Bloomsbury

Thesaurus

Bloomsbury

Thesaurus

Market House Books

BLOOMSBURY

Abbreviations used in the Thesaurus

Aus	Australian	Sp	Spanish
Brit	British	US	United States
Can	Canadian		
Fr	French	Inf	Informal
Ger	German	Sl	Slang
L	Latin	Tab	Taboo
NZ	New Zealand		
Scot	Scottish	Tm	Trademark

First published by Bloomsbury Publishing Limited,
2 Soho Square, London W1V 5DE
Copyright © 1993 by Bloomsbury Publishing Limited
The moral right of the author has been asserted.

British Library Cataloguing in Publication Data
A CIP record for this book is available from the British Library
ISBN 0-7475-1226-4

Compiled and prepared for typesetting by
Market House Books Ltd, Aylesbury

Designed by Paul Fielding
Typeset by Aitch Em, Aylesbury
Printed by The Bath Press, Bath

Contents

Contributors

Editors

John Daintith, BSc, PhD
Elizabeth Martin, MSc
Fran Alexander, BA
John Wright, BA, PhD

Contributors

Callum Brines, BA
Eve Daintith, BSc
Michael Durnin, BA
Rosalind Fergusson, BA
William Gould, BA
Robert Hine, BSc
Valerie Illingworth, MSc
Mandy Isaacs, BA
Pamela Kerr-Frost, BA
Jonathan Law, BA
David Pickering, MA
Megan Remmer, BA
Kathy Rooney, BA, MA, PhD
Mark Salad
Anne Stibbs, BA

Consultant Editors

Betty Kirkpatrick
Cecile Rheinhart Watters

Computer Systems

John Daintith
Anne Stibbs
Edmund Wright

Keyboarding

Elizabeth Bonham
Sandra McQueen
Jessica Scholes
Gwen Shaw
Linda Wells

Introduction

What is a Thesaurus?

The word 'thesaurus' comes from the Greek word for treasure; the original meaning was a place where treasure is stored. As with many words, the sense later changed and a thesaurus became a book that served as a source or repository of information – a treasury of knowledge rather than of material wealth. In 1852, Peter Mark Roget published a new type of reference book, which he entitled *Thesaurus of English Words and Phrases, classified and arranged so as to facilitate the Expression of Ideas and assist in Literary Composition*. Roget arranged words not alphabetically, as in a dictionary, but by concept.

Roget's Thesaurus was immensely successful and 'Roget' has become a generic term for any book in which the words are arranged thematically rather than in the A to Z form familiar from dictionaries and encyclopedias. More recently, with the development of computers and information technology, the term 'thesaurus' has been applied to any collection of words in a particular field, arranged or indexed for use in information processing.

Thesauruses are often contrasted with dictionaries. The user of a dictionary is looking for information about a particular word, usually its meaning – the idea that the word stands for. In a thesaurus, on the other hand, the user starts with an idea and is looking for a word to express it, or for the best word to use in a particular context. A writer may want to avoid using the same word twice – rather than repeat the word 'idea', for example, in several successive sentences, perhaps the occasional use of 'concept' would avoid Mark Twain's stricture '…that the writer's balance at the vocabulary bank has run dry and that he is too lazy to replenish it from the thesaurus'. Alternatively, the user may be seeking a word that expresses a particular kind of intense redness. A list that includes the word 'carmine' may be exactly what is needed.

A thesaurus, then, consists of sets of words connected in some way. In the two examples above the words 'idea–concept' and 'red–carmine' are connected by being synonyms. Of course, they are not exact synonyms. 'Carmine' is a less general word than 'red' and the two can be interchanged only in certain circumstances. 'Idea' and 'concept' are fairly close in meaning in one particular sense of the word 'idea', but 'idea' has an additional range of meanings – impression, belief, viewpoint, or plan.

But a thesaurus is much more than a list of synonyms. It answers other questions than ones of the type 'what is another word for red?' For instance, the user might want to be reminded of things that are typically red – blood, cherries, sunset, etc. The guide to connotation and allusion and the indication of possible metaphors is one of the most useful features of a thesaurus. It extends not only the user's vocabulary but also the user's viewpoint. It opens up whole networks of references which lead the reader, for example, from the synonyms for yellow through all the many types of yellow objects including precious stones and the Yellow Pages to the figurative uses of yellow in its connotations of cowardice.

In addition, a thesaurus can provide information on words, such as musical instruments, chemical elements, breeds of cat, parts of a computer, sails of a ship, bones of the body, countries of the world, types of fear, types of disease, types of pasta, religious sects, gods of love, great lovers, birthstones, the signs of the zodiac, or the seven deadly sins. Over 300 such lists have been included in the *Bloomsbury Thesaurus*.

The Bloomsbury Thesaurus

Our aim in producing the *Bloomsbury Thesaurus* was to reflect the huge richness and variety of the English Language today – as Roget had for his time. The classification system developed by Roget in the mid-nineteenth century was a magnificent creation, grouping words thematically into categories according to the ideas which they expressed. The classification focused on abstract ideas, listing words under general headings such as 'Relation', 'Quantity' and 'Order'.

The world has changed since 1852, and yet the numerous editors of later editions of *Roget's Thesaurus* have been forced to squeeze the thousands of new words, objects, concepts and phrases which have entered the language into the structure devised by Roget all those years ago. So even in the latest revision of Roget's original work, *computer* is listed under *abacus*.

So the main motive behind developing the *Bloomsbury Thesaurus* was to provide a thematic classification of the English language which would be as useful to readers of the 1990s and beyond as the original *Roget* had been in the mid-nineteenth century.

We had the luxury of starting completely from scratch and working out a thematic organization which reflects the huge proliferation of language today. Each and every one of us is surrounded by language, written and spoken – from the latest hi-tech audio gizmos to the babble of TV advertising, from the proliferation of magazines to the latest paperback blockbuster, from job application forms to junk mail. In contrast to Roget's intellectual abstractions, the thousand categories and lists in the *Bloomsbury Thesaurus* reflect the world of computers, of science and technology, of fashion and postmodern culture, of TV and video, of new medicine and drugs, of the boom in sports and leisure, of the worldwide spread of ethnic cuisines, of the earth as a global village.

In our classification we have used two different approaches. The first part of the book covers major branches of knowledge – such subjects as sociology, anthropology, science, technology, the arts, etc., together with plants, animals, countries, places, rivers, seas, etc. This is more like the classification that would be used in an encyclopedia. The second part is a more traditional thesaurus division – existence, the material world, emotions, etc. We believe that these two approaches complement each other.

This approach has allowed us to introduce a number of additional features:

Main Entries

The thesaurus is divided into over 1000 categories and lists. These are itemized in the next section. The first part of the book covers the main branches of knowledge – anthropology, science, technology, sociology, history, the arts, the living world, together with countries, places, rivers and seas. The second part looks at the material world, existence, and the emotions.

Division of Entries

Each main entry is numbered and divided into sections corresponding to parts of speech – nouns, verbs, adjectives, etc. These sections are subdivided into numbered subsections corresponding to different aspects of the main idea. For example, under the noun section of *Hope* we have *hope, expectation, aspiration, comfort*, etc.

For clarity, each of these numbered paragraphs has a subheading in bold type. These subheadings should be regarded as keywords indicating the general content of the paragraph. It is important to realize that all the words in the paragraph are not necessarily synonyms of the keyword, but they are all connected with it.

Within a paragraph words are, as far as is possible, arranged in a logical order – for example, a range from a mild form of an emotion to an intense feeling. In general, informal and slang words and phrases are placed at the end of the relevant paragraph.

Content

A thesaurus is simply a collection of words and phrases. It would not be practical in a book of this size to include all the possible words and phrases in the English language – inevitably a selection has had to be made. We have based our selection on usage, frequency, and usefulness to the reader, focusing on the currency of contemporary English and avoiding for the most part the obsolete or archaic. We have tried to include

a good coverage of idiomatic English, to cover English as it is used throughout the world, and to include informal expression and slang. Where appropriate, labels indicate informal, slang, taboo and offensive terms.

Since English is an international language, the book contains many words and phrases from America, Australia, and other parts of the English-speaking world. These are labelled as such. Foreign words and phrases that are used in English are printed in italic type.

Lists of Words

A new feature of the *Bloomsbury Thesaurus* is the inclusion of highlighted lists of terms relevant to a particular topic. These tend to be quite specific items – countries, places, plants, animals, etc. – and most of them fall in the first section of the book. Names are also part of the language and we have added lists of famous people in various fields. The criterion for inclusion in these biographical lists is partly one of importance but also one of usage. We have included a certain amount of additional information where this may be helpful – for instance, capital cities of countries or symbols for chemical elements. We have not, however, encroached too far on the territory of an encyclopedia.

Cross-references

The book contains over 5000 cross-references to other entries in the book. The reference is to the main category number and title. The user will find other related information at these entries.

Quotations

The book contains a large number of quotations relevant to certain categories. Many of these are a source of common phrases in the language. Others have been included for their general interest. As Doctor Johnson said, 'Every quotation contributes something to the stability or enlargement of the language'.

The Index

Roget said that most people who used his book start with the index. Unlike other thesauruses, which contain only selective indexes, the *Bloomsbury Thesaurus* indexes every occurrence of every word or phrase in the book, no matter how obscure the term or how long the phrase.

It has been a rare privilege to compile a completely new thesaurus. While following in the footsteps of Roget, we have tried to create a new classification that truly reflects the language of our times in a form which is easier for the reader to use – indeed, a treasury of language for the 1990s. The work has involved the compilation and classification of many hundreds of thousands of words. We hope that it proves useful in helping the reader to find the right one.

The Editors

How to Use the Thesaurus

The main text

The text is divided into numbered main categories. Each category contains words listed by *part of speech* (noun, verb, adjective, etc.). The categories are subdivided into *numbered paragraphs*, which group together words of similar meaning and which each have a bold *subheading*. *Cross-references* appear at the end of many paragraphs, indicating other related entries that you may want to refer to. *Quotations* appear at the beginning of many categories.

Main category heading

Main category number — **1 Anthropology**

Quotation (with author)

Know then thyself, presume not God to scan/ The proper study of Mankind is Man.
Alexander Pope.

Part of speech — NOUNS

Subheading number

1 **anthropology**, science of man, human studies, anthropogeny (*or* anthropogenesis), anthropography, ethnology, ethnography, ethnogeny, ethnobotany, ethnomusicology, physical anthropology, biological anthropology, social anthropology, cultural anthropology, symbolic anthropology, economic anthropology, ethnoscientific studies, human geography, anthropogeography, demography, human ecology, behavioural science, anthropometry, craniometry, craniology

Cross-references (to related categories)

▶ *400 Humankind, 59 Life Science, 61 Psychology and Psychiatry, 2 Sociology, 13 Economics, 5 Linguistics*

Subheading

2 **palaeoanthropology**, prehistoric anthropology, archaeological anthropology, palaeoanthropography, palaeoethnography, palaeoethnology, palaeopsychology, Assyriology, Egyptology, Sumerology, epigraphy

A full list of categories, both in the order in which they appear in the book and in alphabetical order, is given in the next section.

The lists

The lists bring together specific groups of related words, e.g. chemical elements, poets, types of pasta, phobias and their causes. These are highlighted in the text for easy reference.

Peoples			Phobias by Topic
African	Fang	Malinke	anaemia - anaemophobia
Afars	Galla	Mandingo	bacteria - bacteriophobia
Afrikaners	Ganda	Masai	beards - pogonophobia
Amhara	Hausa	Nguni	beating - mastigophobia
Ashanti	Herero	Nyoro	bed (going to bed) - clinophobia
Azande	Hottentot	Pondo	bees - apiphobia
Bantu	Ibo	Pygmies	birds - ornithophobia
Baqqarah	Ik	Rif	blood - haemaphobia (or haematophobia or
Barotse	Issas	Somali	haemophobia)
Bemba	Kabyle	Sotho	blushing - erythrophobia
Bushmen	Khoisan	Swazi	body odour - bromidrosiphobia
Dinka	Kikuyu	Teuso	bridges (crossing) - gephyrophobia
Edo	Lozi	Xhosa	bullets - ballistophobia
Efik	Lunda	Yoruba	cancer - cancerphobia (or cancerophobia or car-
Ewe	Luo	Zulu	cinophobia)

Index

Each word in the *Bloomsbury Thesaurus* appears in the index. So if you want to find the word *anthropometrist* in the text, look first in the index, where it is referenced to 1.3 *anthropologist*. This means that it appears in category 1, paragraph 3, under the subheading *anthropologist*.

Reference to a text word ——————————
  (with the paragraph heading in italics)

> **anthropometrically** 1.16 *anthropologically*
> **anthropometrist** 1.3 *anthropologist*
> **anthropometry** 1.1 *anthropology*, 268.2 *micrometry*, 400.5 *study of mankind*

If the index entry is itself a category or a paragraph heading, only the number appears.

Reference to a paragraph subheading ———

Reference to a main category ——————

> **anthropological concept 1**
> **anthropological linguistics** 5.1 *linguistics*
> **anthropologically 1**. 400.15 *humanly*
> **anthropologist 1**, 400.6 *studier of mankind*
> **Anthropology 1**
> **anthropometric** 1.11 *anthropological*, 268.16 *micrometric*
> **anthropometrical** 1.11 *anthropological*

If the index entry refers to a list it appears as follows.

Reference to a list ——————————

> **afar** 263.10 *distantly*
> **a far cry from** 115.4 *dissimilar*
> **Afars 1** Peoples
> **AFC** 19.1 *football*
> **a few** 175.1 *plurality*, 182.1, 182.5 *few*

LIST OF CATEGORIES

SOCIETY

1 Anthropology
2 Sociology
3 History
4 Philosophy
5 Linguistics
6 Education
7 Religion
8 Divinity
9 Worship
10 Ritual
11 Occultism
12 Government and Politics
13 Economics
14 Finance
15 Industrial Relations
16 Law
17 Military Affairs

SPORTS AND PASTIMES

18 Sport
19 American Football
20 Angling
21 Athletics
22 Baseball
23 Basketball
24 Billiards
25 Bowling
26 Combat Sports
27 Cricket
28 Fencing
29 Golf
30 Gymnastics
31 Hockey and Ice Hockey,
    Lacrosse, Etc.
32 Horses
33 Motor Racing
34 Mountaineering
35 Rugby Football
36 Sailing, Rowing, Etc.
37 Shooting
38 Soccer
39 Swimming
40 Tennis, Squash, Badminton,
    Etc.
41 Winter Sports
42 Games and Pastimes

THE ARTS

43 Architecture
44 Ceramics
45 Cookery
46 Dancing and Ballet
47 Furniture and Woodwork
48 Literature
49 Music
50 Painting and Sculpture
51 Performing Arts

SCIENCE AND TECHNOLOGY

52 Mathematics
53 Astronomy, Astronautics,
    and Rocketry
54 Earth Science
55 Meteorology and Climatol-
    ogy
56 Physics
57 Chemistry
58 Biochemistry
59 Life Science
60 Medicine
61 Psychology and Psychiatry
62 Pharmacology
63 Engineering

SPACE

MOTION

Alphabetical Category List

xxvii

Lists

Society

1 Anthropology

*Know then thyself, presume not God to scan/
The proper study of Mankind is Man.*
Alexander Pope.

NOUNS

1 **anthropology**, science of man, human studies, anthropogeny (*or* anthropogenesis), anthropography, ethnology, ethnography, ethnogeny, ethnobotany, ethnomusicology, physical anthropology, biological anthropology, social anthropology, cultural anthropology, symbolic anthropology, economic anthropology, ethnoscientific studies, human geography, anthropogeography, demography, human ecology, behavioural science, anthropometry, craniometry, craniology
▶ *400 Humankind, 59 Life Science, 61 Psychology and Psychiatry, 2 Sociology, 13 Economics, 5 Linguistics*

2 **palaeoanthropology**, prehistoric anthropology, archaeological anthropology, palaeoanthropography, palaeoethnography, palaeoethnology, palaeopsychology, Assyriology, Egyptology, Sumerology, epigraphy
▶ *400 Humankind, 3 History*

3 **anthropologist**, human scientist, ethnologist, ethnographer, ethnogenist, ethnomusicologist, anthropogeographer, demographer, human ecologist, behavioural scientist, anthropometrist, craniometrist, craniologer
▶ *400 Humankind, 61 Psychology and Psychiatry, 2 Sociology, 5 Linguistics*

4 **palaeoanthropologist**, archaeological anthropologist, palaeoethnographer, palaeoethnologist, palaeopsychologist, Assyriologist, Egyptologist, Sumerologist, epigrapher, epigraphist
▶ *400 Humankind, 3 History*

5 **anthropological concept**, structuralism, functionalism, transactionalism, diffusionism, consanguinity, descent, kinship, age set, taboo

6 **race**, ethnic origin, colour, Caucasoid race, Caucasian, White, Nordic type, Alpine type, Aryan, Latino, Negroid race, Negro, Negrito, Negrillo, Nilotic type, Afro-Caribbean, African-American, Afro-American, Anglo-American, Anglo-African, Melanesian, Polynesian, Australasian, Mongoloid race, Oriental, Asian, Anglo-Indian, mixed race, mulatto, quadroon, octaroon, half-caste (Offensive), half-breed (Offensive), indigenous race, native people, native, aborigine, Indian, Amerindian, native American
▶ *91 Countries*

7 **society**, people, nation, nationality, population, folk, tribe, clan, culture, community, race, ethnic group, strain, stock
▶ *163 Class, 91 Countries, 161 Assembly, 400 Humankind, 107 Relatedness*

8 **tradition**, custom, habit, praxis, ritual, rite, symbol, taboo, ancient wisdom, ways of the fathers, common law, immemorial wisdom, Sunna, Talmud, Mishnah, myth, archetypal myth, mythology, legend, lore, folklore, folk tale, folk motif, folk art, folksong, folk history, oral tradition, archetype, racial memory, tribal memory, collective unconscious
▶ *511 Memory, 10 Ritual, 7 Religion, 399 Burial, 812 Celebration, 61 Psychology and Psychiatry, 823 Marriage, 50 Painting and Sculpture, 584 Habit*

9 **physical type**, build, physique, phthisic build, linear build, apoplectic build, stocky build, somatype, endomorphy, endomorph, mesomorphy, mesomorph, ectomorphy, ectomorph

10 **measurement**, anthrometry, anthroscopy, biometrics, craniometry, osteology, growth study, constitutional anthropology, height-weight ratio, Sheldon scale, skinfold, Bergmann's rule

ADJECTIVES

11 **anthropological**, anthropographical, ethnological, ethnographic, ethnogenic, anthropogenic, ethnoscientific, geographic, geographical, anthropogeographic, anthropogeographical, demographic, structuralist, func-

Peoples

African
Afars
Afrikaners
Amhara
Ashanti
Azande
Bantu
Baqqarah
Barotse
Bemba
Bushmen
Dinka
Edo
Efik
Ewe
Fang
Galla
Ganda
Hausa
Herero
Hottentot
Ibo
Ik
Issas
Kabyle
Khoisan
Kikuyu
Lozi
Lunda
Luo
Malinke
Mandingo
Masai
Nguni
Nyoro
Pondo
Pygmies
Rif
Somali
Sotho
Swazi
Teuso
Xhosa
Yoruba
Zulu

European
Achaeans
Angles
Anglo-Saxons
Aryans
Basque
Belgians
Bosnians
Bretons
Britons
Bulgars
Catalonians
Celts
Croatians
Czechs
Dorians
Estonians
Etruscans

Flemings
French
Frisians
Gauls
Germans
Ghegs
Goths
Gypsies (or Gipsies)
Hellenes
Iberians
Jutes
Lapps
Lithuanians
Magyars
Picts
Poles
Saxons
Scots
Serbs
Slavs
Tosks
Visigoths
Walloons

Middle Eastern
Amalekites
Amorites
Arabs
Armenians
Babylonians
Bakhtyari
Bedouin
Cumans
Fulani
Hittites
Hurrians
Israelis
Jews
Kassites
Kazakh
Kurds
Palestinians
Phoenicians
Semites

Asian
Ainu
Andamanese
Bashkir
Bengalis
Burmese
Chinese
Chukchi
Cossacks
Dards
Georgians
Hui
Kaffirs
Karen
Khmer
Maratha (or Mahratta)
Mon
Munda
Pashtuns (or Pathans)

Samoyed
Sherpas
Sinhalese
Tai
Talaing
Tamils
Tatars
Turkmen

Australasian
Aborigines
Dayak
Maoris
Melanesians
Polynesians
Tagalog

Eskimo
Aleut
Inuit
Yupik

North American Indian
Algonquin
Apache
Arapaho
Arikara
Assiniboine
Athapascan
Bannock
Blackfoot
Caddo
Cherokee
Cheyenne
Chickasaw
Chinook
Chippewa
Chitimacha
Choctaw
Comanche
Coushatla
Cree
Creek
Crow
Goshute
Haida
Hidatsa
Hopi
Hupa
Huron
Illinois
Iowa
Iroquois
Karok
Kickapoo
Kiowa
Kutenai
Kwakiutl
Lummi
Maliseet
Mandan
Miccosukee
Mohawk
Mohican

Narraganset
Natchez
Navaho
Nez Percé
Nootka
Ojibwa
Olmec
Omaha
Oneida
Onondaga
Osage
Ottawa
Paiute
Papago
Passamaquoddy
Pawnee
Penobscot
Pequot
Pima
Potawatomi
Powhatan
Pueblo
Quinault
Seminole
Seneca
Shoshoni
Siletz
Sioux
Tiwa
Tlingit
Tsimpshian
Tunica-Biloxi
Umatilla
Ute
Washoe
Winnebago
Yakima
Yavapai
Yurok
Zuñi

Caribbean
Arawaks
Caribs

South American Indian
Araucanians
Aymara
Aztec
Cashinahua
Chibcha
Chimú
Ge
Guarani
Inca
Makuna
Maya
Mixtec
Toltec
Tupi
Zapotec

---

tionalist, transactionalist, diffusionist, ecological, psychological, sociological, anatomical, anthropometric, anthropometrical, anthroposcopic, craniometric, craniometrical, craniological, osteometric

▶ *400 Humankind, 61 Psychology and Psychiatry, 2 Sociology, 5 Linguistics*

12 **palaeoanthropological**, palaeoanthropographic, palaeoanthropographical, palaeoethnographic, palaeoethnological, palaeopsychological, epigraphic, epigraphical

▶ *400 Humankind, 3 History*

13 **racial**, ethnic, Caucasian, Caucasoid, White, Nordic, Alpine, Aryan, albinic, albinistic,

albiniotic, Negroid, Black, Nilotic, Afro-Caribbean, Afro-American, Anglo-African, Melanesian, Polynesian, Australasian, Mongoloid, Oriental, Asian, Anglo-Indian, mixed, mulatto, octaroon, quadroon, half-caste (Offensive), half-breed (Offensive), indigenous, native, aboriginal, Indian, Amerindian

▶ *91 Countries*

14 **societal**, communal, national, tribal, racial, ethnic, cultural, folk, established, time-honoured, immemorial, traditional, customary, received, handed down, unwritten, oral, mythological, legendary, heroic, archetypal

15 **physical**, stocky, apoplectic, lightly built, phthisic, endomorphic, mesomorphic, ectomorphic

ADVERBS

16 **anthropologically**, anthropographically, ethnologically, ethnographically, geographically, anthropogeographically, demographically, anthropometrically, craniometrically, craniologically

17 **palaeoanthropologically**, palaeoanthropographically, palaeoethnographically, palaeoethnologically, palaeopsychologically, epigraphically

18 **societally**, nationally, communally, tribally, racially, ethnically, culturally, traditionally, ritually, customarily, mythologically, mythically, archetypally

2   Sociology

Man was formed for society. William Blackstone.

No man is an island, entire of itself; every man is a piece of the Continent, a part of the main. John Donne.

Man is a social animal. Benedict Spinoza.

NOUNS

1 **sociology**, social science, behavioural science, social anthropology, rural sociology, urban sociology, sociobiology, political sociology, political behaviour, social psychology, macrosociology, comparative macrosociology, social morphology, sociology of knowledge, comparative sociology, human ecology, cultural ecology, applied sociology, pragmatic sociology, demography

▶ *501 Knowledge, 1 Anthropology, 61 Psychology and Psychiatry*

2 **sociological research**, social survey, demographic research, demographic survey, demography, community study, population study, sociological theory, theory of social systems, role theory, locational theory, sociological method, sociometric technique, sociological model, sociological tool, questionnaire, survey, sociological analysis, structural-functionalism, sociological perspective, sociological jargon, sociologese

3 **social environment**, social relations, interaction, social interaction, interpersonal relations, intercourse, human interaction, human communications, social contact, socialization, friendship, marriage, symbolic interaction, human social behaviour, behavioural pattern, social trait, mores, values, value system, social role, sex role, gender, social order, social differences

4 **social organization**, family, group, community, religious organization, political organization, industrial organization, social system, belief system, community, *Gemeinschaft* (Ger), society, *Gesellschaft* (Ger)

▶ *664 Cooperation, 150 Order, 534 Communications, 819 Friendship, 823 Marriage, 543 Sign, 382 Structure, 152 Arrangement, 6 Education, 7 Religion, 12 Government and Politics, 151 Disorder, 611 Importance, 847 Duty, 4 Philosophy*

5 **society**, community, community relations, sense of community, social heterogeneity, homogeneity, collective adaptation, collectivity, mechanical solidarity, organic solidarity, rural sociology, rural society, folk society, rural sector, ruralism, rural-urban migration, urban society, urban sector, urban environment, urbanism, urbanization, suburbanization, urban planning, urban renewal, urban culture, industrialized society

▶ *250 Location, 256 Habitat, 255 Inhabitant*

6 **social group**, small group, primary group, family group, peer group, work group, ethnic group, racial group, age group, status group, group interaction, group behaviour, group solidarity

▶ *161 Assembly, 135 Union*

7 **social stratification**, social pyramid, hierarchy of authority, class boundary, social diversity, social status, prestige, social prestige, occupational prestige, economic status, economic power, educational status, employment status, earning status, class structure, social structure, social class system, social class, A, B, C1, C2, D, E, upper class, privileged class, ruling class, middle class, lower class, working class, class conflict, economic materialism, Marxism, social movement, mobility, social mobility, upward mobility, downward mobility

▶ *163 Class, 235 Power, 224 Changeableness, 13 Economics, 252 Displacement*

8
} **human institution**, social institution, family, kinship, educational institution, school, religious institution, church, industrial institution, factory, political institution, political party, government institution, correctional institution

▶ *6 Education, 7 Religion, 12 Government and Politics, 15 Industrial Relations, 879 Punishment*

9 **social change**, social movement, social engineering, social control, social planning, social transformation, human development, social progress, social obligation, social action, social policy, social benefit

10 **social services**, social security, welfare, welfare organization, welfare state, poor relief, social work, good works, community service

11 **sociologist**, social scientist, empirical sociologist, sociobiologist, social psychologist, demographer, social worker, social reformer, economic determinist, Marxist

▶ *4 Philosophy, 13 Economics*

ADJECTIVES

12 **sociological**, societal, social, behavioural, interactive, symbolic, communal, educational, community-wide, religious, political, bureaucratic, military, environmental, sociobiological

13 **communal**, heterogeneous, collective, organic, rural, rural-urban, urban, urbanized, urbanizing, industrial, industrialized, industrializing governmental, correctional

14 **socioeconomic**, racial, occupational, economic, privileged, ruling, upper, middle, lower, working, Marxist, mobile, upward, downward, unequal, minority, communicative, communication, productive, territorial, demographic(al), locational, structural-functional

VERBS

15 **socialize**, interact, communicate, contact, organize, form a community, have a sense of community, participate, mingle, intermingle, join in, live side by side, work together, work from home, commute, employ, produce, improve living conditions, plan urban renewal, urbanize, industrialize, civilize, reform

ADVERBS

16 **sociologically**, socially, behaviourally, humanly, interactively, heterogeneously, collectively, symbolically, communally, educationally, religiously, politically, bureaucratically, governmentally, militarily, industrially, environmentally, sociobiologically, comparatively, culturally, pragmatically, ethnically, racially, economically, communicatively, socioeconomically, productively, territorially, demographically

3 History

The history of the world is but the biography of great men. Thomas Carlyle.

History is more or less bunk. Henry Ford.

History is past politics, and politics present history. John Robert Seeley.

NOUNS

1 **history**, historiography, philosophy of history, historical methodology, social history, economic history, religious history, political history, constitutional history, legal history, local history, history of ideas, history of science, counterfactual history, historical materialism, Marxist history, revisionist history, counterrevisionist history

2 **archaeology**, prehistoric archaeology, marine archaeology, fossilology, historical geology, Assyriology, Egyptology, Sumerology, palaeology, palaeohistology, palaeontography, palaeontology, human palaeontology, micropalaeontology, palaeogeography, palaeobiogeography, palaeolithy, palaeopotamology, palaeohydrography, palaeolimnology, palaeoeremology, palaeoceanography, palaeoecology, palaeobotany, palaeodendrology, palaeoglaciology, palaeoclimatology, palaeometeorology, palaeocosmology, palaeobiology, palaeoherpetology, palaeomammology, palaeornithology, palaeozoology, palaeophytology, palaeophysiology, palaeophysiography, palaeopathology, palaeography, industrial archaeology

▶ *1 Anthropology, 59 Life Science, 54 Earth Science, 5 Linguistics*

3 **historian**, recorder, biographer, archivist, historiographer

4 **archaeologist**, Assyriologist, Egyptologist, Sumerologist, palaeologist, palaeohistologist, palaeontographer, palaeontologist, micropalaeontologist, palaeogeographer, palaeobiogeographer, palaeopotamologist, palaeohydrographer, palaeolimnologist, palaeoecologist, palaeobotanist, palaeoclimatologist, palaeometeorologist, palaeocosmologist, palaeobiologist, palaeornithologist, palaeozoologist, palaeophytologist, palaeophysiologist, palaeopathologist, palaeographer, epigrapher

5 **chronicle**, history, account, record, diary, journal, log, logbook, recollection, report, reportage, documentary, documentation, recording, annals, archive, historical record, public record, minutes, minute book, notebook, notes, case notes, case history, track record, file, dossier, background, summary, information

6 **biography**, biographical record, autobiography, memoirs, life story, story, past, life, experiences, c.v. (*or* CV) (curriculum vitae), résumé (US)

7 **narrative**, narration, relation, description, tradition, place in history, legend, myth, folk tale, folk history

▶ *750 Accounts, 396 Life, 528 Information, 511 Memory, 533 News, 545 Record*

8 **past time**, history, the past, yesterday, yesteryear, good old days, days of yore, olden days, days of old, old times, foretime, former times, bygone days, bygones, days gone by, long ago, auld lang syne, ancient history, ancien régime, eld (Arch)

9 distant past, dim and distant past, remote age, antiquity, time immemorial, ancient times, way back (Inf), the year dot (Inf)

▶ *207 Age, 200 Past Time*

10 past age, ancient times, prehistory, protohistory, Stone Age, Heroic Age, Bronze Age, Iron Age, Classical Age, Hellenistic Age, Roman Republic, Roman Empire, Holy Roman Empire, Dark Ages, Middle Ages, Medieval times, Time of Troubles, Tudor times, Elizabethan Age, Renaissance, Enlightenment, Age of Reason, Victorian Age, Risorgimento, Reconstruction, Prohibition, the Roaring Twenties, the Swinging Sixties

▶ *207 Age, 200 Past Time*

11 relic, vestige, remains, ruin, remainder, archaism, antiquity, antique, museum piece, heirloom, ancient monument, eolith, neolith, microlith, megalith, monolith, cromlech, dolmen, menhir, earthwork, burial mound, barrow, fogou, cave painting, artefact, flint axe, flint tool, fossil, manuscript, scroll, Dead Sea Scrolls, Pipe rolls, epigraph, inscription, memento, memorabilia, Victoriana, souvenir

▶ *483 Evidence, 528 Information, 207 Age, 400 Humankind*

12 historicism, historical method, excavation, digging up the past, exhumation, medievalism, antiquarianism, archaism

13 looking back, remembrance, reminiscence, flashback, recalling, remembering, reviewing, harking back, nostalgia, déja vu

▶ *511 Memory, 477 Question*

14 historicalness, historicity, reality, matter of fact, factualness, realness, actuality, genuineness, validity, fact, truth, event, deed, act, experience, incident, episode, happening

▶ *537 Truth*

ADJECTIVES

15 historic, ancient, old, ancestral, prehistoric, protohistoric, diachronic, before the Flood, antediluvian, pre-Christian, pre-classical, primordial, primal, aboriginal, antiquated, dated, archaic, former, prior, Classical, Hellenistic, Medieval, Elizabethan, Renaissance, Victorian, atavistic, vestigial, remaining, monumental

▶ *207 Age, 119 Originality, 200 Past Time*

16 historical, historiographical, prehistorical, protohistorical

17 archaeological, Assyriological, Egyptological, Sumerological, palaeological, palaeohistological, palaeontographical, palaeontological, micropalaeontological, palaeogeographical, palaeobiogeographical, palaeopotamological, palaeohydrographical, palaeolimnological, palaeoeremological, palaeoecological, palaeobotanical, palaeoclimatological, palaeometeorological, palaeocosmological, palaeobiological, palaeornithological, palaeozoological, palaeophysiological, palaeopathological, palaeographical, epigraphical

▶ *1 Anthropology, 59 Life Science, 54 Earth Science, 5 Linguistics*

18 in the past, historical, over, finished, old hat, yesterday's news, old story, over and done with, no more, gone, dead and gone, dead and buried, dead as a dodo, extinct, ended, defunct, obsolete, expired, lapsed, passé, has been, retroactive, bygone

▶ *207 Age, 200 Past Time, 157 End*

19 chronicled, recorded, logged, documented, minuted, filed, registered, archival, reported, described, descriptive, recollected, recalled, told, narrated, related, biographical, autobiographical, factual, true, real, actual, authentic, genuine, valid, verifiable, traditional, historical, legendary, famous, mythical

▶ *537 Truth, 511 Memory, 528 Information*

VERBS

20 chronicle, record, log, keep a diary, recollect, report, document, register, minute, file, summarize, inform, store information, narrate, relate, describe

▶ *483 Evidence, 511 Memory, 528 Information, 560 Description, 562 Summary*

21 antiquarianize, archaize, excavate, dig up the past, exhume, look back, trace back

22 remember, reminisce, recall, review, hark back, call to mind

23 turn back time, put the clock back, reconstruct, salvage

▶ *511 Memory, 200 Past Time, 294 Uncovering*

ADVERBS

24 historically, prehistorically, protohistorically, ancestrally, diachronically, primordially, aboriginally, archaically, formerly, aforetime, of old, of yore, ago, long ago, long since, a long time ago, once, some time ago, yesterday, yesteryear, in olden times, in the good old days, in the dim and distant past, in the mists of time, in days gone by, before now, hitherto, from time immemorial, time out of mind, yet, till now, until now, retrospectively, retroactively, with hindsight, from a historical perspective

▶ *200 Past Time, 207 Age, 511 Memory, 194 Priority, 185 Time, 119 Originality*

25 reportedly, summarily, informatively, really, actually, genuinely, validly, vestigially, epigraphically, descriptively, biographically, autobiographically, reminiscently, nostalgically, memorially, monumentally, traditionally, mythically

▶ *537 Truth, 533 News, 528 Information, 396 Life*

4 Philosophy

Do not all charms fly/ At the mere touch of cold philosophy. John Keats.

Philosophy is the product of wonder. A. N. Whitehead.

Philosophy is not a theory but an activity. Ludwig Wittgenstein.

NOUNS

1 **philosophy**, viewpoint, point of view, view, outlook, attitude, opinion, doctrine, philosophical doctrine, feeling, sentiment, idea, thought, notion, conclusion, judgment, tenet, dogma, principle, canon, maxim, axiom, aphorism, statement, assertion, proposition, premise, assumption, precept, presupposition, thesis, postulate, supposition, conjecture, speculation, philosophical speculation, hypothesis, philosophical theory, concept, explanation, theory of knowledge, rationalization, justification

▶ *497 Belief, 759 Feeling, 471 Idea, 505 Maxim, 463 Reason, 518 Supposition, 461 Thought*

2 **philosophical system**, belief system, set of beliefs (*or* values), value system, value judgment, ethical system, ethos, morals, school of thought, code, moral code, code of practice, code of conduct, standards, principles, ideology, world view, *Weltanschauung* (Ger), teaching, creed, credo, stance, position, manifesto, metanarrative

▶ *497 Belief, 759 Feeling, 471 Idea, 492 Judgment, 876 Morality, 7 Religion, 518 Supposition, 461 Thought*

3 **detachment**, stoicism, sang-froid, control, self-control, self-possession, self-restraint, spartanism, dispassion, cool, coolness, coolheadedness, temperance, moderation, sobriety, calmness, inexcitability, imperturbability, aplomb, composure, level-headedness, reasonableness, common sense, rationality, lucidity, objectivity, equanimity, tolerance, balance, patience, thoughtfulness, even temper, good temper, peace of mind, tranquillity, ataraxia, serenity, quietude, placidity, passivity, resignation, horse sense (Inf)

▶ *859 Disinterestedness, 643 Inactivity, 783 Indifference, 242 Moderation, 463 Reason, 869 Self-Restraint, 873 Sobriety*

4 **philosophical investigation**, philosophical inquiry (*or* enquiry), examination, self-examination, introspection, analysis, consideration, scrutiny, investigation, investigation into first causes, search, survey, study, research, asking, challenge, questioning, elenchus, speculation, reflection, reasoning, ratiocination, concentration, contemplation, cogitation, excogitation, pondering, deliberation, musing, brainwork, conceptual thought, intuition, abstract thought, deduction, induction, inference, calculation, computation

▶ *477 Question, 463 Reason, 518 Supposition, 461 Thought, 786 Wonder*

5 **philosophical argument**, discussion, dialogue, symposium, conversation, colloquy, debate, dialectic, Hegelian dialectic, syllogism, thesis, antithesis, synthesis, interlocution, disputation, argument, logomachy, polemic, eristic, rhetoric, oratory

▶ *473 Argument, 568 Conversation, 474 Sophistry*

6 **branch of philosophy**, logic, formal logic, modal logic, deontic logic, axiomatic set theory, moral philosophy, ethics, metaethics, medical ethics, legal ethics, axiology, deontology, analytical philosophy, political philosophy, philosophy of mind, mental philosophy, metaphysics, ontology, epistemology, gnosiology, phenomenology, teleology, cosmology, natural philosophy, casuistry, aesthetics, philosophy of language, semantics, philosophy of signs, semiotics, philosophy of law, philosophy of history, philosophy of psychology, philosophy of commonsense, philosophy of science, quantum physics, quantum mathematics, propositional calculus, philosophy of religion, theology, ontotheology

▶ *471 Idea, 876 Morality, 7 Religion, 459 Intellect, 5 Linguistics*

7 **school of thought**, Platonism, Neo-Platonism, Cambridge Platonism, Pythagoreanism, pre-Socratic philosophy, Eleaticism, euhemerism, eudaemonism, Socraticism, atomism, stoicism, scepticism, lyrenaic philosophy, cynicism, epicureanism, peripatetic philosophy, Aristotelian philosophy, Aristotelianism, Averroism, scholasticism, Thomism, Augustinian philosophy, vitalism, animism, panpsychism, pantheism, deism, theism, dynamism, mechanism, essentialism, holism, hylomorphism, hylozoism, Bergsonism, agnosticism, Gnosticism, Manichaeism, transcendentalism, idealism, mysticism, Sufism, Confucianism, Taoism, Buddhism, Zen Buddhism, Yoga, Vaisesika, Vijnanavada, Nyaya, Sankhya, satyagraha, Lokayata, mimamsa, ahimsa, naturalism, empiricism, Humism, Berkelianism, rationalism, materialism, dialectical materialism, physicalism, mentalism, sensationalism, instrumentalism, pragmatism, conceptualism, pluralism, dualism, monism, Cartesianism, phenomenalism, epiphenomenalism, functionalism, behaviourism, Kantianism (*or* Kantism), intuitionism, relativism, descriptivism, consequentialism, emotivism, boo-hurrah theory, utilitarianism, Benthamism, Nietzscheanism (*or* Nietzscheism), reductionism (*or* reductivism), determinism, fatalism, nihilism, solipsism, existentialism, Sartrism, subjectivism, objectivism, egoism, hedonism, altruism, humanism, utopianism, collectivism, socialism, communism, Marxism, Frankfurt School, syndicalism, anarchism, anarcho-syndicalism, national-

ism, Hobbism, Keyneseanism, monetarism, capitalism, aestheticism, structuralism, post-structuralism, deconstructionism, modernism, contextualism, isolationism, Hegelianism, apriorism, nominalism, individualism, realism, anti-realism, quasi-realism, logical empiricism, logical positivism, Vienna circle, positivism, chaos theory, game theory

▶ *497 Belief, 7 Religion, 13 Economics, 12 Government and Politics*

8 **philosophical term**, axiom, postulate, hypothesis, thesis, antithesis, synthesis, assertion sign, operator, function, reference, sense, quantifier, subaltern, major term (*or* premise), minor term (*or* premise), conjunction, disjunction, antecedent, conditional, biconditional, equivalence, identity, bivalence, categorical proposition, contingent truth, necessary truth, truth value, truth condition, truth function, truth table, verification principle, counterfactual, tautology, negation, dichotomy, counterexample, non sequitur, inference, deduction, salva veritate, argument ad hominem, reductio ad absurdum, argument a fortiori, argument a posteriori, argument a priori, argument from first principles, value judgment, imperative, utility principle, sense data, sensibilia, noumenon, syllogism, analogy, paradox, modality, probability, necessity, Gestalt, Hume's Law, Leibnitz's Law, Ockham's (*or* Occam's) razor

▶ *52 Mathematics*

9 **philosophical problem**, existence of god, a priori knowledge, nature of meaning, referential failure, (radical) indeterminacy of meaning, undistributed middle, anti-private language argument, speech-act theory, artificial intelligence, mental entities, mind-body problem, other minds, personal identity, free will, volition, predestination, categorical imperative, transcendental argument, weakness of will, akrasia, moral relativism, contract theory of morality, primary quality, secondary quality, category mistake, causal theory of perception, first cause, possible worlds, nature of time, beginning of time, end of time, time-travel paradox, Barber paradox, paradox of the unexpected hanging, Zeno's paradoxes, Russell's paradox, Richard's paradox, Schrödinger's cat

▶ *471 Idea, 786 Wonder, 461 Thought, 477 Question, 52 Mathematics, 368 Nonmaterial World, 876 Morality, 7 Religion, 99 Existence*

10 **philosopher**, thinker, academic, logician, dialectician, sophist, syllogist, metaphysician, cosmologist, moralist, theorist, theoretician, theorizer, speculator, hypothesizer, hypothesist, hypothecator, surmiser, investigator, researcher, analyst, inquirer (*or* enquirer), asker, seeker, searcher, dreamer, idealist, ideologue,

visionary, doctrinarian, armchair critic

▶ *507 Wisdom, 459 Intellect, 477 Question, 463 Reason*

11 **follower of a doctrine**, Platonist, Neo-Platonist, Cambridge Platonist, Pythagorean, Eleatic, Euclidian (*or* Euclidean), Protagorean, sophist (*or* sophister), euhemerist, eudaemonist, Socratist, Democritean, Empedoclean, atomist, stoic, Senecan, sceptic, Heraclitean, Cyrenaic, Cynic, epicurean, Lucretian, Pyrrhonist, peripatetic, Aristotelian, Averroist, Thomist, Scholastic, Augustinian, vitalist, animist, panpsychist, pantheist, deist, theist, dynamist, mechanist, essentialist, Bergsonian, agnostic, transcendentalist, idealist, mystic, Sufi, Confucian, Taoist, Buddhist, naturalist, empiricist, Humist, Berkelian, Baconian, rationalist, materialist, physicalist, instrumentalist, conceptualist, pluralist, dualist, monist, Cartesian, compatibilist, phenomenalist, epiphenomenalist, functionalist, behaviourist, Kantian, relativist, descriptivist, axiologist, consequentialist, emotivist, utilitarian, Benthamite, Nietzschean, reductionist (*or* reductivist), determinist, fatalist, nihilist, solipsist, existentialist, Sartrist, subjectivist, objectivist, egoist, hedonist, altruist, humanist, utopian, collectivist, socialist, communist, Marxist, syndicalist, anarchist, anarcho-syndicalist, nationalist, pacifist, Hobbist (*or* Hobbesian), Keynesian, monetarist, capitalist, Kierkegaardian, aesthetic, contextualist, structuralist, post-structuralist, deconstructionist, modernist, isolationist, Hegelian, Leibnitzian, Schellingian, Tregean, apriorist, nominalist, individualist, realist, anti-realist, quasi-realist, Chomskyan (*or* Chomskyite), logical empiricist, logical positivist, positivist, Wittgensteinian

▶ *497 Belief, 7 Religion, 13 Economics, 12 Government and Politics*

12 **sage**, wise man (*or* woman), savant, academic, intellectual, highbrow, pundit, expert, genius, authority, consultant, counsellor, adviser, mentor, teacher, tutor, guru, Socrates, Nestor, Solon, Solomon, boffin (Inf), egghead (Inf), nobody's fool (Inf), wise guy (Inf), know-all (Inf)

▶ *507 Wisdom, 459 Intellect, 688 Authority*

ADJECTIVES

13 **of philosophy**, theoretical, philosophical, notional, abstract, esoteric, ideological, moral, ethical, normative, prescriptive, nomothetic, descriptive, conceptual, conceptive, ideal, ideational, visionary, metaphysical, hypothetical, conjectural, speculative, unapplied, impractical, academic

▶ *471 Idea, 459 Intellect, 518 Supposition, 461 Thought*

14 **of a philosophy**, Platonic, Neo-Platonist,

Philosophers

Abelard, Peter (1079–1142)

Acton, John Emerich Edward Dalberg-Acton, 1st Baron (1834–1902)

Adorno, Theodor Wiesengrund (1903–69)

Alcmaeon (c. 500 BC)

Alexander of Hales (c. 1170–1245)

al-Farabi, Mohammed ibn Tarkhan (d. 950)

al-Ghazālī, Abū Hamid Muhammad (1058–1111)

Al-Kindi, Abu Yusuf Ya'qub ibn Ishaq (died c. 870)

Althusser, Louis (1919–90)

Anaxagoras (c. 500–428 BC)

Anaximander (c. 610–c. 546 BC)

Anaximenes (died c. 528 BC)

Anselm, Saint (1033–1109)

Antisthenes (c. 445–c. 360 BC)

Aquinas, Saint Thomas (c. 1225–74)

Archytas (early 4th century BC)

Arendt, Hannah (1906–75)

Aristippus (c. 435–c. 356 BC)

Aristotle (384–322 BC)

Arnauld, Antoine (1612–94)

Athenagoras (2nd century AD)

Augustine of Hippo, Saint (354–430 AD)

Austin, John (1790–1859)

Austin, John Langshaw (1911–60)

Averroes (Ibn Rushd; 1126–98)

Avicenna (Ibn Sīnā; 980–1037)

Ayer, Sir Alfred (Jules) (1910–89)

Bacon, Francis (1561–1626)

Bacon, Roger (c. 1214–1292)

Baudrillard, Jean (1929–)

Baumgarten, Alexander Gottlieb (1714–62)

Bayle, Pierre (1647–1706)

Beauvoir, Simone de (1908–86)

Bentham, Jeremy (1748–1832)

Berdyaev, Nikolai (1874–1948)

Bergson, Henri (1859–1941)

Berkeley, George (1685–1753)

Berlin, Sir Isaiah (1909–)

Bernard of Chartres (died c. 1130)

Blondel, Maurice (1861–1949)

Bodin, Jean (1530–96)

Boethius, Anicius Manlius Severinus (c. 480–524 AD)

Bosanquet, Bernard (1848–1923)

Bradley, Francis Herbert (1846–1924)

Brentano, Franz (1838–1916)

Bruno, Giordano (1548–1600)

Buchanan, George (1506–82)

Buridan, Jean (c. 1297–c. 1358)

Campanella, Tommaso (1568–1639)

Carnap, Rudolf (1891–1970)

Cassirer, Ernst (1874–1945)

Charron, Pierre (1541–1603)

Chomsky, Avram Noam (1928–)

Chryssipus (c. 280–207 BC)

Cicero, Marcus Tullius (106–43 BC)

Cleanthes (c. 310–230 BC)

Collingwood, Robin George (1889–1943)

Condillac, Étienne Bonnot de (1715–80)

Confucius (Kong Zi or K'ung-fu-tzu; c. 551–479 BC)

Cousin, Victor (1792–1867)

Crescas, Hasdai ben Abraham (d. 1412)

Croce, Benedetto (1866–1952)

Cudworth, Ralph (1617–88)

Cumberland, Richard (1631–1718)

Debray, (Jules) Régis (1940–)

Democritus (c. 460–370 BC)

Derrida, Jacques (1930–)

Descartes, René (1596–1650)

Destutt, Antoine Louis Claude, Comte de Tracy (1754–1836)

Dewey, John (1859–1952)

Diderot, Denis (1713–84)

Dilthey, Wilhelm (1833–1911)

Dio Chrysostom (2nd century AD)

Diogenes Laertius (3rd century AD)

Diogenes of Sinope (412–322 BC)

Duns Scotus, John (c. 1260–1308)

Empedocles (c. 490–430 BC)

Engels, Friedrich (1820–95)

Epictetus (c. 60–110 AD)

Epicurus (341–270 BC)

Erigena, John Scotus (c. 800–c. 877 AD)

Eucken, Rudolf Christoph (1846–1926)

Euclid (c. 360–280 BC)

Euhemerus (4th century BC)

Feuerbach, Ludwig Andreas (1804–72)

Fichte, Johann Gottlieb (1762–1814)

Ficino, Marsilio (1433–99)

Foucault, Michel (1926–84)

Frege, Gottlob (1848–1925)

Gentile, Giovanni (1875–1944)

Geulincx, Arnold (1624–69)

Godwin, William (1756–1836)

Hampshire, Sir Stuart Newton (1914–)

Han fei zi (d. 233 BC)

Hare, Richard Mervyn (1919–)

Harrington, James (1611–77)

Hartmann, (Karl Robert) Eduard von (1842–1906)

Hartmann, Nicolai (1882–1950)

Hegel, Georg Wilhelm Friedrich (1770–1831)

Heidegger, Martin (1889–1976)

Helvétius, Claude Adrien (1715–71)

Heraclitus (c. 535–c. 475 BC)

Herbart, Johann Friedrich (1776–1841)

Herder, Johann Gottfried (1744–1803)

Hobbes, Thomas (1588–1679)

Hume, David (1711–76)

Husserl, Edmund (1859–1938)

Hutcheson, Francis (1694–1746)

Hypatia (d. 415 AD)

Ibn al-'Arabi, Muhyi-l-din (1165–1240)

Ibn Gabirol, Solomon (c. 1021–c. 1058)

Ibn Khaldūn, 'Abd al-Rahmān (1332–1406)

Illich, Ivan (1926–)

Iqbal, Sir Mohammed (?1875–1938)

Jaspers, Karl (Theodor) (1883–1969)

Judah ha-Levi (or Halevy; c. 1075–1141)

Kant, Immanuel (1724–1804)

Kenny, Anthony (1931–)

Keynes, John Neville (1852–1949)

Kierkegaard, Søren (1813–55)

Koffka, Kurt (1886–1941)

Kripke, Saul (1941–)

Kristeva, Julia (1941–)

Lacan, Jacques (1901–81)

Lao Zi (or Lao Tzu; ?6th century BC)

Leibnitz, Gottfried Wilhelm (1646–1716)

Leucippus (5th century BC)

Lewes, George Henry (1817–78)

Locke, John (1632–1704)

Lucretius (c. 95–55 BC)

Lukacs, Giorgi (1885–1971)

Lyotard, Jean François (1924–)

Maimonides, Moses (Mosheh ben Maymun; 1135–1204)

Malebranche, Nicolas (1638–1715)

Marcuse, Herbert (1898–1979)

Maritain, Jacques (1882–1973)
Marsilius of Padua (c. 1280–1342)
Marx, Karl (1818–83)
Mencius (Mengzi or Meng-tzu; 371–289 BC)
Mendelssohn, Moses (1729–86)
Merleau-Ponty, Maurice (1908–61)
Mill, James (1773–1836)
Mill, John Stuart (1806–73)
Montesquieu, Charles Louis de Secondat, Baron de (1689–1755)
Moore, G(eorge) E(dward) (1873–1958)
More, Henry (1614–87)
Murdoch, Dame (Jean) Iris (1919–)
Nagel, Ernest (1901–)
Nietzsche, Friedrich (1844–1900)
Ortega y Gasset, José (1883–1955)
Ouspensky, Peter (1878–1947)
Paine, Thomas (1737–1809)
Parmenides (c. 510–c. 450 BC)
Pascal, Blaise (1623–62)
Peirce, Charles Sanders (1839–1914)
Philo Judaeus (c. 30 BC–45 AD)
Pico della Mirandola, Giovanni, Conte (1463–94)
Plato (429–347 BC)
Plotinus (205–70 AD)

Popper, Sir Karl Raimund (1902–)
Porphyry (232–305 AD)
Posidonius of Apamea (c. 135–51 BC)
Proclus (410–85 AD)
Protagoras (c. 485–415 BC)
Proudhon, Pierre Joseph (1809–65)
Pyrrho (or Pyrrhon; c. 360–c. 270 BC)
Pythagoras (6th century BC)
Quine, Willard van Orman (1908–)
Ramanuja (11th century AD)
Ramus, Petrus (Pierre de la Ramée; 1515–72)
Reid, Thomas (1710–96)
Ricoeur, Paul (1913–)
Rorty, Richard (1931–)
Roscelin (died c. 1125)
Rousseau, Jean Jacques (1712–78)
Russell, Bertrand Arthur William, 3rd Earl (1872–1970)
Ryle, Gilbert (1900–76)
Saint-Simon, Claude Henri de Rouvroy, Comte de (1760–1825)
Samuel, Herbert Louis, 1st Viscount (1870–1963)
Sankara (8th century AD)
Santayana, George (1863–1952)

Sartre, Jean-Paul (1905–80)
Schelling, Friedrich (1775–1854)
Schiller, Johann Christoph Friedrich (1759–1805)
Schlegel, Friedrich von (1772–1829)
Schleiermacher, Friedrich Ernst Daniel (1768–1834)
Schlick, Moritz (1882–1936)
Schopenhauer, Arthur (1788–1860)
Schweitzer, Albert (1875–1965)
Seneca the Elder (Marcus Annaeus Seneca; 55 BC–41 AD)
Sextus Empiricus (2nd century AD)
Sidgwick, Henry (1838–1900)
Siger of Brabant (c. 1240–c. 1284)
Simplicius of Cilicia (4th century AD)
Smith, Adam (1723–90)
Socrates (c. 469–399 BC)
Soloviov, Vladimir Sergevich (1853–1900)
Sorel, Georges (1847–1922)
Spencer, Herbert (1820–1903)
Spengler, Oswald (1880–1936)
Spinoza, Benedict (or Baruch de S.; 1632–77)
Steiner, Rudolf (1861–1925)

Strawson, Sir Peter Frederick (1919–)
Suarez, Francisco de (1548–1617)
Swedenborg, Emanuel (1688–1772)
Taine, Hippolyte Adolphe (1828–93)
Tarski, Alfred (1902–83)
Teilhard de Chardin, Pierre (1881–1955)
Telesio, Bernardino (1509–88)
Thales (c. 624–547 BC)
Theaetetus (c. 414–369 BC)
Theophrastus (c. 370–286 BC)
Thoreau, Henry David (1817–62)
Unamuno y Jugo, Miguel de (1864–1936)
Valla, Lorenzo (1405–57)
Vico, Giambattista (or Giovanni Battista Vico; 1668–1744)
Vivés, Juan Luis (1492–1540)
Weil, Simone (1909–43)
Whitehead, A(lfred) N(orth) (1861–1947)
William of Ockham (c. 1285–1349)
Wittgenstein, Ludwig (1889–1951)
Wolff, Christian (1679–1754)
Xenophanes of Colophon (c. 570–475 BC)
Zeno of Elea (born c. 490 BC)
Zeno of Citium (c. 334–262 BC)

Pythagorean, Eleatic, Euclidian (or Euclidean), Protagorean, sophistical (or sophistic), euhemeristic, eudaemonistic (or eudaemonistical), Socratic, Democritean, Empedoclean, atomistic (or atomistical), stoic, Senecan, sceptical, Heraclitean, Cyrenaic, Cynic, epicurean, Lucretian, Pyrrhonist, peripatetic, Aristotelian, Averroist (or Averroistic), Thomist (or Thomistic or Thomistical), Augustinian, vitalist (or vitalistic), animistic, pantheistic (or pantheistical), deistic (or deistical), theistic (or theistical), dynamistic, mechanistic, essentialist, Bergsonian, agnostic, transcendentalist, idealistic, mystic (or mystical), Sufic, Confucian, Taoist (or Taoistic), Buddhist, naturalistic, empiricist, Berkelian, Baconian, rationalist, materialist (or materialistic), physicalist (or physicalistic), instrumentalist, conceptualistic, pluralist (or pluralistic), dualistic, monist (or mo-

nistic), Cartesian, compatibilist, phenomenalist, epiphenomenalist, functionalist, behaviourist (or behaviouristic), Kantian, Kierkegaardian, relativist, descriptivist, axiological, consequentialist, emotivist, utilitarian, Benthamite, Nietzschean, reductionist (or reductionistic), determinist (or deterministic), fatalistic, nihilist (or nihilistic), solipsist (or solipsistic), existentialist, subjectivistic, objectivist (or objectivistic), egoistic (or egoistical), hedonistic (or hedonic), altruistic, humanistic, utopian, collectivistic, socialist (or socialistic), communist, Marxist, syndicalist (or syndical or syndicalistic), anarchic, anarcho-syndicalist, nationalist (or nationalistic), pacifist, Hobbist (or Hobbesian), Keynesian, monetarist, capitalist, aesthetic, contextualist, isolationist, Hegelian, Leibnitzian, Schellingian, nominalist, individualistic, realist, anti-realist, quasi-

realist, Chomskyan (*or* Chomskyite), Fregean, positivist (*or* positivistic), Wittgensteinian

▶ *471 Idea, 7 Religion, 497 Belief, 13 Economics, 12 Government and Politics*

15 **rational**, reasoned, reasonable, philosophical, logical, objective, impartial, fair, unbiased, unprejudiced, sound, sensible, plausible, practical, pragmatic, down-to-earth, matter-of-fact, no-nonsense, common sensical, realistic, ratiocinative, clear-headed, lucid, well-thought-out, well-reasoned, judicious, discriminating

▶ *481 Discrimination, 459 Intellect, 492 Judgment, 463 Reason*

16 **dialectical**, deictic, cogent, analytic, apodeictic, aporetic, elenctic, a priori, a posteriori, a fortiori, synthetic, dyadic, monadic, polyadic, heuristic

17 **thoughtful**, attentive, studious, studying, concentrated, concentrating, thinking, meditative, cogitative, contemplative, reflective, in a brown study, ruminant, ruminative, deliberative, speculative, musing, pensive, absorbed, lost in thought, introspective, dreaming, brooding, preoccupied, wistful

▶ *459 Intellect, 471 Idea, 461 Thought, 518 Supposition, 786 Wonder*

18 **detached**, unaffected, unemotional, unperturbed, imperturbable, undisturbed, unruffled, unshaken, unconcerned, dispassionate, unimpassioned, cool, cool-headed, pragmatic, sober, calm, collected, composed, level-headed, equable, equanimous, tolerant, controlled, temperate, moderate, self-controlled, self-possessed, self-restrained, restrained, stoical, resigned, patient, enduring, steady, even-tempered, good-tempered, serene, tranquil, placid, pacific

▶ *873 Sobriety, 859 Disinterestedness, 643 Inactivity, 783 Indifference, 242 Moderation, 869 Self-Restraint*

19 **learned**, wise, academic, intellectual, erudite, educated, scholarly, bookish, highbrow, profound, deep, sagacious, intelligent, knowledgeable, expert, skilled, accomplished, informed, well-read, well-versed, lettered, literate, enlightened, cultured, brainy (Inf)

▶ *688 Authority, 277 Depth, 459 Intellect, 507 Wisdom*

VERBS

20 **philosophize**, think about, speculate, conjecture, postulate, suppose, hypothesize, surmise, consider, conceptualize, visualize, contemplate, cogitate, excogitate, ratiocinate, ruminate, reflect, deliberate, ponder, muse, wonder, challenge, analyse, examine, explore, look into, scrutinize, observe, survey, study, research, investigate, question, query, inquire (*or* enquire), ask, seek, search, soul-search, introspect, brood, dream, idealize, have visions

▶ *471 Idea, 459 Intellect, 463 Reason, 518 Supposition, 461 Thought*

21 **rationalize**, philosophize, reason, think through, think out, logicize, logicalize, syllogize, intellectualize, interpret, construe, deduce, infer, work out, evaluate, unscramble, solve, resolve, figure out, calculate, compute, answer, fathom, understand, apprehend, realize, comprehend, follow, grasp, take to mean, take it that, read, define, expound, explicate, explain, elucidate, unfold, clarify, spell out, account for, clear up, make clear, illuminate, demonstrate, show, illustrate, exemplify, justify, vindicate, show sufficient grounds for

▶ *492 Judgment, 478 Answer, 520 Meaning, 461 Thought, 518 Supposition*

22 **propound a philosophy**, state, assert, put forward, propose, expound, aphorize, set forth, pose, posit, lay down, profess, pronounce, moralize, preach, sermonize, declare, proclaim, show, exhibit, demonstrate, espouse a theory, support, maintain, assume, presume, premise, suppose, postulate, judge, feel, conclude, deem, consider, tend to, be disposed to, opine, be of the opinion, hold an opinion, believe in, subscribe to, adhere to, follow, belong to a school of thought, view, take the attitude, look at in the light of

▶ *463 Reason, 518 Supposition, 461 Thought, 497 Belief, 7 Religion, 475 Demonstration, 759 Feeling, 492 Judgment*

23 **discuss philosophically**, debate, exchange ideas, colloquize, engage in dialectic, analyse, comment on, criticize, argue, logomachize, polemicize, contend, contest, dispute, dissent, refute, answer, respond, negate, contradict, deny, put forward a counterargument

▶ *473 Argument, 492 Judgment, 477 Question, 474 Sophistry*

ADVERBS

24 **philosophically**, intellectually, logically, analytically, deductively, dialectically, sophistically, metaphysically, argumentatively, polemically, rhetorically, epistemologically, axiologically, ontologically, phenomenologically, semantically, categorically

25 **theoretically**, notionally, ideally, academically, conceptually, abstractly, in the abstract, esoterically, idealistically, ideologically, morally, ethically, moralistically, proverbially, purportedly, as they say, supposedly, reputedly, seemingly, speculatively, hypothetically, ex hypothesi, assumptively, presumingly, presumptively, on the assumption that

26 **rationally**, philosophically, objectively, impartially, without prejudice, without bias, fairly, reasonably, logically, realistically, pragmatically, practically, sensibly, plausibly, lucidly, soundly, justifiably

▶ *463 Reason*

27 **stoically**, philosophically, dispassionately, imperturbably, restrainedly, moderately, tem-

perately, soberly, coolly, calmly, composedly, unemotionally, equably, fairly, patiently, enduringly, resignedly, passively, quietly, serenely, placidly

▶ *783 Indifference, 242 Moderation*

28 **thoughtfully**, studiously, attentively, carefully, meditatively, ruminatively, cogitatingly, reflectively, contemplatively, deliberatively, introspectively, pensively, broodily, wistfully, dreamily

29 **wisely**, knowledgeably, expertly, authoritatively, advisably, advisedly, profoundly, deeply, inspirationally, inspiringly, discriminatingly, judiciously, judgmentally

▶ *459 Intellect, 507 Wisdom*

5   Linguistics

In the beginning was the Word, and the Word was with God, and the Word was God. Bible: John.

Word's are men's daughters; but God's sons are things. Samuel Madden.

I am always sorry when any language is lost, because languages are the pedigree of nations. Samuel Johnson.

Language is not simply a reporting device for experience but a defining framework for it. Benjamin Lee Whorf.

NOUNS

1 **linguistics**, linguistic science, science of language, linguistic analysis, linguistic geography, linguistic distribution, syntactics, phonetics, pronunciation, phonology, phonography, phonemics, orthoepy, morphophonemics, morphology, morphophonology, lexicology, lexicography, lexicostatistics, philology, comparative grammar, grammatology, etymology, derivation of words, folk etymology, semantics, semasiology, meaning, graphemics, general linguistics, applied linguistics, comparative linguistics, contrastive linguistics, descriptive linguistics, structural linguistics, linguistic structure, structuralism, psycholinguistics, geolinguistics, linguistic typology, dialectology, onomastics (*or* onomasiology), nomenclature, sociolinguistics, philosophical linguistics, computational (*or* mathematical) linguistics, stylistics, areal linguistics, anthropological linguistics, theoretical linguistics, historical linguistics, diachronic linguistics, synchronic linguistics, comparative historical linguistics, glottochronology, palaeography, palaeology, *sprachgefühl* (Ger), foreign-language study, bilingualism, multilingualism, polyglottism, glossology (Arch)

▶ *564 Speech, 520 Meaning, 541 Exaggeration, 534 Communications, 528 Information, 4 Philosophy*

2 **linguist**, linguistician, linguistic scholar, linguistic scientist, linguistic analyst, linguistic geographer, grammarian, phonetician, phonetist, phonemicist, phonologist, orthoepist, morphologist, lexicologist, dictionary compiler, lexicographer, etymologist, semanticist, semasiologist, philologist (*or* philologer), grammatologist, structuralist, psycholinguist, geolinguist, dialectician, dialectologist, onomasiologist, sociolinguist, epigrammatist, palaeographer, epigraphist, language student, foreign-language student, classicist, bilingual, multilingual, polyglot, translator, interpreter, clarifier, expositor, exegete, orthographer, neologist, word-coiner, logophile, phrasemonger, phrasemaker, author, writer, poet, proverbialist, nomenclator, terminologist, namer, namegiver, christener, baptizer, namechild, roll-caller, glossologist (Arch)

▶ *501 Knowledge, 48 Literature, 560 Description, 10 Ritual, 519 Imagination*

3 **spoken language**, tongue, speech, vocalism, talk, parlance, *lingua* (L), *langue* (Fr), *parole* (Fr), living language, natural language, informal language, informal speech, English as she is spoken, vernacular, vernacular language, vernacularism, phraseology, colloquialism, conversationalism, idiom, idiomatic speech, common speech, slang, jargon, argot, patois, vulgate, vulgar tongue, vulgarism

▶ *564 Speech, 827 Curse, 795 Vulgarity, 814 Informality*

4 **parent language**, native language, native tongue, mother tongue, national language, regional language, dialect, basic English, lingo (Inf)

5 **nonstandard language**, personal language, gesture, body language, signal, code, parole, patter, idiolect, idioglossia, childish language, baby talk, empty phrase, empty words, empty talk, substandard language, substandard usage, uneducated speech, illiterate speech, barbarism, corruption, gobbledegook (*or* gobbledygook), language of confusion, confusion of tongues, polyglot medley, glossolalia, non-verbal glossolalia, vocalise semiotics, Babel, babble, jabber, gibberish, rhubarb (Inf), psychobabble (Inf)

▶ *521 Lack of Meaning, 523 Unintelligibility, 506 Nonsense, 133 Mixture, 502 Ignorance*

6 **official language**, standard language, standard usage, Received Pronunciation (RP), Received Standard (US), Queen's (*or* King's) English, BBC English, Oxford English, correct speech, formal language, written language, literary language, legalese

▶ *813 Formality*

7 **international language**, diplomatic language, business language, trade language, lingua franca, koine, International Scientific Vo-

Languages and Groups of Languages

Abkhaz
Abnaki
Aborigine
Achinese
Adamawa
Adygei (or Adyghe)
Afghan (or Afghani)
African
Afrikaans
Afro-Asiatic
Ainu
Akan
Akkadian (or Accadian)
Albanian
Alemannic
Aleut
Algonquian (or Algon-
    kian)
Algonquin (or Algonkin)
Altaic
American
Amharic
Anatolian
Ancient Greek
Anglo-French
Anglo-Irish
Anglo-Norman
Anglo-Saxon
Annamese
Apache
Arabic
Aramaic
Aranda
Arapaho
Araucanian
Arawakan
Armenian
Aryan
Assamese
Assiniboine
Assyrian
Athapascan (or Atha-
    paskan or Athabas-
    can or Athabaskan)
Australian
Austro-Asiatic
Austronesian
Avar
Avestan (or Avestic)
Aymara
Azerbaijani
Aztec
Babylonian
Bahasa Indonesia
Balinese
Baltic
Baluchi (or Balochi)
Bambara
Bantu
Barotse
Bashkir
Basque
Batan
Battak
Beach-la-Mar (or
    bêche-de-mer)
Bemba
Bengali
Benue-Congo
Berber
Biblical Aramaic
Bihari
Bikol

Blackfoot
Bohemian
Bokmål
Brahui
Breton
British
Brythonic
Bugi
Bulgarian
Burmese (or Burman)
Buryat (or Buriat)
Bushman
Byelorussian (or
    Belorussian)
Caddoan
Canaanite
Canaanitic
Cantonese
Carib
Caroline
Castilian
Catalan
Catawba
Caucasian (or
    Caucasic)
Cayuga
Celtiberian
Celtic (or Keltic)
Chadic
Chaldee
Cham
Chamorro
Chari-Nile
Cheremiss (or
    Cheremis)
Cherokee
Chewa
Cheyenne
Chibchan
Chichewa
Chickasaw
Chin
Chinese
Chinook
Chinook Jargon
Choctaw
Chukchi (or Chukchee)
Chuvash
Circassian
Comanche
Coptic
Cornish
Cree
Creek
Crow
Cushitic
Cymric (or Kymric)
Czech
Czechoslovak
Dafia
Damara
Dani
Danish
Dardic
Delaware
Dinka
Divehi
Dravidian
Duala
Dutch
Dyak
Dyula
Dzongka

East Germanic
Edo
Edomite
Efik
Egyptian
Elamite
English
Erie
Eskimo
Estonian (or Esthon-
    ian)
Ethiopian
Ethiopic
Etruscan (or Etrurian)
Evenki
Ewe
Faeroese (or Faroese)
Faliscan
Fang
Fanti
Farsi
Fijian
Finnic
Finnish
Finno-Tartar
Finno-Ugric (or Finno-
    Ugrian)
Flemish
Formosan
Fox
Franconian
Frankish
French
Frisian (or Friesian)
Friulian
Fula (or Fulah)
Fulani
Ga (or Gã)
Gadaba
Gaelic
Gagauzi
Galcha
Galibi
Galician
Galla
Gallo-Romance (or
    Gallo-Roman)
Ganda
Garo
Gaulish
Ge'ez
Georgian
German
Germanic
Gilbertese
Goidelic (or Goidhelic
    or Gadhelic)
Gondi
Gothic
Greek
Griqua (or Grikwa)
Guarani
Gujarati (or Gujerati)
Gur
Gurindji
Gurkhali
Gypsy
Haida
Haitian (or Haytian)
Hamitic
Hamito-Semitic
Hausa
Hawaiian

Hebrew
Hellenic
Herero
High German
Himyaritic
Hindi
Hindustani (or
    Hindoostani or Hin-
    dostani)
Hiri Motu
Hittite
Ho
Hopi
Hottentot
Hun
Hungarian
Huron
Hutu
Ibanag
Ibibio
Ibo (or Igbo)
Icelandic
Ido
Igorot
Illyrian
Ilokano
Inca
Indian
Indic
Indo-Chinese
Indo-European
Indo-Germanic
Indo-Hittite
Indo-Iranian
Indonesian
Indo-Pacific
Ingush
interlingua
Inuktitut
Iranian
Irish
Irish Gaelic
Iroquoian
Iroquois
Italian
Italic
Japanese
Javanese
Kabardian
Kaffir (or Kafir)
Kalmuck (or Kalmyk)
Kamasin
kamilaroi
Kanarese (or Canarese)
Kannada
Kara-Kalpak
Karelian
Karen
Kashmiri
Kasubian
Kavi
Kazakh (or Kazak)
Khalkha
Khasi
Khmer
Khoisan
Khond
Kikuyu
Kingwana
Kirghiz (or Kirgiz)
Kirundi
Kodagu
Koibal

Komi
Kongo
Kordofanian
Korean
Korwa
Krio
Kriol
Kuki
Kurdish
Kurukh
Kwa
Kwakiutl
Ladino
Lahnda
Lampong
Lamut
Langobardic
Lao (or Laotian)
Lapp
Late Greek
Latin
Latvian
Lepcha
Lettish
Libyan
Lithuanian
Livonian
Low German
Lozi
Luba
Luganda
Luo
Lusatian
Lycian
Lydian
Macedonian
Madurese
Magyar
Mahican (or Mohican)
Mahon
Makassar
Malagasy
Malay
Malayalam (or
   Malayalaam)
Malayo-Javanese
Malayo-Polynesian
Malinke (or Maninke)
Maltese
Manchu
Mandarin Chinese (or
   Mandarin)
Mande
Manobo
Manx
Maori
Marathi (or Mahratti)
Masai
Massachuset (or Mas-
   sachusetts)
Matabele
Maya
Mayan
Medieval Greek
Medieval Latin
Melanesian
Melano-Papuan
Menomini (or Me-
   nominee)
Messapian (or
   Messapic)
Micmac
Micronesian
Middle Dutch
Middle English

Middle High German
Middle Low German
Mingrelian
Mishmi
Misima
Mixtec
Modern English
Modern Greek
Modern Hebrew
Mohave (or Mojave)
Mohawk
Mon
Mongol
Mongolic
Mon-Khmer
Mordvin
Moriori
Moro
Mossi
Motu
Mru
Munda
Muong
Murmi
Muskogean (or Mus-
   khogean)
Na-Dene (or Na-Déné)
Naga
Nahuatl
Nama (or Namaqua)
Narraganset (or Nar-
   ragansett)
Navaho (or Navajo)
Ndebele
Negrito
Neo-Latin
Neo-Melanesian
Nepali
Newara
Nez Percé
Nguni
Niasese
Nicobarese
Niger-Congo
Nilo-Saharan
Nilotic
Niue
Nogai
Nootka
Norn
Norse
Northern Sotho
North Germanic
Norwegian
Nuba
Nupe
Nuri
Nyanja
Nyoro
Oceanic
Ojibwa
Okanagan
Old Church Slavonic
   (or Slavic)
Old Dutch
Old English
Old French
Old Frisian
Old High German
Old Icelandic
Old Irish
Old Latin
Old Norse
Old Persian
Old Prussian

Old Slavonic (or Slavic)
Oneida
Onondaga
Oraon
Oriya
Osage
Oscan
Osco-Umbrian
Osmanli
Ossetic (or Ossetian)
Ostyak
Ottoman (or Othman)
Ovambo
Pahari
Pahlavi (or Pehlevi)
Paiute (or Piute)
Palau
Palaung
Pali
Pama-Nyungan
Pampango
Pangasinan
Papuan
Pashto (or Pushto or
   Pushtu)
Pawnee
Pekingese (or Pekinese)
Penutian
Pequot
Permian
Persian
Phoenician
Phrygian
Pictish
Pintubi
Pitjantjatjara (or
   Pitjantjara)
Police Motu
Polish
Polynesian
Pondo
Portuguese
Prakrit
Proto-Germanic
Proto-Indo-European
Proto-Norse
Protosemitic
Provençal
Punic
Punjabi (or Panjabi)
Quechua (or Kechua
   or Quichua)
Rabbinic (or Rabbini-
   cal) Hebrew
Rajasthani
Rejang
Rhaeto-Romanic
Rhaetian
Riksmål
Romaic
Romance
Romanes
Romanian (or Ruman-
   ian or Roumanian)
Romansch (or Romansh)
Romany (or Romani)
Ronga
Russian
Rwanda
Sabaean (or Sabean)
Sabellian
Sabine
Sahaptin (or Sahaptan
   or Sahaptian)
Saharan

Sakai
Salish (or Salishan)
Samoan
Samoyed
San
Sango
Sanskrit
Sanskritic
Santali
Sardinian
Sassak
Savara
Scandinavian
Scottish
Scottish Gaelic
Scythian
Semang
Semi-Bantu
Seminole
Semite
Semitic (or Shemitic)
Semito-Hamitic
Seneca
Serbo-Croat (or Serbo-
   Croatian)
Sesotho
Shan
Shawnee
Shelta
Shilha
Shina
Shona
Shoshone (or Sho-
   shoni)
Siamese
Sindhi
Sinhalese (or Singha-
   lese)
Sinitic
Sino-Tibetan
Siouan
Sioux
Slavonic, Slavic (US)
Slovak
Slovene
Sogdian
Somali
Songhai
Sorbian
Sotho
Southron
Soyot
Spanish
Sudanic
Sumerian
Susu
Swahili
Swazi
Swedish
Syriac
Tadzhiki
Tagalog
Tagula
Tahitian
Tahltan
Taino
Tamashek
Tamil
Tatar (or Tartar)
Tavghi
Teleut
Telugu (or Telegu)
Temne
Teutonic
Thai

Thracian
Thraco-Phrygian
Tibetan
Tibeto-Burman
Tigré
Tigrinya
Tino
Tipura
Tiv
Tlingit
Tocharian (or Tokharian)
Toda
Tokelau
Tonga
Tongan
Trans-New Guinea phylum
Tshiluba
Tsonga

Tswana
Tuamotuan
Tulu
Tungus
Tungusic
Tupi
Tupi-Guarani
Turanian
Turkic
Turkish
Turkmen
Turkoman (or Turkman)
Tuscarora
Twi
Ugaritic
Ugric
Uigur (or Uighur)
Ukrainian
Umbrian

Ural-Altaic
Uralic (or Uralian)
Urdu
Ute
Uto-Aztecan
Uzbek
Vedic
Venda
Venetic
Veps
Vietnamese
Visayan
Vogul
Volapuk (or Volapük)
Volscian
Voltaic
Vote
Votyak
Wa
Wakashan

Warlpiri
Welsh
Wendish
West Atlantic
West Germanic
Winnebago
Wolof
Xhosa
Yakut
Yenisei
Yiddish
Yoruba
Yuman
Yurak
Zapotec
Zenaga
Zulu
Zuñi
Zyrian

cabulary, Esperanto, metalanguage

8 **artificial language**, sign language, semaphore, Morse code, computer language, machine code, data processing language, assembly language
▶ *543 Sign, 65 Computers*

9 **ancient language**, classical language, dead language, lost language, archaism, archaic speech, Wardour Street English
▶ *3 History*

10 **language type**, inflected language, affixing language, analytic language, agglutinative language, polysynthetic language, monosyllabic language, polysyllabic language, symbolic language, tonal language, polytonic language, pidgin, creole

11 **family of languages**, language group, Proto-Indo-European, Indo-European, Indo-Germanic, Germanic, Teutonic, Anatolian, Anatolic, Aryan, Scandinavian, Celtic, Hellenic, Italic, Romance (*or* Romantic), Baltic, Slavonic, Balto-Slavic, Austric, Turkic, Indo-Iranian, Armenian, Tocharian, Turanian, Ural-Altaic, Finno-Ugric (*or* Finno-Ugrian), African, Afro-Asiatic, Paleo-Asiatic, Bushman, Bantu, Zulu-Kaffir, Fijian, Malay, Micronesian, Melanesian, Hamitic, Semitic, Hamito-Semitic, Assam-Burmese, Chinese-Siamese, Sino-Tibetan, Mongolic, Manchu, Dravidian, Austronesian, Malayo-Polynesian, Sabellian, Carib, Tagula, Tarapon, Uralian ndi

12 **translation**, rendering, literal translation, word-for-word translation, verbal translation, faithful translation, free translation, loose translation, paraphrase, rewording, restatement, edition, redaction, transliteration, abridgment, epitome, exegesis, Biblical interpretation, science of interpretation, hermeneutics, exegetics, epigraphy, palaeography, decipherment, decoding
▶ *524 Interpretation, 7 Religion*

13 **letter**, written letter, writing, lexigraphy, lettering, print, type, symbol, character, written character, grapheme, grammatic character, digraph, sign, ideogram, ideograph, pictogram, pictograph, cuneiform, hieroglyph, Chinese character, Pinyin, Kanji, syllabic script, Devanagari, Nagari, rune, wen, initial, monogram, anagram, anagrammatism, acronym, acrostic
▶ *543 Sign, 528 Information*

14 **alphabet**, ABC, Roman alphabet, Cyrillic alphabet, Hebrew alphabet, Arabic alphabet, Cherokee alphabet, Greek alphabet, runic alphabet, runic letter, ogham (*or* ogam) alphabet, phonetic alphabet, phonetic symbol, futhark (*or* futharc), initial teaching alphabet (i.t.a. *or* ITA), International Phonetic Alphabet (IPA), syllabary

15 **type style**, face (*or* typeface), font, fount, bold type, italic type, sans serif type, cursive type, Gothic type, Old English type, Garamond type, Caslon type, big letter, capital letter, capital, cap., upper-case letter, majuscule, uncial, small letter, lower-case letter, minuscule

16 **spoken letter**, speech sound, phone, phonogram, phoneme, grapheme, syllable, vowel, consonant, voiced consonant, gutteral consonant, guttural, nasal, frictionless continuant, labial, labiodental, labionasal, liquid, spirant, sibilant, aspirate, glottal stop, fricative, sonant, polyphone, digraph, diphthong, stress, pitch, inflection (*or* inflexion)
▶ *564 Speech, 554 Emphasis*

17 **word**, written unit, spoken unit, *verbum* (L), Logos, term, name, meaning, glosseme, sememe (*or* semanteme), synonym, cognate word, cognate, paronym, metonym, antonym, homonym, homograph, homophone, tautonym, doublet, palindrome, root, etymon, false root, word form, back formation, clipped word,

morphological unit, morpheme, stem, enclitic, pejorative, intensive, long word, polysyllable, sesquipedalian, short word, monosyllable, one-syllable word, easy word, new word, new term, neologism (*or* neology), coinage, unfamiliar word, newfangled expression, nonce word, loan word, borrowed word, imported word, loan translation, calque, hybrid expression, hybrid, ghost word, rhyming word, echoic word, onomatopoeic word, hard word, difficult word, jawbreaker (Inf)
▶ *560 Description, 660 Easiness, 659 Difficulty, 201 Newness, 119 Originality, 543 Sign, 804 Title, 599 Use*

18 **slang**, slang term, slang word, back slang, rhyming slang, cockney rhyming slang, dog Latin, pig Latin

19 **swearword**, taboo word, naughty word, bad word, rude word, vulgarism, vulgar language, low language, obscene language, coprolalia, billingsgate, scatology, expletive, four-letter word, the f-word, Anglo-Saxon (Inf)
▶ *827 Curse, 795 Vulgarity*

20 **jargon word**, jargon, Pentagonese (US), officialese, legalese, journalese, newspeak, telegraphese, technical word, technical term, technospeak, argot, cant, patter, lingo (Inf), technobabble (Inf), psychobabble (Inf)

21 **catchword**, portmanteau word, counterword, jingo, cliché, vogue word, catchphrase, well-worn phrase, commonplace saying, hackneyed expression, maxim, adage, moral, proverb, Biblical proverb, quotation, quote (Inf), slogan, motto, buzz word (Inf)
▶ *505 Maxim, 796 Fashion*

22 **many words**, pleonasm, wordiness, verbiage, stock of words, verbosity, loquacity, equivocalness, double talk, tautology
▶ *565 Talkativeness, 578 Equivocation, 474 Sophistry*

23 **phrase**, noun phrase (*or* clause), verb phrase (*or* clause), adverbial phrase (*or* clause), adjectival phrase (*or* clause), prepositional phrase (*or* clause), conditional phrase (*or* clause), indirect question, indirect speech, reported speech, subject and predicate, protasis, apodasis, clause, sentence, collocation, frozen collocation, formula

24 **phrasing**, phraseology, choice of words, wording, surface structure, deep structure, rounded phrase, turn of phrase, well-turned phrase, choice of expression, turn of expression, fixed expression, set phrase, set terms, verbalism, locution, trope, metaphor, complimentary phrase, compliments, elegant phrase, elegance, roundabout phrase, circumlocution, periphrasis, diffuseness, paraphrase, translation, phraseogram, phrasegraph
▶ *48 Literature, 558 Elegance, 313 Circularity*

25 **inscription**, lapidary inscription, epitaph, obsequies, legend, corollary
▶ *50 Painting and Sculpture, 562 Summary, 399 Burial*

26 **dialect**, idiom, patois, regional pronunciation, local pronunciation, speech community, argot, isogloss, isophone, isolex, localism, regionism, provincialism, vernacularism, vernacular language, accent, guttural accent, clipped accent, brogue, broagh, burr, Africanism, Americanism, American accent, Southern accent, Boston accent, Brooklyn accent, Midwest accent, New England dialect, Cajun dialect, Texas accent, Mid-Atlantic accent, Briticism, Anglicism, British accent, Geordie dialect, Yorkshire accent, Birmingham (*or* Brummie) accent, Oxford accent, Cornish accent, Welsh accent, Scottish accent, Lallans (*or* Lallan), Scotticism, cockney accent, rhyming slang, Irishism, Hibernicism, Irish accent, Teutonism, Gallicism, French-Canadian dialect, dialectology, hybrid language, broken English, pidgin English, Estuary English, lingua franca, Strine, Franglais
▶ *133 Mixture*

27 **spelling**, orthography, orthographic convention, spelling bee, spelling game, spelling pronunciation, phonetic spelling, incorrect spelling, misspelling, cacography
▶ *843 Right, 166 Rule, 504 Error*

28 **dictionary**, lexicon, wordbook, general dictionary, unabridged dictionary, children's dictionary, illustrated dictionary, school dictionary, college dictionary, learner's dictionary, monolingual dictionary, foreign language dictionary, bilingual dictionary, multilingual dictionary, polyglot dictionary, concise dictionary, compact dictionary, desk dictionary, biographical dictionary, dictionary of (proper) names, dictionary of quotations, dictionary of slang, dictionary of dialects, rhyming dictionary, reverse word dictionary, Dr Johnson's Dictionary, *Oxford English Dictionary*, *Webster's Dictionary*, glossary, gloss, gradus, concordance, synonym dictionary, thesaurus, *Roget's Thesaurus, Bloomsbury Thesaurus*, lexicography, storehouse of words, treasury of words
▶ *532 Publication*

29 **grammar**, good grammar, good English, Standard English, correct English, correct style, grammatical rules, grammaticalness, formal language, formal usage, school grammar, structural linguistics, traditional grammar, descriptive grammar, structural grammar, surface structure, shallow structure, deep structure, underlying structure, systemic grammar, case grammar, phrase-structure grammar, transformational grammar, transformation-generative grammar, bad grammar, incorrect

usage, solecism, malapropism, spoonerism, faulty syntax

▶ *504 Error, 844 Wrong*

30 **syntax**, word order, syntactic structure, syntactic meaning, syntactic analysis, immediate constituent (IC) analysis, agreement, number, gender, case, inflection, declension, conjugation, paradigm, mood, voice, tense, comparative grammar, philology, grammatical studies, grammatical analysis, parsing, construing, punctuation, accentuation, gradation, attraction, assimilation, dissimilation, conjunction, conjunction-reduction, hypotaxis, parataxis, syndeton, asyndeton, ellipsis, apposition

▶ *549 Style, 382 Structure, 503 Accuracy*

31 **case**, nominative, vocative, accusative, genitive, dative, ablative, locative

32 **voice**, active, middle, passive

33 **mood**, indicative, subjunctive, optative, imperative, jussive, infinitive

34 **tense**, present, future, future perfect, perfect, aorist, imperfect, pluperfect, conditional, historic present, past historic

35 **part of speech**, noun, common noun, proper noun, collective noun, substantive, pronoun, adjective, verb, predicate, reflexive verb, transitive verb, intransitive verb, participle, present participle, past participle, perfect participle, ablative absolute, adverb, preposition, copula, conjunction, subordinating conjunction, coordinate conjunction, interjection, subject, object, direct object, indirect object, complement, modifier, article, definite article, indefinite article, particle, affix, prefix, infix, suffix, inflection (*or* inflexion), formative, morpheme, semanteme, diminutive, intensive, augmentative, root, etymon, stem

▶ *477 Question, 166 Rule*

36 **accent**, diacritical work, umlaut, diaeresis, ablaut, grave, acute, circumflex, breve, cedilla, macron, tilde, *háček*, ogonek, caron, alif, hamzah, horn, rude, ayn, apostrophe

37 **linguistic theory**, Grimm's law, Verner's law, bow-wow theory, ding-dong theory, pooh-pooh theory, Sapir-Whorf hypothesis, Great Vowel Shift

ADJECTIVES

38 **linguistic**, lingual, grammatical, comparative, descriptive, structural, analytic(al), syntactic(al), phonetic, pronounced, phonological, phonemic, orthoepic, orthographic, morphophonemic, morphologic(al), diachronic, synchronic, Vernerian, lexicological, lexicographic(al), etymological, derivative, semantic, semasiological, glottological, glottochronological, lexicostatistical, philological, psycholingustic, geolinguistic, dialectological, onomastic, onomasiological, sociolinguistic, palaeographic(al), palaeological, bilingual, multilingual, polyglot, glossological (Arch)

39 **of language**, written, spoken, living, parent, native, mother, national, regional, Queen's (*or* King's), educated, pure, correct, standard, official, formal, literary, politically correct, informal, common, vernacular, colloquial, conversational, childish, holophrastic, personal, dialectal, guttural, burring, slang, slangy, jargonistic, jargonal, jargonish, journalistic, jingoistic, everyday, idiomatic, low, rude, vulgar, scatological, blasphemous, four-letter, obscene, nonstandard, substandard, uneducated, illiterate, ancient, classical, artificial, inflected, affixing, analytic, agglutinative, polysynthetic, monosyllabic, polysyllabic, symbolic, tonal, polytonic

40 **translated**, translating, rendering, literal, word-for-word, verbal, faithful, free, loose, paraphrased, paraphrasing, reworded, rewording, restated, restating, transliterated, abridged, edited, redacted, hermeneutic(al), exegetic(al), epigraphic(al), ciphered, deciphered, decoded, decoding

41 **lettered**, lettering, lexicographical, literal, graphic(al), printed, typed, symbolic(al), alphabetic(al), syllabic, Roman, Cyrillic, Arabic, Greek, runic, ogham (*or* ogam), phonogramic, phonographic, pictographic, ideographic, cuneiform, cuneal, hieroglyphic(al), large-lettered, capital, upper-case, majuscule, uncial, small-lettered, lower-case, minuscule, bold, italic, sans serif, cursive, Gothic, Old English, initial, monogrammatic(al), anagrammatic(al), acronymic, acronymous, acrostic, voiced, vocal, vocalic, consonantal, guttural, frictionless, liquid, labial, nasal, spirant, sibilant, fricative, sonant, polyphonic, polyphonous, digraphic

42 **worded**, wording, verbal, vocabular, lexical, glossarial, named, synonymic(al), cognate, paronymic (*or* paronymous), antonymous, homonymic (*or* homonymous), homographic, homophonic, tautonymic (*or* tautonymous), palindromic, root, back-formed, clipped, morphological, inflectional (*or* inflexional), meaningful, enclitic, pejorative, intensive, sesquipedalian, neologistic(al) (*or* neological), newfangled, (newly) coined, rhyming, echoic, onomatopoeic, argotic, canting, cant, portmanteau, cliché, clichéd, proverbial, commonplace, well-worn, hackneyed, redundant, vogue, pleonastic, wordy, verbose, loquacious, equivocal, pretentious, archaic, obsolete, barbarous (*or* barbaric), corrupted, cacographic(al)

43 **phrasal**, phrased, phrasing, phraseological, clausal, sentential, collocated, collocating, surface, deep, rounded, well-turned, well-rounded, fixed, set, locutionary, metaphoric(al), complimentary, elegant, roundabout, circumlocutory, periphrastic, diffuse,

paraphrastic, paraphrased, paraphrasing, translated, translating, translatable, phraseographic, inscribed, lapidary, epitaphic

44 **grammatical**, structural, descriptive, systemic, transformational, transformational-generative, syntactic, diacritical, substantive, pronominal, adjectival, verbal, predicate, copular, reflexive, transitive, intransitive, regular, irregular, heteroclite (or heteroclitic), participial, adverbial, prepositional, conjunctive, subordinating, coordinate, interjectional (or interjectory), objective, subjective, direct, indirect, complementary, modifying, definite, indefinite, inflectional (or inflexional), inflected, formative, morphemeic, diminutive, intensive, attributive, augmentative, comparative, superlative, masculine, feminine, neuter, singular, plural

VERBS

45 **use language**, communicate, write, speak, pronounce, utter, talk, state, verbalize, vocalize, voice, articulate, have the feel of a language, have a sense of idiom, turn a sentence, rhyme, phrase, express, formulate, anagrammatize, neologize, coin a word, colloquialize, vernacularize, jargonize, cant, patter, swear, blaspheme, curse

▶ 564 Speech, 48 Literature, 532 Publication

46 **translate**, interpret, make a word-for-word translation, give a loose translation, paraphrase, reword, restate, abridge, edit, redact, decipher, decode, transliterate, transcribe, read, gloss

47 **word**, put into words, find words for, verbalize, define, syllabify, syllable, alphabetize, reword, rewrite, rephrase, letter, form letters, carve letters, initial, inscribe, mark, sign, spell, spell out, misspell

ADVERBS

48 **linguistically**, grammatically, comparatively, descriptively, structurally, analytically, syntactically, orthographically, lexicographically, etymologically, semantically, philologically, bilingually, multilingually, literarily, literally, word-for-word, letter-for-letter, verbatim, hermeneutically, exegetically, epigraphically, graphically, alphabetically, hieroglyphically, symbolically, monosyllabically, polysyllabically, anagrammatically, vocally, polyphonically, polyphonously, tonally, phonetically

49 **colloquially**, verbally, conversationally, informally, journalistically, idiomatically, obscenely, blasphemously, scatologically, illiterately

50 **lexically**, glossarially, morphologically, inflectionally (or inflexionally), meaningfully, pejoratively, intensively, pleonastically, wordily, verbosely, loquaciously, equivocally, pretentiously, neologistically (or neologically), archaically, obsoletely

51 **phraseologically**, in set phrases, in set terms, in round terms, in sentences, metaphorically, proverbially, obsequiously, elegantly, periphrastically

52 **grammatically**, syntactically, correctly, formally, descriptively, transitively, intransitively, regularly, irregularly, adverbially, prepositionally, conjunctively, subjunctively, objectively, subjectively, directly, indirectly, morphemically, attributively, comparatively, superlatively, singularly, plurally

6　Education

Education is simply the soul of a society as it passes from one generation to another. G. K. Chesterton.

Education made us what we are. Claude-Adrien Helvéticus.

And seek for truth in the groves of Academe. Horace.

He who can does. He who cannot, teaches. George Bernard Shaw.

NOUNS

1 **education**, teaching, schooling, pedagogy, tuition, coaching, guidance, catechization, private tuition, tutoring, tutelage, training, instruction, drilling, indoctrination, guidance, preparation, advice, illumination, enlightenment, edification, betterment, progress, amelioration, melioration, advancement, acculturation, cultivation, civilization, rearing, raising, upbringing, nurture

▶ 654 Advice, 627 Improvement, 361 Raising, 594 Preparation

2 **educational system**, nursery education, pre-school education, primary education, Froebel system, Montessori system, secondary education, tertiary education, higher education, adult education, moral education, liberal education, remedial education, vocational training, job training, employment training, on-the-job training, in-service training, sandwich course, self-education, home learning, correspondence course, distance learning, autodidactics, recreational education, Open University, teacher training

3 **subject**, discipline, field, area, speciality, province, domain, branch, realm, sphere, department, faculty, curriculum, syllabus, course, module, timetable, core curriculum, National Curriculum, science subject, technical subject, language, humanities, arts, general studies, civics, RE (religious education), RI (religious instruction), PE (physical education), PT (physical training), sex education, interdisciplinary education

▶ 485 Qualification

4 **educator**, teacher, head teacher, headmaster, headmistress, principal, chancellor, vice chancellor, dean, don, professor, professor emeritus, doctor, lecturer, fellow, intern, reader, academic, preceptor, preceptress, tutor, instructor, governess, duenna, dominie (Scot), schoolman, school teacher, schoolmistress, schoolmaster, master, mistress, form teacher, student teacher, supply teacher, home tutor, private tutor, crammer, pedagogue, coach, trainer, mentor, adviser, authority, expert, pundit (*or* pandit), guru, mullah, maestro, docent (US), preacher, homilist

▶ *688 Authority, 696 Master, 507 Wisdom*

5 **educationalist**, educationist, educational psychologist, Educational Welfare Officer, School Attendance Officer, truancy officer, governor, board of governors, governing body, school board

6 **instructorship**, schoolmastery, tutorship, tutorage, tutelage, chair, professorship, professorhood, professorate, readership, lectureship, fellowship, research fellowship, staff, faculty

▶ *696 Master, 688 Authority*

7 **learner**, student, pupil, trainee, apprentice, novice, tiro (*or* tyro), beginner, rookie (Inf), recruit, initiate, neophyte, abecedarian, schoolboy, schoolgirl, classmate, sixth-former, freshman (*or* fresher), sophomore (US), undergraduate, undergrad (Inf), fellow student, tutorial partner, scholar, researcher, postgraduate, alumnus, alumna, autodidact, swot (Inf), bluestocking (Inf), bookworm (Inf), egghead (Inf)

▶ *156 Beginning, 459 Intellect, 201 Newness, 819 Friendship*

8 **learning**, study, acquisition of knowledge, scholarship, storing (*or* stocking) the mind, broadening the mind, absorption, contemplation, perusal, review, reading, brainwork (Inf), conning (Inf), cramming (Inf), swotting (Inf)

▶ *459 Intellect, 501 Knowledge, 461 Thought*

9 **learnedness**, studiousness, scholarliness, scholarship, intellectuality, literacy, bookishness, polymathy, erudition, savvy (Inf), nous (Inf)

10 **educability**, educatability, aptitude, aptness, quickness, cleverness, intelligence, brightness, readiness, willingness to learn, teachability, motivation, receptivity, curiosity, inquisitiveness, susceptibility, malleability, pliability, docility

▶ *465 Curiosity, 459 Intellect, 228 Motive, 572 Willingness*

11 **refinement**, education, taste, discernment, connoisseurship, discrimination, judgment, perception, perceptiveness, insight, acumen, sensitivity, sensibility, cultivation, sophistication, urbanity, suavity, elegance, breeding, background, savoir-faire

▶ *481 Discrimination, 558 Elegance, 459 Intellect, 464 Intuition, 492 Judgment, 794 Refinement, 760 Sensitivity, 380 Sharpness, 411 Taste*

12 **educational institution**, school, *école* (Fr), *scuola* (It), *Schule* (Ger), *escuela* (Sp), kindergarten, play school, playgroup, pre-school playgroup, crèche, nursery school, day nursery, day-care centre, first school, primary school, infant school, grade school (US), middle school, preparatory school, prep school, junior school, secondary school, junior high (US), high school, senior high (US), *lycée* (Fr), lyceum, day school, boarding school, public school, private school, independent school, grant-maintained school, state school, comprehensive school, single-sex school, denominational school, special school, open-classroom school, summer school, night school, college, community college, sixth-form college, further education college, adult-education centre, institute, academy, seminary, finishing school, conservatory, choir school, schola cantorum, music school, ballet school, art college, drama college, riding school, military academy, officer-training school, graduate school, law school, medical school, library school, design school, film school, business school, secretarial college, Bible school, Sunday school, convent school, Talmud Torah, yeshiva, mesivta

13 **university**, polytechnic, college, redbrick university, Oxbridge, Ivy League (US), *Ecole Normale Supérieure* (Fr)

▶ *163 Class, 7 Religion*

14 **school book**, textbook, grammar, grammar book, dictionary, lexicon, encyclopaedia, thesaurus, atlas, primer, abecedarium, crib, answer book, reader, notebook, copybook, exercise book, workbook, rough book, scratchpad (US), manual, handbook, database, literature, publication, examination paper, bibliography, prep book (Inf)

▶ *528 Information, 532 Publication*

15 **schoolroom**, classroom, formroom, staffroom, hall, lecture hall, assembly hall, auditorium, library, laboratory, language laboratory, workshop, music room, art room, dining room, common room, playground, schoolyard (US), gymnasium, sports field, playing field, sickroom, sanatorium, dormitory, hall of residence, fraternity house (US), sorority house (US), campus, schoolhouse

▶ *163 Class, 306 Form*

ADJECTIVES

16 **educational**, educatory, educative, instructive, instructional, informative, informational, revealing, illuminating, enlightening, edifying, improving, remedial, bettering, progressive, revelatory, eye-opening, communicative, helpful, guiding, advisory, authoritative, expert, academic, scholastic, pedagogical, preachy, schoolmarmish

▶ *528 Information, 627 Improvement, 534 Communications, 688 Authority, 507 Wisdom*

17 educable, educatable, teachable, trainable, schoolable, instructable, bright, clever, intelligent, quick, autodidactic, self-taught, apt, willing, motivated, ready, receptive, hungry (*or* thirsty) for knowledge, curious, inquisitive, susceptible, impressionable, malleable, pliable, docile, ESN (educationally subnormal)

▶ *465 Curiosity, 228 Motive, 477 Question, 694 Obedience, 572 Willingness*

18 educated, learned, erudite, literate, literary, numerate, well-read, academic, highbrow, intellectual, sagacious, wise, scholarly, scholastic, gnostic, book-wise, bookish, bibliophagic, polymathic, studious, absorbed, contemplative, clever, brainy, swotty (Inf)

▶ *528 Information, 459 Intellect, 501 Knowledge, 696 Master, 507 Wisdom, 461 Thought*

19 knowledgeable, educated, versed, well-versed, trained, well-trained, grounded, well-grounded, coached, guided, primed, briefed, cognizant, familiar, in the know, conversant with, *au fait* (Fr), at home with, strong in, experienced, practised, accomplished, qualified, skilled, skilful, enlightened, in touch, up to date, *au courant* (Fr), with it (Inf), hip (Inf), genned up (Inf), clued-up (Inf), sussed (Inf), street wise (Inf)

▶ *528 Information, 459 Intellect, 501 Knowledge, 594 Preparation, 655 Skill, 461 Thought, 507 Wisdom*

20 refined, educated, cultivated, cultured, civilized, discerning, critical, sensitive, sensible, discriminating, judicious, perceptive, insightful, shrewd, astute, sharp, polished, sophisticated, elegant, urbane, suave, soigné (*or* soignée), tasteful, advanced, nurtured, reared, raised, well-bred

▶ *481 Discrimination, 558 Elegance, 794 Refinement, 760 Sensitivity, 492 Judgment, 380 Sharpness, 411 Taste*

21 curricular, intramural, extramural, extracurricular, doctoral, graduate, postgraduate, collegiate, varsity, sixth-form, canonical, doctrinal, specialized, technical, classical, liberal

VERBS

22 educate, teach, tutor, train, instruct, school, coach, drill, discipline, indoctrinate, instil, inculcate, make ready, prepare, equip, brief, prime, ground, verse, acquaint, inform, tell, apprise, notify, impart, disclose, divulge, reveal, report, communicate, tip off, guide, advise, illuminate, enlighten, improve, further promote, develop, cultivate, civilize, refine, advance, encourage, mould, shape, form, foster, nurture, rear, raise, bring up

▶ *654 Advice, 534 Communications, 528 Information, 501 Knowledge, 594 Preparation, 361 Raising, 564 Speech*

23 learn, study, attend classes, go to school, take lessons, train, go into training, take part in a training scheme, serve an apprenticeship, be taught, be instructed, acquire knowledge, discover, research, find out, ascertain, become aware of, contemplate, broaden the mind, store (*or* stock) the mind, peruse, read, major (*or* minor) in, read up on, brush up, polish up, rub up, study up on, bone up (Inf), cram (Inf), con (Inf), swot (Inf)

▶ *465 Curiosity, 496 Discovery, 528 Information, 501 Knowledge, 511 Memory*

24 know, be informed, be up on, be grounded in, know by heart, know like a book, know backwards, know inside out, know the ropes, know the score, know what's what, know like the back of one's hand, command, master, get the hang of, be proficient in, understand, perceive, sense, judge, discern, discriminate

▶ *501 Knowledge, 507 Wisdom, 655 Skill, 492 Judgment, 481 Discrimination, 760 Sensitivity, 688 Authority*

ADVERBS

25 educationally, instructively, pedagogically, informatively, informedly, canonically, authoritatively, wisely, sagaciously, expertly, helpfully, advisedly, illuminatingly, revealingly, edifyingly, improvingly, remedially, progressively, encouragingly

▶ *654 Advice, 688 Authority, 528 Information, 627 Improvement, 655 Skill, 507 Wisdom*

26 studiously, academically, scholastically, brainily, bookishly, thoughtfully, contemplatively, intellectually, intelligently, aptly, quickly, cleverly, skilfully, technically, brightly, willingly, receptively, susceptibly, malleably, pliably, docilely

▶ *461 Thought, 459 Intellect, 655 Skill*

27 discerningly, tastefully, discriminatingly, judiciously, judgmentally, insightfully, perceptively, sensitively, sophisticatedly, urbanely, suavely, elegantly

▶ *411 Taste, 481 Discrimination, 492 Judgment, 760 Sensitivity, 558 Elegance, 794 Refinement*

7 Religion

Man is by his constitution a religious animal. Edmund Burke.

To become a popular religion, it is only necessary for a superstition to enslave a philosophy. Dean Inge.

Religion…is the opium of the people. Karl Marx.

Religion is love; in no case is it logic. Beatrice Webb.

NOUNS

1 religion, faith, belief, belief-system, set of beliefs, creed, credo, dogma, doctrine, persuasion, superstition, conviction, religious group,

Christian Movements

Abecedarianism	Arianism	Dyothelites	Melitianism
Abelianism (or Abel-	Arminianism	Eastern Orthodox Church	Mennonitism
ites)	Artemonism	Encratites	Methodism
Abode of Love	Assumptionism	Episcopal Church	Montanism
Abrahamites	Baptism	Evangelicalism	Moral Rearmament
Abstinents	Barclayism	Frankism	Moravian Church
Abyssinian Church	Basildeanism	Free Church of Scot-	Mormonism
Acacianism	Beguines	land	Nestorian Church
Adamites	Biblicism	Fundamentalism	Orthodox Church
Adiaphorism	Bogomils	Generationism	Oxford Movement
Adoptionism	Bonosianism	Gideons	Paulicianism
Adventism	Bosci	Greek Orthodox	Pentecostalism
African Methodism	Bourignianism	Haugeanism	Plymouth Brethren
African Orthodox	Brinsers	Hicksites	Presbyterianism
Church	Broad Church	High Church	Protestantism
Agapemonites	Brownism	Huguenotism	Puritanism
Agnoetae	Brugglers	Hussism (or Hussitism)	Quakerism
Agonizants	Buchanites	Illuminati	Redemptorism
Albigensianism	Calixtines	Infralapsarianism	Roman Catholicism
Alogi	Calvinism	Jacobites	Russian Orthodox
Alombrados	Cameronianism	Jansenism	Church
Amalricianism	Catharism	Jehovah's Witnesses	Rosicrucianism
Ambrosianism	Catholicism	Jumpers	Salvation Army
American Orthodox	Cerdonianism	Laestadianism	Se-baptism
Church	Chiliasm	Latitudinarianism	Shakers
Amish	Christian Science	Levellers	Swedenborgianism
Amyraldianism	Church of England	Lollardy (or Lollardry	Syrian Orthodox
Anabaptism	Church of Ireland	or Lollardism)	Taborites
Anglican Communion	Church of Scotland	Low Church	Templars
(or Anglicanism)	Congregationalism	Lullism	Teutonic Knights
Anglo-Catholicism	Covenanters	Lutheranism	Theopaschites
Annihilationism	Diggers	Macedonianism	Tractarianism
Anomoianism	Docetism	Mandeism	Trinitarianism
Antipaedobaptism	Donatism	Maronism	Tübingen School
Apollinarianism	Dunkers	Mar Thoma	Unification Church
Apostolic Brethren	Dyophysites	Melchites	Unitarianism

religious movement, denomination, church, school, branch, movement, order, sect, cult, faction, chapter, way of life, attitude, outlook, morals, ethics, moral code, philosophy of life, point of view, perspective

▶ *497 Belief, 490 Certainty, 586 Persuasion, 4 Philosophy, 461 Thought, 10 Ritual, 9 Worship, 8 Divinity, 11 Occultism*

2 **religiousness**, piety, piousness, sanctimony, puja, reverence, honour, veneration, observance, strict observance, strictness, faithfulness, ritualism, deism, theism, mysticism, spirituality, chohan, prayerfulness, Kavannah, communion with God, trust in God, self-surrender, self-sacrifice, fear of God, theopathy, humility, prostration, dedication, devotion, adoration, unction, zeal, enthusiasm, fervour, speaking in tongues, glossolalia, sanctimoniousness, religiosity, overpiety, over-orthodoxy, preachiness, churchiness, unctuousness, Bible-bashing (*or* thumping *or* punching), Bible-worship, bibliolatry, literalness, fundamentalism, salvationism, missionary spirit, fanaticism, witch-hunting, heresy-hunting, crusading, bigotry, persecution

▶ *694 Obedience, 673 Submission, 10 Ritual, 503 Accuracy*

3 **religious person**, religious, pietist, child of God, votary, saint, real saint, bodhisattva, marabout, martyr, pilgrim, palmer, hajji, mystic, charismatic, holyman, sadhu, sannyasi, bhikshu, fakir, man (*or* woman) of prayer, believer, worshipper, the faithful, convert, neophyte, catechumen, devotee, disciple, acolyte

▶ *497 Belief, 806 Humility, 861 Good, 694 Obedience, 857 Probity, 134 Purity, 849 Respect, 808 Servility, 863 Virtue*

4 **religionist**, zealot, iconoclast, formalist, precisian, inerrantist, Sabbatarian, bibliolater, preacher, pulpiteer, sermonizer, salvationist, missionary, fanatic, crusader, ghazi, witch-hunter, tyrant, bigot, persecutor

5 **Christian**, practising Christian, communicant, conformist, Catholic, Roman Catholic, papist (Offensive), Protestant, Anglo-Catholic, Anglican, Episcopalian, Unitarian, Trinitarian, Evangelical, born-again Christian, Nonconformist, Lutheran, Calvinist, Presbyterian, Wee Free (Offensive), Methodist, Wesleyan, Baptist, Congregationalist, Quaker, Friend, Puritan, Hussite, Huguenot, Lollard, Mormon, Latter-Day Saint, Mennonite, Jehovah's Witness, Christian Scientist, Moonie (Inf), Adventist, Seventh-Day Adventist, revivalist, evange-

Non-Christian Religions

Judaism
Ashkenazim
Assimilationism
Boethusian
Chazar
Conservative Judaism
Ebionite
Essenes
Falasha
Hasidism
Karaites
Messianic Judaism
Mizrachi
Nazarite
Orthodox Judaism
Pharisaism (or Phari-
  seeism)
Rabbinism
Reconstructionism
Reform Judaism
Sadduceeism
Sephardim
Zionism

Hinduism
Aghorapanthi
Ajivika
Arya Samaj
Brahmanism
Chaitanya Vaishnava
Dadu Panthis
Dakshincharin
Hare Krishna
Lingayata
Lokayata
Madhva
Pancharatra
Rama Krishna
Ramanandi
Saivism
Saktism
Sankar
Satnami
Sittar
Tantrism
Vamcharin
Vedantism

Yogism

Islam
Admadiya
Ahmadiya
Almohades
Almoravides
Babism
Bahaism
Black Muslims
Carmathian (or
  Karmathian)
Druses
Ibadhi
Ja'alin
Malikite
Mohammedanism
Qadarite
Sanusi
Shiah
Sufism
Sunni
Wahhabiyah

Sikhism
Akali
Nirmalin
Udasin

Jainism
Sehanakavasi

**Zoroastrianism (or
  Zoroastrism)**
Mazdaism
Parsee (or Parsi)
Yezidi

Buddhism
Adibuddhism
Hua-yen
Jodo
Kahdam-pa
Kegon
Koan
Lamaism
Mahayanan
Maha Bodhi
Mokusho

Nichiren
Nyigma-pa
Obaku-shu
Sangha
Taoism
Tendai
Vajrayna
Won
Yogacara
Zen

Shinto
Fuso Kyo
Tenri Kyo

African religions
Bantu
Beninese
Hehe
Mtwaran
Voodoo
Xhosa
Yoruba

Nontheistic religions
Confucianism
Humanism
I Am
Spiritualism

Miscellaneous
Algonquin
Andamanese
Araucanian
Caodaism
Cargo Cult
Chuntokyo
Eskimo
Ghost Dance
Guarani
Navaho
Paressi
Peruvian
Pomo
Quiche
Rastafarianism
Sabaism
Scientology (Tm)

Sioux

Ancient religions
Adonism
Aegean
Ainu
Ammonite
Amorite
Ancestor Worship
Ancient and Mystical
  Order of Poahtun
Anglo-Saxon
Assyrian
Aztec
Babylonian
Bön (or Pon)
Canaanite
Carthaginian
Celtic
Chaldean
Druidism
Eleusinianism
Etruscan
Germanic
Incan
Khond
Mammonism
Mayan
Mithraism
Naasene
Norse
Nubian
Ophian
Orphism
Oyomei
Paganism
Phoenician
Roman
Sankhya
Shamanism
Slavonic
Sumerian
Thag (or Thug)
Totemism
Vedic

list, TV evangelist, televangelist, fundamentalist, militant Christian, hot gospeller (Inf),
Jesus freak (Inf), the God squad (Inf), Bible-
basher (or thumper or puncher) (Sl), creeping
Jesus (Sl), holy roller (Sl)

6 non-Christian, Jew, Orthodox Jew, Zionist,
Essene, Pharisee, Sadducee, Muslim, Mohammedan, Mussulman (Arch), infidel (Arch), Shiite, Sunnite, Sufi, Druse, Wahhabi, Black
Muslim, fundamentalist, Baha'i, Hindu, Buddhist, Zen Buddhist, Sikh, Jain (or Jaina or
Jainist), Rastafarian, Rasta (Inf)

7 monk, nun, prior, prioress, abbot, abbess,
mother superior, reverend father, superioress,
reverend mother, canoness, monastic, religious, sister, brother, kalogeros, trapa, talapoin,
bo-san, shonin, bhikku, bhikkunis, bonze,
fakir, dervish, caloyer, coenobite, conventual,
hieromarch, mendicant, friar, pilgrim, palmer,

stylite, pillarist, beadsman, hermit, abbacomes,
anchorite, ascetic, novice, postulant, lay disciple, upasaka, upasika, koji, chela
▶ *871 Fasting, 806 Humility, 861 Good, 694 Obedience, 697 Servant, 863 Virtue*

8 priest, priestess, high priest, pope, papa, pontif, pontifex maximus, chief rabbi, hakam,
Grand hama, Dalai Lama, Panchen Lama, Dastur, Kalif (or Caliph), hierophant, Arch Druid,
Arch Druidess, flamen, Brahman, Gosain,
guru, pundit, purohita, cardinal, bishop, archbishop, primate, patriarch, hierarch, diocesan,
suffragan, prelate, clergyman, clergywoman,
ecclesiastic, ecclesiarch, churchman, cleric,
clerk in holy orders, man (or woman) of the
cloth, minister, ministress, pastor, pastoress,
deacon, deaconess, ordinand, dean, canon,
monsignor, parson, vicar, rector, curate, elder,
father, confessor, chaplain, padre, rabbi (or

Members of Religious Orders

Antonian	Carthusian	Hospitaller	Poor Clare
Augustinian	Cistercian	Jacobin	Premonstratensian
Austin Friar	Cluniac	Jeronymite	Recollect
Barnabite	Crossed Friar	Jesuit	Salesian
Benedictine	Crutched Friar	Loveltine	Servite
Bernadine	Culdee	Loyolite	Studite
Black Friar	Dominican	Marist	Sylvestrine
Black Monk	Fontrevaut	Maryknoll Sister	Templar
Blue Nun	Franciscan	Maryknoll Father	Theatine
Bonhomin	Fratello	Maturine	Trappist
Brigittine	Friar Preacher	Minim	Trinitarian
Camaldolese Monk	Gilbertine	Minorite	Ursuline
Capuchin	Grey Friar	Olivetan	Visitandine
Carmelite	Grey Nun	Oratorian	White Friar

rabbin), kohen (*or* cohen), maggid, koheleth, mullah, imam, ayatollah, qadi, sheikh, qasisha, mujtahid, darshan, rishi, dhammaduta, zen-ji, lama, poonghie, witch doctor, houngan, mamaloi, papaloi, haruspex, augur, churchwarden, almoner, verger, beadle, sexton, acolyte, thurifer, precentor, succentor, cantor, hazzan, muezzin, mukdam, maftir, Levite, scribe, Holy Joe (Sl), Sky Pilot (Sl)
▶ *688 Authority, 696 Master*

9 **priesthood**, priestship, hierocracy, ecclesiasticism (*or* ecclesiasticalism), clericalism, sacerdotalism, Brahmanism, the ministry, pastorate, pastorage, pastoral care, the Church, the clergy, the cloth, holy orders, ordination, ordainment, reading in, election, nomination, appointment, induction, institution, investiture, conferment, preferment, rabbinate, pontificate, papacy, popedom, cardinalship, primacy, prelature, abbacy, bishopric, bishopdom, episcopate, deanery, deanship, curacy, rectorship, rectorate, vicarship, vicariate, pastorship, deaconry, deaconship, chaplaincy, chaplainship, diocese, see, archdiocese, province, parish
▶ *10 Ritual*

10 **priestly dwelling**, vicarage, parsonage, rectory, deanery, manse, presbytery, archdeaconry, bishop's palace, Lambeth Palace, Vatican, ashram, retreat, hermitage, priory, friary, cloister, chapterhouse, monastery, convent, nunnery, lamasery
▶ *10 Ritual, 43 Architecture*

11 **vestment**, canonicals, regalia, habit, veil, robes, cloth, vesture, liturgical garment, ceremonial attire, pontificals, pontificalia, episcopal vestment, frock, mantle, gown, cloak, surplice, scapular, cassock, cope, pallium, amice, chasuble, alb, tunicle, tallith, ephod, apron, soutane, hood, capuche, clerical collar, fanon, headdress, wimple, cardinal's hat, mitre, tiara, triple crown, priest's cap, biretta, prayer cap, skullcap, yarmulke, turban, calotte, zucchetto, Salvation Army bonnet, stole, tippet, cingulum, maniple, crosier, crook, staff, episcopal ring, orphrey (*or* orfray), clericals

(Inf), dog collar (Inf)
▶ *584 Habit, 295 Dress, 10 Ritual*

12 **religious text**, sacred text, scripture, sacred writings, sutra, shastra, word of God, canonical writings, canon, Christian text, Bible, Holy Bible, the Book, the Good Book, the Word, King James' Bible, Authorized Version, Revised Version, New English Bible, Geneva Bible, Breeches Bible, Jerusalem Bible, Good News Bible, Gideon Bible, Septuagint, Old Testament, New Testament, Gospels, Synoptic Gospels, Epistles, Apocrypha, Book of Mormon, Buddhist text, Pitaka, Tripitaka, Theravada, Dhamma, Dhammapada, Jataka, Apadana, Avadana, Lotus of the True Law, Nikaya, Dipavamsa, Mahavastu, Pali Canon, Confucian text, Lun-yu, Shinto text, Nihongi, Yengishiki, Jainist text, Agama, Hindu text, smriti, shruti, Upanishad, Bhagavad-Gita, Purana, Veda, Rigveda, Yajurveda, Samaveda, Atharvaveda, Aranyaka, Granth, Zoroastrian text, Avesta, Zend-Avesta, Islamic text, Koran, Quran, the Glorious Koran, Hadith, Sunna, Jewish text, Torah, Targum, Talmud, Mishnah, Gemara, Masorah, Bahir, Ancient Egyptian text, Book of the Dead
▶ *10 Ritual*

13 **theology**, divinity, dogmatic theology, philosophical theology, theological metaphysics, systematic theology, dialogical theology, patristic theology, patristics, natural theology, physicotheology, crisis theology, scholastic theology, existential theology, ontotheology, phenomenological theology, feminist theology, liberation theology, hierology, hierography, hagiology, hagiography, soteriology, Christology, Mariology, angelology, Buddhology, eschatology, theological hermeneutics, secularism, ecclesiology, doctrinism, doctrinalism, rationalism, apologetics, religious studies, religious education (RE), religious instruction (RI), scripture (Inf)
▶ *524 Interpretation, 520 Meaning, 4 Philosophy*

14 **theologian**, theologist, theologician, theologizer, theologer, theologue, divine, scholastic,

canonist, hierologist, hagiologist, eschatologist, ecclesiologist
▶ *524 Interpretation, 4 Philosophy*
ADJECTIVES
15 **religious**, pious, devout, holy, godly, saintly,
seraphic, cherubic, transcendent, spiritual,
mystic, otherworldly, transcendent, churchgoing, practising, strict, faithful, believing,
holding (*or* keeping) the faith, orthodox, pure,
reverent, worshipful, prayerful, devoted, devotional, reverential, solemn, dedicated, God-
fearing, theopathic, self-surrendering, humble,
prostrate, self-sacrificing, monastic, anchoretic, ascetic, hermit-like, ardent, unctuous,
zealous, overreligious, priest-ridden, formalistic, Pharisaic, overstrict, ritualistic, churchy,
overdevout, overrighteous, holier-than-thou,
self-righteous, sanctimonious, fervent,
preachy, canting, Bible-worshipping, fundamentalist, evangelical, crusading, militant,
missionary, fanatical, witch-hunting, bigoted,
Bible-bashing (*or* thumping *or* punching) (Sl)
▶ *497 Belief, 806 Humility, 861 Good, 694 Obedience, 719 Observance, 849 Respect, 673 Submission, 863 Virtue, 503 Accuracy*
16 **denominational**, sectarian, Christian,
Catholic Roman, Roman Catholic, RC (Inf),
popish, papish, papist (Offensive), Protestant,
Anglican, C of E (Inf), High-Church, Low-
Church, Episcopalian, Nonconformist, Orthodox, Jewish, Judaeo-Christian, Judaic (*or* Juda-
ical), Hebrew, Reform, Conservative, Hasidic,
Sephardic, Islamic, Muslim, fundamentalist,
Hindu, Buddhist, Taoist
17 **priestly**, ecclesiastic(al), sacerdotal, hier-
atic(al), clerical, ministerial, churchly, pastoral, canonical, papal, pontifical, episcopal, rabbinic (*or* rabbinical), prelatic, presbyteral,
hierophantic, druidic (*or* druidical), hierocratic, parochial, diocesan, ordained
▶ *688 Authority, 696 Master*
18 **theological**, religious, divine, patristic, physicotheological, ontotheological, hierological,
hierographical, hagiological, hagiographical,
soteriological, Christological, eschatological,
doctrinal, ecclesiological, canonical, scriptural,
metaphysical
▶ *524 Interpretation, 520 Meaning, 4 Philosophy*
VERBS
19 **be religious**, get religion, meet God, receive
Christ, accept the Lord, enter the church, recant, repent, turn, convert, be converted, be
saved, have a crisis of faith, hold (*or* keep) the
faith, believe, have faith, recite the creed, go to
church, receive communion, support the
church, revere, venerate, honour, observe,
trust in God, worship, adore, obey, devote
oneself, prostrate oneself, humble oneself, surrender oneself, fear God, feel the spirit, be
possessed by the spirit, go on a pilgrimage,

perform the hajj
▶ *220 Conversion, 497 Belief, 10 Ritual, 806 Humility, 861 Good, 694 Obedience, 849 Respect,
673 Submission, 863 Virtue*
20 **preach**, spread the Word, spread the good
news, fight the good fight, speak in tongues,
sermonize, proselytize, evangelize, convert,
convince, win for Christ, receive into the
church, baptize, Christianize, Islamize, Judaize, depaganize, crusade, witch-hunt, heresy-
hunt, persecute, preachify (Inf), Bible bash (*or*
thump *or* punch) (Sl)
▶ *586 Persuasion*
21 **ordain**, consecrate, read in, elect, nominate,
appoint, invest, frock, anoint, call, confer holy
orders on, take holy orders, take vows, take the
veil, wear the cloth
22 **theologize**, study theology, interpret the
scriptures, study the Bible, ponder the nature
of God, philosophize
▶ *524 Interpretation, 520 Meaning, 4 Philosophy*
ADVERBS
23 **religiously**, piously, spiritually, devoutly,
strictly, worshipfully, faithfully, humbly, reverentially, solemnly, ardently, zealously, fanatically, theologically, doctrinally, rabbinically, canonically, ecclesiastically, by the book
▶ *503 Accuracy*

8   Divinity

*For the Kingdom of God is not in word, but in
power.* Bible: I Corinthians.

God's gifts put man's best gifts to shame.
Elizabeth Barrett Browning.

*God moves in a mysterious way/ His wonders to
perform.* William Cowper.

God is subtle but he is not malicious. Albert
Einstein.

The world is charged with the grandeur of God.
Gerard Manley Hopkins.

Man proposes but God disposes. Thomas à
Kempis.

I have no need of that hypothesis. Marquis de
Laplace.

NOUNS
1 **divinity**, divineness, godhood, godhead,
deity, godship, godliness, numinousness,
Brahmahood, Buddhahood, divine essence,
divine principle, divine nature, perfection,
sanctitude, sanctity, holiness, hallowedness,
sacredness, sacrosanctity, transcendence, enlightenment, state of grace, blessed state,
blessedness, nirvana, sublimity
▶ *7 Religion*
2 **divine attribute**, eternity, infinity, immortality, truth, love, mercy, wisdom, power,

Deities

Greek
Aglaia
Ananke
Aphrodite
Apollo
Ares
Artemis
Asclepius
Ate
Athene
Atropos
Castor
Clotho
Cronos
Demeter
Dionysus
Dis
Eos
Eris
Eros
Eumenides
Euphrosyne
Gaia (or Ge or Ga)
Hades
Hebe
Hecate
Helios
Hephaestus
Hera
Hermes
Hestia
Hypnos
Iris
Lachesis
Lyssa
Nemesis
Nike
Ops
Ouranos
Pan
Persephone
Phoebe
Pluto
Plutus
Pollux
Poseidon
Rhea
Selene
Thanatos
Tuche
Zeus

Roman
Acca Larentia
Aesculapius
Apollo
Aurora
Bacchus
Bellona
Ceres
Cupid
Cybele
Diana
Faunus
Fortuna
Hyperion
Iris
Juno
Jupiter (or Jove)
Juventas
Lares
Luna
Mars
Mercury
Minerva
Mors
Neptune
Nox
Penates
Phoebus
Pluto
Pontus
Proserpina
Saturn
Sol
Somnus
Tellus
Uranus
Venus
Vertumnus
Vesta
Vulcan

Etruscan
Cupra
Feronia
Fufluns
Horta
Ilythyia-Leucothea
Losna
Menrva
Nortia
Thalna
Tina
Voltumna

Norse
Aegir
Balder
Bil
Bragi
Eir
Forseti
Frey (or Freya)
Frigg (or Frigga)
Gerda
Heimdal
Hel
Hermod
Hödur
Idun
Lofri
Loki
Nanna
Nerthus
Njord (or Njorth)
Sif
Skuld
Surt
Thor
Tiw (or Tiu)
Urd
Vanir
Verdandi
Vidar
Wotan (or Odin)

Germanic
Eostre (or Estre)
Forseti
Frimla
Hod
Holle
Hulda
Khors

Celtic
Adsullata
Angus
Anu
Artio
Badb
Basso-juan (Basque)
Benzozia (Basque)
Bile
Bormanus
Borvo
Briganta (British)
Brigit
Bussumanus
Ceridwen (British)
Cermait
Cocidius
Cyhiraeth
Dagda
Damona
Danu
Dirona
Dylan
Epona
Fea
Grannos
Hesus (Gallic)
Kelpie
Leucetios
Lir (Gaelic)
Lug
Macha
Moccus
Morrigu
Murigen (Irish)
Nemon
Nodens (British)
Orko (Basque)
Segomo
Shoney
Teutates (Gallic)
Thunar (British)
Tuatha de Danann (Irish)

Egyptian
Aaah-te-huti
Ammon
Amon-ra
Andjeti
Anhur
Anit
Anquet
Anubis
Apep
Apet
Atmu
Aton
Bast
Bes
Chnoumis
Dua
Geb
Hapi
Hathor
Hequet
Hershef
Hey-tau
Horus
Imhotep
Isis
Khensu (or Khons)
Khepera (or Khopri)
Khnemu (or Khnum)
Maat
Mehueret
Menthu
Meshkenit
Min
Munt (or Mont)
Mut
Nekhebit
Nekhen
Neneh
Nephthys
Net
Neter
Nun
Nut
Osiris
Ptah
Ra (Re)
Renpet
Reret
Seb
Sebek
Seker
Sekhmet
Sesheta
Set (or Seth)
Shu
Tatumen
Taueret
Tefnut
Thoth
Upuaut

Babylonian
Ashushu-Namir
Baal Shamain
Belit
Anshar
Kishar
Anu
Aruru
Adad
Allatu
Damkina
Ea
Enki
Enlil
Enmesharra
Enzu
Ga-tum-dag
Gibil
Gula
Haya
Innana
Kingu
Lakhame
Lakhmu
Marduk
Merodach
Mylitta
Nebo
Nergal
Ningal
Ningirsu
Ninib
Nusku
Oannes
Samkhat
Tammuz
Yamm
Zu

Middle Eastern
Adad (Canaanite, Syrian)
Adrammelech (Samaritan)

Allat (Nabatean)
Amor (Amorite)
Anahita (Persian)
Anthat (Ugarit)
Asari (Syrian)
Asheratian (Semitic)
Ashirat (Canaanite)
Ashur (Assyrian)
Astarte (Semitic)
Attar (Arabian)
Atter (Semitic)
Attis (Phrygian)
Baal (Phoenician, Canaanite, Semitic)
Baalat (Semitic)
Babbar (Sumerian)
Belet (Semitic)
Belili (Sumerian)
Berouth (Phoenician)
Buriash (Kassitic)
Cybele (Phrygian)
Dagan (Assyrian)
Dagon (Canaanite)
El (Canaanite, Semitic)
Elat (Semitic)
Elegabalus (Syrian)
Elioun (Phoenician)
Enurta (Assyrian)
Heres (Canaanite)
Ilah (Semitic)
Ilat (Arabian)
Ilmagah (Semitic)
Khoser-et-hasis (Phoenician)
Ma (Turkish)
Milcom (Ammonite)
Molech (Semitic)
Mot (Phoenician)
Nana (Sumerian)
Nannar (Chaldean)
Nikkal (Sumerian)
Ninella (Mesopotamian)
Ninib (Assyrian)
Nisroch (Ninnevan)
Omicle (Phoenician)
Pontus (Phoenician)
Qadesh (Syrian)
Rimman (Syrian)
Sabazios (Phrygian)
Samas (Semitic)
Sinurc (Persian)
Suwa (Arabian)
Teshub (Hittite)
Urbanus (Canaanite)
Uzza (Arabian)
Verethagna (Zoroastrian)
Yaghuth (Arabian)

Hindu

Aditya
Agni
Ahi
Aiyanar
Asura
Bali
Bhairava
Brahma
Devi
Diti
Ganesha
Garuda
Hanuman
Ida
Indra
Jagannath (or Juggernaut)
Jyestha
Kali
Kalki
Kama
Kamashi
Kartikeya
Krishna
Kubera
Kurma
Lakshmi
Mahadeva
Mahadevi
Matsya
Nanda
Narsinh
Parvati
Parshuram
Pasupati
Prajapati
Prithivi
Rama
Rati
Rudra
Saranyu
Sarasvati
Savitri
Sesha
Sitala
Siva (or Shiva)
Sugriva
Surya
Uma
Vaman
Varah
Varuna
Vata
Vayu
Vishnu
Visva-Karma
Visvesvara
Yama

Vedic

Aditi
Asvin
Brihaspati
Daksha
Dhatri
Dyaus
Parjana
Prithivi
Pushan
Sita
Tvastri
Ushas
Vastosh-Pati
Vayu

Far Eastern

Aizen myo-o (Japanese)
Amaterasu-omikami (Japanese)
Amitayus (Tibetan)
Benten (Japanese)
Bimbo-gami (Japanese)
Bishamon (Japanese)
Daikoku (Japanese)
Dakini (Buddhist)
Ebisu (Japanese)
Ema (Japanese)
Fuchi (Japanese)
Fudo (Japanese)
Fukurokuju (Japanese)
Futsunushi (Japanese)
Hachiman (Japanese)
Heu T'U (or Hau-Too) (Chinese)
Hotei (Japanese)
Hsuan-wu (Taoist)
Inari (Shinto)
Infoniwoo (Taiwanese)
Itzanagi (Japanese)
Itzanami (Japanese)
Jade Emperor (Taoist)
Jingo (Japanese)
Jizo (Japanese)
Jorojin (Japanese)
Kagu-Tsuchi (Japanese)
Kishi Bojin (Japanese)
Komoku (Japanese)
Kuan Yin (Chinese)
Nat (Burmese)
Raiden (Japanese)
Sengen (Japanese)
Susa-no-o (Shinto)
Takemikadzuchi (Japanese)
Tou Mu (Chinese)
Tsuki-yumi (Japanese)
W'en-ch'ung (Chinese)

African

Agassou (Beninese)
Amirini (Yoruban)
Fa (Beninese)
Gwalu (Yoruban)
Huntin (Bantu)
Jo-Uk (Sudanese)
Legba (Beninese)
Lissa (Beninese)
Maahes (Nubian)
Maou (Beninese)
Mumbo Jumbo (Sudanese)
Mwari (Mtwaran)
Nguruhe (Hehe)
Obatalla (Yoruban)
Obi (West African)
Olorun (Yoruban)
Orishako (Yoruban)
Quamta (Xhosan)
Tanit (Cathaginian)
Yemaja (Yoruban)

American Indian and Eskimo

Akycha (Alaskan)
Aningan (Eskimo)
Angpetu Wi (Dakota)
Anpao (Dakota)
Anungite (Dakota)
Apisirahts (Blackfoot)
Arnaknagsak (Eskimo)
Asaya-Gigagei (Cherokee)
Ahsonnulti (Navajo)
Aka-kanet (Araucanian)
Awahili (Cherokee)
Awahokshu (Pawnee)
Awonawilona (Zuni)
Begochiddi (Navajo)
Chaharu (Pawnee)
Chasca (Peruvian)
Chia (Muscaya)
Epunamun (Araucanian)
Estanatlehi (Navajo)
Gaoh (Iroquois)
Geyaguga (Cherokee)
Haokah (Sioux)
Heloha (Choctaw)
Hinun (Iroquois)
Hisakitaimisi (Creek)
Hitchi (Hitchiti)
Hunthaca (Chibcha)
Hurakan (Quiche)
Jacy (Tupi-Guarani)
Jurupari (Tupi-Guarani)
Ka-ata-killa (Peruvian)
Kanati (Cherokee)
Katkochila (Wintun)
Kitche Manitou (Algonquin)
Ludjatako (Creek)
Maiso (Paressi)
Marumda (Pomo)
Mixacoatl (Mexican)
Monan (Tupi-Guarani)
Nichant (Algonquin)
Onnion (Huron)
Oonawieh Unggi (Cherokee)
Pautiwa (Hopi)
Pilan (Araucanian)
Quahootze (Nootka)
Sedna (Eskimo)
Selu (Cherokee)
Sus'sistinnako (Sia)
Tohi (Quiche)
Tornarsuk (Eskimo)
Uchtsiti (Acoma)
Ukteni (Natchez)
Winabojo (Chippewa)
Xilonen (Mexican)
Yanauluha (Zuni)

Polynesian

Apu-matangi
Apu-hau
Io
Kiho Tumi
Maui
Oro
Sina
Tangaloa
Tawhiri
Vari-ma-te-takere

Australian

Awhiowhio
B-lame
Bun-jil
Daramulum
Nurrundere

Aztec

Camaxtli
Chacmool
Chantico
Cihuacoatl
Cintzotl
Citallinicue
Coatlicue
Huahuantli
Huitzilopochtli
Huixtocihuatl
Ilamatecuhtli
Itzlacoliuhqui
Itzli
Itzpapalotl
Ixcuina
Ixtlilton
Macuilxochitl
Metztli

Mictlancihvatl	Xochiquetzal	Yum Kaax	Dyaus-Pitar (Aryan)
Mictlantecuhtli	Yacatecutli		Jah (Rastafarian)
Omacatl		**Inca**	Meke Meke (Easter Is-
Omeciuatl	**Mayan**	Ataquchu	land)
Ometecuhtli	Algahom Naum	Huaca	Murugan (Tamil)
Piltzintecuhtli	Bacab	Mama Allpa	Nemu (New Guinea)
Quetzalcoatl	Camazotz	Mama Cocha	Pele (Hawaiian)
Tezcatlipoca	Cauac	Punchau	Perchta (Slavonic)
Tlaloc	Itzamna	Supay	Perkunas (Finnish)
Tlazolteotl	Ix	Visacocha	Ras Tafari Makonnen
Tloque Nahuaque	Ixazalvoh		(Rastafarian)
Tonacatacuhtli	Kabul	**Miscellaneous**	Stribog (Slavonic)
Tonqtiuh	Kan	Asura (Aryan)	Vainamoinen (Finnish)
Xipe	Kinich-ahau	Byelun (Slavonic)	Volos (Serbian)
Xiuhtecuhtli	Kukulcan	Czarnobog (Slavonic)	Zombi (Voodoo)
		Da-bog (Slavonic)	

supremacy, sovereignty, majesty, Shekinah, omnipresence, omniscience, omnipotence, almightiness, theocracy

▶ *688 Authority, 190 Eternity, 861 Good, 184 Infinity, 7 Religion, 619 Perfection, 217 Permanence, 235 Power, 253 Presence, 186 Timelessness*

3 **God**, Lord, the Lord, Providence, Jehovah, Yahweh (*or* Jahweh *or* Yahveh *or* Jahveh), Jah, Adonai, Elohim, Allah, Yuh-hwang-shangte, the Supreme Being, Almighty God, the Almighty, King of Kings, Lord of Lords, the Eternal, Alpha and Omega, the Maker, the Creator, the Father, God the Father, Everlasting Father, First Cause, Prime Mover, *primum mobile* (L), *Ens Entium* (L), Demiourgos, demiurge, the Mother, Great Mother, Mother Nature, the Holy Spirit, the Holy Ghost, Spirit of God, the Great Spirit, the Supreme Soul, oversoul, world soul, Atman, Paramatman, the Preserver, the Universal Self, the Blessed One, the Teacher, Buddha, Bodhisattva, Amida, Dai Nichi, Akshobhya, the Lord of Wisdom, the Wise One, the King of Light, Ahura Mazda (*or* Ormazd), the Trinity, Holy Trinity, Father, Son and Holy Ghost, Trimurti

▶ *688 Authority, 226 Cause, 190 Eternity, 861 Good, 184 Infinity, 7 Religion, 11 Occultism, 619 Perfection, 235 Power, 186 Timelessness*

4 **God the Son**, Son of God, Jesus Christ, Christ, Jesus, Lord Jesus, King of the Jews, Messiah, Emmanuel (*or* Immanuel), The Saviour, The Redeemer, Lamb of God, Son of Man, the Good Shepherd, Prince of Peace, the Way, the Truth, and the Life, the Light of the World

5 **deity**, divinity, god, goddess, deva, devi, the gods, the immortals, the Olympians, fertility god, corn god, rain god, earth goddess, moon goddess, household gods, minor deity, demigod, spirit, guiding spirit, numen, daemon, genius, inspiration, muse, the Muses, animistic spirit, mana, manitou, huaca, nagual, pokunt, tamanoas, wakan, zemi, forest spirit, vegetation spirit, year daemon, faun, satyr, nymph, wood nymph, tree nymph, dryad, hamadryad, oread, water nymph, water spirit, naiad, undine, Anahita, sea nymph, Nereid, object of worship, idol, fetish, totem, supernatural being

▶ *11 Occultism, 10 Ritual*

6 **angel**, angelhood, archangel, archangelship, guardian angel, fairy godmother, seraph, cherub, *putto* (It), celestial, heavenly being, principality, messenger of God, heavenly host, angelic host, choir invisible, thrones, dominations, virtues, powers, ministering spirits, Amesha Spentas, Lha, angel of love, angel of light, Abdiel, Chamuel, Gabriel, Jophiel, Michael, Raphael, Uriel, Zadkiel, Haurvatat, Khshathra Vairya, Rashnu, Sraosha, Vohu Manah, angel of death, Azrael, Israfel, Aesma, fallen angel, Lucifer

▶ *861 Good, 662 Help*

7 **devil**, demon, demonkind, powers of darkness, evil spirit, namtar, kmukamtch, dybbuk, shedu, gyre, incubus, succubus, afreet, fiend, imp, lost soul, fallen angel, rebel angel, the Devil, Satan, Lucifer, the Evil One, the Enemy, the Common Enemy, Prince of Darkness, His Satanic Majesty, Lord of the Flies, Archfiend, Antichrist, The Tempter, Diabolus, Belial, Beelzebub, Mephisto, Mephistopheles, Shaitan, Eblis (*or* Iblis), Apollyon, Abaddon, Ahriman, Angra Mainyu, Sammael, Aeshma, Azidahaka, Pisacha, Putana, Ravana, Mara, Azazil, Tutivillus, Asmodeus, Set, Typhan, Loki, deil (Scot), *diable* (Fr), *diavolo* (It), *diablo* (Sp), *Teukl* (Ger), Old Nick (Inf), Old Harry (Inf), Old Scratchy (Inf), Old Hornie (Dial), Old Clootie (Dial)

▶ *862 Evil, 832 Malevolence, 11 Occultism, 864 Wickedness*

8 **divine manifestation**, epiphany, avatar, materialization, incarnation, embodiment, the Word, the Word made Flesh, appearance, apparition, visitation, vision, annunciation, theophany, angelophany, Christophany, divine revelation, Bat Kol, direct communication, direct intuition, mystical experience, meeting with God, mystical intuition, divination, clairvoyance

▶ *11 Occultism*

9 **deification**, apotheosis, divinization, im-

mortalization, idolization, fetishization, canonization, beatification, sainting, santification, angelization, consecration, enshrinement, exaltation, adulation, glorification, elevation, assumption, dedication, dignification, ennoblement, magnification, lionization

▶ *9 Worship, 10 Ritual, 7 Religion, 851 Approval, 878 Reward*

10 **deified person**, saint, martyr, patron saint, beatified soul, canonized person, redeemed soul, soul in glory, soul in bliss, Madonna, Our Lady, Mother of God, Holy Mary, Queen of Heaven, Queen of Angels, the Blessed Virgin, the Virgin, the Virgin Mary, the Virgin Mother

▶ *861 Good, 863 Virtue, 857 Probity, 7 Religion*

11 **heaven**, sky, firmament, empyrean, welkin, happy hunting ground, the Land of the Leal, the happy land, the Pearly Gates, realm of light, Beulah, Holy City, Zion, New Jerusalem, Celestial City, throne of God, Kingdom of God, Kingdom come, celestial kingdom, telestial kingdom, Gimli, Raj, Tien, Dyu, Sattyaloka, Tushita, Alfardaws, Assama, Falak al Aflak, Dar-el-jannah, Svarog, Swarga, paradise, Bouyan, Sukhavati, Vaikuntha, Amaravati, nirvana, satori, devaloka, Kamavachara, Kamaloka, devachan, Elysium, Elysian fields, Isles of the Blest, Avalon, Kailasa, Valhalla, Abode of the Gods, Olympus, Asgard, Fensalir, Glashem, Vingolf, Valaskjalf, Noatun, Glitnir

▶ *397 Death, 190 Eternity, 861 Good, 512 Oblivion, 279 Summit, 878 Reward*

12 **hell**, place of the dead, limbo, purgatory, Arat Duzzaklı, lower world, underworld, nether world, Hades, Dis, Tartarus, Avernus, Erebus, Orcus, realm of Pluto, sheol, Abaddon, Annwn, Hel, Niflheim, Amenti, Duat (*or* Tuat), Apaya, Aralu, Laza, Naraka, Tophet, Gehenna, jahannan, avici, pit of Acheron, inferno, abyss, bottomless pit, lake of fire and brimstone, perdition, eternal damnation

▶ *827 Curse, 397 Death, 879 Punishment*

ADJECTIVES

13 **divine**, godly, godlike, deistic, theistic, Yahwistic (*or* Jahwistic *or* Yahvistic *or* Jahvistic), Elohistic, Christlike, Christly, messianic, incarnate, theomorphic, epiphanic, numinous, holy, hallowed, sacred, sacrosanct, transcendent, transcendental, enlightened, blessed, full of grace, sublime, perfect, supreme, sovereign, majestic, theocratic, providential, omnipresent, ubiquitous, all-seeing, all-knowing, prescient, omniscient, all-powerful, omnipotent, almighty, absolute, immortal, eternal, infinite, immeasurable, ineffable, mystical, oracular, supernatural, supramundane, extramundane, unearthly

▶ *688 Authority, 190 Eternity, 184 Infinity, 619 Perfection, 217 Permanence, 235 Power*

14 **heavenly**, celestial, empyrean, empyreal, on high, Elysian, paradisiac, paradisical, paradisial, Olympian, supernal, ethereal, angelic, angelical, archangelic, seraphic, cherubic, saintly

▶ *861 Good, 863 Virtue, 279 Summit, 390 Air*

15 **deified**, divinized, immortalized, canonized, beatified, sanctified, angelized, haloed, glorified, saved, redeemed, martyred, consecrated, enshrined, elevated, dedicated, dignified, ennobled, magnified, exalted, adulated, idolized

▶ *851 Approval, 10 Ritual, 9 Worship, 7 Religion, 878 Reward*

16 **devilish**, devil-like, evil, satanic, diabolic, diabolical, demonic (*or* demonical), demoniac (*or* demoniacal), demon-like, Mephistophelean, fiendish, fiendlike, fallen, damned, hellborn, hellish, infernal, sulphurous, chthonian, chthonic, subterranean, pandemonic, Plutonian, Avernal, Tartarean, abysmal, purgatorial

▶ *862 Evil, 832 Malevolence, 864 Wickedness, 879 Punishment, 406 Physical Pain*

VERBS

17 **deify**, apotheosize, divinize, immortalize, canonize, bless, beatify, sanctify, angelize, consecrate, hallow, enshrine, elevate, dedicate, dignify, ennoble, magnify, exalt, adulate, glorify, idolize, go to heaven, ascend, transcend, sublimate, enlighten

▶ *10 Ritual, 9 Worship, 11 Occultism, 878 Reward, 7 Religion, 851 Approval*

18 **devilize**, diabolize, demonize, bedevil, possess, damn, condemn, curse

▶ *827 Curse, 11 Occultism*

ADVERBS

19 **divinely**, numinously, perfectly, sacredly, transcendently, transcendentally, sublimely, supremely, majestically, theocratically, providentially, ineffably, infinitely, absolutely, ubiquitously, omnisciently, almightily, omnipotently, eternally, supernaturally, spiritually, mystically, gracefully, angelically, seraphically, cherubically, celestially, messianically, theistically, Yahwistically, as God, by God's will, *Deo volente* (L), DV, by divine right

▶ *235 Power, 619 Perfection, 7 Religion, 10 Ritual, 688 Authority, 501 Knowledge, 217 Permanence, 184 Infinity*

20 **devilishly**, satanically, diabolically, demonically, fiendishly, infernally, hellishly, in hell, in hellfire, in torment, below, underground

▶ *827 Curse, 862 Evil, 832 Malevolence, 397 Death, 864 Wickedness, 879 Punishment, 11 Occultism*

9　Worship

When two or three are gathered together in thy Name thou will grant their requests. The Book of Common Prayer.

He prayeth well who loveth well/ Both man and

bird and beast. Samuel Taylor Coleridge.

Prayer makes the Christian's armour bright. William Cowper.

More things are wrought by prayer/ Than this world dreams of. Alfred Lord Tennyson.

NOUNS

1 **worship**, honour, reverence, devotion, devotedness, bhakti, dedication, veneration, adoration, adulation, esteem, dignification, glorification, exaltation, magnification, laudation, praise, extolment, celebration, thanksgiving, hymn-singing, psalm-singing, duty, obedience, homage, kneeling, genuflection, prostration, humility, humbling oneself, piety, holy fear, awe, propitiation, appeasement, confession, penitence, atonement, offering, oblation, sacrifice, muda, supplication, petition, praying, contemplation, meditation, communion with God, asceticism, fasting, pilgrimage, hajj, puja

▶ *10 Ritual, 851 Approval, 849 Respect, 837 Gratitude, 812 Celebration, 433 Melody, 49 Music, 806 Humility, 673 Submission, 867 Penitence, 712 Request, 710 Offer, 7 Religion, 8 Divinity, 11 Occultism*

2 **idolatry**, idolism, idolization, iconolatry, superstition, cult, cargo cult, cultism, heathenism, heathenry, paganism, paganry, pagano-Christianism, totemism, fetishism (*or* fetichism), phallicism, priestcraft, bibliolatry, ecclesiolatry, obi (*or* obeah), obiism (*or* abeahism), allotheism, animism, animatism, anthropomorphism, animal worship, zoolatry, zoomorphism, theriolatry, snake worship, ophiolatry, sun worship, heliolatry, star worship, Sabaism, fire worship, pyrolatry, tree worship, dendrolatry, devil worship, diabolism, demonism, Satanism, Mammonism, mammonolatry, ancestor worship, necrolatry, hero worship, anthropolatry

▶ *7 Religion, 8 Divinity, 10 Ritual, 11 Occultism*

3 **idol**, image, graven image, effigy, golden calf, god, deity, Baal, Juggernaut, joss, icon, fetish, symbol, yoni, lingam

▶ *8 Divinity, 11 Occultism*

4 **idolized person**, hero, heroine, celebrity, superstar, megastar, darling, pet, favourite

▶ *8 Divinity, 11 Occultism*

5 **worshipper**, venerator, adorer, praise-singer, celebrant, churchgoer, communicant, supplicant (*or* suppliant), petitioner, penitent, pilgrim, hajji, adherent, votary, follower, admirer, lionizer, idolizer, devotee, aficionado, hero worshipper, fan, groupie (Sl)

▶ *7 Religion, 10 Ritual*

6 **idolater**, idolizer, iconolater, cultist, heathen, pagan, pagano-Christian, totemist, fetishist (*or* fetichist), phallicist, bibliolater,

ecclesiolater, allotheist, animist, animatist, anthropomorphist, animal worshipper, zoolater, theriolater, zoomorphist, snake worshipper, ophiolater, sun worshipper, heliolater, star worshipper, Sabaist, fire worshipper, pyrolater, tree worshipper, dendrolater, devil worshipper, diabolist, Satanist, Mammonist, mammonolater, ancestor worshipper, necrolater

▶ *7 Religion, 1 Anthropology, 11 Occultism, 8 Divinity*

VERBS

7 **worship**, honour, respect, revere, reverence, venerate, hallow, esteem, dignify, adulate, adore, be devoted to, dedicate oneself to, glorify, exalt, magnify, laud, extol, praise, applaud, acclaim, sing (someone's) praises, sing hymns, celebrate, give thanks, pray, say prayers, meditate, contemplate, commune with God, pay homage to, kneel, genuflect, prostrate oneself, humble oneself, obey, fear God, propitiate, appease, atone, make amends, take communion, sacrifice, fast, go on a pilgrimage

▶ *851 Approval, 812 Celebration, 10 Ritual, 806 Humility, 871 Fasting, 7 Religion*

8 **idolatrize**, worship idols, fetishize, totemize, heathenize, paganize, anthropomorphize, idolize, put on a pedestal, idealize, apotheosize, lionize, admire, look up to, hero-worship, make an idol of, deify

▶ *11 Occultism, 8 Divinity*

ADJECTIVES

9 **worshipful**, worshipping, reverential, reverent, venerational, adoring, adorational, praising, full of praises, hero-worshipping, anthropolatrous, devoted, devotional, prostrate, humbled, humble, supplicatory, supplicating, supplicant, penitent, prayerful, dutiful, meditative, meditational, contemplative, ascetic

▶ *851 Approval, 10 Ritual, 837 Gratitude, 806 Humility, 673 Submission, 461 Thought*

10 **idolatrous**, iconolatrous, superstitious, cult, cultish, cultist, heathen, pagan, totemic, totemistic, fetishistic (*or* fetichistic), fetishlike (*or* fetich-like), phallic, bibliolatrous, ecclesiolatrous, allotheistic, animistic, animatistic, anthropomorphic, zoolatrous, animal-worshipping, zoomorphic, theriolatrous, snake-worshipping, ophiolatrous, sun-worshipping, heliolatrous, star-worshipping, Sabaic, fire-worshipping, pyrolatrous, tree-worshipping, dendrolatrous, devil-worshipping, diabolic, diabolical, demonic, Satanic, Mammonistic, mammonolatrous, necrolatrous, ancestor-worshipping

▶ *7 Religion, 1 Anthropology, 400 Humankind, 8 Divinity, 10 Ritual*

11 **worshipped**, honoured, revered, venerated, blessed, esteemed, adored, glorified, extolled,

praised, admired, lionized, idolized

▶ *851 Approval*

ADVERBS

12 **worshipfully**, honorifically, honourably, reverentially, adoringly, devotedly, idolatrously, devotionally, humbly, ascetically, penitentially, sacrificially, meditatively, contemplatively, mystically, mysteriously

▶ *851 Approval, 10 Ritual, 806 Humility, 867 Penitence, 461 Thought, 7 Religion, 673 Submission*

10   Ritual

NOUNS

1 **ritual**, procedure, established practice, custom, praxis, habit, convention, routine, usage, institution, formality, ceremony, ceremonial, ordinance, office, service, form, formula, formulary, duty, order, observance, religious observance, strict observance, solemnity, solemn observance, ritual practice, religious practice, rite, worship, form of worship, order of worship, prescribed form, liturgy, sacrament

▶ *813 Formality, 719 Observance, 584 Habit, 7 Religion*

2 **ritualism**, rituality, ritualization, liturgism, liturgics, liturgology, formalism, ceremonialism, solemnization, symbolism, symbolics, cult, cultism, sacramentalism, sacramentarianism, Sabbatism, Sabbatarianism

▶ *11 Occultism*

3 **rite of worship**, honour, reverence, veneration, adoration, glorification, exaltation, magnification, laudation, praise, celebration, thanksgiving, blessing, benediction, hymn-singing, psalm-singing, confession, astiamnu, penitence, offering, oblation, almsgiving, chalukah, potlatch, sacrifice, asvamedha, muda, supplication, petition, praying, prayer, puja

▶ *9 Worship, 812 Celebration, 433 Melody, 49 Music, 867 Penitence, 712 Request, 710 Offer, 7 Religion, 8 Divinity*

4 **public worship**, prayer meeting, prayers, abodah (*or* avodah), musaph, church service, divine service, divine office, form of worship, liturgy, morning service, morning prayers, matins, evening service, evening prayers, evensong, vespers, minchah, maarib, memorial service, yahrzeit, order of service, canonical hour, lauds, prime, terce, sext, nones, compline (*or* complin), call to prayer, azan, muezzin's cry

5 **Christian rite**, holy rite, sacrament, seven sacraments, baptism, christening, immersion, total immersion, affusion, aspersion, confirmation, first communion, penance, confession, propitiation, penitential rites, Eucharist, Mass, marriage, Holy Matrimony, marriage service, nuptial Mass, holy orders, ordination,

anointing the sick, Chrism (*or* chrisom), unction, Requiem Mass, extreme unction, viaticum, last rites, burial of the dead, ritual act, sign of the Cross, laying on of hands, lustration, purification, cleansing, ablution, thurification, sprinkling, Asperges, recessional, kiss of peace, denunciation, excommunication, exorcism

▶ *867 Penitence, 823 Marriage, 7 Religion, 397 Death, 399 Burial, 621 Cleanness, 827 Curse*

6 **Eucharist**, Holy Communion, Lord's Supper, Mass, High Mass, *Missa solemnis* (L), Low Mass, *Missa bassa* (L), *Missa Brevis* (L), Midnight Mass, order of service, introit, Kyries, Gloria, Lesson, Epistle, Gradual, Collects, Gospel, creed, credo, offertory, lavabo, biddings, thanksgiving, consecration, consecrated elements, bread and wine, breaking of bread, elevation of the Host, transubstantiation, real presence, intinction, consubstantiation, impanation, subpanation, body and blood of Christ, Communion, dismissal, blessing

7 **non-Christian ritual**, initiation rite, passage right (*or* rite of passage), bar mitzvah, bat (*or* bas) mitzvah, ritual mutilation, circumcision, milah, female circumcision, female genital mutilation, clitoridectomy, couvade, circumambulation, cleansing, taslich, oharai, hogahn, bathing, mikvah, abhiseka, fertility rite, rite of spring, spring rounds, ambarvalia, ritual prostitution, dance of Siva, ghost dance, sun dance, potlatch, rain dance, war dance, fetishism, cannibalism, infanticide, suicide, hara-kiri

▶ *11 Occultism*

8 **hymn**, hymning, hymnology, hymnography, hymn-singing, psalm, psalm-singing, psalmody, psalter, chant, niggun, Gregorian chant, kalophonic chant, kontakion, kanon, plainsong, plainchant, Ambrosian chant, mantra, hymnal, hymnary, Rigveda, Samaveda, anthem, cherubicon, carol, exultet, cantata, motet, canticle, doxology, greater doxology, lesser doxology, antiphon, response, Gloria, Gloria Patri, Gloria in Excelsis, Gradual, Te Deum, Benedicite, Sanctus, Jubilate Deo, paean, Magnificat, gospel song, Homeric hymn, Vedic hymn, Alleluia, Hallelujah, Hosanna, maoz tzur, nusach, yigdal, zemitot

▶ *851 Approval, 433 Melody, 49 Music*

9 **prayer**, orison, devotion, impetration, petition, request, petitionary prayer, bidding prayer, invocation, epidesis, nembutsu, gayatri, allocution, intercession, geullah, suffrage, prayer for the dead, anamnesis, vigils, special prayer, comprecation, supplication, intention, rogation, eulogia, blessing, motzi, kol nidre, benediction, nishmat, grace, benison, norito, litany, collect, secret (*or* secreta), Credo, Ange-

lus, the Lord's Prayer, Paternoster, Our Father, rosary, Hail Mary, Ave, Ave Maria, Kyrie Eleison, Pax, Agnus Dei, Nunc Dimittis, Sursum Corda, mantra, alenu, dharani, om (*or* aum), berakah

▶ *837 Gratitude, 806 Humility, 710 Offer, 867 Penitence, 477 Question*

10 **religious manual**, prayer book, Book of Common Prayer, Alternative Prayer Book, breviary, missal, book of hours, farse, lectionary, pontifical, Virginal, ordinal, canon, rubric, church book, mass book, machzor, siddur, menaion

▶ *7 Religion*

11 **place of worship**, house of God, house of prayer, church, kirk, mission, meetinghouse, chapel, conventicle, chantry, Lady chapel, chapel of rest, abbey, cathedral, minster, *duomo* (It), basilica, oratory, oratorium, temple, tabernacle, synagogue, shul, mosque, masjid, wat, pantheon, ziggurat, pagoda, fane (Arch), shrine, cell

▶ *7 Religion*

12 **church**, nave, transept(s), chancel, choir, sanctuary, altar, pulpit, lectern, pew, stall, choirstall, confessional, cloister, aisle, clerestory, triforium, tribune gallery, font, rood screen, crypt, presbytery, sacristy, vestry

▶ *43 Architecture, 7 Religion*

13 **shrine**, chapel, sanctuary, sanctum, sanctum sanctorum, holy of holies, sacrarium, reliquary, tabernacle, dagoba, cella, naos, stupa, tope, sacred place, holy place, Jerusalem, Bethlehem, Wailing Wall, Mount Omei, Mount Tai, Butsuden, Chorten, Myoskinji, Sarnath, Anghkar Wat, Shwe Dagon, Abhayagiri, Tashi Lumpo, Kumbum, Bayon, Adam's Peak, Badrinath, Gangotri, River Ganges, River Narbada, River Godavari, River Kistna, Golden Temple of Amritsar, Kaaba, Mecca, Benares, Zem-Zem, Blue Mosque, Fujiyama, Miya-zaki-jingu, Abydos, Mitla, marae, cromlech, Avebury, Stonehenge, Ayers Rock, Bethel

14 **sacred object**, relic, monstrance, ostensorium, eucharistial, pyx, ciborium, tabernacle, ark, Torah scrolls, aronha-kodesh, phylactery, tefillin, mezuzah, asterisk, crucifix, cross, rood, holy cross, black stone, Bo tree, Banyan tree, osculatory, icon, veronica, *bambino* (It), *pietà* (It), holy water, aspergillum, asperger, incense, thurible, censer, incensory, chrismal, scrobis, cruet, urceole, rosary beads, beadroll, prayerwheel, prayermat, prayer shawl, tallith, chaplet, candle, votive candle, paschal candle, vigil light, menorah, bugia, sanctus bell, sacring bell, chair of Saint Peter, Sangreal, Holy Grail, chalice, juju, totem, talisman, charm, amulet, fetish, totem pole, sacrificial knife

▶ *11 Occultism*

15 **holy day**, holiday, feast, feast day, fast day,

Yob Tom, Lord's Day, Sabbath, Sunday, Saturday, All Hallows' Day, All Saints' Day, All Souls' Day, Lady Day, Purification, Assumption, Candlemas, Lammas, Epiphany, Twelfth Night, Septuagesima, Shrove Tuesday, Mardi Gras, Pancake Day, Ash Wednesday, Quadragesima, Palm Sunday, Maundy Thursday, Good Friday, Ascension Day, Whitsunday, Michaelmas, Martinmas, Shabuoth, Rosh Hashanah, Yom Kippur, Day of Atonement, Rosh Chodesh, summer solstice, winter solstice, autumnal equinox, vernal equinox

▶ *812 Celebration, 773 Rejoicing, 511 Memory, 774 Lamentation, 837 Gratitude*

16 **religious festival**, festival, fiesta, encaenia, festivity, feast, love feast, agape, taanit, celebration, Advent, Christmas, Yuletide, Nativity, Noel, Carnival, Lent, Easter, Eastertide, Whitsun, Harvest Festival, Feast of the Annunciation, Pesach, Passover, Hannukah, Feast of the Dedication, Feast of Weeks, Feast of Tabernacles, Sukkoth, Purim, Feast of Circumcision, Fast of Av (*or* Ab), Eid-ul-Fitr, Eid-ul-Adha, Ramadan, Muharram, Zulhijyah, Baraim, Divali, Festival of Lights, Holi, Dasehra, Durga-puja, Chinese New Year, Beltane, Hallowe'en, Samhain, Saturnalia, Lupercalia, Floralia, Agrionia, Panathenea, Dionysia, Thesmophoria, Delia, Carneia, Anthesteria, Apaturia

▶ *812 Celebration, 350 Eating, 774 Lamentation, 511 Memory, 773 Rejoicing, 837 Gratitude*

17 **worshipper**, venerator, follower, communicant, celebrant, supplicant (*or* suppliant), petitioner, penitent, churchgoer(s), parishioner(s), chapelgoer(s), fold, flock, sheep, congregation, congress, assembly, gathering, concourse, sangha, minyn

▶ *9 Worship, 7 Religion, 161 Assembly*

VERBS

18 **perform rites**, ritualize, observe, celebrate, keep, solemnize, receive the sacrament, commune, oblate, give alms, confess, receive absolution, commune, minister, officiate, anoint, chrism, confirm, lay on hands, bless, baptize, christen, sprinkle, asperse, shrive, absolve, denounce, excommunicate, exorcise, curse

▶ *306 Form, 813 Formality, 719 Observance, 688 Authority, 7 Religion, 11 Occultism, 827 Curse*

19 **offer worship**, honour, revere, reverence, venerate, adore, glorify, exalt, extol, magnify, laud, praise, celebrate, give thanks, sing hymns, say prayers, kneel, genuflect, bow, stoop, cross oneself, make the sign of the cross, sacrifice, propitiate

▶ *9 Worship, 851 Approval, 812 Celebration, 433 Melody, 7 Religion*

20 **pray**, request, invoke, impetrate, petition, rogate, supplicate, implore, beseech, offer a prayer, say one's prayers, say 'Our Father', say

the Lord's Prayer, say grace, invoke a blessing, give thanks, recite the rosary, count (*or* tell *or* say) one's beads, chant, incant
▶ *851 Approval, 712 Request, 183 Repetition, 849 Respect*

ADJECTIVES

21 **ritualistic**, ceremonial, festive, festal, formulaic, official, ordained, impetrational, petitionary, invocational, supplicatory, liturgical, hymnological, hymnographical, comminatory, anthemic, celebratory, laudational, doxological, glorified, glorious, extolled, dignified, consecrated, sacramental, sacral, oblational, libational, libationary, chrismal, sacrificial, nuptial, matrimonial, penitential, funereal, baptismal, symbolic, eucharistic (*or* eucharistical), transubstantial, totemistic, fetishistic, cannibalistic, exorcised, excommunicated, cursed
▶ *399 Burial, 812 Celebration, 183 Repetition, 847 Duty, 306 Form, 813 Formality, 774 Lamentation, 823 Marriage, 719 Observance, 11 Occultism, 8 Divinity, 7 Religion, 477 Question, 150 Order*

22 **worshipping**, reverent, devout, pious, observant, religious, devotional, prayerful, dutiful, solemn, congregational, parochial
▶ *9 Worship, 7 Religion*

ADVERBS

23 **ritually**, ritualistically, observantly, officially, solemnly, dutifully, devoutly, worshipfully, sacramentally, prayerfully, liturgically, doxologically, processionally, festally, communally, congregationally, symbolically

11 Occultism

From ghoulies and ghosties and long-leggety beasties/ And things that go bump in the night/ Good Lord, deliver us! Cornish prayer.

All argument is against it; but all belief is for it. Samuel Johnson.

There are more things in Heaven and Earth, Horatio/ Than are dreamt of in your philosophy. William Shakespeare.

NOUNS

1 **occultism**, esoterics, esotericism, supernaturalism, supranaturalism, preternaturalism, mystery, mystification, mysticism, shamanism, spiritism, animism, Rosicrucianism, hermetics, hermetism, hermeticism, symbolics, symbolism, anagogics, cabbalism (*or* cabalism), cabbala, voodooism, witchcraft, magic, transcendentalism, yoga, yogism, reincarnationism, metaphysics, hyperphysics, transphysical science, psychism, psychics, psychic research, metapsychism, parapsychology, psychosophy, theosophy, anthroposophy, scientology, pseudopsychology, spiritualism, mediumism, poltergeistism, mesmerism, hypnotism, autohypnotism, alchemy, astrology, divination, prophecy, fortune telling, extrasensory perception (ESP), telepathy, telepathic transmission, telergy, thought transference, mind reading, faith healing, astral projection, telekinesis, psychokinesis, fork bending, telaesthesia, teleportation, levitation, pyramidology, ufology, phrenology, Kirlian photography, psychorrhagy, psychography, automatism, automatic writing, spirit writing, trance speaking, ghost dance, spirit rapping (Inf), table tapping (Inf)
▶ *531 Concealment, 529 Secrecy, 516 Foresight, 368 Nonmaterial World, 10 Ritual*

2 **the occult**, the paranormal, the supernatural, the supersensible, supernature, supranature, spirit world, astral plane, esoterica, enigma, arcanum, cabbala, sealed book, code, cipher (*or* cypher), occultness, obscurity, secrecy, mystery, mysteriousness, miraculousness, supernaturalness, supernaturality, supernormalness, supersensitiveness, superphysicalness, superhumanity, unearthliness, unworldliness, otherworldiness, spirituality, eeriness, ghostliness, numinousness
▶ *368 Nonmaterial World, 527 Latency, 551 Obscurity, 529 Secrecy, 531 Concealment, 235 Power*

3 **witchcraft**, witchery, bewitchery, witchwork, Wicca, coven, witches' Sabbath (*or* Sabbat), Walpurgis Night, Hallowe'en, witching hour, sorcery, wizardry, necromancy, spellcraft, spellbinding, spellcasting, enchantment, bedevilment, possession, voodooism, voodoo, hoodoo, wanga, jujuism, obi (*or* obeah), obiism (*or* obeahism), shamanism, magism, magianism, totemism, fetishism (*or* fetichism), vampirism, magic, sortilege, theurgy, gramyre (Arch), thaumaturgy, thaumaturgia, thaumaturgics, alchemy, natural magic, sympathetic magic, white magic, chaos magic, black magic, black art, diablerie
▶ *233 Influence, 862 Evil, 9 Worship, 7 Religion, 235 Power*

4 **witch**, witchwoman, witchman, witch master, witch doctor, obeah (*or* obi) doctor, voodooist, wangateur, medicine man, isangoma, mundunugu, shaman, shamaness, shamanist, sorcerer, sorceress, magician, mage, magus, Merlin, necromancer, wizard, warlock, theurgist, thaumaturge, thaumaturgist, lamia, bewitcher, charmer, enchanter, enchantress, spellbinder, siren, mermaid, lorelei, water witch, white witch, weird sister, Witch of Endor, Hecate, Circe, Medusa, Medea, Stheno, Euryale
▶ *7 Religion, 233 Influence, 235 Power, 507 Wisdom*

5 **spell**, magic spell, charm, love charm, love potion, philtre, rune, glamour (Arch), weird

(Scot), wanga, evil eye, hex, jinx, whammy (US inf), conjuration, conjurement, evocation, invocation, magic words, incantation, chant, hocus-pocus, mumbo jumbo, abracadabra, paternoster, open sesame, abraxas, fee faw fum, glossolalia, pentagram (*or* pentacle)

▶ *827 Curse, 523 Unintelligibility, 551 Obscurity, 235 Power*

6 **talisman**, charm, mascot, amulet, periapt, phylactery (Arch), fetish, totem, juju, obi (*or* obeah), mojo, tiki, medallion, relic, St Christopher (medal), symbol, emblem, mandala, ankh, scarab (*or* scarabaeus), swastika, fylfot, gammadion, lucky charm, crucifix, good-luck charm, luck piece, lucky bean, four-leaf clover, shamrock, horseshoe, rabbit's foot, black cat, antidote, garlic, silver bullet, bell, book, and candle, witch's broomstick, wizard's cap, familiar, familiar spirit, black cat, magic circle, magic ring, ring of invisibility, magic belt, magic sword, magic carpet, seven-league boots, cap of darkness, wishbone, wishing well, wishing stone, fairy ring

▶ *543 Sign, 529 Secrecy, 10 Ritual*

7 **spirit**, soul, geist, atman, mind, inner mind, inner being, psyche, pneuma, animus, anima, the unconscious, the subconscious, id, ego, superego, third eye, astral body, linga sharira, design body, bliss body, Buddhic body, karmic body, kamarupa, mental body, causal body, subtle body, vital body, spiritual body, etheric body, soul body

▶ *396 Life, 368 Nonmaterial World, 527 Latency*

8 **psychic power**, sixth sense, inner sense, intuition, feyness, second sight, psi faculty, third eye, precognition, premonition, clairvoyance, clairaudience, clairsentience, insight, foresight, crystal vision, psychometry, telepathy, telekinesis, metapsychosis, cosmic consciousness

▶ *516 Foresight, 435 Vision, 501 Knowledge, 235 Power*

9 **divination**, divining, prophecy, soothsaying, clairvoyance, prediction, premonition, precognition, forecasting, fortune-telling, tea-leaf reading, Tarot-reading, Tarot cards, dowsing, water-divining, divining rods, dowsing rods, hydromancy, radiaesthesia, augury, sortilege, haruspication, haruspicy, ichthyomancy, ophiomancy, pythonism, mantology, palmistry, palm-reading, chiromancy, chirognomy, crystal-gazing, crystal ball, astrology, horoscopy, sideromancy, astrodiagnosis, astromancy, horoscope, star chart, birth (*or* natal) chart, numerology, arithmomancy, logomancy, dream interpretation, oneiromancy, I Ching, psephomancy, capnomancy, pyromancy, metereomancy, geomancy, hieromancy, hieroscopy, theomancy, necromancy, psycnomancy

▶ *516 Foresight, 464 Intuition, 517 Prediction*

10 **psychic phenomenon**, illusion, hallucination, telepathic hallucination, déjà vu, telepathic dream, premonition, maya, trance, yoga trance, dharana, dhyana, samadhi, hypnosis, hypnotic trance, mediumistic trance, spirit-raising, seance, sitting, Ouija (board) (Tm), planchette, ectoplasm, bioplasma, exteriorized protoplasm, aura, emanation, ectoplasy, effluvium, biofeedback, cosmic vibration, synchronicity, out-of-body experience (Oobe), crop circle, UFO sighting, alien encounter

▶ *723 Possession, 368 Nonmaterial World, 161 Assembly, 10 Ritual*

11 **ghost**, spirit, ghoul, phantom, apparition, manifestation, materialization, poltergeist, shade, manes, lemures, spectre, spook (Inf), phantasm, wraith, presence, undead, vampire, zombie (*or* zombi), fetch, demon, jinni (*or* genie), familiar spirit, elemental spirit, will-o'-the-wisp, fairy, fay, sylph, Mab, Titania, Befana, genius, elf, pixie, piskie (Arch), Puck, alfar, brownie, gnome, dwarf, troll, trow, kobold, orc, werewolf, werecat, goblin, imp, sprite, hobgoblin, leprechaun, changeling, cluricaune, gremlin, little green men (LGM), alien, extraterrestrial (ET), Martian, cosmic being

▶ *457 Appearance, 253 Presence*

12 **occultist**, psychic, esoteric, mystic, mystagogue, cabbalist (*or* cabalist), Rosicrucian, druid, druidess, houngan, supernaturalist, telepathist, mind reader, thought reader, telekinetic, fork bender, telaesthetic, panpsychist, metaphysician, metaphysicist, metapsychist, transcendentalist, spiritualist, spiritist, medium, ecstatic, automatist, psychographist, alchemist, hypnotist, faith healer, psychometer, psychometrist, anthroposophist, theosophist, psychist, psychicist, parapsychologist, pyramidologist, ufologist, phrenologist, adept, mahatma, yogi, fakir, exorcist, exorcizer, unspeller, spirit rapper (Inf), table tapper (Inf), ghostbuster (Inf)

▶ *529 Secrecy, 531 Concealment, 7 Religion, 464 Intuition, 368 Nonmaterial World, 61 Psychology and Psychiatry*

13 **diviner**, dowser, predictor, foreteller, forecaster, psychic, clairvoyant, clairaudient, clairsentient, seer, prophet, soothsayer, *vates* (L), augur, auspex, haruspex, weather prophet, astrologer, fortune teller, tea-leaf reader, Tarot reader, crystal gazer, palmist, palmreader, chiromancer, gypsy, romany, wise woman, sibyl, pythoness, oracle, geomancer, necromancer, psychomancer, icthyomancer, ophiomancer, pythonist, sideromancer, astromancer, numerologist, dream interpreter, oneiromancer, pyromancer, capnomancer, psephomancer,

hieromancer, theomancer

▶ *464 Intuition, 517 Prediction, 516 Foresight, 543 Sign, 501 Knowledge, 507 Wisdom*

ADJECTIVES

14 **occult**, cryptic, paranormal, supersensible, superphysical, supernatural, supranatural, supernormal, preternatural, hermetic, symbolic, anagogic(al), latent, covert, enigmatic, arcane, esoteric, obscure, secret, mysterious, encoded, cabbalistic (*or* cabalistic), runic, Rosicrucian

▶ *527 Latency, 529 Secrecy, 531 Concealment, 551 Obscurity, 524 Interpretation*

15 **witchlike**, wizard-like, wizardly, sorcerous, necromantic, alchemic(al), alchemistic, druidic, shamanic, talismanic, Circean, bewitching, magical, enchanting, charming, spellbinding, entrancing, fascinating, invocational, conjural, incantational, incantatory, hypnotic, autohypnotic, voodooistic, totemistic, totemic, fetishistic (*or* fetichistic), diabolic, diabolical, demonic, demonic(al), fiendish, devilish, Satanic, hellish, undead, vampiric, vampirish

▶ *235 Power, 786 Wonder, 827 Curse, 8 Divinity, 862 Evil*

16 **psychic**, psychical, unconscious, subconscious, transcendental, cosmic, telepathic, telekinetic, psychokinetic, telergic, telaesthetic, radiaesthetic, extrasensory, spiritualistic, mediumistic, psychosensory, transphysical, hyperphysical, metapsychic, metapsychical, panpsychic, parapsychological, theosophical, psychosophical, anthroposophical, scientological, pseudopsychological

▶ *235 Power, 233 Influence*

17 **divinatory**, prophetic, clairvoyant, clairaudient, clairsentient, predictive, predictable, predicted, premonitory, precognitive, augural, haruspical, sibylline, oracular, astrological

▶ *517 Prediction, 516 Foresight, 464 Intuition*

18 **spiritual**, immaterial, nonmaterial, incorporeal, insubstantial, intangible, unembodied, disembodied, unphysical, nonphysical, ethereal, airy, elemental, fairy, fey, ghostly, spectral, shadowy, phantom, phantasmic, phantasmal, wraithy, wraithlike, unearthly, otherworldly, astral, alien, extraterrestrial, ufological, extramundane, supramundane, transmundane, unworldly, eerie, weird, eldritch, uncanny, strange, creepy (Inf), spooky (Inf)

▶ *438 Invisibility, 397 Death, 442 Transparency*

19 **bewitched**, enchanted, charmed, spellbound, entranced, fascinated, hypnotized, mesmerized, hag-ridden, obsessed, possessed, bedevilled, cursed, hexed, jinxed, haunted, ghost-ridden, spooked (Inf)

▶ *827 Curse, 723 Possession*

VERBS

20 **occult**, hide, obscure, veil, cloak, mystify, symbolize, encode, spiritualize, dematerialize,

immaterialize, etherealize

▶ *527 Latency, 551 Obscurity, 529 Secrecy, 531 Concealment, 441 Dimness, 438 Invisibility, 368 Nonmaterial World, 543 Sign*

21 **bewitch**, enchant, incant, charm, mesmerize, hypnotize, practise witchcraft, cast spells, spellbind, say magic words, wave a wand, ride a broomstick, put the evil eye on, hex, jinx, curse, sorcerize, theurgize, thaumaturgize, shamanize, diabolize, demonize, bedevil, possess

▶ *235 Power, 233 Influence, 827 Curse, 10 Ritual*

22 **conjure**, conjure up, invoke, evoke, raise ghosts, wake the dead, practise spiritualism, call up spirits, summon spirits, hold a séance (*or* sitting)

23 **divine**, prophesy, soothsay, predict, forecast, foretell, foresee, intuit, tell fortunes, read tea leaves, read (*or* consult) the Tarot, read palms, crystal-gaze, cast nativities, draw up birth (*or* natal) charts, plot horoscopes, cast the I Ching, interpret dreams, dowse, water-divine, read signs

▶ *517 Prediction, 516 Foresight, 464 Intuition, 760 Sensitivity, 235 Power*

24 **experience psychic phenomena**, see signs, see auras, sense vibrations, hallucinate, transmit thoughts, transfer thoughts, read minds, bend forks, leave one's body, astral-project, travel in the astral plane, levitate, teleport, faith-heal, go into a trance, see the little people, communicate with aliens, encounter aliens

▶ *368 Nonmaterial World, 519 Imagination*

ADVERBS

25 **occultly**, obscurely, mystically, mysteriously, secretly, secretively, enigmatically, arcanely, cabbalistically, esoterically, metaphysically, transcendentally, spiritually, supernaturally, paranormally, psychically, parapsychologically, telepathically, mesmerically, hypnotically, prophetically, clairvoyantly, astrologically, consciously, subconsciously

26 **magically**, eerily, spookily, weirdly, ghoulishly, necromantically, thaumaturgically, theurgically, superstitiously, diabolically, demonically

12 Government and Politics

The right of governing was not property but a trust. Charles James Fox.

Every country has the government it deserves. Joseph de Maistre.

The ballot is stronger than the bullet. Abraham Lincoln.

That government of the people, by the people, and for the people, shall not perish from the earth. Abraham Lincoln.

Man is by nature a political animal. Aristotle.

Politics is not an exact science. Bismarck.

Politics is the art of the possible. R. A. Butler.

NOUNS

1 **government**, direction, management, administration, executive, local government, national government, international government, world government, form of government, state system, political system, hierarchy, political organization, polity, political rule, political authority, political administration, politicking, tribal system, tribalism, feudalism, feudality, physiocracy, Poujadism, benevolent despotism, paternalism, squirearchy, clan system, patriarchy, matriarchy, matriarchate, gynaecocracy, gynarchy, gynocracy, constitutional government, constitutionalism, legal government, rule of law, legality, Senatus Populusque Romanus (SPQR), church government, theocracy, thearchy, priestly government, papal rule, hierocracy, clericalism, ecclesiasticism, medieval government, government by estates, monarchy, monarchical absolutism, constitutional monarchy, monarchical government, kingship (*or* queenship), republicanism, federalism, aristocracy, meritocracy, oligarchy, minority rule, elitism, gerontocracy, senatorial government, duumvirate, triumvirate, rule of wealth, plutocracy, representative government, parliamentary government, government by the ballot box, party system, democracy, independence, people's choice, egalitarianism, democracy unlimited, popular will, public opinion, vox populi, majority rule, one man one vote, proportional representation, isocracy, pantisocracy, pluralism, collectivism, proletarianism, dictatorship of the proletariat, communism, Leninism, Marxism-Leninism, Maoism, Titoism, party rule, Bolshevism, totalitarian dictatorship, totalitarianism, Fascism, Nazism, National Socialism, demagogy, demagoguery, puppet government, instrument, committee rule, sovietism, imperium in imperio, stratocracy, army rule, military government, martial law, ochlocracy, mobocracy, mob rule, mob law, anarchy, misgovernment, syndicalism, socialism, guild socialism, Fabianism, statism, bureaucracy, technocracy, self-government, autocracy, autarchy, self-rule, autonomy, home rule, caretaker government, regency, interregnum, sphere of influence, mandate, mandated territory

▶ *689 Anarchy, 580 Selection, 698 Freedom, 232 Instrumentality*

2 **politics**, political science, public affairs, civil affairs, statecraft, statesmanship, diplomacy

3 **governance**, rule, sway, iron sway, governmental power, reins of government, direction, command, absolute command, directorship, control, supreme control, hold, grip, clutches, domination, mastery, whip hand, effective control, reach, long arm, ascendancy, dominion, joint dominion, joint rule, condominium, sovereignty, suzerainty, raj, overlordship, presidency, supremacy, superiority, reign, regnancy, regency, dynasty, self-rule, autonomy, foreign rule, occupational power, heteronomy, empery, empire, rod of empire, subjection, imperialism, colonialism, neocolonialism, white supremacy, black power, regime, regiment, regimen, state control, statism, dirigisme, paternalism, bureaucracy, apparat, civil service, petty officialdom, officialism, beadledom, bumbledom, Parkinson's law, expansion, red tape, bumph (*or* bumf) (Inf)

▶ *653 Management, 688 Authority, 726 Retention, 126 Superiority, 699 Restraint, 261 Expansion*

4 **governing body**, Parliament, British government, Mother of Parliaments, Westminster, House of Commons, Lower House, Lower Chamber, House of Lords, Upper House, Upper Chamber, House of Peers, Lords Spiritual, Lords Temporal, Scottish Grand Committee, Welsh Grand Committee, US government, Congress, Capitol Hill, Senate, Upper House, Upper Chamber, House of Representatives, House, Lower House, Lower Chamber, Irish government, Oireachtas, Dáil Éireann, Seanad Éireann

▶ *653 Management*

5 **political organization**, body politic, state, nation state, commonwealth, country, realm, kingdom, republic, city-state, Athens, Sparta, Rome, city, free city, polis, temple state, federation, confederation, principality, duchy, archduchy, dukedom, palatinate, empire, dominion, colony, dependency, protectorate, mandate, mandated territory, territory, free world, communist bloc, developing world, Third World, superpower, buffer state, county, region, province, district, corporative state, social state, welfare state, laws, constitution, banana republic (Inf)

▶ *249 Region, 126 Superiority, 127 Inferiority, 298 Interface, 16 Law*

6 **political party**, right, left, centre, Conservative Party, Tories, true blue, Labour Party, Labourite, Liberal Democrat Party, Social Democratic Party (SDP), Social and Liberal Democratic Party, Ulster Democratic Unionist Party (UDUP), Democratic Party (US), Republican Party (US), Grand Old Party (GOP) (US), Fine Gael (Ireland), Fianna Fáil (Ireland), Progressive Democrats (Ireland), Scottish National Party (SNP), Plaid Cymru (Wales), Unionist Parties (Northern Ireland), Social

Democratic and Labour Party (SDLP) (Northern Ireland), Sinn Fein (Northern Ireland), Green Party, Ecologists, National Front (NF), Liberals, Radicals, Whigs, Socialists, Nationalists, Social Democratic Party (Germany), Christian Democratic Union (Germany), New Democratic Party (Canada), Progressive Conservative Party (Canada), Popular Coalition (Spain), Democratic Social Centre (Spain), Christian Democratic Party (Italy), People's Party (Austria), Women's Alliance (Iceland), Workers' Revolutionary Party, International Socialists, Trotskyists, Marxists, Communists, Bolsheviks, Mensheviks, Fascists, Nazis, Falangists, Blackshirts, Brownshirts, Jacobins, Girondists, coalition, popular front, bloc, comrade, tovarisch, Fabian, syndicalist, anarchist, anarcho-syndicalist, revolter, rightwinger, rightist, Tory, reactionary, hard-liner, left-winger, leftist, leftie, pinko (US), populist, democrat, centrist, moderate, party member, party worker, canvasser, Red (Inf), commie (Inf), Trot (Inf), dry (Inf), wet (Inf)
▶ 665 *Party*

7 **governor**, controller, legislator, lawgiver, lawmaker, statesman, stateswoman, president, vice president, prime minister, premier, chancellor governor general
▶ 653 *Management, 696 Master*

8 **politician**, Member of Parliament (MP), Parliamentarian, backbencher, peer, life peer, member of Congress (US), Senator (US), Congressman (*or* Congresswoman) (US), Representative (US), Senate majority leader (US), House majority leader (US), leader of the House of Commons, Father of the House, Senate minority leader (US), House minority leader (US), leader of the Opposition, cabinet minister, cabinet member (US), secretary, minister, undersecretary, junior minister, party chairman, party manager, whip, party whip, majority whip (US), minority whip (US), chief whip, politico (US inf), pol (US sl)
▶ 653 *Management, 696 Master*

ADJECTIVES
9 **governmental**, political, presidential, gubernatorial (US), parliamentary, democratic, republican, independent, constitutional, federal, state, public, civil, civic, administrative, executive, ministerial, senatorial, official, bureaucratic, centralized, technocratic, matriarchal, patriarchal, theocratic, monarchical, feudal, aristocratic, meritocratic, oligarchic, plutocratic, dictatorial, totalitarian, popular, classless, self-governing, self-ruling, autonomous, autarchic, anarchic, Marxist, Leninist, Fascist, Nazi, Socialist, socialistic, Communist, communistic, Conservative, Labour, Liberal, Green
▶ 653 *Management, 665 Party, 698 Freedom, 689 Anarchy*

10 **governing**, ruling, leading, commanding, controlling, dictating, in charge, in power, holding the reins of government, acting, titular, reigning, regnant, regnal, sovereign, holding the sceptre, on the throne, royal, regal, majestic, monarchical, kinglike, kingly, queenlike, queenly, princely, lordly, dynastic, imperial, magisterial
▶ 653 *Management, 802 Aristocrat, 696 Master, 688 Authority*

VERBS
11 **govern**, rule, command, control, lead, be in charge, hold sway, reign, reign supreme, sit on the throne, wear the crown, wield the sceptre, direct, manage, hold the reins, hold office, have a place, occupy a post, fill a post, be in power, occupy 10 Downing Street, occupy the White House (US), have power, have authority, wield power, exert authority, use one's authority, rule absolutely, tyrannize, oppress, dictate, lay down the law, give laws to, legislate for, divide and rule, Balkanize, keep law and order, police
▶ 692 *Command, 688 Authority, 653 Management, 690 Severity, 235 Power, 16 Law*

12 **take authority**, assume authority, seize power, gain power, take control, take command, assume command, take office, take over, take over the reins, form a government, make appointments, mount the throne, ascend the throne, accede to the throne, succeed to the throne, get the power into one's hands, get a hold on, get the whip hand, stage a coup d'état, usurp, usurp the throne
▶ 688 *Authority, 696 Master*

13 **be governed**, owe allegiance, owe fealty, owe loyalty, owe obedience, have laws, have a constitution, be under authority
▶ 699 *Restraint*

ADVERBS
14 **politically**, presidentially, governmentally, democratically, constitutionally, administratively, ministerially, bureaucratically, dictatorially, by law, by authority, in the name of, *de par le Roi* (Fr), by warrant of, in virtue of one's authority

13 Economics

Respectable Professors of the Dismal Science.
Thomas Carlyle.

NOUNS
1 **economics**, economic policy, fiscal policy, monetary policy, welfare economics, economic growth, economic theory, microeconomics, macroeconomics, Keynesian economics, economic system, private enterprise economy, private sector, private enterprise, privatization, denationalization, centrally planned economy, public sector, public utili-

ties, public enterprise, nationalization, public ownership, state-owned industry, mixed economy, fair trade laws (US), interstate commerce (US)

2 **economy**, free-market economy, private sector, personal sector, corporate sector, financial sector, public sector, foreign sector, manufacturing, wholesaling, retailing, selling, marketing, trading, exporting, importing, purchasing power, price controls, goods, producer goods, capital goods, consumer goods, economic upturn, boom, boom/bust cycle, economic downturn, recession, depression, slump, stagflation, inflation, deflation, disinflation, stagnation, deficit financing, deficit spending, black market, black economy

▶ *740 Market, 14 Finance, 737 Trade, 739 Sale, 243 Production, 751 Price*

3 **economic statistics**, econometrics, regression analysis, gross national product (GNP), gross domestic product (GDP), price index, retail price index (RPI), cost of living, economic productivity, prices, vital statistics, economic analysis, supply-side economics, national debt, budget deficit, inflation

4 **economic development**, economic growth, industrialization, natural resources, labour force, developed countries, the West, underdeveloped countries, Third World, International Finance Corporation (IFC), International Development Association, International Bank for Reconstruction and Development (IBRD), World Bank, International Monetary Fund (IMF), capital accumulation, capital investment, public debt, improved technology, improved productivity, restructuring of industry, demographic transition, population growth

▶ *627 Improvement*

5 **international trade**, free trade, free-trade zone, economic zone, commerce, trade agreement, General Agreement on Tariffs and Trade (GATT), restrictive trade agreement, restraint of trade, economic union, trade integration, Exchange Rate Mechanism (ERM), European Free Trade Association (EFTA), European Economic Community (EEC), European Community (EC), Euromarket, Organization of Petroleum-Exporting Countries (OPEC), Benelux, Council for Mutual Economic Assistance (COMECON), Group of Seven (G7), Club of Paris, Caribbean Community and Common Market (CARICOM), Latin American Integration Association (LAIA), visible trade, invisible trade, balance of trade, balance of payments

▶ *737 Trade*

6 **economic factors**, capital, market, buyers' market, sellers' market, bear market, bull market, supply and demand, competition, monopoly, cartel, cooperative, revenue, sales rev-

enue, pricing, profit, profit motive, profit margin, research and development (R and D), technology, automation, commodity, goods, dry goods, durable goods, durables, perishable goods, perishables, productivity, production, production costs, production efficiency, rationalization, distribution, fiscal policy, taxation, progressive taxation, regressive taxation, proportional taxation, income tax, taxable income, standard rate of taxation, tax evasion, tax avoidance, individual retirement account (IRA) (US), Inland Revenue, Internal Revenue (US), sales tax, value-added tax (VAT), excise duty, tariff duty, import duty, protectionism, embargo, sanction, economic sanction, tariff, trade barrier, customs barrier, tariff barrier, protection quota, intervention, free duty, free goods, free port, public expenditure, services, employment, unemployment, wages, real wages, pay increases, business cycle, inflation, inflationary spiral, price-wage spiral, deflation, balance of payments, money supply, exchange rate, standard of living, income, financial security, consumer confidence, price support, subsidy, capitalism, private enterprise, mercantile system, *laissez faire* (Fr), physiocratic school, industrial revolution

▶ *740 Market, 653 Management, 243 Production, 14 Finance, 12 Government and Politics*

7 **corporation**, firm, company, limited company (Ltd), public limited company (plc), incorporated company (Inc) (US), specialized company, costs, fixed costs, marginal costs, indirect costs, budget, budgetary control, budget surplus, budget deficit, profit-and-loss account, balance sheet, profit, gross profit, net profit, excess profit, assets, fixed assets, general audit, liquidation, receivership, takeover, takeover bid, friendly takeover, hostile takeover, buyout, leveraged buyout, management buyout, merger, business affairs, business association, chamber of commerce, junior chamber of commerce (US)

▶ *653 Management, 750 Accounts*

8 **industrial relations**, labour force, workforce, casual labour, labor union (US), trade union, closed shop, labour costs, wages and salaries, working hours, flexitime, industrial safety, working conditions, strike, general strike, go-slow, work to rule, lock-out, pension, retirement benefits, workmen's compensation, unemployment insurance, International Labour Organisation, American Federation of Labor and Congress of Industrial Organizations (AFL-CIO) (US), Trades Union Congress (TUC), Advisory Conciliation and Arbitration Services (ACAS), labour law, the dole (Inf)

▶ *15 Industrial Relations*

9 **economist**, economic expert, businessman

(*or* businesswoman), profiteer, merchant, merchandiser, dealer, trader, seller, barterer, importer, exporter, supplier, employer, chamber of commerce member, junior chamber of commerce member (US), Jaycee (US), liveryman, trade unionist, labor union member (US), spender, consumer, buyer, purchaser, customer, patron, client, clientele

▶ *653 Management, 739 Sale, 738 Purchase, 737 Trade*

VERBS

10 **trade with**, open a trade, traffic in, export, import, market, merchandise, offer for sale, have on offer, sell at a profit, make a profit, realize one's capital, encash, commercialize, corner the market, monopolize, nationalize, privatize

▶ *737 Trade, 740 Market, 739 Sale*

11 **deal**, negotiate, barter, drive a hard bargain, make a bid, raise the bid, take over, act as a white knight, finance, underwrite, bankroll (US inf)

▶ *14 Finance, 716 Negotiation*

12 **cheat**, gazump, gazunder, sell a pig in a poke, cook the books, evade tax, con (Inf), swindle (Inf), fiddle (Inf), rip off (Inf)

ADJECTIVES

13 **economic**, fiscal, monetary, pecuniary, financial, budgetary, inflationary, deflationary, mercantile, commercial, commercialistic, marketable, profitable, taxable, wholesale, retail, export, import, nationalized, privatized

ADVERBS

14 **economically**, fiscally, financially, commercially, profitably

14   Finance

For the love of money is the root of all evil.
Bible: I Timothy.

If possible, honestly, if not, somehow, make money. Horace.

There are few ways in which a man can be more innocently employed than in getting money.
Samuel Johnson.

NOUNS

1 **finance**, world of finance, high finance, international finance, International Monetary Fund (IMF), banking, accounting, financial accounting, financial control, money power, purse strings, power of the purse, money dealings, cash transaction, financial affairs, budget, money management, investment, money market, foreign exchange market, Eurodollar market, European Monetary System (EMS), Exchange Rate Mechanism (ERM), European Currency Unit (ECU), green pound, foreign currency reserves, exchange rate, exchange premium, interest rate, bank rate, minimum

lending rate, effective rate, valuta, parity, par, equality, agio, agiotage, snake, floating currency, devaluation, depreciation, falling exchange rate, deterioration, rising exchange rate, strong currency, rallying, improvement, bimetallism, gold standard, managed currency, equalization fund, sinking fund, revolving fund, deficit finance, inflation, inflationary spiral, disinflation, deflation, stagflation, reflation, financial year

▶ *741 Money, 13 Economics, 750 Accounts, 748 Expenditure, 627 Improvement, 628 Deterioration, 737 Trade*

2 **stock exchange**, exchange, stock market, bull market, bear market, market, Big Bang, Dow Jones Industrial Index (US), Dow (Jones) Industrials (US), the Dow (US), Financial Times Ordinary Share Index (FT Index), Financial Times-Stock Exchange 100 Index (FT-SE 100 Index), Hang Seng Index, Nikkei Dow Index, issue, issue price, bid price, dividends, earnings per share, Footsie (Inf)

▶ *740 Market*

3 **stockbroker**, broker, market maker, stockjobber, financial adviser, speculator, bull, bear, investor, bidder, backer, financier, banker, capitalist, plutocrat

▶ *741 Money, 746 Payment*

4 **personal finance**, savings, deposit, bank account, building society account, TESSA (Tax Exempt Special Savings Account), PEP (Personal Equity Plan), pension, something for a rainy day

▶ *744 Credit, 742 Wealth, 741 Money*

VERBS

5 **invest**, venture, risk, speculate, put one's money to work, sink one's capital in, invest in, fund, finance, go on the stock exchange, float, buy shares, play the stock exchange, play the futures market, deal in futures, bull, bear, stag, bid for, hold the purse strings

▶ *746 Payment*

ADJECTIVES

6 **financial**, monetary, fiscal, economic, rising, bull, falling, bear, devaluated, depreciated, managed, floating, inflationary, deflationary, disinflationary, reflationary

▶ *13 Economics*

15   Industrial Relations

NOUNS

1 **industrial relations**, employee relations, employer-employee relations, management-employee relations, labour relations, union-management relations, work relations, workforce relations, on-the-job relations, employment relationships, social charter, employee rights, employer rights, employee jurisdiction, employer jurisdiction, employers' organiza-

tion, employer's association, Confederation of British Industry (CBI), work (or working) practices, custom and practice, terms and conditions, employment laws, contract of employment, employment contract, employment rules, workplace rules, joint regulations, unfair labour practices, featherbedding, industrial unionism, unionism, (free) collective bargaining, company-wide bargaining, association bargaining, negotiation, salary negotiations, industrial tribunal, collective agreement, the common rule, no strike – no lockout agreement, multiemployer agreement, piecemeal agreement, management practices, employee practices, management demands, employee demands, management, line management, labour-management body, wage council, works council, labour, union labour, non-union labour, workforce, labour force, work group

▶ *644 Work, 653 Management, 667 Agreement, 116 Accord, 692 Command, 737 Trade*

2 **industrial negotiations**, negotiating rights, negotiated points, union recognition, employment standards, conditions of employment, employer's liability, modernization, automation, computerization, seniority, pay differential, wage rates, minimum wages, sliding-scale rates, cost-of-living adjustment, systematic wage structure, method of payment, bonuses, benefits, profit-sharing, nonwage demands, fringe adjustments, training and education, induction training, on-the-job (or in-service) training, hours worked, working hours, minimum hours, make-work rules (US), overtime work, night-shift work, work measurement, work efficiency, work achievement, sports and recreation, promotion, hiring practices, probationary period, contractual obligations, violation of contract, disciplinary procedure, discipline, worker participation, work demarcation, allocation of work, job description, job flexibility, flexitime (or flextime), safety and health, accident prevention, sick leave, holidays, vacation time (US), transfers, grounds for dismissal, dismissal, laying off, sacking, firing, lay-offs, redundancy, guarantee payments, workman's compensation, retraining, retirement, voluntary retirement, early retirement, pension programme

▶ *741 Money, 185 Time, 201 Newness, 845 Entitlement, 632 Safety, 746 Payment, 254 Absence*

3 **organized labour**, trade union, labour union, international union organization, World Federation of Trade Unions (WFTU), International Confederation of Free Trade Unions (ICFTU), International Federation of Christian Trade Unions (IFCTU), national union organization, TUC (Trades Union Congress), AFL-CIO (American Federation of Labor-Congress of Industrial Organizations), independent union, general union, craft union, guild, industrial union, in-company union, white-collar union, blue-collar union, public sector union, union shop, union branch, union demands, union dues, union subscriptions, closed shop, open shop, chapel

4 **industrial dispute**, labour dispute, industrial conflict, industrial strife, employee claim, claim, grievance, complaint, whipsaw tactics (US), political action, industrial action, unofficial action, action, work-to-rule, go-slow, slow-down, work stoppage, stopping work, walkout, sit-in, sit-down strike, stay-in strike, work-in, lightning strike, picketing, picket, picket line, secondary picketing, flying picket, striking, union strike, strike notice, called strike, organized strike, general strike, mass strike, industry-wide strike, official strike, approved strike, sympathy strike, unofficial strike, wildcat strike, spontaneous strike, overtime ban, boycott, management lock-out, sympathy lock-out, strike breaking, crossing the picket lines, strike settlement, pattern settlement, disputes procedure, grievance procedure, joint consultation committee, negotiations, breakdown in negotiations, arbitration, arbitration of rights, arbitration of interests, voluntary arbitration, compulsory arbitration, arbitration tribunal, arbitration court, arbitration award, Advisory Conciliation and Arbitration Service (ACAS), mediation, conciliation, injunction, turn-out (Arch)

▶ *218 Cessation, 586 Persuasion, 568 Conversation*

5 **labour law**, industrial law, uniformlabour law policy, right-to-work law (US), Labour Management Relations (or Taft-Hartley) Act (US), National Labor Relations Act (NLRA) (US), Shops Act, National Labor Relations Board (NLRB) (US), Industrial Relations Act, open shop, closed shop

▶ *16 Law*

6 **employer**, manager, employment manager, director, managing director, boss (Inf), executive, overseer, head of department, training officer, education officer, welfare officer, personnel manager, personnel officer, line manager, production manager, supervisor, arbitrator, mediator, counsellor, conciliator, umpire

▶ *696 Master*

7 **employee**, wage earner, breadwinner, wage worker (US), tax-payer, staff member, white-collar worker, nonmanual worker, skilled worker, semiskilled worker, unskilled worker, blue-collar worker, manual worker, part-time worker, workplace representative, union member, trade union official, national official, district official, elected representative, staff representative, shop steward, father (or mother) of the chapel, councillor, convener,

Trade Unions

Amalgamated Association of Beamers, Twisters and Drawers (Hand and Machine)

Amalgamated Engineering and Electrical Union (AEEU)

Amalgamated Society of Textile Workers and Kindred Trades

Associated Society of Locomotive Engineers and Firemen (ASLEF)

Association of First Division Civil Servants

Association of Professional, Executive, Clerical and Computer Staff (APEX)

Association of University Teachers

Bakers, Food and Allied Workers' Union

Banking, Insurance and Finance Union

British Actors' Equity Association

British Air Line Pilots Association

British Association of Colliery Management

Broadcasting, Entertainment and Cinematograph Technicians' Union (BECTU)

Card Setting Machine Tenters' Society

Ceramic and Allied Trades Union

Civil and Public Services Association

Communication Managers' Association

Confederation of Health Service Employees (COHSE)

Educational Institute of Scotland

Engineering and Fasteners Trade Union

Engineers' and Managers' Association

Film Artistes' Association

Fire Brigades Union

Furniture, Timber and Allied Trades Union

General Union of Associations of Loom Overlookers

GMB (formerly General, Municipal, Boilermakers and Allied Trade Union)

Graphical, Paper and Media Union (GPMU)

Hospital Consultants and Specialists Association

Inland Revenue Staff Federation

Institute of Directors

Institute of Professionals, Managers and Specialists

Iron and Steel Trades Confederation

Manufacturing, Science and Finance Union (MSF)

Military and Orchestral Musical Instrument Makers' Trade Society

Musicians' Union

National and Local Government Officers' Association (NALGO)

National Association of Colliery Overmen, Deputies and Shotfirers

National Association of Co-operative Officials

National Association of Licensed House Managers

National Association of Probation Officers

National Association of Schoolmasters/Union of Women Teachers (NAS/UWT)

National Association of Teachers in Further and Higher Education

National Communications Union

National League of the Blind and Disabled

National Union of Civil and Public Servants (NUCPS)

National Union of Domestic Appliances and General Operatives, The

National Union of Knitwear, Footwear and Apparel Trades

National Union of Insurance Workers

National Union of Journalists (NUJ)

National Union of Lock and Metal Workers

National Union of Marine, Aviation and Shipping Transport Officers

National Union of Mineworkers (NUM)

National Union of Public Employees (NUPE)

National Union of Rail, Maritime and Transport Workers (RMT)

National Union of Scalemakers

National Union of Teachers (NUT)

National Union of the Footwear, Leather and Allied Trades

Power Loom Carpet Weavers' and Textile Workers' Union

Prison Officers' Association

Scottish Prison Officers' Association

Scottish Union of Power-Loom Overlookers

Society of Graphical and Allied Trades (SOGAT)

Society of Shuttlemakers

Society of Telecom Executives

Transport and General Workers' Union (TGWU)

Transport Salaried Staffs' Association

Union of Communication Workers

Union of Construction, Allied Trades and Technicians (UCATT)

Union of Democratic Mineworkers (UDM)

Union of Shop, Distributive and Allied Workers (USDAW)

United Road Transport Union

Writers' Guild of Great Britain

---

health and safety representative, striker, strike-breaker, scab, blackleg

▶ *646 Worker*

ADJECTIVES

8 industrial, employer, employee, labour, work, employment, employed, employing, employable, contractual, contracting, contracted, regulatory, collective, piecemeal, managerial, managed, managing, supervised, supervising, working, worked, wage-earning, staff, manual, nonmanual, skilled, semi-skilled, unskilled

9 negotiated, negotiating, negotiable, modernized, modernizing, automated, computerized, sliding-scale, cost-of-living, systematic, profit-sharing, fringe, on-the-job, make-work (US), featherbedded, featherbedding, over-

time, night-shift, hiring, hired, probationary, promoted, disiplinary, disciplining, disciplined, dismissed, laid off, redundant, fired, sacked, retraining, retrained, retiring, retired

10 unionized, union, organized, independent, in-company, public sector, white-collar, blue-collar, closed, open, work-to-rule, slow-down, sit-in, sit-down, stay-in, work-in, picketed, picketing, striking, industry-wide, official, unofficial, wildcat, lightning, spontaneous, boycotted, boycotting, strike-breaking, arbitrated, arbitrating, mediated, mediating, conciliatory, injunctive

VERBS

11 conduct industrial relations, hire, lay down conditions of employment, train, educate, provide on-the-job (*or* in-service) train-

ing, promote, work overtime, work the night shift, work on flexitime (*or* flextime), meet contractual obligations, featherbed, modernize, automate, computerize, discipline, demote, dismiss, fire, sack, lay off, make redundant, become redundant, retrain

12 **have an industrial dispute**, complain, take industrial action, take action, work to rule, go slow, slow down, stop work, walk out, sit in, sit down, strike, call a strike, call out, boycott, lock out, cross the picket lines, settle a strike, negotiate, arbitrate, mediate

ADVERBS

13 **industrially**, contractually, under contract, collectively, together, managerially, under supervision, with supervision, manually, with one's hands, through negotiations, on the job, independently, officially, unofficially, spontaneously, through arbitration, conciliatorily

16   Law

The law does not concern itself with trifles. Saying.

The good of the people is the chief law. Cicero.

'If the law supposes that,' said Mr Bumble..., *'the law is a ass – a idiot.'* Charles Dickens (Oliver Twist).

Laws grind the poor, and rich men rule the law. Oliver Goldsmith.

NOUNS

1 **the law**, law, body of law, corpus juris, law and equity, constitution, written constitution, unwritten constitution, charter, institution, codification, codified law, statute book, legal code, pandect, Ten Commandments, Decalogue, Pentateuch, Twelve Tables, Corpus Juris Civilis, Digest, Pandects of Justinian, Corpus Juris Canonici, penal code, civil code, Magna Carta, Napoleonic code, written law, lex scripta, statute law, common law, unwritten law, lex non scripta, natural law, jus naturale (Roman Law), equity law, personal law, private law, canon law, jus canonicum, ecclesiastical law, international law, European Community law, EEC law, law of nations, jus gentium (Roman Law), law of the sea, law of the air, law of commerce, commercial law, business law, lex mercatoria, law of contract, law of crime, criminal law, civil law, constitutional law, law of the land, long arm of the law

2 **jurisdiction**, portfolio, function, judicature, magistracy, commission of the peace, mayoralty, shrievalty, bumbledom, competence, legal competence, authority, legal authority, cognizance, mandate, administration of justice, legal administration, Home Office, Justice Department, local jurisdiction, local author-

ity, corporation, municipality, council, town council, city council, board of aldermen (US), aldermanic board (US), county commission (US), county board, county council, regional council, district council, parish council, community council, bailiwick, vigilance committee, watch committee, tribunal, office, bureau, secretariat, workshop

▶ *249 Region, 688 Authority, 703 Commission*

3 **law**, bylaw, statute, decree, ordinance, edict, order, standing order, canon, rule, rescript, precept

4 **bad law**, legal flaw, loophole, let-out, contradictory law, antinomy, error of law, mistake of law, overruled verdict, overturned verdict, bad judgment, misjudgment, miscarriage of justice, injustice, false arrest, wrong verdict, wrong conviction, wrong execution

5 **litigation**, legal action, legal case, legal dispute, legal issue, legal remedy, action, case, cause, dispute, quarrel, issue, contest, lawsuit, suit at law, suit, seeking legal protection, seeking a verdict, seeking justice, going to law, litigiousness, quarrelsomeness, matter for judgment, case for decision, test case, prosecution, arraignment, impeachment, charge, accusation, claim, counter claim, plea, petition, request, pleading, objection, demurrer, affirmation, affidavit, written statement, averment, assertion

▶ *666 Disagreement*

6 **legal process**, proceedings, legal proceedings, legal procedure, due process, course of law, (long) arm of the law, jurisdiction, citation, subpoena, summons, warrant, search warrant, apprehension, arrest, recitation of rights, detention, questioning, committal, restraint, habeas corpus, bail, surety, security, recognizance, personal recognizance, injunction, stay, order, writ, certiorari, mandamus, nisi prius

7 **legal trial**, trial, fair trial, justice seen to be done, trial by law, trial by jury, trial by one's peers, trial at the bar, trial in court, television trial (US), assize, court sessions, sessions, court sitting, court of law, law court, military court, military justice, inquest, inquisition, inquiry, hearing, prosecution, defence, setting of court date, settlement out of court, plea-bargaining, questioning of potential jurors, empanelling a jury, evidence, circumstantial evidence, hearing of evidence, taking of evidence, recording of evidence, insufficient evidence, examination, cross-examination, re-examination, objection sustained, objection overruled, testimony, pleadings, arguments, reasoning, counter-argument, rebutter, rebuttal, rejoinder, proof, demonstration, disproof, confutation, final arguments, summing-up, charge to the jury, charge to the jury, sequestering of the

jury, ruling, finding, decision, judgment, verdict, majority verdict, unanimous verdict, hung jury, reading of the verdict, favourable verdict, not guilty, acquittal, unfavourable verdict, guilty, condemnation, execution of judgment, sentence, prison term, execution, appeal, retrial, precedent, case law, law reports, cause list, case record, dossier, record
▶ *483 Evidence, 473 Argument*

8 **litigant**, litigator, libellant, party, party to a suit, suitor, petitioner, suer claimant, plaintiff, pursuer, defendant, appellant, libellee, respondent, objector, intervener, accused, accused person, prisoner before the court, prisoner at the bar, litigious person, prosecutor, accuser, common informer, informer
▶ *856 Accusation, 528 Information*

9 **lawmaker**, lawgiver, legislator, Supreme Court Justice (US), Law Lord, Chief Justice of the United States (US), associate justice of the Supreme Court (US)

10 **law officer**, legal administrator, public prosecutor, judge advocate, district attorney, Crown Attorney (Canada), judge, mayor, city manager (US), provost general, sheriff, justice of the peace (JP), court officer, clerk of the court, bailiff, procurator fiscal, summoner, process-server, macebearer, official, apparitor, beadle

11 **British law officer**, Lord Chancellor, Attorney General, Solicitor General, Lord Advocate, King's (*or* Queen's) Proctor, Crown Counsel, Crown Prosecution Service (CPS), lord mayor, lord provost, tipstaff, catchpoll, Bow Street runner

12 **US law officer**, Attorney General, Solicitor General, federal marshal, state attorney general, state prosecuting attorney, state prosecutor, district attorney (DA)

13 **lawyer**, solicitor, barrister, attorney (US), attorney-at-law (US), counsel, Queen's (*or* King's) counsel, legal adviser, legal representative, advocate, member of the legal profession, jurist, legal practitioner, judge, recorder, magistrate, jury, trial jury, legal beagle (Inf), legal eagle (Inf), brief (Sl)

14 **police**, police force, the force, forces of law and order, (the long arm of) the law, the boys in blue, constabulary, gendarmerie, military police (MP), shore patrol (US), airport police, mounted police, Royal Canadian Mounted Police (RCMP), Mounties (Inf), international police, Interpol, the fuzz (Sl), Old Bill (Sl), the pigs (Sl), the filth (Sl)

15 **British police**, Metropolitan Police, Scotland Yard, Special Branch, special patrol group (SPG), flying squad, Serious Crime Squad, fraud squad, drugs squad, community police

16 **US police**, Federal Bureau of Investigation (FBI), city police, county sheriff, state highway patrol, special patrol, shotgun patrol

17 **police officer**, policeman (*or* policewoman), law-enforcer, constable, special constable, patrolman (*or* patrolwoman), police sergeant, desk sergeant, police lieutenant, police inspector, police superintendent, chief constable, chief of police (US), commissioner of police, police commissioner, provost marshal, watch, neighbourhood watch, posse (US), posse comitatus (US), detective, plain-clothes officer, private detective (*or* investigator), private police, security officer, copper (Sl), cop (Sl), traffic cop (Sl), bobby (Inf), bizzy (Sl), bull (US sl), flatfoot (Sl), rozzer (Sl), pig (Sl), Smokey (the) Bear (*or* Smokey *or* bear) (US sl), *flic* (Fr sl), Mountie (*or* Mounty) (Inf), dick (US sl), fly dick (*or* ball) (US sl), private eye (Inf)

18 **tribunal**, seat of justice, judgment seat, woolsack, throne, bar, bar of justice, court of conscience, tribunal of penance, confessional, Judgment Day, forum, ecclesia, wardmote, council, public opinion, vox populi, electorate, judicatory, bench, board, bench of judges, panel of judges, judge and jury, judicial assembly, Areopagus, commission of the peace

19 **law court**, court, open court, court of law, court of justice, high court, criminal court, civil court, appellate court, county court, probate court, divorce court, court of equity, court of arbitration, court of session, assizes, police court, juvenile court, children's court, small claims court, coroner's court, court of record, sheriff court, feudal court, manorial court, court-martial, drumhead court-martial, summary court-martial, summary court, kangaroo court, sessions, quarter sessions, petty sessions

20 **British court**, House of Lords, Supreme Court of Judicature, Court of Appeal, High Court (of Justice), King's (*or* Queen's) Bench (Division), Lord Chancellor's Court, Chancery Division (*or* chancery), Admiralty Division (*or* admiralty), crown court, High Court of Justiciary, sheriff court, Central Criminal Court, Old Bailey, magistrates' court, Court of Session, Court of Common Pleas, Court of Exchequer (*or* Exchequer), court of oyer and terminer, assizes, Star Chamber, (court) leet, Eyre of Justice

21 **US court**, US Supreme Court, Federal Court, District Court, state supreme court, court of claims, court of appeals, circuit court of appeals, circuit court, municipal court, night court, family court, court of common pleas, court of chancery, court of oyer and terminer

22 **ecclesiastical court**, Papal Court, Curia, Court of Arches, Inquisition, Holy Office

23 **judge**, justice, justiceship, your Lordship, your Honour, his (*or* her) Honour, his (*or* her) Worship, my lud (*or* m'lud), justiciary, verderer, military judge, judge advocate general,

chief justice, county court judge, recorder, sessions judge, subordinate judge, magistrate, district magistrate, city magistrate, police magistrate, coroner, justice of the peace (JP), bench, judiciary, magistracy, hanging judge, Judge Jeffreys, Judge Roy Bean (US), the Law West of the Pecos (US), umpire, referee, arbiter, arbitrator, ombudsman, assessor, estimator, recorder, Recording Angel, Solomon, Rhadamanthus, Daniel come to judgment, the beak (Sl), his (or her) nibs (Sl)

24 **US judge**, Chief Justice of the United States, federal judge, district judge, circuit judge, state Supreme Court Justice, municipal court judge, night court judge, family court judge, associate justice of the Supreme Court

25 **British judge**, Lord Chancellor, Lord Chief Justice, Master of the Rolls, Lord of Appeal, crown court judge, sheriff, assize judge

26 **jury**, assize, twelve good men and true, twelve just men, twelve men in a box, grand jury, special jury, common jury, petit jury, trial jury, jury panel, juror's panel, jury list, juror, jury man (or woman), jurist, jurat, foreman of the jury

27 **courtroom**, courthouse, law courts, bench, jury box, judgment seat, woolsack, mercy seat, dock, bar, witness box

28 **legality**, lawfulness, licitness, legitimacy, legitimateness, validity, justice, right, keeping within the law, adherence to the law, adherence to the letter of the law, legalism, respect for the law, respect for legal principles

▶ 843 Right

29 **legalization**, legitimization, decriminalization, authorization, sanction, permission, authority, licence, warrant

▶ 708 Permission

30 **legitimacy**, rightfulness, genuineness, authenticity

31 **legislation**, nomology, lawmaking, lawgiving, becoming law, passing into law, codification, ratification, enactment, enacting, validation, confirmation, affirmation, regulation, regulation by law, regulation by statute, constitutionality, constitutionalism, legislature, legislatorship

32 **jurisprudence**, nomology, science of law, knowledge of law, legal learning, law consultancy, legal advice

33 **litigation**, justice, justice under the law, judgment, judgment according to the law, due process of law, jurisdiction, legal process, lawsuit, legal action, writ, summons, trial, verdict, sentence, punishment

▶ 492 Judgment

34 **legal formality**, formality, form of law, form, formula, rite, procedure, workings of the law, letter of the law, four corners of the law

35 **illegality**, illegitimacy, illicitness, unlawful-

ness, ban, proscription, veto, prohibition, impermissibility, unauthorization, irregularity

36 **stolen property**, contraband, black-market goods, haul, hot item (Sl), swag (Sl)

37 **criminology**, penology, criminal statistics, criminologist

38 **lawbreaking**, trespass, transgression, violation, breach, infringement, encroachment, contravention, overstepping, sin, vice, fraud, wickedness, villainy, guilt, culpability, criminality, delinquency, dishonesty, improbity, crookedness (Inf), shadiness (Inf)

▶ 858 Improbity

39 **crime**, capital crime, felony, offence, criminal offence, indictable offence, punishable offence, misdemeanour, misdeed, wrong, wrongdoing, criminality, foul play, criminal activity, malpractice, trespass, tort, civil wrong, malfeasance, misfeasance, theft, robbery, burglary, assault, rape, manslaughter, homicide, justifiable homicide, murder, fraud, corruption, champerty, maintenance, misprision

40 **lawbreaker**, criminal, felon, offender, wrongdoer, miscreant, malefactor, villain, delinquent, culprit, convict, recidivist, thief, car thief, robber, bank robber, burglar, housebreaker, rapist, murderer, crook (Inf), mugger (Inf), jailbird (Inf), lag (Sl)

▶ 844 Wrong, 832 Malevolence

41 **lawlessness**, anarchy, chaos, antinomianism, riot, rioting, hooliganism, ruffianism, rebellion, revolt, sedition, mutiny, insurgence, coup d'etat, usurpation, arrogation, outlawry, breakdown of law and order, crime wave, gang rule, mob law, lynch law, vigilantism, kangaroo court

42 **acquittal**, favourable verdict, verdict of not guilty, verdict of not proven, benefit of the doubt, innocence, clearance, exoneration, exculpation, absolution, discharge, release, let-off, thumbs up, liberation, deliverance, freedom, justification, compurgation, vindication, successful defence, defeat of the prosecution, nonsuit, case dismissed, thrown-out case, dismissal for lack of evidence, no case, withdrawal of the charge, quashing, quietus, reprieve, pardon, forgiveness, nonprosecution, exemption, impunity, nonliability

▶ 865 Innocence, 855 Vindication, 839 Forgiveness, 848 Exemption

43 **conviction**, condemnation, verdict of guilty, unfavourable verdict, hostile verdict, hostile jury, unsuccessful defence, successful prosecution, judgment, sentence, punishment, fine, court costs, prison sentence, going down, death sentence, death warrant, black cap, thumbs down, condemned cell, death row (US), death house (US), execution chamber, electric chair, gas chamber, firing squad, out-

lawry, proscription, blacklisting, attainder, price on one's head
▶ *866 Guilt, 852 Disapproval, 879 Punishment*

ADJECTIVES

44 legal, lawful, licit, legitimate, valid, just, right, proper, within the law, sanctioned, allowable, permissible, permitted, authorized, licensed, warranted, legalized, legitimized, legitimatized, decriminalized, brought within the law, according to law, by right, de jure, legit (Sl)
▶ *708 Permission, 843 Right*

45 legislative, nomothetic, lawmaking, lawgiving, legislatorial, legislational, decretal, nomological, jurisprudential, learned in the law

46 legislated, made law, put into legal effect, enacted, passed, voted, decreed, ordained, ordered, codified, ratified, constitutional, statutory, legally sound, good in law

47 liable to law, amenable to law, fit for legislation, justiciable, cognizable, triable, actionable, accusable
▶ *856 Accusation*

48 jurisdictional, jurisdictive, judicatory, judicatorial, municipal, regional, executive, administrative, administrational, directive, directing, justiciary, judiciary, juridical, justiciable, subject to jurisdiction, liable to the law
▶ *653 Management*

49 judicatory, judicatorial, judicial, judicative, jurisdictional, jurisdictive, jural, jurisprudential, justiciary, curial, inquisitional, forensic, Rhadamanthine, original, appellate, tribunal, magisterial, judicious, critical

50 law-abiding, honest, upright, obedient, authorized, licensed, competent
▶ *694 Obedience*

51 legitimate, rightful, genuine, authentic, real, true

52 legalistic, litigious, disputatious, contentious, quibbling

53 litigating, litigant, suing, accusing, bringing legal action against, at law with, going to law, appearing in court, appearing before the judge, claiming, contesting, objecting, disputing, arguing, quarrelling, litigious, quarrelsome, argumentative
▶ *16 Law, 856 Accusation, 473 Argument, 666 Disagreement*

54 litigated, on trial, up for trial, brought before the court (*or* judge), hauled before the court (*or* judge), *coram judice* (L), *coram populo* (L), argued, disputed, contested, claimed, submitted for judgment, offered for arbitration, sub judice, on the cause list, down for hearing, ready for hearing, litigable, actionable, justiciable, disputable, arguable, suable, accusable, up before the beak (Sl)

55 illegal, not legal, illegitimate, illicit, unlawful, outlawed, banned, proscribed, prohibited, forbidden, *verboten* (Ger), impermissible, contrary to law, against the law, not according to law, outside the law, outwith the law (Scot), on the wrong side of the law, exceeding the law, out of bounds
▶ *736 Stealing*

56 unauthorized, without authority, unlicensed, unofficial, informal, irregular, unconstitutional, unstatutory, unlegislated, unchartered, unwarranted, injudicial, extrajudicial, unknown to law, not covered by law, without legal backing, having no legal protection
▶ *846 Lack of Entitlement*

57 null, null and void, nullified, annulled, abrogated, suspended, superseded, no longer law
▶ *704 Cancellation, 846 Lack of Entitlement*

58 unjust, unwarrantable, wrongful, wrong, tortious, justiciable, cognizable, triable, actionable, accusable, punishable
▶ *844 Wrong, 856 Accusation, 862 Evil*

59 stolen, contraband, smuggled, black-market, nicked (Inf), pinched (Inf), filched (Inf), hot (Sl), too hot to handle (Sl), bent (Sl), off the back of a lorry (Inf)

60 offending, breaking the law, trespassing, transgressing, violating, breaching, infringing, encroaching, sinning, bad, wicked, nefarious, heinous, villainous, guilty, culpable, criminal, felonious, dishonest, fraudulent, corrupt, crooked (Inf), shady (Inf), bent (Sl)
▶ *864 Wickedness, 866 Guilt, 858 Improbity, 357 Overstepping*

61 lawless, without law, anarchic, antinomian, chaotic, every-man-for-himself, ungovernable, licentious, riotous, rebellious, seditious, mutinous, insurgent, violent
▶ *689 Anarchy, 693 Disobedience, 807 Insolence*

62 above the law, acting as a law unto oneself, despotic, tyrannical, dictatorial, oppressive, overmighty
▶ *690 Severity*

63 acquitted, not guilty, not proven, guiltless, innocent, clear, cleared, in the clear, exonerated, exculpated, absolved, vindicated, without a stain on one's character, uncondemned, unpunished, unchastised, let off, let go, let off the hook, discharged, released, liberated, free, reprieved, pardoned, forgiven, recommended for leniency, recommended for mercy, immune, exempted, exempt, nonliable

64 convicted, condemned, guilty, blameworthy, liable, self-convicted, confessing, without a case, having no case, without a leg to stand on, nonsuited, sentenced, sentenced to death, proscribed, outlawed, with a price on one's head, disapproved, lost, damned, in hell, burning in hell, frying in hell (Inf)

VERBS

65 make legal, legalize, legitimize, legitimatize, decriminalize, bring within the law, validate,

sanction, allow, permit, authorize, license, warrant

66 **be legal**, come within the law, stand up in law (*or* in court)

67 **follow the law**, abide by the law, respect the law, follow the letter of the law, keep within the law, stay on the right side of the law

68 **legislate**, make laws, give laws, enact, pass, vote, decree, ordain, order, codify, ratify, confirm, affirm, formalize, endorse, vest, establish

69 **have jurisdiction over**, hold court, administer justice, sit on the bench, sit in judgment, judge, hear a complaint, hear a cause, hear a case, try a case, take cognizance, take judicial notice

70 **litigate**, bring legal action, start an action, bring a lawsuit, bring a suit, file a suit, seek legal protection, seek a verdict, seek justice, go to law, appeal to law, set the law in motion, institute legal proceedings, petition, request, prepare a case, prepare a brief, file a brief, brief counsel, claim, file a claim, contest at law, have the law on, take to court, bring before the court (*or* judge), haul before the court (*or* judge), have up, sue, implead, arraign, impeach, accuse, charge, prefer charges, press charges, indict, cite, summon, serve notice on, prosecute, try, put on trial, bring to trial, bring to justice, bring to the bar, argue one's case (before the jury), take the stand, go to the witness box, swear to tell the truth, advocate, plead, call evidence, argue

▶ *856 Accusation, 473 Argument*

71 **try a case**, take cognizance, put down for hearing, commit for trial, empanel a jury, question potential jurors, hear a case, hear a cause, call witnesses, examine, cross-examine, object, take statements, sit in judgment, rule, find, decide, adjudicate, judge, close the pleadings, close the proceedings, sum up, charge the jury, sequester the jury, bring in a verdict, have the verdict read, pronounce sentence

72 **stand trial**, come before (the court), come up for trial, be on trial, stand in the dock, give evidence, plead guilty, plead not guilty, plead nolo contendere, plead to the charge, ask to be tried, defend an action, put in one's defence, make one's defence, submit to judgment, hear sentence

73 **be illegal**, break the law, violate the law, circumvent the law, bend the law, twist the law, torture the law, defy the law, drive a coach and horses through the law, do wrong, offend, commit a crime

▶ *844 Wrong*

74 **be lawless**, have no law, know no law, take the law into one's own hands, please oneself, exceed one's authority, stand above the law, stand outside the law

▶ *689 Anarchy*

75 **make illegal**, outlaw, criminalize, illegalize, ban, proscribe, veto, prohibit, forbid, punish, bastardize, illegitimize

▶ *709 Veto, 879 Punishment*

76 **judge**, administer justice, exercise judgment, adjudge, adjudicate, hold court, hold the scales, sit on the bench, sit in judgment, preside, hear a case, give a hearing, try (a case), conduct a trial, agree on a verdict, return a verdict, bring in a verdict, pass judgment, decide, pass sentence, pronounce, decree

77 **annul**, nullify, make null and void, abrogate, suspend, cancel

▶ *704 Cancellation*

78 **acquit**, find (*or* pronounce) not guilty, find for, prove innocent, find the case not proven, give the benefit of the doubt, find there is a lack of evidence, find there is no case to answer, clear, exonerate, exculpate, absolve, vindicate, let off, let go, let off the hook, get off, discharge, dismiss charges, release, liberate, free, reprieve, respite, grant a respite, pardon, forgive, not press charges, not prosecute, set aside the sentence, quash, quash the conviction, remit the penalty, reduce the fine, recommend for leniency, recommend for mercy, justify, allow a dismissal, allow an appeal, abrogate, make immune, exempt, make exempt

▶ *855 Vindication, 848 Exemption, 700 Liberation, 839 Forgiveness, 704 Cancellation*

79 **convict**, condemn, find guilty, pronounce guilty, find against, bring in an unfavourable verdict, reject one's defence, prove guilty, bring home the charge, find liable, sentence, give a prison sentence, sentence to death, put on the black cap, sign one's death warrant, reject one's appeal, reject, attaint (Arch), outlaw, bar, proscribe, make illegal, blacklist, attaint (Arch), put a price on one's head, disapprove, damn, curse, excommunicate

80 **convict oneself**, confess, sign a confession, plead guilty, stand condemned out of one's own mouth, be verballed (Sl)

▶ *581 Rejection, 852 Disapproval*

ADVERBS

81 **legally**, lawfully, judicially, judgingly, jurally, jurisdictionally, jurisprudently, juristically, licitly, legitimately, validly, justly, rightly, properly, within the law, by law, according to law, by right, de jure, by order, through the legislative process, through the courts, in court, before the bench (*or* bar *or* court), in the eyes of the law

82 **illegally**, illicitly, illegitimately, unlawfully, criminally, wrongly, against the law, contrary to law, without authority, without legal backing

83 **dishonestly**, fraudulently, on the black market, under the counter (*or* table)

84 **lawlessly**, anarchically, riotously, rebelliously, violently

85 **summarily**, arbitrarily, despotically, tyrannically, dictatorially

86 **jurisdictionally**, municipally, regionally, parochially, communally, administratively, executively, on the council, at the bar, legally, lawfully

87 **in litigation**, at law, in court, before the judge, *coram judice* (L), *coram populo* (L), *sub judice* (L), pendente lite, litigiously

88 **forgivingly**, mercifully, leniently, freely, guiltlessly, innocently, pardonably

89 **guiltily**, culpably, wickedly, illegally, unlawfully, against the law

17   Military Affairs

War is the continuation of politics by other means. Karl von Clausewitz.

The military don't start wars. The politicians start wars. William Westmorland.

NOUNS

1 **military affairs**, military science, military strategy, grand strategy, general policy, war, war plans, warcraft, arms, art of war, siegecraft, military tactics, logistics, campaign, theatre of operations, strategic objectives, command of the sea, command of the air, mobilization, military service, recruiting, compulsory service, conscription, conscripting, the draft (US), impressment, operations, rank, military installations, headquarters (HQ), base, camp, barracks, billet, military equipment
▶ *592 Plan, 594 Preparation, 676 War*

2 **the military**, national defence, military forces, the services, army, land forces, ground forces, navy, air force, marines, special forces, standing army, professional army, regular forces, mercenary forces, nonprofessional army, volunteer army, irregular forces, irregulars, reserve forces, reserves, Territorial Army, Home Guard, US National Guard (US), Senior Service, Special Boat Service (SBS), Special Air Service (SAS), militia, citizen's army, military arm, arm of the service, military branch, branch of the service, military–industrial complex

3 **military training**, national military college, Imperial Defence College, US National War College (US), military academy, United States Military Academy (*or* West Point), United States Naval Academy (*or* Annapolis), Air Force Academy, British military academies: Royal Military Academy (*or* Sandhurst), Royal Naval College (*or* Dartmouth), Royal Air Force Academy (*or* Cranwell), Royal Military College of Canada, Royal Military College (*or* Duntroon) (Aus), *École Spéciale Militaire* (Fr), staff college
▶ *6 Education*

4 **military organization**, national defence headquarters, Ministry of Defence, Government Communications Headquarters (GCHQ), Department of Defense (US), operational command, military unit, tactical unit, support unit, administrative unit, commando unit, medical service, Mobile Army Surgical Hospital (MASH), communication service, maintenance service, supply service, evacuation service, group, battle group, column, rank, file, detail, kitchen police (KP), detachment, combat team, task force, squad, section, platoon, company, troop, battery, battalion, infantry battalion, mechanized battalion, missile battalion, signal battalion, engineer battalion, reconnaissance battalion, regiment, infantry regiment, brigade, artillery brigade, division, infantry division, armoured division, motorized division, mechanized division (US), air division, airborne division, parachute division, aircraft division, destroyer division, cruiser division, submarine division, army corps, armoured corps, medical corps, dental corps, nurse corps, army service corps, drum corps, bugle corps, quartermaster corps, transportation corps, military police corps, field army, flight, squadron, wing, fleet, operational fleet, task group, amphibious force squadron, flotilla, destroyer flotilla, support fleet, auxiliary fleet, reserve fleet, outfit (Inf)

5 **military staff**, general staff, Defence Council, Joint Chiefs of Staff (US), SHAPE (Supreme Headquarters, Allied Powers in Europe), army staff, air force staff, navy staff, military headquarters staff, commander, chief of staff, deputy chief of staff, staff officers, plans and oper-

British Military Ranks

Army	Royal Navy	Royal Air Force	
Field Marshal	Second Lieutenant	Lieutenant Commander	Air Vice-Marshal
General	Cadet	Lieutenant	Air Commodore
Lieutenant General		Sublieutenant	Group Captain
Major General	Royal Navy	Midshipman	Wing Commander
Brigadier	Admiral of the Fleet	Warrant Officer	Squadron Leader
Colonel	Admiral		Flight Lieutenant
Lieutenant Colonel	Vice Admiral	Royal Air Force	Flying Officer
Major	Rear Admiral	Marshal of the Royal	Pilot Officer
Captain	Commodore	Air Force	Cadet
Lieutenant	Captain	Air Chief Marshal	Warrant Officer
	Commander	Air Marshal	

British Military Medals and Decorations

Victoria Cross
Distinguished Service Cross
Military Cross
Distinguished Flying Cross
Air Force Cross
Conspicuous Gallantry Medal
Distinguished Service Medal (Navy)
Distinguished Conduct Medal
Military Medal (Army)
Distinguished Flying Medal
Air Force Medal

ations staff, training staff, supply staff, personnel staff, intelligence staff, commanding officer, company grade officer, junior officer, noncommissioned officer (NCO), platoon commander, company commander, field grade officer, senior officer, battalion commander, regimental commander, brigade commander, cavalry commander, artillery commander, general officer, flag officer, senior commander, divisional commander, corps commander, field army commander, task force commander

▶ *679 Combatant*

6 **military law**, Uniform Code of Military Justice (US), court martial, general court martial, district court martial, field general court martial, special court martial (US), summary court martial (US), military police, military police corps, Royal Military Police (RMP), Military Police (MP) (US)

▶ *16 Law*

7 **miscellaneous terms**, militarism, military government, military tradition, military bearing, military salute, military band, military music, military honours, military spirit, morale, gung-ho attitude (Inf)

ADJECTIVES

8 **military**, martial, militant, naval, airforce, service, fighting, soldierly, gladiatorial, strategic, tactical, offensive, defensive, pre-emptive, aggressive, pugnacious, combative, bellicose, warlike, belligerent, gung-ho (Inf)

9 **enlisted**, conscripted, drafted, volunteer, commissioned, noncommissioned, regular, irregular, reserve, combatant, noncombatant

VERBS

10 **enlist**, join up, join the colours, take the Queen's shilling, recruit, conscript, draft, impress, mobilize, demobilize, demob (Inf)

ADVERBS

11 **militarily**, martially, strategically, tactically, offensively, defensively, pre-emptively

Major Wars

Peloponnesian Wars (431–404 BC)
Samnite Wars (350–200 BC)
Punic War (264–146 BC)
Hundred Years' War (1337–1453)
Wars of the Roses (1455–85)
Thirty Years' War (1618–48)
(English) Civil War (1642–46)
War of the Spanish Succession (1701–13)
War of the Austrian Succession (1740–48)
Seven Years' War (1756–63)

French and Indian War (1754)
War of American Independence (1775–83)
Napoleonic Wars (1805–15)
War of 1812
Opium Wars (1839–42, 1856–60)
Mexican War (1846–48)
Crimean War (1853–56)
(American) Civil War (or War Between the States) (1861–65)
Franco-Prussian War (1870–71)
Sino-Japanese War (1894–95)
Spanish-American War (1898)

Boer War (1880–81, 1899–1902)
Russo-Japanese War (1904–05)
World War I (1914–18)
Spanish Civil War (1936–39)
World War II (1939–45)
Korean War (1950–53)
Vietnam War (1959–75)
Six Day War (1967)
Iran-Iraq War (1980–88)
Falklands War (1982)
Gulf War (1991)

Sports and Recreation

18 Sport

NOUNS

1 **sport**, game, contest, match, event, meeting, meet, bout, round, set, tournament, knock-out, league, division

2 **sportsground**, venue, stadium, field, track, ground, course, links, court, ring, arena, green, alley

3 **sportsman** (*or* sportswoman), player, contender, defender, challenger, opponent, team member, athlete, sporty type

4 **sporting activity**, indoor sport, outdoor sport, participator sport, spectator sport, contact sport, blood sport

ADJECTIVES

5 **sporting**, competitive, agonistic, sportive, sporty, athletic, gymnastic, acrobatic

VERBS

6 **participate**, take part, compete, join in, enter, play

19 American Football

NOUNS

1 **football**, football game, professional football, NFL (National Football League), AFC (American Football Conference), NFC (National Football Conference), exhibition game, playoff game, bowl game, Pro Bowl, Super Bowl, World Bowl, college football, Rose Bowl, Sugar Bowl, Cotton Bowl, Orange Bowl, high-school football, tag football, touch football, pigskin (Sl)

2 **football player**, All-Pro, All-American, varsity player, captain, redshirt, rookie, draft pick, free agent, substitute, sub, coach, head coach, assistant coach, offensive coordinator, defensive coordinator, referee, umpire, head linesman, field judge, back judge, line judge, side judge, zebra (Inf), side-line crew, chain gang (Inf)

3 **uniform**, jersey, helmet, nose guard, flak jacket, facemask, mouthguard, pads

4 **stadium**, bowl, field, Astroturf, artificial grass, rug (Inf), carpet (Inf), gridiron, goal posts, crossbar, uprights, press box, scoreboard, scoreboard clock, 30-second clock, midfield stripe, goal line, end line, end zone, side line, restraining line, hash mark, yard marker, chains

5 **game time**, quarter, half, half time, time-out, officials' time-out, television (*or* commercial) time out, two-minute warning, overtime, sudden death

6 **scoring**, touchdown, extra point, PAT (point after touchdown), conversion, two-point conversion, field goal, safety

7 **offence**, possession, offensive team, offensive drive, forward progress, offensive formation, I-formation, T-formation, shotgun formation, spread formation, slot formation, single-wing formation, double-wing formation, strong side, weak side, balanced line, unbalanced line, offensive backfield, offensive backs, quarterback, signal-caller (Inf), field general (Inf), passer, fullback, halfback, running back, runner, up back, wingback, blocker, offensive line, offensive lineman, centre, guard, tackle, receiver, wide receiver, flanker

8 **huddle**, set, shift, signals, line call, read, audible, snap count, quick count, snap, two-minute offence, two-minute drill, hurry-up offence, run-and-shoot offence

9 **play**, trick play, gadget play, ground game, running game, run, quarterback sneak, option run, pitchout, bootleg, keeper, lateral, draw, cutback, sweep, power sweep, rollout, reverse, end around, inside run, outside run, misdirection, trap, handoff, play-action, play fake, fumble, turnover, passing game, pocket, pass, complete pass, pass reception, incomplete pass, intercepted pass, protection, option pass, screen pass, flare pass, spot pass, square-out pass, square-in pass, hook pass, curl pass, slant-in pass, bomb, hail-Mary, flea-flicker, fly pattern, post pattern, Z pattern, block, cross block, lead block, scissors block, isolation block

10 **defence**, defensive team, defensive formation, zone defence, nickel defence, dime de-

Sporting Activities

Air Sports
aerobatics
air racing
ballooning
freefalling
gliding
hang-gliding
helicopter flying
kiting
parachuting
paragliding
parascending
skydiving

Angling
big-game fish-
 ing
coarse fishing
fly-fishing
game fishing
match fishing
sea fishing

Animal Sports
dressage
falconry
greyhound rac-
 ing
gymkhana
harness horse
 racing
horse racing
pato
pigeon racing
point-to-point
polo
puissance
rodeo
showjumping
sled-dog racing
steeplechasing
three-day event-
 ing
trotting

Athletics
caber tossing
cross-country
 running
decathlon
discus throwing
fell running
hammer throw-
 ing
heptathlon
high jumping
hurdling
javelin throwing
long-distance
 running
long jumping
marathon run-
 ning
middle-distance
 running

modern pentath-
 lon
mountain run-
 ning
polevaulting
relay racing
shot putting
sprinting
steeplechasing
triathlon
triple jump
tug of war
walking events

Hunting
beagling
bullfighting
coursing
deerstalking
ferreting
fox hunting
grouse shooting
mink hunting
otter hunting
pheasant shoot-
 ing
pigeon shooting
wildfowling

Combat Sports
aikido
boxing
fencing
haphido
judo
karate
kendo
kenipo
kick boxing
kung fu
tae kwon do
tang soo do
Thai boxing
wrestling

Court Games
aeroball
badminton
court handball
jai alai (pelota)
lawn tennis
racquetball
rugby fives
short tennis
squash
table tennis
 (ping-pong)
tennis
volleyball

Gymnastics
asymmetric bars
beam
floor exercises
horizontal bar
 (high bar)

parallel bars
pommel horse
rings
rhythmic gym-
 nastics
sports aerobics
trampolining
tumbling
vault

Target Sports
airgun shooting
clay pigeon
 shooting
cross bow
 archery
darts
darts cricket
darts football
down-the-line
 shooting
field archery
free pistol
 shooting
horseshoe pitch-
 ing
Olympic French
 shooting
pistol shooting
rapid-fire pistol
 shooting
rifle shooting
rough shooting
running game
 target shoot-
 ing
sharpshooting
skeet shooting
target archery
trapshooting

**Target Ball
Games**
boules (boccie)
bowling
Canadian 5-pin
 bowling
carom billiards
croquet
crown-green
 bowls
curling
English billiards
flat-green bowls
golf
pool
skittles
snooker
tenpin bowling

Team Games
American football
Australian rules
 football
bandy

baseball
basketball
Canadian foot-
 ball
cricket
field hockey
French cricket
Gaelic football
hurling
ice hockey
kabaddi
korfball
lacrosse
netball
roller hockey
rounders
rugby league
rugby union
sepak takrow
shinty
soccer (Associa-
 tion Football)
softball
speedball
stoolball
team handball
volleyball

Water Sports
Canadian canoe
 racing
canoe polo
canoe sailing
canoe slalom
 racing
canoe sprint rac-
 ing
diving
jet skiing
kayaking
laser sailing
offshore yacht
 racing
Olympic yacht
 classes
powerboat rac-
 ing
rowing
sailplaning
scuba diving
sculling
short board sail-
 ing
snorkelling
surfing
swimming
synchronized
 swimming
underwater div-
 ing
water polo
water skiing
white water raft-
 ing

wild water rac-
 ing
windsurfing
yacht racing

Wheel Sports
autocross
cycle racing
drag racing
karting
motorcycle rac-
 ing
motor racing
mountain biking
rally cross
roller blading
roller derby
roller hockey
roller skating
roller skiing
sidecar racing
skateboarding
stock-car racing

Winter Sports
Alpine com-
 bined event
Alpine skiing
biathlon
bobsleigh racing
cross-country
 (Nordic)
downhill racing
figure skating
freestyle skiing
giant slalom
ice-dancing
langlauf
luge
Nordic com-
 bined event
off-piste skiing
short-track
 speed skating
skibob racing
ski jumping
ski mountaineer-
 ing
slalom
speed skating
super-G
tobogganing

Other
alpine climbing
bunji jumping
caving
hiking
ice climbing
mountaineering
orienteering
potholing
rock climbing
spelunking
weightlifting

---

fence, flex defence, 4-3 defence, 3-4 defence,
prevent defence, man-to-man defence, single
coverage, double coverage, zone coverage,
overshift, undershift, slant, stunt, pinch, penetration, defensive backfield, secondary, defensive backs, linebacker, cornerback, safety,

strong safety, defensive line, defensive lineman, defensive end, defensive tackle, the front
four, the Fearsome Foursome (Sl)

11 **defensive huddle**, pass rush, rush, blitz,
dog, sack, bump and run

12 **special team**, specialty team, kicking team,

Sporting Personalities

Agassi, Andre (1970–) US tennis player

Agostini, Giacomo (1944–) Italian racing motorcyclist

Alekhine, Alexander (1892–1946) French chess player

Ali, Muhammad (Cassius Marcellus Clay; 1942–) US boxer

Ballesteros, Severiano (1957–) Spanish golfer

Bannister, Sir Roger (Gilbert) (1929–) British runner

Barrington, Jonah (1940–) British squash player

Belmonte y García, Juan (1892–1962) Spanish matador

Bonington, Chris (Christian John Storey B.; 1934–) British mountaineer

Borg, Björn (1956–) Swedish tennis player

Botvinnik, Mikhail Moiseivich (1911–) Soviet chess player

Brabham, Jack (John Arthur B.; 1926–) Australian motor-racing driver

Bradman, Sir Donald George (1908–) Australian cricketer

Broome, David (1940–) British show jumper

Brough, Louise (1923–) US tennis player

Bruno, Frank(lyn Roy) (1961–) British boxer

Budge, (James) Don(ald) (1916–) US tennis player

Bueno, Maria (Esther) (1939–) Brazilian tennis player

Busby, Matt (Sir Matthew B.; 1909–) British footballer

Capablanca y Graupera, José Raúl (1888–1942) Cuban chess player

Carnera, Primo (1906–67) Italian boxer

Carpentier, Georges (1894–1975) French boxer

Charlton, Bobby (Robert C.; 1937–) British footballer

Clay, Cassius. See Ali, Muhammad

Comaneci, Nadia (1961–) Romanian gymnast

Compton, Denis (Charles Scott) (1918–) British cricketer

Connors, Jimmy (1952–) US tennis player

Constantine, Learie Nicholas, Baron (1902–71) West Indian cricketer

Cowdrey, (Michael) Colin (1932–) British cricketer

Cruyff, Johann (1947–) Dutch footballer

Culbertson, Ely (1891–1955) US bridge authority

Curry, John (Anthony) (1949–) British ice skater

Dempsey, Jack (William Harrison D.; 1895–1983) US boxer

Duke, Geoffrey E. (1923–) British racing motorcyclist

Edberg, Stefan (1966–) Swedish tennis player

Evert, Chris(tine) (1954–) US tennis player

Faldo, Nick (1957–) British golfer

Fangio, Juan Manuel (1911–) Argentinian motor-racing driver

Fitzsimmons, Bob (1862–1917) New Zealand boxer

Frazier, Joe (1944–) US boxer

Gooch, Graham (Alan) (1953–) British cricketer

Grace, W(illiam) G(ilbert) (1848–1915) British cricketer

Graf, Steffi (1969–) German tennis player

Hadlee, Sir Richard (John) (1951–) New Zealand-born cricketer

Hagen, Walter Charles (1892–1969) US professional golfer

Hailwood, Mike (Stanley Michael Bailey H.; 1940–81) British racing motorcyclist

Hammond, Wally (Walter Reginald H.; 1903–65) British cricketer

Hawthorn, Mike (John Michael H.; 1929–58) British motor-racing driver

Hendry, Stephen (1969–) British snooker player

Hill, Graham (1929–75) British motor-racing driver

Hoad, Lewis Alan (1934–) Australian tennis player

Hobbs, Jack (Sir John Berry H.; 1882–1963) British cricketer

Hogan, Ben (William Benjamin H.; 1912–) US golfer

Hoyle, Edmond (1672–1769) British authority on card games

Hunt, James (1947–93) British motor-racing driver

Hutton, Len (Sir Leonard H.; 1916–90) British cricketer

Imran Khan (1952–) Pakistani cricketer

Jeeps, Dickie (Richard Eric Gantry; 1931–) British Rugby Union footballer

John, Barry (1945–) Welsh Rugby Union footballer

Jones, Bobby (Robert Tyre J.; 1902–71) US amateur golfer

Joselito (José Gómez; 1895–1920) Spanish matador

Karpov, Anatoly (1951–) Russian chess player

Keegan, Kevin (1951–) British footballer

Khan, Hashim (1916–) Pakistani squash player

King, Billie Jean (born Moffitt; 1943–) US tennis player

Korchnoi, Victor (1931–) Soviet-born chess player

Lasker, Emanuel (1868–1941) German chess player

Lauda, Niki (1949–) Austrian motor-racing driver

Laver, Rod(ney George) (1938–) Australian tennis player

Lindwall, Raymond Russell (1921–) Australian cricketer

Llewellyn, Harry (Lt Col Sir Henry Morton L.; 1911–) British show jumper

and equestrian

Lloyd, Chris(tine). See Evert, Chris(tine)

Lloyd, Clive Hubert (1944–) West Indian cricketer

Louis, Joe (Joseph Louis Barrow; 1914–81) US boxer

Lyle, Sandy (1958–) British golfer

McBride, Willie John (1940–) Irish Rugby Union footballer

Matthews, Sir Stanley (1915–) British footballer

Meads, Colin Earl (1935–) New Zealand Rugby Union footballer

Milo (late 6th century BC) Greek wrestler of legendary strength

Moore, Bobby (Robert Frederick M.; 1941–93) British footballer

Moorhouse, Adrian (1964–) British swimmer

Morphy, Paul Charles (1837–84) US chess player

Moss, Stirling (1929–) British motor-racing driver

Newcombe, John (1944–) Australian tennis player

Nicklaus, Jack William (1940–) US golfer

Nurmi, Paavo Johannes (1897–1973) Finnish runner

Owens, Jesse (John Cleveland O.; 1913–80) US sprinter

Palmer, Arnold (1929–) US professional golfer

Pelé (Edson Arantes do Nascimento; 1940–) Brazilian footballer

Perry, Fred(erick John) (1909–) British tennis and table-tennis player

Petrosian, Tigran Vartanovich (1929–84) Soviet chess player

Piggott, Lester Keith (1935–) British jockey

Ramsey, Alf (Sir Alfred Ernest R.; 1922–) British Association footballer

Ranjitsinhji Vibhaji, Kumar Shri, Maharajah Jam Sahib of Nawanagar (1872–1933) Indian cricketer and statesman

Rhodes, Wilfred (1877–1973) British cricketer

Richards, Sir Gordon (1904–86) British jockey

Robinson, Sugar Ray (Walker Smith; 1921–89) US boxer

Schmeling, Max (1905–) German boxer

Scudamore, Peter (1958–) British jockey

Seles, Monica (1973–) Yugoslav tennis player

Senna, Ayrton (1960–) Brazilian motor racing driver

Smith, Harvey (1938–) British showjumper

Sobers, Gary (Sir Garfield Saint Aubrun S.; 1936–) West Indian cricketer

Spassky, Boris (1937–) Russian chess player

Spitz, Mark (Andrew) (1950–) US swimmer

Stewart, Jackie (John Young S.; 1939–) British motor-racing driver

Surtees, John (1934–) British racing motorcyclist and motor-racing driver

Sutcliffe, Herbert (1894–1978) British cricketer

Szewinska, Irena (1946–) Polish athlete

Tenzing Norgay (c. 1914–86) Sherpa mountaineer

Trevino, Lee (1939–) US golfer

Trueman, Freddy (Frederick Sewards T.; 1931–) British cricketer

Tunney, Gene (James Joseph T.; 1897–1978) US boxer

Turishcheva, Ludmilla (1952–) Soviet gymnast

Tyson, Mike (1966–) US boxer

Viren, Lasse Artturi (1949–) Finnish runner

Wade, Virginia (1945–) British tennis player

Weissmuller, Johnny (1904–84) US swimmer

Whymper, Edward (1840–1911) British mountaineer

Williams, J(ohn) P(eter) R(hys) (1949–) Welsh Rugby Union footballer

Wills (Moody), Helen (Helen .W. Roark; 1905–) US tennis player

Winkler, Hans Günter (1926–) West German show jumper

Zátopek, Emil (1922–) Czech long-distance runner

receiving team, kicker, field-goal kicker, place kicker, quick-kicker, holder, kicking tee, kick-off, onside kick, squib kick, quick kick, free kick, fake kick, punt, hang time, catch, fair catch, touchback, run back, return

13 **penalty**, 5-yard penalty, 10-yard penalty, 15-yard penalty, penalty marker, penalty flag, offensive foul, defensive foul, dead-ball foul, spot of enforcement, delay of game, offside, encroachment, holding, faceguarding, clipping, chucking, crackback block, illegal motion, false start, personal foul, unsportsmanlike conduct, ineligible receiver, pass interference, intentional grounding, illegal use of hands, roughing the passer, roughing the kicker, piling on (Inf)

14 **miscellaneous terms**, cheerleader, cointoss, game plan, pep rally, pep squad, spike, training camp, transfer, yardage, waiver

VERBS

15 **play offence**, quarterback, be the field general, call signals, run the offence, run the hurry-up offence, call the plays, be in the shotgun, pass, have possession, lateral, fake, sweep, sneak, run the quarterback sneak, call a draw, call an audible, read the defence, throw a completion, hit a receiver, throw a pass, stick to the ground game, trap, handoff, option, pitchout, bootleg, keep, rollout, leave the pocket, get sacked, score, convert, run a pattern, protect, block, cross block, lead block, centre, cutback, run the power sweep

16 **play defence**, have coverage, overshift, undershift, slant, stunt, pinch, penetrate, rush the passer, red-dog, pass rush, rush, blitz, dog, sack, bump and run, play back

17 **kick**, place kick, quick-kick, split the uprights, hit the crossbar, kick off, quick kick, be awarded a free kick, have good hang time, call

for a fair catch, make a fair catch, have a touchback, run back, return, be on the special team

18 **be penalized**, be offside, have encroachment, hold, faceguard, clip, chuck, throw a crackback block, have illegal motion, have a false start, draw a personal foul, commit unsportsmanlike conduct, throw to an ineligible receiver, interfere, ground intentionally, rough the passer, rough the kicker, pile on, have illegal use of hands, facemask, take too much time, illegally ground the ball

ADJECTIVES

19 **varsity**, collegiate, professional, offensive, defensive, specialist, kicking

20 Angling

NOUNS

1 **angling**, fishing, game fishing, still fishing, bait fishing, fishing with bait, freshwater bait fishing, trolling, float fishing, trotting, ledgering, coarse (or bottom) fishing, casting, spinning, bait casting (US), spin-casting (US), fly-fishing, dapping, natural fly-fishing, natural fly, mayfly, artificial fly-fishing, wet-fly fishing, dry-fly fishing, fishing the water, fishing to the rise, bait, worm, insect, minnow, maggot, bread, ground bait, rubby-dubby, chum (US), catch, bite, strike, take, ice fishing, ice hole, ice bar, ice spoon, surf fishing, beachcasting, saltwater fishing, saltwater bait fishing, saltwater trolling, deep-sea fishing, deep-sea trolling, strip-casting, mooching, big-game fishing, fighting seat, turntable chair, chair socket, harness, throwout level, braided line, sea swivel, competitive fishing, competitive casting, tournament casting, skish, distance event, accuracy event, American Casting Association, International Casting Federation, match fishing, National Anglers Council

2 **artificial fly**, tied fly, dressed fly, lure, artificial lure, jig, streamer, plug, surface plug, floating plug, floating diver, popper, underwater plug, sinking plug, deep diver, jointed plugs, spoon, fly spoon, barspoon, spinner, wagtail, mackerel spinner, artificial minnow, Devon minnow

3 **fishing tackle**, fishing rod (or rod), double-handed rod, single-handed rod, telescopic rod, float rod, ledger rod, spinning rod, fishing pole (or pole), bamboo pole, fly rod, casting rod, handgrip, butt guide, ferrule, tip top, reel, centre-pin reel, single-action reel, multiplier reel, fixed-spool (or spinning) reel, closed-face (or spin-casting) reel, open-face reel, float tackle, float, line, nylon line, sunk line, bobber, sinker, lead sinker, lead, coffin lead, barleycorn lead, plummet lead, fish-hook (or hook), eye, shank, bend, point, double hook, treble hook, shot, split-shot, gaff, cork, bobbin, keepnet, forcep, disgorger

4 **American game fish**, salmon, Atlantic salmon, Pacific salmon, chinook salmon, silver salmon, trout, lake trout, brook trout (or speckled trout), rainbow trout, smallmouth black bass, largemouth black bass, yellow perch, northern pike, muskellunge, walleye, arctic char, sailfish, marlin, blue marlin, swordfish, tuna, tarpon, bonefish, striped bass, bluefish, yellowtail, channel bass, snook, bonito, flounder, sea trout, barracuda, snapper, shark, mackerel, Spanish mackerel

5 **British game fish**, salmon, trout, sea trout, pike, perch, roach, rudd, chub, carp, barbel, tench, bream, eel, grayling, European sea bass, mackerel, grey mullet, skate, plaice, pollack, blue shark, conger eel

6 **angler**, compleat angler, fisher, fly-fisher, fisherman, saltwater fisherman, sea angler, big-game fisherman, deep-sea fisherman, trawlerman (or trawler)

VERBS

7 **angle**, cast, spin-cast, fish, fish the water, fish with bait, fish to the rise, fish with a rod, fish with a pole, fly-fish, entangle one's line, use bait, bait the hook, anchor bait, cast bait, cast a lure, cock the float, pump a fish, watch the float, catch fish, have a bite, hook, reel in, haul in, net, tie a fly, dress a fly, troll, ice fish, deep-sea fish

ADJECTIVES

8 **angling**, fishing, fished, piscatorial (or piscatory), freshwater, coarse, bottom, saltwater, deep-sea, wet-fly, dry-fly, ground, baited, baiting, casting, cast, trolling, trolled, tied, dressed, artificial, natural, floating, surface, underwater, sinking, jointed, double-handed, single-handed, single-action, centre-pin, fixed-spool, spinning, closed-face, open-face

ADVERBS

9 **on the water**, on the surface, by casting, by trolling, underwater, naturally, artificially, piscatorially, competitively

21 Athletics

NOUNS

1 **track events**, indoor track events, race, racing, run, running, heat, preliminary race, semi-final race, final, starting position, set position, start, false start, disqualification, acceleration, curve running, full stride, finishing, finish tape, lane, leg, sprinting, sprint, sprint racing, sprint race, 50-yard dash (US), 50m race, 100m race, 200m race, middle-distance running, middle-distance racing, middle-distance race, 400m race, 800m race, 1500m race, one-mile race, women's 3000m race, 5000m race, long-distance running, long-distance racing, long-distance race, marathon racing, marathon race, relay racing, relay race, 400m relay race (or 4 × 100m relay race), 1600m relay race (or 4 × 400m relay race), medley relay race, baton, baton change, baton changing, changeover, upsweep method, downsweep method, takeover zone, relay box, hurdles, women's 80m hurdles, women's 100m hurdles race, 110m hurdles race, women's 200m hurdles, 400m hurdles, hurdle, barrier, obstacle, steeplechase, 3000m steeplechase, water jump, cross-country racing, 10000m race, racewalking, walking race, walking, walk, 20km walk, 50km walk

▶ *324 Motion, 330 Impulsion*

2 **field events**, jump, jumping, high jump, high jumping, back-layout style, flop, Fosbury flop, straddle style, scissors style, Eastern cut-off style, Western roll style, long jump, long jumping, broad jump (US), broad jumping (US), scratch line, run-up, approach, eight-step approach, plant, take-off point, take-off, clearance, landing, landing area, sand pit, hitchkick technique, hang technique, triple jump, triple jumping, hop, step, and jump, 10-step approach, bounding, hopping, running hop, pole vault, pole-vaulting, take-off point, rockback, pole, fibre pole, vaulting pit, crossbar (or bar), shot, shot put, 16lb shot put, shot-putting, shot velocity, discus, discus throw, discus throwing, preliminary swing, transition, swingback, turn, release, drive-foot landing, hammer, hammer throw, hammer-throwing, hammer glove, circle, lift, early lift, late lift, single-support phase, rotation, acceleration path, javelin, javelin throw, javelin-throwing, javelin-carrying, measuring tape, pentathlon, decathlon, heptathlon

▶ *275 Height, 359 Ascent, 269 Length, 263 Distance, 338 Propulsion*

3 **athlete**, amateur athlete, Olympic athlete, competitor, champion, medallist, gold medallist, silver medallist, bronze medallist, runner, racer, sprinter, middle-distance runner, long-distance runner, miler, marathon runner, marathoner, steeplechaser, cross-country runner, harrier, hurdler, racewalker, walker, starter, timekeeper, vaulter, jumper, high jumper, long jumper, broad jumper (US), triple jumper, pole-vaulter, thrower, shot-putter, discus thrower, hammer-thrower, javelin-thrower, pentathlete, decathlete, heptathlete, coach, judge, field judge

4 **sports equipment**, running shoes, spiked shoes, spikes, starting blocks, blocks, starting pistol, running shorts, running vest, tracksuit, jogging suit, shell suit, athletic support, jock-strap (Inf)

5 **competition**, games, World Games, European Games, Pan-American Games, Commonwealth Games, Olympic Games, record, title, medal, gold medal, silver medal, bronze medal, drug test, anabolic steroid, sex test

VERBS

6 **compete in track and field**, take part, contest, contend, vie, come first, win, set (or break) a record, win in record-breaking time

7 **race**, start, fire the starting gun, make a false start, get off to a fast start, run, run full stride, sprint, accelerate, stay in one's lane, lead, lap, finish first, hit the finish tape, hand over the baton, make a changeover, hurdle (a barrier), knock down a hurdle

8 **jump**, leap, spring, bound, do the Fosbury flop, hop, step, and jump, (pole) vault, land, clear the crossbar, hit the crossbar

ADJECTIVES

9 **track**, track and field, field, Olympic, gold, silver, bronze, record-breaking, racing, sprinting, 50-yard (US), one-mile, middle-distance, long-distance, marathon, relay, medley relay, baton, hurdles, cross-country, walking, jumping, back-layout, take-off, triple, hopping, landing

ADVERBS

10 **fast(ly)**, (at) full stride, with a sprint, at a good pace, rhythmically, with velocity, far, high

22 Baseball

NOUNS

1 **baseball**, the great American game, America's national sport, baseball game, professional baseball, major league baseball, National League, American League, World Series, All-Star Game, pennant winner, world champions, minor league baseball, Triple-A league, Double-A league, farm club, college baseball, NCCA Baseball Championship, Little League baseball, Little League World Series, National Baseball Hall of Fame and Museum, baseball stadium, stands, bleachers, baseball field, diamond, infield, batter's box, catcher's box, pitcher's plate, pitcher's mound, home base, first base, second base, third base, foul line, outfield, left field centre field, right field, outfield fence, fair territory, foul territory, dugout, bullpen, on-deck circle, inning, top of the inning, bottom of the inning, extra innings

2 **baseball player**, the battery, middle position, pitcher, relief pitcher, catcher, fielder, infielder, keystone combination, first-baseman, second-baseman, short stop, third-baseman, outfielder, left fielder, centre fielder, right fielder, batter, hitter, long-distance hitter, home-run hitter, power hitter, left-handed hitter, right-handed hitter, lead-off man, clean-up man, base runner, runner, designated runner, starter, substitute, pinch hitter, designated hitter, batting champion, home-run leader, runs-batted-in leader, RBI leader, earned-run-average leader, All-Star, All-American, Rookie of the Year, manager, head coach, pitching coach, batting coach, home-plate umpire, first-base umpire, third-base umpire, official scorer

3 **baseball equipment**, baseball, baseball bat, bat, Louisville slugger, baseball uniform, stockings, baseball shoes, cap, sliding pads, catcher's glove, catcher's mitt, first baseman's glove, infielder's glove, outfielder's glove, catcher's mask, umpire's mask, chest protectors, shin guards, batter's helmet, horsehide (Inf), apple (Inf)

4 **pitching terms**, catcher's sign, strike zone, strike, ball, wind-up, hard pitch, soft pitch, curve ball, reverse curve, fast ball, knuckle ball, change-up, change-of-pace, slider, breaker, fadeaway, screwball, spit ball, brushing off the batter, brush-off, dusting off the batter, dust-off, strike-out, wild pitch, balk, intentional pass, base on balls, loading the bases, walking a man in, forcing a run, shut-out, perfect game, earned-run average (ERA), win, save, Annie Oakley (Sl)

5 **batting terms**, hit, single, line drive, one you can hang the wash on, pop single, double, triple, home run, inside-the-park home run, grand-slam home run, grand-slammer, fair ball, foul ball, foul tip, ground ball, up-the-middle hit, grounder, bounder, hopper, dribbler, fly ball, fly, pop up, bunt, squeeze play, suicide squeeze, sacrifice fly, perfect sacrifice, sacrifice, hit-and-run play, interference, being hit by a pitched ball, missed third strike, runs batted in (RBI), batting average, Texas Leaguer (Inf), Texas League single (Inf), murderers' row (Inf)

6 **fielding terms**, out, double play, triple play, going around the corner, put-out, throw-out, force play, run-down, tag-out, forced out, infield fly, infield fly rule, stolen base, pickup, fly-out, hot corner

VERBS

7 **play baseball**, take the field, come to bat, pitch, throw a fast ball, throw a curve, throw a slider, throw a wild pitch, balk, brush off the batter, hit the batter, load the bases, give an intentional walk, pitch a shut-out, pitch a perfect game, have a conference on the mound, be relieved, call for a relief pitcher, swing, strike at, foul off, foul, hit, hit a fly, hit a grounder, single, hit a single, double, hit a double, triple, hit a triple, hit a home run, hit a grand-slam home run, hit a grand-slammer, ground out, hit into a double play, force out, fly out, pop up, bunt, sacrifice, squeeze, be thrown out, strike out, walk, be walked, be intentionally walked, be hit by a pitched ball, be brushed off, bat in a run, leave a runner stranded, run bases, slide home, score a run, score, catch a fly, throw out, catch in a run-down, make a double play, take a trip to the showers (Inf)

23 Basketball

NOUNS

1 **basketball**, basketball game, professional basketball, National Basketball Association (NBA), NBA Championship, college basketball, NCCA Basketball Championship, NIT Championship, Basketball Hall of Fame, basketball arena, basketball gymnasium, basketball gym, playing court, centre court, centre line, ten-second line, back court, front court, free-throw lane, quarter, half, half-time, two-minute warning, overtime, sudden death

2 **basketball player**, centre, forward, guard, pivot man, shooter, foul shooter, scorer, passer, blocker, rebounder, All-American, All-Pro, varsity player, first-team player, captain, rookie, draft pick, substitute, draft player, draft, NBA Most Valuable Player, NBA Rookie of the Year, coach, head coach, assistant coach, official, referee, umpire, timer, sub (Inf)

3 **basketball equipment**, basketball, basket, net, rim, backboard, rectangular backboard, fan-shaped backboard, scoring desk, timer's desk, shot-clock, uniform, jersey, shorts, gym shoes, sneakers, knee guard, round ball (Inf), apple (Inf), rock (Inf)

4 **playing terms**, dribbling, shooting, dunking, passing, holding, freezing, rebounding, pivoting, screening, blocking, guarding, dribble, shot, two-pointer, three-pointer, foul, personal foul, technical foul, double foul, free throw, free shot, foul shot, penalty shot, one-pointer, hook shot, jump shot, bank shot, lay-up, dunk, over-the-rim shot, one-hand shot, two-hand shot, set shot, goal, field goal, tip-in, pass, bounce pass, hook pass, baseball pass, behind-the-back pass, rebound, screen, block, loose ball, live ball, held ball, dead ball, jump ball, possession, fast break offence, running offence, shoot-and-run offence, ball-control offence, possession ball, high post, low post, man-to-man defence, zone defence, five-man defence, pressing defence, the press, air ball (Inf), hanger (Inf), whish (Inf)

5 **penalties**, running with the ball, travelling, walking, double-dribbling, kicking the ball, tripping, hacking, three-second lane violation, ten-second backcourt violation, goal-tending, stepping over foul line during free throw, stepping over end line on throw-in, technical foul

VERBS

6 **play basketball**, dribble, shoot, use the backboard, hit a shot, make a field goal, make a bank shot, make a jump shot, make a hook shot, tip in, dunk, slam dunk, pass, make a bounce pass, make a hook pass, hold the ball, freeze the ball, rebound, pivot, screen, block, guard, drive, cut, foul, foul out, travel, walk, double-dribble, kick the ball, trip, hack, goal-tend, draw a penalty, draw a personal foul, draw a technical foul, take a foul shot, shoot a free-throw, play run-and-shoot, play man-to-man, press, can a shot (Sl), knock the bottom out (Inf), shoot an air ball (Inf)

24 Billiards

NOUNS

1 **billiards**, pool (or pocket billiards), English billiards, French billiards, break, inning (US), billiard table, centre spot, cushion, top cushion, pocket, billiard cloth, baize, triangle, rack (US), pool ball, numbered ball, white cue ball, cue stick (or cue), cue rest, triangle, chalk, billiards club, pool hall

2 **billiards play**, run-through, safety, coup, scratch (US), bank shot, cannon, carom (US), dead ball, side, English (US), massé shot (or massé), touching ball, frozen ball (US), full-ball aim, spot stroke, half-ball stroke, screw, hazard, long loser, long in-off, long on-off (US), stun and stab, miscue, miss, pocketing the ball

3 **English billiards**, cue, long-butt cue, half-butt cue, rest, half-butt rest, six-pocket table, pocket, top pocket, centre pocket, bottom pocket, the spot, billiard spot, pyramid spot, centre spot, centre line, baulk-line spot, baulk line, baulk cushion, the D, white ball, spot white ball (or spot), red ball, plain, cue ball, object ball, break, making a break, stroke, foul stroke, push stroke, string, playing from hand, playing up the table, playing down the table, losing hazard (or loser), winning hazard (or pot), cannon, direct cannon, indirect cannon, in-off

4 **carom**, French billiards, pocketless table, head cushion, side rail, diamond, centre spot, head spot, foot spot, foot string, centre string, head string, three-cushion billiards, red ball,

white ball, white object ball, first object ball, striking the cushion, lagging, break shot, carom, carom count, carom score, safety, foul, kiss shot, push shot, shove shot, double stroke, straight-rail billiards, baulk-line, baulk-line game, anchor space

5 **snooker**, volunteer snooker, frame, pocket billiard table, snooker table, baulk, baulk line, baulk spot, billiard spot, pyramid spot, the spot, centre spot, D area, bottom cushion, bottom pocket, centre pocket, top pocket, free ball, nominated ball, cue ball, white ball, red ball, colours, black ball, pink ball, blue ball, brown ball, green ball, yellow ball, potting a ball, stringing, respotting a ball

6 **pool**, American pocket billiards, 15-ball pocket billiards, open table, eight ball, line-up, forty-one, one and nine balls, pool table, foot spot, long string, head spot, head string, break ball, jumped ball, solid-coloured ball, striped ball, called ball, calling the ball, called pocket, calling the pocket, bumper pool (or bumpers), bumper, breaking violation, lag, scratch

7 **billiards player**, pool player, snooker player, striker, referee, marker

VERBS

8 **play billiards**, play pool, play English billiards, take a turn at the table, break, make a break, chalk a stick, make a bank shot, cannon, carom (US), put side on the ball, put English on the ball (US), drive out of baulk, take a shot, take a stroke, have a foul stroke, play up the table, play down the table, miscue, miss, pocket the ball, spot the ball, make a kiss shot, play a frame, hit the bottom cushion, pot a ball, repot a ball, call a ball, call a pocket

ADJECTIVES

9 **billiard**, numbered, cue, miscued, missed, stroked, spotted, pocketed, centred, foul, played, three-cushion, straight-rail, baulk-line, free, nominated, called, snookered, crotched, in baulk, full-ball, half-ball

25 Bowling

NOUNS

1 **green bowling**, bowling, lawn bowls, bowls, level-green bowls, crown-green bowls, bowls match, singles match (or singles), pairs match (or pairs), triples match (or triples), three-on-a-side match, fours match (or fours), end, green, bowling green, slow green, fast green, bowling rink, boundary, backboard, ditch, bank, rolling the jack, wood, bowl, bias, jack, kitty, mat, bowling side, rink

2 **grip**, forehand grip, backhand grip, the claw, the palm, aiming point, delivery, smooth delivery, wobble, head, plant, weight, whip, shot, path, grass, green, backhand shot, controlled shot, yard-on, running shot, reaching

shot, wrestling shot, upshot, onshot, run-through shot, trail shot, block shot, draw shot (or draw), drive, firing shot, cant, tilt, follow-through, front bowls, shot bowl, dead bowl, live bowl, dead jack, live jack, backwood bowl, backest bowl, toucher, wrestling toucher, chalk mark, hit, direct hit, dead end, burnt end (US), shots up, shots down, foot fault

3 **bowls player**, leader, second, third (or vice-skip), skip (or captain), marker, measurer, umpire

4 **bowling**, tenpin bowling (or tenpins), line of tenpins, game of tenpins, ninepins, skittles, duckpins (US), candlepins (US), frame, bowling lane, foul line, gutter, rear cushion, pit, 1–3 strike pocket, ball return, automatic pinsetter, range finder, bowling ball, bowling pin (or pin), head pin (or no. 1 pin), pin spot, bowling shoes, bowling bag

5 **bowling delivery**, four-step delivery, straight-line delivery, hook, curve, backup, follow-through, strike, spare, split, converted split, triple, turkey, error, gutter shot, gutter ball

6 **bowler**, tenpin bowler, professional bowler

VERBS

7 **bowl**, roll the jack, fire a shot, draw a shot, draw close to jack, go for the jack, go short and wide, lay a block, tilt the bowl, drive with the bowl, take more grass, take out

8 **bowl**, play a frame, release the ball, bowl a hook ball, knock down pins, make a strike, score a strike, score a spare, split, score a perfect game, score 300

ADJECTIVES

9 **bowls**, level-green, crown-green, singles, pairs, triples, three-on-a-side, fours, slow, fast, forehand, backhand, aiming, smooth, controlled, yard-on, running, reaching, wrestling, run-through, block, draw, firing, follow-through, front, dead, live, backest, jack-high, draw-weight

10 **bowling**, tenpin, foul, head, split, converted, gutter, four-step, straight-line, hooked, curved, backup, follow-through

26 Combat Sports

NOUNS

1 **combat sports**, combative sport, fighting sport, fighting skill, fighting, boxing, professional boxing, wrestling, professional wrestling, martial art, self-defence, judo, karate, tae kwon do, aikido

2 **boxing**, fighting, prizefighting, pugilism, noble art of self-defence, shadow boxing, fisticuffs, sparring, jabbing, socking, slugging, pummelling, boxing match, prizefight, fight, championship fight, fixed fight, throwing a fight, boxing purse, receipts, boxing rules, Marquess of Queensberry rules, point system, boxing ring,

corner, ropes, bell, round, boxing gloves, boxing scorecard, decision, boxing shorts, mouthpiece, sparring helmet, boxing technique, stance, footwork, dancing, bobbing, bob, feinting, feint, parrying, parry, blocking, block, boxing punch, left jab, left hook, right hook, right cross, straight punch, straight left, left uppercut, right uppercut, swing, knock-down punch, knock-down, knock-out punch, knock-out (KO), count, technical knock-out (TKO), foul, hitting below the belt, butting, butt, rabbit punch, boxing association, International Boxing Federation, European Boxing Union, World Boxing Association (WBA) (US), British Boxing Board of Control (BBBC)

3 **boxing weight divisions**, light-flyweight, flyweight, bantamweight, featherweight, junior-lightweight, lightweight, light-welterweight, welterweight, light-middleweight, middleweight, light-heavyweight, cruiserweight, heavyweight

4 **boxer**, professional boxer, amateur boxer, Olympic boxer, fighter, prizefighter, pugilist, flyweight, bantamweight, featherweight, welterweight, middleweight, cruiserweight, heavyweight, slugger, puncher, jabber, sparring partner, champion, heavyweight champion, world champion, titleholder, challenger, second, manager, trainer, referee, champ (Inf), southpaw (Inf), pug (Sl)

5 **wrestling**, professional wrestling, amateur wrestling, Graeco-Roman wrestling, Olympic wrestling, wrestling weight divisions, 106 pounds, 115 pounds, 126 pounds, 137 pounds, 150 pounds, 163 pounds, 181 pounds, 198 pounds, 220 pounds, 286 pounds, freestyle wrestling, all-in wrestling, catch-as-catch-can wrestling, no-holds-barred wrestling, tag-team wrestling, wrestle, grapple, wrestling match, round, wrestling ring, corner, rope, wrestling hold, full nelson, half-nelson, flying mare, headlock, body slam, fall, pin, illegal hold, choking, choke, strangling, strangle hold, kicking, kick, gouging, gouge, hair-pulling

6 **wrestler**, professional wrestler, amateur wrestler, Olympic wrestler, freestyle wrestler, Graeco-Roman wrestler, NCAA (National Collegiate Athletic Association) wrestler (US), grappler, referee, grunt-and-groaner (US inf)

7 **judo**, the way of gentleness, women's judo, junior judo, judo kata, judo grade, Kyu grade, 1st Kyu, brown belt, Dan grade, black belt, judo technique, nage-waza (throwing techniques), tachi-waza (standing), te-waza (hand), koshi-waza (hip), ashi-waza (foot and leg), sutemi-waza (sacrifice), katame-waza (groundwork), shime-waza (strangle), judo mat, judo club, dojo (practice hall), judo practitioner, judoist, judoka (judo player), tori (attacker), uka (defender), judo match, competition judo, judo referee, corner judge, timekeeper, recorder

8 **karate**, the way of the empty hand, sport karate, recreational karate, karate styles, Shotokan, Shukokai, Wado Kyu, Kyokushinkai, Shotokai, karate grade, Dan grade, beginner (red belt), 8th Kyu (white), 7th Kyu (yellow), 6th Kyu (orange), 5th Kyu (green), 4th–1st Kyu (brown), 3rd Dan (black), karate technique, jun-zuki (punching), gyaku-zuki (punching), kin-geri (kicking), mae-geri (kicking), mawashi-geri (kicking), yoko-geri (kicking), jodan-uke (blocking), gedan-barai (blocking), uchi-ude-uke (blocking), soto-ude-uke (blocking), karate mat, karate club, dojo (practice hall), karate expert, karate combatant, karate referee, judge, arbitrator, timekeeper, scorekeeper

9 **tae kwon do**, the way of the foot and fist, tae kwon do grade, 10th kup (white belt), 8th kup (yellow), 6th kup (green), 4th kup (blue), 2nd kup (red), 1st Dan (black), tae kwon do technique, lunge punch, reverse punch, jab, front kick, turning kick, side kick, back kick, axe kick, crescent kick, flying kick, flying back kick, flying reverse crescent kick, blocking techniques, evasion, block, deflection, blocking with wrist and hand, x-block, knife block, inner block, outer block, blocking kick, tae kwon do combinations, tae kwon do patterns, competitive tae kwon do, competitor, referee, judge, jury

10 **aikido**, the way of harmony of the spirit, aikido grade, 5th Kyu (yellow belt), 4th Kyu (orange), 3rd Kyu (green), 2nd Kyu (blue), 1st Kyu (brown), aikido technique, immobilization techniques, ikkyo, omote, ura, nikkyo, sankyo, yonkyo, aikido throws, shiho nage, kote gaeshi, irimi nage, tenchi nage, kaiten nage, techniques of the bokken (wooden practice sword), ken no kamae, ken suburi, kumi tachi, tachi dori, techniques of the aiki jo (wooden stave), jo suburi, jo kata, kumi jo, competition aikido, tori (thrower), uke (attacker)

VERBS

11 **do a combat sport**, have fighting skills, box, fight, spar, prizefight, practise self-defence, shadow box, engage in fisticuffs, fight as a heavyweight, land a blow, jab, sock, slug, stun, pummel, hold a boxing match, have a prizefight, fix a fight, throw a fight, enter the ring, go to one's corner, have someone on the ropes, save by the bell, box a round, dance about, bob, feint, parry, block, jab throw a left hook, swing, knock down, knock out, win by a TKO, foul, hit below the belt, butt, land a rabbit punch

12 **wrestle**, wrestle freestyle, grapple, hold a wrestling match, last a round, have a full nelson on, secure a fall, pin someone, pin someone's shoulders, choke, strangle, kick,

gouge, pull hair
13 **do martial arts**, practise judo, earn a black belt, become a karate expert, practise tae kwon do, make a flying kick, deflect, block, make a blocking kick, use aikido techniques, immobilize

ADJECTIVES
14 **combat**, combative, fighting, professional, amateur, pugilistic, self-defensive, sparring, jabbed, jabbing, slugged, slugging, hit, hitting, on the ropes, knocked out, in the corner, dancing, bobbing, feinting, parrying, blocking, mixing it up, left, right, straight, knock-down, knock-out, light-flyweight, flyweight, bantamweight, featherweight, junior-lightweight, lightweight, light-welterweight, welterweight, light-middleweight, middleweight, light-heavyweight, cruiserweight, heavyweight, Olympic, champion, world champion
15 **wrestling**, freestyle, Graeco-Roman, all-in, catch-as-catch-can, tag-team, no-holds-barred, grunt-and-groan (US inf), judo, all-red, red-and-white, black, throwing, karate, sport, recreational, punching, kicking, blocking, tae kwon do, lunge, flying, crescent, competitive, aikido, immobilized, wooden

ADVERBS
16 **professionally**, as an amateur, competitively, in the ring, in self-defence, with footwork, by feinting, below the belt, squarely, on the nose, on the chin, for the count, freestyle, evasively, by deflection

27 Cricket

NOUNS
1 **cricket match**, test match, first-class cricket, county cricket, minor-counties cricket, league cricket, village cricket, limited-over match, innings, end of play, rain stopped play, match abandoned
2 **ground**, square, wicket, sight screen, scoreboard, pavilion, Lord's, the Oval, MCC (Marylebone Cricket Club)
3 **official**, umpire, square-leg umpire, scorer
4 **team**, side, eleven, cricketer, player, batting side, all rounder, batter, batsman (or batswoman), opening batsman, opener, first wicket down, striker, runner, night watchman, fielding side, bowler, opening bowler, change bowler, fast bowler, pace bowler, medium-pace bowler, seam bowler, seamer, swing bowler, slow bowler, spin bowler, spinner, fieldsman, fielder, wicketkeeper, keeper, stumper, stumpie (Inf), the slips, slip, first slip, second slip, third slip, gully, square, point, silly point, mid on, silly mid on, third man, the covers, cover, long on, long off, mid off, square leg, deep square, leg slip, on-side fielder, off-side fielder, longstop

5 **wicket**, stump, bail, crease, popping crease, batting crease, sticky wicket, fast wicket, slow wicket, greentop
6 **pad**, glove, cap, helmet, faceguard, elbow protector, boot, box, whites, ducks
7 **bat**, willow, spline, ball, new ball, shine, old ball, seam, stitching, raised seam
8 **delivery**, fast delivery, pace, bounce, swing, lift, seamer, inswinger, outswinger, yorker, long hop, full toss, bodyline bowling, leg theory, leg trap, bouncer, donkey dropper, beamer, slow delivery, spin, flight, leg break, off break, googly, bosie, chinaman, flipper, shooter, cutter, leg cutter, off cutter, daisycutter, over, no-ball, wide, maiden over, maiden, wicket maiden, hat trick, split hat trick
9 **stroke**, defensive stroke, block, stonewalling, attacking stroke, edge, snick, glide, leg glide, glance, leg glance, cut, square cut, drive, on drive, off drive, hook, sweep, reverse sweep
10 **score**, run, one, two, three, boundary, four, six, leg bye, bye, extra, no-ball, wide, overthrow, fifty, century, duck, pair, king pair, nelson
11 **dismissal**, bowling, catch, stumping, lbw (leg before wicket), obstruction, hit wicket, run out

ADJECTIVES
12 **cricketing**, fielding, batting, bowling, in, out
13 **bowling**, fast, pacey, slow, swing, off-break, leg-break, underarm, overarm
14 **positioned**, on, off, on-side, off-side, square, leg, mid, silly

VERBS
15 **play**, take the field, go in (to bat), end play, leave the field, draw stumps
16 **field**, keep wicket, change the field
17 **bat**, go out to the middle, take guard, take stance, receive, pad, pad up to, play, block, stonewall, edge, snick, guide, force, cut, square cut, drive, glide, glance, sweep, loft, hook, slog, knock the cover off, score
18 **bowl**, run in, swing, seam, york, bounce, cut, spin, turn, flight, polish, shine, pick the seam
19 **dismiss**, bowl, stump, run out, catch, appeal

ADVERBS
20 **in**, out, to leg, to off, on the up

INTERJECTIONS
21 **how's that!**, howzat!, owzat!

28 Fencing

NOUNS
1 **fencing**, foil fencing, épée fencing, sabre fencing, fencing bout, fencing assault, swordplay, *escrime* (Fr), *scherma* (It), duelling, historic fencing, singlestick, quarterstaff, cane, *kendo* (Jap), *Schläger-Mensur* (Ger), bayonet fencing, fencing area, piste, fencing association, Fédération Internationale d'Escrime (FIE)
2 **fencing equipment**, fencing weapon, foil,

electrical foil, foil button, foil guard, foil grip, duelling sword, épée, electrical épée, épée prongs, sabre, blade, fencing clothes, wire-mesh mask, chest protector, sailcloth jacket, padded gloves, elbow guard, body cord

▶ *680 Weapon, 295 Dress*

3 **fencing movements**, on guard, *en garde* (Fr), attack, composite attack, straight thrust (*or* cut), lunge, bind, envelopment, jump, march, running attack, *flèche* (Fr), glide, cutover, *coupé* (Fr), line of attack, high-outside, high-inside, low-outside, low-inside, parry, composite parry, redoublement, disengage, false attack, feint, counter (*or* circular) parry, semicircle, *mezzocerchio* (It), beat, counterattack, riposte (*or* ripost), counter-riposte (*or* counter-ripost), stop thrust, remise, time thrust (*or* cut), closing in, *corps à corps* (Fr), clinch, guard, first guard (*or* parry), second guard (*or* parry), third guard (*or* parry), fourth guard (*or* parry), fifth guard (*or* parry), sixth guard (*or* parry), seventh guard (*or* parry), eighth guard (*or* parry), pronation, supination, hit, touch

▶ *670 Attack, 671 Defence, 672 Retaliation*

4 **fencer**, foilsman, épéeist, dueller (*or* duellist)

▶ *679 Combatant*

VERBS

5 **fence**, duel, foil-fence, épée-fence, sabre-fence, bayonet-fence, have a fencing bout, swordplay, be on guard, attack, have a line of attack, thrust, make a straight thrust, lunge, recover from the lunge, recover, make a false attack, use footwork, jump forward, march, make a running attack, glide, parry, avoid a parry, block an attack, feint, make a feint, counterattack, disengage, riposte (*or* ripost), clinch, guard, hit, touch, pronate, supinate

ADJECTIVES

6 **fencing**, foil, épée, sabre, electrical, padded, wire-mesh, attacking, lunging, running, cutover, high-outside, high-inside, low-outside, low-inside, parried, parrying, disengaged, false, feinting, countered, countering, composite, counterattacking, pronated, supinated

ADVERBS

7 **on guard**, with swordplay, with footwork, by parrying, by counterattacking, high-outside, high-inside, low-outside, low-inside

29   Golf

NOUNS

1 **golf**, golfing, golf game, game of golf, golf match, stroke play, medal play, match play, best-ball match, single, threesome, three-ball match, foursome, four-ball match, mixed foursome, golf course, eighteen-hole course, nine-hole course, links, teeing ground, fairway, through the green, approach, pitch-and-run approach, pitch, loose impediments, ob-

struction, bunker, face, water hazard, lateral water hazard, casual water, sand trap, rough, blind, green, putting green, bent grass, hole, dogleg hole, rub of the green, out of bounds, ground under repair, golf bodies, the Royal and Ancient Golf Club (R and A), Professional Golfers Association (PGA), the United States Golf Association (USGA), United States Professional Golfers Association (USPGA), major championships, the Grand Slam, the (British) Open, the US Open, the Masters, the US PGA, major golf courses, St Andrew's, Augusta

2 **golfing terms**, golf ball, dead ball, tee, hole, cup, flag, flagstick, pin, lie of the ball, hole-high ball, hanging ball, divot, par, bogey, birdie, eagle, albatross, score card, Nassau scoring, defaulted match, odd, gross score, net score, handicap score, handicap, halved hole, conceded hole, stroke play, like stroke, square match, all square match, up side, down side, dormie side, bye holes, golf rules, honour system, "Fore!", nineteenth hole

3 **golf shots**, wood shot, iron shot, approaching shot, sand shot, putting, addressing the ball, grounding the club, downswing, backswing, upswing, follow-through, teeing off, driving off, honour, pivot, stance, stroke, carry, line, penalty stroke, handicap stroke, bisque, long game, lofted shot, recovery shot, bunker shot, putt, spot putt, curve putt, gobble, pull, slice, fade, hook, draw, dubbed shot, sclaff, chip, backspin, sidespin, ace, hole in one, hole out

4 **golf club**, wood club, wood, driver, brassie, spoon, baffy, iron club, iron, driving iron, cleek, midiron, mid mashie, mashie iron, mashie, spade mashie, spade, mashie niblick, pitching niblick, niblick, wedge, putter, golf club part, cap, grip, shaft, hosel, neck, face, head, heel, sole, toe

5 **golf ball**, feather ball, special, Gourlay, gutta-percha ball, gutta, OK, Clan, Agrippa, Heley, White Brand, A1, bouncing billy

6 **golfer**, linksman, scratch player, caddie, outside agency, referee, marker, forecaddie, observer, duffer (Inf), dub (US inf)

VERBS

7 **golf**, play golf, have a foursome, tee off, drive, pitch, putt, spot putt, use backspin, pull, slice, fade, hook, chip, sclaff, recover, shoot par, have a birdie, have a bogey, shoot an eagle, hole, ace, have a hole in one, have a penalty stroke, concede a hole, sign one's score card

30   Gymnastics

NOUNS

1 **gymnastics**, Swedish gymnastics, free exercises, rhythmic gymnastics, artistic gymnastics, German gymnastics, strength exercises,

balancing exercises, competitive gymnastics, Olympic gymnastics, gold medal, silver medal, bronze medal, prescribed exercise, optional exercise, gymnastic routine, gymnastic scoring, fluency, correctness, execution, difficulty, originality, gymnasium (*or* gym)

▶ *237 Strength, 324 Motion, 674 Contention*

2 **gymnastic clothing**, leotard, tracksuit, wrist bandage, handstrap, gymnastic (*or* gym) shoes, training shoes (*or* trainers), sneakers (US)

▶ *796 Fashion, 295 Dress*

3 **gymnastic apparatus**, gymnastic mat, springboard, horizontal bar, parallel bars, horse, rings

4 **gymnastic organization**, gymnastics club, gymnastics association, Amateur Athletic Union of the United States (AUU), British Amateur Gymnastics Association, Fédération Internationale de Gymnastique

5 **horizontal bar**, parallel bars, balance, steel poles, guy wires, swinging, swing, backward swing, vaulting, vault, turn, full turn, pirouette, upstarts, back and front, giant circles, handstand position, handstand, inverted grip, dislocated grip, changed grip, straddle, forward somersault, backward somersault, finish, landing

6 **pommel horse**, side horse, pommel, saddle, neck, croup, single-leg circle, double-leg circle, scissors, turn, Moore turn, vaulting (*or* long) horse, vault, elastic board, springboard, run, rebound, straddled-leg vault, squatting vault, stooping vault, handspring, pivot cartwheel, giant cartwheel vault, beam, balance beam, vaulting, jump, jumping, turning, sitting, lying, steps, running, held position, scale, front scale, horizontal scale

7 **stationary rings**, strap, handstand, lever, upstart, forward upstart, backward upstart, uprise, forward uprise, backward uprise, cross, cross hang, hang, straight hang, inverted hang, L position, dislocate circle, forward dislocate circle, backward dislocate circle, uneven parallel bars, swinging, swing, balance movement, cross handstand

8 **floor exercises**, callisthenics, canvas, movement, combined movement, tumbling, handspring, cartwheel, somersault, forward somersault, backward somersault, half-turn, round-off, jump, jumping, holding, splits, backbend, balance, rhythm, harmony

9 **gymnasts**, competitive gymnast, all-round gymnast, vaulter, gymnastics judge, gymnastics coach

VERBS

10 **compete in gymnastics**, exercise, do a prescribed exercise, do an optional exercise, perform a gymnastic routine, execute a gymnastic movement, swing on the horizontal bar, pirouette, do a handstand, somersault, perform a somersault, finish, land, balance, vault, do a cartwheel vault, rebound, jump, turn, sit, lie, hold a position, hang, hold, hold the L position, perform a combined movement, tumble, do a handspring, do a backward somersault, round-off, do the splits

ADJECTIVES

11 **gymnastic**, Swedish, free, rhythmic, artistic, German, balancing, competitive, Olympic, prescribed, optional, training, horizontal, parallel, inverted, dislocated, forward, backward, single-leg, double-leg, vaulting, long, straddled-leg, squatting, stooping, turning, stationary, cross, combined, all-around

ADVERBS

12 **competitively**, optionally, correctly, with balance, forwards, backwards, with rhythm, in the L position

31 Hockey, Ice Hockey, Lacrosse, Etc.

NOUNS

1 **hockey**, field hockey (US), indoor hockey, Olympic hockey, hockey stick, hockey ball, goal, striking circle, shooting circle, penalty spot, hockey technique, stroke, push stroke, pushing, flick stroke, flicking, scoop stroke, scooping, pass, passing, dribble, dribbling, strike, striking, push-in, hit-in, hitting, passing back, pass-back, penalty plays, hook, hooking, hold, holding, interference, high-sticking, tripping, charging, penalty award, penalty corner, corner, penalty stroke, free hit, hockey clothing, goalkeeper's protective clothing, shin guard, glove, pads, abdominal protector, helmet, hockey association, Fédération Internationale de Hockey (FIH), International Hockey Board, All England Women's Hockey Association (AEWHA)

2 **hockey player**, striker, forward, centre forward, back, halfback, centre half, wing half, fullback, goalkeeper, goaltender, goalie (Inf)

▶ *679 Combatant*

3 **ice hockey**, ice hockey stick, hockey stick, left stick, right stick, neutral stick, goalkeeper's stick, ice hockey skates, goal, puck, ice rink, rink, barrier board, sideboards, endboards, red goal line, goal crease, blue line, centre line, centre spot, face-off circle, red face-off spot, zone, defence zone, neutral zone, centre zone, attacking zone, slot, face-off, point, ice hockey tactics, carrying the puck, rushing the puck, puck possession, stealing the puck, triangular offence, three-man combination attack, two-one-two system, power play, check, checking, stickchecking, stickcheck, forechecking, forecheck, pokechecking, pokecheck, assisting, assist, passing, pass, drop-passing, drop pass, headmanning the puck, drawing, draw, fak-

ing, fake, deke, backchecking, backcheck, backhand shot, breakout play, peel-off, give and go, man-to-man assignment, one-on-one assignment, screening, dribbling, dribble, delayed dribbling, delayed dribble, playing short-handed, dead puck, goal, garbage goal, pulling the goalie, penalty plays, offsides, offside pass, icing, charging, bodychecking, boarding, crosschecking, kneeing, elbowing, highsticking, holding, roughing, hooking, tripping, spearing, slashing, butt-ending, interference, fighting, penalty award, five-minute penalty, penalty shot, misconduct penalty, ten-minute penalty, abusive language, penalty box, ice hockey clothing, knee pad, elbow pad, shin guard, protective shoulder, pad, padded glove, helmet, goalkeeper's protective clothing, catching glove, stick glove, face mask, leather leg-guard, shoulder-guard, arm-guard, chest protector, ice hockey association, International Ice Hockey Federation, professional ice hockey, professional team, National Hockey League (NHL) (US), Stanley Cup, sin-bin (Inf)

4 **ice hockey player**, hockey player, forward, centre, winger, left wing, right wing, defender, left defence, right defence, linesman, forechecker, backchecker, puck-carrier, goalminder, goalkeeper, goaltender, goalie (Inf)

5 **lacrosse**, lacrosse stick, crosse, lacrosse ball, helmet, faceguard, shoulder-pad, arm-pad, glove, goal, goal crease, goal area, wing area, centre line, lacrosse techniques, passing, body checking, facing the ball, penalty play, offside, interference, throwing the crosse, entering the crease area, foul, technical foul, personal foul, tripping, pushing, slashing, illegal bodycheck, unnecessary roughness, penalty award, free play, free position, thirty-second suspension, one-minute suspension, three-minute suspension, loss of ball, lacrosse association, United States Intercollegiate Lacrosse Association, United States Women's Lacrosse Association

6 **lacrosse player**, attack player, midfield player, defence player, point, cover point, first defence, right wing, centre, left wing, first attack, inside home, outside home, referee, judge

7 **hurling**, *iomáin* (Gael), Irish hockey, hurling stick, hurley, *camán* (Gael), hurling ball, *sliotar* (Gael), boss, goal, crossbar, hurling association, Gaelic Athletic Association, shinty, *camanachd* (Gael), Scottish hockey, shinty stick, *camán* (Gael)

ADJECTIVES
8 **hockey**, field, indoor, Olympic, striking, shooting, penalty, push, pushed, pushing, flick, flicked, flicking, scoop, scooped, scooping, passed, passing, dribble, dribbled, dribbling, strike, struck, push-in, hit-in, pass-back,

hook, hooked, hooking, held, holding, interfered, interfering, tripped, tripping, charged, charging, ice-hockey, red, blue, face-off, defence, neutral, centre, attacking, carried, carrying, rushed, rushing, stolen, stealing, triangular, three-man combination, two-one-two, checked, checking, assisted, assisting, drop-passed, drop-passing, headmanned, headmanning, drawn, drawing, faked, faking, deked, deking, crosschecked, crosschecking, bodychecked, bodychecking, boarded, boarding, backchecked, backchecking, backhand, breakout, peel-off, give-and-go, man-to-man, one-on-one, screened, screening, short-handed, dead, garbage, offside, iced, icing, kneed, kneeing, elbowed, elbowing, highsticked, highsticking, roughed, roughing, speared, spearing, slashed, slashing, butt-ended, butt-ending, misconduct, lacrosse, technical, personal

VERBS
9 **play hockey**, play field hockey (US), stroke, push, flick, scoop, pass, pass back, dribble, strike, push in, hit in, hit, draw a penalty, hook, hold, interfere, highstick, trip, charge, hit from the penalty corner, have a corner, get a penalty stroke, get a free hit, wear a shinguard, wear a helmet, play ice hockey, face off, hit the puck, carry the puck, rush the puck, keep possession of the puck, steal the puck, use a triangular offence, develop a power play, check, stickcheck, forecheck, pokecheck, assist, drop pass, headman, draw, fake, deke, backcheck, have a breakout play, peel off, give and go, go one-on-one, screen, use a delayed dribble, play short-handed, have a dead puck, score a goal, pull the goalie out, go offsides, ice the puck, bodycheck, use an illegal bodycheck, board, crosscheck, knee, elbow, rough, spear, slash, butt-end, fight, have a penalty shot, go to the penalty box, wear a catching glove, wear a facemask, play lacrosse, face the ball, throw the crosse, enter the crease area, foul, draw a technical foul, draw a personal foul, use unnecessary roughness, have a free play, get a free position, draw a suspension, lose the ball

ADVERBS
10 **on the field**, on the (ice) rink, by scooping, by dribbling, with interference, in a three-man combination, with give-and-go

32 Horses

NOUNS
1 **horse**, equine species, quadruped, horseflesh, dobbin, pony, mount, steed, trusty steed, stallion, gelding, mare, sire, dam, foal, colt, yearling, filly, wild horse, untamed horse, bronco, brumby (Aus), outlaw, trail horse, range horse,

Breeds of Horse and Pony

Akhal Teke
Albino
Alter-Réal
American quarter horse
American saddle horse
American Shetland pony
American thoroughbred
Andalusian
Anglo-Arab
Anglo-Kabardin
Anglo-Norman
Anglo-Persian
Appaloosa
Arab
Ardennes (or Ardennais)
Assateague
Australian pony
Auxois
Avelignese
Balearic
Bali pony
Barb
Barbary
Bashkirsky
Basuto
Batak
Bavarian Warmblood
Belgian Ardennes
Belgian Heavy Draught, Brabant
Bhutia
Bokhara
Bosnian
Boulonnais
Brabant, Belgian Heavy Draught
Brandenburg
Breton
Breton Heavy Draught
Brumby
Budyonny
Burma pony, Shan
Calabrese
Camargue

Campolino
Canadian Cutting Horse
Carthusian
Caspian
Charollais Half-bred
Charro
Chincoteague
Cleveland Bay
Clydesdale
Comtois
Connemara
Corlay
Corsican pony
Criollo
Crioulu Braziliero
Curraleiro
Dales pony
Danubian
Dartmoor pony
Demi-Sang, French Trotter
Dølehest
Don
Dongola
Dosanko
Dülmen
Dutch Draught
Dutch Warmblood
East Bulgarian
East Friesian
Einsiedler
Exmoor pony
Falabella
Faxaflói
Fell
Finnish Horse
Fjord
Frederiksborg
Freiberger
French Saddle Horse
French Trotter, Demi-Sang
Friesian
Furioso
Galiceño
Garranos, Minho
Gayoe
Gelderland
German Trotter

Gidran
Groningen
Guarapuavano
Hackney
Hackney pony
Haflinger
Hanoverian
Highland pony
Hispano Arab
Holstein
Huçul
Hunter
Iceland Pony
Iomud
Irish Draught
Irish Hunter
Isabella
Italian Heavy Draught
Jutland
Kabardin
Karabair
Karabakh
Karadagh
Kathiawari
Kazakh
Kiso
Kladrub
Knabstrup
Kustanair
Landais Pony
Latvian Harness Horse
Limousin Half-bred
Lippizaner
Lithuanian Heavy Draught
Llanero
Lokai
Lundy Island
Lusitano
Mangalarga
Manipur pony
Maremmana, Maremma
Marwari
Masuren
Mecklenburg
Mérens pony
Métis Trotter
Mierzyn
Mimoseano
Minho, Garranos

Morgan
Muraköz
Murgese
Mustang
Nanfan, Tibetan Pony
New Forest pony
New Kirgiz, Novokirghiz
Nonius
Norfold Roadster
Norman
Northlands Pony
North Swedish
Norwegian Racing Trotter
Novokirghiz, New Kirgiz
Oldenburg
Orlov Trotter
Pahlavan
Palomino
Partbred Arabian
Paso Fino
Pechorsky
Percheron
Persian Arab
Peruvian Stepping Horse
Pinkafelder
Pinto
Pinzgauer Noriker
Plateau Persian
Pleven
Poitevin
Polo Pony
Pony of the Americas
Przevalski's Horse
Quarter Horse
Rhineland Heavy Draught
Rottaler
Russ
Russian Heavy Draught
Russian Trotter
Sable Island
Saddlebred
Salerno

Sandalwood Pony
Sardinian
Schleswig
Schwarzwald Heavy Horse
Sertanejo
Shagya
Shan, Belgian pony
Shetland pony
Shire Horse
Skyros pony
Sorraia
Soviet Heavy Draught
Spiti
Standardbred
Suffold Punch
Swedish Half-bred
Swedish Warmblood
Tarpan
Tartar Pony
Tchenaran
Tennessee Walking Horse
Tersky
Thessalian
Thoroughbred
Tibetan Pony, Nanfan
Timor
Toric
Trait du Nord
Trakehner
Turkoman
Viatka
Vladimir Heavy Draught
Voronezh Harness Horse
Waler
Welsh Cob
Welsh Mountain Pony
Welsh Pony
Wielkopolski
Windsor Grey
Württemberg
Yakut
Zemaituka

winter horse, untrainable horse, horse lacking quality, unsound horse, nag, jade, hack, old horse, Rosinante, plug (US), studhorse, stud, brood mare, stable horse, packhorse, beast of burden, circus horse, liberty horse, roan, strawberry roan, grey, dapple-grey, bay, chestnut, sorrel, black, piebald, skewbald, pinto, mustang, dun, bayo coyote, bangtail, quarter horse, Indian horse, cayuse, palomino, cob, montura, hackney, hunter, light horse, winged horse, Pegasus, legendary horse, Al Borak, Bayard, Black Bess, Houyhnhnm, fictional horse, Black Beauty, film horse, Trigger, Champion, Silver, Velvet, gee-gee (Sl), owl-head (Sl), skate (Sl), screw (Sl)

► *77 Mammals*

2 **thoroughbred**, purebred, bloodstock, English thoroughbred, blood-horse, pacer, stepper, high-stepper, trotter, courser, racehorse, racer, goer, stayer, sprinter, speeder, steeplechaser, hurdler, fencer, jumper, hunter, foxhunter, draught horse, plough horse, carthorse, drayhorse, shaft horse, trace horse, carriage horse, coach horse, post horse, pit pony, punch, hackney

3 **warhorse**, cavalry horse, charger, courser, steed, remount, destrier (Arch), Bucephalus, Copenhagen, Marengo

4 **saddle horse**, riding horse, cow pony, (cow-)

cutting horse, mustang, bronco, stockhorse (Aus), mount, roadster, ambler, jennet, palfrey (Arch), hack, jade, nag, pad (Dial), pad-nag (Dial)

5 **pony**, cob, galloway, garron, sheltie, fell pony, dell pony, polo pony, riding pony

6 **horsemanship**, horsewomanship, equitation, equestrianism, riding, horse riding, classical riding, *haute école* (Fr), high school, manège, dressage, horse show, show jumping, eventing, gymkhana, racing, horseracing, steeplechasing, point-to-point racing, polo, bareback riding, pony trekking
▶ *655 Skill, 674 Contention*

7 **horseracing**, racing, sport of kings, flat racing, steeplechasing, hurdle racing, two-horse race, walkover, maiden race, race meeting, meet, mixed meeting, post, start, finish, form, handicap, penalty, odds, evens, price, betting, antepost betting, bet, totalizator, perfecta, exacta, win, place, show (US), each-way bet, double, dividend, weight allowance, weight cloth, weights, weigh in, the field, entry, runner, scratch, favourite, co-favourite, odds-on bet, certainty, dark horse, outsider, maiden, sprinter, stayer, mudder (US), pacemaker, also-ran, starter's orders, dead heat, photo finish, objection, weigh out, winner's enclosure, turf, the Turf, racecourse, racing track, dirt track, bush track (US), training tracks (Aus), weighing room, paddock, English Classics, the Derby, the Oaks, the 1,000 Guineas, the 2,000 Guineas, the St Leger, American Triple Crown, Kentucky Derby, Preakness, Belmont Stakes, race card, silks, point-to-point racing, steeplechase, National Hunt racing, Grand National, Maryland Hunt Cup (US), hurdles, fences, jumps, sticks, leap, the Jockey Club, tote(Inf), sure-thing (Inf), sleeper (US inf), ringer (US sl)
▶ *674 Contention, 324 Motion, 589 Chance*

8 **hunting**, hunt, fox hunting, fox hunt, meet, lawn meet, opening meet, hunter trials, hunter, scent, draghunt, drag, hound, foxhound, foxdog, draghound, hunt terrier, fox, Charley, cry, halloa, baying, tongue, music, hunt master, stale line, country, earth, hunting horn, hunt livery, hunting cap, stock, hunt button, stag hunting, hare hunting
▶ *590 Pursuit, 398 Killing*

9 **jumping**, showjumping, show arena, course, circuit, jumping lane, fence, straight fence, spread fence, gate, wall, parallel bars, triple bar, planks, post and rails, hog's back, water jump, wing, obstacle, combination obstacle, double, treble, clear round, fault, refusal, time allowed, time limit, against-the-clock competition, jump-off, shying, running out, barrage, international show jumping, Prix des Nations
▶ *674 Contention, 361 Raising, 661 Hindrance*

10 **dressage**, dressage movement, quadrille, pas-sage, piaffe, pirouette, caracole, curvet, renvers, travers, volte, half volte, serpenting, two track, turn on the forehand, gait, free-style, kur, Lippizaner stallion, Spanish Riding School, habit

11 **eventing**, three-day event, one-day event, cross-country, course, circuit, fence, straight fence, parallel bars, dressage, speed and endurance, showjumping, Badminton, Burghley, Hickstead, Pan-American Three-Day Event (US)
▶ *361 Raising, 674 Contention*

12 **rodeo**, standard event, calf-roping, saddle-bronc-riding, bareback-(bronc-)riding, bull-riding, steer-wrestling, bull-dogging, barrel-racing, camp-drafting (Aus), All-Around Champion, All-Around Cow Horse, cow horse, calf horse, rope horse, Cheyenne Frontier Days, Pendleton Round Up, Denver Stock Show, Oklahoma City All-American Finals, ground money, mount money
▶ *674 Contention*

13 **breeding**, conformation, pedigree, bloodline, dam, sire, stud, studbook, bred horse, blooded horse, purebred, Orientale, Anglais, thoroughbred

14 **horse-riding terms**, riding school, horse box, horsecloth, horsehair, horseshoe, horsewhip, horse-trading, grooming, grooming kit, currycomb, tack, reins, bit, blinkers, bridle, noseband, neckstrap, cavesson (US), numnah (*or* numdah), tail guard, sweat scraper, saddle, American saddle, English saddle, racing saddle, side saddle, stock saddle (Aus), farriery, livery stable, mucking out, skepping out, stable management, pancake (Sl)

15 **horse person**, breeder, owner, rider, horse rider, horseman (*or* horsewoman), equestrian, equestrienne, postilion, postboy, courier, mounted police, mounted troops, mounted rifles, cavalry regiment, horse, light horse, horse artillery, horse soldier, cavalryman, yeoman, trooper, sowar, hussar, lancer, dragoon, light dragoon, heavy dragoon, Ironsides, Cossack, rough-rider, chivalry, cavalier, knight, knight errant, hunt, hunt master, joint-master, huntsman, hunter, hunt secretary, hunt servant, whipper-in, kennel huntsman, kennel man, racing steward, jockey, jump jockey, steeplechaser, bookmaker, turf accountant, tipster, better, punter, showjumper, eventer, trainer, breaker, roughrider, bareback rider, bronco-buster, buckaroo, cowboy, cowgirl, cowpuncher, rep, drover (Aus), gaucho, rodeo rider, saddler, black saddler, loriner, farrier, blacksmith, vet, veterinarian, horse doctor, ostler (Arch), groom, stud groom, stableboy, stable lad, Mountie (*or* Mounty) (Inf), jockette (Inf), bookie (Inf)
▶ *679 Combatant, 590 Pursuit, 674 Contention*

Formula 1 World Champions

1950 Guiseppe Farina (Italy)	1961 Phil Hill (US)	1972 Emerson Fittipaldi (Brazil)	1983 Nelson Piquet (Brazil)
1951 Juan Manuel Fangio (Argentina)	1962 Graham Hill (England)	1973 Jackie Stewart (Scotland)	1984 Niki Lauda (Austria)
1952 Alberto Ascari (Italy)	1963 Jim Clark (Scotland)	1974 Emerson Fittipaldi (Brazil)	1985 Alain Prost (France)
1953 Alberto Ascari (Italy)	1964 John Surtees (England)	1975 Niki Lauda (Austria)	1986 Alain Prost (France)
1954 Juan Manuel Fangio (Argentina)	1965 Jim Clark (Scotland)	1976 James Hunt (England)	1987 Nelson Piquet (Brazil)
1955 Juan Manuel Fangio (Argentina)	1966 Jack Brabham (Australia)	1977 Niki Lauda (Austria)	1988 Ayrton Senna (Brazil)
1956 Juan Manuel Fangio (Argentina)	1967 Denis Hulme (New Zealand)	1978 Mario Andretti (US)	1989 Alain Prost (France)
1957 Juan Manuel Fangio (Argentina)	1968 Graham Hill (England)	1979 Jody Scheckter (South Africa)	1990 Ayrton Senna (Brazil)
1958 Mike Hawthorn (England)	1969 Jackie Stewart (Scotland)	1980 Alan Jones (Australia)	1991 Ayrton Senna (Brazil)
1959 Jack Brabham (Australia)	1970 Jochen Rindt (Austria)	1981 Nelson Piquet (Brazil)	1992 Nigel Mansell (England)
1960 Jack Brabham (Australia)	1971 Jackie Stewart (Scotland)	1982 Keke Rosberg (Finland)	

VERBS

16 **ride**, ride bareback, ride side-saddle, saddle, mount, trot, canter, gallop, break in, train, race, steeplechase, hunt, jump, groom, curry, muck out

ADJECTIVES

17 **equine**, equestrian, riding, horse-riding, racing, horseracing, hunting, fox-hunting, jumping, showjumping, cross-country, mounted, thoroughbred, purebred

33 Motor Racing

NOUNS

1 **motor racing**, auto (or automobile) racing (US), motor sport, sports car racing, road racing, endurance racing, speedway racing, international racing, Grand Prix Formula One Class, Formula 1 (F1) racing, Grand Prix (GP) racing, Grand Prix World Championship, World Championship points, points table, Formula Super Vee racing, Formula 2 (F2) racing, Formula 3, Formula 3000, Formula Vauxhall Lotus, IndyCar racing, production car racing, stock-car racing, drag racing, midget-car racing, hot-rod racing, rallying, hillclimbing, karting, Go-Karting (Tm), vintage-car racing, racetrack, raceway, race, motor race, automobile race (US), road race, sports-car race, speedway race, stock-car race, drag race, midget-car race, hot-rod race, Formula 1 race, Grand Prix race, hill climb, Pikes Peak climb, motor rally, automobile rally (US), Monte Carlo rally, East African Safari rally, endurance event, maximum-speed event, maximum-acceleration event, sprint, motor trial, automobile trial (US), reliability trial, Scottish Six-Days trial, grasstrack racing, autocross, Formula 1 car, F1 car, Grand Prix car, racing tyre, racing circuit, banger racing (Inf) ▶ *324 Motion, 674 Contention*

2 **Formula 1 race**, Grand Prix (GP), *grandes épreuves* (Fr), United States GP at Phoenix, Brazilian GP at Interlagos, San Marino GP at Imola, Italy, Monaco GP at Monte Carlo, Mexican GP at Mexico City, Canadian GP at Montreal, French GP at Bandol, British GP at Silverstone, German GP at Hockenheim, Hungarian GP at Hungaroring, Belgian GP at Spa Francorchamps, Italian GP at Monza, Portuguese GP at Estoril, Spanish GP at Jerez, Japanese GP at Suzuka, Australian GP at Adelaide

3 **sports car race**, Le Mans 24-hour race, Sebring 12-hour race, Monza 1,000 kilometres, Targa Florio

4 **motor rally**, Monte Carlo, East African Safari, the Alpine, the Acropolis, the San Remo Rally of the Flowers, the Swedish Midnight Sun, the Netherlands' Tulip Rally

5 **motorcycle racing**, motorbike racing, dirt-track racing, motocross, rallycross, scrambling, dirt-track race, motorcycle race, motorbike race, Grand Prix (GP) race, Race of the Year, 500 Italian Grand Prix, Daytona 200, TT (Tourist Trophy) race, Isle of Man TT, Dutch TT, Gran Premio de Barcelona, Macau Grand Prix, motorcycle class, 50 cc, 125 cc, 250 cc, 350 cc (junior), 500 cc (senior), 750 cc, unlimited class, sidecar class, motorcycle, motorbike, superbike, six-wheeler

6 **motor-racing terms**, grid, pole position, scrambling, roughriding, ride height, tyre stagger, active(-ride) suspension system, passive suspension system, set-up, slipstreaming, sliding off, hooking off, clipping, jetting, hacking, gearing, bottom gear, clutch-slip, changing down, cranking over, peeling off, tucking in, spinning out, spin-out, spoiling,

straight-lining, T-boning, run-and-bump tactic, outbraking, sweeping, funnelling, mixed set, ground clearance, wheelie, carburation, powerband, down-force, G-force loading, track, road circuit, circuit, oval, long circuit, short circuit, banked circuit, mountain circuit, ripple, apex, lap, flying lap, starting grid, start, warm-up lap, restart, pit, pit lane, pit wall, pit stop, fuel stop, *parc fermé* (Fr), straight, six-gear straight, corner, off-camber corner, bend, S-bend, right-hander, left-hander, right-hand kink, left-hand kink, hairpin, sweeper, chicane, safety barrier, Armco (Tm), chequered flag, skidpan, hoicking back (Inf), over-rev (Inf), rev limiter (Inf)

▶ *156 Beginning, 313 Circularity*

7 **racing governing body**, Fédération Internationale de l'Automobile (FIA), United States Automobile Club (USAC), National Association for Stock Car Auto Racing (NASCAR) (US), National Hot Rod Association (NHRA) (US), Sports Car Club of America, Royal Automobile Club (RAC), British Racing Drivers' Club (BRDC), motorcycling association, Fédération Internationale Motocycliste (FIM), Auto-Cycle Union, American Motorcycle Association

8 **driver**, Grand Prix driver, Formula 1 driver, number-one driver, number-two driver, racer, Grand Prix racer, Formula 1 racer, motor racer, automobile (*or* auto) racer (US), drag racer, pit mechanic, cornerman, motorcyclist, motorcycle racer, motocrosser

▶ *679 Combatant, 70 Transport*

VERBS

9 **race**, go racing, motor race, auto race (US), race sports cars, road-race, take part in an endurance race, race at a speedway, race internationally, do Formula 1 racing, race stock cars, drag-race, race midget cars, race hot rods, do grasstrack racing, race motorcycles, race motorbikes, do dirt-track racing, scramble, race bangers (Inf)

10 **be on the track**, have the pole position, go to the starting grid, get the green light, start, restart, scramble, roughride, set up, slipstream, slide off, hook off, clip the apex, clip, jet, hack, gear, use the bottom gear, clutch-slip, change down, crank over, peel off, tuck in, spin out, spoil, straight-line, T-bone, outbrake, sweep, funnel, have ground clearance, do a wheelie, have G-force loading, lap, make a pit stop, make a fuel stop, change the tyres, hit a straight, turn a corner, get the chequered flag, hoick back (Inf), over-rev (Inf)

ADJECTIVES

11 **racing**, automobile (*or* auto) (US), motor, endurance, maximum-acceleration, maximum-speed, speedway, international, Grand Prix, Formula 1, Formula 2, stock-car, Go-Kart, reliability, grasstrack, motorcycle, motorbike,

dirt-track, unlimited, active-ride, banked, run-and-bump, T-boned, T-boning, lapped, lapping, spun-out six-gear, off-camber, right-hand, left-hand

ADVERBS

12 **in a race**, in Grand Prix competition, in a Formula 1 car, on a racetrack, at maximum speed, on a motorcycle, internationally

34 Mountaineering

NOUNS

1 **mountaineering**, mountain climbing, alpinism, climbing mountains, climbing, hill climbing, fell walking, rock climbing, bouldering, serious climbing, strenuous climbing, sustained climbing, thin climbing, balance climbing, bold climbing, free climbing, clean climbing, aid climbing, snow and ice climbing, winter climbing, climb, upclimb, climbing expedition, camp, base camp, advance camp, bivouac, route, air route, bolt route, classic route, artificial route

▶ *359 Ascent, 95 Mountains*

2 **climbing dangers**, bad weather, frostbite, mountain hypothermia, avalanche, loose rocks, falling rocks, friable rock, greasy rock, thin ice, concealed crevasse, lack of oxygen

▶ *633 Danger*

3 **climbing technique**, back and knee, back and foot, back rope, ascent, ascending, soloing, cleaning, gardening, prusiking, moving together, committing move, delicate move, desperate move, layaway move, laybacking, bridging, step-cutting, jamming, scrambling, smearing, glissading, top roping, heel hook, swinging, yo-yoing, front-pointing, pendule, pendulum, stomach traverse, toe traverse, tension traverse, Tyrolean traverse, descent, descending, reverse, descending *en rappel* (Fr), abseiling down, abseil, classic abseil, rappel, roping off, belaying, direct belay, dynamic belay, deadman belay, belay braking, waist belay, snow bollard belay, boot-axe belay, running belay, Italian friction hitch, edging, cheating, frigging, chimneying, blind move, combined tactics

▶ *360 Descent*

4 **climbing equipment**, climbing gear, rack of equipment, metal spike, piton, knifeblade piton, RURP (realized ultimate reality piton), bong, peg, metal clip, karabiner (*or* krab), locking karabiner, snaplink, screwgate, skyhook, harness, waist belt, body harness, sit-harness, sit-sling, snap ring, anchor, runner, nut, wedge-shaped nut (*or* wedge), nut key, prodder, hexentric nut (*or* hex), chock, bolt, belay anchor, camming device, hammer, peg hammer, ice hammer, axe, ice axe, adze, knife, ascender, belay brake (*or* plate), sticht plate,

rope, kernmantel rope, live rope, static rope, safety rope, accessory cord, tape, nylon webbing, microwire, extension sling, extender, étrier, stirrup (US), descender, willow wands, aneroid barometer, compass, map, oxygen tank, walkie-talkie, torch, chalk, chalk bag, rucksack, shoulder sling, bandoleer, portable radio, waterproof matchbox, cooking equipment, tent, sleeping bag, climbing boots, cleated boots, kletterschuh (or klett), sticky boots, crampons, skis, goggles, sunglasses, snowglasses, heavy clothing, windproof clothing, parka, thermal underwear, helmet, mittens, heavy socks, sun-block cream, cow's tail (Inf)

▶ *603 Tool, 295 Dress, 632 Safety*

5 **rock face**, wall, ridge, slab, glacis, pitch, ledge, terrace, mantelshelf, ramp, stance, hold, pocket hold, polished hold, fixing point, air point, foothold, corner, groove, shallow groove, V-groove, crack, off-width crack, niche, scoop, cave, amphitheatre, gully, couloir, crevasse, bergschrund, rimaye, chimney, capstone, glacier, neve, firn, flake, spike, arête, knob, bollard, block, pillar, rib, crag, knife edge, outcrop, overhang, roof, prow, bulge, nose, chockstone, gritstone, buttress, sérac, mountaintop, peak, pinnacle, summit

▶ *281 Verticality, 282 Horizontality, 283 Suspension, 277 Depth, 279 Summit*

6 **mountaineering association**, Union Internationale des Associations d'Alpinisme (UIAA), climbing club, British Mountaineering Council (BMC), Scottish Mountaineering Club (SMC), Alpine Club, American Alpine Club, Alpine Club of Canada

7 **mountaineer**, alpinist, climber, rock-climber, ascender, upclimber, cragsman (or cragswoman), fell walker, guide, Sherpa guide, porter

ADJECTIVES

8 **mountaineering**, mountain, hill, rock, bouldering, balance, bold, free, clean, aid, climbed, climbing, back-and-knee, back-and-foot, soloing, cleaning, gardening, prusiking, layaway, laybacking, step-cutting, scrambling, glissading, front-pointing, Tyrolean, deadman, belay, belayed, belaying, boot-axe, blind, bolt, artificial, aneroid, waterproof, goggled, windproof, thermal, sun-block, crevassed, gullied, knifeblade, wedge-shaped, hexentric, camming, peg, live, static, safety, accessory, extension, cleated, sticky, ridged, ledged, terraced, ramped, pocket, polished, fixing, off-width, outcropping, overhanging, knife-edge

VERBS

9 **mountaineer**, go mountaineering, climb a mountain, mountain-climb, do serious climbing, do sustained climbing, do free climbing,

solo, do aid climbing, go fell walking, climb a hill, rock-climb, upclimb, go on a climbing expedition, camp, bivouac, ascend, get a foothold, use the back-and-knee technique, clean, garden, prusik, move together, bridge, stepcut, jam, scramble, smear, glissade, top rope, heel-hook, swing, yo-yo, front-point, traverse, reach the mountaintop, scale a peak, plant a flag on the summit, descend, reverse, descend *en rappel* (Fr), abseil down, abseil, rappel, rope off, belay, edge, cheat, frig, chimney, use combined tactics

ADVERBS

10 **on a climb**, on a climbing expedition, under bad weather, with the back-and-knee technique, with the back-and-foot technique, with cleated boots, by a classic route, by an artificial route

35 Rugby Football

NOUNS

1 **rugger**, rugby, rugby football, Rugby Union, RFU (Rugby Football Union), Rugby League, RFC (Rugby Football Club), rugby side, rugby pack, rugby match, rugby ball, rugby stadium, Twickenham, rugby ground, rugby pitch, goal, goal posts, crossbar, goal line, in-goal area, corner flag, half-way line, 22 metre line, 5 metre line, side line, touch, touch line, touch-in-goal line, dead-ball line

2 **championship**, five-nations championship, triple crown, Calcutta Cup, Rugby World Cup

3 **rugby play**, possession, put-in, scrum (or scrummage), set scrum (or scrummage), tight scrum, loose scrum, collapsing scrum, formation, 3-4-1 formation, 3-3-2 formation, pileup, shove, eight-man shove, ruck, maul, lineout, run, running, dummying, looping, peeling off, grounding the ball, heeling, pass, passing, close-passing, throw-forward, catch, fair catch, interception, rebound, cover, kick, kickoff, kick-ahead, drop kick, drop-out, place kick, clearance kick, free kick, penalty kick, penalty goal, dropped goal, kick at goal, conversion goal, tackle, tackling, fielding (the ball), knock-on, try, ball in touch, touch down, play-the-ball, defence, cover defence, penalty, offside, high tackle, lying on the ball, not playing the ball, handling the ball in a scrum, illegal hooking, tripping, intentional knock-on, penalty try

4 **rugby player**, forward, loose forward, prop forward, prop, scrum half, stand-off half (or fly-half), halfback, fullback, three-quarter back, right wing three-quarter, left wing three-quarter, right centre three-quarter, left centre three-quarter, flanker, hooker, blocker, jumper, front row, back row, second row, second-row forward, lock, No. 8, ball-carrier,

attacker, try scorer, support player, defender, rugby coach, rugby referee

VERBS

5 **play rugby**, attack, form a scrum, form a tight scrum, form a loose scrum, pack a scrum, win a scrum, heel the ball, win the ball, score a try, score, convert a try, kick, take a penalty kick, have a penalty try, peel off, ruck, maul, jump, throw in, drop-kick the ball, tackle, take out a tackler, get one's head in, bend, bind, drive, shove, play the ball, block, protect the ball, go off-sides, make a high tackle, lie on the ball, not play the ball, handle the ball, trip

ADJECTIVES

6 **rugger**, rugby, in-goal, half-way, corner, touch, dead-ball, set, tight, loose, eight-man, collapsing, in touch, running, dummying, looping, peeling, grounding, heeling, passing, drop, clearance, penalty, dropped, converted, tackled, offside

36   Sailing, Rowing, Etc.

NOUNS

1 **sailing**, yachting, international sailing, sailing techniques, beating, bearing off (*or* away), reefing, reaching, fine reaching, close reaching, beam reaching, broad reaching, bottom turn, close hauling, sheeting in, sheeting out, gybe, duck gybe, clew gybe, slam gybe, scissor gybe, flare gybe, stop gybe, tacking, port tacking, starboard tacking, tack, duck tack, clew tack, heading up, luffing, wearing, taking up, competitive sailing, team dinghy racing, regatta, yacht ràcing, Grand Prix yacht racing, yacht race, handicap race, Cowes regatta, Admiral's Cup series, offshore racing, ocean racing, Sydney to Hobart Race, Fastnet Race, Bermuda Race, single-handed racing, dinghy racing, cruiser racing, multihull racing, transatlantic racing, Single-handed Transatlantic Race, the Atlantic Race for Cruisers (ARC), the Whitbread Round the World Race, World Team Racing Championship, sailing trophy, the America's Cup, Congressional Cup, Wilson Trophy, Hinman Cup, tall-ship racing, yachting association, International Yacht Racing Union (IYRU), Intercollegiate Yacht Racing Association (IYRA) (US), the United States Yacht Racing Union (USYRU), Royal Yachting Association (RYA), sailing wind, true wind, apparent wind, anabatic wind, katabatic wind, land breeze, sea breeze, course, wake course

▶ *389 Water, 674 Contention, 390 Air*

2 **sailing boat**, yacht, cruising yacht, ocean-cruising yacht, ocean-racing yacht, yacht class, Formula 40 class, half-tonner class, 50-foot class, Olympic class, Soling class, Star class, Tornado class, Flying Dutchman (FD)

class, 470 class, Finn class, Europe class, Sailboard class, yacht tender, keelboat, two-man keelboat, three-man keelboat, planing keelboat, dinghy, single-handed dinghy, two-man dinghy, catamaran, cruiser, single-masted boat, cutter, sloop, masthead sloop, two-masted boat, two-man trapeze boat, schooner, kedge, yawl, double-ender, square-rigger, lugger, one-design boat, committee boat, stiff boat, tender boat, tide-rode boat, wind-rode boat

3 **parts of a sailing boat**, helm, tiller, wheel, deck, deckhead, bow, prow, stem, pulpit, beam, quarter, amidships, afterpart, stern, transom, pushpit, rudder, rudderpost, cockpit, companionway, hull, carvel-built hull, clinker-built hull, moulded hull, GRP (glass-reinforced plastic) hull, centreboard, daggerboard, keel, fin keel, leeboards, side light, rig, Bermudan rig, Marconi rig, gaff rig, gunter rig, jury rig, rigging, running rigging, standing rigging, tackle, Cunningham tackle, Cunningham hole, purchase, downhaul, uphaul, bulkhead, bulwarks, sail, jib, mainsail, trysail, foresail, Genoa, headsail, spinnaker, gaffsail, fore-and-aft sail, lugsail (*or* lug), loose-footed sail, gaff, forestay, backstay, staysail, bilge, bitts, block, snatch block, sheave, spar, sprit, yard, mast, forward mast, mainmast, aft mast, mizzenmast, deck-stepped mast, keep-stepped mast, boom, boom preventer, vang, boom vang, kicking strap, rope, bolt rope, sheet, shock cord, halyard, hawser, lanyard, warp, outhaul, heaving line, breast line, ratline, reef point, painter, lifeline, mooring line, spring, shroud, lift, topping lift, guy, ballast, chainplates, clew, gasket, fairlead, barber hauler, gooseneck, battens, drogue, cleat, jamming cleat, claw ring, gimbal, hank, cross-tree, sheet winch, bosun's chair, flag, ensign, pennant, burgee, coffee grinder (Inf)

▶ *74 Water Transport*

4 **rowing**, amateur rowing, single-oar rowing, fixed-seat rowing, sweep rowing, sculling, double-oar rowing, single sculling, double sculling, quadruple sculling, competitive rowing, racing, scull racing, skiff racing, regatta, the Henley Royal Regatta, Royal Canadian Henley, Olympic rowing, Olympic regatta, the World Championships, intercollegiate rowing, the boat race, Oxford-Cambridge race, Harvard-Yale race, rowing race, bumping race, open event, pairs, fours, eights, sprint race, sweep (US), racing boat, rowboat, dinghy, skiff, outrigger, coxed fours, coxswainless fours, quadruple sculls, coxed pairs, coxswainless pairs, sculls, double sculls, single sculls, parts of a racing boat, seat, sliding seat, fixed seat, stroke side, bow side, oar, racing oar, spade oar, spoon oar, scull, handle, blade,

loom, collar, button, rowlock, notch, thole-pin, gunwale (*or* gunnel), swivel, thwart, stretcher, rowing technique, catch, stroke, English stroke, American stroke, recovery, feathering, finish, squaring, balance, diving, striking, rate of striking, paddling, blade slip, rowing association, Fédération Internationale Sociétés d'Aviron (FISA), American Rowing Association, catching a crab (Inf)
▶ *330 Impulsion*
5 **Henley trophies**, the Grand Challenge Cup (eights), Thames Cup (eights), Ladies Plate (college and school eights), Princess Elizabeth Cup (schoolboy eights), Prince Philip Cup (coxed fours), Britannia Cup (coxed fours), Stewards' Cup (fours), Visitors' Cup (college and school fours), Wyfold Cup (fours), Silver Goblets (pairs), Diamond Sculls, Double Sculls
▶ *681 Trophy*
6 **canoeing**, recreational canoeing, wild-water canoeing, white-water running, shooting the rapids, competitive canoeing, single-paddle canoeing, double-paddle canoeing, birchbark canoe, dugout canoe, open canoe, Canadian canoe, foldboat, faltboat, paddling canoe, racing canoe, cruising canoe, sailing canoe, outrigger, catamaran, international 10 square metre canoe, V-bottom, war canoe, kayak, decked kayak, folding canoe, paddle, single-bladed paddle, double-bladed paddle, double-ended paddle, softwood paddle, hardwood paddle, parts of a canoe, bow, stern, keel, gunwale (*or* gunnel), seat, sliding outrigger seat, thwart, centreboard, deck, well, cockpit, canoe techniques, stroke, cruising stroke, bow stroke, forward bow stroke, cruising hook, J stroke, draw stroke, turning stroke, pushover stroke, sweep stroke, jamming stroke, stopping stroke, locking the blade, keel lock, Eskimo roll, shaking out, canoe racing, slalom racing, Olympic canoeing, canoe race, one-man (C-1) canoe race, two-man (C-2) canoe race, single kayak (K-1) race, double kayak (K-2) race, four-man kayak (K-4) race, single-blade race, double-blade race, tandem race, open cruising race, decked-canoe race, water course, gate, canoe trophy, International Challenge Cup, canoe association, International Canoe Federation (ICF), British Canoe Union, Royal Canoe Club, British Schools Canoeing Association, American Canoe Association (ACA)
▶ *317 Concavity, 294 Uncovering, 293 Covering, 676 War*
7 **windsurfing**, boardsurfing, sailing, free sailing, freestyle sailing, displacement sailing, windsurf racing, slalom racing, one-design racing, open-class racing, ins-and-outs, wave-sailing, wave riding, wave jumping, ice surfing, sailboard, parts of a sailboard, board, cus-tom board, customs, GRP (glass-reinforced plastic) board, flatboard, displacement board, roundboard, pop-out board, funboard, gun, floater, sinker, marginal, tandem, tridem, rail, fin, skeg, wing, sail, funboard storm sail, rotational sail, RAF (rotating asymmetrical foil), powerhead, fathead, universal joint, boom, wishbone boom, footstrap, harness, harness line, ding, hull, V-shape hull, daggerboard, bowline, bumper, rocker, downhaul line, camber inducer, cleat, clew, windsurfing classes, Division I, Division II, Division III, slalom course, drysuit, windsurfing terms, centre of effort (CE), centre of lateral resistance (CLR), cavatation, railing, spinning out, spin-out, wiping out, wipe-out, windsurfing techniques, Le Mans start, water start, foot steering, planing, pumping, off-the-lip turn
▶ *280 Base, 269 Length, 282 Horizontality*
8 **punting**, pleasure punting, double punting, one-arm punting, punt-racing, competitive punting, Professional Punting Championship, canoe poling, punt, pleasure punt, family punt, racing punt, two-foot punt, Thames punt, *Stocherkahn* (Ger), Mexican *trajinera* (Sp), Dutch *punter*, punt pole, racing pole, parts of a punt, saloon, huff, sheer, swim, knee, tread, grating, rounds, floors, till, locker, deck, counter, shoe, mud shoe, sprit, box, after back rest, punting techniques, climbing the pole, levering, pinching, running, reaching, windmill stroke, shove, C-shape shove, half-shove, after-shove, back-shove, stop-up, throw, drop, recovery, crossover recovery, the bucket, picking up, pole-body-foot movement, trailing
9 **sailor**, yachtsman, helmsman, captain, skipper, crewman, sailing boat designer, yacht designer, rower, oarsman, bow, number one, number two, number three, number four, number five, number six, stroke, sculler, coxswain (*or* cox), Henley stewart, windsurfer, boardsurfer, ice surfer, punter, waterman, sitter

ADJECTIVES
10 **sailing**, yachting, tacking, handicap, offshore, single-handed, multihull, transatlantic, anabatic, katabatic, cruising, ocean-cruising, ocean-racing, half-tonner, 50-foot, Olympic, two-man, three-man, planing, two-masted, square-rigged, one-design, tide-rode, wind-rode, carvel-built, clinker-built, moulded, GRP, Bermudan, Marconi, gaff, gunter, jury, Cunningham, fore-and-aft, forward, aft, deck-stepped, keel-stepped, heaving, mooring, goosenecked, jamming, underway, abeam, adrift, aloft, aweigh, close-hauled, roller-reefed, Bermudan-rigged, Marconi-rigged, gaff-rigged, gunter-rigged, head-to-wind, off-wind, in irons, loose-footed, quartering, stiff, tender, clew, slam, scissor, flare, stop, luffing

11 **rowing**, row, single-oar, single, fixed-seat, sweep (US), double-oar, double, quadruple, scull, skiff, intercollegiate, coxed, coxswainless, stroke, bow, spade, spoon, recovering, feathering, finished, squared, squaring, balanced, balancing, diving, striking, paddling

12 **canoeing**, canoe, wild-water, white-water, single-paddle, double-paddle, birchbark, dugout, open, Canadian, V-bottom, war, decked, folding, paddling, paddled, cruising, sailing, single-bladed, double-bladed, double-ended, softwood, hardwood, bow, forward bow, J, turning, pushover, sweep, jamming, stopping

13 **windsurfing**, windsurf, boardsurfing, freestyle, displacement, pop-out, floater, sinker, marginal, tandem, tridem, rotational, RAF, universal, wishbone, V-shape, downhaul, planing, sub-planing, hooked-in, pumping, off-the-lip

14 **punting**, pleasure, family, racing, one-arm, levered, pinched, running, reaching, trailing, windmill, C-shape, crossover, pole-body-foot

VERBS

15 **sail**, captain, skipper, crew, launch a sailing boat, cast off, shake, slip anchor, sail closehauled, steer, sail close to the wind, harden up, luff up, reach, fetch, sail downwind, goosewing, go about, go astern, heel, careen, miss stays, rig, jury-rig, set a sail, furl a sail, roll a sail, reef a sail, back a sail, tighten, take up, let fly, maintain course, stand on, hitch, bear off (*or* away), bear down, turn head-to-wind, pitchpole, plane, tack, beat, broach to, slew, sail by the lee, run, sail on a run, close-haul, ease out a line, pay out, loose a rope, ride out a storm, lie a sailboat, fix a position, make a dead reckoning, gybe, duck gybe, clew gybe, slam gybe, scissor gybe, flare gybe, stop gybe, port tack, starboard tack, duck tack, clew tack, head up, sheet in, sheet out, wear, bring up, make fast, heave to, come to anchor, sound the depth, lay up a sailboat, splice ropes, quarter (of the wind)

16 **row**, cox, scull, race, have a rowing race, skiffrace, stroke, catch, feather, recover, finish, square, balance, dive, strike, paddle, swing, slide, lift an oar, drop an oar, cover a blade, run level, clear the water, lurch, steer, catch a crab (Inf)

17 **canoe**, do wildwater canoeing, canoe over rapids, shoot the rapids, paddle a canoe, paddle a kayak, single paddle, double paddle, kayak, race a canoe, sail a canoe, use a J stroke, use a turning stroke, lock the blade, shake out

18 **windsurf**, boardsurf, free sail, sail, do freestyle sailing, do displacement sailing, wavesail, ride a wave, wave-ride, jump a wave, wave-jump, ice surf, sailboard, cavatate, have a Le Mans start, have a water start, rail, spin out, wipe out, steer with the foot, plane, sub-plane, pump, hook in, make an off-the-lip turn, tip the board

19 **punt**, punt for pleasure, double punt, punt with one arm, shove, shove around a punt, use the C-shape shove, half shove, run a punt, run, walk a punt, prick a punt, race a punt, punt-race, pole a canoe, climb the pole, lever, pinch, reach, use the windmill stroke, stop up, throw, drop, recover, use the crossover recovery, pick up, trail

ADVERBS

20 **offshore**, on the rail, on the nose, on the tail, inside the boom, back to sail, back to sail inside the boom, to leeward, about, astern, athwart, a-hull, aback, abaft, abeam, adrift, aloft, with an offwind, with a single oar, with two oars, with a cox, without a cox, with a J turn, by the head, by the stern, by the lee, windward, on the quarter, broadside-on

INTERJECTIONS

21 **avast**!, belay!, paddle!, give her ten!, easy!

37 Shooting

NOUNS

1 **target shooting**, pistol shooting, rifle shooting, air-rifle shooting, air-pistol shooting, clay pigeon shooting, skeet shooting, trapshooting

2 **hunting**, game shooting, shoot, field sports, gunning, small-game hunting, hunt, rough shooting, grouse shooting, pheasant shooting, waterfowl shooting, rabbit hunting, squirrel hunting, duck hunting, hare hunting, beagling, big-game hunting, bear hunting, bear hunt, deer hunting, deer hunt, stag hunting, stag hunt, tracking, stalking, woodland stalking, deer stalking, still hunting (US), night lamping, killing, culling, driving, beating, dogging, sitting, calling, sighting-in, shooting party, hunting party (US), hunting season, open season, closed season, hunting limit, bag limit, field trial, hunting lodge, shooting box (*or* lodge), game licence, hunting licence (US), shooting association, hunting association (US), The British Association for Shooting and Conservation (BASC), The British Field Sports Society, The National Rifle Association (US), Ducks Unlimited (US), hunting at force (Arch)

▶ *590 Pursuit, 398 Killing*

3 **hunting equipment**, sporting rifle, hunting rifle (US), high-powered rifle, level-action rifle, bolt-action rifle, auto-loading rifle, single-shot rifle, .22 rimfire rifle, .22 centrefire rifle, shotgun, ammunition round, ammunition, shooting kit, hunting accessories, decoy, telescopic sight, knife, scope sight, shooting stick, stalking stick, binoculars, rifle sling, hunting clothes, hunting jacket, hunting boots

▶ *680 Weapon, 295 Dress*

4 **hunter**, huntress, shooter, sportsman, sports-woman, sportsperson, deer hunter, duck hunter, big-game hunter, dogger (Aus), stalker, deer stalker, tracker, beater, poacher, Diana, Nimrod

5 **game**, quarry, prey, beast of prey, small game, big game, deer, red deer, American elk, moose, antelope, caribou, bear, mountain lion, wild boar, rabbit, game birds, ring-necked pheasant, grouse, partridge, quail, duck, goose, turkey

▶ *77 Mammals, 78 Birds*

6 **sporting dog**, hunting dog, gundog, pointer, English setter, Brittany spaniel, German short-haired pointer, Irish setter, English springer, retriever, golden retriever, flatcoat retriever, Labrador, Chesapeake Bay retriever, Irish water spaniel, American water spaniel

▶ *77 Mammals*

VERBS

7 **shoot**, go shooting, shoot game, hunt, go hunting, hunt for, go big-game hunting, stalk game, stalk, deer-stalk, track, trail, follow the scent, scent out, dog, kill, cull, drive, beat, flush, poach, join a shooting party, sight quarry, scent game, point, retrieve, aim at, draw a bead on, sight in, zero (a rifle), fire (at), pull the trigger, squeeze the trigger

ADJECTIVES

8 **shooting**, hunting, field, small-game, big-game, tracking, stalking, killed, culled, open, closed, high-powered, level-action, single-shot, auto-loading

ADVERBS

9 **on the trail**, on the track, on the scent, hot on the trail, in hot pursuit

passing, back pass, wall pass, one-two, head, heading, foul, fouling, advantage, trip, shoot, shooting, save, miss, tackle, tackling, dribbling, nutmeg, trapping, parrying, handball, throw-in, goal kick, corner kick (*or* corner), drop ball, scoring, score, penalty, handling, deliberate kicking, deliberate tripping, pushing, violent charging, striking, holding, off-side, onside, free kick, direct free kick, indirect free kick

3 **football player**, professional footballer, Footballer of the Year, captain, goalkeeper (*or* goalie), defender, fullback, centre back, centre half, centre forward, wing half, right half, left half, outside left, outside right, inside left, inside right, winger, striker, midfield striker, sweeper, substitute (*or* sub), reserve, football manager, football coach, football trainer, football referee, linesman, football fan

VERBS

4 **play soccer**, play football, kick off, kick, pass, make a pass, make a back pass, head, throw in, throw, shoot, save, miss, tackle, score, foul, trip, push, hold, go offside, go onside, have a free kick, have a goal kick, take a corner, trap, dive, strike, parry, flick, stab, smother, chip

ADJECTIVES

5 **soccer**, football, professional, half-way, six-yard, eighteen-yard, kicked, kicking, passed, passing, headed, heading, fouled, fouling, tripped, tripping, shooting, missed, tackled, tackling, dribbled, dribbling, trapped, trapping, corner, scored, handled, deliberate, pushed, pushing, held, holding, offside, onside, direct, indirect, free, outside, inside, right, left, midfield

38 Soccer

NOUNS

1 **soccer**, Association Football, football, soccer football (US), professional football, football match, football game (US), League match, friendly match, Football League, football team, football side, football, football club, football ground, football stadium (US), football pitch, football field (US), goal, goal area, goal post, crossbar, net, stanchion, scoreboard, perimeter, touchline (*or* by-line), penalty area, penalty spot, six-yard box, eighteen-yard box, half-way line, centre circle, goal line, corner area, corner flag, football kit, football uniform (US), shorts, boots, shinpads, gloves, football championship, World Cup, European Cup, European Cup Winners' Cup, Football Association Challenge Cup (*or* FA Cup), football organization, Football Association (FA), US Soccer Football Association, Fédération Internationale de Football Association (FIFA)

2 **football play**, kickoff, kick, kicking, pass,

39 Swimming

NOUNS

1 **swimming**, natation (Fml), recreational swimming, competitive swimming, swimming team, freestyle event, relay event, medley race, lap, turn, open-water swimming, long-distance swimming, swimming the English Channel, cross-Channel swimming, synchronized swimming, swimming stroke, stroke, breaststroke, sidestroke, backstroke, back crawl, crawl, front crawl, Australian crawl, butterfly, paddling, paddle, doggy-paddling, dog-paddle, treading water, buoyancy, bobbing, head bobbing, floating, back floating, supine floating, float, dead-man's float, swimming under water, underwater swimming, subaqua swimming, skin diving, scuba (self-contained underwater breathing apparatus) diving, snorkeling, swimming equipment, underwater mask, underwater breathing tube, snorkel, fin, flipper

2 **swimming technique**, breath control, al-

ternate breathing, swimming movements, arm stroke, dolphin-butterfly stroke, recovery stroke, single overarm, double-arm movement, double overarm, single-rhythm crawl, trudgen stroke, four-beat trudgen crawl, six-beat crawl, eight-beat crawl, ten-beat crawl, kick, scissors kick, wide scissors kick, upkick, downkick, frog kick, wedge kick, whip kick, fishtail kick, dolphin kick, flutter kick, cross-over kick

▶ *655 Skill*

3   **survival swimming**, drown-proofing (US), swimming in clothes, survival device, floating device, float, inner tube, water wings, arm-band, rubber ring, life preserver (US), life belt, life jacket, life vest (US), life buoy, swimming rescue, lifeguarding, lifesaving, swim-and-tow, artificial respiration, resuscitation, mouth-to-mouth resuscitation, kiss of life, Mae West (Sl)

▶ *632 Safety, 662 Help*

4   **swimmer**, competitive swimmer, long-distance swimmer, underwater swimmer, sub-aqua swimmer, skin-diver, scuba-diver, snor-keler, lifeguard, lifesaver

5   **swimming association**,   International Swimming Federation (FINA), NCAA (National Collegiate Athletic Association) swimming (US), Amateur Swimming Association (ASA)

6   **diving**, recreational diving, competitive diving, springboard diving, platform diving, high diving, dive, take-off, entry dive, entry, swallow dive, duck dive, forward dive, header forward straight, header forward with tuck, tuck dive, backward dive, reverse dive, inward dive, twisting dive, handstand dive, plain jump, tuck jump, somersault, double somersault, diving position, straight position, pike position, tuck position, diving board, springboard, one-metre springboard, three-metre springboard, platform, five-metre platform, ten-metre platform, competitive diving marks, form, execution, difficulty of the dive, variety diving (Arch), fancy diving (Arch)

▶ *360 Descent*

7   **swimming pool**, outdoor swimming pool, indoor swimming pool, natatorium, swimming bath, short-course pool, long-course pool, Olympic-size(d) pool, wading pool, children's swimming pool, swimming area, swimming lake, swimming hole (US), pond, river, beach, swimming beach, leisure pool, wave pool, heated pool

▶ *94 Lakes*

8   **swimwear**, swimsuit, bathing suit (US), swimming (or bathing) costume, one-piece swimsuit, two-piece swimsuit, bikini, mono-kini, swimming trunks, trunks, bathers (Aus), bathing cap, goggles, diving mask, flippers

▶ *295 Dress*

VERBS

9   **swim**, take a dip, dog-paddle, tread water, float, bob, swim under water, snorkel

10 **dive**, plunge, skin-dive, scuba-dive, cannon-ball, belly flop, jump in

ADJECTIVES

11 **swimming**, swim, bathing, natatory (or natatorial), natational (Fml), recreational, competitive, freestyle, relay, medley, open-water, long-distance, cross-Channel, synchronized, paddling, dog-paddling, buoyant, floated, floating, underwater, subaqua, recovery, double, double-arm, trudgen, frog, wedge, whip, fishtail, dolphin, flutter, crossover, survival, drown-proofed, drown-proofing, mouth-to-mouth, entry, swallow, duck, tuck, backward, reverse, inward, twisting, handstand, plain, pike, springboard, platform, outdoor, indoor, short-course, long-course, Olympic-size(d), wading, one-piece, two-piece, variety (Arch), fancy (Arch)

ADVERBS

12 **by swimming**, for recreation, competitively, in competition, in the open water, with synchronization, underwater

40   Tennis, Squash, Badminton, Etc.

NOUNS

1   **tennis**, lawn tennis, real tennis, royal tennis, table tennis, ping pong, *jeu de paume* (Fr), Wimbledon, All-England Championships, Davis Cup, US Open, French Open, Wightman Cup

2   **tennis strokes**, service, serve, ace, slice service, American twist service, reverse twist, drive, forehand drive, backhand drive, ground drive, swing, follow-through, ground stroke, volley, forehand volley, backhand volley, smash, overhead smash, hitting it on the fly, lob

3   **tennis equipment**, tennis racket, tennis ball, net, strap, band, posts, tennis court, singles court, doubles court, umpire's chair, linesman's chair

4   **tennis terms**, singles, doubles, pair, delivery, net position, service line, baseline, tramlines, game, set, match, love deuce, advantage, van, rally, foot fault, fault, let, in, out

5   **real tennis**, tennis, royal tennis, court, net (line), first gallery, door, second gallery, last (winning) gallery, service line, service side, hazard side, main wall, grille penthouse, dedans penthouse, side penthouse, service penthouse, marker's box, net, net post, game terms, grille, tambour, dedans, rough, smooth, server, striker-out, volley, half-volley, not up, chase

6   **tennis player**, singles player, doubles player, net player, server, receiver, volleyer, umpire,

linesman, ball boy

7 **famous tennis players**, Bill Tilden, Fred Perry, Rod Laver, John Newcombe, Jimmy Connors, Arthur Ashe, Björn Borg, John McEnroe, Boris Becker, Ivan Lendl, Andre Agassi, Maureen Connolly, Margaret Smith, Billie Jean King, Chris Evert, Virginia Wade, Martina Navratilova, Steffi Graf, Monica Seles

8 **squash**, squash rackets, squash (US), board, telltale, back wall, service line, service court line, squash court, doubles court

9 **squash terms**, service box, hand in, hand out, in-play wall, out-of-play wall, eight all, set two, sudden death, squash equipment, squash racket, squash ball

10 **badminton**, shuttlecock, battledore, Poona, International Badminton Federation (IBF), Thomas Cup, Uber Cup

11 **badminton equipment**, racket, shuttlecock, shuttle, plastic shuttle, bird, feathers, net posts, badminton court

12 **badminton terms**, shot, clear shot, smash, drop-shot, drive, in side, out side, server, receiver, fault, let, short service line, side boundary line, tramlines, back boundary line, centre line

VERBS

13 **serve**, receive, drive, volley, smash, lob

ADJECTIVES

14 **forehand**, backhand, overhead, singles, doubles

41 Winter Sports

NOUNS

1 **skiing**, snow-skiing (US), alpine skiing, competitive skiing, Olympic skiing, biathlon, freestyle skiing, acrobatic skiing, ballet-skiing, stunt-skiing, mogul skiing, hot-dogging, somersaulting, helicopter skiing (*or* heliskiing), off-piste skiing, birdsnesting, skiing on ice, nordic skiing, mountain skiing, cross-country skiing, touring, *Langlauf* (Ger), *ski du Fond* (Fr), ski-jumping, jump, ski jump, acrobatic jump, aerial, ski-mountaineering, speedskiing, grass-skiing, ski run, downhill ski run, *Abfahrt* (Ger), *descente* (Fr), ski trail, marked trail, piste, moguled piste, motorway, gunbarrel, loipe, ski slope, slope, artificial slope, nursery slope, run, green run, blue run, black run, straight run, *Schuss* (Ger), *Steilhang* (Ger), fall-line, wall, couloir, compression, skiing snow, good piste, hard-surface snow, breakable crust, powder snow, soft damp snow, heavy wet snow, wind crust, windslab, porridge, ice, slush, frozen corn snow, bump, mogul, rut, tramline, ridge, washboard, ledge, season skiing ticket, *abonnement* (Fr), ski-tow, lift, ski lift, gondola lift, bubble, bucket, drag

lift, T-bar lift, button, poma, cable car, cabin lift, *Luftseilbahn* (Ger), *téléphérique* (Fr), chair lift, *Sesselbahn* (Ger), *télésiège* (Fr), funicular, ski teaching method, GLM (graduated length method) (US), skiing association, Fédération Internationale de Ski, British Ski Federation, Canadian Ski Association

2 **cross-country skiing**, *Langlauf* (Ger), ski touring, mountain ski touring, touring, off-track touring, ski rambling, biathlon race, biathlon, biathlon relay race, sprinting race, marathon, American Birkebeiner, Canadian *Coureur des Bois* (Fr), cross-country technique, two-phase walk, two-phase glide, diagonal stride, diagonal stride with pole planting, star turn, kick turn, side-step, stepping a curve, diagonal side-step, double-pole, double-pole with leg kick, swing, herringbone, direct descent, traverse downhill, snowplough glide, snowplough turn, stem turn, parallel turn, telemark, tacking, two-phase uphill, swing to the hill, snowplough brake, cross-country championships, World Grand Prix of Cross-country Skiers, Giant's Ridge International Classic Marathon, *Internationaler Deutscher Skimarathon in Hirschau* (Ger), cross-country equipment, touring ski, racing ski

3 **ski racing**, ski race, racing, race, alpine racing, alpine race, downhill racing, downhill race, slalom racing, slalom race, giant slalom racing, giant slalom race, super giant slalom racing, super giant slalom race, super G race, giant slalom in one run, (ski) skating, single-sided skating, double-sided skating, ski orienteering (*or* Ski-O), ski championship, the World Championship, the World Cup, the Winter Olympic gold medal, slalom pole, rapid slalom pole, gate, open gate, vertical gate, verticale, flush gate, diagonal gate, hairpin, closed gate

4 **skiing technique**, compensation technique, skiing posture, schussing position, tuck, unweighting, up-unweighting, down-unweighting, ski move, snowploughing, snowplough (*or* wedge), reverse snowplough, herringbone, pole plant, ski turn, christiania, christie, parallel christie, stem christie, uphill christie, cornering, stemming, stem turn, step turn, star turn, weldel, basic swing, parallel swing, telemarking, telemark, scissors turn, pressure turn, compression turn, jet turn, rotation turn, inner ski turn, down-motion turn, racing-step turn, snowplough turn (*or* crab), snowplough wedeln, jump turn, kick turn, carved turn, jet, *avalement* (Fr), *projection circulaire* (Fr), edging, sidecutting, sidecut, sideslipping, sideslip, sidestepping, sidestep, traversing, climbing, hockey stop

5 **ski equipment**, ski, downhill ski, cross-country ski, alpine ski, touring ski, outside ski,

uphill ski, inside ski, short ski, compact ski, soft ski, long ski, stiff ski, slalom ski, giant slalom ski, RS-ski, I-ski, instructional ski, wooden ski, metal ski, plastic ski, parablock, safety strap, ski pole, ski stick, safety ski stick, basket, boot, binding, gaiter, slipper pad, toe piece, anti-friction pad, brake, ski stopper, ski wax, klister wax, ski clothes, quilted clothing, anorak, skisuit, racing suit, ski pants, ski jacket, gloves, sunglasses, goggles

6 **ice-skating**, figure skating, free skating, pair-skating, pairs, shadow skating, competitive ice-skating, Olympic skating, compulsory figure, three, paragraph double three, loop, change loop, paragraph loop, bracket, paragraph bracket, rocker, counter, free-skating movement, jump, loop jump, salchow jump, axel jump, toe jump, split jump, spin, camel spin, lay-back spin, one-foot upright spin, sit spin, cross-foot spin, pair-skating movement, death spiral, pairs sit spin, catch-waist camel spin, lift, axel lift, lasso lift, split lutz lift, twist lift, flying axel, throw axel, double throw axel, throw salchow, skating association, International Skating 135 Union, skating equipment, skate, MK skates (Tm), skating boot, Stanzione (Tm)

7 **ice-dancing**, dancing on ice, competitive ice-dancing, Olympic ice-dancing, compulsory dancing, set pattern dancing, free-dancing, ice-dancing move, dance step, arabesque, pivot, pirouette, hold, killian hold, reverse killian hold, waltz hold, turn, three turn, dropped three, dropped mohawk, dance lift, ice-dance music, Viennese waltz, Yankee polka, the blues, Westminster waltz, paso doble, rumba, starlight waltz, killian, tango romantica, Ravensburger waltz, quickstep, Argentine tango, competitive scoring, originality, variety, difficulty, timing, selection of music

8 **speed-skating**, sprint-skating, long-distance racing, middle-distance racing, short-distance racing, short-track racing, speed-skating race, 500-metre race, 1,500-metre race, 5,000-metre race, 10,000-metre race, speed-skating circuit, speed-skating track

9 **bobsledding** (or bobsledging or bobsleighing), bobsled (or bobsledge or bobsleigh), bob, two-man bobsled, four-man bobsled, luge, one-seater toboggan, two-seater toboggan, skeleton, parts of a toboggan, hood, runner, axle, cable, brake, cowling, toboggan racing, toboggan race, luge racing, lugeing, competitive lugeing, Olympic lugeing, European Luge Championships, luge race, luge techniques, steering, lifting, dragging, run, bobrun, toboggan chute, toboggan run, Cresta Run at St. Moritz, Fédération Internationale de Bobsleigh et Tobogganing, International Luge Federation, St. Moritz Tobogganing Club

10 **curling**, curling match, points game, bonspiel, spiel, curling rink, house, hog line, centre line, foot line, tee line, back line, hack, crampit, curling stone, loofie, kuting stone, heavy, light, guard, in-wick, lose handle, narrow, wick, wide, freeze, shot, pad-lid (or pot-lid), cup, arridge (or arris), curling broom, besom, curling tee, button, dolly, curling ice, dour ice, drug ice, swingy ice, bunker, curling technique, curl, sweeping, sooping, running a stone, borrowing, quacking, rubbing, take-out, double take-out, double, hack weight, in-handle turn (or in-turn), out-handle turn (or out-turn), curling championship, the Silver Broom, the World Curling Championship, the Uniroyal World Junior Championship, the Ladies' World Championship, curling association, Royal Caledonian Curling Club, United States Curling Association, Canadian Curling Association, kuting (Arch), cockee (Arch), gogsee (Arch), the roaring game (Inf)

11 **skier**, ski racer, slalom racer, slalomer, individualist, ice-skater, ice-dancer, speed-skater, curling player, skip, lead, tobogganist, bobsledder (or bobsledger or bobsleigher), bobsled captain, oversman (Arch)

ADJECTIVES

12 **ski**, skiing, alpine, nordic, Olympic, freestyle, acrobatic, ballet, stunt, mogul, moguled, hot-dogging, somersaulting, off-piste, mountain, cross-country, aerial, speed, downhill, artificial, nursery, green, blue, black, hard-surface, breakable, powder, rutted, ridged, ledged, T-bar, touring, off-track, biathlon, sprinting, two-phase, diagonal, double-pole, direct, traverse, snowplough, snowploughing, stem, parallel, slalom, single-sided, double-sided, open, vertical, flush, hairpin, closed, compensation, schussing, tucked, tucking, unweighting, step, star, scissors, pressure, compression, jet, rotation, sidecutting, sideslipping, sidestepping, traversing, climbing, jump, kick, carved, short, compact, soft, long, stiff, instructional, wooden, metal, plastic, safety, anti-friction, klister, quilted

13 **ice-skating**, figure, free, free-skating, pair, pair-skating, shadow, compulsory, change, paragraph, catch-waist, lifted, lifting, twist, flying, ice-dancing, ice-dance, dropped, killian, original, varied, difficult, timed, selected, speed-skating, sprint, long-distance, middle-distance, short-distance, short-track, lugeing, steering, dragging, in-wick, hack, in-handle, out-handle

VERBS

14 **ski**, snow ski (US), alpine ski, ski competitively, ski freestyle, do stunt-skiing, hot-dog, somersault, birdsnest, ski on ice, ski cross-country, do cross-country skiing, ski-jump, do

speed-skiing, make a downhill run, take a ski lift, use a diagonal stride, side-step, double-pole, swing, snowplough, turn, do a parallel turn, tack, swing to the hill, race on skis, do alpine racing, win a downhill race, hit a slalom pole, schuss, use the tuck position, do a christie, corner, stem, swing, telemark, make a scissors turn, sideslip, sidestep, traverse, climb, use the hockey stop, wax a ski, wear a skisuit

15 **ice-skate**, figure-skate, free-skate, shadow-skate, do compulsory figures, jump, spin, dance on ice, do set pattern dancing, pivot, pirouette, speed-skate, sprint-skate

16 **bobsled** (*or* bobsledge *or* bobsleigh), luge, toboggan, steer, lift, drag, make a run, do curling, sweep, loop, run a stone, burn a stone, chip a stone, bury a stone, blank an end, chap and lie, out-wick, fill the port, in-turn, out-turn, break an egg (Inf)

ADVERBS

17 **on a ski run**, on a ski jump, on an artificial slope, by a gondola lift, with a cable car, using racing skis, with skis, downhill, acrobatically, artificially, diagonally, vertically, in a slalom race, in a toboggan, in a luge

INTERJECTIONS

18 **danger**!, look out!, *Achtung!* (Ger), *Piste!* (Fr), *Pista!* (It)

42   Games and Pastimes

NOUNS

1 **game**, ball game, board game, card game, darts game, dice game, billiards game, word game, children's game, gambling game, computer game, video game, indoor game, outdoor game

2 **contest**, bout, round, match, session, hand (of cards), competition

▶ *18 Sport*

3 **card game terms**, cards, card game, pack, playing card, heart, club, diamond, spade, picture card, face card, court card, one eye, one-eyed jack, ace, deuce, joker, wildcard, canasta pack, piquet pack, cut, shuffle, deal, shoe, misdeal, hand, banker, pot, ante, limit, raise, cull, kicker, hold, stack, pair, three of a kind, trey, prial, four of a kind, full house, dead man's hand, flush, run, straight, running flush, royal flush, trump, bid, no bid, pass, fold, pre-emptive bid, underbid, undertrick, finesse, contract, rubber, slam, small slam, Yarborough, grand slam

4 **chess terms**, board, square, piece, chess piece, chessman, pawn, castle, rook, knight, bishop, king, queen, opening, fork, pin, castling, check, end game, checkmate, mate

5 **dice**, die, spots, throw, double, snake eyes, craps, Yahtzee (Tm)

6 **darts**, arrow, flight, board, single, double, treble, twenty-five, bull (*or* bull's eye), top, double top, treble top, one hundred and eighty, throw, oche, out, three hundred and one (301), five hundred and one (501), round the clock, shanghai, killer

7 **other games**, dominoes, roulette, skittles, ninepins

8 **pastime**, hobby, activity, recreation, amusement, entertainment

ADJECTIVES

9 **recreational**, entertaining, amusing, competitive

VERBS

10 **play**, compete, gamble, join in, throw, shuffle, cut, deal, misdeal, bank, up the ante, raise, call, hold, pass, stack, throw in, fold, bid, double, pre-empt, ruff, finesse, open, move, castle, queen, crown

ADVERBS

11 **recreationally**, entertainingly

Board Games

backgammon	draughts	Scrabble
checkers	go	(Tm)
(US)	halma	snakes and
chess	ludo	ladders
Chinese	Mah Jong	Trivial Pursuit (Tm)
checkers	Monopoly	suit (Tm)
Cluedo (Tm)	(Tm)	

Card Games

all fours	faro	Pope Joan
auction	find-the-lady	primero
bridge	fish	quadrille
baccarat	five hundred	quinze
banker	flinch	reverse
beggar my	fright	rouge et noir
neighbour	frog	rubber
bezique	gin rummy	bridge
blackjack	(or gin)	rummy
black maria	go fish	Russian brag
blind poker	hearts	seven-card
Boston	high low	brag
brag	keno (or	seven up
bridge	kino)	skat
canasta	knockout	snap
chemin de	whist	snipsnap-
fer	lansquenet	snorum
clubs	loo	solitaire
connections	matrimony	solo whist
contract	monte	(or solo)
bridge	nap (or na-	speculation
cooncan (or	poleon)	straight
conquian)	Newmarket	poker
cribbage (or	nine-card	strip Jack
crib)	brag	naked
draw poker	old maid	strip poker
duplicate	ombre	stud poker
bridge	pairs	tarak
Earl of Coventry	patience	three-card
entry	pelmanism	brag
écarté	penny ante	three-card
eight-five-	pinochle	monte
three	piquet	twenty-one
euchre	poker	vingt-et-un
fan-tan	pontoon	whist

Children's Games and Party Games

blind man's buff
catch
charades
Chinese whispers
consequences
cowboys and Indians
crambo
dumb crambo
doctors and nurses
fivestones
fox and geese

grandmother's footsteps
hangman
hide-and-seek
hopscotch
I-spy
jacks (or jackstones)
jackstraws
kickean
leapfrog
ludo
marbles

mothers and fathers
murder in the dark
musical chairs
noughts and crosses
pass the parcel
pig (or piggy) in the
   middle
pin the tail on the
   donkey
postman's knock
sardines

Simon says
snakes and ladders
spin the bottle
ticktacktoe
tiddlywinks
tig (or tag)
tipcat
wink murder

Hobbies and Pastimes

aerobics
amateur dramatics
appliqué
autograph hunting
bark rubbing
basketry
batik
beachcombing
beekeeping
beer making
birdwatching
book binding
brass rubbing
butterfly collecting
calligraphy
candlemaking
canework
coin collecting

collage
collecting
cookery
crochet
crosswords
découpage
dressmaking
embroidery
enamelling
flower arranging
flower pressing
fossil hunting
fretwork
gardening
genealogy
glass engraving
keep fit
kite flying

knitting
lace making
lampshade making
lapidary
lepidoptery
macramé
marquetry
model making
model railways
mosaics
origami
painting
patchwork
philately
photography
pokerwork
pottery
quilting

raffia work
reading
rug making
shell collecting
spinning
stamp collecting
stencilling
tapestry
tatting
topiary
train spotting
upholstery
weaving
wine making
woodwork

The Arts

No person who is not a great sculptor or painter can be an architect. If he is not a sculptor or painter, he can only be a builder. John Ruskin.

Architecture in general is frozen music.
Friedrich Wilhelm Joseph von Schelling.

In Architecture as in all other Operative Arts, the end must direct the Operation. The end is to build well. Well building hath three Conditions. Commodity, Firmness, and Delight. Henry Wotton.

NOUNS

1 **architecture**, architectonics, tectonics, architectural design, building design, building style, architectural engineering, domestic architecture, civil architecture, governmental architecture, civic architecture, religious architecture, military architecture, industrial architecture, recreational architecture, landscape architecture, rendering, drawing, perspective, skiagraphy

2 **architect**, civil architect, domestic architect, designer, architectural engineer, military architect, industrial architect, landscape architect, master builder, builder, mason, master mason, stone mason

3 **building**, structure, erection, pile, listed building, castle, ranch house (US), colonial home (US), town house, detached house, semi-detached house (*or* semi), terraced house, row house (US), cottage, thatched cottage, country cottage, single-storey building, multistorey building, high-rise building (*or* high-rise), skyscraper, tower, low-rise building (*or* low-rise), half-timbered building, architectural monstrosity, eyesore, carbuncle

▶ 63 Engineering

4 **building material**, stone, building stone, granite, marble, sandstone, brownstone (US), Cotswold stone, slate, brick, rustic brick, engineering brick, brickwork, building block, breeze block, concrete, reinforced concrete, ferroconcrete, prestressed concrete, glass, ferrovitreous construction, aluminium, girder, steel

5 **arch**, rounded arch, lancet arch, parabolic arch, segmental arch, false arch, Norman arch, semicircular arch, ogee arch, Tudor arch, *anse de panier* (Fr), basket arch, horseshoe arch, two (*or* four) centred arch, catenary arch, elliptical arch, corbel arch, depressed arch, lancet arch, keel arch, raking arch, rampant arch, rowlack arch, shouldered arch, skew arch, stilted arch, strainer arch, arcuation

6 **roof**, flat roof, pitch (*or* pitched roof), hip (*or* hipped) roof, gambrel roof (*or* gambrel), imbricated roof (*or* imbricate), mansard roof (*or* mansard), dome, saucer dome, pendentive dome (*or* pendentive), geodesic dome (*or* geodesic)

7 **vault**, vaulting, barrel (*or* tunnel) vault, rib vault, groin vault, fan vault, fan vaulting, lierne vault, parabolic vault, segmental vault, quadripartite vault, intersecting vault, domical vault, voussoir, sexpartite vault, tierceron ridge rib, transverse ridge rib

8 **column**, support, pillar, post, pier, pilaster, buttress, flying buttress, abutment, monolithic column, engaged column, Salomonic column, coupled column, demi-column, columniation, intercolumniation, colonnade, stylobate, diastyle, hexastyle, peristyle, pedestal, shaft, drum, fluting, flute, entasis, capital, chapiter, cap, entablature, impost, Doric order, Tuscan order, Ionic order, Corinthian order, Composite order

9 **miscellaneous architectural features**, abacus, ambulatory, ancon (*or* ancone), anta, arcade, articulation, ashlar, astylar, attic, balcony, base, beak, bolster, bow, cantilever, case, casement, cella, centering, coin (*or* quoin), concha, corbel, cordon, cupola, fenestrated cupola, lantern cupola, dado, die, drip, dripstone, extrados, fantail, fascia (*or* facia), fenestella, fenestra, filler, frieze, frustum, gable, gable end, groin, haunch (*or* hance), head-

Architectural Decoration

abacus	capstone	egg and	lierne	rustication
acanthus	cartouche (or	tongue or egg	list	scotia
accolade	cartouch)	and anchor)	listel	scroll
acroter	caryatid	epistyle	medallion	scrolling
annulet	cavetto	facet	metope	splay
antefix	chevron	fascia	modillion	stria
anthemion	cinquefoil	festoon	moulding	strigil
apophyge	congé	fillet	mullion	stucco
architrave	console	finial	mutule	taenia
astragal	coping stone (or	flute	necking	talon
atlantes	copestone)	foil	neckmould	telemon
atlas	cordon	foliation	ogee	term (or terminal
baguette (or ba-	cornice	fret	ovolo	or terminus)
guet)	corona	frieze	pendant	thumb
band	cove (or coving)	frontispiece	polychromy	topping
banderole (or	crocket (or cro-	gadroon (or go-	poppy head	torus (or tore)
banderol or	chet)	droon)	pulvinate frieze	tracery
bannerol)	crown (or crown-	gorgerin	putto	transome
bas relief (or	piece)	guilloche	quadrega	trefoil
basso rilievo)	cusp	gutta	quarter round	triglyph
bay leaf	cyma	head	quatrefoil	tympanum (or
bead	cyma recta	head mould	quirk	tympan)
beak	cyma reversa	head moulding	quoin	vaulting boss
bezant (or bez-	cymatium	headpiece	reed	vignette
zant or byzant)	dentil	helix	reeding	volute
billet	dogtooth	herms	reglet	zigzag
boss	echinus	hood mould	relief (or relievo	
calotte	ectype	hypophyge	or rilievo)	
canephorae	egg and dart (or	label	respond	

stone, hip, imperia, impost, intrados, invert, lantern, lintel, loggia, louvre, module, naos, neck, pace, pier, podium, portico, propylaeum, prostyle, re-entrant corner, respond, reveal, rib, rotunda, rustication, shafting, spandrel, springer, squint, squinch, string, stringer, table, tailpiece, tail beam, tambour, trumeau, truss, verge, vestibule, voussoir, wall, curtain wall, cheek wall, load-bearing wall, nonbearing wall, window, lancet window (or lancet), lunette, Oriel window

10 **church architecture**, cuniform church, Greek cross plan, Latin cross plan, crossing,

conch, ambulatory, apse, semicircular apse, transept, liturgical east end, chancel, westwork, vestibule, narthex, dome, flèche, spirelet, chevet, triforium, clerestory (or clearstory), blindstorey (or blindstory), basilica, tribune gallery, flying buttress, galilee porch

▶ *50 Painting and Sculpture*

ADJECTIVES

11 **architectural**, edificial, architectonic, tectonic, designed, architecturally designed, architecturally engineered

12 **structural**, erected, listed, designed, colonial (US), detached, semidetached, terraced, single

Architectural Styles

academic	Doric	international	new-brutalist
American	Early Christian	Ionic	Norman
Art Deco	Early English	Islamic	Palladian
Art Nouveau	Early Renaissance	Italian	Perpendicular
baroque	Edwardian	Jacobean	Persian
Bauhaus	Egyptian	Louis Quatorze	postmodernist (or
beaux-arts	Elizabethan	Louis Quinze	post-modern)
brutalist	Empire	Louis Seize	Queen-Anne
Byzantine	English	Louis Treize	Regency
Carolingian	Federation	mannerist	Renaissance
Christian	flamboyant	medieval (or medi-	rococo
churrigueresque (or	French	aeval)	Roman
churrigueresco)	functional	Mesopotamian	Romanesque
cinquecento	Georgian	modern	romantic classical
classical	German	moderne	Saracen
colonial	Gothic	modernist	Spanish
colossal	Gothic Revival	Moorish	transitional (or transi-
Corinthian	Graeco-Roman (or	Moresque	tion)
Cyclopean	Greco-Roman)	Mozarabic	Tudor
Deconstructionism	Grecian (or Greek)	Mudéjar	Tuscan
Decorated	Greek Revival	neoclassical	vernacular
De Stijl	High Renaissance	Neo-Gothic	Victorian

Noted Buildings

Acropolis (Athens)
Battersea Power Station (London)
Blenheim Palace (Woodstock, England)
Blue Mosque (Istanbul)
Bourges Cathedral (France)
British Museum (London)
Buckingham Palace (London)
Casa Milá (Barcelona)
Central Station (Milan)
Chartres Cathedral (France)
Church of the Madeleine (Paris)
Cologne Cathedral
Colosseum (Rome)
Crystal Palace (London)
Edinburgh Castle
Eiffel Tower (Paris)
Empire State Building (New York)
Erectheum (Athens)
Flat Iron Building (New York)
Florence Cathedral
Galleria Vittorio Emanuele II (Milan)
Guggenheim Museum (New York)

Hagia Sophia (Istanbul)
Hermitage (Saint Petersburg)
Houses of Parliament (London)
Jefferson Memorial (Washington)
John Hancock Center (Chicago)
J. Paul Getty Museum (Malibu, California)
King's College Chapel (Cambridge, England)
Law Courts (London)
Leaning Tower of Pisa
Louvre (Paris)
Notre Dame Cathedral (Paris)
Opéra (Paris)
Pagoda (Kew, England)
Pantheon (Rome)
Parliament House (Vienna)
Parthenon (Athens)
Pennsylvania Station (New York)
Pompidou Centre (Paris)
Pyramids (Egypt)
Reims Cathedral (France)
Royal Crescent (Bath, England)
Royal Pavilion (Brighton)

Saint Basil's Cathedral (Moscow)
Sainte-Chapelle (Paris)
Saint Mark's Cathedral (Venice)
Saint Patrick's Cathedral (New York)
Saint Paul's Cathedral (London)
Saint Peter's (Rome)
Sears Tower (Chicago)
Staatsgalerie (Stuttgart)
Sun Temple (Konarak, India)
Taj Mahal (Agra, India)
Temple of Apollo Epicurius (Bassae, Greece)
Tower of London
Transamerica Pyramid (San Francisco)
Trans World Airways Terminal (New York)
US Capitol (Washington)
Versailles (Paris)
Westminster Abbey (London)
Westminster Cathedral (London)
White House (Washington)
World Trade Center (New York)

storey, multistorey, high-rise, low-rise

13 **arched**, arcuated, arcuate, rounded, lancet, parabolic, segmental

14 **roofed**, pitched, hipped, imbricate, domed, pendentive

15 **vaulted**, ribbed, fanned

16 **columned**, columnated, columnar, supported, pilastered, buttressed, fluted, Doric, Tuscan, Corinthian, Composite

17 **structured**, formed, decorated, ornamented, ornamental, abutting, arcuated, articulated, bossed, embossed, corniced, crowned, cuniform, fascial, fenestrated, ferrovitreous, geodesic, intersecting, moulded, parabolic, pendentive, re-entrant, ribbed, rusticated, segmental, scrolled, triglyphic

VERBS

18 **be an architect**, design buildings, design houses, design, draw blueprints, build houses, build buildings, build, construct, structure, erect, prefabricate, package, select building materials, brick, glass

19 **decorate**, ornament, dome, arch, vault, rib, abut, buttress, cantilever, coffer, articulate, flute, mould, boss, fret, crown, cornice, stucco, rusticate

ADVERBS

20 **architecturally**, with an architect, architectonically, tectonically, constructionally, by design, domestically, civilly, industrially, ornamentally, decoratively, structurally

44 Ceramics

NOUNS

1 **ceramics**, ceramic ware, ceramic decoration, sgraffito, ornamental ware, pottery, art pottery, whiteware, redware, stoneware, black

stoneware (*or* blackware), lustreware, agateware, basaltware, marbled ware, slipware, refractory ware, crackle (*or* crackleware), glazed ware, porous pottery, earthenware, ironstone (*or* ironstone china), unglazed earthenware, coarse pottery, ovenware, terracotta, tinglazed earthenware, clayware, faience, creamware, blue and white ware, spongeware, crouch ware, translucent ceramics, porcelain, fired porcelain, biscuit (*or* bisque) ware, softpaste (*or* soft) porcelain, hard-paste (*or* hard) porcelain, salt-glazed porcelain, eggshell porcelain, porcelain enamel, enamelware, tinenamelled ware, stanniferous ware, china, chinaware, crockery, fine china, bone china, English bone china, American household china, glassware, decorative glass, cameo glass, French art nouveau glass, American art glass, Tiffany glass, brown glass, bottle glass, lead crystal, photochromic glass

▶ *792 Decoration, 50 Painting and Sculpture, 258 Container, 543 Sign, 374 Softness, 373 Hardness*

2 **raw material**, potter's clay, clay, primary clay, secondary clay, argil, potter's earth, adobe, porcelain clay, refractory clay, lean clay, fat clay, pipeclay, marl, kaolin, china clay (*or* stone), pegmatite, calcareous clay, slip, engobe, china stone, petuntse (*or* petuntze), ball clay, blue ball clay, feldspar, silica, Cornish stone, flint, flint pebbles, gypsum, bone ash

3 **glaze**, transparent glaze, opaque white glaze, eggshell glaze, smear glaze, soft glaze, matt (*or* matte *or* mat) glaze, semiopaque glaze, raw glaze, fritted glaze, salt-glaze, coloured glaze, underglaze, underglaze decoration, overglaze, overglaze decoration, hare's fur glaze, crackle,

Types of Ceramics

Albion ware	Delft (or delftware)	Lladro	Royal Doulton porce-
Alcora ware	Doulton ware	Lowestoft ware	lain
Allervale pottery	Dresden china	majolica (or maiolica)	Satsuma porcelain
Arita ware	gombroon	Meissen ware	Seto ware
Belleek ware	Hirado ware	Mennecy ware	Sèvres (or Sèvres
Berlin ware	Hispano-Moresque	Mezza-Maiolica (It)	porcelain)
Bonnin and Morris	ware	Ming ware	Spode ware
porcelain	Hizen porcelain	Nabeshima ware	Staffordshire ware
Castleford ware	Imari ware	Nanking ware	Steingut (Ger)
Castor ware	istoriato ware	Neiderviller ware	Sung ware
champlevé (Fr)	Jackfield ware	Old Worcester ware	Talavera ware
Chantilly ware	jasper (or jasper ware)	Palissy ware	Tang ware
Chelsea porcelain	Kakiemon ware	Parian porcelain	Ting ware
Ching (or Ch'ing)	Kinkozan ware	Pennsylvania Dutch	Toft ware
porcelain	Ko-Kutani ware	ware	Tucker porcelain
cloisonné (or	Kubachi ware	Queensware	Vincennes ware
cloisonné enamel)	Leeds pottery	Rockingham ware	Wedgwood ware
Coalport	Limoges (or Limoges	Rockwood pottery	Worcester porcelain
Crown Derby porcelain	ware)		

crazing, slip, body slip, transfer printing, decalcomania, hand-painted decorations, gold decoration, gilded decoration
▶ *792 Decoration, 557 Ornament*

4 **porcelain mark**, earthenware mark, Meissen's crossed swords, Sèvres' royal monogram, factory mark, monogram, seal, trademark

5 **ceramic process**, grinding, plastic mixing, blunging, ball milling, pugging, screening, magnetic separating, filter pressing, de-airing, wedging, throwing, wheel throwing, slip casting, luting, collaring, steaming, smoking, drying chamber, glazing, firing, glaze firing, hard firing, soft firing, biscuit (or bisque) firing, ghost firing, raku firing, soaking, fettling, slab method
▶ *408 Heat*

6 **ceramic workshop**, potter's workplace, pottery factory, pottery, potter's wheel, wheel, slow wheel, hand-turned wheel, kick wheel, pedal wheel, power wheel, electrical wheel, jigger, blunger, dolly (or dolly peg), pug, pug mill, jolly (or jolley), kiln, glaze kiln, acid kiln, brick kiln, cement kiln, enamel kiln, muffle kiln, limekiln, bottle kiln, beehive kiln, tunnel kiln, down-drawn kiln, raku kiln, reverberatory, reverberatory kiln, kiln furniture, ribs, oven, stove, furnace, open hearth, converter, smelter, ore roaster, pyrometer, pyrometric cone, Seger cone, mixing tank, filter press, filter cloth
▶ *647 Workshop*

7 **potter**, ceramist (or ceramicist), turner, firer, glazer, pyroglazer, china decorator, china painter, tile painter, majolica painter, enamellist (or enameller)

8 **ceramic object**, urn, vase, bowl, jar, amphora, jug, toby jug, mug, vessel, ampulla, pipkin, cruse, crock, pot, pitcher, ewer, plate, cup, saucer, figurine, clock case, tile, decorative tile, encaustic tile, inlaid tile, tiling, mosaic, tessera
▶ *258 Container*

9 **industrial ceramics**, porcelain insulation, electrical porcelain, brick, sun-dried brick, adobe, firebrick, refractory brick, mud brick, cement, natural cement, Portland cement, hydrolic cement, concrete, terracotta, drain tile, hollow tile, architectural tile, quarry tile, roofing tile, pantile, wall tile, floor tile, china plumbing ware, chemical porcelain, glass, crystallized glass, devitrified glass, structural glass, window glass, plate glass, safety glass, laminated glass, optical glass, photosensitive glass, glass fibre, foam glass, light bulb, fluorescent tube, lens, television tube, electronic tube
▶ *604 Materials, 439 Light*

ADJECTIVES

10 **ceramic**, enamelled, tin-enamelled, enamelling, stanniferous, ornamental, unglazed, glazed, tin-glazed, salt-glazed, underglazed, underglazing, overglazed, overglazing, glazing, translucent, fired, soft-paste, soft, hardpaste, hard, fine, encaustic, refractory, transparent, opaque, mat (or matte or matt), semiopaque, hand-painted, gilded, blunged, blunging, pugging, screened, screening, handturned, jolly (or jolley), wedged, thrown, down-drawn, reverberatory, pyrometric(al), industrial, bricking, sun-dried, crystallized, devitrified, optical, photosensitive

VERBS

11 **make ceramics**, pot, grind, mix, blunge, pug, screen, filter, de-air, lute, shape, mould clay, mould, cast, wedge, throw, throw a pot, turn a pot, turn, hand-turn, jigger, jolly (or jolley) a cup, roll a slab, dry, fire, bake, glaze, pyroglaze, glaze-fire, hard-fire, soft-fire, ghostfire, draw a kiln, underglaze, overglaze, tinglaze, fettle, enamel, tin-enamel, decorate china, paint china, hand-paint, decorate pottery, paint tile, paint majolica, gild, transfer a decal, mark, monogram, seal, tile, insulate,

Herbs and Spices

allspice	caraway seeds	dill	lovage	sage
amandine	cardamom	dillseed	mace	savory
angelica	cayenne pepper	fennel	marjoram	sesame
anise	celery salt	fenugreek	mint	sorrel
basil	chervil	five spices	mustard	spearmint
bayleaf	chicory	garam masala	nutmeg	sweet cicely
bergamot	chilli	garlic	oregano	tarragon
black pepper	chives	garlic salt	paprika	thyme
borage	cinnamon	ginger	parsley	turmeric
camomile (or	cloves	ginseng	peppermint	vanilla
chamomile)	comfrey	hyssop	pimento	white pepper
campion	coriander	juniper berries	rosemary	
caper	cumin	lavender	rue	
capsicum	curry	lemon mint	saffron	

brick, cement, concrete, glass, devitrify, crystallize, laminate

ADVERBS

12 **ornamentally**, translucently, encaustically, refractorily, transparently, opaquely, semiopaquely, by hand, pyrometrically, industrially, optically

45 Cookery

NOUNS

1 **cookery**, cooking, microwave cooking, pressure cooking, baking, food preparation, food processing, home economics, domestic science, style of cooking, gastronomy, cuisine, haute cuisine, nouvelle cuisine, lean cuisine, catering, provisioning, recipe, cook book (US), cookery book
▶ *606 Provision, 651 Refreshment*

2 **cook**, chef, sous chef, commis chef, apprentice chef, cuisinier, cordon bleu chef, fast-food chef, short-order cook (US), baker, caterer, barbecue cook, ranch-house cook (US), chuckwagon cook (US), cookie (US), cook's helper

3 **kitchen**, cookhouse, bakehouse, bakery, galley, pantry, larder, buttery, still room, cellar

4 **kitchen container**, bread bin, cake tin, biscuit barrel, meat safe, meat compartment, cold store, larder, larder-fridge, refrigerator, freezer, deepfreeze, icebox (US), fridge (Inf)
▶ *605 Store, 258 Container*

5 **cooker**, stove, hob, hotplate, grill, griddle, kitchen range, (conventional) oven, fan oven, kettle, toaster, waffle iron (US), sandwichmaker, barbecue, spit, microwave, Dutch oven, gas ring, Aga (Tm)

6 **kitchen equipment**, *batterie de cuisine* (Fr), cooking utensil, pan, saucepan, frying pan, skillet (US), frier, deep frier, roasting pan, omelette pan, crêpe pan, cooking pot, stew pan, casserole, cocotte, wok, tajine, pressure cooker, ovenproof dish, gratin dish, pie plate, flan dish, flan ring, cake tin, baking sheet, mould, soufflé dish, preserving pan, skimmer, steamer, poacher, mixing bowl, pudding basin, measuring jug, scales, rolling pin, pastry

bag, forcing bag (US), pastry cutter, flour dredger, chopping board, larding needle, trussing needle, vegetable peeler, grater, colander, whisk, beater, hand beater, rotary beater, food mixer, electric mixer, food processor, blender, liquidizer, mincer, grinder (US), coffee grinder, kilner jar, vegetable mill, spatula, wooden spoon, ladle, can (*or* tin) opener, lemon squeezer, juicer, greaseproof paper, waxed paper, aluminium foil, self-adhesive film, Clingfilm (Tm), plastic wrap, oven gloves

7 **basic ingredient**, flour, plain flour, selfraising flour, meal, wheatmeal, wholemeal, cornmeal, cornflour, yeast, leaven, baking powder, fat, butter, margarine, shortening, lard, ghee, suet, grease, dripping, oil, olive oil, vegetable oil, sunflower oil, eggs, sugar, granulated sugar, caster sugar, icing sugar, brown sugar, demerara sugar, salt, cooking salt, table salt, sea salt, pepper, seasoning, vinegar, malt vinegar, wine vinegar, aspic, gelatine, bicarbonate of soda, balsam, herb, spice
▶ *395 Oiliness, 414 Sweetness*

8 **cooking technique**, boiling, parboiling, simmering, poaching, steaming, bain marie, coddling, scrambling, casseroling, baking, roasting, oven-roasting, spit-roasting, potroasting, broiling, charbroiling, grilling, barbecuing, toasting, sautéeing, frying, deep frying, stir-frying, curing, smoking, pickling

9 **dish**, course, hors d'oeuvres, savouries, first course, starter, soup, fish course, entrée, remove, main course, side-dish, salad, cheese, fruit, entremets, dessert, sweet, pudding, pud (Inf), afters (Inf), speciality, speciality of the house, *spécialité de la maison* (Fr), special, *pièce de résistance* (Fr), culinary masterpiece, dish fit for a king (*or* queen), dish of the day, *plat du jour* (Fr), soup of the day

10 **snack**, nibbles, crisps, potato chips (US), nuts, peanuts, salted nuts, cheese straws, pretzels, twiglets (Tm), olives

11 **sandwich**, club sandwich, double-decker, finger sandwich, open sandwich, roast-beef sandwich, barbecue sandwich (US), bacon, let-

tuce, and tomato sandwich (BLT) (US), pastrami sandwich (US), cheese (and pickle) sandwich, ham sandwich, ham and cheese sandwich, turkey sandwich, chicken sandwich, salmon sandwich, tuna sandwich, cucumber sandwich, jam sandwich, peanut butter and jelly sandwich (US), Dagwood sandwich (US), French dip sandwich (US), hero (US), hoagie (US), poor-boy (US), po-boy (US), muffuletta (US), oyster loaf (US), shrimp loaf (US), grinder (US), hamburger, cheeseburger, quarter-pounder, Big Mac (Tm), hot dog, Reuben sandwich (US), toasted sandwich, butty (Inf), sarnie (Sl)

12 **hors d'oeuvre**, appetizer, starter, antipasto, smorgasbord, prawn cocktail, cold cuts, pâté, taramasalata, hummus, raitha, mezze, vol-au-vent, canapé, blini, samosa, pakora

13 **soup**, cream soup, clear soup, broth, Scotch broth, *potage* (Fr), consommé, stock, bouillon, julienne, bisque, lobster bisque, chowder (US), clam chowder, purée, vichysoisse, cock-a-leekie, mulligatawny, minestrone, borscht, gazpacho, fish soup, bouillabaisse, gumbo (US), onion soup, mushroom soup, celery soup, asparagus soup, tomato soup, chicken soup, vegetable soup, oxtail soup, bird's-nest soup

14 **salad**, side salad, tossed salad, green salad, mixed salad, chef's salad (US), potato salad, Russian salad, Waldorf salad (US), Caesar salad, salad niçoise, coleslaw, macedoine

15 **sauce**, tomato sauce, tomato ketchup, catsup, brown sauce, Worcester sauce, soy sauce, Tabasco sauce, tartare sauce, cranberry sauce, apple sauce, mint sauce, horseradish sauce, mayonnaise, salad cream, salad dressing, French dressing, aïoli, vinaigrette, Thousand Island dressing, dip, cheese dip, garlic dip, fondue, bolognese sauce, milanese sauce, barbecue sauce, béarnaise sauce, bordelaise sauce, bourguignonne, sauce espagnole, sauce suprême, hollandaise sauce, béchamel sauce, white sauce, cheese sauce, onion sauce, bread sauce, roux, velouté, demi-glace, chaudfroid, gravy

16 **fish dish**, fresh fish, fried fish, boiled fish, poached fish, fishcake, fish finger, fish pie, fish ball, fish stick, fish and chips, quenelle, gefilte fish, kedgeree, soft roe, hard roe, caviar, Beluga caviar, black caviar, red caviar, lumpfish caviar, taramasalata, jellied eel, smoked fish, smoked haddock, finnan haddock (*or* haddie), smoked mackerel, smoked salmon, smoked trout, kippered fish, kippered herring, kipper, smoky, Arbroath smokey, bloater, cured fish, lox, gravadlax (*or* gravlax), pickled herring, rollmop

17 **freshwater fish**, game fish, salmon, Atlantic salmon, Pacific salmon, trout, brown trout, rainbow trout, sea trout, salmon trout, grayling, coarse fish, eel, carp, perch, pike, bass, catfish

▶ *80 Fishes*

18 **sea fish**, saltwater fish, flatfish, dab, flounder, plaice, lemon sole, Dover sole, coalfish, coley, dogfish, rock salmon , whiting, cod, skate, hake, halibut, haddock (*or* haddie), turbot, brill, mullet, mackerel, herring, sprat, whitebait, sardine, bristling, sild, pilchard, tuna, kingfish, swordfish, hoki, Bombay duck, octopus, squid, calamari

▶ *80 Fishes*

19 **shellfish**, seafood, oyster, bluepoint, scallop, cockle, mussel, winkle, whelk, shrimp, prawn, kingprawn, Dublin bay prawn, crab, lobster, crayfish, crawfish (US), crawdad (US dial), *écrevisse* (Fr), sping lobster, *langouste* (Fr), snail, *escargot* (Fr)

▶ *80 Fishes*

20 **meat**, flesh, red meat, white meat, beef, pork, mutton, lamb, veal, goat, poultry, chicken, turkey, goose, duck, game, rabbit, hare, venison, pheasant, grouse, partridge, pigeon, squab, woodcock, snipe, plover, quail, minced meat, mince, ground meat, meatballs, faggots, rissoles, hamburger, beefburger

21 **meat substitute**, soya, TVP (textured vegetable protein), Quorn (Tm), tofu, bean curd, nut protein

22 **beef (British)**: neck, chuck, blade, fore rib, thick rib, thin rib, rolled ribs, T-bone, sirloin, rump, silverside, topside, leg, flank, brisket, shin, filet steak, undercut steak

23 **beef (US)**: chuck, rib, back rib, short loin, Porterhouse steak, tenderloin, sirloin, round, boneless rump roast, round steak, hind shank, short plate, brisket, fore shank

24 **pork (British)**: spare rib, blade, loin, leg fillet, hock, belly, hand, trotter

25 **pork (US)**: blade shoulder, loin, tenderloin, leg, side, spare rib, shoulder, hock

26 **lamb (British)**: scrag end, middle neck, shoulder, best end of neck, loin, chump, chump chops, leg, breast

27 **lamb (US)**: shoulder, neck slice, rib, loin, loin chop, leg, hind shank, breast, riblets, fore shank

28 **poultry**, white meat, dark meat, breast, leg, drumstick, wing, parson's nose, wishbone

29 **sausage**, sausagemeat, pork sausage, beef sausage, banger (Inf), chipolata, cocktail sausage, saveloy, wiener (US), *wienerwurst* (Ger), wienie (US inf), weenie (USinf), Cumberland sausage, herb sausage, frankfurter, Vienna sausage, liver sausage, garlic sausage, salami, bologna sausage, polony, boloney, *knackwurst* (*or* *knockwurst*) (Ger), *bratwurst* (Ger), black pudding, blood sausage, blood pudding, haggis, pâté, *pâté de foie gras* (Fr)

Vegetables

adzuki bean	collard	manioc	sea kale
asparagus	corn on the cob	marrow	shallot
aubergine	courgette	marrow squash	silver beet
avocado pear	cos lettuce	mung bean	skillet
bamboo shoots	cress	mustard and cress	sorrel
bean	cucumber	neep (Scot)	soya bean
beansprout	curly kale	okra	spinach
beef tomato	dishcloth gourd	onion	spinach beet
beet	eggplant (US)	oyster plant	split pea
beetroot	elephant garlic	pak-choi cabbage	spring cabbage
bhindi	elephant's ear	parsnip	spring onion
black-eyed pea	endive	pea	sprout
bok choy	fennel	pea bean	squash
broad bean	finocchio	pepper	string bean
broccoli	flageolet	petit pois	succory
Brussels sprout	French bean	pe-tsai cabbage	succotash
butter bean	garlic	pimiento	sugar pea
butternut pumpkin	gherkin	pinto bean	Swiss chard
cabbage	gibbon (Dial)	plum tomato	swede
cabbage lettuce	globe artichoke	potato, spud (Inf),	sweet corn
calabrese	gourd	murphy (Inf), tattie	sweet potato
capsicum	gumbo	(or tatty) (Scot)	taro
cardoon	green cabbage	potherb	tomato
carrot	green pepper	pumpkin	tonka bean
cassava	haricot bean	radish	turnip
cauliflower	horse bean	red bean	vegetable marrow
celeriac	Jerusalem artichoke	red beet (US)	water chestnut
celery	kale	red cabbage	watercress
chard	kidney bean	red pepper	wax bean (US)
chayote	kohlrabi	romaine lettuce	white cabbage
cherry tomato	lady's fingers	runner bean	yam
chervil	lentil	rutabaga (US)	yellow pepper
chick pea	lettuce	salsify	zucchini (US)
chicory	lima bean (US)	savoy cabbage	
Chinese cabbage	lotus root	scallion (US)	
Chinese leaves	mangetout	scarlet runner	

30 **bacon**, smoked bacon, unsmoked bacon, green bacon, streaky bacon, back bacon, middle cut, belly pork, sowbelly (US), rasher, side of bacon, flitch, bacon joint, gammon, salt pork, Danish bacon, Canadian bacon, ham, boiled ham

31 **offal**, variety meat, liver, lamb's liver, calf's liver, chicken liver, kidney, steak and kidney, heart, tongue, ox tongue, ox cheek, pig's head, Bath chap, calf's head, brains, brawn, chitterlings, pig's fry, sweetbread, melts, stomach sweetbread, neck sweetbread, pig's feet, pig's knuckles, trotters, cowheel, tripe, thick seam, cow's udder, elder (Dial), oxtail

32 **meat dish**, roast, pot roast, grill, mixed grill, pie, pasty, hash, fricassée, rissole, casserole, stew, goulash, haggis

33 **vegetable**, root vegetable, tuber, green vegetable, greens, spring greens, salad vegetable, pulse, legume, brassica, mushroom, field mushroom, horse mushroom, button mushroom, puffball mushroom, Chinese mushroom, champignon, cep, chanterelle, morel, blewit, boletus, horn of plenty, truffle, earthnut, seaweed, laver, laverbread, samphire, chick pea

▶ *83 Plants (General), 89 Fungi*

34 **vegetarian dish**, vegetable curry, vegetable chilli, vegetable casserole, vegetable flan, nut cutlet, nut roast, cauliflower cheese, macaroni cheese, omelette, aubergine roll, aubergine and tomato pie, stuffed marrow (or peppers or vine leaves), fondue, pease pudding, chilladas, hummus

▶ *350 Eating*

35 **dessert**, sweet, pudding, cake, pie, jelly, blancmange, custard, floating island (US), ice cream, dairy ice cream, sorbet, granita, water ice, knickerbocker glory, Mississippi mud pie, marquise, crème caramel, yoghurt, fool, mousse, soufflé, sundae, banana split, peach melba, trifle, rice pudding, semolina, tapioca, bread-and-butter pudding, steamed pudding, suet pudding, Christmas pudding, plum pudding, summer pudding, brown betty (US), betty (US), roly-poly, spotted dick, Black Forest gateau, pavlova, fruit flan, fruit cup (US), crumble, charlotte, charlotte russe, stewed fruit, compote, fruit salad, fresh fruit, cheese and biscuits, cheese board

▶ *86 Fruits, 414 Sweetness*

36 **cake**, gateau, birthday cake, wedding cake, Christmas cake, yule log, chocolate cake, chocolate gateau, devil's food cake, German chocolate cake (US), coffee cake, fudge cake, brownies (US), angel cake, sponge cake, maids

of honour, madeleine, Swiss roll, upside-down cake (US), carrot cake, fruitcake, spice cake, seed cake, lardy cake, Dundee cake, gingerbread, parkin, Madeira cake, cupcake (US), cheesecake, torte, apple pie, blackbottom (US), lemon meringue pie, Boston cream pie (US), coconut pie (US), pumpkin pie (US), sweet potato pie (US), pecan pie (US), chess pie (US), Bakewell tart, blackberry cobbler (US), peach cobbler (US), turnover, flan, tart, jam tart, mince pie, eclair, macaroon, fritter, apple fritter, Danish pastry, Danish, Eccles cake, sweet roll (US), cinnamon roll (US), Chelsea bun, Bath bun, doughnut, jam doughnut, doughnut hole (US), sinker (US inf)

37 **pastry**, shortcrust pastry, flaky pastry, puff pastry, rough puff pastry, suet crust pastry, hot-water crust pastry, choux pastry, fleur pastry, Genoese pastry, cheese pastry, filo pastry

38 **bread**, dough, crust, crumb, sliced bread, white bread, enriched bread, soda bread, sourdough bread (US), brown bread, wholemeal bread, malt bread, granary bread, black bread, Boston brown bread (US), rye bread, pumpernickel, corn bread (US), corn pone (US), hush puppies (US), spoon bread (US), fried bread, beer bread, banana-nut bread, nut bread, raisin bread, pumpkin bread (US), pitta bread, poppadom, puri, nan, chapatti, toast, cinnamon toast, Melba toast, French toast, rusk, crouton

39 **loaf**, pan loaf, pan, cottage loaf, cob, tin, split tin, farmhouse, bloomer, plait, French bread, baguette, French stick, bread stick, roll, breakfast roll, bridge roll, bap, barm cake, pikelet, bagel, croissant, brioche, bun, currant bun, teacake, English muffin (US), crumpet, muffin, popover (US), blueberry muffin (US), biscuit (US), buttermilk biscuit (US), sourdough biscuit (US), soda biscuit (US), scone, drop scone, pancake, battercake (US), flapjack (US), buttermilk pancake (US), blueberry pan-

cake (US), crêpe, waffle, wafer, biscuit, cookie (US), digestive biscuit, shortbread, flapjack, cracker, soda cracker (US), creamcracker, crispbread, water biscuit, oatcake, bannock (Scot)

40 **breakfast cereal**, cornflakes, bran flakes, bran, wheat germ, muesli, oatmeal, porridge, gruel, skilly, brewis (Dial), brose (Scot), grits (US), mush (US), polenta

41 **sweet**, sweetmeat, bonbon, comfit, confectionary, toffee, taffy, boiled sweet, barley sugar, butterscotch, caramel, chocolate, chocolate bar, fondant, fudge, gobstopper, gum, gumdrop, jelly bean, jujube, liquorice, liquorice allsort, lollipop, marshmallow, marzipan, peppermint, praline, crystallized fruit, toffee apple, sweetie (Inf)

▶ *414 Sweetness*

42 **preserve**, jam, jelly, marmalade, conserve, bottled fruit, pickle, chutney, dried fruit, currant, raisin, sultana, prune

▶ *86 Fruits*

43 **US dish**, New England clam chowder, Waldorf salad, chef's salad, porterhouse steak, barbecued spare ribs, Maine lobster, clam chowder, oysters Rockefeller, Southern fried chicken, jambalaya, stuffed Idaho potato, succotash, corn bread, grits, red beans with rice, pancakes and maple syrup, soul food, hambone soup, cow-pea soup, crackling biscuit, fried catfish, scrambled pork brains, blackplate, Kentucky Fried Chicken (Tm), eggs Benedict

44 **British dish**, cock-a-leekie, English breakfast, Yorkshire pudding, Lancashire hotpot, Welsh rarebit (*or* rabbit), Irish stew, porridge, Scotch broth, fish and chips, Dover sole, smoked salmon, kippers, eel pie and mash, bangers and mash, roast beef, mutton, Aylesbury duck, haggis, ploughman's lunch, mixed grill, toad-in-the-hole, bubble and squeak, devilled kidneys, shepherd's pie, cottage pie

Cheeses

Beaufort	cream cheese	grated cheese	pot cheese
Bel Paese	curd cheese	Gruyère	processed cheese
blue	Danish Blue	Lancashire	Red Leicester
blue cheese	Derby	Leicester	Red Windsor
Blue Stilton	Dolcelatte	Limburger	Reggiano
blue Vinney	Dorset Vinney	Livarot	Roquefort
Boursin	Double Gloucester	Lymeswold	Sage Derby
Brie	Dunlop	Mascarpone	Stilton
Brillat Savarin	Edam	Monterey	Tilamook
Buxton blue	Emmental (or	Monterey Jack	vegetarian cheese
Caerphilly	Emmentaler)	mozarella	Vermont Sage
Camembert	Fontainebleu	Neufchâtel	Vignotte
Cheddar	fromage frais	New York	Wensleydale
Cheshire	Gloucester	Oka	White Stilton
chèvre	Gorgonzola	Oxfordshire	Windsor
Colby	Gouda	Parmesan	
cottage cheese	Grana	Port Salut	

Types of Pasta

agnolotti	fettuccine	penne lisce
annellini	fidelini	penne rig-
bavette	filini	ate
bigoli	fusilli	pennette
bucatini	gnocchi	rigate
cannelloni	gramigna	pipette
capelli	lasagne (or	ravioli
capellini	lasagna)	rigatoni
cappelletti	lasagnette	risoni
chifferi	linguini	rotelle
chifferoni	lumache	sedani
chitarra	macaroni	sedanini
conchiglie	(or mac-	spaghetti
conchigli-	cheroni)	stelline
ette	macche-	tagliatelle
cravattine	roncini	tempesta
ditali	manicotti	tortelli
ditalini	mezza	tortellini
ditalini	noodles	tortiglioni
rigati	orecchiette	trenette
ditaloni	paglia e	tuffoli
eliche	fieno	vermicelli
farfalle	pappardelle	vermicellini
farfalline	penne	zita

45 French dish, onion soup, quiche, quiche Lorraine, soufflé, pâté, pressed duck, chateaubriand, steak tartare, fondue, escargots, frogs legs, petits pois, ratatouille, cassoulet, crêpes suzette, rillettes, coq au vin, steak au poivre, boeuf bourgignon, lobster thermidor

46 German dish, Gemusesuppe, Wiener Schnitzel, Rehschnitzel, Sauerbraten, Sauerkraut, Apfelstrudel, Pfannkuchen, Bratwurst, Rotkohl, Kalbshaxe, Gebratene Huhnerleber

47 Italian dish, minestrone, pasta, antipasto, pizza, risotto, zabaglione, tiramisu

48 Chinese dish, egg drop soup, egg roll, chow mein, chop suey, won ton, dim sum, sweet and sour pork, beef congee, lemon chicken, Peking duck, stir fry, egg fu yung, shrimp balls, fried noodles, fried rice, spring roll

49 Indian dish, pakora, samosa, bhaji, dhal, raitha, biryani, curry, tikka, tandoori, chicken tikka masala, vindaloo, madras, korma, malaya, mughlai, butter chicken, kashmiri, dansak, rogan josh, bhuna, pathia, dopiaza, masala dosa, spiced green bananas, rice pancake, poppadom, nan bread, keema nan, chapatti, paratha, bombay mix, puri, pilau rice, kulfi, lassi

50 Central American dish, black bean soup, taco, tostada, tortilla, tamale, burrito, empanada, enchilada, nacho, guacamole, Montezuma pie, olla podrida, mole poblano, chilli con carne, monteria

51 West Indian dish, asapao, calalou, chiquetaille, féroce, macadam, pasteles, piononos, stoba

52 Greek dish, meze, kefta, moussaka, dolmades, calamari, hummus, tzatziki, taramasalata, spinakoturikopita, souvlaki, ba-

klava, stuffed vine leaves, Greek salad

53 African dish, aitiou, canari, cosidou, dou louf, foutou, gari, nkui, pepe supi, placali, yassa, zegeni

54 other dishes, paella (Spanish), Hungarian goulash, kebabs (Turkish), shish kebab, donner kebab, balti (Pakistani), sushi (Japanese), musi-yaki (Japanese), couscous (Algerian), halvah (Middle East and Asian)

VERBS

55 cook, prepare a meal, put in the oven, bake, put in the microwave (oven), microwave, pressure-cook, heat, heat up, warm through, reheat, roast, spit-roast, pot-roast, brown, toast, grill, charcoal-grill, barbecue, spatchcock, griddle, devil, curry, fry, deep-fry, shallow-fry, sauté, stir-fry, fry sunny side up, fry over lightly (US), double-fry, scramble, coddle, boil, parboil, blanch, scald, seethe, simmer, steam, poach, casserole, stew, braise, baste, lard, bard, flip, whip, whisk, beat, blend, knead, mix, fold in, liquidize, stir, draw, gut, bone, fillet, stuff, dress, garnish, cut, chop, dice, shred, grind, mince, grate, sauce, flavour, spice, season, whip something up (Inf), throw something together (Inf)

▶ *133 Mixture, 136 Separation, 792 Decoration*

ADJECTIVES

56 culinary, gastronomic, epicurean, mensal, prandial, pre-prandial, postprandial, after-dinner, mealtime, dressed, oven-ready, prepared, ready-to-cook, made-up, ready-to-serve, cooked, done, well-done, overcooked, burnt, burnt to a crisp (or cinder), al dente, underdone, undercooked, red, rare, raw, roasted, browned, toasted, grilled, barbecued, devilled, curried, fried, deep-fried, sautéed, stir-fried, scrambled, coddled, boiled, steamed, poached, stewed, braised, beaten, stuffed, chopped, ground, minced, au gratin, au naturel, à la mode, à la carte, table d'hôte

ADVERBS

57 culinarily, gastronomically, palatably, succulently, nutritiously, nutritionally

INTERJECTIONS

58 grub's on!, grub's up!, come and get it!, chow down!, soup's on!, *bon appetit!* (Fr)

46 Dancing and Ballet

NOUNS

1 dancing, dance, promenade (US), ball, *bal masqué* (Fr), masked ball, masquerade, *bal costumé* (Fr), costume ball, fancy dress dance, *thé dansant* (Fr), tea dance, cotillion (or cotillon) (US), ceilidh, barn dance, square dance (US), disco, disco dancing, breakdancing, body popping, robot dancing, robotics, tap dancing, clog dancing, folk dancing, country dancing, Scottish country dancing, Highland dancing,

Irish dancing, morris dancing, old-time dancing, sequence dancing, ballroom dancing, ballet dancing, modern dance, choreography, eurhythmics (or eurythmics), aerobics, muse of dancing, Terpsichore, prom (US inf), hop (Inf), bop (Inf), jam session (Sl), shindig (Inf), knees-up (Inf), rave (Inf)

2 **dance**, ballroom dance, shuffle, soft-shoe shuffle, cakewalk, Castle walk, solo dance, pas seul, clog dance, step dance, tap dance, toe dance, sand dance, fan dance, dance of the seven veils, hula-hula, hula, high kicks, cancan, belly dance, polka, waltz, valse (Fr), last waltz, Viennese waltz, hesitation waltz, St Bernard, valeta, Lancers, excuse-me dance, Paul Jones, snowball, foxtrot, slow foxtrot, fast foxtrot, turkey trot, quickstep, Charleston, black bottom, blues, one-step, English one-step, two-step, Boston two-step, English waltz, military two-step, paso doble, peabody, tango, rumba, samba, mambo, bossanova, habanera, beguine, conga, conga line, bunny hop, cha-cha-cha (or cha-cha), boomps-a-daisy, hokey cokey, Lambeth Walk, Palais Glide, the big apple, stomp, bop, bebop, shimmy, jive, Lindy-hop, jitterbug, rock and roll (or rock'n'roll), twist, mashed potato, jerk, hitch-hike

3 **ballroom dance steps**, chassé, waltz, balance, pivot, walking steps, running steps, syncopated steps

4 **historic dancing**, animal dance, totem dance, hunting dance, trance dance, curative dance, devil dance, agricultural dance, rain dance, harvest dance, courtship dance, fandango, fertility dance, wedding dance, funeral dance, medieval dance, court dance, sword dance, sailor's dance, hornpipe, keel row, war dance, pyrrhic (dance), meke, haka, ritual dance, corroboree (Aus), sacred dance, Indian temple dance, Gypsy dance, flamenco, country dance, morris dance, rapper, long sword, jig, gigue, Irish jig, Walls of Limerick, fling, Highland fling, reel, eightsome reel, foursome reel, Virginia reel, Sir Roger de Coverley, Scottish reel, Strathspey, Gay Gordons, Duke of Perth, Strip the Willow, Dashing White Sergeant, hay (or hey), saraband (or sarabande), set dance, barn dance, military schottische (US), square dance (US), hoedown (US), rigadoon (or rigaudon), folk dance, dionysiac (or bacchic) dance, Russian dance, Cossack dance, farandole, maypole dance, nautch (or nauch), tarantella, bolero, polka, mazurka, polonaise, czardas, dramatic dance, Kabuki, social dance, danse basse (Fr), waltz, galliard, courante, gavotte, contredanse (or contradance), quadrille, pavane (or pavan), minuet, scherzo, écossaise, galop (or gallopade), volta, allemande, cotillion (or cotillon)

5 **dancer**, tap dancer, clog dancer, classical dancer, high-kicker, Radio City Rockettes (US), cancan dancer, go-go dancer, entertainer, waltzer, foxtrotter, shuffler, jiver, jitterbug, bebopper, disco dancer, jumper, choreographer, hoofer (Sl)

6 **famous dancers**, Irene and Vernon Castle, Fred Astaire and Ginger Rogers, Jack Buchanan, Gene Kelly,
▶ 51 Performing Arts

7 **dance hall**, ballroom, palais de danse, discotheque, disco, dance floor

8 **ballet**, dance, ballet dancing, dancing, classical ballet, Russian ballet, romantic ballet, modern ballet, modern dance, toe dance, solo, choreography
▶ 51 Performing Arts

9 **ballet steps**, attitude, chassé, glissade, bourrée, arabesque, arabesque penchée, pirouette, petit allegro, soubresauté, changement, pas de chat, brisé volé, temps de poisson, batterie, cabriole, entrechat, jeté, deboulé, ballong, fouetté, fouetté en tournant, tours en l'air, pas de deux

10 **positions at the barre**, plié, tendus, glissées, ronds de jambes à terre, battement, fondus, ronds de jambes en l'air, développés, petits battements, grands battements

11 **classical ballets**, Swan Lake, The Sleeping Beauty, The Nutcracker, Coppelia, Giselle, Les Sylphides

12 **ballet companies**, Bolshoi Ballet, Kirov Ballet, Paris Opera Ballet, Royal Ballet, Ballet Rambert, Sadler's Wells Ballet, Royal Festival Ballet, New York City Ballet, American Ballet, Royal Danish Ballet

13 **ballet dancer**, danseur (Fr), ballerina, danseuse (Fr), prima ballerina, corps de ballet

14 **famous ballet dancers**, Anna Pavlova, Vaslav Nijinsky, Maria Taglioni, Galina Ulanova, Maya Plisetskaya, George Balanchine, Maria Tallchief, Martha Graham, Edward Villella, Alicia Markova, Ninette de Valois, Marie Rambert, Rudolf Nureyev, Margot Fonteyn, Robert Helpmann, Frederick Ashton, Merle Park, Peter Schaufuss, Mikhail Baryshnikov
▶ 51 Performing Arts

VERBS

15 **dance**, join the dance, go dancing, choreograph, tap-dance, waltz, foxtrot, quickstep, Charleston, tango, rumba, jive, jitterbug, stomp, bop, twist, rock, rock and roll (or rock'n'roll), disco-dance, breakdance, body-pop, whirl, rotate, cavort, gambol, frolic, prance, caper, jig, jig about, bob up and down, shuffle, trip, tread a measure, trip the light fantastic (toe), skip, hop, leap, hoof it (Sl)
▶ 364 Rotation

47   Furniture and Woodwork

NOUNS

1 **furniture**, furnishings, home furnishings, pine furniture, wood furniture, laminated furniture, veneer furniture, veneering, lacquered furniture, lacquering, painted furniture, painting, trompe l'œil, chinoiserie, japanning, inlaid decoration, marquetried furniture, marquetry, parquetried furniture, parquetry, metal furniture, plastic furniture, tubular furniture, upholstery, soft furnishings, built-in furniture, built-in cupboard, unit furniture, designing of furniture, furniture-designing, furniture-making, making of furniture, cabinet-making, furniture factory, furniture store, cabinet shop

▶ *725 Property, 604 Materials, 266 Layer, 293 Covering, 792 Decoration, 740 Market, 647 Workshop*

2 **chair**, wooden chair, bentwood chair, captain's chair, cane chair, box chair, barrel chair, straight chair, Shaker chair, ladder-back chair, wheel-back chair, panel-back chair, rocking chair, Boston rocker, nursing chair, bucket seat, dining chair, upholstered chair, leather chair, armchair, easy chair, Morris chair, Queen-Anne chair, Sheraton chair, Windsor chair, wing chair, club chair, reclining chair, recliner, lounge chair, side chair, carver chair, folding chair, swivel chair, deck chair, highchair, camp chair (*or* seat), stool, milking stool, bar stool, stall, choir stall, bench, settle, couch, studio couch, Grecian couch, sofa, chesterfield, chaise longue, settee, divan, love seat

▶ *284 Support*

3 **chair leg**, scroll leg, twist-turned leg, ball-and-claw leg, cabriole leg, sabre leg

4 **table**, dining table, side table, end table, pier table, drop-leaf table, coffee table, tea table, Pembroke table, gate-leg table, console table (*or* console), bedside table, dressing table, pedestal table, card table, gaming table, worktable, kitchen table, writing table, library table, desk, writing desk, escritoire, secretaire (*or* secretary), davenport, roll-top desk, slant-top (*or* slope-top) desk, knee-hole desk, bureau, reading desk, lectern, board (Arch)

▶ *48 Literature*

5 **cabinet**, dresser, Welsh dresser, double (*or* triple) dresser, mirror cabinet, chest, chest of drawers, cassone, tallboy, highboy, lowboy, bottom drawer, hope chest (US), commode, wardrobe, china cabinet, drinks cabinet, liquor cabinet (US), sideboard, canterbury, cupboard, corner cupboard, press, bookcase, shelves, bookshelf, whatnot

▶ *258 Container*

6 **bed**, single bed, double bed, twin bed, king-size bed, queen-size bed, panelled bed, four-poster bed, feather bed, Colonial bed, canopied bed, Empire bed, day bed, chaise longue, convertible sofa, sofa bed, futon, divan, davenport (US), bunk bed, crib, cot, cradle, berth, hammock, foldaway bed, zed (*or* Z) bed, camp bed, truckle (*or* trundle) bed, water bed, bedstead, headboard, footboard

▶ *284 Support*

7 **furniture style**, Louis Quatorze, Louis Quinze, Louis Seize, Tudor, Elizabethan, Jacobean, Queen-Anne, Chippendale, Adam Hepplewhite, rococo, Georgian, William and Mary, French provincial, colonial, Early American, Early Federal, Shaker, Empire, Sheraton, Regency, chinoiserie, boulle, gothic, baroque, Biedermeier, Victorian, (William) Morris, Art Nouveau, Bauhaus, Scandinavian, modern

▶ *549 Style, 43 Architecture*

8 **woodwork**, woodworking, woodcraft, timberwork, carpentry, joinery, cabinet-making, carving, woodcarving, wood turning, wood sculpting, wood sculpture, treen (*or* treenware), whittling, wood-burning, pyrography, xylopyrography, woodenware, woodcut, cut, black-line woodcut, white-line woodcut, woodcut illustration, wood block, wood-block printing, relief printing, xylography, lignography, wood engraving, woodprint, xylograph, pyrogravure

▶ *50 Painting and Sculpture*

9 **decorative woodwork**, wood inlay, Certosina work, intarsia, horn inlay, mother-of-pearl inlay, tortoiseshell inlay, brass inlay, metal inlay, silver inlay, gold-sheet inlay, true inlay, marquetry, boulle (*or* boullework), floral marquetry, seaweed marquetry, oysterwood marquetry, oyster pieces, brass on shell, *première partie* (Fr), shell on brass, *contre partie* (Fr)

▶ *792 Decoration, 557 Ornament, 267 Juxtaposition, 319 Notch, 321 Furrow*

10 **carpenter's term**, joint, bevel, mitre joint (*or* mitre), timber joint, housed joint, lap joint, fish joint, scarf joint, flitched joint, tusk tenon joint, birdsmouth joint, tenon, mortise, mortise and tenon, dovetailing, cogging, trimming, framing, joist, trimmed joist, strut, strutting, herringbone strutting, truss, king-post truss, queen-post truss, laths, studs, studwork

▶ *135 Union, 138 Adhesion, 382 Structure*

11 **woodworking tool**, lathe, saw, tenon saw, rip saw, crosscut saw, panel saw, plane, smoothing plane, jack plane, drawknife (*or* drawshave), spokeshave, adze, band saw, jigsaw, circular saw, power-driven saw, radial-arm saw, planer (*or* surfacer), jointer, shaper,

router, sander, belt sander, disk sander, spindle sander, drum-bed sander, mortiser, hollow-chisel mortiser, chain-saw mortiser, tenoner, single tenoner, double tenoner, boring machine, borer, drill, wood-engraving tool, chisel, router, burin, graver, tint tool, velo, lamina, sandpaper

▶ *603 Tool*

12 **wood**, timber, lumber, softwood, hardwood, heartwood, sapwood, beam, rafter, joist, board, boarding, plank, planking, deal, red deal, white deal, stick, stave, pole, post, two-by-four, slab, puncheon, slat, splat, lath, lathing, lathwork, timbering, timberwork, sheeting, panelling, panelboard, panelwork, plywood, sheathing, sheathing board, siding, weatherboard, clapboard, hardboard, blockboard, chipboard, shingle, shake, log, cordwood, woodgrain, wood texture, end-grain wood

▶ *85 Trees, 271 Breadth, 383 Texture*

13 **carpenter**, joiner, cabinet-maker, furniture-maker, coach-builder, wheelwright, turner, sawyer, cooper, carver, woodcarver, wood-craftsman, wood engraver, marquetry worker, *ébéniste* (Fr), *marqueteur* (Ger), woodcutter, form engraver, *Formschneider* (Ger), xylographer, xylopyrographer, pyrographer, chippie (Sl)

▶ *646 Worker, 50 Painting and Sculpture*

ADJECTIVES

14 **wooden**, lacquered, painted, inlaid, marquetried, parquetried, upholstered, built-in, straight, ladder-back, panel-back, rocking, reclining, folding, drop-leaf, gate-leg, roll-top, slant-top (*or* slope-top), knee-hole, panelled, canopied, convertible, foldaway

15 **woodcrafted**, carved, woodcarved, wood-turned, wood-sculpted, whittled, wood-burned, woodcut, black-line, white-line, wood-engraved, wood-blocked, woodprinted, xylographic(al), xylopyrographic(al), pyrographic(al)

16 **joined**, joining, jointed, mitred, timbered, housed, flitched, mortised, dovetailed, dovetailing, cogged, cogging, trimmed, trimming, framed, framing, joisted, herringbone, beamed, boarded, boarding, two-by-four, slatted

VERBS

17 **carpenter**, mitre, mortise, dovetail, cog, trim, frame, joist, strut, truss, lathe, saw, cut, crosscut, rip, drill, screw, plane, shape, sand, tenon, bore, chisel, fit a beam, raise a rafter, board, plank, post, slat, lath, timber, sheet, panel, shingle

18 **work wood**, laminate, veneer, lacquer, paint, inlay, build in, upholster, carve, turn wood, sculpt wood, whittle

48   Literature

The reading of all good books is like a conversation with the finest men of past centuries. René Descartes.

The proper study of mankind is books. Aldous Huxley.

Literature flourishes best when it is half a trade and half an art. Dean Inge.

Literature and butterflies are the two sweetest passions known to man. Vladimir Nabokov.

Great Literature is simply language charged with meaning to the utmost possible degree. Ezra Pound.

NOUNS

1 **literature**, writing(s), letters, belles-lettres, *litterae humaniores* (L), republic of letters, polite literature, serious literature, underground literature, popular literature, folk literature, oral literature, wisdom literature, the classics, the arts, the humanities, learning, erudition, culture, lore, civilization

2 **fiction**, prose fiction, narrative fiction, novel,

Literary Groups and Movements

absurdism	expressionism	minimalism	Russian Formalists
Acmeism	Futurism	modernism	Scottish Chaucerians
Aesthetic movement	Georgian poetry	naturalism	Scottish Enlightenment
Alliterative Revival	Gongorism	neoclassicism	sentimentalism
Angry Young Men	graveyard poetry	neorealism	social realism
Augustans	Group, the	Parnassians	socialist realism
Beat Generation	Harlem Renaissance	philosopher	Spasmodic School
Bloomsbury group	hermeticism	Pléiade, la	structuralism
Cavalier Poets	Imagism	postmodernism	Sturm und Drang (Ger)
Celtic Twilight	Kailyard School	post-structuralism	surrealism
Classicism	kitchen-sink drama	Pre-Raphaelitism	Symbolism
Crepuscular school	Lake poets	preromanticism	Transcendentalism
Dadaism	Liverpool poets	primitivism	tremendismo (Sp)
decadence	magic realism	Pylon Poets	verismo (It)
Encyclopédistes	mannerism	realism	Vorticism
Euphuism	Martian poets	Renaissance humanism	Wertherism
existentialism	medievalism	Romanticism	

Shakespeare's plays

Henry VI Part 1	The Merchant of Ven-	Hamlet	The Merry Wives of
Henry VI Part 2	ice	Othello	Windsor
Henry VI Part 3	Much Ado About Noth-	King Lear	Antony and Cleopatra
Richard III	ing	Macbeth	Coriolanus
Love's Labour's Lost	Twelfth Night	The Winter's Tale	Troilus and Cressida
The Two Gentlemen	As You Like It	The Tempest	Measure for Measure
of Verona	Romeo and Juliet	The Comedy of Errors	All's Well That Ends
The Taming of the	Richard II	Titus Andronicus	Well
Shrew	Julius Caesar	King John	Timon of Athens
A Midsummer Night's	Henry IV Part 1	Henry V	Pericles
Dream	Henry IV Part 2	Henry VIII	Cymbeline

novella, *nouvelle* (Fr), novelette, story, short-story, vignette, sketch, *roman* (Fr), thriller, psychological thriller, *roman à clef* (Fr), *roman fleuve* (Fr), novel sequence, stream-of-consciousness novel, psychological novel, *nouveau roman* (Fr), antinovel, metafiction, picaresque novel, Gothic novel, epistolary novel, epic novel, novel of sensibility, regional novel, erotic novel, pornographic novel, *Bildungsroman* (Ger), *Künstlerroman* (Ger), autobiographical novel, fictional biography, historical novel, social novel, thesis novel, *roman à thèse* (Fr), novel of ideas, problem novel, campus novel, love story, Mills & Boon, adventure story, western, science-fiction novel, sci-fi (Inf), fantasy novel, utopia, dystopia, gothic horror, horror story, crime story, spy story, detective story, mystery story, ghost story, supernatural tale, fairy tale, *Märchen* (Ger), legend, myth, mythology, mythopoeia, folk tale, folk story, fable, *fabliau* (Fr), beast fable, parable, *conte* (Fr), geste, romance, whodunit (Inf), cliffhanger (Inf), bodice ripper (Inf), pulp fiction (Inf), shopping and fucking novel (Tab), s and f (Inf), sword and sorcery novel (Inf), blockbuster (Inf), penny dreadful (Inf)

3 **aspect of fiction**, story, storyline, narrative, plot, subplot, scenario, argument, plan, scheme, subject, theme, motif, leitmotiv (*or* leitmotif), development, structure, architecture, continuity, action, incident, episode, complication, turning point, denouement, peripeteia, recognition, anagnonsis, device, contrivance, coincidence, atmosphere, tone, mood, background, description, symbolism, local colour, characterization, dramatic irony, comic relief, catharsis, stream of consciousness, digression, interior monologue, metanarrative, first-person narrative, third-person narrative, point of view, omniscient narrator, unreliable narrator, narrative voice, narratology

4 **nonfiction**, descriptive writing, travel writing, travelogue, history, annals, chronicle, record, life story, life, journal, diary, memoir, confessions, kiss-and-tell confession, profile, biographical sketch, curriculum vitae, autobiography, biography, hagiography, historiography, homily, polemic, anatomy, apology, trea-

tise, discourse, thesis, dissertation, essay, study, commentary, critique, criticism, review

5 **prose**, prose fiction, expository prose, prose style, prose rhythm, prose poetry, poetic prose, polyphonic prose

6 **poetry**, poesy, verse, rhyme, song, numbers (Arch), balladry, versification, poetics, lyric poetry, epic poetry, epos, elegiac poetry, narrative poetry, heroic poetry, mock-heroic poetry, dramatic poetry, pastoral poetry, metaphysical poetry, erotic poetry, didactic poetry, confessional poetry, topographical poetry, satirical poetry, comic poetry, light verse, occasional verse, *verse de société* (Fr), concrete poetry, pattern poetry, nonsense poetry, folk poetry, runic verse, performance poetry, dub poetry, rap poetry, doggerel, lame verse, Hudibrastic verse, jingles, ditties, macaronics

7 **poem**, verse, rhyme, ballade, ballad, epic, epos, lay, saga, dithyramb, epigram, cento, limerick, clerihew, lyric, madrigal, nursery rhyme, ode, epode, choric ode, Pindaric ode, Sapphic ode, Horatian ode, palinode, narrative poem, dramatic monologue, conversation poem, verse epistle, complaint, encomium, satire, sonnet, sonnet sequence, Shakespearean sonnet, English sonnet, Petrarchan sonnet, Italian sonnet, sestina, chanson, tenzone, rondeau, rondel, roundel, roundelay, alba, aubade, reverdie, virelay, triolet, eclogue, idyll, pastoral, georgic, bucolic, prothalamion, epithalamium, elegy, threnody, elegiac poem, pastoral elegy, monody, dirge, song, vilanelle, troubadour poem, hymn, psalm, haiku, tanka

8 **part of poem**, verse, stanza, stave, measure, strain, strophe, antistrophe, epode, line, half line, foot, hemistich, monostich, distich, tristich, tetrastich, pentastich, hexastich, heptastich, octastich, rhyming couplet, closed couplet, couplet, triplet, tercet, quatrain, sestet, septet, octet, octave, verse paragraph, refrain, chorus, envoi, burden, book, canto, fit, bob and wheel

9 **metre**, metrics, measure, numbers (Arch), rhythm, scansion, prosody, quantitative metre, syllabic metre, accentual metre, accentual-syllabic metre, duple metre, triple metre, accent, accentuation, stress, beat, emphasis,

Writers

Adams, Richard
(1920–)
Addison, Joseph
(1672–1719)
Aelfric (c. 955–
c. 1020)
Agee, James (1909–55)
Alcott, Louisa May
(1832–88)
Aldington, Richard
(1892–1962)
Aldiss, Brian W
(1925–)
Aldrich, Thomas Bai-
ley (1836–1907)
Algren, Nelson (1909–
81)
Allingham, Margery
(1904–66)
Ambler, Eric (1909–86)
Amis, Sir Kingsley
(1922–)
Amis, Martin (1949–)
Andersen, Hans Chris-
tian (1805–75)
Anderson, Sherwood
(1876–1941)
Andrić, Ivo (1892–
1975)
Apuleius, Lucius (2nd
century AD)
Asimov, Isaac (1920–
92)
Atwood, Margaret
(1939–)
Aubrey, John (1626–
97)
Austen, Jane (1775–
1817)
Azorín, José Martinéz
Ruíz (1874–1967)
Balchin, Nigel (1908–
70)
Baldwin, James Arthur
(1924–87)
Balzac, Honoré de
(1799–1850)
Bana (7th century AD)
Barbusse, Henri
(1873–1935)
Barth, John (1930–)
Barthes, Roland
(1915–80)
Bates, H E (1905–74)
Baum, L Frank (1856–
1919)
Beauvoir, Simone de
(1908–86)
Beckett, Samuel
(1906–92)
Beerbohm, Sir Max
(1872–1956)
Bellow, Saul (1915–)
Benchley, Robert
Charles (1889–1945)
Benét, Stephen Vin-
cent (1898–1943)
Bennett, Arnold
(1837–1931)
Bentley, Edmund Cleri-
hew (1875–1956)
Bernhard, Thomas
(1931–89)

Bierce, Ambrose
Gwinnett (1842–
1914)
Bilderdijk, Willem
(1756–1831)
Blackmore, R D
(1825–1900)
Blackwood, Algernon
Henry (1869–1951)
Blasco Ibáñez,
Vicente (1867–1928)
Blyton, Enid (1897–
1968)
Boccaccio, Giovanni
(1313–75)
Böll, Heinrich (1917–
85)
Borges, Jorge Luis
(1899–1986)
Borrow, George Henry
(1803–81)
Boswell, James (1740–
95)
Bowen, Elizabeth
(1899–1973)
Bowles, Paul
(1910–)
Bradbury, Malcolm
(1932–)
Bradbury, Ray
(1920–)
Brentano, Clemens
(1778–1842)
Brillat-Savarin, An-
thelme (1755–1826)
Broch, Hermann
(1886–1951)
Brontë, Anne (1820–49)
Brontë, Charlotte
(1816–55)
Brontë, Emily (1818–
48)
Browne, Sir Thomas
(1605–82)
Buchan, John, 1st
Baron Tweedsmuir
(1875–1940)
Buck, Pearl S (1892–
1973)
Bunyan, John (1628–88)
Burgess, Anthony
(John Burgess Wil-
son, 1917–)
Burnett, Frances Eliza
Hodgson (1849–
1924)
Burney, Fanny (Mrs
Frances Burney
D'Arblay, 1752–
1840)
Burroughs, Edgar Rice
(1875–1950)
Burroughs, William S
(1914–)
Butler, Samuel (1835–
1902)
Caldwell, Erskine
(1903–87)
Calvino, Italo (1923–85)
Camus, Albert (1913–
60)
Capote, Truman
(1924–84)

Carroll, Lewis
(Charles Lutwidge
Dodgson, 1832–98)
Carson, Rachel Louise
(1907–64)
Cary, Joyce (1888–
1957)
Castelo Branco,
Camilo (1825–95)
Castiglione,
Baldassare (1478–
1529)
Cela, Camilo José
(1916–)
Céline, Louis Ferdinand
(L F Destouches,
1884–1961)
Cervantes, Miguel de
(1547–1616)
Chandler, Raymond
(1888–1959)
Charteris, Leslie (L
Charles Bowyer Yin,
1907–93)
Chateaubriand, Vi-
comte de (1768–
1848)
Chesterton, G K
(1874–1936)
Christie, Agatha
(1891–1976)
Cleland, John (1709–
89)
Cocteau, Jean (1889–
1963)
Colette (Sidonie-
Gabrielle C, 1873–
1954)
Collins, William Wilkie
(1824–89)
Compton-Burnett,
Dame Ivy (1892–
1969)
Conrad, Joseph (Teo-
dor Josef Konrad
Watęcz Korzeni-
owski, 1857–1924)
Cooper, James
Fenimore (1789–
1851)
Corelli, Marie (1854–
1924)
Crane, Stephen (1871–
1900)
Cronin, A J (1896–
1981)
Cyrano de Bergerac,
Savinien (1619–55)
Dahl, Roald (1916–90)
Daudet, Alphonse
(1840–97)
Defoe, Daniel (1660–
1731)
de la Rôche, Mazo
(1885–1961)
De Quincey, Thomas
(1785–1859)
Dickens, Charles
(1812–70)
Dinesen, Isak (Karen
Blixen, Baroness
Blixen-Finecke,
1885–1962)

Donleavy, J P
(1926–)
Dos Passos, John
(1896–1970)
Dostoievskii, Feodor
Mikhailovich (1821–
81)
Doyle, Sir Arthur
Conan (1859–1930)
Drabble, Margaret
(1939–)
Dreiser, Theodore
(1871–1945)
Du Maurier, Daphne
(1907–89)
Du Maurier, George
(1834–96)
Duras, Marguerite
(1914–)
Durrell, Lawrence
George (1912–90)
Eco, Umberto
(1932–)
Edgeworth, Maria
(1767–1849)
Ehrenberg, Iliya
Grigorievich (1891–
1967)
Eichendorff, Josef,
Freiherr von (1788–
1857)
Eliot, George (Mary
Ann Evans, 1819–80)
Elyot, Sir Thomas (c.
1490–1546)
Evelyn, John (1620–
1706)
Faulkner, William
(1897–1962)
Feuchtwanger, Lion
(1884–1958)
Fielding, Henry (1707–
54)
Firbank, Ronald
(1886–1926)
Fitzgerald, F Scott
(1896–1940)
Flaubert, Gustave
(1821–80)
Fleming, Ian (1908–
64)
Fontane, Theodor
(1819–98)
Ford, Ford Madox
(Ford Hermann Huef-
fer, 1873–1939)
Forester, C S (1899–
1966)
Forster, E M (1879–
1970)
Fouqué, Friedrich
Heinrich Karl, Baron
de la Motte (1777–
1843)
Fowles, John
(1926–)
France, Anatole
(Jacques Anatole
François Thibault,
1844–1924)
Frisch, Max (1911–91)
Fuller, Roy (1912–91)

Roth, Philip (1933–)
Runyon, Damon (1884–1946)
Rushdie, Salman (1947–)
Sade, Donatien Alphonse François, Marquis de (1740–1814)
Sagan, Françoise (Françoise Quoirez, 1935–)
Saint-Exupéry, Antoine de (1900–44)
Saki (H H Munro, 1870–1916)
Salinger, J D (1919–)
Sand, George (Aurore Dupin, Baronne Dudevant, 1804–76)
Saroyan, William (1908–81)
Sarraute, Nathalie (1902–)
Sartre, Jean-Paul (1905–80)
Sayers, Dorothy L (1893–1957)
Sciascia, Leonardo (1921–89)
Scott, Paul (1920–78)
Scott, Sir Walter (1771–1832)
Sholokhov, Mikhail (1905–84)
Shute, Nevil (Nevil Shute Norway, 1899–1960)
Sillitoe, Alan (1928–)
Simenon, Georges (1903–89)
Simonov, Konstantin (1915–79)

Sinclair, Upton (1878–1968)
Singer, Isaac Bashevis (1904–91)
Sitwell, Edith (1887–1964)
Smollett, Tobias (1721–71)
Solzhenitsyn, Aleksandr (1918–)
Spark, Muriel (1918–)
Staël, Anne Louise Germaine Necker, Madame de (1766–1817)
Steele, Sir Richard (1672–1729)
Stein, Gertrude (1874–1946)
Steinbeck, John (1902–68)
Stendhal (Henri Beyle, 1783–1842)
Sterne, Laurence (1713–68)
Stevenson, Robert Louis (1850–94)
Stoker, Bram (Abraham S, 1847–1912)
Storey, David (1933–)
Stowe, Harriet Beecher (1811–96)
Strindberg, August (1849–1912)
Svevo, Italo (Ettore Schmitz, 1861–1928)
Swift, Jonathan (1667–1745)
Thackeray, William Makepeace (1811–63)
Thurber, James (1894–1961)

Tolkien, J R R (1892–1973)
Tolstaia, Tat'iana (1951–)
Tolstoy, Leo, Count (1828–1910)
Traherne, Thomas (c. 1637–74)
Trollope, Anthony (1815–82)
Turgenev, Ivan (1818–83)
Twain, Mark (Samuel Langhorne Clemens, 1835–1910)
Updike, John (1932–)
Van der Post, Sir Laurens (1906–)
Vargas Llosa, Mario (1936–)
Verne, Jules (1828–1905)
Vidal, Gore (1925–)
Vittorini, Elio (1908–66)
Voltaire (François-Marie Arouet, 1694–1778)
Vonnegut, Kurt (1922–)
Wain, John (1925–)
Wallace, Edgar (1875–1932)
Walpole, Sir Hugh (1884–1941)
Walton, Izaak (1593–1683)
Ward, Artemus (Charles Farrar Browne, 1834–67)
Waugh, Evelyn (1903–66)

Webb, Mary (1881–1927)
Weiss, Peter (1916–82)
Wells, H G (1866–1946)
West, Dame Rebecca (Cicely Isabel Fairfield, 1892–1983)
West, Nathanael (Nathan Weinstein, 1903–40)
Wharton, Edith (1862–1937)
White, Patrick (1912–90)
White, T H (1906–64)
Wilder, Thornton (1897–1975)
Williamson, Henry (1895–1977)
Wilson, Sir Angus (1913–91)
Wilson, Colin (1931–)
Wodehouse, Sir P G (1881–1975)
Wolf, Christa (1929–)
Wolfe, Thomas (1900–38)
Woolf, Virginia (1882–1941)
Wright, Richard (1908–60)
Yonge, Charlotte (1823–1901)
Zola, Émile (1840–1902)

Poets

Alberti, Rafael (1902–)
Alcaeus (6th century BC)
Anacreon (6th century BC)
Aneirin (6th century AD)
Angelou, Maya (Marguerite Johnson, 1928–)
Apollinaire, Guillaume (Wilhelm de Kostrowitzky, 1880–1918)
Apollonius of Rhodes (3rd century BC)
Aragon, Louis (1897–1982)
Ariosto, Ludovico (1474–1533)
Auden, W H (1907–73)
Baraka, Imamu Amiri (1934–)
Baudelaire, Charles (1821–67)
Beddoes, Thomas Lovell (1803–49)

Belloc, Hilaire (1870–1953)
Benét, Stephen Vincent (1898–1943)
Benoit de Sainte-Maure (12th century AD)
Betjeman, Sir John (1906–84)
Blok, Aleksandr Aleksandrovich (1880–1921)
Blunden, Edmund Charles (1896–1974)
Boccaccio, Giovanni (1313–75)
Boiardo, Matteo Maria, Conte di Scandiano (1441–94)
Breton, André (1896–1966)
Bridges, Robert Seymour (1844–1930)
Brodsky, Josef (1940–)
Brooke, Rupert (1887–1915)
Browning, Robert (1812–89)

Bryant, William Cullen (1794–1878)
Bunin, Ivan Alekseevich (1879–1953)
Bürger, Gottfried (1747–94)
Burns, Robert (1759–96)
Butler, Samuel (1612–80)
Byron, George Gordon, Lord (1788–1824)
Caedmon (d. c. 680 AD)
Callimachus (c. 305–c. 240 BC)
Camões, Luís de (c. 1524–80)
Campbell, Roy (1901–57)
Campbell, Thomas (1777–1844)
Carew, Thomas (c. 1595–1640)
Castilho, Antonio Feliciano de (1800–75)

Catullus, Valerius (c. 84–c. 54 BC)
Cavafy, Constantine (C Kavafis, 1863–1933)
Cavalcanti, Guido (c. 1255–1300)
Celan, Paul (Paul Antschel, 1920–70)
Chatterton, Thomas (1752–70)
Chaucer, Geoffrey (c. 1342–1400)
Chénier, André de (1762–94)
Chrétien de Troyes (12th century AD)
Clare, John (1793–1864)
Claudian (c. 370–404 AD)
Cocteau, Jean (1889–1963)
Coleridge, Samuel Taylor (1772–1834)
Colum, Padraic (Patrick Colm, 1881–1972)
Cowley, Abraham (1618–67)

Cowper, William
(1731–1800)
Crabbe, George
(1754–1832)
Crashaw, Richard (c.
1613–49)
Creeley, Robert
(1926–)
cummings, e e (1894–
1962)
Cynewulf (early 9th
century AD)
Dafydd ap Gwilym (c.
1320–c. 1380)
D'Annunzio, Gabriele
(1863–1938)
Dante Alighieri (1265–
1321)
Davies, W H (1871–
1940)
Day Lewis, C (1904–
72)
de la Mare, Walter
(1873–1956)
Dickinson, Emily
(1830–86)
Donne, John (1572–
1631)
Doolittle, Hilda (1886–
1961)
Dowson, Ernest
(1867–1900)
Drayton, Michael
(1563–1631)
Dryden, John (1631–
1700)
Dunbar, William (c.
1460–c. 1530)
Eliot, T S (1888–1965)
Elytis, Odysseus
(1912–)
Emerson, Ralph
Waldo (1803–82)
Empson, Sir William
(1906–84)
Ennius, Quintus (238–
169 BC)
Enzensberger, Hans
Magnus (1929–)
Ercilla, Alonso de
(1533–94)
Firdausi (Abul Qasim
Mansur, c. 935–c.
1020)
Fitzgerald, Edward
(1809–83)
Flecker, James Elroy
(1884–1915)
Foscolo, Ugo (1778–
1827)
Freneau, Philip (1752–
1832)
Froissart, Jean (1337–
c. 1400)
Frost, Robert Lee
(1874–1963)
Fuller, Roy (1912–91)
García Lorca, Federico
(1898–1936)
Gautier, Théophile
(1811–72)
Gay, John (1685–1732)
Gibran, Khalil (1883–
1931)

Ginsberg, Allen
(1926–)
Goethe, Johann Wolf-
gang von (1749–
1832)
Góngora y Argote,
Luis de (1561–1627)
Gower, John (c. 1330–
1408)
Goytisolo, Juan
(1931–)
Graves, Robert (1895–
1985)
Gray, Thomas (1716–
71)
Haavikko, Paavo
(1931–)
Hardy, Thomas (1840–
1928)
Harrison, Tony
(1937–)
Heaney, Seamus
(1939–)
Heine, Heinrich (1797–
1856)
Henryson, Robert
(15th century)
Herbert, George
(1593–1633)
Herbert, Zbigniew
(1924–)
Herrick, Robert (1591–
1674)
Hesiod (8th century BC)
Hill, Geoffrey
(1932–)
Holmes, Oliver Wen-
dell (1809–94)
Homer (8th century BC)
Hood, Thomas (1799–
1845)
Hopkins, Gerard
Manley (1844–89)
Horace (Quintus
Horatius Flaccus,
65–68 BC)
Housman, A E (1859–
1936)
Hughes, Ted
(1930–)
Hugo, Victor (1802–
85)
Hunt, Leigh (1784–
1859)
Iqbal, Sir Mohammed
(c. 1875–1938)
Jeffers, Robinson
(1887–1962)
Jonson, Ben (1572–
1637)
Kalidasa (5th century)
Kavanagh, Patrick
(1905–67)
Keats, John (1795–
1821)
Kipling, Rudyard
(1865–1936)
La Fontaine, Jean de
(1621–95)
Laforgue, Jules (1860–
87)
Lamartine, Alphonse
de (1790–1869)
Landor, Walter Sav-
age (1775–1864)

Langland, William (c.
1330–c. 1400)
Lanier, Sidney (1842–
81)
Larkin, Philip (1922–
85)
Lawrence, D H (1885–
1930)
Leconte de Lisle,
Charles Marie René
(1818–94)
Leopardi, Giacomo
(1798–1837)
Lermontov, Mikhail
(1814–41)
Lindsay, Vachel
(1879–1931)
Longfellow, Henry
Wadsworth (1807–
82)
Lovelace, Richard
(1618–57)
Lowell, Amy (1874–
1925)
Lowell, James Russell
(1819–91)
Lowell, Robert (1917–
77)
Lucan (Marcus An-
naeus Lucanus, 39–
65 AD)
Lucretius (Titus Lucre-
tius Carus, c. 95–c.
55 BC)
Macdiarmid, Hugh
(Christopher Murray
Grieve, 1892–1978)
MacNeice, Louis
(1907–63)
Maeterlinck, Maurice
(1862–1949)
Malherbe, François de
(1555–1628)
Mallarmé, Stéphane
(1842–98)
Manzoni, Alessandro
(1785–1873)
Martial (Marcus
Valerius Martialis,
c. 40–c. 104 AD)
Marvell, Andrew
(1621–78)
Masefield, John
(1878–1967)
Masters, Edgar Lee
(1868–1950)
Matsuo Basho
(Matsuo Munefusa,
1644–94)
Mayakovskii, Vladimir
(1893–1930)
Meredith, George
(1828–1909)
Millay, Edna St Vin-
cent (1892–1950)
Milosz, Czeslaw
(1911–)
Milton, John (1608–
74)
Montale, Eugenio
(1896–1981)
Moore, Marianne
(1887–1972)
Moore, Thomas
(1779–1852)

Muir, Edwin (1887–
1959)
Musset, Alfred de
(1810–57)
Nash, Ogden (1902–
71)
Neruda, Pablo (Neftalí
Ricardo Reyes,
1904–73)
Omar Khayyam (c.
1048–c. 1122)
Ovid (Publius Ovidius
Naso, 43 BC–17 AD)
Owen, Wilfred (1893–
1918)
Pasternak, Boris
(1890–1960)
Pavese, Cesare (1908–
50)
Péguy, Charles (1873–
1914)
Petrarch (Francesco
Petrarca, 1304–74)
Pindar (518–438 BC)
Plath, Sylvia (1932–
63)
Pope, Alexander
(1688–1744)
Pound, Ezra (1885–
1972)
Pushkin, Aleksandr
(1799–1837)
Ransom, John Crowe
(1888–1974)
Ratushinskaya, Irina
(1954–)
Read, Sir Herbert
(1893–1968)
Rilke, Rainer Maria
(1875–1926)
Rimbaud, Arthur
(1854–91)
Rochester, John
Wilmot, 2nd Earl of
(1647–80)
Romains, Jules (Louis
Farigoule, 1885–
1972)
Sandburg, Carl (1878–
1967)
Sappho (c. 612–c.
580 BC)
Sassoon, Siegfried
(1886–1967)
Schiller, Friedrich
(1759–1805)
Shelley, Percy Bysshe
(1792–1822)
Shenstone, William
(1714–63)
Sidney, Sir Philip
(1554–86)
Skelton, John (c.
1460–1529)
Smart, Christopher
(1722–71)
Smith, Stevie (Flor-
ence Margaret S,
1902–71)
Southey, Robert
(1774–1843)
Spender, Stephen
(1909–)
Spenser, Edmund (c.
1552–99)

Stevens, Wallace
(1879–1955)
Suckling, Sir John
(1609–42)
Surrey, Henry Howard,
Earl of (1517–47)
Swift, Jonathan (1667–
1745)
Swinburne, Algernon
Charles (1837–1909)
Tagore, Rabindranath
(1861–1941)
Taliesin (6th century AD)
Tannhäuser (c. 1200–
c. 1270)
Tasso, Torquato
(1544–95)
Tate, Allen (1899–
1979)
Tennyson, Alfred,
Lord (1809–92)

Theocritus (c. 310–
250 BC)
Thespis (6th century
BC)
Thomas, Dylan (1914–
53)
Thomas, Edward
(1878–1917)
Thomas, R S (1913–)
Ungaretti, Giuseppe
(1888–1970)
Updike, John
(1932–)
Valéry, Paul (1871–
1945)
Varro, Marcus Ter-
entius (116–27 BC)
Vaughan, Henry (c.
1622–95)
Verlaine, Paul (1844–
96)

Vigny, Alfred de
(1797–1863)
Villon, François (1431–
c. 1463)
Virgil (Publius Vergi-
lius Maro, 70–19 BC)
Voznesensky, Andrei
(1933–)
Walcott, Derek Alton
(1930–)
Waller, Edmund
(1606–87)
Whitman, Walt (1819–
92)
Wilde, Oscar (O
Fingal O'Flahertie
Wills W, 1854–1900)
Williams, William Car-
los (1883–1963)
Wolfe, Charles (1791–
1823)

Wordsworth, William
(1770–1850)
Wotton, Sir Henry
(1568–1639)
Wyatt, Sir Thomas
(1503–42)
Xenophanes (6th cen-
tury BC)
Yeats, William Butler
(1865–1939)
Yesenin, Sergei Al-
eksandrovich (1895–
1925)
Yevtushenko,
Yevgenii (1933–)

Dramatists

Accius, Lucius (170–
c. 85 BC)
Adamov, Arthur
(1908–70)
Aeschylus (c. 525–
456 BC)
Albee, Edward
(1928–)
Anouilh, Jean (1910–
87)
Arden, John (1930–)
Aristophanes (c. 450–
c. 385 BC)
Arrabal, Fernando
(1932–)
Ayckbourn, Alan
(1939–)
Baraka, Imamu Amiri
(1934–)
Barker, Howard
(1946–)
Barrie, Sir James
(1860–1937)
Beaumarchais, Pierre-
Augustin Caron de
(1732–99)
Beaumont, Francis
(1584–1616)
Beckett, Samuel
(1906–92)
Behan, Brendan
(1923–64)
Bennett, Alan
(1934–)
Billetdoux, François
(1927–91)
Bolt, Robert Oxton
(1924–)
Bond, Edward (1934–)
Brecht, Bertolt (1898–
1956)
Brenton, Howard
(1942–)
Büchner, Georg (1813–
37)
Calderón de la Barca,
Pedro (1600–81)

Chekhov, Anton
Pavlovich (1860–
1904)
Churchill, Caryl
(1938–)
Claudel, Paul (1868–
1955)
Congreve, William
(1670–1729)
Corneille, Pierre
(1606–84)
Cyrano de Bergerac,
Savinien (1619–55)
D'Annunzio, Gabriele
(1863–1938)
Davenant, Sir William
(1606–68)
Dekker, Thomas (c.
1572–1632)
Dürrenmatt, Friedrich
(1921–90)
Edgar, David
(1948–)
Eliot, T S (1888–1965)
Etherege, Sir George
(c. 1635–c. 1692)
Eupolis (late 5th cen-
tury BC)
Euripides (c. 480–406
BC)
Farquhar, George
(1678–1707)
Feuchtwanger, Lion
(1884–1958)
Feydeau, Georges
(1862–1921)
Fletcher, John (1579–
1625)
Fo, Dario (1926–)
Ford, John (1586–c.
1640)
Fouqué, Friedrich
Heinrich Karl, Baron
de la Motte (1777–
1843)
Frayn, Michael
(1933–)
Friel, Brian (1929–)

Fry, Christopher (C
Harris, 1907–)
Fugard, Athol
(1932–)
García Lorca, Federico
(1898–1936)
Gay, John (1685–1732)
Genet, Jean (1910–86)
Gilbert, Sir William
Schwenk (1836–
1911)
Giraudoux, Jean
(1882–1944)
Gogol, Nikolai Vas-
ilievich (1809–52)
Goldoni, Carlo (1707–
93)
Griffiths, Trevor
(1935–)
Handke, Peter
(1942–)
Hare, David (1947–)
Hart, Moss (1904–61)
Hauptmann, Gerhart
(1862–1946)
Havel, Václav
(1936–)
Hellman, Lillian
(1905–84)
Hochhuth, Rolf
(1931–)
Ibsen, Henrik (1828–
1906)
Ionesco, Eugène
(1912–)
Jarry, Alfred (1873–
1907)
Jonson, Ben (1572–
1637)
Kaufman, George S
(1889–1961)
Kyd, Thomas (1558–
94)
Leonov, Leonid
(1899–)
Lyly, John (c. 1554–
1606)
Maeterlinck, Maurice
(1862–1949)

Mamet, David (1947–)
Marivaux, Pierre Car-
let de Chamblain de
(1688–1763)
Marlowe, Christopher
(1564–93)
Massinger, Philip
(1583–1640)
Menander (c. 341–
c. 290 BC)
Mercer, David (1928–
80)
Middleton, Thomas
(1580–1627)
Miller, Arthur
(1915–)
Molière (Jean-Baptiste
Poquelin, 1622–73)
Molnár, Ferenc (1878–
1952)
Montherlant, Henry
de (1896–1972)
Musset, Alfred de
(1810–57)
O'Casey, Sean (1880–
1964)
Odets, Clifford (1906–
63)
O'Neill, Eugene
(1888–1953)
Orton, Joe (1933–67)
Osborne, John
(1929–)
Ostrovskii, Aleksandr
Nikolaevich (1823–
86)
Otway, Thomas
(1652–85)
Philemon (c. 368–
c. 264 BC)
Pinero, Sir Arthur
Wing (1855–1934)
Pinter, Harold
(1930–)
Pirandello, Luigi
(1867–1936)
Plautus, Titus
Maccius (c. 254–
184 BC)

Pushkin, Aleksandr (1799–1837)
Racine, Jean (1639–99)
Rattigan, Sir Terence (1911–77)
Rowe, Nicholas (1674–1718)
Russell, Willy (1947–)
Saroyan, William (1908–81)
Schiller, Friedrich (1759–1805)
Shadwell, Thomas (c. 1642–92)
Shaffer, Peter (1926–)
Shakespeare, William (1564–1616)

Shaw, George Bernard (1856–1950)
Sheridan, Richard Brinsley (1751–1816)
Simon, Marvin Neil (1927–)
Simonov, Konstantin (1915–79)
Sophocles (c. 496–406 BC)
Steele, Sir Richard (1672–1729)
Stoppard, Tom (1937–)
Storey, David (1933–)
Strindberg, August (1849–1912)

Synge, John Millington (1871–1909)
Terence (Publius Terentius Afer, c. 185–c. 159 BC)
Tourneur, Cyril (c. 1575–1626)
Travers, Ben (1886–1980)
Vigny, Alfred de (1797–1863)
Walcott, Derek Alton (1930–)
Webster, John (c. 1580–c. 1625)
Wedekind, Frank (1864–1918)

Wesker, Arnold (1932–)
Wilde, Oscar (O Fingal O'Flahertie Wills W, 1854–1900)
Wilder, Thornton (1897–1975)
Williams, Tennessee (1911–83)
Wycherley, William (1640–1716)
Yeats, William Butler (1865–1939)

quantity, metrical unit, foot, dipody, iamb, spondee, trochee, dactyl, anaepest (or anapest), pyrrhic, tribrach, amphibrach, amphimacer, cretic, ionic, paeon, choriamb, dimeter, trimeter, tetrameter, pentameter, hexameter, heptameter, octameter, iambic pentameter, elegiac pentameter, Alexandrine, dactylic hexameter, heroic couplet, elegiac couplet, elegiac distich, distich, sprung rhythm, counterpoint, anacrusis, catalexis, caesura, diaeresis

10 **verse form**, fixed form, ballade, *chant royal* (Fr), rondeau, sestina, triolet, vilanelle, sonnet, terza rima, ottava rima, rhyme royal, Chaucerian stanza, Spenserian stanza, Burns stanza, Sapphics, Anacreontics, Alcaics, alliterative verse, free verse, blank verse

11 **rhyme**, masculine rhyme, feminine rhyme, single rhyme, double rhyme, end rhyme, tail rhyme, eye rhyme, broken rhyme, half rhyme, near rhyme, pararhyme, consonance, internal rhyme, initial rhyme, rhyme scheme, blank verse, unrhymed poetry

12 **poetic language**, poetic diction, poeticism, archaicism, decorum, the grand style, aureate diction, alliteration, repetition, anaphora, epistrophe, assonance, consonance, onomatopoeia, euphony, elision, inversion, chiasmus, periphrasis, figurative language, imagery, conceit, trope, metaphor, simile, Homeric simile, epic simile, Homeric epithet, compound epithet, transferred epithet, kenning, personification, prosopopoeia, apostrophe, metonymy, synecdoche, antonomasia, paronomasia, parallelism, synaesthesia, pathetic fallacy, poetic licence, pseudostatement, irony, pun

13 **poetic genius**, inspiration, afflatus, poesy, creative imagination, the Muse(s), Apollo, Parnassus, Helicon, Hippocrene, Castilian Spring, Pierian Spring, Pegasus

14 **author**, writer, fiction writer, storyteller, novelist, short-story writer, crime writer, fabler, fabulist, mythologist, allegorist, romancer, novelettist, diarist, chronicler, historian, historiographer, biographer, autobiographer, an-

nalist, poet, poetess, major poet, minor poet, poet laureate, minnesinger, Meistersinger, rhapsodist (or rhapsode), dithyrambist, elegist, satirist, sonneteer, symbolist, lyric poet, epic poet, pastoral poet, metaphysical poet, lake poet, romantic poet, modern poet, modernist, beat poet, rap poet, librettist, lyricist, verslibrist, rhymer, rhymester, versemonger, versifier, versesmith, versemaker, poetaster, ballad monger, ballad maker, balladeer, bard, minstrel, jongleur, trouvère, troubadour, scop, skald, comic poet, tragic poet, dramatic poet, playwright, dramatist, dramaturge, screenwriter, wordsmith (Inf), penman (Inf), scribe (Inf)

15 **literary person**, woman of letters, man of letters, belletrist, literary scholar, educator, student of literature, literary critic, Leavisite, New Critic, structuralist, post-structuralist, deconstructor, book reviewer, cultural commentator, the clerisy

ADJECTIVES

16 **literary**, written, humanistic, belletristic, polished, learned, lettered, formal, scholarly, erudite, well-read, critical, interpretive, classical, romantic, surrealistic, realistic, futuristic, decadent, naturalistic, metaphysical

17 **fictional**, fictionalized, mythical, mythological, legendary, fabulous, allegorical, romantic

18 **descriptive**, well-drawn, graphic, depictive, expressive

19 **narrative**, storified, biographical, autobiographical, historiographical, poetic, poetical, Parnassian, Homeric, Dantesque, Miltonic, Pindaric, Sapphic, Horatian, Virgilian, Augustan, Shakespearean, Petrarchan, Spenserian, dramatic, epic, heroic, mock-heroic, elegiac, lyrical, pastoral, bucolic, idyllic, rhapsodic, tragic, comic, doggerel

20 **metrical**, rhythmical, measured, accentual, scanning, scanned, iambic, octosyllabic, hendecasyllabic, trochaic, spondaic, dactylic, anapaestic, catalectic, rhyming, assonant, alliterative, onomatopoeic, dimetic

VERBS

21 **write**, compose, dramatize, make into a play, make into a novel, poetize, versify, compose, poetry, elegize, rhyme, put into verse, compose an epic, write a lyric, write a sonnet, prosify, prose, describe, portray, represent, express, delineate, characterize

ADVERBS

22 **poetically**, lyrically, rhythmically, metrically

23 **descriptively**, expressively, vividly, dramatically

▶ *51 Performing Arts*

49   Music

Nothing is capable of being well set to music that is not nonsense. Joseph Addison.

The English may not like music – but they absolutely love the noise it makes. Thomas Beecham.

Music has charms to soothe a savage breast. William Congreve.

Strange how potent cheap music is. Noël Coward.

Music is the arithmetic of sounds as optics is the geometry of light. Claude Debussy.

There's sure no passion in the human soul,/ But finds its food in music. George Lillo.

If music be the food of love, play on,/ Give me excess of it, that, surfeiting,/ The appetite may sicken and so die. William Shakespeare.

Music that gentlier on the spirit lies,/ Than tir'd eyelids upon tir'd eyes. Alfred, Lord Tennyson.

NOUNS

1 **music**, harmony, melody, musicality, tunefulness, melodiousness, musicalness, musicianship

2 **music making**, playing, performance, improvisation, orchestration, instrumentation, composing, composition, jamming (Sl)

3 **classical music**, romantic music, impressionist music, twelve-tone (*or* dodecaphonic) music, musique concrète, minimalist music, chamber music, contrapuntal music, choral music, operatic music, organ music, modern music, symphonic music, orchestral music, romantic music, madrigal, sonata

4 **opera**, grand opera, opera seria, opera semiseria, opera buffa, opéra bouffe, opéra comique, operetta, music drama, pasticcio, singspiel, aria, recitative, leitmotiv, Sprechgesang, bel canto, sinfonia, overture, prelude, intermezzo, surtitle, libretto

5 **sacred music**, church music, liturgical music, hymn, hymn tune, psalm, chorale, anthem, motet, oratorio, passion, mass, requiem mass, requiem, offertory, cantata, church parable, doxology, introit, canticle, recessional, spiritual, negro spiritual, gospel music, gospel, hymnody, psalmody, hymnology

6 **campanology**, bell ringing, change ringing, peal, change, Bob Major, Grandsire Triple, handbell, carillon

7 **dance music**, ballet music, ballroom music, modern dance music, disco, euro-disco

8 **jazz**, mainstream jazz, progressive jazz, avant-garde jazz, modern jazz, third-stream jazz, cool jazz, acid jazz, fusion, blue note, blues, traditional jazz, trad, Dixieland, syncopation, ragtime, swing, jive, doowop, bebop, Afro-Cuban, bop, boogie-woogie

9 **popular music**, pop music, pop, light music, easy-listening, popular song, pop song, hit, hit tune, charts, top twenty, Karaoke, torch song, rock, rock 'n' roll, hard rock, soft rock, acid rock, folk rock, country rock, rhythm 'n' blues (R and B), AOR (adult-orientated rock), industrial rock (*or* dance), hardcore, death metal, heavy metal, thrash metal, punk rock, New Wave, indie, ska, rap, ragamuffin, ragga, reggae, soul, jazz-funk, fusion, electro, hip-hop, grebo, grunge, garage, house, acid house, techno

10 **world music**, soul, ska, reggae, bhangra, ethnic music, kwela, mbaqanga, township jive, township jazz, marabi, son, salsa, merengue, zouk, qawwali, macumba, marabenta, soca, calypso

11 **folk music**, folksong, folk ballad, folk rock, border ballad, country music, hillbilly music, country and western, bluegrass, skiffle

12 **Tin Pan Alley**, Nashville, Broadway

13 **melody**, tune, air, aria, strain, song, line, descant, harmony, concord, condordance, concert, attunement, chime, diapason, synchronization, unison, euphony, homophony, monody, resolution, cadence, perfect cadence, two- (*or* three-, *or* four-) part harmony, theme, subject, coda

▶ *433 Melody*

14 **harmonics**, melodics, rhythmics, music theory, musicology, musicography

15 **composition**, opus, piece, arrangement, adaptation, setting, transcription, accompaniment

16 **musical note**, note, pitch, keys, keyboard, ivories (Sl), manual, pedal point, black notes, white notes, sharp, flat, double flat, double sharp, accidental, natural, tone, semitone, keynote, fundamental note, partial, overtone, harmonic, tonic, supertonic, mediant, subdominant, dominant, submediant, subtonic, leading note, interval, major (*or* minor) interval, second, third, fourth, fifth, sixth, seventh, octave, ninth, diatessaron, diapason, gamut, scale, chord, common chord, broken chord,

Musical Instruments

accordion
acoustic guitar
adenkum (stamping tube)
aeolian harp
alboka (hornpipe)
alghaita (shawm)
alphorn (or alpenhorn)
altohorn
angel chimes
angle harp
anklung (rattle)
arghul (clarinet)
arpanetta (zither)
atumpan (kettledrum)
auloi (shawm)
autoharp
bagana (lyre)
bagpipe
balalaika (lute)
banana drum
bandoura (lute)
bandurria (lute)
banjo
banjolele
barrel drum
barrel organ
baryton (viol)
bassanello (double reed)
bass drum
bass guitar
basset horn
bass horn
bassonore (bassoon)
bassoon
bata (drum)
bell cittern
bells
bhaya (kettledrum)
bible regal (organ)
bicitrabin (vina)
bin (vina)
biniou (bagpipe)
bird scarer
bivalve bell
biwa (lute)
bladder pipe
board zither
bodhran (drum)
bombarde (shawm)
bombardon (tuba)
bongo drums
bonnang (gong)
bouzouki (lute)
bow harp
bowl lyre
box lyre
buccina (trumpet)
bugle
buisine (trumpet)
bullroarer
bumbass
bumpa (clarinet)
buzz disk
calliope (mechanical organ)
carillon
carnyx (trumpet)
castanets
celeste
cello
chakay (zither)
chalumeau (clarinet)

chang (dulcimer)
changko (drum)
cha pei (lute)
chengcheng (cymbals)
chime
chime bar
ch'in (zither)
Chinese wood block
chitarra battente (guitar)
chitarrone (lute)
cimbalom (dulcimer)
cipactli (flute)
cittern
clapper bell
clappers
clarinet
clarinet d'amore
classical guitar
clave
clavichord
clavicor (brass family)
clavicytherium (harpsichord)
claviorgan
claw bell
cobza (lute)
cocktail drums
cog rattle
colascione (lute)
componium (mechanical organ)
contrabass (double bass)
contrabassoon
cor anglais
cornemuse (bagpipe)
cornet
cornett
cornopean (brass family)
cornu (trumpet)
courtaut (double reed)
cowbell
crecelle (cog rattle)
crook horn
crotals (percussion)
crumhorn (double reed)
crwth (lyre)
curtal (double reed)
cylindrical drums
cymbals
cythara anglica (harp)
da-daiko (drum)
daibyoshi (drum)
darabukke (drum)
darbuk (drum)
dauli (drum)
deutsche schalmei (double reed)
dhola (drum)
didgeridoo (trumpet)
diplice (clarinet)
diplo-kithara (zither)
djunadjan (zither)
dobro (guitar)
double bass
double bassoon (contrabassoon)
drum
dudelsack (bagpipes)
dugdugi (drum)
dulcimer
dvojachka (flute)
dvoynice (flute)

electric guitar
enzenze (zither)
erh-hu (fiddle)
euphonium (brass family)
fandur (fiddle)
fiddle
fidel (fiddle)
fidla (zither)
fife
fipple flute
fithele (fiddle)
flageolet (flute)
flexatone (percussion)
flugelhorn
flute
french horn
fujara (flute)
fuye (flute)
gadulka (fiddle)
gaita (bagpipe)
gajdy (bagpipe)
gambang kaya (xylophone)
gansa gambang (metallophone)
gansa jongkok (metallophone)
geigenwerk (mechanical harpsichord)
gekkin (lute)
gender (metallophone)
gittern
gling-bu (flute)
glockenspiel (metallophone)
gong
gong ageng
gong chimes
gong drum
gongue (percussion)
grand piano
guitar
guitar-banjo
guitar-violin
gusle (fiddle)
hackbrett (dulcimer)
handbell
hand horn
handle drum
hand trumpet
hardangerfele (fiddle)
harmonica
harmonium
harp
harpsichord
hawkbell
heckelclarina (clarinet)
heckelphone (oboe)
helicon
hi-hat cymbals
horn
hu ch'in (fiddle)
hula ipu (percussion)
hummel (zither)
hurdy-gurdy
huruk (drum)
hydraulis (organ)
ingungu (drum)
isigubu (drum)
jew's harp
jingling Johnny
kachapi (zither)
kakko (drum)

kalungu (talking drum)
kamanje (fiddle)
kantele (zither)
kanteleharpe (lyre)
kanun (qanun)
kayakeum (zither)
kazoo (mirliton)
kelontong (drum)
kemanak (clappers)
kena (quena)
kenong (gong)
kerar (lyre)
kettledrum
khen (mouth organ)
khumbgwe (flute)
kissar (lyre)
kit (fiddle)
kithara (lyre)
koboro (drum)
ko-kiu (fiddle)
komungo (zither)
könighorn (brass family)
koto (zither)
langleik (zither)
langspil (zither)
lap organ (melodeon)
launeddas (clarinet)
lira (fiddle)
lirica (fiddle)
lirone (fiddle)
lithophone (percussion)
lituus (trumpet)
lontar (clappers)
lur (horn)
lute
lyra (lyre)
lyre
machete (lute)
mandobass (lute)
mandocello (lute)
mandola (lute)
mandolin (lute)
mandolinetto (ukulele)
mandolone (lute)
maracas (percussion)
masenqo (fiddle)
mayuri (lute)
mbila (xylophone)
mellophone (horn)
melodeon
melodica
metallophone (percussion)
migyaun (zither)
mirliton (kazoo)
mokugyo (drum)
Moog synthesizer (Tm)
morin-chur (fiddle)
moropi (drum)
moshupiane (drum)
mouth organ
mridanga (drum)
murumbu (drum)
musette (bagpipe)
musette (shawm)
mu yü (drum)
mvet (zither)
nakers (drums)
naqara (drums)
ngoma (drum)
nguru (flute)
ntenga (drum)
nyckelharpa

oboe
obukano (lyre)
ocarina (flute)
octavin (wind)
o-daiko (drum)
okedo (drum)
oliphant (horn)
ombgwe (flute)
ophicleide (brass family)
organ
orpharion (cittern)
orphica (piano)
o-tsuzumi (drum)
ottavino (virginal)
oud (ud)
outi (lute)
p'ai hsiao (panpipe)
paimensarvi (horn)
p'ai pan (clappers)
pandora (cittern)
panhuéhuetl (drum)
panpipe
peacock sitar (lute)
penorcon (cittern)
pianino
piano
pianoforte
pianola
pibcorn (hornpipe)
piccolo
picco pipe (flute)
pien ch'ing (lithophone)
piffaro (shawm)
pi nai (shawm)
p'i p'a (lute)
pipe
pochette (kit)
pommer (shawm)
psaltery (zither)
pu-ilu (clappers)
putorino (trumpet)
qanun (zither)
quena (flute)
quinton (viol)
racket (double reed)
ramkie (lute)
ranasringa (horn)
raspa (scraper)
rattle
rauschpfeife (double reed)
rebab (fiddle)
rebec (fiddle)

recorder
reshoto (drum)
rinchik (cymbals)
rkan-dung (trumpet)
rkan-ling (horn)
rommelpot (drum)
ronéat-ek (xylophone)
rote (lyre)
ruan (lute)
sackbut (trombone)
salpinx (trumpet)
samisen (lute)
san hsien (lute)
sansa
santir (dulcimer)
santoor (dulcimer)
sarangi (fiddle)
sarinda (fiddle)
saron demong (metallophone)
saron (metallophone)
sarrusophone (brass)
savernake horn
saw-thai (fiddle)
saxhorn
saxophone
saxotromba
saxtuba
saz (lute)
schrillpfeife (flute)
serpent
shaing (horn)
shaker
shakuhachi (flute)
shanai (shawm)
shawm
sheng (mouth organ)
shield (percussion)
shiwaya (flute)
shô (mouth organ)
shofar (horn)
shoulder harp
side drum
sistrum (rattle)
sitar (lute)
sleigh bells
slide trombone
slit drum
sona (shawm)
sonajero (rattle)
sopile (shawm)
sordine (kit)
sordone (double reed)
sousaphone
spagane (clappers)

spike fiddle
spinet
spitzharfe (zither)
spoons (clappers)
sralay (shawm)
sringara (fiddle)
stock-and-horn (hornpipe)
strumento di porco (zither)
stylophone
surbahar (lute)
surnaj (shawm)
switch (percussion)
symphonium (mouth organ)
synthesizer
syrinx (panpipe)
tabla (drum)
tabor (drum)
taiko (drum)
talambas (drum)
tallharpa (lyre)
tam âm la (gong)
tambourine
tambura (lute)
tam-tam (gong)
tar (drum; lute)
tarabuka (drum)
tarogato (clarinet; shawm)
teponaztli (drum)
terbang (drum)
theorbo (lute)
theorbo-lute
thumb piano (jew's harp)
tibia (shawm)
tiktiri (clarinet)
timbales (drum)
timpani
tin whistle
tiple (shawm)
tippoo's tiger (organ)
ti-tzu (flute)
tlapanhuéhuetl (drum)
tlapiztali (flute)
tom-tom (drum)
totombito (zither)
triangle
triccaballacca (clappers)
tro-khmer (fiddle)
trombone
tro-u (fiddle)

trumpet
tsuri daiko (drum)
tsuzumi (drum)
tuba
tuba-dupré
tubular bells
tudum (drum)
tumyr (drum)
tupan (drum)
turkish crescent (jingling johnny)
txistu (flute)
tympani
uchiwa daiko (drum)
ud (lute)
ujusini (flute)
ukulele (or uke)
urua (clarinet)
uti (lute)
valiha (zither)
vibraphone
vielle (fiddle)
vihuela (guitar)
vina (stringed instrument related to sitar)
viol
viola
viola bastarda (viol)
viola da gamba (viol)
viola d'amore (viol)
violetta (viol)
violin
violoncello
violone (viol)
virginal
whip (percussion)
whistle
whistle flute
wood block
Wurlitzer
xylophone
xylorimba (xylophone)
yangchin (dulcimer)
yangum (dulcimer)
yü (scraper)
yueh ch'in (lute)
yun lo (gong)
yun ngao (gong)
zampogna (bagpipe)
zither
zobo (mirliton)
zummara (clarinet)
zurla (shawm)
zurna (shawm)

Musical Terms

a battuta – return to strict time
accelerando – accelerating
adagietto – quite slow
adagio – slow
ad lib – at will
affettuoso – tender
affrettando – hurrying
agitato – agitated; rapid tempo
al fine – to the end
alla caccia – in hunting style
alla cappella – in church style

allargando – broadening; more dignified
allegretto – quite lively, brisk
allegro – lively, brisk
al segno – as far as the sign
amoroso – loving, emotional
animato – spirited
a piacere – as you please
assai – very
attacca – attack; continue without a pause

bewegt – agitated
bis – repeat
bisbigliando – whispering
brillant – brilliant
buffo – comic
calando – ebbing; lessening of tempo
cantabile – in a singing fashion
cantilena – lyrical, flowing
chiuso – stopped (of a note); closed
coda – final part of a movement

codetta – small coda; to conclude a passage
col canto (or colla voce) – accompaniment to follow solo line
col legno – to strike strings with stick of the bow
con brio – with vigour
con fuoco – fiery; vigorous
da capo – from the beginning
dal segno – from the sign

dehors – outside; prominent
dim – becoming softer
diminuendo – becoming softer
divisi – divided
dolce – sweet
dolente – sorrowful
doppio – double
estinto – extremely softly, almost without tone
f – loud
facile – easy, fluent
ff - very loud
fioritura – decoration of a melody
forte – loud
fortissimo – very loud
giocoso – merry; playful
glissando – sliding scale played on instrument (or sung)
in modo di – in the manner of
largo – very slow
legato – bound, tied (of notes), smoothly
leggeramente – lightly
lento – slowly
maestoso – majestic
marcato – accented
marcia – march
meno mosso – slower pace

mesto – sad, mournful
mezza voce – at half power
mezzo – half
mezzoforte – half loud
mf – half loud
minacciando – menacing
moderato – moderately
molto – very much
morbido – soft, delicate
mosso – moving, fast
moto – motion
niente – nothing
nobile – noble
nobilmente – nobly
obbligato – not to be omitted
p – soft
ped – pedal
perdendosi – dying away gradually
pesante – heavily, firmly
pianissimo – very soft
piano – soft
più – more
piuttosto – somewhat
piz – plucked
pizzicato – plucked
portamento – carrying one note into the next
portando – carrying one note into the next
pp – very soft
quasi – almost, as if

rall – slowing down
rallentando – slowing down
ravvivando – quickening
retenu – held back
rfz – accentuated
rinforzando – accentuated
rit – slowing down, holding back
ritardando – slowing down, holding back
ritenuto – slower, held back
scherzando – joking; playing
schleppend – dragging; deviating from correct speed (Ger)
schnell – fast (Ger)
schneller – faster (Ger)
scorrevole – gliding; fluent
segno – sign
sempre – always, still
senza – without
sf – strongly accented
sfogato – effortless; in a free manner
sforzando – strongly accented
sfz – strongly accented
sin'al fine – up to the end
sino – up to; until

slentando – slowing down
soave – sweet; gentle
sordino – mute
sostenuto – sustained
sotto voce – quiet subdued tone
sourdine – mute (Fr)
staccato – detached
stark – strong, loud (Ger)
stretto – accelerating or intensifying; overlapping of entries of fugue
stringendo – tightening; intensification
subito – immediately
tacet – instrument is silent
tanto – so much
tempo – the speed of a composition
ten – held
tenuto – held
tief – deep; low (Ger)
tutti – all
via – remove mutes
vif – lively (Fr)
vivement – lively (Fr)
zoppa – in syncopated rhythm

primary chord, secondary chord, tertiary chord, triad, tetrachord, arpeggio, grace note, grace, ornament, crush note, appoggiatura, acciaccatura, mordent, turn, shake, trill, tremolo, vibrato, cadenza

17 **notation**, musical note, tonic sol-fa, solfeggio, solfege, solmization, signature, time signature, key signature, clef, treble clef, bass clef, tenor clef, alto clef, bar, measure (US), staff, stave, line, ledger (or leger) line, space, brace, rest, pause, interval, breve, semibreve, minim, crotchet, quarter note (US), quaver, eighth note (US), semiquaver, sixteenth note (US), demisemiquaver, thirty-second note (US), hemidemisemiquaver, sixty-fourth note (US)

18 **written music**, sheet music, score, notation, proportional notation, chart (Sl), paper (Sl)

19 **tempo**, time, beat, rhythm, prosody, measure, pulse, metre, timing, syncopation, counterpoint, counterpoint rhythm, upbeat, downbeat, short note, suspension, suspended note, long note, prolonged note, tempo rubato, rallentando, andante, adagio, metronome, back beat (Sl)

20 **key**, signature, clef, bass clef, C clef, treble clef, modulation, transposition, running changes (Sl), major key, minor key, scale, major scale, gamut, minor scale, harmonic minor scale, diatonic scale, modal scale, chromatic scale, harmonic scale, melodic scale, en-

harmonic scale, twelve-tone scale, series, tone row, mode, Lydian mode, Phrygian mode, Dorian mode, Doric mode, Gregorian mode, mixolydian, Ionian mode, Aeolian mode, Locrian mode, Indian mode, raga

21 **tone**, tonality, register, pitch, concert pitch, high pitch, low pitch, absolute pitch, relative pitch, perfect pitch, high note, stridor, low note, resonance, undertone, overtone, harmonic, upper partial, sustained note, monotone, drone, key centre

22 **phrase**, flourish, sennet, tune, bugle call, call

23 **singer**, songster, vocalist, lead vocalist, backing vocalist, crooner, torch singer, belter (Inf)

24 **musician**, player, instrumentalist, performer, artiste, soloist, virtuoso, singer, songster, vocalist, prima donna, bard, minstrel, troubadour, street musician, busker, composer, scorer, arranger, orchestrator, song writer, librettist, lyricist, balladeer, hymn writer, psalmist, musical director, MD, conductor, maestro, kappelmeister, choir master, chorus master, bandmaster, repetiteur, music teacher, music master, syncopator, jazzman, swinger (Sl), cat (Sl), bluesman (Sl), popster (Sl), funkster (Sl)

25 **musical instrument**, aerophone, idiophone, membranophone, chordophone, woodwind, brass, percussion, timpani, strings, mechanical instrument, electronic instru-

Musicians and Composers

Arne, Thomas Augustine (1710–78; British composer)

Arnold, Malcolm (1921– ; British composer)

Auber, Daniel François Esprit (1782–1871; French composer)

Babbitt, Milton (1916– ; US composer)

Bach, Johann Sebastian (1685–1750; German composer and keyboard player)

Baker, Dame Janet (1933– ; British mezzo-soprano)

Barbirolli, Sir John (1899–1970; British conductor)

Barenboim, Daniel (1942– ; Israeli pianist and composer)

Bartók, Béla (1881–1945; Hungarian composer)

Bax, Sir Arnold Edward Trevor (1883–1953; British composer)

Beecham, Sir Thomas (1879–1961; British conductor)

Beethoven, Ludwig van (1770–1827; German composer)

Bellini, Vincenzo (1801–35; Italian opera composer)

Bennett, Richard Rodney (1936– ; British composer)

Berg, Alban (1885–1935; Austrian composer)

Berlioz, Hector (1803–69; French composer and conductor)

Bernstein, Leonard (1918–90; US conductor, composer, and pianist)

Bizet, Georges (Alexandre César Léopold B, 1838–75; French composer)

Bliss, Sir Arthur Edward Drummond (1891–1975; British composer)

Bloch, Ernest (1880–1959; Swiss-born composer)

Borodin, Aleksandr Porfirevich (1833–87; Russian composer)

Boulanger, Nadia (1887–1979; French composer, teacher, and conductor)

Boult, Sir Adrian (1889–1983; British conductor)

Brahms, Johannes (1833–97; German composer)

Bream, Julian Alexander (1933– ; British guitarist and lutenist)

Britten, Benjamin, Baron (1913–76; British composer and pianist)

Bruch, Max (1838–1920; German composer)

Bruckner, Anton (1824–96; Austrian composer and organist)

Burney, Charles (1726–1814; British musicologist, organist, and composer)

Butt, Dame Clara (1873–1936; British contralto singer)

Byrd, William (?1543–1623; English composer)

Cage, John (1912–92; US composer)

Callas, Maria (Maria Anna Kalageropoulos, 1923–77; US-born soprano)

Campion, Thomas (or Campian, 1567–1620; English composer)

Caruso, Enrico (1873–1921; Italian tenor)

Casals, Pablo (Pau C, 1876–1973; Spanish cellist, conductor, and composer)

Charpentier, Gustave (1860–1956; French composer)

Chausson, Ernest (1855–99; French composer)

Chopin, Frédéric (François, 1810–49; Polish composer)

Clementi, Muzio (1752–1832; Italian pianist and composer)

Coleridge-Taylor, Samuel (1875–1912; British composer)

Copland, Aaron (1900–90; US composer)

Corelli, Arcangelo (1653–1713; Italian violinist and composer)

Couperin, François (1668–1733; French composer)

Curwen, John (1816–80; British teacher who perfected the Tonic Sol-fa system)

Davies, Sir Peter Maxwell (1934– ; British composer)

Davis, Sir Colin (1927– ; British conductor)

Debussy, Claude (1862–1918; French composer)

Delibes, Leo (1836–91; French composer)

Delius, Frederick (1862–1934; British composer)

Dohnányi, Ernö (Ernst von D, 1877–1960; Hungarian composer and pianist)

Dolmetsch, Arnold (1858–1940; British musician and instrument maker)

Domingo, Placido (1941– ; Spanish tenor)

Dowland, John (1563–1626; English composer and lutenist)

Dukas, Paul (1865–1935; French composer)

Dupré, Marcel (1886–1971; French organist and composer)

Dvořák, Antonín (1841–1904; Czech composer)

Elgar, Sir Edward (1857–1934; British composer)

Evans, Sir Geraint (1922–92; Welsh baritone)

Fauré, Gabriel (1845–1924; French composer and organist)

Ferrier, Kathleen (1912–53; British contralto)

Fischer-Dieskau, Dietrich (1925– ; German baritone)

Franck, César Auguste (1822–90; Belgian composer, organist, and teacher)

Gershwin, George (Jacob Gershvin, 1898–1937; US composer)

Gibbons, Orlando (1583–1625; English composer, organist, and virginalist)

Glinka, Mikhail Ivanovich (1804–57; Russian composer)

Gluck, Christoph Willibald (1714–87; German composer)

Goossens, Sir Eugene (1893–1962; British conductor and composer)

Grieg, Edvard Hagerup (1843–1907; Norwegian composer)

Grove, Sir George (1820–1900; British musicologist)

Guido d'Arezzo (c. 990–c. 1050; Italian monk and musical theorist)

Hallé, Sir Charles (Karl Hallé, 1819–1895; German conductor and pianist)

Handel, George Frederick (1685–1759; German composer)

Haydn, Franz Joseph (1732–1809; Austrian composer)

Henze, Hans Werner (1926– ; German composer)

Hess, Dame Myra (1890–1965; British pianist)

Hofmann, Joseph Casimir (1876–1957; Polish-born pianist)

Holst, Gustav (1874–1934; British composer and teacher)

Honegger, Arthur (1892–1955; French composer)

Horowitz, Vladimir (1904–89; Russian pianist)

Humperdinck, Engelbert (1854–1921; German composer)

Ibert, Jacques (1890–1962; French composer)

Ireland, John Nicholson (1879–1962; British composer)

Ives, Charles (1874–1954; US composer)

Janáček, Leo (1854–1928; Czech composer)

Joachim, Joseph (1831–1907; Hungarian violinist and composer)

Khachaturian, Aram Ilich (1903–78; Soviet composer)

Kodály, Zoltan (1882–1967; Hungarian composer)

Kreisler, Fritz (1875–1962; Austrian violinist)

Lill, John (1944– ; British pianist)

Lind, Jenny (1820–87; Swedish soprano)

Liszt, Franz (Ferencz L, 1811–86; Hungarian pianist and composer)

Mahler, Gustav (1860–1911; Austrian composer and conductor)

Massenet, Jules (1842–1912; French composer)

Melba, Dame Nellie (Helen Porter Armstrong, 1861–1931; Australian soprano)

Mendelssohn, Felix (Jacob Ludwig Felix Mendelssohn-Bartholdy, 1809–47; German composer)

Menuhin, Sir Yehudi (1916– ; British violinist)

Messager, André (1853–1929; French composer and conductor)

Messiaen, Olivier (1908– ; French composer, organist, and teacher)

Monteverdi, Claudio (1567–1643; Italian composer)

Mozart, Wolfgang Amadeus (1756–91; Austrian composer)

Mussorgski, Modest Petrovich (1839–81; Russian composer)

Nielsen, Carl (1865–1931; Danish composer and conductor)

Nilsson, Birgit Marta (1918– ; Swedish soprano)

Offenbach, Jacques (J Eberst, 1819–80; French composer)

Ogdon, John (1937–89; British pianist)

Oistrakh, David (1908–74; Russian violinist)

Orff, Carl (1895–1982; German composer and conductor)

Paderewski, Ignacy (1860–1941; Polish pianist and composer)

Paganini, Niccolò (1782–1840; Italian violinist)

Parry, Sir Hubert (1848–1918; British composer)

Pavarotti, Luciano (1935– ; Italian tenor)

Pears, Sir Peter (1910–86; British tenor)

Previn, André (Andreas Ludwig Priwin, 1929– ; German-born conductor, pianist, and composer)

Puccini, Giacomo (1858–1924; Italian opera composer)

Purcell, Henry (1659–95; English composer and organist)

Rachmaninov, Sergei (1873–1943; Russian composer, pianist, and conductor)

Ravel, Maurice (1875–1937; French composer)

Respighi, Ottorino (1879–1936; Italian composer)

Rimsky-Korsakov, Nikolai (1844–1908; Russian composer)

Rossini, Gioacchino Antonio (1792–1868; Italian composer)

Rubinstein, Anton (1829–94; Russian pianist and composer)

Rubinstein, Artur (1888–1982; Polish-born pianist)

Saint-Saëns, Camille (1835–1921; French composer, conductor, pianist, and organist)

Sargent, Sir Malcolm (1895–1967; British conductor)

Satie, Erik (1866–1925; French composer)

Scarlatti, Domenico (1685–1757; Italian composer, harpsichordist, and organist)

Schoenberg, Arnold (1874–1951; Austrian-born composer)

Schubert, Franz (1797–1828; Austrian composer)

Schumann, Elisabeth (1885–1952; German-born soprano)

Schumann, Robert (1810–56; German composer)

Schwarzkopf, Elisabeth (1915– ; German soprano)

Sibelius, Jean (Johan Julius Christian S, 1865–1957; Finnish composer)

Smetana, Bedřich (1824–84; Bohemian composer)

Solti, Sir Georg (1912– ; Hungarian-born British conductor)

Sousa, John Philip (1854–1933; US composer and bandmaster)

Stern, Isaac (1920– ; Russian-born US violinist)

Stockhausen, Karlheinz (1928– ; German composer)

Stradivari, Antonio (?1644–1737; Italian violin maker)

Strauss, Richard (1864–1949; German composer and conductor)

Strauss the Younger, Johann (1825–99; Austrian violinist, conductor, and composer)

Stravinsky, Igor (1882–1971; Russian-born composer)

Sullivan, Sir Arthur (1842–1900; British composer)

Sutherland, Dame Joan (1926– ; Australian soprano)

Tchaikovsky, Peter Ilich (1840–93; Russian composer)

Te Kanawa, Dame Kiri (1944– ; New Zealand soprano)

Tippett, Sir Michael (1905–90; British composer)

Tortelier, Paul (1914– ; French cellist)

Toscanini, Arturo (1867–1957; Italian conductor)

Varèse, Edgard (1883–1965; French composer)

Vaughan Williams, Ralph (1872–1958; British composer)

Verdi, Giuseppe (1813–1901; Italian composer)

Vivaldi, Antonio (1678–1741; Italian composer and violinist)

Wagner, Richard (1813–83; German composer)

Walton, Sir William (1902–83; British composer)

Weber, Carl Maria von (1786–1826; German composer)

Weill, Kurt (1900–50; German composer)

Williams, John (1941– ; Australian guitarist)

Wood, Sir Henry (1869–1944; British conductor)

ment, keyboard instrument

26 **musical group**, orchestra, symphony orchestra, chamber group, chamber orchestra, sinfonietta, duo, trio, quartet, string quartet, quintet, sextet, septet, octet, nonet, ensemble, band, string band, jazz band, ragtime band, brass band, military band, marching band, mounted band, pipe band, skiffle group, steel band, rock band (*or* group), punk band (*or* group), pop group, one-man band

27 **performance**, concert, recital, promenade concert, prom, show, gig (Sl),

28 **concert hall**, opera house, salon

ADJECTIVES

29 **musical**, music loving, musicophile, musicianly, virtuoso, philharmonic

30 **harmonic**, harmonizing, tuneful, attuned, in tune, tonal, symphonious, synchronous, homophonic, harmonious, melodious, mellifluous, mellow, lyric, dulcet, singable, catchy

31 **composed**, orchestrated, improvised

32 **instrumental**, vocal, choral, operatic, liturgical, hymnal, psalmic, psalmodic, romantic, impressionist, twelve-tone, concrete, mini-

malist, contrapuntal, heroic, dramatic, bass, baritone, alto, tenor, soprano, treble, falsetto, castrato

33 **jazz**, syncopated, avant-garde, cool, mainstream, traditional, trad, Dixieland, blue, pop, swinging, punk, folk, folksy, country, soul

VERBS

34 **harmonize**, melodize, attune, assonate, tune, tune up

35 **compose**, write, orchestrate, instrumentate, set to music, score, adapt, arrange, transcribe, transpose

36 **play**, make music, strike up, perform, render, interpret, play by ear, improvise

37 **syncopate**, swing, jam (Inf), riff (Inf), rock

38 **sound**, blow, toot, whistle, lip, tongue, double-tongue, triple-tongue, trumpet, bow, fiddle, pluck, strum, pick, twang, beat, thrum, pound, clash, ring, tickle the ivories

39 **sing**, break into song, vocalize, croon, carol, warble, quaver, trill, pipe, flute, intone, chant, descant, sing together, chorus, harmonize, belt out (Inf)

40 **conduct**, direct, lead, wield (*or* take) the baton

ADVERBS

41 **in tune**, in key, in time, in tempo

50 Painting and Sculpture

Good painters imitate nature, bad ones spew it up. Miguel de Cervantes.

A picture has been said to be something between a thing and a thought. Samuel Palmer.

I paint objects as I think them, not as I see them. Pablo Picasso.

My business is to paint not what I know, but what I see. Joseph Turner.

NOUNS

1 **art**, the arts, the visual arts, fine arts, applied arts, *beaux arts* (Fr), plastic art, graphic arts, decorative arts, decoration, design, arts of design, industrial design, industrial art, commercial art, kinetic art, craft, handicraft, arts and crafts, painting, sculpture, engraving, etching, calligraphy, batik, screen printing, silk-screen printing, embroidery, tapestry, woodcarving, metalwork, enamelling, mosaics, ceramics, stained glass, photography, lithography

▶ *67 Fabrics and Dyeing, 66 Photography, 44 Ceramics*

2 **painting**, colouring, colourizing, the brush (Arch), the pencil (Arch), daubing, washing, underpainting, overpainting, tinting, touching up, illumination, composition, scene painting, sign painting, action painting, finger painting

▶ *444 Colour, 794 Refinement*

3 **drawing**, sketching, drafting, delineating, delineation, limning, outlining, freehand drawing, mechanical drawing, technical drawing, draughtsmanship, tracing, copying, doodling

▶ *299 Outline, 118 Imitation, 547 Representation*

4 **treatment**, tone, values, form, colour, local colour, shadow, shading, *sfumato* (It), *chiaroscuro* (It), scumbling, marbling, ambience, atmosphere, line, composition, balance, arrangement, grouping, design, golden section, golden mean, perspective, scientific perspective, geometric perspective, Renaissance perspective, optical perspective, linear perspective, aerial perspective, foreshortening, vanishing point, illusionism, *trompe l'oeil* (Fr) technique, draughtsmanship, brushwork, painterliness, painterly values, tactile values, significant form

▶ *308 Symmetry, 444 Colour, 306 Form, 152 Arrangement, 382 Structure, 592 Plan, 655 Skill, 439 Light, 383 Texture, 549 Style*

5 **artistry**, art, artistic skill, artistic flair, artistique technique, talent, genius, mastery, invention, artistic invention, artistic quality, artistic taste, virtu, connoisseurship, craftsmanship, artisanship, artistic temperament, artiness, arty-craftiness (Inf), artsy-craftiness (Inf), artsy-fartsiness (Inf)

▶ *655 Skill, 519 Imagination, 119 Originality, 471 Idea, 481 Discrimination, 794 Refinement*

6 **work of art**, artwork, work, *objet d'art* (Fr), art object, artistic production, artistic creation, composition, design, study, piece, masterpiece, masterwork, *chef-d'oeuvre* (Fr), article of virtu, object of virtu, piece of virtu, museum piece, old master

7 **picture**, pictorial equivalent, likeness, image, representation, illustration, painting, drawing, engraving, miniature, tableau, illumination, mosaic, tapestry, stained-glass window, reproduction, copy, plate, print, colour print, block-print, photoprint, photogravure, woodcut, aquatint, poster, picture postcard, montage, photomontage, collage, brass rubbing, frottage

▶ *118 Imitation, 547 Representation, 67 Fabrics and Dyeing, 66 Photography, 114 Similarity*

8 **painting**, canvas, daub, easel painting, cabinet painting, miniature, wall painting, fresco, mural, icon, altarpiece, diptych, triptych, reredos, retable, cave painting, rock painting, action painting, finger painting, spray-can painting, oil painting, oil, airbrush painting, acrylic, watercolour, water, *gouache* (Fr), aquarelle, wash, pastel, tempera, impasto, encaustic, grisaille, monochrome, polychrome

▶ *7 Religion, 43 Architecture, 47 Furniture and Woodwork*

9 **drawing**, line drawing, delineation, black-and-white, sketch, draft, rough draft, outline,

Western Art Styles and Movements

abstract art
abstract ex-
  pression
action art
action painting
aestheticism
analytical cubism
Anglo-Saxon art
Archaic art
art brut (Fr)
Art Deco
arte povera (It)
art informel (Fr)
Art Nouveau
arts and crafts
  movement
baroque
Biedermeier
body art
Bohemian art
Bolognese
  school
Burgundian
  school
Byzantine art
Carolingian art
Celtic art
Classical Greek
  art
classicism
cloisonnisme
Cologne school

conceptual art
concrete art
constructivism
cubism
Dada
Danube school
divisionism
Dutch genre
  painting
Early Christian
  art
Early Renais-
  sance art
earth art
eclecticism
environmental
  art
Etruscan art
expressionism
expressive ab-
  straction
Fauvism
Ferrarese school
figurative art
Florentine
  school
folk art
Fontainebleau
  school
futurism
geometrical ab-
  straction

Gothic art
Graeco-Roman
  art
Grand Manner
Hadrianic art
Hague school
Hellenistic art
high baroque
High Renais-
  sance art
impressionism
International
  Gothic
intimisme
Jugendstil
junk art
kinetic art
kitsch
land art
lyrical abstrac-
  tion
magic realism
mannerism
medieval art
metaphysical
  painting
minimal art
mozarabic art
naive art
naturalism
neoclassicism
neoexpressionism

neoimpressionism
neoromanticism
Neue
  Sachlichkeit
  (Ger)
New York school
nonrepresenta-
  tional art
op art
orphism
performance art
Pergamene
  school
photorealism
plein air paint-
  ing
pointillism
Pompeian art
pop art
postimpression-
  ism
postmodernism
post-painterly
  abstraction
precisionism
pre-Raphaeli-
  tism
primitive art
purism
quattrocento (It)
rayonism
realism

regionalism
Renaissance art
representa-
  tional art
rococo art
romanesque art
Roman school
romanticism
School of Paris
Sienese school
socialist realism
social realism
spatialism
superrealism
suprematism
surrealism
Symbolism
synchronism
synthetic cubism
synthetism
tachisme
transavantgarde,
  the
trecento (It)
Tuscan school
Venetian school
verism
vorticism

rough outline, rough copy, study, design, vignette, thumbnail sketch, lightning sketch, silhouette, doodle, scribble, graffito, caricature, cartoon, comic strip, comic, animated cartoon, amimation, pen-and-ink, pencil drawing, charcoal drawing, charcoal, crayon, pastel drawing, silverpoint drawing, diagram, graph, tracing

▶ *299 Outline, 594 Preparation, 547 Representation, 532 Publication*

10 **art subject**, portrait, profile, head, full-face portrait, *profil perdu* (Fr), full-length portrait, half-length portrait, three-quarter-length portrait, nude, landscape, seascape, marine painting, riverscape, skyscape, cloudscape, scene, townscape, prospect, panorama, view, bird's-eye view, pastoral, nocturne, nightpiece, interior, exterior, historical painting, battle painting, genre painting, *fête champêtre* (Fr), conversation piece, animal painting, equestrian painting, still-life, flower painting, crucifixion, pietà, nativity, annunciation, maestà, vanitas

11 **artist's materials**, pen, pencil, drawing pencil, ink, chalk, charcoal, crayon, pastel, paintbrush, palette, palette knife, spatula, maulstick, mahlstick, spraygun, airbrush, paintbox, paint tube, paints, pigments, oil paint, oils, watercolours, gouache, gesso, tempera, distemper, ground, medium, solvent, thinner, turpentine, white spirit, siccative, fixative, size, varnish, paper, art paper, drawing paper, sketchpad, scratchpad (US), sketchbook, easel, stretcher, drawing frame, camera obscura, camera lucida, Claude glass, studio, atelier, model, sitter, subject, picture frame, picture gallery, salon, art museum

▶ *603 Tool, 604 Materials, 66 Photography, 444 Colour*

12 **sculpture**, plastic art, sculpturing, figuring, modelling, carving, stone-carving, pointing, direct carving, stonecutting, statuary, monumental sculpture, architectural sculpture, statue, statuette, figure, figurine, bust, head, torso, group, caryatid, telemon, atlantes, herm, garden sculpture, portrait sculpture, funerary sculpture, abstract sculpture, stone sculpture, metal sculpture, wire sculpture, paper sculpture, glass sculpture, clay sculpture, earth art, mobile, stabile, kinetic sculpture, minimal sculpture, marble, bronze, terracotta, woodcarving, ivory-carving, bone-carving, whittling, scrimshaw, rock-carving, petroglyph, wax modelling, model, maquette, moulding, ceroplastics, casting, sand casting, plaster casting, cast, plaster cast, *cire-perdue* (Fr), lost-wax casting, waxwork, ready-made, *objet trouvé* (Fr), found object, environment, installation, assemblage

▶ *43 Architecture*

13 **relief-carving**, relief, relievo, low relief, bas-relief, *basso rilievo* (It), half relief, *mezzo rilievo* (It), high relief, *altro relievo* (It), *stiacciato* (It),

Schools and Groups of Artists

Abstraction-Création	Bloomsbury group	Gutai group	Pre-Raphaelite Brother-
Allied Artists Associa-	Brotherhood of	Heidelberg school	hood
tion	Ruralists	Hudson River school	Rocky Mountain School
American Abstract	Brücke	Jeune Peinture Belge	Scottish Colourists
Artists' Group	Camden Town Group	Luminists	Section d'Or
Ancients	Cobra	Nabis	De Stijl
Antwerp Mannerists	the Eight	Nazarenes	Unit One
Ashcan school	Euston Road school	New English Art Club	Les Vingt
Automatistes, Les	Fronte Nuovo delle Arti	Norwich school	Wanderers
Bamboccianati	Glasgow Boys	Novecento Italiano	World of Art group
Barbizon school	Group of Seven	Novembergruppe	
Bauhaus	Groupe de Recherche	Painters Eleven	
Blaue Reiter	d'Art Visuel (GRAV)	Plasticiens	
Blaue Vier	Group Zero	Pont-Aven school	

intaglio, *intaglio rilievo* (It), glyph, anaglyph, anaglyptics, anaglyptography, cameo, medallion, medal, embossment, boss, embossing, engraving, chasing

14 **sculptor's materials**, mallet, chisel, claw chisel, burin, modelling tool, point, spatula, drill, punch, pointing machine, welding torch, cutting torch, soldering iron, armature, modelling clay, sculptor's wax, wax, Plasticine (Tm), plaster, solder, marble, Pathian marble, granite, bronze, terracotta, stucco

▶ *603 Tool, 604 Materials, 306 Form*

15 **engraving**, line engraving, plate engraving, etching, woodcut, drypoint, metal engraving, steel engraving, copper engraving, chalcography, zincography, wood engraving, xylography, lignography, linocut, lithograph, cerography, gem engraving, glyptography, chasing, aquatint, mezzotint, stone, block, woodblock, plate, steel plate, copper plate, chisel, burin, bur-chisel, graver, needle, style, point, etching point

16 **artist**, visual artist, graphic artist, designer, industrial artist, commercial artist, industrial designer, craftsman, artisan, painter, colourist, dauber, easel-painter, action painter, oil painter, watercolour, painter, aquarellist, pastellist, mural painter, icon painter, portrait painter, portraitist, landscape painter, marine painter, historical painter, genre painter, still-life painter, flower painter, animal painter, equestrian painter, religious painter, scene painter, sign painter, pavement artist, drawer, draughtsman, sketcher, limner (Arch), delineator, illustrator, copyist, illuminator, miniaturist, poster artist, cartoonist, political cartoonist, caricaturist, animator, comic-strip artist, doodler, finger painter, enameller, fashion artist, architectural artist, master, old master, modern master, academician, RA, Sunday painter (Inf)

▶ *519 Imagination, 119 Originality, 796 Fashion, 44 Ceramics*

17 **sculptor**, stone-carver, carver, statuary, monumental sculptor, monumental mason, architectural sculptor, figurist, modeller, wax

modeller, moulder, caster, metal sculptor, abstract sculptor

▶ *43 Architecture*

18 **engraver**, etcher, metal engraver, wood engraver, aquatinter, chaser, gem engraver, lapidary, type-cutter, typographer, printer

▶ *532 Publication*

VERBS

19 **paint**, colour, colourize, tint, coat, brush, tone, overpaint, underpaint, scumble, wash, shade, daub, illuminate, ink in, touch up

▶ *444 Colour, 792 Decoration, 557 Ornament*

20 **draw**, sketch, draft, pencil, chalk, limn, outline, doodle, cartoon, caricature, represent, portray, depict, copy, trace, stencil, silhouette, hatch, cross-hatch

▶ *547 Representation, 299 Outline, 118 Imitation*

21 **sculpt**, carve, cut, chisel, chip, whittle, shape, cast, model, mould, form

22 **engrave**, grave, incise, etch, chase, scrape, bite, impress, emboss, aquatint, print

23 **design**, create, visualize, put onto paper, lay out, compose, plan, arrange, group, balance, foreshorten

▶ *119 Originality, 308 Symmetry, 592 Plan, 435 Vision, 152 Arrangement*

ADJECTIVES

24 **pictorial**, pictographic, graphic, calligraphic, geometric(al), linear, optical, illusionist, aerial, atmosphere, photographic, iconic, mosaic

25 **sculptural**, marmoreal, monumental, graven, moulded, ceramic, tactile, plastic, glyptic, anaglyptic, ceroplastic, toreutic

▶ *457 Appearance*

26 **artistic**, painterly, imaginative, illustrative, stylized, decorative, baroque, picturesque, aesthetic, scenic, statuesque, arty (Inf), arty-crafty (Inf), arty-farty (Inf)

▶ *789 Beauty*

27 **painted**, coloured, washed, daubed, tinted, shaded, illuminated, inked, drawn, sketched, drafted, delineated, outlined, designed, foreshortened, traced, copied

28 **sculpted**, sculptured, carved, modelled, moulded, embossed, engraved, *repoussé* (Fr)

29 **realist**, naturalist, photorealist, verist, social-

Non-Western Art

Prehistoric Art	**Mesopotamian art**	**Pre-Columbian Art**	**Song dynasty art**
Palaeolithic art	Ottoman art	Mesoamerican art	Tang dynasty art
cave painting		Aztec art	Yuan dynasty art
rock painting	**Indian art**	Tultec art	Ming dynasty art
	art of the Indus valley		Ch'ing dynasty art
African Art	Gandharan art	**Mediterranean**	
African tribal art	Mogul art	**Cultures**	**Japanese Art**
Benin bronzes	Tamil art	Cycladic art	Japanese scroll paint-
		Minoan art	ing
Middle Eastern Art	**Ancient Egyptian Art**	Mycenean art	Japanese woodblocks
Islamic art	Old Kingdom art		Fujiwara style
Sumerian art	New Kingdom art	**Chinese Art**	Heian style
Assyrian art		Chinese calligraphy	Ukiyo-e
Babylonian art	**Oceanic Art**	Han dynasty art	floating world
	Melanesian art		

ist realist, social realist, regionalist, precisionist, purist, classical, neoclassical, romantic, neoromantic, impressionist, neoimpressionist, postimpressionist, pointillist, divisionist, minimalist, primitive, naive, Fauvist, vorticist, concrete, constructivist, cubist, expressionist, neoexpressionist, figurative, symbolist, Dadaist, abstract, eclectic, mannerist, postmodernist, rayonist, Orphistic, suprematist, synchronic, synthetic, analytic, Renaissance, Baroque, rococo, Gothic, Hellenistic, Etruscan, Celtic, Byzantine, Bohemian

ADVERBS

30 **pictorially**, optically, visually, graphically, sculpturally, photographically, geometrically, realistically, naturalistically, impressionistically, minimally, primitively, concretely, expressionistically, figuratively, symbolically, abstractly, eclectically, in oils, in water colours, in pencil, in pastels, in relief

31 **artistically**, imaginatively, creatively, conceptually, illustratively, decoratively, picturesquely, aesthetically, scenically, atmospherically

51 Performing Arts

NOUNS

1 **drama**, the drama, theatre, the theatre, the stage, the play, the scenes (Arch), traffic of the state, dramatic entertainment, dramatics, amateur dramatics, dramaticism, theatrics, theatricals, amateur theatricals, histrionics, histrionism, dramatic art, histrionic art, Thespian art, Thespis, theatre world, stage world, stage land, stagedom, playland, the West End, Broadway, off-Broadway, off-off-Broadway, the Fringe, fringe theatre, repertory, live theatre, legitimate theatre, straight drama, alternative theatre, street theatre, pub theatre, experimental theatre, rep (Inf), legit (Inf), the boards (Inf), the footlights (Inf), greasepaint (Inf)

▶ *475 Demonstration, 526 Display, 48 Literature*

2 **play**, stage play, drama, dramatic representation, dramatic entertainment, dramatic recital, show, work, piece, vehicle, script, text, lines, libretto, book, book of words, prompt book, monologue, dramatic monologue, monodrama, one-man show, duologue, duodrama, two-hander, dialogue, skit, sketch, playlet, divertissement, charade, burlesque, curtain-raiser, curtain-lifter, intermezzo, entr'acte, double bill, one-act play, five-act play, trilogy, tetralogy, dramatic cycle, Greek drama, *fabula* (L), *Nō* play, *Kyōgen* (Jap), *Kabuki* (Jap), mystery play, mystery, morality play, morality, miracle play, miracle, passion play, Oberammergau, liturgical drama, folk play, mummers' play, sword play, commedia dell'arte, farce, harlequinade, pantomime, mime, dumbshow, masque, antimasque, pastoral, interlude, verse drama, poetic drama, closet drama, melodrama, heroic drama, Grand Guignol, drama of suspense, well-made play, *pièce bien faite* (Fr), problem play, sociodrama, psychodrama, psychological drama, slice of life, kitchen-sink drama, docudrama, documentary drama, drama-documentary, community drama, collective creation, improvised drama, improvisation, happening, broadcast drama, radio drama, radio play, television drama, television play, teleplay, screenplay, scenario, shooting script, serial, soap opera, soap (Inf)

3 **musical drama**, music drama, opera, operetta, musical, Broadway musical, show, musical comedy, comic opera, *opera buffa* (It), *opera seria* (It), ballad opera, rock opera, *Singspiel* (Ger), ballet, Gilbert and Sullivan, cabaret

▶ *49 Music, 46 Dancing and Ballet*

4 **show business**, entertainment industry, vaudeville, variety, burlesque, music hall, song and dance, striptease, the stage, the boards, Broadway, off-Broadway, off-off-Broadway, West End, Hollywood, the silver screen, the big top, showbiz (Inf), strawhat (US inf)

5 **show**, stage show, live show, spectacle, extravaganza, variety show, vaudeville show, vaudeville, burlesque show, burlesque, cabaret, song and dance, revue, review, intimate review, late-night review, minstrel show, music hall, repertory show, Follies, floor show,

strip show, striptease, peepshow, sex show, *tableau vivant* (Fr), tableau, hootchy-kootchy show, raree show, medicine show, road show, magic show, puppet show, puppetry, Punch-and-Judy show, marionette show, *fantoccini* (It), shadow play, shadow show, *ombres chinoises* (Fr), slide show, light show, laser show, *son et lumière* (Fr), circus, travelling circus, the Big Top, the ring, rodeo, ice show, carnival, pageant, sideshow, flea circus, game show, quiz show, panel show, lecture, illustrated lecture, rep show (Inf), girly show (Inf), leg show (Inf), nudie show (Inf), flesh show (Inf)

▶ *526 Display, 475 Demonstration, 296 Undress, 812 Celebration*

6 **scene**, act, speech, monologue, soliloquy, episode, item, piece, number, routine, sketch, turn, bill, top of the bill, bottom of the bill, curtain-music, overture, curtain-raiser, curtain-lifter, rising of the curtain, prologue, introduction, opening scene, expository scene, chorus, interval, intermission, break, intermezzo, entr'acte, interlude, *divertimento* (It), *divertissement* (Fr), climax, catastrophe, denouement, resolution, exposure scene, recognition scene, *deus ex machina*, battle scene, alarums and excursions, love scene, sex scene, transformation scene, set piece, finale, curtain, drop of the curtain, final curtain, curtain call, blackout, epilogue, encore, exode, exodus, afterpiece, jig, applause, ovation, standing ovation, chaser (Inf)

7 **dramaturgy**, dramatic art, dramatic structure, dramatic form, play construction, the well-made play, stagecraft, theatre craft, theatrical convention, dramatic convention, dramatic unities, the unities, dramatic irony, dramatic conflict, *agon* (Gk), dramatic tension, alienation effect, a-effect, *Verfremdungseffekt* (Ger), play writing, script writing, plot, subplot, characterization, story, dialogue, monologue, soliloquy, *stichomythia* (Gk), staging, choreography, action, movement, gesture, business, theatricality, theatrics, dramatics, melodramatics, histrionics, sensationalism, blood and thunder, *Sturm und Drang* (Ger), Grand Guignol, dramatic coup, dramatic stroke, *coup de théâtre* (Fr), spectacle, showmanship, ham (Inf)

▶ *48 Literature, 403 Sensation, 435 Vision, 811 Showiness, 472 Topic, 655 Skill*

8 **theatre movements**, activism, *Aktie Tomaat* (Dutch), Angry Young Men, community theatre, constructivism, *Décentralisation Dramatique* (Fr), documentary theatre, epic theatre, expressionism, feminist theatre, formalism, kitchen-sink drama, naturalism, New Drama, realism, ritual drama, *Sturm und Drang* (Ger), *théâtre du quotidien* (Fr), theatre of the absurd, theatre of cruelty, theatre of fact, theatre of

silence, *théâtre total* (Fr), total theatre, *verismo* (It), *Vormingstoneel* (Dutch)

9 **tragedy**, tragic drama, high tragedy, classical tragedy, Greek tragedy, Aeschylean tragedy, Euripidean tragedy, Sophoclean tragedy, Senecan tragedy, Renaissance tragedy, Shakespearean tragedy, Elizabethan tragedy, Jacobean tragedy, revenge tragedy, domestic tragedy, drama of fate, romantic tragedy, melodrama, tragicomedy, tragic muse, Melpomeme, cothurnus, buskin, tragic flaw, hubris, catharsis, *hamartia* (Gk)

▶ *770 Sorrow, 821 Love*

10 **comedy**, high comedy, low comedy, broad comedy, light comedy, romantic comedy, sentimental comedy, *comédie larmoyante* (Fr), comedy of manners, comedy of ideas, comedy of humours, comedy of intrigue, comedy of morals, comedy of character, comedy of situation, situation comedy, sitcom (Inf), sex comedy, realistic comedy, black comedy, dark comedy, bitter comedy, *comédie rosse* (Fr), tragicomedy, satire, satirical comedy, farce, knockabout farce, knockabout, stand-up comedy, bedroom farce, Feydeau farce, Whitehall farce, French farce, slapstick, slapstick comedy, burlesque, burletta, camp, high camp, low camp, alternative comedy, satyr play, Aristophanean comedy, Old Comedy, Middle Comedy, New Comedy, Roman comedy, *commedia dell'arte* (It), *commedia a soggetto* (It), *commedia erudita* (It), *burla* (It), *lazzo* (It), interlude, Shakespearean comedy, Jonsonian comedy, Restoration comedy, *comédie-ballet* (Fr), drawing-room comedy, comic relief, light relief, comic business, comic muse, Thalia, motley, sock, cap and bells, coxcomb, bladder

▶ *821 Love, 771 Humour*

11 **theatrical performance**, performance, show, production, presentation, stage presentation, presentment, exhibition, bill, first performance, premiere performance, premiere, preview, first night, gala night, debut, farewell performance, personal appearance, command performance, bespeak performance (Arch), benefit performance, benefit, charity performance, charity gala, matinée, first house, second house, successful production, success, critical success, sell-out, full house, hit, box-office hit, smash hit (Inf), long run, failure, short run, flop (Inf), bomb (US inf)

▶ *526 Display, 682 Success, 683 Failure*

12 **production**, direction, staging, mounting, putting on, stage management, *mise en scène* (Fr), audition, casting, rehearsal, readthrough, walkthrough, runthrough, blocking, dress rehearsal, technical rehearsal, new production, revival, modern production, modern-dress production

▶ *243 Production, 594 Preparation*

13 **engagement**, theatrical engagement, playing engagement, booking, date, gig, stand, one-night stand, run, tour, circuit, variety circuit, club circuit, pub circuit, vaudeville circuit, repertory circuit, rep (Inf), strawhat circuit (US inf), borscht belt (US inf), scampi-and-chips circuit (Inf), chicken-in-a-basket circuit (Inf), rubber-chicken circuit (Inf)
▶ *334 Circuit*

14 **theatre**, venue, playhouse, house, hall, hippodrome, auditorium, arena, amphitheatre, stadium, circus, Greek theatre, odeum, odeon, Elizabethan theatre, spectacle theatre, open-air theatre, outdoor theatre, theatre-in-the-round, circle theatre, arena theatre, little theatre, variety theatre, vaudeville theatre, vaudeville house, burlesque theatre, burlesque house, cabaret, music hall, opera house, opera, concert hall, cinema, movie theatre, picture house, nightclub, club, nightspot, *boîte de nuit* (Fr), *boîte* (Fr), booth, showboat, big top, pavilion, end of the pier, toy theatre, *ediophusikon* (Gk), fleapit (Inf)
▶ *43 Architecture*

15 **stage**, the boards, performing area, acting area, playing area, proscenium stage, proscenium, proscenium arch, bridge, picture-frame stage, apron stage, apron, forestage, thrust stage, segment stage, wagon stage, slip stage, revolving stage, trap, stage left, stage L, stage right, stage R, upstage, downstage, centrestage, frontstage, above, below, orchestra pit, orchestra, pit, bandstand, podium, rostrum, dais, soapbox, wings, backstage, dressing room, greenroom, stage door, flies, fly floor, fly gallery, gridiron, grid, lightboard, switchboard, board, sounddesk, prompter's box, scene dock, scene bay
▶ *47 Furniture and Woodwork, 49 Music*

16 **auditorium**, seating, parquet (US), parquet circle (US), stalls, orchestra stalls, front stalls, back stalls, pit, front rows, fauteuil, parterre, loge, box, box seat, stage box, parterre box, proscenium box, royal box, circle, upper circle, dress circle, balcony, gallery, mezzanine, standing room, front of house, foyer, box office, the gods (Inf), heaven (US inf), paradise (US inf), peanut gallery (US inf)

17 **stage set**, stage setting, setting, set, box set, scenery, scene, *mise-en-scène* (Fr), decor, flat, side scene, cyclorama, stage screw, wing, wingcut, border, tormentor, teaser, flipper, batten, drop, drop curtain, drop scene, cloth, backdrop, backcloth, hanging, gauze, scrim, transparency, transformation scene, curtain, drape, house curtain, act curtain, act drop, tabs, safety curtain, fire curtain, advertisement curtain, rag (Inf)

18 **stage lighting**, lights, footlights, limelight, floodlight, flood, spotlight, arc light, arc,

bunch light, battens, houselights, klieg light, colour filter, colour wheel, medium, gelatin, gel (Inf), gobo, diaphragm, iris diaphragm, iris, projector, sciopticon (US), stroboscope, lightboard, lighting board, lighting desk, lighting plot, Varilite (Tm), foots (Inf), spot (Inf), following spot (Inf), strobe (Inf)
▶ *439 Light, 444 Colour*

19 **stage requisite**, stage property, property, prop, handprop, theatrical costume, costume, wardrobe, theatrical make-up, make-up, theatrical cosmetics, greasepaint, spirit gum, whiteface, blackface, clown face
▶ *796 Fashion, 792 Decoration, 557 Ornament*

20 **acting**, play-acting, playing, role-playing, taking a role, taking a part, creating a role, creating a part, impersonation, personation, portrayal, representation, characterization, interpretation, projection, performing, performance, enactment, mimesis, mimicry, mimicking, miming, pantomiming, character acting, method acting, the Method, improvisation, improvising, histrionics, overacting, barnstorming, business, stage business, byplay, stage whisper, aside, entrance, exit, cue, theatrical technique, stage presence, showmanship, star quality, stage fever, first-night nerves, stage fright, ham acting (Inf), hamming (Inf), hamming it up (Inf), camping it up (Inf), hoking it up (US inf), hoking (US inf), mummery (Inf)
▶ *547 Representation, 524 Interpretation, 118 Imitation, 526 Display, 811 Showiness, 541 Exaggeration, 777 Fear, 457 Appearance, 318 Prominence*

21 **role**, part, character, person, personage, *dramatis personae* (L), title role, title part, name part, starring role, leading role, lead role, lead, chief part, good part, principal character, hero, heroine, antihero, villain, protagonist, antagonist, supporting character, deuteragonist, supporting part, supporting role, minor role, bit part, speaking part, walk-on part, walking part, straight part, straight man, cameo, vignette, comic relief, chorus, Greek chorus, stock part, stock character, stereotype, central casting, ingenue, soubrette, juvenile lead, *jeune première* (Fr), love interest, confidante, heavy father, heavy woman, walking lady, walking gentleman, supernumerary, merry widow, injured husband, breeches part, *miles gloriosus* (L), buffoon, fool, stage villain, stage Irishman, stage drunk, Harlequin, Columbine, Pantaloon, Pierrot, Scaramouch, principal boy, principal girl, pantomime dame, heavy (Inf), bad guy (Inf), fat part (Inf), juicy part (Inf), bit (Inf), feeder (Inf), feed (Inf)

22 **actor**, actress, play-actor, player, stage player, strolling player, Thespian, trouper, stage performer, repertory player, Roscius (Arch), barnstormer, actor-manager, tragedian, trage-

dienne, comedian, comedienne, comedy actor, comedy actress, light comedian, low comedian, farcer, character actor, character actress, method actor, improviser, film actor, film actress, film star, star, superstar, starlet, star of stage and screen, matinée idol, idol, icon, leading man, leading lady, lead, juvenile lead, *jeune premier (or première)* (Fr), supporting actor, support, understudy, stand-in, standby, lookalike, substitute, extra, bit player, spear-carrier, supernumerary, super, pantomimist, opera singer, diva, prima donna, prologue, presenter, narrator, speaker, ham (Inf), mummer (Inf), darling (Inf), lovie (Inf)

23 **cast**, characters, *dramatis personae* (L), persons of the drama, chorus, ladies (*or* gentlemen) of the chorus, supporting cast, cast of thousands, ensemble, company, repertory company, stock company, touring company, outfit, troupe, circus troupe, *corps de ballet* (Fr)
▶ *161 Assembly*

24 **dramatist**, dramaturge, dramatizer, playwright, play writer, scenario writer, scenarioist, scenarist, screenwriter, script writer, librettist, radio dramatist, television dramatist, *farceur* (Fr), *farceuse* (Fr), joke writer, tragedian, comedian, tragic poet, comic poet, melodramatist, choreographer, mimographer, play doctor (US inf), play fixer (US inf), jokesmith (Inf), gag man (Inf), gag writer (Inf)
▶ *48 Literature, 119 Originality, 519 Imagination*

25 **producer**, director, auteur, stage manager, manager, actor manager, impresario, exhibitor, promoter, showman, master of ceremonies, ringmaster, choreographer, *régisseur* (Fr), *choregos* (Gr), designer, set designer, costume designer, *costumier* (Fr), *costumière* (Fr), business manager, publicity manager, publicity man, publicity woman, press officer, press agent, booking agent, ticket agent, agent, theatrical agent, advance agent, advance man, playbroker, patron, backer, angel (Inf), ten-per-cent man (US inf), ten-per-center (US inf), MC (Inf), emcee (Inf), SM (Inf)
▶ *243 Production, 688 Authority, 662 Help*

26 **stagehand**, stage technician, state crew, electrician, sound recordist, sound man, lighting man, machinist (Arch), stage carpenter, scene painter, scene shifter, flyman, special effects man, dresser, wardrobe mistress, make-up artist, make-up man, wig maker, callboy, prompter, ticket collector, programme-seller, usher, usherette, doorman, front-of-house staff, box-office staff

27 **entertainer**, public entertainer, artiste, artist, performer, act, vaudeville artist, vaudevillian, variety artist, song and dance man, quick-change artist, drag artist, female impersonator, impersonator, impressionist, mimic, ventriloquist, reciter, monologist, diseuse, diseur, con-

juror, magician, mountebank, prestidigitator, sleight-of-hand artist, hypnotist, escapologist, escape artist, mind reader, memory artist, comedian, comedienne, comic, stand-up comic, humorist, straight man, minstrel, troubadour, goliard (Arch), jongleur (Arch), busker, street performer, show girl, chorus girl, chorus boy, striptease artist, presenter, host, game-show host, quiz-show host, chat show host, radio personality, television personality, burlesque queen (Inf), stripper (Inf), stooge (Inf), foil (Inf), feed (Inf)
▶ *477 Question, 526 Display, 296 Undress, 118 Imitation, 569 Soliloquy*

28 **dancer**, ballet dancer, ballerina, prima ballerina, *danseur* (Fr), *danseuse* (Fr), coryphée, figurante, figurant, Terpsichorean, dancing girl, show girl, chorus girl, cancan dancer, tap dancer, belly dancer, disco dancer, go-go dancer, nautch-girl, geisha girl, geisha, striptease artist, exotic dancer, erotic dancer, ecdysiast, stripper (Inf), hoofer (Inf)
▶ *46 Dancing and Ballet, 296 Undress*

29 **circus performer**, circus artist, tightrope walker, ropewalker, slack-rope artist, high-wire artist, equilibrist, trapeze artist, tumbler, acrobat, *saltimbanco* (It), contortionist, juggler, strongman, stuntman, human cannonball, fire-eater, snake charmer, lion tamer, bareback rider, ringmaster, equestrian director, clown, barker, spiel man (Inf)
▶ *771 Humour, 30 Gymnastics*

30 **clown**, fool, jester, buffoon, *buffo* (Inf), zany, cap and bells, motley, slapstick comedian, slapstick, Punch, Punchinello, Pulcinella, Polichinelle, Harlequin, Columbine, Pantaloon, Pantalone, Scaramouch, Pierrot, Pedrolino, Pasquino, merry-andrew (Arch), pickle-herring (Arch), jack-pudding (Arch)
▶ *771 Humour*

31 **theatregoer**, playgoer, operagoer, filmgoer, balletgoer, spectator, fan, enthusiast, opera buff, buff, balletomane, audience, house, full house, packed house, thin house, stalls, pit, circle, boxes, gallery, balcony, promenader, standee (US), groundling (Arch), pittite (Arch), *claque, claqueur* (Fr), pass holder, critic, reviewer, talent spotter, first-nighter (Inf), stage-door Johnny (Inf), deadhead (Inf), plant (Inf)

VERBS

32 **act**, perform, enact, play, play-act, appear, project, enter, make an entrance, take the stage, tread the boards, face the cameras, play the lead, support, co-star, understudy, see one's name in lights, mimic, mime, imitate, represent, personify, impersonate, take off (Inf), exit, take a bow
▶ *346 Entry, 347 Exit, 526 Display, 118 Imitation, 318 Prominence*

33 **overact**, send up, overplay, rant, roar, play to the gallery, upstage, barnstorm, steal the show, play the fool, improvise, ad lib, wing it (Inf), chew up the scenery (Inf), milk it (Inf), ham (Inf), ham (*or* camp) it up (Inf)
▶ *541 Exaggeration, 610 Excess, 431 Human Cry, 811 Showiness, 357 Overstepping*

34 **underact**, walk on, have a cameo role, miss one's cue, fluff, dry up, go blank, throw away (Inf)
▶ *542 Understatement, 504 Error*

35 **rehearse**, con, learn one's lines, mug up, memorize, recite, run through, read through, walk through, block, interpret the part, get into character, method act
▶ *594 Preparation*

36 **dramatize**, melodramatize, theatricalize, adapt for the stage, write, script, produce, put on, direct, cue, prompt, stage-manage, cast, bill, star, feature, typecast, present, release, preview, premiere, open, raise the curtain
▶ *48 Literature, 322 Opening, 243 Production, 688 Authority, 119 Originality*

ADJECTIVES

37 **dramatic**, dramaturgic, melodramatic, spectacular, theatrical, mimetic, musical, operatic, choral, balletic, choreographic, Terpsichorean, histrionic, Thespian, stagy, staged, enacted, performed, interpreted, characterized, scripted, prompted, directed, improvised, protagonistic, antagonistic

38 **tragic**, tragicomic, buskined, romantic, cathartic, comic, vaudevillian, slapstick, burlesque, farcical, knockabout, sensational, stereotypical, typecast, miscast, hammy (Inf), hammed up (Inf)

39 **stagestruck**, starstruck, all-star, top of the bill, starring, featuring, showing, running

40 **activist**, constructivist, expressionist, formalist, naturalist, realist, Restoration

ADVERBS

41 **onstage**, in the spotlight (*or* limelight), stage left, stage right, upstage, downstage, centrestage, frontstage, offstage, in the wings, backstage, behind the scenes

42 **dramatically**, melodramatically, histrionically, theatrically, tragically, comically, romantically, protagonistically, antagonistically, choreographically, chorally, stereotypically, realistically

Science and Technology

Scientists, Mathematicians, and Engineers

Abel, Sir Frederick Augustus (1827–1902) British chemist

Abel, Niels Henrik (1802–29) Norwegian mathematician

Abu al-Wafa (940–98 AD) Persian mathematician and astronomer

Adams, John Couch (1819–92) English astronomer

Agassiz, Jean Louis Rodolphe (1807–73) Swiss natural historian

Agnesi, Maria Gaetana (1718–99) Italian mathematician and philosopher

Agricola, Georgius (George Bauer; 1494–1555) German physician and mineralogist

Airy, Sir George Biddell (1801–92) British astronomer

Alfvén, Hannes Olof Gösta (1908–) Swedish astrophysicist

al-Khwarizmi, Muhammed ibn Musa (c. 780–c. 850 AD) Arabic mathematician

Alpher, Ralph Asher (1921–) US physicist

Alvarez, Luis Walter (1911–88) US physicist

Amici, Giovanni Battista (1786–1863) Italian astronomer

Ampère, André Marie (1775–1836) French physicist

Anderson, Carl David (1905–) US physicist

Ångström, Anders Jonas (1814–74) Swedish physicist and astronomer

Apollonius of Perga (c. 261–c. 190 BC) Greek mathematician

Arago, (Dominique) François (Jean) (1786–1853) French astronomer and physicist

Archimedes (c. 287–c. 212 BC) Greek mathematician and inventor

Aristarchus of Samos (c. 310–230 BC) Greek astronomer

Arkwright, Sir Richard (1732–92) British inventor and industrialist

Arrhenius, Svante August (1859–1927) Swedish physicist and chemist

Aston, Francis William (1877–1945) British chemist

Audubon, John James (1785–1851) US naturalist and artist

Avery, Oswald Theodore (1877–1955) Canadian bacteriologist

Avogadro, Amedeo, Conte di Quaregna e Ceretto (1776–1856) Italian physicist

Babbage, Charles (1792–1871) British mathematician and inventor

Baer, Karl Ernest von (1792–1876) Russian embryologist

Baily, Francis (1774–1844) British amateur astronomer

Baird, John Logie (1888–1946) British electrical engineer

Banks, Sir Joseph (1743–1820) British botanist and explorer

Bardeen, John (1908–91) US physicist

Barkhausen, Heinrich (1881–1956) German physicist

Barnard, Edward Emerson (1857–1923) US astronomer

Bates, Henry Walter (1825–92) British naturalist and explorer

Bateson, William (1861–1926) British biologist

Beadle, George Wells (1903–) US geneticist

Becquerel, (Antoine) Henri (1852–1908) French physicist

Beebe, Charles William (1877–1962) US explorer and naturalist

Bell, Alexander Graham (1847–1922) Scottish-born US scientist and inventor

Benz, Karl (Friedrich) (1844–1929) German engineer

Bergius, Friedrich (1884–1949) German chemist

Berthelot, (Pierre Eugène) Marcelin (1827–1907) French chemist

Berthollet, Claude Louis, Comte (1748–1822) French chemist

Berzelius, Jöns Jakob, Baron (1779–1848) Swedish chemist

Bessemer, Sir Henry (1813–98) British engineer and inventor

Bethe, Hans Albrecht (1906–) US physicist

Bhaskhara II (1114–c. 1185) Indian mathematician

Birkhoff, George David (1864–1944) US mathematician

Bjerknes, Vilhelm Friman Koren (1862–1951) Norwegian meteorologist and physicist

Black, Sir James (Whyte) (1924–) British biochemist

Black, Joseph (1728–99) Scottish physician and chemist

Blackett, Patrick Maynard Stuart, Baron (1897–1974) British physicist

Bohr, Niels Henrik David (1885–1962) Danish physicist

Boltzmann, Ludwig Eduard (1844–1906) Austrian physicist

Bolyai, János (1802–60) Hungarian mathematician

Bondi, Sir Hermann (1919–) British cosmologist

Bonnet, Charles (1720–93) Swiss naturalist

Boole, George (1815–64) British mathematician

Bordet, Jules Jean Baptiste Vincent (1870–1961) Belgian bacteriologist

Born, Max (1882–1970) British physicist

Bosch, Carl (1874–1940) German chemist

Bose, Sir Jagadis Chandra (1858–1937) Indian physicist

Bourbaki, Nicolas (pseudonym for a group of French mathematicians)

Bovet, Daniel (1907–92) Swiss pharmacologist

Bowen, Norman Levi (1887–1956) Canadian experimental petrologist

Bower, Frederick Orpen (1855–1948) British botanist

Boyle, Robert (1627–91) Irish physicist and chemist

Bragg, Sir William Henry (1862–1942) British physicist

Brahe, Tycho (1546–1601) Danish astronomer

Brewster, Sir David (1781–1868) Scottish physicist

Bridgman, Percy Williams (1882–1961) US physicist

Briggs, Henry (1561–1630) English mathematician

Brindley, James (1716–72) British canal builder

Brouwer, L(uitzen) E(gbertus) J(an) (1881–1966) Dutch mathematician

Brown, Robert (1773–1858) Scottish botanist

Brunel, Isambard Kingdom (1806–59) British engineer

Buffon, Georges Louis Leclerc, Comte de (1707–88) French naturalist

Bunsen, Robert Wilhelm (1811–99) German chemist

Burbank, Luther (1849–1926) US plant breeder

Burbidge, (Eleanor) Margaret (1925–) British astronomer

Calvin, Melvin (1911–) US biochemist

Cannizzaro, Stanislao (1826–1910) Italian chemist

Cantor, Georg (1845–1918) Russian mathematician

Cardano, Girolamo (1501–76) Italian mathematician

Carnot, (Nicolas Léonard) Sadi (1796–1832) French scientist

Cartwright, Edmund (1743–1823) British inventor and industrialist

Carver, George Washington (1864–1943) US agriculturalist

Cauchy, Augustin Louis, Baron (1789–1857) French mathematician

Cavendish, Henry (1731–1810) British physicist

Cayley, Arthur (1821–95) British mathematician

Cayley, Sir George (1773–1857) British engineer

Chadwick, Sir James (1891–1974) British physicist

Chain, Sir Ernst Boris (1906–79) British biochemist

Chamberlain, Owen (1920–) US physicist

Chandrasekhar, Subrahmanyan (1910–) US astronomer

Cherenkov, Pavel Alekseievich (1904–) Russian physicist

Clausius, Rudolf Julius Emanuel (1822–88) German physicist

Cockcroft, Sir John Douglas (1897–1967) British physicist

Cohn, Ferdinand Julius (1839–1884) German botanist

Compton, Arthur Holly (1892–1962) US physicist

Copernicus, Nicolaus (1473–1543) Polish astronomer

Correns, Carl Erich (1864–1933) German botanist and geneticist

Coulomb, Charles Augustin de (1736–1806) French physicist

Crick, Francis Harry Compton (1916–) British biophysicist

Crompton, Samuel (1753–1827) British inventor of the spinning mule

Crookes, Sir William (1832–1919) British physicist

Culpeper, Nicholas (1616–54) English herbalist

Curie, Marie (1867–1934) Polish chemist

Curtiss, Glenn (Hammond) (1878–1930) US aeronautical engineer

Cuvier, Georges, Baron (1769–1832) French zoologist

Daguerre, Louis-Jacques-Mandé (1789–1851) French inventor

Daimler, Gottlieb (Wilhelm) (1834–1900) German inventor

d'Alembert, Jean le Rond (1717–83) French mathematician

Dalton, John (1766–1844) British chemist

Daniell, John Frederic (1790–1845) British chemist

Darwin, Charles Robert (1809–1882) British naturalist

Daubenton, Louis Jean Marie (1716–1800) French naturalist

Davy, Sir Humphry (1778–1829) British chemist

Dawkins, Richard (1941–) British zoologist

de Bary, Heinrich Anton (1831–88) German botanist

de Broglie, Louis Victor, 7th Duc (1892–1987) French physicist

Debye, Peter Joseph Wilhelm (1884–1966) Dutch physicist and chemist

Dedekind, (Julius Wilhelm) Richard (1831–1916) German mathematician

De Forest, Lee (1873–1961) US electrical engineer

De Morgan, Augustus (1806–71) British mathematician and logician

de Vries, Hugo Marie (1848–1935) Dutch botanist

Diels, Otto Paul Hermann (1876–1954) German chemist

Diophantus of Alexandria (mid-3rd century AD) Greek mathematician

Dioscorides Pedanius (c. 40–c. 90 AD) Greek physician

Dirac, Paul Adrien Maurice (1902–84) British physicist

Doppler, Christian Johann (1803–53) Austrian physicist

Dreyer, Johan Ludvig Emil (1852–1926) Danish astronomer

Driesch, Hans Adolf Eduard (1867–1941) German zoologist

Dunlop, John Boyd (1840–1921) Scottish inventor

Eddington, Sir Arthur Stanley (1882–1944) British theoretical astronomer

Edison, Thomas Alva (1847–1931) US inventor

Eichler, August Wilhelm (1839–87) German botanist

Einstein, Albert (1879–1955) US physicist born in Germany

Elton, Charles (1900–91) British zoologist

Enders, John Franklin (1897–1985) US microbiologist

Engler, Gustav Heinrich Adolf (1844–1930) German botanist

Eötvös, Roland von, Baron (1848–1919) Hungarian physicist

Eratosthenes of Cyrene (c. 276–c. 194 BC) Greek astronomer

Euclid (c. 300 BC) Greek mathematician

Eudoxus of Cnidus (c. 408–c. 355 BC) Greek astronomer and mathematician

Euler, Leonhard (1707–83) Swiss mathematician

Fabre, Jean Henri (1823–1915) French entomologist

Faraday, Michael (1791–1867) British chemist and physicist

Fermat, Pierre de (1601–65) French mathematician

Fermi, Enrico (1901–54) US physicist

Feynman, Richard Phillips (1918–88) US physicist

Fibonacci, Leonardo (c. 1170–c. 1230) Italian mathematician

Fischer, Emil Hermann (1852–1919) German chemist

Fischer, Hans (1881–1945) German chemist

Fitzgerald, George Francis (1851–1901) Irish physicist

Flamsteed, John (1646–1719) English astronomer

Fleming, Sir John Ambrose (1849–1945) British electrical engineer

Fokker, Anthony Hermann Gerard (1890–1939) Dutch aircraft manufacturer

Foucault, Jean Bernard Léon (1819–68) French physicist

Fourier, Jean Baptiste Joseph, Baron (1768–1830) French mathematician and physicist

Fraunhofer, Joseph von (1787–1826) German physicist

Frege, Gottlob (1848–1925) German mathematician and logician

Fresnel, Augustin Jean (1788–1827) French physicist

Friese-Greene, William (1855–1921) British photographer

Frisch, Karl von (1886–1982) Austrian zoologist

Frisch, Otto Robert (1904–79) Austrian-born physicist

Fulton, Robert (1765–1815) American inventor

Gabor, Dennis (1900–79) British electrical engineer

Galileo Galilei (1564–1642) Italian mathematician

Galois, Évariste (1811–32) French mathematician

Galton, Sir Francis (1822–1911) British scientist

Galvani, Luigi (1737–98) Italian physician

Gamow, George (1904–68) Russian-born US physicist

Gassendi, Pierre (1592–1655) French physicist and philosopher

Gauss, Karl Friedrich (1777–1855) German mathematician

Gay-Lussac, Joseph Louis (1778–1850) French chemist and physicist

Geber (14th century) Spanish alchemist

Geiger, Hans (1882–1945) German physicist

Gell-Mann, Murray (1929–) US physicist

Gibbs, Josiah Willard (1839–1903) US physicist

Gilbert, William (1544–1603) English physician

Glaser, Donald Arthur (1926–) US physicist

Goddard, Robert Hutchings (1882–1945) US physicist

Gödel, Kurt (1906–78) US mathematician

Gold, Thomas (1920–) Austrian-born astronomer

Goldschmidt, Richard Benedict (1878–1958) US geneticist

Graham, Thomas (1805–69) British physicist

Gray, Asa (1810–88) US botanist

Gregory, James (1638–75) Scottish mathematician and astronomer

Guericke, Otto von (1602–86) German physicist

Haber, Fritz (1868–1934) German chemist

Haeckel, Ernst Heinrich (1834–1919) German zoologist

Hahn, Otto (1879–1968) German chemist and physicist

Halley, Edmund (1656–1742) British astronomer

Hamilton, Sir William Rowan (1805–65) Irish mathematician

Hardy, G(odfrey) H(arold) (1877–1947) British mathematician

Hargreaves, James (d. 1778) English inventor

Heaviside, Oliver (1850–1925) British physicist

Heinkel, Ernst Heinrich (1888–1958) German aircraft designer

Heisenberg, Werner Karl (1901–76) German physicist

Helmholtz, Hermann Ludwig Ferdinand von (1821–94) German physicist and physiologist

Helmont, Jan Baptist van (1580–1644) Belgian alchemist and physician

Henry, Joseph (1797–1878) US physicist

Hermite, Charles (1822–1901) French mathematician

Hero of Alexandria (mid-1st century AD) Greek engineer and mathematician

Herschel, Sir William (1738–1822) British astronomer

Hertz, Heinrich Rudolf (1857–94) German physicist

Hess, Victor Francis (1883–1964) US physicist

Hevesy, George Charles von (1885–1966) Hungarian-born chemist

Hilbert, David (1862–1943) German mathematician

Hipparchus (c. 190–c. 120 BC) Greek astronomer

Hodgkin, Alan Lloyd (1914–) British physiologist

Hodgkin, Dorothy Mary Crowfoot (1910–) British biochemist

Hofmeister, Wilhelm Friedrich Benedict (1824–77) German botanist

Hooke, Robert (1635–1703) British physicist and instrument maker

Hooker, Sir William Jackson (1785–1865) British botanist

Hoyle, Sir Fred (1915–) British astronomer

Hubble, Edwin Powell (1889–1953) US astronomer

Hutton, James (1726–97) Scottish physician

Huxley, Thomas Henry (1825–95) British biologist

Huygens, Christiaan (1629–95) Dutch astronomer and physicist

Ilyushin, Sergei Vladimirovich (1894–1977) Soviet aircraft designer

Ingenhousz, Jan (1730–99) Dutch physician and plant physiologist

Jacquard, Joseph-Marie (1752–1834) French inventor

Jansky, Karl Guthe (1905–50) US radio engineer

Jeans, Sir James Hopwood (1877–1946) British mathematician and astronomer

Josephson, Brian David (1940–) British physicist

Joule, James Prescott (1818–89) British physicist

Junkers, Hugo (1859–1935) German aircraft designer

Kapitza, Peter Leonidovich (1894–1984) Soviet physicist

Kekulé von Stradonitz, (Friedrich) August (1829–96) German chemist

Kelvin, William Thomson, 1st Baron (1824–1907) Scottish physicist

Kendall, Edward Calvin (1886–1972) US biochemist

Kendrew, Sir John Cowdery (1917–) British biochemist

Kennelly, Arthur Edwin (1861–1939) US electrical engineer

Kepler, Johannes (1571–1630) German astronomer

Kinsey, Alfred (1894–1956) US zoologist and sociologist

Kirchhoff, Gustav Robert (1824–87) German physicist

Klaproth, Martin Heinrich (1743–1817) German chemist

Koch, Robert (1843–1910) German bacteriologist

Kolbe, (Adolf Wilhelm) Hermann (1818–84) German chemist

Kolmogorov, Andrei Nikolaevich (1903–87) Soviet mathematician

Krebs, Sir Hans Adolf (1900–81) British biochemist

Kurchatov, Igor Vasilievich (1903–60) Soviet physicist

Lagrange, Joseph Louis, Comte de (1736–1813) French mathematician and astronomer

Lalande, Joseph-Jérôme Le Français de (1732–1807) French astronomer

Lamarck, Jean-Baptiste de Monet, Chevalier de (1744–1829) French naturalist

Lambert, Johann Heinrich (1728–77) German mathematician and astronomer

Land, Edwin Herbert (1909–91) US inventor

Landau, Lev Davidovich (1908–68) Soviet physicist

Langley, Samuel Pierpont (1834–1906) US astronomer

Langmuir, Irving (1881–1957) US chemist

Lankester, Sir Edwin Ray (1847–1929) British zoologist

Laplace, Pierre Simon, Marquis de (1749–1827) French mathematician and astronomer

Laue, Max Theodor Felix von (1879–1960) German physicist

Lavoisier, Antoine Laurent (1743–94) French chemist

Lawrence, Ernest Orlando (1901–58) US physicist

Le Châtelier, Henri-Louis (1850–1936) French chemist

Lecoq de Boisbaudran, Paul-Émile (1838–1912) French chemist

Leeuwenhoek, Antonie van (1632–1723) Dutch scientist

Legendre, Adrien Marie (1752–1833) French mathematician

Lemaître, Georges Édouard, Abbé (1894–1966) Belgian priest and astronomer

Leverrier, Urbain Jean Joseph (1811–77) French astronomer

Liebig, Justus, Baron von (1803–73) German chemist

Linnaeus, Carolus (Carl Linné; 1707–78) Swedish botanist

Liouville, Joseph (1809–82) French mathematician

Lippershey, Hans (died c. 1619) Dutch lens grinder

Lipscomb, William Nunn (1919–) US chemist

Lobachevski, Nikolai Ivanovich (1793–1856) Russian mathematician

Lockyer, Sir Joseph Norman (1836–1920) British astronomer

Lodge, Sir Oliver Joseph (1851–1940) British physicist

Lonsdale, Dame Kathleen (1903–71) Irish physicist

Lorentz, Hendrick Antoon (1853–1928) Dutch physicist

Lorenz, Konrad (1903–89) Austrian zoologist

Lovell, Sir Bernard (1913–) British astronomer

Lowell, Percival (1855–1916) US astronomer

Lumière, Auguste (1862–1954) French photographer

Lyell, Sir Charles (1797–1875) British geologist

Lysenko, Trofim Denisovich (1898–1976) Soviet biologist

McAdam, John Loudon (1756–1836) British inventor

Mach, Ernst (1838–1916) Austrian physicist and philosopher

Macintosh, Charles (1766–1843) Scottish chemist

McMillan, Edwin Mattison (1907–91) US physicist

Marconi, Guglielmo (1874–1937) Italian electrical engineer

Markov, Andrei Andreevich (1856–1922) Russian mathematician

Maudslay, Henry (1771–1831) British engineer

Maupertuis, Pierre Louis Moreau de (1698–1759) French mathematician

Maxim, Sir Hiram Stevens (1840–1916) British inventor

Maxwell, James Clerk (1831–79) Scottish physicist

Mayer, Julius Robert von (1814–78) German physicist

Maynard Smith, John (1920–) British biologist

Meitner, Lise (1878–1968) Austrian physicist

Mendel, Gregor Johann (1822–84) Austrian botanist

Mendeleyev, Dimitrii Ivanovich (1834–1907) Russian chemist

Mercator, Gerardus (Gerhard Kremer; 1512–94) Flemish geographer

Messier, Charles (1730–1817) French astronomer

Metchnikov, Ilya Ilich (or I. I. Mechnikov; 1845–1916) Russian zoologist

Meyerhof, Otto Fritz (1884–1951) US biochemist

Michelson, Albert Abraham (1852–1931) US physicist

Millikan, Robert Andrews (1868–1953) US physicist

Mitchell, R(eginald) J(oseph) (1895–1937) British aeronautical engineer

Monge, Gaspard (1746–1818) French mathematician

Monod, Jacques-Lucien (1910–76) French biochemist

Montgolfier, Jacques-Étienne (1745–99) French balloonist

Morgan, Thomas Hunt (1866–1945) US geneticist

Morse, Samuel Finley Breese (1791–1872) US inventor

Moseley, Henry Gwyn Jeffries (1887–1915) British physicist

Muller, Hermann Joseph (1890–1967) US geneticist

Müller, Paul Hermann (1899–1965) Swiss chemist

Mulliken, Robert Sanderson (1896–1986) US chemist and physicist

Napier, John (1550–1617) Scottish mathematician

Nernst, Walther Hermann (1864–1941) German physical chemist

Neumann, John von (1903–57) US mathematician

Newlands, John Alexander Reina (1837–98) British chemist

Newton, Sir Isaac (1642–1727) British physicist and mathematician

Nirenberg, Marshall Warren (1927–) US biochemist

Nobel, Alfred Bernhard (1833–96) Swedish chemist and businessman

Oersted, Hans Christian (1777–1851) Danish physicist

Ohm, Georg Simon (1787–1854) German physicist

Olbers, Heinrich Wilhelm Matthäus (1758–1840) German astronomer

Oliphant, Sir Mark Laurence Elwin (1901–) Australian physicist

Onsager, Lars (1903–76) US chemist

Oppenheimer, J Robert (1904–67) US physicist

Ostwald, (Friedrich) Wilhelm (1853–1932) German chemist

Otis, Elisha Graves (1811–61) US inventor

Otto, Nikolaus August (1832–91) German engineer

Oughtred, William (1574–1660) English priest and scholar

Pappus of Alexandria (4th century AD) Greek mathematician

Parsons, Sir Charles Algernon (1854–1931) British engineer

Pascal, Blaise (1623–62) French mathematician

Pasteur, Louis (1822–95) French chemist and microbiologist

Pauli, Wolfgang (1900–58) US physicist

Pauling, Linus Carl (1901–) US chemist

Perkin, Sir William Henry (1838–1907) British chemist

Perrin, Jean-Baptiste (1870–1942) French physicist

Perutz, Max Ferdinand (1914–) British chemist

Planck, Max Karl Ernst Ludwig (1858–1947) German physicist

Poincaré, Jules Henri (1854–1912) French mathematician

Poisson, Siméon Dénis (1781–1840) French mathematician

Popov, Aleksandr Stepanovich (1859–1905) Russian physicist

Porsche, Ferdinand (1875–1951) German car designer

Porter, George, Baron (1920–) British physical chemist

Powell, Cecil Frank (1903–69) British physicist

Priestley, Joseph (1733–1804) British chemist

Proust, Joseph-Louis (1754–1826) French chemist

Prout, William (1785–1850) British chemist and physiologist

Ptolemy (or Claudius Ptolemaeus; 2nd century AD) Egyptian mathematician

Purcell, Edward Mills (1912–) US physicist

Rabi, Isidor Isaac (1898–1988) US physicist

Raman, Sir Chandrasekhara Venkata (1888–1970) Indian physicist

Ramsay, Sir William (1852–1916) Scottish chemist

Ray, John (1627–1705) English naturalist

Rayleigh, John William Strutt, 3rd Baron (1842–1919) British physicist

Réaumur, René-Antoine Ferchault de (1683–1757) French physicist

Regiomontanus (Johannes Müller; 1436-76) German astronomer and mathematician

Remington, Eliphalet (1793–1863) US inventor

Rennie, John (1761–1821) British civil engineer

Rheticus (Georg Joachim von Lauchen; 1514–76) German mathematician

Rhine, Joseph Banks (1895–1980) US psychologist

Riemann, Georg Friedrich Bernhard (1826–66) German mathematician

Roebling, John Augustus (1806–69) US engineer

Roentgen, Wilhelm Konrad (1845–1923) German physicist

Rumford, Benjamin Thompson, Count (1753–1814) American-born scientist

Rutherford, Ernest, 1st Baron (1871–1937) English physicist

Ryle, Sir Martin (1918–84) British astronomer

Sabatier, Paul (1854–1941) French chemist

Sakharov, Andrei Dimitrievich (1921–89) Soviet physicist and politician

Sandage, Allan Rex (1926–) US astronomer

Sanger, Frederick (1918–) British biochemist

Savery, Thomas (c. 1650–1715) English engineer

Scheele, Carl Wilhelm (1742–86) Swedish chemist

Schrödinger, Erwin (1887–1961) Austrian physicist

Schwann, Theodor (1810–82) German physiologist

Seaborg, Glenn Theodore (1912–) US physicist

Segrè, Emilio (1905–89) US physicist

Shepard, Jr, Allan Bartlett (1923–) US astronaut

Shockley, William Bradfield (1910–89) US physicist

Sholes, Christopher Latham (1819–90) US inventor

Shrapnel, Henry (1761–1842) British inventor

Siemens, Ernst Werner von (1816–92) German electrical engineer

Sikorsky, Igor Ivan (1889–1972) US aeronautical engineer

Singer, Isaac Merrit (1811–75) US inventor

Sloane, Sir Hans (1660–1753) British physician and naturalist

Soddy, Frederick (1877–1956) British chemist

Sommerfeld, Arnold Johannes Wilhelm (1868–1951) German physicist

Sosigenes of Alexandria (1st century BC) Greek astronomer

Spallanzani, Lazzaro (1729–99) Italian physiologist

Stahl, Georg Ernst (1660–1734) German physician and chemist

Steinmetz, Charles Proteus (1865–1923) US electrical engineer

Stephenson, George (1781–1848) British engineer

Stirling, James (1692–1770) Scottish mathematician

Stokes, Sir George Gabriel (1819–1903) British physicist and mathematician

Struve, Otto (1897–1963) US astronomer

Swammerdam, Jan (1637–80) Dutch naturalist and microscopist

Swan, Sir Joseph Wilson (1828–1914) British physicist

Szilard, Leo (1898–1964) US physicist

Talbot, William Henry Fox (1800–77) British botanist and physicist

Tatum, Edward Lawrie (1909–75) US geneticist

Taylor, Brook (1685–1737) English mathematician

Taylor, Frederick Winslow (1856–1915) US engineer

Telford, Thomas (1757–1834) British civil engineer

Teller, Edward (1908–) US physicist

Tesla, Nikola (1856–1943) US electrical engineer

Thenard, Louis-Jacques (1777–1857) French chemist

Thomson, Sir Joseph John (1856–1940) British physicist

Tinbergen, Niko(laas) (1907–88) Dutch zoologist and pioneer ethologist

Todd, Alexander Robertus, Baron (1907–) British biochemist

Torricelli, Evangelista (1608–47) Italian physicist

Tournefort, Joseph Pitton de (1656–1708) French botanist

Townes, Charles Hard (1915–) US physicist

Trevithick, Richard (1771–1833) British engineer

Tsiolkovski, Konstantin Eduardovich (1857–1935) Russian aeronautical engineer

Tull, Jethro (1674–1741) English agriculturalist

Tyndall, John (1820–93) Irish physicist

Urey, Harold Clayton (1893–1981) US physicist

Van Allen, James Alfred (1914–) US physicist

van der Waals, Johannes Diderik (1837–1923) Dutch physicist

van't Hoff, Jacobus Henricus (1852–1911) Dutch chemist

Vavilov, Nikolai Ivanovich (1887–1943) Soviet plant geneticist

Volta, Alessandro Giuseppe Antonio Anastasio, Count (1745–1827) Italian physicist

Waksman, Selman Abraham (1888–1973) US microbiologist

Wallace, Alfred Russel (1823–1913) British naturalist

Wallis, Sir Barnes (Neville) (1887–1979) British aeronautical engineer

Watson, James Dewey (1928–) US geneticist

Watson-Watt, Sir Robert Alexander (1892–1973) Scottish physicist

Watt, James (1736–1819) British engineer

Weber, Ernst Heinrich (1795–1878) German physiologist

Wegener, Alfred Lothar (1880–1930) German geologist

Weismann, August Friedrich Leopold (1834–1914) German biologist

Wheatstone, Sir Charles (1802–75) British physicist

White, Gilbert (1720–93) English naturalist

Whitney, Eli (1765–1825) American inventor

Whittle, Sir Frank (1907–) British aeronautical engineer

Wiener, Norbert (1894–1964) US mathematician

Wigner, Eugene Paul (1902–) US physicist

Wilkins, Maurice Hugh Frederick (1916–) New Zealand physicist

Wilson, Charles Thomson Rees (1869–1959) British physicist

Wilson, Edmund Beecher (1856–1939) US biologist

Wöhler, Friedrich (1800–82) German chemist

Wright, Orville (1871–1948) US aviator

Young, Thomas (1773–1829) British physician and physicist

Yukawa, Hideki (1907–81) Japanese physicist

Zeeman, Pieter (1865–1943) Dutch physicist

Ziegler, Karl (1898–1973) German chemist

Zuckerman, Solly, Baron (1904–93) British anatomist

Zworykin, Vladimir Kosma (1889–1982) US physicist

---

52 Mathematics

As far as the laws of mathematics refer to reality, they are not certain, and as far as they are certain, they do not refer to reality. Albert Einstein.

There is no 'royal road' to geometry. Euclid.

Let no one ignorant of mathematics enter here. Plato.

Mathematics, rightly viewed, possesses not only truth by supreme beauty – a beauty cold and austere like that of sculpture. Bertrand Russell.

Numbers constitute the only universal language. Nathaniel West.

NOUNS

1 **mathematics**, maths (UK inf), math (US inf), pure mathematics, classical mathematics, new mathematics, higher mathematics, branch, field, study, theory, arithmetic, algebra, calculus, geometry, trigonometry, analysis, numerical analysis, systems analysis, statistics, mathematical logic (or symbolic logic), metamathematics, numeracy, calculation, computation, reckoning, numbers, figures, sums

2 **mathematician**, arithmetician, algebraist, geometrician (or geometer), numerical analyst, systems analyst, statistician

3 **applied mathematics**, mathematical biology, mathematical biophysics, mathematical computing, mathematical ecology, mathematical geography, mathematical physics
▶ *56 Physics, 63 Engineering, 65 Computers*

4 **simple arithmetic**, number work, sums, number theory, higher arithmetic, modular arithmetic

5 **number**, signed number, directed number, positive number, negative number, nonnegative number, even number, odd number, prime number (or prime), composite number, perfect number
▶ *169 Number*

6 **complex number**, real part, imaginary part, modulus, absolute value, argument, complex conjugate, real number, real, imaginary number, rational number, rational, irrational number, irrational, integer, whole number, fraction, mixed number, algebraic number, transcendental number

7 **natural number**, cardinal number, cardinal, ordinal number, ordinal, finite number, infinite number, transfinite number, random number

8 **number system**, counting system, positional notation, place-value notation, decimal notation, decimal system, binary notation, binary system, octal notation, hexadecimal (or hex) notation, duodecimal notation, decimal number, binary number, base, radix point, decimal point, units place, tens place, hundreds place, significant digits, significant figures, fixed-point notation, floating-point notation, precision, accuracy

9 **numeral**, Arabic numeral, Roman numeral, digit, figure, zero, one, two, three, four, five, six, seven, eight, nine, binary digit, bit

10 **zero**, nought, nothing, nill, cypher (Obs), infinitesimal number

11 **infinity**, infinite number, transfinite number, infinitude

12 **numeration**, enumeration, quantification, numbering, counting, reckoning, figuring, quantifying, computation, calculation, mental arithmetic, measurement, count, census, tally, score, whole

13 **mathematical symbol**, plus sign, minus sign, multiplication sign, division sign, equal (or equals) sign, square root sign, radical sign, integral sign, implication sign, operator, operand, arithmetic operator, relational operator, logical operator

14 **operation**, arithmetic operation, algebraic operation, logical operation, associative operation, commutative operation, distributive operation, relation, relationship, formula, solution, result, results, value

15 **addition**, summation, sum, aggregate, total, addend, augend

Mathematical Theories	
catastrophe theory	knot theory
chaos theory	number theory
game theory	queuing theory
group theory	set theory

Theorems and Laws	
associative law	four-colour theorem
binomial theorem	mean-value theorem
commutative law	midpoint theorem
distributive law	remainder theorem

16 **subtraction**, difference, subtrahend, minuend

17 **multiplication**, product, multiplier, multiplicand, multiple, lowest (*or* least) common multiple (LCM), factor, submultiple, highest (*or* greatest) common factor (HCF, GCF), prime factor, power, square, cube, fourth power, exponent, index, square root, cube root, surd, root mean square (rms), factorial, factorization, exponentiation, extraction of roots, multiplication tables

18 **division**, long division, short division, divisibility, quotient, ratio, proportion, percentage, quota, rate, reciprocal, inverse, dividend, divisor, aliquot part, remainder, residue, fraction, numerator, denominator, common denominator, decimal fraction, decimal, recurring decimal, repeated decimal, circular decimal, truncated decimal, vulgar fraction, simple fraction, proper fraction, common fraction, compound fraction, complex fraction, partial fraction, continued fraction, truncation, rounding up, rounding down

19 **logarithm**, log, common logarithm, natural logarithm, base, mantissa, characteristic, antilogarithm, logarithmic scale, logarithm tables, log tables, Napierian (*or* Naperian) logarithm, natural logarithm

20 **sequence**, progression, finite sequence, infinite sequence, arithmetic progression, geometric progression, harmonic progression, series, convergent series, divergent series, arithmetic series, geometric series, binomial series, exponential series, logarithmic series, power series, Fourier series

21 **set**, finite set, infinite set, null set, empty set, universal set, complement, union, intersection, set difference, closure, disjoint sets, ordered set, *n*-tuple, subset, combination, unordered arrangement, permutation, ordered arrangement, element, member, identity element, identity, inverse, bound, upper bound, lower bound, class, group, ring, field

22 **matrix**, row, column, order, square matrix, diagonal matrix, identity matrix, null matrix, inverse, transpose, determinant

23 **algebra**, linear algebra, abstract algebra, set algebra, algebra of propositions, Boolean algebra, set, poset, ring, field, group

24 **evaluation**, simplification, manipulation, expansion, substitution, cross-multiplication, reduction, elimination, cancellation

25 **algebraic expression**, expression, binomial expression, binomial, polynomial expression, polynomial, term, variable, unknown quantity, unknown, coefficient, numerical coefficient, constant, invariant, parameter, brackets, parentheses, square brackets, braces, angle brackets, vinculum, root sign

26 **equality**, inequality, identity, equivalence, conditional

27 **equation**, root, solution, solution set, degree, linear equation, quadratic equation, cubic equation, differential equation, integral equation, functional equation, simultaneous equations

28 **algorithm**, recursive procedure, step-by-step procedure, effective procedure, iteration, recursion, fractal

29 **mathematical function**, function, mapping, transformation, domain, codomain, range, image, dependent variable, independent variable, argument, limit, continuous function, step function, inverse function, composite function, composition, trigonometric function, logarithmic function, exponential function, periodic function, gamma function, beta function, functional

30 **calculus**, infinitesimal calculus, differential calculus, integral calculus, calculus of variations, variational calculus, analysis, real analysis, complex analysis, functional analysis

31 **differentiation**, integration, differential, increment, decrement, derivative, first derivative, second derivative, partial derivative, rate of change, fluxion, integral, indefinite integral, definite integral, limit, upper limit, lower limit, line integral, surface integral, double integral, convolution, differential equation, ordinary differential equation, partial differential equation, integral equation

32 **graph**, chart, plot, graphic representation, curve, bar graph, bar chart, histogram, pie chart, scatter diagram, scattergram, axis, *x*-axis, *y*-axis, *z*-axis, linear scale, logarithmic scale, origin, intercept, graph paper, logarithmic paper, log paper

33 **coordinates**, coordinate system, Cartesian coordinates, polar coordinates, spherical coordinates, cylindrical coordinates, rectangular coordinates, *x*-coordinate, *y*-coordinate, *z*-coordinate, abscissa, ordinate, frame of reference

34 **geometry**, plane geometry, solid geometry, coordinate geometry, analytic geometry, alge-

braic geometry, projective geometry, differential geometry, spherical geometry, Euclidean geometry, non-Euclidean geometry

35 **space**, three-dimensional space, four-dimensional space (*or* space–time continuum), *n*-space, n-dimensional space, hyperspace, hypercube, hypersphere, Euclidean space, Cartesian space, enclosed space, interior, inside, exterior, outside, spatial extension, extent, dimension, dimensions, size, area, volume, capacity

36 **point**, fixed point, reference point, variable point, midpoint, set of points, coordinates (of a point), position, location, point of inflection, stationary point, fiducial point, point at infinity, locus (of a point), path

37 **line**, straight line, curved line, line segment, edge, side, boundary, curve, arc, contour, diagonal, diameter, chord, transversal (*or* transverse), bisector, ray, tangent, asymptote, perpendicular, normal, geodesic, slope (of a line), gradient, parallel lines, intersecting lines, converging lines, diverging lines, skew lines, perpendicular lines, orientation, direction, linear measurement, linear extent, length, width, breadth, height, depth, altitude, radius, perimeter, circumference, linearity, curvature

38 **surface**, flat surface, plane surface, plane, inclined plane, two-dimensional figure, curved surface, concave surface, convex surface, anticlastic surface, synclastic surface, closed surface, solid surface, lamina, face, side, surface measurement, surface area, superficial area, area, extent, flatness, curvature, concavity, convexity, sphericity

39 **angle**, vertex, apex, corner, cusp, node, plane angle, solid angle, dihedral angle, right angle, oblique angle, acute angle, obtuse angle, reflex angle, complementary angle, round angle (*or* perigon), straight angle, interior angle, exterior angle, re-entrant (*or* re-entering) angle, salient angle, conjugate angles, supplementary angles, alternate angles, opposite angles, vertical angles, angle of elevation, angle of depression, angle subtended, angular measurement, angular distance, angular direction, bearing, bearings, latitude, longitude

40 **curve**, sine curve, sinusoid, spiral, Archimedes spiral, logarithmic spiral, hyperbolic spiral, helix, catenary, cardioid, cissoid, cruciform, cycloid, epicycloid, hypocycloid, folium, lemniscate, logistic, trochoid, involute, evolute, trajectory, family (of curves)

41 **geometric figure**, figure, geometric shape, configuration, solid, bounded volume, closed figure, plane figure, solid figure, simplex, fractal, segment, sector, section, cross section, inscribed figure, circumscribed figure, escribed figure, symmetric(al) figure, symmetry, rotational symmetry, mirror symmetry, line (*or* axis) of symmetry, plane of symmetry, centre of symmetry

42 **circle**, annulus, ring, disc, great circle, small circle, circumcircle, incircle, concentric circles, eccentric circles, semicircle, quadrant, sector, crescent, lune, meniscus, circumference, arc, radius, diameter, chord, ellipse, oval, major axis, minor axis, parabola, hyperbola, conic section (or conic), focus, directrix, eccentricity

43 **triangle**, trigon (Obs), right-angled triangle, right triangle, acute-angled triangle, obtuse-angled triangle, equilateral triangle, isosceles triangle, scalene triangle, median triangle, circular triangle, spherical triangle, congruent triangles, similar triangles, equivalent triangles, adjacent, opposite, hypotenuse, base, altitude, median, centroid, orthocentre

44 **polygon**, triangle, square, rectangle, oblong, parallelogram, rhombus, rhomb, diamond, lozenge, rhomboid, quadrilateral, quadrangle, tetragon, trapezoid, trapezium, golden rectangle, golden mean, golden section, pentagon, hexagon, heptagon, octagon, nonagon, decagon, regular polygon, quadrangle, star-shaped figure, pentagram, pentangle, pentacle, hexagram, polyline

45 **curved surface**, closed surface, surface of revolution, solid of revolution, sphere, spheroid, ellipsoid, paraboloid, hyperboloid, cylinder, cone, truncated cone, frustum, torus, anchor ring, toroid, zone

46 **polyhedron**, tetrahedron, pentahedron, hexahedron, cube, cuboid, parallelepiped, octahedron, dodecahedron, icosahedron, pyramid, truncated pyramid, frustum, prism, wedge, prismatoid, prismoid, rhombohedron, regular polyhedron, Platonic solid, irregular polyhedron

47 **topology**, algebraic topology, analysis situs (Obs), continuous distortion, stretching, knotting, knot, Möbius (*or* Moebius) strip, torus, Klein bottle, manifold

48 **transformation**, affine transformation, translation, reflection, rotation, glide reflection, dilation, dilatation, homothety, similitude, congruence, shear, projection, perspective projection, orthogonal projection, isometric projection, mirror image, enantiomorphic figure

49 **geometric construction**, construction, drawing, geometric instrument, compass, compasses, pair of compasses, dividers, ruler, rule, straightedge, protractor, set square, T-square, squaring the circle

50 **scalar quantity**, scalar, vector quantity, vector, magnitude, direction, absolute value, unit vector, position vector, radius vector, component, resultant, parallelogram of forces, vector sum, scalar product, dot product, inner prod-

uct, vector product, cross product, outer product, differential operator, nabla, del, gradient, divergence, curl, tensor

51 **trigonometry**, trig (Inf), plane trigonometry, spherical trigonometry, triangulation, sine rule, cosine rule, tangent rule

52 **trigonometric function**, circular function, hyperbolic function, inverse trigonometric function, sine (sin), cosine (cos), tangent (tan), cosecant (cosec), secant (sec), cotangent (cot), hyperbolic sine (sinh), hyperbolic cosine (cosh), hyperbolic tangent (tanh), inverse sine (arc-sine), inverse cosine (arc-cosine), inverse tangent (arc-tangent)

53 **statistics**, descriptive statistics, statistical inference, statistical analysis, probability theory, vital statistics, parametric statistics, nonparametric statistics

54 **hypothesis testing**, null hypothesis, alternative hypothesis, test statistic, significance level, significance test, one-tailed test, two-tailed test, goodness-of-fit test

55 **statistical methods**, analysis of variance, regression analysis, multivariate analysis, cluster analysis, factor analysis, principle component analysis

56 **nonparametric methods**, ordering, ranking, nominal scale, ordinal scale, interval scale, ratio scale, rank, order number

57 **population**, sample, random sample, biased sample, sample size, data collection, sampling, random sampling, systematic sampling, bias, crude data, data summarization, statistic, sample statistic, random variable, stochastic variable, stochastic process

58 **frequency distribution**, frequency, absolute frequency, relative frequency, event, occurrence, particular instance, success, histogram

59 **probability distribution**, discrete distribution, continuous distribution, normal distribution, Gaussian distribution, binomial distribution, Poisson distribution, exponential distribution, gamma distribution, chi-square distribution, t-distribution, skew distribution, bimodal distribution, skewness, kurtosis, frequency function, probability density function, cumulative distribution function

60 **parameter**, characteristic, average, average value, typical value, expected value, mean, median, mode, arithmetic mean, geometric mean, weighted mean, weighting, variation, spread, dispersion, standard deviation, standard error, mean deviation, covariance, range, interquartile range, percentile, probable error, mean error, confidence level, confidence limits

61 **correlation**, positive correlation, negative correlation, association, correlation coefficient, significance

62 **probability**, chance, mathematical probability, empirical probability, conditional probability, certainty, impossibility, possible outcome, favourable outcome, likelihood, maximum likelihood

63 **mathematical logic**, symbolic logic, formal logic, propositional calculus, predicate calculus, functional calculus, logical proposition, proposition, statement, premise (or premiss), assertion, affirmation, denial, logical expression, logical formula, well-formed formula, logical operation, logical connective, operator, logical operator, relational operator, negation, conjunction, logical product, disjunction, alternation, logical sum, implication, equivalence, conditional, relation, relationship, equivalence relation, ordering relation, transitive relation, reflexive relation, irreflexive relation, symmetric relation, antisymmetric relation, asymmetric relation, truth value, logical value, truth, falsity, truth table, universal quantifier, existential quantifier

64 **reasoning**, mathematical reasoning, logical reasoning, argument, inference, deduction, induction, derivation, premise (or premiss), rules of inference, valid argument, sound argument, invalid argument, unsound argument, conclusion, indication, heuristic solution, validation, verification, validity, soundness, rigour, correctness, truth, completeness, consistency, compatibility, sufficiency, invalidity, falsity, inconsistency, incompatibility, insufficiency, condition, restriction, contingency, necessary and sufficient condition, tautology, contradiction, converse, paradox

65 **theory**, mathematical model, theoretical framework, simulation, generalization, abstraction, idealization, law, general principle, principle, criterion, rule, theorem, hypothesis, general proposition, proposition, lemma, corollary, formal expression, formula, equation, postulate, supposition, presupposition, premise (or premiss), conjecture, axiom, first principles

66 **proof**, rigorous proof, direct proof, indirect proof, QED (quod erat demonstrandum), demonstration, test, procedure, method, evaluation, estimation, approximation, extrapolation, interpolation, error

67 **calculator**, computer, adding machine, abacus, Napier's bones, tally stick, score card, cash register

▶ 65 Computers

ADJECTIVES

68 **mathematical**, arithmetic(al), algebraic, geometric(al), trigonometric(al), analytic(al), topological, statistical

69 **theoretic(al)**, abstract, analytic(al), formal, theorematic, theoremic, hypothetic(al), propositional, axiomatic, self-evident, empiri-

Named Concepts, Theorems, etc.

Abelian group
Agnesi, witch of
Apollonius' theorem
Argand diagram
Banach space
Bayes's theorem
Bernoulli trial
Bessel functions
Boolean algebra
Briggsian logarithms
Cantor set
Cartesian coordinates
Cauchy sequence
Chinese remainder
  theorem
de Moivre's formula
Diophantine equation

Dirichlet series
Eratosthenes, sieve of
Euclidean geometry
Euclid's axioms
Euler's constant
Euler's formula
Fermat's last theorem
French curve
Fibonacci numbers
Fourier analysis
Fourier series
Galois group
Gaussian distribution
Gauss's theorem
Gödel numbers
Green's theorem
Gregory's series

Hanoi, towers of
Heron's (or Hero's)
  formula
Hilbert's problems
Hilbert space
Julia set
Klein bottle
Lagrange's theorem
Laplace operator (or
  Laplacian)
Legendre polynomials
Leibnitz's theorem
L'Hospital's rule
Lie group
Lobachevskian geom-
  etry
Maclaurin series

Markovian chain
Mandelbrot set
Mersenne numbers
Mersenne prime
Möbius strip
Monte Carlo method
Napierian logarithm
Newton's method
Pascal's triangle
Poisson distribution
Pythagoras's theorem
Riemannian geometry
Russell's paradox
Simpson's rule
Stokes's theorem
Taylor series
Venn diagram

cal, observational, experiential, heuristic

70 **universal**, general, fundamental, basic, simple, standard, normal, canonical, uniform, continuous, discrete, noncontinuous, distinct, unique

71 **numerical**, signed, positive, negative, nonnegative, unsigned, even, odd, integral, whole, digital, fractional, decimal, denary, binary, ternary

72 **complex**, real, imaginary, rational, irrational, transcendental, infinitesimal, finite, infinite

73 **numerable**, enumerable, denumerable, countable, quantifiable, measurable, mensurable, calculable, computable, soluble, solvable, insoluble, insolvable, unsolvable, decidable, undecidable

74 **divisible**, indivisible, prime, composite, compound, reciprocal, inverse, in proportion, proportional, percentile, rational, commensurable, irrational, incommensurable

75 **equal**, identical, unequal, ordinal, ordered, partially ordered, ranked, cardinal, first, second, third, fourth, fifth, sixth, seventh, eighth, ninth, tenth, zeroth, maximal, greatest, largest, highest, minimal, least, lowest, smallest, upper, higher, greater, lower, lesser

76 **functional**, relational, exponential, logarithmic, linear, quadratic, cubic, binomial, trinomial, multinomial, polynomial, differential, integral, one-one, one-to-one, one-many, many-one

77 **given**, assumed, known, stipulated, explicit, implicit, characteristic, dependent, variable, variate, independent, invariable, constant, parametric

78 **pictorial**, diagrammatic, graphic, tabular

79 **spatial**, flat, planar, plane, two-dimensional, coplanar, superficial, three-dimensional, solid, symmetric(al), regular, asymmetric(al), irregular, distorted

80 **linear**, lineal, straight, straight-lined, straight-edged, rectilinear, horizontal, flat, vertical, upright, oblique, sloping, slanted, at

an angle, tangential, asymptotic, parallel, perpendicular, normal, orthogonal, orthographic, angular, angled, pointed, intersecting, convergent, divergent, skew, collinear, equidistant, equilateral

81 **curvilinear**, curved, arcuate, convex, concave, round, rounded, circular, annular, ringlike, ring-shaped, spiral, helical, semicircular, quadrantal, crescent-shaped, lunate, lenticular, elliptic(al), oval, parabolic, hyperbolic, central, focal, concentric, confocal, eccentric, radial, diametral, diametric, antipodal

82 **polygonal**, multiangular, triangular, wedge-shaped, three-sided, square, rectangular, oblong, rhombic, rhomboidal, diamond-shaped, quadrilateral, four-sided, tetragonal, pentagonal, five-sided, hexagonal, six-sided, heptagonal, seven-sided, octagonal, eight-sided

83 **spherical**, ellipsoidal, oval, ovoid, oblate, prolate, spheroidal, parabaloid(al), hyperboloid(al), cylindrical, disc-shaped, disclike, rod-shaped, conical, cone-shaped, toric, toroidal

84 **cubic**, cubiform, cuboid, oblong, hexahedral, octahedral, pyramidal, prismatic, wedge-shaped, polyhedral, multifacial

85 **cyclic**, periodic, harmonic, sinusoidal

86 **logical**, deductive, inductive, inferential, valid, sound, correct, true, invalid, unsound, incorrect, false, equivalent, complete, consistent, compatible, necessary, sufficient, inconsistent, incomplete, incompatible, contingent, conditional, tautological, contradictory, converse, paradoxical

ADVERBS

87 **mathematically**, theoretically, analytically, generally, logically, fundamentally, basically, continuously, uniformly, discretely, numerically, positively, negatively, digitally, per cent, infinitesimally, finitely, infinitely, equally, approximately, almost, about, unequally, functionally, exponentially, logarithmically, trigonometrically, spatially, linearly, spherically

PREPOSITIONS

88 **equal to**, not equal to, approximately equal to, proportional to, inversely proportional to, directly proportional to, less than, less than or equal to, much less than, greater than, greater than or equal to, much greater than, plus, minus, divided by, divided into, multiplied by, times

VERBS

89 **theorize**, hypothesize, postulate, presuppose, assume, analyse, reason, deduce, infer, conclude, derive, generalize, prove, validate, demonstrate, satisfy, disprove, invalidate

90 **enumerate**, count, number, reckon up, quantify, measure, compute, calculate, determine, solve, evaluate, resolve

91 **add**, add up, sum, aggregate, subtract, take away, multiply, multiply out, cross multiply, times, raise (to a power), square, cube, extract a root, take the square root, factorize, borrow, carry, divide, subdivide, proportion, decimalize, truncate, round up, round down

92 **manipulate**, simplify, expand, cancel, eliminate, substitute

93 **equate**, equalize, equal, approximate, estimate, sample, extrapolate, interpolate, correct for, correlate

94 **order**, rank, maximize, minimize, vary, approach (a limit), tend to, vanish, standardize, normalize

95 **evaluate**, differentiate, integrate

96 **represent**, draw, configure, construct, generate, plot, graph, project, transform, translate, rotate, reflect

97 **align**, line up, extend, produce (a line), converge, diverge, intersect, disect, bisect, slope, subtend (an angle), curve, circle, encircle, circumscribe, inscribe

53 Astronomy

...in my studies of astronomy and philosophy I hold this opinion about the universe, that the Sun remains fixed in the centre of the circle of heavenly bodies, without changing its place; and the Earth, turning upon itself, moves round the Sun. Galileo Galilei.

Astronomy teaches the correct use of the sun and the planets. Stephen Leacock.

NOUNS

1 **astronomy**, star gazing, star watching, optical astronomy, observational astronomy, radio astronomy, infrared astronomy, X-ray astronomy, ultraviolet astronomy, gamma-ray astronomy, radar astronomy, astrophysics, cosmology, cosmogeny, uranography, astrometry, celestial mechanics, astrodynamics, stellar statistics, astrochemistry, cosmochemistry, astrobiology, exobiology, astrobotany, astrogeology, astrophotography

2 **astronomer**, observer, astrophysicist, cosmologist, cosmogenist, uranographer, cosmochemist, astronomer royal, star gazer

3 **universe**, cosmos, macrocosm, totality, world, heavens, firmament, space, deep space, outer space, sky, empyrean, welkin, vault of heaven

▶ *248 Space, 8 Divinity*

4 **cosmological model**, Ptolemaic universe, Copernican universe, Einstein universe, general relativity, big bang, steady state, expanding universe, inflationary universe, oscillating universe, open universe, closed universe, flat universe, primordial fireball, cosmic background, microwave background, dark matter, gravitational force, gravitational constant

Galaxies

Andromeda
Large Magellanic Cloud (Nubecular Major)
Maffei 1
Maffei 2
Milky Way System
Small Magellanic Cloud (Nubecular Minor)
Sombrero Galaxy
Triangulum Spiral
Whirlpool Galaxy

Clusters

Beehive (Praesepe)
Gould Belt
Great Cluster in Hercules
Hyadese
Jewel Box
Sword Handle

Nebulae

Nebula (Constellation or Direction)
Coalsack (Crux)
Crab Nebula (Taurus)
Dumbbell Nebula (Vulpecula)
Great Looped or Loop or Tarantula Nebula (Dorado)
Great Nebula in Orion
Helix Nebula (Aquarius)
Hind's Nebula (Taurus)
Horsehead Nebula (Orion)
Hubble Nebula (Monoceros)
Keyhole Nebula (Carinus)
Lagoon Nebula (Sagittarius)
Loop or Great Looped or Tarantula Nebula (Dorado)
North American Nebula (Cygnus)
Omega or Swan Nebula (Sagittarius)
Ophiuchus Nebula
Owl Nebula (Ursa Major)
Ring Nebula (Lyra)
Rosette Nebula (Monoceros)
Saturn Nebula (Aquarius)
Swan or Omega Nebula (Sagittarius)
Tarantula or Great Looped or Loop Nebula (Dorado)
Trifid Nebula (Sagittarius)
Veil Nebula (Cygnus)

The Constellations

Technical Name (Common Name)			
Andromeda	Centaurus (Centaur)	Hydrus (Water Snake)	Piscis Volans or
Antlia (Air Pump or Pump)	Cepheus	Indus (Indian)	Volans (Flying Fish)
Apus (Bird of Paradise)	Cetus (Whale)	Lacerta (Lizard)	Puppis (Poop or Stern)
Aquarius (Water Bearer)	Chameleon	Leo (Lion)	Pyxis (Mariner's Compass)
Aquila (Eagle)	Circinus (Compasses)	Leo Minor (Little Lion)	Reticulum (Net)
Ara (Altar)	Columba (Dove)	Lepus (Hare)	Sagitta (Arrow)
Aries (Ram)	Coma Berenices (Bernice's Hair)	Libra (Balance or Scales)	Sagittarius (Archer)
Auriga (Charioteer)	Corona Australis (Southern Crown)	Lupus (Wolf)	Scorpius (Scorpion)
Boötes (Herdsman)	Corona Borealis (Northern Crown)	Lynx	Sculptor
Caelum (Chisel)	Corvus (Crow)	Lyra (Lyre)	Scutum (Shield)
Camelopardalis (Giraffe)	Crater (Cup)	Mensa (Table Mountain)	Serpens (Serpent)
Cancer (Crab, Moon Child (US)	Crux (or Crux Australis) (Southern Cross)	Microscopium (Microscope)	Sextans (Sextant)
Canes Venatici (Hunting Dogs)	Cygnus (Swan)	Monoceros (Unicorn)	Taurus (Bull)
Canis Major (Great Dog)	Delphinus (Dolphin)	Musca (Fly)	Telescopium (Telescope)
Canis Minor (Little Dog)	Dorado (Swordfish)	Norma (Rule or Level)	Triangulum (Triangle)
Capricornus or Capricorn (Sea Goat or Goat)	Draco (Dragon)	Octans (Octant)	Triangulum Australe (Southern Triangle)
Carina (Keel)	Equuleus (Little Horse)	Ophiuchus (Serpent Bearer)	Tucana (Toucan)
Cassiopeia	Eridanus (River)	Orion	Ursa Major (Great Bear)
	Fornax (Furnace)	Pavo (Peacock)	Ursa Minor (Little Bear)
	Gemini (Twins)	Pegasus	Vela (Sails)
	Grus (Crane)	Perseus	Virgo (Virgin or Maiden)
	Hercules	Phoenix	Volans or Piscis Volans (Flying Fish)
	Horologium (Clock)	Pictor (Painter)	Vulpecula (Fox)
	Hydra (Monster or Sea Serpent)	Pisces (Fishes)	
		Piscis Austrinus (Southern Fish)	

5 **celestial sphere**, celestial equator, celestial poles, ecliptic, horizon, meridian, zenith, nadir, equinox, vernal equinox, autumnal equinox, solstice, galactic latitude, galactic longitude, celestial latitude, celestial longitude, right ascension, declination, hour angle, altitude, azimuth

6 **star catalogue**, star atlas, sky survey, Messier Catalogue, New General Catalogue (NGC), ephemeris

7 **galaxy**, island universe, galactic nebula, anagalactic nebula, elliptical galaxy, spiral galaxy, barred spiral galaxy, irregular galaxy, lenticular galaxy, Hubble classification, supergiant elliptical, giant elliptical, giant spiral, dwarf elliptical, cluster, Local Group, supercluster, active galaxy, quasar, radio galaxy, Seyfert galaxy, starburst galaxy, filament, void, galactic centre, nucleus, disc, arm, halo, gravitational redshift, Hubble constant

8 **interstellar medium**, cosmic dust, interstellar dust, interstellar gas, interstellar molecule, HI region, HII region, nebula, emission nebula, reflection nebula, bright nebula, absorption nebula, dark nebula, gaseous nebula, diffuse nebula, planetary nebula, ring nebula, Orion nebula, Crab nebula, Horsehead nebula, Coalsack, cosmic rays

9 **constellation**, zodiac, stellar cluster, globular cluster, open cluster, stellar group, stellar association, stellar population, double star, optical double, binary star, visual binary, eclipsing binary, spectroscopic binary, close binary, X-ray binary, multiple star

10 **star**, luminary, orb, sphere, heavenly body, celestial body, fixed star, evening star, Hesperus, Vesper, morning star, Lucifer, circumpolar star, nebulous star, variable star

11 **stellar birth**, protostar, molecular cloud, stellar evolution, main sequence, gravitational collapse, dying star, red giant, white dwarf, supernova, supernova remnant, neutron star, pulsar, black hole, event horizon, singularity, white hole

12 **variable star**, Algol variable, pulsating variable, Cepheid variable, Mira variable, RR Lyrae star, cataclysmic variable, nova, recurrent nova, flare star

13 **luminosity**, magnitude, apparent magnitude, absolute magnitude, proper motion, radial velocity, parallax, precession, spectral type, O star, B star, A star, F star, G star, K star, M star, luminosity class, supergiant, giant star, giant, subgiant, main-sequence star, Hertzsprung–Russell diagram

14 **solar system**, planetary system, Kepler's laws, interplanetary space, solar wind, zodiacal light, gegenschein, earthshine, the old moon in the new moon's arms

15 **sun**, daystar, Sol, Helios, Hyperion, sunlight, sunshine, midnight sun, solar eclipse, corona, chromosphere, photosphere, solar activity, active sun, quiet sun, solar cycle, sunspot cycle, 11-year cycle, butterfly diagram, solar flare, prominence, sunspot, facula, filament, granule, solar spectrum, Fraunhofer lines

The Constellations

Common Name
(Technical Name)
Air Pump or Pump
  (Antlia)
Altar (Ara)
Andromeda
Archer (Sagittarius)
Arrow (Sagitta)
Balance or Scales
  (Libra)
Bernice's Hair (Coma
  Berenices)
Bird of Paradise
  (Apus)
Bull (Taurus)
Cassiopeia
Centaur (Centaurus)
Cepheus
Chameleon
Charioteer (Auriga)
Chisel (Caelum)
Clock (Horologium)
Compasses (Circinus)
Crab or Moon Child
  (US) (Cancer)
Crane (Grus)
Crow (Corvus)
Cup (Crater)
Dolphin (Delphinus)
Dove (Columba)
Dragon (Draco)
Eagle (Aquila)
Fishes (Pisces)

Fly (Musca)
Flying Fish (Volans or
  Pisces Volans)
Fox (Vulpecula)
Furnace (Fornax)
Giraffe
  (Camelopardalis)
Goat or Sea Goat
  (Capricornus or
  Capricorn)
Great Bear (Ursa
  Major)
Great Dog (Canis
  Major)
Hare (Lepus)
Hercules
Herdsman (Boötes)
Hunting Dogs (Canes
  Venatici)
Indian (Indus)
Keel (Carina)
Level or Rule (Norma)
Lion (Leo)
Little Bear (Ursa
  Minor)
Little Dog (Canis
  Minor)
Little Horse (Equuleus)
Little Lion (Leo Minor)
Lizard (Lacerta)
Lynx
Lyre (Lyra)

Maiden or Virgin
  (Virgo)
Mariner's Compass
  (Pyxis)
Microscope
  (Microscopium)
Monster or Sea Ser-
  pent (Hydra)
Moon Child (US) or
  Crab (Cancer)
Net (Reticulum)
Northern Crown (Co-
  rona Borealis)
Octant (Octans)
Orion
Painter (Pictor)
Peacock (Pavo)
Pegasus
Perseus
Phoenix
Poop or Stern (Puppis)
Pump or Air Pump
  (Antlia)
Ram (Aries)
River (Eridanus)
Rule or Level (Norma)
Sails (Vela)
Scales or Balance
  (Libra)
Scorpion (Scorpius)
Sculptor
Sea Goat or Goat
  (Capricornus)

Serpent (Serpens)
Serpent Bearer (Ophiu-
  chus)
Sextant (Sextans)
Shield (Scutum)
Southern Cross (Crux
  or Crux Australis)
Southern Crown (Co-
  rona Australis)
Southern Fish (Piscis
  Austrinus)
Southern Triangle
  (Triangulum Aus-
  trale)
Stern or Poop (Puppis)
Swan (Cygnus)
Swordfish (Dorado)
Table Mountain
  (Mensa)
Telescope (Telescop-
  ium)
Toucan (Tucana)
Triangulum (Triangle)
Twins (Gemini)
Unicorn (Monoceros)
Virgin or Maiden
  (Virgo)
Water Bearer
  (Aquarius)
Water Snake (Hydrus)
Whale (Ceta)
Wolf (Lupus)

Other Groups of Stars

Diamond of Virgo
False Cross (Carina, Vela)
Great Square of Pegasus
Orion's Belt
Orion's Sword
Pleiades or Seven Sisters
Plough or Big Dipper (US) (Ursa Major)
Pointers (Ursa Major)
Sickle of Leo

16 **planet**, major planet, Mercury, Venus, Earth, Mars (or Red Planet), Jupiter, Saturn, Uranus, Neptune, Pluto, giant planet, Jovian planet, terrestrial planet, inferior planet, superior planet, wandering star, minor planet, asteroid, asteroid belt, planetoid, earthgrazer, opposition, conjunction, greatest elongation, syzygy, albedo, planetary atmosphere, aurora, radiation belt, Van Allen belts, magnetosphere

17 **moon**, moonlight, phase, new moon, full moon, harvest moon, hunter's moon, crescent moon, horned moon, first quarter, last quarter, half-moon, gibbous moon, waxing moon, waning moon, terminator, libration, lunar month, lunar eclipse, crater, mare (pl. maria), sea, basin, highlands, rille, mascon, queen of night, Sister Moon, Selene, Diana, Cynthia, Artemis, man in the moon

18 **satellite**, natural satellite, moon, Galilean satellite

19 **comet**, cometary nucleus, coma, tail, dirty snowball, Oort cloud

20 **meteor**, shooting star, falling star, fireball, bolide, meteor shower, meteor swarm, radiant, meteorite, iron meteorite (or iron), stony meteorite (or stone), aerolite, siderite, siderolite, chondrite, carbonaceous chondrite, achondrite, find, fall, meteorite crater, tektite, meteoroid, micrometeorite

21 **orbit**, elliptical orbit, revolution, trajectory, orbital period, eccentricity, inclination, semimajor axis, perihelion, aphelion, parabolic orbit, hyperbolic orbit, rotation, rotational axis, rotational period, precession, eclipse, transit, occultation, twinkling, scintillation,

Zodiac Constellations

Aries (Ram; 21 Mar – 19 Apr)
Taurus (Bull; 20 Apr – 20 May)
Gemini (Twins; 21 May – 21 June)
Cancer or Moon Child (Crab; 22 June – 22 July)
Leo (Lion; 23 July – 22 Aug)
Virgo (Virgin or Maiden; 23 Aug – 22 Sept)
Libra (Balance or Scales; 24 Sept – 23 Oct)
Scorpio (Scorpion; 24 Oct – 21 Nov)
Sagittarius (Archer; 22 Nov – 21 Dec)
Capricornus or Capricorn (Goat or Sea Goat;
  22 Dec – 19 Jan)
Aquarius (Water Carrier; 20 Jan – 18 Feb)
Pisces (Fishes; 19 Feb – 20 Mar)

Named Stars

Star (Constellation)			
Achernar (Eridanus)	Antares (Scorpius)	Garnet star (Cepheus)	Proxima Centauri (Centaurus)
Acrux or Alpha Crucis (Crux)	Arcturus (Boötes)	Hadar or Beta Centauri (Centaurus)	Ras Algethi (Hercules)
Adhara (Canis Major)	Barnard's Star (Ophiuchus)	Kepler's star (Ophiuchus)	Regulus (Leo)
Albireo (Cygnus)	Bellatrix (Orion)	Kruger	Rigel (Orion)
Alcaid or Alkaid or Benatnasch (Ursa Major)	Beta Centauri or Hadar (Centaurus)	Lalande	Rigil Kent or Alpha Centauri (Centaurus)
Alcor (Ursa Major)	Beta Crucis or Mimosa (Crux)	Luyten	Ross
Alcyone (Taurus)	Betelgeuse (Orion)	Markab (Pegasus)	Saiph (Orion)
Aldebaran (Taurus)	Canopus (Carina)	Merak (Ursa Major)	Scheat (Pegasus)
Algeiba (Leo)	Capella (Auriga)	Mimosa or Beta Crucis (Crux)	Schedar or Shedir (Cassiopeia)
Algenib (Pegasus)	Castor (Gemini)	Mira (Orion)	Shaula (Scorpius)
Algol (Perseus)	Cor Caroli (Canes Venatici)	Mirach (Andromeda)	Shedir or Schedar (Cassiopeia)
Alioth (Ursa Major)	61 Cygni (Cygnus)	Mirfak (Perseus)	Sirius or Dog Star (Canis Major)
Alkaid or Alcaid or Benatnasch (Ursa Major)	Deneb (Cygnus)	Mirzam (Canis Major)	Spica (Virgo)
	Denebola (Leo)	Naos (Puppis)	Tau Ceti (Cetus)
Almach (Andromeda)	Dog Star or Sirius (Canis Major)	North Star or Polaris (Ursa Minor)	Thuban (Draco)
Alpha Centauri or Rigil Kent (Centaurus)	Dubhe (Ursa Major)	Phecda or Phekda (Ursa Major)	Trapezium (Orion)
Alpha Crucis or Acrux (Crux)	El Nath (Taurus)	Polaris or North Star (Ursa Minor)	Tycho's star (Cassiopeia)
Alphard (Hydra)	Epsilon Eridani (Eridanus)	Pollux (Gemini)	Vega (Lyra)
Alpheratz (Andromeda)	Epsilon Indi (Indus)	Porrima (Virgo)	Wolf
Altair (Aquila)	Fomalhaut (Piscis Austrinus)	Procyon (Canis Minor)	Zeta Aurigae (Auriga)

Planets and their Satellites

Planet (Named Satellites)
Mercury
Venus
Earth (Moon)
Mars (Phobos, Deimos)
Jupiter (Metis, Adastea, Amalthea, Thebe, Io, Europa, Ganymede, Callisto, Leda, Milalia, Lysithea, Elara, Ananke, Carme, Pasiphae, Sinope)
Saturn (Mimas, Enceladus, Tethys, Dione, Rhea, Titan, Hyperion, Iapetus, Phoebe, Janus)
Uranus (Miranda, Ariel, Umbriel, Titania, Oberon)
Neptune (Triton, Nereid)
Pluto (Charon)

Minor Planets

Achilles	Euphrosyne
Adonis	Hebe
Amor	Hermes
Apollo	Hidalgo
Astraea	Hygiea
Aten	Icarus
Ceres	Iris
Chiron	Juno
Eros	Pallas
Eunomia	Vesta

zenith, nadir, fiducial point, reddening, redshift, blueshift

22 **astronomical unit**, light-year, parsec, solar mass

23 **observatory**, astronomical observatory, ground-based observatory, optical observatory, infrared observatory, Royal Greenwich Observatory (RGO), Royal Observatory Edinburgh (ROE), Mauna Kea Observatory, Palomar Observatory, Hale Observatories, Kitt Peak National Observatory (KPNO), Anglo-Australian Observatory, European Southern Observatory (ESO), dome, observation, seeing, light pollution, radio observatory, Jodrell Bank, planetarium, planisphere, astrolable, orrery

24 **telescope**, astronomical telescope, optical telescope, reflector (or reflecting telescope), William Herschel Telescope, Anglo-Australian Telescope, Hale Telescope, Hubble Space Telescope, Cassegrain telescope, Newtonian telescope, Schmidt telescope, Dobsonian telescope, refractor (or refracting telescope), Galilean telescope, Keplerian telescope, infrared telescope, flux collector, solar telescope, heliostat

25 **mounting**, equatorial mounting, altazimuth mounting, guide telescope, finder, setting circle, draw tube, collimation, primary mirror, objective lens, eyepiece, spherical aberration, coma, astigmatism, chromatic aberration

26 **radio telescope**, radio dish, antenna, receiver, array, radio interferometer, Very Large Array (VLA), aperture synthesis, very long baseline interferometry (VLBI), X-ray telescope, grazing-incidence telescope

27 **imaging**, wide-angle photography, spectrometry, photometry, interferometry, blink comparator, detector, recording system, imaging system, spectrometer, spectrograph, photometer, radiometer

28 **resolution**, angular resolution, resolving power, aperture, light-gathering power, limiting magnitude, field of view

29 **astronautics**, cosmonautics, space (or aero-

Lunar Features
Craters

Aitken	Jules Verne
Alphonsus	Kepler
Archimedes	Langrenus
Aristarchus	Plato
Aristillus	Proclus
Arzarchel	Ptolemaeus
Autolycus	Reiner
Bailly	Schickard
Clavius	Schiller
Cleomedes	Stevinus
Copernicus	Theophilus
Cyrillas	Tsiolkovsky
Eratosthenes	Tycho
Gassendi	Wargentin
Giordano Bruno	Van de Graaff
Grimaldi	

Seas (Maria)

Oceanus Procellarum (Ocean of Storms)
Mare Imbrium (Sea of Rains)
Mare Serenitatis (Sea of Serenity)
Mare Fecunditatis (Sea of Fertility)
Mare Tranquillitatis (Sea of Tranquillity)
Mare Crisium (Sea of Crises)
Mare Humorum (Sea of Moisture)
Mare Nectaris (Sea of Nectar)
Mare Frigoris (Sea of Cold)
Mare Orientale (Eastern Sea)
Mare Australe (Southern Sea)
Mare Cognitum (Sea of Knowledge)
Mare Nubium (Sea of Clouds)
Mare Marginis (Border Sea)
Mare Smythii (Smyth's Sea)
Mare Spumans (Foaming Sea)
Mare Undarum (Sea of Waves)
Mare Humboldtianum (Humboldt's Sea)
Mare Moscoviense (Sea of Moscow)
Mare Ingenii (Sea of Ingenuity)
Mare Anguis (Serpent Sea)
Mare Vaporum (Sea of Vapours)
Sinus Medii (Central Bay)
Sinus Aestuum (Bay of Heats)
Sinus Roris (Bay of Dews)
Sinus Amoris (Bay of Love)
Sinus Iridum (Bay of Rainbows)
Palus Putredinis (Marsh of Decay)
Palus Somnii (Marsh of Sleep)
Palus Epidemiarum (Marsh of Epidemics)
Palus Nebularum (Marsh of Mists)
Lacus Mortis (Lake of Death)
Lacus Somniorum (Lake of Dreams)
Lacus Veris (Lake of Spring)
Lacus Autumni (Lake of Autumn)

Mountains

Alps	Marius Hills
Altai Scarp	Piton
Apennines	Pyrenees
Apollonius	Riphaeus
Aristarchus Plateau	Rook
Carpathians	Rümker Hills
Caucasus	Spitzbergen
Cordillera	Straight
Haemus	Taurus
Harbinger	Tenerife
La Hire	

Rills and Valleys

Alpine Valley	Posidonius
Aridaeus	Rheita Valley
Byrgius	Schröter's Valley
Cauchy Fault	Schrödinger Canyon
Hadley	Sirsalis
Hyginus	Straight Wall
Lee Lincoln Scarp	

Comets

Arend–Roland	Kohoutek
Bennett	Kopff
Biela	Lexell
Borrelly	Olbers
Bronsen–Metcalf	Pons–Brooks
Comas Solá	Pons–Winnecke
Crommelin	Schaumasse
Daylight Comet	Stephan-Oterma
Encke	Tuttle
Faye	West
Giacobini–Zinner	Westphal
Grigg–Skiellerup	Whipple
Halley	

Meteor Showers

Australids	Ophiuchids
Capricornids	Orionids
Cepheids	Perseids
Cygnids	Phoenicids
Geminids	Quadrantids
Leonids	Taurids
Lyrids	Ursids

space) engineering, space (*or* aerospace) technology, space (*or* aerospace) research, space (*or* aerospace) science, space navigation, space exploration, space (*or* aerospace) medicine, bioastronautics

30 **spacecraft**, space capsule, space probe, module, lunar module, space station, Mir, Salyut, Skylab, space shuttle, shuttle, Columbia, Challenger, 496 Discovery, Atlantis, space laboratory, spacelab, space platform, spaceship

31 **space travel**, trip to the moon, manned flight, spaceflight, space age, NASA (National Aeronautics and Space Administration), ESA (European Space Agency), Vostok, Apollo, Soyuz, astronaut, cosmonaut, spaceman, spacewoman, weightlessness, free fall, microgravity, spacesuit, space helmet, spacewalk, extravehicular activity (EVA), space port, lunar base, moon base

32 **satellite**, artificial satellite, earth satellite, unmanned satellite, sputnik, research satellite, astronomical satellite, X-ray satellite, space observatory, orbiting observatory, geophysical satellite, communications satellite, Telstar, geostationary orbit, geosynchronous orbit, meteorological satellite, weather satellite, navigational satellite, spy satellite, solar cell, solar panel, telemetry, data transmission, satellite tracking, tracking station, relay station

33 **planetary probe**, orbiter, lander, Mariner, Pioneer, Viking, Voyager, Venera
34 **SETI (search for extraterrestrial intelligence)**, flying saucer, UFO (unidentified flying object), alien, LGM (Little Green Man)
35 **rocketry**, rocket propulsion, engine, booster, propellant, liquid fuel, solid fuel, burn, thrust, launch vehicle, launcher, Ariane, Saturn V, Delta, multistage rocket, payload, retrorocket, solid rocket booster (SRB), escape velocity, orbit, earth orbit, perigee, apogee, parking orbit, transfer orbit, insertion, injection, trajectory, flyby, rendezvous, docking, re-entry, splashdown, soft landing, hard landing

ADJECTIVES

36 **astronomical**, astrophysical, cosmological, uranographic(al), cosmic, celestial, heavenly, universal, infinite, boundless, galactic, intergalactic, extragalactic, interstellar, stellar, sidereal, starry, astral, star-studded, solar, heliacal, interplanetary, planetary, Mercurian, Venusian, Martian, Jovian, Saturnian, Neptunian, Uranian, Plutonian, extraterrestrial, extramundane, terrestrial, telluric, tellurian, synodic, lunar, asteroidal, cometary, meteoric, meteoritic, heliocentric, geocentric, telescopic, spectrometric, photometric, astronautic(al)

VERBS

37 **observe**, orbit, revolve, rotate, eclipse, transit, radiate, shine, twinkle, emit, absorb
38 **launch**, enter orbit, travel in space

ADVERBS

39 **astronomically**, astrophysically, cosmologically, cosmically, celestially, universally, infinitely, boundlessly, galactically, intergalactically, extragalactically, sidereally, extraterrestrially, terrestrially, meteorically, heliocentrically

54   Earth Science

NOUNS

1 **earth science**, geoscience, geology, physical geology, structural geology, mineralogy, petrology, hydrology, geochemistry, tectonics, volcanology, marine geology, glaciology, geomorphology, physiography, pedology, geodesy, historical geology, stratigraphy, palaeontology, palaeogeography, palaeoclimatology, geochronology, economic geology, geopolitics, planetology, astrogeology, geography, human geography, physical geography
2 **geophysics**, geomagnetism, geomagnetics, gravity geophysics, gravimetry, solid-earth geophysics, seismology, seismography, volcanology, plate tectonics, physical oceanography, climatology, meteorology
▶ *55 Meteorology and Climatology, 56 Physics*
3 **geologist**, mineralogist, petrologist, hydrologist, geochemist, volcanologist, glaciologist, geomorphologist, physiographer, pedologist, geodesist, stratigrapher (*or* stratigraphist), palaeogeographer, palaeoclimatologist, palaeontologist, geochronologist, planetologist
4 **geophysicist**, geomagnetist, seismologist, volcanologist, oceanographer, climatologist, meteorologist
5 **earth**, planet earth, the world, the globe, earth's surface, surface, atmosphere, hydrosphere, waters of the earth, geosphere, biosphere, ecosphere, geoid, mother earth, Gaia
6 **continent**, subcontinent, continental shelf, continental margin, continental drift, land, mainland, landmass, dry land, ground, topography, relief, elevation, terrain, landscape
7 **landform**, surface feature, natural feature, geomorphic feature, geographical feature, basin, plain, coastal plain, flood plain, shield, valley, rift valley, V-shaped valley, U-shaped valley, glacial valley, fjord, hanging valley, cirque, cwm, valley floor, canyon, gorge, ravine, hill, plateau, scarp (*or* escarpment), mountain, arrête
▶ *95 Mountains, 98 Other Geographical Features*
8 **drainage**, drainage system, river network, drainage channel, stream course, drainage pattern, drainage basin, catchment area, watershed, divide, continental divide
9 **groundwater**, subsurface water, subterranean water, underground water, water table, aquifer, artesian basin, artesian spring
10 **water cycle**, hydrological cycle, evaporation, transpiration, precipitation, runoff, percolation
▶ *55 Meteorology and Climatology, 94 Lakes, 96 Rivers, 97 Seas, 98 Other Geographical Features*

Common Rocks

Igneous Rocks	
andesite	chert
anorthosite	claystone
aplite	coal
appinite	conglomerate
basalt	flint
breccia	limestone
diorite	marl
dolerite	mudstone
gabbro	oolite
granite	sandstone
monzonite	shale
obsidian	siltstone
pegmatite	
peridotite	**Metamorphic Rocks**
porphyrite	epidiorite
porphyry	gneiss
rhyolite	granulite
serpentine	hornblende
syenite	hornfels
trachyte	marble
	mylorite
	phyllite
Sedimentary Rocks	quartzite
argillite	schist
breccia	slate
chalk	

Minerals

actinolite	chalcopyrite	glance	nephrite	sphene
albite	Chile saltpetre	glauconite	niccolite	spherulite
allanite	chlorite	goethite	olivenite	spodumene
allophane	chromite	greenockite	opal	stannite
alunite	chrysoberyl	gummite	orpiment	staurolite
amblygonite	chrysotile	gypsum	ozocerite	stibnite
analcite	cinnabar	halite	pentlandite	stilbite
anatase	cleveite	harmotome	periclase	strontianite
andalusite	cobaltite	hawk's-eye	perovskite	sylvanite
andesine	colemanite	hematite	petuntse	sylvite
andradite	columbite	hemimorphite	phenacite	talc
anglesite	coprolite	hessite	phosgenite	tantalite
anhydrite	cordierite	heulandite	phosphorite	tenorite
ankerite	corundum	hiddenite	piedmontite	tetradymite
annabergite	cristobalite	hornblende	pinite	tetrahedrite
anorthite	crocidolite	hyacinth	pitchblende	thenardite
apatite	crocoite	hypersthene	pollucite	thorianite
apophyllite	cryolite	illite	polybasite	thorite
aragonite	cuprite	ilmenite	proustite	tiemannite
argentite	cyanite	jadeite	psilomelane	topaz
arsenopyrite	datolite	jarosite	pyrargyrite	torbernite
asbestos	diallage	kainite	pyrite	tourmaline
augite	diamond	kaolinite	pyrolusite	tremolite
autunite	diaspore	kernite	pyromorphite	triphylite
axinite	diopside	kieserite	pyrophyllite	trona
azurite	dioptase	kunzite	pyroxenite	troostite
baddeleyite	diorite	lapis lazuli	pyrrhotite	tungstite
barytes	dolomite	lazulite	quartz	turgite
bastnaesite	dumortierite	leucite	realgar	turquoise
beryl	emery	limonite	rhodochrosite	uralite
biotite	enstatite	magnesite	rhodonite	uraninite
bismuthinite	epidote	magnetite	rutile	vanadinite
blackjack	erythrite	malachite	samarskite	variscite
Boehmite	euxenite	manganite	saponite	vermiculite
boracite	fayalite	marcasite	sapphirine	vesuvian
borax	fluorapatite	margarite	scapolite	vesuvianite
bornite	fluorspar	massicot	scheelite	water sapphire
braunite	fool's gold	meerschaum	scolecite	wavellite
brookite	forsterite	microcline	senarmontite	wernerite
calaverite	franklinite	millerite	serpentine	white alkali
calcite	fulgurite	mimetite	siderite	willemite
carnallite	gadolinite	molybdenite	siderolite	witherite
carnotite	gahnite	monazite	sillimanite	wolframite
cassiterite	galena	montmorillonite	smaltite	wollastonite
celestite	garnet	monzonite	smaragdite	wulfenite
cerargyrite	garnierite	mullite	smectite	zeolite
cerussite	gehlenite	muscovite	smithsonite	zincite
chabazite	germanite	natrolite	sodalite	zinkenite
chalcanthite	geyserite	natron	sperrylite	zircon
chalcocite	gibbsite	nepheline	sphalerite	zoisite

11 **coast**, coastline, shore, shoreline, seaside, cliff, stack, beach, shingle, sand dune, sand bar, bar, spit, sandbank, sand wave, barrier island, barrier reef, lagoon, peninsula

12 **ocean**, deep ocean, ocean depths, coastal waters, seawater, ocean water, salinity, sea level

13 **ocean current**, surface current, wind-induced current, tidal current, density current (or subsurface current), circulation pattern, lateral movement, vertical movement, gyre, upwelling, down-welling, Gulf Stream

14 **wave**, seawave, ocean wave, swell, roller, breaker, surf, spume, white horses, whitecap, white foam, storm wave, seiche, tsunami, seismic seawave, tidal wave

15 **tide**, spring tide, neap tide, high tide, low tide, tidal range, intertidal zone

16 **ocean floor**, ocean basin, seafloor, continental margin, continental shelf, continental slope, continental rise, submarine canyon, land bridge, abyssal plain, abyssal hill, mid-oceanic (or midocean) ridge, oceanic ridge, Mid-Atlantic Ridge, oceanic trench, Mariana Trench, Tonga Trench, Kuril Trench, volcanic island, seamount, guyot, atoll

17 **ocean research vessel**, drilling vessel, submersible, bathysphere, bathyscaph (or bathyscape), deep-sea drilling, echo sounding, sub-bottom profiling, bathymetry, hydrography

18 **earth's crust**, crust, continental crust, oceanic crust, mantle, core, bedding-plane, discontinuity, Mohorovičić discontinuity (or Moho or M discontinuity), lithosphere, asthenosphere, isostacy, isostatic equilibrium, sial, sima

Gemstones

adularia	hyacinth
agate	jasper
alexandrite	kunzite
almandine	lapis lazuli
amazonite	Madagascar aquamarine
amber	morganite
amethyst	morion
andalusite	moss agate
andradite	New Zealand green-
aquamarine	stone
aventurine or aventurin	onyx
balas (or balas ruby)	opal
bloodstone	Oriental almandine
bone turquoise	Oriental emerald
cairngorm	Oriental topaz
carbuncle	plasma (or plasm)
carnelian	rhodolite
cat's-eye	rubellite
chalcedony	ruby
chatoyant	ruby spinel
chrysoberyl	sapphire
chrysolite	sard
chrysoprase	sardonyx
citrine	Spanish topaz
corundum	spessartite
diamond	sphene
diopside	spodumene
emerald	staurolite
fire opal	topaz
garnet	turquoise
grossularite	vesuvianite
hawk's-eye	water sapphire
heliodor	white sapphire
hiddenite	zircon

19 plate tectonics, plate, lithospheric plate, plate margin, plate boundary, divergence zone, convergence zone, subduction zone, midoceanic ridge, oceanic trench, transform fault, seafloor spreading, continental drift, Gondwana, Laurasia, Pangaea

20 earth movement, crustal movement, diastrophism, tectonic forces, deformation, strain, folding, fracture, faulting, cleavage, jointing, uplift, subsidence, fold, upright fold, inclined fold, overturned fold, recumbent fold, fold-hinge, anticline, syncline, fault, normal fault, block fault, reverse fault, thrust fault, Moine Thrust, slip-strike fault, joint, fault line, San Andreas fault, mobile belt, mountain belt, island arc

21 mountain building, orogenesis, orogeny, fold mountain, fold-belt mountain, alpine chain, fault-block mountain, oceanic ridge, oceanic rise, volcanic mountain

▶ *95 Mountains, 98 Other Geographical Features*

22 seismic activity, seismicity, earthquake, seism, seismic event, temblor (US), quake, macroseism, major earthquake, microseism, minor earthquake, earth tremor, shock, foreshock, main shock, aftershock, focus, epicentre, earthquake magnitude, Richter scale, earthquake zone

23 seismic wave, body wave, primary wave (*or* P wave), secondary wave (*or* S wave), surface wave, seismograph

24 volcanic activity, volcanism (*or* vulcanism), volcano, active volcano, inactive volcano, shield volcano, volcanic cone, composite volcano (*or* stratovolcano), crater, caldera, vent, fissure, magma chamber, magma, melt

25 eruption, lava, ejecta, tephra, pyroclastic material, ash, pumice, volcanic gas, lava flow, aa, pahoehoe (*or* ropy lava), pillow lava, fumurole, gas vent, geyser, hot spring, thermal spring

▶ *98 Other Geographical Features*

26 mass movement, landslide, slide, glide, slump, mudflow, debris flow, earthflow, plastic flow, lahar, creep, rock fall, avalanche

27 sediment, mud, deposit, organic sediment, inorganic sediment, oceanic sediment, pelagic ooze, ooze, alluvial deposit, delta, lake sediment, glacial deposit, rock, boulder, stone, gravel, granules, pebbles, shingle, chesil, sand, grain of sand, silt, clay, loess, bedrock

28 rock, mineral aggregate, stone, igneous rock, sedimentary rock, metamorphic rock, rock formation, texture, crystalline texture, coarse-grained texture, medium-grained texture, fine-grained texture, porphyritic texture, aphanitic texture, cleavage, slaty cleavage, fabric, facies, rock-forming mineral, xenolith, batholith, laccolith, lopolith

29 petrogenesis, lithification, sedimentation, consolidation, cementation, crystallization, magmatism, metamorphosis, recrystallization, foliation, intrusion, extrusion

30 igneous rock, magmatic rock, plutonic rock, plutonic intrusion, hypabyssal intrusion, dyke, sill, batholith, laccolith, pluton, volcanic rock, extrusive rock, pyroclastic rock, glassy rock, acid rock, intermediate rock, basic rock, ultrabasic rock, mafic rock, felsic rock, ultramafite, peridotite, perknite, picrite

31 sedimentary rock, lithified sediment, stratified rock, clastic rock, nonclastic rock, stratum (*pl.* strata), bed, bedding, breccia

32 metamorphism, regional metamorphism, contact metamorphism, thermal metamorphism, dynamic metamorphism, dislocation metamorphism, metamorphic grade, cataclasis, retrograde metamorphism, autometamorphism

33 metamorphic rock, parent rock, low-grade rock, high-grade rock, primary character, secondary character, foliated rock, schistosity, ultrametamorphic rock

34 mineral, crystalline mineral, noncrystalline mineral, amorphous mineral, rock-forming mineral, silicate, neosilicate, sorosilicate, cyclosilicate, inosilicate, phyllosilicate, tectosilicate, feldspar, alkali feldspar, chromite, magmatite, pegmatite, mica, orthoclase, oligoclase, plagioclase, olivine, chrysolite, pyroxene, orthopyroxene, clinopyroxene,

amphibole, spinel, clay mineral

▶ *57 Chemistry*

35 **weathering**, mechanical weathering, chemical weathering, erosion, wind erosion, wave erosion, rain erosion, river erosion, ice erosion, glacial erosion, denudation, deposition, sedimentation, abrasion, striation

▶ *55 Meteorology and Climatology*

36 **soil**, earth, topsoil, subsoil, regolith, soil profile, soil horizon, A horizon, B horizon, C horizon, soil texture, gravel, sand, loam, silt, clay, soil structure, alluvium, pedalfer, podzol, pedocal, lateritic soil, soil erosion

▶ *69 Horticulture*

37 **dune**, sand dune, coastal dune, desert dune, longitudinal dune, seif, crescent dune, barchan, transverse dune

38 **glacier**, alpine glacier, valley glacier, cirque glacier, continental glacier, continental ice sheet, ice sheet, icecap, ice field, crevasse, icefall, sérac, ice shelf, ice tongue, snout, moraine, till, boulder clay, drift, erratic, meltwater, glacier milk

39 **iceberg**, berg, growler, calf, sea ice, ice floe, floe, pack ice, ice pack, ice raft

40 **glaciation**, glacial advance, glacial surge, glacial period, ice age, glacial maximum, stadial, interglacial, deglaciation, glacial recession (*or* retreat)

41 **geological time**, geological time scale, geological time unit, geochronological unit, eon, olam, era, period, subperiod, epoch, chronostratigraphic unit, time-rock unit, rock division, eonothem, erathem, system, series, stage, relative age, absolute age, uniformitarianism

42 **dating**, radioactive dating, radiometric dating, uranium–lead dating, potassium–argon dating, rubidium–strontium dating, radiocarbon dating, carbon-14 dating, dendrochronology

43 **fossil**, fossil record, fossil man, hominid, fossil animal, fossil plant, ammonite, trilobite, graptolite, coprolite, petrified wood, coal, index fossil, zone fossil, mineralized bone, mineralized shell, cast, mould, fossil track, fossil footprint, fossilization, mineralization, petrification

▶ *76 Animals (General)*

44 **geomagnetism**, terrestrial magnetism, geomagnetic field, magnetosphere, magnetopause, magnetic anomaly, magnetic storm, palaeomagnetism, polarity reversal, magnetic reversal

45 **magnetic pole**, geomagnetic pole, north magnetic pole, south magnetic pole, magnetic equator, aclinic line, agonic line, declination, dip, inclination, polar wandering

46 **aurora**, polar lights, auroral display, aurora borealis, northern lights, aurora australis, southern lights

47 **radiation belt**, Van Allen belts, ozonosphere, ozone layer

ADJECTIVES

48 **geological**, mineralogical, petrological, hydrological, geochemical, volcanological, glaciological, geomorphological, pedological, geodetic, stratigraphical, palaeontological, geochronological, geopolitical

49 **geophysical**, geomagnetic, palaeomagnetic, gravimetric, seismological, seismographic, seismometric, oceanographic, bathymetric, hydrographic, climatological, meteorological

▶ *55 Meteorology and Climatology*

50 **terrestrial**, global, surficial, atmospheric, hydrospheric, geospheric, continental, topographic(al), subsurface, subterranean, underground

51 **oceanic**, deep-sea, marine, maritime, undersea, submarine, suboceanic, thalassic, pelagic, benthic, bathymal, abyssal, hadal, terrigenous

52 **coastal**, littoral, neritic, tidal, intertidal, riverine, alluvial

53 **solid-earth**, crustal, lithospheric, sialic, isostatic

54 **tectonic**, deformational, diastrophic, orogenic, epeirogenic

55 **volcanic**, eruptive, seismic, pyroclastic, molten, laval

56 **petrographic**, petrographical, petrological, petrogenic, lithic, consolidated, unconsolidated, igneous, magmatic, volcanic, plutonic, pyroclastic, intrusive, extrusive, sedimentary, stratified, clastic, detrital, metamorphic, foliated

57 **chalky**, flinty, shaly, slaty, basaltic, granitic, gneissic, gneissoid, gneissose, schistose, calcareous

58 **earthy**, rocky, stony, gravelly, pebbly, sandy, loamy, silty, clayey

59 **weathered**, eroded, abraded, scoured, gouged, striated

Geological Time Intervals

Archaean	Ordovician
Cambrian	Palaeocene
Carboniferous	Palaeogene
Cenozoic	Palaeozoic
Cretaceous	Permian
Devonian	Phanerozoic
Eocene	Pleistocene
Holocene	Pliocene
Jurassic	Precambrian
Lower Carboniferous	Proterozoic
Lower Cretaceous	Quaternary
Lower Jurassic	Recent
Lower Triassic	Silurian
Mesozoic	Tertiary
Middle Jurassic	Triassic
Middle Triassic	Upper Carboniferous
Miocene	Upper Cretaceous
Neogene	Upper Jurassic
Oligocene	Upper Triassic

60 glaciated, glacial, interglacial, postglacial, morainal, morainic
61 fossilized, petrified, mineralized, fossiliferous

VERBS

62 lithify, crystallize, recrystallize, mineralize, fossilize, petrify, consolidate, cement
63 ebb, flow, drain, run off, percolate, well up, spring up, evaporate, transpire, precipitate, ooze, settle
64 fold, fracture, strain, cleave, subside, quake, tremble, shake
65 map, chart, plan, survey, explore, mine, quarry

ADVERBS

66 geographically, geologically, geomorphologically, geodetically, palaeogeographically, topographically, seismologically, petrographically, petrologically, mineralogically, tidally, bathymetrically, hydrologically, meteorologically, continentally, volcanically, on the coast, under the ground

55 Meteorology and Climatology

NOUNS

1 meteorology, aerology, weather science, synoptic meteorology, weather forecasting, micrometeorology, macrometeorology, agricultural meteorology, aviation meteorology, maritime meteorology, atmospheric physics, hydrometeorology, hyetography, nephology, nephanalysis, anemology, climatology, planetary meteorology
2 meteorologist, climatologist, weather forecaster, weatherman, weatherwoman, weather observer, weather prophet
3 weather, weather situation, pattern, conditions, the elements, period, interval, spell, weather lore, St Swithin's day, Groundhog Day, dog days, halcyon days, blackthorn winter, Indian summer
4 weather forecast, forecast, report, bulletin, regional forecast, outlook, general outlook, travel report, road report, short-term forecast, medium-term forecast, long-term forecast, long-range forecast, numerical forecast, shipping forecast, general synopsis, sea area, hurricane (or storm or gale) warning, tornado watch, weather map, synoptic map (or chart), weather symbols, isobar, isotherm, weather bureau, US Weather Bureau, Meteorological Office (or Met. Office)
5 weather station, land station, ground station, field station, coastal station, weather ship, automatic buoy, weather satellite, weather balloon, radiosonde
6 weather data, elements, air pressure, pressure gradient, pressure tendency, rising pressure, falling pressure, air temperature, dew

point, humidity, relative humidity, absolute humidity, damp, dampness, moisture, air density, air movement, wind speed, wind strength, chill factor, wind-chill factor, anemogram
7 weather instruments, barometer, aneroid barometer, barograph, mercury barometer, glass, weatherglass, storm glass, thermometer, thermograph, hygrometer, psychrometer, hygrograph, Stevenson screen, wind gauge, anemometer, cup anemometer, anemograph, wind sock, wind cone, wind sleeve, drogue, weather vane, weathercock, wind rose, rain gauge, pluviometer, udometer, weather radar, sunshine recorder
▶ *56 Physics*
8 atmosphere, earth's atmosphere, air, atmospheric layer, troposphere, stratosphere, upper atmosphere, ionosphere, ozone layer, ozonosphere, exosphere, tropopause, stratopause, atmospheric water vapour, clean dry air, condensation nuclei, atmospheric dust, pollution, pollutant, CFC (chlorofluorocarbon)
▶ *56 Physics*
9 atmospheric process, radiation balance, energy balance, absorption, reflection, scattering, heat transfer, heat transport, convection, radiation, advection, adiabatic process, adiabatic cooling, adiabatic lapse rate, water balance, evaporation, condensation, sublimation, saturation, supercooling, Coriolis force, geostrophic force
10 air movement, atmospheric circulation, air current, airflow, air stream, jetstream, convection cell, thermal, downdraught, updraught, air mass, cold air, warm air, moist air, dry air, polar air, tropical air, front, polar front, cold front, warm front, occlusion, occluded front, warm occlusion, cold occlusion
11 weather system, pressure system, frontal system, depression, area of low pressure, low, cyclone, shallow depression, deepening depression, deep depression, filling depression, stationary depression, warm sector, area of high pressure, high, anticyclone, stationary high, blocking high, Azores high, Icelandic low, trough (or trough of low pressure), ridge (or ridge of high pressure)
12 wind, breeze, zephyr, surface wind, sea breeze, land breeze, onshore wind, offshore wind, local wind, katabatic wind, anabatic wind, mountain wind, valley wind, gust, scud, squall, wind storm, dust storm, sandstorm, upper wind, high-altitude wind, gradient wind, geostrophic wind
13 wind strength, wind force, wind speed, Beaufort scale, calm, light air, breeze, light breeze, gentle breeze, moderate breeze, fresh breeze, strong breeze, near gale, gale, strong gale, storm, violent storm, hurricane, variable wind, wind-chill, wind-chill factor

Winds

berg wind (South Africa)	gregale (or euroclydon or euro-aquilo) (Malta)	nor'wester (New Zealand)
bise (Switzerland, France, Italy)	harmattan (W African coast)	simoom (or samiel) (Arabia, N Africa)
bora (E Adriatic coast)	khamsin (or kamsin or kamseen) (Egypt)	sirocco (N Africa, S Europe)
buran (Central Asia)		southerly buster (SE Australia)
Cape doctor (South Africa)	levanter (W Mediterranean)	tramontane (or tramontana) (Italy and W Mediterranean)
chinook (or snow eater) (Rocky Mountains)	libeccio (or libecchio) (Corsica)	wet chinook (Washington and Oregon coasts)
el Niño (E Pacific)	meltemi (Mediterranean)	williwaw (US and Canada)
etesian (E Mediterranean)	mistral (S France, Mediterranean coast)	
Föhn (or Foehn) (Alps)	monsoon (S Asia)	
ghibli (or gibli) (N Africa)		

14 **windiness**, gustiness, breeziness, puff of wind, breath of wind, zephyr, fresh wind, brisk wind, high wind, strong wind, stiff wind, blow, blast, spanking wind, force eight, force nine, force ten, storm force ten, howling gale, tempest, full gale, half a gale (Inf)

15 **wind direction**, north wind, Boreas (Fml), northerly, norther (US), northeast wind, northeasterly, northeaster, east wind, Eurus (Fml), easterly, southeast wind, southeasterly, southeaster, south wind, Auster (Fml), southerly, southwest wind, southwesterly, southwester, west wind, Zephyr (Fml), westerly, northwest wind, northwesterly, northwester, prevailing wind, head wind, crosswind, tail wind, following wind, favourable wind, wind shift, backing, veering

16 **wind vortex**, eddy, rotating air mass, tropical revolving storm (TRS), tropical storm, cyclone (Indian Ocean), typhoon (N Pacific), hurricane (US and West Indies), Mauritius hurricane (Indian Ocean), South Seas hurricane (S Pacific), baguio (Philippines), willy-willy (Aus), eye of the storm, waterspout, tornado, whirlwind, dust devil, sand column, twister (US inf)

17 **wind system**, trade winds (or trades), northeast trades, southeast trades, intertropical convergence zone (ITCZ), doldrums, horse latitudes, roaring forties, antitrade winds (or antitrades), monsoon, summer monsoon, winter monsoon

18 **cloud**, high cloud, low cloud, cloud base, ice cloud, water cloud, mixed cloud, cirrus, cirrocumulus, altostratus, cirrostratus, altocumulus, nimbostratus, stratocumulus (or cumulostratus), stratus, cumulus, cumulonimbus, rain cloud, rain-bearing cloud, nimbus, scud, storm cloud, thundercloud, anvil cloud, dark cloud, noctilucent cloud

19 **cloud cover**, cloudiness, thin cloud, patchy cloud, broken cloud, thick cloud, dense cloud, widespread cloud, overcast sky

20 **cloud appearance**, filamentary cloud, wispy cloud, billowy cloud, fleecy cloud, feathery cloud, cottony cloud (US), wisp (or billow or patch) of cloud, mare's-tail, heaped cloud, globular cloud, lumpy cloud, band of cloud, belt of cloud, bank of cloud, roll of cloud, sheet of cloud, layer cloud, veil of cloud, cloud tower, cloud street, lenticular cloud, lee-wave cloud, iridescent cloud, mackerel sky, buttermilk sky (US)

21 **thunderstorm**, thunder, thunderclap, clap of thunder, lightning, lightning flash (or stroke), track, fork (or forked) lightning, sheet lightning, ball lightning, summer lightning, thunderbolt, bolt of lightning, electric storm, lightning strike, lightning conductor

22 **sun**, sunshine, strong sun, weak sun, recorded sunshine, clear sky, cloudless sky, blue sky, solar radiation, sunlight, ultraviolet radiation (UV), UVA, UVB, direct radiation, indirect radiation, halo, corona, parhelic circle, parhelion (or mock sun or sundog), anthelion (or countersun), solar power (or energy), sunbathing, sunworshipper, sunstroke, sunburn, suntan, suntanning, suntan lotion (or cream), barrier cream

23 **heat**, hot weather, hot spell, heatwave, Indian summer, humidness, humidity, muggy weather, muggy spell, warm weather, warm spell, sunny weather, sunny period (or interval), sunny spell, scorcher (Inf), sizzler (Inf)

24 **precipitation**, rain, hail, sleet, snow, rainfall, snowfall, rain day, raindrop, hailstone, snowflake, ice crystal, hydrometeor

25 **rain**, rainfall, rainwater, fine rain, drizzle, light rain, shower, light shower, flurry, smir (or smirr or smur) (Scot dial), outbreak of rain, occasional showers (or rain), intermittent showers (or rain), scattered showers, April showers, thundery shower, steady drizzle, persistent rain, rainstorm, torrential rain, driving rain, drenching rain, sheet of rain, stream of rain, downfall, deluge, downpour, cloudburst, spate, belt of rain (or rain belt)

26 **raininess**, showeriness, pluviosity, wetness, rainy season, wet season, monsoon season, the rains, the wet (Aus), rain damage, flood, acid rain, rainmaking, rain dance, cloud-seeding

27 **rainbow**, double rainbow, primary rainbow, secondary rainbow, fogbow (or white rainbow or fogdog or seadog), rainbow's end

28 **dryness**, drought, dry spell

29 **hail**, soft hail (*or* graupel), hailstorm, sleet, freezing rain, glaze ice, glazed frost, silver frost, hoar frost

30 **snow**, snowfall, snow shower, flurry, snow storm, blizzard, drifting snow, driven snow, whiteout, snow cover, mantle of snow, blanket of snow, bank of snow, snowdrift, snow bed, wet snow (*or* papp), powdery snow, granular snow, spindrift, consolidated snow (*or* firn *or* neve), melt, meltage, meltwater, slush, avalanche

31 **coldness**, cold, chill, chilliness, coolness, cold weather (*or* spell), cold snap, cold wave, chill (*or* nip) in the air, wintriness (*or* winteriness *or* winterliness), hard winter, brass-monkey weather (Inf)

32 **freeze**, big freeze, hard freeze, freeze-up, ice, black ice, glacier

33 **fog**, ground fog, hill fog, lake fog, river fog, coastal fog, sea fog, radiation fog, advection fog, dense fog, thick fog, fog bank, pea soup (Inf), peasouper (Inf), freezing fog, smog

34 **mist**, mountain mist, hill mist, fret (*or* haar *or* roke) (Dial), thick mist, Scotch mist, brume, haze, heat haze

35 **visibility**, good visibility, poor visibility, fogginess, haziness, mistiness, har (Scot)

36 **frost**, touch of frost, moderate frost, severe frost, hard frost, sharp frost, ground frost, air frost, radiation frost, advection frost, hoar frost, hoar, white frost, rime, frost hollow, permafrost, frost damage, Jack Frost (Inf)

37 **dew**, fog drip, false dew, dewdrop, dew point

38 **climate**, local climate, microclimate, regional climate, macroclimate, maritime (*or* marine) climate, Mediterranean climate, oceanic climate, continental climate, mountain climate, desert climate, tundra climate, rainforest climate, snow-forest climate, dry climate, arid climate, semiarid climate, humid climate, semihumid climate, hot climate, tropical climate, subtropical climate, temperate climate, moderate climate, cool climate, cold climate, polar climate (*or* arctic climate)

39 **climatic zone**, tropics, equatorial rainy zone, tropical summer rainy zone (*or* marginal tropics), subtropics, subtropical dry zone, subtropical winter rainy zone, temperate zone, continental zone, subpolar zone, polar zone, tundra

40 **climatic change**, climatic variation, climatic trend, ice age, glaciation, interglaciation, interglacial, postglaciation, postglacial, global warming, greenhouse effect, desertification, climate modification

▶ *54 Earth Science, 56 Physics*

ADJECTIVES

41 **meteorologic**, meteorological, synoptic, elemental, climatic, climatological

42 **barometric**, barographic, isobaric, thermometric, thermographic, isothermal, hygrometric, hygrographic, psychrometric, anemometric, anemographic, pluviometric, udometric

43 **atmospheric**, tropospheric, stratospheric, ionospheric, geostrophic, radiative, thermal, convective, advective, adiabatic, isothermal, evaporated, condensed, sublimated, saturated, supercooled

44 **frontal**, cyclonic, anticyclonic

45 **fine**, fair, bright, sunny, dry, rainless, calm, windless, clear, cloudless, brighter, milder, sunnier, drier, settled, fresh, bracing, brisk, crisp, invigorating

46 **seasonal**, springlike, summery, autumnal, wintry (*or* wintery), unseasonal, changeable, unsettled, deteriorating

47 **windy**, breezy, blowy, cooling, windier, fresh, brisk, gusty, blustery, squally, keen, piercing, sharp, biting, cold, freezing, raw, bitter, icy, strong, high, gale-force, storm-force, hurricane-force, northerly, boreal, northeasterly, easterly, southeasterly, southerly, southwesterly, westerly, favonian, northwesterly, prevailing, aeolian, anemological

48 **stormy**, cyclonic, inclement, violent, rough, tempestuous, raging, foul, ugly, dirty, thundery

49 **cloudy**, cloud-flecked, cloud-crossed, cloud-laden, cloud-covered, overcast, overclouded, cloud-capped, cloud-topped, dull, dreich (Scot), gloomy, dark, grey, heavy, cirrose (*or* cirrous), cirriform, cumuliform, cumulous, cirrocumuliform, cirrocumulous, altocumuliform, altocumulous, stratous, stratiform, altostratous, cirrostratous, nimbostratous, cumulonimbiform, nephological

50 **warm**, mild, moderate, temperate, pleasant, balmy, warmer, hotter

51 **hot**, overwarm, overhot, sweltering, sweltry, sizzling, blistering, torrid, boiling (Inf)

52 **humid**, muggy, damp, close, heavy, oppressive, sticky, sweaty

53 **rainy**, showery, wet, drizzly, drizzling, rainier, wetter, steady, persistent, heavy, torrential, driving, streaming, pouring, pelting, drumming, blinding, raining cats and dogs (Inf), coming down in buckets (*or* torrents *or* sheets *or* stair-rods) (Inf), pissing down (Sl)

54 **pluvial**, pluvious (*or* pluviose), hydrometeorologic(al), hyetographic(al)

55 **cool**, chilly, chill, coldish, nippy, cooler, colder, cold, bitterly cold, raw, frigid, frosty, frosted, frost-covered, freezing, icy, below zero, snowy, snow-covered, snow-clad, slushy, sludgy, sleety, bleak, arctic, Siberian, boreal, parky (Inf), perishing (Inf)

56 **foggy**, thick, fogbound, enshrouded, smoggy, misty, hazy, nebulous

VERBS

57 forecast, predict

58 blow, stir, sigh, sough, whisper, murmur, hum, freshen, blow up, get up, whistle, moan, gust, buffet, bluster, roar, howl, screech, wail, scream, shriek, back, veer

59 storm, gather, brew, set in, blow a gale, blow a hurricane, thunder, lightning

60 cloud, cloud over, darken, grow dark, roll, scud, break, thin

61 shine, radiate, glimmer, shimmer, blaze, burn, glare, shine brightly, brighten, lighten, clear

62 rain, precipitate, fall, shower, drizzle, mizzle (Dial), patter, spatter, splatter, plash, pour, pelt, teem, stream, drum, spit (Inf), bucket down (Inf), come down (Inf), come down in buckets (*or* torrents *or* sheets *or* stair-rods) (Inf), rain cats and dogs (Inf), piss down (Sl)

63 snow, blizzard, sleet, hail, frost, ice, ice over, freeze, thaw, melt

64 fog, befog, enshroud, mist, bemist, enmist, haze

ADVERBS

65 meteorologically, synoptically, climatologically, climatically, windily, stormily, cloudily, warmly, mildly, hotly, swelteringly, humidly, rainily, wetly, moistly, coolingly, coldly, frostily, snowily, foggily, mistily, hazily

56 Physics

NOUNS

1 physics, physical science, exact science, natural science, natural philosophy, physicist

2 classical physics, classical mechanics, Newtonian mechanics, dynamics, statics, kinematics, fluid mechanics, hydrodynamics, aerodynamics, sound, acoustics, ultrasonics, phonetics, optics, geometric optics, physical optics, heat, thermodynamics, electricity, magnetism, magnetics, electroacoustics, electrodynamics, electromagnetism, electro-optics

3 modern physics, quantum theory, quantum mechanics, wave mechanics, matrix mechanics, quantum statistics, statistical mechanics, atomic physics, nuclear physics, particle physics, statistical physics, spectroscopy, solid-state physics, crystallography, low-temperature physics, cryogenics, plasma physics, magnetohydrodynamics, radiation physics, relativity theory, relativistic quantum mechanics, quantum gravity, quantum electrothermodynamics

4 experimental physics, theoretical physics, pure physics, applied physics, medical physics, geophysics, meteorology, oceanography, astrophysics, cosmology, physical chemistry, chemical physics, biophysics

▶ *54 Earth Science, 57 Chemistry, 52 Mathematics*

5 theory, kinetic theory, wave theory of light, electromagnetic theory, quantum theory, quantum field theory, special theory of relativity, general theory of relativity

6 law, principle, laws of motion, laws of thermodynamics, laws of reflection, laws of refraction, uncertainty principle, rule, criterion, equation, equation of state, effect, model, atmospheric model, cosmological model, hypothesis, proposition, theorem, premise, thesis, statement, axiom

7 space, position, space coordinates, coordinates, length, breadth, height, altitude, thickness, radius, diameter, area, volume, angle, plane angle, solid angle, vacuum, free space, four-dimensional space, four-dimensional continuum, space-time, space-time continuum

▶ *248 Space, 52 Mathematics*

8 time, period, interval, frequency, angular frequency, phase, motion, linear motion, circular motion, simple harmonic motion, flow, steady flow, turbulence, speed, velocity, relative velocity, angular velocity, acceleration, angular acceleration, acceleration due to gravity (*or* of free fall)

▶ *185 Time, 324 Motion*

9 mass, amount of substance, density, relative density, specific gravity, momentum, angular momentum, inertia, moment of inertia, centre of mass, centre of gravity, conservation of mass

10 force, weight, gravitational force, centripetal force, centrifugal force, couple, moment, torque, torsion, equilibrium, stable equilibrium, unstable equilibrium, metastable equilibrium, buoyancy, field of force, field, flux, flux density, pressure, atmospheric pressure, vapour pressure, stress, strain, elasticity, viscosity, friction, static friction, dynamic friction, rolling friction, abrasion, erosian, osmosis, surface tension

11 energy, potential energy, kinetic energy, chemical energy, solar energy, electrical energy, nuclear energy, conservation of energy, conservation of mass and energy, work, machine, engine, power, power station, nuclear power, fission energy, fusion energy, renewable energy, solar energy, wave power, wind power, tidal power, geothermal energy

12 wave, vibration, oscillation, transient disturbance, undulation, wave motion, longitudinal wave, transverse wave, torsional wave, travelling wave, standing wave, node, antinode, wave propagation, radiation

▶ *365 Oscillation*

13 electromagnetic radiation, radio waves, microwaves, television, radio, radar, infrared (IR) radiation, near infrared, far infrared, light, visible radiation, ultraviolet (UV) radiation,

near ultraviolet, far ultraviolet, UVA, UVB, X-rays, gamma rays, electromagnetic spectrum, visible spectrum, radio spectrum, particle–wave (*or* wave–particle) duality, photon

▶ *534 Communications*

14 **sound wave**, acoustic wave, ultrasonic wave, water wave, ripple, tsunami (*or* tidal wave), seismic wave, bow wave, shock wave, electrical oscillation, mechanical oscillation, vibration, oscillating current, vibrating string, forced vibration, resonance, resonant frequency

15 **wave property**, transmission, attenuation, absorption, dissipation, deflection, diffusion, reflection, refraction, dispersion, scattering, interference, diffraction, polarization, plane polarization, circular polarization

16 **waveform**, waveshape, sine wave, sinusoidal wave, nonsinusoidal wave, pulse, rectangular pulse, square wave, pulse train, wavelength, wave number, frequency, frequency band, frequency spectrum, amplitude, hertz, wave crest, wave trough, wave speed, phase speed, speed of light, speed of sound

▶ *534 Communications*

17 **sound**, noise, white noise, music, ultrasound, infrasound, ear, audibility, inaudibility, loudness

▶ *420 Hearing, 49 Music*

18 **source of sound**, sound generator, musical instrument, amplifier, public-address system (PA), megaphone, loudspeaker, speaker, hearing aid

▶ *64 Electronics and Electrical Engineering, 532 Publication, 49 Music, 420 Hearing*

19 **sound propagation**, speed of sound, subsonic speed, supersonic speed, Mach number, Mach 1, sonic boom, sound (*or* sonic) barrier, audiofrequency, ultrasonic frequency, sound level, sound-pressure level, sound-power level, loudness level, decibel

20 **musical note**, tone, fundamental, overtone, harmonic, partial, pitch, musical interval, musical scale

▶ *49 Music*

21 **architectural acoustics**, auditorium, echo, reverberation, reverberation time, reverberation (*or* echo) chamber, dead room, anechoic chamber, sound insulation, soundproofing

22 **sounding**, echo sounding, depth sounding, sonar, ultrasonic imaging (*or* ultrasonography), ultrasonic cleaning, ultrasonic welding

23 **light**, daylight, sunlight, moonlight, electric light, gaslight, candlelight, vision, colour vision, visual acuity, eye, visibility, brightness, clarity, contrast

▶ *439 Light, 435 Vision*

24 **light emission**, incandescence, luminescence, bioluminescence, thermoluminescence, fluorescence, phosphorescence, radio-luminescence, illumination, shadow, umbra, penumbra, light beam, ray of light, pencil of light, luminous intensity, luminous flux, luminous efficiency, luminous efficacy, illuminance (*or* illumination), luminance

25 **light source**, lamp, light, lighting, incandescent lamp, filament lamp, tungsten lamp, quartz–iodine lamp, light bulb, filament, fluorescent light, strip light, fluorescent tube, mercury-vapour lamp, neon lamp, gas-discharge tube, light-emitting diode (LED)

▶ *439 Light*

26 **laser** (light amplification by stimulated emission of radiation), gas laser, helium-neon laser, carbon dioxide laser, ruby laser, neodymium-glass laser, YAG (yttrium aluminium garnet) laser, semiconductor laser, tunable laser, dye laser, monochromatic radiation, coherent radiation, stimulated emission, population inversion, maser (microwave amplification by stimulated emission of radiation)

27 **polarized light**, plane-polarized light, circularly polarized light, elliptically polarized light, birefringence, Polaroid (Tm)

28 **colour**, pure colour, spectral colour, rainbow, red, orange, yellow, green, blue, indigo, violet, high saturation, low saturation, hue, tint, shade, interference pattern, iridescence, white light, primary colours, secondary colours, red, green, blue, cyan, magenta, yellow, complementary colours, additive process, subtractive process, pigment, paint, dye, lake, colour printing, colour television, colour photography

▶ *444 Colour*

29 **optical element**, mirror, plane mirror, convex mirror, concave mirror, paraboloid (*or* parabolic) mirror, silver coating, aluminium coating, front-surfaced, back surfaced, hand mirror, full-length mirror, shaving mirror, rear-view mirror, wing mirror, lens, converging lens, diverging lens, convex lens, biconvex lens, planoconvex lens, concave lens, spherical lens, cylindrical lens, toric lens, achromatic lens (*or* achromat), antireflection coating, coated lens, bloomed lens, spectacles, glasses, bifocals, dark glasses, sunglasses, photochromic lenses, contact lenses, prism, diffraction grating, grating, reflection grating, optical fibre, light pipe, light guide, reflection, total internal reflection, refraction, refractivity, refractive index, diffraction

▶ *435 Vision*

30 **lens system**, compound lens, mirror system, catadioptric system, eyepiece, objective, condenser, camera lens

▶ *66 Photography*

31 **lens element**, focal length, focal plane, focal point, focus, circle of least confusion, caustic, lens aperture, mirror aperture, f-number (*or*

F-number), relative aperture, object distance, image distance, real image, virtual image, optic axis, axial ray, paraxial ray, aberration, optical aberration, spherical aberration, coma, astigmatism, chromatic aberration

32 **optical instrument**, camera, telescope, binoculars, field glasses, opera glasses, microscope, periscope, electrophotometer, spectrophotometer, spectrometer, photometer, sextant, theodolite, interferometer, focusing, magnification, magnifying power, resolution, resolving power, aperture stop, field stop, field of view, depth of field, depth of focus
▶ *53 Astronomy, Astronautics, and Rocketry, 66 Photography, 435 Vision*

33 **photosensitivity**, photosensitive material, light-sensitive material, photoelectric effect, photoconductivity, photovoltaic effect, electro-optical effect, optical activity, optical rotation

34 **photometry**, photography, photolithography, fibre optics, fibre-optics transmission

35 **heat**, quantity of heat, warmth, hotness, hot body, hot substance, heating device, heater, heating system, furnace, cooker, combustion, burning, fuel, cold, cold body, cold substance, cooling system, refrigeration, refrigerator, freezer
▶ *408 Heat, 409 Cold*

36 **heat flow**, heat transfer, conduction, convection, radiation, heat flow rate, heat exchange, thermal equilibrium, thermal conductivity, heat capacity, specific heat capacity, molar heat capacity

37 **temperature**, temperature scale, phase change, transition, freezing, fusion, melting, boiling, ebullition, liquefaction, vaporization, evaporation, sublimation, transition temperature, freezing point, melting point, boiling point, sublimation point, triple point

38 **thermodynamics**, first law, second law, third law, thermodynamic temperature, absolute zero, triple point of water, volume, pressure, entropy, internal energy, enthalpy, Gibbs function, Helmholtz function, work, external work, latent heat, specific latent heat, standard temperature and pressure (STP), normal temperature and pressure (NTP), standard atmosphere, equation of state, van der Waals equation, critical state, critical temperature, Carnot cycle, Diesel cycle, Otto cycle, Wankel cycle

39 **expansion**, expansion coefficient, compression, compressibility, adiabatic change, isothermal change

40 **heating effect**, incandescence, thermionic emission, thermoelectricity, thermoelectric effect, thermal radiation, black-body radiation, black body, full radiator

41 **thermometry**, pyrometry, thermal imaging

42 **electricity**, current electricity, static electricity (*or* static), frictional electricity, atmospheric electricity, thermoelectricity, photoelectricity, bioelectricity

43 **electrical conduction**, conduction of electricity, conductivity, conducting medium, conductor, metal conductor, liquid conductor, electrolytic conductor, semiconductor, insulator, electrolyte, electrode, anode, cathode, electrolysis, electrolytic cell, primary cell, secondary cell, battery, fuel cell
▶ *57 Chemistry*

44 **semiconductor**, n-type semiconductor, p-type semiconductor, charge carrier, electron, hole, electron conduction, hole conduction, n-type conductivity, p-type conductivity, p–n junction, energy band, conduction band, valence band, energy gap, impurity atom, acceptor impurity, donor impurity, doping, semiconductor device, diode, transistor
▶ *64 Electronics and Electrical Engineering*

45 **superconductivity**, superconductor, transition temperature, high-temperature superconductor, superconducting magnet

46 **electric discharge**, gas discharge, arc discharge, electric arc, arc, glow discharge, transient discharge, spark discharge, spark, gas-discharge tube

47 **electric storm**, thunderstorm, lightning, lightning conductor (*or* rod), lightning arrester
▶ *54 Earth Science*

48 **insulation**, insulator, nonconductor, dielectric, dielectric constant, dielectric coefficient, dielectric polarization, breakdown voltage

49 **electromagnetic induction**, electrostatic induction, thermoelectric effect, photoelectric effect, photovoltaic effect, photoconductivity, piezoelectric effect, electrostriction

50 **electric charge**, quantity of electricity, charge, positive charge, negative charge, charged particle, electron, proton, ion, charged body, charged substance, charge attraction, charge repulsion, conservation of charge, dipole, dipole moment, quadrupole, charge density, electric constant

51 **electric current**, current, flow of electricity, direct current (d.c.), alternating current (a.c.), transient current, pulse, frequency, phase, conduction current, displacement current, induced current, eddy current, current density, juice (Inf)

52 **electric potential**, potential, potential difference (p.d.), voltage, electromotive force (e.m.f.), back e.m.f. ground, earth, live, neutral

53 **resistance**, reactance, impedance, resistivity, conductivity, capacitance, inductance, mutual inductance, self-inductance, conductance, mutual conductance

Named Laws, Effects, Equations, etc.

Amagat's experiments
Ampère–Laplace law
Ampère's law
Andrews' experiments
Archimedes' principle
Aragadro's hypothesis
Balmer series
Barkhausen effect
Bernouilli effect
Biot–Savart law
Bitter pattern
Bloch wall
Bohr atom
Boltzmann constant
Bose–Einstein statistics
Boyle's law
Boy's experiment
Bragg's law
Brewster angle
Bunsen cell
Callendar and Barnes' experiment
Carnot's principle
Cavendish's experiment
Charles' law
Clark cell
Cockroft–Walton accelerator
Compton effect
Coulomb's law
Curie's law
Curie–Weiss law

Dalton's law
Daniell cell
de Broglie principle
Dewar flask
Dirac's equation
Doppler effect
Dulong and Petit's law
Faraday effect
Faraday's laws
Fermat's principle
Fermi level
Fraunhofer diffraction
Fraunhofer lines
Fresnel's biprism
Fresnel diffraction
Fresnel lens
Gay-Lussac's law
Geiger counter
Geiger–Müller counter
Gibbs function
Hall effect
Heisenberg uncertainty principle
Helmholtz coils
Helmholtz function
Hooke's law
Joly steam calorimeter
Joule–Kelvin (or Joule Thomson) effect
Joule's laws
Kepler's laws
Kerr effect

Kirchoff's laws
Lambert's law
Leclanché cell
Lees' disk
Lenz's law
Leslie's cube
Leyden jar
Linde process
Lissajous' figures
Lloyd's mirror
Lorentz–Fitzgerald contraction
Lyman series
Mach number
Maxwell–Boltzmann statistics
Maxwell distribution
Maxwell's equation
Meissner effect
Michelson–Morley experiment
Moseley's law
Néel temperature
Nernst calorimeter
Neumann's law
Newton's law of cooling
Newton's laws of motion
Newton's law of gravitation
Newton's rings
Nicol prism

Ohm's law
Otto cycle
Paschen series
Peltier effect
Planck's radiation law
Poisson ratio
Poynting vector
Prévost's theory of exchanges
Rayleigh scattering
Regnault's apparatus
Reynolds number
Rochon prism
Roentgen rays
Rydberg constant
Searle's bar
Seebeck effect
Stefan's law
Schrödinger's cat
Schrödinger's wave equation
Thomson effect
Van de Graaff generator
van der Waals equation
Weston standard (or cadmium) cell
Wheatstone bridge
Wien's displacement law
Wimshurst machine
Wollaston prism
Young's experiment

54 electric field, electric field strength, electric flux, displacement, permittivity, relative permittivity

55 circuit, electronic circuit, electric circuit, network, interconnected circuits, circuit element, electronic component, electronic device, resistor, capacitor, inductor, diode, transistor, rectifier, amplifier, oscillator, filter, transformer, transducer
▶ *64 Electronics and Electrical Engineering*
56 electrical energy, electric power, generator, electric motor, power station, power supply

57 magnetism, magnetic attaction, magnetic repulsion, electromagnetism

58 geomagnetism, earth's magnetism, terrestrial magnetism, magnetosphere, magnetic North, magnetic South, magnetic North Pole, magnetic South Pole, magnetic equator, magnetic meridian, magnetic declination (*or* magnetic variation), magnetic dip (*or* magnetic inclination, angle of dip), (geo)magnetic storm, palaeomagnetism, magnetic reversal, magnetic epoch
▶ *54 Earth Science*
59 ferromagnetism, ferromagnetic material, iron, nickel, cobalt, magnetic alloy, domain, Permalloy (Tm), Mu metal (Tm), paramagnetism, diamagnetism, antiferromagnetism, ferrimagnetism

60 magnet, permanent magnet, bar magnet, horseshoe magnet, pot magnet, keeper, electromagnet, solenoid, magnetizing coil, coil, ferromagnetic core, superconducting magnet, magnetite, magnetic iron ore, lodestone, ferrite, magnetic monopole

61 magnetic quantity, magnetic variable, magnetomotive force, magnetic potential difference, magnetic field, magnetic field strength, magnetic flux, magnetic induction (*or* magnetic flux density), magnetization, permeability, relative permeability, magnetic dipole moment, magnetic moment, magneton, magnetic constant

62 electromagnetic radiation, electromagnetic wave, electromagnetic spectrum

63 magnetic phenomenon, magnetic hysteresis, hysteresis, residual magnetization, remanence, electromagnetic induction, mutual induction, self-induction, magnetostriction, magneto-optical effect, magnetic damping, magnetic deflection, magnetic focusing, magnetic lens, magnetic mirror, magnetic levitation (*or* maglev)

64 magnetic recording, magnetic tape, video tape, magnetic track, magnetic storage, magnetic memory, magnetic disk, hard disk, floppy disk, magnetic ink character recognition (MICR), magnetic ink, magnetic card, credit card, smart card, phonecard, magnetic stripe, magnetic resonance imaging (MRI)

65 atom, atomic structure, nucleus, proton, neutron, nucleon, binding energy, electron, elec-

tron configuration, electron shell, subshell, s-electron, p-electron, d-electron, f-electron, atomic orbital, energy level

66 **ion**, positive ion, cation, negative ion, anion, charge number, ionization, ionization energy, ionization potential

▶ *57 Chemistry*

67 **excited atom**, excited state, ground state, metastable state, excitation, transition, quantum jump, excitation energy

68 **emission**, absorption, emission spectrum, absorption spectrum, continuous spectrum, line spectrum, band spectrum, optical spectrum, infrared spectrum, ultraviolet spectrum, microwave spectrum, X-ray spectrum

69 **isotope**, nuclide, atomic mass, atomic mass constant, relative atomic mass, atomic weight, atomic number, proton number, mass number, nucleon number, neutron number

70 **radioactivity**, radioactive decay, decay, alpha decay, beta decay, radioactive substance, radioisotope, radionuclide, alpha emitter, beta emitter, parent nuclide, daughter nuclide, daughter product, alpha particle, beta particle, alpha rays, beta rays, gamma rays, radioactive series, half-life, mean life, decay constant, activity, energy imparted, absorbed dose, dose equivalent, ionizing radiation, high-energy radiation, X-rays, particulate radiation, cosmic rays, radiometric dating, radiocarbon dating, potassium–argon dating, radiography, radiology, radiotherapy

▶ *54 Earth Science, 60 Medicine*

71 **nuclear reaction**, disintegration, transmutation, collision, scattering, elastic scattering, inelastic scattering, cross section

72 **nuclear fission**, fission reaction, fission, chain reaction, splitting the atom, atom smashing, fissionable nuclide, fissile nuclide, fertile nuclide, fission product, critical mass, nuclear fusion, fusion reaction, fusion, thermonuclear fusion, controlled nuclear fusion, cold fusion, nuclear energy, atomic energy, nuclear power, nuclear power station, nuclear engineering, nucleonics

73 **nuclear reactor**, reactor, atomic pile, thermal reactor, gas-cooled reactor (GCR), advanced gas-cooled reactor (AGR), high-temperature gas-cooled reactor (HTR), pressurized-water reactor (PWR), boiling-water reactor (BWR), magnox reactor, fast reactor, breeder reactor, fast breeder reactor, reactor core, core, nuclear fuel, uranium, enriched uranium, plutonium, fuel assembly, fuel element, fuel rod, coolant, moderator, control rods, biological shield, shield

74 **nuclear waste**, radioactive waste, high-level waste, low-level waste, intermediate-level waste, waste disposal, waste processing

75 **nuclear accident**, meltdown, fallout, nuclear contamination, decontamination, radiation exposure, Chernobyl, Three Mile Island

76 **fusion reactor**, thermonuclear reactor, tokamak, plasma, plasma containment, plasma confinement

77 **elementary particle**, fundamental particle, subatomic particle, particle, lepton, electron, muon, tauon, neutrino, quark, quark flavour, quark colour, hadron, baryon, meson, proton, neutron, nucleon, pion, pi meson, kaon, K meson, fermion, boson, antiparticle, antiproton, antineutron, positron, antielectron, antiquark

78 **quantum**, quantum of radiation, photon, quantized property, quantum number, charge, spin, isospin, parity, strangeness, charm, beauty, up, down, left, right

79 **fundamental interaction**, gravitational interaction, electromagnetic interaction, nuclear interaction, strong interaction, strong nuclear interaction, weak interaction, weak nuclear interaction, electroweak interaction, exchange force, unified field theory, string, superstring, theory of everything

80 **quantum theory**, quantum mechanics, wave mechanics, matrix mechanics, Dirac notation, wave–particle duality, Copenhagen interpretation, quantum electrodynamics, quantum chromodynamics, Schrödinger's cat, Bell's inequality, Aspect experiment, quantum uncertainty, quantum jump, quantum leap

81 **causality**, cause and effect, causal law, deterministic law, determinism, unpredictability, chaos theory, probability, indeterminacy, uncertainty principle, Heisenberg uncertainty principle

82 **measuring instrument**, instrument, instrumentation, measuring device, gauge, meter, digital meter, indicating instrument, recording instrument, recording device, measurement, observation, recording, measured quantity, measured value, indicated value, meter reading, reading, readout, scale, graduated scale, pointer, needle, digital readout, digital reading

83 **sensitivity**, response, linear response, frequency response, calibration, accuracy, precision, error, systematic error, observational error, personal error, probable error, standard error, standard deviation, estimated value, computed value, specified value

84 **altimeter**, callipers, micrometer, vernier scale, compass, gyroscope, gyrostat, gyrocompass, sextant, theodolite

85 **microscope**, optical microscope, simple microscope, compound microscope, stereomicroscope, phase-contrast microscope, ultramicroscope, polarizing microscope, electron microscope, scanning electron microscope, scanning transmission electron microscope,

atomic-force microscope, field-emission microscope (FEM), field-ion microscope (FIM), telescope, optical telescope, radio telescope, radio interferometer

86 **weighing instrument**, balance, spring balance, scales, steelyard, torsion balance

87 **clock**, atomic clock, caesiumX clock, chronometer, quartz clock, digital clock, analogue clock, pendulum
▶ *185 Time*

88 **barometer**, aneroid barometer, mercury barometer, pressure gauge, vacuum gauge, strain gauge, flowmeter, hygrometer, hydrometer

89 **thermometer**, mercury thermometer, alcohol thermometer, maximum and minimun thermometer, clinical thermometer, gas thermometer, platinum resistance thermometer, thermocouple, thermopile, pyrometer, calorimeter

90 **ammeter**, galvanometer, voltmeter, potentiometer, electrometer, wattmeter, bridge, oscilloscope, stroboscope, magnetometer

91 **spectrometer**, spectrograph, spectroscope, spectrophotometer, monochromator, mass spectrometer, mass spectrograph

92 **light meter**, photometer, radiometer, bolometer, interferometer, polarimeter, colorimeter

93 **radiation detector**, particle detector, particle counter, Geiger counter, Geiger–Müller counter, ionization chamber, scintillation counter, electron multiplier

94 **particle accelerator**, accelerator, collider, particle collider, cyclotron, Beratron, betatron, synchrotron, proton synchrotron, linear accelerator, Van de Graaff accelerator, Joint European Torus (JET)

95 **mensuration**, metrology, telemetry, remote sensing

96 **microscopy**, thermometry, pyrometry, spectrometry, spectroscopy, photometry, interferometry

97 **fundamental constant**, physical constant, universal constant, speed of light (in vacuum) gravitational constant, Planck constant, permeability of vacuum (*or* magnetic constant), permittivity of vacuum (*or* electric constant), elementary charge, electron mass, proton mass, Boltzmann constant, Stefan–Boltzmann constant, fine-structure constant, Rydberg constant, Bohr radius, Avogadro constant, Faraday constant, molar gas constant
▶ *75 Units*

ADJECTIVES

98 **physical**, classical, mechanical, dynamic, static, kinetic, kinematic, hydrodynamic, aerodynamic, acoustic(al), ultrasonic, subsonic, optic, optical, thermal, calorific, thermodynamic, cryogenic, electric, electrical, magnetic, electrodynamic, atomic, crystallographic,

solid-state, spectroscopic, spectrometric, monochrome, polychrome, magnetohydrodynamic nonclassical, quantum, quantum mechanical, quantized, statistical, relativistic

99 **theoretical**, hypothetical, mathematical, experimental, pure, applied

VERBS

100 **physically**, classically, mechanically, dynamically, statically, kinetically, kinematically, hydrodynamically, aerodynamically, acoustically, ultrasonically, subsonically, optically, thermally, calorifically, thermodynamically, cryogenically, electrically, magnetically, electrodynamically, crystallographically, spectroscopically, spectrometrically, magnetohydrodynamically, nonclassically, quantum mechanically, statistically, relativistically

57   Chemistry

NOUNS

1 **chemistry**, organic chemistry, inorganic chemistry, physical chemistry, chemical physics, theoretical chemistry, quantum chemistry, quantum mechanics, thermodynamics, thermochemistry, statistical mechanics, analytical chemistry, analysis, synthesis, kinetics, crystallography, catalysis, photochemistry, radiochemistry, geochemistry, astrochemistry, polymer chemistry, metallurgy, industrial chemistry, chemical engineering, nuclear chemistry, zymurgy, zoochemy, chemurgy, iatrochemistry, biochemistry, alchemy (Arch)
▶ *58 Biochemistry*

2 **chemist**, organic chemist, inorganic chemist, physical chemist, physiochemist, theoretical chemist, statistical mechanic, analytical chemist, analyst, synthetic chemist, kineticist, crystallographer, photochemist, electrochemist, radiochemist, geochemist, astrochemist, polymer chemist, metallurgist, chemical engineer, chemiatrist, alchemist (Arch)

3 **phase**, solid, liquid, melt, gas vapour, phase change, phase diagram, boiling, condensation, melting, freezing, evaporation, sublimation, solution, concentrated solution, dilute solution, saturated solution, unsaturated solution, supersaturated solution, solvent, solute, polar solvent, nonpolar solvent, precipitation, precipitate, flocculent precipitate, colloid, colloidal solution, lyophobic colloid, lyophilic colloid, hydrophobic colloid, hydrophilic colloid, disperse phase, continuous phase, stabilizer, destabilizer, sol, gel, emulsion, hydrosol, aerosol, mist, smoke, fog, thixotropy, colligative property, mixture, eutectic
▶ *367 Material World, 387 Fluid, 388 Gas, 393 Semiliquid, 54 Earth Science*

4 **crystal**, amorphous substance, glass, single crystal, microcrystal, crystallite, crystal

Laboratory Apparatus

alembic	condenser	graduated flask	reflux condenser
aludel	conical flask	hotplate	round-bottomed flask
aspirator	crucible	Kipp's apparatus	separating funnel
balance	deflagrating spoon	Leibig condenser	sintered-glass crucible
beaker	dessicator	measuring cylinder	spatula
Beckmann thermometer	dropper	melting-point apparatus	stand
beehive shelf	Erlenmeyer flask	mortar	still
blowpipe	evaporating dish	muttle furnace	stirrer
boiling tube	filter funnel	oven	thermometer
Bückner funnel	filter paper	pestle	trough
Bunsen burner	filter pump	pipette	U-tube
burette	flask	platinum wire	vacuum still
capillary tube	fluted funnel	pneumatic trough	volumetric flask
centrifuge	fume cupboard	reagent bottle	watchglass
clamp	gas jar	receiver	

boundary, crystallization, supernatant liquid, growth, form, structure, habit, crystal system, lattice, cubic crystal, face-centred-cubic (f.c.c.) crystal, body-centred-cubic (b.c.c.) crystal, cubic close packing, tetragonal crystal, rhombic (or orthorhombic) crystal, hexagonal crystal, hexagonal close packing, trigonal crystal, monoclinic crystal, triclinic crystal, crystallography, X-ray crystallography, Bragg's law

5 **process**, precipitation, crystallization, fractional crystallization, filtration, vacuum filtration, separation, distillation, fractional distillation, refluxing, chromatography, saponification, adsorption

6 **chemical element**, element, metal, heavy metal, nonmetal, semimetal, metalloid, noble gas, inert gas, rare gas, alkali metal, alkaline-earth element, chalconide, halogen, transition element, rare-earth element, lanthanoid (or lanthanon or lanthanide), actinoid (or actinon or actinide), transuranic element, superheavy element, coinage metal, platinum metal, periodic table, Döbereiner's triads, Newland's octaves, diagonal relationship, period, short period, long period, group, s-block, p-block, d-block, f-block

7 **chemical compound**, compound, organic compound, inorganic compound, organometallic compound, covalent compound, ionic compound, coordination compound, interstitial compound, lamellar compound, intercallation compound, clathrate, eutectic, cryohydrate, intermetallic compound, alloy, amalgam, ceramic, refractory, stoichiometric compound, nonstoichiometric compound, polar compound, nonpolar compound, saturated compound, unsaturated compound, electron-deficient compound, cyclic compound, acyclic compound, heterocyclic, homocyclic, aromatic, aliphatic, alicyclic, pseudoaromatic, nonbenzenoid aromatic, complex, coordination complex, ammine, chelate, sandwich compound, binary compound, ternary compound

8 **acid**, mineral acid, organic acid, carboxylic acid, protonic acid, Lewis acid, Lowry–Brønsted acid, strong acid, weak acid, monobasic acid, dibasic acid, tribasic acid

9 **base**, alkali, inorganic base, organic base, quaternary base, Lewis base, Lowry–Brønsted base, strong alkali, weak alkali, monoacidic base, diacidic base, triacidic base, amphoteric compound

10 **salt**, acid salt, basic salt, double salt, alum, hydrate, monohydrate, dihydrate, trihydrate, quadrihydrate, pentahydrate, hexahydrate, heptahydrate, octahydrate, nonahydrate, decahydrate, undecahydrate, dodecahydrate, hemihydrate, sesquihydrate, anhydride, anhydrous salt

11 **chemical bond**, valence bond, ionic bond, electrovalent bond, covalent bond, coordinate bond, ligand, dative bond, donor, acceptor, polar bond, heteropolar bond, homopolar bond, semipolar bond, intermediate bond, pair bond, lone pair, metallic bond, electron-deficient bond, multicentre bond, bent bond, banana bond, dipole–dipole interaction, hydrogen bond, dispersion force, van der Waals force, bond energy, bond strength, bond angle, dissociation energy

12 **valence**, valency, valence-bond (or VB) theory, molecular-orbital (or MO) theory, orbital, molecular orbital, bonding orbital, antibonding orbital, overlap integral, hybridization, hybrid orbital

13 **structure**, formula, chemical formula, empiracle formula, molecular formula, structural formula, stereochemistry, steric effect, steric hindrance, isomerism, isomer, structural isomer(ism), stereoisomer(ism), cis–trans isomer(ism), syn–anti isomer(ism), optical isomer(ism), epimerism, epimer, anomerism, anomer, asymmetric centre, chiral centre, chirality, optical activity, optical rotation, dextro form, d-form, laevo form, l-form, meso-form, racemate, racemic mixture, D-form, L-form, R-form, S-form, CORN rule, resolution, racemization, inversion, invert sugar, polarimetry, ORD (optical rotary dispersion)

Chemical Elements (and Common Allotropes)

actinium (Ac)
aluminium (Al)
americium (Am)
antimony (Sb)
argon (Ar)
arsenic (As)
  grey arsenic
astatine (At)
barium (Ba)
berkelium (Bk)
beryllium (Be)
  (formerly gluci-
  num or glucin-
  ium)
bismuth (Bi)
boron (B)
bromine (Br)
cadmium (Cd)
caesium (Cs)
calcium (Ca)
californium (Cf)
carbon (C)
  graphite
  diamond
cerium (Ce)
chlorine (Cl)
chromium (Cr)

cobalt (Co)
copper (Cu)
curium (Cm)
dysprosium (Dy)
einsteinium (Es)
element 104 (or
  Kurchatovium
  (Ku) or ruther-
  fordium (Rf) or
  unnilquadium
  (Unq)
element 105 (or
  unnilpentium)
element 106 (or
  unnilhexium)
erbium (Er)
europium (Eu)
fermium (Fm)
fluorine (F)
francium (Fr)
gadolinium (Gd)
gallium (Ga)
germanium (Ge)
gold (Au)
hafnium (Hf)
hahnium (Ha)
helium (He)

holmium (Ho)
hydrogen (H)
  dihydrogen
  orthohydrogen
  parahydrogen
  nascent hydrogen
indium (In)
iodine (I)
iridium (Ir)
iron (Fe)
krypton (Kr)
lanthanum (La)
lawrencium (Lr)
lead (Pb)
lithium (Li)
lutetium (Lu)
magnesium (Mg)
manganese (Mn)
mendelevium (Md)
mercury (Hg)
molybdenum (Mo)
neodymium (Nd)
neon (Ne)
neptunium (Np)
nickel (Ni)
niobium (Nb)
nitrogen (N)

nobelium (Nb)
osmium (Os)
oxygen (O)
  dioxygen
  ozone
  trioxygen
palladium (Pd)
phosphorus (P)
  red phosphorus
  white phosphorus
platinum (Pt)
plutonium (Pu)
polonium (Po)
potassium (K)
praseodymium (Pr)
promethium (Pm)
protactinium (Pa)
radium (Ra)
radon (Rn)
rhenium (Re)
rhodium (Rh)
rubidium (Rb)
ruthenium (Ru)
rutherfordium (Rf)
samarium (Sm)
scandium (Sc)
selenium (Se)

silicon (Si)
silver (Ag)
sodium (Na)
strontium (Sr)
sulphur, sulfur
  (US) (S)
tantalum (Ta)
technetium (Tc)
tellurium (Te)
terbium (Tb)
thallium (Tl)
thorium (Th)
thulium (Tm)
tin (Sn)
titanium (Ti)
tungsten (or wol-
  fram) (W)
uranium (U)
vanadium (V)
xenon (Xe)
ytterbium (Yb)
yttrium (Y)
zinc (Zn)
zirconium (Zr)

14 chemical reaction, process, reactant, product, reagent, fast reaction, slow reaction, irreversible reaction, reversible reaction, equilibrium, equilibrium constant, main reaction, side reaction, fission reaction, heterolysis, heterolytic fission, ionization, homolytic fission, homolysis, addition, condensation, substitution, elimination, displacement, disproportionation, rearrangement, ring closure, cyclization, aromatization, ring opening, polymerization, pyrolysis, neutralization, electrophilic reaction, electrophile, nucleophilic reaction, nucleophile, kinetics, unimolecular reaction, bimolecular reaction, reaction order, mechanism, step, rate-determining step, absolute rate theory, collision theory, transition state, activated complex, rate constant, activation energy, isotope effect, photochemical reaction, radiochemical reaction, chain reaction

15 catalysis, catalyst, homogeneous catalysis, heterogeneous catalysis, acid–base catalysis, autocatalysis, deactivation, accelerator, stabilizer, poison, substrate, platinum black, Raney nickel, enzyme

16 synthesis, synthetic compound, synthetic, stoichiometric synthesis, by-product, biosynthesis, biotechnology

17 analysis, qualitative analysis, quantitative

Types of Compounds

acetal
acid anhydride
acyl halide
alcohol
aldehyde
aldohexose
aldol
aldopentose
aldose
alkaloid
alkane
alkene
alkyne
alkoxide
alkyl halide
alkyne
aluminate
amide
amine
amino acid
azide
azine
azo compound

bicarbonate
borane
borate
boride
boron hydride
borosilicate
carbide
carbohydrate
carbonate
carbonyl
carboxylic acid
chlorate
chloride
chlorite
chlorofluorocarbon
  (CFC)
chromate
cresol
cyanide
detergent
diazonium salt
diol
enzyme

epoxide
ester
ether
fluoride
fluorocarbon
furanose
halide
haloalkane
haloform
hexose
hydrogencarbon-
  ate
imine
iodide
ketal
ketohexose
ketone
ketopentose
ketose
lactam
lactate
lactone
mercaptan

metallocene
nitrile
nitrite
nitro compound
oxime
ozonide
paraffin
peptide
permanganate
peroxide
petrochemical
phenol
polymer
protein
pseudohalogen
quaternary com-
  pound
saccharide
Schiff's base
semicarbazone
silane
silicate
silicide

silicone
siloxane
soap
stearate
suboxide
sugar
sulphate
sulphide
sulphite
sulphonamide
sulphonic acid
superoxide
tartrate
terpene
thio alcohol
thio ether
thiosulphate
triol
tungstate
zeolite
zincate

Common Chemical Compounds

acetaldehyde (ethanal)
acetamide
acetic acid (ethanoic acid)
acetone
acetylene (ethene)
alcohol (ethanol)
alum (potash alum)
alumina (aluminium oxide)
ammonia
baking soda (sodium
  hydrogencarbonate)
bicarbonate of soda (sodium
  hydrogencarbonate)
blanc fixe (barium sulphate)
bleaching powder
blue vitriol (copper sulphate)
boracic acid (boric acid)
bromoform (tribromomethane)
butadiene
caliche (sodium nitrate)
calomel (mercurous chloride)
carbolic acid (phenol)
carbon dioxide
carbon moxoxide
carbon tetrachloride (tetrachloro-
  methane)
carborundum (silicon carbide)
chloral (trichloroethanal)
chloral hydrate
Chile saltpetre (sodium nitrate)
chloroform (trichloroethane)
chrome alum
cinnabar (mercuric chloride)
citric acid
common salt (sodium chloride)
corundum (aluminium oxide)

cryalite (sodium hexafluoroalumin-
  ate)
cyanamide (calcium cyanamide)
cyanide (sodium cyanide)
cyanogen
cyclohexane
diethylene glycol
Epsom salt (magnesium sulphate)
ethane
ethanol
ethyl alcohol (ethanol)
ethylene (ethene)
firedamp (methane)
folic acid
formaldehyde (methanal)
formic acid (methanoic acid)
fumaric acid (butenedioic acid)
galena (plumbous sulphide)
gallium arsenide
Glauber's salt (sodium sulphate)
glycerine (glycerol)
gypsum (calcium sulphate)
hexane
hydrazine
hydrochloric acid (hydrogen chloride)
hydrogen peroxide
hydrogen sulphide
jeweller's rouge
killed spirits (zinc chloride)
laughing gas (dinitrogen monoxide)
lithia (lithium hydroxide)
magnesia (magnesium oxide)
malic acid
marsh gas (methane)

naphthalene
nitric acid
nitric oxide (nitrogen monoxide)
nitrous acid
nitrous oxide (dinitrogen monoxide)
octane
oil of vitriol (sulphuric acid)
paraldehyde
pentane
perchloric acid
phosphine
plaster of Paris (calcium sulphate)
plumbane (lead hydride)
potassium permanganate
potassium chloride
propane
propylene (propene)
pyridine
quicklime (calcium oxide)
red lead (lead oxide)
saltpetre (potassium nitrate)
silica (silicon dioxide)
soda (sodium carbonate)
sodamide
sodium bicarbonate (sodium
  hydrogencarbonate)
stannane (tin hydride)
strontia (strontium oxide)
sulphur dioxide
sulphuric acid
sulphurous acid
tetraethyl lead
tetrahydrofuran
washing soda (sodium carbonate)
xylene (dimethylbenzene)

analysis, spectrographic analysis, spectrometry, spectrograph, spectometer, spectrum, mass spectrometry, ultraviolet (or UV) spectrometry, infrared (or IR) spectrometry, X-ray spectroscopy, microwave spectroscopy, electron spectroscopy, PES (photoelectron spectroscopy), UPS (ultraviolet photoelectron spectroscopy), XPS (X-ray photoelectron spectroscopy), NHR (nuclear magnetic resonance), ESR (electron-spin resonance), ENDOR (electron-nuclear double resonance), polarography, polarogram, chromatography, chromatogram, column chromatography, GLC (gas–liquid chromatography), GSC (gas–solid chromatography), TLC (thin-layer chromatography), paper chromatography, electrophoresis, electro-osmosis, gel filtration, ion-exchange chromatography, HPLC (high-performance liquid chromatography), stationary phase, mobile phase, carrier, elution, eluent, solvent front

18 gravimetric analysis, gravimetry, volumetric analysis, titration, titre, indicator, litmus, litmus paper, phenolphthalein, methyl orange, methyl red, mixed indicator, universal indicator, absorption indicator, conductiometric titration, equivalence point, end point, standard solution, standardization, gas analysis

19 electrochemistry, cell, anode, cathode, electrolyte, concentration cell, half cell, electrode potential, electrochemical series, electromotive series, electrolysis, electrolytic cell, electrodeposition, electroplating, electrolytic refining, electrolytic forming, anode sludge, voltaic cell, battery, wet cell, dry cell, polarization, overpotential, Leclanché cell, Daniell cell, Bunsen cell, Weston cell, NIFE cell, fuel cell, electrolytic corrosion, rusting, sacrificial anode, pH, hydrogen electrode, glass electrode

20 surface chemistry, absorption, adsorption, chemisorption, physisorption, sorption, desorption, degassing, outgassing, flash desorption, field desorption, vacuum, high vacuum, low vacuum, hard vacuum, soft vacuum, uhv (ultra-high vacuum), vacuum pump, filter pump, rotary pump, diffusion pump, ion pump, sputtering, sputter-ion pump, gettering, getter-ion pump, cryogenic pump, vacuum gauge, monometer, McLeod gauge, Pirani gauge, ion (or ionization) gauge, Bayerd–Alpert gauge, leak detector, RGA (residual-gas analyser), Tesla coil

21 polymer, polymerization, monomer, macromolecule, addition polymer(ization), condensation polymer(ization), chain, cross linking, homopolymer(ization), copolymer(ization),

Types of Chemical Reaction

acetylation	esterification	nitration
acylation	fermentation	oxidation
benzoylation	fixation	ozonolysis
bromination	fluorination	reduction
calcination	halogenation	saponifica-
carbonation	hydration	tion
carburization	hydrogena-	solvation
chlorination	tion	solvolysis
deuteration	hydrolysis	sulphonation
diazotization	neutralization	tritiation

stereospecific polymerization, stereoregular polymer, atactic polymer, isotactic polymer, syndiotactic polymer, Bakelite (Tm), PVC (polyvinyl chloride *or* polychloroethene), uPVC (ultra-hard PVC), polythene (*or* polyethylene *or* polyethene), polypropylene (*or* polypropene), polyester, nylon, polycarbonate, polyurethane, epoxide resin, polystyrene, expanded polystyrene, PTFE (polytetrafluoroethylene), Teflon (Tm), polymethylmethacrylate, Perspex (Tm), Plexiglass (Tm), vulcanite, isoprene rubber, chloroprene rubber, resin, plasticizer, stabilizer, plastic, thermosetting plastic, thermoplastic material

▶ *377 Elasticity*

22 industrial chemistry, chemical engineering, refining, oil refining, refinery, cracking, cat-cracking reforming, steam reforming, fractionation, fractional distillation, fraction, petrochemicals, plastics, fibres, dyestuffs, fertilizers, explosives, fine chemicals, pharmaceuticals

23 metallurgy, metal, metalloid, alloy extractive metallurgy, production metallurgy, extraction, blast furnace, electrolytic extraction, refining, froth flotation, electrorefining, electroplating

24 ore, deposit, vein, lode, lodestuff, placer, gangue

VERBS

25 solidify, liquefy, vaporize, condense, melt, freeze, evaporate, concentrate, dilute, dissolve, saturate, supersaturate, precipitate, disperse, stabilize, destabilize, flocculate, gel, emulsify, separate, filter, distil, steam-distil, vacuum-distil, fractionate, refine, crystallize, crystallize out

26 react, bond, coordinate, add, substitute, condense, eliminate, transfer, rearrange, dissociate, ionize, heterolyse, neutralize, acidify, cyclize, pyrolyse, irradiate, polymerize, racemize, invert, catalyse, activate, promote, poison, acetylate, acylate, benzoylate, brominate, calcine, calcify, carbonate, carburize, chlorinate, deuterate, diazotize, esterify, ferment, fluormate, fluoridate, halogenate, hydrate, hydrogenate, hydrolyse, nitrate, oxidize, ozonize, reduce, saponify, solvate, sulphonate, sulphurize, tritiate

27 synthesize, analyse, degrade

28 electrolyse, electrodeposit, electroplate, electroform

29 absorb, adsorb, physisorb, chemisorb, sorb, desorb, degass, outgas, getter, sputter, field desorb, field ionize

30 extract, win, concentrate, purify, refine, sinter, alloy, anneal, case-harden, work harden, temper

ADJECTIVES

31 chemical, physiochemical, organic, inorganic, theoretical, thermodynamic, statistico-mechanical, analytic(al), synthetic, kinetic, crystallographic, catalytic, photochemical, radiochemical, biochemical, astrochemical, metallurgical, zymurgic, alchemical (Arch)

32 solid, liquid, gaseous, vapourous, condensed, melted, molten, frozen, evaporated, concentrated, dilute, saturated, unsaturated, supersaturated, flocculent colloidal, lyophobic, lyophilic, hydrophobic, hydrophilic, disperse, continuous, stabilized, destabilized, gelled, emulsoid, thixotropic, colligative, eutectic, precipitated, filtered, distilled, pure, refined

33 crystalline, microcrystalline, crystallized,

Named Reactions, Processes, etc.

Acheson process	Fehling's solution	Kjeldahl's method	Schiff's base
Arrhenius equation	Fischer–Tropsch pro-	Kolbe electrolysis	Schiff's reagent
Beckmann thermometer	cess	Leblanc process	Schoffen–Baumann re-
Born–Haber cycle	Fittig reaction	Le Châtelier's principle	agent
Bosch process	Friedel–Crafts reaction	Lowry–Brønsted theory	Strecker synthesis
Brin process	Gay-Lussac's law	Markovnikoff's rules	Tollen's reagent
Brownian movement	Gibbs function	Mendius reaction	van der Waals force
Cannizzaro reaction	Graham's law	Moseley's law	van't Hoff factor
Corius method	Haber process	Natta process	Victor Meyer's method
Carnot cycle	Hell–Volard–Zelinsky	Newland's law	Wacker process
Claisen condensation	reaction	Ostwald's dilution law	Walden universion
Dewar structure	Helmholtz function	Pauli exclusion principle	Williamson's process
Dow process	Henry's law	Phillip's process	Williamson's synthesis
Downs process	Hesse's law	Raney nickel	Wöhler's synthesis
Dulong and Petit's law	Hofmann degradation	Raoult's law	Wurtz reaction
Dumas' method	Hofmann's method	Rashig process	Zeisel reaction
Fajan's rules	Kekulé structure	Regnault's method	Ziegler process
Faraday's laws	Kipp's apparatus	Sachse reaction	

Common Metal Ores

Ore (Metal)	
anglesite (lead)	haematite (iron)
argentite (silver)	ironstone (iron)
arsenopyrite (iron, arsenic)	limonite (iron)
	litharge (lead)
bauxite (aluminium)	lodestone (iron)
carnotite (uranium)	magnetite (iron)
cassiterite (tin)	mispickel (iron, arsenic)
cerrusite (lead)	pitchblende (uranium)
chalcocite (copper)	siderite (iron)
chalcopyrite (copper)	smithsonite (zinc)
chromite (chromium)	stibnite (antimony)
copper pyrites (copper)	tinstone (tin)
cinnabar (mercury)	zinc blende (zinc)
galena (lead)	zincite (zinc)

crystalloid, noncrystalline, amorphous, irregular, supernatant, structural, cubic, tetragonal, rhombic, orthorhombic, hexagonal, trigonal, monclinic, triclinic, face-centred, body-centred, close packed, cubic close packed, hexagonal close packed

34 **elemental**, native, uncombined, metallic, metalloid, inert, transuranic, superheavy, aluminous, aluminiferous, antimonous, antimonic, arsenous, arsenious, arsenic, bismuthous, bismuthic, bismuthyl, bromous, bromic, brominated, calciferous, carbonic, carboniferous, graphitic, cerous, ceric, chlorous, chloric, chlorinated, chromous, chromic, chromyl, cobaltous, cobaltic, cuprous, cupric, cupriferous, fluoric, fluorinated, fluoridated, germanous, germanic, aurous, auric, auriferous, hydrogenous, iodous, iodic, iridous, iridic, ferrous, ferric, ferrosoferric, ferriferous plumbous, plumbic, plumbiferous, manganous, manganic, mercurous, mercuric, molybdous, molybdenous, molybdic, nickelous, nickelic, nickeliferous, niobous, niobic, columbous, columbic, nitrogenous, osmous, osmious, osmic, oxygenated, oxygenized, phosphorous, phosphoric, platinous, platinic, platinized, platinoid, platiniferous, rhodic, rhodous, scandic, selenous, selenious, selenic, silicic, argentous, argentic, argentiferous, sulphurous, sulphuric, sulphonous, sulphonic, sulphuryl, sulphuretted, tantalous, tantalic, tellurous, telluric, thallous, thallic, stannous, stannic, stanniferous, titanic, titanous, tungstous, tungstic, uranous, uranic, uranyl, vanadous, vanadic, zinciferous

35 **combined**, organic, inorganic, organometallic, covalent, electrovalent, ionic, univalent, monovalent, divalent, trivalent, tervalent, tetravalent, quadrivalent, pentavalent, quinquevalent, hexavalent, sexivalent, heptavalent, septivalent, octavalent, nonstoichiometric, polar, nonpolar, saturated, unsaturated, delocalized, electron-deficient, cyclic, acyclic, heterocyclic, homocyclic, carbocyclic, aromatic, aliphatic, alicyclic, pseudoaromatic,

binary, ternary, molecular, monatomic, diatomic, triatomic, polyatomic, complex, transient, metastable

36 **acid**, acidic, basic, alkaline, weak, strong, monobasic, dibasic, tribasic, monoacidic, diacidic, triacidic, protonic, amphoteric, neutral, saline, hydrated, anhydrous

37 **structural**, steric, conformational, isomeric, stereoisomeric, epimeric, anomeric, asymmetric, chiral, racemized

38 **reactive**, unreactive, inactive, deactivated, passive, fast, slow, reversible, irreversible, equilibrated, homolytic, heterolytic, additive, substitutional, cyclic, electrophilic, nucleophilic, polymeric, monomolecular, bimolecular, first-order, second-order, third-order

39 **catalytic**, autocatalytic, activated, deactivated, poison

40 **synthetic**, synthesized, separative, naturally-occurring

41 **analytic**, quantitative, spectroscopic, spectrographic, polarographic, chromatographic, electrophoretic, stationary, mobile, reversed-phase, gravimetric, volumetric, standardized, neutralized, equivalent

42 **electrochemical**, electrolytic, electromotive, electrovoltaic, electrodeposited, electroplated, electroformed, anodic, cathodic

Alloys

admiralty metal	manganese bronze
alloy steel	misch metal
Alnico (Tm)	Monel metal (Tm)
aluminium bronze	Muntz metal
amalgam	Nichrome (Tm)
babbitt metal	nickel bronze
bearing metal	nickel silver
bell bronze	osmiridium
bell metal	permalloy
brass	perminvar
Britannia metal	pewter
bronze	phosphor bronze
bush metal	pig iron
carbon steel	pig lead
cast iron	pinchbeck
chrome steel	platiniridium
chromel	red brass
coinage metal	Rose's metal
constantan	silicon bronze
cupronickel	silicon steel
damask	silver solder
Duralumin (Tm)	solder
electrum	speculum metal
elinvar	spiegeleisen
ferrochromium	stainless steel
ferromanganese	steel
ferromolybdenum	Stellite (Tm)
ferronickel	sterling silver
ferrosilicon	tombac
fusible alloy	type metal
German silver	white gold
gunmetal	white metal
high-speed steel	Wood's metal
invar	wrought iron
magnolia metal	yellow brass
magnox	zircalloy

43 **absorbed**, adsorbed, physisorbed, chemisorbed, sorbed, desorbed, outgassed, degassed
44 **polymeric**, monomeric, copolymeric, stereospecific, stereoregular, atactic, tactic, isotactic, syndiotactic
45 **metallurgical**, extractive, alloyed

ADVERBS

46 **chemically**, practically, theoretically, thermodynamically, catalytically, photochemically, metallurgically, synthetically, analytically, colloidally, amorphously, covalently, ionically, electrovalently

58 Biochemistry

NOUNS

1 **biochemistry**, biosynthesis, bioenergetics, biomolecule, biochemical taxonomy, biotechnology, enzymology, endocrinology
▶ 59 Life Science
2 **biochemist**, plant biochemist, enzymologist, endocrinologist
3 **carbohydrate**, saccharide, sugar, monosaccharide, simple sugar, triose, tetrose, pentose, hexose, heptose, octose, aldose, ketose, aldotriose, aldotetrose, aldopentose, aldohexose, aldoheptose, aldooctose, ketotriose, ketotetrose, ketopentose, ketohexose, hetoheptose, ketooctose, hemiacetal, pyranose, hemiketal, furanose, complex sugar, disaccharide, trisaccharide, tetrasaccharide, oligosaccharide, sugar alcohol, sorbitol, mannitol, glycerol, glycerine, inositol, sugar acid, aldonic acid, aldaric acid, saccharic acid, uronic acid, sugar derivative, glycoside, glucoside, cardiac glycoside, digitalin
▶ 62 Pharmacology
4 **polysaccharide**, glycan, homopolysaccharide, heteropolysaccharide, storage polysaccharide, starch, amylose, amylopectin, inulin, animal starch, glycogen, dextran, fructan, arabinan, xylon, mannan, structural polysaccharide, cellulose, hemicellulose, pectic substance, pectin, extensin, lignin, agar, gum arabic, chitin, mucopolysaccharide, glycosaminoglycan (GAG)
5 **sugar test**, alpha-naphthol test, Barfoed's test, Benedict's test, Fehling's test, Molisch's test, Schiff's reagent, Seliwanoff's test, Tollen's reagent

Common Fatty Acids

Traditional name (Systematic name)	
formic (methanoic)	palmitic (hexadecanoic)
acetic (ethanoic)	stearic (octadecanoic)
propionic (propanoic)	lactic (hydroxypropanoic)
butyric (butanoic)	acrylic (propenoic)
valeric (pentanoic)	crotonic (trans-buteneoic)
caproic (hexanoic)	malic (hydroxybutanedioic)
oenanthic (heptanoic)	
caprylic (octanoic)	fumaric (trans-butenedioic)
pelargonic (nonanoic)	
capric (decanoic)	maleic (cis-butenedioic)
lauric (dodecanoic)	oxalic (ethanedioic)
myristic (tetradecanoic)	citric

6 **lipid**, complex lipid, saponifiable lipid, fat, oil, wax, glycolipid, cerebroside, phospholipid, phosphatide, phosphoglyceride, glycerophosphatide, lecithin (or phosphatidylcholine), cephalin (or phosphatidylethanolamine), sphingolipid, sphingomyelin, lipoprotein, simple lipid, nonsaponifiable lipid, terpene, steroid, sterol, cholesterol, bile acid
7 **fat**, fatty-acid ester, glyceride, acylglycerol, simple glyceride, mixed glyceride, monoglyceride, diglyceride, triglyceride, fatty acid, carboxylic acid, essential fatty acid, saturated fat, unsaturated fat, monounsaturated fat, polyunsaturated fat, lipolysis, saponification
8 **amino acid**, essential amino acid, nonessential amino acid, imino acid, peptide, peptide bond, disulphide bond, cystine, kinin, bradykinin, kalidin, dipeptide, tripeptide, oligopeptide, polypeptide, amino-acid residue
9 **protein**, protein structure, primary structure, secondary structure, tertiary structure, quaternary structure, oligomeric protein, protomer, globular protein, globulin, fibrous protein, alpha-helix, conjugated protein, nucleoprotein, lipoprotein, glycoprotein, proteoglycan, mucoprotein, mucin, peptidoglycan, phosphoprotein, haemoprotein, flavoprotein, metalloprotein, scleroprotein, sclerotization, prosthetic group, biuret test, denaturization, albumin, albumen, casein, collagen, fibrin, gelatin (or gelatine), gluten, histone, immunoglobulin, insulin, interferon, keratin, myoglobin

Amino Acids

Acid (Abbreviation)	
alanine (ala)	methionine (met)*
arginine (arg)*	phenylalanine (phe)*
asparagine (asn)	proline (pro)
aspartic acid (asp)	serine (ser)
cysteine (cys)	threonine (thr)*
glutamic acid (glu)	tryptophan (trp)*
glutamine (gln)	tyrosine (tyr)
glycine (gly)	valine (val)*
histidine (his)*	ornithine
isoleucine (ile)*	citrulline
leucine (leu)*	
lycine (lys)*	* indicates an essential amino acid

Common Sugars

arabinose	mannose
fructose (or laevulose or fruit sugar)	raffinose
	rhamnose
fucose	ribose
galactose	sorbose
glucose (or dextrose or grape sugar)	sucrose (or cane sugar or beet sugar or saccharose)
lactose (or milk sugar)	
maltose (or malt sugar)	xylose

Hormones

ACTH (or adrenocortico-
trophic hormone or
adrenocorticotrophin
or corticotrophin)
adrenalin(e), epineph-
rine (US)
aldosterone
androgen
androsterone
angiotensin
antidiuretic hormone
(ADH or vasopressin
or pitressin)
bovine somatotrophin
(BST)
calcitonin (or thyrocalcitonin)
cholecystokinin
chorionic gonadotrophin
corticoid
corticosterone
corticotrophin

cortisol
cortisone
deoxycorticosterone
ecdysone (moulting hor-
mone)
enterogastrone
erythropoietin
follicle-stimulating hor-
mone (FSH)
glucagon
growth hormone
hydrocortisone
insulin
intermedin (or melano-
cyte-stimulating hor-
mone)
interstitial-cell-
stimulating hormone
(ICSH)
juvenile hormone
lactogenic hormone
lipotrophin

luteinizing hormone
(LH)
luteotrophic hormone
(or luteotrophin)
melanocyte-stimulating
hormone (MSH or
intermedia)
melatonin
noradrenalin, norepi-
nephrine (US)
oestradiol
oestriol
oestrogen
oestrone
oxytocin
pancreozymin
parathyroid hormone
(or parathormone)
pitressin
progesterone
progestogen (or proges-
tin)

prolactin (or lactogenic
hormone or
luteotrophic hormone
or luteotrophin)
relaxin
secretin
somatotrophin
testosterone
thyrocalcitonin (or calcitonin)
thyroglobulin
thyroid hormone
thyroid-stimulating hor-
mone (TSH or thyro-
trophin)
thyroxine
triiodothyronine
vasotocin
vasopressin (or antidi-
uretic hormone)

10 **nucleoside**, nitrogenous base, purine base, adesnine, guanine, pyrimidine base, thymine, cytosine, uracil, nucleotide, deoxynucleotide, ribonucleotide, nucleic acid, DNA (deoxyribonucleic acid), double helix, RNA (ribonucleic acid), mRNA (messenger RNA), tRNA (transfer RNA)
▶ *59 Life Science*

11 **enzyme**, substrate, active site, apoenzyme, cofactor, coenzyme, prosthetic group, holoenzyme, inhibition, feedback inhibition, enzyme class, oxidoreductase, transferase, hydrolase, lyase, isomerase, ligase, amylase, diastase, dehydrogenase, gastrin, lactase, lipase, lysozyme, papain, protease, peptidase, proteolytic enzyme, proteolysis, pepsin, trypsin, rennin, restriction enzyme, restriction endonuclease, transaminase, zymogen

12 **coenzyme**, CoA (coenzyme A), CoQ (coenzyme Q), NAD (nicotinamide adenine dinucleotide), NADP (nicotinamide adenine dinucleotide phosphate), FAD (flavin adenine dinucleotide), flavoprotein, thiamin (*or* thiamine), pyrophosphate, lipoamide, biocytin, pyridoxal phosphate

13 **vitamin**, vitamin A (retinol), vitamin B complex, vitamin B_1 (thiamin *or* thiamine), vitamin B_2 (riboflavin), vitamin B_6 (pyridoxine), vitamin B_{12} (cyanocobalamin), nicotinic acid, pantothenic acid, folic acid, biotin, lipoic acid, choline, vitamin C (ascorbic acid), vitamin D_2 (ergocalciferol *or* calciferol), vitamin D_3 (cholecalciferol), vitamin E (tocopherol), vitamin K

14 **vitamin deficiency disease**, night blindness, xerophthalmia, beriberi, pernicious anaemia, scurvy, rickets, osteomalacia
▶ *624 Ill Health*

15 **essential element**, major element, macronutrient, carbon, hydrogen, oxygen, nitrogen,

calcium, phosphorus, potassium, sodium, chlorine, sulphur, magnesium, trace element, micronutrient, iron, manganese, zinc, copper, iodine, cobalt, selenium, molybdenum, chromium, silicon

16 **hormone**, neurohormone, releasing hormone, neurohumour, catecholamine, dopamine, steroid hormone, sex hormone, androgen, anabolic steroid, oestrogen, oral contraceptive, corticosteroid, mineralocorticoid, glucocorticoid, gonadotrophin, gonadotrophic hormone, externally acting hormone, ectohormone, pheromone, hormone-like substance, prostaglandin, chemical messenger (Inf)
▶ *352 Secretion, 62 Pharmacology*

17 **plant hormone**, phytohormone, growth substance, auxin, giberellin, ethylene (*or* ethene), abscisic acid, IAA (indolacetic acid), 2,4-D (2,4-dichlorophenoxyacetic acid), 2,4,5-T (2,4,5-trichlorophenoxyacetic acid), cytokinin (*or* kinin), zeatin

18 **pigment**, plant pigment, flavonoid, flavonol, flavone, anthocyanin, phytochrome, photosynthetic pigment, chlorophyll, phycobilin, carotenoid, carotene, xanthophyll, fucoxanthin, respiratory pigment, haemoglobin, bile pigment, bilirubin, biliverdin
▶ *444 Colour*

19 **alkaloid**, morphine, cocaine, atropine, quinine, caffeine, aconite, papaverine, strychnine, coniine, colchicine
▶ *62 Pharmacology*

20 **terpene**, isoprene unit, monoterpene, sesquiterpene, diterpene, triterpene, tetraterpene, geraniol, limonene, menthol, pinene, camphor, carvone, farnesol, phytol, carotenoid, squalene, vitamin A, vitamin E, vitamin K

21 **metabolism**, catabolism, anabolism, meta-

bolic pathway, metabolite
▶ *59 Life Science*
22 **bioenergetics**, ATP (adenosine triphosphate), ADP (adenosine diphosphate), AMP (adenosine monophosphate), phosphorylation, phosphate bond, energy-rich bond, phosphagen, creatine phosphate, ATP cycle
23 **photosynthesis**, light reaction, dark reaction, chlorophyll a, chlorophyll b, photophosphorylation, Calvin cycle
▶ *59 Life Science, 83 Plants (General)*
24 **respiration**, aerobic respiration, anaerobic respiration, photorespiration, external respiration, internal respiration, cell respiration, haemoglobin, myoglobin, haem, glycolysis, Embden–Meyerhof pathway, Krebs cycle, citric acid cycle, TCA cycle (tricarboxylic acid cycle), respiratory chain, electron-transport chain
▶ *59 Life Science, 390 Air*

VERBS
25 **metabolize**, photosynthesize, synthesize, catalyse

ADJECTIVES
26 **biochemical**, biosynthetic, biomolecular, enzymic, hormonal, metabolic, catabolic, anabolic, bioenergetic, photosynthetic, glycolytic

ADVERBS
27 **biochemically**, biosynthetically, photosynthetically, enzymically, hormonally, metabolically, catabolically, anabolically

59 Life Science

NOUNS
1 **life science**, biological science, natural science, biology, zoology, botany, palaeobotany, dendrology, pomology, phytochemistry, phytoecology, phytobiology, phytography, phytology, vegetable (*or* plant) pathology, vegetable (*or* plant) physiology, microbiology, algology, bryology, fungology, epidemiology, bacteriology, virology, gnotobiotics, parasitology, anatomy, morphology, physiology, biochemistry (*or* biochemy *or* biochemics), enzymology, endocrinology, neuroscience, immunology, histology, cell biology, cytology, molecular biology, genetics, biogenetics, genetic engineering, biotechnology, developmental biology, embryology, evolution, palaeontology, taxonomy, systematics, natural history, marine biology, ecology, bioecology, bionomics, biophysics, biometry (*or* biometrics), bionics, cybernetics, cryobiology, electrobiology, radiobiology, space biology, astrobiology, exobiology, xenobiology, ethnobiology, sociobiology
▶ *76 Animals (General), 83 Plants (General), 68 Agriculture, 69 Horticulture, 58 Biochemistry, 60 Medicine, 1 Anthropology, 2 Sociology, 54 Earth Science*

2 **living world**, natural world, nature, plant and animal life, flora and fauna, biota, biosphere, ecosphere
▶ *396 Life*
3 **organism**, living organism, being, living being, organic being, living thing, creature, entity, body, individual, animal, plant, eukaryote (*or* eucaryote), prokaryote (*or* procaryote), aerobe, anaerobe, microorganism, microbe, animalcule, microphyte, protist, monad, germ, bacterium, coccus, bacillus, spirillum, rickettsia, mycoplasma, virus, filtrable virus, bacteriophage, phage, retrovirus, virion, viroid, plasmid, provirus, organic remains, fossil
▶ *76 Animals (General), 81 Invertebrates, 83 Plants (General), 624 Ill Health*
4 **anatomy**, form, structure, gross structure, morphology, comparative anatomy, dissection, zootomy, tissue structure, histology
▶ *382 Structure, 290 Interior, 387 Fluid*
5 **physiology**, vital functions, nutrition, absorption, respiration, photosynthesis, metabolism, anabolism, catabolism, transpiration, guttation, osmoregulation, secretion, excretion, sensation, reproduction, growth, locomotion
▶ *350 Eating, 390 Air, 352 Secretion, 353 Excretion, 403 Sensation, 245 Reproduction, 324 Motion*
6 **cell biology**, cytology, cell structure, ultrastructure, microscopical examination, light microscopy, electron microscopy, phase-contrast microscopy, fixation, sectioning, staining, counterstaining, cytochemistry, histochemistry, tissue culture, histology, cytological test, smear test, cell physiology, biochemistry, internal respiration, aerobic respiration, anaerobic respiration, glycolysis, Krebs cycle
▶ *60 Medicine, 58 Biochemistry*
7 **cell**, prokaryotic (*or* procaryotic) cell, eukaryotic (*or* eucaryotic) cell, plant cell, animal cell, bacterial cell, protoplast, cellule, germ cell, germen, reproductive cell, gamete, spore, somatic cell, blood cell, corpuscle, muscle cell, bone cell, pigment cell, unicellular organism, unicell, cell membrane, plasma membrane, plasmalemma, microvillus, cell wall, cellulose, lignin, chitin, cell plate, middle lamella, plasmodesma, cellular tissue, protoplasm, cytoplasm, bioplasm, cytosome, hyaloplasm, energid, trophoplasm, ectoplasm, endoplasm, reticulum, coenocyte, syncytium, idioplasm, germ plasm
▶ *245 Reproduction*
8 **cell organ**, organelle, nucleus, mitochondrion, chondriosome, Golgi apparatus, Golgi body, Golgi vesicle, Golgi complex, cisternum, microtubule, endoplasmic reticulum (ER), rough endoplasmic reticulum, smooth

endoplasmic reticulum, microsome, mesosome, microfibril, ribosome, polysome (*or* polyribosome), spherosome, centrosome, centrosphere, central body, microcentrum, centriole, basal body, kinetosome, flagellum, cilium, pilum, lysosome, peroxisome, plastid, chromatophore, chromoplast, chloroplast, leucoplast, plastosome, vacuole, tonoplast

9   **cell nucleus**, macronucleus, meganucleus, micronucleus, nucleolus, plasmosome, nuclear membrane, nuclear envelope, nuclear pore, nucleoplasm, karyoplasm, nuclear sap, chromatin, chromatin strands, karyotin, karyosome, nucleosome, basichromatin, heterochromatin, oxychromatin, nucleoprotein, nucleopeptide, nucleic acid, DNA (deoxyribonucleic acid), RNA (ribonucleic acid)

10   **cell division**, cell cycle, mitosis, meiosis, reduction division, amitosis, endomitosis, metamitosis, eumitosis, promitosis, haplomitosis, mesomitosis, karyomitosis, karyokinesis, interphase, prophase, metaphase, anaphase, telophase, diaster, cytokinesis, spindle, equator, centrosome, centromere, aster, spindle fibres, linkage, crossing over

11   **genetics**, classical genetics, Mendelian genetics (*or* Mendelism), Mendel's laws, heredity, inheritance, hereditary character, factor, gene, chromosome, dominance, recessiveness, double recessiveness, genetic constitution, genotype, biotype, phenotype, population genetics, genecology, gene flow, gene frequency, gene pool, genetic drift, gene complex, cytogenetics, molecular genetics, biochemical genetics, microbial genetics, genetic engineering, eugenics

▶ *60 Medicine*

12   **molecular biology**, biological molecule, macromolecule, protein, nucleic acid, macromolecular structure, protein structure, polypeptide chain, amino-acid sequence, protein sequencing, nucleic-acid structure, DNA double helix, nitrogenous base, adenosine, cytosine, guanine, thymine, uracil, nucleoside, nucleotide, polynucleotide, molecular genetics, gene structure, gene sequencing, genetic mapping, recombinant DNA technology, biotechnology, genetic engineering, genetic (*or* DNA) fingerprinting, gene (*or* DNA) probe, restriction enzyme, gene cloning, cloning vector, gene splicing, designer gene, genotype, phenotype

▶ *58 Biochemistry*

13   **genetic material**, DNA, RNA, genetic element, gene, factor, allele, operon, structural gene, regulator gene, operator gene, gene complement, genome, genetic code, codon, anticodon, messenger RNA (mRNA), transfer RNA (tRNA), ribosomal RNA, protein synthesis, extrachromosomal genetic element, plasma-

gene, plasmid, transposon, gene mutation, gene sequence, exon, intron, gene splicing

14   **chromosome**, heterosome, autosome, heterochromosome, allerome, idiochromosome, sex chromosome, W chromosome, X chromosome, Y chromosome, Z chromosome, euchromosome, homologous chromosome, univalent chromosome, chromatid, centromere, kinetochore, chromomere, chromonema, gene string, chromatin, chromosome, complement, chromosome number, diploid number, haploid number, diploidy, haploidy, polyploidy, autopolyploidy, allopolyploidy, chromosome mutation

15   **developmental biology**, embryology, ontogeny, embryogenesis, embryogeny, germination, cleavage, blastulation, gastrulation, induction, evocation, embryo, germ, primordium, rudiment, zygote, oosperm, morula, blastomere, blastula, blastocyst, gastrula, germ layer, ectoderm, endoderm, mesoderm, fetus (*or* foetus), extra-embryonic membrane, amnion, chorion, allantois, juvenile, larva, nymph, pupa, chrysalis, metamorphosis, paedogenesis, neoteny

▶ *82 Insects and Arachnids, 79 Reptiles and Amphibians*

16   **evolution**, phylogeny, speciation, convergent evolution, parallel evolution, natural selection, survival of the fittest, Darwinism, Weismannism, continuity of germ plasm, neo-Darwinism, Lamarckism, inheritance of acquired characteristics, neo-Lamarckism, Lysenkoism, uniformitarianism, catastrophism, palaeontology, fossil record, recapitulation, Haeckel's law

17   **taxonomy**, systematics, biological classification, classical taxonomy, cytotaxonomy, numerical taxonomy, experimental taxonomy, biosystematics, cladistics, cladism, clade, taxonomic group, taxon, kingdom, subkingdom, division, subdivision, phylum, subphylum, superclass, class, subclass, order, suborder, superfamily, family, subfamily, tribe, subtribe, genus, section, series, species, subspecies, variety, cultivar, race, form, binomial nomenclature, Linnaean system

18   **ecology**, synecology, autecology, plant ecology, phytoecology, animal ecology, zooecology, ecosystem, community, population, niche, ecophysiology, food chain, food web, food pyramid, producer, primary producer, consumer, primary consumer, secondary consumer, parasitism, parasite, host, mutualism, symbiosis, symbiont, symbiote (US), commensalism, commensal, competition, succession, sere, climax, human ecology, conservation, pollution

▶ *76 Animals (General)*

19   **life scientist**, biologist, natural scientist, zo-

ologist, botanist, microbiologist, bacteriologist, virologist, parasitologist, anatomist, morphologist, physiologist, biochemist, endocrinologist, immunologist, histologist, cell biologist, cytologist, molecular biologist, geneticist, developmental biologist, embryologist, palaeontologist, evolutionist, Darwinist, Neo-Darwinist, taxonomist, cladist, naturalist, marine biologist, ecologist, biophysicist, biometrist, cryobiologist, space biologist, ethnobiologist, sociobiologist

ADJECTIVES

20 biological, zoological, botanical, microbiological, bacteriological virological, gnotobiotic, parasitological, anatomical, morphological, physiological, biochemical, endocrinological, endocrine, immunological, histological, cytological, genetic, biotechnological, embryological, evolutionary, palaeontological, taxonomic, systematic, ecological, bionomic, biophysical, biometric, bionic, cryobiological, ethnobiological, sociobiological

21 living, live, alive, animate, vital, viable, organic, natural, biotic, plant, animal, microbial, bacterial, rickettsial, viral

▶ *396 Life*

22 physiological, metabolic, anabolic, catabolic, alimentary, respiratory, aerobic, anaerobic, photosynthetic, secretory, excretory, reproductive, locomotory

▶ *350 Eating, 390 Air, 352 Secretion, 353 Excretion, 403 Sensation, 245 Reproduction, 324 Motion*

23 cellular, cell, cellulus, prokaryotic (*or* procaryotic), eukaryotic (*or* eucaryotic), multicellular, unicellular, single-celled, acellular, plasmic, protoplasmic, cytoplasmic, ectoplasmic, endoplasmic, reticular, coenocytic, syncytial, mitochondrial, ribosomal

24 nuclear, nucleal, nucleary, nucleic, nucleate, uninucleate, multinucleate, nucleolar, nucleolate(d)

25 genetic, genotypic(al), genomic, gene, genic, factorial, hereditary, Mendelian, dominant, recessive, mutant, mutational, chromosomal, mitotic, meiotic, haploid, diploid, polyploid

26 developmental, ontogenic (*or* ontogenetic), developing, primordial, rudimentary, germ, germinal, germinating, germinant, germinative, in the bud, embryonic, ectodermal (*or* ectodermic), endodermal (*or* endodermic), mesodermal (*or* mesodermic), fetal (*or* foetal), amniotic, chorionic, allantoic, juvenile, larval, pupal, neotenous, paedogenetic (*or* paedogenic)

27 evolutionary, phylogenetic (*or* phyletic), Darwinian, neo-Darwinian, Lamarckian, neo-Lamarckian, uniformitarian

28 taxonomic, systematic, biosystematic, cladistic, generic, specific, subspecific

ADVERBS

29 biologically, zoologically, botanically, anatomically, morphologically, physiologically, biochemically, immunologically, histologically, cytologically, genetically, embryologically, taxonomically, generically, systematically, specifically, ecologically

6o Medicine

The art of medicine is generally a question of time. Ovid.

Not even medicine can master incurable diseases. Seneca.

Formerly, when religion was strong and science weak, men mistook magic for medicine, now, when science is strong and religion weak, men mistake medicine for magic. Thomas Szasz.

NOUNS

1 medicine, medical practice, medical profession, medical ethics, Hippocratic oath, medical jurisprudence, orthodox medicine, allopathic medicine, conventional medicine, general medicine, internal medicine, tropical medicine, industrial medicine, occupational medicine, community medicine, public-health medicine, preventive medicine, medical care, health care, primary health (*or* medical) care, general practice, group practice, practice, National Health Service, Medicare (US), Medicaid (US), private medicine, medical insurance, BUPA (British United Provident Association), Blue Cross (US trademark), Blue Shield (US trademark)

▶ *61 Psychology and Psychiatry, 624 Ill Health*

2 natural medicine, traditional medicine, folk medicine, old wives' medicine, healing, faith healing, holistic medicine, alternative medicine, complementary medicine, supplementary medicine, unorthodox medicine, unconventional medicine, fringe medicine, herbalism, homeopathy, naturopathy, osteopathy, chiropractic, acupuncture, acupressure, shiatsu, aromatherapy, reflexology, Ayurvedic medicine

▶ *630 Remedy*

3 medical specialty, clinical medicine, internal medicine, surgery, anaesthetics, anaesthesiology, gynaecology, obstetrics, paediatrics, teratology, embryology, geriatrics, gerontology, nostology, orthopaedics, rheumatology, physical medicine, osteology, gastroenterology, nephrology, urology, venereology, genitourinary medicine, dermatology, neurology, ophthalmology, otology, ENT (ear, nose, and throat), otorhinolaryngology, otolaryngology, eye, ear, nose, and throat (US), nuclear medicine, cardiology, nuclear cardiology, oncology, radiology, haematology, serology,

medical science, immunology, endocrinology, biochemistry, medical genetics, eugenics, bacteriology, microbiology, virology, parasitology, toxicology, epidemiology, posology, nosology, aetiology, symptomatology, semeiology, pathology, forensic medicine, space medicine, biomedicine, psychiatry

▶ *59 Life Science, 62 Pharmacology, 16 Law, 61 Psychology and Psychiatry*

4 **dentistry**, dental surgery, oral surgery, exodontics, endodontics, orthodontics, prosthetic dentistry, prosthodontics, periodontics, periodontology, oral pathology, fillings, root canal work, crowning, capping, scaling, polishing, extraction, fissure sealing

5 **veterinary medicine**, veterinary practice, small-animal practice, large-animal practice, veterinary clinic, veterinary surgery, animal welfare

▶ *76 Animals (General), 68 Agriculture*

6 **health care**, health promotion, health education, community medicine, public-health medicine, preventive medicine, prophylaxis, immunization, inoculation, vaccination, fluoridation, nutrition, dietetics, hygiene, genetic counselling, midwifery, chiropody, podiatry, medical consultation, call-out, home visit, medical history, case history, medical examination, medical, check-up (Inf), physical examination, physical, internal examination, second-opinion, referral, prognosis, follow-up

▶ *623 Health, 625 Hygiene, 630 Remedy, 58 Biochemistry*

7 **diagnosis**, diagnostics, differential diagnosis, prognosis, diagnostic test, test, medical test, laboratory test, screening test, screening, mass screening, genetic screening, battery of tests, eye test, hearing test, blood test, serotest, sputum test, skin test, patch test, sample, blood sample, stool sample, urine sample, semen sample, tissue sample, biopsy, puncture, lumbar puncture, smear test, cervical smear, Pap test, pregnancy test, prenatal diagnosis, amniocentesis, chorionic villus sampling (CVS), fetoscopy, diagnostic procedure, electrocardiography, ECG (electrocardiogram), electroencephalogy, EEG (electroencephalogram), radiography, diagnostic radiology, barium meal, barium enema, radiograph, X-ray, mass X-ray, chest X-ray, arteriography, angiography, angiogram, lymphography, lymphogram, venography, venogram, thermography, mammothermography, mammography, mammogram, pyelography, pyelogram, intravenous (IV) pyelogram, scanning, scan, ultrasound scan, body scan, Grain scan, tomography, tomogram, CT (or CAT) scan, PET scan, MUGA scan, thallium scan, MRI (magnetic resonance imaging), NMR (nuclear magnetic resonance) scan, endoscopy, bronchoscopy, laparoscopy,

gastroscopy, colposcopy, ureteroscopy, cystoscopy, diagnostic instrument, stethoscope, ophthalmoscope, auriscope, otoscope, endoscope, fibrescope, fetoscope, bronchoscope, gastroscope, laparoscope, colposcope, ureteroscope, cystoscope, postmortem (examination) (PM), autopsy

8 **treatment**, therapy, therapeutics, medical treatment, medical care, intensive therapy (or care), nursing care, nursing, medical intervention, clinical treatment, allopathy, conservative (or palliative) treatment, radical treatment, active treatment, drug treatment, medication, prescription, hormone replacement therapy, naturopathy, homeopathy, herbalism, chemotherapy, immunotherapy, radiotherapy, therapeutic radiology, gene therapy, gene replacement therapy, dialysis, surgical treatment, surgery, manipulative treatment, physiotherapy, orthontics, osteopathy, chiropractic, speech therapy, occupational therapy, rehabilitation, aftercare

▶ *62 Pharmacology, 630 Remedy*

9 **surgery**, surgical treatment, surgical intervention, general surgery, heart surgery, open-heart surgery, bypass surgery, brain surgery, neurosurgery, plastic surgery, dental surgery, psychosurgery, major surgery, minor surgery, keyhole surgery, laser surgery, surgical operation, operation, op (Inf), premedication, premed (Inf), sedation, induction, anaesthesia, acupuncture, incision, section, resection, division, excision, amputation, advancement, transplantation, grafting, transfusion, perfusion, suture

▶ *630 Remedy, 61 Psychology and Psychiatry, 62 Pharmacology*

10 **hospital**, general hospital, teaching hospital, university hospital (US), women's hospital, maternity hospital, children's hospital, day hospital, community hospital, cottage hospital, county hospital (US), cooperative hospital (US), NHS hospital, private hospital, NHS trust hospital, municipal hospital, city hospital, voluntary hospital, infirmary, sanatorium, nursing home, convalescent home, rest home, hospice, hospital ward, ward, isolation ward, operating theatre, intensive therapy (or care) unit (ITU or ICU), dispensary, clinic, polyclinic, out-patient clinic, antenatal clinic, prenatal clinic (US), well-woman clinic, child-health clinic, well-baby clinic, health centre, surgery, consulting room

▶ *630 Remedy*

11 **doctor**, physician, surgeon, medical doctor (MD), medical practitioner, general practitioner (GP), family doctor, family practitioner (US), locum (or locum tenens), medical student, hospital doctor, intern, resident, houseman, house physician, house surgeon, senior

Surgical Operations

Surgical Incision
amniotomy (amniotic membranes)
arteriotomy (artery)
arthrotomy (joint capsule)
capsulotomy (lens capsule of eye)
cardiomyotomy (stomach opening)
cholecystotomy (gall bladder)
choledochotomy (bile duct)
colpotomy (vagina)
cordotomy (part of spinal cord)
craniotomy (skull)
cystotomy (bladder)
embryotomy (fetus)
enterotomy (intestine)
episiotomy (vaginal opening)
gastrotomy (stomach)
goniotomy, trabeculotomy (duct in eye)
hymenotomy (hymen)
hysterotomy (womb)
iridotomy (iris)
jejunotomy (jejunum)
keratotomy (cornea)
laparotomy (abdomen)
laryngotomy (larynx)
leucotomy (nerve fibres in brain)
lithotomy, lithonephrotomy, nephrolithotomy, pyelolithotomy (kidney stone)
lobotomy, prefrontal leucotomy (nerve fibres from frontal lobe of brain)
mastoidotomy (mastoid bone)
myotomy (muscle)
myringotomy, tympanotomy (eardrum)
nephrotomy (kidney)
neurotomy (nerve)
oesophagotomy (gullet)
ophthalmotomy (eye)
orbitotomy (bone around eye)
orchidotomy (testis)
osteotomy (bone)
ovariotomy (ovary)
pancreatotomy (pancreas)
papillotomy (part of bile duct)
pericardiotomy, pericardotomy (membrane around heart)
phlebotomy (vein)
pleurotomy (pleural membrane)
proctotomy (rectum or anus)
pubiotomy (pubic bone)
pyelotomy (pelvis of kidney)
pyloromyotomy (stomach outlet)
rachiotomy (backbone)
rhizotomy (nerve roots)
sclerotomy (white of eye)
scrototomy (scrotum)
sphincterotomy (sphincter muscle)
sternotomy (breastbone)
symphysiotomy (front of pelvis)
tenotomy (tendon)
thalamotomy (part of brain)
thoracotomy (chest cavity)
thyrotomy (thyroid gland)
tonsillotomy (tonsil)
tracheotomy (windpipe)
ureterotomy (ureter)
urethrotomy (urethra)
vagotomy (vagus nerve)
valvotomy, valvulotomy (heart valve)
varicotomy (varicose vein)
vasotomy (sperm duct)

Surgical Opening or Surgical Joining (of two organs)
antrostomy (bone cavity)
appendicostomy (appendix)
caecostomy (caecum)
cholecystenterostomy (gall bladder and small intestine)
cholecystoduodenostomy (gall bladder and duodenum)
cholecystogastrostomy (gall bladder and stomach)
colostomy (colon)
cystostomy, vesicostomy (bladder)
dacryocystorhinostomy (tear sac and nose)
duodenostomy (duodenum)
enterostomy (small intestine)
epididymovasostomy (sperm ducts)
gastroduodenostomy (stomach and duodenum)
gastroenterostomy (stomach and small intestine)
gastrojejunostomy (stomach and jejunum)
gastro-oesophagostomy (stomach and gullet)
gastrostomy (stomach)
hepaticostomy (liver)
ileocolostomy (ileum and colon)
ileoproctostomy (ileum and rectum)
ileostomy (ileum)
jejunoileostomy (jejunum and ileum)
jejunostomy (jejunum)
nephrostomy (kidney)
oesophagostomy (gullet)
pericardiostomy (membrane around heart)
salpingostomy (fallopian tube)
tracheostomy (wind pipe)
transuretero- ureterostomy (one ureter to the other)
ureteroenterostomy (ureter and bowel)
ureteroneocystostomy (ureter and bladder)
ureterosigmoidostomy (ureter and part of bowel)
ureterostomy (ureter)
urethrostomy (urethra)
vaso-epididymostomy (sperm ducts)
vasovasostomy (rejoining of severed sperm duct)
ventriculostomy (cavity of brain)

Surgical Removal
adenoidectomy (adenoids)
antrectomy (part of stomach)
apicectomy (root of tooth)
appendicectomy, appendectomy (US)
arteriectomy (artery)
arthrectomy (joint)
cholecystectomy (gall bladder)
cingulectomy (part of brain)
clitoridectomy (clitoris)
colectomy (colon)
cordectomy (vocal cord)
cystectomy (bladder)
embolectomy (embolus, blood clot)

endarterectomy (inner wall of artery)
enterectomy (intestine)
epididymectomy (sperm duct)
fraenectomy (tissue beneath tongue)
gastrectomy (stomach)
gingivectomy (gum tissue)
glossectomy (tongue)
haemorrhoidectomy (haemorrhoids)
hemicolectomy (part of colon)
hepatectomy (liver)
hypophysectomy (pituitary gland)
hysterectomy (womb)
ileectomy (ileum)
incudectomy (middle ear osside)
iridectomy (iris)
jejunectomy (jejunum)
keratectomy (cornea)
laryngectomy (larynx)
lobectomy (lobe of an organ)
lumpectomy (breast tumour)
lymphadenectomy (lymph node)
mastectomy (breast)
mastoidectomy (mastoid)
meniscectomy (knee cartilage)
myectomy (muscle)
myomectomy (fibroids)
nephrectomy (kidney)
nephroureterectomy, ureteronephrectomy (kidney and ureter)
neurectomy (nerve)
omentectomy (peritoneum of stomach)
oophorectomy, ovariectomy (ovary)
ophthalmectomy (eye)
orchidectomy (testis)
ostectomy (bone)
pallidectomy (part of brain)
pancreatectomy (pancreas)
parathyroidectomy (parathyroid gland)
pericardiectomy, pericardectomy (membrane around heart)
phalangectomy (finger or toe bones)
pharyngectomy (pharynx)
phlebectomy (vein)
phrenicectomy (phrenic nerve)
pleurectomy (pleural membrane)
pneumonectomy (lung)
polypectomy (polyp)
proctectomy (rectum)
proctocolectomy (rectum and colon)
prostatectomy (prostate gland)
pylorectomy (part of stomach)
salpingectomy (fallopian tube)
sclerectomy (white of eye)
sequestrectomy (dead bone)
sigmoidectomy (part of colon)
sphincterectomy (sphincter muscle)
splenectomy (spleen)
stapedectomy (third ear ossicle)
staphylectomy, uvulectomy (uvula)
sympathectomy (sympathetic nerve)
synovectomy (membrane around joint)

	Surgical Repair	myoplasty (muscle)
tarsectomy (ankle bones or eyelid tissue)	angioplasty (blood vessel)	myringoplasty, tympanoplasty (eardrum)
thoracectomy (rib or ribs)	arterioplasty (artery)	neuronoplasty (nerves)
thrombectomy (blood clot)	arthroplasty (joint)	otoplasty (ear)
thymectomy (thymus gland)	blepharoplasty, tarsoplasty (eyelid)	palatoplasty (cleft palate)
thyroidectomy (thyroid gland)	colpoperineoplasty (vaginal opening)	perineoplasty (vaginal opening)
tonsillectomy (tonsils)	cystoplasty (bladder)	phalloplasty (penis)
topectomy (part of brain)	dermatoplasty (skin)	pyeloplasty (pelvis of kidney)
trabeculectomy (part of eye)	gastroplasty (stomach)	pyloroplasty (stomach outlet)
turbinectomy (bone in nose)	genioplasty (chin)	rhinoplasty (nose)
ureterectomy (ureter)	helcoplasty (skin ulcers)	stricturoplasty (stricture)
varicectomy (varicose veins)	hernioplasty (hernia)	tenoplasty (tendon)
vasectomy (sperm duct)	keratoplasty (cornea)	thoracoplasty (chest cavity)
vesiculectomy (seminal vesicle)	labioplasty, cheiloplasty (lips)	ureteroplasty (ureter)
vitrectomy (vitreus humour)	mammoplasty (breast)	urethroplasty (urethra)
vulvectomy (vulva)		vaginoplasty, colpoplasty (vagina)

house officer, registrar, medical registrar, surgical registrar, senior registrar, consultant, medical officer (MO), health officer, community physician, public-health physican, psychiatrist, doc (Inf), medic (or medico) (Inf), quack (Inf), sawbones (Inf), trick cyclist (Sl), leech (Arch)

▶ *630 Remedy, 61 Psychology and Psychiatry*

12 **healer**, therapist, faith healer, alternative practitioner, acupuncturist, homeopath, naturopath, aromatherapist, reflexologist, osteopath, chiropractor, bonesetter, herbalist, hakim

13 **medical specialist**, specialist, consultant, clinician, diagnostician, surgeon, general surgeon, heart surgeon, brain surgeon, neurosurgeon, plastic surgeon, radiotherapist, anaesthetist, anaesthesiologist (US), gynaecologist, obstetrician, paediatrician, teratologist, embryologist, geriatrician, gerontologist, nostologist, orthopaedist, rheumatologist, osteologist, gastroenterologist, nephrologist, urologist, venereologist, dermatologist, neurologist, ophthalmologist, otologist, aurist, otorhinolaryngologist, otolaryngologist, cardiologist, oncologist, radiologist, haematologist, serologist, immunologist, endocrinologist, bacteriologist, microbiologist, virologist, parasitologist, toxicologist, epidemiologist, nosologist, posologist, pathologist, forensic pathologist, medical examiner (US)

14 **dentist**, dental surgeon, oral surgeon, children's dentist, exodontist, endodontist, orthodontist, prosthodontist, periodontist, periodontologist, oral pathologist

15 **veterinarian**, veterinary, vet (Inf), veterinary practitioner, veterinary surgeon, veterinary student, veterinary nurse, veterinary technician (US), animal doctor, horse doctor (Inf), horseleech (Arch)

16 **nurse**, male nurse, student nurse, trainee nurse (US), probationer (nurse), staff nurse, head nurse (US), charge nurse, sister, night sister, ward sister, theatre sister, head nurse (US), nursing officer, senior nursing officer, principal nursing officer, matron, Licensed Practical Nurse (LPN) (US), Registered Nurse (RN) (US), private nurse (US), visiting nurse (US), Enrolled Nurse, Registered General Nurse (RGN), State Enrolled Nurse (SEN), State Registered Nurse (SRN), special nurse, children's nurse, school nurse, day nurse, night nurse, district nurse, home nurse, health visitor, occupational-health nurse, nurse practitioner, midwife, domiciliary midwife, Florence Nightingale, lady with a lamp, ministering angel, angel of mercy

17 **paramedic**, paramedical, anaesthetist (US), radiographer, physiotherapist, occupational therapist, speech therapist, dental therapist, dietician, nutritionist, chiropodist, hygienist, dental (or oral) hygienist, medical attendant, nurse, midwife, carer, care attendant, ambulanceman, stretcher-bearer, medical assistant, surgical assistant, dresser, dental surgery assistant, medical auxiliary, dental auxiliary, nursing auxiliary, orderly, ward orderly, medical technician, dental technician, hospital social worker, hospital administrator

▶ *630 Remedy*

18 **patient**, in-patient, out-patient, client, case, terminal case, invalid, sick person

▶ *624 Ill Health*

VERBS

19 **practise medicine**, hold surgery, attend, advise, examine, refer, seek a second opinion, consult, diagnose, prognosticate, immunize, inoculate, vaccinate, test for, screen (for), X-ray, scan, treat, doctor, prescribe, medicate, administer, inject, care for, look after, minister to, nurse, tend, support, relieve, ease, palliate, restore, cure, heal, rehabilitate, follow up, make a house call, be called out

▶ *630 Remedy, 62 Pharmacology, 767 Relief, 625 Hygiene*

20 **practise surgery**, prepare for surgery, prep (Inf), sedate, anaesthetize, operate, induce, maintain, make an incision, incise, divide, excise, amputate, transfuse, perfuse, suture, dialyse, transplant

▶ *630 Remedy*

21 **practise dentistry**, treat teeth, descale, polish, fill, stop, crown, extract, pull (Inf)

ADJECTIVES

22 **medical**, iatric, Hippocratic, clinical, allopathic, homeopathic, surgical, osteopathic, gynaecological, obstetric, paediatric, geriatric, neurological, dermatological, urological, genitourinary, ophthalmological, cardiac, radiological, epidemiological, forensic, pathological, veterinary
▶ *630 Remedy*

23 **dental**, oral, orthodontic, exodontic, endodontic, prosthodontic, periodontic, periodontal

24 **diagnostic**, symptomatological, symptomatic, prognostic, indicative

25 **therapeutic**, medicinal, preventive (*or* preventative), prophylactic, remedial, curative, healing, nursing, tending
▶ *630 Remedy, 767 Relief*

ADVERBS

26 **medically**, clinically, surgically

61 Psychology and Psychiatry

What progress we are making. In the Middle Ages they would have burned me. Now they are content with burning my books. Sigmund Freud.

NOUNS

1 **psychology**, science of the mind, science of human and animal behaviour, abnormal psychology, academic psychology, Freudian psychology, psychoanalysis, Freudianism, psychoanalytic theory, Jungian psychology, analytic(al) psychology, Adlerian psychology, individual psychology, apperceptionism, applied psychology, associationism, association psychology, mental chemistry, animal psychology, ethology, animal behaviour, behavioural psychology, behaviourism, stimulus-response psychology, Skinnerian psychology, Watsonian psychology, Pavlovian psychology, Lacanian psychology, clinical psychology, child psychology, cognitive psychology, comparative psychology, constitutional psychology, criminal psychology, depth psychology, developmental psychology, dianetics, differential psychology, dynamic psychology, ecological psychology, educational psychology, empirical psychology, existential psychology, experimental psychology, faculty psychology, folk psychology, functional psychology, genetic psychology, Gestaltism, Gestalt psychology, Gestalt theory, configurationism, group psychology, hedontics, hormic psychology, Horneyan psychology, humanistic psychology, industrial psychology, introspection psychology, metaphysics, metapsychology, morbid psychology, neuropsy-

chology, object-relations theory, objective psychology, phenomenological psychology, physiological psychology, popular psychology, psychic determinism, psychoacoustics, psychobiochemistry, psychobiology, psychodynamics, psychogenesis, psychogenetics, psychognosis, psychography, psycholinguistics, psychologism, psychometrics, psychometry, psychoneurosis, psychopathology, psychopharmacology, psychophysics, psychophysiology, psychosociology, psychosomatics, psychotechnics, psychotechnology, psychological warfare, psychosexuality, psychosexual development, race psychology, rational psychology, reactology, reflexology, Reichian psychology, orgone theory, self psychology, social psychology, structuralism, structural psychology, parapsychology, psychokinesis (PK)
▶ *60 Medicine, 11 Occultism*

2 **psychiatry**, medicopsychology, prophylactic psychiatry, psychodiagnostics, psychodiagnosis, antipsychiatry, neuropsychiatry, orthopsychiatry, psychogeriatrics, psychological medicine, psychosocial medicine, psychosomatic medicine
▶ *60 Medicine*

3 **psychiatric treatment**, psychiatric care, drug treatment, psychotropic drug, psychosurgery, leucotomy, prefrontal leucotomy (*or* lobotomy), cingulectomy, amygdalectomy, stereotaxy, psychoanalysis, analysis, ego analysis, Freudian analysis, psychoanalytic method, the couch, James-Lange theory, transactional analysis (TA), assertiveness training, psychotherapeutics, psychotherapy, behaviour modification, behaviour therapy, New Consciousness, bioenergetics, autosuggestion, biofeedback, client-centred therapy, aversion therapy, confrontation therapy, desensitization, conditioning, relaxation therapy, counselling, psychological counselling, pastoral counselling, directive therapy, ego therapy, est (Erhard seminars training), existential therapy, evocative psychotherapy, Gestalt therapy, group psychotherapy, group dynamics, marathon group, family therapy, family training, conjoint therapy, co-counselling, encounter group, consciousness raising, sensitivity training, sensitivity training group (*or* T-group), group relations training, sensory awareness training (SAT), marriage encounter, marriage guidance, humanistic therapy, logotherapy, mind cure, modelling, nondirective therapy, occupational therapy, play therapy, recreational therapy, primal therapy, regression therapy, scream therapy, psychodrama, drama therapy, radical therapy, feminist therapy, rational-emotive therapy, reality therapy, release therapy, abreaction, catharsis, psy-

chocatharsis, reminiscence therapy, Rogerian therapy, role playing, sex therapy, supportive theory, token economy, transcendental meditation (TM), transpersonal theory, Arica movement, vocational therapy, suggestion therapy, suggestionism, hypnotherapy, hypnotic suggestion, post-hypnotic suggestion, narcohypnosis, autohypnosis, self-hypnosis, sleep treatment, sleep therapy, narcotherapy, pentothal interview, narcoanalysis, shock treatment, shock therapy, convulsive therapy, electroconvulsive therapy (ECT), electroconvulsive shock therapy (EST), electroshock, electroshock therapy, electronarcosis, metrazol shock therapy, hypoglycaemic shock therapy, insulin shock therapy, nonconvulsive electric treatment

▶ *630 Remedy, 60 Medicine, 62 Pharmacology*

4 **psychometrics**, psychometry, intelligence testing, mental test, psychological screening, psychography, psychogram, psychometer, lie detector, polygraph, psychogalvanometer, psychogalvanic skin response, psychogalvanic response (PGR), IQ meter (Inf)

5 **psychological test**, mental test, aptitude test, intelligence test, general aptitude test battery (GATB), Allport-Vernon draw-a-person test, Allport-Vernon study of values, association test, word-association test, controlled-association test, free-association test, personality test, personality adjustment test, personality inventory, personality research form, Bernreuter personality inventory, Brown personality inventory, Minnesota multiphasic personality inventory (MMPI), Candle problem, frustration test, Gesell's development schedule, graduated reciprocation in tension reduction (GRIT), group test, inkblot test, Rorschach test, Holtzman inkblot technique, Lüscher colour test, individual test, Oseretsky test, projective test, Szondi test, house-tree-person (HTP) projective test, Rogers' process scale, Rotter incomplete sentences blank, scientific aptitude test, strong vocational interest test, thematic apperception test (TAT)

6 **intelligence test**, intelligence quotient (IQ), IQ test, Army General Classification Test (AGCT), alpha test, beta test, Army Alpha test, Army Beta test, Weschler-Bellvue intelligence test, Weschler intelligence scale for children (WISC), Weschler Adult Intelligence Scale (WAIS), Stanford-Binet Intelligence Scale, Stanford revision, Stanford-Binet test, Binet (or Binet-Simon) test, Babcock-Levy test, Cattell's Infant Intelligence Scale, Minnesota preschool scale, Goldstein-Sheerer test, Kent mental test

7 **personality type**, personality tendency, introvert, introversion, introvertedness, ingoingness, extrovert, extroversion, extro-

vertedness, outgoingness, other-directedness, syntone, syntony, ambivert, ambiversion, choleric, melancholic, sanguine, phlegmatic, ectomorph, ectomorphy, ectomorphism, endomorph, endomorphy, endomorphism, mesomorph, mesomorphism, mesomorphy

▶ *510 Insanity*

8 **disordered personality**, personality disorder, neurotic personality, neurotic, neuropath, psychoneurotic, disturbed person, emotionally disturbed person, unstable person, hysterical personality, weak personality, inferior personality, immature personality, antisocial personality, sociopath, shut-in personality, escapist, mentally defective personality, maladjusted personality, hostile personality, perverse personality, paranoid personality, schizoid, schizoid personality, dual personality, double personality, multiple personality, split personality, alternating personality, schizothyme, schyzothymia, schizothymic personality, cyclothyme, cyclothymic personality, cyclothymia, cycloid, cycloid personality, psychopath, psychopathic personality, psychotic, psychotic personality, lunatic, loony (Inf), schizo (Inf), psycho (Inf), wacko (Inf)

9 **psychological disorder**, mental disorder, nervous disorder, psychogenic disorder, functional nervous disorder, neurosis, psychosis, mental subnormality, intellectual subnormality

▶ *510 Insanity, 460 Lack of Intellect*

10 **neurosis**, psychoneurosis, neuroticism, neurotic disorder, accident neurosis, anxiety neurosis, anxiety reaction, neurotic-depressive reaction, deviation, blast neurosis, compensation neurosis, conversion neurosis, expectation neurosis, dissociation reaction, fixation neurosis, fright neurosis, flight reaction, homosexual neurosis, hypochondria, depression, melancholia, hysteria, occupational neurosis, pathoneurosis, regression neurosis, traumatic neurosis, transference neurosis, compulsion neurosis, obsessional neurosis, obsessive-compulsive neurosis (*or* reaction), phobia, reactive neurosis, situational neurosis, combat neurosis, battle fatigue, shell shock, psychopathia martialis, breakdown, nervous breakdown, mental breakdown

▶ *777 Fear*

11 **psychosis**, psychopathy, organic psychosis, functional psychosis, affective psychosis, schizoaffective psychosis, cycloid psychosis, manic-depressive psychosis, onecroid psychosis, puerperal psychosis, schizophrenia, dementia praecox, hebephrenia, catatonia, cyclothymia, alcoholic psychosis, Korsakoff's psychosis

▶ *510 Insanity*

12 **stress**, mental stress, psychological stress, pre-menstrual syndrome, emotional strain (*or* tension), stress reaction, anxiety, panic attack, psychalgia, anxiety state, anxiety equivalent, free-floating anxiety, hysteria, anxiety hysteria, conversion hysteria, dissociative hysteria, hysterics, trauma, traumatism, shock, shock reaction, post-traumatic stress disorder, frustration, conflict, ambivalence (of impulse), mental (*or* emotional) shock, decompensation, nervous tic, nerves (Inf)
▶ *777 Fear*

13 **depression**, clinical depression, melancholia, involutional melancholia, endogenous depression, reactive depression, depressive reaction, SAD syndrome (seasonal affective disorder), agitated depression, dejection, detachment, alienation, withdrawal, abstraction, preoccupation, apathy, lethargy, indifference, unresponsiveness, insensibility, stupor, catatonic stupor
▶ *770 Sorrow*

14 **trance**, stupor, daze, hypnotic trance, catatonic trance, hysterical trance, trance state, catalepsy, cataplexy, dream state, reverie, daydreaming, sleepwalking, somnambulism, fugue, fugue state, amnesia, meditation, religious ecstasy, aphonia, aphasia

15 **compulsion**, urge, craving, addiction, bulimia nervosa, anorexia nervosa, dipsomania, passion, obsession, impulsion, craze, mania, megalomania, monomania, egomania, paranoia, nymphomania, satyriasis
▶ *510 Insanity, 584 Habit*

16 **dissociation**, disconnection, dissociation of personality, disintegration of personality, schizoidism, schizoid personality, double personality, split personality, multiple personality, alternating personality, knight's-move thought, schizothymia, schizophrenia, depersonalization, paranoia, paranoid personality

17 **fixation**, libido fixation, libido arrest, arrested development, fixation of affect, infantile fixation, Freudian fixation, parent fixation, mother fixation, father fixation

18 **complex**, inferiority complex, superiority complex, parent complex, Oedipus complex, mother complex, Electra complex, father complex, Diana complex, persecution complex, castration complex, compulsion complex

19 **defence mechanism**, defence reaction, censor, repression, suppression, inhibition, block, blocking, blockage, resistance, avoidance, denial, negation, rejection, reaction formation, splitting, rigid control, suppressed desire, sublimation, regression, reversion, projection, identification, fantasy, escapism, flight, withdrawal, isolation, negativism, alienation, dreamlike thinking, wishful thinking, autism, dereism, compensation, overcompensation,

decompensation, substitution, blame-shifting, displacement, rationalization

20 **conditioning**, Pavlovian conditioning, classical conditioning, operant conditioning, psychogogy, re-education, reorientation, conditioned reflex, reinforcement, positive reinforcement, negative reinforcement, simple reflex, unconditioned reflex, reflex, suggestion, counterconditioning, avoidance conditioning

21 **psyche**, psychic apparatus, self, psychological me, mind, pneuma, soul, personality, preconscious, foreconscious, stream of consciousness, coconscious, subconscious, unconscious, subliminal, subliminal self, unconscious mind, primitive self, id, conscious mind, conscious self, ego, ethical self, superego, ego ideal, ego-id conflict, anima, animus, persona, collective unconscious, racial unconscious

22 **libido**, sex(ual) drive, life instinct, Eros, vital force, motive force, psychic energy, sex instinct, libidinal energy, libidinal (*or* libido) object, libido analogue, erotic desire, eroticism, pleasure principle, death instinct, death wish, Thanatos

23 **memory**, engram, recall, reproduction, recognition, recollection, retention, memory trace, unconscious memory, forgetting

24 **symbolism**, symbolization, symbol, universal symbol, father symbol, mother symbol, phallic symbol, fertility symbol, dream-symbol interpretation, imago, image, archetype, archetypal image (*or* symbol), father (*or* mother *or* child) image

25 **surrogate**, substitute, parent surrogate, father figure, mother figure, father (*or* mother) image, mother surrogate

26 **gestalt**, pattern, figure, form, perceptual concept, configuration, sensory pattern, figure-ground

27 **association of ideas**, association, linking, reinforcement, controlled association, free association, association by contiguity, word association, association by sound, clang association, stream of consciousness, transference, negative transference, synaesthesia

28 **cathexis**, cathection, desire concentration, charge, energy charge, cathectic energy, anticathexis, countercathexis, counterinvestment, hypercathexis, overcharge

29 **psychologist**, psychologue, clinical psychologist, clinician, child psychologist, psychiatrist, psychotherapist, therapist, psychoanalyst, analyst, psychopathologist, psychotechnologist, industrial psychologist, psychobiologist, psychochemist, psychophysiologist, psychophysicist, psychographer, psychosociologist, Freud, Jung, Adler, Horney, James, Janrt, Lange, Pavlov, Reich, Skinner, Watson, Laing, Lacan, Klein, Piaget

30 **psychiatrist**, mental specialist, neuropsychiatrist, psychogeriatrician, clinical psychologist, alienist, analyst, psychotherapist, psychotherapeutist, hypnotherapist, narcotherapist, dramatherapist, behaviour therapist, psychiatric social worker, counsellor, mad doctor, shrink (Sl), headshrinker (Sl), trick cyclist (Sl), men in white coats (Sl), barred-window boys (Sl)

▶ *510 Insanity*

31 **psychiatric hospital**, psychiatric unit, psychiatric ward, special hospital, mental hospital

▶ *510 Insanity, 630 Remedy*

ADJECTIVES

32 **psychological**, psychiatric, neuropsychiatric, psychotherapeutic, hypnotherapeutic, psychoanalytical, psychodiagnostic, psychometric, psychopathological, psychosocial, psychosomatic, psychophysical, psychobiological, psychoneurological, psychosexual, psychogenic, psychogenetic, psychotechnical, psychogeriatric, psychopharmacological

33 **Freudian**, Jungian, Adlerian, Horneyan, Pavlovian, Reichian, Skinnerian, Watsonian, Lacanian, Laingian, Kleinian

34 **introverted**, introvert, introversive, ingoing, in-directed, withdrawn, isolated

35 **extroverted**, extrovert, extroversive, outgoing, out-directed

36 **psychologically disturbed**, neurotic, disturbed, nervous, traumatized, emotional, schizoid, sociopathic, psychopathic, psychotic, hypochondriacal, paranoid, dissociated, disconnected

37 **subconscious**, subliminal, unconscious, co-conscious, repressed, suppressed, inhibited, restrained, blocked, controlled

VERBS

38 **psychologize**, psychoanalyse, analyse, counsel, condition

ADVERBS

39 **psychologically**, psychiatrically, unconsciously, subconsciously, subliminally, neurotically, hysterically, inhibitedly, depressively

62   Pharmacology

NOUNS

1 **pharmacology**, pharmacy, pharmaceutics, pharmacodynamics, pharmacokinetics, pharmocognosy, therapeutics, chemotherapy, pharmacopocia, materia medica, posology, dosology

▶ *630 Remedy, 60 Medicine*

2 **pharmacologist**, pharmacist, pharmaceutist, chemist, druggist (US), dispenser, drug store (US)

3 **drug**, medicine, medication, medicinal, preparation, potion, dose, draught, tonic, healing

agent, pharmaceutical, generic name, proprietary name, brand name, ethical drug, prescription (*or* prescribed) drug, nonprescription drug, over-the-counter drug, premedication, broad-spectrum drug, wonder drug, panacea, cure-all, catholicon, elixir, placebo, tolerance, side effect, drug dependence

▶ *630 Remedy, 875 Drug-Taking*

4 **drug type**, abortifacient, alkaloid, alkylating agent, anabolic steroid, androgen, antiviral drug, antipsychotic drug, anaesthetic, painkiller, analeptic, analgesic, antihydrotic, anodyne, antacid, anthelmintic, antibiotic, anticholinergic drug, anticoagulant, anticonvulsant, antidepressant, antidote, antiemetic, antifebrile, antifungal drug, antihistamine, anti-inflammatory, antimalarial drug, antimetabolite, antimycotic, antipyretic, antipruritic, antiseptic, antiserum, antispasmodic, antispastic, antithrombin, antitussive, antivenene (*or* antivenin), aperient, astringent, bactericide, bacteriostatic, barbiturate, beta blocker, bromide, bronchoconstrictor, bronchodilator, carminative, cathartic, caustic, choleretic, coagulant, collyrium, corticosteroid, counterirritant, cytoxic drug, decongestant, demulcent, deobstruent, deodorant, depilatory, depressant, diaphoretic, dilator, disinfectant, diuretic, emetic, epispastic, expectorant, febrifuge, fungicide, germicide, hallucinogen, hidrotic, humectant, hydragogue, hypnotic, immunosuppressive, inhibitor, insecticide, lachrymator, lactifuge, laxative, lithagogue, MAO inhibitor, muscle relaxant, narcotic, natriuretic, neuroleptic, opiate, oral contraceptive, palliative, parasiticide, parasympatholytic, parasympathomimetic, paregoric, pediculicide, penicillin, pressor, prophylactic, psychedelic drug, pulicide, purgative, pyrogen, relaxant, rubefacient, scabicide, sedative, somnifacient, sleeping pill, soporific, spasmolytic, spermicide, sporicide, sternutator, steroid, sulpha drug, sulphonamide, sulphone, sympatholytic, sympathomimetic, taeniacide, tetracycline, tonic, tranquillizer, vasoconstrictor, vasodilator, vasopressor, vermicide, vermifuge, vesicant

5 **prescription**, formula, dose, effective dose, course, active principle, essence, vehicle, excipient, galenical, confection, antagonist

6 **pill**, tablet, capsule, cachet, lozenge, pastille, dragée, troche, powder, gel

7 **ointment**, salve, cream, balm, balsam, lotion, ungent, embrocation, paint, poultice, fomentation, unguent, unction, oil, liniment, emollient, demulcent, abirritant, arquebusade

8 **drops**, guttae, ear drops, nose drops, eye drops, eyewash, dropper

9 **pessary**, suppository

10 **inhalant**, spray, atomizer, nebulizer, aerosol

Medication

Antiseptics and Disinfectants
ABC powder
aminacrine
benzalkonium
benzelthonium
benzoic acid
borax
boracic acid
calomel
cetrimide
chloramine
chlorhexidine
chlorocresol
chlorooxylenol
clotrimazole
cresol
Dettol (Tm)
dequalinium
diiodohydroxyquinoline
diloxanide
domiphen
formaldehyde
hexachlorophane
hexamine
hydrogen peroxide
iodochlorhydroxyquin
iodoform
lye
peroxide
sodium hypochlorite
thimeracol
trimethroprim

Antipyretics
acetanilide
aspirin
benorylate
mepacrine
phenacetin
phenazone

Antihistamines
antazoline
bromodiphenylhydraine
bromopheniramine
buclizine
carbinoxamine
chlorcyclizine
chloropyrilene
chlorpheniramine
chlorphenoxamine
clemizole
cyclizine
cyproheptadine
dimenhydrinate
dimethothiazine
diphenhydramine
hydroxyzine
meclozine
mepyramine
methapyrilene
pheniramine
promethazine
trimeprazine

Antidepressants
amitriptyline
clomipramine
desipramine
dipenzepin
doxepin
imipramine
iprindole
iproniazid
maprotiline
mianserin
nialamide
nortryptyline
phenelzine
protriptyline
pulvule
tranylcypromine
trimipramine

Antibiotics
actinomycin
amphotericin
ampicillin
basitracin
benthazine penicillin
benzyl penicillin
bleomycin
capreomycin
carbenicillin
carbomycin
cephalexin
cephaloglycin
cephaloridine
cephalosporin
cephalothin sodium
chloramphenicol
chlortetracycline
clindamycin
cloxacillin sodium
colistin
co-trimoxazole
cycloserine
dimethylchlortetra-
 cycline
dihydrostreptomycin
doxorubicin
doxycycline
erythromycin
fradicin
framycetin
gentamycin
griseofulvin
hydrargaphen
hydroxystilbamidine
kanamycin
lincomycin
methicillin
mithramycin
mycomycin
nalidixic acid
neomycin
nifuratel
nitrofurantoin
novobiocin
oleandomycin
oxacillin
oxolinic acid
oxytetracycline
paromomycin
penicillin
phenethicillin
phenoxymethylpenicillin
podophylline
polymixin
procaine penicillin
pyocyanase
pyocyanin
rifampicin
rifamycin
spectinomycin
subtilin
streptomycin
tetracycline
tylocin
tyrothrycin
vanomycin
viomycin

Sulpha Drugs (Sulphonamides)
sulphacetamide
sulphadiazine
sulphadidimine
sulphadoxine
sulphafurazole
sulphaquanidine
sulphamethizole
sulphamethoxazole
sulphisoxazole

Analgesics
acetanilide
aloxiprin
anileridine
aspirin
barbitone
benorylate
carisprodol
chlormezanone
choline salicylate
codeine
dextromoramide
dextropropoxyphene
diamorphine or heroin
 (narcotic)
dihydrocodeine
dipipanone
fenoprofen
flufenamic acid
heroin or diamorphine
 (narcotic)
indomethacin
ketoprofen
levorphanol (narcotic)
mefanamic acid
meperidine
methadone (narcotic)
morphine (narcotic)
naproxen
opium (narcotic)
oxyphenbutazone
papaveretum
paracetamol
pentazocine
pethidine
phenacetin
phenazocine
phenazopyridine
phenylbutazone
salicylamide

Anaesthetics
ACE mixture
amethocaine
benzocaine (local)
bupivacaine (local)
butacaine (local)
CE mixture
chloroform
cinchocaine (local)
cocaine (local)
cyclomethycaine
cyclopropane
dibucaine
ethychloride (local)
ethylene
halocaine
halothane
hydroflumethiazide
laughing gas
lignocaine (local)
nitrous oxide
oxythiazine (local)
piperocaine
prilocaine
procaine (local)
propanidid
tetracaine
tribromoethanol (local)
trichloromethane
urethane
vinyl ether

Vasodilators
aminophylline
azapetine
buphenine
cyclandelate
erythritol
glycerine trinitrate
isoxuprine
nicotinyl
pentaerythritol
phenoxybenzamine
phentolamine
prenylamine
tetrahydrozoline
thymoxamine
tolazoline

Tranquillizers
amobarbital
amylobarbitone
benzodiazepine
carisprodol
chlordiazepoxide
chlormezanone
chlorpromazine
chlorprothixene
chlorazepate potassium
diazepam
doxepin
fluphenazine
fluspirilene
haloperidol
hyoscine
lorazepam
meprobamate
methotrimeprazine
oxazepam
oxypertine
perphenazine
phenothiazine
pimozide
prochlorperazine
promazine
prothipendyl
thiopropazate
thioridazine
trifluoperazine

Stimulants
amphetamine
colcynth
cyclopentamine
dexamphetamine
methylamphetamine
nikethamide
nux vomica
oubain
picrotoxin
strychnine

Sedatives
barbitone
buclizine
butobarbitone
carbromal
chloral
chloral hydrate
chlordiazepoxide
chlorhexadol
chlormethiazole
cyclobarbitone
dichloralphenazone
ethinamate
flurazepam
hydroxyzine
methaqualone
methyprylone
prothipendyl
thalidomide (former)
thiopentone (oral)
triclofos

Laxatives
aloes
bisacodyl
calomel
cascara
castor oil
colcynth
Epsom salt
Glauber's salt
jalap
liquid paraffin
magnesium sulphate
methylcellulose
phenolphthalein
Rochelle salt
Seidlitz powder
senna
sodium sulphate

Antacids
Alka Seltzer (Tm)
bicarbonate of soda
Bromo Seltzer (Tm)
magnesium carbonate
magnesium hydroxide
Milk of Magnesia (Tm)
seltzer water
sodium bicarbonate

Diuretics
acetazolamide
amiloride
aminophylline
bendrofluazide
chlorothiazide
chlorthalidone
clopamide
clorexolone
cyclopenthiazide
dichlorophenamide
ethacrynic acid
frusemide
hydrochlorothiazide
mannitol
metolazone
theobromine
triamterene
trometamol

Steroids
allylestrenol
chlorotrianisene
cortisone
cyproterone
dienoestrol

diethylstilbesterol
dimethisterone
drostanolone
dydrogesterone
ethinyloestradiol
ethisterone
ethyloestrenol
ethynodiol
fludrocortisone
hydrocortisone
hydroxyprogesterone
liothyronine
lynoestrenol
medroxyprogesterone
megestrol
mestranol
methanderione
methandrione
methenolone
methyltestosterone
nadrolone
norethandrolone
norethisterone
oestrogen
oxymesterone
progestogen
stanolone
stilboestrol

Hallucinogens
dimethyltriptomine
jimson weed
LSD (lysergic acid
   diethylamide)
mescal
mescaline
psilocyloin

Depressants
aconite
biperiden
bromide

Treatment of Gout
allopurinol
colchicine
ethebenecid
probenecid
sulphinpyrazole

Treatment of High
   Blood Pressure
alprenolol
bethanidine
clonidine
debrisoquine
deserpidine
dihydralazine
guanethidine
hydrallazine
mecamylamine
methoserpidine
methyldopa
metoprolol
oxprenadol
propanolol
sotalol

Cancer Treatments
bisulphan (leukaemia)
chlorambucil (leukae-
   mia)
cyclophosphamide
cytarabine (leukaemia)
etoglucid
fluoxuridine
hydroxyurea (leukae-
   mia)

laetrile
mannomustine
melphalan
mercaptopurine
methotrexate
mitrobronitol
mustine
nitrogen mustard
procarbazine
thioguanine
triaziquone
uramustine
urethane
vinblastine
vincristine

Anticonvulsants
barbitone or barbital
beclamide
carbamazepine
clonazepam
ethosuximide
ethotoin
methoin
paraldehyde
paramethadione
pheneturide
phensuximide
phenetoin
primidone
sulthiame
troxidone
valproic acid

Balms
balm of Gilead
balsam
blue ointment
glycerine or glycerin
melissa
olive oil
petrolatum

Miscellaneous Drugs
acetohexamide (diabe-
   tes mellitus)
acetylcysteine (respira-
   tory diseases)
amantadine (influenza,
   parkinsonism)
amodiaquine (malaria)
amyl nitrite (angina
   pectoris)
Antabuse (Tm) (alcohol-
   ism)
apomorphine (emetic)
azathioprine (immuno-
   suppressive)
beclomethasone (skin
   disorders)
benzhexol (parkinsonism)
betamethasone (rheu-
   matic diseases)
candicidin (fungicide)
carbachol (glaucoma)
carbimazole (hyperthy-
   roidism)
chlorbutanol (fungicide)
chlordantoin (fungicide)
chlorphentermine (ap-
   petite suppressor)
chlorpropamide (diabe-
   tes)
choline theophyllinate
   (asthma, bronchitis)
clofibrate (reduces cho-
   lesterol level)

clorindole (anticoagu-
   lant)
cromolyn sodium
   (asthma, bronchitis)
crotamiton (skin infec-
   tions)
cyclopentolate (eye in-
   fections)
dapsone (leprosy, der-
   matitis)
dexamethasone (aller-
   gies, inflammatory
   conditions)
dextromethorphan (anti-
   tussive)
dextrothyroxine (re-
   duces cholesterol
   level)
dichlorophen (anthel-
   mintic)
dicoumarol (anticoagu-
   lant)
diethylpropion (appe-
   tite suppressor)
digitalis (heart failure)
digitoxin (heart failure)
digoxin (heart failure)
dihydrocodeine (antitus-
   sive)
dihydroergotamine (mi-
   graine)
dimethylsulphoxide or
   DMSO (skin disor-
   ders)
diphenoxylate (diarrhoea)
diprophylline
   (bronchodilator)
disopyramide (heart
   conditions)
disulfiram (alcoholism)
dithiazinine (anthelmin-
   tic)
dithranol (skin disorders)
dopa (parkinsonism)
emetine (liver and gut
   infections)
ethambutol (tuberculosis)
ethionamide (tuberculo-
   sis)
ethyl biscoumacetate
   (anticoagulant)
fenfluridine (obesity)
gallamine (muscle re-
   laxant)
glibenclamide (diabetes)
glucagon (diabetic
   hypoglycaemia)
glutethimidine (insomnia)
glymidine (diabetes)
guaiphenesin (expecto-
   rant)
heparin (anticoagulant)
heptabarbitone (insom-
   nia)
hexobarbitone (insomnia)
hirudin (anticoagulant)
hydroxyamphetamine
   (decongestant)
hyoscyamine (muscle
   spasm)
ichthammol (skin dis-
   eases)
idoxuridine (antiviral
   agent)

insulin (diabetes mellitus)
ipecacuanha (expectorant)
isoniazid (tuberculosis)
isoprenaline (bronchial conditions)
L-dopa or levodopa (parkinsonism)
lithium carbonate (schizophrenia)
menthol (cold relief)
mephenesin (muscle relaxant)
metformin (diabetes)
mathimazole (reduces thyroid activity)
mazindol (appetite suppressor)
methoxamine (low blood pressure)
methoxyphenamine (asthma)
methylene blue (urinary infections)
methysergide (migraine)
Mogadon (Tm), insomnia)
naphazoline (decongestant)

nitrazapam (insomnia)
orciprenaline (asthma, bronchitis)
orphenadrine (muscle spasm)
papaverine (muscle relaxant, asthma)
para-aminosalicylic acid (tuberculosis)
paraformaldehyde (skin disorders)
penicillamine (rheumatoid arthritis)
pentobarbitone (insomnia)
phenindione (anticoagulant)
phenmetrazine (appetite suppressor)
phentermine (appetite suppressor)
phenylephrine (vasoconstrictor, decongestant)
phenylpropanolamine (asthma, allergies)
pholcodine (antitussive)
phthalylsulphathiazole (bowel infections)

physostigmine (constricts eye pupil)
philocarpine (constricts eye pupil)
piperazine (anthelmintic)
piperidolate (colic)
prednisolone (rheumatic diseases, inflammatory conditions)
prednisone (rheumatic diseases, inflammatory conditions)
primaquine (malaria)
procyclidine (muscle relaxant, parkinsonism)
proquanil (malaria)
propantheline (heart conditions)
prothionamide (tuberculosis)
pyrazinamide (tuberculosis)
quinidine (heart conditions)
quinine (malaria)
resorcinol (acne, dandruff)

rimiterol (asthma, bronchitis)
salbutamol (asthma, bronchitis)
salicylic acid (skin disorders)
suramin (sleeping sickness)
terbutaline (bronchodilator)
tetrahydrozoline (decongestant)
theophylline (asthma)
thiacetazone (leprosy, tuberculosis)
thyrocalcitonin (hypercalcaemia)
tolazamide (diabetes)
triamcinolone (inflammation)
tryparsamide (sleeping sickness)
vasopressin (diabetes insipidus)
warfarin (thrombosis)
xylometazoline (decongestant)

11 **linctus**, gargle, mouthwash, wash, eyebath, undine, douche

12 **injection**, intracutaneous injection, intradermal injection, subcutaneous injection, intramuscular injection, intravenous injection, venoclysis, intubation, drip, implant, pellet, translumbar injection, transdermal injection, patch, epidural

13 **administration**, topical administration, inhalation, oral administration, enteral administration, peroral administration, rectal administration, parenteral administration, infusion

ADJECTIVES

14 **counteracting**, suppressing, inhibiting, destroying, antipsychotic, anaesthetic, analgesic, antihydrotic, antacid, anthelmintic, vermicidal, vermifugal, antibiotic, antibacterial, antifungal, antimycotic, antiviral, bacteriostatic, bacteriocidal, fungicidal, germicidal, antiseptic, disinfectant, anticholinergic, anticoagulant, antidepressant, antidotal, antiemetic, anti-inflammatory, antimalarial, antimitotic, cytotoxic, antipruritic, antipyretic, febrifugal, antispasmodic, spasmolytic, antispastic, antitussive, counterirritant, decongestant, immunosuppressive, lactifugal, parasympatholytic, sympatholytic, spermicidal, antiscorbutic

15 **sedative**, calmative, depressant, soporific, hypnotic, tranquillizing, neuroleptic, narcotic

16 **soothing**, relieving, anodyne, demulcent, emollient, balsamic

17 **stimulating**, enhancing, tonic, invigorating, astringent, anabolic, analeptic, aperient, purging, purgative, cathartic, laxative, choleretic,

diaphoretic, sudorific, diuretic, natriuretic, uricosumic, emetic, expectorant, hallucinogenic, psychedelic, hidrotic, parasympathomimetic, sympathomimetic, rubefacient, abortifacient

18 **pharmacological**, pharmaceutic(al), pharmacodynamic, pharmacokinetic, pharmacognostic, therapeutic

▶ *630 Remedy, 60 Medicine*

VERBS

19 **administer**, inject, inoculate, instil, infuse, perfuse, apply, anoint, insert, implant, take in, inhale, ingest, swallow

63 Engineering

NOUNS

1 **engineering**, civil engineering, mechanical engineering, aeronautical engineering, automotive engineering, naval engineering, agricultural engineering, electrical engineering, electronics engineering, chemical engineering, mining engineering, metallurgical engineering, metallurgy, nuclear engineering, production engineering, environmental engineering, engineering geology, engineering design, engineering drawing, CAE (computer-aided engineering), CAD (computer-aided design), management engineering, bioengineering

2 **engineer**, mechanical engineer, civil engineer, electrical engineer, chartered engineer

▶ *57 Chemistry, 64 Electronics and Electrical Engineering, 70 Transport, 54 Earth Science, 56 Physics*

3 **mechanical engineering**, machine-design engineering, industrial engineering, automo-

tive engineering, aeronautical engineering, marine engineering

▶ *70 Transport*

4 **mechanical engineer**, mechanic, technician, fitter

5 **dynamic structure**, dynamic system, machinery, mechanical device, machine, engine, motor, mechanism, tool, servomechanism

6 **simple machine**, lever, wheel and axle, pulley, block and tackle, inclined plane, wedge, screw, gear drive, hydraulic press

7 **gear**, spur gear, rack and pinion, helical gear, bevel gear, skew gear, worm gear, gear train, pinion, internal gear, external gear, gear tooth, diametral pitch, pitch diameter

8 **machine element**, machine part, wheel, gear, gearwheel, pulley, shaft, crank, rod, axle, hub, cam, belt, coupling, bearing, ball bearing, roller bearing, journal, bush, differential

9 **machine tool**, horizontal machine, vertical machine, drill, drilling machine, press drill, boring machine, lathe, engine lathe, turret lathe, capstan lathe, milling machine, broaching machine, grinder, planer, shaper, saw, circular saw, band saw, single-point tool, multipoint tool, speed, feed, cutting fluid, cooling fluid, coolant, high-speed steel

▶ *603 Tool*

10 **work**, useful work, efficiency, load, effort, mechanical advantage, velocity ratio, erg

11 **engine**, internal-combustion engine, Wankel engine, external-combustion engine, reciprocating engine, steam engine, petrol engine, car engine, automotive engine, diesel engine, aeroengine, jet engine, rocket engine, Stirling engine, piston, cylinder, crank, crankshaft, prime mover, governor

▶ *64 Electronics and Electrical Engineering*

12 **turbine**, water turbine, steam turbine, gas turbine, impulse turbine, reaction turbine, impulse-reaction turbine

13 **engine cycle**, heat-engine cycle, four-stroke cycle, two-stroke cycle, Carnot cycle, Otto cycle, Diesel cycle, Rankine cycle, thermal efficiency

▶ *57 Chemistry*

14 **load**, applied load, static load, dynamic load, live load, dead load, transverse load, stress, normal stress, tension, compression, shear stress, strain, longitudinal strain, linear strain, volume strain, bulk strain, shear strain, elastic strain, inelastic strain, plastic strain, structural loading, forces, stability, centre of gravity

15 **strength of materials**, cohesive strength, yield strength, ultimate tensile strength, resistance to compaction, resistance to sliding, stiffness, elasticity, modulus of elasticity, bending moment

16 **deformation**, distortion, elongation, compression, bending, sliding, angular deforma-

tion, torsion, plastic deformation, creep, instability, failure, rupture, fracture, metal fatigue, corrosion

▶ *56 Physics*

17 **civil engineering**, structural engineering, transportation engineering, highway engineering, railway engineering, airport engineering, traffic engineering, river engineering, coastal engineering, water-supply engineering, geotechnical engineering, rock mechanics, soil mechanics, construction engineering, construction, architectural engineering, urban planning, community planning, land-use planning, photogrammetry, surveying, theodolite, level, clinometer, alidade, topographic surveying, mapping, photoelastic modelling

18 **civil engineer**, structural engineer, surveyor, quantity surveyor, contractor

19 **structure**, construction, building, bridge, tunnel, tunnelling, dam, retaining wall, embankment, bulkhead, road, railway, runway, pylon

▶ *70 Transport*

20 **building**, public building, auditorium, church, theatre, stadium, institutional building, hospital, school, prison, residential building, house, apartment building (*or* complex *or* block) (US), block of flats, hotel, commercial building, store, shop, department store, factory, office building, storage building, garage, warehouse, multistorey building, high-rise building, tower block, skyscraper

▶ *256 Habitat, 737 Trade, 43 Architecture*

21 **bridge**, road bridge, railway bridge, flyover, overpass, humpback bridge, viaduct, aqueduct, canal bridge, causeway, ford, toll bridge, footbridge, pedestrian bridge, walkway, catwalk, rope bridge, stepping stones, duckboard, gangway, gangplank, fixed bridge, beam bridge, girder bridge, box-girder bridge, plate-girder bridge, truss bridge, arch bridge, suspension bridge, cantilever bridge, cable-stayed bridge, concrete bridge, movable bridge, lift bridge, vertical-lift bridge, swing bridge, bascule bridge, drawbridge, ferry bridge, transporter bridge, Bailey bridge, pontoon bridge, trestle bridge, deck bridge, through bridge, square bridge, skewed bridge, span, single span, multiple span, deck, flooring, pier, abutment

22 **tunnel**, road tunnel, railway (*or* rail) tunnel, cut-and-cover tunnel, bored tunnel, subway, underpass, channel, culvert, drain, sewer, cloaca

23 **dam**, concrete dam, arch dam, buttress dam, gravity dam, earth dam, reservoir, impoundment, weir, barrage, embankment

24 **water system**, water-supply system, drainage system, sewage system, irrigation system,

flood-control system, seawall, barrage, floodgate, sluicegate, breakwater, mole, groyne, canal, lock, harbour, port, dock, wharf, pier, quay, jetty

▶ *54 Earth Science*

25 **construction material**, structural material, building material, stone, brick, steel, rolled steel, sheet steel, plate steel, cast steel, stainless steel, cast iron, wrought iron, aluminium alloy, magnesium alloy, concrete, reinforced concrete, prestressed concrete, precast concrete, cement, mortar, wood, timber, lumber (US), plywood, glulam (glued-laminated) timber, plastic, reinforced plastic, carbon fibre, glass fibre, composite, tarmac (*or* tarmacadam), asphalt, bitumen, hard core

▶ *57 Chemistry, 47 Furniture and Woodwork, 85 Trees*

26 **masonry**, stonework, brickwork, building stone, stone, limestone, sandstone, granite, marble, brick, bricklaying, header, stretcher, bond, stretcher bond, English bond, Flemish bond, breeze block, tile, slate, mortar, grout, plaster, cement, Portland cement, gravel, sand, clay, terracotta, pavior

27 **superstructure**, structural framework, skeletal frame, frame, space frame, truss, structural member, supporting member, horizontal member, vertical member, strut, tie, beam, girder, stringer, joist, boom, cantilever, RSJ (rolled steel joist), plate girder, I-beam, H-beam, T-beam, continuous beam, concrete slab, column, pillar, pier, tower, rib, spar, abutment, buttress, arch, vault, dome, shell, bearing, bearing plate, flange, shoe, structural connection, rivet, bolt, weld, web connection, seat connection, pin connection, geodesic dome

28 **substructure**, foundation, foundations, spread foundation, footing, mat, raft, slab, pile, caisson, cofferdam, underpinning, fill, backfill

29 **construction equipment**, excavator, digger, trenching machine, trencher, power shovel, front-end loader, backhoe, dragline, clamshell, grab bucket, belt loader, dredge, dredger, JCB (Tm), bulldozer, dozer (Inf), scraper, hauler, earthmover, dump truck, rear-dump truck, pile-driver, pile hammer, auger, compactor, hoist, crane, mobile crane, tower crane, derrick, guy derrick, cableway, elevator, conveyor, excavation, hauling, drilling, hoisting, grading, paving

VERBS

30 **engineer**, construct, build, erect, plan, design, survey, map, excavate, dig, dredge, drill, tunnel, blast, lay, haul, hoist

31 **load**, stress, strain, deform, bend, slide, fail, fracture, rupture, shear

ADJECTIVES

32 **structural**, constructional, edificial, architectural, architectonic, skeletal, superstructural, substructural, foundational, mechanical, fabricated, precast, prestressed

ADVERBS

33 **structurally**, mechanically, architecturally, architectonically, constructionally

64 Electronics and Electrical Engineering

NOUNS

1 **electronics**, microelectronics, computer electronics, optoelectronics, telecommunications, electronics engineering, electrical engineering, electrotechnology, electrotechnics

2 **electronics engineer**, electrical engineer, electrotechnician, electrician

▶ *65 Computers, 534 Communications*

3 **electricity**, current electricity, static electricity, static electrical conduction, conduction, conductivity, conducting medium, conductor, metallic conductor, copper, aluminium, liquid conductor, electrolyte

4 **semiconductor**, silicon, germanium, gallium arsenide, n-type semiconductor, p-type semiconductor, charge carrier, electron, hole, electron conduction, hole conduction, n-type conductivity, p-type conductivity, p–n junction, impurity atom, acceptor impurity, donor impurity, doping, dopant

5 **electrolytic conduction**, electrolyte, electrode, anode, cathode, ion, anion, cation, electrolytic cell, cell, primary cell, voltaic cell, secondary cell, battery

▶ *57 Chemistry*

6 **electric discharge**, gas discharge, arc discharge, arc, glow discharge, corona discharge, silent discharge, transient discharge, spark discharge, spark, disruptive discharge, gas-discharge tube

7 **nonconductor**, insulator, dielectric, dielectric constant, insulating material, insulation

8 **electric charge**, charge, charge density, charge carrier

▶ *56 Physics*

9 **electric current**, current, direct current (d.c.), alternating current (a.c.), instantaneous current, frequency, phase, phase difference, phase angle, induced current, eddy current, current density, juice (Inf)

10 **electric potential**, potential, potential difference (p.d.), voltage, alternating voltage, instantaneous voltage, bias voltage, bias, electromotive force (e.m.f.), back e.m.f., earth (*or* esp. US) ground) potential, earth, earthed conductor, live conductor, live circuit

11 **electric field**, field strength, flux, displacement, permittivity, relative permittivity

12 **resistance**, internal resistance, reactance, impedance, input impedance, characteristic impedance, resistivity, conductivity, capaci-

tance, capacity, stray capacitance, inductance, mutual inductance, self-inductance, conductance, mutual conductance

13 **circuit**, electronic circuit, electric circuit, network, printed circuit, printed circuit board (*or* card), microcircuit, chip, microchip, silicon chip, integrated circuit (IC), LSI (large-scale integration), VLSI (very large-scale integration), equivalent circuit, closed circuit, open circuit, short circuit (*or* short), linear circuit, nonlinear circuit, digital circuit, logic circuit, gate, bistable circuit, flip-flop, resonant circuit, tuned circuit, resonant (*or* resonance) frequency, coupling circuit, switching circuit, bridge, Wheatstone bridge, circuit diagram, circuit design, circuitry, electronics

14 **terminal**, input terminal, output terminal, signal, waveform, pulse train, input signal, output signal, input (*or* output) voltage (*or* power *or* current), load, noise, spurious signal, signal-to-noise ratio, distortion

15 **circuit function**, amplification, gain, feedback, negative feedback, oscillation, positive feedback, negative resistance, rectification, switching, filtering

16 **circuit element**, component, discrete component, electronic device, semiconductor device, solid-state device, series connection, parallel connection

17 **resistor**, variable resistor, rheostat, potentiometer (*or* pot), capacitor, condenser, ceramic capacitor, mica capacitor, electrolytic capacitor, inductor, induction coil, winding, choke

18 **diode**, p–n junction diode, photodiode, LED (light-emitting diode), Zener diode, Schottky diode, diode rectifier

19 **transistor**, bipolar transistor, pnp transistor, npn transistor, base, base electrode, emitter, emitter electrode, collector, collector electrode, FET (field-effect transistor), MOS (metal–oxide–silicon) transistor, MOSFET, source, source electrode, drain, drain electrode, gate, gate electrode, channel, transistor amplifier, transistor switch, power transistor

20 **electron tube**, gas-discharge tube, fluorescent lamp, mercury-vapour lamp, glow lamp, CRT (cathode-ray tube), television receiver, VDU, microwave generator, klystron, magnetron, thermionic valve, valve, triode, tetrode, pentode, anode, cathode, grid, neon light

21 **rectifier**, full-wave rectifier, half-wave rectifier, amplifier, voltage amplifier, power amplifier, audio amplifier, radio amplifier, microwave amplifier, maser, oscillator, radio oscillator, microwave oscillator, piezoelectric oscillator, crystal oscillator, crystal-controlled oscillator, quartz oscillator

22 **transformer**, primary coil, secondary coil, step-up transformer, step-down transformer, voltage transformer, current transformer, instrument transformer, transducer, electroacoustic transducer, pickup, microphone, loudspeaker, filter, band-pass filter, low-pass filter, high-pass filter, band-stop filter

23 **electrical instrument**, ammeter, galvanometer, voltmeter, potentiometer, electrometer, wattmeter, oscilloscope

24 **electron emission**, thermionic emission, thermionic cathode, electron lens, electron gun, electron tube, electron multiplier, photoelectric effect, photoelectric emission, photoelectron, photocathode, photomultiplier, secondary emission, secondary electron, field emission

25 **photoconductivity**, photocurrent, photodetector, photocell, photodiode, photovoltaic effect, photovoltaic cell, solar cell

26 **electrical energy**, electric power, apparent power, active power, reactive power, power factor

27 **wire**, multistranded wire, lead, flex, cord (US), electric filament, electric cable, coaxial cable (*or* coax), paired cable, twin cable, twisted pair, bus, waveguide, cordless appliance

28 **plug**, socket, power point, fuse, circuit breaker, switch, trip switch, dimmer, dimming switch, termination, interface

29 **power source**, cell, primary cell, secondary cell, dry cell, wet cell, battery, dry battery, alkaline battery, accumulator, storage battery, secondary battery, rechargable battery, battery charger, fuel cell, solar cell, solar battery, solar panel, solar energy

30 **generator**, a.c. generator, alternator, oscillator, dynamo, magneto, armature, windings, electrostatic generator, Van de Graaff generator, wind-driven generator, thermoelectric generator

31 **electric motor**, induction motor, stator, rotor, cage rotor, slip-ring rotor, synchronous motor, synchronous-induction motor, asynchronous motor, universal motor, commutator, vibrator

32 **power station**, generating station, powerhouse, thermal power station, nuclear power station, hydroelectric power station, geothermal power station, power generation, power production, power plant, generator, turbine

33 **power distribution**, distribution network, national grid, a.c. (alternating current) transmission, high-voltage a.c. transmission, extra-high-voltage a.c. transmission, d.c. (direct current) transmission, high-voltage d.c. transmission, power line, transmission line, overhead wire, underground cable, feeder, pylon (*or* tower), substation

34 **power supply**, mains supply (*or* mains), three-phase supply, two-phase supply, single-phase supply, power conversion, power regulation, voltage regulator, transformer, recti-

fier, filter, converter, inverter, power pack, peak load, power cut, electric meter, watt-hour meter, domestic wiring, ring main, off-peak supply, white meter, blackout, brownout (Inf)

VERBS

35 **conduct**, insulate, earth, ground, charge, discharge, amplify, oscillate, connect, disconnect, switch (or turn) on (or off), plug in, wire (or wire up), fuse, input, output, electrocute, generate, transmit

ADJECTIVES

36 **electronic**, electric, electrical, photoelectric, thermoelectric, piezoelectric, hydroelectric, electrodynamic, electrolytic, electromagnetic, electromechanical, electromotive, electrostatic, negative, positive, neutral, live, resistive, capacitive, inductive, rechargeable, cordless, solid-state

ADVERBS

37 **electronically**, electrically, photoelectrically, thermoelectrically, electrodynamically, electrolytically, electromagnetically, electromechanically, electrostatically, negatively, positively, in series, in parallel

65 Computers

NOUNS

1 **computing**, computer science, systems analysis, programming, DP (data processing), EDP (electronic data processing), data entry, information technology (IT), DTP (desk-top publishing), CIM (computer-integrated manufacture), CMI (computer-managed instruction), CAD (computer-aided design), CAM (computer-aided manufacturing), CAI (computer-aided instruction), CAT (computer-aided testing), CAL (computer-assisted learning), CBL (computer-based learning), cybernetics, robotics

2 **operator**, programmer, DP manager, systems analyst, hacker, liveware

3 **computer**, digital computer, hybrid computer, supercomputer, parallel computer, mainframe, minicomputer, mini, microcomputer, micro, PC (personal computer), home computer, games computer, lap-top computer, personal organizer, smart card, calculator, programmable calculator, machine, electronic computer, electronic brain, ABC (Atanasoff–Berry computer), Turing machine, Analytical Engine, ACE (Automatic Computing Engine), ATLAS, ENIAC, UNIVAC, Cray, ERNIE, adding machine, calculating machine, abacus, Napier's bones

4 **computer part**, hardware, architecture, processor, memory, peripheral, software

5 **processor**, central processor, CPU (central processing unit), ALU (arithmetic and logic unit), CU (control unit), microprocessor, math co-processor

6 **memory**, store, storage, main memory, primary memory, register, cache, semiconductor memory, core store, solid-state memory, cryogenic memory, backing store, auxiliary (or secondary) memory, bulk memory, bubble memory, buffer, scratchpad, volatile memory, nonvolatile memory, dynamic memory, RAM (random access memory), DRAM (dynamic RAM), ROM (read-only memory), EAROM (electrically alterable read-only memory), CD-ROM (compact-disk ROM), Diskman (Tm)

7 **peripheral**, backing store, disk, disk pack, disk reader, hard disk, Winchester, floppy disk, floppy, diskette, microfloppy, microdiskette, minifloppy, minidiskette, optical disk, CD-ROM, MTU (magnetic-tape unit), tape streamer, ATU (automatic tape unit) tape, cartridge, cassette, VDU (visual display unit), flat screen, keyboard, console, terminal, monitor, card punch, punched card, tape punch, paper tape, reader, input-output device, I/O device, port, printer, band printer, belt printer, barrel printer, drum printer, chain printer, letter-quality printer, daisywheel printer, dot-matrix printer, electrophotographic printer, electrostatic printer, golfball printer, impact printer, ink-jet printer, bubble-jet printer, thermal ink jet printer, serial printer, ionographic printer, laserprinter, line printer, matrix printer, colour printer, plotter, flat-bed plotter, x-y plotter, printout, pretty printing, scanner, wand, bar-code reader, light pen, digitizer, data tablet, joystick, mouse, tailless mouse, modem, acoustic coupler, voice synthesizer

8 **software**, operating system (OS), UNIX (Tm), DOS (Tm), disk operating system), MSDOS (Tm), Microsoft DOS), OS/2 (Tm), CP/M (Tm), program, programming language, language, compiler, interpreter, driver, filter, pipe, analyser, parser, applications program, package

9 **programming language**, language, machine code, high-level language, low-level language, compiled language, interpreted language, source code, object code, syntax, semantics, trace program, JCL (job-control lan-

Programming Languages

Ada	COMAL	ML
AED	Common Lisp	Modula
Algol	CORAL	OBERON
APL	CPL	PARLOG
B	Forth	Pascal
Babbage	Fortran	Pascal-Plus
Basic	Franzlisp	PL/I (or PL/1)
BCPL	HOPE	POP
C	IAL	POPLOG
C-plus	ICON	Prolog
CHILL	JOVIAL	SCHEME
CIS-COBOL	Logo	SIMULA
Clear	Maclisp	Smalltalk
Cobol	MIRANDA	SNOBOL

guage), DML (data manipulation language), query language, pseudolanguage, Turbo language (Tm)

10 **character**, alphanumeric character, code, character set, ASCII (American standard code for information interchange), EBSIDIC (extended binary-coded decimal interchange code), ISO-7 (International Standards Organization 7-bit code), printable character, nonprintable character, control character, escape character, escape sequence, CR (carriage return), graphic character, binary code, hexadecimal code, decimal code, octal code

11 **application**, word processing (or word processor) (WP), text editor, editor, Wordstar (Tm), Word Perfect (Tm), Word (Tm), spelling checker, dictionary, thesaurus, database, hierarchical database, network database, relational database, database management system (DBMS), data manipulation language (DML), dBase (Tm), spreadsheet, Visicale (Tm), Supercalc (Tm), Lotus-123 (Tm), DTP (desktop publishing), Ventura (Tm), Pagemaker (Tm), Quark Xpress (Tm), TEX, window, window manager, wimp (windows icons menus pointers), Windows (Tm), MIDI (musical instrument digital interface)

12 **electronic office**, ACU (automatic calling unit), facsimile, fax, electronic mail (or email), bulletin board, mailbox, teleconferencing, EFTS (electronic funds transfer system), EPOS (electronic point of sale), ATM (automatic teller machine), PIN (personal identification number), smart card, modem

13 **character recognition**, scanner, OCR (optical character reader or recognition), ICR (intelligent character recognition), MICR (magnetic ink character recognition)

14 **data transfer**, multiplexing, modem (modulator and demodulator), codec (coder–decoder), acoustic coupler, telecommunications, EDI (electronic data interchange), packet switching, handshake, protocol, acknowledgment, ACK, NCK, fibre optics

15 **network**, network architecture, ring, star, bus, server, node, LAN (local-area network), Ethernet, Euronet, Arpanet (Advanced Research Projects Agency Network), BITNET, JANET (Joint Academic Network), SOSENET (Social Security Network), Telenet, bridge, gateway, internetworking, telecommuting, file server, multitasking, fax

16 **artificial intelligence** (AI), game-playing, perceptual computing, natural-language understanding, theorem proving, means-ends analysis, semantic net, game theory, expert system, cybernetics, robotics, neurocomputer, neural computer, neural net (or network)

17 **computing term**, access, address, algorithm, archive, backup, batch processing, band rate, baud rate, benchmark, bisection search, bit, bit map, block, bootstrap, branch, bug, byte, carriage return (CR), channel, chip, clock, clock rate, command, compatibility, controller, counter, crash, cross talk, cursor, data, debugging, diagnostics, direct access, directory, display, download, downsize, downtime, dump, emulator, field, file, flip-flop, floating point operation, flops, format, function, gateway, gigabyte, goto, handshake, hard return, hard sector, header, help, icon, input, interface, job, kilobyte, leader, login, logon, logout, logoff, loop, megabyte, menu, multiplexing, middleware, nesting, nibble, output, packet, parallel access, parity, password, patch, pixel, protocol, queue, random access, raster, real time, record, scanner, sector, sequential access, soft return, soft sector, sortkey, sprite, suite of programs, time sharing, toolbox, Trojan horse, turnkey operation, virus, write ring, wysiwyg (what you see is what you get)

18 **computer game**, video game, arcade game, hand-held computer game, Gameboy (Tm), Space Invaders (Tm), shoot 'em up (Inf)

VERBS

19 **abort**, access, address, archive, backup, bootstrap, boot, branch, compile, copy, crash, debug, decode, decompile, delete, downgrade, download, dump, emulate, erase, format, hardwire, input, interface, load, login, logon, logoff, logout, loop, output, patch, read, scroll, spool, upgrade, write

ADJECTIVES

20 **on-line**, off-line, user-friendly, erasable, rewritable, read-only, write-enabled

ADVERBS

21 **on-line**, off-line

66 Photography

NOUNS

1 **photography**, picture taking, colour photography, black-and-white photography, aerial photography, astrophotography, landscape photography, architectural photography, underwater photography, wildlife photography, documentary photography, fashion photography, portraiture, photojournalism, time-lapse photography, telephotography, macrophotography, microphotography, flash photography, infrared photography, cine photography, cinematography, stereophotography, holography, phototopography, radiography

2 **photoreproduction**, photocopying, Xerography, photogrammetry, photolithography, photogravure, photointaglio

3 **photograph**, photo, picture, image, shot, snapshot, take, daguerreotype, colour photo(graph), black and white, monotone,

half tone, transparency, slide, radiograph, X-ray, shadowgraph, photograph album, snap (Inf)

4 **portrait**, close-up, long shot, medium shot, pin-up, Photofit (Tm), mug shot (Sl), beefcake (Sl), cheesecake (Sl), group photograph, rogues' gallery, photobiography, landscape, cloudscape, silhouette, action shot, studio photograph, still-life, abstract, split image, multiple image, action sequence, photomontage, photomural

5 **stereoscopic image**, holographic image, hologram, colour hologram, reflection hologram

6 **microphotograph**, microcopy, microfilm, microfiche

7 **photocopy**, Photostat (Tm), Xerox (Tm), photomicrograph, PMT (photo mechanical transfer)

8 **composition**, framing, perspective, colour balance, contrast, highlights, tonal range, high key, low key, sharpness, focus, depth of field, image blur, acutance, overexposure, underexposure, colour cast, flare, fog, red-eye

9 **film**, photographic plate, photographic paper, bromide paper, roll film, black-and-white film, colour film, panchromatic film, chromogenic film, Polaroid film (Tm), X-ray film, infrared film, spool, reel, cassette, cartridge

10 **graininess**, fine grain, coarse grain, film speed, fast film, slow film, sensitivity, photosensitivity, ISO rating, ASA number, DIN number, DX code, hypersensitization, photographic density, transmission density, opacity, characteristic curve, H-D (Hurter-Driffield) curve, dynamic range, gamma, reciprocity failure, saturation level, fog level

11 **emulsion**, silver halide, gelatin, backing, latent image

12 **development**, processing, colour processing, printing, enlargement, darkroom, safelight, enlarger, developer, acid stop, stop bath, fixing solution, fixer, hypo, frame, exposure, negative, colour negative, print, colour print, slide, transparency, diapositive, sepia, lantern-slide, contact print, silver print, gum print, sun print, enprint, enlargement, blow-up, reprint, gloss finish, matt finish, semimatt finish, slide projector, overhead projector, slide carrier, screen, magic lantern

13 **framing**, cropping, bracketing, soft focusing, differential focusing, controlled blur, panning, pulling, pushing (or uprating), solarization

14 **cine film**, Super-8, home movie, cine camera, projector, screen, camcorder (Tm)

15 **lighting**, light source, daylight, natural light, ambient light, white light, soft light, hard light, backlighting, textured lighting, artificial light (or lighting), tungsten light (or lighting),

studio lighting, studio flash, spotlight (or spot), photoflood, bounced light, fill-in light, diffuser, reflector, floodlight, colour temperature, guide number

16 **camera**, single-lens reflex (SLR), twin-lens reflex, large-format camera, box Brownie, automatic camera, compact camera, miniature camera, disc camera, disposable camera, plate camera, camera obscura, cine camera, pinhole camera, video camera, camcorder (Tm), TV camera, security camera, film camera, gamma camera, Instamatic (Tm), Polaroid (Tm), photo booth

17 **lens**, lens system, standard (or normal) lens, fixed-focus lens, long-focus lens, telephoto lens, mirror lens, reflex lens, catadioptric lens, zoom lens, short zoom (or wide-angle zoom), mid-range zoom, telephoto zoom, wide-angle lens, ultrawide lens, shift lens, fisheye lens, macro lens, focal length, focus, angle of view, prism, pentaprism, lens mount, lens attachment, lens cap, lens cover, lens hood

18 **exposure time**, shutter, shutter release, cable release, shutter speed, B setting, self-timer, motordrive, aperture, diaphragm, iris diaphragm, aperture setting, f-stop (or F-stop), f-number (or F-number), viewfinder, rangefinder, infinity, vanishing point, hyperfocal distance, light meter, TTL (through-the-lens) meter, CdS meter, selenium meter, spot meter, autofocus, autoexposure, aperture priority, shutter priority, film advance, film rewind, take-up spool, film plane, focusing screen, depth of focus, tripod

19 **flash**, electronic flash, synchronized flash, flashgun, flash bulb, flash cube, hot-shoe, slave unit

20 **filter**, colour-balancing filter, colour-correcting (or compensating) filter, UV (or haze) filter, skylight filter, polarizing (PL) filter, neutral-density (ND) filter, diffusing filter

VERBS

21 **photograph**, shoot, take a photograph (or photo or picture), focus, stop down, open up, zoom in, zoom out, pan, expose, develop, process, print, enlarge, blow up, reduce, project, video, photo (Inf), snap (Inf), vid (Inf)

ADJECTIVES

22 **photographic**, photogenic, camera-shy, photosensitive

ADVERBS

23 **photographically**, photogenically

67   Fabrics and Dyeing

NOUNS

1 **fibre**, thread, filament, yarn, natural fibre, synthetic fibre, braided fibre, monofilament, denier

2 **spinning**, twining, intertwining, braiding, interbraiding, braid, plaiting, plait, spinning

Natural Fabrics

alpaca (wool)
astrakhan (wool)
baize (wool)
balbriggan (cotton)
batiste (cotton)
brocade
brocatelle
buckram (cotton, linen)
bunting (cotton)
burlap (jute, hemp)
calico (cotton)
cambric (cotton, linen)
camel hair or camel's hair
Canton crepe
canvas (cotton, hemp, jute)
cashmere or Kashmir (wool)
cassimere or casimere (wool)
castor (beaver fur)
challis (wool, cotton)
chambray (cotton, linen)
cheesecloth (cotton)
chenille (silk, wool)
cheviot (wool)
chiffon
chinchilla (wool)
chino (cotton)
chintz (cotton)
cord
corduroy (cotton)
cotton
crash (cotton, linen)
crepe (cotton, silk, etc.)
crepe de Chine
cretonne (cotton, linen)
crinoline
damask (silk, linen)
denim (cotton)
dimity (cotton)
doeskin
Donegal tweed
drill (cotton)

drugget
duck (cotton)
duffel (wool)
dungaree (cotton)
duvetine or duvetyne or duvetyn
faille (silk, rayon, taffeta)
felt (wool, hair)
flannel (wool, cotton)
flannelette (cotton)
fleece
foulard (silk, rayon)
frieze (wool)
fustian (cotton/wool)
gaberdine or gabardine (cotton, rayon)
gauze
Georgette crepe
gingham (cotton)
gossamer (silk)
grenadine
grogram
grosgrain (silk, rayon)
gunny (jute)
haircloth
Harris tweed
herringbone
hessian (jute)
homespun
hopsacking or hopsack (wool, cotton)
horsehair
huck or huckaback (linen, cotton)
Jacquard or Jacquard weave
jean (cotton)
jersey
lamé (silk, cotton, wool)
lawn (linen, cotton)
linen
linsey-woolsey (linen–wool)
lisle (cotton)
loden (wool)

longcloth (cotton)
mackinaw (US)
mackintosh
madras (cotton, silk)
malines or maline (silk)
marquisette
marseille or marseilles (cotton)
matting
melton (wool)
messaline (silk)
mohair (wool)
moiré (silk)
moleskin (cotton)
moquette
mousseline (rayon, silk)
mousseline de laine (wool)
mousseline de soie (rayon, silk)
muslin (cotton)
nainsook (cotton)
nankeen (cotton)
net
netting
oil silk
organdy or organdie (cotton)
organza
paisley (wool)
panne velvet
percale (cotton)
piqué (cotton, silk, rayon)
plaid
plush
pongee (silk)
poplin (cotton)
rep
russet
sackcloth
sacking
sailcloth
samite (silk)
sarcenet or sarsenet (silk)

sateen (linen, cotton)
satin
say (wool)
scrim
seersucker (cotton, linen)
serge
shalloon (wool)
shantung (silk, cotton, rayon)
sharkskin (acetate rayon)
sheer
shoddy (wool)
shot silk
silk
stammel (wool)
stockinet or stockinette
suede or suede leather
swansdown or swan's-down (wool, cotton)
tabaret (silk)
tabby (silk, taffeta)
tapestry
tarpaulin
terry
ticking or tick (cotton)
toile (linen, cotton)
towelling
tricot (rayon, nylon)
tricotine (wool)
tulle (silk, rayon)
tussore (silk)
tweed (wool)
twill
velours or velour
velure
velvet
velveteen (cotton)
vicuña (wool)
webbing (hemp, cotton, jute)
wool
worsted (wool)

Synthetic Fibres and Fabrics

acetate
acetate rayon
acrylic
artificial silk
Acrilan (Tm)

Celanese (Tm)
Crimplene (Tm)
Dacron (Tm)
Leatherette (Tm)
Lycra (Tm)

microfibre
nylon
Orlon (Tm)
polyacetate
polyamide

PVC (polyvinyl chloride)
polyester
rayon
Terylene (Tm)
viscose (rayon)

wheel, spinning mule, spinning jenny, spinner, extrusion, extruder, spinerette

3 **fabric**, cloth, textile, material, drapery, rag, natural fabric, synthetic fabric, synthetic, woven fabric, knitted fabric, soft furnishing, print, screen print, carpet, carpeting, Axminster, Wilton, broadcloth, broadloom

4 **weaving**, weave, plain weave, twill weave, warp, weft (or woof), selvage (or selvedge), list, web, webbing, lace, lacing, interweaving, shoot, weaving frame, loom, hand loom, machine loom, Jacquard loom, shuttle, bobbin, weaver, texture, nap, pattern

5 **knitting**, stitch, interlock stitch, plain stitch, purl stitch, cable stitch, moss stitch, stocking stitch, knit, machine knitting, knitting machine, pattern, needle, gauge

▶ *796 Fashion, 295 Dress*

6 **dye**, colourant, dyestuff, natural dye, vegetable dye, mineral dye, synthetic dye, chemical dye, acid dye, basic dye, vat dye, direct dye, mordant, lake, soluble dye, fast dye, absorption, chromophore, acridine dye, alizarin dye, aniline dye, azo dye, phthalocyanine dye, rhodamine dye, xanthine dye, crocein, eosin, fuchsine, madder, mauveine (or Perkin's

mauve), Tyrian purple, woad, bleach, chromotrope, garance, lake naphthol, pincoffin

7 **dyeing**, colouring, staining, patterning, printing, screen printing, tie-dyeing, batik (*or* battik)

8 **fabric treatment**, cleaning, washing, laundering, dry-cleaning, stain removal, bleaching, flameproofing, preshrinking, Sanforizing (Tm), wrinkleproofing, waterproofing, vulcanizing

ADJECTIVES

9 **spun**, twisted, braided, twined, plaited, extrudable, extruded

10 **woven**, knitted, cloth, fabric, fine, sheer, coarse, netted, fine-weave, open-weave, ikat weave, twill, felted, brushed, napped, looped, uncut, cut

11 **treated**, washed, bleached, dyed, coloured, dyed-in-the-wool, dyed-in-the-yarn, tie-dyed, coated, flameproof, preshrunk, Sanforized (Tm), waterproof (*or* waterproofed), showerproof (*or* showerproofed), drip-dry, crease-resistant, rubberized, vulcanized

12 **natural**, wool, woollen, woolly, silk, silky, silken, cotton, linen, rayon

VERBS

13 **spin**, twist, braid, plait, extrude

14 **weave**, knit, felt, mat, brush, nap

15 **treat**, wash, bleach, dye, tie-dye, flameproof, preshrink, Sanforize (Tm), waterproof, showerproof, rubberize, vulcanize

68 Agriculture

NOUNS

1 **agriculture**, farming, husbandry, intensive farming, factory farming, extensive farming, subsistence farming, mixed farming, share farming, sharecropping, arable farming, livestock farming, organic farming, ecofarming, biodynamic farming, agroecology, agroecosystem, agricultural science, agroscience (*or* agriscience), agronomy, agrology, agrobiology, agrogeology, agroforestry, geoponics, agronomics, rural economics, agrarianism, estate management, agribusiness, farm business, agricultural sale, Smithfield, farm-gate sale
▶ *69 Horticulture, 85 Trees*

2 **Common Agricultural Policy (CAP)**, green pound, quota, subsidy, grant, premium, marketing board, levy, set-aside, butter mountain, beef mountain, wine (*or* milk) lake

3 **livestock farming**, herding, stock rearing, ranching, dairy farming, dairying, beef farming, sheep farming, grazing, strip grazing, paddock grazing, zero grazing, folding, pig farming, poultry farming, chicken farming, fish farming, pisciculture, rabbit farming, mink farming, duck farming, animal husbandry, animal breeding, artificial insemination (AI), thremmatology, zootechnics, gnotobiotics, animal nutrition, animal health, animal production

4 **arable farming**, grain farming, dry farming, dirt farming (US inf), Green Revolution, crop rotation, monoculture, monocropping, slash-and-burn, crop husbandry, plant breeding, hydroponics, tank farming, fruit farming, truck farming (US), market gardening, tree farming, forestry
▶ *69 Horticulture, 85 Trees*

5 **cultivation**, culture, tillage, tilth, ploughing, harrowing, sowing, planting, hedge-laying, hedging, pleaching, plashing, heathering, ethering, irrigation, fertilizing, muckraking, muckspreading, dunging, weeding, cropspraying, insurance spraying, harvesting, haymaking, turning, bale-carting, straw-burning, silaging
▶ *69 Horticulture, 85 Trees*

Breeds of Cattle

Aberdeen Angus	Brahman	German Red Pied	Longhorn	Red Ruby Devon
Africander	Bangus (hybrid)	German Yellow	Luing	Red Steppe
Ala-Tau	British White	Gir	Maine Anjou	Red Welsh
Andalusian	Brown Swiss	Groningen	Marchigiana	Romagnola
Angeln	Canadian	Whiteheaded	Meuse-Rhine-Ijssel	Salers
Ankole	Charbray	Guernsey	Miranda	Santa Gertrudis
Aubrac	Charollais	Hereford	Mongolian	Shetland
Australian Illa-	Chianina	Highland	Murray Grey	Shorthorn
warra Shorthorn	Danish Red	Holstein-Friesian	N'Dama	Simmental
Ayrshire	Devon	(or Holstein)	Nguni	South Devon
Bapedi	Dexter	Irish Moiled	Normandy	Sussex
Barrosã	Drakensberger	Jamaica Hope	Old Gloucester-	Swedish Red-and-
Beefalo (hybrid)	Droughtmaster	Jersey	shire	White
Beef Shorthorn	Durham	Kankre	Pembroke	Tarentaise
Belgian Blue	Dutch Belted	Kerry	Piemontese	Telemark
Belted Galloway	Fighting Bull	Khillari	Pinzgauer	Texas Longhorn
Belted Welsh	Finncattle	Kholmogor	Polled Hereford	Tharparkar
Blacksided Trond-	Finnish Ayrshire	Kuri	Polled Welsh	Welsh Black
heim and Nord-	Friesian	Kyloe	Black	West Highland
land	Fulani	Limousin	Red-and-White	White Galloway
Blonde d'Aquitaine	Galician Blond	Line-Backed	Friesian	White Fulani
Blue Albian	Galloway	Welsh	Red Poll	White Park
Boran	Gascony	Lincoln Red	Red Sindhu	White Welsh

Breeds of Sheep

Awassi	Cambridge	Gritstone	Panama	Teeswater
Baalwen	Cannock Chase	Hampshire Down	Polled Dorset	Texel
Beulah Speckled	Cardy	Hebridean	Polwarth	Torddu
Face	Castlemilk Moorit	Herdwick	Portland	Torwen
Blackface	Cheviot	Hill Radnor	Radnor	Vendeen
Blackhead Per-	Chios	Ile de France	Rambouillet	Welsh Hill Speck-
sian	Clun Forest	Jacob	Rhiw Hill	led Face
Black Welsh	Colbred	Karakul	Romanov	Welsh Mountain
Mountain	Columbia	Kerry Hill	Romeldale	– Badger Faced
Bluefaced Leices-	Corriedale	Lacaune	Romney Marsh	(Rare breed)
ter (Hexham	Cotswold	Leicester	Rough Fell	Welsh Mountain
Leicester)	Dalesbred	Longwool	Ryeland	– Hill Flock
Boreray	Dartmoor	Lincoln	Scottish Blackface	Welsh Mountain
Border Leicester	Derbyshire	Llanwenog	Shetland	Wensleydale
Brecknock Hill	Gritstone	Lleyn	Shropshire	Whiteface Dart-
Cheviot	Devon Closewool	Lonk	Soay	moor
British Bleu du	Devon and Corn-	Manx Loghtan	Southdown	Whiteface Wood-
Maine	wall Longwool	Merino	South Devon	lands
British Charolais	Dorset Down	Norfolk Horn	South Wales	Wicklow Cheviot
British Friesland	Dorset Horn	North Country	Mountain	Wiltshire Horn
British Milksheep	English Longwool	Cheviot	Suffolk	
British Oldenburg	Exmoor Horn	North Ronaldsay	Swaledale	
British Texel	Galway	Oxford Down	Targhee	

6 **farm**, mixed farm, family farm, factory farm, organic farm, state farm, collective farm, kolkhoz, kibbutz, livestock farm, stock farm, dairy farm, poultry farm, chicken farm, beef farm, sheep farm, deer farm, fish farm, trout farm, ranch, rancho (US), spread (US), station (Aus), sheep ranch, cattle ranch, beef ranch, dude ranch, hacienda, hill farm, arable farm, grain farm, fruit farm, tree farm, mushroom farm, truck farm (US), plantation, tea plantation, coffee plantation, estate, tea estate, coffee estate, holding, smallholding, croft, farmstead, homestead, steading, toft (Arch), demesne, home farm, farmtoun, city farm

7 **farm building**, grange, farmhouse, yard, covered yard, farmyard, barton (Arch), barnyard, barn, granary, smokehouse, oast house, cowshed, dairy, milking parlour, hayloft, haybarn, Dutch barn, collecting yard, stable, pen, loosebox, box, stall, cubicle, byre, feedlot (US), piggery, pigsty, sty, pigpen (US), farrowing crate, farrowing house, pig ark, fattening house, lambing house, fold, sheepfold, pinfold, corral, hen-house, chicken house, broiler house, hutch, coop, hen coop, battery house, deep-litter house, aviary, chicken run, hen run, tractor shed, silo, grain elevator, workshop, farm office

▶ *301 Enclosure*

8 **livestock**, stock, beasts, fatstock, cattle, cow, heifer, calf, stirk, tatling, veal calf, yearling, milker, dry cow, suckler cow, milch cow, nurse cow, barren cow, bull, steer, bullock, store, store cattle, fat cattle, bull beef, barley beef, suckler beef, sheep, ewe, lamb, hogget, hogg, teg, ram, wether, tup, fat lamb, pig, hog, swine, sow, piglet, weaner, gilt, boar, porker, baconer, cutter, heavy hog, barrow (US), goat,

nanny goat, billy goat, kid, poultry, chick, poult, pullet, chicken, hen, battery hen (*or* chicken), free-range hen (*or* chicken), fowl, laying hen, layer, broiler, boiler, roaster, cock, capon, rooster, goose, gander, gosling, duck, drake, duckling

▶ *77 Mammals, 32 Horses, 78 Birds*

9 **animal feedstuff**, feed, ration, fodder, roughage, hay, haylage, silage, grass silage, maize silage, bale, big-bale silage, dried grass, straw, barley straw, wheat straw, oat straw, sugar-beet pulp, molasses, brewers' grains, malt culms, brewers' yeast, flaked maize, bran, coconut meal, groundnut meal, cottonseed cake, linseed meal, palm-kernel meal, soyabean meal, sunflower-seed meal, fishmeal, whey, meat-and-bone meal

10 **farm tool**, farm implement, farm machinery, deadstock, tractor, trailer, drill, corn drill, seed drill, plough, chisel plough, harrows, spring-tine harrows, chain harrows, draw harrows, disc harrows, power harrow, roll, flat roll, Cambridge roll, disc, cultivator, breaker (US), Rotavator (Tm), subsoiler, potato planter, beet planter, ridger, sprayer, harvester, combine harvester, combine, potato harvester, beet harvester, pea viner, scythe, sickle, reaping hook, swather, binder, baler, bale sledge, bale carrier, bale wrapper, mower, mowing machine, flail mower, rotary mower, conditioner, topper, forage harvester, hay turner, tedder, haywain, haystack, hayrick, rick, haycock, stook, buckrake, transport box, front-end loader, telescopic loader, all-terrain vehicle (ATV), farm bike, fertilizer spreader, muckspreader, pitchfork, pikle (Inf), muckfork, shovel, scubbin, slurry tanker, slurry tank, slurry pit, muckheap, midden, manure

Breeds of Pig

Berkshire	Duroc	"Iron Age" pig	Meishan	Poland-China
British Lop	Gloucester Old	Landrace	Middle White	Tamworth
British Saddle-	Spot	Large Black	Oxford Sandy-	Vietnamese Pot-
back	Hampshire	Large White	and-Black	Bellied
Chester White	Hereford	Mangalitsa	Pietrain	Welsh

heap, slurry scraper, silage clamp, irrigator, hedgecutter, plasher, electric fencer, trough, feeder, drinker, water bowl, feedbin, feedstore, grain bin, grain drier, hayrack, crush, race, milking machine, milk tank, bulk tank, churn

▶ *603 Tool*

11 **farmland**, arable land, arable, glebe (Arch), farm belt, corn belt, wheat belt, cotton belt, tobacco belt, black belt, fruit belt, citrus belt, plot (*or* piece) of land, acreage (US), field, hedgerow, hedge, quick, quickset, plot, piece, patch, parcel, paddock, strip, clearing, terrace, paddy, paddy field, rice paddy, potato field, cornfield, wheatfield, hayfield, grassland, meadow, mead (Arch), lea, pasture, grazing, rough grazing, enclosed land, enclosure, fence, hurdle, electric fence, barbed wire, post, stake, rail, gate, five-barred gate, wicket gate, wire netting, pig netting, sheep netting, ploughed land, cultivated land, furrow, drill, row, ridge, seedbed, tramline, headland, swathe, windrow, stubble

▶ *87 Grasses, 301 Enclosure*

12 **crop**, cash crop, catch crop, break crop, cover crop, cereal crop, corn, winter wheat, spring wheat, barley, winter barley, spring barley, oats, winter oats, spring oats, rye, triticale, millet, maize, rice, sorghum, root crop, fodder crop, green manure, turnips, swedes, fodder beet, sugar beet, mangels (*or* mangolds), potatoes, early potatoes, earlies, first early, second early, maincrop potatoes, peas, fodder peas, field peas, beans, field beans, black beans, soyabeans (*or* soybeans), groundnuts, peanuts, kale, cabbage, rape, oilseed rape, fodder rape, linseed, mustard, clover, red clover, white clover, alfalfa, lucerne, lupin, sainfoin, vetch, flax, okra, tobacco, cotton, fescue, ryegrass, Italian ryegrass, timothy, cocksfoot

▶ *69 Horticulture, 87 Grasses, 45 Cookery*

13 **fertilizer**, manure, muck, dung, slurry, effluent, farmyard manure, green manure, organic manure, dried-blood meal, hoof-and-horn meal, meat-and-bone meal, fishmeal, bonemeal, seaweed meal, compost, sewage, sludge, compound fertilizer, straight fertilizer, nitrate, phosphate, potash, granule, prill, dust, lime, limestone, quicklime, slaked lime, basic slag, bagmuck (Inf)

14 **pest control**, rat trap, mousetrap, mole trap, snare, gintrap, hang, scarecrow, bird scarer, gas gun, sheep-dip, pesticide, rodenticide, rat poison, insecticide, contact insecticide, resid-

ual insecticide, molluscicide, slug pellet, fungicide, contact herbicide, systemic herbicide, spray, wetting agent, herbicide, weedkiller, agrochemicals, DDT, aldrin, dieldrin, parathion, warfarin, Paraquat (Tm), 2,4-D

15 **agriculturist**, agriculturalist, agronomist, agrologist, agrobiologist, agrogeologist, agroecologist, rural economist, farmer, yeoman, granger, husbandman, tiller, tiller of the soil, gentleman farmer, tenant farmer, peasant farmer, hill farmer, crofter, smallholder, kibbutznik, livestock farmer, stock farmer, dairy farmer, beef farmer, poultry farmer, pig farmer, sheep farmer, stockkeeper (Aus), stock raiser, stockbreeder, breeder, cattle breeder, sheep breeder, pig breeder, cattleman, grazier, rancher, ranchman, ranchero (US), arable farmer, grower, raiser, cultivator, sharecropper, tank farmer, dirt farmer, dry farmer, truck farmer (US), fruit farmer, planter, tea planter, coffee planter, barley baron

16 **farm worker**, farm manager, bailiff, farm agent, (migrant) farm labourer, farmhand, farmboy, stockman, stockperson, cowman, cowherd, cowboy, cowgirl, cowpuncher, puncher, herdsman, herd manager, cowhand, dairyhand, milkmaid, dairymaid, pigman, swineherd, shepherd, shepherdess, goatherd, broncobuster (US), buckaroo (US), gaucho, wrangler (US), groom, ostler, hostler, stableboy, stableman, herder, drover, gooseboy, goosegirl, swanherd, tractor driver, ploughman, potato picker, hop picker, fruit picker, crew (US)

VERBS

17 **farm**, work the land, cultivate, grow, sharecrop, till, till the soil, plough, rotavate, dig, delve, spade, harrow, rake, plant, sow, drill, direct drill, scatter seed, broadcast, top-dress, fertilize, muck, manure, dung, mulch, irrigate, spray, weed, hoe, mow, cut, harvest, reap, glean, gather, swathe, turn, crop, bale

▶ *69 Horticulture*

18 **practise livestock farming**, ranch, raise, rear, grow, breed, feed, nurture, suckle, wean, fatten, run, graze, fodder, water, muck out, bed, drench, worm, groom, comb, rub down, castrate, dehorn, brand, milk, hand-milk, machine-milk, dry off, calve, lamb, harness, bridle, yoke, hitch, drive, herd, tend, drove, punch cattle, wrangle (US), round up, corral, shepherd, stable, pen

Breeds of Fowl

Large Fowl	Leghorn	Sicilian Buttercup	Guinea Fowl	Pilgrim
Ancona	Malay	Silkie	Lavender	Roman
Andalusian	Malines	Spanish	Pearl Grey	Sebastopol
Araucana	Marans	Sultan	White	Toulouse
Aseel	Marsh Daisy	Sumatra Game		
Australorp	Minorca	Sussex	Ducks	Turkeys
Barnevelder	Modern Game	Transylvanian	Aylesbury	Arnewood Inter-
Brahma	Modern Langshan	Naked Necks	Black East Indian	national Dou-
Bresse	New Hampshire	Welsummer	Cayuga	ble AA
Campine	Red	Wyandotte	Crested	Arnewood Inter-
Cochin	Norfolk Grey	Yokohama	Decoy	national Treble
Creve-coeur	North Holland	Bantam	Indian Runner	CCC
Croad Langshan	Blue	Belgian, Barbu	Khaki Campbell	Beltsville
Dorking	Old English Game	d'Anvers	Magpie	Black Norfolk
Faverolle	Old English	Belgian, Barbu	Muscovy	Bourbon Red
Frizzle	Pheasant Fowl	d'Uccles	Orpington	Broad-Breasted
Hamburgh	Orloff	Booted	Pekin	Bronze
Houdan	Orpington	Frizzles	Rouen	Broad-Breasted
Indian Game	Phoenix	Japanese	Welsh Harlequin	White
Jubilee Indian	Plymouth Rock	Nankin	Whalesbury	Cambridge Bronze
Game	Poland	Old English Game		Mammoth Bronze
Ixworth	Redcap	Pekin (or Cochin)	Geese	Narragansett
Jersey Giant	Rhode Island Red	Rosecomb	African	Nicholas
La Fleche	Scots Dumpy	Rumpless	Brecon Buff	White Austrian
Lakenfelder	Scots Grey	Sebright	Chinese	White Holland
			Embden	

ADJECTIVES

19 **agricultural**, agrarian, agronomic, agrological, agroecological, agrobiological, geoponic, farm, farming, farmhouse, rustic, rural, pastoral, peasant, bucolic, agrestic, praedial (*or* predial), georgic (Arch)

20 **farmable**, arable, cultivable, ploughable, tillable, fertile, productive, fruitful, farmed, cropped, ploughed, broken down, tilled, grazed, fallow, undersown

21 **domesticated**, domestic, broken in, reared, raised, bred, milked, dry, fat, bought-in, purebred, cross-bred, thoroughbred, half-bred, inbred

ADVERBS

22 **agriculturally**, hydroponically, pisciculturally, gnotobiotically, organically, ecologically, rurally, pastorally, rustically, bucolically, productively, fruitfully, down on the farm

69 Horticulture

NOUNS

1 **horticulture**, gardening, landscape gardening, landscape architecture, flower growing, floriculture, rose growing, market gardening, truck farming (*or* gardening) (US), vegetable growing, mushroom growing, fruit growing, soft-fruit growing, pomiculture, citriculture, fruitage, viticulture, viniculture, indoor gardening, arboriculture, silviculture

▶ 86 Fruits, 85 Trees, 68 Agriculture

2 **garden**, pleasure garden, formal garden, flower garden, botanic(al) garden, ornamental garden, rock garden, alpine garden, rose garden, water garden, knot garden, parterre, Japanese garden, sunken garden, indoor garden, winter garden, bottle garden, hanging garden, bonsai, herb garden, garden centre, garden shop, vegetable garden, kitchen garden, allotment, cabbage patch, market garden, truck garden (*or* farm) (US), fruit farm, orchard, hop garden, lemon grove, olive grove, orange grove, vineyard, arboretum, tea garden, beer garden, roof garden, civic garden, municipal garden, public garden, zoological garden, botanical garden, garden city, garden suburb, victory garden, garden of remembrance, garden of rest, Hanging Gardens of Babylon, Garden of the Hesperides, Garden of Eden, Kew Gardens

▶ 85 Trees

3 **ornamental garden**, flower garden, bed, flowerbed, rose bed, rosery (*or* rosary), rosarium, herbaceous border, border, rockery, lawn, pond, lily pond, fountain, birdbath, bird table, garden gnome, bench, garden seat, garden chair, sun lounger, shrubbery, hedge, topiary, fence, trellis, rustic fence, lap fence, bower, arbour, grotto, summerhouse, gazebo, pergola, belvedere, ha-ha (*or* haw-haw), water butt, garden path, paving, crazy paving, patio, terrace, hanging basket, window box, patio set, barbecue, barbie (Inf)

4 **nursery**, glasshouse, greenhouse, conservatory, orangery, garden shed, potting shed, polytunnel, hothouse, coolhouse, forcing house, forcing bed, hotbed, frame, cold frame, propagator, cloche, module, seed tray, grow bag, compost heap, flowerpot, planter, jardinière

5 **gardening**, growing plants, green fingers, repotting, potting on, bedding out, pruning, pinching out, cutting back, hard pruning,

feeding, watering, weeding, composting, aquiculture, hydroponics, propagation, planting, grafting, budding, layering, stooling, graft, rootstock, stock, scion, graft union, cutting, stem cutting, leaf cutting, offset, budstick, maiden, whip, sucker, runner, plant breeding, variety, strain, cultivar, diploid, triploid, polyploid

6 **garden tool**, spade, fork, hoe, Dutch hoe, draw hoe, Canterbury hoe, onion hoe, rake, lawn rake, trowel, handfork, dibble, dibber, drill, seed drill, lopper, pruner, secateurs, lawn mower, cylinder mower, power mower, rotary mower, hover mower, Strimmer (Tm), edger, edging tool, cultivator, Rotavator (Tm), distributor, spreader, flame gun, garden line, shears, hedge trimmer, sprinkler, hose, leaf sweeper, roller, sprayer, knapsack sprayer, nozzle, lance, trug, watering can, rose, wheelbarrow, stake, tie, rabbit guard, beanpole, peastick

7 **fertilizer**, manure, compost, potting compost, mulch, peat, fish meal, foliar feed

8 **weedkiller**, herbicide, moss killer, fungicide, systemic fungicide, Bordeaux mixture, pesticide, spray, slug pellet, insecticide, pyrethrum, derris, benzene hexachloride (BHC), Malathion (Tm), primicarb, dimethoate, dinitro ortho cresol (DNOC)

9 **garden plant**, seedling, cutting, bulb, corm, rhizome, tuber, rock plant, alpine, bedding plant, annual, biennial, perennial, herb, flower, succulent, creeper, ground cover, turf, climber, climbing plant, rambler, woody plant, shrub, tree, specimen shrub, specimen tree

▶ 83 Plants (General), 84 Flowers, 85 Trees

10 **fruit tree**, bush tree, dwarf bush tree, cordon, dwarf pyramid, fan-trained tree, espalier, half standard, standard, fruit, soft fruit, stone fruit, citrus fruit

▶ 86 Fruits

11 **vegetable**, green vegetable, brassica, salad vegetable, root vegetable, root, tuber, legume, bean, pulse, dried vegetable, herb, culinary herb, sweet herb, potherb, mushroom

▶ 45 Cookery, 89 Fungi

12 **pests and diseases**, beetle, wireworm, asparagus beetle, flea beetle, raspberry beetle, thrips, weevil, apple blossom weevil, scale insect, leaf-hopper, leaf miner, aphid, apple aphid, cabbage aphid, root aphid, greenfly, whitefly, blackfly, black bean aphid, woolly aphid, raspberry midge, blackcurrant midge, cabbage fly, carrot fly, celery fly, onion fly, caterpillar, cutworm, leatherjacket, Colorado beetle, cabbage white, pea moth, codling moth (or codlin moth), apple sawfly, plum sawfly, gooseberry sawfly, red spider mite, big bud mite, mealy bug, eelworm, slug, snail, earwig, club root,

mildew, powdery mildew, downy mildew, blight, brown rot, canker, damping-off, sooty mould, grey mould, botrytis, leaf curl, leaf mould, leaf spot, ring spot, honey fungus, rust, scab, silver leaf, root rot, wilt, crown rot, stem rot, crown gall, fireblight, heart rot, blackleg, soft rot, chlorosis, scald, bitter pit, dieback, mosaic, yellow edge, crinkle, spotted wilt, fruit drop

▶ 89 Fungi

13 **horticulturist**, gardener, plantsman, landscape gardener, landscapist, topiarist, landscape architect, floriculturist, flower grower, rose grower, rosarian, seedsman, nurseryman (or -woman), market gardener, truck gardener (or farmer) (US), fruit grower, fruiter, fruit farmer, pomologist, orchardist, vine grower, viniculturist, vigneron (Fr), vegetable grower, mushroom grower, hop grower, fruit picker, hop picker, under-gardener, arboriculturist

▶ 84 Flowers, 85 Trees

VERBS

14 **practise horticulture**, garden, landscape, cultivate, grow fruit, grow vegetables, market garden, truck garden (or farm) (US)

15 **cultivate**, plant, pot, sow, seed, put in, set, drill, heel in, dib, dibble, puddle in, transplant, pot on, prick out, plant out, bed out, dig, double-dig, trench, bastard-trench, delve, spade, fork, rotavate, hoe, rake, weed, thin, thin out, train, tie in, stake, prune, cut, mow, strim, crop, top, lop, deadhead, debud, deblossom, mulch, muck, dung, manure, straw, top-dress, fertilize, compost, sprinkle, water, spray, dust, propagate, breed, pollinate, graft, bud, take cuttings, layer

▶ 68 Agriculture

ADJECTIVES

16 **horticultural**, floricultural, floral, flowery, florescent, efflorescent, in bloom, uniflorous, multiflorous, herbaceous, herbal, vegetable, vegetal, vegetative, leguminous, cereal, farinaceous, arboricultural, arboreal, arborical, dendroid, sylvan, silvicultural, pomological, viticultural, vinicultural, aquicultural, hydroponic

17 **botanical**, annual, biennial, perennial, hardy, half-hardy, succulent, verdant, verdurous, mossy, grassy, bushy, fruity, woody, shrubby, scrubby, mildewy, rotten, mouldy, blighted, wilting, weed-choked, bug-infested, gone to seed

18 **herbicidal**, pesticidal, fungicidal, insecticidal

19 **ornamental**, alpine, exotic, tropical, subtropical, landscaped, cultivated, cultured, forced, trained, pruned, grafted, cut, watered, hoed, raked

ADVERBS

20 **horticulturally**, hydroponically, pomologi-

cally, florally, botanically, annually, biennially, perennially, succulently, verdantly, ornamentally, exotically, tropically, subtropically
▶ *84 Flowers, 86 Fruits, 85 Trees*

70 Transport

NOUNS

1 **transport**, transportation, transport system, passenger transport, commuting, personal transport, commercial transport, freight carriage, carriage, haulage, hauling freightage, portage, shipment, transshipment, cartage, carting, distribution, forwarding, sending, loading, unloading, off-loading, intermodal transportation, containerization, palletization, road, rail, air, water
▶ *326 Transfer, 324 Motion, 252 Displacement, 356 Passage*

2 **thing transported**, cargo, freight, goods, load, payload, consignment, shipment, contents, mail, luggage, baggage, container, pallet

3 **transporter**, shipper, conveyor, distributer, carrier, consignee, courier, loader, unloader, docker, stevedore

VERBS

4 **transport**, transport goods, transport door-to-door, haul, freight (US), portage, ship, cart, convey, consign, carry, act as a freight carrier, distribute, deliver, forward, dispatch, export, send, move, remove, load, unload, off-load (US), handle cargo, handle a consignment, transship, reship, bus, fly, commute, ride

ADJECTIVES

5 **transportable**, transported, transporting, movable, portable, roadworthy, airworthy, seaworthy, transport, transportation (US), door-to-door, urban, commercial, shipped, shipping, freight, private, forwarded, forwarding, loaded, loading, unloaded, unloading, bussed, bussing, commuting, road, rail, air, water, biking, biked, main, rural, farm (US), motorway, interstate (US), lorry, truck (US), railway, passenger, express, goods, piggyback, elevated (US), monorail, air-cargo (or cargo), aeroplane, short-range, medium-range, long-range, jumbo, supersonic, waterborne, towed, towing, river, navigational, navigated, navigable, inland, canal, ocean, ocean-going, merchant, dry-cargo, container, oil, piped, piping, pumped, pumping, pack, consigned

ADVERBS

6 **commercially**, as freight, door-to-door, hand-to-hand, by road, by motorway, by lorry, by bus, by rail, by train, with British Rail, by air, by aeroplane, supersonically, by water, by sea, by ship, by tanker, with the merchant navy, by pipeline, in the pipeline, in transit, en route, on the way

71 Road Transport

NOUNS

1 **road transport**, road transportation, foot transport, horse transport, cycling, motorcycling, motor transport, driving, trucking, motor haulage

2 **road**, road system, route, highway, Queen's highway, main road, trunk road, A road, clearway, urban clearway, motorway, freeway (US), interstate highway (US), superhighway (US), expressway (US), autobahn (Ger), autoroute (Fr), autopista (Sp), autostrada (It), toll road, turnpike (US), side road, B road, single track, rural road, farm road (US), farm track, beef road (Aus), dirt road (or track), rat run (Inf)

3 **carriageway**, lane, single lane, dual carriageway, slow lane, fast lane, hard shoulder, soft shoulder, crawler lane, escape lane, corner, bend, S-bend, hairpin bend, chicane, camber, intersection, T-junction, crossroads, box junction, roundabout, traffic circle (US), cloverleaf (or cloverleaf junction), spaghetti junction, slip road, feeder road, filter, one-way system, lights, traffic lights, crossing, pedestrian crossing, zebra crossing, panda crossing, pelican crossing, Belisha beacon

4 **personal transport**, walking, shanks's pony, people mover, driverless car, moving pavement, travolator (or travelator), lift, elevator (US), paternoster

Carriages and Carts

barouche	chaise	fly	phaeton	trap
brake	chariot	four-in-hand	post chaise	trishaw
britzka	clarence	gharry	prairie schooner	tumbrel (or tumbril)
brougham	coach	gig	randem	
buckboard	Conestoga wagon	Gladstone	ratha	victoria
buggy	coupé	hackney	rickshaw	vis-à-vis
cab	covered wagon	hansom	rig	voiturette
cabriolet	curricle	haywain	rockaway	wagon
calash	dogcart	herdic	spider phaeton	wagonette
Cape cart	drag	jaunting car	stagecoach	wain
cariole	dray	landau	sulky	whim
carriage	droshky	one-horse car-	surrey	
carryall	equipage	riage	tarantass	
cart	fiacre	oxcart	tilbury	

Motor Vehicles

ambulance	crawler tractor	jigger (NZ)	runabout
amphibian	delivery truck	juggernaut	RV (recreational vehi-
armoured car	digger	kart	cle) (US)
articulated lorry	Dormobile (Tm)	landau	saloon
automatic	dragster	Land Rover (Tm)	scout car
automobile	dray	limousine	sedan
autorickshaw	duck	lorry	semitrailer
beach buggy	dune buggy	loudspeaker van	shooting brake
bloodmobile (US)	dustcart	low-loader	snowmobile
bookmobile (US)	electric car	mammy wagon (or wag-	snowplough
bowser	estate car	gon) (W Africa)	sports car
breakdown van (or	farm tractor	milk float	steamroller
truck)	fastback	mini (Tm)	stock car
bubble car	fire engine	mobile home	streetcar
buggy	float	mobile library	swamp buggy
bulldozer	fork-lift truck	motor caravan	taxi
bumper car	garbage truck (US)	moving van	tourer
bus	go-kart (or go-cart)	phaeton	tracklayer
camper	golf cart	postbus	tractor
car	gritter	PSV (public service ve-	trailer
carryall	half-track	hicle)	tram
car transporter	hardtop	racing car	transporter
caterpillar	hatchback	rally car	trolley
coach	hearse	refrigerator (or refriger-	trolleybus
convertible	HGV	ated) van	truck
coupé	hot rod	removal van	van
crash wagon (or wag-	JCB	roadroller	wagon (or waggon)
gon) (US)	Jeep (Tm)	rocket car	weasel

5 **pack**, carrier, saddlebag, backpack, bearer

6 **litter**, stretcher, pallet, bier, sedan (or sedan chair), dooly (or doolie) (East Indies), jainpan (India), muncheel (India), norimon (Japan), palanquin (or palankeen) (Orient), tonjon (Sri Lanka), horse litter, camel litter

7 **handcart**, cart, pushcart, dumpcart (US), barrow, handbarrow, wheelbarrow, coster's barrow, push car, trolley, bag trolley, luggage trolley, shopping trolley, tea trolley, dolly

8 **baby carriage**, pram, perambulator, go cart (US), baby walker, baby buggy, pushchair, stroller, carrycot

9 **animal transport**, horse, riding, pack animal, packhorse, mule train, dispatch rider, pony express, wagon train, draught animal, carthorse, draught horse, carriage, dray

10 **sled**, sledge, sleigh, toboggan, luge, snowboard, bobsled (or bobsleigh or bob), jumper, pung (US), scoot (US), drag, dray, dogsled, troika, motorized sled, snowmobile, bombardier, Sno-Cat, Skimobile, weasel, cat-train (Canad)

11 **bicycle part**, frame, fork, crossbar, mixte frame, wheel, spoke, disc wheel, brake, hub brake, brake block, rod brake, cable brake, caliper brake, cantilever brake, crank, pedal, rat trap, toeclip, bicycle chain, chainguard, gear, clanger, hub gear, derailleur, handlebars, drop handlebars, racing handlebars, straight handlebars, saddle, saddlebag, pannier, kickstand, mudguard, mud flap, bicycle pump, bicycle clips

12 **bicycle**, bike, cycle, push-bike, wheel (US), racing bicycle, roadster, sit-up-and-beg, minibike, trailbike, BMX (bicycle motocross), mountain bike, chopper, ATB (all-terrain bike), hobbyhorse (or hobby), velocipede, boneshaker, penny-farthing, safety bicycle, tandem, bicycle-made-for-two, tricycle, trike, fairy cycle, quadricycle, monocycle, unicycle, folding cycle, trick cycle, bicycle rickshaw, trishaw, iron horse (Inf)

13 **motorcycle**, motorbike, bike, motorbicycle, motorscooter, scooter, moped, autocycle, motorbike and sidecar, combination, autorickshaw, superbike

14 **cyclist**, bicyclist, motorcyclist, bike rider, motorcycle courier, bicycle courier, motocross racer, biker (Inf), bikie (Aus inf), rocker (Inf), greaser (Sl), easy rider (Inf)

15 **motor transport**, driving, motoring, bussing, road transport, road haulage

16 **car**, motorcar, (motor) vehicle, automobile, auto, private car, family car, runabout, tourer, roadster, saloon, hatchback, coupé, fixedhead coupé, drophead coupé, estate (or estate car), station wagon, shooting brake, sports car, convertible, limousine, limo (Inf), stretch limo (Inf), buggy (Inf), motor (Inf), wheels (Inf), jalopy (Inf), tin lizzie (Inf), crate (Inf), bomb (US inf), heap (Inf), banger (or old banger) (Inf), put put (Inf), rattletrap (Inf)

17 **police car**, patrol car, squad car, prowl car, panda car, unmarked car, police van, wagon (or waggon), Black Maria, paddy wagon (or waggon) (Inf), jam sandwich (Sl)

Motor Vehicle Parts

ABS brake
accelerator
air bag
alternator
antidazzle mirror
antilock brake
anti-roll bar
anti-theft device
automatic choke
automatic transmission
axle
bench seat
bezel
blinker
bodywork
bonnet
boot
brake
brake drum
brake light
bucket seat
bumper
camshaft
carburettor (or carburetter)
catalytic converter (cat)
central locking
chassis
clutch
connecting rod
courtesy light
cowl
crank
crankcase
cruise control
cylinder
cylinder head
dashboard (or dash)

death seat
differential gear
dimmer
disc brake
distributor
driving wheel
drum brake
emergency light
fender (US)
fifth gear
fifth wheel
filler cap
flasher
fluid drive
flywheel
fog light
four-wheel drive
freewheel
gate
gauge (or gage)
gear
gearbox
gear lever (or gearshift)
generator
grille (or grill)
hazard warning light
headlight (or headlamp)
headrest
hood (US)
horn
hydraulic brake
hydraulic suspension
hypoid gear
ignition
ignition key
indicator
jump leads

jump seat
license plate (US)
kingpin
manifold
mileometer (or milom-
   eter)
monocoque
motive power
muffler
numberplate
odometer (US)
oil gauge
overrider
overrun brake
parking light (or lamp)
pintle
piston
pneumatic tyre
power brakes
power steering
propeller shaft
rack and pinion
radial tyre
radiator
radius rod (or arm)
reach
rear light (or lamp)
rear-view mirror
reflector
reverse
reversing light
roof rack
rumble seat
running board
seat belt
shaft
shift

shock absorber
sidelight
side mirror
silencer
solenoid
spare tyre
spare wheel
spark plug (or sparking
   plug)
speedometer
splashboard
sprag
starter
starter motor
steering column
steering gear
steering wheel
stick
stick shift (US)
stoplight
sun roof
suspension
tachograph (or tacho)
tail light
tailpipe
tail wheel
top gear
towbar
track rod
trafficator
transmission
tyre
wheel
windscreen
windshield
winker
wing

18 **cab**, taxi, taxicab, minicab, hackney cab (*or* hackney), hack (US), hire car (*or* hired car)

19 **bus**, omnibus, single-decker, double-decker, coach, motor coach, luxury coach, charabanc, trolleybus (*or* trolley)

20 **truck**, lorry, wagon (*or* waggon), cart, transporter, articulated vehicle, tractor, trailer, van

21 **miscellaneous motoring terms**, autocade, aquaplaning, automobilia, automotive engineering, body shop, brake-fade, bump start, carnet, carsickness, coach building, *concours d'élégance*, cornering, crash barrier, crashworthiness, deathtrap, double declutch, double parking, driving licence, endorsement, fade, garage, garaging, gas, grab, green card, gridlock (US), gritter, gritting, handbrake turn, hard standing, hit-and-run accident, hitchhiker, hitchhiking, hot-wiring, jack, jaws of life, jerrycan, judder, knock-for-knock, lighting-up time, lock, logbook, lubritorium, mechanic, mileage (*or* milage), misfiring, MOT, motel, motion sickness, motorcade, nearside, no-claims bonus, offside, overdrive, oversteer, overtaking, panel beater, parking, parking meter, parking space, pile up, piston slap, pit, pull in, rack and pinion, registration, registration document, registration number, road-

fund licence, roadholding, road tax, road test, shimmy, shunt, sideslip, skid, skidpan, slip, speed limit, speed trap, stall, tailskid, tailspin, tax disc, test drive, three-point turn, tow, traction, trade plate, traffic, traffic jam, triptyque, turning circle, underseal, understeer, U-turn, weighbridge, wheelbase, wheel wobble

72 Rail Transport

NOUNS

1 **railway**, railroad (US), railway system, mainline railway, overground railway, light railway, tramway, tramcar, tram, cog railway, rack railway, inclined railway, cable railway, cable car, funicular, monorail, telpher (*or* telfer *or* telpherage *or* telferage), scenic railway, elevated railway, elevated (US), el (US inf), underground railway, underground, tube, subway (US), metro, metritis, rapid-transit system (RTS)

2 **track**, main line, up line, down line, section, branch line, spur (*or* spur track), loop, siding, sidetrack (US), switch (US), lay-by, cutting, embankment, gradient, gradient post, crossing, level crossing, gated crossing, manned crossing, unmanned crossing, signal, lights, semaphore, signal box, fog signal, highball

Types of Aircraft

aerodyne	drone	jumbo jet	ramjet
amphibian	fighter	jump jet	rotaplane
autogiro	fighter–bomber	lifting body	seaplane
bomber	flying wing	microlite	swing wing
canard	freighter	MRCA (multirole com-	taxiplane
coleopter	gyrocopter	bat aircraft)	turbofan
convertiplane	gyrodyne	multiplane	turbojet
cyclogiro	interceptor	night fighter	turboprop
dive bomber	jet plane (or jet)	pusher	

(US), torpedo (US), water tower, water trough

3 **rail**, rails, metals, gauge, narrow gauge, standard gauge, broad gauge, roadbed, permanent way, ballast, sleeper, tie (US), fish joint, fishplate, frog, points, catch points, switch (US), crossover, turntable, buffer, end of steel

4 **locomotive**, engine, diesel locomotive, diesel-electric, electric locomotive, steam locomotive, steamer, iron horse, tank engine, tanker, shunting engine, shunter, light engine, wildcat (US), jerkwater engine (US), jigger (NZ), loco (Inf), choo choo (Inf), chuffer (Inf), chuff chuff (Inf), puffer (Inf), puff puff (Inf)

5 **locomotive part**, traction unit, motorcar, pantograph, dead man's handle, boiler, tank, side tank, saddle tank, tender, footplate, firebox, funnel, piston, sandbox

6 **rolling stock**, car, carriage, railcar, observation car, *coupé* (Fr), parlor car (US), dog box (Aus), dining car, restaurant car, sleeping car, sleeper, roomette (US), *couchette* (Fr), *wagon lit* (Fr), luggage van, baggage car (US), caboose (US), guard's van, mailcoach, mail van, Pullman (or Pullman car), freight car, freightliner, wagon (or waggon), truck, van, gondola, lowloader, hoppercar (or hopper), tank wagon (or waggon)

7 **train**, passenger train, express, slow train, stopping train, milk train, mail train, night mail, freight train, goods train, rake (NZ), double header, twin bill, bogie, coupling, drawbar, draw gear, king bolt (or king rod)

8 **railway station**, rail station, station, terminus, railhead, end of the line, main-line station, halt, whistle stop (US), platform, bay, booking office, waiting room, left-luggage office (or locker), barrier, depot, shed, yard, marshalling yard, switch yard (US), snow shed (US)

9 **railway worker**, railwayman (or woman), engine driver, engineer (US), motorman, fireman, conductor (US), guard, inspector (or ticket inspector), platelayer, lengthman, trackman (US), pointsman, signalman, station manager, stationmaster, porter, gandy dancer (Sl)

10 **miscellaneous**, British Rail (BR), Amtrak, Canadian Pacific, Trans-Siberian Railway, APT (advanced passenger train), TGV (*train à grande vitesse*) (Fr), Bullet Train (Japan), Orient Express, Brighton Belle, Stephenson's Rocket, Locomotion, Puffing Billy, train spotting, train spotter, gricer (Sl)

73 Aviation

NOUNS

1 **aviation**, flying, flight, gliding, piloting, pilotage, aerial reconnaissance, air transport, air travel, scheduled flight, sortie, air route, air corridor, air freight, air cargo, air mail (or airmail), payload, airlift, airdrop, paradrop, mercy flight, flying doctor, flying circus, aerobatics, crop dusting, skywriting, skyjack, jet lag

2 **aeronautics**, aeronautical engineering, aircraft design, avionics, aerothermodynamics, aeroballistics, aero-optics, bioaeronautics

3 **aircraft personnel**, aviator, flyer, pilot, airline pilot, glider pilot, test pilot, aircrew, crew, captain, copilot, first officer, flight engineer, navigator, observer, pathfinder, purser, steward, stewardess, air hostess, groundcrew, aircraftsman (or aircraftswoman), ground engineer, air-traffic controller, groundling

4 **airport**, airfield, airbase, air station, aerodrome, airstrip, landing strip, landing field, terminal, apron, hard standing, hangar, control tower, taxiway, runway, clearway, flight line, airside, landside

5 **flight**, takeoff, climb, flight level, flight formation, airspeed, groundspeed, heading, headwind, tailwind, terminal velocity, ceiling, aeropause, absolute ceiling, service ceiling, descent, approach, flare, glide path, landing, touchdown, belly landing, pancake landing, three-point landing, ground run, overflight, overshoot, undershoot, crash landing, manoeuvre, bank, banking, barrel roll, buffeting, bunting, chandelle, crab, dive, crash-dive, figure of eight (or figure eight), flat spin, flutter, hunting, hedgehopping, low-level flying, Immelann turn, loop, looping the loop, nose dive, pitching, rolling, stall, stalling, shock stall, sideslip, skidding, snap roll, soaring, spin, spiral, turn, roll, vectoring, VIFF (vector in flight), victory roll, wingover, whipstall, yawing, zooming

6 **flight control**, ground control, air-traffic

Aircraft Parts

aerodynamic brake	bombsight	engine pod	plane
aero engine	bucket seat	fairing	pod
aeroplane cloth	bulkhead	flap	pressure cabin
aerostructure	bypass ratio	flight deck	prop
afterburner	cabin	flight recorder	propeller
aileron	canopy	frame	pusher
air brake	cantilever	fuselage	pylon
air dam	chassis	galley	ram-air turbine
airframe	clamshell	gull wing	ramjet
air intake	cockpit	head-up display	rudder
air scoop	control column	hold	seat belt
all-flying tail	control stick	horn balance	slinger ring
altimeter	control surface	inclinometer	spinner
anti-icer	cowling (or cowl)	jet engine	spoiler
arrester	dashboard (or dash)	jet pipe	stabilizer
artificial horizon	de-icer	joystick	tailplane
astrocompass	dive brake	kymograph (or cymo-	tailskid
astrodome	drogue	graph)	tail wheel
automatic pilot	drop tank	longeron	trim tab
auxilliary power unit	ejector seat	Machmeter	turbofan
backwash	electronic flight informa-	main plane	turbojet engine
barostat	tion system	monocoque	undercarriage
bay	elevator	nacelle	windmill
black box	elevon	nose	wing
blister	empennage	nose wheel	winglet

control, AEW (airborne early warning), ASDE (airport surface detection equipment), fly-by-light, fly-by-wire, landing beam, loran, navar, radar beacon, SBA (standard beam approach), shortan, talk down, Teleran (Tm), traffic pattern, stack, stacking

7 **miscellaneous aviation terms**, air flow, air miss, air pocket, airsickness, angle of bank, angle of incidence, anhedral, bird strike, boarding card, dihedral, dip, downwash, drag, drift, driftage, feathering, flameout, fly-past, footprint, gremlin, hook-up, icing, load factor, loading, parasite drag, rake, reheating, slipstream, spread, STOL (short take-off and landing), sweepback, trim, turbulence, clear-air turbulence, VTOL (vertical take-off and landing), washin, wind shear, wind tunnel, wing loading, wingspan

8 **aircraft**, heavier-than-air craft, airplane, aeroplane, airliner, kite (Inf), glider, hang glider, rogallo, helicopter, copter (Inf), chopper (Sl), eggbeater (Sl), lighter-than-air craft, balloon, hot-air balloon, helium balloon, dirigible, blimp, Zeppelin

74 Water Transport

NOUNS

1 **water travel**, shipping, boating, sailing, rowing, sea travel, seafaring, cruising, sea trip, boat trip, life on the ocean wave, voyage, voyaging, passage, crossing, river travel, canal travel, inland navigation, navigation, circumnavigation

▶ *17 Military Affairs*

2 **waterway**, navigable water, sea lane, seaway, ocean track, steamer route, crossing, ferry

crossing, inland waterway, river, lake, canal, cut

3 **vessel**, ship, boat, craft, rowing boat, rowboat, skull, sailing boat, sailboat, pleasure boat, yacht, steamship, steamboat, passenger ship, liner, ferry, canal boat, narrow boat, barge, merchant ship, merchantman, freighter, tanker, fishing boat, trawler, drifter, whaler, warship

4 **shipbuilding**, ship design, naval architecture, naval engineering, ship materials, wood, steel, medium steel, high-tensile steel, special-treatment steel, aluminium alloy, reinforced concrete, shipbuilding skill, ship specifications, structural design, structural model, structural test, launching, launching ceremony, christening, shipbuilding contract, shipbuilding yard

▶ *382 Structure, 306 Form*

5 **navigation**, celestial navigation, astronavigation, inertial navigation, compass reading, piloting, pilotage, pilotship, helmsmanship, seamanship, steering, plane sailing, plain sailing, spherical sailing, great-circle sailing, parallel sailing, dead reckoning, dead-reckoning position, estimated position, plotting, navigational aid, sailing aid, navigational instrument, marine sextant, sextant, quadrant, angular measure, traverse table, log, ship's log, towed log, submerged log, compass, ship's compass, magnetic compass, gyrocompass (or gyroscopic compass), astrocompass, needle, magnetic needle, card, compass card (or rose), binnacle, chronometer, ship's chronometer, ship's timekeeper, chart, Admiralty chart, nautical almanac, ephemeris, directional reference, bearings, sea mark, buoy, lighthouse,

Ships and Boats

amphibious land-
ing craft
ark
banana boat
barge
bateau
battleship
boatel (or botel)
bulk carrier
bumboat
cabin cruiser
cable ship
caïque
canal boat
canoe
cargo boat
catamaran
catboat
cockleboat
cockleshell
collier
coracle
crabber
cruiser
currach (or
curagh)

cutter
dinghy
dory
dredger
drifter
DUKW (duck)
E-boat
factory ship
faltboat
fishing boat
flagship
flatboat
flotel (or floatel)
freighter
galley
gig
gondola
hooker
houseboat
hovercraft
hydrofoil
icebreaker
Indiaman
inflatable
jet-boat
jolly boat

kayak (or kaiak)
keelboat
launch
liberty ship
lifeboat
lighter
lightship (or
light vessel)
longboat
lugger
mail boat
merchantman
mosquito boat
motorboat
narrow boat
nuggar
oiler
outboard
outrigger
oyster crab
packet
paddle boat (or
steamer)
pearler
pilot (or pilot
boat)

pinnace
pontoon
post boat
powerboat
PT boat
punt
Q-ship
racing shell
randan
refrigeration ship
revenue cutter
roll-on/roll-off
rowing boat (or
rowboat)
runabout
sabot
sailing boat (or
sailboat)
sailing ship
sampan
school ship
scow
scull
sealer
shallop
shell

ship's boat
slaver
slave ship
steamboat
steamer
steamship
supertanker
surfboat
swamp boat
tanker
tender
torpedo boat
towboat
tramp steamer
trawler
trimaran
troop carrier
tug (or tugboat)
umiak (or oomiak)
weather ship
whaleboat
wherry
yawl

Sailing Ships and Boats

barque (or bark)
barquentine (or
barquantine)
brig
brigantine
caïque
caravel (or car-
vel)
carrack
cat
catamaran
catboat
clipper
corsair
corvette
cutter
dhow
dragon
dromond (or
dromon)
felucca
four-master
frigate
gabert
galiot (or
galliot)
galleon
hermaphrodite
brig
hooker
jolly boat
junk
keelboat
ketch
lateen
longboat
longship
lugger

monohull
multihull
nuggar
ocean racer
outrigger
pink
pinnace
piragua
pirogue
polacre
proa (or prau)
púcán
razee
rigger
sabot
sailboard
sailer
sailing boat (or sail-
boat)
sailing dinghy
schooner
scow
shallop
skiff
skipjack
sloop
sloop of war
smack
square rigger
tall ship
tartan
tea clipper
trimaran
windjammer
xebec (or zebec or
zebeck)
yacht
yawl

Sails

Bermuda rig
canvas
course
foreroyal
foresail
forestaysail
foretop
fore-topgallant
fore-topsail
Genoa
headsail
jenny

jib
jigger
kite
lateen sail
lugsail
main course
mainsail
maintopsail
mizzen
moonraker
rig
royal

skysail
spanker
spinnaker
spritsail
square sail
staysail
studdingsail
topgallant
topsail
trysail

Rigging

arm
backstay
bibb
bitt
boom
bull's-eye
burton
cable
clamp
clinch
club
club foot
crosshead
crossjack
crowfoot
eye
fall
foremast
fore-topmast
fox
gaff
garland

gasket
gooseneck
gripe
hank
horse
hound
jack
jigger
lanyard (or
laniard)
lead
leader (or
fairlead)
mainstay
martingale
mizzenmast
(or mizen-
mast)
messenger
moorings
mouse (or
mousing)

pendant (or
pennant)
pole
preventer
service
shroud
sling
snub
spider
spring
stick
stirrup
stop
tabernacle
thimble
topmast
traveller
truck
truss
warp
whelp
yolk

Knots

becket knot	clove hitch	half hitch	prusik	surgeon's knot
bend	diamond knot	hangman's knot	reef knot	sword knot
Blackwall hitch	Englishman's tie	harness hitch	rolling hitch	thumb knot
blood knot	(or knot)	hawser bend	round turn and	tie
bow	figure of eight	hitch	two half hitches	timber hitch
bowknot	(or figure eight)	Hunter's bend	running bowline	truelove knot (or
bowline	fisherman's bend	loop knot	sheepshank	true-lover's
bowline on the	fisherman's knot	love knot	sheet bend	knot)
bight	flat knot	magnus hitch	shroud knot	Turk's-head
builder's knot	French knot	Matthew Walker	slipknot	wall knot
carrick bend	granny knot (or	mesh knot	square knot	weaver's knot
cat's-paw	granny's knot)	overhand knot	stevedore's knot	Windsor knot

pharos, lightship, lead, line, lead line, shore direction-finding (DF) station, radio-beacon station, automatic direction finder, single-loop goniometer, crossed-loop goniometer, loran (long range navigation) system, loran-A system, loran-B system, decca system, decca phasemeter, consol system, radar, navigational radar, sonar, navigational satellite, Transit system, NAVSTAR Global Positioning System (GPS), ship's steering, helm, wheel, tiller, rudder, steering oar, navigation laws, rules of the sea

▶ 528 Information, 334 Circuit, 335 Deviation

6 **nautical speed**, ship's speed, knot, log-line knot, nautical mile per hour

7 **nautical person**, navyman, naval man (or woman), naval officer, admiral, Sea Lord, Admiral of the Fleet, Fleet Admiral (US), sailor, sailorman, seaman, able-bodied seaman (AB), able seaman, coastguardsman, marine, seafarer, seafaring man (or woman), Wren, Wran (Aus), mariner, master mariner, master, ship's master, sailing master, quartermaster, captain, skipper, navigator, pilot, helmsman, steersman, wheelman, man at the wheel, circumnavigator, ship's steward, boatswain (or bosun), bosun's mate, coxswain (or cox), shipmate (or mate), deckhand (or hand), leadsman, lookout man, foretopman, reefer, cabin boy, (ship's) crew, (ship's) complement, watch, fisherman, deep-sea fisherman, trawler, whaler, sea scout, sea cadet, bad sailor, fair-weather sailor, salt, old salt, sea dog, pirate, piratess, privateer, buccaneer, sea king, Viking, mythical seaman, argonaut, Jason, Ancient Mariner, Flying Dutchman, Captain Ahab, Sinbad the Sailor, sea god, Neptune, Poseidon, sea rover (Arch), hearty (Inf), tar (Inf), Jack Tar (Inf), matelot (Sl), swabbie (or swab) (US sl), marine scientist, shipbuilder, ship designer, naval architect

8 **boatman**, waterman, yachtsman (or yachtswoman), canoeist, paddler, rower, oarsman (or oar), sculler, galley slave, punter, gondolier, ferryman, Charon, wherryman, bargee, bargeman (US)

Parts of a Ship

accommodation	companion ladder	hawsehole	pintle	stanchion
ladder	companionway	head	planking	starboard
after deck	counter	hold	Plimsoll line	stateroom
berth	crow's nest	keel	poop	stern
bilge	daggerboard	keelson	poop deck	sternpost
bitt	davit	larboard	port	strake
board	engine room	lazaretto (or laza-	porthole	strecher
boat deck	false keel	ret or lazarette)	portside	stringer
boiler room	figurehead	leeward	promenade deck	superstructure
bollard	fin keel	limber	propeller	thole
bow	flight deck	limber hole	propeller shaft	tiller
bridge	forecastle (or	lower deck	prow	top deck
brig	fo'c'sle)	main deck	quarters	transom
bulkhead	freeboard	maintop	radio room	turtleback
bull's-eye	futtock	middle deck	rail	wardroom
bulwarks	galley	mizzentop	riding lamp	washboard
cabin	gangplank	monkey rail	rigger	water line
capstan	gangway	oar	round house	weatherboard
carling (or car-	glory hole	orlop (or orlop	rowlock	weather deck
line)	gudgeon	deck)	rudder	wheel
cathead	gun deck	outboard	rudderpost	winch
cat hole	gunwale (or gun-	outrigger	scupper	windlass
centreboard	nel)	paddle wheel	sea ladder	windward
chain locker	half deck	painter	skeg	
chart room	hatch	paint locker	stabilizer	
cleat	hatchway	pilot house	stack	

VERBS

9 **navigate**, circumnavigate, use dead reckoning, plot, use a sextant, use a compass, chart, find one's bearings, travel by water, take on a pilot, pilot a ship, steer, hold the helm, man a ship, crew, ship out, sail, set sail, hoist sail, trim the sails, square (away), spread canvas, launch, push off, cast off, boom off, unmoor, get under way, weigh anchor, get up steam, raise steam, put to sea, set a course, steer for, make for, head for, make way, gather way, carry sail, read the chart, go by the card, take soundings, heave the lead, bring into the wind, sail close to the wind, haul, beat to windward, run before the wind, run before a gale, scud, put the helm up, fall to leeward, luff, pay off, put the helm down, head into the wind, change course, turn round, veer, back, go astern, regress, crab, put about, tack, weather, back and fill, wear, gybe, yaw, race, cross one's bows, outmanoeuvre, gain the weather gauge, foul, collide

10 **sail**, set sail, heave to, lie to, lay to, bring to rest, surface, break water, flood the tanks, dive, plunge, run for port, weather the storm, ride out the storm, ride, ride on an even keel, take the wind out of one's sails, keep afloat, list, overturn, capsize, heel over, keel over, careen, turn turtle, ground, run aground, wreck, be cast away, sight land, make a landfall, land, make port, drop anchor, cast anchor, wedge, clubhaul, warp, draw, moor, tie up, dock, disembark, get one's sea legs (Inf)

ADJECTIVES

11 **nautical**, naval, marine, seafaring, seaworthy, sea-going, ocean-going, at the helm, on board, sea, deep-sea, at sea, on the high seas, seaborne, floating, afloat, launched, waterborne, salty, sailing, steaming, plying, ferrying, coasting, rolling, pitching, tossing, wallowing, yawing, aquatic, like a sailor, sailorly, sailor-like, seaman-like, able-bodied, able, fishing, trawling, like a fish, amphibious, amphibian, seasick, green, natatory (or natatorial), swimming, buoyant, fleet, water, shipping, boating, yachting, rowing, cruising, river, canal, inland, special-treatment (steel), shipbuilding

ADVERBS

12 **nautically**, at sea, on the high seas, afloat, like a sailor, amphibiously, under way, under sail, under canvas, under steam, before the mast, on board, on deck, on the bridge, on the quarterdeck, at the helm, at the wheel

75 Units

NOUNS

1 **unit**, unit of measurement, measure, linear measure, square measure, cubic measure, liquid measure, dry measure, surveyor's measure, board measure, avoirdupois weight (or measure), troy weight (or measure), apothecaries' weight (or measure)

2 **unit system**, base unit, derived unit, supplementary unit, compound unit, fundamental unit, absolute unit, coherent units (or system), rationalized units (or system), Imperial units, f.p.s. (foot–pound–second) system, f.p.s. unit, metric system, metric unit, m.k.s. (metre–kilogram–second) system, m.k.s. unit, MKSA (metre–kilgram–second–ampere) system, Giorgi system, e.m.u. (electromagnetic unit), e.s.u. (electrostatic unit), *Système International d'Unités* (Fr), SI unit

3 **scale**, linear scale, logarithmic scale, log scale, temperature scale, Celsius scale, centigrade scale, Fahrenheit scale, Rankine scale, Réaumur scale, absolute scale, thermodynamic scale, Kelvin scale, IPTS (International Practical Temperature Scale)

4 **standard**, fundamental standard, substandard, standardization, BIPM (*Bureau International des poids et mésures*) (Fr), ISO (International Standards Organization), NBS (National Bureau of Standards) (US), BSI (British Standards Institution), NPL (National Physical Laboratory), Deutsche Industrie Normen (DIN), Kitemark

5 **dimension**, mass, length, time, physical quantity, dimensional analysis

SI Units

Base and Supplementary Units		Decimal Prefixes
metre (m, length)	pascal (Pa, pressure)	deci (d, 10^{-1})
kilogram (kg, mass)	coulomb (C, electric charge)	centi (c, 10^{-2})
second (s, time)	volt (V, electric potential difference)	milli (m, 10^{-3})
ampere (A, electric current)	ohm (Ω, electric resistance)	micro (μ, 10^{-6})
kelvin (K, thermodynamic temperature)	siemens (S, electric conductance)	nano (n, 10^{-9})
candela (cd, luminous intensity)	farad (F, electric capacitance)	pico (p, 10^{-12})
mole (mol, amount of substance)	weber (Wb, magnetic flux)	femto (f, 10^{-15})
radian (rad, plane angle)	henry (H, inductance)	atto (a, 10^{-18})
steradian (sr, solid angle)	tesla (T, magnetic flux density or magnetic induction)	deca (da, 10)
		hecto (h, 10^2)
Derived Units	lumen (lm, luminous flux)	kilo (k, 10^3)
hertz (Hz, frequency)	lux (lx, illuminance)	mega (M, 10^6)
joule (J, energy)	gray (Gy, absorbed dose)	giga (G, 10^9)
newton (N, force)	becquerel (Bq, activity)	tera (T, 10^{12})
watt (W, power)	sievert (Sv, dose equivalent)	peta (P, 10^{15})
		exa (E, 10^{18})

Scientific and Technical Units

abampere
abcoulomb
abfarad
abhenry
abohm
abvolt
abwatt
ampere
ampere-hour
ampere-turn
amu
angstrom
astronomical unit
atmosphere
atomic mass
atomic mass unit
barn
barye
baud
becquerel
bel
bit
Board of Trade Unit
British thermal
   unit
bucket
byte
calorie (or calory)
Calorie
candela
candle

centimetre-gram-
   second
centimetre-gram-
   second
centimorgan
centner
chronon
circular mil
coulomb
curie
cusec (flow rate)
cycle
dalton
daraf
darcy
decibel
degree-day
dioptre (or diop-
   ter)
dyne
epoch
erg
farad
faraday
fathom
fermi
foot-candle
foot-lambert
foot-pound
foot-poundal
foot-ton

fresnel
gal
gallon
gamma
gauge (or gage)
gauss
gigahertz
gilbert
grade
gram (or gramme)
gram atom (or
   gram-atomic
   weight)
gram calorie
gram molecule
   (or gram-
   molecular
   weight)
grav
gray
henry
hertz
international candle
jansky
joule
kelvin
kilocycle
kilogram (or
   kilogramme)
kilogram calorie
kiloton

kilowatt-hour
light year
line
lumen
Mach number
magneton (or
   Bohr magneton)
maxwell
measurement ton
megaton
metre
mho
micrometre
micromicron
micron
mil
millibar
millimicron
mmHg
mole
neper
nit
oersted
ohm
okta (or octa)
parsec
pascal
perceived noise
   decibel
phon
phot

poise
poundal
rad
radian
roentgen (or
   röntgen)
rutherford
sabin
shed
siemens
sievert
slug
small calorie
standard candle
steradian
stilb
stokes (or stoke)
tesla
therm
torr
unit pole
var
volt
volt-ampere
watt-hour
weber
x-unit

General Units

acre
acre-foot
acre-inch
air mile
are
bar
barleycorn
barrel
board foot
board rule
bushel
butt (US)
cable
carat
cental
centiare (or centare)
chain
column inch
cord (wood)
cup
degree
denier

DIN (photogra-
   phy)
em (printing)
en (printing)
fathom
firkin
fluid dram
fluid ounce
foot
freight ton
furlong
gallon
gallonage
geographical mile
gill
grain
gross ton
Gunter's chain
hank (cloth)
hogshead
Hoppus foot
   (wood)

horsepower
horsepower-hour
hundredweight
   (or long hun-
   dredweight)
inch
international nau-
   tical mile
kilderkin
kilo
kip
knot
last (weight or
   capacity)
lea (length of
   yarn)
league
link (length)
man-hour
metric ton
mile (or statute
   mile)

milline (advertising)
minim
minute
nail (length of
   cloth)
nautical mile
net ton
noggin
ounce
peck (dry meas-
   ure)
pennyweight
perch
pica (printing)
pint
pipe
point (printing)
point (jewellery,
   weight)
pole
pound
puncheon

quart
quarter
quartern
quintal
rod (length, area)
rood
scruple
sea mile
second
short hundred-
   weight
short ton
shot (length)
span (length)
stere (volume of
   timber)
stone
surveyor's chain
tog (insulation)
ton
tonne
yard

Some Foreign Units

archine (Russia,
   length)
ardeb (Middle East,
   dry measure)
arpent (former
   French, length
   or area)
arroba (Spain,
   weight, volume)
congius (ancient
   Rome, liquid)
drachma (ancient
   Greece, weight)

lepton (Greek)
li (Chinese,
   length)
libra (ancient
   Rome, weight)
maund (Asia,
   weight)
mina (Asia
   Minor, weight)
morgen (South
   Africa, area)
morgen (formerly
   Prussia, area)

mutchkin (Scot-
   tish, liquids)
obolus (Greek,
   weight)
oka or oke
   (Turkey, liq-
   uids)
Olympiad (an-
   cient Greece,
   time)
omer (ancient
   Hebrew, dry
   measure)

parasang (Persia,
   distance)
picul (Far East,
   weight)
pood (Russia,
   weight)
reed (ancient He-
   brew, length)
Roman mile
Roman pace
rotl (Muslim
   countries,
   weight)

ser or seer
   (India, weight)
Swedish mile
tael (Far East,
   weight)
talent (ancient
   world, weight)
tical (Thailand,
   weight)
tola (India,
   weight)
vara (Spain,
   length)

Animals and Plants

76 Animals (General)

And God said, Let the earth bring forth the living creature after his kind, cattle, and creeping thing, and beast of the earth after his kind: and it was so. Bible: Genesis.

There are two things for which animals are to be envied: they know nothing of future evils, or of what people say about them. Voltaire.

NOUNS

1 **animals**, animal life, animal kingdom, Animalia, fauna, the bird, beast, and fish, the beasts of the field, the fowl of the air, and the fish of the sea, wildlife, endangered species, game, big game, small game
▶ *59 Life Science*

2 **animal**, creature, beast, brute, dumb animal, dumb friend, furry friend, four-legged friend, creeping thing, varmint (Inf), critter (US dial)

3 **domesticated animal**, beast of burden, pack animal, draught animal, farm animal, livestock, stock, circus animal, experimental animal, laboratory animal, tame animal, pet animal, pet, house pet
▶ *68 Agriculture, 77 Mammals*

4 **type of animal**, invertebrate, animalcule, zooid, protist, protozoan, worm, mollusc, gastropod, arthropod, insect, chordate, vertebrate, fish, amphibian, reptile, bird, mammal, biped, quadruped, herbivore, browser, grazer, filter-feeder, scavenger, omnivore, carnivore, flesh-eater, meat-eater, insectivore, predator, prey, parasite, bloodsucker, ectoparasite, endoparasite, host, intermediate host, vector, symbiont, commensal
▶ *77 Mammals, 78 Birds, 79 Reptiles and Amphibians, 80 Fishes, 81 Invertebrates*

5 **aquatic animal**, marine animal, marine mammal, cetacean, whale, dolphin, seal, fish, starfish, echinoderm, cuttlefish, cephalopod, octopus, shellfish, bivalve, jellyfish, coelenterate, coral, sponge, plankton, zooplankton, nekton, benthos (or benthon), fry, krill, larva
▶ *77 Mammals, 80 Fishes, 81 Invertebrates*

6 **flying animal**, flier, bird, flying insect, fly, butterfly, flying fish, flying mammal, flying fox, bat
▶ *78 Birds, 82 Insects and Arachnids, 80 Fishes, 77 Mammals*

7 **legendary beast**, unicorn, Pegasus, Cerberus, dragon, drake (Arch), firedrake (or firedragon), griffin (or griffon or gryphon), chimera, banshee, siren, lamia, harpy, manticore, behemoth, centaur, minotaur, cyclops, elf, gnome, goblin, orc, troll, jinn, hippogriff (or hippogryph), wyvern, cockatrice, basilisk, phoenix, roc, snark, kraken, Loch Ness monster, Sasquatch, Bigfoot, Yeti, Abominable Snowman, zoomorphism, therianthropism, bestiary
▶ *78 Birds, 11 Occultism*

8 **animal welfare**, animal health, veterinary science, animal breeding, zootechnics, thremmatology, animal conservation, zoological garden, zoo, safari park, wildlife park, game reserve (or preserve), dolphinarium, animal protection, Royal Society for the Prevention of Cruelty to Animals (RSPCA), animal rights movement, animal liberation, Animal Liberation Front (ALF)
▶ *60 Medicine, 68 Agriculture*

9 **animal science(s)**, zoology, animal taxonomy, systematic zoology, zoography, zoometry, animal anatomy, comparative anatomy, zootomy, animal physiology, zoonomy, embryology, animal biochemistry, zoochemistry, animal ecology, parasitology, marine biology, animal behaviour, animal psychology, ethology, sociobiology, zoogeography, animal pathology, zoopathology, palaeozoology, palaeontology, vertebrate zoology, mammology, ornithology, herpetology, ichthyology, invertebrate zoology, entomology, malacology, helminthology, protozoology
▶ *59 Life Science, 61 Psychology and Psychiatry, 54 Earth Science, 77 Mammals, 78 Birds, 79 Reptiles and Amphibians, 80 Fishes, 81 Invertebrates, 82 Insects and Arachnids*

10 animal welfarist, veterinarian, vet (Inf), thremmatologist, conservationist, zoo-keeper, game warden, animal lover, zoophile, pet owner, dog lover, cat lover, antivivisectionist, animal-rights activist, animal liberationist, hunt saboteur, hunt sab (Inf)

11 zoologist, animal taxonomist, systematic zoologist, zoographer, zoometrist, comparative anatomist, zootomist, animal physiologist, zoonomist, embryologist, zoochemist, animal ecologist, paransitologist, marine biologist, ethologist, behaviourist zoographer, zoopathologist, palaeozoologist, vertebrate zoologist, mammologist, ornithologist, herpetologist, ichthyologist, invertebrate zoologist, entomologist, malacologist, helminthologist, protozoologist

▶ *59 Life Science, 61 Psychology and Psychiatry, 54 Earth Science, 77 Mammals, 78 Birds, 79 Reptiles and Amphibians, 80 Fishes, 81 Invertebrates, 82 Insects and Arachnids*

12 zoophilism, zoophilia, bestiality, animality, animalism

▶ *821 Love*

13 fear of animals, zoophobia

▶ *777 Fear*

ADJECTIVES

14 animalian, animal, animalic, animalistic, zoic, brutish, subhuman, dumb, brutal, bestial, beastly, beastlike, animal-like, zoomorphic, therianthropic, theriomorphic (*or* theriomorphous)

▶ *241 Violence*

15 of animals, invertebrate, animalcular, zooidal, chordate, vertebrate, bipedal, quadrupedal, domesticated, tamed, feral, wild, solitary, social, colonial, terrestrial, arboreal, aquatic, marine, planktonic, benthic, pelagic, littoral, diurnal, nocturnal, carnivorous, herbivorous, omnivorous, insectivorous, predacious, parasitic, bloodsucking, ectoparasitic, endoparasitic, symbiotic, commensal

16 zoological, zoographic(al), zoometric(al), zoonomic(al), zoogeographic(al), zoochemical, embryological, ethological, zoopathological, palaeozoological

17 animal-loving, zoophilic

18 animal-fearing, zoophobic

77   Mammals

NOUNS

1 mammal, Mammalia, warm-blooded animal, homoiotherm, study of mammals, mammology

2 mammalian characteristic, mammary gland, mamilla, mamma, udder, dug, nipple, teat, pap, papilla, milk, colostrum, beestings, sweat gland, sebaceous gland, scent gland, musk gland, hair, spine, bristle, whisker, vibrissa, wool, fur, pelage

3 egg-laying mammal, prototherian, Prototheria, monotreme, Monotremata (platypus *or* duck-billed platypus *or* duckbill, echidna *or* spiny anteater)

4 pouched mammal, metatherian, Metatheria, marsupial, Marsupialia, marsupial characteristic, marsupium, pouch

5 placental mammal, eutherian, Eutheria, eutherian characteristic, placenta, uterus

6 insect-eating mammal, insectivore, Insectivora (hedgehogs, shrews, moles, etc.), anteater, scaly anteater, pangolin, pholidote, spiny anteater, echidna, ant bear, aardvark, tubulidentate

7 flying mammal, chiropteran (*or* chiropter), Chiroptera (bats), dermopteran, Dermoptera (flying lemur)

8 flesh-eating mammal, carnivore, Carnivora, canine, canid, Canidae (dogs, wolves, foxes, jackals, etc.), ursid, Ursidae (bears), mustelid, Mustelidae (weasels, otters, badgers, etc.), procyonid, Procyonidae (raccoons), viverrid, Viverridae (mongooses, civets, etc.), hyaenid, Hyaenidae (hyenas *or* hyaenas), feline, felid, Felidae (cats)

9 dog, canine, bitch, whelp, pup, puppy, puppy-dog, mongrel, cross-breed, lurcher, cur, tyke, pariah dog, pi-dog, hound, hunting dog, gundog, working dog, guard dog, watchdog, police dog, tracker dog, sniffer dog, guide dog, sheepdog, show dog, toy dog, lapdog, man's best friend, Fido, bow-wow (Inf), mutt (Sl), pooch (US sl)

10 cat, feline, wildcat, big cat, domestic cat, mouser, ratter, house cat, tom (*or* tomcat), gib, queen, grimalkin, kitten, kit (*or* kitty) (Inf), puss (*or* pussy *or* pussycat) (Inf), mog (*or* moggy) (Sl)

Marsupials

bandicoot	koala	planigale	tree kangaroo
cuscus	marsupial mole	quokka	wallaby
dasyure	marsupial mouse	rat kangaroo	wallaroo
Diprotodon*	marsupial rat	rat opossum	wombat
flying phalanger	mouse opossum	rock wallaby	yapok
hare wallaby	numbat	sminthopsis	
honey mouse (or honey	opossum, possum (Inf)	Tasmanian devil	*extinct marsupial
phalanger)	pademelon	thylacine, Tasmanian	
kangaroo	phalanger	wolf	

Breeds of Dogs

Aberdeen (or Scottish)
terrier
affenpinscher
Afghan hound
Airedale terrier
Alaskan malamute
Alsatian, German shep-
herd
American cocker spaniel
Australian terrier
basenji
basset hound
beagle
Bedlington terrier
Belgian shepherd dog
Bernese mountain dog
Blenheim spaniel
bloodhound
Border collie
Border terrier
borzoi
Boston terrier
Bouvier des Flandres
boxer
briard
bulldog
bull mastiff
bull terrier
Cairn terrier
chihuahua
chow (or chow chow)
clumber spaniel
cocker spaniel

collie
coonhound
corgi
dachshund
Dalmatian, carriage (or
coach) dog
Dandie Dinmont terrier
deerhound
Doberman pinscher
elkhound
English setter
Eskimo dog, husky
field spaniel
Finnish spitz
foxhound
fox terrier
French bulldog
German shepherd, Al-
satian
golden retriever
Gordon setter
Great Dane
greyhound
griffon
Groenendael
harrier
Hungarian puli
Hungarian vizsla
husky, Eskimo dog
Ibizan hound
Irish setter
Irish terrier
Irish wolfhound

Jack Russell terrier
Japanese chin
keeshond
kelpie
Kerry blue terrier
King Charles spaniel
Komondor
Kuvasz
Labrador retriever
Lakeland terrier
Large Munsterlander
Lhasa apso
Löwchen
Maltese
Manchester terrier
mastiff
Mexican hairless
Newfoundland
Norfolk terrier
Norwich terrier
Old English sheepdog
otterhound
papillon
pekingese
pharaoh hound
pit bull terrier
pointer
Pomeranian
poodle
pug
puli
Pyrennean mountain
dog

retriever
Rhodesian ridgeback
Rottweiler
Saluki
Samoyed
schipperke
schnauzer
Scottish (or Aberdeen)
terrier
Sealyham terrier
setter
Shetland sheepdog,
sheltie
shih tzu
silky terrier
Skye terrier
spaniel
spitz
springer spaniel
Staffordshire bull terrier
staghound
St Bernard
terrier
vizsla
Weimaraner
Welsh corgi
Welsh terrier
West Highland white
terrier
whippet
wire-haired pointing
griffon
Yorkshire terrier

---

11 **marine mammal**, cetacean, Cetacea (whales, dolphins, porpoises), pinniped, Pinnipedia (seals, phocids, sealions, walrus), sirenian, Sirenia (dugong, sea cow, manatee)

12 **gnawing mammal**, rodent, Rodentia, sciuromorphs (beavers, squirrels, chipmunks, etc.), myomorphs (murids, rats, mice, lemmings, gerbils, voles, etc.), histricomorphs (porcupines, cavies, etc.), lagomorph, Lagomorpha (pika (or cony), leporids, rabbits, hares)

13 **toothless mammal**, edentate, Edentata (anteaters, sloths, armadillos)

14 **pachyderm**, subungulate, proboscidean, Proboscidea (elephant, Jumbo, mastodon, mammoth), rhinoceros, hippopotamus, river horse (Inf)

15 **hoofed mammal**, ungulate, ungulant, odd-toed ungulate, perissodactyl, Perissodactyla (equines, equids, Equidae (horses), tapirs, rhinoceroses), even-toed ungulate, artiodactyl,

Artiodactyla, suid, Suidae (pigs, hogs, swine), hippopotamus, ruminant, cud-chewer, Ruminantia, camelid, Camelidae (camels, llamas, etc.), cervid, Cervidae (deer), giraffe, camelopard (Arch), okapi, bovid, bovine, Bovidae (cattle, antelopes, gazelles, goats, ovines, sheep, etc.), hyracoid, Hyracoidea (hyraxes or conies)

▶ *32 Horses, 68 Agriculture*

16 **primate**, Primates, prosimians (lemurs, lorises, bushbabies, tarsiers, etc.), anthropoids, monkeys, New World monkeys (capuchins, howlers, marmosets, tamarins, etc.), Old World monkeys (macaques, baboons, etc.), apes, anthropoid apes, pongids, Pongidae (gibbons, great apes, orangutan, chimpanzee, gorilla), hominids, Hominidae (man, *Homo sapiens*, human, human being), study of primates, primatology

▶ *400 Humankind*

Breeds of Cats

Abyssinian
Birman
blue Burmese
blue cream
blue-pointed Siamese
British blue
brown Burmese
brown tabby
Burmese
chestnut brown
chinchilla

chocolate-pointed
Siamese
colourpoint
Cornish rex
cream
Devon rex
domestic long-hair
domestic tabby
Havana
lilac-pointed Siamese
long-haired blue

Manx
Persian
red Abyssinian
red-pointed Siamese
red self
red tabby
rex
Russian blue
seal-pointed Siamese
Siamese
silver tabby

smoke
tabby
tabby-pointed Siamese
tortoiseshell
tortoiseshell and white
tortoiseshell-pointed
Siamese
Turkish

Placental Mammals

aardvark, ant bear
aardwolf
acouchi
addax
African elephant
agouti
ai
alpaca
angwantibo
anoa
ant bear, aardvark
anteater
antelope
aoudad
ape
Arctic fox
Arctic hare
argali
armadillo
ass
aurochs, urus
axis deer
aye-aye
babirusa
baboon
Bactrian camel
badger
Baluchitherium*
bamboo rat
banteng
Barbary ape
barbastelle
barking deer, muntjac
bat
bear
beaver
bettong
bighorn
binturong
bison, buffalo (US)
black bear
blackbuck
blesbok
blue fox
blue whale
boar, wild boar
bobcat
bongo
bontebok
bottlenose
Brontotherium*
brown bear
buffalo
bushbaby
bushbuck
cachalot
cacomistle
camel
camelopard (Arch)
cane rat
Cape buffalo
capuchin monkey
capybara
caracal
carcajou (US), wolver-
   ine, glutton
caribou
cat
catamount (or cata-
   mountain)
cattle
cavy
chamois
cheetah

chevrotain, mouse deer
chickaree, American
   red squirrel
chigetai
chimpanzee
chinchilla
Chinese water deer
chipmunk
chiru
chital
cinnamon bear
civet
clouded leopard
coati (or coatimundi)
colobus
colugo
cony
cottontail
cougar, puma, moun-
   tain lion
cow
coyote
coypu
crabeater seal
creodont*
deer
deer mouse
desert rat
desman
dhole
dik-dik
dingo
dog
dolphin
donkey
Dorcas gazelle
dormouse
douroucouli
drill
dromedary
Dryopithecus*
dugong
duiker
eland
elephant
elephant seal (or sea el-
   ephant)
elk
entellus
eohippus*
ermine
eyra
fallow deer
fennec
ferret
fieldmouse
fisher
flying fox
flying lemur
flying squirrel
fossa
foumart, polecat
fox
fruit bat
galago
gaur
gayal
gazelle
gelada
gemsbok
genet
gerbil
gerenuk
gibbon

giraffe, camelopard
   (Arch)
glutton, wolverine
Glyptodon*
gnu
goat
goat antelope
golden cat
golden mole
gopher
goral
gorilla
grampus
grass monkey
grey squirrel
grey wolf
grison
grizzly bear
groundhog
ground squirrel
guanaco
guenon
guinea pig
gymnure, hairy hedge-
   hog
hamadryas
hamster
harbour seal
hare
hartebeest
harvest mouse
hedgehog
hinny
Hipparion*
hippopotamus, hippo
   (Inf)
hog
honey badger, ratel
honey bear
hooded seal
horse
horseshoe bat
howler monkey
humpback whale
hutia
hyena (or hyaena)
hyrax
ibex
impala
Indian elephant
indri
Irish elk*
jackal
jackrabbit
jaguar
jaguarundi
jerboa
jumping mouse
kangaroo rat
kiang
killer whale
kinkajou
kit fox (or swift fox)
klipspringer
kob
Kodiak bear
kudu
langur
lemming
lemur
leopard
leopard seal
liger
linsang

lion
llama
loris
lynx
macaque
mammoth*
manatee
mandrill
mangabey
mara
margay
markhor
marmoset
marmot
marten
mastodon*
meerkat
Megaloceros*
Megatherium*
mink
mole
mole rat
mona monkey
mongoose
monkey
moon rat
moose
mouflon
mountain beaver
mountain cat
mountain goat (or
   Rocky Mountain goat)
mountain lion, puma,
   cougar
mountain sheep
mouse
mouse deer, chevrotain
mule
mule deer
muntjac, barking deer
musk deer
musk ox
muskrat, musquash
Mylodon*
narwhal
New World monkey
nilgai
noctule
nyala
ocelot
okapi
Old World monkey
olingo
onager
orang-utan
oribi
oryx
otter
otter shrew
ounce, snow leopard
ox
paca
pack (or wood rat)
Pallas's cat
palm civet
pampas cat
panda
pangolin, scaly anteater
panther
patas monkey
peccary
Père David's deer
pig
pika

pilot whale	roe deer	souslik (or suslik)	vervet
pine marten	rorqual	spectacled bear	vicuna
pipistrelle	royal antelope	sperm whale	Virginia (or white-tailed
pocket gopher	sable	spider monkey	deer)
pocket mouse	sable antelope	spiny dormouse	viscacha
polar bear	sabre-toothed tiger (or	springbok	vole
polecat, foumart	cat), Smilodon*	springhaas	walrus
porcupine	saiga	squirrel	wapiti
porpoise	saki	squirrel monkey	warthog
potto	sambar (or sambur)	Stegodon*	waterbuck
pouched rat	scaly anteater, pangolin	steinbok	water buffalo
prairie dog (or prairie	scaly-tailed squirrel	stoat	water rat
marmot)	sea cow	stone marten	water shrew
prairie wolf	sea elephant (or ele-	sun bear	water vole
proboscis monkey	phant seal)	suslik (or souslik)	weasel
Proconsul*	seal	swine	whale
pronghorn (or prong-	sea lion	tahr	white rhinoceros
horn antelope)	sea otter	takin	white whale
puma, cougar, moun-	sei whale	talapoin	wild boar
tain lion	serotine bat	tamandua	wildcat
pygmy hippopotamus	serow	tamarin	wild dog
quagga*	serval	tamarou	wildebeest
rabbit	sheep	tapir	wisent, European bison
raccoon	shrew	tarpan*	wolf
raccoon dog	siamang	tarsier	wolverine, glutton, car-
rat	sifaka	tatouay	cajou (US)
ratel, honey badger	sika	tayra	woodchuck
red deer	silver fox	tenrec	wood (or pack) rat
red fox	sitatunga	tiger	woolly monkey
red squirrel	skunk	tigon	woolly rhinoceros
reedbuck	sloth	timber wolf	woolly spider monkey
reindeer	sloth bear	titanothere*	yak
rhesus monkey	Smilodon, sabre-	titi	zebra
rhinoceros, rhino (Inf)	toothed tiger*	tucotuco	zebu
right whale	snow leopard, ounce	tree shrew	zorilla
roan antelope	snowshoe hare (or	unau	
Rocky Mountain goat	snowshoe rabbit)	urus, aurochs	*extinct mammal
(or mountain goat)	solenodon	vampire bat	

17 **male mammal**, dog [dog, wolf, fox, coyote], buck [reindeer, antelope, hare, rabbit, kangaroo], stag [deer, caribou], hart [deer, red deer], stallion [horse, zebra], colt [horse], bull [buffalo, camel, cattle, elephant, giraffe, moose, elk, ox, rhinoceros, seal, walrus, whale], boar [pig, badger, bear, weasel], ram [sheep, impala], tom [cat, bobcat, cougar], billy goat [goat], roebuck [roe deer], jackass [ass, donkey], jack [ferret]

18 **female mammal**, bitch [dog, wolf], doe [deer, antelope, hare, rabbit, kangaroo], hind [deer, red deer], mare [horse, zebra], filly [horse], cow [buffalo, camel, cattle, elephant, giraffe, moose, elk, ox, rhinoceros, weasel, seal, walrus, whale], heifer [cattle], sow [pig, badger, bear], gilt [pig], ewe [sheep, impala], vixen [fox], tigress [tiger], leopardess [leopard], lioness [lion], nanny goat [goat], jenny [ass, donkey], queen [cat], jill [ferret]

▶ *402 Female*

19 **young mammal**, kitten [cat, bobcat, beaver, rabbit, skunk], kit [weasel], pup (or puppy) [dog], whelp [wolf, dog], cub [bear, fox, lion, tiger, leopard, badger], calf [cattle, buffalo, camel, elephant, elk, giraffe, rhinoceros, seal, whale], dogie (US), weaner [any weaned animal], foal [horse, zebra], colt [horse], filly [horse], piglet [pig], lamb [sheep], lambkin [sheep], kid [goat, antelope, roedeer], yeanling [goat, sheep], fawn [deer, caribou, reindeer], leveret [hare], joey [kangaroo]

20 **abode of mammals**, lair, den, covert, form, burrow, earth, sett (or set), lodge, couch, run, drey, sty, pen, pound, cage, corral, stable, stall, hutch

21 **assemblage of mammals**, pack, herd, drove, train, troop, team, flock, school [porpoises], bevy [roedeer], leap, pride [lions]

22 **mammologist**, primatologist, zoologist

23 **mammal hunting**, big-game hunting, foxhunting, staghunting, deerstalking, chase, chivy (or chevy), venery, hare coursing, beagling, otter hunting, pigsticking, boar hunting, bear-baiting, bullfighting, dog-fighting, whaling, trapping, ratting, ferreting, rabbiting, mole-catching

24 **hunter**, big-game hunter, white hunter, foxhunter, deerstalker, trapper, rat-catcher, rodent operative

ADJECTIVES

25 **mammalian**, mammal-like, warm-blooded, homoiothermic, prototherian, monotrematous, metatherian, marsupial, marsupialian (or marsupian), eutherian, placental (or placentate)

26 **insectivorous**, anteating, pholidote, tubulidentate, edentate, toothless

27 **chiropteran**, dermopteran, winged, flying

28 carnivorous, flesh-eating, clawed, unguiculate, canine, doglike, doggy, doggish, puppyish, foxy, foxlike, vulpine, vulpecular, wolflike, wolfish, lupine, bearish, bearlike, ursine, weaselly, musteline, viverrine, feline, catlike, cattish, catty, kittenish, leonine, lion-like, tigerish, tiger-like

29 cetacean, cetaceous, whalelike, pinniped, pinnipedian, seal-like, sirenian

30 rodent-like, rodentian, gnawing, murine, rat-like, rattish, ratty, mouselike, mousy (*or* mousey), squirrel-like, sciurine

31 rabbit-like, rabbity, harelike, lagomorphic, lagomorphous, leporid, leporine

32 pachydermatous, subungulate, proboscidean (*or* proboscidian), elephantine, elephantoid, rhinocerotic

33 ungulate, hoofed, unguligrade, cloven-hoofed, perissodactyl, odd-toed, equine, horselike, horsy (*or* horsey), asinine, mulish, artiodactyl, artiodactylous, even-toed, piglike, piggy, piggish, por-cine, hoggish, swinish, ruminant, cud-chewing, camel-like, camelid, deerlike, cervid, cervine, oxlike, bovid, bovine, cowlike, cowish, bull-like, bullish, taurine, sheeplike, ovine, goatlike, caprine, hircine, cavicorn, hyrax-like, hyracoid

34 primate, primatial, prosimian, anthropoid, simian, simious, pongid, hominid

VERBS

35 give birth, drop, farrow, lamb, foal, calve, cub, pup, whelp, kitten, litter, kindle

36 lactate, milk, nurse, suckle, breast-feed

37 graze, ruminate, chew the cud, browse, grass

78   Birds

NOUNS

1 birds, birdlife, avifauna, Aves, wildfowl, fowl of the air, fowl, birdie (Inf), feathered friend, bird of peace, dove, bird of passage, migratory bird, migrant

2 flightless bird, ratite, ostrich, rhea, cassowary, emu, kiwi, takahe, penguin

Birds

accentor	brambling	cowbird	finch	guinea fowl
adjutant stork	brent goose,	crake	finfoot	gull, seagull,
Aepyornis, ele-	brent, brant	crane	firecrest	mew, sea mew
phant bird*	(US)	creeper (US),	fish hawk, osprey	gyrfalcon
albatross	broadbill	treecreeper	fish owl	hammerhead
American (or	brush turkey	crested tit	flamingo	harlequin duck
bald) eagle	budgerigar,	crocodile bird	flicker	harpy eagle
antbird	budgie (Inf)	crossbill	flowerpecker	harrier
apteryx, kiwi	bulbul	crow	flycatcher	Hawaiian goose
Archaeopteryx*	bullfinch	cuckoo	francolin	hawfinch
Arctic tern	bunting	cuckoo-shrike	friarbird	hawk
auk	burrowing owl	curassow	frigate bird, man-	hawk owl
auklet	bushtit	curlew	of-war (or man-	hedge sparrow,
avadavat (or	bush wren	currawong	o'-war) bird	dunnock
amadavat)	bustard	dabchick	frogmouth	heron
avocet	butcherbird	darter	fulmar	herring gull
babbler	button quail	demoiselle crane	gadwall	Hesperornis*
bald (or Ameri-	buzzard	diamondbird	gallinule	hill mynah
can) eagle	Canada goose	dipper	gannet, solan	hoatzin
Baltimore oriole	canary	diver	goose (Arch)	hobby
barbet	canvasback (or	dodo*	garganey	honeycreeper
barnacle goose	canvasback	dotterel	gnatcatcher	honeyeater
barn owl	duck)	dove	goatsucker (US),	honey guide
bateleur	capercaillie	drongo	nightjar	hooded crow
bearded tit, reed-	caracara	duck	godwit	hoopoe
ling	cardinal (or	dunlin	goldcrest	hoot owl
bearded vulture,	cardinal bird)	dunnock, hedge	golden eagle	hornbill
lammergeier	carrion crow	sparrow	goldeneye	horned owl
bee-eater	cassowary	eagle	golden pheasant	house martin
bird of paradise	catbird	eagle owl	goldfinch	house sparrow
bittern	chaffinch	egret	goose	huia
blackbird	chat	eider (or eider	goosander	hummingbird
blackcap	chickadee	duck)	goshawk	ibis
black grouse	chiffchaff	elephant bird,	grackle	Ichthyornis*
black swan	chipping sparrow	Aepyornis*	grassfinch	ivory-billed wood-
bluebill (US),	chough	emperor penguin	great crested	pecker
scaup	coal tit	emu	grebe	jabiru
bluebird	cockatiel	emu wren	great tit	jacamar
bluetit	cockatoo	erne (or ern), sea	grebe	jacana
boatbill	coly	eagle	greenfinch	jackdaw
bobolink	condor	fairy bluebird	greenshank	jay
bobwhite (or bob-	coot	fairy penguin	greylag goose	junco
white quail)	cormorant	falcon	griffon vulture	jungle fowl
booby	corncrake	fantail	grosbeak	kagu
bowerbird	courser	fieldfare	guillemot	kakapo

kea	mourning dove	puffin	sheathbill	trogon
kestrel	mousebird	pygmy owl	shelduck	tropic bird
killdeer	murre	quail	shoebill	trumpeter
kingbird	Muscovy duck	quelea	shoveler duck	tui
kingfisher	mute swan	quetzal	shrike	turaco (or tou-
kinglet	muttonbird	rail	siskin	raco)
kite	mynah (or	raven	skimmer	turkey
kittiwake	myna), mynah	razorbill	skua	turkey buzzard
kiwi, apteryx	(or myna) bird	red grouse	skylark	(or turkey vul-
knot	night hawk	redhead	smew	ture)
kookaburra	night heron	redpoll	snakebird	turnstone
lammergeier,	nightingale	redshank	snipe	turtledove
bearded vulture	nightjar, goat-	redstart	snow bunting (or	tyrant flycatcher
lanner falcon	sucker (US)	redwing	snowbird)	umbrella bird
lapwing, peewit	noddy	reedbird	snow goose	vulture
lark	nutcracker	reedling,	snowy owl	wagtail
laughing jackass	nuthatch	bearded tit	solan or solan	wallcreeper
laughing owl	oilbird	reed warbler	goose (Arch),	warbler
linnet	oriole	rhea	gannet	waxbill
little owl	ortolan	ricebird	song thrush,	waxwing
long-tailed tit	osprey, fish hawk	riflebird	mavis (Dial)	weaverbird (or
lory	ostrich	rifleman	sparrow	weaver)
lovebird	ouzel	ringdove	sparrowhawk	weaverfinch
lyrebird	ovenbird	ring-necked	spoonbill	wheatear
macaw	owl	pheasant	standardwing	whidah (or
magpie	owlet frogmouth	ring ouzel	starling	whydah)
mallard	oxpecker	roadrunner	stilt	whimbrel
mallee fowl	oystercatcher	robin	stonechat	whinchat
manakin	parakeet	rock dove	stone curlew	whipbird
mandarin duck	parrot	roller	stork	whippoorwill
mannikin	partridge	rook	storm (or stormy)	whistler
man-of-war (or	passenger pi-	rosella	petrel, Mother	white-eye
man-o'-war)	geon*	ruddy duck	Carey's chicken	whitethroat
bird, frigate	peacock	ruff	sunbird	whooping crane
bird	peafowl	ruffed grouse	sun bittern	whydah (or
marabou (or	peewee (or	sacred ibis	swallow	whidah)
marabou stork)	pewee)	saddleback	swan	wigeon (or wid-
marsh harrier	peewit, lapwing	sage grouse	swiftlet	geon)
martin	pelican	sanderling	tailorbird	willet
mavis (Dial),	penguin	sandgrouse	takahe	willow warbler
song thrush	peregrine falcon	sand martin	tanager	woodchat
meadowlark	petrel	sandpiper	tawny owl	woodcock
megapode	pewee (or pee-	sapsucker	teal	woodcreeper
merganser	wee)	scaup, bluebill	tern	wood duck
merlin	phalarope	(US)	thickhead	woodpecker
mew, mew gull,	pheasant	scops owl	thornbill	wood pigeon
sea mew	Philippine eagle	scrub bird	thrasher	wren
minivet	phoebe	screamer	thrush	wren babbler
mistle (or missel)	pigeon	screech owl	tinamou	wrybill
thrush	pigeon hawk	scrub bird	tit, titmouse	wryneck thers
moa*	pintail	sea eagle, erne	titlark, pipit	yellowhammer
mockingbird	pipit, titlark	(or ern)	toucan	yellowlegs
moorhen	plains-wanderer	seagull, gull, sea	touraco (or tu-	zebra finch
Mother Carey's	plover	mew	raco)	
chicken, storm	pochard	secretary bird	towhee	*extinct or fossil
(or stormy) pet-	pratincole	seriema	tragopan	bird
rel	prion	serin	tree creeper,	
motmot	ptarmigan	shag	creeper (US)	
		shearwater		

3 **water bird**, seabird, oceanic bird, gull, seagull, shag, tern, skua, puffin, auk, albatross, petrel, fulmar, shearwater, frigate bird, gannet, cormorant, fishing bird, pelican, kingfisher, diving bird, diver, loon, grebe, wading bird, wader, marsh bird, mud hen, shore bird, plover, sandpiper, lapwing, curlew, snipe, avocet, oystercatcher, crane, rail, crake, coot, heron, bittern, stork, flamingo, spoonbill, ibis, waterfowl, duck, dabbling duck, diving duck, perching duck, whistling duck, sea duck, swan, goose

4 **table bird**, game bird, game fowl, pheasant, partridge, grouse, quail, snipe, woodcock, guinea fowl, pigeon, turkey, domestic fowl
▶ *68 Agriculture, 45 Cookery*

5 **bird of prey**, raptor, falcon, hawk, goshawk, eagle, osprey, kestrel, harrier, kite, vulture, condor, buzzard, owl, barn owl, screech owl, hoot owl, horned owl

6 **songbird**, passerine (bird), perching bird, lark, wren, warbler, flycatcher, thrush, tit, shrike, wagtail, pipit, bunting, finch, Darwin's (*or* Galapagos) finches, weaverbird, sparrow, starling, oriole, crow, magpie, jackdaw, rook, raven, nightingale

7 **cagebird**, canary, songster, talking bird, parrot, parakeet, budgerigar, budgie (Inf), mynah bird, cockatoo

8 **extinct bird**, fossil bird, Archaeopteryx, Aepyornis, elephant bird, moa, dodo, great auk, passenger pigeon

9 **fabulous bird**, mythological bird, phoenix, roc, garuda, senmurv, simurg, cockatrice, griffin (or griffon or gryphon), harpy, bird god, Horus, heraldic bird, martlet

10 **male bird**, cock, cockerel, chanticleer, rooster, tom turkey, turkey cock, gobbler (Inf), bubby-jock (Scot), peacock, guinea cock, drake, gander, cob, blackcock, heathcock, cock-sparrow, cock-robin

11 **female bird**, hen, peahen, pen, greyhen, heath hen, goose, duck

12 **young bird**, chick, poult, pullet, eaglet, owlet, cygnet, duckling, gosling, eyas, squab, nestling, fledgling, clutch, hatch, brood

13 **assemblage of birds**, flock, flight, gaggle [geese], skein [geese], covey [grouse, partridge], covert [coots], wing, charm, exaltation [larks], murder [crows]

14 **nest**, perch, roost, eyrie, aerie (US), rookery, covert, mew, lek, nest site, nestbox, bird box, birdhouse (US), hatchery, nest building, nidification

15 **eggs**, hatch, clutch, egg, shell, eggshell, white, yolk, vitelline membrane, chalaza

16 **avian anatomy**, bill, beak, feathers, wings, talons, syrinx, carina, keel, wishbone, crop, gizzard, webbed feet

17 **plumage**, feathers, ruff, crest, plume, frill, feather, contour feather, quill, vane, rachis, barbule, barbicel, aftershaft, down feathers, plumulae, down, eiderdown, swan's-down, flight feather, wing feather, primary, secondary, tail feather, rectrix (pl. rectrices), remex (pl. remiges), alula, bastard wing, filoplume, covert, tectrix (pl. tectrices), pteryla, apterium

18 **birdsong**, bird call, dawn chorus, chirp, chirrup, cheep, peep, tweet, twitter, warble, hoot, cock-a-doodle-doo

▶ *432 Animal Cry*

19 **ornithology**, birdwatching, ringing, bird-banding (US), aviculture, aviary, swannery, bird sanctuary, bird reserve, birdhouse, birdcage, dovecote, pigeon loft, columbarium, nestbox, birdbox, hatchery

20 **bird sport**, hawking, falconry, fowling, wildfowling, duck shoot, cock-fighting, bird's-nesting

21 **ornithologist**, aviculturist, fancier, pigeon fancier, ringer, birdwatcher, birder (Inf), twitcher (Inf)

22 **hunter**, hawker, falconer, wildfowler

ADJECTIVES

23 **avian**, birdlike, birdy, flightless, ratite, ostrich-like, struthious, struthioniform, gooselike, goosy, anserine (or anserous), anseriform fowl-like, gallinaceous, galliform, rasorial, dovelike, pigeon-like, columbine, columbiform, parrot-like, psittacine, psittaciform, cuckoo-like, cuculiform, raptorial, predatory, hawkish, aquiline, vulturine, owl-like, owlish, strigiform, swallow-like, hirundine, perching, passerine, passeriform, singing, oscine, finchlike, fringilline (or fringillid), thrushlike, turdine, crowlike, corvine

24 **newly hatched**, unfledged, altricial, newly fledged, precocial, nidicolous, nidifugous

25 **ornithological**, avicultural

VERBS

26 **nest**, nidify, brood, hatch, perch, peck, preen

▶ *245 Reproduction*

27 **fly**, take wing, wing, soar, hover

▶ *70 Transport, 324 Motion, 359 Ascent*

28 **sing**, warble, chirp, chirrup, cheep, peep, tweet, twitter, hoot

79 Reptiles and Amphibians

NOUNS

1 **reptile**, reptilian, cold-blooded animal, poikilotherm, Reptilia, Squamata (lizards and snakes), Rhynocephalia (tuatara), Crocodilia (crocodilians)

2 **lizard**, saurian, lacertilian (or lacertian), Sauria, Lacertilia, iguana, chameleon, gecko, skink, monitor, glass snake, Komodo dragon, basilisk, legless lizard, slow worm, lizard-like reptile, rhynocephalian, tuatara

3 **snake**, serpent, ophidian, Serpentes, Ophidia, nonvenomous snake, constrictor, boa, python, anaconda, venomous snake, viper, asp, cobra, mamba, rattlesnake, rattler (US inf), legendary serpent, basilisk, cockatrice

4 **chelonian**, chelonid, tortoise, turtle, terrapin

5 **crocodilian**, crocodile, alligator, cayman, croc (Inf), gator (US inf)

6 **extinct reptile**, fossil reptile, giant reptile, terrestrial reptile, dinosaur, ornithischian, ornithopod, saurischian, sauropod, marine reptile, ichthyopterygian, ichthyosaur, sauropterygian, plesiosaur, nothosaur, mosasaur, flying reptile, pterosaur, mammal-like reptile, therapsid

7 **amphibian**, batrachian, Amphibia, limbless amphibian, caecilian, apodan, Apoda (or Gymnophiona), tailed amphibian, urodele, caudate, Urodela or Caudata (salamanders, newts), tailless amphibian, salientian, anuran, Salienta or Anura (frogs, toads), paddock (Dial)

8 **young amphibian**, frogspawn, tadpole, polliwog, froglet, toadlet, metamorphosis, immature amphibian, neotenous amphibian, axolotl, neoteny, paedogenesis

9 **herpetology**, ophiology, reptile house, reptilarium, reptiliary

10 herpetologist, ophiologist, snake charmer

ADJECTIVES

11 reptilian, reptilelike, reptiliform, reptiloid, apodal (*or* apodous), cold-blooded, poikilothermic, creeping, slithering, reptant, lizardlike, saurian, lacertilian, snakelike, ophidian, turtlelike, chelonian, crocodilian, scaly, squamous

12 snakelike, snaky, serpentine, serpentiform, sinuous, twisting, ophidian, ophiomorphic, colubrine, colubriform, anguine, viper-like, viperish, viperous (*or* viperine), hissing

13 amphibian, batrachian, apodan, salamandrian, newtlike, caudate, neotenous, froglike, froggy, toadlike, toadish, anuran, salientian

14 herpetological, herpetology, ophiological

VERBS

15 live as a reptile, creep, crawl, glide, twist, hiss
▶ *335 Deviation, 429 Hissing Sound*

16 live as an amphibian, creep, crawl, hop, croak, grunt
▶ *328 Slowness, 432 Animal Cry, 430 Harsh Sound*

Reptiles

adder	diamondback (rattle-	krait	sidewinder
agama	snake or terrapin)	leatherback (or leather-	skink
alligator	fer-de-lance	back turtle)	slow-worm
amphisbaena	flying lizard (or flying	lizard	smooth snake
anaconda	dragon)	loggerhead (or logger-	snake
anole	flying snake	head turtle)	snake-necked turtle,
asp	frilled lizard	mamba	matamata
basilisk	gaboon viper	mangrove snake	snapping turtle
bearded lizard	Galápagos giant tortoise	matamata, snake-	soft-shelled turtle
black snake	garter snake	necked turtle	sphenodon, tuatara
blind snake	gavial (or gharial)	milk snake	taipan
blindworm	gecko	moccasin, water mocca-	terrapin
boa	Gila monster	sin, cottonmouth	tokay
boa constrictor	glass snake	moloch	tortoise
boomslang	grass snake	monitor lizard	tree snake
box turtle	green turtle	mugger	tuatara, sphenodon
bull snake	hamadryad, king cobra	pit viper	turtle
bushmaster	harlequin snake	pond turtle	vine snake
cayman	hawksbill turtle	puff adder	viper
chameleon	hognose snake	python	wart snake
chuckwalla	horned toad (or horned	racer	water moccasin, cotton-
cobra	lizard)	rat snake	mouth
constrictor	horned viper	rattlesnake, rattler (US	water snake
copperhead	iguana	inf)	whip snake
coral snake	jacaré	ringhals	worm lizard
cottonmouth, water	king cobra, hamadryad	Russell's viper	
moccasin	king snake	sand lizard	
crocodile	Komodo dragon	sea snake	

Fossil Reptiles

allosaur, Allosaurus	dicynodon(t), Dicynodon	Mesosaurus	pterosaur (or ptero-
ankylosaur, Ankylo-	Dimetrodon	mosasaur, Mosasaurus	dactyl)
saurus	Diplodocus	nothosaur, Nothosaurus	stegodon(t), Stegodon
apatosaur, Apatosaurus	elasmosaur	Ornitholestes	stegosaur, Stegosaurus
atlantosaur, Atlanto-	hadrosaur, Hadrosaurus	pelycosaur	titanosaur
saurus	ichthyosaur,	phytosaur	Triceratops
brachiosaur, Brachio-	Ichthyosaurus	plesiosaur, Plesiosaurus	tyrannosaur, Tyranno-
saurus	iguanodon(t), Iguano-	pliosaur, Pliosaurus	saurus
brontosaur, Brontosau-	don	Protoceratops	
rus	megalosaur,	pteranodon(t), Pterano-	
cotylosaur	Megalosaurus	don	

Amphibians

arrow-poison frog	fire salamander	natterjack (or natterjack	Surinam toad, pipa
axolotl	frog	toad)	toad
bullfrog	goliath frog	newt, eft (Dial)	tree frog
caecilian	hairy frog	olm	Xenopus, clawed frog
clawed frog, Xenopus	hellbender	pipa, Surinam toad	
congo eel (or congo	labyrinthodont*	salamander	*extinct amphibian
snake)	midwife toad	siren	
eft	mudpuppy	spadefoot toad	

Fishes

albacore
alewife
amberjack
anchovy
anemone fish
angelfish
anglerfish
archer fish
barbel
barracuda
barramunda
basking shark
bass
batfish
beluga
bichir
black bass
blackfish
bleak
blenny
blindfish
blowfish, puffer
bluefish
blue shark
Bombay duck
bonito
bonefish
bowfin
boxfish, trunkfish
bream
brill
brisling
brook trout
brotulid
brown trout
buffalo fish
bullhead
burbot
butterfish
butterfly fish
candlefish
capelin
carp
catfish
cave fish
char
characin
chimera
Chinook salmon
chub
cichlid
cisco
climbing perch
clingfish
cobia
cod (or codfish)
coelacanth, Lati-
  meria
conger eel
cornetfish

crappie
croaker
cutlass fish
dab
dace
damselfish
danio
darter
dealfish
devil ray (or
  fish), manta ray
dogfish
Dolly Varden
  (trout)
dorado
dory
dragonet
dragonfish
drumfish
eel
eelpout
electric eel
electric ray
fighting fish
filefish
flatfish
flathead
flounder
fluke
flying fish
flying gurnard
four-eyed fish
frogfish
gar (or garfish or
  garpike)
ghost shark
glassfish
globefish
goblin shark
goby
goldfish
goosefish
gourami
grayling
Greenland shark
grenadier
grey mullet
grouper
grunion
grunt
gudgeon
guitar fish
gunnel
guppy
gurnard
haddock
hagfish
hake
halfbeak
halibut

hammerhead
  shark
hatchetfish
herring
hippocampus,
  sea horse
hogfish
horse mackerel
icefish
ide
jewfish
John Dory
killifish
kingfish
labyrinth fish
lake trout
lamprey
lancet fish
lantern fish
Latimeria, coela-
  canth
lemon sole
ling
lizard fish
loach
lumpsucker
lungfish
mackerel
mackerel shark,
  porbeagle
mako shark
man-eating shark
manta ray, devil
  ray (or fish)
marlin
menhaden
midshipman
miller's thumb
minnow
molly
monkfish
moonfish
Moorish idol
moray eel
mudfish
mudskipper
mullet
Murray cod
muskellunge
needlefish
nurse shark
oarfish
opah
orfe
paddlefish
parrot fish
pearlfish
perch
pickerel
pike

pikeperch
pilchard
pilot fish
pink salmon
pipefish
piranha
plaice
pollack
pompano
porbeagle, mack-
  erel shark
porcupine fish
porgy
powan
puffer, blowfish
rabbitfish
rainbow trout
ratfish
ray
redfin
redfish
red mullet
red (or sockeye)
  salmon
remora, sucker-
  fish
requiem shark
ribbonfish
roach
rock bass
rudd
sailfish
saithe
salmon
salmon trout
sardine
saury
sawfish
scorpion fish
sculpin
scup
sea bass
sea bream
sea horse, hippo-
  campus
sea perch
sea robin
sea trout
sergeant fish
shad
shark
shovelhead
shovelnose
silverside
skate
skipjack (or skip-
  jack tuna)
smelt
snapper
snook

sockeye (or red
  salmon)
sole
sprat
stargazer
steelhead (or
  steelhead trout)
stickleback
stingray
stone bass
stonefish
sturgeon
sucker
suckerfish,
  remora
sunfish
surgeonfish
swamp eel
swordfish
swordtail
tarpon
tautog
tench
tetra
thornback (or
  thornback ray)
threadfin
thresher (or
  thresher shark)
tigerfish
tiger shark
toadfish
tooth carp
tope
top minnow
torpedo fish
triggerfish
trout
trunkfish, boxfish
tuna, tunny
turbot
wahoo
walleye (or wall-
  eyed pike)
weakfish
weever
wels
whale shark
whitebait
whitefish
white shark
whiting
wolf fish
wrasse
wreckfish
yellowfin tuna
yellowtail
zebra fish

80   Fishes

NOUNS

1   **fishes**, fish, Pisces, sea fish(es), saltwater fish(es), marine fish(es), shoal, school, fresh-water fish(es)

2   **fish**, jawless fish, cyclostome, cartilaginous fish, Chondrichthyes, elasmobranch, selachian, holocephalan, bony fish, lobe-finned fish, crossopterygian, dipnoan, ray-finned fish, teleost fish, flying fish, mouthbrooder, flatfish, food fish, game fish, aquarium fish, tropical fish

3   **young fish**, fry, elver, alevin, fingerling, parr, smolt, grilse

4   **fossil fish**, placoderm, arthrodire, ostracoderm, Pteraspis, crossopterygian, Osteolepis, living fossil, coelacanth

5 **fish anatomy**, fin, pectoral fin, pelvic fin, dorsal fin, anal fin, caudal fin, tail fin, scale, placoid scale, ganoid scale, cosmoid scale, gill, gill cover, operculum, gill slit, spiracle, swim bladder, air bladder, lateral line, roe, soft roe, hard roe

6 **study of fish**, ichthyology, fish breeding, fish farm, aquarium, fish pond, fishtank, fishbowl

7 **fishing**, piscatology, fishability, angling, game fishing, coarse fishing, fly fishing, sea fishing, big-game fishing, deep-sea fishing, shark fishing, whaling, fish farming, pisciculture, fishery, fishing bank, fishing ground, piscary, fishing fleet, trawler, shrimper, fishfinder, fish-hold, fishing line, fish line (US), fishnet, trawl, drift net, seine, catch, tonnara, eel basket, fishgig, fishtrap, fish weir, fish ladder, fish way (US), gill net, shark net, fish-hook
▶ *20 Angling*

8 **food fish**, cod, haddock, mackerel, herring, whitebait, sprat, sardine, flatfish, plaice, sole, halibut, turbot, game fish, salmon, trout, wet fish, pan fish, preserved fish, smoked fish, kipper, bloater, brisling, smoked haddock, finnan haddock (*or* haddie), stockfish, jellied eel, rollmop

9 **fish product**, fish roe, herring roe, caviar, fish-liver oil, cod-liver oil, fishmeal, fish glue, isinglass
▶ *45 Cookery, 20 Angling*

10 **fisher**, angler, whaler, fisherman, trawlerman, piscator, fisherfolk, fish farmer, pisciculturalist, fish seller, fishmonger, fishman, fishwife

11 **fishing animal**, otter, sea otter, polar bear, fishing cat, fish eagle (*or* hawk), osprey, kingfisher

12 **ichthyologist**, aquarist, fish lover, ichthyophile

ADJECTIVES
13 **fishlike**, fishy, cold-blooded, poikilothermic, piscine, pisciform, piscatorial (*or* piscatory), ichthyic, ichthyoid(al), ichthyomorphic, sharklike, sharkish, selachian, herring-like, clu-

peoid, codlike, gadoid, perchlike, percoid, carplike, cyprinoid, eel-like, anguilliform

14 **ichthyological**, piscicultural, piscatorial (*or* piscatory), scaly, squamous

VERBS
15 **fish**, angle, fly-fish, trawl, net, shrimp, seine
▶ *20 Angling, 590 Pursuit*

81 Invertebrates

NOUNS
1 **invertebrate**, lower animal, invertebrate chordate, protochordate, many-celled invertebrate, metazoan, Metazoa, nonchordate invertebrate, mesozoan, parazoan, single-celled invertebrate, protozoan, protist

2 **protochordate**, hemichordate, Hemichordata, acorn worm, chordate, Chordata, urochordate, Urochordata, tunicate, ascidian, sea squirt, salp, cephalochordate, Cephalochordata (*or* Acrania), lancelet, amphioxus, craniate, Craniata (vertebrates)
▶ *80 Fishes, 79 Reptiles and Amphibians, 78 Birds, 77 Mammals*

3 **echinoderm**, Echinodermata, crinoid, sea lily, feather star, asteroid (*or* asteroidean), starfish, crown-of-thorns, sea star, ophiuroid, brittle star, echinoid, sea urchin, heart urchin, sand dollar, sea biscuit, holothurian, sea cucumber, trepang, bêche-de-mer

4 **arthropod**, Arthropoda, extinct arthropod, trilobite, eurypterid, living fossil, horseshoe (*or* king) crab, limulus, arachnid, Arachnida (scorpions, spiders, ticks, mites, etc.), insect, Insecta, pycnogonid, Pycnogonida (sea spiders), crustacean, Crustacea, branchiopod, fairy shrimp, brine shrimp, tadpole shrimp, water flea, daphnia, ostracod, mussel shrimp, seed shrimp, copepod, cyclops, branchiuran, fish louse, cirripede, barnacle, acorn barnacle, stalked barnacle, goose barnacle, malacostracan, amphipod, mantis shrimp, Tasmanian shrimp, opossum shrimp, sand hopper (*or* beach hopper *or* sand flea *or* beach flea), skeleton shrimp, whale louse, isopod, water louse, woodlouse, pill bug, sow bug (US), slater (Aus),

Molluscs

abalone	cowrie	mussel	sea butterfly	top shell
ammonite*	cuttlefish	nautilus	sea hare	triton shell
argonaut	elephant's-tusk	nudibranch	sea lemon	tusk shell
ark shell	shell	octopus	sea slug	venus clam
auger shell	geoduck	olive shell	shipworm	volute
belemnite*	giant clam	oyster	slipper shell	wentletrap
bleeding tooth	hard-shell (or	paper nautilus	slit shell	whelk
chiton, coat-of-	hard-shell	pearly nautilus	slug	winkle (or peri-
mail shell	clam), quahog	periwinkle (or	snail	winkle)
clam	helmet shell	winkle)	soft-shell clam	worm shell
coat-of-mail	keyhole limpet	piddock	spider conch	
shell, chiton	limpet	quahog, hard-	squid	*extinct mollusc
cockle	mitre shell	shell clam	teredo	
conch	money cowrie	razor shell	tiger cowrie	
cone shell	murex	scallop	tooth shell	

gribble, shrimp, prawn, crab, hermit crab, robber (*or* coconut) crab, fiddler crab, pea crab, spider crab, land crab, lobster, crayfish, spiny lobster, crawfish (US), shellfish, seafood, myriapod, Myriapoda, diplopod, Diplopoda (millipedes), thousand-leggers (Inf), chilopod, Chilopoda (centipedes), pauropod, symphylan, arthropod-like invertebrate, tardigrade, water bear, Tardigrada, pentastomid, Pentastomida, onychophoran, Onychophora
▶ *82 Insects and Arachnids, 45 Cookery*

5 **mollusc**, Mollusca, amphineuran, Amphineura (chitons), gastropod (*or* gasteropod), Gastropoda (limpets, snails, slugs, etc.), bivalve, lamellibranch, Bivalvia *or* Lamellibranchia (shellfish, clams, mussels, scallops, oysters, etc.), scaphopod, Scaphopoda (tusk shells), cephalopod, Cephalopoda (cuttlefish, squids, octopods, octopuses, etc.), mollusclike invertebrate, lampshell, brachiopod, Brachiopoda
▶ *45 Cookery*

6 **worm**, parasitic worm, helminth, flatworm, platyhelminth, Platyhelminthes, free-living flatworm, planarian, turbellarian, Turbellaria, parasitic flatworm, fluke, liver fluke, blood fluke, trematode, Trematoda, tapeworm, cestode, Cestoda, ribbon worm, nemertean (*or* nemertine), Nemertea (*or* Nemertina), aschelminth, roundworm, nematode, Nematoda, horsehair worm, nematomorph, Nematomorpha, wheel animacule (*or* worm), rotifer (*or* rotiferan), Rotifera, kinorhynch, Kinorhyncha, gastrotrich, Gastrotricha, spiny-headed worm, acanthocephalan, Acanthocephala, segmented worm, annelid worm, Annelida, bristle worm, polychaete, Polychaeta, earthworm, oligochaete, Oligochaeta, leech, medicinal leech, hirudinean, Hirudinea, wormlike invertebrate, peanut worm, sipunculid, Sipunculida, beard worm, pogonophoran, Pogonophora, peripatus, phoronid, Phoronida, onychophoran, Onychophora, arrow worm, chaetognath, Chaetognatha, acorn worm, hemichordate, insect, glow-worm, bookworm, insect larva, woodworm, wireworm, caterpillar, silkworm
▶ *82 Insects and Arachnids*

7 **coelenterate**, cnidarian, Cnidaria, polyp, medusa, hydrozoan, Hydrozoa (sea fir, *Hydra*, Portuguese man-of-war, etc.), scyphozoan, Scyphozoa (jellyfish, box jellyfish, sea wasp, etc.), anthozoan, Anthozoa (coral, organ-pipe coral, dead-men's fingers, sea fan, sea pen, sea pansy, sea anemone, etc.), ctenophore (*or* ctenophoran), comb jelly, Ctenophora (sea gooseberry, Venus's girdle, etc.), polypoid invertebrate, bryozoan, Bryozoa, ectoproct, Ectoprocta (sea mats, moss animals), entoproct, Entoprocta

8 **sponge**, bath sponge, Venus's flower basket, poriferan, Porifera, parazoan, Parazoa

9 **protozoan** (*or* **protozoon**), Protozoa, flagellate protozoan, flagellate, mastigophoran, Mastigophora (*Euglena, Chlamydomonas, Volvox,* dinoflagellate, trypanosome, trichomonad, etc.), amoeboid protozoan, Sarcodina (amoeba, foraminiferan, radiolarian, heliozoan), spore-producing protozoan, sporozoan, Sporozoa (malaria parasite, *Plasmodium,* etc.), ciliate protozoan, ciliate, Ciliata (*Paramecium,* etc.)

10 **parasite**, fish louse, whale louse, sand hopper, helminth, fluke, blood fluke, liver fluke, tapeworm, pinworm, guinea worm, hookworm, protozoan, entamoeba, trypanosome, piroplasm, leishmania, giardia, toxoplasma, bloodsucker, leech

11 **helminthic disease**, fascioliasis, schistosomiasis, hookworm disease, ascariasis, filariasis, dirofilariasis, onchocerciasis, river blindness, toxocariasis
▶ *624 Ill Health*

12 **protozoal disease**, amoebiasis, amoebic dysentery, sleeping sickness, trypanosomiasis, leishmaniasis, trichomoniasis, giardiasis, coccidiosis, malaria, babesiosis, piroplasmosis, theileriosis, toxoplasmosis
▶ *624 Ill Health*

13 **invertebrate larva**, tornaria, nauplius, trochophore, veliger, microfilaria, redia, cercaria, miracidium, hydatid, cysticercus, caenurus, onchosphere, hexacanth
▶ *82 Insects and Arachnids*

14 **invertebrate zoology**, arachnology, entomology, malacology, conchology, helminthology, protozoology, parasitology
▶ *82 Insects and Arachnids*

15 **invertebrate zoologist**, arachnologist, en-

Worms

annelid worm	eelworm	hookworm	parchment worm	scaleworm
arrow worm	eyeworm	horsehair worm	peacock worm	schistosome
Ascaris	fanworm	kidney worm	peanut worm	sea mouse
bamboo worm	Fasciola	leech	pinworm	serpulid
beard worm	feather duster	liver fluke	planarian	sipunculid
blood fluke	filaria	lugworm	platyhelminth	tapeworm
bootlace worm	flatworm	lungworm	pogonophoran	threadworm
bristle worm	fluke	nematode	proboscis worm	Trematoda
Cestoda	guinea worm	Nemertina	ragworm	tubifex
cone worm	hairworm	paddleworm	ribbonworm	vinegar eel
earthworm	heartworm	palolo worm	roundworm	whipworm

tomologist, malacologist, conchologist, helminthologist, protozoologist, parasitologist

▶ *82 Insects and Arachnids*

ADJECTIVES

16 **invertebrate**, protochordate, hemichordate, urochordate, cephalochordate, acraniate, coelomate, pseudocoelomate, acoelomate, metazoan, mesozoan, protozoan

17 **echinodermal**, echinodermatous, crinoidal, asteroid (*or* asteroidal), ophiuroid, echinoid, holothurian

18 **arthropodous**, arthropodial, jointed, chelicerate, arachnidan, arachnoid, spider-like, spidery, insect-like, insectile, crustacean, crustaceous, shrimplike, crablike, arachnological, entomological

▶ *82 Insects and Arachnids*

19 **molluscan**, gastropodan, gastropodous, snail-like, univalve(d), sluglike, bivalve(d), bivalvular, clamlike, oyster-like, cephalopodic, cephalopodous, cephalopodan, octopod, malcological, conchological

20 **wormlike**, vermicular, vermiform, helminthic, helminthoid, platyhelminthic, fluky, cestoid, annelid, annelidan, segmented, polychaetous, oligochaetous, lumbricoid, hirudinean, leechlike, helminthological

21 **coelenterate**, hydroid, polypoid, medusoid, hydrozoan, scyphozoan, anthrozoan, coralline, coralloid, ctenophoran

22 **spongelike**, poriferan, poriferous, spongy, fibrous, calcareous

23 **protozoan**, protozoic, amoebic, amoeboid, flagellate, ciliate, sporozoan, protozoological

Orders of Insects

Thysanura (bristletails), thysanuran	Hemiptera (bugs), hemipteran (or hemipteron)
Diplura (bristletails), dipluran	Thysanoptera (thrips), thysanopteran
Collembola (springtails), collembolan	
Protura, proturan	Grylloblatodea, grylloblatodean
Ephemeroptera (mayflies), ephemerid (or ephemeropteran)	Zoraptera, zorapteran
	Neuroptera (lacewings), neuropteran (or neuropteron)
Odonata (dragonflies)	
Plecoptera (stoneflies), plecopteran	Megaloptera (alderflies), megalopteran
Orthoptera (grasshoppers), orthopteran (or orthopteron)	Mecoptera (scorpion flies), mecopteran
Phasmida (stick insects), phasmid	Lepidoptera (butterflies and moths), lepidopteran (or lepidopteron)
Dermaptera (earwigs), dermapteran	
Embioptera (footspinners or webspinners), embiopteran	Trichoptera (caddis flies), trichopteran
	Diptera (flies), dipteran (or dipteron)
Dictyoptera (cockroaches and mantids), dictyopteran	Siphonaptera (fleas), siphonapteran
Isoptera (termites), isopteran	Hymenoptera (ants, bees, and wasps), hymenopteran (or hymenopteron)
Psocoptera (book lice), psocopteran	
Mallophaga (biting lice), mallophagan	Coleoptera (beetles), coleopteran (or coleopteron)
Anoplura (sucking lice), anopluran	Strepsiptera (stylops), strepsipteran

82 Insects and Arachnids

NOUNS

1 **insect**, Insecta, Hexapoda, winged insect, fly, gnat, midge, mosquito, cranefly, dragonfly, caddis fly, butterfly, moth, bee, wasp, ant, beetle, cockroach, earwig, stick insect, mantis, hopper, grasshopper, locust, leaf hopper, creepy-crawly (Inf), roach (US inf), skeeter (US inf), mozzy (Aus inf), daddy longlegs (Inf)

2 **arachnid**, Arachnida, scorpion, pseudoscorpion, false scorpion, spider, black widow, tarantula, phalangid, opilionid, harvestman, acarid (*or* acardian), mite, tick, hard tick, soft tick

3 **pest**, parasite, vermin, cockroach, weevil, boll weevil, grain weevil, borer, woodborer, corn borer, deathwatch beetle, woodworm, bookworm, wireworm, cutworm, screwworm, chafer, cockchafer, corn chafer, scale insect, scale, locust, seventeen-year locust, bug, plant bug, aphid, greenfly, blackfly, louse, head louse, nit, body louse, crab louse, crab, flea, rat flea, dog flea, cat flea, human flea, sand flea, chigoe, chigger, red bug (US), jigger, mite, harvest

mite, itch mite, bloodsucker, bedbug, tick, sheep tick, dog tick, wood tick, mosquito, midge, cootie (US sl)

4 **social insect**, bee, honeybee, wasp, yellow jacket (US), ant, emmet (Dial), pismire (Dial), red ant, army ant, white ant, termite, caste, reproductive, queen, queen bee, drone, king (termite), worker, soldier, soldier ant, hive, beehive, apiary, beeswax, honey, wasps' nest, vespiary, anthill, antheap, termite colony, termitarium, swarm, army, plague

▶ *161 Assembly*

5 **larva**, grub, maggot, nest, nidus, spiderling, caterpillar, woolly bear, looper, army worm, bagworm, silkworm, cutworm, antlion, doodlebug (US), leatherjacket, caddis worm, bloodworm, glow-worm, mealworm, wireworm, screwworm, nymph, pupa, chrysalis, cocoon, metamorphosis, imago

6 **spinner**, spider, silkworm, silk, silk gland, spinneret, cocoon, web, spider's web, cobweb

7 **study**, entomology, beekeeping, sericulture, arachnology, acarology

8 **entomologist**, lepidopterist, bug hunter, beekeeper, apiarist, sericulturalist

9 **arachnologist**, acarologist

Insects

aedes (mosquito)
alderfly
Amazon ant
ambrosia beetle
anopheles (mosquito)
ant
antlion
aphid
army ant
army worm
assassin bug
backswimmer
bagworm moth
bark beetle
bedbug
bee
bee fly
beetle
black beetle
black fly, buffalo gnat
blackfly
blister beetle
bloodworm
blowfly, bluebottle
body louse, cootie (US sl)
boll weevil
bombardier beetle
booklouse
bookworm
borer
botfly
brimstone butterfly
bristletail
buffalo gnat, black fly
bug
bumblebee
burying (or sexton) beetle
bush cricket
cabbage root fly
cabbage white butterfly
Cactoblastis (moth)
cactus moth
caddis fly
Camberwell beauty
capsid
carpenter bee
carpet beetle
cat flea

cecropia moth
chafer
chigoe, chigger, jigger, sand flea
chinch bug
cicada
cinnabar moth
clearwing moth
click beetle
clothes moth
cockchafer
cockroach, roach (US inf)
codling moth
Colorado potato beetle
cootie (US sl), body louse
corn borer
corn chafer
cotton stainer
crab (louse)
cranefly, daddy longlegs (Inf)
cricket
croton bug
cuckoo-spit insect
culex (mosquito)
cutworm
daddy longlegs (Inf), cranefly
damselfly
darkling beetle
death's-head moth
deathwatch beetle
deer fly
devil's coach horse
digger wasp
diving beetle
dobsonfly
dog flea
dor beetle
dragonfly
driver ant
drosophila (fruit fly)
dung beetle
earwig
elm bark beetle
emperor moth
fire ant
firebrat
firefly
flea

flea beetle
fly
foot-spinner (or webspinner)
fritillary
froghopper
fruit fly
gad fly
gall midge
gall wasp
geometrid moth
giant water bug
glow worm
goat moth
goliath beetle
grain weevil
grasshopper
greenbottle (fly)
greenfly
ground beetle
ground bug
gypsy moth
hairstreak
harlequin bug
hawk moth
head louse
hercules beetle
hercules moth
honey ant
honeybee
hornet
horntail
horse fly
housefly
hoverfly
ichneumon
io moth
jigger, sand flea
June beetle (or bug)
katydid
kissing bug
lacewing
lac insect
ladybird beetle
lantern fly
leaf beetle
leafcutter ant
leafcutter bee
leaf-hopper
leaf insect
leatherjacket
locust
louse
luna moth
mantis, praying mantis
mason bee
mayfly

mealworm
mealy bug
midge
milkweed butterfly
miller (moth)
mole cricket
monarch butterfly
mosquito, skeeter (US inf), mozzy (Aus inf)
noctuid moth
nymphalid butterfly
oil beetle
owlet moth
painted lady
papilionid butterfly
peacock butterfly
peppered moth
phylloxera
plant bug
plant hopper
pond skater
potato beetle
potter wasp
praying mantis
puss moth
pyralid moth
red admiral
red ant
red bug (US)
rhinoceros beetle
ringlet (butterfly)
roach (US inf), cockroach
robber fly
rove beetle
sand flea, jigger, chigoe, chigger
sandfly
saturniid moth
satyrid butterfly
sawfly
scale insect
scarab beetle
scorpion fly
screwworm
seventeen-year locust
sexton (or burying) beetle
sheep ked
shield bug
silkworm moth
silverfish

skipper (butterfly)
slave-making ant
snakefly
snout beetle, weevil
soldier beetle
Spanish fly
spider wasp
spittlebug
springtail
squash bug
stag beetle
stick insect, walking stick (US)
stink bug
stonefly
stylops
swallowtail butterfly
swift moth
termite, white ant
thrips
tiger beetle
tiger moth
tineid moth
tortoise beetle
tortoiseshell butterfly
treehopper
tsetse fly
tussock moth
underwing moth
walking stick (US), stick insect
warble fly
wasp
water beetle
water boatman
water bug
water scorpion
water strider
wax moth
webspinner (or foot-spinner)
weevil, snout beetle
whirligig
white ant, termite
whitefly
wireworm
woodborer
woodwasp
woodworm
yellow jacket (US), wasp

ADJECTIVES

10 **insectan** (or **insectean**), insectile, insectiform, insect-like, thysanuran, dipluran, collembolan, proturan, ephemeropteran, plecopteran, orthopteran (or orthopterous), phasmid, dermapteran, embiopteran, dictyopteran, isopteran, psocopteran, mallophagan, anopluran, hemipteran (or hemipterous), homopteran, heteropteran, thysanopteran, grylloblatodean, zorapteran, neuropteran (or neuropterous), megalopteran, mecopteran, lepidopteran (or lepidopterous), trichopteran, dipteran (or dipterous), siphonapteran, hymenopteran (or hymenopterous), coleopteran (or coleopterous), strepsipteran

11 **arachnidan**, spider-like, spidery, arachnoid, mitelike, ticklike, acarid (or acaridan), acaroid

12 **verminous**, infested, buggy, weevilly, maggoty, grubby, lousy, flea-bitten, mothy, moth-eaten, flyblown

Arachnids

bird spider	harvestman, daddy	pseudoscorpion, false	tarantula
black widow	longlegs (US inf)	scorpion	tick
chigger, harvest mite	harvest mite, scrub	red mite	trap-door spider
daddy longlegs (US	mite, chigger	scorpion	water spider
inf), harvestman	hunting spider, wolf	scorpion spider	whip scorpion
dog tick	spider	scrubmite, harvest mite	wind scorpion
false scorpion, pseudo-	itch mite	sheep tick	wolf spider, hunting
scorpion	microwhip scorpion	spider	spider
follicle mite	mite	spider mite	wood tick
fowl tick	money spider	sun spider (or sun	
funnel weaver	orb weaver	scorpion)	

13 **immature**, larval, pupal, chrysalid (or chrysalidal)
▶ *206 Youth*
14 **entomological**, apiarian, sericultural
15 **arachnological**, acarological

VERBS
16 **infest**, invade, swarm, buzz, drone, plague, sting, bite, parasitize, swarm with, crawl with, teem with, contaminate, flyblow
▶ *622 Dirtiness, 670 Attack*
17 **develop**, hatch, pupate, metamorphose

83 Plants (General)

NOUNS
1 **plants**, plant life, flora, plant kingdom, Plantae, vegetable kingdom, vegetable life, vegetation, green plants, growth, herbage, verdure, greenery, forest, jungle, grassland, savanna (or savannah), steppe, scrub, chaparral
▶ *453 Greenness, 85 Trees, 87 Grasses*
2 **plant**, green plant, vascular plant, herbaceous plant, seedling, herb, flower, wild flower, weed, escape, cultivated plant, garden plant, house plant, pot plant, hot-house plant, exotic, food plant, cereal, vegetable, potherb, culinary herb, medicinal plant, medicinal herb, wort, succulent (plant), cactus, xerophyte, aquatic (plant), hydrophyte, air plant, epiphyte, parasite, ephemeral, annual, biennial, perennial, herbaceous perennial, woody perennial, woody plant, tree, sapling, shrub, bush, evergreen, climber, twiner, vine, liana
▶ *84 Flowers, 69 Horticulture, 45 Cookery, 630 Remedy, 85 Trees*
3 **seed plant**, spermatophyte, Spermatophyta, phanerogam, gymnosperm, Gymnospermae (conifers, softwoods, cycads, gnetums, welwitschia, etc.), flowering plant, angiosperm, Angiospermae, monocotyledon (or monocot), Monocotyledonae, palms, grasses, cereals, reeds, sedge family (Cyperaceae), rush family (Juncaceae), orchids, lily family (Liliaceae), pineapple family (Bromeliaceae, bromeliads, etc.), dicotyledon (or dicot), Dicotyledonae (hardwoods), rose family (Rosaceae), daisy family (Compositae, composites), buttercup family (Ranunculaceae), mustard family (Cruciferae, Brassicaceae, crucifers, brassicas),

parsley family (Umbelliferae, umbellifers), nettle family (Labiatae, labiates), pea family (Leguminosae, legumes), goosefoot family (Chenopodiaceae, chenopods, etc.)
▶ *85 Trees, 84 Flowers, 87 Grasses*
4 **lower plant**, nonseed-bearing plant, cryptogam, pteridophyte, Pteridophyta (ferns, horsetails, clubmosses, etc.), bryophyte, Bryophyta (mosses, liverworts), thallophyte, Thallophyta, fungus, saprophyte, parasite, lichen, alga, seaweed
▶ *88 Ferns and Mosses, 89 Fungi, 90 Algae and Lichens*
5 **stem**, axis, caulis, caudex, trunk, caulid, shoot, sprout, plumule, internode, node, axil, offshoot, scion, branch, twig, spray, stalk, stipe, seta, leafstalk, petiole, rachis, rachilla, flower stalk, peduncle, pedicel, seed stalk, funicle (or funiculus), underground stem (or shoot), rhizome, runner, stolon, sucker, rootstock, stock, corm, bulb, tuber, stem tuber, stem tissue, epidermis, cortex, pith, medulla, cambium, vascular bundle, xylem, phloem
▶ *85 Trees, 87 Grasses*
6 **leaf**, leaflet, needle, frond, megaphyll, microphyll, leaf blade, lamina, vein, leafstalk, petiole, leaves, foliage, greenery, leaflike part, bract, bracteole, cladode, phylloclade, phyllode, involucre, scale leaf, ligule, stipule, modified leaf, tendril, spine, floral leaf, petal, sepal, seed leaf, cotyledon, leaf tissue, palisade, mesophyll, stoma (pl. stomata), guard cell, leaf fall, abscission
▶ *453 Greenness, 87 Grasses, 84 Flowers*
7 **root**, radix, rootlet, radicle, taproot, lateral root, fibrous root, prop root, buttress root, stilt root, adventitious root, aerial root, tuberous root, root tuber, tuber, root cap, calyptra, root hair, root nodule, rootlike part, rootstock, rhizoid, rhizomorph
8 **bud**, burgeon, leaf bud, foliage bud, flower bud, apical bud, terminal bud, axillary bud, lateral bud, adventitious bud, winter bud, resting bud, dormancy, gemma, gemmule, budding, gemmation, gemmulation
▶ *245 Reproduction, 246 Fertility, 643 Inactivity*
9 **seed**, grain, kernel, pip, hayseed, rapeseed, flaxseed, linseed, cottonseed, birdseed, seed-

case, seed capsule, seed pod, seed coat, testa, micropyle, hilum, seed stalk, funicle (*or* funiculus), seed leaf, cotyledon, embryo, ovule, endosperm, germinating seed, germination, seedling, shoot, bamboo shoot, mustard and cress, plumule, acrospire, coleoptile, radicle, coleorhiza

▶ *86 Fruits, 245 Reproduction, 246 Fertility*

10 **plant science(s)**, botany, phytology, plant taxonomy, phytography, plant biochemistry, phytochemistry, phytogenesis, plant anatomy, plant physiology, plant cytology, plant ecology, phytosociology, plant geography, phytogeography, plant pathology, phytopathology, palaeobotany, palynology, pollen analysis, palaeoethnobotany, ethnobotany, pteridology, bryology, mycology, phycology, algology, lichenology, dendrology, economic botany, arboriculture, silviculture, horticulture, forestry, pomology, crop husbandry, agrobiology

▶ *59 Life Science, 85 Trees, 84 Flowers, 69 Horticulture, 68 Agriculture, 89 Fungi, 90 Algae and Lichens*

11 **herbarium**, hortus siccus, botanic garden, seed bank, flora, florilegium, herbal

12 **plant scientist**, botanist, plant hunter, herbalist, naturalist, phytologist, phytographer, phytochemist, phytogeneticist, phytogeographer, phytopathologist, ethnobotanist, phytosociologist, palaeobotanist, agrobiologist, dendrologist, pomologist, pteridologist, bryologist, mycologist, phycologist, algologist, lichenologist

▶ *59 Life Science*

ADJECTIVES

13 **plantlike**, vegetable, vegetal, vegetative, herbal, herbaceous, green, grassy, leafy, verdant, flourishing, planted, plant-covered, wooded, forested, growing, luxuriant, lush, dense, overgrown, rank, weedy, unweeded, weed-choked, gone to seed

▶ *87 Grasses, 85 Trees*

14 **of plants**, green, herbaceous, ephemeral, annual, biennial, perennial, bulbous, cormous, tuberous, woody, deciduous, evergreen, leafy, foliate, branched, succulent, xerophytic, aquatic, hydrophytic, terrestrial, land, creeping, prostrate, erect, twining, climbing, epiphytic, parasitic, saprophytic, insectivorous, carnivorous, photosynthetic

15 **wild**, native, indigenous, cultivated, alien, exotic, introduced, escaped, naturalized, hardy, half-hardy

16 **taxonomic**, vascular, seed-bearing, phanerogamic, cone-bearing, coniferous, flowering, monocotyledonous, cyperaceous, juncaceous, orchidaceous, liliaceous, bromeliaceous, dicotyledonous, rosaceous, composite, ranunculaceous, cruciferous, brassicaceous, umbellifer-

ous, labiate, leguminous, chenopodiaceous, nonseed-bearing, cryptogamic, thallophytic

17 **of stems**, axial, cauline, rachial (*or* rachidial), axillary

18 **of leaves**, simple, entire, ovate, lanceolate, linear, orbicular, cordate, lobed, toothed, serrate, dentate, crenate, hastate, sagittate, stalked, unstalked, sessile, peltate, compound, trifoliate, palmate, pinnate, bipinnate

19 **of roots**, radical, radicular, rooted, fibrous-rooted, tuberous-rooted, rootlike, rhizoid

20 **botanical**, botanic, plant, phytological, phytographic(al), phytochemical, phytogeographic(al), phytopathological, ethnobotanical, phytosociological

▶ *59 Life Science, 69 Horticulture, 68 Agriculture, 85 Trees, 84 Flowers, 88 Ferns and Mosses, 89 Fungi, 90 Algae and Lichens*

VERBS

21 **vegetate**, grow, germinate, root, take root, sprout, sprout up, shoot, shoot up, bud, gemmate, unfold, leaf, flower, flourish, burgeon, overgrow, overrun, run to seed, shed seeds, dehisce, photosynthesize

▶ *128 Increase*

22 **be dormant**, shed leaves, abscise, wilt, wither, suspend growth, overwinter, perennate, survive, exist, rest, vegetate

▶ *643 Inactivity*

23 **study plants**, collect plants, botanize, be a botanist

ADVERBS

24 **herbaceously**, exotically, succulently, ephemerally, annually, biennially, perennially, xerophytically, epiphytically, saprophytically, photosynthetically

25 **botanically**, phytologically, horticulturally, ecologically, phytogenetically, phytosociologically, algologically, dendrologically

84   Flowers

Gather the flowers, but spare the buds. Andrew Marvell.

Say it with flowers. Patrick O'Keefe.

NOUNS

1 **flower**, floweret, floret, bloom, blossom, blow (Arch), flowers, may blossom, apple blossom, orange blossom, cherry blossom, wild flower, garden flower, pot plant, flower arrangement, spray, cut flowers, posy, bouquet, garland, wreath, nosegay, daisy chain, buttonhole, boutonniere, dried flower, everlasting flower, pressed flower

▶ *792 Decoration, 557 Ornament*

2 **flowering plant**, flowerer, bloomer, annual, biennial, ephemeral, perennial, bulb, corm, angiosperm

▶ *83 Plants (General)*

Flowers and Flowering Plants

Aaron's rod
acacia
acanthus
aconite
Adam's-needle
aechmea
African violet
agapanthus
agave
agrimony
alfalfa
alkanet
allamanda
allium
althaea
alsike
amaranthus
amaryllis
Amazon lily
anchusa
anemone
anthurium
antirrhinum
aquilegia
arrowroot
arum lily
asphodel
aspidistra
aster
astilbe
aubrietia
auricula
autumn crocus
avens
azalea
baby's-breath
bachelor's-
  button
bedstraw
begonia
belladonna
belladonna lily
bellflower
bergenia
bindweed
bird-of-paradise
  flower
bird's-nest
  orchid
bishop's weed
bistort
bittersweet
blackberry lily
black-eyed
  Susan
black night-
  shade
bladderwort
bleeding heart
bluebell
bluets
bougainvillea
briar (or briar
  rose)
bridal wreath
broom
broomrape
bryony
buddleia
bugloss
burdock
busy Lizzie
buttercup
butterwort

cabbage rose
cactus
calceolaria
calendula
California lilac
calla lily
calypso orchid
camellia
camomile (or
  chamomile)
campanula
campion
candytuft
canna
Canterbury bell
cardinal flower
carnation
carrion flower
catbrier
catmint
ceanothus
celandine
century plant
charlock
chickweed
Chinese lantern
  plant
Christmas cactus
Christmas rose
chrysanthemum
cineraria
cinquefoil
clarkia
cleavers
clematis
clianthus
clove pink
clover
cocklebur
cockscomb
coleus
coltsfoot
columbine
coneflower
convolvulus
corncockle
cornflower
corn poppy
corydalis
cosmos
cow parsley
cowpea
cowslip
cranesbill
creeping Jenny
crocus
crowfoot
crown of thorns
cuckoopint
cylcamen
cymbidium
daffodil, daff
  (Inf)
dahlia
daisy
damask rose
dandelion
darnel
datura
day lily
deadly night-
  shade
deadnettle
delphinium

dianthus
dock
dogbane
dog rose
dog's-tooth vio-
  let
dog violet
Dutchman's
  breeches
Dutchman's pipe
dyer's broom
edelweiss
eglantine
enchanter's
  nightshade
epiphyllum
erica
eucharis
euphorbia
eyebright
fig marigold
figwort
firethorn
fireweed
flag
flax
fleabane
fleawort
flowering cur-
  rant
flowering quince
forget-me-not
forsythia
foxglove
frangipani
freesia
fritillary
frog-bit
fuchsia
fumitory
furze
gaillardia
gardenia
garlic mustard
gentian
geranium
germander
gillyflower
gladden
gladiolus, glad
  (or gladdie)
  (Inf)
glasswort
globe flower
globe thistle
gloxinia
goatsbeard
golden bell
goldenrod
goosefoot
goosegrass
gorse
goutweed
granadilla
grape hyacinth
grass of
  Parnassus
ground elder
groundsel
guelder rose
gypsophila
harebell
hawkbit
hawkweed

heath
heather
hedgehog cac-
  tus
heliotrope
hellebore
helleborine
hemlock
henbane
henequen
herb Paris
herb Robert
hibiscus
hollyhock
honesty
honeysuckle
horehound
houseleek
hoya
hyacinth
hydrangea
hypericum
hyssop
ice plant
impatiens
Indian paint-
  brush
iris
jack-by-the-
  hedge
jack-in-the-
  pulpit
japonica
jimson weed
jonquil
kalanchoe
kangaroo paw
kingcup
knapweed
knotweed
laburnum
lady's slipper
lady's smock
larkspur
lavender
leopard lily
lilac
lily
lily-of-the-valley
lobelia
London pride
lords-and-ladies
lotus
love-in-a-mist
love-lies-
  bleeding
lungwort
lupin
Madonna lily
magnolia
mallow
marguerite
marigold
marsh mallow
marsh marigold
martagon (or
  martagon lily)
marvel-of-Peru
may (or may-
  flower)
meadow saffron
meadowsweet
mecanopsis
medick

mesembryan-
  themum
Michaelmas
  daisy
mignonette
milfoil
milkweed
milkwort
mimosa
moccasin flower
mock orange
moneywort
monkeyflower
monkshood
montbretia
moonflower
morning glory
moschatel
moss pink
moss rose
motherwort
mullein
musk rose
narcissus
nasturtium
nemesia
nettle
nicotiana
night-scented
  stock
old man cactus
old man's beard
oleander
opium poppy
opuntia
orchid
organ-pipe cac-
  tus
orpine
oxeye daisy
oxlip
pansy
passionflower
patchouli
pelargonium
pennyroyal
peony
periwinkle
petrea
petunia
peyote
philadelphus
phlox
pigweed
pimpernel
pink
plantain
plumbago
poinsettia
polyanthus
pontentilla
poppy
portulaca
pot marigold
prickly pear
prickly poppy
primrose
primula
protea
pyracantha
pyrethrum
Queen Anne's
  lace
ragged robin

ragwort	self heal	spurrey	thistle	viburnum
ranunculus	shamrock	squill	thorn apple	viola
rape	shrimp plant	star of Bethle-	thrift	violet
red-hot poker	slipper orchid	hem	thunbergia	wallflower
rhododendron,	slipperwort	stephanotis	tiger lily	water lily
rhodie (Inf)	snakeroot	stitchwort	toad lily	waxplant
rock rose	snake's head	St John's wort	tormentil	Welsh poppy
rose	snapdragon	stock	touch-me-not	wichuraiana
rose of China	snowdrop	stonecrop	townhall clock	(rose)
rose of Jericho	snow-on-the-	strawflower	tradescantia	willowherb
rose of Sharon	mountain	strelitzia	traveller's joy	winter aconite
rudbeckia	soapwort	streptocarpus	trefoil	winter jasmine
safflower	Solomon's seal	sundew	trumpet creeper	wisteria
saguaro	sorrel	sunflower	tuberose	witchweed
sainfoin	sow thistle	sun rose	tulip	wolfsbane
salvia	speedwell	sweet briar	Turk's-cap lily	wood sorrel
samphire	spider flower	sweet flag	valerian	wormwood
sanicle	spider plant	sweet pea	Venus flytrap	woundwort
saxifrage	spiderwort	sweet william	verbena	yarrow
scabious	spikenard	syringa	veronica	yucca
sea lavender	spiraea	tea rose	vervain	zinnia
sedum	spurge	teasel	vetch	

3 **flower part**, sepal, calyx, petal, nectary, corolla, perianth, floral envelope, epicalyx, involucre (or involucrum), bract, whorl, spathe, stamen, filament, anther, androecium, pollen, pollen grain, stigma, style, ovary, carpel, gynoecium, pistil, pollen tube, ovule, micropyle, receptacle, floral diagram, floral formula
▶ *86 Fruits, 83 Plants (General)*

4 **flower head**, flower cluster, inflorescence, racemose inflorescence, raceme, panicle, corymb, spadix, spike, spikelet, catkin, ament, umbel, capitulum, ray floret, disc floret, cyme, cymose inflorescence, monochasium, monochasial cyme, dichasium, dichasial cyme, thyrse, verticillaster

5 **flowering**, florescence, efflorescence, blossoming, blooming, flowerage, unfolding, anthesis, blowing, blow, full blow, full bloom

6 **pollination**, cross-pollination, self-pollination, selfing
▶ *245 Reproduction*

7 **flower culture**, floriculture, flower growing, flower selling, floristics, floriculturist, flower grower, florist, flower seller, flower girl
▶ *69 Horticulture*

8 **flower product**, nectar, rose water, attar of roses, rose (or primrose) oil, lavender water, oil of lavender, camomile tea, elderflower (or dandelion) wine, crystallized (or jellied) rose petals
▶ *418 Fragrance, 351 Drinking*

9 **figurative usage**, floral dance, flower child, flower power, daisycutter, daisywheel, Poppy Day, primrose path, rose window, rosette, Sunflower State, bed of roses, shrinking violet (Inf)

ADJECTIVES

10 **floral**, flowered, flowery, bloomy, floristic, flower-like, fragrant, florid, ornate, floreate, floriate(d)
▶ *418 Fragrance, 557 Ornament*

11 **flowering**, in flower, in bloom, in full bloom, in full blow, in blossom, blossoming, blooming, flourishing, florescent, inflorescent, efflorescent
▶ *686 Prosperity*

12 **of flowers**, staminate, male, pistillate, female, imperfect, perfect, monoecious, dioecious, regular, irregular, synsepalous, synpetalous, synandrous, aposepalous, apopetalous, apoandrous, hypogynous, epigynous, perigynous, racemose, cymose, corymbose, umbelliferous
▶ *83 Plants (General)*

VERBS

13 **flower**, bud, bloom, blossom, blow, be in flower, be in bloom, effloresce, flourish
▶ *686 Prosperity*

ADVERBS

14 **florally**, floristically, floridly, fragrantly

85   Trees

I think that I shall never see/ A poem lovely as a tree. Alfred Joyce Kilmer.

NOUNS

1 **tree**, shrub, bush, sapling, coniferous tree, conifer, evergreen (tree), deciduous tree, broadleaf, broadleaved tree, palm (tree), fan palm, feather palm, tree fern, tree mallow, shade tree, timber tree, softwood (tree), hardwood (tree), tropical hardwood, amenity tree, ornamental (tree), Christmas tree, fruit tree, fruiter, bonsai tree, dwarf tree, hedgerow tree, specimen tree, standard, maiden, pollard, coppice, stool

2 **tree part**, trunk, collar, bole, gnarl, knot, burl, burr, crutch, fork, crown, limb, branch, bough, twig, spur, leader, leaf, palm leaf, palm frond, needle, pine needle, cone, pine cone, fir cone, tree stump, stump, snag (US)
▶ *83 Plants (General)*

3 **timber**, wood, lumber (US), cordwood, cord, cordage, log, pole, flitch, faggot, brushwood,

Trees and Shrubs

Conifers and Related Trees
alerce
araucaria
arbor vitae
bald cypress
balsam fir
big tree
black pine
black spruce
blue spruce
bristlecone pine
bunya
cade
cedar
cedar of Lebanon
celery pine
cryptomeria
cupressus
cypress
cypress pine
dawn redwood
deodar
Douglas fir
fir
ginkgo
hemlock (or hemlock spruce)
hoop pine
Huon pine
incense cedar
jack pine
Japanese cedar
juniper
kahikatea
kauri (or kauri pine)
larch
lignum vitae
loblolly
longleaf pine
macrocarpa
maidenhair tree
matai
monkey puzzle
Norway spruce
nut pine
Paraná pine
pencil cedar
pinaster
pine
radiata pine
red cedar
red fir
red pine
redwood
sandarac
savin
Scots pine
sequoia
silver fir
sitka spruce
spruce
spruce pine
stone pine
sugar pine
swamp cypress
tamarack
thuja
totara
umbrella pine

wellingtonia
western hemlock
western red cedar
white cedar
white pine
white spruce
yew

Palms
babassu
betel palm
cabbage palm
coco de mer
coconut palm
coquito
date palm
doum palm
gomuti
ivory palm
nikau (or nikau palm)
nipa
oil palm
palmyra
sago palm
talipot (or talipot palm)
Washington palm
wax palm
wine palm

Hardwoods, Ornamentals, and Others
acacia
acer
ailanthus
alder
almond
ambatch
amboyna
apple
apple box
arbutus
ash
aspen
assegai
axe-breaker
balata
balsa
balsam poplar
banak
banksia
banyan
baobab
basswood
bayberry
bay rum tree
bay (or bay tree)
baywood
bean tree
beech
bebeeru
beefwood
belah
ben
birch, birk (Scot)
black bean
blackjack

black walnut
blackthorn
blackwood
bladdernut
blue gum
bo tree
bottlebrush
bottle tree
box (or box-wood)
box elder
bulletwood
butcher's broom
butternut
buttonball
buttonwood
cabbage tree
cacao
calabash
camphor tree
camwood
candleberry (or candle-tree)
candlewood
canoewood
cassia
casuarina
catalpa
champac (or champak)
chaste tree
chaulmoogra
chestnut
chinaberry (or China tree)
coachwood
cockspur
cocuswood
coffee tree
coolabah
coral tree
cork oak
corkwood
cornel
cottonwood
courbaril
cow tree
crabwood
croton
cucumber tree
cudgerie
daphne
desert oak
dhak
divi-divi
dogwood
dragon tree
durmast (or dur-mast oak)
Dutch elm
eaglewood
ebony
elder
elm
eucalyptus
eucryphia
euonymus
false acacia
fever tree
flame-of-the-forest
flame tree
flowering ash

fringe tree
gaboon
gean
ghost gum
gidgee
greasewood
greenheart
guaiacum
guayule
gum (or gum tree)
gympie
haematoxylon
hakea
hawthorn
hazel
Hercules'-club
hevea
hickory
holly
holm oak (or holly oak)
honey locust
hop-hornbeam
hornbeam
horse chestnut
Indian mulberry
inkberry
iroko
ironwood
ivorywood
jacaranda
Japanese maple
jarrah
jelutong
jojoba
Joshua tree
Judas tree
kaffirboom
kalmia
kamala
karri
kawakawa
Kentucky coffee tree
kiaat
kingwood
koa
kowhai
kurrajong
lacquer tree
lancewood
lantana
laurel
lemonwood
lilly-pilly
lime
linden
liquidambar
liriodendron
locust
logwood
Lombardy pop-lar
madroña
mahogany
mako
mallee tree
manchineel
mangrove
manna
manuka
maple

marblewood
marmalade tree
maté
may tree
mazzard
melaleuca
mesquite
mountain ash
myrtle
needle bush
neem
ngaio
Norway maple
nux vomica
oak
ocotillo
osier
pagoda tree
paper mulberry
partridge-wood
paulownia
pedunculate oak
peepul
pepper tree
plane (or plane tree), platan
pohutukawa
poinciana
poison oak
poison sumac
poplar
prickly ash
privet
puriri
pussy willow
pyinkado
quassia
quebracho
rain tree
rangiora
redbud
red gum
red oak
rewa-rewa
ribbonwood
robinia
roble
rosewood
rowan
royal poinciana
rubber plant
rubber tree
sallee
sallow
sandalwood
sandbox tree
sapele
sappan (or sap-panwood)
saskatoon
sassafras
sassy (or sass-wood or sassy wood)
satin walnut
satinwood
screw pine
seringa
serviceberry
service tree
shagbark
shea
silk-cotton tree

silky oak	Spanish cedar	sycamore	tupelo	white oak
silver birch	spindle tree	tallow wood	Turkey oak	white poplar
silver maple	spotted gum	tamarind	turpentine tree	wilga
simarouba	stinkwood	tamarisk	umbrella tree	willow
slippery elm	strawberry bush	tawa	upas	witch hazel
smoke tree	strawberry tree	teak	varnish tree	wych-elm
sneezewood	styrax	tea tree	wahoo	yarran
snowball tree	sugar gum	terebinth	walnut	yaupon
snowdrop tree	sugar maple	thorn tree	wandoo	yellow poplar
soapbark	sumach (or	toon	wattle	yellowwood
sorb	sumac)	toothache tree	wax tree	ylang-ylang
sorrel tree	sweet bay	tree of heaven	wayfaring tree	yucca
sour gum	sweet gum	tuart	weeping willow	zanthoxylum
sourwood	sycamine	tulip tree	whitebeam	zebrawood

firewood, kindling, pulpwood, sapwood, alburum, wetwood, heartwood, duramen, reaction wood, tension wood, compression wood, spring wood, summer wood, autumn wood, early wood, late wood, trunkwood, branchwood, woody tissue, bark, cork, phellem, lignin, tree ring, annual ring, growth ring, tree-ring dating, dendrochronology

▶ *373 Hardness*

4 **trees**, tree line (*or* zone), timber line, forest, rainforest, tropical forest, jungle, thorn forest, cloud forest, gallery forest, virgin forest, primeval forest, coniferous forest, taiga, woodland, woods, ancient woodland, chaparral, brush, bocage, wood, greenwood, copse, spinney, coppice, thicket, clearing, glade, bower, arbour, underwood, undergrowth, tree litter, leaf litter, leaf mould, beech mast, brake, covert, bosket (*or* bosquet), bosk, holt (Arch), hurst (Arch), shelter belt, plantation, stand, timberland (US), wood lot, bush lot (Can), tree farm, arboretum, pinetum, pinery, tree nursery, orchard, orangery

▶ *69 Horticulture*

5 **forestry**, tree farming, agroforestry, tree planting, afforestation, reforestation, deforestation, conservation, dendrology, arboriculture, silviculture, woodcraft (US), treen, treenware, cabinet-making

▶ *68 Agriculture, 47 Furniture and Woodwork*

6 **tree management**, beating up, brashing, thinning, pruning, lopping, topping, dropcrotching, coppicing, pollarding, tree surgery, tapping, rubber tapping, felling, tree felling, logging, lumbering (US), felling licence

7 **timber production**, timber yard, lumber yard (US), saw, chain saw, power-saw, bowsaw, felling saw, axe, hatchet, billhook, wedge, splitter, chipper, sawmill, sawbench, circular saw, band saw, skidder, forwarder, grapple

▶ *603 Tool*

8 **forester**, forest manager, ranger, forest ranger, verderer, woodlander, woodcutter, lumberjack, timberman, woodsman, woodman, logger, lumberer (US), tapper, tapster, tree farmer, tree surgeon, arboriculturist, arborist, silviculturist, dendrologist

9 **tree product**, wood alcohol, wood coal, wood pitch, wood spirit, wood sugar, wood tar, pine tar, wood vinegar, gum turpentine, oil, pinewood oil, palm oil, resin, gum, wax, rubber, fruit, nuts

▶ *394 Viscosity, 376 Smoothness, 395 Oiliness, 393 Semiliquid, 377 Elasticity, 630 Remedy, 62 Pharmacology, 86 Fruits, 45 Cookery*

10 **tree disease**, defoliation, mosaic, mottle, ring spot, leaf curl, dieback, witches' broom, soft rot, wilt, canker, butt rot, blight, mildew, rust, heart rot, pocket rot, leaf cast, needle cast, crown gall, oak apple, oak gall, Dutch elm disease

▶ *69 Horticulture, 89 Fungi*

11 **tree-related animal**, tree creeper, tree frog, treehopper, tree kangaroo, tree shrew, tree snake, tree sparrow, wood ant, woodborer, wood duck, woodcock, woodchat, woodgrouse, woodchuck, woodlark, woodlouse, woodpecker, wood pigeon, wood rat, wood warbler, woodwasp, woodworm, pine marten, willow grouse, willow tit, willow warbler

▶ *82 Insects and Arachnids, 78 Birds, 77 Mammals*

12 **figurative usage**, family tree, genealogical tree, shoetree, axeltree, manteltree, rooftree, ridgetree, summer tree, saddletree, swingle-

Tree Products

acaroid gum	cajuput	cinchona	percha	myrrh	storax
animē	calisaya	copalm	haematoxy-	ouabain	tacamahac
annatto	camphor	dragon's	lin	pereira bark	tolu
araroba	canella	blood	henna	rauwolfia	tragacanth
balm of	carnauba	frankin-	kapok	rubber	tung oil
Gilead	cascara	cense	kermes	sassafras	turpentine
balsam	cassia bark	fustic	kino	sassafras	yohimbine
benzoin	catechu	gamboge	latex	oil	
borneol	chicle	gutta-	mastic	senna pods	

Fruits

ackee (or akee)
alligator pear
amarelle (cherry)
ananas
anchovy pear
apple
apricot
Asian pear
assai
avocado
babaco
bael
bakeapple
banana
barberry
bayberry
beach plum
bearberry
bergamot
bilberry
blackberry
blackcurrant
blackheart (cherry)
blaeberry
Blenheim (apple)
blueberry
boysenberry
Bramley (or Bramley's seedling) (apple)
breadfruit
bullace
calamondin
canistel
cantaloupe (melon)
capulin
carambola
carob
casaba

chayote
chempaduk
cherimoya
cherry
cherry plum
chinaberry
Chinese gooseberry (kiwi fruit)
chokeberry
chokecherry
choko
citron
clementine
clingstone (peach)
coconut
Concord (grape)
Conference (pear)
costard
Cox's Orange Pippin (apple)
crab apple
cranberry
crowberry
currant
custard apple
damson
date
Delaware (grape)
dewberry
durian (or durion)
elderberry
feijoa
fig
fox grape
geebung
genipap (or genip)
gingerbread plum

Golden Delicious (apple)
gooseberry, goosegog (Inf)
gourd
granadilla
grape
grapefruit
greengage
guava
hackberry (or hagberry)
hanepoot (grape)
hautboy (strawberry)
honeydew (melon)
huckleberry
icaco plum
imbu
jaboticaba
jackfruit
Jaffa (orange)
Japanese quince
Japanese persimmon
Jerusalem cherry
jujube
kaki
kiwi fruit
kumquat (or cumquat)
lemon
lime
lingonberry
litchi (or lichee or lichi or lychee)
loganberry
longan (or lungan)
loquat

love apple (Arch)
mammee apple
mandarin
mango
mangosteen
manzanilla
marang
marasca (cherry)
May apple
medlar
melon
minneola
mombin
morello (cherry)
mulberry
muscadine (grape)
muscat (or muscatel) (grape)
muskmelon
myrobalan
nashi
navel orange
nectarine
nipa
olive
orange
Osage orange
papaw
papaya
passion fruit
peach
pear
Persian melon
persimmon
pineapple
pippin
plantain
plum
pomegranate
pomelo
prickly pear

quandong (or quandang or quantong)
queen olive
quince
rambutan
raspberry
redcurrant
rhubarb
rose apple
russet (apple)
salmonberry
sapodilla
satsuma
serviceberry
Seville orange
sharon fruit
sloe
sorb apple
sour cherry
sour gourd
soursop
spiceberry
star-apple
star fruit
strawberry
sweet cherry
sweetsop
tamarillo
tamarind
tangelo
tangerine
tayberry
tomato, love apple (Arch)
tree tomato
ugli fruit
watermelon
whitecurrant
whortleberry
Williams (pear)
winter melon
youngberry

---

tree, whippletree (or whiffletree), cross tree, trestletree, olive branch

13 **tree mythology**, tree of knowledge, tree of life, tree of Jesse, Yggdrasil, Bo tree, wood nymph, tree nymph, dryad, hamadryad, Daphne

▶ *47 Furniture and Woodwork, 32 Horses*

ADJECTIVES

14 **treelike**, arboreal, arboraceous, arborescent, dendritic, dendroid (or dendroidal), dendriform, palmate, palmaceous, branching, slender, willowy, shrubby, bushy, gnarled, coniferous, evergreen, piny, resinous

15 **woody**, wood, ligneous, ligniform, hardwood, softwood, hard-grained, soft-grained, wooden, treen, oaken, beechen, ashen, solid, massive

16 **wooded**, forested, forestal, timbered, afforested, reafforested, planted, tree-covered, arboreous, woodland, sylvan (or silvan), sylvatic, sylvestral, shaded, shady, bosky, copsy, braky, woodsy (US inf)

17 **arboricultural**, silvicultural, silvical (US), dendrologic(al), dendrologous

VERBS

18 **manage trees**, practise forestry, thin, prune, grub, lop, top, pollard, coppice, tap, cut timber, fell, clear, log, lumber (US), build a tree house

19 **grow**, spread, bloom, flower, leaf out, lose (or drop or shed) leaves, branch out, provide shade, (produce) fruit, whisper (aspen), weep (willow)

ADVERBS

20 **arboriculturally**, silviculturally, dendrologically

86   Fruits

NOUNS

1 **fruits**, fruits of the earth, produce, crop, yield, soft fruit, stone fruit, citrus fruit, dried fruit, nuts, kernels, grain, seeds, pulses, vegetables, legumes, root vegetables, roots, tubers, green vegetables, salad vegetables

▶ *246 Fertility, 69 Horticulture, 68 Agriculture, 87 Grasses, 45 Cookery*

Nuts

acorn	cashew	dwarf chestnut	macadamia nut	quandang or
almond	chestnut	earthnut	marron (Fr)	quantong)
areca	chinquapin (or	filbert	mockernut	Queensland nut
beechnut	chincapin or	groundnut	monkey nut	sal nut
betel nut	chinkapin)	grugru nut	palm nut	souari nut
bitternut	cob (or cobnut)	gum nut	peanut	sweet (or Span-
black walnut	coco de mer	hazelnut	pecan	ish) chestnut
brazil (or brasil)	coconut	hickory	pignut	walnut
nut	coffee nut	hognut	pili nut	water chestnut
breadnut	cola (or kola) nut	horse chestnut	pine nut (or	(or caltrop)
burrawang nut	conker	ivory nut	piñon)	water chinquapin
butternut	coquilla nut	kola nut	pistachio	white walnut
candlenut	double coconut	litchi nut	quandong (or	

2 **botanical fruit**, simple fruit, true fruit, composite fruit, aggregate fruit, multiple fruit, false fruit, succulent fruit, citrus fruit, drupe, berry, pome, pepo, sorosis, syconus, hesperidium, dry fruit, dehiscent fruit, legume, pod, capsule, follicle, siliqua, silicula, pyxidium, indehiscent fruit, nut, achene, samara, caryopsis, cypsela, schizocarpic fruit, schizocarp, carcerulus, cremocarp, lomentum, regma, fruiting body
▶ 83 Plants (General), 89 Fungi

3 **fruit structure**, fruit wall, pericarp, exocarp (or epicarp), skin, rind, peel, shell, shuck, husk, seed pod, seed capsule, mesocarp, endocarp, flesh, pulp, meat, pith, stone, pit (US), nutlet, seed, pip, kernel, grain
▶ 83 Plants (General), 245 Reproduction

4 **fruit eating**, fruit-eater, fruit-eating animal, fruit bat, frugivore, fruit-eating person, fruitarian, vegetarian, vegan, frugivorousness, fruitarianism, vegetarianism, fruit growing, market gardening, truck farming (or gardening) (US), fruit selling, fruit seller, fruiterer, greengrocer
▶ 350 Eating, 69 Horticulture, 739 Sale

5 **figurative usage**, forbidden fruit, apple of one's eye, Adam's apple, apple of discord, lotus-eater, cherry picker, strawberry mark, grapevine (Inf), raspberry (Inf), peanuts (Sl), banana skin (Inf), lemon (Sl), melon (Sl), limey (US sl), apples (or apples and pears) (Sl), apple sauce (US sl), apple polisher (US sl), banana republic (Inf), Banana bender (Aus sl), lemon squeezer (NZ sl), cherry (Tab sl)

ADJECTIVES

6 **fruiting**, fruit-bearing, fructiferous, pomiferous, leguminous, fructuous, fruitful, productive, fertile
▶ 246 Fertility

7 **fruitlike**, fruity, citrus, citrous, citric, citrine

8 **fruit-eating**, frugivorous, vegetarian

9 **of a fruit**, fleshy, succulent, ripe, unripe, indehiscent, dehiscent, monocarpellary, bicarpellary, polycarpellary, syncarpous, apocarpous, monocarpic, schizocarpic, parthenocarpic

VERBS

10 **fruit**, bear fruit, fructify, ripen, be fruitful, yield, release seeds, dehisce
▶ 246 Fertility, 245 Reproduction, 686 Prosperity

ADVERBS

11 **fructiferously**, fruitily, fructuously, succulently, fruitfully, productively

87 Grasses

NOUNS

1 **grass**, true grass, grass family, Gramineae, Poaceae, graminaceous plant, ornamental grass, mowing grass, lawn grass, fodder grass, meadow grass, pasture grass, ley grass, cereal grass, grasslike plant, rush, sedge

2 **grassland**, meadow, field, meadow land, mead (Arch), lea (Arch), pasture land, permanent pasture, pasturage, herbage, verdure, ley, grazing, plain, range (US), pampas (South America), savanna (or savannah) (Africa), llano (South America), campo (Brazil), veld (or veldt) (South Africa), prairie (US), steppe (Russia), champaign (France), campagna (Italy), common, moor, moorland, heath, downs, downland, wold (Arch), park, parkland, lawn, green, sward (Arch), greensward (Arch), turf, grass, sod, divot, clump, tussock, tuft, hassock
▶ 68 Agriculture, 453 Greenness

3 **grass plant**, stem, culm, haulm, cane, reed, straw, spear, spire, blade, blade of grass, leaf, sheath, ligule, auricle, grass flower, spike, panicle, spikelet, glume, rachilla, lemma, palea (or pale), awn, lodicule, tassel

4 **cereal grass**, cereal, grain, ear, ear of corn, cob, corncob, barleycorn, husk, bran, chaff, stubble, straw
▶ 86 Fruits, 68 Agriculture, 45 Cookery

5 **grass-cutter**, mower, mowing machine, lawn mower, scythe, reedcutter, thatcher
▶ 603 Tool, 68 Agriculture, 69 Horticulture

6 **grass-eater**, browser, grazer, graminivore, herbivore

7 **figurative usage**, bamboo curtain, grass roots, grass widow, broken reed (Inf)

Grasses

True grasses	cordgrass	Japanese (or Korean) lawn grass	reed grass	Yorkshire fog
bamboo	corn		rice	zoysia
barley	cotton grass		rye	**Grasslike Plants**
beach grass (US)	couch (or couch grass)	Kentucky bluegrass	rye-brome	bulrush
beard grass	crab grass	lesser quaking grass	ryegrass	Dutch rush
bent (or bent grass)	creeping bent	lovegrass	scutch (or scutch grass)	eelgrass
Bermuda grass	cut-grass	lyme grass	sheep's fescue	elephant grass
black bent	darnel	maize	sorghum	goosegrass
bluegrass	dog's-tail	marram grass	spelt	grass of
bog hair grass	durra	meadow fescue	squirrel-tail grass	Parnassus
bristle grass	emmer	meadow foxtail	sugar cane	grass tree
brome (or brome grass)	English ryegrass	meadow grass	switch grass	horsetail
broomcorn	feather grass	melick	sword grass	paper reed
buckwheat	fescue	millet	timothy (or timothy grass)	papyrus
buffalo grass	fiorin	oat grass	tufted hair grass	reedmace
bunch grass (US)	finger grass	oats	twitch grass	rush
canary grass	foxtail	orchard grass	vernal grass	scouring rush
cane	gama grass	paddy	wheat	sedge
cat's-tail	grama grass	pampas grass	wild oat	spear grass
China grass	hair grass	quack grass	wild rice	star grass
citronella	hare's-tail	quaking grass	wild rye	tape grass
cocksfoot	herd's grass (US)	quitch grass	wire grass	woodrush
cockspur	Indian corn	rattan	wood meadow grass	worm grass
	Indian rice	redtop (US)		
	Italian ryegrass	reed		

ADJECTIVES

8 **grasslike**, gramineous, graminaceous, poaceous, graminiferous, farinaceous, wheaten, oaten

9 **grassy**, verdant, green, grass-green, grass-covered, verdured, meadowy, swardy, turfy, reedy, rushy, sedgy

▶ *453 Greenness, 83 Plants (General)*

10 **grass-eating**, graminivorous, herbivorous, grazing, browsing

VERBS

11 **eat grass**, graze, browse, crop, forage, pasture, ruminate, chew the cud, put out to grass (*or* pasture), forage, fodder

12 **manage grassland**, cut, mow, scythe, top, grass, grass over, turf, sod, seed, sow seed, fertilize, feed, water, weed, top-dress, spray, roll

ADVERBS

13 **herbivorously**, verdantly

88   Ferns and Mosses

NOUNS

1 **fern**, true fern, pteridophyte, filicopsid, Filicinae, Filicopsida, bracken, brake, tropical fern, tree fern, fern ally, sphenopsid, horsetail, equisetum, Dutch rush, calamite, lycopsid, clubmoss, lycopodium, lycopod, ground pine, quillwort, fernlike plant, asparagus fern, seed fern, pteridosperm, cycad, cycad fern

▶ *83 Plants (General)*

2 **fern plant**, stem, rachis, leaf, frond, leaflet, pinna, plant body, sporophyte, fern seed, spore, spore case, sporangium, sorus, indusium, prothallus, reproductive organ, archegonium, antheridium, study of ferns, pteridology, pteridologist

3 **moss**, true moss, bryophyte, Musci, Bryopsida, bryopsid, peat moss, bog moss, sphagnum, granite moss, wall moss, wood moss, hair moss, tree moss, moss ally, liverwort, Hepaticae, Hepaticopsida, leafy liverwort, thallose liverwort, horned liverwort, hornwort, mosslike plant, lichen, Spanish moss, long moss, reindeer moss, oak moss, alga, Irish moss

▶ *90 Algae and Lichens*

4 **moss plant**, plant body, gametophyte, root, rhizoid, spore capsule, seta, stalk, calyptra, cap, elater, foot, propagation, gemma, gemma cup, reproductive organ, archegonium, venter, antheridium, study of mosses, bryology, bryologist

Ferns

adder's-tongue	moonwort
beech fern	oak fern
bird's-nest fern	osmunda
bladder fern	pepperwort
Boston fern	pillwort
bracken	polypody
buckler fern	ponga
cliffbrake	rock brake
dryopteris	royal fern
grape fern (US)	shield fern
hard fern	spleenwort
hart's-tongue	staghorn
holly fern	tree fern
lady fern	walking fern (US)
maidenhair fern	wall rue
male fern	woodsia
marsh fern	

ADJECTIVES

5 **fernlike**, ferny, pteridophyte, pteridophytic, pteridophytous, pteridological
6 **mosslike**, mossy, moss-covered, moss-grown, bryophyte, bryophytic, hepatic, bryological

89 Fungi

NOUNS

1 **fungus**, fungosity, mould, must, mildew, rot, dry rot, wet rot, blight, canker
▶ *631 Blight*
2 **mushroom**, toadstool, *champignon* (Fr), cultivated mushroom, button mushroom, wild mushroom, field mushroom, fairy ring, magic mushroom, mushroom cloud
▶ *45 Cookery, 69 Horticulture*
3 **fungi**, Fungi (*or* Mycota), true fungi, Eumycota, basidiomycetes, Basidiomycotina, agarics, bracket fungi, pore fungi, tooth fungi, club fungi, skin fungi, jelly fungi, rusts, smuts, ascomycetes, Ascomycotina, sac fungi, cup fungi, flask fungi, deuteromycetes, imperfect fungi, Deuteromycotina (*or* Fungi Imperfecta), phycomycetes, Mastigomycotina, Zygomycotina, myxomycetes, Myxomycota, slime moulds, cellular slime moulds
4 **fungal body**, thallus, mycelium, hypha, haustorium, rhizoid, rhizomorph, plasmodium, reproductive body, carpophore, fruiting body, mushroom, cap, pileus, gill, lamella, stalk, stipe, veil, volva, annulus, bracket, conk, sporophore, basidiocarp, basidium, sterigma, hymenium, ascocarp, ascus, spore, basidiospore, ascospore, conidium

5 **fungal association**, symbiosis, mycorrhiza, ectotrophic mycorrhiza, endotrophic mycorrhiza, lichen, symbiotic fungus, mycobiont, parasitism, parasitic fungus, parasite, dermatophyte, saprophyte, pathogen, fungal disease, mycosis, dermatophytosis, ringworm, tinea, athlete's foot, dhobi itch, favus, thrush, candidiasis, moniliasis, phycomycosis, aspergillosis, ergotism, histoplasmosis, farmer's lung, mycetoma, Madura foot, blastomycosis, coccidioidomycosis, plant disease, damping-off, dieback, Dutch elm disease
▶ *90 Algae and Lichens, 624 Ill Health, 69 Horticulture, 85 Trees, 68 Agriculture*
6 **fungal antibiotic**, penicillin, streptomycin, actinomycin, neomycin, chloramphenical
▶ *62 Pharmacology*
7 **antifungal agent**, fungicide, fungistat, antimycotic
▶ *630 Remedy, 398 Killing*
8 **study of fungi**, mycology, mycologist, mushroom grower, mushroom farmer, mushroom farm, truffle hunter, mushroom eating, mycophagy, mycophagist

ADJECTIVES

9 **fungal**, fungous, fungoid, fungiform, mildewed, mildewy, mouldy, musty, rotten, blighted, cankered, yeasty, fermented
10 **of fungi**, saprophytic, parasitic, homothallic, heterothallic, mycelial, hyphal, ascogenous, mycotic, mycologic(al), coprophilous, decurrent, epigeal, deliquescent, adnate, adnexed, alveolate, amyloid, aeriolate, bulbous, cespitose, fusiform, reticulate, sessile

Fungi

Mushrooms, Toadstools, etc.			
agaric	false morel	panther cap	botrytis
agrocybe	field mushroom	parasol mushroom	bread mould
amanita	fly agaric	pluteus	brewers' (or bakers')
ascomycetes	funnel cap	polypore	yeast
beefsteak fungus	hare's ear	psilocybe	brown rot (of apples)
bird's-nest fungus	helvella	psathyrella	bunt
blewits	honey fungus (or aga-	puffball	candida
blusher	ric)	russula	corn smut
boletus	horn of plenty	St George's mushroom	cramp ball
bootlace fungus	horsehair toadstool (or	Satan's (or devil's) bo-	downy mildew
bracket fungus	fungus)	letus	ergot
brain fungus	horse mushroom	shaggy inkcap	mucor
cep	hydnum	stag's-horn fungus	penicillium
chanterelle	hydrocybe	stinkhorn	pin mould
collybia	ink cap	truffle	potato blight
coprinus	inocybe	tuckahoe	powdery mildew
cortinarius	jew's ear	velvet shank	rhizopus
death cap	lactarius	verdigris toadstool	rust
destroying angel	lepista	wax cap	smut
earth ball	leptonia	witches' butter	sooty mould
earthstar	liberty cap	wood hedgehog	stinking smut
earth tongue	meadow mushroom	wood woollyfoot	streptomyces
elf-cup	milk cap		verticillium
entoloma	miller	**Moulds, Mildews, and**	water mould
fairy-ring mushroom	morel	**Pathogens**	yeast
(or champignon)	orange-peel fungus	aspergillus	
	oyster mushroom	black rust (of wheat)	
	panaeolus	blue (or green) mould	

VERBS

11 **moulder**, mildew, rot, putrefy, decompose, ferment, deliquesce

▶ *628 Deterioration*

12 **mushroom**, germinate, spring up, flourish, burgeon, proliferate, multiply

▶ *128 Increase, 259 Size*

ADVERBS

13 **saprophytically**, parasitically, symbiotically

90   Algae and Lichens

NOUNS

1 **alga**, thallophyte, seaweed, wrack, kelp, phytoplankton, algal bloom, eutrophication, red tide, mat, pond scum, frog spit, symbiotic alga, phycobiont, lichen

2 **algae**, blue-green algae, cyanobacteria, Cyanophyta, golden-brown algae, Chrysophyta, chrysophyte, yellow-green algae, Xanthophyta, xanthophyte, green algae, Chlorophyta, chlorophyte, isokont, brown algae (*or* seaweeds), Phaeophyta, phaeophyte, red algae (*or* seaweeds), Rhodophyta, rhodophyte, study of algae, algology, phycology, algologist, phycologist

3 **plant body**, thallus, frond, holdfast, hapteron, stem, stipe, branch, branchlet, lamina, blade, float, air bladder, thread, rhizoid, protonema, frustule, theca, epitheca, hypotheca, algal pigment, chlorophyll, carotene, xanthophyll, fucoxanthin, phycocyanin, phycoerythrin, eyespot, stigma, blepharoplast, food store, pyrenoid, starch, paramylum

4 **reproductive body**, zoospore, aplanospore, hypnospore, autospore, cyst, propagule, hormogonium, coenobium, sexual reproduction, isogamy, anisogamy, oogamy, gamete, spermatozoid, antherozoid, oosphere, gonidium, antheridium, oogonium, manubrium, conceptacle, spermatangium, spermatium, carpogonium, carpospore

5 **algal product**, agar, algin, alginate, laver

Algae

anabaena	laminaria
badderlocks	laver
bladderwrack	nostoc
bull kelp	nullipore
carrageen, carragheen,	oarweed
or carageen	peacock's tail
Ceylon moss	redware
chlorella	rockweed
conferva	sargassum
desmid	sea lace
diatom	sea lettuce
dinoflagellate	sea tangle
dulse	seaware
euglena	sea wrack
fucoid	spirogyra
fucus	stonewort
gulfweed	wrack
kelp	

bread, miru (Jap), kombu (Jap), fossil algae, diatomaceous earth, stromatolite

6 **lichen**, reindeer moss, rock tripe, oak moss, Spanish moss, crustose lichen, foliose lichen, fruticose lichen, symbiosis, fungal constituent, mycobiont, algal constituent, phycobiont, root, rhizine, propagation, podetium, isidium, soredium, study of lichens, lichenology, lichenometry, lichenologist

▶ *88 Ferns and Mosses, 89 Fungi*

ADJECTIVES

7 **algal**, algoid, diatomaceous, conferval, confervoid, fucoid, unicellular, colonial, coenobial, filamentous, thalloid, siphonaceous, palmelloid, dendroid, sessile, motile, symbiotic, epiphytic, epilithic, flagellate, uniflagellate, biflagellate, multiflagellate, parenchymatous, pseudoparenchymatous, algological, phycological

8 **lichenoid**, lichenous, lichenose, lichened, lichenized, licheniform, crustose, foliose, fruticose, corticolous, saxicolous, lichenological

ADVERBS

9 **algologically**, colonially, epiphytically, symbiotically

Places

NOUNS

1 **country**, nation, nationhood, state, statehood, land, body politic, sovereign state (*or* nation), sovereignty, self-governing state, independent state, free country (*or* nation), self-determination, democracy, parliamentary democracy, dictatorship, oligarchy, monarchy, republic, people's republic, capitalist country, socialist country, communist country, Iron Curtain country, power, superpower, Western nation, third-world country, nonaligned (*or* unaligned) country, neutral nation, isolationist nation

2 **union of nations**, federation, confederation, commonwealth, commonweal, British Commonwealth, EC (European Community), CIS (Commonwealth of Independent States), UN (United Nations), Western bloc, Eastern bloc, Soviet bloc

▶ *12 Government and Politics, 249 Region, 135 Union*

3 **dominion**, domain, realm, kingdom, principality, principate, duchy, dukedom, grand duchy, archduchy, archdukedom, earldom, palatinate, sultanate, chieftaincy, toparchy, empire, British Empire, Roman Empire, Holy Roman Empire, Ottoman Empire, Mogul Empire, province, territory, occupied country, colony, settlement, protectorate, mandate, mandated territory (*or* mandate), mandatory, captive nation, Lebensraum, buffer state, ally, satellite nation, puppet regime, sphere of influence, imperialism, colonialism

▶ *688 Authority, 166 Rule, 692 Command, 701 Subjection*

4 **nationalism**, nationality, ultranationalism, national consciousness, patriotism, chauvinism, jingoism, isolationism, protectionism, xenophobia, racism, gung-ho nationalism (Inf)

▶ *805 Pride*

5 **internationalism**, internationality, global outlook, universality, universalism, cosmopolitanism

Names for Inhabitants (mostly offensive)

Abo (Aus; Aborigine)
Anglo (Aus; person of British descent)
Argie (Argentinian)
Aussie (Australian)
Balt (Aus; person of Baltic descent)
binghi (Aus; Aborigine)
bogtrotter (Irish)
bohunk (US; person from E or central Europe)
buck (US; young male Indian or Negro)
Canuck (Can; French Canadian)
Chink (or Chinky) (Chinese)
coon (Negro)
crunchie (South African; Afrikaner)
dago (person of Latin descent)
ding (Aus; Italian or Greek)

dinge (US; Negro)
Eyetie (Brit; Italian)
Frog (French person)
gook (US; person from Far East)
goy (gentile)
greaseball (US; Italian)
greaser (US; Mexican)
gringo (person from English-speaking country)
guinea (US; Italian)
gyppo (Brit; Egyptian)
honky (US; White person)
hori (NZ; Maori)
Hun (German)
Hunk (or Hunkie) (US; person from E or central Europe)
Jackie (or Jacky) (Aus; Aborigine)
Jap (Japanese)
Jerry (German)

jim crow (US; Negro)
Jock (Brit; Scots person)
kike (Jew)
kipper (Aus; English person)
Kraut (German)
limey (US; British person)
Mick (Irish person)
munt (Zimbabwe; Black African)
Nip (Japanese)
ofay (US; White person)
Paddy (Irish person)
Paki (Brit; Pakistani)
Pepsi (Can; French Canadian)
polak (Pole)
pom (or pommie) (Aus; English person)
redleg (Carib; poor White)
Ruskie (Russian)
Sawney (Scots person)

sheeny (Jew)
shiksa (non-Jewish girl)
Siwash (US; North American Indian)
spade (Negro)
spic (or spick or spik) (US; Latin American)
Taffy (Brit; Welsh person)
Uncle Tom (servile or obsequious Negro)
Wasp (US; White Anglo-Saxon Protestant)
wetback (US; Mexican)
whitey (or whity) (US; White person)
wog (Brit; non-White)
wop (Italian, Spanish, or Portuguese)
Yank (or Yankee) (American)
yid (Jew)

Countries (with capitals)

Afghanistan (Kabul)
Albania (Tirana)
Algeria (Algiers)
Angola (Luanda)
Antigua and Barbuda
 (St John's)
Argentina (Buenos
 Aires)
Armenia (Yerevan)
Australia (Canberra)
Austria (Vienna)
Azerbaijan (Baku)
Bahamas, The (Nassau)
Bahrain (Manama)
Bangladesh (Dhaka)
Barbados (Bridgetown)
Belarus (Minsk)
Belgium (Brussels)
Belize (Belmopan)
Benin (Porto Novo)
Bhutan (Thamphu)
Bolivia (La Paz)
Bosnia-Hercegovina
 (Sarajevo)
Botswana (Gaborone)
Brazil (Brasilia)
Brunei (Bandar Seri
 Begawan)
Bulgaria (Sofia)
Burkina Faso
 (Ouagadougou)
Burma (Rangoon)
Burundi (Bujumbura)
Byelorussia (Minsk)
Cambodia (Phnom
 Penh)
Cameroon (Yaoundé)
Canada (Ottawa)
Cape Verde (Praia)
Central African Repub-
 lic (Bangui)
Chad (Ndjamena)
Chile (Santiago)
China (Beijing or
 Peking)
Colombia (Bogota)
Comoros (Moroni)
Congo (Brazzaville)
Costa Rica (San José)
Croatia (Zagreb)
Cuba (Havana)
Cyprus (Nicosia)
Czech Republic (Prague)
Denmark (Copenhagen)

Djibouti (Djibouti)
Dominica (Roseau)
Dominican Republic
 (Santo Domingo)
Ecuador (Quito)
Egypt (Cairo)
El Salvador (San Salva-
 dor)
Equatorial Guinea
 (Malabo)
Estonia (Tallinn)
Ethiopia (Addis Ababa)
Fiji (Suva)
Finland (Helsinki)
France (Paris)
Gabon (Libreville)
Gambia, The (Banjul)
Georgia (Tbilisi)
Germany (Bonn)
Ghana (Accra)
Greece (Athens)
Grenada (St George's)
Guatemala (Guatemala
 City)
Guinea (Conakry)
Guinea-Bissau (Bissau)
Guyana (Georgetown)
Haiti (Port-au-Prince)
Honduras (Tegucigalpa)
Hungary (Budapest)
Iceland (Reykjavik)
India (New Delhi)
Indonesia (Jakarta)
Iran (Tehran)
Iraq (Baghdad)
Ireland (Dublin)
Israel (Jerusalem)
Italy (Rome)
Jamaica (Kingston)
Japan (Tokyo)
Jordan (Amman)
Kazakhstan (Alma-Ata)
Kenya (Nairobi)
Kirghizia (Frunze)
Korea, North
 (Pyongyang)
Korea, South (Seoul)
Kuwait (Kuwait)
Laos (Vientiane)
Latvia (Riga)
Lebanon (Beirut)
Lesotho (Maseru)
Liberia (Monrovia)
Libya (Tripoli)

Liechtenstein (Vaduz)
Lithuania (Vilnius)
Luxembourg (Luxem-
 bourg)
Madagascar (An-
 tananarivo)
Malawi (Lilongwe)
Malaysia (Kuala Lum-
 pur)
Maldives (Malé)
Mali (Bamako)
Malta (Valletta)
Mauritania (Nouakchott)
Mauritius (Port Louis)
Mexico (Mexico City)
Moldavia (Kishinev)
Monaco (Monaco-Ville)
Mongolia (Ulan Bator)
Morocco (Rabat)
Mozambique (Maputo)
Namibia (Windhoek)
Nauru (Yaren)
Nepal (Kathmandu)
Netherlands, The (Am-
 sterdam)
New Zealand (Welling-
 ton)
Nicaragua (Managua)
Niger (Niamey)
Nigeria (Abuja)
Norway (Oslo)
Oman (Muscat)
Pakistan (Islamabad)
Panama (Panama City)
Papua New Guinea
 (Port Moresby)
Paraguay (Asunción)
Peru (Lima)
Philippines (Manila)
Poland (Warsaw)
Portugal (Lisbon)
Qatar (Doha)
Romania (Bucharest)
Russia (Moscow)
Rwanda (Kigali)
St Christopher and
 Nevis (or St Kitts-
 Nevis) (Basseterre)
St Lucia (Castries)
St Vincent and the
 Grenadines (Kings-
 town)
San Marino (San Ma-
 rino)

São Tomé e Principe
 (São Tomé)
Saudi Arabia (Riyadh)
Senegal (Dakar)
Serbia (Belgrade)
Seychelles (Victoria)
Sierra Leone (Freetown)
Singapore (Singapore)
Slovakia (Bratislava)
Slovenia (Ljubljana)
Solomon Islands
 (Honiara)
Somalia (Mogadishu)
South Africa (Pretoria)
South Yemen (Aden)
Spain (Madrid)
Sri Lanka (Colombo)
Sudan (Khartoum)
Surinam (Paramaribo)
Swaziland (Mbabane)
Sweden (Stockholm)
Syria (Damascus)
Tadzhikistan
 (Dushanbe)
Taiwan (Taipei)
Tanzania (Dodoma)
Thailand (Bangkok)
Togo (Lomé)
Tonga (Nuku'alofa)
Trinidad and Tobago
 (Port of Spain)
Tunisia (Tunis)
Turkey (Ankara)
Turkmenistan
 (Ashkhabad)
Uganda (Kampala)
Ukraine (Kiev)
United Arab Emirates
 (Abu Dhabi)
United Kingdom (Lon-
 don)
United States of Amer-
 ica (Washington)
Uruguay (Montevideo)
Uzbekistan (Tashkent)
Vanuatu (Vila)
Venezuela (Caracas)
Vietnam (Hanoi)
Western Samoa (Apia)
Yemen (or North
 Yemen) (San'a)
Zaïre (Kinshasa)
Zambia (Lusaka)
Zimbabwe (Harare)

6 **native land**, native soil, country of origin, mother country, motherland, fatherland, *Vaterland* (Ger), *patria* (L), the old country, one's native ground, birthplace, cradle, home, homeland, home ground, God's (own) country (Inf)

▶ *256 Habitat, 156 Beginning*

7 **United States (US)**, United States of America (USA), America, the States, Stateside, Columbia, Land of Liberty, the Land of the Free, the Americans, Americanism, Americana, Americanization, American eagle, Stars and Stripes, Yankee (Doodle), the Melting Pot (Inf), Uncle Sugar (US inf), Yank (Inf), US of A (Inf), Uncle Sam (Inf)

8 **Great Britain**, the British Isles, United Kingdom (UK), Britain, (Perfidious) Albion (Lit), Britannia, Britishism, Briticism, the British, Briton, Brit (Inf), British bulldog (Inf), Limeyland (US sl)

9 **England**, (Perfidious) Albion (Lit), the English, Englishman (*or* woman), Northerner, Southerner, Englishness, Anglicization, Anglicism, Anglophile, Anglophobe, John Bull

10 **Ireland**, the Emerald Isle, Erin (Lit), Hibernia (Lit), Eire, the Republic of Ireland, the Republic, the South, Northern Ireland, Ulster, the Six Counties, the North, the Irish, the Northern Irish, Irishman (*or* woman), Irishness, Irishism

11 **Scotland**, Caledonia (Lit), the Highlands, the Lowlands, the Scottish, Scotsman (or woman), Scot, Caledonian, Highlander, Lowlander, Scottishness

12 **Wales**, *Cymru* (Welsh), *Cambria* (L), the Principality, North Wales, South Wales, the Welsh, North Walian, South Walian, Welshman (or woman), Welshness

13 **native**, countryman (or -woman), citizen, national, local

▶ *255 Inhabitant*

14 **nationalist**, ultranationalist, colonialist, patriot, jingoist, isolationist, protectionist, xenophobe, racist

15 **internationalist**, universalist, cosmopolitan, citizen of the world

ADJECTIVES

16 **national**, federal, state, sovereign, self-governing, independent, self-determining, democratic, republican, welfare, socialist, socialistic, communist, communistic, non-aligned (or unaligned), international, imperialistic, colonial, mandated, buffer, satellite, puppet, nationalistic, ultranational, ultranationalistic, chauvinistic, jingoistic, gung-ho (Inf)

VERBS

17 **become a nation**, become independent, declare independence, become self-governing, gain self-determination, have sovereignty, democratize, socialize, communize

18 **exert sovereignty**, rule, occupy, colonize, settle, mandate, Americanize, Anglicize

ADVERBS

19 **nationally**, federally, independently, democratically, socialistically, communistically, internationally, imperialistically, colonially, nationalistically, patriotically, in a patriotic way, chauvinistically, jingoistically

92　Administrative Areas

NOUNS

1 **administrative area**, governmental area, state, enclave, county, metropolitan county, province, region, division, district, congressional district (US), urban district, rural district, borough, constituency, area, township, community, parish, sheading (Isle of Man)

2 **former British divisions**, hundred, riding, tithing, wapentake, soke, shire

3 **other**, barony (Ireland), department, arondissement (France), canton (Switzerland), ep-

Counties

English Counties (and Administrative Centres)
Avon (Bristol)
Bedfordshire (Bedford)
Berkshire (Reading)
Buckinghamshire (Aylesbury)
Cambridgeshire (Cambridge)
Cheshire (Chester)
Cleveland (Middlesbrough)
Cornwall (Truro)
Cumbria (Carlisle)
Derbyshire (Matlock)
Devon (or Devonshire) (Exeter)
Dorset (Dorchester)
Durham (Durham)
East Sussex (Lewes)
Essex (Chelmsford)
Gloucestershire (Gloucester)
Hampshire (Winchester)
Hereford and Worcester (Worcester)
Hertfordshire (Hertford)
Humberside (Beverley)
Kent (Maidstone)
Lancashire (Preston)
Leicestershire (Leicester)
Lincolnshire (Lincoln)
Norfolk (Norwich)
Northamptonshire (Northampton)
Northumberland (Morpeth)
North Yorkshire (Northallerton)
Nottinghamshire (Nottingham)
Oxfordshire (Oxford)
Shropshire (Shrewsbury)
Somerset (Taunton)
South Yorkshire (Barnsley)
Staffordshire (Stafford)
Suffolk (Ipswich)

Surrey (Kingston upon Thames)
Tyne and Wear (Newcastle-on-Tyne)
Warwickshire (Warwick)
West Sussex (Chichester)
West Yorkshire (Wakefield)
Wight, Isle of (Newport)
Wiltshire (Trowbridge)

Welsh Counties (and Administrative Centres)
Clwyd (Mold)
Dyfed (Carmarthen)
Gwent (Cwmbran)
Gwynedd (Caernarfon)
Mid Glamorgan (Cardiff)
Powys (Llandrindod Wells)
South Glamorgan (Cardiff)
West Glamorgan (Swansea)

Scottish Regions and Counties (and Administrative Centres)
Borders (Newton St Boswells)
Central (Stirling)
Dumfries and Galloway (Dumfries)
Fife (Glenrothes)
Grampian (Aberdeen)
Highland (Inverness)
Lothian (Edinburgh)
Orkney (Kirkwall)
Shetland (Lerwick)
Strathclyde (Glasgow)
Tayside (Dundee)
Western Isles (Stornoway)

Northern Ireland Counties (and County Towns)
Antrim (Belfast)
Armagh (Armagh)

Down (Downpatrick)
Fermanagh (Enniskillen)
Londonderry (Londonderry)
Tyrone (Omagh)

Republic of Ireland Provinces
Connacht (or Connaught)
Leinster
Munster
Ulster

Republic of Ireland Counties (and County Towns)
Carlow (Carlow)
Cavan (Cavan)
Clare (Ennis)
Cork (Cork)
Donegal (Lifford)
Dublin (Dublin)
Galway (Galway)
Kerry (Tralee)
Kildare (Naas)
Kilkenny (Kilkenny)
Laois (Portlaoise)
Leitrim (Carrick-on-Shannon)
Limerick (Limerick)
Longford (Longford)
Louth (Dundalk)
Mayo (Castlebar)
Meath (Trim)
Monaghan (Monaghan)
Offaly (Tullamore)
Roscommon (Roscommon)
Sligo (Sligo)
Tipperary (Clonmel)
Waterford (Waterford)
Westmeath (Mullingar)
Wexford (Wexford)
Wicklow (Wicklow)

American States

State (Capital)	
Alabama (Montgomery)	New Hampshire (Concord)
Alaska (Juneau)	New Jersey (Trenton)
Arizona (Phoenix)	New Mexico (Santa Fe)
Arkansas (Little Rock)	New York (Albany)
California (Sacramento)	North Carolina (Raleigh)
Colorado (Denver)	North Dakota (Bismarck)
Connecticut (Hartford)	
Delaware (Dover)	Ohio (Columbus)
Florida (Tallahassee)	Oklahoma (Oklahoma City)
Georgia (Atlanta)	
Hawaii (Honolulu)	Oregon (Salem)
Idaho (Boise)	Pennsylvania (Harrisburg)
Illinois (Springfield)	
Indiana (Indianapolis)	Rhode Island (Providence)
Iowa (Des Moines)	
Kansas (Topeka)	South Carolina (Columbia)
Kentucky (Frankfort)	
Louisiana (Baton Rouge)	South Dakota (Pierre)
	Tennessee (Nashville)
Maine (Augusta)	Texas (Austin)
Maryland (Annapolis)	Utah (Salt Lake City)
Massachusetts (Boston)	Vermont (Montpelier)
Michigan (Lansing)	Virginia (Richmond)
Minnesota (St Paul)	Washington (Olympia)
Mississippi (Jackson)	West Virginia (Charleston)
Missouri (Jefferson City)	
Montana (Helena)	Wisconsin (Madison)
Nebraska (Lincoln)	Wyoming (Cheyenne)
Nevada (Carson City)	

Australian States and Territories

State/Territory (Capital)
New South Wales (Sydney)
Queensland (Brisbane)
South Australia (Adelaide)
Tasmania (Hobart)
The Australian Capital Territory (Canberra)
The Northern Territory (Darwin)
Victoria (Melbourne)
Western Australia (Perth)

New Zealand Regions and Territories

Region/Territory (Administrative Centre)
Aorangi (Timaru)
Auckland (Auckland)
Bay of Plenty (Tauranga)
Canterbury (Christchurch)
Cook Islands (Avarua)
East Cape (Gisborne)
Hawke's Bay (Napier, Hastings)
Horowhenua (Levin)
Manawatu (Palmerston North)
Marlborough (Blenheim)
Nelson Bays (Nelson)
Niue (Alofi)
Northland (Whangarei)
Otago (Dunedin)
Southland (Invercargil)
Taranaki (New Plymouth)
Thames Valley (Thames-Coromandel)
Tongariro (Taupo)
Waikato (Hamilton)
Wairarapa (Masterton)
Wanganui (Wanganui)
Wellington (Wellington)
West Coast (Greymouth)

Canadian Provinces and Territories

Province/Territory (Capital)
Alberta (Edmonton)
British Colombia (Victoria)
Manitoba (Winnipeg)
New Brunswick (Fredericton)
Newfoundland (St John's)
Northwest Territories (Yellowknife)
Nova Scotia (Halifax)
Ontario (Toronto)
Prince Edward Island (Charlottetown)
Quebec (Quebec)
Saskatchewan (Regina)
Yukon Territory (Whitehouse)

archy, prefecture (Greece), guberniya, oblast (former USSR), commune (Iceland), fylker (Norway), Län (Sweden), Land (Germany)
▶ *12 Government and Politics, 249 Region, 301 Enclosure, 688 Authority*

4 **community**, municipality, city, metropolis, borough, town, township, village, hamlet, quarter, hinterland
▶ *93 Cities, Towns, and Villages*

5 **administrative headquarters**, headquarters, administrative centre, station, seat of government, capital, national capital, state capital, provincial capital, territorial capital, county town, county seat (US)
▶ *256 Habitat, 592 Plan*

ADJECTIVES

6 **administrative**, divisional, governmental, departmental, congressional, constituent, metropolitan, municipal, provincial, rural, territorial, national

VERBS

7 **administer**, govern, have jurisdiction, rule, organize

ADVERBS

8 **administratively**, governmentally, divisionally, zonally, departmentally, sectionally, regionally, territorially, municipally, parochially, provincially

93 Cities, Towns, and Villages

NOUNS

1 **city**, municipality, metropolis, metropolitan area, greater city, megalopolis, conurbation, urban complex, urban spread (*or* sprawl), seat of government, capital, industrial city, commercial city, twinned city, sister city (US), town, country town, holiday town, community, village, hamlet, urbanization, gentrification, suburbanization, countrification
▶ *256 Habitat, 260 Littleness, 143 Part*

2 **American cities**, state capital, county seat, New York, Chicago, Los Angeles, Hollywood, San Francisco, Philadelphia, Pittsburgh, Boston, Miami, Atlanta, New Orleans, Houston, Dallas, St Louis, Seattle, Detroit, Washington, Denver, Nashville, Las Vegas

Cities, Towns, and Villages

Afghanistan
Herat
Kabul
Kandahar

Albania
Durrës
Tirana

Algeria
Algiers
Constantine
El Djazair
Qacentina
Oran
Wahran

Angola
Lobito
Luanda

Argentina
Buenos Aires
Cordoba
La Plata
Mendoza
Rosario

Armenia
Kirovakan
Yerevan

Australia
Adelaide
Alice Springs
Brisbane
Canberra
Darwin
Hobart
Melbourne
Newcastle
Perth
Sydney
Wollongong

Austria
Graz
Innsbruck
Salzburg
Vienna

Azerbaijan
Baku
Kirovabad

Bahamas, The
Nassau
New Providence

Bangladesh
Chittagong
Dhaka
Khulna

Belgium
Antwerp
Bruges
Brussels
Ghent
Liège
Namur
Ostend
Ypres
Zeebrugge

Bolivia
Cochabamba

La Paz
Santa Cruz

Bosnia-Hercegovina
Sarajevo
Zenica

Brazil
Brasilia
Fortaleza
Porto Alegre
Recife
Rio de Janeiro
São Paulo

Bulgaria
Plovdiv
Sofia
Varna

Burma
Mandalay
Moulmein
Rangoon

Byelorussia
Brest
Minsk
Pinsk

Cambodia
Kampot
Phnom Penh

Cameroon
Douala
Yaoundé

Canada
Calgary
Charlottetown
Edmonton
Fredericton
Halifax
Hamilton
Kingston
Montreal
Moose Jaw
Niagara Falls
Ottawa
Quebec
Regina
St John's
Saskatoon
Thunder Bay
Toronto
Vancouver
Victoria
Whitehouse
Windsor
Winnipeg
Yellowknife

Chile
Concepción
Santiago
Valparaíso

China
Anshan
Beijing (or Peking)
Canton
Changchun
Chengdu
Chongquig
Fushun

Harbin
Jinan
Kunming
Lanchow
Lüda
Lüshun
Nanjing
Shanghai
Shenyang
Taiyuan
Tianjin
Wuhan
Xi An

Colombia
Barranquilla
Bogotá
Cali
Cartagena
Medellin

Congo
Brazzaville
Pointe-Noire

Costa Rica
San José

Croatia
Osijek
Zagreb

Cuba
Guantánamo
Havana
Santiago de Cuba

Cyprus
Nicosia

Czech Republic
Brno
Ceské Budějovice
Ostrava
Prague

Denmark
Aalborg (or Ålborg)
Copenhagen
Esbjerg

Dominican Republic
Santo Domingo

Ecuador
Guayaquil
Quito

Egypt
Alexandria
Aswan
Cairo
El Giza
Ismailia
Luxor
Port Said
Suez
Tanta
Thebes

El Salvador
San Salvador
Santa Ana

England
Arundel
Aylesbury
Barnsley
Bath
Bedford
Berwick-on-Tweed
Beverley
Birmingham
Blackburn
Blackpool
Bournemouth
Bradford
Brighton
Bristol
Buckingham
Cambridge
Canterbury
Carlisle
Cheltenham
Chester
Chesterfield
Chichester
Colchester
Coventry
Cowes
Crewe
Darlington
Dartmouth
Deal
Derby
Devizes
Doncaster
Dorchester
Douglas
Dover
Durham
Exeter
Folkestone
Gloucester
Great Yarmouth
Grimsby
Halifax
Harrogate
Harwich
Hastings
Hereford
Hertford
Huddersfield
Hull
Ipswich
King's Lynn
Lancaster
Leeds
Leicester
Lincoln
Liverpool
London
Luton
Maidenhead
Maidstone
Manchester
Matlock
Middlesbrough
Milton Keynes
Morpeth
Newark
Newcastle-upon-Tyne

Newmarket
Newport
Northampton
Norwich
Nottingham
Oldham
Oxford
Penzance
Peterborough
Plymouth
Poole
Portsmouth
Preston
Reading
Richmond
Rugby
St Ives
Salisbury
Scarborough
Sheffield
Shrewsbury
Southampton
Southport
Stafford
Stoke-on-Trent
Stratford-on-Avon
Sunderland
Swindon
Taunton
Torquay
Trowbridge
Truro
Tunbridge Wells
Wakefield
Warrington
Warwick
Wells
Weymouth
Whitby
Wigan
Winchester
Windsor
Wolverhampton
Worcester
York

Estonia
Tallinn (or Tallin)
Tartu

Ethiopia
Addis Ababa
Asmara

Finland
Helsinki
Tampere
Turku

France
Abbeville
Aix-en-Provence
Alençon
Amiens
Avignon
Bayeux
Bayonne
Biarritz
Bordeaux

Boulogne
Brest
Caen
Calais
Cannes
Chartres
Cherbourg
Cluny
Dieppe
Dijon
Dunkirk (or Dunkerque)
Grenoble
Le Havre
Le Mans
Lille
Limoges
Lourdes
Lyons (or Lyon)
Mâcon
Marseilles (or Marseille)
Metz
Montélimar
Montpellier
Nancy
Nîmes
Nantes
Nice
Orléans
Paris
Perpignan
Reims (or Rheims)
Rouen
St Étienne
St Malo
St Tropez
Strasbourg
Toulon
Toulouse
Tours
Verdun
Versailles
Vichy

Germany
Aachen
Augsburg
Baden-Baden
Berlin
Bonn
Brandenburg
Bremen
Brunswick
Cologne (or Köln)
Darmstadt
Dortmund
Dresden
Düsseldorf
Erfurt
Essen
Frankfurt am Main
Frankfurt an der Oder
Halle
Hamburg
Hanover (or Hannover)
Heidelberg

Homburg
Ingolstadt
Kassel
Kiel
Koblenz
Leipzig
Lübeck
Magdeburg
Mainz
Mannheim
Meissen
Munich (or
  München)
Neuburg an
  der Donau
Nuremberg
  (or Nürnberg)
Potsdam
Rostock
Saarbrücken
Spandau
Stuttgart
Wiesbaden
Worms

Ghana
Accra
Kumasi

Greece
Athens
Canea
Corinth
Kaválla
Patras
Piraeus
Salonika (or
  Thessaloníki)

Guatemala
Guatemala
  City

Haiti
Port-au-Prince

Honduras
San Pedro
  Sula
Tegucigalpa

Hungary
Budapest
Debrecen
Miskolc
Pécs

Iceland
Reykjavik

India
Agartala
Agra
Ahmedabad
Ajmer
Allahabad
Amritsar
Bangalore
Bhopal
Bhubaneswar
Bombay
Calcutta
Chandigarh
Darjeeling
Gwalior
Howrah
Hyderabad
Imphal
Indore

Jaipur
Jamshedpur
Jhansi
Jodhpur
Kanpur
Kohima
Lucknow
Madras
Meerut
Mysore
Nagpur
New Delhi
Old Delhi
Patna
Poona (or
  Pune)
Rampur
Shillong
Simla
Srinagar
Trivandrum
Vadodara
Varanasi

Indonesia
Bandung
Jakarta
Medan
Palembang
Surabaya

Iran
Abadan
Shiraz
Tabriz
Tehran

Iraq
Baghdad
Basra
Kirkuk
Mosul

Ireland
Balla
Ballymurphy
Blarney
Carlow
Carrick-on-
  Shannon
Castlebar
Cavan
Clare
Clonmel
Connemara
Cork
Dublin
Dundalk
Ennis
Galway
Kells
Kildare
Kilkenny
Killarney
Lifford
Limerick
Longford
Monaghan
Mullingar
Naas
Portlaoise
Roscommon
Shannon
Shillelagh
Sligo
Tipperary
Tralee

Trim
Tullamore
Waterford
Wexford
Wicklow

Israel
Beersheba
Bethlehem
Gaza
Haifa
Jaffa
Jerusalem
Tel Aviv

Italy
Agrigento
Bologna
Brindisi
Florence
Genoa
Messina
Milan
Naples
Padua
Palermo
Parma
Pisa
Ravenna
Reggio di
  Calabria
Rome
Salerno
San Remo
Siena
Syracuse
Trento (or
  Trent)
Trieste
Turin
Vatican City
Venice
Verona

Jamaica
Kingston

Japan
Fukuoka
Hiroshima
Kitakyushu
Kobe
Kyoto
Nagasaki
Nagoya
Osaka
Sapporo
Tokyo
Yokohama

Jordan
Amman
Az-Zarqu

Kazakhstan
Alma-Ata
Karaganda

Kenya
Mombasa
Nairobi

Korea, North
Pyongyang
Wŏnsan

Korea, South
Pusan
Seoul
Taegu

Kuwait
Kuwait

Latvia
Daugavpils
Riga

Lebanon
Beirut
Tripoli

Liberia
Monrovia

Libya
Benghazi
Tobruk
Tripoli

Lithuania
Kaunas
Siauliai
Vilnius

Luxembourg
Luxembourg

Madagascar
Antananarivo

Malawi
Blantyre-
  Limbe
Lilongwe

Malaysia
Kuala Lumpur

Mali
Bamako
Timbuktu

Malta
Valletta

Mauritania
Nouakchott

Mauritius
Port Louis

Mexico
Acapulco
Guadalajara
Juárez
Matamoros
Mérida
Mexico City
Monterrey
Puebla
Tampico
Tijuana
Veracruz

Monaco
Monaco-Ville
Monte Carlo

Mongolia
Ulan Bator

Morocco
Casablanca
Marrakech
  (or Marra-
  kesh)
Rabat
Tangier

Mozambique
Maputo

**Netherlands,
  The**
Amsterdam
Arnhem
Dordrecht (or
  Dort)
Eindhoven
Hague, The
Leiden (or
  Leyden)
Maastricht
Rotterdam
Utrecht

New Zealand
Auckland
Christchurch
Dunedin
Manukau
Napier
Nelson
Wellington

Nicaragua
Managua

Nigeria
Abuja
Enugu
Ibadan
Kano
Lagos

**Northern
  Ireland**
Antrim
Armagh
Ballymena
Belfast
Coleraine
Downpatrick
Dunmore
Enniskillen
Kilconnell
Larne
Lisburn
Londonderry
  (or Derry)
Lurgan
Newcastle
Newry
Newtown-
  abbey
Omagh
Portadown
Portrush
Strabane
Trillick

Norway
Bergen
Oslo
Trondheim

Oman
Muscat

Pakistan
Faisalabad
Hyderabad
Islamabad
Karachi
Lahore
Peshawar
Quetta
Rawalpindi

Panama
Panama City

Peru
Arequipa
Callao
Cuzco (or
  Cusco)
Lima

**Philippines,
  The**
Manila
Quezon City

Poland
Cracow
Gdansk (or
  Danzig)
Lodz
Lublin
Poznań
Przemyśl
Warsaw
Wroclaw

Portugal
Coimbra
Lisbon
Oporto

Romania
Braşov
Bucharest
Constanţa

Russia
Astrakhan
Gorky
Irkutsk
Kalinin
Kaliningrad
Moscow
Novgorod
Omsk
Pskov
St Petersburg
Smolensk
Sverdlovsk
Volgograd
Yakutsk

Saudi Arabia
Jidda
Mecca
Medina
Riyadh

Scotland
Aberdeen
Ayr
Banff
Bannockburn
Bonar Bridge
Braemar
Coldstream
Douglas
Dumbarton
Dumfries
Dunbar
Dundee
Dunfermline
Dunoon
Duns
East Kilbride
Edinburgh
Falkirk
Forfar
Fort William
Galashiels
Glasgow
Glencoe

Glenrothes	Barcelona	**Trinidad and**	Des Moines	New Haven	Waco
Greenock	Bilbao	**Tobago**	Detroit	New London	Washington
Hamilton	Cádiz	Plymouth	Dover	New Orleans	Waterbury
Hawick	Córdoba	Port of Spain	Duluth	Newport	Wheeling
Inverness	Granada		El Paso	News	Wichita
Islay	Madrid	**Tunisia**	Eugene	New York	Worcester
John o'Groats	Málaga	Tunis	Evansville	Niagara Falls	Yonkers
Kelso	Pamplona		Fairbanks	Norfolk	Youngstown
Kilmarnock	San	**Turkey**	Fayetteville	Oakland	
Kinross	Sebastián	Ankara	Flint	Oak Ridge	**Ukraine**
Kirkcaldy	Santiago de	Erzurum	Fort Lauder-	Oklahoma	Chernobyl
Kirkcudbright	Compostela	Istanbul	dale	City	Chernovtsy
Kirkwall	Saragossa (or	Izmir	Fort Wayne	Olympia	Donetsk
Lanark	Zaragoza)	Tarsus	Fort Worth	Omaha	Kharkov
Lerwick	Seville		Frankfurt	Orlando	Kiev
Lockerbie	Toledo	**Uganda**	Fresno	Oxnard	Krivoy Rog
Lossiemouth	Valencia	Entebbe	Galveston	Ozark	Lvov
Montrose		Kampala	Garland	Palm Springs	Odessa
Motherwell	**Sri Lanka**		Gary	Palo Alto	Sevastopol
Newton St	Colombo	**United Arab**	Gettysburg	Pasadena	(or
Boswells	Kandy	**Emirates**	Grand Rapids	Peoria	Sebastopol)
Newport	Trincomalee	Abu Dhabi	Green Bay	Philadelphia	Yalta
Oban			Greensboro	Phoenix	
Paisley	**Sudan**	**USA**	Greenville	Pierre	**Uruguay**
Perth	Dongola	Abilene	Hampton	Pittsburgh	Maldonado
Ronaldsay	Khartoum	Akron	Hannibal	Portland	Montevideo
St Andrews	Omdurman	Albany	Harrisburg	Poughkeepsie	Salto
Selkirk	Port Sudan	Albuquerque	Hartford	Princeton	
Stirling		Amarillo	Helena	Providence	**Uzbekistan**
Stornoway	**Swaziland**	Anaheim	Hoboken	Raleigh	Samarkand
Strathblane	Lavumisa	Anchorage	Hollywood	Reading	Tashkent
Thurso	Mbabane	Annapolis	Honolulu	Reno	
Troon	Stegi	Ann Arbor	Houston	Richmond	**Venezuela**
Wick		Appomattox	Huntingdon	Riverside	Caracas
	Sweden	Arlington		Roanoke	Maracaibo
Senegal	Boden	Atlantic City	Beach	Rochester	San Cristóbal
Dakar	Göteborg (or	Atlanta	Huntsville	Sacramento	
Kaolack	Gothen-	Augusta	Independence	Saginaw	**Vietnam**
	burg)	Aurora	Indianapolis	St Louis	Dien Bien
Serbia	Hälsingborg	Austin	Jackson	St Paul	Phu
Belgrade	Malmö	Baltimore	Jacksonville	St Petersburg	Haiphong
Kruševac	Stockholm	Bangor	Jefferson City	Salem	Hanoi
	Uppsala	Baton Rouge	Jersey City	Salt Lake City	Ho Chi Minh
Sierra Leone		Berkeley	Johnstown	San Antonio	City
Freetown	**Switzerland**	Bethlehem	Juneau	San Diego	My Lai
	Basel (or	Beverly Hills	Kalamazoo	San Francisco	
Singapore	Basle)	Biloxi	Kansas City	San Jose	**Wales**
Singapore	Bern	Birmingham	Key West	Santa Ana	Aberdare
	Geneva	Bismarck	Knoxville	Santa Barbara	Abergavenny
Slovakia	Lausanne	Boise	Lancaster	Santa Fe	Aberystwyth
Bratislava	Lucerne	Boston	Lansing	Savannah	Bala
Košice	Lugano	Boulder	Las Vegas	Schenectady	Bangor
	St Moritz	Brooklyn	Lexington	Seattle	Barry
Slovenia	Zürich	Buffalo	Lima	Selma	Brecon
Kranj		Butte	Lincoln	Shreveport	Bridgend
Ljubljana	**Syria**	Cambridge	Little Rock	Spokane	Caernarfon
	Aleppo	Camden	Long Beach	Springfield	(or
Somalia	Damascus	Canton	Los Angeles	Stamford	Caernarvon)
Mogadishu	Homs (or	Carson	Louisville	Stockton	Cardiff
	Hums)	Cedar Rapids	Lowell	Syracuse	Cardigan
South Africa	Palmyra	Champaign	Lubbock	Tacoma	Carmarthen
Bloemfontein		Charleston	Madison	Tallahassee	Colwyn Bay
Cape Town	**Taiwan**	Charlotte	Memphis	Tampa	Cwmbran
Durban	Kaohsiung	Chattanooga	Mesa	Toledo	Ebbw Vale
Johannesburg	Taipei	Cheyenne	Miami	Tombstone	Fishguard
Kimberley		Chicago	Milwaukee	Topeka	Flint
Ladysmith	**Tanzania**	Cincinatti	Minneapolis	Trenton	Haverford-
Mafikeng (for-	Dar es Sa-	Cleveland	Mobile	Troy	west
merly	laam	Colorado	Modesto	Tucson	Holyhead
Mafeking)	Dodoma	Springs	Montgomery	Tulsa	Holywell
Pietermaritz-	Zanzibar	Columbia	Montpelier	Tuscaloosa	Llandudno
burg		Columbus	Nashville	Urbana	Llanelly
Port Elizabeth	**Thailand**	Concord	Nassau	Utica	Llandrindod
Pretoria	Bangkok	Corpus Christi	Newark	Virginia	Wells
Sharpeville	Chumphon	Dallas	New Bedford	Beach	Llangollen
Soweto	Lampang	Dayton	New Brunswick		Maesteg
Springbok		Dearborn			Merthyr Tydfil
	Togo	Denver			Monmouth
Spain	Lomé				
Alicante	Mango				

Montgomery	Pwllheli	Usk	San'a (or	Zambia	Harare
Newport	Rhondda	Welshpool	Sanaa)	Kitwe	Hwange
Newtown	Rhyl	Wrexham		Lusaka	
Pembroke	Swansea		Zaïre	Ndola	
Pontypool	Tenby	Yemen	Kananga		
Pontypridd	Towyn	Aden	Kinshasa	Zimbabwe	
Port Talbot	Treorchy	Hodeida	Lubumbashi	Bulawayo	

3 **New York**, the Big Apple, Gotham, Manhattan, the Bronx, Queens, Brooklyn, Richmond (*or* Staten Island), Central Park, the Bowery, Harlem, Greenwich Village, Wall Street, East Side, West Side, Chinatown, Little Italy, the Bowry, Hell's Kitchen, Times Square, Greater New York

4 **British cities**, garden city, cathedral city, county town, shire town, London, Birmingham, Manchester, Leeds, Liverpool, Plymouth, Portsmouth, Canterbury, Oxford, Lincoln, Newcastle-upon-Tyne, York, Edinburgh, Glasgow, Aberdeen, Inverness, Cardiff, Swansea, Belfast

5 **London**, the Smoke, the Great Wen, East End, West End, Mayfair, Soho, Docklands, the Isle of Dogs, the City, the Square Mile, Hyde Park, Regent's Park, Knightsbridge, Paddington, Kensington, South Kensington, Holborn, Barbican, Earl's Court, Belgravia, Westminster, Hampstead, Highgate, Lambeth, Southwark, Greater London

6 **other cities**, Paris, Rome, Madrid, Lisbon, Ankara, Athens, Moscow, Vienna, Budapest, Prague, Belgrade, Beijing (*or* Peking), Cairo, Calcutta, Mexico City, Rio de Janeiro, Tokyo, Hong Kong, Berlin, Quebec, Toronto, Sydney, Melbourne, Pretoria

7 **city district**, district, quarter, precinct, voting precinct (US), shopping precinct, ward, central city, city centre, inner city, high street, main street (US), block, square, marketplace, market square, market, mart, forum, plaza, *piazza* (It), uptown (US), midtown (US), downtown (US), shopping area, shopping centre, shopping arcade, shopping mall, financial district, business district, business (*or* commercial) zone (US), residential area, residential zone (US), tenement district, housing estate, ghetto, Black ghetto, niggertown (Offensive), Jewish ghetto, Jewtown (Offensive), barrio (US), slum (*or* slums), blighted area, blighted neighbourhood, no-go area, Tenderloin (US), red-light district, skid row (*or* road) (US sl), the other side of the tracks (US inf)

▶ *12 Government and Politics, 291 Centre, 611 Importance, 740 Market, 743 Poverty*

8 **suburb**, suburbia, subtopia, outskirts, built-up area, exurb (US), exurbia (US), green belt, dormitory suburb (*or* town), bedroom suburb (US), garden suburb, stockbroker belt (Inf)

▶ *297 Surroundings, 300 Edge, 313 Circularity*

9 **town**, township, community, country town, market town, new town, county town, county

seat (US), boom town, ghost town (US), borough, burgh (Scot), burg (US inf)

10 **village**, country village, rural village, hamlet, tanktown (US), crossroads (US), whistle stop (US), wide place in the road (US), jumping-off place (US), village green, one-horse town (Inf), hick town (US inf), jerkwater town (US sl), rube town (US sl)

11 **urbanite**, urban dweller, city dweller, burgher, burgess, freeman, downtowner (US), uptowner (US), city father, city manager (US), slum-dweller, suburbanite, suburban dweller, commuter, townsman (*or* townswoman), local, oppidan, villager, parishioner, city slicker (Inf), townee (Inf)

12 **rural dweller**, countryman (*or* countrywoman), country bumpkin, rustic, yokel, hayseed (US inf), rube (US sl)

▶ *255 Inhabitant*

13 **municipal building**, city hall, town hall, fire station, firehouse (US), police station (*or* headquarters), precinct station (US), courthouse, county courthouse (US), community centre, county building

ADJECTIVES

14 **urban**, interurban, metropolitan, civic, municipal, city, citified, financial, business, residential, suburbanized, gentrified, blighted, no-go, red-light, suburban, subtopian, exurban (US), oppidan, town, high-street, main street (US), downtown (US), midtown (US), uptown (US), village, village-like, community, communal, county, parochial, country, countrified, rural, local, public, civil, hick (US inf), skid-row (US sl)

VERBS

15 **urbanize**, citify, gentrify, suburbanize, commute, countrify

ADVERBS

16 **municipally**, communally, parochially, rurally, locally, publicly, civically

94 Lakes

NOUNS

1 **lake**, loch (Scot), lough (Irish), llyn (Welsh), natural lake, artificial lake, man-made lake, reservoir, freshwater lake, mountain lake, tarn, volcanic lake, glacial lake, oxbow lake, broad, flash (Dial), sea loch, salt lake, salina, lagoon, inland sea, the Dead Sea, the Great Salt Lake

2 **small lake**, lakelet, pool, linn (Scot), tidal pool, clear pool, muddy pool, pond, millpond,

Lakes

Albert (Uganda, Zaïre)
Athabasca (Canada)
Awe (Scotland)
Baikal (Russia)
Balaton (Hungary)
Bala (Wales)
Balkhash (Kazakhstan)
Bangweulu (Zambia)
Bassenthwaite (England)
Bear (USA)
Becharof (USA)
Breydon (England)
Buttermere (England)
Celyn (Wales)
Central Park Lake (USA)
Chad (Chad, Niger, Nigeria, Cameroon)
Champlain (USA)
Chiemsee (Germany)
Clark (USA)
Clywedog (Wales)
Como (Italy)
Coniston (England)
Constance (Germany)
Cwellyn (Wales)
Dall (USA)
Derwent Water (England)
Dongting (or Tungting) (China)
Edward (Uganda, Zaïre)
Ennerdale (England)
Ericht (Scotland)
Erie (Canada, USA)
Erne (Northern Ireland)
Esthwaite (England)
Eyre (Australia)
Flathead (USA)
Foyle (Ireland)
Garda (Italy)
Geneva (Switzerland, France)
Grasmere (England)

Great Lake (USA, Canada; Australia)
Great Bear (Canada)
Great Salt Lake (USA)
Great Slave (Canada)
Hawes Water (England)
Hickling Broad (England)
Huron (USA, Canada)
Ijsselmeer (or Ysselmeer) (Netherlands)
Iliamna (USA)
Issyk-kul (Kirghizia)
Kariba (Zambia, Zimbabwe)
Katrine (Scotland)
Kivu (Zaïre, Rwanda)
Kyoga (or Kioga) (Uganda)
Ladoga (Russia)
Lake of the Woods (Canada)
Leech (USA)
Léman (Switzerland, France)
Leven (Scotland)
Lochy (Scotland)
Lomond (Scotland)
Lop Nur (or Lop Nor) (China)
Lucerne (Switzerland)
Maggiore (Italy, Switzerland)
Malawi (Malawi, Tanzania, Mozambique)
Manitoba (Canada)
Maracaibo (Venezuela)
Maree (Scotland)
Martin (USA)
Menindee (Australia)
Michigan (USA)
Mille Lacs (USA)

Mobutu (Uganda, Zaïre)
Moosehead (USA)
Naknek (USA)
Nasser (Egypt)
Natron (Tanzania)
Neagh (Northern Ireland)
Nemi (Italy)
Ness (Scotland)
Neusiedl (Austria, Hungary)
Nicaragua (Nicaragua)
Nipigon (Canada)
Nu Jiang (China, Burma)
Nyasa (or Nyassa) (Malawi, Tanzania, Mozambique)
Okeechobee (USA)
Onega (Russia)
Ontario (Canada, USA)
Oulton Broad (England)
Padarn (Wales)
Pend Oreille (USA)
Peipus (Russia, Estonia)
Pontchartrain (USA)
Poyang (or P'o-yang) (China)
Pyramid (USA)
Qinghai Hu (or Koko Nor) (China)
Rainy (USA)
Rannoch (Scotland)
Red Tarn (England)
Reindeer (Canada)
Rudolf (Kenya, Ethiopia)
Rutland (England)
Rydal Water (England)
Saimaa (Finland)
St Clair (USA, Canada)
St James's Park Lake (England)
Salton Sea (USA)

Serpentine, The (England)
Superior (USA, Canada)
Tahoe (USA)
Tana (or Tsana) (Ethiopia)
Tanganyika (Zaïre, Burundi, Tanzania, Zambia)
Taupo (New Zealand)
Tay (Scotland)
Tegid (Wales)
Teshekpuk (USA)
Thirlmere (England)
Titicaca (Peru, Bolivia)
Tonle Sap (Kampuchea)
Torrens (Australia)
Trasimeno (Italy)
Tungting (or Tungt'ing) (China)
Turkana (Kenya, Ethiopia)
Tustumena (USA)
Ugashik (USA)
Ullswater (England)
Upper Klamath (USA)
Urmia (Iran)
Utah (USA)
Vänern (Sweden)
Van (Turkey)
Victoria (Uganda, Tanzania, Kenya)
Vierwaldstättersee (Switzerland)
Volta (Ghana)
Vyrnwy (Wales)
Wast Water (England)
Windermere (England)
Winnebago (USA)
Winnibigoshish (USA)
Winnipeg (Canada)
Yellowstone (USA)

farm pond, village pond, fishpond, dew pond, water hole, swimming hole (US), swimming pool, swimming bath, landlocked water, standing water, backwater, water pocket, still water, stagnant water, dead water, bayou, wash, marsh, mere

▶ *389 Water, 54 Earth Science, 55 Meteorology and Climatology*

3 **US lakes**, the Great Lakes, Erie, Superior, Huron, Michigan, Ontario, Great Salt Lake, Tahoe, Bear, Yellowstone

4 **British lakes**, English lakes, the Lake District (*or* Lakeland), Windermere, Grasmere, Hawes Water, Coniston Water, Wast Water, Derwent Water, Rydal Water, Ullswater, Buttermere, Thirlmere, Bassenthwaite, Rutland Water, Breydon Water, the Broads, Hickling Broad, Oulton Broad, The Serpentine, Bala, Vyrnwy, Loch Lomond, Loch Ness, Loch Rannoch, Loch Leven, Loch Tay, Lough Neagh, Strangford Lough, Lower Lough Erne, Upper Lough Erne

5 **other major lakes**, Manitoba, Caspian Sea, Aral Sea, Tanganyika, Baykal, Great Bear, Malawi, Great Slave, Winnipeg, Balkhash, Ladoga, Chad, Maracaibo, Onega, Eyre, Volta, Titicaca, Nicaragua, Athabasca, Albert, Kariba, Nipigon, Urmia, Victoria

6 **lake dweller**, lakeside dweller, lacustrine dweller, lacustrian, pile dweller, pile builder, laker

7 **lake dwelling**, lacustrine dwelling, lake house, lakeside house, lake lodge, lakeside village, pile house, stilt house, Cajun cabin (US), crannog (Scot), stilt village, kampong

8 **limnology**, limnologist, limnometer, limnograph, limnetic zone

ADJECTIVES

9 **lakelike**, pondlike, landlocked, tidal, clear, muddy, standing, still, stagnant, marshy, lacustrine, lacustrian, lacustral, lacuscular, limnologic(al), limnophilous, lake-dwelling

ADVERBS

10 **limnologically**, stagnantly, muddily, clearly

Mountains, Mountain Ranges, and Hills

Aconcagua (Mt) (Argentina)
Adirondack (Mts) (USA)
Allegheny (Mts) (USA)
Alps (Range) (France, Switzerland, Italy, Austria)
Altai (Mts) (Russia, China, Mongolia)
Andes (Range) (South America)
Annapurna (Mt) (Nepal)
An Teallach (Mt) (Scotland)
Apennine (Hills) (Italy)
Appalachian (Mts) (USA)
Ararat (Mt) (Turkey)
Aso (Mt) (Japan)
Athos (Mt) (Greece)
Atlas (Mts) (Morocco, Algeria)
Balkan (Mts) (Bulgaria)
Bernese Alps (or Oberland) (Range) (Switzerland)
Bernina (Mt) (Switzerland)
Black (Mts) (Wales)
Blanc (Mt) (France, Italy)
Blue (Mts) (Australia)
Blue Ridge (Mts) (USA)
Boundary Peak (Mt) (USA)
Brecon Beacons (Mts) (Wales)
Brocken (Mt) (Germany)
Cader Idris (Mt) (Wales)
Cairngorm (Mts) (Scotland)
Cambrian (Mts) (Wales)
Cantabrian (Mts) (Spain)
Carmel (Mt) (Israel)
Carnedd Llywelyn (Mt) (Wales)
Carpathian (Mts) (Czechoslovakia, Poland, Romania, Ukraine)
Carrantuohill (Mt) (Ireland)
Caucasus (Mts) (Russia, Georgia, Azerbaijan)
Cévennes (Range) (France)
Cheviot (Hills) (England, Scotland)
Chianti (Range) (Italy)

Chiltern (Hills) (England)
Chimborazo (Mt) (Ecuador)
Citlaltépetl (Mt) (Mexico)
Coast (Mts) (Canada)
Cook (Mt) (New Zealand)
Cotopaxi (Mt) (Ecuador)
Cotswold (Hills) (or Cotswolds) (England)
Cumbrian (Mts) (England)
Dolomites (Mts) (Italy)
Drakensberg (Mts) (South Africa)
Dunsinane (Hill) (Scotland)
Egmont (Mt) (New Zealand)
Eiger (Mt) (Switzerland)
Elbert (Mt) (USA)
Elbrus (Mt) (Russia)
Elgon (Mt) (Uganda, Kenya)
Etna (Mt) (Sicily)
Everest (Mt) (Nepal, Tibet)
Finsteraarhorn (Mt) (Switzerland)
Flinders (Range) (Australia)
Fujiyama (or Fuji) (Mt) (Japan)
Ghats (Range) (India)
Godwin Austen (or K2) (Mt) (India)
Golan Heights (Hills) (Israel)
Grampian (Mts) (Scotland)
Granite Peak (Mt) (USA)
Gran Paradiso (Mt) (Italy)
Hamersley (Range) (Australia)
Harz (Mts) (Germany)
Helvellyn (Mt) (England)
Hermon (Mt) (Syria, Lebanon)
Himalayas (Range) (S Asia)
Hindu Kush (Range) (Afghanistan, Pakistan)
Hoggar (or Ahaggar) (Mts) (Algeria)
Hood (Mt) (USA)

Humphreys Peak (Mt) (USA)
Hymettus (Mt) (Greece)
Ida (Mt) (Turkey, Greece)
Ingleborough (Mt) (England)
Jungfrau (Switzerland)
Jura (Mts) (France, Switzerland)
Kaikoura (Ranges) (New Zealand)
Kamet (Mt) (India)
Kanchenjunga (Mt) (Nepal, India)
Karakoram (Range) (China, India)
Kenya (Mt) (Kenya)
Kilimanjaro (Mt) (Tanzania)
Kings Peak (Mt) (USA)
Kosciusko (Mt) (Australia)
Kunlun (Range) (China)
Ladakh (Range) (India)
Lammermuir (Hills) (Scotland)
Lenin (Peak) (Tadzhikistan)
Logan, Ben (Mt) (Canada)
Lomond, Ben (Mt) (Scotland)
Macdonnell (Ranges) (Australia)
McKinley (Mt) (USA)
Malvern (Hills) (England)
Matopo (Hills) (Zimbabwe)
Matterhorn (Mt) (Switzerland, Italy)
Mauna Kea (Mt) (USA)
Mendip (Hills) (England)
Middleback (Range) (Australia)
Moelwyn (Mts) (Wales)
Montserrat (Range) (Spain)
Mount Elbert (Mt) (USA)
Mourne (Mts) (Northern Ireland)
Musgrave (Ranges) (Australia)
Nevis, Ben (Mt) (Scotland)
North West Highlands (Mts) (Scotland)

Ojos del Salado (Mt) (Argentina, Chile)
Olives (Mt of) (Israel)
Olympic (Mts) (USA)
Olympus (Mt) (Greece, USA)
Ossa (Mt) (Australia)
Palomar (Mt) (USA)
Pamirs (Range) (Tadzhikistan, China, Afghanistan)
Parnassus (Mt) (Greece)
Peak District (Hills) (England)
Pennines (Hills) (England)
Pikes Peak (Mt) (USA)
Pindus (Mts) (Greece, Albania)
Popocatepetl (Mt) (Mexico)
Pyrenees (Mts) (France, Spain)
Rainier (Mt) (USA)
Rhinog Fawr (Mt) (Wales)
Rigi (Mt) (Switzerland)
Rocky (Mts) (or Rockies) (USA, Canada)
St Elias (Mts) (Alaska, Canada)
Sayan (Mts) (Russia)
Scafell Pike (Mt) (England)
Shropshire (Hills) (England)
Siding Spring (Mt) (Australia)
Sierra Madre (Range) (Mexico)
Sierra Morena (Range) (Spain)
Sierra Nevada (Range) (USA, Spain)
Smoky (Mts) (or Smokies) (USA)
Snowdon (Mt) (Wales)
Snowy (Mts) (Australia)
Taurus (Mts) (Turkey)
Tian Shan (Kirghizia) (China, Mongolia)
Ural (Mts) (Russia)
Vesuvius (Mt) (Italy)
Vosges (Range) (France)
Wheeler Peak (Mt) (USA)
Whitney (Mt) (USA)
Wilson (Mt) (USA)
Zagros (Mts) (Iran)
Zugspitze (Peak) (Germany)

95 Mountains

Mountains are the beginning and the end of all natural scenery. John Ruskin.

NOUNS

1 **mountain**, mount, alp, snow-capped mountain, mountain range, range, chain, sierra, cordillera, massif, highlands, heights, mountaintop, precipice, summit, peak, ben (Scot), cloud-capped peak, snow-clad peak, pike (Dial), tor, crag, pinnacle, crest, ridge, saddle, spur, hill, brae (Scot), hillock, hummock, downs, hilltop, fell, monticule, foothill, steepness, climb, mountaineering, mountain climbing, rock climbing

▶ *286 Obliqueness, 318 Prominence, 282 Horizontality, 275 Height, 279 Summit*

2 **orology**, orometer, orologist

▶ *54 Earth Science*

3 **mountaineer**, mountain climber, rock

climber, Alpinist, mountain-dweller, mountain man, hill-dweller, hillbilly (US), abominable snowman, yeti, Bigfoot, Sasquatch, Brocken Spectre

▶ *256 Habitat, 538 Untruth*

4 **US mountains**, Wheeler Peak, Rocky Mountains, Sierra Nevada Mountains, Cascade Range, Olympic Mountains, Appalachian Mountains, Smoky Mountains, Adirondack Mountains, Allegheny Mountains, Bighorn Mountains, Mount McKinley, Mount Whitney, Mount Wilson, Mount Palomar, Pikes Peak

5 **British mountains**, Scottish mountains, Grampian Mountains, Monadhliath Mountains, North West Highlands, Cairngorm Mountains, Ben Nevis, Ben Lomond, Welsh mountains, Snowdonia, Brecon Beacons, Molewyn Mountains, Cambrian Mountains, Snowdon, Cader Idris, English mountains, Pennines, Cumbrian Mountains, Cheviot Hills, Shropshire Hills, Malvern Hills, Cotswolds, Mendip Hills, Peak District, Helvellyn

6 **other major mountains and ranges**, Himalayas, Alps, Pyrenees, Caucasus, Andes Mountains, Everest, K2 (*or* Godwin Austen), Annapurna, Matterhorn, Mont Blanc, Eiger, Ararat, Kilimanjaro, Mount Logan, Mount Cook, Mount Olympus, Aconcagua, Atlas Mountains

▶ *54 Earth Science*

ADJECTIVES

7 **mountainous**, mountained, alpine, alpestrine, alpigene, subalpine, Himalayan, Olympian, mountain-dwelling, altitudinous, elevated, mounting, ascending, towering, soaring, lofty, topping, monumental, highest, topmost, cloud-capped, snow-capped, snow-clad, high, highland, hilly, upland, rolling, monticulous, hill-dwelling

8 **orogenic**, orographic, orogenetic, orological, orometric

▶ *275 Height*

VERBS

9 **tower**, soar, spire, rise, rise above (*or* over), tower above (*or* over), overtop, top, surmount, overlook, look down upon, command, dominate, overshadow

10 **climb a mountain**, mountaineer, climb, mount, scale, conquer a mountain, dwell (*or* live) on a mountain

ADVERBS

11 **on the mountain**, on the summit, on the peak, on the crest, on the pinnacle, atop, on high, high up, high, aloft, straight up, above, in the clouds, on (*or* at the) top of the world

96 Rivers

NOUNS

1 **river**, flowing river, meandering river, lazy river, racing river, navigable river, river running to the sea, braided river, freshet (*or* fresh), running water, polluted river, open sewer, watercourse, waterway, canal, cut (Dial), stream, mountain stream, small stream, streamlet, rivulet, freshet, millstream, rillet, brook, babbling brook, bourn (*or* bourne), burn (Scot), runnel (*or* runlet), run (US), rill, gill (Dial), kill (US), beck, arroyo (US), brooklet, creek, crick (US dial), sike (Dial), wadi, underground (*or* subterranean) river, tributary, confluent stream, confluent, confluence, bayou (US), branch, feeder, affluent, distributary, fork, effluent, anabranch, billabong (Aus), river system, water system

▶ *54 Earth Science, 324 Motion*

2 **channel**, midchannel, midstream, sandbank, (river) bend, meander, (river) bank, embankment, levee (US), riverside, waterside, water's edge, source of a river, headwaters, headstream, head, riverhead, fountainhead, backwater, waterfall, falls (*or* fall), cataract, linn (Scot), cascade, force, rapids, chute, shoot, nappe, sault (US), spillway (*or* spill), overflow, sluiceway (*or* sluice), bore, tidal bore, river's end, river's mouth, delta, river crossing, ford, bridge, ferry

▶ *54 Earth Science, 70 Transport*

3 **US rivers**, Mississippi, Missouri, Rio Grande, Alabama, Colorado, Columbia, Hudson, Potomac, Red, Tennessee, Yukon, Old Man River (Inf)

4 **British rivers**, Thames, Severn, Mersey, Avon, Ouse, Trent, Tees, Humber, Cam, Isis, Old Father Thames (Inf), Conwy, Clwyd, Taff, Forth, Clyde, Dee, Spey

5 **other major rivers**, Seine, Danube, Rhine, Rhône, St Lawrence, Nile, Amazon, Congo, Elbe, Po, Moselle, Tiber, Shannon, Jordan, Ganges, Tigris, Euphrates, Don, Volga, Yellow (*or* Huang He), Chang Jiang, Zaïre, Mackenzie, Mekong, Niger, Oxus, Styx

6 **river flow**, water flow, water power, stream, millstream, millrace, coure, onward course, current, undercurrent, undertow, eddy, whirlpool, whirl, swirl, twirl, gulf, vortex, maelstrom, Maelstrom, Charybdis, flowing, flowage, flux, fluency, afflux, drift, driftage, ripple, riffle (US), washing, wash, wake, splash, plash, slosh, lapping, lap, inflow, ingress, affluence, flowing together, confluence, convergence, concourse, conflux, outflow, egress, effluence, crossflow, crosscurrent, counterflow, countercurrent, counterflux, backflow, ebb, reflux, refluence, backwash, back stream, profluence, surge, gush, rush, onrush, spate, race, run,

Rivers

Adige (Italy)
Ain (France)
Aire (England, France)
Aisne (France)
Alabama (USA)
Allier (France)
Amazon (Peru, Brazil)
Amu Darya (Turkmenistan, Uzbekistan)
Amur (Mongolia, Russia, China)
Angara (Russia)
Annan (Scotland)
Arkansas (USA)
Arno (Italy)
Assiniboine (Canada)
Athabasca (Canada)
Aube (France)
Avon (England)
Beas (India)
Bermejo (Argentina)
Bío-Bío (Chile)
Brahmaputra (Tibet, India)
Bug (Ukraine, Poland, Germany)
Bure (England)
Cam (England)
Canadian (USA)
Cauvery (India)
Charente (France)
Chari (Central African Republic, Cameroon, Chad)
Chenab (Pakistan)
Churchill (Canada)
Clutha (New Zealand)
Clwyd (Wales)
Clyde (Scotland, Canada)
Colorado (USA)
Columbia (USA)
Congo (or Zaïre) (Congo, Zaïre)
Connecticut (USA)
Conwy (Wales)
Cooper (Australia)
Coppermine (Canada)
Crouch (England)
Damodar (India)
Danube (Germany, Austria, Romania, Hungary, Czechoslovakia, Serbia, Bulgaria)
Darling (Australia)
Dart (England)
Dee (Scotland, Wales, England)
Demerara (Guyana)
Derwent (England)
Dnieper (or Dnepr) (Ukraine)
Dniester (or Dnestr) (Ukraine)
Don (Russia; Scotland; England; France; Australia)
Doon (Scotland)

Dordogne (France)
Doubs (France, Switzerland)
Douro (or Duero) (Spain, Portugal)
Dove (England)
Dovey (Wales)
Drava (Italy, Austria, Croatia, Hungary)
Ebro (Spain)
Elbe (Germany)
Ems (Germany, Netherlands)
Esk (Australia)
Essequibo (Guyana)
Euphrates (Iraq)
Exe (England)
Fal (England)
Forth (Scotland)
Fraser (Canada)
Frome (Australia)
Gambia (The Gambia, Senegal)
Ganges (India)
Garonne (France)
Gironde (France)
Glomma (Norway)
Godavari (India)
Great Ouse (England)
Han (China)
Hawkesbury (Australia)
Hooghly (India)
Hsi Chiang (China)
Hudson (USA)
Humber (England)
Hunter (Australia)
Illinois (USA)
Indus (India, Pakistan, China)
Irrawaddy (Burma)
Irtysh (China, Russia, Kazakistan)
Isis (England)
Itchen (England)
James (USA; Australia)
Jordan (Israel, Jordan)
Juba (Ethiopia, Somalia)
Jumna (India)
Juruá (Brazil)
Kama (Russia)
Kasai (Angola, Zaïre)
Kolyma (Russia)
Kuban (Russia)
Kura (Turkey, Georgia, Azerbaijan)
Lachlan (Australia)
Lea (England)
Lena (Russia)
Liffey (Ireland)
Limpopo (South Africa, Zimbabwe, Mozambique)
Lippe (Germany)
Loire (France)
Lualaba (Zaïre)
Lune (England)
Lüne (Germany)

Maas (Netherlands)
Mackenzie (Australia)
Madeira (Brazil)
Magdalena (Colombia)
Main (Germany; Northern Ireland)
Manawatu (New Zealand)
Maritsa (Bulgaria, Turkey)
Marne (France)
Medina (USA)
Medway (England)
Mekong (Laos, China, Vietnam)
Menderes (Turkey)
Mersey (England)
Meuse (France, Belgium)
Miño (or Minho) (Spain, Portugal)
Mississippi (USA)
Missouri (USA)
Moselle (or Mosel) (France, Germany)
Murray (Australia; Canada)
Murrumbidgee (Australia)
Neckar (Germany)
Neisse (Poland, Czechoslovakia, Germany)
Niger (Nigeria, Mali, Guinea)
Nile (Sudan, Egypt)
Ob (Russia)
Oder (Germany, Czechoslovakia, Poland)
Ohio (USA)
Oise (France)
Orange (South Africa)
Orontes (Syria, Turkey)
Ouachita (USA)
Ouse (England)
Paraguay (Paraguay)
Paraná (Brazil)
Pecos (USA)
Peel (Australia, USA)
Piave (Italy)
Platte (USA)
Po (Italy)
Potomac (USA)
Ravi (India, Pakistan)
Rede (England)
Red (USA)
Rhine (Switzerland, France, Germany, Netherlands)
Ribble (England)
Río de la Plata (Argentina, Uruguay)
Rio Grande (or Río Bravo) (USA, Mexico)
Ruhr (Germany)
Saar (Germany, France)
St John (Canada, USA)

St Lawrence (USA)
Saskatchewan (Canada)
Savannah (USA)
Seine (France)
Severn (England)
Shannon (Ireland)
Shenandoah (USA)
Slave (Canada)
Snake (USA)
Somme (France)
Songhua (or Sungari) (China)
Spey (Scotland)
Stour (England)
Susquehanna (USA)
Suwannee (or Swanee) (USA)
Swale (England)
Taff (Wales)
Tagus (or Tajo or Tejo) (Portugal, Spain)
Tallahatchie (USA)
Tamar (England)
Tawe (Wales)
Tay (Scotland)
Tees (England)
Teifi (Wales)
Tennessee (USA)
Test (England)
Thames (England)
Tiber (Italy)
Tigris (Iraq, Turkey)
Trent (England)
Tunguska (Russia)
Tweed (England, Scotland)
Tyne (England)
Ural (Russia, Kazakhstan)
Ure (England)
Uruguay (Uruguay, Brazil, Argentina)
Usk (Wales, England)
Vistula (Poland)
Volga (Russia)
Volta (Ghana)
Volturno (Italy)
Wabash (USA)
Waikato (New Zealand)
Wear (England)
Weaver (England)
Weser (Germany)
Windrush (England)
Witham (England)
Wye (Wales, England)
Yangtze (China)
Yare (England)
Yellow (or Huang Ho) (China, USA)
Yellowstone (USA)
Yenisei (Russia)
Yeo (England)
Yukon (USA)
Zambezi (Zambia, Angola, Zimbabwe, Mozambique)

rapids, torrent, mountain torrent, freshet (*or* fresh), flood, flash food, deluge, overflow, overflowing, overrunning, spillage, spillover (US), washout, flush, inundation, engulfment, submersion, alluvium, cataclysm, the Flood, the Deluge

▶ *54 Earth Science, 55 Meteorology and Climatology, 235 Power, 336 Forward Motion, 364 Rotation, 314 Convolution, 337 Backward Motion*

VERBS

7 **flow**, meander, race, braid, run, course, channel, pour, stream, drift, glide, slide, flow over, babble, bubble, burble, gurgle, purl, trill, murmur, trickle, dribble, eddy, rotate, whirl, swirl, twirl, engulf, ripple, riffle (US), wash, swash, splash, plash, slosh, lap, flow together, converge, flow in, surge, gush, rush, flood, overflow, overrun, spill (over), cascade, fall, flush, inundate, submerge, swamp, flow out, flow back, ebb

8 **cause to flow**, open the sluice gates, drain, divert a river, irrigate

9 **stop the flow**, stem the flow, staunch, obstruct a river, dam (up), build a breakwater

ADJECTIVES

10 **fluvial**, fluviomarine, flowing, fluent, effluent, profluent, affluent, confluent, convergent, streaming, running, coursing, winding, meandering, sluggish, snaking, serpentine, rippling, ripply, purling, racing, gushing, rushing, surging, torrential, dam-breaking, vortical, inundant (*or* inundatory), falling, ebbing, refluent

11 **flooded**, deluged, inundated, engulfed, swamped, drowned, afloat, awash, washed, in (*or* at) flood, in spate

12 **hydrologic(al)**, hydrospheric, hydrostatic, fluvioterrestrial

ADVERBS

13 **fluently**, affluently, convergently, sluggishly, torrentially, like a torrent, in (*or* at) flood, vortically, inundatorily, cataclysmically, hydrologically

97 Seas

For all at last return to the sea – to Oceanus, the ocean river, like the ever-flowing stream of time, the beginning and the end. Rachel Carson.

NOUNS

1 **sea**, ocean, deep sea, deep blue sea, seven seas, the deep, high seas, ocean blue, the blue, main, bounding main, the billow, sea water, salt water, brine, salt sea, blue water, tide, wave, ocean depths, ocean floor, sea bed, sea bottom, benthos, Davy Jones's Locker, Mariana Trench, sea lane, shipping lane, the briny (Inf), the briny deep (Inf), the (big) drink (Inf), watery waste (Inf), great waters (Inf), herring pond (Inf)

▶ *70 Transport*

2 **tide**, tidal current, tidal flow, tidal flood, tidal stream, tide race, tidewater, tideway, tide gate, riptide (*or* tide-rip *or* rip), direct tide, opposite tide, high tide, high water, full tide, lunar tide, solar tide, flood tide, spring tide, equinoctial tide, ebb tide (*or* ebb), rising tide, flux, flow, flood, low tide, low water, neap tide (*or* neap), reflux, refluence, tidal rise and fall, ebb and flow, flux and reflux, tidal range, tide chart, tidal table, tide gauge, thalassometer, tidal power, tideland (US)

▶ *324 Motion, 336 Forward Motion, 337 Backward Motion, 361 Raising, 362 Lowering*

3 **wave**, billow, swell, heavy swell, surge, heave, undulation, waviness, rise, trough, wavelet, ripple, riffle (US), spume, foam, froth, surf, breaker, comber (US), roller, roll, peak, wave crest, whitecap, white horses, broken water, rough water, rough sea, heavy sea, choppy sea, choppiness, turbulent sea, overfall, angry sea, (tidal) bore, eagre (*or* eager), rogue wave, tidal wave, tsunami, undertow, undercurrent

▶ *365 Oscillation*

4 **sea god**, Neptune, Triton, Oceanus, Poseidon, Nereus, Varuna, merman, sea nymph, Oceanid, Nereid, siren, Amphitrite, Thetis, Dylan, Calypso, undine, mermaid, water sprite, water spirit, sea serpent

▶ *7 Religion*

5 **oceanography**, thalassography, hydrography, bathymetry, marine biology, aquaculture (*or* aquiculture), sea survey, Admiralty chart, diving bell, bathysphere, diving vessel, bathyscaph (*or* bathyscaphe), bathythermograph

▶ *54 Earth Science, 55 Meteorology and Climatology*

Oceans and Seas

Adriatic (Sea)	Indian (Ocean)
Aegean (Sea)	Inland (or Seto Naikai)
Amundsen (Sea)	(Sea)
Andaman (Sea)	Ionian (Sea)
Antarctic (Ocean)	Irish (Sea)
Arabian (Sea)	Japan (Sea of)
Arafura (Sea)	Java (Sea)
Aral (Sea) (or Lake	Kara (Sea)
Aral)	Laptev (Sea)
Arctic (Ocean)	Ligurian (Sea)
Atlantic (Ocean)	Marmara (Sea of)
Azov (Sea of)	Mediterranean (Sea)
Baltic (Sea)	North (Sea)
Banda (Sea)	Okhotsk (Sea of)
Barents (Sea)	Pacific (Ocean)
Beaufort (Sea)	Philippine (Sea)
Bellingshausen (Sea)	Red (Sea)
Bering (Sea)	Ross (Sea)
Black (Sea)	Sargasso (Sea)
Caribbean (Sea)	South China (or
Caspian (Sea)	Nanhai) (Sea)
China (Sea)	Tasman (Sea)
Coral (Sea)	Timor (Sea)
Dead (Sea)	Weddell (Sea)
East China (Sea)	White (Sea)
Galilee (Sea of) (or	Yellow (or Huang Hai)
Tiberias Lake)	(Sea)
Greenland (Sea)	

6 **oceanographer**, thalassographer, hydrographer, marine biologist, deep-sea diver, underwater explorer, Jacques Cousteau

ADJECTIVES

7 **oceanic**, nautical, tidal, sea, salty, briny, equinoctial, lunar, solar, ebb, ebbing, neap, billowing, swelling, surging, breaking, rolling, choppy, heavy, turbulent, angry, dirty, marine, maritime, ocean-going, sea-going, seaworthy, seafaring, undersea, underwater, deep, deep-sea, submarine, subaqueous, subaquatic, subaqua, thalassic, pelagic, pelagian, benthic, estuarine, littoral, sublittoral, intertidal, abyssal, terriginous

8 **oceanographic(al)**, thalassographic(al), hydrographic(al), bathymetric(al)

VERBS

9 **sail the high seas**, sail the ocean (blue), go over the bounding main, conduct a sea survey, explore underwater, descend in a diving bell, plumb the ocean depths

10 **billow**, swell, surge, heave, toss, popple, become choppy, become turbulent, undulate, rise, peak, draw to a peak, scend (or send), ripple, riffle (US), wave, foam, froth, break, dash, crash, comb (US), roll, flow in, flow out, surge back, ebb, rise and fall, ebb and flow

ADVERBS

11 **nautically**, at sea, on the sea, on the high seas, afloat, by sea, by water, over the water, across the sea, oversea, overseas, beyond seas, oceanwards (or oceanward), seawards (or seaward), offshore, off soundings, out of soundings, in blue water, tidally

12 **oceanographically**, hydrographically, bathymetrically

98 Other Geographical Features

NOUNS

1 **continent**, America, Africa, Europe, Asia, Antarctica, landmass, North America, South America, Eurasia, Oceania, Australasia, subcontinent, India

▶ *54 Earth Science, 55 Meteorology and Climatology, 249 Region*

2 **island**, isle, islet, river island, holm (Dial) (or eyot) (Dial), inch (Scot), skerry (Scot), coral island, lagoon, island, atoll, reef, coral reef, Great Barrier Reef, cay, key, Key West, sandbank (or bank), sandbar (or bar), floating island, iceberg, ice floe, island continent, continental island, archipelago, island group, island chain

▶ *249 Region*

3 **marsh**, marshland, wetlands, fen, fenland, flat, mud flat, salt flat, salt marsh, saltpan, salina, playa, bog, peat bog, moss, moor, carr, swamp, swampland, the Everglades, swampforest, bayou (US), morass, quag, quagmire, quicksand, mudhole, mud, mire, ooze, wallow, slough, sudd, mangrove sudd, (river) delta

▶ *389 Water, 391 Moisture*

Islands

Alderney (UK)	Hainan (China)	Mauritius	Santa Catalina (USA)
Australia	Haiti	Melville (Canada)	Sardinia (Italy)
Baffin (Canada)	Halmahera (Indonesia)	Mindanao (Philippines)	Sark (UK)
Bali (Indonesia)	Hawaii (USA)	Mindoro (Philippines)	Seram (or Ceram) (Indonesia)
Banks (Canada)	Hispaniola (Haiti, the	Nantucket (USA)	nesia)
Barbados	Dominican Republic)	Negros (Philippines)	Shikoku (Japan)
Bermuda (UK)	Hokkaido (Japan)	New Britain (Papua	Sicily (Italy)
Borneo (Indonesia, Ma-	Hong Kong (UK)	New Guinea)	Singapore
laysia, Brunei)	Honshu (Japan)	New Caledonia (France)	Skye (UK)
Bougainville (Papua	Iceland	Newfoundland (Canada)	Somerset (Canada)
New Guinea)	Ireland (Ireland, UK)	New Guinea (Indonesia,	Southampton (Canada)
Cape Breton (Canada)	Isle of Man	Papua New Guinea)	South Georgia (UK)
Cebú (Philippines)	Isle of Wight (UK)	New Ireland (Papua	Spitsbergen (Norway)
Corfu (Greece)	Isle of Youth (Cuba)	New Guinea)	Sri Lanka
Corsica (France)	Jamaica	New Zealand	Sulawesi (Indonesia)
Crete (Greece)	Java (Indonesia)	Novaya Zemlya (Russia)	Sumatra (Indonesia)
Cuba	Jersey (UK)	Oahu (USA)	Tahiti (France)
Curaçao (The Nether-	Key West (USA)	Okinawa (Japan)	Taiwan (China)
lands)	Kodiak (USA)	Palawan (Philippines)	Tasmania (Australia)
Cyprus	Kyushu (or Kiushu)	Panay (Philippines)	Tenerife (Spain)
Devon (Canada)	(Japan)	Penang (Malaysia)	Tierra del Fuego
Dominica	Leyte (Philippines)	Prince Edward Island	Timor (Indonesia)
Ellesmere (Canada)	Long Island (USA)	(Canada)	Trinidad (Trinidad and
Flores (Indonesia)	Luzon (Philippines)	Prince of Wales (Canada)	Tobago)
Gotland (Sweden)	Madagascar	Puerto Rico (USA)	Unalaska (USA)
Great Britain	Madeira (Portugal)	Rhodes (Greece)	Vancouver (Canada)
Greenland (Denmark)	Madura (Indonesia)	St Lucia	Victoria (Canada)
Grenada	Majorca (Spain)	St Vincent (St Vincent	Viti Levu (Fiji)
Guadalcanal (Solomon	Malta	and the Grenadines)	Wrangel (Russia)
Islands)	Manhattan (USA)	Sakhalin (or Saghalien)	Zanzibar (Tanzania)
Guam (USA)	Martha's Vineyard (USA)	(Russia)	
Guernsey (UK)	Martinique (France)	Samar (Philippines)	

4 **coast**, coastline, shoreline, coastland, rocky coast, ironbound coast, sea wall, sea cliff, beach, shore, ocean shore, seashore, seaboard, seaside, strand, sand, pebbles, shingle, submerged coast, continental shelf, coastal plain, the Riviera, Costa Brava, Costa del Sol
▶ *300 Edge, 302 Limit, 298 Interface*

5 **peninsula**, point of land, point, tongue, neck, spit, sandspit, hook, spur, cape, promontory, bill, foreland, headland, head, mull (Scot), chersonese (Fml), projection, isthmus, land bridge, Hook of Holland, Cape of Good Hope, Cape Horn, Portland Bill
▶ *318 Prominence, 135 Union*

6 **lowland**, flat country, flats, level, meadow, field, mead (Fml), weald (Fml), lea, water meadow, bottom land (US), plain, the plains, alluvial plain, flood plain, polder, vale, strath (Scot), open country, wide-open spaces, range, heath, grassland, prairie, pampas, llano, veld (*or* veldt), savanna (*or* savannah), campos, steppe (*or* steppes), moor, moorland, grouse moor, inch (Scot)
▶ *276 Lowness, 112 Uniformity, 282 Horizontality*

7 **upland**, high country, highland, heights, wold (Fml), plateau, mesa, tableland, undulating land, downs, downland
▶ *95 Mountains*

8 **valley**, vale, dale, dell, dingle, dip, coomb (*or* combe *or* comb), cirque, corrie (Scot), cwm (Welsh), glen, ravine, gorge, canyon, gully, crevasse, chimney, ditch, chine, clough, couloir, Grand Canyon
▶ *317 Concavity, 322 Opening, 321 Furrow*

9 **inlet**, bay, gulf, arm of the sea, natural harbour, port, bight, fleet (Dial), cove, fiord (*or* fjord), firth (Scot), sound, backwater, bayou (US), outlet, estuary, mouth, delta, channel, gut, straits, Bay of Biscay, Persian Gulf, Great Australian Bight, Bay of Bengal, Firth of Forth, Kyle of Lochalsh, Plymouth Sound, Strait of Messina, Dardanelles, Hellespont, Bight of Benin, Chesapeake Bay, Gulf of Mexico, Gulf of California, Gulf of Saint Lawrence, Gulf of Alaska, Hudson Bay, Gulf of Campeche, Gulf of Guinea
▶ *97 Seas, 634 Refuge*

10 **miscellaneous**, desert, desert sands, sands, geyser, Old Faithful, hot spring, warm spring, thermal spring, thermae, fault, San Andreas Fault, volcano
▶ *349 Expulsion, 408 Heat, 241 Violence*

ADJECTIVES

11 **continental**, subcontinental, insular, islander, isleted, archipelagic, marooned, ashore, submerged, estuarial, coastal, littoral, ashore, sandy, pebbled, shingled, swampy, boggy, marshy, paludal, deltaic, soggy, poached, squashy, squishy, spongy, oozy, quaggy, undrained, waterlogged, muddy, alluvial, miry, flat, plain, rocky, peninsular, isthmian, promontory, downland, lowland, rolling, open, campestral, moorish, fenny, upland, highland, volcanic, thermal

VERBS

12 **be marooned**, become stranded on an island, hit a sandbar, hit a reef, hit an iceberg, fall into quicksand, become stuck in a quagmire, wallow in the mud, sight a coastline, land on a beach, round a cape, cross a land bridge, cross an isthmus, farm bottom land (US), start a prairie fire, fall into a gorge, dock at a port

ADVERBS

13 **continentally**, on land, ashore, adrift, subcontinentally, insularly, with insularity, soggily, muddily, with mud, rockily, with rocks, openly, volcanically, like a volcano, thermally, with heat

Deserts

Arabian (Egypt)	Gobi (Mongolia, China)	Negev (Israel)	Sturt Stony (Australia)
Atacama (Chile)	Great Salt Lake (USA)	Nubian (Sudan)	Syrian (Syria, Iraq, Jordan, Saudi Arabia)
Australian (Australia)	Great Sandy (Australia)	Painted (USA)	
Betpak-Dala (Kazakhstan)	Great Victoria (Australia)	Patagonian (Argentina)	Taklimakan (China)
	Kalahari (South Africa, Namibia, Botswana)	Rub' al Khali (Saudi Arabia, Oman, Yemen, United Arab Emirates)	Thar (or Indian or Great Indian) (India, Pakistan)
Black Rock (USA)			
Chihuahuan (USA, Mexico)	Kara Kum (Turkmenistan)		Turfan Depression (China)
Colorado (USA)	Mojave (USA)	Sahara (North Africa)	
Death Valley (USA)	Namib (Namibia)	Simpson (Australia)	Ustyurt (or Ust Urt) (Kazakhstan)
Gibson (Australia)	Nefud (Saudi Arabia)	Sonotan (USA, Mexico)	

Existence and Reality

99 Existence

NOUNS

1 **existence**, being, life, subsistence, coexistence, entity, ens, esse, occurrence, presence, metaphysics, metaphysics of presence, monadism, existentialism
▶ *396 Life, 4 Philosophy, 253 Presence*

2 **thing**, something, entity, being, body, object, substance, item, monad, phenomenon, happening

3 **nature**, fundamental nature, essential nature, essence, quiddity, innateness, ontology, materiality, substantiality
▶ *103 Essence*

4 **demonstrable existence**, reality, actuality, factuality, truth, authenticity, necessity, historicity, the real thing, facticity (Sl)
▶ *101 Reality, 537 Truth*

5 **fact**, fact (*or* truth) of the matter, matter of fact, *fait accompli* (Fr), the case, the basic fact(s), the basics, the realities, the specifics, the fundamentals, the essentials, what's what (Inf), the whole story (Inf), the picture (Inf), the gen (Inf), nitty-gritty (Inf), brass tacks (Inf), nuts and bolts (Inf), the dope (Sl), the scoop (Sl), the score (Sl), the dirt (Sl)
▶ *528 Information*

6 **continuing existence**, duration, endurance, persistence, continuance, survival, perpetuity

7 **self-existence**, aseity, uncreated being, deity, divinity
▶ *7 Religion*

8 **creation**, coming into being, materialization, actualization, birth, evolution, big-bang theory, ontogeny
▶ *156 Beginning, 226 Cause*

9 **mere existence**, vegetable existence, vegetation, stagnation, inertia, indolence, sloth, torpor, PVS (persistent vegetative state *or* syndrome)
▶ *240 Inertness*

ADJECTIVES

10 **existing**, existent, being, living, subsistent, coexistent, occurring, present, prevalent, current, extant, manifest, necessary, obvious, in force, in effect

11 **intrinsic**, innate, inherent, essential, basic, fundamental, natural, material, substantial, substantive, concrete, ontological

12 **lasting**, enduring, persisting, persistent, abiding, continual, continuous, surviving, perpetual

13 **real**, actual, factual, de facto, true, authentic, veritable, undeniable, indisputable, positive, provable, empirical, historical, phenomenal, well-known, honest-to-God (Inf), for real (Sl)

14 **self-existent**, self-existing, uncreated, god-like, divine

15 **created**, materialized, made, actualized, evolved

16 **vegetating**, stagnating, stagnant, inert, torpid, indolent, slothful

VERBS

17 **exist**, be, live, breathe, coexist, subsist, live in, inhabit, dwell, occur, be there, be found, be true

18 **come to be**, become, materialize, take shape (*or* form), be born, evolve, arise, come about, grow, develop, unfold

19 **continue to be**, endure, last, persist, continue, survive, prevail, live on, stand, hold, remain, stay

20 **bring into being**, create, make, form, make up, compose, devise, invent, cause, realize, actualize, factualize, reify
▶ *156 Beginning, 226 Cause*

21 **merely exist**, vegetate, stagnate

ADVERBS

22 **really**, actually, basically, fundamentally, necessarily, essentially, existentially, inherently, truly, demonstrably, manifestly, positively, in fact, as a matter of fact, in point of fact, ipso facto, de facto, to all intents and purposes, as it happens, no ifs or buts (Inf)

23 **now**, at the moment, currently, presently, immediately
▶ *185 Time*

100 Nonexistence

NOUNS

1 **nonexistence**, nonbeing, nonentity, unbeing, nonsubsistence, nonoccurrence, nonhappening

2 **nothingness**, nullity, nihility, nothing, nil, nought, zero, love, naught, nowt (Dial), nothing whatever, nothing at all, nothing on earth (*or* under the sun), no such thing, zilch (Sl), sweet Fanny Adams (*or* sweet FA) (Sl)

3 **negativeness**, negativity, negation, denial, refusal, *via negativa* (L)
▶ *536 Negation, 476 Refutation*

4 **emptiness**, vacuity, vacancy, vacuum, void, limbo, blank, hole, gap, break, lacuna, interval, space
▶ *265 Interval, 248 Space*

5 **nonreality**, unreality, imagination, fantasy, make-believe
▶ *519 Imagination, 102 Unreality*

6 **absence**, none, no-one, nobody, not a one, never a one, ne'er a one, nary a one (Dial), not a blessed one (Inf)
▶ *254 Absence*

7 **not any**, not a bit, not a whit, not a hint, not a speck, not a mite, not a particle, not an iota, not a jot, not a scrap, not a trace, not a suspicion, not a shadow of a suspicion (*or* doubt), neither hide nor hair, not a lick (Inf), not a lick or smell (Inf), not a smidgen (Inf)

8 **extinction**, obliteration, annihilation, obsolescence, oblivion, death
▶ *546 Obliteration, 512 Oblivion*

ADJECTIVES

9 **nonexistent**, absent, missing, minus, negative, null, void, vacant, empty, blank, devoid, lacking

10 **unreal**, imaginary, illusory, fanciful, fantastical

11 **no more**, extinct, died out, vanished, dead, passed away, dead and gone, all over, all over and done with, defunct, obsolete, dead as a dodo, past, finished, ended, annihilated, obliterated, destroyed, wiped out, kaput (Inf)
▶ *397 Death, 546 Obliteration, 3 History, 244 Destruction*

VERBS

12 **not exist**, have no existence, be null and void

13 **cease to exist**, vanish, disappear, end, leave no trace, sink without trace, melt, dissolve, evaporate, melt into thin air, go up in a puff of smoke, die, expire, pass away, die out, die away, peter out, fade away, turn to nothing, pass out of the picture (Inf), snuff it (Sl), kick the bucket (Sl)

14 **cause not to exist**, annihilate, destroy, exterminate, eradicate, wipe out, stamp out, extinguish, snuff out, kill, slay, murder, abort, miscarry, cancel, invalidate, annul, negate, end, veto, vaporize, nuke (Sl)
▶ *398 Killing*

ADVERBS

15 **not at all**, by no means, absolutely not, to no extent, on no account, under no circumstances, not by any stretch of the imagination, in no way, no way (Sl)

16 **not ever**, never, at no time, not at any time, not in a million years (Inf)

17 **nowhere**, in no place, neither here nor there, not on this earth

101 Reality

Human kind/ Cannot bear very much reality.
T. S. Eliot.

If this were play'd upon a stage now, I could condemn it as an improbable fiction. William Shakespeare.

NOUNS

1 **reality**, objective existence, actuality, occurrence, presence, entelechy, material existence, materiality, corporeality, substance, matter, thing, solidity, substantiality, tangibility, substantivity, validity, fact, factuality, matter of fact, historicity, the here and now, practicality
▶ *490 Certainty, 99 Existence*

2 **real world**, universe, cosmos, physical world, natural world, earth matter
▶ *367 Material World*

3 **realism**, real life, naturalism, authenticity, pragmatism, verisimilitude, documentary, cinema vérité, kitchen-sink drama, slice of life
▶ *503 Accuracy, 537 Truth*

4 **realist**, pragmatist

5 **realities**, basics, fundamentals, facts of life, home truths, bottom line (Inf), crunch (Inf)

ADJECTIVES

6 **real**, actual, occurring, existing, entelechial, true, factual, valid, historical, material, corporeal, tangible, solid, substantial, substantive

7 **realistic**, natural, naturalistic, lifelike, real-life, true-to-life, truthful, authentic, genuine, faithful, graphic

8 **practical**, realistic, pragmatic, expedient, sensible, matter-of-fact, no-nonsense, no-frills, down-to-earth, businesslike, hardheaded, level-headed, sound, functional, utilitarian, usable, serviceable, workable, in working order, operative

9 **realizable**, achievable, attainable, practicable, plausible, feasible, possible, probable, likely

VERBS

10 **be real**, exist, occur, loom large, happen

11 **make real**, actualize, materialize, factualize, realize, reify, visualize

12 **establish reality**, validate, authenticate, verify, prove, demonstrate, establish, settle

the matter, set at rest, prove one's point, nail down, ascertain, substantiate, corroborate, bear out, confirm, attest, uphold, certify, sustain, reinforce, back up, ratify, endorse, clinch (Inf)

ADVERBS

13 **really**, actually, in reality, in fact, de facto, in effect, in actuality, in practice, in all likelihood, when it comes to the crunch (Inf), when the chips are down (Inf), when the push comes to the shove (Inf)

14 **certainly**, indeed, truly, honestly, in truth, undoubtedly, indubitably, no buts about it, nothing else but, really-truly (Inf), honest to God (Inf)

102 Unreality

NOUNS

1 **unreality**, nonexistence, unactuality, subjective existence, subjectivity, unsubstantiality, intangibility, impalpability, incorporeality, ethereality, immateriality, immaterialism

2 **illusion**, fantasy, chimera, phantasmagoria, fancy, flight of fancy, figment, castle in the air (*or* Spain), pipe dream, daydream, dream, nightmare, hallucination, mirage, Fata Morgana, will-o'-the-wisp, jack-o'-lantern, ignis fatuus, vision, appearance, phantasm, phantom, ghost, spectre, spirit, wraith, shade, shadow, fetch, doppelgänger, simulacrum (Arch), spook (Inf)

▶ *519 Imagination*

3 **delusion**, misconception, self-deception, fallacy, false impression, optical illusion, trompe l'oeil, trick of the light, sleight of hand, illusionism, magic, conjuring, trick

▶ *539 Deception, 504 Error*

4 **theorization**, theory, hypothesis, assumption, speculation, conjecture, guesswork, fiction, empty talk, empty promises, fool's paradise, false dawn, wishful thinking, idealism, utopianism, pie in the sky (Inf), hot air (Inf), wind (Inf), gas (Inf)

▶ *518 Supposition, 538 Untruth*

5 **insubstantial person**, a nobody, a nothing, nonperson, unperson, nonentity, hollow man, straw man (US), man of straw, broken reed, paper tiger, puppet, dummy, jackstraw, windbag (Sl), dud (Sl)

6 **unrealistic person**, speculator, theorizer, idealist, romantic, visionary, dreamer

7 **artificiality**, imitation, simulation, shadow, image, fake, sham, artifact

▶ *540 Falsehood*

ADJECTIVES

8 **unreal**, nonexistent, incorporeal, intangible, impalpable, insubstantial, unsubstantial, ethereal, elusive, fugitive, fleeting, obscure, nebulous, tenuous, vague, flimsy, hollow, airy, hazy, indeterminate, indefinite, undefined, blurred, shadowy, ghostly, spectral, phantasmal

9 **illusory**, imaginary, subjective, fantastic, dreamlike, chimerical, phantasmagorical, fanciful, fancied, hallucinatory, figmental, visional, delusory

10 **theoretical**, hypothetical, abstract, ideal, speculative, assumed, putative, mythical, fanciful, imaginary, fictional, fictitious, made-up, make-believe

11 **unrealistic**, idealistic, utopian, visionary, romantic

12 **not the real thing**, artificial, synthetic, man-made, simulated, imitation, mock, pretend, pretended, dummy, sham, fake, false, spurious, specious, phony, bogus, counterfeit, so-called, put-on, quasi, pseudo (Inf)

VERBS

13 **imagine**, fantasize, conjure up, dream, daydream, hallucinate, hear things, see things

14 **theorize**, hypothesize, conceptualize, conjecture, guess

15 **idealize**, romanticize, see through rose-coloured glasses (Inf), build castles in the air (Inf)

16 **delude**, deceive, mislead, give a wrong idea (*or* impression), misrepresent, belie, distort, pervert, twist, fudge, embroider, embellish, gild, varnish, whitewash, spin a yarn (Inf), waffle (Inf)

17 **fabricate**, manufacture, simulate, imitate, make up, invent, hatch, concoct, cook up (Inf)

ADVERBS

18 **ideally**, in theory, theoretically, hypothetically, perfectly

19 **apparently**, to all appearances, seemingly, ostensibly, allegedly, putatively, purportedly, professedly, avowedly, superficially, in name only

103 Essence

NOUNS

1 **essence**, quiddity, quid, subject, substance, structure, stuff, material, matter, fabric, medium, building blocks

2 **essential content**, basis, core, kernel, gist, meat, heart, backbone, nub, nucleus, marrow, pith, sap, lifeblood, crux, subject matter, principle, issue, gravamen, highlight, high point, centre, focus, pivot, keystone, cornerstone, landmark, benchmark, milestone, nuts and bolts (Inf), nitty-gritty (Inf), name of the game (Inf), bottom line (Inf)

3 **quintessence**, embodiment, incarnation, personification, epitome, archetype, soul, spirit, entelechy, flower, elixir, extract, concentrate, distillate, distillation

4 **nature**, distinguishing feature(s), character,

suchness, makeup, constitution, composition, complexion, temperament, disposition, mould, pattern, stamp, type, breed, strain, stripe, humour, mood, trait, hue, quality, attribute, property, nature of the beast (Inf), thusness (Sl)

ADJECTIVES

5 **essential**, crucial, vital, necessary, paramount, indispensable, of the essence, prerequisite, requisite, obligatory, mandatory, compulsory, imperative, inalienable, unalienable, uninfringeable, unquestionable

▶ *611 Importance*

6 **intrinsic**, inherent, basic, primary, fundamental, immanent, innate, inborn, inbred, deep-seated, deep-rooted, ingrained, bred-in-the-bone

7 **integral**, inseparable, ineradicable, built-in, component, constituent, indivisible, integrated

8 **quintessential**, constitutional, structural, organic, peerless, singular, unique, consummate, archetypical (*or* archetypal)

9 **characteristic**, distinctive, distinguishing, typical, specific, particular, peculiar, defining, discriminating, idiosyncratic

VERBS

10 **be essential**, be central to, be part and parcel of

11 **characterize**, stamp, inform, mark, identify, depict, portray, represent, delineate, designate, distinguish, differentiate, demarcate

12 **embody**, incarnate, personify, epitomize, constitute, comprise, incorporate, assimilate, include, embrace, encompass

ADVERBS

13 **in essence**, essentially, intrinsically, per se, primarily, in the main, substantially, materially, by and large, mainly, mostly, chiefly, effectually, for the most part, almost entirely, for all practical purposes, necessarily

14 **at heart**, basically, at bottom, *au fond* (Fr), fundamentally, radically, at the core, in substance

104   Extraneousness

NOUNS

1 **extraneousness**, irrelevance, irrelevancy, immateriality, inessentiality, superfluity, pleonasm, superficiality, redundancy, pointlessness, inapplicability, incidentalness, secondariness, insignificance, triviality, lack of importance

▶ *136 Separation, 130 Addition, 612 Unimportance*

2 **foreignness**, alienism, alienage, unrelatedness, unconnectedness, disconnectedness, difference, otherness, exoticness, strangeness, the unknown

3 **separateness**, segregation, dissociation, dis-

affiliation, nonassimilation, discreteness, apartheid, isolation, insularity, detachment, noninvolvement, independence, nonconformity

▶ *111 Oppositeness, 147 Exclusion, 168 Nonconformity*

4 **externality**, extrinsicality, exteriority, coming from without, outside, outwardness, surface, periphery, circumference, the external, foreign product, importation, incoming, invasion, infringement, interloping, intrusion, trespassing, gate-crashing, externalization, projection, the supernatural, the paranormal

▶ *670 Attack, 346 Entry*

5 **nonconformist**, rebel, maverick, anarchist, outlaw, gypsy, nomad, eccentric, bohemian, hippie, New-Age traveller, beatnik, crank (Inf), weirdo (Inf)

6 **outsider**, alien, stranger, foreigner, outlander, ultramontane, tramontane (*or* transmontane), extraterrestrial (being), E.T., space invader, Martian, man from Mars, cosmic being, little green man

▶ *263 Distance*

7 **new arrival**, newcomer, exile, refugee, emigrant, emigré, displaced person (DP), the Wandering Jew, Diaspora, settler, new resident, expatriate, guest worker, *Gastarbeiter* (Ger), migrant worker, economic migrant, political refugee, homeless person, stateless person, immigrant, new face, new boy, new kid on the block (US), tenderfoot, greenhorn

8 **intruder**, gate-crasher, interloper, trespasser, squatter, uninvited guest, stowaway, cuckoo in the nest,

▶ *201 Newness, 68 Agriculture, 12 Government and Politics*

ADJECTIVES

9 **extraneous**, irrelevant, irrelative, immaterial, inessential, unessential, superfluous, extra, superficial, redundant, pleonastic, pointless, inapplicable, unrelated, disrelated, unconnected, disconnected, incidental, adventitious, secondary, insignificant, trivial

10 **foreign**, alien, unrelated, other, continental, overseas, transatlantic, ultramontane, tramontane (*or* transmontane), strange, different, deviating, outlandish, unknown, exotic, barbaric, barbarian, wandering, travelling, rambling, roaming, nomadic, gypsy, migrant, homeless, stateless

11 **separate**, separated, apart, dissociated, unaffiliated, disaffiliated, nonassimilated, segregated, removed, isolated, discrete, detached, independent, nonconforming, anarchic, anarchistic, rebellious

12 **external**, extrinsic, exterior, extraterrestrial, not of this world, distant, outward, outer, outside, ulterior, peripheral, superficial, foreignmade, imported, importing, incoming, invad-

ing, invasive, infringing, interloping, intrusive, trespassing, gate-crashing, externalizing, externalized, projecting, projected, supernatural, paranormal

VERBS

13 **be extraneous**, be irrelevant, miss the point, not come to the point, digress, talk off the subject, ramble, go off at (or on) a tangent, beat about the bush, beat around the bush (US), have no point, have no relevance, have no relation to, not relate, not apply, not fit

14 **be foreign**, come from another country, live in another land, emigrate, immigrate, flee one's homeland, travel, wander, ramble, roam, live on the road

15 **separate**, keep apart, segregate, isolate, remove, detach, divide

16 **be external**, come from without, exist outside, import, invade, infringe, interlope, squat, intrude, trespass, stowaway, gate-crash, externalize, project, delve into the supernatural

17 **not conform**, be different, be independent, live one's own life, do one's own thing (Inf)

ADVERBS

18 **extraneously**, irrelevantly, immaterially, superfluously, superficially, prima facie, pointlessly, beside the point, neither here nor there, inapplicably, without application, incidentally, adventitiously, secondarily, insignificantly, without significance, trivially, strangely, in a strange way, differently, outlandishly, exotically, nomadically, like a nomad, discretely, separately, independently, externally, extrinsically, distantly, from a distance, on one's travels, abroad, in a foreign country, in foreign lands, in foreign parts, overseas, from outer space, outwardly, on the outside, away from, apart, peripherally, intrusively, with an intrusive manner, supernaturally

105 State

NOUNS

1 **state**, condition, situation, circumstances, lot, fettle, form, order, repair, estate, social position, position, station in life, role, status, standing, rank, ranking, place, posture, footing, walk of life, class, echelon, category, structure, aspect, guise, shape, phase, light, mode, manner, way, style, lifestyle, fashion, complexion, appearance, tone, modality, modus vivendi, modus operandi, trend, stamp, fit, mould, street credibility, cred (Inf)

▶ 106 Circumstances, 251 Situation, 103 Essence, 306 Form, 382 Structure, 457 Appearance, 234 Tendency, 92 Administrative Areas, 564 Speech, 535 Affirmation, 526 Display, 12 Government and Politics

2 **predicament**, problem, dilemma, plight, trouble, difficulties, hot water (Inf), jam (Inf),

fix (Inf), pickle (Inf)

▶ 659 Difficulty, 661 Hindrance, 663 Opposition

3 **state of affairs**, the nature of things, the shape of things, the way things shape up, the way things are, how things stand, the way of the world, the lie of the land, the lay of the land (US), how it is (Inf), where it's at (Inf), the size of it (Inf), how things stack up (Sl)

4 **state of mind**, frame of mind, mood, humour, disposition, temper, temperament, attitude, vein, morale, fettle, fine fettle, spirits, good spirits, high spirits, good humour, bad spirits, low spirits, bad humour

▶ 769 Cheerfulness

5 **physical state**, state of health, physical form, physical condition, shape, good condition (or shape), bad (or poor) condition (or shape), trim, kilter (or kelter), fettle, fine fettle, fig (Sl)

▶ 623 Health

VERBS

6 **be in a state of**, be so, have a standing, stand, maintain a certain footing, maintain one's status, lie, sit, occupy (or enjoy) a certain social position, occupy (or enjoy) a certain standing, occupy a certain walk of life, have a station in life, play a role, fare, manage, do well, do poorly, get on (or along), come on (or along), live a certain way, follow a trend, fit a mould, come through, turn out, come out, make out (Inf), get by (Inf), shape up (Inf), stack up (Sl)

7 **be in a predicament**, have a predicament, have a problem, have a dilemma, run into trouble, have difficulties, labour under, need help, see no way out, get into a jam (Inf), get into a fix (Inf), be up shit creek (without a paddle) (Tab sl)

ADJECTIVES

8 **in a state of**, in a certain state, on form, in form, in good form, in bad form, conditional, modal, ranking, ranked, placed, situated, classed, in fine fettle, in good spirits, in a good mood, high-spirited, good-humoured, in bad spirits, low-spirited, in a bad mood, bad-humoured, temperamental, in condition, in order, in good condition (or shape), in bad condition (or shape), out of order, out of sorts, out of kilter (or kelter), stylish, fashionable, trendy, cred (Inf)

ADVERBS

9 **conditionally**, as it is, as it stands, in a state of, in a certain state, such being the case, as things are, as the matter stands, in the circumstances, in the present case, in fine fettle, in good form, in good spirits, good-humouredly, in bad form, in bad spirits, bad-humouredly, temperamentally, provisionally, contingently, stylishly, in style, fashionable, in fashion, trendily

106   Circumstances

NOUNS

1 **circumstances**, conditions, condition, relative condition, situation, total situation, existing conditions, environment, surroundings, setting, milieu, background, the times, context, the whole picture, the picture, status quo, status, state of affairs, state of play, position, means, resources, state, posture, attitude, terms, footing, standing, lie of the land, lay of the land (US), full particulars, ins and outs, story so far, the way it is, contingency, eventuality, setup (Inf), how it goes (Inf), the score (Inf)

▶ *251 Situation, 297 Surroundings, 107 Relatedness, 105 State, 154 Precedence, 150 Order, 845 Entitlement*

2 **occurrence**, event, episode, incident, case, happening, occasion, instance, juncture, conjuncture, stage, point, milestone, moment, hour, right time, opportunity, stepping-stone

▶ *185 Timeliness*

3 **critical moment**, hour of decision, crossroads, turning point, match point, point of no return, Rubicon

▶ *216 Change, 189 Transience*

4 **difficult circumstances**, awkward situation, trouble, catch-22, plight, dilemma, predicament, crisis, emergency, exigency, quandary, pretty pass, pinch, corner, hole, jam (Inf), fix (Inf), pickle (Inf), time when the chips are down (Inf)

▶ *659 Difficulty, 661 Hindrance, 743 Poverty, 633 Danger*

5 **comfortable circumstances**, comfort, ease, security, well-being, prosperity, success, luck, luckiness, good fortune, life of ease, the good life, lap of luxury, halcyon days, golden age

▶ *742 Wealth, 686 Prosperity, 632 Safety, 589 Chance, 765 Satisfaction*

6 **aspect**, element, factor, fact, facet, datum, detail, minor detail, minutia, incidental, item, particular, point, thing

▶ *537 Truth*

ADJECTIVES

7 **circumstantial**, dependent on circumstances, relative, given, contingent, conditional, indirect, inferential, hearsay, conjectural, presumed, implied, provisional, fitting the circumstances, adventitious, situational, surrounding, environmental, background, situated, placed, contextual, changeful, variable, transient, incidental, eventual, eventful

8 **difficult**, awkward, critical, crucial, pivotal, decisive, troublesome, exigent, in a jam (Inf), in a fix (Inf), in a pickle (Inf), up shit creek (without a paddle) (Tab sl)

9 **comfortable**, easy, secure, well, prosperous, lucky, opportune, suitable, auspicious, favourable

10 **detailed**, meticulous, elaborate, minute, incidental, particular, full, precise, exact, specific, special, fussy, finicky, pernickety, nit-picking (Inf)

VERBS

11 **circumstantiate**, itemize, specify, particularize, substantiate, put in context, see the whole picture, get the lie of the land, get the lay of the land (US), get the full particulars, detail, go (*or* enter) into detail, cite, instance, adduce, document, spell out, quote chapter and verse, atomize, anatomize, know the ins and outs, see how it goes (Inf)

12 **come to a juncture**, come to a crossroads, reach a stage, reach the turning point, reach a milestone, play match point, come to the point of no return, cross one's Rubicon

13 **get into difficulties**, get into trouble, be in a catch-22 situation, reach a crisis, have an emergency, get into a jam (Inf), get into a fix (Inf), get into hot water (Inf), get in a pickle (Inf), find oneself up shit creek (without a paddle) (Tab sl)

14 **be comfortable**, prosper, enjoy good fortune, get lucky, live a life of ease, live in the lap of luxury, be smiled on by fate, fare well, succeed, flourish

ADVERBS

15 **under the circumstances**, according to circumstances, circumstantially, accordingly, as it is, as it happened, as things stand, as it turns out, as matters stand, as the winds blow, as the case may be, that (*or* such) being the case, in that case, in this way, that (*or* it) being so, given that, from that angle, at that rate, taking it that, and so, thus, so, in the event, in the case, if, if so, provided that, supposing, assuming, granting, allowing, as it may happen, as things may fall, like this, like that, should it so happen, should it be that, by the same token, equally, similarly, consequently, if not, unless, except, without, like so (Inf)

16 **relatively**, in a relative way, conditionally, under certain conditions, provisionally, with provisions, indirectly, inferentially, conjecturally, adventitiously, environmentally, contextually, changefully, with many changes, variably, incidentally, contingently, eventually

17 **difficultly**, awkwardly, critically, crucially, at a crucial time, at a crucial point, exigently, when the chips are down (Inf)

18 **comfortably**, easily, safely, securely, prosperously, luckily, opportunely, suitably, auspiciously, favourably

19 **meticulously**, with a fine-tooth (*or* fine-toothed) comb, elaborately, in an elaborate

manner, minutely, incidentally, particularly, fully, in full, precisely, exactly, just so, specifically, specially, fussily, sedulously, assiduously

107 Relatedness

NOUNS

1 **relatedness**, relation, relationship, relevance, pertinence, germaneness, bearing, appositeness, connectedness, connection, affinity, friendship, propinquity, kinship, bond, tie, rapport, family relationship, blood relationship, consanguinity, partnership, marriage relationship, link, tie-up, involvement, implication, casual relationship, merger, association, affiliation, alliance, linkage, liaison, interconnection, mutuality, combination, correspondence, agreement, similarity, something in common, parallel, comparison, reference, cross-reference, analogy, correlation, homology, addition, adjunct, attachment, appendix, accompaniment

▶ *137 Connection, 611 Importance, 819 Friendship, 823 Marriage, 520 Meaning, 114 Similarity, 167 Conformity, 110 Sameness*

2 **interrelatedness**, similar relation, similarity, equality, comparability, homology, correlation, reciprocity, reciprocation, interdependence, cross-reference, reference, citation, complementarity, interconnection, association, mutuality, relativity, proportionality, interlocking, interlinkage, interalliance, interassociation, covariation, interaction, interplaying, interworking, intercourse, intercommunication, interweaving, intertwining, interlacing, interpenetration, interchanging, interchange, tit for tat, blow for blow, engagement, intermeshing, mesh, alternation, seesaw, relativeness, ratio, proportion, scale, direct ratio, inverse ratio, direct proportion, inverse proportion, contrast

▶ *122 Equality, 664 Cooperation, 109 Reciprocity*

3 **relative position**, rank, class, classification, order, degree, echelon, rating, status, level

▶ *152 Arrangement, 121 Degree*

ADJECTIVES

4 **related**, relevant, pertinent, germane, apposite, connected, associated, affiliated, allied, linked, bonded, kindred, cognate, agnate, akin to, consanguineous, consanguine, wedded, bound, joined, tied, tied up with, twinned, paired, involved, implicated, merged, combined, added, attached, accompanied, spliced (Inf)

5 **interrelated**, correlated, reciprocal, interdependent, complementary, interconnected, associated, mutual, relative, proportional, interlocked, interlinked, interallied, interassociated, interwoven, intertwined, inter-

changed, interacting, interworking, engaged, intermeshed, cross-referred, corresponding, agreed, similar, parallel, comparable, analogous, equal, homologous, relational, commensurate, opposite

6 **ranked**, classed, classified, ordered, rated, given status

VERBS

7 **relate to**, relate, have a relationship, stand in relation to, have relevance, apply to, apply, bear upon, pertain to, pertain, appertain, affect, interest, have to do with, have a bearing on, refer to, make a reference to, touch upon, touch, associate, connect, establish a connection, put in its context, juxtapose, bracket, bracket together, couple, tie up, tie together, tie, bring to bear upon, reconcile, contrast, cross-refer, answer to, have a connection with, liaise with, deal with, pair up with, belong to, link with, tie in with, tie into, become a factor, have a point, support an analogy, serve as an example, sketch in, provide a background, come to the point, stick to the point, address the question, get down to the nitty-gritty (Inf), get down to brass tacks (Inf)

8 **be proportionate to**, correspond to, correlate, compare, have a mutual relationship, interconnect, interlock, interpenetrate, interlink, interassociate, interact, interplay, interwork, balance, liken, parallel, draw a parallel with (or between), equalize, proportion, symmetrize, match, equate, accord, fit, tally

9 **have a relative position**, have a classification, hold a certain position, rank, rate, belong to a class, have certain status, fit into a category (or pigeonhole)

ADVERBS

10 **relevantly**, pertinently, germanely, concerning, touching, regarding, as to, as regards, in regard to, in relation to, appositely, mutually, equally, on equal terms, reciprocally, interdependently, respectively, correspondingly, proportionally, proportionately, in proportion to, to scale, similarly, comparably, comparatively, in (or by) comparison, analogously, commensurately, consanguineously, consanguinely, in a context, in some degree, to some extent, oppositely, in contrast

108 Unrelatedness

NOUNS

1 **unrelatedness**, irrelation, irrelevance, irrelevancy, pointlessness, inappositeness, extraneousness, randomness, arbitrariness, coincidence, illogicality, inapplicability, inaptitude, inaptness, inappropriateness, unconnectedness, difference, heterogeneity, disconnection, disassociation, disjuncture, foreignness, separateness, independence, nonconformity,

singularity, unilateralism, neutrality, individuality, freedom, homelessness, no fixed abode, rootlessness, divorce, insularity, isolation, isolationism

▶ *136 Separation, 335 Deviation, 117 Disparity, 612 Unimportance, 111 Opppositeness, 115 Dissimilarity, 113 Diversity, 698 Freedom*

2   **unrelated thing**, non sequitur, fish out of water, square peg in a round hole, cuckoo in the nest, red herring

▶ *149 Foreign Body*

3   **unconnected person**, hermit, recluse, dropout, misfit, stranger, alien, foreigner, draft dodger (US), displaced person (DP), expatriate, refugee, tenderfoot, uninvited guest, gatecrasher, gooseberry, stowaway

4   **distortion**, disparity, imbalance, asymmetry, disproportion, dissimilarity, inequality

▶ *309 Distortion, 168 Nonconformity, 151 Disorder, 123 Inequality*

5   **misconnection**, no connection, bad connection, misrelation, no relation, wrong association, misalliance, *mésalliance* (Fr), misapplication, misreference, wrong reference

▶ *211 Untimeliness, 504 Error*

ADJECTIVES

6   **unrelated**, irrelevant, inapposite, inapplicable, inapt, inappropriate, unconnected, separate, separated, unilateral, disconnected, disassociated, extraneous, difference, heterogenous, independent, singular, individual, unallied, unaffiliated, disrelated, detached, reclusive, discrete, disjunct, removed, segregated, apart, other, floating, uninvolved, divorced, foreign, alien, strange, exotic, owing nothing to, free, rootless, homeless, carefree, fancy-free

7   **illogical**, improbable, impractical, immaterial, incommensurable, beside the point, off the subject, nothing to do with, something else, nonessential, extrinsic, aleatoric, neither here nor there, unimportant, random, arbitrary, coincidental, incidental, remote, far-fetched, distant, out-of-the-way, strained, laboured, forced

8   **distorted**, disproportionate, out of (all) proportion, imbalanced, asymmetrical, dissimilar, unequal, discordant, incongruent

9   **misconnected**, not connected, not related, unrelated, not associated, not allied, misapplied, misreferred

VERBS

10 **be unrelated**, not concern, not involve, not relate to, not connect with, become irrelevant, have no bearing on, go off the point, stray from the topic, digress, get sidetracked, lose the thread, ramble, wander, miss the point, avoid the issue, cloud the issue, draw a red herring, throw dust in one's eyes, strain, labour

11 **be unconcerned**, have no concern with (*or* for), have no interest in, have nothing to do with, owe nothing to, disown, not be one's business, not give (*or* care) a toss (Inf), not give a monkey's (Inf)

ADVERBS

12 **irrelevantly**, without relevance, irrelatively, without reference, without regard, inapplicably, inaptly, inappositely, inappropriately, extraneously, incidentally, coincidentally, by the way, beside the point, off the point, separately, independently, with an independent manner, freely, singularly, individually, as an individual, strangely, exotically

13 **disproportionately**, asymmetrically, dissimilarly, without similarities, unequally, discordantly, incongruently

109   Reciprocity

NOUNS

1   **interchange**, interchangeability, reciprocation, interplay, interaction, interacting, give and take, compromise, exchange, equal exchange, fair exchange, balance, justice, change, bartering, barter, swap, trade-off, alternation, turn and turn about, compensation, retaliation, payment in kind, tit for tat, an eye for an eye, blow for blow, measure for measure, *quid pro quo* (L), *tu quoque* (L), return, retort, reaction, requital, counteraction, recoil, counterstroke, comeback (Inf)

▶ *737 Trade, 223 Exchange, 125 Compensation, 672 Retaliation, 365 Oscillation, 216 Change, 717 Compromise, 231 Counteraction, 111 Oppositeness, 331 Recoil*

2   **interconnection**, interrelationship (*or* interrelation), interdependence, mutual relationship (*or* relation), mutual dependence, mutual influence, mutuality, mutualism, mutualization, symbiosis, cooperation, partnership, sharing, each other, one another, opposite number, complement, counterpart, alter ego

▶ *116 Accord, 137 Connection, 664 Cooperation*

3   **correlation**, correlativity, correspondence, similarity, parallelism, comparability, comparison, analogy, analogue, allegory, equivalence, symmetry, proportionality, proportion, proportionment, pattern, tally, match, identity

▶ *110 Sameness, 114 Similarity, 308 Symmetry, 122 Equality, 544 Identification*

ADJECTIVES

4   **reciprocal**, reciprocative, reciprocatory, reciprocating, interacting, interchangeable, interchanged, interplaying, give-and-take, compromising, exchanged, exchangeable, changed, bartered, swapped, trade-off, alternative, alternate, alternating, balancing, seesaw, compensatory, retaliatory, tit-for-tat, eye-for-eye, blow-for-blow, reacting, recoiling, re-

quited, requitable, counteracting, counteractive

5 **interconnected**, interrelated, interlocking, interlinked, interdependent, mutual, symbiotic, cooperative, two-way, bilateral, complementary, complemental, opposite

6 **correlative**, correlational, correlating, correlated, correspondent, corresponding, comparable, analogous, allegorical, parallel, symmetric(al), proportional, proportionate, proportioned, patterned, matching, equivalent, similar, identical

VERBS

7 **reciprocate**, interchange, interplay, interact, give and take, compromise, exchange, give an equal exchange, change, give in exchange, counterchange, barter, swap, trade off, trade, alternate, compensate, balance, seesaw, take turn and turn about, take turns, retaliate, pay in kind, give tit for tat, take an eye for an eye, give blow for blow, react, counteract, recoil, counterstrike, requite, return, retort

8 **interrelate**, establish an interrelationship, interconnect, interlock, interlink, interdepend, interassociate, neutralize, cooperate, partner, pair, twin, participate, share, complement, act as a foil to

▶ 288 Interweaving

9 **correlate**, correspond, identify with, parallel, parallelize, compare, proportion, tally, answer, match, resemble, equalize

▶ 478 Answer

ADVERBS

10 **reciprocally**, interchangeably, compromisingly, proportionally, proportionately, in (mutual) exchange, alternatively, to and fro, by turns, turn and turn about, first one and then the other, interdependently, mutually, equally, bilaterally, cooperatively, symbiotically, contrariwise, vice versa, complementally, oppositely

11 **correlatively**, correspondingly, comparably, analogously, allegorically, symmetrically, proportionally, proportionately, equivalently, similarly, identically

110 Sameness

NOUNS

1 **sameness**, the same, the very same, the exact same, *idem* (L), very thing, actual thing, selfsameness, one and the same, no other, none other, uniformity, identicalness, isotrophy, indistinguishability, no difference, oneness, oneness with, unity, solidarity, mergence, coalescence, assimilation, agreement, repetition, redundancy, tautology, the very words, *ipsissima verba* (L), verbatim, homoousia, consubstantiality, consubstantiation, birds of a feather

▶ 112 Uniformity, 183 Repetition, 116 Accord, 348 Admittance, 135 Union, 667 Agreement, 7 Religion, 10 Ritual, 167 Conformity, 544 Identification, 174 One

2 **equivalence**, equivalent, correspondence, concordance, accordance, harmony, agreement, congruence (*or* congruency), equipollence, interchangeability, reciprocation, equal exchange, representation, similarity, homoiousia, parallelism, coincidence, synchronicity, synonymousness, synonymy, synonymity, homogeneity, homonym, homograph, homophone, analogy, analogue, analog (US), simile, metaphor, reflection, shadow

▶ 114 Similarity, 520 Meaning, 109 Reciprocity, 5 Linguistics, 116 Accord, 667 Agreement, 198 Same Time, 285 Parallelism

3 **lookalike**, double, doppelgänger, alter ego, other self, ka, ba, twin, Siamese twin, family resemblance, homophyly, very image, (exact) counterpart, reflection, two of a kind, two peas in a pod, Tweedledum and Tweedledee, pair, match, suit, portrait, clone, chip off the old block (Inf), spit (Inf), dead spit (Inf), spitting image (Inf), picture of (Inf), living image (Inf), dead ringer (Sl)

▶ 176 Two, 796 Fashion, 457 Appearance, 544 Identification

4 **duplicate**, duplication, triplicate, imitation, copy, carbon copy, photocopy, Xerox (Tm), Photostat (Tm), Mimeograph (Tm), hectograph copy, microcopy, facsimile, fax, photograph, positive, negative, enlargement, print, contact print, PMT (photomechanical transfer), reprint, offprint, separate (US), second printing, second edition, reproduction, impression, hologram, replication, replica, representation, model, mould, moulding, stamp, seal, ditto (Inf), dupe (US inf)

▶ 118 Imitation, 547 Representation, 50 Painting and Sculpture, 66 Photography, 243 Production, 245 Reproduction

5 **equality**, coequality, parity, symmetry, balance, equilibration, equiponderance, equal standing, equal rights, equal opportunity, impartiality, justice, equal value, even money, six of one and half a dozen of the other, six and two threes, nothing to choose between, nothing in it, par, tie, draw, drawn match, tied game, love-all score, deuce, stalemate, deadlock, dead heat, neck-and-neck race, half-and-half split, fifty-fifty split (Inf), level pegging (Inf), quits (Inf), even break (Inf)

▶ 122 Equality, 482 Lack of Discrimination

6 **regularity**, clockwork regularity, routine, daily routine, daily round, constancy, changelessness, smoothness, even pace, evenness, levelness, equilibrium, homeostasis (*or* homoeostasis), homogeneity, consistency, invariability, unvariableness (*or* invariableness),

invariant, no change, uniformity, standardization, conformity, conformance, monotonousness, monotony, repetition, flatness, treadmill, mass production, assembly line, automation, regimentation, same old thing, same old story

▶ *214 Regularity, 376 Smoothness, 282 Horizontality, 225 Stability, 112 Uniformity, 788 Boredom, 124 Average, 166 Rule, 490 Certainty, 219 Continuity, 342 Convergence, 150 Order, 217 Permanence, 584 Habit, 133 Mixture*

VERBS

7 **be the same**, be identical, be as like as two peas in a pod, correspond, agree, harmonize, merge, coalesce, coincide, match, tally, answer, interchange, reciprocate, imitate, look alike, shadow, reflect, repeat, quote, tell the same (old) story

8 **make the same**, unify, unite, join, merge, homogenize, coalesce, assimilate, synthesize, synchronize, consubstantiate, parallel, equate, pair, twin, symmetrize, balance, harmonize, smooth, level, flatten, even up, stereotype, standardize, regulate, regularize, phase, mass-produce, automate, clone

▶ *133 Mixture, 167 Conformity, 135 Union, 125 Compensation*

9 **duplicate**, triplicate, copy, imitate, ape, photocopy, Xerox (Tm), Photostat (Tm), Mimeograph (Tm), fax, photograph, shoot, enlarge, print, reprint, offprint, run a second edition, reproduce, make an impression, replicate, mould, stamp, ditto (Inf)

10 **be equal**, equal, match, balance, measure up to, equalize, equiponderate, equilibrate, draw a match, tie a game, stalemate, deadlock, come to the same thing, break even, race neck-and-neck, split half-and-half, go fifty-fifty (Inf)

11 **be regular**, continue the same, fall into a routine, repeat, iterate, persist, drag on, harp on, hum, drone, keep an even pace, typify, conform, toe the line, get in a rut

▶ *217 Permanence, 575 Perseverance*

ADJECTIVES

12 **same**, *idem* (L), selfsame, one and the same, identical, isotrophic (*or* isotropous), indistinguishable, undifferentiated, repetitious, repetitive, unvarying, repeated, redundant, tautologic(al) (*or* tautologous), verbatim, united, solid, all the same, one, all one, homogeneous, merging, merged, of that ilk, absorbed, coalescent, coalesced, assimilated, agreed, consubstantial, homoousian, of the same kidney, tarred with the same brush

13 **equivalent**, corresponding, concordant, accordant, harmonious, agreeing, agreeable, congruent, equipollent, interchangeable, reciprocal, representative, parallel, similar, ho-

moiousian, coincidental, synchronous, synonymous, homogeneous, homographic, homonymic (*or* homonymous), homophonic (*or* homophonous), analogous, metaphoric(al), reflective, shadowing

14 **lookalike**, twin, homophyllic, matching, matched, like, alike, paired, like two peas in a pod, cloned

15 **duplicate**, triplicate, copied, photocopied, Xeroxed (Tm), Photostated (Tm), Mimeographed (Tm), microcopied, faxed, photographic, photographed, positive, negative, printed, reprinted, offprinted, reproduced, holographic, replicated, moulded, cast out of the same mould, stamped

16 **equal**, coequal, symmetrical, balanced, equiponderant, equidistant, on equal terms, on the same footing, as good as, no better and no worse, neither more nor less, level, impartial, par, on par, on a par, tied, drawn, love-all, stalemated, deadlocked, neck-and-neck, half-and-half, fifty-fifty (Inf), level-pegging (Inf), quits (Inf)

17 **regular**, clockwork, routine, hourly, daily, weekly, monthly, yearly, annual, constant, smooth, steady, even, level, changeless, homeostatic (*or* homoeostatic), homogenous, consistent, unvariable, unvarying, unvaried, unaltered, invariant, invariable, always the same, unchanging, unchanged, unchangeable, undeviating, undiversified, uniform, flat, standardized, conforming, mundane, repetitive, repetitious, monotonous, automative, automated, regimented

▶ *185 Time, 192 Timekeeping*

ADVERBS

18 **identically**, alike, just the same, in the same way, in the same place, ibid, *ibidem* (L), at the same time, coincidentally, synchronously, again, ditto, likewise, isotrophically, indistinguishably, repetitiously, repetitively, in duplicate, in triplicate, tautologically, homogenously, consubstantially, equivalently, correspondently, correspondingly, congruently, agreeably, concordantly, harmoniously, synonymously, analogously, metaphorically, reflectively, imitatively, holographically, photographically

19 **equally**, coequally, on equal terms, on the same footing, levelly, impartially, in par, on a par, neck and neck, fifty-fifty (Inf)

20 **regularly**, routinely, like clockwork, hourly, daily, weekly, monthly, yearly, annually, days, mornings, afternoons, evenings, nights, constantly, smoothly, steadily, in phase, evenly, levelly, on a level, unvariably, invariably, changelessly, always, without exception, uniformly, monotonously, flatly, repetitively, in a rut, in a groove

111 Oppositeness

The poet and the dreamer are distinct,/ Diverse, sheer opposite, antipodes./ The one pours out a balm upon the world,/ The other vexes it. John Keats.

Doublethink means the power of holding two contradictory beliefs in one's mind simultaneously, and accepting both of them. Geoge Orwell.

NOUNS

1 **oppositeness**, opposite side, other side, opposing side, opposition, opposite number, contraposition, opposure, antithesis, contrariety, contraries, contradiction, contrariness, confrontment, contrast, reverse, reversal, inverse, inversion, obverse, converse, back, rear, polarity, polarization, polar opposition, opposite pole, counterpole, poles apart, antipodes, antipodal points, extremes, other side of the fence, other side of the coin, other side of the picture
▶ *287 Inversion, 303 Front, 304 Rear*

2 **opposites**, east and west, north and south, night and day, black and white, good and evil, high and low, rich and poor, hill and dale, great and small, hot and cold, sweet and sour, fair and foul, laughter and tears, land and sea, Yin and Yang, ancient and modern, feast and famine, heads and tails, man and beast, Jekyll and Hyde, chalk and cheese, oil and water, sheep and goats, beauty and the beast, the lion and the lamb, the hare and the tortoise, cat and mouse, Tom and Jerry, the prince and the pauper, Dives and Lazarus, the lady and the tramp, Socrates and the fool, saints and sinners, cops and robbers, cowboys and Indians, goodies and baddies (Inf)

3 **opposition**, resistance, obstruction, hindrance, confrontation, disapproval, defiance, antagonism, hostility, contention, impugnation, impugnment, conflict, disagreement, argument, antipathy, enmity, inimicality, animosity, rivalry, counteraction, crosscurrent, headwind
▶ *663 Opposition, 687 Adversity, 473 Argument, 670 Attack, 231 Counteraction, 820 Enmity*

ADJECTIVES

4 **opposite**, opposing, opposed, oppositional, diametrically opposite (*or* opposed), diametric(al), other, contrapositive, antithetic(al), antipodal (*or* antipodean), contrary, contrariwise, contrasting, reverse, reversed, inverse, inverted, obverse, converse, subcontrary, confronting, oncoming, facing, face-to-face, vis-à-vis, nose-to-nose, eyeball-to-eyeball, polarized, polar, poles apart

5 **opposing**, resistant, resisting, resisted, obstructive, obstructing, obstructed, hindering, hindered, confrontational, confronting, confronted, disapproving, disapproved, antipathetic, antagonistic, antagonizing, antagonized, hostile, defiant, contentious, rival, inimical

ADVERBS

6 **oppositely**, diametrically, antithetically, contrarily, contrastively, inversely, obversely, conversely, contrariwise, counter, vice versa, poles apart, poles asunder, at opposite extremes, against, over the way, over against, facing, face to face, nose to nose, eyeball to eyeball, vis-à-vis, belly to belly, toe to toe, head to head, back to back, overleaf, on the other side, on the other side of the fence

7 **disapprovingly**, antagonistically, hostilely, defiantly, confrontationally, contentiously, argumentatively, inimically

VERBS

8 **be opposite**, oppose, stand on the opposite side, take the opposing side, lie opposite, set against (*or* over), polarize, subtend, face, traverse, run counter, counteract, contradict, contrapose, contrast, reverse, invert, confront, meet head-on, meet a crosscurrent, meet a headwind

9 **oppose**, resist, obstruct, hinder, confront, contradict, disapprove, antagonize, show hostility, defy, contend against (*or* with), impugn, argue, disagree, protest, vote against, militate against, fight

112 Uniformity

NOUNS

1 **uniformity**, uniformness, similarity, evenness, consistency, lack of variety, sameness, homogeneity, symmetry, steadiness, steadfastness, stability, permanence, inevitability, persistence, levelness, smoothness, roundness, constancy, continuousness, continuity, regularity, routine, habit, repetition, even rhythm, even pace, jog trot
▶ *114 Similarity, 219 Continuity, 308 Symmetry, 225 Stability, 159 Consecutiveness, 217 Permanence, 584 Habit, 183 Repetition*

2 **conformity**, equality, correspondence, identicalness, regimentation, standardization, normalization, uniformity, plainness, blankness, automation, mass production, conveyor belt, orderliness, order, method, computerization, pattern, stereotype, cliché, typecasting mould, copy, stamp, set, suit, standard
▶ *122 Equality, 214 Regularity, 150 Order*

3 **agreement**, accord, equanimity, consensus, unison, unity, solidarity, unanimous vote
▶ *116 Accord*

4 **monotony**, monotonousness, repetition, lack of change, invariability, identicalness,

sameness, same old story, routine, dullness, drabness, tediousness, humdrumness, boredom, greyness, drone, droning, round, daily round, daily beat, groove, rut, drill, singsong, ding-dong, monotone, monotonous life, treadmill, military training, totalitarianism, communism

▶ *788 Boredom*

ADJECTIVES

5 **uniform**, identical, even, consistent, same, alike, homogeneous, constant, continuous, regular, inevitable, unchanging, unvarying, permanent, steady, steadfast, stable, persistent, equal, level, flat, flush, smooth, symmetric(al), round, continuing, unruffled, unbroken, immutable, routine, habitual, repetitious

6 **conforming**, equal, correspondent, corresponding, standard, standardized, normalized, uniform, mechanical, identical, regimented, mass-produced, ready-to-wear, off-the-peg, undifferentiated, monolithic, plain, faceless, characterless, featureless, blank, bland, normal, automatic, automated, orderly, ordered, aligned, in line, computerized, stereotyped, typecast, patterned, copied, stamped

7 **agreeing**, agreed, equanimous, united, solid, unanimous

8 **monotonous**, repetitious, repetitive, planned, invariable, unvaried, unvarying, identical, same, lack of change, methodical, routine, dull, drab, humdrum, tedious, unrelieved, boring, grey, droning, singsong, ding-dong, monotone

VERBS

9 **be uniform**, stay the same, make uniform, make similar, even up (*or* out *or* off), make consistent, homogenize, equalize, regulate, regularize, stabilize, steady, remain steadfast, persist, continue, level off (*or* up), smooth, round off, make symmetric(al), balance, make a habit of, repeat, keep an even rhythm, keep an even pace, sing in unison

10 **conform**, correspond to, regiment, standardize, normalize, harmonize, make uniform, lack variety, align, bring into line, drill, grade, size, homogenize, automate, mass-produce, order, computerize, pattern, stereotype, run true to type, typecast, mould, copy, stamp, toe the line, fall in, follow the crowd, climb (*or* jump) on the bandwagon

11 **agree**, reach an accord, reach a consensus, unite, vote unanimously

12 **be monotonous**, repeat, persist, continue the same way, remain unchanged, stay the same, tell the same old story, bore, drone on, drag on, follow one's routine, make one's daily round, walk one's daily beat, stay in a rut, lead a monotonous life

ADVERBS

13 **uniformly**, identically, just the same, correspondingly, evenly, consistently, homogeneously, constantly, continuingly, continuously, methodically, normally, regularly, repetitiously, repetitively, permanently, inevitably, invariably, without exception, always, like clockwork, steadily, steadfastly, persistently, endlessly, without stopping, equally, levelly, smoothly, symmetrically, habitually, routinely, mechanically, automatically, in line, in keeping with, in the groove (US)

14 **equanimously**, unanimously, solidly, across the board, from Land's End to John o'Groat's, from coast to coast (US)

15 **monotonously**, dully, drably, plainly, blankly, tediously, in a rut

113   Diversity

NOUNS

1 **diversity**, difference, variety, multiplicity, heterogeneity, miscellany, diversification, variation, versatility, dissimilarity, contrast, disorder, deviation, variousness, divergence, variegation, incongruity, nonconformity, exception, exception to the rule, special case, odd man out, nonuniformity, inconsistency, inequality, discontinuity, variability, unevenness, bumpiness, raggedness, irregularity, changeability, instability, unpredictability, haphazardness, fitfulness, modifiability, alterability, abnormality, mutation, individuality, uniqueness, freak, one-off (Inf)

▶ *115 Dissimilarity, 160 Discontinuity, 215 Irregularity, 456 Variegation, 224 Changeableness, 168 Nonconformity, 151 Disorder, 335 Deviation*

2 **assortment**, mixture, medley, miscellany, *e pluribus unum* (L), all shapes and sizes, all sorts and conditions, hotchpotch, hodgepodge (US), odds and ends, motley, variegation, dappleness, multiplicity, multiformity, omnifariousness, allotropy (*or* allotropism), heteromorphism, Proteus, all colours of the rainbow, everything but the kitchen sink

▶ *133 Mixture*

3 **diverse thing**, motley collection, miscellanea, ragbag, lucky dip, grab bag (US), mosaic, stained-glass window, crazy paving, patchwork quilt, coat of many colours, rainbow, kaleidoscope, chequered career, mixed bag (Inf)

4 **dissension**, disagreement, controversy, discordance, different opinions, various opinions, many voices

▶ *111 Oppositeness*

ADJECTIVES

5 **diverse**, varied, variable, nonuniform, heterogeneous, dissimilar, contrasting, deviant, diverging, diversiform, different, manifold, in-

congruous, variegated, chequered, exceptional, abnormal, freakish, unique, individual, unusual, inconsistent, changeable, unstable, uneven, bumpy, versatile, all-round, all-around (US), unpredictable, spasmodic, sporadic, erratic, haphazard, fitful, inconstant, never the same, out of step

6 **assorted**, mixed, chequered, miscellaneous, motley, dapple, omnifarious, multifarious, allotropic, kaleidoscopic, sundry, all and sundry, various, multipurpose, multifaceted, multiform, diversiform, polymorphous, heteromorphous, of many kinds, of all sorts, multicoloured, divers (Arch)

7 **dissenting**, disagreeing, controversial, discordant, of different opinions

VERBS

8 **be diverse**, diverge, branch out, differ, variegate, deviate, mutate, make diverse, differentiate, vary, contrast, chequer, diversify, mix, stir, jumble, shake up, shuffle, scramble, tangle, blend, intermix, intersperse, interleave, ring the changes, have many irons in the fire, have many strings to one's bow, spread one's wings

9 **dissent**, disagree, have discord, vote against, hold opposite opinions, have different opinions

ADVERBS

10 **diversely**, differently, variably, nonuniformly, heterogeneously, miscellaneously, omnifariously, kaleidoscopically, variously, in different ways, dissimilarly, dissentingly, out of step, differently, exceptionally, individually, abnormally, freakishly, uniquely, unusually, untidily, changeably, unequally, unevenly, bumpily, versatilely, unpredictably, inconsistently, without consistency, inconstantly, unsteadily

11 **irregularly**, spasmodically, sporadically, erratically, haphazardly, fitfully, chaotically, without order, in turmoil, in confusion, all over the place (or shop), here, there, and everywhere, in all manner of ways, willynilly, helter-skelter, harum-scarum, huggermugger, topsy-turvy, every which way (US inf), at sixes and sevens (Inf), higgledy-piggledy (Inf)

114 Similarity

NOUNS

1 **similarity**, sameness, resemblance, synonymy, homonymy, likeness, alikeness, similitude, affinity, kinship, seeming, analogy, correspondence, equivalence, comparability, common feature, point in common, parallel, parallelism, uniformity, conformity, parity, equality, proportionality, accordance, agreement, nearness, approximation, near likeness, closeness, close likeness, similar look, family resemblance, family likeness, genetic likeness, good likeness, faithful likeness, faint resemblance, the like(s) of, suchlike, duplication, similation, imitation, semblance, assimilation, simile, metaphor, parable, allegory, portrayal, copying, aping, mimicking

▶ *457 Appearance, 107 Relatedness, 116 Accord, 122 Equality, 308 Symmetry, 547 Representation, 183 Repetition, 118 Imitation, 503 Accuracy*

2 **copy**, photocopy, facsimile (*or* fax) (copy), stencil, duplicate, Mimeograph, photomechanical transfer (PMT), reproduction, imitation, close imitation, pirated record, twin, clone, trend, style, fashion, fad, bootleg copy (Inf)

▶ *796 Fashion, 167 Conformity*

3 **copier**, photocopier, facsimile (*or* fax) machine, duplicator, stenciller, press, printer, computer printer, laser printer, camera, video cassette recorder (VCR) (*or* video), camcorder, tape recorder, Xerox machine (Tm), Photostat (Tm)

▶ *65 Computers*

4 **person who copies**, copyist, transcriber, forger, counterfeiter, plagiarist, mimic, impersonator, imitator, painter, sketcher, printer, photographer, record pirate, follower of fashion, clotheshorse (Inf), fashion victim (Inf), copycat (Inf)

▶ *539 Deception*

5 **counterpart**, equivalent, correspondent, pendant, reciprocal, coordinate, twin, copy, clone, alter ego, kindred spirit, soul mate, second self, doppelgänger, image, living image, another edition, brother (*or* sister) under the skin, blood brother, double, lookalike, reflection, shadow, understudy, stunt man (*or* woman), better half, other half, other, fellow, mate, companion, ka, chip off the old block (Inf), spitting image (Inf), spit (Inf), (dead) ringer (Sl)

6 **couple**, pair, twins, matched pair, matching set, two of a kind, two peas in a pod, birds of a feather, Tweedledum and Tweedledee

ADJECTIVES

7 **similar**, same, synonymous, symmetrical, akin, like, alike, something like, not unlike, resembling, allied, connected, related, matching, corresponding, analogous, equivalent, comparable, commensurable, parallel, identical, of a piece, uniform with, duplicated, approximate, approximating, near, close, much the same, nearly the same, quasi, bracketed with, connatural, homogeneous, assonant, alliterative, rhyming, much of a muchness, favouring, following, pretty much the same, damned little difference (Inf)

8 **simulated**, artificial, false, imitation, imitative, cultured, ersatz, synthetic, aped, mim-

icked, imitated, mocked, mock, phoney, counterfeit, copied, duplicated, duplicate, replicated, spurious, pseudo (Inf)

9 **lifelike**, realistic, photographic, exact, faithful, true to life, true to nature, true to type, graphic, vivid, eidetic, natural, living, breathing, speaking

VERBS

10 **be similar**, be like, resemble, bear resemblance, correspond, coincide, agree, accord, tally, compare, take after, favour, suggest, evoke, put one in mind of, bring to mind, call to mind, seem like, smack of, savour of, have all the signs of, have all the appearances (or features) of, have all the earmarks of, have all the hallmarks of, reflect, mirror, echo, match, parallel

11 **make similar**, equalize, homogenize, assimilate, compare, liken, draw a parallel between, compare with, approximate to, not tell apart, not tell one from the other, see no difference

12 **imitate**, emulate, copy, reproduce, duplicate, Mimeograph, Photostat, Xerox, fax, clone, simulate, camouflage, portray, make like, ape, mimic, counterfeit, replicate, alliterate, rhyme

ADVERBS

13 **similarly**, in a similar situation, likewise, in like manner, like, by the same token, as, just as, as if, as it were, so to speak, so, correspondingly, metaphorically, in a way, in the same category, in the same boat, as in a mirror, like father like son, like a chip off the old block (Inf), like the spitting image (Inf)

14 **comparably**, synonymously, symmetrically, correspondingly, at the same time, in the same way, analogously, equivalently, equally, with equal measures, identically, approximately, nearly, almost the same way, closely, homogeneously, alliteratively, realistically, photographically, like a photograph, exactly, with the exact touch, faithfully, graphically, vividly, eidetically, naturally, with a natural look, artificially, falsely, imitatively, synthetically, spuriously

115   Dissimilarity

NOUNS

1 **dissimilarity**, dissimilitude, difference, disparity, diversity, discrepancy, divergence, unsimilarity, extraneousness, nonuniformity, differentiation, variation, multiformity, discrimination, distinction, variance, variety, contrast, heterogeneity

2 **unlikeness**, unrelatedness, incongruity, incompatibility, contrast, asymmetry, incommensurability, no comparison, nothing in common, a different kettle of fish, another matter, another story, no common ground, no

match, not a pair, misfit, odd man out, odd bod (Inf)

▶ *113 Diversity, 111 Oppositeness, 108 Unrelatedness, 117 Disparity*

3 **disguise**, camouflage, caricature, bad likeness, concealment, misrepresentation, poor imitation, copy, counterfeit, make up, cosmetic (or plastic) surgery

▶ *531 Concealment, 548 Misrepresentation, 540 Falsehood, 309 Distortion*

ADJECTIVES

4 **dissimilar**, different, disparate, divergent, diverse, various, multiform, unequal, asymmetrical, nonuniform, not true to life, unresembling, unlike, unalike, unidentical, nothing like, incongruous, incompatible, contrasting, poles apart, strange, unrealistic, scarcely like, hardly like, discrepant, far from it, way off, a mile off, no such thing, distinctive, unusual, peculiar, out of the ordinary, original, singular, unrelated, far above, superior, far below, inferior, new, unique, peerless, matchless, nonpareil, untypical, atypical, unprecedented, incomparable, incommensurate, incommensurable, novel, cast in a different mould, a far cry from, not a bit alike, not a bit of it, nothing of the sort (or kind), something else, quite another thing, way out (Inf)

VERBS

5 **be dissimilar**, be unlike, differ, not resemble, bear no resemblance, have nothing in common, have little in common, diverge, deviate, depart from, contrast, conflict, not look like, not compare with, look superior, look inferior, stand out, stand out in a crowd, stick out like a sore thumb

6 **differentiate**, make unlike, distinguish, discriminate, split hairs, innovate, vary, modify, change, convert, distort, caricature, misrepresent, dissemble, disguise, deceive, conceal, camouflage, tell the men from the boys, separate the sheep from the goats, nit-pick (Inf)

ADVERBS

7 **dissimilarly**, differently, discordantly, contrastingly, variously, at different times, disparately, divergently, in different directions, diversely, unequally, without equal, incongruously, incompatibly, strangely, in a strange way, unrealistically, distinctively, unusually, peculiarly, singularly, incomparably, without comparison, incommensurately

116   Accord

NOUNS

1 **accord**, accordance, unanimity, unanimousness, harmony, unity, agreement, consensus, concert, consentaneity, concurrence, confluence, concourse, concord, concordance, one

voice, vox populi, meeting of minds, like-mindedness, one (*or* same) mind, mutual understanding, sympathy, acceptance, acquiescence, accedence, accommodation, concession, reconciliation, capitulation, compromise, compliance, solidarity, kinship, compatibility, affinity, rapport, empathy, identity, similarity, mutuality, closeness, communion, peace, happy family, team spirit, *esprit de corps* (Fr)

▶ *667 Agreement, 717 Compromise, 664 Cooperation, 819 Friendship, 675 Peace*

2 **alliance**, league, union, federation, entente (cordiale), affiliation, guild, coalition, collusion, conspiracy, collaboration, synergy, partnership, fellowship, society, community, association, cartel, consortium, team, crew, group, band, bunch, gang, posse, mob, combo (Inf)

▶ *161 Assembly, 12 Government and Politics, 665 Party, 135 Union*

3 **arrangement**, settlement, compact, pact, treaty, covenant, contract, convention, bargain, deal, bond, transaction, pledge, promise

▶ *667 Agreement, 717 Compromise, 715 Contract, 664 Cooperation, 716 Negotiation, 135 Union*

4 **harmony**, harmonization, coordination, synchronization, synchronism, coincidence, concomitance, conjunction, symmetry, balance, equilibrium, regularity, consonance, consonancy, assonance, resonance, echo, rhyme, alliteration, melody, counterpoint, chime, chiming, homophony, euphony, euphoniousness, symphony, unison, chorus, choir, resolution (of a discord), blend, modulation, attunement, adjustment, orchestration

▶ *433 Melody, 49 Music, 427 Resonance, 308 Symmetry*

5 **conformity**, conformance, conformation, uniformity, uniformness, constancy, continuity, consistency, coherence, homogeneity, homology, sameness, oneness, equipollence, parity, isotropy, synonymity, synonymy, indistinguishability, equivalence, interchangeability, congruence, congruity, correspondence, correlation, reciprocation, parallelism, likeness, similarity, analogousness, analogy, match, twin, brother, sister, complement, counterpart, alter ego, doppelgänger, clone, look-alike, spitting image, birds of a feather

▶ *167 Conformity, 118 Imitation, 285 Parallelism, 109 Reciprocity, 110 Sameness, 114 Similarity, 112 Uniformity*

6 **convention**, orthodoxy, tradition, institution, custom, habit, praxis, pattern, order, system, method, routine, stereotype, type, norm, standard

▶ *167 Conformity, 584 Habit, 214 Regularity*

7 **consent**, assent, hearty assent, affirmation, blessing, approval, agreement, authorization, authority, ratification, certification, vouch-

safement, endorsement, recognition, support, leave, liberty, attestation, tick, check (US), okay (OK) (Inf), go-ahead (Inf), green light (Inf)

▶ *535 Affirmation, 667 Agreement, 851 Approval, 499 Assent*

8 **permit**, permission, sanction, allowance, clearance, licence, charter, warrant, warranty, certificate, patent, exemption, entitlement, dispensation

▶ *851 Approval, 845 Entitlement, 848 Exemption, 485 Qualification*

9 **grant**, gift, present, donation, bestowal, presentment, conferment, conferral, provision, privilege, investiture, endowment, perquisite, perk

▶ *729 Giving*

ADJECTIVES

10 **in accord**, accordant, unanimous, harmonious, united, agreeing, agreed, *en rapport* (Fr), in rapport, consenting, consentient, consentaneous, in concert, concerted, concurrent, confluent, concordant, at one, with one voice, sympathetic, like-minded, understanding, empathizing, identifying with, amicable, frictionless, congenial, compatible, conciliatory, reconciling, reconcilable, complying, compliant, conceding, concessive, compromising, accepting, accepted, accommodating, acquiescing, acquiescent

▶ *667 Agreement, 717 Compromise, 819 Friendship, 110 Sameness, 135 Union*

11 **allied**, corporate, affiliated, filiated, associated, bonded, joint, conjoint, combined, combining, connected, linked, merged, in communion, communal, contributing, coactive, synergic, colluding, conspiring, conspiratorial, collaborating, collaborative, fraternal, fraternizing, coexisting, ganging up (Inf)

▶ *161 Assembly, 664 Cooperation, 12 Government and Politics, 665 Party, 135 Union*

12 **arranged**, settled, negotiated, negotiating, covenanted, covenantal, contractual, bargaining, pledged, promised

▶ *152 Arrangement, 715 Contract, 716 Negotiation*

13 **harmonious**, coordinated, synchronized, synchronous, coincident, coinciding, conjoint, concomitant, symmetrical, balanced, in equilibrium, regular, regulated, shaped, adjusted, attuned, homophonic, euphonious, euphonic, symphonious, symphonic, unisonous, blended, merged, orchestrated, modulated, modulating, in concert, choral, melodic, melodious, contrapuntal, harmonic, enharmonic, sounding, chiming, echoing, resounding, resonant, resonating, assonant, consonant, rhyming, alliterative, in tune (Inf), in sync (Inf)

▶ *433 Melody, 49 Music, 427 Resonance, 308 Symmetry*

14 **conforming**, conformable, uniform, homogenous, homogenetic, homologous, level, equal, isotropic, identical, indistinguishable, same, constant, steady, unbroken, consistent, coherent, continuous, undeviating, orderly, straight, even, monotonous, unvarying, invariable, undifferentiated, equipollent, equivalent, interchangeable, synonymous, reciprocal, parallel, correspondent, corresponding, congruous, congruent, correlated, correlative, interrelated, commensurate, complementary, reflecting, resembling, like, similar, analogous, analogical, matching, paired, twinned, twin, held together, hanging together (Inf), all of a piece (Inf)

▶ *167 Conformity, 118 Imitation, 285 Parallelism, 109 Reciprocity, 110 Sameness, 112 Uniformity*

15 **conventional**, orthodox, strict, conservative, typical, typifying, traditional, customary, stock, usual, habitual, mundane, normal, ordinary, commonplace, stereotypical, quintessential, regular, regulated, standard, standardized, institutional, institutionalized, *comme il faut (Fr)*

▶ *167 Conformity, 584 Habit, 214 Regularity*

16 **fitting**, befitting, relevant, belonging, pertaining, appertaining, germane, pertinent, apposite, expedient, suitable, serving the purpose, qualified for, cut out for (Inf)

▶ *485 Qualification*

17 **consenting**, consentient, consentaneous, assenting, assentient, assentatious, affirming, affirmative, confirming, confirmed, approving, approved, recognized, agreeing, agreed, ratifying, ratified, ratificatory, authorizing, authorized, accredited, supported, seconded, backed, underwritten, endorsed, signed, sealed, stamped, rubberstamped, ticked, checked (US)

▶ *535 Affirmation, 667 Agreement, 851 Approval, 499 Assent*

18 **permitting**, permitted, entitled, cleared, validated, valid, passed, certificated, licensed, chartered, vouchsafed, sanctioned, warranted, allowing, allowed, legalized, legal, licit, decriminalized, exempt, exempted

▶ *851 Approval, 845 Entitlement, 848 Exemption, Legality, 485 Qualification*

19 **granted**, donated, bestowed, presented, conferred, afforded, privileged, vested, rendered, enabled

▶ *729 Giving*

20 **agreeable**, uncontested, acceptable, uncontradicted, incontrovertible, unopposed, unobjectionable, viable, bipartisan, apolitical

▶ *667 Agreement*

VERBS

21 **be in accord**, be in accordance, accord, concord, concur, agree, have no objection, be at one, be in harmony, see eye to eye (with), empathize, identify with, go along with, comply, accede, concede, acquiesce, be reconciled, hit it off with (Inf)

▶ *667 Agreement, 819 Friendship*

22 **form an alliance**, ally, affiliate, unite, collude, conspire, collaborate, pull together, associate with, side with, team up (with), partner, fraternize, combine with, join with, conjoin, coact, cowork, synergize, gang up (with) (Inf), be in cahoots (with) (Inf)

▶ *161 Assembly, 665 Party, 135 Union*

23 **arrange**, settle, make terms, bargain, deal, negotiate, compromise, contract, transact, covenant, pledge, promise, shake hands on

▶ *152 Arrangement, 715 Contract, 716 Negotiation*

24 **harmonize**, coordinate, synchronize, coincide, conjoin, symmetrize, balance, shape, regulate, equalize, equilibrate, blend, merge, concert, orchestrate, symphonize, melodize, modulate, counterpoise, attune, tune in, adjust, resolve, rhyme, alliterate, assonate, resonate, chime, sound, resound, echo

▶ *433 Melody, 49 Music, 427 Resonance, 308 Symmetry*

25 **conform**, be uniform, match, mirror, tally, square with, be like, resemble, look like, sound like, reflect, interrelate, correlate, correspond, complement, parallel, reciprocate, be consistent, cohere, hold together, hang together, tie in with, be conventional, follow, take one's place, line up, fall in, know one's place, go with the flow (Inf), follow the crowd (Inf), jump on the band wagon (Inf), toe the line (Inf)

▶ *167 Conformity, 285 Parallelism, 109 Reciprocity, 110 Sameness, 114 Similarity, 112 Uniformity*

26 **make uniform**, standardize, normalize, regularize, systematize, order, equalize, level, even out (*or* up), homogenize, assimilate, habituate, conventionalize, institutionalize, align, liken, stereotype

▶ *167 Conformity, 584 Habit, 214 Regularity*

27 **fit**, serve, suit, belong, appertain, pertain, qualify for, be just the thing (Inf), fill the bill (Inf), check (Inf), jibe (Inf), be just the job (Inf)

▶ *485 Qualification*

28 **consent**, assent, affirm, agree, approve, give one's blessing, authorize, ratify, confirm, certify, vouchsafe, endorse, accredit, validate, authenticate, recognize, tick, check (US), attest, sign, seal, stamp, rubberstamp, underwrite, second, back, back up, support, bless, nod, give the nod, say aye, say hear hear, say the word, OK (Inf), give the OK (Inf), give the thumbs up (Inf), tip the wink (Inf), give the all clear (*or* green light) (Inf), give the go ahead (Inf)

▶ *535 Affirmation, 667 Agreement, 851 Approval, 499 Assent*

29 permit, sanction, allow, warrant, license, pass, charter, patent, clear, give (*or* grant) leave, entitle, exempt, legalize, decriminalize

▶ *851 Approval, 845 Entitlement, 848 Exemption, 485 Qualification*

30 grant, donate, give, bestow, present, confer, rend, render, afford, provide, privilege, vest, invest with, endow, patronize, enable, give someone a chance

▶ *729 Giving*

ADVERBS

31 in accord, with one accord, unanimously, harmoniously, *en rapport* (Fr), in concert, concertedly, unitedly, with one voice, of one mind, *nem. con.* (*nemine contradicente*) (L), together, all together, as one, solidly, by consensus, sympathetically, understandingly, compatibly, closely, communally, *en masse* (Fr), *en bloc* (Fr), like sheep

▶ *667 Agreement, 717 Compromise, 819 Friendship, 110 Sameness, 135 Union*

32 in alliance, corporately, in league, federally, in partnership, conspiratorially, hand in hand, shoulder to shoulder, cheek by jowl, in cahoots (Inf)

▶ *161 Assembly, 664 Cooperation, 12 Government and Politics, 665 Party, 135 Union*

33 harmoniously, agreeably, synchronously, resonantly, homophonically, euphonically, euphoniously, symphonically, melodically, soundingly, resoundingly, chorally, in chorus, in unison, in concert

▶ *433 Melody, 49 Music, 427 Resonance*

34 uniformly, identically, equally, indistinguishably, similarly, like, likewise, thus, in the same way, in like manner, by the same token

35 consistently, regularly, evenly, steadily, constantly, invariably, continually, continuously, always, without exception

36 accordingly, consequently, therefore, *ergo* (L), so, it follows that, hence, whence, wherefore, wherefrom, that (*or* such) being the case, in that case, at that rate, that being so, as it happens, in that way, thus, like that, for that (*or* which) reason, on that ground, under the circumstances, as the matter stands

▶ *159 Consecutiveness*

37 conventionally, traditionally, customarily, ordinarily, usually, routinely, habitually, typically, normally, as a rule

38 fittingly, befittingly, relevantly, pertinently, expediently, suitably, in keeping, appropriately, aptly, appositely

39 with consent, consentingly, assentingly, affirmingly, affirmatively, in the affirmative, approvingly, as agreed upon, as promised, as contracted for, as arranged, with permission, by (*or* with) someone's leave

▶ *535 Affirmation, 667 Agreement*

117 Disparity

NOUNS

1 disparity, dissimilarity, dissimilitude, difference, contrast, unlikeness, unrelatedness, diversity, divergence, variance, variety, discrepancy, nonuniformity, inconsonance, incongruence, incongruity, incommensurability, heterogeneity, disproportionateness, disproportion, asymmetry, irregularity, inconsistency, gap, credibility gap, generation gap, ambiguity, ambivalence, equivocality, equivocalness, two voices, inequality

▶ *113 Diversity, 108 Unrelatedness, 123 Inequality, 115 Dissimilarity, 343 Divergence, 578 Equivocation, 265 Interval, 215 Irregularity, 168 Nonconformity, 456 Variegation, 844 Wrong, 224 Changeableness*

2 contradiction, contrariety, oppositeness, negation, jarring, jar, grating, false note, paradox, self-contradiction, antinomy, oxymoron, misfit, bad fit, bad match, misalliance, misjoinder (Fml), *mésalliance* (Fr), maladjustment, distortion, mutation, abnormality, oddity, anomaly, non sequitur

▶ *111 Oppositeness, 666 Disagreement, 309 Distortion, 123 Inequality*

3 nonconformity, unconformity, nonconformability (*or* unconformability), unconventionality, individuality, distinctness, uniqueness, idiosyncrasy, singularity, peculiarity, inner-directedness, eccentricity, freakishness, weirdness, mannerism, unorthodoxy, heterodoxy, heresy

▶ *168 Nonconformity, 7 Religion*

4 disagreement, nonagreement, discordance, discordancy, discord, disaccord, disaccordance, disharmony, inharmoniousness (*or* unharmoniousness), controversy, argument, argumentation, challenge, dissension, dissidence, dissent, samizdat, dissonance, disunity, disunion, conflict of opinion, divergent opinions, incompatibility, uncongeniality, irreconcilability, wrangle, wrangling, confrontation, opposition, defiance, antagonism, enmity, hostility, bickering, bicker, squabbling, squabble, quarrelling, quarrel, conflict, clashing, clash, fighting, fight, faction, schism, rupture, breach, rebellion, war

▶ *666 Disagreement, 500 Dissent, 434 Dissonance, 820 Enmity, 668 Defiance, 676 War, 687 Adversity, 768 Aggravation, 473 Argument, 231 Counteraction, 852 Disapproval, 854 Disparagement, 766 Dissatisfaction, 824 Divorce; Widowhood, 536 Negation, 663 Opposition, 713 Protest, 711 Refusal, 476 Refutation, 669 Resistance, 581 Rejection*

5 unfitness, unfittingness, unsuitability, inappropriateness, wrongness, inappositeness, inaptitude, inaptness, inapplicability, inadmis-

sibility, irrelevance, irrelevancy, incapacity, incompetence, unskilfulness, inexpedience, undecorousness, inelegance, infelicity, impropriety, bad taste, untimeliness, intrusiveness, intrusion, interruption

▶ *656 Unskilfulness, 559 Inelegance, 211 Untimeliness, 151 Disorder, 601 Misuse, 193 Wrong Time, 614 Uselessness*

6 **misfit**, odd man out, outsider, stranger, alien, foreigner, fish out of water, square peg (in a round hole), eccentric, individualist, one of a kind, inner-directed person, loner, maverick, bohemian, beatnik, nonconformist, dissident, anarchist, dissenter, arguer, rebel, heretic, pretender, hypocrite, Tartuffe, sham, wolf in sheep's clothing, laughing stock, oddball (Inf), weirdo (Inf), freak (Inf)

▶ *539 Deception, 540 Falsehood, 510 Insanity, 579 Caprice, 679 Combatant, 104 Extraneousness, 519 Imagination, 168 Nonconformity, 119 Originality, 136 Separation*

ADJECTIVES

7 **disparate**, dissimilar, different, contrasting, unrelated, unlikely, unusual, strange, foreign, alien, exotic, diverse, divergent, various, variant, varied, varying, discrepant, nonuniform, inconsonant, incongruent, immiscible, incommensurate, incommensurable, heterogeneous, disproportionate, disproportional, out of proportion, unsymmetric(al), asymmetric(al), irregular, odd, inconsistent, ambiguous, ambivalent, equivocal, unequal

▶ *115 Dissimilarity*

8 **contradictory**, jarring, grating, paradoxical, absurd, oxymoronic, antinomic, self-contradictory, self-contradicting, contrary, opposite, ill-matching, ill-matched, badly matched, mismatched, mismated, ill-mated, misjoined (Fml), misallied, ill-sorted, illassorted, ill-chosen, maladjusted, against nature, unnatural, abnormal, mutant, distorted, anomalous, odd, against one's nature, against the grain, out of character, uncharacteristic, out of keeping, out of whack (US inf)

▶ *111 Oppositeness*

9 **nonconforming**, nonconformist, unconventional, individual, distinct, unique, singular, peculiar, idiosyncratic, inner-directed, eccentric, maverick, outlandish, weird, bizarre, odd, freakish, unorthodox, heterodox, heretic(al), rebellious, freaky (Inf), nutty (Inf), wacky (Sl)

▶ *168 Nonconformity*

10 **disagreeing**, disagreeable, nonagreeing, unagreed, moot, discordant, disaccordant, inaccordant, disharmonious, inharmonious (or unharmonious), disunited, controversial, incompatible, uncongenial, irreconcilable, at cross-purposes, differing, dissenting, dissident, dissonant, at variance, at odds, confron-

tational, confronting, challenging, disparaging, antipathetic(al), opposite, in opposition, defiant, antagonistic, argumentative, hostile, inimical, at loggerheads, wrangling, bickering, squabbling, snapping, quarrelling, quarrelsome, clashing, conflicting, fighting, factional, schismatic(al), warring, at war, at one another's throats

▶ *666 Disagreement*

11 **unfit**, unfitted, unfitting, ill-fitted, unsuitable, unsuited, ill-suited, incompatible, wrong, out of tune, out of step, out of phase, out of joint, malapropos, *mal à propos* (Fr), inapposite, inapt, impracticable, ill-adapted, unadapted, unadaptable, out of line, out of order, incapable, ineligible, unqualified, incompetent, inept, unskilful, unskilled, clumsy, untimely, out of time, ill-timed, unfortunate, inopportune, unseasonable, out of season, irrelevant, extraneous, inconsequential (*or* inconsequent), inapplicable, inadmissible, inexpedient, inappropriate, undecorous, inelegant, unbefitting, unbecoming, unseemly, improper, infelicitous, intrusive, intruding, out of place, outside, out of one's element, alien, pretending, fake, sham, hypocritical

▶ *844 Wrong*

VERBS

12 **be disparate**, contrast, diversify, diverge, vary, differ, mutate, deviate, distort, misfit, misalign, miscast, misjoin, misally, mismatch, mismate, mistime, interrupt, talk out of turn, fake, sham, pretend, equivocate, speak with two voices, jar, grate, strike a false note, negate, contradict oneself, draw attention to oneself, have no business with, stick out a mile (Inf), stick out like a sore thumb (Inf)

▶ *115 Dissimilarity*

13 **not conform**, individualize, peculiarize, march out of step, march to (*or* hear) a different drummer, go off the beaten track, rock the boat, not play ball (Inf), do one's own thing (Inf), drop out (Inf)

14 **disagree**, differ, contradict, confront, challenge, counter, dissent, demur, object, oppose, defy, dispute, argue, antagonize, wrangle, bicker, squabble, have words, clash, quarrel, conflict, square off, cross swords, fight, divide, disunite, put the cat among the pigeons, set at odds, break into factions, schismatize, rupture, breach, rebel, declare war, come to blows, fall out (Inf)

▶ *666 Disagreement*

ADVERBS

15 **dissimilarly**, differently, diversely, incongruently, out of step, out of place, out of time, out of phase, out of line, out of order, inconsistently, disproportionately, asymmetrically, irregularly, abnormally, unnaturally, oddly,

absurdly, anomalously, unconventionally, individually, eccentrically, uniquely, idiosyncratically, peculiarly, singularly, outlandishly, weirdly, strangely, ambiguously, ambivalently, equivocally, antinomically, unequally, paradoxically, oppositely

16 **disagreeably**, against, discordantly, disharmoniously, inconsonantly, controversially, contradictorily, contrarily, in spite of, despite, disparagingly, dissonantly, schismatically, heretically, defiantly, antagonistically, argumentatively, hostilely, rebelliously, incompatibly, irreconcilably

17 **unsuitably**, wrongly, inadmissibly, irrelevantly, inappropriately, malapropos, *mal à propos* (Fr), infelicitously, unfortunately, inexpediently, inopportunely, impracticably, inaptly, ineptly, incompetently, unskilfully, clumsily, amiss, unseasonably, inelegantly, improperly, intrusively, hypocritically

118   Imitation

Imitation is the sincerest form of flattery.
Charles Caleb Colton.

It is an infallible sign of the second-rate in nature and intellect to make use of everything and everyone. Ada Beddington Leverson.

NOUNS

1 **imitation**, copying, simulation, repetition, mimesis, parody, onomatopoeia, emulation, impersonation, imposture, the sincerest form of flattery, conformity, slavishness, slavish, literalism, representation, reflection, mirror, echo, canon, fugue, mirroring, following
▶ *547 Representation, 167 Conformity, 183 Repetition*

2 **copy**, reproduction, image, likeness, replica, model, working model, duplication, duplicate, imitation, dummy, mock-up, facsimile, photocopy, picture, portrait, pastiche (*or* pasticcio), fair copy, faithful copy, carbon copy, clone, doppelgänger, simulation, fake, forgery, sham, bootleg, counterfeit, plagiarism, disguise, camouflage, crib (Inf), pony (US inf), phoney (Inf), rip-off (Sl)
▶ *245 Reproduction, 114 Similarity*

3 **mockery**, mimicry, pantomime, mime, satire, caricature, travesty, burlesque, impersonation, parody, apery, parrotry, spoof (Inf), takeoff (Inf), send-up (Inf), wind-up (Inf)
▶ *771 Humour, 524 Interpretation*

4 **camouflage**, protective colouration, mimicry, simulation, cosmetics, make-up, disguise, dissimulation, playing possum, playing dead
▶ *548 Misrepresentation, 540 Falsehood, 531 Concealment, 309 Distortion*

5 **duplicate**, photocopy, Xerox (Tm), Mimeograph (Tm), Photostat (Tm), pantograph, graph, stencil, facsimile, fax, carbon copy, replica, model, tracing, rubbing, transfer, transcript, video recording, tape recording, print, offprint, Photostat, photograph, negative, enlargement

6 **photocopier**, copier, duplicator, facsimile (*or* fax) machine, telex machine, stenciller, computer printer, camera, camcorder, video cassette recorder (VCR) (*or* video), tape recorder

7 **imitator**, ventriloquist, impersonator, female impersonator, mimic, imposter, poseur, charlatan, mountebank, hypocrite, Tartuffe, illusionist, follower, disciple, slave to fashion, sheep, ape, parrot, phoney (Inf), drag artist (Sl)

8 **copier**, copyist, plagiarist, counterfeiter, record pirate, forger, faker, painter, sketcher, printer, photographer, bootlegger

VERBS

9 **imitate**, emulate, follow, model oneself upon, ape, parrot, flatter, mirror, repeat, echo, reflect, copy after, model after, take after, take as a model, pattern after, take a leaf out of one's book, mimic, mock, caricature, satirize, burlesque, parody, travesty, impersonate, mime, spoof (Inf), take off (Inf), send up (Inf)

10 **copy**, reproduce, duplicate, clone, photocopy, Mimeograph, stencil, plagiarize, borrow, replicate, counterfeit, fake, forge, pirate, crib (Inf)

11 **emulate**, follow, follow on, follow in the (foot)steps of, walk in the shoes of, follow in the wake of, follow the example of, follow suit, follow the herd, follow like sheep, play follow-my-leader, play follow-the-leader, climb (*or* jump) on the bandwagon

ADJECTIVES

12 **imitative**, imitated, derivative, unoriginal, parodied, transcribed, mimetic, onomatopoeic, emulating, echoing, aping, parrot-like, parroting, following, posing, apish, echoic, fugal

13 **imitation**, mock, sham, fake, forged, plagiarized, copied, counterfeit, ersatz, artificial, synthetic, cultured, man-made, pseudo (Inf), phoney (Inf), so-called, copycat (Inf), hokey (US sl)

ADVERBS

14 **imitatively**, apishly, like an ape, mockingly, onomatopoeically, onomatopoetically, unoriginally, artificially, synthetically, derivatively, quasi, verbatim, word for word, ditto, parrot-fashion, like a parrot, to the life, truly, to the letter, letter for letter, literally, literatim

119   Originality

An original writer is not one who imitates nobody, but one whom nobody can imitate.
Vicomte de Chateaubriand.

A thought is often original, though you have uttered it a hundred times. Oliver Wendell Holmes.

All good things which exist are the fruits of originality. John Stuart Mill.

NOUNS

1 **originality**, creativity, creativeness, creation, nonimitation, dissimilarity, genuineness, authenticity, inventiveness, innovation, initiation, imagination, original thought, individuality, independence, idiosyncrasy, eccentricity, novelty, newness, uniqueness, freshness, the one and only, new departure, precedence, beginning, something new, all my own work, a poor thing but my own
▶ *519 Imagination, 115 Dissimilarity, 201 Newness, 108 Unrelatedness, 698 Freedom*

2 **original**, autograph, holograph, signature, one's own hand, manuscript, first edition, source, model, paradigm, blueprint, pattern, mould, prototype, archetype, test case, precedent, pilot (film), invention, patented invention, trademarked product, copyrighted work, the real thing, the real article, the genuine article, it (Inf), absolutely it (Inf), the real McCoy (Sl)
▶ *194 Priority, 103 Essence*

3 **originator**, inventor, creator, innovator, deviser, source, creative writer, composer, designer
▶ *165 Speciality*

ADJECTIVES

4 **original**, creative, inventive, imaginative, innovative, unimitated, first, first-hand, first in the field, pioneering, seminal, prototypal, archetypal

5 **novel**, unique, different, personal, individual, one-off, one and only, one of a kind, unparalleled, unprecedented, unheard-of, offbeat, sui generis, inimitable, incomparable, new, fresh, avant-garde, revolutionary, transcendent, unmatched, out of reach

6 **authentic**, genuine, real, *echt* (Ger), bona fide, verified, unimitated, true, natural, sincere, unadulterated, uncopied, unduplicated, patented, copyrighted, trademarked

VERBS

7 **originate**, invent, innovate, create, devise, design, imagine, dream up, conceive, generate, pioneer, start, initiate, begin, auspicate (Arch), revolutionize, patent, blueprint, copyright, trademark

ADVERBS

8 **originally**, seminally, first, innovatively, conceptually, creatively, inventively, newly, freshly, imaginatively, with imagination, individually, personally, uniquely, differently, with a difference, inimitably, incomparably, without comparison, naturally, sincerely, truly, honestly

120 Quantity

NOUNS

1 **quantity**, amount, measurement, measure, measured quantity, measuring, extent, dimension, proportions, size, space, area, magnitude, multitude, amplitude, length, width, breadth, thickness, thinness, height, altitude, depth, deepness, capacity, volume, weighing, weight, mass, matter, substance, body, bulk, gravity, heaviness, lightness
▶ *142 Whole, 144 Completeness, 268 Measurement, 259 Size, 269 Length, 271 Breadth, 275 Height, 277 Depth, 248 Space, 369 Heaviness, 370 Lightness, 75 Units*

2 **certain amount**, portion, piece, share, lot, load, batch, bunch, pack, packet, parcel, part, mess, limit, stint, quota, quorum, dosage, dose, ration, quantum, upper limit, ceiling, lower limit, floor, great quantity, large amount, mass, mountain, lake, chunk, hunk, majority, increase, addition, extension, more, most, small quantity, small amount, some, somewhat, few, fewness, pittance, dribble, fraction, minority, decrease, subtraction, less, least, heap (Inf), gob (Inf), whack (Inf)
▶ *257 Contents, 302 Limit, 128 Increase, 130 Addition, 182 Few, 129 Decrease, 131 Subtraction, 181 Multitude, 169 Number*

3 **container(ful)**, armful, handful, mouthful, pocketful, spoon(ful), teaspoon(ful), tablespoon(ful), cup(ful), glass(ful), bottle(ful), jar(ful), pitcher(ful), bowl(ful), pot(ful), plate(ful), bag(ful), sack(ful), basket(ful), box(ful), carton(ful), case(ful), can(ful), bin(ful), crate(ful), barrel(ful), bucket(ful), shovel(ful), roomful, lorryload, truckload
▶ *258 Container*

4 **total**, whole, all, lock, stock, and barrel, totality, entirety, aggregate, sum, count, number, nett (total), gross (total), the whole thing, the whole caboodle (Inf)
▶ *142 Whole, 144 Completeness*

5 **numbers**, integers, variable, plurality, zero, infinity, mean, average
▶ *169 Number, 181 Multitude, 175 Plurality, 184 Infinity, 124 Average, 170 Calculation, 52 Mathematics, 174 One, 176 Two, 177 Three, 178 Four, 179 Five and Over, 75 Units, 172 Zero*

ADJECTIVES

6 **quantitative**, quantified, quantized, measured, measuring, weighed, weighing, counted, sized, ample, high, deep, long, wide, massive, voluminous, thick, thin, heavy, light, bunched, packed, sparse, mountainous, increased, added, extended, greater, majority,

most, many, so many, so much, any, about, approximate, more or less, plural, infinite, all, total, whole, entire, enough, small, some, certain, limited, rationed, finite, few, smaller, least, numbered, fractional, variable, average
▶ *174 One, 608 Sufficiency, 268 Measurement, 52 Mathematics, 259 Size, 490 Certainty, 184 Infinity, 181 Multitude, 169 Number, 175 Plurality*

ADVERBS

7 **quantitatively**, to such an extent, finitely, about, approximately, some, nearly, as much as, more or less, wholely, entirely, totally, infinitely, amply, highly, deeply, widely, massively, hugely, enormously, voluminously, thickly, heavily, variably, fractionally, slightly, thinly, sparsely, lightly, mathematically, to the tune of (Inf), all of (Inf)

VERBS

8 **quantify**, quantize, measure, weigh, count, number, rate, fix, size, piece, portion, apportion, allot, allocate, divide, share, pack, parcel, limit, set a quota, take a dose, ration, set an upper limit, set a ceiling, set a lower limit, set a floor, increase, add, extend, decrease, reduce, subtract
▶ *731 Allocation, 302 Limit, 130 Addition, 261 Expansion, 128 Increase, 131 Subtraction, 262 Contraction, 129 Decrease, 169 Number*

121 Degree

NOUNS

1 **degree**, extent, measure, amount, frequency, intensity, rate, amplitude, magnitude, value, calibre, quantity, depth, height, altitude, size, breadth, speed, gradualism, gradualness, slowness, scope, range, duration, reach, compass, limitation, stint, scale, pitch, tenor, register, key
▶ *433 Melody, 120 Quantity, 271 Breadth, 188 Duration, 49 Music, 259 Size, 277 Depth, 275 Height, 324 Motion, 328 Slowness, 302 Limit, 268 Measurement*

2 **rank**, level, hierarchy, grading, grade, echelon, precedence, order, place, position, power structure, station, circumstance, footing, standing, status, social rank, class, caste, authority, military rank, generalship, leadership, ecclesiastical rank
▶ *731 Allocation, 106 Circumstances, 163 Class, 688 Authority, 679 Combatant, 7 Religion*

3 **gradation**, graduation, measurement, calibration, valuation, differentiation, differential, degree of difference, classification, rating, ranking, remove, relativeness, relative quantity, comparison, ratio, proportion, ration, standard, grading, shading, notation, bar, line, mark, notch, peg, score

▶ *111 Oppositeness, 107 Relatedness, 143 Part, 268 Measurement*

4 **interval**, period, time, stint, shift, portion, part, shade, shadow, nuance, majority, minority, point, place, step, rung, tread, stair, stage, plane, level, plateau, space, steppingstone, milestone, turning point, juncture, crisis
▶ *359 Ascent, 248 Space, 265 Interval*

VERBS

5 **measure**, classify, evaluate, rate, rank, order, class, grade, sort, mark, peg, score, scale, shade, graduate, place, position, estimate, quantify, calibrate, calculate, clock speed, compare, differentiate, precede, lead

6 **change gradually**, lower, taper off, shade off, cut back, trim, pare, whittle down, abate, die away, melt away, fade out, fade, diminish, decrease, wane, dissolve, evolve, melt into, increase, augment, build up, crescendo, grow, expand, inflate, swell, wax, unfold
▶ *129 Decrease, 128 Increase, 130 Addition, 131 Subtraction, 261 Expansion, 262 Contraction*

ADJECTIVES

7 **gradational**, graduated, graded, measured, rated, scaled, in scale, calibrated, classified, valued, sized, sorted, differentiated, differential, relative, comparative, comparable, proportional, proportionable, portioned, standard, within the bounds of, encompassing, limited, majority, minority, level, regular, frequent, extensive, progressive, gradual, slow-ranging, slow-changing, growing, increasing, waxing, reaching, waning, shading off, tapering, fading, fading out, diminishing

8 **ranked**, hierarchic, hierarchical, leading, preceding, authoritative, ecclesiastical

ADVERBS

9 **differentially**, relatively, comparatively, by comparison, comparably, proportionally, levelly, regularly, routinely, frequently, often, extensively, hierarchically, authoritatively

10 **by degrees**, progressively, gradually, slowly, by inches, inchmeal, piecemeal, slowly but surely, a little at a time, in slight measure, inch by inch, just a bit, bit by bit, little by little, by stages, step by step, drop by drop, however little, however much, increasingly, more and more, decreasingly, less and less

11 **to a degree**, to (or in) some degree, to some extent, in a way, in a measure, in some measure, somewhat, sort of, kind of, fairly, quite, rather, to a great degree, extremely, very, to a small degree, scarcely, slightly, a little, a bit, pretty (Inf)

122 Equality

Equality may perhaps be a right, but no power on Earth can turn it into a fact. Honoré de Balzac.

All animals are equal but some animals are more equal than others. George Orwell (Animal Farm).

NOUNS

1 **equality**, equivalence, equivalency, sameness, equal footing, same quantity, same degree, correspondence, parallelism, coequality, sharing, going halves, likeness, equiponderance, egalitarianism, fairness, democracy, equal rights, equal opportunity, justice, evenness, levelness, parity, par, even money, nothing in it, nothing to choose between, six of one and half a dozen of the other, quits (Inf), level pegging (Inf), going Dutch (Inf), an eye for an eye
▶ *116 Accord, 112 Uniformity, 114 Similarity, 285 Parallelism, 223 Exchange*

2 **equilibrium**, balance, poise, counterpoise, equipoise, even keel, evenness, steadiness, stable state, steady state, balance of power, balance of terror, mutually assured destruction, homeostasis, symmetry, proportion, stability, the same, status quo, stop, stasis, stalemate, deadlock, standstill, log jam (US), hung jury, hung parliament, tie, tied score, knotted score, tied game, draw, drawn game, drawn match, drawn battle, dead heat, photo finish, neck-and-neck race, nip-and-tuck race (US), ding-dong race, cliffhanger, touch and go, Greek meets Greek, deuce (Tennis), love all (Tennis), a distinction without a difference, even break (Inf), fair shake (US inf)
▶ *674 Contention*

3 **equalization**, equation, equilibration, balancing, weighing, adjustment, readjustment, weighing up, levelling up (*or* down), evening up (*or* down), rounding up (*or* down), compensation, positive discrimination, affirmative action, counteraction, offset, exchange, interchange, interchangeability, equipollence (*or* equipollency), isotropy, synonymity, synonym, reciprocation, fair exchange, barter, trade-off, exchange value, fair value, value, fair price, just price
▶ *629 Repair, 125 Compensation, 737 Trade, 751 Price*

4 **equilizer**, counterweight, ballast, makeweight, stopgap, counterpoise, stabilizer, rudder, fin, aileron, spoiler

5 **equal**, peer, twin, match, mate, fellow, counterpart, opposite number, coequal, compeer, comrade, companion, brother, sister, shadow, competitor, parallel, oppo (Inf)
▶ *819 Friendship*

ADJECTIVES

6 **equal**, equalized, same, similar, parallel, convertible, identical, equivalent, corresponding, coequal, egalitarian, democratic, equitable, just, fair, impartial, sharing, co-sharing, homologous, congruent, coextensive, equilateral, equidistant, coordinate, coincident, symmetrical, equable, stable, static, homeostatic, self-regulating, steady, balanced, fixed, round, rounded, square, squared, flush, even-sided, regular, well-ordered, commensurate, tantamount, equipollent, correspondent, proportionate, uniform, unvarying, monotonous, much the same, as broad as long, neither more no less, Dutch (Inf)

7 **dividing line**, radius, diameter, coordinate, equator, bisector, longitudinal line, latitudinal line

8 **on equal terms**, equally divided, even, par, on a par, at par, level, one-to-one, on the same level, on the same plane, on the same footing, half-and-half, neck-and-neck, nip-and-tuck (US), ding-dong, abreast, all one, all the same, drawn, tied, parallel, well-matched, evenly matched, matched, Greek meeting Greek, fifty-fifty (Inf), level pegged (Inf)

9 **adequate**, capable, fit, able, competent, suitable, apt, appropriate, up to, up to the mark

VERBS

10 **be equal**, be equal to, correspond to, accord with, agree with, coincide with, tie, draw, measure up to, come up to, match up with, parallel, break even, hold one's own, keep up with, keep in step with, keep pace with, keep abreast with, cope with, run abreast, run neck and neck, run nip and tuck (US), run level, make it all square, go shares, go halves, go Dutch (Inf), stack up with (Sl)

11 **equalize**, synchronize, even, redress the balance, balance, tally, make good, set off, accommodate, adjust, readjust, even up (*or* down), level, level up (*or* down), round, round up (*or* down), square (up), equate, strike a balance, poise, counterpoise, counterbalance, countervail, offset, cancel out, coordinate, integrate, proportion, fit, smooth, stabilize, compensate, come to the same thing, add up to the same thing, add nothing, detract nothing, leave no remainder, make no difference, right oneself, hold the road, rob Peter to pay Paul

ADVERBS

12 **equally**, on equal terms, similarly, coequally, correspondingly, equivalently, evenly, as good as, other things being equal, *ceteris paribus* (L), by the same token, identically, to all intents and purposes, as much as to say, to the same degree, *ad eundem* (L), at the same rate, *pari passu* (L), abreast, neck and neck, nip and tuck (US), in equilibrium, on an even keel

13 **equitably**, justly, with justice, fairly, in a fair way, impartially, without prejudice, democratically, congruently, coextensively, equidistantly, coincidentally, symmetrically,

equably, stably, steadily, with a steady pace, roundly, squarely, regularly, uniformly, monotonously

123 Inequality

Men are by nature unequal. It is vain, therefore, to treat them as if they were equal. J. A. Froude.

NOUNS

1 **inequality**, disparity, difference, difference of degree, discrepancy, disproportion, heterogeneity, imparity, unlikeness, dissimilarity, nonuniformity, diversity, variability, patchiness, overbalance, overcompensation, addition, subtraction, imbalance, unbalance, odds, overload, overkill, top-heaviness, extra, shortage, shortfall, deficiency, inclination of balance, tilt, camber, list, superiority, inferiority, unevenness, oddness, odd number, casting (*or* deciding) vote, distortion, roughness, irregularity, asymmetry, lopsidedness, skewness, obliquity, disequilibrium, dizziness, the staggers, tilting of the scales, preponderance, overweight, underweight, lightness, insufficiency, insufficience, defect, disadvantage, handicap, loaded dice
▶ *117 Disparity, 115 Dissimilarity, 113 Diversity, 125 Compensation, 130 Addition, 131 Subtraction, 126 Superiority, 127 Inferiority, 609 Insufficiency, 309 Distortion, 369 Heaviness, 370 Lightness*

2 **injustice**, inequity, discrimination, prejudice, bias, partiality, lack of fairness, lack of democracy
▶ *493 Misjudgment*

ADJECTIVES

3 **unequal**, disparate, different, disproportionate, disproportioned, incongruent, dissimilar, diverse, disagreeing, unlike, uneven, odd, asymmetrical, distorted, irregular, scalene, unique, unequalled, at an advantage, at a disadvantage, inferior, below par, unequable, variable, variegated, deficient, defective, patchy, inadequate, insufficient, falling short, mismatched, ill-matched, ill-sorted, unbalanced, ill-balanced, lopsided, unwieldy, listing, leaning, canting, heeling, off balance, overbalanced, top-heavy, overweight, underweight, overloaded, underloaded, overshot, undershot, askew, awry, in disequilibrium, swinging, swaying, rocking, unstable, untrimmed, unballasted, uncompensated, losing balance, dizzy, giddy, toppling, falling, skewwhiff (Inf)

4 **unjust**, unfair, inequitable, discriminatory, prejudiced, biased, partial, undemocratic

VERBS

5 **be unequal**, not match, not equate, not balance, disagree, have the advantage, have superiority, preponderate, outclass, outstrip, outrank, outvote, outweigh, outdo, surpass, play below par, overtop, give points to, have the disadvantage, not suffice, fall short, play above par, disadvantage, handicap, tip the scales, throw the casting vote, cast the deciding vote, throw off (*or* out of) balance, unbalance, disbalance, overbalance, unequalize, leave a remainder, make disproportionate, disproportion, skew, destabilize, upset, list, tilt, lean, heel, rock, swing, sway, lilt, fluctuate, vary, change, capsize, miss, overcompensate, overshoot, undershoot

6 **be unjust**, lack fairness, discriminate, be prejudiced, show prejudice, be biased, show bias, show partiality, be undemocratic

ADVERBS

7 **unequally**, disparately, differently, disproportionately, dissimilarly, diversely, nonuniformly, unevenly, off balance, off-centre, all at sea, asymmetrically, irregularly, variously, uniquely, variably, on the heavy side, at (*or* with) an advantage, out in front, at (*or* with) a disadvantage, on the light side, up against it, from behind, from the rear, deficiently, defectively, inadequately, insufficiently, with a handicap, with the odds stacked against one

8 **unjustly**, without justice, unfairly, without fairness, inequitably, discriminatorily, prejudicially, undemocratically

124 Average

ADJECTIVES

1 **average**, usual, normal, par, typical, general, common, prevailing, current, popular, prevalent, predominant, across the board, sweeping, universal, generic, representative, characteristic, ordinary, everyday, familiar, household, common or garden, routine, habitual, customary, accustomed, wonted, traditional, accepted, conventional, middlebrow, standard, stock, set, established, regular, regulation, regulated, classic, orthodox, normative, prescriptive
▶ *167 Conformity, 164 Generality, 214 Regularity, 112 Uniformity*

2 **medium**, median, medial, mesial, mesiad, mean, average, middle, middling, mid-, midmost, middlemost, midway, intermediate, intermediary, balanced, halfway, half and half, fifty-fifty, central, middle-of-the-road, sitting on the fence, moderate, nonextremist
▶ *291 Centre, 158 Middle, 333 Middle Way, 242 Moderation*

3 **mediocre**, average, passable, fair, fairish, fair to middling, middling, moderate, tolerable, adequate, not bad, neither good nor bad, alright, indifferent, lukewarm, unremarkable, undistinguished, unexceptional, unnote-

worthy, unspectacular, commonplace, pedestrian, prosaic, second-class, second-best, second-division, second-rate, inferior, downmarket, banal, grey, dull, run-of-the-mill, *comme ci comme ça* (Fr), *così-così* (It), so-so (Inf), okay (OK) (Inf), nothing to write home about (Inf), no great shakes (Inf), small-time (Inf)

▶ *167 Conformity, 555 Lack of Emphasis, 612 Unimportance, 127 Inferiority*

NOUNS

4 **average**, norm, standard, par, rule, measure, criterion, yardstick, model, type, class, category, run, averageness, generality, commonness, commonality, prevalence, popularity, predominance, universality, ordinariness, familiarity, normality, normalcy, common or garden variety, conventionality, conformity, standardness, regularity, the usual, the ordinary, the common lot, the way things are, the way of the world

▶ *167 Conformity, 164 Generality, 214 Regularity, 112 Uniformity*

5 **medium**, happy medium, intermedium, average, mean, golden mean, *juste milieu* (Fr), balance, middle, mid (Arch), midpoint, median, halfway point, halfway house, centre, midsection, middle ground, midterm, middle term, middle course, middle of the road, *via media* (L), moderation, moderateness

▶ *291 Centre, 158 Middle, 333 Middle Way, 52 Mathematics, 242 Moderation*

6 **mediocrity**, mediocreness, averageness, fairishness, passableness, tolerableness, adequacy, mixed blessing, half-measure, indifference, unremarkableness, second best, second division, beta minus, C grade, inferiority, small change, small fry, small potatoes (US inf), small beer (Inf), nothing to boast (*or* brag) about (Inf), nothing special (Inf), nothing to write home about (Inf), no oil painting (Inf)

▶ *127 Inferiority, 555 Lack of Emphasis, 608 Sufficiency, 612 Unimportance*

7 **average person**, Mr (*or* Mrs) Average, commoner, boy (*or* girl) next door, man (*or* woman) in (*or* on) the street, man (*or* woman) on the Clapham omnibus, ordinary Joe, plain Jane, Joe Soap, Joe Bloggs, GI Joe, Joe Public, John Q. Public, everyman, everywoman, Tom, Dick, or Harry, Brown, Jones, and Robinson, Uncle Tom Cobbley and all, rank and file, masses, ruck, common folk, common (Arch), people, hoi polloi, the great unwashed (Offensive), proletariat, working classes, secondrater, unskilled worker, semiskilled worker, manual worker, labourer

▶ *163 Class, 803 Commoner, 181 Multitude, 646 Worker*

8 **middle classes**, bourgeois, bourgeoisie, Bab-

bitt (US), Pooter, burgher, burgherdom, respectability, suburb, suburbia, suburbanite, villadom, small town, Middle America, Home Counties, commuter, commuter belt, dormitory town, semidetached house, family car, middle-income earner, white-collar worker, skilled worker, C1, C2, semiprofessional, professional, middle manager, nonextremist, moderate, middle-of-the-roader

▶ *163 Class, 158 Middle, 167 Conformity*

VERBS

9 **be average**, be the norm, prevail, predominate, be about right, suffice, be enough, get by, make do, be moderate, sit on the fence, not cause a stir, conform, go with the crowd, go unnoticed, blend with the crowd, blur, take a back seat, stay in the background, be a nobody, play second fiddle

▶ *112 Uniformity, 164 Generality, 555 Lack of Emphasis, 608 Sufficiency, 127 Inferiority*

10 **make average**, even out (*or* up), average out, level, level up (*or* down), normalize, generalize, conventionalize, standardize, equalize, equate, balance, balance out, strike a balance, symmetrize, regularize, proportion, smooth out, share out, distribute, allocate, divide, take the mean, establish a mean, split down the middle, split the difference, halve, bisect, make it all square, go shares, go fifty-fifty, go halves, go halfway, go Dutch (Inf)

▶ *731 Allocation, 170 Calculation, 291 Centre, 724 Joint Possession, 52 Mathematics, 158 Middle, 333 Middle Way, 214 Regularity*

ADVERBS

11 **on average**, chiefly, mainly, commonly, generally, in general, generally speaking, broadly, broadly speaking, as a rule, roughly, roughly speaking, at a guess, as an approximation, as a general rule, about, round about, just about, more or less, mostly, for the most part, on the whole, as a whole, by and large, altogether, taking all things together, all things considered, all things being equal, on balance, in the long run, all in all, overall, prevailingly, predominantly, usually, normally, ordinarily, typically, habitually, routinely, as a matter of course, to be expected, as per usual (Inf)

▶ *167 Conformity, 164 Generality, 214 Regularity, 112 Uniformity*

12 **mediumly**, medianly, medially, intermediately, centrally, midway, halfway, half and half, midmost, middlemost, in the middle, moderately, neither here nor there, in between, betwixt and between (Inf)

▶ *291 Centre, 158 Middle, 333 Middle Way*

125   Compensation

NOUNS

1 **compensation**, recompense, amends, amend-

ment, reparation, indemnity, indemnification, distraint, damages, replevin, reimbursement, refund, repayment, reward, guerdon (Arch), meed (Arch), remuneration, remittance, remittal, costs, money back, payoff, golden handshake, golden parachute, redundancy money, settlement, redemption, requital, requitement, replacement, restoration, restitution, recoupment, redeemability, recovery, retrieval, rectification, redress, remedy, satisfaction, propitiation, expiation, atonement, penance, overcompensation, penalty, ransom, blood money, wergild (Arch), eric (Arch)

▶ *840 Atonement, 735 Giving Back, 741 Money, 746 Payment, 630 Remedy*

2 **counterbalance**, compensation, set off, offset, balance, counterweight, ballast, makeweight, counterpoise, equilibrium, equilibration, equilibrant, equalization, equiponderance (*or* equiponderancy), correction, self-correction, attunement, tuning, adjustment, readjustment, allowance, countermeasure, contraposition, counteraction, return action, retroaction, neutralization, cancellation, nullification, deactivation, antidote, reprisal, atonement, retaliation, revenge, vengeance, an eye for an eye, measure for measure, *quid pro quo* (L), tit for tat (Inf)

▶ *704 Cancellation, 231 Counteraction, 122 Equality*

3 **compensator**, amender, indemnifier, remitter, rewarder, guerdoner (Arch), requiter, restorer, satisfier, propitiator, redeemer

VERBS

4 **compensate**, recompense, make amends, indemnify, replevy, reimburse, refund, repay, pay back, pay up, pay off, reward, guerdon (Arch), remunerate, remit, settle, settle accounts, settle the score, distrain, redeem, requite, replace, restore, restitute, make restitution, rectify, redress, remedy, mend, satisfy, propitiate, expiate, atone, do penance, overcompensate, lean over backwards, make up for, make good, make it up, put (*or* set) straight, put (*or* set) right, cough up (Inf)

▶ *840 Atonement, 735 Giving Back, 746 Payment*

5 **counterbalance**, compensate, offset, balance, counterweigh, countervail, counterpoise, counterpose, contrapose, equipoise, equilibrate, equalize, equiponderate, restore to equilibrium, set on an even keel, level, even up (*or* out), correct, square, square up, adjust, readjust, attune, counteract, countermeasure, cancel out, write off, nullify, neutralize, deactivate, counterblast, return action, retaliate, avenge, revenge

▶ *704 Cancellation, 231 Counteraction, 630 Remedy, 122 Equality*

6 **be compensated**, take back, get back, get

compensation, recover, retrieve, regain, repossess, recoup, reclaim, retake, redeem, receive satisfaction, be avenged

ADJECTIVES

7 **compensated**, recompensed, indemnified, reimbursed, refunded, repaid, paid back, paid off, rewarded, remunerated, remitted, requited, satisfied, propitiated, overcompensated, avenged, revenged, replaced, restored, restituted, recouped, recovered, rectified, redressed, remedied, expiated, redeemed, atoned

▶ *840 Atonement, 735 Giving Back, 746 Payment*

8 **compensable**, amendable, rectifiable, recoupable, reclaimable, repleviable, redeemable, redemptible, remittable, requitable, restorable, recoverable, satisfiable, propitiable, atonable

9 **compensatory**, compensative, compensating, compensational, reparatory, reparative, restitutory, restitutive, restorative, restoring, indemnificatory, indemnifying, amendatory, amending, retributive, redemptory, redemptive, redeeming, remedial, expiatory, expiating, propitiative, propitiatious, propitiating, piacular, penitential, penitentiary

▶ *840 Atonement, 735 Giving Back, 746 Payment*

10 **counterbalancing**, balancing, compensating, counterbalanced, counterweighted, counterweighing, counterpoised, equipoised, in equilibrium, equiponderant, equilibrated, equilibrating, equalized, equalizing, countervailing, levelled, levelling, evening up (*or* out), evened up (*or* out), offsetting, corrected, corrective, correcting, self-correcting, attuned, adjusted, readjusted, return, counter, counterposed, counterposing, contraposed, contraposing, counteracted, counteracting, counteractive, retroactive, neutralized, neutralizing, cancelled out, written off, nullified, deactivated, antidotal, retaliating, retaliatory, avenging

▶ *704 Cancellation, 231 Counteraction, 630 Remedy, 122 Equality*

ADVERBS

11 **in compensation**, remedially, remediably, redemptively, counteractively, correctively, redeemably, propitiatorily, penitentially, vengefully

126 Superiority

NOUNS

1 **superiority**, precedence, eminence, preeminence, primacy, greatness, preponderance, predominance, predomination, prepotence, prepotency, transcendence, transcendency, prestige, ascendancy, loftiness, altitude, sublimity, pride of place, first place, priority, seniority, influence, leverage, say, effectiveness,

excellence, quality, perfection, high calibre, virtuosity, inimitability, incomparability, majority, supremacy, paramountcy, prominence, success, domination, privilege, right, prerogative, be-all and end-all (Inf), clout (Inf), pull (Inf)

▶ *154 Precedence, 619 Perfection, 682 Success, 194 Priority*

2 **leadership**, authority, jurisdiction, power, authorization, rule, sway, control, hegemony, sovereignty, kingship, imperium, dominion, lordship, command, generalship, captaincy, directorship, management, prime ministership (*or* prime ministry), presidency, premiership, headship, mastership, top, spot (Inf)

▶ *688 Authority, 653 Management, 12 Government and Politics*

3 **advantage**, vantage, odds, points, handicap, edge, lead, commanding lead, being ahead, start, head start, running start, flying start, upper hand, whip hand, trump hand, something in hand, vantage point, vantage ground, coign of vantage, favour, lion's share, seeded position, winning position, pole position, inside track (Inf), bulge (Inf), drop (US), something extra, something in reserve, second wind, one-upmanship (Inf), card up one's sleeve (Inf), ace in the hole (Inf), jump (Sl)

4 **summit**, top, top of the pyramid, height, the heights, high ground, lofty ground, acme, zenith, pinnacle, peak, Everest, Nob Hill (US), climax, crest, crest of the wave, new high, record high, top rung of the ladder

▶ *279 Summit, 275 Height*

5 **superior**, master, prophet, leader, chief, chief executive officer (CEO) (US), executive, manager, head, superintendent, foreman, commander, general, captain, ruler, king, emperor, sheik, sultan, prime minister, president, premier, governor, mayor, bishop, archbishop, cardinal, pope, rabbi, imam, elder, senior, principal, VIP (very important person), fugleman, headmaster, headmistress, head boy (*or* girl), first among equals, *primus inter pares* (L), boss (Inf), gaffer (Inf), Mr Big (Inf), the main man (Sl), the big cheese (Inf), the big enchilada (Inf), higher-up (Inf), brass hat (Inf), top dog (Inf), cock of the walk (Inf), Triton among the minnows (Inf), big fish (*or* frog) in a small pond (Inf), bigwig (Inf), big gun (Inf), big cheese (Inf), big noise (Sl), big enchilada (US sl), head honcho (Sl)

▶ *696 Master, 611 Importance*

6 **paragon**, genius, prodigy, nonpareil, virtuoso, prima donna, diva, first lady, expert, specialist, laureate, poet laureate, high-flier, mastermind, superman, superwoman, wonder woman, champion, victor, star, superstar, celebrity, winner, prizewinner, world-beater,

record-holder, cup-holder, record-breaker, ace (Inf), whiz kid (Inf), pop star (Inf), chart-topper (Inf), the greatest (Inf), number one (Inf), numero uno (US inf), the most (US sl), the biz (Sl)

▶ *507 Wisdom, 655 Skill*

7 **the best people**, the best, the elite, top people, nobility, aristocracy, cream, cream of the crop (US), upper class, one's (elders and) betters, chosen few, select few, happy few, *crème de la crème* (Fr), the brightest and best, the pick of the bunch, the ruling class, the Establishment, the power structure, upper crust (Inf), the brass (Inf), top brass (Inf), big boys (Inf), top drawer (Inf), nobs (Sl), aristos (Sl)

▶ *802 Aristocrat, 2 Sociology*

VERBS

8 **be superior**, excel, exceed, predominate, transcend, prevail, better, get the better of, surpass, go one better, have it over one, get ahead of, shoot ahead of, win, triumph, defeat, overcome, best, beat, take command, rise above, tower above (*or* over), prove too much for, steal the show, come to the front, steal a march on, have the edge on (*or* over), beat the record, set a record, set a new record, improve on, reach new heights, reach a new high, rise to a peak, peak, culminate, climax, pass, outdistance, top, trump, overtrump, overplay, overstep, override, overjump, overleap, overtop, overlook, overshadow, eclipse, throw into the shade, extinguish, carry the day, batter, thrash, trounce, put to shame, have the whip hand, have the last laugh, carry off the laurels, wear the crown, bear the palm, win the prize, win the championship, win the blue ribbon, win the cup, hold all the cards, hold all the aces, steal someone's thunder, out-Herod Herod, cap (Inf), cap it all (Inf), hammer (Inf), lick (Inf), beat (*or* lick) someone hollow (Inf), run rings (*or* circles) around, clobber (Sl), get (*or* have) the jump on (Sl), make mincemeat of someone (Inf)

▶ *357 Overstepping*

9 **outdo**, outplay, outrank, outvie, outbid, outshine, outstrip, outwit, outgo, outtrump, outrace, outpace, outmarch, outrun, outride, outjump, outleap, outstep, outrange, outdistance, outreach, outperform, outmanoeuvre

10 **lead**, take the lead, hold (*or* have) the lead, hold (*or* have) a healthy lead, head, direct, manage, run, front, spearhead, captain, take precedence, come first, rank first, rank, lead the dance, play the lead, star

11 **get ahead**, be ahead, hold (*or* have) an advantage, hold (*or* have) the edge, get a head start, get a running start, get off to a flying start, hold the upper hand, hold the whip hand, hold the trump hand, have something in hand, have a vantage point, have the lion's

share, have the pole position, get the drop on someone (US), have something extra, have something in reserve, get a second wind, have the inside track (Inf), have a card up one's sleeve (Inf), have an ace in the hole (Inf), get the jump on someone (Sl)

ADJECTIVES

12 **superior**, greater, better, finer, higher, over, super, above, surpassing, eclipsing, overtopping, arch, exceeding, leading, outclassing, more than a match for, ahead, in a different class, more so, (always) one step ahead, above average, head and shoulders above, ascendant, in the ascendant, in ascendancy, preferred, favourite, top-drawer, cut above (Inf), one-up (on) (Inf), capping (Inf), streets ahead (Inf)

13 **dominant**, dominating, dictatorial, magisterial, authoritative, in authority, ruling, overruling, overriding, governing, ordering, imperial, sovereign, royal

14 **best**, best ever, greatest, supreme, superlative, crowning, cardinal, capital, matchless, unmatched, unmatchable, peerless, unparalleled, unrivalled, unequalled, unapproachable, unsurpassed, unsurpassable, unexcelled, inimitable, incomparable, beyond compare, beyond criticism, unique, without equal, *sans pareil* (Fr), *nulli secundus* (L), unbeatable, invincible, perfect, highest, maximal, maximum, max, most, uppermost, utmost, top, topmost, tiptop, prime, primary, dominant, predominant, preponderant, hegemonic, prevailing, paramount, foremost, headmost, main, chief, principal, central, focal, first, record, record-breaking, top-ranking, top-ranked, champion, gold-medal, victorious, winning, triumphant, world-beating, record-holding, A1, number-one, pre-eminent, supereminent, supernormal, immortal, ultimate, transcendent, transcending, transcendental, the last word in, upmost (Inf), topnotch (Inf), chart-topping (Inf), chart-busting (Inf), out of this world (Inf)

15 **excellent**, major, first-rate, first-class, top-flight, prestigious, elder, senior, master, superb, upper, prominent, eminent, important, distinguished, singular, outstanding, banner (US), star, blue-chip, rare, classic, marked, chosen, of choice, not like the rest, every inch a king (*or* queen)

ADVERBS

16 **superiorly**, with superiority, superlatively, surpassingly, exceedingly, dominantly, dominatingly, with a dominating manner, dictatorially, magisterially, authoritatively, with authority, royally, predominantly, preponderantly, mainly, in the main, chiefly, primarily, principally, paramountly, centrally, victoriously, triumphantly, eminently, transcend-

ently, transcendentally, excellently, prestigiously, masterly, superbly, prominently, extremely, importantly, outstandingly, above average, above par, especially, rarely, advantageously, with an advantage, favourably, out of the common run, out of the top drawer

17 **supremely**, superlatively, *par excellence* (Fr), incomparably, without comparison, inimitably, peerlessly, unmatchably, matchlessly, unsurpassedly, unsurpassably, at the top of the scale, on the crest, at the peak, at the zenith, above all, to crown all, to the highest degree, far and away, by far, the most, even more, all the more, still more, more than ever, uniquely, first of all, second to none, *nulli secundus* (L), invincibly, out of this world, singularly, perfectly, in a perfect way

127 Inferiority

No one can make you feel inferior without your consent. Eleanor Roosevelt.

NOUNS

1 **inferiority**, secondariness, supporting role, second rank, second class, lower class, inferior standing, inferior status, subordinate position, second best, ordinariness, obscurity, lowliness, baseness, subordination, abasement, dependence, humbleness, humility, subservience, insignificance, unimportance, back seat (Inf), second fiddle (Inf), second eleven (Inf), second string (US inf)
▶ *612 Unimportance, 806 Humility*

2 **deficiency**, disadvantage, handicap, impairment, stain, blemish, defect, fault, faultiness, imperfection, failure, failing, decline, worsening, deterioration, reversion, insufficiency, shortfall, poverty, beggarliness
▶ *609 Insufficiency, 358 Shortfall, 683 Failure, 628 Deterioration, 129 Decrease*

3 **inferior numbers**, minority, fewness, littleness, smallness, meanness, meagreness, inadequacy
▶ *276 Lowness, 182 Few*

4 **poor quality**, badness, cheapness, shoddiness, worthlessness, shabbiness, vulgarity, bad taste, kitsch
▶ *617 Worthlessness, 795 Vulgarity*

5 **inferior state**, reduced circumstances, straitened circumstances, low point, low ebb, low, record low, all-time low, nadir, lowest point, minimum, floor, base, bottom, rock bottom, trough, depression, lowness, level, plain, flatness, sameness, mediocrity

6 **inferior**, younger, minor, junior, subordinate, subaltern, assistant, satellite, vassal, tributary, underling, henchman, menial, servant, retainer, subject, slave, hireling, agent, subsidiary, deputy, dupe, pawn, flunky, tool, instru-

ment, dependant, follower, camp follower, supporter, backbencher, nonentity, poor relation, private, other ranks, lower classes, hoi polloi, lower orders, low life, criminal classes, scum, the masses, the mob, rabble, *canaille* (Fr), lesser creation, beasts of the field, beast, worm, serpent, loser, second, poor second, poor third, also-ran, second-stringer, second-rater, third-rater, reject, failure, lowest of the low, small fry (Inf), small beer (Inf), small potatoes (US inf), sidekick (Inf), no-hoper (Inf), groupie (Sl), gofer (US sl)

▶ *697 Servant, 803 Commoner, 673 Submission*

7 **inferior thing**, sweepings, leavings, remains, leftovers, crumbs, (load of) rubbish, seconds, rejects, B-movie, one-horse town (Inf), hick town (US inf), jerkwater town (US sl), lemon (Sl), (old) clunker (US sl), clinker (US inf), (load of) crap (Tab sl), (load of) cobblers (*or* old cobblers) (Tab sl)

VERBS

8 **be inferior**, fail, fall short, come short of, fall below, not come up to, not come up to scratch, not come up to the mark, not come up to standard, lag, trail, fall behind, drag one's feet, not make the grade, not pass, not pass the test, not be up to it (Inf)

9 **yield to**, give in to, cede to, concede the victory to, have to hand it to, hand to on a plate, bow to, knuckle under, submit, lose face, lose the upper hand, not hold a candle to (Inf), have (got) nothing on (Inf)

10 **follow**, take (*or* play) a supporting role, withdraw into the background, sink into obscurity, lapse into oblivion, be dependent upon, play second fiddle (Inf), take a back seat (Inf)

11 **become inferior**, get worse, worsen, go from bad to worse, lack, want, deteriorate, decline, diminish, descend, plunge, sink, sink low, sink without trace, plumb the depths, touch rock bottom, reach one's nadir, hit the skids (Sl), have the skids put under one (Sl)

ADJECTIVES

12 **inferior**, lesser, least, lower, lowest, bottommost, low-grade, not up to much, low-class, below the salt, second-best, second-rate, third-rate, low-caste, secondary, second-class, third-class, unworthy, nothing special, nothing to shout about, nothing out of the ordinary, nothing to write home about (Inf)

13 **insignificant**, minimal, minimum, small, inconsiderable, smaller, smallest, diminished, small-time, unimportant, lightweight, small-town, one-horse (Inf), hick (US inf), jerkwater (US inf)

14 **poor**, worthless, bad, shoddy, poor-quality, substandard, subnormal, tatty, cheap, scratch, makeshift, jerry-built, patchy, crummy (Sl),

crappy (Sl), duff (Inf)

15 **subordinate**, minor, junior, dependent, subsidiary, subject, subservient, humble, tributary, ancillary, auxiliary, untouchable, criminal, low-life

16 **ordinary**, middling, mediocre, common, vulgar, base, plebeian

17 **defective**, deficient, marred, spoilt, shop-soiled, shopworn (US), like the curate's egg, failed, failing, faulty, imperfect, weak, slight, feeble, unsound, underweight, not up to snuff (*or* scratch) (Inf)

18 **outclassed**, outshone, bested, worsted, trounced, beaten, defeated, humiliated, humbled, ruined, on one's beam-ends, not fit to hold a candle to (Inf), not in the same league (Inf), not a patch on (Inf)

ADVERBS

19 **inferiorly**, in an inferior state, in an inferior place, minimally, at a low ebb, in the lowest position, at one's lowest ebb, below standard, below the mark, under par, short of, less, less than, minus, beneath, under, below

20 **insignificantly**, inconsiderably, unimportantly, worthlessly, commonly, ordinarily, middlingly

21 **badly**, shoddily, unsoundly, cheaply, defectively, imperfectly, weakly, slightly, feebly, poorly, subnormally

22 **basely**, subordinately, dependently, subserviently, humbly, unworthily

128 Increase

NOUNS

1 **increase**, addition, increment, augmentation, enlargement, growth, development, progress, advancement, advance, accumulation, cumulativeness, cumulative effect, build-up, accretion, snowballing effect, gain, waxing, bulging, swelling, dilation, expansion, fattening, thickening, broadening, widening, deepening, improvement, prosperity, profitability, appreciation, excess, overenlargement, magnification, doubling, redoubling, duplication, trebling, triplication, quadruplication, multiplication, reproduction, propagation, proliferation, amplification, extension, prolongation, protraction, intensification, escalation, acceleration, speeding, stepping up, concentration, condensation, enrichment, supplement, added contribution, accrual, heightening, enhancement, exaltation, elevation, aggrandizement, glorification, exaggeration, reinforcement, invigoration, stimulation, stimulus, spur, aggravation, exacerbation, culmination, climax

▶ *261 Expansion, 336 Forward Motion, 130 Addition, 176 Two, 243 Production, 245 Reproduction, 246 Fertility, 541 Exaggeration*

2 **spread**, spiral, upswing, upturn, upward curve, upward trend, upsurge, uprush, push, swell, swelling, intumescence, surge, gush, boost, boom, rise, climb, crescendo, leap, jump, takeoff
▶ *273 Thickness, 361 Raising, 359 Ascent, 275 Height*

3 **increasing thing**, snowball, spring tide, flood tide, rising tide, waxing moon, bull market, inflation, interest, simple interest, compound interest, rising price

VERBS

4 **increase**, grow, gain, develop, escalate, wax, bulge, swell, dilate, distend, expand, fill, fill out, fatten, thicken, broaden, become larger, grow larger, put on weight, bud, sprout, burgeon, blossom, flower, flourish, thrive, breed, swarm, spawn, proliferate, mushroom, multiply, spread, swell, intumesce, grow up, shoot up, spring up, grow by leaps and bounds, climb, spiral, mount, rise, soar, accumulate, snowball, take off, take off in a big way, rocket, flare up, gain strength, improve, grow rich, prosper, profit, be profitable, earn interest, gain in value, appreciate, rise in price, boom, surge, exceed, rise to a peak, rise to a maximum, crescendo, progress, gain ground, advance, hit the roof (Inf), go through the roof (*or* ceiling) (Inf), skyrocket (Inf)

5 **make bigger**, make more, augment, supplement, add to, contribute to, bring to, increase, increase numbers, enlist, recruit, enlarge, magnify, double, triple, quadruple, redouble, multiply, duplicate, square, cube, raise to the power of, reproduce, propagate, breed, grow, rear, raise from seed, raise from cuttings, develop, build up, fill up, fill in, fill out, pad out, expand, amplify, extend, prolong, stretch, lengthen, broaden, thicken, concentrate, condense, deepen, enrich, accrue to, repay with interest, widen, inflate, blow up, heighten, enhance, raise, exalt, erect, elevate, aggrandize, glorify, overrate, exaggerate, raise one's sights, set one's sights higher, raise the stakes, spur on, speed up, accelerate, intensify, escalate, step up, energize, stimulate, invigorate, reinforce, boost, give a boost to, maximize, stoke, fuel, add fuel to, aggravate, exacerbate, bring to the boil, bring to a head, culminate, climax, heat up (Inf), hot up (Inf), hike up (Inf), jack up (Inf), bump up (Inf), beef up (Inf), hop up (Sl), jazz up (Sl)

ADJECTIVES

6 **increasing**, progressive, progressing, expanding, growing, spreading, spreading like wildfire, escalating, bigger and better, crescent, waxing, filling, on the up and up, on the increase, ever-increasing, cumulative, snowballing, augmentative, prolific, additional, supplementary

7 **increased**, enlarged, magnified, accelerated, swollen, bloated, expanded, extended, stretched, intensified, heightened, enhanced, augmented, supplemented, hiked (Inf), jazzed up (Sl)

ADVERBS

8 **increasingly**, to an increasing extent, additionally, in addition, progressively, more and more, all the more, more so, even more so, greater and greater, bigger and bigger, bigger and better, cumulatively, prolifically, supplementarily

129 Decrease

NOUNS

1 **decrease**, deduction, subtraction, lessening, decrement, regression, de-escalation, abatement, slackening, moderation, growing soft, diminuendo, decrescendo, dimming, fading, fade-out, evanescence, diminution, waning, shrinking, shrinkage, contraction, detumescence, dwindling, ebb, drain, wasting away, degeneration, atrophy, failure, subsidence, loss of value, depreciation, enfeeblement, weakening, impoverishment, shortage, scarcity, exhaustion, diminishing returns, slowdown, deceleration, retardation, weight loss, reduction, disappearance, evaporation, deliquescence, erosion, attrition, wear, wear and tear, decay, dilapidation, damage, wastage, waste, leakage, loss, extinction, consumption, limitation, restriction, curtailment, squeeze, compression, retrenchment, rationalization, cutback, rollback (US), economization, economizing, shortening, abbreviation, abridgment, precis, mitigation, extenuation, belittlement, underestimation, undervaluation
▶ *131 Subtraction, 262 Contraction, 360 Descent, 276 Lowness, 337 Backward Motion, 743 Poverty, 609 Insufficiency, 722 Loss, 182 Few*

2 **decline**, downturn, downward trend, downward curve, fall, drop, falling off, sinking, plunge, collapse, slump, downward spiral, deflation, depression, levelling off, levelling out, bottoming out, nose dive (Inf), tailspin (Inf)
▶ *360 Descent, 276 Lowness, 752 Discount, 14 Finance*

3 **decreasing thing**, punctured tyre, ebb tide, neap tide, waning moon, bear market, deflation, recession, slump, crash, falling price

VERBS

4 **decrease**, grow less, lessen, de-escalate, ease, abate, slacken, moderate, die down, fade, fade away, evanesce, grow soft, grow dim, grow smaller, wane, wither, shrink, contract, shrivel, diminish, dwindle, ebb, ebb away, drain, drain away, dry up, waste away, wear away, eat away, corrode, run down, run low,

fail, degenerate, atrophy, die away, tail off, taper off, peter out, decline, drop (off), fall (off), subside, sink, go down, come down, take a turn for the worse, plunge, collapse, slump, spiral, downwards, go into recession, depreciate, not increase, not grow, level off, level out, bottom out, slow down, decelerate, lose, shed, cast off, cast away, lose one's voice, become invisible, fade from sight (*or* view), disappear, evaporate, melt away, become scarce, thin out, thin, detumesce, become endangered, become extinct, die out, pass away, pass into history, pass into oblivion, take a nosedive (Inf), go into a tailspin (Inf)

5 **make smaller**, make less, decrease, whittle, pare down, scrape, shave, trim, prune, dock, clip, slash, reduce, lose weight, become anorexic, cut, cut down, thin out, weed out, rid oneself of, run down, impoverish, cut back, roll back (US), limit, restrict, curtail, scale down, squeeze, compress, contract, retrench, economize, rationalize, shorten, abbreviate, abridge, condense, precis, edit down, slow down, reduce speed, decelerate, retard, depress, lower, hush, quieten, turn down, weaken, enfeeble, debilitate, dilute, water down, extenuate, mitigate, alleviate, belittle, minimize, undervalue, underestimate, degrade, downgrade, play down

ADJECTIVES
6 **decreasing**, declining, falling, dwindling, waning, wasting away, fading, evanescent, abating, moderation, softening, diminuendo, decrescendo, sinking, going down, subsiding, detumescent, ebbing, decaying, diminished, decreased, belittled, on the slide (Inf), on a downer (Sl)

7 **decrescent**, declinate, reductive, depressive, debilitative, deflationary, deflationist, depreciatory, depreciative, loss-making, regressive, corrosive, deliquescent, decompressive, decadent, decayable, declinable, deductible, depreciable (US)

ADVERBS
8 **decreasingly**, diminishingly, in decline, on the wane, at low ebb, less and less, less so, ever less, even less, in descending order, downwards, down and down, on a declining scale, at a lower rate, at a lower price

130 Addition

NOUNS
1 **addition**, adding, joining, annexation, admixture, agglutination, superaddition, load, extra load, encumbrance, burden, imposition, superimposition, superposition, interjection, interposition, supervention, insertion, inclusion, attachment, affixture, prefixion, suffixion, supplementation, augmentation, acces-

sion, accrual, accretion, increase, increment, supplement, complement, enlargement, extension, addendum, accessory, appurtenance, appendage, appanage, reinforcement, continuation, prolongation

▶ *135 Union, 661 Hindrance, 354 Insertion, 128 Increase, 104 Extraneousness, 610 Excess, 261 Expansion*

2 **mathematical addition**, arithmetic, adding-up, summation, computation, calculation, totalling, counting-up, ringing-up, total, toll, tally

▶ *170 Calculation*

3 **additional item**, addition, add-on (US), adjunct, augmentation, augment, inflection, affix, prefix, suffix, infix, adjective, adverb, additive, attachment, addendum, additament, carry-over, leftover, contribution, reinforcement, patch, padding, stuffing, lining, tail, tailpiece, coda, appendix, postscript, PS, PPS, ending, epilogue, envoy, codicil, rider, annotation, footnote, marginal note, marginalia, interpolation, interlineation, interlude, intermezzo, ingredient, component, flap, lapel, tag, tab, ticket, lappet, frill, fringe, edging, border, decoration, ornamentation, garnish, garnishing, seasoning, flavouring, sauce, dressing, trimmings, all the trimmings, all that goes with it, accoutrements, furnishings, trappings, finish, finishing touch, icing on the cake, conclusion, corollary, side effect, side issue, additional part, aftereffect, annexe, wing, ell, outhouse, shed, the works (Sl)

▶ *149 Foreign Body, 188 Duration, 144 Completeness, 293 Covering, 45 Cookery*

4 **extra**, little extra, added extra, peripheral (computer), by-product, interest, gain, benefit, bonus, plus, perquisite, tip, gratuity, lagniappe (US), graft, free gift, giveaway (US), windfall, find, lucky find, serendipity, supernumerary, surplus, superfluity, superaddition, extras, sundries, reserves, reserve equipment, spare parts, spares, provisions, items, oddment, odd items, odds and ends, extra help, auxiliaries, auxiliary forces, reinforcements, extra time, injury time, sudden death, extra inning(s), odds and sods (Inf), golden handshake (Inf), bit on the side (Inf), perk (Inf), freebie (US sl)

5 **extra person**, extra pair of hands, substitute, relief, auxiliary, reinforcement, backup, stand-in, locum, extra mouth to feed, the other man (*or* woman), co-respondent (Fml)

▶ *51 Performing Arts, 16 Law*

VERBS
6 **add**, add up, count, count up, calculate, total, total up, sum, sum up, do sums, do (the) addition, compute, carry, carry over, add to, append, annex, subjoin, attach, pin to, staple to, clip to, stick to, stick onto (*or* on), glue onto,

tag, tag on, tack on, hitch to, hitch up to, hook up to, yoke to, join, tie to, unite to, conjoin, glue together, agglutinate, accrete, preface, prefix, affix, suffix, infix, interpolate, insert, stick in, introduce, interject, interpose, engraft, let in, bring to, contribute to, make one's contribution, add one's share, add (*or* put in) one's two penn'orth (Inf), swell, augment, expand, extend, supplement, crown, complete, put the finishing touch(es) to, make up the shortfall, fill a space, fill the gap, lay on, place on, put upon, impose, burden, load, overload, saddle with, burden (*or* load) with, heap on, pile on, superadd, superimpose, overlay, paint, paint over, coat, plaster, decorate, ornament, embellish, garnish, season, spice, flavour, mix with, mix in, take to oneself, take in, encompass, absorb, include, add value, accrue, bear interest, tote up (Inf), tot up (Inf)

7 **support**, add one's support, adhere to, combine with, mix with, join, make an addition to, make one more, reinforce, recruit, make up the numbers, swell the ranks

▶ *161 Assembly, 237 Strength*

ADJECTIVES

8 **additional**, added, included, interpolated, lined, inclusive, annexed, loaded, reinforced, additive, cumulative, adjunctive, adjunct, conjunctive, attached, adjoined, joined, subjoined, inserted, prefixed, adscititious, adventitious, supplemental (*or* supplementary), complementary, accretive, accretionary, agglutinative, subsidiary, incremental, auxiliary, collateral, contributory, another, yet another, further, more

9 **extra**, new, fresh, supererogatory, supernumerary, surplus, spare, superfluous, decorative, ornamental, padded, stuffed, dressed-up

ADVERBS

10 **additionally**, in addition (to), plus, and, extra, cumulatively, adjunctly, supplementarily, collaterally, superfluously, et cetera (*or* etc.), and so on, and so forth, more, over and above, on top of, as a tip, as a lagniappe (US), with interest, with a vengeance, also, as well (as), too, to boot, into the bargain, not to mention, let alone, not forgetting, moreover, furthermore, further, (or) else, besides, on the side, apart from, together with, along with, conjointly, jointly, at the same time, in collaboration, in conjunction with, coupled with, including, inclusive of, even with, despite, in spite of, for all that, beside (Arch), with (brass) knobs on (Inf)

131 Subtraction

NOUNS

1 **subtraction**, deduction, taking away, minus, discounting, detraction, devaluation, diminu-

tion, decrease, cut, cutting, cutting back, retrenchment, shrinkage, decimation, price cutting, discount, offset, exception, abstraction, exclusion, withdrawal, elimination, expulsion, ejection, extraction, precipitation, sedimentation, removal, alleviation, relief, erosion, corrosion, wear and tear, rubbing out, deletion, erasure, obliteration, eradication, editing, bowdlerization, expurgation, striking out, extirpation, chopping, lopping, mutilation, cutting off, amputation, beheading, decapitation, severance, excision, circumcision, docking, curtailment, condensation, abridgment, abbreviation, shortening, castration, emasculation, fixing (Inf), altering (US inf)

▶ *129 Decrease, 752 Discount, 734 Taking, 349 Expulsion, 147 Exclusion, 252 Displacement, 355 Extraction, 580 Selection, 532 Publication, 533 News, 245 Reproduction, 270 Shortness*

2 **subtracted item**, thing deducted, decrement, subtrahend, minuend, allowance, remission, discount, price cut, refund, rebate, cut, cutback, limitation, restriction, drawback, shortfall, loss, forfeit, sacrifice, clawback (Inf), rake-off (Sl)

▶ *169 Number, 358 Shortfall*

VERBS

3 **subtract**, deduct, take away, do subtraction, detract from, devalue, diminish, decrease, condense, abbreviate, abridge, decimate, cut, cut prices, discount, allow, set off, offset, leave out, take out, except, make an exception, abstract, exclude, omit, eliminate, withdraw, throw out, expel, eject, remove, unload, alleviate, relieve, shift, draw off, drain, empty, void, file down, corrode, erode, rub out, cross out, cancel, delete, erase, obliterate, cull, eradicate, thin, thin out, weed, uproot, pull up by the roots, extirpate, pull out, root out, rip out, hoick out (Inf), extract, precipitate, pick, pick out, hand-pick, pick a pocket, put on one side, censor, blue-pencil, bowdlerize, expurgate, garble, mutilate

4 **take off**, sever, cut off, amputate, behead, decapitate, excise, chop off, lop, prune, dock, curtail, shorten, circumcise, castrate, geld, caponize, emasculate, unman, spay, uncover, strip, strip off (*or* away), doff, denude, divest, skin, peel, pluck, fleece, kill (Inf), knock off (Inf), fix (Inf), alter (US inf), de-ball (US taboo sl)

▶ *736 Stealing*

ADJECTIVES

5 **subtracted**, taken away, removed, deducted, excepted, abstracted, withdrawn, extracted, excluded, expelled, ejected, eliminated, eradicated, deleted, rubbed out, erased, obliterated

6 **subtractive**, reductive, extirpative, deductive, abstract, removable, eradicable

7 **reduced**, decreased, minus, curtailed, muti-

lated, headless, beheaded, decapitated, tailless, docked, chopped, lopped, severed, limbless, short, shortened, condensed, abridged, abbreviated, cut-price, cut-rate (US), discounted, devalued, diminished, lessened, decimated, eroded, corroded, worn

ADVERBS

8 **by subtraction**, at a discount, deductively, in deduction, less, short of, minus, without, bar, barring, save, exclusive of, excluding, except, excepting, with the exception of, save and except (Fml)

9 **decreasingly**, diminishingly, less and less, in a downward curve (or spiral), deductively, corrosively, removably, eradicably

132 Remainder

NOUNS

1 **remainder**, remains, rest, relic, relict, remnant, frustum, piece, chunk, shard (or sherd), shell, empty shell, husk, stump, rump, stub, plug, dottle (or dottel), cigarette end, butt, cigarette butt, butt end, fag end, roach (Sl), scrag end, body, torso, trunk, corpse, mortal remains, skeleton, bones, fossil, fragments, bits, debris, wreckage, ruins, all that is left, record, vestige, trace, track, trail, wake, footprint, fingerprint, afterglow, memory, tribal memory, memorabilia, souvenir, reminder, remembrance, survival, effect, aftereffect, result

▶ *143 Part, 157 End, 270 Shortness, 182 Few, 399 Burial, 545 Record, 610 Excess, 244 Destruction, 170 Calculation, 3 History*

2 **residue**, deposit, sediment, silt, precipitate, alluvium, moraine, loess, detritus, residual, residuum (Fml), leavings, leftovers, grounds, dregs, lees, dross, heeltaps, skimmings, offscourings, scum, slag, ashes, cinders, scoria, sludge, bilge, powder, sawdust, shavings, filings, scrapings, crumbs, husks, bran, chaff, stubble, scourings, sweepings, peelings, peel, skin, slough, scurf, dandruff, combings, clippings, trimmings, remnants, castoffs, offcuts, scraps, oddments, odds and ends, bits and pieces, bits and bobs, lumber, jumble, junk, rubbish, trash (US), rejects, refuse, litter, dirt, waste, excrement, sewage

3 **difference**, discrepancy, surplus, margin, amount (or sum) outstanding, (net) balance, balance carried forward, carry-over, credit, profit, excess, loss, deficit, debit

▶ *14 Finance, 13 Economics*

4 **surplus**, excess, overgrowth, abundance, superabundance, overabundance, oversupply, redundancy, pleonasm, surfeit, superfluity, overload, glut, leftovers, extras, spares, bonus, dividend, something for a rainy day (Inf)

▶ *130 Addition*

5 **estate**, effects, hereditament, acquest, bequest, inheritance, patrimony

▶ *227 Effect, 384 Powderiness, 581 Rejection, 622 Dirtiness, 353 Excretion*

6 **person remaining**, person left, survivor, sole survivor, last one out, heir, inheritor, successor, widow, widower, orphan, descendant, offspring, line, lineage

▶ *397 Death, 245 Reproduction*

VERBS

7 **be left**, be left over, remain, survive, result, continue, subsist, stay, rest

8 **leave**, leave over, owe, leave behind, deposit, bequeath, leave out, exclude, reject, abandon, discard, cast off, cast away, except, not choose

ADJECTIVES

9 **remaining**, residual, residuary, resultant, resting, left, hereditary, patrimonial, left behind, vestigial, precipitated, deposited, sedimentary, surviving, bereft, widowed, orphan, orphaned, abandoned, discarded, rejected, cast-off

10 **surplus**, net, unused, unspent, unexpired, unconsumed, outcast, on the shelf, over, left over, passed over, unwanted, odd, still remaining, outstanding, owed, carried over, extra, spare, to spare, excess, excessive, overabundant, superabundant, overloaded, redundant, superfluous, pleonastic, otiose

ADVERBS

11 **residually**, vestigially, memorably, discrepantly, excessively, superfluously, abundantly, overabundantly, superabundantly, pleonastically, redundantly

12 **with a remainder**, with the rest, among those remaining, in arrears, in default, outstandingly, sparely, redundantly, superfluously, like a relic, like a fossil, on the shelf

133 Mixture

NOUNS

1 **mixture**, admixture, commixture, intermixture, mixing, mingling, intermingling, stirring, shaking, blending, harmonization, association, combination, integration, syncretism, eclecticism, fusion, merger, union, amalgamation, conglomeration, composition, miscibility, solubility, infusion, interfusion, suffusion, transfusion, instillation, infiltration, pervasion, permeation, saturation, penetration, impregnation, contamination, pollution, contagion, infection, adulteration, dilution, watering down, qualification, sophistication, involvement, complexity, complication, entanglement, confusion, disorder, jumble, muddle, scramble, chaos, entropy, randomness, nonuniformity, patchiness, heterogeneity, hybridization, mongrelism, cross-breeding, interbreeding, miscegenation, intermarriage,

syngamy, allogamy

2 **mixed thing**, mix, mixture, blend, mélange, composition, harmony, association, synthesis, marriage, interracial marriage, interfaith marriage, combination, compound, alloy, bronze, brass, pewter, billon, electrum, steel, magma, amalgam, fusion, infusion, solution, colloid, suspension, cocktail, punch, brew, witch's brew, medicinal compound, linctus, cough linctus, cough mixture, patent medicine, potion, concoction, confection, potpourri, pastiche, pasticcio, paste, stew, Irish stew, gumbo (US), soup, broth, goulash, Hungarian goulash, hash, ragout, salmagundi, olla podrida, bubble and squeak, fry-up (Inf), combo (Inf), Mickey Finn (Sl)

3 **miscellany**, miscellaneous collection, medley, miscellanea, anthology, collection, thesaurus, chrestomathy (Lit), variety, patchwork, mosaic, variegation, dappling, speckling, speckled effect, mottled effect, motley, job lot hotchpotch, hash, mess, farrago, gallimaufry, potpourri, mishmash, linsey-woolsey, ragbag, jumble, lucky dip, grab bag (US), tombola, conglomeration, muddle, tangle, entanglement, imbroglio, confusion, complexity, kaleidoscope, phantasmagoria, babel, Tower of Babel, topsy-turvydom (US), bear garden, clatter, clamour, pandemonium, omniumgatherum, motley crew, menagerie, zoo, circus, variety show, assortment, all sorts, bits and pieces, bits and bobs, oddments, snippets, paraphernalia, odds and ends, odds and sods (Inf), dog's dinner (*or* breakfast) (Inf)

4 **admixture**, ingredient, element, vein, streak, strain, dash, tincture, tinge, infusion, sprinkling, *soupçon* (Fr), touch, pinch, smack, modicum, suspicion, flavour, seasoning, condiment, herb, spice, bouquet garni, colouring, colour, dye, hue, stain, blot, smidgen (US inf)

5 **hybrid**, cross, hybrid flower, hybrid rose, cross-breed, half-breed (Offensive), half-blood (Offensive), half-caste (Offensive), mestizo, métis, quadroon, octaroon, mulatto, high yellow (Sl), Creole, Cape Coloured (*or* Coloured) (S Afr), Eurasian, mongrel, cur, alley cat (US), mule, hinny, tigon (*or* tiglon), loganberry, boysenberry, tayberry, clementine

6 **mixer**, electric mixer, beater, shaker, cocktail shaker, stirrer, spoon, wooden spoon, blender, liquidizer, food processor, whisk, churn, cream-maker, creamer, scrambler, mixing bowl, crucible, melting pot
▶ 45 Cookery

7 **person who mixes**, chef, cook, baker, bartender, chemist, alchemist, witch, socialite, stirrer, mixer (Inf), mixologist (US inf)

VERBS

8 **mix**, admix, commix, immix, mix up, mix and match, stir, shake, knead, pound, pulverize, mash, brew, infuse, instil, imbue, impregnate, tinge, dye, colour, speckle, bespeckle, dapple, variegate, suffuse, combine, integrate, fuse, compound, alloy, amalgamate, merge, blend, harmonize, mingle, commingle, intermingle, intersperse, intermix, interlard, interleave, interlay, intertwine, intertwist, interweave, interlace, plait, braid, sprinkle, besprinkle, dash, dilute, water, water down, qualify, weaken, adulterate, sophisticate, temper, spice, season, fortify, lace, spike, pep up, doctor, meddle with, interfere with, tamper with, spoil, mar, debase, contaminate, cross, cross-fertilize, crossbreed, interbreed, hybridize, mongrelize

9 **mix up**, muddle, scramble, jumble, shuffle, confuse, bewilder, puzzle, confound, mistake, entangle, do wrong, mess up (Inf)

10 **become mixed**, blend, mix together, integrate, run through, penetrate, permeate, pervade, stain, infiltrate, infect, pollute, contaminate, become tainted with, become inextricably linked with, become entangled with, become involved with, intermarry, interbreed

11 **be mixed up**, misunderstand, not understand, puzzle over, get wrong, forget

ADJECTIVES

12 **mixed**, mixed-up, intermixed, mingled, intermingled, interracial, interfaith, interspersed, interlaced, interwoven, intertwisted, intertwined, plaited, braided, miscible, soluble, colloidal, dissolved, stirred, shaken, blended, harmonized, combined, integrated, syncretic, eclectic, fused, mashed, alloyed, merged, amalgamated, conglomerated, composite, half-and-half, tempered, sophisticated, adulterated, dilute, diluted, watered-down, weakened, qualified, involved, involved in, complex, complicated, in the melting pot, tangled, entangled, unclassified, unsorted, unordered, disordered, jumbled, confused, out of order, orderless, shuffled, scrambled, chaotic, topsyturvy, miscellaneous, random, nonuniform, patchy, patched, heterogeneous, hybrid, mongrel, half-breed (*or* half-bred) (Offensive), cross-bred, crossed, half-caste (Offensive), half-blooded (Offensive), of mixed blood, miscegenetic, interbred, intermarried, multiracial, multicultural, kaleidoscopic, phantasmagoric(al), variegated, dappled, speckled, mottled, motley, shot, shot through with, tinged, dyed, coloured, pervasive, all-pervading, fifty-fifty (Inf), higgledy-piggledy (Inf)

13 **mixed-up**, muddled, jumbled, scrambled, confused, bewildered, puzzled, confounded, mistaken, forgetful

ADVERBS

14 **in the midst**, among many, among others, *inter alios* (L), among other things, *inter alia* (L), among (*or* amongst), amidst, in the midst of, in

the middle of, interracially, between races, complexly, complicatedly, with complications, out of order, chaotically, miscellaneously, randomly, at random, patchily, heterogeneously, with different parts, kaleidoscopically, phantasmagorically, pervasively, contagiously, infectiously, higgledy-piggledy (Inf)

134 Purity

I'm as pure as the driven slush. Tallulah Bankhead.

It is one of the superstitions of the human mind to have imagined that virginity could be a virtue. Voltaire.

NOUNS

1 **purity**, pureness, cleanness, cleanliness, freshness, clearness, clarity, spotlessness, immaculacy, stainlessness, sinlessness, innocence, faultlessness, flawlessness, perfection, moral purity, morals, morality, high moral tone, high-mindedness, moral rectitude, virtue, decency, honesty, honour, integrity, piety, virginity, chastity, delicacy, propriety, good taste, simplicity, modesty, pudency, false modesty, primness, priggishness, prudery, prudishness, censorship, bowdlerization, expurgation, euphemism, coyness, sanctimoniousness, sanctimony, Puritanism, Grundyism, Victorian values
▶ *621 Cleanness, 865 Innocence, 619 Perfection, 863 Virtue, 794 Refinement, 869 Self-Restraint, 810 Modesty, 876 Morality*

2 **purification**, cleansing, cleaning, washing, lustration, Asperges, purgation, washing out, flushing, dialysis, purging, clearance, riddance, expulsion, elimination, ventilation, airing, fumigation, deodorization, antisepsis, disinfection, sterilization, decontamination, disinfestation, delousing, sanitation
▶ *625 Hygiene, 353 Excretion*

3 **purifier**, cleanser, cleaner, cleansing agent, soda, washing soda, carbolic acid, detergent, washing powder, soapflakes, washing-up liquid, dishwashing liquid (US), soap, soap and water, water, hot water, shampoo, mouthwash, gargle, toothpaste, dentifrice, lotion, hand lotion, hand cream, cleansing cream, cold cream, vanishing cream, disinfectant, deodorant, air-freshener, filter, water filter, strainer

4 **purgative**, purgative agent, purge, cathartic, enema, diuretic, nauseant, emetic, laxative, aperient, evacuant

5 **pure person**, saint, virgin, maid, maiden, virgo intacta, vestal, vestal virgin, spinster, old maid, religious celibate, monk, nun, Puritan, Quaker, paragon, paragon of virtue, Lancelot, Knight in Shining Armour, angel (Inf), goody-goody (Inf), wowser (Aus and NZ sl)
▶ *7 Religion*

6 **prude**, prig, Victorian, moral guardian, Mrs Grundy, Mary Whitehouse, censor, Watch Committee
▶ *852 Disapproval, 876 Morality*

7 **purebred**, thoroughbred, pedigree

8 **simplicity**, simpleness, homogeneity, uniformity, oneness, absoluteness, bedrock, indivisibility, essence, no mixture, no dilution

VERBS

9 **be pure**, have no sin, have no faults, live purely, live honourably, keep a high moral tone, have morals, have integrity, have (*or* lead a life of) virtue, stay virtuous, stay innocent, live like a monk, live like a nun, live like a Puritan, resist temptation, control oneself, keep to (*or* on) the straight and narrow (path)

10 **purify**, clean, cleanse, purge, wash, lave, lustrate, purify oneself, wash clean, wipe clean, freshen, fumigate, deodorize, edulcorate, ventilate, desalinate, decontaminate, disinfect, chlorinate, pasteurize, sanitize, sanitate, sterilize, free from impurities, refine, sublimate, distil, strain, filter, percolate, leach, lixiviate, sift, sieve, winnow, depurate, clarify, clear, skim, scum, despumate, rack, decarbonize, decoke, elutriate, flush, dialyse, catheterize, wash out, drain, flush out, clean out, censor, expurgate, blue-pencil, bowdlerize

11 **simplify**, make simple, make uniform, unify, make one, reduce to its constituent parts, reduce to its elements, not mix, not dilute, unscramble, unravel, sort out, weed out, eliminate, get rid of, expel, eject, clear out, exclude

ADJECTIVES

12 **morally pure**, pure, virtuous, righteous, decent, moral, chaste, virginal, faithful, high-minded, unerring, perfect, noble, spotless, sinless, innocent, uncorrupt, uncorrupted, honourable, angelic, modest, prudish, prim, priggish, coy, euphemistic, Christian, sanctimonious, Puritanical, Victorian, on the side of the angels

13 **pure**, purified, cleansed, clean, cleanly, spotless, stainless, unblemished, immaculate, unmuddied, unsullied, untarnished, unspoilt, unpolluted, uncontaminated, unadulterated, undiluted, neat, unfortified, unmedicated, unflavoured, unfragranced, unspiced, unseasoned, uncoloured, undyed, untinged, free from, clear, clarified, refined, blank, purebred, thoroughbred, pedigreed

14 **purified**, cleansed, cleaned, clean, spick-and-span, shining, shiny, polished, scrubbed, snowy, white, snow-white, pure as the driven snow, dainty, nice, fresh, fresh as a daisy, bright (*or* clean) as a new pin, bright, deodorized, disinfected, aseptic, antiseptic, sterilized, sterile, ritually clean, kosher (Judaism), halal

15 **purifying**, cleansing, purificatory, lustral, hygienic, sterilizing, germicidal, sanitary, disinfectant, detergent, purging, purgative, purgatory, ablutionary

16 **simple**, one, single, homogeneous, unified, all of a piece, monolithic, uniform, undifferentiated, indivisible, elemental, entire, nothing but, unadulterated, undefiled, unalloyed, uncompounded, uncombined, unblended, mere, sheer, utter, irreducible, basic, fundamental, elementary, intrinsic, simplified, unmixed, unmingled, pure and simple, no frills, unravelled, disentangled, intelligible, comprehensible

17 **direct**, unsophisticated, simplistic, homespun, straight, straight from the shoulder, unqualified, unmitigated, wholehearted, single-minded, downright, sincere, unpretentious, honest, honourable, unaffected, undisguised, naked, bare

ADVERBS

18 **virtuously**, righteously, decently, morally, chastely, virginally, faithfully, with faith, high-mindedly, unerringly, perfectly, in a perfect way, nobly, innocently, in all innocence, uncorruptibly, honourably, angelically, modestly, prudishly, primly, priggishly, coyly, sanctimoniously, Puritanically, like a Puritan

19 **purely**, cleanly, spotlessly, without a spot, immaculately, aseptically, antiseptically, sterilely, hygienically, purgatively

20 **homogenously**, irreducibly, fundamentally, intrinsically, directly, in a direct fashion, simplistically, wholeheartedly, with all one's heart, single-mindedly, sincerely, unpretentiously, without pretence, honestly, honourably

135 Union

NOUNS

1 **union**, unity, coming together, joining, junction, conjunction, concurrence, confluence, convergence, meeting, rendezvous, liaison, concrescence, coalescence, fusion, nuclear fusion, synthesis, merger, combination, cohesion, coherence, tenacity, agglutination, concretion, consolidation, solidification, coagulation, condensation, concentration, compaction, close union, closeness, nearness, touching, touch, contact, contiguity, contiguousness, compactness, concentratedness, tightness, association, collection, congress, concourse, gathering, forgathering, assembly, crowd, mob, throng, reunion, alliance, coalition, symbiosis, bond, bonding, ligature, link, linkage, concatenation, hyphenation, connection, tie-up, hook-up, yoke, interconnection, cross-connection, anastomosis, inosculation, interlocking, network, net, communications

network, communication, computer network, local area network (LAN), wide area network (WAN), intercommunication, exchange, interchange, intercourse, trade, commerce, traffic, cross-communication, involvement
▶ *267 Juxtaposition, 133 Mixture, 140 Combination, 138 Adhesion, 371 Density, 137 Connection, 737 Trade*

2 **agreement**, accord, unity, concurrence, unison, unanimity, solidarity, brotherhood, sisterhood, harmony, peace, concord, concert, entente (cordiale)
▶ *667 Agreement, 675 Peace, 116 Accord*

3 **unification**, bringing together, joining together, assemblage, collection, jointing, articulation, structure, organization, composition, knitting, weaving, sewing, stitching, suture, tightening, contraction, ligation, knotting, welding, astriction (Arch)
▶ *161 Assembly, 288 Interweaving*

4 **sexual union**, mating, coupling, sleeping with, copulation, intercourse, sexual intercourse, coition, coitus, coitus interruptus, sex, fornication, carnal knowledge, knowing (carnally), intimacy, generation, procreation, propagation, reproduction, syngenesis, syngamy, pairing, pair-bonding, wedlock, wedding, marriage, consummation, fucking (Tab), screwing (Sl), shagging (Tab sl), bonking (Sl), balling (US tab sl), a roll in the hay (Sl), rumpy-pumpy (Sl)
▶ *823 Marriage, 877 Immorality*

5 **joint**, join, hyphen, conjunction, copula, junction, juncture, tie, knot, hitch, splice, node, link, crease, fold, seam, stitching, suture, bond, weld, welded joint, rivet, screw, staple, pivot, ball-and-socket joint, dovetail joint, dovetail and mortise joint, mortise and tenon joint, mitre joint, hasp, latch, sneck (Dial), catch, hook, fastening, fastener, clasp, clip, paperclip, hinge, bracket, ginglymus, ankle, toe, finger, thumb, knuckle, wrist, knee, hip, elbow, shoulder
▶ *320 Fold, 298 Interface*

6 **point of union**, junction, junction box, juncture, meeting place, rendezvous, meeting point, focus, intersection, crossroads, decussation

7 **joiner**, carpenter, welder, riveter, weaver, tailor, seamstress, dressmaker, creative artist, composer and lyricist, organizer, communicator, continuity person, linkman, middleman, intermediary, agent, go-between, pander (or panderer), pimp, matchmaker, entrepreneur

VERBS

8 **unite**, join, conjoin, link, hyphenate, tie in, couple, pair, pair up, have a twin town, have a sister city (US), pair off, harness together, match, marry, bracket, bracket together, assemble, collect, bring together, draw together, piece together, fit together, put together, lay

together, throw together, lump together, gather together, gather, mobilize, combine, mix, mass, amass, mass together, accumulate, add to, merge, consolidate, associate, incorporate, make one, unify, roll into one, include, comprise, embrace, unite closely, pack, compact, impact, compress, condense, concentrate, narrow, constrict, tighten, make firm, make fast, tauten, pull tight, draw tight, truss, lace (*or* do) up tight(ly), brail, frap, trice up, unite with, join (*or* link) with, come together, converge, meet, hold together, hang together, stick together, coalesce, fit well, cohere, adhere, make a good fit, mesh together, interlock, engage, grip, grapple, clinch, hold hands, go with, go steady with, go out with, walk out with, partner, accompany, associate with, liaise, link up with, mix with, be in league with, join (a group)

9 **agree**, reach an agreement, unite, reach an accord, concur, vote unanimously, have solidarity, have harmony, have concord

10 **link**, attach, annex, affix, suffix, prefix, infix, fix, stick, tape, staple, pin, pin to, pin on, clip, hang on, hook on, nail, bolt, screw, screw up (*or* down), rivet, hammer in, knock in, connect, thread, thread through, thread together, string together, rope together, link together, chain together, concatenate, contact, put in contact with, make contact, plug in, earth, earth, ground (US), network, interconnect, link, span, bestride, straddle, bridge, connect with, put through to, put in touch, get in touch, communicate, intercommunicate, hook up with, tie up with, link up with, yoke, yoke together, harness, leash, tie, splice, knot, lash, hitch, belay, tie together, entwine, intertwine, braid, baste, plait, twist, crochet, lace, interlace, interweave, truss, tie up, strap, lace up, lash up, tie to, tie up to, moor to, anchor, tether, pinion, fetter, handcuff, manacle, hobble, shackle, bind, gird, girdle, bandage, swaddle, swathe, wrap, enfold, embrace, clasp, clinch, grip, grapple, articulate, dovetail, mortise, mitre, rabbet, fit, wedge, jam, clamp, lock, lock together, interlock, set, gear to, engage, wed, join, weld, solder, fuse, braze, cement, glue, knit, weave, sew, suture, stitch, seam, tack, fasten, fasten up, button, button up, do up, zip up, buckle, close, lock up, seal up, patch, darn, mend, heal over (*or* up), form a scab, knit together

11 **make love**, marry, wed, live with, cohabit, have sexual relations, have sex with, go to bed with, lie with, sleep with, consummate a marriage (*or* union), have sexual intercourse, have carnal knowledge, know (Arch), enjoy, possess, bed, have one's wicked (*or* evil) way with, couple, copulate, mate, pair, pair-bond, serve, cover, mount, tup, breed with, fuck (Tab), live in sin (Inf), get spliced (Inf), get hitched (Sl), lay (Sl), have (Sl), make someone (Sl), make it with (Sl), have it off (*or* away) (Sl), knock off (Sl), ball (US tab sl), screw (Sl), shag (Tab sl)

ADJECTIVES

12 **united**, joined, connected, conjoined, accompanied, partnered, betrothed, promised, engaged, married, wedded, hand in hand, arm in arm, intimate, involved, inextricable, inseparable, intricate, indissoluble, indivisible, thick as thieves, associated, symbiotic, (all) rolled into one, incorporated, corporate, cooperative, merged, unified, conjoint, composite, combined, coalescent, collected, cohesive, adhesive, concretive, put-together, made-up, assembled, jointed, articulated, seamed, stitched, sewn, woven through, patched, darned

13 **agreeable**, agreed, united, unanimous, solid, harmonious, peaceful, concordant, in concert

14 **conjunctive**, adjunctive, connective, copulative, coagulating, solidifying, condensing, concentrative, astringent, possessive, possessed, copulatory, coital, venereal, sexual, fucked (Tab), hitched (Sl), hooked (Sl), laid (Sl), screwed (Sl)

15 **tied**, tied down, tied up, bound, knotted, lashed, hitched, yoked, spliced, gathered, sewn, stitched, woven, interwoven, braided, plaited, well-tied, roped, secured, fastened, attached, adhering, cohesive, glued, bonded, cemented, rooted, tight, fast, taut, tense, firm, secure, close, close-set, close-packed, tightly packed, tight-fitting, wedged, jammed, stuck, immovable

ADVERBS

16 **as one**, together, jointly, cooperatively, conjointly, all together, altogether, in conjunction (with), in union (with), in partnership (with), in league (with), inseparably, indissolubly, indivisibly, cohesively, with cohesion, adhesively, inextricably, intricately, intimately, conjunctively, connectively, possessively, in a possessive way, copulatively, sexually, with sexual undertones, in a sexual way, in cahoots (with) (US sl)

17 **agreeably**, unanimously, solidly, harmoniously, peacefully, concordantly, in concert

18 **inextricably**, inseparably, intimately, firmly, tightly, tight, fast, tautly, tensely, securely, closely, immovably, without moving

136 Separation

Absence from whom we love is worse than death. William Cowper.

Every parting gives a foretaste of death; every coming together again a foretaste of the resurrection. Arthur Schopenhauer.

NOUNS

1 **separation**, disconnection, disunion, disunity, discontinuity, disjunction, disjuncture, dislocation, separability, disintegration, breakage, breakup, dispersion, dispersal, scattering, dissolution, decomposition, breakdown, dissection, analysis, resolution, resolving power, high resolution, low resolution, disruption, fragmentation, shattering, splitting, fission, nuclear fission, separating, parting, severance, uncoupling, divorce, divorcement, moving apart, growing apart, divergence, spreading, spread, deviation, split, schism, detachment, unfastening, undoing, untying, unbuttoning, unthreading, unravelling, loosening, loosing, liberating, freeing

▶ *160 Discontinuity, 162 Dispersion, 139 Nonadhesion, 628 Deterioration, 141 Disintegration, 666 Disagreement, 824 Divorce; Widowhood, 700 Liberation*

2 **setting apart**, setting aside, ejection, expulsion, exception, exemption, rejection, boycott, avoidance, exclusion, selection, choice, division, severance, discrimination, apartheid, segregation, zoning, zone, compartment, no-go area, off-limits area (US), ghetto, box, cage, prison, isolation, loneliness, seclusion, quarantine, putting aside, keeping to one side, conservation, preservation, reservation, taking away, deprivation, expropriation, removal, withdrawal, resignation, retirement, nonattachment, nonalignment, insularity

▶ *147 Exclusion, 580 Selection, 591 Avoidance, 349 Expulsion, 131 Subtraction, 816 Unsociability, 705 Resignation*

3 **separateness**, separability, immiscibility, oil and water, severalty, separatism, nationalism, isolationism, difference, dichotomy, division, subdivision, segmentation, partition, cutting, scission, section, break, tear, laceration, dilaceration, tearing apart, rip, rent, fissure, split, gap, breach, rift, crack, cleft, chasm, cleavage, slit, slot, gash, incision, hole, rupture, opening, ladder, run(US), abscission, offcut (Brit), decapitation, beheading, amputation, castration, circumcision, docking, curtailment, retrenchment, cutting away, resection

4 **disunity**, disagreement, lack of unity, lack of harmony, dissension, opposition, hostility, no common ground, poles apart

▶ *111 Oppositeness*

5 **separator**, dividing line, caesura, comma, slash, solidus, dash, hyphen, partition, diaeresis, umlaut, full stop, period (US)

6 **boundary**, fence, hedge, wall, ha-ha, screen, curtain, limit, frontier, border, barrier, barricade, Berlin Wall, Iron Curtain, Mason-Dixon line (US)

7 **separates**, coordinates, accessories, peripherals, add-ons (US)

8 **person who separates**, surgeon, judge, Moses, Solomon, critic, selector, chemist, separatist, segregationist, isolationist

VERBS

9 **separate**, part, sever, break, fracture, chip, crack, rupture, snap, break in two, split up, disunite, dissociate, disassociate, divorce, unhitch, uncouple, disconnect, unplug, disengage, displace, wrench, dislocate, throw out of gear, detach, unseat, unhorse, dismount, throw, unstick, untie, unfasten, undo, unbutton, unlace, unhook, unclasp, unzip, unstring, unlock, unlatch, unchain, unbind, unfetter, sever ties, cut the knot, cut the ties that bind, break the link, disentangle, unravel, unstitch, unpick, ladder, run (US), loosen, slacken, relax, loose, set free, liberate, release, eject, expel, dispel, scatter, disband, demobilize, disperse, disintegrate, break up, break down, come undone, come unstuck, spring apart, fall apart, come apart, come (or fall) to pieces (or bits), take to pieces (or bits), take apart, cannibalize, slit, split, rive, cleave, rend, tear, tear apart, rip, tear (or rip) to bits (or pieces), lacerate, dilacerate, hack, hew, cut, chop, stab, slash, gash, cut through, saw, slice, shred, mince, mash, grind, crunch, bite, bite into, bite through, gnaw, carve, carve up, disassemble, dismantle, disjoin, dissolve, unmake, decompose, decay, degrade, blow up, blow to pieces (or bits), smash, shatter, shiver, splinter, crumble, cave in, pulverize, destroy, sunder (Arch)

10 **set apart**, set aside, put aside, lay up, store, conserve, preserve, reserve, mark out, select, sort, tick off, check off (US), pick out, single out, distinguish, differentiate, discern, resolve (images), discriminate, exclude, except, boycott, ban, bar, blacklist, blackball, banish, ostracize, send to Coventry, isolate, insulate, cut off, hive off, remove, take away, detract, subtract, deduct, strip, strip bare, denude, peel, pare, flake, skin, flay, fleece, shear, clip, pluck, behead, decapitate, amputate, curtail, dock, lop, prune

11 **divide**, divide up, subdivide, sectionalize, separate the sheep from the goats, separate the wheat from the chaff, segment, fragment, fractionalize, fractionate, fractionize, factorize, analyse, cut up, anatomize, dissect, bisect, halve, apportion, share out, dismember, disembowel, quarter, partition, screen off, compartmentalize, circumscribe, keep apart, segregate, sequester, seclude, quarantine, maroon, keep (or hold) apart, set against, estrange, alienate, divorce, make enemies, become enemies

12 **disagree**, lack unity, lack harmony, have dissention, dissent, oppose, show hostility, find no common ground, stand poles apart

13 **diverge**, go away, go separate (*or* different) ways, follow separate paths, depart, scatter, disperse, deviate, bifurcate, part, part company, cast adrift, set (*or* cut) adrift, cut loose, get loose, get free, free oneself, get away, break away, fall away, escape, quit, leave, relinquish, abandon, wash one's hands of, get shot of

14 **come between**, step between, put asunder, divide, keep (*or* hold) apart, interpose, flow between, drive apart, drive a wedge between, sunder (Arch)

ADJECTIVES

15 **separate**, separated, disunited, disjointed, disjunctive, dislocated, divorced, broken up, disconnected, unplugged, unstuck, untied, undone, unzipped, unloosed, loosened, loose, liberated, released, expelled, ejected, unfettered, unchained, free, open, discontinuous, interrupted, partitioned, bipartite, multipartite, dichotomous, dividing, divided, subdivided, halved, quartered, dismembered, disembowelled, cut, torn, severed, ruptured

16 **apart**, in pieces (*or* bits), asunder, broken, shattered, split, schizoid, cut up, cut to pieces (*or* bits), shot to pieces, rent, riven, cloven, cleft, dispersed, scattered, fugitive, divergent, radiating, sundered (Arch)

17 **unjoined**, unfastened, adrift, detached, unattached, nonattached, nonaligned, neutral, unfixed, unconnected, discrete, distinct, distinctive, differentiated, separative, hived off, excluded, excepted, exempt, abstracted, absent-minded, withdrawn, uninvolved, unmixed, immiscible, unassimilated, unassimilable, not belonging, unrelated, alien, foreign, external, extrinsic, self-sufficient, insular, isolated, secluded, lonely, alone, cast off, cast out, left, abandoned, rejected, selective, picked out, set apart, reclusive

18 **disagreeable**, disagreeing, unharmonious, dissenting, hostile, adverse, opposed, opposite, antipathetic, inimical

19 **separable**, severable, partiable, divisible, fissionable, fissile, scissile, tearable, breakable, biodegradable, dissolvable, dissoluble, resolvable (image), high-resolution, low-resolution, discernible, distinguishable

ADVERBS

20 **separately**, severally, singly, one at a time, one by one, piecemeal, piece by piece, bit by bit, in bits, in pieces, in halves, in two, dichotomously, discontinuously, disjunctively, loosely, freely, in twain (Arch)

21 **apart**, asunder, divergently, brokenly, in pieces, in bits, to bits, to smithereens, to shreds, to tatters, to matchwood, limb from limb, never the twain shall meet

22 **in isolation**, in splendid isolation, aloof, apart, away, adrift, separatively, distinctly, distinctively, discretely, self-sufficiently, neu-

trally, abstractly, absent-mindedly, externally, in an alien way, extrinsically, selectively, diagnostically

23 **disagreeably**, antipathetically, inimically, hostilely, with hostility, unharmoniously, with dissent, adversely, oppositely

137   Connection

NOUNS

1 **connection**, union, merger, conjunction, interconnection, attachment, graft, linking, joining, coupling, fastening, meeting, cohesion, adhesion, involvement, entanglement
▶ *135 Union, 323 Closure, 138 Adhesion*

2 **association**, relationship, relation, liaison, nexus, network, intercourse, commerce, communication network, communication, intercommunication, satellite link
▶ *534 Communications*

3 **associate**, business associate, contact, ally, friend, kith, relation, relative, family member, kin, kinsman, blood kin, clan, tribe
▶ *819 Friendship, 815 Sociability, 107 Relatedness, 284 Support*

4 **means of connection**, bond, chain, fetter, shackle, tie, band, hoop, yoke, link, junction, arch, joint, hinge, ramification, branching, branch, nexus, connective, bonding agent, intermedium, tie beam, beam, girder, stay, stretcher, strut, interconnection, stairway, stairs, ladder, stepladder, steps, stepping stone, canal, isthmus, neck, col, ridge, copula, punctuation mark, hyphen, dash, slash, solidus, parenthesis, bracket, square bracket, angle bracket, brace, zeugma, en-rule
▶ *699 Restraint, 5 Linguistics*

5 **road**, main road, arterial road, A-road, motorway, highway (US), interstate (highway) (US), expressway (US), freeway (US), turnpike (US), toll road, toll bridge, bridge, span, causeway, access road, exit, slip road, service road (US), interchange, highway ramp (US), cloverleaf, spaghetti junction, intersecting road, flyover (*or* overpass), underpass, bypass, street, main street, lane, path, track
▶ *70 Transport*

6 **line**, cable, hawser, cord, whipcord, rope, painter, moorings, guy, guy rope, guest rope, towline, towrope, lifeline, umbilical cord, communication cord, ripcord, string, wire, tape, adhesive tape, twine, binder, binding twine, fibre, ligature, connective tissue, ligament, tendon, muscle, withe (*or* withy), raffia, bast (*or* bass), osier, lashing, binding, thread, band, ribband, bandage, tourniquet, roller bandage, braid, plait, thong, drawstring, lace, shoelace, bootlace, tag, tie, cravat, stock, knot, granny knot, slipknot, stitch

7 **tackle**, chain, anchor chain, rope, cordage,

rig, rigging, sheets, ratline, shroud, clew line, stay, guy, garnet, halyard (or halliard), bowline, harness, lanyard

8 **fastening**, fastener, zip (fastener), zipper (US), button, buttonhole, eyelet, loop, frog, toggle, hook, hook and eye, stud, press stud, snaps (US), stitch, basting, Velcro, collar stud, cufflink, tiepin, suspender, garter (US), braces, suspenders (US), brooch, clasp, clip, tie clasp (or clip), grip, hairgrip, bobby pin (US), (hair) slide, barrette (US), curlers, rollers, hairpin, hatpin, skewer, spit, brochette, drawing pin, pushpin (US), thumbtack (US), tack, safety pin, straight pin (US), toggle pin, cotter pin, linchpin, kingpin (or swivel pin), peg, dowel, nail, treenail, brad, holdfast, staple, brace, batten, clamp, cramp, nut, bolt, rivet, screw, buckle, hasp, hinge, catch, safety catch, spring catch, latch, lock, lock and key, combination lock, mortise lock, Yale lock, Yale key, padlock, manacles, handcuffs, ring, cleat, bollard, post, stake, pile, pale, bar, popper (Inf), bracelets (Sl)

▶ *796 Fashion, 718 Security, 138 Adhesion*

9 **yoke**, coupling, coupler, traces, drawbar, hook, claw, grapple, grappling iron, anchor, sheet anchor, harness, reins, ribbons, halter, collar, lead, leash, tether, lasso, lariat (US), noose, loop

10 **band**, girdle, belt, strap, waistband, cummerbund, bellyband, girth, cinch, sash, shoulder belt, bandoleer (or bandolier), Sam Brown belt, collar, neckband, headband, fillet, ribbon

VERBS

11 **connect**, link, join, conjoin, unite, unify, merge, couple, fasten, attach, interconnect, interweave, entwine, entangle, lace, braid, plait, knot, lash, bind, ligate, bandage, tie, stitch, sew, tack, zip (up), snap (US), button (up), buckle, hook, clip, pin, nail, staple, peg, rivet, screw, skewer, bolt, hinge, stick, bond, glue, tape, bracket, bridge, graft

12 **bind**, tie, chain, fetter, shackle, yoke, harness, leash, tether, lasso, manacle, handcuff, secure, lock, bolt, latch, padlock, batten, clamp, clasp, grip, moor, anchor

13 **intercommunicate**, communicate, contact, meet, liaise, network, interface, associate, relate, cohere, adhere, stick together, involve, entangle, form an alliance, pair up, match

ADJECTIVES

14 **connective**, conjunctive, cohesive, adhesive, sticky, interconnective, communicative, in contact, liaising, associated, related, joint, coherent

15 **connected**, tied, linked, joined, united, merged, coupled, interfaced, fastened, attached, interconnected, interwoven, entangled, laced, braided, plaited, knotted, lashed, bound, stitched, sewn, tacked, zipped

(up), buttoned (up), buckled, hooked, wired (up), pinned, nailed, stapled, pegged, riveted, screwed, hinged, stuck, bonded, glued, bracketed, hyphenated, bridged

16 **bound**, tied, chained, fettered, shackled, yoked, harnessed, leashed, tethered, lassoed, manacled, handcuffed, secured, locked, bolted, latched, padlocked, battened, clamped, clasped, gripped

ADVERBS

17 **in connection with**, connectively, in relation to (or with), jointly, conjunctively, cohesively, adhesively, with a rope, with a hook, with a pin, with a lock, securely

138 Adhesion

NOUNS

1 **adhesion**, adhesiveness, holding together, sticking (together), cohesion, cohesiveness, attachment, bonding, connection, connectedness, linkage, continuity, coherence, unity, stickiness, cementation, agglutination, conglutination, soldering, welding, agglomeration, conglomeration, consolidation, congealment, condensation, concentration, compaction, inseparability, indivisibility, birds of a feather

▶ *135 Union, 137 Connection, 371 Density, 140 Combination, 161 Assembly, 159 Consecutiveness*

2 **tenacity**, tenaciousness, pertinacious, perseverance, persistence, determination, endurance, stubbornness, obstinacy, headstrongness, bull-headedness, holding on, attachment, adherence, loyalty, fidelity, stick-to-itiveness (US inf)

▶ *378 Toughness, 726 Retention*

3 **adhesive**, glue, superglue, fish glue, gum, birdlime, lime, epoxy resin, fixative, paste, size, clay, lute (or luting), cement, putty, mortar, plaster, grout, sealing wax, solder, flypaper, sticky tape, masking tape, Scotch tape, Sellotape, Blu-tack, sticking plaster, adhesive tape (US), Elastoplast, Band-Aid (US), magnet

4 **adherent**, sticky label, decal, stamp, barnacle, limpet, remora, leech, parasite, bur, brier, bramble, clinging vine, gum, chewing gum, toffee, taffy (US), treacle, molasses (US)

5 **follower**, disciple, apostle, adherent, supporter, suitor, fan, satellite, dependent, parasite, hanger-on, clinger, sycophant, sucker (Inf), sponger (Inf), clinging vine (US inf), groupie (Sl)

VERBS

6 **adhere**, cohere, hang together, hold together, grow together, hold, hold fast, bunch, bunch up, bunch together, close ranks, stand side by side, stand shoulder to shoulder, sit cheek by jowl, stick, stick close(ly), stick to-

gether, grip, clasp, grasp, take hold of, hug, embrace, squeeze, cling to, twine around, close with, grapple with, clinch, fit, fit tight(ly), fit like a glove, mould the figure, stick like glue, stick onto, cleave to, come (or rub) off on, freeze onto, stick like a leech, stick like a limpet, cling like ivy, condense, coagulate, solidify, consolidate, agglomerate, conglomerate, freeze

7 **cause to adhere**, stick, stick to, affix to, stick together, hold together, gum, glue, superglue, agglutinate, conglutinate, paste, lute, cement, weld, solder, braze, unite, join

8 **be tenacious**, persevere, adhere, hold on, hang on, stick to, cling to, attach oneself to, hold on like a bulldog, show loyalty to

ADJECTIVES

9 **adhesive**, adherent, coherent, cohesive, connective, sessile, sticky, gummy, tacky, gluey, viscous, viscid, colloidal, dense, condensed, concentrated, compact, solid, congealed, coagulated, concrete, indivisible, infrangible, inseparable, inextricable, linked, bonded, cemented, close, side-by-side, shoulder-to-shoulder, cheek-by-jowl, close-fitting, close-packed, continuous, tight, clinging, figure-hugging, moulding, skintight

10 **tenacious**, pertinacious, persevering, persistent, determined, enduring, stubborn, obstinate, bull-headed, attached, loyal, faithful, supportive, stick-to-itive (US inf), dependent, parasitic, sycophantic, clingy (Inf)

ADVERBS

11 **cohesively**, unitedly, in unison, coherently, indivisibly, solidly, compactly, densely, concretely, inseparably, inextricably, tightly, side-by-side, closely, shoulder-to-shoulder, cheek-by-jowl, stickily, viscously, like a limpet, like ivy

12 **tenaciously**, pertinaciously, persistently, determinedly, enduringly, stubbornly, obstinately, loyally, faithfully, parasitically, sycophantically

139 Nonadhesion

NOUNS

1 **nonadhesion**, noncohesion, noncoherence, incoherence, noncombination, separation, separability, immiscibility, lack of unity, non-uniformity, lack of order, disorder, confusion, chaos, entropy, looseness, bagginess, floppiness, uncondensed state, wateriness, runniness, liquid, liquidity, fluidity, lack of viscosity, slipperiness, frangibility, fragileness, crumbliness, friability, atomization

▶ *160 Discontinuity, 162 Dispersion, 136 Separation, 387 Fluid*

2 **aloofness**, privacy, discreteness, separateness, independence, freedom, isolation, seclusion, solitude, unsociability

▶ *700 Liberation, 168 Nonconformity*

3 **nonadhesive thing**, nonadherent, nonstick frying pan, Teflon (Tm), slick tyre, used stamp

4 **individualist**, nonconformist, dissenter, one's own man, free spirit, independent, bohemian, maverick, eccentric, separatist, isolationist, hermit, ascetic, anchorite, monk, nun, lone wolf, loner (Inf)

VERBS

5 **unstick**, unglue, peel off, unpeel, pull off, pull apart, detach, unfasten, unpin, undo, free, loose, loosen, separate, knock off, shake off, unseat, isolate

6 **come unstuck**, come off, fall off, drop off, peel off, come undone, liquefy, melt, thaw, run, become runny, come adrift, totter, tumble, dangle, flap, flop, wave, rock

7 **be aloof**, stay alone, seek privacy, separate from, seek solitude, go into seclusion, hide, resign one's membership, become unsociable, keep oneself to oneself, mind one's own business

ADJECTIVES

8 **nonadhesive**, nonadhering, noncohesive, immiscible, decomposed, broken up, frangible, fragile, noncoherent, uncombined, unconnected, incoherent, not held together, not sticky, nonstick, dry, smooth, slippery, unconsolidated, loose, undone, friable, crumbly, like grains of sand, free, wide-ranging, not closely packed, not stuck on, lax, slack, relaxed, loose-fitting, baggy, flapping, flapping in the breeze, flopping, floppy, dangling, hanging, peeling off, pulling off, pendulous, waving, flying, streaming, running, runny, watery, liquid, fluid

9 **aloof**, private, discrete, separate, independent, free, isolated, unassimilated, secluded, solitary, unsociable, antisocial

ADVERBS

10 **noncohesively**, without adhesion, noncoherently, incoherently, fragilely, loosely, in a loose manner, laxly, baggily, pendulously, like a pendulum, liquidly, fluidly, immiscibly

11 **aloofly**, privately, in private, discretely, with discretion, separately, alone, independently, without help, freely, in seclusion, in isolation, solitarily, at large, without assimilation, unsociably

140 Combination

NOUNS

1 **combination**, combining, joining together, growing together, symphysis, symbiosis, synthesis, bringing together, composition, fusion, coalescence, conflation, blending, blend, mingling, mixing, mixture, mix, syncretism, amalgamation, merger, unification, uniting,

assimilation, absorption, digestion, integration, embodiment, incorporation, centralization, coincidence, concurrence, conjunction, synchronicity
▶ *135 Union, 133 Mixture*

2 **cooperation**, collaboration, concurrence, conjunction, synchronization, union, coagency, alliance, league, marriage, federation, confederation, confederacy, association, plot, conspiracy, cabal, agreement, unity, concord, harmony, chord, counterpoint, music, orchestration, jigsaw, mosaic, tessellation, collage, patchwork
▶ *664 Cooperation, 135 Union, 116 Accord, 667 Agreement, 592 Plan, 49 Music, 198 Same Time*

3 **assembly**, assemblage, collection, set, compendium, anthology, aggregation, aggregate, agglomeration, conglomeration, conglomerate, combine, syndicate, consortium, bloc, corporation, company, society, association, club, party, force, army, regiment, brigade, division, squadron, air squadron, wing, flotilla, fleet, team, group, grouping, pressure group, rock group, pop group, band, wind band, brass band, orchestra, symphony orchestra, chamber orchestra, duo, dynamic duo, duet, trio, quartet, string quartet, quintet, sextet, septet, octet, nonet, chorus, choir, congregation, audience
▶ *161 Assembly, 152 Arrangement, 562 Summary, 665 Party, 17 Military Affairs, 49 Music*

4 **compound**, mixture, suspension, solution, blend, alloy, amalgam, composite, make-up, hybrid, cocktail, portmanteau word
▶ *133 Mixture*

VERBS

5 **combine**, join together, unite, fit together, put together, assemble, make up, compose, synthesize, integrate, fuse, merge, coalesce, consolidate, grow together, run together, converge, have an affinity, blend, mingle, commingle, mix, mix together, syncretize, mix with water, add water, dilute, hydrate, interweave, intertwine, network, connect, join, conjoin, link, conjugate, yoke, centralize, unify, incorporate, embody, impregnate, imbue, infuse, instil, inoculate, inculcate, absorb, digest, assimilate, soak up, take in with one's mother's milk, amalgamate, pool, collect, heap up, lay up, store, aggregate, congregate, compound, lump together, bracket together, group, regroup, rally, bring together
▶ *135 Union, 133 Mixture, 130 Addition, 354 Insertion*

6 **come together**, band together, brigade, associate, partner, go into partnership with, league with, federate, confederate, join hands, join forces with, team up with, cooperate, come to an agreement, agree, concur, make a pact, make an alliance, ally, collaborate, act

together, harmonize, synchronize, make friends with, fraternize, bond, cement a relationship, marry, wed, mate, couple, copulate, put heads together, conspire, plot
▶ *161 Assembly, 665 Party, 667 Agreement, 116 Accord, 664 Cooperation, 592 Plan, 815 Sociability, 819 Friendship, 823 Marriage, 245 Reproduction*

ADJECTIVES

7 **combined**, combinatory, combinative, integrated, fused, composed, blended, mingled, mixed, syncretic, harmonized, interwoven, intertwined, networked, connected, joined, joint, conjugate, conjoined, conjoint, yoked, linked, united, unified, centralized, incorporated, embodied, bred into, bred in the bone, inbred, ingrained, impregnated, absorbed, digested, coalescent, symphystic

8 **cooperative**, symbiotic, in agreement, in harmony, harmonious, on the same wavelength, associated, in association, orchestrated, leagued, in league, conspiratorial, cabbalistic, in partnership, allied, federated, confederate, coagent, concurrent, synchronized, synchronous, coincident, conjunctive
▶ *135 Union, 133 Mixture, 667 Agreement, 116 Accord, 198 Same Time*

9 **assembled**, collected, heaped up, congregated, aggregated, amalgamated, merged, collective, aggregate, conglomerate, associative, congregational
▶ *161 Assembly*

ADVERBS

10 **in combination**, in concert, in league (with), in partnership (with), jointly, cooperatively, harmoniously, conspiratorially, cabbalistically, collectively, associatively, congregationally, concurrently, coincidentally, synchronously, symbiotically, syncretically, together, as one

141 Disintegration

NOUNS

1 **disintegration**, breakup, disorder, chaos, disturbance, derangement, explosion, collapse, wear, wear and tear, erosion, death, decomposition, corruption, corrosion, rust, decay, mould, mouldering, fungus, rot, rotting, compost, putrefaction, mortification, necrosis, gangrene, caries, adipocere, grave-wax, carrion
▶ *151 Disorder, 153 Disturbance, 628 Deterioration, 397 Death*

2 **deconstruction**, demolition, destruction, breakdown, taking apart, dismantling, decentralization, devolution, delegation, demerging, demerger, regionalization, compartmentation, compartmentalization, division, partition, disunion, separation, dispersal, scatter-

ing, dissolution, melting, liquefaction, deliquescence, reduction, simplification, resolution, analysis, parsing, syllabification, dissection, dismemberment, anatomization, electrolysis, hydrolysis, catalysis, photolysis, catabolism, atom-smashing, fission, nuclear fission, atomization

▶ *244 Destruction, 136 Separation, 162 Dispersion, 5 Linguistics, 56 Physics, 57 Chemistry*

VERBS

3 disintegrate, come apart, come to pieces, break up, break down, collapse, fall apart, fall to pieces, go to pieces, explode, blow up, smash to pieces, shatter, splinter, crumble, decompose, corrupt, corrode, rust, perish, decay, moulder, rot, rot down, putrefy, mortify, gangrene, necrose, consume, waste away, erode, wear away, wear out

▶ *136 Separation, 628 Deterioration*

4 deconstruct, demolish, pull down, wreck, smash, break up, destroy, unsettle, disorder, cause chaos, disturb, derange, pull apart, pull to pieces, take apart, take to pieces, dismantle, disband, decentralize, devolve, delegate, demerge, regionalize, compartmentalize, partition, divide, disperse, scatter, dissolve, melt, liquefy, deliquesce, reduce, simplify, unscramble, resolve, decompound, separate, separate out, break down, analyse, parse, syllabify, dissect, dismember, electrolyse, hydrolyse, catalyse, split, fission, atomize

▶ *244 Destruction, 151 Disorder, 153 Disturbance, 136 Separation, 162 Dispersion, 5 Linguistics, 56 Physics, 57 Chemistry*

ADJECTIVES

5 disintegrated, in pieces, in bits, smashed, shattered, destroyed, demolished, uncombined, chaotic, disordered, broken down, dissolved, melted, molten, liquefied, separated, curdled, decomposed, deconstructed, high, well hung, bad, off, rotted, rotten, putrid, rancid, sour, gangrenous, corrupted, decayed, composted, mouldering, rusty, corroded, dilapidated, ruined, in ruins, decomposable, compostable, biodegradable, recyclable, disposable

▶ *244 Destruction, 136 Separation, 628 Deterioration*

6 disintegrating, crumbling, falling apart, tumbledown, dilapidated, decomposing, rotting, decaying, melting, deliquescent, catabolic, gangrenous, necrotic, rusty, corroding

ADVERBS

7 to pieces, to bits, to smithereens, in parts, partitively, analytically, on (*or* by) analysis, electrolytically, hydrolytically, catalytically, photolytically, catabolically

8 destructively, divisively, separately, reductively, explosively, corrosively, chaotically, disturbingly, necrotically, gangrenously, putridly

142 Whole

NOUNS

1 whole, wholeness, totality, integrality, integrity, integration, fullness, completeness, indivisibility, oneness, unity, universality, generality, holism, holistic approach, comprehensiveness, inclusiveness, generalization

▶ *144 Completeness, 164 Generality*

2 whole thing, entity, whole number, integer, unit, entirety, Gestalt, totality, sum, total sum, sum total, summation, total, aggregate, corpus, complete works, complex, ensemble, system, four corners of the Earth, world, globe, universe, cosmos, macrocosm, microcosm, *Lebensraum* (Ger), life space

▶ *174 One, 140 Combination*

3 whole situation, grand design, full view, grand view, panorama, bird's-eye view, overview, survey, conspectus, synopsis, world view, world picture, full course, circuit, lap, round

▶ *435 Vision, 363 Orbital Motion*

4 all, everything, everybody, everyone, one and all, everyone and everything, everything but the kitchen sink, the world, the whole world, all the world, the world and his wife, the whole, the aggregate, the total, the lot, the whole lot, *le tout ensemble* (Fr), the gross amount, one hundred per cent, Alpha and Omega, be-all and end-all, the rough with the smooth, the length and breadth, the sum and substance

▶ *181 Multitude, 161 Assembly, 164 Generality*

5 unit, family, ensemble, set, complete set, series, pack, kit, outfit, inventory, full list, complete list, whole list, rind, pips, and all, the whole caboodle (Inf), the whole kit and caboodle (Inf), the whole bang shoot (Inf), the whole shooting match (Inf), the whole shebang (Sl)

▶ *171 List, 140 Combination*

ADJECTIVES

6 whole, integral, total, holistic, general, universal, complete, full, integrated, unified, all, every, any, each, individual, single, one, in one piece, all of a piece, all-inclusive, comprehensive, fully comprehensive, gross, all-embracing, across-the-board, global, worldwide, international

▶ *164 Generality, 144 Completeness, 174 One, 146 Inclusion*

7 uncut, entire, unabridged, unexpurgated, undivided, undiminished, unbroken, intact, unharmed, unscathed, unhurt, uninjured, undamaged, unimpaired, unspoiled, unadulterated, uncontaminated, untouched, inviolate, virgin, pure, faultless, flawless, perfect

▶ *144 Completeness, 134 Purity, 619 Perfection*

8 sound, sound in wind and limb, able-bodied,

strong, fit, well, healthy, in good health, hale, hale and hearty, in fine fettle, recovered, fully restored, better

▶ *623 Health, 629 Repair*

VERBS

9 **be whole**, form a whole, unite, unify, integrate, total, sum up, add up to, amount to, come to, number, comprise, embrace, encompass

▶ *135 Union, 169 Number*

10 **complete**, fulfill, succeed, accomplish, reach one's goal, achieve (one's purpose), leave no loose ends, bring to a head, culminate, climax, take to the limit, carry through, finish (off), polish off (Inf), round off, end, finalize, perfect, put the finishing touches on, put the icing on the cake

▶ *684 Completion*

ADVERBS

11 **wholly**, entirely, integrally, holistically, completely, body and soul, heart and soul, totally, utterly, absolutely, fully, every bit, every inch, pound for pound, in every respect, without exception, without exemption, one hundred per cent, universally, *in toto* (L), hook, line, and sinker, lock, stock, and barrel, root and branch, rind, pips, and all

12 **one and all**, as a whole, as a team, as a group, as a unit, comprehensively, collectively, all together, corporately, bodily, and all, in sum, altogether, in the aggregate, in the mass, in bulk, *en masse* (Fr), *en bloc* (Fr)

13 **on the whole**, generally, in general, all in all, by and large, as a rule, predominantly, mostly, for the most part, mainly, in the main, largely, taking everything into consideration, all things considered, when all is said and done, in all truth, essentially, in essence, altogether, quite, substantially, in substance, virtually, practically, almost, nearly, all but, to all intents and purposes, as far as one can tell, in effect, effectively, as good as

▶ *164 Generality, 103 Essence, 264 Nearness*

143 Part

NOUNS

1 **part**, fragment, small fragment, particle, portion, proportion, certain proportion, majority, minority, fraction, half, moiety, third, quarter, eighth, tenth, tithe, percentage, aliquot, aliquant, divisor, factor, quotient, dividend, share, whack (Inf), quota, remainder, balance, surplus, element, better element, worse element, faction, class, subclass, category, subcategory, group, subgroup, family, subfamily, genus, subgenus, species, subspecies, phylum, division, subdivision, segment, sector, arc, curve, semicircle, hemisphere, partition, compartment, department, ward, community,

parish, district, county, region, area

▶ *173 Fraction, 132 Remainder, 136 Separation, 731 Allocation, 665 Party, 163 Class, 161 Assembly, 152 Arrangement, 249 Region*

2 **particular**, detail, item, article, chapter, episode, instalment, fascicule (*or* fascicle), part, number, issue, edition, canto, verse, section, subsection, paragraph, sentence, clause, coordinate clause, subordinate clause, phrase, word, part of speech, page, folio, sheet, leaf, volume, passage, quotation, citation, sound bite, gobbet, extract, text, part payment, down payment, deposit, tranche, advance, earnest, earnest of good faith, foretaste, preview, appetizer, sample, example, quote (Inf)

▶ *532 Publication, 746 Payment*

3 **stage**, phase, leg, lap, round, heat

▶ *187 Period*

4 **component**, constituent, ingredient, particle, element, molecule, member, appendage, organ, feeler, antenna, limb, hindlimb, leg, foot, forelimb, hand, arm, forearm, wing, flipper, fin, privates, private parts

▶ *148 Component*

5 **largest part**, principal part, main part, main body, the main, chief part, greater part, major part, ninety-nine per cent, bulk, mass, majority, vast majority, lion's share, biggest slice of the cake, essential part, the essentials, bare essentials, nuts and bolts, gist, summary, almost all, nearly all, all but, all but the kitchen sink, best part, best bit, nitty-gritty (Inf), the long and the short of it (Inf)

▶ *611 Importance, 181 Multitude, 103 Essence, 562 Summary*

6 **branch**, subbranch, offshoot, ramification, flower head, petal, sepal, stamen, anther, calyx, tendril, leaf, leaflet, shoot, switch, scion, sucker, sprig, spray, slip, foliage, bough, limb, spur, twig, stem, stalk, trunk, bole, stump, torso

7 **piece**, bit, segment, section, patch, insertion, interpolation, addition, length, roll, swatch, scrap, offcut, rag, shred, wisp, speck, morsel, bite, crust, crumb, sliver, splinter, snip, snippet, chip, cut, slice, tranche, wedge, finger, rasher, cutlet, collop, chop, steak, gobbet, chunk, hunk, lump, slab, bar, block, mass, heap, tump (Dial), clod, sod, turf, divot, shard, sherd, potsherd, flake, scale, drop, dose, portion, helping, piece of land, allotment, parcel, wodge (Inf), dollop (Inf), smidgin (Inf)

▶ *274 Thinness, 266 Layer, 130 Addition, 354 Insertion, 731 Allocation*

8 **bits and pieces**, bits and bobs, miscellanea, oddments, flotsam and jetsam, *disjecta membra* (L), bin ends, shavings, filings, swarf, clippings, parings, peelings, leavings, rubble,

trash, detritus, moraine, debris, rags, tatters, odds and ends, odds and sods (Inf)

▶ *607 Waste, 132 Remainder*

9 **participation**, role, character, duty, responsibility, function

▶ *51 Performing Arts, 847 Duty*

VERBS

10 **part**, divide, subdivide, share, apportion, cut up, dissect, segment, sectionalize, compartmentalize, partition, separate, split, bisect, sever, fragment, dismantle, break, break up

▶ *136 Separation, 731 Allocation, 141 Disintegration*

ADJECTIVES

11 **partial**, part, not whole, broken, fragmented, fragmentary, in bits, in pieces, in smithereens, brashy, crumbly, incomplete, with bits missing, armless, legless, limbless, headless, imperfect, inadequate, insufficient, scrappy, bitty, piecemeal, unfinished, half-finished, fractional, aliquot, proportional, proportionate, partitive, segmental, sectional, compartmental, departmental, divided, molecular, atomic, elemental, departmentalized, compartmentalized, sectionalized, sliced, diced, minced, ground, shredded, wispy

▶ *136 Separation, 145 Incompleteness, 620 Imperfection, 609 Insufficiency, 173 Fraction*

ADVERBS

12 **partly**, in part, in some measure, to some extent, to a certain extent, to a (*or* some) degree, a little, a bit, somewhat, quasi, slightly, moderately, partially, half, half and half, fractionally, not wholly, not fully, incompletely, inadequately, scrappily, piecemeal, part by part, bit by bit, little by little, a little at a time, in (*or* by) instalments, in dribs and drabs, by fits and starts, drop by drop, by degrees, gradually, in parts, in detail, in lots, part for part, proportionally, proportionately, pro rata

144 Completeness

NOUNS

1 **completeness**, finished state, nothing lacking, nothing missing, nothing to add, sufficiency, self-sufficiency, entirety, totality, wholeness, unity, integrality, universality, comprehensiveness, solidarity, solidity, balance, harmony, concord, fulfilment, consummation, finishing touch, final touch, last touch, icing on the cake, finish, the end, the limit, *ne plus ultra* (L), the utmost, summit, peak, zenith, culmination, ideal, perfection, the whole hog (Inf)

▶ *142 Whole, 608 Sufficiency, 157 End, 116 Accord, 279 Summit, 619 Perfection*

2 **fullness**, plenitude, pregnancy, capacity, full capacity, full size, full length, full extent, full volume, full value, maximum, saturation, saturation point, satiety, repletion, filling, refilling, replenishment, refill, filling up, brimming, overfilling, overflowing, overflow, overfulfilment, full complement, full crew, requisite number, quorum, quota, full quota, full house, full load, full measure, bumper, brimmer, bellyful, skinful (Sl), makeweight, complement, supplement, fill-up, compensation

▶ *608 Sufficiency, 610 Excess, 130 Addition, 125 Compensation*

3 **completion**, completing, end, ending, finish, finishing, finishing off, finalization, close, conclusion, termination, expiration, culmination, attainment, accomplishment, achievement, fulfilment, consummation, realization, fruition, topping-out ceremony

▶ *157 End, 684 Completion*

VERBS

4 **complete**, make complete, make into a whole, integrate, unite, join, make whole, complement, supplement, eke out, fill a gap, fill a need, fill in, fill out, build up, make up, construct, piece together, compose, do, perform, execute, discharge, fulfil, realize, accomplish, achieve, do thoroughly, leave nothing out (*or* undone), have nothing to add, leave nothing to chance, carry through, carry out, carry out to the full, carry out to the letter, crown, cap, overfulfil, overdo, put the icing on the cake, put the finishing touch (*or* touches) to, finalize, perfect, finish, end, terminate, close, conclude, round off, wrap up (Inf)

▶ *135 Union, 140 Combination, 243 Production, 640 Action, 619 Perfection, 684 Completion, 157 End*

5 **be complete**, make a whole, have everything, have it all, say it all, reach (*or* touch) perfection, climax, culminate, come to an end, come to a close, end, finish, close, terminate, have enough, want (*or* lack) nothing, become complete, fill out, develop fully, reach full growth, become grown-up, become adult, reach maturity, realize one's potential, be full (*or* filled), brim with, overflow, run over, slop over, bulge, swell, have one's fill, eat (*or* drink) one's fill

▶ *608 Sufficiency, 610 Excess, 157 End, 684 Completion, 261 Expansion*

6 **fill**, refill, replenish, fill up, top up, top off, satisfy, sate, saturate, overfill, soak, drench, overwhelm, swamp, drown, pervade, suffuse, fill to capacity, cram, jam, stuff, bloat, pack in, pile in, pile on, ram in, ram down, squeeze in, pack, stow, load, charge, lade, freight, stock, supply, fill a space (*or* gap), cover, occupy, line, spread over, extend (*or* reach) to, overrun

▶ *765 Satisfaction, 606 Provision, 257 Contents, 354 Insertion, 293 Covering, 253 Presence*

ADJECTIVES

7 **complete**, entire, integral, intact, unbroken,

unimpaired, undivided, individual, united, self-contained, self-sufficient, whole, plenary, quorate, sufficient, adequate, effective, effectual, lacking nothing, all there, unexpurgated, unabridged, uncut, unabbreviated, all-in, all-inclusive, all-embracing, comprehensive, absolute, utter, total, exhaustive, full-scale, detailed, thorough, thoroughgoing, all-out, wholesale, sweeping, unconfined, unrestricted, unlimited, unqualified, plain, plumb, downright, pure, unadulterated, out-and-out, unmitigating, unmitigated, dyed-in-the-wool, consummate, full-blown, full-grown, fully grown, full-fledged, fully fledged, mature, perfect, faultless, perfected, finished, accomplished, achieved, compleat (Arch), crowning, culminating, supplementary, complementary, finalized, ended, concluded, closed, terminated, over, done

▶ *142 Whole, 174 One, 608 Sufficiency, 134 Purity, 619 Perfection, 684 Completion*

8 **full**, filled, refilled, replenished, replete, satisfied, topped up, topped off, full up, filled up, well-filled, well-stocked, well-lined, bulging, brimming, brimful, full to the brim, level with, flush, overfilled, overfull, overflowing, full to overflowing, running over, slopping over, oozing, leaking, swamped, overwhelmed, drowned, saturated, coming out of one's ears, full to bursting, bursting at the seams, stuffed, gorged, sickened with, up to here with, sated, satiated, chock-full, chock-a-block, no room to spare, no room to turn round, no room to swing a cat, crowded, congested, solid, crop-full, cram-full, crammed, packed, packed like sardines, jammed, jam-packed, tight, jammed tight, loaded, laden, fully laden, overloaded, heavy-laden, freighted, fraught, fully charged, all seats taken, standing room only, sold out, full of, stiff with, seething with, teeming with, jumping with, alive with, lousy with, crawling with, infested, overrun, rolling in, dripping with, fit to bust (Inf)

▶ *608 Sufficiency, 610 Excess, 181 Multitude*

ADVERBS

9 **completely**, entirely, wholly, totally, absolutely, utterly, quite, thoroughly, clean, plain, plumb, downright, perfectly, in every way, in all, in all respects, on all counts, outright, stark, hollow, unequivocally, unconditionally, root and branch, neck and crop, all round, all around, all the way, heart and soul, body and soul, head over heels, solidly, *en masse* (Fr), *en bloc* (Fr), all in all, *in toto* (L), all told, from wall to wall, from A to Z, from first to last, throughout, from beginning to end, from end to end, from one end to the other, the length and breadth of, from sea to sea, from sea to shining sea, from coast to coast, from Land's End to John o' Groats, from the four points of the compass, from the four corners of the world, from far and near, (from) far and wide, high and low, fore and aft, from stem to stern, from top to bottom, from top to toe, from head to foot, altogether, hook, line, and sinker, lock, stock, and barrel, rind, pips, and all, warts and all

▶ *142 Whole, 263 Distance, 271 Breadth*

10 **fully**, in full, every inch, every whit, to capacity, to the maximum, as … as can be, as … as possible, to the utmost, to the top of one's bent, (up) to the hilt, up to the neck, up to the ears, up to the eyes, to the full, to the brim, to the top, over the top, with knobs on, with a vengeance, with all the trimmings, and then some, through and through, to the heart, to the marrow, to the core, (down) to the quick, (down) to the ground, full out, at full stretch, through thick and thin, to the last breath, to the last man, for good, for good and all, for ever, to the end, to the bitter end, to the end of the chapter, to the end of the road, to the end of the line

145 Incompleteness

NOUNS

1 **incompleteness**, partialness, partiality, defectiveness, deficiency, falling short, insufficiency, poverty, scantness, scantiness, inadequacy, lack, want, need, ineffectiveness, ineffectuality, imperfection, unfinished state, interrupted state, unpreparedness, unreadiness, under-development, unripeness, immaturity, rawness, roughness, sketchiness, scrappiness, bittiness, hollowness, superficiality, insubstantiality, perfunctoriness, half-heartedness, negligence, default, arrears, non-completion, nonfulfilment, broken state, mutilation, impairment, nonsatisfaction, dissatisfaction

▶ *143 Part, 609 Insufficiency, 358 Shortfall, 620 Imperfection, 595 Lack of Preparation, 685 Non-completion, 766 Dissatisfaction*

2 **omission**, gap, lacuna, void, interval, break, breakage, missing link, loss, deficit, lack, want, need, deficiency, insufficiency, shortfall, slippage, ullage, defalcation, arrears, default, part missing, screw loose, a few sandwiches short of a picnic (Inf), not sixteen ounces to the pound (Inf), not the full pound (*or* shilling) note (Inf)

▶ *265 Interval, 160 Discontinuity, 620 Imperfection, 609 Insufficiency, 358 Shortfall, 722 Loss, 147 Exclusion*

3 **incomplete thing**, part, fraction, proportion, part payment instalment, sketch, draft, rough, embryo

▶ *143 Part, 746 Payment*

ADJECTIVES

4 **incomplete**, defective, deficient, scant, scanty, skimpy, short, insufficient, inadequate, ineffective, ineffectual, like Hamlet without the Prince, missing, omitting, lacking, wanting, needing, in need of, requiring, short of, shy of, shortened, abbreviated, abridged, truncated, curtailed, cropped, docked, lopped, maimed, mutilated, mangled, lame, limping, halting, marred, spoiled, impaired, garbled, broken, fragmentary, eyeless, legless, armless, limbless, one-armed, one-legged, one-eyed, unsatisfactory, blemished, stained, flawed, imperfect, half, partial, unfinished, not finished, going on, continuing, developing, in progress, in the pipeline, on the stocks, begun, in embryo, in preparation, left unfinished, half-finished, half-done, neglected, uncompleted, under-developed, undeveloped, unprepared, unready, unripe, immature, raw, underdone, undercooked, rude, rough, crude, rough-hewn, sketchy, scrappy, bitty, thin, poor, meagre, hollow, superficial, insubstantial, perfunctory, half-hearted, left hanging, left in the air, interrupted, omitted, lost, missed, *manqué* (Fr), in default, defaulting in arrears, not up to date, not all there

▶ *609 Insufficiency, 358 Shortfall, 593 Requirement, 270 Shortness, 620 Imperfection, 685 Noncompletion, 143 Part, 470 Negligence, 747 Nonpayment*

VERBS

5 **be incomplete**, need, want, be wanting, lack, be lacking, miss, fall short, skimp on, give a lick and a promise (Inf), fail to fulfil, default, leave undone, begin, sketch, draft, rough (out), leave unfinished, not complete, interrupt, leave hanging, leave dangling, leave in the air, neglect, omit, miss out, exclude

▶ *609 Insufficiency, 358 Shortfall, 620 Imperfection, 685 Noncompletion, 470 Negligence, 147 Exclusion, 156 Beginning, 594 Preparation*

ADVERBS

6 **incompletely**, partially, partly, in part, in (or by) instalments, by halves, half, insufficiently, poorly, inadequately, ineffectually, ineffectively, deficiently, insubstantially, scantily, roughly, embryonically, sketchily, superficially, scrappily, crudely, improperly, in default, negligently, neglectfully, in arrears, without, minus

146   Inclusion

NOUNS

1 **inclusion**, enclosure, encirclement, encapsulation, containment, comprisal, comprehension, involvement, implication, concern, reception, admission, admittance, admissibility, elegibility, participation, membership, presence, accommodation, room, space, capacity, volume, inclusiveness, coverage, full coverage, blanket coverage, wall-to-wall coverage, global approach, universality, generality, versatility, comprehensiveness, no exception, no omission, nothing left out, set, full set, complete set, package, package deal, complement, full complement, full quota, allowance, comprising, composition, composing, construction, make-up, constitution, constituting, incorporation, integration, embodiment

▶ *301 Enclosure, 348 Admittance, 253 Presence, 248 Space, 164 Generality, 142 Whole, 144 Completeness, 243 Production*

2 **thing included**, inclusion, enclosure, ingredient, constituent, factor, additive, appurtenance, feature, component, component part, item, element, part, piece, bit, contents

3 **person included**, insider, participant, member, brother, sister, one of us, co-worker, staff member, staff, crew member, crew, team, workforce, complement, company, personnel, citizen

▶ *148 Component, 143 Part, 257 Contents, 130 Addition, 646 Worker*

VERBS

4 **include**, contain, hold, have, enclose, encircle, envelop, encapsulate, comprehend, involve, implicate, embrace, cover, encompass, take in, receive, admit, find room for, find space for, accommodate, count, number, boast, take into account, take into consideration, allow for, take account of, take cognizance of, recognize, allow (of), admit of, consist of, comprise, compose, be made up of, incorporate, integrate, embody, constitute, mean

▶ *258 Container, 723 Possession, 301 Enclosure, 730 Receiving, 348 Admittance, 142 Whole, 144 Completeness*

5 **be included**, be one of, be part of, make up, belong, enter into, become involved with, be mixed up in, be implicated in, participate, take part, share, merge, belong to, appertain to, pertain to, relate to

▶ *107 Relatedness, 723 Possession, 724 Joint Possession*

6 **subsume**, place under, count with, reckon among, number with, enumerate with, class with, classify as, categorize as (or with), enter, list, enter as, put in, put among, arrange in, add to

▶ *163 Class, 152 Arrangement, 130 Addition, 354 Insertion*

ADJECTIVES

7 **including**, inclusive, containing, holding, accommodating, having, allowing, considering, counting, consisting of, comprising, composed of, made up of, incorporating, incorporative, all-in, all-inclusive, all-embracing,

comprehensive, wholesale, blanket, extensive, widespread, across-the-board, wall-to-wall, sweeping, global, worldwide, universal, expansive, broad-based, covering, umbrella, overall, general, encyclopedic, nonexclusive, nondiscriminatory, without exception, without omission

▶ *142 Whole, 144 Completeness, 164 Generality*

8 **included**, built-in, integrated, unsegregated, unseparated, constituent, component, part of, part and parcel of, inherent, intrinsic, belonging, pertinent, pertaining, appurtenant, admissible, admitted, allowed, eligible, in the same class, in the same league, classed with, classified with, related, akin, congenerous, congeneric, entered, listed, on the list, noted, recorded, added, linked, joined, combined, merged, inner, interior

▶ *148 Component, 723 Possession, 348 Admittance, 163 Class, 107 Relatedness, 140 Combination, 135 Union, 171 List, 545 Record, 290 Interior, 130 Addition, 103 Essence*

ADVERBS

9 **inclusively**, inherently, intrinsically, pertinently, as well as, comprehensively, universally, globally, generally, from A to Z, alpha to omega, et cetera, etc., and so on, and so forth, inside, within

▶ *290 Interior, 257 Contents*

147 Exclusion

NOUNS

1 **exclusion**, noninclusion, omission, suppression, rejection, refusal, denial, forbiddance, prohibition, veto, proscription, interdiction, ban, taboo, embargo, bar, exception, an exception in favour of, exemption, special case, dispensation, special dispensation, relegation, exclusion order, lockout, picket line, closed door, no entry, nonadmission, shunning, blacklisting, blacklist, blackball, limitation, circumscription, segregation, sequestration, seclusion, ghettoization, discrimination, boycott, ostracism, preclusion, pre-emption, prevention

▶ *134 Purity, 709 Veto, 711 Refusal, 581 Rejection, 848 Exemption, 493 Misjudgment, 302 Limit*

2 **ejection**, eviction, expulsion, dismissal, redundancy, firing, suspension, disqualification, disbarment, removal, riddance, deletion, cancellation, elimination, obliteration, censorship, bowdlerization, expurgation, eradication, excommunication, deportation, extradition, banishment, exile, expatriation, the sack (Inf), sacking (Inf), the heave-ho (Inf), the elbow (Inf), the big E (Inf), the push (Inf), the shove (Inf), the boot (Inf)

▶ *349 Expulsion, 546 Obliteration*

3 **exclusion zone**, ghetto, no-go area, no-

man's-land, outer darkness, the outside, pale, enclosure, dam, cofferdam, wall, fence, partition, screen, curtain, Iron Curtain, Bamboo Curtain, barricade, defensive wall, ditch, moat, rampart, barrier, customs barrier, tariff wall, economic zone, quarantine, isolation

▶ *301 Enclosure, 289 Exterior*

4 **exclusiveness**, exclusivity, restrictiveness, closed shop, private club, clique, inner circle, members only, possessiveness, sole rights, monopoly, dog-in-the-manger policy, social discrimination, apartheid, colour bar, racial discrimination, xenophobia, sexual discrimination

▶ *860 Selfishness, 481 Discrimination, 493 Misjudgment*

5 **excluded person**, nonmember, victim of discrimination, outsider, alien, odd man out, forgotten man, exile, outcast, pariah, outlaw, incomer, intruder, interloper, trespasser, burglar, invader, besieger

6 **thing excluded**, foreign body, contaminant, impurity, reject

▶ *149 Foreign Body, 104 Extraneousness*

VERBS

7 **exclude**, leave out, count out, not include, omit, miss, miss out, disregard, ignore, pass over, exempt, excuse, except, make an exception (of), treat as a special case, keep out, warn off, forbid, prohibit, disallow, veto, proscribe, interdict, ban, taboo, embargo, place under an embargo, put an embargo on, bar, suppress, stifle, relegate, put (or lay) aside, leave, give up, abandon, reject, refuse, deny, vote against, vote out, vote down, shut out, shut the door on, deny entry, spurn, blacklist, blackball, rule out, draw the line at, limit, circumscribe, enclose, wall off, fence off, screen off, curtain off, box off, segregate, discriminate against, sequester, quarantine, isolate, seclude, ghettoize, boycott, shun, cold-shoulder, send to Coventry, ostracize, preclude, forestall, pre-empt, prevent, not entertain (the possibility of), count out (Inf), include out (Inf)

▶ *848 Exemption, 709 Veto, 581 Rejection, 711 Refusal, 134 Purity, 302 Limit, 301 Enclosure*

8 **eject**, evict, expel, throw out, cast out, dismiss, make redundant, suspend, disqualify, disbar, unfrock, defrock, strike off, remove, dispense with, oust, thrust out, get rid of, take out, delete, cross out, strike out, rub out, blot out, cancel, eliminate, obliterate, censor, edit out, blue-pencil, bowdlerize, expurgate, eradicate, uproot, excommunicate, deport, extradite, banish, exile, outlaw, expatriate, sack (Inf), fire (Inf), send packing (Inf), kick out (Inf), give the elbow (or boot or push or shove) (Inf), give the big E (or heave-ho) (Inf)

▶ *349 Expulsion, 546 Obliteration*

9 **be excluded**, not belong, stay out, stay out-

side, go into exile, go into voluntary exile
▶ *289 Exterior*

ADJECTIVES

10 **excluding**, exclusive, exclusionary, exclusory, close, closed, close-knit, clannish, cliquish, cliquey, narrow, restrictive, xenophobic, racist, sexist, restricted, limited, private, elite, select, choice, unique, sole, exemptive, interdictory, prohibitive, preventive, preclusive, pre-emptive, silent about
▶ *709 Veto, 665 Party, 580 Selection, 165 Speciality*

11 **excluded**, not included, absent, missing, not counted, left out, omitted, missed out, excepted, excused, exempt, exempted, barred, banned, embargoed, forbidden, taboo, prohibited, rejected, deleted, dismissed, evicted, expelled, shut out, shunned, blackballed, blacklisted, disbarred, struck off, outcast, exiled, untold, unsaid, unrecounted, unreported, inadmissible, beyond the pale, peripheral, extra, extraneous, foreign, not considered, disregarded, out of account, not in contention, outclassed, not in the same league, out in left field (US), out in the cold, precluded, pre-empted, forestalled, prevented
▶ *254 Absence, 848 Exemption, 709 Veto, 104 Extraneousness*

ADVERBS

12 **exclusively**, narrowly, with reservations, with restrictions, outside, excluding, exclusive of, except, excepting, except for, with the exception of, bar, barring, save, not counting, ignoring, omitting, outside of, short of, apart from, let alone

148   Component

NOUNS

1 **component**, content, constituent, part, integral part, integrant, ingredient, element, aspect, feature, facet, detail, particular, factor, item, link, part and parcel
▶ *143 Part*

2 **piece**, bit, portion, part, fragment, fraction, segment, section, sector, division, subdivision, category, faction, class, branch, department, unit
▶ *143 Part*

3 **unit**, module, building block, building brick, cell, particle, molecule, atom, jigsaw piece, Meccano (Tm), Lego (Tm), spare part, basic materials

4 **components**, works, workings, mechanism, machinery, engine, innards, guts, insides (Inf)
▶ *290 Interior, 257 Contents*

5 **member**, team member, member of staff, one of, one of us, co-worker, colleague, associate, fellow, cog in the wheel
▶ *644 Worker*

ADJECTIVES

6 **component**, constituent, integral, integrant, ingredient, elemental, elementary, formative, fractional, segmental, departmental, categorical
▶ *143 Part*

7 **modular**, cellular, molecular, atomic, integral, joined, linked, fitted, built-in

8 **belonging**, appurtenant, part of, one of, essential, fundamental, intrinsic, inherent, integral, particular
▶ *103 Essence*

9 **composing**, constituting, comprising, including, inclusive of, containing, embodying, incorporating
▶ *146 Inclusion, 142 Whole*

VERBS

10 **compose**, constitute, comprise, make up, form part of, combine in, merge in, amalgamate, participate in, join, contribute
▶ *140 Combination*

11 **consist of**, comprise, contain, include, embrace, encompass, subsume, embody, incorporate, be made up of, be composed of, involve, cover
▶ *142 Whole, 146 Inclusion*

12 **be one of**, belong to, be part of, inhere, reside in, consist in
▶ *143 Part*

13 **make**, make up, construct, build, build up, erect, structure, assemble, put together, piece together, connect together, fit together, set up, compound, fabricate, fashion, form, compile, compose, knock together (Inf)
▶ *243 Production*

ADVERBS

14 **constituently**, elementally, atomically, inclusively, integrally, inherently, essentially, fundamentally, constructively, departmentally, fractionally

149   Foreign Body

NOUNS

1 **foreign body**, foreign element, foreign matter, foreign substance, extraneous element, xenolith
▶ *104 Extraneousness*

2 **impurity**, contaminant, pollutant, blemish, spot, mark, birthmark, naevus, pimple, wart, stain, speck, sliver, splinter, fragment
▶ *793 Blemish*

3 **foreignness**, alienness, extraneousness, extrinsicality, exteriority, strangeness, exoticness, exoticism
▶ *104 Extraneousness, 289 Exterior, 168 Nonconformity, 113 Diversity*

4 **foreigner**, stranger, alien, outsider, outlander, tramontane, ultramontane, barbarian
▶ *91 Countries*

5 **extraterrestrial**, alien, Martian, thing from outer space, cosmic being, little green man (Inf)
▶ *11 Occultism*

6 **immigrant**, incomer, guest, refugee, settler, tenderfoot, expatriate, foreign resident, colonial, migrant, traveller, wanderer, wandering minstrel, migrant worker, guest worker, *Gastarbeiter* (Ger)
▶ *346 Entry, 255 Inhabitant*

7 **newcomer**, new arrival, new boy, new girl, new face, apprentice, fresher (*or* freshman), *nouveau arrivé* (Fr), new kid (on the block) (Inf), Johnny come lately (Inf), greenhorn (Inf), rookie (Inf)
▶ *156 Beginning*

8 **exile**, émigré, emigrant, refugee, evacuee, outlaw
▶ *347 Exit, 252 Displacement*

9 **misfit**, odd man out, eccentric, black sheep, fish out of water, square peg in a round hole, outcast, pariah, oddball (US inf), odd (*or* queer) fish (Inf)

10 **intruder**, interloper, invader, gate-crasher, trespasser, squatter, uninvited guest, *persona non grata* (L), cuckoo in the nest, stowaway

ADJECTIVES

11 **foreign**, strange, unfamiliar, unknown, extraneous, extrinsic, alien, exotic, ethnic, outlandish, barbarian, out of place, xenolithic
▶ *104 Extraneousness, 289 Exterior, 168 Nonconformity*

12 **extraterrestrial**, alien, unearthly, supernatural, cosmic, not of this world

13 **immigrant**, incoming, foreign-born, migrant, expatriate, colonial

14 **imported**, foreign-made, not indigenous, brought in

VERBS

15 **be foreign**, be out of place, stick out like a sore thumb (Inf)

16 **migrate**, travel, roam, wander, settle, live abroad, work abroad, emigrate, immigrate, seek political asylum

17 **intrude**, interlope, invade, gate-crash, trespass, squat, stow away

ADVERBS

18 **extraneously**, exotically, extrinsically, xenolithically, extraterrestrially, cosmically, supernaturally, strangely, unfamiliarly, eccentrically

19 **abroad**, overseas, oversea, beyond seas, in foreign parts, on one's travels, from outer space

150 Order

Order is heaven's first law. Alexander Pope.

How sour sweet music is/ When time is broke and no proportion kept!/ So is it in the music of men's lives. William Shakespeare.

A place for everything, and everything in its place. Samuel Smiles.

NOUNS

1 **order**, organization, formalization, formalism, arrangement, array, disposition, layout, pattern, composition, formation, structure, setup, distribution, line-up, putting in order, prioritization, system, scheme, schedule
▶ *152 Arrangement, 382 Structure, 306 Form*

2 **grouping**, categorization, classification, codification, specification, pigeonholing, cataloguing, indexing, listing, taxonomy
▶ *163 Class*

3 **hierarchy**, pecking order, series, sequence, gradation, progression, alphabetical order, numerical order, serial order, ascending (*or* descending) order, reverse order, logical order
▶ *159 Consecutiveness, 155 Sequence*

4 **position**, place, class, grade, category, degree, rank, ranking, status, subordination
▶ *163 Class*

5 **orderliness**, state of order, tidiness, neatness, cleanness, smoothness, straightness, correctness, good condition, good trim, fine fettle, a place for everything and everything in its place, apple-pie order (Inf), good nick (Inf), (all ship-shape and) Bristol fashion (Inf)
▶ *843 Right, 621 Cleanness*

6 **methodicalness**, methodology, meticulousness, punctiliousness, accuracy, straightness, systematization, systematism, systematics, systematology
▶ *503 Accuracy*

7 **method**, system, discipline, organization, routine, custom, habit, rule, pattern, plan, scheme, structure, coherence, coordination, uniformity, regularity, symmetry, proportion
▶ *602 Means, 592 Plan, 584 Habit, 308 Symmetry, 112 Uniformity*

8 **harmony**, concord, stability, quiet, quietude, peace, peace and quiet, calm, tranquillity, stillness, quietness, detachment
▶ *116 Accord, 422 Silence, 325 Motionlessness, 4 Philosophy*

9 **discipline**, law, law and order, rule of law, control, stability
▶ *16 Law*

ADJECTIVES

10 **ordered**, organized, formalized, formal, formalistic, arranged, arrayed, disposed, composed, structured, schematic, systematic, symmetrical, balanced, ordained
▶ *152 Arrangement, 382 Structure, 308 Symmetry, 592 Plan*

11 **grouped**, categorized, categorical, classified, classificatory, codified, specified, pigeonholed, indexed, indexical, catalogued, listed
▶ *163 Class*

12 **hierarchical**, serial, sequential, gradational, taxonomic(al), progressive, alphabetical, numerical, in order, graded, ranked
▶ *159 Consecutiveness, 155 Sequence*

13 **orderly**, tidy, neat, neat and tidy, spick and span, clean, smooth, straight, correct, trim, spruce, dapper, smart, sleek, slick, groomed, well-groomed, not a hair out of place, kempt, well-kept, well-cared for, in good order, in perfect order, in good trim, in good condition, in the pink, in fine fettle, shipshape, all shipshape and Bristol fashion, neat as a button (*or* pin), dinky (Inf), in apple-pie order (Inf), in good nick (Inf)
▶ *843 Right, 621 Cleanness*

14 **well-ordered**, well-organized, methodical, meticulous, punctilious, systematic, scientific, businesslike, formal, accurate, straight, regular, uniform, coherent, intelligible
▶ *503 Accuracy, 522 Intelligibility, 112 Uniformity*

15 **habitual**, routine, usual, regular, customary
▶ *584 Habit*

16 **harmonious**, concordant, stable, steady, quiet, peaceful, calm, tranquil
▶ *116 Accord, 422 Silence, 325 Motionlessness*

17 **disciplined**, controlled, under control, restrained, lawful, law-abiding, peaceable, docile, obedient, well-behaved, well-drilled, well-regulated, according to rule, decorous, mannerly
▶ *16 Law, 694 Obedience, 673 Submission, 652 Conduct*

VERBS

18 **order**, put in order, set in order, arrange, array, dispose, lay out, organize, marshal, manage, compose, form, structure, set up, line up, align, ordain
▶ *152 Arrangement, 653 Management, 382 Structure*

19 **systematize**, methodize, rationalize, standardize, sort, sort out, sift, group, categorize, class, classify, catalogue, codify, index, pigeonhole, rank, grade, place, position, tabulate, prioritize
▶ *163 Class*

20 **harmonize**, stabilize, regularize, regulate, synchronize, accord
▶ *116 Accord*

21 **tidy**, tidy up, neaten, clean, straighten, smooth, straighten up, correct, put (*or* set) to rights, smarten up, spruce up, groom, lick (*or* knock *or* whip) into shape

22 **pacify**, calm, cool down, cool off, pour oil on troubled water, restore order, keep order, discipline, take in hand, control, govern, police, clean up, tighten up on, clamp down on
▶ *677 Pacification, 688 Authority*

23 **be in order**, be in working order, work, function, operate, go like clockwork, go
▶ *230 Operation*

24 **line up**, fall in, take one's place, queue up, place oneself, draw up, fall into place, find one's level

ADVERBS

25 **in order**, in turn, hierarchically, taxonomically, formalistically, in series, step by step, by stages, progressively, sequentially, alphabetically, numerically, according to plan

26 **orderly**, in orderly fashion, in order, neatly, tidily, just so

27 **methodically**, systematically, symmetrically, uniformly, regularly, routinely, by the book

151   Disorder

NOUNS

1 **disorder**, disorderliness, disorganization, disarrangement, disarray, derangement, disjunction, disharmony, discord, disruption, disturbance, upset, discomposure, discomfiture, disconcertedness, disintegration, incoherence, unintelligibility, confusion
▶ *153 Disturbance, 523 Unintelligibility, 141 Disintegration, 666 Disagreement*

2 **irregular order**, irregularity, randomness, haphazardness, nonuniformity, unsymmetry, nonsymmetry, disproportion, misshapenness, shapelessness, no pattern, no rhyme or reason
▶ *307 Shapelessness, 113 Diversity*

3 **untidiness**, dirtiness, uncleanness, grubbiness, messiness, unkemptness, dishevelment, scruffiness, shabbiness, neglect, negligence, carelessness, slipshodness, shoddiness, sloppiness, sluttishness, slovenliness, slatternliness, sordidness, squalidness, slobbishness (Inf)
▶ *622 Dirtiness, 470 Negligence*

4 **litter**, rubbish, garbage, trash, mess, clutter, muddle, jumble, lumber, hodgepodge (*or* hotchpotch), hash, mishmash, pickle, topsy-turvy, topsy-turviness, shambles, rat's nest, pigsty, midden, dump, tip, slum, (junk) heap, higgledy-piggledy (Inf), unholy (*or* god-awful) mess (Sl)
▶ *607 Waste, 614 Uselessness, 133 Mixture, 727 Disposal*

5 **confusion**, chaos, muddle, mess, jumble, welter, bedlam, pandemonium, hell, all hell let loose, inferno, madhouse, bear-garden, tumult, turmoil, turbulence, upheaval, ferment, hullabaloo (*or* hullaballoo), hubbub, racket, cacophony, uproar
▶ *423 Loudness, 434 Dissonance*

6 **mix-up**, snarl-up, foul-up, mess, hash (Inf), pig's ear (Inf), cock-up (Sl), balls-up (Sl), screw-up (Sl), fuck-up (Tab sl), snafu (situation normal: all fucked up) (Sl)
▶ *656 Unskilfulness*

7 **tangle**, snarl, labyrinth, maze, web, jungle
▶ *659 Difficulty*

8 **lawlessness**, anarchy, chaos, disorder, disobedience, disorderly behaviour, unruliness, boisterousness, rowdiness, laddishness, disruptiveness, no discipline, nihilism, amorality, lack of discipline, rebelliousness, revolution, uprising, upheaval, vandalism, hooliganism
▶ *689 Anarchy, 693 Disobedience*

9 **disorder**, disturbance, disruption, commotion, pother, stir, fuss, bother, spot of bother, trouble, ado, to-do, hurly-burly, all hell let loose, fight, argument, brawl, row, fistfight, fisticuffs, rumpus, ruckus, ruction, mêlée, rough and tumble, free-for-all, donnybrook, affray, fray, breach of the peace, riot, rampage, anarchy, mob rule, set-to (Inf), shindig (*or* shindy) (Inf), argy-bargy (Inf), punch-up (Sl), roughhouse (Sl), aggro (Sl), dust-up (Inf)
▶ *674 Contention, 689 Anarchy*

10 **slattern**, sloven, slut, slob (Inf), slag (Sl), litterbug (Sl), litter lout (Sl)

11 **troublemaker**, rioter, lord of misrule, nihilist, amorality, anarchist, pest, nuisance, irritant, agitator, loot, hooligan, vandal, pain in the neck (Inf), stirrer (Inf)

ADJECTIVES

12 **disordered**, orderless, in disorder, in disarray, disarranged, deranged, disrupted, disorganized, muddled, jumbled, shuffled, out of order, displaced, misplaced, out of place, out of joint, disjointed, dislocated
▶ *252 Displacement*

13 **unordered**, unorganized, unarranged, ungraded, unsorted, unsifted, unclassified

14 **irregular**, random, haphazard, erratic, hit-or-miss, sporadic, spasmodic, desultory, nonuniform, unsymmetrical, nonsymmetrical, misshapen, disproportionate, shapeless, formless
▶ *307 Shapelessness*

15 **untidy**, dirty, filthy, unclean, grubby, messy, in a mess, scruffy, shabby, ragged, in rags, down at heel, unsightly, unkempt, dishevelled, bedraggled, tousled, uncombed, windblown, pulled through a hedge backwards, like something the cat brought in, ruffled, crumpled, frumpish, sluttish, slovenly, slatternly, neglectful, negligent, careless, slipshod, shoddy, slack, sordid, squalid, shambolic (Inf), slobbish (Inf)
▶ *622 Dirtiness, 628 Deterioration, 470 Negligence*

16 **confused**, incoherent, convoluted, disorganized, muddleheaded, scatterbrained, featherbrained, unsystematic, unmethodical
▶ *523 Unintelligibility*

17 **discomposed**, discomfited, disconcerted, unsettled, disturbed, perturbed, upset, deranged, convulsed

18 **muddled**, jumbled, scrambled, confused, chaotic, tangled, labyrinthine, awry, askew, amiss, topsy-turvy, upside-down, at sixes and sevens, head over heals, higgledy-piggledy (Inf), arsy-versy (Sl), cockeyed (Sl), haywire (Inf)
▶ *659 Difficulty*

19 **mixed-up**, snarled-up, fouled-up, messed-up, mucked-up (Sl), ballsed-up (Sl), screwed-up (Sl), fucked-up (Tab sl), snafu (Sl)
▶ *656 Unskilfulness*

20 **disorderly**, chaotic, lawless, unruly, undisciplined, uncontrolled, out of control, unmanageable, boisterous, disruptive, stroppy (Inf), laddish (Inf), rowdy, hell-raising, harum-scarum, wild, turbulent, rampageous, riotous, rebellious, insubordinate, contumacious, mutinous, obstreperous, disobedient, anarchic, nihilistic
▶ *693 Disobedience, 689 Anarchy, 577 Obstinacy*

VERBS

21 **disorder**, disorganize, disarrange, derange, throw into disarray, muddle, jumble, shuffle, mix up, scramble, disperse, scatter, break up, disrupt, disturb
▶ *252 Displacement, 162 Dispersion, 153 Disturbance*

22 **discompose**, disconcert, disturb, perturb, upset, hassle (Inf), pester, unsettle, disorient, addle, befuddle, confuse, tie in knots, knock galley-west (US sl)

23 **confuse**, muddle (up), mess (up), hash (up), botch, bungle, mix up, snarl up, foul up, make a hash (*or* mess) of (Inf), make a pig's ear of (Inf), cock up (Sl), screw up (Sl), balls-up (Sl), fuck up (Tab sl), bollix up (Tab sl)
▶ *656 Unskilfulness*

24 **make disordered**, untidy, mess up, dishevel, bedraggle, tousle, ruffle, rumple, crumple, crease, turn upside down, tangle, snarl

25 **be disordered**, lapse into disorder, fall into confusion, fall into disarray, degenerate, disintegrate, come apart, come unstuck, dissolve into chaos
▶ *628 Deterioration, 141 Disintegration*

26 **be disorderly**, get out of hand, get out of control, disobey, throw off discipline, make trouble, raise a rumpus, run wild, run amok (*or* amuck), riot, run riot, rampage, go on the rampage, roister, storm, mob, kick up a row (Inf), raise hell (Inf), raise the devil (Inf), horse around (Inf), cut up rough (Inf)
▶ *689 Anarchy, 693 Disobedience, 423 Loudness*

ADVERBS

27 **in disorder**, in disarray, in confusion, in a muddle, in a mess, in a jumble, by chance, unmethodically, unsystematically, irregularly, haphazardly, erratically, indiscriminately, randomly, at random, sporadically, spasmodically, by fits and starts, without rhyme or reason, chaotically, confusedly

28 **anyhow**, all anyhow, all over, all over the

place, upside-down, topsy-turvy, pell-mell, helter-skelter, harum-scarum, off the rails, at sixes and sevens, at cross-purposes, all over the shop (Inf), arsy-versy (Sl), higgledy-piggledy (Inf), every which way (Inf)

29 **riotously**, on the rampage, anarchically, rebelliously, boisterously, disruptively

152 Arrangement

NOUNS

1 **arrangement**, order, ordering, putting in order, arranging, arraying, marshalling, disposition, disposal, placing, placement, location, structuring, composition, grouping, alignment, line-up
▶ *150 Order, 250 Location, 382 Structure*

2 **array**, assemblage, arrangement, display, pattern, design, decoration, style, layout, structure, composition, flower arrangement
▶ *526 Display, 792 Decoration*

3 **organization**, method, methodization, system, systematization, structuring, planning, charting, routinization, rationalization, standardization, centralization, coordination
▶ *602 Means, 653 Management, 592 Plan*

4 **rearrangement**, reordering, reorganization, restructuring, realignment, regrouping, simplification, streamlining, shake-up (Inf)
▶ *216 Change, 382 Structure, 163 Class*

5 **categorization**, classification, codification, taxonomy, grouping, placing, placement, pigeonholing, compartmentalization, grading, gradation, ranking, rating, seeding (sport), hierarchy, stratification, graduation, sorting, sorting out, sifting, screening, selection, analysis, tabulation, alphabetization, alpha-sorting, cataloguing, listing, indexing, filing
▶ *150 Order, 163 Class, 580 Selection, 171 List*

6 **category**, subcategory, class, subclass, group, subgroup, order, suborder, division, subdivision, family, set, bracket, head, heading, department, section, grade, rank, level, position, place, status, slot, niche, pigeonhole, compartment
▶ *163 Class*

7 **catalogue**, directory, gazetteer, register, digest, compendium, index, list, inventory, record, file, computer file, computer listing
▶ *171 List, 545 Record, 65 Computers*

8 **chart**, diagram, table, graph, flow chart, pie chart, bar chart, scatter diagram, flow sheet, spreadsheet, Venn diagram, plan, scheme, schema, schedule, programme
▶ *592 Plan*

9 **musical arrangement**, adaptation, interpretation, version, orchestration, score, instrumentation, choreography
▶ *49 Music*

10 **agreement**, understanding, arrangement,

settlement, deal, compact, contract, covenant, terms
▶ *715 Contract, 667 Agreement, 717 Compromise*

11 **arrangements**, plans, preparations, making arrangements, planning, preparing, groundwork
▶ *592 Plan, 594 Preparation*

VERBS

12 **arrange**, order, put (*or* set) in order, reduce to order, structure, range, array, marshal, dispose, place, position, locate, set, set out, lay out, display, align, line up, put into shape, compose, group, space, space out, distribute, allocate, settle
▶ *150 Order, 382 Structure, 250 Location, 731 Allocation, 526 Display*

13 **organize**, methodize, systematize, rationalize, standardize, normalize, centralize, coordinate, plan, schematize
▶ *653 Management, 592 Plan*

14 **rearrange**, reorder, reorganize, restructure, shake up, realign, adjust, simplify, streamline
▶ *216 Change*

15 **categorize**, classify, class, codify, digest, program, group, pigeonhole, compartmentalize, place, place in order, put in order, grade, rank, rate, seed, sort, sort out, assort, sift, sift out, sieve, screen, select, analyse, process, process data, tabulate, alphabetize, catalogue, index, list, inventory, record, register, file
▶ *163 Class, 171 List, 545 Record, 580 Selection*

16 **adapt**, arrange, interpret, compose, orchestrate, score, instrument, choreograph
▶ *49 Music*

17 **come to an arrangement**, come to an agreement, compromise, agree, settle, make a deal, come to terms, fix up (Inf)
▶ *667 Agreement, 717 Compromise*

18 **make arrangements**, arrange for, prearrange, prepare, plan, schedule, organize, manage, contrive, devise
▶ *594 Preparation, 592 Plan, 653 Management*

19 **tidy**, tidy up, neaten, rearrange, straighten, straighten up, clean up, put to rights, put in trim, clear up, clear the decks, untangle, disentangle, unravel, unsnarl, iron out, smooth, debug
▶ *150 Order, 376 Smoothness*

ADJECTIVES

20 **arranged**, ordered, in order, orderly, structured, ranged, arrayed, marshalled, disposed, placed, aligned, grouped
▶ *150 Order, 382 Structure, 250 Location, 526 Display*

21 **organized**, methodized, systematized, rationalized, planned, prearranged
▶ *592 Plan*

22 **organizational**, methodical, systematic, schematic, rational, formational
▶ *653 Management*

23 rearranged, reordered, reorganized, restructured, realigned, adjusted, simplified, streamlined
▶ *216 Change*
24 categorized, classified, codified, grouped, pigeonholed, compartmentalized, placed, graded, ranked, rated, seeded, stratified, sorted, sorted out, assorted, sifted, screened, selected, analysed, processed, tabulated, alphabetized, catalogued, indexed, listed, filed, on file, on record
▶ *163 Class, 171 List, 545 Record*
25 categorical, classificatory, hierarchical, taxonomic(al)
▶ *150 Order*
26 diagrammatic, graphic, tabular, schematic, analytic
27 tidied, tidy, neatened, neat, straightened, straightened out, cleared up, untangled, disentangled, unravelled, unsnarled

ADVERBS
28 in place, in order, rationally, tidily, neatly, methodically, systematically, schematically, taxonomically, diagrammatically, indexically, analytically

153 Disturbance

NOUNS
1 disturbance, perturbation, agitation, convulsion, upheaval, upset, disconcertedness, disquiet, discomfiture, discomposure, worry, anxiety, annoyance, bother, nuisance
▶ *366 Agitation*
2 disarrangement, derangement, disorder, disorganization, muddle, confusion
▶ *151 Disorder*
3 dispersion, displacement, dislodgment, dislocation, disorientation, derailment
▶ *162 Dispersion, 252 Displacement*
4 disruption, disturbance, interruption, intrusion, interference, intervention, molestation, perversion, sabotage, hindrance, obstruction, inconvenience, untimeliness, distraction
▶ *211 Untimeliness, 661 Hindrance, 616 Inconvenience*
5 commotion, disturbance, disorder, breach of the peace, tumult, turmoil, ferment, furore, outcry, outburst, clamour, uproar, fuss, rumpus, bedlam, hubbub, hurly-burly, hullabaloo (*or* hullaballoo), brouhaha, to-do, ado, racket, din, noise, bother, trouble, scuffle, fracas, fray, riot, ruction (Inf), shemozzle (Sl), spot of bother (Inf)
▶ *151 Disorder, 423 Loudness, 674 Contention*
6 derangement, mental derangement, mental disorder, insanity, madness, instability, screw loose (Inf)
▶ *510 Insanity*

VERBS
7 disturb, perturb, agitate, stir, convulse, upset, distress, unsettle, disconcert, disquiet, discomfit, discompose, throw into confusion, fluster, ruffle, shake, rattle, alarm, concern, worry, trouble, bother, pester, harass, annoy, irritate, vex, irk, throw into a tizzy (Inf), hassle (Inf), spook (Sl), bug (Sl)
▶ *366 Agitation, 770 Sorrow, 777 Fear*
8 disarrange, derange, disorder, throw into disorder, disorganize, muddle, confuse, put out of gear, roil (the waters)
▶ *151 Disorder, 659 Difficulty*
9 disperse, displace, dislodge, dislocate, disorient, derail
▶ *162 Dispersion, 252 Displacement*
10 disrupt, interrupt, intrude, butt in on, break in on, interfere, intervene, molest, pervert, tamper with, sabotage, hinder, obstruct, inconvenience, put out, distract, put off
▶ *616 Inconvenience, 211 Untimeliness, 661 Hindrance*
11 derange, unhinge, unbalance, drive insane, drive mad, enrage, drive round the bend (*or* the twist) (Inf), drive up the wall (Inf)
▶ *510 Insanity*

ADJECTIVES
12 disturbed, perturbed, agitated, convulsed, upset, distressed, unsettled, disconcerted, disquieted, discomfited, discomposed, uncomfortable, uneasy, confused, flustered, ruffled, shaken, rattled, alarmed, concerned, worried, anxious, troubled, bothered, annoyed, irritated, vexed, in a tizzy (Inf), bugged (Sl)
▶ *366 Agitation, 770 Sorrow, 777 Fear*
13 disarranged, deranged, disordered, disorganized, muddled, confused, roiled
▶ *151 Disorder*
14 dispersed, displaced, dislodged, dislocated, disorientated, derailed
▶ *162 Dispersion, 252 Displacement*
15 disrupted, interrupted, interfered with, molested, sabotaged, hindered, obstructed, inconvenienced, distracted
▶ *616 Inconvenience, 661 Hindrance*
16 deranged, mentally deranged, disordered, unhinged, unbalanced, maladjusted, disturbed, demented, neurotic, psychotic, unstable, mad, insane, hung-up (Sl), gaga (Sl), off one's head (*or* trolley *or* rocker *or* box) (Inf), round the bend (*or* twist) (Inf), out to lunch (Inf)
▶ *510 Insanity*
17 disturbing, upsetting, distressing, unsettling, disconcerting, alarming, worrying, bothersome, annoying, vexatious, muddling, disruptive, distracting, off-putting (Inf)

ADVERBS
18 disturbingly, disconcertingly, confusingly, alarmingly, disquietingly, worryingly, annoy-

ingly, irritatingly, inconveniently, disruptively, intrusively, obstructively, perversely, off the rails, on the wrong track, off course

19 **distractedly**, uneasily, anxiously, nervously, neurotically, crazily, insanely, psychotically

154   Precedence

NOUNS

1 **precedence**, antecedence, antecedency, preceding, going before, coming before, precession, anteriority, anteposition, taking precedence, pre-emption
▶ *208 Earliness, 156 Beginning*

2 **priority**, primacy, supremacy, dominion, pre-eminence, superiority, higher position, higher rank, seniority, prerogative, privilege, front, front position, forefront, vanguard, front of the queue, pole position, first place, the lead, pride of place, top of the tree, top priority, urgency, importance, preference, first concern
▶ *194 Priority, 126 Superiority, 303 Front, 611 Importance*

3 **preparation**, groundwork, foundation, development, exploration, pioneering, innovation, avant-gardism, breakthrough, discovery, leap
▶ *594 Preparation, 496 Discovery*

4 **precedent**, antecedent, lead, example, standard, prototype, model, pattern, paradigm, yardstick, criterion

5 **preface**, foreword, proem, prologue, frontispiece, introduction, opening, opener, preliminaries, prelims, front matter, prelude, overture, curtain raiser, apéritif, appetizer, hors d'oeuvre
▶ *156 Beginning*

6 **preview**, trailer, foretaste, taster, premonition, omen, warning
▶ *517 Prediction, 636 Warning*

7 **prefix**, prefixion, prefixation, prothesis

8 **precursor**, forerunner, foregoer, herald, harbinger, messenger, announcer, crier, frontrunner, lead runner, leader, vanguard, scout, reconnaisance party, guide, pilot, explorer, pathfinder, trailblazer, avant-garde, avant-gardist, groundbreaker, pioneer, frontiersman, founding father, trendsetter, innovator, inventor, discoverer
▶ *532 Publication, 688 Authority, 303 Front, 496 Discovery, 201 Newness*

9 **predecessor**, forebear, forefather, ancestor, firstborn, eldest, senior

ADJECTIVES

10 **preceding**, precedent, antecedent, anterior, precessional, leading, first, pre-emptive, earliest
▶ *303 Front*

11 **prior**, former, ex, late, erstwhile, one-time, previous, last, earlier, foregoing, above, abovementioned, aforementioned, beforementioned, aforenamed, forenamed, aforesaid
▶ *208 Earliness, 200 Past Time, 194 Priority*

12 **primary**, senior, superior, supreme, leading, pre-eminent, first, foremost, headmost, chief, elder
▶ *688 Authority, 653 Management, 126 Superiority, 611 Importance*

13 **precursory**, preliminary, initial, initiatory, introductory, elementary, basic, inaugural, baptismal, prefatory, prefatorial, proemial
▶ *156 Beginning*

14 **preparatory**, foundational, developmental, leading, guiding, piloting, exploratory, reconnoitring, founding, discovering, innovatory, innovative, avant-garde, pioneering, trailblazing, ground-breaking
▶ *594 Preparation, 496 Discovery, 201 Newness*

VERBS

15 **precede**, antecede, predate, antedate, come before, go before, lead, go first, go ahead of, guide, pilot, indicate, show (*or* lead) the way, point the way, head, spearhead, stand at the head, front, head up (Inf)
▶ *303 Front, 653 Management*

16 **take precedence**, have precedence, outrank, be superior, have priority, take priority, pre-empt
▶ *194 Priority, 126 Superiority, 611 Importance*

17 **give priority**, put first, prioritize

18 **forerun**, pioneer, explore, reconnoitre, discover, invent, found, inaugurate, initiate, innovate, blaze a trail, set a trend, set the fashion, lead the dance, set the example, influence, pave the way, map out
▶ *496 Discovery, 156 Beginning, 201 Newness, 233 Influence*

19 **forecast**, foretell, presage, introduce, herald, usher in, ring in, predict, warn
▶ *517 Prediction, 11 Occultism*

ADVERBS

20 **before**, prior to, formerly, previously, earlier, beforehand

21 **first**, first and foremost, ahead, in front, in advance

22 **in anticipation**, in preparation, preparatorily, as a prelude, as a preliminary

23 **primarily**, supremely, pre-eminently, first, pre-emptively

155   Sequence

NOUNS

1 **sequence**, logical sequence, succession, successiveness, consecution, consecutiveness, progression, procession, serialization, following, coming after, going after
▶ *159 Consecutiveness, 195 Succession, 590 Pursuit, 150 Order*

2 **series**, chain, string, train, line, run, course, cycle, rotation, alternation
▶ *109 Reciprocity*

3 **continuity**, continuation, extension, prolongation, protraction, follow-through, segue, follow-up
▶ *219 Continuity*

4 **sequel**, continuation, series, saga, soap opera, next instalment

5 **consequence**, sequel, effect, result, end result, product, end product, outcome, upshot, payoff (Inf)
▶ *227 Effect, 243 Production*

6 **aftermath**, aftereffect(s), afterglow, aftertaste, legacy, by-product, spin-off, fallout, hangover, morning after

7 **afterthought**, second thoughts, better thoughts, second chance, second try, second bite at the cherry, double take (Inf)

8 **addition**, insert, supplement, adjunct, addendum, codicil, appendix, end matter, back matter, conclusion, postscript (PS), afterword, afterpiece, refrain, chorus, coda, postlude, subscript, suffixation, subjunction, postposition, add-on (Inf)
▶ *130 Addition*

9 **conclusion**, end, finish, completion, termination, last words, parting shot, dying words, swan song
▶ *157 End*

10 **rear**, back, last place, posterior, tail, tailpiece, train, trail, wake, tab, tag
▶ *304 Rear*

11 **progeny**, offspring, issue, child, children, fruit, seed, kids (Inf)
▶ *245 Reproduction*

12 **successor**, descendant, heir, inheritor, beneficiary, later generations, future generations, the unborn
▶ *199 Future Time*

13 **replacement**, substitute, locum (tenens), fill-in, stand-in, backup, understudy, fresh blood, new broom, supplanter, usurper, temp (Inf), sub (Inf)
▶ *222 Substitution*

14 **follower**, following, followers, camp followers, attendant, retainer, retinue, procession, cortège, adherent, believer, disciple, apostle, sycophant, hanger-on, enthusiast, fan, devotee, groupie (Inf)
▶ *159 Consecutiveness*

ADJECTIVES

15 **sequential**, sequent, succeeding, successive, successional, following, serial, consecutive, in order, sequacious, continuous, in a row, progressive
▶ *159 Consecutiveness, 195 Succession, 150 Order, 219 Continuity*

16 **alternating**, alternate, every second, every other, antiphonal, cyclical

17 **next**, near, later, latter, proximate, proximal

18 **consequent**, consequential, resulting, ensuing, caused
▶ *227 Effect*

19 **additional**, supplementary, appendant, suffixed, postpositive, postpositional, another
▶ *130 Addition*

20 **rear**, back, last, end, posterior, hindmost, tail
▶ *304 Rear, 157 End*

VERBS

21 **follow in sequence**, follow, follow on, segue, succeed, come after, go after, come next, come in the wake of, follow in the footsteps of, tread on the heels of
▶ *195 Succession*

22 **succeed**, inherit, supersede, supplant, usurp, substitute, replace, relieve, take over, take the place of, take the role of, take the mantle of, step into the shoes of, step into the place of
▶ *222 Substitution*

23 **follow close**, trail, shadow, dog someone's footsteps, sit on someone's tail (Inf), tail (Inf)
▶ *590 Pursuit*

24 **alternate**, take turns, take it in turns, take turn and turn about, follow in turn

25 **result**, ensue, arise, spring, emanate, issue, flow, turn out, come to pass
▶ *227 Effect, 156 Beginning*

26 **bring up the rear**, come last, lag, lag behind, dawdle, tag along, follow
▶ *328 Slowness, 157 End, 304 Rear*

ADVERBS

27 **in sequence**, sequentially, in order, in succession, successively, consecutively, one after the other, running, in waves, in relays, alternately, in turn, on the trot (Inf)

28 **after**, afterwards, following, subsequently, in the aftermath, next, then, later, at a later date

29 **consequently**, as a result, in consequence, as a consequence

30 **behind**, rearward, at the end, bringing up the rear, below, finally, in the end

156 Beginning

The distance doesn't matter; it is only the first step that is difficult. Marquise du Deffand.

NOUNS

1 **beginning**, start, commencement, opening, launch, onset, outset, outbreak, day one, square one
▶ *303 Front, 154 Precedence*

2 **creation**, the Creation, genesis, origin, origination, emergence, appearance, arrival, first beginnings, dawn, daybreak, break of day, morning
▶ *457 Appearance, 344 Arrival, 204 Daytime*

3 **source**, origin, provenance, fountainhead, wellspring, root, seed, seedbed, bud, germ, embryo, egg, nucleus, primordial soup, proto-

plasm, nest, womb, cradle
▶ *226 Cause*

4 **conception**, pregnancy, birth, nativity, delivery, parturition, pullulation, babyhood, cradle, infancy, first steps, childhood, youth
▶ *245 Reproduction, 206 Youth*

5 **invention**, discovery, formation, creation, origin, origination, conception, innovation, coinage
▶ *496 Discovery, 119 Originality*

6 **inauguration**, inception, inchoation, incipience, foundation, institution, establishment, setting up, installation, instigation, setting in motion, launch, embarkation
▶ *324 Motion, 496 Discovery*

7 **rudiments**, basics, elements, principles, first principles, preparation, groundwork, spadework (Inf)
▶ *103 Essence, 594 Preparation*

8 **enrolment**, investiture, induction, ordination, installation, initiation, initiation ceremony, christening, baptism, baptism of fire, honeymoon, house-warming
▶ *346 Entry*

9 **premiere**, first night, first time, first appearance, debut, coming out, curtain rise, curtain raiser, maiden speech, inaugural address, presentation, launch, launching, flotation, opening, opening ceremony, unveiling, cutting the ribbon, laying the first stone, maiden voyage
▶ *322 Opening*

10 **introduction**, gambit, opening gambit, opener, opening line, lead-in, prelude, preamble, exordium, preface, foreword, front matter, preliminaries, prelims, title page, frontispiece
▶ *154 Precedence*

11 **starting point**, point of departure, starting post, starting block, starting pistol, zero hour, blast-off, opening, initiative, kickoff, bully-off, jump-off, start, flying start, false start, square one (Inf)
▶ *345 Departure*

12 **first move**, commencing (*or* opening) move, first step, first base, first lap, first round, first stage, first leg, first innings, early stages, early days, first course, starter
▶ *154 Precedence, 45 Cookery, 208 Earliness*

13 **new beginnings**, fresh start, new departure, new tack, fresh fields, pastures new, new leaf, new page, new chapter
▶ *201 Newness, 216 Change*

14 **beginner**, starter, novice, learner, trainee, student, pupil, apprentice, probationer, recruit, raw recruit, tenderfoot, initiate, new boy, new girl, freshman, fresher, neophyte, tyro, debutante, greenhorn (Inf), rookie (Inf), deb (Inf)

15 **baby**, newborn, infant, fledgling, nestling,

babe in arms, rug rat (Sl), ankle-biter (Sl)
▶ *206 Youth*

16 **originator**, initiator, maker, creator, inventor, architect, prime mover, the Creator, God
▶ *243 Production*

VERBS

17 **begin**, start, commence, open, originate, initiate, establish
▶ *322 Opening*

18 **make a beginning**, make a start, get started, debut, set to work, put one's hand to the plough, go to it, go at it, embark on, set to (*or* about), turn to, fall to, go ahead, tackle, broach, face, get off to a good start, kick off, bully off, tee off, blast off, fire away (Inf), blast away (Inf), take the plunge (Inf), get one's feet wet (Inf), plunge into (Inf), head into (Inf), dive in (Inf), pitch in (Inf), get going (Inf), get weaving (Inf), get cracking (Inf), pull one's finger out (Inf), get the show on the road (Inf), put one's shoulder to the wheel (Inf)
▶ *640 Action, 642 Activity, 644 Work*

19 **start off**, start out, set off (*or* out), sally forth, make a move, get moving, get under way, set sail, take off, get on the road, hit the road (Inf)
▶ *345 Departure*

20 **activate**, start up, start going, turn on, switch on, set in motion, prompt, provoke, spark off, trigger off, apply the match, light the fuse, launch, set the ball rolling, kick-start, boot (*or* boot up)
▶ *226 Cause*

21 **pioneer**, explore, guide, pilot, lead, lead the way, set a precedent, head, spearhead, break new ground, open up, blaze a trail, trailblaze, take the first step, take the initiative, make the first move, break the ice
▶ *154 Precedence, 653 Management*

22 **invent**, discover, innovate, form, create, dream up, call into being, originate, generate, conceive, think of, coin, come up with, sow the seeds
▶ *496 Discovery, 243 Production*

23 **inaugurate**, initiate, auspicate (Arch), establish, found, institute, set up, start up, install, induct, instigate, cause, commission, launch, float, present, be a founder member, be in at the beginning, be in on the ground floor
▶ *226 Cause*

24 **open**, unveil, cut the ribbon, declare open, lay the foundation stone, lay the first stone, cut the first turf

25 **enrol**, invest, crown, induct, ordain, install, institute, initiate, blood, baptize, christen

26 **produce**, give birth, bear, mother, father, sire, engender, bring into being, bring into the world, pullulate, breed, teem, bud, germinate
▶ *245 Reproduction*

27 **emerge**, appear, arrive, originate, arise, issue, issue forth, burst forth, erupt, spring, spring

up, crop up, sprout, germinate, be born, come into the world, come into being, come into existence, come to be, come forth, see the light of day, dawn, come out, make one's debut

▶ *457 Appearance, 344 Arrival, 347 Exit*

28 **begin again**, recommence, make a fresh start, start afresh, start anew, turn over a new leaf, go back to square one, go back to the drawing board, return to go (Inf)

▶ *201 Newness, 216 Change*

ADJECTIVES

29 **beginning**, starting, commencing, opening, first, primary, initial, initiatory, initiative, maiden, early, formative

▶ *322 Opening, 208 Earliness*

30 **front**, frontal, leading, foremost, head

31 **prime**, primal, primordial, primeval, primitive, aboriginal, earliest, original, pristine

▶ *208 Earliness*

32 **embryonic**, budding, in the bud, nascent, germinal, inchoate, developing, fetal, pregnant, gestatory, parturient, dawning, emergent, new, fresh, raw, newborn, baby, infant, unfledged, young

▶ *245 Reproduction, 206 Youth, 201 Newness*

33 **inventive**, innovative, creative, original, conceptional, conceptive

34 **inaugural**, inauguratory, incipient, inceptive, inchoative, inchoate, foundational, institutionary, establishing, instigatory, instigative

35 **rudimentary**, rudimental, basic, elementary, fundamental

▶ *103 Essence*

36 **introductory**, preliminary, preparatory, precursory, initiatory, baptismal, prefatory, proemial, preludial, prepositive, prefixed

▶ *154 Precedence*

37 **enrolled**, installed, initiated, baptized, christened, premiered, inaugurated, presented, launched, opened, newly opened, unveiled

ADVERBS

38 **in the beginning**, at the beginning, at the first, at the very start, originally, initially

39 **from the beginning**, from the first, from the foundations, from its inception, from its birth, *ab ovo* (L), *ab initio* (L), *ab origine* (L), from scratch (Inf), from the word go (Inf)

40 **first**, firstly, primarily, at first, first thing, in the first place, first of all, first and foremost, before everything, for a start, as a start, for a beginning, for starters (Sl), for a kick-off (Inf)

41 **in the bud**, in embryo, in its infancy

42 **principally**, primarily, mainly, chiefly, basically, fundamentally

157 End

This is the way the world ends/ Not with a bang but a whimper. T. S. Eliot.

NOUNS

1 **end**, ending, conclusion, finish, close, finis, finale, completion, wind-up (Inf)

▶ *684 Completion*

2 **cessation**, ceasing, expiry, expiration, termination, stop, stoppage, halt, abrogation, cancellation, annulment

▶ *218 Cessation*

3 **death**, demise, decease, expiration, passing, departure, exit, release, quietus, last gasp, last breath, last words, swan song, end of the line, curtains (Inf)

▶ *397 Death*

4 **annihilation**, destruction, extermination, extinction, elimination, dissolution, liquidation, ruin

▶ *244 Destruction, 546 Obliteration*

5 **fate**, destiny, doom, doomsday, crack of doom, end of time, end of the world, eschatology, last judgment, Day of Judgment, apocalypse, twilight of the gods, Götterdämmerung

6 **end point**, terminus, terminal, end of the line, last stop, journey's end, destination

7 **limit**, boundary, frontier, border, rim, edge, fringe, verge, extent, extreme, extremity, pole, point, tip, peak, cusp, summit, zenith, top, last frontier, ends of the earth, where the rainbow ends

▶ *302 Limit, 300 Edge, 279 Summit*

8 **tail**, tail end, butt, butt end, fag end, scrag end, bin end, bitter end, last penny, last cent, bottom dollar, dregs, lees, bottom of the barrel (Inf)

▶ *304 Rear*

9 **close**, closing stages, last stage, final stage, last lap, home stretch, last round, last innings, last ball, last over, end of the day, evening, dusk, twilight, decline, end of the road, beginning of the end

▶ *628 Deterioration, 205 Night-Time*

10 **ending**, finale, finish, last act, climax, culmination, crowning glory, denouement, catastrophe, final curtain, epilogue, envoy (or envoi), coda, postscript (PS), end matter, back matter, appendix, suffix, last word, last laugh, punch line, sting in the tail, parting shot, Parthian shot

▶ *155 Sequence*

11 **finality**, deadline, time up, closing time, close of play, last orders, throwing (or chucking) out time, stop tap (Inf)

12 **end result**, result, effect, consequence, issue, outcome, upshot, payoff (Inf)

▶ *227 Effect*

13 **ender**, stopper, finisher, clincher, settler, crusher, knockout, knockout blow, death-

blow, mortal blow, death stroke, finishing stroke, coup de grâce, the end (Sl), the limit (Inf), the last straw (Inf), the final blow (Inf)

14 **aim**, intent, intention, aspiration, goal, target, object, objective, purpose, reason, drift
▶ *588 Intention*

VERBS

15 **end**, conclude, finish, close, achieve, complete, finalize, resolve, decide, settle, finish off, round off, culminate, consummate, crown, cap, wind up (Inf), wrap up (Inf), be done with (Inf)
▶ *684 Completion*

16 **cease**, stop, halt, terminate, discontinue, put an end to, put a stop to, scotch, bring to an end, call a halt, close down, shut down, shut up shop, ring down (*or* drop) the curtain, make an end of, finish off, kill off, polish off, dispose of, abort, annul, cancel, abrogate, put paid to, scrap (Inf), scratch (Inf), put the (tin) lid on (Sl), fold up (Inf), pull the plug on (Inf), put the stoppers on (Inf), draw stumps (Inf)
▶ *218 Cessation, 160 Discontinuity, 704 Cancellation*

17 **kill**, extinguish, annihilate, destroy, exterminate, eliminate, dissolve, liquidate, wipe out, knock out, shoot down, kayo (*or* KO) (Sl), shoot down in flames (Sl), zap (Sl)
▶ *398 Killing, 244 Destruction, 546 Obliteration*

18 **come to an end**, draw to a close, go out, run out, run out of time, be over, be no more, fade out, fade away, peter out, fizzle out, tail off, die away, come to the end of the road
▶ *458 Disappearance*

19 **expire**, pass away, pass on, give up the ghost, draw one's last breath, die, die out, become extinct, end it all, commit suicide, come to a sticky end (Inf)
▶ *397 Death*

ADJECTIVES

20 **ending**, last, final, ultimate, terminal, concluding, conclusive, completing, completive, closing, finishing, definitive, culminating, culminative, consummative, consummatory, crowning, capping, apocalyptic, catastrophic, eschatological

21 **ended**, at an end, finished, complete, finalized, terminated, concluded, decided, settled, done, done with, through, over, all over, over and done with, dead and buried, all up (Sl), wound up (Inf), washed up (Sl), all over bar the shouting (Inf)
▶ *684 Completion, 218 Cessation*

22 **cancelled**, off, all off, played out, called off, scrapped

23 **annihilated**, destroyed, exterminated, eliminated, dissolved, liquidated, ruined, doomed, fated, destined
▶ *244 Destruction*

24 **limiting**, boundary, frontier, bordering,

fringing, furthest, extreme, polar, eventual, last

25 **hindmost**, rear, back, tail, end, endmost
▶ *304 Rear*

ADVERBS

26 **finally**, lastly, in conclusion, eventually, ultimately, at last, at long last, in the end, at the end of the day, when all is said and done, in the final analysis, in the long run, when the chips are down (Inf)

27 **to the end**, to the bitter end, to the last gasp, for always, to the end of the road, till hell freezes over (Inf)

28 **conclusively**, definitively, once and for all, for good, for good and all, never again

158 Middle

NOUNS

1 **middle**, centre, epicentre, midst, midpoint, halfway point (*or* stage), halfway house
▶ *291 Centre, 333 Middle Way, 298 Interface*

2 **core**, nucleus, heart, hub, focus, pivot, fulcrum, bull's-eye, kernel, marrow, inside, interior, heartland, midst, thick, thick of things, focal point, keystone, linchpin, nub, heart of the matter, *in media res* (L)
▶ *290 Interior*

3 **median**, mean, golden mean, balance, par, average, medium, happy medium, intermediate
▶ *124 Average*

4 **midline**, equator, the Line, diameter, bisection, midsection, waist, waistline, midriff

5 **middle distance**, equidistance, midfield, midcourse, midstream, halfway, moiety, mideity

6 **middle ground**, no-man's-land, grey area, compromise, mediation, arbitration
▶ *717 Compromise, 678 Mediation, 492 Judgment*

7 **middle age**, middle life, middle years, the wrong side of forty, midlife crisis

8 **middle class**, upper middle class, lower middle class, bourgeoisie, professional class, white-collar class, merchant class, suburbia, burgherdom, Babbittry
▶ *163 Class, 2 Sociology, 124 Average*

9 **middleman**, broker, distributor, intermediary, third party, interventionist, intercessor, counsellor, ombudsman, negotiator, spokesperson, mouthpiece, go-between, mediator, arbitrator, moderator, umpire, referee, pig-in-the-middle (Inf), medium, messenger, agent, panderer, pimp (Inf)
▶ *678 Mediation, 737 Trade*

ADJECTIVES

10 **middle**, mid, central, centre, medial, middlemost, midmost
▶ *291 Centre*

11 **midway**, halfway, equidistant, mezzanine,

midstream, equatorial, diametric
12 **core**, nuclear, focal, pivotal, inner, inside, interior
▶ *290 Interior*
13 **median**, medial, mesial, mean, average, medium, balanced
▶ *124 Average*
14 **mediatory**, intermediary, interim, intermediate, neutral, moderate, middle-of-the-road, noncommittal
▶ *678 Mediation, 333 Middle Way*
15 **middling**, average, mediocre, ordinary, indifferent, undistinguished, fair, fairish, run-of-the-mill, so-so (Inf)
▶ *124 Average*

VERBS
16 **place in the middle**, centre, focus, pivot, centre on, balance, interpose, sandwich, interpolate
▶ *291 Centre*
17 **average**, bisect, cut in half, halve, divide fifty-fifty, split down the middle, split in two, split the difference, strike a balance, compromise, pair off, double, fold in two
▶ *124 Average, 173 Fraction, 176 Two, 136 Separation*
18 **stand in the middle**, straddle, lie betwixt and between, stand on middle ground, sit on the fence, fall between two stools, be neither one thing nor the other, be neither fish nor fowl, run with the hare and hunt with the hounds
▶ *158 Middle Way, 298 Interface*
19 **mediate**, arbitrate, umpire, referee, intervene, intercede, come between, compromise, negotiate, bargain, meet halfway, speak for, act for pander, pimp (Inf)
▶ *678 Mediation, 717 Compromise*

ADVERBS
20 **in the middle**, centrally, medially, in the midst of, in the thick of, amid, amidst, among, amongst, between, in between, meanwhile
21 **midway**, halfway, midstream, midships, amidships, smack (or bang or slap-bang) in the middle (Inf)
22 **half and half**, neither one thing nor the other, neither here nor there, between the devil and the deep blue sea, between Scylla and Charybdis, between a rock and a hard place, betwixt and between (Inf)

159 Consecutiveness

NOUNS
1 **consecutiveness**, successiveness, succession, progression, queue, line-up, procession
▶ *155 Sequence, 195 Succession*
2 **consecution**, sequence, series, nexus, run, course, turn, one thing after another, order, ascending order, descending order, chrono-

logical order, catenation, concatenation, chain, chaining, train, file, line, queue, string, thread, ladder, stairs, staircase, steps, colonnade, scale, arpeggio, gamut, spectrum, rainbow, suite, suit of cards
▶ *150 Order*
3 **line**, lineage, bloodline, descent, pedigree, dynasty, family tree, genealogy
▶ *154 Precedence, 107 Relatedness*
4 **repercussion**, result, consequence, effect, causality, cause and effect, domino theory, knock-on effect, snowball effect, chain reaction, aftermath, backlash, reverberation
▶ *226 Cause, 227 Effect, 231 Counteraction*
5 **continuity**, continuousness, continualness, continuance, uninterruption, unbrokenness, uniformity, sameness, undifferentiation, monotony, endlessness, ceaselessness, incessancy, constancy, constant flow
▶ *219 Continuity, 112 Uniformity, 110 Sameness, 190 Eternity*
6 **continuum**, continuous motion, cycle, circle, round, endless round, rotation, periodicity, recurrence, assembly line, conveyor belt, treadmill, vicious circle (or cycle), endless band, Möbius strip (or band), Klein bottle
▶ *313 Circularity, 364 Rotation, 183 Repetition*
7 **stability**, steadiness, steady state, equilibrium, balance, routine, rut, flow, trend
▶ *225 Stability, 584 Habit*
8 **procession**, parade, pageant, promenade, march past, cortège, funeral procession, cavalcade, motorcade, caravan, train, line, column, file, crocodile, stream, steady stream, queue, traffic jam, tailback, gridlock

ADJECTIVES
9 **consecutive**, successive, succeeding, following, serial, seriate, sequential, in order, running, ongoing, progressive, chronological, catenary, ordinal, linear, lineal
▶ *155 Sequence, 195 Succession, 150 Order*
10 **repercussive**, causal, resultant, knock-on, consequential, reverberatory
▶ *226 Cause, 227 Effect*
11 **continuous**, continual, constant, incessant, perpetual, nonstop, endless, unending, never-ending, ceaseless, unremitting, interminable, unrelieved, unbroken, solid, smooth, serried, seamless, uninterrupted, uniform, undifferentiated, featureless, monotonous
▶ *219 Continuity, 112 Uniformity, 110 Sameness, 190 Eternity*
12 **cyclical**, periodic, rhythmic, recurrent, repetitive
▶ *313 Circularity, 183 Repetition*

VERBS
13 **be consecutive**, succeed, come after, follow on, follow in a series, run on, progress
▶ *155 Sequence, 195 Succession*
14 **continue**, be continuous, not stop, extend,

run, run and run, go on (and on), carry on

▶ *219 Continuity*

15 **concatenate**, catenate, connect, connect up, join, link, string, string together, thread, chain

▶ *137 Connection*

16 **arrange consecutively**, arrange in succession, array, range, rank, line, line up, align, string out

▶ *150 Order, 152 Arrangement*

17 **line up**, get in line, fall in, form a line, queue, queue up, form a queue, form a crocodile, parade, promenade, march past, file, file past, stream past

ADVERBS

18 **consecutively**, successively, in succession, serially, in a series, sequentially, in order, chronologically, progressively, on the run, one after another, one after the other, one behind the other, in turn, turn and turn about, on the trot (Inf)

19 **continuously**, continually, constantly, incessantly, perpetually, nonstop, without stopping, at one go, endlessly, ceaselessly, day in day out, round the clock, night and day

20 **in a line**, in a row (*or* queue), in file, in single file, in Indian file, in a crocodile, end to end, bumper to bumper, nose to tail

160   Discontinuity

NOUNS

1 **discontinuity**, discontinuousness, discontinuation, discontinuance, lack of continuity, disconnectedness, disconnection, disjunction, disjointedness, irregularity, intermittence, brokenness, fitfulness, spasmodicalness, sporadicalness, disorder, incoherence, confusion, nonuniformity, unevenness, roughness, jerkiness, bumpiness, joltiness, choppiness

▶ *151 Disorder, 136 Separation, 215 Irregularity, 113 Diversity*

2 **cessation**, cease, ceasing, end, stop, halt, termination, finish

▶ *218 Cessation, 157 End*

3 **interval**, interim, intermission, lull, pause, pause for thought, time-out, break, rest, stopover, time lag, time warp, jump in time, let-up (Inf)

▶ *265 Interval*

4 **interruption**, break, suspension, breach, gap, fissure, crevasse, fault, split, crack, fracture, cut, wound

▶ *153 Disturbance, 265 Interval*

5 **caesura**, hiatus, lacuna, diaeresis, ellipsis, pause, rest, fermata

6 **intervention**, interruption, interjection, interpolation, disturbance, disruption

▶ *153 Disturbance*

7 **broken thread**, broken train of thought,

digression, non sequitur, parenthesis, nonseriality, nonlinearity, missing link, lost connection

ADJECTIVES

8 **discontinuous**, noncontinuous, unsuccessive, disconnected, disjointed, disunited, discrete, fragmented, broken, unjoined, unconnected, irregular, intermittent, fitful, spasmodic, sporadic, erratic, random, desultory, episodic, periodic, alternate, alternating, stopgo, on-off, gappy, incoherent, confused, nonuniform, uneven, rough, choppy, jerky, snatchy, bumpy, jolty, scrappy, bitty, patchy, spotty, dotted

▶ *136 Separation, 215 Irregularity, 523 Unintelligibility, 113 Diversity*

9 **discontinued**, nonrecurrent, unrepeated, ended, ceased, stopped, halted, terminated, finished, given up, no longer made

▶ *218 Cessation, 157 End*

10 **interrupted**, disturbed, disrupted, broken off, suspended

11 **digressive**, parenthetic, nonserial, nonlinear, nonsequential

VERBS

12 **discontinue**, end, put an end to, cease, stop, halt, terminate, finish, quit, give up, suspend, break off, cut off, cut short, leave off, refrain from, drop, call it a day (Inf), pack it in (Inf), call it quits (Inf)

▶ *218 Cessation, 157 End, 684 Completion*

13 **pause**, pause for thought, take time out, take a sabbatical (*or* vacation *or* holiday), rest, have a break, lay over, stop over, let up, take five (Inf)

14 **disconnect**, break the connection, break (off), disjoin, disunite, separate, sever, cut

15 **lose one's train of thought**, digress, stray (from the subject), ramble, go off at a tangent, wander, go off the point

16 **interrupt**, disturb, disrupt, break one's chain of thought, intervene, interject, interpolate, interpose, put between, chip in (Inf), chime in (Inf), butt in (Inf), cut in (Inf), barge in on (Inf), put one's oar in (Inf)

▶ *153 Disturbance, 298 Interface*

ADVERBS

17 **discontinuously**, periodically, at intervals, intermittently, fitfully, spasmodically, sporadically, irregularly, occasionally, infrequently, once in a while, now and then, off and on, by fits, in fits and starts, by degrees, here and there, *passim* (L), in spots, in dribs and drabs (Inf)

18 **disconnectedly**, disjointedly, brokenly, desultorily, by catches, by jerks, by skips, by fits and starts

161 Assembly

NOUNS

1 **assembly**, assemblage, bringing together, coming together, convergence, confluence, collection, collecting, gathering, ingathering, forgathering, grouping, congregation, mobilization, muster, rally, call-up, combination, joining together, junction, collocation, colligation
▶ *135 Union, 137 Connection, 140 Combination*

2 **herding**, whipping in, round-up, shepherding, driving, corralling, marshalling, rodeo

3 **meeting**, assembly, gathering, meet, concourse, turnout

4 **rally**, mass meeting, demonstration, protest meeting, sit-in, demo (Inf)
▶ *713 Protest, 475 Demonstration*

5 **conference**, symposium, convention, convocation, congregation, congress, caucus, synod, diet, council, legislature, conclave
▶ *143 Party, 12 Government and Politics*

6 **sitting**, session, board meeting, business meeting, discussion group

7 **committee**, commission, council, panel, board, cabinet, body

8 **rendezvous**, tryst, assignation, date, appointment

9 **social gathering**, get-together, reunion, gathering of the clans, party, celebration, festival, fiesta, festivity, social, reception, function, wedding breakfast, wedding reception, stag party, hen party, at-home, soirée, housewarming, do (Inf), bash (Inf), thrash (Inf), shindig (Inf), shindy (Inf), beanfeast (Inf), beano (Inf), bunfight (Inf)
▶ *812 Celebration, 815 Sociability*

10 **dance**, ball, hunt ball, charity ball, prom (US), disco, acid-house party, rave, hop, barn dance, ceilidh, knees-up (Inf), bop (Inf)
▶ *46 Dancing and Ballet*

11 **group**, grouping, party, company, body, band, gang, pack, ring, circle, posse, bevy, bunch (Inf), crowd (Inf)

12 **team**, squad, crew, outfit, complement, corps, troupe, cast, company, orchestra, band, rock group, pop group
▶ *51 Performing Arts, 49 Music*

13 **workforce**, staff, personnel, manpower, crew, factory floor, shop floor
▶ *644 Worker*

14 **force**, armed force, army, navy, air force, troop, squadron, squad, platoon, unit, regiment, corps, battalion, division, brigade, legion, fleet
▶ *17 Military Affairs, 679 Combatant*

15 **association**, organization, society, club, union, trade union, guild, syndicate, fellowship, brotherhood, fraternity, sisterhood, sorority
▶ *815 Sociability*

16 **party**, faction, movement, wing, junta, cabal, cell, unit
▶ *665 Party, 143 Part*

17 **family**, nuclear family, extended family, household, kith and kin, folks (Inf), relatives, social group, peer group, community, class, clan, tribe, speech community, people
▶ *107 Relatedness, 2 Sociology, 163 Class*

18 **generation**, age group, peer group, cohort (US), compeers

19 **clique**, circle, set, coterie, in-crowd, in-group, them and us

20 **crowd**, mob, mass, throng, multitude, horde, host, swarm, ruck, rabble, the masses, the hoi polloi, all and then some, all the world and his wife (Inf), the great unwashed (Inf), every mother's son (Inf), every Tom, Dick, and Harry (Inf)
▶ *181 Multitude, 164 Generality, 400 Humankind*

21 **scrum**, scrummage (*or* scrimmage), huddle, crush, squeeze, jam, press

Collective Names for Birds and Animals

bask (crocodiles)
bevy (roe deer, quails, larks, pheasants)
bloat (hippopotami)
brood (chickens)
bury (rabbits)
busyness (ferrets)
charm (finches, goldfinches)
chattering (choughs)
clowder (cats)
covey (partridges)
crash (rhinoceros)
descent (woodpeckers)
desert (lapwings)
dout (wild cats)
down (hares)
doylt (swine)
drove (horses, ponies, bullocks)

flock (sheep)
fluther (jellyfish)
gaggle (geese on land)
gam (whales)
gang (elk)
gulp (swallows)
herd (cattle, elephants, bison)
hive (bees)
hover (trout)
kennel (dogs)
labour (moles)
leap (leopards)
lepe (leopards)
litter (kittens, pigs)
murder (crows)
murmuration (starlings)
muster (peacocks, penguins)
mute (hares)

obstinacy (buffalo)
pack (hounds, dogs, grouse)
paddling (ducks on water)
pandemonium (parrots)
parade (elephants)
parcel (penguins)
parliament (owls)
pod (seals)
pride (lions)
rafter (turkeys)
rookery (rooks, seals)
safe (ducks)
sawt (lions)
school (whales, porpoises, dolphins)
serge (herons)
shoal (fish)
skein (geese in flight)

skulk (foxes)
sloth (bears)
smack (jellyfish)
sowse (lions)
span (mules)
spring (teal)
stare (owls)
string (horses)
stud (mares)
swarm (flies, locusts, bees)
tittering (magpies)
tribe (goats)
turmoil (porpoises)
turn (turtles)
unkindness (ravens)
watch (nightingales)
zeal (zebras)

Collective Names by Animal

bears (sloth)	finches (charm)	lions (pride, sawt, sowse)	rabbits (bury)
bees (hive, swarm)	fish (shoal)		ravens (unkindness)
bison (herd)	flies (swarm)	locusts (swarm)	rhinoceros (crash)
buffalo (obstinacy)	foxes (skulk)	magpies (tittering)	roe deer (bevy)
bullocks (drove)	geese (gaggle, skein)	mares (stud)	rooks (rookery)
cats (clowder)	goats (tribe)	moles (labour)	seals (pod, rookery)
cattle (herd)	goldfinches (charm)	mules (span)	sheep (flock)
chickens (brood)	grouse (pack)	owls (parliament, stare)	starlings (murmuration)
choughs (chattering)	hares (down, mute)	parrots (pandemonium)	swallows (gulp)
crocodiles (bask)	herons (serge)	partridges (covey)	swine (doylt)
crows (murder)	hippopotami (bloat)	peacocks (muster)	teal (spring)
dogs (kennel, pack)	horses (drove)	penguins (muster)	trout (hover)
dolphins (school)	hounds (pack)	pheasants (bevy)	turkeys (rafter)
ducks (paddling, safe)	jellyfish (smack, fluther)	pigs (litter)	turtles (turn)
elephants (herd, pa-rade)	kittens (litter)	ponies (drove)	woodpeckers (descent)
	larks (bevy)	porpoises (school, turmoil)	wildcats (dout)
elk (gang)	lapwings (desert)		whales (school, gam)
ferrets (busyness)	leopards (leap, lepe)	quails (bevy)	zebras (zeal)

22 **flood**, deluge, spate, surge, stream, volley, shower, hail, storm
▸ *610 Excess*

23 **flock**, herd, pack, kennel, drove, drive, stable, string, colony, set, host, troop, army, swarm, school, shoal

24 **brace**, pair, clutch, batch, litter, brood
▸ *176 Two, 245 Reproduction*

25 **assemblage**, collection, set, batch, group, accumulation, congeries, agglomeration, conglomeration, aggregation, hoard, store, stockpile, food mountain, fund, holdings
▸ *140 Combination, 605 Store, 610 Excess*

26 **mass**, heap, pile, stack, mound, mountain, embankment, bank, sandbank, dune, drift, snowdrift, deposit, sediment
▸ *132 Remainder*

27 **bundle**, wad, batch, clump, cluster, bunch, knot, parcel, package, bale, truss, rick, hayrick, haystack, roll, bolt, quiver, sheaf, skein, hank, tussock, hassock, crop

28 **cluster**, galaxy, constellation, nebula, star system
▸ *53 Astronomy, Astronautics, and Rocketry*

29 **bunch**, bouquet, posy, nosegay, spray
▸ *84 Flowers*

30 **compilation**, collection, corpus, compendium, anthology, composition, roundup (Inf)
▸ *133 Mixture*

31 **exhibition**, show, display, collection, gallery, museum, library, zoo, menagerie, aviary, aquarium

32 **miscellany**, miscellanea, collectanea, chrestomathy (Lit), medley, assortment, mixture, mixed bag, mixed lot, potpourri, smorgasbord, jumble, hotchpotch (*or* hodgepodge), sundries, oddments, bits and pieces, odds and ends, bits and bobs (Inf)
▸ *133 Mixture*

33 **putting together**, assembly, assemblage, collage, montage, construction, erection, connection, fitting (*or* joining *or* piecing) together, manufacture, fabrication, assembly line, production line
▸ *137 Connection, 243 Production*

34 **assembler**, convener (*or* convenor), whip, whipper-in, herdsman, shepherd, sheepdog

35 **collector**, accumulator, gatherer, gleaner, beachcomber, harvester, reaper, tax collector, rent collector, debt collector, stamp collector, philatelist, coin collector, numismatist
▸ *746 Payment, 68 Agriculture*

36 **hoarder**, squirrel, magpie, miser, penny-pincher, niggard, Scrooge
▸ *758 Meanness, 605 Store*

VERBS

37 **assemble**, collect, gather, bring together, draw together, group, group together, accumulate, agglomerate, aggregate, mass, amass, hoard, store, stockpile, heap, pile, stack, build up, mound, bank, bank up
▸ *605 Store*

38 **group**, batch, clump, cluster, bunch, bundle, parcel, package, wrap, bale, truss, bind

39 **come together**, collect together, gather together, forgather, meet, rendezvous, congregate, group, flock together, gather round, rally round, huddle, go into a huddle, cluster, bunch

40 **crowd**, mass, throng, pack, cram, mill, mill around, seethe, teem, crawl, swarm, horde, troop, flood, stream, pour, surge, sweep, flow, rush
▸ *181 Multitude*

41 **band together**, get together, join forces, unite, team up, join up, link up, gang up, fall in, swell the ranks
▸ *664 Cooperation*

42 **call together**, convene, convoke, summon, call a meeting, hold a meeting, muster, marshal, rally, mobilize, call up

43 **herd**, shepherd, round up, corral, drive, drive together, whip in, call in

44 **put together**, compose, compile, colligate,

connect, join, unite, combine, fit (*or* join *or* piece) together, construct, erect, fabricate, manufacture, make

▶ *243 Production, 137 Connection, 135 Union, 140 Combination*

45 **reassemble**, rejoin, put back together

ADJECTIVES

46 **assembled**, gathered, congregate, congregated, convened, summoned, mobilized, called up, herded, mustered, shepherded, rounded up

47 **collected**, amassed, massed, accumulated, hoarded, stockpiled, heaped, piled, stacked, put together

48 **cumulate**, glomerate, conglomerate, agglomerate, aggregate, convergent, confluent, collective, combined, joined, united, connected

49 **grouped**, clumped, clustered, bunched, bundled, packaged, baled, trussed, wrapped, parcelled, wrapped up, fascicled, fascicular, congressional, congregational, factional, cabalistic

50 **crowded**, packed, crammed, congested, dense, close, serried, swarming, seething, teeming, bristling, milling, crawling, jam-packed (Inf), chock-a-block (Inf), thick as flies (Inf), thick on the ground (Inf)

ADVERBS

51 **together**, unitedly, collectively, all together, en masse, in a mass, in a body, as one

162 Dispersion

NOUNS

1 **dispersion**, dispersal, diffusion, distribution, dissemination, sowing, strewing, casting, seeding, scattering, scatterment, circulation, publication, broadcast, broadcasting, spread, deployment, propagation, issuance, giving out, dispensation

▶ *532 Publication, 731 Allocation*

2 **disbandment**, dissolution, demobilization, deactivation, dismissal, sending home, going home, demob (Inf)

▶ *345 Departure*

3 **dilution**, watering down, attenuation, liquefaction, deliquescence, evaporation, boiling away, vaporization, volatilization, dissipation, disappearance

▶ *458 Disappearance*

4 **sprinkling**, spraying, spattering, splattering, smattering, dusting, powdering, peppering, circumfusion, studding, spotting, dotting, speckling, freckling

5 **divergence**, radiation, branching, branching out, ramification, fanning out, splaying, deflection, diffraction, disintegration, fragmentation, decomposition, break-up, separation, parting, split-up (Inf)

▶ *343 Divergence, 136 Separation, 141 Disintegration*

6 **decentralization**, deconcentration, regionalization, localization, federalization, subsidiarity

7 **sprawl**, urban sprawl, ribbon development, dispersed population, population drift, diaspora, emigration

8 **driftwood**, flotsam and jetsam

VERBS

9 **be dispersed**, disperse, scatter, separate, part, break up, split up, part company, go one's separate ways, move apart, drift apart, drift off, stray, straggle, spread, spread out, sprawl

▶ *136 Separation, 345 Departure*

10 **diverge**, fork, branch out (*or* off), ramify, radiate, fan out, splay

11 **explode**, burst, fly apart, fly in all directions, come apart, come unstuck, break up, disintegrate, fragment, decompose, evaporate, dissipate, disappear, vanish

▶ *141 Disintegration, 458 Disappearance*

12 **disperse**, scatter, diffract, diffuse, dispel, separate, part, divide, sunder, hive off, detach

▶ *136 Separation*

13 **dismiss**, send away, send off, disband, dissolve, demobilize, deactivate, discharge, send home, muster out (US), rout, put to flight, demob (Inf)

14 **dilute**, water down, dissolve, thin, thin out, attenuate, liquefy, evaporate, boil away, vaporize, volatilize, dissipate

15 **decentralize**, deconcentrate, regionalize, localize, depopulate

16 **distribute**, disseminate, circulate, put into circulation, publish, broadcast, spread, deploy, propagate, issue, dispense, deal, deal out, dole out

▶ *532 Publication, 731 Allocation*

17 **sow**, seed, strew, scatter around, scatter to the winds, throw around, cast, fling, litter

18 **sprinkle**, spray, splash, shower, spatter, splatter, smatter, dust, powder, flour, dredge, pepper, stud, spot, dot, speckle, speck, freckle

ADJECTIVES

19 **dispersed**, scattered, diffuse, widespread, sparse, infrequent, sporadic, dotted about, few and far between

▶ *213 Infrequency, 182 Few*

20 **separated**, separate, discrete, disintegrated, fragmented, decomposed, broken-up, split-up

▶ *136 Separation, 141 Disintegration*

21 **disbanded**, dissolved, unassembled, dismissed, demobilized, deactivated, demobbed (Inf)

22 **distributed**, disseminated, diffused, broadcast, spread, deployed, strewn, sown, propagated, circulated, published, issued, given out, dispensed

▶ *532 Publication, 731 Allocation*

23 **sprinkled**, sprayed, spattered, splattered,

smattered, dusted, powdered, peppered, studded, spotted, dotted, speckled, freckled
24 **divergent**, forking, radiating, branching, ramiform, dendriform, dendritic, centrifugal
25 **sprawled**, sprawling, straggling, straggly, drifting, adrift, astray, wandering, stray, loose, all over the lot (Inf)
26 **decentralized**, deconcentrated, regionalized, localized, federalized
27 **dilute**, diluted, watered-down, liquefied, evaporated, boiled away, vaporized, dissipated
28 **dispersive**, scattering, spreading, diffractive, diffusive, distributive, disseminative, dissipative

ADVERBS

29 **dispersively**, diffractively, diffusively, distributively, disseminatively, dissipatively
30 **diffusely**, sparsely, infrequently, sporadically, here and there, in places
31 **everywhere**, in all quarters, wherever you look (or turn), in all directions, to the four winds, to the four corners of the earth

163　Class

O let us love our occupations,/ Bless the squire and his relations, /Live upon our daily rations, /And always know our proper stations. Charles Dickens.

All the world over, I will back the masses against the classes. William Ewart Gladstone.

The history of all hitherto existing society is the history of class struggles. Karl Marx.

NOUNS

1 **classification**, categorization, grouping, ordering, ranking, grading, hierarchy, taxonomy
2 **class**, subclass, category, subcategory, division, subdivision, bracket, set, subset, slot, niche, pigeonhole, compartment, pocket, section, subsection, group, subgroup, grouping, head, heading, list, listing, order, branch, department
▶ *171 List, 150 Order, 161 Assembly, 665 Party, 143 Part, 258 Container*
3 **kingdom**, subkingdom, phylum, subphylum, branch, subbranch, class, subclass, order, suborder, family, subfamily, genus, subgenus, species, subspecies, variety, subvariety, sex, gender
▶ *592 Plants, 76 Animals (General)*
4 **type**, sort, kind, genre, variety, version, style, ilk, strain, species, genus, league, realm, domain, sphere, brand, make, mark, marque, label, shape, cast, form, mould, frame, stripe, feather, line, grain, kidney, stamp, colour, complexion, hue, character, nature, manner, persuasion, the like (or likes) of (Inf)
▶ *306 Form, 114 Similarity*

5 **social class**, social status, standing, station, position, grade, rating, pecking order, rank, tier, level, stratum, band, league, order, sphere, caste, group, set, clique, coterie
▶ *2 Sociology, 161 Assembly*
6 **students**, class, pupils, grade, form, year, track, year-group, subject-group, stream, discussion group
7 **lecture**, class, seminar, lesson, presentation, discussion
▶ *6 Education*
8 **genealogy**, line, lineage, birth, descent, ancestry, extraction, stock, strain, breed, pedigree, blood, kin, ilk, family, clan, tribe, race, religion, denomination, sect
▶ *107 Relatedness, 7 Religion*
9 **distinction**, prestige, merit, excellence, presence, bearing, breeding, style, chic
▶ *617 Worth, 794 Refinement*

ADJECTIVES

10 **classificatory**, classificational, categorical, hierarchical, taxonomic(al), indexical, tabular
11 **typical**, characteristic, representative, generic, stereotypical, special, specific, particular, peculiar, distinctive, defining, definitive
▶ *165 Speciality*
12 **classed**, classified, categorized, grouped, ranked, graded, rated, sorted, ordered, placed, pigeonholed

VERBS

13 **class**, classify, categorize, group, type, place, pigeonhole, catalogue, designate, fix, assign, dispose, distribute, label, brand
▶ *544 Identification*
14 **sort**, organize, assort, arrange, range, order, grade, rank, rate, divide, subdivide, analyse, tabulate, index, codify
▶ *152 Arrangement, 150 Order, 136 Separation*
15 **be in a class of one's own**, stand out, shine, be head and shoulders above the rest

ADVERBS

16 **taxonomically**, hierarchically, categorically, characteristically, typically, generically, specifically, distinctively, definitively

164　Generality

All generalizations are dangerous, even this one. Alexandre Dumas, fils.

NOUNS

1 **generality**, universality, general applicability, comprehensiveness, inclusiveness, globality, cosmopolitanism, internationalism
▶ *146 Inclusion*
2 **catholicity**, catholicism, ecumenicalism, ecumenicism, ecumenicity, Broad Church, eclecticism
3 **nonspecificness**, broadness, sweepingness, looseness, imprecision, inexactitude, broad canvas, broad spectrum, blanket coverage,

dragnet, catch-all, open house, open letter, circular

▶ *271 Breadth, 504 Error*

4 **widespreadness**, extensiveness, rifeness, rampantness, pervasiveness, ubiquity, omnipresence

▶ *253 Presence*

5 **averageness**, ordinariness, standardness, rule, general rule, commonness, commonality, routineness, routine, habitualness, habit, usualness

▶ *124 Average, 167 Conformity, 584 Habit, 166 Rule*

6 **average**, run of the mill, run, general run, ordinary run, common run, ruck, lowest common denominator

7 **global view**, world view, panorama, bird's-eye view, overview, overall picture

▶ *142 Whole, 435 Vision*

8 **generalization**, general idea, abstract, abstraction, sweeping (*or* loose *or* vague) statement, cliché, platitude, trite (*or* hackneyed *or* jaded) expression

▶ *505 Maxim*

9 **everyman**, everywoman, common man (*or* woman), common type, Mr (*or* Mrs) Average, man (*or* woman) in the street, man (*or* woman) on the Clapham omnibus, Joe Bloggs, Joe Public, John Q. Public, ordinary Joe, Joe Six-Pack (US), John Doe (US), girl (*or* boy) next door, little man

▶ *400 Humankind, 803 Commoner*

10 **everyone**, everybody, everything, all, one and all, all hands, the long, the short, and the tall, all and sundry, each one, each and every one, every mother's son, every man Jack, every Tom, Dick, and Harry, all the world and his wife (*or* brother), the whole world, *tout le monde* (Fr), everybody under the sun, Uncle Tom Cobbley and all, all and then some, the whole kit and caboodle (Inf), the whole shooting match (Inf), the whole shebang (Sl)

▶ *144 Completeness, 142 Whole*

11 **general public**, populace, common people, grass roots, rank and file, masses, multitude, hoi polloi, vox populi, rabble, mob, the great unwashed (Sl)

▶ *181 Multitude, 803 Commoner, 161 Assembly*

12 **any**, anything, anyone, anybody

13 **whoever**, whosoever, whomever, whomsoever, no matter who

14 **whatever**, whatsoever, what, which, what have you, what you will, no matter what (*or* which)

ADJECTIVES

15 **general**, universal, whole, comprehensive, fully comprehensive, inclusive, all-inclusive, nonexclusive, all-embracing, all-encompassing, all-covering, all-comprehending, all-pervading, overall, synoptic, heterogenous, diversified, miscellaneous, eclectic, liberal, catholic, ecumenical, cosmopolitan, broad-based, encyclopedic, blanket, extensive, sweeping, wide, broad, across-the-board, panoramic, bird's-eye

▶ *146 Inclusion, 271 Breadth, 142 Whole, 133 Mixture*

16 **universal**, cosmic, galactic, planetary, worldwide, global, international, cosmopolitan, national, nationwide, countrywide

17 **widespread**, extensive, rife, rampant, pervasive, ubiquitous, omnipresent, endemic, epidemic, pandemic

▶ *253 Presence*

18 **far-reaching**, wide-reaching, far-ranging, wide-ranging, far-flung

▶ *263 Distance*

19 **prevailing**, prevalent, widespread, common, popular, accepted, predominant, dominant, predominating, public, communal, community, unrestricted

20 **generalized**, nonspecific, unspecific, generic, approximate, inexact, imprecise, indefinite, indeterminate, undetermined, unspecified, ill-defined, broad, loose, vague, sweeping, abstract, nebulous

▶ *271 Breadth, 504 Error*

21 **common**, regular, standard, normal, usual, ordinary, average, unexceptional, run-of-the-mill, customary, habitual, routine, everyday, equotidian, familiar, accustomed, middle-brow, middle-of-the-road, conventional, pedestrian, vernacular, vulgar, down-market, plebeian

▶ *167 Conformity, 584 Habit, 803 Commoner*

22 **commonplace**, trite, platitudinous, hackneyed, uninspired, unimaginative, jaded, overused, overworked, stereotyped, stereotypical, common or garden

▶ *505 Maxim*

VERBS

23 **generalize**, universalize, globalize, catholicize, ecumenicize

24 **broaden**, widen, spread, expand, extend

▶ *271 Breadth, 261 Expansion*

25 **broadcast**, diffuse, disperse, disseminate, sow

▶ *162 Dispersion*

26 **popularize**, vulgarize, take to the masses

27 **make a generalization**, make a sweeping statement, generalize, deal in generalities, paint with a broad brush

28 **prevail**, predominate, dominate, obtain, reign, rule, be the rule, have currency, be the rage (Sl), be in (Sl), be the in thing (Sl)

▶ *796 Fashion, 688 Authority, 235 Power*

ADVERBS

29 **generally**, in general, generally speaking, broadly, broadly speaking, loosely, approximately

30 **usually**, as a rule, almost always, normally, ordinarily, typically, invariably, routinely, habitually, as a matter of course, in the usual course, without exception
▶ *584 Habit*

31 **overall**, on balance, on average, all things considered, all in all, on the whole, as a whole, in the long run, for the most part, in the main, mainly, mostly, largely, wholly
▶ *142 Whole, 143 Part*

32 **universally**, cosmically, internationally, nationally, widely, extensively, commonly, predominantly, invariably, everywhere, the world over

165   Speciality

NOUNS

1 **speciality**, specialness, specific quality, specificity, particularity, individuality, originality, uniqueness, distinctiveness, differentness, differentiation
▶ *119 Originality, 117 Disparity, 174 One, 544 Identification*

2 **personality**, character, nature, temperament, identity, persona, psyche, make-up
▶ *103 Essence*

3 **characteristic**, feature, distinctive feature, singularity, attribute, quality, property, trait, quirk, mannerism, peculiarity, idiosyncrasy, eccentricity, trick, mark, earmark, hallmark, trademark, stamp, seal, brand, cachet, token, mould, cut, shape, figure, configuration, taste, flavour, savour, smell, odour, aroma, touch, feel
▶ *411 Taste, 416 Odour, 306 Form*

4 **specifications**, conditions, qualifications, particulars, details, minutiae, essentials, essential facts, fundamentals, specs (Inf), nitty-gritty (Inf), fine print (Inf), nuts and bolts (Inf), ins and outs (Inf)
▶ *485 Qualification*

5 **the special**, the specific, the particular, the individual, the unique
▶ *174 One*

6 **exception**, exception to the rule, isolated instance, special case, anomaly, irregularity, peculiarity, departure, one-off
▶ *215 Irregularity, 168 Nonconformity*

7 **special skill**, expertise, métier, forte, strong point, genius, gift, talent, aptitude, skill
▶ *655 Skill*

8 **specialization**, special study, particularization, concentration, special interest, pursuit, line, field, area, sphere, school, subject, pet subject, special subject, major (US), vocation, trade, craft, bag (Sl), scene (Inf), thing (Sl), cup of tea (Inf), baby (Inf), claim to fame (Inf)
▶ *644 Work*

9 **special**, speciality of the house, *spécialité de la maison* (Fr), chef's special, dish of the day, feature, main feature, leader, leading item

10 **specialized language**, technical language, code, jargon, idiom, dialect, patois, idiolect, argot, technobabble (Inf), psychobabble (Inf)
▶ *5 Linguistics*

11 **identity**, id, ego, self, oneself, real self, inner self, inner man (*or* woman), true self, subliminal self, subconscious self, hidden self, other self, alter ego, *alter* (L), outward self, outer self, psyche, soul, spirit

12 **I**, me, myself, I myself, my humble self, we, I and I, us, ourselves, yourself, yourselves, himself, herself, itself, themselves, yours truly (Inf), number one (Inf)

13 **person**, character, individual, being
▶ *400 Humankind, 174 One*

14 **specialist**, authority, consultant, expert, master, connoisseur, professional, scholar
▶ *655 Skill, 501 Knowledge*

ADJECTIVES

15 **special**, especial, specific, particular, express, precise, individual, respective, individualistic, original, unique, quintessential, intrinsic, single, singular, distinct, distinctive, different
▶ *119 Originality, 103 Essence, 117 Disparity, 174 One, 503 Accuracy, 550 Clarity*

16 **characteristic**, distinguishing, personal, peculiar, idiosyncratic, idiomatic, unusual, out of the ordinary, extraordinary, uncommon, curious, marked, quirky, eccentric, typical, in character, true to form
▶ *544 Identification, 168 Nonconformity*

17 **exceptional**, special, one of a kind, unique, sui generis, inimitable, distinguished, remarkable, notable, noteworthy, esoteric, exotic, ageneric, way-out (Inf)

18 **subjective**, individualistic, solipsistic, egotistical, self-centred, selfish
▶ *860 Selfishness*

19 **personal**, private, intimate, inner
▶ *103 Essence*

20 **personalized**, individualized, custom-built, made to measure, bespoke, one-off

21 **specialized**, technical, specialist, expert, authoritative, knowledgeable, professional, scholarly
▶ *501 Knowledge, 655 Skill*

VERBS

22 **characterize**, distinguish, mark, differentiate, identify, brand, label, earmark, set apart, select, single out, pick out, point out, highlight, pinpoint, put one's finger on (Inf)
▶ *117 Disparity, 544 Identification, 580 Selection, 554 Emphasis*

23 **particularize**, descend to particulars, give details of, treat in detail, go into detail, spell out, come to the point, get down to brass tacks (Inf), get down to the nitty gritty (Inf)

24 **specify**, stipulate, designate, determine, fix,

set, assign, pin down, define, describe, delineate, depict, enumerate, quantify, itemize, list, denominate, name, signify, name names, point to (or out), mention, cite, quote
▶ *560 Description, 171 List*
25 **excel**, stand out, shine, in a class of one's own
▶ *617 Worth, 126 Superiority*
26 **personalize**, individualize, make one's own, put one's mark upon
27 **specialize**, specialize in, pursue, follow, study, major in (US), go in for, be into (Sl)

ADVERBS

28 **specially**, especially, specifically, particularly, expressly, exactly, precisely, distinctly, in particular, to be specific
29 **personally**, privately, individually, for one's own part, as far as one is concerned, in person, in the flesh
30 **characteristically**, peculiarly, uniquely, singularly, distinctively, markedly, exceptionally, remarkably, like no other, in its own way
31 **namely**, that is to say, *videlicet* (L), viz, to wit, i.e., e.g., *scilicet* (L), scil., sc
32 **severally**, each, apiece, respectively, singly, one by one, in turn, in detail, bit by bit

166   Rule

The exception proves the rule. Saying.

Rules and models destroy genius and art. William Hazlitt.

The golden rule is that there are no golden rules. George Bernard Shaw.

NOUNS

1 **rule**, regulation, law, directive, ruling, injunction, statute, bylaw, order, prescription, standing order, decree, edict, ukase, fiat, commandment, act, covenant, ordinance, enactment
▶ *16 Law, 692 Command*
2 **canon**, code, rulebook, statute book, constitution, charter, jurisprudence
3 **rule** (*or* **law**) **of nature**, law of the jungle, sod's law, Murphy's law, Parkinson's law, law of averages, rule of thumb, natural (*or* universal) law, Procrustean law
4 **guide**, guideline, direction, instruction, prescription, precept, principle, tenet, keynote, axiom, maxim, canon, norm, standard, criterion, firm principle, hard and fast rule, condition
▶ *505 Maxim*
5 **precedent**, forerunner, example, model, pattern, prototype, formula
▶ *167 Conformity*
6 **custom**, habit, convention, tradition, wont, praxis, way, method, system, practice, procedure, routine, drill, rut, groove, policy, form, done thing, way of things, order of things, way things are

▶ *584 Habit, 327 Way, 167 Conformity*
7 **uniformity**, constancy, consistency, regularity, harmony
▶ *112 Uniformity, 214 Regularity*
8 **authority**, command, direction, management, administration, influence, control, sway, dominion, domination, power, supremacy, mastery, reign, sovereignty
▶ *688 Authority, 653 Management, 235 Power, 233 Influence*

ADJECTIVES

9 **legal**, statutory, mandatory, compulsory, obligatory, de rigueur, regulatory, injunctive, prescriptive, procedural, administrative, official
▶ *16 Law*
10 **customary**, habitual, accustomed, wonted, conventional, traditional, regulation, standard, routine, usual, normal, typical, copybook, regulated, methodical, systematic, orderly
▶ *584 Habit*
11 **uniform**, constant, consistent, regular, harmonious
▶ *112 Uniformity, 214 Regularity*
12 **ruling**, authoritative, commanding, influential, controlling, powerful, dominant, supreme, masterful, reigning, sovereign

VERBS

13 **rule**, ordain, decree, prescribe, lay down, lay down the law, make a ruling, decide, determine, adjudicate, judge, deem, find, resolve, settle, hand down a judgment, pronounce, declare, establish
▶ *492 Judgment*
14 **regulate**, standardize, normalize, systematize, organize, order, bring into line
▶ *150 Order, 152 Arrangement*
15 **be the rule**, hold sway, prevail, predominate
16 **direct**, guide, steer, control, regulate, lead, administer, manage, run, preside over, superintend, supervise, oversee, govern, rule, rule over, hold sway over, dominate, command, be in power, reign, wear the crown, sit on the throne, wield the sceptre, rule the roost
▶ *653 Management, 688 Authority, 235 Power, 233 Influence*
17 **obey orders**, follow the party line, go by the book (*or* rulebook), stick to the rules, watch one's step, stay (*or* keep) on the straight and narrow, mind one's p's and q's, toe the line (Inf), keep one's nose clean (Inf)
▶ *694 Obedience*

ADVERBS

18 **as a rule**, habitually, customarily, normally, ordinarily, usually, generally, as is one's wont, on the whole, for the most part, mostly, more often than not, mainly, in the main, chiefly, commonly
19 **to rule**, according to the rules, by the book, methodically, systematically

167 Conformity

When in Rome, live as the Romans do: when elsewhere, live as they live elsewhere. St Ambrose.

NOUNS

1 **conformity**, conformance, conformation, accord, accordance, agreement, harmony, compatibility, consistency, uniformity, congruity, correspondence, concurrence, line, keeping, similarity, likeness, imitation, emulation, parrotry
▶ *116 Accord, 667 Agreement, 112 Uniformity, 114 Similarity, 118 Imitation*

2 **compliance**, obedience, observance, respect, abidance, acquiescence, submission, subordination
▶ *694 Obedience, 673 Submission*

3 **pliancy**, flexibility, malleability, plasticity, softness, adaptability, adaption, adaptation, accommodation, adjustment, assimilation, naturalization, acclimatization, rehabilitation
▶ *220 Conversion, 374 Softness*

4 **conventionalism**, conservatism, conformism, orthodoxy, traditionalism, Babbittry, bourgeois ethic, etiquette, formality, formalism, strictness, severity, primness, prudery
▶ *306 Formality, 690 Severity*

5 **convention**, practice, form, done thing, order of the day, received idea, party line, policy, rule, tradition, custom, fashion, trend, vogue, style
▶ *584 Habit, 166 Rule*

6 **conformist**, conformer, traditionalist, conventionalist, formalist, pedant, precisian, prude, bourgeois, burgher, Babbitt, Philistine, Mrs Grundy, Middle American, herd, sheep, company man, organization man, follower, loyalist, party hack, running dog, trimmer, lapdog, timeserver, yes-man, flatterer, parrot, copycat, imitator, square (Inf), stick-in-the-mud (Inf), square John (Inf), grey (Inf), do-right man (Inf)
▶ *847 Duty, 808 Servility, 853 Flattery, 118 Imitation, 7 Religion*

VERBS

7 **conform**, conform to, accord, agree, concur, correspond, match, tally, fit, square with, harmonize, suit, meet, run true to form
▶ *667 Agreement, 116 Accord*

8 **comply**, comply with, adapt, adapt oneself, adjust, accommodate oneself, fit in, fall in with, go along with, play the game, submit, yield, acquiesce, accede, consent, agree, go by, abide by, follow, observe, respect, obey, obey regulations, stick to the rules, toe the line (*or* mark), stay in line, keep in step, follow suit, go with the flow, go with the stream (*or* current *or* tide), swim with the stream (*or* tide), run with the pack (*or* herd), follow the beaten path, imitate, emulate, copy, do as others do, do as the Romans do, follow the fashion, follow the trend, keep up with the Joneses, jump on the bandwagon
▶ *694 Obedience, 673 Submission, 118 Imitation*

9 **make conform**, conform, accommodate, adjust, straighten, align, bring into line, fit, fit in, trim, cut (*or* trim) down to size, form, shape, mould, force into a mould, press, standardize, stereotype

10 **assimilate**, naturalize, acclimatize, rehabilitate, reeducate, indoctrinate, brainwash, imbue, instil, implant, drill, school, teach, train, coach, instruct, correct, discipline, knock (*or* lick) into shape

ADJECTIVES

11 **conformable**, adaptable, adaptive, adjustable, flexible, pliant, malleable, soft, plastic

12 **conforming**, accordant, concordant, harmonious, compatible, consistent, consonant, congruous, congruent, corresponding, agreeing, in agreement, in accord, in keeping, in line, in step
▶ *116 Accord, 667 Agreement*

13 **compliant**, willing, obedient, acquiescent, submissive, yielding, sheep-like, lemming-like, tractable, complaisant, accommodating, agreeable, passive
▶ *694 Obedience, 673 Submission*

14 **conformist**, orthodox, kosher, conservative, law-abiding, conventional, traditional, traditionalist, traditionalistic, bourgeois, provincial, correct, proper, pedantic, formal, old-fashioned, staid, strait-laced, prim, prudish, square (Inf), stuffy (Inf), stodgy (Inf), grey (Inf), uptight (Inf)
▶ *584 Habit*

15 **everyday**, quotidian, ordinary, unexceptional, common, commonplace, common or garden, familiar, household, typical, stock, standard, general, usual, identikit, stereotyped, average, median, middling, normal, straight

ADVERBS

16 **adaptably**, conformably, pliantly, malleably, flexibly, willingly, yieldingly, complaisantly, submissively, compliantly, obediently, passively

17 **conformingly**, harmoniously, compatibly, consistently, congruously, in harmony, in accord, in keeping, in line, in place, in accordance

18 **as usual**, as a matter of course, of course, as always, as before

19 **according to rule**, by the book, conventionally, traditionally, by the numbers (Inf)

168 Nonconformity

NOUNS

1 **nonconformity**, unconformity, noncon-

formance, disaccord, disaccordance, disagreement, inconsistency, incongruity, incompatibility, disparity, contrast, difference, diversity
▶ *117 Disparity, 666 Disagreement, 113 Diversity, 115 Dissimilarity*

2 **dissent**, nonconcurrence, disagreement, dissidence, noncompliance, infringement, infraction, nonobservance, disobedience, recalcitrance, contrariety, contumely, protest, recusance, revolt, rebellion, breaking away
▶ *500 Dissent, 693 Disobedience, 713 Protest*

3 **nonconformism**, unorthodoxy, heterodoxy, heresy, iconoclasm, schism, revisionism, deviationism, unconventionality, unconventional behaviour, eccentricity, Bohemianism, hippiedom

4 **unusualness**, uncommonness, exceptionality, extraordinariness, uniqueness, rareness, rarity, individuality, singularity, originality, oddity, queerness, curiosity, peculiarity, strangeness, bizarreness, weirdness, outlandishness, freakishness, quirkiness, grotesqueness, grotesquerie, monstrousness

5 **idiosyncrasy**, quirk, peculiar trait, peculiarity, mannerism, kink

6 **deviation**, deviance, aberration, vagary, abnormality, anomaly, anomalousness, unnaturalness, mutation, perversion, variant, exception, special case
▶ *113 Diversity*

7 **nonconformist**, nonconformer, maverick, unconventionalist, *enfant terrible* (Fr), Bohemian, free spirit, dropout, hippie, beatnik, flower child, traveller, New-Age traveller, tramp, vagrant, hobo, gentleman of the road, bag lady, independent, free-thinker, outsider, odd man out, misfit, fish out of water, square peg in a round hole
▶ *698 Freedom*

8 **dissenter**, dissentient, dissident, protester, radical, revolutionary, zealot, fanatic, crank, iconoclast, schismatic, apostate, heretic, recusant, rebel, anarchist, renegade, young Turk, angry young man, punk, outlaw

9 **hermit**, loner, lone wolf, solitary, solitudinarian, solitaire, eremite, anchorite, marabout, ascetic, stylite, recluse, isolationist, seclusionist

10 **eccentric**, character, natural, original, oddity, odd fellow, odd customer, odd stick, queer specimen, freak, deviant, mutant, monster, wacko (Sl), weirdo (Inf), crackpot (Inf), rum one (*or* customer) (Sl), odd (*or* queer) fish (Inf), odd bod (Inf), oddball (Inf), screwball (US sl), one-off (Inf), card (Inf), case (Inf), headcase (Inf), nutcase (Sl), basketcase (Sl), loony (Inf), nut (Sl), fruitcake (Sl)
▶ *510 Insanity*

ADJECTIVES

11 **nonconforming**, unconformable, inconsistent, incongruous, incompatible, contrasting, different
▶ *117 Disparity, 104 Extraneousness*

12 **nonconformist**, unorthodox, heterodox, heretical, iconoclastic, schismatic, schismatical, dissident, dissenting, dissentient, contumacious, recusant, radical, revolutionary, rebellious, anarchic, renegade, uncompliant, unsubmissive, recalcitrant, contrary, defiant
▶ *693 Disobedience, 668 Defiance*

13 **unconventional**, maverick, independent, free-thinking, Bohemian, fringe, beat, hippie, wandering, nomadic, travelling, off the wall (Inf)

14 **eccentric**, offbeat, idiosyncratic, quirky, individual, individualistic, singular, original, rare, unusual, exotic, unique, exceptional, far-out, way-out, extraordinary, out of the ordinary, out of this world, out of the common, out on a limb, odd, queer, curious, peculiar, strange, bizarre, outlandish, weird, freakish, grotesque, monstrous, oddball (Inf), freaky (Inf), kooky (Inf), funny (Inf), rum (Sl), dolally (Inf)
▶ *510 Insanity, 786 Wonder*

15 **irregular**, nonstandard, against the rules, not done, out of place, out of line, out of step, out of tune, out of one's element, misplaced, displaced, stray, not cricket (Inf)
▶ *844 Wrong*

16 **solitary**, standoffish, unsociable, antisocial, lone, reclusive, isolated, aloof

17 **abnormal**, anomalous, unnatural, deviant, aberrant, mutant, variant

VERBS

18 **not conform**, dissent, protest, rebel, revolt, kick over the traces, get out of line, rock the boat, make waves
▶ *713 Protest*

19 **be independent**, break away, break step, break bounds, drop out, opt out, go one's own way, do one's own thing, go against the grain, swim against the tide, go out on a limb, buck the trend, march to a different drum, leave the beaten path, go off the beaten track, deviate, break with custom, break the habit, break the mould, not fit in, stick out like a sore thumb

20 **infringe a law**, break a law, commit crime, violate, disobey, break the rules, transgress
▶ *693 Disobedience*

ADVERBS

21 **unconformably**, inconsistently, incongruously, rebelliously, unconventionally, unusually, uncommonly, singularly, unnaturally, abnormally, queerly, peculiarly, strangely, oddly, outlandishly

22 **out of step**, out of keeping, out of line, out on a limb, independently, off the beaten track, out of the way

169   Number

Round numbers are always false. Samuel Johnson.

NOUNS

1   **number**, numeral, no. (*or* n.), figure, digit, cipher, character, decimal, symbol, sign, constant, variable, notation, Arabic numeral, Roman numeral, decimal system, binary system

2   **kind of number**, whole number, integer, odd number, even number, prime number, complex number, imaginary number, real number, rational number, irrational number, transcendental number, algebraic number, cardinal number, ordinal number

3   **large number**, astronomical number, million, milliard, billion, trillion, quadrillion, quintillion, sextillion, septillion, octillion, nonillion, decillion, undecillion, duodecillion, tredecillion, quattuordecillion, quindecillion, sexdecillion, septendecillion, octodecillion, novemdecillion, vigintillion, centrillion, googol, googolplex, infinity, umpteen (Inf), zillion (Inf), jillion (Inf), squillion (Inf)

▶ *179 Five and Over, 181 Multitude, 184 Infinity*

4   **mathematical result**, sum, summation, total, running total, score, reckoning, tally, bill, aggregate, whole, amount, quantity, difference, residual, remainder, product, factor

▶ *170 Calculation, 142 Whole, 132 Remainder*

5   **ratio**, proportion, percentage, percent, fraction, proper fraction, improper fraction, simple fraction, vulgar fraction, common fraction, compound fraction, numerator, denominator, decimal fraction, decimal

▶ *173 Fraction, 143 Part*

6   **power**, exponent, index, root, square root, cube root, surd, logarithm, common logarithm, log, natural logarithm, mantissa, antilogarithm, antilog

▶ *52 Mathematics*

ADJECTIVES

7   **numerical**, numeric, numerary, numerative, numerate, digital, figurate, figural

8   **odd**, impair, even, pair, cardinal, ordinal, imaginary, real, rational, irrational, arithmetical, geometrical, algorithmic (*or* algorismic), digital, round, whole, prime, positive, negative

9   **fractional**, decimal, exponential, logarithmic, logometric, differential, integral, surd, radical, finite, infinite, aliquot

VERBS

10   **number**, enumerate, count, tell, reckon, tally, notch up, tot up, sum up, add, tote up (Inf), tick off (Inf), figure out (Inf), dope out (US sl)

11   **total**, come to, make, equal, amount to

▶ *170 Calculation*

ADVERBS

12   **numerically**, in numerical order, arithmetically, geometrically, digitally

170   Calculation

NOUNS

1   **calculation**, computation, numeration, enumeration, reckoning, figuring, determining, estimation, assessment, figure work, number work, sums, addition, subtraction, multiplication, division, algebra, geometry, trigonometry, calculus, differentiation, integration, analysis, extraction of roots, reduction, inversion, involution, evolution, convolution, approximation, interpolation, extrapolation, permutation, transformation, equation, algorithm, logarithm

▶ *130 Addition, 131 Subtraction, 52 Mathematics, 169 Number, 268 Measurement, 492 Judgment*

2   **statistics**, figures, vital statistics, indexes (*or* indices), tables, averages, psephology

3   **count**, tally, census, poll, opinion poll, head count, inventory, stocktaking, numbering, counting, accounting, telling, tallying, calculating, ciphering, reckoning, adding, totalling, yan tan tethera, one-two-three

4   **computing**, computation, data processing (DP), electronic data processing, computer technology, information technology (IT), information processing, information retrieval, numbercrunching (Inf)

▶ *65 Computers*

5   **computer**, calculator, pocket calculator, Comptometer (Tm), adding machine, cash register, till, abacus, ready reckoner, table, multiplication table, log table, rule, ruler, slide rule, Napier's bones (*or* rods), tabulator, tape measure, yardstick, gauge, dividers, compass, difference machine, suan pan, totalizer, numbercruncher (Inf)

▶ *268 Measurement*

6   **calculator**, computer, counter, teller, enumerator, census-taker, pollster, reckoner, estimator, abacist, computer operator, computer programmer, systems analyst, liveware

▶ *65 Computers*

7   **mathematician**, arithmetician, algebraist, geometrician, geometer, trigonometrician, geodesist, surveyor, statistician, actuary, pollster, psephologist, accountant, bookkeeper

▶ *750 Accounts*

VERBS

8   **calculate**, compute, work out, solve, cipher, reckon, figure, determine, estimate, tally, notch up, score, keep the score, count, keep a count, figure out (Inf), dope out (US sl), guesstimate (Inf)

▶ *169 Number*

9   **add**, add up, sum, sum up, tot up, totalize,

subtract, take away, deduct, multiply, divide, square, cube, extract roots, integrate, differentiate, extrapolate, interpolate

10 **total**, aggregate, add up to, tot up to, amount to, come to, make, equal

11 **number**, numerate, enumerate, count, count up, tell, tally, poll, count heads, count hands, count noses, call the roll, take stock, inventory, list, quantify, quantize, measure, gauge

▶ *171 List, 268 Measurement*

12 **check**, verify, audit, balance, balance the books, account, keep accounts

▶ *750 Accounts*

ADJECTIVES

13 **calculative**, computative, numerative, enumerative, estimative, calculating, computing, computational, numerical, quantifying, statistical, actuarial, psephological

14 **calculable**, computable, reckonable, estimable, countable, numerable, measurable, mensurable, quantifiable

15 **mathematical**, arithmetical, algebraic(al), geometric(al), logarithmic, algorithmic, trigonometrical, differential, integral, analytical

ADVERBS

16 **mathematically**, arithmetically, algebraically, geometrically, trigonometrically, numerically, calculably, computably, estimably, measurably, quantifiably, logarithmically, exponentially

171 List

NOUNS

1 **list**, listing, enumeration, series, items, itemization, inventory, tally, stock, repertory, register, registry, table, chart, check list

▶ *545 Record*

2 **table**, table of contents, contents, index, card index, file, filing system, catalogue, reference list, bibliography, book list, reading list, syllabus, filmography, discography, publisher's catalogue (*or* list), computer listing, menu, window, database, spreadsheet

▶ *152 Arrangement, 150 Order, 65 Computers*

3 **dictionary**, lexicon, glossary, word list, vocabulary, terminology, nomenclature, thesaurus, gazetteer, atlas, encyclopedia, almanac, yearbook, reference book, directory, guidebook, who's who, telephone directory, phone book, Yellow Pages, address book

▶ *5 Linguistics*

4 **bill**, invoice, account, itemized account, statement, ledger, books, account books, daybook, journal, bill of lading, manifest, docket, price list, tariff, bill of fare, menu, carte, wine list, shopping list

▶ *750 Accounts, 751 Price, 45 Cookery*

5 **list of appointments**, diary, engagement

diary, engagement book, daybook, Filofax (Tm), calendar, agenda, order of business, docket (US), programme, timetable, schedule, itinerary, prospectus, syllabus, curriculum, synopsis, compendium

▶ *562 Summary*

6 **list of names**, roll, register, rota, roster, scroll, panel, census, poll, head count, roll call, muster roll, tax roll, electoral roll, electorate, voting list, property roll, cadaster, payroll, active list, retired list, civil list, waiting list, sick list, short list, blacklist, cast list, dramatis personae, credits, lineup

7 **listing**, enumeration, itemization, registration, filing, indexing, cataloguing, tabulation, charting, classification, taxonomy

VERBS

8 **list**, make a list, enumerate, itemize, inventory, register, record, note, write down, put down, set down, chronicle, enter, book, post, file, pigeonhole, classify, catalogue, index, tabulate, chart, diarize, timetable, schedule, bill, invoice, short-list, blacklist

▶ *545 Record, 163 Class*

9 **enlist**, enrol, matriculate, sign up

10 **score**, keep score, tally, keep a tally of, keep count

▶ *169 Number*

ADJECTIVES

11 **listed**, enumerated, itemized, inventoried, registered, recorded, entered, noted, filed, catalogued, taxonomic, classificatory, indexed, tabulated, charted, scheduled, programmed, timetabled

12 **inventorial**, glossarial, cadastral

ADVERBS

13 **inventorially**, glossarially, tabularly, terminologically, encyclopedically, taxonomically, alphabetically, numerically, in order, in series, in sequence

172 Zero

NOUNS

1 **zero**, nought, 0, cipher, nothing, none, nil, love, duck, no score, absolute zero, blob (Sl), goose egg (US sl)

2 **nothing**, naught, aught, *nihil* (L), *nada* (Sp), *nichts* (Ger), nothing at all, not any, none, not a one, nobody, no one, not a soul, not a mite, not an iota, not a jot, not a whit, not a blessed one (Inf), not a lick (Inf), not a smell (Inf), not a sausage (Inf), zilch (Inf), nix (Sl), damn all (Sl), bugger all (Sl), sod all (Sl), fuck all (Tab sl), sweet fuck all (Tab sl), sweet FA (Sl), sweet Fanny Adams (Sl), Jack shit (Sl)

3 **nothingness**, nullity, nonexistence, nonbeing, nihility, floccinaucinihilipilification (Lit)

▶ *100 Nonexistence*

4 **zero level**, nadir, rock bottom, lowest point, last moment, zero hour, crisis point
▶ *280 Base*

5 **nonentity**, anonymity, nobody, unknown, unperson, nothing (Inf)

ADJECTIVES

6 **zero**, nil, no, not one, not any, infinitesimal, all gone

7 **null**, void, nonexistent, missing, lacking, gone, vanished

VERBS

8 **not exist**, not occur, be absent, be fictitious, vanish, disappear

9 **annihilate**, eradicate, nullify, wipe out, put an end to

10 **hit rock bottom**, reach an all-time low

ADVERBS

11 **none**, no, not at all, in no way

12 **absently**, anonymously, by proxy

173 Fraction

NOUNS

1 **fraction**, simple fraction, common fraction, vulgar fraction, compound fraction, proper fraction, improper fraction, decimal fraction, decimal
▶ *169 Number*

2 **fractional part**, part, percentage, proportion, portion, share, piece, section, segment, division, subdivision, ration
▶ *143 Part*

3 **fragment**, particle, chip, shard, sherd, splinter, sliver, scrap, shred, bit, speck, morsel, crumb, atom, iota, whit, jot, tittle

4 **less than one**, half, third, two thirds, quarter, fourth, three quarters, fifth, sixth, seventh, eighth, ninth, tenth, eleventh, twelfth, thirteenth, fourteenth, fifteenth, sixteenth, seventeenth, eighteenth, nineteenth, twentieth, thirtieth, fortieth, fiftieth, sixtieth, seventieth, eightieth, ninetieth, hundredth, thousandth, millionth, billionth, thou (Inf), mil (Inf)

ADJECTIVES

5 **fractional**, half, quarter, three-quarter, part, partial, fragmentary, incomplete, proportional, sectional, segmental, divisional, subdivisional
▶ *143 Part, 145 Incompleteness*

6 **small**, tiny, infinitesimal, insignificant

ADVERBS

7 **fractionally**, partially, partly, part, half, three-quarters, two-thirds, slightly, marginally

VERBS

8 **divide**, subdivide, split, part, share, fragment
▶ *136 Separation, 731 Allocation*

174 One

NOUNS

1 **one**, unity, unit, integer, ace, entity, singleton, single, monad, atom, point, item, article, module, individual, person, persona, soul, one and only, no other, nothing else, naught beside, nobody else

2 **item**, detail, bit, piece, single instance, isolated instance, isolated case, only exception

3 **oneness**, singleness, wholeness, integrality, unity, union, undividedness, indivisibility, solidarity, solidity, indissolubility, coherence, integrity
▶ *135 Union, 142 Whole*

4 **singularity**, individuality, uniqueness, specialness, speciality, particularity, identity, distinctiveness

5 **aloneness**, loneness, solitude, solitariness, isolation, apartness, separateness, separatism, isolationism, unilateralism, aloofness, detachment, insularity, privacy, seclusion, loneliness, lonesomeness, friendlessness
▶ *816 Unsociability*

6 **singleness**, celibacy, divorce, separation, widowhood, chastity
▶ *825 Celibacy, 824 Divorce; Widowhood*

7 **single person**, single, unmarried man, bachelor, unmarried woman, bachelor girl, spinster, maiden aunt, single parent, divorcé(e), widow, widower

8 **loner**, lone wolf, only child, solitary, hermit, eremite, anchorite, marabout, stylite, ascetic, recluse, isolationist, seclusionist
▶ *168 Nonconformity*

9 **soloist**, one-man band, one-man show, one-woman show, solo effort, solo, monologue, soliloquy, monologist, soliloquist
▶ *569 Soliloquy*

10 **single thing**, unicycle, uniped, monocle, monohull, singleton, solitaire, patience, single ticket, single file, single cream, single track, single decker

ADJECTIVES

11 **one**, single, solo, mono, monadic, atomic, individual, solitary, sole, lone, only, one and the same, first, primary

12 **one-sided**, unilateral, uniplanar, one-way, unidirectional, one-size, one-piece, unisex, unisexual, unicellular, unipolar, unicameral, monolingual, monochromatic

13 **whole**, entire, complete, integral, unified, united, joined, rolled into one, undivided, indivisible, inseparable, indissoluble, solid, unanimous
▶ *135 Union, 142 Whole, 144 Completeness*

14 **singular**, individual, special, particular, distinct, unique, one and only, only-begotten, first and last, unrepeated, one-off, once-in-a-lifetime

15 **solo**, one-man, one-woman, independent, single-handed, on one's own, alone, unaided, unassisted, unabetted, unsupported, unaccompanied, unescorted, unchaperoned

16 **alone**, lone, solitary, isolated, apart, separate, separated, separatist, isolationist, unilateralist, detached, aloof, insular, withdrawn, reclusive, lonely, lonesome, friendless, companionless, deserted, abandoned, forsaken
▶ *816 Unsociability*

17 **single**, unmarried, unwedded, divorced, separated, widowed, chaste, celibate
▶ *825 Celibacy, 824 Divorce; Widowhood*

VERBS

18 **be one**, stand alone, stand by oneself, stand on one's own two feet, go solo, stand apart, stand aloof, isolate oneself, withdraw, retreat, plough a lonely furrow, go it alone (Inf), go one's own sweet way (Inf), do one's own thing (Inf), paddle one's own canoe (Inf), hoe one's own row (Inf), roll one's own (Inf), look after number one (Inf), take care of number one (Inf)

19 **become one**, make one, unite, unify, integrate, cohere, merge, combine, fuse, join, blend
▶ *140 Combination, 142 Whole, 135 Union*

20 **single out**, pick out, isolate, separate, detach
▶ *136 Separation, 580 Selection*

ADVERBS

21 **alone**, on its own, uniquely, by itself, *per se* (L), on one's own, by oneself, all by oneself, independently, solo, single-handedly, under one's own steam, on one's lonesome (Inf), on one's Jack (Inf), on one's tod (Inf)

22 **one by one**, one at a time, singly, individually, separately, apart, in the singular

23 **wholly**, completely, integrally, indivisibly, unanimously, as one

24 **once**, once only, just once, just this once, never again, once and for all, only, solely, exclusively, simply, purely

175 Plurality

NOUNS

1 **plurality**, pluralness, the plural, plural number, many, several, some, a number, a few, a couple, a handful, more than one, (the odd) one or two, two or three, more, a greater number

2 **multiplicity**, multitude, numerousness, multitudinousness, multifariousness, variety, diversity, compositeness, multiformity, many-sidedness, polygon, polyhedron, multilateralism, polygamy, polygyny, polyandry, polytheism, pluralism, multiple personality
▶ *181 Multitude, 113 Diversity*

3 **majority**, greater number, more, greatest number, most, more than half, greater (*or* best)

part, greater proportion, bulk, mass, preponderance, lion's share
▶ *143 Part*

4 **multiplication**, proliferation, increase, multiple, product, multiplier, multiplicand, multiplication table
▶ *128 Increase, 170 Calculation*

5 **pluralist**, all-rounder, polymath, Renaissance man (*or* woman), polyglot, multilateralist, polygamist, polytheist

ADJECTIVES

6 **plural**, in the plural, not singular, more than one, multiple, nonsingle, many, several, some, certain, few, upwards of, more, most, majority, numerous, multitudinous
▶ *181 Multitude, 143 Part*

7 **various**, divers, diverse, sundry, multifarious, multiform, composite, multilateral, polygonal, many-sided, multifaceted, versatile, multipurpose, multirole, polymorphous (*or* polymorphic), multinational, multiracial, multilingual, polyglot
▶ *113 Diversity*

8 **multiplicative**, multiplied, multiple, manifold, multifold, increasing, increased, proliferative, proliferating, proliferated
▶ *128 Increase*

VERBS

9 **pluralize**, plurify, multiply, proliferate, increase, propagate, replicate, clone
▶ *128 Increase*

ADVERBS

10 **plurally**, severally, multitudinously, multiply, variously, diversely, multifariously, multilaterally

11 **in majority**, in the majority, more, most

12 **et cetera**, etc., and so on, *et al.* (L), and others, and the rest

176 Two

NOUNS

1 **two**, deuce, twain (Arch), set of two, pair, couple, brace, span, yoke, team, double harness, duet, duo, twosome, Darby and Joan, dyad, power of two, square, squared, me and you (Sl)

2 **double**, doublet, couplet, distich, duet, two-hander, diptych, double-decker, tandem, two-seater, two-wheeler, bicycle, biplane, catamaran, two-piece, duplex, bivalve, biped, bipod, binoculars, biathlon

3 **duality**, doubleness, dualism, duplexity, bilingualism, bisexuality, ambidexterity, ambiguity, double meaning, double entendre, irony, ambivalence, dual personality, split personality, Jekyll and Hyde, double life, double agent, two-facedness, double-dealing, double-crossing, double-sidedness, duplicity, Janus
▶ *578 Equivocation*

4 doubling, pairing, twinning, gemination, cloning, duplication, reproduction, repetition, double exposure
▶ *183 Repetition, 245 Reproduction*

5 twin, double, lookalike, doppelgänger, clone, duplicate, copy, carbon-copy, photocopy, counterpart, ringer (Sl), dead ringer (Sl), spitting image (Inf), dead spit (Inf)
▶ *110 Sameness, 114 Similarity, 118 Imitation*

6 twins, identical twins, fraternal twins, Siamese twins, Tweedledum and Tweedledee, Castor and Pollux, Gemini, Twin Stars

7 halving, dichotomy, bisection, bipartition, dividing by two, splitting (*or* cutting) in two, splitting (*or* cutting) in half, bifurcation, forking, ramification, branching
▶ *136 Separation*

8 half, fifty percent, moiety, hemisphere, semicircle, diameter, equator, great circle, bisector, fork, swallowtail, branch, prong
▶ *143 Part*

ADJECTIVES

9 two, dual, dualistic, double, duple, duplex, binary, dyadic, twofold, bifold, paired, coupled, yoked, bracketed, twinned, matched, mated, doubled, squared, two by two, two abreast, in pairs, in twos, *à deux* (Fr), both, the two, second, secondary

10 two-sided, double-sided, two-way, two-ply, dual-purpose, two-stroke, two-storey, two-level, two-dimensional, biennial, biannual, biform, bipartite, bifurcate, biped, bipedal, binocular, bifocal, bilateral, bicameral, bilingual, ambidextrous, bisexual, AC/DC (Sl)

11 double-edged, double-barrelled, ambiguous, ironic, ambivalent, duplicitous, two-faced, hypocritical, double-faced, double-dealing, double-crossing, Janus-like, two-timing (Inf)
▶ *578 Equivocation*

12 double, twin, duplicate, geminate, repeat, second, duplicated, geminated, copied, photocopied, repeated, cloned
▶ *110 Sameness, 114 Similarity, 118 Imitation, 183 Repetition, 245 Reproduction*

13 half, halved, bisected, divided by two, split in half, split two ways, dichotomous, dichotomic, bifurcated, forked, ramified, branched, cloven, cleft, halfway, mid, middle, midway
▶ *158 Middle, 136 Separation*

VERBS

14 pair, couple, bracket, yoke, span, double-harness, twin, match, mate, matchmake, pair off, couple up, team (up)

15 double, multiply by two, square, duplicate, replicate, clone, twin, geminate, copy, mirror, echo, repeat
▶ *245 Reproduction, 183 Repetition*

16 halve, bisect, transect, divide in half, divide by two, split (*or* cut) in half, split (*or* cut) in two, cleave, sunder, dichotomize, bifurcate,

fork, ramify, branch
▶ *136 Separation*

17 go halves, go fifty-fifty, share, split two ways, split down the middle, go Dutch (Inf)
▶ *731 Allocation*

18 have it both ways, have the best of both worlds, have one's cake and eat it (Inf)

ADVERBS

19 twice, twofold, doubly, dually, twice as much, as much again, twice over, two times, once more, again, over again, yet again, encore, *bis* (Fr)

20 two by two, two abreast, in pairs, in twos

21 second, secondly, in the second place, secondarily

22 in half, in halves, in two, in twain (Arch), down the middle, half, fifty percent, half-and-half (Inf), fifty-fifty (Inf)

177 Three

NOUNS

1 three, trey, set of three, trio, threesome, triad, trinity, trine, triune, triple, treble, power of three, cube

2 trident, tripod, trivet, tricorn, triangle, trihedron, three-wheeler, tricycle, trimaran, three-decker, three-hander, triumvirate, trihebdomadary, troika, triennial, triennium, trimester, trinomial, trilogy, triptych, trimeter, tristich, triplet, trefoil, shamrock, *ménage à trois* (Fr), hat trick

3 threeness, triality, trimorphism, triplicity, tripleness, trebleness, threefoldness

4 triplication, tripling, triplicating, trebling, multiplying by three

5 trisection, tripartition, trichotomy, trifurcation, dividing by three, splitting in three
▶ *136 Separation*

6 third, tierce, third part, one third, *tertium quid* (L), third party, third person, third power, major third, minor third, Third World, third age, third eye, third degree

ADJECTIVES

7 three, triple, triplex, triadic, trinal, trine, triform, trimorphic, ternary, trinary, triune, treble, triplicate, threefold, trifold, three times as much, cubed, third, tertiary

8 three-sided, triangular, triangulate, trigonal, trilateral, trihedral, deltoid, fan-shaped, three-pointed, three-pronged, trident, tridentate, three-cornered, tricorn, tricornered, three-leaved, trifoliate, three-legged, three-footed, tripedal, tripodic, three-ply, three-way, three-dimensional (3-D), tridimensional, trilingual, trimetric, triennial, trimestrial

9 trisected, tripartite, three-part, three-parted, triparted, trichotomous, trifid, trifurcated

VERBS

10 triple, triplicate, treble, multiply by three,

increase threefold, cube

11 **trisect**, divide by three, split (*or* cut) in three, trichotomize, trifurcate, split three ways (Inf)

ADVERBS

12 **thrice**, threefold, three times, trebly, triply, trinely, in triplicate

13 **in threes**, three by three, three abreast

14 **third**, thirdly, in the third place

178 Four

NOUNS

1 **four**, quatre, set of four, quartet, foursome, tetrad, quaternity, quadruple, quadruplet, quad

2 **quadrilateral**, tetragon, quadrangle, square, rectangle, oblong, parallelogram, rhombus, trapezium, trapezoid, tetrahedron

3 **foursome**, quadruped, tetrapod, tetradactyl, quadrennium, quadrennial, quadrille, square dance, quatrefoil, four-leaf (*or* four-leaved) clover, four-in-hand, four-poster, four winds, four seasons, four corners of the earth, tetrameter, quatrain, tetragram, tetragrammation, tetralogy, four-letter word

4 **quadruplication**, quadruplicature, quadrupling, quadruplicating, quadruplicity, fourfoldness

5 **quadrisection**, quadripartition, quartering, dividing by four, splitting in four

6 **quarter**, fourth, fourth part, one fourth, twenty-five percent, quadrant

ADJECTIVES

7 **four**, quaternary, quadratic, quadruple, quadruplex, quadruplicate, fourfold, fourth

8 **quadrilateral**, four-sided, square, rectangular, quadrate, tetrahedral, foursquare

9 **tetramerous**, quadruped, four-legged, four-footed, quadraphonic, quadrennial, tetravalent, quadrivalent

10 **quartered**, quadrisected, quadripartite, fourpart, four-parted, four-handed, four-stroke, quarterly, quadrifid

VERBS

11 **quadruple**, quadruplicate, multiply by four, increase fourfold, quadrate

12 **quadrisect**, quarter, divide by four, divide into four, split four ways (Inf)

ADVERBS

13 **four times**, fourfold, quadruply, quadrennially, quarterly, squarely, foursquare

14 **in fours**, four by four, on all fours

15 **fourth**, fourthly, in the fourth place

179 Five and Over

NOUNS

1 **five**, cinque, quintet, fivesome, quintuplicate, quintuple, quintuplet, quin, fifth, fifth part, one fifth, pentagon, pentahedron, pentagram, pentacle, pentameter, pentastich, Pen-

tateuch, pentarchy, pentathlon, pentachord, quint, quinquereme, quincunx, cinquefoil, five-finger, quinquennium, quinquennial, pentathlon, five-a-side, five-by-five, five stones, a bunch of fives, five-dollar bill (US), five-pound note, fiver (Inf), five-spot (US inf), fin (US sl)

2 **six**, half-a-dozen, hexad, sextet, sextuplicate, sextuple, sextuplet, sixth, sixth part, one sixth, sextile, hexagon, hexahedron, hexagram, hexameter, sixain, Hexateuch, hexachord, hexapod, sixth sense, six-footer, sixshooter, sixth form (*or* year), sixer (Sl), Captain Hicks (Sl), Jimmy Hix (Sl)

3 **seven**, heptad, septet, septenary, septuplicate, septuple, septuplet, seventh, seventh part, one seventh, heptagon, heptahedron, heptameter, Heptateuch, seven deadly sins, Seven Wonders of the World, diminished seventh, seven days, week, sevener (Sl), God's in heaven (Sl)

4 **eight**, octad, octet, octonary, octuple, octuplet, octagon, octahedron, octave, Octateuch, octopus, octarchy, octavo (8vo), figure of eight, piece of eight, eighth, eighth part, one eighth, one over the eight (Inf), eighter (Sl), eighter from Decatur (US sl), garden gate (Sl), Harry Tate (Sl)

5 **nine**, ennead, nonet, nonary, novena, nonuplet, nonagon, enneagon, enneahedron, ninth, ninth part, one ninth, nine-days wonder, niner (Sl), Nina from Carolina (US sl)

6 **ten**, decade, decennium, decagon, decahedron, decapod, decagram, decathlon, Decalogue, Ten Commandments, tenth, tenth part, one tenth, tithe, tenner (Sl), big Dick (Sl), cock and hen (Sl), Downing Street (Sl)

7 **double figures**, eleven, undecagon, hendecagon, hendecahedron, twelve, dozen, dodecagon, dodecahedron, duodecimal, duodecimo, twelfth man, Twelfth Night, Twelfth Day, twelvemonth, teens, teenager, thirteen, baker's dozen, long dozen, fourteen, two weeks, fortnight, fifteen, quindecaplet, quindecagon, quindecennial, sixteen, hexadecimal, legs eleven (Sl), boxcar (Sl), monkey's cousin (Sl)

8 **twenty and over**, score, twenty-four, four and twenty, two dozen, twenty-five, five and twenty, pony, silver jubilee, forty, twoscore, quadragenarian, fifty, half a hundred, half century, jubilee, quinquagenarian, sixty, threescore, sexagenary, sexagenarian, seventy, threescore and ten, septuagenarian, eighty, fourscore, octogenarian, ninety, fourscore and ten, nonagenarian

9 **treble figures**, hundred, one hundred, century, one hundredfold, centuple, centuplicate, hundred percent, centennial, centenary, centennium, centenarian, centurion, centimetre,

centigrade, hundredweight (cwt), centipede, the hundred days, hundred and twenty, great (*or* long) hundred, hundred and forty-four, gross, two-hundred, bicentennial, bicentenary, three hundred, tercentennial, tercentenary, four hundred, quatercentenary, five hundred, five centuries, quincentenary, six centuries, sexcentenary, seven centuries, eight centuries, octocentenary, nine centuries, ten centuries, millennium, hundreds and hundreds, hundreds and thousands, one C (Sl), ton (Sl), five C's (Sl), monkey (Sl)

10 **thousand**, K, chiliad, millennium, millenary, milligram, millilitre, millimetre, kilometre, kilogram, kilo, kilobyte, gigabyte, millipede, ten thousand, myriad, hundred thousand, lakh, G (Sl), grand (Sl), yard (Sl)

11 **million**, ten million, crore, thousand million, billion, milliard, million million, trillion, quadrillion, quintillion, sextillion, septillion, octillion, nonillion, decillion, undecillion, duodecillion, tredecillion, quattuordecillion, quindecillion, sexdecillion, septendecillion, octodecillion, novemdecillion, vigintillion, centrillion, googol, googolplex, multimillion, millionaire, multimillionaire, billionaire, milliardaire, zillion (Inf), jillion (Inf), squillion (Inf)

▶ *181 Multitude, 65 Computers*

ADJECTIVES

12 **fifth**, five, fivefold, quintuple, quintuplicate, quinary, quinquennial, quintic, quinquepartite, pentadic, pentagonal, pentangular, pentahedral, pentatonic

13 **sixth**, six, sixfold, sextuple, sextuplicate, sexennial, sexpartite, hexadic, hexagonal, hexangular, hexahedral, hexatonic

14 **seventh**, seven, sevenfold, septuple, septuplicate, septenary, septennial, heptadic, heptagonal, heptangular, heptahedral, heptatonic

15 **eighth**, eight, eightfold, octuple, octonary, octennial, octadic, octagonal, octangular, octahedral, octatonic

16 **ninth**, nine, ninefold, nonuple, novenary, nonary, enneadic, nonagonal, enneagonal, enneahedral

17 **tenth**, ten, tenfold, decuple, decimal, denary, decennial, decagonal, decahedral

18 **eleventh**, undecennial, hendecagonal, twelfth, duodenary, duodecimal, thirteenth, fourteenth, fifteenth, quindecagonal, quindecennial, sixteenth, hexadecimal, in one's teens, umpteenth

19 **twentieth**, vigesimal, vicenary, vicennial, thirtieth, fortieth, fiftieth, sixtieth, seventieth, eightieth, ninetieth

20 **hundredth**, centesimal, centennial, centenary, centenarian, hundredfold, centuple, centuplicate

21 **thousandth**, millenary, millenarian, millen-

ial, thousandfold, four-figure, five-figure, six-figure

22 **millionth**, billionth, trillionth

VERBS

23 **quintuple**, quintuplicate, sextuple, sextuplicate, septuple, octuple, centuple, centuplicate, decimalize, decimate

ADVERBS

24 **fivefold**, fifth, fifthly, quinquennially, sixfold, sixth, sixthly, sexennially, sevenfold, seventh, seventhly, septennially, tenfold, tenth, tenthly, decennially, hundredfold, centennially

180 Accompaniment

NOUNS

1 **accompaniment**, concomitance, coexistence, symbiosis, cohabitation, combination, conjunction, association, union, coagency, convoy

▶ *140 Combination, 135 Union*

2 **synchronism**, simultaneity, contemporaneity, coincidence, concurrence, conjunction, co-occurrence

▶ *198 Same Time*

3 **companionship**, company, togetherness, fellowship, friendship, partnership, consortship, cohabitation, marriage, society, community, mateyness (Inf)

▶ *815 Sociability, 819 Friendship, 823 Marriage*

4 **concomitant**, attribute, feature, fixture, accessory, appendage, adjunct, appurtenance, ornament, attendant, corollary, symptom, syndrome, indication, sign, background, context

▶ *103 Essence, 130 Addition, 543 Sign*

5 **side dish**, salad, vegetables, condiments, sauce, dressing, drinks

▶ *45 Cookery*

6 **accompanier**, accompanist, repetiteur, backing band (*or* group), backing vocalists (*or* singers), rhythm section, string (*or* brass *or* wind) section, *Nebenstimme* (Ger)

▶ *49 Music*

7 **attendant**, squire, cavalier, escort, outrider, chaperon (*or* chaperone), duenna, protector, keeper, guard, bodyguard, minder (Inf), heavy (Inf), muscle (Inf)

▶ *632 Safety*

8 **usher**, shepherd, marshal, conductor, leader, guide, pilot

▶ *653 Management*

9 **follower**, shadow, tail, satellite, dependant, hanger-on, parasite, sycophant, camp follower, groupie (Sl)

▶ *155 Sequence, 697 Servant*

10 **attendance**, cortege, retinue, following, entourage, court, suite, retainers

11 **companion**, colleague, partner, associate,

co-worker, fellow, classmate, flatmate, comrade, friend, best friend, travelling companion, fellow traveller, mate (Inf), buddy (Inf)
▶ *664 Cooperation, 819 Friendship*
12 **partner**, constant companion, escort, date, girlfriend, boyfriend, lover, consort, cohabitant, cohabitee, live-in lover, common-law spouse, spouse, husband, wife, better half, hubbie (Inf), trouble and strife (Sl)
▶ *821 Love, 823 Marriage*

VERBS
13 **accompany**, go together, go with, belong with, complement, go together with, come with, be linked with, go hand in hand with, go hand in glove with, concur, coincide, synchronize, keep time with
14 **keep company with**, travel with, run with, work with, partner, escort, go out with, date (US), consort with, associate with, frequent, befriend, socialize, club together, team up, gang up, pair up, couple, live together, live with, cohabit, hobnob (Inf), hang around with (Inf), hang out with (Inf)
▶ *815 Sociability, 664 Cooperation, 819 Friendship*
15 **escort**, squire, chaperone, protect, guard, safeguard, guide, lead, pilot, usher, shepherd, marshal, conduct, convoy, bring (*or* take) in tow, mind (Inf)
▶ *632 Safety, 653 Management*
16 **attend**, dance attendance on, wait on, follow, tag along, attach oneself to, dog the footsteps of, shadow, tail, track
▶ *155 Sequence, 697 Servant*

ADJECTIVES
17 **accompanying**, concomitant, attending, attendant, belonging, complementary, accessory, collateral, incidental, background, contextual
18 **concurrent**, concurring, coincident, coinciding, simultaneous, contemporary, contemporaneous, parallel, correlative, coexistent, coexisting, symbiotic, cohabiting
19 **associated**, partnered, coupled, paired, wedded, married, combined, joined, inseparable, thick as thieves, hand-in-glove
▶ *135 Union, 140 Combination*
20 **accompanied**, attended, escorted, chaperoned, protected, guarded, ushered, shepherded, marshalled, guided, led, conducted, minded (Inf)

ADVERBS
21 **together**, in a body, all together, in unison, collectively, inseparably, unitedly, in convoy, in a crocodile, in tow, in someone's wake
22 **hand in hand**, arm in arm, side by side, cheek by jowl, hand in glove
23 **concurrently**, simultaneously, contemporaneously, symbiotically

PREPOSITIONS
24 **with**, together with, along with, in company with, in association with, coupled with, paired with, partnered with, in tandem with, in conjunction with

181 Multitude

NOUNS
1 **multiplicity**, multitudinousness, numerousness, multifoldness, countlessness, innumerability, infinity
▶ *184 Infinity*
2 **multitude**, many, great number, large numbers, quite a few, a lot, lots, large amount, tidy sum, dozens, scores, hundreds, hundreds and thousands, thousands, tens of thousands, hundreds of thousands, millions, billions, trillions, myriads, umpteen (Inf), zillions (Inf), jillions (Inf), big bucks (Inf), telephone numbers (Inf), scads (Inf), wads (Inf)
▶ *169 Number, 179 Five and Over, 175 Plurality*
3 **profuseness**, profusion, rifeness, abundance, plenty, tons (Inf), oodles (Inf), bags (Inf), barrels (Inf), heaps (Inf), loads (Inf), heck of a lot (Inf), hell of a lot (Inf), devil of a lot (Inf)
▶ *608 Sufficiency, 610 Excess*
4 **throng**, multitude, mass, mob, crowd, congregation, horde, host, army, troop, legion, fleet, high turnout, large turnout, rout, ruck, jam, clutter, press, crush, swarm, flock, flight, cloud, hail, bevy, covey, shoal, hive, colony, nest, brood, pack, bunch, drove, array, galaxy, mass of, masses of, sea of, world of, worlds of, forest of
▶ *161 Assembly*

ADJECTIVES
5 **multitudinous**, multitudinal, numerous, legion, multiple, multifold, multifarious, manifold
6 **many**, a good few, not a few, a good many, very many, ever so many, considerable, umpteen (Inf), quite some (Inf)
7 **myriad**, hundred, a hundred and one, thousand, a thousand and one, million, billion, trillion, zillion (Inf), jillion (Inf)
▶ *169 Number, 175 Plurality, 179 Five and Over*
8 **numberless**, innumerable, countless, uncountable, incalculable, immeasurable, measureless, beyond measure, unnumbered, uncounted, untold, infinite, endless, without end, limitless, without limit, boundless, inexhaustible, countless as the stars (*or* sand on the seashore), countless as the hairs on one's head, no end of (Inf), more than you can shake a stick at (Inf)
▶ *184 Infinity, 190 Eternity*
9 **ample**, abundant, superabundant, profuse, rife, plentiful, plenteous, copious, bumper, thick on the ground, in abundance, in plenty, in profusion, galore (Inf)
▶ *608 Sufficiency, 610 Excess*

10 **crowded**, thronged, mobbed, congested, massed, packed, jammed, jam-packed, high-density, pressed, crushed, packed like sardines in a can (*or* tin), cluttered, overcrowded, over-populated, overmanned, overstaffed, overrun

VERBS

11 **crowd**, throng, mob, mass, congregate, pack, jam, press, crush, swarm, teem, crawl, pullu-late, hum, buzz, bristle, seethe, mill, troop, flock, pour, stream, flood, brim, overflow, burst, swarm like flies, swarm like ants, swarm like bees around a honey-pot

▶ *161 Assembly*

12 **overcrowd**, overpopulate, overman, over-staff, outnumber, overrun, infest, swamp, overwhelm, snow under

▶ *610 Excess*

ADVERBS

13 **numerously**, aplenty, multitudinously, mul-tiply, multifariously, innumerably, count-lessly, incalculably, immeasurably, beyond measure, beyond count, infinitely, no end (Inf), by leaps and bounds (Inf)

14 **in crowds**, in swarms, in masses, en masse, in heaps, in loads, thick and fast

182   Few

NOUNS

1 **few**, a few, only a few, just a few, not many, some, small number, one or two, two or three, couple, handful, mere handful, almost none, too few to mention, not enough to count (*or* matter), low turnout, poor turnout, low attendance, scattering, sprinkling, trickle, small quantity, small amount, little, a little, soupçon, derisory amount, dash, hint, suspi-cion, smidgen (Inf)

▶ *169 Number*

2 **least**, minimum, less, minority, the minority, minority group

3 **fewness**, sparsity, sparseness, scarcity, scarce-ness, scantiness, exiguity, paucity, dearth, lack, deficiency, skimpiness, meagreness, shortage, undersupply, underpopulation, skel-eton staff

▶ *609 Insufficiency, 358 Shortfall*

4 **rarity**, rareness, infrequency, intermittence, sporadicness

▶ *213 Infrequency*

ADJECTIVES

5 **few**, a few, some, not many, hardly any, scarcely any, precious few, too few, little, a little, not much, precious little, to be counted on one's fingers, to be counted on the fingers of one hand, soon counted

6 **sparse**, scant, scanty, light, thin, little, mini-mal, meagre, exiguous, measly, niggardly, in-frequent, occasional, sporadic, intermittent, rare, seldom seen, seldom met with, uncom-

mon, near extinction, scarce, thin on the ground, few and far between, strung out, spread out, widely spaced, at great intervals, dispersed, scattered, sprinkled, dotted about, underpopulated, low-density, understaffed, undermanned

▶ *609 Insufficiency, 358 Shortfall, 213 Infrequency*

7 **fewer**, less, reduced, diminished, diminish-ing, least, minimum, minimal, minority, in a minority, too few, inquorate

VERBS

8 **reduce**, diminish, rarefy, thin, thin out, weed out, eliminate, decimate, pare (*or* cut) down, scale down, downsize (US), cut back, prune, trim, rationalize, underman, understaff

9 **scatter**, sprinkle, dot, dot about, string out, space out, spread out, disperse

ADVERBS

10 **in ones and twos**, in twos and threes, here and there, in places, in spots, in a trickle, in dribs and drabs (Inf)

11 **sparsely**, scantily, lightly, thinly, meagrely, exiguously, little, rarely, infrequently, seldom, occasionally, scarcely, hardly, barely

183   Repetition

NOUNS

1 **repetition**, repeating, doing again, rehearsal, practice, practising, recital, duplication, redu-plication, doubling, redoubling, reproduction, replication, recurrence, imitation, copying, plagiarism, echo, echolalia, reecho, ditto, anaphora, epistrophe

▶ *176 Two, 118 Imitation, 245 Reproduction*

2 **iteration**, reiteration, repeating, saying again, relating, relation, recounting, retelling, recapitulation, going over again, review, résumé, summary, summing up, peroration, restatement, tautology, redundancy, padding, filling, quotation, plagiarism, recap (Inf), waf-fle (Inf)

▶ *562 Summary, 553 Diffuseness*

3 **repetitiveness**, repetitiousness, repetition, stale repetition, monotony, tedium, unifor-mity, regularity, invariability, familiarity, daily grind, same old round, humdrum, rut, routine, habit, cliché, same old story, old joke, (old) chestnut (Inf)

▶ *112 Uniformity, 584 Habit, 225 Stability*

4 **return**, reappearance, comeback, renewal, starting again, beginning again, starting afresh, reprise, recurrence, rebirth, reincarna-tion, renaissance, revival, restoration, recycl-ing, cycle, round, eternal return

5 **repeat**, repetition, repeat performance, en-core, curtain call, rerun, reshowing, replay, replaying, return match, repeat order, second helping, reprint, offprint, reissue, new edition, remake, rehash (Inf)

6 **reverberation**, echo, reecho, resonance, vibration, oscillation, rhythm, beat, pulse, pulsation, throb, throbbing, drumming, hammering, rhyme, alliteration, assonance
▶ *426 Repeated Sound, 427 Resonance*
7 **replica**, double, duplicate, copy, carbon-copy, photocopy, print
▶ *110 Sameness*
8 **creature of habit**, copycat, parrot, mimic, automaton, robot
▶ *584 Habit, 118 Imitation*

ADJECTIVES
9 **repeated**, duplicated, reduplicated, doubled, redoubled, reproduced, replicated, echoed, reechoed, mirrored, imitative, parrot-like, plagiarized
▶ *118 Imitation, 245 Reproduction*
10 **iterated**, reiterated, said again, retold, twice-told, said before, recounted, related, restated, quoted, cited
11 **reprinted**, reissued, remade, replayed, reshown, revived, restored, renewed, reborn, reincarnated, reheated, warmed-up, recycled, reprocessed, rehashed (Inf)
12 **repetitious**, repetitive, repetitional, repeating, duplicative, reproductive, doubling, redoubling, echoing, reechoing, iterative, reiterative, reiterant, tautological, redundant, otiose, pleonastic, recapitulative, harping, stuck-in-a-groove, wordy, prolix
▶ *553 Diffuseness*
13 **monotonous**, tedious, boring, uniform, invariable, changeless, monotone, singsong, familiar, habitual, humdrum, mundane, routine, stale, cliché-ridden, clichéd, hackneyed, trite, yawn-making (Inf)
▶ *788 Boredom, 584 Habit, 112 Uniformity, 225 Stability*
14 **recurrent**, regular, periodic, cyclical, returning, recurring, reoccurring, reappearing, ubiquitous, haunting, continual, continuous, constant, nonstop, incessant, ceaseless, unremitting
▶ *219 Continuity, 217 Permanence*
15 **reverberatory**, resonant, vibrational, oscillatory, rhythmical, rhythmic, beating, pulsing, pulsating, throbbing, drumming, hammering, chiming, chanting, rhymed, rhyming, alliterative, alliterating, assonant
▶ *426 Repeated Sound, 427 Resonance*

VERBS
16 **repeat**, redo, do again, do a repeat, rehearse, practise, duplicate, reduplicate, double, redouble, reproduce, replicate, plagiarize, copy, echo, mirror, parrot, imitate, mimic
▶ *176 Two, 245 Reproduction, 118 Imitation*
17 **iterate**, reiterate, repeat, say again, say over again, relate, recite, recount, retell, recapitulate, perorate, go over again, review, resume, summarize, sum up, restate, reemphasize,

quote, cite, quote oneself, repeat oneself, go over the same ground, give an encore, recap (Inf)
▶ *562 Summary*
18 **harp**, harp on, go on about, plug, labour, belabour, go on at, hammer away at, churn out, trot out, sing the same old song, play the same old record, tell the same old story, go over again and again, say over and over, hammer into, din (or drum) into, nag, go on and on, never hear the last of
▶ *553 Diffuseness*
19 **return to**, go back, retrace one's steps, go over the same ground, relapse, regress, revert, remember, recall
▶ *511 Memory*
20 **renew**, resume, restart, start again, begin again, start afresh, go back to the beginning, come back, stage a comeback, revive, restore, recycle, reprocess, reheat, warm up, reprint, reissue, rerun, replay, play back, remake, rehash (Inf)
21 **be repeated**, recur, reoccur, happen again, return, reappear, pop up, crop up, show up again, keep coming, come again and again, turn up like a bad penny
22 **resound**, reverberate, echo, reecho, vibrate, oscillate, beat, pulse, pulsate, throb, drum, thrum, hammer, pound, rhyme, alliterate
▶ *426 Repeated Sound, 427 Resonance*

ADVERBS
23 **repeatedly**, reiteratively, repetitively, repetitiously, monotonously, recurrently, frequently, often, continually, incessantly, again and again, over and over, over and over again, time after time, time and again, many times over, day after day, year after year, day in day out, year in year out, ad nauseam
24 **again**, once more, once again, encore, bis, da capo, from the beginning, afresh, anew, twice over, ditto

184 Infinity

I cannot help it; – in spite of myself, infinity torments me. Alfred de Musset.

ADJECTIVES
1 **infinite**, boundless, limitless, unlimited, without limit (or end), illimitable, bottomless, endless, interminable, recurring
2 **immeasurable**, measureless, vast, immense, enormous, astronomical, incalculable, uncountable, countless, innumerable, myriad, numberless, unnumbered, without number, beyond reckoning, untold, indeterminable, inestimable, unfathomable, incomprehensible, beyond comprehension, transcendent, mind-boggling (Inf)
▶ *181 Multitude*
3 **eternal**, perpetual, everlasting, immortal, un-

dying, forever, ceaseless, endless, unending, never-ending, constant, continual, continuous, unremitting, open-ended, without beginning or end, no end of

▶ *190 Eternity, 217 Permanence*

NOUNS

4 **infinity**, infiniteness, infinitude, boundlessness, limitlessness, illimitability, endlessness, interminability, infinite supply, bottomless pit

5 **immeasurability**, measurelessness, incalculability, countlessness, innumerability, numberlessness, indeterminableness, incomprehensibility

▶ *181 Multitude*

6 **vastness**, immenseness, immensity, space, outer space, infinite space

7 **eternity**, perpetuity, forever, everlastingness, immortality, perpetual motion

▶ *190 Eternity, 217 Permanence*

VERBS

8 **have no limit**, have no bounds, know no limit (*or* bounds *or* end)

9 **be infinite**, last forever, never end, go on and on, never die, never cease, recur, perpetuate, continue, be eternal, gain immortality, discover the secret of eternal life

ADVERBS

10 **infinitely**, boundlessly, limitlessly, illimitably, endlessly, interminably, indefinitely, without end, without limit, to infinity, ad infinitum

11 **immeasurably**, measurelessly, vastly, immensely, astronomically, incalculably, innumerably, indeterminably, inestimably

12 **eternally**, perpetually, constantly, immortally, forever, in perpetuity, until the end of time, until the rivers run uphill, until all the seas run dry, until the sun ceases to shine, for keeps (Inf), till hell freezes over (Inf), till the cows come home (Inf)

Time

Except Time all other things are created. Time is the creator; and Time has no limit, neither top nor bottom. The Persian Rivayat.

To choose time is to save time. Francis Bacon.

Time is a great teacher, but unfortunately it kills all its pupils. Hector Berlioz.

To every thing there is a season, and a time to every purpose under the heaven:/ A time to be born, and a time to die; a time to plant, and a time to pluck up that which is planted;/ A time to kill, and a time to heal; a time to break down, and a time to build up;/ A time to weep, and a time to laugh; a time to mourn, and a time to dance;/ A time to cast away stones, and a time to gather stones together; a time to embrace, and a time to refrain from embracing;/ A time to get, and a time to lose; a time to keep, and a time to cast away;/ A time to rend, and a time to sew; a time to keep silence, and a time to speak;/ A time to love, and a time to hate; a time of war, and a time of peace. Bible: Ecclesiastes.

Men talk of killing time, while time quietly kills them. Dion Boucicault.

O aching time! O moments big as years! John Keats.

They do that to pass the time, nothing more. But Time is too large, it refuses to let itself be filled up. Jean-Paul Sartre.

Come what come may,/ Time and the hour runs through the roughest day. William Shakespeare.

Th' inaudible and noiseless foot of Time. William Shakespeare.

Time is but the stream I go a-fishing in. Henry David Thoreau.

But meanwhile it is flying, irretrievable time is flying. Virgil.

Time flies, death urges, knells call, heaven invites,/ Hell threatens. Edward Young.

Time is like a river made up of the events which happen, and its current is strong; no sooner does anything appear than it is swept away, and another comes in its place, and will be swept away too. Marcus Aurelius.

NOUNS

1 **time**, space-time, space-time continuum, the fourth dimension, arrow of time, time warp, time travel, time machine, timeslip, chronon, tachyon, ontological time, psychological time, sense of time
   ▶ *56 Physics*

2 **passage of time**, lapse of time, ravages of time, time and tide, (Old) Father Time, time's winged chariot, time the enemy, time the great healer, the sands of time

3 **duration**, continuation, extent, time span, span, allotted span, life span, threescore years and ten, course, course of time, stretch, space, spell, period, limited period, fixed term, stint, reign, office, tenure, tenancy, tour of duty, shift, a bit, a while, a short while

4 **term**, semester, quarter, cycle, season, year, month, calendar month, lunar month, fortnight, week, day, hour, minute, second, millisecond, microsecond, nanosecond, aeon, millennium, century, decade, olympiad, epoch, era, geological period
   ▶ *54 Earth Science, 75 Units*

5 **indefinite period**, indefinite time, some time, age, aeon, ages, days, a while, heyday, palmy days, salad days

6 **interval**, interlude, lull, break, tea (*or* coffee) break, breather, respite, pause, interim, interregnum, meantime, breathing space, interim period, pause for breath, time-out

7 **time measurement**, clock time, real time, right time, exact time, chronology, chronography

8 **dating**, radiometric dating, carbon dating, thermoluminescent dating, tree-ring dating, dendrochronology

9 time zone, local time, daylight saving, International Date Line, sidereal time, solar time, ephemeris time, equation of time, Greenwich Mean Time, British Summer Time, Double Summer Time, Central European Time, Atlantic Standard Time, Atlantic Daylight Time, Eastern Standard Time, Eastern Daylight Time, Central Standard Time, Central Daylight Time, Mountain Standard Time, Mountain Daylight Time, Pacific Standard Time, Pacific Daylight Time, Yukon Standard Time, Yukon Daylight Time, Alaska–Hawaii Standard Time, Alaska–Hawaii Daylight Time, Bering Standard Time, Bering Daylight Time

10 chronometry, chronoscopy, horology, timekeeping, watchmaking, clockmaking

11 date, day, Calends, Nones, Ides, birthday, name day, saint's day, anniversary, occasion, red-letter day, moment, instant, juncture, point, appointed day, fixed day, right time, right moment, zero hour, H-hour, D-day

12 musical time, rhythm, metre, beat, tempo, polyrhythm, pulse, syncopation, time signature

▶ *49 Music*

13 timer, counter, timing device, time clock, timepiece, clock, watch, chronometer, horologe, chronograph, chronogram, calendar, Julian calendar, Gregorian calendar, perpetual calendar, diary, daybook

14 timekeeper, chronologist, chronographer, chronicler, annalist, diarist, calendar-maker, calendarist, horologist, clockmaker, watchmaker, clock watcher

VERBS

15 pass, pass by, elapse, roll by, roll on, flow, flow by, flow onwards, drag, drag by, drag on, fly, fly by, intervene

16 time, keep time, measure time, clock, monitor, record, count, judge, set, set a date for, set a time for, settle on a date, settle on a time, schedule, timetable, time it right, mark time, beat time

17 date, calendar, chronologize, assign a date to, be dated, carry (*or* bear) a date

18 adjust the clock, synchronize, synchronize watches, set the alarm, the hands of the clock, put the clocks forward, put the clocks back

19 clock on, clock off, clock in (*or* out), watch the clock, clockwatch, count the hours (*or* minutes)

ADJECTIVES

20 temporal, time-based, time-related, temporary

21 lasting through time, long-lasting, constant, chronic, eternal, perpetual, everlasting, immemorial, time-honoured, horological, pending, throughout

22 periodic, periodical, cyclic, repetitive, annual, yearly, biannual, biennial, monthly, weekly, daily, hourly

23 occasional, sporadic, intermittent, infrequent

24 between times, interim, intermediate, intercalary, intercalated, intervallic, interwar, interglacial, interlunar

25 of known date, dated, in date order, chronological, chronometric, chronographic, chronogrammatic, calendrical, annalistic

ADVERBS

26 all the time, while, whilst, between whiles, during, in the course of, all along, all through, so long as, till, until, for now, for the time being, in the meantime, meanwhile, in the interim, for the interim, for a time, for a season, for the duration, the whole time, always, ever, forever, day by day, from day to day, day in day out, week in week out

27 at what time, when, at the time, then, whereupon, at that moment, now, at this moment, at this moment in time, yesterday, today, tonight, tomorrow, this morning, this afternoon, this evening, sometime, someday, any day, anytime

28 sometimes, often, now and then, now and again, on and off, occasionally, infrequently, sporadically, intermittently, from time to time, once in a while

29 one day, once upon a time, in the days (*or* time) of, in the year of, AD (Anno Domini), BC (Before Christ), AC (Ante Christum), AH (Anno Hegirae *or* Anno Hebraico), AUC (Anno urbis conditae), CE (Common Era), BCE (before the Common Era)

30 chronologically, temporally, annually, biannually, perennially, perpetually, eternally, for ever, for always

▶ *190 Eternity*

186 Timelessness

NOUNS

1 timelessness, eternity, changelessness, sempiternity (Fml), no time, neverness (Inf)

▶ *190 Eternity*

2 agelessness, datelessness, immortality, deathlessness, everlastingness

3 immutability, permanence, perpetuity, perpetuation, continuance, continuity

▶ *188 Duration, 217 Permanence*

VERBS

4 perpetuate, hold (*or* keep) in perpetuity, immortalize, eternalize, keep alive, memorialize, preserve, maintain, make time stand still

ADJECTIVES

5 timeless, eternal, sempiternal (Fml), ageless, dateless, immortal, undying, lasting, everlasting, continuous, perpetual, unceasing, never out of date, never out of fashion

6 changeless, permanent, immutable, imperishable, incorruptible, indestructible

ADVERBS

7 **beyond time**, out of time, outside time

8 **ever**, evermore, forever, forever more, always, eternally, everlastingly, endlessly, incessantly, unceasingly, until hell freezes over, until the twelfth of never, until the Greek Calends (Fml), till the cows come home (Inf)

9 **never**, ne'er, not ever, at no time, never (*or* not) in a million years, not (*or* never) in a month of Sundays

10 **seldom**, rarely, hardly ever, scarcely, scarcely ever, once in a blue moon

187 Period

NOUNS

1 **period**, interval, span, time, time span, term, stretch, space, fit, spell, break, pause, breather (Inf)

▶ *185 Time*

2 **time period**, era, aeon, age, generation, epoch, millennium, chiliad, century, decade, decennium, quinquennium, year, quarter, month, fortnight, week, day, weekday, hour, minute, second, moment, instant, millisecond, microsecond, nanosecond

3 **geological period**, era, epoch, eon, olam

▶ *54 Earth Science*

4 **period of activity**, stint, spell, phase, turn, watch, session, shift, work shift, overtime, half-time, working day, man-hour, tour, tour of duty, term, school term, academic year, semester, tenure, term (*or* tenure) of office, fiscal (*or* financial) year, term of imprisonment, sentence, bout, innings, inning (US), go (Inf), whack (Inf)

5 **recurrent period**, series, season, cycle, iteration, periodic function, recurrent pattern, menstrual cycle, menstruation, biorhythm, circadian rhythm, biological clock, photoperiodism

▶ *97 Season*

6 **periodicity**, recurrence, return, repetition, repetitiveness, regularity

7 **periodical**, periodical publication, magazine, journal, learned journal, academic journal, newsletter, bulletin, weekly, monthly, annual

ADJECTIVES

8 **periodical**, regular, repetitive, repetitious, iterative, returning, recurrent, quinquennial, millennial, millenary (*or* millenarian), cyclic, seasonal, yearly, annual, biannual, biennial, monthly, weekly, daily

▶ *214 Regularity*

9 **periodic**, intermittent, sporadic, discontinuous, fitful, irregular

▶ *215 Irregularity*

VERBS

10 **be periodical**, recur, reappear, repeat, iter-

ate, reiterate, return, come round again

11 **make periodical**, regulate, regularize, modulate

ADVERBS

12 **periodically**, regularly, recurrently, repeatedly, repetitively, repetitiously

13 **for specified periods**, quinquennially, biennially, biannually, yearly, annually, quarterly, monthly, weekly, daily, hourly

14 **for short periods**, on occasion, occasionally, at odd times, now and again, now and then, fitfully, irregularly, off and on, on and off, by fits and starts

188 Duration

NOUNS

1 **duration**, period, term, course, course of time

2 **time**, length of time, passage of time, lapse of time, march of time, river of time, tide of time, flow of time, time flies, *tempus fugit* (L)

3 **continuity**, continuation, continuousness, progress, progression, process, due process (of law)

4 **long-lastingness**, endurance, permanence, fixity, permanency, constancy, durableness, durability, perdurability (Fml), stability, staying power, survival, will to live

5 **long duration**, a long time, an age, ages, aeons, generations, a lifetime, a life sentence, a long stretch, an eternity, days, years, years on end, a month of Sundays, time immemorial, donkey's years (Inf), yonks (Inf)

VERBS

6 **last**, endure, stay, stay the course, stand, stand the test of time, abide, remain, last out, hold out, survive, outlive, outlast, hang on, hang on in there (Sl)

7 **go on**, move on, continue, progress, proceed, run, run its course, elapse, pass

ADJECTIVES

8 **lasting**, durable, enduring, long-lasting, long-lived, abiding, continuing, continuous, continual, longstanding, evergreen, long-term, lifelong

9 **permanent**, unceasing, incessant, everlasting, eternal, perpetual, perennial, undying, immortal

ADVERBS

10 **for the duration**, to the end, to (*or* till) the bitter end, for ever, for evermore, for good, for good and all

11 **long**, for long, for a long time, till the cows come home (Inf), till one is blue in the face (Inf)

12 **everlastingly**, permanently, perennially, without end, eternally, without stopping, without pausing for breath, incessantly, continually, continuously

189 Transience

Faith, Sir, we are here to-day, and gone tomorrow. Aphra Behn.

They are not long, the days of wine and roses. Ernest Dowson.

The Worldly Hope men set their Hearts upon/ Turns Ashes – or it prospers; and anon,/ Like Snow upon the Desert's dusty face,/ Lighting a little Hour or two – is gone. Edward Fitzgerald *The Rubaiyat of Omar Khayyám.*

Fair daffodils, we weep to see/ You haste away so soon:/ As yet the early-rising sun/ Has not attain'd his noon./ Stay, stay,/ Until the hasting day/ Has run/ But to the even-song;/ And, having pray'd together, we/ Will go with you along./ We have short time to stay, as you,/ We have as short a Spring;/ As quick a growth to meet decay,/ As you or any thing. Robert Herrick.

Not to hope for things to last for ever, is what the year teaches and even the hour which snatches a nice day away. Horace.

Ships that pass in the night, and speak each other in passing;/ Only a signal shown and a distant voice in the darkness;/ So on the ocean of life we pass and speak one another,/ Only a look and a voice; then darkness again and a silence. Henry Wadsworth Longfellow.

NOUNS

1 **transience**, transitoriness, impermanence, fugacity (Fml), momentariness, suddenness, quickness, brevity, ephemerality, instability, evanescence, volatility

2 **transient thing**, passing fashion, nine-days wonder, flash in the pan, shooting star, meteor, bird of passage, brief encounter, a ship that passes in the night, *sic transit gloria mundi* (L)

3 **short duration**, brief span, short time, short space of time, moment, instant, a second or two, a minute or two, just a minute, just a second, just a tick (Inf), half a mo (Inf)

VERBS

4 **be transient**, pass, pass away, flit, fly, fly away, be fleeting, melt, melt away, decay, rot, turn to ashes, come to dust, fade, evanesce, evaporate, vanish, vanish into thin air, disappear, disappear in a puff of smoke, burst like a bubble, burst like a balloon, crumble away, fall to pieces, fall apart, shatter

5 **make transient**, shorten the life of, cut off, curtail, make disappear, bring to an end, put an end to, shatter the dreams of, burst someone's bubble (or balloon)

ADJECTIVES

6 **transient**, fleeting, flying, fugitive, fugacious (Fml), quick, ephemeral, perishable, unstable, brief, short, short-term, shortlived, evanescent, volatile, disappearing, fading, decaying, passing, transitory, meteoric, momentary, sudden, here today and gone tomorrow

7 **impermanent**, temporary, one-off, single-use, throwaway, biodegradable, nondurable, brittle, fragile, mortal

ADVERBS

8 **transiently**, transitorily, ephemerally, quickly, fleetingly, temporarily, impermanently, not long, briefly, shortly, momentarily, for a moment, in a moment, suddenly, in an instant, in a trice, in a twinkling, in the twinkling of an eye

9 **for the time being**, meantime, in the meantime, meanwhile, between whiles, for the nonce (Fml)

190 Eternity

NOUNS

1 **eternity**, endlessness, infinity, infinitude, everlastingness, time without end, timelessness, perpetuity, sempiternity (Fml), permanence, continuity, incorruptibility, imperishability
▶ *185 Timelessness*

2 **a long time**, age, aeon, olam, millennium
▶ *187 Period, 185 Time*

3 **life without end**, life everlasting, deathlessness, immortality, heaven, paradise, the hereafter, the afterlife, the next world, eternal rest (or rest eternal)

4 **eternalization**, perpetuation, memorialization, remembrance

VERBS

5 **be eternal**, last forever, outlast, outlive, remain forever, endure forever, go on forever, continue forever, never cease, be permanent, have no end

6 **make eternal**, perpetuate, immortalize, memorialize, remember forever

7 **make permanent**, establish, set up, continue

ADJECTIVES

8 **eternal**, everlasting, never-ending, unending, infinite, perpetual, timeless, sempiternal, permanent, enduring, durable, incorruptible, imperishable, immortal, undying, deathless, unchanging, immutable, evergreen

9 **agelong**, aeonian, millennial, immemorial

10 **continuing forever**, ceaseless, unceasing, continuous, constant, unending, nonstop, interminable, incessant, going on and on

ADVERBS

11 **eternally**, throughout eternity, forever, for always, for aye (Fml), evermore, for evermore, for ever and ever, for ever and a day, until the end of time, till the crack of doom, till doomsday, to infinity, until the twelfth of never, until the Greek Calends (Fml), until hell

freezes over, without end, on and on, through thick and thin, for better or worse, from age to age, from generation to generation, world without end, for good, for good and all, for keeps (Sl)

191 Immediacy

NOUNS

1 **immediacy**, immediateness, lack of delay, instantaneousness, instantaneity, directness, urgency, emergency, exigency, promptness, promptitude

2 **closeness**, nearness, proximity, contiguity

3 **instant**, second, split second, a sec, half a sec, moment, twinkling, twinkling of an eye, flash, jiffy (Inf), mo (Inf), half a mo (Inf), tick (Inf), half a tick (Inf)

4 **point in time**, point, moment, juncture, occasion, instant

ADJECTIVES

5 **immediate**, instantaneous, instant, prompt, quick, fast, rapid, swifty, speedy, direct, split-second, urgent, on-the-spot

6 **allowing no delay**, demanding, importunate, burning, imperative, exigent, urgent

7 **prepared for immediate use**, ready to wear, off the peg, ready to eat, fast (of food), convenience (of food), precooked

ADVERBS

8 **immediately**, instantaneously, instantly, without delay, at once, now, right now, on the spot, swiftly, speedily, rapidly, quick, as quick as lightning, as quick as a flash, promptly, right away, straight away, forthwith, before one knows it, before you can say Jack Robinson (Inf), like greased lightning (Inf), in two shakes of a lamb's tail (Inf), yesterday (Inf)

9 **in the shortest possible time**, in no time, in an instant, in the same breath, in a twinkling, in the twinkling of an eye, in a trice, in a flash, on the instant, ASAP (as soon as possible), posthaste

192 Timekeeping

NOUNS

1 **timekeeping**, timing, dating, scheduling, timetabling, calendar-making
▶ *185 Time, 188 Duration, 152 Arrangement, 150 Order, 187 Period*

2 **timetable**, calendar, schedule, diary, journal, order of the day, order of service, programme, course, curriculum, list
▶ *152 Arrangement, 592 Plan, 171 List*

3 **chronology**, chronography, dendrochronology (*or* tree-ring dating), radiocarbon dating, thermoluminescence, calendar, Julian calendar, Gregorian calendar, era, epoch, date, date line, International Date Line, time zone, clock time, local time, civil time, astronomical time,

solar time, sidereal time, Universal Time (UT), the time now, the exact time, time of day, time of night, hour, summer time, daylight saving time, 12-hour clock, 24-hour clock
▶ *185 Time*

4 **horology**, clockmaking, watchmaking

5 **timekeeper**, timepiece, horologe, chronometer

6 **clock**, grandfather clock, grandmother clock, longcase clock, carriage clock, travelling clock, wall clock, bracket clock, electric clock, quartz clock, digital clock, alarm clock, clock radio, cuckoo clock, water clock, clepsydra, speaking clock, Tim (Inf), atomic clock, caesium clock, body clock, biological clock

7 **watch**, wristwatch, analogue watch, digital watch, quartz watch, pocket watch, fob, turnip, hunter, half-hunter, repeater, clip watch

8 **face**, clockface, watchface, dial, analog dial, hands, gnomon, digital display, chronogram

9 **hourglass**, sandglass, egg timer, sundial, chronograph, chronoscope

10 **signal**, time signal, hooter, siren, four-minute warning, gong, bell, minute gun, starting gun, stopwatch, timer, timing device, time switch, time fuse, time bomb
▶ *543 Sign*

11 **person keeping time**, timekeeper, referee, time beater, conductor, bandleader

12 **chronologist**, chronologer, chronographer, calendrist, calendar-maker, clockmaker, watchmaker, horologist

13 **chronicler**, diarist, annalist, historian, historiographer, scribe, recorder
▶ *3 History, 545 Record*

VERBS

14 **keep time**, clock, time, monitor, set a date for, set a time for, fix the time, fix the date, fix the day, schedule, timetable, slate, adjust the

Timepieces and Timers

alarm clock (or watch)	half-hunter (watch)
	hourglass
Albert (watch)	hunter (watch)
ammonia clock	isochronon
analogue clock (or watch)	journeyman (watch)
	marine chronometer
astronomical clock	metronome
atomic clock	pendulum clock
box chronometer	pocket watch
calendar clock	quartz (or quartz-crystal) clock
Caesium clock	
clepystra (or water clock)	repeater
	sandglass
clock radio	stemwinder (watch)
cuckoo clock	stopwatch
digital clock (or watch)	sundial
egg timer	travelling clock
electric clock	wall clock
electronic clock	water clock
gnomon	wristwatch or wristlet watch
grandfather clock	
grandmother clock	

hands of the clock, put the clock forward, put the clock back, set the alarm, synchronize watches

15 chronologize, calendar, date, be dated, carry a date, bear a date, record, chronicle, diarize, keep a journal

16 measure time, count the hours, count the minutes, mark time, beat time, keep time, watch the clock, clock in (*or* clock on), clock out (*or* clock off)

ADJECTIVES

17 timekeeping, horological, chronometric, chronographic, chronologic, chronological, annalistic, diaristic, calendrical, chronogrammatic, temporal

ADVERBS

18 horologically, by the clock, chronologically, chronographically, annalistically, at this hour, at that hour, at this time, at that time, o'clock, a.m., p.m.

193   Wrong Time

NOUNS

1 wrong time, wrong date, wrong day, mix-up in dates, misdating, chronological error, dating error, mistiming, untimeliness, lateness, tardiness, earliness, pre-emption, anticipation, prolepsis, anachronism, parachronism, metachronism, prochronism

▶ *504 Error, 211 Untimeliness*

VERBS

2 be untimely, mistake the date, mistake the day, mistake the time, arrive late, be too early

3 mistime, antedate, anticipate, jump the gun, pre-empt, go off at half cock, (of clocks) gain, be fast, postdate, lag behind, take no note of time, (of clocks) lose, be slow

ADJECTIVES

4 mistimed, untimely, misdated, wrongly dated, undated, anachronistic, metachronistic

5 too early, antedated, previous, ahead of time, precipitate, overhasty, ahead of one's time, prochronistic, pre-emptive, proleptic

▶ *208 Earliness*

6 too late, tardy, overdue, unpunctual, behind time, postdated, out of date, behind the times, parachronistic

▶ *209 Lateness*

ADVERBS

7 out of chronological order, out of sequence, anachronistically, metachronistically, too soon, too early, ahead of time, ahead of one's time, pre-emptively, prochronistically, too late, behind time, unpunctually, behind the times, out of fashion, out of date, parachronistically

194   Priority

NOUNS

1 priority, precedence, pre-existence, antecedence, previousness, anteriority

2 greater importance, seniority, supremacy, superiority, lead, pre-eminence, first class, first place, first division, first eleven

3 matter of priority, first concern, primary issue, question of highest importance

4 claim to priority, prerogative, privi-lege, primogeniture, birthright, *droit de seigneur* (Fr)

5 gift of priority, advantage, head start, flying start

6 person having priority, ancestor, antecedent, predecessor, forerunner, precursor, elder, chief, leader, trailblazer, pathfinder, member of the avant garde

7 foretaste, preview, prerelease, trailer, presage, presentiment, prediction, precursor, herald, forerunner, prequel, preface, foreword, introduction, prelude, prologue

VERBS

8 be before, precede, anticipate, foreshadow, antedate, come before, go before, antecede, forerun, take precedence, take priority, lead, take the lead, lead the world, head, head up, be first, be out in front, be more important

9 do before, pre-empt, anticipate, give precedence to, forestall, jump the queue, get in first, steal a march on, have a start on, precede, preface, introduce, preview, prepare beforehand, prefabricate, prearrange, predecease

ADJECTIVES

10 prior, previous, former, earlier, earliest, first, first in the field, first of its kind, first among equals, leading, forward, foremost, first-class, first-division, avant garde, advanced, primal, elder, eldest

ADVERBS

11 before, just before, prior to, before now, before then, beforehand, afore (Dial), ere (Fml), first, firstly, in first place, in the first place, earlier, earliest, in front, in front of, in the lead, in the vanguard, up to this time, up to now, up to that time, up to then, till now, till then, hitherto, heretofore

195   Succession

NOUNS

1 succession, sequence, order, arrangement, cycle, rota, list, turn, hierarchy, pecking order, Buggins's turn, queue, line (US), tailback, series, run, chain, train, retinue, entourage, suite, wake, following, subsequence, procession, process, progression, flow, flux, continuation, course, progress, forward movement, forward motion, successiveness

▶ *155 Sequence, 150 Order, 152 Arrangement, 159 Consecutiveness, 219 Continuity, 324 Motion*

2 **descent**, line of descent, lineage, family, family tree, tribe, race

3 **subordination**, inferiority, lesser importance, lower merit, no priority, little worth, second place, second class, second eleven, second division, last place

4 **accession**, takeover, inauguration, assumption, assumption of office, entry upon, entry into office, taking up the post of, taking over, transfer, changeover, elevation, promotion, inheritance

▶ *132 Remainder, 156 Beginning, 119 Originality*

5 **successor**, descendant, inheritor, heir, heir apparent, heir presumptive, heiress, beneficiary, replacement, substitute, next in line, next man in, new boy, new broom, new arrival, new kid on the block, new blood, fresh blood, newcomer

6 **posterity**, the unborn, later generations, future generations

▶ *245 Reproduction, 199 Future Time*

7 **subordinate**, inferior, the person in second place, assistant, right hand man, subaltern, second fiddle, always the bridesmaid but never the bride

▶ *127 Inferiority*

8 **follower**, camp follower, groupie (Inf), hanger-on, sycophant, dependant, dependent relative, poor relation, last in the field, latecomer, incomer, upstart, last man in, no-hoper, also-ran

▶ *180 Accompaniment, 132 Remainder, 209 Lateness, 107 Relatedness*

9 **sequel**, continuation, development, follow-up, conclusion, end, result, net result, denouement, consequence, outcome, upshot, aftermath, post mortem, afterword, postlude, coda, epilogue, postscript, payoff (Inf), the way things pan out (Inf), the way the cookie crumbles (Inf)

▶ *155 Sequence*

VERBS

10 **succeed**, follow, follow in sequence, come next, come after, come last, bring up the rear, be subsequent to, be consequent upon, result, result from, ensue, supervene

11 **follow in office**, follow in the position of, accede to, succeed, succeed to, assume, assume office, assume the mantle, embark upon office, take over, take over the mantle, take over the reins, take the helm, replace, supplant, take up, enter upon, come into, become possessed of, come into possession of, come into ownership of

ADJECTIVES

12 **succeeding**, successive, successional, following, next, proximate, close, near, sequential, consecutive, ordered, arranged, second, another, every, every other, every second, alternate, subsequent, consequent, ensuing, pursu-

ant, late, later, latter, last, latest

13 **subordinate**, inferior, less important, second-class, second-division

ADVERBS

14 **in succession**, successively, one after the other, one after another, one behind the other, in line, in a row, in sequence, in order, consecutively, running, on the trot (Inf)

15 **as follows**, secondly, in second place, in the second place, lastly, last

196 Present Time

NOUNS

1 **present time**, the present, the here and now, the present moment, this moment, this moment in time, this very minute, this second, this instant, this hour, this very day, today, tonight, this morning, this afternoon, this evening

2 **the present day**, the time being, this time, the nonce (Fml), this day, this day and age, the present time, the present situation, the current situation, contemporary life, the modern day, our day, our own day, the present generation, modern times, the modern world, the world of today, the contemporary world, one's contemporaries

▶ *198 Same Time*

3 **actuality**, happening, existence, present tense

4 **up-to-dateness**, modernity, modernism, currency, topicality, the height of fashion

▶ *201 Newness*

VERBS

5 **be present**, exist, be, live, not be absent, be now, live in the present, live for today, live for the day, *carpe diem* (L), live in the modern world, be modern, modernize

ADJECTIVES

6 **present**, current, existent, existing, extant, of today, of this date, of today's date, topical, actual, contemporary, contemporaneous, modern, fashionable, in fashion, up-to-date, bang up-to-date, instant

▶ *198 Same Time, 191 Immediacy*

7 **occasional**, temporary, provisional, interim, passing, pro tem (or *pro tempore*)

8 **available**, at hand, to hand, ready, ready to hand, here, there, in attendance, nearby, close by, standing by, accounted for, present and correct

ADVERBS

9 **at present**, at this moment, now, at this time, at this moment in time, right now, just now, presently, today, tonight, nowadays, these days

10 **for the present**, for the moment, for a while, meanwhile, in the meantime, in the interim, for this occasion, for the occasion, for the time

being, for the nonce, not for long, provisionally, temporarily

197 Different Time

NOUNS

1 **different time**, another time, asynchronism, archaism, some other time, other times,
distant time, better time, more convenient
time, any time but this (or now), the past, past
time, former time, future time, the future,
later time, wrong time, mistiming, wrong
date, misdating, chronological error, anachronism, parachronism, prochronism, time shift,
time warp
▶ 211 Untimeliness, 193 Wrong Time

ADJECTIVES

2 **occurring at a different time**, asynchronous, unsynchronized, out of sync (Inf), of (or
from) another time, of (or from) another age,
not contemporary, not modern, unmodern,
behind the times, out of date, archaic, ahead
of the times, avant-garde, mistimed, misdated, anachronistic, parachronistic, prochronistic

ADVERBS

3 **another time**, asynchronously, some other
time, not now, not today, not at the moment,
not just this minute, sometime, someday,
sooner or later, any (old) time, tomorrow, in
the future, later, soon, one of these days,
mañana (Sp), yesterday, in the past, previously, earlier, then, once upon a time

VERBS

4 **be a different time**, mistime, misdate

198 Same Time

NOUNS

1 **same time**, same date, same day, simultaneity, contemporaneousness, contemporaneity, contemporariness, coevality, accompaniment, coexistence, existing together, concomitance, concurrence, coincidence, photo
finish

2 **present time**, present age, present day, present moment, today, now
▶ 196 Present Time

3 **synchronism**, synchronization, isochronism, sync (Inf), lip-sync (Inf)

4 **equal race**, dead heat, tie, draw, neck and
neck, nip and tuck (US), level pegging (Inf),
lock step (US)

5 **contemporary**, coeval, compeer, friend,
classmate, one of the boys, one of the girls,
one's contemporaries, one's peers, one's own
generation, brother, sister, men (or women) of
today, people of today, peer group, one of the
lads, one of the lasses, one of the gang, age
group, class, class of (a certain year)

VERBS

6 **be simultaneous**, exist simultaneously, be
contemporary, happen at the same time, live
at the same time, coexist, exist together, accompany, concur, coincide, encounter

7 **synchronize**, keep the same beat, keep in
time, keep time with, stay in time, keep in
step, keep in step with, keep pace with, march
in lock step (US), go hand in hand, say together, sing together, chorus, sync (Inf)

8 **run equally**, run a dead heat, tie, draw, run
neck and neck, run nip and tuck (US), be level
pegging (Inf)

ADJECTIVES

9 **simultaneous**, coeval, contemporary, contemporaneous, coexistent, coexisting, coeternal, concomitant, coincident, coincidental,
concurrent, photo-finish, accompanying, of
the same generation, of the same year, of the
same age, matched in age, twinned, of the
same vintage

10 **synchronized**, synchronous, isochronal, isochronous, timed, phased, on (or with) the
beat, in time, in step, in lock step (US), in sync
(Inf)

11 **equal**, level, dead-heat, neck-and-neck, nip-
and-tuck (US), level-pegging (Inf), on a par
with

ADVERBS

12 **simultaneously**, at the same time, together,
all together, coevally, contemporarily, contemporaneously, coeternally, concomitantly,
concomitant with, coincidentally, concurrently, concurrent with

13 **synchronously**, isochronally, isochronously, in time, in step, pari passu (L), on (or with)
the beat, in unison, in chorus, in concert, at
one time, with one voice, as one man, as one,
in sync (Inf)

14 **equal with**, level with, in a dead heat, neck
and neck, nip and tuck(US), level pegged (Inf)

15 **as**, just as, even as, as soon as, at the moment
of, just when, in the very moment that, in the
same breath as, while (or whilst)

199 Future Time

NOUNS

1 **future time**, future, the future, futurity, time
to come, days and years to come, the years
ahead, the time ahead, future years, the near
future, tomorrow, mañana (Sp), tomorrow
morning, tomorrow afternoon, tomorrow evening, tomorrow night, the day after tomorrow, next week, next month, next year, the far
future, the distant future, the remote future,
the long run, the long term, after ages, the
womb of time, the morrow (Arch), by-and-by
(US), sweet by-and-by (US inf)
▶ 264 Nearness, 263 Distance

2 **future generation**, descendants, heirs, inheritors, successors, posterity

3 **future condition**, future state, what the future brings, what the future holds, better days, jam tomorrow, uncertain future, fate, destiny, coming events, what fate has in store, latter days, doomsday, the crack of doom, the end of the world, the end of time, the millennium, Judgment Day, Day of Judgment, Last Judgment, post-existence, good time coming, life after death, life to come, the hereafter, the next world, kingdom come, paradise, nirvana, heaven, damnation, the underworld, hell, hellfire, eternal fire

▶ *7 Religion, 571 Necessity, 8 Divinity*

4 **looking to the future**, eschatology, teleology, looking ahead, waiting, expectancy, expectation, great expectations, anticipation, foresight, foreknowledge, prescience, preparation, prospect, prospects, likelihood, outlook, forecast, prediction, prophecy, premonition, astrology, horoscope, fortune-telling, crystal-ball gazing, crystal-gazing, second sight

5 **predictor**, forecaster, prophet, prophetess, soothsayer, oracle, seer, diviner, augur, geomancer, astrologer, fortune teller, crystal gazer

▶ *513 Expectation, 517 Prediction, 594 Preparation, 11 Occultism*

6 **future event**, forthcoming event, scheduled event, advent, coming, approach of time

▶ *336 Forward Motion*

VERBS

7 **be in the future**, be to come, lie ahead, lie in the future, lie just around the corner, draw near, approach, come soon, overhang, threaten, stare one in the face, cast a shadow before, draw nigh (Arch)

8 **intend**, have every intention to, be about to, plan to, have in mind to, have an eye to, mean to, shall, will

9 **look ahead**, look forward, think of the future, hope for, foresee, predict, presage, prophesy, have a premonition, divine, foretell, augur, look into a crystal, read tea leaves, cast bones, haruspicate

10 **expect**, await, wait for, see it coming, prepare for, have prospects, put by for a rainy day, anticipate, forestall, forewarn, take thought for tomorrow, take the long view, take the long-term view

ADJECTIVES

11 **future**, forthcoming, upcoming (US), coming, to come, yet to come, to be, yet to be, eventual, later, ahead, near, at hand, near at hand, close at hand, just round the corner, approaching, oncoming, due, fated, destined, imminent, threatening, overhanging, impending, pending, waiting, waiting in the wings, nigh (Arch)

12 **predictable**, foreseeable, probable, possible, potential, likely, certain, sure

13 **foreseen**, foretold, predicted, expected, anticipated, awaited, looked for, hoped for, promised

ADVERBS

14 **in the future**, in future, tomorrow, next week, next month, next year, someday, one fine day, some other time, not now, soon, imminently, just round the corner, in the offing, in the wind, on the horizon, getting on for, heading for, at the right time, in the fullness of time, eventually, later, later on, ultimately, when the time is right, when the time is ripe, by and by, in due course, on the morrow (Arch)

15 **after**, afterwards, hereafter, hereinafter (Fml), henceforth, henceforward, from this time forth, from now on, from this moment on

16 **predictably**, probably, possibly, potentially, likely, in the stars

200 Past Time

Even God cannot change the past. Agathon.

Study the past, if you would divine the future. Confucius.

The past is a foreign country: they do things differently there. L. P. Hartley.

Keep off your thoughts from things that are past and done;/ For thinking of the past wakes regret and pain. Arthur Waley.

NOUNS

1 **past time**, past times, the past, times past, times gone by, former times, recent past, yesterday, yesterday morning, yesterday afternoon, yesterday evening, last night, the day before yesterday, last week, last month, last year, yesteryear (Fml), years gone by, the far past, prehistory, protohistory, history, the remote past, ancient times, antiquity, high antiquity, remote ages, time immemorial, a bygone age, bygone days, days of old, good old days, days of yore, olden days, auld lang syne (Scot), golden age, the ancient world

▶ *202 Oldness, 3 History*

2 **retrospection**, retrospective, remembrance, reminiscence, review, reprise, looking back

▶ *511 Memory*

3 **geological period**, geological epoch, Precambrian era, Palaeozoic era, Mesozoic era, Cenozoic era, Cambrian period, Ordovician period, Silurian period, Devonian period, Carboniferous period, Permian period, Triassic period, Jurassic period, Cretaceous period, Tertiary period, Palaeocene period, Eocene period, Oligocene period, Miocene period, Pliocene period, Quaternary period, Plistocene period, Holocene period, the age of amphibians, the

age of reptiles, glacial period, ice age
▶ *187 Period*
4 **prehistoric age**, Stone Age, Palaeolithic period, Mesolithic period, Neolithic period, Chalcolithic period, Bronze Age, Iron Age
5 **historical period**, heroic age, Classical Age, Dark Ages, Middle Ages, Renaissance, Age of Reason, Age of Enlightenment, *ancien régime* (Fr), Industrial Revolution
6 **people of the past**, people of antiquity, prehistoric people, cave-dweller, caveman, Neanderthal man, Neanderthaler, Peking man, Cro-Magnon man, the ancients, Egyptians, Babylonians, Sumerians, Ethiopians, Phoenicians, Persians, ancient Greeks, ancient Romans, Etruscans, Parthians, Huns, Incas, Mayas, Toltecs, Aztecs, Picts, Vandals, Goths, Visigoths, Saxons, Angles, Caribs, Arawaks, Maori, Aborigines, American Indians
▶ *3 History, 1 Anthropology*
7 **thing of the past**, survival, remainder, museum piece, antique, relic, relict, remains, vestiges, fossilized remains, monument, ancient monument, ruin, ancient ruin, artefact (*or* artifact), megalith, dolmen, cromlech, menhir, standing stone(s), Stonehenge, ancient flint, arrowhead, eolith, microlith, earthwork, barrow, burial chamber, tholos, beehive tomb, fogou, pyramid, ziggurat, King Tutankhamen's tomb
▶ *3 History, 132 Remainder, 543 Sign, 43 Architecture, 399 Burial*
8 **excavation**, archaeological dig (Inf), dig (Inf)
▶ *496 Discovery*
9 **antiquarianism**, classicism, medievalism, archaeology, industrial archaeology, palaeontology, palaeozoology, palaeoanthropology, palaeogeography, palaeontography, palaeography, palaeethnology, palaeoclimatology, palaeometeorology, prehistoric anthropology, prehistoric archaeology
▶ *3 History*
10 **fossilization**, petrification, petrified forest, fossil, ammonite, trilobite, dinosaur, mammoth, fossil record, amber, fossil fuel, coal, coal measures, brown coal, peat, oil, petroleum
11 **antiquarian**, antiquary, palaeontologist, archaeologist, Egyptologist, Assyriologist, Hebraist, Arabist, classicist, medievalist, palaeozoologist, palaeoanthropologist, palaeogeographer, palaeontographer, palaeographer, palaeethnologist, palaeoclimatologist, palaeometeorologist, prehistoric anthropologist, prehistoric archaeologist
▶ *3 History*
12 **genealogy**, lineage, ancient lineage, pedigree, family history, family tree
▶ *195 Succession, 155 Sequence, 159 Consecutiveness*

VERBS
13 **be past**, be over, be over and done with, have expired, have had one's day, be in the past, be history, be lost and gone, have gone out with the Ark (Inf)
14 **pass**, pass away, pass into history, finish, end, elapse, expire, become extinct, die out, run out, run its course
15 **look back**, trace back, remember, reminisce, review, reprise, regress, antiquarianize, put the clock back, turn back the clock, turn back time, archaize, return to the past, go back to the past, hark back, relive, live in the past, look over one's shoulder, cast one's eyes backwards
16 **excavate**, excavate the past, unearth the past, exhume, unearth, dig up the past, archaeologize, conduct a dig (Inf)

ADJECTIVES
17 **past**, historical, historic, old, olden, prehistoric, prehistorical, protohistoric, ancient, early, earlier, elder, primitive, primal, primeval
18 **over**, over and done with, gone, gone for good, gone forever, lost forever, lost and gone, completely past, past and gone, bygone, finished, exhausted, ended, done, spent, completed, irrecoverable, dead, dead and gone, dead and buried, extinct, dead as a dodo
▶ *397 Death*
19 **antiquarian**, ancestral, antecedent, preceding, foregoing, out of date, outdated, outworn, outmoded, old hat, behind the times, anachronistic, belonging to the past, antiquated, fossilized, old-fashioned, obsolete, passé, past its sell-by date, long past, stale, moth-eaten
20 **former**, late, quondam, sometime, obsolescent, retired, emeritus, superannuated, deceased, no longer present, no longer serving, ex (Inf)
21 **retrospective**, retroactive, diachronic, remembering, reminiscing, looking back, backward-looking

ADVERBS
22 **in the past**, during the past, in past times, in times gone by, formerly, of old, in days of yore, ago, long ago, long since, once upon a time, years ago, ages ago, some time ago, a while ago, a while back, some while back, far back in the past, in the mists of time, at (*or* from) the dawn of time, from time immemorial, time out of mind, lately, recently, yesterday, yesterday evening, yestreen (Scot), the day before yesterday, last week, last month, last season, last year, yesteryear, within living memory, only yesterday, the other day, aforetime (Arch)
23 **before now**, hitherto, heretofore, yet, as yet, until now, till now, up to now, up to this moment, up to this time, *ex post facto* (L), already, no longer, not any more

24 retrospectively, historically, with hindsight, with the wisdom of hindsight, from experience, from past experience

201 Newness

NOUNS

1 **newness**, recentness, recency, recent occurrence, contemporaneity, topicality, currency, up-to-dateness, new production, mint condition, state of the art, modernism, modernity, innovation, invention, originality, usualness, unfamiliarity, unknownness, newfangledness, gimmickry, unknownness, novelty, neology, neologism, neophilia, new (*or* latest) wrinkle (Inf)
▶ *196 Present Time, 119 Originality*

2 **trendiness**, the latest craze, the latest fashion, fad (Inf), high fashion, artistic movement, modernism, postmodernism, New Wave, *Nouvelle Vague* (Fr), New Look, New Age, New Thought (US), futurism, *nouvelle cuisine* (Fr), the rage (Inf), the last word (Inf), the latest thing (Inf), the in thing (Inf), what's in (Inf)
▶ *796 Fashion, 549 Style*

3 **immaturity**, inexperience, youth, virginity, dewiness, callowness, greenness, rawness, naivety, ingenuousness, innocence, freshness, cleanness, cleanliness
▶ *206 Youth, 595 Lack of Preparation, 621 Cleanness*

4 **beginning**, birth, start, inception, commencement, inauguration, initiation, generating, generation, opening, auspication, grand opening, house-warming, unveiling, launching, maiden voyage, first night, premiere
▶ *156 Beginning*

5 **fresh start**, new start, clean slate, tabula rasa (L), renewal, regeneration, renovation, restoration, refurbishment, rejuvenation, repainting, resurrection, revival, revivification, remake, change, reconstruction, rebuilding, restructure, redesign, reorganization, alteration, modernization, updating, upgrading, revisal, new look, new leaf, addition, extra, supplement, doing up (Inf)
▶ *629 Repair*

6 **avant-garde**, advance guard, vanguard, van, fashionable set, in-group, in-set, in-crowd, jet set, beautiful people, trendsetting group, younger generation, young generation, new generation, next generation

7 **new thing**, trend, gimmick, new wrinkle, new moon, new town, new maths, New Year, New Deal (US), New American Bible (US)

8 **new arrival**, newborn baby, newcomer, beginner, fledgling, amateur, novice, tyro, greenhorn, raw recruit, new recruit, new member, freshman, fresher, new convert, neophyte, new boy, new kid on the block (US), new broom, debutante, latecomer, upstart,

parvenu, nouveau riche, incomer, immigrant, foreigner, alien, illegal alien, *novus homo* (L), Johnny-come-lately (Inf), rookie (Inf)

9 **modern person**, modern man (*or* woman), new man (*or* woman), trendsetter, avant-garde artist, avant-gardist, modernist, ultramodernist, postmodernist, futurist, advanced thinker, bright young thing, yuppie, faddist, neophiliac, neologist, neoteric

ADJECTIVES

10 **new**, brand new, newly, recent, contemporary, topical, current, up-to-date, modern, modernistic, futuristic, ultramodern, postmodern, innovative, revolutionary, inventive, advanced, original, first, latest, most recent, state-of-the-art, newly produced, just out, new-made, oven-fresh, mint condition, trendy, gimmicky, neological, neologistic, neologistical, neophytic, brand spanking new (Inf), bang up-to-date (Inf), hot off the press (Inf), in (Inf), faddish (Inf)

11 **unfamiliar**, unknown, not seen before, unheard of, unprecedented, unused, untried, untested, untrodden, unbeaten, unexplored, out of the ordinary, newfangled, novel, nontraditional, mould-breaking

12 **immature**, inexperienced, budding, aspiring, upstart, parvenu (*or* parvenue), nouveau riche, amateurish, amateur, novice, apprentice, new to the job, embryonic, inchoate, newborn, young, youthful, virginal, virgin, maiden, dewy, callow, green, raw, naive, naïf, ingenuous, innocent, fresh, fresh as a daisy, fresh as paint, clean, clean as a new pin, spick-and-span, rookie (Inf)

13 **inaugurated**, initiated, opened, unveiled, launched, premiered, premiere

14 **renewed**, renovated, restored, refurbished, regenerated, rejuvenated, refreshed, freshened up, touched up, repainted, resurrected, revived, revivified, remade, good as new, changed, reconstructed, rebuilt, restructured, redesigned, reorganized, altered, modernized, new-look, updated, upgraded, revised, added, additional, extra, supplementary, done up (Inf)

15 **renewable**, restorable, reconstructible, rebuildable, redesignable, alterable, updateable, upgradeable, revisable

16 **avant-garde**, advanced, advance, trendsetting, trendy, fashionable, modish, à la mode, all the rage, with it (Inf)

VERBS

17 **become new**, begin again, start anew, start from the beginning, renew oneself, get up to date, start afresh, have a fresh start, have a new start, wipe the slate clean, reform, have a new look, turn over a new leaf

18 **be trendy**, follow the trend, try the latest craze, move with the times, get the new look,

go contemporary, go modern, innovate, invent, originate, set a trend, try something new, get with it (Inf)

19 **begin**, give birth to, commence, generate, inaugurate, initiate, open, have a grand opening, have a house-warming, unveil, launch, take a maiden voyage, premiere

20 **make new**, renew, renovate, restore, refresh, freshen up, touch up, refurbish, rejuvenate, regenerate, repaint, resurrect, give a new lease of life, revive, revivify, remake, change, reconstruct, rebuild, restructure, redesign, reorganize, alter, modernize, update, bring up to date, upgrade, revise, add on, supplement, do up (Inf)

ADVERBS

21 **newly**, like new, as new, new, lately, latterly, of late, only yesterday, not long ago, a short time ago, just, just now, recently, contemporarily, topically, currently, modernistically, futuristically, innovatively, revolutionarily, inventively, originally, first, firstly, nontraditionally, unusually, neologically, neologistically

22 **again**, anew, afresh, once more, from the top, from the ground up, from the start, from the beginning, all over again, from scratch

23 **trendily**, fashionably, in fashion, modishly, in the current mode

24 **immaturely**, aspiringly, amateurishly, youthfully, virginally, maidenly, dewily, rawly, freshly, fresh, cleanly, clean

202   Oldness

NOUNS

1 **oldness**, elderliness, age, hoary age, old age, ripe old age, mellowness, venerableness, maturity, seniority, dotage, senility, decrepitude, the autumn of one's life, the burden of years, retirement

2 **old people**, the elderly, elders, elders and betters, older generation, grandparents, ancestors, forebears, senior citizens, pensioners, wrinklies (Sl), crumblies (Sl), Methuselah, Nestor, Sibyl of Cumae, Tithonus, Father Time
▶ *207 Age*

3 **antiquity**, primitiveness, ancientness, *ancien régime* (Fr), dust of antiquity, cobwebs of antiquity, rust, decay, olden days, olden times, ancient times, distant past, time out of mind, time immemorial

4 **antiquarianism**, classicism, medievalism, archaism, archaeology
▶ *200 Past Time, 207 Age*

5 **old thing**, thing of the past, archaism, antique, Victoriana, heirloom, museum piece, artefact (*or* artifact), relic, relic of the past, ancient monument, Stonehenge, ancient manuscript, Dead Sea Scrolls, historic build-

ing, listed building, Historic District (US), fossil, petrified wood, dinosaur

6 **tradition**, custom, common law, lore, folklore, legend, myth, mythology, ancient wisdom, ancient tale
▶ *3 History*

7 **ancient people**, prehistoric man, primitive man, early man, humanoid, protohuman, apeman, hominid, Homo erectus, Homo sapiens, caveman, cave dweller, Australopithecus, Pithecanthropus, Neanderthal man, Cro-Magnon man, Heidelberg man, Java man, Peking man, Stone-Age man, Bronze-Age man, Iron-Age man

8 **prehistoric animal**, woolly mammoth, mastodon, sabre-toothed tiger (*or* cat), dinosaur, brontosaurus, tyrannosaurus, ichthyosaurus, pterodactyl, giant sloth, ammonite, trilobite

9 **antiquarian**, antiquary, classicist, medievalist, archaeologist, archaist, antique dealer, antique collector

10 **staleness**, sourness, rottenness, overripeness, rankness, spoilage

ADJECTIVES

11 **old**, older, elderly, elder, aged, full of years, venerable, veteran, senior, patriarchal, of advanced years, advanced in years, getting on, getting on in years, mature, mellow, ripe, grey, old and grey, grey-haired, white-haired, grizzled, hoary, decrepit, senile, senescent, past one's prime, past one's best, doddering, past it (Inf), over the hill (Inf)

12 **olden**, antiquarian, antique, antiqued, ancient, timeworn, archaic, archaistic, antiquated, outdated, outmoded, moth-eaten, musty, crumbling, mouldering, mouldy, stale, time-honoured, rooted, established, long established, longstanding, traditional, age-old, ancestral, immemorial, antediluvian, from before the Flood, out of the Ark, as old as the hills, as old as time, as old as Adam, adamic, as old as Methuselah, old-world, olde-worlde (Arch), ye olde (Arch), prewar, antebellum, venerable, inveterate, vintage, classic, classical

13 **former**, previous, prior, erstwhile, one-time, sometime, quondam, retired, emeritus

14 **historic**, historical, of historical interest, heroic, Helladic, Hellenic, classical, Hellenistic, Roman, Etruscan, Ottoman, Persian, Byzantine, medieval, Saxon, Norman, feudal, Romanesque, Gothic, Tudor, Elizabethan, Jacobean, Georgian, Hanoverian, Colonial, Victorian, Edwardian

15 **primal**, primordial, primitive, primeval, early, antediluvian, prelapsarian, Precambrian, Palaeozoic, Mesozoic, Cenozoic, preglacial, glacial, prehistoric, Palaeolithic, Mesolithic, Neolithic, Chalcolithic, Stone-Age, Bronze-Age, Iron-Age

VERBS

16 **be old**, belong to the past, survive from the past, go back a long way, go back in time

17 **grow old**, age, decline, deteriorate, fade, burn out, decay, rot, spoil, wither, moulder, decompose, rust, crumble, crumble into dust, become obsolete, go out of style, lose currency, dodder

ADVERBS

18 **venerably**, patriarchally, maturely, mellowly, ripely, mustily, stalely, greyly, decrepitly, senilely

19 **anciently**, in ancient times, in olden days, in the good old days, of old, of yore, since long ago, since days of yore, ages ago, way back when, since the big bang, since the world was young, since the world was new, since before the Flood, since the year one, since God knows when (Sl), since Adam was a lad (Inf)

20 **formerly**, previously, earlier, before, before now

21 **archaically**, ancestrally, immemorially, oldworldly, inveterately, venerably, classically, historically, primordially, primitively, primevally, primarily, originally, early

203 Season

NOUNS

1 **season**, season of the year, time of year, time, period, annual period, quarterly period, spell, term, interval, dry season, rainy season, snow season, social season, the season, the English season, the New York season, tourist season, football season, baseball season (US), cricket season, basketball season, hunting season, shooting season, open season, duck season, deer season, grouse season, pheasant season, fishing season, close (or closed) season, ecclesiastical season, Easter season, Advent season, the Season (Christmas), silly season
▶ 185 Time, 187 Period, 815 Sociability

2 **spring**, springtime, springtide, vernal season, vernal equinox, point of Aries, seedtime, Easter, Eastertide, blossom time, budtime, Maytime, the merry month of May, the month of Maying, May Day, first cuckoo, rustle of spring

3 **summer**, summertime, good old summertime, summertide, growing season, Whitsuntide, Whitsun, midsummer, Midsummer (or Midsummer's) Day, summer solstice, high summer, dog days, haymaking, Indian summer, St Martin's summer, aestivation
▶ 408 Heat

4 **autumn**, fall (US), fall of the leaf, back end (Dial), harvest, harvest time, harvest moon, hunter's moon, autumnal equinox, point of Libra, Michaelmas
▶ 209 Lateness, 68 Agriculture

5 **winter**, wintertime, wintertide, midwinter,

winter solstice, Christmas, Christmas time, the Season, yuletide, yule (Arch), hibernation
▶ 409 Cold, 7 Religion, 9 Worship, 10 Ritual

VERBS

6 **spend the season**, summer, spend the summer aestivate, winter, overwinter, spend the winter, pass the winter, hibernate, have a long winter's sleep, celebrate Christmas, celebrate the yuletide, send Season's greetings

7 **season**, harden, anneal, inure, discipline, toughen, mature, acclimatize, acclimate, accustom

8 **mitigate**, temper, leaven, mollify, moderate

ADJECTIVES

9 **seasonal**, in season, out of season, equinoctial, solstitial

10 **spring**, vernal, springlike, flowery, sappy, juicy, young

11 **summer**, summery, summerlike, aestival, midsummer

12 **autumn**, autumnal, autumnlike, golden

13 **winter**, wintry, wintery, hibernal, winterlike, midwinter, hiemal, brumal

14 **seasonable**, suited to the weather, appropriate, suitable, convenient, timely, well-timed, welcome, providential, opportune

15 **seasoned**, hardened, toughened, matured, inured, accustomed

16 **mitigated**, tempered, leavened, mollified, moderated

17 **in season**, in (or on) heat, oestrous, rutting, lusting, leching (Inf)

ADVERBS

18 **seasonally**, equinoctially, vernally, in spring, summerly, in summer, autumnally, in autumn, wintrily, in winter

204 Daytime

NOUNS

1 **morning**, morning time, forenoon, a.m. (ante meridiem), dawn, false dawn, waking time, daybreak, break of day, crack of dawn, sunrise, sunup, morning light, first light, daylight, matins, prime, terce (or tierce), cockcrow, dawn chorus, rosy-fingered dawn, Aurora, Eos, morn (Arch), morrow (Arch)
▶ 208 Earliness, 439 Light

2 **morning thing**, morning star, Venus, morning glory, morning sickness, crowing cock, early bird, breakfast, rush hour, elevenses

3 **noon**, 12 noon, 12 o'clock, 1200 hours, noonday, noontime, high noon, noontide, midday, middle of the day, eight bells, meridian (Arch)

4 **afternoon**, p.m. (post meridiem), matinée, five o'clock, afternoon tea, siesta, after (Inf)

ADJECTIVES

5 **morning**, matin, matinal, matutinal, fore-

noon, dawn, dawning, early, fresh, morning-fresh, dewy, antemeridian, auroral (Arch)

6 **noon**, high-noon, midday, meridian

7 **afternoon**, postmeridian

ADVERBS

8 **in the morning**, of a morning, at sunrise, at sunup, at dawn, at the crack of dawn, by the dawn's early light, at daybreak, at first light, at break of day, at the dawning of the day, at cockcrow, with the sun, with the lark, ante meridiem, every morning, mornings, aurorally (Arch)

205 Night-time

NOUNS

1 **evening**, evening time, eve, early evening, p.m. (post meridiem), vespers, sunset, sundown, setting of the sun, going down of the sun, lighting-up time, dusk, twilight, evening twilight, gloaming (Scot), nightfall, close of day, day's end, moonrise, moonset, darkfall, eventide, evensong

▶ *441 Dimness, 209 Lateness*

2 **night**, night-time, bedtime, the cloak of night, (the) dark, darktime, darkness, the dark of night, blackness

▶ *447 Blackness*

3 **midnight**, 12 midnight, 12 o'clock, 2400 hours, the witching hour, the dead of night, night watch, small hours, wee small hours

4 **evening thing**, sunset, evening star, Venus, Hesperus, evening news, evening class, evening primrose, rush hour, afternoon tea, dogwatch, soiree

5 **night thing**, owl, night shift, night school, nightlife, nightclub, dinner, sleep, dreams, nightmare

ADJECTIVES

6 **evening**, afternoon, postmeridian, vesperine, vesperal, twilight, dusky, crepuscular, nocturnal, dark, nightly, night-time, benighted (Arch)

ADVERBS

7 **evening**, every evening, in the evening, during the evening, afternoon, in the afternoon, every afternoon, post meridiem, every night, at night, after dark, nocturnally, in the dead of night, through the night, all through the night, overnight, by night, nightly, late, late at night, in the small hours, in the wee small hours, evenings, nights

206 Youth

Better is a poor and a wise child than an old and foolish king, who will no more be admonished. Bible: Ecclesiastes.

It is good for a man that he bear the yoke in his youth. Bible: Lamentations.

Les enfants terribles./ The embarrassing young. Paul Gavarni.

Youth is a malady of which one becomes cured a little every day. Benito Mussolini.

My salad days,/ When I was green in judgment, cold in blood,/ To say as I said then! William Shakespeare

NOUNS

1 **youth**, adolescence, pubescence, puberty, age of puberty, teens, preteens, boyhood, girlhood, maidenhood, childhood, babyhood, infancy, young days, younger days, school age, schooldays, college days, student days, pupilage, apprenticeship, wardship, happiest days of one's life, salad days, the prime of life, heyday of the blood, early life, springtime of life, bloom of youth, tender age, awkward age, immaturity, puerility, nonage, minority

▶ *201 Newness, 156 Beginning*

2 **youthfulness**, juvenescence, juvenility, juvenilia, youngness, childishness, boyishness, girlishness, maidenliness, young blood, vigour, freshness, sappiness, juiciness, growing pains

3 **immaturity**, inexperience, undevelopment, greenness, rawness, naivety, ingenuousness, awkwardness, callowness, unreadiness, unpreparedness

▶ *595 Lack of Preparation*

4 **young animal**, young, yearling, fawn, kitten, puppy, pup, kid, lamb, lambkin, cub, whelp, piglet, duckling, cygnet, chick, fry, fledgling, nestling, calf, colt, foal, filly, larva, grub, nymph, pupa, chrysalis, cocoon, caterpillar, tadpole, polliwog, brood, clutch, spawn, farrow, litter

5 **young plant**, sprout, seedling, set, shoot, offshoot, sucker, twig, sprig, scion, sapling

6 **young person**, youngster, youth, youngling (Fml), young'un (Inf), minor, adolescent, teenager, young adult, juvenile, junior, young hopeful, kid (Inf), teenybopper (Sl), weenybopper (Sl), groupie (Sl)

7 **young man**, youth, boy, lad, laddie (Scot), stripling, schoolboy, urchin, street urchin, cub, kid (Inf), young shaver (Inf), pup (Inf), young pup (Inf)

8 **young woman**, girl, young lady, miss, lass, lassie (Scot), chit of a girl, slip of a girl, schoolgirl, maid, maiden, virgin, tomboy, hoyden, mademoiselle, minx, hussy, nymph, nymphet, missy (Inf), baggage (Derog), chick (Sl), bird (Sl), baby (Sl), babe (US sl)

9 **child**, baby, babe, bairn (Scot), bouncing baby, nursling (or nurseling), bundle of joy, babe in arms, infant, tiny tot, mite, toddler, little one, darling, little angel, little monkey, little cherub, little imp, youngster, boy, lad,

laddie (Scot), girl, lass, lassie (Scot), kid (Inf), kiddie (Inf), peewee (US inf), nipper (Inf), brat (Inf), moppet (Inf), poppet (Inf), whipper-snapper (Inf), rugrat (Sl), ankle-biter (Sl)

10 **the young**, young people, youth, young blood, children, schoolchildren, the rising young, the rising generation, the younger generation, the new generation, kids (Inf)

ADJECTIVES

11 **young**, youthful, juvenile, juvenescent, childlike, childish, boylike, boyish, beardless, girllike, girlish, maidenly, virginal, innocent, underage, underaged, undeveloped, minor, pre-school, school-age, junior, teenage, teen-aged, in one's teens, sweet sixteen, adolescent, pubescent, sweet and twenty, in the flower of youth, infantile, infant, in one's infancy, baby, babyish, unfledged, fledgling, new-fledged, in the cradle, at the breast, in arms, in nappies, knee-high, knee-high to a grasshopper

12 **immature**, inexperienced, undeveloped, green, raw, naive, naïf, ingenuous, awkward, callow, unready, unprepared

13 **maturing**, growing, budding, pullulating, burgeoning, developing, rounding out, flowering, blooming, in bloom

ADVERBS

14 **youthfully**, juvenilely, childishly, boyishly, girlishly, virginally, innocently, in one's infancy, in one's teens, in the flower of youth, in the cradle, at the breast

15 **immaturely**, greenly, rawly, awkwardly, unreadily, unpreparedly

VERBS

16 **be young**, have the bloom of youth, stay young

17 **make young**, youthen, rejuvenate, reinvigorate

18 **grow**, have growing pains, bud, pullulate, burgeon, develop, round out, flower, bloom, mature

207 Age

I am past thirty, and three parts iced over. Matthew Arnold.

What is an adult? A child blown up by age. Simone de Beauvoir.

If thou hast gathered nothing in thy youth, how canst thou find any thing in thine age? Bible: Ecclesiasticus.

Being now come to the years of discretion. The Book of Common Prayer.

Therefore I summon age/ To grant youth's heritage. Robert Browning.

Youth is a blunder; manhood a struggle; old age a regret. Benjamin Disraeli.

Here I am, an old man in a dry month,/ Being read to by a boy, waiting for rain. T. S. Eliot.

Si jeunesse savait; si vieillesse pouvait./ If only youth knew, if only age could. Henri Estienne.

But at my back I always hear/ Time's winged chariot hurrying near;/ And yonder all before us lie/ Deserts of vast eternity. Andrew Marvell.

How soon hath Time, the subtle thief of youth,/ Stolen on his wing my three-and-twentieth year! John Milton.

Doth not the appetite alter? A man loves the meat in his youth that he cannot endure in his age. William Shakespeare.

Life begins at forty. Sophie Tucker.

Be wise with speed,/ A fool at forty is a fool indeed. Edward Young.

NOUNS

1 **age**, time span, lifetime, life span, (number of) years, one's age, one's time of life
▶ *188 Duration*

2 **adulthood**, adultness, maturity, maturation, manhood, womanhood, matronliness, middle age, prime of life, seniority, oldness, old age, ripeness
▶ *202 Oldness*

3 **maturity**, matureness, experience, professionalism, confidence, readiness, preparedness, leadership
▶ *154 Precedence, 594 Preparation*

4 **middle age**, middle life, middle years, maturity, mellowness, ripeness, the riper years, years of discretion, one's prime, the prime of life, change of life, menopause, male menopause, climacteric, midlife crisis, dangerous age, wrong side of forty (Inf)

5 **old age**, elderliness, senescence, longevity, seniority, retirement age, pensionable age, ripe old age, green old age, golden years, third age, advanced years, allotted span, threescore years and ten, declining years, decline, hoariness, greyness, frailty, infirmity, anility, senility, second childhood, dotage, anecdotage, evening of one's life, autumn of one's life, winter of one's life
▶ *238 Weakness, 510 Insanity*

6 **gerontology**, geriatric medicine, gerontologist, geriatrician
▶ *60 Medicine*

7 **older person**, adult, grown-up, elder, senior, doyen (or doyenne), retired person, pensioner, old person, old age pensioner (OAP), retiree (US), senior citizen, veteran, geriatric, greybeard, sexagenarian, septuagenarian, octogenarian, nonagenarian, centenarian, Methuselah, old fogy, dotard, the old folks, Darby

and Joan, gray panther (US), oldster (Inf), oldie (Inf), golden oldie (Inf), no spring chicken (Inf), crumbly (Inf), wrinkly (Inf), dodderer (Inf)

8 **man**, husband, father, grandfather, patron, widower, old bachelor, man of the world, older man, old man, old boy, veteran, greybeard, old guy (Inf), old codger (Inf), old buffer (Inf), old duffer (Inf), old-timer (US inf), old geezer (Sl), old git (Sl)

9 **woman**, wife, mother, grandmother, matron, widow, old spinster, older woman, old woman, old witch, woman of the world, granny (Inf), old gal (Sl), old bag (Sl), old bat (Sl)

10 **the old**, the elderly, old people, the older generation, the over-the-hill gang (Inf), woopies (well-off older people) (Inf)

ADJECTIVES

11 **adult**, mature, senior, experienced, prepared, grown-up, ripe, developed, full-grown, in full bloom, in one's prime

12 **ageing**, growing old, getting old, senescent, getting on (or along), getting on (or along) in years, going grey, greying, getting crow's-feet, getting a middle-aged spread, declining, weakening, waning, on the wane, running (or going) to seed, sinking, moribund

13 **middle-aged**, mature, of mature years, fatherly, motherly, matronly, menopausal, climacteric, overblown, run (or gone) to seed, gone to pot, not as young as one was, long in the tooth, thirtysomething (Inf), fortysomething (Inf), no chicken (Inf), no spring chicken (Inf)

14 **aged**, old, grown old, elderly, venerable, patriarchal, matriarchal, geriatric, advanced in years, at an advanced age, past one's prime, well-preserved, white-haired, grey-haired, old and grey, hoary, wrinkled, wizened, shrivelled, lined, decrepit, failing, senile, anile, burdened with age, stricken in years, moribund, living on borrowed time, not long for this world, with one foot in the grave, ancient, old as the hills, old as Methuselah, still in full possession of one's faculties, doddering, past it (Inf), too old to cut the mustard (US sl), gaga (Sl)

15 **age-related**, geriatric, gerontologic, ageist

ADVERBS

16 **maturely**, with maturity, preparedly, ripely, in full bloom, in one's prime, venerably, patriarchally, matriarchally, past one's prime, at an advanced age, in one's old age, climacterically, hoarily, senilely, burdened with age, stricken in years, moribundly, on borrowed time, with one foot in the grave

VERBS

17 **age**, be (some) years old, see one's (specified) summer, grow up, grow old, get old, mature, ripen, mellow, pass one's prime, get on, get on in years, show one's years, go to seed, go to pot, decline, sink, weaken, deteriorate, get a middle-aged spread, get crow's-feet, wrinkle, wizen, shrivel, wither, grey, go grey, turn white, live to a ripe old age, become long in the tooth, dodder, have a second childhood, have had one's day, have seen better days, have one foot in the grave, become too old to cut the mustard (US inf)

18 **mature**, grow up, grow, develop, ripen, mellow, flower, bloom, come of age, leave the nest, come to maturity, attain majority, reach one's majority, assume responsibility, reach manhood (or womanhood), reach the prime of one's life

208   Earliness

NOUNS

1 **earliness**, promptness, promptitude, punctuality, punctualness, immediacy, dispatch, expedition, early start, head start, time to spare, readiness, alacrity, quickness, hastiness, haste, hurriedness, hurry, timeliness

▶ *191 Immediacy, 194 Priority, 210 Timeliness, 648 Haste*

2 **early hour**, early time, early morning, unearthly hour, sunrise, sunup (US), dawn, first crack of dawn, first crack, daybreak, the small hours, the wee small hours

▶ *204 Daytime*

3 **early stage**, earliest stage, advanced stage, first step, early warning, early warning system, primeval stage, primitive stage, primitiveness, early history, ancient history, early man, beginning, very beginning, creation, big bang

▶ *156 Beginning, 200 Past Time*

4 **early comer**, early arrival, first arrival, advance man (US), premature baby, early riser, precursor, predecessor, ancestor, forefather, prophet, earliest inhabitant, primitive, aborigine, Aborigine (or Aboriginal) (Aus), American Indian, earliest settler, colonist, scout, explorer, discoverer, early bird (Inf), Johnny on the spot (Inf)

▶ *496 Discovery*

5 **prematurity**, prematureness, precipitance, prevenience, preparation, foresight, anticipation, expectation, impetuosity, haste, hastiness, early maturity, precociousness, precocity, pre-emption

▶ *594 Preparation, 516 Foresight*

6 **getting ahead**, getting in early, getting in on the ground floor, seizing one's chance, seizing the moment, seizing the occasion, taking the opportunity, jumping at the chance, moving with the times

▶ *154 Precedence*

VERBS

7 **be early**, arrive early, arrive first, arrive ahead of time, arrive ahead of schedule, get there early, get there ahead of time, get there first, start early, start too soon, jump the gun, pre-empt, anticipate, get a head start, gain a flying start, rise at the crack of dawn, gain time, be fast (of clocks), have time to spare, be ready and waiting, show readiness, hasten, hurry, dispatch, expedite

8 **precede**, precede in time, predate, get ahead of, go before, colonize, settle, scout ahead, explore, discover

9 **prepare**, precipitate, reserve, order, book, book in advance, engage, anticipate, expect, foresee, pre-empt, forestall, nip in the bud, prevent, catch napping, steal a march on, take the words out of one's mouth, step on someone's lines (US)

10 **hasten**, lose no time, jump to it (Inf), hop to it (Inf), get one's finger out (Inf), get a wiggle on (Inf), go off half-cocked (*or* at half-cock) (Inf), be half-baked (Inf), jump the gun (Inf)

11 **get ahead**, get in early, get in on the ground floor, seize one's chance, seize the moment, seize the occasion, take the opportunity, jump at the chance, move with the times

ADJECTIVES

12 **early**, first, earliest, prompt, punctual, on time, timely, immediate, expeditious, ready, ahead of time, ahead of schedule, advanced, alacritous, fast (of clocks), quick, hurried, hasty, summary, good and early (Inf), bright and early (Inf)

13 **imminent**, forthcoming, impending, looming, expected soon, at hand, near at hand, just round the corner

14 **primeval**, primitive, ancient

15 **precursory**, precursive, preceding, ancestral, aboriginal, indigenous, colonial, exploratory

16 **premature**, precipitate, precipitative, precipitous, precocious, forward, ahead of one's time, beforehand, forehand, too early, prevenient, preparatory, prophetic, foresighted, anticipatory, anticipative, expectative, impetuous, hasty, overhasty, too soon, pre-emptive, half-cocked (Inf), half-baked (Inf)

ADVERBS

17 **early**, at an early time, at the earliest, firstly, first, as soon as possible, soon, promptly, punctually, immediately, without delay, forthwith, directly, right away, expeditiously, readily, in advance, ahead of time, ahead of schedule, ahead of oneself, first thing, at the first opportunity, before time, forehand, ahead of its time, in the small hours, in the wee small hours, in time, in good time, on time, on schedule, to the minute, to the second, with plenty of time, with time to spare, quickly, hurriedly, hastily, summarily, before

the ink was dry, betimes (Arch), anon (Arch), good and early (Inf), bright and early (Inf)

18 **soon**, presently, shortly, directly, imminently, before long, in a short time, in a while, in a short while, by and by, at short notice, suddenly, without notice, at the drop of a hat (Inf)

▶ *264 Nearness*

19 **primevally**, primitively, anciently, aboriginally, indigenously, colonially, ancestrally

20 **prematurely**, precipitately, precipitously, precociously, forwardly, ahead of one's time, beforehand, forehand, too early, preveniently, preparatorily, prophetically, foresightedly, anticipatorily, anticipatively, hastily, impetuously, overhastily, too soon

209 Lateness

NOUNS

1 **lateness**, unpunctuality, belatedness, tardiness, late arrival, last arrival, slowness, retardation, lag, time lag, lagging, delay, unreadiness, unpreparedness, slow development

▶ *328 Slowness, 595 Lack of Preparation*

2 **late hour**, the lateness of the hour, advanced hour, small hours, wee small hours, day's end, sunset, night-time, last minute, eleventh hour, high time (Inf)

3 **delayed action**, delay, wait, delayed reaction, last-minute preparations, dilatoriness, procrastination, *mañana* (Sp), putting off, putting on hold, pigeonholing, tabling, postponement, deferment, deferral, adjournment, prorogation, prolongation, extension, protraction, filibuster, stonewalling, delaying tactics, prevention, hindrance, obstruction, jam, log jam (US), suspension, hold-up, red tape, blockage, block, restraint, detention, remand, moratorium, halt, pause, cooling-off period, truce, cease-fire, lull, respite, rest and recreation (R & R) (US), days of grace, stay of execution, stay, reprieve, last-ditch stand, last word, afterthought, esprit d'escalier, mothballing, putting on ice (Inf), putting in cold storage (Inf), putting on the back burner (Inf)

▶ *661 Hindrance, 218 Cessation, 704 Cancellation, 643 Inactivity, 188 Duration*

4 **latecomer**, late arriver, last arriver, Johnny-come-lately, laggard, late developer, late bloomer, slow starter, slow learner, late riser, slugabed, sluggard, idler, delayer, slowpoke (US inf), slowcoach (Inf)

5 **delayer**, procrastinator, filibusterer, stonewaller, bureaucrat

VERBS

6 **be late**, arrive late, arrive last, stay up late, sit up late, stay out late, keep late hours, burn the candle at both ends, burn the midnight oil, awake late, oversleep, lag, lag behind, be be-

hindhand, develop late, lose time, be slow (of clocks), drag one's feet, take one's time, take ages, drag on

7 **wait**, pause, stop, stay, tarry, linger, dawdle, waste time, loiter, hang around, hang about, await, be kept waiting, kick one's heels, cool one's heels, delay, dally, dilly-dally, hang fire, hang back, miss the boat, lose (or miss) one's chance

8 **delay**, stall, retard, set back, hold back, hold up, obstruct, jam, create a log jam (US), suspend, halt, block, stonewall, prevent, hinder, restrain, remand, detain, hold over, put off, postpone, reprieve, stay, adjourn, prorogue, defer, gain time, buy time, play for time, play the waiting game, filibuster, prolong, extend, protract, spin out, procrastinate, temporize, sleep on it, hold one's horses, bide one's time, wait and see, reserve, keep for later, have the last word, keep (or save) for a rainy day, withhold, file, shelve, pigeonhole, table, lay on the table, hold, hold on, hold the line, make a last-ditch stand, hang on, stand by, put on hold, mothball, put on ice (Inf), put in cold storage (Inf), put on the back burner (Inf)

ADJECTIVES

9 **late**, belated, happening late, delayed, not on time, never on time, overdue, unpunctual, dilatory, unready, unprepared, tardy, behind schedule, behind time, behindhand, slow, sluggish

10 **held up**, postponed, deferred, adjourned, prorogued, prolonged, extended, protracted, stonewalled, hindered, obstructed, held-up, suspended, blocked, tabled, stalled, restrained, detained, remanded, halted, jammed, log-jammed (US), bogged down, on hold, mothballed, on ice (Inf), in cold storage (Inf), on the back burner (Inf)

11 **late in the day**, last-minute, eleventh-hour, deathbed

12 **delaying**, slowing, procrastinating, obstructive, obstructing, hindering, retarding, blocking, restraining, detaining, lagging, lagging behind, late-running, following, coming later

13 **later**, future, distant, upcoming

14 **dead**, deceased, late, late lamented, former, previous, past, erstwhile, sometime, old, posthumous

ADVERBS

15 **late**, lately, belatedly, unpunctually, dilatorily, unreadily, unpreparedly, tardily, behind schedule, behind time, behindhand, slowly, leisurely, at one's leisure, sluggishly, extendedly, protractedly, obstructively

16 **at a late hour**, at such a late hour, none too soon, at the last minute, at the eleventh hour, at last, at long last, on one's deathbed, too late

17 **later**, later on, much later on, in the future, at a later time, in time, in due course, in a while, after a while

18 **formerly**, lately, posthumously

210   Timeliness

NOUNS

1 **timeliness**, opportuneness, providence, providentiality, suitability, convenience, appropriateness, propitiousness, auspiciousness, favourableness, aptness, fitness, right time, right moment, just the time, perfect moment, readiness, ripeness, maturity, proper time, auspicious moment, good occasion, happy coincidence

▶ 615 Convenience

2 **opportunity**, good opportunity, fine opportunity, favourable opportunity, golden opportunity, chance, good chance, happy chance, best chance, only chance, luck, good luck, opening, break, lucky break, piece of luck, stroke of luck, elbow room, clear field, clear run, clear view, scope, stepping stone, look-in (Inf)

▶ 589 Chance

3 **critical time**, critical moment, crucial time, crucial moment, critical juncture, crisis, key point, turning point, pivotal point, nexus, pinch, rub, crux, moment of truth, decisive moment, point of no return, pregnant moment, emergency, eleventh hour, last minute, nick of time

▶ 659 Difficulty, 209 Lateness

VERBS

4 **be timely**, suit the occasion, fit the occasion, come at the right time (or moment), befit the occasion, befit the time, offer an opportunity, provide a chance

5 **take the opportunity**, profit by, cash in on, capitalize on, turn to good account, exploit, improve the occasion, take time by the forelock, carpe diem (L), take one's chance, seize one's chance, seize one's opportunity, grab one's opportunity, seize the day, create an opening for oneself, make hay while the sun shines, strike while the iron is hot, not be caught flatfooted (Inf)

ADJECTIVES

6 **timely**, opportune, seasonable, providential, propitious, auspicious, appropriate, apropos, suitable, suited, befitting, fitting, fit, convenient, apt, for the occasion, heaven-sent, welcome, favourable, fortunate, lucky, happy, felicitous

7 **critical**, crucial, decisive, momentous, pivotal, key, vital to the occasion

8 **in time**, on time, punctual, within the time limit, well-timed, well-judged, eleventh-hour, last-minute, deathbed

ADVERBS

9 **opportunely**, seasonably, providentially, propitiously, auspiciously, appropriate, apropos, suitably, befittingly, fittingly, fitly, conveniently, aptly, for the occasion, favourably, fortunately, luckily, happily, as (good) luck would have it

10 **critically**, crucially, decisively, momentously, pivotally

11 **in time**, on time, punctually, within the time limit, just in time, in the nick of time, at the last minute, at the eleventh hour, on one's deathbed

211 Untimeliness

NOUNS

1 **untimeliness**, mistiming, inopportuneness, inauspiciousness, unpropitiousness, unfavourableness, unseasonableness, ominousness, immaturity, unripeness, poor timing, bad timing, bad time, wrong time, unsuitable time, prematurity, earliness, lateness, unpunctuality, bad time of the month, inopportune moment, untimely occurrence, awkward occurrence, untimely action, inexpedience, inappropriateness, unsuitableness, awkwardness, inconvenience, intrusion, interruption, disturbance, disruption

▶ *193 Wrong Time, 117 Disparity, 208 Earliness, 209 Lateness, 616 Inconvenience*

2 **anachronism**, chronological error, misdating, parachronism, prochronism

3 **lost chance**, lost opportunity, missed opportunity, misfortune, ill fortune, ill luck, bad luck, hard luck, mischance, misjudgment, mistake, error, blunder, bungle, boo-boo (Sl), boob (Sl)

▶ *683 Failure, 656 Unskilfulness, 470 Negligence, 493 Misjudgment*

4 **mishap**, misadventure, contretemps, accident, disaster, calamity, death

▶ *687 Adversity*

VERBS

5 **take untimely action**, mistime, time badly, arrive at the wrong time, arrive early, arrive late, lose time, waste time, be late, misjudge, intrude, disturb, disrupt, interrupt, break in upon, bust in on, butt in, find engaged, shut the stable door after the horse has bolted

6 **lose one's chance**, be unlucky, have misfortune, have bad luck, lose an opportunity, waste an opportunity, spoil one's chances, wreck one's chances, throw away an opportunity, throw it all away, let an opportunity slip, let slip through one's fingers, allow the occasion to go by, miss the boat, miss the bus, blow one's chance (Sl), blow it (Sl)

7 **be busy**, be engaged, have a prior engagement, not have time, have other things to do,

have other fish to fry (Inf)

8 **make a mistake**, err, misjudge, blunder, bungle, put one's foot in it (Inf), put one's foot in one's mouth (US inf), drop a clanger (Inf), make a boo-boo (Sl), boob (Sl)

9 **have a mishap**, have a misadventure, have an accident, suffer injury, die

ADJECTIVES

10 **untimely**, mistimed, ill-timed, inopportune, inauspicious, unpropitious, unfavourable, unseasonable, immature, unripe, ill-starred, ill-omened, ominous, poorly timed, badly timed, premature, early, late, not in time, unpunctual, out of turn, out of order, inexpedient, inappropriate, malapropos, unsuited, inapt, unsuitable, unbefitting, awkward, inconvenient, intrusive, interrupting, disturbing, disrupting

11 **anachronistic**, misdated, parachronistic, prochronistic, out of season

12 **busy**, engaged, having a prior engagement, not having time, having other things to do, having other fish to fry (Inf)

13 **mistaken**, erroneous, mistaking, erring, misjudging, blundering, bungling

14 **accidental**, unlucky, unfortunate, infelicitous, disastrous, calamitous, fatal, deadly, deathly

ADVERBS

15 **at the wrong time**, at just the wrong time, too soon, immaturely, prematurely, inopportunely, inauspiciously, unpropitiously, unfavourably, unseasonably, unripely, ominously, lately, unpunctually, too late, inexpediently, inappropriately, malapropos, unsuitably, unbefittingly, awkwardly, inconveniently, intrusively, disturbingly, disruptively

16 **anachronistically**, parachronistically, prochronistically

17 **mistakenly**, erroneously, accidentally, unluckily, unfortunately, blunderingly, disastrously, calamitously

212 Frequency

ADVERBS

1 **frequently**, often, many a time, repeatedly, repetitively, recurrently, regularly, periodically, cyclically, commonly, usually, generally, constantly, continually, consecutively, perpetually, ordinarily, routinely, habitually, incessantly, persistently, sustainingly, steadily, numerously, crowdedly, multitudinously, prevalently, assiduously, hauntingly, without ceasing, without stopping, without stop, thick and fast, all the time, times without number, as often as one likes, daily, hourly, every hour, every minute, every second, morning, noon, and night, day and night, night and day, day in, day out, day after day, as often as not, more

often than not, in quick succession, in rapid succession, time after time, time and again, again and again, over and over, many times, many a time, oft (Arch), oftentimes (Arch), many a time and oft (Arch), ever and anon (Arch)

▶ *183 Repetition, 214 Regularity, 219 Continuity, 159 Consecutiveness, 181 Multitude*

2 **sometimes**, occasionally, from time to time, every so often, now and again, every now and again, now and then, once in a while

ADJECTIVES

3 **frequent**, recurrent, recurring, repetitive, repeated, repetitious, regular, periodic, cyclic, cyclical, continual, consecutive, persistent, sustained, steady, constant, nonstop, incessant, common, of common occurrence, run-of-the-mill, many, numerous, crowded, multitudinous, prevalent, often encountered, assiduous, habitual, haunting

NOUNS

4 **frequency**, frequence, frequentness, oftenness, recurrence, repetition, periodicity, continuity, consecutiveness, constancy, persistence, sustainment, steadiness, commonness, numerousness, crowdedness, multitudinousness, incessancy, prevalence, regularity, assiduity, assiduousness, habitualness, frequent occurrence, regular occurrence, common occurrence, cycle, speed, pulse, everyday occurrence

5 **frequenting**, patronizing, visiting often, coming to often, attending regularly, being a regular customer, hanging out, haunting

▶ *815 Sociability*

6 **radio frequency**, radio-frequency band, frequency band, citizens band (CB), frequency spectrum, long wave (LW), medium wave (MW), short wave (SW), very high frequency (VHF), ultrahigh frequency (UHF), frequency modulation (FM), amplitude modulation (AM), wavelength, wave, cycles per second, hertz (Hz), kilohertz (kHz), megahertz (MHz)

VERBS

7 **be frequent**, happen often, recur, reoccur, repeat itself, happen every day, occur regularly, occur periodically, have continuity, continue, go on, prevail, repeat oneself, do habitually, do nothing but

8 **frequent**, be often seen at, be found at, visit often, come to often, attend regularly, be a regular customer of, patronize, haunt, hang out at (Inf)

213   Infrequency

ADVERBS

1 **infrequently**, irregularly, intermittently, not often, very occasionally, (only) now and then, only occasionally, only sometimes,

hardly ever, hardly, seldom, very seldom, little, rarely, sparsely, scarcely, scarcely ever, uncommonly, unusually, once in a while, once or twice, uniquely, once, only once, just this once, once and for all, discontinuously, fitfully, at infrequent intervals, few and far between, once in a blue moon (Inf), once in a month of Sundays (Inf), once in a coon's age (US inf)

ADJECTIVES

2 **infrequent**, occasional, sparse, uncommon, unusual, rare, irregular, sporadic, discontinuous, fitful, few and far between, few, intermittent, scarce, seldom seen, seldom met with, almost unheard-of, one of a kind, unique, unprecedented, like gold dust, like snow in August, rare as hen's teeth

NOUNS

3 **infrequency**, infrequence, intermittence, seldomness, irregularity, discontinuity, fitfulness, rareness, scarcity, scarceness, uncommonness, unusualness, sparsity, paucity, fewness, uniqueness, infrequent occurrence, rare occurrence, rarity, unrepeatable offer, one-time offer

▶ *160 Discontinuity, 182 Few*

4 **rare things**, phoenix, rare bird, rara avis, miracle, sun's total eclipse, supernova, comet, Halley's Comet, leap year, four-leaf clover, pearl in an oyster

214   Regularity

NOUNS

1 **regularity**, frequency, recurrence, regular recurrence, regular occurrence, clockwork regularity, periodicity, repetition, repetitiveness, return, serialization, timing, phasing, pattern, symmetry, alternation, reciprocity, tidal flow, ebb and flow, wave motion, wave frequency, oscillation, to-and-fro movement, pendulum movement, piston movement, shuttle movement, undulating motion, undulation, simple harmonic motion, swing, rhythm, tempo, meassure, beat, pulsation, throb, tick

▶ *183 Repetition, 159 Consecutiveness, 365 Oscillation, 426 Repeated Sound*

2 **cycle**, return, circular return, revolution, rotation, orbital motion, regular return, life cycle, yearly cycle, biorhythm, alpha rhythm, alpha wave, circadian rhythm, menstrual cycle, oestrous cycle, menstruation, menses, period, routine, daily round, round, beat, wheel of life, orbit, circuit, lap, shift, relay, turn, go, rota

▶ *364 Rotation, 363 Orbital Motion, 187 Period*

3 **anniversary**, commemoration, annual occurrence, centenary (*or* centennial), sesquicentennial (*or* sesquicentenary), bicentenary (*or* bicentennial), tricentenary (*or* tricenten-

nial or tercentenary or tercentennial), millennium

4 **orderliness**, regularity, balance, uniformity, evenness, steadiness, levelness, flatness, ordinariness, continuity, continuousness, constance, constancy, consistency, normality, regulation, rule, order, law, custom, tradition, routine

▶ *150 Order, 112 Uniformity, 584 Habit*

5 **regular thing**, death and taxes, pendulum, metronome, metre, rhythm, beat, tempo, drumbeat, heartbeat, pulsebeat, pulse, breathing, alternating current (AC), shuttle service, comet, Halley's Comet, tide, spring tide, neap tide, incoming tide, ebb tide, Old Faithful (US), serial, holiday, vacation, annual vacation, summer holiday, bank holiday, day and night, sunrise and sunset, calendar, days of the week, months of the year, leap year, seasons of the year, spring, summer, winter, autumn, fall (US)

▶ *203 Season, 204 Daytime, 205 Night-Time, 185 Time*

6 **annually celebrated day**, wedding anniversary, silver wedding anniversary, ruby wedding anniversary, golden wedding anniversary, birthday, saint's day, holy day, jubilee, silver jubilee, diamond jubilee, New Year's Day, Australia Day (Aus), St. Valentine's Day, Easter, April Fools' Day (or All Fools' Day), May Day, V-E Day, Mother's Day, Father's Day, Memorial Day (US), D-day, Canada Day, Fourth of July (US), Independence Day (US), Bastille Day (Fr), V-J Day, Labor Day (US), Hallowe'en, Guy Fawkes Day, Remembrance Sunday (or Day), Poppy Day, Thanksgiving Day (US), Christmas, Boxing Day

VERBS

7 **be regular**, recur, reoccur, reoccur constantly, repeat, be in order, run on in order, succeed, follow a pattern, intermit, reciprocate, alternate, take one's turn, work a shift, have a turn, have a go, beat time, tick, throb, pulse, pulsate, have a rapid (or slow) heartbeat, breathe regularly, undulate, oscillate, swing, sway, swing and sway, go to and fro, come and go, ebb and flow, go back and forth, ply, commute, shuttle, holiday, vacation, take a summer holiday

8 **be cyclic**, cycle, circle, orbit, cycle round, come again, go and return, come round again, return once again, return, walk one's beat, make one's daily round, run a lap, turn, spin, revolve, rotate, occur monthly, menstruate, have one's period, occur annually, happen yearly

9 **commemorate**, celebrate Christmas, have an anniversary, celebrate an anniversary, have a birthday, celebrate a birthday, honour the dead, burn the guy

10 **make regular**, regularize, make consistent, make uniform, balance, make routine, regulate, time, adjust, set (a clock), order, impose order upon, bring order out of chaos, rule, make ordinary, normalize, rationalize, systematize, steady, serialize, make continual, make constant, level, level out, make even, flatten, flatten out

ADJECTIVES

11 **regular**, frequent, periodic, periodical, recurrent, recurring, repeating, repetitive, tidal, reciprocal, alternating, alternate, alternative, to-and-fro, oscillatory, oscillating, revolving, returning, timed, isochronal, isochronous, phasic, phaseal, phased, serial, serialized, rhythmic, rhythmical, measured, swinging, steady, stable, clockwork, beating, ticking, throbbing, pulsating, pulsatory, pulsatile, undulating, constant, even, symmetric, symmetrical, consistent, level, flat, featureless

12 **cyclic**, cyclical, circular, circling, orbital, revolving, rotational, rotative, rotating, routine, hourly, daily, diurnal, quotidian, nightly, tertian, semiweekly, weekly, hebdomadary, hebdomadal, biweekly, fortnightly, semimonthly, monthly, bimonthly, seasonal, semiannual, biannual, annual, yearly, perennial, bissextile, biennial, Metonic cycle, biorhythmic, menstrual, oestrous

13 **anniversary**, commemorative, annual, yearly, centenary (or centennial), sesquicentennial (or sesquicentenary), bicentenary (or bicentennial), tricentenary (or tricentennial or tercentenary or tercentennial), Metonic, millennial, secular

14 **orderly**, regular, balanced, uniform, even, steady, level, flat, ordinary, everyday, typical, routine, continual, constant, methodical, metrical, consistent, normal, legal, customary, traditional

ADVERBS

15 **regularly**, frequently, periodically, at regular intervals, at fixed intervals, at stated times, at specified times, at fixed periods, repeatedly, repetitiously, reciprocally, alternately, alternatively, by turns, turn and turn about, in a swinging motion, up and down, from side to side, to and fro, serially, rhythmically, steadily, like clockwork, pulsatingly, undulatingly, constantly, evenly, symmetrically, consistently, flatly

16 **cyclically**, circularly, orbitally, round and round, routinely, hourly, hour by hour, daily, every day, day by day, diurnally, per diem, nightly, every night, every other day, every other night, semiweekly, twice a week, weekly, every week, biweekly, every other week, fortnightly, semimonthly, twice a month, monthly, every month, bimonthly, every other month, seasonally, semiannually, bian-

nually, twice a year, annually, yearly, per annum, every year, perennially, biennially, every other year, centennially, sesquicentennially, bicentennially, tricentennially, tercentennially, millennially, secularly, commemoratively

17 **orderly**, regularly, uniformly, evenly, steadily, flatly, ordinarily, routinely, in an everyday manner, continually, constantly, consistently, normally, legally, according to law, according to order, customarily, by custom, according to rule, traditionally, according to tradition

215   Irregularity

NOUNS

1 **irregularity**, unregularity, nonuniformity, unequalness, inequality, asymmetry, unevenness, roughness, choppiness, spottiness, patchiness, brokenness, disconnection, discontinuation, discontinuity, sporadicalness, infrequency, intermittence, fluctuation, changeableness, change, waver, wavering, variability, variableness, variety, diversity, inconsistency, inconstancy, unpredictability, randomness, randomness of recurrence, fitfulness, fits and starts, capriciousness, caprice, restlessness, desultoriness, unmethodicalness, haphazardness, disorder, instability, unsteadiness, oscillation, wobbliness, shakiness, jerkiness, flickering, staggering, lurching, careening, veering, bumping, wobble, shake, jerk, flicker, stagger, lurch, careen, veer, bump

▶ *123 Inequality, 213 Infrequency, 160 Discontinuity, 224 Changeableness, 216 Change, 113 Diversity, 579 Caprice, 151 Disorder, 366 Agitation, 365 Oscillation*

2 **unusualness**, uncommonness, exceptionalness, anomalousness, incongruousness, aberrance, aberration, abnormality, eccentricity, nonconformity, unconventionality, unorthodoxy, oddness, peculiarity, whimsicality, whimsy, moodiness

3 **irregular thing**, unpaved road, mountain range, stormy sea, British weather, stock exchange, gambling, crooked teeth

▶ *168 Nonconformity*

ADJECTIVES

4 **irregular**, unregular, nonuniform, unequal, asymmetric, asymmetrical, unsymmetrical, uneven, rough, choppy, spotty, patchy, broken, disconnected, discontinuous, sporadic, spasmodic, halting, off and on, on and off, on-again-off-again, stop and go, stop-go, infrequent, intermittent, fluctuating, changeable, changeful, wavering, variable, varying, diverse, inconsistent, erratic, inconstant, unpredictable, random, fitful, capricious, restless, desultory, unmethodically, unsystematic, unsystematical, unrhythmic, unrhythmical,

haphazard, disorderly, disordered, unstable, unsteady, oscillatory, oscillating, wobbly, wobbling, shaky, shaking, jerky, jerking, flickering, staggering, lurching, careening, veering, bumpy, bumping, herky-jerky (US inf)

5 **unusual**, uncommon, exceptional, anomalous, incongruous, incoherent, aberrant, erratic, abnormal, eccentric, idiosyncratic, unique, individual, nonconforming, unconventional, unorthodox, odd, peculiar, whimsical, moody

VERBS

6 **be irregular**, lack regularity, intermit, break, disconnect, fluctuate, change, change directions, change speed, vary, waver, oscillate, wobble, shake, jerk, go by fits and starts, flicker, stagger, lurch, careen, veer, bump

7 **be unusual**, be eccentric, act erratic, act odd

ADVERBS

8 **irregularly**, unregularly, unequally, asymmetrically, unevenly, roughly, discontinuously, spasmodically, sporadically, in spots, haltingly, off and on, on and off, on again off again, stop and go, infrequently, once in a while, now and then, every now and again, intermittently, changeably, waveringly, variably, inconsistently, erratically, in a disorderly manner, inconstantly, unpredictably, randomly, at random, fitfully, by fits and starts, unrhythmically, capriciously, restlessly, desultorily, unmethodically, unsystematically, haphazardly, unsteadily, shakily, jerkily, flickeringly, bumpily

9 **unusually**, uncommonly, exceptionally, anomalously, abnormally, eccentrically, unconventionally, oddly, peculiarly, whimsically, moodily

216   Change

NOUNS

1 **change**, variation, variety, mutability, alteration, difference, diversity, fluctuation, vicissitude, inconsistency, inconstancy, waxing and waning, modification, adjustment, qualification, variegation, process, activation, fermentation, leavening, modulation, inflection, declension, change of course, change of direction, deviation, diversion, detour, turn, U-turn, reversal, shift, eversion, inversion, change of position, change of scenery, change of place, relocation, passage, transference, transition, translation, interpretation, adaptation, transcription, sea change, sudden change, violent change, revolution, revolt, coup, subversion, reformation, break with the past, break, change for the better, invention, innovation, diversification, modernization, renewal, redecoration, rearrangement, reorganization, restructuring, reordering, remould-

ing, reshaping, restyling, remodelling, revision, emendation, amendment, improvement, betterment, restoration, revival, repairing, repair, amelioration, change for the worse, adulteration, dilution, distortion, deterioration, degeneration, perversion

▶ *224 Changeableness, 111 Oppositeness, 335 Deviation, 337 Backward Motion, 356 Passage, 524 Interpretation, 485 Qualification, 201 Newness, 627 Improvement, 628 Deterioration*

2 **change of mind**, change of opinion, change of belief, change of stance, change of heart, conversion, tergiversation, desultoriness, vacillation, fickleness, capriciousness, caprice, whimsicality, flip-flop

▶ *220 Conversion, 578 Equivocation*

3 **transformation**, mutation, transmutation, transfiguration, transubstantiation, metamorphosis, transmogrification, transmigration of souls, metempsychosis, metabolism, conversion

▶ *220 Conversion*

4 **exchange**, interchange, trade, substitution, commutability, permutation, transposition, alternation, replacement, exchange of gifts, exchange of goods, barter, swap, change of clothes, displacement

▶ *223 Exchange*

5 **changer**, modifier, kaleidoscope, activator, converter, transformer, agent, catalytic agent, catalytic converter, catalyst, enzyme, yeast, ferment, leaven, leavening agent, adapter

6 **editor**, reviser, censor, bowdlerizer, innovator, alterer, tailor, dressmaker, decorator, chemist, alchemist, magician, conjurer, sorcerer, good influence, restorer, reformer, revolutionary, improver, destroyer, bad influence, bad apple

VERBS

7 **be changed**, change, become different, undergo a change, reform, adapt, vary, alter, wax and wane, modify, reorganize, modernize, diversify, adjust, fluctuate, turn, shift, change course, divert, deviate, detour, change position, relocate, change places, change direction, do a U-turn, turn back, reverse, revert, revolt, change one's mind, change one's opinion, change one's belief, change one's stance, change one's heart, change for the worse, deteriorate, degenerate, change for the better, improve, get better, pass the crisis, get over the worst, turn the corner, better oneself, be converted, convert, vacillate, tergiversate, flip-flop, blow hot and cold, change one's expression, change one's tune, sing a different tune, break with the past, make a break, move with the times, turn over a new leaf

8 **cause change**, make a change, effect a change, work a change, make different, convert, influence, cause, affect, alter, diversify,

divert, reform, innovate, invent, modify, inflect (a word), decline (a word), activate, ferment, leaven, qualify, modulate, commute, modernize, renew, remodel, restyle, reorganize, restructure, redecorate, rearrange, reorder, remould, reshape, bring in new blood, turn upside down, subvert, revolt, revolutionize, evert, turn inside out, invert, adapt, shift, move, transfer, arrange, change round, translate, interpret, perform magic, conjure, dabble in sorcery, variegate, adjust, influence in a good way, better, change for the better, make better, improve, ameliorate, process, edit, revise, censor, bowdlerize, amend, revamp, rehash, influence in a bad way, change for the worse, worsen, impair, wreck, destroy, pervert, spoil, mark, interfere with, tamper with, meddle with, tinker with, mess with, adulterate, doctor, dilute, weaken, warp, distort, discolour, change back, repair, reset, restore, revive, turn back, ring the changes, chop and change, fiddle with (Inf)

9 **transform**, transmute, transfigure, transubstantiate, transmogrify, mutate, metamorphose, metabolize

10 **exchange**, interchange, trade, substitute, commute, transpose, change round, permute, shuffle the cards, alternate, replace, exchange gifts, exchange goods, barter, swap, change one's clothes, displace

ADJECTIVES

11 **changeable**, changeful, mutable, variable, alterable, different, diverse, fluctuating, vacillating, wavering, inconsistent, inconstant, shifty, shifting, waxing and waning, kaleidoscopic, deviatory, turning, reverse, transitional, transitory, transient, revolutionary, subversive, reformative, reformational, inventive, innovative, innovational, ameliorative, better, worse, perverse, desultory, indecisive, fickle, capricious, whimsical, ever-changing, flip-flop

12 **changed**, varied, altered, modified, qualified, diversified, modernized, renewed, redecorated, rearranged, reorganized, restructured, reordered, restyled, remodelled, remoulded, reshaped, revised, emended, amended, improved, repaired, restored, revived, deteriorated, degenerated

13 **transformative**, mutative, transmutative, transubstantial, metabolic, metamorphic, metamorphous, convertive

14 **exchangeable**, interchangeable, tradeable, substitutable, commutable, permutable, transpositional, replaceable

ADVERBS

15 **changeably**, mutably, variably, alterably, differently, diversely, vacillatingly, inconsistently, inconstantly, shiftily, kaleidoscopically, transitionally, subversively, inventively, in-

novatively, desultorily, indecisively, capriciously, whimsically, back and forth, off and on, on and off, in and out, *mutatis mutandis* (L), with amendments, with emendations

217 Permanence

NOUNS

1 **permanence**, permanency, continuance, continuity, no change, the status quo, everlastingness, perpetuity, long standing, establishment, entrenchment, persistence, perseverance, dependability, steadfastness, reliability, endurance, abidance, durability, survival, subsistence, conservation, conservancy, preservation, environmentalism, indestructibility, imperishability, immortality, changelessness, eternity, constancy, immutability, finality, fixedness, fixity, firmness, solidity, steadiness, stability, immobility, rigidity

▶ *225 Stability, 188 Duration, 219 Continuity, 637 Preservation, 202 Oldness, 190 Eternity, 325 Motionlessness*

2 **conservatism**, conservative attitude, conservative politics, right-wing politics, the political right, rightism, the right wing, the hard right, the Conservative Party, stubbornness, obstinacy

▶ *577 Obstinacy*

3 **conservative person**, conservative, traditionalist, Conservative, Tory, Republican (US), right-winger, true blue, obstinate person, hard-liner, reactionary, die-hard, dyed-in-the-wool conservative, dry (Inf), stick-in-the-mud (Inf)

4 **conservationist**, conservator, environmentalist, ecologist, green, Green Party member

VERBS

5 **be permanent**, last, continue, persist, persevere, stand fast, stand firm, stand pat (US), stand one's ground, resist change, be the same as ever, be always the same, remain the same, look as young as ever, not look a day older, endure, abide, survive, subsist, outlive, be here for good, last forever, last an eternity, be here for the duration, stay, be here to stay, come to stay, set in, take root, remain unchanged, remain at rest, refuse to budge, dig in one's heels (*or* toes)

6 **make permanent**, perpetuate, conserve, preserve, maintain the status quo, oppose change, sustain, keep, keep up, immortalize, fix, finalize, establish, stabilize, immobilize, let (*or* leave) be, let (*or* leave) alone, let well enough alone, let sleeping dogs lie, live and let live

ADJECTIVES

7 **permanent**, lasting, unchanging, unchangeable, everlasting, long-lasting, perpetual, persistent, persisting, persevering, continuing, continuous, constant, changeless, invariable, unalterable, immutable, unfailing, dependable, reliable, steadfast, sustained, perennial, evergreen, abiding, enduring, surviving, subsisting, durable, stable, standing, fixed, established, well-established, entrenched, longstanding, still standing, indestructible, conserved, preserved, well-preserved, imperishable, unbreakable, inviolable, immortal, undying, eternal, sempiternal, unfading, firm, solid, steady, rock-steady, rocklike, immobile, immovable, rigid, static, stationary, part of the furniture

8 **conservative**, traditional, traditionalist, right-wing, rightist, hard-right, true-blue, reactionary, obstinate, stubborn, old-fashioned, unprogressive, die-hard, dyed-in-the-wool, stick-in-the-mud (Inf)

ADVERBS

9 **permanently**, lastingly, changelessly, in statu quo (L), as is, as usual, as ever, still the same, as before, persistently, perseveringly, continuously, constantly, invariably, unalterably, immutably, unfailingly, reliably, steadfastly, perennially, abidingly, enduringly, firmly, solidly, steadily, rigidly, fixedly, at a standstill, indestructibly, imperishably, inviolably, immortally, undyingly, perpetually, eternally, sempiternally, forever, for ever and ever, everlastingly, always, for good, for good and all, once and for all

10 **conservatively**, traditionally, reactionarily, obstinately, stubbornly, old-fashionedly, unprogressively

218 Cessation

NOUNS

1 **cessation**, termination, ceasing, stopping, closing, desistance, discontinuance, discontinuation, discontinuity, relinquishment, withdrawal, abandonment, breakoff, death

2 **stop**, dead stop, halt, holdup, standstill, standoff, deadlock, stalemate, draw, checkmate, defeat, failure, breakdown, shutting down, shutdown, closing down, close-down, stoppage, temporary stoppage, blockage, log jam (US), gridlock (US), interruption, stay, check, hitch, technical hitch, hindrance, work stoppage, retirement, resignation, dismissal, lay-off, strike, general strike, industrial action, walkout, lockout, permanent stoppage, end, ending, finish, conclusion, hanging up, ringing off, breaking off, breaking off of negotiations, closure, closure of debate, cloture (US), guillotine, firing (Inf), sacking (Inf), shutting up (Inf), piping down (Inf), glitch (Sl)

▶ *325 Motionlessness, 643 Inactivity, 661 Hindrance, 666 Disagreement, 323 Closure, 683 Failure, 705 Resignation, 669 Resistance*

3 **pause**, break, lull, letup, respite, rest, sleep, nap, interruption, lacuna, gap, breathing space, interim, interim period, cooling-off period, interlude, interval, fermata, caesura, time-out (US), time off, day off, holiday, vacation, leisure, leisure time, close (*or* closed) season, delay, truce, moratorium, suspension, suspension of hostilities, ceasefire, armistice, breather (Inf)
▶ *651 Refreshment, 645 Leisure, 265 Interval*

4 **stopping place**, stop, bus stop, request stop, station, railway station, train station, taxi rank, halt, railway halt, tube station, bus station, service station, petrol station, lay-by, motorway services, highway restaurant (US), port, port of call, harbour, terminal, terminus, ferry terminal, air terminal, airport, waiting room
▶ *344 Arrival*

5 **resting place**, bed, bedroom couch, hospital, nursing home, retirement home, lodging, hotel, motel, billet, prison, prison cell, jail, final resting place, cemetery, graveyard, grave
▶ *157 End*

VERBS

6 **cease**, stop, come to a stop, halt, come to a halt, stop abruptly, stop dead, stop short, stop in one's tracks, freeze in one's tracks, grind to a halt, brake, put on the brake, pull up, draw up, come to a standstill, stall, stick, jam, discontinue, break down, quit, hold up, refrain from, desist, relinquish, give up, give in, admit defeat, leave off, disappear, fade out, fade away, blow over, run out, run down, peter out, let up, slacken off, tail off (*or* away), die off, die away, end, come to an end, finish, conclude, terminate, break off, break off negotiations, stop talking, hang up, ring off, put the phone down, be quiet, be silent, stop breathing, die, shut up (Inf), pipe down (Inf), fold (Inf), fold up (Inf), give over (Inf), call it a day (Inf), call it quits (Inf), run out of gas (US inf)

7 **stop working**, stop work, leave one's job, retire, resign, stand down, be laid off, be made redundant, strike, go on strike, come out on strike, call a strike, stage a strike, walk out, vote with one's feet, close down, close, shut up shop, put up the shutters, shut down, cease trading, go out of business, ring down the curtain, wind up, fail, collapse, go bankrupt, go into liquidation, go into receivership, call in the receiver, be sacked (Inf), be fired (Inf), go belly up (US sl)

8 **cause to cease**, put a stop to, stay, freeze, call a halt, cancel, call off, cut short, interrupt, bring to a standstill, catch, hinder, thwart, block, check, stem, arrest, restrain, hold, hold up, stalemate, checkmate, defeat, closure, cloture (US), guillotine, shut down, quieten down, close down, lock out, dismiss, lay off,

make redundant, exhaust, use up, bring to an end, end, disconnect, break off, see the last of, cut off, cut someone off in his (*or* her) prime, kill, murder, shut up (Inf), fire (Inf), sack (Inf), see off (Inf)

9 **pause**, pause for breath, relax, rest, fall asleep, sleep, nap, interrupt, suspend, stay, adjourn, recess, break, take a break, take five (*or* ten) (US), call time-out (US), take a day off, take a holiday, holiday, take a vacation, vacation, let up, cool off, hold up, hold back, hang fire, stay one's hand, call a truce, suspend hostilities, cease fire, make peace, hold one's horses, rest on one's oars, rest on one's laurels, hang loose (US inf), take a breather (Inf)

ADJECTIVES

10 **finished**, ended, at an end, stopped, over, complete, closed, in recess, adjourned, interrupted, pending, on hold, on ice, redundant, fired (Inf), sacked (Inf)

ADVERBS

11 **finally**, in the end, at the end, at the finish, in his (*or* her) prime, when all is said and done

INTERJECTIONS

12 **stop!**, whoa!, enough!, that's enough!, stop it!, quit it!, that's it!, stop thief!, break it up!, leave off!, get off!, come off it!, drop it!, forget it!, let up! (Inf), lay off! (Inf), give over! (Inf), shut up! (Inf), shut your face! (Inf), can it! (US inf), knock it off! (Inf), cut it out! (Inf), uncle! (US inf), pack it in! (Inf), chuck it! (Inf), cool it (Sl), stow it! (Sl), shut your trap! (Sl), naff off! (Sl)

219 Continuity

NOUNS

1 **continuity**, continuance, continuation, continuousness, constancy, progression, progress, succession, sequence, supplement, sequel, follow-up, postscript, repetition, recurrence, regular recurrence, flow, run, uninterrupted course, connectedness, connection, interconnection, interrelatedness, interrelation, cohesion, preservation, maintenance, sustenance, support
▶ *159 Consecutiveness, 336 Forward Motion, 183 Repetition, 217 Permanence, 225 Stability*

2 **protraction**, prolongation, long duration, extension, addition, furtherance, perpetuation, perpetuity, endurance, persistence, perseverance, survival, pursuit, resumption, recommencement, return
▶ *188 Duration, 575 Perseverance*

VERBS

3 **continue**, not stop, proceed, advance, make progress, progress, succeed, recur, repeat, connect, interconnect, interrelate, add, supplement, cohere, flow, run on, go on, follow through, maintain, keep up, sustain, support, uphold, preserve, harp on, keep on, keep alive,

keep going, keep things moving, keep the ball rolling, keep the ball in play, keep the pot boiling, not interfere, let nature take its course, let things take their course, let sleeping dogs lie, let (*or* leave) alone, let be, keep on keeping on (US inf)

4 **protract**, prolong, further, extend, draw out, spin out, maintain, perpetuate, persist, persist in, persevere, pursue, pursue one's course, resume, follow up, pick up, take up again, continue, recommence, restart, return to, pick up where one left off, last, endure, remain, abide, live on, survive, stay, stay on, haunt, frequent, carry on, keep on, march on, roll on, plod on, keep at it, peg away, stick at it, stick to, go on for a long time, stand the test of time, live out one's time (*or* life), see the end of, hang on, hang on in there (US inf), stick it out to the bitter end (Inf), sit it out (Inf), carry one's bat (Inf)

ADJECTIVES

5 **continual**, continuous, continuing, in progress, ongoing, constant, steady, incessant, progressive, sequent, sequential, additional, supplemental, repetitive, recurrent, flowing, running, connected, unbroken, undivided, uninterrupted, interconnected, interrelated, cohesive, sustained, supported, not out (Inf)

6 **protracted**, prolonged, extended, lengthened, drawn-out, interminable, unvarying, unending, unceasing, undying, unstoppable, unremitting, unrelenting, persistent, unfailing, inexhaustible, without respite, with no letup, nonstop, endless, enduring, lasting, everlasting, eternal, perpetual

ADVERBS

7 **continually**, continuously, constantly, repeatedly, endlessly, steadily, incessantly, progressively, sequentially, additionally, supplementally, repetitively, recurrently, without interruption, protractedly, interminably, unendingly, unceasingly, unremittingly, unrelentingly, persistently, inexhaustibly, enduringly, lastingly, everlastingly, eternally, perpetually, without respite, with no letup, nonstop, all the time, always, forever, on and on

INTERJECTIONS

8 **go on!**, carry on!, drive on!, keep it up!, keep going!, keep up the good work!, keep moving!, stick with it!, never say die!, onward and upward!

220 Conversion

NOUNS

1 **conversion**, converting, changeableness, convertibility, change, transition, transposition, movement, shift, transfer, transference, translation, interpretation, misinterpretation, alteration, modification, reorganization, rationalization, transformation, metamorphosis, mutation, processing, chemical change, chemistry, reduction, resolution, fermentation, ferment, leaven, dehydration, crystallization, melting, physical change, transmutation, transfiguration, magic, enchantment, bewitchment, alchemy

▶ *216 Change, 243 Production, 227 Effect*

2 **evolution**, evolving, growth, life cycle, development, progress, revolution, reformation, re-education, rebirth, regeneration, rehabilitation, improvement, naturalization, assimilation, degeneration, deterioration, perversion, denaturalization, alienation

▶ *128 Increase, 627 Improvement, 336 Forward Motion, 629 Repair, 628 Deterioration*

3 **persuasion**, indoctrination, brainwashing, religious conversion, proselytizing, proselytization, evangelism, evangelization, revivalism, revival, spiritual rebirth

▶ *586 Persuasion, 233 Influence, 7 Religion*

4 **medium of conversion**, Bible, church, school, laboratory, melting pot, crucible, cauldron, test tube, retort, alembic, fermentation vat, workshop, lathe, potter's wheel, sculptor's tools, foundry, anvil

5 **converter**, indoctrinator, teacher, preacher, minister, priest, vicar, evangelist, television evangelist (US), proselyter, proselytizer, missionary, apostle, televangelist (US inf)

6 **convert**, changed person, proselyte, catechumen, neophyte, new man (*or* woman), apostate, tergiversator, backslider, renegade, turncoat, traitor

VERBS

7 **convert into**, metamorphose, mutate, transpose, move, shift, transfer, translate, alter, transform, process, reduce, resolve, ferment, leaven, dehydrate, crystallize, melt, transmute, transfigure, become, be turned into (*or* to), change into, turn into (*or* to), get, come to, develop into, evolve into, pass into, shift into, slide into, mellow into, mature into, ripen into, ferment into, melt into, merge into, dissolve into, sink into

8 **be transformed**, be changed, evolve, develop, wax, grow, ripen, mature, mellow, age, progress, improve, naturalize, assimilate, regenerate, be rejuvenated, denaturalize, deteriorate, degenerate, take the shape of, assume the shape of, assume the character of, assume the nature of, undergo a personality change, not know oneself, suffer a sea change, reform, revolt, enter a new phase, enter a different phase, reach a stage, turn over a new leaf

9 **transform**, transfigure, change the face of, make into, ferment, leaven, process, reduce, reduce to, turn into, convert into, resolve into, conjure into, metamorphose, transmute, alchemize, mould, shape, lick into shape, knock

into shape, rehabilitate, paper over, paper over the cracks, paint over, render, translate, interpret, misinterpret, reinterpret, modify, decorate, redecorate, reshape, remodel, reform, reorganize, restructure, re-educate, rationalize, deform, distort, twist, pervert

10 **be converted**, be saved, be born again, turn to God, change one's ways, turn against, renege, apostatize, desert, turn traitor, turn to sin

11 **persuade**, influence, indoctrinate, brainwash, win over, proselytize, preach, evangelize, convert, save, revive

12 **naturalize**, internationalize, assimilate, orientalize, Indianize, Russify, westernize, Americanize, Anglicize, Frenchify, Germanize, Europeanize, Africanize, denaturalize

ADJECTIVES

13 **converted**, changed, transformed, turned into, transposed, transfigured, transmuted, metamorphosed, mutated, translated, enchanted, bewitched, changed beyond recognition, unrecognizable, brainwashed, proselytized, assimilated, naturalized, improved, regenerated, degenerated

14 **converting**, changing, becoming, growing, developing, maturing, transferring, altering, transforming, mutating, processing, fermenting, leavening, crystallizing, melting, transmuting, transfiguring, evolving, progressing, regenerating, improving, degenerating, deteriorating

15 **convertible**, changeable, transformable, impressionable, influenceable, persuadable, transmutable, transposable, transferable, translatable, alterable, improvable, reducible, resolvable

16 **influenced**, persuaded, brainwashed, converted, saved, revived, born again, reborn, proselytized, evangelized

17 **naturalized**, internationalized, assimilated, orientalized, westernized, Americanized, Anglicized, Frenchified, Germanized, Europeanized, Africanized, denaturalized

ADVERBS

18 **convertibly**, in transition, in transit, en route, on the way to

221 Reversion

NOUNS

1 **reversion**, reversal, turning back, turning backwards, going back, return, regression, recession, retrogression, retrograde state, withdrawal, apostasy, retraction, recantation, repentance, backing down, retreat, retirement, retroversion, retroflexion, looking back, retrospection, reaction, retroaction, retrospective action, counteraction, backfire, ricochet, recoil, boomerang effect, backlash, counter-

revolution, counter-reformation, about-turn, right about-turn, U-turn, volte-face, atavism, recidivism, backsliding, relapse

▶ *337 Backward Motion, 331 Recoil, 183 Repetition, 202 Oldness, 226 Cause, 511 Memory*

2 **restoration**, reconversion, changing back, giving back, reinstatement, transfer, restitution, compensation, revival, new beginning, resumption, recommencement, recovery, retrieval, recycling, taking back, retaliation, reprisal, getting back

▶ *735 Giving Back, 125 Compensation, 156 Beginning, 734 Taking, 721 Gain*

3 **turning point**, pivotal point, crucial point, crucial moment, crisis point, crisis, watershed, turn of the tide

4 **return**, swing, swing of the pendulum, give and take, comings and goings, shuttling, shuttle, commuting, returning home, round trip, return ticket, commute (US inf)

▶ *311 Curve*

5 **reply**, retort, retortion, answer, response, feedback, confutation, refutation

▶ *478 Answer, 476 Refutation*

VERBS

6 **reverse**, turn back, turn about, turn, go back, return, revert, regress, recede, retrogress, recidivate, withdraw, retract, back down, retreat, retire, recant, renege, backslide, slide back, slip back, relapse, turn backwards, look back, hark back, archaize, turn back the clock, react, counteract, backfire, ricochet, recoil, boomerang, do (*or* make) an about-turn, do (*or* make) a U-turn

7 **restore**, restore the status quo, reconvert, revive, resume, change back, give back, make restitution, compensate, reinstate, restart, recommence, start again, begin again, go back to the beginning, undo, do again, unmake, remake, start afresh, start anew, recover, retrieve, recycle, take back, retaliate, get back at, get one's own back (Inf), take it from the top (Inf)

8 **return**, swing back, swing around, swing, trace back, rebound, recoil, kick back, give and take, come and go, shuttle, commute, return home, make a round trip, buy a return-trip ticket

9 **reply**, retort, answer, respond, give feedback, confute, refute, recant, repent

ADJECTIVES

10 **regressive**, recessive, reversionary, reversional, retroverse, retrograde, restitutive, restitutory, compensatory, retrospective, reflexive, reactive, reactionary, retroactive, atavistic, recidivist, recidivistic, recidivous

11 **reversed**, regressed, retracted, recanted, retreated, retired, reverted, reacted, recoiled, backfired, returned, restored, reinstated, revived, resumed, recovered, retrieved, recycled,

replied, retorted, answered, responded, refuted

12 **reversible**, returnable, restorable, recoverable, retrievable, recyclable, refutable

ADVERBS

13 **reversibly**, regressively, retrospectively, reflexively, reactively, retroactively, atavistically, retrievably, refutably, invertedly, inside out, wrong side out, back to front, back to the beginning, as you were, from the top (Inf)

222 Substitution

NOUNS

1 **substitution**, change, exchange, quid pro quo, commutation, alternation, switch, swap, shuffle, representation, replacement, deputing, deputizing, power of attorney, vicariousness, supplanting, supersession, surrogation, surrogacy, alternative choice, equivalence, equivalent, alternative, worse alternative, the lesser of two evils, second best, *pis aller* (Fr), expedient, compromise, modus vivendi, temporary measure, stopgap, compensation, expiation

▶ *223 Exchange, 122 Equality, 547 Representation, 717 Compromise, 707 Deputy*

2 **substitute person**, sub, alternate, proxy, agent, representative, deputy, depute (Scot), surrogate, surrogate mother, locum, locum tenens, fill-in, stand-in, understudy, stuntman (*or* stuntwoman), double, ringer, lookalike, soundalike, impostor, changeling, Doppelgänger, ghostwriter, reserve, reservist, pinch hitter (US), twelfth man, supply, supply teacher, relief, replacement, successor, supplanter, foster parent, father figure, father substitute, mother figure, mother substitute, scapegoat, whipping boy, fall guy (US sl), patsy (Sl)

▶ *664 Cooperation*

3 **substitute thing**, symbol, representation, synonym, doublet, metaphor, analogy, transplant, artificial limb, prosthesis, pacemaker, succedaneum, bandage, sticking plaster, Elastoplast, Band-Aid (US), remount, guilt-offering, sacrifice, lamb to the slaughter

▶ *5 Linguistics, 630 Remedy*

VERBS

4 **be a substitute**, relieve, succeed, supplant, supersede, oust, displace, replace, take the place of, ghostwrite, pinch hit (US), serve as proxy, act as deputy for, represent, act for, do duty for, double for, imitate, fill in, stand in, understudy, deputize, cover, cover for, hold the fort, take over, foster, take responsibility, take on responsibility, shoulder responsibility, take the blame, take the rap, step into the shoes of (Inf)

5 **take a substitute**, exchange for, exchange,

commute, choose an alternative, compromise, take in exchange, take second best, make do with, put up with, count as, treat as, regard as, take a rain check (US inf)

6 **give a substitute**, give in exchange, exchange, switch, swap, shuffle, change for, change, interchange, put in place of, compensate for, symbolize, fob off, palm off

ADJECTIVES

7 **substitute**, substitutive, substitutional, alternate, alternative, acting, deputy, proxy, reserve, replacement, equivalent, lookalike, soundalike, surrogate, second, additional, stopgap, makeshift, temporary, provisional

8 **substituted**, changed, exchanged, switched, swapped, replaced, deputized, supplanted, superseded, compensated

ADVERBS

9 **instead**, instead of, in place of, in lieu of, on behalf of, in one's behalf, in one's place, in favour of, at the expense of, as an alternative, alternatively, equivalently, additionally, temporarily, provisionally, for want of anything better, *faux de mieux* (Fr), in default of, by default, by proxy, per pro (p.p.), *in loco parentis* (L), by (*or* through) the agency of, in one's shoes (Inf)

223 Exchange

NOUNS

1 **exchange**, interchange, change, trade, barter, conversion, commutation, permutation, substitution, transposition, shuffle, shuffling, switch, switching, swap, swapping, pawning, castling (chess), mutuality, reciprocity, reciprocation, give-and-take, tit for tat, quid pro quo, retaliation, blow for blow, eye for an eye, tooth for a tooth, measure for measure, cooperation, logrolling (US), interplay, two-way traffic, repartee, equivalent, correlation, compensation, recompense, consideration, small consideration, redemption, ransom, trade-off, dealing, financial dealing, transaction, truck

▶ *737 Trade, 664 Cooperation, 717 Compromise, 478 Answer, 672 Retaliation*

2 **place of exchange**, place of trade, market, marketplace, stock exchange, Bourse, rialto, bank, bureau de change, *cambio* (It), *Weschel* (Ger), pawnshop

3 **something in exchange**, new lamps for old, pawn ticket, change, small change, money, cash, bill of exchange, banker's draft, cheque, business cards, valentines, telephone numbers

4 **person who exchanges**, banker, money-changer, stockbroker, pawnbroker, exchange student, au pair, substitute, wife swapper

VERBS

5 exchange, give in exchange, give an equivalent, interchange, shuffle, switch, swap, castle (chess), reciprocate, cooperate, logroll (US), correlate, requite, give as good as one gets, answer back, retort, bandy words with, return the compliment, pay in kind, compensate, recompense, exchange for, change places, transpose, shuttle, commute, substitute, convert, pawn, convert into, change money, barter, trade, trade off, traffic, truck, transact, deal, give in return, give and take, give tit for tat, give blow for blow, take an eye for an eye, rob Peter to pay Paul, take in one another's washing, scratch each other's back

ADJECTIVES

6 in exchange, equivalent, complementary, reciprocal, reciprocative, mutual, two-way, tit-for-tat, retaliatory, compensatory, exchangeable, changeable, interchangeable, convertible, commutative, substitutive, substitutable

7 exchanged, changed, interchanged, substituted, transposed, traded, bartered, converted, switched, swapped, pawned, reciprocated, requited, compensated, ransomed

ADVERBS

8 in exchange, mutually, reciprocally, equivalently, correlatively, changeably, interchangeably, commutatively, au pair, vice versa, back and forth, backwards and forwards, to and fro, by turns, turn and turn about, turn about (US), each in his (*or* her) turn, in kind, in return, in return for, in exchange for

224 Changeableness

NOUNS

1 changeableness, changeability, changefulness, mutability, mobility, flexibility, versatility, variety, variegation, iridescence, inconsistency, inconstancy, variability, irregularity, imbalance, disequilibrium, plasticity, pliancy, softness, suppleness, fluidity, flux, fluctuation, alternation, turning, veering, oscillation, uncertainty, unreliability, unpredictability, vicissitude, unsteadiness, instability, wobbliness, rockiness, shakiness, impermanence, transience, metamorphosis

2 irresolution, vacillation, uncertainty, tergiversation, wavering, hesitation, procrastination, fickleness, whim, whimsicality, moodiness, capriciousness, caprice, desultoriness, flightiness, light-mindedness, volatility, erraticism, restlessness, agitation, fitfulness, disquiet, inquietude, fidgeting, chopping and changing, bobbing and weaving, ducking and diving, darting, shiftiness, equivocation, slipperiness, disloyalty, infidelity, treacherousness

▶ *216 Change, 324 Motion, 456 Variegation, 123*

Inequality, 374 Softness, 387 Fluid, 113 Diversity, 215 Irregularity, 365 Oscillation, 189 Transience, 576 Vacillation, 578 Equivocation, 229 Lack of Motive, 579 Caprice, 468 Inattention, 366 Agitation

3 changeable thing, moon, phases of the moon, chameleon, kaleidoscope, changing scene, shifting sands, mercury, quicksilver, wind, wind of change, weathercock, weather vane, luck, chance, fortune, wheel of fortune, variable, random number, Ernie (Electronic Random Number Indicator Equipment), April shower, proteus, free radical

▶ *169 Number*

4 editor, amender, corrector, reformer, revisionist, revolutionary, swapper, dealer, exchanger, trader, replacer, chemist, alchemist, magician

▶ *223 Exchange*

5 changeable person, moody person, temperamental person, Doctor Jekyll and Mister Hyde, manic-depressive, schizophrenic

6 fickle person, ladies' man, philanderer, adulterer, two-timer, double-dealer, hypocrite, turncoat, traitor, counterspy, Vicar of Bray

7 person who moves around, wanderer, traveller, New-Age traveller, vagrant, tramp, hobo, explorer, adventurer, voyager, tourist

8 person who changes costume, actor, actress, mimic, quick-change artist, impersonator, female impersonator

9 person who changes sex, transsexual

10 person who is exchanged, changeling, hostage

VERBS

11 be changeable, change, metamorphose, vary, fluctuate, alternate, oscillate, show variety, show phases, go through phases, ring the changes, flash, flicker, twinkle, gutter, wave, wave in the wind, flutter, whiffle, flap, falter, stagger, teeter, totter, sway, reel, rock, tremble, vibrate, shake, wobble, swing, shuttle, pitch, roll, yaw, tack, turn, veer, back, ebb and flow, wax and wane, have as many phases as the moon

12 be irresolute, tergiversate, vacillate, seesaw, blow hot and cold, waver, hesitate, hover, drift, float, chop and change, dodge about, dart, duck and dive, bob and weave, flit, flitter, fidget, shillyshally, play fast and loose, change one's mind, change the rules, move the goal posts

ADJECTIVES

13 changeable, changeful, mutable, alterable, mobile, versatile, varied, variant, variegated, protean, kaleidoscopic, iridescent, inconsistent, inconstant, variable, irregular, imbalanced, plastic, pliant, soft, supple, flowing, melting, fluid, fluctuating, in a state of flux,

ever-changing, never the same, alternating, tidal, vibrating, oscillating, uncertain, unreliable, unpredictable, unstable, unsteady, floating, loose, unattached, labile, wobbly, rocky, shaky, swaying, tottering, teetering, built on sand, built on weak foundations, unsettled, impermanent, transient, rootless, homeless, of no fixed abode, vagrant, rambling, wandering, roving, precarious, touch and go, fitful, shifting, ephemeral, spasmodic, flickering, wavering

14 **irresolute**, hesitating, vacillating, seesawing, fickle, whimsical, moody, wayward, capricious, desultory, malleable, impressionable, yielding, flighty, dizzy, giddy, scatterbrained, light-headed, light-minded, volatile, mercurial, restless, tossing and turning, fidgety, shitty, disloyal, unfaithful, traitorous, like putty in someone's hands, scatty (Inf)

ADVERBS

15 **changeably**, alterably, back and forth, to and fro, in and out, inconsistently, off and on, on and off, inconstantly, variably, irregularly, iridescently, pliantly, softly, fluidly, alternatively, now this, now that, uncertainly, unreliably, unpredictably, unsteadily, shakily, precariously, fitfully, impermanently, now here, now there, waveringly, ephemerally, spasmodically, irresolutely, round and round, whimsically, moodily, waywardly, capriciously, desultorily, impressionably, dizzily, shiftily, disloyally, unfaithfully, traitorously

225   Stability

NOUNS

1 **stability**, stabilization, steadiness, steadfastness, rootedness, fixedness, fixity, solidity, soundness, secureness, strength, durability, permanence, consistency, reliability, constancy, rest, quietude, quiet, calm, immobilization, immobility, immovability, hardening, stiffening, stiffness, firmness, firming up, inflexibility, steady state, stable equilibrium, homeostasis, balance, equality, stasis, immutability, unchangeableness, unchangeability, changelessness, invariability, irreversibility, indestructibility, deathlessness

▶ *217 Permanence, 371 Density, 112 Uniformity, 373 Hardness, 325 Motionlessness, 122 Equality, 188 Duration, 190 Eternity*

2 **determination**, resolution, resolve, nerve, nerves of steel, iron nerve, iron will, inflexibility, toughness, hardness, steeliness, obstinacy, stubbornness, obduracy, aplomb, imperturbability, coolness (Sl)

▶ *574 Resolution, 490 Certainty, 577 Obstinacy*

3 **stabilizer**, keel, centreboard, fin, aerofoil, wing flap, spoiler, counterbalance, counter-

weight, ballast, support, prop, buttress, beam, crossbeam, joist, buttress, aileron

▶ *284 Support*

4 **stable thing**, perpetual motion, the Establishment, fixture, firm fixture, firm foundation, strong foundation, solid foundations, solid footing, cornerstone, rock, bedrock, pillar, tower, pyramid, granite rock, mountain, constant, invariable, invariable quantity, immutable law, the Code of Hammurabi, law of the Medes and the Persians, Ten Commandments, Twelve Tables, Justinian's Code, written constitution, US Constitution, the Bill of Rights (US), prescriptive right, rights under law, droit de seigneur, indelible ink, fast colour, engraving

▶ *166 Rule*

5 **stable person**, born leader, a man of his word, pillar of society, pillar of the community, pillar of the church, tower of strength, rock of Gibraltar, Victorian, Darby and Joan, square (Inf), straight (Sl)

VERBS

6 **be stable**, not change, stay in one place, stick fast, hold, remain fixed, adhere, stand, stand up well, hold up, stand firm, stay put, harden, stiffen, stabilize, keep one's balance, set in, settle in, settle down, stay, take root, strike root, quieten down, rest, keep one's cool (Sl)

7 **make stable**, stabilize, steady, transfix, freeze, balance, equalize, fix, establish, confirm, validate, ratify, make sure, ensure, secure, firm up, set up, set on its feet, found, erect, build on a rock, build on a firm foundation, support, buttress, engrave, stamp, print, stereotype, set, set in stone, set in concrete, set in granite, keep stable, bind, make fast, root, entrench, tie, fasten down, batten down (the hatches), put at rest, quieten, quieten down

8 **show determination**, persist, persevere, stand firm, stand pat (US), stiffen, not budge, show stubbornness, hold out, hold out to the bitter end, stay with it, stick with it, stick fast, hold the road, stand (*or* hold) one's ground, hang on by one's teeth (Inf), weather the storm (Inf), not bat an eyelid (Inf), put one's foot down (Inf), stick it out (Inf), stick to one's guns (Inf)

ADJECTIVES

9 **stable**, steady, steadfast, solid, sound, firm, stiff, secure, strong, durable, permanent, consistent, reliable, constant, dependable, predictable, unchangeable, unchanging, unvarying, inalterable, irrevocable, irreversible, restful, quiet, calm, immobile, immovable, held, at rest, at anchor, riding at anchor, aground, stuck fast, high and dry, written in stone, well-founded, frozen, frozen like a statue, hard, inflexible, unshakable, incontrovertible, indisputable, indefeasible, equal, homeostatic,

immutable, changeless, invariable, incommutable, intransmutable, indissoluble, imperishable, inextinguishable, invulnerable, indestructible, ineradicable, indelible, perennial, evergreen, enduring, long-lasting, deathless, perpetual, rocklike, steady as a rock, like the Rock of Gibraltar

10 **stabilized**, unchanged, unaltered, settled, transfixed, stereotyped, fixed, anchored, moored, tethered, tied, chained, grounded, stranded, pinned down, rooted, rooted to the spot, deep-rooted, well-rooted, established, well-established, ingrained, entrenched, engraved, balanced

11 **determined**, resolute, resolved, certain, sure, nerved, iron-nerved, iron-willed, inflexible, unwavering, tough, hard, steely, obstinate, stubborn, obdurate, imperturbable, cool (Sl)

ADVERBS

12 **stably**, unalterably, steadily, steadfastly, solidly, soundly, securely, strongly, permanently, consistently, reliably, constantly, dependably, predictably, irrevocably, irreversibly, restfully, quietly, calmly, stiffly, firmly, on a firm basis, on a firm footing, on a strong foundation, inflexibly, unshakably, indisputably, equally, immutably, indissolubly, imperishably, invulnerably, indestructibly, indelibly, perennially, enduringly, perpetually

13 **determinedly**, with determination, resolutely, in a resolute manner, inflexibly, unwaveringly, toughly, obstinately, stubbornly, obdurately, imperturbably, coolly (Sl)

226 Cause

NOUNS

1 **cause**, causation, causality, formal cause, underlying cause, motivation, initiation, instigation, determinant, creation, authorship, attribution, origination, occasion, invention, derivation, production, propagation, cultivation, generation, evocation, provocation, compulsion, temptation, impulsion, stimulation, inspiration, fomentation, encouragement, force, spark, etiology, etymology

▶ *156 Beginning, 119 Originality, 228 Motive, 695 Compulsion*

2 **source**, spring, wellspring, mainspring, wellhead, fountainhead, fountain, fount, *fons et origo* (L), headwaters, mine, quarry, home, birthplace, breeding ground, genitalia, womb, fertile soil, grow bag, growing medium, greenhouse, hothouse, propagator, seedbed, hotbed, incubator, hatchery, cradle, nursery

▶ *206 Youth, 256 Habitat*

3 **rudiment**, principle, first principle, element, first step, first thing, hypothesis, raw material, nucleus, germ, spore, seed, sperm, egg, embryo, fetus, larva, chrysalis, pupa, cocoon,

bud, stem, stock, rootstock, root, taproot, bulb, tuber, radical, radix, etymon, base, basis, foundation, bedrock, fundamentals, basics, building blocks, beginnings, groundwork, spadework, the nitty-gritty (Inf), nuts and bolts (Inf)

4 **contributing factor**, contributory cause, contribution, agent, leaven, stimulus, factor, hidden cause, influence, planetary influence, stars, astrological influence, destiny, fate

▶ *586 Persuasion*

5 **reason**, reason why, reason behind, idea behind, the why, the why and wherefore, key, explanation, answer, basis, ground, grounds, rationale, idea, *raison d'être* (Fr), occasion, motive, object, purpose, aim, opportunity, excuse, pretext

▶ *478 Answer*

6 **undertaking**, enterprise, attempt, action, case, subject, matter, topic, purpose, principle, ideal, worthy cause

7 **Prime Mover**, God, Father, Maker, the Creator, Divine Creator, the Deity, deity, Supreme Being, *primum mobile* (L), producer, begetter, only begetter, sire, father, mother, parent, ancestor, progenitor, propagator, instigator, originator, author, founder, inventor, motivator, inspirer

▶ *8 Divinity*

8 **contributor**, accessory, abettor, helper, aider, fomenter, agent, astrologer, power behind the throne, boys in the back-room

VERBS

9 **be the cause of**, cause, create, originate, be the author of, author, beget, propagate, father, bring into the world, bring into being, make, produce, invent, derive, cultivate, generate, lie at the bottom of, make or mar, result in, bring about, bring off, bring to pass, make happen, effect, effectuate, have the effect of, lead to, give rise to, occasion, give occasion for

10 **awaken**, stimulate, tempt, excite, kindle, inspire, encourage, motivate, influence, impel, compel, force, make, foment, provoke, incite, set off, touch off, trigger off, spark off, evoke, bring on, bring out, draw out, induce, precipitate, hasten, elicit, plan, contrive, procure, find means, find the means, engineer, manage

11 **inaugurate**, initiate, start, begin, launch, instigate, institute, found, lay the foundations, erect, establish, open, broach, set up, set going, set on foot, set afloat, set in motion, sow the seeds of, open the door to, be an open sesame to

12 **determine**, decide, decide the result, decide the outcome, decide the issue, turn (or tip) the scale, have the casting vote, come down on one side or the other, come (or climb) down off the fence, help decide, contribute to, have

a hand in, have a large part in, have an effect, promote, advance, foster, aid, abet, help

ADJECTIVES

13 **causal**, causative, etiological, explanatory, creative, inventive, original, aboriginal, primary, primal, primordial, primitive, basic, fundamental, intrinsic, foundational, elemental, elementary, ultimate, radical, effectual, effective, pivotal, determinant, decisive, crucial, central, significant, productive, genetic, generative, germinal, seminal, embryonic, inceptive, rudimentary, formative, initiatory, suggestive, inspiring, inspirational, influential, impelling, compelling, responsible, answerable, blameworthy, at the bottom of, behind the scenes

ADVERBS

14 **causally**, because, by reason of, causatively, creatively, inventively, originally, primarily, primordially, primitively, basically, fundamentally, intrinsically, ultimately, radically, effectually, effectively, pivotally, decisively, crucially, centrally, significantly, productively, genetically, inceptively, suggestively, inspiringly, inspirationally, influentially, compelling, responsibly, answerably, behind the scenes, in the background

227 Effect

NOUNS

1 **effect**, outcome, logical outcome, counteraction, reaction, action, event, happening, achievement, issue, end, denouement, result, final result, net result, end result, upshot, termination, completion, conclusion, aftermath, aftereffect, culmination, consequence, impact, product, by-product, repercussion, side effect, spin-off, sequel, corollary, inference, derivation, derivative, precipitate, remainder, residue, payoff (Inf)

▶ *155 Sequence, 640 Action, 132 Remainder, 684 Completion, 545 Record, 624 Ill Health*

2 **visible effect**, handiwork, print, imprint, impress, mark, trace, side effect, fingerprint, footprint, backwash, wake, legacy, inheritance, hereditament, property, belongings, effects, personal effects

3 **growth**, development, expansion, increase, swelling, outgrowth, bud, blossom, florescence, flower, fruit, ear, crop, harvest, produce, gain, profit, malignant growth, lump, carcinoma, cancer

▶ *128 Increase, 721 Gain*

4 **significance**, import, meaning, purport, sense, tendency, trend, drift

VERBS

5 **show an effect**, affect, have an effect, have a side effect, have consequence, have impact,

impact upon, counteract, react, act, happen, achieve, effect, accomplish, issue, end in, result in, eventuate in, terminate, complete, conclude, culminate, produce, precipitate, spin off, pay off

6 **have a visible effect**, print, imprint, impress upon, mark, leave a trace, have a side effect, leave a footprint, leave a fingerprint, inherit

7 **follow from**, follow on from, follow, ensure, supervene, result, result from, spin off from, be the result of, be due to, owe everything to, borrow from, derive from, be derived from, inherit, descend from, have its roots in, originate in (*or* from), come of, come out of, emanate from, emerge, proceed from, issue from, begin from, arise from, spring from, flow from, unfold, evolve, develop, bear the stamp of, depend on, hang upon, turn on, pivot on, centre on, be subject to

8 **grow**, grow from, accrue, develop, develop from, expand, increase, swell, sprout, germinate, bud, blossom, flower, bear fruit, harvest, produce, gain, profit, have a malignant growth, have cancer

9 **take effect**, come into effect, become law, come about, transpire, arise, happen, occur, take place, end up, turn out, fall out, come to pass, work out, come off (Inf), crop up (Inf), pan out (Inf)

ADJECTIVES

10 **caused**, caused by, effected by, effected, reacting to, reacting, resulting from, resulting, resultant, ensuing, following from, following, coming from, due to, owing to, developing from, developed, deriving from, derived, derivative, evolving from, evolved, arising from, descending from, descended, inheriting from, inherited, hereditary, genetic, depending on, dependent on, dependent, attributed to, attributable to, consequent, consequent upon, consequential, contingent, contingent upon, subject to, subsequent, sequential, secondary, second-generation, next-generation, unoriginal, emergent, eventual, born of, out of, by

11 **growing**, developing, expanding, increasing, swelling, budding, blossoming, flowering, fruit-bearing

ADVERBS

12 **with the effect of**, in consequence, as a consequence, consequently, consequentially, derivatively, dependently, attributively, contingently, secondarily, unoriginally, subsequently, eventually, because of, as a result, with the result that, necessarily, naturally, accordingly, of course, and so, and there, ergo, hence, following upon, it follows that

228 Motive

Never ascribe to an opponent motives meaner than your own. J. M. Barrie.

Nobody ever did anything very foolish except from some strong principle. Lord Melbourne.

NOUNS

1 **motive**, cause, reason, rationale, grounds, excuse, pretext, motivation, driving force, guiding principle, guiding light, guiding star, lodestar, ideal, intention, objective, object, design, purpose, aim, goal, hope, desire, ambition, driving ambition, impetus, stimulation, impulse, compulsion, inspiration, bright idea, call, calling, vocation, aspiration, selfish motive, ulterior motive, what makes one tick (Inf), brainwave (Inf)

▶ *226 Cause, 775 Hope, 588 Intention, 847 Duty, 860 Selfishness*

2 **inducement**, influence, encouragement, invitation, incentive, provocation, enticement, lure, allurement, attraction, attractiveness, charm, fascination, bewitchment, magnetism, magnetic personality, seductiveness, seduction, blandishment, cajolery, coaxing, flattering, teasing, wheedling, pleading, advocacy, advice, persuasion, persuasiveness, propaganda, agitprop, pressure, lobbying, solicitation, advertising, hard sell (Inf), soft sell (Inf), sales talk, patter, promises

▶ *340 Attraction, 853 Flattery, 826 Endearment, 654 Advice, 712 Request*

3 **stimulus**, stimulant, fillip, tonic, sop, prod, goad, spur, carrot and stick (Inf)

4 **negative stimulus**, threat, castigation, big stick, whip, lash, crack of the whip, threat of dismissal

5 **positive stimulus**, flattery, carrot, charm, spell, lure, bait, loss leader, special offer, limited offer, added attraction, profit, money, cash, pay, payment, salary, wages, benefits, pay increase, rise, raise (US), bonus, hand-out, gift, donation, gratuity, tip, bribe, kickback, baksheesh, slush fund, political favours, spoils system (US), tempting offer, offer one cannot refuse, golden apple, perk (Inf), sweet talk (Inf), come-on (Inf), turn-on (Sl), freebie (US sl), pork barrel (US sl), hush money (Sl)

▶ *662 Help, 777 Fear*

6 **suggestibility**, susceptibility, receptivity, impressibility, tractability, malleability, adaptability, docility, compliance, willingness, putty in one's hands

▶ *572 Willingness*

7 **motivator**, prime mover, moving spirit, orator, rhetorician, preacher, lawyer, politician, instigator, rabble-rouser, demagogue, agitator, troublemaker, firebrand, ringleader, manipulator, manoeuvrer, strategist, tactician, manager, prompter, adviser, counsellor, aider and abettor, *agent provocateur* (Fr), tempter, temptress, seducer, seductress, *femme fatale* (Fr), siren, flatterer, coaxer, Svengali, Rasputin, hypnotizer, hypnotist, persuader, advertiser, salesman (*or* saleswoman), propagandist, public relations person, publicist, press agent, lobbyist, lobby, pressure group, special interest group, ginger group, vamp (Inf), sexpot (Sl), flack (US sl)

VERBS

8 **be motivated**, be induced, succumb, submit, concede, give in, come (*or* fall) under the influence of, fall for, heed the call, feel the urge, be infected, have self-motivation, follow (*or* obey) one's conscience, follow (*or* obey) one's instincts, catch the bug (Inf), be bitten by the bug (Inf), get it bad (Inf)

9 **motivate**, start, initiate, begin, set in motion, instigate, bring about, induce, prompt, actuate, move, cause, bring on, influence, persuade, convince, suggest, recommend, advocate, advise, counsel, talk into, bring (*or* talk) someone round, bring over, win over, enlist, recruit, bring to one's side, procure, carry with one, make one's point, carry one's point, have an impact with, interest, intrigue, prevail upon, act upon, appeal to, attract, captivate, fascinate, charm, coax, cajole, blandish, flatter, tantalize, make things easy for, energize, galvanize, electrify, encourage, cheer on, sound the trumpet, rally, inspire, inspirit, animate, rouse, arouse, exhort, stimulate, excite, evoke, call forth, challenge, provoke, impel, impress, jolt, jog, prick, spur, spur on, drive on, hurry, hustle, bend, incline, dispose, pull, draw, direct, lead, give a lead, set the pace, set a trend, set the fashion, be a trendsetter, hold out a carrot, make someone's mouth water, sugar the pill, sweet-talk (Inf), root for (Inf), turn on (Sl)

10 **manipulate**, play on (*or* upon), operate on (*or* upon), call the tune, put up to, abet, aid and abet, lobby, prejudice, bias, predetermine, predispose, lead astray, misdirect, mislead, insinuate, hint, lead into temptation, tempt, entice, seduce, lure, hypnotize, mesmerize, bewitch, infect, exert pressure, bring pressure to bear, force, compel, nag, drive, push, bully, browbeat, override, prevail upon, press, prod, goad, whip, lash, inveigle, incite, egg on, ensnare, entrap, get round someone, twist someone's arm (Inf), needle (Inf)

ADJECTIVES

11 **motivational**, influential, directional, directive, incentive, attractive, magnetic, persuasive, hortatory, hortative, provocative, incitive, instigative, inflammatory, hypnotic, mesmeric, irresistible, suggestive, motivating, influencing, convincing, compelling, encour-

aging, challenging, provoking, stimulating, electrifying, inciting, instigating, energizing, kinetic, galvanizing, inflaming, rousing, insinuating, teasing, tantalizing, alluring, tempting, inviting, charming, fascinating, bewitching, spellbinding

12 **motivated**, persuaded, moved, influenced, induced, prompted, impelled, caused, directed, encouraged, exhorted, challenged, urged, egged on, spurred on, pressured, lobbied, prodded, goaded, whipped, provoked, stimulated, electrified, energized, animated, inspired, inflamed, incited, roused, galvanized, charmed, enticed, lured, attracted, seduced, bewitched, coaxed, flattered, spellbound, hypnotized, mesmerized, self-motivated, goal-oriented

13 **suggestible**, susceptible, receptive, impressible, tractable, malleable, adaptable, docile, compliant, willing, easily led

▶ 572 Willingness

ADVERBS

14 **influentially**, in order to influence, persuasively, provocatively, hypnotically, irresistibly, suggestively, convincingly, to convince, compellingly, rousingly, hortatorily, hortatively, insinuatingly, teasingly, tantalizingly, alluringly, temptingly, as a temptation, invitingly, charmingly, fascinatingly, bewitchingly, stimulatingly, inspirationally, encouragingly, seductively, in a seductive manner, susceptibly, receptively, tractably, docilely, compliantly, willingly

229   Lack of Motive

NOUNS

1 **lack of motive**, lack of cause, no attributable cause, lack of intention, nonintention, aimlessness, haphazardness, randomness, no reason, purposelessness, no good reason, arbitrariness, fortuity, fortuitousness, indeterminacy, unpredictability, uncertainty, uncertainty principle, inexplicability, unaccountability, inconsistency, illogicality, irrationality, quirkiness

▶ 486 Possibility, 488 Probability, 489 Improbability, 523 Unintelligibility

2 **chance**, lot, luck, Lady Luck, good luck, bad luck, the luck of the draw, fortune, Dame Fortune, good fortune, misfortune, ill-fortune, wheel of fortune, risk, even chance, equal chance, fifty fifty chance, toss-up, toss of the coin, spin of the coin, heads or tails, spin of the wheel, throw of the dice, turn of the card, random sample, game of chance, gamble, raffle, lottery, bingo, tombola, sweepstake, sweep, fair chance, sporting chance, fighting chance, small chance, remote chance, outside chance, long shot, ghost of a chance, no

chance, good chance, best chance, favourable chance, main chance, long odds, short odds, safe bet, sure thing, pot luck (Inf)

▶ 589 Chance, 517 Prediction, 122 Equality, 213 Infrequency, 686 Prosperity, 687 Adversity, 491 Uncertainty

3 **coincidence**, chance happening, chance encounter, chance meeting, chance hit, shot in the dark, lucky shot, lucky strike, lucky break, one chance in a million, fluke, wild guess, chance discovery, accidental discovery, serendipity, misadventure, accident, casualty, chapter of accidents

▶ 514 Surprise, 496 Discovery

VERBS

4 **chance**, risk, risk it, take a risk, try one's luck, leave to chance, chance it, have good luck, get lucky, strike it lucky, have bad luck, have a fair chance, stand a chance, take an even chance, take a long shot, toss up, toss a coin, spin a coin, call heads or tails, spin a wheel, throw the dice, turn a card, take a random sample, play a game of chance, gamble, bet, raffle, take long odds, take pot luck (Inf), go out on a limb (Inf), stick one's neck out (Inf), chance one's arm (Inf)

5 **happen by chance**, happen, hap, happen by coincidence, befall, fall to one's lot, turn up, come upon, happen upon, chance upon, light upon, stumble into (of upon), blunder into (or upon), run (or come) across, meet unexpectedly, discover by chance, take a wild guess, take a shot in the dark, crop up (Inf), bump into (Inf)

ADJECTIVES

6 **motiveless**, groundless, unintended, unintentional, unmeant, noncausal, aimless, purposeless, unplanned, unmotivated, arbitrary, fortuitous, indeterminant, undetermined, random, stochastic, unpredictable, haphazard, uncertain, inexplicable, unaccountable, unexpected, unreasonable, inconsistent, hit-or-miss, illogical, irrational, coincidental, accidental, chance, casual, stray, incidental, adventitious, serendipitous, aleatory, aleatoric, quirky, risky, fifty-fifty, toss-up, fluky (Inf), chancy (Inf), dicey (Inf), wacky (Inf)

7 **adventurous**, gambling, lucky, fortunate, unlucky, misfortunate

ADVERBS

8 **by chance**, at random, randomly, possibly, perchance, unintentionally, without design, aimlessly, purposelessly, arbitrarily, according to chance, as the case may be, fortuitously, indeterminantly, unpredictably, haphazardly, uncertainly, inexplicably, unaccountably, for no good reason, unexpectedly, unreasonably, inconsistently, illogically, irrationally, coincidentally, accidentally, by accident, casually, incidentally, adventitiously, riskily

9 **luckily**, fortunately, as luck would have it, as good luck would have it, unluckily, unfortunately, as bad (or ill) luck would have it

230 Operation

NOUNS

1 **operation**, implementation, execution, action, performance, exercise, treatment, work, working, doing, course of action, course, procedure, measure, process, movement, motion, power, force, stress, strain, swing, play
▶ 640 Action, 642 Activity, 239 Vigour

2 **joint operation**, joint venture, cooperation, coordination, interaction, takeover, merger, buy-out

3 **business**, office, production, undertaking, venture, matter, cause, affair, task, work, job, position, post
▶ 243 Production, 684 Completion

4 **management**, responsibility, effectiveness, effectuality, efficiency, direction, handling, manipulation, manoeuvring, maintenance, service, support
▶ 233 Influence

5 **operator**, dealer, trader, handler, speculator, agent, worker, employee, co-worker, skilled worker, driver, mechanic, technician, computer operator, telephone operator, telephonist, conductor, manager, director, administrator, executive

6 **operative**, labourer, hand, unskilled worker, semiskilled worker, machinist

VERBS

7 **be operational**, be in action, operate, work, go, run, act, play, be in play, do, idle, tick over, serve, perform, function, do one's job, come into operation, come into effect, take effect, be in force, do one's thing (Inf), do one's stuff (Inf)

8 **activate**, actuate, bring into action, bring into operation, make operational, make operate, make work, bring into effect, bring into force, bring into play, make happen, effectuate, influence, stimulate, motivate, wind up, plug in, turn on, switch on, flip the switch, press the button, set going, start up, rev up

9 **take action**, use, handle, deal with, manage, manipulate, manoeuvre, wield, process, treat, employ, implement, execute, move, power, drive, cause, act upon, work upon, bear upon, play upon, maintain, service, sustain, support, crew, man, procure, get done
▶ 599 Use

ADJECTIVES

10 **operational**, operating, in operation, functional, functioning, going, working, in working order, usable, running, in running order, in play, in use, up and going, up and doing, active, on the active list

11 **workable**, operable, doable, manageable, manipulatable, manoeuvrable, negotiable, practicable, practical, useful, viable

12 **operative**, in force, carrying force, relevant, significant, important, crucial, critical, key, influential, efficacious, efficient, effective, effectual

ADVERBS

13 **operationally**, functionally, actively, in an active manner, usefully, readily, efficaciously, efficiently, with efficiency, effectively, effectually, practically, relevantly, significantly, importantly, crucially, critically, influentially

231 Counteraction

NOUNS

1 **counteraction**, opposing action (or cause), polarity, polarization, opposition, prevention, remedy, compensation, contravention, reaction, counter, retroaction, return action, repercussion, kickback, boomerang effect, backlash, backfire, recoil, kick, recalcitrance, conflict, clash, antagonism, antipathy, hostility, resistance, opposing force, countermove, counterintelligence, counteroffensive, counterattack, counterpunch, counterblast, deterrent, defence, defensive measure, inhibitor, preventive, preventative, friction, drag, check, block, hindrance, obstruction, obstacle, barrier, frustration, interference, counterpressure, repression, intolerance, persecution, suppression, restraint, moderation, neutralization, derestriction, deregulation, decriminalization, demagnetization, deactivation, invalidation, cancellation, abrogation, negation, nullification, veto, offset, counterweight, counterpoise, counterbalance, counterirritant, neutralizer, countermeasure, countercharm, counterspell
▶ 125 Compensation, 663 Opposition, 331 Recoil, 330 Impulsion, 820 Enmity, 661 Hindrance, 701 Subjection, 709 Veto, 671 Defence

2 **counteracting thing**, headwind, crosscurrent, crossfire, antidote, antitoxin, antivenin, antivenom, cure, remedy, degausser (US), burglar alarm, Mace, defender, protection, prophylactic, contraceptive, condom

VERBS

3 **counteract**, counter, run counter to, obviate, contravene, oppose, cause opposition, polarize, react against, go against, militate against, agitate against, work against, cross, traverse, thwart, hinder, inhibit, prevent, prohibit, drag, block, check, obstruct, not be conducive to, frustrate, interfere with, repress, persecute, suppress, restrain, resist, fight against, defend against, withstand, conflict with, antagonize, clash, react, recoil, backfire, boomerang, counter-

vail, counterbalance, counterpoise, compensate for, kick back, cancel out, cancel, annul, undo, invalidate, negate, nullify, veto, abrogate, decontrol, derestrict, deregulate, decriminalize, deactivate, demagnetize, degauss, neutralize, moderate, cure, find a remedy, recover, get back, retrieve, find a way round

ADJECTIVES

4 **counteracting**, counteractive, counter, oppositional, opposing, contravening, opposed to, polarized, contrary, conflicting, clashing, antipathetic, antagonistic, inimical, hostile, resistant, resisting, recalcitrant, intractable, reactionary, retroactive, reactive, frictional, restraining, frustrating, interfering, repressive, suppressive, intolerant, obstructive, preventive, preventative, antidotal, contraceptive, remedial, corrective, balancing, offsetting, moderating, neutralizing, invalidating, nullifying, compensatory

ADVERBS

5 **counter**, counteractively, contrarily, contrary to, counter to, against, conflictingly, antipathetically, antagonistically, inimically, hostilely, resistantly, resistingly, in opposition to, in contrast, in spite of, despite, although, notwithstanding, intractably, retroactively, reactively, repressively, intolerantly, preventively, antidotally, remedially, correctively

232   Instrumentality

NOUNS

1 **instrumentality**, agency, operation, occasion, opportunity, responsibility, cause, effect, result, influence, significance, power, weight, effectiveness, efficacy, performance, achievement, functionality, function, service, promotion, advancement, aid, assistance, support, help, midwifery, intermediacy, intermediateness, intervention, interposition, intercession, mediation, interference, pressure, cooperation, subordination, subservience, employment, use, medium, means, mechanical means, electronic means, use of machinery, instrumentation, mechanization, computerization, automation, application, practicality, serviceability, utility, usefulness, handiness

▶ *226 Cause, 227 Effect, 235 Power, 662 Help, 664 Cooperation, 678 Mediation, 694 Obedience, 642 Activity, 602 Means, 613 Usefulness*

2 **instrument**, means, medium, catalyst, vehicle, agency, influence, mechanism, force, factor, organ, implement, device, tool, machine, apparatus, appliance, equipment, gadget, contrivance, expedient, compromise, contraption (Inf), gizmo (*or* gismo) (US sl)

▶ *603 Tool, 49 Music, 185 Time, 192 Timekeeping, 120 Quantity, 70 Transport*

3 **assistant**, helper, help, aide, hand, man (*or*

girl) Friday, the hand of God, agent, amanuensis, midwife, handmaid, servant, lackey, slave, slave of the lamp, genie of the lamp, intermediary, mediator, go-between, pander, pimp, procurer, puppet, creature, cat's-paw, pawn

▶ *697 Servant*

VERBS

4 **be an instrument**, be instrumental, function, operate, work, act, perform, do, serve, be useful, work for, lend oneself to, minister to, pander to, pander, pimp, procure, help, assist, aid, support, cooperate, promote, advance, have a hand in, cause, control, be responsible for, bridge, channel, interpose, intervene, intercede for, intermediate, mediate, compromise, influence, use one's influence, use one's good offices, pressure, pull strings, implement, effect, bring into effect, carry into effect, carry through, carry out, expedite, achieve, save someone's bacon (Inf), pull someone's chestnuts out of the fire (Inf)

5 **find means**, find a way, obtain assistance, use one's connections, network, get by hook or (by) crook

ADJECTIVES

6 **instrumental**, useful, applicable, employable, utilizable, handy, helping, helpful, assisting, cooperative, advancing, promoting, promotive, promotional, aiding, supportive, subordinate, subservient, effective, efficient, effectual, efficacious, performance-oriented

7 **causal**, responsible, instrumental, central, powerful, weighty, significant, telling, influential, mediative, intermediate, intervening, interventional, intercessional, interfering, pressuring, maieutic, Socratic, agential

8 **practical**, applied, servicing, serviceable, general-purpose, working, functioning, functional, operating, operational, operative, hand-operated, manual, mechanical, automatic, automated, electronic, computerized, pushbutton

ADVERBS

9 **instrumentally**, through the instrumentality of, by means of, by virtue of, usefully, handily, helpfully, with the help of, with the aid of, by way of, by, via, thanks to, with, herewith (Fml), through, per, cooperatively, supportively, subserviently, effectively, efficiently, effectually, efficaciously, powerfully, significantly, influentially, by (*or* through) the good offices of, manually, by the hand of, at the hands of, mechanically, automatically, electronically

233   Influence

How to Win Friends and Influence People. Dale Carnegie.

The hand that rocks the cradle/ Is the hand that rules the world. William Ross Wallace.

NOUNS

1 influence, power, powerful influence, potency, potentiality, ability, capability, superior power, strength, might, mightiness, force, force to be reckoned with, predominance, prevalence, greatness, magnitude, importance, significance, advantage, authority, whip hand, upper hand, final say, casting vote, vital role, leading part, leverage, grip, hold, footing, play, weight, impact, pressure, pull, drag, magnetism, gravity, attraction, fascination, repulsion, drive, push, thrust, impulse, motive, motivation, interest, vested interest, emotion, impression, inspiration, persuasion, encouragement, cause, contagion, infection, climate, atmosphere, circumstances, fate, destiny, clout (Inf)

▶ *235 Power, 126 Superiority, 800 Repute, 611 Importance, 467 Attention, 340 Attraction, 341 Repulsion, 330 Impulsion, 688 Authority, 586 Persuasion, 695 Compulsion*

2 occult influence, magic, magic spell, witchcraft, sorcery, charm, mesmerism, hypnotism, planetary influence, heaven, stars, astrology, horoscope, malevolence, malign influence, curse, voodoo (or hoodoo)

▶ *11 Occultism*

3 personal influence, personality, magnetic personality, charisma, repute, reputation, credit, prestige, leadership, ascendancy, hegemony, domination, dominance, dominion, tyranny, authority, sway, control, reign

4 indirect influence, favour, friend at court, amicus curiae (Fml), patronage, wires, wire-pulling (US), strings, lever, hold, hidden influence, secret influence, hidden hand, power broker, kingmaker, *éminence grise* (Fr), grey eminence, power behind the throne, woman behind the (great) man, hand that rocks the cradle, pull (Inf)

5 influential person, president, prime minister, premier, chairman (or chairwoman), director, parent, best friend, priest, preacher, doctor, lawyer, lobbyist, manager, manipulator, uncrowned king (or queen), big noise (Inf), big shot (Inf), bigwig (Inf), big wheel (Inf), big cheese (Inf), queen bee (Inf), brass hat (Inf), top brass (Inf), wheeler-dealer (Inf), influence pedlar (Inf)

▶ *662 Help*

6 group influence, pressure group, self-help group, lobby, public opinion, the powers that be, the Establishment, Big Brother, multinational company, superpower

7 sphere of influence, area (or field) of influence, territory, orbit, ambit, bailiwick, turf (US sl)

VERBS

8 influence, have influence, exercise influence, exert influence, command influence, have charisma, impress, motivate, actuate, activate, encourage, suggest, persuade, carry weight, have importance, be recognized, be listened to, have a voice, make one's voice heard, have a say in, play a role (or part) in, have a part to play, gain a footing (or foothold), take root, strike root in, gain a hearing, make oneself felt, affect, bear upon, tell upon, work upon, have the right connections, know the right people, have friends in high places, have the ear of, pressurize, put pressure on, lobby, pull (the) strings, pull (the) wires (US), guide, direct, lead, establish the trend, set the trend, set the fashion, serve as a model, promote, prejudice, bias, brainwash, predispose, dispose, colour, lure, tempt, appeal, have pull (Inf), have pulling power (Inf), have clout (Inf), carry clout (Inf), wheel and deal (Inf), weigh in (Inf)

9 change, change for better or for worse, make or mar, counterbalance, tip (or turn) the scale(s), influence positively, make better, improve, leaven, influence negatively, discourage, repulse, disgust, repel, put off, militate against, infect, dilute, contaminate, adulterate, mar, spoil, impair, ruin

10 be a prevailing influence, be prevalent, prevail, predominate, fascinate, mesmerize, hypnotize, practise witchcraft, outweigh, override, overbear, gain (or have) the upper hand, have the final say, have the casting vote, have sway, force, compel, pull, drag, tyrannize, dominate, have power over, tower over, have a hold over (or on), have in one's power, bestride, subdue, subjugate, overawe, overcome, gain full play, master, gain mastery, overmaster, reign supreme, rule, run, control, monopolize, take over, take a firm grip, take (a) hold, rage, be all the rage, be rife, spread, spread like wildfire, run through, pervade, permeate, hold all the cards, hold all the aces, hold the whip hand, be in the driving seat, lead by the nose, have under one's thumb, wind (or twist) around one's little finger, wear the trousers (Inf), wear the pants (US inf), throw one's weight around (Inf), catch on (Inf)

ADJECTIVES

11 influential, causal, effectual, effective, persuasive, important, vital, significant, contributing, contributory, decisive, momentous, world-shattering, earth-shaking, telling, prestigious, impressive, potent, powerful, strong, active, busy, meddling, interfering, mighty, forceful, great, superior, ruling, leading, guiding, directing, instructive, educative, reigning, regnant, in the ascendant, rising, in authority,

of authority, commanding, authoritative, tyrannical

12 **appealing**, emotional, moving, affecting,
charming, attractive, gripping, fascinating, irresistible, charismatic, magnetic, mesmeric,
hypnotic, compelling, inspirational, encouraging, inspiring, motivating, suggestive, seductive, tempting, addictive, habit-forming,
infectious, contagious, catching

13 **dominant**, predominant, wide-ranging, international, multinational, monopolistic, prevailing, prevalent, ubiquitous, pervasive, all-
pervading, in the driving seat, on the up and
up (Inf)

ADVERBS

14 **influentially**, causally, effectually, to good
effect, with great (or telling) effect, persuasively, importantly, vitally, significantly, prestigiously, impressively, potently, powerfully,
strongly, forcefully, predominantly, commandingly, authoritatively, with (or by) authority, under someone's influence, within
someone's orbit, tyrannically, internationally,
encouragingly, decisively, momentously,
emotionally, charmingly, irresistibly, charismatically, hypnotically, inspirationally, suggestively, seductively, infectiously, contagiously, ubiquitously, pervasively

234   Tendency

NOUNS

1 **tendency**, tenor, drift, trend, course, current,
stream, fashion, taste, the way things are
going, sign of the times, spirit of the age,
Zeitgeist (Ger), turn, cast, climate, climate of
opinion, influence, contribution
▶ *332 Direction, 340 Attraction, 116 Accord*

2 **attitude**, cast of mind, turn of mind, mind
set, disposition, predisposition, proclivity, susceptibility, affinity, attraction, liability, probability, proneness, bent, inclination, gravitation, leaning, bias, prejudice, partiality, weakness, readiness, preparedness, propensity, predilection, liking, penchant, humour, mood,
vein, grain, strain, tincture, tone, quality,
character, genius, idiosyncrasy
▶ *488 Probability, 588 Intention, 594 Preparation*

3 **aptitude**, ability, talent, natural talent, gift,
instinct
▶ *655 Skill*

VERBS

4 **tend**, have a tendency, show a tendency,
show a trend, bend, have a bent, develop an
attitude, incline, lean, have a leaning, like,
show an affinity, have a propensity, have an
aptitude, have a genius for, show talent, have
natural talent, have a gift, have an instinct,
be biased, show prejudice, have a predisposition, be disposed, gravitate towards, incline

towards, lean towards, prepare, approach, affect, contribute, redound, influence, turn to,
point to, lead to, conduce to, bid fair, bode
well

ADJECTIVES

5 **tending to**, trending, leading, leading to, inclined towards, inclining towards, inclining,
leaning, leaning towards, intending, working
towards, aiming at, pointing to, conducive to,
calculated, calculated to, prejudiced, prejudicial, partial, biased, tendentious, probable,
likely, liable to, apt to, prone to, ready, ready
to, about to, prepared

ADVERBS

6 **probably**, readily, with a strong tendency,
prejudicially, tendentiously, from a biased
standpoint

235   Power

*Power tends to corrupt, and absolute power
corrupts absolutely. Great men are almost
always bad men...There is no worse heresy than
that the office sanctifies the holder of it.* Lord
Acton.

*The greater the power, the more dangerous the
abuse.* Edmund Burke.

Power is the ultimate aphrodisiac. Henry
Kissinger.

*Unlimited power is apt to corrupt the minds of
those who possess it.* William Pitt the Elder.

The balance of power. Robert Walpole.

NOUNS

1 **power**, powerfulness, potency, forcefulness,
might, mightiness, greatness, puissance
(Arch), omnipotence, governance, government, authority, sovereignty, hegemony, control, sway, superiority, ascendancy, prevalence, predominance, influence, persuasion,
charisma, mana, special power, special gift,
occult power, magical power, magic, witchcraft, sorcery, staying power, endurance, stamina, force, driving force, main force, virility,
muscle, brute force, strength, brute strength,
effort, exertion, right arm, right hand, endeavour, stress, strain, gravitation, gravity, weight,
weight of numbers, manpower, staff, personnel, position of power, position of strength,
strong position, vantage ground, high ground,
truth, validity, cogency, emphasis, accent, additional power, extra power, overdrive
▶ *126 Superiority, 688 Authority, 233 Influence,
586 Persuasion, 225 Stability, 237 Strength, 181
Multitude, 646 Worker, 535 Affirmation, 11 Occultism*

2 **ability**, potentiality, potential, capability,
competence, effectuality, effectiveness, efficiency, efficacy, proficiency, capacity, faculty,

property, virtue, attribute, endowment, gift, flair, native wit, talent, skill, qualification, aptitude, fitness, scope, range, reach, compass, grasp, what it takes, know-how (Inf), the real stuff (Inf), the right stuff (Inf), street smarts (US inf)

▶ *486 Possibility, 655 Skill*

3 **vitality**, dynamism, vigour, energy, vivacity, animation, verve, liveliness, drive, spirit, get-up-and-go (Inf), spunk (Inf), pep (Inf), zip (Inf)

4 **energy**, internal energy, chemical energy, mass energy, rest energy, potential energy, work, binding energy, kinetic energy, heat, electrical energy, radiant energy, atomic energy, nuclear energy, mechanical energy, muscle power, pedal power, engine power, horsepower, manpower, electric power, hydroelectric power, hydraulic power, water power, steam power, nuclear power, atomic power, force of inertia, resistance, friction, force, field of force, force of gravity, centrifugal force, buoyancy, compression, spring, springiness, elasticity, pressure, head, steam pressure, full head of steam, electricity, magnetism, magnetic force, magnetic field, attraction, repulsion, polarity, electromagnetism, electromagnetic field, charge, electromotive force, potential, electrical potential, tension, high tension, potential difference, motive power, pulling power, traction, pushing power, thrust, jet, jet propulsion, momentum, angular momentum, impetus, suction, expulsion

▶ *340 Attraction, 338 Propulsion, 341 Repulsion*

5 **unit of work**, erg, joule, calorie, foot-pound, poundal, unit of electrical power, voltage, volt, wattage, watt, kilowatt, megawatt, ohm, amperage, ampere, amp

▶ *56 Physics*

6 **source of energy**, fossil fuel, coal, gas, natural gas, oil, nuclear fuel, nuclear power, renewable energy source, wind power, solar power, solar energy, geothermal power, hydroelectricity, wave power, tidal power, powerhouse, power plant, power station, generating station, electricity substation, pumped storage scheme, hydroelectric station, waterfall, tidal barrage, water wheel, windmill, wind farm, solar cell, solar battery, solar panel, heat exchanger, heater, generator, motor, oscillator, alternator, commutator, magneto, dynamo, turbine, turbocharger, turbosupercharger

▶ *410 Fuel, 408 Heat, 409 Cold, 439 Light, 365 Oscillation, 364 Rotation*

7 **electrical power**, electricity, electric light, induced electricity, photoelectricity, thermoelectricity, piezoelectricity, voltaic electricity, galvanic electricity, static electricity, lightning, electrodynamics, electrostatics, induc-tion, inductance, capacitance, resistance, conduction, conductivity, superconductivity, oscillation, frequency, pulse, electric charge, electric shock, electrocution, electric current, direct current, alternating current, circuit, closed circuit, short circuit, electrode, positive electrode, positive, anode, negative electrode, negative, cathode, electrolysis, conductor, semiconductor, superconductor, nonconductor, insulator, lightning conductor, earth, ground (US), live wire, electrification, electricity supply, power line, lead, flex, cord (US), power cord (US), cable, distributor, junction box, pylon, grid, national grid, transformer, power pack, battery, storage battery, accumulator, cell, wet cell, dry cell, fuel cell, photoelectric cell, photocell, valve, tube, vacuum tube, cathode-ray tube, transistor

▶ *64 Electronics*

8 **nuclear power**, atomic power, nucleonics, nuclear physics, thermonuclear reaction, chain reaction, fission, fusion, atom smasher, particle accelerator, linear accelerator, cyclotron, synchrotron, ZETA (Zero-Energy Thermonuclear Apparatus), JET (Joint European Torus), CERN (Conceil européen pour la recherche nucléaire), European Organization for Nuclear Research, International Atomic Energy Agency (IAEA), Nuclear Regulatory Commission (US), Energy Information Administration (US), superconductor, supercollider, atomic pile, nuclear reactor, fast-breeder reactor, advanced gas-cooled reactor (AGR), light water reactor (LWR), pressurized water reactor (PWR), coolant, fuel rod, moderator, radioactivity, fallout, radioactive waste, waste reprocessing, nuclear weapon, nuclear warhead, nuclear missile, atomic bomb, hydrogen bomb, fusion bomb, neutron bomb

▶ *56 Physics, 680 Weapon*

9 **electronics**, electron physics, optics, light, electromagnetic radiation, laser, integrated circuit, microprocessor, microelectronics, microcircuit, computerization, computing, data processing, word processing, desktop publishing (DTP), telecommunications, telegraph, telephone, radio, television, automation

▶ *633 Danger, 534 Communications, 64 Electronics, 56 Physics*

VERBS

10 **be powerful**, have power, be able, lie in one's power, have it in one's power, be capable of, have the talent for, measure up to, exercise power, govern, have authority, manage, control, maintain control, have sway, dominate, compel, use force, force, use brute force, use one's brute strength, exert energy, endeavour, stress, strain, enjoy the power of, win power, come into power, gain power, ascend, prevail, predominate, influence, exert influence, show

potential, have a gift, have a flair, have charisma, show talent, have aptitude, qualify, be fit for, have vitality, have stamina, have drive, have staying power, possess spirit, possess special power, possess magical power, practise witchcraft, have what it takes, have know-how (Inf), be made of the right stuff (Inf), muscle in (Inf)

11 **give power**, empower, enable, authorize, invest with power, vest power in, endow, endow with power, give teeth, arm, strengthen, energize, animate, electrify, charge, transistorize, magnetize, plug in, switch on, turn on, power up, charge up, power, drive, go into overdrive, step on it (Inf), step on the gas (US inf), give it some welly (Inf), give it the gun (Sl), put the hammer down (US sl), soup up (Sl)

12 **generate power**, produce power, power, fuel, pump, radiate, heat, cool, light, transform energy, amplify, store energy, compute

ADJECTIVES

13 **powerful**, potent, mighty, virile, strong, puissant (Arch), great, prevailing, prevalent, predominant, superior, influential, omnipotent, almighty, irresistible, in full control, empowered, endowed, authoritative, sovereign, hegemonic, with full powers, plenipotentiary, at the height of one's powers, potential, virtual, possible, competent, capable, fit, adequate, able, gifted, talented, qualified, equal to, up to, more than a match for, effectual, effective, efficacious, efficient, proficient, forceful, compelling, charismatic, compulsive, cogent, forcible, violent

14 **operative**, working, switched on, workable, armed, having teeth, in force, valid, established

15 **full of energy**, energetic, dynamic, vigorous, lively, vivacious, animated, spirited, attractive, drawing, pulling, impelling, propulsive, moving, motive, locomotive, kinetic, driven, automated, powered up, on-line, pro-active, on stream, live

16 **charged**, supercharged, high-tension, magnetic, polarized, mechanized, mechanical, electric, electrical, electronic, souped-up (Inf)

17 **powered**, electrical, atomic, nuclear, thermonuclear, geothermal, hydroelectric, wave-powered, solar, wind-powered, wind-driven, steam-powered, steam-operated

ADVERBS

18 **powerfully**, potently, strongly, mightily, with telling effect, with might and main, with all one's might, by dint of, by virtue of, prevailingly, prevalently, predominantly, influentially, omnipotently, irresistibly, authoritatively, potentially, virtually, possibly, competently, adequately, effectually, effectively, efficaciously, efficiently, proficiently, forcefully, compellingly, compulsively, co-

gently, forcibly, by force, by force of arms, violently

19 **energetically**, dynamically, vigorously, magnetically, electrically, electronically

236   Powerlessness

NOUNS

1 **powerlessness**, lack of power, absence of power, lack of authority, ineffectiveness, ineffectuality, inefficiency, impotence, inability, incapacity, incompetence, emptiness, barrenness, sterility, sterilization, vasectomy, futility, uselessness, inutility, incapability, ineptitude, unfitness, disqualification, invalidation, decrepitude, frailty, fragility, power vacuum, power failure, energy depletion, neutralization, disarmament, demilitarization

▶ *238 Weakness, 683 Failure, 656 Unskilfulness, 117 Disparity, 614 Uselessness, 699 Restraint*

2 **futile effort**, futile exploit, labour of Sisyphus, dead letter, empty threats, bluster, impotent fury, frustration, all talk and no action

3 **helplessness**, defencelessness, lack of protection, vulnerability, harmlessness, innocence, babyhood, infancy, weakness, softness, meekness

▶ *633 Danger, 865 Innocence, 206 Youth*

4 **disability**, physical weakness, invalidity, weakness, mental handicap, physical handicap, physical disability, sexual impotence, sterility, infertility, prostration, exhaustion, tiredness, fatigue, collapse, breakdown, faint, dead faint, swoon, loss of consciousness, unconsciousness, coma, catatonic fit, catatonia, narcosis, stroke, heart attack, apoplexy, debilitating illness, paralysis, hemiplegia, paraplegia, quadriplegia, tetraplegia, atrophy, ataxia, loss of control, incontinence, mental decay, hardening of the arteries, softening of the brain, dementia, senile dementia, senility, Alzheimer's disease

▶ *207 Age, 650 Fatigue, 624 Ill Health, 628 Deterioration, 510 Insanity*

5 **powerless person**, unauthorized person, figurehead, titular head, invalid, sick (or sickly) person, hermaphrodite, man of straw (or straw man), broken reed, shut-in (US), pushover (Inf), easy mark (US inf), easy meat (Inf), patsy (US sl), schnook (US sl)

VERBS

6 **be powerless**, be impotent, stand defenceless, cannot, not work, not operate, not do, not help, be of no help, not change anything, not alter things, avail nothing, be of no avail, strive in vain, fail, have no power, have no influence, have no say, have no control, get nowhere, have no resistance, feel helpless, wring one's hands, stamp one's feet, gnash one's teeth, do nothing, look on, stand by,

have a hopeless case, have no chance, become unconscious, lose consciousness, lapse into unconsciousness, faint, pass out, collapse, not have a leg to stand on, be like putty in someone's hands, not make the grade (Inf), cut no ice (Inf), not be able to cut the mustard (US inf)

7 **remove power from**, remove authority from, deprive of power, deprive of authority, invalidate, incapacitate, disable, disqualify, abrogate, disarm, demilitarize, neutralize, weaken, emaciate, debilitate, sap, undermine, consume, exhaust, use up

8 **overpower**, disarm, put out of action, knock down, prostrate, bowl over, wind, knock out, tie up, tie hand and foot, numb, benumb, paralyse, cripple, lame, maim, hobble, hamstring, stifle, smother, choke, throttle, suffocate, strangle, garrotte (or garrote), kill, deaden, muzzle, silence, spike someone's guns, put a spoke in someone's wheel, deflate, power down, switch off, put out of commission, take the wind out of someone's sails, throw a spanner in the works (Inf), throw a monkey wrench into (US inf), KO (Sl), nobble (Sl), put the kibosh on (Sl)

▶ 701 Subjection

9 **make impotent**, sterilize, make barren, vasectomize, castrate, geld, spay, neuter, unsex, emasculate, evirate, effeminize, unman, unnerve, enervate, devitalize, fix (Inf), de-ball (US tab sl), de-nut (US tab sl)

ADJECTIVES

10 **powerless**, unable, not able, not enabled, incapable, not empowered, unauthorized, invalid, invalidated, null and void, not lawful, illegal, disfranchised (or disenfranchised), inoperative, unemployed, deactivated, not working, switched off, suspended, out of action, out of order, in abeyance, mothballed, out of circulation, broken, broken down, deposed, disqualified, unqualified, unfit, inept, good-for-nothing, unworkable, worthless, useless, ineffective, ineffectual, inefficacious, inefficient, incompetent, unpowered, without a leg to stand on, dud (Inf), duff (Inf), laid up (Inf), kaput (Sl), buggered (Tab sl), fucked (Tab sl), fucked up (Tab sl)

11 **unprotected**, undefended, unguarded, defenceless, indefensible, ill-equipped, weaponless, unarmed, disarmed, unfortified, exposed, pregnable, untenable, dependent, subject, without resource, orphaned, friendless, vulnerable, harmless, innocent, meek

12 **impotent**, weak, feeble, frail, debilitated, etiolated, tired, fatigued, worn out, tired out, exhausted, used up, decrepit, senile, paraplegic, hemiplegic, paralytic, unconscious, comatose, catatonic, drugged, insensible, incapacitated, disabled, paralysed, quadriplegic, crippled, in-

continent, lacking self-control, prostrate, supine, irresolute, spineless, nerveless, unnerved, demoralized, shell-shocked, hors de combat (Fr), out of the running, helpless, out of control, drifting, rudderless, swamped, waterlogged, on one's beam-ends, grounded, on one's back, all in (Inf), done in (or up) (Inf), beat (Inf), dead beat (Inf), clapped out (Inf), fixed (Inf), belly up (US sl), zonked (Sl)

13 **unsexed**, sterilized, sterile, barren, infertile, vasectomized, emasculated, castrated, gelded, neutered, spayed, caponized, unmanned, effete, sexless, de-balled (US tab sl), de-nutted (US tab sl)

ADVERBS

14 **powerlessly**, illegally, without authority, ineptly, worthlessly, uselessly, ineffectively, ineffectually, inefficiently, incompetently, beyond one, beyond one's power, above one's head, too much for, defencelessly, indefensibly, dependently, harmlessly, innocently, impotently, weakly, feebly, irresolutely, helplessly, in over one's head, out of one's league (US inf)

237 Strength

NOUNS

1 **strength**, power, potency, might, force, mechanical strength, load-bearing capacity, tensile strength, compressive strengh, torsional strength, physical strength, athleticism, physical force, brute force, assertiveness, aggressiveness, aggression, bellicosity, brute strength, virility, manliness, musculature, muscularity, muscle, biceps, triceps, pectorals, laterals, sinews, thews, brawn, burliness, greatness, superiority, effectuality, effectiveness, firmness, steadfastness, determination, stability, durability, endurance, survivability, staying power, stamina, resourcefulness, resolution, stoutheartedness, backbone, courage, pluck, grit, nerve, bravery, toughness, tenacity, resilience, resistance, fortification, protection, impregnability, impenetrability, inviolability, invincibility, invulnerability, unassailability, beefiness (Inf), spunk (Inf), guts (Inf)

▶ 235 Power, 259 Size, 239 Vigour, 690 Severity, 373 Hardness, 378 Toughness, 778 Courage, 574 Resolution, 676 War, 632 Safety, 56 Physics

2 **healthiness**, soundness, fitness, physical fitness, vitality, liveliness, energy, enthusiasm, zeal, compulsion, vehemence, vim, vigour, youth, acuity, keenness, dedication

▶ 623 Health, 396 Life, 769 Cheerfulness, 206 Youth

3 **intensity**, concentration, depth, emphasis, stress, urgency, rashness, cogency, weight, pressure, severity

▶ 780 Rashness

4 **strengthening**, toughening, tempering, reinforcing, hardening, stiffening, fortifying, protecting, invigorating, restoring, convalescing, refreshing, reviving, revivifying, revival, reinforcement, invigoration, restoration, refreshment, tonic, revivification, convalescence
▶ *651 Refreshment, 629 Repair, 623 Health*

5 **athlete**, sportsman (*or* sportswoman), sporty person, amateur athlete, letterman (US), professional athlete, footballer, football player (US), baseball player (US), all-American (US), cricketer, all-round player, all-rounder, gymnast, tumbler, circus performer, acrobat, contortionist, funambulist, tightrope walker, trapeze artist, bareback rider, strongman, weightlifter, boxer, wrestler, sumo wrestler, runner, sprinter, marathon runner, high jumper, pole-vaulter, contender, champion, gold-medallist, runner-up, silver-medallist, bronze-medallist, challenger
▶ *674 Contention, 21 Athletics*

6 **muscleman**, bodybuilder, Mr Universe, superhero, Superman, Supergirl, Batman and Robin, Captain America, Wonder Woman, Tarzan, Rambo, mythical hero, Atlas, Hercules, Titan, Biblical strong men, Samson, Goliath, giant, strong woman, amazon, virago (Arch), tower of strength, bully, bullyboy, bruiser, he-man (Inf), strong-arm man (Inf), tough guy (Inf), heavy (Sl), hunk of a man (Sl), hunk (Sl), hulk (Sl), beefcake (Sl), meathead (Sl), bouncer (Sl), chucker-out (Sl)

VERBS

7 **be strong**, possess strength, have what it takes, come in force, overwhelm, overpower, outmatch, be more than a match for, overmaster, become stronger, rally, recover, revive, convalesce, not weaken, hold out, hold up, bear up, gird (up) one's loins, never say die (Inf), come down (on) like a ton of bricks (Inf), pack a punch (Sl)

8 **strengthen**, make strong, give strength to, lend force to, confirm, underline, underscore, emphasize, stress, reinforce, fortify, protect, entrench, pad, stuff, buttress, prop up, sustain, support, brace, toughen, harden, case-harden, temper, energize, animate, quicken, enliven, invigorate, boost, revive, revivify, reinvigorate, refresh, set someone up properly, set someone on his (*or* her) feet (*or* legs), build up, tune up, strengthen oneself, steel oneself, temper oneself, nerve oneself, screw up one's courage, stiffen, stiffen one's resolve, stiffen the sinews, put life into, put body into, put one's back into, use force, use muscle, beef up (Inf), soup up (Sl)

ADJECTIVES

9 **physically strong**, strong, powerful, athletic, muscular, sinewy, burly, brawny, virile, manly, Herculean, amazonian, strapping,

healthy, hale, hale and hearty, robust, sound, sound in wind and limb, sound as a bell, fit, fit as a fiddle, fit as a flea, in fine fettle, in good health, in good shape, in the pink (of health), hardy, lusty, feisty, vigorous, sturdy, tough, stalwart, stout, strong as a horse, strong as a bull, strong as an ox, strong as a lion, beefy (Inf), red-blooded (Inf), in good nick (Inf)

10 **potent**, forceful, powerful, puissant (Arch), mighty, redoubtable, formidable, great, high-powered, overpowering, overwhelming, superior, compelling, convincing, persuasive, effective, cogent, telling, trenchant, weighty, clear, clear-cut, distinct, marked, unmistakable, urgent, pressing, severe, intense, vehement, extreme, drastic, Draconian, thoroughgoing, deep-rooted, well-established, well-founded, firm, staunch, fervent, fervid, fierce

11 **strong in spirit**, firm, steadfast, determined, resolute, stouthearted, courageous, plucky, resilient, resourceful, acute, keen, dedicated, enthusiastic, energetic, zealous, eager, tough, tenacious, unyielding, brave, assertive, self-assertive, aggressive, bellicose, warlike

12 **strong to the senses**, striking, bold, daring, stark, brilliant, bright, dazzling, glaring, loud, strong-smelling, strong-tasting, biting, mordant, sharp, pungent, piquant, spicy, highly flavoured, highly seasoned, hot, concentrated, undiluted, pure, neat, intoxicating, heady

13 **strengthened**, toughened, reinforced, fortified, armed, well-armed, well-protected, protective, hard-wearing, heavy-duty, on a firm footing, on a firm foundation, well-built, stout, substantial, durable, tough, resistant, restored, revived, braced, buttressed

ADVERBS

14 **strongly**, powerfully, energetically, forcefully, forcibly, by force, by sheer force, in force, with might and main, soundly, hardily, sturdily, stoutly, robustly, ruggedly, fiercely, courageously, tenaciously, bravely, assertively, aggressively, boldly, invulnerably, unyieldingly

15 **acutely**, keenly, enthusiastically, energetically, vigorously, zealously, lustily, resolutely, eagerly, heartily, firmly, fervently, urgently, compulsively, by compulsion, intensely, extremely, drastically, brilliantly, brightly, loudly, sharply, pungently, potently, compellingly, convincingly, persuasively, effectively, distinctly, unmistakably

238   Weakness

Oh, your precious 'lame ducks'! John Galsworthy.

NOUNS

1 **weakness**, lack of strength, feebleness, impotence, enfeeblement, softness, limpness,

flaccidity, floppiness, slackness, looseness, weak foundation, dilapidation, impairment, damage, decay, rust, wear, deactivation, neutralization, adulteration, dilution, feet of clay, instability, fragility, delicateness, delicacy, puniness, smallness, helplessness, innocence, harmlessness, vulnerability, defencelessness, defect, Achilles' heel

▶ 236 *Powerlessness*, 370 *Lightness*, 374 *Softness*, 612 *Unimportance*, 628 *Deterioration*, 620 *Imperfection*, 687 *Adversity*, 206 *Youth*

2 **indecisiveness**, indecision, irresolution, hesitance, doubtfulness, pusillanimity, ineffectuality, slowness, sheepishness, spinelessness, nervelessness, nervousness, timorousness, cowardliness, cowardice, gutlessness (Inf)

▶ 576 *Vacillation*, 224 *Changeableness*, 779 *Cowardice*, 491 *Uncertainty*

3 **poor health**, sickliness, debility, frailty, infirmity, weakliness, faintness, paleness, anaemia, asthenia, thinness, anorexia, anorexia nervosa, senility, caducity, decrepitude, dizziness, giddiness, vertigo, shakiness, lameness, blindness, deafness, loss of strength, weakened state, enervation, deflation, depletion, dissipation, impoverishment, burnout, failure, waning, flagging, weariness, exhaustion, fatigue, tiredness

▶ 624 *Ill Health*, 274 *Thinness*, 207 *Age*, 650 *Fatigue*

4 **weakling**, seven-stone weakling, ninety-pound weakling (US), broken reed, small fry, dupe, victim, milksop, namby-pamby, hypochondriac, invalid, sick person, poor dab (Welsh dial), lame duck, lame dog, kitten, infant, baby, babe-in-arms, big baby, crybaby, coward, teacher's pet, mummy's boy, man of straw, straw man (US), easy mark (US inf), easy meat (Inf), weed (Inf), softy (Inf), pushover (Inf), doormat (Inf), drip (Inf), lightweight (Inf), jellyfish (Inf), (poor) fish (Inf), wimp (Inf), twit (Inf), wet (Inf), patsy (US sl), sissy (Inf), pansy (Sl), nerd (US sl), chicken (Sl)

5 **weak thing**, flimsy item, insubstantial thing, reed, cobweb, gossamer, thread, gossamer thread, sand castle, house built on sand, house of cards, castle in the air, castle in Spain, fragile item, paper, tissue paper, matchstick, matchwood, glass, china, eggshell, water, thin gruel, watered-down soup, dishwater, milk and water, slops (Inf)

VERBS

6 **be weak**, be ill, grow weak, weaken, sicken, faint, languish, flag, fail, fall, drop, droop, flop, wilt, fade, decrease, diminish, decline, dwindle, crumble, wear, wear out, wear thin, yield, sag, give way, break, split, come apart at the seams, fall apart at the seams, shake, tremble, totter, teeter, stagger, dodder, go lame, limp, halt

7 **weaken**, make weak, enfeeble, debilitate, enervate, unnerve, rattle, alarm, shake, relax, slacken, loosen, deflate, diminish, reduce, reduce in number, decimate, extenuate, thin, thin out, lessen, deplete, drain, impoverish, starve, deprive, rob, sap, undermine, impair, damage, invalidate, spoil, mar, disarm, disable, strain, sprain, lame, maim, cripple, hurt, harm, injure, wound, strip, strip bare, denude, expose, adulterate, dilute, water down, shake up, soften up, soften, muffle, mute

ADJECTIVES

8 **weak**, lacking strength, not strong, impotent, powerless, feeble, deprived of strength, enfeebled, unhardened, untempered, soft, limp, flaccid, floppy, drooping, hanging, sagging, unstrung, slack, loose, relaxed, gimcrack, shoddy, jerry-built, rickety, tottery, tottering, teetering, wobbly, creaky, run down, seedy, breakable, brittle, fragile, delicate, puny, small, lightweight, ineffectual, helpless, defenceless, unsafe, unprotected, unguarded, unfortified, untenable, wonky (Inf)

9 **dilapidated**, broken, broken-down, tumbledown, weather-beaten, laid bare, worn, worn out, the worse for wear, on its last legs, rotten, decayed, rusted, withered, diminished, deflated, wasted, depleted, drained, spent, used up, laid up

10 **ill**, sickly, faint, pale, pallid, bloodless, white as a sheet, anaemic, asthenic, groggy, below par, languid, feeble, weakly, weak as a child, weak as a baby, weak as a kitten, weak as water, wasted, thin, skinny, emaciated, skin-and-bone, skeletal, anorexic, frail, decrepit, infirm, crippled, lame, game, limping, hobbling, shaky, unsteady, unsound, feeble-minded, imbecile, slow, dim-witted (Inf), poorly (Inf), under the weather (Inf), green about the gills (Inf), gammy (Sl), gimpy (US sl)

11 **weakened**, debilitated, enervated, dissipated, burnt out, sapped, wearied, exhausted, fatigued, tired, laid low, weary, worn out, on one's last legs, on the wane, failed, impoverished

12 **weak-willed**, indecisive, irresolute, wavering, dithering, pusillanimous, vacillating, hesitant, doubtful, half-hearted, nerveless, unnerved, nervous, timid, timorous, cowardly, sheepish, effete, mealy-mouthed, spineless, lily-livered, chicken-hearted, sissy, namby-pamby, limp-wristed, weak-kneed, scared, yellow (Inf), gutless (Inf), chicken (Sl)

13 **insufficient**, inadequate, insubstantial, inconclusive, invalid, unconvincing, unsatisfactory, lacking, wanting, deficient, flimsy, slight, small, little, thin, light, shallow, hollow, faulty, substandard, poor, pathetic, under strength, below par, imperceptible, inaudible, invisible, faint, low, distant, muffled, soft,

muted, quiet, diluted, runny, tasteless, insipid, watery, milk-and-water, wishy-washy (Inf)

ADVERBS

14 **weakly**, impotently, softly, ineffectually, without effect, helplessly, unsafely, faintly, languidly, feebly, weakly, unsteadily, while ill, on one's last legs, unsoundly, indecisively, irresolutely, half-heartedly, nervously, timidly, cowardly, in a cowardly way, sheepishly, insufficiently, inadequately, inconclusively, unsatisfactorily, slightly, thinly, lightly, poorly, pathetically, imperceptibly, inaudibly, quietly, tastelessly, insipidly

239   Vigour

NOUNS

1 **vigour**, energy, physical energy, exertion, effort, activity, excitement, enthusiasm, stimulation, inspiration, dynamism, strength, power, robustness, force, forcefulness, life, animation, exhilaration, spirit, pluck, mettle, liveliness, intensity, impetus, dash, élan, éclat, vitality, health, invigoration, refreshment, revitalization, freshness, zest, verve, sparkle, drive, keenness, lustiness, gusto, pep (Inf), spunk (Inf), guts (Inf), kick (Inf), pepper (US inf), punch (Inf), snap (Inf), pizzazz (or pizazz) (Inf), zip (Inf), go (Inf), get-up-and-go (Inf), wallop (Inf), welly (Inf), vim (Sl), oomph (Sl), piss and vinegar (Tab sl), balls (Tab sl)

▶ *642 Activity, 235 Power, 237 Strength, 648 Haste, 554 Emphasis, 762 Joy, 778 Courage, 241 Violence, 574 Resolution, 575 Perseverance, 366 Agitation*

VERBS

2 **be full of vigour**, thrive, have zest, enjoy life, enthuse, burst with energy, burst with health, never stop, rush around, be up and doing, exert oneself, drive, push, raise the pressure, put on a spurt, pull out all the stops, strike hard, hit hard, tell upon, make an impression, rush around like a chicken with its head cut off, steam away (Inf), get up a good head of steam (Inf), give it some welly (Inf), have a lot of pizzazz (or pizazz) (Inf), have a lot of get-up-and-go (Inf), give it the gun (Sl), go like a bat out of hell (Sl), go like gangbusters (US sl), be full of piss and vinegar (Tab sl), have balls (Tab sl)

3 **invigorate**, activate, energize, galvanize, exhilarate, electrify, intensify, double, redouble, rouse, kindle, inflame, excite, stimulate, enliven, put life into, pep up, ginger up, boost, fire up, hike up, step up, wind up, act like a tonic, give heart to, hearten, put heart into, egg on, cheer on, inspire, intoxicate, freshen, refresh, revive, restore, reinvigorate, revitalize, give an edge to, sharpen, make glow, fertilize,

bump up (Inf), psych up (Inf), root for (Inf), pep up (Inf), step on the gas (Inf), turn up the juice (Sl), soup up (Sl)

ADJECTIVES

4 **vigorous**, energetic, active, dynamic, powerful, strong, forceful, forcible, strenuous, vehement, intense, animated, spirited, vibrant, brisk, lively, vital, healthy, spry, hale, hale and hearty, hardy, zestful, lusty, feisty, mettlesome, strapping, virile, extrovert, extroverted, outgoing, robust, effective, efficient, enterprising, go-ahead, thrusting, aggressive, keen, enthusiastic, flourishing, growing, red-blooded (Inf), full of beans (Inf), full of pep (Inf), peppy (Inf), nippy (Inf), spunky (Inf), snappy (Inf), punchy (Inf), zippy (Sl), pushy (Inf), go-getting (Inf)

5 **invigorating**, healthy, bouncy, bouncing, fresh, exhilarating, rousing, stimulating, inspiring, exciting, bracing, strengthening, reinvigorating, reviving, revivifying, restoring, rejuvenating, refreshing, revitalizing

ADVERBS

6 **with vigour**, vigorously, energetically, forcefully, forcibly, with telling effect, straight from the shoulder, con brio, lustily, zestfully, hard, at full tilt, all out, hammer and tongs, firing on all cylinders, with the throttle wide open, full pelt, with a vengeance, with a will, like a chicken with its head cut off, flat out (Inf), full steam ahead (Inf), like mad (Inf), like crazy (Inf), like hell (Inf), like a bat out of hell (Sl), like gangbusters (US sl)

240   Inertness

NOUNS

1 **inertness**, inertia, inactivity, inaction, stillness, motionlessness, indolence, idleness, lifelessness, deathliness, languor, torpor, torpidity, paralysis, insensibility, numbness, vegetation, stagnation, quiescence, dormancy, latency, fallowness, apathy, indifference, dullness, sloth, slowness, sluggishness, laziness, sleepiness, hibernation, laxity, slackness, passivity, passiveness, peacefulness, impassivity, immobility, stolidity, inexcitability, indecisiveness, indecision, irresolution, gutlessness (Inf)

▶ *641 Inaction, 643 Inactivity, 325 Motionlessness, 527 Latency, 783 Indifference, 761 Insensitivity, 404 Insensibility, 328 Slowness, 247 Infertility, 576 Vacillation, 675 Peace, 238 Weakness, 236 Powerlessness*

2 **inert person**, heavy sleeper, dolt, dullard, comatose patient, vegetable (Inf), cabbage (Inf)

3 **inert thing**, extinct volcano, dormant volcano, inanimate object, sailboat on calm waters, flag on a windless day, broken clock, ghost town, unexploded bomb, dud (Inf)

VERBS

4 **be inert**, sleep, slumber, doze, laze around, lie, lie still, lie idle, lie in wait, lurk, smoulder, hang fire, hold one's fire, hold one's breath, hold one's horses, stagnate, vegetate, just sit there, just stand there, just lie there, not stir, freeze, snooze (Inf), have (or take) forty winks (Inf), nod off (Inf), lie doggo (Inf)

ADJECTIVES

5 **inert**, inactive, passive, impassive, apathetic, indifferent, unexcitable, pacific, unaggressive, unwarlike, peaceful, unreactive, indecisive, irresolute, unresponsive, stolid, idle, lazy, indolent, slack, lax, limp, flaccid, heavy, slothful, lumpish, doltish, sluggish, slow, slumberous (Fml), dull, numb, dormant, smouldering, latent, dead, lifeless, languid, torpid, insensible, hibernating, sleepy, immobile, unmoving, motionless, still, static, stagnant, stagnating, vegetating, paralysed, quiet, quiescent, fallow, gutless (Inf)

6 **suspended**, pending, in abeyance, switched off, on hold, on ice, in reserve, abrogated, off the active list, deactivated, uninfluential, powerless

ADVERBS

7 **inertly**, inactively, passively, impassively, apathetically, indifferently, peacefully, idly, lazily, indolently, limply, sluggishly, slowly, numbly, latently, lifelessly, languidly, insensibly, sleepily, motionlessly, quietly, at rest, in suspense, in abeyance, on hold, on ice, in reserve, in cold storage (Inf), in the deepfreeze (Inf)

241 Violence

So soon as the man overtook me, he was but a word and a blow. John Bunyan.

NOUNS

1 **violence**, ferocity, vehemence, excess, force, severity, virulence, intensity, power, strength, vigour, bluster, roughness, rough handling, harshness, fierceness, aggression, wildness, fury, frenzy, passion, ferment, effervescence, agitation, turbulence, storminess, impetuosity, forcefulness, might, energy, boisterousness, destructiveness, murderousness

▶ *235 Power, 237 Strength, 239 Vigour, 690 Severity, 366 Agitation, 244 Destruction*

2 **physical violence**, physical cruelty, physical abuse, child abuse, torture, hammer blows, strong-arm tactics, thuggery, hooliganism, vandalism, terrorism, brute force, brutality, bestiality, savagery, barbarity, bloodlust, bloodthirstiness, blood-letting, slaughter, homicide, murder, rape, sexual assault, indecent assault, violation, gang rape, male rape

▶ *832 Malevolence, 406 Physical Pain, 398 Killing*

3 **instance of violence**, onrush, assault, charge, sortie, attack, outburst, outbreak, rush, commotion, disturbance, tumult, brouhaha, riot, row, uproar, roughhouse, fisticuffs, fracas, clash, crash, twist, sprain, fracture, wrench, dislocation, shock, outrage, atrocity, murder, bloodbath, throe, paroxysm, fit, convulsion, spasm, tremor, earthquake, quake, tidal wave, flood, cataclysm, eruption, explosion, detonation, blow-up, flare-up, blast, burst, bursting open, dissilience, rumpus (Sl), ruckus (US sl), punch-up (Inf)

▶ *670 Attack, 423 Loudness, 674 Contention, 309 Distortion*

4 **violent person or animal**, savage, beast, savage beast, wild beast, brute, monster, dragon, demon, devil, hellhound, hound of Hell, Hound of the Baskervilles, mad dog, wolf, she-wolf, tiger, tigress, hellcat, he-man, hulk, caveman, Neanderthal, barbarian, vandal, rough, tough, tough guy, ruffian, mugger, thug, hooligan, bully, bullyboy, bovver boy, terror, holy terror, terrorist, revolutionary, militant, anarchist, agitator, assassin, murderer, mass murderer, sex murderer, serial killer, rapist, hangman, executioner, butcher, slaughterer, man of blood, Herod, Boadicea, psychopath, homicidal maniac, madman, thunderer, fire raiser, arsonist, pyromaniac, firebrand, fire-eater, hotspur (Arch), madcap, hell-raiser, bravo, desperado, termagant, fury, spitfire, shrew, virago, Amazon

▶ *398 Killing, 510 Insanity, 689 Anarchy*

5 **violent weather**, storm, tempest, cloudburst, downpour, rainstorm, hailstorm, snowstorm, blizzard, flood, flash flood, gully washer (US dial), thunder, thunder and lightning, fulguration, squall, tornado, cyclone, hurricane, typhoon, gale, strong wind, war of the elements, weather, bad weather, inclement weather, rough weather, dirty weather, foul weather, magnetic storm, dust storm, sandstorm, sirocco

ADJECTIVES

6 **violent**, ferocious, vehement, excessive, outrageous, severe, virulent, intense, extreme, acute, unmitigated, sharp, blustering, blustery, brisk, abrupt, brusque, rude, bluff, rough, harsh, fierce, aggressive, tyrannical, heavy-handed, forceful, forcible, strong, powerful, mighty, vigorous, energetic, wild, furious, infuriated, angry, on the rampage, on the warpath, fuming, frenzied, frantic, frenetic, in hysterics, hysterical, kicking, struggling, thrashing, mad, insane, maddened, crazed, enraged, berserk, intemperate, immoderate, unbridled, unrestrained, out of control, uncontrollable, ungovernable, unruly, untamed, raging, rabid, like a mad dog, like a mad bull, like a raging bull, inextinguishable, irrepressible, ebullient, heated, inflamed, hot, red-

hot, flaming, scorching, fiery, impassioned, passionate, ardent, fervent, eruptive, bursting, convulsive, spasmodic, destructive, ruinous, catastrophic, cataclysmic, overwhelming, devastating, explosive, volcanic, seismic, boiling, effervescent, agitated, disturbed, turbulent, tumultuous, tempestuous, stormy, impetuous, riotous, uproarious, boisterous, rampant, charging, roaring, desperate, gnashing, howling, murderous, barbarous, savage, brutal, bestial, cruel, vicious, bloody, bloodthirsty, ravening, hot-blooded, hotheaded, headstrong, bellicose, warlike, threatening, tigerish, waspish

▶ *237 Strength, 235 Power, 239 Vigour, 366 Agitation, 690 Severity, 423 Loudness, 832 Malevolence, 244 Destruction, 398 Killing, 510 Insanity*

VERBS

7 **be violent**, rush about, run riot, run wild, run amok, dash, rush headlong, hurtle, hurl oneself, crash in, burst in, break out, burst out, surge forward, charge, stampede, break the peace, raise a storm, riot, roughhouse, kick up a row, kick up a shindig, rampage, go on the rampage, go on the warpath, rage, storm, bluster, roar, come in like a lion, see red, go berserk, lose control, resort to violence, resort to fisticuffs, take up arms, take to arms, rebel

▶ *648 Haste, 423 Loudness*

8 **use violence**, force, use force, strike, hit, mug, beat up, do violence to, assault, abuse, violate, rape, ravish, torture, ill-treat, break, smash, destroy, strain, pull, wrench, twist, sprain, dislocate, fracture, force open, blow open, break open, break in, burst in, shock, shake, clobber (Sl)

▶ *406 Physical Pain, 244 Destruction, 309 Distortion, 366 Agitation, 832 Malevolence, 601 Misuse, 670 Attack*

9 **make violent**, stir up, jolt, goad, whip, whip up, lash, incite, fire, fire up, inflame, blow on the embers, add fuel to the flames, foment, exacerbate, aggravate, whet, sharpen, irritate, exasperate, anger, infuriate, lash (or whip up) into a fury, enrage, madden, make mad, wave a red flag before a bull

▶ *768 Aggravation*

ADVERBS

10 **violently**, ferociously, vehemently, severely, intensely, abruptly, rudely, harshly, fiercely, forcefully, forcibly, powerfully, vigorously, by storm, by force, hammer and tongs, tooth and nail, like mad, headlong, precipitately, head first, head foremost, like Gadarene swine, like a bull at a gate, like a battering ram, at the point of a sword (or gun or knife), at gunpoint, at knifepoint, tyrannously, tyrannically, highhandedly, neck and crop, bodily, at one fell swoop, with a vengeance, beyond all reason

242 Moderation

By God, Mr Chairman, at this moment I stand astonished at my own moderation! Clive of India.

Not too much zeal. Talleyrand.

Moderation is a fatal thing, Lady Hunstanton. Nothing succeeds like excess. Oscar Wilde.

NOUNS

1 **moderation**, moderateness, reasonableness, restraint, check, control, self-control, equanimity, composure, sang-froid, sedateness, self-possession, sobriety, coolness, calmness, quietness, mildness, gentleness, nonviolence, temperance, steadiness, impartiality, neutrality, fairness, justness, judiciousness, justice, due measure, golden mean, average, happy medium, middle way, halfway house, correction, adjustment, modulation, regulation, mutual concession, trade-off, give and take, compromise, mitigation, relaxation, relief, letup, remission, alleviation, easing, assuagement, mollification, calming, quietening, sedation, tranquillization, abatement, lessening, reduction, diminution, decrease

▶ *873 Sobriety, 422 Silence, 325 Motionlessness, 124 Average, 717 Compromise, 630 Remedy, 649 Ease, 629 Repair, 129 Decrease*

2 **moderator**, controller, calming influence, restraining hand, mollifier, peacemaker, pacifier, mediator, arbitrator, arbiter, judge, referee, umpire, chairperson, cushion, buffer, shock absorber, damper, restraint, brake, clamp, killjoy, wet blanket, stopper, downer, dummy, sedative, tranquillizer, soporific, sleeping pill, barbiturate, bromide, nightcap, lullaby, soothing influence, palliative, lenitive, demulcent, alleviative, rosewater, painkiller, analgesic, anodyne, anaesthetic, opiate, opium, laudanum, oil on troubled waters, balm, balm of Gilead

▶ *678 Mediation, 699 Restraint, 630 Remedy*

VERBS

3 **be moderate**, take the middle way, follow the golden mean, stay on an even keel, stay within bounds, sober up, calm down, settle, settle down, keep the peace, give up arms, disarm, go quietly, go out like a lamb, remit, relent, relax, ease off, go easy, compromise

▶ *873 Sobriety, 649 Ease, 717 Compromise*

4 **moderate**, correct, adjust, modulate, regulate, mediate, judge, arbitrate, chair, take the chair, preside, referee, umpire, curb, tame, check, keep within bounds, restrict, constrict, constrain, limit, keep within limits, repress, restrain, chasten, govern, control, clamp, clamp down on, calm, pour oil on troubled waters, temper, mollify, soften, cushion, break the fall of, put a damper on, damp, dampen,

deaden, cool, subdue, sedate, tranquillize, anaesthetize, still, quiet, quieten, hush, lull, rock, rock to sleep, sweeten, keep sweet, dulcify, mitigate, palliate, extenuate, qualify, weaken, obtund, blunt, dull, take the edge off, assuage, ease, soothe, relieve, alleviate, lighten, neutralize, take the sting out of, deactivate, smooth over, bring round, talk round, disarm, appease, pacify, allay, abate, lessen, reduce, diminish, decrease, play down, moderate one's language, censor, blue-pencil, tone down, euphemize, sober, sober down, throw cold water on, reduce the temperature, bank down the fires, slacken, relax, comfort, softpedal (Inf)

▶ *678 Mediation, 677 Pacification, 699 Restraint, 630 Remedy, 649 Ease, 231 Counteraction, 629 Repair, 129 Decrease, 653 Management*

5 **moderate one's hunger**, assuage one's hunger, satisfy one's appetite, assuage one's thirst, quench one's thirst, slake one's thirst

ADJECTIVES

6 **moderate**, medium, equable, balanced, steady, not extreme, not excessive, modest, judicious, just, fair, nonviolent, harmless, gentle, gentle as a lamb, mild, mild as milk, milk-and-water, weak, poor, middling, fair to middling, mediocre, indifferent, average, ordinary, passable, unexceptional, unremarkable, limited, restricted, measured, sensible, rational, reasonable, within reason, within limits (*or* bounds), restrained, controlled, chastened, subdued, quiet, peaceable, pacific, still, untroubled, peaceful, tranquil, self-controlled, low-key, temperate, tempered, sober, calm, cool, composed, cool, calm, and collected, so-so (Inf)

▶ *124 Average, 422 Silence, 325 Motionlessness, 873 Sobriety*

7 **politically moderate**, neutral, liberal, tolerant, middle-of-the-road, centre, left of centre, nonextreme, non-radical, non-reactionary, mugwumpish, noncommittal, wishy-washy

8 **moderating**, lenitive, soothing, nonirritant, alleviative, assuaging, easing, painkilling, analgesic, anodyne, calming, calmative, sedative, tranquillizing, narcotic, hypnotic, mesmeric, soporific, smooth, soft, bland, emollient, demulcent, lubricating, comforting, disarming, pacificatory

▶ *630 Remedy, 677 Pacification*

ADVERBS

9 **moderately**, in moderation, with moderation, within limits, within bounds, within reason, reasonably, within range, to a degree, to some extent, fairly, pretty, quite, rather, somewhat, slightly, at half speed, equably, judiciously, gently, weakly, temperately, calmly, half-heartedly, nervously

243 Production

NOUNS

1 **production**, making, producing, preparation, creation, invention, innovation, origination, original work, originality, creative impulse, creative urge, inspiration, discovery, doing, productivity, productiveness, output, throughput, turnout, effort, endeavour, attempt, try, undertaking, project, enterprise, performance, execution, accomplishment, achievement, art, painting, sculpture, writing, composition, musicianship, musical composition, authorship, literary composition, literary work, assembly of materials, cogitation, conception, formulation, concoction, brewing, fermenting, moulding, forming, shaping, casting, technology, workmanship, skill, handiwork, craftsmanship, design, planning, organization, structure

▶ *201 Newness, 246 Fertility, 640 Action, 644 Work, 596 Attempt, 655 Skill*

2 **manufacture**, manufacturing, making, fabrication, construction, building, engineering, civil engineering, tectonics, architecture, erection, setting up, establishment, business, industry, heavy industry, light industry, sunrise industry, processing, process, treatment, machining, assembly, machine, machinery, plant, conveyor belt, assembly line, production line, workshop, factory, workshop practice, technology, low technology, intermediate technology, ecodevelopment, industrialization, increased output, mass production, automation, high technology, new technology, computerization, robotics, development, growth, agriculture, growing, market gardening, farming, factory farming, stockbreeding, animal husbandry

▶ *63 Engineering, 43 Architecture, 361 Raising, 647 Workshop, 68 Agriculture, 245 Reproduction*

3 **product**, manufacture, artefact (*or* artifact), article, finished article, item, manufactured item, thing, object, creation, creature, result, consequence, effect, outcome, issue, output, turnout, extract, essence, decoction, concoction, confection, compound, end-product, by-product, spin-off, offshoot, waste product, waste, slag, leavings, fallout

4 **mental product**, brainchild, brainwave, figment, figment of the imagination, fiction, idea

5 **work of art**, production, performance, work, *oeuvre* (Fr), composition, piece, musical composition, opus, sonata, symphony, concerto, ballet, opera, literary composition, literary work, work of literature, piece of writing, book, pamphlet, article, poem, work of fiction, story, short story, short novel, novella, novel, full-length novel, theatrical production, play,

sketch, film, movie, short, feature film, B-feature, B-movie, travelogue

6 **great work**, magnum opus, *chef-d'oeuvre* (Fr), masterwork, masterpiece, crowning achievement

▶ *227 Effect, 644 Work, 48 Literature, 49 Music, 50 Painting and Sculpture, 51 Performing Arts, 46 Dancing and Ballet*

7 **produce**, goods and services, gross national product (GNP), gross domestic product (GDP), goods, merchandise, wares, commodity, pottery, earthenware, porcelain, china, stoneware, ironware, kitchenware, hardware, ironmongery, brown goods, fabric, cloth, textile, drapery, white goods, hosiery, animal products, meat, dairy products, milk, butter, cheese, cream, yoghurt, eggs, skin, fur, leather, hide, plant products, fruit, flower, blossom, berry, stalk, leaf, heart, head, crop, harvest, vintage, yield, interest, return, increase, dividend, gain, profit, revenue, income, offspring, baby, child, young, egg, seed, spawn, young creature

▶ *44 Ceramics, 67 Fabrics and Dyeing, 45 Cookery, 128 Increase, 721 Gain, 746 Payment, 206 Youth, 245 Reproduction*

8 **construction**, structure, building, edifice, piece of architecture, pile, dome, tower, high-rise building, skyscraper, office block, block of flats, apartment building, church, chapel, cathedral, temple, mausoleum, tomb, cenotaph, monument, ancient monument, pyramid, ziggurat, acropolis, Colosseum, Coliseum, theatre, hospital, college, school, hall, habitation, house, great house, mansion, stately home, palace, castle, fort, fortress, folly, stonework, brickwork, bricks and mortar, timbering, half-timbering, wattle and daub

▶ *382 Structure, 256 Habitat, 399 Burial, 7 Religion, 671 Defence*

9 **producer**, maker, creator, God, Nature, Mother Nature, originator, inventor, discoverer, prime mover, instigator, innovator, founder, founding father, founder member, establisher, begetter, onlie begetter (Arch), father, mother, parent, creative artist, author, writer, poet, playwright, dramatist, artist, painter, sculptor, composer, musician, director, stage director, film director, television director, play producer, film producer, programme-maker, radio producer, television producer, designer, planner, developer, builder, constructor, contractor, architect, engineer, fabricator, manufacturer, industrialist, entrepreneur, business executive, businessman, businesswoman, worker, labourer, artificer, artisan, craftsman, craftswoman, craftworker, planter, grower, cultivator, gardener, plantsman, plantswoman, farmer, stockbreeder, sheep farmer, rancher (US), grazier

(Aus), miner, prospector

▶ *156 Beginning, 226 Cause, 228 Motive, 245 Reproduction, 646 Worker, 653 Management, 68 Agriculture*

VERBS

10 **produce**, make, create, originate, invent, innovate, fabricate, engineer, manufacture, output, mine, quarry, extract, exploit, process, industrialize, develop industrially, mechanize, automate, computerize, mass-produce, synthesize, blend, concoct, combine, put together, cobble together, make up, assemble, build, construct, erect, set up, establish, found, institute, constitute, organize, structure, arrange, stage, direct, bring about, set in motion, cause, beget, bear, give birth to, spawn, bring into the world, bring into being, bring into existence, generate, engender, breed, hatch, sow, grow, farm, cultivate, raise, rear, bring up, educate, train, develop, evolve, cogitate, cogitate upon, think of, imagine, think up, conceive, dream up, plan, devise, formulate, do, perform, achieve, accomplish, implement, carry out, execute, effect, yield, supply, provide, furnish, give, present, bring out, take out, show, reveal, unfold, uncover, find, discover, write, author (US), compose, paint, shape, form, mould, fashion, frame, design, spin, weave, knit, sew, run up, carve, chisel, sculpt, forge, cast, coin, mint, mill, machine, prefabricate, turn out, knock out, churn out, multiply, reproduce, propagate, make by hand, craft, custom-build, customize, bash out (Inf), get up (Inf)

▶ *226 Cause, 245 Reproduction, 382 Structure, 152 Arrangement, 519 Imagination, 461 Thought, 48 Literature, 49 Music, 50 Painting and Sculpture, 606 Provision, 729 Giving*

ADJECTIVES

11 **productive**, creative, innovative, inventive, original, formative, structural, constructive, architectonic, manufacturing, industrial, industrialized, developed, mechanized, automated, high-technology, computerized, robotic, postindustrial, nonindustrial, underdeveloped, developing, low-technology, agricultural, fertile, fruitful, fecund, prolific, rich, profitable, remunerative, lucrative, paying, high-yielding, interest-bearing, worthwhile, high-tech (Inf), low-tech (Inf)

▶ *246 Fertility, 606 Provision, 610 Excess, 128 Increase, 721 Gain, 617 Worth*

12 **produced**, created, made, man-made, synthetic, artificial, manufactured, processed, ready-made, machine-made, untouched by human hand, mass-produced, factory-made, handmade, done by hand, home-made, homespun, tailor-made, architect-designed, craftsman-built, custom-built, invented, thought of, dreamed up, imagined, devised, worked

out, discovered, begotten, born, bred, hatched, sown, grown, raised, reared, brought up, educated

ADVERBS

13 **productively**, creatively, innovatively, inventively, fruitfully, prolifically, profitably, remuneratively

244 Destruction

NOUNS

1 **destruction**, unmaking, undoing, nullification, annihilation, obliteration, deletion, erasure, liquidation, elimination, extermination, extinction, abolition, abolishment, repression, suppression, silencing, stifling, smothering, suffocation, threatening, insidiousness, subversion, overturning, overthrow, prostration, precipitation

▶ *100 Nonexistence, 546 Obliteration, 699 Restraint*

2 **destroying**, demolition, demolishment, flattening, razing, knocking down, decomposition, dissolution, breaking up, disruption, shattering, crushing, grinding, pulverization, disintegration, shredding, incineration, defoliation, eradication, uprooting, deracination, extirpation, decimation, slaughter, massacre, genocide, mass murder, mass destruction, killing, murder, hatchet job (Inf)

▶ *141 Disintegration, 398 Killing, 384 Powderiness, 408 Heat*

3 **destructiveness**, wanton destructiveness, wanton destruction, vandalism, sabotage, arson, fire-raising, iconoclasm

4 **ruin**, downfall, someone's undoing, crushing blow, knockout blow, knockout punch, fatal blow, ruination, perdition, disaster, calamity, catastrophe, act of God, collapse, debacle, upheaval, cataclysm, breakdown, irretrievable breakdown, crack-up, failure, utter failure, meltdown, China syndrome, break-up, crash, smash, smash-up, write-off, wreck, shipwreck, sinking, wreckage, ruins, ancient ruins, dilapidation, wrack, rack and ruin, loss, total loss, Waterloo, bankruptcy, insolvency, road to ruin, slippery slope, the beginning of the end, *coup de grâce* (Fr), end, end of the world, apocalypse, doom, doomsday, crack of doom, knell, death knell

▶ *683 Failure, 722 Loss, 362 Lowering, 136 Separation, 157 End*

5 **havoc**, damage, turmoil, confusion, mayhem, chaos, devastation, laying waste, raid, raiding, despoiling, spoliation, pillage, looting, rape, rapine, depredation, explosion, blitz, nuclear blast, nuclear winter, desolation, scene of desolation, scene of destruction, disaster area, wasteland, desert, desert waste, wilderness, scorched earth, shambles, carnage, slaughterhouse, holocaust, hecatomb

▶ *151 Disorder*

6 **destroyer**, wrecker, spoiler, despoiler, raider, ravager, pillager, looter, arsonist, pyromaniac, demolisher, leveller, Luddite, iconoclast, destructionist, annihilationist, nihilist, anarchist, revolutionary, revolutionist, saboteur, vandal, defacer, eraser, rubber, extinguisher, liquidator, exterminator, killer, murderer, assassin, executioner, hangman, barbarian, Hun, Vandal, Viking, berserker, death, the grim reaper, the angel of death, time, the scythe of time, time's scythe, the hand of time, hatchet man (Inf), hit man (Sl)

▶ *689 Anarchy, 398 Killing, 397 Death*

7 **agent of destruction**, plague, pestilence, disease, bubonic plague, the Black Death, cholera, AIDS, locusts, moth, woodworm, dry rot, wet rot, rust, mildew, blight, potato blight, wear, wear and tear, erosion, decay, corrosion, corrosive, acid, poison, pesticide, defoliant, Agent Orange, radiation, nuclear fallout, natural disaster, landslide, landslip, avalanche, earthquake, fire, flood, inundation, storm, the Four Horsemen of the Apocalypse (conquest, war, famine, disease), Fury, avenging angel, weapon, dagger, sword, bow and arrow, crossbow, longbow, slingshot, catapult, gun, cannon, machine gun, explosive, gunpowder, dynamite, blasting powder, nitroglycerine, TNT, Semtex, bomb, nuclear missile, nuclear warhead, nuclear weapon, blockbuster, bulldozer, battering ram, juggernaut

▶ *631 Blight, 624 Ill Health, 628 Deterioration, 680 Weapon*

VERBS

8 **destroy**, unmake, undo, bankrupt, destruct, annihilate, liquidate, terminate, end, put an end to, exterminate, put down, put out of his (*or* her) misery, put away, do away with, make away with, get rid of, dispose of, dispatch, decimate, massacre, slaughter, kill, murder, quell, extinguish, quench, put out, snuff out, blow out, blow away, stamp out, extirpate, eradicate, deracinate, uproot, root up, abolish, axe, invalidate, tear up, revoke, abrogate, cancel, obliterate, efface, expunge, wipe out, wipe off the map, erase, rub out, blot out, strike out, delete, scratch out, nullify, annul, quash, squash, suppress, repress, sit on, keep down, clamp down on, silence, muzzle, muffle, blanket, stifle, smother, suffocate, strangle, drown, submerge, overturn, subvert, overthrow, throw out, precipitate, scatter, disperse, dispel, dissipate, dissolve, vaporize, evaporate, lose, sacrifice, neutralize, counteract, negate, zap (Sl), do in (Inf), do for (Inf), chuck out (Inf)

▶ *100 Nonexistence, 398 Killing, 546 Obliteration, 162 Dispersion, 231 Counteraction, 536 Negation*

9 **demolish**, dismantle, take apart, take to pieces, take to bits, tear apart, rend asunder, tear (or rend) to pieces, tear (or rend) to bits, tear to rags, tear to shreds, tear limb from limb, pick (or pluck) to pieces, pull to pieces, pull apart, unbuild, break, break down, break up, blow away, carry away, blow down, knock down, fell, cut down, pull down, tear down, throw down, bulldoze, steamroller, flatten, level, raze, raze to the ground, lay in the dust, mow down, cut to pieces, butcher, slaughter, knock over, topple, kick over, overturn, upset, overthrow, subvert, cause the downfall of, turn upside down, invert, sap (or undermine) the foundations of, mine, blast, explode, dynamite, blow up, blow to bits, blow to smithereens, blow to kingdom come, bombard, bomb, blitz, shatter, smash, smash up, shiver, smash to matchwood, smash to smithereens, wreck, pulp, crush, crush to pieces, grind, grind (or turn) to dust, grind to powder, pulverize, shred, grind into the dust, trample underfoot, grind underfoot, grind under one's heel, atomize, make mincemeat of, shake to pieces, batter, beat down, ram

▶ *136 Separation, 141 Disintegration, 282 Horizontality, 384 Powderiness, 241 Violence*

10 **lay waste**, devastate, waste, desolate, defoliate, deforest, denude, strip, strip bare, gut, damage, vandalize, run amok, bring destruction, deal destruction, wreak havoc, cause a shambles, lay waste with fire and the sword, lay in ruins, lay in ashes, make a wilderness and call it peace, despoil, depopulate, put to the sword, raid, sack, ransack, pillage, rape, ravage, violate, loot, plunder

11 **ruin**, bring to ruin, spoil, mar, bedevil, play hell with, play merry hell with, play the devil with, wreck, shipwreck, sink, scupper, torpedo, shoot down in flames, mutilate, deface, knock out, knock flat, floor, flatten, make short work of, make mincemeat of, defeat comprehensively, trounce, hamstring, hobble, nip in the bud, abort, cut off, cut short, KO (Sl), put the kibosh on (Inf), put the skids under (Inf), dish (Inf), spifflicate (Inf), clobber (Inf)

▶ *683 Failure*

12 **consume**, eat up, gobble up, devour, swallow up, engulf, envelop, drown, swamp, overwhelm, burn, burn up, incinerate, waste, squander, throw away, fling to the four winds, run through, play ducks and drakes with, throw to the dogs, cast pearls before swine

▶ *607 Waste, 599 Use, 75 Extravagance*

13 **be destroyed**, self-destruct, go to waste, perish, go down, go under, plunge, sink, sink without trace, disappear, fail, founder, go on the rocks, disintegrate, split, break up, go to pieces, crumple up, turn to dust, end, come to an end, come to a sticky end, have had it, fall,

fall into ruin, go to rack and ruin, tumble, tumble down, crumble, crumble away, crumble to dust, go to the dogs, go to the wall, go downhill, go downhill fast, go to pot, bite the dust, go to blazes (Inf), go to hell (Inf), have bought it (Sl), have bought the farm (Sl), go west (Inf)

▶ *458 Disappearance, 683 Failure, 157 End, 628 Deterioration, 141 Disintegration*

ADJECTIVES

14 **destructive**, destroying, devastating, ruinous, internecine, cutthroat, annihilating, consuming, all-consuming, raging, rampaging, suicidal, sacrificial, mortal, life-threatening, deadly, lethal, fatal, disastrous, catastrophic, apocalyptic, cataclysmic, overwhelming, subversive, revolutionary, anarchistic, incendiary, mischievous, threatening, insidious, pernicious, noxious, harmful, injurious, baneful, negative, adverse, unfavourable

▶ *631 Blight, 854 Disparagement*

15 **destroyed**, wiped out, ruined, devastated, undone, fallen, crushed, ground, pulverized, pulped, shredded, broken up, broken, disintegrated, shattered, wrecked, torpedoed, sunk, done for, dished, in tatters, in ruins, crumbling, dilapidated, falling down, falling apart, tumble down, coming apart at the seams, failing, not long for this world, sinking fast, doomed, for the chop, heading for the scrap heap, marked out for destruction, due for demolition, on the way to the breaker's yard, bankrupt, bust, in liquidation, in receivership, in the hands of the receiver, down-and-out, up the chute (Inf), buggered (Sl), fucked (Tab sl), kaput (Inf)

▶ *100 Nonexistence*

ADVERBS

16 **destructively**, fatally, lethally, ruinously, devastatingly, catastrophically, disastrously, with crushing effect, with a sledge hammer, with one blow, at a stroke, root and branch

245   Reproduction

NOUNS

1 **reproduction**, multiplication, proliferation, repetition, replication, duplication, reduplication, copying, photocopying, photocopy, Xerox (Tm), photoreproduction, PMT (photomechanical transfer), printing, letterpress printing, hot-metal printing, offset lithography, publishing, mass production, reconstruction, renovation, renewal, restoration, revival, resuscitation, reanimation, regeneration, resurrection, resurgence, reincarnation, rebirth, palingenesis

▶ *175 Plurality, 118 Imitation, 183 Repetition, 110 Sameness, 532 Publication, 629 Repair*

2 **print**, reprint, offprint, photocopy, copy, du-

plicate, facsimile, edition, new edition, revised edition, clone, replica

▶ *50 Painting and Sculpture, 66 Photography*

3 **propagation**, generation, procreation, sex, facts of life, the birds and the bees, sexual intercourse, copulation, coition, breeding, spawning, genetic engineering, gene manipulation, eugenics, genesis, biogenesis, abiogenesis, autogenesis, spontaneous generation, parthenogenesis, virgin birth, fertilization, impregnation, pollination, fecundation, insemination, artificial insemination (AI), AID (artificial insemination by donor), DI (donor insemination), AIH (artificial insemination by husband), IVF (in vitro fertilization), GIFT (gamete intra-Fallopian transfer), test-tube baby, conception, germination, pregnancy, gestation, incubation, hatching, birth, parturition, nativity, happy event, the patter of tiny feet, childbirth, birth rate, natality, fructification, fruition, florescence, efflorescence, flowering

4 **development**, growth, adolescence, sexual awakening, puberty, adulthood, parenthood, parentage, paternity, maternity, fatherhood, motherhood, loins, womb

▶ *246 Fertility, 877 Immorality, 156 Beginning, 206 Youth*

5 **propagator**, pollinator, fertilizer, cultivator, procreator, begetter, parent, father, mother, sire, dam

6 **progeny**, offspring, child, baby, young, fruit of someone's loins, kid (Inf), nipper (Inf), sprog (Inf)

▶ *107 Relatedness, 243 Production*

7 **obstetrics**, midwifery, childbirth, natural childbirth, childbed, lying-in, confinement, labour, accouchement, travail (Arch), contractions, labour pains, epidural, amniotic fluid, waters, breaking of the waters, birth pangs, breech presentation, delivery, forceps delivery, Caesarian section, Caesarian, embryo, fetus, amniotic sac, bag of waters, caul, umbilical cord, placenta, afterbirth, amniocentesis, alpha-fetoprotein test, afp test, obstetrician, gynaecologist, midwife, pregnant woman, mother-to-be, primigravida, unigravida, multigravida, gooseberry bush, stork

▶ *353 Excretion, 60 Medicine*

8 **organs of reproduction**, reproductive organs, genitalia, genitals, pudenda, private parts, privates, female sex organs, vulva, clitoris, labia majora, labia minora, vagina, uterus, womb, cervix, neck of the womb, ovary, Fallopian tubes, ovipositor, ovum, egg, male sex organs, penis, phallus, intromittent organ, male member, privvy member, glans penis, foreskin, testicles, testes, scrotum, prostate, prostate gland, vas deferens, semen, seminal fluid, sperm, spermatozoa, seed, pollen, stigma, style, gynoecium, stamen, anther, cunt (Tab sl), quim (Tab sl), pussy (Tab sl), fanny (Tab sl), twat (Tab sl), slit (Tab sl), cock (Tab sl), knob (Tab sl), prick (Tab sl), dick (Tab sl), weapon (Sl), tool (Sl), pecker (US tab sl), willy (*or* willie) (Inf), chopper (Inf), John Thomas (Sl), balls (Tab sl), nuts (Tab sl), goolies (Tab sl), bollocks (Tab sl), rocks (Tab sl)

VERBS

9 **reproduce**, repeat, echo, duplicate, replicate, clone, copy, make a copy of, photocopy, Xerox (Tm), mass-produce, print, reprint, print off, bash off, bash out, turn out, churn out

10 **reproduce oneself**, conceive, get (*or* become) pregnant, fall, carry, give birth, bring to birth, bring forth, bear, be brought to bed of (Arch), have a baby, have children, drop sprogs (Inf)

11 **have young**, have progeny, have offspring, lay (eggs), spawn, hatch, drop, foal, lamb, farrow, pup, whelp, calve, cub, kitten, litter, have one's birth, be born, seed oneself, germinate, sprout, bloom, flower, fruit, bear fruit, fructify

12 **multiply**, burgeon, proliferate, spring up like mushrooms, crop up all over the place, recreate

▶ *175 Plurality, 118 Imitation, 110 Sameness, 532 Publication, 246 Fertility, 107 Relatedness*

13 **propagate**, generate, produce, produce offspring, procreate, breed, bring into existence, bring (*or* call) into being, bring into the world, give life to, beget, spawn, engender, father, sire, carry on the line, make pregnant, impregnate, fertilize, fecundate, inseminate, pollinate, hatch, incubate, raise, rear, bring up, raise from seed, bud, graft, take cuttings, layer, air-layer, knock up (Sl)

▶ *246 Fertility, 243 Production, 107 Relatedness*

14 **have sex**, have sexual intercourse, make love, copulate, do it, fuck (Tab sl), shag (Tab sl), screw (Tab sl), shaft (Tab sl), roger (Tab sl), lay (Tab sl), knock (Sl), knock off (Sl), bonk (Sl), have it off (Tab sl), have it away (Tab sl)

▶ *877 Immorality*

ADJECTIVES

15 **reproduced**, printed, duplicated, copied, repeated, renewed, renewing, re-created, re-creating, reborn, renascent, resurgent, resurrectional, resurrectionary, reappearing, hydra-headed, Phoenix-like

16 **reproductive**, generative, procreative, procreant, life-giving, originative, seminal, spermatic, germinal, genetic, sexual, unisexual, bisexual, genital, vulvar, clitoral, vaginal, cervical, ovarian, penile, phallic, scrotal, in season, on (*or* in) heat, pregnant, impregnated, fertilized, fecundated, breeding, broody, enceinte, with child, big with, heavy with, gravid, expecting, expecting a baby, expecting a happy

event, expectant, in the family way, in an interesting condition, in a delicate condition, eating for two, about to give birth, parturient, in labour, antenatal, perinatal, postnatal, puerperal, obstetric, live-bearing, viviparous, oviparous, parthenogenetic, up the spout (Sl), up the stick (Sl), up the pole (Sl), in the club (Sl), in the pudding club (Sl), with a bun in the oven (Sl), preggers (Sl)

▶ *353 Excretion, 60 Medicine*

ADVERBS

17 **repeatedly**, in duplicate, in triplicate

18 **reproductively**, genetically, sexually, genitally

246   Fertility

NOUNS

1 **fertility**, fecundity, fruitfulness, exuberance, luxuriance, lushness, richness, embarrassment of riches, *embarras de richesses* (Fr), abundance, plenty, plenitude, wealth, riot, profusion, rich harvest, bounty, nature's bounty, rich soil, rich earth, Mother Earth, hotbed, seedbed, nursery, propagator, cornucopia, horn of plenty, land flowing with milk and honey, milch cow, second crop, aftermath, aftergrowth, Green Revolution

▶ *608 Sufficiency, 610 Excess, 68 Agriculture*

2 **productiveness**, mass production, productivity, high productivity, boom, economic boom, economic upturn, booming economy, prosperity, overproductiveness, superabundance, superfluity, glut, butter mountain, wine lake, high birth rate, population explosion, baby boom, biotic potential, productive capacity, menarche, menstruation, procreation, reproduction, propagation, fructification, fecundation, fertilization, pollination, resourcefulness, inventiveness, imaginativeness, fertile imagination

▶ *243 Production, 245 Reproduction, 610 Excess, 13 Economics, 686 Prosperity, 353 Excretion, 519 Imagination*

3 **fertilizer**, organic fertilizer, manure, farmyard manure, dung, cow dung, guano, compost, bonemeal, hoof and horn, fishmeal, slurry, artificial fertilizer, chemical fertilizer, phosphates, nitrates, potash, ammonium salts, sulphates, lime, marl, dressing, top dressing, mulch, seed, semen, sperm, fertility drug, gonadotrophin

▶ *68 Agriculture, 353 Excretion, 622 Dirtiness, 245 Reproduction*

4 **fertility cult**, fertility rite, fertility symbol, phallic symbol, phallus, lingam, yoni, Earth Goddess, Earth Mother, Demeter, Ceres

ADJECTIVES

5 **fertile**, fecund, fruitful, fructiferous, fruitbearing, productive, highly productive, profit-

able, paying, lucrative, remunerative, highyielding, generative, prolific, philoprogenitive (Rare), multiparous, teeming, streaming, pouring, copious, abundant, plentiful, plenteous, profuse, bountiful, bounteous, fat, lush, verdant, luxuriant, rich, rife, exuberant, thriving, flourishing, prosperous, booming, pregnant, parturient, heavy with, big with, procreant, procreative, propagatory, regenerative, creative, inventive, resourceful

▶ *243 Production, 245 Reproduction, 608 Sufficiency, 610 Excess, 686 Prosperity, 519 Imagination*

VERBS

6 **be fertile**, thrive, flourish, burgeon, bloom, blossom, fructify, produce seeds, seed itself, germinate, conceive, give birth, bear, teem, swarm, pullulate, proliferate, mushroom, spring up like mushrooms, multiply, boom, populate, overpopulate, prosper

▶ *245 Reproduction, 686 Prosperity, 181 Multitude*

7 **make fertile**, fecundate, fructify, green the desert, make the desert bloom, plant, fertilize, manure, compost, dress, top-dress, mulch, marl, enrich, feed, water, irrigate, impregnate, inseminate, pollinate, propagate, produce, procreate, generate

▶ *245 Reproduction, 68 Agriculture*

ADVERBS

8 **fruitfully**, productively, profitably, prolifically, abundantly, through nature's bounty, thanks to Mother Nature, creatively, inventively, resourcefully

247   Infertility

NOUNS

1 **infertility**, infecundity, fruitlessness, unproductiveness, unproductivity, barrenness, sterility, impotence, celibacy, childlessness, fallowness, aridity, aridness, dryness, droughtstricken land, desert, desert sands, sand dunes, dust bowl, desert island, waste, wasteland, lunar landscape, Arctic waste, Antarctic waste, barren waste, wild, wilderness, desolation, desertification, soil erosion, deforestation, defoliation, scorched earth policy, waste of waters, dying race, menopause, change of life, abortion, spontaneous abortion, miscarriage, falling birth rate, low birth rate, zero population growth, economic decline, recession, stagnation, economic stagnation, slump, depression, unprofitableness, unprofitability, poor return, low yield, dearth, famine, waste of time, waste of effort

▶ *244 Destruction, 609 Insufficiency, 129 Decrease, 722 Loss, 607 Waste, 614 Uselessness, 392 Dryness*

2 **making infertile**, sterilization, tying the tubes (Inf), hysterectomy, vasectomy, castration, neutering, spaying, gelding

3 **birth control**, contraception, prophylactic, planned parenthood, family planning, contraceptive, IUD (intrauterine device), IUCD (intrauterine contraceptive device), coil, loop, barrier contraceptive, diaphragm, Dutch cap, condom, sheath, French letter (Sl), rubber (Sl), johnny (Sl), female condom, femidom, contraceptive sponge, spermicide, contraceptive pill, the pill, minipill, morning-after pill, male pill, contraceptive injection, rhythm method, coitus interruptus,

ADJECTIVES

4 **infertile**, infecund, fruitless, unfruitful, unproductive, unprolific, barren, sterile, impotent, celibate, childless, fallow, arid, dry, drought-stricken, desert, poor, empty, treeless, gaunt, bleak, stark, bare, sparse, uncultivated, stony, shallow, eroded, withered, shrivelled, dead, blasted, waste, wild, desolate, wasted, stagnating, stagnant, recessionary, unprofitable, depressed, low-yield
▶ *609 Insufficiency, 392 Dryness*

5 **rendered infertile**, unfertilized, on the pill, sterilized, vasectomized, castrated, gelded, neutered, spayed

6 **having no effect**, ineffective, unsuccessful, failed, null and void, addled, abortive
▶ *614 Uselessness, 618 Worthlessness, 236 Powerlessness, 683 Failure*

VERBS

7 **be infertile**, lie fallow, stagnate, rust, rot, run to seed, hide one's abilities, bury one's talents, hide one's light under a bushel, hang fire, prove infertile, fail, come to nothing, come to naught, abort, miscarry, lose the baby, have no issue, have no offspring, die without issue (or offspring), be childless
▶ *628 Deterioration, 683 Failure, 614 Uselessness*

8 **make infertile**, sterilize, vasectomize, unman, emasculate, castrate, geld, spay, neuter

9 **practise birth control**, plan one's family, take precautions, use a condom, go on the pill

10 **waste**, lay waste, desolate, deforest, overgraze, overfish
▶ *625 Hygiene, 244 Destruction*

ADVERBS

11 **unproductively**, fruitlessly, impotently, unprofitably

12 **without issue**, without offspring, o.s.p. (obit sine prole)

Space

That's one small step for man, one giant leap for mankind. Neil Armstrong.

Outer space is no place for a person of breeding. Violet Bonham Carter.

I am a passenger on the spaceship, Earth. Richard Buckminster Fuller.

NOUNS

1 **space**, expanse, expansion, extent, extension, spatial extension, measure, dimension(s), proportion(s), size, length, breadth, width, height, depth, depth of space, surface, area, diameter, circumference, tract, volume, cubic content, capacity
▶ *277 Depth, 263 Distance, 261 Expansion, 269 Length, 268 Measurement, 120 Quantity*

2 **empty space**, emptiness, void, nothingness, infinite space, infinity, unlimited space, sky, heavens, aerospace, airspace, outer space, interplanetary space, interstellar space, intergalactic space, space the final frontier (Inf)
▶ *368 Nonmaterial World, 184 Infinity, 53 Astronomy, Astronautics, and Rocketry, 512 Oblivion*

3 **geographical space**, region, open space, clear space, clearing, glade, open country, wide-open space, wide horizons, expanse, stretch, tract, reach, green belt, hinterland, grassland, prairie, steppe, veld, plain, upland, moorland, back country, outback (Aus), wild, wilderness, waste, desert, back of beyond
▶ *249 Region, 54 Earth Science, 250 Location*

4 **spaciousness**, roominess, extensiveness, expansiveness, capaciousness, voluminousness, vastness, immensity
▶ *259 Size*

5 **reserved space**, room, accommodation, capacity, stowage, storage, storage space, seating capacity, seating, standing room, berthage, place, seat, berth, parking space

6 **available space**, room, latitude, leeway, scope, swing, play, margin, clearance, windage, amplitude, headroom, room overhead, head-way, elbowroom, legroom, room to spare, sea room, seaway, airspace, breathing space, living space, *Lebensraum* (Ger), turning space, room to manoeuvre, room to swing a cat (Inf)
▶ *258 Container*

7 **range**, reach, coverage, scope, compass, radius, sweep, stretch, grasp, sphere, field, area, gamut, spectrum, array
▶ *302 Limit*

8 **intervening space**, distance, interval, gap, remove, break, hiatus, lacuna, blank, pause, interruption, intermission, lapse, time lapse, while, duration, span, spell, stretch, period, turn, go (Inf), trick (Inf)
▶ *265 Interval, 263 Distance, 136 Separation, 188 Duration, 187 Period, 185 Time*

9 **fourth dimension**, space-time, time-space, space-time continuum, continuum, relativity, Einstein theory, general theory of relativity
▶ *56 Physics, 185 Time*

10 **spaceman**, spacewoman, space traveller, astronaut, cosmonaut, rocket pilot, astronavigator, rocket man (Inf)
▶ *53 Astronomy, Astronautics, and Rocketry*

ADJECTIVES

11 **spatial**, spacial, space, dimensional, proportional, two-dimensional, surface, radial, superficial, flat, three-dimensional (3-D), cubic, volumetric, stereoscopic, fourth-dimensional, space-time, spatiotemporal

12 **extensive**, regional, widespread, far-flung, far-reaching, wide-ranging, global, worldwide, interstellar, intergalactic, universal, boundless, infinite, unconfined, uncircumscribed, unrestricted

13 **spacious**, roomy, airy, lofty, capacious, voluminous, commodious, cavernous, sizeable, ample, vast, great, immense, enormous, outsized, oversized, expansive, extended, long, broad, wide, deep, high, amplitudinous
▶ *259 Size, 390 Air*

ADVERBS

14 **spatially**, three-dimensionally, spatiotemporally

15 **spaciously**, sizeably, amply, voluminously, capaciously, immensely, vastly, deeply, expansively, spatially, spatiotemporally, three-dimensionally

16 **extensively**, widely, everywhere, globally, universally, intergalactically, here there and everywhere, in every place, in all places, in every quarter, in all lands, in all areas, the (whole) world over, throughout the world, on the face of the earth, under the sun, high and low, upstairs and downstairs, near and far, far and wide, inside and out, no stone unturned, in every nook and cranny, all round the globe, all around, all over, all over the map (Inf), all over the shop (Inf), all over hell (Sl), every which way (Inf), hell west and crooked (Inf), six ways from Sunday (Inf)

17 **from end to end**, from pole to pole, from coast to coast, from top to bottom, from north to south, from Land's End to John O'Groats (Inf), from here to the back of beyond (Inf), from hell to breakfast (Sl), from here to eternity (Inf), from here until kingdom come (Inf)

18 **from everywhere**, from the four corners of the earth (*or* world), from every place, from the furthest corners of the earth (*or* world), from all points of the compass

19 **to all places**, to the four winds, to the ends of the earth (*or* world), to hell and back

VERBS

20 **extend**, expand, lengthen, widen, dilate, distend, deepen, raise, spread out, spread, range, sweep, reach, stretch, cover, encompass, span, straddle, enclose, surround, environ, contain, hold
▶ *301 Enclosure*

21 **space**, space out, spread out, place at intervals, organize, empty, make room for, order, rank, array, lay out, set out, measure out, proportion, time, mark time, pause, wait, break, lapse, omit, leave out
▶ *150 Order, 152 Arrangement*

249   Region

NOUNS

1 **region**, area, territory, terrain, zone, belt, section, sector, place, space, ground, geographical unit, land, landmass, continent, peninsula, island, islet

2 **geographical region**, zone, longitude, meridian, prime meridian, latitude, parallel, equator, the Line, tropic, tropics, subtropics, horse latitudes, roaring forties

3 **regional boundary**, boundary, outer limit, bounds, pale, confines, marches, shore, territorial limits, territorial waters, continental shelf, offshore rights, 3-mile limit, 12-mile limit, 200-mile limit, exclusion zone, airspace, economic zone

4 **territorial division**, political entity, nation, nation state, sovereign state, power, superpower, territory, country, state, republic, democratic republic, people's republic, kingdom, realm, domain, principality, sultanate, dominion, protectorate, mandate, possession, colony, dependency, commonwealth, union of nations, empire, homeland, fatherland, land of our fathers, motherland, mother country, native land, country of origin, old country
▶ *12 Government and Politics, 91 Countries*

5 **state**, territory, province, region, country, shire, metropolitan district, division, district, canton, duchy, *département* (Fr), *Kreis* (Ger), borough, ward, enumeration district, riding, bailiwick, hundred, wapentake, soke, congressional district, electoral district, constituency, electorate, precinct, diocese, archdiocese, bishopric, archbishopric, parish
▶ *92 Administrative Areas, 7 Religion*

6 **regions**, highlands, lowlands, borders, borderland, march, panhandle (US), corridor, rural area, country, countryside, green belt, hinterland, heartland, back-country, provinces, outback, bush, brush, backwoods, backwater, outpost, back of beyond, wilderness, virgin territory, wasteland, the sticks (Inf), boondocks (US sl), boonies (US sl), yokeldom (Sl), hickdom (Sl)

7 **regions of the world**, Old World, New World, East and West, North and South, North-South divide, Western Hemisphere, Occident, Eastern Hemisphere, Orient, Middle East, Far East, Antipodes, down under (Inf), Third World, developed world, undeveloped world, underdeveloped world, developing nations
▶ *91 Countries*

8 **regions of the US**, Wild West, the Coast, Middle West (*or* Midwest), Dixie, Dixieland, Sunbelt, Silicon Valley, Yankeeland (Inf)

9 **regions of Britain**, Home Counties, Midlands, the Highlands, the North, the South, north of Watford, Fens, Broads, Marches, Borders, West Country

10 **urban area**, built-up area, urban sprawl, city, metropolitan area, megalopolis, metropolis, capital city, cathedral city, new city, garden city, inner city, city centre, central business district (CBD), precinct, uptown, downtown, ghetto, no-go area, slums, skid row (US sl), nowhere city (Sl), wrong side of the tracks (US sl), burg (US inf), big smoke (Aus inf), New York, Big Apple (Inf), Gotham (Inf), London, the Smoke (Inf)
▶ *93 Cities, Towns, and Villages*

11 **settlement**, village, hamlet, town, township, municipality, market town, county town, new town, dormitory town (*or* village), boom

town, ghost town, shanty town, small town, one-horse town (Inf), suburbs, suburbia, outskirts, stockbroker belt (Inf), exurbia (US), gin and Jaguar belt (Inf)

12 **plot**, plot of land, parcel of land, enclosure, patch, lot, acreage, block, section, tract, allotment, holding, claim

▶ *301 Enclosure, 723 Possession*

13 **locality**, locale, neighbourhood, vicinity, area, haunt, circuit, beat, round, orbit, walk, environs, back yard (Inf), neck of the woods (Inf), stamping ground (Inf), turf (Inf), manor (Inf), patch (Inf)

▶ *250 Location, 297 Surroundings*

14 **sphere**, field, arena, province, ambit, theatre, territory, pale, jurisdiction, scope, realm, domain, bailiwick, interest, line, discipline, forte, métier, pigeon (Inf)

15 **regionalism**, provincialism, parochialism, nationalism, patriotism

▶ *12 Government and Politics*

ADJECTIVES

16 **regional**, areal, spatial (*or* spacial), geographical, topographic (*or* topographical), territorial, zonal, longitudinal, latitudinal, meridian, highland, lowland, peninsular, insular, tropical, subtropical, continental, eastern, western, northern, southern, Occidental, Oriental, antipodean

17 **national**, state, provincial, sectional, divisional, district, municipal, urban, metropolitan, suburban, rural, up-country, colonial, dependent, republican, democratic, patriotic

18 **local**, localized, next-door, neighbouring, nearby, provincial, parochial, diocesan, insular, confined, limited, back-country, backwoods, small-town, uptown, downtown, ghettoized, slummy

ADVERBS

19 **geographically**, spatially, longitudinally, latitudinally, regionally, territorially, continentally, equatorially, tropically, subtropically

20 **nationally**, internationally, divisionally, provincially, municipally, locally, nearby, colonially, politically, democratically, nationalistically, patriotically

250   Location

NOUNS

1 **location**, locality, situation, place, site, position, whereabouts, locale, spot, setting, environs, environment, habitat, parts, haunt, patch, pitch, beat, territory, seat, station, post, base, neck of the woods (Inf), stamping ground (Inf), hole (Inf), turf (Inf), manor (Inf)

▶ *251 Situation, 256 Habitat, 297 Surroundings*

2 **exact location**, spot, point, pinpoint, dot, bench mark, grid reference, map reference,

coordinates, bearings, compass direction, eastings and northings, latitude and longitude, declination, chart, map, plan, address, postal address, postal district, postcode, zip code (US)

▶ *54 Earth Science, 567 Address, 592 Plan*

3 **locating**, pinpointing, finding the spot (*or* place), homing in on, finding, discovering, detecting, unearthing, running to earth, laying one's hands (*or* fingers) on, turning up, tracking down, pinning down, coming across, chancing upon, hitting on

▶ *496 Discovery, 294 Uncovering*

4 **placing**, locating, situating, siting, placement, emplacement, establishment, installation, settling, fixation, fixing, posting, stationing

5 **topography**, geography, cartography, chorography, surveying, triangulation, navigation, orienteering, geodesy

▶ *54 Earth Science, 268 Measurement, 249 Region*

ADJECTIVES

6 **located**, situated, placed, positioned, sited, set, stationed, posted, established, installed, settled, fixed, emplaced, planted, ensconced

7 **found**, located, locatable, discovered, pinpointed, detected, unearthed, tracked down, pinned down

8 **locational**, situated, positional, topographical, geographical, cartographical, navigational, geodetic, surveyed

VERBS

9 **locate**, situate, place, site, position, emplace, put, put in place, install (*or* instal), establish, set up, plant, ensconce, station, post, billet, quarter, base, fix, spot (Inf), stick (Inf)

10 **settle**, take up residence, establish residence, move in, ensconce oneself, stay at, inhabit, dwell, reside in, locate (Inf), relocate, change address, move, move house

▶ *252 Displacement, 255 Inhabitant*

11 **find**, find the spot, pinpoint, zero in on, home in on, discover, detect, unearth, run to earth, lay one's hands (*or* fingers) on, turn up, track down, pin down, come across, chance upon (*or* on), hit upon (*or* on), get a fix, get a bearing, calculate (*or* fix) one's position, navigate, survey, triangulate

▶ *170 Calculation*

ADVERBS

12 **where**, whereabouts, whither, here, hereat, hereabouts, just here, on this spot, at this point, in this vicinity (*or* neighbourhood), in place, *in situ* (L), *in loco* (L), on location, on site, on the spot, there, thereat, in that place, thereabouts, thither, to that place, here and there, in places, in spots, *passim* (L)

13 **topographically**, geographically, cartographically, geodetically

251 Situation

NOUNS

1 **situation**, position, orientation, direction, bearings, latitude, longitude, aspect, side, frontage, altitude, topography, geography, location, site, setting, place, spot, point, seat, venue, scene, scenery, locale, locality
▶ *250 Location*

2 **circumstances**, setting, ground, background, footing, basis, stand, standing, standpoint, viewpoint, position, place, context, factor, contingency, condition, juncture, case, state, state of affairs, status quo, climate, atmosphere, scene, scenario, lay of the land, the way of the world, how things stand, how it is, outfit, layout (Inf), ball game (Inf), kettle of fish (Inf), set-up (Inf), picture (Inf), whole picture (Inf), the size of it (Inf)
▶ *106 Circumstances, 105 State, 297 Surroundings*

3 **difficult circumstances**, tricky situation, plight, predicament, fix, jam, trouble, pickle (Inf), hot water (Inf)
▶ *687 Adversity, 659 Difficulty*

4 **employment**, post, position, job, service, station, office, place, livelihood, occupation, situations vacant, sitvac column (Inf), berth (Inf), billet (Inf)
▶ *644 Work*

5 **rank**, sphere, status, standing, station, position, position in society, estate
▶ *150 Order*

ADJECTIVES

6 **situated**, positioned, located, set, placed, sited, seated, stationed, orientated, directed towards, pointed, appointed, posted, employed, occupational

7 **situational**, directional, topographical, geographical, local

8 **circumstantial**, contextual, contingent, grounded, based, climatic, atmospheric, surrounding, troublesome, difficult

VERBS

9 **be situated**, be located, be, lie, stand, rest, sit, take up a position
▶ *99 Existence*

10 **situate**, place in a situation (*or* position *or* location), place, position, locate, site, put, install (*or* instal), stand, fix, set, set up, station, post, deploy, direct, orientate

ADVERBS

11 **geographically**, topographically, locally, round about, around, round here, in place, in position, on site, *in situ* (L), on location

12 **circumstantially**, contingently, contextually, as it stands, under the circumstances

252 Displacement

NOUNS

1 **displacement**, dislocation, dislodgment, disturbance, disarrangement, derangement, derailment, shift, shunt, move, movement, motion, removal, relocation, translocation, transference, transshipment, switch, swerve, veer, deflection, knocking off course (*or* out of place), aberration, perturbation
▶ *153 Disturbance, 335 Deviation*

2 **removal**, extraction, extrication, taking away, uprooting, ripping out, tearing out, pulling up, plucking out, pulling out by the roots
▶ *355 Extraction, 131 Subtraction, 704 Cancellation*

3 **replacement**, substitution, supplantation, transfer, relocation, removal, forcible removal, overthrow, coup, deposition (*or* deposal), unseating, takeover, evacuation, ejection, banishment, expulsion, eviction, deportation, diaspora, enforced repatriation, ethnic cleansing
▶ *222 Substitution, 670 Attack, 216 Change, 349 Expulsion, 341 Repulsion*

4 **relegation**, demotion, downgrading, dismissal, discharge, lay-off, redundancy, marching orders, the sack, the boot (Inf), one's cards (Inf), the elbow (Inf), the big E (Inf), the (old) heave-ho (Inf), the bounce (Inf), boot-out (Inf), kicking downstairs (Inf), kicking upstairs (Inf)
▶ *345 Departure, 581 Rejection, 727 Disposal*

5 **disconnection**, separation, detachment, unhinging, disjointedness, dislocation, putting out of joint, disarticulation, disengagement, luxation, dismemberment
▶ *136 Separation, 141 Disintegration*

6 **misplacement**, mislaying, mislocation, misputting, losing, wrong place

7 **displaced person**, refugee, evacuee, exile, deportee, outcast, stateless person, homeless person, waif, stray, fish out of water, square peg in a round hole
▶ *349 Expulsion*

ADJECTIVES

8 **displaced**, dislocated, dislodged, disturbed, disarranged, deranged, derailed, shifted, shunted, moved, removed, relocated, transferred, switched, swerved, veered, deflected, knocked off course (*or* out of place), disturbing, shifting, moving, swerving, veering

9 **removed**, extracted, extricated, uprooted, ripped, torn, wrested, pulled, drawn, plucked, pulled out by the roots

10 **replaced**, overthrown, deposed, substitute, supplanted, transferred, removed, relocated, banished, thrown out, expelled, deported, exiled, ostracized, stateless, outcast, refugee, evicted, evacuated, unhoused, unharboured, houseless, homeless, rootless, of no fixed abode, of no fixed address, out of place, in the wrong place, like a fish out of water, like a

square peg in a round hole, out of one's element

11 **relegated**, demoted, downgraded, dismissed, discharged, laid off, sacked, out of a job, booted out (Inf), out on one's ear (Inf), out on one's arse (Sl)

12 **disconnected**, disjointed, out of joint, disarticulated, dislocated, unhinged, disengaged, dismembered, detached, separated

13 **misplaced**, mislaid, misput, mislocated, lost, missing, gone missing (*or* astray)

VERBS

14 **displace**, dislodge, dislocate, unseat, upset, disturb, disarrange, disorder, disorganize, disrupt, derail, knock (*or* throw) off course, throw out of gear, switch, swerve, veer, deflect, shift, move, shunt, transfer, transport, relocate, move lock, stock, and barrel, translocate, transship

15 **remove**, extract, extricate, draw out, pull out, pull up, uproot, root out (*or* up), pull up by the roots, rip out, tear out, pluck out

16 **replace**, substitute, supplant, overthrow, dethrone, unseat, depose, oust, usurp, stage a coup, take over, banish, expel, exile, ostracize, deport, cast out, turn out, evict, eject, boot out (Inf), boot out on one's ear (*or* arse) (Inf)

17 **relegate**, demote, downgrade, discharge, dismiss, let go, make redundant, lay off, sack, fire, kick downstairs (Inf), kick upstairs (Inf), kick out (Inf), boot (Inf), give the (old) heave-ho (Inf), give the elbow (Inf), give the big E (Inf), give one's cards (Inf), give the brown envelope (Inf), give one's walking papers (Inf), give one's marching orders (Inf), show the door (Inf)

18 **disconnect**, unhinge, disjoint, put out of joint, disarticulate, dislocate, luxate, dismember, separate, detach

19 **misplace**, mislay, misput, mislocate, put in the wrong place, lose, lose track of

ADVERBS

20 **out of place**, in the wrong place, on the move, in transit, on the run, instead, in place of, in lieu, as an alternative

21 **disconnectedly**, disjointedly, detachedly, separately

253 Presence

NOUNS

1 **presence**, physical presence, bodily presence, existence, being, manifestation, manifestness, reality, actuality, materialness, materiality, solidity, ontology, metaphysics of presence, thusness (Inf)

▶ *101 Reality, 99 Existence, 367 Material World, 103 Essence*

2 **omnipresence**, ubiquitousness, ubiquity, all-presence, pervasiveness, pervasion, perme-

ation, diffusion, diffusiveness, attendance, personal attendance, appearance, frequenting, visiting, participation, accompaniment, company, companionship, society, association

▶ *184 Infinity, 553 Diffuseness, 8 Divinity, 457 Appearance*

3 **residence**, occupancy, inhabitance, habitation

▶ *255 Inhabitant, 256 Habitat*

4 **availability**, plenty, sufficiency, accessibility, readiness, handiness, convenience, proximity, nearness, immediacy, propinquity, vicinity, neighbourhood, immediate circle

▶ *608 Sufficiency, 297 Surroundings, 250 Location, 251 Situation*

5 **someone present**, participant, spectator, audience, theatregoer, cinemagoer, bystander, onlooker, looker-on, witness, eyewitness, watcher, observer, beholder, viewer, passerby, attender, attendee, visitor, patron, frequenter, haunter, habitué, regular customer, regular (Inf)

▶ *719 Observance, 51 Performing Arts*

6 **ghostly presence**, presence, ghost, apparition, manifestation, spectre, phantom, vision, spook (Inf)

▶ *11 Occultism, 435 Vision*

ADJECTIVES

7 **present**, existent, existing, extant, in being, real, actual, material, solid, manifest, omnipresent, all-present, all-over, present throughout, ubiquitous, infinite, everywhere, pervasive, all-pervasive, pervading, diffusive, penetrating, permeating, permeative, suffusive, suffusing, ghostly, spectral, haunted

▶ *185 Time, 537 Truth, 99 Existence*

8 **attendant**, in attendance, on hand, participating, watching, witnessed, associated, accompanying, concomitant, companionable, sociable, regular, habituated

▶ *180 Accompaniment, 815 Sociability*

9 **resident**, residential, in residence, on the premises, on the spot, occupying, in occupation, live-in, in-house, at home

10 **available**, plenty, sufficient, accessible, at hand, on, on tap, ready, handy, convenient, within reach (*or* sight *or* call), to hand, near, nearby, nearest, close, closest, immediate, in view, at one's fingertips (*or* elbow), under one's nose, before one's eyes

VERBS

11 **be present**, be, exist, occur, live, breathe, be here, be there, be everywhere, pervade, permeate, penetrate, suffuse, diffuse, imbue, impregnate, fill, soak, saturate, leave no space (*or* void), run through, filter through, infiltrate, overrun, overswarm, meet one at every turn, appear, materialize, solidify

12 **attend**, be present at, be there in person, sit in on, be on hand, make one's presence felt,

participate, take part, join in, stand by, spectate, look on, witness, see, watch, observe, view, visit, appear, turn up, show up, put in an appearance, show one's face, look in on, grace the occasion, honour with one's presence, present oneself, report, report for duty, be all present and correct (*or* all present and accounted for), frequent, haunt, hang around (Sl), hang out (Sl)

▶ *318 Prominence, 815 Sociability*

13 **reside**, be in residence, occupy, inhabit, live in, dwell

ADVERBS

14 **in person**, personally, live, in existence, really, actually, solidly, materially, bodily, *in propria persona* (L), in the flesh (Inf)

15 **here**, there, where, everywhere, somewhere, anywhere

16 **on the spot**, on the ground, on location, on site, *in situ* (L), in place, to hand, near at hand, within reach, on call, on tap, before one's very eyes, under one's nose, in the face of, in the presence of, before

17 **at home**, in residence, on the premises, in

254 Absence

Absence makes the heart grow fonder,/ Isle of Beauty, Fare thee well! Thomas Haynes Bayly.

Absence is to love what wind is to fire; it extinguishes the small, it inflames the great. Bussy-Rabutin.

NOUNS

1 **absence**, nonpresence, nonentity, nonbeing, unbeing, inexistence, nonexistence, unreality, nonoccurrence, nullity, nihility

▶ *100 Nonexistence, 368 Nonmaterial World, 102 Unreality*

2 **disappearance**, dematerialization, vanishment, departure, loss, lack, want, deficiency, shortage, scarcity, dearth, insufficiency, paucity, scantiness

▶ *458 Disappearance, 722 Loss, 609 Insufficiency*

3 **emptiness**, voidness, vacancy, vacuity, bareness, blankness, hollowness, barrenness, nothingness, void, gap, vacuum, nothing, empty space, empty shell, husk, clean sheet, clean slate, blank paper, blank slate, *tabula rasa* (L)

▶ *248 Space*

4 **absenteeism**, absentation, nonappearance, nonattendance, truantism, truancy, desertion, defection, French leave, unauthorized absence, AWOL (absence without leave), hooky (*or* hookey) (Inf), cut (Inf), bunk (Inf)

▶ *638 Escape, 136 Separation, 345 Departure*

5 **leave of absence**, leave, holiday, vacation, furlough, break, time off, day off, compassionate leave, sabbatical, sabbatical leave, sick leave, sickie (Aus inf)

▶ *812 Celebration*

6 **absentee**, nonperson, missing person, defector, deserter, truant, runaway, no-show (Inf), skiver (Sl)

7 **nobody**, no one, no man, no woman, nobody present, nobody there, not one, not a soul, not a single person, not a living thing

ADJECTIVES

8 **absent**, not present, nonattendant, unavailable, nonexistent, inexistent, unreal, nonoccurrent, null, void

9 **away**, out, no longer among us, gone, departed, dematerialized, out of sight, missing, lost, nowhere to be found, disappeared, vanished, absconded, flown, fled, vamoosed (Inf), off (Inf)

10 **nonresident**, not resident, not in residence, away from home, not at home, out of town, on tour, on the road, on location, on leave, on holiday, on vacation, on furlough, on sabbatical, not at work, on sick leave, on compassionate leave

▶ *397 Death*

11 **truant**, absentee, defected, deserted, jumped ship, AWOL (absent without leave)

12 **missing**, lacking, wanting, wanted, deficient, minus, short, taken away, deleted, subtracted, omitted, mislaid, excluded, left out, not included

13 **vacant**, vacuous, void, devoid, empty, without content, hollow, barren, bare, blank, clean, clear, featureless, characterless

14 **unoccupied**, empty, vacant, available, unfilled, unlived-in, uninhabited, untenanted, unpeopled, unsettled, unmanned, unstaffed, depopulated, deserted, abandoned, forsaken, godforsaken

VERBS

15 **be absent**, keep away, stay away, take no part in, not come, fail to appear, not turn up, not show up, be conspicuous by one's absence, vote with one's feet, turn up missing (Inf), stay away in droves (Inf)

16 **absent oneself**, take one's leave, leave, take leave, withdraw, retire, retreat, depart, exit, leave the scene, bow out, vacate, slip away, slip out, sneak out (Inf), make oneself scarce (Inf)

▶ *347 Exit*

17 **take leave of absence**, go on leave, go on vacation, go on holiday, go on furlough, go on sabbatical, take time off, take a day off, go out of town, go on location

18 **abscond**, decamp, disappear, vanish, dematerialize, go missing, fly the nest, escape, fly, flee, run away, desert, defect, jump ship, go AWOL (absent without leave), take French leave, play truant, bunk off (Inf), do a bunk

(Inf), vamoose (US sl), skive off (Sl), cut (Inf), skip (Inf), play hooky (or hookey) (Inf)

19 **leave empty**, evacuate, vacate, desert, depopulate, abandon, forsake

ADVERBS

20 **absently**, vacantly, vacuously, emptily, hollowly, blankly, in one's absence, behind one's back, in absentia

21 **away**, elsewhere, not here, out of house, off the premises, on tour, on location, on leave, on vacation, on holiday, on furlough, on sabbatical, out of town, somewhere else, not there, neither here nor there, nowhere, no place

255 Inhabitant

NOUNS

1 **inhabitant**, inhabiter, native, aborigine, autochthon, indigene, Indian, earliest inhabitant, first comer, local, occupant, occupier, dweller, resident, resider, residentiary, denizen, indweller, inmate, incumbent

▶ *256 Habitat, 400 Humankind, 702 Prison*

2 **inhabitants**, population, native population, populace, people, people at large, public, general public, citizenry, colony, commune, community, neighbourhood, dwellers, residents, household, family, ménage, tribe, clan

▶ *803 Commoner, 400 Humankind, 1 Anthropology*

3 **householder**, head of the household, owner-occupier, freeholder, tenant, sitting tenant, renter, lessee, leaseholder, lodger, roomer, paying guest, boarder, roommate, flatmate, addressee, guest, visitor

▶ *723 Possession, 725 Property, 567 Address*

4 **townsman**, townswoman, townsfolk, townspeople, townsperson, towndweller, burgess, burgher, oppidan, citizen, city-dweller, city person, metropolitan, urbanite, suburbanite, commuter, townee (Inf), city slicker (Inf), slicker (Inf)

▶ *93 Cities, Towns, and Villages*

5 **countryman**, countrywoman, country gentleman, country-dweller, country cousin, country bumpkin, ruralist, provincial, rustic, peasant, yokel, villager, parishioner, cottager, farmer, smallholder, crofter, highlander, lowlander, backsettler, bushman (Aus), frontiersman, backwoodsman, apple-knocker (Inf), clod (Inf), hick (US inf), redneck (Inf), cracker (US inf), hayseed (US inf), hillbilly (US inf)

6 **illegal occupant**, squatter, trespasser, illegal immigrant, uninvited guest, invader, gatecrasher, cuckoo (Inf)

7 **settler**, pioneer, precursor, incomer, immigrant, colonist, colonizer, colonial, planter

▶ *119 Originality*

8 **national**, subject, citizen, naturalized citizen, citizen by adoption, holder of dual nationality, citizen of the world, compatriot, fellow countryman (or countrywoman), fellow citizen, home towner (US inf)

9 **British inhabitant**, Brit, Briton, John Bull, Englishman (or Englishwoman), Pom (Aus sl), Limey (US sl), Scot, Jock (Sl), Jimmy (Sl), Welshman (or Welshwoman), Taffy (Sl), Celt, Gael, Northerner, Southerner, Westcountryman (or Westcountrywoman), Londoner, cockney, Bristolian, Brummie (Inf), Mancunian, Geordie, Liverpudlian, Scouse (Inf), Glaswegian, Aberdonian

▶ *93 Cities, Towns, and Villages 249 Region, 91 Countries, 250 Location, 251 Situation*

10 **US inhabitant**, American, Uncle Sam, Easterner, Eastlander, Westerner, Westlander, Northerner, New Englander, New Yorker, Yankee (Inf), Yank (Sl), GI Joe (Inf)

ADJECTIVES

11 **inhabited**, occupied, occupied by, populated, lived in, indwelt, residential, tenanted, rented, leased, let, freehold, squatted, communal

12 **native**, indigenous, aboriginal, autochthonous (or autochthonic or autochthonal), ethnic, tribal, local, metropolitan, urban, suburban, rustic, provincial

13 **resident**, residing, living in, dwelling, settled, domiciled, colonial, colonized, naturalized, immigrant

VERBS

14 **inhabit**, dwell, reside, live in, abide in, occupy, lease, rent, lodge, board, take rooms, stay, sojourn, visit

▶ *256 Habitat*

15 **settle**, move in, set up house, domicile, pioneer, immigrate, colonize, people, populate, squat, trespass, gate-crash, crash down (Inf)

256 Habitat

NOUNS

1 **habitat**, habitation, abode, dwelling, dwelling place, domicile, place, place where one lives (or resides), residence, place of residence, house, home, roof over one's head, accommodation, quarters, living quarters, lodgings, lodging, billet, rooms, sleeping place, squat, crash pad (Inf), digs (diggings) (Inf), pad (Inf), crib (Inf)

▶ *255 Inhabitant*

2 **environment**, surroundings, habitat, microhabitat, ecosystem, niche, abode, locality, locale, haunt, domain, range, territory, terrain, element, home ground, base, bailiwick, own back yard, neighbourhood, hangout (Sl), stamping ground (Inf)

▶ *250 Location, 251 Situation, 106 Circumstances, 297 Surroundings, 54 Earth Science*

3 **home**, homestead, home-sweet-home, hearth and home, hearth, fireside, inglenook, base, nest, place where one hangs one's hat, home town, birthplace, cradle, homeland, native land, motherland, fatherland
▶ *280 Base*

4 **official residence**, presidential palace, governor's mansion, White House, 10 Downing Street, Chequers, Mansion House, Buckingham Palace, Windsor Castle, Balmoral, embassy, consulate, vicarage, rectory, parsonage, deanery, manse, mansion, palace, castle, château, villa, manor house, grange, hall, lodge, stately home, ancestral hall (*or* seat), estate, pile (Inf)
▶ *7 Religion, 43 Architecture, 802 Aristocrat*

5 **house**, town house, semidetached house, semi, duplex (US), detached house, terraced house, row house, back-to-back, two-up-two-down , split-level house, ranch house, farmhouse, villa, bungalow, dormer bungalow, chalet, cottage, cabin, log cabin, flat, apartment, maisonette, penthouse, duplex apartment, bedsit (*or* bedsitter), studio, granny flat, *pied-à-terre* (Fr), snuggery, love nest

6 **apartment block**, tower block, high-rise flats (*or* apartments), tenement, condominium (US), housing estate
▶ *258 Container, 382 Structure, 248 Space*

7 **room**, chamber, hall, entrance hall, lobby, vestibule, anteroom, gallery, porch, portico, foyer, corridor, passage, landing, mezzanine, living room, sitting room, lounge, reception room, drawing room, front room, best room, parlour, salon, dining room, breakfast room, dinette, dining hall, dining kitchen, canteen, mess, mess room, restaurant, cafeteria, kitchen, kitchenette, back kitchen, galley, utility room, laundry room, larder, pantry, scullery, still room, study, library, studio, workroom, office, den, snuggery, snug, games room, family room, rumpus room (US), playroom, recreation room, bedroom, bedchamber, boudoir, sleeping room, nursery, dormitory, dressing room, bathroom, shower room, washroom, cloakroom, toilet, lavatory, WC, water closet, comfort station (US), smallest room, loo (Inf), lav (Inf), bog (Sl), store room, junk room, box room, lumber room, glory hole, cellar, bunker, basement, subbasement, coal hole, attic, garret, loft, garden room, conservatory, sun lounge, solarium, sun porch, greenhouse, glasshouse, orangery, lean-to, outhouse, summer house, gazebo, belvedere, garage, carport, boathouse, hangar, veranda, balcony, patio, piazza
▶ *43 Architecture, 350 Eating*

8 **shelter**, shed, shack, hut, lean-to, outhouse, hutch, booth, bothy (Scot), shanty, hovel, tumbledown shack, squat, derelict house, slum, deri (Inf), hole (Inf), dump (Inf), pigsty (Inf), pigpen (Inf), dive (Sl), joint (Sl), dosshouse (doss) (Sl), flophouse (US sl), kiphouse (Sl), fleabag (US sl)
▶ *743 Poverty*

9 **mobile home**, caravan, trailer, camper, campervan, houseboat, tent, tepee (*or* tipi), wigwam, pavilion

10 **hotel**, motel, motor inn, inn, hostelry, guest house, boarding house, *pension* (Fr), bed and breakfast (B & B), bed and board, board and lodging, hostel, youth hostel, pub (public house), tavern, local (Inf), boozer (Inf)

11 **retreat**, haven, refuge, sanctuary, hideaway, halfway house, sheltered housing, hospice
▶ *634 Refuge*

12 **stall**, fold, barn, stable, byre, sty, pigsty, cowshed, cowhouse, kennel, pound, cattery, coop, henhouse, chicken coop, run, battery, cage, zoo, zoological garden, menagerie, aquarium, fish tank, marine park, sea zoo, aviary, birdhouse, birdcage, dovecote, pigeon loft
▶ *78 Birds, 80 Fishes, 82 Insects and Arachnids, 77 Mammals, 301 Enclosure*

13 **lair**, den, cave, hole, covert, sett, holt, burrow, warren, tunnel, earth, drey, nest, eyrie, perch, roost, beehive, anthill

ADJECTIVES

14 **inhabiting**, abiding, residing, residential, fit for habitation, residentiary, resident, in residence, at home, dwelling, living, staying, domiciled, housed, roofed, lodged, billeted, sheltered

15 **environmental**, surrounding, neighbourhood, territorial, local, urban, suburban, built-up, metropolitan, towny, inner-city
▶ *54 Earth Science, 93 Cities, Towns, and Villages*

16 **manorial**, palatial, presidential, grand, detached, semidetached, terraced, back-to-back, duplex, split-level, single-storey, multistorey, high-rise

VERBS

17 **inhabit**, abide in, dwell, dwell in, reside in, live in, occupy, squat, stay, sojourn, settle, colonize, populate, people

18 **take up residence**, hang up one's hat, move in, make one's nest, nest, nestle, perch, roost, burrow, stable, pitch one's tent, camp, encamp, bivouac, quarter, room, board, lodge, put up at (Inf), doss down (Sl), crash (Inf), park one's carcass (Inf), drop anchor (Inf)

19 **frequent**, haunt, visit, hang out at (Inf)

ADVERBS

20 **environmentally**, territorially, locally, around, in the vicinity, in the neighbourhood

257 Contents

NOUNS

1 **contents**, content, what is contained, things

contained, ingredients, components, constituents, constitution, composition, make-up, structure, embodiment, parts, elements, factors, features, substance, stuff, material, matter, spirit, essence, quintessence, gist, meat, nub

▶ *148 Component, 152 Arrangement, 103 Essence, 520 Meaning, 382 Structure*

2 **load**, lading, cargo, payload, freight, burden, charge, containerload, carload, truckload, busload, trainload, boatload, shipment, stowage, tonnage

▶ *120 Quantity, 259 Size, 258 Container, 70 Transport, 248 Space, 726 Retention*

3 **insides**, inside, inner workings, guts, pith, marrow, heart, core, kernel, entrails, bowels, offal, innards (Inf)

▶ *290 Interior, 158 Middle*

4 **stuffing**, filling, filler, wadding, padding, packing, lining, interlining

▶ *292 Lining, 604 Materials*

5 **divisions**, subdivisions, sections, chapters, subject matter, themes, topics, items, index, inventory, code, table, list, checklist, tally, chart, catalogue, glossary, register, schedule, scheme, agenda

▶ *171 List, 532 Publication, 163 Class, 731 Allocation*

VERBS

6 **contain**, hold, enclose, conceal, package, parcel, box up, containerize, load, lade, freight, take on board

▶ *258 Container, 726 Retention*

7 **stuff**, fill, pad, pack, pack in (*or* into), cram, jam, squeeze in, insert, pour in, make full, fill up, top up

8 **embody**, subsume, include, compose, constitute, make up, structure, build, assemble, put together

▶ *146 Inclusion*

9 **itemize**, index, list, enumerate, tabulate, catalogue, classify, divide, subdivide, section, register, file, tally, schedule, schematize, programme

ADJECTIVES

10 **containing**, component, constituent, constituted, composed, made-up, embodying, subsuming, including, inclusive, structured, featuring, elemental, substantial, material, essential, quintessential

11 **loaded**, laden, holding, containing, charged, burdened, burdensome, stuffed, full, lined, padded, packed, crammed, squeezed, topped up

12 **itemized**, indexed, listed, coded, tabled, tabular, tabulated, charted, catalogued, registered, scheduled, programmed, sectioned, divided, subdivided, thematic, topical, schematic

ADVERBS

13 **structurally**, elementally, substantially, materially, in essence, essentially, quintessentially

14 **internally**, inside, within, to the core, inclusively, fully, to the brim, to the top

15 **thematically**, indexically, topically, schematically, sectionally, divisionally

258   Container

NOUNS

1 **container**, receptacle, holder, frame, vessel, repository, depository, reservoir, store

▶ *257 Contents, 531 Concealment, 259 Size, 120 Quantity, 248 Space, 302 Limit, 301 Enclosure*

2 **compartment**, cell, cage, cubicle, booth, stall, box, pew, niche, recess, nook, inglenook, cranny, bay, alcove, cubby, cubbyhole, snuggery, hole in the wall (Inf)

3 **cabinet**, cupboard, built-in cupboard, fitted unit, highboy (US), lowboy (US), tallboy, whatnot, chest, commode, chest of drawers, drawer, shelf, bookshelf, bookcase, unit, wall unit, hi-fi unit, dresser, Welsh dresser, drinks cabinet, sideboard, bureau, davenport, escritoire, secretaire, desk, writing desk, filing cabinet, kitchen unit (*or* cabinet), freezer, fridge-freezer, fridge, refrigerator, dishwasher

▶ *47 Furniture and Woodwork, 605 Store*

4 **rack**, shelf, shelving, layer, level, storey, floor, deck

5 **packet**, pack, packaging, cover, wrapper, sheath, envelope, jacket, document, wallet, file, folder, parcel, bundle

▶ *644 Work, 647 Workshop*

6 **box**, chest, coffer, casket, caddy, case, locker, canister, tin can, tin, can, carton, punnet, cardboard box, shoe box, cool box, Esky (Aus), moneybox, safe, jewellery box, cigarette case, snuff box, matchbox, tinderbox, ammunition box, powder box, file, boxfile, dispatch box, packing box (*or* case), crate, (freight) container, tea chest, coffin, sarcophagus

▶ *605 Store*

7 **basket**, shopping basket, hamper, picnic hamper (*or* basket), rush basket, reed basket, wicker basket, wire basket, flower basket, fruit basket, bread basket, laundry basket, clothes basket, wastepaper basket, wastebasket, log basket, pannier, punnet, Moses basket, bassinet, creel, skep, trug

8 **bag**, sack, string bag, carrier bag, plastic bag, polythene bag, freezer bag, paper bag, shopping bag, carryall, holdall, grip, poke (Dial), pouch, diplomatic pouch, purse, handbag, shoulder bag, duffel bag, clutch bag, tote bag, bum bag, evening bag, sponge bag, carpetbag, overnight bag, school bag, satchel, sports bag,

kitbag, golf bag, game bag, cool bag, tucker bag (Aus), swag (Aus), bundle, saddlebag, nosebag

9 **baggage**, luggage, suitcase, travel bag, grip, holdall, carryall, Gladstone bag, Boston bag, portmanteau, valise, trunk, overnight bag, flight bag, carry on bag, backpack, knapsack, rucksack, haversack, daysack, briefcase, attaché case, portfolio, wallet, money belt

10 **cart**, pushcart, handcart, trolley, shopping trolley, barrow, wheelbarrow, wagon, truck, lorry, van, transit van, removal van, freight train, boot, luggage rack, overhead locker

▶ 70 Transport

11 **vessel**, urn, jar, tea caddy, coffee jar, kilner jar, vase, ewer, pitcher, jug, amphora, cask, vat, barrel, keg, drum, wine cask, pipe, beer barrel, puncheon, hogshead, firkin, tun, mash tun, tank, cistern, bucket, pail, watering can, dustbin, bin, litter bin, rubbish bin, trash can (US inf), wheelie bin, scuttle, coal scuttle, silo, hopper

12 **bath**, bathtub, hip bath, footbath, eyebath, sitzbath, jacuzzi, tin bath, bidet, tub, washtub, sink, kitchen sink, basin, washbasin, bowl, vat, trough

13 **drinking vessel**, cup, teacup, coffee cup, eggcup, mug, stoup (Dial), beaker, drinking cup, glass, tumbler, highball glass, beer glass, *Stein* (Ger), pint glass, half pint glass, straight glass, lager glass, tankard, toby jug, horn, drinking horn, cannikin, pannikin, noggin, chalice, goblet, wineglass, champagne flute, schooner, rummer, brandy balloon, brandy snifter, jigger, liqueur glass, pony, sherry glass, loving cup

14 **bottle**, flask, flagon, vial, phial, decanter, carafe, wine bottle, demijohn, magnum, jeroboam, rehoboam, methuselah, balthazar, gourd, calabash, wineskin, beer bottle, milk bottle, hip flask, hot-water bottle, thermos (flask)

15 **pot**, pan, pots and pans, cooking pot, cauldron, saucepan, wok, frying pan, skillet, steamer, fish kettle, roasting tin, double boiler, bain-marie, casserole, roaster, cake tin, bread tin, boiler, brazier, kettle, jug kettle, coffeepot, coffee urn, percolator, coffee maker, *cafetière* (Fr), teapot, tea urn, jamjar, honeypot, storage jar, plastic container, warming pan, chamber pot, potty

16 **crockery**, china, chinaware, dishware, pottery, teaset, dinner service, glassware, Tupperware (Tm), utensils, bowl, finger bowl, mixing bowl, cereal bowl, soup bowl, porringer, sugar bowl, salad bowl, punch bowl, tureen, ramekin, terrine, jelly mould, gravy (or sauce) boat, rose bowl, plate, dinner plate, platter, dish, saucer, charger, salver, tray

17 **ladle**, ice-cream scoop, scoop, dipper, spatula, spoon, wooden spoon, tablespoon, dessertspoon, soupspoon, teaspoon, eggspoon, sugar spoon, shovel, spade, trowel

▶ 45 Cookery

18 **stomach**, belly, gut, paunch, midriff, tummy (tum) (Inf), bread basket (Inf), pot belly (Inf), beer gut (Inf), spare tyre (Inf), bay window (Inf)

▶ 350 Eating

19 **inflatable**, balloon, inner tube, football, gasbag, bubble, blister, sac

ADJECTIVES

20 **containing**, contained, holding, held, enclosing, enclosed, covering, covered, enveloping, enveloped, wrapping, wrapped, sheathed, surrounded, cocooning, cocooned, stabling, stabled, sheltering, sheltered, storing, storage, stored, reserved, packing, packed, bundled, boxed, caged, canning, canned, tinning, tinned, potting, potted, bottling, bottled, ladled, scooped, spooned, shovelled, binned, shelved, garaged, bagged, in the bag, locked up, entombed

VERBS

21 **put** (or **place**) **in a container**, store, reserve, containerize, crate up, bundle, can, tin, pot, box up, pour in, bottle, cover, wrap, pack, package, sheath, cocoon, envelope, enclose, cage, surround, shelter, stable, garage, entomb

259 Size

NOUNS

1 **size**, magnitude, order of magnitude, amplitude, dimension(s), proportion(s), measurement(s), measure, gauge, scale, extent, extension, scope, range, reach, limit, expanse, spread, coverage, area, length, breadth, width, height, depth, radius, diameter, calibre, scantling, girth, circumference, mass, bulk, volume, capacity, cubature, cubage, content, room, space, accommodation, stowage, tonnage, displacement, burden, tankage

▶ 503 Accuracy, 269 Length, 275 Height, 277 Depth, 273 Thickness, 299 Outline, 369 Heaviness, 248 Space

2 **bigness**, largeness, greatness, full size, full growth, life size, sizableness, ampleness, generousness, voluminousness, bagginess, capaciousness, spaciousness, roominess, hugeness, enormity, immenseness, immensity, massiveness, grandness, grandeur, prodigiousness, tallness, bulkiness, unwieldiness, cumbersomeness, broadness, wideness, comprehensiveness, expansiveness, extensiveness, vastness

▶ 144 Completeness, 142 Whole

3 **large scale**, good size, fair size, large size, family size, economy size, king-size, queen-size, giant size, record size, outsize, oversize, overgrowth

4 **gigantism**, giantism, hypertrophy, hyperplasia, acromegaly, elephantiasis

5 **fatness**, obesity, overweight, corpulence, portliness, rotundity, roundness, endomorphy, grossness, fleshiness, flabbiness, bloatedness, puffiness, fullness, plumpness, fattishness, paunchiness, buxomness, bustiness, plumpishness, podginess, tubbiness, chubbiness, adiposity, stoutness, *embonpoint* (Fr)

6 **squatness**, dumpiness, stockiness, squareness, heavy build, burliness, brawniness, beefiness, meatiness, chunkiness, heaviness, heftiness, hulkiness, lumpishness, lumpiness

7 **mass**, lump, chunk, hunk, block, clump, cluster, wad, heap, mountain, clod, cake, glob, gob, wodge (Inf), gobs (Inf), dollop (Inf)

8 **fat**, cellulite, double chin, potbelly, paunch, flab (Inf), blubber (Inf), lard (Inf), corporation (Brit inf), beer belly (Sl), spare tyre (Sl)

9 **big thing**, giant, monster, whale, dinosaur, mammoth, mastodon, elephant, hippopotamus, leviathan, behemoth, King Kong, Empire State Building, redwood tree, whopper (Inf), spanker (Inf), lunker (US inf), jumbo (Inf), humdinger (Sl)

10 **big person**, hulk, man mountain, monster man, giant, giantess, ogre, ogress, Titan, Titaness, colossus, amazon, Goliath, Brobdingnagian, Gargantua, Pantagruel, Cyclops, Polyphemus, Atlas, Hercules, Typhon, heavy (Inf)

11 **tall person**, six footer, colossus, giant, longlegs (Inf), highpockets (Inf), beanpole (Sl), long drink of water (Sl)

12 **fat person**, roly-poly, heavyweight, Falstaff, fatty (Inf), tub of lard (Inf), dumpling (Inf), blimp (Inf), hippo (Inf), fatso (Sl)

ADJECTIVES

13 **this size**, about this size, so big, this big, about this big, of that order

14 **medium**, medium-size(d), average, average-size(d), standard, regular

15 **big**, large, great, full-size(d), full-grown, full-blown, full-scale, life-size(d), large as life, sizable, good-size(d), fair-size(d), large-size(d), large-scale, considerable, substantial, goodly, bumper, ample, generous, voluminous, baggy, capacious, spacious, roomy, family-size(d), economy-size(d), man-size(d), king-size(d), queen-size(d), giant-size(d), record-size(d), huge, enormous, immense, massive, massy, gigantic, gigantesque, colossal, titanic, monstrous, great big, larger than life, mammoth, giant, monster, Gargantuan, Brobdingnagian, Cyclopean, towering, monumental, grand, imposing, Homeric, epic, tremendous, stupendous, prodigious, mountainous, megalithic, macroscopic, astronomical, outsize, extra large, oversized, too big, overlarge, overgrown, bulky, mighty, broad, wide, comprehensive, expansive, extensive, vast, limitless, infinite,

tidy (Inf), healthy (Inf), jumbo (Inf), almighty (Inf), whopping (Inf), walloping (Inf), whacking (Inf), spanking (Inf), thumping (Sl), thundering (Sl), mega (Sl), ginormous (Sl)

16 **fat**, obese, overweight, endomorphic, gross, fleshy, flabby, bloated, puffy, swollen, distended, full, plump, podgy, tubby, chubby, bonny, adipose, stout, corpulent, portly, rotund, round, roly-poly, well-fed, overfed, fat as a pig, plump as a dumpling, plump as a partridge, squab, dumpy, round-faced, moonfaced, full-faced, chubby-faced, chubby-cheeked, double-chinned, big-bellied, full-bellied, potbellied, paunchy, abdominous, big-bottomed, buxom, busty, bosomy, full-bosomed, well-endowed, top-heavy, steatopygic, steatopygous, hippy (Inf), broad in the beam (Inf), well-upholstered (Inf), fat-arsed (Sl)

17 **stocky**, stout, thickset, heavyset, squat, square, well-built, heavily built, burly, strapping, lusty, brawny, beefy, meaty, heavy, chunky, hefty, hulking, hulky, lumbering, lumpish, lumpy, elephantine

VERBS

18 **measure**, gauge, size, grade, group, rank, sort, match, graduate, adjust, proportion, enlarge

19 **be big**, bulk, loom, loom large, fill space, tower, soar

ADVERBS

20 **largely**, on a large scale, in the large, greatly, considerably, substantially, amply, generously, voluminously, baggily, capaciously, spaciously, hugely, in a big way, enormously, immensely, massively, monstrously, mightily, limitlessly, infinitely, as can be, fatly, obesely, plumply, stoutly, roundly, buxomly

260 Littleness

NOUNS

1 **littleness**, smallness, smallishness, diminutiveness, shortness, petiteness, squatness, dumpiness, dwarfishness, daintiness, dinkiness, small scale, compactness, handiness, portability, tininess, minuteness, fineness, thinness, slightness, exiguity, tenuousness, imperceptibility, intangibility, impalpability, imponderability, inappreciability, invisibility, undersize, stuntedness, puniness, runtiness, shrunkenness, scrubbiness, scrawniness, scragginess, meagreness, scantness, scantiness, skimpiness, pokiness, snugness, cosiness, paltriness, pettiness, miniaturization, microminiaturization, microscopy, micrography, microscope, micrometer

2 **little thing**, particle, grain, grain of sand, seed, mustard seed, granule, corpuscle, molecule, cell, nucleus, monad, atom, subatomic particle, ion, electron, proton, neutron, neu-

trino, parton, meson, muon, quark, point, pinpoint, pinhead, dot, microdot, pixel, microbe, bacterium, virus, germ, bacillus, microorganism, animalcule, protozoan, zoospore, microphyte, amoeba, euglena, plankton, miniature, mini, baby, toy, doll, puppet, model, microcosm, microphotograph, microfilm, microfiche, thumbnail sketch, pocket edition, Elzevir edition, duodecimo, twelvemo, chip, silicon chip, microchip, integrated circuit

3 **little piece**, bit, fragment, sliver, shaving, filing, jot, tittle, iota, speck, fleck, mote, scrap, crumb, morsel, snippet, minutia, minim, drop, droplet

4 **little person**, dwarf, midget, pygmy, manikin, homunculus, Hop-o'-my-thumb, Tom Thumb, Thumbelina, Pinocchio, Alberich, Nibelung, hobbit, elf, gnome, fairy, sprite, brownie, leprechaun, halfling, runt, weakling, shrimp (Inf), minnow (Inf), tiddler (Inf), squirt (Inf), squit (Inf), fingerling, slip, chit, wisp, snip (US inf), small fry, titch (Inf), half-pint (Sl), pipsqueak (Inf), peewee (Inf), bantam, lightweight, featherweight, mouse, tot, mite

5 **little space**, hole, pigeonhole, cubbyhole, doll's house, tight squeeze, tight spot, pinch

VERBS

6 **be little**, be small, take up no room, fit on the head of a pin

ADJECTIVES

7 **little**, small, smallish, diminutive, short, petite, squat, dumpy, dwarfish, dwarfed, elfin, dainty, dinky, pint-size(d) (Inf), knee-high (to a grasshopper), Lilliputian, miniature, subminiature, mini, dwarf, midget, pygmy, bantam, baby, model, small-scale, miniaturized, microcosmic, compact, handy, portable, pocket-size(d), pocket, vest-pocket (US), duodecimo, twelvemo, tiny, minute, minuscule, infinitesimal, microscopic, ultramicroscopic, rudimentary, rudimental, incipient, embryonic, germinal, fine, thin, slight, exiguous, tenuous, imperceptible, intangible, impalpable, imponderable, inappreciable, negligible, indiscernible, invisible, undersize(d), stunted, puny, runty, pindling (US inf), shrunk, contracted, shrunken, wizened, shrivelled, scrubby, scrawny, scraggy, meagre, scant, scanty, skimpy, inadequate, poky, cramped, limited, restricted, no room to swing a cat, snug, cosy, bijou, two-by-four (Inf), one-horse (Inf), piddling (Inf), paltry, petty, trifling, trivial, inconsiderable, insignificant, unimportant, minimal, granular, corpuscular, molecular, atomic, subatomic, microbic, microbial, bacterial, animalcular, protozoan, amoebic, amoeboid, wee (Inf), teeny (Inf), weeny (Inf), teeny-weeny (Inf), titchy (Sl), tiddly (Sl), bitsy (Inf), itsy-bitsy (Inf), itty-bitty (Inf)

ADVERBS

8 **in a small way**, on a small scale, in a nutshell, in miniature, diminutively, daintily, slightly, minimally, tinily, minutely, punily, finely, tenuously, inappreciably, negligibly, inconsiderably, insignificantly, unimportantly

9 **microscopically**, microcosmically, atomically, subatomically, infinitesimally, indiscernibly, imperceptibly, invisibly, intangibly, impalpably, imponderably

261 Expansion

NOUNS

1 **growth**, enlargement, increase in size, extension, lengthening, drawing out, stretch, stretching, stretching out, outstretching, spread, spreading, spreading out, outspreading, sprawl, sprawling, splay, splaying, branching, ramification, fanning, fanning out, dispersion, expansion, widening, broadening, flare, flaring, dilation, dilatation, diastole, opening, unfolding, distension, distention, swell, swelling, swollenness, bloat, bloating, bloatedness, tumefaction, tumescence, intumescence, tumidity, tumidness, turgescence, turgidity, turgidness, dropsy, oedema, puffiness, inflation, reflation, blowing up, bulging, bulbousness, stuffing, padding, fattening, increase, building, build-up, augmentation, addition, heightening, rising, raising, elevation, hiking, magnification, aggrandizement, amplification, development, overdevelopment, hypertrophy, overgrowth, waxing, crescendo, germination, budding, shooting, sprouting, vegetation, burgeoning, blossoming, blooming, flowering, maturation, flourishing, thriving, multiplication, reproduction, procreation, breeding, pullulation

2 **enlargeability**, extendability, extendibility, extensibility, extensibleness, stretch, stretchability, elasticity, spreadability, expansibility, dilatability, dilatableness, distensibility

3 **enlarged thing**, enlargement, extension, swelling, tumour, bulge, balloon, bubble, inflatable

4 **enlarger**, extensor, lengthener, stretcher, spreader, disperser, expander, widener, broadener, dilater, dilator, distender, stuffing, padding, inflater, inflator, pump, increaser, augmenter, augmentor, developer

VERBS

5 **make bigger**, make larger, enlarge, increase in size, extend, lengthen, draw out, stretch, stretch out, outstretch, spread, spread out, outspread, sprawl, splay, ramify, fan, fan out, disperse, expand, widen, broaden, flare, dilate, open, distend, swell, bloat, puff up, inflate, blow up, pump, pump up, stuff, pad, fatten,

fat, plump, plump up, increase, build, build up, augment, add to, heighten, raise, elevate, hike, hike up, up, magnify, aggandize, amplify, develop, overdevelop, hypertrophy

6 **become bigger**, become larger, grow, enlarge, increase in size, extend, lengthen, draw out, stretch, stretch out, spread, spread out, outspread, sprawl, splay, branch, branch out, ramify, fan, fan out, disperse, expand, widen, broaden, flare, dilate, open up, unfold, distend, swell, bloat, tumify, puff up, inflate, balloon, belly, bulge, fatten, fat, plump, plump out, fill out, get fat, gain weight, put on weight, become overweight, increase, build, build up, augment, mushroom, snowball, overdevelop, hypertrophy, outgrow, overgrow, grow like a weed, spread like wildfire, magnify, amplify, develop, wax, greaten, crescendo, gather, brew, rise, grow up, shoot up, spring up, upspring, sprout up, germinate, bud, shoot, sprout, vegetate, burgeon, blossom, bloom, flower, flourish, thrive, multiply, reproduce, procreate, breed, pullulate

ADJECTIVES
7 **bigger**, larger, enlarged, extended, lengthened, drawn-out, stretched, stretched-out, outstretched, spread, spread-out, outspread, widespread, splayed, fanned, fanned out, dispersed, expanded, widened, broadened, flared, dilated, open, wide-open, unfolded, distended, swelled, swollen, bloated, tumid, turgid, incrassate, dropsical, oedematous, puffed-up, puffy, inflated, blown-up, pumped-up, stuffed, padded, fatter, fattened, fatted, overweight, increased, built-up, augmented, heightened, raised, elevated, magnified, amplified, developed, mature, grown, full-grown, fully grown, full-fledged, fully fledged, full-blown, fully developed, overdeveloped, hypertrophied, overgrown

8 **growing**, crescent, extending, lengthening, stretching, spreading, sprawling, sprawly, splaying, patulous, branching, fanning, fanlike, fan-shape(d), flabellate, flabelliform, deltoid, expanding, widening, broadening, flaring, dilating, opening, unfolding, swelling, tumescent, turgescent, bulging, bulbous, increasing, waxing, gathering, brewing, mushrooming, snowballing, heightening, rising, developing, germinating, budding, shooting, sprouting, burgeoning, blossoming, blooming, flowering, flourishing, thriving, multiplying, pullulating

9 **enlargeable**, extendable, extendible, extensible, extensive, extensile, extensional, stretchable, stretchy, elastic, spreadable, dispersive, expandable, expansible, expansive, expansile, expansionary, dilatable, dilational, dilatant, dilative, distensible, distensive, inflatable, inflationary, augmentative, eleva-

tory, multipliable, magnifiable, amplifiable, developable

ADVERBS
10 **largely**, broadly, widely, extensively, expansively, increasingly, additionally, reproductively, procreatively, bulbously, puffily, turgidly, tumidly

262   Contraction

NOUNS
1 **contraction**, decrease in size, systole, syneresis, synizesis, shrinking, shrinkage, shrunkenness, preshrinking, preshrinkage, constringency, astringency, astringence, compression, compaction, compactedness, condensation, concentration, miniaturization, scaling-down, squeeze, squeezing, tightening, tightness, pressing, pressure, crush, crushing, pinch, pinching, clenching, clamping, cramping, constriction, coarctation, limitation, restriction, circumscription, strangling, strangulation, stenosis, deflation, flattening, flatness, implosion, collapse, cave-in, shortening, abbreviation, elision, curtailment, abridgment, pruning, trimming, clipping, shearing shaving, filing, grinding, narrowing, drawing in, drawing together, closing up, taking in, gathering, puckering, puckering up, pursing, knitting, wrinkling, shrivelling, withering, searing, wasting, consumption, tabescence, atrophy, marasmus, emaciation, thinning, slimming, losing weight, decrease, reduction, lessening, diminuendo, wane, waning, levelling off, bottoming out

2 **contractibility**, contractility, shrinkability, compressibility, compactability, condensibility, crushability, limitability, circumscribability, deflatability, collapsibility

3 **contracted thing**, epitome, compendium, digest, bottleneck, neck, isthmus, hourglass, hourglass figure, wasp waist

4 **contractor**, astringent, styptic, compressor, compacter, condenser, tourniquet, squeezer, press, crusher, foller, mangle, clamp, vice, corset, straigjacket, constrictor, trimmer, grinder

VERBS
5 **make smaller**, contract, decrease in size, shrink, preshrink, Sanforize (Tm), constringe, compress, compact, condense, concentrate, boil down, miniaturize, scale down, squeeze, tighten, press, crush, pinch, cram, jam, roll up, rool up into a ball, clench, clamp, cramp, constrict, limit, restrict, circumscribe, strangle, strangulate, deflate, flatten, implode, collapse, telescope, shorten, abbreviate, curtail, abridge, stunt, prune, trim, clip, shear, shave, whittle away, file, grind, narrow, draw, draw in, draw together, close up, take in, gather, smock, tuck, pucker, pucker up, purse, knit, wrinkle,

shrivel, sear, waste, emaciate, thin, slim, decrease, reduce, lessen

6 **become smaller**, contract, shrink, condense, concentrate, boil down, tighten, roll up, rool up into a ball, curl up, huddle, crowd together, deflate, go down, implode, collapse, cave in, fall in, fold up, telescope, shorten, narrow, draw in, close up, pucker, pucker up, knit, wrinkle, shrivel, shrivel up, wither, wizen, waste, waste away, emaciate, thin, slim, diet, lose weight, decrease, reduce, lessen, wane level off, bottom out

ADJECTIVES

7 **smaller**, contracted, shrunk, shrunken, preshrunk, Sanforized (Tm), compressed, compact, compacted, condensed, concentrated, boiled-down, miniaturized, scaled-down, squeezed, tight, tightened, pressed, crushed, pinched, rolled-up, curled-up, huddled, clenched, cramped, constricted, coarctate, limited, restricted, circumscribed, strangled, strangulated, deflated, flat, collapsed, telescoped, shortened, abbreviated, curtailed, abridged, stunted, pruned, trimmed, clipped, shorn, narrow, narrowed, drawn-in, drawn-together, closed-up, gathered, smocked, tucked, puckered, puckered up, pursed, knitted, wrinkled, shrivelled, shrivelled-up, withered, wizen, wizened, sear, seared, wasted, consumptive, emaciated, thin, slim, decreased, reduced

8 **contracting**, contractive, contractional, shrinking, constringent, astringent, styptic, compressive, tightening, crushing, pinching, cramping, constricting, constrictive, limiting, restricting, restrictive, circumscriptive, strangling, deflationary, implosive, collapsing, shortening, stunting, narrowing, gathering, puckering, pursing, shrivelling, searing, wasting, tabescent, emaciating, thinning, slimming, decreasing, reducing, lessening, waning

9 **contractible**, contractile, shrinkable, compressible, compactable, condensible, crushable, limitable, circumscribable, deflatable, collapsible, foldable, telescopic

263 Distance

NOUNS

1 **distance**, farness, remoteness, inaccessibility, aloofness, removal, separation, divergence, deviation, dispersion, perspective, long range, astronomical distance, deep space, depths of space, light years, infinity
▶ *269 Length, 136 Separation, 343 Divergence, 248 Space, 265 Interval*

2 **great distance**, step, long way, great way, good way, fair way, long run, long haul, long trail, day's march, marathon, far cry, tidy step (Inf), miles away (Inf), long chalk (Inf)

3 **distant place**, background, periphery, circumference, horizon, skyline, offing, vanishing point, where the earth meets the sky, godforsaken place, the back of beyond, back o'Bourke (Aus), outback, outskirts, outpost, antipodes, pole, the North Pole, the South Pole, Thule, ultima Thule, Pillars of Hercules, Timbuktu, Outer Mongolia, Darkest Africa, Siberia, Pago Pago, the Great Divide, Far East, Far West, four corners of the earth, ends of the earth, world's end, end of the rainbow, outer space, the moon, the middle of nowhere (Inf), God knows where (Inf), the sticks (Inf), the boondocks (US sl), the boonies (US sl)
▶ *299 Outline, 304 Rear, 302 Limit*

4 **reserve**, aloofness, standoffishness, shyness, coldness, coolness
▶ *591 Avoidance, 816 Unsociability*

VERBS

5 **be distant**, outlie, outrange, outdistance, stand far away, lie out of the way, stretch to the ends of the earth

6 **keep away**, keep off, keep one's distance, keep at a distance, remain at a distance, stand off, stand away, stand aloof, stand back, distance onself, keep away from, keep out of the way of, keep a safe distance from, keep clear of, stand clear of, steer clear of, give a wide berth to, keep at arm's length, keep apart, separate, space out

7 **reach**, stretch, extend, go, carry, reach out, stretch out, outreach, outstretch, reach to, stretch to, extend to, go to, lead to, run to, carry to, get to, come to

ADJECTIVES

8 **distant**, far, far off, far away, far-flung, remote, yonder, yon (Dial), ulterior, farther, further, outlying, offshore, inaccessible, out-of-the-way, godforsaken, exotic, antipodean, hyperborean, overseas, transatlantic, transpacific, transoceanic, transmarine, ultramarine, transcontinental, transalpine, transmontane, tramontane, ultramontane, transpolar, transpontine, transmundane, ultramundane, out of this world, away, apart, asunder, separated, distal, peripheral, long-distance, long-range, out of sight, out of range, out of reach, farthest, farthermost, furthest, furthermost, ultimate, extreme, terminal, unget-at-able (Inf)

9 **reserved**, aloof, standoffish, unapproachable, untouchable, shy, cold, cool

ADVERBS

10 **distantly**, remotely, far, afar, far off, far away, a long way off, a long way away, over the hills and far away, overseas, abroad, afield, far afield, far and wide, far and near, widely, broadly, to the ends of the earth, out of this world, in the distance, yonder, yon (Dial), in the background, in the offing, on the horizon, as far as the eye can see, out of sight, out of

hearing, out of earshot, out of range, out of reach, beyond reach, out of bounds, too far, further, farther, ahead, in front, behind, way behind, way in front, away, off, at a distance, at arm's length, apart, asunder, aloof, aside, astray, clear, wide, wide of the mark, in the back of beyond, out of the way, in the sticks (Inf), in the boondocks (US sl), in the boonies (US sl)

11 **reservedly**, aloofly, standoffishly, in a stand-offish mood, shyly, coldly, coolly, with an unapproachable manner

264   Nearness

NOUNS

1 **nearness**, closeness, proximity, propinquity, immediacy, intimacy, inseparability, handiness, convenience, accessibility, approximation, approach, convergence, juncture, collision course, conjunction, syzygy, appulse, perigee, perihelion

▶ *342 Convergence, 253 Presence, 267 Juxtaposition, 191 Immediacy*

2 **short distance**, no distance, little way, short way, short cut, step, stone's throw, spitting distance, striking distance, earshot, gunshot, bowshot, close range, close quarters, brink, verge, hair's-breadth, fingerbreadth, finger's-breadth, finger's width, inch, millimetre, ace, near miss, photo finish, near thing (Inf), narrow squeak (Inf), level pegging (Inf)

▶ *300 Edge, 674 Contention*

3 **near place**, vicinity, vicinage, neighbourhood, locality, precinct, environs, surroundings, purlieus, confines, approaches, foreground, front, ringside seat

▶ *297 Surroundings*

4 **neighbour**, next-door neighbour, bystander, onlooker

ADJECTIVES

5 **near**, nigh, close, proximate, proximal, side-by-side, shoulder-to-shoulder, cheek-by-jowl, hand-in-hand, arm-in-arm, intimate, elbow-to-elbow, bumper-to-bumper, inseparable, neck-and-neck, close-run, nearby, in the vicinity, in the neighbourhood, local, home, wayside, roadside, inshore, neighbouring, vicinal, next-door, next, adjoining, contiguous, immediate, nearest, closest, on the spot, to hand, at hand, handy, convenient, accessible, at one's fingertips, nearer, closer, approximate, approximating, nearing, approaching, converging, convergent, forthcoming, warm (Inf), hot (Inf), level pegging (Inf), get-at-able (Inf)

ADVERBS

6 **near**, nigh (Fml), close, closely, at close quarters, at close range, not far, nearby, close by, hard by, fast by, in the vicinity, in the neighbourhood, locally, next door, hereabouts, thereabouts, about, around, around and about, at hand, near at hand, close at hand, at one's fingertips, at one's elbow, at one's side, at one's feet, under one's nose, within reach, within range, within earshot, within hearing, within call, within sight, a stone's throw away, only a step, just around the corner, on one's doorstep, in one's own back yard, in spitting distance, as near as makes no difference, verging on, on the verge of, on the brink of, by a hair's-breadth, by the skin of one's teeth, by a whisker, on the tip of one's tongue

7 **nearly**, almost, well-nigh, not quite, just about, all but, as good as, near enough, virtually, practically, for all practical purposes, to all intents and purposes, more or less, give or take a little, approximately, roughly, in round numbers, generally speaking, say

VERBS

8 **be near**, stand close to, lie in the vicinity of, lie in the neighbourhood of

9 **near**, come near, get near, get close, move close, bring near, draw near, draw nigh, approach, converge, verge on, close up, move up, get warm (Inf), get hot (Inf)

10 **stay near**, keep close to, follow, shadow, dog, sit on the tail of, tread on the heels of, breathe down the neck of, hover over, tailgate, go with, hang around, hang about, stick to, cling to, hug, embrace, skirt, tail (Inf)

265   Interval

NOUNS

1 **interval**, gap, space, distance, room, margin, clearance, headroom, leeway, freeboard, distance between, space between, intervening space, interspace, spacing, single space, double space, half space, en space, em space, thin space, hair space, interruption, daylight, firebreak, passage, separation, time interval, discontinuity, hiatus, lacuna, caesura, jump, leap

▶ *248 Space, 185 Time, 322 Opening, 136 Separation, 160 Discontinuity, 49 Music*

2 **crack**, crevice, cleft, fissure, scissure, interstice, chink, cranny, check, flaw, hairline crack, notch, nick, cut, incision, gash, slit, split, rift, fault, rupture, rent, tear, break, fracture, breach, hole, opening, aperture, orifice, cavity, groove, slot, furrow, trench, ditch, dyke, moat, ha-ha

▶ *277 Depth, 321 Furrow, 319 Notch*

3 **gulf**, abyss, chasm, void, gape, gorge, ravine, canyon, box canyon, crevasse, chimney, gully, gulch, ghat, pass, defile, col, couloir, coulee (US), flume, kloof (S Africa), donga (Aus and NZ), draw, clough (Dial), valley, dell, cwm (Welsh)

▶ *317 Concavity, 356 Passage*

VERBS

4 space, space out, interspace, separate, break up, part, set apart, keep apart, place at intervals, make a space, make room, clear

5 crack, cleave, check, notch, nick, cut, incise, gash, slit, split, split apart, rive, rupture, rend, tear, break, fracture, breach, open, gape, groove, slot, furrow, trench, ditch

ADJECTIVES

6 spaced, spaced out, interspaced, interspatial, interstitial, separate, separated, parted, set apart, removed, placed at intervals, intervallic, discontinuous

7 cracked, cleft, cloven, fissured, fissile, cut, slit, split, riven, ruptured, rent, torn, broken, fractured, open, gaping, gappy, grooved, furrowed, rimose, dehiscent

ADVERBS

8 apart, separately, discontinuously, at intervals, with a break, with an intermission, with an interval, off and on, now and then, now and again, every so often, interspatially, interstitially

266 Layer

NOUNS

1 layer, stratum, seam, zone, vein, lode, bed, belt, strip, band, course, table, thickness, ply, interlining, fold, pleat, lap, flap, superstratum, overlayer, topcoat, topsoil, overlap, substratum, underlayer, underlay, lining, undercoat, bedding

▶ *293 Covering, 273 Thickness, 282 Horizontality, 292 Lining*

2 level, tier, row, storey, floor, landing, deck, terrace, ledge, shelf, step, stage

▶ *284 Support, 280 Base*

3 coat, coating, covering, sheet, blanket, foil, leaf, lamina, lamella, plate, plating, veneer, facing, fascia, overlay, sheathe, bark, membrane, skin, peel, pellicle, film, patina, bloom, scum, dross

▶ *604 Materials, 274 Thinness*

4 slice, sliver, wafer, disc, chip, rasher, collop (Dial), cut, slab, tablet, plaque, plank, slat, lath, panel, pane, tile, slate, shaving, paring, scale, squama, flake, dandruff, scurf, flock, floccus

5 layered thing, laminate, Formica (Tm), laminated wood, plywood, laminated glass, safety glass, sandwich, club sandwich (US), double-decker, layer cake, onion, nest of tables, Russian doll, coal mine, shingled roof, clapboard house (US), atmosphere

6 layering, stratification, lamination, lamellation, foliation, scaliness, flakiness, squamation, delamination, exfoliation, desquamation

ADJECTIVES

7 layered, in layers, stratified, stratiform, straticulate, foliated, laminate, laminated, two-ply, three-ply, two-tiered, three-tiered, two-storeyed, three-storeyed, double-decker, terraced, multistage

8 coated, undercoated, plated, veneered, faced, lined, overlaid, overlaying, overlapped, overlapping, sheathed, laminated

9 platelike, leaflike, foliate, lamellar, lamellate, lamellated, lamelliform, placoid, membranous, pellicular, filmy, scummy, drossy, scaly, furfuraceous, squamous, squamose, squamulose, flaky, scurfy, flocculent, floccose

VERBS

10 layer, lay, lay down, arrange in layers, stratify, laminate, tier, deck, shingle, sandwich, coat, spread, cover, plate, veneer, face, line, overlay, overlap

11 scale, peel off, peel, flake off, flake, strip, shave, delaminate, exfoliate, desquamate

ADVERBS

12 in layers, in strips, on several levels, membraneously, furfuraceously, squamously, squamosely, flocculently

267 Juxtaposition

NOUNS

1 juxtaposition, apposition, adjacency, nearness, closeness, contiguity, contiguousness, abuttal, abutment, tangency, touching, touch, contact, continuity, junction, joining, connection, union, bordering, border, borderland, frontier, buffer state

▶ *264 Nearness, 407 Touch, 159 Consecutiveness, 135 Union, 138 Adhesion, 300 Edge, 302 Limit*

2 meeting, encounter, confrontation, interface, intercommunication, impingement, touch, nudge, brush, graze, glance

▶ *298 Interface*

VERBS

3 juxtapose, appose, adjoin, abut, butt, touch, make contact, come into contact, bring into contact, join, connect, border, neighbour, be next to, be beside, be side by side, place side by side

4 meet, encounter, confront, interface, intercommunicate, impinge, hit, nudge, jostle, elbow, rub, brush, kiss, graze, scrape, shave, skim, glance, rub shoulders (or elbows) with (Inf)

ADJECTIVES

5 juxtaposed, juxtapositional, juxtapositive, adjacent, near, close, tangent, tangential, contiguous, adjoining, abutting, touching, in contact, continuous, joined, connecting, intercommunicating, linking, bordering, conterminous, coterminous, side-by-side, cheek-by-jowl, face-to-face, nose-to-nose, eyeball-to-

eyeball, end-to-end, elbow-to-elbow, bumper-to-bumper, nose-to-tail

6 **meeting**, impinging, rubbing, brushing, grazing, glancing

ADVERBS

7 **beside**, alongside, in juxtaposition, adjacently, tangentially, in contact, contiguously, continuously, side by side, cheek by jowl, face to face, nose to nose, eyeball to eyeball, end to end, elbow to elbow, bumper to bumper, nose to tail

268   Measurement

NOUNS

1 **measurement**, mensuration, measure, measuring, admeasurement, metage, quantification, quantitation, gauging, calibration, reading, read-out, calculation, computation, reckoning, metrology, assessment, valuation, rating, evaluation, appraisal, appraisement, estimation, estimate, approximation, rough measure, determination, survey, surveying, triangulation, geodesy, geodetics, topography, cartography, oceanography

▶ *120 Quantity, 170 Calculation, 275 Height, 269 Length, 248 Space*

2 **micrometry**, telemetry, tacheometry, tachymetry, odometry, cyclometry, photogrammetry, dilatometry, planimetry, goniometry, clinometry, altimetry, hypsometry, bathometry, bathymetry, stereometry, volumetry, densimetry, hydrometry, viscometry, plastometry, acidimetry, alkalimetry, stoichiometry, oxidimetry, iodometry, saccharimetry, salinometry, salimetry, atmometry, aerometry, hygrometry, colorimetry, thermometry, tasimetry, calorimetry, cryometry, pyrometry, photometry, spectrophotometry, spectrometry, sensitometry, refractometry, fluorometry, polarimetry, bolometry, actinometry, dosimetry, radiometry, anemometry, barometry, piezometry, manometry, dynamometry, chronometry, tachometry, magnetometry, coulometry, galvanometry, potentiometry, electrometry, interferometry, astrometry, heliometry, biometry, biometrics, zoometry, anthropometry, cephalometry, craniometry, optometry, spirometry, pneumatometry, rheometry, psychometry, dolorimetry, algometry, audiometry, tonometry

3 **measurability**, mensurability, quantifiability, determinability

4 **size**, magnitude, height, altitude, depth, length, distance, range, scope, breadth, width, volume, capacity, weight, quantity, amount, dosage, degree, extent, value, coordinates, ordinate, abscissa, latitude, longitude, azimuth, right ascension, declination

▶ *259 Size*

5 **measuring system**, metric system, imperial system, Système International d'Unités (SI), apothecaries' measure, apothecaries' weight, troy weight, avoirdupois weight

▶ *75 Units*

6 **measuring instrument**, measuring rod, yardstick, foot rule, feeler gauge, line, plumb line, lead, chain, Gunter's chain, rule, ruler, tape measure, steel rule, scale, graduated scale, calibrated scale, vernier, dividers, callipers, set square, try square, T-square, protractor, quadrant, sextant, octant, astrolabe, log, echo sounder, dipstick, watermark, water line, tidemark, high-water mark, Plimsoll line, load line, milestone

7 **standard**, norm, yardstick, touchstone, benchmark, criterion, rule of thumb, canon, test, check, type, model, pattern, prototype, weighing machine, weighbridge, scales, balance

8 **meter**, gauge, dial gauge, indicator, chart recorder, micrometer, micrometer gauge, micrometer calliper, telemeter, tellurometer, tacheometer, tachymeter, theodolite, alidade, pedometer, mileometer, odometer, cyclometer, dilatometer, planimeter, goniometer, clinometer, altimeter, hypsometer, bathometer, volumeter, densimeter, densitometer, hydrometer, viscometer, plastometer, acidimeter, alkalimeter, nitrometer, saccharimeter, saccharometer, salinometer, salimeter, alcoholometer, vaporimeter, atmometer, evaporimeter, tensimeter, tensiometer, aerometer, hygrometer, colorimeter, tintometer, thermometer, tasimeter, calorimeter, cryometer, pyrometer, photometer, spectrophotometer, spectrometer, sensitometer, refractometer, fluorometer, polarimeter, solarimeter, pyranometer, bolometer, thermopile, actinometer, dosimeter, Geiger counter, radiometer, anemometer, wind gauge, barometer, pressure gauge, thermobarometer, piezometer, manometer, dynamometer, seismometer, chronometer, tachometer, speedometer, rev counter, accelerometer, decelerometer, magnetometer, variometer, voltmeter, ammeter, voltammeter, voltameter, coulometer, galvanometer, potentiometer, electrometer, interferometer, heliometer, cephalometer, craniometer, optometer, spirometer, pneumatometer, rheometer, pulsimeter, algometer, audiometer, tonometer, phonometer, water meter, gas meter, electricity meter

9 **measurer**, researcher, scientist, gauger, assessor, valuer, valuator, appraiser, estimator, surveyor, geodesist, topographer, cartographer, oceanographer, timekeeper, quantifier, actuary

▶ *52 Mathematics*

VERBS

10 **measure**, measure up, take the measurements of, admeasure, quantify, meter, gauge, calibrate, grade, graduate, calculate, compute, count, reckon, assess, value, cost, rate, evaluate, appraise, estimate, determine, survey, triangulate, plumb, sound, fathom, probe, assay, weigh, time, size up, measure off, measure out, mark off, pace off

11 **measure out**, mete out, weigh out, dole out, share, share out, apportion, allot

ADJECTIVES

12 **metrical**, metric, imperial, avoirdupois, SI, linear, cubic, measuring, mensural, mensurational, mensurative, quantitative, metrological, geodetic, topographic, cartographic, oceanographic

13 **measured**, admeasured, quantified, metered, gauged, calibrated, graduated, reckoned, assessed, valued, rated, estimated, determined, surveyed, triangulated, plotted, mapped

14 **measurable**, mensurable, quantifiable, meterable, gaugeable, calculable, computable, assessable, appraisable, estimable, determinable, perceptible, fathomable

15 **deliberate**, unhurried, leisurely, slow, studied, planned, calculated

16 **micrometric**, telemetric, tacheometric, tachymetric, photogrammetric, dilatometric, planimetric, goniometric, clinometric, altimetric, hypsometric, bathometric, bathymetric, stereometric, volumetric, densimetric, densitometric, hydrometric, viscometric, plastometric, acidimetric, alkalimetric, stoichiometric, oxidimetric, iodometric, nitrometric, salinometric, salimetric, aerometric, hygrometric, colorimetric, thermometric, tasimetric, calorimetric, pyrometric, photometric, spectrophotometric, spectrometric, refractometric, fluorometric, polarimetric, bolometric, actinometric, dosimetric, radiometric, anemometric, barometric, piezometric, manometric, dynamometric, chronometric, tachometric, magnetometric, voltametric, coulometric, galvanometric, electrometric, interferometric, astrometric, heliometric, biometric, zoometric, anthropometric, cephalometric, craniometric, optometric, spirometric, rheometric, psychometric, audiometric, tonometric, phonometric

ADVERBS

17 **measurably**, with precise measurements, perceptibly, noticeably, metrically, quantitatively, metrologically, geodetically, topographically, cartographically, oceanographically

269 Length

ADJECTIVES

1 **long**, lengthy, tall, high, lengthened, extended, prolonged, protracted, drawn out, long-drawn-out, dragged out, stretched, outstretched, stretched out, spun out, strung out, straggling, overlong, extensive, far-reaching, far, sustained, polysyllabic, sesquipedalian, sesquipedal, interminable, endless, no end to, without end, long-winded, verbose, as long as one's arm, a mile long, shoulder-length, waist-length, knee-length, ankle-length, full-length, unabridged

▶ *259 Size, 263 Distance, 275 Height, 277 Depth, 188 Duration, 155 Sequence, 261 Expansion, 144 Completeness, 553 Diffuseness, 565 Talkativeness*

2 **elongated**, oblong, rectangular, elliptical

▶ *312 Straightness*

3 **longitudinal**, lengthways (*or* lengthwise), longways (*or* longwise), endways (*or* endwise), linear

NOUNS

4 **length**, longitude, longness, overall length, lengthiness, tallness, height, distance, measure, mileage, yardage, footage, extent, reach, span, stretch, duration, stretching out, spinning out, stringing out, drawing out, dragging out, lengthening, elongation, extension, prolongation, protraction, sesquipedalianism, infinity, interminability, endlessness, full length

5 **piece**, portion, section, measure, roll, bolt, coil, run, strip, band, stripe, bar, streak, line, string, queue, crocodile (Inf), single file

▶ *75 Units*

6 **oblong**, rectangle, ellipse

7 **measure of length**, inch, foot, yard, mile, nautical mile, knot, millimetre, centimetre, metre, kilometre, light-year, parsec

▶ *268 Measurement*

8 **measure of time**, millisecond, second, minute, hour, day, week, month, year, decade, lifetime, century, millenium

VERBS

9 **be long**, extend, stretch, stretch out, outstretch, reach out, outreach, spreadeagle, stretch oneself, crane, crane one's neck, stand on tiptoe

10 **lengthen**, extend, stretch, produce, continue, increase, elongate, unroll, uncoil, unfurl, unfold, drop, let down, take up time, prolong, protract, draw, draw out, drag out, spin out, string out

ADVERBS

11 **lengthily**, extensively, in length, end to end, stem to stern, at (full) length, *in extenso* (L), interminably, endlessly, without end, ad infinitum

12 **longitudinally**, lengthways (*or* lengthwise), longways (*or* longwise), endways (*or* endwise), along, in a line, in single file, in tandem, one behind the other

270 Shortness

NOUNS

1 **shortness**, diminutiveness, littleness, stubbiness, stumpiness, stockiness, dumpiness, lowness, squatness, stuntedness, snubness, transience, briefness, brevity, skimpiness, scantiness, curtness, terseness, conciseness, succinctness, compendiousness
▶ *260 Littleness, 276 Lowness, 264 Nearness, 552 Conciseness, 189 Transience*

2 **shortening**, abbreviation, abridgment, compression, capsulization, encapsulation, epitomization, elision, aphaeresis, syncope, apocope, foreshortening, cutting, truncation, curtailment, retrenchment, reduction, cut, cutback, docking, clipping, trimming, pruning, mowing, shearing, shaving, decapitation, beheading
▶ *262 Contraction, 131 Subtraction, 129 Decrease, 879 Punishment*

3 **shortened version**, synopsis, summary, precis, résumé, conspectus, compendium, abbreviation, digest, abridgment, abstract, capsule, outline, epitome, ellipsis

4 **short thing**, short cut, shorts, short legs, miniskirt, crew cut, February, shorthand, one-hit wonder, nine-day wonder, flash in the pan
▶ *189 Transience*

5 **short person**, dwarf, midget, midge, pygmy, elf, gnome, brownie, bantam, small fry, runt, Lilliputian, Tom Thumb, Thumbelina, banty (US inf), shorty (Inf), short stuff (Inf), squirt (Inf), shrimp (Inf), tiddler (Inf), titch (Inf), peewee (Inf), half-pint (Sl)

6 **abruptness**, curtness, brusqueness, gruffness, rudeness, irascibility
▶ *818 Discourtesy, 829 Irascibility*

ADJECTIVES

7 **short**, diminutive, little, stubby, stumpy, thickset, stocky, dumpy, squat, stunted, low, snub, turned-up, retroussé, snub-nosed, pugnosed, short and sweet, transient, brief, skimpy, scanty, curt, terse, concise, succinct, synoptic, summary, compendious

8 **shortened**, abbreviated, abridged, condensed, compressed, digested, abstracted, capsulized, encapsulated, epitomized, elliptical, elided, foreshortened, cut, sawn-off, truncated, cut short, curtailed, curtal, curtate, docked, bobbed, clipped, trimmed, cropped, pruned, mown, mowed, sheared, shorn, shaved, shaven, polled, decapitated, beheaded

9 **abrupt**, curt, brusque, gruff, rude, irascible, short-tempered

VERBS

10 **shorten**, abbreviate, abridge, condense, compress, digest, abstract, boil down, capsulize, encapsulate, epitomize, synopsize (US), summarize, sum up, elide, telescope, foreshorten, truncate, cut, cut short, curtail, retrench, reduce, cut back, cut down, cut off, dock, bob, clip, trim, crop, reap, prune, lop, mow, shear, shave, poll, decapitate, behead, axe, slash, stunt, skimp, take up, turn up

11 **short-cut**, take a short cut, cut across, cut through, cut a corner, go as the crow flies

ADVERBS

12 **short**, shortly, briefly, abruptly, suddenly, all of a sudden, in short, in brief, in a word, in a nutshell, to summarize, curtly, tersely, concisely, succinctly, elliptically, diminutively

271 Breadth

ADJECTIVES

1 **broad**, wide, wide-set, wide-spaced, splayed, splay, patulous, transverse, extensive, expansive, roomy, ample, deep, widespread, wide-ranging, spread-out, beamy, broadcast, open, wide-open, full, baggy, wide-cut, flared, bell-bottomed, wide-angle, wide-screen, broad-gauge, broad-gauged, broadloom, as wide as a barn door, as wide as a truck (US)
▶ *273 Thickness, 261 Expansion, 263 Distance*

2 **broad-shaped**, broad-faced, broad-based, broad-bottomed, wide-bottomed, broad in the beam (Inf), broad-beamed, wide-hipped, broad-tailed, wide-bodied, broad-brimmed, broad-leaved, broad-billed, wide-billed, broad-toothed, broad-lipped, wide-mouthed, wide-eyed, broad-nosed, broad-headed, broad-backed, broad-shouldered, broad-chested, broad-breasted, broad-winged

3 **broad-minded**, open-minded, liberal, open, unprejudiced, unbiased, impartial, disinterested, unbigoted, free-thinking, free, direct, frank, candid, explicit

NOUNS

4 **breadth**, broadness, width, wideness, span, wingspan, gauge, radius, diameter, bore, calibre, handbreadth, range, scope, beam, latitude, extent, extensiveness, catholicity, expanse, expansiveness, spaciousness, roominess, amplitude, ampleness, bagginess, fullness, flare, splay, openness, opening, dilation

5 **broad (or wide) thing**, wide screen, Cinemascope (Tm), Cinerama (Tm), broad gauge, broadsword, broadcloth, broadleaf, broadbill, crossbeam, ocean, Pacific Ocean, desert, Sahara

6 **broad-mindedness**, open-mindedness, liberality, openness, lack of prejudice, impartiality, freedom, free-thinker, directness, explicitness

ADVERBS

7 **broadly**, widely, extensively, generally, by and large, on the whole, openly, freely, obscenely, in an explicit way

8 **breadthwise**, breadthways, broadwise,

broadways, widthwise, widthways, across, athwart, transversely, crosswise, crossways, sideways, broadside, through, from one side to the other, all the way across, clear across

VERBS

9 **be broad** (*or* **wide**), extend, flare, splay
10 **span**, straddle, bestride, cross, link
11 **broaden**, widen, expand, enlarge, spread, diverge, open, dilate
12 **be broad-minded**, keep an open mind, be unbiased, lack prejudice, speak directly

272 Narrowness

ADJECTIVES

1 **narrow**, slender, thin, close, tight, strait, clinging, cramped, pinched, compressed, contracted, pent, pent-up, close-fitting, figure-hugging, limited, restricted, straitened, confined, constricted, circumscribed, incommodious
▶ *262 Contraction, 274 Thinness*
2 **fine**, finespun, fine-drawn, wire-drawn, threadlike, hairlike, filamentous, filiform, spindle-shaped, spindling, spindly, bacillary, bacilliform, spidery, wispy, scanty, tenuous, exiguous, delicate, fragile
3 **tapered**, tapering, convergent, attenuated, attenuate, pointed, peaked, conical, cone-shaped, wedge-shaped, fusiform
4 **narrow-leaved**, angustifoliate, stenophyllous, leptophyllous, narrow-petalled, stenopetalous, narrow-beaked, angustirostrate, narrow-nosed, leptorrhine, catarrhine, narrow-skulled, leptocephalic, narrow-gauge, narrow-gauged, single-track, isthmian

NOUNS

5 **narrowness**, slenderness, thinness, closeness, tightness, straitness, limitation, restriction, confinement, constriction, circumspection, incommodiousness
6 **narrow place**, confined space, small gap, tight squeeze, chink, crack, narrows, strait, straits, channel, slip (US), tunnel, passage, corridor, bottleneck, bridge, ridge, pass, ford, defile, ravine, gully, ditch, isthmus, peninsula, spit
7 **fineness**, spideriness, wispiness, tenuity, exiguity, fragility
8 **narrow thing**, neck, waist, fingers, strip, band, stripe, taper, spindle, stick, rod, pipe, tube, wire, thread, strand, hair, filament, splinter, wisp, streak, line, knife-edge, razor's edge, point, peak, spire, cone, wedge, narrow gauge, single track
9 **narrowing**, shrinking, tapering, taper, convergence, contraction, stricture, attenuation, stenosis

VERBS

10 **narrow**, tighten, cramp, pinch, compress, contract, limit, restrict, straiten, confine, constrict, circumscribe, taper, converge, attenuate, draw, stretch

VERBS

11 **narrowly**, tightly, closely, nearly, only just, barely, hardly, by the skin of one's teeth, by a hair's-breadth, by a whisker

273 Thickness

ADJECTIVES

1 **thick**, broad, wide, deep, massive, substantial, bulky, ample, chunky, heavy, stout, buxom, endomorphic, fat, corpulent, obese, overweight, well-fed, plump, portly, round, rotund, flabby, chubby, podgy, tubby, potbellied, fat as a pig (*or* hog), big as a house, like the back of a bus (Inf), solid, padded, swollen, incrassate, stocky, sturdy, thick-bodied, thickset, barrel-chested, thick-necked, bull-necked, thickheaded, thick-lipped, thick-jawed, thick-legged, thick-ankled, thick-fingered, thick-wristed, thick-leaved, thick-stemmed, thick-stalked, thick-ribbed, thick-barked, pachydermatous, thick-skinned, thick-coated, thick-walled
▶ *271 Breadth, 259 Size*
2 **dense**, full-bodied, semiliquid, viscous, condensed, congealed, coagulated, clotted, thickened, intensified, boiled-down, reduced, thick with, crowded, abundant, packed, swarming, teeming, jammed, chock-a-block, impenetrable
▶ *371 Density, 394 Viscosity*
3 **thick-witted**, slow-witted, dull-witted, dull, dense, stupid, obtuse, dim, dumb, boneheaded (Sl), thick (Sl)
▶ *508 Folly*
4 **thick-skinned**, callous, insensitive, hard, coarse

NOUNS

5 **thickness**, breadth, width, depth, mass, massiveness, bulk, bulkiness, chunkiness, heaviness, stoutness, buxomness, fatness, corpulence, obesity, plumpness, portliness, roundness, rotundity, flabbiness, chubbiness, podginess, tubbiness, potbelly, fat, blubber, padding, upholstery, solidity, body, fullness, viscosity, density, slab, thick slice, doorstep (Inf)
6 **denseness**, density, viscosity, condensation, congealment, coagulation, thickening, intensity, abundance, impenetrability, closeness, friendship

VERBS

7 **thicken**, congeal, condense, coagulate, clot, boil down, reduce, gel, set, solidify, harden, firm up, intensify, compress, crowd, swarm
8 **fatten**, coarsen, thicken, fill out, put on weight, pad, upholster

ADVERBS
9 **thick**, thickly, densely, coarsely

274 Thinness

ADJECTIVES
1 **thin**, slender, slim, svelte, gracile, sylphlike, sylphic, willowy, twiggy, slight, slightly built, small-framed, leptosomic, ectomorphic, narrow-waisted, wasp-waisted, flat-chested, girlish, boyish, lean-limbed, thin-legged, spindle-legged (or spindle-shanked), hatchet-faced, thin-faced, lantern-jawed, lean, spare, wiry, bony, rawboned, rangy, lanky, gawky, underweight, skinny, scrawny, scraggy, puny, gangling (or gangly), weedy (Inf)
▶ *272 Narrowness, 871 Fasting*
2 **emaciated**, malnourished, undernourished, underfed, starved, starving, anorexic (or anorectic), wizened, shrivelled, withered, wasted, peaked, tabescent, wasting away, tabetic, marasmic, gaunt, haggard, hollow-cheeked, hollow-eyed, sunken-eyed, drawn, pinched, cadaverous, corpselike, skeletal, skin and bones, frail, wraithlike, thin as a lath (rake, or rail), worn to a shadow
3 **slimming**, dieting, reducing, slenderizing, weight-watching, calorie-counting
4 **fine**, delicate, light, insubstantial, flimsy, sheer, diaphanous, gossamer, gauzy, lacy, papery, wafer-thin
▶ *266 Layer*
5 **thinned**, diluted, watered-down, watery, runny, weak, attenuated, attenuate, rarefied, rare, flattened, pressed, rolled out
6 **scant**, scanty, sparse, meagre, few in number, few, thin on the ground
NOUNS
7 **thinness**, slenderness, slimness, gracility, willowiness, twigginess, slightness, slight build, small frame, hourglass figure, narrow waist, wasp waist, flat chest, girlish figure, boyish figure, hatchet face, lantern jaws, leanness, spareness, wiriness, boniness, ranginess, lankiness, gawkiness, skinniness, scrawniness, scragginess, puniness, gangliness, weediness (Inf)
8 **emaciation**, malnutrition, starvation, anorexia nervosa, anorexia, wasting, atrophy, tabescence, tabes, marasmus, gauntness, haggardness, hollow cheeks, hollow eyes, sunken eyes, cadaverousness, boniness, frailty, lean and hungry look
9 **thin person**, slip, sylph, leptosome, ectomorph, spindlelegs (or spindleshanks), weakling, runt, slimmer, dieter, weight watcher, calorie-counter, anorexic (or anorectic), wraith, shadow, bag of bones (Inf), skeleton (Inf), walking skeleton (Inf), beanpole (Inf), long drink of water (Inf), broomstick (Inf), scarecrow (Inf)

10 **diet**, dieting, slimming, weight-watching, watching one's figure, calorie-counting, crash-dieting, slimming pills, diet plan, diet programme
11 **fineness**, delicacy, lightness, insubstantiality, flimsiness, sheerness, diaphanousness, gauziness, laciness, paperiness, gossamer, gauze, muslin, lace, paper, tissue, wafer, lath, slat, shaving, film
12 **thinning**, dilution, watering down, wateriness, runniness, weakness, rarefaction, attenuation, meagreness, paucity, scantiness, sparseness, fewness
13 **thinner**, diluter, solvent
VERBS
14 **become thin**, slim, slim down, slenderize, reduce, diet, watch one's weight, lose weight, count the calories
15 **be emaciated**, starve, undereat, waste away
16 **make thin**, thin, thin down, thin out, dilute, water down, weaken, rarefy, attenuate, flatten, press, roll out
ADVERBS
17 **thin**, thinly, meagrely, scantily, sparsely

275 Height

NOUNS
1 **height**, altitude, highness, tallness, stature, lankiness, ranginess, pitch, loftiness, elevation, rise, lift, uprise, uplift, exaltation, eminence, prominence, sublimity
▶ *259 Size*
2 **heights**, highland(s), upland(s), moorland, moor(s), down(s), wold, fell, foothills, rising ground, acclivity, incline, escarpment, climb, zenith, acme, apex, pinnacle, summit, peak, top, mountaintop, hilltop, knap, tableland, plateau, mesa
▶ *279 Summit, 286 Obliqueness*
3 **mountain**, mount, alp, tor, ben, Olympus, Everest, Matterhorn, Mont Blanc, McKinley, Ben Nevis, hill, brae, pike, butte, cliff, bluff, crag, scar, precipice, hillock, hummock, monticule, knoll, kop, kopje, inselberg, roche moutonnée, drumlin, knob, hump, dune, sand dune, mound, tump, barrow, tumulus, motte
4 **mountain range**, massif, sierra, chain, cordillera, Himalayas, Alps, Andes, Rockies, Urals, Caucasus, Snowdonia, ridge, arête, chine, spur, kame, esker, os, moraine, col, saddleback, hogback, hog's back, watershed, divide, Continental Divide, Great Divide, bank, bench, crest, spine, comb, saddle
▶ *98 Other Geographical Features, 54 Earth Science*
5 **height measure**, relief, topography, orography, hypsography, hypsometry, altimetry, altimeter, hypsometer
6 **tall thing**, telegraph pole, street light, stee-

ple, spire, flèche, tower, turret, bell tower, campanile, belfry, watchtower, barbican, Martello tower, water tower, observation tower, Eiffel Tower, minaret, pagoda, ziggurat, lighthouse, windmill, pile, skyscraper, Empire State Building, tower block, office block, highrise flats, multistorey car park, mast, radio mast, chimney, smokestack, pillar, column, shaft, pilaster, pole, telegraph pole, maypole, flagstaff, post, lamppost, pylon, crane, derrick, obelisk, Cleopatra's Needle, monument, sequoia, redwood, giraffe, elephant

7 **tall person**, six-footer, seven-footer, basketball player, giant, Goliath, colossus, Amazon, beanpole (Inf), longlegs (or longshanks) (Inf), long drink of water (Inf)

8 **high thing**, ceiling, roof, vault, cupola, dome, lantern, attic, garret, loft, cockloft, mansard, penthouse, top floor, clerestory, weathercock, weather vane, topmast, topgallant mast, masthead, crow's-nest, eyrie, vantage point, viewpoint, triangulation station, sky, heaven, heavens, ether, stratosphere, mesosphere, thermosphere, exosphere, highchair, ladder, steps, stilts, high heels, platform soles, high tide, high water, flood, flood tide, spring tide, equinoctial tide, tidal wave, tsunami, trig point (Inf)

ADJECTIVES

9 **high**, tall, altitudinal, altitudinous, high-up, sky-high, lofty, elevated, uplifted, upreared, upraised, high-rise, multistorey, towering, skyscraping, ascending, rising, uprising, mounting, aspiring, soaring, flying, hovering, topping, overtopping, overlooking, dominating, overshadowing, overhanging, beetling, cloud-topped, cloud-capped, aerial, supernal, ethereal, airy, as high as a steeple, vertiginous, dizzy, giddy

10 **higher**, taller, highest, tallest, superior, upper, upmost, uppermost, topmost, nearest the top

11 **exalted**, elevated, eminent, prominent, sublime, supreme, superlative

12 **tall**, lanky, rangy, leggy, long-legged, longlimbed, long-necked, giant, gigantic, colossal, statuesque, monumental, Amazonian, Olympian, as tall as a maypole, knee-high, thighhigh, waist-high, chest-high, shoulder-high, gangling (Inf), gangly (Inf)

13 **mountainous**, hilly, rolling, undulating, hillocky, hummocky, orogenic, orogenetic, alpine, alpestrine, subalpine, Himalayan, Andean, mountain-dwelling, hill-dwelling

14 **altimetric**, topographic, orographic, hypsometric, hypsographic

VERBS

15 **be high**, tower, tower above, spire, aspire, soar, fly, hover over, top, overtop, clear, surmount, overlook, look down on, dominate,

command, overshadow, overarch, bestride, overhang, beetle

16 **rise**, rise up, uprise, climb, ascend, mount, rear, rear up, uprear, stand on tiptoe, grow, shoot up, culminate, peak

▶ *359 Ascent*

17 **raise**, heighten, elevate, hoist, lift, lift up, uplift, exalt, hold up

▶ *361 Raising*

18 **erect**, construct, build, put up

ADVERBS

19 **high**, high up, on high, aloft, above, over, overhead, above one's head, in the air, in the clouds, in orbit, at the top, on top, upstairs, above stairs, as high as a kite, toweringly, sublimely, on stilts, on tiptoe, up to the knees, up to the waist, up to the shoulders

20 **higher**, up, straight up, vertically, upward(s), skyward(s), heavenward(s)

276 Lowness

NOUNS

1 **lowness**, shortness, squatness, stumpiness, stuntedness, shallowness, lowering, flattening, lying down, prostration, proneness, supineness, recumbency, reclining, subordination, inferiority

▶ *270 Shortness*

2 **lowland(s)**, foothills, hillock, hummock, molehill, nursery slope, plain, flats, level ground, flatness, sea level, depression, hollow, valley

▶ *277 Depth, 280 Base, 282 Horizontality*

3 **lowest point**, lowest level, nadir, low tide, low water, ebb, ebb tide, neap tide

4 **low thing**, nether regions, subjacency, subscript, subcortex, submucosa, hypolimnion, underlay, underfelt, substratum, subsoil, undersoil, bedrock, floor, bottom, foot, base, subbase, subfloor, subgrade, basement, cellar, underneath, underside, undersurface, underbelly, underpart, underbody, undercarriage, bungalow, coffee table, low-cut neckline, décolletage, dachshund, low heels, flats, flatties (Inf)

▶ *127 Inferiority*

ADJECTIVES

5 **low**, short, squat, stumpy, stunted, shallow, ankle-high, knee-high, lowered, low-slung, flattened, laid low, knocked down, knocked over, knocked flat, lying down, prostrate, prone, supine, recumbent, reclining, couchant, crouched, crouching, stooped, stooping, low-level, low-set, low-hung, low-heeled, lownecked, low-cut, décolleté, low-built, low-rise, single-storey, knee-high to a grasshopper (Inf)

6 **lower**, lowest, inferior, nether, bottom, bottommost, undermost, subjacent, underlying, underlaid, subscript, subcutaneous, hypoder-

mic, subcartilaginous, subcranial, subcortical, suborbital, subauricular, submental, subglottal, subclavian, subscapular, subaxillary, infracostal, subdorsal, subabdominal, hypogastric

7 **lowland**, subalpine, submontane, piedmont, low-lying, flat, at sea level, below sea level, submerged, sunken, depressed

VERBS

8 **be low**, bottom out, underlie, underlay, look up to, lie down, prostrate oneself, recline, couch, crouch, squat, stoop, slouch, bend, bow, crawl, creep, grovel, lie low, go below
▶ *360 Descent*

9 **lower**, flatten, depress, lay low, knock down, knock over, knock flat, squash flat
▶ *362 Lowering*

ADVERBS

10 **low**, low down, under, below, underneath, beneath, neath, down, downwards, down below, downstairs, underground, underfoot, at the bottom, at the foot

277　Depth

NOUNS

1 **depth**, deepness, drop, fall, bottomlessness, unfathomableness, fathomlessness, soundlessness, cavernousness, deepening, lowering, sinking, sinkage, diving, deep-sea diving, submersion, immersion, excavation, spelunking, potholing, digging, burial, interment, mining, drilling, tunnelling, subterraneity
▶ *276 Lowness, 280 Base*

2 **intensity**, strength, extent, measure, deep-seatedness, deep-rootedness

3 **profundity**, profoundness, understanding, wisdom, sagacity, insight, perspicacity, penetration, acuity, discernment, astuteness
▶ *507 Wisdom*

4 **deep thing**, the deeps, the depths, lower depths, pit, mine, shaft, well, hole, basin, cavity, crater, pothole, crevasse, valley, ravine, coombe, corrie, cwm, cirque, chasm, gulf, abyss, subway, underpass, underground, tunnel, grave, vault, crypt, hypogeum, catacomb, dungeon, underworld, hell, bowels of the earth, bottomless pit, nadir, bottom of the sea, sea-bed, sea-bottom, sea-floor, ocean-bottom, ocean-floor, ocean depths, deep water, deep sea, benthos, Davy Jones's locker, Marianas Trench, submarine, submersible, bathysphere, bathyscaph, diving bell, benthoscope, bathometer, depth sounder, echo sounder, Fathometer (Tm), lead, lead line, plumb, plumb line, sounding line, sound, probe, sounder, fathomer

5 **submariner**, deep-sea diver, spelunker, potholer, miner

6 **bathymetry**, bathometry, oceanography, sounding, depth sounding, probing, echosounding, sonar, echolocation, draught, displacement

7 **deep thinking**, profundity, wisdom, wise man, wise woman, sage, intellectual

ADJECTIVES

8 **deep**, bottomless, unfathomable, fathomless, unfathomed, unsoundable, soundless, unsounded, unplumbed, abysmal, abyssal, cavernous, plunging, yawning, gaping, as deep as the ocean (*or* the sea), as deep as a well, as deep as hell, ankle-deep, knee-deep, waist-deep, deep-down, deep-lying, deep-laid, deep-set, sunken, deep-reaching, engraved, incised, deep-cut, deep-dish, deep-pan

9 **deep-seated**, deep-rooted, intense, extreme, sincere, profound, serious, heartfelt, earnest

10 **deeper**, deepest, deepmost, lowest, bottom, rock-bottom

11 **wise**, profound, deep, understanding, knowledgeable, perspicacious, acute, astute, discerning

12 **under**, underground, subterranean, subterraneous, subterrestrial, hypogeal, hypogeous, hypogene, buried, sunk, submerged, immersed, underwater, subaqua, subaquatic, subaqueous, undersea, submarine, suboceanic, deep-sea, deep-water, bathyal, bathypelagic, benthic, benthal, benthonic

13 **bathymetric**, bathometric, oceanographic, sounding, depth-sounding, probing, echolocating

VERBS

14 **deepen**, lower, go lower, drop, fall, sink, founder, descend, dive, plunge, yawn, gape, submerge, immerse, excavate, dig, bury, inter, mine, drill, tunnel, fathom, sound, take soundings, heave the lead, plumb, plumb the depths, probe, touch bottom, reach the bottom, sink to the bottom

15 **be profound**, understand, have deep understanding, be wise, be knowledgeable

ADVERBS

16 **deep**, deeply, deep down, out of one's depth, up to one's eyes (*or* ears), at the lowest point, at rock bottom

17 **profoundly**, deeply, in depth, in detail, extensively, thoroughly, exhaustively, comprehensively

278　Shallowness

ADJECTIVES

1 **shallow**, not deep, shoal, shoaly, reefy, unnavigable, ankle-deep, knee-deep, waist-deep, shallow-bottomed, shallow-rooted

2 **superficial**, surface, one-dimensional, cursory, hasty, slight, light, skin-deep, epidermal, thin, flat, low, trivial, trifling, lightweight, unimportant, petty, meaningless, empty, flimsy, frivolous, foolish, idle, silly
▶ *612 Unimportance*

NOUNS

3 **shallowness**, lack of depth, shoaliness, superficiality, triviality, cursoriness, slightness, lightness, surface, sprinkling, dusting, superficies (Fml)

4 **shallow thing**, skin, epidermis, cuticle, veneer, film, shallows, shallow, shoal, shoals, ford, shallow water, low water, low tide, puddle, pool, wetlands, swamp, shelf, reef, coral reef, bank, sandbank, mudbank, bar, sand bar, flat, flats, mud flat, tidal flats, pool, puddle, shallow-bottomed boat, shallow cut, superficial wound, scratch, graze, abrasion, pinprick

▶ *266 Layer, 274 Thinness, 276 Lowness, 277 Depth, 289 Exterior*

5 **shallow person**, man of straw, lightweight, mediocrity, nonentity, nobody

VERBS

6 **be shallow**, skim, skim over, touch, touch the surface, scratch the surface, scrape, graze

7 **make shallow**, shallow, shoal, silt up

ADVERBS

8 **shallowly**, near the surface, within one's depth, on the surface, superficially, cursorily, lightly, once-over, with a lick and a promise

279 Summit

NOUNS

1 **summit**, top, mountaintop, hilltop, peak, pinnacle, acme, zenith, meridian, pole, apogee, climax, culmination, maximum, limit, apex, vertex, cusp, point, tip, extremity, crest, brow, ridge, pitch, highest point, highest level, upper extremity, utmost height, tiptop, very top, top of the world, crest of the wave, upper regions, exosphere, sky, heaven, heavens, seventh heaven, cloud nine (Inf)

▶ *275 Height*

2 **head**, crown, cap, topknot, pinhead, heading, headpiece, crownpiece, masthead, topmast, topgallant, topgallant mast, topsail, topgallant sail, spire, treetop

3 **architectural summit**, capital, chapiter, necking, gorgerin, abacus, architrave, epistyle, taenia, entablature, cornice, cymatium, finial, fastigium, headstone, keystone, quoin, capstone, copestone, coping stone, coping, cope, gable, pediment, frontispiece, tympanum, lintel, frieze, picture rail, ceiling, roof, rooftop, housetop, ridgepole, top floor, top storey, penthouse, stairhead, landing

▶ *293 Covering*

4 **top layer**, topping, icing, frosting, superstratum, topsoil, top dressing, topside, upper side, upside, surface, top surface, upper surface

ADJECTIVES

5 **top**, tiptop, topmost, upmost, uppermost, highest, ultimate, maximum, maximal, consummate, climactic, culminating, crowning,

meridian, meridional, polar, head, leading, chief, capital, supreme, paramount, summital, zenithal, apical, vertical

6 **topped**, capped, crowned, tipped, crested, headed, covered, roofed, iced, frosted

VERBS

7 **top**, top off, top out, cap, crown, head, lead, peak, culminate, climax, surmount, overtop, overarch, cover, roof, ice, frost

ADVERBS

8 **on top**, on the top, at the top, at the summit, at the highest level, tiptop, on top of the world, on the crest of the wave, at the top of the ladder (*or* tree), in seventh heaven, on cloud nine (Inf)

280 Base

NOUNS

1 **base**, bottom, fundus, fundament, foundation, support, basis, root, footing, ground, earth, sea level, lowest point, lowest level, nadir, floor, bed, bedrock, hardpan, rock bottom, river bed, sea-bed, sea-floor, ocean-floor, substratum, underlayer, deck, pavement, paving, flagstone, concrete, Tarmac (Tm), flooring, floor covering, rug, carpet, parquet, tile, linoleum

▶ *103 Essence, 276 Lowness, 277 Depth*

2 **foot**, sole, toe, heel, footnote, baseboard, skirting board, mopboard (US), baseplate, keel, chassis, undercarriage, frame, substructure, infrastructure, stand, plinth, pedestal, sill, threshold, dampcourse, wainscot, dado, ground floor, first floor (US), underneath, underside, undersurface, lower ground floor, basement, cellar, lower deck, hold, bilge, sump

▶ *284 Support*

ADJECTIVES

3 **base**, ground, ground-level, supporting, underlying, basal, basilar, basilary, bottom, rock-bottom, bottommost, undermost, nethermost, lowest, basic, fundamental, essential, inherent, radical, rudimentary, vestigial

VERBS

4 **base**, found, build, establish, anchor, fix, root, ground, underlie, support, underpin

ADVERBS

5 **basically**, fundamentally, essentially

281 Verticality

NOUNS

1 **verticality**, verticalness, uprightness, erectness, erection, straightness, perpendicularity, squareness, sheerness, precipitousness, steepness, fall, drop, plunge, dive

▶ *312 Straightness*

2 **making vertical**, upending, standing up,

straightening, rearing, uprearing, rising, uprising, raising, upraising, elevating, elevation,
building, erecting, erection
▶ *361 Raising, 283 Suspension, 284 Support*

3 **vertical thing**, upright, post, newel post,
newel, pole, pillar, pylon, column, lighthouse,
stake, palisade, wall, skyscraper, face, cliff,
precipice, scarp, escarpment, scar, crag, bluff,
stack, stalagmite, stalactite, vertical line, vertical axis, vertical, plumb, perpendicular, right
angle, normal

4 **plumb line**, plumb, square, set square, try
square, T-square

VERBS

5 **be vertical**, stand, stand up, stand upright,
stand erect, stand up straight, hold oneself
straight, stand to attention, rear, rear up, uprear, rise, rise up, get up, arise, uprise, rise (*or*
get) to one's feet, be upstanding, straighten
up, sit up

6 **make vertical**, erect, build, elevate, raise,
raise up, upraise, stick up, cock up, prick up,
bristle, pitch (camp), set up, upend, stand on
end, straighten, plumb, square

7 **fall vertically**, drop, drop like a stone, plummet, plunge, dive

ADJECTIVES

8 **vertical**, upright, erect, upended, standing,
standing up, upstanding, straight, bolt upright, up-and-down, straight-up-and-down,
straight up, straight down, plumb, sheer, precipitous, plunging, very steep

9 **unbowed**, rampant, rearing, reared, upreared, raising, raised, upraised, cocked up,
pricked up

10 **perpendicular**, orthogonal, right-angled,
square, normal, rectangular

ADVERBS

11 **vertically**, upright, uprightly, erectly,
straight, up, on end, endways, endwise, bolt
upright, on one's feet, on its hindlegs, on top
of each other

12 **perpendicularly**, at (*or* with) right angles,
up and down, straight up and down, up,
down, plumb, sheer, very steeply

282 Horizontality

NOUNS

1 **horizontality**, horizontalness, flatness, levelness, planeness, plainness, smoothness,
evenness, flushness, lying, reclining, reclination, recumbency, decumbency, accumbency,
prostration, proneness, supineness, sprawling,
sprawl
▶ *276 Lowness, 376 Smoothness, 649 Ease*

2 **horizontal surface**, horizontal, flat, level,
plane, plane surface, homaloid, horizontal
line, horizontal axis, water level, sea level,
horizontal angle, azimuth

3 **flat thing**, disc, slab, layer, stratum, tablet,
pancake, flatfish, flounder, flatware, saucer,
plate, platter, tray, gridiron, flat tyre, flat surface, flat land, level ground, flats, plain, prairie, pampas, steppe, green, bowling green,
bedding plane, bed, esplanade, plateau, tableland, terrace, ledge, platform, table, billiard
table, floor, ceiling, horizon, skyline

4 **flattener**, plane, press, trouser press, iron,
flatiron, steam iron, mangle, rolling pin,
roller, garden roller, steamroller, bulldozer

5 **planometer**, planimeter, spirit level, ruler,
rule

VERBS

6 **be horizontal**, recline, lie, lie down, lie flat,
lie on one's back (*or* face), sprawl, spread-eagle,
prostrate oneself, grovel

7 **make horizontal**, level, level out, flatten,
grade, plane, flush, even, equalize, smooth,
smoothen, smooth out, smooth down, iron,
press, roll, roll out, beat flat, squash flat, tread
flat, trample down, lay, lay down, spread,
knock down, knock flat, prostrate, fell, raze,
raze to the ground

ADJECTIVES

8 **horizontal**, flat, level, plane, plain, planar,
two-dimensional, tabular, homaloidal, even,
smooth, unwrinkled, flush, flat as a pancake
(*or* board, flounder, fluke, billiard table, bowling green)

9 **flattened**, levelled, smoothed, smoothened,
pressed, ironed, rolled, consolidated, beaten
flat, squashed flat, well-trodden, trodden flat,
trampled down, spread

10 **lying**, lying down, lying flat, flat out, recumbent, decumbent, accumbent, prostrate, procumbent, prone, face down, supine, couchant,
reclining, sprawling, sprawled, spread-eagled,
knocked down, knocked flat, razed to the
ground

ADVERBS

11 **horizontally**, flat, flat on one's back (*or*
face), flatly, flatways, flatwise, lengthways,
lengthwise, on its side, level, plane, evenly,
smoothly, flush

283 Suspension

NOUNS

1 **suspension**, suspendibility, suspensiveness,
hanging, dangling, pendency, pendulousness,
pensileness, hang, swing, dangle, drape,
droop, sag
▶ *365 Oscillation, 137 Connection, 377 Elasticity*

2 **projection**, projecting part, overhang, overlie, protruberance
▶ *318 Prominence*

3 **suspended object**, hanging object, pendulum, pendant, plumb bob, tassel, curtain, pigtail, ponytail, earring, bell rope, icicle, chande-

lier, picture, coat-tail, fringe, suspended cymbal, hammock, trapeze, swing, suspension bridge

▶ *792 Decoration*

4 **hanger**, suspender, hook, peg, clothes peg, nail, knob, coat hanger, hat rack, clothesline, clotheshorse, picture hook, curtain rod, braces, suspender belt, gallows, gibbet, crane

5 **projecting object**, diving board, balcony, mantelpiece, hat brim, nose, pier, buttress, gable, cantilever

▶ *43 Architecture*

6 **interruption**, pause, postponement, suspension, deferment, adjournment, moratorium, cooling-off period, shelving, tabling, delay, procrastination, putting off, stopping, withholding, stay, discontinuance, abeyance, dormancy

▶ *160 Discontinuity, 641 Inaction, 209 Lateness, 218 Cessation, 527 Latency, 349 Expulsion*

ADJECTIVES

7 **suspended**, hanging, hung, dangling, swinging, sagging, pendulous, pendent, pensile, suspendible (*or* suspensible), suspensive

8 **projecting**, overhanging, jutting, sticking out, beetling, beetle-browed

9 **interrupted**, postponed, delayed, suspended, deferred, adjourned, put off, shelved, tabled, withheld, stopped, stayed, discontinued, abeyant, dormant, pending

VERBS

10 **suspend**, hang, hang up, hook up, fasten (up), put up, drape, hang down, dangle, swing, swing from, droop, trail, bungee jump, hang glide

11 **project**, overhang, hang over, overlie, jut, beetle, stick out over, hover

12 **interrupt**, postpone, suspend, defer, adjourn, shelve, table, delay, procrastinate, hold up, pause, put off, withhold, stop, discontinue, stay, arrest, put on hold (Inf)

ADVERBS

13 **pendulously**, pendently, suspensively, on a string, in mid air, in suspense

284 Support

NOUNS

1 **support**, buttress, abutment, reinforcement, underpinning, strengthening, holding up, propping up, backing up

▶ *382 Structure*

2 **supporting part**, support, mainstay, prop, fulcrum, brace, buttress, flying buttress, abutment, bulwark, rampart, wall, retaining wall, embankment, mounting, scaffolding, frame, framework, skeleton, backbone, spine, ribs, A-frame, transom, chassis, underframe, undercarriage, underpinning, underlay, bracket, strut, pier, girder, rafter, beam, crossbeam,

crossbar, lintel, king post, balustrade, pilaster, column, post, pillar, caryatid, shaft, stem, pile, foundation, foundation stone, cornerstone, keystone, bedrock, basement, groundwork, substructure, pedestal, base, stand, music stand, tripod, table, worktable, mantelpiece, shelf

▶ *63 Engineering, 282 Horizontality, 281 Verticality, 280 Base, 135 Union, 137 Connection*

3 **body support**, sling, bandage, splint, crutch, cane, stick, walking stick, walking frame, walker, Zimmer (Tm), staff, alpenstock

4 **rest**, headrest, footrest, footstool, back rest, chair, easy chair, dentist's chair, shooting stick, saddle, sofa, couch, ottoman, davenport, bed, cradle, crib, mattress, springs, box springs, pillow, bolster

5 **supporting garment**, girdle, corset, brassiere, bra, athletic belt, athletic support, jockstrap

▶ *796 Fashion, 634 Refuge*

6 **moral support**, encouragement, furtherance, backing, advocacy, championship, protection, friendship, sympathy, empathy, aid, abetment, help, succour, assistance, cooperation, corroboration, collaboration, approval, endorsement, preferential treatment, intercession, favour, security blanket (US)

▶ *664 Cooperation, 667 Agreement, 671 Defence*

7 **financial support**, financial aid, pecuniary assistance, provision, sponsorship, backing, patronage, sustenance, sustainment, maintenance, subsistence, contribution, grant, allowance, stipend, pension, subsidy, upkeep, child support, alimony

▶ *741 Money, 746 Payment, 662 Help*

8 **supporter**, helper, aide, auxiliary, assistant, sidekick, spear carrier, helpmate, helping hand, fund-raiser, charity worker, tower of strength, substitute, backup (US), well-wisher, disciple, adherent, follower, fan, admirer, attendant, acolyte, collaborator, colleague, ally, corroborator, cooperator, sympathizer, fellow traveller, advocate, upholder, defender, protector, champion, proposer, seconder, benefactor, backer, underwriter, patron, sponsor, angel, sustainer, maintainer, friend, guardian, guardian angel, fairy godmother

▶ *755 Generosity, 767 Relief*

ADJECTIVES

9 **supportive**, supporting, retaining, foundational, ground, basal, upholding, sustaining, maintaining, helpful, encouraging, kindly, sympathetic, empathetic, understanding, reassuring, cooperative, corroborative, collaborative, benevolent, patronal, well-disposed, favourable, contributory, stipendiary, advocatory, preferential, intercessional, auxiliary, subsidiary, ancillary, substitute, discipular, attending, guardian

10 **supportable**, bearable, tolerable, endurable, sufferable, acceptable, manageable, passable, average, not (so) bad, so-so (Inf)

VERBS

11 **support**, bear, carry, hold up, prop up, prop, back up, shore up, strengthen, buttress, reinforce, bolster, brace, abut, bulwark, rampart, wall, embank, scaffold, frame, underframe, underpin, bracket, post, dig (or sink) a foundation, lay a foundation stone, lay a cornerstone

12 **bear**, tolerate, endure, stomach, brook, abide, countenance, suffer, submit to, undergo, stand (for), put up with (Inf), stick (Inf)

13 **support financially**, finance, pay for, fund, provide for, back, subsidize, sponsor, patronize, underwrite, maintain, keep, pension, contribute, grant, bankroll (US sl)

14 **give moral support**, stand by, back up, encourage, wish well, strengthen, buoy up, carry, back, champion, stand up for, stand behind, uphold, defend, assist, substitute for, lend a helping hand, aid, further, forward, abet, help, succour, sustain, foster, cooperate, corroborate, collaborate, intercede (on behalf of), propose, second, favour, praise, honour, approve of, endorse, advocate, recommend, give the seal of approval to, give one's blessing to, stick up for (Inf)

285   Parallelism

NOUNS

1 **parallelism**, parallel, equidistance, concentricity, coextension, collimation, nonconvergence, nondivergence, correlation, correspondence, balance, alignment, equality, uniformity, harmony
▶ *122 Equality, 114 Similarity*

2 **parallel thing**, parallelogram, parallelepiped, parallel bars, railway tracks, aligned wheels, dual carriageway, World Trade Center twin towers (US)

ADJECTIVES

3 **parallel**, equidistant, concentric, coextensive, nonconvergent, nondivergent, antiparallel

4 **correlated**, correlative, correspondent, corresponding, balanced, aligned, equal, uniform, harmonious

VERBS

5 **parallel**, lie parallel, run parallel, run abreast, coextend, collimate

6 **correlate**, correspond, balance, align, equal, harmonize

ADVERBS

7 **in parallel**, abreast, alongside, side-by-side, collaterally, coextensively

286   Obliqueness

NOUNS

1 **obliqueness**, obliquity, deviation, divergence, skewness, diagonal, deflection, indirection, indirectness, transverseness, crookedness, convolution, digression, meandering, twist, turn, veer, bend, bias, swerve, zigzag, inclination, leaning, curvature, slope, grade, slant, cant, bank, ramp, slide, camber, pitch, tip, tilt, list, tangent
▶ *335 Deviation, 310 Angle, 311 Curve, 275 Height, 281 Verticality*

2 **oblique line**, diagonal, slash, oblique, solidus, separatrix, stroke, virgule, bevelled edge, oblique angle, rakish angle, rhomboid, hairpin curve, dogleg, slide, ski jump, Tower of Pisa

3 **deviousness**, circumlocution, periphrasis, circuitousness, indirection, furtiveness, backhandedness, evasion, equivocation, prevarication, hedging, deception, distortion, dissemblance, euphemism, fraudulence, spuriousness, shadiness (Inf), fishiness (Inf)
▶ *309 Distortion, 578 Equivocation*

ADJECTIVES

4 **oblique**, deviating, divergent, skewed, askew, diagonal, on the diagonal, deflected, deflective, indirect, sidelong, transverse, sideways, crosswise (or crossways), cater-cornered (or cater-corner) (US), kitty-cornered (or kitty-corner) (US), crooked, convoluted, digressive, meandering, tangent, bevelled, twisted, turning, bending, zigzag, zigzagged, inclining, inclined, inclinational, sloping, sloped, on the slope, slanting, slanted, pitched, tilting, atilt, on the tilt, leaning, listing, off course, off-target, skewwhiff (Inf)

5 **devious**, deviant, circumlocutory, periphrastic, circuitous, roundabout, indirect, sidelong, furtive, backhand, backhanded, evasive, deceptive, equivocal, hedging, distorted, distortive, euphemistic, dissembling, fraudulent, spurious, shady (Inf), fishy (Inf)

VERBS

6 **be oblique**, oblique, transect, deviate, diverge, bear off, angle off, skew, deflect, crook, digress, meander, twist, turn, veer, bend, swerve, zigzag, wind in and out, incline, camber, curve, slope, slant, cant, bank, pitch, tip, tilt, lean, list, tip to one side

7 **deviate**, circumlocute, evade, equivocate, prevaricate, hedge, deceive, distort, dissemble, bend the truth

ADVERBS

8 **obliquely**, diagonally, at an angle, askew, askance, transversely, sideways, crosswise (or crossways), across, on the bias, cater-cornered (or cater-corner) (US), kitty-cornered (or kitty-corner) (US), off course, off-target

9 **deviously**, circuitously, periphrastically, indirectly, euphemistically, sidelong, furtively, equivocally, spuriously

287 Inversion

NOUNS

1 **inversion**, reversion, reversal, reverse, converse, transposition, inverted order, contrary, opposite, antithesis, turning upside down, turning inside out, turning back to front, turning backwards, introversion, retroversion, evagination, invagination, capsizing, overturning, upset, spill, cartwheel, somersault, handspring, headstand, undermining, palindrome, counterpoint, other side of the coin
▶ *221 Reversion, 337 Backward Motion, 223 Exchange, 282 Horizontality*

ADJECTIVES

2 **inverted**, reversed, transpositional, in inverted order, inside-out and back-to-front, inside-out, back-to-front, upside-down, head-over-heels, bottom-up, topsy-turvy, wrong way in, wrong way out, capsized, capsizing, arsy-versy (Sl)

VERBS

3 **invert**, reverse, transpose, put in inverted order, turn upside down, turn inside out, turn back to front, turn backwards, introvert, retrovert, evaginate, invaginate, capsize, overturn, upset, spill, cartwheel, somersault, handspring, stand on one's head, undermine, turn the tables, put the cart before the horse, try to run before one can walk

ADVERBS

4 **inversely**, conversely, backwards, the other way around, turned around, topsy-turvy, upside-down, head-over-heels, contrariwise, vice versa, in reverse, arsy-versy (Sl), arse over tit (Tab sl), ass backwards (US tab sl)

288 Interweaving

NOUNS

1 **interweaving**, weaving, crisscross, interlacing, interlacement, intertexture, interwork, lacing, intertwining, intertwinement, twining, entanglement, webbing, braiding, plaiting, pleaching (*or* plashing), interlocking, intercommunication, interfusion, interlineation, interdigitation, reticulation, interpenetration
▶ *792 Decoration, 314 Convolution, 151 Disorder, 133 Mixture*

2 **braid**, plait, pigtail, wreath, arabesque, filigree, cat's cradle, web, skein, network, webbing, netting, net, fishnet, mesh, spider's web, wickerwork, trellis, espalier, lattice, wattle, grid, tracery, fretwork, knitting, tatting, macramé, crochet, lace, laciness, lace making, lacework, knotting

3 **weaving**, loom, hand loom, warp, weft, woof, shuttle, distaff, spinning wheel, sewing machine, weaver, knitter, spinner, spider, weaverbird

4 **textile**, woven cloth, cloth, material, fabric, broadcloth, suiting, sacking, sackcloth, jute, linen, cheesecloth, muslin, towelling, flannel, flannelette, wool, mohair, cashmere, tweed, vicuna, alpaca, merino, angora, cotton, khaddar (*or* khadi), homespun, drill, twill, moleskin, denim, voile, poplin, madras, seersucker, chintz, cotton jersey, silk, satin, tussore, taffeta, shantung, chiffon, velvet, velveteen, corduroy, lace, chenille
▶ *67 Fabrics and Dyeing*

5 **crossroads**, crossing, intersection, interchange, road junction, cloverleaf, spaghetti junction
▶ *70 Transport, 356 Passage*

ADJECTIVES

6 **interwoven**, woven, handwoven, crisscross, interlaced, laced, lacy, intertwined, twined, webbed, webby, interdigitated, braided, plaited, pleached, wreathed, reticulate (*or* reticular), loomed, woollen, woolly, tweedy

7 **crossing**, intersecting, interchanging, interconnecting, intersectional

VERBS

8 **interweave**, inweave, weave, crisscross, enlace, interlace, lace, intertwine, entwine (*or* intwine), twine, entangle, web, braid, plait, pleach (*or* plash), interlock, interdigitate, reticulate, filigree, net, mesh, mesh together, knit, tat, macramé, crochet, knot, twist, warp, shuttle, spin, sew, intercrop, espalier, interfile, interfuse, intermingle, interlay, interline, interpenetrate

9 **cross**, intersect, interchange, come to a junction

ADVERBS

10 **interlacedly**, interlinearly, interlineally, interspatially, intertwiningly, interpenetratively, interchangeably

289 Exterior

NOUNS

1 **exterior**, exteriority, external, externality, externalness, surface, outer side, façade, front, face, outer face, facet, shell, rind, pod, crust, covering, coating, outer wall, envelope, integument, superstratum, superficies, outer layer, skin, epidermis, cuticle, exoskeleton, cortex, hull, husk, periphery, circumference, outline, fringe, surroundings, border
▶ *293 Covering, 303 Front, 297 Surroundings*

2 **outside**, outwardness, out of doors, the great outdoors, open air, the open, hinterland, outland, outback (Aus)
▶ *263 Distance*

3 appearance, surface appearance, outward appearance, apparentness, aspect, image, mien, impression, public persona, guise, seemingness, superficiality, shallowness

▶ *457 Appearance*

4 externalization, exteriorization, projection, openness, outwardness, extroversion, extrovert

5 extraneousness, foreignness, strangeness, otherworldliness, the other side, others, outsiders, strangers, foreigners

▶ *104 Extraneousness*

ADJECTIVES

6 exterior, external, surface, outer, front, facing, faceted, shelly, podded, crusty, crusted, covered, enveloped, integumental, epidermal, epidermic, epidermoid, cuticular, exoskeletal

7 outside, outward, out-of-doors, outdoor, open, open-air, alfresco, outermost, outlying, extramural

8 apparent, surface, outward, ostensible, superficial, shallow, seeming, imaginal, imaginary, impressional

9 externalized, exteriorized, projected, open, outward, extroverted

10 extraneous, foreign, alien, exotic, strange, otherworldly

VERBS

11 be exterior, cover, surface, overlie, front, face, encrust, skin over, envelop, outline, fringe, surround, border

12 be outside, be out-of-doors, enjoy the open air, dine alfresco, picnic, take to the road

13 appear outwardly, appear, seem, look, give an impression

14 externalize, exteriorize, project, reveal, bring out, bring into the open

ADVERBS

15 externally, outwardly, outwards, outside, on the outside, in the open air, in the open, out of doors, without, alfresco, on the surface, on the face of it, apparently, to all appearances, seemingly, superficially

290   Interior

NOUNS

1 interior, interiority, internal, internality, internalness, inwardness, centrality, inner surface, inner layer, inner side, inner wall, undersurface, endodermis, endoderm, subcortex, substratum, subsoil, depth, cave, pothole

▶ *301 Enclosure, 280 Base, 277 Depth*

2 inside, indoors, home, room, confinement, cell, prison, jail, solitary confinement, inner part, centre, middle, heart, core, depths, recesses, secret place, seclusion, retreat, sanctuary

▶ *291 Centre*

3 inland, inlands, the interior, hinterland, heartland, upstate, upcountry, the Midwest (US), the Midlands

▶ *54 Earth Science, 55 Meteorology and Climatology*

4 insides, contents, internal organs, bodily organs, vital organs, the vitals, viscera, gland, heart, lung, liver, kidney, spleen, abdomen, stomach, belly, paunch, womb, uterus, entrails, intestines, duodenum, jejunum, colon, rectum, offal, tripe, tummy (Inf), innards (Inf), guts (Sl)

▶ *60 Medicine*

5 inner nature, inner life, intrinsicality, inner person, inner man (*or* woman), innermost being, heart, soul, animus, anima, core, marrow, pith, nitty-gritty (Inf)

▶ *103 Essence*

6 internalization, secretiveness, secrecy, privacy, inwardness, self-absorption, engrossment, egocentrism, introversion, introvert

▶ *531 Concealment, 529 Secrecy*

ADJECTIVES

7 interior, internal, central, inside, inward, inner, undersurfaced, enclosed, endemic, endodermal, endodermic, subcutaneous, subcortical, intravenous, substrative (*or* substratal), deep

8 internal, inward, indoor, homelike, homy, home, in-house, domestic, local, civil, national

9 inland, interior, landlocked, central, upstate, upcountry, midland, continental

10 visceral, internal, bodily, vital, splanchnic, glandular, cardiac, pulmonary, cardiovascular, renal, intestinal, enteric, gastric, duodenal, jejunal, uterine, intrauterine, abdominal, colonic, rectal

11 intrinsic, innate, inherent, innermost, fundamental, radical, constitutional

12 internalized, intimate, personal, private, secret, hidden, veiled, inmost, inward, self-absorbed, engrossed, egocentric, secretive, introverted

VERBS

13 be interior, lie within, lie beneath, underlie, lie below the surface, be at the bottom of

14 go inside, enter, retreat into, take refuge, seclude oneself, home

15 keep inside, internalize, bottle up, contain, absorb, hold within, hide, conceal, confine, imprison, jail

ADVERBS

16 inwardly, internally, inside, deeply, intimately, secretively, innately, intrinsically

291   Centre

NOUNS

1 centre, dead centre, centre point, centre of gravity, middle, mean, median, midpoint,

focal point, focus, epicentre, centroid, nucleus, heart, core, hub, nub, pivot, fulcrum, axis, kernel, pith, backbone, marrow, omphalos

▶ *158 Middle, 371 Density, 103 Essence, 290 Interior*

2 **central thing**, centrepiece, sun, centrosphere, eye of the hurricane, nave, bull's-eye, gold, bull, pupil, midriff, navel, belly button, umbilical cord

3 **centrality**, centricity, centralness, centralization, centralism, centring, concentricity, focusing, focalization, focalizing, convergence, confluence, concentration, pinpointing, locating

4 **centre of activity**, hotbed, main place, place of pilgrimage, holy place, Jerusalem, Lourdes, Mecca, capital city, capital, town centre, Piccadilly Circus, Times Square, shopping centre, mall, shopping mall, medical centre, civic centre, market town, marketplace, mart, forum, airport, train station, depot, central office, main office, nerve centre, headquarters (HQ), general headquarters (GHQ), where the action is (Inf), where it's at (Inf)

▶ *250 Location, 740 Market*

5 **focus**, focal point, main interest, centre of interest, centre of attention (*or* attraction), star, cynosure, personality, chief, head, principal, key figure, primary source

▶ *235 Power*

ADJECTIVES

6 **central**, middle, mean, median, average, midmost, midpoint, epicentral, geocentric, heliocentric, centripetal, nuclear, nucleate, umbilical, pivotal, key, axial, omphalic

7 **centralized**, centred, centric, centrical, concentric, homocentric, focalized, convergent, converging, confluent, concentrated, pinpointed, pinpointing

8 **focal**, cynosural, favourite, chief, head, principal, main, key, primary, crucial

VERBS

9 **centre**, centralize, nucleate, focus, bring into focus, focalize, centre on, converge, converge on, flow together, concentrate, concentrate on, pivot on, zero in on, home in on, come to a point, pinpoint, focus on, locate, headquarter (US)

ADVERBS

10 **centrally**, in the centre of, in the middle of, in the midst of, at the core, at the heart of

292 Lining

NOUNS

1 **lining**, interlining, coating, undercoating, facing, interfacing, interlining, insulating, insulation, soundproofing, double glazing, liner, lining paper, wallpaper, panelling, wainscot,

backing, lined coat, petticoat, slip

▶ *293 Covering, 298 Interface, 604 Materials*

2 **filling**, stuffing, padding, packing, packaging, filler, wadding, quilting, foam, polystyrene, kapok, down, feathers

▶ *354 Insertion*

VERBS

3 **line**, interline, coat, undercoat, face, interface, insulate, soundproof, double glaze, paper, wallpaper, panel, wainscot, back

4 **fill**, stuff, pad, pack, package, wad, quilt

293 Covering

NOUNS

1 **covering**, covering up, covering over, coverage, cover, overarching, spanning, overlaying, laying on, stratification, superimposition, overlapping, imbrication, coating, topping, paving, blanketing, cloaking, enclosement, walling in, walling up, envelopment, enfoldment, enwrapment, wrapping, casing, screening, shielding, overshadowing, eclipsing, blotting out, flooding over, obscuring, hiding

▶ *531 Concealment*

2 **cover**, top, lid, cap, cork, plug, stopper, bung, crust, piecrust, flap, shutter, gravestone, shroud, pall, topsoil, mulch, cloud, smoke screen

3 **coating**, coat, layer, film, plastering, topping, icing, frosting, glaze, varnish, veneer, enamel, lacquer, japan, stain, creosote, paint, wax, furniture polish, plate, silver plate, electroplate, copperplate, gold plate

4 **wrapping**, wrapping paper, giftwrapping, wrapper, tissue paper, packaging, box, envelope, involucre, shroud, sheath, sheathing, book cover, dust jacket, binding, binder, foil, Cellophane (Tm), polythene, wax paper, aluminium foil, plastic wrap, clingfilm

5 **body covering**, hat, hard hat, coat, jacket, cloak, robe, vestment, sweater, cowl, hood, veil, scarf, comforter, shroud, sunbonnet, afghan, lap robe, rug

▶ *295 Dress*

6 **medical covering**, dressing, bandage, bandaging, elastic bandage, adhesive tape, plaster, Elastoplast, cast, plaster cast, surgical dressing, surgical mask

▶ *60 Medicine, 630 Remedy*

7 **overhead covering**, roof, pitched roof, gable roof, flat roof, rooftop, housetop, dome, cupola, roofing, slates, tiles, shingles, thatch, ceiling plaster, ceiling, overhead, overhead beam, rafters, canopy, awning, marquee, tent, big top, tepee (*or* teepee *or* tipi), wigwam, ciborium, canvas, tarpaulin, tarp (US inf), mosquito netting

8 **wall covering**, facing, revetment, rendering, cladding, bricks, adobe, mortar, grout, pebble

dash, panelling, plywood, wallboard, planking, boarding, weatherboard, clapboard, wall tiles, ceramic tiles, paint, whitewash, plaster work, plaster, size (*or* sizing), stucco, parget (*or* pargeting), wallpaper, curtain, drape, drapery, hanging, tapestry, soft furnishings, mould, encrustation (*or* incrustation)

9 **floor covering**, rug, hooked rug, throw rug (US), area rug, hearth rug, braided rug, drugget, carpet, wall-to-wall carpet, fitted carpet, carpeting, broadloom carpet, pile carpet, Persian carpet (*or* rug), Turkish carpet (*or* rug), stair carpet, runner, mat, doormat, bathmat, matting, dropcloth (US), groundsheet (*or* ground cloth), tiles, tiling, linoleum, lino, vinyl, floorboards, duckboards, parquet, parquet floor, wax

10 **bed covering**, bed cover, mattress cover, dust ruffle (US), bedding, bedclothes, bed linen, blanket, duvet, continental quilt, quilt, patchwork quilt, eiderdown, comforter (US), bedspread, spread, counterpane, coverlet, cover, bedsheet, fitted sheet, sheet, pillowcase (*or* pillowslip), pillow sham (US), bed canopy, valance

11 **paving**, surfacing, road surface, pavement, sidewalk (US), crazy paving, concrete, cement, Portland cement, tar, blacktop (US), Tarmac (Tm), asphalt, macadam, gravel, chippings, cobble, cobblestone, flagstone, stepping stone

12 **protective covering**, shield, sunshade, parasol, sun hat, pith helmet, topee, visor, eyeshade, sunglasses, shades (Inf), suntan lotion, sunscreen, life jacket, life belt, umbrella, brolly (Inf), bumbershoot (US inf), insulation, lagging, fibreglass, awning, blind, Venetian blind, shade, lampshade, placemat, tablecloth, doily, Formica (Tm), upholstery, furniture cover, chair cover, slipcover, antimacassar, cushion cover, bullet-proof glass, unbreakable glass, watch glass, screen, fire curtain, car bonnet, car silencer, housing, armour, mail

13 **casing**, case, watchcase, ammunition case, crate, box, capsule, shell, nutshell, artillery shell, pastry shell, egg shell, pod, hull, husk, chaff, cornhusk (US), shuck, skin, jacket, peel, rind, bark, seed coat, testa, integument, tegumen

14 **animal covering**, cortex, skin, outer skin, epidermis, scar, eschar, scab, scalp, cuticle, eyelid, hair, fell, hide, rawhide, horsehide, pigskin, leather, kid, calf, suede, chamois, morocco, buckskin, doeskin, fur, mink, sable, ermine, chinchilla, fleece, pelt, beaver pelt, feathers, plumage, shell, oyster shell, clam shell, snail shell, turtle shell, conch, scallop, scale, scute, carapace, lorica, operculum, cocoon, chrysalis, horse blanket, saddlecloth

15 **shelter**, protection, secrecy, concealment, hiding place, hideout, hideaway, safe house, retreat, refuge, den, lair, secret drawer, secret passageway, hidden panel, cache, cover, screen, covert, hide

16 **disguise**, mask, domino, veil, camouflage, protective colouring, false beard, masquerade

17 **coverer**, tailor, furrier, painter, whitewasher, plasterer, roofer, thatcher, draper, wallpaperer, bricklayer, carpetlayer, upholsterer, bookbinder, electroplater, giftwrapper, packager, tiler, paver, tanner, quilter, disguiser, camouflager, masker, masquerader, incorporator

18 **fixer**, handler, publicist, journalist, public relations man (*or* woman), spin doctor

19 **inclusion**, embodiment, incorporation, comprehension, comprehensive insurance policy, blanket coverage

20 **fixing**, handling, news coverage, news item, publicity

21 **substitution**, substitute, replacement, alternative, alternate, surrogate, surrogate mother, stepmother, stepfather, foster parent, proxy, fill-in, stand-in, backup, relief, locum, reserve, understudy, double, stunt man (*or* woman), ghostwriter

▶ *284 Support*

22 **progression**, making progress, traversal, traversing, continuation, continuing, continuing on, passing through, travelling through, traveller, tourist, traverser, wanderer, student, reader

VERBS

23 **cover**, lay on, superimpose, lay over, put a lid on, top, crown, cap, cork, plug, bung, stopper, stop

24 **coat**, spread, spread on, spread over, overlay, carpet, blanket, tile, parquet, upholster, layer, daub, plaster, top, ice, frost, glaze, varnish, veneer, enamel, lacquer, japan, stain, tan, creosote, paint, whitewash, wax, polish, plate, silver, silver-plate, gold-plate, gild, electroplate, copperplate

25 **wrap**, enwrap, wrap up, wrap round, surround, envelop, enfold, shroud, enshroud, giftwrap, package, box, pack, enclose, case, encase, crate, sheathe, bandage, bind, swathe, dress

26 **overlie**, lie over, overlap, lap, imbricate, jut, shingle, span, bridge, overarch, overhang, overshadow

27 **roof**, roof in (*or* over), dome, tile, thatch, plaster, ceil, canopy

28 **face**, front, revet, render, clad, brick, lay bricks, mortar, grout, pebble-dash, panel, plank, board, paint, whitewash, plaster, size, stucco, parget, wallpaper, paper, curtain, drape, mould, encrust (*or* incrust)

29 **surface**, pave, concrete, cement, tar, blacktop (US), Tarmac (Tm), macadamize, gravel, cobble

30 **protect**, shield, screen, shade, insulate, lag,

house, guard, defend, armour, watch over, hide out, retreat

31 **hide**, conceal, keep under cover, cover up, mask, veil, cloak, cowl, shroud, hood, disguise, camouflage, masquerade, cloud, obscure, blot out, eclipse, blot, flood, inundate

32 **include**, embody, incorporate, contain, comprise, encompass

33 **fix**, handle, take care of, pay attention to, give news coverage to, report, publicize

34 **cover for**, substitute for, replace, alternate, surrogate, foster, fill in, stand in, back up, relieve, understudy, double for, ghostwrite

35 **progress**, traverse, continue, continue on, pass through, travel through, study, read

ADJECTIVES

36 **covered**, covered up, topped, capped, corked, glazed, varnished, stained, painted, whitewashed, copperplated, roofed, tiled, thatched, tented, faced, bricked, panelled, papered, wallpapered, covered over, roofed in (or over)

37 **protected**, shielded, enclosed, wrapped, packaged, boxed, crated, encased, bound, sheathed, swathed, bandaged, hidden, concealed, screened, masked, veiled, shrouded, enshrouded, cloaked, robed, hooded, camouflaged, disguised, secret, obscured, walled in, walled up

38 **covering**, overlaying, overlying, spanning, superimposed, epidermal, cuticular, integumental

39 **inclusive**, embodied, incorporated (or incorporate), comprehensive, encompassing

40 **substitutive**, substitutable, substitute, alternative, surrogate, foster, stand-in, back-up, relief, locum, reserve

41 **progressing**, continuous, passing, travelling, studious, well-read

ADVERBS

42 **inclusively**, comprehensively, universally, all around, on all sides, from all directions, over, above, around, under, below, above and below

43 **alternatively**, as substitute, on behalf of, in behalf of, per pro (p.p.)

294 Uncovering

NOUNS

1 **uncovering**, opening, laying bare, bareness, nakedness, nudity, nudism, naturism, denudation, exposure, indecent exposure, exhibitionism, flashing, divestment, divestiture

2 **undressing**, undress, dishabille, unclothing, disrobement, peeling, striptease, stripping, streaking, strip poker

3 **nakedness**, nudity, the nude, birthday suit (Inf), the altogether (Inf), the buff (Inf), the raw (Inf), mooning (Sl), debagging (Sl)

▶ 530 Disclosure, 295 Dress, 526 Display, 795 Vulgarity

4 **exposer**, streaker, stripper, stripteaser, striptease dancer (or artist), exotic dancer, fan dancer, topless dancer, ecdysiast, nudist, naturist, nude, nude model, denuder, skinny-dipper, mooner (Sl), flasher (Sl)

5 **shedding**, moulting, moult, shaving, scalping, depilation, hair remover, depilatory, exfoliation, excoriation, flaying, skinning, exuviation, desquamation

6 **baldness**, bald head, hairlessness, receding hair, falling hair, alopecia, tonsure

7 **shedder**, moulter, barber, shaver, scalper, flayer, skinner

ADJECTIVES

8 **uncovered**, opened, exposed, bare, laid bare, hatless, bareheaded, barefoot (or barefooted), bare-chested, bare-legged, bare-bottomed, naked, stark-naked, nude, divested, unclad, undressed, unclothed, au naturel (Fr), stripped, topless, naked as the day one was born, naked as a jaybird, starkers (Inf), not a stitch on (Inf), in one's birthday suit (Inf), in the altogether (Inf), in the buff (Inf), in the raw (Inf), nuddy (Inf), debagged (Sl), bare-ass (or bare-assed) (Tab sl), bare-bollock (Tab sl)

9 **shed**, moulted, unfledged, shaven, clean-shaven, shaved, smooth-shaven, smooth-faced, scalped, flayed, skinned

10 **bald**, hairless, thin on top, receding, bald as a billiard ball (Inf), bald as an egg (or a coot) (Inf), follicularly challenged (Inf)

VERBS

11 **uncover**, open, open up, lay bare, bare, uncover one's head, raise one's hat, doff one's cap, go hatless, expose, exhibit, divest, undress, unclothe, disrobe, undo, unbutton, unlace, peel, peel off, tear off, strip, streak, moon (Sl), flash (Sl), debag (Sl)

12 **shed**, shed skin, shed a layer, moult, slough off, lose hair, recede, go bald

13 **remove**, pluck, shave, scalp, depilate, tonsure, exfoliate, excoriate, flay, skin, exuviate, desquamate

295 Dress

NOUNS

1 **dress**, clothing, clothes, suit of clothes, wear, apparel, accoutrement, article of clothing, garment, garb, frock, creation, linen, habiliments, attire, kit, rig, outfit, wardrobe, tailor-made clothes, bespoke clothes, ready-to-wear clothes, off-the-peg clothes, wash-and-wear clothes, store-bought clothes (Dial), unisex clothes, men's clothing, menswear, women's clothing, womenswear, trousseau, wedding clothes, bridal outfit, maternity wear, work (or working) clothes, formal clothes, best clothes, Sunday best, Sunday go-to-meeting clothes (US), best bib and tucker, finery, regalia,

caparison, panoply, array, frippery, ostrich feathers, informal clothes, sportswear, old clothes, worn clothes, cast-offs, second-hand clothes, tatters, slops, seconds, (fine) raiment (Arch), vesture (Arch), number (Inf), rag (Inf), rags (Inf), glad rags (Inf), togs (Inf), toggery (Inf), get-up (Inf), rigout (Inf), (full) fig (Sl), duds (Inf), front (US sl), gear (Inf), hand-me-down (Inf), reach-me-down (Inf), threads (Sl), clobber, dry goods (US sl)

▶ *293 Covering, 792 Decoration, 811 Showiness*

2 **dressing**, covering, vestiture, investiture, investment, toilet, toilette (Fml), wardrobe, turnout, dressing up, overdressing, foppishness, underdressing, casualness, fashion, the latest fashion, the latest style, the fashion world, fashion designing, Paris fashion, high fashion, couture, *haute couture* (Fr), Savile Row, Carnaby Street, Garment District (US), Fifth Avenue (US), Rodeo Drive (US), the clothing business, tailoring, dressmaking, garment-making, habilimentation, millinery, hosiery, hatmaking, hatting, shoemaking, bootmaking, cobbling, the rag trade (Inf)

▶ *796 Fashion, 558 Elegance, 201 Newness, 792 Decoration, 811 Showiness, 737 Trade*

3 **formal dress**, formal (US), correct dress, court dress, full dress, dress suit, morning dress, tail coat (*or* swallow-tailed coat), tails (Inf), white tie and tails (Inf), soup and fish (Sl), morning coat, dinner dress, party dress, evening dress, evening gown, dinner jacket, tuxedo (US), tux (US), black tie, bow tie, dicky bow, cummerbund, academic dress, academicals, cap and gown, academic robe, vestment, vesture, subfusc, the tartan, kilt, pearlies, uniform, military uniform, dress uniform, full-dress uniform, blues, dress blues, whites, dress whites, mess kit, uniform slops, battledress, khaki uniform, khakis (US), regimentals, fatigues, school uniform, clerical dress, clerical garb, canonicals, nun's habit, nurse's uniform, policeman's (*or* policewoman's) uniform, servant's uniform, livery, riding habit, national dress, national costume, folk costume, mourning clothes, black, (widow's) weeds

▶ *813 Formality, 544 Identification, 7 Religion*

4 **informal dress**, casual clothes, plain clothes, leisure wear, sportswear, tracksuit, shell suit, dishabille, slacks, lounge suit, slack suit (US), blazer, sports jacket, denims, sweat shirt, T-shirt, blouson, smoking jacket, housecoat, lounging pyjamas, bed jacket, wrapper, dressing gown, bathrobe, slippers, mufti, civvies (Sl)

▶ *645 Leisure, 18 Sport, 296 Undress*

5 **fancy dress**, costume, guise, masquerade, bedizenment (Arch), motley, silks, colours, character dress, outfit, rig, gear, disguise, camouflage, theatrical costume, ballet costume,

dance costume, Hollywood costume, Broadway costume, symbolic costume, animal costume, antique costume, novelty costume, medieval costume, classical costume, baroque costume, neoclassic costume, Wagnerian costume, Kabuki costume, buskin, cothurnus, sock and buskin, cap and bells, mask, wooden mask, papier mâché mask, rubber mask, tunic, plume, gown, armour, make-up, greasepaint, powder, lipstick, wig, beard

▶ *531 Concealment, 46 Dancing and Ballet, 51 Performing Arts*

6 **skirt**, maxiskirt (*or* maxi), midiskirt (*or* midi), miniskirt (*or* mini), microskirt (*or* micro), pleated skirt, full skirt, flared skirt, A-line skirt, gored skirt, dirndl, kilt, filibeg (*or* fillibeg), straight skirt, slit skirt, divided skirt, culottes, sarong, tight skirt, hobble skirt, sports skirt, riding habit, tennis skirt, ballet skirt, tutu, overskirt, hoop skirt, crinoline, grass skirt, kirtle (Arch)

▶ *46 Dancing and Ballet*

7 **frock**, dress, cocktail dress, dinner dress, gown, ballgown, dinner gown, tea gown, evening gown, overdress, shirtdress, mantua, cheongsam, muu-muu, Mother Hubbard, maxidress (*or* maxi), minidress (*or* mini), pinafore dress, jumper (US), tube dress, sheath dress, sack, shirtwaister, shirtwaist (US), gymslip, sundress, backless dress, strapless dress, topless dress, maternity dress, wedding dress, little black dress, little black number (Inf)

8 **shirt**, long-sleeved shirt, dress shirt, evening shirt, office shirt, body shirt (*or* bodysuit) (US), olive-drab shirt (*or* OD shirt) (US), short-sleeved shirt, sports shirt, pullover shirt, blouse, middy blouse (*or* middy), overblouse, top, tank top, halter, bustier, smock, dashiki, polo shirt, T-shirt, sweat shirt, sark (Scot), dicky, hair shirt, doublet (Arch)

9 **trousers**, pants (US), trews (Scot), long trousers, long pants (US), cords, flannels, pinstripes, hipsters, hip-huggers (US), Capri pants (*or* Capris), toreador pants, bell-bottoms, slacks, Oxford bags, pegged trousers, pegged pants (US), knickerbockers, knickers (US), plus fours, galligaskins, breeches, breeks (Scot), knee breeches, riding breeches, riding pants (US), buckskins (US), overalls, jodhpurs, pedal pushers, dungarees, denims, jeans, bluejeans, Levi's (Tm), lederhosen, bloomers, pantaloons, gym pants (US), ski pants, shorts, short pants (US), Bermuda shorts, hot pants, short shorts, cycling shorts, britches (Inf), drainpipes (Inf), flares (Inf), bags (Inf), striders (*or* strides) (US sl), pistols (US sl), joggers (Inf)

10 **suit**, outfit, costume, ensemble, coordinates, separates, dress suit, one-piece suit, two-piece suit, three-piece suit, business suit, lounge suit, pinstripe suit, tweed suit, tweeds, trouser

suit, pantsuit (US), catsuit, slack suit (US), leisure suit (US), zoot suit, jump suit, leotard, coveralls, boiler suit, tracksuit, shell suit, jog suit, jogging suit (US), wet suit, G-suit, spacesuit

11 **jacket**, cutaway, morning (or tail or swallowtailed) coat, tails (Inf), claw-hammer coat (US), tweed coat, sack coat (US), topper (US), midicoat, sports jacket, sports coat (US), blazer, sporting jacket, Eton jacket, mess jacket, shell jacket, cardigan (jacket), cardie (Inf), Nehru jacket, Mao jacket, loden, dolman jacket, Mackinaw coat (US), lumber-jacket, lumberjack (US), leather jacket, bomber jacket, parka, anorak, cagoule, reefer, windcheater, windbreaker (US), hunting jacket, shooting jacket, Norfolk jacket, donkey jacket, riding jacket, hacking jacket (or coat), Eisenhower jacket (US), jerkin, spencer, bolero, tunic, tabard, waistcoat, vest (US), monkey jacket (Inf), bumfreezer (Sl), boolhipper (US sl)

12 **coat**, overcoat, topcoat, surcoat, fur, mink, greatcoat, frock coat (or frock), Prince Albert, chesterfield, redingote, paletot, surtout, raglan, ulster, duffel (or duffle) coat, pea jacket (or pea coat), fearnought (or fearnaught), dreadnought (or dreadnaught), light coat, duster, raincoat, waterproof, mackintosh, Burberry (Tm), Barbour (Tm), gaberdine (or gabardine) coat, trench coat, oilskins, slicker (US), southwester (or sou'wester), mac (Inf), crombie (Sl)
▶ *293 Covering*

13 **sweater**, jersey, cardigan, pullover, slipover, woolly, cashmere sweater, knitted sweater, knit, hand-knit (or hand-knitted) sweater, jumper, V-neck, polo-neck (or polo), ski sweater, turtleneck, crew-neck, Guernsey, Aran sweater, fisherman's jersey, Fair Isle, twinset, sloppy joe (Inf), cardie (Inf)

14 **neckwear**, scarf, muffler, comforter, fichu, stock, neckpiece, neckerchief, bandanna (or bandana), kerchief, shawl, tallith, stole, fur, boa, tippet, jabot, tucker, chemisette, guimpe, cravat, neckcloth, ascot, tie, necktie (US), bow tie, dicky bow, Windsor tie, four-in-hand, string tie, necklace, neckband, band, collar, starched collar, stiff collar, high collar, choker, Vandyke collar, Peter Pan collar, bertha collar, Eton collar, Mandarin collar, stand-up collar, rabato, button-down collar, shawl collar, clerical (or Roman) collar, ruff, dog collar (Inf)
▶ *7 Religion*

15 **headgear**, headdress, millinery, hat, chapeau, top hat, high hat, silk hat, stovepipe hat, bowler, derby (US), felt hat, homburg, fedora, trilby, pork-pie hat, deerstalker, Tyrolean hat, straw hat, boater, panama, cowboy hat, stetson, ten-gallon hat, sombrero, slouch hat, beaver, beaverskin, coonskin hat (or cap), busby, cocked hat, tricorn (or tricorne), mortarboard,

bonnet, Easter bonnet, poke bonnet, sunbonnet, sunhat, picture hat, pillbox, toque, cloche, rain hat, southwester (or sou'wester), clerical hat, biretta, shovel hat, woolly hat, bobble hat, helmet, pith helmet (or topee), hard hat, safety hat, crash helmet, work hat, coolie hat, witch's hat, wizard's hat, cap, cloth cap, beanie (or beany) (US), baseball cap (US), jockey cap, beret, tam-o'shanter, (or tam), glengarry, balmoral, skullcap, coif, mobcap (or mob), Juliet cap, Dutch cap, stocking cap, military cap, forage cap, kepi, shako, fez, dunce cap (or dunce's cap or fool's cap), jester's cap, coxcomb, balaclava helmet, scarf, mantilla, plumes, crown, coronet, tiara, net, snood, headscarf, headband, ribbon, fillet, sweatband, turban, hood, cowl, wimple, veil, yashmak, wig, hairpiece, toupee, false hair, peruke, periwig, barrister's wig, bagwig (Arch), powdered wig, hair transplant, topper (Inf), tin hat (Inf), lid (Sl), tile (Sl), titfer, skid lid (Sl), plug hat (US sl), rug (Sl)
▶ *646 Worker, 697 Servant, 22 Baseball, 679 Combatant, 16 Law*

16 **robe**, bathrobe, lounging robe, gown, dressing gown, robe-de-chambre (Fr), peignoir, negligée, housecoat, wrapper, bed jacket, boudoir dress, tunic, sari, kimono, caftan (or kaftan), jubbah, burka, kanga, chiton, himation, toga, toga virilis, pallium, clerical robe, cassock
▶ *7 Religion, 10 Ritual*

17 **grave clothes**, shroud, winding sheet
▶ *399 Burial*

18 **underwear**, undergarments, underclothes, underthings, scanties, lingerie, unmentionables, thermal underwear, long underwear, combinations (or combs), union suit (US), drawers (or underdrawers), pants (or underpants), shorts (or undershorts) (US), boxer shorts, trunks, briefs, Y-fronts, BVD's (US), jockey shorts (US), jockstrap (or athletic support), panties, pantalets (or pantalettes), bloomers, knickers, French knickers, camiknickers (or camiknicks), vest (or undervest), singlet, undershirt (US), T-shirt (US), semmit (Scot), camisole, chemise, shift, stepins, slip, half-slip, underskirt, petticoat, crinoline, Balmoral, teddy, crop top, body stocking, body, foundation garment, corset, stays, girdle, panty girdle, roll-on, supporter, brassiere, bra, suspender belt, garter belt (US), braces, bustle, hoop, farthingale, pannier, smock (Arch), long johns (Inf), undies (Inf), smalls, skivvy shirt (or skivvy) (US sl), skivvies (US sl)
▶ *408 Heat, 284 Support, 296 Undress*

19 **footwear**, footgear, shoes, leather shoes, lace-ups, Oxfords, pumps, court shoes, winklepickers, buckled shoes, square-toed shoes, pointed shoes, high heels, spike (or stiletto)

heels, platform heels, Cuban heels, wedge heels, wedgies (US), canvas shoes, plimsolls (or plimsoles), trainers, sneakers (US), gym shoes, running shoes, spikes, football boots, rugby boots, tennis shoes, trainers, espadrilles, rubber-soled shoes, crepe-soled shoes, ballet shoes (or slippers), casuals, flat shoes, sling (or slingback) shoes, walking shoes, brogues, moccasins, loafers (US), Hush Puppies (Tm), slippers, mules, slip-ons, scuffs, sandals, open-toed sandals, buskins, chappals, flip-flops, thongs (US), zoris, wooden shoes, clogs, sabots, pattens, work shoes, boots, riding boots, fashion boots, high boots, top boots, thigh boots, hip boots, waders, Wellington boots (or wellingtons or gumboots), hobnail boots, walking boots, fell boots, Doc Martens (DMs) (Tm), stogies (US), cowboy boots, ski boots, paratrooper boots, combat boots, desert boots, jackboots, chukka boots, snow-shoes, overshoes, galoshes, gumshoes, rubbers (US), bumpers (Inf), daps (Inf), clodhoppers (Inf), flatties (Inf), wellies (Inf), Jesus boots (Sl), brothel creepers (Sl), beetle-crushers (Sl)

20 **legwear**, hosiery, hose, stockings, sheer stockings, seamless stockings, seamed stockings, silk stockings, lisle stockings, nylons, tights, fishnet tights, pantyhose (US and Aus), fleshings, half-hose, socks, argyles, crew socks, knee-length (or knee) socks, over-the-knee socks, bobby socks, ankle socks, anklets (US), sweat socks, ski socks, galligaskins, leggings, legwarmers, chaps (US), gaiters, spats, suspender, garter (US), puttees, spatterdashes

21 **beachwear**, swimsuit, swimming (or bathing) costume, bathing (or swimming) suit, (swimming) trunks, bathers (Aus), bikini, tanga, one-piece swimsuit, monokini, maillot, two-piece swimsuit, wet suit, sundress, beach robe, sunglasses, shades (Inf)

▶ *39 Swimming, 296 Undress*

22 **nightwear**, sleepwear, nightclothes, nightdress (or nightgown), nightshirt, bedgown, negligée, pyjamas, baby doll pyjamas, dressing gown, bed jacket, nightcap, bedsocks, nightie (Inf), PJs (Inf)

▶ *643 Inactivity, 296 Undress*

23 **children's clothes**, infants' wear, baby clothes, layette, rompers, jumpers (US), creepers (US), matinée coat (or jacket), coatee, playsuit, sunsuit, bootees, bib, nappy (or napkin), diaper (US), swaddling clothes, beanie (US), babygro (Tm), sleepsuit

24 **part of garment**, neck, yoke, collar, top, bodice, bosom, corsage, bib, stomacher, shirtfront, waistline, peplum, train, gusset, crotch, codpiece, arm, armhole, sleeve, short sleeve, long sleeve, dolmen sleeve, raglan sleeve, puff sleeve, leg-of-mutton sleeve, flap, coat-tail, placket, opening, pocket, patch pocket, gore,

pleat, kick pleat, lapel, fold, turn-up, cuff, hemline, edging, garniture, trim, button, fly, zip, hook and eye, Velcro (Tm)

▶ *320 Fold, 300 Edge, 137 Connection, 135 Union, 791 Beautification*

25 **accessories**, accoutrements, paraphernalia, muff, earmuffs, cloak, capote, cape, mantle, shawl, wrap, poncho, afghan, apron, pinafore, pinny (Inf), overall, armlet, armband, shoulder pad, belt, cincture, bandoleer, sash, baldric, codpiece, obi, gloves, kid gloves, suede gloves, driving gloves, long gloves, evening gloves, gauntlets, mittens, mitts, wristband, sunglasses, shades (Inf), handkerchief, loincloth, waistcloth, lungi (or lungee), dhoti, fig leaf, G-string, jockstrap, falsies (Inf)

▶ *143 Part, 148 Component, 296 Undress*

26 **fashion designer**, couturier (or couturiere), costumier (or costumer), costume designer, dressmaker, tailor, sartor (Fml), garment-maker, clothier, outfitter, milliner, modiste, hatter, hosier, glover, furrier, haberdasher (US), draper, fabric dealer (US), mercer, dry-goods dealer (US), shoemaker, cobbler, souter (Scot), bootmaker, booter, garmentworker, cutter, needleworker, needlewoman, seamstress, sewer, stitcher, finisher, fitter, busheller, cordwainer (Arch)

▶ *792 Decoration, 243 Production, 604 Materials, 737 Trade, 67 Fabrics and Dyeing*

27 **model**, fashion model, male model, Beau, Beau Brummel, dandy, fop, trendsetter, snappy dresser (Inf), poser (Inf), clotheshorse (Inf), coat hanger (Inf), face (Sl)

28 **valet**, dresser, batman, lady's maid, wardrobe mistress

▶ *697 Servant*

ADJECTIVES

29 **dressed**, clothed, clad, attired, garbed, apparelled, bedecked, arrayed, vested, invested, habited, habilimented, wrapped, draped, robed, frocked, mantled, cloaked, gowned, hatted, capped, bonneted, hooded, bewigged, gloved, shod, shoed, booted, decked out, turned out, rigged, kitted out, costumed, uniformed, liveried

▶ *531 Concealment*

30 **dressed up**, smart, clothes-conscious, fashionable, stylish, modish, à la mode, chic, dapper, spruced up, spruce, well-dressed, groomed, well turned out, tricked out (or up), *soigné* (or *soignée*), *en grande tenue* (Fr), *en grande toilette* (Fr), in Sunday best, in Sunday go-to-meeting clothes (US), in full dress, in white tie and tails, in tails, bedight (Arch), bedizened (Arch), natty (Inf), dressed to kill (Inf), dressed up to the nines (Inf), in fine feather (Inf), in one's best bib and tucker (Inf), done (or got) up like a dog's dinner (Inf), togged (Inf), fancied up (Inf), slicked up (US inf), tarted up (Inf),

tarty (Inf), gussied up (US sl), dolled up (Sl), spiffed up (Sl), dap (US sl)

▶ *796 Fashion, 558 Elegance*

31 **styled**, tailored, sartorial, tailor-made, bespoke, made-to-measure, made-to-order, custom-made, designer, store-bought (Dial), off-the-peg, ready-made, ready-to-wear, single-breasted, double-breasted, one-piece, two-piece, unisex, well-cut, fully fashioned, stylish, dressy, smart, matching, colour-coordinated, classic, princess-line, Empire-line, A-line, step-in, pull-on, button-through, buttoned-up, zip-up, casual, informal, sporty, baggy, sloppy, gathered, rucked, ruched, tucked, darted, hemmed, laced, long-sleeved, short-sleeved, gusseted, pleated, trimmed, folded, bloused, bouffant, skintight, slinky (Inf), natty (Inf), snazzy (Inf)

VERBS

32 **dress**, clothe, clad, garment, apparel, accoutre, attire, robe, enrobe, gown, drape, cloak, mantle, garb, enfold, envelop, wrap, roll up in, swaddle, swathe, shroud, sheathe, cover, vest, invest, cap, hood, glove, shoe, uniform, costume

33 **dress up**, deck out, turn out, rig out, spruce up, titivate, bedeck, array, beautify, primp, prink, comparison, dight (Arch), bedizen (Arch), dress to kill (Inf), dress up to the nines (Inf), dress in one's best bib and tucker (Inf), fancy up (Inf), tart up (Inf), gussy up (US sl), doll up (Sl), spiff up (Sl)

34 **wear**, dress in, have on, don, clothe oneself, attire oneself, get dressed, get one's clothes on, put on, pull on, slip on, slip (*or* get) into, step in, button up, zip up, do up, lace up, tie, get changed, change one's clothes, change, try on

35 **make clothing**, outfit, tailor, tailor-make, custom-make, make to order, accoutre, costume, powder, bewig, uniform, equip, rig out, fit out, design, style, cobble, measure, adjust, gather, fold, blouse, seam, sew, stitch, pleat, finish, fit, bushel (US)

ADVERBS

36 **dressily**, fashionably, stylishly, modishly, in vogue, chicly, elegantly, smartly, glamorously, casually, informally, sportily, nattily (Inf), snazzily (Inf)

296 Undress

NOUNS

1 **undress**, undressing, unclothing, uncovering, disrobing, disrobement, divestment, denuding, denudation, stripping, stripping bare, laying bare, baring, bareness, nudism, naturism, gymnosophy, revealing, exposing, exposure, toplessness, indecent exposure, striptease, dance of the seven veils, exhibitionism,

streaking, strip poker, strip-search (*or* skin-search), skinny-dipping (Inf), flashing (Sl), mooning (Sl)

▶ *294 Uncovering, 530 Disclosure, 295 Dress, 526 Display, 46 Dancing and Ballet, 811 Showiness*

2 **nudity**, nakedness, bareness, state of nature, the nude, the buff (Inf), the raw (Inf), the altogether (Inf), birthday suit (Inf), not a stitch on (Inf), not a stitch to one's name (Inf), nudie (US sl)

3 **pornography**, pornographic picture, pornographic film, X-rated film, blue film, pornographic magazine, erotica, nude painting, soft porn, strip (*or* striptease) club, strip-o-gram (Inf), skin flick (Sl), skin magazine (US sl), strip (*or* striptease) joint (US sl)

▶ *51 Performing Arts, 50 Painting and Sculpture, 66 Photography*

4 **dishabille** (*or* **deshabille**), informality, informal dress, nightwear, nightdress, nightgown, nightie (Inf), pyjamas, dressing gown, bathrobe, housecoat, kimono, underwear, swimwear, revealing dress, miniskirt, microskirt, shorts, hot pants, G-string, thong, posing pouch, jockstrap, décolletage, plunging neckline, careless dress, negligent dress, poor dress, second-hand clothes, hand me downs, rags, tatters

▶ *814 Informality, 470 Negligence, 796 Fashion*

5 **baldness**, hairlessness, alopecia, calvities, premature baldness, baldheadedness, bare head, baldpatedness, bald top, beardlessness, bald person, baldhead, baldpate, skinhead, baldy (Inf), slaphead (Inf)

▶ *376 Smoothness*

6 **peeling**, shedding, moulting, moult, decortication, excoriation, desquamation, exfoliation, abscission, ecdysis, exuviation

▶ *136 Separation, 82 Insects and Arachnids, 78 Birds*

7 **depilation**, falling hair, alopecia, hair remover, denuder, depilatory, electrolysis, wax, razor, shaving, shave, plucking, shearing, shear, haircut, tonsure

8 **nude person**, naked person, naked lady, disrober, nude, nude model, nude figure, nudist, naturist, gymnosophist, stripper, male stripper, stripteaser, striptease dancer, striptease artiste (*or* artist), exotic dancer, topless dancer, topless waitress, ecdysiast, exhibitionist, streaker, exposer, skinny-dipper (Inf), strip-o-gram (Inf), flasher (Sl), peeler (US sl)

▶ *50 Painting and Sculpture*

ADJECTIVES

9 **undressed**, unclothed, clothesless, uncovered, unclad, without a stitch on, bared, bare, nude, in the nude, naked, stark-naked (*or* stark), stripped, stripped naked (*or* bare *or* nude), strip-searched (*or* skin-searched), disrobed, unrobed, unattired, undraped, un-

garbed, in a state of nature, *au naturel* (Fr), *in puris naturalibus* (L), in nature's garb, naked as the day one was born, naked as a jaybird (US), nudist, naturistic, gymnosophical, buck naked (US inf), nuddy (Inf), raw (Inf), in the raw (Inf), in the buff (Inf), stripped to the buff (Inf), in the altogether (Inf), starkers (Inf), in one's birthday suit (Inf), bare-ass (*or* bare-assed) (US sl), bare-bollock (Sl)

10 **in dishabille**, *en deshabille* (Fr), under-dressed, underclothed, half-dressed, half-clothed, informally dressed, bareheaded, hat-less, topless, décolleté, low-necked, low-cut, off-the-shoulder, strapless, miniskirted, micro-skirted, swimsuited, bikini-clad, casually dressed, negligently dressed, in one's shirt-sleeves, poorly dressed, tattered, threadbare, out-at-elbows, ragged, barefoot, barelegged

11 **exposed**, exposable, divested, unveiled, de-nuded (*or* denudated), laid bare, barebacked, barebreasted, topless, barechested, barelegged, barefoot (*or* barefooted), discalced (*or* discal-ceate), barenecked, indecently dressed, por-nographic, X-rated, stripped, peeled, skinny-dipping (Inf), debagged (Sl), flashing (Sl), mooning (Sl)
▶ *795 Vulgarity*

12 **peeling**, peeled, shedding, shed, sloughy, exuvial, exfoliatory (*or* exfoliative), leafless, desquamative, ecdysial, moulting, moulted, unfledged, unfeathered, plucked

13 **hairless**, bald, baldheaded, bald-pated, thin, thin on top, tonsured, shaved, shaven, clean-shaven, beardless, smooth-shaven, smooth-faced, smooth, glabrous (*or* glabrate), hair-removing, depilatory, bald as a coot, bald as an egg, bald as a billiard ball, bare as the back of one's hand

VERBS

14 **undress**, unclothe, uncover, disrobe, unrobe, unveil, uncloak, undrape, divest, doff, take off, strip off, slip off, slip out of, step out of, re-move, put off, drop, undo, unbutton, unzip, unhook, unlace, untie, change one's clothes, change, strip, bare, strip bare, lay bare, expose, lay open, disclose, reveal, expose oneself, streak, go topless, practise nudism, peel off (Sl), strip to the buff (Inf), wear a smile (US inf), skinny-dip (Inf), flash (Sl), moon (Sl)

15 **make nude**, denude, denudate, strip, force someone to strip, pull (*or* rip) off someone's clothes, disrobe, strip-search (*or* skin-search), unwrap, fleece, shear, shave, pluck, deplume, tear off, scrape off, peel, pare, flay, abrade, rub off, scalp, debark, debag (Sl)

16 **peel**, shed, slough, lose feathers, moult, throw off, cast off skin, scale off, scale, flake off, flake, decorticate, excoriate, desquamate, exfoliate, exuviate

ADVERBS

17 **nakedly**, with nothing on, without a stitch on, barely, in the nude, pornographically, ex-plicitly, indecently, in one's shirtsleeves, in-formally, casually, revealingly, baldly, in the raw (Inf), in the buff (Inf), in the altogether (Inf), in one's birthday suit (Inf)

297　Surroundings

NOUNS

1 **surroundings**, environment, environs, area, neighbourhood, confines, locale, background, backdrop, setting, arena, stage, scene, scenery, outskirts, outposts, perimeter, periphery, pre-cincts, vicinity, suburb, green belt
▶ *289 Exterior, 301 Enclosure, 299 Outline*

2 **encirclement**, envelopment, enfoldment, encompassment, circumambience (*or* circum-ambiency)

3 **atmosphere**, ambience, milieu, aura, feeling, tone, overtone, undertone, situation, vibra-tions (Sl), vibes (Sl)
▶ *251 Situation*

ADJECTIVES

4 **surrounding**, environmental, neighbour-hood, background, outlying, perimetric (*or* perimetrical), peripheral, suburban

5 **surrounded**, encircled, enveloped, wrapped, enfolded, encompassed, girded, circum-scribed, circumambient, on all sides, round-about, round and about, hemmed-in, en-closed

6 **atmospheric**, ambient, in the air, aural, situational

VERBS

7 **surround**, lie around, environ, outlie, encir-cle, circle, go round, envelop, enfold, encom-pass, surround, be around, enclose, contain, keep in, edge, border, frame

ADVERBS

8 **round**, about, round about, on all sides, right and left, all round, in the neighbourhood, in the vicinity

298　Interface

NOUNS

1 **interface**, place of contact, meeting point, adjoining section, contiguity, adjacency, abut-ment, place of interaction, threshold, place of confrontation, battlefront, division line, shared frontier, common boundary, common border, political border, Iron Curtain, Bamboo Curtain, forty-ninth parallel, Mason-Dixon Line, Berlin Wall, Hadrian's wall, Antonine wall, Maginot line, Siegfried line
▶ *342 Convergence, 407 Touch, 264 Nearness, 302 Limit, 663 Opposition, 671 Defence*

2 **interaction**, common ground, cooperation, compatibility, working together, permeation,

interpenetration, blend, dovetail, fitting together

▶ *158 Middle, 135 Union, 138 Adhesion*

3 interfacer, confronter, frontbencher, front-line soldier, frontiersman, pioneer, intermediary, middleman, mediator, negotiator, referee, umpire, director, continuity girl (*or* man), linkman

▶ *678 Mediation*

VERBS

4 interface, meet, contact, make contact, touch, adjoin, be contiguous, be adjacent, abut, abut on, interact, confront, divide, share, hold in common, border, border on

5 cooperate, find common ground, be compatible, work together, blend, dovetail, permeate, interpenetrate, fit together

ADJECTIVES

6 interfacial, contiguous, adjacent, adjoining, meeting, abutting, liminal, interactive, confrontational, divisive, shared, common, same, cooperative, compatible, blended, dovetailed, permeated, interpenetrative, intermediary

ADVERBS

7 interfacially, contiguously, adjacently, on the threshold, interactively, commonly, cooperatively, compatibly

299 Outline

NOUNS

1 outline, plan, summary, synopsis, abstract, epitome, precis, notes, class notes, brief impression, single aspect, bare essentials, frame, profile, projection, ground plan, layout, blueprint, representation, limning, emblem, sample, representative sample, random sample, survey, contour line, contour, brief description, illustration, etching, engraving, delineation, depiction, chart, graph, line graph, bar graph, diagram, portrayal, picture, simple picture, sketch, thumbnail sketch, tracing, cartoon, stick figure, matchstick man, skeleton, bare bones, reduction, abridgment, digest, condensation, contraction, abbreviation, long story made short

▶ *592 Plan, 457 Appearance, 50 Painting and Sculpture, 306 Form, 560 Description*

2 shadow, silhouette, shape, form, relief, profile, contour, figure, frame, framework

▶ *305 Side, 382 Structure*

3 edge, upper edge, horizon, skyline, coastline, outside edge, perimeter, border, fringe, flange, margin, circumference, surround, rim, circumscription

▶ *300 Edge, 313 Circularity*

4 map, road map, world map, city map, town plan, A to Z, treasure map, sketch map, relief map, political map, historical map, projection map, Mercator projection, Peters' projection,

globe, atlas, cartography

▶ *547 Representation*

VERBS

5 outline, plan, sketch out, rough out, block out, summarize, synopsize (US), abstract, epitomize, precis, present the main points, note, frame, profile, project, lay out, blueprint, draw an outline, picture, portray, sketch, limn, represent, sample, survey, describe briefly, boil down, illustrate, etch, engrave, delineate, depict, chart, graph, diagram, make a thumbnail sketch, trace, reduce, abridge, digest, condense, contract, abbreviate, cut a long story short

ADJECTIVES

6 outlined, in outline, summarized, synopsized (US), brief, impressionistic, representative, emblematic, sample, random, descriptive, delineative, depictive, thumbnail, skeletal, abridged, abbreviated, circumscriptive, projectional, peripheral, marginal

ADVERBS

7 essentially, skeletally, depictively, in outline, in brief, marginally, peripherally

300 Edge

NOUNS

1 edge, border, rim, brim, margin, limit, periphery, lip, skirt, fringe, brink, verge, extremity, bounds, confines, limits, frontier, boundary, water's edge, shoreline, shore, seaside, coast, tideline, waterfront, littoral, strand, beach, riverside, waterside, bank, verge, hard shoulder, soft shoulder, roadside, wayside, sideline, kerb, ragged edge

▶ *157 End, 302 Limit, 389 Water, 70 Transport, 299 Outline*

2 edging, hem, hemline, border, selvage (*or* selvedge), fringe, flounce, piping, trimming, valance, furbelow, gimp (*or* guimpe), crenellation

▶ *792 Decoration, 796 Fashion*

3 cutting edge, sharp edge, knife edge, razor's edge, blade, sharpness, steel, point of action

▶ *380 Sharpness, 642 Activity*

4 advantage, upper hand, whip hand, little something extra, head start, flying (*or* running) start, the jump (Inf), inside track (Inf), ace in the hole (Inf)

▶ *126 Superiority, 459 Intellect, 235 Power, 233 Influence*

VERBS

5 border, verge, rim, be limiting, skirt, be at the brink, verge on, bind, confine, be on the beach, be on the sideline

6 edge, border, hem, fringe, pipe, trim, furbelow, decorate, crenellate, marginalize

7 have an advantage, be ahead, outwit, outthink, outmanoeuvre, outstrip, outshine, have

a head start, have a flying (*or* running) start, have that little extra something (Inf), have the jump on (Inf), have the inside track (Inf), have an ace in the hole (Inf)

ADJECTIVES

8 **edging**, edged, bordered, marginal, extreme, seaside, waterfront, coastal, littoral, beach, riverside, waterside, roadside, wayside, sideline, peripheral

9 **skirting**, skirted, edged, fringed, valanced

10 **advantaged**, ahead, keen, sharp, acute, biting, pungent, effective, forceful, incisive, powerful

ADVERBS

11 **marginally**, peripherally, on the edge, at the limit, on the border, at the extreme, extremely, on the threshold

12 **at an advantage**, powerfully, forcefully, incisively, effectively, acutely, keenly, sharply, pungently

301   Enclosure

NOUNS

1 **enclosure** (*or* **inclosure**), enclosing, closing in, ringing round, circumvallation, circumscription, envelopment, encirclement, appropriation of land

▶ *293 Covering, 258 Container, 299 Outline, 313 Circularity*

2 **enclosed place**, enclosure, confine, precinct, close, pen, pigpen, pigsty, paddock, field, corral (US), reserve, enclave, special area, compound, fold, pound, quadrangle, quad, courtyard, walled garden, royal enclosure, reserved section, holy of holies, sanctum sanctorum, high table, cloister, monastery, convent, backyard, yard, park, patio, stockade, prison, palisade, harbour, marina

▶ *323 Closure, 531 Concealment, 250 Location, 7 Religion*

3 **enclosing thing**, wall, fence, post and rail, railing, paling, pale, moat, trench, hedge, hedgerow, mole, ditch, dyke, fosse, ha-ha, balustrade, barrier

▶ *661 Hindrance, 671 Defence, 298 Interface*

4 **wrapper**, wrapping, bandage, cast, wrapping paper, Cellophane (Tm), clingfilm (Tm), bubblewrap, foil, scarf, wraparound skirt, sheath, net, dustsheet, dust cover, container, envelope, folder, dust jacket, frame, framework

▶ *48 Literature*

VERBS

5 **enclose**, surround, close, close in, fence, fence in, wall, wall in, rail, pale, moat, dyke, shut, shut in, hem in, build in, pen, pen up, paddock, corral (US), reserve, cloister, confine, imprison

6 **wrap**, bandage, bind, sheath, net, contain,

envelop, enfold, encompass, circumscribe, frame

ADJECTIVES

7 **enclosed**, closed-in, fenced-in, walled-in, shut-in, hemmed-in, built-in, penned, pent-up, indoor, cloistered, monastic, conventual, intramural, confined, imprisoned, claustrophobic

ADVERBS

8 **confinedly**, cloisteredly, intramurally, monastically, claustrophobically

302   Limit

NOUNS

1 **limitation**, limit, restriction, proscription, circumscription, demarcation, definition, moderation, mitigation, exclusion, restraint, constraint, control, containment, inhibition

2 **limiting factor**, upper limit, lower limit, self-control, self-restraint, check, prohibition, restricted area, no-go area, off-limits area (US), specification, ceiling, speed limit, high-water mark, bottom, threshold, failing grade, low-water mark, hindrance, brake, drag, repression, censorship, narrow outlook, veto, ban, stricture, rationing, price freeze, curtailment, curb, curfew, restrictive practice, closed shop, trading ring, monopoly, cartel, trust, quota, embargo, tariff, allotment, finite quantity, extent, measure, dose, lot, copyright, patent

▶ *699 Restraint, 701 Subjection, 485 Qualification, 731 Allocation, 711 Refusal, 218 Cessation*

3 **furthest point**, extremity, farness, boundary, verge, margin, edge, outside edge, brink, three-mile limit, frontier, outpost, last outpost, back of beyond

▶ *263 Distance, 300 Edge, 157 End*

4 **boundary marker**, boundary stone, partition wall, fence, stone wall, hedge, river, checkpoint, line, line in the sand, time zone, international date line, longitude, latitude

▶ *75 Units, 298 Interface*

ADJECTIVES

5 **limited**, restricted, restrictive, proscripted, prohibitive, repressive, inhibiting, no-go, off-limits (US), exclusive, definite, under control, under restraint, held back, in check, confined, frozen, under curfew, curtailed, finite, narrow, cramped, hidebound, copyrighted, patented, tight (US)

6 **furthest**, extreme, far, verging, on the brink, at the three-mile limit, boundary, border, bordering, longitudinal, latitudinal

VERBS

7 **limit**, restrict, proscribe, circumscribe, demarcate, draw the line at, define, moderate, be exclusive, exclude, restrain, constrain, control, lay down guidelines, mitigate, be inhibited, inhibit, have self-control, have self-

restraint, check, hamper, hold in, confine, prohibit, specify, set parameters, limit one's speed, reach one's threshold, hinder, brake, drag, repress, put a stop to, curb, bottle up, censor, have a narrow outlook, veto, ban, place strictures on, ration, freeze prices, curtail, set a curfew, contain, hold one back, monopolize, set a quota, embargo, allot, measure out, copyright, patent

ADVERBS

8 **within limits**, under control, under restrictions, when forbidden, to a certain extent, off-limits, out of bounds

303 Front

NOUNS

1 **front**, forefront, fore, frontage, front elevation, façade, foreground, front door, entrance, main entrance, entrance hall, foyer, vestibule, lobby, forecourt, antechamber, anteroom, proscenium, seafront, waterfront, shore, marina, promenade, esplanade, strand, front line, forward line, battlefront, battleground, theatre of war, first, beginning, introduction, preliminaries, prefix, preface, foreword, frontispiece, front page, front matter, prelims, prologue, avant-garde, advance guard, vanguard, spearhead, figurehead, prow, bowsprit, forecastle (or fo'c'sle), foredeck, foremast

▶ *154 Precedence, 194 Priority, 322 Opening, 670 Attack*

2 **face**, visage, façade, physiognomy, countenance, profile, fullface picture, head-and-shoulders shot, mug shot (Sl), mug (Sl), pan (Sl), puss (Sl), kisser (Sl), phiz (Sl), clock (Sl), dial (Sl), index (US Sl)

▶ *457 Appearance, 279 Summit*

3 **show**, surface show, outward appearance, projected image, persona, mask, façade, display

4 **assurance**, self-assurance, confidence, self-confidence, composure, equanimity, authority

5 **boldness**, cheek, nerve, audacity, brazenness, brassiness, arrogance, sauce, effrontery, brass neck (Inf), front (Inf), sass (US inf), bottle (Sl), chutzpah (US inf)

ADJECTIVES

6 **front**, fore, foreground, frontal, fronting, entrance, obverse, anterior, preceding, forward, physiognomic, physiognomical, full-faced, head-and-shoulders, full-frontal (Inf)

7 **outward**, surface, facial, superficial, displayed, projected, assumed

8 **assured**, self-assured, self-confident, composed, authoritative

9 **arrogant**, overconfident, bold, brazen, sassy (US inf)

VERBS

10 **be in front,** stand in front, front, come to the front, come forward, be ahead of, be first, be

in the vanguard (or van), put up front, put in advance, ante, take the lead, lead, take the helm, head, introduce, prefix, preface, prelude, spearhead, challenge, face, confront, face up to, front up to

ADVERBS

11 **in front**, up front, to the fore, forward, ahead, before, in advance, in the lead, in the vanguard (or van)

304 Rear

NOUNS

1 **rear**, behind, background, hinterland, backstage, rear part, back part, rear entrance, back door, postern, tradesman's entrance, back end, afterpart, wake, train, tail end, tailpiece, pigtail, heel, heel piece, coda, endpiece, back matter, end matter, colophon, afterword, verso, afterpiece, epilogue, afterthought, postscript (PS), continuation, appendix, supplement, suffix, stern, afterquarters, poop deck, mizzenmast (or mizenmast), rear mast

▶ *157 End, 49 Music, 48 Literature, 155 Sequence, 159 Consecutiveness*

2 **rear end**, end, rump, behind, stern, bottom, anus, posterior, backside, buttocks, back, lower back, fundament, lumbar region, dorsal region, hindquarters, haunches, hunkers, tail, latter end, derriere, sitter (Inf), sit-upon (Inf), tush (or tushie) (US inf), cheeks (Inf), butt (US inf), back passage (Sl), fanny (US sl), rusty-dusty (US sl), arse (Tab sl), bum (Sl), keister (or keester) (US sl) Gary Glitter (Sl)

3 **rearing up**, rising up, leaning backwards, going backwards, elevating oneself, going up on hind legs, lifting front legs

▶ *275 Height, 594 Preparation, 128 Increase*

ADJECTIVES

4 **rear**, rearward, back, hind, hindmost, postern, posterior, mizzen (or mizen), dorsal, lumbar, tail, end, continued, supplemental, anal, caudal, latter, lower

5 **bred**, well-bred, fattened-up, grown

VERBS

6 **be in the rear**, be behind, trail, tag along, lag behind, drop behind, follow, follow in the wake, bring up the rear, be last

7 **rear up**, rise up, lean backwards, go backwards, elevate oneself, go up on hind legs, lift front legs

8 **nurture**, raise children, bring up children, rear, raise, breed, stock, incubate, fatten up, farm, grow plants

ADVERBS

9 **in the rear**, to the rear, at the end, rearward, behind, behind the scenes, in back of, in the background, after, aftermost, sternmost, aft, backward

305   Side

NOUNS

1 **side**, laterality, edge, side entrance, side door, siding, side elevation, hillside, flank, right hand, dexter side, starboard, left hand, sinister side, port, ribs, hip, side of the face, cheek, jowl, temple, jaw, side whiskers, sideboards, profile, side view

▶ *300 Edge, 286 Obliqueness*

2 **surface**, facing, front side, back side, top side, bottom side, far side of the moon, side of a coin

3 **side direction**, windward side, right-hand side, left-hand side, lee side, south side, east side, west side, north side, right side, left side, other side, far side, near side, offside

▶ *332 Direction*

4 **aspect**, feature, facet, element, bright side, funny side, dark side, cruel side

▶ *457 Appearance*

5 **team**, group, circle, camp, coterie, home side, away side, visiting side, our side, opposing side, opposite side

▶ *665 Party, 161 Assembly*

ADJECTIVES

6 **side**, sidelong, oblique, lateral, flanking, skirting, facing, southern, eastern, western, northern, right, left, far, near, two-sided, many-sided, multifaceted, bilateral, trilateral, quadrilateral, collateral

VERBS

7 **be alongside**, side, side up to, edge, flank, be next to, stand side-by-side, skirt, face

8 **move sideways**, go sideways, step aside, sidestep, sidle, make a side move, avoid, deviate

▶ *335 Deviation*

9 **side with**, side, support, back, take sides, be partisan, conspire with

ADVERBS

10 **laterally**, sideways, sidewards, obliquely, to one side, to the side, sidewise, alongside, side-by-side, hand-in-hand

306   Form

NOUNS

1 **form**, structure, order, system, formation, forming, conformation, format, configuration, construction, composition, composure, gestalt, Gestalt whole, shape, shaping, figure, profile, contour, frame, lines, outline, silhouette, relief, pattern, patterning, arrangement, design, designing, significant form, inner form, essence, substance, nominalism, Platonism, Platonic form, idea, morphology, isomorphism

▶ *142 Whole, 382 Structure, 152 Arrangement, 299 Outline, 243 Production, 101 Reality, 103 Essence, 457 Appearance, 150 Order, 214 Regularity*

2 **prototype**, form, formula, format, model, dummy, mould, example, paradigm, pattern, jig, template, stencil, matrix, frame, blank, punch, stamp, cast, die, blueprint

▶ *594 Preparation, 592 Plan, 119 Originality*

3 **kind**, form, type, sort, variety, character, order, genre, art form, inscape, verse form, word form, sonata form

▶ *163 Class, 50 Painting and Sculpture, 48 Literature, 49 Music, 150 Order, 549 Style*

4 **forming**, formulation, creation, morphogenesis, construction, production, expression, fashioning, modelling, moulding, tailoring, knitting, weaving, shaping, setup, make-up, composition

▶ *644 Work, 604 Materials, 243 Production*

5 **formality**, good form, decorum, etiquette, protocol, behaviour, conduct, practice, routine, habit, fashion, trend, style, custom, tradition, convention, procedure, form of law, litigation, ceremony, ritual, solemnity

▶ *811 Showiness, 796 Fashion, 584 Habit, 10 Ritual, 116 Accord, 167 Conformity, 652 Conduct, 817 Courtesy, 813 Formality, 549 Style*

6 **nature**, health, fitness, condition, shape, fettle, soundness, character, attitude, turn, appearance, features, lineament, face, expression, look, mein, aspect, demeanour, cast, set, physiognomy, physique, anatomy, body, build, ectomorph, endomorph, mesomorph, figure, trim, posture, stance, cut, cut of one's jib (Inf), get-up (Inf)

▶ *457 Appearance, 303 Front, 549 Style, 623 Health*

VERBS

7 **form**, structure, order, systematize, formalize, arrange, pattern, figure, design, draft, sketch, formulate, draw, format, lay out, rough out, block out, shape, turn, round, square, frame, outline, silhouette, cut out, cut, whittle, hew, rough-hew, carve, chisel, sculpt (or sculpture), mould, model, knead, throw (pots), blow (glass), cast, coin, mint, stamp, found, hammer out, punch out, forge, smith, fashion, work up, work, build, construct, create, bring into being, make, produce, express, verbalize, put into words, put into shape, knock into shape, lick into shape (Inf)

8 **be formal**, conform, comply, toe the line, stick to the rules, follow protocol, practise etiquette, behave well, mind one's manners, mind one's p's and q's, maintain tradition, stand on ceremony, observe a ritual, solemnize

ADJECTIVES

9 **formed**, formative, formal, orderly, systematic, conformable, configurational, configurative, creative, created, made, constructed, produced, shaped, sculptured, carved, moulded, modelled, tailored, thrown (pot), blown

(glass), turned, rounded, squared, fashioned, set-up, composed, styled, stylized, stylish, expressive, morphologic (*or* morphological), morphogenic (*or* morphogenetic), isomorphic, isomorphous, Platonic, concrete, solid, plastic, fictile

10 **prototypical**, original, exemplary, dummy, paradigmatic, generic, model, custom-built, ready-made, off the rack, off the peg, tailor-made, designer

11 **formal**, conventional, procedural, protocol, decorous, behavioural, traditional, ceremonial, solemn, ritual, customary, routine, habitual, litigious, ritualistic, fashionable, trendy, stylish

12 **on form**, in shape, in good condition, fit, able, capable, healthy, salubrious, hale, in fine fettle, hearty, in the pink, in good nick (Inf)

ADVERBS

13 **formatively**, formally, systematically, by design, conformably, configurationally, concretely, solidly, plastically, stylishly, creatively, constructively, productively, prototypically, originally, paradigmatically, generically, healthily, heartily, expressively, morphologically, Platonically

14 **conventionally**, procedurally, routinely, habitually, traditionally, fashionably, stylishly, ceremonially, solemnly, litigiously, ritually

307 Shapelessness

NOUNS

1 **shapelessness**, formlessness, featurelessness, amorphousness, amorphism, undevelopment, incompleteness, incompletion, rawness, lack of definition, obscurity, vagueness, obscureness, unclearness, fuzziness, blurriness, haziness, mistiness, fog, fogginess, chaos

▶ *309 Distortion, 595 Lack of Preparation, 441 Dimness, 151 Disorder*

2 **shapeless thing**, diamond in the rough, old pillow, sack dress, sloppy sweater, blob, amoeba, jellyfish

VERBS

3 **make shapeless**, deform, distort, misform, unform, misshape, unshape, unmake, knock out of shape, twist, bend, leave undeveloped, keep incomplete, remain raw, lack definition, be vague, obscure, be unclear, blur, fog

4 **disorder**, put into disorder, cause chaos, muddle, jumble, obfuscate

▶ *244 Destruction, 153 Disturbance, 133 Mixture*

ADJECTIVES

5 **shapeless**, unshaped, formless, unformed, amorphous, unfinished, undefined, lacking definition, indefinite, undeveloped, underdeveloped, incomplete, raw, uncut, unhewn, unlicked, vague, obscure, unclear, shadowed, fuzzy, blurred, hazy, misty, ill-defined, featureless

ADVERBS

6 **shapelessly**, formlessly, amorphously, indefinitely, obscurely, unclearly, fuzzily, hazily, mistily, foggily

308 Symmetry

NOUNS

1 **symmetry**, symmetricalness, uniformity, balance, balance of form, bilateral symmetry, proportion, proportionality, rhyme, harmony, chiasmus, counterbalance, equality, equilibrium, equipose, even sides, congruence, congruity, correspondence, parallelism, correlation, coordinateness, interrelation, interconnectedness, interdependence, interaction, reciprocity, reciprocation

▶ *112 Uniformity, 116 Accord, 122 Equality, 285 Parallelism*

2 **symmetry operation**, reflection, rotation, inversion, translation, symmetry element, mirror plane, axis of symmetry, glide plane, rotational symmetry, bilateral symmetry

▶ *57 Chemistry*

3 **evenness**, regularity, conformity, regular features, consistency, uniformity, eurhythmy, harmony, beauty, shapeliness

▶ *789 Beauty, 167 Conformity*

ADJECTIVES

4 **symmetrical**, symmetric, uniform, balanced, well-balanced, proportional, proportionate, well-proportioned, proportioned, harmonious, counterbalanced, equal, equilateral, even-sided, bisymmetric(al), isosceles, congruent, correspondent, corresponding, correlational, coordinate, interdependent, interacting, reciprocal, enantiomorphic, chiastic

5 **even**, even-sided, regular, consistent, uniform, eurhythmic, eurhythmical, harmonious, beautiful, shapely

VERBS

6 **symmetrize**, make uniform, balance, proportion, harmonize, counterbalance, equalize, equilibrate, correlate, coordinate, even, even up, regularize, make consistent

ADVERBS

7 **symmetrically**, uniformly, proportionally, equilaterally, proportionately, correspondingly

8 **equally**, evenly, even-sidedly, reciprocally, on the one hand and on the other, even Stevens (Inf)

309 Distortion

NOUNS

1 **distortion**, asymmetry, disproportion, lopsidedness, imbalance, difference, irregularity, crookedness, warp, strain, stress, contortion, bias, skewness, twist, torsion, twistedness

▶ *123 Inequality, 286 Obliqueness, 215 Irregularity*

2 **facial distortion**, contortion, grimace, girn (Dial), scowl, frown, snarl, sneer, leer, pout, *moue* (Fr), rictus, tic, squint

3 **deformity**, malformation, hunchback, clubfoot, cleft palate, mutation, misshapenness, ugliness, hideousness, disfigurement, grotesquerie, defacement, imperfection, scar, cicatrix, spot, stain, mark, welt, weal, pockmark, blemish, pimple, zit (Sl)
▶ *168 Nonconformity, 790 Ugliness, 793 Blemish*

4 **distortion of the truth**, exaggeration, misrepresentation, perversion, misconstruction, false reading, fiction, deception, fabrication, falsity, spuriousness, perfidy, mendacity, deceitfulness, misinformation, disinformation, brainwashing, whitewashing, untruthfulness, lie, falsehood, travesty, burlesque, parody, propaganda, economy with the truth, terminological inexactitude, selective facts, imaginative journalism, poetic truth, pork pie (Sl), porky (Sl), cock-and-bull story (Inf), bull (Sl), bullshit (Tab sl), tall story (Inf)

5 **defacer**, spoiler, distorter, propagandist, spin doctor, hypocrite, liar, vandal, hooligan, thug, pervert, bullshitter (Tab sl)
▶ *540 Falsehood, 541 Exaggeration, 525 Misinterpretation, 474 Sophistry*

ADJECTIVES

6 **distorted**, asymmetric, unsymmetrical, unbalanced, out of balance, out of kilter, out of true alignment, out of shape, misshapen, irregular, lopsided, crooked, askew, disproportionate, unequal, out of context, off-target, off-centre, skewwhiff (Inf), cockeyed (Inf)

7 **deformed**, malformed, hunchbacked, clubfooted, disfigured, imperfect, ugly, hideous, grotesque, defaced, scarred, marked, pockmarked, spotty, pitted, blemished, ill-made, zitty (Sl)

8 **exaggerated**, false, perfidious, evasive, fake, misrepresented, perverted, fictitious, deceptive, fabricated, spurious, misinformed, misguided, misleading, untruthful, deceitful, deceiving, mendacious, lying, economical with the truth, burlesqued, parodied, creative (Sl), bullshitting (Tab sl)

VERBS

9 **distort**, warp, twist, strain, stress, contort, bias, disproportion, imbalance, misshape, knock out of true alignment, put out of kilter

10 **make faces**, grimace, girn (Dial), leer, scowl, frown, snarl, sneer, pout, contort

11 **deform**, malform, disfigure, deface, damage, impair, stain, spot, mark, welt, weal, pit, pockmark, warp, cicatrize, blemish

12 **distort the truth**, exaggerate, reshape, deform, misrepresent, pervert, misconceive, misconstrue, give a false reading, twist words, read something into it, falsify, fabricate, dissemble, embroider, fake, deceive, dress up, forge, concoct, rig, misinform, mislead, misguide, be false, lie, brainwash, whitewash, propagandize, be economical with the truth, translate the truth, stretch the truth, take out of context, tell porkies (Sl), tell a cock-and-bull story (Inf), bullshit (Tab sl), speak with forked tongue (Inf), lead up the garden path (Inf)

ADVERBS

13 **asymmetrically**, unsymmetrically, differently, irregularly, disproportionately, lopsidedly, crookedly, contortedly, misshapenly, hideously, grotesquely, imperfectly

14 **distortedly**, evasively, deceptively, hypocritically, falsely, spuriously, deceitfully, untruthfully, mendaciously, perfidiously, perversely

310   Angle

NOUNS

1 **angle**, bend, fork, corner, sharp corner, intersection, junction, zigzag, obtuse angle, oblique angle, acute angle, right angle, circumflex angle, perpendicular, A-frame, V-shape, T-shape, U-shape, chevron, V-sign, hairpin bend, dogleg, angle iron, elbow-joint, knee-joint, gonion, mitre joint
▶ *288 Interweaving, 52 Mathematics, 316 Convexity*

2 **obliquity**, skewness, bias slope, bevel, cant, bezel, edge, wedge, slant, ramp, hill, slope, tilt, declivity, steepness, escarpment, scarp, tangent
▶ *286 Obliqueness*

3 **angled figure**, triangle, equilateral triangle, isosceles triangle, scalene triangle, right-angled triangle, quadrangle, quadrilateral, square, rectangle, parallelogram, tetragon, rhombus, lozenge, rhomboid, pentagon, hexagon, hexagram, heptagon, octagon, decagon, decahedron, duodecahedron, polyhedron, prism, pyramid, diamond

4 **angular measurement**, trigonometry, goniometry, geometry, goniometer, protractor, sextant, sundial, bevel square, set square, T-square, theodolite, quadrant, astrological angle, semi-sextile, sextile, biquintile, square, quintile, trine, quincunx, opposition

5 **viewpoint**, aspect, standpoint, stand, view, impression, slant, bias, premise, theory
▶ *497 Belief, 501 Knowledge, 4 Philosophy*

6 **motive**, personal motive, purpose, angle (Inf)
▶ *860 Selfishness, 228 Motive*

ADJECTIVES

7 **angular**, cornered, pointed, sharp-cornered, bent, hooked, jointed, forked, bifurcate, V-shaped, A-framed, doglegged, mitred

8 **oblique**, skew, skewed, sloping, bevelled, slanting, hilly, sloped, inclined, tilted, steep, tangential, diagonal, transverse, thwart, skewwhiff (Inf)

9 **angled**, acute-angled, oblique-angled, obtuse-angled, scalene, triangular, square, right-angled, perpendicular, rectangular, quadrilateral, quadrangular, polygonal, pentagonal, rhomboidal, hexagonal, heptagonal, hexagrammoid, octagonal, decagonal, trilateral, cuneate, cuneiform, decahedral, polyhedral, prismatic, pyramidal, faceted, diamond

10 **biased**, slanted, angled toward

VERBS

11 **angle**, fork, intersect, zigzag, bend, hook over, tip, tilt, slope, lean, cant, bevel, bank, mitre, incline, careen, twist, warp, camber, go off on (*or* at) a tangent

ADVERBS

12 **askew**, aslant, obliquely, diagonally, at an angle, (off) on (*or* at) a tangent, on the bias

311 Curve

NOUNS

1 **curvature**, incurvature, concavity, convexity, bending, arching, circularity, circularness, curliness, curvilinearity, sinuousity

▶ *317 Concavity, 316 Convexity, 314 Convolution*

2 **bend**, camber, turn, U-turn, S-curve, detour, curl, arc, arch, crescent, coil, loop, spiral, circuit, circle, oval, rondure, semicircle, meniscus, parabola, hyperbola, roundness, wave, undulation

▶ *313 Circularity*

3 **curved things**, horseshoe, dome, half-moon, archer's bow, figure (of) eight, bend in the road, rainbow, horizon, earth's orbit, sine wave

ADJECTIVES

4 **curved**, curving, cambered, curviform, curvilinear, bent, concave, convex, turning, sloping, sloped, stooped, bowed, vaulted, arciform, arched, archiform, spiraled, curled, coiled, looped, round, oval, semicircular, circular, crescentic, lunar, meniscal, parabolic, hyperbolic, domical, sinusoidal

5 **well-rounded**, rounded, curvy, wavy, undulatory, pear-shaped, sinuous, curvaceous

VERBS

6 **curve**, bend, loop, arc, arch, turn, detour, curl, coil, spiral, bow, circle, twine, entwine

ADVERBS

7 **curvedly**, curvilinearly, sinuously, sinusoidally, convexly, concavely, parabolically, hyperbolically, circularly, circuitously, roundly, curvaceously, wavily

312 Straightness

ADJECTIVES

1 **straight**, linear, rectilinear, straight-lined, perpendicular, horizontal, vertical, true, right, plumb, rigid, dead straight, straightened, straightened out, uncurled, unbent, direct, as

the crow flies, straight as an arrow

2 **straightforward**, simple, direct, plain, clear, uncomplicated, easy to understand

3 **continuous**, straight through, uninterrupted, nonstop, one-hop (Inf)

4 **traditional**, conventional, conservative, moderate, old-fashioned, cautious, heterosexual, not using drugs, square (Inf)

5 **honourable**, straightforward, candid, plain, frank, open, overt, manifest, direct, unambiguous, truthful, trustworthy, fair and square, as good as one's word, honest, straight down the line (Inf), straight up (Sl), upfront (Sl)

NOUNS

6 **straightness**, directness, linearity, rectilinearity, perpendicularity

▶ *269 Length*

7 **straight line**, beeline, vertical line, horizontal line, unbroken line, plumbline, perpendicular, ascending order, descending order, row, colonnade

▶ *281 Verticality, 282 Horizontality*

8 **directness**, plainness, plain speaking, straight talking, truth, honesty, straightforwardness, simplicity, clarity, fairness, scrupulousness, fair dealing, truthfulness, candour

9 **straight person**, conservative, moderate, heterosexual, nonuser of drugs, straight-shooter (US sl)

▶ *857 Probity, 167 Conformity*

VERBS

10 **straighten**, make straight, unravel, iron out, flatten out, straighten out, uncurl, unbend, unroll, unfurl, untangle, unfold, disentangle, comb out, uncoil, untwist, smooth out, unscramble, tidy up, neaten, make shipshape

11 **be straight**, talk straight, talk plainly, speak the truth, stick to the truth, speak one's mind, give it to someone straight, make a clean breast of, mean what one says, keep to the point, not deviate

ADVERBS

12 **straight**, straightly, horizontally, vertically, directly, unswervingly, as the crow flies, on the beam (Inf)

13 **straightforwardly**, honourably, honestly, directly, plainly, truthfully, frankly, openly

313 Circularity

NOUNS

1 **circularity**, roundness, orbicularity, sphericalness, curvedness, rotundity, annularity

▶ *315 Roundness, 311 Curve*

2 **circle**, full circle, circumference, ambit, curve, orb, sphere, cycle, full cycle, orbit, epicycle, annulus, semicircle, half circle, oval, zodiac, mandala, circular path, circular road, circuit, annulation, loop, ring, figure of eight,

roundabout, roundabout way, circuitous route, racecourse, detour, bypass, arc, round trip, lap
▶ *70 Transport*

3 **circular thing**, headband, hairband, crown, coronet, collar, neckband, dog collar, necklace, choker, belt, waistband, cummerbund, sash, girdle, bracelet, wristband, anklet, discus, plate, saucer, disc, ring, hoop, band, tyre, wheel, noose, wreath, equator, halo, corona

4 **parts of a circle**, centre, circumference, radius, diameter, quadrant, sextant, sector, segment, chord, crescent, arc

ADJECTIVES

5 **circular**, annular, annulate, discoid, spherical, orbital, orbicular, spheric, spherelike, spheroidal, rounded, round, ring-shaped, semicircular, cyclic, elliptic, ovate, oval, ovoid, egg-shaped, rotund, circulatory, circumferential

VERBS

6 **circle**, encircle, surround, go round, travel in a circle, make a round trip, make a circle, circulate, circumambulate, circumnavigate, lap, take a turn, orbit, go into orbit, revolve, rotate, detour, make a detour, bypass, skirt around

7 **make circular**, circularize, draw a circle, arrange in a circle, make round, girdle, encompass, round, turn

ADVERBS

8 **circularly**, circuitously, circumferentially, cyclically, orbitally, orbicularly, annularly, elliptically, ovately, ovally, spherically, spheroidally, roundly, rotundly

314 Convolution

NOUNS

1 **convolution**, convolutedness, involution, circumvolution, circling upon itself, intricacy, intricateness, twistedness, sinuousness, undulation, anfractuosity
▶ *151 Disorder, 313 Circularity, 335 Deviation*

2 **coil**, turn, twist, twirl, intricacy, spiral, turbination, screwthread, corkscrew, spring, whorl, (double) helix, curl, curlicue, ringlet, loop, meandering, squiggle, kink, corrugation, squirm, shimmy, wriggle
▶ *311 Curve, 320 Fold*

3 **convoluted thing**, snailshell, ammonite, nautilus, scallop (*or* scollop) shell, snake, whirlpool, vortex, tornado, twister (US inf), labyrinth, maze, braid, intestines, cochlea

ADJECTIVES

4 **convolutional**, convoluted, winding, twisted, involutional, circumlocutory, sinuous, undulatory, intricate, braided, wavy, twirled, entwined, corrugated, tortuous, meandering, labyrinthine, like a maze, serpentine, vermiform, wriggling, squirming, squiggly, coiled, spiral, helical, cochleate, whorled, turbinate

5 **ambiguous**, equivocal, difficult to comprehend, involved, complicated, complex, contorted
▶ *578 Equivocation, 474 Sophistry*

VERBS

6 **convolute**, convolve, circle upon itself, wind together, twist together, weave together, enlace, twine, entwine, coil, roll, braid, corkscrew, spiral, twirl, curl, wave, undulate, corrugate, scallop (*or* scollop), distort, meander, loop, snake, twist, turn, twist and turn, wriggle, writhe, squirm, squiggle, shimmy

7 **be ambiguous**, equivocate, complicate, make complex

ADVERBS

8 **circularly**, circuitously, all around the houses, ambiguously, equivocally, complexly, intricately, tortuously, spirally, helically, sinuously, wavily

315 Roundness

NOUNS

1 **roundness**, rotundity, orbicularity, sphericity, sphericalness, globosity, globularity, gibbousness, convexity, cylindricality
▶ *313 Circularity, 316 Convexity*

2 **round body**, well-rounded shape, shapeliness, pear shape, fatness, corpulence, obesity, fleshiness, stoutness, plumpness, portliness, paunchiness podginess, tubbiness, chubbiness, potbelly, curvaceousness
▶ *259 Size*

3 **round thing**, circle, circuit, orbit, sphere, globe, orb, egg, spheroid, hemisphere, ball, bubble, balloon, marble, pellet, bead, pill, pea, bulb, globule, drop, droplet, dewdrop

4 **cylinder**, roller, rod, rung, tube, cigar, pipe, stalk, trunk, bole, column, rolling-pin
▶ *322 Opening*

5 **cone**, cornet, horn, trumpet, bell shape, top, spinning top

6 **round**, turn, bowl, lap, round trip, circuit, chukker, daily round, orbit, ambit, circumambulation, circumnavigation, groove, rut

7 **round**, part song, madrigal

8 **round**, live ammunition

ADJECTIVES

9 **round**, rotund, orbicular, gibbous, spherical, globose, globous, globular, convex, egg-shaped, ovoid, cylindrical, tubular, conical, conic, bell-shaped, bulbous, spherelike, spheric, hemispherical, round as a ball

10 **well-rounded**, rounded out, round, pear-shaped, shapely, well-proportioned, well-turned, fleshy, fat, overweight, obese, corpulent, stout, plump, portly, paunchy, podgy,

tubby, chubby, potbellied, curvaceous

VERBS

11 **make round**, roll, smooth, turn, make spherical, balloon out, ball up, coil up, roll up, ball, round off, round out, fill out

12 **move round**, orbit, circle, circulate, circumambulate, circumnavigate, lap, complete a circuit

ADVERBS

13 **roundly**, rotundly, orbicularly, spherically, globosely, globularly, convexly, cylindrically, conically, bulbously, curvaceously

316 Convexity

NOUNS

1 **convexity**, convexness, bulbousness, bulginess, bulging, swelling, gibbousness, billowing, distention, protrusion, protuberance, prominence, excrescence, tumescence, meniscus, camber

▶ *311 Curve, 315 Roundness, 318 Prominence*

2 **bulge**, hump, lens, arc, bubble, knob, button, boss, bud, nose, bump, wart, knot, oedema, swelling, erection, bubo, carbuncle, boil, blister, corn, bunion, tumour, cyst, pregnancy, beergut, muscle, biceps, pectoral, pecks (Inf), nipple, papilla, mamilla, bosom, breast, bust, boobs (Sl), knockers (Sl), tits (Sl), testicles, balls (Sl), rocks (Sl), bollocks (Tab sl)

▶ *624 Ill Health, 259 Size*

3 **dome**, cupola, vault, arc, arch, beehive, barrow, mound, hillock, hummock, hump (Dial)

▶ *293 Covering, 275 Height*

ADJECTIVES

4 **convex**, bulbous, bulgy, bulging, swelling, gibbous, billowing, protruding, distended, humped, prominent, excrescent, tumescent, swollen, meniscoid, arcuated, bowed out, arched, vaulted, lenticular, lentiform

VERBS

5 **be convex**, arcuate, arch, curve, camber, bow, protrude, bulge, stick out, swell out, swell, hump, balloon out, round out, distend, billow

ADVERBS

6 **convexly**, bulbously, bulgingly, protuberantly, prominently, excrescently

317 Concavity

NOUNS

1 **concavity**, hollowness, curving inwards, sinking, incurvation, indentation, indention, depression, impression

▶ *311 Curve, 254 Absence, 319 Notch, 277 Depth*

2 **concave land**, hollow, cove, dip, hole, pothole, borehole, foxhole, crater, valley, vale, dell, glen, dingle, col, combe, gap, pass, ravine, gorge, abyss, crevasse, canyon, gully, den, burrow, warren, cave, cavern, trough,

sap, tunnel, tube, trench, fosse (or foss), moat, grave, quarry, pit, mine, coal mine, colliery, gold mine, diamond mine, cutting, excavation, canal, inlet, gulf

▶ *54 Earth Science, 55 Meteorology and Climatology*

3 **cavity**, dent, nook, cranny, niche, recess, alcove, basin, trough, bowl, cup, sump, socket, footprint, dimple, honeycomb, pockmark (or pock)

▶ *258 Container, 322 Opening*

4 **digger**, miner, excavator, quarryman, tunneller, burrower, grave digger, sapper, archaeologist, driller, borer, dredger, dredge

ADJECTIVES

5 **concave**, hollow, curved inwards, incurvate, depressed, sunken, cavernous, indented, cup-shaped, bowl-shaped, dented, dimpled, pocked, pockmarked, pitted, full of holes, porous, spongy

VERBS

6 **be concave**, curve inwards, sink, cave in, collapse, settle

7 **make concave**, hollow, press (or push) inwards, press, impress, imprint, indent, punch in, depress, dent, stamp, stave in, excavate, delve into, tunnel, burrow, bore, bore into, dig out, scoop out, gouge out, hollow out, dig, spade, mine, sink a shaft, pockmark, honeycomb

ADVERBS

8 **concavely**, hollowly, cavernously

318 Prominence

NOUNS

1 **prominence**, eminence, distinction, importance, salience, mark, repute, esteem, prestige, kudos, cachet, glory, position, impressiveness, exaltedness, primacy, clout (Inf)

▶ *849 Respect, 851 Approval, 744 Credit*

2 **projection**, spit, headland, promontory, cape, cliff, ness, point, peninsula, island, breakwater, mole, jetty, pier, mountain, foothill, peak, fortification, projection, overhang, outcrop, shelf, ledge, balcony

▶ *310 Angle, 634 Refuge*

3 **protuberance**, bump, swelling, protrusion, prominent feature, face, forehead, brow, proboscis, trunk, antenna, beak, nose, snout (Sl), snoot (Sl), conk (Sl), hooter (Sl), bugle (Sl), schnozzle (or schnozz) (US sl)

▶ *316 Convexity, 303 Front*

4 **conspicuousness**, obviousness, distinctness, clear visibility, clearness, clarity

▶ *437 Visibility*

ADJECTIVES

5 **protuberant**, protrudent, swelling, sticking out, proud, standing out, poking out, jutting out, bumpy, beaked, beaky

6 **eminent**, prominent, distinctive, important,

salient, reputable, esteemed, glorious, impressive, exalted, primary

7 **conspicuous**, distinct, clearly visible, plainly visible, easily seen, well defined, unblurred, clear-cut, obvious, eye-catching

VERBS

8 **protrude**, swell, stick out, stick out like a sore thumb, stand out, poke out, project, jut out, overhang, have a prominent feature, be conspicuous, catch one's eye

9 **be prominent**, have distinction, be exalted, have clout (Inf)

ADVERBS

10 **protuberantly**, juttingly, conspicuously, visibly, obviously, distinctly

11 **eminently**, prominently, importantly, exaltedly, distinctively, impressively, proudly, gloriously

319   Notch

NOUNS

1 **notch**, indentation, nick, nock, hack, cut, incision, incisure, dent, groove, cleft, slit, split, gash, gouge, tooth, score, kerf, serration, serrulation, crenel (or crenelle), crenation, crenulation, crenature

▶ *380 Sharpness, 265 Interval, 317 Concavity, 671 Defence*

2 **notched thing**, arrow, leaf, shell, scallop, Vandyke collar, jack-o'-lantern, saw blade, pinking shears, cog, dogtooth, zigzag, battlements

3 **rung**, peg, notch, step, level, stage, grade, degree, gradation

▶ *121 Degree*

ADJECTIVES

4 **notched**, notchy, indented, crenate, crenated, cut, slit, split, toothed, cogged, dentate, scalloped, pinked, jagged, jaggy, incisural, sawlike, saw-toothed, serrated, serriform, zigzag, zigzagged, uneven

VERBS

5 **notch**, indent, nick, nock, cog, hack, cut, incise, dent, slit, split, gash, gouge, score, kerf, serrate, pink, crenellate

6 **notch up**, score, achieve, accomplish, add to, win, gain

ADVERBS

7 **jaggedly**, crenately, dentately, denticulately, unevenly

320   Fold

NOUNS

1 **fold**, bend, turn, overlap, layer, roll, furl, coil, doubling, doubling over, dog-ear, plication, plicature, plica, flexure, flection, buckling, geological fold, anticline, syncline

▶ *310 Angle*

2 **pleat**, plait, accordion pleat, knife pleat, box

pleat, crease, pucker, tuck, gather, ruche (or rouche), ruffle, shirr, flounce, ruck, rumple, wrinkle, crinkle, crumple, crimp, ripple, furrow, corrugation

▶ *321 Furrow, 314 Convolution, 153 Disturbance*

3 **enfoldment**, envelopment, enclosure, wrapping, swathing, entwining, hug, embrace, clasp

▶ *301 Enclosure*

4 **closure**, closing, close-down, shutting, shutdown, financial failure, business failure, going out of business, bankruptcy, collapse, bust (US inf), folding up (Inf), going under (Inf), striking out (US inf)

▶ *218 Cessation, 244 Destruction, 747 Nonpayment*

ADJECTIVES

5 **folded**, folded over, bent, pleated, plicate, plical, flexuous, flectional, doubled over, turned over (or down), dog-eared, rolled, creased, creasy, rucked up, ruched, flexed, corrugated

6 **closed**, close-down, shut-down, failed, bankrupt, busted (US inf)

VERBS

7 **fold**, fold up, fold over, fold around, lap, double, double over (or under), turn over (or under), turn up (or down), dog-ear, bend, buckle, overlap, layer, roll, roll up, furl, coil

8 **pleat**, crease, pucker, tuck, tuck up, gather, ruffle, shirr, flounce, ruck, rumple, wrinkle, crinkle, crumple, crimp, ripple, furrow, corrugate

9 **enfold**, envelop, enclose, wrap, swathe, entwine, intertwine, hug, embrace, clasp

10 **close**, close down, shut, shut down, collapse, fail, go out of business, go bust (US inf), fold up (Inf), go under (Inf), go to the wall (Inf), strike out (US inf), cave in (Inf), take it on the chin (Inf)

ADVERBS

11 **doubly**, in two, plicately, flexuously, ripplingly

12 **in the red**, in liquidation, in receivership

321   Furrow

NOUNS

1 **furrow**, trench, trough, scratch, seam, groove, wheel-track, slot, fissure, chink, cut, slit, channel, conduit, rut, ditch, gutter, canal, flute, score, corrugation

▶ *320 Fold, 271 Breadth, 317 Concavity, 136 Separation, 545 Record, 389 Water*

2 **wrinkle**, crinkle, crease, pucker, line, laughline, crow's-foot, knitted brow

▶ *207 Age, 293 Covering, 303 Front*

3 **furrowed thing**, corduroy material, pleated dress, washboard, corrugated paper, corrugated iron, etching, engraving, ploughed field,

rippled lake, choppy sea

▶ *796 Fashion, 50 Painting and Sculpture, 68 Agriculture*

ADJECTIVES

4 **furrowed**, scratched, grooved, wheel-tracked, slotted, chinky, rutty, rutted, rimose, fluted, scored, corrugated, etched, engraved, ploughed

5 **wrinkly**, wrinkled, crinkly, crinkled, creased, puckered, lined, seamed, knitted

VERBS

6 **furrow**, trench, trough, scratch, seam, groove, track, slot, fissure, chink (US), cut, etch, engrave, slit, channel, rut, plough, ditch, gutter, canal, flute, score, corrugate

7 **wrinkle**, crinkle, crease, pucker, line, knit

ADVERBS

8 **ruttily**, rimosely, ripplingly

322 Opening

NOUNS

1 **opening**, gap, hole, hollow, cavity, aperture, orifice, gape, duct, passageway, passage, space, open space, interval, slot, split, crack, hairline crack, crevice, chasm, pass, fault, flaw, breach, break, fracture, rupture, cut, tear, cleft, fissure, perforation, piercing, pricking, puncture, bore

▶ *317 Concavity, 319 Notch, 258 Container, 261 Expansion, 248 Space, 265 Interval, 356 Passage, 680 Weapon*

2 **opener**, key, master key, skeleton key, passkey, key card, smart card, password, open sesame, tin-opener, bottle-opener, corkscrew, drill, brace and bit, reamer, awl, needle, hypodermic needle, pin, bodkin, punch, leather punch, auger, bit, probe, pick, pickaxe, axe, saw, trephine, trepan, lance, lancet, bayonet, knife

3 **person who opens**, locksmith, doorman, warder, excavator, tunneller, digger, miner, plumber, carpenter, surgeon, wine steward, Pandora

4 **body orifice**, pore, sweat gland, aural cavity, ear, nasal cavity, nostril, nose, anus, cloaca, urethra, vagina, oral cavity, mouth, maw, trap (Sl), kisser (Sl), gob (Sl), lug (Inf or Scot), arse (Tab sl), arsehole (Tab sl)

5 **hole**, keyhole, peephole, knothole, eyehole, eyelet, eye, buttonhole, pinhole, porthole, borehole, blowhole, airhole, shaft, well, mine, mineshaft, excavation, cavern, cave, volcano

6 **porous thing**, sponge, sieve, colander, teabag, honeycomb, screen, mosquito net, nylon stockings, lattice, grate, grille, filter

7 **passageway**, gangway, hallway, corridor, aisle, entrance, exit, doorway, postern, pass, gorge, defile, window, skylight, dormer, fanlight, arch, gate, porch, portal, manhole, tunnel, underpass, tube, mousehole, rabbithole,

molehole, foxhole, conduit, funnel, hose, sewer, drain, pipe, pipeline, windpipe, throat, oesophagus, artery, vein, colon, intestines, alimentary canal, anal canal, ureter, sperm duct, stoma, vent, flue, chimney, chimneystack, smokestack, smokehole

▶ *346 Entry, 347 Exit, 60 Medicine*

8 **open space**, open country, open sea, clearing, meadow, beach, desert, court, yard, glade, stage

9 **openness**, opening up, frankness, bluntness, explicitness, plain words, candour, honesty, sincerity, artlessness, open heart, open face, ingenuousness, naivety

10 **opportunity**, opening, open door, toe (or foot) in the door, toehold, foothold, chance, possibility, golden opportunity, occasion, available post, vacancy, position, job, lucky break, break (Inf)

11 **beginning**, start, commencement, initiation, inception, dawn, birth, inauguration, launch, debut

▶ *156 Beginning*

ADJECTIVES

12 **open**, wide-open, pushed open, pulled open, unclosed, uncovered, unwrapped, unfolded, exposed, visible, ajar, punched open, cut open, split, torn, cracked, creviced, cleft, fissured, breached, gaping, open-mouthed, agape, hacked, hewn, cut, sawed (or sawn), broken, fractured, ruptured

▶ *530 Disclosure*

13 **opened up**, unblocked, unlocked, unbolted, unbarred, unlatched, unfastened, unsealed, uncovered, uncorked, unstopped, unobstructed, patent, clear, evident, obvious, apparent, manifest, free, unimpeded, unhindered, unhampered, unrestricted, accessible, open-door, available, vacant, public, unenclosed, unfenced, unprotected, unshielded, extended, extensive, bare, open-plan

14 **holed**, perforated, porous, permeated, riddled with holes, punched full of holes, filled with holes, sievelike, cribriform, honeycombed, spongy, leaky, injected, penetrated, probed, pierced, pricked, punctured, lanced, bayoneted, knifed, stabbed, stuck, slashed, gashed, shot, peppered with shot, bored, hollowed, drilled, reamed, dug, burrowed, tunnelled, sunk, excavated, cavernous, spacial, volcanic

15 **providing passage**, gated, draining, arterial, venous, colonic, intestinal, alimentary, anal

16 **open**, frank, blunt, explicit, plain, candid, unreserved, open-hearted, open-faced, honest, sincere, ingenuous, naive, artless

17 **beginning**, starting, commencing, dawning, initial, inceptive, inaugural, introductory, first, newborn, debut

VERBS

18 **open**, push open, pull open, open up, open

out, unclose, uncover, unwrap, unfold, expose, disclose, reveal, show, leave ajar, punch open, cut open, split, tear, crack, cleave, breach, hack, hew, cut, saw, break, fracture, rupture, burst open, gape, erupt, explode

19 **open up**, unblock, unlock, unbolt, unbar, unlatch, unfasten, unseal, uncover, uncork, unstop, not obstruct, clear, free, gain access, access, not enclose, extend, spread

20 **hole**, make porous, perforate, permeate, riddle with holes, punch full of holes, fill with holes, honeycomb, fissure, slot, break the skin, trephine, trepan, inject, penetrate, probe, pierce, prick, puncture, lance, bayonet, knife, stab, run through, stick, slash, gash, shoot, pepper with shot, bore, hollow, drill, ream, dig a hole, burrow, tunnel, sink a mineshaft, excavate

21 **provide passage for**, drain, pipe, funnel, vent, sieve, screen

22 **be open**, have openness, open up, speak straight from the shoulder, use plain words, open one's heart

23 **find an opening**, gain a foothold, be in the right place at the right time, get a (lucky) break (Inf)

24 **begin**, start, commence, initiate, dawn, inaugurate, launch, debut

ADVERBS

25 **obviously**, apparently, manifestly, visibly, patently, clearly, evidently, plainly, in the open, publicly, availably, accessibly, extensively, widely

26 **openly**, candidly, bluntly, plainly, explicitly, frankly, sincerely, honestly, straight from the shoulder, in plain words, ingenuously, naively, artlessly, vacantly, blankly

27 **cavernously**, gapingly, porously, volcanically, intestinally, arterially, venously, anally

323 Closure

NOUNS

1 **closure**, closing, closing up, closing down, close-down, shutdown, finish, cessation, discontinuance, stop, stoppage, conclusion, resolution, fulfilment, completion, termination, end, foreclosure, imperviousness, impermeability, impenetrability, impassability, obstruction, occlusion, contraction, constriction, congestion, strangulation, blockage, constipation, blockade, block, chock, barrier, bar, hindrance, let, impasse, sealing off, standstill, deadlock, stalemate

▶ *218 Cessation, 262 Contraction, 302 Limit, 661 Hindrance*

2 **stopper**, stop, cap, lid, top, cork, covering, cover, seal, plug, bandage, tourniquet, bung, peg, pin, spigot, valve, tap, faucet, stopcock, wad, wadding, stuffing, tampion, wedge,

blood clot, thrombus, embolus, infarct, tampon, damper, choke, trip switch, cutout switch, piston

▶ *293 Covering, 292 Lining, 137 Connection*

3 **restrainer**, lock, padlock, latch, bolt, bar, clamp, clasp, hasp, catch, safety catch, straitjacket, handcuffs, chain, rope, leash, lead, muzzle

▶ *632 Safety*

4 **closed place**, enclosed place, dead end, cul-de-sac, blind alley, road block, enclosure, courtyard, quadrangle, reserve, sanctuary, zoo, walled garden, pen, hutch, cage, kennel, coop, pigsty, corral, paddock, fold, ghetto, grave, tomb, sepulchre, trap, prison, jail, dungeon, cell, oubliette, reformatory, borstal, can (Sl), clink (Sl), nick (Sl), cooler (Sl), slammer (Sl), the big house (US sl)

▶ *301 Enclosure, 702 Prison*

5 **person who closes**, doorman, doorkeeper, porter, concierge, gatekeeper, commissionaire, warder, turnkey, jailer, caretaker, sentry, sentinel, night watchman, screw (Sl)

6 **closed-in person**, prisoner, inmate, detainee, internee, miner, submariner, shut-in (US)

VERBS

7 **close**, close up, shut, shut up, seal, fasten, secure, lock, lock up, bolt, bar, latch, padlock, do up, button, button up, zip up, seal off, batten down, batten down the hatches, put the lid on, cover, contain

8 **stop**, stopper, plug, cap, top, cork, dam, staunch, bandage, tampon, stop up, bar, stay, block, block up, clog, clog up, bung, bung up, obstruct, occlude, constipate, contract, constrict, congest, strangle, throttle, choke, blockade, hinder

9 **close down**, close up, shut down, finish, cease, discontinue, terminate, end, foreclose, conclude, resolve, fulfil, complete, wind up

10 **enclose**, confine, keep in, lock up (or in), shut up (or in), imprison, jail, cage, impound, pen, hutch, kennel, coop, corral, fold, intern, immure, incarcerate, bury, entomb, throw in the slammer (Sl), bang up (Sl), send down (Sl), send to the big house (US sl)

11 **restrain**, handcuff, chain, shackle, rope, bind, tie, leash, muzzle, straitjacket

ADJECTIVES

12 **closed**, unopened, shut, shut up, locked, bolted, barred, latched, padlocked, burglarproof, fastened, secured, buttoned, buttoned up, zipped up, sealed, hermetically sealed, airtight, vacuum-packed, watertight, waterproof, lightproof, nonporous, impermeable, impervious

13 **stopped**, stopped up, plugged, capped, corked, dammed, staunched, bandaged, blocked, obstructed, occluded, blocked up,

clogged, clogged up, impenetrable, impassable, bunged up, stuffed up, constipated, costive, constricted, congested, choked, choked up, full, stuffed, packed, jammed

14 **closed down**, closed up, shut down, wound up, finished, resolved, completed, ended

15 **enclosed**, closed in, shut up, jailed, imprisoned, confined

ADVERBS

16 **impermeably**, imperviously, impenetrably, impassably, nonporously, hermetically, costively

17 **finally**, at last, in the end, completely, over, over (and done) with

Motion

NOUNS

1 **motion**, movement, moving, change of position, migration, movability, movableness, mobility, motility, locomotion, walking, perambulation, pedestrianism, going, running, rushing, marching, kinetic energy, motivity, actuation, motive power, laws of motion, kinetics, dynamics, kinesis, kinematics, kinesiatrics, kinesipathy, kinesitherapy
▶ *56 Physics*

2 **momentum**, propulsion, impulsion, mobilization, motivation, actuation, impetus, stir, stirring, restlessness, unrest, action, activity, agitation, bustle, course, passage, set, trend, career, stream, flow, flux, flight, current, rush, onrush, run, drift, driftage, transit, traffic, flow of traffic, transport, transportation, travel, riding, equitation, land travel, water travel, air travel
▶ *338 Propulsion, 366 Agitation, 326 Transfer, 640 Action, 330 Impulsion*

3 **motion towards**, advance, approach, arrival, progress, progression, headway, evolution, motion into, ingress
▶ *336 Forward Motion, 344 Arrival, 346 Entry*

4 **backward motion**, regression, backing, backflowing, reflowing, refluence, reflux, retreat, withdrawal, departure, exit, motion out of, egress, sternway, recession
▶ *337 Backward Motion, 347 Exit, 345 Departure*

5 **circuition**, motion round, circumnavigation, rotation, axial motion, radial motion, oscillation, fluctuation, vibration, gyration, agitation, to-and-fro movement, irregular motion, sideward (*or* sideways) motion, oblique motion, angular motion, random motion, Brownian movement
▶ *334 Circuit, 364 Rotation, 365 Oscillation, 363 Orbital Motion, 335 Deviation, 366 Agitation*

6 **descending motion**, descent, downward motion, subsiding motion, sinking, plunging
▶ *360 Descent*

7 **ascending motion**, upward motion, ascent, ascending, rising, soaring, mounting, climbing
▶ *359 Ascent*

8 **rapid motion**, rapidity, speed, velocity
▶ *329 Swiftness*

9 **slow motion**, slowness, pottering
▶ *328 Slowness*

10 **regular movement**, recurring movement, rhythm, uniform movement, continual movement, motion in front, precession, motion after, following, pursuit
▶ *214 Regularity, 183 Repetition*

11 **bodily movement**, exercise, athletics, gymnastics, aerobics, gesticulation, wave, gesture, thumbs up, V-sign

12 **gait**, walk, carriage, bearing, tread, pace, step, stride, stroll, saunter, tramp, stamp, run, lope, jog, jog trot, dogtrot, trot, amble, dance step, hop, skip, jump, leap, waddle, swagger, shuffle, creep, stalk, strut, goosestep, march, quick march, scamper, scramble, canter, gallop, clip (Inf), lick (Inf)
▶ *46 Dancing and Ballet*

VERBS

13 **be in motion**, move, have mobility, change position, stir, budge, go, flow, drift, stream, progress, advance, develop, drive forward, evolve, make one's way, proceed, gather way, keep going, go on, pick (*or* fight) one's way, wade through, back, back up, regress, retrogress, subside, ebb, wane, change direction, deviate, soar, mount, rise, ascend, climb, descend, sink, plunge, oscillate, go sidewards (*or* sideways), gyrate, go round, rotate, spin, whirl, move over, get over, shift, change, change place
▶ *336 Forward Motion, 337 Backward Motion, 343 Divergence, 359 Ascent, 360 Descent, 365 Oscillation, 364 Rotation*

14 **set in motion**, move, actuate, push, nudge, shove, drive, hustle, motivate, pull, tug, draw, haul, propel, impel, throw, mobilize, send, dispatch, scatter, disperse, bring together, gather, transfer, transport, convey, transpose,

displace

▶ *330 Impulsion, 338 Propulsion, 339 Traction, 326 Transfer*

15 **walk**, march, stride, tramp, lope, tread, trip, amble, jog, stroll, saunter, shuffle, waddle, dance, leap, toddle, patter, potter, strut, stagger, mince, stalk, run, rush, gallop, hare, fly, dash, dart, roll, cruise, freewheel, coast, trundle, taxi, chug, stream, travel, roam, wander, drift, stray, shift, dodge, duck, weave, tack, manoeuvre, make a move, change (places), interchange, move over, move house, remove, change one's address, motion, gesture, gesticulate, wave

▶ *328 Slowness, 329 Swiftness*

ADJECTIVES

16 **moving**, having motion, in motion, motive, motory, motor, motile, motional, movable, mobile, motivational, locomotive, automotive, self-propelled, shifting, impelling, propelling, propellant, driving, travelling, riding, running, rushing, going, passing, fluent, flowing, streaming, flying, transitional, fleeting, mercurial, restless, active, agitated, bustling, scurrying, stirring, wandering, drifting, nomadic, peripatetic, ambulant, erratic, runaway

17 **directional**, advancing, advance, progressive, progressing, backward, regressive, retrogressive, back, backtracking, backflowing, refluent, reflowing, downward, sinking, plunging, descending, subsiding, upward, ascending, rising, soaring, mounting, climbing, rapid, speedy, speeding, slow, toddling, pottering, regular, recurring, rhythmic, periodic, uniform, continuous, continual, circuitous, rotary, rotatory, rotational, centripetal, centrifugal, axial, radial, oscillating, fluctuating, vibrating, agitating, irregular, sideward (*or* sideways), oblique, angular, random, to and fro, Brownian, gyratory, gyrational, gyrating, kinetic, kinesodic, dynamic, kinematic, kinesipathic

ADVERBS

18 **in motion**, kinetically, dynamically, on the move, on the go, up and about, astir, on the march, on the run, on the wing, on the hop (Inf), under way, on the road, en route, in transit, under sail, from pillar to post, transitionally, movably, motivationally, progressively, regressively, automotively, mercurially, restlessly, actively, nomadically, peripatetically, rapidly, slowly, circuitously, centripetally, centrifugally

INTERJECTIONS

19 **go!**, move it!, faster!, forward!, advance!, retreat!, step on it!

325 Motionlessness

NOUNS

1 **motionlessness**, immobility, stillness, inactivity, inaction, fixity, fixation, rigidity, stiffness, standstill, stand, stop, halt, pause, dead stop (*or* stand), full stop, lock, dead set, stability, equilibrium, poise, equipoise, balance, stasis, steadiness, inertness, inertia, dormancy, passiveness, passivity, apathy, latency, torpor, indifference, indolence, lotus-eating, languor, stagnancy, vegetation, coma, deathliness, deadliness, numbness, trance, catalepsy, catatonia, suspension, cessation, stagnation, deadlock, gridlock (US), stalemate, truce, lull, suspense, abeyance, stoppage, embargo, freeze, strike

▶ *643 Inactivity, 641 Inaction, 783 Indifference, 218 Cessation, 527 Latency, 122 Equality*

2 **repose**, rest, sleep, slumber, insensibility, silken repose, eternal rest, death, quiescence, quiescency, silence, quietness, quiet, quietude, placidity, placidness, tranquillity, serenity, peace, composure, quietism, contemplation, satori, nirvana, ataraxia, calmness, calm, restfulness, peacefulness, imperturbability, stillness, still, hush, lull, calm (*or* lull) before the storm, dead (*or* flat) calm, deathlike calm, windlessness, doldrums, eye of the hurricane, horse latitudes, anticyclone, not a breath of air, airlessness, nothing stirring, not a mouse stirring

▶ *422 Silence, 397 Death, 675 Peace, 527 Latency*

3 **resting place**, refuge, shelter, journey's end, home, haven, quarters, bivouac, bed, pillow, hammock, final resting place, last rest, grave, tomb, mausoleum, cemetery, graveyard, burial ground, heaven, paradise, happy hunting ground (US)

▶ *399 Burial*

ADJECTIVES

4 **motionless**, immobile, still, inactive, unmoving, immotive, static, stationary, stagnant, standing, steady, poised, balanced, immovable, unmovable, fixed, stiff, stuck, paralysed, unmoved, petrified, transfixed, rooted to the spot, sedentary, stock-still, spellbound, frozen, still as a statue, quiet as a mouse, still as death, airless, windless, becalmed, at anchor

▶ *643 Inactivity*

5 **sedentary**, stay-at-home, housebound, shut-in (US), home-loving, domesticated, supine, bedridden, disabled, on one's back, untravelled, stick in the mud, idle, unemployed, out of commission, inert, dormant, passive, latent, languid, languorous, apathetic, indifferent, indolent, phlegmatic, sluggish, vegetating, unaroused, suspended, abeyant, sleeping, slumbering, smouldering, groggy, heavy, leaden, dull, flat, slack, tame, dead, lifeless, catatonic, cataleptic, numb, dopey (Inf)

▶ *641 Inaction, 783 Indifference, 397 Death*

6 **quiescent**, silent, quiet, still, hushed, insen-

sible, soundless, placid, tranquil, calm, serene, easygoing, peaceful, restful, composed, contemplative, smooth, unruffled, untroubled, unperturbed, unagitated, unhurried, unmoved, unstirring, stolid, stoic, impassive, calm as a mill pond, quiet as death, inexcitable, imperturbable, cool, cool as a cucumber, pacific, halcyon, undisturbed, sequestered, leisured, at rest, resting, reposing, reposeful, sleepy

▶ *422 Silence, 675 Peace, 783 Indifference*

7 **sedentary person**, shut-in (US), stick-in-the-mud, sluggard, couch potato (US sl)

VERBS

8 **be motionless**, stand still, stand, not budge, freeze, remain, abide, stay, stay put, sit, sit down, sit tight, remain seated, remain *in situ* (L), perch, land, alight, mark time, wait, stand firm, stand like a post, not stir (a step), not breathe, hold one's breath, tread water, coast, cease, stop, halt, stop short, stop in one's tracks, slow down, decelerate, pull up, check, brake, come to a standstill, come to a halt, come to journey's end, stand fast, stick fast, remain at anchor, subside, settle, settle down, die down, come to rest, pause, rest, tarry, relax, rest on one's oars, keep still, keep quiet, rest and be thankful, stagnate, vegetate, idle, hang fire, sleep, slumber, repose, retire, go to bed, stay at home, stay indoors, not go out, die, go to one's eternal rest, go to the happy hunting ground, take a breather (Inf), doss down (Sl), cool it (Sl)

9 **make motionless**, bring to a standstill, immobilize, suspend, stalemate, call a truce, lock, jam, catch, stick, lodge, put a stop to, embargo, lay an embargo on, prohibit, freeze, soothe, lull, calm (down), tranquillize, pacify, assuage, becalm, take the wind out of someone's sails

ADVERBS

10 **motionlessly**, fixedly, stationarily, inertly, inactively, statically, dormantly, passively, latently, stagnantly, calmly, quietly, still, tranquilly, peacefully, placidly, restfully, smoothly, unperturbedly, languidly, languorously, sluggishly, heavily, lifelessly, apathetically, coldly, phlegmatically, stoically, stolidly, impassively, in repose, at a halt, at a stand, far from the madding crowd, after death, posthumously, after life's fitful fever, stilly (Arch)

INTERJECTIONS

11 **stop!**, stay!, halt!, whoa!, hold!, hold hard!, hold it!, don't move!, lay off! (Inf), pipe down! (Inf), no way! (Inf), cool it! (Sl)

326 Transfer

NOUNS

1 **transfer**, transference, transferral (US), trans-

location, transmittal, transmittance, transposition, metathesis, transposal, transplacement, transmigration (of souls), metempsychosis, transplantation, removal, relocation, moving, movement, removement, displacement, delocalization, deportation, expulsion, extradition, relegation, shift, shifting, transition, mutual transfer, interchange, trade, exchange, barter, swap

▶ *737 Trade, 324 Motion*

2 **transportation**, transport, conveyance, transshipment, dispatch, sending, posting, mailing (US), export, exportation, import, importation, transit, transition, bridge, passage, vection, vectitation, vecture, carriage, delivery, handover, haulage, hauling, cartage, carry, portage, porterage, waft, waftage, truckage, waggonage, drayage, ferriage, lighterage, telpherage, freightage, freight, expressage, railway express, air express, air freight, airlift, shipment, shipping, asportation (Fml), humping (Sl)

▶ *70 Transport*

3 **transmission**, conduction, convection, osmosis, transpiration, throughput, electromagnetic conduction, diapedesis, transduction, transfusion, perfusion, decantation, dispersal, transmission of disease, contagion, infection, contamination, communication, contact, dissemination, spread, spreading, diffusion, metastasis, dispersion

▶ *624 Ill Health*

4 **translation**, transcription, literary conversion, transumption, transliteration, copying, photocopying, plagiarism

5 **means of transport**, conveyance, public transport, rail transport, road transport, sea transport, air transport, car, automobile, vehicle, truck, lorry, juggernaut, trailer, bus, postbus, taxi, tram, carriage, van, delivery van, train, goods train, freight train (US), Pullman, cargo vessel, freighter, tramp steamer, (oil) tanker, bicycle, motorcycle, conveyor belt, escalator, travolator, moving pavement, lift, sleigh, sledge, sled (US), trolley, stretcher, litter, roller (*or* ice) skates, rollerblades, skateboard

▶ *70 Transport*

6 **beast of burden**, pack (*or* draught) animal, pack (*or* draught) horse, pack mule, ass, donkey, cuddy (Scot), burro, ox, coach horse, sledge dog, husky, malamute, reindeer, llama, camel, dromedary, elephant, sumpter (Arch), moke (Sl)

7 **transferor** (*or* **transferrer**), testator, conveyor (*or* conveyer), conveyancer, carrier, transporter, hauler, carter, drayman, common carrier, trucker, driver, truck driver, bus driver (*or* busman), taxi driver, tram driver, chauffeur, waggoner, boatman, gondolier, ferry-

man, importer, exporter, freighter, stevedore, cargo handler, bearer, porter, retainer, redcap (US), skycap (US), bellboy, page, bus boy (US), litter bearer, coolie, stretcher-bearer, shield-bearer, gunbearer, cupbearer, Ganymede, water carrier (*or* bearer), Aquarius, the Water Carrier, water boy, caddy, pallbearer

8 **messenger**, letter carrier, mail carrier (US), Royal Mail, Pony Express, postman, mailman (US), expressman, courier, carrier pigeon, homing pigeon, winged messenger, Mercury, Hermes, Iris
▶ *534 Communications*

9 **disease carrier**, sick person, infectious person, vector, transmitter, diffuser, contaminator
▶ *624 Ill Health*

10 **transferred thing**, passenger, fare, freight, freightage, consignment, shipment, goods, load, cargo, cargo load, payload, baggage, luggage, impedimenta, personal belongings, everything but the kitchen sink, container, pack, backpack, knapsack, rucksack, carrier bag, shopping bag, handbag, message, post, mail (US), letters, card, postcard, telegram, telegraph, gift, security, trust, legacy, bequest, pledge, driftwood, flotsam, jetsam, sediment, silt, drift, alluvium, alluvion, loess, moraine, scree, sinter, detritus, debris, infectious disease, contagious disease
▶ *258 Container, 257 Contents*

VERBS

11 **transfer**, transmit, translocate, transpose, metathesize, transplant, consign, assign, turn over, hand over, make over, conduct, convect, radiate, transpire, transfuse, diffuse, perfuse, spread, disseminate, disperse, metastasize, infect, contaminate, strain, decant, siphon, tap, funnel, channel, interchange, exchange, barter, swap, switch, shuffle, castle

12 **transport**, take, convey, freight, dispatch, send, send off (*or* away), send forth, remit, consign, transmit, forward, expedite, ship, import, export, carry, deliver, hand over, bear, haul, cart, heave, pack, tote, lug, manhandle, push, propel, lift, waft, whisk, wing, fly, send flying, airlift, truck, bus, ship, ferry, raft, boat, barge, sledge, sled (US), hump (Sl), schlep (US sl)

13 **post**, mail (US), airmail, forward, drop a line to, express, air-express, send by hand, fax, telex, address, readdress

14 **bring back**, fetch, get, bring, go and get, go after, go for, pick up, call for, procure, obtain, secure, retain, retrieve, chase, chase after, run after, fetch and carry, disperse, bequeath, commit, assign, leave, entrust, hand on (*or* down), pass on, scatter, deport, expel, eject, extradite, send

15 **take away**, cart away, carry off (*or* away), manhandle, set aside, lay (*or* put) aside, side, relegate, remove, relocate, move, displace, ladle, scoop, dip, bail, bucket, dish, spoon (out), shovel, spade, fork, dig, dislodge, unload, shift, shunt

16 **translate**, transcribe, transliterate, copy, make a copy, photocopy, plagiarize
▶ *5 Linguistics, 118 Imitation*

ADJECTIVES

17 **transferable**, transmittable, transmissible, transmissive, communicable, contagious, infectious, transfusable, importable, metastatic(al), metathetic(al), shifting, conveyable, mailable, consignable, conductive, conductional, interchangeable, exchangeable, negotiable, removable, movable, portable, portative, transportable, transportative, transportive, transposable, displaceable, carriageable, roadworthy, airworthy, seaworthy

ADVERBS

18 **in transit**, en route, on (*or* along) the way, on the (high) road, on the (high) sea, on the wing, as one goes, in passing, *en passant* (Fr), in mid-stream, by hand, *per manus* (L), by transfer, from door to door, by express, by rail, by special delivery, by remittance, from hand to hand, from pillar to post, conductively, interchangeably, exchangeably, contagiously, infectiously, communicably, metastatically

327 Way

NOUNS

1 **way**, ways and means, mode, manner, wise (Arch), means, form, method, methodology, system, technique, procedure, process, proceeding, *modus operandi* (L), line, line of action, order, mode of operation (MO), manner of working, way of doing things, *modus vivendi* (L), practice, skill, conduct, algorithm, approach, tack, line of attack, tactics, routine, the how, the drill, the way of, operation, working arrangement, usual way, fashion, style, tone, guise, progress, progression, way of life, behaviour, know-how (Inf)
▶ *602 Means, 150 Order*

2 **route**, itinerary, course, track, trail, direction, way to, way in, way out, way through, way over, line, march, beaten track, beat, road, run, trajectory, orbit, lane, traffic lane, flight lane, sea lane, sea path, primrose path, path of least resistance, line of advance, line of retreat, detour, roundabout way, short cut, bypass, circumlocution, circumbendibus, circumference, circuit, access, means of access, right of way, approach, direct approach, doorway, door, entrance, side entrance, back door, side door, tradesman's entrance, adit, drive, path, garden path, hall, hallway, lobby, porch, vestibule, corridor, gangway, gangplank, passage,

aisle, staircase, flight of stairs, step, tread, step-ladder, ladder, fireman's ladder

▶ *70 Transport*

3 **road**, high road, roadway, main road, A road, carriageway, thoroughfare, arterial road, artery, highway (US), King's (*or* Queen's) highway, royal road, highways and by-ways, trunk road, motorway, freeway (US), superhighway (US), interstate highway (US), expressway (US), *Autobahn* (Ger), *autostrada* (It), *autoroute* (Fr), state highway (US), throughway (US), parkway (US), dual carriageway, controlled access highway, toll road, turnpike (*or* pike) (US), ring road, beltway (*or* belt) (US), clearway, overpass, causeway, underpass, flyover, clover leaf, spaghetti junction, (road) junction, crossroads, intersection, roundabout, traffic circle (US), secondary road, local road, B road, private road, country road, byway, driveway, dirt road, gravel road, paved road, *pavé* (Fr), plank road, corduroy road, street, through street, arterial street, one-way street, high street, main street (US), drive, avenue, boulevard, crescent, circus, close, place, court, row, terrace, lane, alley, blind alley, alleyway, side street, cul-de-sac, dead end, mews, wynd (Scot)

4 **road surface**, surface, Tarmac (Tm), Tarmacadam (Tm), bitumen, asphalt, blacktop (US), cement, concrete, road metal, paving stone, flagstone (*or* flag), tile, brick, stone, cobblestone (*or* cobble), causey (Scot), kerb, kerbstone

5 **crossing**, pedestrian crossing, zebra crossing, pelican crossing, panda crossing, main drag (US sl)

▶ *70 Transport, 63 Engineering*

6 **path**, pathway, footpath, footway, pavement, sidewalk (US), bypath, towpath, side-path, bridle path, bicycle (*or* cycle) path, track, racing track, athletics track, racecourse, trail, hiking trail, rut, groove, berm, sea path, sea lane, shipping lane

▶ *356 Passage*

7 **arcade**, colonnade, covered way, gallery, portico, aisle, cloister, triforium, nave, loggia, ambulatory, (shopping) mall, promenade, esplanade, parade, *prado* (Sp), seafront

8 **tunnel**, underpass, way under, subway, underground, tube, *métro* (Fr), railway (*or* railroad) tunnel, Channel Tunnel, Chunnel (Inf)

9 **bridge**, span, viaduct, aqueduct, overpass, overcrossing, way over, footbridge, overbridge, suspension bridge, cantilever bridge, humpback bridge, arched bridge, railway bridge, floating bridge, pontoon bridge, Bailey bridge, drawbridge, steppingstones, catwalk, rope bridge, toll bridge, Bifrost

▶ *63 Engineering*

10 **railway**, railroad, track, line, railway (*or* railroad) line, tram (*or* tramcar), streetcar (US), tramline, streetcar line (US), trolley line, street railway, elevated railway, underground, subway (US), tube, metro, *métro* (Fr), electric railway, horse railway, cog railway, rack railway, rack-and-pinion railway, cable (*or* rope) railway, gravity-operated railway, light railway, main line, branch line (*or* branch), trunk line (*or* trunk), feeder line (*or* feeder), turnout, switchback, gauge, standard gauge, junction, turntable, level crossing, grade crossing (US), embankment, trestle, cutting, siding, sidetrack (US), marshalling yard, shunting yard, railroad yard (US), stop, station, platform, whistle, signal, signal box, rails, points, switch (US), sleeper, tie (US), tracks, roadbed, terminus (*or* terminal), end of the line, el (*or* L) (US inf)

11 **channel**, canal, conduit, aisle, alley, lane, inlet, exit, outlet, gulf, culvert, strait, sound, dike (*or* dyke), ditch, sewer, waterway, watercourse, river, navigable river, estuary, delta, stream, lock

12 **cableway**, wire ropeway, wireway, cable (*or* rope) railway, funicular (railway), monorail, telpher (railway), telpher way, telpher line, ski lift, chair lift, gondola

13 **flight path**, flight lane, airlane, air route, skyway, air corridor, path, landing field, runway, taxiway, air strip, flight strip, take-off strip, launching site, blastoff, trajectory, orbit, earth orbit, parking orbit, docking, re-entry, splashdown

VERBS

14 **find one's way**, find a way, make a way, have a method, do things the usual way, enter, use the side entrance, use the tradesman's entrance, have a route, draw up an itinerary, approach, take the high road, take to the road, come to a crossroads, detour, take a short cut, bypass, go round, go up a blind alley, cross the street, use a pedestrian crossing, use a footpath, bridge a river, take the train, take a plane, fly, blast off, orbit, splash down, come to the end of the line, reach one's destination

ADJECTIVES

15 **accessible**, through, connecting, connected, communicating, linked, bridged, flyover, spanned, arched, main, arterial, trunk, paved, cobbled, well-paved, well-laid, smooth, skidproof, signposted, marked, signalled, well-lit, lit, floodlit, well-used, busy, crowded, overcrowded, jammed, beaten, trodden, bumper-to-bumper

ADVERBS

16 **how**, in this way, after this fashion, along these lines, on the lines of, thus, so, as, like, anyway, anyhow, anywise, by any (manner of) means, in any event, in any case, at any rate, nevertheless, nonetheless, however, regardless, irregardless, at all, somehow, in some way (or other), by some means, somehow or

other (*or* another), in one way or another, after a fashion, no matter how, by hook or (by) crook, by fair means or foul

17 **via**, by way of, through, by, passing by (*or* through), over, around, round about, here and there, all through, towards, in the direction of, to, up, on, over against, on the way to, on the (high) road, in transit to, en route to (*or* for), on route to, in passage to

328 Slowness

VERBS

1 **move slowly**, walk slowly, barely move, go slow, go at a snail's pace, amble, saunter, march in slow-time, take it easy, stroll, get nowhere fast, laze, creep, crawl, inch along, ease along, trickle, ooze, drip, idle, go dead slow, shuffle along, stagger along, poke along, wobble, totter along, toddle along, scuff, take short steps, mince, plod, trudge, shamble, peg away, plod along, chug on, stump along, jogtrot, dogtrot, limp, hobble, hirple, traipse (Inf), mosey along (*or* on) (Inf), plug along (*or* away) (Inf), mooch around (Sl)

2 **hesitate**, barely move, grope (*or* feel) one's way, show caution, speak slowly, drawl, pause, falter, flag, dawdle, linger, loiter, tarry, hover, hang over, delay, dally, waste time, lag, drag, drag one's feet, take one's time, run out of steam, go lame, trail, halt, not get started, dilly-dally (Inf), shillyshally (Inf), lollygag (*or* lallygag) (US inf), goof off (US sl)
▶ *491 Uncertainty, 576 Vacillation, 781 Caution*

3 **slow down**, slow up, slow, let up, ease off (*or* up), slacken (*or* slack) off, relax, moderate, lose speed, reduce speed, lose momentum, decelerate, retard, delay, detain, impede, arrest, obstruct, hinder, stay, check, curb, hold back, keep back, set back, hold in check, rein in, draw rein, throttle down, take one's foot off the gas (US), brake, put on the drag, reef, take in sail, shorten sail, back water, back-pedal, lose ground, clip the wings, reverse, regress
▶ *699 Restraint, 661 Hindrance*

ADJECTIVES

4 **slow**, slow-moving, slow-paced, slow-footed, slow-running, ambling, strolling, sauntering, lumbering, easy-paced, snail-paced, snail-like, faltering, flagging, slow-as-slow, slow as death, creeping, crawling, walking, dragging, waddling, slouching, shuffling, plodding, clumsy, limping, halting, hobbling, shambling, tottering, staggering, poking, poky (US inf)
▶ *643 Inactivity, 240 Inertness*

5 **unhurried**, leisurely, sluggish, languorous, lethargic, inert, slack, slothful, languid, lazy, indolent, sluggardly, listless, idle, apathetic, phlegmatic, methodical, patient, deliberate, circumspect, gradual, Fabian, meticulous, re-strained, easy, moderate, gentle, relaxed, taking one's time, imperceptible, stealthy
▶ *491 Uncertainty, 781 Caution*

6 **hesitant**, tentative, softly-softly, cautious, reluctant, lagging, dawdling, drawling, procrastinating, unwilling, slow off the mark, groping, foot-dragging (Inf)

7 **delayed**, held-up, detained, checked, arrested, obstructed, impeded, set back, slowed down, retarded, restrained, slack, backward, behind, late, tardy, tardigrade, hysteretic, dilatory, lingering, dawdling, loitering, dallying, dilly-dallying (Inf), shillyshallying (Inf), lollygagging (*or* lallygagging) (US inf)

NOUNS

8 **slowness**, leisureliness, unhurriedness, lack of haste, no hurry, sluggishness, languor, lethargy, inertia, slackness, sloth, laziness, indolence, inertness, lentitude, dilatoriness, wasting time, methodicalness, patience, deliberation, deliberateness, circumspection, *festina lente* (L), gradualism, Fabianism, leisurely progress, meticulousness, restraint, time to spare, easy stages

9 **deceleration**, brake, curb, restraint, friction, retardation, retardment, slackening, flagging, slowing down (*or* up), easing off (*or* up), negative (*or* minus) acceleration

10 **slow motion**, leisurely gait, walk, amble, stroll, saunter, dawdle, low gear, piaffer, dragging, lumbering, creeping, snail's pace, tortoise's pace, creep, crawl, pace, trudge, waddle, slouch, shuffle, plod, limp, hobble, shamble, trot, dogtrot, jog trot, jog, single-foot, rack, mincing steps
▶ *699 Restraint*

11 **lingering**, lagging, dawdling, loitering, dallying, dalliance, dilly-dallying (Inf), shillyshallying (Inf), lollygagging (*or* lallygagging) (US inf), goofing off (US sl)

12 **hesitation**, tentativeness, caution, cautiousness, reluctance, drawling, tardiness, procrastination, unwillingness, standing start, slow start, delay, hold-up, go slow, slowdown (US), work-to-rule, detention, setback, check, arrest, obstruction, hysteresis, foot-dragging (Inf)
▶ *781 Caution*

13 **slow thing**, slow clock, funeral march, funeral procession, fugue, slow train, stopping train

14 **slow creature**, sloth, tortoise, slug, snail, creepy-crawly (Inf)
▶ *79 Reptiles and Amphibians, 82 Insects and Arachnids*

15 **slow person**, plodder, slow-goer, lingerer, loiterer, sloth, tortoise, snail, dawdler, dawdle, laggard, sloucher, slacker, idler, procrastinator, slug, sluggard, stick-in-the-mud, drone, slow starter, slowcoach (Inf), slowpoke (US inf), sleepyhead (Inf), foot-dragger (Inf), stick-

in-the-mud (Inf), goof-off (US sl), gold brick (US sl)

ADVERBS

16 **slowly**, slow, leisurely, unhurriedly, patiently, easily, moderately, gently, adagio, largo, larghetto, andante, languidly, sluggishly, languorously, lazily, idly, indolently, lingeringly, dilatorily, loiteringly, haltingly, falteringly, cautiously, deliberately, circumspectly, tentatively, reluctantly, gradually, by degrees, inch by inch, little by little, step by step, bit by bit, by easy stages

17 **in slow motion**, creepingly, crawlingly, pokingly, pokily, softly-softly, at a slow pace, at a snail's pace, at a funeral pace, in low gear, at half-speed, allargando, ritenuto, ritardando

329 Swiftness

ADJECTIVES

1 **swift**, swift-moving, fast, quick, rapid, fleet, speedy, speeding, high-speed, high-velocity, darting, dashing, snappy, round, smart, wasting no time, expeditious, hustling, hurrying, hurried, hasty, double-quick, rapid-fire, alacritous, prompt, sudden, early, immediate, instantaneous, express, meteoric, jet-propelled, faster than sound, supersonic, hypersonic, ultrasonic, electric, high-geared, high-velocity, high-speed, adapted for speed, streamlined, running, runaway, charging, racing, galloping, cantering, fleet of foot, light-footed, nimble-footed, nimble, agile, volant (Fml), quick-footed, wing-footed, winged, eagle-winged, like an eagle, like a bird, flying, hurtling, whirling, rattling, headlong, tempestuous, pelting, breakneck, precipitate, precipitous, expeditious, darting, flashing, quick as lightning, quick as a wink, quick as a flash, quick as the wind, faster than a speeding bullet, quick on the draw (Inf), quick on the trigger (Inf), hair-trigger (Inf), like greased lightning (Inf), nifty (Inf), zippy (Inf), whizzing (Inf), spanking (Inf), all-out (Inf), flat-out (Inf), wide-open (Inf), barrelling (Inf), go-go (US inf), ton-up (Inf), scorching, souped-up (Sl), hotted-up (Sl), hopped-up (US sl)

▶ *648 Haste, 191 Immediacy, 324 Motion, 330 Impulsion, 338 Propulsion*

2 **mentally quick**, quick-thinking, nimble-witted, quick-witted, bright, lively, brisk, vigorous, mercurial, quicksilver, reckless, rash

▶ *459 Intellect, 780 Rashness*

3 **accelerating**, accelerated, quickening, speeding-up, getaway, overtaking, passing, passed, lapping, lapped

▶ *638 Escape, 674 Contention*

VERBS

4 **be swift**, move fast, really move, drive quickly, speed, run, lope, race, chase, hurtle, bowl along, tear along, sweep along, scoot, scamper, scuttle, scurry, rush, dash, whisk, skirr, scour (territory), charge, stampede, ride hard, gallop, canter, trot, expedite, precipitate, hasten, hurry, career, careen, break the speed limit, fly, wing, move at the speed of sound, break the sound barrier, move at the speed of light, travel at maximum speed, go full tilt, go full pelt, go full steam, storm along, thunder along, rattle along, streak, dark, flit, zoom, zip, zing, whizz, hustle, expedite, lunge, spring, bound, leap, jump, pounce, swoop, dive, plunge, show a clean pair of heels, hie (Arch), skedaddle (Inf), get a move on (Inf), get cracking (Inf), get (or pull) one's finger out (Inf), step on it (Inf), hotfoot it (Inf), cut and run (Inf), go all out (Inf), make tracks (Inf), tear up the road (Inf), burn up the miles (Inf), rip along (Inf), nip along (Inf), barrel along (US inf), hare off (or after) (Inf), vroom (Inf), burn rubber (Sl), grayhound (US sl), put the hammer down (US sl), go full bat (Sl), zap along (Sl), shift (Sl), scorch (Sl), shag ass (US tab sl), haul ass (US tab sl)

▶ *648 Haste*

5 **run like a shot**, run like the wind, run like a hare, run like a scared rabbit, run like wildfire, run like (or in) a flash, run like lightning, run like a streak of lightning, run like a streak, run like the devil, run like a bat out of hell, run like a blue-streak (US inf), run like greased lightning (Inf), run like the clappers (Inf), run like a house on fire (or afire) (Inf), run like sixty (US inf), run like mad (Inf), run like crazy (Inf), run like sin (Inf), run to beat the band (US sl), pour it on (US sl), highball it (US sl), ball the jack (US sl)

6 **accelerate**, quicken, quicken one's speed, gather speed, speed up, pick up speed, put on speed, spurt, sprint, burst ahead, have a burst of speed, have a burst of energy, gather momentum, impart momentum, step up the pace, raise the tempo, open the throttle, thrust ahead, flash by, run away, dash forward, dash off, dart off, tear off (or away or out), set off at a run, get off to a flying start, make up time, make up for lost time, bolt, jump ahead, spring forward, spring, bound forward, dash, scamper, run, leave standing, leave at the starting post, gain on, overtake, overhaul, catch up (with), make the running, pass, lap, shake off, lose someone, outdistance, outrun, outpace, outstrip, outmarch, outsail, outdrive, outclass, outdo, leave behind, romp home, win the race, get a move on (Inf), step on it (Inf), let it rip (Inf), step on the gas (Inf), put one's foot down (Inf), put on one's running shoes (Inf), open up (Inf), whizz by (Inf)

7 **hurry someone up**, hasten, urge on, urge forward, drive, spur, chivy (or chivvy) along,

lend wings to, put dynamite under (Inf), put a bomb under (Inf)

▶ *648 Haste*

NOUNS

8 **speed**, velocity, speediness, swiftness, quickness, fastness, fleetness, promptness, promptitude, rapidity, celerity, quick pace, round pace, smart pace, snappy pace, briskness, rattling pace, rapid tempo, fast rate, fast motion, speeding, driving, hard driving, racing, bowling along, dispatch, expedition, expeditiousness, precipitation, hastiness, haste, hurry, flurry, no loss of time, instantaneity, instantaneousness, agility, nimbleness, rashness, career, full career, full pelt, full sail, press of sail, great speed, speed of light, speed of sound, sonic speed, sound barrier, supersonic speed, ultrasonic speed, hypersonic speed, express speed, utmost speed, full speed, top speed, maximum speed, lightning speed, excessive speed, dangerous speed, breakneck speed, reckless speed, illegal speed, speed trap, radar trap, rate of speed (*or* speed-rate), air speed, ground speed, miles per hour (mph), kilometres per hour (kph), rpm (revolutions per minute), knot, Mach number, speed measurement, tachometer, speedometer, mileometer, odometer (US), accelerometer, cyclometer, gauge, wind gauge, anemometer, log, chip log, flat-out speed (Inf), wide-open speed (Inf), pickup (US inf), good (*or* fair) clip (Inf), nifty pace (Inf), full lick (Inf), blue streak (Inf), spanking rate (Inf), making tracks (Inf), barrelling (along) (US inf), burning rubber (Sl), bat (Sl), burn-up (Sl), scorching (Sl)

9 **acceleration**, quickening, speed-up, spurt, burst, burst of speed, burst of energy, thrust, drive, impetus, impulse, jump, spring, bound, pounce, leap, swoop, swoosh, vroom, zip, zoom, dive, power dive, flying start, getaway, rush, headlong rush, headlong plunge, dash, scamper, run, sprint, canter, gallop, tantivy, overtaking, passing, lapping, whizz (Inf), zing (Inf), zap (Sl)

10 **quickness of mind**, quick-wittedness, speed of thought, alacrity, mental quickness, mental agility, brightness, liveliness

▶ *459 Intellect*

11 **swift thing**, lightning, lightning flash, streak of lightning, hurricane, gale, tempest, torrent, arrow, express, pony express, express train, racing car, sports car, speedboat, clipper, jet, jet flight, supersonic flight, rocket, missile, bullet, cannonball, electricity, telegraph, telephone, magic carpet, seven-league boots, race, forced march, quick march, double march, quick retreat, greased lightning (Inf)

12 **swift animal**, racehorse, racer, thoroughbred, galloper, courser, greyhound, cheetah, hare, scared rabbit, fox, deer, doe, gazelle, antelope, ostrich, eagle, swallow, swift, roadrunner, bat out of hell (Inf)

▶ *32 Horses*

13 **swift person**, runner, sprinter, harrier, speeder, racer, racing driver, Jehu, hustler, courser, courier, messenger, express messenger, messenger of the gods, Mercury, Hermes, Iris, Ariel, speed maniac (Inf), speed demon (Inf), speed freak (US sl), hell-driver (US sl), scorcher (Sl)

ADVERBS

14 **swiftly**, quickly, rapidly, fleetly, apace, speedily, snappily, allegro, at express speed, headlong, with all speed, at full speed, prestissimo, at full throttle, full speed ahead, at one's top speed, at full tilt, at full blast, in full sail, under press of sail, in full career, in high gear, under full steam, for all one is worth, in full gallop, *ventre à terre* (Fr), with whip and spur, with giant strides, with giant leaps, on eagle's wings, roundly, smartly, on (*or* at) the double, double-quick, in double-quick time, in double-time, accelerando, in no time, by leaps and bounds, helter-skelter, expeditiously, posthaste, hurryingly, hastily, presto, quickwittedly, promptly, suddenly, immediately, instantaneously, meteorically, supersonically, hypersonically, ultrasonically, in high gear, in high, nimbly, agilely, as fast as one's legs would carry one, before one could (*or* can) say Jack Robinson, amain (Arch), niftily (Inf), lickety-split (US inf), all out (Inf), flat out (Inf), in nothing flat (Inf), wide open (Inf), at a good (*or* fair) slip (Inf), at a rate of knots (Inf), pronto (Inf), hell for leather (Inf), pdq (pretty damn quick) (Sl), ASAP (as soon as possible) (Sl)

330 Impulsion

VERBS

1 **impel**, give an impetus to, import momentum, accelerate, drive, propel, compel, motivate, incite, urge, spur, start, run, set going, set in motion, move, animate, actuate, galvanize, power, goad, drive on (*or* forward), project, traject, thrust, press, stress, push, shove, heave, prod, poke, dig, jostle, push around, jolt, jog, tug, wrench, joggle, jerk, elbow, shoulder, hustle, butt, thwack, press on, bear, bear upon, bring pressure to bear on, throw out, run out, push out of the way, expel, eject, frogmarch

▶ *338 Propulsion, 324 Motion, 235 Power*

2 **collide**, impact, crash, crash into, bump into, smash, impinge upon, crunch, crump, clash, cannon into, carom into (US), jolt, nudge, bump, meet, encounter, confront, charge, attack, converge, careen, bang, percuss, concuss, foul, run foul of, hurtle, smash up, cross swords, fence, run one's head against, run up

against a brick wall, knock heads together, ram, ram down, tamp, hammer, bulldoze, sledgehammer, pile-drive, shoulder, butt, bash, slam into, brunt (Arch), pile up (Inf), whomp (US inf)

3 **hit**, strike, stroke, rap, punch, thwack, pound, slam, bang, smack, swipe, dash, belt, clout, swat, swing, buffet, hit over the head, box, box someone's ears, jab, knock, bat, poke, thump, pelt, biff, sock, cut, slog, slug, bash, bonk, dent, aim a blow, deal a blow, strike at, clip round the ear, dint (Arch), let have it (Inf), knock cold (Inf), plunk (Inf), whop (Inf), bop (Sl), deck (Sl), coldcock (Sl), clobber (Sl), paste (Sl)

▶ *670 Attack*

4 **throw**, throw stones at, fling, hurl, toss, launch, propel, pitch, cast, hurtle, heave, lob, fire, catapult, let fly (Inf)

5 **beat**, trounce, leather, hammer, spank, pound, pummel, rain blows down on, give a good hiding, whip, flog, flail, thrash, cut, lash, stripe, cane, baste, lambaste, batter, pulverize, beat up (Inf), wallop (Inf), lick (Inf), dust off (US inf)

6 **tap**, rap, touch, chuck (under the chin), tip, pat, dab, flick, flip, peck, pick, brush, whisk

7 **kick**, boot, drop-kick, penalty-kick, place-kick, punt, knee, stamp, clump, clop, drub, trample, tread on, stamp on, kneel on, ride roughshod over, stomp (Inf)

8 **club**, cudgel, blackjack, sandbag, cosh, hit over the head, crown, concuss, assail, attack

9 **fight**, go at it hammer and tongs, cut and thrust, box, knock out, knock down, give someone a bloody nose, give someone a black eye, leave senseless (Inf)

10 **bat**, strike a ball, drive, hit, lift, smash, volley, slice, cut, pull

NOUNS

11 **impulsion**, impulse, impellent, impelling force, impetus, momentum, moment, moment of force, force, irresistible force, driving force, power, motive power, propulsion, compulsion, incentive, incitement, science of forces, mechanics, dynamics, transmission (mechanics)

12 **collision**, head-on collision, meeting, encounter, charge, attack, convergence, multiple collision, pile-up, smash-up, percussion, concussion, scrape, friction, crash, impact, shock, smash, crunch, cannon, carom (US), jolt, nudge, bump, ramming, hammering, drumming, rapping, tapping, beating, thrusting, bulling, bulldozing, shouldering, smashing, sledgehammering, butting, bashing, spanking, trouncing, leathering, paddling, pummelling, raining (of blows), hiding, whipping, flogging, corporal punishment, thrashing, assault, assault and battery, grievous bodily

harm (GBH), attack, exchange of blows, fisticuffs, boxing, hammer and tongs, cut and thrust, dusting off (US inf), licking (Inf)

13 **blow**, hit, strike, stroke, rap, punch, thwack, pound, slam, bang, butt, smack, swipe, dash, belt, clout, swat, swing, buffet, blow on the ears, body blow, jab, knock, poke, thump, pelt, cut, slog, slug, bash, bonk, dent, thrust, press, stress, pressure, pressing, push, shove, heave, prod, nudge, dig, biff, jostle, jolt, jog, joggle, hustle, tap, touch, chuck, tip, pat, dab, flick, flip, fillip, peck, brush, whisk, slap, spank, cuff, box, whip, lash, stripe, kick, boot, drop kick, penalty kick, place kick, punt, stamp, clump, clop, drub, dint (Arch), brunt (Arch), plunk (Inf), whop (Inf), stomp (Inf)

14 **sporting hit**, boxing blow, hook, jab, punch, left, right uppercut, swing, backhand(er), backstroke, sidewinder, short-arm blow, round-arm blow, round house, Long Melford, bolopunch, knock-out punch, haymaker, straight left, body blow, batting hit, drive, on (*or* off) drive, straight drive, hit, cut, pull, slice, bunt, line drive, home run

▶ *18 Sport*

15 **ram**, rammer, ramrod, battering ram, bulldozer, pile-driver, monkey, tamper, tamp, tamping iron, pusher, shover, cue, billiard cue, hammer, sledge, sledgehammer (*or* sledge), hammer head, peen, hammerstone, punch, puncher, knocker, door-knocker, carpetbeater, tapper, bat, mallet, hockey stick, baseball bat, rounders bat, tennis racket

16 **weapons**, cudgel, mace, truncheon, whip, flail, cosh, knuckle-duster, brass knuckles (US), bicycle chain, boxing glove

ADJECTIVES

17 **impelling**, impellent, impulsive, pulsive, dynamic, motive, moving, thrusting, thrustful, driving, ramming, smashing, thrashing, flogging

ADVERBS

18 **dynamically**, impulsively, with momentum, with power, percussively, forcefully, violently, shockingly

331 Recoil

VERBS

1 **recoil**, rebound, cannon, carom (US), ricochet, boomerang, kick, kick back, backfire, backlash, lash back, spring, spring back, bounce, bounce back, bound, bound back, uncoil, return, swing back, revert, reflect, mirror, reverberate, resound, echo, oscillate

▶ *221 Reversion, 427 Resonance, 663 Opposition*

2 **respond**, react, counteract, reply, retort, rebuff, answer, answer back, riposte, snap back, come back at, retaliate, give as good as one gets, flinch, shrink, wince, cringe, blink,

blench, quail, draw back, pull back, recoil, retreat, avoid, evade, sidestep, duck, shy, dodge, swerve, sheer off, jib

▶ *478 Answer, 672 Retaliation, 735 Giving Back*

3 **get a response**, get a reaction, strike a chord, ring a bell, hit (*or* strike) home, hit a nerve, get a rise out of

NOUNS

4 **recoil**, rebound, bounce, bound, spring, swing of pendulum, elasticity, resilience, *contrecoup* (Fr), reflex, reflex action, kickback, bounce-back, ricochet, boomerang, cannon, carom (US), oscillation, ducks and drakes, return, reflux, refluence, backfire, echo, reflection, reverberation, repercussion, reversion, backlash, resonance, sympathetic vibration

▶ *109 Reciprocity*

5 **reflector**, mirror, sounding board, echo chamber, springboard, trampoline, pendulum

6 **response**, reaction, reply, retort, riposte, rebuff, repercussion, predictable response, automatic response, spontaneous response, spur-of-the-moment response, conditioned reflex, retroaction, retreat, drawing aside, recoil, falling back, fall-back, pulling out, pull out, evasion, avoidance, sidestepping, duck, shy, dodge, sidestep, flinch, wince, cringe, revulsion

▶ *478 Answer*

7 **responder**, rebuffer, reactionary, reactionist, recalcitrant

ADJECTIVES

8 **recoiling**, rebounding, resilient, springy, springing, bouncing, bounding, elastic, resonant, vibrating, reverberative, reflective, reflecting, repercussive, backfiring

9 **reactive**, reacting, responsive, responding, respondent, retortive, retorting, antiphonal, reflex, knee-jerk, reactionary, retroactive, recalcitrant, revulsive

ADVERBS

10 **on the rebound**, on the return, on the bounce, off the top of one's head, on the spur of the moment, resiliently, elastically, resonantly, reflectively, reactively, retroactively, recalcitrantly

332 Direction

NOUNS

1 **direction**, bearing, bearings, location, situation, position, lie of the land, set, quarter, line, line of direction, aim, goal, target, objective, steering, steerage, navigation, piloting, helmsmanship

▶ *250 Location*

2 **bearing**, heading, trend, tendency, run, set, inclination, bent, tenor, drift, thrust, course, route, line, track, path, way, lay, lie, short cut, beeline, line of sight, compass direction, compass bearing (*or* heading), relative bearing (*or* heading), true bearing (*or* heading), relative (*or* true) course, tack, vector

▶ *234 Tendency, 327 Way*

3 **orientation**, bearings, collimation, adaptation, adjustment, alignment, accommodation, direction finder (D/F), compass, signpost, map, tracking device, rangefinder, gauge, degrees, compass rose, compass card, lubber line, rhumb line, azimuth

▶ *543 Sign*

4 **compass point**, cardinal point, half-point, north (N), magnetic North, northward, nor', south (S), southward, east (E), eastward, the Orient, sunrise, west (W), westward, the Occident, sunset, southeast, southwest, northeast, northwest, easting, westing, northing, southing

5 **directions**, direction, pointing (out), guiding, leading, guidance, instruction, education, supervising, managing

▶ *6 Education, 654 Advice, 653 Management*

VERBS

6 **direct**, direct to, give directions, point (*or* show) the way, indicate, guide, signpost, steer, point, aim, determine, set, fix, present, point to (*or* at), point out to, push in the right direction, lead, conduct, steer towards, put on the right track, set straight (*or* right), put right

7 **take a direction**, bear, aim, navigate, collimate, set one's sights on, fix on, train upon, sight on, aim at, point, turn, head, lead, go, hold a heading, direct (*or* align) oneself, incline, tend, tend to go, trend, set, dispose, verge, head for, go for, bear for, hit for, steer for, make for, put for, set out (*or* off) for, strike out for, take off for, lay for, bear up to (*or* for), set in towards, set one's course for, direct one's course for, set one's compass for, sail for, align one's march, dash for, make a break for, run for, go straight, go directly, head straight on, follow one's nose, make a beeline for, get straight to the point, steer a straight course, hold steady, cleave to the line, keep pointed, take the airline (US), stay on the beam, hold the line, keep the nose down

8 **orient** (*or* **orientate**), orient onself, take (*or* get) one's bearings, get the lay (*or* lie) of the land, see which way the wind blows, see which way the land lies, adapt, adjust, accommodate, box the compass, take (*or* shoot) the sun, check one's course

ADVERBS

9 **directly**, direct, straight, point blank, straightly, straightforward (*or* straightforwards), full tilt, unswervingly, undeviatingly, unveeringly, due, due north, right, forthright, in a direct (*or* straight) line, in line with, in a beeline, as the crow flies, straight as a dye, straight as an arrow, straight across, on course,

on the right track, squarely, square, dead right, dead ahead, dead, straight ahead, full, flush, exactly, precisely, kerplunk (Inf), plop, plumb (Inf), plump (Inf), plunk (Inf), smack (Inf), smack-dab (Inf), spang (US inf)

▶ *336 Forward Motion, 312 Straightness*

10 **clockwise**, anticlockwise, counterclockwise, withershins (*or* widdershins) (Scot), leftward (*or* leftwards), rightward (*or* rightwards), homeward, landward, seaward, leeward, earthward, heavenward, windward

▶ *364 Rotation*

11 **in all directions**, in every direction, in all manner of ways, every way, everywhere, every which way, in all directions at once, in every quarter, on every side, around, all round, round and about, from every quarter, from (*or* to) the four corners of the earth, from (*or* to) the four winds, upstream, downstream, upwind, downwind, before the wind, close to the wind, near the wind, against the wind, in the wind's eye, close hauled, downtown (US), uptown (US)

12 **north**, northerly, northwards, northwardly, south, southerly, southwards, southwardly, east, easterly, eastwards, eastwardly, west, westerly, westernly, westwards, westwardly, northeast, northeasterly, northeastwards, north-northeast, northeast by east, northeast by north, northwest, northwesterly, northwestwards, northwestwardly, north-northwest, northwest by west, northwest by north, southeast, southeasterly, southeastwards, southeastwardly, south-southeast, southeast by east, southeast by south, southwest, southwesterly, southwestwards, southwestwardly, south-southwest, southwest by west, southwest by south

ADJECTIVES

13 **directional**, northern, north, northward, northerly, northernmost, northbound, arctic, boreal, hyperborean, southern, south, southward, southerly, southernmost, southbound, meridional, antarctic, austral, eastern, east, eastward, easterly, easternmost, eastbound, Oriental, western, west, westward, westerly, westernmost, westbound, Occidental, northeastern, northeast, northeasterly, southeastern, southeast, southeasterly, northwestern, northwest, northwesterly, southwestern, southwest, southwesterly

14 **directed**, directable, steerable, guidable, dirigible, leadable, aligned, parallel, oblique, axial, cross-country, downwind, upwind, downtown (US), uptown (US), orientated towards, directed towards, pointed for, headed for, bound for, set, signposted, aimed, well-aimed, well-directed, on the mark, on the nose (US sl), on the money (US sl)

15 **direct**, immediate, straight, straightforward, straightaway, undeviating, unswerving, un-

veering, uninterrupted, unbroken, one-way, unidirectional, irreversible

16 **directing**, directive, guiding, steering, leading, instructing, educating

333 Middle Way

NOUNS

1 **middle way**, midway, midpoint, central position, centre, diameter, radius, nondeviation, straight line, short cut, beeline, short circuit, middle course, mid-course, median, medium, happy medium, average, golden mean

▶ *158 Middle, 124 Average, 291 Centre*

2 **middle of the road**, *via media* (L), middle ground, neutral ground, neutrality, noncommittal, impartiality, compromise, moderation, moderateness, balance, halfway measures, half measures, half-and-half measures, lukewarmness, mutuality, mutual concessions, reciprocity, symbiosis

▶ *242 Moderation, 109 Reciprocity*

3 **moderate person**, moderate, nonextremist, liberal, minimalist, Menshevist, middle-of-the-roader, half-and-halfer, neutral person, third party, objective observer, arbitrator, referee, neutralist, uncommitted person, 'don't know', agnostic, Laodicean, nonpartisan, centrist, mugwump

▶ *242 Moderation, 124 Average, 167 Conformity, 491 Uncertainty*

ADJECTIVES

4 **middle**, central, equidistant, midway, halfway, medial, intermediate, sitting on the fence, lukewarm, half-and-half, even, fifty-fifty, neutral, moderate, middle-of-the-road, unextreme, nonextreme, noncommittal, uncommitted, unattached, detached, indifferent, independent, nonpartisan, nonaligned, impartial, irresolute, neither one thing nor the other, grey, neither hot nor cold

▶ *124 Average, 242 Moderation, 158 Middle, 291 Centre, 783 Indifference*

5 **undeviating**, direct, straight, unswerving, keeping to the middle, looking neither left nor right

▶ *332 Direction, 312 Straightness*

VERBS

6 **be in the middle**, keep to the middle, steer a middle course, keep to mid-stream, hold straight, not deviate, not swerve, look neither right nor left, make a beeline for

7 **be halfway**, be in-between, go halfway, meet halfway, compromise, equalize, occupy the centre (ground), hold the scales, sit on the fence, equivocate, hedge one's bets, balance, preserve a balance, keep a happy medium, keep the golden mean, show moderation, avoid both Scylla and Charybdis

▶ *578 Equivocation*

334 Circuit

ADVERBS

8 **medially**, midway, in the middle, moderately, in moderation, neutrally, equally, centrally, intermediately, impartially

NOUNS

1 **circuit**, round, revolution, lap, the rounds, beat, walk, turn, tour, gyre (Fml), circle, full circle, ring, ellipse, oval, loop, looping the loop, circumference, cycle, orbit, ambit, round trip, *aller-retour* (Fr), roundabout, traffic circle (US), circling, circulation, wheeling, whirling, spinning, reeling, twirling
▶ *364 Rotation, 313 Circularity*

2 **detour**, diversion, bypass, loop, loop line, ring road, beltway (or belt) (US), roundabout way, circuitous route, longest way, long way round, circumlocution, circumbendibus, digression, periphrasis, deviation, excursion, divagation, circumnavigation, circumambience, circummigration, ambage (Arch), circuitousness, circuitry, circuition, roundaboutness, meandering, deviance, deviancy
▶ *335 Deviation, 327 Way, 474 Sophistry, 578 Equivocation*

VERBS

3 **circuit**, make a circuit, circle, move in a circle, describe a circle, lap, loop, ring, loop the loop, keep to the circumference, skirt, edge round, circulate, go round (or around), orbit, revolve, come full circle, close the circle, make a round trip, go the round, make one's rounds, circumvent, circumambulate, circummigrate, circumnavigate, return to the starting point, cycle, spiral, gyre (Fml), go round in circles, go round and round, chase one's tail
▶ *363 Orbital Motion, 364 Rotation*

4 **detour**, make a detour, make a diversion, diverge, deviate, digress, go out of one's way, go the long way round, go all round the houses, bypass, avoid, give a wide berth to, short-circuit, beat about the bush, go off at a tangent, miss the point, divagate, zigzag
▶ *335 Deviation, 591 Avoidance*

5 **encircle**, encompass, surround, skirt, flank, girdle, embrace
▶ *313 Circularity*

ADJECTIVES

6 **circular**, round, wheel-shaped, O-shaped, oval, egg-shaped, ovate, elliptical, orbital, rotary, spiral, helical, circulatory, circulating, circumambient, circumambulatory, circumfluent, circumnavigatory, circumnavigable
▶ *313 Circularity*

7 **circuitous**, roundabout, out of the way, deviating, digressive, periphrastic, discursive, excursive, indirect, circumlocutory, long-winded, devious, diffuse, oblique, meandering, backhanded, ambagious (Arch)
▶ *335 Deviation*

ADVERBS

8 **circuitously**, round about, deviously, obliquely, discursively, indirectly, backhandedly, in a roundabout way, periphrastically, from pillar to post, by the side door

335 Deviation

VERBS

1 **deviate**, diverge, divert, divaricate, vary, depart from, digress, branch, branch out, tralineate, detour, go off at a tangent, sheer, curve, heel, trend, bear off, filter, swerve, turn a corner, leave the straight and narrow, turn (or go) out of one's way, alter (or depart) from one's course, change direction, tack, yaw, veer, back, navigate

2 **divert**, change course (or the course of), put rudder on, pull (or push or draw) aside, put screw on, slice, pull, hook, glance, bowl wide

3 **go astray**, stray, get lost, lose (or miss) one's way, lose one's bearings, lose one's sense of direction, take a wrong turn (or the wrong turning), foul the line, go adrift, drift, get sidetracked, err, ramble, wander, rove, straggle, excurse, pererrate, divagate

4 **lose track of**, lose the thread, blunder, be inattentive, miss the point, daydream

5 **twist**, turn, bend, meander, wind, weave, twine, snake, curve, twist and turn, zigzag, hairpin, pull, crook, dogleg

6 **distort**, warp, bias, twist, skew, screw

7 **misdirect**, put off the scent, divert, avert, mislead, misaddress, misinform

8 **sidestep**, sidetrack, turn (or move or draw or step) aside (or to one side), side, sidle, make way for, avoid, turn away, shy, shy off, jib, avert, avoid, gee, haw, be oblique, steer clear of, get out of the way of, go (or bear or sheer or veer or ease or edge) off, fly off, passage

9 **shove aside**, sidetrack, shunt, switch, shuffle, put on one side

10 **slide**, slip, sideslip, skid, swing, wobble, oscillate

11 **turn round**, turn about, about-turn, wheel, face about, face the other way, reverse, reverse direction, return, revert, turn back, go back

12 **deflect**, diffract, bend, diverge, scatter, disperse, diffuse, refract

NOUNS

13 **deviation**, deviance, deviancy, deviousness, disorientation, misdirection, aberration, aberrancy, nonconformism, eccentricity, exorbitation, wrong course (or turning), digression, excursion, departure, declension, tangent, diversion, deflection, divergence, divarication, curvature, branching off, aside, parenthesis, divagation, declination, variation, indirec-

tion, obliqueness, obliquity, skew, slant, bias

▶ *343 Divergence, 286 Obliqueness, 311 Curve, 168 Nonconformity, 334 Circuit*

14 **deviating course**, curve, turn, flexure, double, declension, bend, corner, hairpin bend, dogleg, zigzag, slope, slant, sheer, sweep, pitch, tack, indirect course, detour, diversion, bypass, bypath, long way round, winding course, slalom course

▶ *332 Direction*

15 **deviating motion**, indirect motion, swerve, swerving, veer(ing), skid, sideslip, sidestep, crabwalk, shift, drift, leeway, roll, pitch, yaw, swing, break, leg break, off break, knight's-move

16 **wandering**, drifting, circuitousness, circumlocution, circumbendibus, rambling, digression, discursion, discursiveness, excursus, straying, errantry, pererration, vagrancy, lapse, error, wandering mind, abstractedness

17 **torsion**, twisting, torque, distortion, warp

▶ *309 Distortion*

18 **diffraction**, scatter, refraction, reflection, diffusion, dispersion, diaspora, fanning out

▶ *162 Dispersion, 56 Physics*

19 **deviant person**, deviant, deviate, deviationist, nonconformist, unconformist, Bohemian, dropout, misfit, oddity, freak, square peg in a round hole, fish out of water, ugly duckling, black swan, odd man out, joker in the pack, one in a million, character, eccentric, dissident, dissenter, heretic, tergiversator, rebel, marginal, renegade, outsider, outcast, pariah, outlaw, criminal, hermit, lone wolf, loner, solitary, extremist, fanatic, lunatic fringe, blackleg, scab, sexual deviant, pervert, queer fish (Inf), crank (Inf), weirdo (Inf), oddball (Inf)

▶ *168 Nonconformity, 877 Immorality*

ADJECTIVES

20 **deviant**, deviative, deviatory, deviating, misdirected, nonconformist, aberrant, aberrational, eccentric, off-centre, out of orbit, exorbitant

▶ *168 Nonconformity*

21 **indirect**, turning, curving, roundabout, winding, bending, meandering, snaking, serpentine, labyrinthine, mazy, shifting, swerving, deflected, deflective, twisting, veering, zigzag, crooked, out-of-the-way, off course, off the beam, off target, off the mark, wide, wide of the mark, lost, stray, astray, off the fairway, in the rough

▶ *332 Direction*

22 **undirected**, unguided, random

▶ *589 Chance*

23 **oblique**, skewed, biased, slanted, distorted, twisted

▶ *286 Obliqueness, 309 Distortion*

24 **diverging**, divaricating, branching, diver-

gent, once (*or* twice) removed

▶ *343 Divergence*

25 **wandering**, drifting, digressive, circuitous, devious, divagatory, rambling, digressing, discursive, straying, errant, erratic, desultory, abstracted, inattentive, off the point, off the subject, vagrant, loose, footloose, footloose and fancy free

26 **diffractive**, refractive, refractile, refrangible, refracted, diffracted, scattered, reflected, diffuse, diffused, dispersed

▶ *162 Dispersion, 56 Physics*

ADVERBS

27 **astray**, adrift, off the mark, wide of the mark, round about, discursively

28 **indirectly**, obliquely, sideways, diagonally, at one remove, at a tangent

29 **erratically**, eccentrically, oddly, strangely

336   Forward Motion

VERBS

1 **go forward**, proceed, progress, make progress, advance, go (*or* move) forward, step forward, pass on, move, be in motion, travel, get along, come along, roll, roll on, make headway (Inf)

▶ *324 Motion*

2 **start**, make a good start, make initial progress, make good progress, break the back of

▶ *156 Beginning*

3 **press on**, push, press forward, drive on, keep on, make leeway, make (rapid) strides, push on, gain ground, cover ground, gather way, forge (*or* shoot) ahead, go ahead, climb, gain height, rise, rise higher

▶ *359 Ascent, 361 Raising*

4 **make good time**, make the best of one's way, make up for lost time, make up leeway, recover lost ground, recoup, gain time

▶ *185 Time*

5 **develop**, evolve, move with the times, show promise, come on, get on, do well, prosper

▶ *686 Prosperity*

6 **march on**, rub (*or* run) on, jog on, roll on, flow, flow on, drift along, go (*or* move) with the stream

7 **make one's way**, work one's way, weave (*or* worm *or* thread) one's way, inch forward, muddle through, carve (*or* force *or* fight) one's way, further oneself, get somewhere, climb, reach towards, reach out, raise one's sights

8 **further**, bring on, foster, contribute to, advance, aid, raise, lift, elevate, bounce up, promote, upgrade, improve, better, forward, hasten, modernize, bring forward, push, force, develop, grow, augment, step up, accelerate, put ahead, put in front, put forward, propose, favour, make for, conduce

9 **maintain progress**, never look back, hold

one's lead, overtake, gain on, distance, outdistance, outstrip, leave behind, move fast, go fast, go ahead, get a move on, get ahead, advance by leaps and bounds

NOUNS

10 **forward motion**, going forward, progress, steady progress, progression, progressiveness, advance, headway, arithmetic progression, geometric progression, forward march, forwarding, forwardal, roll, rolling on, travel

▶ *324 Motion*

11 **course**, march, passage, way, ongoing, career, march (*or* passage *or* course) of time, tide, current, flood, onward course, ongo, go ahead, way forward

▶ *185 Time*

12 **advance**, advancement, promotion, preferment, leg-up, furtherance, furthering, rise, raise, lift, ascent, elevation, gain, ground gained, enterprise, success, achievement, economic progress, prosperity, go-getting (Inf)

▶ *361 Raising, 359 Ascent*

13 **step**, stride, jump, leap, spurt, sudden progress, leaps and bounds, step on the ladder

14 **development**, growth, evolution, furtherance, next step

15 **improvement**, betterment, reform, perfectibility, majestic progress, irreversibility, irresistible progress, getting ahead, overtaking, overstepping, encroachment

▶ *627 Improvement, 357 Overstepping*

16 **progressive person**, progressive, improver, reformer, coming man (*or* woman), made man (*or* woman), upstart, man (*or* woman) of action, doer, hustler, bustler, go-getter (Inf), ball of fire (Inf), live wire (Sl), whiz kid (Inf)

ADJECTIVES

17 **forward**, progressive, progressing, advanced, advancing, go-ahead, forward-looking, up-to-date, abreast of the times, enterprising, reformist, go-getting (Inf)

18 **ongoing**, continuing, inexorable, irreversible, onward, oncoming, proceeding, moving, profluent, flowing on, unbroken

ADVERBS

19 **forward**, forwards, onward, onwards, forth, on, along, ahead, forrard (Dial), on the way to, on the road, en route to (*or* for), on one's way

20 **in progress**, in mid-progress, in transit, going on, progressively, by leaps and bounds, underway, in sight of

337 Backward Motion

VERBS

1 **go backward(s)**, regress, return, revert, relapse, backslide, slip back, lose ground, slide down the slippery slope, lapse, fall off, decline, recidivate, retrogress, retrograde, retroflex, retrocede, go down the tubes (*or* chute *or* drain), go back to the drawing board

▶ *221 Reversion, 628 Deterioration*

2 **retreat**, withdraw, retire, sound (*or* beat) a retreat, pull back, pull out, advance to the rear, disengage, fall back, fall behind, draw back, run back, move back, stand back, back out, back out of, back down, give way, give ground, give place, run away, resign, recede into the distance, back into a corner

▶ *673 Submission*

3 **reverse**, back, turn, backtrack, take the backtrack, back up, go into reverse, back off, back-pedal, back away, backtrail, countermarch, reverse one's field, retrace one's steps, double back, take the reciprocal course, back water, run back, flow back, ebb, regurgitate, crawfish (US inf)

4 **slip back**, ebb, fall, drop, decline, descend

▶ *360 Descent*

5 **turn back**, put back, double, double back, retrace one's steps, turn, return, go (*or* come) back, go (*or* come) home, remigrate

6 **shrink back**, avoid, shy, shy away, shrink, jib

▶ *591 Avoidance*

7 **recoil**, bounce back, come back to where one started, box the compass

▶ *231 Counteraction*

8 **look back**, look over one's shoulder, hark back, reminisce

▶ *3 History, 200 Past Time*

9 **turn round**, turn around (*or* about), face about, about-face (US), about-turn, *volte-face* (Fr), right-about-face, turn on one's heel, turn one's back, come (*or* go *or* fetch) about, make a U-turn, turn tail, double, wheel, turn on a dime (US), veer, veer around, swivel, pivot, swing round, crane one's neck

NOUNS

10 **backward motion**, going back, regression, regress, recession, infinite regress, reverse direction, backward step (*or* motion), retroflexion (*or* retroflection), retrocession, retrogression, retrogradation, retroaction

▶ *221 Reversion*

11 **retreat**, motion from, recess, withdrawal, *reculade* (Fr), retirement, fallback, pullout, pullback, pulling (*or* falling *or* drawing) back, advance to the rear, disengagement, resigning, resignation

▶ *673 Submission*

12 **reversal**, reverse, reversing, reversion, inversion, backing, backing up (*or* off *or* out), backup, regurgitation, voidance, re-entrance, re-entry, turn of the tide, reflux, refluence, ebb

▶ *221 Reversion*

13 **about-turn**, about-face (US), *volte-face* (Fr), right-about, right-about-face, U-turn, turnaround, turnabout, swingaround, backtrack, backtracking, back trail

14 **decline**, fall off, ebb, falling away, drop, fall, slump, downturn, downward trend, deterioration
▶ *628 Deterioration*
15 **looking back**, reminiscing, harking-back, reminiscence, nostalgia
16 **countermotion**, counteraction, countermovement, countermarching, reversion, turn, turning point
17 **resilience**, reflex, elasticity, recoil, return to base (*or* starting point), circular argument
▶ *313 Circularity*
18 **setback**, backset, throwback, rollback
19 **backsliding**, lapse, relapse, recidivism, recidivation, sliding down the slippery slope, going down the tubes (*or* chute *or* drain *or* pan) (Inf)
20 **return**, home-coming, homeward journey
21 **backslider**, tergiversator, recidivist, failure, no-hoper (Sl)
▶ *683 Failure*

ADJECTIVES

22 **backward**, retrograde, retrogressive, retrocessive
23 **receding**, recessive, retreating, retractile, regressive, declining, ebbing, refluent, backsliding, lapsing, relapsing
24 **retroactive**, nostalgic, reactionary, backward-looking, retrospective
25 **reversed**, reverse, reversible, reflex, turned around, wrong way, wrong way round, counter, recoiling, counterclockwise (US), anticlockwise
26 **resilient**, elastic, reflexive
27 **returning**, homing, homeward-bound, remigrating

ADVERBS

28 **backward(s)**, hindward(s), in reverse, rearward(s), retrally, arear, astern, reflexively, back to where one started
29 **in reverse**, counterclockwise (US), anticlockwise, withershins (*or* widdershins) (Dial), against the grain, *à rebours* (Fr),

338　Propulsion

NOUNS

1 **propulsion**, impulsion, pulsion, propelling, propelment, drive, driving (*or* propulsive *or* propelling) force, momentum, motive power, thrust, impetus, push, shove, butt, bunt, shunt, kick, jaculation
▶ *330 Impulsion*
2 **method of propulsion**, steam propulsion, gas propulsion, petrol propulsion, diesel propulsion, diesel-electric propulsion, jet propulsion, turbojet propulsion, turboprop propulsion, rocket propulsion, pulsejet propulsion, plasmajet propulsion, ramjet propulsion, resojet propulsion, reaction propulsion, wind propulsion
▶ *70 Transport*
3 **throwing**, projection, trajection, jaculation, flinging, slinging, pelting, stone-throwing, precipitation, pitching, casting, hurling, lobbing, heaving, chucking (Inf)
4 **ejection**, expulsion, ejector seat, defenestration
5 **throw**, toss, pitch, pitch and toss, cast, bowl, fling, sling, swipe, shy, cockshy, hurl, chuck, chunk, lob, heave, flip, knock, peg (Inf), put, shot-put, pass, forward (*or* lateral) pass, kick, punt, dribble, throw-in, full toss (*or* pitch), yorker, stroke, drive, fastball, curve, upcurve, downcurve, sinker, slider, knuckle-ball, spitball, spitter, service, return, volley, smash, rally, kill, slice, pull
▶ *18 Sport*
6 **shooting**, gunnery, ballistics, artillery, firing, musketry, trapshooting, skeet, skeet shooting, archery, toxophily
7 **shot**, discharge, shooting, gunfire, gunshot, potshot, volley, fusillade, salvo, bombardment, cannonade, tattoo, spray, ejection, detonation, bowshot, stoneshot
▶ *670 Attack*
8 **missile**, projectile, weapon, ballistic missile, shot, small shot, grapeshot, grape, ball, pellet, bullet, slug, shell, mortar, cannon, cannonball, torpedo, Exocet, Scud, heat-seeking missile, rocket, trajectile, ejector, ejectamenta, arrow, dart, shaft, bolt, slingstone, slingshot, brickbat, stone
9 **firearm**, gun, shotgun, rifle, musket, blunderbus, double-barrelled shotgun, elephant gun, revolver, six-shooter, pistol, shooter (Inf), toy gun, pop gun, water gun (*or* pistol), blowpipe, peashooter, catapult, sling, mangonel, bow, longbow, crossbow
▶ *680 Weapon*
10 **ball**, tennis ball, hockey ball, golf ball, cricket ball, football, rugby ball, floater, bowl, wood, puck, curling stone, discus, shot, javelin, dart, arrow, quarrel, quoit, hammer, caber, snowball
11 **propeller**, prop, pedal, lever, oar, turbo, turbine, booster, thruster, propellant, propulsor, driver, screw, blade, wheel, paddle wheel, screw propeller, twin screws, fan, impeller, rotor, piston
12 **propellant**, driving force, energy, thrust, charge, explosive device, detonator, jet, steam, tail wind, following wind
13 **fuel**, coal, wood, peat, petrol, gas, oil, diesel, electricity, dynamite, cordite, guncotton, gunpowder, solid fuel, rocket fuel, nuclear fuel, hydrogen, helium
14 **thrower**, pitcher, hurler, heaver, tosser, flinger, slinger, bowler, shot-putter, javelin thrower, discus thrower, discobolus, snow-

baller, knife-thrower, server, striker, curler, stone-slinger, chucker (Inf)

15 **shooter**, marksman, markswoman, target shooter, shot, crack shot, good shot, dead shot, deadeye (Inf), gun, gunner, gunman, sniper, rifleman, musketeer, pistoleer, carabineer, cannoneer, artillery man, trapshooter

16 **archer**, toxophilite (Fml), bowman, hunter, Nimrod, Artemis, Sagittarius

ADJECTIVES

17 **propulsive**, propellant, propulsory, pulsive, propelling, motive, driving, shoving, pushing

18 **projectile**, trajectile, jaculatory, ejective, ballistic, missile, expulsive, explosive

19 **propelled**, petrol-propelled, diesel-propelled, jet-propelled, steam-propelled, gas-propelled, wind-propelled, self-propelled

VERBS

20 **propel**, push, shove, thrust, impel, launch, move, traject, project, jaculate, drive, kick, pedal, row, pole, treadle, wheel

21 **move forward**, advance, sweep, sweep before one, move on, hustle, drive, drive like leaves, put to flight, butt, bunt, shunt

22 **roll**, bowl, bowl a hoop, trundle, troll

23 **throw**, toss, pitch, cast, hurl, fling, sling, lob, heave, shy, york, catapult, pelt, lapidate, stone, shower, snowball, jerk, flip, snap, pass, serve, return, volley, slice, smash, put, put the shot, dart, lance, throw the javelin, tilt, chuck (Inf), peg (Inf), bung (Sl)

24 **push**, shove, send flying, send headlong, shoulder, ease along, fork, pitchfork, pitch forward

25 **eject**, expel, defenestrate

26 **bat**, slam, slog, drive, loft, cut, pull, glance, shank, slice, strike

27 **kick**, dribble, punt, pass

28 **shoot**, discharge, explode, fire, fire at, open fire, fire off, loose off, volley, fire a volley, volley and thunder, bombard, cannonade, detonate, let off, let fly, send off, gun, gun down, gun for (Inf), pistol, shoot at, pull the trigger, strike, hit, shoot down, fell, drop, blast, blow away, puff away, stop in one's tracks, draw a bead on, shower with arrows, plug (Sl)

▶ *670 Attack*

29 **riddle**, pepper, pelt, pump (*or* blast) full of lead (Sl)

30 **blow up**, fulminate, put dynamite under

31 **snipe**, pick off, pot, potshoot, potshot, take a pot shot, torpedo

32 **load**, prime, charge, cock, send off

33 **start**, start off (*or* up), give a start, set (*or* put) in motion, launch, set going, start going, set out on foot, start the ball rolling, kick off, bully off, bundle, bundle off, set afloat, float

ADVERBS

34 **forward**, onward, progressively, impulsively,

forcefully, powerfully, thrustingly, pushily, explosively, ballistically

339 Traction

NOUNS

1 **traction**, pulling, draught, drawing, heaving, tugging, pulling (*or* tractive) power, pulling back, retractiveness, retraction, retractility, retractability, towage, towing, haulage, hauling, drayage

2 **pull**, tug, tow, heave, draw, draught, haul, lug, drag, strain, trawl, tug of war, rowing

3 **jerk**, yerk (Dial), yank, twitch, sudden pull, tweak, pluck, wrench, snatch, hitch, start, bob, flip, flick, flirt, flounce, jig, jiggle, jolt, jog, joggle

▶ *366 Agitation*

4 **friction**, drag, grip, purchase, adhesion

▶ *138 Adhesion*

5 **magnetism**, attraction, pulling towards, drawing power, charisma

▶ *340 Attraction*

6 **towline**, towrope, drawer, puller, tower, hauler, haulier, dragnet, windlass, tugboat, tractor, traction engine, locomotive

7 **magnet**, magnetizer, lodestone (*or* loadstone)

ADJECTIVES

8 **tractional**, tractive, pulling, drawing, hauling, tugging, towing, pulling back, attracting, drawn, horse-drawn

9 **retractive**, retractable, retractile, ductile

10 **magnetic**, attractive, charismatic

VERBS

11 **pull**, haul, draw, heave, tow, take in tow, hale, lug, tug, trail, train, trice, warp, kedge

12 **drag**, trawl, dredge, winch, reel in, wind in, wind up, lift, tug, draggle, snake, troll, rake, rake in, rake out, drag up, elevate, drag down

13 **pull at**, pull out, tug, yank, jerk, tweak, yerk (Dial), twitch, pluck, snatch, snatch at, wrench, hitch, flip, flick, flirt, flounce, jig, jiggle, jolt, joggle, jog

14 **draw in**, draw back, retract, withdraw, sheathe, pull back, pull in

15 **pull towards**, attract, magnetize, spellbind

▶ *11 Occultism*

ADVERBS

16 **magnetically**, charismatically, attractively, adhesively, retractably

340 Attraction

NOUNS

1 **attraction**, attractiveness, attractivity, attractance, attractancy, mutual attraction, pull, draw, drag, tug, itch, desire, affinity, sympathy

▶ *339 Traction, 782 Desire*

2 **pulling power**, magnetism, magnetization, gravity, force of gravity, centripetal force, cap-

illarity, capillary attraction, adhesion, cohesion, adduction, inducement, hypnotism, mesmerism

3 **magnet**, bar magnet, horseshoe magnet, coil magnet, electromagnet, field magnet, artificial magnet, solenoid, paramagnet, magnetic needle, lodestone (*or* loadstone), lodestar, pole star, magnetite, siderite, magnetized iron
▶ *56 Physics, 54 Earth Science*

4 **allurement**, allure, fascination, charm, charisma, seduction, seductiveness, temptation, appeal, enticement, sex appeal, animal magnetism (Inf), come-on (Inf), pull (Inf)

5 **lure**, bait, decoy, charm, siren, siren song, snare

6 **charmer**, temptress, seductress, seducer, enchantress, enchanter, vamp, *femme fatale* (Fr), Lothario, ladies' man, Don Juan, Casanova, favourite, siren, Circe, Adonis, sex symbol, screen idol, teen idol, man-eater (Sl), foxy lady (US sl), stud (Sl), hunk (Inf)

7 **centre of attraction**, centre of attention, focal point, cynosure, focus, centre
▶ *318 Prominence, 158 Middle*

ADJECTIVES

8 **attracting**, pulling, drawing, dragging, tugging, adductive, associative, adducent

9 **attractive**, seductive, enticing, tempting, charming, fascinating, captivating, charismatic, irresistible, alluring, fetching, appealing, good-looking, sexually attractive, sexy (Inf), dishy (Inf), hunky (Inf)
▶ *789 Beauty, 782 Desire*

10 **magnetic**, magnetized, gravitational, centripetal, convergent, inductive, influential

VERBS

11 **attract**, pull, draw, adduct, drag, tug, have an attraction, draw towards, influence, persuade, magnetize, be magnetic, exercise a pull, pull towards, appeal, charm, move, pluck at one's heartstrings, induce
▶ *233 Influence*

12 **lure**, allure, draw in, coax, bait, ensnare, seduce, decoy, lead on, tempt, entice, tantalize, fascinate, captivate, enthral, hypnotize, mesmerize

ADVERBS

13 **attractionally**, attractively, centripetally, adhesively, cohesively inductively, magnetically, mesmerically, hypnotically, irresistibly

14 **attractively**, influentially, sympathetically, appealingly, charismatically, charmingly, enchantingly, seductively, sexily (Inf)

341   Repulsion

VERBS

1 **repel**, drive (*or* push *or* put) away, head off, repulse, turn back, drive (*or* push *or* thrust) back, chase off (*or* away), reject, rebuff, snub,

cold-shoulder, slight, cut, spurn, refuse, say no to, reject someone's advances, show someone the door, give someone the bird, make someone keep his (*or* her) distance, brush off (Inf)
▶ *581 Rejection*

2 **eject**, expel, throw out, send packing, pack off, send someone about his (*or* her) business, give someone his (*or* her) marching (*or* walking) orders, dismiss, sack (Inf), boot out (Inf)
▶ *349 Expulsion*

3 **fend off**, deflect, ward off, keep at bay, put off, head off, parry, keep at arm's length, beat (*or* fight) off, make unwelcome, send someone off with a flea in his (*or* her) ear
▶ *231 Counteraction*

4 **be repulsive**, disgust, revolt, sicken, nauseate, repel, upset, offend, appal, turn one's stomach, make one's gorge rise
▶ *764 Unpleasantness*

NOUNS

5 **repulsion**, repellence, repellency, repelling, ugliness, repellent quality, repulsiveness, recoil, mutual repulsion, repulsive force, centrifugal force, polarization, disaffinity, magnetic repulsion, diamagnetism, antigravity
▶ *790 Ugliness, 111 Oppositeness, 56 Physics*

6 **repulse**, rebuff, dismissal, snub, cut, cold shoulder, spurning, refusal, rejection, ejection, expulsion, brush-off (Inf), the big E (Sl)
▶ *581 Rejection, 349 Expulsion*

7 **deflection**, defence, foil, counterstroke, parry, counterattack, resistance
▶ *671 Defence, 669 Resistance*

ADJECTIVES

8 **repulsive**, repellent, repugnant, offensive, noisome, off-putting, antipathetic, ugly, abhorrent, obnoxious, disgusting, nauseating, sickening, foul, loathsome, horrible, appalling, hideous, obscene
▶ *764 Unpleasantness, 790 Ugliness*

9 **abducent**, abductive, centrifugal, repelling, diamagnetic, of opposite polarity
▶ *56 Physics*

10 **defensive**, resistant, hostile, dismissive
▶ *671 Defence, 669 Resistance, 581 Rejection*

ADVERBS

11 **repulsively**, repellently, repugnantly, offensively, antipathetically, abhorrently, noisomely, obnoxiously, horribly, hideously, obscenely

12 **defensively**, resistantly, dismissively, against

342   Convergence

NOUNS

1 **convergence**, converging, confluence, conflux, concurrence, concourse, collision, mutual approach, concentration, meeting, coming together
▶ *116 Accord*

2 **approach**, advance, confrontation, collision course, narrowing gap

3 **convergent view**, perspective, vanishing point (*or* line *or* plane)

4 **meeting place**, congress, congregation, assembly, union, junction, crossing
▶ *161 Assembly, 135 Union*

5 **focus**, centre, hub, pivot, centring, coming to the point, concentralization, focalization, asymptote, converging line, radius, tangent, spokes
▶ *158 Middle*

6 **narrowing**, narrowing gap, taper, tapering, funnel, bottleneck
▶ *272 Narrowness*

ADJECTIVES

7 **convergent**, converging, confluent, uniting, concurrent, meeting, focal, focusing, focused, confocal, centrolineal, centripetal, asymptotic(al), radial, radiating, tangent, tangential, centring, pointed, tapering, narrowing, conical, pyramidal, knock-kneed

8 **advancing**, oncoming, approaching, mutually approaching, connivent

VERBS

9 **converge**, close in, approach, draw near, intersect, be on a collision course, narrow the gap, close with, close, close up, funnel, taper, pinch, nip
▶ *135 Union, 336 Forward Motion, 272 Narrowness*

10 **come together**, assemble, congregate, concentrate, gather, cluster, run together, meet, unite, fall in with, get together, roll up, roll in, pour in
▶ *135 Union*

11 **focus**, bring into focus, centre, home in, zero in, centralize, taper, concentralize, concentre, come to a focus, concentrate, corradiate, come to the point

ADVERBS

12 **convergently**, confluently, concurrently, congruently, mutually, together

343 Divergence

NOUNS

1 **divergence**, divergency, divarication, aberration, declination, deviation, difference, contradiction, contrariety
▶ *115 Dissimilarity, 335 Deviation, 476 Refutation*

2 **parting**, moving (*or* going) apart, drifting apart, spread, spreading out, splaying, fanning, fanning out, deployment, separation, centrifugence, division, decentralization
▶ *136 Separation*

3 **radiation**, ray, radius, spoke, radiance, scattering, diffusion, dispersion, emanation
▶ *162 Dispersion*

4 **branching**, branching out, ramification, arborescence, arborization, treelikeness, forking,

furcation, bifurcation, biforking, trifurcation, triforking, parting of the ways, intersection, crossroads, crossing

5 **fork**, prong, trident, branch, Y-shape, V-shape, stem, offshoot, fan, delta, groin, inguen, furcula, furculum, wishbone

ADJECTIVES

6 **divergent**, diverging, divaricate, separated, separate, aberrant, different, contradictory, centrifugal, deviating
▶ *335 Deviation, 136 Separation, 115 Dissimilarity*

7 **radiating**, radial, radiate(d), radiant, rayed, spoked
▶ *162 Dispersion*

8 **fanlike**, fan-shaped, deltoid(al), delta-like, delta-shaped, palmate(d), splayed, spread-eagled

9 **branched**, branching, arborescent, arboreal, arboriform, treelike, tree-shaped, dendriform, dendritic, branchlike, ramose, ramous, Y-shaped, V-shaped, forking, forked, furcate, forklike, biforked, bifurcate(d), trifurcate(d), pronged, trident-like

VERBS

10 **diverge**, divaricate, aberrate, deviate

11 **move apart**, part, spread, spread out (*or* apart), outspread, fan, fan out, deploy, go off (*or* away)

12 **separate**, divide, splay, splay apart, go separate ways, split, split off, part company, be disjoined
▶ *136 Separation*

13 **radiate**, ray, diffuse, emanate, disperse, scatter
▶ *162 Dispersion*

14 **branch**, stem, ramify, branch off (*or* out), spread-eagle, straddle, step wide, fork, furcate, bifurcate, trifurcate

15 **change direction**, switch, fly (*or* go) off at a tangent, glance, fly off

ADVERBS

16 **divergently**, apart, radiantly, radially, diffusely, ramosely, ramously, aberrantly, differently, separately

344 Arrival

VERBS

1 **arrive**, appear, come, make (*or* put in) an appearance, be present, be found, turn up, show up (Inf), roll up (Inf), drop in (Inf), blow in (Inf), pop up (Inf), bob up (Inf), hit (Inf), hit town (Inf)
▶ *457 Appearance*

2 **reach**, reach there, get there, get to, come to, fetch, fetch up in (*or* at), end up in (*or* at), make it, reach one's destination (*or* goal), come to one's journey's end, find, discover, arrive at (*or* upon), come upon, strike upon, hit upon, fall upon, light upon, pitch upon, stumble upon

(*or* on), come to rest, finish the race, breast the tape, be in at the death, be received

▶ *496 Discovery*

3 **approach**, draw up, sight, stand at the door, be on the threshold, knock at the door, look for a welcome

4 **land**, make port, put into port, dock, beach, berth, moor, tie up, drop anchor, ground, run aground, make a landfall, set foot on dry land, step (*or* go) ashore, disembark, debark, unboat, alight, touch down, disemplane, deplane, get off, detrain, debus, dismount, get down, unharness, unhitch, quit the saddle, emerge, surrender one's ticket, home, return, come (*or* get *or* return) home, perch, discharge, unload

5 **get in**, come in, set foot in, enter, burst upon, make an entrance, check in, clock in, punch in, ring in, sign in

▶ *346 Entry*

6 **stop at**, visit, put in, pull in, stop over, stop off, break one's journey, pause

7 **be brought**, be delivered, come to hand

8 **meet**, join, rejoin, see again, go (*or* come) to meet, be at the station, keep a date, rendezvous, come upon (*or* across), encounter, come into contact, run into (*or* across), bump into, meet by chance, butt into, knock into, collide with, gather, assemble, congregate

▶ *161 Assembly*

9 **achieve**, accomplish, attain, gain, succeed, be successful, prosper, get to the top, reach the top, get ahead, make good, make it (Inf), make the grade (Inf), get somewhere (Inf), get there (Inf)

▶ *682 Success, 686 Prosperity*

NOUNS

10 **arrival**, coming, advent, approach, onset, advance, appearance, entrance, emergence, presence, debut, beginning

▶ *156 Beginning, 346 Entry*

11 **landing**, landfall, docking, touchdown, mooring, disembarkation, disembarkment, debarkation, coming (*or* going) ashore, tying up, dropping (*or* weighing) anchor

12 **reception**, hospitality, welcome, greeting, handshake, aloha, hello

▶ *815 Sociability*

13 **return**, homecoming, coming back, recursion, re-entrance, re-entry, prodigal's return

14 **meeting**, encounter, recounter, rejoining, rendezvous, meeting place

15 **destination**, goal, objective, bourn (Arch), terra firma, harbour, haven, home, end, stop, last stop, terminal point, point of arrival, journey's end, end of the line, terminus, terminal, stopping place, arrival at the winning post, finish, close finish, photo finish, last lap, port, aerodrome, airport, heliport, air terminal, depot, junction, railway station

▶ *157 End*

16 **stopover**, stage, halt, billet, shelter, dock, port in a storm, dry dock, berth, stable

17 **achievement**, accomplishment, attainment, accession, fulfilment, reaching, making

▶ *682 Success*

ADJECTIVES

18 **arriving**, incoming, immigrant, entering, emerging, appearing

▶ *346 Entry, 457 Appearance*

19 **approaching**, impending, imminent, oncoming, advancing, coming, incoming, inbound, inwardbound, homeward, homewardbound, nearing, terminal

▶ *156 Beginning*

20 **attainable**, achievable, approachable, accessible, get-at-able (Inf)

21 **welcoming**, inviting, hospitable

▶ *815 Sociability*

ADVERBS

22 **on arrival**, on the doorstep (*or* threshold), at the door, here, home, back home, home again, aground, ashore, at journey's end

INTERJECTIONS

23 **hello!**, hail!, hi!, hiya!, *ciao*! (It), *salut*! (Fr), how do you do?, how are you?, alright? (Inf)

24 **welcome!**, greetings!, (do) come in!, make yourself at home!, have a seat!, help yourself!

345 Departure

Come, dear children, let us away;/ Down and away below. Matthew Arnold.

Once I leave, I leave. I am not going to speak to the man on the bridge, and I am not going to spit on the deck. Stanley Baldwin.

VERBS

1 **depart**, leave, take (*or* make) one's leave, take (*or* make) one's departure, go, go away, get away, get away (*or* off), get (*or* go) along, make tracks, go (*or* get) on, toddle along, trot along, stagger along, gang along (Scot), walk away, slink off, slope off, flounce off (*or* out), fling off (*or* out), leave in high dudgeon, stamp off, storm out, up and go (Inf), mosey along (Inf), push off (Inf), clear off (Inf), buzz off (Inf), piss off (Tab sl), fuck off (Tab sl), bugger off (Tab sl), sod (*or* bog *or* mog) off (Sl)

2 **withdraw**, retreat, beat a retreat, turn back, turn one's back on, pull out, exit, make one's exit, leave the stage, bow out, leave work, clock out, punch out, cease work, retire, receive a golden handshake, resign, sign off, sign out, check out, vacate, evacuate, abandon, relinquish, die, depart this life, pass away, pass over

▶ *337 Backward Motion, 347 Exit, 705 Resignation, 218 Cessation, 598 Relinquishment, 397 Death*

3 **quit**, quit the scene, leave the country, emigrate, expatriate, move house, remove, relo-

cate, leave home, leave the nest, leave the neighbourhood, disappear, vanish, leave no trace, take wing, slip away, elope, escape, give someone the slip, abscond, absent oneself, march out, debouch, decamp, break camp, strike camp (or tent), up sticks, pull up stakes, sling one's hook (Sl), flit (Inf), do a moonlight flit (Inf)

▶ *638 Escape, 458 Disappearance, 254 Absence*

4 **hurry off**, move fast, take off, make off, run away, run off, flee, bolt, take flight (or wing), take to one's heels, run for one's life, cut and run, decamp, absquatulate, rush off, hasten off, scamper away, skip, skip off, dash, dash off, nip, nip off, whip off, whiz off, tear off (or out), cut, cut away, make oneself scarce, beetle off-(Inf), vamoose (Sl), skedaddle (Inf), scarper (Sl), beat it (Sl), scram (Inf), hightail (Inf), split (Sl), lam (US sl), take it on the lam (US sl), take a powder (US sl)

▶ *648 Haste*

5 **set out**, set forth (or forward), put (or go) forth, be off, be on one's way, emerge, sally forth, issue, issue forth, start, start out (or off), strike out, get off, move off, march off, march away, embark, board, entrain, embus, enplane, emplane, go aboard (or on board), jump on, hop on, mount, set sail, spread sail, spread canvas, hoist the Blue Peter, weigh anchor, unmoor, cast off, drop the pilot, push off, put to sea, get under way, leave land behind, take off, pull out of the station, hit the road (Inf)

▶ *70 Transport, 156 Beginning, 347 Exit, 349 Expulsion*

6 **part**, separate, part company, take (or break) oneself off, tear oneself away, take one's leave, say farewell, bid farewell, bid (or say) goodbye (or goodnight or Godspeed), make one's adieus, wave goodbye, speed the parting guest, give someone a good sendoff, have one for the road

NOUNS

7 **departure**, leaving, going, going away, exit, egress, exodus, emigration, migration, Hegira (or Hejira), flight, escape, getaway, flit, moonlight flit, elopement, decampment, abandonment, withdrawal, retreat, retirement, evacuation, pulling out, remigration, going back, return

▶ *337 Backward Motion, 347 Exit, 638 Escape*

8 **start**, starting, startoff, outset, embarkation, embarkment, boarding, going on board, entrainment, enplanement, emplanement, takeoff, ascent, liftoff, blastoff, zero hour

▶ *156 Beginning, 70 Transport*

9 **parting**, separation, leavetaking, leave, congé, farewell, goodbye, goodnight, adieu, one's adieus, parting shot, valediction, valedictory, valedictory address, farewell address,

last words, funeral oration, obituary, epitaph, last post, last handshake, golden handshake, dismissal, viaticum, one for the road, nightcap, stirrup cup, deoch-an-doruis (or doch-andoris) (Scot), sendoff (Inf)

10 **place of departure**, port, dock, place of embarkation, airport, gate, station, railway station, departure platform, bus station, bus stop, starting point, outset, base, springboard, jumping-off point

▶ *70 Transport*

ADJECTIVES

11 **departing**, leaving, farewell, valedictory, parting, leave-taking, last, final

12 **departed**, gone, gone away, gone off, left

13 **outgoing**, outward-bound, emigratory

INTERJECTIONS

14 **goodbye!**, goodnight!, farewell!, adieu!, *au revoir!* (Fr), *auf Wiedersehn* (Ger), *ciao!* (It), *adios!* (Sp), so long!, bye-bye!, bye!, cheerio!, see you!, see you later!, have a nice day!, bon voyage!, cheers!

15 **go!**, go away!, begone!, never darken my door again!, get thee hence! (Arch), get out!, clear out!, shoo! (Inf), get lost! (Sl), get going! (Sl), shove off! (Sl), push off! (Sl), clear off! (Sl), buzz off! (Sl), piss off! (Tab sl), naff off! (Sl), sod off! (Sl), bog off! (Sl), bugger off! (Sl), fuck off! (Tab sl), beat it! (Sl), scram! (Sl), vamoose! (Sl), get! (Sl), git! (Sl)

346 Entry

1 **entry**, entrance, ingress, ingression, intergression, *entrée* (Fr), access, incoming, ingoing, import, input, re-entry, re-entrance, admission, reception, enrolment, enlistment, induction, initiation, introduction, debut, appearance, arrival

▶ *348 Admittance, 326 Transfer, 344 Arrival, 457 Appearance*

2 **influx**, inflow, flood, inflooding, stream, indraught, inhalation, indrawing, indrawal, intake, inrush, inrun, afflux, affluxion, affluence

3 **inroad**, encroachment, insertion, penetration, interpenetration, insinuation, infiltration, percolation, seepage, leakage, intrusion, invasion, forced entry, raid, irruption, incursion, attack, illegal entry, trespassing, housebreaking, breaking and entering, burglary

▶ *354 Insertion, 670 Attack, 153 Disturbance*

4 **right of entry**, non-restriction, admission, admittance, access, permission, permit, ticket, pass, passport, visa, immigration, inmigration, foreign influx, importation, importing, trade, free trade, free port, open-door policy, free market, expansionism

▶ *348 Admittance, 708 Permission, 737 Trade, 740 Market*

5 **entrance**, way in, entry, access, inlet, ingress,

approach, adit, mouth, opening, orifice, conduit, channel, passage

▶ *322 Opening, 327 Way, 356 Passage*

6 **means of entry** (*or* **access**), porch, propylaeum, portico, portal, porte-cochere, doorway, threshold, lintel, doorpost (*or* -jamb), door, front door, side door, French door (*or* window), patio door, back door, postern, storm door, cellar door, trap door, hatch, hatchway, scuttle, gate, gateway, gate post, lychgate, archway, tollgate, turnstile, turnpike, stile, lobby, vestibule, foyer

7 **entrant**, incomer, comer, arrival, visitor, visitant, caller, guest, immigrant, inmigrant, newcomer, new face, new member, new boy, new girl, intake, beginner, debutante, settler, colonist, competitor, contender, ticketholder, cardholder, audience, house

▶ *156 Beginning, 815 Sociability, 674 Contention*

8 **intruder**, invader, raider, attacker, gatecrasher, unwelcome guest, trespasser, burglar, housebreaker, picklock, thief

▶ *153 Disturbance, 736 Stealing*

VERBS

9 **enter**, go in (*or* into), come in (*or* into), get in (*or* into), gain admittance, be admitted, open the door, let oneself in, cross the threshold, set foot in, arrive, make an entrance, visit, call, call in, look in, pop in, find one's way into, have an in, turn into, put in (*or* into), board, embark, go aboard, mount

▶ *348 Admittance, 815 Sociability, 344 Arrival*

10 **invade**, irrupt, raid, attack, storm, escalade, encroach, trespass, gate-crash, barge in, rush in, burst in, storm in, butt in, interrupt, muscle in, horn in, outstay one's welcome, put one's foot in it, break in, break and enter, pick the lock, burgle

▶ *153 Disturbance*

11 **infiltrate**, permeate, percolate, filter in, soak in, leak in, seep, drip, work (*or* worm) one's way into, insinuate, creep in, slip in, sneak in, slink in, penetrate, interpenetrate, break through, get (*or* pass *or* go) through, bore in, pierce, puncture, insert, bite into, eat into, cut into

▶ *354 Insertion*

12 **flood in**, inflood, flow in, inflow, rush in, inrush, pour in, swarm in, pack in, crowd in, throng in, press in, cram in, squeeze in, wedge in, jam in, congregate

▶ *161 Assembly*

13 **fall into**, drop into, plunge into, dive into, sink into

▶ *360 Descent, 362 Lowering*

14 **enrol**, join, admit, take in, enlist, inscribe, sign on, enter for, contend, induct, initiate, introduce, immigrate, settle, settle in, colonize

▶ *674 Contention, 156 Beginning*

ADJECTIVES

15 **entering**, ingressive, inward, incoming, in-

going, inbound, immigrant, imported, allowed in, homing

16 **invasive**, incursive, intrusive, trespassing, attacking, penetrating, irruptive, ingrowing, inflowing, inflooding, inpouring, inrushing

ADVERBS

17 **in**, inward(s), inwardly, invasively, intrusively, incursively

PREPOSITIONS

18 **into**, in, to

347   Exit

NOUNS

1 **exit**, egress, egression, going out, outgoing, outgo, coming out, outcoming, outcome, emergence, emerging, emersion, issue, issuance, extrusion, exodus, departure, walk-out, walk-off, evacuation, outbreak, breakout, eruption, proruption, outburst

▶ *345 Departure, 355 Extraction, 349 Expulsion*

2 **outflow**, outflowing, outpouring, outpour, flood, inundation, spill, waste, effluence, effusion, outflux, efflux, effluxion, defluxion, outfall, waterfall, gush, gushing, stream, streaming, jet, fountain, well, spring, gusher, exhaust, emission, discharge, emanation, exudation, secretion, voidance, excretion, evaporation, perspiration, sweating, sweat, transudation, diaphoresis, running sore, streaming eyes, runny nose, haemorrhage

▶ *353 Excretion, 607 Waste*

3 **leakage**, leak, leaking, seepage, seep, seeping, drip, dripping, dribble, dribbling, trickle, trickling, filtration, filtering, exfiltration, straining, percolation, percolating, leaching, lixiviation, effusion, extravasation, ooze, oozing, weep, weeping

4 **emigration**, outmigration, migration, expatriation, deportation, exile, expulsion, dismissal

▶ *349 Expulsion*

5 **export**, exporting, exportation, transference, outgoings, outlay, expenditure, spending, loss

▶ *737 Trade, 326 Transfer, 748 Expenditure, 722 Loss*

6 **way out**, exit, egress, door, back door, gate, outgate, port, emergency exit, fire escape, escape hatch, escape route, path, avenue, channel, loophole

▶ *638 Escape, 327 Way*

7 **outlet**, outfall, chute, spout, tap, drain, drainpipe, gutter, conduit, gargoyle, overflow, flume, sluice, weir, floodgate, opening, orifice, vent, ventage, venthole, pore, blowhole, spiracle, anus

▶ *322 Opening, 356 Passage*

8 **outgoer**, goer, leaver, departer, emigrant, émigré (Fr), outmigrant, migrant, colonist, settler, expellee, exile, expatriate, remittance man

VERBS

9 exit, make an (or one's) exit, egress, go, leave, depart, withdraw, go out, pass out, get out, walk out, run out, pop out, march out, bow out, walk off, die, pass over
▶ 345 Departure, 397 Death

10 emerge, come out, issue, issue forth, debouch, sally, sally forth, emanate, effuse, come out in the open, appear, surface, arise, erupt, break out, break forth, project, protrude, jut, break cover, burst out, escape, evacuate, bale out, jump out
▶ 457 Appearance, 359 Ascent, 638 Escape

11 run out, drain, drain out, flow out, outflow, flood, flood out, inundate, pour, outpour, pour out, disembogue, surge, well out (or up or over), gush, gush out, jet, spurt, spurt out, spout, spout out, vomit, spew, spew out, blow out, overflow, spill, spill over, slop, slop over

12 leak, leak out, drip, dribble, trickle, seep, seep out, weep, ooze, ooze out, extravasate, filter, filtrate, exfiltrate, strain, percolate, leach, lixiviate, effuse, drivel, drool, slaver, slobber, salivate, water at the mouth, emanate, exude, emit, discharge, secrete, excrete, exudate, perspire, sweat, exhale, breathe out
▶ 353 Excretion

13 emigrate, outmigrate, migrate, expatriate, deport, exile, expel, dismiss, export, send abroad
▶ 349 Expulsion

14 be dismissed, leave, resign, retire, walk out, get the boot (Inf), get the sack (Inf), get fired (Inf), get the bird (Inf)
▶ 349 Expulsion

ADJECTIVES

15 outgoing, outbound, outward-bound, going, departing, leaving, forthcoming, issuing, egressive, emerging, emergent, coming out, arising, surfacing, erupting, eruptive, volcanic, explosive, expulsive, emanating, emanent, emanative, transeunt, transient
▶ 189 Transience

16 outflowing, outpouring, effluent, effusive, effused, extravasated, expended, spent

17 leaky, oozy, weeping, runny, excretory, porous, permeable, exudative, transudative

ADVERBS

18 forth, out, outward(s), apart, away, outwardly, effusively, eruptively, explosively

PREPOSITIONS

19 out of, from

348 Admittance

NOUNS

1 admittance, admission, readmission, taking in, receipt, receiving, reception, acceptance, import, importing, importation, introception, immission, intromission, insertion, interjection, invitation, inclusion, interjacence
▶ 730 Receiving, 354 Insertion, 146 Inclusion, 298 Interface

2 receptivity, receptiveness, openness, recipience, recipiency, hospitality, welcome, welcoming, effusive welcome, welcoming with open arms, refuge, sanctuary, asylum, shelter, protection, open door, access, entrance, entrée, entry
▶ 815 Sociability, 632 Safety, 346 Entry

3 introduction, bringing in, initiation, baptism, rite of passage, enrolment, investiture, ordination, induction, registration, enlistment, instatement, installation, inauguration, naturalization, admissibility, acceptability
▶ 156 Beginning

4 intake, indrawal, indraught, engulfing, engulfment, ingestion, consumption, eating, drinking, fluid intake, imbibition, ingurgitation, engorgement, swallow, swallowing, gulp, gulping, suck, sucking, suction, aspiration, respiration, breathing in, inspiration, inhalement, inhalation, sniff, sniffing, snuff, snuffle, sniffle, slurp (Inf), slurping (Inf)
▶ 350 Eating, 351 Drinking, 411 Taste, 416 Odour

5 absorption, adsorption, sorption, chemisorption, resorption, digestion, engrossment, assimilation, incorporation, absorbency, resorbence, sponging, blotting, seeping, percolation, osmosis, endosmosis, exosmosis

6 sponge, blotter, blotting paper, chromatography paper, absorbent, adsorbent

VERBS

7 admit, receive, take in, include, readmit, let in, allow in, allow access, give a ticket (or pass) to, give admittance (or entrance) to, intromit, open the door to, open the hatches, insert, import, bring in
▶ 730 Receiving, 146 Inclusion, 354 Insertion

8 show in, usher, usher in, introduce, go before, come before, send in
▶ 154 Precedence

9 welcome, embrace, adopt, accept, fling wide the gates, welcome with open arms, put the flags out, invite, call in, give refuge to, give sanctuary to, grant asylum, naturalize, shelter, accommodate, protect, safeguard
▶ 815 Sociability, 632 Safety

10 introduce, bring in, initiate, baptize, register, inscribe, enlist, take on, install, inaugurate, enrol, invest, ordain, show the ropes (Inf)

11 ingest, eat, imbibe, drink, drink up (or in), lap up, engulf, engorge, ingurgitate, swallow, gulp, gulp down, wolf down, gobble, slurp (Inf)
▶ 350 Eating, 351 Drinking, 411 Taste

12 draw in, suck, suck in (or up), suckle, aspirate, respire, inhale, inspire, breathe in, sniff, sniffle, snuff, snuffle, smell, scent, scent (or

smell) out, detect

▶ *416 Odour*

13 **absorb**, adsorb, sorb, chemisorb, digest, incorporate, assimilate, internalize, engross, take up, blot, blot up, soak, soak up, sponge, osmose, soak in, seep in, permeate, percolate, infiltrate, reabsorb, resorb

ADJECTIVES

14 **admissive**, admissory, admissible, acceptable, suitable, receivable, receptible, introceptive, intromissive, intromittent

15 **receptive**, recipient, open, accessible, welcoming, hospitable, inviting, invitatory

16 **introductory**, introductive, initiatory, initiative, baptismal

17 **absorbent**, absorptive, adsorbent, sorbent, chemisorptive, assimilative, digestive, ingestive, imbibitory, bibulous, soaking, blotting, spongy, spongeous, osmotic, endosmotic, exosmotic

ADVERBS

18 **receptively**, welcomingly, hospitably, invitingly, with open arms

349 Expulsion

VERBS

1 **expel**, eject, put out, turn out, throw out, cast out, toss out, heave out, hustle out, show someone the door, bounce (Sl), chuck out (Inf), turf out (Inf), kick out (Inf), boot out (Inf), give the bum's rush (US sl), give the old heave-ho (Inf), throw out on one's ear (Inf)

▶ *338 Propulsion*

2 **dismiss**, discharge, disemploy, suspend, lay off, furlough (US), make redundant, drop, let go, release, let out, retire, superannuate, pension off, sack (Inf), give the sack (Inf), fire (Inf), give one's marching orders (*or* walking papers) (Inf), kick out (Inf), boot out (Inf), give the boot (Sl), give the hook (US sl), axe (Inf), give the axe (Inf), kick upstairs (Inf)

3 **disbar**, excommunicate, unfrock, defrock, strip, deplume, displume, disqualify, strike off, strike off the roll, drum out, cashier, depose, dethrone, expel, suspend, send down, rusticate, demote, degrade, downgrade, relegate, bust (US), kick downstairs (Inf)

▶ *879 Punishment*

4 **ostracize**, exclude, seclude, blackball, spurn, snub, cut, send to Coventry, give the silent treatment, brush off, give the cold shoulder, make unwelcome, outlaw, fugitate, ban, proscribe, prohibit, banish, rusticate, exile, expatriate, repatriate, deport, transport, extradite, send away

▶ *147 Exclusion, 581 Rejection, 816 Unsociability*

5 **take the place of**, usurp, supplant, supersede, substitute, replace, displace

▶ *222 Substitution, 252 Displacement*

6 **send away**, send off, see off, order off (*or* away), turn away, bundle away, bundle off, pack off, send about one's business, send to the showers, shake off, shoo off (*or* away), send away with a flea in one's ear (Inf), send packing (Inf)

7 **drive out**, drum out, chase out, rout out, push out, force out, hunt out, smoke out, freeze out, drive into the open, run out of town, ride on a rail

8 **evict**, oust, remove, dispossess, repossess, expropriate, deprive, dislodge, extirpate, uproot, put out, turn out, turn out of doors, turn out of house and home, turn (*or* put) out bag and baggage, unhouse, unkennel

▶ *734 Taking*

9 **depopulate**, unpeople, depeople, dispeople, desolate, devastate

▶ *398 Killing*

10 **exterminate**, do away with, purge, liquidate, dispel, eradicate, root out, deracinate, eliminate, get rid of, reject, throw off, cast off, fling off, shake off, shed, destroy, rub out, erase, obliterate, exorcise

▶ *546 Obliteration, 581 Rejection*

11 **void**, evacuate, eliminate, remove, deplete, exhaust, empty, empty out, vent, drain, drink up, drain to the dregs, siphon off, pump out, clear out, clean out, curette, purge, gut, disembowel, eviscerate, draw, bone, fillet, unclog, unfoul, blow, blow out, clear off, clear away, sweep out, make a clean sweep, clear the decks

12 **unload**, unburden, disburden, off-load, unlade, unpack, discharge, dump, unship

13 **throw away**, throw out, jettison, throw overboard, discard, scrap, precipitate, defenestrate, get rid of, rid oneself of, junk (Inf), bin (Sl), get shot (*or* shut) of (Sl)

▶ *727 Disposal*

14 **let out**, give out (*or* off), emit, send out, radiate, emit rays, perfume, scent, exhaust, give vent to, exhale, expire, respire, breathe (out), let one's breath out, blow, puff, fume, smoke, reek, steam, vaporize, stream, turn on the tap, open the flood (*or* sluice) gates, disgorge, debouch, disembogue, discharge, ejaculate, cast forth, cast out, send forth, extrude, detrude, obtrude, erupt, eruct, blow out, pour out, outpour, spew, spout, jet, spurt, squirt, sputter, splutter, extravasate, bleed, defecate, urinate, excrete, egest, secrete, sweat, perspire, ooze, suppurate, dribble, drool, slaver, slobber

▶ *353 Excretion, 347 Exit, 338 Propulsion*

15 **vomit**, spew, regurgitate, spit, spit out, bring up, be sick, retch, heave, gag, puke (Sl), barf (US sl), throw up (Inf), sick up (Inf), chuck up (Sl), upchuck (Sl), shoot (*or* toss) one's cookies (US sl), shoot a cat (Sl), cat (Sl), cry (*or* call for) Hughie (*or* Ralph) (Sl), talk on the big white telephone (Sl), chunder (Sl)

16 belch, hiccup, eruct, eructate, fart, break wind, blow a raspberry, burp (Inf), gurk (Sl), drop one (Sl), drop one's guts (Sl), blow off (Sl), let rip (Sl)

NOUNS

17 expulsion, ejection, ejectment, throwing out, rejection, propulsion, kicking out (Inf), booting out (Inf), the push (Inf), the bounce (Sl), the chuck (Inf), the boot (Sl), the bum's rush (US sl), the old heave-ho (Inf)

18 dismissal, discharge, congé, suspension, laying off, furlough (US), redundancy, drumming out, cashiering, demotion, degradation, relegation, stripping, depluming, displuming, externment, exclusion, excommunication, unfrocking, defrocking, disqualification, disfellowship, striking off, the sack (Inf), sacking (Inf), firing (Inf), axing (Inf), the axe (Inf), the boot (Sl), the gate (Inf), one's marching orders (Inf), one's walking papers (Inf), one's cards (Inf), pink slip (US inf)

19 ostracism, ostracization, exclusion, seclusion, blackballing, sending to Coventry, the cold shoulder, the brushoff, outlawing, outlawry, fugitation, banning, proscription, banishment, rustication, exile, exilement, expatriation, repatriation, deportation, transportation, extradition

20 eviction, ousting, removal, dispossession, repossession, expropriation, deprivation, dislodgment, throwing overboard, jettison, precipitation, defenestration, unloading, offloading

21 removal, elimination, evacuation, voidance, voiding, clearance, clearing, clearage, cleaning out, scouring out, purging, purgation, catharsis, unfouling, emptying, depletion, exhaustion, draining, drainage, egress

22 disgorgement, disemboguement, ejaculation, extrusion, detrusion, obtrusion, eruption, eruptiveness, blowout, outburst, outpour, effusion, jet, spout, spurt, squirt, excretion, secretion, extravasation, blood-letting, cupping, bleeding, venesection, phlebotomy, paracentesis, tapping, spilling, shedding, libation, oblation

23 vomiting, vomition, vomit, sickness, sick, regurgitation, egestion, emesis, heaving, retching, gagging, nausea, puking (Sl), puke (Sl), multicolour (or technicolour) yawn (Sl), pavement pizza (Sl), tactical vom (Sl)

24 belch, belching, hiccup, ructation, eructation, wind, gas, flatulence, flatulency, flatuosity, flatus, fart, farting, breaking wind

25 emission, emissivity, radioactivity, radiation, fall-out

26 ejector, expeller, ouster, evictor, dispossessor, depriver, taker, displacer, supplanter, superseder, substitute, cuckoo, cuckoo in the nest, bouncer (Sl), chucker out (Inf)

27 expellee, deportee, refugee, outlaw, outcast, outcaste

28 propellant, explosive, emitter, radiator, ejecting mechanism, ejector seat, volcano, emetic, aperient, purgative, laxative

ADJECTIVES

29 expulsive, expellent, ejective, ejaculative, eliminant, explosive, eruptive, radiating, emitting, emissive, secretory, sweaty, sudatory, sudorific, salivary, salivant, sickening, emetic, purgative, laxative, cathartic, emetocathartic, sialagogue, emmenagogic

30 vomiting, sick, sickened, nauseated, seasick, airsick, carsick, travel-sick, vomitive, vomitory, pukey (Inf)

31 eructative, flatulent, flatulous, belching

ADVERBS

32 expulsively, explosively, eruptively, emetically, cathartically

INTERJECTIONS

33 go away!, begone!, get thee hence!, get you gone!, run along!, away!, away with you!, off with you!, off you go!, be off!, on your way!, get out!, get out of here!, get the hell out of here!, clear out!, clear off!, buzz off! (Sl), push off! (Sl), shove off! (Sl), bug off! (Sl), bugger off! (Sl), piss off! (Sl), naff off! (Sl), fuck off! (Tab sl), beat it! (Sl), scram! (Sl), vamoose! (Sl), skidoo! (Sl), skedaddle! (Sl), get lost! (Sl), walk! (Sl), take a walk! (Sl), take a running jump! (Sl), go chase yourself! (Sl), cheese it! (Sl), take a powder! (Sl), blow! (Sl)

▶ *345 Departure*

350 Eating

NOUNS

1 eating, consuming, consumption, feeding, taking (in) food, ingesting, ingestion, ingurgitation, chewing, mastication, munching, manducation, biting, gnashing, champing, chomping, swallowing, deglutition, downing, getting down, gulping, slurping, engulfment, digestion, absorption

2 appetite, hunger, craving, voracity, voraciousness, wolfishness, gluttony, greed, gormandizing, gourmandism, voracious eating, devouring, devourment, engorgement, gobbling, bolting, guzzling, overeating, overindulgence, feasting, gorging, bingeing, binge, stuffing oneself, excessive consumption, compulsive eating, bulimia, bulimia nervosa, bulimarexia, pigout (US sl)

▶ *872 Gluttony, 870 Self-Indulgence, 782 Desire*

3 delicate eating, tasting, relishing, savouring, palate-tickling, refined palate, educated palate, epicurism, gourmandism, dainty palate, nibbling, licking, pecking, lack of appetite, picking at one's food, playing with one's food, toying with one's food, dieting, patho-

logical dieting, anorexia, anorexia nervosa, starving
▶ *45 Cookery, 274 Thinness, 871 Fasting*

4 **eating meals**, dining, lunching, breakfasting, supping, having tea, snacking, grazing, eating on the run, eating in bed, breakfast in bed, eating alone, eating out, dining out, communal eating, eating together, messing, partaking, formal dining, feasting, banqueting, regalement, hospitality, entertainment, table manners
▶ *651 Refreshment, 815 Sociability, 584 Habit*

5 **eating habit**, meat-eating, flesh-eating, carnivorousness, omophagy, creophagy, ichthyophagy, insectivorousness, anthropophagy, man-eating, cannibalism, vegetarianism, veganism, herbivorousness, rumination, chewing the cud, grazing, pasturing, cropping, graminivorousness, frugivorousness, omnivorousness

6 **nutrition**, diet, dietetics, healthy eating, proper eating, balanced diet, recommended diet, special diet, macrobiotic diet, vegetarian diet, protein diet, carbohydrate diet, fruit diet, salt-free diet, low-fat diet, fat-free diet, low-cholesterol diet, diabetic diet, sugar-free diet, calorie-controlled diet, slimming diet, crash diet, liquid diet, Cambridge Diet (Tm), food-combining diet, Hay Diet (Tm), slimming, dieting, weight-watching, losing weight, reducing, regaining one's figure, regulated diet, diet regimen, regimen, regime, course, dietary plan, dietary, diet sheet, calorie counter

7 **food**, sustenance, nourishment, aliment, alimentation, nutriment, nutrition, nurture, fare, baby food, Pablum (Tm), pabulum, pap, food for the body, food for the mind, food for the spirit, manna, food of the gods, ambrosia, amrita, bread, daily bread, staff of life, meat, staple food, foodstuffs, groceries, provisions, stores, supplies, commissariat, comestibles, edibles, eatables, victuals, vittles (Dial), viands, provender, rations, emergency rations, wartime rations, iron rations, emergency food supply, tack, hard tack, biscuit, salt pork, pemmican, rich food, heavy food, bulk, stodge, packaged food, vacuum-packed food, tinned food, frozen food, freezer stock, freeze-dried food, dried food, dehydrated food, long-life food, processed food, convenience food, junk food, fast food, short-order food (US), microwave food, healthy food, health food, wholefood, organic food, hydroponic food, home-grown food, high-fibre food, low-fat food, low-salt food, good food, savoury food, good cheer (Arch), cheer (Arch), fat of the land, creature comforts, cakes and ale, delicacies, dainties, luxuries, titbits, snacks, eats (Inf), grub (Sl), tuck (Inf), tucker (Aus inf), nosh (Sl), scoff (Sl), chow (Sl), chuck (US sl),

peckings (US sl), soul food (US sl), goodies (Inf)
▶ *45 Cookery, 86 Fruits, 605 Store, 606 Provision, 731 Allocation, 686 Prosperity, 628 Deterioration*

8 **animal food**, pet food, dog food, cat food, rabbit food, gerbil food, hamster food, fish food, bird food, birdseed, feed, feedstuff, chicken feed, provender, fodder, pasture, pasturage, forage, corn, oats, barley, grain, hay, grass, clover, alfalfa, lucerne, silage, nuts, acorns, beechmast, dry feed, winter feed, pigswill, cattle cake, saltlick
▶ *68 Agriculture*

9 **plenty**, oversupply of food, food mountain, cornucopia, milk and honey, fleshpots, good table, loaded table, festal cheer, festive board, groaning board
▶ *608 Sufficiency, 610 Excess*

10 **scarcity**, lack of food, insufficient diet, meagre diet, bread-and-water diet, poor table, bare cupboard, malnutrition, rickets, beriberi, pellagra, scurvy, starvation, famine
▶ *609 Insufficiency, 782 Desire, 624 Ill Health*

11 **food content**, vitamins, calories, roughage, bulk, fibre, water, minerals, salt, calcium, iron, protein, amino acid, carbohydrates, cholesterol, oil, fat, saturated fats, polyunsaturates, starch, sugar, glucose, sucrose, lactose, fructose, (food) additive, E number, preservative, flavour enhancer (*or* intensifier), monosodium glutamate, (artificial) flavouring, (artificial) colouring, artificial sweetener, emulsifier
▶ *130 Addition, 411 Taste*

12 **meal**, refreshment, refection, repast, collation, informal meal, light meal, stand-up meal, buffet, snack, bite to eat, piece to eat, chance meal, potluck, full meal, square meal, three-course meal, formal meal, sit-down meal, family meal, breakfast, English breakfast, continental breakfast, brunch, elevenses, lunch, luncheon, Sunday lunch, light lunch, austerity lunch, bread-and-cheese lunch, ploughman's lunch, packed lunch, pack-lunch, tiffin, tea, afternoon tea, five o'clock, high tea, cream tea, tea for two, evening meal, dinner, TV dinner, supper, fork supper

13 **feast**, banquet, state banquet, regale (Arch), harvest supper, harvest home, reception, wedding reception, wedding breakfast, formal dinner, formal occasion, annual dinner, annual company get-together, employee dinner (*or* party), dinner dance, Christmas dinner, festive gathering, party, tea party, picnic, *fête champêtre* (Fr), tailgate picnic (US), barbecue, cookout (US), wiener roast (US), weenie roast (US inf), clambake (US), spread, junket, orgy, Roman orgy, bacchanalia, Lucullan banquet, beanfeast (Inf), beano (Sl), do (Inf), bun fight (Sl), nosh-up (Sl), thrash (Inf), blowout (Sl)
▶ *812 Celebration, 815 Sociability*

14 **mouthful**, bite, nibble, piece, morsel, bolus,

gobbet, slice, sliver, appetizer, hors d'oeuvre, titbit, helping, serving, portion, second helping, seconds (Inf), dish, course, first course, starter, soup, fish course, entrée, remove, main course, side-dish, entremets, dessert, sweet, pudding, afters (Inf)

▸ *45 Cookery*

15 **eating place**, dining room, dinette, dining hall, banquet hall, banqueting hall, refectory, refreshment room, lunchroom (US), canteen, company canteen, mess room, military canteen, military mess, Naafi, restaurant, health-food restaurant, wholefood restaurant, fastfood restaurant, hamburger place, McDonald's (Tm), café, cafeteria, self-service restaurant, automat (US), eating house, diner (US), luncheonette (US), beanery (US), kebab house, crêperie, trattoria, spaghetti house, pizzeria, bistro, brasserie, steakhouse, chophouse, grill room, rotisserie, carvery, coffee house, espresso café, coffee bar, milk bar, ice-cream parlour, soda fountain (US), drug-store counter (US), lunch counter, fast-food counter, snack bar, sandwich bar, teahouse, teashop, tearoom, pancake house, waffle house (US), drive-in (US), drive-in window (US), take-away window, fish-and-chip shop, coffee stall, hot-dog stand, motorway restaurant, pull-in, transport café, roadside café (US), buffet, dining car, diner, vending machine, takeaway, eatery (US inf), greasy spoon (Sl), chippy (Inf)

16 **eating utensil**, knife, carving knife, fish knife, steak knife, butter knife, fork, fish fork, salad fork, fondue fork, spoon, teaspoon, tablespoon, dessertspoon, soup spoon, chopsticks, plate, dish, bowl, feeding organ, teeth, jaws, mandibles, mouth, tongue, throat, gullet, stomach, belly, paunch, crop, maw, intestines, bowels, guts

▸ *258 Container*

17 **food shop**, supermarket, hypermarket, grocery (store), grocer's (shop), fish store (US), fishmonger, bakery, baker's (shop), butcher's (shop), butcher, greengrocer('s), fruit stall, delicatessen, deli (Inf), health-food shop, food department, food hall, market, confectionary('s), sweet shop, tuck shop, commissary (US), commissariat

▸ *740 Market, 739 Sale*

18 **eater**, feeder, consumer, partaker, diner, luncher, small eater, light eater, dainty eater, taster, nibbler, dieter, slimmer, weight watcher, anorexic, big eater, hearty eater, heavy eater, feaster, banqueter, glutton, gourmand, bulimic, *bon vivant* (Fr), trencherman (*or* trencherwoman), Lucullus, bacchanal, bacchant, diner-in, boarder, messer, messmate, diner-out, frequenter of restaurants, dining-club member, picnicker, gourmet, epicure, connoisseur, meat-eater, flesh-eater, carni-

vore, man-eater, cannibal, anthropophagite, insectivore, omnivore, vegetarian, vegan, herbivore, fussy eater (Inf), picky eater (Inf), picker (Inf), pecker (Inf), gobbler (Inf), pig (Sl), hog (Sl), wolf (Sl), hyena (Sl), gannet (Sl), locust (Sl), foodie (Inf), veggie (Inf)

▸ *872 Gluttony, 481 Discrimination, 815 Sociability*

19 **dietitian**, dietician, dietary expert, nutritionist, nutrition expert

20 **food provider**, farmer, fisherman, rancher, grocer, greengrocer, fishmonger, butcher, baker, confectioner, milkman, restaurateur, chef, cook, caterer

▸ *45 Cookery*

VERBS

21 **eat**, take nourishment, subsist, fare (Arch), consume, feed, ingest, ingurgitate, engulf, take in food, graze, browse, pasture, crop, chew, chew up, munch, crunch, scrunch, masticate, manducate, gnash, champ, chomp, mouth, worry, gnaw, grind, bite, nibble, peck, tear, rend, ruminate, chew the cud, swallow, gulp, gulp down, slurp, suck, devour, take down, get down, digest, absorb

22 **eat well**, have a good appetite, water at the mouth, drool, salivate, raven, hunger, starve, fall to, pitch in, set to, tuck in to, lay into, get one's teeth into, sink one's teeth into, devour, gobble, snap up, dispatch, bolt, wolf (down), overeat, overindulge, gorge oneself, engorge, stuff oneself, binge, fill one's stomach, feed oneself full (US dial), sate, guzzle, gormandize, gluttonize, eat like a pig, take every course, eat everything in sight, eat up, clean one's plate, leave a clean plate, lick the platter clean, put away, polish off, make short work of, ask for seconds, ask for more, fatten on, batten on, prey on, nosh (Sl), scoff (Inf), put on the feedbag (Sl), lay it on (Inf), do justice to (Sl), get the hungries (US sl), fork in (Inf), spoon in (Inf), shovel in (Sl), feed one's face (Sl), feed one's tapeworm (Sl), pig out (US sl), scarf up (*or* down) (US sl)

23 **taste**, relish, savour, nibble (at), lick, sample, peck at, pick at, play with one's food, toy with one's food, have a poor appetite, sniff at, eat less, diet, count the calories, reduce

▸ *274 Thinness*

24 **have a meal**, board, mess, partake, have a feed, break bread, break one's fast, breakfast, brunch, lunch, have (*or* take) tea, dine, sup, snack, graze, eat between meals, eat out, dine out, regale, feast, banquet, carouse, revel

25 **provide food**, feed, give to eat, nourish, nurture, sustain, aliment, take care of, board, victual, provision, cater, purvey, dine, wine and dine, feast, banquet, fête, regale, have to dinner, invite over, cook for, nurse, breast-feed, suckle, give suck, force-feed, drip-feed, graze,

pasture, put out to grass, fatten, fatten up
▶ *606 Provision, 815 Sociability, 45 Cookery*

ADJECTIVES

26 **eating**, feeding, dining, grazing, meat-eating, flesh-eating, carnivorous, creophagous, man-eating, cannibalistic, omophagic, omophagous, insectivorous, herbivorous, graminivorous, frugivorous, vegetarian, vegan, omnivorous, greedy, gluttonous, hungry, ravenous, voracious, devouring, guzzling, bulimic, wolfish, gannet-like, well-fed, well-nourished, full, full-up, bloated, stuffed, sated
▶ *872 Gluttony, 782 Desire, 871 Fasting*

27 **edible**, eatable, consumable, esculent, comestible, digestible, predigested, nourishing, nutritious, nutritive, nutritional, feeding, sustaining, alimental, alimentary, dietary, dietetic, slimming, low-calorie, low-fat, wholesome, good, appetizing, palate-tickling, palatable, mouth-watering, dainty, tasty, savoury, sweet, calorific, high-calorie, fattening, bodybuilding, protein-rich, rich, succulent, delicious, scrumptious, moreish (Inf), finger-licking (US inf)
▶ *411 Taste, 623 Health*

ADVERBS

28 **carnivorously**, creophagously, cannibalistically, omophagically, omophagously, insectivorously, herbivorously, omnivorously, gluttonously, hungrily, ravenously, voraciously, greedily

29 **edibly**, eatably, consumably, digestibly, nutritiously, calorifically, succulently, tastily, deliciously

351 Drinking

NOUNS

1 **drinking**, imbibing, imbibition, fluid intake, potation, sucking, lapping, sipping, tasting, nipping, supping, gulping, swallowing, swilling, swigging, quaffing, toping, soaking, pulling, wine tasting, wine bibbing, drinking to excess, drunkenness, alcoholism, dipsomania
▶ *874 Drunkenness, 624 Ill Health, 812 Celebration, 815 Sociability*

2 **drink**, beverage, potation, libation, oblation, toast, health, mixed drink, concoction, cocktail, potion, decoction, infusion, cup of tea, cuppa (Inf), drink of the gods, nectar, thirst-quencher, draught, gulp, swallow, sip, sup (Dial), bottleful, can, glass, glassful, cup, cupful, pint (Dial), long drink, tall drink, bumper, stiff one, two fingers, short drink, short one, short, quick one (US sl), snifter (Inf), sundowner (Inf), pick-me-up (Inf)
▶ *133 Mixture, 630 Remedy, 651 Refreshment*

3 **tea**, green tea, black tea, iced tea, lemon tea, herbal tea, jasmine tea, camomile tea, peppermint tea, Earl Grey, Indian tea, Darjeeling,

Assam, China tea, pekoe, orange pekoe, Keemun, Lapsang Souchong, gunpowder, Ceylon tea, Russian tea, mate, tisane, char (Sl)

4 **coffee**, white coffee (Inf), java (US inf)

5 **milk**, fresh milk, pint of milk, pinta (Inf), quart of milk (US), cow's milk, goat's milk, mare's milk, kumiss (*or* koumiss), camel's milk, pasteurized milk, homogenized milk, long-life milk, UHT milk, beestings, mother's milk, breast milk, colostrum, dried milk, powdered milk, skimmed milk, semiskimmed milk, condensed milk, evaporated milk, Pet Milk (US trademark), ice milk (US), milk shake, milky drink, malted milk, chocolate milk, hot chocolate, cocoa, Horlicks (Tm), top of the milk, cream, drinking yoghurt, lassi
▶ *350 Eating, 45 Cookery*

6 **soft drink**, nonalcoholic beverage, thirst-quencher, water, drinking water, filtered water, *eau potable* (Fr), spring water, mineral water, Perrier (Tm), sparkling water, carbonated water, fizzy water, soda water, soda, cream soda, soda fountain, tonic water, barley water, squash, cordial, mixer, low-calorie drink, ginger beer, sarasparilla, root beer, near beer, cream soda, ginger ale, cola, Coca-Cola (Tm), Coke (Tm), Pepsi (Cola) (Tm), fizz, fizzy drink, lemonade, bitter lemon, orangeade, fruit juice, apple juice, orange juice, grapefruit juice, pineapple juice, tomato juice, Virgin Mary, vegetable juice, V-8 juice (US trademark), coconut milk, julep, sherbet (US), pop (Inf), black cow (US inf)

7 **alcoholic drink**, alcohol, liquor, wood alcohol, fermented drink, wine, corn liquor, corn whisky, corn, malt liquor, John Barleycorn, beer, hops, bottled beer, draught beer, keg beer, bitter, mild, ale, strong ale, pale ale, real ale, stout, porterwhisky, usquebaugh, Scotch whisky, Scotch, rye (US), rye whiskey (US), bourbon (US), bourbon whiskey (US), Irish whiskey, poteen, vodka, aquavit, absinthe, raki, arrack, ouzo, rum, dark rum, light rum, Jamaica rum, demerara rum, white rum, Bacardi (Tm), grog, hot grog, toddy, hot toddy, punch, rum punch, milk punch, eggnog, egg flip, advocaat, cordial, grenadine, spiced wine, mulled wine, negus, posset, hippocras, caudle, cup, claret cup, apéritif, liqueur, frappé, Cointreau (Tm), Tia Maria (Tm), Drambuie (Tm), crème de menthe, cassis, booze (Inf), poison (Inf), hooch (US inf), rotgut (Sl), moonshine (US inf), mountain dew (US inf), mother's ruin (Inf)

8 **mixed drink**, gin and tonic, gin and It, pink gin, brandy and soda, whisky and soda, rum and Coke, rum and pep, rum and black, vodka and tonic, cocktail, Bucks fizz, Bloody Mary, brandy Alexander, collins, Tom Collins, Rum Collins, daiquiri, sling, gin sling, Singapore

sling, highball, julep, mint julep, kir, kir rose, black velvet, Manhattan, margarita, martini, Old Fashioned, Pimms (Tm), pina colada, red eye, sangria, screwdriver, snakebite, snowball, spritzer, tequila sunrise, whiskey sour, whisky mac, white lady, mixer, tonic, soda, vermouth, angostura bitters, Worcester sauce, Tabasco (Tm)

9 **wine**, the grape, juice of the grape, blood of the grape, red wine, white wine, rosé, vin rosé, Rhine wine, sparkling wine, spumante, champagne, still wine, sweet wine, dessert wine, dry wine, light wine, heavy wine, full-bodied wine, vintage wine, vin ordinaire, vin de table, table wine, vin du pays, Bordeaux, claret, white Bordeaux, Sauternes, burgundy, chablis, sparkling burgundy, beaujolais, Muscadet, chardonnay, hock, Moselle, riesling, Tokay, chianti, Bulls Blood, rioja, retsina, vinho verde, cabernet sauvignon, vermouth, fortified wine, sherry, sweet sherry, cream sherry, dry sherry, sack, port, white port, ruby port, tawny port, vintage port, crusted port, madeira, marsala, vermouth, Martini (Tm), vino (Inf), plonk (Inf), bubbly (Inf), champers (Sl)

10 **drink container**, bottle, flask, hip flask, Thermos (flask) (Tm), vacuum flask (*or* bottle *or* jug), canteen, can, decanter, glass, tumbler, rummer, wineglass, sherry glass, tankard, stein, mug, cup, coffee cup, teacup, Styrofoam cup (US Trademark), loving cup, stirrup cup, bowl
▶ *258 Container*

11 **drink provider**, drinking place, teashop, coffee bar, licensed premises, public house (US), liquor store (US)
▶ *651 Refreshment, 737 Trade, 740 Market*

12 **drinker**, light drinker, social drinker, sipper, wine taster, heavy drinker, hard drinker, guzzler, bibber, swiller, quaffer, toper, drunkard, wino (Inf), boozer (Inf), pisshead (Tab sl), alehead (Sl), lush (Sl), alkie (Inf)

VERBS

13 **drink**, imbibe, potate, suck, lap, sip, taste, nip, have a drink, wet one's lips, wet one's whistle (Inf), draw the cork, crack a bottle, drink up, quaff, sup, swallow, gulp, gulp down, down, drain, knock back, put away, lap up, soak up, sponge up, wash down, swill, swig, slake one's thirst, drink one's fill, toss off one's glass, empty the glass (*or* bottle), drain one's glass, have a refill, sweeten (US), have another, have one for the road, tipple, tope,

get drunk, drink like a fish, indulge (Inf), booze (Inf), chug (Sl), get pissed (Tab sl), go out on the ale (Sl)
▶ *874 Drunkenness, 812 Celebration*

14 **drink to**, drink the health of, raise one's glass, pledge, toast, salute

15 **provide drink**, water, wine, suckle, give suck, nurse, lay in drink, lay down a cellar, give someone a refill, sweeten (US)

ADJECTIVES

16 **drinking**, nursed, suckled, breast-fed, imbibing, swilling, tippling, drunken, bibulous, vinous, dipsomaniacal, off the wagon (Inf), boozing (Inf)
▶ *874 Drunkenness, 873 Sobriety*

17 **drinkable**, potable, milky, lactic, white, diluted, weak, strong, undiluted, black, nonalcoholic, soft, fizzy, alcoholic, fermented, distilled, spiritous, hard, vinous, sparkling, still, sweet, dry, light, full-bodied, vintage

INTERJECTIONS

18 **cheers!**, here's health!, to us!, here's to you!, here's looking at you!, here's mud in your eye!, bottoms up!, down the hatch!, slàinte!, *prosit!*, (Ger), skol!, chug-a-lug! (Sl)

352 Secretion

NOUNS

1 **secretion**, exudation, emission, transudation, excretion, discharge, release, voidance, ejection, emanation, secernment, lactation, lacrimation, crying, weeping, guttation, salivation, sweating, perspiration, secretory mechanism, merocrine secretion, eccrine secretion, apocrine secretion, holocrine secretion
▶ *353 Excretion*

2 **secreted substance**, secretion, internal secretion, hormone, chalone, digestive juice, gastric juice, succus entericus, pancreatic juice, bile, gall, mucus, external secretion, phlegm, sputum, saliva, tears, rheum, seminal fluid, semen, milk, colostrum, sweat, sebum, musk, pheromone, ectohormone, honeydew, plant secretion, nectar, latex, resin, tannin, gum
▶ *58 Biochemistry, 353 Excretion, 85 Trees, 387 Fluid, 393 Semiliquid*

3 **gland**, endocrine gland, ductless gland, exocrine gland, eccrine gland, intestinal gland, sweat gland, mammary gland, lacrimal (*or* lachrymal) gland, scent gland, plant gland, oil gland, salt gland, nectary, laticifer, hydathode

Endocrine Glands

adrenal gland, suprarenal gland	ovary	suprarenal gland, adrenal gland
corpora allata	parathyroid gland	testis
corpora cardiaca	pineal gland	thyroid gland
corpus luteum	pituitary gland	
islets of Langerhans	placenta	

Exocrine Glands

Bartholin's gland	lacrimal gland	pancreas	submandibular gland,
breast	Lieberkühn's gland	parotid gland	submaxillary gland
Brunner's gland	liver	preputial gland	sweat gland
buccal gland	mammary gland	prostate gland	tarsal gland, meibo-
Cowper's gland,	meibomian gland, tar-	salivary gland	mian gland
bulbourethral gland	sal gland	sebaceous gland	vestibular gland
gastric gland	nabothian gland	sublingual gland	

ADJECTIVES

4 **secretory**, secretionary, secretive, exudative, transudatory, emissive, excretory, emanative, emanatory, emanational, glandular, merocrine, eccrine, apocrine, holocrine, secreting, lactating, lactational, lactescent, lactiferous, laticiferous, lacrimatory, crying, weeping, sebaceous, sebiferous, sweating, sweaty, sudatory, salivating

5 **of a secretion**, glandular, glandulous, hormonal, endocrine, adrenal, ovarian, testicular, seminal, pineal, pituitary, placental, luteal, thyroidal, exocrine, eccrine, lacrimal (or lachrymal), lacrimatory, mammary, lacteal (or lacteous), mucous (or mucose), mucoid, sudoral, sebaceous, salivary, parotid, sialoid, gastric, pyloric, pancreatic, prostatic

6 **inducing secretion**, lactogenic, sialogogic, lacrimatory, sudatory, sudorific, cholagogic
▶ 62 Pharmacology

VERBS

7 **secrete**, exude, transude, produce, emit, excrete, discharge, release, liberate, void, eject, give up, give off, emanate, secern, produce, produce secretion, lactate, lacrimate, cry, weep, salivate, sweat, perspire
▶ 353 Excretion, 349 Expulsion

ADVERBS

8 **glandularly**, glandulously, lactationally, lacteally, weepily, tearfully, sweatily

353 Excretion

NOUNS

1 **excretion**, egestion, elimination, expulsion, discharge, ejection, extrusion, emission, emanation, secretion, transudation, exudation, extravasation, flux, flow, expectoration, ejaculation, ecchymosis, effusion
▶ 349 Expulsion

2 **defecation**, evacuation, voidance, dejection, purge, purgation, catharsis, clearance, bowel movement (BM), movement, motion, regular motion, diarrhoea, loose bowels, flux, bloody flux, dysentery, lientery, copremesis, constipation, the runs (Sl), the trots (Inf), the shits (Sl), Delhi belly (Sl), GI's (or GI shits) (US sl), turistas (US sl), Montezuma's revenge (Sl), Aztec two-step (Sl)
▶ 624 Ill Health, 60 Medicine, 630 Remedy

3 **urination**, micturation, call of nature, incontinence, weak bladder, enuresis, bed-wetting,

nocturnal enuresis, urinalysis, urinometer, wee (Inf), pee (Inf), piss (Sl), slash (Sl), Jimmy Riddle (Sl), leak (Sl)

4 **excrement**, excreta, egesta, ejecta, ejectamenta, waste, waste matter, dejection, dejecture, dejecta, exudation, exudate, transudation, transudate, extravasation, extravasate, effluent, sewage, sewerage
▶ 607 Waste

5 **faeces**, stool, motion, turd (Tab), feculence, ordure, night soil, jakes (Dial), dung, muck, manure, cow pats, cow flops, cow chips, buffalo chips, guano, dirt, droppings, sheep's currants, coprolite, coprolith, shit (Tab sl), crap (Tab sl), poo (Inf), poo-poo (Inf), poop (Inf), ca-ca (Inf), number twos (Inf), big jobs (Inf), dingleberry (Sl), clinker (Sl)
▶ 622 Dirtiness

6 **urine**, water, urea, uric acid, number ones (Inf), little jobs (Inf), pee (Inf), pee-pee (Inf), wee (Inf), wee-wee (Inf), piss (Tab sl), piddle (Inf), widdle (Inf)
▶ 389 Water

7 **pus**, discharge, matter, pustule, mucopus, seropus, ichor, sanies, purulence, pussiness, suppuration, festering, mattering, running, weeping, rankling, gleet, leucorrhoea

8 **sweat**, perspiration, sudor, sweating, perspiring, sudation, sudoresis, diaphoresis, exudation, exudate, induced sweat, honest sweat, cold sweat, sweat of one's brows, beads of sweat, streams of sweat, BO (body odour)

9 **saliva**, spit, spittle, salivation, salivary gland, ptyalism, sialorrhoea, dribble, drivel, slaver, slobber, slabber, froth, foam, cough, coughing, expectoration, spitting, phlegm, catarrh, mucus, rheum, snot

10 **bleeding**, extravasation of blood, nosebleed, ecchymosis, petechia, bruising, bruise, haemorrhage, haemorrhoea, haematemesis, haemoptysis, haematuria, haemophilia

11 **menstruation**, menses, menstrual flow (or flux or discharge), monthly discharge, catamenia, catamenial discharge, period(s), monthlies, courses, the curse, the Curse of Eve, time of the month, menopause, menarche, amenorrhoea, dysmenorrhoea, epimenorrhoea, hypomenorrhoea, menorrhagia, oligomenorrhoea

12 **dead tissue**, slough, cast, exuviae, ecdysis, moulting, desquamation

13 **lavatory**, toilet, convenience, public convenience, WC (water closet), latrine, head, bathroom, washroom, basement, rest room, comfort station (US), ladies, ladies' (*or* women's) room, little girls' room, powder room, gents, little boys' room, urinal, privy, outhouse, backhouse, earth closet, chemical toilet, loo (Inf), bog (Sl), john (US sl), can (US sl), crapper (Sl), khazi (Sl), shithouse (Tab sl)

14 **toilet**, stool, throne, commode, closestool, chamber pot, chamber, potty, bedpan, po (*or* poe) (Inf), jerry (Inf), thunderbox (Sl), gazunder (Sl), pisspot (Sl)

VERBS

15 **excrete**, egest, eliminate, pass, expel, discharge, eject, extrude, emit, give off, secrete, transude, exude, extravasate, weep, expectorate, ejaculate, relieve (*or* ease) oneself, go to the toilet, go, answer the call of nature, pay a call (Inf)

▶ *349 Expulsion*

16 **defecate**, have a bowel movement (BM), move one's bowels, move, pass, evacuate, void, purge, shit, have (*or* take) a shit, shit oneself, be caught short, foul, soil, crap (Tab sl), poo (Inf), do a poo (Inf), ca-ca (Inf), do number twos (Inf), have the runs (*or* trots *or* shits) (Sl)

17 **urinate**, micturate, pass (*or* make) water, wet, wet oneself, wet the bed, stale, piss (Tab sl), pee (Inf), pee-pee (Inf), wee (Inf), wee-wee (Inf), piddle (Inf), widdle (Inf), do number ones (Inf), spend a penny (Inf), have a slash (Sl), take a leak (Sl), have a Jimmy Riddle (Sl), pump bilge (Sl), siphon the python (Sl), point Percy at the porcelain (Sl), pee oneself (Inf)

18 **fester**, suppurate, run, weep, rankle, matter, come to a head

19 **sweat**, perspire, exude, break out in a sweat, sweat like a trooper (*or* horse *or* pig), swelter, wilt, steam, glow

▶ *408 Heat*

20 **salivate**, water at the mouth, spit, splutter, slobber, slabber, slaver, dribble, drivel, drool, froth (*or* foam) at the mouth, cough, cough up, expectorate, hawk, clear one's throat, blow one's nose

21 **bleed**, spill (*or* lose) blood, bloody, ecchymose, extravasate, haemorrhage

22 **menstruate**, bleed, be on, come on, have one's period, have the curse, have visitors, have one's friends and relations

23 **cast**, slough, shed one's skin, ecdyse, moult, desquamate

ADJECTIVES

24 **excretory**, excretive, excretionary, egestive, eliminative, eliminant, ejective, exudative, transudative, secretory

25 **faecal**, feculent, excremental, excrementary, scatologic, scatological, stercoral, stercorous, stercoraceous, shitty, dungy, cathartic, purgative, laxative, aperient

26 **urinary**, urinative, diuretic, enuretic, incontinent, continent, potty-trained, toilet-trained, house-trained

27 **purulent**, suppurative, festering, pussy, mattering, running

28 **sweaty**, sudatory, sudoric, sudorific, diaphoretic, sweating, perspiring, bathed in sweat, drenched with sweat, wet with sweat, clammy, sticky, wilting, glowing

29 **salivating**, spitting, coughing, spluttering, slobbering, slavering, dribbling, drooling, frothing, foaming, rheumy, watery, mucous, expectorant

30 **bleeding**, haemorrhaging, blood-soaked, bloody, ecchymosed

31 **menstrual**, catamenial, monthly, menopausal, menstruating, on, on the rag (Sl)

32 **cast-off**, shed, exuvial, moulting, ecdysial, desquamated

ADVERBS

33 **scatologically**, shittily, crappily, diuretically, bloodily, sweatily, clammily, stickily

354 Insertion

VERBS

1 **insert**, put in, stick in, introduce, introject, insinuate, add, interject, interpolate, intercalate, put between, intromit, include, drag in, import, bring in, drop in, pot, hole, put in the slot

▶ *146 Inclusion, 298 Interface, 130 Addition*

2 **inject**, inoculate, vaccinate, implant, impregnate, enter, penetrate, pierce, poke in, squirt in, introduce, pop in, infuse, instil, imbue, perfuse, transfuse, pour in, decant, shoot (Sl)

▶ *346 Entry*

3 **impact**, thrust in, drive in, plunge in, run in, push in, force in, hammer in, knock in, pound in, ram in, jam in, cram in, press in, squeeze in, crowd in, stuff in, pack in

▶ *257 Contents, 258 Container*

4 **immerse**, immerge (Arch), submerge, dip, plunge, dunk, duck, baptize, steep, souse, drench, flood, bury, inter, immerse oneself in, bury oneself in

▶ *362 Lowering, 399 Burial*

5 **inset**, set in, inlay, slip in, slide in, ease in, wedge in, infix, dovetail, embed, bed in, encapsulate, ensheathe, sheathe, encase, case, box, cover, mount, frame, circumscribe

▶ *297 Surroundings, 293 Covering*

6 **plant**, implant, transplant, plant out, bed out, graft, engraft, ingraft, imp, bud

▶ *68 Agriculture*

7 **install**, instate, inaugurate, initiate, invest,

ordain, induct, enrol, enlist, sign up, sign on, admit

▶ *348 Admittance*

NOUNS

8 **insertion**, introduction, introjection, insinuation, addition, interjection, interpolation, intercalation, intromission, embolism, parenthesis, import, importation, infixion, impaction, impactment, planting, implantation, transplantation, transplant, graft, grafting, embedment, tessellation

▶ *130 Addition*

9 **injection**, inoculation, vaccination, implantation, impregnation, entry, ingress, penetration, infusion, perfusion, transfusion, shot (Inf)

▶ *346 Entry*

10 **immersion**, submersion, submergence, dip, plunge, bath, ducking, baptism, interment, burial, burial at sea

▶ *399 Burial*

11 **thing inserted**, insert, insertion, inset, inlay, inclusion, supplement, filling, stuffing, syringe, tampon, tampion, suppository, enema, clyster

▶ *146 Inclusion*

ADJECTIVES

12 **inserted**, introduced, introjected, insinuated, added, interpolated, intercalated, interpolative, intercalative, parenthetical, by-the-by, imported, infixed, impacted, planted, transplanted, grafted, embedded, tessellated, inlaid, included

13 **injected**, inoculated, vaccinated, implanted, impregnated, infused, perfused

14 **immersed**, submersed, submerged, baptized, interred, buried

ADVERBS

15 **in**, inside, parenthetically, in parenthesis, in brackets

355 Extraction

NOUNS

1 **extraction**, removal, withdrawal, pull, pulling out, drawing, drawing out, tug, tugging out, wrench, wrenching out, wresting out, evulsion, avulsion, ripping out, tearing out, rooting out, uprooting, deracination, eradication, elimination, dredging, fishing, extrication, disengagement, liberation

▶ *339 Traction, 639 Deliverance, 700 Liberation, 244 Destruction, 546 Obliteration*

2 **displacement**, dislodgment, expulsion, expression, squeezing out, pruning, thinning, thinning out, weeding, deforestation

▶ *349 Expulsion, 252 Displacement*

3 **digging out**, digging up, unearthing, disinterment, exhumation, disentombment, graverobbing, cutting out, excision, exsection, ex-

cavation, mining, quarrying, drilling

▶ *317 Concavity, 136 Separation*

4 **sucking**, sucking out, suction, exsuction, drawing, drawing off, draught, vacuuming, aspiration, pumping, siphoning, tapping, milking, pipetting, broaching, emptying, draining, cupping, bleeding, blood-letting, phlebotomy, venesection, evisceration, gutting, disembowelment, shelling

5 **drawing out**, bringing forth, elicitation, evocation, eduction, calling forth, arousal, stimulation, obtaining, derivation

▶ *721 Gain*

6 **extorsion**, wresting, wrenching, wringing, tearing, ripping, wrest, wrench, wring, exaction, demand, claim

▶ *734 Taking*

7 **obtaining an extract**, extraction, separation, refinement, purification, distillation, sublimation, condensation, vaporization, decoction, infusion, squeezing, pressing, expressing, rendering, rendition, steeping, soaking, marinating, concentration

8 **extract**, essence, quintessence, spirit, elixir, decoction, infusion, distillate, sublimate, concentrate, juice

▶ *103 Essence, 143 Part*

9 **extractor**, separator, siphon, pump, syringe, pipette, aspirator, vacuum pump, press, wringer, mangle, lemon squeezer, juice extractor, cherry stoner, apple corer

10 **excavator**, miner, quarrier, digger, mechanical digger, JCB, shovel, pick, pickaxe, toothpick, rake, dredge, dredger, shadoof, Persian wheel, scoop, spoon, lever, crowbar, wrench, corkscrew, screwdriver, forceps, pliers, tweezers, pincers

▶ *603 Tool*

VERBS

11 **extract**, remove, withdraw, pull out, draw out, take out, get out, tug out, wrench out, wrest out, evulse, avulse, rip out, tear out, root out, uproot, deracinate, eradicate, eliminate, pluck out, pick out, rake out, dredge, fish, fish out, grub out, winkle out, extricate, disengage, free, liberate

▶ *339 Traction, 580 Selection, 639 Deliverance, 700 Liberation*

12 **displace**, dislodge, lever out, smoke out, expel, express, squeeze out, wring out, prune, thin, thin out, weed out, deforest

▶ *349 Expulsion, 252 Displacement*

13 **dig out**, dig up, unearth, disinter, exhume, disentomb, gouge out, cut out, excise, excavate, mine, quarry, drill

▶ *317 Concavity, 136 Separation*

14 **suck**, suck out, draw, draw off, aspirate, vacuum, pump, pump out, siphon, siphon off, tap, milk, pipette, broach, empty, drain, cup, bleed, eviscerate, gut, disembowel, shell

15 **draw out**, bring forth, elicit, evoke, educe, worm out, bring to light, summon up, call up, rouse, arouse, stimulate, obtain, get, procure, secure, derive, induce, deduce, glean
▶ *721 Gain*

16 **extort**, wrest, wrench, wring, force out, tear out, rip out, exact, demand, claim
▶ *734 Taking*

17 **obtain an extract**, separate, refine, purify, cream off, distil, condense, vaporize, decoct, infuse, squeeze, press, melt down, render, steep, soak, marinate, concentrate, essentialize

ADJECTIVES

18 **extractive**, eductive, educible, eradicative, eradicable, removable, uprooting, elicitory, evocative, arousing, stimulating

19 **dislodged**, displaced, uprooted, deracinated, extricated, disengaged, liberated, eliminated, extracted

20 **exacting**, exactive, extortionate, extortionary, extortive

ADVERBS

21 **away**, apart, asunder, removably, exactingly, exigently

22 **expressively**, evocatively, stimulatingly

356 Passage

NOUNS

1 **passage**, passing, passing through, movement, transit, transmission, transference, transduction, transfusion, crossing, traversing, traverse, transcursion, journey, voyage, trip, perambulation, patrol, round, beat
▶ *326 Transfer, 324 Motion*

2 **passing along**, walking, driving, riding, cycling, sailing, flying, progress, thoroughfare, road, highway, clearway, motorway, airlane, sea lane, route, course, track, path, orbit, traffic, circulation, traffic flow, traffic pattern, traffic load, traffic jam, loading, unloading, waiting, parking, kerbside parking, offstreet parking, lay-by, parking place (*or* area *or* zone), car park, diversion, alternative route
▶ *70 Transport*

3 **passage into**, entrance, entry, ingress, penetration, interpenetration, intervention, infiltration, transudation, permeation, percolation, osmosis, endosmosis
▶ *346 Entry*

4 **access**, approach, road, right of way, path, pathway, footpath, bridle path, stepping stones, pass, channel, passageway
▶ *327 Way*

5 **crossing point**, crossing, intercrossing, intersection, junction, crossroads, roundabout, clover leaf, Spaghetti Junction, overcrossing, overpass, flyover, bridge, pontoon, viaduct, undercrossing, underpass, tunnel, level crossing, ford, pedestrian crossing, zebra crossing, pelican crossing, traffic lights, Belisha beacon, island, central reservation, frontier post, checkpoint
▶ *63 Engineering, 288 Interweaving*

6 **passport**, visa, pass, safe conduct, *laissez passer* (Fr), ID, clearance, clearance papers, papers, documentation, permit

7 **traffic controller**, air-traffic controller, traffic police, road patrol, traffic engineer, traffic warden, metermaid, traffic cop (Sl)

VERBS

8 **pass**, pass by, flash by, overtake, get past, leave on one side, skirt, pass through, get through, move through, shoot through, come out the other side

9 **proceed**, go, move along, travel, journey, voyage, circulate, patrol, do the rounds, join the traffic, weave
▶ *324 Motion*

10 **enter**, penetrate, infiltrate, permeate, percolate, osmose, soak through, open a way, force a passage, elbow through, worm one's way in, clear the ground, progress
▶ *346 Entry, 327 Way*

11 **cross**, traverse, transit, negotiate, go across, cross over, make a crossing, reach the other side, ford, wade across, step over, bridge, straddle, bestride, span, overfly, traject, transmit, carry across, move across, transport, convey, hand over, transfer, translate
▶ *326 Transfer, 70 Transport*

ADJECTIVES

12 **passing**, overtaking, moving, proceeding, transferring, transducing, crossing, traversing, transitional, transilient

13 **penetrating**, infiltrating, transudating, permeating, percolating, osmotic, intervening

ADVERBS

14 **by the way**, en passant, via, by way of, en route, in transit, transitionally, through, across

357 Overstepping

VERBS

1 **overstep**, overrun, overpass, overreach, overgrow, overgo, overstride, overleap, leapfrog, overjump, go beyond, go too far, overstep the mark (*or* bounds), aim too high, overspread, overflow, irrupt, flood, spill over, brim over
▶ *610 Excess, 128 Increase, 261 Expansion*

2 **cross**, cross over, cross the border, cross the Rubicon, pass the point of no return
▶ *300 Edge, 302 Limit*

3 **exceed**, surpass, outdo, outclass, excel, transcend, surmount, rise above, sow above, outrival, overbid, outbid, outmanoeuvre, outflank, outstrip, steal a march on, make the running, outdistance, outride, outrun, overtake, come in front, shoot ahead, lap, leave

standing, leave behind, race, beat hollow

▶ *336 Forward Motion, 648 Haste, 126 Superiority, 627 Improvement, 154 Precedence, 324 Motion, 590 Pursuit, 263 Distance, 682 Success*

4 **exaggerate**, overdo, superabound, overrate, overestimate, strain, stretch, stretch a point, go over the limit, overbid, overcall one's hand, overact, overplay, overindulge, go over the top, go OTT (Inf)

▶ *541 Exaggeration, 870 Self-Indulgence, 811 Showiness, 494 Overestimation*

5 **transgress**, trespass, infringe, encroach, entrench, impinge, violate, breach, usurp, squat, poach, break bounds, make inroads, barge in, intrude, invade, overrun, impair, infest

▶ *241 Violence, 734 Taking, 736 Stealing*

NOUNS

6 **overstepping**, overrunning, overrun, overpassing, overtaking, overgrowth, overspreading, inundation, overflowing, irruption, flooding, flood

7 **crossing**, crossing-over, transcursion, transilience, transcendence, leapfrog, jump, excursion, extravagation

8 **transgression**, trespass, incursion, infringement, infraction, encroachment, intrusion, invasion, breach, infestation, plague, violation, usurpation, taking liberties

9 **excessiveness**, exaggeration, overplaying, overacting, overestimation, overrating, arrogation, hyperbole, excess, overfulfilment, surplus, redundance, overindulgence, intemperance, greed

▶ *870 Self-Indulgence, 610 Excess, 541 Exaggeration*

10 **expansionism**, overextension, ribbon development, empire building, imperialism

▶ *261 Expansion*

ADJECTIVES

11 **overrun**, overspread, overgrown, overflowing, brimming, flooding, flooded, inundated, infested, beset, teeming, swarming, plagued, encroaching, trespassing, intrusive, invasive

12 **excessive**, unwarranted, overreaching, undue, uncalled-for, exorbitant, surplus

13 **exaggerated**, overdone, pretentious, affected, hyperbolic, overrated, overindulgent, overambitious, strained, far-fetched, grandiose, grandiloquent, bombastic, over-the-top (OTT) (Inf)

14 **surpassing**, overextended, overlong, one up on, in the lead, overtaken, outclassed, outdone, outbid, transcended, surmounted, outmanoeuvred

15 **out of reach**, unreachable, far away, cut off, secluded, out of bounds, forbidden

ADVERBS

16 **excessively**, overindulgently, hyperbolically, greedily, intrusively, invasively

17 **ahead**, in front, in the lead, across the line, over the border, on the other side, over the hills and far away

▶ *263 Distance*

358 Shortfall

VERBS

1 **fall short**, miss, want, lack, be found wanting, require, not answer, need, cry out for, not measure up, not fill the bill, not suffice, not stretch, not reach to, lose, make a loss, run (or stop) short, lag, not make, miss the mark, fall by the wayside, not stay the course, break down, stick in the mud, get bogged (or mired) down, fall down, lose ground, slip back, regress

▶ *360 Descent, 776 Hopelessness, 571 Necessity, 620 Imperfection, 127 Inferiority, 609 Insufficiency, 238 Weakness*

2 **fail**, fizzle out, disappoint, leave something to be desired, not come up to scratch (or expectations), not make it, not make the grade, waste effort, labour in vain

▶ *683 Failure, 129 Decrease, 515 Disappointment, 766 Dissatisfaction, 145 Incompleteness, 362 Lowering, 685 Noncompletion, 236 Powerlessness, 673 Submission, 607 Waste*

3 **fall through**, fall down, fall to the ground, fall flat, slump, collapse, break down, get hung up, come to naught (or nothing), end up, end (or go up) in smoke

▶ *628 Deterioration, 141 Disintegration, 162 Dispersion*

4 **miss**, miscarry, go amiss, go astray, miss the mark, misfire, miss the bus (or boat), miss out, miss one's mooring

▶ *211 Untimeliness, 193 Wrong Time, 209 Lateness, 844 Wrong*

NOUNS

5 **shortfall**, insufficiency, shortage, famine, dearth, scarcity, lack, loss, deficit, want, need, requirement, short measure, half measure, unfinished state, incompleteness, perfunctoriness, cursoriness, noncompletion, no go (Inf)

▶ *254 Absence, 552 Conciseness, 182 Few, 145 Incompleteness, 722 Loss, 260 Littleness, 685 Noncompletion, 743 Poverty, 270 Shortness, 372 Sparseness*

6 **shortcoming**, inadequacy, minus, falling short, fault, imperfection, inferiority, blemish, defect, deficiency, default, defalcation, arrear, arrears, arrearage, decline, slump, failure, nonfulfilment, something missing

▶ *793 Blemish, 631 Blight, 504 Error, 127 Inferiority, 661 Hindrance, 620 Imperfection, 609 Insufficiency, 614 Uselessness, 618 Worthlessness*

ADJECTIVES

7 **short**, short of, deficient, needy, wanting, lacking, scarce, missing, amiss, minus, inadequate, insufficient, unreached, unfulfilled, un-

finished, incomplete, half-done, vain

8 **defective**, broken, faulty, poor, disappointing, blemished, shop-soiled, imperfect, inadequate, perfunctory, cursory, substandard, inferior, catalectic, not up to scratch, failing, running short, not good enough, out of one's depth

▶ *124 Average, 793 Blemish*

ADVERBS

9 **behind**, behindhand, in arrears, arrear

▶ *747 Nonpayment*

10 **not enough**, inadequately, deficiently, defectively, under par, below the mark, beside the point, far from it, amiss, astray

11 **in vain**, to no purpose, vainly, fruitlessly, bootlessly

359 Ascent

NOUNS

1 **ascent**, ascension, rise, rising, levitation, assumption, uprise, uprising, uprisal, upward motion, uphill, upslope, upgo, upgoing, upcoming, upping, upgang (Dial), gaining height, defying gravity, surfacing, breaking surface, floating up

▶ *361 Raising, 281 Verticality, 39 Swimming*

2 **upturn**, upsurge, surge, spurt, gush, jet, spout, fountain, upsurgence, uptrend, upswing, upsweep, upbend, upcurve, upcast, upgrowth, upgrade, upleap, upshoot, uprush, updraught, increase, spiral, uplift, elevation, rising air, rising current, upthrow, gradient, incline, slope, hill, ramp, rising ground, high land

▶ *311 Curve, 338 Propulsion, 279 Summit*

3 **sun rise**, sun-up, dawn, first light, morning, morn, moonrise, star-rise

▶ *204 Daytime, 205 Night-Time*

4 **taking off**, leaving ground, takeoff, liftoff, departure, flying up, soaring, gaining altitude, zoom, zooming up, spiralling up, gyring up, shooting up, rocketing up, mushrooming

▶ *53 Astronomy, Astronautics, and Rocketry, 345 Departure*

5 **jump**, vault, leap, bound, leapfrog, quantum leap (*or* jump), spring, handspring, saltation, bounce, hop, skip, hop, skip, and jump, high jump, pole-vault, pole-jump, recoil, hurdle, hurdling, steeplechase, steeplechasing, standing (*or* running *or* flying) jump, ski-jump

▶ *46 Dancing and Ballet*

6 **mounting**, mount, upclimb, climb, climbing, scaling, scaling the heights, clamber, ladder-climbing, hill-climbing, mountaineering, alpinism, anabasis, going up, skylarking, attack, culmination

▶ *275 Height*

7 **means of ascent**, stairway, stairs, staircase, *escalier* (Fr), steps, treads and risers, flight of stairs (*or* steps), spiral (*or* winding) staircase,

companionway, companion, backstairs, perron, fire escape, landing, landing stage

▶ *47 Furniture and Woodwork*

8 **lift**, escalator, elevator, ski-lift, chair lift, cable car, funicular (railway), springboard, vault, trampoline

▶ *361 Raising, 30 Gymnastics*

9 **ladder**, scale, stepladder, folding ladder, loft ladder, extension ladder, roof ladder, companion ladder, accommodation ladder, side ladder, gangway ladder, quarter ladder, stern ladder, rope ladder, Jacob's ladder, ratlin(e)

10 **step**, stair, footstep, rest, footrest, rung, rundle, round, spoke, stave, scale, doorstep, tread, riser, bridgeboard, string, stepstool, kickstool, stepping-stone

11 **ascender**, rocket, skylark, laverock (Dial), skyrocket, lark, eagle, soarer, climber, upclimber, mountaineer, mountain climber, alpinist, rock climber, cragsman, excelsior figure, steeplejack, stegophilist, foretopman

▶ *78 Birds, 34 Mountaineering*

12 **geyser**, gusher, fountain, spouter

VERBS

13 **ascend**, climb, lift, rise, rise up, arise, uprise, mount, levitate, soar, spiral, spire, aspire, curl upwards, upwind, upspin, upgo, go up, upsurge, surge, upstream, upheave, swarm up, upswarm, sweep up, upgrow, grow up, reach the top, reach the zenith, culminate

▶ *279 Summit*

14 **climb**, upclimb, mount, walk up, struggle up, climb hand over fist, shin up, shinny up, monkey up, scale, escalade, scale the heights, top, breast, clear, hurdle, clamber, clamber up, scramble, scrabble up, claw one's way up, ramp, work one's way up, climb over, surmount, skylark, go over the top, go OTT (Inf)

15 **mount**, get on, climb on, back, bestride, climb into the saddle, bestraddle, board, go aboard, go on board, hop in, pile in, hop aboard, jump in, go upstairs

16 **stand up**, get up, rise to one's feet, vacate one's seat, rear, rear up, ramp

17 **spring up**, surface, float up, break water, shoot up, jump up, leap up, vault up, start up, fly up, pop up, bob up, upshoot, upspring, upstart, upleap, spurt, gush, jet, spout, fountain, play, dance, flow out, blow up, explode

18 **jump**, spring, leap, vault, hurdle, bound, bounce, hop, skip, push up, grow up, upheave

19 **take off**, lift off, rocket, skyrocket, leave the ground, leave the earth, launch, gain altitude, gain height, claw skyward, become airborne, soar, zoom, fly, plane, kite, fly aloft, spire, gyre upward

20 **hover**, levitate, float, hang, poise, float in the air, tower, loom, loom over

▶ *283 Suspension*

21 **upturn**, turn up, take an upturn, improve,

get better, trend upwards, slope up, upcast, upsweep, upbend, upcurve, steepen
▶ *627 Improvement*

ADJECTIVES

22 **ascending**, upward, uphill, uphillward, in the ascendant, climbing, scansorial, scandent, steep, upgrade (US), uparching, upwith (Dial), upturned, upcast, uplifted, turned-up, retroussé

23 **rising**, mounting, buoyant, rampant, rearing, on the up and up, bullish, escalating, uprising, upgoing, upcoming, ascendant, ascensional, ascentive, anabatic, soaring, zooming, rocketing, lifting, gaining height, light, floating, airborne
▶ *370 Lightness, 13 Economics*

24 **leaping**, springing, vaulting, jumping, hopping, saltatory, saltant, saltatorial, skipping, prancing, bounding, bouncing, spiralling, skyrocketing

25 **ladder-like**, scalar, scalariform, scalable, climbable, stepped

ADVERBS

26 **up**, upwards, upwith (Dial), upstairs, uphill, uphillward, upstream, upstreamward, uplong, upalong, uptown, up north, excelsior, ever higher, skyward, heavenward, hand over fist, onward and upward
▶ *332 Direction, 281 Verticality*

INTERJECTIONS

27 **alley-oop!**, upsy-daisy!, lift off!

360   Descent

NOUNS

1 **descent**, going down, descension, descending, lowering, declension, decline, declination, downcome, comedown, way down, down, downturn, downcurve, downbend, downdraught, downthrow, demotion, contraction, downer (Inf)
▶ *362 Lowering, 129 Decrease, 311 Curve, 54 Earth Science, 327 Way*

2 **sinkage**, decline, decrease, lowering, downward trend, depression, subsidence, droop, drooping, sag, sagging, catenary, slump, immersion, drowning, submergence, lapse, decurrence, cadence, gravitation, downgrade
▶ *317 Concavity, 234 Tendency, 628 Deterioration, 369 Heaviness*

3 **downflow**, downrush, pour, downpour, shower, rain, cascade, nappe, waterfall, rapids, cataract, chute, precipice, defluxion, landslide, landslip, subsidence, avalanche, snowslide, snowslip
▶ *300 Edge, 389 Water, 54 Earth Science*

4 **fall**, falling, dropping, plummeting, plunging, swooping, dipping, tumble, overturning, stumble, stumbling, titubation, trip, *culbute* (Fr), sprawl, crash, flop, spill, header, fate of

Icarus, downfall, collapse, debacle, failure, comedown, demotion, humiliation, ruin, end, nightfall, sunset, curtains (Inf), pratfall (US sl)
▶ *440 Darkness, 205 Night-Time, 244 Destruction, 546 Obliteration, 157 End, 504 Error, 683 Failure, 806 Humility*

5 **dive**, duck, stoop, dip, plunge, swoop, pounce, header, belly flop, nose-dive, powerdive, drop, fall, *chute* (Fr), landing, touchdown, forced landing, crash-landing, crash
▶ *39 Swimming, 53 Astronomy, Astronautics, and Rocketry*

6 **slide**, sliding, slip, slippage, slither, slid, glide, coast, glissade, glissando, inclination, declivity, hill, slope, tilt, dip, acclivity, precipice, sheer drop

7 **tunnelling**, boring, mining, burrowing, caving, speleology, digging, excavation, potholing, sapping, undermining
▶ *277 Depth, 63 Engineering*

8 **descender**, faller, free-faller, parachutist, paratrooper, aeronaut, sky-diver, hang-glider, diver, frogman, submariner, submarine, diving bell, bathysphere, underwater swimmer, diving bird, merganser, kingfisher
▶ *39 Swimming, 78 Birds*

VERBS

9 **descend**, come (or go) down, down, dip down, lose height (or altitude), gravitate, lower, get lower, get lower and lower, decrease, decline, abate, ebb, fall off, drop off, tread downward, go downhill, sink, sink down, seep, seep down, soak in, subside, settle, set, submerge, go under, drown, founder, go under water, dive, reach a lower level, alight, get down, get off, climb down, abseil, rappel, dismount

10 **droop**, sag, slouch, swag, slump, slump down, sit down, flop, flop down, plump, plop, plump down, plop down, come down a peg, hang down, prolapse, collapse, cave, cave in, crash, give way, fail, fall down, fall in, touch depth, reach the depths, touch bottom, sink to the bottom, reach one's nadir

11 **trip**, fall, fall over, fall down, take a fall (or spill), slip, slip up, totter, career, pitch, topple, topple over, overbalance, overturn, capsize, tumble, take a tumble, stumble, stagger, lurch, sprawl, spreadeagle, fall headlong, fall flat on one's face, take a header, take a nosedive, measure one's length, fall prostrate, miss one's footing, take a running jump, crash, bite the dust, go for a burton (Sl)

12 **drop**, fall, fall (or drop) down, plummet, pitch, toss, roll, plunge, swoop, dip, bow down, titubate, flutter down, spiral, spiral down, dive, drop, drop from the sky, fall through the air, parachute, skydive, fly down, pounce, duck, belly flop, nose dive, powerdive, prang, drop on, dump upon, hit (or

strike) upon, land, light upon, alight upon, come down on, settle on, descend on, perch, touch down, get down, crashland, crash

13 **drip**, drizzle, patter, shower, cascade, flow down, pour, pour down, rain, rain cats and dogs, precipitate, snow, avalanche, overflow

14 **slide**, slide down, slip, slither, slidder (Dial), skid, glide, skim, coast, glissade, toboggan, incline, sideslip, slope, tilt, dip, list, be oblique

15 **tunnel**, bore, mine, burrow, excavate, go underground, dig down, sink into the earth, sap, undermine

ADJECTIVES

16 **descending**, descendant, on the descendant, down, downward, downhill, decurrent, declivitous, deciduous, downflowing, pouring, downrushing, downturning, sinking, declining, bearish, decreasing, lowering, subsiding, slumping, drowning, foundering, tottering, tumbling, crashing, collapsing, tumbledown, submersible, sinkable

▶ *13 Economics*

17 **drooping**, droopy, sagging, on the downgrade, depressed, downcast, demoted, down at heart, down in the mouth (Inf)

▶ *770 Sorrow*

18 **falling**, tumbling, stumbling, titubant, tripping, sprawling, flopping, spilling, lurching, plunging, plummeting, diving, dipping, nosediving, dropping, falling, swooping, stooping, ducking, sliding, slipping, slithering, skidding, gliding, coasting

ADVERBS

19 **down**, downwards, down with (Dial), adown, down below, downright, downhill, downstairs, downstream, downstreet, downtown, down south, downgrade, nosedown

▶ *332 Direction*

361 Raising

VERBS

1 **raise**, erect, build, up, put up, upraise, raise up, set up, lift, levitate, uplift, lift up, hoist, heist, hike, hoick, heft, heave, upheave, uphoist, upthrow, upcast, lever, jack up, prop up, shoulder, boost, hold up, uphold, stick up, support, prevent from falling, perk up, buoy up, upbuoy, help up, put on, mount

▶ *359 Ascent, 275 Height, 284 Support*

2 **send up**, throw in the air, lob, loft, knock up, flight, sky, shoot up, propel, blow up, puff up, swell, increase, escalate

▶ *627 Improvement, 128 Increase, 359 Ascent, 338 Propulsion, 330 Impulsion, 324 Motion*

3 **promote**, heighten, give a lift, give a leg-up, aid, perk, perk up, elevate, enshrine, put on a pedestal, exalt, enhance, apotheosize, lionize, deify, beatify, canonize, sublimate,

chair, shoulder, crown

▶ *318 Prominence, 627 Improvement, 662 Help, 279 Summit, 8 Divinity*

4 **gather up**, pick up, pluck up, take up, draw up, fish up, haul up, drag up, dredge up, weigh, trip (anchor)

5 **arise**, rise, rise up, rear, uprear, lift oneself, stand up, be upstanding, get up, jump up, jump to one's feet, leap up, leap (*or* spring) to one's feet, pull oneself up, hold oneself up, hold one's head up, draw oneself to one's full height, stand on tiptoe, be vertical

▶ *281 Verticality*

NOUNS

6 **raising**, elevation, lifting, erection, escalation, rearing, uprearing, uplifting, upbuoying, uptrending, uplift, levitation, hoist, heave, upheaval, sublevation, upthrow, upcast, upthrust, picking up, ascent, defiance of gravity, antigravity

7 **lift**, boost, upswinging, upgrading, aid, leg-up (Inf), promotion, exaltation, apotheosis, godmaking, deification, canonization, beatification, enshrinement, assumption, bodily assumption, *sursum corda* (L), lionization

8 **height**, eminence, sublimity, loftiness, prominence

▶ *279 Summit, 275 Height*

9 **lifter**, crane, dredger, derrick, hoist, gantry crane, lever, jack, jackscrew, crab, lift, hydraulic lift, forklift, hydraulic tailgate, windlass, winch, tackle, capstan, jeer capstan, purchase, rope and pulley, block and tackle, luff-tackle, jeers

▶ *34 Mountaineering, 603 Tool, 63 Engineering*

10 **elevator**, lift, escalator, moving staircase, dumb waiter, spring, springboard, trampoline, ski lift, funicular, chair lift, conveyor, hot-air balloon, helium balloon, barrage balloon, hydrogen balloon, hot air, gas, hydrogen, helium, raising agent, yeast, leven, raiser, lightener, fermentation

▶ *359 Ascent*

ADJECTIVES

11 **raised**, lifted, upraised, elevated, levitated, erected, erectile, set up, escalated, upreared, uplifted, upcast, upbuoyed, attolent, supportive, upstanding, vertical, hoisted, heaved, mounted, lobbed, thrown, shot up, blown up, swollen

▶ *284 Support*

12 **exalted**, eminent, prominent, promoted, upgraded, lofty, sublime, high-flown, elevated, enshrined, on high, deified, canonized, lionized, beatified, apotheosized

ADVERBS

13 **highly**, sublimely, on stilts, on tiptoe, on one's hind legs, on high, aloft, on the shoulders of, on the back of

362   Lowering

VERBS

1 **lower**, depress, deflate, let down, take down, lay down, set down, put down, reduce, decrease, deteriorate, worsen
▶ *628 Deterioration, 360 Descent, 129 Decrease, 276 Lowness, 609 Insufficiency*

2 **flatten**, level, demolish, rase, raze, raze to the ground, fell, cut down, hew, chop, hew down, chop down, wack down, mow down, lumber, ground, fetch down, down, pull down, tear down, dash down, pull down about one's ears, trample in the dust, dent, crush, stave in, hollow
▶ *244 Destruction, 546 Obliteration, 676 War, 157 End, 317 Concavity*

3 **bring down**, overthrow, overturn, shoot down, shoot down in flames, couch, pull down, take down, overset, upset, topple, subvert, floor, send headlong, deck, lay out, bowl over, spreadeagle, torpedo, scuttle, sink, submerge, drown, duck, souse, douse, dip, plunge, send to the bottom
▶ *287 Inversion, 676 War*

4 **debase**, abase, degrade, downgrade, lower standards, demote, put down, humble, reduce to the ranks, cashier, humiliate, snub, deflate, debunk, take the wind out of one's sails, take the rise out of, water down, dilute, adulterate
▶ *127 Inferiority, 806 Humility, 238 Weakness*

5 **bear down on**, downbear, push down, thrust down, weigh on, press, press on, suppress, keep down, keep under, hold down, squash, detrude, put a lid on

6 **throw down**, throw, cast down, fling, fling down, blow over, blow down, pitch, throw overboard, drop over the side, let fall, drop, let drop, shed, let go, let slip (*or* slide), slip (*or* slide) through one's fingers, scatter, dust, sow, broadcast, disperse, pour out, pour, decant, void, spill, slop, moisten, sprinkle, shower
▶ *162 Dispersion, 391 Moisture*

7 **lean**, incline, lean over backward(s), lean forward(s), bend forward(s), bend backward(s), bend over, trip, topple, tumble, fall headlong, capsize, roll over, tip, tilt
▶ *337 Backward Motion*

8 **sit**, sit down, seat oneself, be seated, park oneself, perch, alight, squat, get down on one's haunches (*or* hunkers), crouch, hunch, stoop, bend, duck, get down, hunch down, scrooch (*or* scrunch) down, prostrate, supinate, lie down, prone, flatten oneself, couch, recline, drape oneself, spreadeagle
▶ *643 Inactivity*

9 **bow**, bend, genuflect, make a bow, bow low, bow down, kneel, kowtow, salaam, kiss hands, revere, pay respects, do reverence, curtsy, bob, duck, nod, incline one's head, make obeisance, prostrate oneself, grovel, cower, cringe, wallow, welter
▶ *808 Servility, 806 Humility, 694 Obedience*

10 **lower the flag**, lower the standard, haul down, half-mast, strike
▶ *17 Military Affairs*

NOUNS

11 **lowering**, depression, deflation, sinking, levelling, demolition, reduction, decrease, deterioration, worsening, de-escalation, diminution, descent, drop, downfall, rainfall, shower, fall, trip, tumble, spillage
▶ *389 Water, 54 Earth Science, 360 Descent*

12 **downthrow**, downcast, flattening, levelling, grounding, overthrow, overturn, overset, upset, toppling, subversion, revolution, overturning, precipitation, defenestration

13 **submergence**, sinking, ducking, sousing, pushing under, thrusting under, pushing down, detrusion, plunging, keeping down, keeping under, suppression, oppression

14 **depression**, indentation, hollow, cavity, concavity, dip, dent, sinkhole, well

15 **debasement**, degradation, downgrading, demotion, deterioration, humiliation, bowing and scraping, grovelling, Uriah Heep

16 **courtesy**, courteous act, deference, respect, comity, bow, genuflect, kneeling, kowtow, salaam, kissing hands, reverence, obeisance, curtsy, bob, duck, nod, crouch, hunch, stoop, bend, squat, prostration, supination

ADJECTIVES

17 **lowered**, depressed, deflated, flattened, grounded, levelled, demolished, reduced, decreased, deteriorated, worse
▶ *628 Deterioration, 129 Decrease*

18 **lowering**, descendent, descending, depressing, humiliating, demeaning, debasing, low, at a low ebb

19 **fallen**, sunk, sunken, soused, submerged, downcast, downthrown, defenestrated

20 **falling**, toppling, tumbling, tripping, showering, sprinkling, scattering, spilling, dropping, precipitous

21 **degraded**, debased, downgraded, demoted, humiliated, cast down, downcast, depressed, depressive, kowtowing, kneeling, grovelling, courteous, deferential

22 **overthrown**, cast down, overturned, overset, upset, toppled, subverted, suppressed, oppressed, subversive, revolutionary
▶ *701 Subjection*

23 **sedentary**, sitting, crouching, stooping, squatting, hunched, bent, bent double, prostrate, supine

ADVERBS

24 **down**, downwards, to the ground, decreasingly, reductively, subversively, oppressively, on the ground, on the floor, in the dirt, on the bottom, at rock bottom, in Davy Jones' locker,

at a low ebb, at half-mast
▶ *280 Base, 97 Seas, 277 Depth*
25 **courteously**, humbly, degradingly, on one's knees, on one's back

363 Orbital Motion

NOUNS
1 **orbital motion**, orbiting, wheeling, circling, rounding, orbit, circularity, rotation, turning, spiralling, spiral, gyre, gyring, helix, coil, ellipse, revolution, circulation, circumnavigation, circumambulation, circumambience (*or* circumambiency), circumflexion, circummigration
▶ *364 Rotation, 311 Curve, 331 Recoil, 545 Record*
2 **circuitousness**, circuitry, circuition, circulation, roundaboutness, indirection, meandering, deviance, deviation, digression, circumlocution, excursion, circumbendibus, ambages (Arch), turning, cornering, turn, U-turn
▶ *313 Circularity, 314 Convolution, 335 Deviation, 343 Divergence*
3 **orbit**, cycle, circle, full circle, wheel, circuit, ambit, round trip, lap, loop, walk, turn, rounds, beat, tour
▶ *334 Circuit, 297 Surroundings*
4 **orbiting body**, satellite, moon, planet, sun, star, asteroid, planetesimal, planetoid, Sputnik, spaceship
▶ *53 Astronomy, Astronautics, and Rocketry, 248 Space, 364 Rotation*
5 **ringroad**, orbital, bypass, M25, *péripherique* (Fr), detour, roundabout way, scenic route, tourist route, long way round, country route, the pretty way (Inf)
▶ *327 Way, 356 Passage, 335 Deviation*
VERBS
6 **orbit**, go into orbit, circuit, revolve, turn, make a circuit, describe (*or* move in) a circle, circulate, go around, go about, spiral, gyre, wheel, come full circle, make a round trip, return to the starting point, go round in circles, chase one's tail, U-turn
7 **ring**, circle, encircle, compass, encompass, surround, skirt, gird, girdle, loop, bend, curve, flank, go the round, make one's rounds, lap, circumvent, circumambulate, circummigrate, circumnavigate, girdle the earth
▶ *311 Curve, 301 Enclosure, 302 Limit, 54 Earth Science*
8 **detour**, make a detour, turn a corner, go the long way round, go all round the houses, go out of one's way, go the pretty way, deviate, bypass, digress, meander, circumlocute, beat about the bush, wander off the point
▶ *474 Sophistry, 314 Convolution*
ADJECTIVES
9 **orbital**, rotatory, rotary, revolutionary, circuitous, circulatory, turning, roundabout, in-

direct, oblique, meandering, ambagious (Arch), deviating, circumnavigable, circumambient, circumlocutory
10 **circular**, round, O-shaped, wheel-shaped, curved, spiral, heliacal, elliptical, cyclical, gyratory, coiled, looped
▶ *313 Circularity*
11 **orbiting**, wheeling, circling, spiralling, turning, spinning, gyring, gyrating
ADVERBS
12 **circuitously**, indirectly, roundabout, in a roundabout way, deviously, obliquely, by a side door (*or* wind), circlewise, wheelwise

364 Rotation

NOUNS
1 **rotation**, rotational motion, revolution, revolutions, revs (Inf), revolutions per minute (rpm), revolving, volution, orbit, orbiting, orbital motion, cycle, full circle, circulation, turbination, circumference, circumrotation, circumnutation, circumvolution, gyration, spin, spinning motion, axial motion, angular motion (*or* momentum *or* velocity), dizziness, giddiness, vertigo
▶ *363 Orbital Motion, 313 Circularity, 334 Circuit, 314 Convolution*
2 **turning**, whirling, swirling, twirling, spinning, pivoting, pirouetting, wheeling, whir, whirring, reeling, centrifugation, rolling, bowling, trolling, trundling, volutation, spiral, spiralling, twisting, torsion, torque
3 **reel**, pirouette, turn, roll, whirl, wheel, swirl, twirl, spin, dance, whirlabout, round, dizzy round, rat race
▶ *46 Dancing and Ballet*
4 **vortex**, whirl, whirlwind, whirlblast, maelstrom, charybdis, cyclone, tornado, whirlpool, eddy, swirl, surge, gurge, waterspout, twister (US inf),
▶ *54 Earth Science, 389 Water, 97 Seas, 96 Rivers, 390 Air*
5 **axle**, axis, shaft, axle shaft, spindle, axle spindle, axlebar, axle-true, axlebox, journal, journal box, hotbox, swivel, pivot, gudgeon, trunnion, pole, radiant, fulcrum, pin, pintle, hinge, hingle, rowlock, oarlock, hub, nave, distaff, mandrel, gimbal, bearing, ball bearing, roller bearing, thrust bearing, needle bearing, bevel bearing, bushing, jewel, headstock
▶ *63 Engineering*
6 **rotator**, wheel, cartwheel, wagon wheel, steering wheel, drive wheel, gearwheel, gear, spur wheel (*or* gear), worm gear (*or* wheel), cog, cogwheel, pinwheel, flywheel, ratchet wheel, idler wheel, crown wheel, balance wheel, escape wheel, sprocket wheel, mill wheel, paddle wheel, water wheel, spinning wheel, charka, spinning jenny, potter's wheel, buff-

ing wheel, roulette wheel, Catherine wheel, Ferris wheel, prayer wheel, wheel of fortune, Ixion's wheel, top, spinning top, peg top, humming top, bobbin, spindle, spool, drill, rotary drill, Archimedes' screw, rotor, circular saw, gyro, gyroscope, gyrocompass, gyrostabilizer, gyroplane, autogyro, spin-dryer, centrifuge, ultracentrifuge, impeller, turbine, propeller, prop, screw, airscrew, winder, capstan, extractor fan, turntable, gramophone record, disc (*or* disk), compact disk, floppy disk, windmill, treadmill, spit, turnspit, whisk, egg whisk, eggbeater, food processor, revolving door, rolling pin

▶ *53 Astronomy, Astronautics, and Rocketry, 45 Cookery 63 Engineering, 338 Propulsion, 47 Furniture and Woodwork*

7 **science of rotation (*or* rotatory motion)**, gyrostatics, trochilics

▶ *56 Physics, 63 Engineering*

VERBS

8 **rotate**, revolve, spin, turn, orbit, go round, circle, circulate, circuit, turn right round, chase one's own tail, spin (like a top), spin like a teetotum, twirl, pirouette, gyre, gyrate, swing, waltz, circumnutate, circumvolve, circumvolute, swing round, spin round, whirl, whirl like a dervish, go into orbit, wheel, pivot, swivel, hinge

▶ *53 Astronomy, Astronautics, and Rocketry, 46 Dancing and Ballet*

9 **roll**, wind, roll up, fold, scroll, furl, reel, spin, spin yarn, twist, screw, crank, yarn, wamble, roll along, bowl, trundle, troll, trill, set rolling

10 **swirl**, eddy, whirlpool, surge, gurge, seethe, mill around (*or* about), stir, roil, moil, mix, flounder, wallow, roll about in, welter, grovel, roll, tumble

▶ *133 Mixture, 806 Humility, 153 Disturbance*

ADJECTIVES

11 **rotating**, revolving, gyrating, turning, orbiting, swivelling, pivoting, whirling, spinning, swirling, twirling, reeling, wheeling, rolling, trolling, bowling

12 **rotary**, rotational, rotatory, rotative, orbital, pivotal, trochilic, circumrotatory, circumgyratory, gyratory, gyrational, gyroscopic, gyrostatic, centrifugal, centripetal, circling, cyclic, cyclical, circulatory, torsional, vortical, vorticose, vorticular, cyclonic, turbinated, vertiginous, dizzy, giddy, tornadic, whirlwindy, whirlwindish

ADVERBS

13 **round**, around, in a circle, round and round, in circles, in a whirl, in a spin, head over heels, heels over head, like a horse in a mill, clockwise, anticlockwise, counterclockwise, widdershins

365 Oscillation

NOUNS

1 **oscillation**, fluctuation, alternation, (simple) harmonic motion, pendular motion, swing, swing of the pendulum, pendulation, lunar motion, libration, nutation, reciprocation, periodicity, frequency, coming and going, toing and froing, shuttle service, ebb and flow, *va-et-vien* (Fr), ups and downs, boom and bust, wax and wane, flux and reflux, systole and diastole, night and day

▶ *109 Reciprocity, 212 Frequency, 214 Regularity, 285 Parallelism, 363 Orbital Motion*

2 **vibration**, vibratility, vibrancy, resonance, pulsation, rhythm, tempo, pulse, throb, beat, heartbeat, heart-throb, beating, throbbing, staccato, rat-a-tat, rataplan, drumming, flickering, shaking, quivering, shivering, palpitation, flutter, tremor, agitation, pitter-patter, pitapat, arrhythmia

▶ *426 Repeated Sound, 427 Resonance, 366 Agitation, 777 Fear, 624 Ill Health*

3 **vacillation**, wavering, equivocation, indecision, hesitation, irresolution, dubiety, mental fluctuation

▶ *576 Vacillation, 491 Uncertainty, 578 Equivocation*

4 **rock**, roll, reel, lurch, careen, pitch, shake, dance, swing, swinging, sway, swag, wag, waggle, wave, waver, waving, wave motion, undulation, undulancy, brandishing, flourishing, shaking, flaunting

▶ *324 Motion, 364 Rotation, 363 Orbital Motion, 46 Dancing and Ballet, 526 Display*

5 **wave**, ray, transverse wave, longitudinal wave, electromagnetic wave (*or* radiation), light, radio wave, sky wave, mechanical wave, radiation, heat wave, acoustic wave, sound wave, sawtooth wave, square wave, sine wave, seismic wave, seismicity, earthquake, shock wave, ground work, tremor, de Broglie wave, diffracted wave, guided wave, one- (*or* two- *or* three-)dimensional wave, node, antinode, surface wave, tidal wave, tsunami, amplitude, crest, trough, wavelength, frequency, frequency band, frequency spectrum, resonance, resonant (*or* resonance) frequency, period, wave number, diffraction, reinforcement, interference, beat, in phase, out of phase, wave equation, Schrödinger equation, Huygens' principle

▶ *56 Physics, 52 Mathematics, 54 Earth Science*

6 **measuring instrument**, oscilloscope, oscillograph, oscillometer, harmonograph, vibroscope, vibrograph, kymograph, seismoscope, seismograph, seismometer

▶ *56 Physics*

7 **oscillator**, bob, pendulum, vibrator, pendulum wheel, metronome, swing, teeter, teeter-

totter, teeterboard, teetery-bender, rocker, rocking chair, rocking stone, logan stone, seesaw, cradle, shuttle, shuttlecock
▶ *47 Furniture and Woodwork, 49 Music, 192 Timekeeping*

VERBS

8 **oscillate**, fluctuate, alternate, vary, swing, sway, move to and fro, pendulate, nutate, reciprocate, come and go, ebb and flow, wax and wane, ride and tie, hitch and hike, back and fill, seesaw, teeter, teeter-totter, shuttle, shuttlecock, wigwag, wibble-wobble, zigzag, pass and repass, leapfrog
▶ *109 Reciprocity, 212 Frequency, 214 Regularity*

9 **vibrate**, resonate, pulsate, pulse, beat, beat time, drum, tick, ticktock, throb, flutter, agitate, shake, quiver, rattle, shiver, flicker, tremble, palpitate, pant, heave, go pitapat
▶ *366 Agitation, 324 Motion, 777 Fear, 426 Repeated Sound, 192 Timekeeping*

10 **vacillate**, waver, hesitate, fluctuate, dither
▶ *576 Vacillation, 491 Uncertainty*

11 **rock**, roll, reel, lurch, career, pitch, shake, dance, stagger, totter, tumble, swing, sway, swag, waggle, waddle, wave, waver, dangle, nod, flutter, bob, bob up and down, bounce
▶ *46 Dancing and Ballet, 324 Motion*

12 **wave**, undulate, brandish, flourish, shake, wield, float, fly, flutter, flap, wag, wave to and fro, wave up and down, wallow, flounder
▶ *338 Propulsion, 526 Display*

ADJECTIVES

13 **oscillating**, oscillatory, swinging, fluctuating, fluctuant, alternating, alternate, alternative, reciprocal, reciprocative, back-and-forth, to-and-fro, up-and-down, seesaw, periodic(al), harmonic, libratory, nutational

14 **vibrating**, vibratory, vibratile, resonant, pulsating, pulsatory, pulsatile, pulsing, pulsative, beating, throbbing, staccato, rhythmic, rhythmical, flickering, quivering, shivering, shaking, agitating, palpitating, palpitant

15 **vacillating**, vacillatory, wavering, hesitant, dithering

16 **rocking**, rolling, reeling, lurching, careening, pitching, shaking, dancing, tossing, staggering, swaying

17 **waving**, undulating, undulatory, undulant, sinusoidal, sinuous, shaking, tremulous, seismic, seismatical, seismological, seismographic, seismometric, successive, successatory, sussultatory, earth-shaking

ADVERBS

18 **to and fro**, back and forth, backward(s) and forward(s), in and out, up and down, side to side, left to right, right to left, zigzag, seesaw, wibble-wobble, shuttlewise, like a bucket in a well, from pillar to post, ride and tie, hitch and hike, round and round
▶ *363 Orbital Motion, 364 Rotation, 313 Circularity*

366 Agitation

NOUNS

1 **agitation**, perturbation, mental agitation, conturbation (Arch), embarrassment, discomposure, disquiet, disquietude, inquietude, unease, nervousness, jerkiness, jumpiness, edginess, nerviness, nervosity, twitter, dither, flap, upset, unsteadiness, fits and starts, the channels (Inf), jitters (Inf), butterflies (Inf), heebie-jeebies (Inf), collywobbles (Inf)
▶ *642 Activity, 659 Difficulty, 777 Fear, 365 Oscillation, 576 Vacillation, 491 Uncertainty*

2 **tumult**, turmoil, commotion, racket, din, confusion, stir, bustle, moil, tumultation, disturbance, hubbub, hurly-burly, rout, rush, furore, frenzy, fever, excitement, maelstrom, disorder, bobbery (Inf), brouhaha (Inf)
▶ *151 Disorder, 689 Anarchy, 153 Disturbance, 676 War, 473 Argument, 666 Disagreement, 423 Loudness*

3 **turbulence**, turbidity, ferment, fermentation, effervescence, seethe, seething, swell, squall, swirl, choppiness, changeableness, pitching, rolling, joltiness, bumpiness, stir, churn, ebullition, boil, boiling, embroilment, roil, fume
▶ *153 Disturbance, 97 Seas, 389 Water, 54 Earth Science, 133 Mixture*

4 **fuss**, bother, fluster, bluster, flap, flurry, flutteration, bustle, row, song and dance, to-do, tizz (Inf), tizzy (Inf), tiz-woz (Inf)

5 **restlessness**, unrest, fever, feverishness, the fidgets, fidgetiness, hopping, twitchiness, itchiness, tossing and turning, jactation, jactitation, formication, pruritus, itching
▶ *788 Boredom, 61 Psychology and Psychiatry, 624 Ill Health, 224 Changeableness*

6 **shaking**, vibrating, quaking, quivering, quavering, shivering, shuddering, juddering, faltering, dancing, throbbing, trembling, aspen (Arch), tremulousness, vibration, succussion
▶ *427 Resonance*

7 **shake**, tremor, quiver, wriggle, squirm, wag, waggle, wiggle, shudder, judder, falter, throb, the shakes, delirium tremens (DTs), shivers, cold shivers, rigor, ague, chorea, St Vitus's dance, trembling palsy, uncontrollable tremor, shaking palsy, parkinsonism
▶ *624 Ill Health*

8 **spasm**, orgasm, ejaculation, climax, cramp, convulsion, paroxysm, fit, seizure, throes, twitch, tic, nervous tic, rictus, vellication, attack, pang, access, grip, the jerks, falling sickness, epilepsy, catalepsy, tarantism, megrims, frenzy, staggers, stroke, apoplexy, eclampsia
▶ *510 Insanity, 624 Ill Health*

9 **jolt**, jar, knock, tremor, shock, throb, jerk,

jump, sudden motion, start, judder, bump, nudge, dig, jog, joggle, jostle, jounce, bounce, bob, bobbing, jig, jigget (Inf)
▶ *425 Sudden Sound*
10 **beat**, beating, throb, throbbing, thrill, *frisson* (Fr), palpitation, flutter, pitapat, pitter-patter
▶ *425 Sudden Sound, 426 Repeated Sound, 183 Repetition*
11 **stagger**, stumble, totter, falter, flounder, flounce, rock, roll, lurch, careen, swing, sway, pitch, toss, tumble, plunge, wallow, welter, volution
12 **flicker**, flutter, twinkle, flash, flit, waver, quiver, sputter
▶ *365 Oscillation*
13 **tempest**, storm, swell, ground swell, squall, heavy sea, magnetic storm, vortex, whirlwind, disturbance, atmospherics
▶ *54 Earth Science*
14 **agitator**, shaker, vibrator, beater, jiggler, paddle, whisk, eggbeater, food processor, churn
▶ *364 Rotation*

ADJECTIVES
15 **agitated**, perturbed, troubled, disturbed, discomposed, embarrassed, nervous, nervy, edgy, uneasy, jittery, upset, unsteady, confused, ruffled, flurried, flustered, shaken, shaken up, shocked, stirred up, worked up, in a lather, troublous (Arch), hopping, leaping, aspen
16 **restless**, feverish, fevered, fidgety, itchy, unquiet, unpeaceful, twitchy, all of a tizz, all of a flutter, excited, flustered, fussing, fluttering, fluttery, hot and bothered, in a flap, panting, breathless, giddy, in a spin
17 **turbulent**, choppy, rough, bumpy, bouncy, pitching, rolling, stormy, tempestuous, boiling, seething, fuming, effervescent
18 **shaky**, shaking, quaky, quaking, quivery, quivering, quavery, quavering, unsteady, doddering, shivery, shivering, aguey, shuddering, juddering, joggling, wriggling, squirming, wiggling, wriggly, squirmy, wiggly, faltering, trembling, tremulous, wobbly, successive, successatory, vibratory, vibrating, pulsating, throbbing
19 **convulsive**, jerky, jolting, jarring, jolty, twitchy, twitchety, jumping, jumpy, palsied, fitful, spasmodic, paroxysmic, eclamptic, spastic, vellicative, orgasmic, saltatory, choreic, choreal, epileptic, cataleptic
20 **flickering**, flickery, sputtering, spluttering, guttering, sputtery, wavery

VERBS
21 **be agitated**, fuss, flap, flutter, twitter, dither, bustle, rush, mill around, jerk, jump, jump about, hop about, bounce, dance, ripple, effervesce, be in turmoil, bubble, ferment, foam at the mouth, spit tacks, seethe, simmer, boil, boil over, throw a fit, convulse, writhe,

squirm, thresh, toss and turn, jactitate, thrash about, rampage, be angry
▶ *829 Irascibility, 768 Aggravation, 642 Activity*
22 **agitate**, shake, wag, waggle, wave, flourish, brandish, fly a flag, flutter, fluster, perturb, disturb, perturbate, discompose, upset, untidy, disquiet, worry, stir, ruffle, rumple, move, trouble, swirl, churn, whip, whisk, beat, paddle, mix, stir up, rile, work up, roil, beat up, churn up, whip up, excite, muddy the waters
23 **jolt**, judder, shudder, shock, jar, jerk, twitch, bump, jog, joggle, jostle, jounce, bounce, bob, hustle, jump
▶ *338 Propulsion, 330 Impulsion*
24 **shake**, vibrate, quake, quiver, quaver, shiver, falter, shudder, judder, throb, drum, beat, pulse, thrill, pulsate, palpitate, tremble, go pitapat, twitter, didder, fidget, twitch, jerk, itch, vellicate, jig, jiggle, jigger, shake in one's shoes (*or* boots), tremble like an aspen leaf, shake like a leaf, have an ague, wriggle, squirm, wiggle, twist and turn, have ants in one's pants (Inf), jigget (Inf)
25 **pitch**, rock, wobble, waggle, totter, teeter, dither, stagger, swing, sway, lurch, swag, roll, reel, careen, plunge, toss and turn, toss and tumble, pitch and plunge, be the sport of wind and waves, flounder, founder, flounce, wallow, welter, stumble, falter, blunder, wallop, struggle, labour, thrash about
26 **flicker**, flutter, twinkle, flash, splutter, sputter, spatter, spit, flick, gutter, bicker, wave, waver, dance

ADVERBS
27 **agitatedly**, restlessly, uneasily, troublously (Arch), unquietly, unpeacefully, nervously, feverishly, in a dither, in a tizzy (Inf)
28 **shakily**, quiveringly, tremulously, quakily, tremblingly, unsteadily, waveringly, all of a twitter
29 **jerkily**, convulsively, spasmodically, in fits, in spasms, by fits and starts, with a hop, skip, and a jump, by snatches, saltatorily, like a cat on hot bricks, like a cat on a hot tin roof

367 Material World

NOUNS
1 **material world**, physical world, empirical world, real world, world of experience, world of nature, nature, laws of nature, material existence, materiality, materialness, existence, corporeity, corporeality, corporality, bodiliness, substantiality, physical being, physical existence, physical condition, concreteness, tangibility, palpability, solidity, density, weight, gravity, personality, individuality
▶ *101 Reality, 99 Existence, 289 Exterior, 369 Heaviness, 371 Density, 382 Structure*

2 **materialization**, embodiment, incarnation, corporation, epiphany, manifestation, reincarnation, metempsychosis, realization, positivism, materialism, dialectical materialism, empiricism, scientism, unspirituality, worldliness, sensuality, sensualism
▶ *8 Divinity*

3 **materialist**, dialectical materialist, Marxist, realist, humanist, positivist, chemist, physicist, geophysicist, atomist, scientist
▶ *4 Philosophy, 57 Chemistry, 56 Physics, 54 Earth Science*

4 **matter**, prime matter, brute matter, material, raw material, basic materials, materials, materiality, stuff, mass, fabric, body, frame, structure, substance, solid substance, corpus, organic matter, flesh, flesh and blood, plasma, protoplasm, cells, organism, element, elementary unit, fundamental particle, building block, principle, first principle, unit of being, origin, the four elements, earth, air, fire, and water, ingredient, factor, component, constituent, mineral, monad, chemical element, basic substance, isotope, physical element, atom, molecule, elementary particle, electron, neutron, meson, proton, quark, nucleus, nucleon, photon, quantum, ion, minuteness, nuts and bolts (Inf), the nitty-gritty (Inf)
▶ *59 Life Science, 103 Essence, 56 Physics, 57 Chemistry, 148 Component*

5 **object**, inanimate object, tangible object, still life, physical presence, body, human object, person, real person, flesh and blood, thing, something, commodity, article, item, artefact, gadget, thingumabob (Inf), thingumajig (Inf), thingummy (Inf), what's-its-name (Inf)
▶ *396 Life, 400 Humankind, 101 Reality, 99 Existence*

6 **natural science**, physical science, science of matter, science of physical properties, science, biology, chemistry, organic chemistry, inorganic chemistry, physical chemistry, geophysics, physics, mechanics, Newtonian mechanics, quantum mechanics, theory of relativity, thermodynamics, electromagnetism, applied physics, technology, atomic physics, nuclear physics, nucleonics

ADJECTIVES

7 **material**, tangible, substantial, sensible, real, natural, massy, solid, massive, concrete, palpable, ponderable, weighty, physical, empirical, spatiotemporal, objective, impersonal, clinical, neuter, incarnate, embodied, somatic, corporal, corporeal, bodily, fleshly, of flesh and blood, in the flesh, carnal, reincarnated, realized, materialized, materialistic, worldly, earthly, unspiritual, nonspiritual, sensual
▶ *101 Reality*

VERBS

8 **be material**, exist, materialize, substantialize, substantiate, make concrete, reify, objectify, externalize, realize, make real, corporealize, embody, incarnate, personify, reincarnate
▶ *99 Existence*

ADVERBS

9 **materially**, of material, with material, tangibly, substantially, sensibly, naturally, in a natural way, solidly, concretely, palpably, physically, objectively, with objectivity, impersonally, clinically, corporally, sensually

368 Nonmaterial World

NOUNS

1 **nonmaterial world**, nonphysical world, metaphysical world, ethereal world, other world, another world, imaginary world, heaven, heavenly kingdom, Elysium (or Elysian Fields), Valhalla, Olympus, happy hunting ground, hell, lower world, nether world, nether regions, place of the damned, underworld, other place, Hades, eternity, eternal life, afterlife, life after death, perpetuity, hereafter
▶ *102 Unreality, 519 Imagination, 7 Religion, 8 Divinity, 190 Eternity, 397 Death*

2 **unworldliness**, otherworldliness, unearthliness, spiritualness, spiritualization, spirituality, religion, immateriality, immaterialness, immaterialism, unreality, incorporeity (or incorporeality), incorporealness, insubstantiality (or unsubstantiality), unsubstantialness, intangibility, disembodiment, disincarnation, dematerialization, impalpability, imponderability, shadowiness, ghostliness
▶ *397 Death*

3 **spiritual world**, spirit world, world of spirits, the other side, occult phenomena, the occult, spiritualism (or spiritism), supernaturalism, animism, animatism, astral plane, astral body, spirit, ghost, phantom, ESP (extrasensory perception), sixth sense

4 **parapsychology**, psychokinesis, precognition, clairvoyance, telepathy, psychic phenomena, psychic(al) research
▶ *11 Occultism*

5 **idealism**, philosophical idealism, metaphysical idealism, absolute idealism, transcendental idealism, transcendentalism, Platonism, Neo-Platonism, Hegelianism, Kantianism
▶ *4 Philosophy, 459 Intellect, 461 Thought, 471 Idea*

6 **internal world**, nonexternality, subjectivity, solipsism, selfhood, consciousness, the conscious, myself, me, yours truly, self, ego, superego, subconscious, unconsciousness, the unconscious, id, psyche, spirit, soul, mind, intellect, psychoanalysis
▶ *61 Psychology and Psychiatry*

7 believer in a nonmaterial world, spiritualist, medium, supernaturalist, psychic, occultist, animist, parapsychologist, clairvoyant, crystal-gazer, fortune-teller, mind reader, telepathist, solipsist, idealist, religious believer, philosopher, Platonist, Neo-Platonist, Hegelian, Kantian, psychoanalyst

▶ *11 Occultism, 7 Religion*

ADJECTIVES

8 nonmaterial, nonphysical, unphysical, metaphysical, imaginary, illusory, ethereal, heavenly, eternal, perpetual, unworldly, otherworldly, other, unearthly, transcendent, transmundane, extramundane, spiritual, celestial, supernal (Fml), religious, higher, psychic(al), immaterial, immaterialist, immaterialistic, unreal, incorporeal, incorporate (Arch), insubstantial (*or* unsubstantial), intangible, airy, without mass, disincarnated, disembodied, unembodied, bodiless, without body, unfleshly, dematerializing, dematerialized, impalpable, imponderable, shadowy, ghostly

9 parapsychological, extrasensory, supersensible (*or* supersensory), precognitive, clairvoyant, telepathic, psychokinetic, psychic(al), occult, spiritual, spiritualist, spiritualistic (*or* spiritistic), supernatural, animist, animistic, astral, phantom

10 idealistic, idealist, Platonic, Neo-Platonic, Hegelian, Kantian

11 internal, nonexternal, subjective, personal, solipsist, solipsistic, conscious, subconscious, unconscious, psychoanalytic, mental, abstract

VERBS

12 enter a nonmaterial world, go to heaven, go to hell, spiritualize (*or* spiritize), dematerialize, immaterialize, disembody, disincarnate, insubstantialize (*or* unsubstantialize), practise one's religion, dabble in occultism, psychoanalyse

ADVERBS

13 metaphysically, illusorily, like an illusion, ethereally, eternally, for eternity, perpetually, forever, transcendently, spiritually, celestially, religiously, immaterially, incorporeally, insubstantially (*or* unsubstantially), intangibly, airily, impalpably, imponderably, occultly, supernaturally, clairvoyantly, telepathically, psychically

14 subjectively, personally, internally, within, nonexternally, psychoanalytically, mentally, consciously, unconsciously, abstractly, idealistically, with idealism, Platonically, Neo-Platonically

369 Heaviness

ADJECTIVES

1 heavy, weighty, having weight, weighted, with a weight of, weighing, weigh-in, weigh-

out, weighed, heavyweight, middleweight, lightweight, featherweight, leaden, solid, dense, massive, massy (Fml), considerable, great, stout, large, lumpish, lumpy, bulky, fat, overweight, obese, corpulent, heavy as a horse, heavy as lead, hefty (Inf), beefy (Inf), chunky (Inf)

2 loaded, laden, charged, overloaded, overladen, overweighed, overweighted

▶ *259 Size, 371 Density, 273 Thickness*

3 ponderous, onerous, heavy-handed, cumbersome, cumbrous, weighed (*or* weighted) down, burdensome, burdened, taxed, saddled, overburdened, overloaded, overladen, oppressive, oppressed, taxing, overtaxing, overtaxed, overbalanced, top-heavy, unwieldy, pressing, incumbent on, pressurized, handicapped

▶ *687 Adversity*

NOUNS

4 heaviness, weightiness, weight, poundage, tonnage, body weight, solid body, massiveness, mass, lumpiness, lump, bulkiness, bulk, extra weight, fatness, obesity, corpulence, brawn, beefiness (Inf), beef (Inf), heftiness (Inf), heft (Inf)

▶ *259 Size, 371 Density, 273 Thickness*

5 gravity, specific gravity, gravitation, force of gravity, gravitational pull, G, G-force

6 displacement, draught, sinkage, load, loading, freight, cargo, bale, ballast, lading, charging, charge, overload, overloading, overweighting, surcharge

▶ *70 Transport, 257 Contents*

7 weighing, weighing-in, weigh-in, weighing-out, weigh-out, dead weight, dead load, live load, gross weight, net weight, neat weight, overweight, underweight, boxing weight, heavyweight, light heavyweight, middleweight, welterweight, lightweight, featherweight, cruiserweight, bantamweight, flyweight, hefting (US inf)

▶ *32 Horses, 26 Combat Sports*

8 weighing down, weighting down, saddling, burdensomeness, burdening, burden, overburdening, ponderousness, ponderosity, incubus, onerousness, oppressiveness, oppression, taxing, tax, overtaxing, overbalance, unwieldiness, pressure, cumbersomeness, cumbrance, encumbrance, handicap, drag, stone, millstone

▶ *360 Descent, 362 Lowering, 123 Inequality, 659 Difficulty, 661 Hindrance*

9 avoirdupois weight, troy weight, apothecaries' weight, atomic weight, molecular weight, ounce, pound, stone, ton, pennyweight, hundredweight, milligram, gram, kilogram, kilo, dram, drachm, carat, scruple, axle load, laden weight

▶ *268 Measurement*

10 scales, pair of scales, scale, calibrator, weigh-

ing machine, weighbridge, bathroom scales, kitchen scales, counter scale, platform scale, spring scale, torsion scale, barrel scale, drum scale, fan scale, steelyard, balance, spring balance, spiral balance, Roman balance, counterbalance, counterpoise, makeweight, ballast, ballasting

▶ *603 Tool*

11 **weight**, sinker, lead, plumb, plumb bob, plummet, heavy weight (*or* object), lead balloon, ton of bricks (Inf)

VERBS

12 **be heavy**, have weight, gain weight, put on weight, exert weight, carry weight, weigh the same, balance, counterweigh, counterpoise, outweigh, overweigh, outbalance, overbalance, tip the scales, turn the scales, tip the balance, wallow, sink, gravitate, settle, founder, descend, weigh a ton (Inf)

13 **weigh on**, weigh (*or* lie) heavy upon, press upon, weigh one down, oppress, hang like a millstone

▶ *122 Equality*

14 **make heavy**, load, lade, weigh down, weigh one down, hang weights on, ballast, burden, make overweight, overburden, overload, encumber, cumber, charge, tax, hinder, handicap, hamper, saddle, oppress, lie heavy upon, bear (*or* rest) hard upon, overweigh, overtax

15 **weigh**, take (*or* find) the weight of, put (*or* stand) on the scales, lay on the scale, measure, weigh oneself, weigh in, weigh out, weigh in the balance, strike a balance, heft (US inf)

ADVERBS

16 **heavily**, heavy, weightily, with great weight, massively, greatly, stoutly, largely, densely, leadenly, like a ton of bricks, like a lead balloon, like lead, like a horse

17 **burdensomely**, under a burden, oppressively, with oppression, ponderously, onerously, cumbersomely, cumbrously

370 Lightness

ADJECTIVES

1 **light**, unheavy, weighing little, portable, handy, low-weight, lightweight, featherweight, bantamweight, underweight, light-footed, light on one's feet, light-handed, light-fingered, having a light touch, light as air, lighter than air, light as a feather, light as thistledown, light as a fairy, weightless, without weight, unweighable, imponderable, imponderous

▶ *274 Thinness*

2 **insubstantial**, ethereal, rare, sublime, airy, gaseous, volatile, frothy, foamy, foaming, whipped, whisked, bubbly, bubbling, effervescent, *pétillant* (Fr), sparkling, downy, feathery,

cobwebby, gossamery, fluffy, uncompressed, soft, gentle, delicate, dainty, tender, flimsy, floaty, floating, floatable, buoyant, buoyed up, unsinkable, levitative, levitational, levitating

▶ *274 Thinness*

3 **lightening**, unloading, unloaded, offloaded, aerating, aerated, easing, relieving, alleviating, alleviative, disburdening, unburdening, disencumbering

4 **leavening**, fermenting, fermentative, raising, self-raising, yeasty, enzymic, diastasic, zymotic

NOUNS

5 **lightness**, rarity, thinness, unheaviness, portability, airiness, ethereality, gaseousness, volatileness, volatility, vaporization, foaminess, frothiness, bubbliness, effervescence, sparkling, yeastiness, downiness, fluffiness, softness, gentleness, tenderness, flimsiness, delicacy, daintiness, unweighableness, imponderableness, imponderability, lack of weight, weightlessness, defiance of gravity, levitation, levitating, floating, floatability, ascent, buoyancy, levity (Arch)

▶ *260 Littleness, 372 Sparseness, 390 Air, 102 Unreality, 388 Gas, 374 Softness, 359 Ascent*

6 **lightening**, easing, easement, aeration, alleviation, relief, unburdening, unloading, unlading, unsaddling, untaxing

▶ *349 Expulsion, 660 Easiness*

7 **light thing**, air, hot air, helium, ether, bubble, balloon, snowflake, feather, down, thistledown, fluff, fuzz, oose (Scot), gossamer, cobweb, straw, dust, mote, cork, froth, foam, spume, soufflé, mousse, sponge, floating thing, float, life buoy, life belt, life jacket, life preserver (US), mae west (Sl)

8 **leavening**, leaven, fermentation, ferment, raising agent, yeast, enzyme, barm (Arch), baking powder, self-raising flour

▶ *45 Cookery, 361 Raising*

VERBS

9 **be light**, weigh little, have little weight, lack weight, defy gravity, levitate, ascend, rise, elevate, surface, float to the surface, float, swim, drift, waft, glide, soar, hover

10 **lighten**, make light, make lighter, gasify, vaporize, aerate, volatilize, buoy, buoy up, hold up, uplift, fluff, upraise, leaven, ferment, work, raise, empty, unload, off-load, unlade, lighten ship, unballast, throw overboard, jettison, disencumber, disburden, unburden, unsaddle, untax, relieve, alleviate, ease, reduce weight, lose weight

ADVERBS

11 **lightly**, with a light touch, insubstantially, without substance, ethereally, sublimely, effervescently, softly, gently, with gentleness, delicately, daintily, tenderly, with tenderness,

flimsily, fluffily, imponderably, zymotically

371 Density

NOUNS

1 **density**, denseness, solidity, solidness, bulk, mass, thickness, thickening, compactness, concreteness, toughness, hardness, hardening, closeness, cohesion, coalescence, consistency, impenetrability, impermeability, imperviousness, indissolubility, indivisibility, inseparability, coherence, incompressibility
▶ *138 Adhesion, 367 Material World, 273 Thickness, 369 Heaviness, 373 Hardness, 237 Strength, 378 Toughness*

2 **concentration**, consolidation, condensation, coagulation, constriction, haemostasis, thrombosis, concretion, concretization, solidification, congealment, constipation, nucleation, gelatinization, glaciation, ossification, petrifaction, fossilization, crystallization, sedimentation, precipitation

3 **relative density**, specific gravity, densimeter, hydrometer, aerometer
▶ *603 Tool*

4 **solid body**, solid mass, solid, mass, aggregate, conglomerate, hard core, nucleus, precipitate, deposit, sediment, coagulum, curd, clot, blood clot, thrombosis, thrombus, embolus, concretion, concrete, cement, earth, clay, hardpan, block, rock, crystal, stone, lump, chunk, clod, clump, cluster, cake, nugget, knot, node, nodule, burl, bone, gristle, cartilage, ossicle, obstacle, wall, forest, thicket
▶ *661 Hindrance, 624 Ill Health*

5 **condenser**, compressor, thickener, thickening, gelatine, rennet, pepsin

ADJECTIVES

6 **dense**, thick, compact, cohesive, close-knit, close-packed, close-textured, close-woven, incompressible, close, firm-packed, firm, full, densely arrayed, assembled, serried, massed, thick on the ground, massive, massy, heavy, weighty, monolithic, solid, concrete, rigid, inelastic, constrictive, styptic, astringent, haemostatic, strong, unbreakable, infrangible, indivisible, inseparable, consistent, impenetrable, thickset, thick-growing, bushy, luxuriant, plenteous, impermeable, impervious, without holes

7 **condensed**, consolidated, concentrated, solidified, solidifying, binding, congealed, congealing, coagulated, coagulating, constipated, constipating, costive, curdled, clotted, clotting, jelled (*or* gelled), jelling (*or* gelling), set, setting, freezing, frozen, deep-frozen, unthawed, unmelted, undissolved, insoluble, indissoluble, infusible, crystalline, crystallized, caked, matted, knotted, knotty, ropy, tangled, gnarled, lumpy, close, stuffy, foggy, murky,

smoky, thick enough to be cut with a knife

VERBS

8 **be dense**, densify, become thick, thicken, cohere, solidify, become solid, harden, cement, set, gelatinize, jellify, jell (*or* gell), congeal, coagulate, clot, curdle, cake, crust, consolidate, constipate, conglomerate, contract, form a core, form a kernel, nucleate, crystallize, fossilize, petrify, ossify, freeze, glaciate, deposit, condense, evaporate, precipitate, inspissate (Arch)

9 **make dense**, bring together, bind, crowd, mass, squeeze (*or* pack) together, pack, squeeze in, squeeze, load tightly, cram, tamp, ram down, make smaller, compact, compress, concentrate, firm up (*or* down)

ADVERBS

10 **densely**, thickly, compactly, cohesively, firmly, with firmness, fully, massively, heavily, solidly, concretely, rigidly, constrictively, strongly, plenteously, imperviously, costively, insolubly

372 Sparseness

ADJECTIVES

1 **sparse**, thin, empty, vacuous, vacuum, void, scarce, rare, tenuous, delicate, fine, wispy, light, low-pressure, windy, airy, gaseous, vaporous, volatilizable, volatilized, ethereal, buoyant, insubstantial (*or* unsubstantial), immaterial, slight, flimsy, incorporeal, uncompressed, uncompact, spongy, compressible, soft, airy-fairy (Inf)
▶ *254 Absence, 100 Nonexistence, 370 Lightness, 102 Unreality, 368 Nonmaterial World, 374 Softness*

2 **rarefied**, rarefactional (*or* rarefactive), expansive, expanding, expanded, extensive, extending, extended, attenuated, attenuate, dilative, dilatational, dilatable, dilatant, dilating, etherealized, thinning, thinned, thinned-out, diluted, dilute, weak, adulterated, watered, watered-down, cut
▶ *262 Contraction, 261 Expansion, 162 Dispersion, 238 Weakness*

NOUNS

3 **sparseness**, thinness, emptiness, vacuity, vacuousness, voidness, scarcity, scarceness, rarity, rareness, tenuity, tenuousness, delicacy, fineness, wispiness, lightness, low pressure, windiness, airiness, gaseousness, volatility, volatileness, ethereality, buoyancy, lack of substance, insubstantiality (*or* unsubstantiality), immateriality, lack of solidity, slightness, flimsiness, incorporeality, reduced pressure, compressibility, sponginess, softness

4 **rarefaction**, expansion, extension, attenuation, dilation, dilatation, etherealization, thinning, dilution, weakness, adulteration

5 gas, air, atmosphere, oxygen, hydrogen, ether, wind, vacuum, near vacuum
▶ *390 Air, 388 Gas*

VERBS
6 make sparse, thin, thin out, rarefy, gasify, vaporize, volatilize, reduce pressure, create a vacuum, hermetically seal, pump out, empty, exhaust, expand, extend, attenuate, dilate, etherealize, dilute, water, water down, cut, weaken, adulterate

ADVERBS
7 sparsely, thinly, emptily, with emptiness, vacuously, in a vacuum, tenuously, delicately, finely, lightly, airily, ethereally, insubstantially (*or* unsubstantially), expansively, by expanding, extensively

373 Hardness

ADJECTIVES
1 hard, hard as steel, hard as nails, steely, steel, diamond-like, iron, wrought-iron, cast-iron, hard as iron, stone, stony, hard as stone, lithic, granite, granitic, marble, rock, rocky, rockhard, hard as a rock, rocklike, lapideous, lithoid (*or* lithoidal), lithic, flinty, pebbly, gravelly, gritty, lumpy, horny, corneous, callous, leathery, bony, osseous, ossific, cartilaginous, gristly, sclerotic, crusty, incrusted, glassy, crystalline, vitreous, petrifactive, petrifying
▶ *237 Strength, 371 Density, 407 Touch*
2 tough, strong, firm, solid, rock-solid, unbreakable, adamant, indestructible, shatterproof, resistant, starchy, starched, boned, whaleboned, stark, stiff, rigid, inflexible, inelastic, unsprung, unrelaxed, tight, taut, tense, pokerlike, muscle-bound, muscular, stiff as a board, stiff as a poker, stiff as a ramrod, stiff as buckram
▶ *378 Toughness*
3 hardened, toughened, fortified, strengthened, stiffened, reinforced, backed, braced, buttressed, proofed, tempered, heat-treated, annealed, oil-tempered, indurate, indurated, case-hardened, hard-boiled, steeled, armoured, armour-plated, callous, calloused, ossified, hornified, calcified, crusted, crystallized, granulated, vitrified, petrified, fossilized, sunbaked, solidified, set, frozen, frozen solid, frozen over, icy
4 mentally hard, inflexible, stubborn, obdurate, obstinate, firm, tough, intransigent, unadaptable, unpliable, unpliant, unmalleable, intractable, intractile, unbending, unyielding, ungiving, unalterable, immutable, difficult, callous, case-hardened, hardhearted, stonyhearted, heartless, insensitive, thick-skinned, hard-boiled, tough as old boots (Inf)

NOUNS
5 hardness, strength, firmness, solidity, impenetrability, resistance, density, hard core, hard centre, toughness, toughening, steeliness, stoniness, rockiness, cragginess, grittiness, lumpiness, nodularity, nodosity, rigidity, rigidness, rigour, temper, stiffness, stiffening, starchiness, starching, tautness, tightness, inflexibility, inelasticity, inextensibility, tension, tenseness, tensity, backing
6 solidification, hardening, setting, crystallization, granulation, petrifaction (*or* petrification), fossilization, lapidification, ossification, vitrification, glaciation, steeling, tempering, vulcanization, calcification, sclerosis, atherosclerosis, multiple sclerosis, arteriosclerosis, hardening of the arteries
▶ *54 Earth Science, 624 Ill Health*
7 hard substance, diamond, steel, hard steel, hammer, iron, wrought iron, cast iron, metal, aluminium, Duralumin (Tm), nail, hardware, stoneware, rock, stone, stone wall, adamant, pebble, grit, boulder, silica, flint, granite, quartz, marble, brick, cement, concrete, concrete block, reinforced concrete, ferroconcrete, baked brick, brick wall, brick house, bulletproof glass, armour, wood, hardwood, heartwood, duramen, oak, heart of oak, teak, board, bone, gristle, cartilage, spine, backbone, fingernail, toenail, horn, ivory, shell, wart, corn, callus, node, nodule, lump, crust, jawbreaker (*or* jawcrusher)
▶ *54 Earth Science*
8 mental hardness, toughness, hardness of heart, hardheartedness, callousness, obduracy, obstinacy, intractability, intransigence, inflexibility, unpliability, unmalleability, unbendingness, unyieldingness, immovability, stubbornness, asperity
▶ *577 Obstinacy*

VERBS
9 harden, make hard, render hard, toughen, case-harden, strengthen, steel, temper, reinforce, brace, buttress, shore, shore up, back, tighten, stiffen, tauten, starch, wax, tense, vulcanize, crisp, bake, heat, heat-treat, hard-boil, anneal, freeze, refrigerate
10 solidify, petrify, fossilize, ossify, calcify, vitrify, crystallize, glaciate, granulate, candy, set, firm, stiffen, condense, thicken, jell (*or* gel)
11 be stubborn, remain intransigent, not yield, not bend, not give, not alter

ADVERBS
12 toughly, strongly, resistantly, by offering resistance, starkly, stiffly, with stiffness, rigidly, tightly, tautly, tensely, in a tense manner, stonily, grittily, crustily, icily
13 inflexibly, without flexibility, stubbornly, in a stubborn manner, firmly, with firmness, intransigently, intractably, unalterably, im-

mutably, callously, hardheartedly

374   Softness

ADJECTIVES

1 **soft**, softening, softened, unstarched, un-stiffened, nonrigid, flaccid, limp, rubbery, flabby, floppy, flimsy, unstrung, relaxed, slack, lax, loose, sprung, fluid
▶ *387 Fluid*

2 **pliant**, pliable, giving, yielding, melting, flexible, flexile, bendable, stretchable, elastic, lithe, lithesome, willowy, supple, lissom, limber, loose-limbed, double-jointed, springy, acrobatic, athletic, plastic, extensile, extensible, extendible, ductile, tractile, tractable, adaptable, malleable, mouldable, shapable, impressible, waxy, doughy, pasty, putty-like
▶ *377 Elasticity*

3 **smooth**, satiny, satinlike, silky, silken, velvety, velvet, velvetlike, plushy, plush, downy, feathery, fluffy, flossy, woolly, fleecy, flocculent, furry
▶ *376 Smoothness*

4 **compressible**, squeezable, padded, foam-filled, cushiony, pneumatic, pillowed, podgy, pudgy, spongy, mashy, soggy, squashy, squishy, squelchy, juicy, overripe, pulpy, pithy, medullary, muddy, boggy, marshy, mossy, grassy, turfy, loamy, clayey, argillaceous

5 **soft as butter**, soft as wax, soft as soap, soft as down, soft as velvet, soft as silk, soft as putty, soft as dough, soft (*or* smooth) as a baby's bottom, soft as a kiss, soft as a whisper, soft as a sigh, tender as a spring chicken

6 **softhearted**, tender-hearted, kind-hearted, warm-hearted, sympathetic, compassionate, gentle, tender, kind, delicate, mild, easy, easygoing, relaxed, lenient, lax, complaisant, mellow, laid-back (Inf)

7 **impressionable**, susceptible, formable, sensitive, formative, nonresistive, easing, mollifying, mollified, showing leniency, appeasing, complying, adapting, adaptable

NOUNS

8 **softness**, softening, softening-up, pliability, pliableness, pliancy, flexibility, bendability, give, suppleness, willowiness, limberness, litheness, nonrigidity, springiness, springing, elasticity, plasticity, ductility, tensileness, tractability, malleability, impressibility, rubberiness, extendibility, extensibility, looseness, slackness, flaccidity, flaccidness, flabbiness, floppiness, limpness

9 **smoothness**, downiness, fluffiness, furriness, woolliness, flocculence, flossiness, featheriness, silkiness, velvetiness, satininess, plushiness

10 **compressibility**, sponginess, pulpiness,

doughiness, semiliquidity, sogginess, marshiness, bogginess, squashiness, squelchiness

11 **soft thing**, feather, feather bed, eiderdown, swan's-down, duvet, continental quilt, pillow, cushion, armchair, easy chair, sofa, pad, padding, upholstery, wadding, foam-filling, foam, fluff, puff, fur, cotton wool, wool, fleece, silk, satin, velvet, velveteen, plush, down, thistledown, kapok, hair, paste, modelling clay, Plasticine (Tm), play dough, dough, putty, wax, soap, butter, pulp, mousse, mud, marsh, bog, snowflake, snow, breeze, zephyr
▶ *405 Physical Pleasure, 78 Birds, 55 Meteorology and Climatology*

12 **gentleness**, tenderness, delicacy, mellowness, mildness, kindness, sensitiveness, easiness, easing up, leniency, laxity, laxness, laxation, mollification, mollifying, appeasement, compliance, complying, obedience, adaptability
▶ *691 Leniency, 689 Anarchy, 673 Submission*

VERBS

13 **soften**, soften up, unstiffen, sag, flop, unstring, relax, slacken, loosen, bend, unbend, spring, mould, shape, make an impression in, impress, wax, smooth out, pad, cushion, plump up, plump, fluff up, fluff, shake up, featherbed, render soft, tenderize, mellow, mature, ripen, overripen, oil, grease, lubricate, knead, massage, mash, whip, pulp, squash, pulverize, chew, masticate, macerate, marinate, steep, drench, melt, thaw, liquefy

14 **ease**, relax, unwind, mellow, temper, lessen, mitigate, demulce, assuage, soothe, subdue, soften the tone, tone down, turn down, simmer down, mollify, limber up, massage, loosen, loosen up, hang loose (Sl), cool it (Sl), cool (*or* chill) out (Sl)

15 **be kind**, show gentleness, show tenderness, show leniency, have compassion, ease up

16 **yield**, give way, give in, give, relent, appease, comply, obey, adapt, submit

ADVERBS

17 **softly**, with softness, limply, flaccidly, flimsily, slackly, loosely, laxly, fluidly, pliantly, flexibly, elastically, lithely, lissomly, limberly, acrobatically, like an acrobat, athletically, like an athlete, waxily, smoothly, pneumatically, silkily, fluffily, soggily

18 **softheartedly**, gently, tenderly, with tenderness, sensitively, delicately, easily, leniently, laxly, compassionately, with compassion, mildly, complaisantly, impressionably, susceptibly, compliantly, submissively

375   Roughness

ADJECTIVES

1 **rough**, roughened, rough-hewn, roughcast, unsmooth, textured, rippled, rippling, ripply,

undulatory, wrinkled, wrinkly, crinkled, crinkly, crumpled, crumply, rugose (or rugous), uneven, corrugated, nonuniform, irregular, ruffled, muricate (or muricated), inequal, rugged, ragged, unsifted

▶ *383 Texture, 385 Friction*

2 **coarse**, coarse-grained, rough-grained, cross-grained, grainy, granulated, gravelly, stony, rocky, rockbound, ironbound, craggy, cragged, scraggly, scraggy, snaggy, snagged, snaggled, nodose (or nodous), nodular, lumpy, slubbed, hispid, villous, spiny, nubby, studded, knobby, knobbly, knotted, knotty, gnarled, gnarly, knurled, bouclé, shattered, broken, jagged, jaggy, sharp, serrated, ridged, rough-edged, deckle-edged, corrugated, grated, tweed, tweedy, potholed, furrowed, rutty, rutted, pitted, pockmarked, pocked, pocky, pimply, scabby, scabrous, encrusted, scaly, warty, blistered, cracked, chapped

3 **barbed**, prickly, scratchy, notched, hacked, hairy, unshorn, hirsute, shockheaded, pigtailed, ponytailed, bushy, woolly, flocculent, lanate, furry, matted, curly, frizzy, fuzzy, shaggy, shagged, bristly, bristling, bristled, barbellate, setiform, setose, strigose, hispid, unkempt, unshaven, stubbled, stubbly, bearded, bewhiskered, moustached

▶ *380 Sharpness*

4 **bumpy**, jolting, agitated, turbulent, choppy, tempestuous, storm-tossed

5 **unfinished**, incomplete, unpolished, unrefined, shapeless, rudimentary, preliminary, cursory, crude, raw, rough-and-ready, sketchy, vague, approximate

NOUNS

6 **roughness**, unsmoothness, wrinkliness, rugosity, unevenness, corrugation, nonuniformity, irregularity, inequality, rough going, joltiness, bumpiness, rough surface, rough ground, ruggedness, raggedness, granulation, coarseness, coarse grain, coarse cloth, cragginess, scraggliness, nodosity, lumpiness, rough air, strong wind, turbulence, rough water, choppiness, hispidity, bristliness, horripilation, villosity, spininess, nubbiness, nubbliness, rough skin, scaliness, scabrousness, hairiness, rough hair, shagginess, knobbliness, scratchiness, rough texture, rough fibre, shattered surface, brokenness, jaggedness, sharp edge, serration, saw edge, rough edge, deckle edge, scalloped edge

▶ *385 Friction, 383 Texture, 390 Air, 389 Water, 293 Covering, 300 Edge*

7 **rough thing**, roughcast, sandpaper, glasspaper, emery paper, emery board, emery wheel, file, corrugated iron, washboard, grater, steel wool, scrubbing brush, nailbrush, sackcloth, homespun, tweed, linsey-woolsey, corduroy, knot, kink, bouclé, chapped hands, bumpy face,

acne, creeping flesh, goose flesh, goose pimples, goose bumps, barbed wire, broken glass, notched wood, splinter, burr, bristle, awn, thistle, prickle, barb, thorn, scale, scab, matted hair, shag, stubble, five-o'clock shadow, plaid, braid, pigtail, ponytail, dreadlocks, beard, goatee, whiskers, muttonchops, moustache, handlebars, horsehair, designer stubble (Inf)

▶ *295 Dress, 793 Blemish, 321 Furrow, 319 Notch, 314 Convolution*

8 **rough ground**, broken ground, canyon, mountain, sierra, rough road, potholed road (or street), dirt road, dirt track, sheeptrack, furrow, rut, crack, undergrowth, overgrowth

▶ *70 Transport*

9 **broken water**, ripple, big wave, tidal wave, tsunami, choppy sea, air pocket, hurricane, tornado, cyclone, twister (US inf)

▶ *54 Earth Science*

10 **rough idea**, rough working, rough copy, rough approximation, rough, mock-up, draft, preliminary sketch, unfinished piece, crudeness, incompleteness, shapelessness, rudiment, cursoriness, sketchiness, vagueness, approximateness

▶ *471 Idea, 118 Imitation, 553 Diffuseness, 555 Lack of Emphasis*

VERBS

11 **be rough**, lack uniformity, lack regularity, lack equality, have a rough surface (or texture), ripple, crack, chap, have a bumpy face, have acne, creep (of flesh), horripilate, bristle, bristle up, prickle, scale, bump, jolt, jerk

12 **make rough**, rough, rough up, roughen, roughen up, roughcast, rough-hew, ruffle, wrinkle, crease, fold, crinkle, crumple, rumple, corrugate, granulate, coarsen, stud, emboss, boss, break, crack, hack, serrate, crenate, notch, engrail, indent, mill, sandpaper, grate, go against the grain, rub up the wrong way, set on edge, knot, kink, tousle, tangle, gnarl, pothole, furrow, plaid, braid

13 **be unfinished**, leave unfinished (or incomplete), give a rough idea, make a rough copy, approximate, sketch, make a preliminary sketch, draft, rough out, mock-up

ADVERBS

14 **roughly**, rough, in the rough, unsmoothly, against the grain, against the nap, the wrong way, choppily, unevenly, rugosely, irregularly, without regularity, inequally, without equality, ruggedly, coarsely, stonily, lumpily, turbulently, bumpily, villously, sharply, brokenly, jaggedly

15 **incompletely**, in unfinished form, shapelessly, without shape, preliminarily, crudely, sketchily, vaguely, approximately

376   Smoothness

ADJECTIVES

1 **smooth**, smoothing, smoothed, smooth-surfaced, smooth-textured, streamlined, non-frictional, frictionless, even, unrough, flush, sleek, slick (US), bald, clean-shaven, hairless, glabrous (or glabrate), smooth-haired, well-brushed, combed, brushed, groomed, carded, silken, silky, satiny, velvety, smooth-skinned, peachlike, fleecy, woolly, soft, downy

2 **uniform**, even, regular, horizontal, plane, level, harrowed, rolled, steamrolled, flattened, unsharpened, blunt, edgeless, rounded, curved, waterworn, flat, ironed, unwrinkled, uncrumpled, unruffled, unbroken

▶ *381 Bluntness, 311 Curve, 315 Roundness*

3 **soothing**, peaceful, still, quiet, calm, dead, quiescent

4 **polished**, varnished, burnished, waxed, enamelled, lacquered, glazed, glacé, gleaming, shiny, glossy, glassy, mirror-like, reflective, slippery, slick (US), skiddy, slithery, buttery, lubricated, lubricious, oily, oiled, greasy, greased, soapy

5 **smooth as a peach**, smooth as a baby's bottom, smooth as glass, smooth as velvet, smooth as satin, satin-smooth, smooth as marble, slippery as an eel, slippery as a greased pig, calm as a mill pond

6 **smooth-mannered**, well-mannered, suave, smooth-spoken, sophisticated, urbane, glib, slick, sleek, sycophantic, unctuous, ingratiating, creepy (Inf), smarmy (Inf)

NOUNS

7 **smoothness**, evenness, flushness, smooth texture, smooth surface, uniformity, regularity, horizontality, levelness, flatness, peacefulness, stillness, calmness, serenity, calm, dead calm, unruffled surface, quiescence, making smooth, levigation, sleekness, silkiness, satininess, velvetiness, fleeciness, softness, shininess, shine, lustre, finish, glossiness, glassiness, slickness (US), slipperiness, slitheriness, unctuousness, lubrication, lubricity, oiliness, greasiness

▶ *282 Horizontality, 112 Uniformity, 325 Motionlessness, 439 Light*

8 **smooth thing**, silk, satin, velvet, velveteen, velour, down, swan's-down, hair, baby's bottom, bald head, mahogany, marble, alabaster, ivory, glass, mirror, ice, dance floor, ice rink, lawn, plumb wicket, bowling alley, bowling green, artificial turf, Astroturf (Tm), desert, plain, billiard table, billiard ball, tennis court, paving, asphalt, Tarmac (Tm), flagstone, slide, chute, slipway, millpond, smooth water, dead water, calm water

9 **smoother**, roller, garden roller, steamroller, bulldozer, rolling pin, flattener, trowel, iron,

electric iron, smoothing iron, flatiron, tailor's goose, mangle, wringer, press, hot press, trouser press, plane, spokeshave, drawknife, rake, harrow, card, comb, brush, hairbrush, sandpaper, glasspaper, emery paper, emery board, file, nailfile, buffer, floor polisher, sander, burnisher, chamois, waxer

▶ *385 Friction, 796 Fashion, 621 Cleanness*

10 **polish**, shoe polish, car polish, floor polish, furniture polish, silver polish, French polish, varnish, burnish, enamel, gloss, glaze, patina, wax, facing, lubricant, grease, oil, lubricator, grease gun, oilcan

▶ *386 Lubrication*

VERBS

11 **smooth**, smoothen, smooth out (or away), remove friction, streamline, plane, planish, even, level, harrow, mow, rake, flatten, flatten down, plaster down, comb, rub down, rub, roll, calender, press, hot-press, uncrease, iron, iron out, unravel, mangle, shave, cut, shorten, smooth down, file down, sand, sandpaper, emery, levigate, slick down (US), slick (US), starch, launder, clean, shine, burnish, make bright, buff, polish, glaze, glacé, butter, gloss, wax, varnish, paint, coat, finish, pave, Tarmac (Tm), overlay, Astroturf (Tm), lubricate, oil, grease

12 **go smoothly**, feel no friction, glide, skate, ice-skate, roller-skate, roll, ski, float, bowl along, run on rails, slip, slide, skid, coast, freewheel

▶ *324 Motion*

13 **smooth over**, soothe, calm, appease, pacify, allay, ameliorate, assuage, mitigate, alleviate, charm, ingratiate, toady, creep up to (Inf), suck up to (Inf)

ADVERBS

14 **smoothly**, evenly, unroughly, without roughness, flushly, sleekly, slickly (US), uniformly, on an even keel, regularly, horizontally, levelly, flatly, bluntly

15 **soothingly**, peacefully, without trouble, stilly, quietly, calmly, softly, quiescently

16 **suavely**, sophisticatedly, glibly, urbanely, sleekly, sycophantically, unctuously, creepily (Inf), smarmily (Inf)

377   Elasticity

NOUNS

1 **elasticity**, stretch, stretchability, stretchiness, stretching, suppleness, plasticity, rubberiness, extensibility, extension, distension, flexibility, pliancy, pliability, tensibility, tension, strain, ductility, tonicity, tonus, tone, springiness, spring, resilience (or resiliency), give, snap, snapback, recoil, rebound, bounciness, bounce, flex (Inf)

▶ *252 Displacement, 216 Change, 374 Softness, 331 Recoil*

2 **adaptability**, resilience (*or* resiliency), buoyance (*or* buoyancy), flexibility, adjustability, responsiveness, liveliness, compliance, accommodation, yielding
▶ *224 Changeableness, 116 Accord, 467 Attention, 664 Cooperation, 660 Easiness*

3 **elastic thing**, elastic tissue, whalebone, baleen, elastic band, rubber band, rubber ball, tennis ball, handball, basketball, stretch fabric, Lycra (Tm), spandex, stretch jeans, gum, chewing gum, bubble gum, spring, springboard, diving board, trampoline, pogo stick, bungee rope, racket, jumping jack, catapult, slingshot (US), condom
▶ *796 Fashion, 50 Painting and Sculpture*

4 **rubber**, gum elastic, elastomer, crude rubber, natural rubber, latex, caoutchouc, guttapercha, plantation rubber, india rubber, foam rubber, sponge rubber, hard rubber, vulcanized rubber, vulcanite, ebonite, synthetic rubber, Thiokol (Tm), cold rubber, Buna (Tm), nitrile, neoprene, silicone rubber, crepe rubber, Butyl (rubber) (Tm), polyurethane rubber, reclaimed rubber, rubber plantation, rubber plant, rubber tree

5 **spring**, mainspring, hairspring, coil spring, spiral spring, volute spring, leaf spring, bedspring (US), box spring, suspension system, shock absorber
▶ *314 Convolution*

ADJECTIVES

6 **elastic**, rubber, rubbery, rubberlike, rubberized, stretchable, stretchy, stretching, stretch, stretched, supple, plastic, extensible (*or* extensile), extending, extended, distensible, distending, distended, flexible, flexing, flexed, pliant, pliable, tensile, tensible, ductile, tonic, springy, springing, sprung, well-sprung, coiling, coiled, resilient, giving, yielding, snapping, recoiling, rebounding, bouncy, bouncing

7 **adaptive**, adaptable, adapting, adapted, resilient, buoyant, flexible, adjustable, adjusting, adjusted, responsive, responding, lively, compliant, complying, yielding, accommodating

VERBS

8 **be elastic**, stretch, extend, expand, distend, flex, have flexibility, have tone, show resilience, give, spring, snap, snap back, recoil, rebound, bounce

9 **make elastic**, elasticize, elasticate, rubberize, rubber, vulcanize, plasticize

10 **be adaptable**, adapt, have resilience, have buoyancy, stay flexible, comply, adjust, respond quickly, accommodate, yield, bounce back

ADVERBS

11 **elastically**, supplely, with suppleness, plastically, flexibly, pliantly, springily, bouncily

12 **adaptably**, resiliently, flexibly, responsively, compliantly, accommodatingly

378 Toughness

ADJECTIVES

1 **tough**, strong, rugged, solid, sturdy, resistant, resisting, durable, hard-wearing, lasting, long-lasting, infrangible, untearable, unbreakable, nonbreakable, unshatterable, shatterproof, shockproof, chip-proof, fractureproof, bulletproof, bombproof, fireproof, indestructible

2 **toughened**, case-hardened, tanned, hardened, tempered, annealed, vulcanized, strengthened

3 **hard**, rock-hard, rigid, stiff, nonelastic, inelastic, unsprung, leathery, leatherlike, coriaceous, firm, clinging, stuck, cohesive, coherent, viscid, chewy, fibrous, woody, ligneous, gristly, cartilaginous, rubbery, overdone, hard-boiled, inedible, indigestible, tough as nails, tough as old boots, tough as (shoe) leather
▶ *373 Hardness*

4 **powerful**, athletic, muscular, brawny, burly, sinewy, strapping, weather-beaten, lean, wiry, stringy, full of vitality, blessed with stamina, robust, enduring, untiring, unflagging, indefatigable, tenacious, resilient, hardy, stalwart, rough, brutal, vicious, bullying
▶ *237 Strength*

5 **mentally tough**, mentally strong, resolved, single-minded, unyielding, stubborn, obstinate, obdurate, inflexible, hardhearted, stern, unfeeling, callous, cynical, case-hardened, thick-skinned, hard-boiled (Inf), hard-nosed (Inf)
▶ *570 Will, 575 Perseverance, 498 Disbelief*

NOUNS

6 **toughness**, strength, ruggedness, solidness, sturdiness, resistance, durability, survivability, lastingness, infrangibility, unbreakableness, unbreakability, hardness, rigidness, stiffness, firmness, clinging, cohesiveness, cohesion, coherence, viscidity, leatheriness, stringiness, rubberiness, chewiness, inedibility, indigestibility
▶ *371 Density, 188 Duration, 373 Hardness, 138 Adhesion*

7 **tough thing**, leather, gristle, cartilage, bulletproof glass, bulletproof vest, air-raid shelter, nut, coconut

8 **physical strength**, physical power, powerful build, athletic build, muscularity, muscles, sinews, brawn, leanness, wiriness, stringiness, vitality, vigorousness, vigour, stamina, robustness, stalwartness, tenacity, endurance, resilience, hardiness, lasting power, physical roughness, brutality, brute force, viciousness, bullying
▶ *239 Vigour, 241 Violence*

9 **mental toughness**, mental strength, resolve, single-mindedness, unyieldingness, stubbornness, obstinacy, obdurateness, inflexibility, hardheartedness, sternness, unfeelingness, callousness, cynicalness

▶ *570 Will, 575 Perseverance, 498 Disbelief*

VERBS

10 **be tough**, show strength, resist, last, outlast, survive, have survivability, endure, stay the course, resist breaking, toughen, harden, stiffen, cling, stick fast, have physical strength, have an athletic build, flex one's muscles, show stamina, have tenacity, refuse to yield, have no feelings, act rough, brutalize, use brute force, bully, hang tough (Sl), tough something out (Inf)

▶ *188 Duration, 768 Aggravation*

11 **make tough**, strengthen, harden, tan, mercerize, vulcanize, temper, anneal, case-harden, make unbreakable, shatterproof, bulletproof, bombproof, fireproof

ADVERBS

12 **toughly**, strongly, using strength, ruggedly, solidly, sturdily, resistantly, resistingly, durably, lastingly, infrangibly, indestructibly, rigidly, stiffly, firmly, cohesively, coherently, viscidly, indigestibly

13 **powerfully**, athletically, muscularly, leanly, robustly, enduringly, untiringly, tenaciously, resiliently, hardily, stalwartly, roughly, brutally, with brute force

14 **single-mindedly**, stubbornly, obstinately, obdurately, inflexibly, hardheartedly, sternly, unfeelingly, callously, cynically

379 Brittleness

ADJECTIVES

1 **brittle**, brittle as glass, fragile, fragile as an eggshell, frangible, delicate, papery, wafer-thin, flimsy, frail, unsturdy, unsteady, insubstantial, shoddy, gimcrack, jerry-built, dilapidated, tumbledown, weak, vulnerable, breakable, ready to break, breaking, broken, ready to burst, bursting, burst, explosive, crackable, ready to crack, cracking, cracked, crackled, chipping, chipped, shatterable, shattering, shattered, ready to split, splitting, split, splintery, splintering, scissile, tearable, tearing, torn, crushable, crushing, crushed, crumbly, crumbling, crumbled, short, friable, fissile, flaky, flaking, powdery, crispy, crisp, inelastic, rigid, like parchment, crazy (Arch)

▶ *238 Weakness, 136 Separation, 628 Deterioration, 380 Sharpness, 373 Hardness*

NOUNS

2 **brittleness**, fragility, fragileness, frangibility, frangibleness, delicacy, flimsiness, frailty, unsturdiness, weakness, vulnerability, breakableness, breakability, breaking, break-up, cracking, crackup, splitting, split, splintering, scission, crushability, crumbliness, crumbling, deterioration, friability, friableness, fissility, flakiness, crispness, crispiness, inelasticity, rigidness

3 **brittle thing**, eggshell, icicle, thin ice, ice sculpture, old paper, parchment, rice paper, old bone, lamina, dead leaf, piecrust, pastry, matchwood, balsa (or balsawood), shale, slate, glass, windowpane, glasshouse, greenhouse, crystal, porcelain, pottery, weak thing, jerry-built house, house of cards, sand castle, snowman, bubble

VERBS

4 **be brittle**, be fragile, deteriorate, wear thin, crash, give way, fall in, tumble, fall to pieces, break, break down, break apart (or up), craze (Dial), disintegrate, burst, explode, crack, crack off, fracture, shatter, break off, snap off, snap, split, splinter, chip, chip off, crush, crumble, flake, fragment, shiver, live in a glass house

ADVERBS

5 **fragilely**, delicately, flimsily, frailly, unsteadily, insubstantially, shoddily, weakly, vulnerably, explosively, crispily, rigidly, without flexibility

6 **by cracking**, by chipping, by shattering, by bursting

380 Sharpness

ADJECTIVES

1 **sharp**, sharpened, pointed, pointy, sharp-pointed, needle-pointed, needle-like, acicular, aciculate (or aciculated), mucronate, acuminate, needle-sharp, sharp as a needle, spearlike, lanceolate, lance-shaped, hastate, arrow-like, sagittal, sagittate (or sagittiform), unblunted, tapered, tapering, fastigiate, conic(al), pyramidal, convergent, spindle-shaped, fusiform, wedge-shaped, wedgy

2 **spiked**, spiky, star-pointed, star-shaped, star-like, stellate, stellular, barbed, spiny, spinose, spinous, acanthoid, acanthous, prickly, pricky, pricking, bristly, bristling, hispid, awned, stinging, stingy, thorny, brambly, briery, thistly, sharp as broken glass

▶ *379 Brittleness*

3 **sharp-edged**, sharp-set, honed, razor-edged, razor-sharp, sharp as a razor, knife-edged, knifelike, cultrate, keen, keen as a razor, keen-edged, double-edged, cutting, swordlike, ensiform, saw-edged

4 **toothed**, toothy, fanged, fanglike, tusked, tusklike, horned, hornlike, corniculate, cornute (or cornuted), toothlike, odontoid, dentiform, denticulate, cusped, cuspidate (or cuspate), muricate (or muricated), serrated, notched, emarginate (or emarginated), comblike, pectinate (or pectinated), snagged, snaggy,

snaggle-toothed, craggy, rough, jagged
▶ *319 Notch*

5 **mentally sharp**, sharp-witted, quick-witted, keen-minded, acute, astute, alert, bright, shrewd, clever, smart, intelligent, perspicacious, discerning, observant, perceptive, sharp-eyed, keen, acuminous, sharp as a tack, razor-sharp, sharp-tongued, acerbic
▶ *459 Intellect*

NOUNS

6 **sharpness**, pointedness, acumination, mucronation, spininess, spinosity, thorniness, bristliness, prickliness, denticulation, dentition, serration
▶ *342 Convergence*

7 **sharp point**, point, knife point, pencil point, sword point, cusp, vertex, prong, tine, sting, dent, notch, sharp edge, saw-edge, cutting edge, knife edge, razor edge, jagged edge
▶ *319 Notch, 680 Weapon*

8 **sharp-pointed thing**, pyramid, summit, peak, crag, arête, projection, spire, steeple, flèche, nail, tack, stylus, pin, hatpin, drawing pin, thumbtack (US), pushpin (US), burin, rowel, staple, nib, needle, knitting needle, bodkin, hypodermic needle, pick, pickaxe, icepick, toothpick, fork, pitchfork, harrow, rake, comb, cog, sprocket, ratchet, awl, auger, drill, borer, gimlet, broach, perforator, spear, spearhead, bayonet, lance, lancet, fleam, marlinespike (or marlinspike), caltrop, cheval-de-frise, bodkin, barb, barbed wire, barbwire (US), harpoon, fluke, hook, fish-hook, gaff, nippers, sword, dagger, dirk, stiletto, rapier, pike, skewer, spit, arrowhead, arrow, quarrel, goad, ankus, prod, sticker (US inf), horn, antler, claw, talon, cockspur (or spur), porcupine, hedgehog, quill, spine, prick, sting, spicule (or spiculum), pine needle, prickle, thorn, brier, burr, bramble, thistle, nettle, awn, cactus, yucca, Adam's-needle, Spanish bayonet, bristle, hair, beard, moustache
▶ *279 Summit, 295 Dress, 603 Tool, 680 Weapon, 293 Covering*

9 **sharp-edged thing**, broken glass, razor, razor blade, blade, wedge, fingernail, edge tool, chisel, plane, scraper, drawknife, spokeshave, cutter, saw, scissors, shears, pinking shears, pruning shears, pruner, clippers, secateurs, billhook, grass cutter, lawn mower, scythe, sickle, shovel, spade, trowel, adze, adz (US), mattock, ploughshare, share, coulter, colter (US), hatchet, axe
▶ *68 Agriculture*

10 **knife**, surgical knife, scalpel, bistoury, cook's knife, cleaver, chopper, carving knife, carver, whittle (Dial), slicer, kitchen knife, bread knife, fish knife, paring knife, skiver, penknife, pocketknife, craft knife, clasp knife, flick knife, switchblade (US), sheath knife, jack-

knife, hunting knife, bowie knife, bush knife, machete, kris, parang, panga, sword, broadsword, cutlass, scimitar
▶ *60 Medicine, 45 Cookery*

11 **tooth**, first tooth, milk tooth, baby tooth, deciduous tooth, permanent tooth, front tooth, incisor, cutter, canine (tooth), eyetooth, carnassial, bicuspid, premolar, back tooth, grinder, molar, wisdom tooth, bucktooth, snaggletooth, gold tooth, crown, false tooth, fang, tusk, denticle, set of teeth, uppers and lowers (Inf), fangs (Inf), ivories (Sl), pearls (Sl)

12 **sharpener**, knife sharpener, steel, pencil sharpener, whetstone, grindstone, oilstone, hone, file, emery, emery board, emery paper, sandpaper, glasspaper, Carborundum (Tm), strap, strop

13 **mental sharpness**, sharp-wittedness, quick-wittedness, acuteness, acuity, astuteness, alertness, brightness, shrewdness, cleverness, intelligence, smartness, perspicacity, perspicaciousness, keenness, discernment, acumen
▶ *459 Intellect*

VERBS

14 **be sharp**, be pointed, have a point, end in a point, taper (or come) to a point, peak, converge, acuminate, spiculate, bristle, bristle with, prickle, prick, stick, pierce, sting, have prongs, have an edge, have a jagged edge, cut, needle, have horns, gore, bite, chew, cut a tooth

15 **make sharp**, sharpen, hone, file, sandpaper, grind, oilstone, strop, strap, whet, taper, edge, put an edge on, point, make pointed, put a point on, notch, serrate, barb, spur, break glass

16 **use a sharp tool** (or **weapon**), scrape, chisel, plane, cut, scissor, saw, shear, clip, prune, cut (or mow) the lawn (or grass), fork, harrow, rake, comb, scythe, sickle, shovel, spade, trowel, plough, axe, knife, razor, cleave, chop, carve, whittle, slice, skive, drill, bore, perforate, spear, bayonet, lance, spike, harpoon, hook, gaff, nip, stick, skewer, shoot an arrow, shoot with an arrow, goad, prod, claw, scratch
▶ *670 Attack*

17 **be mentally sharp**, have sharp wits, have quick wits, show acuteness, stay alert, show intelligence, discern
▶ *459 Intellect*

ADVERBS

18 **sharply**, pointedly, acutely, smartly, astutely, alertly, brightly, shrewdly, cleverly, intelligently, perspicaciously, discerningly, keenly

19 **suddenly**, sharply, cleanly, without warning
▶ *514 Surprise*

381 Bluntness

ADJECTIVES

1 **blunt**, bluntish, blunted, dull, unsharp, un-sharpened, unwhetted, worn, smooth, smoothed, faired, stub, stubby, snub, blunt-nosed, rounded, square, curving, flat, flattened, unedged, edgeless, unpointed, pointless, blunt-edged, blunt-ended, blunt-pointed, dull-edged, dull-pointed, bated
▶ *376 Smoothness, 315 Roundness, 311 Curve*

2 **outspoken**, straightforward, frank, direct, plain-spoken, candid, curt, bluff, abrupt
▶ *857 Probity, 552 Conciseness, 807 Insolence*

3 **dull**, obtuse, insensitive, unperceptive, hebetudinous, dense, slow, numb, unfeeling
▶ *761 Insensitivity, 404 Insensibility*

4 **toothless**, edentate, edental, edentulous, teethless, biteless

NOUNS

5 **bluntness**, unsharpness, dullness, smoothness, flatness, stubbiness, roundness

6 **outspokenness**, straightforwardness, frankness, directness, plain-spokenness, candidness, curtness, bluffness, abruptness

7 **dullness**, obtuseness, obtundity, insensitivity, insensitiveness, hebetude, impercipience, numbness

8 **toothlessness**, lack of bite, lack of incisiveness, toothless tiger

9 **blunt instrument**, blunt edge, foil, spatula, palette knife

VERBS

10 **blunt**, dull, obtund, take the edge off, disedge, flatten, round, smooth, turn, turn the edge, bate (a foil), draw the teeth (*or* fangs) of

ADVERBS

11 **smoothly**, dully, stubbily, flatly, roundly, pointlessly, toothlessly

12 **bluntly**, frankly, to the point, candidly, curtly, plainly, straightforwardly, directly, abruptly

13 **obtusely**, insensitively, imperceptively, numbly

382 Structure

NOUNS

1 **structure**, arrangement, organization, organic structure, plan, pattern, tectonics, architecture, architectonics
▶ *152 Arrangement, 592 Plan*

2 **fabric**, build, texture, contexture, tissue, warp, weft, weave, content, substance, materials, work, brickwork
▶ *604 Materials, 383 Texture*

3 **form**, formation, morphology, shape, mould, architecture, physique, build, setup, make-up, fashion, fabrication, conformation, configuration, format, composition, constitution, creation, body, anatomy, get-up (Inf)
▶ *306 Form*

4 **framework**, frame, framing, bodywork, skeleton, lattice, latticework, scaffold, rack, shell, chassis, cadre, doorframe, window case (*or* frame), casement, picture frame, cantilever, space frame

5 **structuring**, formation, making, shaping, creation, building, production, forging, patterning, moulding
▶ *156 Beginning, 243 Production*

6 **construction**, building, edifice, construct, erection, elevation, establishment, house, skyscraper, tower, pyramid, pile, prefab, prefabrication, superstructure, complex, works, workings, substructure, infrastructure, understructure, foundations, underbuilding
▶ *43 Architecture, 63 Engineering*

7 **skeleton**, exoskeleton, carapace, endoskeleton, axial skeleton, appendicular skeleton, bone, horn, cartilage, keratin, ossicle, ossification, osteoblast, osteoclast, osteocyte, chondroblast, tendon, ligament

8 **science of structure**, adenography, adeno-

Bones

anklebone	frontal bone	maxilla	shoulder blade
anvil	funny bone	maxillary	skull
astragalus	hallux	metacarpal, metacarpus	sphenoid
backbone	hammer	metatarsal, metatarsus	spinal column
breastbone	haunch bone	nasal bone	spine
calcancus	heel bone	occipital bone	stapes
cannon bone	hipbone	parietal bone	sternum
carpal, carpus	humerus	patella	stirrup
cheekbone	hyoid bone	pelvis	talus
clavicle	ilium	phalanx, phalanges (pl)	tarsal, tarsus
coccyx	incus	pubis	temporal bone
collarbone	innominate bone	rachis	thighbone
costa	ischium	radius	tibia
cranium	jawbone	rib	ulna
cuboid	kneecap	sacrum	vertebra
ethmoid bone	kneepan	scaphoid	vertebral column
femur	malleus	scapula	vomer
fibula	mandible	sesamoid bones	wristbone
floating rib	mastoid	shinbone	zygomatic bone

logy, anatomy, angiography, angiology, anthropotomy, histology, morphology, myology, neurology, organology, osteography, osteology, promorphology, splanchnography, splanchnology, zootomy, geomorphology, plate tectonics, tectology
▶ *60 Medicine, 59 Life Science, 54 Earth Science*
9 **artistic structure**, musical structure, structuralism, post-structuralism, constructionism, deconstructionism, composition, choreography, design, balance, unity, rhythm, theme, subject
▶ *49 Music, 50 Painting and Sculpture, 46 Dancing and Ballet, 51 Performing Arts, 48 Literature*
10 **anatomist**, histologist, morphologist, geomorphologist
ADJECTIVES
11 **structural**, constructional, organizational, superstructural, substructural, infrastructural, textural, architectural, tectonic, architectonic
12 **organic**, organismal, organological, morphologic(al), anatomic(al), formal
13 **skeletal**, bony, osteal, osseous, ossiferous, ossicular, ossified
VERBS
14 **structure**, organize, plan, pattern, arrange, prepare, design, draw up, invent
15 **shape**, form, formulate, evolve, raise, make, manufacture, fashion, fabricate, elaborate, mould, frame, compose, create, unify
16 **construct**, build, erect, devise, concoct, put up, set up, get up
17 **assemble**, put together, piece together, patch together
ADVERBS
18 **structurally**, architecturally, constructionally, superstructurally, substructurally, tectonically, architectonically, organically, skeletally, morphologically, anatomically
19 **in production**, under construction, in hand

383 Texture

NOUNS
1 **texture**, surface texture, surface, finish, feel, touch, sensation, intertexture, contexture, structure, constitution, consistency
▶ *382 Structure, 403 Sensation, 407 Touch*
2 **grain**, denier, fineness (*or* coarseness) of grain, smoothness, fineness, refinement, softness, delicacy, daintiness, filminess, gossameriness, fluffiness, fluff, downiness, down, fuzziness, peachiness, satin, satininess, silk, silkiness, roughness, graininess, granular texture, granulation, grittiness, grit, hardness
▶ *373 Hardness, 374 Softness, 376 Smoothness, 794 Refinement*
3 **nap**, pile, shag, nub, knub, protuberance, indentation, pit, pock
4 **weave**, weaving, web, network, weftage, warp

and woof (*or* weft)
5 **textile**, fabric, cloth, stuff, staple, material, tissue
▶ *604 Materials*
6 **fibre**, yarn, thread, string, tow, filament
ADJECTIVES
7 **textural**, textured, woven
8 **rough**, coarse, coarse-woven, coarse-grained, grained, grainy, granular, granulated, gritty, ribbed, twilled, tweedy, woolly, hairy, fibrous, homespun, hodden, linsey-woolsey
9 **smooth**, fine, fine-grained, close-woven, finewoven, refined, satin, satiny, silky, cottony
10 **delicate**, dainty, filmy, gossamer, gossamery, finespun, thin-spun, subtle, fine-drawn, wiredrawn
11 **fluffy**, downy, fuzzy, velvety, velutinous
VERBS
12 **coarsen**, roughen, rough up, granulate, grain, gnarl, knob
13 **smooth**, smooth out, flatten, iron out, press
14 **go against the grain**, rub the wrong way, rumple, wrinkle
ADVERBS
15 **texturally**, structurally, roughly, fuzzily, coarsely, fibrously, smoothly, finely, silkily, delicately, daintily, subtly, on the surface, to the touch

384 Powderiness

NOUNS
1 **powderiness**, pulverulence, dustiness, chalkiness, flouriness, efflorescence, bloom
2 **crumbliness**, flakiness, friability, friableness, pulverableness, brittleness, looseness
▶ *379 Brittleness*
3 **graininess**, granularity, granulation, mealiness, branniness, grittiness, sandiness, sabulosity, gravelliness
▶ *383 Texture*
4 **pulverization**, powdering, milling, multure, reducing to dust, dusting, frosting, grinding, trituration, crushing, mashing, smashing, beating, pounding, contusion, grating, shredding, crumbling, flaking, levigation, granulation, granulization, comminution, erosion, abrasion, attrition, detrition, brecciation, fragmentation, sharding, atomization, micronization, disintegration, attenuation, decomposition, limation
▶ *141 Disintegration, 162 Dispersion*
5 **powder**, dust, dirt, chalk, efflorescence, flowers, flowers of sulphur, pounce, talc (talcum powder), face powder, cosmetics, attritus, dustball, fluff, pussies, kittens, slut's wool, lint, soot, smut(s), ash, sawdust, coal dust, airborne particles, fallout, air pollution, smog, cosmic dust, dust cloud, dust storm, dust devil
6 **crumb**, flake, crumble, dandruff, scurf, fil-

ings, raspings, snowflake, fragment, smithereens
7 **grain**, granule, granulet, speck, mote, particle
8 **meal**, groats, bran, flour, atta, farina, grist
9 **grit**, sand, gravel, shingle, detritus, debris, breccia, collapse breccia
▶ *54 Earth Science*
10 **spore**, pollen, pollen grain, microspore, sporule
▶ *84 Flowers, 245 Reproduction*
11 **pulverizer**, comminutor, kominuter, triturator, levigator, crusher, rock crusher, food processor, mill, grinder, coffee grinder (*or* mill), pepper mill, atomizer, grindstone, bulldozer, masher, pounder, millstone, pestle, pestle and mortar, muller, quern, quernstone, roller, steamroller
12 **abrasive**, file, sandpaper, glasspaper, emery paper, emery board, nailfile
13 **grater**, cheese grater, nutmeg grater, shredder
14 **hammer**, sledgehammer, sledge, ram, mallet
▶ *603 Tool*
15 **koniology**, konimeter
ADJECTIVES
16 **powdery**, dusty, dust-covered, pulverulent, pulverous, scobiform, scobicula, dirty, sooty, chalky, chalklike, calcareous, flocculent
17 **mealy**, branny, floury, farinaceous, furfuraceous
18 **grainy**, gritty, granular, sandy, sabulous, arenose, arenaceous, arenarious, gravelly, shingly, shingled, pebbly, pebbled, breccial, brecciated, detrited, detrital
19 **pulverized**, powdered, ground, granulated, disintegrated, ground to dust, crushed, grated, shredded, sifted, pestled, comminuted, triturated, levigated, sharded
20 **crumbly**, friable, crumbled, crumbling, crisp, flaky, scaly, scurfy
21 **pulverizable**, pulverable, pulverulent, triturable
VERBS
22 **powder**, dust, flour, sand, sprinkle, scatter, dredge
23 **pulverize**, powder, comminute, reduce (*or* grind) to powder (*or* dust), triturate, contriturate, levigate, bray, pestle, disintegrate, fragment, shard, brecciate, atomize, micronize
24 **crumble**, crumb, chip, flake
25 **grind**, granulate, granulize, grain, mill, flour, mince
26 **grate**, shred, abrade, rub down, scrape, rasp, file
27 **beat**, pound, bray, smash, mash, hammer, bruise, knead, crush, squash, crunch, kibble, kevel, scrunch (Inf)
28 **come** (*or* **fall**) **to dust**, crumble into dust, disintegrate, fall to bits (*or* pieces), break up, granulate, decompose, effloresce

29 **weather**, erode, wear down, rust
ADVERBS
30 **flakily**, granularly, grittily, dustily, abrasively, dirtily

385 Friction

NOUNS
1 **friction**, rubbing, drag, force, resistance, viscosity, static friction, rolling friction, internal friction, sliding friction, slip friction, coefficient of friction, skin friction, roughness, rub, affriction, frottage, frication (Arch), confrication (Arch), perfrication (Arch)
▶ *669 Resistance, 56 Physics*
2 **wearing away**, attrition, abrasion, rubbing against, rubbing together, erosion, wear, corrosion, detrition, ablation, collision, rubbing out (*or* off *or* away), erasure, obliteration, sandblasting
▶ *384 Powderiness, 244 Destruction, 546 Obliteration*
3 **grinding**, filing, rasping, fretting, limation, chafing, galling, chafe, levigation
▶ *384 Powderiness*
4 **scraping**, scratching, grazing, scuffing, scrub, scrubbing, scouring, scrape, scratch, scuff
5 **polishing**, rubbing, burnishing, sanding, smoothing, buffing, shining, dressing, elbow grease
6 **massage**, massaging, massotherapy, stroking, rubdown, kneading, facial massage, facial, shampoo, whirlpool bath, Jacuzzi (Tm), vibrator
▶ *791 Beautification*
7 **eraser**, rubber, scraper, sander, sanding disc, sandpaper, glasspaper, emery paper, emery board, nailfile, file, rasp, pumice (pumice stone), facemask, facial scrub
▶ *603 Tool*
8 **masseur**, masseuse, massotherapist, shampooer, beautician
▶ *791 Beautification*
9 **irritation**, grating, prickliness, irascibility, tension
▶ *829 Irascibility, 366 Agitation*
ADJECTIVES
10 **frictional**, friction, abrasive, anatriptic, irritant, rubbing, attritive, erosive, ablative, gnawing
11 **rough**, rasping, grating, grinding, chafing, fretting, galling
VERBS
12 **rub**, rub up, smooth, polish, wax, levigate, burnish, furbish, buff, scour, scrub, sandpaper, sand, sandblast, dress, brush, curry, currycomb
13 **abrade**, frictionize, abrase, rub against, scrape, scuff, graze, raze, bark, scratch, gnaw, gnaw away, strike (a match)

14 erode, corrode, wear, wear away, fray, frazzle, skin, erase, rub out (*or* away *or* off), obliterate
▶ *546 Obliteration*

15 grind, rasp, file, plane, grate, catch, stick, chafe, gall, fret, irritate, rub up the wrong way

16 massage, knead, rub down, pulverize, shampoo, rub gently, smooth, iron out, iron, stroke, caress, pet

ADVERBS

17 abrasively, roughly, raspingly, irritatingly, harshly

386 Lubrication

NOUNS

1 lubrication, nonfriction, lubricating, lubrification (Arch), smoothness, slickness, sleekness, slipperiness, lubricity, grease job (Inf), lube (Inf)
▶ *376 Smoothness, 139 Nonadhesion*

2 oiliness, greasiness, waxiness, unctuousness, unctuosity, soapiness, saponacity (*or* saponaceousness), fattiness, fatness, pinguidity
▶ *395 Oiliness*

3 anointment, unction, oiling, inunction, chrismation
▶ *10 Ritual*

4 lubricant, lubricator, lubricating oil, lubricating agent, antifriction, graphite, plumbago, black lead, silicone, glycerine (*or* glycerine), wax, grease, tallow, cart grease, motor oil, oil, *oleum* (L), soap, lather, mucilage, mucus, synovia, saliva, spit, spittle
▶ *395 Oiliness, 387 Fluid, 393 Semiliquid*

5 ointment, salve, balm, lotion, cream, unguent, unguentum, inunction, inunctum, unction, chrism, emollient, lenitive, soothing syrup, embrocation, demulcent, spikenard, nard, balsam, macassar
▶ *395 Oiliness, 630 Remedy*

6 pomade, pomatum, brilliantine, hair conditioner, setting lotion, styling mousse, styling gel, cleanser, cold cream, face cream, hand lotion (*or* cream), lanolin, eye lotion, eyewash, collyrium, eyebath
▶ *791 Beautification*

7 lubricator, oilcan, grease gun
▶ *603 Tool*

ADJECTIVES

8 lubricated, oiled, well-oiled, well-greased, smooth-running, not rusty, silent

9 lubricant, lubricative, lubricating, lubricatory, lubricational, lenitive, emollient, soothing

10 oily, greasy, waxy, slippery, slithery, unctuous, unctional, unguinous, oleaginous, oleic, fat, fatty, adipose, pinguid, pinguidinous, pinguescent, lardy, lardaceous, blubbery, tallowy, suety, sebaceous, rich, buttery, butyraceous, soapy, saponaceous, mucoid

11 unguent, unguentary, unguentous, chrismal, chrismatory

12 smooth, slick, sleek, slippery, slithery, slimy

VERBS

13 lubricate, lubrify (Arch), lubricitate, oil, grease, wax, beeswax, soap, lather, grease leather, butter, lard, glycerolate, glycerinate, glycerinize

14 anoint, salve, unguent, embrocate, dress, pour oil (*or* balm) upon, smear, daub, cream, pomade, lard

15 ease, smooth over, smooth the way, oil (*or* grease) the wheels, pour oil on troubled waters, soap the ways

ADVERBS

16 oilily, greasily, soapily, slickly, unctuously

387 Fluid

NOUNS

1 fluid, liquid, liquid state, liquor, water, drink, beverage, liquid extract, fluid extract, condensation, elastic fluid, nonelastic fluid
▶ *389 Water, 391 Moisture, 351 Drinking*

2 juice, sap, extract, latex, milk, whey, buttermilk, ghee, water, running water, gravy, stock, meat juice, sauce, gippo, soup
▶ *393 Semiliquid, 45 Cookery, 85 Trees*

3 body fluid, lymph, plasma, blood, humour, chyle, rheum, serous fluid, serum, pus, matter, purulence, suppuration, ichor, sanies, discharge, gleet, leucorrhoea, the whites (Inf), mucus, mucor, phlegm, snot (Sl), saliva, spittle, urine, piss (Sl), pee (Inf), wee (Inf), excrement, shit (Sl), semen, menstrual flow, sweat, perspiration, tear, tears, teardrop, milk, mother's milk, colostrum, lactation, dropsy, oedema, hydrocele
▶ *353 Excretion*

4 blood, lifeblood, arterial blood, venous blood, gore, claret, blood serum, blood substitute, blood plasma, plasma substitute, synthetic plasma, dextran, clinical dextran, blood cell (*or* corpuscle), red blood cell (*or* corpuscle), erythrocyte, white blood cell (*or* corpuscle), leucocyte, lymphocyte, neutrophil, phagocyte, blood platelet, haemoglobin, clot, blood clot, thrombosis, blood pressure, blood group (*or* type), O (*or* A *or* B *or* AB) blood groups, Rhesus factor, Rh factor, Rh-positive, Rh-negative, antigen, antibody, isoantibody, globulin, opsonin, blood count, blood picture, circulation, bloodstream, blood bank, bloodmobile (US), blood transfusion
▶ *60 Medicine, 630 Remedy*

5 fluidity, fluidness, liquidity, liquidness, fluxure, fluxility, liquefaction, colliquation, juiciness, sappiness, pulpiness, wateriness, runniness, rheuminess, nonviscosity, noncoagulation, haemophilia, solubleness, liquidescence,

bloodiness, goriness, semiliquidity

6 **flow**, fluency, flux, fluxion, fluxility (Arch), haemorrhage, suppuration, secretion

7 **juiciness**, sappiness, milkiness, succulence, lactescence, lactation, chylifaction, chylification, serosity, moisture

8 **fluidification**, liquefaction, liquidization, liquescence, colliquefaction, solubility, deliquation, liquescency, deliquescence, fluxibility, dissolution, solution, dissolving, decoagulation, unclotting, melting, thaw, thawing, unfreezing, running, fusing, fusion, solubilization, lixiviation, percolation, leaching

9 **solvent**, liquifier, liquefacient, dissolvent, dissolver, dissolving agent, menstruum, anticoagulent, hydragogue, resolvent, resolutive, thinner, diluent (or dilutant), flux, universal solvent, alkahest (or alcahest)

10 **solution**, infusion, decoction, suspension, emulsion, apozem, flux, lixivium, lye

▶ 393 Semiliquid, 133 Mixture

11 **liquidizer**, blender, food processor, juice extractor

▶ 45 Cookery

12 **flowmeter**, fluidmeter, hydrometer

13 **fluid mechanics**, hydraulics, hydrogeology, hydrology, hydrometry, hydrostatics, hydrodynamics, hydrokinetics

▶ 56 Physics

ADJECTIVES

14 **fluid**, liquid, fluidal, fluidic, liquiform, uncongealed, unclotted

15 **flowing**, fluent, fluxive, fluxible (Arch), fluxile (Arch), fluxional, fluxionary (Arch), watery, runny, juicy, sappy, moist, succulent, squashy

16 **rheumy**, weeping, pussy, purulent, suppurating, suppurative, suppurated, sanious, ichorous, phlegmy, humoral, serous, chylific, chylifactive, chylifactory, tearlike, lachrymal, lachrymatory

17 **milky**, lacteal, lacteous, lactic, lactescent, lactiferous

18 **bloody**, gory, bleeding, sanguineous, haemic, haemal, haemogenic, haemophilic

19 **liquefied**, dissolved, deliquescent, melted, molten, thawed, decoagulated, in solution, in suspension, liquescent, liquefacient, solvent

20 **liquefying**, liquefactive, colliquative, thawing, melting, fusing, dissolving, dissolutional, anticoagulant

21 **liquefiable**, soluble, meltable, fusible, thawable, dissolvable, dissoluble

VERBS

22 **make fluid**, liquefy, liquate, liquidize, fluidize, fluidify, liquesce, blend, emulsify

23 **dissolve**, solve, thin, solubilize, decoagulate, unclot, hold in solution, leach, lixiviate, percolate, decoct, infuse, resolve

24 **melt**, run, thaw, melt down, smelt, defrost, unfreeze, render, clarify, deliquesce, fuse, flux

25 **flow**, run, stream, pour, well up, gush, spout, vomit forth, spew out, bleed, flood, weep, seep, sweat, ooze

ADVERBS

26 **fluidly**, liquidly, fluently, runnily, juicily, moistly, succulently, purulently, weepily, tearfully, lacteally, sanguinely, sanguinarily, sweatily, oozily

388   Gas

NOUNS

1 **gas**, rare (or inert or noble) gas, air, atmosphere, atmospheric air, vapour, elastic fluid, ether, volatile

▶ 57 Chemistry, 390 Air

2 **exhalation**, breath, exspiration, effluvium

3 **miasma**, mephitis, malaria (Arch), foetid air, rank air fume(s), reek, smoke, wisp (or puff or plume) of smoke, smog, poisonous gas, damp, firedamp, blackdamp, afterdamp, chokedamp

▶ 416 Odour

4 **water vapour**, steam, cloud, mist, fog

▶ 55 Meteorology and Climatology, 389 Water

5 **belch**, ructation, eructation, hiccup, flatulence, flatulency, flatuosity, flatus, wind, windiness, gas, burp (Inf), fart (Sl)

6 **aerogastria**, aerogenesis, aerodontalgia, aeroneurosis, aerophagia, gas gangrene

▶ 624 Ill Health

7 **gaseousness**, gassiness, gaseity, gaseous state, fizziness, effervescence, fermentation, vaporousness, vaporosity, vapouriness, vapour, pressure (or tension)

8 **volatility**, vapourability, vapourizability, evaporability

▶ 370 Lightness

9 **aeriness**, etherealism, etheriability

10 **vaporization**, evaporation, volatilization, gasification, aeration, etherification, aerification, sublimation, distillation, fractionation, atomization, exhalation, etherealization, steaming, smoking, fumigation

11 **vaporizer**, spray, aerosol, aerosol spray, CFC (chlorofluorocarbon), Freon (Tm), propellant, atomizer, condenser, retort, still

12 **aerostatics**, aerodynamics, pneumatostatics, pneumatics, pneumodynamics

▶ 56 Physics

13 **gas balloon**, air balloon, helium balloon, hydrogen balloon, airship, bladder, air bladder, bicycle tube, inner tube

14 **gasworks**, gas plant, gasholder, gasometer, gasolier, gaslight, gaslamp

15 **vaporimeter**, manometer, pressure gauge, gasometer, gas meter, airometer, aerometer, spirometer, eudiometer, pneumatometer

ADJECTIVES

16 **gaseous**, gaslike, gasiform, gassy, gasified, in

the gaseous state, vaporous, vapour-like, va-poury, vapourish

17 **airy**, aery, aerial, ethereal, atmospheric

18 **miasmic**, miasmal, miasmatic, mephitic, foetid, reeking, fumy, fuming, effluvial

19 **smoky**, smoking, smoggy, steamy, steaming, vaporing, cloudy, misty, foggy

20 **flatulent**, windy, gassy

21 **gassy**, fizzy, effervescent, bubbly, sparkling, carbonated, aerated

22 **aerostatic**, aerodynamic, pneumatic

23 **volatile**, volatilizable, vapourable, vaporific, vaporizable, vaporescent, evaporable, evapo-rative

24 **oxygenous**, oxygenic, ozonous, ozonic, ozone-friendly

VERBS

25 **gasify**, evaporate, vaporize, volatilize, atom-ize, sublimate, sublime, distil, fractionate, etherify

26 **aerate**, fumigate, aerify, etherize, carbonate, oxygenate, hydrogenate, atomize, spray, per-fume, fluidize

27 **give off**, emit, exhale, reek, fume, send out, smoke, steam, let off (or blow off) steam, turn on the gas, combine with gas

ADVERBS

28 **aerily**, ethereally, atmospherically, vapor-ously

29 **aerostatically**, aerodynamically, pneumati-cally, pneumodynamically

30 **smokily**, steamily, mistily, effervescently, effervescingly

389 Water

NOUNS

1 **water**, H_2O, aqua (L), eau (Fr), Adam's ale, Adam's wine, hydrol, fluid, liquid, moisture, heavy water (D_2O), distilled water, hard water, soft water, mineral water(s), limewater, rain(s), rain water, running water, spring, fountain, spring water, well water, hydrothermal water, fresh water, sea water, salt water, brine, the briny (Inf), meltwater, ice, standing water
▶ 55 Meteorology and Climatology, 387 Fluid, 391 Moisture, 96 Rivers, 97 Seas, 94 Lakes

2 **drinking water**, tap water, bottled water, spa water, mineral water, soda water, carbon-ated water, fizzy water
▶ 351 Drinking

3 **wateriness**, wet, wetness, wettishness, damp, dampness, runniness, moistness, raini-ness, rainfall, dewiness, vapour, water vapour, steam, condensation, haze, mist, fog, cloud
▶ 388 Gas

4 **exudate**, exudation, tears, weeping, sweat, perspiration, saliva, spittle, urine, urination, piss (Sl), pee (Inf), wee (Inf)
▶ 353 Excretion, 774 Lamentation, 770 Sorrow

5 **dilution**, solution, adulteration, saturation, watering down

6 **hydrate**, hydration, hydrolysis, wetting agent, wetting-out agent

7 **hydrotherapeutics**, hydropathy, hydro-therapy, irrigation, water cure, taking the wa-ters
▶ 630 Remedy

8 **watering**, irrigation, wetting, hosing, hosing down, sprinkling, spraying, squirting, sparg-ing, spargefaction, aspersion, aspergation, splashing, spattering, swashing, affusion
▶ 162 Dispersion

9 **soaking**, soakage, soak, drenching, drench, sousing, souse, drowning, flooding, inunda-tion, immersion, submersion, imbruement, ducking, saturation, permeation, percolation, leaching, lixiviation, dunking (Inf)

10 **steeping**, infusion, brewing, maceration, seething, impregnation, infiltration, injec-tion, pulping

11 **wash**, washing, rinse, rinsing, laving, bath, bathing, dip, soap and water, splash, ablution, cleansing, balneation, bidet, shower, shower-ing, shower bath, shower head, needle bath, Jacuzzi (Tm), whirlpool bath, douche, syringe, fountain syringe, enema, clyster
▶ 621 Cleanness

12 **sprinkler**, watering can, spray can, rose, nozzle, sparger, sparge, sprayer, speed sprayer, mist, concentrate sprayer, spray, aspergillum (or aspergill), sprinkling system, sprinkler head, aerosol, atomizer, vaporizer, water pistol (or gun), squirt gun
▶ 603 Tool

13 **irrigator**, well, oasis, conduit, hydrant, water hydrant, garden hose, hosepipe, tap, standpipe, water pipe, pump, fire engine, sha-doof (or shaduf), Persian wheel, Archimedes' screw
▶ 68 Agriculture, 69 Horticulture

14 **lavender water**, rose water, scent, perfume, eau de Cologne
▶ 418 Fragrance

15 **holy water**, baptism, immersion, christen-ing, hydromancy, religious rite
▶ 10 Ritual

16 **water carrier**, water cart, watering cart, water jug, ewer, pitcher, jug, reservoir, dam, cistern, water tank
▶ 258 Container

17 **water cycle**, hydrologic cycle, hydrosphere, hydrometeor, head, hydrostatic head, head of pressure
▶ 96 Rivers, 97 Seas

18 **hydrography**, hydrology, hydrometry, hy-grometry, hydraulics, hydrodynamics, hydro-mechanics, hydrokinetics, hydrostatics, hy-droponics, aquiculture
▶ 56 Physics, 69 Horticulture

19 measuring instrument, hygrometer, hair hygrometer, hygrograph, hydrograph, hygrodeik, hygroscope, hygrothermagraph, psychrometer, wet-and-dry bulb thermometer, sling psychrometer, humidor, hydrostat, rain gauge, udometer, pluviometer, Nilometer, weather house

20 hydrologist, hydrographer, water diviner

▶ *11 Occultism*

ADJECTIVES

21 watery, waterish, fluid, liquid, aqueous, aquatic, moist, hydrous, hydrated, hydraulic, hydrodynamic, hydrometric, hydrostatic

22 diluted, saturated, watered-down, thinned, adulterated, weak, wishy-washy (Inf)

▶ *274 Thinness*

23 wet, soaked, drenched, soaking wet, soaked to the skin, like a drowned rat, sodden, wringing, wringing wet, sopping, sopping wet, saturated, soused, waterlogged, watersoaked, streaming, dripping, dripping wet, awash, soggy, bathed, steeped

24 flooded, overflowed, awash, whelmed, inundated, swamped, engulfed, deluged, drowned, submerged, submersed, immersed, dipped, ducked, dunked, weltering

25 seeping, weeping, oozing, dribbling, dripping

26 wetting, watering, moistening, damping, humectant, irrigational, irriguous (Arch)

27 cleansing, hydrotherapeutic

28 hygric, hygrometric, hygroscopic, hygrophilous, hygrothermal

VERBS

29 water, moisten, sprinkle, irrigate, hydrate, wet, soak, drench, douse, souse, drown, drouk (Scot), immerse, submerse, imbrue, permeate, percolate, leach, lixiviate, flood, inundate, saturate, waterlog, deluge, swamp, submerge, pour on, flow on, duck, dunk, sluice, come down cats and dogs

30 dilute, water down, add water, thin, adulterate, cut, dissolve

31 steep, infuse, imbue, macerate, pickle, brine, impregnate, infiltrate, seethe, inject

32 seep, weep, bleed, ooze, percolate, dribble, drip, exude, perspire, sweat, salivate, spit, dribble, cry, weep, urinate, pass water, piss (Sl), pee (Inf), wee (Inf)

33 sprinkle, spray, sparge, asperge, mist, atomize, shower, scatter, splash, splatter, spatter, bespatter, clash, paddle, slop, slobber

34 hose, hose down, syringe, squirt, inject, douche, sponge, wash, rinse, lave (Arch), (take a) bath, bathe, (take a) shower, perform one's ablutions

ADVERBS

35 wetly, moistly, damply, fluidly (*or* fluidally), liquidly, weepily, runnily, oozily

36 hydraulically, hydrodynamically, hydrometrically, hydrostatically, hydroscopically

390 Air

NOUNS

1 air, ether, atmosphere, oxygen, gas, thin air, rarity, airspace, gaseous medium (*or* environment *or* envelope), the sky, blue sky, the heavens, welkin (Arch), lift (Dial), ozone (Inf)

▶ *388 Gas*

2 aerosphere, ecosphere, biosphere, noosphere

3 atmospheric layers, troposphere, substratosphere, tropopause, stratosphere, stratoisothermal region, isothermal layer, ozone layer (*or* ozonosphere), ionosphere, exosphere, D region, Heaviside (*or* Heaviside-Kennelly *or* Kennelly-Heaviside) layer (*or* region), E region, Appleton layer, F region, Van Allen belt (*or* radiation belt), photosphere, chemosphere, lower atmosphere, upper atmosphere, outer atmosphere, stratum, layer, belt

▶ *54 Earth Science*

4 air flow, wind, breeze, blast, gust, air current, current of air, updraught, downdraught, crosscurrent, monsoon, head wind, tail wind, following wind, jetstream

▶ *55 Meteorology and Climatology, 359 Ascent, 360 Descent*

5 open air, fresh air, out-of-doors, exposure, the great outdoors, sea air, ozone (Inf)

6 ventilation, airing, fanning, aeration, aerage, cross-ventilation, refreshment, perflation, air conditioning, air cooling, refrigeration, oxygenation, oxygenization

▶ *409 Cold*

7 ventilator, aerator, fan, blower, air conditioner, AC (Aus inf), air filter, air cooler, ventilating system, air passage

8 respiration, breathing, inhalation, inspiration, exhalation, expiration, air flow, windpipe, trachea, bronchus, bronchiole, exchange of gases, respiratory organ, lung, alveoli, gills

9 airiness, lightness, weightlessness, buoyancy, ethereality

▶ *370 Lightness*

10 air bubble, froth, foam, fluff, sponge, lather, suds, spray, spume, spindrift, cushion of air, air pocket, soufflé, mousse, meringue, balloon, air balloon, air bladder

11 aeration, fermentation, leavening, raising agent, yeast, leaven, ferment

ADJECTIVES

12 airy, aery, aerial, aeriform, aeriferous, airlike, ethereal, insubstantial, light, lighter-than-air, weightless, exposed, roomy, rare, rarified, thin

13 atmospheric, stratospheric, tropospheric

14 aerial, buoyant, inflated, blown-up, flatulent, pneumatic

15 **breezy**, windy, blowy, fresh, gusty
16 **open-air**, outdoor, out-of-doors, alfresco
17 **ventilated**, well-ventilated, fresh, fanned, air-conditioned, cooled, air-cooled
18 **bubbly**, foamy, frothy, fizzy, effervescent, aerated, yeasty
19 **respiratory**, breathing, respiring, inhaling, exhaling, bronchial, pulmonary, pneumonic

VERBS

20 **aerate**, aerify, oxygenate, air, ventilate, air-condition, air-cool, expose, freshen, deodorize, clean, take an airing
21 **respire**, breathe, breathe in, inhale, inspire, breathe out, exhale, expire
22 **blow**, blast, gust, huff, puff, make a draught, fan
23 **whisk**, aerate, whip, beat
24 **bubble**, froth, foam, fizz, effervesce, sparkle, gurgle, ferment, simmer

ADVERBS

25 **airily**, lightly, frothily, effervescently, effervescingly, atmospherically, pneumatically
26 **out-of-doors**, outside, in the open, in the open air, alfresco, under the open sky, in the sun, abroad, *en plein air* (Fr)

391 Moisture

NOUNS

1 **moisture**, moistness, moistiness, dampness, wetness, wettishness, wateriness, humour (Arch), humectation (Arch), sogginess, soddenness, soppiness
▶ *389 Water, 387 Fluid*
2 **mistiness**, fogginess, fog, fog band, cloud, rain, raininess, rainfall, pluviosity, showeriness, scotch mist, drizzle, mizzle, wet weather
▶ *55 Meteorology and Climatology*
3 **humidity**, humidness, dankness, dankishness, mugginess, stickiness, clamminess, closeness, humidification, absolute humidity, relative humidity, dew point, saturation, saturation point
4 **seepage**, percolation, permeation, rising damp, wet rot
5 **sprinkle**, sprinkling, spraying, sparge, asperge, aspersion, hosing, splash, spatter, splatter, affusion
▶ *162 Dispersion*
6 **dew**, dewdrops, night dew, dawn dew, rain dew, evening damp, fog drip, false dew, tear dew, guttation
7 **bogginess**, swampiness, marshiness, muddiness, dewiness
8 **marsh**, swamp, fen, bog, quagmire, wetland(s), salt marsh, flood plain, quicksand, mud, slime, ooze, mire, wet, sludge, squelch
▶ *393 Semiliquid*

ADJECTIVES

9 **moist**, damp, wet, moisty, dampish, wettish, soggy, sodden, humid, clammy, sticky, muggy, close, dank, tacky, humectant
10 **misty**, foggy, cloudy, watery, rainy, showery, drizzling, drizzly, mizzly, dewy, bedewed, roric
11 **marshy**, swampy, boggy, fenny, soggy, oozy, squashy, squelchy, splashy, sludgy, slushy, muddy, sodden, waterlogged, flooded
12 **seeping**, dripping, drip-dropping, percolating, splashed, spattered, weeping, tear-stained, tearful, dribbling, drivelling, drooling, sweating, perspiring
▶ *389 Water*

VERBS

13 **moisten**, dampen, wet, add water, humidify, humectate (Arch), humect (Arch)
14 **sprinkle**, spatter, spray, hose, splash, dabble, slosh (Inf)
15 **be moist**, be damp, be soggy, squelch, not have a dry thread (*or* stitch), drizzle, mizzle
16 **seep**, drip, percolate, leak, ooze, trickle, shed tears, weep, sweat, perspire, exude, bleed, salivate, dribble, drool, slobber
▶ *389 Water*

ADVERBS

17 **moistly**, wetly, succulently, damply, clammily, humidly, stickily, dankly, soggily, oozily

392 Dryness

ADJECTIVES

1 **dry**, arid, waterless, moistureless, unwatered, unirrigated, unmoistened, needing water, undamped, anhydrous, droughty, high and dry
2 **thirsty**, thirsting, athirst, dry, dry as a bone, parched, drouthy (Scot)
3 **dried-up**, dried, dehydrated, desiccated, exsiccated, withered, shrivelled, sere (*or* sear) (Arch), faded, wizened, weazened, parchment-like, mummified, corky, juiceless, sapless, dry as a bone, bone-dry, dry as dust, dry as parchment, dry as a stick, dry as a biscuit, dry as a mummy
4 **dried-out**, drained, evaporated, squeezed dry, mangled
5 **rainless**, fair, set fair, hot, sunny, fine, cloudless, pleasant
▶ *55 Meteorology and Climatology*
6 **desert**, arid, Saharan, dusty, powdery, sandy, barren, bare, brown, grassless
▶ *384 Powderiness*
7 **adapted to drought**, xerophilous, xerophytic, xeromorphic
8 **baked**, parched, sun-dried, sun-baked, burnt, scorched, bleached, sunned, insolated, aired, wind-dried, air-dried
▶ *408 Heat*
9 **drying**, desiccative, desiccant, dehydrating, exsiccative, exsiccant, siccative, siccant, evaporative

10 **waterproof**, protected from wet, water-proofed, proof, moistureproof, rainproof, stormproof, flood proof, showerproof, damp-proof, leakproof, watertight, snug, dry-shod

NOUNS

11 **dryness**, aridness, aridity, siccity, parched-ness, waterlessness, drought

12 **thirst**, thirstiness, drought (Scot), dryness, dehydration, xerostomia

13 **drying**, drying up, desiccation, exsiccation, dehydration, airing, anhydration, air-drying, dehumidification, withering, fading, bleaching, searing, mummification, insolation, sunning, blotting, mopping-up

14 **desert**, sand dune, barren land, badlands, dust bowl, salt flat, wasteland, Death Valley, Sahara, Kalahari, Gobi, Sinai, karoo (Africa), dry (or arid) climate, sun, heat, sunniness, sunny South

15 **dryer (or drier)**, absorbent, blotting paper, blotter, mop, sponge, swab, swabber, brush, towel, towelling, desiccator, desiccative, siccative, exsiccative, exsiccator, dehydrator, dehydrant, dehumidifier, evaporator, hair-dryer, wringer, mangle, spin-dryer, tumble-dryer, clothes-dryer, clotheshorse

16 **dry skin**, xeroderma (or xerodermia), ichthyosis, fishskin disease, xerophthalmia

VERBS

17 **dry**, become dry, dry up, dry off, dry out, dehydrate, anhydrate, drain, evaporate, vaporize, desiccate, exsiccate, freeze-dry, dehumidify, air-dry, wind-dry, smoke, smoke-dry, kipper, cure

18 **thirst**, be thirsty, thirst for, parch

19 **bake**, sun, expose to sunlight, insolate, sun-dry, toast, roast, scorch, bleach, apricate, burn, fire, kiln, torrefy

20 **absorb**, drink up, soak up, blot, blot up, mop, mop up, swab, wipe, wipe up, wipe dry, sponge, towel, rub, brush

21 **dry up**, parch, wither, shrivel, wilt, wizen, weazen, mummify, preserve

22 **keep dry**, keep watertight, wear a macintosh, hold off the wet, waterproof

23 **drip-dry**, spin-dry, tumble-dry, wring, mangle, hang out to dry, hang out, peg out, air, evaporate

ADVERBS

24 **drily**, aridly, anhydrously, thirstily, dustily, xerically, xerophytically

393   Semiliquid

NOUNS

1 **semiliquid**, semifluid, emulsion, emulsoid, colloid, paste, slime, goo (Inf), gunk (Inf), gunge (Inf), gook (Inf), goop (Inf), glop (Inf), guck (Inf)

2 **semiliquidity**, semifluidity, erassitude,

spissitude, viscosity, viscidity, stickiness, gaum (Dial)

▶ *394 Viscosity*

3 **muddiness**, slushiness, sloshiness, sloppiness, slabbiness (Arch), slobbiness, ooziness, miriness, turbidity, turbidness, dirtiness

▶ *391 Moisture*

4 **pulpiness**, pulpousness, softness, sponginess, doughiness, pastiness, pithiness, squashiness, thickness, heaviness, stodginess, sogginess, mushiness, mashiness, flabbiness, creaminess, butteriness, juiciness, succulence, fleshiness, sappiness, overripeness

▶ *374 Softness, 387 Fluid, 273 Thickness, 369 Heaviness*

5 **pulping**, pulpification, pulpefaction, blending, steeping, maceration, mastication, digestion

▶ *350 Eating*

6 **thickening**, coagulation, curdling, clotting, gelation, gelefaction, inspissation, incrassation, emulsification, colloidality

7 **soup**, stew, gravy, gruel, porridge, slops, loblolly (US dial), gumbo

▶ *45 Cookery*

8 **pulp**, purée, pap, mush, mash, stodge, squash, dough, clabber, bonnyclabber, curd, batter, paste, mousse, fool, pudding, pith, butter, cream, crème fraîche, junket, yoghurt (or yogurt or yoghourt), fromage frais

▶ *45 Cookery*

9 **jelly**, jell, gel, gelatin (or gelatine), agar (or agar-agar), aspic, jam, treacle, syrup, honey, molasses, rob, isinglass

▶ *394 Viscosity*

10 **mucus**, mucilage, phlegm, pituita, clot, grume, gore, pus, matter, glue, size, gluten, egg white, albumen, glair

▶ *387 Fluid*

11 **thickener**, starch, paste, flour, cornflour, rennet, curdler, emulsifier, colloider

12 **poultice**, cataplasm, plaster, putty, slip, glaze

13 **mud**, slush, muck, slosh, sludge, slob (Ir), slop, slough, ooze, slime, mire, swill, silt, clay, lava, ash, slip, sediment, grounds, coffee grounds, dirt, dregs, lees

14 **puddle**, mudhole, muckhole, loblolly (US dial), chuckhole, chughole, hog wallow

15 **pulper**, pulpifier, blender, masher, macerator, potato masher, garlic press, steak tenderizer, beetle, pulp engine (or machine), food processor

ADJECTIVES

16 **semiliquid**, semifluid, emulsive, colloidal, sticky, pasty, slimy, incrassate, inspissate, viscous (or viscose), viscid, gooey (Inf), gunky (Inf), gungy (Inf)

17 **muddy**, slushy, sloshy, sludgy, squelchy, sloppy, slabby (Arch), oozy, miry, turbid, dirty, waterlogged, marshy, slimy, silty, sedimentary

18 **pulpy**, soft, spongy, doughy, pasty, squashy, stodgy, soggy, mushy, flabby, creamy, buttery, soupy, starchy, amylaceous
19 **juicy**, succulent, fleshy, sappy, overripe, runny, watery, milky, lactescent, lacteal, lactiferous
20 **thick**, thickened, coagulated, curdled, clotted, gelled, heavy, lumpy, clabbered (Dial), loppered (Dial)
21 **gelatinous**, jelly-like, treacly, syrupy
22 **mucilaginous**, pussy, gluey, glutinous, gory, slimy, mucous, snotty (Sl)
23 **thawing**, half-melted, half-frozen, slushy
VERBS
24 **pulp**, purée, mash, liquidize, blend, stew, beat up, pulverize
25 **thicken**, curdle, clot, churn, whip, congeal, emulsify, inspissate, incrassate, coagulate, clabber (Dial), lopper (Dial)
26 **gelatinize**, gelatinify, gel, jell, jelly, jellify
ADVERBS
27 **slimily**, stickily, gelatinously, viscidly, viscously, thickly, mucilaginously, oozily, slushily, sloppily, damply

394 Viscosity

NOUNS
1 **viscosity**, viscidity, viscousness, thickening, spissitude, inspissation, incrassation, stickiness, tackiness, glueyness, gluelikeness, adhesiveness, glutinousness, glutinosity, gumminess, gummosity, gauminess (Dial), gumlikeness, syrupiness, treacliness, mucilaginousness, gelatinousness, jelly-likeness, jellification, gelatinity, clabbering (Dial), loppering (Dial), colloidality, doughiness, pastiness, clamminess, slabbinness (Arch), lentor (Arch), ropiness, stringiness, toughness, tenacity, tenaciousness, gooeyness (Inf)
▶ 393 Semiliquid, 138 Adhesion, 273 Thickness, 378 Toughness
2 **adhesive**, glue, gluten, mastic, wax, beeswax, gum, chewing gum, bubble gum, chicle, chicle gum, guar gum, resin, paste, size, birdlime, tar
▶ 138 Adhesion
3 **paste**, size, glair, glaze
4 **emulsion**, collodion (or collodium), colloid
▶ 393 Semiliquid
5 **mucus**, phlegm, albumen, pus, matter, snot (Sl)
▶ 393 Semiliquid, 387 Fluid
6 **gelatin**, gel, jelly, syrup, honey, treacle, jam
▶ 393 Semiliquid, 45 Cookery
7 **slime**, goo (Inf), gunge (Inf), gunk (Inf), gook (Inf), glop (Inf), guck (Inf)
▶ 393 Semiliquid
ADJECTIVES
8 **viscous**, viscose, viscid, inspissate, incrassate, sticky, tacky, adhesive, gluey, gluelike, waxy, glutinous, glutinose, glutenous, colloidal, emulsive, gumbo, gumbolike, gummy, gaumy (Dial), gummous, gumlike, slabby (Arch), thick, stodgy, heavy, mucilaginous, clammy, ropy, stringy, tough
▶ 393 Semiliquid
9 **gelatinous**, jelly-like, jellied, jelled, syrupy, treacly, jammy, tremelloid (or tremellose)
VERBS
10 **stick**, glue, gum, gum up, paste, adhere
▶ 138 Adhesion
11 **thicken**, jellify, jelly, gelatinize, emulsify, clabber (Dial), lopper (Dial), incrassate (Arch), inspissate (Arch)
▶ 273 Thickness, 393 Semiliquid
ADVERBS
12 **viscously**, viscidly, thickly, stickily, tackily, adhesively, tenaciously

395 Oiliness

NOUNS
1 **oiliness**, unctuousness, unctuosity, greasiness, lubricity, fatness, fattiness, pinguidity, pinguescence, richness, creaminess, butteriness, sebaceousness, adiposis, adiposity, soapiness, saponacity (or saponaceousness)
▶ 393 Semiliquid, 394 Viscosity
2 **smoothness**, slickness, slipperiness, sleekness
▶ 376 Smoothness, 139 Nonadhesion
3 **lubrication**, lubricating, lubrification, oiling, greasing, grease job (Inf), lube (Inf)
▶ 386 Lubrication
4 **anointment**, unction, inunction, inunctum, chrism, chrismatory, chrismation
▶ 10 Ritual
5 **lubricant**, lubricator, lubricating oil, lubricating agent, antifriction, black lead, plumbago, graphite, glycerine (or glycerin), silicone, wax, grease, mucilage, mucus, spit, spittle, synovia, saliva, soap, lather, grease gun, oilcan, lubritorium, lubritary, grease rack, grease pit
▶ 387 Fluid, 393 Semiliquid, 386 Lubrication
6 **ointment**, unguent, salve, balm, lotion, cream, face cream, cold cream, hand cream (or lotion), pomade, pomatum, brilliantine, hair oil, spike oil, spikenard, nard, lanolin, embrocation, liniment, emollient, soothing syrup, lenitive, demulcent, eyewash, collyrium
▶ 630 Remedy
7 **oil**, oleum (L), mineral oil, fuel oil, vegetable oil, animal oil, fixed oil, fatty oil, grease, ester, volatile oil, nonvolatile oil, essential oil, glyceryl ester, wax, drying oil, non-drying oil
▶ 63 Engineering, 57 Chemistry
8 **fat**, adeps, adipocere, ester, tallow, animal fat, lanolin, blubber, sebum, ceresin, wax, saturated fat, unsaturated fat, polyunsaturated fat,

hydrogenated fat, soap, carbolic soap, washing soap, scented soap, soapflakes, soap powder, suet, lard, butter, margarine, cream, double cream, single cream, whipping cream, Devonshire cream, Cornish cream, top of the milk, buttermilk

▶ 45 Cookery

9 **petroleum**, fossil oil, rock oil, shale oil, coal oil, fuel oil, crude, crude oil, petrol, premium gas (US), high-test gas (US), high-octane petrol, leaded petrol, unleaded petrol, regular, regular petrol, two-star, four-star, white gas, kerosene, paraffin, diesel oil (or fuel), motor oil

▶ 57 Chemistry

10 **resin**, rosin, gum rosin, resinoid, resina, resene, resinate, gum(s), gum resin, oleoresin, tar, bitumen, asphalt, varnish, japan, synthetic resin, Bakelite (Tm), hard resin, acaroid gum (or resin), gum acaroides, coumarone resin, fossil resin, amber, lac resin, pine resin, vegetable resin, plastic

ADJECTIVES

11 **oily**, unctuous, unctional, unguinous, greasy, oleic, oleaginous, fat, fatty, fleshy, adipose, pinguid, pinguedinous, pinguescent, blubbery, tallowy, suety, lardy, lardaceous, rich, creamy, buttery, butyric, butyraceous, milky, paraffinic, mucoid, waxy, waxen, sebaceous, cereous, cerated, soapy, saponaceous, smooth, slick, slippery, slithery, sleek

12 **unguent**, unguentary, unguentous, chrismal, chrismatory, anointed

13 **lubricant**, lubricating, lubricative, lubricatory, lubricational, lenitive, emollient, soothing, moist

14 **resinous**, resiny, rosiny, resinic, resiniform, resinoid, resinaceous, resiniferous, bituminous, pitchy, tarry, asphaltic, varnished, japanned, myrrhy, masticic, gummy, gummic, gummiferous, gummous, gumlike

15 **basted**, greased, oiled, dripping with oil

16 **lubricated**, well-oiled, well-greased, smooth-running, slippery, oily, greasy, oiled, greased

VERBS

17 **oil**, grease, lubricate, lubrify (Arch), oleaginize, wax, soap, lather, soap the ways, moisten, smooth, smooth the way, grease the wheels, grease leather

18 **anoint**, salve, unguent, embrocate, dress, pour oil (or balm) on, smear, daub, slick, slick on, pomade, spread, baste, butter, butter up, cream, lard, glycerolate, glycerinize, wax, beeswax

19 **resinify**, resin, rosin, resinize, resinate

ADVERBS

20 **oilily**, greasily, unctuously, deaginously, pinguidly, resinously, richly, creamily, soapily, smoothly, slickly, sleekly, moistly

396   Life

Before this strange disease of modern life,/ With its sick hurry, its divided aims. Matthew Arnold.

Remember that no man loses any other life than this which he now lives, nor lives any other than this which he now loses. Marcus Aurelius.

At last awake/ From life, that insane dream we take/ For waking now. Robert Browning.

Life is a tragedy when seen in close-up, but a comedy in long-shot. Charlie Chaplin.

Life is an incurable disease. Abraham Cowley.

Life is like a sewer. What you get out of it depends on what you put into it. Tom Lehrer.

Life is as tedious as a twice-told tale/ Vexing the dull ear of a drowsy man. William Shakespeare.

Life's but a walking shadow, a poor player,/ That struts and frets his hour upon the stage,/ And then is heard no more; it is a tale/ Told by an idiot, full of sound and fury,/ Signifying nothing. William Shakespeare.

Lift not the painted veil which those who live/ Call life. Percy Bysshe Shelley.

Oh, isn't life a terrible thing, thank God? Dylan Thomas.

NOUNS

1 **life**, living, being alive, being, existing, existence, subsistence, entity, animate existence, animation, living things, animal life, the animal kingdom, human life, humankind, mankind, vegetable life, plant life, life on earth, the living and breathing world, the living, living being, human being, living person, person, individual, survivor, living soul, soul, spirit, animal spirits, life force, vital force, vital spark, vital flame, élan vital (Fr), seat of life, essential part, beating heart, strong pulse, liveliness, vivacity, energy, sprightliness, vitality, vitalization, vivification, sensation, sentience, sensibility, moral sensibility, imparting of life, cooperative living, symbiosis, association, ginger (Inf)

▶ 99 Existence, 400 Humankind, 76 Animals (General), 83 Plants (General), 642 Activity, 239 Vigour, 235 Power, 237 Strength, 103 Essence, 664 Cooperation

2 **living matter**, protoplasm, bioplasm, tissue, living tissue, macromolecule, bioplast, cell, gene, unicellular organism, organism

3 **life requirements**, vital necessities, subsistence, sustenance, nourishment, food, staff of life, bread, daily bread, manna, water, oxygen, air, vital air, breath of life, breath of one's nostrils, lifeblood, heart's blood, heart, artery

4 **biological function**, life senses, sight, smell, touch, taste, hearing, breathing, respiration, life activity, biological clock, fertility, parenthood, motherhood, fatherhood, procreation, propagation, reproduction, sexual reproduction, sex, sexual activity, coition, copulation, sexual intercourse, conception, pregnancy, confinement, delivery, birth, gift of life, nativity, viability, viableness, origin
▶ *403 Sensation, 246 Fertility, 245 Reproduction, 135 Union, 156 Beginning*

5 **life cycle**, seven ages of man, birth, childhood, youth, adolescence, adulthood, middle age, old age, death, lifetime, life span, life expectancy, average life, allotted span, allotted days, one's born days, threescore years and ten, biometry, longevity, survival, survivability, capacity for life, hold on life, will to live, life-support system, cat's nine lives, new birth, renaissance, revivification, revival, reanimation, reincarnation, resurrection, Lazarus, life to come, immortal life, immortality, eternal life, eternity, future state, the hereafter, afterlife, heaven, paradise
▶ *207 Age, 397 Death, 156 Beginning, 629 Repair, 190 Eternity, 188 Duration, 185 Time*

6 **things brought to life**, Pinocchio, Frankenstein's monster, the portrait of Dorian Gray, nutcracker, witch's broom, magic carpet, scarecrow and tin man in *The Wizard of Oz*, Pygmalion's statue

7 **studies of life**, life sciences, biology, genetics, botany, zoology, anthropology, humanities, sociology
▶ *1 Anthropology*

8 **theories of life**, creation, evolution, Bhavachakra, reincarnation, samsara

9 **classifications of life**, taxonomy, viruses, bacteria, plants, algae, fungi, bryophytes, pteridophytes, spermatophytes, animals, protozoa, parazoa, metazoa, vertebrates, amphibians, mammals
▶ *163 Class*

10 **lifestyle**, way of life, existence
▶ *652 Conduct, 584 Habit, 327 Way*

11 **life story**, history, biography, autobiography, memoirs
▶ *545 Record, 48 Literature, 3 History, 560 Description*

ADJECTIVES

12 **alive**, live, living, quick (Arch), alive and kicking, animate, conscious, breathing, in life, incarnate, in the flesh, not dead, existent, extant, surviving, ongoing, in the land of the living, (still) with us, still breathing, above ground, on this side of the grave, long-lived, old, aged, ancient, tenacious of life, lasting, lifelong, capable of life, viable, vital, vivifying, life-giving, Promethean, vivified, enlivened,

revived, restored, reborn
▶ *99 Existence, 207 Age, 397 Death, 629 Repair, 101 Reality*

13 **lively**, animated, vivacious, spirited, energetic, vigorous, dynamic, active, sprightly, gingery (Inf)
▶ *642 Activity, 239 Vigour, 235 Power, 237 Strength*

14 **biotic**, biotical (US), symbiotic, biological, biologic (US), biogenetic, biogenetical, protoplasmatic, protoplasmic, protoplastic, bioplastic

15 **born**, born alive, newly born, newborn, begotten, out of, by, fathered, sired, mothered, dammed, foaled, dropped, spawned, littered, laid, new-laid, hatched, produced
▶ *156 Beginning, 245 Reproduction, 243 Production, 107 Relatedness*

VERBS

16 **live**, be alive, have life, be, have being, exist, draw breath, breathe, respire, subsist, walk the earth, live one's life, live life to the fullest, liven (up), quicken, come to life, come to, come round, regain consciousness, revive, not die, be spared, survive, endure, come through, carry on, continue, last, persist, cheat death, have nine lives, be reborn
▶ *99 Existence, 629 Repair*

17 **dwell**, live at (or in), reside at (or in), inhabit, lodge, stay, abide
▶ *256 Habitat*

18 **be born**, come into the world, have one's nativity, come into existence, first see the light (of day), begin, draw breath, draw first breath, fetch breath
▶ *156 Beginning*

19 **give birth to**, give life to, create life, impart life, beget, hear the patter of little (or tiny) feet, have an extra mouth to feed, breed, spawn, procreate, reproduce, conceive, generate, vitalize, vivify, liven (up), breathe life into, bring (back) to life, raise up, raise from the dead, resuscitate, revive, bring round, restore to consciousness
▶ *245 Reproduction, 629 Repair*

20 **support life**, provide for, provide a living for, support, maintain, keep alive, save the life of, keep body and soul together, make ends meet, keep the wolf from the door, feed, nourish

21 **invigorate**, revitalize, put new life into, rejuvenate, give hope, give a shot in the arm, give a new lease of (or on) life, put zest into, reanimate, revive the spirit, resurrect, restore
▶ *651 Refreshment*

ADVERBS

22 **vitally**, viably, lively, animatedly, vivaciously, biologically, biotically

397   Death

God grants an easy death only to the just.
Svetlana Alliluyeva.

*O Death, where is thy sting-a-ling-a-ling,/ O
Grave, thy victoree?/ The bells of hell go
ting-a-ling-a-ling/ For you but not for me.*
Anonymous.

*I have often thought upon death, and I find it
the least of all evils.* Francis Bacon.

*I do not believe that any man fears to be dead,
but only the stroke of death.* Francis Bacon.

*Men fear death, as children fear to go in the
dark; and as that natural fear in children is
increased with tales, so is the other.* Francis
Bacon.

To die will be an awfully big adventure. J. M.
Barrie.

*And I looked, and behold a pale horse: and his
name that sat on him was Death, and Hell
followed with him.* Bible: Revelations.

*In the hour of death, and in the day of
judgement.* The Book of Common Prayer.

Alack he's gone the way of all flesh. William
Congreve.

*Any man's death diminishes me, because I am
involved in Mankind; And therefore never send
to know for whom the bell tolls; it tolls for thee.*
John Donne.

*It hath been often said, that it is not death, but
dying, which is terrible.* Henry Fielding.

*Darkling I listen; and, for many a time/ I have
been half in love with easeful Death,/* John
Keats.

*That is the road we all have to take – over the
Bridge of Sighs into eternity.* Søren Kierkegaard.

Whom the gods love dies young. Menander.

*I care not; a man can die but once; we owe God
a death.* William Shakespeare.

*Death is the veil which those who live call life:/
They sleep, and it is lifted.* Percy Bysshe
Shelley.

*Sleep after toil, port after stormy seas,/ Ease after
war, death after life does greatly please.*
Edmund Spenser.

NOUNS

1 **death**, biological death, clinical death, brain
death, cerebral death, dying, act of dying, expiration, expiry, decease, demise, mortality,
extinction, end of life, end, no life, stillbirth,
loss of life, exit, departure, passing, passing
away (*or* over), process of death, perishability,

putrefaction, mortification, necrosis, decay,
deathliness, cadaverousness, ephemerality,
transience, transiency, hand of death, cold
fingers of death, jaws of death, dance of death,
shadow of death, shades of death, the beyond,
the other side, the great divide, rest, eternal
rest, quietude, the great adventure (Inf), the
last debt (Inf), the final thrill (US inf), curtains
(Sl), crossing the bar (Inf), crossing the Styx (*or*
Lethe *or* River Jordan) (Inf), the long sleep
(Inf), the big sleep (Inf)

▶ *628 Deterioration, 189 Transience, 100 Nonexistence, 445 Colourlessness*

2 **death personified**, Death, the Grim Reaper,
the Great Leveller, the Thief in the Night, the
Last Summoner, Angel of Death, Azrael, King
of Death, King of Terrors

3 **symbol of death**, death's-head, skull, skull
and crossbones, memento mori

4 **death sentence**, doom, crack of doom, knell,
death knell, martyrdom, quietus, execution,
capital punishment, legalized killing, hanging, electric chair, electrocution, gas chamber,
lethal injection, guillotine, firing squad, crucifixion, death row (US), death chamber, death
house (US sl)

▶ *879 Punishment, 398 Killing*

5 **ways of dying**, natural death, old-age death,
easy death, quiet end, euthanasia, release,
happy release, welcome end, suicide, violent
death, sudden death, unexpected loss of life,
untimely end, accidental death, death by misadventure, fatality, fatal accident, drowning,
watery grave, road fatality, traffic accident,
starvation, fatal disease, mortal illness, terminal illness (*or* disease)

6 **killing**, murder, poisoning, stabbing, shooting

▶ *398 Killing*

7 **dying day**, last hour, valley of the shadow of
death, deathbed, deathwatch, deathbed repentance, deathbed confession, final words,
last words, death scene, last breath, last gasp,
dying breath, death rattle, death throes, last
agony, finality, extreme unction, passing bell,
last rites, funeral rites, obsequies, swan song
(Sl)

▶ *157 End, 399 Burial*

8 **after death**, rigor mortis, post-mortem, post-
mortem examination, autopsy, necropsy, inquest, mortuary, morgue, charnel house,
embalming, mourning, lamentation, wake,
Irish wake, viewing the body, funeral, funeral
parlour, crematorium, cemetery, graveyard,
graveside services, eulogy, coffin, grave, tomb,
dead-house (Inf), cold meat party (US sl), pine
drape (US sl), deep six (US sl), six (US sl)

▶ *399 Burial*

9 **person dealing with the dead**, doctor,
coroner, police, undertaker, mortician (US),

funeral director, embalmer
▶ *399 Burial*
10 **dying person**, dying patient, terminal patient, hopeless case, condemned man (*or* woman), the condemned, dead duck (Sl), dead pigeon (Sl), goner (Sl)
▶ *624 Ill Health*
11 **dead person**, fatality, casualty, victim, stillbirth, the deceased, the defunct, the late lamented, dead body, body, corpse, cadaver, carcass, mummy, embalmed body, skeleton, fossil, remains, mortal remains, relics, ashes, carrion, stiff (Sl), food for worms (Sl)
12 **death count**, mortality rate, mortality table, bill of mortality, mortality, death rate, death register, death roll, death toll, fatality list, casualty list, martyrology, necrology, deaths column, obituary (obit), death notice, death record, death certificate, fatalities, casualties, the dead, the dead and dying, the fallen (Inf), the lost (Inf)
13 **the dead**, ancestors, forefathers, precursors, those who have gone before, loved ones, dear (*or* dearly) departed
14 **the spiritual world**, world of spirits, unseen world, next world, future state, afterlife, hereafter, the shades, saints, souls, spirits, ghosts, phantoms, underworld, the lower regions, nether world, nether regions, Sheol, Styx, Stygian shore, Stygian darkness, Hades, hell, mythic hell, Elysian fields, meads of asphodel, happy hunting grounds, Abraham's bosom, Davy Jones's locker, heaven, paradise, mythic heaven, halls of death (Inf)
▶ *7 Religion, 199 Future Time, 8 Divinity*

VERBS

15 **die**, be dead, lose one's life, succumb, expire, perish, decease, pass away (*or* over), pass, depart this life, depart, be taken, meet one's death, meet one's end, meet one's fate, be no more, cease to be, cease to live, be gone, stop breathing, breathe one's last, give up the ghost, curl up and die, drop off, close one's eyes, fall asleep, predecease, become extinct, come (*or* turn) to dust, decompose, lie in the grave, sleep one's last sleep (Inf), turn up one's toes (Inf), push up daisies (Inf), be six feet under (Inf), ring down the curtain (Inf), shuffle off this mortal coil (Inf), pay the debt of nature (Inf), go the way of all flesh (Inf), go to one's reward (Inf), go to one's last home (Inf), go west (Inf), go to the last roundup (US inf), go to one's long account (Inf), cash in one's chips (Inf), have had one's chips (Inf), quit the scene (US inf), quit it (US inf), cross the bar (Inf), cross the Styx (*or* Lethe *or* River Jordan) (Inf), go up Salt River (US inf), join the majority (Inf), join the choir invisible (Inf), join the angels (Inf), meet one's Maker (Inf), meet Saint Peter (Inf), enter the Golden Gate (Inf),

go to glory (Inf), reach a better world (Inf), awake to life immortal (Inf), kick the bucket (Sl), kick it (Sl), bite the dust (Sl), croak (Sl), peg it (Sl), peg out (Sl), snuff it (Sl), cop it (Sl), buy it (Sl), buy the farm (US sl), conk out (Sl), go for a burton (Sl), pop off (Sl), pop one's clogs (Sl), hop the twig (US sl), go belly up (US sl)
▶ *100 Nonexistence, 157 End, 628 Deterioration, 129 Decrease, 218 Cessation*
16 **meet one's fate**, die peacefully, die in one's sleep, die in bed, drop (down) dead, die a natural death, die in poverty, die well, die with honour, die young, die before one's time, die prematurely, come to an untimely end, die of old age, catch one's death, die of neglect, starve to death, die hard, die fighting (for one's country), die in combat, die in action, fall, get cut down, get killed, surrender one's life, lay down one's life, relinquish one's life, give (up) one's life for another, make the supreme sacrifice, die (*or* meet) a violent death, break one's neck, bleed to death, drown, go to Davy Jones's locker, founder, receive one's death warrant, receive a death sentence, be put to death, suffer execution, die the death, hang, walk the plank, commit euthanasia, commit suicide, end one's life, kill oneself, die by one's own hand, snuff out like a candle (Inf), die in harness (Inf), die with one's boots on (Inf), meet a sticky end (Inf)
▶ *398 Killing*
17 **bury**, entomb, embalm, view the body, mourn, grieve, lament, bemoan, regret, eulogize, plant (Sl), deep six (US sl)
▶ *399 Burial, 770 Sorrow*

ADJECTIVES

18 **dying**, expiring, deathly, deathlike, deathly pale, white as a sheet, cadaverous, skeletal, on the danger list, in intensive care, in a critical condition, terminally ill, sick unto death, hopeless, doomed (to die), fated (to die), fey (Scot), condemned to die, condemned to death, sentenced to death, under sentence of death, on one's deathbed, at the point of death, moribund, *in extremis* (L), half-dead, slipping away, slipping, sinking, sinking fast, fading, fading fast, hanging by a thread, struggling for breath, at one's last gasp, not long for this world, not long to go, going, about gone, far gone, done for (Inf), having had it (Inf), on one's last legs (Inf), with one foot in the grave (Inf), at death's door (Inf), death knocking at the door (Inf), sands of time running out (Inf), one's hour having come (Inf), one's time being up (Inf), one's number being up (Sl)
▶ *624 Ill Health, 879 Punishment, 157 End*
19 **dead**, deceased, defunct, demised, lifeless, breathless, still, inanimate, exanimate, bereft of life, no more, passed away, passed over, passed, released, out of one's misery, departed

this life, departed, gone, dead on arrival (DOA), born dead, stillborn, extinct, finished, out of this world, numbered with the dead, taken by God, called by God, called to one's eternal rest, gathered to one's fathers, in Abraham's bosom, asleep in Jesus, in Paradise, at the Pearly Gates, gone before, gone to join one's ancestors, long gone, gone but not forgotten, late, lamented, late lamented, regretted, dead and gone, dead and buried, buried, in the grave, killed, murdered, slaughtered, massacred, sacrificed, martyred, sainted, (as) dead as a doornail, (as) dead as mutton, (as) dead as a dodo, done for (Inf), kaput (Inf), six feet under (Inf), under hatches (Inf), beyond the grave (Inf), launched into eternity (Inf), on the other side (Inf), behind the veil (Inf), beyond mortal ken (Inf), gone to Elysium (Inf), gone to the Elysian fields (Inf), gone to the happy hunting grounds (US inf), gone for a burton (Sl), cold (Sl), stiff (Sl), stone dead (Sl)

▶ *157 End, 100 Nonexistence, 399 Burial, 404 Insensibility*

20 **deadly**, mortal, fatal, terminal, lethal, murderous, perishable, ephemeral, transient

▶ *398 Killing, 626 Lack of Hygiene, 189 Transience*

21 **deathly**, deathlike, corpse-like, cadaverous, ghastly, livid, pale, pallid, wan, ghostly, ashen, haggard, skeletal

▶ *445 Colourlessness, 274 Thinness*

22 **post-mortem**, post-obit, posthumous, funereal, embalmed, mummified, fossilized

ADVERBS

23 **fatally**, terminally, moribundly, lifelessly, inanimately, post-mortem, after death, posthumously, in the event of death

INTERJECTIONS

24 **I'm dying!**, I'm done for!, I've had it!, it's curtains!, this is it!, it's all over!, it is all up with me!

398   Killing

Killing/ Is the ultimate simplification of life.
Hugh MacDiarmid.

…there's no difference between one's killing and making decisions that will send others to kill. It's exactly the same thing, or even worse. Golda Meir.

Yet each man kills the thing he loves,/ By each let this be heard,/ Some do it with a bitter look,/ Some with a flattering word./ The coward does it with a kiss,/ The brave man with a sword! Oscar Wilde.

NOUNS

1 **killing**, slaying, murder, manslaughter, revenge killing, senseless killing, destruction, destruction of life, taking life, causing death, dealing death, execution, blood-shedding, blood-letting, ritual killing, accidental killing, mercy killing, euthanasia

▶ *397 Death, 244 Destruction*

2 **murder**, first-degree murder, second-degree murder, premeditated murder, capital murder, assassination, contract murder, mass murder, gang murder, St Valentine's Day murder, terrorist killing, brutal murder, murder most foul, classic murder, crime of passion, manslaughter, unlawful killing, thuggery, shooting, knifing, poisoning, drowning, suffocation, asphyxiation, strangulation, garrotting, hanging, murder weapon, gun, knife, blunt instrument, rope, (terrorist) bomb, bumping off (Sl), rubbing out (Sl), blowing away (Sl), wasting (Sl)

3 **homicide**, regicide, tyrannicide, parricide, patricide, matricide, uxoricide, fratricide, sororicide, infanticide, exposure of infants, genocide, ethnic cleansing

4 **slaughter**, massacre, bloodbath, carnage, butchery, wholesale murder, high casualties, great bloodshed, noyade, battue, holocaust, pogrom, purge, annihilation, liquidation, decimation, extermination, destruction, genocide, the Holocaust, Final Solution, war, battle, Custer's Last Stand, Roman holiday, gladiatorial combat, duel, Massacre of the Innocents, Sicilian Vespers, St Bartholomew's Day Massacre, Night of the Long Knives

▶ *244 Destruction, 676 War*

5 **execution**, capital punishment, death penalty, legalized killing, judicial murder, auto-da-fé, hanging, rope, scaffold, gallows, gibbet, electrocution, electric chair, shooting, firing squad, lethal injection, gas chamber, beheading, guillotine, axe, burning alive, the stake, stoning, extrajudicial execution, lynching, dispatch, deathblow, *coup de grâce* (Fr), final stroke, quietus

▶ *879 Punishment*

6 **ritual killing**, sacrifice, religious sacrifice, martyrdom, martyrization, immolation, crucifixion, field of blood, Aceldama

▶ *7 Religion*

7 **suicide**, self-destruction, self-slaughter, killing oneself, doing away with oneself, dying by one's own hand, felo-de-se, slashing one's wrists, jumping from a high place, hanging oneself, shooting oneself, taking an overdose, overdose of sleeping pills, drug overdose, gas, gassing oneself, self-immolation, suttee, seppuku, hara-kiri, kamikaze, attempted suicide, mass suicide, parasuicide, fake suicide, suicide pact

8 **accidental killing**, death by misadventure, manslaughter, violent death, fatal accident, traffic death, death on the roads, fatal car crash, fatal train crash, fatal plane crash

▶ *397 Death*

9 **animal killing**, blood sports, bullfighting, hunting, fox hunting, deer hunting, rabbit hunting, duck hunting, wildfowling, chase, shooting, grouse shooting, pheasant shooting, trapping, selective killing, cull, extermination, slaughtering, knackery, vivisection, animal suicide, lemmings, Gadarene swine, whale (*or* dolphin) beaching

▶ *32 Horses*

10 **killer**, slayer, murderer, man of blood, mercy killer, soldier, combatant, guerrilla, urban guerrilla, terrorist, slaughterer, butcher, executioner, hangman, punisher, tribal killer, head-hunter, cannibal, killer dog, poisonous snake, rabid animal, shark, man-eater

▶ *679 Combatant*

11 **murderer**, murderess, cold-blooded murderer, killer, assassin, hired killer, hired assassin, contract killer, professional killer, professional murderer, mass murderer, serial killer, psychopathic killer, psychopath, pathological killer, homicidal maniac, Cain, terrorist, bomber, poisoner, strangler, garrotter, axe murderer, hatchet man, gangster, gang member, gunman, hired gun, bravo, desperado, cutthroat, thug, ruffian, homicide, regicide, tyrannicide, parricide, patricide, matricide, uxoricide, fratricide, sororicide, infanticide, hit man (Sl), Mafia hit man (Sl), psycho (Inf)

12 **executioner**, hangman, firing squad member, axeman

13 **animal killer**, hunter, huntsman, fox hunter, beagler, deer hunter, rabbit hunter, duck hunter, wildfowler, grouse shooter, pheasant shooter, trapper, slaughterman, knacker, bullfighter, matador, toreador, picador, pest exterminator, rat-catcher, mole-catcher, knacker, vivisectionist, predator, bird of prey, beast of prey, poison, pesticide, insecticide, ratsbane, rodenticide, vermicide, germicide

14 **plant killer**, weedkiller, herbicide, fungicide, algicide

▶ *68 Agriculture*

15 **slaughterhouse**, abattoir, knacker's yard, shambles, bullring, arena, battleground, field of battle, battlefield, killing fields, the Alamo, Little Bighorn, Wounded Knee, the Somme, Pearl Harbor, Stalingrad, Mylai, civilian targets, Dresden, Hiroshima, Nagasaki, gas chamber, gas oven, Auschwitz, Dachau, Belsen

VERBS

16 **kill**, slay, murder, shed blood, take life, deprive of life, rob of life, shorten someone's life, hasten someone's end, end someone's life, dispatch, destroy, do away with, make away with, get rid of, cut off, nip in the bud, put down, put to sleep, bring down to the grave, drive to death, work to death, send out of the world, send to one's account, send to one's Maker, launch into eternity, snuff (Sl), put out of one's misery (Inf)

▶ *397 Death*

17 **murder**, commit murder, assassinate, poison, stab, stab to death, knife, sabre, spear, put to the sword, lance, bayonet, run through, shoot, shoot down, gun down, pick off, pistol, blow out the brains of, bomb, strangle, wring the neck of, garrotte, choke, smother, burke, suffocate, asphyxiate, stifle, drown, wall up, bury alive, strike, smite, brain, spill the brains of, poleaxe, sandbag, beat to death, burn, burn alive, roast alive, gas, electrocute, starve to death, arrange a fatal accident, eliminate (Sl), waste (US sl), do in (Sl), do for (Sl), bump off (Sl), rub out (Sl), take for a ride (Sl), make to walk the plank (Sl)

18 **slaughter**, butcher, poleaxe, cut the throat of, drain the lifeblood of, massacre, slay en masse, smite hip and thigh, put to the sword, cut to pieces, cut to ribbons, cut down, decimate, mow down, shoot down, gun down, steep one's hands in blood, wade in blood, give no quarter, spare none, take no prisoners, destroy, wipe out, wipe off the face of the earth, annihilate, exterminate, liquidate, purge, send to the gas chamber, commit genocide

▶ *244 Destruction*

19 **execute**, condemn to death, condemn, sign the death warrant, put to death, hang, send to the scaffold, electrocute, gas, give a lethal injection, shoot, behead, guillotine, send to the stake, burn alive, stone to death, lynch, garrotte, deal a deathblow, give one's quietus, string up (Inf)

▶ *879 Punishment*

20 **kill ritually**, sacrifice, offer up, martyr, martyrize, crucify, immolate, burn

▶ *7 Religion*

21 **commit suicide**, kill oneself, take one's own life, put an end to one's life, do away with oneself, die by one's own hand, make away with oneself, commit hara-kiri, commit suttee, hang oneself, shoot oneself, blow out one's brains, cut one's throat, slash one's wrists, fall on one's sword, die Roman fashion, put one's head in the oven, gas oneself, take poison, take an overdose, jump from a high place, jump overboard, drown oneself, get oneself killed, request euthanasia, do oneself in (Sl), top oneself (Sl)

22 **kill animals**, hunt, shoot, trap, fish, angle, poison, cull, exterminate, put to sleep, put down, experiment on, perform vivisection on

ADJECTIVES

23 **deadly**, lethal, killing, mortal, fatal, deathly, fell (Arch), life-threatening, capital, death-bringing, malignant, poisonous, toxic, as-

phyxiant, suffocating, stifling, unhealthy, miasmic, pathological, insalubrious, inoperable, incurable, terminal

▶ *397 Death, 626 Lack of Hygiene, 624 Ill Health*

24 **murderous**, homicidal, psychopathic, genocidal, internecine, slaughterous, destructive, death-dealing, trigger-happy, cold-blooded, sanguinary, ensanguined, bloody, gory, bloodstained, red-handed, bloodthirsty, thirsting for blood, cruel, savage, brutal, head-hunting, man-eating, cannibalistic, self-destructive, suicidal

▶ *832 Malevolence, 244 Destruction*

ADVERBS

25 **lethally**, mortally, fatally, malignantly, terminally, murderously, homicidally, bloodthirstly, suicidally, in at the death, in at the kill

INTERJECTIONS

26 **no quarter!,** take no prisoners!, cry havoc!, shoot to kill!, string him up!, hang 'em high!, nuke 'em! (Inf)

399   Burial

NOUNS

1 **burial**, burying, disposal of the dead, burial customs, interment, inhumation, entombment, sepulture, urn burial, cremation, incineration, scattering of the ashes, mass burial, burial at sea, military burial, full military rites, embalmment, embalming, mummification, myrrh, spices, natron, mummy-case, sarcophagus, pyre, funeral pile, crematorium, mortuary, morgue, charnel house, dead-house (Inf)

▶ *397 Death*

2 **funeral**, funeral rites, funeral ceremony, funeral service, burial service, graveside service, memorial service, requiem, obsequies, exequies, obituary, funeral parlour, crematorium, mourning, weeping and wailing, keen, lamentation, wake, Irish wake, lying-in-state, viewing the body, receiving family friends, funeral procession, cortege, dead march, knell, passing bell, muffled drum, last post, taps, funeral hymn, *Dies Irae* (L), funeral oration, funeral sermon, eulogy, elegy, dirge, lament, lowering the body, closing the grave, cold meat party (US sl), obit (Inf)

▶ *397 Death, 774 Lamentation*

3 **funeral director**, undertaker, mortician (US), pallbearer, grave digger, sexton, priest, minister, mourner, weeper, keener, hired mourner, mute, embalmer, monument mason, eulogist, eulogizer, elegist, epitaphist, obituary writer, obituarist, necrologist

▶ *7 Religion, 774 Lamentation*

4 **funeral objects**, hearse, coffin, casket, shell, cist, bier, pall, catafalque, urn, cinerary urn,

funeral urn, bone urn, ossuary, canopic urn (*or* jar *or* vase), inscription, Rest in Peace (RIP), here lies, *hic jacet* (L), epitaph, lapidary phrases, monument, sepulchral monument, tombstone, gravestone, headstone, footstone, brass, hatchment, cross, memorial, war memorial, cenotaph, burial clothes, grave clothes, cerements, cerecloth, shroud, winding sheet, mummy wrapping, flowers, wreath, pine drape (US sl)

▶ *511 Memory*

5 **cemetery**, graveyard, churchyard, burial place, burial ground, plot, family plot, final resting place, God's acre, catacomb, columbarium, cinerarium, necropolis, city of the dead, golgotha, chapel of remembrance, garden of remembrance, garden of rest, military cemetery, pet cemetery, boneyard (Sl)

6 **grave**, grave pit, plague pit, common grave, mass grave, open grave, tomb, mausoleum, vault, crypt, burial chamber, sepulchre, mummy chamber, King Tut's tomb, pyramid, mastaba, pantheon, dakhma, fogou, Tower of Silence, narrow house, long home, beehive tomb, shaft tomb, barrow, mound, tumulus, earthwork, cromlech, dolmen, menhir, cairn, shrine, memorial, cenotaph, deep six (US sl), six (US sl)

▶ *316 Convexity*

7 **inquest**, autopsy, necropsy, post-mortem examination, post-mortem, exhumation, disinterment, disentombment, removal of the body, digging up the body

▶ *477 Question*

VERBS

8 **bury**, inter, inhume, lay to rest, lay in the grave, consign to earth, lower the body, put to bed with a shovel, lay out, prepare for burial, close the eyes, embalm, mummify, coffin, encoffin, entomb, ensepulchre, urn, cremate, incinerate, burn on the pyre, pay one's last respects, go to a funeral, toll the knell, sing a requiem, sound the last post, mourn, keen, lament, hold a wake, plant (Sl), deep six (US sl)

▶ *397 Death, 774 Lamentation*

9 **exhume**, disinter, dig up, unearth, unbury, disentomb

ADJECTIVES

10 **buried**, dead and buried, interred, inhumed, laid to rest, entombed, coffined, urned, cremated, embalmed, mummified, in the grave, below ground, six feet under, pushing up daisies (Inf)

▶ *397 Death*

11 **funeral**, burial, funerary, funebrial, funereal, sombre, black, dark, sad, mournful, mourning, lamenting, dirgelike, dirgeful, mortuary, cinerary, crematory, crematorial (US), sepulchral, memorial, obsequial, eulogistic, eulo-

gistical (US), elegiac, elegiacal (US), obituary, necrological, lapidary, epitaphic
▶ *447 Blackness, 440 Darkness, 774 Lamentation, 770 Sorrow*

ADVERBS

12 **funereally**, sombrely, sepulchrally, eulogistically, elegiacally, necrologically, in memoriam, post-obitum, post-mortem, beneath the sod, six feet deep

---

400   Humankind

NOUNS

1 **humankind**, mankind, womankind, humanity, human race, human species, Homo sapiens, hominid, man, generations of man, peoples of the earth, earthlings, the world, the world population, everyone, everybody, every living soul, the living, us, ourselves, grains of sand, blades of grass, fish in the sea

2 **human nature**, human fallibility, human failing, human frailty, human weakness, mortality, flesh
▶ *238 Weakness*

3 **uncivilized human**, primitive human, primitive humanity, backward peoples, barbarians, pagans, savages, bushmen, aborigines, ancient man, early man, early humanity, primeval man, primeval humanity, Homo erectus, Stone-age man, Cro-Magnon man, Homo neanderthalensis, Neanderthal man, anthropoid ape, apeman (*or* apewoman), caveman (*or* cavewoman), cave dweller, troglodytes, Ramapithecus, Pithecanthropus, Peking man, Java man
▶ *3 History*

4 **civilized human**, civilized humanity, modern man, modern woman, well-bred person, gentleman, lady, educated person, scientific man (*or* woman), political animal, the civilized world, culture, civilization, early civilizations, the ancients, Sumerian, Egyptian, Ethiopian, Babylonian, Assyrian, Persian, Hittite, Hebrew, Aegean, Phoenician, Greek, Roman, Mogul, Chinese, Aztec, Inca
▶ *627 Improvement, 794 Refinement*

5 **study of mankind**, anthropology, anthropography, anthropometry, craniometry, craniology, anthropogenesis, somatology, social anthropology, demography, social science, sociology, humanitarianism, humanism, anthroposophy, anthropomorphism, ethnology, ethnography, folklore, mythology
▶ *1 Anthropology, 2 Sociology*

6 **studier of mankind**, anthropologist, craniologist, social anthropologist, demographer, sociologist, humanist, ethnographer, folklorist, mythologist

7 **person**, individual, human being, human, being, man, woman, adult, girl, boy, teenager,

adolescent, child, baby, Adamite, mortal, creature, fellow creature, body, soul, living soul, flesh and blood, average person, ordinary person, common man, everyman, everywoman, man (*or* woman) in the street, man on the Clapham omnibus, John Doe, the noble animal, the naked ape, earthling, tellurian, Lord of Creation, God's image, God's creation, I, one, somebody, someone, so and so, such a one, party, customer, character, type, element, important figure, important person, personage, person of note, VIP, man (*or* woman) at the top, celebrity, star, favourite, all (those) concerned, personnel, cast, list of characters, dramatis personae, counted person, head, hand, nose, unit, bod (Inf), guy (US inf), chap (Inf), bugger (Sl), sod (Sl), joe (US sl), Joe Bloggs (Sl), Joe Soap (Sl), the average punter (Sl), top dog (Sl), suit (US sl), the man (US sl), cele (Inf)
▶ *206 Youth, 207 Age, 401 Male, 402 Female, 611 Importance*

8 **humanlike machine**, robot, automaton, android, humanoid, cyborg, bionic man, bionic woman

9 **group**, kinship group, family, clan, brotherhood, fraternity, sorority, clique, set, social group, society, organized society, stratified society, class, social classes, nobility, aristocracy, gentility, upper class, bourgeoisie, middle class(es), upper middle class, lower middle class, working class, lower class, public, general public, general population, generality, populace, citizenry, inhabitants, the masses, commonalty, plebs, hoi polloi, common people, common persons, people, folk, you and me, community at large, community, neighbourhood, ghetto, ethnic minority, ethnic group, racial group (*or* type), race, primitive society, tribe, tribalism, the human family, socio-political group, international society, community of nations, European Community (EC), European Economic Community (EEC), comity of nations, United Nations (UN), international cooperation, Joe Public (Sl)
▶ *107 Relatedness, 802 Aristocrat, 803 Commoner, 255 Inhabitant, 664 Cooperation, 161 Assembly, 2 Sociology*

10 **member of society**, citizen, nobleman, noblewoman, aristocrat, patrician, gentleman, lady, bourgeois, white-collar worker, commoner, blue-collar worker, worker, co-worker, colleague, comrade
▶ *802 Aristocrat, 803 Commoner, 646 Worker*

11 **nation**, people, state, country, realm, kingdom, national entity, nationality, statehood, civil society, body politic, political entity, demos, city state, welfare state, civil state, nation state, multiracial state, melting pot, isolationism, noninvolvement, neutrality, Swiss neutrality, Austrian neutrality, alliance of

states, commonwealth, Commonwealth of Nations, the Commonwealth, polity, democratic state, democracy, republican state, republic, socialist state, socialism, communistic state, communism, totalitarian state, totalitarianism, dictatorship, nationalism, national consciousness, race consciousness, Pan-Africanism, ultranationalism, chauvinism, jingoism, expansionism, imperialism, colonialism, Lebensraum

▶ *91 Countries, 12 Government and Politics*

ADJECTIVES

12 **human**, mortal, creaturely, fleshly, earthborn, tellurian, anthropoid, humanoid, hominoid, humanlike, subhuman, civilized, anthropological, ethnographical, racial, ethnic, anthropocentric, anthropomorphic, personal, individual, humanistic, bionic

▶ *1 Anthropology*

13 **national**, state, civic, civil, governmental, democratic, republican, socialistic, communistic, totalitarian, public, general, communal, tribal, social, societal, cosmopolitan, international, interracial

▶ *2 Sociology*

VERBS

14 **make human**, humanize, anthropomorphize, civilize

ADVERBS

15 **humanly**, mortally, anthropologically, ethnographically, racially, ethnically, personally, individually, personally, humanistically, socially, nationally, internationally

401 Male

NOUNS

1 **male sex**, masculine gender, man, mankind, manhood, masculinity, manliness, mannishness, virility, virilism, machismo, male chauvinism, misogyny, male exclusiveness, male-dominated society, patriarchy, laddishness (Sl)

2 **male**, male person, man, gentleman, old man, young man, youth, boy, little boy, lad, fellow, he, him, himself, Adam, blade (Arch), swain (Arch), bloke (Inf), guy (US inf), chap (Inf), chappie (Inf), dude (US inf), bozo (US sl), prick (Tab sl), joker (Sl), card (Inf), cove (Sl), gay dog (Sl), gent (Inf), (old) geezer (Inf), (old) gaffer (Inf), (old) codger (Inf), (old) buffer (Inf), blue-eyed boy (Inf), yob (Sl), young buck (Sl), young Turk (Sl)

▶ *206 Youth, 207 Age*

3 **male title of address**, Mr, mister, Sir (*or* sir), esquire, Esq., Father, master, Lord (*or* lord), my lord (*or* m'lud), his lordship, my good man, my dear man (*or* sir), gentleman, goodman (Arch), monsieur, Herr, Don, dom, señor, senhor, signor, sahib, Sri, babu, tovarisch, com-

rade, boy, son, sonny, lad, boyo (Inf), man (US sl), fellow (US inf), Mac (Inf), mate (Inf), pal (Inf), chum (Inf), buddy (US inf), bud (US inf), buster (US inf), sport (Aus sl), cock (Inf), squire (Inf), governor (Inf), guvnor (Inf), guv (Inf), Jock (Inf), Jimmy (Inf), Johnny (Inf), pop (Inf), old man (Inf), Mister Charlie (US sl)

▶ *804 Title, 819 Friendship*

4 **boyfriend**, boy, sweetheart, engaged man, fiancé, bridegroom, groom, beau, escort, date, partner, lover, Adonis, lover boy, toy boy (Sl), sugar daddy (Sl), beefcake (Sl), dish (Sl), hunk (Sl), prime beef (Sl), choice meat (Sl)

▶ *821 Love*

5 **single man**, unmarried man, bachelor, available man, unattached male, divorcé, ex-husband, widower

6 **macho man**, muscleman, he-man, cocksman (Tab sl), caveman (Inf), male chauvinist pig (MCP) (Inf)

7 **libertine**, rake, cad, bounder, philanderer, heartbreaker, Casanova, Don Juan, buck, stallion, man of the world, worldly man, gigolo, ladies' man, male prostitute, rent boy, stud (Sl), slag (Sl)

▶ *877 Immorality, 168 Nonconformity*

8 **homosexual**, gay

9 **offensive terms for homosexual**, sissy, pretty boy (Inf), mummy's boy (Inf), nancy (boy) (Inf), homo (Inf), queer (Inf), queen (Sl), faggot (US sl), fag (US sl), pansy (Sl)

10 **bisexual**, AC/DC guy, bi-guy (Sl)

11 **transsexual**, transvestite, cross-dresser

12 **eunuch**, castrate, castrato, capon (US sl)

▶ *238 Weakness*

13 **man in the family**, family man, married man, husband, spouse, live-in lover, widower, house husband, man about the house, father, patriarch, paterfamilias, paternity, fatherhood, son, boy, brother, uncle, nephew, godfather, godson, grandfather, grandson, old man (Inf), daddy (Inf), dad (Inf), pop (Inf), pater (Sl)

▶ *107 Relatedness, 823 Marriage*

14 **liberated man**, new man, male feminist, sensitive man, caring father

15 **menfolk**, men, the boys, the boys in the back room, spear side, stag party (Inf), the lads (Inf)

16 **male animal**, lion, tiger, bull, bullock, bull-calf, ox, steer, stallion, stud horse, stud, entire horse, colt, gelding, stag, buck, hart, boar, hog, ram, tup, he-goat, billy goat, dog, dog fox, tom cat, jack, cock, cockerel, rooster, capon, drake, gander

ADJECTIVES

17 **male**, masculine, manly, macho, virile, muscular, gentlemanly, chivalrous, mannish, manlike, unmanly, effeminate, gay, homosexual, laddish (Sl), butch (Sl), homo (Inf), queer (Inf)

402 Female

NOUNS

1 **female sex**, feminine gender, second sex, weaker sex, gentle sex, fair sex, woman, womankind, womanhood, femininity, feminineness, feminality, muliebrity, womanliness, womanishness, the eternal feminine, girlishness, feminism, women's rights, equal rights, Women's Movement, Women's Liberation, women's lib, gynography, matriarchy, gynarchy, gynocracy, effeminacy, androgyny, gynaecology, gyniatrics, gyniatry, obstetrics

▶ *60 Medicine, 245 Reproduction, 122 Equality*

2 **female**, female person, woman, lady, old woman, matron, dowager, young woman, girl, little girl, she, her, herself, Eve, maiden (Arch), damsel (Arch), colleen, grisette, midinette, virago, Amazon, sheila (Aus inf), gal (Sl), lassie (Inf)

▶ *206 Youth, 207 Age*

3 **female title of address**, Miss (*or* miss), Mrs, Ms, Madam (*or* madam), ma'am, marm, mistress, missus, goody (Arch), goodwife (Arch), Dame, Lady, lady, milady, her ladyship, my good lady, my dear woman (*or* lady), mademoiselle, madame, Frau, Fraulein, Donna, signora, signorina, señora, señorita, memsahib, hinny (Dial), lass, lassie (Inf), sister (US sl)

4 **girlfriend**, girl, sweetheart, bride, escort, date, lover, engaged woman, fiancée, mistress, kept woman

5 **single girl**, single woman, unmarried woman, virgin, maiden, unmarried mother, bachelor girl, spinster, old maid, unattached female, divorcée, widow

6 **loose woman**, nymph, nymphet, hussy, *femme fatale* (Fr), nymphomaniac, goer (Inf), slag (Sl), nympho (Sl)

7 **prostitute**, whore, sex-worker, lady of the night, call girl, harlot, strumpet, tart (Sl), tom (Sl)

▶ *877 Immorality*

8 **nasty woman**, jade, shrew, minx, nag, witch, bitch (Sl), (old) cow (Inf), (old) bag (Inf)

9 **woman considered as a sex object**, skirt (Inf), bit of skirt (Sl), doll (Sl), dolly bird (Sl), bird (Sl), chick (Sl), fine fryer (US sl), honey (US inf), a real honey (US inf), cupcake (US inf), baby (Sl), babe (US sl), little mama (US sl), moll (Sl), bint (Sl), crumpet (Sl), cheesecake (Sl), bit of fluff (Sl), piece of fluff (US sl), broad (US sl), dame (US sl), baggage (Inf), tart (Inf), ball-breaker (Tab sl), cunt (Tab sl)

10 **homosexual**, gay, lesbian, Sapphic, tribade, les (Inf), lez (Inf), dyke (Sl), butch (Sl), bulldyke (US sl), bisexual, transsexual, female transvestite

▶ *821 Love, 168 Nonconformity*

11 **liberated woman**, modern woman, feminist, sister, women's libber, bra burner, suffragette, career woman, working woman, working wife (*or* mother), superwoman

▶ *644 Work, 700 Liberation*

12 **woman in the family**, married woman, wife, spouse, live-in lover, ex-wife, widow, housewife, mother, matriarch, materfamilias, maternity, motherhood, daughter, girl, sister, aunt, auntie, niece, godmother, goddaughter, grandmother, granddaughter, old lady (Inf), old woman (Inf), trouble and strife (Inf), ball and chain (Inf), squaw (Sl), mummy (Inf), mum (Inf), mom (Inf), mater (Sl), sis (Inf)

▶ *107 Relatedness, 823 Marriage*

13 **womenfolk**, women, the girls, the sisterhood, matronage, distaff side, women's quarters, harem, seraglio, zenana, purdah, hen party (Inf), the second (*or* weaker *or* lesser *or* subordinate) sex (Offensive)

14 **female animal**, lioness, tigress, cow, heifer, mare, filly, hind, doe, vixen, sow, gilt, ewe, ewe-lamb, she-goat, nanny goat, bitch, hen, pen

ADJECTIVES

15 **female**, feminine, womanly, womanish, effeminate, ladylike, girlish, maidenly, matronly, child-bearing, feminist, feministic, virago-like, Amazonian, lesbian, butch (Sl), dykey (Sl)

403 Sensation

O for a life of sensations rather than of thoughts! John Keats.

NOUNS

1 **sensation**, feeling, awareness, sentience, perception, experience, sense-perception, impression, sense-datum, sensum, response, reaction, receptivity, receptiveness, consciousness, emotion, sentiment, the senses, sight, hearing, touch, taste, smell, sixth sense, second sight, extrasensory perception, ESP, telepathy, clairvoyance, agitation, excitement, thrill

2 **ability to sense**, sensitivity, feelings, susceptibility, threshold of pain, irritability, tenderness, thin skin, vulnerability, soft underbelly, prickliness, ticklishness, touchiness, delicacy, sensuousness, sensuality, warm-bloodedness, oversensitivity, hyperaesthesia, allergy

3 **stimulus**, goad, prick, stimulant, heightener, thrill, throb, prickle, tingle, frisson, fluttering, buzz, kick, tickle, itch, horripilation, goose pimples, goose flesh, the shivers, formication, pins and needles, sore spot, titillation, stimulation, the creeps (Inf), heebie-jeebies (Inf)

4 **someone or something that feels**, aesthete, epicure, epicurean, shrinking violet, sensitive plant, cry-baby, sense organ, sensorium, nervous system, nerve, nerve fibre, raw

nerve, nerve-end(ing), nerve cell, neurone, whisker, tentacle, proboscis, finger, finger-tip, antenna, nerve centre

ADJECTIVES

5 **sensible**, sensitive, aware, aware of, alive to, sentient, feeling, percipient, switched on (Inf), clued up (*or* in) (Inf), in the picture (Inf)

6 **conscious**, awake, wide awake, sleepless, insomniac

7 **susceptible**, impressionable, perceptive, responsive, oversensitive, thin-skinned, allergic, delicate, tender, touchy, irritable, tetchy, jumpy, excited, temperamental, agitated, irritated, thrilled, stirred, overexcited, hyperactive, hyped up (Inf), hot-blooded, carnal, epicurean, sensuous, aesthetic

8 **sensate**, perceptible, tactile, palpable, tangible, audible, visible, noticeable

9 **exciting**, sensational, titillating, thrilling, stimulating, keen, breath-taking, impressive, stirring, emotive, poignant, striking, electric, electrifying, hair-raising, itchy, prickly, tingly, tickly

10 **sensory**, sensorial, nerval, nervous, neurological

VERBS

11 **sense**, be sensitive, be alive to, respond, react, tingle, prickle, tickle, itch, be itchy, be irritated, be irritable, have gooseflesh, have goose-pimples, horripilate, be aware, be aware of, detect, feel, have one's senses, perceive, see, hear, touch, taste, smell, realize, experience

12 **awake**, wake up, regain consciousness, come to one's senses, be on a high, have one's wits about one, be on the ball, have one's nerves stretched, be on tenterhooks

13 **arouse sensation**, wake, wake up, enliven, activate, stir, disturb, agitate, impress, invigorate, quicken, animate, stimulate, titillate, whet, galvanize, cause a sensation, thrill, excite, arouse, touch a raw nerve, heighten awareness, raise one's consciousness

ADVERBS

14 **sensationally**, feelingly, emotionally, excitingly, melodramatically

404 Insensibility

NOUNS

1 **lack of feeling**, lack of awareness, ignorance, lack of sensation, analgesia, paralysis, anaesthesia, clumsiness, heavy-handedness, dullness, insensitiveness, apathy

2 **unconsciousness**, coma, faint, swoon, sleep, doze, snooze, torpor, daydream, nap, cat-nap, stupor, trance, suspended animation, etherism, sleepiness, somnolence, numbness

3 **heedlessness**, impassivity, hardness, callousness, hard-heartedness, heartlessness, thick skin

4 **anaesthetic**, painkiller, analgesic, narcotic, opium, laudanum, dope, drug, ether, novocaine, cocaine, pethidine, barbiturate, halothane, lignocaine, acupuncture, hypnosis, Mickey Finn, sleeping pill, somnifer, sleeping draught, knockout drops, tranquillizer

5 **unfeeling person**, sleepwalker, somnambulist, robot, android, zombie, hearty, pachyderm, Sleeping Beauty

ADJECTIVES

6 **unfeeling**, blind, deaf, insentient, nerveless, senseless, insensitive, clumsy, heavy-handed, unresponsive, impassive, cold-blooded, apathetic, heedless, oblivious, unmindful, forgetful, unwary, impervious, unemotional, hardened, stolid, blockish

7 **anaesthetized**, etherized, frozen, hypnotized, insensible, numb, knocked out (Inf), deadened, inured

8 **unconscious**, stunned, concussed, in a coma, comatose, asleep, out cold, catatonic, away with the fairies, out for the count, dead to the world, wigged out (Sl), zonked out (Sl), knocked out (Inf)

▶ *874 Drunkenness*

9 **anaesthetic**, analgesic, deadening, numbing, hypnotic, narcotic, soporific, somnific, somniferous

10 **sleepy**, somnolent, dopey, drowsy, fuzzy, woozy (Inf)

VERBS

11 **be unfeeling**, be impassive, be apathetic, drowse, doze, sleep, sleepwalk, somnabulate, fall asleep, go to sleep, nod off, drop off, faint, pass out, black out, shut off, shut oneself off, switch off, ignore, be oblivious

12 **anaesthetize**, render insensible, etherize, put to sleep, put under, desensitize, deaden, blunt, benumb, freeze, hypnotize, mesmerize, narcotize, stun, stupefy, knock out, brain, render unconscious, concuss

ADVERBS

13 **insensibly**, unfeelingly, bluntly, insensitively, sleepily, somnolently, unconsciously, obliviously, imperceptibly, in one's sleep

405 Physical Pleasure

NOUNS

1 **physical pleasure**, pleasant sensation, feeling good, well-being, ease, contentment, comfort, pleasantness, cosiness, enjoyment, conviviality, fun, zest, *joie de vivre* (Fr), happiness, felicity, delight, bliss, euphoria, indulgence, the good life, luxury, opulence, sensuousness, loveliness, softness, smoothness, tastiness, sweetness, fragrance, self-indulgence, self-gratification, profligacy, gourmandising, epicureanism, *la dolce vita* (It), sensual pleasure, sensualism, hedonism, pleasure principle, dis-

sipation, carnality, voluptuousness, sexual pleasure, eroticism, titillation, arousal, satisfaction, gratification, orgasm, climax, masturbation, sexual intercourse

2 **good time**, happy hour, fun time, whale of a time, wine, women and song, bread and circuses, just what the doctor ordered, just the ticket (Inf), the life of Riley (Inf)

▶ *763 Pleasantness, 374 Softness, 649 Ease, 742 Wealth, 686 Prosperity, 651 Refreshment, 821 Love, 782 Desire*

3 **pleasure-seeker**, jet-setter, connoisseur, *bon viveur* (Fr), epicure, epicurean, gourmet, gourmand, lotus-eater, sybarite, playboy, sensualist, hedonist, voluptuary, roué, libertine, philanderer, rake, seducer, seductress, *fille de joie* (Fr), mistress, nymphomaniac, courtesan, good-time girl, sexpot (Inf), swinger (Sl)

▶ *782 Desire*

4 **pleasurable things**, comforter, amenity, cushion, comfort blanket, feather-bed, snuggery, entertainment, feast, treat, banquet, beanfeast (Inf), spread, jamboree, splurge, sweetmeats, ambrosia, nectar, creature comforts, wall-to-wall carpeting, free lunch, luxury goods, revelry, carnival, spree, orgy, a good time, love-in, aphrodisiac, love-potion, philtre, flesh pots

5 **idealized pleasure**, easy street, bed of roses, land of milk and honey, Elysium, Elysian fields, heaven, heaven on earth, earthly paradise

ADJECTIVES

6 **pleasant**, comfortable, easeful, restful, relaxing, soothing, comforting, warm, congenial, agreeable, likable, nice, pleasing, pleasurable, pleasure-giving, satisfying, gratifying, attractive, refreshing, enjoyable, convivial, delectable, charming, delightful, idyllic, Elysian, paradisiacal (*or* paradisiac), generous, luscious, opulent, luxuriant, luxurious, exquisite, sumptuous, de luxe, lush, lovely, silken, smooth, fun, welcome, inviting, snug, cosy, soft, cuddly, cuddlesome, heart-warming, lovable, blissful, palatable, delicious, mouthwatering, ambrosial, sweet, succulent, juicy, sweet-smelling, perfumed, fragrant, euphonious, dulcet, mellifluous, titillating, seductive, sensual, sexy, erotic, carnal, voluptuous, to one's taste, to one's liking, scrumptious (Inf), cushy (Inf)

7 **pleased**, relaxed, comfortable, warm, snug, cosy, content, contented, happy, delighted, at ease, sensual, self-indulgent, profligate, voluptuous, pleasure-seeking, licentious, hedonistic, fun-loving, wanton, sybaritic, nymphomaniac, aroused, excited, titillated, gratified, satisfied, coddled, mollycoddled, cosseted, pampered, spoiled, merry, euphoric, chuffed (Sl), gruntled (Brit), tickled pink (Inf), tickled

to death (Inf), snug as a bug in a rug (Inf), in clover (Inf), in the pink (Inf), high (Sl), turned on (Sl), on a high (Sl), high as a kite (Sl)

VERBS

8 **feel pleasure**, feel good, enjoy, relish, revel in, take pleasure in, delight in, enjoy oneself, please oneself, have fun, make merry, bask, bask in, indulge oneself, gormandize, splurge, luxuriate, wallow, purr, nestle, snuggle, enjoy sex, have an orgasm, climax, kill the fatted calf, feather one's nest, have a ball (Sl), get a kick out of (Sl), paint the town red (Sl)

9 **give pleasure**, please, cheer, gladden, delight, charm, gratify, indulge, entertain, amuse, treat, regale, wine and dine, cuddle, hug, fondle, pet, stimulate, arouse, tickle, titillate, thrill, excite, satisfy, sate, satiate, make love to, warm the cockles of one's heart, take one's fancy, sugar the pill, gild the pill, tickle pink (Inf)

10 **comfort**, ease, relieve, slake, alleviate, appease, salve, soothe, soften, sympathize with, offer sympathy to, refresh, content, hug, cuddle, warm, mother, pet, make comfortable, coddle, mollycoddle, cosset, pamper, spoil, featherbed

ADVERBS

11 **pleasingly**, satisfyingly, luxuriously, indulgently, enjoyably, comfortably, happily, painlessly, warmly, cosily, blissfully, with pleasure, for kicks

406 Physical Pain

NOUNS

1 **pain**, hurt, painfulness, hurtfulness, soreness, suffering, dolour (Fml), malaise, affliction, misery, discomfort, distress, irritation, tenderness, sore spot, inflammation, pinprick, pins and needles, twinge, pang, pangs, smarting, prick, throes, cramp, spasm, stitch, ache, aching, aches and pains, throb, throbbing, agony, convulsion, anguish, ordeal, hell, martyrdom, passion, purgatory, lancination, stab, torment, hell on earth, punishment, physical punishment, flogging, torture

▶ *764 Unpleasantness, 879 Punishment*

2 **painful condition**, headache, splitting headache (*or* head), migraine, megrim (Arch), sick headache, toothache, earache, sore throat, laryngitis, ulcer, hunger pains, indigestion, heartburn, pyrosis, upset stomach, dyspepsia, stomachache, colic, grips, hernia, rupture, backache, lumbago, sciatica, rheumatism, arthritis, myalgia, neuralgia, heart pain, angina pectoris, angina, dysmenorrhoea, period pains, labour pains, afterpains, crick in the neck (Inf), tummyache (Inf), bellyache (Inf), gut-ache (Sl)

▶ *624 Ill Health, 760 Sensitivity*

3 **injury**, wound, lesion, trauma, scratch, scrape, graze, abrasion, bruise, contusion, bump, hit, sprain, burn, scald, cut, stab, puncture, jab, tear, slash, gash, laceration, bite, fracture, broken bone, broken jaw, mauling, savaging, bloody nose, black eye, shiner (Inf)

4 **pain relief**, analgesia

▶ *630 Remedy, 62 Pharmacology*

ADJECTIVES

5 **painful**, sore, hurting, uncomfortable, distressing, miserable, chronic, acute, stinging, tingling, smarting, cramping, lancinating, aching, tender, raw, throbbing, biting, gnawing, gripping, stabbing, shooting, grinding, splitting, pounding, agonizing, purgatorial, excruciating, exquisite, racking, harrowing, burning, searing, scalding, traumatic, extreme, unbearable, intolerable

6 **injured**, wounded, bruised, grazed, cut, punctured, scraped, sprained, lacerated, torn, fractured, broken, blackened

7 **feeling pain**, pained, suffering, hurting, distressed, sore, hurt, aching, anguished, in agony, agonized, convulsed, wincing, writhing, aching all over, tormented, tortured, afflicted, martyred, raw, black-and-blue, bleeding, blistered, traumatized

8 **inflicting pain**, painful, hurtful, hurting, torturing, tormenting, brutal, cruel, sadistic

VERBS

9 **feel pain**, suffer, hurt, ache, agonize, be afflicted, smart, wince, flinch, twitch, chafe, writhe, squirm, go through hell, be a martyr, show fortitude, bite the bullet

10 **be painful**, hurt, sting, tingle, smart, cramp, ache, throb, bite, gnaw, grip, stab, shoot, grind, pound, burn, sear

11 **inflict pain**, pain, hurt, injure, wound, hit, scratch, scrape, graze, prick, pinch, nip, tweak, sting, bruise, contuse, bump, sprain, burn, scald, jab, cut, tear, slash, gash, draw blood, bloody, puncture, run through, impale, fracture, punish, shoot, maul, mangle, savage, bite, claw, knife, stab, beat, beat up, beat black-and-blue, batter, smash, flog, thrash, convulse, traumatize, excruciate, wring, harrow, torment, torture, rack, martyr, crucify, touch a raw nerve, cut to the quick, give someone a bad time, carve up (Inf)

12 **express pain**, cry sob, wail, moan, gasp, whimper, groan, squeal, squawk, yelp, scream, shriek, screech, howl, yowl, yell

ADVERBS

13 **painfully**, throbbingly, achingly, excruciatingly, hurtfully, to the quick

407   Touch

NOUNS

1 **touch**, sense of touch, feeling, tactile, sensa-

tion, impression, sense perception, aesthesia, aesthesis, sensitivity, tactility, tangibility, solidity, concreteness, reality, palpability, texture, consistency, feel, vibration

▶ *403 Sensation, 383 Texture, 376 Smoothness*

2 **touching**, physical contact, handling, fingering, palpating, manipulating, applying pressure, massaging, stroking, rubbing, fondling, holding, grasping, gripping, clutching, laying on of hands, osteopothy, chiropractic, fondling, caressing, petting (Inf), groping (Sl), goosing (Sl)

3 **press**, brush, graze, skim, flick, tickle, pinch, nip, tweak, twitch, pull, tug, yang, top, pot, dab, nudge, push, poke, prod, blow, hit, knock, strike, jab, bump, slap, punch, bot, smash, kick

4 **kiss**, caress, fondle, rub, stroke, nuzzle, maul, paw, pet (Inf), grope (Sl), goose (Sl)

5 **toucher**, massager, massagist, masseur, masseuse, osteopath, chiropractor, bonesetter, right-handed, left-handed

▶ *60 Medicine*

6 **contiguity**, convergence, confluence, conjunction, meeting, joining, node, connection, nexus, meeting place, meeting point, joint, junction, intersection, overlap, seam, interface

▶ *267 Juxtaposition, 298 Interface, 138 Adhesion*

7 **sense organ**, nerve, nerve-ending, feeler, toucher, whisker, antenna, proboscis, tentacle, palpus, palp, paw, claw, flipper, hand, right-handedness, dextrality, left-handedness, sinistrality, thumb, finger, first finger, forefinger, index finger, second finger, middle finger, third finger, ring finger, fourth finger, little finger, fingernail, fingertip, fist, toe, big toe, hallux, little toe, pinkie (Inf), dukes (Sl), knuckle sandwich (Sl)

ADJECTIVES

8 **touchable**, palpable, tangible, solid, concrete, material, real, substantial, perceptible, sensuous, attainable, at hand, handy, reachable, gettable, sensory, tactual, tactile, touch-sensitive, sensitive to touch, sensitive, tender, get-at-able (Inf)

9 **touching**, adjacent, adjoining, meeting, contiguous, bordering, abutting, intersecting, glancing, colliding, crashing, overlapping, interfacing, connecting, hand-in-hand, hand-in-glove

10 **handed**, right-handed, dextral, left-handed, sinistral, ambidextrous, light-handed, neat, delicate, heavy-handed, clumsy, manual, hand-operated, touch-operated, hands-on, able, artistic, skilful

VERBS

11 **touch**, contact, feel, finger, handle, palpate, manipulate, manoeuvre, massage, rub, rub noses, nuzzle, knead, caress, kiss, stroke, fum-

ble, fondle, maul, paw, grope, graze, skim, shave, brush, flick, tickle, nip, pinch, stick, tweak, twitch, pull, pluck, tug, yank, hit, strike, pat, tap, dab, knock, slap, bat, punch, smash, kick, press, jab, poke, prod, nudge, elbow, play with, tamper with, tinker, tinker with, toy with, fiddle, fiddle with, buttonhole, pick up, seize, catch, hold, hold fast, hold on, lay hands on, grab, snatch, clutch, grasp, grip, pet (Inf), touch up (Inf), feel up (Inf), grope (Sl), goose (Sl), collar (Inf), nab (Inf), cop (Sl)

12 **abut**, adjoin, border, verge on, contact, come into contact, make contact, meet, touch, reach, converge, interface, come together, join, connect, overlap, attach, couple, splice, conjoin, impinge, brush, skim, graze, glance, kiss, collide, impact, bump into, bump, clash, crash, crunch, run into, intersect, link up, amalgamate, keep in touch, come to hand, shake hands, touch a sore point, make someone's hackles rise

13 **be touched by**, feel, be sensitive, tingle, itch, have goose flesh (*or* bumps *or* pimples), bruise, become black-and-blue

ADVERBS

14 **palpably**, tangibly, solidly, substantially

15 **insensitively**, clumsily, heavy-handedly, with a heavy hand

16 **sensitively**, perceptibly, caressingly, light-handedly, with a light touch

17 **manually**, by hand, hand to hand

408 Heat

NOUNS

1 **heat**, hotness, warmness, warmth, lukewarmness, tepidity, tepidness, temperature, room temperature, radiant heat, body heat, blood heat, warm-bloodedness, raised temperature, calescence, high temperature, fever, pyrexia, feverishness, inflammation, flush, hot flush, blush, fug, stuffiness, steam, steaminess, overheating, sweatiness, sweat, perspiration, white heat, incandescence, flash point, melting point, boiling point, first-degree burn, second-degree burn, third-degree burn, burn

▶ *410 Fuel, 60 Medicine*

2 **heat measurement**, temperature, calorific value, joule, calorie, kilocalorie, heat unit, BTU (British thermal unit), therm, calorimeter, thermometer, clinical thermometer, thermograph, Fahrenheit scale, Celsius scale, centigrade scale, Réaumur scale, specific heat, latent heat

▶ *268 Measurement*

3 **heater**, warmer, heating element, space heater, space heating, fan heater, convection heater, gas heater, central heating, radiator, hot-water tank, hot-water pipes, boiler, copper, immersion heater, geyser, thermostat, underfloor heating, hypocaust, hot-air vent (*or* duct), solar heating, solar panel, antifreeze, ethylene glycol, de-icer, double glazing, lagging, insulation, polystyrene, Thermos (Tm), winter clothes, thermal wear, winter woollies, overcoat, British warm, fur coat, fur hat, parka, foot-warmer, poultice, fomentation, warming pan, hot-water bottle, electric blanket, blanket, duvet, quilt, iron, electric iron, steam iron, branding iron, soldering iron, crucible, long johns (Inf), hottie (Aus and NZ inf)

▶ *295 Dress*

4 **burner**, cooker, stove, hob, hotplate, grill, griddle, kitchen range, oven, kettle, toaster, waffle iron (US), sandwich-maker, barbecue pit, spit, microwave oven, haybox, Dutch oven, gas ring

▶ *45 Cookery*

5 **hot weather**, summer, summertime, high summer, flaming June, midsummer, dog days, warm spell, hot spell, long hot summer, heat-haze, midday sun, sunbathing, sunbath, sunbed, sunlamp, solarium, suntan, tan, tanning, browning, bronzing, sunburn, peeling, redness, blister, heat rash, sunstroke, heat exhaustion, heatstroke, sunbather, sun-worshipper, nudist, warm front, summer drought, heat wave, tropical heat, sultriness, Indian summer, St Luke's summer, St Martin's summer, thaw, melting, global warming, greenhouse effect, greenhouse gases, warming of the earth's atmosphere, sizzler (Inf), scorcher (Inf)

▶ *439 Light*

6 **fire**, combustion, fireplace, hearth, chimney corner, inglenook, grate, hearthstone, flue, chimney, brazier, firebrand, flame, flames, blaze, glow, conflagration, holocaust, fireball, smoke, embers, ash, cinders, clinker, coke, charcoal, bonfire, beacon fire, kiln, furnace, smelter, forge, oast house (*or* oast), incinerator, torch, blowtorch, flamethrower, oxyacetylene burner, pyre, funeral pyre, coal fire, open fire, wood fire, campfire, wood stove, firebox, gas fire, gas jet, pilot light, gas oven, paraffin stove, Bunsen burner, electric fire, heat lamp, forest fire, house fire, arson, pyromania, firebomb, incendiary bomb, Greek fire, wildfire, firestorm, sheet of fire, sea of flames, towering inferno, flammability, inflammability, combustibility, spontaneous combustion, ignition, the stake, crematorium

▶ *322 Opening, 879 Punishment, 397 Death*

7 **fireman**, fire fighter, arsonist, pyromaniac, incendiary, firebomber, fire raiser, firebug (Inf)

8 **hot place**, hot spot, sun deck, sun lounge, thermae (L), calidarium (L), sauna, Jacuzzi, Turkish bath, boiler room, greenhouse, hothouse, hotbed, conservatory, equator, tropics, Tropic of Cancer, Tropic of Capricorn, Africa, South Pacific, rain forest, equatorial rain for-

est, jungle, Amazon Basin, desert, Sahara, Kalahari, Gobi, Death Valley, Sunbelt, Deep South Torrid Zone, subtropics, Mediterranean, hot spring, geyser, Old Faithful, warm current, Gulf Stream, hot-air current, thermal, south wind, Zephyr, sirocco, volcano, magma, lava, Vesuvius, Etna, Hell, inferno, hellfire

ADJECTIVES

9 **hot**, thermal, thermic, feeling hot, warm, mild, tepid, lukewarm room-temperature, chambré, snug, fuggy, stuffy, heating, warming, calefacient, calorific, overheated, suffocating, piping hot, baking hot, fiery, fierce, scalding, searing, scorching, cauterizing, roasting, boiling, on the boil, simmering, steaming, sizzling, smoking, smouldering, red-hot, white-hot, incandescent, candent (Arch), molten, glowing

10 **on fire**, alight, flaming, in flames, burning, ablaze, flaring, burnt to a crisp, burnt to a cinder, inflammable, flammable, combustible, incendiary, igneous, caustic, thermonuclear, volcanic, pyrogenic, warm as toast, hot as hell, hot enough to fry an egg on, frazzled (Inf)

11 **warm**, balmy, temperate, spring-like, mild, fair, clement, summery, sunny, sunbaked, blistering, scorching, humid, muggy, close, steamy, sticky, sizzling, sweltering, stifling, sultry subtropical, tropical, equatorial

12 **warm-hearted**, cordial, heart-warming, hot-blooded, ebullient, warm-blooded, homoiothermic, blushing, pyrexial (*or* pyrexic), fevered, feverish, flushed, hot and bothered, passionate, ardent, vehement, hot-tempered, fire-breathing, burning, torrid, seething, inflaming

13 **heated**, insulated, lined, padded, fur-lined, double-glazed, lagged, centrally heated, coal-fired, coal-burning, wood-burning, gas-fired, oil-fired, warmed up, warmed through, defrosted, heated up, preheated, baked, roasted, boiled, toasted, reheated, burnt, fired, burnt out, burnt down, singed, scorched, molten

VERBS

14 **be hot**, heat, heat up, glow, heat through, defrost, thaw, melt, de-ice, warm, warm up, reheat, cook, roast, toast, simmer, boil, scald, parboil, steam, bake, stew, braise, grill, fry, parch, wither, shrivel (up), melt down, smelt, solder, weld, fuse, lag, insulate, line, pad, double glaze, rub, chafe, take the chill off, stamp one's feet

15 **burn**, set fire to, set on fire, fire, set alight, torch, kindle, ignite, put a match to, catch fire, be on fire, flame, flare, blaze, crackle, smoke, fume, smoulder, burn up, burn down, burn out, singe, scorch, sear, calcine, char, carbonize, cremate, incinerate, vaporize, cauterize, brand, reduce to ashes, burn to a cinder, burn at the stake, burn to the ground, burst into flames, go up in flames

16 **feel hot**, keep warm, dress warmly, get overheated, blush, flush, sweat, perspire, run a temperature, be feverish, swelter, bask, sunbathe, sun oneself, suntan, tan, get a tan, brown, burn, peel, blister

ADVERBS

17 **warmly**, hotly, ardently, fierily, feverishly, to the boiling point, to a cinder

409 Cold

NOUNS

1 **coldness**, lack of heat, chill, chilliness, coolness, cooling, low temperature, freshness, nippiness

2 **freezing**, frost, freezing cold, icing, iciness, frigidity, gelidity, algidity, sub-zero temperature, absolute zero

▶ *56 Physics*

3 **chill**, common cold, pneumonia, coryza, hypothermia, exposure, chilblain, frostbite

4 **cooler**, chiller, fan, air-conditioning, air-conditioner, ventilator, punkah, cooling tower, refrigerator, fridge, icebox (US), cool box, cool bag, Esky (Aus), ice bag, ice bucket, ice pack, chilled counter, chill cupboard, ice house, ice machine, freezer, deep-freezer, deep-freeze, fridge-freezer, refrigerant, coolant, liquid oxygen, lox, cryogenics, cryogen, cryonics, cryostat, cryosurgery

▶ *45 Cookery*

5 **ice**, ice cube, cracked ice, frosting, glaze, dry ice, glacier, ice sheet, pack ice, icecap, ice field, ice floe, frost, frostiness, hoar frost, white frost, frost hollow, rime, freeze-up, Jack Frost, black frost, hard frost, black ice, icicle, wintry shower, frozen rain, sleet, snow, snow flurry, flurry, snowfall, snowstorm, blizzard, whiteout, snowflake, snow crystal, wet snow, slush, powder snow, granular snow, dry snow, snowball, driven snow, snowdrift, avalanche, hail, hailstorm, hailstone, snowman, Snow Queen

6 **Arctic**, North Pole, Antarctic, South Pole, Siberia, Arctic Circle, Land of the Midnight Sun, permafrost, snowline, snow house, igloo, Eskimo, iceberg, frigidarium, hibernacle, hibernaculum, winter quarters, frigid zone

7 **cold weather**, cold spell, cold snap, nippiness, severe weather, nip in the air, cold season, inclemency, cold front, chill factor, wind-chill factor, North Wind, Boreas, ice age, winter, December, January, February, wintriness, arctic conditions, dead of winter, depths of winter, brass monkey weather (Sl)

ADJECTIVES

8 **cold**, fresh, bracing, nippy, sharp, inclement, parky, breezy, invigorating, raw, chill, chilly, cool, coolish, unheated, chilled, shivery, pinched, biting, bitter, bleak, wintry, severe,

snowy, sleety, frosty, icy, snowbound, snowed in, iced up, ice-bound, blue with cold, stiff with cold, perishing, ice-cold, algid, glacial, frigid, freezing, frozen, gelid, polar, Arctic, Siberian, frost-bitten, frozen solid (*or* stiff), frosted, hoar, frappé, iced, glazed, on ice, on the rocks, chilled to the bone, chilled to the marrow, cold as the grave, cold as marble, cold as charity, cold enough to freeze the balls off a brass monkey (Inf)

9 **heat-resistant**, heat-proof, insulated, air-conditioned, air-cooled, water-cooled, cooling, chilling, refrigerant, frigorific, freezable, freezing, refrigerated, unmelted, quick-frozen, freeze-dried, cryogenic, cryonic

VERBS

10 **be cold**, shiver, tremble, shudder, perish, quiver, have gooseflesh (*or* goose-pimples), freeze, catch cold, take a chill, have the shivers, stamp one's feet, one's teeth chatter

11 **become cold**, cool down, lose heat, cool off, freeze, freeze over, congeal, ice over, ice up, be snowed in, be snowed under, freeze to death, get frostbite, be so cold one's toes (*or* fingers) drop off

12 **make cold**, chill, freshen, sharpen, ventilate, air-condition, fan, benumb, freeze, refrigerate, glaciate, freeze-dry

ADVERBS

13 **coldly**, coolly, wintrily, frigidly, icily, bitterly, frostily

410 Fuel

NOUNS

1 **fuel**, fossil fuel, gas, oil, solid fuel, coal, wood, charcoal, peat, peat bog, peat moss, electricity, nuclear power, renewable energy source, non-renewable energy source

2 **lighter**, firelighter, tinder, tinderbox, kindling, wood, firewood, log, Yule log, faggot, charcoal, turf, dung, brushwood, spunk, punk, touchpaper, taper, match, spill, vesta, lucifer, safety match, matchbox, wick, spark, scintilla, flint, burning glass, torch, firebrand, brand (Arch), cigarette lighter, cap, percussion cap, ignition system, sparking plug, detonator, fuse, time-fuse, explosive, high explosive, firebomb *or* incendiary bomb, fire ship

▶ *408 Heat*

3 **gas**, coal, gas, natural gas, town gas, producer gas, North Sea gas, Calor gas, propane, butane, methane, lighter fuel, gasfield, gasworks, gasholder, gasometer, gas tank, gas main, gas pipe, gas meter, gas poker, gas burner, gas turbine, rocket fuel, liquid oxygen, lox

▶ *388 Gas, 387 Fluid, 70 Transport, 338 Propulsion*

4 **electricity**, hydroelectricity, generating station, power station, generator, turbine, power pack, magneto, dynamo, electricity supply, electric current, national grid, pylon, underground cable, power cable, electric lead, flex, power point, socket, electric switch, light switch, electricity meter, fuel cell, electric battery, battery, electrification, electrocution, electric chair, electric motor, power cut, blackout, brownout (US)

5 **coal**, bituminous coal, brown coal, cannel coal, lignite, coke, anthracite, briquette (*or* briquet), coal dust, slack, coal-bed, Coal Measures, coalfield, coalmine, pit, coalface, coal cellar, coal bunker, coal hole (Inf), coal box, coal bin, coal scuttle, black diamonds

▶ *54 Earth Science*

6 **oil**, petroleum, mineral oil, crude oil, crude, petrol, gasoline (*or* gas) (US), unleaded petrol, diesel oil (*or* fuel), derv, paraffin, coal oil (US), aviation fuel, methylated spirits (*or* spirit), naphtha, gas oil, oil reserves, oilfield, Alaskan oil, oil well, oil rig, offshore rig, oil platform, North Sea oil, oil refinery, refining, fractionation, cracking, oil pipeline, oil tanker, oil drum, oilcan, petrol can, octane number (*or* rating), petrol station, filling station, petrol pump, oil shale, oil slick, fuel injection, petrodollar diesel (Inf), meths (Inf), nodding donkey (Inf)

▶ *395 Oiliness, 386 Lubrication, 133 Mixture*

7 **nuclear power**, nuclear energy, nuclear generating station, Windscale, Sellafield, nuclear reactor, thermal reactor, gas-cooled reactor, magnox reactor, advanced gas-cooled reactor (AGR), water-cooled reactor, pressurized-water reactor (PWR), boiling-water reactor (BWR), fast-breeder reactor, nuclear fuel, core, fuel rod, uranium, enriched uranium, plutonium, nuclear fission, nuclear fusion, nuclear waste, nuclear accident, Chernobyl, Three Mile Island

8 **renewable energy**, solar power, solar energy, solar battery, photovoltaic cell, wind power, windmill, wind pump, wind generator, wind turbine, geothermal energy, water mill, water turbine, wave power, tidal power, tidal energy, biomass

9 **power-worker**, stoker, charcoal-burner, coal merchant, coal miner, gas-fitter, gasman, boilermaker, meter-reader, electrician, oil-worker, oilman, lumberjack, woodcutter, peat cutter, firebomber

▶ *644 Work*

ADJECTIVES

10 **powered**, charged, combustible, inflammable, flammable, explosive, incendiary, raw, refined, carbonaceous, carboniferous, coaly, bituminous, lignitic, coal-fired, gaseous, gas-fired, fuel-efficient, electric, hydroelectric, electrical, electrifying, woody, ligneous, wood-burning, oil-fired, petrol-driven, high-octane, unleaded, thermal, nuclear, thermo-

nuclear, nuclear-powered, wind-driven, wind-powered, geothermal, water-driven, steam-operated, solar, solar-powered, renewable, gas-guzzling (US inf)

VERBS

11 **fuel**, stoke, fill up, refuel, light, light the touchpaper, strike, put a match to, kindle, fire up, fire, burn gas, detonate, set off, touch off, trigger (off), explode, power, charge, recharge, electrify, plug in, switch on, dig coal, mine coal, burn coal, strike oil, pump oil, refine oil, pump petrol, have a meltdown, heat with solar power, step on the gas (Inf)

ADVERBS

12 **powerfully**, combustibly, explosively, electrically, hydroelectrically, thermally, at full power, at full steam

411   Taste

Good taste is better than bad taste, but bad taste is better than no taste. Arnold Bennett.

Taste is the feminine of genius. Edward Fitzgerald.

What is food to one man is bitter poison to others. Lucretius.

NOUNS

1 **taste**, sense of taste, palate, tastiness, pleasant taste, sapidity, deliciousness, palatability, unpleasant taste, unpalatability, sharp taste, acid taste, tart taste, salty taste, spicy taste, sweet taste, sour taste, bitter taste, pungent taste, aftertaste

2 **taste of life**, experience, liking, preference, inclination, predilection, good taste, refinement, discrimination, elegance, cultivation, bad taste, vulgarity, lack of style, sweet taste, enjoyment, success, sour taste, bitter taste, disappointment, failure

▶ *45 Cookery, 492 Judgment, 481 Discrimination, 794 Refinement, 763 Pleasantness, 784 Liking, 785 Dislike, 414 Sweetness, 415 Sourness, 413 Piquancy*

3 **appetizer**, starter, hors d'oeuvre, *bonne bouche* (Fr), apéritif, delicacy, dainty, titbit, sample, sampler, drop, morsel, mouthful, nibble, nip, soupçon (Fr), tasting, sampling, gustation, degustation

4 **flavour**, gusto, relish, savour, richness, sweetness, saltiness, sourness, bitterness, strong flavour, delicate flavour, flavouring, seasoning, flavour enhancer, monosodium glutamate (MSG)

5 **taster**, sampler, nibbler, eater, drinker, wine taster, diner, connoisseur, gourmet, epicure, gourmand, *bon vivant* (Fr), foodie (Inf),

▶ *350 Eating*

6 **taste bud**, appetite, taste test, taste treat, tasting cup, tester

ADJECTIVES

7 **tasty**, palatable, delicious, having flavour, tastable, edible (*or* eatable), esculent, comestible, sapid, tasteful, savorous, savoury, appetizing, inviting, relishable, delectable, dainty, epicurean, flavourful (*or* flavoursome), ambrosial, potable, drinkable, toothsome, mouth-watering, succulent, sharp, unpleasant, unpalatable, acid, spicy, sweet, sour, tart, bitter, pungent, salty, scrumptious (Inf), yummy (Sl), finger-lickin' good (Inf), done to a turn (Inf), moreish (*or* morish) (Inf)

8 **tasteful**, having good taste, cultivated, refined, discriminating, elegant, having bad taste, vulgar, lacking style, experiencing the sweet taste of success, experiencing the sour (*or* bitter) taste of failure

▶ *794 Refinement*

VERBS

9 **taste**, try, sample, eat, nibble, drink, test, experience, savour, degust, smack, enjoy, appreciate, relish, tickle one's palate, tickle one's fancy

10 **make taste**, add taste to, enhance, flavour, dress, garnish, spice, sauce

ADVERBS

11 **tastily**, deliciously, full of flavour, palatably, succulently, sweetly, bitterly, pungently, scrumptiously (Inf), mouthwateringly, tastefully, elegantly, tastelessly, vulgarly

412   Tastelessness

NOUNS

1 **tastelessness**, blandness, mildness, insipidity, insipidness, plainness, unsavouriness, tameness, dullness, vapidness, vapidity, weakness, weakening, thinness, feebleness, adulteration, dilution, wateriness,

2 **dilution**, watering, watering down, staleness, flatness, banality, triteness, lifelessness, dryness, aridity, monotony, boredom, wishy-washiness (Inf), jejuneness, dissatisfaction, indifference

▶ *45 Cookery, 238 Weakness, 202 Oldness, 766 Dissatisfaction, 788 Boredom, 783 Indifference*

3 **tasteless items**, pap, mash, pulp, gruel, skilly, bread and milk, bread and water, weak coffee, dishwater, slop (Sl)

4 **bad taste**, tastelessness, lack of (good) taste, lack of refinement, inelegance, insensitivity, raciness, coarseness, crudeness, crassness, tackiness, tawdriness, gaucheness, vulgarity, indecency, obscenity

▶ *559 Inelegance, 795 Vulgarity*

ADJECTIVES

5 **tasteless**, bland, mild, insipid, plain, tame, dull, rapid, weak, thin, feeble, flat, stale, dry, arid, humdrum, monotonous, nondescript, unexciting, uninviting, lifeless, flavourless,

unflavoured, unsalted, unseasoned, watered, watered-down, diluted, adulterated, dilute, milk-and-water, unappetizing, banal, trite, uninspired, boring, jejune, unsatisfying, indifferent, characterless, as dull as ditchwater, dry as dust, wishy-washy (Inf)

6 **coarse**, lacking refinement, having bad taste, tasteless, lacking (good) taste, inelegant, insensitive, undiscriminating, racy, tacky, tawdry, gauche, gaudy, vulgar, crude, crass, indecent, obscene, sick (Inf), gross (Inf)

VERBS

7 **be tasteless**, have no taste, taste stale, taste flat, lose taste, lose interest, show indifference, bore, pall

8 **dilute**, water down, thin, weaken, adulterate

9 **have bad taste**, lack (good) taste, lack refinement, act vulgar

ADVERBS

10 **without taste**, blandly, insipidly, mildly, dully, weakly, flatly, drily, aridly, monotonously

11 **tastelessly**, coarsely, inelegantly, insensitively, racily, tackily, gauchely, vulgarly, crudely, crassly, indecently, obscenely

413 Piquancy

NOUNS

1 **piquancy**, pungency, strong flavour, spiciness, sting, tang, tanginess, smokiness, tartness, bite, kick, sourness, bitterness, gaminess, raciness, poignancy, aroma
▶ 45 Cookery, 411 Taste

2 **seasoning**, flavouring, condiment, salt, sea salt, pepper, black pepper, white pepper, peppercorn, garnish, dressing, salad dressing, mayonnaise, French dressing, vinaigrette, marinade, relish, sauce, soy (or soya) sauce, Worcestershire sauce, ketchup, barbecue sauce, horseradish sauce, mint sauce, cranberry sauce, chutney, pickle, dill pickle, gherkin, piccalilli, Tabasco (Tm), onion, pickled onion, garlic, garlic salt, curry, Madras, curry powder

3 **curing**, smoking

4 **stimulation**, titillation, liveliness, spirit, zest, archness, harshness, roughness, poignancy

5 **herbs**, spices, allspice, angelica, aniseed, balm, basil, bay leaf, borage, camomile, caper, caraway seeds, cassia, cayenne, chervil, chilli, chives, cinnamon, clove, coriander, cumin, dill, fennel, fenugreek, gentian, ginger, horseradish, hyssop, juniper, lemon thyme, lemon verbena, liquorice, lovage, mace, marjoram, mint, mustard, French mustard, English mustard, myrrh, nutmeg, oregano, paprika, parsley, peppermint, rosemary, rue, saffron, sage, savory, sesame seeds, sorrel, tarragon, thyme,

vanilla, verbena, wormwood, *bouquet garni* (Fr), mixed herbs, *fines herbes* (Fr)

6 **cordial**, stimulant, reviver, restorative, tonic, medicinal drink, nip, toddy, smelling salts, sal volatile, pick-me-up (Inf)

7 **tobacco**, Virginia tobacco, Turkish tobacco, nicotine, tar, cigar, Havana, corona, panatella, cheroot, cigarillo, humidor, cigarette, filter-tip, cork-tip, king-size, high tar, low tar, menthol, cigarette case, cigarette lighter, packet, carton, box, cigarette end, stub, butt, cigarette paper, roll-your-own, rolling tobacco, cigarette machine, ashtray, snuff, snuffbox, pinch of snuff, oral tobacco, chewing tobacoo, plug, quid, tobacco sachet, pipe tobacco, shag, flake, clay pipe, meerschaum, churchwarden, water pipe, hubble-bubble, narghile, hookah, pipe of peace, culumet, tobacco pouch, stem, pbow, the weed (Inf), baccy, cig (Inf), ciggie (Inf), fag (Sl), cancer stick (Sl), coffin nail (Sl), fag end (Sl), dog-end (Sl)

8 **smoking**, draw, puff, drag, chain-smoking, passive smoking, smoking area, smoking compartment, smoker, nonsmoker, smoke-free area, smoker's requisites, tobacconist, smoker's cough, bronchitis, lung cancer

ADJECTIVES

9 **piquant**, pungent, aromatic, flavourful, appetizing, stinging, biting, hot, peppery, seasoned, spiced, herby, savoury, tangy, tart, sharp, sour, bitter, minty, highly flavoured, highly seasoned, spicy, salty, strong, smoky, smoked, cured, kippered, pickled, soused, gamy, racy

10 **stimulating**, interesting, intriguing, titillating, exciting, lively, restorative, medicinal, provocative, spirited, thought-provoking, poignant, arch

11 **tobacco**, smoking, smoke-free, smoking-related, filter-tip, cork-tip, king-size, high-tar, low-tar, roll-your-own

VERBS

12 **season**, flavour, salt, pepper, marinate, souse, smoke, kipper, cure, dry, pickle, curry

13 **be piquant**, sting, bite, pique, goad, interest, stimulate, revive, restore, titillate, intrigue, excite, provoke, stir

14 **smoke**, smoke cigarettes, smoke cigars, smoke a pipe, draw, puff, drag, inhale, chain-smoke

ADVERBS

15 **piquantly**, pungently, aromatically, tartly, sharply, bitterly, medicinally

16 **stimulatingly**, interestingly, intriguingly, provocatively, spiritedly, poignantly

414 Sweetness

NOUNS

1 **sweetness**, sugariness, syrupiness, cloying, sweetness, sickliness, saccharinity, sweet

tooth, fragrance, pleasantness, melodiousness, freshness, smoothness

▶ *45 Cookery, 418 Fragrance, 433 Melody, 763 Pleasantness, 376 Smoothness, 784 Liking*

2 **sweetener**, sweetening, sugar, sucrose, glucose, fructose, dextrose, lactose, cane sugar, beet sugar, sugar lump, sugar loaf, caster sugar, granulated sugar, powdered sugar, icing sugar, refined sugar, unrefined sugar, brown sugar, demerara sugar, syrup, maple syrup, treacle, molasses, glycerine, artificial sweetener, saccharine, aspartame, Nutrasweet (Tm), cyclamate, honey, honeycomb, Hymettus honey, clover honey, honeydew, jam, jelly, preserve, conserve, marmalade, nectar, delicacies, sweetmeats, fruit, candied fruit, glacé fruit, ambrosia, a spoonful of sugar, sugar and spice and all things nice

3 **dessert**, pudding, sweet, ice cream, chocolate mousse, custard, whipped cream, cake, chocolate cake, fruit cake, cheesecake, sponge cake, gateau, brownie, pie, apple pie, pastry, Danish pastry, patisserie, icing, frosting (US), marzipan, afters (Inf)

4 **confectionery**, sweets, sweeties (Inf), comfit, candy (US), bonbon, dragée, chocolate, milk chocolate, white chocolate, toffee, fudge, boiled sweet, jawbreaker (US), lollipop, liquorice, dolly mixture, peppermint, gumdrop, fruit gum, fondant, candyfloss, confectioner's shop, sweet shop

5 **sweet drink**, cocoa, hot chocolate, cordial, fruit juice, fruit squash, fruit crush, lemonade, orangeade, soft drink, Coca-Cola (Tm), cream soda, ice-cream soda (US), sherbet, mead, sweet wine, dessert wine, muscatel, Sauternes, mulled wine, spiced wine, gluhwein, hot toddy, fruit cup, punch, liqueur

ADJECTIVES

6 **sweet**, sweetish, sweetened, saccharine, cloying, sickly, sickly-sweet, honeyed, sugared, sugary, sugar-coated, treacly, syrupy, ambrosial, nectared, nectareous, candied, crystallized, glazed, iced, frosted (US), bittersweet, sweet-and-sour, sweet as a nut

7 **pleasant**, fresh, smooth, fragrant, melodious

VERBS

8 **sweeten**, sugar, sugar-coat, honey, ice, frost (US), glaze, candy, mull, make pleasant, make fragrant, sugar the pill

ADVERBS

9 **sweetly**, pleasantly, freshly, smoothly, fragrantly, melodiously

415 Sourness

NOUNS

1 **sourness**, sour taste, tartness, bitterness, sharp flavouring, sharpness, dryness, acerbity, acidity, astringency, acidulousness, subacid-

ity, vinegariness, unripeness, greenness

2 **unpalatability**, bitterness, gall, acridity, bile, nasty taste, foul taste, staleness, rancidness, mould, rottenness, unwholesomeness, rankness, brackishness, dankness

3 **sour thing**, crab apple, green apple, lemon, lime, aloes, sloe, vinegar, vinaigrette, bitters, Angostura bitters, wormwood, sour milk, sour cream, soured cream, sloe gin, whisky sour, dry wine, sour wine, acid rain, tartaric acid, acetic acid, gall and wormwood

4 **spleen**, rancour, bile, biliousness, crabbedness, moroseness, sullenness, bitterness, sour grapes, crosspatch (Inf), sourpuss (Inf)

ADJECTIVES

5 **acid**, acidic, sharp, sour, tangy, tart, pungent, acerbic, acidulous, lemony, vinegary, acidulated, subacid, unripe, green, immature, hard, unsweetened, dry, acrid, biting, bitter

6 **unpalatable**, unappetizing, uninviting, unsavoury, unpleasant, disagreeable, nasty, disgusting, foul-tasting, nauseating, uneatable, inedible, dank, brackish, undrinkable, corked, harsh, stale, rough, rancid, overripe, mouldy, rotten, high, bad, off, curdled, fermented, on the turn, turned, unwholesome, contaminated, poisonous, toxic

7 **splenetic**, rancorous, bilious, sarcastic, harsh, crabbed, crabby, bitter, morose, sullen, grumpy

VERBS

8 **sour**, be sour, go sour, turn sour, acidify, sharpen, taste bad, taste foul, curdle, spoil, turn, ferment, go off, go bad, go mouldy, moulder, set one's teeth on edge

9 **disgust**, nauseate, sicken, embitter, turn one's stomach, get up one's nose (Inf)

ADVERBS

10 **sourly**, bitterly, tartly, sharply, drily, pungently, harshly, unpleasantly, inedibly, nauseatingly

11 **splenetically**, rancorously, harshly, sarcastically, morosely, sullenly, grumpily

416 Odour

NOUNS

1 **odour**, smell, smelliness, odorousness, scent, sweet smell, fragrance, perfume, unpleasant smell, stench, stink, slight smell, faint smell, aroma, aromaticity, bouquet, nose, savour, breath, air, suggestion, whiff, waft, smoke, vapour, exhalation, emanation, heady scent, redolence, strong smell, fruitiness, pungency, fresh smell, olfactology, olfactologist, olfactronics, odorimetry, olfactometry

▶ *418 Fragrance, 419 Stench, 103 Essence, 388 Gas*

2 **sense of smell**, smelling, act of smelling, olfaction, inhalation, sniff, sniffing, sniffle, nosing, nose, nostril, naris, nasal cavity, olfactory nerve, smelling bottle, smelling salts,

herbs, spices, sniffer dog, bloodhound, keen nose, good nose, snuffler, snout (Sl), hooter (Sl), schnozzle (Sl), snoot (Sl), smeller (Sl), conk (Sl), proboscis (Inf), beak (Sl)
▶ *390 Air, 318 Prominence, 481 Discrimination*
3 **scent**, trail, scent-gland, pheromone
▶ *545 Record, 590 Pursuit*
4 **reputation**, repute, regard, aura, tone, character, savour, emanation, good odour, bad odour, odour of sanctity, smell of success

ADJECTIVES
5 **odorous**, odoriferous, smelling, olent, redolent, pungent, heady, fragrant, perfumed, scented, smelly, stinking, noisome, noxious, whiffy (Inf), aromatic, savorous, herby, spicy, downwind of, emanative, olfactible, pheromonal, keen-scented, sharp-nosed
▶ *418 Fragrance, 419 Stench, 481 Discrimination*
6 **olfactory**, olfactive, nasal, rhinological

VERBS
7 **smell**, breathe, breathe in, inhale, sniff, nose, sniff at, smell at, snuff, snuffle, sniffle, sniff out, smell out, nose out, catch a whiff of, get wind of, follow the scent, follow one's nose
▶ *390 Air, 590 Pursuit*
8 **have odour**, smell, smell of, emanate, exhale, stink, reek, pong (Inf), whiff (Inf)
▶ *419 Stench*
9 **impart odour to**, perfume, scent, aromatize
▶ *418 Fragrance*

ADVERBS
10 **odorously**, odoriferously, olfactorily, nasally, aromatically, headily

417 Odourlessness

NOUNS
1 **odourlessness**, inodorousness, lack of smell, scentlessness, deodorization, fumigation, freshness, cleanness, fresh air, ventilation, lack of sense of smell, anosmia, bad nose, nasal congestion, blocked nose, cold in the nose (*or* head), head cold, a breath of fresh air, smoke-free zone (*or* area), smokeless zone, no-smoking area
▶ *621 Cleanness, 390 Air, 404 Insensibility, 254 Absence, 100 Nonexistence*
2 **deodorant**, anti-perspirant, spray deodorant, roll-on, stick, mouthwash, breath-freshener, breath-sweetener, cachou, deodorizer, fumigator, ventilator, extractor fan, exhaust fan (US), air-filter, air-purifier, air-freshener, cooker hood, disinfectant, drain cleaner, smell trap, stench trap, stink trap
▶ *625 Hygiene, 134 Purity, 412 Tastelessness, 418 Fragrance*

ADJECTIVES
3 **odourless**, inodorous, scentless, unperfumed, unscented, fragrance-free, odour-free, smoke-free, smokeless, smell-less, noseless, deodor-

ized, disinfected, fumigated, clean, fresh, ventilated, upwind of, in the fresh air
▶ *621 Cleanness, 390 Air, 625 Hygiene, 134 Purity*
4 **deodorizing**, deodorant, cleansing, freshening, disinfectant

VERBS
5 **deodorize**, disinfect, fumigate, ventilate, freshen, clean, cleanse, clear the air, open a window, put off the scent
6 **have no smell**, lose one's sense of smell, have a cold in the nose, hold one's nose, be upwind of, lose the scent

ADVERBS
7 **odourlessly**, cleanly, freshly, upwind, in the fresh air

418 Fragrance

NOUNS
1 **fragrance**, fragrancy, sweet smell, bouquet, aroma, scent, perfume, *parfum* (Fr), musk, muskiness, spice, spiciness, balm, balminess, perfume dynamics, aromatherapy, aromatherapist
▶ *416 Odour, 414 Sweetness, 621 Cleanness*
2 **fragrant thing**, new-baked bread, fresh coffee, wax polish, sea air, new-mown hay, flower garden, herb garden, herbs, spices, flower, bunch of flowers, bouquet, posy, nosegay, buttonhole, corsage, orange blossom, honeysuckle, lily, sweet pea, gardenia, lavender, jasmine, rose, bed of roses, rose garden, stephanotis, violet, carnation, tuberose, cloves, vanilla, sweet cicely, essence, essential oil, fixative, toiletries, body lotion, talcum powder, bath oil, shower gel, scented soap, rose water, lavender water, eau de Cologne, cologne, toilet water, *eau de toilette* (Fr), scent, perfume, French perfume, Chanel No. 5 (Tm), after-shave, pomade, scent bottle, perfume bottle, flacon, atomizer, perfume spray, lavender bag, lavender sachet, perfumer, *parfumier* (Fr), perfumery, all the perfumes of Arabia, pomander, potpourri, pastille, cachou
▶ *84 Flowers, 103 Essence, 789 Beauty, 791 Beautification, 405 Physical Pleasure, 763 Pleasantness*
3 **incense**, frangipani, resin, olibanum, frankincense, myrrh, camphor, eucalyptus, spikenard, musk, civet, otto (*or* attar), ambergris, patchouli, sandalwood, vetiver, chypre, censer, thurible, thurifer, joss stick
▶ *7 Religion, 10 Ritual*

ADJECTIVES
4 **fragrant**, sweet-smelling, scented, sweet-scented, perfumed, aromatic, flowery, floral, spicy, musky, fruity, pungent, heady, camphorated, balmy, ambrosial, aromatherapeutic
▶ *416 Odour, 414 Sweetness, 763 Pleasantness, 413 Piquancy*

VERBS

5 **be fragrant**, smell sweet, smell like a flower garden
▶ *416 Odour, 414 Sweetness*

6 **perfume**, scent, aromatize, spray, burn incense, cense, thurify, embalm, lay up in lavender
▶ *7 Religion*

ADVERBS

7 **fragrantly**, aromatically, florally, spicily, muskily, pungently

419   Stench

NOUNS

1 **stench**, stink, unpleasant smell, bad odour, malodour, malodorousness, smelliness, fetor (*or* foetor), fetidness (*or* foetidness), mephitis, miasma, gas, effluvium, reek, exhalation, osmidrosis, sweatiness, fug, staleness, mustiness, frowstiness, frowziness, fustiness, fust, lack of ventilation, whiff (Inf), hum (Inf), pong (Inf), niff (Inf)
▶ *416 Odour, 764 Unpleasantness*

2 **something that makes an unpleasant smell**, bad drains, smell of drains, sewer, sewer gas, cesspit, cesspool, latrine, exhaust fumes, air pollution, cigarette smoke, cooking smells, boiled cabbage, rotting vegetables, sour milk, strong cheese, stinker, stink-bomb, hydrogen sulphide, sulphur dioxide, bad egg, rotten egg, body odour (BO), sweat, armpits, smelly feet, sweaty socks, halitosis, bad breath, dogbreath, ammonia, urine, excrement, sewage, dung, farmyard smells, breaking wind, flatus, fart (Tab), skunk, polecat, billy goat, stinkard, stinkhorn, garlic, asafoetida (*or* asafetida), putrefaction, putrescence, decomposition, decay, rancidity, gaminess, corruption, the great unwashed
▶ *622 Dirtiness, 353 Excretion, 68 Agriculture, 57 Chemistry, 388 Gas, 628 Deterioration, 202 Oldness, 415 Sourness*

ADJECTIVES

3 **stinking**, smelly, reeking, noisome, offensive, malodorous, foul-smelling, evil-smelling, mephitic, miasmic, miasmal, overpowering, unwholesome, sweaty, unwashed, fetid (*or* foetid), frowsty, frowzy, musty, unventilated, fusty, fuggy, stale, rank, olid, graveolent, gassy, asphyxiating, sulphurous, ammoniacal, whiffy (Inf), niffy (Inf), pongy (Inf)
▶ *416 Odour, 622 Dirtiness, 202 Oldness*

4 **putrid**, putrescent, decaying, rotting, rotten, decomposed, high, off, gamy, rancid, sour, tainted
▶ *628 Deterioration, 415 Sourness*

VERBS

5 **stink**, smell, smell bad, smell foul, reek, stink out, have bad breath, have halitosis, have BO, stink to high heaven, smell like a drain, smell like a midden, smell of rotten eggs, whiff (Inf), pong (Inf), hum (Inf), niff (Inf), break wind, fart (Tab), let off (Sl), let fly (Sl), drop one (Sl)
▶ *416 Odour, 353 Excretion, 622 Dirtiness*

ADVERBS

6 **stinkingly**, smellily, malodorously, sourly, mustily, fustily, rankly

420   Hearing

NOUNS

1 **hearing**, sense of hearing, audition, sharp ear, keen sense of hearing, good ear, musical ear, musicality, perfect pitch, absolute pitch, bad ear, poor ear, earshot, hearing distance, auditory range, range, audibility, listening, listening in, eavesdropping, attention, heed, heeding, mind, auscultation, sounding, acoustics, radiophonics
▶ *421 Deafness, 423 Loudness, 522 Intelligibility, 49 Music, 56 Physics*

2 **hearer**, listener, auditor, hearkener, ear witness, audience, congregation, house, audiophile, hi-fi enthusiast, eavesdropper, listener in, telephone tapper, monitor

3 **auditorium**, hall, concert hall, opera house, music room, listening post

4 **ear**, outer ear, earlobe, earhole, cauliflower ear, jug ears, bat ears, pierced ears, lug (Sl), lughole (Sl), shell-like (Sl)

5 **internal ear**, middle ear, tympanic cavity, eardrum, tympanum, tympanic membrane, auditory ossicle, incus, anvil, malleus, hammer, stapes, stirrup bone, Eustachian tube, inner ear, labyrinth, cochlea, cochlear nerve, semicircular canals

6 **otology**, otolaryngology, otorhinolaryngology, ENT (ear, nose, and throat), audiology, ear wax, ear drops, earache, otalgia, otitis, labyrinthitis, otologist, otolaryngologist, otorhinolaryngologist, ENT specialist, audiologist, aurist, hearing specialist, auriscope, audiometer

7 **ear attachments**, earmuffs, ear flaps, earring, ear clip, ear stud, ear plug, grommet, hearing aid, ear trumpet, earphone

8 **something heard**, noise, sound, speech, conversation, talk, hearsay, hearsay evidence, report, rumour, gossip, *on dit* (Fr), grapevine, jungle telegraph, word of mouth, word (*or* whisper) in one's ear, Chinese whisper, tattle, tittle-tattle, ringing in the ears, tinnitus, reflected sound, echo, reverberation, alarm clock, clock radio, doorbell, Entryphone (Tm), earful (Inf)
▶ *564 Speech, 568 Conversation, 427 Resonance, 56 Physics*

9 **audio device**, sound receiver, hearing aid, deaf aid, ear trumpet, earphones, headphones,

headset, telephone tap, wiretap, auscultator, stethoscope, audio, amplification, amplifier, volume control, broadcasting device, pickup, microphone, megaphone, loud-hailer, bullhorn (US), loudspeaker, speaker, loudspeaker van, public address system (PA), Tannoy (Tm), ultrasound scanner, echolocation, radar, sonar, asdic, sonic depth finder, sonobuoy, radio, radio receiver, wireless, transistor radio, car radio, spoken radio, talk radio, Citizens' Band radio (CB), telephone, phone, handset, earpiece, mobile (tele)phone, car phone, Cellnet (Tm), cellphone, cellular telephone, cellular radio, connection, call, radiotelephone, radiotelephony, radiophone, transceiver, intercom, telephone answering machine, answering machine, answerphone, Ansafone (Tm), answering service, bleeper, pager, radiopager, radiopaging, tape recorder, cassette recorder, personal stereo, Walkman (Tm), cassette, tape, record, disc, vinyl disc, compact disc (CD), bug (Inf), cans (Inf), mike (Inf), amp (Inf), steam radio (Inf), walkie-talkie (Inf), ghetto blaster (Inf), boom box (US inf)

▶ *534 Communications, 49 Music*

10 **sound quality**, monophonic sound, stereophonic sound, quadraphonic sound, listenability, reception, tone control, graphic equalizer, equalization, bias, phase, bass, treble, range, level, echo, reverb (Inf)

ADJECTIVES

11 **aural**, auricular, auditory, audile, auditive, acoustic, audio, radio, wireless, broadcast, transmitted, telephone, telephonic, radiophonic, audiovisual, hearing, audient, listening, attentive, musical, all ears (Inf), bugged (Inf)

▶ *467 Attention, 49 Music, 481 Discrimination, 56 Physics*

12 **eared**, having ears, auricular, auriculate, ear-shaped, earlike, auriform, big-eared, long-eared, jug-eared, cauliflower-eared, lop-eared, crop-eared

13 **otological**, audiological, otolaryngological, otorhinolaryngological, ENT (ear, nose, and throat), otalgic, otoscopic

▶ *60 Medicine*

14 **hearable**, audible, reachable, within range, within earshot, loud, soft, resonant, sonorous, echoing, echoic, carrying, listenable, easy-listening, easy on the ear, harsh, ear-splitting, loud enough to wake the dead

▶ *423 Loudness, 424 Faintness, 427 Resonance, 428 Mutedness, 430 Harsh Sound*

VERBS

15 **hear**, hear things, hear voices, perceive, catch, have an ear for, have a good ear, have perfect (*or* absolute) pitch, have a poor ear, have no ear, hear of, hear tell, hear tell of, hear on the grapevine, hear from, be in touch with, listen, give ear, lend an ear, hearken, hark,

listen to, give a hearing, hear out, attend, pay attention, concentrate, heed, mind, learn, gather, auscultate, sound, listen in, tune in, pick up, overhear, eavesdrop, tape, tap, wiretap, intercept, monitor, pin back one's ears, prick up one's ears, be all ears, keep one's ear to the ground, keep one's ears open, have long ears, make someone's ears burn, have someone's ear, hang on someone's words (*or* lips), bug (Inf), get an earful (Inf)

▶ *467 Attention, 534 Communications*

16 **be heard**, fall on the ear, reach, carry, come within earshot, sound, resound, reverberate, echo, transmit, broadcast, go on the air

▶ *427 Resonance*

ADVERBS

17 **aurally**, auricularly, within earshot, within range, within hearing, within call, hearably, audibly, aloud, out loud, telephonically, by telephone, on the air, on the radio, audiovisually, attentively, auscultatorily, by ear, at first hearing

INTERJECTIONS

18 **hear hear!,** listen!, hark!, oyez!, hist!

421 Deafness

NOUNS

1 **deafness**, hearing loss, hearing impairment, partial deafness, total deafness, deaf-mutism, poor hearing, defective hearing, failure to hear, tone deafness, unmusicalness, inattention, lack of attention, daydreaming, indifference, heedlessness, oblivion, insensitivity, deaf ears, lip-reading, lip-reader, sign language, American Sign Language (AMSLAN), signing, dactylology, finger alphabet, smoke signals, semaphore, hearing aid, deaf aid, ear trumpet

▶ *420 Hearing, 422 Silence, 60 Medicine, 534 Communications, 207 Age, 404 Insensibility, 783 Indifference, 761 Insensitivity, 512 Oblivion*

2 **deaf people**, the deaf, the hard of hearing, deaf-mute

3 **inaudibility**, faintness, faint sound, earplug, silencer, damper, mute, sordino, sourdine, soft pedal, soundproofing, sound insulation, baffle, threshold of hearing, ultrasound, poor reception, interference, jamming, mute button

▶ *424 Faintness, 428 Mutedness, 64 Electronics and Electrical Engineering*

ADJECTIVES

4 **deaf**, unhearing, without hearing, hard of hearing, hearing-impaired, partially deaf, totally deaf, stone deaf, deaf as a post, deaf-mute, deaf and dumb, tone deaf, unmusical, earless, deafened, stunned, wearing earplugs

▶ *420 Hearing, 60 Medicine*

5 **unhearing**, unaware, oblivious, deaf to, heedless, unheeding, unconcerned, indiffer-

ent, insensitive, inattentive, dead to the world
▶ *783 Indifference, 468 Inattention, 761 Insensitivity, 512 Oblivion*
6 **deafening**, ear-splitting, piercing, ear-shattering
▶ *423 Loudness*
7 **unheard**, inaudible, toneless, faint, difficult to hear, muted, soundproof, ultrasonic, out of range, out of earshot, off-air, off the air, turned off, switched off, unheard-of, deaf to all pleas, none so deaf as those who will not hear
▶ *424 Faintness, 428 Mutedness, 422 Silence, 783 Indifference*

VERBS
8 **be deaf**, go deaf, lose one's hearing, fail to hear, miss, ignore, turn a deaf ear, close one's ears, not listen, tune out, lip-read, use sign language, sign, have no ear for
▶ *420 Hearing, 534 Communications, 468 Inattention, 512 Oblivion*
9 **deafen**, make deaf, burst the eardrums, stun
▶ *423 Loudness*
10 **muffle**, mute, baffle, deaden, silence, soundproof, insulate, jam, drown out, use earplugs, put one's fingers in one's ears, turn the sound down (or off)
▶ *428 Mutedness, 422 Silence*
11 **be unheard**, fall on deaf ears, go in (at) one ear and out (of) the other, go off the air

ADVERBS
12 **deafly**, deafeningly, inaudibly, tonelessly, out of earshot, out of range

422 Silence

When you have nothing to say, say nothing. Charles Caleb Colton.

Silence is as full of potential wisdom and wit as the unhewn marble of great sculpture. Aldous Huxley.

Thou still unravish'd bride of quietness,/ Thou foster-child of silence and slow time. John Keats.

Silence is the best tactic for him who distrusts himself. Duc de la Rochefoucauld.

Whereof one cannot speak, thereon one must remain silent. Ludwig Wittgenstein.

VERBS
1 **be silent**, be quiet, keep silent, keep quiet, keep mum, not speak, not say a word, not open one's mouth, hold one's tongue, clench one's teeth, hold one's breath, make no noise, not make a sound, not make a peep, not utter a squeak, become silent, fall silent, stop talking, relapse into silence, lose one's voice, be struck dumb, get laryngitis, clam up (Inf), pipe down (Inf), knock it off (Inf)
▶ *566 Taciturnity, 563 Voicelessness, 428 Mutedness, 424 Faintness*

2 **silence**, make silent, quiet, make quiet, quieten, hush, still, lull, quell, subdue, mute, stifle, smother, muffle, muzzle, gag, stop, put to silence, soft-pedal, play down, drown the noise, drown (out), can it (US inf), put the lid on (Inf), stop someone's mouth (Inf)
▶ *563 Voicelessness, 428 Mutedness, 325 Motionlessness, 423 Loudness*

ADJECTIVES
3 **silent**, quiet, inaudible, noiseless, soundless, taciturn, mute, mum, tight-lipped, dumb, voiceless, aphonic, aphasic, tongueless, speechless, dumbfounded, wordless, hushed, still, stilly (Arch), calm, peaceful, quiescent, soft, faint, muted, soundproof, unsounded, unuttered, unspoken, tacit, solemn, awful, deathlike, quiet as a mouse, quiet as a lamb, silent as the grave, silent as the tomb, so silent one could hear a pin drop, clammed up (Inf)
▶ *325 Motionlessness, 424 Faintness, 428 Mutedness, 563 Voicelessness, 566 Taciturnity, 675 Peace*

NOUNS
4 **silence**, quiet, quietness, noiselessness, inaudibility, soundlessness, taciturnity, muteness, dumbness, voicelessness, aphonia, laryngitis, speechlessness, wordlessness, hush, stillness, lull, rest, calm, peace, quietude, quiescence, softness, faintness, mutedness, solemnity, solemnness, solemn silence, awful silence, dead silence, deathlike silence, deathly hush, uncanny silence, perfect silence, total silence, not a sound, not a squeak
▶ *325 Motionlessness, 424 Faintness, 428 Mutedness, 563 Voicelessness, 566 Taciturnity, 675 Peace*

ADVERBS
5 **silently**, in silence, quietly, inaudibly, noiselessly, soundlessly, calmly, peacefully, softly, faintly

INTERJECTIONS
6 **hush!**, sh!, silence!, quiet!, shut up!, that's enough!, peace!, soft!, mum's the word!, whist! (Dial), hold your tongue!, keep your mouth shut!, keep your trap shut! (Inf), dry up! (Inf), pipe down! (Inf), cut the cackle! (Inf), stow it! (Inf), can it! (US inf), knock it off! (Inf)

423 Loudness

NOUNS
1 **loudness**, high volume, noise, loud noise, ear-splitting noise, shattered silence, burst of sound, report, loud report, explosion, bang, blast, boom, sonic boom, burst, shell burst, slam, clap, thunderclap, alarm, siren, honk, toot, prolonged noise, reverberation, loud laughter, cachinnation, laughter, loud breathing, stertorousness, snoring, rumble, roll, rattle, thunder, storm, thundering storm, rum-

bling thunder, rattling thunder, thunderbolts of Thor, war in heaven, dashing, surging, hissing, sibilation, retort, fire, gunfire, artillery, bombardment, blitz, dissonance, cacophony, stridency, stridor, brassiness, shrillness, blare, bray, fanfare, flourish, trumpet blast, clarion call, call, view halloo, sonority, sonorousness, organ notes, clang, clangour, stentorian tones, plangency, resonance, ringing tones, bells, peal, chimes, campanology, diapason, swell, surge, crescendo, forte, fortissimo, tutti, full blast, full chorus
▶ *425 Sudden Sound, 426 Repeated Sound, 427 Resonance, 429 Hissing Sound, 430 Harsh Sound, 636 Warning, 49 Music, 434 Dissonance*

2 **outcry**, vociferation, clamour, shouting, screaming, roaring, bawling, yelling, hooting, chanting, shout, scream, shriek, cry, roar, whoop, howl, ululation, hubbub, hullabaloo, song and dance, slamming, banging, stamping, crash, clash, clatter, din, row, uproar, tumult, deafening row, noisiness, racket, bedlam, pandemonium, turmoil, rumpus, all hell let loose, enough noise to wake the dead, stramash (Scot), ballyhoo (Inf), shemozzle (Sl)
▶ *431 Human Cry, 432 Animal Cry, 241 Violence, 773 Rejoicing, 151 Disorder*

3 **audibility**, distinctness, sound, noise, broken silence
▶ *420 Hearing*

4 **sound maker**, voice, larynx, voice box, vocal chords, loud pedal, amplifier, public-address system, PA (system), loudspeaker, speaker, megaphone, loud-hailer, microphone, ear trumpet, hearing aid, loud instrument, gong, whistle, siren, horn, hooter, klaxon, rattle, bullroarer, buzzer, bell, alarm, door knocker, brass horn, trumpet, bugle, portable stereo player, stentorian voice, lungs, good lungs, good pair of lungs, lungs of brass, iron throat, mike (Inf), amp (Inf), ghetto blaster (Inf)

5 **loud person**, opera singer, Shakespearean actor, hog caller, drill sergeant, tobacco auctioneer, Stentor, Hermes, town crier

ADJECTIVES
6 **loud**, noisy, full of noise, on full volume, at full pitch, full, booming, ringing, carrying, deafening, ear-splitting, ear-rending, thundering, thunderous, rattling, crashing, pealing, clangorous, dinning, rackety, shrill, piercing, high-sounding, strident, braying, blaring, brassy, echoing, resounding, resonant, sonorous, plangent, deep, discordant, cacophonous, shouting, yelling, whooping, screaming, bellowing, crying, big-mouthed, loud-mouthed, lusty, powerful, full-throated, at the top of one's voice (or lungs), stentorian, brazen-mouthed, trumpet-tongued, uproarious, rowdy, rumbustious, rambunctious, boister-

ous, disorderly, multisonous, many-tongued, vociferous, clamorous, clamant, swelling, crescendo, forte, fortissimo, enough to wake the dead
▶ *151 Disorder, 434 Dissonance, 431 Human Cry, 432 Animal Cry, 430 Harsh Sound, 427 Resonance*

7 **heard**, hearable, audible, distinct
▶ *420 Hearing*

VERBS
8 **be loud**, sound, break the silence, speak, give tongue, speak up, raise one's voice, strain one's voice, crack one's voice, vociferate, shout, yell, roar, bellow, call, catcall, caterwaul, yowl, howl, ululate, shriek, cry, scream, squawk, skirl (Scot dial), trumpet, bugle, blare, whistle, shrill, bray, cachinnate, laugh, snore, clap, stamp, reverberate, resound, ring, peal, clang, rattle, thunder, fulminate, storm, clash, crash, clatter, slam, bang, blast, burst, boom, explode, detonate, go off, knock, knock hard, hammer, drill, din, shatter the peace, stun, deafen, split the ears, rend the eardrums, shatter the eardrums, ring in the ear, swell, fill the air, rend the skies, make the welkin ring (Arch), rattle the windows, bring the house down, raise the roof, blow the roof off, raise the rafters, raise all hell, awake the echoes, wake the dead, raise Cain, make a devil of a row, rampage, go on a rampage, kick up a shindy (Inf)
▶ *430 Harsh Sound, 431 Human Cry, 773 Rejoicing, 432 Animal Cry, 427 Resonance, 425 Sudden Sound, 151 Disorder*

ADVERBS
9 **loudly**, noisily, stridently, sonorously, uproariously, vociferously, lustily, at the top of one's voice, in full cry, full blast, full chorus, tutti, with a deafening roar, like all hell let loose, forte, fortissimo, crescendo

10 **aloud**, audibly, distinctly

424 Faintness

NOUNS
1 **faintness**, softness, soft sound, less sound, low volume, sound reduction, noise abatement, muffled sound, muted sound, mutedness, distant sound, indistinctness, inaudibility, soundproofing, dull sound, clunk, plunk, thud, thump, bump, plonk, nonresonance, voicelessness, hoarseness, whisper, susurration, breath, bated breath, soft voice, quiet tone, muffled tones, hushed tones, undertone, undercurrent of sound, murmur, hum, drone, roll, sigh, sough, moan, scratch, squeak, creak, pop, tick, click, tinkle, clink, chink, buzz, whirr, purr, purl, ripple, plash, plop, babble, burble, gurgle, rustle, swoosh, swish, froufrou,

squish, squash, fizz, sizzle, hiss, patter, pitter-patter, pitapat, soft footfall, pad

▶ *428 Mutedness, 422 Silence, 563 Voicelessness, 426 Repeated Sound, 429 Hissing Sound, 441 Dimness, 523 Unintelligibility, 260 Littleness*

2 **sound reducer**, silencer, car silencer, firearm silencer, soft pedal, mute, damper, dampener, filter, cork, double glazing, soundproofing, rubber heel, rubber soles, grease, oil, lubricant, earplugs, gag, cough drop, laryngitis

▶ *49 Music, 428 Mutedness, 386 Lubrication*

3 **faint-sounding thing**, bare feet, heartbeat, raindrops, light breeze, rustling leaves, gurgling brook, pin dropping

ADJECTIVES

4 **faint**, soft, quiet, low, gentle, distant, indistinct, inaudible, barely audible, soundproof, soundproofed, just caught, just heard, half-heard, barely heard, weak, feeble, trembling in the air, dying away, unemphatic, unstressed, unaccented, piano, hushed, muted, muffled, damped, dampened, nonresonant, dead, deadened, dull, soft-pedalled, subdued, suppressed, stifled, bated, voiceless, whispered, hoarse, husky, wheezy, rasping, gravelly, murmuring, sighing, purring, gurgling, rustling, hissing, pattering, stealthy

▶ *428 Mutedness, 422 Silence, 563 Voicelessness, 430 Harsh Sound, 429 Hissing Sound*

VERBS

5 **sound faint**, speak low, speak softly, say sotto voce, sing low, sing softly, play piano, drop one's voice, lower one's voice, breathe, whisper, murmur, mutter, hum, croon, drone, purr, buzz, whirr, purl, ripple, plash, splash, lap, plop, babble, burble, gurgle, flow, sputter, splutter, patter, squeak, creak, tick, click, tinkle, clink, chink, clunk, plunk, thud, thump, bump, plonk, moan, sigh, sough, hiss, wheeze, blow, rustle, swish, swoosh, squish, squash, fizz, sizzle, tremble, float on the air, steal on the air, become inaudible, melt on the air, melt, die on the ear, die away, fade away, sink into silence, sound dead

▶ *563 Voicelessness, 428 Mutedness, 389 Water, 390 Air*

6 **mute**, soften, dull, deaden, dampen, damp down, soft-pedal, turn down the volume, soundproof, muffle, stifle, hush, silence, stop

▶ *422 Silence, 428 Mutedness*

ADVERBS

7 **faintly**, softly, quietly, low, indistinctly, in a whisper, in an undertone, sotto voce, aside, under one's breath, between the teeth, distantly, out of earshot, piano, pianissimo, à la sourdine

425   Sudden Sound

NOUNS

1 **bang**, slam, wham, whack, thump, thud,

blast, report, discharge, explosion, burst, volley, round, salvo, shot, pistol-shot, detonation, blowout, backfire, boom, sonic boom, peal, thunderclap, clap of thunder, crash, clash, kaboom (Inf), kapow (Inf), zap (Inf), Kazam (Inf)

▶ *423 Loudness*

2 **crack**, crackle, crackling, crepitation, sizzling, spitting, click, snap, slap, smack, clap, tap, rap, rat-tat-tat, knock, pop, plop, plunk

▶ *426 Repeated Sound*

3 **banger**, cracker, firecracker, squib, explosive, bomb, grenade, firearm, gun, shot gun, pop gun, rifle, air rifle, air gun

4 **belch**, hiccup, eructation, flatulence, burp (Inf), fart (Sl)

▶ *349 Expulsion*

VERBS

5 **bang**, slam, wham, blast, discharge, burst, burst on the ear, explode, blow up, detonate, backfire, boom, thunder, resound, echo, rumble, peal, crash, clash

6 **crack**, crackle, crepitate, sizzle, fizzle, spit, effervesce, click, clunk, clatter, rattle, snap, clap, rap, tap, slap, smack, pop, plop, plonk, plunk

7 **belch**, hiccup, eruct, break wind, burp (Inf), fart (Sl)

ADJECTIVES

8 **banging**, crashing, slamming, bursting, exploding, explosive, booming, thundering, thundrous, ear-splitting, deafening

9 **crackling**, crepitant, sizzling, spitting, clicking, rattling, popping, staccato

ADVERBS

10 **explosively**, like a bolt from the blue, bang, abruptly, suddenly, staccato

▶ *514 Surprise*

426   Repeated Sound

NOUNS

1 **drumming**, thrumming, roll, rumble, rumbling, grumbling, booming, reverberation, echo, vibration, pulsation, palpitation, throbbing, pounding, beat, pulse, beating, drum, drumbeat, drum roll, tattoo, devil's tattoo, tom-tom

▶ *183 Repetition, 427 Resonance, 423 Loudness*

2 **humming**, whirring, buzzing, hum, whirr, buzz, purr, drone, bombination (or bombilation) (Fml), mutter, murmur, background murmur, blah-blah

3 **rattle**, clatter, clitter-clatter, chatter, babble, clack, racket

▶ *425 Sudden Sound*

4 **knocking**, knock-knock, rat-a-tat, rat-tat-tat, rub-a-dub, pitter-patter, pit-a-pat, tick, tick-tock, drip-drop

5 **ringing**, pinging, ping, pip, ring-ring, chim-

ing, pealing, carillon, ding-dong

6 **musical repetition**, rhythm, trill, tremolo, vibrato, refrain, burden, chorus, canon, round
▶ *433 Melody, 49 Music*

7 **repeated word**, reiteration, restatement, anaphora, epistrophe, catchword, buzz word, cliché, truism, catchphrase, slogan, rhyme, assonance
▶ *48 Literature, 5 Linguistics, 796 Fashion*

VERBS

8 **drum**, thrum, roll, rumble, grumble, boom, reverberate, resound, resonate, echo, re-echo, vibrate, pulse, pulsate, throb, pound, beat, beat (*or* sound) a tattoo, tattoo

9 **hum**, whirr, buzz, purr, drone, bombinate (*or* bombilate) (Fml), mutter, murmur, witter

10 **rattle**, clatter, clack, chatter, babble, sputter, chug, rev up (Inf)

11 **knock**, tap, tick, ticktock, patter, drip

12 **ring**, ping, clang, chime, peal, toll, carillon

13 **trill**, quaver, warble, chorus, sing in a round

14 **repeat**, reiterate, restate, say it again, trot out clichés, talk in clichés

ADJECTIVES

15 **drumming**, rolling, thrumming, reverberant, reverberative, resonant, throbbing, pounding, beating, loud, insistent, persistent, incessant, repeated

16 **humming**, whirring, buzzing, droning, monotonous, repetitive, unvaried

17 **rattling**, clattering, chattering, sputtering, clicking, ticking, knocking

18 **pealing**, chiming, repeating

ADVERBS

19 **repeatedly**, resonantly, over and over again, rhythmically, insistently, persistently, repetitively, monotonously, incessantly

427 Resonance

NOUNS

1 **resonance**, resonation, reverberation, resounding, rebounding, hollowness, echo, re-echo, lingering note, reflection, recurrence, vibration, whirring, humming, buzzing, oscillation, sympathetic resonance, morphogenetic resonance
▶ *426 Repeated Sound, 365 Oscillation*

2 **ringing**, bell ringing, tintinnabulation, campanology, peal, toll, knell, chime, tinkle, jingle, chink, clink, ping, ting-a-ling, clang, clangour, sounding brass, brass, blare, flourish, fanfare, tucket
▶ *423 Loudness*

3 **deepness**, lowness, profundity, booming, thundering, fillness, richness, sonorousness, sonority, plangency, deep note, low note, bass note, (*or* grave note, pedal note, low voice, bass, basso, basso profondo, baritone, bass baritone, contralto

4 **sources of resonance**, tube, tunnel, bell, handbell, church bell, doorbell, chimes, telephone bell, firebell, cowbell, clapper, gong, triangle, trumpet, horn, stringed instrument

5 **resonator**, sounding board, sound box, resonating chamber (*or* cavity), sustaining pedal

ADJECTIVES

6 **resonant**, resonating, reverberating, reverberative, reboant, stentorian, resounding, rebounding, hollow, echoing, re-echoing, vibrating, pulsating, carrying, echoic, lingering, persisting, persistent, humming, whirring, buzzing

7 **ringing**, tintinnabular (*or* tintinnabulary), pealing, tolling, sounding, chiming, tinkling, jingling, pinging, clanging, loud

8 **deep**, low, deep-toned, deep-pitched, deep-sounding, deep-voiced, sepulchral, sonorous, vibrant, booming, thundering, full, rich, plangent, mellow, melodious, rounded, orotund, full-throated
▶ *433 Melody*

VERBS

9 **resonate**, reverberate, resound, rebound, boom, echo, re-echo, be repeated, be reflected, recur, vibrate, whir, hum, buzz, oscillate

10 **ring**, ring in the ear, tintinnabulate, peal, toll, sound, knell, chime, tinkle, jingle, jangle, chink, clink, ping, twang, clang, blare, trumpet, tootle, toot

ADVERBS

11 **resonantly**, reverberantly, resoundingly, reflectively, recurrently, deeply, profoundly, richly, vibrantly, sonorously, plangently

428 Mutedness

ADJECTIVES

1 **faint-sounding**, faint, subdued, hushed, muted, low, quiet, soft, gentle, piano, pianissimo, indistinct, unclear, distant, weak, muffled, stifled, whispered, murmured, muttered, mumbled, half-heard, inaudible, imperceptible
▶ *424 Faintness, 422 Silence, 563 Voicelessness*

2 **nonresonant**, deadened, dulled, damped, dampened, muted, muffled, stifled, smothered, silenced, soundproof(ed), dull, heavy, flat, dead

NOUNS

3 **mutedness**, faintness, lowness, softness, indistinctness, lack of clarity, nonresonance

4 **faint sound**, soft sound, undertone, bated breath, murmur(ing), murmuration, mutter(ing), mumble, mumbling, whisper(ing), susurration, rustle, rustling, crackle, sigh(ing), moan(ing), whine, whining, humming, drone, droning, purring
▶ *424 Faintness, 429 Hissing Sound*

5 **dull sound**, heavy sound, thud, clunk,

thump, bump, plump, plunk, plonk, plop

6 **silencer**, mute, damper, soft pedal, sordino

VERBS

7 **mute**, lower, subdue, dampen, damp down, soft-pedal, deaden, dull, muffle, stifle, hush, quieten, quiet, soften, still, silence

8 **sound faint**, drop (*or* lower) one's voice, murmur, mutter, mumble, whisper, breathe, susurrate, rustle, crackle, sigh, moan, whine, hum, croon, drone, purr

9 **be nonresonant**, sound dead, fall dead on the ear, arouse no echoes, thud, clunk, thump, plump, plunk, plonk, plop

ADVERBS

10 **faintly**, softly, quietly, piano, pianissimo, in an undertone, with bated breath, sotto voce, aside, in an aside, out of earshot

429 Hissing Sound

NOUNS

1 **hiss**, hissing, sibilation, sibilance, assibilation, lisp(ing), whisper(ing), stage whisper, susurration, shush(ing), hush(ing), rustle, rustling, swish, swoosh, froufrou, sputter, splutter, splash, plash, wheezing, whistling, white noise, rhonchus, rale (*or* râle), sneeze, sneezing, wheeze, fizz(ing), effervescence, sizzle, sizzling, whiz(zing), squish, squash, squelch

2 **catcall**, jeer, boo, hoot, raspberry, derision, Bronx cheer (US sl)

▶ *852 Disapproval, 827 Curse*

3 **hisser**, snake, serpent, cat, goose, leaking tyre, sibilant, letter *s*, sigma

VERBS

4 **hiss**, sibilate, assibilate, lisp, whisper, shush, hush, rustle, susurrate, swish, swoosh, sputter, splutter, splash, plash, wheeze, rasp, whistle, snuffle, sneeze, fizz, effervesce, fizzle, sizzle, whiz, squish, squash, squelch

5 **catcall**, jeer, boo, hoot, blow a raspberry, deride, disparage

ADJECTIVES

6 **hissing**, sibilant, rustling, whispering, sneezing, wheezy, asthmatic, fizzy, effervescent, sizzling, fizzling

7 **catcalling**, jeering, booing, hooting, disapproving, derisive, scornful

ADVERBS

8 **sibilantly**, swishingly, squashily, effervescently, asthmatically, wheezily

INTERJECTIONS

9 **sh!**, hist!, whist!, whisht!, wheesh!, tsk!, tush!

430 Harsh Sound

NOUNS

1 **stridency** (*or* stridence), harshness, discord, discordance, clamour, harsh sound, stridor, cacophony, raucousness, dissonance, squawk, yawp, yelp, yell, howl, wail, ululation, bray,

brassiness, brass, blare, skirl, blast, tantara

▶ *434 Dissonance, 423 Loudness*

2 **hoarseness**, roughness, huskiness, gruffness, lowness, gutteralness, throatiness, gutteral sound, rasping sound, caw, croak, grunt, snort, snore, stertor, cough, belch, cracked voice, frog in the throat, rustiness, friction, scrape, scratch, nasality, nasal tone, twang, drone

3 **shrillness**, high pitch, shriek, scream, squeal, screech, squeak, piping, whistling, whistle, catcall, wolf whistle, penny whistle, tin whistle, bleep, bleeper, high note, falsetto, acute note, sharp note, squeakiness, creakiness, creak, creaking door, rusty hinge

VERBS

4 **be strident**, jar, clash, discord, jangle, rasp, grind, grate, grate on one's ears, set one's teeth on edge, go right through one, squawk, yawp, yelp, yawl, yell, howl, wail, ululate, bray, blare, skirl, blast, split one's ears, lift the roof (Inf)

5 **sound hoarse**, rasp, grate, grind, crunch, scrunch, gutteralize, caw, croak, grunt, snort, snore, cough, hawk, clear one's throat, hem, belch, choke, gasp, crack one's voice, have a frog in one's throat, scrape, saw, scratch, twang, drone, clank, clink

6 **be shrill**, shriek, scream, screech, squeal, squeak, creak, pipe, whistle, wolf-whistle, catcall

ADJECTIVES

7 **strident**, stridulous (*or* stridulant), harsh, raucous, discordant, grating, jarring, flat, inharmonious, unmelodious, unmusical, metallic, twangy, penetrating, loud, clamorous, cacophonous, dissonant, ear-splitting, squawky, squawking, howling, ululant, brassy, brazen, braying, blaring

8 **hoarse**, husky, rough, gruff, low, gutteral, throaty, gravelly, rasping, cawing, croaky, croaking, grunting, snorting, snoring, stertorous, cracked, nonresonant, dry, rusty, unoiled, scraping, scratchy, droning, clanking, clinking

9 **shrill**, high, high-pitched, sharp, acute, piercing, ear-piercing, squeaky, squeaking, creaky, creaking, tinny, reedy, piping, whistling, bleeping

ADVERBS

10 **stridently**, loudly, harshly, discordantly, raspingly, gutterally, shrilly

431 Human Cry

NOUNS

1 **cry**, call, loud cry, outcry, outburst, battle cry, war cry, rallying cry, vociferation, clamour, uproar, hullabaloo, hubbub, shout, scream, screech, shriek, yell, roar, bellow, bawl, yawl,

caterwaul, holler (Inf)

▶ *423 Loudness*

2 **cry of joy**, laugh, laughter, cachinnation, horse laugh, guffaw, hoot, whoop, yippee, chortle, chuckle, giggle, titter, snigger

▶ *762 Joy, 773 Rejoicing, 771 Humour*

3 **cry of praise**, acclamation, paean, hallelujah, alleluia, hosanna, glossolalia, applause, cheer, whoop, bravo, hurrah, hooray, hip-hip hurrah (*or* hooray), huzzah (Arch)

▶ *851 Approval*

4 **cry of greeting**, hello (*or* hullo), hail, greetings, salutation

▶ *815 Sociability, 817 Courtesy*

5 **hunting cry**, cry of the chase, hue and cry, halloo (or halloa), whoa, view halloo, tally-ho, yoicks (Arch)

6 **cry of pain**, scream, shriek, squeal, gasp, whine, whimper, groan, moan, crying, weeping, weeping and wailing, keening, ululation, lamentation, wail, howl, bawl, sob, sigh, boohoo, ouch, ow

▶ *774 Lamentation, 770 Sorrow*

7 **cry of disapproval**, exclamation, ejaculation, interjection, expletive, hoot, jeer, boo, hiss, catcall, curse, raspberry, bird (US sl), Bronx cheer (US sl)

▶ *852 Disapproval, 827 Curse*

8 **musical cry**, song, yodel, chant, chorus, solo

▶ *433 Melody, 49 Music*

9 **crier**, town crier, barker, street trader, hawker, huntsman, master of hounds, yodeller, shouter, yeller, bawler, cheerer, cheerleader, rooter (Inf)

VERBS

10 **cry out**, call, call out, vociferate, raise a cry, raise one's voice, strain one's lungs (*or* voice, vocal cords), crack one's throat, shout, shout out, shout oneself hoarse, shout at the top of one's voice (*or* lungs), blast out, thunder out, explode, scream, shriek, yell, roar, bellow, bawl, yawl, yowl, squall, caterwaul, holler (Inf), yawp (US inf)

11 **laugh**, cachinnate, guffaw, hoot, whoop, chortle, chuckle, giggle, titter, snigger, split one's sides, blow a gut (US sl)

▶ *771 Humour*

12 **cheer**, cheer for, give three cheers, hurrah, horray, sing the praises of, shout for, root for (Inf), pull for (US inf)

13 **cry**, sob, sigh, groan, moan, whine, whimper, yammer, mewl, pule, gasp, fret, lament, weep, wail, keen, ululate, howl, bawl, blubber, blub (Inf)

14 **hiss**, hoot, boo, jeer, catcall, exclaim, ejaculate, curse, tell off, shout down, bawl out

15 **sing out**, give voice, yodel, chant, chorus, belt out (Inf)

ADJECTIVES

16 **vociferous**, noisy, loud, vocal, stentorian, full-throated, thundering, thunderous, boom-

ing, deafening, shouting, screaming, yelling, bellowing, roaring, uproarious, clamorous, obstreperous, loudmouthed (Inf)

17 **cheering**, rousing, shooping, laughing, chuckling, giggling

18 **crying**, sobbing, sighing, groaning, moaning, whimpering, weeping, wailing, howling, ululant, blubbering, blubbing (Inf)

19 **hissing**, booing, jeering, cursing, exclamatory, ejaculatory

ADVERBS

20 **vociferously**, noisily, loudly, vocally, thunderously, deafeningly, uproariously, clamorously, obstreperously, at the top of one's voice

432 Animal Cry

NOUNS

1 **animal cry**, warning cry, mating call, animal call, barking, baying, howling, belling, wailing, yowling, yawling, bleating, bellowing, roaring, ululation, bark, yelp, yap, snap, snarl, growl, woof, hiss, meow (*or* miaow, miaou), mew, purr, baa, moo, neigh, whinny, heehaw, yawp (US inf)

2 **bird song**, bird call, note, woodnote, chirping, chirruping, chattering, twittering, warble, squeak, cheep, twitter, tweet-tweet, cuckoo, hoot, tu-whit tu-whoo, cock-a-doodle-doo, croak, caw, coo, whoop, hiss, quack, cluck, squawk, screech

3 **insect noise**, buzzing, humming, droning, whining, stridulation, bombination (*or* bombilation) (Fml)

VERBS

4 **cry**, call, ululate, give tongue, bay, bay at the moon, howl, bell, troat, wail, yowl, yawl, caterwaul, bark, yelp, yap, whine, snap, snarl, growl, meow (*or* miaow, miaou), purr, mew, mewl, hiss, bleat, baa, moo, low, bellow, roar, trumpet, neigh, bray, whinny, whicker, nicker, grunt, snort, croak, squeal, squeak, gibber, yawp (US inf)

5 **sing**, sing like a bird, warble, carol, whistle, chirp, chirr, chirrup, cheep, peep, pule, pipe, tweet, twitter, chatter, whirr, coo, caw, hoot, screech, honk, oink, quack, cluck, clack, crow, cackle, chuckle, gaggle, gobble, squawk

6 **buzz**, hum, drone, whine, stridulate, grate, rasp, bombinate (*or* bombilate) (Fml)

ADJECTIVES

7 **ululant**, howling, yowling, wailing, wailful, bellowing, full-throated, deep-throated

8 **singing**, warbling, carolling, tweeting, twittering, twittery, chattering

9 **humming**, buzzing, droning, stridulous (*or* stridulant)

ADVERBS

10 **howlingly**, wailfully, stridulously, stridulantly, chattily, croakily

433 Melody

NOUNS

1 **melody**, tune, air, song, aria, strain, measure, theme, subject, motif, leitmotif, line, melodic line, cantus, cantus firmus, canto, refrain, reprise, descant, chorus, solo, theme song, signature tune, Broadway melody, simple melody, popular melody, lost melody

2 **song**, lied, chanson, aubade, serenade, lullaby, cradle song, berceuse, barcarolle, part song, round, madrigal, folk song, glee, lay, roundelay, lilt, shanty, yodel, popular song, lyric, calypso, spiritual, love song, torch song, chant, plainchant, cantide, chorale, carol, Christmas carol, hymn, psalm, anthem, national anthem, cavatina

3 **melodiousness**, musicality, musicalness, musical quality, musical texture, euphony, euphoniousness, harmoniousness, harmony, chime, concord, consonance, attunement,

4 **harmonics**, harmonization, harmonic progression, unison, homophony, monophony, monody, counterpoint, polyphony, heterophony, cantus firmus, tonality, resolution, cadence, perfect cadence, fauxbourdon, faburden, thorough bass, basso continuo, continuo, figured bass, ground bass, walking bass, syncopation, timing, rhythm, tempo, beat, phrasing, phrase, passage, figure, sequence, tonal sequence, orchestration, instrumentation, arrangement, passacaglia, chaconne, musica ficta
▶ *49 Music*

5 **melodist**, harmonist, songwriter, lyricist, psalmist, singer, balladeer, minstrel, lieder singer, Meistersinger, minnesinger, troubadour, trouvère, serenader, chanteuse, crooner, soprano, contralto, alto, tenor, bass, soloist, chorister, songster, warbler, songbird, nightingale, canary
▶ *49 Music*

ADJECTIVES

6 **melodious**, melodic, musical, tuneful, lyrical, canorous, lilting, singable, catchy, tripping, soft, sweet, dulcet, velvety, mellow, smooth, sweet-sounding, honeyed, mellifluous, mellifluent, Orphean, silvery, silvertoned, golden-toned, fine-toned, true, well-pitched, clear, clear as a bell, chiming, full-toned, resonant, full, rich, euphonious, euphonic, harmonious

7 **harmonious**, harmonizing, harmonic, in harmony, concordant, consonant, agreeing, in concord, in consent, *en rapport* (Fr), unanimous, attuned, in tune, in unison, in chorus, homophonic, monophonic, monodic, polyphonic, synchronous, synchronized, syncopated, corresponding, assonant, rhyming, matching
▶ *116 Accord, 667 Agreement, 49 Music*

VERBS

8 **harmonize**, accord, chime in, be in harmony, synchronize, attune, tune, tune up, be together, be in unison, agree, be at one, conform, correspond, rhyme, match

9 **set to music**, melodize, harmonize, symphonize, orchestrate, syncopate, score, accompany

10 **sing**, vocalize, lilt, warble, trill, carol, croon
▶ *432 Animal Cry*

ADVERBS

11 **melodiously**, melodically, tunefully, lyrically, sweetly, mellifluously, euphoniously, resonantly

12 **harmoniously**, in harmony, in accord, in concord, in consent, *en rapport*, unanimously, in tune, in unison, in chorus, synchronously, in sync (Inf)

434 Dissonance

NOUNS

1 **dissonance**, discord, discordance, disharmony, harshness, jarring, jangling, clashing, stridency, hoarseness

2 **dissonant noise**, cacophony, Babel, cat's concert, caterwauling, yowling, row, din, noise, clamour, uproar, racket, hullabaloo, hubbub, pandemonium, bedlam, tumult, turmoil
▶ *430 Harsh Sound, 423 Loudness*

3 **musical dissonance**, tunelessness, unmelodiousness, flatness, sharpness, dissonant chord, wrong note, clinker (US sl)

4 **atonality**, twelve-note (*or* twelve-tone) composition, twelve-note (*or* twelve-tone) scale, note (*or* tone) row, series, serialism, dodecaphony, total serialism, preparation (of dissonance), imperfect cadence, emancipation of the dissonance
▶ *49 Music*

5 **atmospheric dissonance**, static, wow, flutter, hiss, white noise, interference

6 **disagreement**, disaccord, discord, dissension, dissent, difference, conflict, clash, argument, quarrel
▶ *666 Disagreement, 500 Dissent*

ADJECTIVES

7 **dissonant**, discordant, inharmonious, jangling, jarring, clashing, grating, scraping, rasping, harsh, raucous, cacophonous, strident, shrill

8 **disagreeing**, conflicting, at variance, contrary, unresolved

9 **unmelodious**, unmusical, unharmonized, untuneful, tuneless, droning, singsong, untuned, cracked, off-pitch, off-key, off, out of tune, sharp, flat, flat-toned, toneless, atonal, serial

VERBS

10 **lack harmony**, jangle, jar, grate, clash, crash, saw, scrape, rasp, drone, whine, thrum, play sharp, play flat, hurt the ears, fluff (Inf), hit a clinker (US sl)

11 **disagree**, differ, conflict, be in conflict, be at odds, clash, argue, quarrel, cross swords
▶ *666 Disagreement, 500 Dissent*

ADVERBS

12 **dissonantly**, discordantly, disharmoniously, cacophonously, tunelessly, unmelodiously, raucously, atonally, harshly, stridently, hoarsely, hissingly, raspingly

435   Vision

NOUNS

1 **vision**, seeing, sight, eyesight, visual sense, visual acuity, sense of sight, faculty of sight, power of seeing, normal sight, normal vision, perfect vision, 20/20 vision, night vision, scotopia, good eyesight, long sight, far sight (US), short sight, near sight (US)

2 **eye**, orb, eyeball, eyesocket, orbit, white of the eye, sclera, cornea, iris, pupil, lens, aqueous humour, vitreous humour, light-sensitive cell, retina, cone, rod, blind spot, optic nerve, eye muscle, eyebrow, eyelid, conjunctiva, eyelash, sharp eye, keen eye, penetrating eye, gimlet eye, x-ray eye, eagle eye, eagle, hawk, cat, lynx, Argus, basilisk, Gorgon, gazehound, optic (Inf), peepers (Inf), sparklers (Inf)

3 **observation**, examination, scanning, inspection, supervision, perusal, scrutiny, scan, study, survey, watching, watchfulness, surveillance, espionage, spying, peering, prying, voyeurism, I-spy, reconnaissance, recce (Inf), look-see (Sl), once-over (Sl)

4 **visualization**, consideration, contemplation, imagination, mind's eye, insight, prevision, anticipation, foresight, farsightedness, planning, perception, discernment, awareness, understanding, perspicacity, perspicuity
▶ *516 Foresight, 550 Clarity*

5 **imagination**, dreaming, daydreaming, stargazing, dream, daydream, pipe dream, second sight, the sight, clairvoyance, crystal-gazing, scrying, illusion, *déjà vu* (Fr), optical illusion, mirage, hallucination, will-o'-the-wisp, *ignis fatuus* (L), Fata Morgana, pink elephant, chimera, figment, apparition, semblance, phantom, phantasm, spectre, phantasmagoria, wraith, ghost, vision, fantasy
▶ *519 Imagination, 504 Error, 102 Unreality*

6 **look**, glance, glimpse, *coup d'oeil* (Fr), peep, peek, squint, sideways look, sidelong look, gaze, stare, gape, grimace, black look, glare, glower, scowl, evil eye, dirty look, leer, ogle, old-fashioned look, glad eye, roving eye, come-hither look, sheep's eyes, melting look, gander (Sl), dekko (Sl), butcher's (Sl), shufty (Sl)

7 **view**, sight, aspect, vista, panorama, prospect, outlook, scene, scenery, landscape, townscape, cityscape, seascape, show, peepshow, spectacle, pageant, display, tableau, exhibition, spectator sport, performance, showing, picture, painting, drawing, photograph, film, overview, eyesore, blemish, blot (on the landscape), eyeful (Inf), eye-opener (Inf), sight for sore eyes (Inf), sight (Inf), fright (Inf)

8 **reflection**, image, mirror image, likeness, representation, mirror, glass, looking glass, hand mirror, magnifying mirror, shaving mirror, dressing-table mirror, full-length mirror, cheval glass, pier glass, reflector, wing mirror, rear-view mirror, cat's eye, speculum, distorting mirror, image recorder, camera, cine camera, video camera, telephoto lens, zoom lens, wide-angle lens, fisheye lens, slide, projector, magic lantern
▶ *66 Photography*

9 **viewpoint**, perspective, scope, range, eyeshot, field of vision, bird's-eye view, worm's-eye view, point of view, peephole, sight hole, spyhole, window, windscreen, picture window, shop window, judas-window, squint, belvedere, mirador, gazebo, watchtower, observation point, conning tower, bridge, crow's nest, observatory, planetarium, observation car, theatre, stalls, pit, dress circle, circle, gallery, gods (Inf), cinema, stadium, amphitheatre, arena, ringside seat, terrace, stand, grandstand, bleachers (Inf)

10 **visual aid**, eyeglass, reading glass, spectacles, pair of spectacles, specs (Inf), glasses, frames, lenses, contact lenses, hard (*or* soft *or* gas permeable) lenses, disposable lenses, contacts (Inf), gold-rimmed glasses, steel-rimmed glasses, horn-rimmed glasses, reading glasses, pebble glasses, granny glasses, bifocals, half-moon glasses, contact lenses, monocle, lorgnette, pince-nez, quizzing glass, eyeshade, sightscreen, sunglasses, dark glasses, night glasses, tinted glasses, polaroid glasses, shades (Inf), protective glasses, goggles, magnifier, magnifying glass, loupe, microfilm reader, microreader, opera glasses, binoculars, field glasses, optical instrument, spyglass, telescope, telescopic sight, gunsight, foresight, backsight, cross hairs, peep sight, microscope, optics, magnification, microscopy, telescopy, stereoscopy, spectroscopy
▶ *56 Physics, 436 Blindness*

11 **observer**, spectator, audience, sightseer, tourist, beholder, viewer, looker, onlooker, looker-on, witness, eyewitness, bystander, watcher, birdwatcher, spotter, train spotter, lookout, sentry, sentinel, scout, watchman, night watchman, caretaker, janitor, guard,

watchdog, vigilante, patrolman, security man, inspector, supervisor, overseer, monitor, scanner, invigilator, scrutinizer, scrutineer, scrutator, gazer, stargazer, crystal-gazer, clairvoyant, seer, seeress, visionary, starer, gaper, peerer, nosy parker, prier, peeping Tom, voyeur, gawper (Sl), rubbernecker (US sl)

VERBS

12 **see**, use one's eyes, behold (Arch), sight, catch sight of, glimpse, catch a glimpse of, espy, spy, notice, witness, spot, perceive, see with the naked eye, see with half an eye, have x-ray eyes, have eyes in the back of one's head, see through a brick wall, see round corners, discern, distinguish, descry, make out, recognize, pick out, discover, sightsee, spectate, see the sights, rubberneck (US sl), keep one's eye in (Inf), lay eyes on (Inf), clap eyes on (Inf)

13 **look**, look at, regard, focus (on), eye, look straight at, look someone in the face (or eye), feast one's eyes on, devour with one's eyes, gaze (at), stare (at), gape (at), goggle (at), look sideways (at), glance (at), steal a glance (at), peep (at), peek (at), squint (at), grimace, give someone a black (or dirty) look, glare (at), glower (at), scowl (at), look down one's nose (at), look askance (at), look daggers (at), leer (at), ogle, eye up, flutter one's eyelashes (at), make (sheep's) eyes at (Inf), give someone the glad eye (Inf), be all eyes (Inf), gawk (Inf), gawp (Inf)

14 **inspect**, examine, view, reconnoitre, scout, look closely at, scrutinize, study, pore over, look over, survey, scan, peruse, read, cast (or run) one's eye(s) over, have (or take) a look at, give someone (or something) the once-over (Sl), have a look-see (Sl), take (or have) a gander (at) (Sl), have a dekko (Sl), have a butcher's (Sl), take a shufty (at) (Sl), eyeball (Sl)

15 **watch**, observe, keep under observation, keep one's eyes (or an eye) on, monitor, watch over, oversee, invigilate, supervise, watch out for, keep a lookout for, keep an eye out for (or open for), spy on, watch like a hawk, keep one's eyes skinned (or peeled)

16 **visualize**, picture, imagine, see in the mind's eye, consider, contemplate, take stock of, anticipate, foresee, plan, perceive, discern, be aware of, understand

17 **imagine**, fancy, dream, dream up, conjure up, daydream, stargaze, crystal-gaze, scry, foresee, have second sight, hallucinate, see things (Inf)

18 **make visible**, reveal, reflect, mirror, show, display, exhibit, bring to light, demonstrate, point out, uncover, unmask, expose

▶ *530 Disclosure*

19 **be visible**, appear, come into view, come to light, emerge, catch the eye, loom up, loom large, show, show through, stand out

▶ *437 Visibility*

ADJECTIVES

20 **visual**, optical, optic, ophthalmic, eyelike, ocular, binocular, mirror-like, reflecting, two-dimensional, telescopic, microscopic, stereoscopic, three-dimensional, panoramic, scenic, visional, illusionary, illusory, imaginary

21 **seeing**, sighted, eyed, sharp-eyed, lynx-eyed, eagle-eyed, hawk-eyed, gimlet-eyed, Argus-eyed, staring, glaring, goggle-eyed, popeyed, noticing, watching, looking, on the lookout, observant, watchful, vigilant, aware, perceptive, clear-sighted, clear-eyed, far-seeing, far-sighted, perspicacious, discerning, imaginative, visionary

22 **bespectacled**, long-sighted, far-sighted (US), short-sighted, near-sighted (US), four-eyed (Inf)

23 **visible**, perceivable, in view, before one's eyes, perceptible, discernible, detectable, recognizable, apparent, observable, distinct, clear, clear-cut, evident, manifest, plain, obvious, patent, conspicuous, noticeable, watchable, viewable, worth watching, easy on the eye, eye-catching, eye-opening, spectacular

ADVERBS

24 **visually**, optically, by eye, by sight, in sight, within sight, at sight, at first sight, prima facie, eye to eye, eyeball to eyeball (Inf)

25 **visibly**, perceptibly, recognizably, apparently, observably, distinctly, clearly, at a glance, evidently, manifestly, plainly, obviously, patently, conspicuously, noticeably

26 **watchfully**, observantly, vigilantly, sideways, sidelong, glancingly, out of the corner of one's eye

436 Blindness

My darkness has been filled with the light of intelligence, and behold, the outer day-light world was stumbling and groping in social blindness. Helen Keller.

Ask for this great deliverer now, and find him/ Eyeless in Gaza at the mill with slaves. John Milton.

NOUNS

1 **blindness**, sightlessness, eyelessness, lack of sight, stone-blindness, loss of vision, amaurosis, ablepsia, glaucoma, river blindness, onchocerciasis, trachoma, cataract, going blind, darkness, white-out, snow blindness, blackout

2 **poor sight**, failing sight, visual handicap, faulty vision, defective sight, impaired vision, day blindness, hemeralopia, night blindness, nyctalopia, colour-blindness, daltonism, red-blindness, protanopia, deuteranopia, tritanopia, poor vision, amblyopia, dim sight, sand-blindness, purblindness, long sight, long-

sightedness, far sight (US), far-sightedness (US), hypermetropia, presbyopia, short sight, near sight (US), near-sightedness (US), short-sightedness, myopia, astigmatism, tunnel vision, detached retina, squint, strabismus, heterotropia, wandering eye, cast, cockeye (Inf), walleye, divergent strabismus, exotropia, cross-eye, convergent strabismus, esotropia, nystagmus, winking, blinking, nictitation, (eye)tic, eyestrain, double vision, diplopia, seeing double, blurred vision, bleariness, bloodshot eyes, red eyes, eye disease, ophthalmia, ophthalmitis, retinopathy, diabetic retinopathy, conjunctivitis, pink eye

3 **aid for poor sight**, eye hospital, eye clinic, ophthalmology, ophthalmologist, eyewash, eye drops, optometry, optometrist, optician, large-print book, spectacles, glasses, Braille, talking book, guide dog, white stick (or cane), glass eye, artificial eye, blind register, partially sighted register
▶ 435 Vision

4 **blind people**, the blind, the sightless, mole, bat, the visually handicapped, the visually impaired, the partially sighted

5 **visual distortion**, prism, refraction, reflection, optical illusion, distorting mirror, hall of mirrors
▶ 309 Distortion

6 **blinder**, blindfold, blinkers, eyepatch, patch, cover, covering, cloak, screen, smoke, smoke-screen, curtain, blind, eclipse, camouflage, façade
▶ 293 Covering

7 **figurative blindness**, lack of perception, inability to see, blind side, blind flying, fly-by-wire, unawareness, unconcern, disregard, obliviousness, unconsciousness, blind eye, thoughtlessness, lack of consideration, ignorance, invincible ignorance, prejudice, unenlightenment, lack of enlightenment, blind spot, lack of discernment, benightedness
▶ 502 Ignorance, 468 Inattention

ADJECTIVES

8 **blind**, lacking sight, sightless, unsighted, deprived of vision, unseeing, eyeless, amaurotic, glaucomatous, registered blind, visionless, stone-blind, snow-blind, blind as a bat, blind as a mole

9 **weak-sighted**, having poor sight (or vision), visually handicapped, visually impaired, partially sighted, one-eyed, day-blind, hemeralopic, night-blind, nyctalopic, colour-blind, red-blind, protanopic, deuteranopic, tritanopic, amblyopic, dim-sighted, purblind, sand-blind, long-sighted, far-sighted (US), hypermetropic, presbyopic, short-sighted, near-sighted (US), myopic, astigmatic, squinting, stabismic, wall-eyed, cross-eyed, cockeyed (Inf), boss-eyed

(Inf), blinking, winking, nystagmatic, bleary, bleary-eyed, bloodshot, blurry, watery-eyed, red-eyed, seeing double

10 **blinded**, snow-blind, snow-blinded, dazzled, blindfold(ed), blinkered

11 **blinding**, dazzling, bedazzling, stunning, darkening, obscuring, hiding, masking, deceptive, misleading
▶ 539 Deception

12 **blind to**, imperceptive, unaware (of), unconcerned, oblivious (of), unconscious (of), thoughtless, inconsiderate, unobservant, unmindful, ignorant, in the dark, unenlightened, blinkered, undiscerning, benighted

13 **hidden**, dark, obscure, indistinct, camouflaged, invisible, unseen
▶ 531 Concealment

VERBS

14 **be blind**, not see, go blind, lose one's sight, black out, see badly, feel one's way, grope, have defective sight, squint, blink, wink, screw up one's eyes, see double, have something in one's eye, have spots in front of one's eyes, be unable to see straight, be unable to see something under one's nose (or in front of one's eyes), be unable to see the wood for the trees, have a blind spot

15 **blind**, deprive of sight, make blind, strike blind, put (or gouge) someone's eyes out, darken, obscure, blur, eclipse, dazzle, bedazzle, blindfold, blinker, camouflage, mask, screen, deceive, hoodwink

16 **be blind to**, ignore, disregard, overlook, look away, look the other way, drop one's eyes, avert one's gaze (or eyes), shut one's eyes to, turn a blind eye (to), take no notice of, wink at, blink at

ADVERBS

17 **blindly**, blindfold, without looking, by touch, by feel, by ear

18 **blindingly**, dazzlingly

437 Visibility

ADJECTIVES

1 **visible**, seeable, in sight, viewable, in view, in full view, observable, distinguishable, discernible, perceptible, perceivable, discoverable, detectable, above the horizon, noticeable, conspicuous, clear, open, overt, plain, evident, manifest, obvious, patent, unhidden, unconcealed, undisguised, exposed, showing, apparent, distinct, easily distinguished, identifiable, recognizable, unmistakable, public, available, present, concrete, material, tangible, palpable, external, outward, superficial, surface, in focus, visible to the naked eye
▶ 435 Vision, 457 Appearance, 550 Clarity, 544 Identification, 289 Exterior, 294 Uncovering, 530 Disclosure, 367 Material World, 253 Presence

2 **clear**, plain, easy to see, bright, light, signed, signposted, clear-cut, distinct, defined, in focus, sharp, high-definition, open, exposed, exposed to view, uncovered, naked, showy, garish, gaudy, lurid, vivid, brilliant, spectacular, glitzy, glaring, unmissable, eye-catching, remarkable, outstanding, striking, blatant, salient, prominent, stark, crystal-clear, lucid, visual, lit (up), well lit, highlighted, spotlighted, illuminated, picked out, in high relief, in bold relief, on show, on display, high-profile, as clear as day, in front of one's face (*or* eyes), staring one in the face, under one's nose, plain to see, open to view, open to the public, in the public eye, for all to see, plain as a pikestaff, plain as the nose on one's face

▶ *550 Clarity, 526 Display, 811 Showiness, 439 Light, 294 Uncovering, 530 Disclosure, 554 Emphasis*

NOUNS

3 **visibility**, visibleness, eyesight, eyeshot, naked eye, range, horizon, visible horizon, skyline, sightline, line of sight, observability, discernibility, perceptibility, perceivability, detectability, identifiability, recognizability, distinctness, conspicuousness, overtness, evidence, availability, presence, tangibility, lack of concealment, revelation

▶ *435 Vision, 457 Appearance, 544 Identification, 253 Presence, 294 Uncovering, 530 Disclosure*

4 **clarity**, clearness, plainness, brightness, brilliance, definition, focus, sharpness, ease of viewing, publicity, exposure, high profile, prominence, starkness, obviousness, blatancy, showiness, vividness, gaudiness, glitz

▶ *550 Clarity, 811 Showiness*

5 **manifestation**, display, demonstration, exposition, exhibition, show, performance, exposure, pointing out

▶ *526 Display, 51 Performing Arts*

6 **visible thing**, sight, field of vision, field of view, light, visible radiation, outside, exterior, surface, skin, façade, feature, badge, insignia, packaging, sign, signpost, signboard, signal, landmark, outcrop, illustration, high relief, bold relief, exhibit, attraction, cynosure

▶ *289 Exterior, 544 Identification, 457 Appearance*

7 **that which makes visible**, visual aid, light, illumination, spotlight, highlighter, underlining, pointer, sign, signpost, high relief, bold relief, fluorescent paint, fluorescent clothing, reflector, shop window, showcase, rangefinder, optical instrument, spectacles, telescope, microscope, x-rays

▶ *439 Light, 435 Vision, 554 Emphasis, 261 Expansion, 60 Medicine*

VERBS

8 **be visible**, be seen, show, stand out, stick out, be obvious, have a high profile, hit one in the eye, stare one in the face, strike one in the face (*or* eye), stick out like a sore thumb (Inf)

▶ *435 Vision, 811 Showiness*

9 **appear**, materialize, become visible, manifest (itself), come to light, crop up, open (out), meet the eye, show up, turn up, show through, shine through, come to the surface, loom, heave in sight, come over the horizon, come into focus, come out from the woodwork, make an entrance, put in an appearance, pop up (Inf), pop out (Inf)

▶ *457 Appearance, 530 Disclosure, 344 Arrival, 346 Entry*

10 **make visible**, focus, focus on, show, reveal, disclose, demonstrate, manifest, put on view, display, put on display, exhibit, signal, indicate, sign, signpost, point out, open (up), bring to light, uncover, unwrap, expose, illuminate, light (up), unmask, lay bare, raise the curtain on, take the lid off, spotlight, highlight, underline, clarify, elucidate, illustrate, keep sight of, keep in sight, keep in view, not let out of one's sight

▶ *530 Disclosure, 294 Uncovering, 544 Identification, 439 Light, 550 Clarity*

ADVERBS

11 **visibly**, in sight, in view, into sight, into view, out of hiding, outward, outwardly, externally, superficially, on the surface, apparently, ostensibly, to all appearances, evidently, seemingly, in public, openly, in plain view, clearly, plainly, distinctly, obviously, patently, blatantly, manifestly, conspicuously, noticeably, perceptibly, discernibly

438   Invisibility

ADJECTIVES

1 **invisible**, unable to be seen, unseeable, out of sight, unperceivable, imperceptible, indistinguishable, indiscernible, unnoticeable, undetectable, unrecognizable, unidentifiable, unrecognized, unidentified, unmarked, not signposted, not apparent, unapparent, inappreciable, immaterial, insubstantial, unsubstantial, transparent, unseen, unsighted, unobserved, unwitnessed, unnoticed, unperceived, eclipsed, latent, buried, submerged, lurking, in ambush, over the horizon, below the horizon, out of range, out of sight, out of mind

▶ *368 Nonmaterial World, 442 Transparency, 527 Latency, 263 Distance*

2 **difficult to see**, partly visible, half-seen, inconspicuous, low-profile, very small, infinitesimal, microscopic, subliminal, distant, remote, lost in the distance, dark, darkened, faint, pale, indefinite, unclear, indistinct, unfocused, undefined, blurred, blurry, bleared, bleary, hazy, misty, foggy, filmy, shadowy, obscured, dim, low-definition, out of focus,

ill-defined, fuzzy, clear as mud (Sl)

▶ *441 Dimness, 440 Darkness, 551 Obscurity, 443 Opaqueness*

3 private, internal, inward, hidden, concealed, covert, secret, clandestine, disguised, camouflaged, screened, masked, covered, veiled, recondite, under wraps, dark, blacked out, obscure, obscured, obstructed, behind the scenes, backstage, in camera

▶ *531 Concealment, 529 Secrecy, 440 Darkness, 293 Covering, 551 Obscurity*

NOUNS

4 invisibility, disappearance, vanishing, nonappearance, nonpresence, absence, transparency, insubstantiality, darkness, blackness, obscurity, poor visibility, bad visibility, haze, haziness, mist, mistiness, fog, fogginess, fuzziness, indistinctness, faintness, paleness, low definition, poor definition, imperceptibility, indistinguishability, indiscernibility, undetectability, zero visibility, low profile, latency, concealment, hiding, secrecy, privacy

▶ *458 Disappearance, 254 Absence, 443 Opaqueness, 441 Dimness, 531 Concealment, 529 Secrecy*

5 invisible thing, the unseen, vanisher, dark corner, blind corner, blind spot, black hole, hidden camera, secret surveillance system, vanishing cream, black ice, invisible ink, the invisible man, back-room boys (*or* girls), spirit world, the fourth dimension, invisible imports (*or* exports), more than meets the eye, hide-and-seek, blind man's buff

▶ *368 Nonmaterial World*

6 that which makes invisible, darkness, night, mist, fog, peasouper, haze, smoke, smokescreen, film, membrane, muddy waters, black light, eraser, rubber, correction fluid, Tippex (Tm), masking tape, eclipse, distance, remoteness, horizon, edge of sight, vanishing point, veil, yashmak, chador, purdah, mask, domino, disguise, front, camouflage, protective colouring, shroud, curtain, blind, shade, shutter, screen, partition, brick wall, blank wall, plain wrapper, hide, hiding place, hideyhole, interference, jamming, snow (Inf)

▶ *440 Darkness, 441 Dimness, 443 Opaqueness, 546 Obliteration, 531 Concealment, 293 Covering*

VERBS

7 become invisible, disappear, vanish, fade, fade away, blur, dim, darken, escape notice, hide, retreat, go into purdah, go into hiding, play hide-and-seek, lurk, lie low, keep one's head down, keep a low profile, blend into the background, sink without trace, lose sight of, cease to see, see through a glass darkly, now you see it now you don't

▶ *458 Disappearance, 441 Dimness, 531 Concealment*

8 make invisible, put out of sight, hide, hide away, bury, conceal, mask, screen, cloak, veil, eclipse, cover (up), put under wraps, obscure, disguise, erase, delete, rub out, white out, Tippex (Tm), black out, blank out, blur, dim, darken, put a lid on, hide under a bushel, sweep under the carpet

▶ *531 Concealment, 293 Covering, 546 Obliteration, 440 Darkness, 551 Obscurity*

ADVERBS

9 invisibly, out of view, out of sight, out of range, imperceptibly, indistinguishably, indiscernibly, unnoticeably, unrecognizably, unidentifiably, sight unseen, under plain cover, in hiding, behind the scenes, backstage, in camera, in private, secretly, under cover, internally, inwardly, inwards, underneath, indistinctly, dimly, indefinitely, hazily, on the blind side

439 Light

NOUNS

1 light, luminosity, luminousness, lucency, phosphorescence, fluorescence, luminescence, illumination, candescence, incandescence, lustre, radiance, radiation, refulgence, splendour, resplendence, brightness, brilliance, vividness, visible radiation, light ray, light wave, ray, beam, rays of the sun, sunlight, sunbeam, electromagnetic radiation, ultraviolet light, infrared radiation, photon, monochromatic light, coherent light, visible spectrum

▶ *56 Physics, 435 Vision, 437 Visibility*

2 quality of light, soft light, glow, shimmer, shimmering, gleam, glint, glister, sheen, gloss, patina, polish, lustre, iridescence, opalescence, shine, shininess, glassiness, glistening, shining, beam, bright light, brightness, effulgence, glare, dazzle, flare, brilliance, sparkle, twinkle, twinkling, scintillation, glitter, spangle, tinsel, sequin, diamanté, Lurex (Tm), cloth of gold, spark, flash, coruscation, flashing, flicker, flickering

3 lightening, illumination, making light, giving light, shedding light, brightening, bleaching, peroxide, overexposure

▶ *204 Daytime*

4 natural light, daylight, sun, sunlight, sunshine, rays of the sun, sunbeam, moon, moonlight, moonshine, moonbeam, moonrise, full moon, harvest moon, star, starlight, starshine, nova, supernova, Pole Star, North Star, Polaris, Star of Bethlehem, Milky Way, meteor, falling star, shooting star, comet, Halley's comet, northern lights, aurora borealis, southern lights, aurora australis, merry dancers, streamers, *gegenschein* (Ger), counterglow, zodiacal light, earthshine, lightning, sheet (*or* forked *or*

ball) lightning, summer lightning, flash, thunderbolt, streak

▶ *53 Astronomy, Astronautics, and Rocketry, 54 Earth Science, 55 Meteorology and Climatology*

5 **incandescent light**, artificial light, lightsource, lighting, lamp, lamplight, candle, candlelight, tallow candle, wax candle, cake candle, church candle, rush light, dip, wick, candlestick, candleholder, candelabrum, candelabra, oil lamp, paraffin lamp, hurricane lamp, spirit lamp, acetylene lamp, gaslamp, gaslight, gas mantle, gas jet, gasolier

6 **electric light**, light bulb, bulb, mushroom bulb, pearl bulb, clear bulb, light socket, lampholder, ceiling rose, light switch, light fitting, ceiling light, wall light, sconce, standard lamp, table lamp, bedside lamp, reading lamp, desk lamp, Anglepoise (Tm), strip light, fluorescent light, halogen light, quartz–iodine light, sun lamp, sunray lamp, stroboscope, strobe lighting, searchlight, floodlight, spotlight, limelight, klieg light, footlights, house lights, one's name in lights, neon light, neon lighting, illuminated sign, fairy lights, Christmas tree lights, headlight, headlamp, dipped headlights, dimmed headlights, dims (US inf), sidelight, parking light, rear light, tail light, brake light, reversing light, indicator light, indicator, trafficator, fog lamp, interior light, courtesy light, lighting-up time, streetlight, streetlamp, mercury-vapour lamp, sodium lamp, lamppost, lamp-standard, traffic lights, traffic signals, red light, amber light, green light, stop light, pedestrian lights, green (*or* red) man, Belisha beacon, beacon, lighthouse, pharos, flashing light, occulting light, lightship, light buoy, navigation lights, masthead light, stern light, anchor light, riding lights, running lights, aviation beacon, flare path, approach light, runway lights, light signal, warning light, winker (Inf)

▶ *70 Transport, 636 Warning*

7 **lantern**, horn lantern, dark lantern, link, link-boy, lamplighter, torch, torchlight, flambeau, brand, flashlight (US), pocket torch, pumpkin lantern, turnip lantern, Chinese lantern, nightlight, miner's lamp, safety lamp, Davy lamp, flashlamp, flashgun, flashbulb, photoflood, arc lamp

▶ *66 Photography, 56 Physics*

8 **fire**, flame, firelight, embers, glow, red glow, red heat, white heat, blaze, conflagration, wildfire, fireball, bonfire, watch fire, bale-fire, signal fire, beacon, spill, match, friction match, vesta, lucifer, safety match, taper, firelighter, lighter, spark, scintilla, ignition, pyrophoric alloy, fireworks, pyrotechnics, Bengal light, sparkler, Roman candle, Catherine wheel, pinwheel, banger, jumping jack,

rocket, Very light, flare

▶ *408 Heat, 410 Fuel*

9 **firefly**, glow-worm, corposant, St Elmo's fire, will-o'-the-wisp, Jack-o'-lantern, marshlight, corpse candle, ignis fatuus

10 **window**, windowpane, skylight, fanlight, rose window, stained glass, clear glass, frosted glass, bad light, poor light, good light, north light

▶ *442 Transparency, 322 Opening, 443 Opaqueness*

11 **photoelectricity**, photoemission, photoconduction, photosensor, photometer, photoelectric cell, photosensitivity, exposure meter, LED (light-emitting diode), LCD (liquid-crystal display), light pen, solar energy

12 **highlight**, downlight, uplighting, uplighter, reflection, chiaroscuro, black-and-white, halftone, light show, *son et lumière* (Fr), laser, laser show, holography, hologram, halo, aureole, gloriole, nimbus, corona, rainbow, spectrum

▶ *50 Painting and Sculpture, 444 Colour*

13 **enlightenment**, elucidation, illumination, clarification, clarity, knowledge, understanding, comprehension, insight, clue, guiding star, leading light, star, shining light, Illuminati

▶ *550 Clarity, 501 Knowledge, 459 Intellect*

14 **light colour**, pale colour, lightness, colourlessness, paleness, pallor, pastiness, blondness, fairness, pastel colour, cream, ivory, off-white

▶ *446 Whiteness, 445 Colourlessness*

ADJECTIVES

15 **lucent**, luminous, radiant, refulgent, glowing, glimmering, burning, candescent, incandescent, aglow, phosphorescent, fluorescent, shining, lambent, flickering, flickery, blinking, winking, flashing, occulting, stroboscopic, lighting, lightening, illuminating, shedding light on, brightening, beaming

▶ *435 Vision, 437 Visibility*

16 **bright**, vivid, brilliant, flamboyant, garish, lurid, flashy, effulgent, splendid, resplendent, kaleidoscopic, shining, dazzling, fluorescent, Day-Glo (Tm), blinding, glaring, flashing, sparking, coruscating, glinting, sparkling, scintillating, twinkling, glittering, glittery, tinselly, spangly, sequined, diamanté, Lurex (Tm), fiery, flaming, aflame, alight, blazing, ablaze, flaring

▶ *811 Showiness, 137 Visibility, 408 Heat*

17 **lustrous**, glossy, gleaming, shiny, polished, burnished, *glacé* (Fr), glassy, glistening, shimmering, shimmery, opalescent, iridescent, pearly, pearlized, haloed

18 **lit**, illuminated, lightened, brightened, lit up, well-lit, light, bright, lamplit, candlelit, torchlit, firelit, spotlit, floodlit, flashlit, highlighted, sunlit, starlit, moonlit

19 **sunny**, daylight, light as day, sunshiny, cloudless, unclouded, clear, daylight-saving

20 **starry**, starbright, star-spangled, star-studded

21 **light**, lightish, pale, light-coloured, pastel, cream-coloured, ivory, pallid, pasty, colourless, white, whitish, albino, blond, blonde, fair, flaxen, tow-headed, faded, bleached, peroxided, lightened, overexposed

▶ *446 Whiteness, 445 Colourlessness*

22 **enlightened**, elucidated, clarified, (crystal) clear, lucid, illuminated, bright, brilliant, intelligent, sparky (Inf)

▶ *550 Clarity, 459 Intellect*

23 **photoelectric**, photoconductive, photoemissive, photometric, photosensitive, light-sensitive, phototropic, photophobic, spectral, photic, optic

▶ *66 Photography, 56 Physics*

VERBS

24 **light**, give light, illuminate, illumine, light up, lighten, brighten, switch (*or* turn *or* put) on a light, switch on, turn on, put on, strike a light, strike, ignite, set alight, kindle, fire, set fire to, floodlight, spotlight, highlight, irradiate, dazzle, bedazzle, blind

▶ *408 Heat*

25 **light up**, gleam, glint, glance, glisten, glimmer, blink, wink, flicker, twinkle, sparkle, spark, flash, coruscate, scintillate, glitter, spangle, shine, glow, glare, flare, flare up, flame, blaze, burn, incandesce, radiate, radiate light, beam, fluoresce, phosphoresce, iridesce

26 **grow light**, get light, dawn, break, lighten, brighten

27 **glaze**, polish, burnish, rub up, take a shine, shine like a new pin, reflect, refract

28 **bleach**, lighten, whiten, dye, peroxide, overexpose, fade, pale, grow pale, lose colour, blench, blanch

▶ *446 Whiteness, 445 Colourlessness*

29 **clarify**, elucidate, throw light on, shed light on, draw back the curtains, open the shutters, roll up the blind

ADVERBS

30 **lightly**, brightly, palely, radiantly, incandescently, gleamingly, twinklingly, scintillatingly, glowingly, luminously, illuminatingly, dazzlingly, brilliantly, vividly, flamboyantly, at first light, by day, by daylight, by artificial light

440 Darkness

NOUNS

1 **darkness**, dark, lack of light, sunlessness, dimness, shadow, shadows, shade, gloom, gloominess, murk, murkiness, lividness, leadenness, sombreness, drabness, obscurity, bad light, poor light, twilight, blindness, blackout, eclipse, total eclipse, eclipse of the sun, solar eclipse, eclipse of the moon, lunar eclipse, blackness, pitch-darkness, Stygian gloom, night-blindness, darkest hour

▶ *447 Blackness, 441 Dimness, 551 Obscurity, 438 Invisibility, 436 Blindness, 205 Night-Time, 531 Concealment, 293 Covering, 439 Light, 371 Density, 295 Dress*

2 **darkening**, dimming, turning the lights down (*or* off *or* out), extinguishment, obscuration, obfuscation, occultation, underexposure, blackening, blackout, eclipse, fadeout, lights out, power cut, dimmer switch, dip switch, dipper, cut-out, shading, shading-in, hatching, cross-hatching, benday

▶ *439 Light, 50 Painting and Sculpture*

3 **dark colour**, deep colour, dark hair, brunette, dark skin, swarthiness, dark brown, slate grey, aubergine, navy blue, midnight blue, black, blackness, dirt, grime, stain, drabness

▶ *444 Colour, 447 Blackness, 449 Brownness, 448 Greyness, 454 Blueness, 455 Purpleness, 622 Dirtiness*

4 **dark thing**, dark glasses, dark lantern, cloud, thundercloud, soot, smut, ink, jet, obsidian, pitch, raven, ebony, darkroom, dungeon, cellar, dark clothes, business suit, man's evening dress, little black dress, mourning clothes, black, silhouette, shadow, the man in black, dark star, dark matter

▶ *447 Blackness, 66 Photography, 295 Dress*

5 **figurative dark thing**, Dark Ages, Darkest Africa, Dark Continent, dark horse

6 **shade**, parasol, beach umbrella, sunshade, awning, smoked glass, eyeshade, sun visor, dark glasses, sunglasses, sun-hat, shutters, curtain, blind, roller blind, Venetian blind, festoon blind, blackout, blindfold, hood, shroud, cover, lid, shades (Sl)

▶ *293 Covering, 632 Safety, 443 Opaqueness*

7 **spiritual darkness**, dark powers, black magic, malignity, evil, ignorance, blindness, oblivion, dejection, depression, despair, gloom, murk, obscurity, shadow, sombreness, grimness, deadness

▶ *529 Secrecy, 862 Evil, 502 Ignorance, 551 Obscurity, 512 Oblivion, 770 Sorrow, 436 Blindness*

ADJECTIVES

8 **dark**, unlit, unlighted, unilluminated, darkish, dim, badly lit, ill-lit, underexposed, lighttight, lightproof, lightless, sunless, moonless, starless, pitch-dark, shady, shaded, umbrageous, overcast, cloudy, stormy, thundery, louring (*or* lowering), dusky, gloomy, dingy, murky, tenebrous, black, Stygian, Cimmerian, nocturnal

▶ *441 Dimness, 439 Light, 443 Opaqueness*

9 **darkening**, extinguishing, shading, shadowing, screening, obscuring, dimming, dipping, dyeing, casting a shadow

▶ *531 Concealment, 67 Fabrics and Dyeing, 293 Covering*

10 **dark-coloured**, dark, deep-coloured, deep, subfusc, dark-haired, brunette, dark-skinned, swarthy, black-skinned, dusky, darkling, black, pitch-black, pitchy, jet-black, inky, black as ink, black as night, ebony, melanic, melanous, sable, livid, leaden, grimy, dirty, stained, drab, funereal
▶ *447 Blackness, 622 Dirtiness*

11 **benighted**, dismal, gloomy, cheerless, depressed, dejected, mournful, clouded, murky, wicked, evil, ominous, menacing, threatening, sinister, shadowy, shady, sombre, grim, forbidding, unenlightened, ignorant, blind, oblivious, obfuscated, obscure, cryptic, mysterious, enigmatic, mystic, inscrutable, secret, arcane, hidden, occult, esoteric
▶ *770 Sorrow, 862 Evil, 551 Obscurity, 502 Ignorance, 529 Secrecy, 531 Concealment, 11 Occultism*

VERBS

12 **be dark**, lack light, wear mourning, lurk in the shadows

13 **become dark**, darken, deepen, blacken, grow dark, cloud over, look like rain, lour (*or* lower), dim, be extinguished, go out, night falls, the sun sets (*or goes down*), the light fails
▶ *447 Blackness, 441 Dimness*

14 **make dark**, darken, obscure, obfuscate, turn (*or switch*) the lights out (*or off*), extinguish, douse, quench, snuff, snuff out, blow out (the candle), dim, dip, shade, shadow, adumbrate, overshadow, cast a shadow over, put in the shade, occult, eclipse, shutter, close the shutters, draw the curtains, pull down the blind, black out, block out light, blot out light, underexpose, blindfold, hood, cover (over), veil, shroud, silhouette, shade in, hatch, crosshatch, deject, depress, keep dark, keep in the dark
▶ *447 Blackness, 441 Dimness, 551 Obscurity, 293 Covering, 531 Concealment, 50 Painting and Sculpture, 770 Sorrow, 529 Secrecy*

ADVERBS

15 **darkly**, dimly, obscurely, blackly, at nightfall, by night, in the night, at midnight, nocturnally, in the dark, in the shade, shadily, gloomily, mournfully, sombrely, grimly, ominously, mysteriously, inscrutably

441 Dimness

NOUNS

1 **dimness**, faintness, paleness, half-light, semi-darkness, twilight, gloaming, evening light, late evening, dusk, duskiness, first light, early morning, thick cloud, waning of the moon, partial eclipse, penumbra, oblique light, bad light, poor light, shadiness, shade, shadow, dim lighting, romantic lighting, dimmed lights, dipped lights, sidelights, lampshade, light filter, dimmer switch
▶ *440 Darkness, 439 Light, 204 Daytime, 205 Night-Time*

2 **murk**, murkiness, fog, fogginess, dense fog, peasouper, smog, mist, mistiness, sea mist, haar, fret vapour, condensation, steam, miasma, exhalation, smoke, cloudiness, haze, haziness, dusty air, sandstorm, low visibility, poor visibility, impaired visibility, obscurity, distance, remoteness, vagueness, indistinctness, low definition, soft focus, blur, blurriness, fuzziness, bleariness, poor sight, cataract, dullness, matt finish, tarnish, greyness, dinginess, drabness, opaqueness, semitransparency, smoked glass, frosted glass, film, filminess, veil, muslin, sheer fabric
▶ *443 Opaqueness, 551 Obscurity, 437 Visibility, 438 Invisibility, 435 Vision, 436 Blindness, 448 Greyness*

3 **dimming**, making dim, becoming dim, clouding over, shading, shadowing, overshadowing, blackening

4 **stupidity**, dimness, dim-wittedness, thickness, denseness, lack of intelligence, obtuseness
▶ *508 Folly, 460 Lack of Intellect*

ADJECTIVES

5 **dim**, half-lit, half-dark, semidark, twilit, crepuscular, waning, dimly lit, ill-lit, dark, darkish, sombre, livid, leaden, dusky, grey, dull, overcast, cloudy, louring (*or* lowering), stormy, sunless, shady, shadowy, tenebrous
▶ *440 Darkness, 448 Greyness*

6 **murky**, foggy, smoggy, smog-laden, thick, dusty, smoky, smoke-laden, smoke-filled, misty, steamy, steamed up, miasmal, miasmic, cloudy, nebulous, hazy, distant, remote, vague, indistinct, unclear, low-definition, soft-focus, blurred, blurry, fuzzy, blear, bleary, bleared, muzzy, opaque, smoked, frosted, milky, veiled, filmy, obscured, obscure, shadowy, ill-defined, indistinguishable, faint, feeble, weak, muted, diffused, pale, white, clear as mud (Inf)
▶ *443 Opaqueness, 551 Obscurity, 446 Whiteness*

7 **dimmed**, clouded, dull, dulled, faded, drab, dingy, gloomy, lacklustre, lustreless, matt, unpolished, tarnished, rusty, dusty, dirty
▶ *622 Dirtiness*

8 **stupid**, dim, dull, dense, thick, unintelligent, obtuse, doltish, dim-witted
▶ *160 Lack of Intellect, 508 Folly*

VERBS

9 **be dim**, become dim, grow dim, darken, cloud over, film over, glaze over, mist over, steam up, lour (*or* lower), become grey, pale, grow pale (*or faint*), wane, fade, fade out, gutter
▶ *440 Darkness, 448 Greyness, 443 Opaqueness*

10 **make dim**, bedim, fade, cloud, becloud, fog,

befog, blur, blear, mist, film, smear, glaze, darken, lower (the lights), turn (the lights) down, dip, shade, shadow, cast a shadow, obscure, obfuscate, veil, shroud

▶ *551 Obscurity, 443 Opaqueness, 531 Concealment*

11 **tarnish**, rust, dull, lose (its) shine, deaden, tone down, dirty, sully, muddy

▶ *622 Dirtiness*

ADVERBS

12 **dimly**, cloudily, hazily, foggily, mistily, blearily, muzzily, obscurely, darkly, vaguely, indistinctly, faintly, dingily, drably, in the twilight, in the gloaming, through a glass darkly

442 Transparency

ADJECTIVES

1 **transparent**, clear, limpid, pellucid, colourless, crystal, crystalline, crystal-clear, glassy, vitreous, glass-like, hyaline, transpicuous, dioptric, refractive, nonreflective, watery, liquid, clarified, pure, cloudless, unclouded, unobstructed, as clear as crystal, clear as air

▶ *438 Invisibility, 389 Water, 390 Air, 134 Purity, 439 Light, 621 Cleanness, 445 Colourlessness*

2 **translucent**, see-through, revealing, diaphanous, lucent, gauzy, open-textured, sheer, thin, flimsy, filmy, fine, insubstantial, vaporous

▶ *274 Thinness, 100 Nonexistence*

3 **semitransparent**, translucent, milky, misty, smoky, smoked, tinted, stained, frosted, pearly, opalescent, opaline, semiopaque

▶ *443 Opaqueness*

4 **easily seen through**, open, guileless, ingenuous, direct, forthright, straightforward, frank, candid, open-hearted, undisguised, evident, obvious, patent, easily detected, manifest, plain, unambiguous, lucid

▶ *550 Clarity, 437 Visibility, 522 Intelligibility, 530 Disclosure*

NOUNS

5 **transparency**, clarity, clearness, limpidity, limpidness, pellucidity, pellucidness, colourlessness, glassiness, vitreousness, vitreosity, crystallinity, wateriness, purity, cleanness, unobstructed view, cloudlessness

▶ *438 Invisibility, 389 Water, 134 Purity, 621 Cleanness*

6 **translucency**, translucence, diaphanousness, gauziness, open texture, sheerness, thinness, flimsiness, filminess, fineness, insubstantiality, vaporousness

▶ *274 Thinness, 100 Nonexistence*

7 **semitransparency**, translucency, milkiness, pearliness, mistiness, smokiness, opalescence

▶ *443 Opaqueness*

8 **transparent thing**, water, ice, vapour, air, glass, window, shop window, showcase, glass

case, display case, goldfish bowl, glasshouse, greenhouse, conservatory, watch glass, lens, eyeglass, spectacles, glasses, crystal ball, hyalite, hyalin, clear varnish, Perspex (Tm), Plexiglass (US trademark), Cellophane (Tm), plastic wrap, clingfilm, bubble pack, blister pack, window envelope, slide, transparency, negative, film, gossamer, sheer fabric, muslin, scrim, gauze, chiffon, organdie, organza, tiffany, voile, net, lace, smoke, mist, haze

▶ *322 Opening, 435 Vision, 443 Opaqueness*

9 **glass**, clear glass, crystal, crystal glass, rock crystal, lead glass, lead crystal, bottle glass, crown glass, flint glass, plate glass, sheet glass, window glass, bullet-proof glass, laminated glass, safety glass, toughened glass, reinforced glass, opal glass, frosted glass, ground glass, stained glass, fibreglass, quartz glass, glassware, window, windowpane, pane, window light, light, windshield, windscreen, two-way mirror

▶ *439 Light, 322 Opening*

10 **openness**, apparentness, obviousness, plainness, lucidity, guilelessness, ingenuousness, straightforwardness, forthrightness, frankness, open-heartedness

▶ *437 Visibility, 530 Disclosure, 550 Clarity, 522 Intelligibility*

VERBS

11 **be transparent**, reveal, show through, shine through, transmit light, become transparent, crystallize, liquefy, vaporize

12 **make transparent**, crystallize, purify, clarify, refine, brighten, wipe, clean, cleanse, open, open out, demist, uncloud, see through, see through a brick wall, see round corners, have x-ray eyes (Inf)

▶ *134 Purity, 621 Cleanness*

ADVERBS

13 **transparently**, clearly, limpidly, pellucidly, translucently, diaphanously, flimsily, insubstantially, mistily, smokily, openly, directly, obviously, plainly

443 Opaqueness

ADJECTIVES

1 **opaque**, nontransparent, nontranslucent, dense, thick, solid, impenetrable, impermeable, impervious, light-tight, lightproof, dark, black, windowless, blank, covered, coated

▶ *371 Density, 273 Thickness, 440 Darkness, 447 Blackness, 293 Covering*

2 **shady**, obscure, dark, murky, dirty, grimy, dusty, dull, lustreless, matt, muddy, muddied, turbid, cloudy, milky, fuzzy, blurred, vague, dim, hazy, smoky, foggy, misty, misted, steamed up, clouded, obfuscated, opaline, frosted, smoked, filmy, semiopaque

▶ *440 Darkness, 622 Dirtiness, 441 Dimness, 442 Transparency, 551 Obscurity*

3 **mirror-like**, mirrored, reflecting, reflective, mirroring, shiny, glassy
▶ *56 Physics*

4 **inscrutable**, baffling, mystifying, cryptic, enigmatic, arcane, recondite, unclear, ambiguous, indefinite, unknowable, unfathomable, unintelligible, clear as mud (Inf)
▶ *531 Concealment, 523 Unintelligibility, 529 Secrecy*

5 **unintelligent**, dim, dim-witted, stupid, dense, thick, thickheaded, dull, dull-witted, obtuse, doltish, stolid, having a closed mind, not open to new ideas, thick as a plank (*or* two short planks) (Sl)

NOUNS

6 **opaqueness**, opacity, filminess, density, thickness, solidity, impenetrability, impermeability, imperviousness, darkness, blackness, murkiness, dirtiness, dullness, muddiness, turbidity, cloudiness, milkiness, fuzziness, dimness, haziness, fogginess, obfuscation, reflection, mirroring
▶ *371 Density, 273 Thickness, 440 Darkness, 447 Blackness, 622 Dirtiness, 441 Dimness, 442 Transparency, 56 Physics*

7 **opaque thing**, brick wall, muddy water, haze, mist, film, steam, smoke, cloud, fog, peasouper, blizzard, dust storm, sandstorm, smokescreen, frosted glass, ground glass, screen, curtain, drapes (US), blind, shutter
▶ *441 Dimness, 531 Concealment*

8 **obscurity**, inscrutability, abstruseness, ambiguity, unclearness, unintelligibility, opacity
▶ *551 Obscurity, 523 Unintelligibility*

9 **stupidity**, thickheadedness, stolidity, dull-wittedness, hebetude
▶ *460 Lack of Intellect*

VERBS

10 **be opaque**, become opaque, cloud over, steam up, mist, fog, thicken

11 **make opaque**, thicken, muddy, stir up, cloud, darken, dim, frost, smoke, devitrify, screen, cover, coat, obfuscate, obscure
▶ *273 Thickness, 440 Darkness, 441 Dimness, 293 Covering*

12 **obscure**, mystify, puzzle, baffle, perplex
▶ *551 Obscurity, 523 Unintelligibility*

ADVERBS

13 **opaquely**, densely, solidly, impenetrably, impermeably, imperviously, obscurely, cloudily, foggily, mistily, inscrutably, cryptically, ambiguously, unintelligibly, stupidly, stolidly

444 Colour

NOUNS

1 **colour**, colouring, coloration, biological coloration, pigmentation, monochrome, spectral colour, primary colour, primary triads, secondary colour, secondary triads, natural colour, complementary colour, neutral colour, heraldic colour, chromatic colour, chromaticism, chromatism, chromatic aberration, colour vision, colour perception, colour-blindness
▶ *446 Whiteness, 447 Blackness, 448 Greyness, 449 Brownness, 450 Redness, 451 Orangeness, 452 Yellowness, 453 Greenness, 454 Blueness, 455 Purpleness*

2 **colourfulness**, spectrum, rainbow, prism, refracted colour, range of colour, variegation, multicolour, polychrome, polychromatism, riot of colour, splash of colour, colour disk, colour wheel, colour circle, colour scheme, colour harmony, colour coordination, colour chart, pigment chart, colour code, colourcast
▶ *456 Variegation*

3 **hue**, colour temperature, warm hue, cool hue, chroma, chromaticity, saturation, purity, colour quality, tone, value, tint, tincture, tinge, shade, cast, darkness, loudness, intensity, brilliance, luminosity, softness, warmth, dullness, deadness, paleness, faded hue, discoloration, patina, half-tone, half-light, mezzotint
▶ *439 Light*

4 **pigment**, colorant, staining pigment, organic pigment, inorganic pigment, opaque pigment, semi-transparent pigment, transparent pigment, metallic pigment, colouring, colouring matter, additive colour, subtractive colour, artificial colouring, dye, dyestuff, stain, fast dye, natural dye, vegetable dye, artificial dye, synthetic dye, aniline, red dye, cochineal, grain, purple dye, indigo, madder, blue dye, woad, tint, paint, varnish, lacquer, enamel, glaze, luminous glaze, wash, colourwash, whitewash, distemper, fixative, mordant, colourfastness

5 **paint**, medium, emulsion paint, gloss paint, undercoat, primer, oil paints, acrylic paints, gouache, poster paint, watercolours, watercolour pigments, artist colours, basic palette, standard palette, expanded palette, coloured pencil, coloured crayon, coloured chalk, coloured paper, art equipment, art supplies
▶ *50 Painting and Sculpture*

6 **painter**, colourist, watercolourist, chromatist, chromatic painter, colour-field painter, colour photographer, chromolithographer, colour coordinator

7 **colour painting**, chromatic painting, colour-field painting, colour photography, colour film, colour slides, colour transparencies, colour negative, colour prints, colour printing, colour reproduction, colour filter, colourization, chromolithography, Technicolor (Tm)
▶ *50 Painting and Sculpture, 66 Photography*

8 **chromatics**, chromatology, science of colour, colour theory, colorimetry, spectrum analysis, spectrography, spectrophotometry, spectroscope, chromascope, colorimeter, spec-

trometer, tintometer, spectrophotometer, spectrograph, chromaticity chart, chromaticity diagram

9 **complexion**, natural colour, healthy hue, flush, blush, glow, rosy cheeks, ruddiness, sickly hue, paleness, pallor, cosmetics, make-up, rouge, blusher, lipstick, eye-shadow, war paint (Sl)
▶ *791 Beautification, 623 Health, 624 Ill Health*

ADJECTIVES

10 **coloured**, in colour, in Technicolor (Tm), painted, pigmented, stained, dyed, tinted, tinct, tinged, toned, shaded, technicoloured, colourized, multicoloured, many-coloured, polychrome, polychromatic, variegated, kaleidoscopic, prismatic, spectroscopic, chromatic, monochromatic, colourable, colorific, tinctorial, colourfast, fast, unfading, constant

11 **colourful**, full-coloured, uniform, matching, agreeing, harmonious, toning, intense, strong, emphatic, florid, high-coloured, deep, deep-coloured, rich, warm, glowing, bright, brilliant, vivid, gay
▶ *439 Light, 116 Accord*

12 **gaudy**, garish, overstated, showy, flashy, lurid, loud, glaring, flaring, flaunting, spectacular, clashing, disagreeing, discordant, screaming, shrieking, harsh, stark, raw, crude
▶ *811 Showiness, 434 Dissonance*

13 **soft-hued**, soft, quiet, understated, mellow, delicate, refined, discreet, whitish, pearly, creamy, light, pale, pastel, muted, dull, flat, matt, dead, simple, plain, sober, sombre, dark, drab, dingy, black, faded, discoloured, patinated, weathered
▶ *446 Whiteness, 440 Darkness*

14 **chromolithographic**, colorimetric, spectrophotometric, spectrographic, chromatological, photochromic, calorochromic

VERBS

15 **colour**, colour in, paint, watercolour, crayon, colour print, colourize, variegate, pigment, stain, dye, tie-dye, imbue, imbrue, tint, tincture, tinge, tone, shade, wash, colourwash, distemper, lacquer, enamel, coat, discolour, fade, weather, mellow, tone down, whiten, whitewash, silver, yellow, gild, redden, rouge, tan, darken, blacken, brighten, illuminate, emblazon

16 **make up**, powder, rouge, flush, blush, redden, glow, pale
▶ *791 Beautification*

17 **colourcast**, transmit colour

ADVERBS

18 **colourfully**, colouristically, brightly, brilliantly, gaudily, garishly, polychromatically, in technicolour

445 Colourlessness

NOUNS

1 **colourlessness**, achromatism, achromatic-ity, neutral hue, decoloration, decolorization, etiolation, bleaching, blanching, fading, weathering, whitening, whiteness, neutral tint

2 **paleness**, pallor, pallidity, lightness, faintness, anaemia, bloodlessness, albinism, albinoism, pigment deficiency

3 **pen-and-ink sketch**, black-and-white drawing, overexposed photograph, overexposed negative, overexposure, underexposed photograph, underexposed negative, underexposure, black-and-white photograph, black-and-white print

4 **colour remover,** bleacher, bleach, bleaching powder, blancher, whitener, decolorant, hydrogen peroxide, peroxide, lime, chloride of lime, chlorinated lime

VERBS

5 **lose colour**, pale, fade, run, bleach, blanch, whiten, come out in the wash, turn pale, peak, change countenance, go as white as a sheet, go white around the gills

6 **decolour**, achromatize, fade, etiolate, bleach, blanch, peroxide, whiten, drain of colour, wash out, tone down, deaden, weaken, pale, dim, bedim, dull, tarnish, discolour

ADJECTIVES

7 **colourless**, hueless, toneless, neutral, uncoloured, achromatic, decoloured, discoloured, bleached, etiolated, overexposed, underexposed, weathered, faint, faded, fading, washed out, washy, wishy-washy, unpigmented, whitish, yellowish, lustreless, mousy, dingy, milky, dull, leaden, grey, lacklustre, without gloss, dim

8 **drained of colour**, white-skinned, light-skinned, white, faint-coloured, bloodless, anaemic, albino, albinotic, emaciated, peaky, peakish, peaked (US), pale, pallid, mousy, ashy, ashen, ashen-hued, livid, tallow-faced, pasty, doughy, mealy, sallow, sickly, unhealthy, blank, glassy, lacklustre, insipid, lurid, ghastly, wan, deathly, deathlike, deathly pale, pale as death, dead, pale as ashes, white as a sheet, white (or green) around the gills, cadaverous, ghostlike, ghostly

ADVERBS

9 **colourlessly**, tonelessly, achromatically, neutrally, faintly, dimly, dully, dingily, blankly

446 Whiteness

ADJECTIVES

1 **white**, pure-white, snow-white, snowy, lily-white, milk-white, milky, lactescent, whitish, albescent, off-white, half-white, oyster-white, pearly, ivory, alabaster, marble, chalky, creamy, magnolia, ecru, unbleached, undyed, greige, mushroom, beige, silver, silvery, silvered, argent, argentine, argental, white as the

driven snow, white as a lily, white as milk, white as marble, white like ivory, fair-skinned, light- (*or* pale-) complexioned, albinotic, albinistic, Caucasian

▶ *449 Brownness, 1 Anthropology, 2 Sociology, 457 Appearance*

2 **whitened**, bleached, blanched, decolorized, faded, colourless, achromatic, semitransparent, whitewashed, snow-capped, snow-covered, ice-covered, hoary, frosty, frosted, foam-flecked, foaming, spumy, soapy, lathery, white with dust, dusty, white-hot

▶ *445 Colourlessness, 408 Heat*

3 **white-haired**, fair-haired, fair, blond(e), ash-blond(e), platinum-blond(e), golden-haired, flaxen-haired, tow-headed, Nordic, grey-haired, grey, canescent, hoary, grizzled, pepper-and-salt, mottled

▶ *448 Greyness*

4 **pale**, pallid, sallow, waxen, ashen, ashy, livid, ghastly, white as a sheet

▶ *445 Colourlessness*

5 **pure**, chaste, virginal, clean, spotless, immaculate

▶ *621 Cleanness, 134 Purity*

6 **light**, luminous, bright, dazzling

▶ *439 Light*

NOUNS

7 **whiteness**, snowiness, milkiness, lactescence, whitishness, albescence, off-whiteness, pearliness, chalkiness, creaminess, silveriness, fairness, greyness, canescence, hoariness, colourlessness, achromatism, etiolation, semitransparency, paleness, pallor, sallowness, albinism, albinoism, lack of pigment, leucoderma

▶ *445 Colourlessness, 1 Anthropology, 2 Sociology, 122 Equality*

8 **whitener**, whiting, blanco, white alkali, white arsenic, white lead, pipeclay, whitewash, calcimine, white paint, Chinese white, Luma white, Paris white, flake white, zinc white, titanium white, achromatic hue

9 **white thing**, whites, white goods, white sale, white tie, hoar, frost, snow, driven snow, new-fallen snow, chalk, paper, white paper, teeth, milk, flour, white flag, white wall, white light, white heat, marble, alabaster, ivory, pearl, lily, whitecap, white water, white horse, white dwarf, white blood cell, silver, white metal, white gold, pewter, platinum, white oak, white spruce, white poplar, white rose, whitethorn, white clover, swan, white fish, white whale, white shark, whitetail, white-tailed deer, whitethroat, white admiral, white-fly, white ant, whitebait, white flour, white bread, white sauce, white wine, white coffee, white pepper, white meat, White House, White Friar, White Cliffs of Dover

10 **figurative usage**, white-collar worker, white elephant, white hat, white knight, white feather, white hope, white lie, whited sepulchre, White Nile, White Mountains, White Russia, White Sea, White Volta, white lightning (US sl), white stuff (Sl)

11 **purity**, chastity, cleanness, spotlessness

▶ *621 Cleanness, 134 Purity*

12 **light**, luminosity, brightness

▶ *439 Light*

VERBS

13 **whiten**, white, bleach, blanch, blanco, pipeclay, whitewash, calcimine, wash, clean, pale, blench, fade, decolorize, etiolate, frost, silver, grizzle

ADVERBS

14 **whitely**, palely, pallidly, achromatically, lightly, luminously, chalkily, creamily, semitransparently, foamily

447   Blackness

ADJECTIVES

1 **black**, sable, raven, ebon, ebony, jet, jet-black, jetty, pitch-black, pitchy, inky, sooty, fuliginous, coal-black, sloe-black, blackish, nigrescent, blue-black, grey-black, brown-black, black as coal, black as soot, black as jet, black as pitch, black as night, black as midnight, black as ink, black as my hat, black as a tinker's pot, black as thunder, black as hell

2 **dark**, deep, of the deepest dye, achromatic, low-toned, low in tone, dim, dingy, murky, smudgy, smoky, dusky, swarthy, swart (Arch), pigmented, melanistic, dark-complexioned, Black, Negro, Negroid

▶ *440 Darkness, 457 Appearance, 1 Anthropology, 2 Sociology*

3 **blackened**, singed, charred, tanned, sun-tanned, sunburnt, black-and-blue

▶ *408 Heat, 449 Brownness*

4 **black-haired**, black-locked, raven-haired, dark-haired, dark-headed, brunette, black-eyed, sloe-eyed

5 **black-hearted**, evil, wicked, nefarious, heinous, villainous, blackguardly

▶ *862 Evil*

6 **sad**, sombre, gloomy, depressed, depressing, mournful, mourning, funereal

▶ *770 Sorrow, 774 Lamentation, 399 Burial*

NOUNS

7 **blackness**, inkiness, blackishness, nigrescence, nigritude, darkness, dark, night, dark colour, dark colouring, pigmentation, pigment, colour, depth, deep tone, black and white, chiaroscuro, chequer, blackening, darkening, obscuration, Negroism, melanism, melanosis, swarthiness, swartness, duskiness

▶ *440 Darkness, 1 Anthropology*

8 **black pigment**, melanin, blacking, lampblack, blacklead, ivory black, blue-black, ni-

grosine, japan, niello, burnt cork, ink, Indian ink, China ink, printer's ink, newsprint ink, indelible ink

9 **black thing**, ink, tar, pitch, coal, charcoal, silhouette, shadow, ebony, jet, obsidian, soot, smut, sable, black face, black eye, bruise, blackhead, black belt, black tie, crepe, mourning clothes, black hat, blacktop (US), black flag, blackboard, blackjack, blackout, black light, black hole, black pudding, black coffee, black pepper, crow, raven, blackbird, black swan, black Angus, blacksnake, black bear, black grouse, black widow, blacktail deer, black fish, black bass, blackfly, blackberry, blackcurrant, black spruce, black nightshade, blackthorn, sloe, black-eyed Susan, Black Friar, Black Rod, Black and Tan, Black Watch, Black Shirt, Black Maria

10 **figurative usage**, blackmail, blackball, blacklist, blackguard, black magic, black art, black market, black economy, black sheep, black ice, black spot, black box, black book, black bottom, Black Mass, Black Death, Black Prince, Black Forest, Black Hills, Black Sea, Black Country, blackleg (Sl), black stuff (Sl), black diamonds (Sl)

VERBS

11 **blacken**, black, blacklead, japan, niello, ink, ink in, dirty, blot, smudge, smirch, sully, darken, deepen, singe, char, burn, tan, suntan, blackball, blacklist, boycott

ADVERBS

12 **blackly**, darkly, deeply, inkily, duskily, swarthily, obscurely, gloomily

448 Greyness

ADJECTIVES

1 **grey**, greyish, canescent, griseous, silver-grey, silver, silvery, silvered, light-grey, pale-grey, powder-grey, dove-grey, pearl-grey, pearly, mouse-coloured, mousy, taupe, dun, brown-grey, donkey-grey, steel-grey, steely, iron-grey, leaden, charcoal-grey, dark-grey, blue-grey, slate-grey, slate-coloured, ash-grey, ashen, ashy, cinereous, smoky, fuliginous, dapple-grey, neutral, unbleached, undyed, greige, ecru
▶ *446 Whiteness*

2 **grey-haired**, grey-headed, grizzled, grizzly, pepper-and-salt, hoary, hoar, greying, elderly, old, aged
▶ *446 Whiteness, 207 Age*

3 **dull**, drab, dreary, gloomy, sombre, dark, leaden, overcast, cloudy, murky, misty, foggy

NOUNS

4 **greyness**, grey colour, greyishness, canescence, grey pigment, Payne's grey, neutral tint, grisaille, oyster, taupe, greige

5 **grey thing**, slate, silver, pewter, iron, steel,

lead, gunmetal, ashes, Grey Friar, greyhound, grey wolf, grey whale, greyhen, grey squirrel, greylag, greywacke, grey hair

6 **figurative usage**, grey area, grey matter, grey population, Old Grey Whistle Test, grey-beard, grey market, grey knight, Gray Panther (US), grey man (Inf)

7 **dullness**, drabness, dreariness, gloominess, darkness, cloudiness, murk

VERBS

8 **grey**, turn grey, go grey, silver, frost

ADVERBS

9 **greyly**, dully, drably, drearily, gloomily, sombrely, cloudily, mistily, murkily, foggily, smokily

449 Brownness

ADJECTIVES

1 **brown**, pale brown, oatmeal, beige, buff, fawn, biscuit, mushroom, café-au-lait, ecru, snuff-coloured, yellow-brown, dun, khaki, hazel, walnut, orange-brown, amber, bronze, tawny, fulvous, sorrel, reddish-brown, nut-brown, tan, foxy, bay, roan, chestnut, auburn, mahogany, copper, coppery, copper-coloured, cupreous, russet, rust-coloured, rusty, rubiginous, ferruginous, liver-coloured, maroon, purple-brown, puce, dark brown, peat-brown, mocha, chocolate, coffee, coffee-coloured, fuscous

2 **browned**, bronzed, dark, brunette, tanned, suntanned, brown as a berry, brown as a nut, sunburnt, toasted, grilled, charred, singed

NOUNS

3 **brownness**, brown colour, brown pigmentation, melanin, mole, freckle, suntan, sunburn, brunette, dark skin, dark complexion
▶ *400 Humankind*

4 **brown pigment**, bistre, ochre, sepia, raw sienna, burnt sienna, raw umber, burnt umber, Vandyke brown, brown dye, Bismarck brown

5 **brown thing**, cinnamon, coffee, chocolate, butterscotch, caramel, toffee, burnt almond, brown sugar, demerara, muscovado, brown bread, wholemeal bread, brown rice, brownie, brown betty (US), tobacco leaf, dead leaf, autumn colours, fall colours (US), brown coal, lignite, brownstone (US), brown algae, brown fat, brown rot, brown-lung disease, brown bear, brown trout, brown recluse spider (US), brown-tail moth, Brown Swiss cattle, Burmese cat, seal-point (Siamese cat), chocolate-point (Siamese cat), brown paper bag, brown belt, shit (Sl)

6 **figurative usage**, brownie, brown study, brown-out (US), Brown Owl, Brownie Guide, Brownie Girl Scout (US), Brownie point, Brown Shirt, brown stuff (Sl), brown-bagger

(US sl), brown-noser (US tab sl), brown-trousers (Tab sl)

VERBS

7 **brown**, embrown, tan, suntan, bronze, sunburn, burn, singe, char, grill, toast

450   Redness

ADJECTIVES

1 **red**, pink, coral, coral-pink, orange-pink, shell-pink, flesh-pink, flesh-coloured, peach-coloured, salmon-pink, shocking pink, rose-pink, damask, carnation, rosy, roseate, rose-coloured, rose-red, cherry, cherry-red, cerise, bright red, blood-red, carmine, crimson, cramoisy (Arch), scarlet, cardinal red, Turkey red, vermilion, vermeil, gules, brick-red, pillarbox red, flame-coloured, deep red, ruby, wine-coloured, purple-red, beetroot-red, fuchsia, cyclamen, magenta, maroon, murrey (Arch), brownish-red, oxblood, rust-coloured, rufous, rufescent, russet

▶ *449 Brownness, 455 Purpleness*

2 **red-faced**, red-cheeked, rosy-cheeked, rosy, glowing, blooming, flushing, blushing, rubescent (Fml), ruddy, sanguine, rubicund, florid, blowzy, rouged, reddened, flushed, red as a beetroot, red as a lobster, sunburnt, hectic, fevered, feverish, fiery, red-hot

▶ *408 Heat, 624 Ill Health*

3 **red-haired**, ginger-haired, carroty, sandy, Titian, auburn, chestnut

4 **bloody**, blood-stained, bloodshot, gory, sanguineous, sanguinary, ensanguined, incarnadine (Arch)

NOUNS

5 **redness**, reddening, rubescence, rubefaction, rubefacient, rufescence, red colour, red complexion, blush, flush, hectic flush, red rash, scarlet fever, glow, warmth, rosiness, bloom, ruddiness, floridness, rubicundity

6 **red pigment**, red dye, cadmium red, cadmium scarlet, Windsor red, Grumbacher red, Thalo red, Indian red, murex, cochineal, carmine, kermes, dragon's blood, cinnabar, vermilion, minium, red lead, ruddle, madder, rose madder, brown madder, alizarin, alizarin crimson, crimson lake, Venetian red, rosaniline, solferino, red ochre, light red oxide, red cosmetic, henna, rouge, blusher, lipstick, nail polish

7 **red thing**, ruby, garnet, carnelian, fire, flame, fireglow, sunset, dawn, rust, brick, blood, gore, red blood cell (*or* corpuscle), rose, geranium, carnation, poppy, peony, cherry, strawberry, raspberry, mulberry, redcurrant, plum, peach, tomato, beetroot, red clover, red pepper, redwood, red bird, cardinal, robin redbreast, redwing, red deer, red fox, red squirrel, red salmon, red snapper, red admiral, redbug

(US), red grouse, red meat, red wine, claret, port, burgundy, red planet, Mars, red giant, red dwarf, red card, red ink, red light, danger signal, fire engine, pillarbox, red cheeks, rosy cheeks, apple cheeks, cherry lips, high colour, strawberry mark, red hair, redhead, carrot-top (Inf), gingernob (Inf)

8 **figurative usage**, red carpet, red herring, red-letter day, red tape, red alert, red-light district, red-hot mama, Red Cross, Red Crescent, Red Sea, Communist, Red (Inf), better red than dead, reds under the bed, redcoat, redneck (US sl), red-eye flight (US sl)

VERBS

9 **redden**, flush, blush, glow, colour, colour up, crimson, make red, rubefy, ruddle, rouge, raddle, rubricate, mantle, incarnadine (Arch)

ADVERBS

10 **ruddily**, rosily, blushingly, in the pink, floridly, sanguineously, sanguinarily, warmly

451   Orangeness

ADJECTIVES

1 **orange**, reddish-yellow, yellowish-red, ochreous, amber, saffron, apricot, peach, golden, old-gold, or, carroty, Titian, ginger, tan, bronze, brassy, flame-coloured, coppery

▶ *450 Redness, 452 Yellowness, 449 Brownness*

NOUNS

2 **orangeness**, orange colour, orange pigment, ochre, raw sienna, Mars orange, cadmium orange, henna, carotene

3 **orange thing**, orange, marmalade, orangeade, orange squash, orange juice, tangerine, mandarin, clementine, satsuma, peach, apricot, nectarine, carrot, pumpkin, marigold, sunflower, saffron, orange hawkweed, goldfish, amber, amber light, brass, copper, sand, tequila sunrise, orange sunshine (Sl)

4 **figurative usage**, orange blossom, orangewood, orangery, orange pekoe, orange stick, orange-flower water, Orangeman, Orangeman's Day, Orange March, Orange Free State

452   Yellowness

ADJECTIVES

1 **yellow**, pale yellow, cream-coloured, creamy, beige, honey-coloured, straw-coloured, fallow, champagne, greenish-yellow, citron, chartreuse, primrose-yellow, lemon-yellow, citrine, bright yellow, canary-yellow, sunshine-yellow, gold, golden, golden-yellow, gilt, gilded, aureate, or, amber, honey-coloured, brownish-yellow, old-gold, mustard-yellow, mustard, buff, tawny

2 **yellowish**, xanthous, luteous, fulvous, flavescent, sulphurous

3 **yellow-haired**, fair-haired, flaxen-haired, golden-haired, tow-haired, blond, ash-blond,

platinum-blond, strawberry-blond, honey-blond

4 **yellow-faced**, sallow, jaundiced, bilious

5 **cowardly**, craven, spineless, chicken-hearted, lily-livered, yellow (Inf), chicken (Inf)

▶ *779 Cowardice*

NOUNS

6 **yellowness**, yellow colour, yellow hair, fair hair, blond(e), towhead, yellow skin, jaundice, icterus, yellow fever, biliousness

7 **yellow pigment**, cadmium yellow, cadmium lemon, gamboge, chrome yellow, Windsor yellow, Indian yellow, Naples yellow, lemon yellow, orpiment, yellow ochre, Claude tint, massicot, weld, luteolin, xanthene, xanthophyll

8 **yellow thing**, gold, topaz, amber, old ivory, yellow metal, sulphur, brimstone, lemon, citron, banana, mustard, honey, butter, buttercup, daffodil, crocus, primrose, cowslip, dandelion, winter jasmine, yellowhammer, yellowtail, yellowthroat, yellow underwing, yellow jacket (US), Yellow Pages, yellow line, yellow rain, yellow card, yellow spot, yellow jacket (US sl), yellows (Sl), yellow sunshine (Sl)

9 **figurative usage**, Yellow Sea, Yellowstone National Park, yellow journalism, yellow peril, yellow streak, yellow press, yellow-belly (Sl)

VERBS

10 **make** (*or* **become**) **yellow**, yellow, gild

ADVERBS

11 **yellowly**, goldenly, creamily

453 Greenness

ADJECTIVES

1 **green**, emerald, jade, vert, grass-green, leaf-green, pea-green, leek-green, greenish, virescent, viridescent, yellow-green, lime-green, chartreuse, eau-de-nil, Lincoln green, bice-green, olive-green, grey-green, sage-green, avocado, celadon, reseda, mignonette, blue-green, glaucous, sea-green, Nile green, loden green, aquamarine, dull green, dark green, bottle green, jungle green, forest green

▶ *454 Blueness, 452 Yellowness*

2 **verdant**, grassy, leafy, green, fresh, rural

3 **raw**, unripe, unseasoned, immature, callow, green, inexperienced, unskilled, inexpert, untrained, untried, untested, unsophisticated, naive, ingenuous, artless, innocent, credulous, gullible, gauche, awkward, wet behind the ears (Inf)

▶ *502 Ignorance, 206 Youth*

4 **fresh**, new, young, youthful, evergreen, sappy, springlike, vernal, vigorous, flourishing, blooming

▶ *206 Youth*

5 **green-eyed**, jealous, envious, green with envy, covetous, resentful

▶ *842 Envy, 841 Jealousy*

6 **sick**, nauseated, green, bilious, greensick, green around the gills (Inf)

▶ *624 Ill Health*

7 **environmental**, conservationist, green, environment-friendly, ozone-friendly

NOUNS

8 **greenness**, viridity, viridescence, virescence, verdancy, verdure, greenery, woodland, greenwood, evergreen, foliage, leaves, grass, moss, turf, sward, grassland, farmland, pasture, common, green belt, park, lawn, green, village green, bowling green, greenkeeper, green fingers

9 **greenstuff**, greens, spring greens, cabbage, lettuce, broccoli, green leek, green bean, green pepper, greengage, lime, avocado, greengrocer

10 **green pigment**, chlorophyll, terre verte, celadonite, viridian, verditer, Paris green, Windsor green, Thalo yellow green, Hooker's green

11 **green thing**, greenstone, jade, emerald, malachite, beryl, chrysoprase, olivine, verd antique, green porphyry, aquamarine, greensand, verdigris, patina, green turtle, green snake, greenfinch, greenshank, greenlet, greenfly, greenheart, green card, little green men, green paper, green ice (US sl), green dragon (Sl), green hornet (Sl)

12 **figurative usage**, Greenland, Greenland Sea, Green Mountains, Green River, Green Bay, Green Berets, greenroom, greenhouse, greenhouse effect, green pound, greenback (US inf), greenmail (US sl), the green stuff (US sl)

13 **young thing**, immature thing, greenhorn, greenstick fracture, green tea

14 **green-eyed monster**, jealousy, envy, covetousness, green envy

15 **green light**, traffic light, go-ahead, all clear, permission, approval, consent

▶ *708 Permission, 851 Approval*

16 **green politics**, Green Party, Greens, environmentalism, ecology, preservationism, conservationism, greening, green labelling, Greenpeace, Friends of the Earth

VERBS

17 **green**, become green, make green

ADVERBS

18 **greenly**, verdantly, freshly, youthfully

454 Blueness

ADJECTIVES

1 **blue**, light blue, sky blue, pale blue, ice blue, powder blue, Cambridge blue, Wedgwood blue, grey-blue, saxe blue, slate blue, smoke blue, steel blue, green-blue, robin's-egg blue (US), duck-egg blue, eggshell blue, aquamarine, turquoise, peacock blue, kingfisher blue, cobalt blue, cyan, cyanic, bright blue, ceru-

lean, sapphire, air-force blue, electric blue, ultramarine, deep blue, royal blue, dark blue, Oxford blue, midnight blue, navy blue, navy, French navy, perse, purplish-blue, azure, indigo, hyacinthine

▶ *453 Greenness, 455 Purpleness*

2 **bluish**, black-and-blue, livid, bruised, cyanotic, cyanosed, caesious, blue with cold, freezing, blue around the gills (Inf), blue in the face

3 **depressed**, dejected, downcast, despondent, blue, unhappy, sad, melancholy, gloomy, glum

4 **indecent**, smutty, risqué, bawdy, blue, coarse, obscene, near the knuckle

▶ *877 Immorality*

NOUNS

5 **blueness**, blue colour, blue pigment, blue dye, azure, cyan, indigo, woad, bice, Prussian blue, Saxon blue, French blue, ultramarine, cobalt blue, cerulean blue, Antwerp blue, phthalocyanine blue zaffre, smalt, methylene blue, gentian blue

6 **blue thing**, sky, sea, bluejeans, blueprint, blue pencil, blue ribbon, bluebook, blue peter, bluestone, sapphire, aquamarine, turquoise, lapis lazuli, beryl, bluebonnet, bluegrass, bluebell, cornflower, forget-me-not, iris, hyacinth, blueberry, blue cheese, Stilton, blue mould, bluebird, bluetit, blue jay, bluebill, bluefish, blue whale, bluegill, blue crab, bluepoint oyster (US), blue fox, blue racer, Blue Cross (US), Bluebeard, Blue Ridge Mountains, Blue Mountains, Blue Nile, blue cheer (Sl), blue velvet (Sl)

7 **figurative usage**, blues, blue devils, blue note, blue streak, blue murder, blue blood, bluestocking, blueprint, bluejacket, blue chip, blue-collar worker, blue-eyed boy, bluegrass (US), blue moon, blue film, blue pencil, blue law (US), blue-sky law (US), blue-plate special (US), blue language, blue funk (Sl), blue balls (Sl), blue flu (US sl)

8 **bluishness**, cyanosis, blue baby, lividness, lividity, bruising

VERBS

9 **blue**, turn blue, dye blue, woad, azure

10 **blue-pencil**, edit

455   Purpleness

NOUNS

1 **purpleness**, purplishness, blue and red, purple colour, imperial purple, bishop's purple, mourning colour, funeral colour

2 **purple pigment**, purple dye, Tyrian purple, gentian violet, Parma violet, cobalt violet, methyl violet, mauveine, amaranth, permanent magenta, Windsor violet, Thalo purple, Thio violet

3 **purple thing**, lavender, lilac, violet, pansy, heather, foxglove, hyancinth, heliotrope,

clematis, rhododendron, purple-fringed orchid, plum, damson, aubergine, beetroot, purple gallinule, purple grackle, purple martin, purple emperor, amethyst, Purple Heart (US), purple heart (Sl), purple haze (Sl)

4 **figurative usage**, purple prose, purple patch, purple passage, born to the purple

5 **lividness**, lividity, bruising, bruise

ADJECTIVES

6 **purple**, purplish, purply, purpled, pale purple, lavender, lilac, mauve, purple-red, fuchsia, magenta, maroon, plum, plum-coloured, damson-coloured, puce, amaranthine, hyacinthine, heliotrope, violet, violaceous, amethystine, purpure, deep purple, dark purple, aubergine, mulberry, murrey (Arch), purple bluc, indigo

▶ *450 Redness, 454 Blueness*

7 **livid**, black-and-blue, bruised

8 **furious**, livid, purple with rage

VERBS

9 **empurple**, purple, bruise

456   Variegation

NOUNS

1 **variegation**, variety, difference, diversification, diversity, diversity of colours, dichroism (*or* dichromatism), trichroism, trichromatism, polychromatism, polychromy, motley, medley of colour, riot of colour, spectrum, rainbow effect, play of colour, iridescence, opalescence, pearliness, chatoyancy, moiré

2 **check**, chequer, Prince of Wales chequer, hound's tooth check, plaid, tartan, mosaic, patch, patchiness, patchwork, inlay, damascene, marquetry, parquetry, tessellation, tessera

3 **striping**, striation, stripe, stria, band, bar, line, streak, streakiness, marbling, crack, craze, crackle, reticulation

4 **maculation**, mottling, mottle, mottlement, dappling, brindling, stippling, pointillism, freckling, spottiness, patchiness patch, speck, speckle, spot, sunspot, dot, polka dot, macula, foxing, brindle, fleck, freckle, pimple, blotch, splotch, birthmark, strawberry mark, splodge, splash

5 **variegated thing**, stained glass, kaleidoscope, spectrum, prism, rainbow, Joseph's coat, Harlequin, motley, patchwork quilt, tartan, collage, confetti, peacock, peacock's tail, zebra, tiger, leopard, jaguar, tortoiseshell cat, calico cat, tabby cat, Dalmatian, chameleon, tortoiseshell butterfly, dragonfly, mackerel sky, buttermilk sky, dancing light, glancing light, shot silk, watered silk, moiré, opal, mother-of-pearl, nacre, tiger's-eye, agate, jasper, cymophane, tortoiseshell, serpentine, spangle, sequin, marbled paper, parquet floor,

enamelwork, chessboard, draughtboard, tri-colour, bar code, crazy paving, cracked glass

ADJECTIVES

6 **variegated**, bicolour (*or* bicoloured), dichroic (*or* dichromatic), trichoic, trichomatic, poly-chrome, polychromatic, multicoloured, parti-coloured, pied, varicoloured, versicolour, many-coloured, many-hued, rainbow-coloured, mot-ley, kaleidoscopic, spectral, prismatic, colourful, florid, ornamental, patterned, embroidered, worked, chameleonic, changeable

7 **iridescent**, opalescent, opaline, nacreous, pearly, semitransparent, shot, shot through with, pavonine, moiré, chatoyant

8 **checked**, chequered, plaid, tartan, tortoise-shell, inlaid, tessellated, patched, patchy, pied, black-and-white, piebald, pinto, skewbald, fas-ciate, stripy

9 **striped**, stripy, striate (*or* striated), banded, barred, lined, streaked, marbled, marbly, veined, jaspé, reticulate, panelled, paned

10 **mottled**, dappled, brindled, tabby, grizzled, pepper-and-salt, roan, spotted, maculate, macular, dotted, studded, peppered, sprin-kled, powdered, dusted, dusty, cloudy, hazy, blemished, fly-spotted, speckled, speckledy, freckled, spotty, pimply, pocked, pockmarked

VERBS

11 **variegate**, diversify, pattern, chequer, check, patch, spangle, damascene, inlay, enamel, tes-sellate, mottle, dapple, brindle, stipple, grizzle, spot, maculate, dot (with), stud, pepper, sprin-kle, powder, dust, speckle, freckle, stripe, stri-ate, band, bar, streak, marble, vein, craze, crack, cloud, stain, blot, discolour, fox

ADVERBS

12 **variedly**, diversely, polychromatically, kaleido-scopically, floridly, ornamentally, iridescently, nacreously, patchily, fasciately, reticulately

457 Appearance

Alas, after a certain age every man is responsible for his face. Albert Camus.

The Lord prefers common-looking people. That is why he makes so many of them. Abraham Lincoln.

Gentlemen always seem to remember blondes. Anita Loos.

Had Cleopatra's nose been shorter, the whole face of the world would have changed. Blaise Pascal.

Enclosing every thin man, there's a fat man demanding elbow-room. Evelyn Waugh.

NOUNS

1 **appearance**, appearing, coming into view, coming into being, materialization, manifes-tation, embodiment, incarnation, realization, birth, formation, dawning, dawn, beginning, emergence, onset, arising, rise, coming, ad-vent, arrival, debut, entrance, introduction, presentation, first appearance, publication, issue, issuing forth, launch, release, preview, opening, opening night, first night, premiere, first screening, opening up, unfolding, bloom-ing, waxing, disclosure, revelation, exposure

▷ *344 Arrival, 156 Beginning, 526 Display, 367 Material World, 101 Reality, 532 Publication, 322 Opening, 530 Disclosure*

2 **being in view**, visibility, presence, attend-ance, court appearance, existence, being, being there, occurrence, happening, phenom-enon, performance, stage appearance, show-ing, show, parade, display, exhibition

▷ *437 Visibility, 253 Presence, 99 Existence, 51 Performing Arts, 526 Display, 811 Showiness*

3 **external appearance**, look, outward form, superficies, surface, form, shape, format, di-mensions, outline, contour, silhouette, relief, elevation, section, aspect, side, facet, angle, point of view, facies, outside, exterior, exter-nals, front, façade, fascia, facing, covering, ve-neer, dress, clothes, clothing, garb, fashion, dressing up, cut, style, demeanour, manner, mien, bearing, posture, carriage, deportment, air, feature, characteristic, marking, trait, fig-ure, body, body type, physical type, face, physiognomy, visage, countenance, linea-ments, features, forehead, brow, eye, nose, mouth, lips, cheek, cheekbone, jaw, chin, ear, full-face, half-face, profile, back-view, expres-sion, facial expression, body language, skin, skin colour, complexion, looks, good looks, beauty, ugliness, homeliness

▷ *289 Exterior, 306 Form, 303 Front, 293 Covering, 295 Dress, 796 Fashion, 789 Beauty, 790 Ugli-ness*

4 **something that appears**, spectacle, sight, revelation, apocalypse, theophany, epiphany, miracle, marvel, prodigy, apparition, ghost, spectre, phantom, emanation, ectoplasm, illu-sion, hallucination, vision, dream, chimera, image, after-image, mirage, hologram, seem-ing, semblance, pretence, pose, guise, disguise

5 **impression**, effect, first impression, impact, visual appeal, face value, public persona, pub-lic image, reflection, mirror image, likeness, similarity, match, look-alike, double, copy, clone, imitation, ringer, representation, pic-ture, photograph, model, replica

▷ *435 Vision, 368 Nonmaterial World, 102 Unreal-ity, 539 Deception, 458 Disappearance, 531 Con-cealment, 293 Covering, 114 Similarity, 118 Imi-tation, 66 Photography, 50 Painting and Sculpture*

6 **reappearance**, return, reissue, republica-tion, second showing, repeat, recurrence, sec-ond coming, déjà vu (Fr)

▷ *183 Repetition*

7 **appearing**, apparent, material, embodied, incarnate, realized, there, present, all there, obvious, evident, patent, manifest, showing, visible, in sight, on show, on view, exposed, displayed, revealed, epiphanic, theophanic, salient, prominent, conspicuous, jutting, impressive, effective, spectacular, phenomenal, apocalyptic, coming into sight, coming into view, coming into being, beginning, coming, arriving, entering, coming on the scene, emergent, arising, developing, unfolding, waxing, recurring, repeated
▶ *253 Presence, 437 Visibility, 344 Arrival, 156 Beginning*

8 **outer**, outward, superficial, surface, external, exterior, visual, reflected, mirrored, reflecting, mirroring, visible

9 **ostensible**, seeming, deceptive, specious, illusory, visionary, dreamlike, chimerical, imaginary, hallucinatory
▶ *289 Exterior, 368 Nonmaterial World, 102 Unreality, 539 Deception*

10 **aspectual**, beautiful, attractive, sightly, decorated, decorative, well-dressed, fashionable, ugly, unattractive, homely, unsightly, plain, ill-dressed, unfashionable, easy on the eye (Inf)
▶ *789 Beauty, 790 Ugliness, 792 Decoration, 796 Fashion*

11 **appear**, show, show up, be present, attend, be at, be there, be, look, seem, appear like, look like, seem like, seem to be, look to be, appear to be, have a look of, have the appearance of, take the shape of, take the guise of, disguise oneself as, dress up as, imitate, copy, reflect, mirror, match, resemble
▶ *437 Visibility, 253 Presence, 114 Similarity, 118 Imitation*

12 **become visible**, materialize, appear, come to light, see the light, begin, dawn, come forth, come forward, come out, emerge, issue, rise, arise, surface, come to the surface, come up, crop up, show, show up, show oneself, turn up, come, arrive, enter, present itself (*or* oneself), make (*or* put in) an appearance, come into the picture, come on the scene, reveal itself (*or* oneself), peep, peep out, crawl out of the woodwork, come over the horizon, loom, wax, fade in, heave in sight, come in sight, rear its (ugly) head, pop up (Inf)
▶ *367 Material World, 156 Beginning, 344 Arrival, 437 Visibility*

13 **occur**, happen, perform, play, act, appear in, act in, star in, appear on stage, come on the stage, appear on film (*or* screen), be published, come out, become available, appear in the shops, appear in court, recur, reappear, come round again
▶ *51 Performing Arts, 532 Publication*

14 **present**, put forward, make apparent, realize, show, show up, reveal, disclose, expose, display, exhibit, expose oneself, publish, issue, launch, release, screen, point out, point up, highlight, silhouette, outline, wrap, giftwrap, wrap up in clean linen, disguise, flash (Sl), prettify (Inf), tart up (Sl)
▶ *530 Disclosure, 526 Display, 532 Publication, 791 Beautification*

15 **apparently**, evidently, obviously, plainly, clearly, manifestly, to all appearances, seemingly, ostensibly, on the face of it, on the surface, superficially, outwardly, externally, facially, for the sake of appearances, at face value, at sight, at first sight, at first blush, on sight, into sight, in outline

458 Disappearance

1 **disappear**, cease, end, cease to be, cease to exist, become extinct, die out, die, expire, perish, pass away, pass, wane, ebb, recede, vanish, dematerialize, become invisible, evanesce, evaporate, dissolve, melt, fade, fade away, fade out, dwindle, dwindle away, peter out, disguise oneself, hide, lie low, go to ground, lurk, disappear into thin air, blend into the background, sink below the horizon, sink without trace, go out of use, become obsolete, cease publication, go out of print, go off the air, close, close down
▶ *218 Cessation, 157 End, 397 Death, 100 Nonexistence, 438 Invisibility, 129 Decrease, 531 Concealment*

2 **depart**, decamp, go, go away, escape, run, run away, flee, fly, withdraw, retire, go into retirement, retreat, go into retreat, melt away, absent oneself, play (Dial), go AWOL, take French leave, play truant, not appear, fail to appear, stay away, play hooky (Inf), do a runner (Sl), scarper (Sl), vamoose (Sl)
▶ *345 Departure, 347 Exit, 254 Absence*

3 **cause to disappear**, vaporize, liquidate, disembody, destroy, annihilate, waste, disperse, dissipate, dispel, scatter, dismiss, send away, expel, hide, conceal, obscure, bury, disguise, camouflage, erase, blot out, obliterate, rub, rub out, wipe, wipe out, scrub, cancel, get rid of, eliminate, remove, take away, spirit away, steal, rip off (Sl)
▶ *531 Concealment, 399 Burial, 546 Obliteration, 704 Cancellation, 244 Destruction, 349 Expulsion*

4 **disappearance**, disappearing, cessation, end, extinction, dying out, death, dying, passing away, passing, wane, ebb, vanishing, dematerialization, disembodiment, vaporiza-

tion, evaporation, evanescence, dissolution, melting, fading, fading away, fading out, dwindling, erosion, wearing away, dispersal, dispersion, dissipation, scattering, departure, exit, going, going away, escape, running away, flight, withdrawal, retreat, desertion, truancy, nonappearance, staying away, absence, nonexistence, invisibility, vanishing trick, escapology, escapee, missing person, runaway, truant, fade-out, blackout, vanishing point, horizon, disappearing act (Inf)

▶ *218 Cessation, 157 End, 397 Death, 345 Departure, 347 Exit, 254 Absence, 100 Nonexistence*

5 **disguise**, protective coloration, camouflage, blacking up, blacking out, occultation, eclipse, obscuring, obscuration, hiding, concealment, burial, erasure, obliteration, cancellation, elimination, annihilation, destruction, loss

▶ *440 Darkness, 531 Concealment, 399 Burial, 457 Appearance, 546 Obliteration, 704 Cancellation*

ADJECTIVES

6 **disappearing**, vanishing, evanescent, fugi-

tive, going, departing, escaping, transient, fleeting, passing, fading, waning, dying, dissolving, evaporating, hiding, obsolescent, here today gone tomorrow, now you see it now you don't

▶ *189 Transience*

7 **disappeared**, vanished, absent, not present, gone, gone away, away, missing, lost, dead, extinct, obsolete, past, past and gone, nonexistent, invisible, eclipsed, occulted, hidden, gone to ground, concealed, buried, disguised, camouflaged, dispersed, dissipated, worn away, eroded, out of the picture, out of sight, lost to sight, out of range

▶ *254 Absence, 345 Departure, 100 Nonexistence, 438 Invisibility, 531 Concealment*

ADVERBS

8 **fleetingly**, transiently, evanescently, meltingly, fugitively, away, absently, invisibly, inwardly, below the surface, below the horizon, in hiding, in disguise, underground, obsolescently

Intellect

459   Intellect

We should take care not to make the intellect our god; it has, of course, powerful muscles, but no personality. Albert Einstein.

The voice of the intellect is a soft one, but it does not rest till it has gained a hearing. Sigmund Freud.

The highest intellects, like the tops of mountains, are the first to catch and to reflect the dawn. Lord Macaulay.

The higher the voice the smaller the intellect. Ernest Newman.

Intellect is invisible to the man who has none. Arthur Schopenhauer.

NOUNS

1   **mind**, mentality, rationality, ratiocination, conception, intellectualism, intellectuality, consciousness, awareness, cognition, perception, perceptiveness, apperception, percipience
▶ *461 Thought, 511 Memory, 61 Psychology and Psychiatry, 509 Sanity*

2   **ways of thinking**, logic, formal reasoning, deduction, induction, reasoning, insight, acumen, inspiration, instinct, rationale, ratiocination, intuition, sixth sense, extrasensory perception (ESP), quantum leap (Inf)
▶ *463 Reason, 464 Intuition, 4 Philosophy, 11 Occultism*

3   **intelligence**, intellect, understanding, comprehension, sense, judgment, mentality, mind, brain, brains, wit, wits, reason, nous, IQ (intelligence quotient)

4   **cleverness**, genius, flair, brains, wit, wisdom, sagacity, sapience, erudition, knowledgeableness, brightness, incisiveness, shrewdness, astuteness, aptitude, brilliance, alertness, sharpness, acuity, acuteness, quickness, quick-wittedness, keen-wittedness, canniness, subtlety, braininess (Inf)
▶ *507 Wisdom, 501 Knowledge*

5   **common sense**, sense, sensibleness, sound judgment, discernment, clear thinking, horse sense, native wit, mother wit, savvy, nous (Inf), street smarts (US inf)

6   **thoughtfulness**, judiciousness, consideration, reflection, reflectiveness, circumspection, profundity, profoundness, depth

7   **brain**, head, cerebrum, grey matter, seat of thought, upper storey (Inf), noddle (Inf), noodle (US inf), noggin (Inf)

8   **intellectual person**, intellectual, scholar, academic, academician, thinker, genius, wise man, sage, savant, master, guru, elder statesman, oracle, pundit, polymath, littérateur, illuminati, bookman, bookworm, bibliophile, bluestocking, highbrow, egghead (Inf), intellect (Inf), boffin (Inf), brainbox (Inf), know-all (Inf), know-it-all (US inf), clever clogs (Inf), swot (Inf), smart aleck (Inf), smarty pants (Inf), smartarse (Inf)

ADJECTIVES

9   **mental**, intellectual, rational, reasoning, thinking, conceptual, conceptive, cerebral, cephalic, noetic, phrenic, psychological, logical, deductive, instinctive, intuitive

10   **intelligent**, understanding, clever, learned, erudite, knowledgeable, wise, sage, sagacious, bright, smart, shrewd, astute, brilliant, alert, sharp, acute, quick-witted, keen-witted, gifted, brainy (Inf)

11   **thoughtful**, judicious, reflective, circumspect, sapient, profound, sensible, reasonable, sound, deep

VERBS

12   **think**, reason, rationalize, ratiocinate, conceptualize, cognize, perceive, apperceive, ideate, deduce, induce, intuit

13   **be intelligent**, use one's head (Inf), have one's head screwed on (Inf), have one's wits about one (Inf), have a head on one's shoulders (Inf), know what's what (Inf)

ADVERBS

14   **mentally**, intellectually, cerebrally, conceptually, instinctively, intuitively

15 intelligently, sensibly, reasonably, rationally, logically, knowledgeably, wisely, cleverly, sagaciously, profoundly, reflectively, judiciously, thoughtfully, shrewdly, astutely, alertly, acutely, smartly

460 Lack of Intellect

NOUNS

1 lack of intellect, absence of intellect, poverty of intellect, intellectual weakness, mental weakness, lack of brains, low IQ, low mental age, low reading age, feeble-mindedness, simple-mindedness, backwardness, slowness, imbecility, idiocy, mindlessness, senselessness, brainlessness, vacancy, vacuity, mental deficiency, mental retardation, mental handicap, brain damage, senility, dementia, lack of reason, unreason, irrationality, insanity
▶ *462 Lack of Thought, 510 Insanity*

2 unintelligence, ignorance, stupidity, denseness, lack of knowledge, lack of wisdom, foolishness, folly, thoughtlessness, illogicality, empty-headedness, inanity, fatuity, puerility, childishness, immaturity, lack of understanding, incomprehension, unperceptiveness (*or* imperceptiveness), obtuseness, stolidity, thickheadedness, hebetude, oafishness, boorishness, lack of wit, witlessness, dim-wittedness, dimness, unoriginality, uninventiveness, unimaginativeness, imitativeness, imitation
▶ *462 Lack of Thought, 502 Ignorance, 468 Inattention, 508 Folly, 118 Imitation, 658 Naivety, 206 Youth, 556 Simplicity, 656 Unskilfulness*

3 unintelligent person, ignoramus, fool, dunce, simpleton, Simple Simon, idiot, complete idiot, imbecile, moron, cretin, dolt, dullard, blockhead, clod, oaf, boor, numbskull (*or* numskull), halfwit, dunderhead, bumpkin, ninny, nincompoop, silly idiot (Inf), scatterbrain (Inf), dummy (Inf), dumbo (Inf), thickie (*or* thicky) (Inf), twit (Inf), nitwit (Inf), dimwit (Inf), wally (Inf), dope (Inf), lamebrain (Inf), pinhead (Inf), peabrain (Inf), birdbrain (Inf), vegetable (Inf), dumbbell (US sl), klutz (US sl), plonker (Sl), prat (Sl)

4 nonhuman existence, irrationality, unreason, animality, instinct, brute instinct, brute creation, vegetation, vegetable life, inanimate nature, inanimate objects, sticks and stones
▶ *76 Animals (General), 83 Plants (General), 54 Earth Science, 99 Existence*

ADJECTIVES

5 lacking intellect, intellectually weak, mentally weak, feeble-minded, simple, simple-minded, slow, backward, educationally subnormal (ESN), dull, vacuous, vacant, mindless, senseless, brainless, imbecilic, idiotic, cretinous, moronic, mentally deficient, mentally

retarded, mentally handicapped, brain-damaged, senile, in one's second childhood, demented, insane, irrational

6 unintelligent, ignorant, stupid, dense, foolish, thoughtless, unthinking, illogical, inane, fatuous, empty-headed, puerile, childish, childlike, infantile, immature, unwise, unperceptive (*or* imperceptive), obtuse, stolid, thickheaded, blockheaded, oafish, boorish, doltish, witless, unoriginal, uninventive, unimaginative, imitative, dim-witted (Inf), dim (Inf), thick (Inf), thick as two short planks (Inf), dumb (Inf), dopey (Inf), silly (Inf), daft (Inf), loony (*or* looney) (Sl), nutty (Sl), klutzy (US sl), soft (Inf), soft in the head (Inf), not all there (Inf), not sixteen ounces to the pound (Inf), not playing with a full deck (Inf), not sixteen annas to the rupee (Inf), a brick short of a load (Inf), two sandwiches short of a picnic (Inf), not the full pound note (Inf), two bangers short of a barbie (Aus inf), out to lunch (Sl)
▶ *798 Ridiculousness, 510 Insanity, 502 Ignorance*

7 intellectually subnormal, mentally subnormal, educationally subnormal (ESN), subnormal, mentally deficient, mentally handicapped, retarded, backward, simple, simple-minded, feeble-minded, imbecilic, idiotic, moronic, cretinous, autistic, brain-damaged, senile, confused, incoherent, witless, gaga (Inf)

8 nonhuman, irrational, without reason, dumb, brute, animal, instinctive, instinctual, vegetable, vegetative, inanimate, inorganic, mineral
▶ *641 Inaction, 643 Inactivity, 240 Inertness*

VERBS

9 lack intellect, have a low IQ, lack reason, be of unsound mind, be out of one's mind, show ignorance, be stupid, not have enough sense to come in out of the rain, not see an inch beyond one's nose, not find one's way to first base (US), fail to see, play the fool, be not all there (Inf)

10 bemuse, confound, confuse, muddle, befuddle, fuddle, bewilder, mystify, perplex, flummox, baffle, bedazzle, addle, stump, stun, knock out, paralyse, make one's head spin, drive to one's wits end, blunt, dull, obscure, drug, anaesthetize
▶ *151 Disorder, 366 Agitation, 875 Drug-Taking, 153 Disturbance, 404 Insensibility, 523 Unintelligibility, 563 Voicelessness*

ADVERBS

11 unintelligently, without intelligence, unthinkingly, without thinking, emptyheadedly, absently, vacantly, vacuously, inanely, fatuously, ignorantly, stupidly, mindlessly, senselessly, brainlessly, feeble-mindedly, simple-mindedly, idiotically, moronically, insanely, senilely, irrationally, illogically, unwisely, fool-

ishly, imperceptively, obtusely, stolidly, childishly, puerilely, immaturely, imitatively, uninventively, unimaginatively

12 **nonhumanly**, irrationally, unreasoningly, without rationality, without reason, instinctively, instinctually, from instinct, inanimately

461 Thought

NOUNS

1 **thought**, thinking, cognition, reasoning, reason, cogitation, mental process, thought process, mental activity, cerebration, deduction, ratiocination, rumination, workings of the mind

2 **intellcctual exercise**, deep thinking, hard thinking, profound thought, headwork, brainwork, ideation
▶ *471 Idea*

3 **thoughtfulness**, concentration, contemplation, reflection, consideration, speculation, retrospection, pensiveness, reverie, brown study, introspection, musing, daydreaming, innermost thought, meditation, meditativeness
▶ *4 Philosophy*

4 **deliberation**, pondering, abstract thought, abstractedness, profundity

5 **creative thought**, lateral thinking, inventiveness, originality, inventive power, flow of ideas, inspiration, train of thoughts, stream of consciousness, thinking cap (Inf)
▶ *459 Intellect, 467 Attention, 507 Wisdom, 519 Imagination, 511 Memory*

6 **idea**, thought, notion, concept, conception, belief, premise, theory, hypothesis, conjecture, fancy, supposition, surmise, intuition, inkling, conclusion, principle, precept, point of view, attitude, novel idea, crazy idea, good idea, quantum leap, flash of inspiration, brainwave (Inf), brainstorm (US inf), good wheeze (Sl)
▶ *472 Topic, 497 Belief, 473 Argument, 477 Question, 518 Supposition, 471 Idea*

7 **thinker**, logical thinker, rational person, wise man, philosopher, professor, academic, intellectual, highbrow, genius, scholar, student, ideologist, dreamer, egghead (Inf), walking encyclopaedia (Inf), brainbox (Inf)
▶ *501 Knowledge*

ADJECTIVES

8 **thoughtful**, thinking, reasoning, mental, intellectual, cognitive, cerebral, ruminative, philosophical, considerate

9 **concentrating**, contemplative, pensive, reflective, absorbed, lost in thought

10 **speculative**, introspective, meditative, profound, deliberative, pondered, pondering, musing, inventive, dreamy, notional, concep-

tual, fanciful, theoretical, conjectural, suppositional, in a brown study, in a world of one's own, miles away (Inf)

11 **reasoning**, intelligent, rational, logical, intellectual, philosophical, professorial, scholarly, ideological, highbrow

VERBS

12 **think**, reason, cogitate, ruminate, ponder, consider, meditate, exercise one's intellect, cerebrate, ratiocinate, think deeply, think hard, think profoundly, use one's head, use one's brain, rack one's brains, ideate, speculate, imagine

13 **concentrate**, contemplate, mull over, reflect, reflect upon, study, apply one's mind

14 **have second thoughts**, think ovcr, rethink, reconsider, think again, sleep on it

15 **think about**, work out, weigh up, take stock of, deliberate, ponder, use lateral thinking, get one's brain into gear (Inf)

16 **have an idea**, conceive of, premise, theorize, conjecture, hypothesize, deduce, infer, speculate, suppose, surmise, conclude, hold a point of view, defend one's attitude, originate, invent, have a good idea, have a brainwave (Inf)

17 **philosophize**, intellectualize, internalize, introspect, show genius

ADVERBS

18 **thoughtfully**, reflectively, philosophically, contemplatively, on reconsideration, on second thoughts, rationally, logically, intuitively, introspectively, creatively, inventively

462 Lack of Thought

NOUNS

1 **lack of thought**, thoughtlessness, mindlessness, vacancy, inanity, fatuity, vacuity, blankness, empty-headedness, empty head, blank mind, absent-mindedness, folly, head in the clouds, fallow mind, tranquillity, calm, oblivion

2 **ignorance**, unintelligence, unawareness, nescience, stupidity
▶ *460 Lack of Intellect, 468 Inattention, 254 Absence, 502 Ignorance*

3 **instinct**, instinctiveness, intuition, conditioned reflex, kneejerk response, Pavlovian reaction, gut reaction (Inf)
▶ *464 Intuition*

4 **inconsideration**, thoughtlessness, insensitivity, insensitiveness, inattention, neglect, selfishness, unkindness, tactlessness
▶ *860 Selfishness*

5 **mental block**, blank spot, blind spot, brainstorm, amnesia, lack of memory

6 **daydream**, reverie, fantasizing, pensiveness, deep thought, brown study, woolgathering

7 **inconsiderate person**, hothead, pesterer, pest, bother, nuisance, braggart, queue-

jumper, discourteous driver, road hog (Inf)

ADJECTIVES

8 **thoughtless**, mindless, unthinking, incapable of thought, unreflective, inane, fatuous, vacuous, vacant, blank, empty-headed, absent-minded, abstracted, fallow, oblivious, ignorant, foolish, carefree, easygoing, happy-go-lucky, devil-may-care

9 **instinctive**, intuitive, automatic, involuntary, reflex, impulsive

10 **inconsiderate**, thoughtless, insensitive, heedless, inattentive, neglectful, uncaring, selfish, oblivious to, unkind, tactless, pestering, bothering, discourteous

11 **unthought**, unconsidered, unconceived, unimagined, undreamed-of

VERBS

12 **lack thought**, forget, act without thinking, speak without thinking, not stop and think, suffer from absent-mindedness, have one's head in the clouds, hit a mental block, blank out, have a brainstorm (Inf), daydream, suffer from amnesia, lose one's memory, ignore the consequences, rush in where angels fear to tread

13 **be inconsiderate**, pester, bother, queue-jump

ADVERBS

14 **thoughtlessly**, instinctively, through ignorance, insensitively, mindlessly, obliviously, selfishly, discourteously, with one's head in the clouds (Inf), without a care in the world (Inf)

463 Reason

Reason is itself a matter of faith. It is an act of faith to assert that our thoughts have any relation to reality at all. G. K. Chesterton.

NOUNS

1 **reason**, mind, intellect, power of reason, rationality, intelligence, understanding, perception, judgment, wisdom, sense, sanity, saneness, power of conception

▶ *459 Intellect, 461 Thought, 501 Knowledge, 481 Discrimination, 509 Sanity*

2 **reasoning**, rationalizing, rationalism, rationality, rationalization, logical process, logical thought, logic, ratiocination, plain reason, generalization, inference, deductive reasoning, deduction, inductive reasoning, induction, *a priori* reasoning, *a posteriori* reasoning, syllogism, analysis, discursive reasoning

▶ *464 Intuition, 52 Mathematics*

3 **debate**, polemics, dialectics, dialecticism, apologetics, argumentation, argument, formal argument, legal argument, dissent, dispute, disputation, litigation

▶ *500 Dissent, 666 Disagreement*

4 **explanation**, cause, motive, grounds, premise, pretext, theory, basis, assumption, justifi-

cation, defence, speculation, hypothesis, valid point, excuse

▶ *226 Cause, 518 Supposition, 491 Uncertainty, 505 Maxim*

5 **reasoner**, thinker, intellectual, academic, philosopher, logician, rationalist, apologist, dialectician, syllogist

6 **arguer**, debater, litigator, disputant, plaintiff, defendant, jurist, polemicist (*or* polemist), casuist, proponent, wrangler, barrack-room lawyer, jailhouse lawyer (US), Philadelphia lawyer (US), ambulance chaser (US)

▶ *473 Argument*

ADJECTIVES

7 **reasoning**, reasonable, rational, thinking, intellectual, intelligent, understanding, perceptive, knowledgeable, judgmental, wise, sensible, sane

8 **rational**, rationalistic, logical, ratiocinative, analytical, inferential, deductive, inductive, *a priori, a posteriori*

9 **argumentative**, dissenting, disputing, litigious, polemic (*or* polemical), dialectical

10 **causal**, theoretical, assumptive, valid, explanatory, justified, defended, defensive, excused

VERBS

11 **reason**, rationalize, analyse, think, think logically, logicalize, understand, perceive, judge, ratiocinate, generalize, synthesize, infer, deduce, induce

12 **be reasonable**, show wisdom, make sense, hold water (Inf)

13 **debate**, argue, dissent, dispute, litigate, enter into argument, exchange opinions

14 **premise**, theorize, postulate, philosophize, assume, explain, justify, defend, excuse

ADVERBS

15 **reasonably**, rationally, logically, sensibly, sanely, within bounds, as far as possible

464 Intuition

NOUNS

1 **intuition**, intuitiveness, intuitive reasoning, feminine intuition, feeling, insight, perception, inspiration

2 **precognition**, *a priori* knowledge, sixth sense, second sight, clairvoyance, divination, telepathy, extrasensory perception (ESP), presentiment

▶ *462 Lack of Thought, 459 Intellect, 759 Feeling, 583 Improvisation*

3 **insight**, foreboding, impression, feeling, impulse, hunch, flash

4 **instinct**, innate reaction, proclivity, subconscious, unconscious, automatic reaction, Pavlovian response, knee-jerk (Inf), gut reaction (Inf)

5 **intuitive person**, feeling person, medium,

clairvoyant, seer, prophet, diviner, sibyl, carer

ADJECTIVES

6 **intuitive**, insightful, perceptive, sensitive, sensing, inspired

7 **precognitive**, *a priori*, unmediated, second-sighted, clairvoyant, divinatory, telepathic, extrasensory, presentient

8 **instinctive**, instinctual, automatic, spontaneous, reflex, innate, Pavlovian, knee-jerk (Inf)

VERBS

9 **be intuitive**, intuit, feel, have a feeling about, go on one's feelings, perceive, divine, work on a hunch, follow one's hunch, feel it in one's bones (*or* water), have a funny feeling about, just know

10 **be instinctive**, react automatically, give a knee-jerk reaction

ADVERBS

11 **intuitively**, by intuition, instinctively, by (*or* on) instinct, automatically, spontaneously

465   Curiosity

NOUNS

1 **curiosity**, curiousness, inquisitiveness, questioning, interest, inquisition, inquiry (*or* enquiry), desire (*or* thirst) for knowledge, inquiring mind

2 **prying**, nosiness, snooping, meddling, officiousness, gossip, tittle-tattle, morbid curiosity, prurience, voyeurism, rubbernecking (Sl)

▶ *477 Question, 467 Attention, 642 Activity, 533 News*

3 **curious person**, inquirer (*or* enquirer), inquisitor, investigator, examiner, questioner, detective, lawyer, teacher, explorer, adventurer, sightseer, tourist, spectator, traveller, journalist

4 **meddler**, gossip, gossipmonger, scandalmonger, stirrer, prier, pry, spy, tittle-tattler, eavesdropper, voyeur, Peeping Tom, quidnunc, kibitzer (US), Paul Pry, busybody (Inf), snoop (Inf), nosy parker (Inf), mole (Inf), big-ears (Inf), rubbernecker (Sl)

ADJECTIVES

5 **curious**, inquisitive, inquiring, inquisitorial, questioning, interested, with ears burning, wanting to know, keen to learn, keen, adventurous, sightseeing

6 **prying**, officious, meddlesome, meddling, prurient, gossipy, snooping (Inf), snoopy (Inf), nosy (Inf)

VERBS

7 **be curious**, inquire (*or* enquire), inquire (*or* enquire) after, question, quiz, interrogate, search for, show interest, desire knowledge, thirst for knowledge, want to know, seek out, feel concern for, show interest in, gossip, tittle-tattle, sightsee, eavesdrop, pry, meddle, poke one's nose in, prick up one's ears, sniff

out (Inf), nose around (Inf), snoop (Inf), rubberneck (Sl)

ADVERBS

8 **curiously**, inquisitively, inquisitorially, questioningly, keenly, adventurously

9 **officiously**, pruriently, nosily (Inf)

466   Lack of Curiosity

NOUNS

1 **incuriousness**, incuriosity, total trust, blind faith, credulity, credulousness, gullibility

2 **lack of interest**, disinterest, unconcern, boredom, insouciance, indifference, apathy, impassivity, imperturbability, uninvolvement, numbness, stupor, insensibility, inactivity, stagnation, idleness, sluggishness, slowness, mental inertia, complacency, nonchalance, pococurantism

▶ *783 Indifference, 787 Lack of Wonder, 788 Boredom, 761 Insensitivity*

ADJECTIVES

3 **incurious**, uninquisitive, trusting, unquestioning, credulous, gullible

4 **uninterested**, unthinking, unconcerned, heedless, nonchalant, bored, insouciant, indifferent, dull, imperturbable, unresponsive, aloof, insensible, apathetic, complacent, phlegmatic, impassive, uninvolved, unmoved, detached, distant, disengaged, unenthusiastic, unstirred, numb, inactive, slow, stagnating, deadpan, idle, lackadaisical, sluggish, brain-dead (Inf), cool (Sl)

VERBS

5 **not ask**, not question, take on trust, believe, be taken in

6 **be incurious**, disregard, take (*or* show) no interest in, feel no concern for, not care, could not care less, disengage, detach oneself, not mind, be easy about, be able to take it or leave it, be neutral about, leave one cold, not trouble oneself, mind one's own business, live in an ivory tower

ADVERBS

7 **incuriously**, uninquisitively, unquestioningly, credulously, gullibly, without a doubt, without a second thought

8 **disinterestedly**, unconcernedly, heedlessly, indifferently, apathetically, impassively, imperturbably, numbly, insensitively, inertly, stagnantly, idly, complacently

467   Attention

NOUNS

1 **attention**, attentiveness, notice, regard, concern, consideration, mindfulness

2 **close attention**, undivided attention, attention to detail, close observance, examination, watchfulness, alertness, finickiness, nit picking (Inf)

3 **carefulness**, meticulousness, fastidiousness, sedulousness, circumspection, scrutiny, surveillance, vigilance, wariness, heed, concentration, application, assiduousness

4 **diligence**, studiousness, single-mindedness, fixation, pedantry, purism, obsession, preoccupation, tunnel vision, hang-up (Inf)

▶ *461 Thought, 469 Carefulness, 465 Curiosity, 781 Caution*

5 **solicitude**, care, consideration, protection, indulgence, attendance, courtesy, gallantry, spoiling, fussing over (Inf)

6 **attentive person**, doctor, lawyer, examiner, scholar, lover, suitor, chaperon

ADJECTIVES

7 **watchful**, alert, attentive, observant, sharp-eyed, vigilant, on guard, careful, wary, circumspect, scrutinizing, surveying, heedful, curious

8 **diligent**, studious, painstaking, meticulous, fastidious, sedulous, assiduous, undistracted, single-minded, rapt, engrossed, obsessed, fixated, pedantic, preoccupied, purist, hung-up (Inf), all eyes (Inf), all ears (Inf)

9 **solicitous**, caring, concerned, protective, considerate, mindful, indulgent, attentive, courteous, gallant

VERBS

10 **be attentive**, regard, consider, notice, note, pay attention to, hover over, dance attendance on, attend, care for

11 **take note of**, register, mark, keep an eye on, give undivided attention to, watch, observe, examine, miss nothing, stay alert, guard against, prick up one's ears (Inf)

12 **scrutinize**, survey, heed, study, fix upon, nit-pick (Inf)

13 **attract attention**, draw attention, excite the attention of, be the centre of attention, catch the eye of, act as a magnet

14 **be solicitous**, indulge, pay attention to, show consideration for, shower attention on, court, spoil, flirt, grovel, toady, fawn over, crawl, fuss over (Inf), suck up to (Sl), brown-nose (Tab sl), arse-lick (Tab sl)

ADVERBS

15 **attentively**, mindfully, observantly, watchfully, alertly, carefully, meticulously, fastidiously, sedulously, circumspectly, vigilantly, warily, assiduously, diligently, studiously, pedantically

468   Inattention

NOUNS

1 **inattention**, inattentiveness, incuriosity, thoughtlessness, unmindfulness, forgetfulness, aberration, heedlessness, unconcern, detachment, obliviousness, apathy, disregard, distraction, nonobservance, carelessness, rashness, desultoriness, superficiality, indifference, cold shoulder

2 **impetuosity**, precipitance, impulsiveness, rashness, recklessness, foolhardiness, flightiness

3 **absent-mindedness**, daydreaming, dizziness, frivolity, woolgathering, stargazing, head in the clouds, castles in the air, Walter Mitty

▶ *466 Lack of Curiosity, 783 Indifference, 462 Lack of Thought, 278 Shallowness*

4 **thoughtlessness**, inconsideration, disregard, indifference, ignoring, insensitivity, selfishness

▶ *860 Selfishness*

5 **inattentive act**, oversight, lapse, slip, error, mistake, blunder, mishap, forgotten name, forgotten anniversary, forgotten birthday, slip-up (Inf)

▶ *504 Error*

6 **inattentive person**, daydreamer, dreamer, scatterbrain, woolgatherer, absent-minded professor

ADJECTIVES

7 **inattentive**, thoughtless, unthinking, not concentrating, incurious, unmindful, forgetful, heedless, unheeding, unconcerned, detached, oblivious, apathetic, listless, disregarding, distracted, unobservant

8 **absent-minded**, lost in thought, daydreaming, woolgathering, stargazing, in a brown study, in a world of one's own (Inf), out to lunch (Inf), not with it (Inf)

9 **thoughtless**, inconsiderate, uncaring, selfish, insensitive, unthinking

10 **careless**, negligent, neglectful, slack, remiss, sloppy, slapdash, slipshod, hit-or-miss, dizzy, flighty, rash, precipitous

11 **perfunctory**, casual, lackadaisical, desultory, superficial

VERBS

12 **be inattentive**, show unconcern, disregard, ignore, not notice, not listen, pay no attention, take no notice (*or* note) of, pay no heed to, overlook, put out of mind, allow one's mind to wander, daydream, stargaze, woolgather, be elsewhere (Inf), build castles in the air (Inf)

13 **be thoughtless**, be inattentive, show inconsideration for, disregard, ignore, slight, turn one's back on, make unwelcome, cold-shoulder, give someone the cold shoulder

ADVERBS

14 **inattentively**, incuriously, thoughtlessly, unmindfully, forgetfully, heedlessly, selfishly, inconsiderately, indifferently, obliviously, apathetically, carelessly, rashly, impetuously, recklessly, impulsively

469 Carefulness

NOUNS

1 **carefulness**, care, caution, attentiveness, attention, mindfulness, diligence, heed, assiduity, thoroughness, exactness, precision, meticulousness

2 **consideration**, solicitude, compassion, mindfulness, care, loving care, tender loving care (TLC)

3 **circumspection**, watchfulness, alertness, vigilance, readiness, preparation, prudence, scruples, scrupulousness

4 **fastidiousness**, particularity, exactitude, perfectionism, orderliness, tidiness, neatness, perfection, attention to detail, niceness, pedantry, pernicketiness, faddiness

▶ *503 Accuracy, 467 Attention, 642 Activity, 150 Order, 594 Preparation, 516 Foresight, 781 Caution*

5 **watchfulness**, surveillance, vigilance, wariness, guarding, guardedness, watching, watch, lookout, inspection, invigilation, vigil, guard-duty, baby-sitting, baby-minding, neighbourhood watch, stake-out

▶ *632 Safety*

6 **careful person**, perfectionist, pedant, miser, hoarder, Scrooge, bomb-disposal expert, shrewd businessman (*or* businesswoman)

7 **caring person**, carer, nurse, doctor, social worker

8 **watchful person**, baby-sitter, baby-minder, guard, caretaker, guardian, chaperon, bodyguard, sentry, sentinel, vigilante, neighbourhood watchman, Guardian Angel (US)

ADJECTIVES

9 **careful**, attentive, mindful, diligent, heedful, assiduous, thorough, meticulous, circumspect, watchful, wide-awake, alert, vigilant, observant, guarding, watching, on guard, ready, prepared, prudent, scrupulous, precise, painstaking, pedantic, perfect, perfectionist, fastidious, nice, pernickety, faddy, particular, exact, orderly, tidy, neat

VERBS

10 **be careful**, mind, heed, watch, prepare, be vigilant, be cautious, tread carefully, pay attention to, tread warily, walk on eggshells (Inf)

11 **care for**, take charge of, safeguard, guard, stand guard, look out for, survey, check, inspect, invigilate, watch over, keep an eye on, attend to, take care of, chaperon, baby-sit, baby-mind, nurse, keep tabs on (Inf)

ADVERBS

12 **carefully**, with care, cautiously, gingerly, diligently, with precision, in detail, with exactitude, thoroughly, precisely, perfectly, alertly, warily

13 **caringly**, tenderly

470 Negligence

NOUNS

1 **negligence**, carelessness, inattention, thoughtlessness, unmindfulness, nonchalance, unconcern, oblivion, insouciance, disregard, neglectfulness, dereliction, forgetfulness, heedlessness, remissness

2 **indifference**, informality, casualness, *laissez faire* (Fr), inexactitude, unscrupulousness, superficiality, shallowness, offhandedness, slackness, shoddiness, laziness, untidiness, messiness, slovenliness, sloppiness, sluttishness, procrastination, avoidance, delay

3 **negligent person**, procrastinator, idler, shirker, sloven, slut, slob (Inf)

ADJECTIVES

4 **negligent**, neglectful, careless, inattentive, thoughtless, unmindful, nonchalant, unconcerned, uncaring, oblivious, insouciant, disregardful, forgetful, heedless, remiss

5 **indifferent**, informal, casual, lackadaisical, inexact, unscrupulous, superficial, shallow, offhanded, procrastinating, avoiding, delaying, slack, lax, half-done, slipshod, slapdash, incomplete, shoddy, lazy, untidy, dirty, messy, slovenly, sluttish, sloppy (Inf), grotty (Sl)

VERBS

6 **be neglectful**, neglect, disregard, take no notice of, not care for, ignore, turn a blind eye to, forget, not heed, procrastinate, take things slowly, put off until tomorrow, take it easy, put one's feet up, avoid, delay, leave undone, leave half-done, not complete, give a lick and a promise (Inf)

ADVERBS

7 **negligently**, neglectfully, carelessly, cursorily, any old way (Inf), sloppily (Inf)

471 Idea

NOUNS

1 **idea**, notion, abstraction, thought, thinking, concept, conception, observation, perception, understanding, awareness, apprehension, comprehension, reflection, assumption, presumption, reaction, estimation, feeling, sentiment, memory, construct, mental picture, mental image, mental object, imago, ideatum, noumenon, essence, Platonic Idea, the Absolute Idea

▶ *7 Religion, 8 Divinity, 4 Philosophy, 461 Thought, 459 Intellect, 103 Essence, 518 Supposition, 464 Intuition, 511 Memory, 760 Sensitivity, 368 Nonmaterial World*

2 **theory**, idea, hypothesis, suggestion, conjecture, speculation, supposition, suspicion, indication, fancy, clue, hint, guess, feeling, intuition, hunch (Inf)

▶ *518 Supposition, 4 Philosophy*

3 **plan**, intention, scheme, project, proposal, invention, idea, brainwave, bright idea, brainstorm, brainchild, cunning plan, wizard wheeze (Inf)
▶ *592 Plan, 588 Intention, 119 Originality*

4 **purpose**, aim, design, function, goal, object, objective, target, end, point, reason, significance, meaning
▶ *592 Plan, 588 Intention, 157 End, 463 Reason, 228 Motive, 520 Meaning, 570 Will*

5 **ideology**, opinion, view, viewpoint, stand, stance, position, philosophy, ideas, beliefs, principles, creed, credo, teachings, tenets, ideals, morals, standards, prejudices
▶ *4 Philosophy, 7 Religion, 497 Belief*

6 **ideal**, model, example, exemplar, paragon, paradigm, standard, pattern, quintessence, epitome, prototype, archetype, vision, dream, Utopia, fantasy, fancy, wishful thinking, castle in the air (*or* in Spain)
▶ *619 Perfection, 775 Hope, 519 Imagination*

7 **idealism**, idealization, optimism, visionariness, utopianism, romanticism, daydreaming, wishful thinking, impracticality, ideality, idealness
▶ *619 Perfection, 775 Hope, 4 Philosophy*

8 **imagination**, imaginativeness, inventiveness, originality, creativity, ingenuity, inspiration, perception, visualization, conceptualization
▶ *519 Imagination, 760 Sensitivity, 119 Originality, 786 Wonder*

9 **person of ideas**, thinker, philosopher, theorizer, theoretician, idealist, ideologue, ideologist, dreamer, optimist, utopian, visionary, creator, mentor, romantic, creative artist, inventor, boffin (Inf), egghead (Inf), backroom boy (Inf), ideas person (Inf)
▶ *4 Philosophy, 459 Intellect, 48 Literature, 49 Music, 51 Performing Arts, 6 Education, 50 Painting and Sculpture, 11 Occultism, 435 Vision, 507 Wisdom*

ADJECTIVES

10 **theoretical**, notional, abstract, putative, conceptual, perceptual, philosophical, hypothetical, conjectural, speculative, suppositional, propositional, suggestive, indicative, suspected, assumed, presumed, estimated, guesstimated (*or* guestimated) (Inf)

11 **ideational**, mental, cerebral, intellectual, in the mind, in the mind's eye, in one's head, imagined, visualized, conceived, conceptualized, inspired, aware, reflective, imaginative, inventive, creative, original, ingenious, fanciful

12 **purposive**, functional, goal-directed, teleological, aiming, functioning, targeting, intentional, proposed, aimed, targeted, schematic, designed, planned, reasoned, well-reasoned, reasonable, significant, meaningful
▶ *226 Cause*

13 **ideal**, model, exemplary, paradigmatic, epitomical, quintessential, prototypical, archetypical, visionary, fantastic, idealistic, idealized, optimistic, utopian, romantic, sentimental, dreamy, impractical, ideological
▶ *619 Perfection, 775 Hope, 4 Philosophy*

VERBS

14 **have an idea**, come to mind, enter one's head, cross one's mind, suggest itself, dawn upon, realize, perceive, remember, come to one, occur to one, hit one, strike one, be struck by, deduce, understand, apprehend, intuit, see, grasp, grab one (Inf), get (Inf), suss (out) (Inf), pop into one's head (Inf)
▶ *478 Answer*

15 **imagine**, ideate, think, reflect, deliberate, feel, conceive, visualize, conceptualize, picture, envision, envisage, formulate, create, invent, originate, think up, conjure up, dream up, dream, fancy, fantasize, idealize, romanticize, daydream, pipe dream, see through rose-coloured (*or* tinted) glasses, build castles in the air
▶ *459 Intellect, 461 Thought, 519 Imagination*

16 **inspire**, inspirit, fire one's imagination, animate, exhilarate, enliven

17 **theorize**, hypothesize, conjecture, suggest, suspect, guess, reckon, estimate, suppose, opine, believe, assume, presume, have a hunch (Inf), guesstimate (*or* guestimate) (Inf)
▶ *4 Philosophy, 461 Thought*

18 **aim**, plan, plot, scheme, design, propose, intend, target, point to, head for, get ideas, set one's sights on, aspire, aim high, overreach, overstep oneself, have thoughts above one's station, go all out for (Inf)
▶ *588 Intention, 357 Overstepping, 228 Motive, 570 Will, 592 Plan, 590 Pursuit*

19 **epitomize**, exemplify, set an example, model, pattern, indicate, represent, signify, mean

ADVERBS

20 **theoretically**, notionally, in theory, abstractly, abstractedly, putatively, philosophically, thoughtfully, conceptually, hypothetically, conjecturally, reflectively, mentally, in the mind, in the mind's eye, in one's head, upstairs (Inf)

21 **purposively**, intentionally, schematically, indicatively, functionally, significantly, meaningfully, reasonably, to the point, with an aim in mind, with a view to, on purpose, deliberately

22 **imaginatively**, originally, inventively, creatively, ingeniously, perceptively, inspirationally, optimistically, romantically, sentimentally, impractically, dreamily, fantastically, idealistically, through rose-coloured (*or* -tinted) glasses

23 **ideally**, perfectly, under the best circum-

stances, in a perfect world, at best, all things being equal

24 **ideologically**, standardly, archetypally, paradigmatically, so it seems, as one sees it, to one's way of thinking, in one's opinion

INTERJECTIONS

25 **got it!**, eureka!, I see!, that's it!, aha!, that's the idea!

472 Topic

NOUNS

1 **topic**, subject, contents, text, subject matter, matter, theme, plot, angle, interest, concern, point, motif, leitmotiv, programme, statement, message, argument, thesis, theorem, proposition, supposition, heart of the matter, main point, keynote, essence, idea, gist, drift, pith, meat, basis, foundation, rubric
▶ *471 Idea, 562 Summary, 518 Supposition, 257 Contents, 520 Meaning, 103 Essence, 561 Dissertation, 310 Angle*

2 **issue**, point at issue, concern, focus, question, topic, problem, bone of contention, moot point, living issue, matter for discussion, case, point, item, motion, agenda, business on hand, any other business
▶ *477 Question, 473 Argument, 674 Contention, 666 Disagreement, 716 Negotiation*

3 **matter of interest**, topic for discussion, events, news, happenings, rumour, gossip, story, affair, business, proceedings, goings-on (Inf)
▶ *533 News, 528 Information, 565 Talkativeness*

4 **sphere**, domain, business, concern, area, branch, course, discipline, topic, field, field of inquiry, subject of investigation
▶ *251 Situation, 477 Question*

5 **educational topic**, subject, field of study, course, project, class project, individual project, art project, special topic, nature topic, science topic, local-history topic, tract, treatise, lecture course
▶ *561 Dissertation, 6 Education*

ADJECTIVES

6 **topical**, in the news, current, present, immediate, contemporary, up-to-date, up-to-the-minute, hot off the press, straight from the horse's mouth, timely, happening (Sl)
▶ *533 News*

7 **focused**, subjective, angled, pointed, founded, based, concerned with, dealing with, supposed, proposed, programmed, thematic, central, basic

8 **problematic**, moot, mooted, undecided, questioned, challenged, challenging, curious, interesting, thought-provoking, debatable, worthy of discussion, on the agenda

9 **local**, familiar, domestic, nearby, local-interest, gossipy, tell-tale

VERBS

10 **focus on**, concentrate on, centre on, point to, be concerned with, contain, include, state, argue, propose, suppose
▶ *103 Essence, 146 Inclusion*

11 **raise the point**, raise the issue, point out, make a point, put on the agenda, put forward (a suggestion), deal with, discuss, debate, contend, question, inquire, study, get to the heart of the matter, do a project on (Inf)
▶ *666 Disagreement, 716 Negotiation, 473 Argument, 4 Philosophy*

ADVERBS

12 **topically**, locally, domestically, currently, in the news, as it happens, up to date, up to the minute, in the mind, on the brain, in one's thoughts
▶ *250 Location, 297 Surroundings, 185 Time*

13 **problematically**, curiously, interestingly, challengingly, questionably, debatably, in question, under consideration, under discussion, afoot, on the agenda, on the table, before the house, before the committee
▶ *716 Negotiation*

14 **thematically**, essentially, basically, centrally, supposedly, pointedly, to the point, in essence, in short
▶ *103 Essence, 562 Summary*

473 Argument

NOUNS

1 **argument**, disagreement, dispute, quarrel, controversy, discord, misunderstanding, incompatibility, diversity, difference, altercation, wrangle, squabble, bickering, tiff, spat, row, scuffle, clash, brawl, conflict, feud, fight, fray, affray, fracas, scrimmage, donnybrook, strife, argy-bargy (Inf), set to (Inf), scrap (Inf), fisticuffs (Inf), barney (Inf), falling-out (Inf), to-do (Inf), slanging match (Inf), name calling (Inf)
▶ *666 Disagreement, 117 Disparity, 670 Attack, 500 Dissent, 153 Disturbance, 820 Enmity, 223 Exchange, 385 Friction, 676 War*

2 **logical argument**, debate, discussion, disputation, dialogue, dialectic, eristic, polemic, maieutic, hermeneutic, heuristic, elenchus, logic, sophistry, argumentation, discourse, reasoning, ratiocination, deliberation, deduction, induction, consideration, reflection, thought, challenge, *reductio ad absurdum* (L), questioning, inquiry, doubt
▶ *4 Philosophy, 477 Question, 52 Mathematics, 568 Conversation, 716 Negotiation, 463 Reason, 474 Sophistry, 461 Thought*

3 **line of argument**, line of reasoning, reasoning, rationale, contention, topic, issue, thesis, hypothesis, postulate, proposition, premise, pretext, point, case, claim, assertion, state-

ment, affirmation, attestation, testimony, position, opinion, stance, grounds, evidence
▶ *472 Topic, 471 Idea, 674 Contention, 490 Certainty, 483 Evidence, 518 Supposition*

4 **gist**, outline, summary, essence, theme, subject, topic, idea, point, nub, argument, issue, plot, subplot, scenario, setting, story, moral, allegory, parable
▶ *472 Topic, 103 Essence, 520 Meaning*

5 **plea**, pleading, argument, request, entreaty, cry, suit, consideration, excuse, answer, apology, defence, claim, justification, explanation, rationalization, vindication, cause
▶ *855 Vindication, 712 Request, 478 Answer, 226 Cause*

6 **arguer**, argumentative type, debater, disputant, pleader, lawyer, barrister, disputer, quarreller, troublemaker, wrangler, polemicist, polemist, controversialist, logician, eristic, sophist
▶ *4 Philosophy, 16 Law, 679 Combatant*

ADJECTIVES

7 **arguing**, quibbling, quarrelling, wrangling, squabbling, bickering, at odds, at cross purposes, different, diverse, discordant, incompatible, dissenting, dissentient, rowing, scuffling, clashing, at loggerheads, scrapping (Inf)
▶ *500 Dissent, 153 Disturbance, 113 Diversity*

8 **argumentative**, quarrelsome, disagreeable, disputatious, litigious, dissentious, factious, querulous, peevish, irritable, contrary, testy, petulant, fractious, choleric, cross, irascible, cantankerous, grouchy (Inf)
▶ *829 Irascibility, 577 Obstinacy, 768 Aggravation*

9 **hostile**, antagonistic, provocative, polemical, eristic, inimical, pugnacious, belligerent, bellicose, warlike, brawling, conflicting, feuding, fighting, at war, at each other's throats, in battle
▶ *670 Attack, 241 Violence, 663 Opposition, 669 Resistance*

10 **arguable**, debatable, disputable, contentious, topical, controversial, questionable, doubtful, dubious, challenging, problematic, refutable, open to question, in question, moot, unsettled, undecided, misunderstood

11 **logical**, elenctic, sophistic (or sophistical), heuristic, hypothetical, propositional, proposed, postulated, claimed, asserted, stated, affirmed, attested

12 **apologetic**, in defence, defensive, pleading, justifiable, explicable, vindicated, justified, rational, explained, causal, caused

VERBS

13 **argue**, disagree, bicker, wrangle, quarrel, quibble, squabble, fall out (Inf), remonstrate, altercate, have words (Inf), gainsay, contradict, polemicize, oppose, dissent, differ, dispute, contest, spar, scuffle, have a set to (Inf),

clash, conflict, brawl, feud, fight, go to war
▶ *536 Negation*

14 **discuss**, debate, exchange opinions, reason, ratiocinate, logicize, logomachize, deliberate, consider, weigh up, reflect, doubt, question, inquire, challenge, moot, deduce, induce, chop logic, cavil, argue the toss
▶ *474 Sophistry, 223 Exchange, 716 Negotiation*

15 **state**, argue, maintain, say, affirm, attest, hold, claim, hypothesize, propose, postulate, suggest, imply, indicate, signify, betoken, denote, show, demonstrate, establish, evince, prove
▶ *490 Certainty, 518 Supposition*

16 **plead**, argue, request, entreat, prevail upon, persuade, canvass, put one's case, apologize, defend, claim, answer, justify, explain, rationalize, vindicate
▶ *712 Request, 855 Vindication*

ADVERBS

17 **argumentatively**, disagreeably, irritably, petulantly, crossly, discordantly, incompatibly, diversely, differently, at odds, at cross purposes, at loggerheads, polemically, antagonistically, provocatively, inimically, belligerently, in conflict, at each other's throats, at war

18 **arguably**, disputedly, topically, controversially, contrarily, on the contrary, on the other hand, at issue, under investigation, in question, doubtfully, hypothetically, plausibly

19 **logically**, dialectically, deductively, inductively, reflectively, thoughtfully, deliberately

20 **apologetically**, in defence, as a defence, in answer, in response, justifiably, explicably, rationally, reasonably, causally

474 Sophistry

NOUNS

1 **sophistry**, casuistry, philosophism, jesuitry, false reasoning, specious reasoning, logic chopping, faulty logic, illogicality, illogicalness, fallaciousness, fallacy, speciousness, invalidity, untenableness, unsoundness, irrationality, inconsistency, circularity, equivocation, subterfuge, sleight, distortion, misapplication, solecism, mere rhetoric, empty words, moonshine
▶ *4 Philosophy, 473 Argument, 313 Circularity, 578 Equivocation, 548 Misrepresentation, 506 Nonsense, 286 Obliqueness, 309 Distortion, 538 Untruth, 844 Wrong, 504 Error*

2 **sophism**, paralogism, pseudosyllogism, solecism, flawed argument, circular argument, *non sequitur* (L), paradox, contradiction in terms, antilogy, fallacy, dodge, trick, ruse, shuffle, quibble, quip, quirk, cavil, contrivance, stratagem, subterfuge, red herring, scheme, misinformation, disinformation,

propaganda, hogwash, baloney, bosh (Inf), bunkum (Inf), hooey (Inf), hokum (Inf), scam (Inf), blag (Sl), bullshit (Tab sl)

▶ *531 Concealment, 539 Deception, 540 Falsehood, 551 Obscurity, 592 Plan*

3 **cunning**, sophistication, craftiness, artfulness, art, artifice, slyness, foxiness, slipperiness, shiftiness, trickiness, sneakiness, insidiousness, machination, manipulation, demagoguery, pulling the wool over someone's eyes, mystification, obfuscation

▶ *657 Cunning, 293 Covering, 539 Deception, 551 Obscurity, 11 Occultism, 443 Opaqueness, 586 Persuasion, 811 Showiness, 655 Skill, 233 Influence*

4 **quibbling**, captiousness, hair-splitting, nit-picking, cavilling, subtlety, oversubtlety, paltering, prevarication, hedging, shuffling, beating about the bush, pettifoggery, pussyfooting (Inf), jiggery-pokery (Inf)

▶ *521 Lack of Meaning, 578 Equivocation*

5 **hypocrisy**, deceit, deception, duplicity, pretence, humbug, double-dealing, insincerity, disingenuousness, guile, evasion, mendacity, fakery, chicanery, quackery, charlatanism, mountebankery, Pharisaism, Tartuffery

▶ *539 Deception, 540 Falsehood, 11 Occultism, 538 Untruth, 278 Shallowness*

6 **sophist**, sophister, sophisticator, paralogist, philosophist, casuist, Jesuit, solecist, logic chopper, equivocator, prevaricator, caviller, quibbler, nit-picker, hair-splitter, pussyfooter, pettifogger, waffler, charmer, demagogue, propagandist, sweet-talker, trickster, schemer, hypocrite, faker, liar, quack, charlatan, mountebank, con man (Inf), shyster (Inf)

▶ *4 Philosophy, 539 Deception*

ADJECTIVES

7 **sophistic**, sophistical, casuistic(al), jesuitic(al), solecistic(al), rhetorical, logic-chopping, paralogistic, pseudosyllogistic, specious, fallacious, spurious, faulty, flawed, inconsistent, circular, equivocal, erroneous, illogical, paradoxical, contradictory, unreasonable, irrational, unfounded, baseless, groundless, invalid, untenable, unsound, distorted, misapplied, contrived, tortuous, misleading, spurious, inconsequential, dubious, fictitious, illusory, superficial, empty, misinformed, economical with the truth

▶ *844 Wrong, 506 Nonsense, 168 Nonconformity, 548 Misrepresentation, 521 Lack of Meaning*

8 **cunning**, sophisticated, crafty, artful, sly, foxy, sneaky, shifty, dodgy, tricky, insidious, underhand, perfidious, evasive, elusive, manipulating, demagogic, mystifying, obfuscated

▶ *657 Cunning, 655 Skill, 539 Deception, 551 Obscurity, 233 Influence, 586 Persuasion*

9 **quibbling**, cavilling, captious, hair-splitting,

nit-picking, shuffling, hedging, equivocal, equivocating, prevaricating, pettifogging, pussyfooting (Inf)

10 **hypocritical**, deceptive, deceitful, pretended, in pretence, feigning, dissembling, dissimulating, double-dealing, unreliable, insincere, disingenuous, tongue in cheek, fraudulent, dishonest, lying, mendacious, false, bogus, sham, counterfeit, fake, faking, sweet-talking, Pharisaic, pseudo (Inf), so-called (Inf), two-timing (Inf), phoney (*or* phony) (Inf)

▶ *540 Falsehood, 538 Untruth*

VERBS

11 **practise sophistry**, chop logic, misapply, misconstrue, misrepresent, misquote, contradict oneself, falsify, distort, strain, warp, slant, twist, gild, gloss, whitewash, dress up, embroider, disguise, camouflage, mask, juggle, rig, contrive, scheme, manipulate, machinate, propagandize, sway the crowd, misinform, mislead, pull the wool over someone's eyes, mystify, obfuscate, fudge (Inf)

▶ *557 Ornament, 548 Misrepresentation, 565 Talkativeness*

12 **deceive**, dissimulate, dissemble, pretend, feign, bluff, masquerade, put on an act, put up a front, lie, fake, dodge, trick, elude, evade, charm, sweet-talk, have it both ways, double-deal, cheat, work both sides of the street (Inf), con (Inf), two-time (Inf), blag (Sl), talk with one's fingers crossed (Inf), talk shit (Tab sl), bullshit (Tab sl)

▶ *539 Deception, 529 Secrecy, 531 Concealment, 118 Imitation*

13 **quibble**, cavil, split hairs, nit-pick, palter, bandy words, hedge, shuffle, pettifog, equivocate, beg the question, prevaricate, beat about the bush, avoid the issue, filibuster, pussyfoot (Inf), argue all round the houses (Inf), argue the hind legs off a donkey (Inf)

▶ *314 Convolution, 578 Equivocation, 565 Talkativeness, 473 Argument, 811 Showiness, 564 Speech*

ADVERBS

14 **sophistically**, casuistically, jesuitically, solecistically, speciously, falsely, fallaciously, illogically, irrationally, unsoundly, inconsistently, paradoxically, erroneously, groundlessly, circularly, equivocally, captiously, subtly, dubiously, spuriously, rhetorically

15 **hypocritically**, deceitfully, deceptively, dishonestly, insincerely, disingenuously, with tongue in cheek, unreliably, dodgily, sneakily, craftily, artfully, slyly, on the sly, cunningly, insidiously, perfidiously, evasively, elusively, as a gloss, strategically, demagogically, as a con (Inf), behind someone's back (Inf), with fingers crossed (Inf)

475 Demonstration

NOUNS

1 **demonstration**, display, manifestation, showing, show, exhibition, exposition, presentation, disclosure, revelation, presentment, publication, performance, expo
▶ *530 Disclosure, 526 Display, 532 Publication, 294 Uncovering, 457 Appearance*

2 **demonstrativeness**, openness, frankness, candour, emotionality, affection, effusiveness, expansiveness, ostentation, showiness, flashiness, flamboyance, exhibitionism, showing off, dramatics, theatrics, staginess, emotionalism, overemotionalism, histrionics
▶ *526 Display, 51 Performing Arts, 61 Psychology and Psychiatry*

3 **explanation**, demonstration, clarification, elucidation, exposition, indication, illustration, description, depiction, delineation, illumination, exemplification, expounding, exegesis, briefing, instructions, lecture, talk, discourse, example, model, sample, specimen
▶ *528 Information, 560 Description, 6 Education, 561 Dissertation*

4 **proof**, demonstration, evidence, *quod erat demonstrandum* (L) (QED), substantiation, confirmation, verification, determination, ascertainment, settlement, ratification, bearing out, corroboration, justification, affirmation, attestation, testimonial, testimony
▶ *483 Evidence, 543 Sign, 535 Affirmation, 480 Verification*

5 **demonstrability**, demonstrableness, provability, verifiability, confirmability, accountability, certainty, likelihood, probability
▶ *490 Certainty, 488 Probability, 480 Verification*

6 **mass demonstration**, parade, pageant, spectacle, march, protest march, rally, protest, picket, strike, industrial action, boycott, occupation, takeover, sit-in (Inf), sleep-in (Inf), work-in (Inf), demo (Inf)
▶ *15 Industrial Relations, 161 Assembly, 153 Disturbance, 713 Protest*

7 **demonstrator**, explainer, explicator, clarifier, exponent, expositor, expounder, exegetist, illustrator, instructor, lecturer, experimenter, producer, presenter, performer, showman, show-off, exhibitionist, emotionalist, poser (Inf)
▶ *811 Showiness, 51 Performing Arts, 479 Experiment, 6 Education*

8 **protester**, dissenter, dissident, objector, demonstrator, political activist, agitator, minority voice, voice of opposition, picket, striker
▶ *366 Agitation, 668 Defiance, 500 Dissent, 663 Opposition, 669 Resistance, 713 Protest*

ADJECTIVES

9 **demonstrated**, on show, on display, obvious, manifest, plain, clear, express, explicit, displayed, exhibited, disclosed, exposed, revealed, made public, published, publicized, expository, expositional, exhibitional, revelatory, apodeictic
▶ *437 Visibility, 526 Display, 530 Disclosure, 532 Publication*

10 **demonstrative**, open, unrestrained, frank, candid, warm, affectionate, effusive, expansive, ostentatious, showy, flashy, flamboyant, dramatic, stagy, theatrical, exhibitionist, emotional, exhibitionistic, emotionalistic, histrionic
▶ *811 Showiness, 51 Performing Arts, 759 Feeling, 821 Love*

11 **explanatory**, explicatory, illustrative, indicative, descriptive, representative, exemplificatory, exemplifying, illuminating, exegetic, explained, demonstrated, clarified, cleared up, elucidated, illustrated, described, depicted, delineated, illuminated, exemplified, expounded
▶ *560 Description*

12 **demonstrable**, provable, confirmable, attestable, verifiable, evident, self-evident, obvious, undeniable, apparent, perspicuous, distinct, indisputable, unquestionable, positive, certain, conclusive, clear-cut
▶ *483 Evidence, 490 Certainty, 437 Visibility*

13 **proven**, demonstrated, shown, substantiated, confirmed, verified, determined, ascertained, settled, ratified, corroborated, borne out, justified, affirmed, attested, evidential, probative, probatory, corroborative, relevant
▶ *480 Verification, 535 Affirmation*

14 **demonstrating**, protesting, objecting, opposing, dissenting, agitating, rallying, marching, parading, on parade, striking, picketing, boycotting
▶ *663 Opposition, 500 Dissent, 161 Assembly*

VERBS

15 **demonstrate**, show, display, exhibit, manifest, disclose, expose, point out, bring out, roll out, reveal, produce, air, put forward, publish, perform, flaunt, brandish, flourish
▶ *532 Publication, 530 Disclosure, 51 Performing Arts, 526 Display*

16 **explain**, expound, show how, elucidate, express, indicate, unfold, make clear, clarify, illuminate, exemplify, illustrate, quote, cite, itemize, particularize, give instances, delineate, depict, describe, brief, instruct, lecture
▶ *6 Education, 560 Description*

17 **prove**, evince, substantiate, establish, evidence, validate, ratify, verify, corroborate, support, bear out, circumstantiate, justify, determine, ascertain, fix, settle, confirm, affirm, attest, prove one's point, remove all doubt, clinch (Inf)
▶ *483 Evidence, 480 Verification, 535 Affirmation*

18 appear, materialize, come forth, take a stand, stand up and be counted, speak out, raise one's voice, speak one's mind, assert oneself, draw attention to oneself, play to the gallery, perform, show off, dramatize, emotionalize
▶ *457 Appearance, 51 Performing Arts, 318 Prominence*

19 protest, dissent, object, complain about, oppose, agitate, demonstrate, rally, march, march for, parade, strike, picket, boycott, occupy, take over, stage a demo (Inf), stage a sit-in (Inf), sit in (Inf)
▶ *663 Opposition*

ADVERBS

20 manifestly, obviously, plainly, clearly, publicly, in public, for all to see, in broad daylight, under one's nose, to one's face, as plain as the nose on one's face

21 demonstratively, openly, frankly, candidly, emotionally, expressively, affectionately, warmly, effusively, expansively, ostentatiously, flamboyantly, dramatically, theatrically, histrionically

22 demonstrably, verifiably, justifiably, accountably, certainly, likely, probably, in all likelihood, illuminatingly, illustratively, indicatively, descriptively, exegetically, as an example, in proof, as proof, as evidence, in evidence, in other words, that is, *id est* (L), that is to say

23 in protest, in opposition, on parade, on a demo (Inf)

476 Refutation

NOUNS

1 refutation, disproof, disproval, invalidation, negation, negativity, naysaying, nullification, annulment, disaffirmation, disconfirmation, confounding, discrediting, abrogation, disallowal, dismissal, reversal, undermining, subversion, overthrow, destruction, demolition, *reductio ad absurdum* (L), conclusive argument, knockdown argument, floorer (Inf), clincher (Inf)
▶ *473 Argument, 704 Cancellation, 244 Destruction, 666 Disagreement, 536 Negation, 709 Veto, 856 Accusation, 799 Derision, 587 Dissuasion*

2 denial, refutation, rebuttal, contradiction, confutation, contravention, contention, negation, disaffirmation, rejection, repudiation, renunciation, abnegation, recantation, recusance, withdrawal, reversal, disclaimer, disavowal, disownment, apostasy
▶ *674 Contention, 536 Negation, 581 Rejection, 221 Reversion, 670 Attack*

3 countercharge, refutation, counterclaim, counteraccusation, counterstatement, counterblast, counteraction, comeback, reply, counterargument, rebuttal, rejoinder, answer, response, retort, riposte, retaliation, objection, defence, statement of defence, demurrer, demurral
▶ *478 Answer, 125 Compensation, 231 Counteraction, 484 Counterevidence, 671 Defence, 672 Retaliation, 500 Dissent, 663 Opposition, 711 Refusal, 16 Law*

4 refutability, confutability, disprovability, defeasibility, weakness, unsoundness, groundlessness
▶ *491 Uncertainty, 238 Weakness, 683 Failure, 540 Falsehood, 844 Wrong*

5 refuter, confuter, negator, nullifier, naysayer, abrogator, denier, repudiator, abnegator, recanter, recusant, responder, defendant, destroyer
▶ *679 Combatant, 663 Opposition, 713 Protest, 855 Vindication*

ADJECTIVES

6 refutable, confutable, disprovable, defeasible, weak, faulty, flawed, unfounded, groundless, unsound, objectionable, inconclusive, without a leg to stand on
▶ *238 Weakness, 504 Error, 540 Falsehood, 844 Wrong, 491 Uncertainty*

7 refuting, confuting, confounding, confutative, refutative, refutatory, contradictory, contrary, counteractive, retaliatory, answering, responding, contravening, rebutting, repudiating, renouncing, abnegating, disclaiming, disowning, discrediting, exploding, disproving, negating, invalidating, overturning, destroying
▶ *663 Opposition, 711 Refusal, 536 Negation, 801 Disrepute, 244 Destruction*

VERBS

8 refute, confute, confound, disprove, prove the contrary, invalidate, nullify, annul, negate, disallow, forbid, dismiss, abrogate, dispose of, disconfirm, discredit, expose, show up, belie, deflate, undermine, overturn, overthrow, defeat, outsmart, outwit, demolish, destroy, explode, crush, squash, quash, floor, silence, have the last word, argue into a corner, argue down, knock down, shout down, not leave a leg to stand on, score points against, force to step down, show them what's what (Inf)
▶ *799 Derision, 244 Destruction, 801 Disrepute, 546 Obliteration, 422 Silence, 673 Submission*

9 deny, refute, contradict, gainsay, naysay, argue against, argue with, raise doubts about, question, dispute, oppose, controvert, contravene, disaffirm, reject, repudiate, renounce, abnegate, recant, reverse, withdraw, disclaim, disavow, disown, repugn
▶ *477 Question, 473 Argument, 491 Uncertainty*

10 countercharge, counter, counterclaim, counterblast, rebut, parry, retaliate, retort, answer, answer back, reply, rejoin, respond,

object, offer in defence, demur

▶ *231 Counteraction, 484 Counterevidence, 16 Law*

ADVERBS

11 **in reply**, in response, in answer, as an answer, as a defence, in defence, defensively, dismissively, negatively, destructively, conclusively

12 **refutably**, confutably, disprovably, defeasibly, weakly, unsoundly, groundlessly, without grounds, without a leg to stand on, inconclusively, disputedly

INTERJECTIONS

13 **no!**, nay!, wrong!, I disagree!, I object!, nonsense!, not at all!, no way!

▶ *844 Wrong, 506 Nonsense, 504 Error, 540 Falsehood*

477 Question

NOUNS

1 **question**, query, doubt, uncertainty, reservation, problem, difficulty, confusion, puzzle, challenge, objection, issue, point, proposition, request, entreaty, plea

▶ *659 Difficulty, 471 Idea, 472 Topic, 498 Disbelief, 502 Ignorance, 712 Request, 593 Requirement, 491 Uncertainty*

2 **questioning**, inquiry (*or* enquiry), querying, interrogation, interpellation, inquisition, cross-questioning, cross-examination, challenge, Socratic elenchus, philosophical inquiry, argument, investigation, analysis, inspection, scrutiny, survey, review, study, probe, inquest, criminal investigation, scientific investigation, research, poll, market research, search, quest, pumping (Inf), grilling (Inf), the third degree (Inf)

▶ *16 Law, 4 Philosophy, 473 Argument, 479 Experiment*

3 **questionnaire**, question paper, quiz, examination, test, poll, census, checklist, trial, catechism, oral examination, viva voce examination, hearing, audition, question-time, question and answer session, interview, viva (Inf)

▶ *485 Qualification, 6 Education, 51 Performing Arts, 2 Sociology, 7 Religion, 492 Judgment, 478 Answer*

4 **difficult question**, awkward question, personal question, burning question, sixty-four (thousand) dollar question, leading question, bone of contention, controversy, moot point, catch, trick question, knotty problem, poser, stumper, mystery, tough nut to crack, mind boggler, brain-teaser, conundrum, riddle, enigma, dilemma, moral dilemma, crux, crisis, Hobson's choice, catch-22, sticky moment (Inf)

▶ *659 Difficulty, 551 Obscurity, 473 Argument, 666 Disagreement, 635 Trap, 876 Morality, 523 Unintelligibility*

5 **easy question**, silly question, stupid question, rhetorical question, formality, trivia quiz, child's play, doddle (Inf), cinch (Inf), breeze (Inf), pushover (Inf), piece of cake (Inf)

▶ *649 Ease, 660 Easiness, 813 Formality, 612 Unimportance*

6 **uncertainty**, questioning, doubt, doubtfulness, scepticism, Pyrrhonism, agnosticism, misgiving, mistrust, distrust, hesitation, conjecture, guesswork, anybody's guess (Inf)

▶ *491 Uncertainty, 4 Philosophy, 498 Disbelief, 502 Ignorance, 518 Supposition, 576 Vacillation*

7 **questionableness**, dubiousness, doubtfulness, implausibility, unlikelihood, improbability, uncertainty, wild chance, faint hope, risk, riskiness, unreliability, untrustworthiness, deceptiveness, deceitfulness, ambiguity

▶ *539 Deception, 578 Equivocation, 489 Improbability, 551 Obscurity, 474 Sophistry, 491 Uncertainty*

8 **curiosity**, inquisitiveness, inquiring (*or* enquiring) mind, insatiable curiosity, desire (*or* thirst) for knowledge, wonder, puzzlement, soul-searching, probing, prying

▶ *786 Wonder, 465 Curiosity, 6 Education*

9 **questioner**, asker, interrogator, interpellator, investigator, journalist, interviewer, chat show host (*or* hostess), quiz master, game show presenter, prober, examiner, inquisitor, cross-examiner, interlocutor, lawyer, barrister, coroner, detective, inspector, scrutineer, student, researcher, tester, experimenter, scientist, surveyor, reviewer, analyst, pollster, canvasser, market researcher, seeker, doubter, philosopher, sceptic, doubting Thomas, agnostic, dissenter, detractor

▶ *4 Philosophy, 7 Religion, 6 Education, 461 Thought, 786 Wonder, 16 Law, 532 Publication, 51 Performing Arts, 479 Experiment, 2 Sociology, 471 Idea, 663 Opposition, 713 Protest*

10 **person questioned**, interviewee, chat (*or* game) show guest, examinee, candidate, defendant, suspect, witness, plaintiff

▶ *856 Accusation, 485 Qualification, 16 Law*

11 **question mark**, query, interrogation mark, interrogation point, note of interrogation, interrogative pronoun, interrogative clause, future interrogative, indirect question

▶ *5 Linguistics*

ADJECTIVES

12 **questioning**, requesting, pleading, inquiring, interrogative, curious, inquisitive, elenctic, investigative, examining, fact-finding, knowledge-seeking, exploratory, analytic, interpellant, probing, searching, researching, questing, prying, introspective, wondering, doubting

▶ *528 Information, 479 Experiment, 465 Curiosity*

13 **problematic**, difficult, confusing, confused,

puzzling, challenging, quizzical, tricky, sticky, knotty, tough, mysterious, riddling, enigmatic, in a dilemma, on the horns of a dilemma, crucial, examinational, catechismic
▶ *659 Difficulty, 11 Occultism, 876 Morality, 551 Obscurity*

14 **questionable**, doubtful, uncertain, moot, at issue, open to question, in question, in doubt, open to debate, debatable, under discussion, controversial, borderline, arguable, disputable, equivocal, suspicious, dubious, implausible, unlikely, improbable, chancy, risky, unreliable, unverifiable, untrustworthy, deceptive, deceitful, ambiguous, shady, spurious
▶ *473 Argument, 539 Deception, 589 Chance, 489 Improbability, 578 Equivocation, 474 Sophistry*

15 **sceptical**, doubting, Pyrrhonist, agnostic, distrustful, journalistic, scientific, criminal, philosophical, legal, experimental, conjectural, guessing, hesitating
▶ *4 Philosophy, 498 Disbelief, 16 Law, 479 Experiment*

16 **questioned**, asked, interrogated, examined, cross-examined, cross-questioned, quizzed, analysed, researched, challenged, investigated, inspected, scrutinized, reviewed, surveyed, studied, probed, polled, canvassed, sought, grilled (Inf), pumped (Inf), given the third degree (Inf)
▶ *16 Law, 2 Sociology, 712 Request*

VERBS
17 **question**, inquire (*or* enquire), ask, quiz, query, plead, entreat, request, appeal, interpellate, examine, test, try, check, catechize, hear, give a viva voce examination, give an audition, interview, sound out, pick the brains of, investigate, analyse, conduct an inquiry into, inspect, scrutinize, survey, scan, review, study, fact-find, hunt the facts, probe, research, poll, canvass, search, wonder, introspect, soul-search, pry, hunt, pursue, search out, seek, quest
▶ *712 Request, 528 Information, 2 Sociology, 4 Philosophy, 7 Religion, 479 Experiment*

18 **interrogate**, question, examine, hold for questioning, cross-question, cross-examine, pump (Inf), grill (Inf), give someone the third degree (Inf), put through the hoop (Inf), torture, witchhunt
▶ *16 Law, 7 Religion*

19 **be questioned**, help the police with their inquiries, appear on a chat show, sit an examination, take part in a survey
▶ *16 Law, 6 Education, 51 Performing Arts, 2 Sociology, 478 Answer*

20 **doubt**, question, have one's doubts, have misgivings, mistrust, distrust, suspect, disbelieve, cast doubt upon, call into question, moot, raise the issue, make the point, propose, debate, discuss, dispute, contest, impugn, refute, confute, disagree, dissent, object, hesi-

tate, conjecture, guess, risk, chance
▶ *473 Argument, 666 Disagreement, 491 Uncertainty, 713 Protest, 663 Opposition, 589 Chance*

21 **confuse**, challenge, puzzle, pose, set a riddle, boggle, mystify, stump, trick, deceive
▶ *460 Lack of Intellect, 539 Deception, 659 Difficulty, 523 Unintelligibility*

22 **pop the question**, ask for someone's hand in marriage, ask to marry, propose, get engaged, plight one's troth
▶ *823 Marriage, 712 Request*

ADVERBS
23 **questioningly**, curiously, quizzically, inquisitively, probingly, searchingly, on a quest, on a mission, on a fact-finding mission, analytically, investigatively, scientifically, experimentally, agnostically, sceptically, philosophically, introspectively

24 **questionably**, hesitatingly, doubtfully, in doubt, dubiously, challengingly, puzzlingly, arguably, debatably, disputably, in question, under discussion, on the horns of a dilemma, on the borderline, controversially, conjecturally, riskily, suspiciously, equivocally, unreliably, problematically, trickily, enigmatically, deceptively, deceitfully, ambiguously, implausibly, improbably

25 **what?**, how much?, when?, at what time?, where?, at what place?, in what position?, whence?, from what place?, why?, for what reason?, how?, in what way?

478 Answer

NOUNS
1 **answer**, reply, response, rejoinder, responsion, respondence, replication, retort, riposte, comeback, repartee, witty repartee, short answer, back talk, backchat, insolence, smart alec answer (Inf)
▶ *459 Intellect, 807 Insolence, 564 Speech, 818 Discourtesy, 568 Conversation, 735 Giving Back*

2 **acknowledgment**, answer, return correspondence, written reply, official reply, rescript, receipt, confirmation, RSVP
▶ *534 Communications, 535 Affirmation, 735 Giving Back, 749 Receipt, 730 Receiving*

3 **question and answer**, dialogue, interchange, interlocution, interview, exchange, interaction
▶ *223 Exchange, 477 Question, 4 Philosophy, 109 Reciprocity, 568 Conversation*

4 **reaction**, answer, retroaction, recoil, reflex, return, reflux, rebuff, backlash, kickback, recalcitration, bounceback, repercussion, reverberation, echo, response, responsory, antiphon, antiphonal chant, antistrophe, antithesis
▶ *331 Recoil, 426 Repeated Sound, 183 Repetition, 427 Resonance, 49 Music, 10 Ritual, 48 Literature, 267 Juxtaposition, 231 Counteraction*

5 **counterstatement**, answer, countercharge, counterblast, retaliation, defence, plea, argu-

ment, refutation, rebuttal, contradiction, objection, vindication, last word, parting shot, interjection

▶ *476 Refutation, 855 Vindication, 672 Retaliation, 473 Argument, 157 End, 125 Compensation, 484 Counterevidence*

6 **solution**, answer, result, issue, outcome, upshot, denouement, resolution, conclusion, discovery, resolving, working out, unscrambling, clearing up, sorting out, decoding, interpretation, explanation, reason, resource, contrivance, measure, plan, remedy, antidote

▶ *157 End, 574 Resolution, 496 Discovery, 524 Interpretation, 463 Reason, 592 Plan, 630 Remedy, 327 Way, 227 Effect*

7 **numerical result**, answer, solution, product, sum, total, difference, equation, remainder, score, tally

▶ *52 Mathematics, 169 Number, 170 Calculation, 684 Completion*

8 **correspondence**, answerableness, correlation, parallelism, symmetry, equivalence, congruence, conformity, twin, match, tally, agreement, aptness, fitness, suitability, relevance, usefulness

▶ *285 Parallelism, 667 Agreement, 613 Usefulness, 167 Conformity, 110 Sameness, 116 Accord, 608 Sufficiency*

9 **answerability**, responsibility, liability, accountability, obligation, duty, requirement

▶ *593 Requirement, 847 Duty*

10 **answerer**, respondent, replier, correspondent, interlocutor, dialectician, talker, chatterer, conversationalist, addressee, interviewee, inquirer, objector, defendant, solver, planner, decoder, mathematician

▶ *16 Law, 4 Philosophy, 815 Sociability, 565 Talkativeness, 477 Question*

ADJECTIVES

11 **answering**, replying, responsive, responding, respondent, acknowledged, confirmed, returned, retorted, backchatting, insolent

▶ *807 Insolence*

12 **reactive**, interlocutory, interactive, retroactive, recoiling, reflexive, returning, refluent, rebuffed, recalcitrant, repercussive, reverberatory, echoing, antiphonal, antithetical

13 **retaliatory**, counterstated, countercharged, counterblasted, defensive, pleading, argumentative, refutative, refutatory, rebutted, objectionable, objecting, vindicating, vindicated, interjecting, interjected

▶ *473 Argument, 672 Retaliation, 476 Refutation, 855 Vindication*

14 **solved**, soluble, resultant, issuing, resolved, concluded, discovered, worked out, unscrambled, cleared up, sorted out, decoded, interpreted, interpretational, explanatory, explained, reasoned, contrived, measured,

planned, remedial, antidotal

▶ *574 Resolution, 592 Plan, 496 Discovery, 630 Remedy*

15 **correspondent**, corresponding, correlative, parallel, reciprocal, symmetrical, equivalent, congruent, conforming, twin, matching, tallying, agreeing, apt, fitting, suitable, relevant, useful

▶ *613 Usefulness, 110 Sameness, 109 Reciprocity, 285 Parallelism*

16 **answerable**, responsible, liable, accountable, required, obliged, obligatory, under obligation, duty-bound, beholden, dutiful

▶ *847 Duty, 593 Requirement*

VERBS

17 **answer**, reply, respond, rejoin, riposte, retort, return, acknowledge, confirm, come back (Inf), get back (Inf)

18 **answer back**, talk back, contradict, confute, counterstate, countercharge, counterblast, refute, rebut, defend, vindicate, plead, argue, object, backchat, butt in, interject, insult, taunt, provoke, have the last word, fire the parting shot, have the final say, forget one's manners, be lippy (Inf), give some lip (Inf), lip off (US inf), mouth off (Sl)

▶ *818 Discourtesy, 807 Insolence, 768 Aggravation, 476 Refutation*

19 **react**, exchange, interact, converse, interview, interlocute, interchange, retroact, recoil, return, rebuff, kick back, recalcitrate, bounce back, reverberate, echo

▶ *331 Recoil, 125 Compensation, 427 Resonance*

20 **solve**, sum, score, equate, total, resolve, conclude, discover, work out, unscramble, clear up, sort out, decode, interpret, explain, reason, contrive, measure, plan, remedy

▶ *630 Remedy, 463 Reason, 684 Completion, 170 Calculation, 524 Interpretation, 496 Discovery, 471 Idea, 544 Identification*

21 **answer to**, correspond, correlate, parallel, reciprocate, conform, twin, match, tally, agree, oblige, require

▶ *110 Sameness, 167 Conformity, 116 Accord, 109 Reciprocity, 285 Parallelism, 667 Agreement*

22 **be the answer**, pertain, fit, suit, fulfil expectations, rise to the occasion, turn up trumps (Inf), be just the job (or thing) (Inf), do the trick (Inf)

▶ *608 Sufficiency, 765 Satisfaction, 775 Hope*

23 **answer for**, be responsible, act on behalf of, represent, speak for, appear for, replace, stand in for, deputize, understudy

▶ *706 Delegate, 707 Deputy, 547 Representation, 597 Undertaking, 847 Duty, 593 Requirement*

ADVERBS

24 **in answer**, in reply, in response, responsively, reflexively, reactively, retroactively, interactively, interchangeably, reciprocally, exchangeably, conversationally, dialectically,

in conversation, argumentatively, insolently, defensively, in defence, recalcitrantly, antithetically, reverberantly, echoingly, on the rebound, on the bounce

25 **conclusively**, in conclusion, in the end, as it turns out, solubly

26 **correspondingly**, answerably, correlatively, in parallel, symmetrically, equivalently, congruently, conformingly, agreeably, aptly, fittingly, suitably, relevantly, usefully, reasonably, remedially

27 **answerably**, responsibly, representatively, accountably, dutifully, instead, in lieu, in place, as a replacement

479   Experiment

NOUNS

1 **experiment**, investigation, probe, analysis, diagnosis, assay, essay, test, acid test, blood test, trial, inquiry (or enquiry), probation, sounding out, sounder, sound, feeler, check, tentation, venture, bid, endeavour, effort, gambit, risk, try, trial and error, hit and miss, cut and try (Inf), shot (Inf), go (Inf), fling (Inf), crack (Sl), whack (Sl), stab (Sl)
▶ 596 Attempt, 496 Discovery, 483 Evidence, 492 Judgment, 719 Observance, 230 Operation, 575 Perseverance, 60 Medicine

2 **rehearsal**, practice, audition, hearing, model, mock-up, rough draft, sketch, trial, trial run, single-blind trial, double-blind trial, tryout, dummy run, practice run, pilot run, dry run, road test, flight test, test flight, trial balloon, sample, control
▶ 118 Imitation

3 **experimentation**, experimentalism, empiricism, pragmatism, instrumentalism, testing, trying, research, research and development (R and D), vivisection, investigation, examination, exploration, verification, determination, ascertainment, speculation, conjecture, guesswork, estimation, rule of thumb
▶ 477 Question, 4 Philosophy, 786 Wonder, 480 Verification, 544 Identification, 517 Prediction, 475 Demonstration, 268 Measurement, 227 Effect, 483 Evidence

4 **originality**, experimentation, inventiveness, creativity, innovation, novelty, newness, unfamiliarity, strangeness, avant-garde, modernism, daring, recklessness, risk, nothing ventured, nothing gained
▶ 519 Imagination, 471 Idea, 119 Originality, 201 Newness, 50 Painting and Sculpture, 49 Music, 48 Literature, 51 Performing Arts

5 **experimenter**, experimentalist, empiricist, investigator, scientist, researcher, research scientist, research worker, vivisectionist, R and D worker, analyst, assayer, quester, striver, inquirer (or enquirer), trier, tester, test-driver,

test-pilot, speculator, inventor, innovator, creator, creative artist
▶ 57 Chemistry, 56 Physics, 53 Astronomy, Astronautics, and Rocketry, 62 Pharmacology, 50 Painting and Sculpture

6 **place of experimentation**, laboratory, lab (Inf), research establishment, field station, proving ground, think tank, workshop, studio
▶ 6 Education, 57 Chemistry, 56 Physics

7 **experimentee**, testee, patient, subject, guinea pig, laboratory animal, lab rat (Inf)
▶ 62 Pharmacology, 76 Animals (General)

ADJECTIVES

8 **experimental**, empirical, pragmatic, scientific, analytic, instrumental, probational, probationary, exploratory, investigative, trying, experimenting, inquiring, testing, researching, verifying, verifiable, determining, determinable, speculative, conjectural, tentative, provisional, mock, rough, trial, test, dummy, practice, model, simulated
▶ 118 Imitation

9 **original**, experimental, inventive, creative, innovative, novel, modern, new, unfamiliar, strange, avant-garde, modernist, venturesome, daring, enterprising, reckless, risky, chancy
▶ 519 Imagination, 201 Newness

10 **tested**, experimented upon, tried, researched, determined, verified, checked, essayed, ventured, estimated, risked, chanced

VERBS

11 **experiment**, experimentalize, conduct an experiment, test, try, essay, assay, try out, put on trial, put to the test (or proof), research, sound out, test the water, explore, analyse, feel the pulse, test the depth, investigate, probe, sample, examine, inquire (or enquire), verify, substantiate, confirm, check, check out, determine, prove, ascertain, speculate, prospect, conjecture, guess, estimate
▶ 268 Measurement, 477 Question

12 **rehearse**, practise, audition, mock up, sketch, try out, road-test, flight-test, simulate, model
▶ 118 Imitation

13 **invent**, create, innovate, dare, risk, chance, take chances, gamble, try one's luck, try one's hand, try one's strength, venture, attempt, endeavour, try, undertake, take the bull by the horns, have a go (Inf), have a fling (Inf), give it a go (Inf), have a stab at (Inf), take a crack at (Inf)
▶ 596 Attempt, 119 Originality, 519 Imagination, 589 Chance

ADVERBS

14 **experimentally**, empirically, scientifically, analytically, investigatively, provisionally, conjecturally, speculatively, on spec, by rule of thumb, by trial and error, by hit and miss, by guess and God, on trial, on probation, under

examination, on the slab (Inf)

15 **inventively**, experimentally, creatively, innovatively, daringly, recklessly, riskily, strangely, for the first time, as never before

480 Verification

VERBS

1 **verify**, validate, confirm, ratify, authenticate, certify, record, document, assure, guarantee, warrant, second, support, sign, countersign, endorse, vindicate, make certain, remove doubt, make good, ensure, check, doublecheck, crosscheck, recheck, collate

▶ *855 Vindication, 718 Security*

2 **prove**, demonstrate, illustrate, clarify, clear up, show, evince, corroborate, sustain, bear out, support, substantiate, circumstantiate, determine, ascertain, establish, witness

▶ *475 Demonstration*

3 **testify**, attest, affirm, state, assert, avow, aver, give evidence, turn queen's evidence, witness, inform, grass (Sl), rat (US sl), squeal (Sl), sing (Sl), lag (Aus sl), dob (Aus sl)

▶ *719 Observance, 856 Accusation, 483 Evidence*

NOUNS

4 **verification**, validation, confirmation, ratification, authentication, certification, documentation, attestation, affirmation, avouchment, avowal, averment, assurance, surety, check, double-check, crosscheck, collation

▶ *535 Affirmation, 503 Accuracy, 490 Certainty, 544 Identification, 718 Security, 855 Vindication, 485 Qualification, 537 Truth*

5 **proof**, proving, demonstration, illustration, clarification, corroboration, support, substantiation, circumstantiation, determination, ascertainment, establishment

▶ *473 Argument, 479 Experiment, 475 Demonstration, 496 Discovery*

6 **evidence**, counterevidence, confirmation, statement, credential, testimonial, reference, character reference, recommendation, seal, signature, documentation, documents, ticket, passport, visa, permit

▶ *483 Evidence, 485 Qualification, 484 Counterevidence, 543 Sign, 528 Information*

7 **verifier**, testifier, voucher, swearer, attestant, signatory, witness, eyewitness, spectator, bystander, passer-by, informant, informer, snout (Sl), grass (Sl), rat (US sl), squealer (Sl), nark (Sl), dobber (Aus sl), lagger (Aus sl)

▶ *719 Observance, 528 Information*

ADJECTIVES

8 **verifiable**, certifiable, documented, authentic, recorded, seconded, proved, witnessed

▶ *537 Truth, 3 History, 560 Description*

9 **verificatory**, verificative, demonstrative, illustrative, evidential, determining, validating, assuring, establishing, confirming, testificatory, ratificatory, prima facie, corroborative, supportive, substantial, circumstantial, probative, collative, checking, cross-checking, double-checking

10 **verified**, validated, confirmed, ratified, authenticated, certified, documented, attested, affirmed, avouched, avowed, averred, assured, sure, certain, checked, doublechecked, cross-checked, collated

ADVERBS

11 **verifiably**, corroboratively, demonstratively, illustratively, supportively, circumstantially, authentically, genuinely, certifiably, with appropriate papers, with all documents

▶ *101 Reality, 845 Entitlement*

12 **assuredly**, certainly, surely, indisputably, really, for certain, for sure, in truth, most certainly, indeed, to be sure, sure enough, beyond question, no two ways about it

▶ *537 Truth, 501 Knowledge, 490 Certainty*

INTERJECTIONS

13 **really!**, honestly!, honest!, that's the one!, I swear!, marry! (Arch)

481 Discrimination

NOUNS

1 **discrimination**, selection, selectivity, selectiveness, distinction, differentiation, appraisal, sorting, graduation, separation, demarcation, division, segregation, diagnosis, interpretation

▶ *152 Arrangement, 121 Degree, 268 Measurement, 580 Selection, 136 Separation, 524 Interpretation*

2 **judiciousness**, judgment, discrimination, discretion, taste, good taste, sensitivity, sensibility, discernment, criticism, appreciation, feel, perception, insight, connoisseurship, acumen, flair, dilettantism, palate, refined palate, refinement, delicacy, finesse, fastidiousness, meticulousness, perfectionism, quibbling, hair-splitting (Inf)

▶ *492 Judgment, 411 Taste, 474 Sophistry, 760 Sensitivity, 619 Perfection*

3 **prejudice**, discrimination, bias, bigotry, narrow-mindedness, narrowness, pettiness, small-mindedness, intolerance, insularism, parochialism, one-sidedness, partisanship, jaundice, prejudgment, inequity, unfairness, foul play (Inf), not cricket (Inf)

▶ *123 Inequality, 233 Influence, 577 Obstinacy*

4 **social discrimination**, sexual discrimination, sexism, male chauvinism, misogyny, misandry, homophobia, racial discrimination, racism, racialism, race hatred, anti-semitism, apartheid, segregation (US), ghettoization, xenophobia, ethnocentricity, ethnic cleansing, pogrom, political persecution, McCarthyism, elitism, class prejudice, class discrimination, classism, class war, fascism, Nazism,

Aryanism, jingoism, chauvinism, ultranationalism, superpatriotism, religious persecution, fundamentalism, fanaticism, witch-hunting, heresy-hunting, ageism, granny-bashing (Sl), queer-bashing (Sl), Paki-bashing (Sl), red-baiting (US sl)

▶ *822 Hate, 670 Attack, 241 Violence, 7 Religion, 163 Class, 601 Misuse*

5 **favouritism**, nepotism, partisanship, positive discrimination, preferential treatment

6 **discriminating person**, critic, selector, judge, connoisseur, dilettante, gourmet, epicure, idealist, purist, pedant, perfectionist, quibbler, hair-splitter (Inf), fuss-pot (Inf)

▶ *350 Eating*

7 **bigot**, dogmatist, partisan, elitist, fanatic, persecutor, ageist, sexist, male chauvinist, misogynist, misandrist, homophobe, racist, racialist, anti-semite, xenophobe, fascist, Nazi, jingo, jingoist, ultranationalist, chauvinist, superpatriot, fundamentalist, witch-hunter, male chauvinist pig (Inf), pig (Inf), redneck (Inf), granny-basher (Sl), queer-basher (Sl), Paki-basher (Sl), red-baiter (US sl)

▶ *577 Obstinacy*

8 **victim of discrimination**, victim of oppression, sufferer, prey, martyr, unlucky person, unfortunate, scapegoat, the persecuted, the exploited, the oppressed, slave, underdog (Inf)

▶ *687 Adversity*

ADJECTIVES

9 **discriminating**, judicious, selective, tasteful, sensitive, differential, separating, discerning, divisional, critical, diagnostic, interpretational, appreciative, epicurean, perceptive, insightful, refined, delicate, fastidious, meticulous, perfectionist, pedantic, quibbling, hair-splitting (Inf), choosy (Inf), picky (Inf)

▶ *580 Selection, 474 Sophistry, 136 Separation, 469 Carefulness*

10 **discriminatory**, prejudicial, one-sided, partisan, jaundiced, inequitable, unfair, partial, preferential, nepotistic, prejudiced, biased, bigoted, narrow-minded, blinkered, small-minded, petty, intolerant, dogmatic, insular, parochial, elitist, classist, ageist, sexist, misogynist, misogynous, misandrist, misandrous, homophobic, racist, racialist, anti-semitic, xenophobic, jingoistic, ethnocentric, fascist, Nazi, ultranationalistic, superpatriotic, chauvinist(ic), fundamentalist, fanatical

11 **judged**, selected, distinct, discrete, diagnosed, interpreted, differentiated, sorted, graded, graduated, separate, demarcated, divided, segregated, discriminated against, persecuted, exploited, oppressed

VERBS

12 **discriminate**, select, choose, favour, prefer, judge, distinguish, differentiate, discern, pick,

pick out, pick and choose, compare and contrast, sort, analyse, grade, graduate, separate, demarcate, divide, segregate, diagnose, interpret, quibble, split hairs (Inf), sort the sheep from the goats (Inf), sort the grain (*or* wheat) from the chaff (Inf)

▶ *580 Selection, 492 Judgment*

13 **prejudge**, forejudge, precondemn, bias, prejudice, warp, not see beyond one's nose, put on blinkers, blind oneself, close one's mind, listen with deaf ears

▶ *502 Ignorance, 421 Deafness, 233 Influence, 309 Distortion*

14 **discriminate against**, criticize, persecute, harass, be hard on, treat unfairly, oppress, exploit, witch-hunt, pick on (Inf), granny-bash (Sl), queer-bash (Sl), red-bait (US sl), Paki-bash (Sl)

ADVERBS

15 **discriminatingly**, selectively, distinctly, separately, differentially, divisively, diagnostically

16 **judiciously**, judgmentally, with discretion, tastefully, sensitively, discerningly, critically, analytically, appreciatively, perceptively, insightfully, delicately, fastidiously, meticulously, pedantically

17 **prejudicially**, preferentially, dogmatically, inequitably, unfairly, narrow-mindedly, small-mindedly, intolerantly, parochially, fanatically, homophobically, xenophobically, ethnocentrically, racially, chauvinistically, ultranationalistically, superpatriotically, jingoistically

482 Lack of Discrimination

ADJECTIVES

1 **undiscriminating**, unselective, catholic, omnivorous, undiscerning, undifferentiating, colour-blind, tone-deaf, uncritical, indifferent, unfussy, unfastidious, unrefined, tasteless, indelicate, insensitive, coarse, vulgar, promiscuous, unrestrained, loose, sloppy, casual, lax, negligent, thoughtless, indiscreet, slipshod, careless, unmeticulous, inaccurate, cursory, perfunctory

▶ *783 Indifference, 870 Self-Indulgence, 872 Gluttony, 795 Vulgarity, 877 Immorality, 470 Negligence, 761 Insensitivity*

2 **impartial**, equanimous, fair, fair-minded, neutral, nonaligned, mugwumpish, nonpartisan, disinterested, unbiased, unprejudiced, nonjudgmental, uncriticizing, tolerant, liberal, broad-minded

▶ *857 Probity, 859 Disinterestedness, 242 Moderation*

3 **indiscriminate**, random, haphazard, unsystematic, mixed, assorted, unsorted, unselected, miscellaneous, motley, unorganized,

disorganized, confused, jumbled, muddled, intermingled, disordered, mixed-up, chaotic, scrambled, higgledy-piggledy (Inf)
▶ *133 Mixture*

4 **wholesale**, broad, wide, general, all-embracing, wide-ranging, all-inclusive, comprehensive, catholic, widespread, worldwide, global, universal, blanket (Inf), carpet (Inf)
▶ *146 Inclusion, 164 Generality*

5 **vague**, indistinct, indistinctive, inexact, desultory, undefined, ill-defined, undifferentiated, undistinguished, undistinguishable, interchangeable, standard, average, alike
▶ *164 Generality, 124 Average*

NOUNS

6 **lack of discrimination**, indiscrimination, unselectiveness, catholicity, catholic tastes, uncriticalness, indifference, bad taste, tastelessness, insensitivity, indelicacy, vulgarity, promiscuity, lack of restraint, negligence, thoughtlessness, indiscretion, carelessness, inaccuracy
▶ *783 Indifference, 795 Vulgarity, 761 Insensitivity, 870 Self-Indulgence, 877 Immorality*

7 **impartiality**, equanimity, fairness, justice, neutrality, nonalignment, mugwumpism, disinterestedness, tolerance, fair-mindedness, broad-mindedness
▶ *122 Equality, 859 Disinterestedness, 698 Freedom*

8 **indiscriminateness**, randomness, generality, universality, vagueness, inexactitude, confusion, muddle, jumble, mixture, heap, any old thing (Inf)
▶ *133 Mixture, 146 Inclusion, 164 Generality*

9 **undiscriminating person**, vulgarian, omnivore, glutton, gourmand, barbarian, philistine, lecher, Don Juan, satyr, nymphomaniac
▶ *795 Vulgarity, 872 Gluttony, 877 Immorality, 870 Self-Indulgence*

10 **impartial person**, judge, referee, moderate, liberal, mugwump
▶ *242 Moderation*

VERBS

11 **not discriminate**, see no difference between, make no distinction between, disregard, generalize, universalize, swallow lock, stock, and barrel, take as one, roll into one, muddle up, confound, jumble, mix, heap, lump together, smooth over the differences, average out
▶ *142 Whole, 133 Mixture, 146 Inclusion*

12 **be fair**, remain neutral, sit on the fence, refuse to judge (*or* take sides), keep an open mind, see both sides, tolerate, live with, accept
▶ *122 Equality, 158 Middle, 242 Moderation*

ADVERBS

13 **unselectively**, indifferently, imperceptively, uncritically, insensitively, tastelessly, coarsely, indelicately, promiscuously

14 **indiscriminately**, vaguely, universally, generally, commonly, indistinguishably, haphazardly, inexactly, randomly, inaccurately, in a muddle, in a mess, in a heap, all mixed up together

15 **impartially**, fairly, neutrally, equanimously, tolerantly, disinterestedly

483 Evidence

NOUNS

1 **evidence**, grounds, reasons, premises, basis for belief, data, information, facts, relevant facts, record, reference, report, intelligence, gen (Inf), the low-down (Inf)
▶ *463 Reason, 528 Information, 545 Record, 3 History, 497 Belief, 501 Knowledge, 560 Description*

2 **proof**, verification, demonstration, corroboration, substantiation, confirmation, certainty
▶ *480 Verification, 475 Demonstration, 490 Certainty, 473 Argument*

3 **evidentness**, manifestation, obviousness, appearance, self-evidence, visibility, prominence
▶ *457 Appearance, 437 Visibility, 318 Prominence*

4 **indication**, indicator, pointer, tell-tale sign, token, symptom, clue, remains, mark, track, trail, footprint, wake, vapour trail, spoor, scent
▶ *590 Pursuit, 496 Discovery*

5 **legal evidence**, evidence in chief (US), prima-facie evidence, external (*or* extrinsic) evidence, internal (*or* intrinsic) evidence, primary evidence, secondary evidence, direct evidence, indirect evidence, testimonial evidence, testimony, statement, declaration, admission, deposition, documentary evidence, exhibit, confession, affidavit, collateral evidence, cumulative evidence, circumstantial evidence, hearsay evidence, word-of-mouth evidence, incriminating evidence, counter-evidence, inadmissible evidence
▶ *16 Law, 535 Affirmation, 530 Disclosure, 532 Publication, 484 Counterevidence*

6 **documentation**, document, authority, papers, case history, record, testimonial, recommendation, character reference, reference, credential, *curriculum vitae* (L), CV, résumé (US), warrant, warranty, ticket, chit, receipt, voucher, passport, identity card, i.d., visa, permit, security pass
▶ *3 History, 545 Record, 544 Identification, 688 Authority, 485 Qualification, 845 Entitlement*

7 **person who gives evidence**, witness, eyewitness, bystander, passer-by, attestant, defendant, plaintiff, spectator, spy, informant, tell-tale, stool pigeon (Inf), rat (US sl), squealer (Sl), snout (Sl), mole (Sl), nark (Sl), grass (Sl), supergrass (Sl), lagger (Aus sl), dobber (Aus sl)
▶ *480 Verification, 528 Information, 719 Observance*

ADJECTIVES

8 **evidential**, prima facie, significant, factual,

relevant, informed, witnessed, attested, circumstantial, direct, documented, recorded, documentary, reported, corroborative, probative, constructive, indicative, pointing, demonstrative, tell-tale, authentic, empirical, verified, confirmed, proved, certain

9 **evident**, apparent, manifest, obvious, self-evident, visible, prominent, ostensible

▶ *457 Appearance*

VERBS

10 **make evident**, show, show signs of, represent, speak for itself, suggest, indicate, imply

11 **give evidence**, witness, testify, swear, take the oath, attest, affirm, assert, declare, state, bear witness to, swear to, allege

12 **prove**, verify, validate, corroborate, support, sustain, back up, circumstantiate, authenticate, confirm, certify, countersign, endorse

13 **turn queen's evidence**, inform, betray, save one's own skin, tell tales, nark (Sl), squeal (Sl), sing (Sl), rat (US sl), grass on (Sl), grass (someone) up (Sl), lag (Aus sl), dob (Aus sl)

ADVERBS

14 **as evidence**, in evidence, in proof, certainly, factually, authentically, relevantly, significantly, circumstantially, indicatively, demonstratively, reportedly, with reason, on good grounds

15 **evidently**, manifestly, obviously, apparently, self-evidently, visibly, ostensibly, prominently, on display, for all to see, in broad daylight

484   Counterevidence

NOUNS

1 **counterevidence**, answer, defence, apology, appeal, retort, rebuttal, surrebuttal, rejoinder, surrejoinder, retaliation, contradiction, confutation, refutation, denial, demurrer, comeback, contraindication, counterstatement, countercharge, counterblast, counterreply, counteraccusation, counterclaim, counterdemand, contraremonstrance, countermand, counterorder, equivocation, annulment, nullification, negation, invalidation, opposition, protest, resistance

▶ *473 Argument, 483 Evidence, 476 Refutation, 478 Answer, 663 Opposition, 713 Protest, 669 Resistance, 16 Law, 125 Compensation, 672 Retaliation, 704 Cancellation, 674 Contention, 578 Equivocation, 536 Negation, 855 Vindication*

2 **reversal**, tergiversation, turnaround, about-face, U-turn, second thoughts, after thoughts, backtracking, back-pedalling, repentance, recantation, disavowal, denial, reneging, unsaying, repudiation, retraction, palinody, disclamation, disownment, abjuration, abnegation, abrogation, cassation, revocation, renunciation, forswearing, apostasy, treason, self-

contradiction, hypocrisy, false promise

▶ *474 Sophistry, 216 Change, 224 Changeableness, 231 Counteraction, 539 Deception, 540 Falsehood, 287 Inversion, 867 Penitence, 581 Rejection, 221 Reversion, 326 Transfer, 538 Untruth*

3 **counterclaimant**, rebutter, refuter, denier, devil's advocate

4 **tergiversator**, tergiversant, traitor, equivocator, deserter, apostate, recusant, renegade, hypocrite, hostile witness

ADJECTIVES

5 **countering**, answering, defensive, apologetic, retaliatory, confutative, refutative, refutatory, contrary, counteractive, rebutting, denying, contradictory, oppositional, apostatic, self-contradictory, hypocritical, equivocal

6 **countered**, repudiated, retracted, disclaimed, disowned, abjured, abnegated, abrogated, revoked, renounced, denied, disavowed, reneged, retorted, refuted, confuted, negated, invalidated, annulled

VERBS

7 **counter**, answer, apologize, appeal, retort, rebut, rejoin, retaliate, contradict, confute, refute, deny, demur, contraindicate, counterstate, countercharge, counterblast, counterreply, counteraccuse, counterclaim, counterdemand, contraremonstrate, countermand, counterorder, annul, nullify, negate, invalidate, turn the tables, protest, oppose, resist, play devil's advocate

8 **reverse**, tergiversate, turn around, have second thoughts, change one's mind, waver, vacillate, equivocate, think again, change one's tune, backtrack, back-pedal, recant, repent, disavow, renege, unsay, repudiate, retract, disclaim, disown, abjure, abnegate, abrogate, revoke, renounce, forswear, apostasize, desert, betray, swear falsely, contradict oneself, do a U-turn

▶ *576 Vacillation*

ADVERBS

9 **to the contrary**, on the contrary, contrarily, *au contraire* (Fr), on the other hand, in response, in reply, counteractively, defensively, apologetically, equivocally, hypocritically

485   Qualification

NOUNS

1 **qualification**, qualifiedness, eligibility, suitability, suitableness, suitedness, acceptability, appropriateness, propriety, fitness, fittedness, preparedness, readiness, adequacy, sufficiency, efficacy, appositeness, relevance, applicability, aptness, aptitude, ability, ableness, capability, capableness, worthiness, deservedness, meritedness, dueness, entitlement, competence, efficiency, proficiency, potentiality, equipment

▶ *845 Entitlement, 655 Skill, 486 Possibility, 608 Sufficiency, 235 Power, 617 Worth, 843 Right, 594 Preparation, 613 Usefulness*

Educational Qualifications

Advanced level (A level)	Certificate of the Business and Technician Education Council (BTEC)	Doctor of Medicine (MD)	Master of Fine Arts (MFA)
Advanced Ordinary level (AO level)		Doctor of Music (MusD, DMus)	Master of Library Science (MLS)
Advanced Supplementary level (AS level)	Certificate of Prevocational Education (CPVE)	Doctor of Philosophy (PhD, DPhil)	Master of Philosophy (MPhil)
Associate of Arts (AA)	Certificate of Secondary Education (CSE)	General Certificate of Secondary Education (GCSE)	Master of Science (MS, MSc)
Bachelor of Arts (BA, AB)	Diploma in Education (DipEd)	Higher National Certificate (HNC)	National Vocational Qualification (NVQ)
Bachelor of Divinity (BD)	Diploma in Higher Education (DipHE)	Higher National Diploma (HND)	Ordinary level (O level)
Bachelor of Education (BEd)	Doctor of Divinity (DD)	Higher Grade (or Highers)	Postgraduate Certificate (PG Cert)
Bachelor of Laws (LLB)	Doctor of Education (DEd, EdD)	Master of Arts (AM, MA)	Postgraduate Certificate of Education (PGCE)
Bachelor of Medicine (MB)	Doctor of Jurisprudence (JD)	Master of Business Administration (MBA)	Scottish Certificate of Education (SCE)
Bachelor of Music (BMus)	Doctor of Letters (LittD, DLitt)	Master of Divinity (MDiv)	Sixth Year Studies
Bachelor of Science (BS, SB, BSc)	Doctor of Laws (LLD)		Special level (S level)
			Standard grade

2 **ability**, facility, faculty, capability, capacity, quality, mastery, attribute, tendency, endowment, natural power, innate ability, talent, skill, genius, flair, gift, bent, knack, what it takes (Inf), green fingers (Inf), know-how (Inf)
▶ *528 Information, 501 Knowledge, 507 Wisdom, 655 Skill, 234 Tendency*

3 **qualifications**, authorization, permit, licence, documentation, certification, certificate, diploma, degree, licentiate, baccalaureate, examinations, skills, expertise, experience, record, background, history, references, credentials, testimonial
▶ *688 Authority, 708 Permission, 655 Skill, 6 Education, 3 History*

4 **permission**, authorization, empowerment, enablement, investment, endowment, equipment
▶ *708 Permission, 851 Approval, 688 Authority, 235 Power, 729 Giving, 116 Accord*

5 **modification**, qualification, adjustment, adaptation, alteration, change, variation, modulation, coordination, regulation, attunement, improvement, reconciliation, palliation, mitigation, softening, allowance, extenuating circumstances
▶ *116 Accord, 125 Compensation, 627 Improvement, 794 Refinement*

6 **specification**, qualification, frame of reference, terms of reference, definition, determination, limitation, restriction, circumscription, bounding, confinement, control, check, demarcation, delimitation, prescription, proscription, mandate, bounds, conditions
▶ *302 Limit, 715 Contract, 301 Enclosure*

7 **condition**, qualification, grounds, reservation, parameter, stipulation, obligation, requisite, prerequisite, provision, proviso, *sine qua non* (L), limiting condition, boundary condition, escape clause, saving clause, small print
▶ *302 Limit, 301 Enclosure, 715 Contract, 606 Provision, 593 Requirement*

8 **qualified person**, graduate, postgraduate, specialist, professor, expert, professional, ace, doctor, technician, skilled worker, consultant, adviser, boffin, connoisseur, virtuoso, perfect candidate, right man (*or* woman) for the job (Inf), old hand (Inf)
▶ *655 Skill, 507 Wisdom, 501 Knowledge*

ADJECTIVES

9 **qualified**, capable, able, eligible, suitable, suited, well-adapted, acceptable, appropriate, fit, fitting, fitted, prepared, ready, apt, worthy, deserved, merited, competent, efficient, professional, businesslike, proficient, equipped, endowed, talented, gifted, masterful, expert, skilled, skilful, experienced, practised, versed, tried and tested, cut out for (Inf)

10 **authorized**, certified, empowered, enabled, permitted, licensed, entitled, allowed, documented

11 **modified**, adjusted, adapted, altered, changed, varied, variational, modulated, coordinated, conditioned, regulated, attuned, improved, reconciled, palliative, palliated, mitigatory, mitigated, softened, moderated

12 **conditional**, qualificatory, reserved, stipulatory, stipulated, parametric, obligatory, requisitional, provisional, provisory, specified, defined, definitional, mandatory, determined, limiting, limited, restricted, restrictive, circumscribed, contingent, bound, confined, controlled, checked, curbed, demarcated, delimited, prescribed, prescriptive, proscribed, proscriptive

VERBS

13 **qualify**, permit, authorize, empower, enable, invest, endow, equip, license, certify, pass, get into the final, get through
▶ *682 Success*

14 **be qualified**, suit, fit, suffice, apply, deserve, merit, know how, know one's job, have the knack, be trained (in)

15 **modify**, qualify, adjust, adapt, alter, change, vary, colour, modulate, coordinate, regulate, attune, improve, reconcile, temper, palliate, tone down, mitigate, moderate, soften, allow, extenuate, make allowances, make exception, set apart, split hairs

16 **specify**, qualify, frame, define, determine, limit, restrain, restrict, circumscribe, bind, confine, control, check, demarcate, delimit, prescribe, proscribe, stipulate, reserve, oblige, require, state terms, propose conditions

ADVERBS

17 **capably**, ably, masterfully, competently, efficiently, proficiently, professionally, skilfully, acceptably, aptly, appropriately, properly, fittingly, readily, worthily, deservedly

18 **with qualification**, conditionally, provisionally, contingently, restrictively, proscriptively, prescriptively, with the proviso, with strings attached

486 Possibility

The grand Perhaps! Robert Browning.

Your If is the only peace-maker; much virtue in If. William Shakespeare.

NOUNS

1 **possibility**, potential, potentiality, plausibility, likelihood, prospect, promise, chance, odds, opportunity, virtuality, eventuality, contingency
▶ *589 Chance, 488 Probability*

2 **possibleness**, the realms of possibility, conceivability, conceivableness, credibility, feasibility, viableness, practicability, practicality, workability, operability, accessibility, admissibility, flexibility, approachability, availability, aptitude, ability, capacity, facility
▶ *461 Thought, 640 Action, 642 Activity, 99 Existence, 527 Latency, 101 Reality*

3 **strong possibility**, good chance, sporting chance, best chance, even chance, half a chance, opening, luck, good opportunity, sure bet, evens, odds-on, sure thing (Inf)
▶ *488 Probability, 199 Future Time*

4 **remote possibility**, hope, faint hope, outside hope, small chance, off chance, slim chance, poor prospect, long odds, long shot, outside chance (Inf)
▶ *775 Hope, 589 Chance, 489 Improbability*

ADJECTIVES

5 **possible**, potential, conceivable, imaginable, thinkable, credible, believable, feasible, admissible, viable, tenable, reasonable, practical, practicable, doable, workable, performable, operable, achievable, attainable, realizable, likely, accessible, approachable, reachable, available, flexible, able, capable, apt
▶ *488 Probability*

6 **potential**, possible, promising, undeveloped, future, prospective, eventual, virtual, dormant
▶ *527 Latency*

VERBS

7 **make possible**, enable, empower, permit, allow, clear the way for, give a chance to, take a chance, gamble, hope
▶ *327 Way, 235 Power*

8 **be possible**, could be, might be, stand a chance, stand a good chance

ADVERBS

9 **possibly**, perhaps, perchance, peradventure (Arch), haply, maybe, for all one knows, if possible, by chance, on the off chance, by any means

10 **practically**, workably, tenably, reasonably, within reach, within sight, within one's power
▶ *488 Probability*

11 **potentially**, virtually, conceivably, imaginably, credibly, believably, feasibly, plausibly, prospectively, eventually, in all likelihood, somehow
▶ *527 Latency*

487 Impossibility

ADJECTIVES

1 **impossible**, not possible, beyond the bounds of possibility, inconceivable, unthinkable, not to be thought of, unimaginable, out of the question, unquestionable, unreasonable, contrary to reason, absurd, ridiculous, preposterous, illogical, irrational, paradoxical, self-contradictory, self-defeating
▶ *100 Nonexistence, 462 Lack of Thought, 536 Negation, 476 Refutation, 798 Ridiculousness, 523 Unintelligibility*

2 **unbelievable**, incredible, counterintuitive, beyond belief, fantastic, miraculous, fabulous, bizarre, weird, ineffable, mysterious, mystical
▶ *498 Disbelief, 102 Unreality*

3 **hopeless**, impractical, unfeasible, unworkable, unachievable, untenable, irrecoverable, unviable, inoperable, broken, irreparable, irrevocable, unattainable, insurmountable, insuperable, inaccessible, unaccessible, unapproachable, unreachable, impenetrable, impervious, unobtainable, unavailable, out, away, over, finished, gone
▶ *687 Adversity, 659 Difficulty, 157 End, 3 History, 722 Loss, 614 Uselessness, 218 Cessation*

4 **forbidden**, prohibited, denied, disallowed, blocked, barred, banned, stopped, cancelled, ruled out
▶ *704 Cancellation, 147 Exclusion, 709 Veto*

NOUNS

5 **impossibility**, impossibleness, inconceivability, unthinkability, unimaginability, nonexistence, unreality, self-contradiction, absurdity, paradox, logical impossibility, illogicality, what cannot be
▶ *462 Lack of Thought, 498 Disbelief, 489 Improbability, 521 Lack of Meaning, 506 Nonsense, 100 Nonexistence, 536 Negation, 476 Refutation, 523 Unintelligibility, 102 Unreality*

6 **hopelessness**, impossibility, impracticality, impracticability, unfeasibility, unworkability, inoperability, unattainability, insuperability, insurmountability, inaccessibility, unaccessibility, impenetrability, imperviousness, unobtainability, unavailability
▶ *776 Hopelessness, 236 Powerlessness*

7 **obstacle**, prohibition, no-go area, deadlock, block, impasse, barrier, problem, Sisyphean task, no-no (Inf)
▶ *687 Adversity, 659 Difficulty, 709 Veto*

VERBS

8 **make impossible**, prohibit, block, bar, ban, forbid, rule out, disqualify, exclude, deny, withhold, negate, disenable, disable, put out of reach, make things difficult, scupper (Inf), put (*or* throw) a spanner in the works (Inf)

9 **be impossible**, fly in the face of reason, be a waste of time, not stand a chance

10 **attempt the impossible**, waste time, cry for the moon, try for a miracle, look for a needle in a haystack, seek the end of the rainbow, teach an old dog new tricks, make the leopard change its spots, turn back time, turn back the tide, stop the world from turning, make hell freeze over, make rivers run uphill, make a silk purse from a sow's ear, fetch water in a sieve, walk on water, catch the wind, draw blood from a stone
▶ *798 Ridiculousness*

ADVERBS

11 **impossibly**, inconceivably, unthinkably, unimaginably, unquestionably, incredibly, illogically, irrationally, absurdly, ridiculously, paradoxically

12 **hopelessly**, impractically, unworkably, inoperably, irreparably, irrecoverably, irrevocably, unattainably, insurmountably, insuperably, unapproachably

INTERJECTIONS

13 **impossible!**, no way! (Inf), no fear! (Inf), no can do! (Inf), not on your life! (Inf), not on your nelly! (Inf), no chance! (Inf), not a hope in hell! (Inf)

488 Probability

NOUNS

1 **probability**, likelihood, likeliness, chance, odds, liability, liableness, proneness, predictability, prospect, forecast, outlook, expectation, presumption, anticipation, prognosis, prediction
▶ *589 Chance, 513 Expectation, 516 Foresight, 517 Prediction, 199 Future Time, 234 Tendency*

2 **tendency**, propensity, trend, drift, tenor, tone, swing, bearing, tending, general tendency, the way it looks
▶ *234 Tendency, 219 Continuity, 155 Sequence, 327 Way*

3 **plausibility**, probability, possibility, reasonability, credibility, verisimilitude
▶ *486 Possibility, 497 Belief, 114 Similarity, 463 Reason*

4 **chance**, good chance, sporting chance, main chance, even chance, strong possibility, odds-on chance, best bet, well-grounded hope, fair expectation, favourable prospect
▶ *775 Hope, 486 Possibility, 589 Chance, 513 Expectation*

5 **probability theory**, mathematical probability, statistical probability, empirical probability, subjective probability, probability distribution, probability function, probability density function, probability curve, uncertainty principle, law of averages, probabilism
▶ *52 Mathematics, 170 Calculation*

ADJECTIVES

6 **probable**, likely, expected, undoubted, indubitable, unquestioned, apparent, ostensible, evident, presumable, presumed, presumptive, predictive, predictable, prone, liable, apt, anticipated, prospective, tending, drifting, on the cards
▶ *513 Expectation, 234 Tendency*

7 **plausible**, probable, possible, reasonable, credible, believable, persuasive
▶ *497 Belief, 463 Reason, 486 Possibility, 457 Appearance*

VERBS

8 **be probable**, seem likely, lead one to expect, promise, show a tendency, show signs of, have the makings of, be on the cards, stand a good chance, be in the running, bid fair to, stand a fair chance, impend, come as no surprise, be bound to happen (Inf)
▶ *199 Future Time, 234 Tendency, 714 Promise*

9 **make probable**, smooth the way for, make likely, increase the odds, increase the chances
▶ *662 Help, 327 Way*

10 **think likely**, expect, anticipate, presume, suppose, daresay, predict, prognosticate, foresee, look for, count on, reckon, take for granted, risk, gamble, bet on, bet one's bottom

dollar on, take a chance, not put it past (Inf)

▶ *497 Belief, 516 Foresight, 517 Prediction, 589 Chance, 513 Expectation, 775 Hope, 518 Supposition*

ADVERBS

11 **probably**, in all probability, in all likelihood, likely, most likely, as likely as not, doubtless (*or* doubtlessly), indubitably, unquestionably, to all intents and purposes, all things considered, ten to one, presumably, apparently, ostensibly, predictably, expectedly, to be expected, as expected, as usual, on average, in anticipation

▶ *124 Average, 584 Habit, 513 Expectation, 110 Sameness*

489   Improbability

ADJECTIVES

1 **improbable**, unlikely, uncertain, doubtful, dubious, dubitable, unpromising, inauspicious, scarcely to be expected, unrealistic, remote, far-fetched, unexpected

▶ *491 Uncertainty*

2 **questionable**, implausible, unbelievable, fanciful, extraordinary, exceptional, wild, too good to be true, hard to believe, incredible, beyond belief, hard to swallow (Inf)

▶ *498 Disbelief*

3 **unexpected**, unforeseeable, unpredictable, unanticipated, unguessed, unpredicted, unforeseen, fortuitous, rare, accidental, freakish, chance, fluky (Inf)

▶ *589 Chance*

NOUNS

4 **improbability**, unlikeliness, unlikelihood, uncertainty, doubt, doubtfulness, poor prospect, remote possibility, foolish hope, castle in the air (*or* in Spain), pipe dream, small chance, hardly a chance, outside chance, ghost of a chance, slim chance, long shot, long odds, a chance in a million, million-to-one chance (*or* shot), hundred-to-one chance (*or* shot), fat chance (Inf)

▶ *491 Uncertainty, 776 Hopelessness, 487 Impossibility*

5 **unexpectedness**, unforeseeableness, unpredictability, miraculousness, rarity, oddity, the unforeseen, the last thing one would expect, more than one bargained for, freak accident, miracle, prodigy, wonder, surprise, lucky shot, fluke, chance

▶ *589 Chance, 514 Surprise*

6 **implausibility**, incredibility, unbelievability, questionableness, tall story, fib, lie, porky (Sl), whopper (Inf)

▶ *498 Disbelief, 538 Untruth*

VERBS

7 **be improbable**, go beyond belief, strain one's credulity, go beyond the bounds of rea-

son, be economical with the truth, build castles in the air (*or* in Spain), dream, fib, lie, spin a yarn, tell tales

▶ *498 Disbelief, 540 Falsehood, 538 Untruth*

ADVERBS

8 **improbably**, incredibly, unbelievably, questionably, doubtfully, dubiously, uncertainly

9 **unexpectedly**, unpredictably, unforeseeably, contrary to expectation, by accident, without warning, out of the blue, never in a month of Sundays

10 **rarely**, exceptionally, seldom if ever, once in a blue moon, once in a lifetime, hardly ever, uncommonly, uniquely

11 **luckily**, happily, fortuitously, by chance, by accident

490   Certainty

ADJECTIVES

1 **certain**, known, factual, actual, historical, real, true, veracious, definite, sure, secure, absolute, given, verifiable, demonstrable, well-grounded, well-founded, proved, documented, certified, ascertained, demonstrated, established, tried and tested, safe, self-evident, unmistakable, unmistaken, ostensible, obvious, necessary, realistic, accurate, authoritative

▶ *501 Knowledge, 101 Reality, 843 Right, 503 Accuracy, 479 Experiment, 437 Visibility, 505 Maxim, 475 Demonstration, 480 Verification, 688 Authority, 550 Clarity*

2 **convinced**, certain, sure, positive, believing, accepting, trusting, unquestioning, undoubting, unswerving, unhesitating, undeviating, assured, satisfied, persuaded, confident, self-assured, self-confident, opinionated, cocksure, assertive, overconfident, doctrinaire, dogmatic, orthodox, narrow-minded, obstinate, stubborn, bigoted, biased, partisan, fanatical

▶ *497 Belief, 811 Showiness, 481 Discrimination, 577 Obstinacy, 7 Religion*

3 **decided**, settled, fixed, established, open and shut, undisputed, unrefuted, irrefutable, undeniable, uncontestable, unchallengeable, incontrovertible, indubitable, unimpeachable, unambiguous, unequivocal

▶ *483 Evidence*

4 **guaranteed**, assured, insured, warranted, pledged, promised

▶ *714 Promise*

5 **inevitable**, destined, predestined, determined, predetermined, fixed, set, fated, fateful, unstoppable, ineluctable, necessary, inescapable, unavoidable, inevasible, unpreventable, relentless, inflexible, inexorable, unyielding, directed, headed for

▶ *582 Predetermination, 571 Necessity*

6 **infallible**, reliable, dependable, trustworthy,

predictable, regular, stable, solid, secure, unshakable, unwavering, unchanging, undeviating, steady, steadfast, firm, sound, staunch, faithful, loyal, stoical

▶ *217 Permanence, 718 Security, 225 Stability, 214 Regularity*

7 **particular**, specific, specified, definite, determined, stipulated, indicated, named, fixed, pinned down, distinct, singular, single, individual

▶ *174 One, 544 Identification, 242 Moderation*

8 **unspecified**, indeterminate, undetermined, indefinite, unnamed, unmentioned, several, few, many

▶ *182 Few, 120 Quantity, 175 Plurality, 491 Uncertainty*

NOUNS

9 **certainty**, surety, knowledge, factuality, reality, actuality, historicity, truth, trueness, verity, veracity, absoluteness, authoritativeness, indubitability, indisputability, definiteness, validity, accuracy, evidence, proof, obviousness, necessity

▶ *501 Knowledge, 483 Evidence, 479 Experiment, 571 Necessity, 318 Prominence, 437 Visibility, 503 Accuracy, 537 Truth, 3 History, 101 Reality, 99 Existence, 688 Authority*

10 **conviction**, certainty, certainness, certitude, belief, acceptance, credence, trust, faith, assurance, assuredness, sureness, surety, positiveness, confidence, self-assurance, cocksureness, self-confidence, assertiveness, overconfidence, dogmatism, positivism, orthodoxy, narrow-mindedness, obstinacy, stubbornness, bigotry, bias, partisanship, fanaticism, fideism

▶ *497 Belief, 577 Obstinacy, 481 Discrimination, 7 Religion, 811 Showiness*

11 **opinionist**, convinced person, believer, overconfident person, show-off, exhibitionist, positivist, doctrinaire, dogmatist, bigot, zealot, fanatic, partisan, stick-in-the-mud (Inf), old fogy (Inf)

▶ *577 Obstinacy, 7 Religion, 497 Belief*

12 **something certain**, fact, foregone conclusion, open-and-shut case, winner, safe bet, dead certainty, dead cert (Inf), cinch (Inf), sure thing (Inf)

▶ *101 Reality, 488 Probability, 537 Truth*

13 **confirmation**, assurance, verification, affirmation, affirmativeness, demonstration, proof, ascertainment, establishment, evidence, grounds, facts, signs

▶ *480 Verification, 475 Demonstration, 535 Affirmation, 483 Evidence, 543 Sign*

14 **guarantee**, assurance, insurance, warrant, warranty, pledge, promise

▶ *714 Promise, 851 Approval*

15 **guarantor**, insurer, warrantor, pledger, promiser

16 **inevitability**, inevitableness, certainty, fate, destiny, fatefulness, predestination, determination, predetermination, ineluctability, necessity, unavoidability, inescapableness, inevasibleness, unpreventability, irrevocability, relentlessness, inexorability, force majeure, *vis major* (L), act of God

▶ *571 Necessity, 157 End, 235 Power, 582 Predetermination*

17 **infallibility**, reliability, dependability, trustworthiness, predictability, regularity, stability, solidity, security, steadiness, steadfastness, firmness, soundness, staunchness, fidelity, loyalty, stoicism

▶ *214 Regularity, 225 Stability, 718 Security, 4 Philosophy, 517 Prediction*

18 **particularity**, particularization, specification, specificness, definiteness, determination, stipulation, indication, fixing, pinning down, distinctness, singularity, the specific, the particular, the case in point, quantity, amount, number, measure

▶ *174 One, 606 Provision, 302 Limit*

19 **indeterminacy**, inexactness, imprecision, generality, vagueness

▶ *491 Uncertainty*

VERBS

20 **be certain**, know, know for sure, feel sure, have no doubt, believe, be convinced, accept, credit, rely on, depend on, have faith in, assert oneself, lay down the law, pontificate, stick to one's guns, dogmatize, dig in one's heels

21 **make certain**, make sure, ensure, confirm, verify, affirm, demonstrate, prove, ascertain, establish, determine, find out, settle, fix, pin down, clear up, check, decide, convince, evince, ground, guarantee, warrant, pledge, promise, authenticate, certify, endorse, substantiate, secure, stabilize, steady, solidify

22 **specify**, particularize, define, determine, stipulate, indicate, measure, quantify

ADVERBS

23 **certainly**, surely, really, truly, actually, absolutely, positively, firmly, definitely, undoubtedly, indubitably, unquestionably, without question, without a shadow of doubt

24 **with certainty**, confidently, assuredly, assertively, dogmatically, obstinately, stubbornly

25 **inevitably**, certainly, ineluctably, unavoidably, inescapably, irrevocably, relentlessly, inexorably, surely, fatefully, in the end

INTERJECTIONS

26 **certainly**!, naturally!, definitely!, of course!, by all means!, be my guest!, go ahead!, help yourself!

491 Uncertainty

ADJECTIVES

1 **uncertain**, unsure, unknown, doubtful, du-

bious, speculative, conjectural, hypothetical, provisional, disputable, contestable, controversial, controvertible, moot, questionable, suspicious, distrustful, mistrustful, unbelieving, sceptical, agnostic, open-minded

▶ *477 Question, 498 Disbelief, 7 Religion, 502 Ignorance, 473 Argument*

2 **irresolute**, indecisive, vacillating, wavering, hesitant, hesitating, hanging (*or* holding) back, faltering, undecided, unsettled, ambivalent, unresolved, unanswered

▶ *576 Vacillation, 365 Oscillation, 578 Equivocation*

3 **confused**, bewildered, disconcerted, worried, perplexed, nonplussed, confounded, baffled, puzzled, discomposed, in a quandary, at a loss for words, embarrassed, shy, timid, bewildering, disconcerting, worrying, perplexing, baffling, puzzling, difficult, enigmatic, problematic, cryptic

▶ *477 Question, 659 Difficulty, 523 Unintelligibility, 661 Hindrance, 153 Disturbance*

4 **indemonstrable**, unverifiable, unprovable, unconfirmable, unlikely, improbable, unpredictable

▶ *489 Improbability, 844 Wrong, 538 Untruth*

5 **uncertified**, undocumented, unchecked, uncorroborated, unverified, unauthenticated, unsigned, unratified, unascertained, unofficial, unproved, untried, untested, speculative, experimental, apocryphal

▶ *479 Experiment*

6 **indeterminate**, indefinite, vague, unclear, undefined, borderline, ambiguous, equivocal, indistinct, faint, hazy, foggy, misty, fuzzy, obscure, inaccurate, inexact, imprecise, loose, lax, broad, general, amorphous, incoherent

▶ *307 Shapelessness, 164 Generality, 424 Faintness, 441 Dimness, 443 Opaqueness, 578 Equivocation, 551 Obscurity, 474 Sophistry, 151 Disorder, 553 Diffuseness, 482 Lack of Discrimination*

7 **unreliable**, fallible, undependable, untrustworthy, treacherous, dishonest, perfidious, insecure, transient, infirm, insubstantial, unsound, unstable, unsteady, inconsistent, shifty, shaky, precarious, slippery, risky, hazardous, dangerous, perilous, eccentric, erratic, irregular, unpredictable

▶ *633 Danger, 238 Weakness, 189 Transience, 539 Deception, 215 Irregularity, 683 Failure*

8 **capricious**, whimsical, fickle, irresponsible, skittish, volatile, mercurial, fitful, changeable, mutable, fluid, fluctuating, wavering, flexible, mobile, aleatoric, inconstant, variable, random, chancy, haphazard

▶ *589 Chance, 579 Caprice, 324 Motion, 456 Variegation, 216 Change, 224 Changeableness, 335 Deviation, 160 Discontinuity, 377 Elasticity*

NOUNS

9 **uncertainty**, incertitude, unsureness, uncer-

tainness, contestability, controvertibility, doubtfulness, dubiousness, disputability, questionableness, open mind, open verdict, question mark, guesswork, guess, anyone's guess, wild guess, enigma

▶ *477 Question, 473 Argument, 498 Disbelief*

10 **suspicion**, suspiciousness, conjecture, doubt, distrust, mistrust, caution, disbelief, incredulity, denial, rejection, scepticism, agnosticism, atheism

▶ *581 Rejection, 476 Refutation, 4 Philosophy, 7 Religion*

11 **irresoluteness**, irresolution, indecision, indecisiveness, unsettledness, vacillation, wavering, hesitation, ambivalence, faltering, cleft stick, horns of a dilemma, borderline case

▶ *576 Vacillation*

12 **confusion**, bewilderment, disconcertion, disconcertedness, confoundment, perplexity, bafflement, puzzlement, predicament, quandary, embarrassment, discomposure, shyness, timidity

▶ *659 Difficulty, 477 Question*

13 **indemonstrability**, unverifiability, unprovability, unconfirmability, unlikelihood, unlikeliness, improbability

▶ *487 Impossibility, 489 Improbability, 536 Negation*

14 **indeterminacy**, indefiniteness, vagueness, unclearness, ambiguity, equivocalness, indistinctness, neither one thing nor the other, faintness, haziness, fogginess, mistiness, fuzziness, obscurity, inaccuracy, inexactness, imprecision, looseness, laxity, broadness, generality, amorphousness, incoherence

▶ *307 Shapelessness, 164 Generality*

15 **unreliability**, fallibility, untrustworthiness, treacherousness, insecurity, transience, infirmity, insubstantiality, unsoundness, instability, unstableness, unsteadiness, inconsistency, shiftiness, shakiness, precariousness, eccentricity, irregularity, unpredictability, risk, hazard, adventure, gamble

▶ *683 Failure, 215 Irregularity, 489 Improbability, 238 Weakness, 633 Danger*

16 **capriciousness**, whimsicality, fickleness, volatility, volatileness, fitfulness, changeableness, mutability, fluidity, fluctuation, wavering, inconstancy, flexibility, mobility, variability, randomness, chance

▶ *579 Caprice, 589 Chance, 324 Motion, 224 Changeableness, 365 Oscillation*

17 **uncertain person**, agnostic, doubting Thomas, doubter, worrier, questioner, sceptic, erratic

▶ *477 Question*

VERBS

18 **be uncertain**, have one's doubts, doubt, question, moot, distrust, mistrust, disbelieve, have a suspicion about, suspect, wait and see,

wonder about, speculate, conjecture, dispute, contest, controvert
▶ *477 Question, 473 Argument*

19 **hesitate**, vacillate, dither, waver, hang (*or* hold) back, falter, be irresolute, be in two minds about, equivocate, prevaricate, sit on the fence, keep an open mind
▶ *482 Lack of Discrimination, 576 Vacillation, 474 Sophistry*

20 **make uncertain**, obscure, mystify, baffle, faze, confound, confuse, perplex, daze, haze, fog, disturb, disconcert, embarrass, worry, bewilder, flummox, nonplus, puzzle, stump, keep someone guessing
▶ *551 Obscurity, 460 Lack of Intellect*

21 **change**, mutate, fluctuate, vary, move, shift, shake, slip, fail, betray
▶ *683 Failure, 324 Motion*

22 **risk**, chance, gamble, hazard, venture, dare, speculate
▶ *589 Chance*

ADVERBS

23 **uncertainly**, doubtfully, dubiously, suspiciously, sceptically, irresolutely, hesitantly, indecisively, speculatively, conjecturally, disputably, controversially, questionably, in question
▶ *477 Question, 473 Argument, 498 Disbelief*

24 **confusingly**, bewilderingly, worryingly, puzzlingly, problematically, enigmatically, embarrassingly, in a quandary, on the horns of a dilemma
▶ *514 Surprise, 477 Question, 563 Voicelessness, 659 Difficulty, 153 Disturbance*

25 **indeterminately**, indefinitely, vaguely, ambiguously, equivocally, indistinctly, faintly, hazily, foggily, mistily, fuzzily, obscurely, inaccurately, imprecisely, loosely, broadly, generally, amorphously, incoherently
▶ *307 Shapelessness, 551 Obscurity*

26 **unreliably**, fallibly, treacherously, dishonestly, insecurely, transiently, insubstantially, unsteadily, inconsistently, shiftily, shakily, precariously, dangerously, perilously, riskily, hazardously, eccentrically, erratically, irregularly, unpredictably, improbably
▶ *633 Danger, 589 Chance, 489 Improbability, 215 Irregularity*

27 **capriciously**, on a whim, whimsically, irresponsibly, fitfully, intermittently, changeably, fluidly, flexibly, inconstantly, variably, randomly
▶ *579 Caprice, 224 Changeableness*

492 Judgment

NOUNS

1 **judgment**, discrimination, discernment, distinction, differentiation, selection, choice, discretion, taste, wisdom, sense, judging, adjudication, arbitration, umpirage, faculty of judgment, reasoning, deduction, inference, dissertation, corollary, consideration, view, belief, opinion, assessment, evaluation, speculation, conjecture, surmise, sensibility, guesswork, guess, estimate, estimation, calculation, rating, valuation, appraisal, appreciation, survey, inspection, report, review, notice, remark, comment, critique, criticism, constructive criticism, censure, value judgment, second opinion, public opinion, vox populi, vote, referendum, plebiscite
▶ *481 Discrimination, 117 Disparity, 580 Selection, 507 Wisdom, 497 Belief, 463 Reason, 170 Calculation, 268 Measurement, 851 Approval, 852 Disapproval*

2 **verdict**, judgment, adjudication, summing up, recapitulation, decision, conclusion, ruling, finding, award, sentence, pronouncement, order, edict, decree, decree nisi, decree absolute, acquittal, condemnation, execution of judgment, law, canon, act, legislation
▶ *16 Law, 692 Command, 562 Summary*

3 **place of judgment**, judgment seat, seat of justice, tribunal, the Woolsack, law court, court of law, criminal court, civil court, Court of Appeal, Star Chamber, High Court, Queen's Bench, circuit court, assizes, assize sessions, quarter sessions, crown court, petty sessions, magistrate's court, police court, coroner's court, court martial, kangaroo court, courtroom, the bench, jury box, dock, witness box, chair
▶ *16 Law*

4 **judgment day**, day of judgment, Last Judgment, the Last Day, Doomsday, millennium, resurrection day, afterlife, hereafter
▶ *7 Religion*

5 **judge**, adjudicator, arbitrator, jurist, arbiter, umpire, referee, mediator, assessor, valuer, appraiser, surveyor, inspector, examiner, tester, reporter, commentator, censor, editor, critic, reviewer, expert, connoisseur, adviser, counsellor, panel of judges, panel, jury
▶ *481 Discrimination, 654 Advice, 678 Mediation*

6 **justice**, judge, judge advocate general, his Lordship, his Worship, judge advocate, chief justice, crown court judge, public prosecutor, procurator fiscal, district attorney, county court judge, trial judge, sessions judge, assize judge, recorder, magistrate, coroner, stipendiary magistrate, justice of the peace (JP), associate justice, the bench, the judiciary, the magistracy, the beak (Sl)
▶ *16 Law*

7 **jury**, jury, juryman, jurywoman, juror, foreman of the jury, grand jury, special jury, coroner's jury, jury list, trial jury, twelve good men and true (Inf)
▶ *16 Law*

ADJECTIVES

8 judging, discriminating, discerning, selecting, selective, criticizing, critical, judgmental, inquisitional, moralistic, sententious, approving, appreciative, disapproving, condemnatory, censorious

▶ *481 Discrimination, 580 Selection, 851 Approval, 852 Disapproval*

9 judicious, discerning, discriminating, sensitive, accurate, right, just, fair, unbiased, dispassionate, wise, shrewd, judicial, judicatory, juridical

▶ *481 Discrimination, 507 Wisdom, 843 Right, 859 Disinterestedness*

10 judged, submitted for judgment, under consideration, on trial, up for trial, sub judice, before the bar, up before the beak (Sl)

VERBS

11 judge, umpire, referee, sit in judgment, arbitrate, hear, hear the case, commit for trial, try, sum up, award, decree, adjudge, adjudicate, decide, conclude, find, find for, find against, determine, settle, settle the matter, rule, pronounce sentence, pass judgment, charge the jury, bring a verdict, acquit, condemn, censure, censor, criticize, disapprove of, approve of

▶ *16 Law, 851 Approval, 852 Disapproval*

12 estimate, judge, gauge, calculate, reckon, size up, evaluate, assess, value, appraise, rate, regard, deem, esteem, think, believe, guess, surmise, conjecture, judge by eye, weigh up, ponder over, consider, reason, deduce, infer, examine, investigate, inspect, survey, vet, make a report on, review, criticize, comment on, scan, check, check out (Sl)

▶ *170 Calculation, 463 Reason*

ADVERBS

13 judicially, judiciously, selectively, critically, approvingly, disapprovingly

14 considering, taking into account, all things considered, everything being equal

493 Misjudgment

NOUNS

1 misjudgment, poor judgment, miscalculation, misconception, misconstruction, misinterpretation, misunderstanding, wrong impression, cross purposes, inexactness, underestimation, overestimation, undervaluation, overvaluation, false reading, distortion, fallacy, deception, fallibility, gullibility, self-deception, fool's paradise, wrong end of the stick (Inf)

▶ *494 Overestimation, 495 Underestimation, 482 Lack of Discrimination, 539 Deception*

2 mistake, error, blunder, bungling, clanger (Inf), howler (Inf), blooper (Sl), boob (Sl), booboo (Sl), bloomer (Inf), dog's breakfast (Sl)

▶ *504 Error*

3 injustice, miscarriage of justice, mistrial, packed jury, partiality, partisanship, onesidedness, predilection, predisposition, preferential treatment, favouritism, nepotism, intolerance, discrimination, unfairness, inequality, unlawfulness, bias, prejudice, prejudicial treatment, chauvinism, sectarianism, provincialism, parochialism, insularity, xenophobia, racism, racialism, racial prejudice, racial intolerance, Aryanism, apartheid, anti-Semitism, sexism, ageism, homophobia, bigotry, fanaticism, narrow-mindedness, tunnel vision, overspecialization, narrow mind, closed mind, jaundiced eye, foul play (Inf), not cricket (Sl), one-track mind (Inf)

▶ *481 Discrimination, 822 Hate, 123 Inequality*

4 prejudgment, preconception, preconceived idea, *parti pris* (Fr), mind made up, *idée fixe* (Fr), fixed idea, fixation, obsession, predetermination, foregone conclusion, presupposition

▶ *582 Predetermination*

5 misjudging person, bigot, zealot, fanatic, partisan, chauvinist, xenophobe, racist, racialist, Nazi, sexist, homophobe, pervert, fool, bungler

6 misjudged person, victim, scapegoat, prey, guy, butt

ADJECTIVES

7 misjudging, in error, mistaken, wrong, wrong-headed, muddled, fallible, gullible, misguided, misled, deluded, deceived

▶ *504 Error, 539 Deception*

8 unjust, unfair, discriminatory, prejudicial, partial, partisan, subjective, one-sided, predisposed, preferential, intolerant, prejudiced, biased, jaundiced, warped, twisted, chauvinistic, sectarian, provincial, parochial, insular, xenophobic, racist, colour-prejudiced, anti-Semitic, sexist, ageist, class-prejudiced, homophobic, snobbish, bigoted, fanatical, narrow-minded, narrow, hidebound, pedantic, unimaginative, prejudged, preconceived, fixed

▶ *481 Discrimination, 309 Distortion, 582 Predetermination*

9 misjudged, misunderstood, wrongly accused, unfairly treated, misconstrued, misinterpreted, underestimated, overestimated, undervalued, overvalued, underrated, overrated, out, wrong, mistaken, ill-timed, untimely, inconvenient, ill-advised, foolish

▶ *494 Overestimation, 495 Underestimation, 504 Error, 211 Untimeliness, 616 Inconvenience, 508 Folly*

VERBS

10 misjudge, miscalculate, misreckon, misinterpret, misconstrue, misunderstand, misconceive, misread, get wrong, mistake, twist, distort, let slip, waste an opportunity, miss, trip, slip, stumble, blunder, bungle, time badly, mistime, overestimate, underestimate, over-

value, undervalue, overrate, underrate, be unable to see the wood for the trees, get hold of the wrong end of the stick (Inf)
▶ *504 Error, 309 Distortion, 494 Overestimation, 495 Underestimation*

11 **be unjust**, treat unfairly, discriminate, take sides, prejudge, preconceive
▶ *481 Discrimination*

12 **bias**, prejudice, jaundice, warp, twist, predispose
▶ *309 Distortion*

ADVERBS

13 **misguidedly**, mistakenly, in error, wrongly, fallibly, gullibly, foolishly

14 **unjustly**, unfairly, partially, subjectively, preferentially, intolerantly, chauvinistically, parochially, fanatically, narrow-mindedly

494 Overestimation

NOUNS

1 **overestimation**, overvaluation, overrating, misjudgment, miscalculation, overconfidence, rashness, overoptimism, idealism, overweening pride, conceit, hubris, arrogance, egomania, exaggeration, overstatement, hype, hyperbole, megalomania, vanity, showing off, blowing one's own trumpet (Inf)
▶ *493 Misjudgment, 541 Exaggeration, 780 Rashness, 809 Vanity, 811 Showiness*

2 **overestimate**, much ado about nothing, storm in a teacup, pipe dream, castles in Spain, castles in the air, fool's paradise, Utopia, panegyric, fuss, hue and cry, hot air (Inf), big deal (Sl)
▶ *775 Hope*

3 **optimist**, young hopeful, idealist, megalomaniac, panjandrum, exaggerator, promoter

VERBS

4 **overestimate**, overvalue, overrate, overprize, overprice, price oneself out of the market, overcharge, misjudge, miscalculate, exaggerate, overstate, make a mountain out of a molehill, make a fuss about, hype, overpraise, panegyrize, maximize, make the most of, be too good to be true
▶ *753 Dearness, 493 Misjudgment, 541 Exaggeration*

ADJECTIVES

5 **overestimating**, overconfident, rash, overoptimistic, overenthusiastic, hubristic, arrogant
▶ *780 Rashness, 775 Hope*

6 **overestimated**, overvalued, overrated, overpriced, dear, expensive, misjudged, exaggerated, overpraised, not all it's cracked up to be (Inf)
▶ *541 Exaggeration, 753 Dearness*

ADVERBS

7 **overoptimistically**, idealistically, over-

enthusiastically, hyperbolically, arrogantly, overconfidently, rashly, vainly

495 Underestimation

NOUNS

1 **underestimation**, undervaluation, underrating, misjudgment, miscalculation, underestimate, conservative estimate, minimization, deprecation, self-deprecation, depreciation, self-depreciation, detraction, understatement, litotes, self-effacement, humility, modesty, false modesty, affectation, pessimism, defeatism, negative outlook, cynicism
▶ *493 Misjudgment, 854 Disparagement, 542 Understatement, 806 Humility, 810 Modesty, 797 Affectation, 776 Hopelessness*

2 **pessimist**, defeatist, minimizer, detractor, cynic

VERBS

3 **underestimate**, undervalue, underrate, misprize, misjudge, miscalculate, minimize, play down, understate, make little of, make light of, shrug off, pooh-pooh, belittle, disparage, underpraise, underprice, discount, mark down, hold cheap, scorn, set no store by, not do justice to, soft-pedal (Inf)
▶ *493 Misjudgment, 754 Cheapness, 542 Understatement, 854 Disparagement, 799 Derision*

ADJECTIVES

4 **underestimating**, deprecating, depreciatory, detracting, disparaging, scornful, minimizing, conservative, moderate, pessimistic, defeatist, modest, humble
▶ *854 Disparagement, 806 Humility, 810 Modesty, 776 Hopelessness*

5 **underestimated**, undervalued, underrated, misjudged, miscalculated, underpriced, cheap
▶ *493 Misjudgment, 754 Cheapness*

ADVERBS

6 **pessimistically**, cynically, scornfully, disparagingly, affectedly, conservatively, moderately, modestly, humbly

496 Discovery

VERBS

1 **discover**, find, locate, place, come across, come upon, happen upon, stumble on, hit upon, encounter, meet with, meet, see, spy, espy, spot, descry, perceive, sight, glimpse, catch a glimpse of, set eyes on, notice, observe, watch, recognize, identify
▶ *250 Location, 435 Vision, 544 Identification*

2 **detect**, ferret out, worm out, track down, run down, run to earth, hunt, seek, smell out, sniff out, get wind of, get warm, find a clue, set a trap for, ensnare, catch, catch red-handed, catch in the act, acquire, unearth, disinter, dig up, uncover, bring to light, expose, lay bare, unveil, lift the veil on, unmask, disclose, re-

veal, divulge, betray, show up, show in one's true colours, spill the beans (Inf)

▶ *590 Pursuit, 477 Question, 721 Gain, 530 Disclosure, 294 Uncovering*

3 **find out**, find out about, learn, ascertain, determine, realize, understand, see the light, catch on (Inf), get it (Inf)

▶ *522 Intelligibility, 501 Knowledge, 528 Information*

4 **invent**, design, devise, contrive, hit upon an idea, originate, create, pioneer, herald, be in the vanguard, lead the way to, explore, rediscover

▶ *156 Beginning, 243 Production, 479 Experiment*

5 **be discovered**, be unmasked, come to light, appear, show up, turn up

▶ *457 Appearance*

NOUNS

6 **discovery**, finding, location, accidental discovery, serendipity, encounter, meeting, spotting, perception, sight, sighting, glimpse, observation, recognition, identification

▶ *250 Location, 435 Vision, 544 Identification*

7 **detection**, ferreting out, tracking down, search, hunt, hunting, pursuit, catching, catch, acquisition, excavation, archaeology (*or* archeology), uncovering, exposure, unveiling, unmasking, disclosure, leak, manifestation, revelation, divulgence, betrayal, eye-opener (Inf), showdown (Inf)

▶ *590 Pursuit, 477 Question, 530 Disclosure, 294 Uncovering*

8 **finding out**, learning, ascertaining, realization, understanding, enlightenment, illumination

▶ *522 Intelligibility, 501 Knowledge, 528 Information*

9 **invention**, designing, design, device, idea, contrivance, inspiration, origination, creation, pioneering, exploration, experiment, rediscovery

▶ *156 Beginning, 243 Production, 479 Experiment*

10 **find**, discovery, lucky find, *trouvaille* (Fr), treasure-trove, strike

11 **detector**, metal detector, divining rod, lie detector, sonar, radar, probe, sensor, scanner

12 **discoverer**, finder, spotter, scout, spy, observer, dowser, water diviner, prospector, archaeologist (*or* archeologist), detective, private detective, sniffer dog, inventor, designer, author, founder, parent, producer, agent, motivator, originator, forerunner, herald, pioneer, pathfinder, explorer, traveller, mole (Inf), private eye (Inf), gumshoe (US sl)

▶ *435 Vision, 156 Beginning, 243 Production*

ADJECTIVES

13 **discovering**, finding, on the trail of, on the right track, warm, revelatory, revealing, inventive, pioneering, exploratory, experimental

▶ *530 Disclosure, 479 Experiment*

14 **discovered**, found, located, seen, spotted, unearthed, uncovered, exposed, unmasked, revealed

▶ *250 Location, 435 Vision, 294 Uncovering*

15 **discoverable**, findable, recognizable, identifiable, perceptible, detectable, heuristic

ADVERBS

16 **originally**, experimentally, inventively, at first sight, at a glance, apparently, identifiably, recognizably, obviously, manifestly, revealingly

497 Belief

NOUNS

1 **belief**, opinion, view, point of view, angle, viewpoint, stand, standpoint, position, attitude, stance, impression, feeling, sentiment, intuition, thought, idea, notion, premise (*or* premiss), principle, proposition, theory, hypothesis, judgment, conjecture, supposition, surmise, speculation, popular belief, climate of opinion, persuasion, conviction, certainty, truth

▶ *759 Feeling, 464 Intuition, 471 Idea, 461 Thought, 518 Supposition, 492 Judgment, 490 Certainty, 537 Truth*

2 **religious belief**, religion, faith, religious feeling, persuasion, creed, credo, dogma, canon, principle, tenet, *aberglaube* (Ger), articles of faith, declaration of faith, statement of belief, catechism, manifesto, doctrine, school, cult, philosophy, ideology, traditional belief, superstition, old wives' tale, folklore, obi, obeah, pishogue, voodoo, myalisma, ism (Inf)

▶ *7 Religion, 505 Maxim, 4 Philosophy*

3 **believing**, faith, trust, confidence, assurance, reliance, dependence, credence, credit, credulity, credulousness, gullibility, blind faith, suspension of disbelief, expectation, hope, acceptance, pledge, word of honour

▶ *775 Hope, 857 Probity*

4 **believability**, credibility, plausibility, trustworthiness, reliability

5 **believer**, true believer, conformer, conformist, traditionalist, theist, deist, pilgrim, sanyasin, devotee, hajji, communicant, worshipper, church member, churchgoer, practising Christian, man (*or* woman) of prayer, nun, monk, contemplative, mystic, convert, born-again Christian, Jesus-freak (Sl)

▶ *7 Religion*

6 **trusting person**, innocent, ingenue, lamb to the slaughter (Inf), sucker (Inf)

VERBS

7 **believe**, have faith in, put one's faith in, have no doubts about, credit, accept, be led to believe, take someone's word for, accept on faith, take on trust, trust, confide in, rely on, depend on, count on, bank on, swear by, take

for granted, rest assured, know, maintain, hold, declare, affirm, profess, confess, fall for (Inf), buy (Inf), swallow (Inf), swallow (*or* fall for) hook, line, and sinker (Inf)

▶ *535 Affirmation, 501 Knowledge*

8 be of the opinion, opine, presume, assume, surmise, guess, suppose, think, suspect, understand, be under the impression, get it into one's head, have in mind, imagine, fancy, regard, consider, deem, esteem

▶ *461 Thought, 518 Supposition*

9 make someone believe, assure, convince, persuade, influence, convert, win over, evangelize, proselytize, propagandize, spread the word, indoctrinate, brainwash, deceive, dupe, take in (Inf)

▶ *233 Influence, 539 Deception*

10 be believed, gain acceptance, go down well, find credence

ADJECTIVES

11 believing, assured, confident, convinced, sure, certain, positive, opinionated, dogmatic, trusting, trustful, unhesitating, unquestioning, undoubting, unsuspecting, credulous, gullible, faithful, conformist, orthodox, converted, born-again

▶ *490 Certainty, 658 Naivety, 7 Religion*

12 gullible, credulous, innocent, naive, green, wet behind the ears (Inf)

13 believable, credible, creditable, tenable, plausible, reasonable, realistic, possible, probable, likely, convincing, persuasive, impressive, commanding, reliable, trustworthy

▶ *486 Possibility, 488 Probability*

14 believed, undisputed, unquestioned, authoritative, accredited, doctrinal, creedal, received, accepted, maintained, putative, supposed, alleged, hypothetical

ADVERBS

15 believingly, confidently, positively, dogmatically, trustfully, unhesitatingly, unsuspectingly, faithfully, credulously, gullibly, like a lamb to the slaughter (Inf)

16 believably, credibly, plausibly, reasonably, convincingly, persuasively, supposedly, allegedly, hypothetically

498 Disbelief

NOUNS

1 disbelief, doubt, doubtfulness, dubiousness, dubiety, uncertainty, hesitancy, hesitation, distrust, mistrust, misgiving, qualm, scruple, reservation, scepticism, scorn, suspiciousness, suspicion, disagreement, dissent, demur

▶ *491 Uncertainty, 799 Derision, 666 Disagreement, 500 Dissent*

2 unbelievability, incredibility, impossibility, improbability, implausibility, untenability

▶ *487 Impossibility, 489 Improbability*

3 incredulity, amazement, bewilderment, bafflement, perplexity, nonbelief, discredit, rejection, denial

▶ *514 Surprise, 536 Negation*

4 unbelief, infidelity, paganism, heathenism, misbelief, heresy, agnosticism, atheism, irreligion, loss of faith

▶ *7 Religion*

5 disbeliever, unbeliever, nonbeliever, heretic, pagan, heathen, infidel, agnostic, atheist, doubter, doubting Thomas, apostate, dissenter, dissident, nonconformist, sceptic, mocker, detractor, irreligionist, secularist, rationalist, free-thinker, materialist, Marxist, conscientious objector

▶ *7 Religion*

ADJECTIVES

6 disbelieving, unbelieving, incredulous, sceptical, scornful, doubtful, doubting, dubious, uncertain, hesitant, distrustful, mistrustful, suspicious, dissenting, heretical, atheistic, agnostic, pagan, heathen, faithless, unfaithful

▶ *491 Uncertainty, 799 Derision, 500 Dissent, 7 Religion*

7 disbelieved, unbelieved, discredited, exploded, unbelievable, incredible, beyond belief, impossible, improbable, implausible, untenable, hard to believe, far-fetched, unreliable, suspect, suspected, suspicious, so-called, self-styled, questionable, disputable

▶ *487 Impossibility, 489 Improbability, 798 Ridiculousness*

VERBS

8 disbelieve, discredit, refuse to believe, dissent, disagree, scorn, ridicule, mock, scoff at, deny, negate, challenge, dispute, question, doubt, have doubts about, hesitate, waver, half-believe, have reservations, distrust, mistrust, suspect, smell a rat, take with a pinch (*or* grain) of salt, apostatize, lapse

▶ *799 Derision, 536 Negation, 477 Question*

9 cause disbelief, cast doubt, call into question, discredit, raise suspicions, amaze, stagger

▶ *477 Question, 514 Surprise*

ADVERBS

10 disbelievingly, unbelievingly, incredulously, sceptically, doubtfully, dubiously, uncertainly, hesitantly, distrustfully, mistrustfully, suspiciously

11 unbelievably, incredibly, implausibly, unreliably, questionably, disputably

499 Assent

NOUNS

1 assent, corroboration, confirmation, affirmation, consent, general consent, agreement, acquiescence, compliance, acceptance, approval, approbation, admission, acknowledgment, recognition, confession, sanction, per-

mission, concordance, harmony, accord, concurrence, consensus, unanimity, single voice, meeting of minds, like-mindedness

▶ *535 Affirmation, 667 Agreement, 572 Willingness, 851 Approval, 708 Permission, 116 Accord, 114 Similarity*

2 **yes**, affirmative, ratification, validation, certification, endorsement, nod of approval, seal of approval, rubber stamp, thumbs up, green light, aye, yea, amen, yeah (Inf), the OK (Inf), the nod (Inf)

▶ *535 Affirmation, 851 Approval, 708 Permission*

3 **assenter**, conformist, fellow traveller, ally, collaborator, sympathizer, supporter, subscriber, endorser, seconder, signatory, underwriter, consenter, yes-man, flatterer, sycophant, toady, fawner, backscratcher, hypocrite, fair-weather friend, assenters, the ayes, brown-noser (Sl), arse-licker (Sl)

▶ *664 Cooperation, 167 Conformity, 284 Support, 853 Flattery, 808 Servility*

VERBS

4 **assent**, agree, concur, see eye to eye, agree with, go along with, agree in principle, like the idea of, welcome, jump at the chance, go all the way with, echo, say the same as, chime in with, say ditto to, corroborate, confirm, affirm, approve, say yes, nod, give the thumbs up, give the green light, consent to, sanction, authorize, permit, allow, concede, give in, grant, admit, acknowledge, recognize, confess, support, subscribe to, second, vote for, endorse, authenticate, ratify, validate, countersign, underwrite, give the OK (Inf), rubber-stamp (Inf)

▶ *667 Agreement, 116 Accord, 535 Affirmation, 851 Approval, 708 Permission, 284 Support*

5 **assent to**, acquiesce, accede, comply, accept, tolerate, bear, put up with, submit, yield, defer, let the ayes have it, sign on the dotted line, conform, jump on the bandwagon, follow the crowd

▶ *673 Submission, 167 Conformity*

ADJECTIVES

6 **assenting**, agreeing, in agreement, concurring, concordant, unanimous, solid, like-minded, confirmative, affirmative, approving, consenting, supportive, sympathetic, cooperative, collaborating, willing, acquiescent, compliant

7 **agreed**, carried, signed, sealed, ratified, validated, countersigned, underwritten

ADVERBS

8 **unanimously**, with one voice, as one, to a man, with one accord, affirmatively, in the affirmative, willingly, acquiescently, compliantly

INTERJECTIONS

9 **yes!**, aye-aye!, affirmative!, hear, hear!, ditto!, amen to that!, amen!, so be it!, absolutely!, I

couldn't agree more!, you can say that again!, OK!, Roger!

500 Dissent

NOUNS

1 **dissent**, difference of opinion, variance, difference, differences, conflict, friction, disagreement, dispute, controversy, quarrel, feud, war, strife, clash, squabble, spat, tiff, scrap, fracas, brawl, fisticuffs, altercation, set-to, spot of bother (Inf)

▶ *666 Disagreement, 117 Disparity, 674 Contention, 676 War, 153 Disturbance*

2 **disapproval**, disapprobation, rejection, refusal, denial, negation, no, nay, negative, thumbs down, red light, objection, demur, protest, complaint, dissatisfaction

▶ *852 Disapproval, 581 Rejection, 711 Refusal, 536 Negation, 709 Veto, 766 Dissatisfaction*

3 **dissentience**, quarrelsomeness, dissidence, dissension, discordance, discord, disharmony, disunion, intolerance, recrimination, unpleasantness, disobedience, noncooperation, opposition, rebellion, sedition, strike, walkout, nonconformity, nonconformism, unorthodoxy, counterculture, sectarianism, separatism, factionalism, disaffection, secession, withdrawal

▶ *666 Disagreement, 693 Disobedience, 663 Opposition, 168 Nonconformity, 136 Separation*

4 **faction**, split, schism, separation, parting of the ways, rift, breach, rupture, severance of relations, division

▶ *136 Separation*

5 **dissenter**, dissident, dissentient, nonconformist, protestant, sectarian, partisan, separatist, schismatic, factionalist, malcontent, protester, recusant, caviller, critic, detractor, conscientious objector, passive resister, opponent, rebel, revolutionary, tergiversator, disputer, aggressor, agitator, troublemaker, mischief maker, heckler, scold, shrew, odd man out, unconventionalist, angry young man, bohemian, hippie, dropout, blackleg (Sl), scab (Sl)

6 **dissenters**, the opposition, the noes, the nays, splinter group, breakaway group, dissidents, separatists, faction, minority

▶ *663 Opposition, 136 Separation, 665 Party*

ADJECTIVES

7 **dissenting**, dissentient, differing, of another opinion, at odds, opposing, conflicting, heterodox, unorthodox, heretical, sceptical, unconvinced, dissatisfied, protesting, unwilling, resistant, intolerant, dissident, seditious, divisive, separatist, schismatic, party-minded, partisan, clannish, sectarian, nonconformist, protestant, schismatical, secessionist, seceding, breakaway, rebel, recusant, rebellious,

quarrelling, arguing, cantankerous, irascible, bellicose, warlike, contentious, disputatious

▶ *666 Disagreement, 117 Disparity, 674 Contention, 136 Separation, 168 Nonconformity, 573 Unwillingness*

VERBS

8 **dissent**, disagree, differ, agree to differ, beg to differ, take issue, quarrel, clash, conflict, dispute, confute, be at odds with, fall out with, have differences with, have a difference of opinion with, argue with, schismatize, separate, divide, secede, break away from, rebel, strike, walk out

▶ *666 Disagreement, 117 Disparity, 136 Separation, 674 Contention, 668 Defiance, 713 Protest, 343 Divergence*

9 **refuse**, say no, shake one's head, disapprove, object, demur, protest, complain, oppose, contradict, negate, deny, reject, give the thumbs down, give the red light

▶ *711 Refusal, 852 Disapproval, 766 Dissatisfaction, 663 Opposition, 536 Negation, 581 Rejection, 709 Veto, 474 Sophistry, 669 Resistance, 473 Argument*

ADVERBS

10 **dissentiently**, in protest, unwillingly, divisively, rebelliously, contentiously

INTERJECTIONS

11 **no!**, not likely!, over my dead body!, not on your life!, no way!

▶ *536 Negation*

501 Knowledge

Nam et ipsa scientia potestas est./ Knowledge itself is power. Francis Bacon.

I have taken all knowledge to be my province. Francis Bacon.

For in much wisdom is much grief: and he that increaseth knowledge increaseth sorrow. Bible: Ecclesiastes.

But of the tree of the knowledge of good and evil, thou shalt not eat of it: for in the day that thou eatest thereof thou shalt surely die. Bible: Genesis.

Knowledge dwells/ In heads replete with thoughts of other men;/ Wisdom in minds attentive to their own. William Cowper.

Knowledge is of two kinds. We know a subject ourselves, or we know where we can find information upon it. Samuel Johnson.

Knowledge advances by steps, and not by leaps. Lord Macaulay.

His had been an intellectual decision founded on his conviction that if a little knowledge was a dangerous thing, a lot was lethal. Tom Sharpe.

NOUNS

1 **knowledge**, knowing, ken, cognition, cognizance, gnosis, realization, perception, understanding, comprehension, apprehension, grasp, mastery, awareness, consciousness, acquaintance, familiarity, illumination, enlightenment, foresight, foreknowledge, intuition, savoir-faire, *Aufklärung* (Ger), savvy (Sl)

▶ *522 Intelligibility, 516 Foresight, 464 Intuition*

2 **information**, data, common knowledge, general knowledge, facts, know-how, expertise, skill, aptitude, forte, métier, touch, technique, accomplishment, partial knowledge, half-knowledge, smattering, inkling, intimation, suspicion

▶ *528 Information, 655 Skill, 502 Ignorance*

3 **learning**, lore, erudition, sagacity, wisdom, scholarship, letters, omniscience, polymathy, proficiency, mastery, craftsmanship, literacy, numeracy, cleverness, intelligence, acquired knowledge, booklearning, bookishness, education, schooling, instruction, teaching, culture, cultivation, civilization, self-education, self-instruction, autodidactism, accomplishments, acquirements, attainments, attainment targets, experience, practical experience, practice

▶ *507 Wisdom*

4 **intellect**, mind, brain, intelligence, wit, faculty, brains (Inf), smarts (US sl), street smarts (US sl), suss (Sl)

▶ *459 Intellect*

5 **science**, natural science, applied science, technology, the arts, the humanities, letters, literature, ology (Inf)

6 **knowledgeable person**, mastermind, genius, sage, wise man, savant(e), mine of information, walking encyclopedia, expert, authority, scholar, don, academic, pedant, scientist, teacher, intellectual, highbrow, egghead (Inf), bluestocking (Inf), know-all (Inf), clever dick (Sl), clever clogs (Sl), smartarse (Sl), smartypants (Sl), smart alec (Sl), wise guy (Inf), brainbox (Inf), bright spark (Inf), boffin (Inf)

▶ *507 Wisdom, 459 Intellect*

7 **academia**, groves of academe, intelligentsia, literati, illuminati

ADJECTIVES

8 **knowledgeable**, knowing, well-informed, all-knowing, omniscient, polymathic, encyclopedic, clever, intelligent, sagacious, wise, enlightened, informed, instructed, trained, cognizant, qualified, experienced, practised, versed, competent, skilled, proficient, efficient, expert, well versed, gifted, talented, good at, aware, conscious, mindful, attentive, acquainted with, no stranger to, familiar with, conversant with, briefed, primed *au fait* (Fr), *au courant* (Fr), in the picture, streetwise, shrewd, astute, perceptive, smart, brainy (Inf),

wise to (Sl), in the know (Inf), sussed (Sl)

▶ *507 Wisdom, 459 Intellect, 528 Information, 655 Skill*

9 **literate**, numerate, schooled, educated, well-educated, erudite, scholarly, donnish, academic, intellectual, highbrow, cultured, cultivated, sophisticated, worldly, pedantic, well-qualified, highly qualified, overqualified

▶ *459 Intellect*

10 **known**, verified, proved, true, certain, discovered, explored, recognized, perceived, seen, knowable, heard of, well-known, famous, infamous, notorious, celebrated, renowned, common, public, no secret

▶ *537 Truth, 490 Certainty, 483 Evidence*

VERBS

11 **know**, understand, comprehend, apprehend, realize, conceive, appreciate, recognize, identify, distinguish, discern, perceive, see, ken (Dial), master, retain, savvy (Sl), twig (Sl), catch on (Inf)

▶ *459 Intellect, 522 Intelligibility, 544 Identification*

12 **know by heart**, know inside out, know backwards, know forward and backward (US), learn by rote, memorize, know all the answers, know one's stuff, know the ropes, know from A to Z, know like the back of one's hand, know full well

▶ *511 Memory*

13 **get to know**, acquaint oneself with, familiarize oneself with, experience, study, con, learn, discover, find out, take in, grasp, get wise to (Inf), suss (out) (Sl)

▶ *496 Discovery*

14 **cause to know**, tell, inform, brief, prime, teach, instruct, train, school, educate, coach

▶ *528 Information*

ADVERBS

15 **knowledgeably**, knowingly, intelligently, wisely, proficiently, consciously, intellectually, academically, pedantically, cognitively, as far as one knows, as every schoolboy (*or* schoolgirl) knows

502　Ignorance

Yet ah! why should they know their fate?/ Since sorrow never comes too late,/ And happiness too swiftly flies./ Thought would destroy their paradise./ No more; where ignorance is bliss,/ 'Tis folly to be wise. Thomas Gray.

The ignorant man always adores what he cannot understand. Cesare Lombroso.

I count religion but a childish toy,/ And hold there is no sin but ignorance. Christopher Marlowe.

From ignorance our comfort flows,/ The only wretched are the wise. Matthew Prior.

Ignorance is like a delicate exotic fruit; touch it, and the bloom is gone. Oscar Wilde.

NOUNS

1 **ignorance**, lack of knowledge, nescience, incognizance, incomprehension, unawareness, insensibility, unconsciousness, blankness, nonrecognition, unfamiliarity, awkwardness, gaucherie, uncertainty, illiteracy, backwardness, unenlightenment, unskilfulness, artlessness, naivety, innocence, unintelligence, empty-headedness, folly, stupidity

▶ *460 Lack of Intellect, 656 Unskilfulness, 658 Naivety, 508 Folly, 404 Insensibility*

2 **half-knowledge**, inexperience, inexpertness, amateurism, amateurishness, semiliteracy, smattering of knowledge, dabbling, superficiality, sciolism, dilettantism, quackery, charlatanism, bluff

3 **unknown thing**, unknown quantity, mystery, enigma, secret, anonymity, the unknown, unknown territory, *terra incognita* (L), guesswork, anybody's guess, complete blank, closed (*or* sealed) book, all Greek, pig in a poke, mystery tour, UFO (unidentified flying object)

▶ *523 Unintelligibility, 529 Secrecy*

4 **unknown person**, anonymous person, person(s) unknown, John (*or* Jane) Doe, dark horse, anon., Mr X, A. N. Other, any Tom, Dick, or Harry, Mr Nobody, blind date

5 **ignorant person**, ignoramus, simpleton, fool, bungler, charlatan, quack, amateur, dilettante, dabbler, layman, Philistine, humbug, bluffer, illiterate, dunce, blockhead, novice, greenhorn, duffer (Inf), berk (Sl), thicko (Sl), dickhead (Sl), fuckwit (Tab sl), smeghead (Sl), dumbo (Sl), plonker (Sl), dimbo (Sl), bimbo (Sl), himbo (Sl), dummy (Sl), dum-dum (Sl), dumbbell (Sl), dumb cluck (Sl), nerd (Sl)

ADJECTIVES

6 **ignorant**, unknowing, nescient, incognizant, unwitting, unaware, oblivious, unconscious, blank, uninformed, in the dark, misinformed, misled, unskilled, uninitiated, green, naive, simple, innocent, gauche, awkward, unenlightened, backward, illiterate, unlettered, unschooled, untutored, uneducated, untaught, uninstructed, unscholarly, lowbrow, Philistine, stupid, dull, dim, dim-witted, slow, slow-witted, thick, thickheaded, thick as two short planks, empty-headed, clueless (Sl), dumb (Inf), nerdy (Sl), pig ignorant (Inf), dead from the neck up (Inf), fuckwitted (Tab sl)

▶ *460 Lack of Intellect, 508 Folly, 658 Naivety, 656 Unskilfulness*

7 **semiskilled**, semi-literate, semi-schooled, lay, amateur, amateurish, inexperienced, inexpert, unqualified, quack, shallow, superficial, dilettante, half-baked (Inf)

8 unknown, mysterious, strange, unfamiliar, unrecognized, unnamed, anonymous, un-identified, secret, obscure, unbeknown, un-seen, unheard of, unspoken, ineffable, untold, unrealized, unperceived, unexplored, un-charted, unknowable, beyond the frontiers of knowledge
▶ *523 Unintelligibility, 529 Secrecy*

VERBS

9 be ignorant, not know, know nothing, wal-low in ignorance, be in the dark, lack informa-tion, have nothing to go on, have a lot to learn, be stumped, give up, not have a clue, not have the foggiest idea, shrug one's shoul-ders

10 know little, have a smattering of knowl-edge, dabble in, have a go at

11 make ignorant, keep in the dark, mystify, mislead, misinform

ADVERBS

12 ignorantly, unknowingly, unwittingly, un-consciously, stupidly, in ignorance, for all one knows

INTERJECTIONS

13 who knows?, God knows!, search me!, I give up!

503 Accuracy

NOUNS

1 accuracy, precision, preciseness, exactness, exactitude, meticulousness, fastidiousness, scrupulousness, subtlety, nicety, refinement, strictness, rigidity, pedantry, rigour, rigorous-ness, acuity, attention to detail, hairsplitting, pinpoint accuracy, mathematical precision, clockwork precision, perfect pitch, fine tuning
▶ *813 Formality*

2 correctness, attention to fact, truth, literal-ness, literalism, the literal truth, the letter, faithfulness, fidelity, high fidelity, realism, naturalism
▶ *101 Reality, 537 Truth*

3 accurate thing, precise measurement, preci-sion instrument, fine adjustment, dead centre, micrometer, metronome, atomic clock, fine detail, finer points, fine distinction, nice dis-tinction, quibble, legal quibble, fine line, *mot juste* (Fr), proven fact, documented fact, pho-tographic memory, bull's-eye (Inf), hole in one (Inf)
▶ *56 Physics, 192 Timekeeping*

4 accurate person, pedant, hairsplitter, quib-bler, nit-picker (Inf)
▶ *474 Sophistry*

ADJECTIVES

5 accurate, precise, exact, perfect, pinpoint, detailed, meticulous, scrupulous, rigorous, pe-dantic, hairsplitting, subtle, nice, point-blank, dead right (Inf), spot on (Inf), on the button

(Inf), bang-on (Inf), nit-picking (Inf)

6 correct, factual, truthful, literal, true-to-the-letter, word-perfect, true-to-life, unerring, ver-batim, faithful, lifelike, high-fidelity, realistic, naturalistic, photographic

VERBS

7 be accurate, go into details, go into particu-lars, particularize, refine, hone, split hairs, stick to the facts, stick to the letter, go by the book (Inf), dot the i's and cross the t's (Inf), hit the nail on the head (Inf), score a bull's-eye (Inf)

ADVERBS

8 accurately, precisely, exactly, just, just so, dead, squarely, on the mark, right, to a nicety, correctly, literally, faithfully, verbatim, word for word, letter by letter, by the book, (accord-ing) to the letter, to the nth degree, plumb (Inf), plumb on (Inf), to a hair (Inf), to a T (Inf)

504 Error

NOUNS

1 mistake, error, fault, miscalculation, miscon-struction, misconception, misinterpretation, misjudgment, misapprehension, misunder-standing, false conclusion, wrong turning, false move, bad move, false step

2 inaccuracy, imprecision, inexactness, inex-actitude, looseness, sloppiness, carelessness, laxity, negligence, approximation, guesswork, speculation, generalization, randomness, shooting in the dark (Inf), hit or miss (*or hit and miss*) (Inf)

3 erroneousness, wrongness, untrueness, un-truth, falsity, falseness, incorrectness, falla-ciousness, fallacy
▶ *538 Untruth, 540 Falsehood*

4 faulty reasoning, fallacy, sophistry, flawed logic, circular argument, inconsistency, self-contradiction, sloppy thinking, choplogic
▶ *4 Philosophy*

5 misrepresentation, distortion, falsification, misquotation, misstatement, travesty, parody, caricature

6 fallibility, human error, subjectivity, preju-dice, bias, self-deception, wishful thinking, de-lusion, illusion, hallucination, false impres-sion, popular misconception, superstition, old wives' tale
▶ *497 Belief*

7 errancy, wrongdoing, culpability, guiltiness, aberrancy, deviancy, perversion, heresy, heterodoxy, unorthodoxy
▶ *844 Wrong*

8 moral error, transgression, misdeed, sin, of-fence, crime
▶ *877 Immorality*

9 trivial error, slip, slip-up, lapse, oversight, omission, slip of the tongue, *lapsus linguae* (L),

slip of the pen, *lapsus calami* (L), Freudian slip, miscue (Inf)

10 **blunder**, bungle, gaffe, faux pas, glaring error, bloomer (Inf), blooper (Inf), clanger (Inf), boner (Inf), howler (Inf), screamer (Inf), boob (Inf), boo-boo (Inf), muff (Inf), fluff (Inf), goof (Inf), banana skin (Inf), botch-up (Inf), balls-up (or ball up) (Sl), foul-up (Sl), louse-up (Sl), cock-up (Sl), screw-up (Sl), fuck-up (Tab sl)

11 **grammatical error**, solecism, spelling mistake, misspelling, dropping one's aitches, mispronunciation, bad grammar, incorrect usage, faulty syntax, misusage, abuse of language, abuse of terms, cacology, barbarism, spoonerism, malapropism, Goldwynism, bull, Irish bull, ambiguity, tautology, double negative, split infinitive, dangling participle, folk etymology, anacoluthia (Fml), catachresis (Fml), murdering the Queen's English (Inf)

12 **typing error**, typographical error, literal, printing error, misprint, erratum, corrigendum, clerical error, typo (Inf)

13 **sporting error**, miss, mishit, miscue, no-ball, own goal, wide, dropped catch, hit wicket, double fault

14 **computer error**, bug, glitch, virus

ADJECTIVES

15 **erroneous**, wrong, untrue, incorrect, false, fallacious, illogical, faulty, flawed, falsified, inaccurate, inexact, loose, inconsistent, self-contradictory, distorted

16 **errant**, erring, fallible, culpable, guilty, sinful, aberrant, deviant, perverse, perverted, heretical, unorthodox

17 **mistaken**, in error, at fault, wrong, all wrong, self-contradicting, prejudiced, biased, deluded, wide of the mark (Inf), way off the mark (Inf), off the track (or rails) (Inf)

VERBS

18 **be in error**, misunderstand, misapprehend, get it wrong, labour under a false impression, bark up the wrong tree (Inf), back the wrong horse (Inf), have another think coming (Inf)

19 **make a mistake**, err, miscalculate, misconstrue, misinterpret, misjudge, misrepresent, distort, parody, caricature, falsify, misstate, misquote, overlook, omit, misspell, mispronounce, misprint, mishit, misfield, miscue, slip, slip up, lapse, bungle, blunder, boob (Inf), muff (Inf), botch up (Inf), balls up (or ball up) (Sl), foul up (Sl), louse up (Sl), cock up (Sl), screw up (Sl), fuck up (Tab sl)

20 **transgress**, err, sin, deviate, lapse, fall

ADVERBS

21 **erroneously**, in error, mistakenly, by mistake

22 **wrongly**, incorrectly, badly, faultily, awry, amiss, inaccurately, approximately, imprecisely, out of true, inexactly, loosely, carelessly, without thinking

505 Maxim

NOUNS

1 **maxim**, saying, proverb, adage, aphorism, apophthegm (or apothegm), words of wisdom, saw, gnome, gnomic formula, oracle, mot, witticism, epigram, epigraph, motto, slogan, catchphrase, catchword, watchword, byword, epithet, tag, moral, axiom, truth, truism, banality, cliché, platitude, commonplace, bromide, hackneyed phrase, stock phrase, precept, order, dictum, formula, mantra, theorem, rule, law, observation, principle, old chestnut (Inf)

▶ *552 Conciseness, 771 Humour, 654 Advice, 507 Wisdom*

ADJECTIVES

2 **proverbial**, aphoristic, gnomic, epigrammatic, axiomatic, banal, clichéd, platitudinous, commonplace, trite, hackneyed, stock, stereotyped, sententious, moralistic, moralizing, preceptive, witty, pithy, enigmatic, oracular

VERBS

3 **aphorize**, epigrammatize, coin a phrase, proverb, moralize, pronounce, utter, theorize, formulate, observe, propose, remark

ADVERBS

4 **proverbially**, aphoristically, epigrammatically, axiomatically, platitudinously, as they say, as the saying goes, to coin a phrase, in a nutshell

506 Nonsense

NOUNS

1 **nonsense**, rubbish, trash, stuff and nonsense, balderdash, rot, twaddle, drivel, gibberish, gobbledegook, absurdity, senselessness, bombast, empty talk, bunkum, amphigory (or amphigouri), nonsense verse, doggerel, blah (Sl), hooey (Sl), bilge (Inf), claptrap (Inf), piffle (Inf), bosh (Inf), tosh (Sl), tripe (Inf), poppycock (Inf), crap (Sl), shit (Tab sl), bullshit (Tab sl), bull (Sl), cobblers (Tab sl), balls (Tab sl), bollocks (Tab sl)

▶ *508 Folly, 798 Ridiculousness, 521 Lack of Meaning, 540 Falsehood*

2 **solecism**, malapropism, Freudian slip, spoonerism, wellerism, howler, witticism, *bon mot* (Fr), epigram, riddle, pun, play on words, joke, quip, crack (Inf), gag (Inf), wisecrack (Inf), scream (Inf), laugh (Inf)

▶ *504 Error, 771 Humour*

3 **tomfoolery**, horseplay, antics, capers, high jinks, silliness, silly season, vagary, whimsicality, banter, buffoonery, drollery, clowning, burlesque, farce, scrape, prank, trick, practical joke, mucking about (Inf), shenanigans (Inf), skylarking (Inf)

▶ *799 Derision, 508 Folly*

4 **buffoon**, fool, jester, clown, joker, practical joker, prankster, japer, humorist, wit, wag, comedian, tease, teaser, *farceur* (Fr), wisecracker (Inf)

▶ *771 Humour*

ADJECTIVES

5 **nonsensical**, foolish, silly, absurd, meaningless, senseless, idiotic, mad, crazy, ridiculous, ludicrous, asinine, anserine, preposterous, fanciful, imaginative, fatuous, funny, jocular, humorous, droll, waggish, comic, merry, farcical, laughable, piffling (Inf)

▶ *508 Folly, 510 Insanity, 771 Humour, 798 Ridiculousness*

VERBS

6 **talk nonsense**, rave, rant, gabble, garble, blarney, talk through one's hat, rhapsodize, romance, joke, pun, play on words, quip, crack jokes, gag (Inf), blah (Sl), bullshit (Tab sl)

▶ *521 Lack of Meaning, 771 Humour, 540 Falsehood*

7 **be nonsense**, mean nothing, have no meaning

▶ *521 Lack of Meaning*

8 **fool**, fool around, play the fool, act the fool, clown, lark about, skylark, monkey around, horse about, act the goat

▶ *508 Folly*

ADVERBS

9 **nonsensically**, foolishly, absurdly, meaninglessly, ridiculously, preposterously, humorously

507   Wisdom

For in much wisdom is much grief: and he that increaseth knowledge increaseth sorrow. Bible: Ecclesiastes.

The words of wise men are heard in quiet more than the cry of him that ruleth among fools. Bible: Ecclesiastes.

No mention shall be made of coral, or of pearls: for the price of wisdom is above rubies. Bible: Job.

Wisdom is the principal thing; therefore get wisdom: and with all thy getting get understanding. Bible: Proverbs.

I care not whether a man is Good or Evil; all that I care/ Is whether he is a Wise Man or a Fool. Go! put off Holiness,/ And put on Intellect. William Blake.

Knowledge dwells/ In heads replete with thoughts of other men;/ Wisdom in minds attentive to their own. William Cowper.

It is the province of knowledge to speak and it is the privilege of wisdom to listen. Oliver Wendell Holmes.

NOUNS

1 **wisdom**, sagacity, sagaciousness, sapience, reason, judgment, discretion, discernment, discrimination, perspicacity, penetration, perception, insight, intuition, understanding, comprehension, breadth of vision, profundity, knowledge, erudition, learning, experience, enlightenment, objectivity, soundness of mind, shrewdness, acumen, astuteness, tact, level-headedness, prudence, judiciousness, farsightedness, foresight, forethought, cunning, craftiness

▶ *492 Judgment, 481 Discrimination, 501 Knowledge, 516 Foresight, 781 Caution, 657 Cunning*

2 **intelligence**, intellectualism, intellect, mind, understanding, quick-wittedness, cleverness, smartness, brightness, brilliance, aptitude, talent, genius, high IQ (intelligence quotient), inspiration, bright idea, brainwave, wit, wits, mother wit, sense, common sense, horse sense, good sense, brain (Inf), brains (Inf), little grey cells (Inf), grey matter (Inf), gumption (Inf), nous (Sl)

▶ *459 Intellect*

3 **wise man**, wise woman, sage, guru, witch, shaman, sibyl, oracle, seer, prophet, thinker, philosopher, Solomon

▶ *517 Prediction, 4 Philosophy*

4 **intellectual**, scholar, academic, genius, Mensa member, bright spark (Inf), brainbox (Inf), clever dick (Sl), smartarse (Sl), smart alec (Sl), wise guy (Inf)

▶ *501 Knowledge, 459 Intellect*

ADJECTIVES

5 **wise**, sagacious, sapient, thoughtful, thinking, reflecting, reasoning, rational, sensible, profound, deep, intellectual, highbrow, knowledgeable, knowing, erudite, learned, perspicacious, perceptive, oracular, level-headed, prudent, judicious, balanced, objective, impartial, just, fair-minded, broad-minded, circumspect, unprejudiced, statesmanlike, diplomatic, discreet, tactful, politic, well-advised

▶ *492 Judgment, 859 Disinterestedness, 516 Foresight, 781 Caution, 509 Sanity*

6 **intelligent**, clever, smart, bright, brilliant, talented, gifted, highly capable, able, skilful, skilled, quick, quick-witted, sharp, sharp-witted, alert, astute, shrewd, streetwise, canny, farsighted, clear-headed, calculating, crafty, cunning, brainy (Inf), all there (Inf), on the ball (Inf), too clever by half (Inf), clever-clever (Inf), smartarse (Sl)

▶ *459 Intellect, 655 Skill, 657 Cunning*

VERBS

7 **be wise**, understand, grasp, fathom, discern, see through, distinguish, discriminate, judge, intuit, use one's head, use one's intelligence, have one's wits about one, know the score,

know what's what
▶ *492 Judgment, 481 Discrimination, 522 Intelligibility*
8 **be intelligent**, have brains, know, shine, scintillate, know how many beans make five, have one's head screwed on the right way (Inf)
▶ *459 Intellect, 501 Knowledge*

ADVERBS
9 **wisely**, sagaciously, thoughtfully, rationally, sensibly, perspicaciously, prudently, judiciously, objectively, diplomatically, discreetly
10 **intelligently**, cleverly, brilliantly, astutely, shrewdly

508   Folly

NOUNS
1 **folly**, foolishness, stupidity, ineptitude, inanity, rashness, recklessness, madness, senselessness, silliness, absurdity, ridiculousness, ludicrousness, asininity, childishness, puerility, fatuousness, pointlessness, extravagance, frivolity, flippancy, giddiness, thoughtlessness, irresponsibility, · imprudence, indiscretion, conceit, heedlessness, ignorance, unintelligence, low IQ (intelligence quotient), eccentricity, insanity, lunacy, idiocy, imbecility, feeble-mindedness, empty-headedness, senility, dotage, craziness (Inf), daftness (Inf)
▶ *798 Ridiculousness, 780 Rashness, 502 Ignorance, 460 Lack of Intellect, 510 Insanity*
2 **act of folly**, foolery, tomfoolery, mistake, error, misjudgment, gaffe, blunder, bloomer (Inf), blooper (US inf)
▶ *504 Error, 493 Misjudgment, 506 Nonsense*
3 **foolish person**, fool, simpleton, imbecile, idiot, moron, cretin, halfwit, ass, jackass, dolt, blockhead, dunce, dotard, dimwit (Inf), dumbo (Sl), dimbo (Sl), birdbrain (Inf), dope (Inf), nincompoop (Inf), ninny (Inf), nitwit (Inf), twit (Inf), dingbat (US sl), noodle (Inf), pinhead (Sl), pillock (Sl), right Charlie (Inf), wally (Sl), meathead (Sl), jerk (Sl), asshole (US tab sl), sucker (Sl), prat (Sl), fuckwit (Tab sl)
▶ *510 Insanity, 502 Ignorance*
4 **rash person**, hothead, daredevil, adventurer, madcap, eccentric

ADJECTIVES
5 **foolish**, stupid, inept, inane, mad, ill-advised, ill-considered, unwise, imprudent, injudicious, uncircumspect, incautious, rash, reckless, foolhardy, harebrained, heedless, inattentive, hotheaded, hellbent, headstrong, wild, prodigal, devil-may-care, couldn't-care-less, frivolous, flippant, silly, asinine, idiotic, imbecilic, moronic, anserine, lunatic, insane, senseless, brainless, ignorant, unintelligent, dim-witted, feeble-minded, empty-headed, simple, slow, doltish, dull, gormless, fatuous, pointless, absurd, ludicrous, ridiculous, non-sensical, preposterous, childish, puerile, senile, eccentric, bird-brained (Inf), nutty (Inf), daft (Inf), crazy (Inf), barmy (Sl), spaced-out (Sl), potty (Inf), gaga (Inf)
▶ *780 Rashness, 502 Ignorance, 460 Lack of Intellect, 510 Insanity, 798 Ridiculousness*

VERBS
6 **be foolish**, take leave of one's senses, go mad, lose one's head, throw caution to the wind, stick one's neck out, take a leap in the dark, play with fire, have no thought for the consequences, ask for trouble, tempt fate, buy a pig in a poke, never learn, not have the sense one was born with
▶ *780 Rashness, 502 Ignorance, 510 Insanity*
7 **play the fool**, act the goat, make a fool of oneself, clown around, play silly buggers (Sl)
▶ *506 Nonsense*

ADVERBS
8 **foolishly**, stupidly, unwisely, imprudently, rashly, recklessly, idiotically, insanely, senselessly, brainlessly, unintelligently, absurdly, ludicrously, ridiculously, nonsensically

509   Sanity

NOUNS
1 **sanity**, saneness, sound mind, soundness of mind, *mens sana* (L), stability, balanced mind, mental equilibrium, mental health, normality, sobriety
▶ *873 Sobriety*
2 **rationality**, reasonableness, reason, intelligibility, lucidity, coherence, good sense, common sense, wits, intelligence
▶ *522 Intelligibility, 507 Wisdom*
3 **sane person**, Mr (or Mrs) Normal, reasonable person, voice of reason, rock (of Gibraltar)

ADJECTIVES
4 **sane**, not mad, *compos mentis* (L), in one's right mind, in full possession of one's faculties, of sound mind, mentally sound, normal, sober, all there (Inf), together (Inf), with both oars in the water (Sl), right in the head (Inf)
▶ *873 Sobriety*
5 **rational**, reasonable, coherent, intelligible, lucid, clear-headed, balanced, well-balanced, level-headed, stable, steady, sound, sensible, common-sensical, intelligent
▶ *522 Intelligibility, 507 Wisdom*

VERBS
6 **be sane**, have one's wits about one, become sane, ratiocinate, come to one's senses, sober down, sober up, make sane, restore to sanity

ADVERBS
7 **sanely**, soberly, rationally, reasonably, coherently, lucidly

510   Insanity

NOUNS

1 insanity, madness, lunacy, idiocy, irrationality, unsound mind, sick mind, mental illness (*or* disorder), (mental) derangement, mental instability, unbalanced mind, balance of mind disturbed, criminal insanity, McNaghten Rules, diminished responsibility, abnormality, aberration, incoherence, eccentricity, oddness, freakishness, crankiness, craziness, kinkiness (Inf), nuttiness (Inf), battiness (Inf), bats in the belfry (Inf), screw loose (Sl), slate loose (Sl)

▶ *61 Psychology and Psychiatry, 508 Folly, 16 Law, 168 Nonconformity*

2 subnormality, mental subnormality, intellectual subnormality, (mental) retardation, mental deficiency, amentia, aphrenia, mental handicap, oligophrenia, mental impairment, backwardness, learning difficulties, Down's syndrome, autism, cretinism, feeblemindedness, imbecility, idiocy

▶ *61 Psychology and Psychiatry, 624 Ill Health, 460 Lack of Intellect*

3 mental deterioration, dementia, confusion, softening of the brain, senile dementia, presenile dementia, Alzheimer's disease, Pick's disease, brain damage, brain disease, brain disorder, encephalopathy, spongiform encephalopathy, mad-cow disease, Creutzfeld-Jacob disease, kuru, general paralysis of the insane (GPI), fit, convulsion, paroxysm, seizure, stroke, rabies, hydrophobia, epilepsy, epileptic fit, grand mal, tonic-clonic fit, petit mal

▶ *624 Ill Health*

4 delusion, illusion, hallucination, paraphrenia, shared delusions, communicated insanity, folie à deux, personality disorder, paranoia, monomania, obsessive behaviour, hypochondria, obsession, complex (Inf), phobia, persecution mania, fixation, compulsion, urge, craving, craze, passion, elation, ecstasy, hypomania, mania, frenzy, hysteria, ravings, delirium, delirium tremens, DT's (Inf), dipsomania, megalomania, delusions of grandeur, kleptomania, pyromania, agromania, onomatomania, theomania, religious mania, nymphomania, satyriasis, erotomania, necromania, fetishism, homicidal mania

▶ *102 Unreality, 777 Fear, 519 Imagination, 61 Psychology and Psychiatry, 877 Immorality*

5 psychosis, psychopathy, schizophrenia, dementia praecox, split personality, schizoid personality, hebephrenia, catatonia, manic-depressive psychosis, cyclothymia, alcoholic psychosis, Korsakoff's psychosis (*or* syndrome)

▶ *61 Psychology and Psychiatry*

6 mental breakdown, nervous breakdown, neurosis, psychoneurosis, neuroticism, neurasthenia, anxiety, (personal) crisis, depression, clinical depression, melancholia, involutional melancholia, hysteria, shell shock, nervous tic, nerves (Inf), attack of nerves (Inf), brainstorm (Inf), crack-up (Sl)

▶ *770 Sorrow, 777 Fear, 366 Agitation, 61 Psychology and Psychiatry*

7 insane person, madman, madwoman, lunatic, mental case, maniac, manic-depressive, homicidal maniac, megalomaniac, monomaniac, hypomaniac, kleptomaniac, nymphomaniac, sex maniac, psychopath, psychotic, paranoiac, obsessive, hysteric, neurotic, hypochondriac, schizoid, schizophrenic, melancholic, depressive, idiot, idiot savant, cretin, moron, imbecile, eccentric, crank (Inf), crackpot (Inf), kook (US inf), headcase (Inf), nut (Inf), nutcase (Inf), nutter (Sl), screwball (Sl), oddball (Sl), fruitcake (Sl), booby (Sl), dummy (Sl), loony (Sl), loony tune (US sl), loon (Sl), psycho (Sl), sicko (Sl), space-case (US sl), space cadet (US sl)

8 mental hospital, mental institution, mental home, lunatic asylum, insane asylum, madhouse, Bedlam, psychiatric hospital, special hospital, psychiatric unit, psychiatric ward, padded cell, special school, loony bin (Sl), bin (Sl), nuthouse (Sl), funny farm (Sl), funny place (Sl), funny house (Sl), nut college (Sl), nut farm (Sl), nut hatch (Sl), screw factory (Sl), squirrel tank (Sl), acorn academy (Sl), bughouse (US sl), booby hutch (Sl), loony school (Sl)

▶ *61 Psychology and Psychiatry*

9 treatment, psychiatric care, psychoanalysis, analysis, psychotherapy, counselling, electroconvulsive therapy (ECT), shock therapy (*or* treatment)

10 psychiatrist, psychoanalyst, psychotherapist, mad doctor (Inf), head doctor (Inf), headshrinker (Sl), shrink (Sl), trick cyclist (Sl), barred-window boys (Sl), men in white coats (Sl)

▶ *630 Remedy, 60 Medicine*

ADJECTIVES

11 insane, mad, of unsound mind, *non compos mentis* (L), deranged, demented, abnormal, disturbed, unbalanced, unhinged, alienated, weird, peculiar, odd, anile, doited, out of one's mind (*or* senses), raving mad, stark raving mad, stark staring mad, mad as a march hare, mad as a hatter, mental (Inf), certifiable (Inf), funny (in the head) (Inf), wacky (Inf), screwy (Inf), kinky (Inf), cranky (Inf), crazy (Inf), daft (Inf), queer in the head (Inf), touched (Inf), daft as a brush (Inf), cracked (Inf), crackers (Inf), crackbrained (Inf), cuckoo (Inf), dolally (*or* dolallytap) (Dial), bonkers (Inf), nutty (Inf), nutty as a fruitcake (Inf), nuts (Inf), barmy (*or* balmy) (Inf), bananas (Sl), bats (Inf), batty (Inf), dotty (Inf), barking mad (Sl), (clean) round the bend (*or* twist) (Inf), dippy (Sl), loco (US sl), loopy (Sl), loose in the attic (Sl), loose in the head (Sl),

in left field (US sl), off one's head (Sl), off one's chump (Sl), off one's trolley (Sl), off one's rocker (Sl), off one's nuts (Sl), off one's block (Sl), off one's crust (Sl), off one's onion (Sl), off the side (US sl), off the wall (US sl), up the pole (Sl), out of one's head (Sl), out of one's skull (Sl), out of one's tree (Sl), ape (US sl)

12 **manic**, ranting, raving, frenzied, frenetic, frantic, hysterical, demented, rabid, foaming at the mouth, wild, berserk, delirious, deluded, hallucinating

13 **mentally ill**, disturbed, sick, abnormal, neurotic, depressed, depressive, melancholic, paranoid (*or* paranoiac), fixated, psychotic, schizophrenic, schizoid, catatonic, psychopathic, certified, schizo (Inf)

▶ *61 Psychology and Psychiatry, 624 Ill Health*

VERBS

14 **become insane**, go mad, lose one's wits, be insane, rave, ramble, run amok, have a screw loose (Inf), have bats in the belfry (Inf), lose one's marbles (Inf), go off one's head (Inf), go round the bend (Inf), start climbing the wall (Inf), go ape (Sl)

15 **make insane**, madden, drive mad, derange, dement, unbalance, unhinge, confuse, drive crazy, drive up the wall (Inf), drive round the bend (Inf), send over the edge (Inf)

16 **certify**, commit, section, put away

ADVERBS

17 **insanely**, madly, dementedly, psychotically, abnormally, neurotically, crazily (Inf)

511 Memory

Memories are hunting horns whose sound dies on the wind. Guillaume Apollinaire.

The taste was that of the little crumb of madeleine which on Sunday mornings at Combray…, when I used to say good-day to her in her bedroom, my aunt Léonie used to give me, dipping it first in her own cup of real or of lime-flower tea. Marcel Proust.

Thanks For the Memory. Leo Robin.

Better by far you should forget and smile/ Than that you should remember and be sad. Christina Rossetti.

Old men forget; yet all shall be forgot,/ But he'll remember, with advantages,/ What feats he did that day. William Shakespeare.

NOUNS

1 **memory**, recollection, remembrance, remembering, recall, total recall, good memory, photographic memory, retention, retentiveness, memorization, learning by heart (*or* rote), reminiscence, anamnesis, retrospection, reflection, hindsight, evocation, mind's eye, nostalgia, recognition, identification, collec-tive memory, race memory, Mother of the Muses, Mnemosyne

▶ *544 Identification, 501 Knowledge*

2 **retrospect**, retrospective, review, flashback, *déjà vu* (Fr), history, memoirs, autobiography, anecdote

▶ *545 Record, 3 History*

3 **memento**, souvenir, token, keepsake, memorabilia, trophy, relic, commemoration, memorial, monument, statue, plaque, tribute

4 **reminder**, memorandum, memo, note, diary, engagement diary, album, photograph album, scrapbook, record, mnemonic, *aide-mémoire* (Fr), cue, prompt, prompter

▶ *545 Record, 528 Information*

5 **day to remember**, memory, centenary, bicentenary, tercentenary, quatercentenary, quincentenary, sexcentenary, anniversary, place in history, fame, notoriety

▶ *812 Celebration, 800 Repute*

6 **artificial memory**, computer memory, RAM (random access memory), ROM (read only memory), data bank, database

▶ *65 Computers, 605 Store*

ADJECTIVES

7 **memorable**, unforgettable, notable, noteworthy, remembered, unforgotten, indelible, stamped on one's memory, forever in one's memory, haunting, evocative, reminiscent, nostalgic, reminding, mnemonic

▶ *611 Importance*

8 **remembering**, unable to forget, retrospective, mindful, bearing (*or* keeping) in mind

9 **memorized**, learnt by heart (*or* rote), committed to memory

10 **memorial**, commemorative, celebratory

VERBS

11 **memorize**, fix in one's mind, commit to memory, learn by heart, learn by rote, learn, remember, retain, hold in one's mind, bear (*or* keep) in mind, store in one's heart

▶ *501 Knowledge*

12 **remember**, recall, call to mind, recollect, think of, call up, summon up, conjure up, recognize, identify, know again, review, retrace, recapture, hark back, look back, think back, reminisce, reflect, rake up the past, write one's memoirs

▶ *544 Identification*

13 **remind**, bring to mind, bring back, take back, prompt, jog one's memory, ring a bell, refresh one's memory, brush up, recapitulate, review, haunt, not allow to forget, remind oneself, tie a knot in one's handkerchief, make a note

▶ *183 Repetition, 545 Record*

14 **commemorate**, memorialize, remember, honour, pay tribute to, toast, observe, celebrate, mark the occasion

▶ *812 Celebration*

15 **be remembered**, make history, live on, make an impression, stick in the mind, be engraved on one's memory, recur, come back, be unforgotten

ADVERBS

16 **memorably**, unforgettably, reminiscently, mnemonically, retrospectively, commemoratively, in memory of, *in memoriam* (L), by heart, by rote

512   Oblivion

Many brave men lived before Agamemnon's time; but they are all, unmourned and unknown, covered by the long night, because they lack their sacred poet. Horace.

Annihilating all that's made/ To a green thought in a green shade. Andrew Marvell.

NOUNS

1 **oblivion**, obliviousness, abstractedness, detachment, ataraxia, withdrawal, absorption, self-absorption, introspection, self-loss, depersonalization, catatonia, senselessness, insensibility, unconsciousness, coma, stupor, narcosis, trance, meditative trance, yoga trance, rapture, ecstasy, ecstasis, hypnosis
▶ *468 Inattention, 404 Insensibility, 551 Obscurity*
2 **blankness**, vacancy, vacuity, emptiness of mind, empty-headedness, absent-mindedness, forgetfulness, loss of memory, amnesia, total blank, mental block, blackout
▶ *468 Inattention*
3 **poor memory**, dim memory, hazy recollection, lapse of memory, mind (*or* brain) like a sieve
4 **unthinkingness**, thoughtlessness, unmindfulness, heedlessness, inattention, disregard, neglect, carelessness, selfishness, ingratitude, indifference
▶ *860 Selfishness, 838 Ingratitude*
5 **death**, annihilation, obliteration, nirvana
▶ *397 Death, 8 Divinity*
6 **amnesty**, pardon, forgiveness, absolution
▶ *839 Forgiveness*
7 **forgetful person**, absent-minded professor, scatterbrain, amnesiac

ADJECTIVES

8 **oblivious**, abstracted, detached, withdrawn, (self-)absorbed, introspective, head in the clouds, wandering, distracted, preoccupied, otherwise engaged, blind, deaf, unaware, in a world of one's own, depersonalized, catatonic, senseless, insensible, unconscious, rapturous, ecstatic, hypnotic, trance-like, spaced-out (Sl), out to lunch (Sl), miles away (Inf)
▶ *468 Inattention, 470 Negligence*
9 **blank**, vacant, vacuous, empty-headed, absent-minded, forgetful, forgetting, amnesic, Lethean, nirvanic

10 **unthinking**, thoughtless, unmindful, heedless, inattentive, disregarding, neglectful, negligent, careless, selfish, ungrateful, indifferent
11 **forgotten**, not remembered, out of sight, out of mind, not missed, forgettable, unmemorable, best forgotten, dead and buried, lost to oblivion, past, gone, lost, beyond recall, half-remembered, on the tip of one's tongue

VERBS

12 **be forgotten**, slip one's mind, fade from one's memory, sink into oblivion, sink without trace, drop from view, go in one ear and out of the other
13 **forget**, have no recollection of, not remember, miss, overlook, neglect, omit, think no more of, not give another thought to, erase (*or* efface) from one's memory, unlearn, leave behind, break with the past, consign to oblivion, clean forget (Inf)
▶ *546 Obliteration, 468 Inattention*
14 **be forgetful**, have a mind (*or* brain) like a sieve, have a short memory, misremember, remember wrongly, forget one's lines, fluff one's lines, dry
15 **forgive**, forgive and forget, let bygones be bygones, bury the hatchet
▶ *839 Forgiveness*

ADVERBS

16 **obliviously**, unconsciously, senselessly, blankly, vacantly, vacuously, forgetfully, absent-mindedly, abstractedly, distractedly, negligently, inattentively, unthinkingly, thoughtlessly, heedlessly, carelessly, indifferently, hypnotically, ecstatically, in a dream, in a trance

513   Expectation

NOUNS

1 **expectation**, expectancy, expectance, anticipation, contemplation, prospect, hope, hopefulness, optimism, presumption, assumption, confidence, assurance, reliance, trust, belief, waiting, suspense, apprehension, apprehensiveness, pessimism, dread, fear, foreboding, anxiety, uncertainty, possibility, probability, likelihood, certainty
▶ *775 Hope, 497 Belief, 208 Earliness, 209 Lateness, 777 Fear, 776 Hopelessness, 491 Uncertainty, 486 Possibility, 488 Probability, 490 Certainty*
2 **expectations**, demands, desires, hopes, prospects, outlook, forecast, prognosis, prediction, accountability, responsibility, contingency, possibility, dream, aspiration, ambition, castles in Spain, castles in the air
▶ *775 Hope, 517 Prediction, 199 Future Time*
3 **the expected thing**, the done thing, the usual, the normal, normal behaviour, custom,

tradition, habit, just what one would have expected
▶ *584 Habit*

4 **expectant person**, expectant, anticipant, omen, portent, augury, heir, heiress, beneficiary, recipient, inheritor, successor, next of kin, expectant mother, mother-to-be, prospective parents
▶ *730 Receiving, 245 Reproduction*

ADJECTIVES

5 **expecting**, expectant, in expectation, in high hopes, full of hope, hopeful, confident, sanguine, optimistic, desiring, wanting, on the waiting list, sure, certain, anticipating, anticipant, anticipative, anticipatory, prepared, ready, waiting, on stand-by, forewarned, forearmed, unsurprised, on the lookout, vigilant, watchful, on tenterhooks, in suspense, excited, eager, prognostic, apprehensive, dreading, pessimistic, anxious
▶ *775 Hope, 782 Desire, 490 Certainty, 787 Lack of Wonder, 594 Preparation, 777 Fear, 776 Hopelessness*

6 **expectant**, expecting, pregnant, gravid, with child, in the family way

7 **expected**, predicted, foreseen, unsurprising, designated, chosen, promised, due, anticipated, probable, likely, apparent, predictable, foreseeable, sure, certain, long-awaited, future, prospective, contemplated, impending, imminent, on the cards, hoped for, desired, feared, dreaded
▶ *517 Prediction, 580 Selection, 199 Future Time, 782 Desire, 777 Fear*

VERBS

8 **expect**, anticipate, look forward to, look for, see coming, look at, contemplate, face, have in prospect, intend, plan, envisage, hope, hope for, apprehend, dread, fear, expect the worst
▶ *588 Intention, 592 Plan, 775 Hope, 777 Fear*

9 **predict**, foresee, forecast, think, believe, estimate, reckon, calculate, bargain for, count on, bank on, take for granted, assume, presume, count one's chickens before they are hatched
▶ *517 Prediction, 492 Judgment, 497 Belief, 775 Hope*

10 **wait**, bide one's time, wait for, await, be on the waiting list for, queue up for, stand by, be on stand-by, be on call, look out for, watch out for

11 **demand**, insist on, call for, require, need, want, wish
▶ *593 Requirement, 571 Necessity, 782 Desire*

ADVERBS

12 **expectantly**, hopefully, confidently, optimistically, anticipatively, anticipatorily, apprehensively, pessimistically, anxiously, in suspense, on tenterhooks, with bated breath

13 **expectedly**, unsurprisingly, predictably, foreseeably

514 Surprise

NOUNS

1 **surprise**, lack of warning, lack of expectation, unexpectedness, unpredictability, unpreparedness, unreadiness, miscalculation, misjudgment, improbability
▶ *595 Lack of Preparation*

2 **amazement**, wonder, astonishment, astoundment, stupefaction, incredulity, disconcertment, disappointment, anticlimax
▶ *786 Wonder, 498 Disbelief, 515 Disappointment*

3 **shock**, horror, surprisal, start, jump, fright, turn, jolt, blow, bolt from the blue, thunderbolt, bombshell, facer
▶ *777 Fear*

4 **surprising thing**, wonder, the unexpected, the unforeseen, serendipity, the unpredictable, unexpected gift, treat, special treat, windfall, unexpected occurrence, unforeseen result, twist, reversal, revelation, eye-opener
▶ *721 Gain, 216 Change*

5 **surpriser**, wonderman, wonderwoman, superman, superwoman, miracle worker, thaumaturge, magician

ADJECTIVES

6 **surprised**, off guard, unprepared, unsuspecting, unaware, caught unawares, caught napping, taken aback, startled, ambushed, trapped
▶ *595 Lack of Preparation, 777 Fear*

7 **amazed**, awed, awestruck, marvelling, admiring, impressed, astonished, astounded, stupefied, stunned, stunned into silence, struck dumb, speechless, dumbfounded, thunderstruck, staggered, shocked, disconcerted, disappointed, flabbergasted (Inf), bowled over (Inf), gobsmacked (Sl)
▶ *786 Wonder, 515 Disappointment*

8 **surprising**, sudden, unexpected, unforeseen, unpredictable, unanticipated, unannounced, amazing, astounding, astonishing, staggering, shocking, out of the ordinary, full of surprises, serendipitous, unusual, unprecedented, odd, abnormal, freakish, weird and wonderful, peculiar, freaky (Sl)
▶ *168 Nonconformity, 786 Wonder*

VERBS

9 **surprise**, discover, take unawares, take by surprise, catch out, catch off-guard, catch unawares, catch napping, catch red-handed, startle, jolt, frighten, give one a fright, make one jump, give one (quite) a turn, take aback, spring on, catch with one's pants (or trousers) down (Inf)
▶ *777 Fear, 595 Lack of Preparation, 496 Discovery*

10 **ambush**, capture, ensnare, trap, creep up on, pounce on, spring upon
▶ *635 Trap*

11 **amaze**, astonish, astound, dumbfound, strike

dumb, leave speechless, stupefy, stagger, boggle, stun, shock, disconcert, disappoint, electrify, impress, come out of the blue, be a surprise, be one in the eye for, flabbergast (Inf), bowl over (Inf), floor (Inf), gobsmack (Sl), knock for six (Inf), knock for a loop (US inf)

▶ *786 Wonder, 515 Disappointment*

12 **be surprised**, not expect, start, jump, jump out of one's skin, shy, be taken aback, fall into a trap

▶ *777 Fear, 595 Lack of Preparation*

ADVERBS

13 **surprisingly**, amazingly, astoundingly, unexpectedly, suddenly, without warning, out of the blue, like a bolt from the blue, unawares, off (one's) guard

▶ *191 Immediacy*

INTERJECTIONS

14 **good heavens!**, well I never!, you don't say!, I don't believe it!, you could have knocked me down with a feather!, marry! (Arch)

▶ *786 Wonder*

515 Disappointment

Unhappiness is best defined as the difference between our talents and our expectations. Edward de Bono.

The best laid schemes o' mice an' men/ Gang aft a-gley,/ An' lea'e us nought but grief an' pain/ For promis'd joy. Robert Burns.

Mountains will heave in childbirth, and a silly little mouse will be born. Horace.

Look in my face; my name is Might-have-been./ I am also called No-more, Too-late, Farewell. Dante Gabriel Rossetti.

Oh, I wish that God had not given me what I prayed for! It was not so good as I thought. Johanna Spyri.

He said that he was too old to cry, but it hurt too much to laugh. Adlai Stevenson.

NOUNS

1 **disappointment**, bitter disappointment, discouragement, mortification, chagrin, regret, regrets, frustration, feeling of frustration, frustrated expectations, partial success, near failure, noncompletion, nonfulfilment, unfulfilled expectations, tantalization, tease, raised expectations, false hopes, blighted hopes, unsatisfied hopes, hopes unrealized, betrayed hopes, hopelessness, despair, bafflement, false expectation, vain expectation, forlorn hope, overestimation, miscalculation, misjudgment

▶ *770 Sorrow, 776 Hopelessness, 494 Overestimation, 685 Noncompletion, 493 Misjudgment*

2 **bad outcome**, bad result, bad news, not what one had hoped for, not what one had

expected, disenchantment, disillusionment, disillusion, discontent, dissatisfaction, shock, blow, setback, balk, hitch, impediment, obstacle, bad luck, misfortune, trick of fortune, slip 'twixt the cup and the lip, anticlimax, damp squib, comedown, letdown, bringing down to earth, humiliation, humbling, failure, defeat, disaster, fiasco, one in the eye for (Inf), bummer (Sl)

▶ *533 News, 766 Dissatisfaction, 661 Hindrance, 681 Trophy, 687 Adversity, 514 Surprise, 806 Humility, 683 Failure*

3 **mirage**, trick of the light, false dawn, fool's paradise, fool's gold

VERBS

4 **be disappointed**, try in vain, fail, come up short, fall short, not realize one's expectations, miscalculate, misjudge, expect more, expect better, have hoped for better, have hoped for something better, have hoped better of, expect otherwise, have one's plans ruined, have a bad outcome, have a bad result, find to one's cost, regret, follow bad advice, listen to a false prophet, be duped, be led astray

▶ *683 Failure, 358 Shortfall, 539 Deception*

5 **be crestfallen**, look blue, look blank, laugh on the other side of one's face, be sick with disappointment, be sick at heart, despair

▶ *806 Humility, 776 Hopelessness, 770 Sorrow*

6 **disappoint**, fall short, fail to deliver, not come up to expectations, belie one's expectations, ruin one's plans, go wrong, turn sour, defeat one's hopes, dash one's hopes, crush one's hopes, blight one's hopes, deceive one's hopes, betray one's hopes, burst the bubble, bring down to earth, disenchant, disillusion, serve badly, fail, let down, leave in the lurch, not come up to scratch, dash the cup from one's lips, tantalize, tease, raise one's expectations, leave unsatisfied, dissatisfy, dishearten, sadden, upset, spoil one's pleasure, dumbfound, boggle one's mind, surprise, amaze

▶ *358 Shortfall, 661 Hindrance, 514 Surprise, 806 Humility, 770 Sorrow*

7 **thwart**, frustrate, balk, bilk, foil, baffle, confound, hinder, hamper, refuse, deny, stonewall, turn away, reject, jilt, befool, humble, humiliate, put one's nose out of joint, disconcert, discontent, sour, embitter with disappointment, cause discontent, stand up (Inf)

▶ *766 Dissatisfaction, 581 Rejection, 806 Humility, 415 Sourness*

8 **be dishonest**, betray, cheat, deceive, mislead, delude, dupe, trick, swindle, play false, betray one's trust, play a trick, con (Inf), flimflam (Inf), sting (Inf), take to the cleaners (Inf)

▶ *858 Improbity, 539 Deception*

ADJECTIVES

9 **disappointed**, disenchanted, disillusioned, expecting more, expecting better, expecting

otherwise, badly served, let down, frustrated, thwarted, balked, bilked, foiled, baffled, confounded, confused, hindered, hampered, denied, refused, stonewalled, rejected, turned away, jilted, defeated, disconcerted, crestfallen, dejected, depressed, disheartened, discouraged, mortified, chagrined, humiliated, humbled, disgruntled, soured, dissatisfied, sad, discontented, upset, sick with disappointment, hopeless, heartbroken, crushed, devastated

▶ *514 Surprise, 661 Hindrance, 683 Failure, 806 Humility, 766 Dissatisfaction, 776 Hopelessness, 770 Sorrow, 581 Rejection*

10 **deceived**, misled, deluded, duped, betrayed, tricked, cheated, swindled, conned (Inf), taken to the cleaners (Inf)

▶ *539 Deception*

11 **disappointing**, frustrating, unfulfilling, unsatisfying, unsatisfactory, insufficient, inadequate, falling short, not up to expectations, less than one's hopes, second-best, second-rate, poor, inferior, discontenting, miscarried, abortive, unsuccessful

▶ *609 Insufficiency, 766 Dissatisfaction, 683 Failure*

12 **deceptive**, misleading, deceiving, dishonest, untrustworthy, cheating

▶ *539 Deception*

ADVERBS

13 **disappointingly**, with a disappointing result, without meeting expectations, frustratingly, tantalizingly, so near and yet so far, deceptively, misleadingly

516   Foresight

VERBS

1 **foresee**, see ahead, know in advance, foreknow, have advance knowledge, have prior information, predict, forecast, prophesy, divine, augur, forewarn, warn, see (or peep or pry) into the future, read the future, look into one's crystal ball, read one's palm, read tea leaves, read the runes, read the cards, read one's astrology chart, consult the Ouija board (Tm), have second sight, have extrasensory perception (ESP), have clairvoyance, be clairvoyant, feel (or see) it coming, feel it in one's bones (or water), scent, scent from afar, look for, expect, envisage, envision, be prepared, anticipate, forestall, surmise, make a good guess, suppose, presume, forejudge, portend, foreshadow, forebode, promise, presage, foretell, predetermine, predestine

▶ *517 Prediction, 636 Warning, 528 Information, 513 Expectation, 208 Earliness, 594 Preparation, 518 Supposition, 582 Predetermination*

2 **show prudence**, be cautious, keep a sharp lookout, feel one's way, look ahead, plan

ahead, plan, prepare, prepare for the future, guard against, take precautions, provide against, make provisions, lay up for a rainy day, look to the future, have an eye to the future, have an eye on the main chance, test the waters, send up a trial balloon, see how the wind blows, see the lay of the land, see how the cat jumps, look before one leaps

▶ *592 Plan, 594 Preparation, 199 Future Time, 507 Wisdom, 467 Attention, 606 Provision, 781 Caution*

NOUNS

3 **foresight**, prevision, prediction, forecast, prophecy, prognosis, prognostication, foregone conclusion, certainty, expectation, anticipation, foretaste, precognition, foreknowledge, prescience, second sight, extrasensory perception (ESP), clairvoyancy, telepathy, premonition, presentiment, foreboding, forewarning, divination, augury, portent, *abnung* (Ger), omen, something in the air, eerie feeling, astrology, horoscope, fortune, fortunetelling, palm-reading, palmistry, crystalgazing, I Ching

▶ *517 Prediction, 490 Certainty, 513 Expectation, 11 Occultism*

4 **prudence**, caution, care, circumspection, wisdom, sagacity, forethought, precaution, plan, long-range plan, emergency plan, contingency plan, forward planning, longsightedness, farsightedness, providence, provision, readiness, preparation, intelligent anticipation, perspicacity, insight, vision, futurology, premeditation, predetermination, predestination, appointments calendar, calendar of events, programme, prospectus

▶ *592 Plan, 507 Wisdom, 582 Predetermination, 781 Caution, 469 Carefulness, 594 Preparation*

5 **predictor**, forecaster, prophet, prognosticator, soothsayer, augur, sibyl, clairvoyant, visionary, astrologer, fortune-teller, crystal gazer, palm-reader, palmist, telepathist, planner, preparer, futurologist, Cassandra

▶ *517 Prediction*

ADJECTIVES

6 **foreseeing**, foresighted, predictive, predicting, prophetic, prognostic, precognitive, prospective, clairvoyant, intuitive, telepathic, second-sighted, prescient, farsighted, longsighted, weather-wise, planning ahead, looking ahead, expectant, anticipant, anticipatory, prudent, provident, cautious, careful, circumspect, wise, sagacious

▶ *517 Prediction, 507 Wisdom, 781 Caution, 513 Expectation*

7 **foreseeable**, predictable, probable, forecast, predicted

▶ *517 Prediction*

ADVERBS

8 **foresightedly**, with foresight, prophetically,

clairvoyantly, in one's crystal ball, telepathically, farsightedly, longsightedly, expectantly, prudently, providently, cautiously, wisely, for a rainy day

517 Prediction

NOUNS

1 **prediction**, forecast, forecasting, foretelling, forewarning, prophecy, apocalypse, revelation, prognosis, prognostication, presentiment, premonition, hunch, feeling, foreboding, foresight, presage, prefiguration, prefigurement, prior consideration, expectation, prospect, weather forecast, horoscope, fortune
▶ *516 Foresight, 513 Expectation, 199 Future Time*

2 **divination**, clairvoyance, augury, taking the auspices, soothsaying, astrology, horoscopy, haruspicy, vaticination, casting nativities, fortune-telling, palmistry, chiromancy, crystal-gazing, reading cards, cartomancy, I Ching, casting lots, sortilege, bibliomancy, interpreting dreams, oneiromancy, hydromancy, pyromancy, geomancy, necromancy, occultism, dowsing, discovery, guesswork, speculation

3 **plan**, planning, forward planning, long-range plan, emergency plan, contingency plan, programme, prospectus, schedule, itinerary, appointments calendar, calendar of events, almanac, preview, announcement, notice, advance notice, publication, prepublication, warning, preliminary warning, warning sign, warning shot, danger signal, hint, suggestion, intimation
▶ *592 Plan, 532 Publication, 636 Warning*

4 **model**, working model, test model, test design, prototype, shape of things to come

5 **omen**, good omen, bad omen, sign, indication, portent, presage, augury, auspice, writing on the wall, prognostic, prognostication, syndrome, symptom, caution, warning, forewarning, harbinger, precursor, forerunner, herald, messenger, prefigurement, foretoken, type, ominousness, portentousness, signs of the times
▶ *544 Identification, 636 Warning, 533 News, 633 Danger, 154 Precedence*

6 **good-luck sign**, good-luck charm, talisman, mascot, horseshoe, four-leaf (*or* four-leaved) clover, rabbit's foot, Saint Christopher's medal, shooting star, amber, bloodstone, lodestone, black cat, finding a penny, touching a sailor, seeing a bride, seeing a chimney sweep, knocking on wood
▶ *589 Chance*

7 **bad-luck sign**, broken mirror, clock that stops, spilt salt, gathering clouds, peacock feather, bird of ill omen, owl, raven, walking under a ladder, opening an umbrella indoors, stepping on a crack, telling one's dream before breakfast
▶ *589 Chance*

8 **oracle**, sage, prophet, prophetess, prophet of doom, doom merchant, doomster, doomwatcher, Cassandra, warner, seer, visionary, vaticinator, soothsayer, clairvoyant, telepathist, medium, occultist, pythoness, sorcerer, witch, warlock, Delphic oracle, Pythian oracle, Pythia, sibyl, Sibylline books, Nostradamus, Witch of Endor
▶ *492 Judgment, 636 Warning*

9 **forecaster**, consultant, weather forecaster, meteorologist, weatherman (*or* weatherwoman), financial forecaster, sports forecaster, racing forecaster, odds-maker, tipster, gambler, speculator, prognosticator, futurologist, diviner, water diviner, dowser, astrologer, caster of nativities, fortune-teller, palm-reader, palmist, crystal-gazer, interpreter of dreams, augur, auspex, haruspex
▶ *516 Foresight*

10 **cards**, Tarot cards, Ouija board (Tm), runes, dice, lot, tripod, crystal ball, mirror, tea leaves, palm, head, entrails, texts, Bible, *sortes Biblicae* (L), *sortes Virgilianae* (L), *sortes Homericae* (L)

VERBS

11 **predict**, foresee, forecast, foretell, prophesy, reveal, make a prediction, make an educated guess, guess, guesstimate, speculate, prognosticate, make a prognosis, vaticinate, forebode, bode, augur, foretoken, presage, portend, foreshow, foreshadow, prefigure, shadow forth, forerun, herald, harbinger, usher in, go before, come before, point to, indicate, signify, betoken, represent, typify, hint, suggest, announce, give notice, notify, advertise, forewarn, warn, give warning, look black, look ominous, lower (*or* lour), menace, threaten, depress, promise, augur well, bid fair, give hope, hold out hopes, build up hopes, raise expectations, excite expectations, cheer up
▶ *516 Foresight, 154 Precedence, 544 Identification, 532 Publication, 636 Warning, 775 Hope*

12 **divine**, soothsay, take (*or* read) the auspices, take (*or* read) the omens, interpret dreams, vaticinate, cast a horoscope, cast a nativity, cast lots, gamble, tell fortunes, gaze into a crystal ball, read the future, read the signs, read the stars, read the cards, read the runes, read the entrails, read one's hand, read one's palm

ADJECTIVES

13 **predicting**, predictive, foretelling, forewarning, presentient, prescient, foreseeing, clairvoyant, fortune-telling, weather-wise, prophetic, oracular, mantic, vatic (*or* vaticinal), fatidic (*or* fatidical), apocalyptic, sibylline, sibyllic (*or* sibylic), monitory, premonitory, foreboding, cautionary, heralding, prefigur-

ing, precursory, signifying, indicative, symptomatic

▶ *516 Foresight, 636 Warning, 154 Precedence*

14 **predicted**, foretold, forecast, predictable, foreseeable

▶ *516 Foresight*

15 **presageful**, portentous, significant, fateful, augural, auspicial, haruspical, of good omen, auspicious, propitious, promising, fortunate, favourable, prosperous, of ill omen, ominous, big with fate, pregnant with doom, inauspicious, sinister, adverse, unfavourable

▶ *686 Prosperity, 687 Adversity, 589 Chance*

ADVERBS

16 **predictively**, prophetically, predictably, foreseeably, portentously, significantly, fatefully, auspiciously, promisingly, inauspiciously, ominously

518 Supposition

NOUNS

1 **supposition**, assumption, presumption, notion, idea, the idea of, fancy, conceit, ideality, pretence, pretending, affectation, presupposition, condition, stipulation, *sine qua non* (L), conditions, proposal, proposition, offer, submission, argument, hypothetical argument, postulation, postulate, premise, theory, hypothesis, working hypothesis, explanation, tentative explanation, model, theorem, mathematical theorem, topic, thesis, position, stand, attitude, orientation, point of view, standpoint, opinion, suggestion, casual suggestion, suggestiveness

▶ *471 Idea, 519 Imagination, 797 Affectation, 473 Argument, 716 Negotiation, 710 Offer, 472 Topic, 497 Belief, 528 Information*

2 **basis of supposition**, hint, clue, evidence, data, research data, datum, deduction, induction, inference, suspicion, sneaking suspicion, hunch, inkling, intimation, intuition, instinct, association of ideas, causal relationship, thought, thinking, lateral thinking, supposability, conjecturability, probability, possibility

▶ *483 Evidence, 464 Intuition, 461 Thought, 486 Possibility, 488 Probability*

3 **conjecture**, unverified supposition, bare supposition, speculation, pure speculation, vague suspicion, suspicion, guess, surmise, mere notion, gamble, try, shot, shot in the dark, gambling, guessing, guesswork, rough guess, crude estimate, shrewd idea, intuition, construction, reconstruction, guesstimate (Inf)

▶ *464 Intuition, 492 Judgment*

4 **theorist**, theorizer, theoretician, hypothesist, thinker, philosopher, academic, researcher, research worker, academic researcher, scientific researcher, experimenter, experimental scientist, scientist, theory builder, model builder, supposer, surmiser, guesser, critic, armchair critic, armchair strategist, armchair detective, armchair quarterback (US), doctrinarian, doctrinaire, speculator, gambler, planner, boffin (Inf)

▶ *490 Certainty, 461 Thought, 592 Plan*

VERBS

5 **suppose**, assume, presume, have a notion, have an idea, imagine, pretend, fancy, dream, think, conceive, draw a mental picture, take into one's head, get into one's head, opine, divine, suspect, have a hunch, have an inkling, intuit, infer, deduce, conclude, surmise, conjecture, guess, make a guess, hazard a guess, guesstimate, suppose so, dare say, convince oneself, persuade oneself, believe, understand, gather, presuppose, presurmise, premise, posit, postulate, lay down, assert, affirm, predicate, take for granted, take, take it, reason, speculate, form a hypothesis, hypothesize, have a theory, theorize, let, sketch, draft, outline, plan, rely on supposition, gamble

▶ *519 Imagination, 497 Belief, 464 Intuition, 463 Reason, 535 Affirmation, 473 Argument, 461 Thought, 592 Plan*

6 **propound**, propose, suggest, make a suggestion, mean seriously, offer, put on the agenda, moot, move, propose a motion, bring up for debate, request, plead (*or* argue) a case, put a case, submit, make one's submission, argue, put forth, put forward, advance, venture to say, make a point, put forward a notion, throw out an idea, throw into the melting pot, advise, outline, adumbrate, allude, hint, put an idea into one's head, persuade, urge, motivate, influence

▶ *710 Offer, 712 Request, 463 Reason, 654 Advice, 528 Information, 586 Persuasion*

ADJECTIVES

7 **suppositional**, suppositive, supposing, assumptive, presumptive, notional, conjectural, guessing, intuitive, propositional, hypothetical, theoretical, postulatory, putative, suppositious (*or* supposititious), unverified, moot, armchair, speculative, wildly speculative, blue-sky (US), gratuitous, suggestive, hinting, allusive, hard to pin down, stimulating, thought-provoking, of academic interest, academic, guesstimating (Inf)

▶ *464 Intuition, 497 Belief*

8 **supposed**, assumed, presumed, premised, *a priori* (L), postulated, surmised, conjectured, guessed, hypothesized, understood, taken, taken as read, taken for granted, proposed, suggested, mooted, topical, given, granted, granted for the sake of argument, assented, suppositive, putative, inferred, deduced, pretended, alleged, reputed, so-called, titular, quasi, not real, unreal, abstract, fanciful, fan-

cied, imagined, imaginary, fabled, untrue, supposable, assumable, presumable, surmisable, imaginable

▶ *472 Topic, 499 Assent, 100 Nonexistence, 538 Untruth, 519 Imagination*

9 **meant**, intended, designed, expected, obliged, required

▶ *588 Intention, 593 Requirement*

ADVERBS

10 **supposedly**, allegedly, reputedly, as rumour has it, seemingly, possibly, conjecturally, hypothetically, theoretically, speculatively, in a speculative way, for the sake of argument, as an academic exercise, ex hypothesi, in theory, as it were, at a guess

CONJUNCTIONS

11 **supposing**, if, in the event that, assuming that, on the assumption that, even if, though, although, as if, as though

▶ *485 Qualification, 106 Circumstances*

519 Imagination

Art is ruled uniquely by the imagination. Benedetto Croce.

Imagination and fiction make up more than three quarters of our real life. Simone Weil.

NOUNS

1 **imagination**, imaginativeness, perception, vision, creativity, creativeness, invention, inventiveness, originality, ingenuity, resourcefulness, enterprise, skill, fancy, fancifulness, fantasy, fantasticality (*or* fantasticalness), stretch of the imagination, power of imagination, visual imagination, vivid imagination, highly-coloured imagination, bold imagination, fertile imagination, lively imagination, poetic imagination, the mind's eye, visualization, objectification, conceptualization, imagery, image-building, word-painting, artistry, creative thought, creative work, creative force

▶ *119 Originality, 655 Skill*

2 **inspiration**, muse, inspiration from the muse, afflatus, divine afflatus, frenzy, poetic frenzy, ecstasy, genius

3 **insight**, understanding, empathy, sympathy, moral sensibility, sensitivity

▶ *760 Sensitivity*

4 **ideality**, mental image, mental picture, impression, concept, conception, thought, idealization, ideal, ego ideal, appearance, image, picture, projection, fancy, conceit (Arch), coinage of the brain, brain-creation, brainchild, notion, idea, whim, maggot, vagary, caprice, whimsy (*or* whimsey), whimsical notion, whim-wham (Arch), crinkum-crankum, absurdity, unreality, figment, figment of the imagination, fiction, work of fiction, creative writing, story, novel, romance, science fiction, fantasy, fairy tale, imaginary world, imaginative exercise, creative exercise, flight of fancy, play of fancy, daydream, uncontrolled imagination, extravaganza, rhapsody, exaggeration, falsehood, poetic licence, poetry, quixotry, knight errantry, tilting at windmills, shadow-boxing, sciamachy

▶ *461 Thought, 457 Appearance, 471 Idea, 506 Nonsense, 102 Unreality, 579 Caprice, 540 Falsehood, 560 Description, 541 Exaggeration, 48 Literature*

5 **fantasy**, fabrication, improvisation, make-believe, vision, wildest dreams, dream, bad dream, nightmare, bogey (*or* bogy), phantom, ghost, apparition, spectre, shadow, vapour (Rare), dimness, mirage, *Fata Morgana* (It), visual fallacy, fancy, illusion, optical illusion, trompe l'oeil, delusion, hallucination, chimera, error

▶ *168 Nonconformity, 441 Dimness, 435 Vision, 504 Error*

6 **reverie**, daydream, brown study, abstractedness, abstraction, head in the clouds, sleepwalking, somnambulism, trance, insensibility, delirium, frenzy, subjectivism, autosuggestion, wishful thinking, sophistry, window-shopping, golden dream, pipe dream, fantasia, wish, desire, romance, stardust, romanticism, escapism

▶ *468 Inattention, 404 Insensibility, 510 Insanity, 474 Sophistry, 782 Desire*

7 **idealism**, Utopianism, castles in the air, castles in Spain, castles in the sand, pie in the sky, end of the rainbow, good times coming, millennium, idle fancy, myth, fable, jam tomorrow (Inf)

▶ *782 Desire, 199 Future Time*

8 **dreamland**, dream world, Utopia, Erewhon, promised land, land of milk and honey, Garden of Eden, El Dorado, Happy Valley, Fortunate Isles, Isles of the Blest, Cockaigne, Ruritania, Arcadia, Shangri-la, Atlantis, Lyonnesse, Middle-earth, Narnia, Oz, never-never land, wonderland, fairyland, cloud-cuckoo land, the end of the rainbow

▶ *199 Future Time, 538 Untruth*

9 **visionary**, seer, diviner, dreamer, daydreamer, somnambulist, fantast, fantasist, idealist, Utopian, philanthropist, escapist, ostrich, avoider, lotus-eater, wishful thinker, romantic, romancer, romanticist, myth-maker, rhapsodist, enthusiast, knight errant, Don Quixote, eccentric, crank, creative worker, artist, poet

▶ *517 Prediction, 468 Inattention, 591 Avoidance, 510 Insanity*

ADJECTIVES

10 **imaginative**, creative, inventive, innovative, original, ingenious, resourceful, clever, enterprising, skilful, eidetic, visualizing, per-

ceptive, fertile, fecund, productive, inspired, fancy-led, romancing, romantic, high-flown, rhapsodic (*or* rhapsodical), enthusiastic, carried away, exaggerated, lively, vivid, poetic, fictional, Utopian, idealistic, dreamy, dreaming, daydreaming, in a brown study, in a trance

▶ *655 Skill, 541 Exaggeration, 468 Inattention, 246 Fertility*

11 **fantastical**, fantastic, unreal, bizarre, grotesque, extravagant, whimsical, fanciful, airy-fairy (Inf), preposterous, absurd, outlandish, impractical, Heath Robinson, Rube Goldberg (US), visionary, otherworldly, starry-eyed, quixotic, Laputan

▶ *506 Nonsense, 102 Unreality*

12 **imaginary**, imagined, unreal, abstract, illusory, illusive, fanciful, fancied, chimerical, ethereal, unsubstantial, insubstantial, lacking substance, subjective, hypothetical, suppositional, conceptual, notional, ideal, dreamy, dreamlike, visionary, not of this world, of another world, cloudy, vaporous, shadowy, fictitious, fictional, fictive, storybook, make-believe, thought-up, dreamed-up, created, invented, fabricated, contrived, devised, pretend, not real, simulated, imitated, non-existent, untrue, unhistorical, mythical (*or* mythic), mythological, legendary, fabulous, fabled

▶ *102 Unreality, 504 Error, 441 Dimness, 538 Untruth, 518 Supposition*

13 **imaginable**, conceivable, thinkable, fanciable

VERBS

14 **imagine**, perceive, conceive, create, invent, think, suppose, think of, think up, conjure up, fancy, dream, dream up, make up, devise, concoct, coin, hatch, produce, fabricate, originate, excogitate, have an inspiration, improvise, visualize, envisage, envision, see in the mind's eye, see, picture, conceptualize, conjure up a vision, form an image of, get a mental picture of, picture to oneself, represent to oneself, represent, paint, write, compose, paint in words, write a portrait of, realize, objectify, capture, recapture, call to mind, call up, summon up, use one's imagination, give rein to one's imagination, let one's imagination run riot, exaggerate, play with one's thoughts, pretend, make believe, hallucinate

▶ *461 Thought, 518 Supposition, 583 Improvisation, 243 Production, 435 Vision, 547 Representation*

15 **fantasize**, live in a dream world, build Utopias, build castles in the air, build castles in Spain, build castles in the sand, see visions, dream of other worlds, dream dreams, daydream, muse, go into a brown study, idealize, see through rose-coloured glasses (*or* specta-

cles), romanticize, poeticize, fictionalize, rhapsodize, exaggerate

▶ *468 Inattention, 541 Exaggeration*

16 **have insight**, have understanding, understand, empathize, sympathize

▶ *522 Intelligibility, 760 Sensitivity*

ADVERBS

17 **imaginatively**, creatively, inventively, ingeniously, resourcefully, with imagination, with a flight of fancy, in the mind's eye, with one's head in the clouds, fancifully, romantically, idealistically

520 Meaning

The least of things with a meaning is worth more in life than the greatest of things without it. Carl Gustav Jung.

NOUNS

1 **meaning**, signification, sense, message, idea, message conveyed, idea conveyed, denotation, substance, essence, spirit, sum, sum and substance, gist, pith, core, contents, text, matter, subject matter, topic, semantic content, deep structure, value, drift, tenor, purport, import, implication, connotation, colouring, effect, force, relevance, bearing, scope, context, meaningfulness, semantic flow, expression, mode of expression, diction, style, semantics, general semantics, semasiology, sematology, semiotics, semiology, linguistics, nuts and bolts (Inf), nitty-gritty (Inf)

▶ *472 Topic, 549 Style, 5 Linguistics, 543 Sign*

2 **significance**, seriousness, importance, import, substance, pith

▶ *611 Importance*

3 **comprehension**, clarity, plainness, explicitness, clear message, single meaning, univocal, monosemy, unambiguity, unambiguousness, unambiguous passage, lack of clarity, confused message, double meaning, extended meaning, multivocal, polysemy, ambiguity, ambiguousness, ambiguous passage, equivocal passage, equivocalness

▶ *556 Simplicity, 522 Intelligibility, 578 Equivocation*

4 **type of meaning**, level of meaning, denotation, literal meaning, plainness, literality, connotation, interpretation, explanation, definition, reference, application, construction, context, intention, intelligibility, meaningfulness, semantic field, original meaning, main meaning, derivation, etymology, chief meaning, leading sense, received meaning, accepted meaning, allegorical meaning, usage, practice, lexical meaning, grammatical meaning, technical meaning, specialized meaning, special meaning, jargon, idiom, same meaning, equivalent meaning, equivalence, synonym, synonymousness, synonymity, synonymy,

identity, opposite meaning, contradictory meaning, opposite, antonym, changed meaning, semantic shift, figurative meaning, metaphorical meaning, metaphor, trope, hidden meaning, latent meaning, tropical meaning, latency, esoteric sense, implied sense, no sense, nonsense, absurdity

▶ *524 Interpretation, 556 Simplicity, 226 Cause, 584 Habit, 522 Intelligibility, 165 Speciality, 527 Latency, 506 Nonsense*

5 **point**, purpose, aim, object, end, idea, plan, design, intention, intent, value, worth, use

▶ *588 Intention, 617 Worth, 613 Usefulness, 592 Plan*

ADJECTIVES

6 **meaningful**, full of meaning, replete with meaning, packed with meaning, pregnant with meaning, having meaning, having sense, etymological, denotative, comprehensible, intelligible, unambiguous, univocal, monosemous, clear, plain, lucid, perspicuous, literal, express, explicit, pointed, declaratory, affirmative, indicative, repeated, tautological (*or* tautologous), identical, similar, synonymous, equivalent, paraphrastic, tantamount, connotative, implied, implicit, inferred, tacit, suggestive, unclear, obscure, confused, technical, professional, special, specialized, contrary, opposite, antonymous, homonymous, extended, transferred, ambiguous, multivocal, polysemous, equivocal, symbolic, figurative, metaphorical, allegorical, idiomatic, significative, importing, purporting, indicating, tell-tale, evocative, expressive, interpretative, interpretive, telling, eloquent, allusive, without meaning, meaningless, nonsensical, absurd

▶ *544 Identification, 522 Intelligibility, 550 Clarity, 556 Simplicity, 535 Affirmation, 543 Sign, 183 Repetition, 114 Similarity, 524 Interpretation, 578 Equivocation, 527 Latency, 523 Unintelligibility, 551 Obscurity, 506 Nonsense*

7 **significant**, consequential, serious, important, weighty, substantial, pithy, meaty, of moment

▶ *611 Importance*

8 **semantic**, semasiological, semiotic, semiological, linguistic, philological, verbal, lexical

▶ *5 Linguistics*

9 **meant**, implied, intended, deliberate, designed, planned, destined, predestined

▶ *588 Intention, 582 Predetermination*

VERBS

10 **mean**, signify, have a meaning, have a sense, mean something, convey a meaning, convey a message, convey an idea, get across, communicate, denote, say clearly, say plainly, use plain words, say directly, spell out, declare, assert, affirm, express, inform, tell, connote, imply, indicate, symbolize, stand for, represent, betoken, designate, import, purport, intend, point

to, add up to, boil down to, spell, convey, bespeak, tell of, speak of, breathe of, savour of, speak volumes, evidence, mean to say, try to say, be getting at, be driving at, really mean, have in mind, contemplate, allude to, refer to, hint at, suggest, intimate, say in other words, put another way, rephrase, paraphrase, repeat, tautologize, have the same meaning, agree in meaning, mean the same thing, coincide, accord, conflict in meaning, mean something else, mean the opposite, mean the reverse, contradict, disagree, talk turkey (US inf)

▶ *528 Information, 544 Identification, 547 Representation, 527 Latency, 535 Affirmation, 483 Evidence, 183 Repetition, 116 Accord, 117 Disparity, 522 Intelligibility*

11 **infer**, draw a meaning, deduce, understand, understand by

▶ *518 Supposition*

12 **intend**, aim, purpose, plan, design, destine, predestine, cause, result in, bring about, entail, involve, portend, presage, augur

▶ *588 Intention, 592 Plan, 226 Cause, 582 Predetermination, 517 Prediction*

ADVERBS

13 **meaningfully**, meaningly, with meaning, significantly, intelligibly, clearly, directly, explicitly, plainly, unambiguously, in plain words, to the effect that, in the sense that (*or* of), in a sense, in some sense, as meant, as intended, as understood, according to the book, from the context, literally, verbatim, word for word, in other words, so to speak, ambiguously, figuratively, metaphorically, symbolically

▶ *524 Interpretation*

521 Lack of Meaning

NOUNS

1 **lack of meaning**, meaninglessness, absence of meaning, no meaning, no context, no bearing, irrelevance, nonsignificance, insignificance, unimportance, nonsense, nonsensical writing, nonsensicality, amphigory, absurdity, inanity, vacuity, emptiness, triteness, truism, platitude, commonplace, cliché, mere words, empty words, verbalism, unreason, lack of reason, illogicality, sophistry, invalidity, dead letter, nullity, ineffectuality, illegibility, scribble, doodle, scribbling, scrawl, daub, misrepresentation, empty sound, meaningless noise, strumming, sounding brass, tinkling cymbal, loudness, jargon, mystification, abracadabra, hocus-pocus, mumbo jumbo, unintelligibility, incoherence, raving, delirium, frenzy

▶ *108 Unrelatedness, 612 Unimportance, 506 Nonsense, 505 Maxim, 474 Sophistry, 236 Powerlessness, 548 Misrepresentation, 423 Loudness, 523 Unintelligibility, 510 Insanity, 529 Secrecy*

2 **aimlessness**, purposelessness, lack of purpose, pointlessness, futility, worthlessness, ineffectuality
▶ *614 Uselessness, 618 Worthlessness*
3 **meaningless thing**, meaningless gesture, empty gesture, insincerity, flattery, liar's promise, senseless killing, motiveless murder
▶ *853 Flattery*
4 **senseless talk**, foolish talk, silly talk, empty talk, nonsense, utter nonsense, absurdity, stuff, stuff and nonsense, balderdash, gibberish, gobbledegook, rigmarole (*or* rigamarole), double talk, Babel, rubbish, drivel, twaddle, load of rubbish (Inf), Greek (Inf), double Dutch (Inf), rot (Sl), tommyrot (Sl), bosh (Inf), tosh (Inf), tripe (Sl), piffle (Inf), bilge (Sl), bull (Sl), load of bull (Sl), bullshit (Tab sl), crap (Tab sl)
▶ *506 Nonsense*
5 **empty talk**, empty chatter, idle speech, verbiage, diffuseness, jabber, jaw, babble, gabble, prattle, prate, sweet nothings, endearments, flattery, blarney, flummery, trumpery, bunkum (*or* buncombe), bunk, moonshine, humbug, claptrap, drivel, wind, vapouring, galimatias, fable, falsehood, exaggeration, blether (*or* blather), sales talk, sales blandishment, sales patter, patter, glib talk, spiel, line, PR (public relations) line, gas (Sl), hot air (Sl), spouting (US sl), psychobabble (Inf), yammer (Inf), blah (*or* blah blah) (Sl), flapdoodle (Inf), flimflam (Inf), jazz (US sl), jive (US sl), junk (Inf), guff (Sl), eyewash (Sl), poppycock (Inf), malarkey (*or* malarky) (Sl), hokum (US sl), baloney (Sl), hooey (Sl), drool (Sl), flannel (Inf), yackety-yak (*or* yak *or* yak-yak) (Sl)
▶ *553 Diffuseness, 538 Untruth, 540 Falsehood, 853 Flattery, 565 Talkativeness*
6 **aimlessness**, purposelessness, lack of purpose, pointlessness, futility
▶ *614 Uselessness*

VERBS

7 **mean nothing**, have no meaning, have no bearing, make no sense, make nonsense of, act aimlessly, scribble, daub, fiddle, tap, drum, strum, scratch
▶ *506 Nonsense, 612 Unimportance*
8 **not understand**, misinterpret, miss the meaning of, miss the point of, have no meaning for, pass over one's head, puzzle, confuse, be Greek to (Inf)
▶ *523 Unintelligibility, 491 Uncertainty*
9 **talk nonsense**, not mean what one says, talk rubbish, talk bunkum, talk like an idiot, rant, rave, rant and rave, twaddle, jabber, jaw, babble, gabble, blather (*or* blether), prattle, prate, gibber, talk gibberish, drivel, double talk, flatter, blarney, gush, spiel, psychobabble (US inf), vapour (Sl), talk double Dutch (Inf), yammer (Inf), waffle (Inf), drool (Sl), blah (*or* blah

blah) (Sl), jive (US sl), yackety-yak (*or* yak *or* yak-yak) (Sl), spread the bull (Sl), bullshit (Tab sl)
▶ *506 Nonsense, 565 Talkativeness, 523 Unintelligibility, 541 Exaggeration, 508 Folly, 853 Flattery, 525 Misinterpretation, 491 Uncertainty*

ADJECTIVES

10 **meaningless**, senseless, unmeaning, without meaning, irrelevant, nonsignificant, insignificant, unimportant, trite, commonplace, platitudinous, hackneyed, clichéd, banal, trivial, trifling, nonsense, nonsensical, amphigoric, absurd, inane, foolish, fatuous, illogical, sophistic (*or* sophistical), incoherent, unintelligible, illegible, mystifying, without rhyme or reason, piffling, ineffectual, ineffective, invalid, null, empty, vacuous, hollow, unexpressive, unidiomatic, unapt, rubbishy, trashy, delirious, frenzied, ranting, raving, prattling, gibbering, blithering, windy, exaggerated, Pickwickian
▶ *506 Nonsense, 508 Folly, 505 Maxim, 117 Disparity, 612 Unimportance, 541 Exaggeration, 510 Insanity*
11 **aimless**, purposeless, pointless, futile, vain, worthless, inconsequential, ineffectual
▶ *614 Uselessness, 618 Worthlessness*
12 **unmeant**, unintentional, unintended, involuntary, unimplied, misunderstood, misread, mistranslated, misinterpreted, misrepresented, mistaken, insincere, flattering, tongue-in-cheek
▶ *525 Misinterpretation, 548 Misrepresentation, 853 Flattery*

ADVERBS

13 **meaninglessly**, senselessly, irrelevantly, insignificantly, nonsensically, illogically, unintelligibly, aimlessly, purposelessly

INTERJECTIONS

14 **nonsense!**, bunk!, humbug!, hooey!, fiddlefaddle!, fiddlesticks!, rubbish!, poppycock!, blah!, rot!, what rot!, stuff and nonsense!, baloney! (Sl), bull! (Sl), bullshit! (Tab sl), crap! (Tab sl), bollocks! (Tab sl)
▶ *506 Nonsense*

522   Intelligibility

ADJECTIVES

1 **intelligible**, comprehensible, understandable, knowable, apprehensible, fathomable, penetrable, scrutable, interpretable, realizable, coherent, making sense, sane, audible, coming through loud and clear, visible, luminous, unambiguous, unambivalent, unequivocal, univocal, meaningful, explicable, teachable, unblurred, focused, clear-cut, precise, definite, certain, positive, telling, striking, vivid, graphic, highly coloured, descriptive, illustrative, explanatory, explicatory, interpretative,

interpretive, informative

▶ *509 Sanity, 501 Knowledge, 520 Meaning, 437 Visibility, 560 Description*

2 **simple**, clear, crystal-clear, plain, plainly stated, explicit, articulate, well-spoken, distinct, direct, straightforward, unevasive, unadorned, downright, forthright, uninvolved, uncomplicated, obvious, self-explanatory, self-evident, easy, easily understood, easy to comprehend, easy to follow, easy to grasp, made easy, made simple, clear to anyone, easy to read, readable, legible, *lisible* (Fr), decipherable, beautifully handwritten, clearly printed, uncoded, decoded, explained, interpreted, simplified, popularized, popular, exoteric, for everyone, for the layman, for the general public, reaching a mass audience, aiming for the lowest common denominator, available to all, apodeictic, using short words, using simple language, limpid, transparent, lucid, pellucid, perspicuous, as simple as pie, as clear as day, as plain as the nose on one's face

▶ *556 Simplicity, 660 Easiness, 550 Clarity, 524 Interpretation, 442 Transparency*

3 **recognizable**, distinguishable, identifiable, distinct, defined, well-defined, standing out, definite, unmistakable, knowable

▶ *490 Certainty, 165 Speciality*

VERBS

4 **be intelligible**, make sense, come through loud and clear, come alive, take on depth, offer readability, read easily, add up, speak to one's understanding, tell its own tale, speak for itself, speak volumes, have no secrets, become apparent, sink in, penetrate, dawn on, register, open one's eyes, come over (Inf), get across (Inf)

▶ *473 Argument, 483 Evidence, 437 Visibility*

5 **simplify**, make clear, make crystal-clear, make plain, state plainly, speak clearly, articulate, repeat, recapitulate, make easy, predigest, make easily understood, popularize, write for the layman, address the general public, reach a mass audience, aim for the lowest common denominator, make available to all, spell out, put in plain words, state in plain English, use short words, use simple language, avoid gobbledegook, offer an easy read, facilitate, explain, explicate, interpret, elucidate, clarify, clear up, labour the obvious, emphasize, put over (Inf)

▶ *183 Repetition, 556 Simplicity, 660 Easiness, 550 Clarity, 524 Interpretation*

6 **understand**, comprehend, know, realize, apprehend, fathom, penetrate, master, learn, have, hold, retain, remember, have understanding, get to the bottom of, grasp, grasp the meaning, get the gist of, get the idea, get hold of, seize, be on to, take in, follow, get, begin to understand, come to understand, have insight,

have one's eyes opened, see the light, see through, see it all, be undeceived, get to know, be told, be informed, be with it (Inf), be with one (Inf), twig (Inf), latch on to (Inf), catch on (Inf), get wise to (Inf), get the picture (Inf), see the lay of the land (Inf), catch the drift of (Inf), get the hang of (Inf), tumble to (Inf), rumble (Sl), dig (Sl), savvy (Sl), colly (US sl)

▶ *501 Knowledge, 511 Memory, 507 Wisdom, 496 Discovery, 435 Vision, 528 Information*

7 **recognize**, detect, identify, spot, descry, distinguish, discern, make out, perceive, ken (Scot), conceive, see at a glance, see with half an eye, see, make no mistake

▶ *535 Affirmation, 490 Certainty, 435 Vision, 544 Identification*

8 **be recognizable**, have a distinctive appearance, stand out, leap out

NOUNS

9 **intelligibility**, comprehensibility, understandability, knowability, apprehensibility, fathomableness, penetrability, scrutability, interpretability, explicability, teachability, coherence, unambiguity, unambivalence, precision, preciseness, definiteness, positiveness, certainty, sense, meaningfulness, informativeness, vividness, graphicness, descriptiveness

▶ *501 Knowledge, 520 Meaning*

10 **simplicity**, clarity, clearness, plainness, plain speaking, plain speech, explicitness, articulateness, articulacy, distinctness, directness, straightforwardness, downrightness, forthrightness, uninvolvement, unadornment, unadorned style, simple eloquence, readability, legibility, beautiful handwriting, decipherability, clear printing, decoding, easiness, facility, obviousness, self-evidence, explanation, amplification, interpretation, simplification, popularization, lowest common denominator (LCD), short words, words of one syllable, plain words, simple language, plain English, mother tongue, limpidity, transparency, lucidity, pellucidity, perspicuity

▶ *556 Simplicity, 660 Easiness, 550 Clarity, 524 Interpretation, 442 Transparency*

11 **recognizability**, cognizability, distinction, distinguishability, distinctiveness, definiteness, definition

▶ *490 Certainty*

12 **understanding**, comprehension, mastery, realization, apprehension, grasp, learning, knowledge, perception, recognition

▶ *501 Knowledge, 544 Identification*

ADVERBS

13 **intelligibly**, comprehensibly, understandably, coherently, articulately, expressively, simply, clearly, lucidly, plainly, distinctly, unmistakably, explicitly, concisely, in words of one syllable, with clarity, in a clear style, in plain terms, in no uncertain terms, in plain

English, unambiguously, for the layman, for the general public

523   Unintelligibility

ADJECTIVES

1 **unintelligible**, incomprehensible, unclear, meaningless, obscure, esoteric, inconceivable, not understandable, impossible to explain, inexplicable, unexplainable, unaccountable, so much nonsense, gibbering, incoherent, rambling, inarticulate, unknown, undiscoverable, unfathomable, inapprehensible, unbridgeable, impenetrable, unsearchable, inscrutable, blank, expressionless, deadpan, impassive, inaudible, muted, scrambled, garbled, scrawly, scribbled, cramped, crabbed, encoded, hard to decode, undecipherable, unreadable, illegible, undiscernible, unseen, invisible, hidden, unknowable, private, arcane, cryptic, mysterious, shrouded in mystery, enigmatic, esoteric, gnostic, sphinxlike, oracular, profound, deep, occult, mystic, mystical, transcendental, inexpressible, unspeakable, unpronounceable, unutterable, ineffable, incommunicable, untranslatable, indefinable, like double Dutch (Inf), poker-faced (Inf)

▶ *551 Obscurity, 521 Lack of Meaning, 531 Concealment, 566 Taciturnity, 277 Depth, 7 Religion*

2 **unexplained**, never solved, without a solution, without a clue, unsolvable, insoluble, unsolved, unresolved, uncertain, shrouded in mystery

3 **unrecognizable**, incognizable, indistinguishable, unidentifiable, indistinct, poorly defined, undefined, hidden, indefinite, easily mistaken, unknowable

▶ *502 Ignorance, 761 Insensitivity, 424 Faintness*

4 **difficult**, confusing, puzzling, baffling, perplexing, hard to understand, complex, complicated, beyond one's comprehension, defying comprehension, beyond one, over one's head, recondite, abstruse, elusive, amorphous, shadowy, obscure, sphinxlike, enigmatic, inscrutable, mysterious, occult, nebulous, vague, murky, muddy, misty, foggy, hazy, fuzzy, dim, clear as mud, unclear, ambiguous, equivocal, paradoxical, of doubtful meaning, oracular

▶ *659 Difficulty, 527 Latency, 441 Dimness, 551 Obscurity, 578 Equivocation*

5 **strange**, odd, weird, abnormal, unexpected, bizarre, quaint, eccentric, oddball (Inf)

▶ *514 Surprise, 168 Nonconformity, 491 Uncertainty*

6 **confused**, puzzled, baffled, perplexed, mystified, unable to understand, wondering, bewildered, flummoxed, stumped, confounded, nonplussed, out of one's depth, out of it (Inf), not getting it (Inf)

VERBS

7 **be unintelligible**, defy comprehension, not make sense, elude one, escape one, lose one, make one's head swim (*or* ache), need an interpreter, present a puzzle, keep one guessing, talk in riddles, speak in tongues, talk nonsense, gibber, ramble, mean nothing, speak badly, speak gobbledegook, talk like an idiot, babble, look blank, look expressionless, look deadpan, scribble, doodle, scrawl, cause doubt, puzzle, baffle, perplex, mystify, bewilder, flummox, confound, stump, confuse, bedevil, entangle, go over one's head, be beyond one's reach, talk double Dutch (Inf)

▶ *521 Lack of Meaning, 498 Disbelief, 153 Disturbance, 491 Uncertainty*

8 **make unintelligible**, scribble, scrawl, scramble, garble, encode, encipher, shroud in mystery, obscure, complicate, confuse

9 **find unintelligible**, not understand, find hard to understand, find too difficult, misjudge, misunderstand, get wrong, get the wrong idea, not know, not register, have a blind spot, have no grasp of, not have the first idea, not make out, not know what to make of, make neither head nor tail of, make nothing of, puzzle, wonder, rack one's brains, be out of one's depth, not know what one is about, be lost, be at sea, not get it (Inf), not grasp it (Inf), throw up one's hands (Inf), be on a different wavelength (Inf)

▶ *483 Evidence, 656 Unskilfulness, 436 Blindness, 504 Error, 493 Misjudgment, 468 Inattention*

10 **be unexplained**, require explanation, remain unsolved, have no answer, have no solution, give no clue

NOUNS

11 **unintelligibility**, incomprehensibility, inapprehensibility, meaninglessness, lack of meaning, lack of sense, nonsense, unclearness, lack of clarity, obscurity, uncertainty, ambiguity, equivocalness, esotericism, difficulty, perplexity, bafflement, confusion, mystification, impenetrability, inscrutability, the unknown, inconceivability, lack of understanding, inexplicability, unaccountability, impossibility of discovery, secrecy, babbling, mumbling, stuttering, stammering, blankness, lack of expression, impassivity, inaudibility, faintness, muteness, illegibility, unreadability, invisibility, privacy, arcaneness, mystery, profoundness, deepness, occultism, mysticism, transcendentalism, inexpressibility, unspeakableness, ineffability, incommunicability, indefinableness, poker face (Inf)

▶ *521 Lack of Meaning, 506 Nonsense, 491 Uncertainty, 510 Insanity, 564 Speech, 424 Faintness, 529 Secrecy*

12 **unintelligible thing**, obscure point, per-

plexing question, puzzle, puzzler, problem, conundrum, knotty problem, hard (or tough) nut to crack, baffling attitude, mysterious message, secret, secret book, code, cipher (or cypher), secret language, idiolect, gibberish, scrawl, scribble, mystery, enigma, enigmatic question, riddle, paradox, double Dutch (Inf)
▶ *551 Obscurity, 491 Uncertainty, 529 Secrecy*

ADVERBS
13 **unintelligibly**, incomprehensibly, meaninglessly, inconceivably, inexplicably, unaccountably, incoherently, inarticulately, unfathomably, impenetrably, expressionlessly, inscrutably, blankly, impassively, inaudibly, unreadably, illegibly, cryptically, esoterically, mysteriously, enigmatically

524 Interpretation

NOUNS
1 **interpretation**, construction, rendering, way of putting something, explanation, definition, description, explication, emendation, amendment, editing, simplification, exposition, exegesis, epexegesis, eisegesis, isogesis, judgment, estimate, personal feeling, understanding, enlightenment, light, clarification, insight, elucidation, illumination, illustration, exemplification, demonstration, example, resolution, solution, answer, key, clue, the secret, decipherment, decoding, code cracking, analysis, conflation, application, particular interpretation, twist, turn, reading, lection, meaning, subaudition, connotation, euhemerism, demythologization, allegorization, metaphor, accepted reading, usual text, vulgate, edited text, alternative reading, variant reading, rendition, deconstruction, version, edition, critical edition
▶ *478 Answer, 496 Discovery, 627 Improvement, 520 Meaning, 556 Simplicity, 550 Clarity, 522 Intelligibility, 5 Linguistics, 48 Literature, 492 Judgment, 760 Sensitivity*
2 **annotation**, gloss, footnote, textual note, marginalia, variorum, scholium, apparatus criticus, note, note of explanation, exegesis, legend, appendix, explanatory remark, word of explanation, inscription, comment, editorial comment, additional comment, commentary
▶ *130 Addition*
3 **criticism**, literary criticism, critique, review, notice, theatre review, art review, music review, book review, film review, television review, rave review, puff, favourable review, good review, negative review, bad review, panning, textual criticism, form criticism, higher criticism, New Criticism, lower criticism, practical criticism, personal criticism, critical

power, critic's gift
▶ *654 Advice, 561 Dissertation*
4 **translation**, transcription, rendering, literal translation, faithful translation, word-for-word translation, loose translation, free translation, bilingual text, version, rewording, paraphrase, adaptation, simplification, amplification, transliteration, decoding, unscrambling, decipherment, sign-language reading, lip-reading, key, crib (Inf), pony (Inf), trot (US sl)
▶ *503 Accuracy, 562 Summary, 522 Intelligibility, 547 Representation*
5 **science of interpretation**, exegetics, hermeneutics, tropology, epigraphy, cryptology, cryptography, cryptanalysis, palaeography, semiology (or semeiology), lexicography, linguistics, diagnostics, symptomatology, physiognomy, phrenology, graphology, prophecy, divination, criticism
▶ *517 Prediction, 5 Linguistics*
6 **interpreter**, translator, linguist, explainer, clarifier, paraphraser, paraphrast, simplifier, popularizer, lexicographer, definer, teacher, religious teacher, expounder, exponent, reviewer, critic, textual critic, literary critic, Leavisite, editor, copy editor, emender, emendator, annotator, glossator, glossarist, scholiast, commentator, exegete, exegetist (or exegesist), isogete, euhemerist, demythologizer, cryptographer, cryptologist, cryptanalyst, decoder, code-breaker, cipher clerk, signlanguage reader, lip-reader, oneirocritic, medium, spiritualist, diviner, epigraphist, palaeographer
▶ *501 Knowledge, 7 Religion, 517 Prediction, 200 Past Time, 48 Literature, 5 Linguistics*
7 **news interpreter**, journalist, reporter, commentator, editorial writer, leader writer, columnist, news source, specialist source, public relations (PR) man (or woman), PR representative (or officer), press officer, press agent, public information officer, publicizer, spokesman (or spokeswoman), company spokesman (or spokeswoman), mouthpiece, flack (US sl), spin doctor (Sl)
▶ *528 Information, 532 Publication, 533 News, 534 Communications*
VERBS
8 **interpret**, construe, put a construction on, render, put, explain, explicate, inform, expound, comment on, give a sense to, ascribe a meaning to, make sense of, understand, take to mean, read, read into, read between the lines, deduce, infer, reason, define, describe, emend, amend, twist, turn, conflate, edit, copy-edit, simplify, spell out, popularize, facilitate, judge, estimate, give insight, give enlightenment, clarify, make clear, elucidate, disambiguate, analyse, illuminate, throw (or

shed) light on, illustrate, exemplify, give an example, demonstrate, show, act as guide

▶ *520 Meaning, 556 Simplicity, 550 Clarity, 522 Intelligibility, 627 Improvement, 496 Discovery, 492 Judgment*

9 **decipher**, crack, crack a code, unlock a code, crack the cipher, decode, unscramble, find the meaning, read hieroglyphics, read, spell out, puzzle out, make out, work out, sort out, piece together, find the sense of, find the key to, solve, resolve, find a solution, find a resolution, enucleate, unravel, unriddle, demystify, disentangle

▶ *478 Answer, 522 Intelligibility*

10 **annotate**, gloss, footnote, add commentary, add explanation, write notes for, inscribe, comment on

▶ *130 Addition*

11 **criticize**, review, critique, evaluate, give criticism, offer criticism, pan, slate, give (*or* offer) constructive criticism, puff

▶ *654 Advice, 48 Literature*

12 **translate**, transcribe, transliterate, render, paraphrase, rephrase, reword, restate, rehash, make a new version, put into, turn into, give a literal translation of, adapt, simplify, amplify, encode, decode, put into code, cipher, decipher, use sign language, sign, read sign language, read lips, lip-read, interpret, act as interpreter, offer an interpretation, use a crib (Inf), use a pony (Inf), use a trot (US sl)

▶ *562 Summary, 547 Representation*

13 **interpret news**, report, cover, slant, comment on, write an editorial, write a leader, write a column, do public relations, serve as press officer for, act as spokesman (*or* woman) for, spin, give a spin (to)

▶ *528 Information, 532 Publication, 533 News, 534 Communications*

ADJECTIVES

14 **interpretive**, interpretative, interpretational, constructive, explanatory, explicatory, explicative, explaining, descriptive, expositive, expository, insightful, illustrative, demonstrative, definitional, definitive, defining, exemplary, exegetic, exegetical, hermeneutic, clarifying, elucidative, elucidatory, illuminating, semiological (*or* semeiological), euhemeristic, demythologizing

▶ *556 Simplicity, 550 Clarity, 520 Meaning*

15 **interpreted**, glossed, explained, defined, illustrated, elucidated, clarified, simplified, annotated, commented on, edited, emended, amended, conflated, translated, rendered, deciphered, decoded, unscrambled, cracked, unlocked, coded, encoded, scrambled

▶ *522 Intelligibility*

16 **annotative**, glossarial, scholiastic, explanatory, critical, editorial, commentarial

▶ *130 Addition*

17 **translational**, paraphrastic, metaphrastic, polyglot, multilingual, bilingual, synonymous, equivalent, literal, word-for-word, verbatim, faithful, free, loose

▶ *5 Linguistics*

ADVERBS

18 **in other words**, in words to that effect, that is to say, that is, i.e., *id est* (L), namely, viz, *videlicet* (L), to wit, to put it another way, plainly, in plain words, in plain English, to be clear, to explain, in explanation, interpretively, interpretatively, illustratively, exegetically

525   Misinterpretation

VERBS

1 **misinterpret**, misunderstand, misapprehend, mistranslate, render incorrectly, misread, misconstrue, put a wrong construction on, get wrong, get one wrong, take wrong, misconceive, misjudge, miscompute, misdiagnose, mistake, get hold of the wrong end of the stick, err, blunder, misspell, put in a false light, misteach, miseducate, explain wrongly, misrepresent, stretch the meaning, strain the sense, put a false sense on, put a false construction on, give a false idea, give a false impression, pervert, distort, change the meaning, do violence to the meaning, wrench, twist, give a twist (*or* turn) to, twist the words, manipulate the truth, misquote, equivocate, play upon words, read into, write into, take out of context, add a meaning, add, omit, leave out, suppress, subtract, repeat wrongly, falsify, garble, exaggerate, inflate, overpraise, overrate, overestimate, underpraise, underrate, underestimate, depict falsely, traduce, travesty, parody, caricature, burlesque, ridicule, defame, libel, slander, guy (Inf)

▶ *493 Misjudgment, 504 Error, 502 Ignorance, 309 Distortion, 578 Equivocation, 130 Addition, 131 Subtraction, 548 Misrepresentation, 494 Overestimation, 495 Underestimation, 541 Exaggeration, 799 Derision, 854 Disparagement*

NOUNS

2 **misinterpretation**, wrong interpretation, misunderstanding, misapprehension, mistranslation, translator's error, misreading, false reading, wrong words, misconstruction, false construction, misapplication, misdiagnosis, misconception, misjudgment, miscomputation, mistake, wrong end of the stick, error, blunder, solecism, misspelling, false light, misteaching, wrong instruction, wrong explanation, misrepresentation, stretching the meaning, straining the sense, overdoing it, strained sense, false sense, false idea, false impression, colouring the truth, lying, perversion, distortion, wrenching, twisting, twist,

turn, manipulation, misquotation, equivocalness, circumlocution, wordplay, misuse of words, catachresis, abuse of language, addition, omission, suppression, subtraction, falsification, garbling, garble, overestimation, underestimation, exaggeration, inflation, different wavelength, false depiction, traducement, travesty, parody, caricature, burlesque, ridiculing, defamation, libel, slander

▶ *493 Misjudgment, 504 Error, 502 Ignorance, 309 Distortion, 578 Equivocation, 130 Addition, 131 Subtraction, 548 Misrepresentation, 494 Overestimation, 495 Underestimation, 541 Exaggeration, 799 Derision, 854 Disparagement*

ADJECTIVES

3 **misinterpreted**, misunderstood, mistranslated, misread, misconstrued, misconceived, mistaken, wrong, misspelt, solecistic, catachrestic, misquoted, garbled, falsified, distorted, exaggerated, inflated, misrepresented, libellous, slanderous

ADVERBS

4 **mistakenly**, erroneously, in error, wrongly, falsely

5 **misrepresentedly**, distortedly, exaggeratedly, libellously, slanderously

526 Display

VERBS

1 **display**, show, put on display, put on view, put on show, exhibit, manifest, present, bring forward, reveal to the public, expose, expose to view, disclose, offer for approval, set out, set before someone's eyes, give a guided tour, show round, bring to notice, draw attention to, feature, spotlight, illuminate, put in bold (*or* high) relief, headline, emphasize, point out, indicate, teach, instruct, explain, make a show of, flourish, brandish, wave, dangle, flaunt, vaunt, show off, parade, air, sport, model, demonstrate, perform, act, enact, dramatize, put on, stage, release, publish, flash (Inf)

▶ *365 Oscillation, 295 Dress, 811 Showiness, 797 Affectation, 467 Attention, 547 Representation, 475 Demonstration, 51 Performing Arts, 501 Knowledge, 544 Identification, 554 Emphasis, 118 Imitation, 530 Disclosure*

2 **display something**, screen, televise, put on television, broadcast, put on radio, stage a play, hold an exhibition, exhibit, hang a picture, show photographs, place in a shop window, advertise

▶ *51 Performing Arts, 50 Painting and Sculpture*

3 **reveal**, manifest, divulge, disclose, discover, uncover, unearth, bring to light, illuminate, throw light on, make plain, make obvious, bring to notice, bring up, point up, point out, indicate, accentuate, enhance, make impor-

tant, throw into relief, emphasize, highlight, spotlight, place in the spotlight, place in the foreground, proclaim, publicize, promote, advertise, publish, cite, mention, make reference to, adduce, quote, extract, invent, develop, formulate, produce, bring out, bring forth, expose, open up, lay bare, lay open, throw open, unmask, unveil, drag out, draw out, draw forth, express, trot out, come out with, show off, evidence, show, evince, give away, betray, draw attention to, unfurl, unroll, unfold, spread out, solve, decipher, decode, explain, interpret

▶ *530 Disclosure, 483 Evidence, 496 Discovery, 524 Interpretation, 294 Uncovering, 322 Opening, 355 Extraction, 243 Production, 289 Exterior, 128 Increase, 439 Light, 535 Affirmation, 611 Importance, 532 Publication*

4 **show oneself**, show one's face, reveal oneself, appear, materialize, rear one's head, show up, be seen, show the flag, come out into the open, come forth, unmask oneself, unveil oneself, tear off the mask, show (oneself in) one's true colours, stand in the open, stand in full view, confront, force a confrontation, come face to face, come eyeball to eyeball, assert onself, speak up, speak out, raise one's voice, stand up, stand up and be counted, take a stand, speak plainly, put one's cards on the table, have no secrets, make no mystery, make no secret of, not try to hide, have no shame, wash one's dirty linen in public, wear one's heart on one's sleeve, reveal one's mind, reveal one's thoughts, reveal one's opinions, tell to one's face, give straight from the shoulder, make no bones about

▶ *457 Appearance, 537 Truth*

5 **be visible**, attract attention, attract notice, stand out, stand out a mile, have the spotlight on one, be in the limelight, hold centre stage, show up, show up well, require no explanation, go without saying, stand to reason, tell its own story, speak for itself, make an impression, loom large, stare one in the face, openly happen, come to light, transpire, emanate

▶ *556 Simplicity, 522 Intelligibility, 475 Demonstration, 437 Visibility, 467 Attention, 264 Nearness*

NOUNS

6 **display**, show, exhibition, exposition, expo, demonstration, presentation, spectacle, showing, viewing, collection, retrospective, fair, market, fashion show, motor show, boat show, dog show, cat show, art show, craft show, crafts fair, antique show, antiques fair, parade, array

▶ *167 Conformity, 605 Store, 740 Market, 50 Painting and Sculpture, 475 Demonstration, 295 Dress*

7 **showpiece**, exhibit, collector's piece, pride, jewel in the crown, collectable (*or* collectible),

curio, antique, museum piece, model, sample, specimen, example, mock-up, dummy, piece of evidence

8 **showplace**, showroom, exhibition hall, exhibition centre, gallery, museum, hall, auditorium, scene, showcase, display case, display cabinet, dumpbin, store window, shop window, notice board, bulletin board, pegboard, hoarding, sign, advertisement, poster, placard, sandwich boards, label, bill, citation

9 **production**, performance, presentation, enactment, show, spectacle, musical, concert, play, ballet, film, motion picture, cinema, television programme, TV programme, radio programme, preview

▶ *51 Performing Arts, 547 Representation*

10 **manifestation**, manifestness, revelation, disclosure, exposure, laying open, unfolding, unrolling, discovery, uncovering, bringing to light, shedding of daylight on, visibility, publicity, promotion, advertising, flagrancy, blatancy, conspicuousness, ostentation, showing off, accentuation, emphasis, highlight, spotlight, ceremony, pageant, pageantry, pomp, expression, formulation, affirmation, proof, evidence, confrontation, comparison, projection, representation, symbolization, typification, personification, indication, sign, token, signal, symptom, syndrome, omen, press conference, proclamation, publication, apparition, appearance, materialization, epiphany, incarnation, theophany, avatar, seance, occultism, splash (Inf)

▶ *530 Disclosure, 811 Showiness, 467 Attention, 544 Identification, 554 Emphasis, 517 Prediction, 435 Vision, 7 Religion*

11 **openness**, obviousness, plainness, candour, glasnost, plain speech, unadulterated truth, simple truth, home truth, open-and-shut case

▶ *537 Truth*

12 **displayer**, exhibitor, demonstrator, presenter, publicist, publicizer, advertiser, press agent, flack (US sl), public relations (PR) man (*or* woman), promotional manager, barker, showman, master of ceremonies (MC), impresario, stage manager, exhibitionist, flaunter, striptease artiste, stripteaser, stripper, model, male model, mannequin, vain person, peacock

▶ *51 Performing Arts, 809 Vanity, 811 Showiness, 295 Dress*

ADJECTIVES

13 **displayed**, on display, exhibited, presented, shown, on show, on view, on, made public, brought to public notice, brought to one's notice, brought to attention, manifested, apodeictic, featured, visible, apparent, brought forth, produced, mentioned, adduced, cited, quoted, confronted, brought face to face, worn, sported, paraded, shown off, flaunted, waved, unfurled, brandished, flourished, advertised, publicized, promoted, published, expressible, producible, showable

▶ *457 Appearance, 165 Speciality, 811 Showiness, 365 Oscillation*

14 **manifest**, revealed, disclosed, divulged, exposed, uncovered, discovered, declared, overt, palpable, open, in the open, public, on the surface, staring one in the face, unconcealed, uncamouflaged, undisguised, noticeable, conspicuous, notable, apparent, visible, obvious, ostensible, open-and-shut, appearing, token, indicative, typical, symbolic, personified, representative, definite, defined, identifiable, recognizable, certain, unmistakable, incontestable, pronounced, prominent, clear as daylight, intelligible, signal, marked, striking, in relief, bold, in bold (*or* high) relief, salient, highlighted, accentuated, emphasized, in the foreground, in the limelight, patent, evident, self-evident, written all over one for all to see, obtrusive, flagrant, blatant, arrant, glaring, stark-staring, ostentatious, catching the eye, eye-catching, well-known, notorious, famous, infamous, gaudy, showy, loud, shouting from the rooftops

▶ *490 Certainty, 483 Evidence, 811 Showiness, 544 Identification, 554 Emphasis*

15 **open**, candid, frank, explicit, plain, plain-speaking, plain-spoken, plain as the nose on one's face, clear, crystal-clear, truthful, honest, veracious, free, unreserved, honest to goodness, honest to God, downright, forthright, straightforward, blunt, heart-to-heart, off-the-record, outspoken, emphatic, no-nonsense, bold, daring, brazen, immodest, shameless, impudent, defiant, barefaced, bare, uncovered, naked, flaunting

▶ *537 Truth, 857 Probity, 668 Defiance, 877 Immorality*

ADVERBS

16 **manifestly**, obviously, evidently, plainly, apparently, openly, overtly, publicly, in public, for public notice, for all to see, conspicuously, flagrantly, undisguisedly, palpably, notoriously, at first blush, externally, on the face of it, on the surface, superficially, open and above-board, with one's cards on the table, before one, before all, before God, under the eye of heaven, on exhibition, in full view, in broad daylight, out in the open, in open court, on the stage

17 **frankly**, candidly, honestly, forthrightly, to one's face, face-to-face, in a heart-to-heart way, off-the-record, boldly, defiantly

527 Latency

ADJECTIVES

1 **latent**, dormant, sleeping, hibernating, aestivating, inactive, passive, quiescent, in abey-

ance, inert, delitescent, undeveloped, potential, possible, virtual, subconscious, subliminal, submerged, underlying, archityp(ic)al, unacknowledged, subterranean, below the surface, deep

▶ *643 Inactivity, 240 Inertness, 325 Motionlessness, 486 Possibility, 277 Depth*

2 **concealed**, hidden, covert, unseen, unmanifested, unexposed, invisible, screened, behind the scenes, backroom, in the background, underground, skulking, lurking, stealthy, hiding, lying low, private, not public, secluded, sequestered, tucked away, hidden away, unspied, undetected, undisclosed, undercover, under wraps, veiled, muffled, masked, disguised, coded, cryptographic, secret, top-secret, classified, restricted, kept quiet, off-the-record, obscure, murky, dark, arcane, unintelligible, impenetrable, undiscoverable, undiscovered, awaiting discovery, closed, cloaked in secrecy

▶ *531 Concealment, 529 Secrecy, 502 Ignorance, 438 Invisibility, 440 Darkness, 816 Unsociability, 523 Unintelligibility*

3 **unsolved**, unknown, undiscovered, unexplained, unrevealed, undivulged, unguessed, unsuspected, untold, unspoken, unexplored, untracked, untraced, uninvented, hush-hush (Inf)

▶ *523 Unintelligibility*

4 **unsaid**, unspoken, unvoiced, unpronounced, unuttered, unexpressed, unarticulated, unmentioned, untold of, undivulged, unsung, unpromoted, unproclaimed, undeclared, unprofessed, unwritten, unpublished, tacit, half-spoken, understood, implied, inferred, inferential, implicit, meant, indicated, suggested, hinted, intimated, insinuated, insinuating, implicative, between the lines, suggestive, allusive, allusory

▶ *520 Meaning, 422 Silence, 566 Taciturnity*

5 **mysterious**, mystic, occult, symbolic, allegorical, tropic (*or* tropical), anagogical, metaphorical, figurative, cryptic, esoteric, secret, cabbalistic, gnostic, indirect, oblique, clandestine, insidious, treacherous, perfidious, underhand, crooked (Inf), bent (Sl)

▶ *5 Linguistics, 286 Obliqueness, 858 Improbity, 165 Speciality*

NOUNS

6 **latency**, latentness, dormancy, dormant condition, sleep, hibernation, aestivation, inactivity, passivity, quiescence, abeyance, inertness, delitescence, underdevelopment, potentiality, possibility, virtuality, subconsciousness, subconscious, sublimity, anonymity, no name, unknown man (*or* woman), mystery man (*or* woman), secret society, cabal, clandestineness, depth, hidden depths, deep structure, trope, figure, metaphor, allegory, the tip of the

iceberg, more than meets the eye, deceptive appearance, hidden fires

▶ *643 Inactivity, 240 Inertness, 325 Motionlessness, 486 Possibility, 277 Depth*

7 **latent things**, dormant disease, cancer, sleeping dog, sleeping giant, sleeping baby, dormant volcano, dark horse, snake in the grass, iron hand in a velvet glove, hidden danger, covered pit, undercurrent, undertow, subliminal influence, subliminal advertising

▶ *635 Trap, 633 Danger*

8 **concealment**, hiding, invisibility, imperceptibility, submergence, skulking, lurking, stealth, privacy, seclusion, sequestration, secrecy, secret document, top-secret document, classified document, restriction, obscurity, code, invisible writing, cryptography, intrigue, undercurrent, plot, ambush

▶ *531 Concealment, 529 Secrecy, 438 Invisibility, 816 Unsociability, 523 Unintelligibility, 592 Plan*

9 **backstage manipulator**, secret influencer, power behind the throne, hidden hand, puller of strings, wirepuller (US), friend at court, *amicus curiae* (L), friends in high places, *éminence grise*, (Fr), old boy network, boys in the backroom, Freemason, puppeteer

▶ *233 Influence*

10 **quietness**, taciturnity, muteness, sealed lips, closed lips, half-spoken word, whisper, stage whisper, undertone, nuance, faintness, mutter, hint, suggestion, innuendo, insinuation, aside, connotation, adumbration, implication, inference, inner person, innermost recesses, interiority

▶ *520 Meaning, 422 Silence, 566 Taciturnity, 290 Interior, 424 Faintness*

11 **mysteriousness**, mysticism, occultism, occultness, symbolism, symbolization, allegory, anagoge, metaphor, esotericism, cabbala, latent meaning, veiled meaning, hidden meaning, occult meaning, unintelligibility, oracle, secret, mystery, dimness, darkness, shadowiness, riddle of the Sphinx

▶ *517 Prediction, 441 Dimness, 440 Darkness, 528 Information, 520 Meaning, 523 Unintelligibility*

VERBS

12 **be latent**, lie dormant, lie under the surface, lie beneath, sleep, hibernate, smoke, smoulder, keep quiet, keep mum (Inf)

▶ *643 Inactivity, 325 Motionlessness*

13 **hide**, conceal, submerge, go below the surface, lie below the surface, skulk, lurk, creep, slink, tiptoe, walk on tiptoe, burrow, go underground, lie low, lie hidden, stow away, lie in ambush, keep quiet, make no sign, await discovery, avoid notice, escape observation, evade detection, avoid recognition, stay behind the scenes, dissemble, secretly cause, influence, underlie, pull the strings, stage-

manage, lie doggo (Inf), go on the lam (US sl)

▶ *531 Concealment, 540 Falsehood, 226 Cause, 233 Influence, 240 Inertness*

14 **imply**, mean, indicate, spell, suggest, carry a suggestion, imply, connote, hint, intimate, insinuate, mean to say, whisper, murmur, understand, allude, symbolize, implicate, involve

▶ *520 Meaning*

ADVERBS

15 **latently**, passively, quiescently, potentially, virtually, subconsciously, subliminally, secretly, covertly, implicity, indirectly

528   Information

NOUNS

1 **information**, facts, facts and figures, data, knowledge, intelligence, acquaintance, news, tidings, word, info (Inf), the know (Inf), gen (Inf), low-down (Inf), dope (Sl), dirt (Sl)

2 **communication**, transmission, dissemination, diffusion, notification, announcement, broadcast, publication, narration, account, eyewitness account, statement, review, report, dispatch, communiqué, bulletin, message, wire, fax, telegram, telemessage, telex, cable, cablegram, notice, order, briefing, instruction

3 **document**, paper, certificate, record, report, medical report, police report, review, *compte rendu* (Fr), annual report, progress report, term report, statement, estimate, specification, statement of account, financial statement, return, annual return, tax return, government documents, white paper, green paper, classified information, file, dossier, official documents, bumph (Inf)

4 **mass communication**, mass media, the media, broadcasting, radio, television, journalism, the press, serious press, tabloid press, yellow press, news, news coverage, blanket coverage, news item, newscast, feature story, scoop, publicity, press release, news release, hand-out, news conference, press conference, mention, obituary, regular feature, letters to the editor, advertisement, advert, ad, classified ad, small ad, births, marriages, and deaths, hatches, matches, and dispatches (Inf), magazines, journals, mailing list, subscription list, correspondence, circular, mailshot, junk mail

▶ *534 Communications, 532 Publication, 533 News*

5 **reference book**, encyclopaedia, almanac, yearbook, dictionary, thesaurus, directory, index, guidebook, Baedeker, Fodor, Michelin, travelogue, handbook, manual, vade mecum, ABC, A–Z, timetable, Bradshaw, map, atlas, roadbook, road map, route map, itinerary,

chart, plan, gazetteer, nautical almanac, astronomical almanac, ephemeris, catalogue, telephone directory, phone book, Yellow Pages

6 **information technology**, IT, computerized information, data communications, information retrieval, database, viewdata, data processing, information processing, word processing, information theory, statistics

▶ *65 Computers*

7 **advice**, tip, word, passing word, word in the ear, word to the wise, subtle word, hint, whisper, aside, suggestion, inference, intimation, insinuation, indication, inside information, pointer, tip-off, word of mouth, rumour, leak, gossip, gesture, prompt, reminder, signal, nod, wink, look, nudge, pinch, kick, kick under the table, caution, warning, scuttlebutt (US sl)

▶ *654 Advice, 529 Secrecy, 530 Disclosure*

8 **source of information**, source, authority, grapevine, channel, quarter(s), information centre, information office, press office, news agency, news syndicate, press service, wire service (US), Reuters, Press Association, Associated Press, United Press International, Agence France Presse

9 **informant**, informer, messenger, herald, teller, witness, eyewitness, testifier, narrator, communicator, announcer, broadcaster, newsreader, newscaster, anchorman (*or* anchor woman), spokesman (*or* spokeswoman), spokesperson, mouthpiece, news commentator, weather forecaster, notifier, advertiser, adviser, promoter, publicizer, publicist, public relations officer, publicity agent, press agent, flack (US), publisher, journalist, correspondent, special correspondent, foreign correspondent, reporter, freelance reporter, freelancer, stringer, feature writer, columnist, gossip columnist, gossip writer, chequebook journalist, newshound (Inf), hack (Sl)

10 **informer**, contact, source, adviser, tipster, tipper, talebearer, telltale, blabber, tattler, gossip, newsmonger, inside agent, betrayer, fifth columnist, accuser, stool pigeon, mole (Inf), nark (Sl), copper's nark (Sl), squealer (Sl), squeaker (Sl), whistle-blower (Sl), rat (Sl), snitch (Sl), fink (US sl), nose (US sl), grass (Sl), supergrass (Sl), delator (Arch)

VERBS

11 **inform**, tell, apprise, acquaint, advise, confide, notify, certify, testify, brief, instruct, teach, enlighten, educate, point out, correct, put right, disabuse, undeceive, disillusion, let know, have know, keep posted, give to understand, put in the picture (Inf), fill in (Inf), put wise (Inf), clue up (Inf), wise up (US inf)

12 **communicate**, make known, impart, transmit, disseminate, convey, recount, narrate, describe, publicize, break the news, broadcast, announce, televise, publish, report, docu-

ment, post, wire, telegraph, fax, telex, telephone, phone, call, call up

▶ *532 Publication, 534 Communications*

13 **inform on** (*or* **against**), betray, denounce, accuse, turn queen's (*or* king's) evidence, tergiversate, tell, tell on, blab, spill the beans (Inf), let the cat out of the bag (Inf), stool (US inf), sell down the river (Inf), spill one's guts (Sl), sing (Sl), split (Sl), grass (Sl), shop (Sl), snitch (Sl), peach (Sl), squeal (Sl), blow (Sl), blow the lid off (Sl), blow the gaff (Sl), blow the whistle on (Sl), rat (Sl), delate (Arch)

▶ *530 Disclosure*

14 **tip**, tip off, hint, breathe, whisper, indicate, signal, suggest, imply, intimate, insinuate

15 **be informed**, come to know, realize, understand, know, learn, discover, be in the know, infer, get wind of, scent, hear, overhear, be a fly on the wall, get to hear of, become alive to, have it from, have it on good authority, have it from the horse's mouth, be told by a little bird

ADJECTIVES

16 **informative**, informatory, informational, revealing, illuminating, enlightening, explicit, clear, definite, expressive, expository, instructive, instructional, educational, advisory, cautionary, monitory, indicating, insinuating, suggesting, candid, plain-spoken, communicative, overcommunicative, indiscreet, loquacious, talkative, chatty, gossipy, big-mouthed (Sl)

▶ *530 Disclosure, 565 Talkativeness*

17 **newsworthy**, front-page, headline, newsy

▶ *533 News*

18 **informed**, enlightened, alert (to), aware (of), advised (of), briefed, posted, in touch, au fait, *au courant* (Fr), up to date, in the know (Inf), in on (Inf), in the picture (Inf), clued up (Inf), wised up (US inf), genned up (Inf)

ADVERBS

19 **reportedly**, as stated, on information received, as it is said, from the grapevine, by word of mouth, straight from the horse's mouth, as the story goes, apparently, from what one can gather, if one can trust one's ears

529 Secrecy

Stolen waters are sweet, and bread eaten in secret is pleasant. Bible: Proverbs.

Mum's the word. George Colman, the Younger.

O fie miss, you must not kiss and tell. William Congreve.

Three may keep a secret, if two of them are dead. Benjamin Franklin.

NOUNS

1 **secrecy**, silence, privacy, confidentiality, confidence, secret, confidant (*or* confidante), seal of the confessional, family secret, skeleton in the cupboard, secret meeting, private meeting, closed session, meeting in camera, confidential information, sealed orders, state secret, classified information, Official Secrets Act, top-secret file, censorship, suppression

▶ *531 Concealment*

2 **secretiveness**, stealth, stealthiness, furtiveness, clandestineness, covertness, secret service, intelligence service, MI5, MI6, CIA, KGB, espionage, counterintelligence, undercover agent, secret agent, spy, double agent, mole, industrial espionage, underhand dealing, intrigue, plot, conspiracy, cabal, *omertà* (It)

3 **mystification**, mystery, enigma, puzzle, problem, poser, intricacy, complexity, difficulty

4 **brain-teaser**, teaser, brain-twister, charade, Chinese puzzle, tangram, Rubik Cube (Tm), maze, labyrinth, word-puzzle, crossword, anagram, acrostic, riddle, riddle-me-ree, conundrum, rebus, cipher, code, cryptogram, cryptography, cryptographer, coder, public-key cryptography, decoder, hieroglyphics

5 **difficult problem**, knotty problem, hard nut to crack, Gordian knot, Hyrcanian wood, squaring the circle, duplicating the cube, riddle of the sphinx

6 **natural mystery**, ghosts, Bermuda Triangle, Atlantis, Stonehenge, Lourdes, Easter Island, flying saucers, UFOs (unidentified flying objects), crop circles, Fortean animals, Loch Ness Monster, Yeti, abominable snowman, bigfoot

7 **esotericism**, mystery, obscurity, secrecy, secret society, Freemasonry, Freemason, lodge, Ku Klux Klan, Klansman, initiate, Mafia, mafioso, Know-Nothings (US), occultism, gnosis, cabbalism, cabbala, arcanum, esoterica, secret lore, secret art, secret formula, alchemy, alchemist

8 **anonymity**, unknown quantity, unknown person, mysterious stranger, no name, Unknown Warrior, invisible man, code name, X, Anon., assumed name, stage name, pen name, pseudonym, nom de plume, alias, unknown country, terra incognita, Dark Continent

ADJECTIVES

9 **secret**, private, privy, intimate, confidential, closed, secluded, sealed, isolated, unrevealed, undisclosed, undivulged, unspoken, untold, top-secret, classified, restricted, censored, suppressed, off-the-record, hush-hush (Inf)

10 **secretive**, silent, close, reticent, surreptitious, stealthy, furtive, sly, clandestine, covert, undercover, underhand, conspirational, cabalistic, cloak-and-dagger (Inf)

11 **mysterious**, enigmatic, inscrutable, un-

knowable, esoteric, cabbalistic, arcane, occult, abstruse, mystifying, confusing, bewildering, puzzling, perplexing, unresolved, unintelligible, problematic, complex, intricate, labyrinthine, difficult, knotty, cryptic, hidden, concealed, camouflaged, disguised, incognito, unknown, anonymous

VERBS

12 **keep secret**, conceal, hide, withhold, keep back, suppress, censor, seal, ban, restrict, classify, put a D-notice on, keep under wraps, keep close, keep (it) to oneself, keep under one's hat, play (it) close to one's chest, keep (it) dark, give nothing away, keep one's mouth shut, hold one's tongue, not breathe a word, keep mum, keep one's counsel, make no sign, neither confirm nor deny, make no comment, let (it) go no further, hush up, cover up, clam up (Inf), put (or keep) the lid on (Inf), black out (Inf)

▶ *531 Concealment*

13 **mystify**, puzzle, baffle, perplex, bewilder, confuse, deceive, keep (someone) in the dark, stump (Inf)

14 **make mysterious**, obscure, obfuscate, code, encode, cipher, encipher

ADVERBS

15 **in secret**, secretly, privately, behind closed doors, in camera, sub rosa, confidentially, in confidence, (just *or* strictly) between ourselves, *entre nous* (Fr), off the record, between you, me, and the gatepost, for your ears only, *sotto voce* (It), in a whisper, in an undertone, anonymously, incognito, with nobody (any) the wiser

16 **stealthily**, furtively, conspiratorially, in secrecy, like a thief in the night, under cloak of darkness, invisibly, behind one's back, by the back door, under the counter, huggermugger (Arch), in a hole-and-corner way (Inf), on the sly, on the quiet, on the q.t. (Inf)

530   Disclosure

NOUNS

1 **disclosure**, exposure, uncovering, unveiling, revelation, manifestation, epiphany, anagnorisis, discovery, diagnosis, denouement, resolution, explanation, showdown, catastrophe, apocalypse

▶ *496 Discovery*

2 **divulgence** (*or* **divulgement**), communication, broadcast, announcement, declaration, publication, full report, investigative journalism, exposé, betrayal, leak, hint, telltale sign, giveaway, state's evidence (US), queen's (*or* king's) evidence, tergiversation, admission, acknowledgment, avowal, affirmation, confession

3 **openness**, full details, no holds barred, plain

speaking, downrightness, candour, frankness, truth, honesty, unreservedness, outspokenness, indiscretion

▶ *537 Truth, 565 Talkativeness*

4 **discloser**, revealer, discoverer, researcher, exposer, investigator, investigative journalist, reporter, communicator, publicizer, broadcaster, announcer, source, informant, confessor, informer, betrayer, maieusis, telltale (Inf), blabberer (Inf), blabbermouth (Inf), whistleblower (Sl), squealer (Sl), peacher (Sl), grass (Sl), supergrass (Sl)

▶ *528 Information*

VERBS

5 **disclose**, reveal, expose, show, make known, bring to light, bring into the open, open the windows, discover, diagnose, take the lid off, let out, unleash, unkennel, hold up to view, take the wraps off, bare, lay bare, strip bare, denude, unfold, unroll, unfurl, unpack, unwrap, uncover, unshroud, unscreen, uncurtain, unveil, lift (*or* draw) the veil, raise the curtain, shine some light on, let in daylight, let some light in, unclose, unseal, break the seal, break the wax, open, lay open, open up, dig up, disinter, show up, manifest, uncloak, unmask, tear off the mask, go public, let slip, show for what it is, show oneself in one's true colours

6 **divulge**, declare, broadcast, announce, communicate, inform, educate, publicize, publish, break the news, break it to, give out, vent, give vent to, ventilate, air, speak out, come out with, tell all, let on, tell, talk, speak, utter, breathe, hint, confide, leak, let one in on, let drop, let fall, let out, open the books, set straight (*or* right), set the record straight, straighten the record, show one's hand, show one's cards, put one's cards on the table, talk straight, talk turkey (US Inf), blow the lid off (Sl), blow the gaff (Sl), let it all hang out (US sl)

7 **betray**, give away, tell on, inform on, accuse, name names, turn state's evidence (US), turn queen's (*or* king's) evidence, tergiversate, blurt out, talk out of turn, blab, tell tales out of school (Inf), let the cat out of the bag (Inf), spill the beans (Inf), give the game away (Inf), blow the whistle on (Inf), shoot off one's mouth (Sl), blow someone's cover (Sl), split (Sl), sing (US sl), sing like a canary (US sl), peach (Sl), squeal (Sl), grass (Sl), rat (on) (Sl)

8 **admit**, allow, acknowledge, concede, grant, assent, affirm, avow, own, confess, own up, plead guilty, come clean, make a clean breast of it, get it off one's chest, open one's heart to, unbosom oneself, unburden oneself, bare one's breast to

9 **be disclosed**, appear, stand revealed, emerge, transpire, come to light, become known, come

out, break, blow up, get out, leak out, become public knowledge, break forth, break through the clouds, show through, show its face, show its true colours, come as a revelation, come with a blinding flash, flash on the mind, dawn upon

ADJECTIVES

10 **disclosed**, revealed, shown, showing, visible, clear, obvious, transparent, open, laid bare, exposed, leaked, confessed, admitted, avowed, acknowledged, uncovered, unearthed, unmasked

11 **disclosing**, revealing, divulging, maieutic, open, candid, frank, downright, unreserved, outspoken, forthcoming, informative, communicative, talkative, garrulous, loquacious, indiscreet, imprudent, chatty, leaky

12 **revelatory**, expository, explicatory, explanatory, interpretive, apocalyptic, manifesting, epiphanic

ADVERBS

13 **openly**, unreservedly, in the open, with no holds barred, outright, freely, frankly, plainly, candidly, forthrightly, indiscreetly

531 Concealment

NOUNS

1 **concealment**, invisibility, disappearance, eclipse, occultation, hiding, secretion, reconditeness

2 **hiding place**, mother's skirt, foxhole, dugout, bolt hole, bomb shelter, refuge, shelter, sanctuary, asylum, safe house, hidden cave, nook, cranny, niche, hide-out, hideaway, cubbyhole, hidy-hole, cache, stash, closet, attic, cellar, doormat, mattress, secret compartment, secret panel, secret passage, fake book, hollow tree, safe, safe-deposit, bank vault

3 **covering up**, purdah, masking, screening, veiling, anonymity, disguise, mask, masked ball, *bal masqué* (Fr), costume party, camouflage, screen, smoke screen, ambush, trap

4 **silence**, reticence, taciturnity, reserve, closeness, discretion, confidentiality, privacy, suppression, censorship, clampdown, national security, classified information, D-notice, Official Secrets Act, Privy Councillor's oath
▶ *529 Secrecy*

5 **evasion**, evasiveness, equivocation, equivocality, equivocalness, prevarication, vagueness, obscurity, mystification, obfuscation, deception, misinformation, disinformation, lie, untruth, cover-up, Watergate, Irangate, Chernobyl, dishonesty, false evidence, perjury, deceitfulness, dissimulation, duplicity, trickery, subterfuge
▶ *539 Deception, 538 Untruth, 540 Falsehood*

6 **privacy**, seclusion, retreat, sanctum, monas-

tery, convent, nunnery, closed order, private garden, private club, lair, den, study, library, boudoir, bedroom, bath, toilet, desert island, lighthouse, mountaintop, ivory tower

7 **concealer**, hider, hermit, recluse, lone wolf, power behind the throne, *éminence grise* (Fr), undercover agent, face in the crowd, no name, X, code name, alias, stage name, pen name, pseudonym, nom de plume, masquerader, evader, Freemason, Klansman, mafioso, dissembler, deceiver, conspirator, boogerboo (US sl)
▶ *529 Secrecy*

VERBS

8 **conceal**, hide, hide away, secrete, bury, inter, confine, seclude, ensconce, stow away, lock up, seal up, wall up, bottle up, store, stash (away), sweep under the carpet (mat or rug), cover up, cover, wrap up, paper over, whitewash, varnish, gloss over, overlay, paint over, smother, stifle, suppress, censor, screen, cloak, shroud, curtain, blanket, veil, draw a veil over, keep under wraps, muffle, mask

9 **disguise**, camouflage, encode, obscure, eclipse, darken, fog, befog, cloud, becloud, muddle, obfuscate, dim, bedim, muddy the waters,

10 **deceive**, dissemble, masquerade, blindfold, mislead, confuse, pull the wool over someone's eyes, bamboozle (Inf)

11 **conceal oneself**, evade, shun, hide from, retreat into one's shell, keep (fade or stay) in the background, keep a low profile, stay out of the limelight, stay in the shadows, dodge, avoid, play hide-and-seek, steal away, slip by, slink, glide, creep, tiptoe, leave no address, cover one's tracks, lay a false scent (or trail), take cover, go to earth, go underground, lie low, hide out, be on the run, take to the hills, vanish, vanish into thin air, disappear, exit, skip town (US inf), hit the road (US inf), lie doggo (Inf), go on the lam (US sl)

12 **be silent**, keep one's mouth shut, hold one's tongue, look blank, look natural, keep a straight face, keep mum, shut up, act dumb (Inf), shut one's trap (or face) (Sl), zip (or button) one's lips (or mouth) (Sl), zip it (Sl)
▶ *422 Silence, 529 Secrecy*

13 **equivocate**, prevaricate, evade, hedge, fence, stonewall, beat about the bush (Inf)

ADJECTIVES

14 **concealed**, hidden, unseen, secluded, sequestered, reclusive, incommunicado, out-of-touch, private, screened, hooded, masked, recondite, veiled, covered, overprinted, eclipsed, obscured, blotted out, under wraps, smothered, stifled, suppressed, censored

15 **disguised**, distorted, camouflaged, unrecognized, unrecognizable, incognito, anonymous, cryptic, secret, covert, occult, latent,

coded, codified, cryptographic, unintelligible
16 **silent**, taciturn, reticent, reserved, aloof, unsociable, withdrawn
17 **noncommittal**, uncommunicative, uninformative, clamlike, tight-lipped, poker-faced, vague, evasive, close, discreet, secretive, cagey (Inf), buttoned-up (Sl)

ADVERBS
18 **privately**, in private, secretly, in secret, behind closed doors
▶ *529 Secrecy*

532 Publication

NOUNS
1 **publication**, publishing, dissemination, circulation, ventilation, divulgence (*or* divulgency), divulgation, disclosure, promulgation, broadcasting, public-address system, loudspeaker, Tannoy (Tm), loud hailer, bullhorn (US), spreading the word, spreading abroad, broadcast, announcement, declaration, proclamation, pronouncement, public notice, speech, statement, sermon, notification, official notice, report, communiqué, bulletin, manifesto, pronunciamento, edict, decree, encyclical, ukase, ban, unconfirmed report, rumour, hearsay, gossip, trial ballon
▶ *530 Disclosure, 564 Speech*
2 **mass media**, the media, communication, mass communication, telecommunication, television, radio, broadcasting, telecasting, cable television, narrowcasting, cablecasting, cable-vision (US), readership, audience, viewership, viewing figures, ratings, television ratings, A.C. Nielsen ratings (US), BARB (Broadcasters' Audience Research Board) ratings, radio audience measurement, BBC's BRD (Broadcasting Research Department) Daily Survey of Listening, audience survey
▶ *534 Communications*
3 **journalism**, the press, fourth estate, newspaper world, Fleet Street, Street of Shame (Inf), serious press, tabloid press, popular press, gutter press, yellow press, underground press, reporting, rapportage, newspapering (US), coverage, report, notice, write-up, broadsheet, scoop, editorial comment, editorial, leader, leading article, gossip column, advice column, agony column (Inf), personal column, personals (Inf), public comment, correspondence column, open letter, letters to the editor, headline, banner headline, streamer, screamer (US sl)
▶ *533 News*
4 **newspaper**, paper, international paper, national paper, provincial paper, local paper, freesheet, giveaway, morning paper, evening paper, weekly paper, Sunday paper, daily paper, daily, quality daily, broadsheet, the

heavies (Inf), tabloid, sheet, rag (Inf), edition, early edition, late edition, stop-press edition, extra edition, extra, late extra, special edition, sports edition, magazine section, supplement, colour supplement, feuilleton, trade supplement
5 **journal**, periodical, review, gazette, magazine, glossy magazine, picture magazine, newsmagazine, women's magazine, men's magazine, business magazine, comic magazine, comic, comic strip, in-flight magazine, literary magazine, pulp magazine, serial, series, part work, daily, weekly, biweekly, fortnightly, semimonthly, monthly, quarterly, seasonal, annual, specialist publication, organ, academic journal, professional journal, technical journal, trade journal, trade paper, trade organ, house magazine, in-house magazine, house organ, newsletter, newssheet, pamphlet
6 **book publishing**, publishing, book trade, bookselling, bookshop, library, Public Lending Right (PLR), book club, book, hardback, paperback, coffee-table book, textbook, trade book, reference book, dictionary, thesaurus, guidebook, cookbook, cookery book, sports book, children's book, novel, best-seller, romantic novel, Mills & Boon, bodice ripper, thriller, general fiction, adult fiction, juvenile fiction, pulp fiction, book serialization, book review, book fair, Frankfurt Book Fair, promotion tour, Pulitzer Prize (US), Booker Prize
▶ *528 Information*
7 **publicity**, limelight, spotlight, coverage, public recognition, public eye, fame, famousness, renown, blaze of publicity, the talk of the town, the flavour of the month, the cover of *Time*, notoriety, infamy, common knowledge, public knowledge, openness, manifestation, publicness, currency, wide currency, wide circulation, nationwide circulation, countrywide circulation, public discussion, conference, public forum, town-hall meeting, pulpit, platform, soapbox, rostrum, hustings, ballyhoo (Inf)
8 **public relations** (PR), press office, press conference, news conference, press release, press announcement, propaganda, media event, staged event, exhibition, media blitz, photocall, photo-opportunity, display, name in (bright) lights, letters a foot high, letters of fire (*or* gold), top billing, showmanship, P. T. Barnum, medicine show (US), window dressing, ostentation, sensationalism, exaggeration, puff, three-ring circus, The Greatest Show on Earth, promo (Inf), flackery (US sl), hype (Sl), media hype (Sl)
9 **advertisement**, notice, announcement, commercial, trailer, poster, flier (US), *affiche* (Fr), insertion, insert, leaflet, pamphlet, flyer,

blad, brochure, blurb, circular, hand out, handbill, bill, billboard, hoarding, placard, banner, sandwich board, display board, notice board, classified advertisement, commercial listing, Yellow Pages, advertorial, advert (Inf), ad (Inf), small ad (Inf), classified ad (Inf), want ad (Inf), plug (Inf), teaser (Inf), puff job (Inf), puff piece (Inf)

10 **publicizer**, publicist, promoter, propagandist, publicity agent, press agent, image-maker, advertiser, advertising agent, advertising account executive, hidden persuader, copywriter, blurb writer, public relations officer (PRO), PR man, PR woman, PR person, notifier, announcer, messenger, proclaimer, crier, herald, barker, spieler, tout, pamphleteer, bill poster, bill sticker, sandwichman, spin doctor (Inf), flack (US sl), shill (US sl)

11 **newspaperman**, newsman, newspaperwoman, newswoman, newspaper proprietor, press baron, journalist, reporter, news reporter, correspondent, special correspondent, foreign correspondent, war correspondent, investigative journalist, chequebook journalist, editorial writer, leader writer, columnist, gossip columnist, agony aunt, freelancer, stringer, press photographer, critic, editor, news editor, city editor, features editor, sports editor, copy editor, subeditor, hack (Sl)

12 **publisher**, book publisher, university press, bookperson, author, writer, novelist, ghostwriter, literary agent, agent, editor, managing editor, editor-in-chief, copy editor, manuscript editor, desk editor, fiction editor, reference editor, proofreader, printer, typesetter, compositor, comp (Inf), bookbinder, bookseller, librarian

VERBS

13 **make public**, bring to public notice, bring into the open, tell the world, inform, go public, let it be known, make known, divulge, reveal, disclose, expose, ventilate, air, communicate, broadcast, transmit, relay, telecast, televise, radio, narrowcast, cablecast (US), disseminate, diffuse, propagate, get out, put out, give out, promulgate, release, circulate, spread, spread the word, spread abroad, put about, rumour, spread a rumour, fly a kite, launch a trial balloon, bruit (about), bruit abroad, noise abroad, bring up, mention, talk about, gossip, retail, pass round, bandy about, hawk about, buzz about

14 **proclaim**, publish, announce, notify, pronounce, declare, declaim, herald, trumpet, blast, blazon, blaze, blaze abroad, cry, shout, scream, thunder, shout from the rooftops, beat the big drum, announce with a flourish of trumpets, raise a hue and cry, raise the roof, raise hell, come on like gangbusters (US), pitch a bitch (US sl)

15 **publish**, prepare for publication, report, cover, write, write up, serialize, syndicate, edit, copy-edit, subedit, sub(Inf), typeset, set, print, put to bed, go to press, issue a publication, issue, bring out, break a story, scoop, put out, distribute, circularize

16 **publicize**, advertise, advertise for, request, place (*or* insert) an advertisement, bill, post bills, placard, pamphleteer, propagandize, promote, build up, boost, sell, push, feature, highlight, spotlight, pinpoint, emphasize, headline, put in headlines, splash, blitz the media, make famous, put on the map, make one's name (known), make someone, make a cynosure of, make much of, extol, glorify, rave about, overrate, puff, tout, plug (Inf), ballyhoo (Inf), hype (up) (Sl), shill (US sl)

17 **be published**, become public knowledge, come out, see oneself in print, get in print, circulate, spread, pass round, go the rounds, get around (*or* about), spread abroad, spread like wildfire, fly about, buzz about

18 **become famous**, be in the news, get into the papers, hit the headlines, make the front page, make it to the top, become known from coast to coast (US) be sold, have a circulation, sell well, sell like hotcakes (Inf)

ADJECTIVES

19 **published**, in print, printed, in circulation, circulating, in the air, current, in the news, in the open, open, public, made public, revealed, disclosed, exposed, announced, declared, proclaimed, ventilated, aired, communicated, disseminated, distributed, circularized, spread around (*or* about), broadcast, on the air, televised

20 **well-known**, widely known, on everyone's lips, in the headlines, in the public eye, celebrated, renowned, famed, famous, popular, infamous, notorious, crying, flagrant, blatant, glaring, sensational, manifest

21 **publishing**, declaratory, notificatory

ADVERBS

22 **publicly**, openly, blatantly, (out) in the open, out front, in open court, with open doors, in full view, on stage, in the public eye, for all to see, in the limelight

533 News

NOUNS

1 **news**, breaking news, hard news, straight news, facts, information, intelligence, current affairs, journalism, print journalism, electronic journalism, Fourth Estate, public relations (PR)

▶ *532 Publication, 534 Communications*

2 **news event**, news happening, news account, eyewitness account, press conference, news conference

3 **reporting**, news reporting, reportage, news gathering, coverage, live coverage, newscasting, sportscasting, newspapering, investigative reporting, in-depth reporting, political reporting, parliamentary reporting, interpretive reporting, analytical journalism, objective reporting, scoop, exclusive, spoiler, leg-work (Inf), muckraking (Inf), doorstopping (Inf), knee-jerk journalism (Inf)

4 **journalist**, broadcast journalist, news reporter, reporter, cub reporter, newspaperman (*or* -woman), newsman (*or* -woman), newshound, journo (Aus sl), newscaster, news staff, news crew, news pool, news photographer, news cameraman (*or* -woman), news camera crew, sports reporter, sportscaster, fashion reporter, free-lance reporter, free-lance writer, correspondent, foreign correspondent, lobby correspondent, columnist, gossip columnist, critic, chequebook journalism, hack, scandalmonger, muckraker, leader writer, editor, gatekeeper (US), managing editor, subeditor, foreign editor, sports editor, anchorman (*or* -woman), newsreader, news commentator, news bureau chief, press secretary, press officer, press agent, public relations practitioner, spokesman (*or* -woman)

5 **mass communication**, mass media, news organization, news outlet, news media, print media, electronic media, press, quality press, tabloid press, popular press, yellow press, gutter press, newspaper, broadsheet, heavy, scandal sheet, popular newspaper, national newspaper, provincial newspaper, local newspaper, Sunday newspaper, weekly newspaper, special edition, special issue, extra, newsmagazine, colour supplement

6 **radio news**, television news, newscast, sportscast, evening news, 6 o'clock news, 10 o'clock news, documentary, newsreel

7 **press agency**, news agency, news service, wire service, syndicate, Reuters, Press Association, Associated Press, United Press International, Agence France Presse

8 **newsroom**, press room, news desk, sports desk, press office, copy desk

9 **news story**, news article, news item, news report, news review, running story, feature story, feature article, editorial, leader, column, opinion column, gossip column, humour column, news programme, latest news, news update, news brief, news flash, news bulletin, scoop, exclusive, extra, news dispatch, news release, press release, press notice, hand out, hard news, straight news, fresh news, breaking news, hot news (Inf), feature news, news analysis, news style, media hype, journalese (Inf), Timese (US inf)

10 **copy**, feature copy, time copy (US), evergreen copy (US), subbed copy, take

11 **news source**, newsstand, newsdealer (US), news stall, newsagent, news vendor, newsboy (*or* -girl), newsie (US), newsletter, newssheet, newsprint, news beat

12 **headline**, head, by-line, banner head, masthead, flag

VERBS

13 **report**, broadcast, transmit, document, cover, disclose, break, issue, dispatch, scoop, publish, publicize, circulate, interview, write, freelance, edit, subedit, sub (Brit inf), syndicate

ADJECTIVES

14 **journalistic**, reportorial, reportable, editorial, newsworthy, newsy, full of news, informative, reported, going the rounds, hot off the press

ADVERBS

15 **journalistically**, reportorially, reportedly, editorially, informatively, as reported, as stated

534   Communications

NOUNS

1 **communications**, means of communication, speech, talking, writing, correspondence, long-distance communication, electronic communication, telecommunications, signalling, radio communication, broadcasting, mass communication, communications medium, mass media, radio, television, the press

▶ *564 Speech, 532 Publication, 533 News, 528 Information*

2 **postal communication**, postal service, Post Office, US Postal Service, GPO (General Post Office), Postal Union, post office, sorting office, dead-letter office, returned-letter office, Royal Mail, letter post, domestic mail (US), inland post, international mail, overseas mail, air mail, Swiftair, surface mail, express mail (US), priority mail (US), special handling (US), special delivery, Data Post, first-class mail, second-class mail, third-class mail (US), sea mail, parcel post, Parcel Force (Tm), fourth-class mail (US), COD, collect on delivery (US), cash on delivery, Freepost (Tm), registered mail, recorded delivery, return receipt (US), express delivery, Red Star delivery, insured mail (US), metered mail, forwarded mail, general delivery (US), poste restante, Pony Express

3 **correspondence**, mail, post, letter, air-mail letter, air letter, aerogram, registered letter, dead letter, postcard, postal card (US), money order (US), postal order, packet, parcel, envelope, name and address, address, zip code (US), postcode, stamp, postage stamp, air-mail stamp, first-class stamp, second-class stamp, mailbox (US), pillarbox, postbox, letterbox, post-office box, private box, pigeonhole, pi-

geon box, mailbag, mailsack, mail pouch (US), postbag, diplomatic bag, dispatch box, postage (*or* postal) meter (US), franking machine, postmark

4 **postal worker**, postmaster general, postmaster, postmistress, mailman (US), mailwoman (US), mail carrier (US), letter carrier, postman, postwoman, sorter, special-delivery messenger, messenger, courier, Queen's Messenger

5 **correspondent**, letter writer, pen friend, pen pal (Inf)

6 **telecommunication**, transmission, propagation, two-way communication, one-way communication, telephony, radiotelephony, computer networking, telegraphy, radiotelegraphy, teleinformatics, communications technology, communications engineering, radio engineering, telephone engineering, communications system, network, communications network, communications channel, communications link, telecottage, communications line, transmission line, cable, coaxial cable (*or* coax), multiwire cable, fibre cable, fibre-optic cable

7 **satellite communication**, communications satellite, geostationary satellite, Comsat (Tm), Telstar (Tm), Astra (Tm), Marcopole (Tm), Intelsat (Tm), Eutelsat (Tm)

8 **data transmission**, text transmission, telegraph, radiotelegraph, Morse code, dot, dash, dit, dah, heliograph, telegram, overseas telegram, cablegram, cable, wire, Telemessage (Tm), telex, telex machine, teleprinter, teletypewriter (US), Teletex (Tm), facsimile transmission, fax, fax machine, fax number, electronic mail, email (*or* e-mail), electronic office

9 **telephone**, phone, telephone set, handset, receiver, earpiece, mouthpiece, microphone, headset, headphones, extension, intercom, answering machine, pushbutton telephone, dial telephone, cordless telephone, mobile telephone, car telephone, radiotelephone, radiophone, ship-to-shore telephone, videophone, cellular phone, cellphone, Cellnet (Tm), Vodaphone (Tm), public telephone, pay station (US), payphone, cardphone, phonecard, Mercurycard (Tm), telephone box, telephone booth, call box, telephone kiosk, blower (Inf), dog and bone (Sl)

10 **telephone call**, phone call, call, local call, long-distance call, toll call, overseas call, reverse-charge call, collect call (US), personal call, person-to-person call (US), nuisance call, diverted call, hunging, waiting, conference call, Freefone call, buzz (Inf), tinkle (Inf), bell (Sl)

11 **dialling**, direct distance dialing (DDD) (US), direct dialling, international direct dialling (IDD), subscriber trunk dialling (STD), telephone number, phone number, dialling code, area code (US), local code, national code, international code, dial tone (US), dialling tone, tone, ring tone, busy signal (US), engaged tone, telephone book, phone book, telephone directory, Yellow Pages

12 **public telephone system**, public telephone (*or* network), telephoneline, subscriber line, party line, trunk line, hot line, chat line, telephone wire, telephone pole, telegraph pole, telephone exchange, exchange, local exchange, tandem exchange, trunk exchange, automatic exchange, crossbar exchange, private exchange (PX), private branch exchange (PBX), private automatic branch exchange (PABX), private manual branch exchange (PMBX), switchboard

13 **telephoner**, subscriber, caller, phoner, telephone operator, switchboard operator, operator, telephonist, telephone mechanic (US), telephone engineer, linesman

14 **radio transmission**, radio wave, long wave (LW), short wave (SW), medium wave (MW), radio spectrum, microwaves, radio frequency (RF), frequency band, waveband, band, bandwidth, frequency allocation, radio beam, radio signal, pulsed signal, radio link, microwave link, radio channel, modulation, carrier, modulated carrier, demodulation, modulator, demodulator, carrier transmission, frequency modulation (FM), amplitude modulation (AM), phase modulation (PM), sideband, single sideband transmission, pulse code modulation (PCM), multiplex transmission, frequency-division multiplex (FDM), time-division multiplex (TDM)

15 **transmitted wave**, line-of-sight transmission, direct wave, ground wave, ground-reflected wave, ionosphere, F-layer (*or* F-region), E-layer (*or* E-region), D-layer (*or* D-region), ionospheric reflection, ionospheric wave, indirect wave, sky wave, space wave, ionospheric disturbance, ionospheric storm

16 **transmitter**, radio transmitter, FM (frequency-modulated) transmitter, LW (long-wave) transmitter, AM (amplitude-modulated) transmitter, MW (medium-wave) transmitter, UHF (ultra-high-frequency) transmitter, SHF (superhigh-frequency) transmitter, VHF (very high-frequency) transmitter, radio microphone, radio phone, mobile phone, car phone, cellular phone, short-wave radio, Citizens' Band (CB)

Radio-frequency Bands

EHF extremely high frequency
SHF superhigh frequency
UHF ultrahigh frequency
HF high frequency
MF medium frequency
LF low frequency
VF very low frequency

17 **antenna**, aerial, transmitting antenna, receiving antenna, directional antenna, dipole antenna, dipole, folded dipole, Yagi antenna, loop (or frame) antenna, whip antenna, longwire antenna, dish antenna, dish, horn antenna, omnidirectional antenna, radiator, director, reflector

18 **radio**, radio receiver, receiver, tuned radio-frequency (TRF) receiver, superhet receiver, amplifier, booster, intermediate-frequency (IF) amplifier, audiofrequency (AF) amplifier, loudspeaker, speaker, tuner, tuning, preset tuning, volume control, tone control, wireless, radio set, crystal set, cat's whisker, clock radio, car radio, VHF radio, mobile radio, walkie-talkie, radiopager, pager, bleep (or bleeper), portable radio, battery radio, transistor radio, trannie (Inf), Walkman (Tm), personal stereo, ghetto blaster (Inf), boom box (US inf)

19 **radio reception**, reception, fading (or fade), drift, creeping, crawling, distortion, interference, noise, atmospherics, static, white noise, crosstalk, him, hiss

20 **radio broadcasting**, broadcasting authority, broadcasting station, BBC (British Broadcasting Corporation), Beeb (Inf), Auntie (Inf), BBC Radio, Radio 1, Radio 2, Radio 3, Radio 4, Radio 5, BBC World Service, National Public Radio (NPR) (US), local radio, college radio, commercial radio, satellite radio (US), pirate radio, Citizen's Band radio, CB radio, amateur radio, radio station, relay station, booster station, radio mast, radio tower, mobile radio station, mobile unit, radio car, radio-mobile, station identification, call sign, call letters (US)

21 **television** (TV), black-and-white television, monochrome television, colour television, small screen, high-definition television (HDTV), broadcast television, closed-circuit television (CCTV), cable television, pay (or subscription) television, satellite television, television camera, telecamera, mobile camera, television tube (or picture tube), cathode-ray tube, tube, video signal, audio signal, sequential scanning, interlaced scanning, line, field, frame, lines per frame, frame frequency, field frequency

22 **television set**, receiver, screen, controls, volume, brightness, colour, contrast, preset tuning, remote control, colour television, black-and-white television, portable television, TV, small screen, telly (Inf), the box (Inf), idiot box (Inf), boob tube (US inf)

23 **television reception**, reception, picture quality (or picture), video, sound quality (or sound), test card, grainy picture, snowy picture, snow, vertical roll, fipples, interference, noise, distortion, picture clarity, definition, high definition

24 **television broadcasting**, broadcasting authority, BBC Television, independent television, commercial television, Independent Broadcasting Authority (IBA), Independent Television Authority (ITA), Independent Television Commission (ITC), FOX (US), broadcasting station, television channel, BBC1, BBC2, ITV (Independent Television), Channel 4 (C4), Federal Communications Commission (FCC) (US), network television (US), ABC (American Broadcasting), CBS (Columbia Broadcasting System), NBC (National Broadcasting Corporation), public broadcasting (US), PBS (Public Broadcasting Service) (US), local television, cable television, satellite television, Sky, CNN (Cable News Network) (US), television station, relay station, booster station, television mast, television tower, mobile station, TV mobile

25 **broadcast material**, transmission, telecast, simulcast, on-site broadcast (US), outside broadcast (OB), relay, live relay, recording, repeat, rerun, transcription, programme, prime-time programme, syndicated programme (US), audience participation, phone-in, telethon, quiz show, game show, chat show, talk show, variety show, series, miniseries, serial, costume drama, saga, docudrama, faction, soap opera, soap, situation comedy, sitcom (Inf), news, news summary, news roundup, news documentary, news report, live coverage, commercial break, commercial, station break (US), public service announcement (PSA) (US), Teletext (Tm), viewdata, Ceefax (Tm), Oracle (Tm), Prestel (Tm), Skytext (Tm), Viewtron (Tm), CableText (Tm), Antiope (Tm), educational broadcasting, Open University, religious broadcasting, Christian Broadcasting Network (US)

26 **recording**, tape recording, tape recorder, tapedeck cassette, audio cassette, tape, video

recording, video, video cassette, video cassette recorder (VCR), video tape, video game, TV game, video nasty, videodisc, video camera, camcorder

27 **signalling**, signal, semaphore, flag signals, Morse code, railway signals, smoke signals, radio signalling, radio control, radio navigation, radiobeacon, navigational beacon, radio marker, radio direction-finding (RDF), radio compass, radiogoniometer, radio bearing, radio astronomy

28 **radar**, pulse (or pulsed) radar, continuous-wave (CW) radar, primary radar, secondary radar, MTI (moving-target indication, phrased-array radar, radar station, radar beacon, radar transponder beacon, racon, radar antenna, radar dish, transmit-receive (TR) switch, anti-transmit-receive (ATR) switch, fixed array, radar beam, target, return signal, echo, radar screen, radar indicator, plan-position indicator (PPI), radarscope, display, scan, military radar, weather radar, radar navigation, radar guidance, radar tracking, radar surveillance, radar astronomy

29 **broadcaster**, telegrapher, telegraphist, radio operator, amateur radio operator, radio ham (Inf), radio broadcaster, television broadcaster, announcer, commentator, talking head, newscaster, anchorman, anchorwoman, newsreader, presenter, newsman, newswoman, informant, master of ceremonies (MC), emcee (US), host, compere, question master, disc jockey (DJ), deejay, televangelist (US), media personality

VERBS

30 **communicate**, communicate with, be in touch, get in touch, make contact, speak (to), talk (to), write (to), signal, transmit, link up, relay, propagate, amplify, modulate, demodulate, radio, page, bleep, broadcast, announce, inform, televise, telecast, repeat, rerun, advertise, receive, tune in, listen in, watch, record, tape-record, tape, video

▶ *564 Speech, 532 Publication, 533 News, 528 Information*

31 **correspond**, correspond with, exchange letters, write (to), send a letter to, drop a line to, reply (to), answer, acknowledge, address, stamp, frank, mail, post, airmail, send, send on, forward, dispatch, sort, deliver, send a telegram (to), telegraph, cable, wire, telex, fax

▶ *326 Transfer*

32 **telephone**, phone, call (up), ring (up), make a (phone) call, give someone a call (or ring), give someone a buzz (Inf), give someone a tinkle (Inf), give someone a bell (Sl), hang up, ring off

ADJECTIVES

33 **communicational**, communicating, transmissional, oral, verbal, epistolary (or epistola-

tory), postal, relecommunicational, telephonic, telegraphic

▶ *564 Speech, 48 Literature*

34 **communicated**, spoken, written, signalled, posted, post-paid, registered, sent, transmitted, relayed, propagated, amplified, modulated, demodulated, broadcast, announced, advertised, radioed, televised, repeated, received, read, seen, heard, transcribed, recorded, taped, videoed

▶ *532 Publication*

35 **communicable**, transmittable, transmissible

▶ *326 Transfer*

535 Affirmation

NOUNS

1 **affirmation**, affirmance, assertion, attestation, declaration, averment, asseveration, allegation, swearing, vouching, certification, vouch (Arch)

▶ *530 Disclosure, 490 Certainty*

2 **statement**, pronouncement, profession, utterance, word, say, saying, dictum, *ipse dixit* (L), proposition, maxim, positive declaration, proclamation, enunciation, annunciation, announcement, press announcement, public relations release, position, position paper, stand, stance, manifesto, creed, submission, prepared text, thesis, supposition, predication, conclusion, say-so (Inf)

▶ *505 Maxim, 518 Supposition, 492 Judgment*

3 **vow**, oath, word, pledge, promise, guarantee, solemn word, solemn oath, sworn statement, statement under (or on) oath, deposition, affidavit, sworn testimony, solemn affirmation, declaration of truth, assurance, commitment, word of honour, word of a gentleman, swearing in, charging, adjuration, swearing on the Bible, Bible oath, judicial oath, oath of office, official oath, oath of allegiance, loyalty oath, test (Arch)

▶ *483 Evidence, 714 Promise*

4 **confirmation**, corroboration, substantiation, ratification, authentication, proof, establishment, assurance, endorsement, second, support, supportive statement, written statement, backing, backing-up, attestation, validation, verification, certification, fortification, reinforcement, lack of retraction, buttressing

5 **admission**, avowal, avouchment, disclosure, deposition, confession

6 **assertiveness**, forcefulness, self-assertion, assurance, decisiveness, incisiveness, pointedness, explicitness, expressness, outspokenness, bluntness, plainness, strong words, thrust, drive, push, pushiness, insistence, peremptoriness, vehemence, vigorousness, vig-

our, positiveness, chutzpah (US), zip (Inf), go (Inf), get-up-and-go (Inf), oomph (Inf)
▶ *239 Vigour*

7 **emphasis**, stress, stressed point, overstatement
▶ *554 Emphasis*

8 **definiteness**, absoluteness, categoricalness, unequivocalness, certainty, unquestionability, unquestionableness, undisputedness, indubitability, indubitableness
▶ *713 Protest, 668 Defiance, 856 Accusation*

9 **affirmer**, affirmant, asserter (*or* assertor), witness, eyewitness, testifier, attestant, declarer, professor, proclaimer, enunciator, announcer, public relations man (*or* woman), submitter, voucher, vower, discloser, confessor, pledger, swearer, oath-taker, oath administrator, guarantor, authenticator, backer, corroborator, certifier, verifier, ratifier, advocate, assurer, supporter, sponsor, endorser, seconder, promoter, patron, ally, helpmate, tower of strength, champion, fortifier, pusher, insister

ADJECTIVES

10 **affirmative**, affirming, affirmatory, assertive, assertory, supportive, declarative, declaratory, proclamatory, annunciative, annunciatory, enunciative, enunciatory, validatory, creedal, suppositional, predicative, predicational, propositional, conclusive

11 **stated**, declared, asserted, pronounced, professed, uttered, proclaimed, affirmed, attested, alleged, averred, asseverated, enunciated, annunciated, announced, released, read, submitted, admitted, confessed, avowed, avouched, disclosed

12 **vowed**, pledged, promised, assured, guaranteed, committed, vouched, vouched for, sworn, sworn to, on oath, depositional, true, veridical

13 **supported**, confirmed, corroborated, substantiated, ratified, authenticated, attested, validated, verified, certified, established, assured, unretracted, unretractable, endorsed, supported, backed, reinforced, fortified, buttressed

14 **assertive**, self-assertive, assertory, assured, confident, forceful, decisive, decided, incisive, pointed, explicit, express, outspoken, blunt, plain, strongly worded, thrustful, driven, insistent, dogmatic, peremptory, pontifical, ex cathedra, vehement, emphatic, vigorous, positive, not negative, brooking no denial, straight from the shoulder, pushy (Inf)

15 **emphasized**, stressed, strongly worded, pointed, underlined, underscored, overstated, exaggerated

16 **definite**, absolute, categorical, unequivocal, unquestionable, undisputed, indisputable, indubitable

VERBS

17 **affirm**, assert, attest, declare, state, make a statement, pronounce, aver, asseverate, profess, utter, give the word, propose, declare positively, proclaim, enunciate, annunciate, announce, make a press announcement, issue a public relations release, say, speak, give voice to, have one's say, release a paper, issue a manifesto, issue a press release, live by a creed, submit, put forward, write a thesis, set down, predicate, conclude, certify, allege, swear, vouch

18 **vow**, swear (to), swear an oath, swear on oath, state under (*or* on) oath, give one's (solemn) word, give one's (solemn) oath, pledge, promise, guarantee, commit oneself, vouch for, administer an oath, place (*or* put) under oath, swear in, charge, adjure, give a sworn statement, make a deposition, sign an affidavit, give sworn testimony, testify, bear witness, declare as true, assure, commit, give one's word of honour, give one's word as a gentleman, take the oath of office, swear an oath of allegiance, swear on the Bible, kiss the book, swear to God, swear by all that is holy, cross one's heart (and hope to die)

19 **confirm**, corroborate, substantiate, ratify, authenticate, prove, establish, assure, endorse, second, support, issue a supportive statement, back, back up, attest, validate, verify, certify, fortify, reinforce, fail to retract, buttress, stick to one's guns (Inf)

20 **admit**, avow, avouch, disclose, depose, confess, own up

21 **be assertive**, assert, assure, act forcefully, act decisively, speak ex cathedra, speak out (*or* up), have one's say, say so, have the last word, use strong words, put it bluntly, thrust, drive, push, insist, brook no denial, get on one's soapbox, hold the floor, lay down the law, make no bones about

22 **emphasize**, stress, stress a point, overstate, mean what one says, be definite, not equivocate, not question, not dispute

ADVERBS

23 **affirmatively**, positively, absolutely, definitely, categorically, assertively, allegedly, avowedly, undoubtedly, unequivocally, unquestionably, indisputably, indubitably, conclusively, authentically, assuredly, emphatically, with emphasis, without fear of contradiction

24 **truthfully**, truly, assuredly, decidedly, seriously, in all seriousness, in earnest, in all conscience, upon one's word, upon one's honour, in sworn testimony, on the Bible, under (*or* on) oath

25 **explicitly**, bluntly, insistently, plainly, dogmatically, ex cathedra, vehemently, pointedly, vigorously, provocatively, defiantly, critically

26 as God is my witness!, honest to God!, on my word of honour!, as I stand here!, cross my heart and hope to die!, scout's honour!, on my mother's life!

536 Negation

NOUNS

1 negation, abnegation, negative, negativism, negativeness, negativity, negative attitude, pessimism, defeatism, despondence, despondency, noncorroboration, no, nay, naysaying (Arch), nix (US sl)
▶ *776 Hopelessness*

2 rejection, refusal, denial, disavowal, disallowance, prohibition, invalidation, disclaimer, nonacceptance, declining, refusal of consent, veto, refusal of belief, nonbelief, disbelief, atheism, unbelief, agnosticism, apostasy, nonobservance, disobedience, recusance, recusancy, disownment, repudiation, renunciation, disclamation, dissociation, disassociation, nonassociation
▶ *581 Rejection, 693 Disobedience, 720 Nonobservance, 498 Disbelief, 711 Refusal*

3 rebuttal, refutation, rejoinder, retortion, retort, challenge, objection, demurral, demur, defiance, obstruction, deprecation, dissent, doubtfulness, questioning, protest, denial, flat denial, emphatic denial, contradiction, flat contradiction, contravention, contrary assertion, disagreement, impugnation, disaffirmation, antithesis, reverse, opposite, contrary, contrariness, countering, contesting, taking issue with, disproving, crossing, disproof, appeal, cross-appeal, gainsaying (Arch)
▶ *500 Dissent, 713 Protest, 668 Defiance, 111 Oppositeness*

4 renunciation, abrogation, recantation, repudiation, abjuration, forswearing, swearing-off, relinquishment, revocation, repeal, rescindment, retraction, retractation, cancellation, nullification, annulment, countermand, invalidation
▶ *598 Relinquishment, 704 Cancellation, 578 Equivocation*

5 nonexistence, nothingness, nothing, nullity, nonentity, void, vacuity, vacuum, emptiness
▶ *100 Nonexistence*

6 negativist, pessimist, refuser, vetoer, atheist, agnostic, apostate, rebutter, challenger, protestant, objector, dissenter, protester, recanter, repealer, retractor, nonentity, gainsayer (Arch)

VERBS

7 be negative, be pessimistic, negate, abnegate, not corroborate, shake one's head, say no, reject, refuse, refuse to accept, not accept, deny, not admit, disavow, disallow, prohibit, make impossible, invalidate, decline, refuse consent, veto, not believe, disbelieve, practise atheism, be agnostic, not observe, disobey, disown, repudiate, renunciate, disclaim, dissociate oneself, disassociate oneself, not associate, naysay (Arch)

8 rebut, refute, rejoin, retort, challenge, object, demur, defy, obstruct, deprecate, stand up to, dissent, doubt, express doubts, question, call into question, refuse credence, protest, deny, deny the possibility, issue a flat denial, emphatically deny, contradict, issue a flat contradiction, controvert, contravene, disagree, impugn, disaffirm, reverse, be opposite, affirm the contrary, counter, contest, take issue with, disprove, cross, appeal, cross-appeal, belie, give the lie to, gainsay (Arch)

9 renounce, abrogate, recant, repudiate, abjure, forswear, swear off, relinquish, revoke, repeal, rescind, retract, cancel, nullify, annul, countermand, invalidate, apostatize, tergiversate, take back, go back on one's word, change one's mind, do a U-turn, make a 180-degree turn, do a turn-around, eat one's words (Inf), eat one's hat (Inf)

10 be nothing, have no existence, not exist, not be, be null and void

ADJECTIVES

11 negative, pessimistic, defeatist, despondent, abnegative, atheistic, agnostic, recusant, doubtful, protestant, defiant, contrary, obstructive, contradictive, contradictory, repudiative, renunciative, renunciatory, abrogative, revocatory, abjuratory, deprecative, dissociative, disassociative, nonassociative

12 rejected, refused, denied, refuted, rebutted, disobeyed, disavowed, disallowed, prohibited, obstructed, contravened, invalidated, nonaccepted, declined, vetoed, disbelieved, nonobserved, disowned, disclaimed, relinquished, renounced, negated, deprecated, repudiated, repealed, rescinded, retracted, reversed, recanted, cancelled, nullified, annulled, countermanded, challenged, questioned, contested, disproved, crossed, appealed, cross-appealed, nixed (US sl)

13 rebutting, refuting, rejecting, prohibiting, refusing, denying, forswearing, rejoining, retorting, objecting, opposing, obstructing, deprecating, dissenting, doubting, questioning, challenging, contradicting, countering, disagreeing, impugning, disaffirming, gainsaying (Arch)

14 nonexistent, unexisting, null and void, vacant, vacuous, empty

ADVERBS

15 negatively, in the negative, not at all, (in) no way, pessimistically, despondently, atheistically, doubtfully, deniably, in denial, defiantly, contrarily, in contradiction, contradic-

torily, prohibitively, obstructively, invalidly, in opposition, opposingly, deprecatively, dissentingly, questionably, challengingly

INTERJECTIONS

16 **no!**, nay!, *non!* (Fr), *nein!* (Ger), *nyet!* (Russian), certainly not!, absolutely not!, I think not!, not so!, not really!, not likely!, not if I can help it!, not for the world!, not for the love of money!, not for the life of me!, not at all!, noway!, in no case!, a thousand times no!, to the contrary!, *au contraire!* (Fr), quite the contrary!, far from it!, nothing of the kind!, nothing of the sort!, nothing doing! (Inf), nope! (Inf), nix! (US sl)

17 **never!**, anything but!, out of the question!, you must be joking!, God forbid!, forget it!, not by a long shot! (Inf), not by a long chalk! (Inf), no sirree! (US inf), fat chance! (Inf), over my dead body! (Inf)

537 Truth

The truth that makes men free is for the most part the truth which men prefer not to hear. Herbert Sebastian Agar.

Truth sits upon the lips of dying men. Matthew Arnold.

And ye shall know the truth, and the truth shall make you free. Bible: John.

'Tis strange – but true; for truth is always strange;/ Stranger than fiction: if it could be told,/ How much would novels gain by the exchange! Lord Byron.

It is an old maxim of mine that when you have excluded the impossible, whatever remains, however improbable, must be the truth. Arthur Conan Doyle.

Ethical axioms are found and tested not very differently from the axioms of science. Truth is what stands the test of experience. Albert Einstein.

'Beauty is truth, truth beauty,' – that is all/ Ye know on earth, and all ye need to know. John Keats.

It is one thing to show a man that he is in an error, and another to put him in possession of truth. John Locke.

It is hard to believe that a man is telling the truth when you know that you would lie if you were in his place. Henry Louis Mencken.

It takes two to speak the truth – one to speak, and another to hear. Henry David Thoreau.

I believe that in the end the truth will conquer. John Wycliffe.

NOUNS

1 **truth**, trueness, fact, verity, eternal verities, rightness, unerroneousness, unmistakenness, unfalseness, unfallaciousness, unspeciousness, unspuriousness, unfictitiousness, (good) sooth (Arch), dinkum oil (Aus and NZ inf)

2 **reality**, actuality, existence, substance, substantiality, tangibility, the real world, things as they are

▶ *101 Reality, 99 Existence*

3 **the truth**, the facts, facts of the matter, facts of life, facts, the case, the plain truth, the simple truth, the honest truth, the actual truth, the very truth, the absolute truth, the objective truth, the ultimate truth, home truths, the unalloyed truth, the unvarnished truth, the naked truth, the unqualified truth, the sober truth, the exact truth, the straight truth, the honest-to-goodness truth, the honest-to-God truth, God's truth, gospel, the gospel truth, Holy Writ, Biblical truth, the revealed truth, revelation, the heart of the matter, the whole truth and nothing but the truth, how it is (Inf), the low-down (Sl)

4 **truism**, basic truth, intrinsic truth, primary premise, axiom, maxim, aphorism, platitude, proverb, precept, principle, dictum

▶ *505 Maxim*

5 **truthfulness**, frankness, veracity, honesty, lack of disguise, lack of exaggeration, objectivity, lack of bias, probity, candour, sincerity, openness, open-heartedness, forthrightness, straightforwardness, directness, bluntness, lack of flattery, warts and all, plainness, baldness, outspokenness, ingenuousness, naivety, artlessness, guilelessness, simpleness, lack of pretension, lack of pretence, lack of assumption, unaffectedness, downrightness

▶ *857 Probity*

6 **authenticity**, realness, no illusion, genuineness, officialness, originality, inimitability, uniqueness, purity, unadulteration, sterling silver, hallmarked silver, twenty-four-carat gold, validity, bona fideness, legitimacy, rightfulness, the real thing, the genuine article, the very thing, not a fake, no imitation, soundness, solidity, unquestionability, unquestionableness, unqualifiedness, unrefutability, unconfutability, undeniableness, it (Inf), all wool and a yard wide (US inf), the (real) McCoy (Sl), the real Simon Pure (Sl)

▶ *119 Originality, 483 Evidence*

7 **confirmation**, determination, ascertainment, authentication, verification, validation, certification, demonstration, establishment, attestation, substantiality, substantiation, corroboration, proof, facts, logic, evidence, statistics

▶ *475 Demonstration*

8 **accuracy**, perfection, preciseness, precision,

exactness, exactitude, meticulousness, pinpoint accuracy, detail, microscopic detail, definition, fastidiousness, correctness, rightness, aptness, rigour, rigorousness, faultlessness, absoluteness, flawlessness, care for the truth, attention to details (*or* facts), particularization, punctiliousness, mathematical exactness, mechanical precision, micrometry, scientific exactness, documentation, fine adjustment, squaring, setting, truing, trimming, delicateness, delicacy, refinement, fineness, niceness, nicety, subtleness, subtlety, faithfulness, fidelity, high fidelity, true report, true representation, hitting the nail on the head, scoring a bull's-eye

▶ *467 Attention*

9 **uniformity**, regularity, constancy, straightness, lack of deviation, unchangeableness, unerringness

▶ *112 Uniformity*

10 **literalness**, literality, literalism, literal meaning, denotation, following the letter, true to the letter, the very words, verbatim account, textualism, chapter and verse, word-for-word translation

▶ *48 Literature*

11 **pedantry**, strictness, rigidity, severity, rigour, rigorousness, literal-mindedness, closeness, authority, authoritativeness, cogency, weight, force, legality, lawfulness, legitimacy, acting according to the book, going by the letter of the law

▶ *688 Authority, 16 Law*

12 **true to life**, lifelikeness, true look, true sound, ring of truth, look of reality, verisimilitude, veraciousness, appearance of truth, absolute likeness, realism, absolute realism, photographic realism, realistic representation, representationalism, naturalism, naturalness, true to nature, faithful rendering, true to scale

▶ *50 Painting and Sculpture*

13 **faithfulness**, loyalty, fidelity, faith, trueness

▶ *694 Obedience*

14 **truthful person**, honest John, George Washington

ADJECTIVES

15 **true**, veritable, veracious, factual, right, unmistaken, not in error, unfictitious, honest-to-goodness, honest-to-God, gospel, Biblical, revealed, holding true, holding good, holding water, holding up, standing up, standing the test, standing the test of time, holding up in the wash (Inf)

16 **existing**, real, actual, substantial, tangible

17 **truistic**, intrinsic, primary, axiomatic, aphoristic, platitudinous, proverbial, preceptive, principled

18 **truthful**, frank, veracious, honest, veridical, undisguised, unexaggerated, objective, unbiased, candid, sincere, open, open-hearted, above board, forthright, straightforward, direct, blunt, unflattering, warts-and-all, plain, bald, outspoken, ingenuous, naive, artless, guileless, simple, unpretending, unpretentious, unassuming, unaffected, downright, straight from the shoulder

19 **authentic**, real, without illusion, genuine, official, original, unimitated, inimitable, unique, pure, unadulterated, sterling, hallmarked, twenty-four carat, valid, bona fide, legitimate, rightful, by birth, sound, solid, substantial, undoubted, unquestionable, unquestioned, unqualified, unrefuted, unconfuted, undenied, honest-to-goodness, honest-to-God, pukka (*or* pucka) (Inf), sure-enough (Inf), dinkum (Aus and NZ sl)

20 **proved**, proven, factually proven, logically proven, statistically proven, authenticated, ascertained, verified, validated, certified, demonstrated, logically demonstrated, confirmed, determined, established, attested, substantiated, corroborated

21 **accurate**, precise, exact, perfect, word-perfect, definitive, meticulous, pinpoint, pin-pointed, detailed, particularized, defined, microscopic, correct, right, apt, rigorous, faultless, absolute, flawless, punctilious, mathematical, mathematically exact, mechanically precise, scientific, documented, documentary, documental, fine, finely adjusted, squared, trued, set, trimmed, delicate, refined, nice, subtle, faithful, straight, well-aimed, dead right, true to the facts, OK (*or* okay) (Inf), dead-on (Inf), on the button (Inf), A-OK (*or* A-okay) (US inf), bang-on (Inf), spot-on (Inf), on the nose (US sl), straight up (Sl)

22 **uniform**, regular, constant, straight, undeviating, unchanging, unerring

23 **literal**, denotative, verbatim, textual, word-for-word, chapter-and-verse, following the letter, true to the letter

24 **pedantic**, strict, rigid, severe, literal-minded, rigorous, close, authoritative, cogent, weighty, forceful, legal, lawful, legitimate

25 **lifelike**, true to life, ringing true, looking true, sounding true, appearing true, seeming real, verisimilar, realistic, veracious, unmistaken, naturalistic, representative, true to nature, faithfully rendered, just right, true to the spirit, coming alive, true to scale

26 **faithful**, loyal, true, true-blue

VERBS

27 **be true**, be the case, conform to facts, square with facts, square with the evidence, hold true, hold good, hold water, hold up, stand up, stand the test, stand the test of time, hold up in the wash (Inf), wash (Inf)

28 **bring into existence**, actualize, make tangible, know the real world, see things as they are

29 **be truthful**, tell the truth, speak the truth,

confess the truth, give the true story, stick to the facts, square with the facts (*or* evidence), lack disguise, lack bias, show sincerity, be open, open up, open one's heart, make a clean breast of it, make no bones about it, call a spade a spade

30 **prove (to be) true**, prove real, confirm, determine, ascertain, authenticate, verify, validate, certify, demonstrate, establish, attest, substantiate, corroborate, offer factual evidence, present the facts

31 **be accurate**, perfect, pinpoint, detail, define, correct, care for the truth, give attention to details (*or* facts), particularize, document, make fine adjustments, adjust, square, true, set, trim, refine, make fine, make uniform, regularize, straighten, not allow to deviate, aim well, give a true report, make a true representation, get at the truth, hit the nail on the head, score a bull's-eye, dot one's i's and cross one's t's, hit it on the nose (US sl)

32 **be literal**, give a verbatim account, follow the letter, be a pedant, act according to the book, go by the letter of the law

33 **seem lifelike**, seem true to life, ring true, hold the ring of truth, look true, sound true, carry conviction, give the appearance of truth, seem real, seem true to nature, come alive

34 **render**, render faithfully, copy nature, represent, bring alive

ADVERBS

35 **truly**, really, actually, factually, in point of fact, verily, veritably, in truth, indeed, with truth, to tell the truth, in reality, in fact, as a matter of fact, really-truly (Inf), no buts (about it) (Inf), forsooth (Arch)

36 **truthfully**, frankly, honestly, veridically, objectively, candidly, sincerely, openly, directly, bluntly, warts and all, simply, not to mince words (*or* matters)

37 **authentically**, genuinely, really, truly, officially, uniquely, purely, indubitably, undoubtedly, undeniably, certainly, indeed, nothing else but, rightfully, logically, naturally, legitimately

38 **literally**, strictly speaking, verbatim, word for word, letter for letter, *verbatim et litteratim* (L), by the book, in the same words, to the letter, pedantically, rigorously, legitimately, as it reads, *sic* (L)

39 **accurately**, correctly, rightly, properly, precisely, exactly, perfectly, straight, expressly, dead right, even, square, plumb, directly, squarely, point-blank, unerringly, undeviatingly, right to an inch, right to a hair, right to a turn, right to a T, in every detail, in all respects, neither more nor less, *tout à fait* (Fr), to be exact, spot on (Inf)

INTERJECTIONS

40 **right!**, fine!, right you are!, that's it!, you've got it!, that's for sure!, ain't it the truth! (Inf), righto! (Inf), fair dinkum! (Aus and NZ inf)

538   Untruth

NOUNS

1 **untruth**, untrueness, untruism, untruthfulness, falsehood, falseness, falsity, falsification, prevarication, libel, slander, perjury, fallaciousness, fallacy, inaccuracy, erroneousness, inexactness, distortion, concoction, fabrication, fiction, fictionalization, romanticized version, faction, perversion, bad estimation, overestimation, exaggeration, overstatement, more than the truth, underestimation, understatement, less than the truth, misrepresentation, misconstruction, misstatement, misinformation, disinformation, reverse of the truth, thing that is not, false excuse, *suggestio falsi* (L), *suppressio veri* (L)

▶ *540 Falsehood, 309 Distortion, 541 Exaggeration, 495 Underestimation*

2 **unrealness**, phoniness, bogusness, spuriousness, forgery, counterfeitness, unauthenticity, artificiality, syntheticness, invention, myth, mythology, figment

3 **lying**, untruthfulness, fibbing, fibbery, fabrication, falsification, mendaceousness, mendacity, pseudology, pathological lying, habitual lying, shameless lying, barefaced lying, perfidy, libel, slander, perjury, false oath, false plea, pack of lies, tissue of lies, trumped-up story, frame-up (Sl)

▶ *483 Evidence*

4 **lie**, fib, fable, story, tall story, tale, tall tale, fairy tale, fantasy, the big lie, downright lie, shameless lie, monstrous lie, barefaced lie, taradiddle (*or* tarradiddle), breach of promise, broken promise, broken word, terminological inexactitude, traveller's tale, flam (Dial), flimflam (Inf), cock-and-bull story (Inf), yarn (Inf), fisherman's yarn (Inf), fish story (US inf), shaggy dog story (Inf), whopper (Inf), all my eye (and Betty Martin) (Inf), dirty lie (Sl)

5 **half-truth**, half-lie, partial truth, near-truth, equivocation, (little) white lie, economy with the truth, false rumour, empty gossip (*or* talk), canard, old wives' tale, diplomatic excuse, misinterpretation, distorted truth, propaganda, propaganda machine, factory of lies (Inf), gate of ivory (Inf)

▶ *531 Concealment, 525 Misinterpretation, 533 News, 519 Imagination*

6 **nonsense**, nonsensical talk, moonshine, hogwash, eyewash (Inf), claptrap (Inf), bunkum (*or* buncombe) (Inf), bosh (Inf), bunk (Sl), hooey (Sl), hokum (US sl), baloney (Sl), guff (Sl), bull (Sl), bullshit (Tab sl), crap (Tab sl), balls (Tab sl)

▶ *506 Nonsense, 521 Lack of Meaning*

7 **duplicity**, doubleness, equivocalness, double-dealing, doublethink, irony, backhanded compliment, tongue-in-cheek statement, ambidexterity, Judas kiss, falseness, false-heartedness
▶ *578 Equivocation*

8 **pretence**, pretending, pretension, deception, concealment, evasion, pretext, subterfuge, shift, shuffle, ambiguity, ambivalence, show, false show, insincerity, meretriciousness, uncandidness, make-believe, unfrankness, excuse, feigning, imposture, bluff, bluffing, speciousness, hollowness, affectation, artificiality, unnaturalness, sham, hoax, flummery, empty words, tokenism, lip service, posture, pose, posing, impersonating, attitudinizing, cheating, humbuggery, gammon (Inf), whitewash (job) (Inf), flimflam (Inf), jiggery-pokery (Inf), put-on (US sl)
▶ *797 Affectation, 539 Deception*

9 **hypocrisy**, hypocriticalness, delusion, dissembling, insincerity, disingenuousness, artifice, acting, play-acting, representation, window-dressing, false face, false front, varnish, Tartuffery, Tartuffism, Pecksniffery, Pharisaism, mealy-mouthedness, lip service, flattery, unctuousness, crocodile tears, sweet-talk (Inf), soft soap (Inf)

10 **dishonesty**, falseness, duplicity, lack of integrity, deceitfulness, treachery, faithlessness, mendaciousness, improbity, (piece of) sharp practice, illicit practice, fraud, fraudulence, cozenage, counterfeitness, forgery, put-up job, racket, dodge, cheat, swindle, confidence trick, con (Inf), Machiavellianism, bad faith, low cunning, wile
▶ *858 Improbity*

11 **liar**, fibber, fibster, fabricator, fabulist, phoney, perjurer, false witness, falsifier, propagandist, prevaricator, pseudologist, pathological liar, confirmed liar, habitual liar, consummate liar, palterer, equivocator, storyteller, romancer, Ananias, Satan, Father of Lies, Baron Münchhausen, Sir John Mandeville, yarn-spinner (Inf), dirty liar (Sl), bullshitter (Tab sl)

12 **cheat**, fraud, defrauder, cozener, counterfeiter, forger, swindler, imposter, impersonator, ringer (US), pretender, humbug, fake, faker, shark, phoney, sham, shammer, quack, quackster, mountebank, *saltinbanco* (It), bluff, bluffer, charlatan, poser, poseur, hypocrite, Pharisee, whited sepulchre, Tartuffe, Pecksniff, Joseph Surface, false friend, fair-weather friend, summer soldier, wolf in sheep's clothing, ass in a lion's skin, four-flusher (US sl), mealy-mouth (Inf)

ADJECTIVES

13 **untrue**, false, libellous, slanderous, perjurious, fallacious, erroneous, fictionalized, romanticized, factionalized, imagined, concocted, fabricated, dreamed-up, misconstructed, misstated, misrepresented, inaccurate, inexact, nonsensical, bad, distorted, perverted, exaggerated, overstated, overestimated, understated, underestimated

14 **unreal**, fake, faked, bogus, phoney, sham, false, spurious, forged, counterfeit, bootleg, inauthentic, unauthentic, artificial, synthetic, invented, nonexistent, make-believe, mythical, mythological, hokey (US sl)

15 **lying**, untruthful, fibbing, fabricating, prevaricating, mendacious, perfidious, falsifying, propagandizing, libelling, slandering, perjuring, paltering, storytelling, equivocating, evasive, shifty, ambiguous, ambivalent, flimflamming (Inf), bullshitting (Tab sl)

16 **misinformed**, disinformed, misled, deceived, duped, outsmarted, fooled, cheated, tricked

17 **duplicitous**, deceiving, deceptive, dissembling, double-dealing, equivocal, backhanded, tongue-in-cheek, ambidextrous, false, false-hearted

18 **pretentious**, pretend, deceptive, showy, hypocritical, insincere, meretricious, pretending, posing, posturing, impostrous (*or* imposturous), acting, play-acting, dissembling, feigning, bluffing, uncandid, unfrank, unnatural, false, phoney, hollow, affected, sanctimonious, Tartuffian, Pecksniffian, Pharisaic, mealy-mouthed, artificial, false-faced, tokenistic, unctuous, sweet-talking (Inf)

19 **dishonest**, false, duplicitous, deceitful, treacherous, mendacious, insincere, disingenuous, Machiavellian, cunning, sly, wily, cheating, defrauding, swindling, impersonating, pretending, shamming, humbug, fraudulent, fake, flimflamming (Inf), four-flushing (US sl)

20 **unfaithful**, faithless, promiscuous, adulterous, fickle, deceitful, false, cheating, philandering, running around (Inf), sneaking around (Inf), cruising (Inf)
▶ *877 Immorality*

VERBS

21 **lie**, be untruthful, tell lies, fib, fabricate, fictionalize, romanticize, imagine, dream up, palter, prevaricate, distort, pervert, concoct, misrepresent, misstate, libel, slander, perjure, bear false witness, swear a false oath, give a false plea, falsify, tell a pack of lies, break one's promise, break one's word, frame someone (Inf), tell the half-truth, half-lie, tell a (little) white lie, speak the partial truth, tell the near-truth, rumour, spread a rumour, gossip, repeat old wives' tales, use a diplomatic excuse, misinterpret, distort the truth, be economical with the truth, propagandize, spin yarns (Inf), tell tall stories (Inf), tell a fish story (US inf), tell a shaggy dog story (Inf), tell a whopper (Inf), tell a dirty lie (Sl)

22 **make unreal**, make artificial, fake, falsify, forge, counterfeit, fabricate, invent, mythologize

23 **talk nonsense**, talk hogwash, dish out claptrap (Inf), talk bunkum (or buncombe) (Inf), talk bunk (Sl), be full of hokum (US sl), be full of baloney (Sl), talk guff (Sl), give out the bull (Sl), bullshit (Tab sl), be full of bullshit (Tab sl), talk crap (Tab sl), be full of crap (Tab sl)

24 **pretend**, deceive, conceal, be hypocritical, show, show falsely, make believe, feign, bluff, posture, pose, attitudinize, humbug, delude, dissemble, act, play-act, imitate, impersonate, represent, evade, use a pretext, use a subterfuge, shift, shuffle, be ambivalent, affect, speak empty words, give (or pay) lip service, be mealy-mouthed, cry crocodile tears, gammon (Inf), whitewash (Inf), sweet-talk (Inf), soft-soap (Inf), put on (US sl)

25 **be dishonest**, falsify, deceive, lack integrity, lack sincerity, act Machiavellian, show bad faith, practise artifice, hoax, sham, cheat, fraud, defraud, cozen, counterfeit, forge, swindle, fake, flimflam (Inf), four-flush (US sl)

ADVERBS

26 **untruthfully**, untruly, falsely, fallaciously, inaccurately, inexactly, erroneously, mendaciously, libellously, slanderously, perjuriously, mythically, mythologically, half-truthfully, equivocally, equivocatingly, backhandedly, nonsensically, badly, distortedly, pervertedly, exaggeratedly, tongue-in-cheek

27 **pretentiously**, evasively, shiftily, ambiguously, ambivalently, insincerely, meretriciously, uncandidly, unfrankly, feigningly, speciously, affectedly, artificially, unnaturally, hypocritically, delusively, disingenuously, representationally, flatteringly, unctuously

28 **dishonestly**, fraudulently, illicitly, fakely, bogusly, phonily, unreally, unauthentically, artificially, synthetically, spuriously, duplicitously, ironically, ambidextrously, false-heartedly, deceitfully, deceptively, treacherously, perfidiously, faithlessly, cheatingly, cunningly

539 Deception

Beware of false prophets, which come to you in sheep's clothing, but inwardly they are ravening wolves. Bible: Matthew.

You can fool some of the people all the time and all the people some of the time; but you can't fool all the people all the time. Abraham Lincoln.

False face must hide what the false heart doth know. William Shakespeare.

NOUNS

1 **deception**, calculated deception, deceptiveness, deceit, deceiving, lying, falsehood, falseness, dishonesty, duplicity, double-dealing, circumvention, fraudulence, fraudulency, craftiness, artfulness, guile, cunning, craft, insidiousness, underhandedness, sneakiness, deviousness, shiftiness, furtiveness, surreptitiousness, indirection, subterfuge, tongue in cheek
▶ *540 Falsehood, 657 Cunning, 538 Untruth*

2 **self-deception**, wishful thinking, fond illusion, delusion, delusiveness, make-believe, living in one's own little world, living in an ivory tower, living in cloud-cuckoo land, living in a fool's paradise
▶ *508 Folly, 504 Error*

3 **hypocrisy**, falseness, hypocriticalness, insincerity, mealy-mouthedness, lip service, empty gesture, veneer, hollowness, bubble, sham, pretence, Tartuffery, Tartuffism, Pecksniffery, Pharisaism, artificiality, false face, false front, show, false show, outward show, tokenism, soft soap (Inf), sweet talk (Inf)
▶ *531 Concealment*

4 **false-heartedness**, duplicity, hypocrisy, treachery, treacherousness, treason, betrayal, perfidy, machination
▶ *864 Wickedness, 858 Improbity*

5 **falseness**, deceit, trickiness, imposture, fallaciousness, fallacy, misleading, misguidance, misdirection, misinformation, misconception, mockery, false reputation, feet of clay, insubstantiality, hallucination, illusion, phantasm, mirage, will-o'-the-wisp, bum steer (US sl)

6 **imitation**, rubbish, tinsel, paste, ormolu, fool's gold, mosaic gold, nickel silver, German silver, Britannia metal, cultured pearl, synthetic rubber, simulated wood, plastic spoon, man-made lake
▶ *118 Imitation*

7 **tricking**, trickery, fooling, befooling, outsmarting, outmanoeuvring, taking advantage of, bluffing, shamming, circumvention, outwitting, ensnarement, entrapment, entanglement, enmeshment, whitewashing, dupery, hoodwinking, victimization (or victimisation), manipulation, quackery, chicanery, chicane, sleight (of hand), wheeling and dealing, sharp practice, dodgery, artifice, machination, sorcery, witchcraft, bag of tricks, connivance, collusion, conspiracy, covin (Arch), tricks of the trade, kidding (Inf), conning (Inf), burning (Inf), putting on (US inf), snow job (US sl), flimflam (Inf), flimflammery (Inf), blag (Inf), blagging (Inf), bamboozlement (Inf), diddling (Inf), fishy transaction (Inf), skulduggery (Inf), shenanigan (Inf), hanky-panky (Inf), monkey business (Inf), jiggery-pokery (Inf), hornswoggling (Sl), boiler room (Sl)

8 **trick**, dirty trick, ploy, gambit, ruse, strata-

gem, contrivance, catch, artifice, device, scheme, design, *ficelle* (Fr), blind, wile, shift, dodge, artful dodge, sleight, fetch, feint, pass, bluff, gimmick, diversion, joker (US), bag of tricks, confidence trick, gold brick, wrinkle (Inf), put-on (US inf), diddle (Inf), con (Inf), bunco (game) (US inf), rip-off (Sl), (good) wheeze (Sl), sting (Sl)

9 **sleight of hand**, legerdemain, juggling, jugglery, illusion, trickery, subterfuge, conjuring, conjuration, prestidigitation, ventriloquism, magic, mumbo jumbo, hocus-pocus, curve (US), curveball (US), thimblerig, three-card trick, googly (Inf), bosey (Inf), wrong'un (Inf)

10 **fraud**, fraudulence, pious fraud, racket, dodge, swindle, cheat, cheating, dishonesty, foul play, imposture, (piece of) sharp practice, illicit practice, underhanded deal, legal chicanery, insider dealing, counterfeiting, forgery, ballot-box stuffing, ballot rigging, gerrymandering, cardsharping, forcing a card, wangle (Inf), sell (Inf), con (Inf), fix (Inf), flimflam (Inf), diddle (Inf), fiddle (Inf), swizzle (Inf), swiz (Inf), ramp (Sl), scam (Sl), gyp (*or* gip) (Sl), rip-off (Sl)

11 **hoax**, deception, sham, spoof, game, bluff, sport, joke, practical joke, April fool hoax, rag, humbug, Piltdown Man, Loch Ness monster, pulling one's leg, leg-pull (Inf)

▶ *771 Humour*

12 **disguise**, concealment, camouflage, protective coloration, false colours, borrowed plumes, false front, incognito, mask, domino, visor (*or* vizor) (Arch), veil, cloak, masquerade, masque, mummery, diversion, smoke screen, red herring, tub to a whale, trap door, sliding panel, fake bottom, secret passage, secret drawer (*or* compartment), varnish, paint, whitewash, gloss

▶ *531 Concealment, 527 Latency*

13 **snare**, trap, gin, deathtrap, ambush, pitfall, deadfall, pit, trapdoor, mousetrap, moletrap, rat trap, flytrap, flypaper, Venus flytrap, pitcher plant, Dionaea, spring gun, set gun, baited trap, Longworth trap, booby trap, mine, tripwire, decoy, diversion, sprat to catch a mackerel, kidnapping, hijacking (*or* highjacking), car bomb, letter bomb, parcel bomb, net, mesh, trawl, dragnet, seine, purse seine, pound net, gill net, web, cobweb, hook, fish hook, bait, sniggle, ground bait, lure, fly, jig, squid, plug, wobbler, spinner, lime twig, birdlime, shanghaiing (Sl)

14 **fatal gift**, poisoned apple, Trojan horse, Greek gift

15 **deceiver**, hypocrite, liar, deluder, duper, misleader, beguiler, kidder, ragger, leg-puller, practical joker, Puck, Loki, trickster, swindler, hoaxer, spoofer, cheat, imposter, fake, faker, charlatan, impersonator, pretender, sham, shammer, fraud, ringer (US), humbug, bluff, bluffer, mountebank, *saltinbanco* (It), poser, poseur, malingerer, hypochondriac, masquerader, mummer, guiser, guisard (Scot), incognito (*or* incognita), phoney, quack, quackster, rogue, seducer, Don Juan, Casanova, wolf in sheep's clothing, ass in a lion's skin, jackdaw in peacock's feathers, quacksalver (Arch), pseud (Inf), bamboozler (Inf), four-flusher (US sl)

16 **liar**, fibber, fibster, consumate liar, pathological liar, confirmed liar, habitual liar, perjurer, false witness, mythomaniac, pseudologue, prevaricator, fabricator, equivocator, fabulist, falsifier, story teller, yarner, yarn-spinner, Ananias, Satan, Father of Lies, Baron Münchhausen, Sir John Mandeville, dirty liar (Sl), bullshitter (Tab sl)

17 **cheat**, cheater, swindler, defrauder, confidence man, trickster, cozener, gyp, gypper, bilker, crook, short-changer, counterfeiter, horsetrader, horse coper, cardsharp, cardsharper, pettifogger, land pirate, land shark, shark, land-grabber, mortgage shark, crimp, thimblerigger, con man (Inf), con artist (Inf), bunco artist (US inf), bunco steerer (US inf), shyster (US inf), diddler (Inf), wide boy (Inf), cowboy (Inf), two-timer (Inf), flimflammer (Inf), flimflam man (Inf), blackleg (Inf), magsman (Sl), chiseller (Sl), spiv (Sl)

18 **decoy**, *agent provocateur* (Fr), stool pigeon (US sl), stoolie (US sl), shill (Sl), come-on man (Sl), plant (Sl)

19 **hypocrite**, phoney, sham, sanctimonious fraud, false friend, fair-weather friend, summer soldier, pharisee, whited sepulchre, canter, snuffler, mealy-mouth, Tartuffe, Pecksniff, Joseph Surface

20 **plotter**, schemer, intriguer, *intrigant* (Fr), conspirer, conspirator, Guy Fawkes, machinator, subversive, saboteur, fifth columnist, fellow traveller, security risk, collaborator, collaborationist, fraternizer

21 **traitor**, treasonist, quisling, betrayer, serpent, snake, snake in the grass, double-crosser, double-dealer, double agent, trimmer, timeserver, turncoat, informer, archtraitor, Judas, Judas Iscariot, Benedict Arnold, Brutus, rat (Sl)

22 **dupe**, victim, fool, April fool, laughing stock, fair game, greenhorn, innocent, beginner, trusting soul, puppet, cat's-paw, toy, plaything, pawn, instrument, tool, gull (Arch), soft touch (Inf), easy pickings (Inf), easy mark (US inf), pushover (Inf), babe (Inf), babe in arms (Inf), babe in the woods (Inf), dude (US inf), sitting duck (Inf), pigeon (Sl), mug (Sl), patsy (Sl), cinch (Sl), stooge (Sl), sucker (US sl), fall guy (US sl), schmuck (US sl), schnook (US sl), schlemiel (US sl), sap (Sl), monkey (Sl)

VERBS

23 **deceive**, be dishonest, give a false impression,

sneak, double-cross, double-deal, circumvent, pull a fast one (Inf), two-time (Inf), sell someone a bill of goods (Inf), pull the wool over someone's eyes (Inf)

24 **be deceived**, fall victim to, fall for, be had (Inf), get taken for a ride (Inf), buy a pig in a poke (Inf)

25 **deceive oneself**, indulge in wishful thinking, have fond illusions, delude oneself, hallucinate, make-believe, live in one's own little world, live in cloud-cuckoo land (or an ivory tower or a fool's paradise)

26 **be a hypocrite**, pay lip service, make an empty gesture, pretend, show a false face, show a false front, show, belie, talk sweetly, soft-soap (Inf)

27 **be false**, betray, trick, deceive, delude, beguile, mock, misinform, mislead, misguide, misdirect, throw off the scent, lay a false scent, have feet of clay, send on a wild goose chase (Inf), lead up the garden path (Inf), string along (Inf), give someone a bum steer (US sl)

28 **trick**, play a trick on, fool, befool, make a fool of, make an ass of, make one look silly, mock, make fun of, take advantage of, ridicule, outsmart, outmanoeuvre, spoof, bluff, sham, circumvent, contrive, catch, devise, scheme, design, shift, dodge, fetch, feint, pass, fudge, divert, outwit, ensnare, entrap, entangle, enmesh, whitewash, dupe, swindle, hoodwink, victimize, manipulate, chicane, wheel and deal, machinate, sell a gold brick, practise sorcery, practise witchcraft, have a bag of tricks, connive, collude, conspire, use tricks of the trade, play a confidence trick, fake someone out (US inf), take for a ride (Inf), diddle (Inf), kid (Inf), con (Inf), have (or put) someone on (Inf), flimflam (Inf), bamboozle (Inf), snow (US sl), hornswoggle (Sl), make a wally of (Sl), rip off (Sl)

29 **juggle**, trick, conjure, ventriloquize, practise magic, throw someone a curve (US), throw someone a curveball (US), thimblerig, bowl a googly (Inf), bowl a bosey (Inf), bowl a wrong'un (Inf)

30 **be fraudulent**, defraud, dodge, swindle, fleece, bilk, cheat, do out of, cheat on, deal on inside information, counterfeit, forge, force a card, mark the cards, stack the deck, deal off the bottom of the deck, load the dice, throw a fight, obtain under false pretenses, leave in the lurch, leave holding the baby, wangle (Inf), sell (Inf), gull (Inf), con (Inf), burn (Inf), fix (Inf), flimflam (Inf), fiddle (Inf), swizzle (or swiz) (Inf), short-change (Inf), cook the books (Inf), scam (Sl), gyp (or gip) (Sl), rip off (Sl), nick someone for (US sl), screw (Sl), take a dive (Sl)

31 **hoax**, deceive, spoof, bluff, play a joke on, play a practical joke on, play an April fool joke on, rag, pull one's leg

32 **disguise**, conceal, camouflage, show false colours, have a false front, mask, veil, cloak, masquerade, divert, throw up a smoke screen, introduce a red herring, varnish, paint, whitewash, gloss

33 **snare**, ensnare, trap, entrap, lay a trap for, gin, catch, ambush, waylay, kidnap, hijack (or highjack), set a gun, bait a trap, set a booby trap, mine, tripwire, trip up, trip, lime, birdlime, decoy, lure, divert, plant a car bomb, post a letter bomb, post a parcel bomb, net, trawl, seine, entangle, ensnarl, tangle, hook, hook in, bait, bait a hook, dangle the bait, sniggle, nab (Inf), nick (Sl), shanghai (Sl)

ADJECTIVES

34 **deceiving**, misleading, double-dealing, conniving, contriving, covering up, whitewashing, colluding, dodging, feinting, designing, scheming, cheating, calculating, cunning, sharp, artful, guileful, wily, crafty, tricky, shifty, devious, dishonest, sneaky, furtive, surreptitious, indirect, smooth, slippery, slick (US inf), conning (Inf), wangling (Inf), dodgy (Inf)

35 **deceptive**, deceitful, false, fallacious, duplicitous, dishonest, conspiratorial, fraudulent, sorcerous, insidious, illicit, underhand, ballot-rigged, gerrymandered, contrived, gimmicky, misleading, tongue-in-cheek, fixed (Inf)

36 **deceived**, duped, tricked, hoaxed, fooled, befooled, outsmarted, hookwinked, victimized, outmanoeuvred, bluffed, cheated, outwitted, ensnared, entrapped, entangled, enmeshed, manipulated, misled, misguided, misdirected, misinformed, self-deceived, mocked, ridiculed, made sport of, made a joke of, ragged, flimflammed (Inf), spoofed (Inf), diddled (Inf), done (Inf), swizzled (Inf), taken in (Inf), taken for a ride (Inf), sold a pig in a poke (Inf), sold a pup (Inf), had (Sl)

37 **hypocritical**, false, insincere, phoney, sanctimonious, Pharisaic, Tartuffian, Pecksniffian, mealy-mouthed, hollow, pretending, artificial, false-faced, false-fronted, tokenistic

38 **treacherous**, false-hearted, duplicitous, faithless, unfaithful, inconstant, double-dealing, betraying, treasonous, perfidious, dangerous

39 **imitative**, imitation, artificial, phoney, synthetic, simulated, substituted, cultured, unnatural, unoriginal, copied, plastic, manmade, fake, bogus, sham, mock, quack, counterfeit, forged, shoddy, rubbishy

40 **illusory**, illusive, unreal, insubstantial, tricky, conjured, juggled, magic, magical, sleight-of-hand, mumbo-jumbo, hocus-pocus, delusive, delusory, make-believe, imagined, dreamed-up, chimerical, hallucinatory, phantasmic

41 **disguised**, concealed, hidden, camouflaged, incognito (or incognita), masquerading,

masked, veiled, cloaked, varnished, painted, whitewashed, glossed, visored (or vizored) (Arch)

42 **trapped**, snared, ginned, ambushed, mined, kidnapped, hijacked (or highjacked), baited, trawled, hooked, netted, meshed, webbed, cobwebbed

540   Falsehood

NOUNS

1 **falsehood**, falseness, falsity, error, mendaciousness, mendacity, inveracity, untruth, untruthfulness, truthlessness, untrueness, unverity, fallaciousness, fallacy, erroneousness, ungenuineness, spuriousness, false conduct, improbity, dissemblance, dishonesty, bad faith, lack of integrity, deception, delusion, Machiavellianism

▶ *309 Distortion, 538 Untruth, 539 Deception, 858 Improbity*

2 **duplicity**, doubleness, two-facedness, double life, double-mindedness, double facade, double-tongue, forked tongue, double-dealing, ambidexterity

3 **hypocrisy**, hypocriticalness, insincerity, deception, delusion, disguise, camouflage, concealment, sanctimony, sanctimoniousness, religiosity, false piety, ostentatiousness, uncandidness, uncandour, unfrankness, tokenism, flattery, unctuousness, oiliness, cant, lip service, mummery, mouthing, mealy-mouthedness, empty gesture, emptiness, disingenuousness, mockery, unseriousness, meretriciousness, crossed fingers, tongue in cheek, cupboard love, crocodile tears, Tartuffery, Pecksniffery, Pharisaism, blandishments, blarney, sweet talk (Inf), soft soap (Inf)

4 **spuriousness**, bogusness, falseness, ungenuineness, unauthenticity, unrealness, forgery, counterfeiting, artificiality, factitiousness, hollowness, humbug, humbuggery, speciousness, sophistry, casuistry, Jesuitism, charlatanism, charlatanry, quackery, quackishness, quackism, mountebankery, imposture, illegitimacy, phoniness (Inf)

▶ *474 Sophistry*

5 **deceitfulness**, duplicity, fraudulence, false-heartedness, cunning, low cunning, sneakiness, artfulness, artifice, guile, wile, fake conduct, malingering, improbity, lying, treason, treachery, Judas kiss

6 **lying**, fibbing, fibbery, fabrication, pseudology, pathological lying, habitual lying, shameless lying, barefaced lying, mythomania, perjury, false witness, false swearing, forswearing, perfidy, defamation, libel, slander

▶ *538 Untruth*

7 **pretence**, pretending, pretension, dissimulation, impersonation, imitation, acting, play-acting, representation, feigning, feint, pretext, posture, pose, posing, affectation, apparentness, ostensibility, attitudinizing

8 **fraud**, fraudulence, swindle, dishonesty, cheating, trickery, fakery, faking, falsity, imposture, sharp practice, illicit practice, confidence trick, underhanded deal, insider dealing, adulteration, packed jury, stacked deck, loaded dice, salted mine, juggled figures, counterfeiting, forgery, put-up job, hoax, canard, con (Inf), crookedness (Inf), whitewash job (Inf), frame-up (Sl), put-on (US sl), sting (Sl), rip-off (Sl)

9 **falsification**, falsifying, faking, misrepresentation, misstatement, overstatement, understatement, misquote, misinterpretation, misreporting, misciting, perversion, distortion, straining, warping, slanting, slant, twisting, twist, garbling, garble, sharp practice, nod and a wink, collusion, manipulation, tampering with, doctoring, rigging, juggling, retouching, counterfeiting, forgery, fabrication, trumping up, confabulation, invention, imagination, concoction, canard, fiction, figment, myth, legend, fable, wangle (Inf), fiddle (Inf), fix (Inf), plant (Inf), frame (Sl), frame-up (Sl)

▶ *525 Misinterpretation, 519 Imagination*

10 **fake**, sham, mock, imitation, copy, counterfeit, bootleg, dummy, tinsel, paste, rubbish, junk, phoney (Inf), pseud (Inf), pseudo (Inf)

11 **evasion**, equivocation, ambivalence, double-talk, shiftiness, dodging, shuffling, fencing, fudging the issue

12 **façade**, front, mask, show, masquerade, disguise, ostentation, false front, outward show, false show, dressing up, false air, false light, face, appearance, fanfaronade, semblance, seeming, sham, fake, act, bluff, bluffing, simulation, dissimulation, dissemblance, window-dressing, whitewash, gloss, varnish, gild, embellishment, embroidery, touch-up, touching-up, deodorization, colour, colouring, false colour, falsely colouring, simulacrum (Arch)

▶ *811 Showiness*

13 **nonsense**, humbug, humbuggery, moonshine, hogwash, eyewash (Inf), bosh (Inf), baloney (Inf), flimflam (Inf), claptrap (Inf), gammon (Inf), bunkum (or buncombe) (Inf), bunk (Sl), hooey (Sl), hoke (US sl), hokum (US sl), bull (Sl), bullshit (Tab sl), crap (Tab sl), balls (Tab sl)

▶ *521 Lack of Meaning*

14 **false thing**, forged passport, counterfeit note, Hitler diaries, plagiarized book, simulated wood, paste gem, fool's gold, nine-bob note, Trojan horse, mirage

15 **false person**, humbug, hoaxer, hypocrite, whited sepulchre, pretender, imposter, charlatan, liar, perjurer, fraud, cheat, swindler, confidence man, counterfeiter, plotter, schemer,

saboteur, informer, traitor, betrayer, double-crosser, double agent, Pharisee, Judas Iscariot, Benedict Arnold, seducer, Don Juan, Casanova, goody-goody (Inf), con man (Inf), pseud (Inf)

VERBS

16 **be false**, ring false, not ring true, falsify, lie, not speak the truth, dissemble, show bad faith, lack integrity, deceive, delude, make an error

17 **double-deal**, play a double role, have it both ways, play both ends against the middle, have one's cake and eat it too, have a foot in both camps, run with the hare and hunt with the hounds, two-time (Inf)

18 **be hypocritical**, be insincere, deceive, delude, act sanctimoniously, have false piety, be holier than thou, be holier than the Pope, disguise, camouflage, conceal, lack candour, cant, render (or pay) lip service, mouth, make an empty gesture, flatter, mock, say one thing and mean another, cross one's fingers, put one's tongue in one's cheek, shed crocodile tears, blandish, be full of blarney, sweet-talk (Inf), soft-soap (Inf)

19 **be deceitful**, malinger, sneak, show treachery, give a Judas kiss

20 **pretend**, make a pretense of, make a show of, make like, make as if, dissimulate, impersonate, imitate, act, play-act, play, play a part, dissemble, represent, feign, feint, posture, pose, pose as, assume the guise of, pass oneself off as, affect, attitudinize, assume, put on, put on a (false) front, sail under false colours, play possum, roll over and play dead

21 **be fraudulent**, swindle, cheat, trick, fake, copy, falsify, deal underhandedly, deal on inside information, pack (a jury), stack, juggle, load, salt, salt a mine, adulterate, counterfeit, forge, hoax, whitewash, con (Inf), put on (Sl), sting (Sl), rip off (Sl), nobble (Sl)

22 **falsify**, fake, misrepresent, misstate, overstate, understate, misquote, misinterpret, put a false construction on, misreport, miscite, pervert, distort, strain, warp, slant, twist, garble, collude, give a nod and a wink, manipulate, tamper with, retouch, counterfeit, forge, fabricate, trump up, confabulate, invent, imagine, cry wolf, concoct, mythologize, fable, doctor, rig, wangle (Inf), fiddle (Inf), cook the books (Inf), fix (Inf), plant (Inf), frame (Sl)

23 **evade**, equivocate, be ambivalent, double-talk, shuffle, fence, fudge the issue

24 **mask**, show, masquerade, disguise, impersonate, show a false front, make an outward show, put up a (false) front, give a false show, present a false air, put in a false light, face, appear, seem, fake, act, bluff, simulate, dissimulate, dissemble, window-dress, embellish, embroider, touch up, dress up, overdo, deodorize, make smell like roses, gloss, gloss over, whitewash, varnish, gilt, colour, colour falsely

ADJECTIVES

25 **false**, fallacious, erroneous, mendaceous, inveracious, untrue, untruthful, truthless, not true, ungenuine, spurious, dissembling, dishonest, deceptive, delusive, Machiavellian

26 **duplicitous**, two-faced, Janus-faced, double-minded, double-dealing, double-tongued, ambidextrous

27 **hypocritical**, insincere, disingenuous, meretricious, deceptive, delusive, sanctimonious, religiose, falsely pious, empty, Pharisaic, ostentatious, uncandid, unfrank, unctuous, oily, mealy-mouthed, flattering, Pecksniffian, mocking, unserious, tongue-in-cheek, nonsensical, goody-goody (Inf), sweet-talking (Inf), soft-soaping (Inf)

28 **spurious**, bogus, ungenuine, unauthentic, unreal, apocryphal, forged, counterfeited, artificial, factitious, hollow, humbug, specious, sophistic, casuistic, charlatan, charlatanistic, quackish, impostrous, illegitimate, phoney (Inf)

29 **deceitful**, duplicitous, fraudulent, fake, artificial, false-hearted, cunning, sneaky, artful, guileful, wily, crafty, manipulative, malingering, lying, fibbing, fabricating, prevaricating, slandering, libelling, perjuring, falsely swearing, forswearing, perfidious, collusive, treasonous, treacherous, flimflam (Inf)

30 **pretending**, pretentious, dissembling, dissimulating, acting, play-acting, masquerading, feigning, bluffing, affecting, attitudinizing, posturing, posing, seeming, apparent, so-called, ostensible, put-on (US sl)

31 **fraudulent**, swindling, dishonest, cheating, tricky, false, fake, impostrous, illicit, underhanded, counterfeit, forged, copied, put-up, whitewashed, crooked (Inf), put-on (US sl), rip-off (Sl)

32 **falsified**, faked, fake, misrepresented, exaggerated, distorted, twisted, stretched, half-true, counterfeit, forged, fabricated, made-up, confabulated, invented, slanderous, libellous, perjurious, manipulated, concocted, fictional, fictionalized, imaginative, mythologized, fabled, legendary, cock-and-bull, trumped-up, contrary-to-fact

33 **fake**, sham, mock, artificial, imitative, bogus, counterfeit, tinselled, rubbishy, junky, phoney (Inf), not all it's cracked up to be (Inf)

34 **evasive**, equivocal, ambivalent, double-talking, shifty, shuffling, dodging, fencing

35 **disguised**, false, seeming, sham, imitative, fake, imitation, simulated, dissembled, dissimulated, glossed, varnished, gilded, embellished, embroidered, overdone, dressed-up, touched-up, coloured, falsely coloured

ADVERBS

36 **falsely**, mendaciously, untruthfully, truthlessly, unveraciously, deceitfully, deceptively, fallaciously, under false pretences, erroneously, hypocritically, ungenuinely, bogusly, dishonestly

37 **spuriously**, artificially, synthetically, unnaturally, ungenuinely, factitiously, speciously, seemingly, apparently, plausibly, ostensibly, nominally, in name only

38 **hypocritically**, insincerely, uncandidly, emptily, unseriously, unctuously, mealymouthedly

541 Exaggeration

NOUNS

1 **exaggeration**, exaggerating, overemphasis, overstatement, excessiveness, intensification, overenthusiasm, overstress, overexposure, extremism, extreme(s), exacerbation, exorbitance, inordinacy, overkill, aggravation, hyperbolism, hyperbole, superlative, sensationalism, sensation, overdoing, excitement, hype (Inf), overselling, embellishment, embroidery, touching up, varnish, overcolouring, prodigality, overreaction, fuss, pother, commotion, to-do, leaning (or bending) over backwards, stretching, straining, labouring, overestimation, overvaluation, exaggerated lengths, overcompensation, enhancement, gilding the lily, overacting, histrionics, hamming, overdrawing, overwriting, purple patch, melodrama, burlesque, travesty, caricature, making a mountain out of a molehill, storm in a teacup, ballyhoo (Inf), puffery (Inf)
▶ *309 Distortion, 538 Untruth, 768 Aggravation, 494 Overestimation, 493 Misjudgment, 557 Ornament, 519 Imagination, 366 Agitation, 799 Derision*

2 **enlargement**, magnification, amplification, dilation, dilatation, maximization, inflation, expansion, aggrandizement, heightening, blowing up, puffing up
▶ *261 Expansion, 130 Addition*

3 **extravagance**, excessiveness, flamboyance, ostentation, outrageousness, profuseness, profusion, lavishness, overindulgence, overspending, pound-foolishness, intemperance, inordinacy, exorbitance, going to extremes, running riot, overdoing it, carrying too far, going too far, overshooting, overstepping the mark, piling Ossa upon Pelion, piling it on (Inf)
▶ *870 Self-Indulgence*

4 **bombast**, pomposity, inflatedness, magniloquence, grandiloquence, boasting, boast, bragging, self-glorification, ranting, raving, huckstering, talking in superlatives, hype, overpraise, flattery, overrating, depiction in glowing terms, purple prose, making much of, excessive loyalty, chauvinism, hot air (Inf)
▶ *853 Flattery, 532 Publication*

5 **tall story**, traveller's tale, fisherman's (or angler's) tale, flight of fancy, stretch of the imagination, drawing on the imagination, dealing in the marvellous, teratology, yarn (Inf), fish story (US inf), fisherman's tale (Inf), shaggy dog story (Inf)

6 **exaggerator**, extremist, miracle-monger, teratologist, panjandrum, liar, Baron Münchhausen, sensationalist, radical, fanatic, boaster, braggart, braggadocio, brag, blusterer, hector, fanfaron, windbag (Sl), bullshitter (Tab sl)

VERBS

7 **exaggerate**, overemphasize, intensify, overstate, overenthuse, overstress, hyperbolize, sensationalize, overdo, hype, embellish, embroider, touch up, varnish, colour highly, overcolour, overexpose, exacerbate, overkill, aggravate, overreact, fuss, pother, make a commotion, make a to-do, lean (or bend) over backwards, stretch, strain, labour, go to exaggerated lengths, overestimate, overvalue, overcompensate, enhance, gild the lily, overact, have histrionics, ham, ham it up, chew the scenery (Inf), overdraw, overwrite, write a purple patch, burlesque, travesty, caricature, make a mountain out of a molehill, be a storm in a teacup, ballyhoo (Inf)

8 **enlarge**, magnify, amplify, dilate, maximize, inflate, expand, distend, heighten, aggrandize, blow up, puff up

9 **be extravagant**, overdo, overdo it, lavish, overindulge, overspend, run riot, go to extremes, carry too far, go too far, overshoot, overstep the mark, not know when to stop, pile Ossa upon Pelion, pile it on (Inf)

10 **boast**, brag, bombast, rant, rave, huckster, hype, talk in superlatives, blow up (out of all proportion), oversell, overrate, overpraise, flatter, inflate, depict in glowing terms, make much of, self-glorify, out-Herod Herod, pile it on (Inf), lay it on (Inf), lay it on thick (Inf), lay it on with a trowel (Inf)

11 **tell a tall story**, have a flight of fancy, stretch the imagination, draw on the imagination, deal in the marvellous, spin a yarn (Inf)

ADJECTIVES

12 **exaggerated**, overemphasized, overstated, sensationalized, overdone, inflated, hyped, puffed, overrated, overpraised, oversold, flattered, embellished, embroidered, touched-up, blown-up, varnished, highly coloured, overcoloured, overdrawn, far-fetched, excessive, intensified, overstressed, overenthusiastic, overemphatic, hyperbolic, overexposed, exacerbated, exorbitant, extreme, inordinate, aggravated, superlative, prodigious, stretched,

strained, laboured, overestimated, overvalued, overcompensated, enhanced, overwritten, purple patch, overacted, histrionic, histrionical, melodramatic, teratologic, teratological, ballyhooed (Inf)

13 **enlarged**, magnified, amplified, dilated, maximized, inflated, expanded, aggrandized, heightened, blown-up, puffed-up

14 **extravagant**, excessive, flamboyant, ostentatious, outrageous, profuse, lavish, grandiose, overindulgent, overspending, pound-foolish, intemperate, inordinate, exorbitant, overdone, overshot, overstepped, meretricious, piled-on (Inf)

15 **bombastic**, boasting, bragging, raving, inflating, self-glorifying, hyping, magniloquent, grandiloquent, pompous, fustian

ADVERBS

16 **exaggeratedly**, hyperbolically, superlatively, overenthusiastically, overemphatically, excitedly, sensationally, histrionically, melodramatically, magniloquently, grandiloquently, bombastically, pompously

17 **excessively**, extremely, outrageously, extravagantly, exorbitantly, inordinately, prodigiously, flamboyantly, ostentatiously, lavishly, profusely, intemperately, too much, *in extremis* (L)

542   Understatement

NOUNS

1 **understatement**, underemphasis, conservativeness, minimization, underestimation, unobtrusiveness, unsubstantiality, undervaluation, conservative estimate, underreckoning
▶ *495 Underestimation*

2 **detraction**, belittlement, faint praise, two cheers

3 **subtlety**, delicacy, restraint, restrainedness, elegance, refinement, good taste, finesse, discrimination, fastidiousness
▶ *794 Refinement, 481 Discrimination*

4 **simplicity**, simpleness, plainness, clinicalness, modesty, Spartan simplicity, bareness, austerity, austereness, starkness, unelaborateness, unfanciness, unfussiness, minimalism, beauty unadorned, unpretentiousness, unostentatiousness, unaffectedness
▶ *556 Simplicity*

5 **reserve**, reticence, restraint, constraint, diffidence, modesty, quietness, subduedness, retiring disposition
▶ *699 Restraint, 810 Modesty*

6 **suggestion**, trace, touch, dash, smattering, sprinkling, tinge, taste, jot, iota, suspicion, *soupçon* (Fr), inkling, intimation, smack, taint, thought, shade, tempering, smidgen (*or* smidgin) (US inf)

7 **imperceptibility**, imperceptibleness, inconspicuousness, unimpressiveness, faintness, shadowiness, vagueness

8 **insipidness**, insipidity, pallidness, blandness, tastelessness, flavourlessness, vapidity, wateriness, half-heartedness, wishy-washiness (Inf)

9 **downplaying**, de-emphasis, dilution, watering down, diminishment, curtailment, moderation, restraint, constraint, disregard, playing down, deprecation, underplaying, making light of, shrugging off, paring down, cutting down to size

10 **deflation**, puncturing, depreciation, cutting down, cutting back

11 **modest person**, quiet person, shy person, introvert, mouse, shrinking violet (Inf)

ADJECTIVES

12 **understated**, underemphasized, conservative, minimized, underestimated, unobtrusive, unsubstantial, undervalued, underreckoned, underrated

13 **subtle**, delicate, restrained, elegant, refined, tasteful, discriminating, fastidious, pastel

14 **simple**, plain, modest, bare, austere, stark, clinical, unelaborate, unfancy, unfussy, unpretentious, unostentatious, unadorned, unaffected, minimal

15 **reserved**, reticent, restrained, constrained, diffident, modest, quiet, subdued, retiring, unassuming, low-profile

16 **imperceptible**, inconspicuous, unimpressive, faint, shadowy, vague, indistinct, impalpable, slight, underwhelming (Inf)

17 **insipid**, pallid, bland, diluted, watered-down, tasteless, flavourless, half-hearted, vapid, watery, wersh (Scot), wishy-washy (Inf)

18 **deflated**, punctured, depreciated, cut-down, cut-back

19 **downplayed**, played-down, underplayed, toned-down, moderated, de-emphasized, diluted, watered-down, reduced, diminished, curtailed, restrained, constrained, disregarded, made light of, shrugged-off, pared, pared-down

VERBS

20 **understate**, underemphasize, underreckon, minimize, underplay, underestimate, undervalue, underrate, sell short (Inf)

21 **detract from**, underpraise, belittle, damn with faint praise, give two cheers, deflate, puncture, depreciate, cut down, cut back, bring down to earth, cut down to size, let the air out of, take the wind out of one's sails

22 **play down**, downplay, underplay, tone down, moderate, de-emphasize, deprecate, dilute, water down, reduce, diminish, curtail, restrain, constrain, disregard, make light of, set no store by, shrug off, pare, pare down, spare one's blushes

23 **unobtrusively**, conservatively, unnoticeably

24 **simply**, plainly, austerely, starkly, unelaborately, unfussily, unpretentiously, unostentatiously, minimally

25 **reservedly**, reticently, diffidently, modestly, quietly, unassumingly

26 **insipidly**, pallidly, vapidly, blandly, tastelessly, half-heartedly

27 **imperceptibly**, inconspicuously, unimpressively, faintly, vaguely, indistinctly

28 **moderately**, with restraint, in a constrained manner

543 Sign

NOUNS

1 **sign**, symbol, signification, meaning, connotation, representation, signal, indicator, indication, pointing out, identification sign, signature, autograph, mark, 'X', fingerprint, name tag, directional sign, signpost, road sign, motorway sign, highway sign (US), banner, poster, placard, protest sign, 'for sale' sign, warning sign, 'no parking' sign, 'no trespassing' sign, danger sign, rallying symbol, fiery cross, political symbol, emblem, eagle, hammer and sickle, sun, swastika, religious symbol, sacred symbol, cross, crescent, mandala, magic symbol, talisman, mojo (US), conventional symbol, image, token, letter, sure sign, evidence, telltale sign, omen, sign of the times, identifying sign, brand, trademark, hallmark, imprint, track, trail, *piste* (Fr), condensation trail, signs, traces, scent, clue, cue, key, lead, marker, weather sign, dark clouds, falling leaves, thunder and lightning, sign of illness, symptom, syndrome, fever, pain, dizziness, nausea, secret symbol, secret sign, shibboleth, high sign, countersign, password, cipher, code, picture writing, hieroglyphics, hieroglyph, rune, gypsy signs, scout signs, musical notation, mathematical notation, plus sign, minus sign, multiplication sign, division sign, equal (or equals) sign, decimal point, symbol list, sigla

▶ *547 Representation, 520 Meaning, 528 Information, 544 Identification, 526 Display, 70 Transport, 529 Secrecy, 524 Interpretation, 49 Music, 52 Mathematics, 171 List*

2 **symbolism**, symbology, symbolization, semiotics, semiology, symptomatology, iconology, iconography

3 **gesture**, gesticulation, body language, sign language, signing, dactylology, deaf-and-dumb language, ticktack, baseball sign (US), kinesics, demeanour, look, beckoning look, come-hither look, twinkle, glance, smile, blush, ogle, leer, wink, fluttering eyelashes, raised eyebrows, tic, twitch, frown, scowl, pout, moue, pursed lips, grimace, clenched jaw, clenched teeth, arms akimbo, stuck-out tongue, nod of the head, shake of the head, laugh, cheer, hiss, sigh, moan, hoot, boo, whistle, catcall, hand signal, fist, clenched fist, wringing hands, hands on hips, hands in pockets, praying gesture, tearing one's hair, pointing, point, wave, hat waving, flag waving, V-sign, two-finger gesture, middle-finger gesture, wagging forefinger, drumming fingers, clapping, applause, touch, handshake, grip, shoulder clasping, head patting, bottom patting, bottom pinching, poking someone in the ribs, hug, nudge, push, shove, slap, tapping foot, stamping foot, kick, kick under the table, crossed legs, folded arms, wolf whistle (Inf), raspberry (Inf), Bronx cheer (US inf), Harvey Smith salute (Inf), footsie (Inf), goose (Sl)

▶ *324 Motion, 22 Baseball, 812 Celebration, 769 Cheerfulness, 762 Joy, 773 Rejoicing, 330 Impulsion, 829 Irascibility, 770 Sorrow, 830 Sullenness, 766 Dissatisfaction*

4 **signal**, message, time signal, pips, telegraph signal, Morse code, heliograph, semaphore, wigwag flag, signal lamp, fire, watch fire, smoke signal, danger signal, warning signal, warning flag, red flag, signal lamp (or light), traffic light (or signal), green light, go light, red light, stop light, amber light, caution light, warning light, beacon, beacon fire, balefire, flashing light, lighthouse beacon, railway signal, Belisha beacon, distress signal, SOS, rocket, signal rocket, flare, Very light, Very pistol, minute gun, warning sound, horn, hooter, foghorn, starter's gun, whistle, referee's whistle, police whistle, alarm, fire alarm, burglar alarm, car alarm, alarm clock, siren, police siren, ambulance siren, fire-engine siren, air-raid siren, all-clear siren, alarm bell, Lutine bell, summoning sound, telephone ring, bleep, bleeper, door buzzer, door knocker, doorbell, bell, church bell, Angelus bell, sacring bell, dinner bell, dinner gong, passing knell, knell, muffled drum, manifestation, signalling, alarum (Arch)

▶ *534 Communications, 410 Fuel, 408 Heat, 637 Preservation*

5 **indicator**, guide, index, gauge, thermometer, barometer, speedometer, mileometer, odometer (US), cynosure, pointer, finger, index finger, forefinger, arm, needle, arrow, cursor, time indicator, timekeeper, clock, watch, stopwatch, hour hand, minute hand, second hand, direction indicator, turn indicator, blinker, winker, compass, compass needle, magnetic needle, radar, weather vane, weathercock, windsock, wind sleeve, white line, Catseye (Tm), signpost, roadsign, motor-

way sign, highway sign (US), guidepost, crossroad sign, finger post, milepost, milestone, landmark, bench mark, earthwork, cairn, monument, sea mark, lighthouse, lightship, buoy, star, guiding star, lodestar, North Star, Pole Star, Polaris, Southern Cross, depth indicator, water line, watermark, tidemark, load line, Plimsoll line, triangulation point

▶ *268 Measurement, 192 Timekeeping*

6 **word**, catchword, slogan, watchword, shibboleth, call, cry, hue and cry, shout, hail, proclamation, publication, announcement, marriage banns, invitation, summons, call to prayer, church bell, muezzin's call, command, word of command, rallying cry, war cry, battle cry, rebel yell (US), call to arms, bugle-call, trumpet call, fanfare, sennet, flourish, reveille, assemble, charge, advance, rally, tattoo, retreat, lights out, last post, taps (US), drumbeat, cry for help, distress call, SOS, Mayday, Hey rube! (US sl)

▶ *423 Loudness, 533 News, 532 Publication, 676 War, 662 Help*

7 **punctuation**, punctuation mark, point, stop, full stop, period, comma, colon, semicolon, quotation mark, inverted comma, turned comma, quotes (Inf), single quotes, double quotes, exclamation mark, question mark, query, interrobang, apostrophe, parentheses, brackets, square brackets, braces, hyphen, dash, en rule, em rule, blank, ellipsis, swung dash, reference mark, asterisk, star, asterism, cross-reference mark, dagger, obelus, solidus, stroke, virgule, omission mark, caret, accent, grave accent, acute accent, circumflex, breve, umlaut, tilde, cedilla, háček, hamse, dieresis, diacritical mark, diacritic, macron, vowel point, indention, paragraph, printing mark, hand, fist, index, underlining

▶ *550 Clarity, 552 Conciseness*

8 **signer**, autographer, signatory, orthologist, symbolist, symbologist, symbolizer, iconographer, semiologist, semiotician, iconologist, letterer, sign-maker, imprinter, marker, communicator, gesturer, gesticulator, telegraph operator, telegrapher, telegraphist, telegraph messenger, heliographer, telecommunicator, signaller, timekeeper, lighthouse operator, shouter, hailer, proclaimer, messenger, publisher, announcer, inviter, summoner, bellringer, muezzin, commander, bugler, trumpeter, alarmist, referee, policeman (*or* policewoman), fireman, air-raid warden

▶ *532 Publication, 534 Communications, 530 Disclosure*

VERBS

9 **use signs**, sign, sign one's name, put one's signature to, sign on the dotted line, autograph, initial, countersign, use symbols, signal, gesture, indicate, point to, point out, sign-

post, mark, mark the way, point the way, show the way, direct, guide, blaze, demarcate, mark out, chalk out, lay out, delineate, fingerprint, carry a protest sign, burn a cross, give someone a secret sign, give a password, code, put the finger on (US inf), finger (US inf)

10 **signify**, represent, symbolize, stand for, mean, denote, connote, imply, indicate, suggest, intimate, hint at, give evidence of, show signs of, symptomize, characterize, bear the marks of, bear the stamp of, smack of, smell of, witness to, bear witness to, typify, betoken, disclose, reveal, signalize, emphasize, highlight, blazon

11 **gesture**, use body language, gesture, motion, gesticulate, attract notice, pantomime, mime, mimic, imitate, use sign language, sign, suit the action to the word, give a look, shrug, nod one's head, shake one's head, beckon, gaze, glance, look (*or* speak) volumes, ogle, leer, look daggers (at), wink, flutter (*or* bat) one's eyelashes, raise one's eyebrows, frown, scowl, pout, moue, purse one's lips, grimace, show anger, curl one's lip, snap, bite, clench one's jaw, clench one's teeth, grit one's teeth, gnash one's teeth, stick out one's tongue, pull faces, twinkle, smile, laugh, hiss, sigh, moan, hoot, boo, whistle, give a catcall, give a hand-signal, clench one's fist, wring one's hands, raise one's hand, wave, chop the air, flag down, wave to, wave on, wave by, wave through, wave one's hat, tear one's hair, point, point one's finger, point at (*or* to), give the V-sign, drum one's fingers, clap, applaud, hold out one's hand, salute, greet, squeeze someone's hand, clasp someone's shoulder, clap someone on the back, pat someone's head, pat someone's bottom, pinch someone's bottom, poke someone in the ribs, hug, nudge, pat, stroke, caress, jog, push, shove, poke, prod, slap, tap one's foot, stamp, stomp, kick, shuffle, scrape one's feet, paw the ground, cross one's legs, fold one's arms, give a wolf whistle (Inf), play footsie (Inf), blow a raspberry (Inf), cock a snook (Inf), goose someone (Sl)

12 **signal**, make a signal, hang out a signal, send a signal, semaphore, wigwag, send smoke signals, exchange signals, communicate, publish, inform, announce, declare, herald, hail, proclaim, call, cry, shout, summon, command, call to prayer, send a message, tap out a message, use Morse code, call for help, send out a distress call, send an SOS, warn, fire a warning shot, alert, honk, whistle, set off an alarm, raise the alarm, ring the church bells, sound the trumpets, beat the drum, beat a retreat

▶ *534 Communications, 532 Publication*

13 **punctuate**, abbreviate, accent, indent, parenthesize, underline, italicize, underscore, stress, emphasize, dot, dash, hyphenate, cross,

cross out, obelize, asterisk, dot one's i's and cross one's t's, put in quotes (Inf)

ADJECTIVES

14 **signifying**, indicative, indicatory, significative, identifying, directional, pointing, connotative, denotative, signalizing, disclosing, revealing, explanatory, betraying, giving away, telltale, signalling, symbolic, symbolical, symbolistic, symbological, semiotic, semiological, symptomatic, symptomatological, diagnostic, expressive, implicative, demonstrative, meaningful, suggestive, suggesting, representative, representing, evidential, nominal, diagrammatic, typical, characteristic, individual, special, interpretive, prophetic, presageful, ominous

15 **gestural**, gesticulative, dactylographic, pantomimic, signing, thumbing, looking, glancing, smiling, winking, grimacing, laughing, sighing, moaning, whistling, clapping, patting, pushing, slapping, stamping

16 **signalling**, telegraphic, heliographic(al), semaphoric(al), flashing, warning, summoning, ringing, bell-ringing, bleeping, shouting, hailing, proclaiming, publishing, announcing, inviting, calling, commanding

17 **punctuated**, quoted, hyphenated, referenced, cross-referenced, accented, abbreviated, apostrophized, indented, paragraphed, underlined, italicized

ADVERBS

18 **indicatively**, revealingly, symptomatically, diagnostically, expressively, with expression, demonstratively, meaningfully, signficantly, with meaning, suggestively, in a suggestive manner, evidentially, by this token, in token of, representatively, symbolically, as a symbol, symbolistically, semiologically, in pantomime, in sign language, diagrammatically, typically, characteristically, individually, specially, interpretively, prophetically, as a sign, ominously, telegraphically, semaphorically

544   Identification

NOUNS

1 **identification**, recognition, detection, distinguishing, differentiation, diagnosis, indicating, indication, pointing out, pinpointing, designation, naming, labelling, characterization, characteristic, form, shape, outline, size, colour, colouring, mannerism, trait, denomination, classifying, classification, analysis, categorization, cataloguing, establishing, establishment, authentication, verification, substantiation, corroboration

▶ *535 Affirmation, 547 Representation, 560 Description, 306 Form, 299 Outline, 169 Number, 60 Medicine*

2 **identity**, particularity, individuality, distinc-

tiveness, uniqueness, personality, self, name

▶ *103 Essence*

3 **means of identification**, ID, name, title, letters after one's name, name and address, signature, autograph, paraph, initials, mark, 'X', monogram, identification papers, identity (*or* ID) card, passport, visa, letter of introduction, permit, credentials, endorsement, fingerprint, thumbprint, footprint, dental record, genetic fingerprinting, DNA fingerprinting, photograph, passport photograph, Identikit, identity number, National Insurance number, Social Security number (US), student number, military service number, driving licence number, bank-account number, telephone number, credit-card number, numberplate registration number, license plate number (US), personalized numberplate, ISBN (International Standard Book Number), call sign, call letters (US), secret word, password, 'open sesame,' watchword, token, countersign, shibboleth, secret signal, dactylography (US), trademark, brand, brand name, tradename, copyright, logo, logotype, hallmark, cachet, official stamp, seal, great seal, privy seal, signet, sigil, superscription, impress (*or* impression), imprint, watermark, letterhead, masthead, colophon, bookplate, ex-libris, marque, model, earmark, caste mark, tattoo, birthmark, strawberry mark, blemish, scar, stigma, label, luggage label, tie-on label, clothes marking, prisoner's broad arrow, clothes label, tag, tally, tessera, counter, chip, adhesive label, sticker, badge, emblem, name badge, nametape, plate, nameplate, brass plate, card, visiting card, business card, place card, sign, signboard, trade sign, fascia, inn sign, pub sign, tavern's bush, barber's striped pole, pawnshop's three balls, certificate, birth certificate, marriage certificate, death certificate, ticket, airline ticket, train ticket, bus ticket, theatre ticket, cinema ticket, raffle ticket, cloakroom ticket, ticket counterfoil, ticket stub (US), chit, chitty, docket, invoice, bill, bill of lading, waybill, copy, duplicate, dog tag (US sl)

▶ *804 Title, 529 Secrecy, 543 Sign*

4 **insignia**, badge, markings, military markings, badge of sovereignty, throne, sceptre, orb, crown, regalia, robes of office, badge of office, chain of office, mark of authority, sword of state, gavel, mace, staff, pastoral staff, wand, baton, keys, military insignia, badge of rank, spread eagle (US), star, bar, stripe, chevron, wings, epaulette, brassard (*or* brassart), aiguillette, cockade, hackle, sash, medal, Congressional Medal of Honor (US), ribbon, decoration, cross, Victoria Cross (VC), George Cross, Iron Cross, *Croix de Guerre* (Fr), badge of merit, victory laurels, garland, wreath, bays, chaplet, trophy, gold medal, silver medal,

bronze medal, silver cup, silver plate, rosette, blue ribbon, school letter (US), pip (Inf), gong (Sl), chicken (US sl), hash mark (US sl), Hershey bar (US sl)

▶ *804 Title, 681 Trophy*

5 **uniform**, military uniform, army uniform, navy uniform, air force uniform, marine's uniform, regimentals, school uniform, sports outfit, sports uniform (US), baseball uniform (US), nurse's uniform, Boy Scout uniform, chauffeur's uniform, livery, stable colours, jockey's colours, national dress, tartan, kilt, stetson, lederhosen, prison clothes, mourning clothes, widow's weeds, crepe, black dress, black armband, cardinal's cap, dunce's cap, cap and gown, mortarboard, tie, club tie, old school tie, school ring (US), class ring (US), signet ring, lapel pin, sphragistics

▶ *295 Dress, 796 Fashion*

6 **national emblem**, national device, American spread eagle, British lion and unicorn, English rose, Scottish thistle, Welsh leek, Welsh daffodil, Irish shamrock, Canadian maple leaf, French fleur-de-lis, Russian bear, Soviet hammer and sickle, Japanese rising sun, Turkish crescent and star, Swiss cross, Nazi swastika, fylfot, Roman eagle

▶ *91 Countries*

7 **flag**, standard, banner, ensign, bunting, colours, national colours, national flag, Stars and Stripes, Star-Spangled Banner, Old Glory, the red, white, and blue, jack, Union Jack, Union flag, St Andrew's cross, St George's cross, St Patrick's cross, Tricolour, *drapeau tricolore* (Fr), Confederate flag, Stars and Bars, red flag, regimental colours, ship's colours, King's (*or* Queen's) Colour, Red Ensign, White Ensign, Blue Ensign, pilot jack, merchant jack, blue peter, flag of convenience, pirate flag, skull and crossbones, black flag, Jolly Roger, military flag, vexillum, labarum, gonfalon, guidon, oriflamme, bannerette (*or* banneret), streamer, pennon, banderole, bannerol, pennant, swallowtail, burgee, quarantine flag, yellow flag, flag of truce, flag of surrender, white flag, flagpole, flagstaff, canton, hoist, fly, grommet, halyard, heading, sleeve, truck, clip, red duster (Inf)

8 **heraldic device**, armory, blazonry, blazon, armorial bearings, coat of arms, arms, achievement, hatchment, shield, escutcheon (*or* scutcheon), crest, torse, wreath, helmet, crown, coronet, mantling, garland, chaplet, bandeau, lambrequin, supporters, motto, field, quarter, rustre, tresure, dexter, bar, bar sinister, chief, base, charge, device, bearing, ordinary, label, pale, bend, bend sinister, chevron, pile, saltire, cross, canton, bordure, lozenge, fusil, gyron, flanch, fret, marshalling, quartering, impaling, impalement, dimidi-

ation, differencing, difference, fesse point, honour point, nombril point, animal charge, lion, lion rampant, lion couchant, antelope, bear and ragged staff, unicorn, griffin, cockatrice, eagle, spread eagle, falcon, martlet, crescent, mullet, annulet, floral charge, fleur-de-lis, Tudor rose, cinquefoil, trefoil, planta genista, badge, rebus, baton, portcullis, heraldic tincture, gules, azure, vert, sable, purpore, tenne, murrey, metal, or, argent, fur, ermine, ermines, erminites, erminois, pean, vair, potent

9 **herald**, heraldist, heraldic official, herald extraordinary, Earl Marshal, king of arms, Clarenceux, Lyon King of Arms, Lord Lyon, pursuivant, Rouge Croix, Rouge Dragon, heraldic register, Roll of Arms, College of Arms, College of Heralds

VERBS

10 **identify**, recognize, detect, distinguish, differentiate, diagnose, analyse, indicate, show, exhibit, point out, pinpoint, establish, authenticate, verify, substantiate, corroborate, designate, name, give a name to, specify, characterize, hallmark, earmark, label, docket, tag, tab, keep tabs on, classify, categorize, catalogue, reference, number, letter, page, paginate, record, photograph, picture, fingerprint, register, ticket, delimit, limit, note, annotate, mark, put a mark on, underline, underscore, tick, check (US), tick off, check off (US), mark off, etch, engrave, imprint, tattoo, pierce, notch, chalk, chalk up, scar, disfigure, blaze, brand, burn in, stamp, seal, punch, impress, emboss, overprint, emblazon, blazon, impale, dimidiate, quarter, difference, marshal, charge

11 **identify oneself**, sign, ratify, countersign, endorse, autograph, write one's signature, write one's name, inscribe, put one's hand to, subscribe, undersign, initial, paraph, put one's mark on, put one's cross on, be identified, leave fingerprints, leave footprints, have a birthmark, be conspicuous, stand out, stick out

ADJECTIVES

12 **identified**, recognized, established, authenticated, verified, substantiated, corroborated, identifiable, recognizable, shown, shown up, known, known by, known as, designated, denoted, named, labelled, tagged, marked, hallmarked, trademarked, earmarked, characterized, classified, categorized, referenced, catalogued, indexed, lettered, numbered, patterned, signed, signatory, symbolic(al), sigillary, titled, imprinted, fingerprinted, photographed, pictured, stigmatized, scarred, branded, tattooed

13 **heraldic**, emblematic, crested, armorial, blazoned, emblazoned, paly, barry, dexter, sinister, gules, azure, vert, purpure, sable, tenne,

murrey, or, argent, ermine, fleury, seme, pomme, rampant, gardant, regardant, couchant, statant, sejant, passant

ADVERBS

14 **identifiably**, indicatively, symbolically, as a symbol, emblematically, heraldically

545 Record

NOUNS

1 **record**, recording, documentation, document, form, documents, papers, chronicle, history, historical record, historical documents, annals, archives, account, narrative, memoir, autobiography, biography, biographical record, case history, obituary, personal history, curriculum vitae (CV), vita (US), resumé, correspondence, memorabilia, cutting, press cutting, visual record, photograph, picture, snapshot, portrait, sketch, representation, list, inventory, waiting list, jury list, file, dossier, portfolio, personal file, public record, public file, police record, criminal record, official record, official publication, Congressional Record (US), Hansard, government papers, recorded material, recorded proceedings, transactions, minutes, report, official report, company report, annual report, school report, report card, office memorandum, memo, reminder, note, entry, item, return, income tax return, invoice, bill, check (US), statement, receipt, voucher, docket, counterfoil, stub, cheque stub, tally, scoresheet, scoreboard

▶ *560 Description, 547 Representation, 511 Memory, 528 Information, 483 Evidence, 718 Security, 171 List, 544 Identification, 3 History*

2 **certificate**, credential, charter, authorization, birth certificate, marriage certificate, death certificate, passport, ID (identification), diploma, muniments, deed, title, title deed, ownership papers, car papers, registration document, insurance papers, insurance certificate, ticket, warranty, testimonial, sworn statement, affidavit, notarized statement, deposition, daybook

3 **notes**, school notes, annotations, margin notes, marginalia, adversaria, jottings, writing

▶ *524 Interpretation*

4 **inscription**, personal note, signature, autograph, initials, legend, wall writing, graffiti

5 **copy**, photocopy, Xerox (Tm), Xerox copy, laser copy, carbon copy, spare copy, duplicate copy, duplicate

6 **record book**, notebook, scrapbook, album, commonplace book, minute book, registry, register, roll, rollbook, directory, address book, logbook, log, diary, journal, calendar, cartulary, tablet, table, notepad, memo pad, scratch pad, jotter, ledger, cashbook, account book, chequebook, catalogue, index, card, index

card, microfilm, microfiche, microcard, tape, magnetic tape, computer tape, disk, database, data processing

▶ *170 Calculation, 750 Accounts, 260 Littleness, 65 Computers*

7 **recording**, phonograph record, gramophone record, record, LP (long-playing record), single, EP (extended-play record), CD (compact disc), pressing, cassette tape, cassette, tape, magnetic tape, film, motion-picture film, video tape, vid (Inf)

8 **registration**, registry, record-keeping, recording, writing, printing, inscribing, engraving, epigraphy, enrolment, enlistment, empanelment, booking, reservation, entry, double entry, bookkeeping, accountancy, accounts, filing, indexing, cataloguing, listing

▶ *750 Accounts*

9 **recorder**, record-keeper, registrar, chronicler, annalist, archivist, historian, archaeologist, antiquarian, diarist, columnist, journalist, reporter, newsman (or newswoman), press photographer, writer, biographer, autobiographer, amanuensis, notary, stenographer, typist, computer operator, keyboarder, scribe, secretary, receptionist, clerk, filing clerk, bookkeeper, accountant, petitioner, artist, engraver, draughtsman, photographer, cameraman, scorekeeper, timekeeper

▶ *3 History, 533 News, 66 Photography*

10 **recording instrument**, photocopier, camera, video camera, camcorder, recorder, tape recorder, tape machine, cassette recorder, electronic listening device, wiretap, bug (Inf), answering machine, video tape recorder, video cassette recorder (VCR), dictaphone, cash register, seismograph, speedometer, gauge, flight recorder, black box, stopwatch

▶ *534 Communications, 192 Timekeeping, 268 Measurement, 66 Photography*

11 **monument**, memorial, war memorial, memorial arch, victory arch, column, pillar, national monument, tomb of an unknown soldier, tomb, mausoleum, pyramid, shrine, statue, bust, plaque, tablet, slab, memorial inscription, gravestone, tombstone, ancient monument, monolith, obelisk, megalith, dolmen, menhir, cromlech, cairn, barrow, earthwork, mound, testimonial, cup, trophy, prize, ribbon, medal, decoration, memento, souvenir

▶ *399 Burial, 200 Past Time, 681 Trophy, 511 Memory*

12 **vestige**, trace, track, trail, piste, scent, spoor, mark, print, footprint, footstep, fingermark, tyremark, tidemark, stain, relic, remains

▶ *483 Evidence, 543 Sign, 607 Waste, 793 Blemish*

VERBS

13 **record**, document, chronicle, log, put (or place) on record, put in the minutes, inscribe, register, enrol, file, index, catalogue, tabulate,

list, empanel, copy, photocopy, print, store in a database, input, tape, tape-record, videotape, film, photograph, take a picture, capture on film, preserve for posterity, store in the archives, paint, represent, relate, narrate, recount, recite

▶ *560 Description, 547 Representation, 528 Information, 3 History*

14 **inscribe**, transcribe, write, write down, commit to writing, put on paper, put (*or* set) down, set down in black and white, enter in a book, take minutes, make notes, note, note down, take down, mark down, jot, jot down, engrave, cut, incise, etch, carve

▶ *48 Literature*

15 **register**, enter, docket, enter names, tick off names, put on the list, put on the waiting list, enrol, enlist, empanel, book, reserve, list, itemize, tabulate, score, tally, notch up (Inf)

▶ *171 List*

ADJECTIVES

16 **recorded**, on record, in the minutes, documented, chronicled, logged, noted, inscribed, written down, on paper, in black and white, printed, entered, registered, enrolled, on the books, in the book, filed, in the file, indexed, in the index, listed, on the list, on the waiting list, copied, photographed, photocopied, input, in the database, taped, on tape, videotaped, filmed, on film, official, documentary

▶ *171 List, 528 Information*

ADVERBS

17 **on the record**, in black and white, on paper, officially

546   Obliteration

VERBS

1 **obliterate**, erase, expunge, eliminate, delete, dele, take out, remove, efface, deface, write over, print over, overprint, paint over, make illegible, scribble out, cover up, cover, conceal, remove any trace, scratch out, scratch through, score out, score through, strike out, strike through, cross out, cross through, rule out, rub out, rub off, sponge off, sponge out, wash out, wash off, wipe out, wipe off, blot, blot out, black out, white out, brush off, cancel, annul, abrogate, edit out, blue-pencil, censor, take out of print, leave on the cutting-room floor, destroy, eradicate, extirpate, annihilate, demolish, raze, burn to the ground, liquidate, exterminate, purge, leave no survivors, leave no trace, vaporize, wipe off the map, bury, force into oblivion, submerge, sink without trace, drown, silence, scrub (Inf)

▶ *531 Concealment, 293 Covering, 385 Friction, 621 Cleanness, 704 Cancellation, 399 Burial, 244 Destruction, 398 Killing, 422 Silence, 458 Disappearance*

2 **forget**, have a mental block, block out, repress, suppress

▶ *511 Memory, 512 Oblivion*

NOUNS

3 **obliteration**, erasure, erasing, expunction, elimination, deletion, dele, removal, effacement, defacement, writing over, printing over, overprinting, painting over, illegibility, covering up, cover, concealment, crossing out, rubbing out, cancellation, annulment, abrogation, cessation, amnesty, editorial change, editing, blue pencil, censorship, destruction, eradication, extirpation, annihilation, demolition, liquidation, extermination, purge, interment, burial, oblivion

4 **eraser**, rubber, correction fluid, cleanser, abrasive, paint-stripper, duster, sponge, clean slate, tabula rasa

▶ *622 Dirtiness, 621 Cleanness*

5 **forgetfulness**, forgetting, amnesia, loss of memory, memory gap, absentmindedness, mental block, repression, suppression

▶ *511 Memory, 512 Oblivion*

ADJECTIVES

6 **obliterated**, erased, expunged, eliminated, deleted, effaced, illegible, scribbled out, covered, concealed, crossed out, rubbed out, vaporized, liquidated, extirpated, cancelled, edited, censored, out of print, destroyed, eradicated, annihilated, demolished, razed to the ground, exterminated, buried, forgotten, unrecorded, unregistered, unwritten, intestate

▶ *704 Cancellation, 531 Concealment, 293 Covering, 244 Destruction, 512 Oblivion*

547   Representation

Taxation without representation is tyranny.
James Otis.

No annihilation without representation. Arnold Toynbee.

NOUNS

1 **representation**, depiction, delineation, portrayal, rendering, embodiment, personification, incarnation, realization, typification, epitome, quintessence, type, figuration, symbolization, indication, conventional representation, manifestation, evocation, presentation, presentment, imitation, impersonation, impression, exemplar, similarity, semblance, likeness, realism, photographic likeness, striking likeness, speaking likeness, lookalike, exact likeness, true picture, spitting image, double, doppelgänger, copy, duplicate, facsimile, fax (Inf), replica, reflection, mirror image, outline, description, writing, picture writing, pictogram, hieroglyphics, runes, notation, mathematical notation, musical notation, bad likeness, poor representation,

misrepresentation, dead ringer (Inf)
▶ *526 Display, 114 Similarity, 118 Imitation, 539 Deception, 544 Identification, 560 Description, 48 Literature, 299 Outline, 548 Misrepresentation*

2 **reproduction**, photograph, carbon copy, photocopy, Xerox (Tm), Identikit (Tm), Photofit (Tm), print, graphics, etching, engraving, lithograph, collotype, blueprint, diagram, chart, graph, plan, draft, rough draft, sketch, cartoon, caricature, picture, illustration, book illustration, tracing, drawing, isometric drawing, isometric projection, axiometric drawing, technical drawing, mechanical drawing, artwork, painting, oil painting, oil, watercolour, portraiture, portrait, fine art, illumination, calligraphy, film, video
▶ *306 Form, 592 Plan, 792 Decoration, 50 Painting and Sculpture, 66 Photography*

3 **acting**, portraying, portrayal, playing, playing a character, playing the part of, impersonating, impersonation, posing, characterizing, characterization, performing, performance, enactment, role-playing, mimicry, charade, mime, dumb show, masquerade
▶ *51 Performing Arts, 118 Imitation, 243 Production*

4 **person who makes a representation**, artist, painter, watercolourist, copyist, illustrator, graphic artist, cartoonist, sketcher, caricaturist, etcher, engraver, printmaker, mapmaker, cartographer, photographer, sculptor, sculptress, modeller, model maker, forger, counterfeiter

5 **performer**, player, actor, actress, mime artist, mime, mimic, impersonator, female impersonator, drag artist

6 **image**, symbol, likeness, very image, clear image, exact image, very picture, exact picture, spitting image, visual, visual aid, photograph, duplicate, eidetic image, mental image, idea, thought, afterthought, after-image, reflected image, reflection, mirror image, projection, hologram, shadow figure, silhouette, painted image, icon, idol, graven image, effigy, gargoyle, sculpture, statue, statuette, bust, torso, head, figure, figurine, wax figure, waxwork, model, working model, replica, manikin, dummy, tailor's dummy, doll, china doll, rag doll, golliwog, soft toy, teddy bear, puppet, marionette, fantoccini, finger puppet, glove puppet, snowman, gingerbread man, scarecrow, guy, Guy Fawkes, robot, automaton
▶ *439 Light, 471 Idea, 543 Sign, 457 Appearance, 7 Religion*

7 **map**, world map, county map, city map, town plan, A to Z, road map, relief map, survey map, Ordnance Survey map, sketch map, elevation, projection, Mercator's projection, orthographic projection, conic projection, gnomonic projection, chart, cartogram, statistics, atlas, world atlas, globe, map of the heavens, star map, mapmaking, cartography
▶ *170 Calculation, 592 Plan*

8 **representative**, example, sample, specimen, cross-section, agent, agency, proxy, substitute, replacement, stand-in, deputy, delegate, ambassador, envoy, spokesman (*or* spokeswoman), spokesperson
▶ *707 Deputy, 222 Substitution, 739 Sale*

VERBS
9 **represent**, depict, delineate, portray, render, embody, personify, incarnate, realize, typify, symbolize, epitomize, manifest, evoke, present, imitate, impersonate, personate, pretend to be, resemble, look like, copy, duplicate, reproduce, reflect, mirror, image, catch, capture, catch exactly, catch a likeness, register, record, photograph, film, snap, shoot, take a picture, take a photo, shoot a picture, scan, X-ray, process, print, enlarge, blow up, project
▶ *114 Similarity, 118 Imitation, 539 Deception, 544 Identification, 66 Photography, 545 Record*

10 **act**, portray, present, dramatize, play, play a character, play the part of, act the part of, assume the role of, role-play, characterize, perform, enact, impersonate, take off, pose as, go as, mimic, mime, masquerade, improvise
▶ *51 Performing Arts, 118 Imitation, 583 Improvisation*

11 **paint**, draw, sketch, caricature, picture, illustrate, draft, sketch out, rough out, block out, plan, diagram, make a diagram, draw a blueprint, design, outline, describe, trace, shape, form, mould, carve, sculpt, cast, cut, engrave, etch, print, plot, map, chart, survey
▶ *50 Painting and Sculpture, 306 Form, 299 Outline, 560 Description, 592 Plan*

12 **stand for**, mean, denote, exemplify, show, pass for, pass as, replace, substitute for, stand in for, act for
▶ *520 Meaning, 707 Deputy, 222 Substitution, 526 Display*

ADJECTIVES
13 **representational**, representing, representative, depictive, delineatory, portraying, symbolic, emblematic, figurative, typical, quintessential, archetypal, characteristic, exemplary, evocative, descriptive, illustrative, graphic, pictorial, hieroglyphic, reflecting, similar, like, imitative, iconic, diagrammatic, vivid, realistic, naturalistic, true-to-life, impressionistic, abstract, nonrepresentational, surrealistic, surreal, artistic, painterly, paintable, photogenic, photographic
▶ *50 Painting and Sculpture, 118 Imitation, 114 Similarity, 543 Sign, 66 Photography, 560 Description, 592 Plan*

ADVERBS
14 **representationally**, representatively, sym-

bolically, emblematically, figuratively, typically, characteristically, descriptively, illustratively, graphically, pictorially, vividly, realistically

548 Misrepresentation

NOUNS

1 **misrepresentation**, distortion, deformation, twist, dissimilarity, perversion, falsification, lie, fib, not a true picture, false light, falsehood, unfair representation, bad likeness, poor likeness, exaggeration, grotesquerie, colouring, overemphasis, overdramatization, caricature, travesty, parody, burlesque, guy, flattering, flattery, nonrealism, bad art, daubing, daub, botch, anamorphosis, false image, distorted image, distorting mirror

▶ *309 Distortion, 115 Dissimilarity, 540 Falsehood, 538 Untruth, 844 Wrong, 541 Exaggeration, 799 Derision, 853 Flattery, 50 Painting and Sculpture*

2 **misinformation**, false information, disinformation, misteaching, misevaluation, misinterpretation, garbling, misstatement, misquotation

▶ *525 Misinterpretation, 528 Information*

3 **deceiver**, liar, dissembler, dissimulator, fraud, cheat, swindler, hoaxer, trickster, adulterer, cardsharp, confidence trickster, Tartuffe, con man (Inf)

VERBS

4 **misrepresent**, distort, deform, twist, make dissimilar, pervert, falsify, slant, put in a false light, lie, belie, represent unfairly, make a poor likeness, make a false image, exaggerate, colour, overemphasize, overdramatize, caricature, parody, travesty, burlesque, guy, flatter, overembellish, gild the lily, create nonrepresentational art, overdraw, daub, botch

▶ *309 Distortion, 115 Dissimilarity, 540 Falsehood, 538 Untruth, 844 Wrong, 541 Exaggeration, 799 Derision, 853 Flattery, 50 Painting and Sculpture*

5 **misinform**, give false information, disinform, misteach, misevaluate, misinterpret, garble, misstate, misquote

▶ *525 Misinterpretation, 528 Information*

ADJECTIVES

6 **misrepresented**, misrepresenting, biased, slanted, not representative, unrepresentative, distorted, deformed, twisted, perverted, false, untrue, wrong, incorrect, inaccurate, dissimilar, unlike, unfair, unjust, exaggerated, caricatured, parodied, grotesque, flattering, nonrepresentational, cardboard

▶ *309 Distortion, 115 Dissimilarity, 540 Falsehood, 538 Untruth, 844 Wrong, 541 Exaggeration, 799 Derision, 853 Flattery*

7 **misinformed**, mistaught, misinterpreted, garbled, misstated, misquoted

▶ *525 Misinterpretation, 528 Information*

ADVERBS

8 **unrepresentatively**, falsely, wrongly, incorrectly, inaccurately, unfairly, unjustly, in a false light

549 Style

Style is the man himself. Comte de Buffon.

Style, like sheer silk, too often hides eczema. Albert Camus.

All styles are good except the tiresome sort. Voltaire.

In matters of grave importance, style, not sincerity, is the vital thing. Oscar Wilde.

NOUNS

1 **style**, fashion, mode, manner, way, technique, approach, tone, tenor, idiom, vein, strain, quality, character, personal style, mannerism, speciality, peculiarity, affectation, idiosyncrasy

▶ *602 Means, 796 Fashion, 165 Speciality, 554 Emphasis*

2 **stylishness**, elegance, grace, charm, flair, panache, élan, chic, perfect touch

▶ *796 Fashion, 558 Elegance, 794 Refinement, 557 Ornament, 556 Simplicity*

3 **inelegance**, plainness, lack of refinement, affectation, overelaboration, heaviness, heavyhandedness, lumpishness, commonness

▶ *559 Inelegance*

4 **literary style**, mode of expression, manner of speaking, form of speech, diction, phrasing, wording, sentence structure, phraseology, phrase, choice of words, idiolect, vocabulary, language, expression of ideas, command of language, oratory, rhetoric, word power, command of idiom, feeling for language, sense of language, word magic

5 **stylist**, stylish writer, fine writer, classical author, rhetorician, orator, phrasemonger, wordsmith, word-spinner (Inf)

▶ *558 Elegance, 557 Ornament*

ADJECTIVES

6 **styled**, phrased, worded, expressed, put

7 **stylish**, elegant, graceful, chic, sophisticated, fashionable

8 **inelegant**, common, vernacular, heavy, heavy-handed, clumsy, plain, dowdy, dumpy, frumpy, overelaborate

▶ *48 Literature, 5 Linguistics, 564 Speech, 796 Fashion, 558 Elegance, 794 Refinement, 557 Ornament, 559 Inelegance, 556 Simplicity, 550 Clarity*

VERBS

9 **style**, show style, demonstrate style, develop a literary style, state, put, express, express in

words, find words to express, choose one's words carefully, phrase, word, formulate, frame, couch, set out, present, use the vernacular, overwrite, spin words (Inf)

ADVERBS

10 **stylistically**, linguistically, rhetorically, idiomatically, idiosyncratically, ornately, elaborately, gracefully, elegantly, stylishly, with style, with flair, fluently, plainly

550 Clarity

NOUNS

1 **clarity**, clearness, lucidity, pellucidity, perspicuity, perspicuousness, transparency, purity, limpidity, coherence, intelligibility, comprehensibility, plainness, simplicity, austerity, starkness, straightforwardness, directness, unambiguousness, explicitness, definition, definiteness, distinctness, obviousness, exactness, accuracy

▶ *442 Transparency, 439 Light, 437 Visibility, 522 Intelligibility, 556 Simplicity, 503 Accuracy*

VERBS

2 **clarify**, make clear, disambiguate, define, demonstrate, explicate, interpret, decipher, elucidate, illuminate, enlighten, fill in

ADJECTIVES

3 **clear**, lucid, pellucid, perspicuous, limpid, transparent, pure, coherent, intelligible, comprehensible, apodeictic, plain, unadorned, simple, austere, stark, straightforward, direct, unambiguous, explicit, clear-cut, definite, distinct, obvious, exact, accurate, uninvolved

▶ *442 Transparency, 439 Light, 437 Visibility, 522 Intelligibility, 556 Simplicity, 503 Accuracy*

ADVERBS

4 **clearly**, lucidly, pellucidly, perspicuously, limpidly, transparently, purely, coherently, intelligibly, comprehensibly, plainly, simply, straightforwardly, directly, unambiguously, explicitly, distinctly, obviously, exactly, accurately

551 Obscurity

NOUNS

1 **obscurity**, obscuration, lack of clarity, obfuscation, unintelligibility, incomprehensibility, opacity, lack of transparency, cloudiness, obsidian, fogginess, fuzziness, murkiness, muddiness, difficulty, hard words, Johnsonese, ornament, purple prose, tortuousness, convolution, involved style, complexity, muddle, gobbledegook, confusion, indistinctness, vagueness, uncertainty, imprecision, impreciseness, inexactness, inaccuracy, indefiniteness, abstraction, indirectness, allusion, ambiguity, equivocalness, shapelessness, amorphousness, convolution, mysteriousness, enigma, abstruseness, profundity, depth,

overcompression, ellipsis, flood of words, verbiage, diffuseness, jibberish, mumbo jumbo, inelegance, lack of naturalness, stiffness

▶ *523 Unintelligibility, 443 Opaqueness, 441 Dimness, 440 Darkness, 531 Concealment, 557 Ornament, 659 Difficulty, 491 Uncertainty, 504 Error, 277 Depth, 552 Conciseness, 553 Diffuseness, 527 Latency, 559 Inelegance, 151 Disorder, 502 Ignorance, 612 Unimportance*

ADJECTIVES

2 **obscure**, unclear, obfuscatory, unintelligible, incomprehensible, opaque, not transparent, cloudy, foggy, fuzzy, murky, muddy, as clear as mud, hard, obsidian, difficult, full of difficult words, Johnsonian, ornamental, purple, tortuous, convoluted, involved, complex, confused, gnostic, muddled, indistinct, vague, uncertain, imprecise, inexact, inaccurate, indefinite, abstract, indirect, allusive, ambiguous, Cimmerian, cabalistic, equivocal, shapeless, amorphous, mysterious, enigmatic, cryptic, abstruse, esoteric, arcane, recondite, profound, deep, overcompressed, elliptical, diffuse, jibbering, mumbo-jumbo, inelegant, not natural, stiff, crabbed

▶ *523 Unintelligibility, 443 Opaqueness, 441 Dimness, 440 Darkness, 531 Concealment, 557 Ornament, 659 Difficulty, 491 Uncertainty, 504 Error, 277 Depth, 552 Conciseness, 553 Diffuseness, 527 Latency, 559 Inelegance, 151 Disorder, 502 Ignorance, 612 Unimportance*

VERBS

3 **make obscure**, obscure, obfuscate, make abstruse, complicate, confound, muddy, confuse, muddle, mix up, use gobbledegook

ADVERBS

4 **obscurely**, unintelligibly, incomprehensibly, fuzzily, murkily, ornamentally, tortuously, indistinctly, vaguely, imprecisely, inexactly, inaccurately, indefinitely, indirectly, allusively, ambiguously, equivocally, mysteriously, enigmatically, cryptically, abstrusely, profoundly, elliptically, inelegantly, stiffly

552 Conciseness

NOUNS

1 **conciseness**, concision, brevity, briefness, shortness, succinctness, pithiness, pithy saying, crispness, compactness, terseness, curtness, brusqueness, taciturnity, monosyllabism, words of one syllable, laconism, laconicism, briskness, exactness, incisiveness, pointedness, nutshell, the long and the short of it, the heart of the matter, witticism, soul of wit, brachylogy, concise style, economy of words, no words wasted, few words, clipped speech, portmanteau word, compression, telegraphese, ellipsis, elision, syncope, apocope, abbreviation, contraction, truncation, short-

ening, compendiousness, sententiousness, abridgment

▶ *270 Shortness, 566 Taciturnity, 818 Discourtesy*

2 **outline**, summary, synopsis, precis, résumé, brief sketch, compendium, condensation, monostich, haiku, epitome, maxim, aphorism, epigram, clerihew

▶ *505 Maxim, 562 Summary*

ADJECTIVES

3 **concise**, brief, short, succinct, pithy, crisp, compact, terse, curt, brusque, taciturn, monosyllabic, laconic, sparing of words, brisk, exact, incisive, trenchant, pointed, to the point, in a nutshell, short and sweet, brachylogous, concisely styled, economically worded, tight-knit, portmanteau, compressed, telegraphic, elliptic, syncopal, clipped, abbreviated, contracted, truncated, shortened, compendious, epitomical, aphoristic, epigrammatic, sententious, outlined, summarized, summary, condensed, abridged, cut, not long in the telling

▶ *270 Shortness, 566 Taciturnity, 818 Discourtesy*

VERBS

4 **be concise**, waste no words, need few words, put in a nutshell, express pithily, cut a long story short, put it bluntly, not beat about the bush, come (straight) to the point, telescope, compress, compact, condense, abridge, cut, abbreviate, truncate, clip, shorten, contract, outline, sketch, epitomize, synopsize (US), sum up, summarize, abstract, precis, cut short, cut off, epigrammatize, pull no punches, talk turkey (US inf), give it straight (Inf), tell it like it is, cut the cackle (Inf), get down to brass tacks (Inf), get down to the nuts and bolts (*or* nitty-gritty) (Inf)

▶ *270 Shortness, 562 Summary*

ADVERBS

5 **concisely**, briefly, succinctly, pithily, crisply, compactly, tersely, curtly, brusquely, laconically, briskly, exactly, incisively, trenchantly, pointedly, telegraphically, elliptically, compendiously, sententiously, summarily, with few words, without wasting words, in brief, in short, in a word, in a nutshell, to the point, in outline, to sum up, to put it succinctly, to cut a long story short, in words of one syllable

553　Diffuseness

NOUNS

1 **diffuseness**, diffusion, diffusiveness, profuseness, copiousness, abundance, superabundance, amplitude, amplification, elaboration, expansion, extension, protraction, enlargement, expatiation, filler, expletive, padding, extra, circumstantiality, minuteness, detail, detailed account, blow-by-blow account, superfluity, repetitiveness, repetition, reiterativeness, reiteration, twice-told tales, redun-

dancy, redundance, tautology, pleonasm, excess, richness, rich vocabulary, fertility, output, productivity, productiveness, vein, flow, outpouring, exuberance, gush, effusiveness, effusion, verboseness, verbosity, loquacity, talkativeness, nonstop talking, wordiness, verbiage, long-windedness, waffle, prolixity, cloud of words, epic length, tedium, rigmarole, empty talk, rhetoric, oration, tirade, sermon, disquisition, dissertation, logorrhoea, verbal diarrhoea (Inf), blah (Sl)

▶ *261 Expansion, 269 Length, 188 Duration, 246 Fertility, 610 Excess, 565 Talkativeness, 183 Repetition, 788 Boredom, 521 Lack of Meaning, 564 Speech, 561 Dissertation*

2 **circumlocution**, circuitous writing, periphrasis, ambage (Arch), roundabout phrase, digression, deviation, discursion, excursion, excursus, rambling, wandering, indirectness, irrelevance, pointlessness, aimlessness, sidetrack, departure, beating about the bush, equivocalness

▶ *130 Addition, 108 Unrelatedness, 578 Equivocation, 335 Deviation, 151 Disorder*

ADJECTIVES

3 **diffuse**, diffusive, profuse, prolific, copious, abundant, superabundant, detailed, minute, amplified, expanded, extended, protracted, drawn out, long-drawn-out, spun out, padded out, padded, long, loose-knit, lengthy, neverending, nonstop, going on and on, repetitive, reiterative, epic, repeated, tautologous, tautological, redundant, pleonastic, superfluous, excessive, talkative, verbose, loquacious, fluent, gushing, effuse, effusive, inspired, wordy, exuberant, rich, fertile, flowing, overflowing, polysyllabic, sesquipedalian, waffling, prosy, prolix, long-winded, windy, fustian, flatulent, pretentious, empty, incoherent, ornate, rhetorical, magniloquent, bombastic, turgid, voluminous, tedious, boring, in love with one's own voice, of many words

▶ *610 Excess, 246 Fertility, 261 Expansion, 269 Length, 188 Duration, 565 Talkativeness, 183 Repetition, 557 Ornament, 788 Boredom, 521 Lack of Meaning, 564 Speech, 561 Dissertation*

4 **circumlocutory**, circuitous, periphrastic, ambagious (Arch), roundabout, deviating, digressive, discursive, excursive, rambling, wandering, oblique, indirect, irrelevant, pointless, aimless, sidetracked

▶ *108 Unrelatedness, 130 Addition, 335 Deviation, 151 Disorder*

VERBS

5 **be diffuse**, amplify, enlarge upon, expatiate, dilate, expand, extend, lengthen, protract, draw out, spin out, pad out, pad, repeat, repeat oneself, reiterate, tautologize, gush, flow, overflow, pour out, let oneself go, wax eloquent, elaborate, particularize, detail, go into

detail, go on and on, never end, discourse at length, waffle, orate, harangue, rant, rant and rave, use long words, bore, spin a long tale, ramble on, blether on, rabbit on (Inf)

▶ *261 Expansion, 269 Length, 565 Talkativeness, 183 Repetition, 788 Boredom, 564 Speech, 561 Dissertation*

6 **be circuitous**, digress, diverge, deviate, ramble, maunder, wander, make no point, not come to the point, beat about the bush, get sidetracked, get off the subject, go off on (*or* at) a tangent

▶ *108 Unrelatedness, 335 Deviation*

ADVERBS

7 **diffusely**, diffusively, profusely, prolifically, copiously, abundantly, minutely, in detail, repetitively, tautologously, tautologically, verbosely, loquaciously, effusively, in full, longwindedly, bombastically, turgidly, with many words, at length, at great length, on and on, ad nauseam, *in extenso* (L)

8 **circuitously**, periphrastically, in a roundabout way, digressively, discursively, obliquely, indirectly, on (*or* at) a tangent

554 Emphasis

NOUNS

1 **emphasis**, stress, accent, accentuation, underlining, underscoring, italics, vehemence, insistence, urgency, priority, iteration, reiteration, repetition, enthusiasm, fervour, passion, feeling, ardour, fire, warmth, glow, spirit, inspiration, vigour, vigorousness, vim, gusto, zest, verve, boldness, dash, raciness, sparkle, panache, liveliness, vitality, vivaciousness, vivacity, vividness, positive outlook, affirmation, piquancy, poignancy, bite, sharpness, mordancy, pungency, penetration, asperity, acuity, intensity, incisiveness, keenness, trenchancy, strength, strong language, power, force, forcefulness, energy, drive, punch, oomph (Sl)

▶ *535 Affirmation, 239 Vigour, 235 Power, 237 Strength, 380 Sharpness, 413 Piquancy, 183 Repetition, 557 Ornament, 564 Speech, 695 Compulsion, 547 Representation, 541 Exaggeration*

2 **seriousness**, solemnity, gravity, weight, importance, significance, attention, prominence, impressiveness, loftiness, elevation, sublimity, eloquence, grandeur, grandiloquence, magniloquence

▶ *611 Importance, 467 Attention*

ADJECTIVES

3 **emphatic**, vehement, earnest, insistent, urgent, firm, uncompromising, dogmatic, iterative, reiterative, repetitive, enthusiastic, fervent, passionate, impassioned, ardent, fiery, glowing, warm, spirited, inspired, vigorous, zestful, bold, dashing, racy, sparkling, lively,

vivacious, positive, affirmative, categorical, unequivocal, definite, sure, certain, incisive, cutting, slashing, pulling no punches, penetrating, keen, trenchant, pointed, sententious, pithy, meaty, thought-provoking, pungent, sharp, mordant, piquant, poignant, vivid, graphic, strong, strongly-worded, eloquent, compelling, convincing, effective, cogent, forceful, powerful, strenuous, energetic, brisk, peppy (Inf), punchy (Inf), zingy (Sl)

▶ *239 Vigour, 235 Power, 237 Strength, 760 Sensitivity, 695 Compulsion, 547 Representation, 380 Sharpness, 413 Piquancy, 183 Repetition, 557 Ornament, 564 Speech, 490 Certainty*

4 **emphasized**, stressed, accentuated, highlighted, enhanced, underlined, in italics, pointed out, pointed up, marked, pronounced, *accusé* (Fr)

▶ *535 Affirmation*

5 **serious**, solemn, grave, weighty, important, significant, heavy, intense, solid, impressive, lofty, elevated, sublime, grand, grandiloquent, majestic, magniloquent

▶ *611 Importance*

VERBS

6 **emphasize**, stress, accent, accentuate, highlight, enhance, spotlight, feature, underline, underscore, italicize, put in italics, point out, call (*or* draw) attention to, point up, insist, urge, reaffirm, reassert, reiterate, repeat, dwell on, plug, raise one's voice, shout, roar, thunder, bellow, glow, dash, sparkle, pull no punches, penetrate, provoke thought, convince, impress on, press home, drive home, din in, rub in, hammer home

▶ *535 Affirmation, 183 Repetition, 611 Importance, 564 Speech, 467 Attention, 541 Exaggeration*

ADVERBS

7 **emphatically**, vehemently, earnestly, insistently, urgently, dogmatically, enthusiastically, fervently, passionately, ardently, positively, incisively, strongly, forcefully, vigorously, energetically, strenuously, solemnly, gravely, with conviction, in no uncertain terms, with eloquence, in glowing terms, grandiloquently, magniloquently, majestically

555 Lack of Emphasis

ADJECTIVES

1 **unemphatic**, unimpassioned, unspirited, unexciting, uninspiring, tame, undramatic, inane, empty, pointless, lame, uninspired, boring, monotonous, stale, prosaic, prosy, commonplace, platitudinous, hackneyed, cliché-ridden, clichéd, conventional, insipid, wan, colourless, dull, dry, vapid, flat, thin, watery, wersh (Scot), poorly done, careless, inexact, slovenly, slipshod, rambling, prolix,

flatulent, disjointed, disconnected, garbled, amorphous, shapeless, smooth, loose, limp, unconvincing, ineffective, feeble, weak, meagre, languid, flaccid, exhausted, spent, vapouring, sloppy (Inf), wishy-washy (Inf), schmaltzy (Sl)

▶ *788 Boredom, 412 Tastelessness, 556 Simplicity, 542 Understatement, 474 Sophistry, 553 Diffuseness, 795 Vulgarity, 238 Weakness*

NOUNS

2 **lack of emphasis**, lack of passion, lack of spirit, lack of force, lack of inspiration, lack of sparkle, lack of style, tameness, emptiness, pointlessness, lameness, boredom, monotony, sameness, staleness, prosiness, plainness, commonplace, platitude, cliché, convention, insipidity, wanness, dullness, vapidity, flatness, thinness, wateriness, carelessness, inexactitude, flatulence, disconnection, garble, looseness, limpness, ineffectiveness, feebleness, weakness, weak style, enervation, enervated style, anticlimax, meagreness, flaccidity, exhaustion, sloppiness (Inf), schmaltz (Sl)

▶ *788 Boredom, 412 Tastelessness, 556 Simplicity, 542 Understatement, 474 Sophistry, 553 Diffuseness, 795 Vulgarity, 238 Weakness*

ADVERBS

3 **unemphatically**, uninspiringly, tamely, lamely, prosaically, platitudinously, conventionally, sentimentally, tastelessly, plainly, colourlessly, vapidly, carelessly, inexactly, loosely, unconvincingly, feebly, weakly

VERBS

4 **de-emphasize**, blur, dim, obfuscate

556   Simplicity

'Excellent!' I cried. 'Elementary,' said he. Arthur Conan Doyle.

The ability to simplify means to eliminate the unnecessary so that the necessary may speak. Hans Hofmann.

O holy simplicity! John Huss.

A child of five would understand this./ Send somebody to fetch a child of five. Groucho Marx.

Our life is frittered away by detail…Simplify, simplify. Henry David Thoreau.

ADJECTIVES

1 **simple**, plain, basic, ordinary, common, commonplace, common-variety, garden-variety, everyday, workaday, homy, homely, homespun, humble, lowly, austere, severe, Spartan, spare, ascetic, stark, bald, bare, naked, classic, neat, uncluttered, stripped-down, clear, clean, pure, unadulterated, unmixed, uninvolved, uncomplicated, unpretentious, unaffected, unassuming, modest, chaste, uninflated,

played down, unemphatic, undramatic, unsensational, restrained, sober, serious, dry, stodgy, tedious, boring, humdrum, mundane, usual, vernacular, matter-of-fact, prosaic, quotidian, mundane, unimaginative, uninspired, unpoetical, common-or-garden

▶ *550 Clarity, 621 Cleanness, 134 Purity, 810 Modesty, 296 Undress, 806 Humility, 558 Elegance, 788 Boredom, 584 Habit, 164 Generality, 166 Rule, 542 Understatement, 522 Intelligibility, 660 Easiness, 803 Commoner, 795 Vulgarity*

2 **unadorned**, unembellished, undecorated, unornamented, untrimmed, ungarnished, unpainted, uncoloured, unvarnished

3 **natural**, artless, simple-hearted, candid, frank, blunt, open, guileless, ingenuous, honest, veracious, direct, straightforward, plainspeaking, forthright, unpretentious, unaffected, unassuming, unfeigning, unsophisticated

▶ *658 Naivety, 537 Truth*

NOUNS

4 **simplicity**, unadorned simplicity, simpleness, plainness, ordinariness, commonness, homeyness, homeliness, humbleness, lowliness, austerity, severity, spareness, asceticism, ascesis, starkness, baldness, bareness, nakedness, neatness, clarity, cleanness, cleanliness, purity, unpretentiousness, modesty, chastity, restraint, soberness, seriousness, dryness, stodginess, tediousness, boredom, usualness, matter-of-factness, mundaneness, common speech, everyday speech, idiom, natural idiom, vernacular, prose, plain prose, plain words, plain English, household words, intelligibility

▶ *550 Clarity, 621 Cleanness, 134 Purity, 810 Modesty, 296 Undress, 806 Humility, 788 Boredom, 584 Habit, 522 Intelligibility, 795 Vulgarity*

5 **unadornment**, unembellishment, lack of decoration, lack of ornamentation, lack of colour

6 **naturalness**, artlessness, candidness, candour, frankness, bluntness, openness, honesty, veracity, directness, straightforwardness, unpretentiousness, unaffectedness, plain speech, plain speaking, home truth, speaking straight from the shoulder, mincing no words

▶ *658 Naivety, 537 Truth*

VERBS

7 **be simple**, make simple, simplify, use common speech, use plain English, speak plainly, speak simply, come to the point, say outright, call a spade a spade, speak straight from the shoulder, mince no words, make no bones about it, tell it like it is, tell one straight to his (*or* her) face, get down to brass tacks (Inf), talk turkey (US inf)

▶ *550 Clarity, 524 Interpretation, 522 Intelligibility, 537 Truth*

ADVERBS
8 **simply**, plainly, basically, starkly, baldly, purely, unpretentiously, undramatically, candidly, frankly, bluntly, openly, directly, point-blank, intelligibly, clearly, matter-of-factly, prosaically, in the vernacular, in plain words, in common parlance, in prose, not to put too fine a point upon it, in words of one syllable

557 Ornament

NOUNS
1 **ornament**, ornamentation, adornment, decoration, garnish, trimming, embellishment, colour, flourish, embroidery, frills, *épergne* (Fr), arrangement, flower arrangement, floral arrangement, table setting, interior decoration, colour decoration, colour design, floridness, floweriness, flowers of speech, arabesques, purple passages, preciosity, preciousness, euphuism, euphemism, rhetoric, figurativeness, figure of speech, metaphor, simile, trope, alliteration, assonance, hyperbaton, antithesis
▶ *792 Decoration, 48 Literature, 49 Music, 791 Beautification*
2 **affectation**, pomposity, pretension, pretentiousness, ostentation, showiness, false show, false front, putting on airs, magniloquence, grandiloquence, loftiness, high tone, high-sounding words, eloquence, rhetoric, orotundity, vigour, extravagance, overstatement, exaggeration, hyperbole, turgidity, turgescence, flatulence, talking big, boasting, bombast, rant, fustian, rodomontade, empty talk, Johnsonese, long words, diffuseness, circumlocution, convolution, tortuousness
▶ *554 Emphasis, 541 Exaggeration, 797 Affectation, 811 Showiness, 423 Loudness, 521 Lack of Meaning, 553 Diffuseness*
3 **phrasemonger**, stylist, euphuist, flowery writer, flowery speaker, speaker, orator, rhetorician, politician, word-spinner (Inf)
▶ *558 Elegance, 564 Speech, 549 Style*
ADJECTIVES
4 **ornate**, elaborate, fancy, ornamented, ornamental, decorated, richly decorated, decorative, adorned, garnished, trimmed, embellished, beautified, gilded, coloured, rich, luxuriant, florid, flowery, precious, euphuistic, euphemistic, extravagant, overstated, exaggerated, hyperbolic, affected, pompous, pretentious, ostentatious, flashy, flamboyant, showy, meretricious, frothy, fussy, overloaded, stiff, stilted, pedantic, ponderous, long-worded, Latinate, sesquipedalian, Johnsonian, diffuse, circumlocutory, convoluted, tortuous, rhetorical, declamatory, oratorical, eloquent, grandiloquent, magniloquent, lofty, high-flown, high-flying, loud, brassy,

resonant, sonorous, ringing, singing, ranting, orotund, high-pitched, high-sounding, grandiose, stately, bombastic, fustian, inflated, tumid, turgid, swollen, antithetical, alliterative, metaphorical, figurative, highfalutin (Inf)
▶ *792 Decoration, 791 Beautification, 797 Affectation, 423 Loudness, 811 Showiness, 541 Exaggeration, 554 Emphasis, 553 Diffuseness*
VERBS
5 **ornament**, adorn, decorate, garnish, trim, deck, festoon, embellish, beautify, enhance, grace, embroider, enrich, gild, overlay, load with ornament, overload, gild the lily, euphuize, euphemize, elaborate, overelaborate, overstate, use long words, ring, sing, boast, rant, rave
▶ *792 Decoration, 791 Beautification, 797 Affectation, 423 Loudness*
ADVERBS
6 **ornately**, elaborately, floridly, preciously, extravagantly, hyperbolically, pompously, pretentiously, ostentatiously, flamboyantly, pedantically, ponderously, grandiloquently, magniloquently, bombastically, turgidly, metaphorically, figuratively

558 Elegance

NOUNS
1 **elegance**, elegancy, style, stylishness, perfect style, grace, gracefulness, delicacy, harmony, euphony, taste, tastefulness, good taste, propriety, beauty, politeness, gentility, refinement, sophistication, suavity, suaveness, culture, purity, perspicuity, clarity, plainness, simplicity, restraint, dignity, distinction, grandeur, naturalness, classicism, Atticism, proportion, symmetry, balance, rhythm, ease, readability, flow, fluidity, smoothness, fluency, aptness, fittingness, felicity, the right word in the right place, *mot juste* (Fr), polish, finish, neatness, well-turned phrase, elaboration, ornament, flourish, florid style, artificiality
▶ *549 Style, 796 Fashion, 789 Beauty, 794 Refinement, 550 Clarity, 556 Simplicity, 308 Symmetry, 557 Ornament, 619 Perfection, 655 Skill, 295 Dress*
2 **stylist**, stylish writer, euphuist, classical author, classic, classicist, purist
▶ *48 Literature, 557 Ornament, 549 Style*
ADJECTIVES
3 **elegant**, stylish, smart, graceful, delicate, harmonious, euphonious, tasteful, fine, beautiful, majestic, stately, exquisite, polite, courtly, refined, sophisticated, suave, cultivated, pure, perspicacious, clear, plain, simple, restrained, dignified, distinguished, distinctive, natural, idiomatic, good, correct, expressive, sensitive,

readable, classic, well-proportioned, proportional, symmetrical, balanced, gracile, rhythmic, tripping, easy, fluid, smooth, flawless, mellifluous, fluent, apt, fitting, felicitous, polished, manicured, soigné, well-groomed, finished, unlaboured, well-turned, round, neat, neatly put, neatly wrought, artistic, artistically done, elaborate, ornamented, artificial, classical, Attic, Augustan, Ciceronian

▶ *549 Style, 796 Fashion, 789 Beauty, 794 Refinement, 550 Clarity, 556 Simplicity, 308 Symmetry, 557 Ornament, 655 Skill, 619 Perfection, 295 Dress, 48 Literature*

VERBS

4 **be elegant**, have a good style, show style, be stylish, write well, show taste, have taste, have a light touch, turn a phrase, perfect, polish, refine, edit, rewrite, elaborate, ornament, do artistically

▶ *48 Literature, 619 Perfection, 557 Ornament, 549 Style, 794 Refinement, 796 Fashion, 789 Beauty*

ADVERBS

5 **elegantly**, stylishly, smartly, gracefully, delicately, harmoniously, euphoniously, tastefully, beautifully, suavely, perspicaciously, clearly, plainly, simply, naturally, expressively, readably, symmetrically, rhythmically, easily, smoothly, mellifluously, fluently, aptly, felicitously, neatly, artistically, elaborately, artificially

559 Inelegance

NOUNS

1 **inelegance**, inelegancy, gracelessness, clumsiness, awkwardness, gaucheness, lack of finesse, gaucherie, gawkiness, gawkishness, lack of style, lack of polish, cack-handedness (Sl), klutziness (US sl)

▶ *656 Unskilfulness, 620 Imperfection*

2 **impropriety**, indelicacy, crudeness, vulgarity, tastelessness, bad taste, rudeness, discourtesy, grossness, coarseness, roughness, boorishness, churlishness, uncouthness, unrefinement

▶ *795 Vulgarity, 818 Discourtesy, 807 Insolence*

3 **ugliness**, plainness, drabness, shabbiness, bad taste, garishness, gaudiness, loudness, tawdriness, vulgarity, commonness, tackiness (Inf)

▶ *795 Vulgarity, 790 Ugliness, 412 Tastelessness*

4 **inelegance of speech**, incorrectness, bad grammar, solecism, lack of polish, vulgarism, vulgarity, dysphemism, clumsy construction, clumsiness, long-windedness, sesquipedalianism, stiffness, stiltedness, cumbrousness, ponderousness, turgidity, bombast, pomposity, grandiloquence, cacology, bad language, cursing, effing and blinding (Sl)

▶ *474 Sophistry, 578 Equivocation, 5 Linguistics*

5 **mispronunciation**, poor diction, speech defect, speech impediment

6 **blunder**, faux pas, gaffe, gaucherie, bloomer (Inf), clanger (Inf), howler (Inf), cock up (Sl), dog's breakfast (Sl), pig's ear (Sl), balls-up (Tab sl)

▶ *504 Error*

ADJECTIVES

7 **graceless**, ungraceful, inelegant, clumsy, awkward, cumbersome, ill-proportioned, ungainly, dumpy, clownish, gauche, gawky, gawkish, undignified, ham-fisted, heavy-handed, heavy-footed, all fingers and thumbs (Inf), cack-handed (Sl), klutzy (US sl)

▶ *656 Unskilfulness, 620 Imperfection*

8 **indecorous**, unseemly, improper, indelicate, crude, vulgar, tasteless, in bad taste, beyond the pale, rude, discourteous, impolite, gross, coarse, boorish, churlish, uncouth, barbaric, barbarous, unrefined, unpolished, *infra dignitatem* (L), infra dig

▶ *795 Vulgarity, 818 Discourtesy*

9 **inelegant**, dysphemistic, cacological, turgid, pompous, rhetorical, grandiloquent, formal, stiff, stilted, wooden, unfluent, ill-sounding, cacophonous, uneuphonious, jarring, grating, incorrect, solecistic, doggerel, artless, unnatural, artificial, mannered, affected, laboured, tortuous, ludicrous, grotesque

▶ *813 Formality, 797 Affectation*

10 **ugly**, unattractive, unaesthetic, plain, drab, dingy, dreary, dull, shabby, seedy, squalid, rough, mousy, lank, dowdy, badly dressed, unfashionable, in bad taste, tasteless, common, vulgar, garish, gaudy, loud, tawdry, meretricious, overdressed, tacky (Inf), tarty (Inf), dressed up like a dog's dinner (Sl), common as muck (Inf)

▶ *790 Ugliness, 795 Vulgarity, 811 Showiness*

ADVERBS

11 **inelegantly**, gracelessly, clumsily, awkwardly, indecorously, indelicately, grossly, coarsely, shabbily, unfashionably, tastelessly

560 Description

NOUNS

1 **description**, account, detailed description, detailed account, statement, statement of facts, details, particulars, specification, report, record, delineation, depiction, picture, portrait, portrayal, characterization, profile, character sketch, case history, version, explanation

▶ *528 Information, 545 Record*

2 **brief description**, caption, legend, indication, heading, subtitle, word portrait, thumbnail sketch, summary, outline, cameo, vignette, exposé

▶ *562 Summary*

3 **narration**, narrative, narrative writing, account, essay, story, storyline, plot, subplot, scenario, tale, *conte* (Fr), yarn, fairy tale, folk tale, myth, legend, saga, epic, narrative poem, serial, soap opera, kitchen-sink drama, fable, cautionary tale, parable, allegory, metaphor, simile, stream of consciousness, ballad, anecdote, reminiscence, chronicle, annals, history, record, journal, diary, drama, documentary, documentary drama, docudrama, faction, reportage, travelogue, fiction, fantasy, tall story (Inf), soap (Inf)
▶ *48 Literature, 3 History*

4 **factual account**, nonfiction, documentary, documentary account, report, journalism, biography, autobiography, life story, curriculum vitae (CV), résumé (US), hagiography, obituary, real-life story, personal account, confessions, memoirs, diary, journal, letter, personal correspondence
▶ *545 Record, 561 Dissertation*

5 **fiction**, descriptive writing, creative writing, creative composition, novel, short story, novella, historical novel, picaresque novel, *roman à clef* (Fr), fictional biography, *Bildungsroman* (Ger), crime fiction, detective novel, thriller, spy story, science fiction, sci-fi, adventure story, western, romance, love story, gothic novel, ghost story, pulp fiction, bestseller, blockbuster (Inf), whodunit (Inf), potboiler (Sl)
▶ *48 Literature*

6 **sort**, kind, type, genre, variety, breed, species, ilk, kidney
▶ *163 Class*

7 **nomenclature**, naming, addressing, calling, roll call, appellation, denomination, terminology, taxonomy, classification, designation, description, identification, indication, antonomasia, naming ceremony, christening, baptising, baptism, nicknaming, study of names, eponymy, onomastics, onomatology, orismology, study of place names, toponymy, misnaming, pseudonymity
▶ *544 Identification*

8 **name**, nomen, noun, proper noun, appellation, apellative, full name, forename, first name, praenomen, Christian name, baptismal name, given name, Confirmation name, middle name, second name, agnomen, last name, married name, surname, family name, patronymic, matronymic, cognomen, maiden name, pet name, diminutive, sweetheart name, familiar name, pen name, *nom de plume* (Fr), false name, alias, assumed name, pseudonym, allonym, stage name, sobriquet, nickname, tautonym, namesake, epithet, title, autograph, signature, label, tag, term, technical term, password, place name, eponym, toponym, trademark, tradename, hallmark,

markings, moniker (*or* monicker) (Sl), handle (Sl)
▶ *544 Identification, 804 Title, 567 Address, 821 Love, 10 Ritual*

9 **representation**, imitation, likeness, striking likeness, impression, picture, true picture, portrait, sketch, drawing, mechanical drawing, freehand drawing, technical drawing, duplicate, double, spitting image, facsimile, tracing, photocopy, Xerox (Tm), lithograph
▶ *547 Representation, 50 Painting and Sculpture, 110 Sameness*

10 **descriptive writer**, creative writer, wordsmith, literary person, man (*or* woman) of letters, writer, author, novelist, fiction writer, fictionist, crime writer, essayist, poet, playwright, dramatist, librettist, script writer, fabulist, teller of tales, storyteller, raconteur, anecdotist, biographer, hagiographer, diarist, historian, chronicler, annalist, recorder, historiographer, journalist, reporter, correspondent, special correspondent, war correspondent, sports correspondent, columnist, gossip columnist, agony aunt, scribbler, pen pusher, ghostwriter, hack (Inf)
▶ *48 Literature, 532 Publication, 533 News*
ADJECTIVES

11 **descriptive**, representational, graphic, vivid, detailed, full, informative, illustrative, explicatory, explanatory, elucidatory, illuminating, expository, expositive, interpretive, amplifying, well-drawn, true-to-life, real-life, realistic, naturalistic, photographic, eidetic, convincing, picturesque, expressive, impressionistic, suggestive, evocative, moving, poignant, thrilling, exciting, striking, highly coloured, forceful
▶ *528 Information*

12 **narrative**, fictional, imaginative, kitchen-sink, factual, documentary, biographical, autobiographical, factional, mythological, epic, heroic, romantic, picaresque
▶ *48 Literature*

13 **representing**, representative, iconic, pictorial, emblematic, symbolic, figurative, diagrammatic, representational, realistic, true-to-life, photographic, artistic, primitive, naive, impressionistic, surrealistic, surreal, abstract
▶ *50 Painting and Sculpture, 66 Photography*
VERBS

14 **describe**, delineate, draw, sketch, picture, depict, portray, limn, paint, represent, illustrate, characterize, form, shape, fashion, design, draft, sketch out, adumbrate, rough out, outline, make a diagram of, do a portrait, catch a likeness, capture an expression, doodle, scribble

15 **recount**, relate, tell, retell, narrate, tell a story, tell a tale, spin a yarn, reminisce, evoke, bring to life, characterize, detail, recapitulate,

review, record, chronicle, repeat, recite, rehearse, pass on the information, communicate, report, cover, submit a report, make a statement, testify, keep posted, correspond, write an account of, write a story about, fictionalize, dramatize, romanticize, mythologize, imagine
▶ 528 Information, 519 Imagination

16 **define**, specify, name, mention, detail, particularize, itemize, inventorize, explain, interpret

17 **describe a circle**, draw a circle, circumscribe, mark out, trace

ADVERBS

18 **descriptively**, graphically, vividly, realistically, illustratively, imaginatively

561 Dissertation

NOUNS

1 **dissertation**, discourse, disquisition, treatise, tract, tractate, exposition, summary, theme, argument, descant, thesis, essay, composition, study, lucubration, examination, survey, inquiry, discussion, symposium, paper, monograph, memoir, screed, harangue, homily, sermon, oration, peroration, tirade, lecture, lesson, prolegomenon, exegesis, interpretation, explanation, gloss, annotation, comment, commentary
▶ 562 Summary, 473 Argument, 564 Speech

2 **article**, leading article, leader, editorial comment, editorial, column, news item, review, notice, critique, criticism, write-up, puff (Inf)
▶ 533 News, 532 Publication

3 **dissertator**, essayist, pamphleteer, propagandist, preacher, orator, speaker, lecturer, teacher, publicizer, publicist, writer, author, editor, leader writer, journalist, contributor, reviewer, critic, commentator, exponent, expounder, expositor, proselytizer, proselyte, interpreter, Leavisite, exegete, glossarist, annotator

VERBS

4 **dissertate**, discourse, descant, speak about, write about, put forward an argument about, argue, develop a thesis, go into, deal with in depth, do a paper on, write a treatise on, hold a symposium, inquire into, survey, discuss, comment on, criticize, commentate, gloss, annotate, interpret, explain, elucidate, define, expound, proselytize, harangue, orate, perorate, sermonize, preach, pontificate
▶ 473 Argument, 524 Interpretation, 564 Speech

ADJECTIVES

5 **expository**, discursive, disquisitional, critical, interpretive, interpretative, exegetical, illuminating, editorial, glossarial, annotative

562 Summary

NOUNS

1 **summary**, synopsis, precis, résumé, aperçu (Fr), digest, epitome, abstract, review, recapitulation, gist, drift, conspectus, survey, bird's-eye view, overview, rundown, sketch, thumbnail sketch, CV (curriculum vitae), recap (Inf)

2 **outline**, skeleton, plan, blueprint, syllabus, prospectus, brochure, abridgment (or abridgement), concise version, potted version, abbreviation, shortening, diminution, contraction, truncation, pruning, compression, apheresis, apocope, syncope, elision
▶ 552 Conciseness, 262 Contraction, 592 Plan, 171 List

3 **compendium**, anthology, treasury, collection, compilation, corpus, chrestomathy, miscellany, miscellanea, album, scrapbook, ephemera, cuttings, extracts, excerpts, selection
▶ 161 Assembly, 580 Selection

4 **summariness**, briefness, brevity, shortness, terseness, brusqueness, conciseness, pithiness, succinctness, compactness, pointedness, compendiousness, laconism, laconicism
▶ 270 Shortness, 552 Conciseness

5 **summarizer**, precis writer, abridger, epitomizer, abbreviator, shortener, cutter, editor

ADJECTIVES

6 **summary**, brief, short, short and sweet, curt, brusque, terse, concise, pithy, compendious, succinct, compact, pointed, short and to the point, epigrammatic, epigrammatical, laconic, irreducible
▶ 552 Conciseness, 270 Shortness, 648 Haste

7 **shortened**, abbreviated, abridged, summarized, synopsized, clipped, pruned, docked, truncated, cut short, cut, contracted, compacted, potted, collected
▶ 262 Contraction, 270 Shortness

VERBS

8 **summarize**, precis, make a résumé, synopsize, make a synopsis of, condense, digest, epitomize, encapsulate, reduce, shorten, abbreviate, abridge, contract, pot, truncate, cut short, give an outline of, outline, sketch, sketch out, boil down, sum up, resume, recapitulate, abstract, express pithily, epigrammatize, recap (Inf)
▶ 552 Conciseness, 270 Shortness, 262 Contraction

9 **compile**, consolidate, collect together, anthologize, excerpt, select
▶ 580 Selection, 161 Assembly

10 **be brief**, come to the point, cut a long story short

ADVERBS

11 **summarily**, briefly, shortly, brusquely, tersely, crisply, laconically, concisely, pithily, succintly, pointedly

12 **in brief**, in short, without wasting words, in a word, in a nutshell, in a few words, epigrammatically

563 Voicelessness

NOUNS

1 **voicelessness**, loss of voice, no voice, aphonia, dysphonia

2 **inarticulation**, inarticulateness, difficulty in speaking, hoarseness, huskiness, croakiness, changing voice, breaking voice, thickness of voice, raucousness, harsh voice, unmusicality, tuneless voice
▶ 430 Harsh Sound

3 **speech defect**, speech impediment, aphasia, dysphasia, dysphemia, stammer, stammering, stutter, stuttering, unintelligible speech, paraphasia, lallation, babbling, lisping, sibilation
▶ 429 Hissing Sound, 523 Unintelligibility, 506 Nonsense

4 **whispering**, whisper, stage whisper, murmur, mumble, muffled voice, low voice, undertone, aside, mutter, voiceless consonant, surd, sigh, hiss
▶ 428 Mutedness, 424 Faintness

5 **mutism**, deaf-mutism, muteness, dumbness, speechlessness, taciturnity, reticence, silence
▶ 566 Taciturnity, 422 Silence, 421 Deafness

6 **voiceless speech**, sign language, deaf and dumb language, gesture, gesticulation, meaningful look
▶ 543 Sign

7 **voiceless person**, mute, deaf-mute, deaf-and-dumb person, infant, fracastorius

8 **mute**, damper, soft pedal

ADJECTIVES

9 **voiceless**, unvoiced, aphonic, dysphonic, surd, silent, infant
▶ 422 Silence

10 **low-voiced**, whispering, whispered, inaudible, muted, muttering, murmuring, mumbling, muffled, faint, low, breaking, cracked, hoarse, husky, croaking, with a frog in one's throat
▶ 428 Mutedness, 424 Faintness

11 **speechless**, inarticulate, mute, dumb, deaf and dumb, tongue-tied, taciturn, reticent, silent, silenced, gagged, choked, dumbfounded, struck dumb, mum (Inf), shtoom (Sl), gobsmacked (Sl)
▶ 422 Silence, 421 Deafness, 566 Taciturnity, 514 Surprise

12 **inarticulate**, unintelligible, aphasic, dysphasic, dysphemic, stammering, stuttering, paraphasic, babbling, lisping, sibilant, hissing, sighing
▶ 523 Unintelligibility

VERBS

13 **be voiceless**, not speak, be silent, keep quiet, hold one's tongue, not breathe a word, button one's lip (Sl), keep mum (Inf), keep shtoom (Sl)

14 **have difficulty speaking**, stammer, stutter, babble, lisp, hiss, lose one's voice, be struck dumb, lose one's powers of speech, lose one's tongue, let the cat get one's tongue, use sign language, sign, exchange meaningful looks, gesture, gesticulate
▶ 543 Sign

15 **strike dumb**, make mute, dumbfound, take one's breath away, muffle, mute, deaden, silence, hush, gag, suppress, reduce to silence, cut short, hang up on, shout down, gobsmack (Sl)
▶ 422 Silence

16 **speak in a low voice**, speak softly, whisper, stage whisper, whisper in one's ear, mutter, mumble, murmur, speak *sotto voce*, drop one's voice, speak under one's breath, speak in muted tones, sound faint, sigh
▶ 428 Mutedness, 424 Faintness

ADVERBS

17 **voicelessly**, silently, hoarsely, huskily, low, in an undertone, *sotto voce* (It), under one's breath, in a whisper, with bated breath

564 Speech

Let your speech be alway with grace, seasoned with salt, that ye may know how ye ought to answer every man. Bible: Colossians.

Let thy speech be short, comprehending much in few words; be as one that knoweth and yet holdeth his tongue. Bible: Ecclesiasticus.

Most men make little use of their speech than to give evidence against their own understanding. Lord Halifax.

But words once spoke can never be recall'd. Earl of Roscommon.

NOUNS

1 **faculty of speech**, oral communication, language, talk, talking, speaking, verbal intercourse, dialogue, conversation, colloquy, discourse, voice, speaking voice, tongue, langue, parole, vocabulary, spoken language, living language, mother tongue, native tongue, Queen's English, English as she is spoken, vernacular, vulgar tongue, colloquial speech, idiomatic speech, idiom, dialect, patois, parlance, private language, code, idiolect, slang, cant, jargon, gobbledegook, computerspeak, technobabble, newspeak, patter, chat, natter, chatter, psychobabble (Inf), lingo (Inf), yakking (Inf), yakkety-yak (Inf), chinwag (Inf), rabbit (Sl), spiel (Sl), rap (Sl)
▶ 567 Address, 568 Conversation, 5 Linguistics, 534 Communications

2 **power of speech**, articulateness, articulacy,

eloquence, fluency, command of language, way with words, word power, style, rich vocabulary, grandiloquence, magniloquence, orotundity, purple passage, flowery speech, talkativeness, volubility, loquacity, glossolalia, speaking in tongues, prolixity, logorrhoea, verbosity, verbiage, wordiness, verbal diarrhoea, long-windedness, repetitiveness, blah (Sl), blarney (Sl), gift of the gab (Sl)

▶ *565 Talkativeness, 549 Style, 553 Diffuseness, 183 Repetition*

3 mode of speech, tone of voice, voice, tone, voice quality, timbre, intonation, pitch, modulation, inflection, stress, emphasis, pronunciation, accent, regional accent, native accent, foreign accent, broad accent, brogue, twang, burr, trill, drawl, suburban whine, nasality, stridor, lisping, stammer, stutter, speech impediment, speech defect, mispronunciation, cacoepy

4 articulation, diction, elocution, voicing, enunciation, phonation, vocalization, utterance, delivery, attack, ventriloquism, sign language, meaningful looks, gesticulation, gesture

▶ *543 Sign, 563 Voicelessness*

5 organ of speech, articulator, voice, mouth, tongue, teeth, lips, vocal organs, vocal chords, vocal folds, voice box, larynx, Adam's apple, glottis, epiglottis, hard palate, alveolar palate, soft palate, uvula, nasal cavity, oral cavity, pharynx, throat

6 phonetics, phonology, articulatory phonetics, acoustic phonetics, orthoepy, pronunciation, accentuation, rhythmic pattern, cadence, prosody, prosodics, metrics, linguistics, agogics

▶ *5 Linguistics*

7 utterance, vocalization, spoken word, word of mouth, word, phrase, sentence, expression, locution, articulate sound, speech sound, phoneme, vowel, diphthong, voiced consonant, syllable, remark, observation, comment, dictum, statement, affirmation, assertion, averment, declaration, pronouncement, allegation, thought, reflection, interjection, exclamation, ejaculation, gasp, mutter, murmur, whisper, aside, question, answer, reply, response, address, greeting, opinion, contribution, say, crack (Dial), one's two cents' worth (US inf), one's two-pennyworth (Inf), one's bit (Inf), one's piece (Inf)

▶ *535 Affirmation*

8 speech, oration, address, welcoming address, panegyric, eulogy, encomium, farewell oration, farewell address, valedictory, obsequies, after-dinner speech, vote of thanks, reading, recital, declaration, broadcast, sermon, exhortation, homily, harangue, mouthful, earful, tirade, diatribe, invective, obloquy, flea in

one's ear, lecture, dissertation, peroration, preamble, proem, prologue, foreword, monologue, soliloquy

▶ *561 Dissertation, 567 Address, 569 Soliloquy, 156 Beginning*

9 art of public speaking, oratory, rhetoric, stump oratory, speech-making, speechifying, tub-thumping, declamation, ranting, rant, blarney, vituperation, address, soap-box oratory

10 speaker, utterer, talker, sayer, chatterer, prattler, gossip, gossiper, communicator, conversationalist, interlocutor, monologist, soliloquizer, soliloquist, public speaker, after-dinner speaker, speech-maker, speechifier, orator, oratrix, rhetorician, ranter, soap-box orator, tub-thumper, haranguer, demagogue, sermonizer, preacher, lecturer, presenter, announcer, broadcaster, narrator, chorus, spokesperson, spokesman, spokeswoman, delegate, advocate, mediator, intermediary, salesperson, salesman, saleswoman, representative, rep, smooth-talker (Inf), blabbermouth (Inf), bigmouth (Inf)

▶ *568 Conversation, 569 Soliloquy, 678 Mediation*

VERBS

11 speak, talk, say, utter, declare, proclaim, state, aver, assert, affirm, allege, tell, relate, recite, quote, cite, give utterance to, enunciate, voice, express, verbalize, put into words, find words for, find words to express, formulate, convey, impart, communicate, disclose, blurt out, interject, exclaim, ejaculate, interrupt, have one's say, answer, reply, respond, call attention to, refer to, allude to, mention

▶ *535 Affirmation, 530 Disclosure*

12 speak loudly, speak up, shout, yell, cry, bawl, roar, boom, thunder, trumpet, blare, scream, shriek, screech, exclaim

▶ *423 Loudness, 430 Harsh Sound*

13 speak in a particular way, breathe, whisper, murmur, mutter, mumble, sigh, gasp, pant, pipe, flute, warble, coo, sing out, chant, cackle, crow, bark, yelp, growl, snap, snarl, squeak, whine, sob, wail, drawl, sibilate

▶ *431 Human Cry, 424 Faintness, 429 Hissing Sound*

14 speak to, address, talk to, apostrophize, discourse, lecture, sermonize, preach to, hold forth, orate, deliver a speech, make speeches, speechify, take the floor, perorate, rant, tub-thump, rail, harangue, invoke, appeal to

▶ *567 Address, 568 Conversation, 565 Talkativeness, 583 Improvisation, 853 Flattery*

15 talk to oneself, soliloquize, monologize

▶ *569 Soliloquy*

ADJECTIVES

16 speech, lingual, linguistic, vocal, spoken, uttered, said, articulated, voiced, vocalized, pronounced, enunciated

17 oral, verbal, unwritten, *viva voce* (L), nuncupative, parol

18 phonetic, phonic, tonic, tonal, pitched, accented, stressed, unstressed, unaccented, nasal, twangy, throaty, guttural, aspirated, aspirate, voiced, voiceless

▶ *5 Linguistics*

19 speaking, talking, able to speak, with a tongue in one's head, articulate, fluent, talkative, loquacious, voluble, free-speaking, true-speaking, plain-speaking, plain-spoken, outspoken, out-speaking, loud-spoken, loud-speaking, soft-spoken, soft-speaking, quietly spoken, well-spoken, Anglophone, English-speaking, monolingual, unilingual, bilingual, trilingual, multilingual, polyglot, monoglot

▶ *565 Talkativeness*

20 eloquent, silver-tongued, smooth-talking, rhetorical, grandiloquent, magniloquent, tub-thumping, ranting, declamatory, bombastic, dithyrambic

ADVERBS

21 orally, vocally, verbally, *viva voce* (L), by word of mouth, phonetically, linguistically, eloquently, articulately, rhetorically, grandiloquently, magniloquently

565   Talkativeness

NOUNS

1 talkativeness, loquacity, loquaciousness, volubility, garrulousness, garrulity, verbosity, wordiness, prolixity, logorrhoea, logomania, verbal diarrhoea, runaway tongue, long-windedness, windiness, fluency, glibness, fluent tongue, multiloquence, multiloquy, eloquence, flow of words, chattiness, gabbiness (Inf), gassiness (Inf), big mouth (Inf), gift of the gab (Inf), spiel (Inf)

▶ *553 Diffuseness, 564 Speech*

2 effusiveness, effusion, gushiness, gush, candour, openness, frankness, communicativeness, sociability

▶ *815 Sociability*

3 talk, chat, chatter, chattering, babble, gabble, jabber, jabbering, rap, prattle, prating, palaver, gab, blab, blabber, small talk, gossip, idle gossip, tittle-tattle, waffle, gas, hot air, empty talk, chinwag (Inf), yak (Inf), yakkety-yak (Inf), witter (Inf), jaw (Sl), jaw-jaw (Sl), guff (Sl), blah (Sl), blah-blah (Sl)

▶ *568 Conversation, 564 Speech, 506 Nonsense*

4 talker, speaker, nonstop talker, chatterer, chatterbox, babbler, jabberer, gossip, tattler, tittle-tattler, driveller, waffler, ranter, quacker, gasser, magpie, jay, gabber, blabber, informer, blabbermouth (Inf), grass (Sl), bigmouth (Inf), windbag (Sl), gasbag (Sl), motor-mouth (Sl)

▶ *528 Information*

ADJECTIVES

5 talkative, loquacious, voluble, garrulous, verbose, wordy, prolix, long-winded, windy, chattering, babbling, gabbling, jabbering, jibbering, running on, fluent, glib, multiloquent, eloquent, gassy (Inf), gabby (Inf)

▶ *553 Diffuseness, 564 Speech*

6 effusive, gushing, expansive, candid, frank, communicative, sociable, chatty, conversational, gossipy, tattling, prattling, prating, blabbing, yakking (Inf), big-mouthed (Inf), all mouth (Inf), mouthy (Inf), lippy (Inf), flip (Sl)

▶ *815 Sociability, 568 Conversation*

VERBS

7 be talkative, talk at length, talk, chat, chatter, babble, gabble, jabber, gibber, prate, gab, natter, gas, prattle on, rattle on, ramble on, blab, blabber, waffle, blah (Sl), rabbit on (Sl), witter (Inf), jaw (Inf), go on and on (Inf), run off at the mouth (Sl)

8 talk too much, talk nineteen to the dozen, talk the hind leg(s) off a donkey, talk one's head off, oil one's tongue, have a big mouth, spin out, expatiate, gush, spout, hold forth, drone on, bore, buttonhole, monopolize the conversation, not let anyone get a word in edgeways, like the sound of one's own voice, talk until one is blue in the face, shoot one's mouth off (Sl)

9 out-talk, shout down, bamboozle, filibuster, stonewall

▶ *474 Sophistry*

ADVERBS

10 talkatively, loquaciously, volubly, garrulously, fluently, glibly, eloquently

11 effusively, gushingly, expansively, candidly, frankly, sociably, communicatively, chattily

INTERJECTIONS

12 rhubarb! rhubarb! , blah! blah!, yak! yak!, yakkety-yak!

566   Taciturnity

ADJECTIVES

1 taciturn, quiet, reserved, reticent, withdrawn, shy, incommunicative, uncommunicative, unforthcoming, diffident, reserved, not to be drawn, tight-lipped, antisocial, unsociable, sullen, self-contained, mum (Sl), shtoom (Sl)

▶ *816 Unsociability*

2 silent, mute, dumb, voiceless, speechless, inarticulate

▶ *422 Silence, 563 Voicelessness*

3 sparing with words, saying little, laconic, monosyllabic, guarded, cautious, playing one's cards close to one's chest, secretive, with sealed lips, uninformative, vague, evasive, cagey (Inf), brusque, short, curt, terse, concise

▶ *781 Caution, 529 Secrecy*

NOUNS

4 **taciturnity**, quietness, reticence, reserve, diffidence, shyness, incommunicativeness, uncommunicativeness, shortness, brevity, brusqueness, curtness, gruffness, sullenness, evasiveness, secrecy
▶ *529 Secrecy*

5 **silence**, muteness, dumbness, voicelessness, speechlessness, inarticulacy
▶ *422 Silence, 563 Voicelessness*

6 **guarded speech**, laconism, laconicism, laconicness, conciseness, succinctness, terseness
▶ *552 Conciseness*

7 **taciturn person**, person of few words, no speaker, no orator, not a great talker, strong silent type, clam, Trappist

VERBS

8 **be taciturn**, spare one's words, use few words, have little to say, stay silent, keep quiet, say nothing, make no answer, keep one's counsel, refuse to comment, neither confirm nor deny, hold one's tongue, keep one's mouth shut, keep oneself to oneself, keep one's trap shut (Inf), keep shtoom (Sl)

9 **lapse into silence**, pipe down, have the words taken out of one's mouth, lose one's voice, dry up, not mention, leave out, pass over, waste no words over, save one's breath

ADVERBS

10 **taciturnly**, quietly, reticently, incommunicatively, uncommunicatively, silently, voicelessly, without speaking, without a word

INTERJECTIONS

11 **hush!**, mum's the word!, shut up!, hold your tongue!, say no more!, no comment!

567 Address

NOUNS

1 **address**, allocution, apostrophe, lecture, discourse, recitation, recital, reading, talk, presentation, speech, oration, public speech, formal speech, set speech, prepared speech, disquisition, declamation, tirade, diatribe, jeremiad, invective, harangue, screed, rodomontade, philippic, sermon, homily, rant (Sl), earful (Inf), mouthful (Inf)
▶ *564 Speech*

2 **salutation**, greeting, salaam, hail, salutatory address, address of welcome, valedictory address, valedictory, valediction, inaugural address, pep talk, exhortation, peroration, appeal, invocation, interpellation, interjection, advances, suit, court
▶ *817 Courtesy, 712 Request*

3 **skill**, address, adroitness, dexterity, deftness, neatness, expertness, expertise, ability, cleverness, ingenuity, art, tact
▶ *655 Skill*

4 **approach**, method, way, mode, line, attack
▶ *602 Means, 327 Way*

5 **place of residence**, residence, domicile, habitation, abode, home, house, habitat, location, whereabouts, house number, number, road name, street name, district, postcode, zip code (US), no fixed abode (NFA)
▶ *256 Habitat, 250 Location*

6 **public speaker**, speechmaker, spokesperson, spokesman, spokeswoman, lecturer, discourser, reader, orator, declaimer, ranter, tub-thumper, rhetorician, silver-tongued orator, soapbox orator, stump orator, rabble-rouser, demagogue, pulpiteer, preacher, sermonizer, sermoner, sermonist, pontificator, expositor, expounder

VERBS

7 **address**, speak to, talk to, lecture, apostrophize, take the floor, give a talk, make a speech (*or* presentation), deliver an address, discourse, speechify, hold forth, declaim, orate, harangue, perorate, pontificate, rant, tub-thump, rabble-rouse, sermonize, preach at
▶ *564 Speech*

8 **appeal to**, invoke, entreat, pray to, apply to, petition, go cap in hand to
▶ *712 Request*

9 **approach**, accost, buttonhole, call to, salute, hail, greet, say good morning to, pass the time of day with, parley with, converse with
▶ *568 Conversation, 817 Courtesy*

10 **send**, direct, address, consign, transmit, dispatch, post, mail, seal, stamp, frank, send on, forward, redirect, readdress

11 **title**, entitle, style, term, call sir, call madam
▶ *804 Title, 817 Courtesy*

12 **address oneself to**, go in for, take up, undertake, engage in, apply oneself to, devote oneself to
▶ *597 Undertaking*

ADJECTIVES

13 **oratorical**, rhetorical, declamatory, demagogic, demagogical

14 **vocative**, invocatory, salutatory, valedictory

INTERJECTIONS

15 **hail!**, greetings!, hello!, hi!

568 Conversation

NOUNS

1 **conversation**, talk, chat, dialogue, duologue, two-hander, interlocution, colloquy, converse, discourse, intercourse, verbal intercourse, social intercourse, communication, intercommunication, communion

2 **chat**, natter, crack (Dial), small talk, table talk, friendly talk, heart-to-heart, *tête-à-tête* (Fr), fireside chat, cosy chat, causerie, idle talk, prattle, tattle, tittle-tattle, gossip, idle gossip, chit-chat, backchat, repartee, banter, confabu-

lation, confab (Inf), conflab (Sl), chinwag (Inf)
► *565 Talkativeness*

3 **social gathering**, social, party, soirée, *conversazione* (It)
► *815 Sociability, 665 Party*

4 **conference**, parley, powwow, congress, conclave, meeting, gathering, assembly, convention, forum, open forum, symposium, talk-in, teach-in, seminar, polemics, dialectic, exchange of views, discussion, debate, debating, colloquium, *convivio* (It), consultation, council, council of war, round-table conference, huddle, putting one's heads together
► *161 Assembly*

5 **talks**, high-level talks, summit meeting, summit talks, summit, negotiations, bargaining, treaty-making
► *716 Negotiation*

6 **interview**, audience, audition, interrogation, interlocution, examination, investigation, analysis, review, consideration, question and answer session
► *477 Question*

7 **conversationalist**, converser, talker, discourser, confabulator, colloquist, collocutor, interlocutor, interviewer, examiner, cross-examiner, interrogator, interpellator, inquirer, respondent

8 **chatterer**, natterer, gossip, tittle-tattler, gasser (Inf), gasbag (Inf), windbag (Inf)

VERBS

9 **converse**, discourse, talk together, talk, speak, parley, communicate, commune, confabulate, have a talk, hold a conversation, engage in conversation, carry on a conversation, have a word with, have a quick word with, exchange words, exchange pleasantries, pass the time of day, chew the fat (Sl)

10 **chat**, natter, chatter, prattle, prate, gossip, have a cosy chat, have a little chat, have a heart-to-heart, talk *tête-à-tête*, go in a huddle, talk privately, whisper together, have a chinwag (Inf)

11 **confer**, hold a conference, parley, powwow, sit down together, meet around a conference table, get round the table, talk over, thrash out, debate, discuss, exchange views, sit in council, sit in committee, consider the pros and cons, deliberate over, analyse, canvass, consult, refer to, negotiate, bargain, hold talks, hold a summit, hold a council of war

ADJECTIVES

12 **conversing**, talking, chatting, interlocutory, confabulatory, talkative, loquacious, communicative, unreserved
► *565 Talkativeness*

13 **discussing**, conferring, conferential, in conference, in committee, consultatory, consultative, advisory

14 **conversational**, chatty, colloquial, informal, gossipy, newsy, informative

ADVERBS

15 **conversationally**, colloquially, informally, *tête-à-tête* (Fr), loquaciously, communicatively, unreservedly, off the record

569 Soliloquy

NOUNS

1 **soliloquy**, monologue, monology, monody, monodrama, interior monologue, stream of consciousness, apostrophe, aside, one-man show, one-woman show, ravings (Inf)
► *174 One*

2 **soliloquist**, soliloquizer, monologist, monodist

VERBS

3 **soliloquize**, monologize, talk to oneself, talk to the wall, have an audience of one, say to oneself, tell oneself, think aloud, apostrophize

4 **monopolize the conversation**, do all the talking, hold forth without interruption, rabbit on (Sl), rave on (Inf), run off at the mouth (Sl)
► *565 Talkativeness*

ADJECTIVES

5 **soliloquizing**, monologic, monological, apostrophic, monodramatic, soloistic, thinking aloud, talking to oneself, raving (Inf)

Will

570 Will

NOUNS

1 **will**, volition, conation, willing, intention, intent, purpose, wish, desire, pleasure, fancy, choice, option, preference, inclination, disposition, mind
▶ *782 Desire*

2 **willpower**, strength of will, strength of purpose, firmness of purpose, iron will, determination, steadfastness, resoluteness, resolution, resolve, tenacity, single-mindedness, mind over matter, self-control

3 **wilfulness**, self-will, one's own sweet will, will of one's own, waywardness, obstinacy, obduracy, doggedness, intransigence, stubbornness, pig-headedness, mulishness, bloody-mindedness (Inf)
▶ *860 Selfishness*

4 **free will**, independence, self-determination, autonomy, freedom of choice, personal freedom, discretion, free hand, free spirit

5 **will**, testament, last will and testament, codicil, privileged will, inheritance, estate, legacy, bequest
▶ *16 Law*

ADJECTIVES

6 **willed**, volitional, volitive, intentional, deliberate, willing, disposed, conative
▶ *572 Willingness*

7 **iron-willed**, determined, purposeful, steadfast, resolute, adamant, unyielding, tenacious, single-minded, self-controlled

8 **wilful**, self-willed, headstrong, wayward, stubborn, dogged, obstinate, obdurate, intransigent, pig-headed, bull-headed, mulish, bloody-minded (Inf)

9 **autocratic**, authoritarian, arbitrary, dictatorial

10 **free**, independent, self-determined, autonomous, discretionary, optional

VERBS

11 **wish**, will, want, desire

12 **choose**, decide, select, opt for, plump for, favour, think best, see fit

13 **intend**, determine, purpose, plan, cause, bring about, effect, be (hell) bent on (Inf)

14 **follow one's own will**, do as one likes (chooses *or* pleases), do what one likes (chooses *or* pleases), please oneself, go one's own way, know one's own mind, have a mind of one's own, be one's own man (*or* woman)

15 **impose one's will**, assert oneself, dominate, command, demand, order, ordain, decree, have one's own way, have it all one's own way, trample over, bulldoze, bully, force

16 **bequeath**, will, leave, pass on, hand down, transfer, give, confer

ADVERBS

17 **at will**, as one pleases (*or* wishes), when and how one pleases, at one's pleasure, as one thinks fit (*or* best), ad libitum, ad lib

571 Necessity

Necessity is the plea for every infringement of human freedom. It is the argument of tyrants; it is the creed of slaves. William Pitt the Younger.

Teach thy necessity to reason thus:/ There is no virtue like necessity. William Shakespeare.

Necessity knows no law. Publilius Syrus.

NOUNS

1 **necessity**, essential, fundamental, must, necessary, prerequisite, imperative, precondition, requisite, requirement, want, need, *sine qua non* (L), desideratum, matter of life and death, urgency
▶ *611 Importance*

2 **indispensability**, indispensableness, essentialness, needfulness

3 **lack of choice**, obligation, constraint, duty, compulsion, coercion, no choice, no alternative, no option, Hobson's choice

4 **need**, poverty, penury, want, hardship, indigence, privation, destitution
▶ *743 Poverty*

5 **inevitability**, certainty, unavoidability, inexorability, ineluctability, what must be, one's lot, destiny, fate, nemesis, doom, karma, God's will, will of Allah, sword of Damocles
▶ *490 Certainty*

6 **necessitarianism**, determinism, fatalism, predetermination, predestination, circumstances beyond one's control, force of circumstances, force majeure, act of God, fatality

7 **necessitarian**, fatalist, predeterminist

8 **involuntariness**, compulsion, instinctiveness, reflex, reflex action, Pavlovian reaction, impulse, knee-jerk reaction

ADJECTIVES

9 **necessary**, essential, required, requisite, indispensable, fundamental, needed, imperative, urgent, vital
▶ *103 Essence*

10 **obligatory**, compulsory, *de rigueur* (Fr), mandatory, binding, imperative

11 **needy**, needful, necessitous, poor, destitute, indigent, poverty-striken, hard up

12 **inevitable**, certain, inescapable, unavoidable, ordained, preordained, inexorable, ineluctable, fated, doomed, karmic, predestined, destined, necessitarian, deterministic

13 **involuntary**, compulsory, impulsive, automatic, instinctive, intuitive, mechanical, autonomic, reflex

VERBS

14 **necessitate**, require, need, want, demand, call for, entail, involve, cause

15 **compel**, force, coerce, impel, mandate, oblige, impose, dictate, leave no choice (*or* option *or* alternative), push into a corner, trap

16 **be compelled**, have no alternative (*or* option *or* choice), bow to fate, submit to fate, take it or leave it, be cornered, have no way out, be pushed against the wall

17 **preordain**, ordain, predetermine, predestine, destine, fate, doom

18 **make a virtue of necessity**, make the best of it

ADVERBS

19 **necessarily**, of necessity, from necessity, imperatively, fatedly, by force of circumstances, come what may, inevitably, unavoidably, certainly, surely, whether one will or not, perforce, *nolens volens* (L), willy-nilly

20 **with need**, urgently, vitally

572 Willingness

ADJECTIVES

1 **willing**, agreeable, content, disposed, inclined, prone, ready, game, receptive, assenting, consenting, in favour, prepared

2 **eager**, enthusiastic, keen, prompt, ready and willing, willing and able, alacritous, zealous, overzealous, overenthusiastic, overeager, over-

keen, fanatical, no holding back, keen as mustard (Inf), raring to go (Inf), spoiling for, gungho (Inf), champing at the bit (Inf)

3 **amenable**, compliant, acquiescent, biddable, persuadable, pliable, pliant, tractable, manageable, obedient, docile

4 **helpful**, cooperative, collaborative, cordial, gracious, benevolent, philanthropic
▶ *831 Benevolence, 833 Philanthropy*

5 **voluntary**, unprompted, spontaneous, offered, unbidden, unforced, volunteering, offering, self-appointed

NOUNS

6 **willingness**, readiness, cheerful compliance, gameness, consent, receptiveness

7 **eagerness**, enthusiasm, keenness, promptness, alacrity, ardour, fervour, zeal, zealousness, overeagerness, overenthusiasm, overzealousness, excessive zeal, zealotry, ardour of the chase, fanaticism

8 **acquiescence**, amenability, compliance, pliancy, pliability, tractability, persuasability, docility, obedience

9 **goodwill**, benevolence, graciousness, cordiality, helpfulness, cooperation, collaboration, right mood

10 **voluntary work**, voluntary service, voluntary aid, unpaid work, self-appointed task, labour of love, charitable work, community work, voluntaryism (*or* voluntarism)
▶ *767 Relief*

11 **willing worker**, willing hands, helping hand, volunteer, unpaid worker, aid worker, charity worker, eager beaver (Inf)

12 **philanthropist**, do-gooder (Inf)
▶ *755 Generosity*

VERBS

13 **be willing**, agree, assent, comply, acquiesce, consent, abide by, accept, go along with, have a mind to, have a good mind to, be ready, show willing, go off like a shot, go off at the drop of a hat, jump at, leap at, catch at, go out of one's way to, bend over backwards, lean over backwards

14 **cooperate**, collaborate, help, aid, assist, lend a hand

15 **volunteer**, offer, put forward, put oneself in the firing line, sacrifice oneself

ADVERBS

16 **willingly**, with a will, without demur, cheerfully, readily, agreeably, gladly, with (great) gusto, with good grace, with all one's heart, with open arms

17 **spontaneously**, at the drop of a hat, without hesitation, like a shot

18 **voluntarily**, of one's own free will, off one's own bat, without prompting, of one's own accord, on one's own initiative, on one's own volition

573   Unwillingness

ADJECTIVES

1 **unwilling**, disinclined, indisposed, loath, reluctant, demurring, averse, not prepared, not so minded, not in the mood, not feeling like, not ready

2 **refusing**, unconsenting, unreconciled, unconvinced, dissenting, dissident, adverse, opposed, opting out, disagreeing, antipathetic, digging in one's toes (or heels) (Inf)

3 **cautious**, wary, chary, hesitant, shy, bashful, modest, shrinking, shirking, unzealous, unenthusiastic, unsympathetic, half-hearted, lukewarm, backward, unhelpful, uncooperative, apathetic

4 **procrastinating**, postponing, delaying, sluggish, lazy, neglectful, negligent, remiss

5 **reluctant**, resistant, protesting, sulky, dissenting, sceptical, atheistic

VERBS

6 **be unwilling**, resist, reject, disagree, dissent, protest, not have the heart to, have no stomach for, stickle, stick, have scruples, boggle at (Inf), give the thumbs down to (Inf), give the red light to (Inf)

▶ 666 Disagreement, 500 Dissent, 713 Protest, 581 Rejection

7 **refuse**, recoil, turn away, back away, edge away, not face, blench, flinch, fight, shy away, shrink from, duck, jib, shirk, elude, neglect

▶ 711 Refusal

8 **hold back**, postpone, delay, demur, procrastinate, shelve, hang back, drag one's feet, look over one's shoulder, sit back, sit tight, hesitate, balk, tread warily, look before one leaps, put off (till tomorrow), put on the back burner, hang fire (Inf)

9 **not cooperate**, dissent, obstruct, not do one's part, not pull one's weight, not play, not play ball, dissociate oneself, have no truck with, turn one's back, drop out, abstain, opt out, stonewall

10 **grudge**, begrudge, turn up one's nose, show one's distaste, force oneself, make oneself, do with a heavy heart, sulk

NOUNS

11 **unwillingness**, loathness, reluctance, disinclination, indisposition, dislike, disagreement, demur, objection, protest

▶ 666 Disagreement, 713 Protest

12 **opposition**, resistance, renitency, recalcitrance, filibuster, balking, refusal, rejection, opt-out, rebuff, turndown (US), unhelpfulness, noncooperation, hindrance

▶ 663 Opposition, 711 Refusal, 661 Hindrance

13 **dissociation**, nonassociation, abstention, unenthusiasm, lack of zeal, half-heartedness, apathy, indifference, lifelessness, faintheartedness, want of alacrity, backwardness,

slowness, hesitation, wariness, scruple, qualm, doubt, repugnance, abhorrence, recoil, aversion, averseness, no stomach for, shrinking, shyness, bashfulness, modesty

▶ 783 Indifference, 328 Slowness, 591 Avoidance, 810 Modesty

14 **disobedience**, nonobservance, noncompliance, indocility, refractoriness, fractiousness, the sulks, sulkiness, sullenness, grudging service, perfunctoriness, undependability, unreliability, dereliction

▶ 693 Disobedience, 830 Sullenness

15 **delay**, shelving, postponement, putting on the back burner, putting off (till tomorrow), procrastination, mañana attitude, sluggishness, laziness, neglect, negligence, remissness

▶ 643 Inactivity, 470 Negligence

16 **reluctant person**, objector, resister, protester, abstainer, dropout, shirker, sulker, nonactivist, procrastinator, dissenter, dissident, sceptic, nonbeliever, atheist

ADVERBS

17 **unwillingly**, reluctantly, under protest, under duress, under pressure, with a bad grace, in spite of oneself, against one's will, against the grain, regretfully, with regret, without enthusiasm, unenthusiastically, half-heartedly, with dragging feet, with a heavy heart, with a long face, hesitantly, warily

574   Resolution

ADJECTIVES

1 **resolute**, resolved, determined, decided, decisive, deliberate, single-minded, concentrated, purposive, purposeful, intent, (dead) set, intent upon, set upon, bent upon, obsessed, hell-bent (Inf)

▶ 588 Intention

2 **tenacious**, persevering, persistent, dogged, zealous, thorough, all-consuming, earnest, serious, insistent, pressing, urgent, driving, forceful, energetic, vigorous, hard-hitting, desperate, stopping at nothing, all out, wholehearted, committed, devoted, dedicated, tireless, indefatigable, whole hog (Sl), gung-ho (Inf), bodacious (US inf)

▶ 575 Perseverance, 467 Attention, 239 Vigour

3 **strong-willed**, iron-willed, strong-minded, uncompromising, unbending, inflexible, unyielding, intransigent, adamant, obstinate, stubborn, relentless, ruthless, merciless, pitiless, inexorable, implacable, stern, grim, unfeeling, stony, icy, hard, rock-hard, hard as iron, iron, cast-iron, steely, tough as steel

▶ 577 Obstinacy, 836 Pitilessness, 373 Hardness, 378 Toughness

4 **undaunted**, nothing daunted, heroic, game, unfearing, unshaken, unshakable, unshrinking, unflinching, unwavering, unhesitant, stead-

fast, indomitable, unconquered, unbeaten, steeled, armoured

▶ *778 Courage, 682 Success*

5 **steady**, constant, firm, solid, like the Rock of Gibraltar, immovable, unchangeable, reliable, staunch, dependable, self-controlled, self-restrained, self-mastered, self-possessed

▶ *225 Stability, 869 Self-Restraint*

VERBS

6 **be resolute**, know one's own mind, mean business, stop at nothing, stick at nothing, not stop at trifles, go through fire and water, go to all lengths, go to any length, push to extremes, see through, carry through, go the whole hog (Sl)

▶ *684 Completion*

7 **resolve**, make up one's mind, decide, determine, purpose, intend, will, make a resolution, take a resolution, fix, settle, seal, conclude, terminate

▶ *588 Intention, 570 Will, 157 End*

8 **brace oneself**, steel oneself, clench one's teeth, grit one's teeth, face, face the issue, face the odds, rise to the occasion, dare, defy, take on all comers, bell the cat, outface, stare down, take the bull by the horns, take the bit between one's teeth, bite the bullet, take the plunge, throw down the gauntlet, cross the Rubicon, burn one's boats, burn one's bridges, show one's colours, nail one's colours to the mast, set one's face (Inf), go for it (Inf), go for broke (Sl)

▶ *633 Danger, 668 Defiance*

9 **undertake**, take on, take up, go in for, get down to, set to, buckle to, roll one's sleeves up, put one's shoulder to the wheel, tackle, grapple with, commit oneself, devote oneself, dedicate oneself, give oneself to, put one's heart into, grasp the nettle, give up everything for, set one's heart on, pursue, go after, bear down on, get a move on (Inf), get weaving (Inf), stir the possum (Aus sl), get on the stick (Sl), get one's ass moving (Tab sl), get one's ass in gear (Tab sl), go to it (Inf), get after (Inf), go get it (Inf), get going (Inf)

▶ *642 Activity*

10 **insist**, urge, press, make something happen, not take no for an answer, put one's foot down, stand no nonsense, stand firm, dig in, dig one's toes (*or* heels) in, hold (*or* stand) one's ground, stay put, not budge, not yield, not compromise, not give an inch, stand up for one's principles, stand fast, hold fast, stick fast, adhere

11 **persist**, persevere, soldier on, stick it out, endure, grin and bear it, hold out, hold out one's own, never despair, never say die, never surrender, fight to the finish, fight to the death, die fighting, die with one's boots on, go down with (colours) flying, go down with one's ship,

die hard, hang in (Inf)

▶ *575 Perseverance*

NOUNS

12 **resolution**, resolve, fixed resolve, resoluteness, determination, grim determination, doggedness, decidedness, mind made up, decisiveness, decision, purposefulness, purpose, intention

▶ *588 Intention*

13 **concentration**, seriousness, fixity of purpose, single-mindedness, commitment, total commitment, devotion, utter devotion, self-devotion, devotedness, dedication, earnestness, zeal, ardour, eagerness, drive, vigour, energy, desperation

▶ *239 Vigour, 642 Activity*

14 **tenacity**, persistence, perseverance, stubbornness, obstinacy, relentlessness, ruthlessness, inexorability, implacability, sternness, pitilessness, hardness, steeliness, inflexibility, insistence, pressure, compulsion

▶ *575 Perseverance, 577 Obstinacy, 836 Pitilessness, 695 Compulsion*

15 **will**, iron will, willpower, intent, strength of character, self-control, self-restraint, self-mastery, self-command, self-possession, steadiness, constancy, firmness, stability, staunchness, reliability, steadfastness

▶ *570 Will, 869 Self-Restraint, 225 Stability*

16 **fortitude**, spirit, grit, backbone, mettle, daring, dauntlessness, courage, pluck, dash, aplomb, élan, moral fibre, stiff upper lip, gritted teeth, clenched teeth, clenched jaw, rock, iron, cast iron, steel, backbone of steel, hearts of oak, bulldog breed, spunk (Inf), guts (Sl), moxie (US sl), bottle (Sl)

▶ *778 Courage*

ADVERBS

17 **resolutely**, decisively, purposefully, deliberately, single-mindedly, intently, seriously, earnestly, in earnest, with body and soul, with tooth and nail, with might and main, at all costs, at any price, come what may, come rain or shine, come hell or high water, persistently, doggedly, manfully, like a man, live or die, neck or nothing, once and for all

INTERJECTIONS

18 **here goes!**, go for it!, once more unto the breach!, damn the consequences!, full speed ahead!

575 Perseverance

NOUNS

1 **perseverance**, persistence, doggedness, determination, resolution, tenacity, pertinacity, pertinaciousness, stubbornness, obstinacy, insistence, patience, plodding

▶ *574 Resolution, 577 Obstinacy*

2 **commitment**, total commitment, single-

mindedness, singleness of purpose, concentration, attention, application, sedulity, sedulousness, assiduity, assiduousness, industriousness, tirelessness, indefatigability, effort, exertion, hard work, repeated efforts, unflagging efforts

▶ *644 Work, 642 Activity, 467 Attention*

3 **constancy**, steadfastness, fidelity, staunchness, maintenance, continuance, ceaselessness, diligence, permanence, iteration, reiteration, repetition

▶ *219 Continuity, 217 Permanence, 183 Repetition*

4 **stamina**, endurance, staying power, fortitude, strength, courage, bulldog courage, grit, true grit, backbone, gameness, pluck, guts (Sl), gutsiness (Sl), moxie (US sl), bottle (Sl)

▶ *778 Courage, 237 Strength*

5 **tenacious person**, loyal supporter, hardcore supporter, diehard, old guard, trier, willing worker, workaholic, workhorse (Inf), stayer (Inf)

VERBS

6 **persevere**, persist, keep at it, keep on trying, try and try again, repeat, iterate, reiterate, renew one's efforts, double one's efforts, plod, slog, slog away, peg away, hammer away at, work at, work round the clock, work one's fingers to the bone, work till one drops, die in harness, die with one's boots on, move heaven and earth, work miracles, keep on keeping on (US inf), plug away (Inf), work one's ass (*or* butt *or* tail) off (Tab sl)

▶ *596 Attempt, 644 Work*

7 **maintain**, sustain, keep up, follow through, continue, carry on, go on, keep on, keep going, keep the pot boiling (Inf), keep the ball rolling (Inf)

▶ *219 Continuity*

8 **hold out**, hold out for, not take no for an answer, stand firm, maintain one's ground, not budge, dig in one's toes (*or* heels), hold out to the last, die at one's post, go down with one's ship, not despair, never despair, never say die, never give up hope, hope on, grit one's teeth, hang on, not let go, hold fast, maintain one's grip, cling, stick like glue, hang on by one's teeth, hang on for dear life, hang on like grim death, sink or swim, stick to one's guns (Inf)

▶ *574 Resolution, 775 Hope, 726 Retention*

9 **endure**, have what it takes, come up (*or* back) for more, survive, remain, stick it out, see it through, stay till the bitter end, carry through, complete, take a licking and keep on ticking (US sl)

▶ *684 Completion*

ADJECTIVES

10 **persevering**, persistent, tenacious, sedulous, assiduous, dogged, determined, resolute, stubborn, obstinate, enduring, staunch, faithful,

diligent, surviving, patient, trying hard, plodding, slogging away, industrious, strenuous, hanging in there (Inf)

▶ *574 Resolution, 577 Obstinacy, 644 Work, 642 Activity, 596 Attempt*

11 **steady**, unfaltering, unwavering, unflagging, undrooping, unwearied, untiring, indefatigable, unsleeping, sleepless, vigilant, unfailing, unremitting, constant, continual, unceasing, renewed, iterated, reiterated, repeated

▶ *219 Continuity, 183 Repetition*

12 **indomitable**, undefeated, unconquerable, unconquered, unbeaten, undaunted, undiscouraged, undeterred, game, plucky, game to the last (*or* end), going down fighting, going down with guns blazing, true to the bitter end, gutsy (Sl)

▶ *682 Success, 778 Courage*

ADVERBS

13 **persistently**, perseveringly, doggedly, tenaciously, resolutely, patiently, for better or for worse, through thick and thin, through fire and water, to the last man, to the bitter end

14 **continually**, repeatedly, unendingly, ceaselessly, till the cows come home (Inf)

576 Vacillation

ADJECTIVES

1 **vacillating**, wavering, irresolute, unresolved, undecided, uncommitted, equivocal, tergiversating, noncommittal, undetermined, of (*or* in) two minds, unable to make up one's mind, indecisive, unsure, uncertain, hesitating, hesitant, dithering, wobbling, boggling, stalling, evasive, shifty, wobbly

▶ *578 Equivocation, 491 Uncertainty, 573 Unwillingness*

2 **changeable**, variable, unstable, inconstant, temperamental, mercurial, fickle, whimsical, capricious, not to be pinned down, without ballast, restless, fidgety, irresponsible, giddy, flighty, feather-brained, light-minded, superficial, unpersevering, unfaithful, adulterous, as changeable as a weathercock (*or* the weather *or* the moon)

▶ *224 Changeableness, 579 Caprice*

3 **timid**, tremulous, nervy, jumpy, jittery, panicky, shaken, rattled, faint-hearted, cowardly, unheroic, nerveless, squeamish, weak, weakwilled, pusillanimous, weak-minded, weakkneed, spineless, insipid, ineffectual, wimpish (Sl), wet (Inf), wishy-washy (Inf)

▶ *777 Fear, 779 Cowardice, 238 Weakness*

4 **unsteady**, unreliable, unstaunch, unsteadfast, teetering, tottering, apathetic, indifferent, characterless, featureless, suggestible, impressionable, flexible, pliant, putty-like, easygoing, good-natured

VERBS

5 **vacillate**, waver, fluctuate, vary, oscillate, seesaw, wobble, teeter, sway, go back and forth, go to and fro, boggle, dither, stall, equivocate, tergiversate, quibble, palter, shuffle, shillyshally (Inf)

▶ *365 Oscillation, 578 Equivocation, 224 Changeableness*

6 **hesitate**, have second thoughts, change one's mind, blow hot and cold, back away, balk, shy, jib, shirk, evade, avoid

▶ *591 Avoidance*

7 **be irresolute**, be of (or in) two minds, not know one's own mind, not know what to do, sit on the fence, go where the wind blows, go round in circles, put off a decision, delay, put off (till tomorrow), procrastinate, dally, dillydally, leave undecided, leave in suspense

▶ *491 Uncertainty, 209 Lateness*

8 **balance**, weigh up the pros and cons, discuss, debate, argue, hum (or hem) and haw, will and will not

▶ *473 Argument*

9 **change sides**, go over, apostatize, cross the floor, shift one's ground, be unfaithful, commit adultery, play around, go catting (Sl), jump ship (Inf), sell out (Inf)

10 **compromise**, yield, give way, take half measures, meet halfway, give up, not persevere

▶ *717 Compromise, 673 Submission*

NOUNS

11 **vacillation**, irresolution, indecision, uncertainty, equivocation, tergiversation, doubt, hesitation, hesitancy, infirmity of purpose, lack of resolution, lack of commitment, nonperseverance, broken resolve, broken promise, uncommitted vote, floating vote

▶ *491 Uncertainty, 578 Equivocation*

12 **inconstancy**, fluctuation, changeableness, variability, blowing hot and cold, fickleness, whimsicality, capriciousness, irresponsibility, levity, lack of willpower, lack of drive

▶ *224 Changeableness, 579 Caprice*

13 **timidity**, tremulousness, nervousness, nerviness, jumpiness, jitteriness, faint-heartedness, cowardice, loss of nerve, squeamishness, weakness, pusillanimity, weak will, spinelessness, no backbone, no grit, wishy-washiness (Inf)

▶ *777 Fear, 779 Cowardice, 238 Weakness*

14 **apathy**, indifference, no strong feelings, lukewarmness, half-heartedness, listlessness, no will of one's own, impressibility, impressionability, suggestibility, pliancy, easygoing nature, putty in one's hands, passivity, inertness, submission, submissiveness, servitude

▶ *783 Indifference, 673 Submission*

15 **indecisive person**, uncommitted voter, floating voter, independent (US), dabbler, dilettante, weakling, compromiser, waverer, wobbler, ditherer, staller, tergiversator, turncoat, adulterer, butterfly, feather, weathercock, chameleon, don't-know (Inf), man of straw (Inf), funker (Inf), wimp (Sl), wet (Inf), piss-ant (US sl)

ADVERBS

16 **irresolutely**, indecisively, equivocally, noncommittally, uncertainly, hesitantly, nervously, pusillanimously, from pillar to post, between the devil and the deep blue sea, between Scylla and Charybdis, between a rock and a hard place, in a catch-22 situation

577 Obstinacy

ADJECTIVES

1 **obstinate**, stubborn, obdurate, headstrong, bull-headed, pig-headed, mulish, stubborn as a mule, pertinacious, wilful, self-willed, froward (Arch), *entêté* (Fr), awkward, dog-in-the-manger, bloody-minded (Inf)

2 **refractory**, recalcitrant, wayward, arbitrary, perverse, contrary, contumacious, disobedient, unruly, restive, unmanageable, intractable, uncontrollable, ungovernable, unpersuadable, incorrigible, irrepressible, indocile, stiff-necked, hard-mouthed, cross-grained, crotchety, irascible

▶ *693 Disobedience, 868 Impenitence, 830 Sullenness, 829 Irascibility, 669 Resistance, 668 Defiance*

3 **unyielding**, firm, determined, resolute, dogged, bulldog-like, tenacious, persevering, stiff, wooden, rigid, adamant, inelastic, inflexible, unbending, obdurate, hardened, hard (or tough) as nails, case-hardened, hard-headed, uncompromising, hard-core, intransigent, unmoved; uninfluenced, unrelenting, with heels dug in, immovable, irremovable, irreversible, persistent, incurable, chronic, dour, grim, inexorable, unappeasable, implacable, merciless, pitiless, hard-nosed (Inf), hard-boiled (Inf)

▶ *574 Resolution, 575 Perseverance, 373 Hardness, 217 Permanence, 836 Pitilessness*

4 **set**, set in one's ways, habituated, hidebound, conservative, ultraconservative, obscurantist, reactionary, blimpish, unteachable, impervious, blind, blinded, deaf, opinionated, dogmatic, hard-line, hard-shelled (US), pedantic, obsessed, bigoted, fanatical, dry (Inf), blinkered (Inf)

▶ *584 Habit, 493 Misjudgment*

NOUNS

5 **obstinacy**, stubbornness, obduracy, obdurateness, adamantine, bull-headedness, pigheadedness, mulishness, pertinaciousness, pertinacity, self-will, mind of one's own, perversity, contumacy, disobedience, resistance,

intractability, incorrigibility, stiff neck, wrong-headedness, cussedness, dourness, indocility, bloody-mindedness (Inf)

▶ *570 Will, 669 Resistance, 693 Disobedience, 830 Sullenness*

6 **determination**, will, single-mindedness, resolution, grimness, doggedness, tenacity, bulldog tenacity, perseverance, stubborn persistence, inelasticity, inflexibility, woodenness, toughness, hardness, intransigence, immovability, hard line, no compromise, irreversibility, fixity

▶ *574 Resolution, 575 Perseverance, 373 Hardness*

7 **opinionatedness**, opiniativeness, self-opinion, dogmatism, rigorism, intolerance, prejudice, bias, bigotry, zealotry, fanaticism, ruling passion, obsession, *idée fixe* (Fr), blind side, blindness, closed mind, narrow-mindedness, illiberality, obscurantism, ignorance, old school, *ancien régime* (Fr)

▶ *490 Certainty, 493 Misjudgment, 502 Ignorance, 436 Blindness*

8 **obstinate person**, hardliner, hard-head, rigorist, stickler, pedant, dogmatist, fanatic, zealot, bigot, persecutor, stayer, die-hard, old fogy, conservative, obscurantist, reactionary, Colonel Blimp, blimp, mule (Inf), stick-in-the-mud (Inf), hard-nose (Inf), hard-ass (US tab sl), dry (Inf), last-ditcher (Inf), bitter-ender (US inf)

VERBS

9 **be obstinate**, persist, persevere, brazen it out, stick to one's guns, dig in one's toes (*or* heels), not budge, sit tight, stay put, stand firm, insist, brook no denial, not take no for an answer, not change one's mind, go one's own way, want one's own way, dogmatize, have a closed mind, stay in a rut, cling to custom, ignore, not listen, turn a deaf ear, take no advice,

▶ *575 Perseverance, 868 Impenitence, 669 Resistance, 574 Resolution, 860 Selfishness, 490 Certainty, 584 Habit, 780 Rashness*

ADVERBS

10 **obstinately**, stubbornly, obdurately, pigheadedly, mulishly, like a mule, wilfully, doggedly, tenaciously, for oneself, in an uncompromising way, intransigently, inexorably

578 Equivocation

VERBS

1 **be equivocal**, be ambiguous, cut both ways, play on words, pun, have two meanings, have a double meaning, have a second meaning, speak oracles, speak with two voices, double talk, dissemble, deceive, mislead, fudge, hedge, beat about the bush, fence, sit on the fence, quibble, equivocate, avoid, evade, dodge, sidestep, trim, prevaricate, change the subject, waffle (Inf), speak with forked tongue (US inf), weasel (out) (Inf), change the channel (US inf), pussyfoot (Inf), shillyshally (Inf)

▶ *520 Meaning, 591 Avoidance, 540 Falsehood, 539 Deception, 474 Sophistry*

2 **equivocate**, tergiversate, change one's mind, think again, think better of it, change one's tune, shift one's ground, shift gears, move the goalposts, vacillate, shuffle, face both ways, be two-faced, run with the hare and hunt with the hounds, change round, swerve, tack, do a U-turn, wheel about, change front, turn one's back on, turn against, back out, withdraw, get cold feet, resign, forsake, wash one's hands of, turn over a new leaf, become a new man (*or* woman)

▶ *576 Vacillation, 216 Change, 705 Resignation, 867 Penitence, 627 Improvement, 628 Deterioration, 598 Relinquishment*

3 **apostatize**, change sides, change one's colours, change one's allegiance, turn one's coat, let the side down, turn renegade, turn traitor, switch, switch over, cross over, cross the floor, join the opposition, go over, desert, defect, blackleg, collaborate, betray, jump ship, jump (*or* climb) on the bandwagon, follow the rising star, stool (on) (US inf), rat (on) (Sl)

4 **recant**, unsay, take back (one's words), recall one's words, withdraw, retract, apologize, eat one's words, crawl, cringe, back down, backpedal, go back on, renege, disavow, disclaim, repudiate, refute, deny, negate, renounce, abjure, forswear, swear off, recall, revoke, rescind, abrogate, eat one's hat (Inf), eat humble pie (Inf), eat crow (US inf)

▶ *704 Cancellation, 806 Humility, 808 Servility, 536 Negation*

NOUNS

5 **equivocalness**, equivocation, ambiguity, ambivalence, indefiniteness, vagueness, uncertainty, mental reservation, concealment, prevarication, evasion, balancing act, white lie, untruth, quibble, quibbling, sophistry, two voices, contrariety, double meaning, amphibology, enigma, wordplay, play upon words, *double entendre* (Fr), pun, paronomasia, calembour, equivoque, newspeak, Pentagonese (US), double talk, gobbledegook, circumlocution, conundrum, riddle, oracle, oracular utterance, parable, polysemy, weasel word (Inf)

▶ *523 Unintelligibility, 491 Uncertainty, 520 Meaning, 521 Lack of Meaning, 474 Sophistry, 771 Humour, 538 Untruth, 531 Concealment, 591 Avoidance, 5 Linguistics*

6 **equivocation**, tergiversation, change of mind, irresolution, vacillation, inconsistency, better thoughts, afterthought, second thoughts, change of purpose, alteration of plan, change of direction, deviation, shifting one's ground, versatility, back-pedalling, reversal, about-

turn, U-turn, volte-face, withdrawal, change of mood, temperament, whim, caprice

▶ *576 Vacillation, 216 Change, 867 Penitence, 335 Deviation, 579 Caprice, 598 Relinquishment*

7 **apostasy**, change of allegiance, conversion, turning renegade, turning traitor, going over, recreancy, desertion, defection, collaboration, betrayal, treachery, perfidy, unreliableness, untrustworthiness, improbity, ratting (Sl)

▶ *858 Improbity*

8 **recantation**, taking back one's words, withdrawal, retraction, retractation, apology, eating one's words, disavowal, disclaimer, repudiation, denial, negation, renunciation, abjuration, forswearing, revocation, revoking, recall, abrogation, humble pie (Inf), eating crow (US inf)

▶ *704 Cancellation, 536 Negation*

9 **equivocator**, tergiversator, opportunist, timeserver, toady, Vicar of Bray, double-dealer, weasel, two-faced person, trimmer, Janus, jilt, flirt, coquette, weathercock, recanter, forswearer, recreant, apostate, renegade, turncoat, reneger, traitor, Judas, betrayer, disloyal (*or* fair-weather) friend, quisling, fifth columnist, collaborationist, collaborator, lost leader, deserter, defector, quitter, runaway, informer, telltale, tattler, strike-breaker, blackleg, deviationist, secessionist, seceder, recidivist, backslider, proselyte, slippery customer (Inf), rat (Sl), ratter (Sl), grass (Sl), squealer (Sl), stool pigeon (Inf), scab (Sl)

▶ *539 Deception, 224 Changeableness, 664 Cooperation, 528 Information, 591 Avoidance*

ADJECTIVES

10 **equivocal**, ambiguous, ambivalent, epicene, not univocal, double, double-tongued, two-edged, facing both ways, left-handed, backhanded, equivocating, prevaricating, vague, evasive, misleading, roundabout, circumlocutory, oracular, amphibolous, homonymous, anagrammatic

▶ *313 Circularity*

11 **equivocating**, tergiversating, shuffling, slippery, supple, versatile, perfidious, double-dealing, hypocritical, two-faced, false, unfaithful, disloyal, traitorous, treacherous, apostate, recanting, renegade, recidivist, relapsed, going back, back-pedalling, vacillating, irresolute, fickle, whimsical, capricious, timeserving, flattering

▶ *540 Falsehood, 579 Caprice, 576 Vacillation, 853 Flattery*

ADVERBS

12 **equivocally**, ambiguously, ambivalently, evasively, amphibolously

13 **perfidiously**, traitorously, treacherously, unfaithfully, disloyally

579 Caprice

ADJECTIVES

1 **capricious**, arbitrary, erratic, fitful, uncertain, unpredictable, idiosyncratic, unexpected, volatile, mercurial, inconsistent, inconstant, variable, changeable, unstable, unreliable, fickle, feckless, irresponsible, flighty, flirtatious, coquettish, frivolous, skittish, giddy, featherbrained, light-minded, whimsical, fanciful, fantastic, eccentric, offbeat, freakish, quirky, humoursome, temperamental, moody, crotchety, irascible, fretful, hysterical, mad, weird, crazy, playful, mischievous, prankish, wanton, motiveless, purposeless, wayward, perverse, contrary, undisciplined, refractory, wilful, particular, faddy, faddish, captious, unreasonable

▶ *491 Uncertainty, 514 Surprise, 468 Inattention, 224 Changeableness, 510 Insanity*

NOUNS

2 **caprice**, capriciousness, arbitrariness, fitfulness, flightiness, uncertainty, unpredictability, inconsistency, inconstancy, changeableness, changeability, variability, instability, unreliability, fickleness, fecklessness, irresponsibility, coquettishness, flirtatiousness, frivolousness, frivolity, giddiness, levity, lightmindedness, whimsicality, eccentricity, crankiness, freakishness, quirkiness, fretfulness, pettishness, irascibility, playfulness, mischief, waywardness, motivelessness, purposelessness, faddishness, faddism

3 **whim**, whimsy, caprice, megrim (Arch), idea, notion, fancy, passing fancy, impulse, change of mind, flip-flop, vagary, outlandish notion, crotchet, maggot, bee in the bonnet, humour, mood, temperament, fit, peculiarity, idiosyncrasy, quirk, kink, fad, craze, freak, escapade, prank, boutade, wild-goose chase, coquetry, flirtation, the whim-whams (US inf), brainstorm (Inf)

▶ *519 Imagination, 583 Improvisation, 510 Insanity, 508 Folly*

4 **capricious person**, man (*or* woman) of impulse, eccentric, freak, oddball (Inf), crank, flirt, coquette, tease, trifler, featherbrain, butterfly, fair-weather friend, prankster, imp (Inf), monkey (Inf)

VERBS

5 **be capricious**, submit to a whim, take it into one's head, have a sudden flight of fancy, pick and choose, chop and change, blow hot and cold, flip-flop, vary, change, vacillate, fluctuate, have a bee in one's bonnet, show fickleness, trifle with, take up a thing and drop it, do by fits and starts, tease, flirt, coquet

▶ *224 Changeableness, 576 Vacillation, 508 Folly*

ADVERBS

6 **capriciously**, arbitrarily, erratically, fitfully,

by fits and starts, by dribs and drabs, now this, now that, from one extreme to the other, frivolously, fancifully, on impulse, as the mood takes one, as the fancy takes one, at the drop of a hat, at one's own sweet will

580 Selection

VERBS

1 **select**, choose, make a choice, eliminate the alternatives, decide, determine, make up one's mind, decide on, settle on, plump for, opt, opt for, take up an option, take up, accept, adopt, coopt, have a choice, have a voice, have free will, judge, exercise one's discretion
▷ *492 Judgment, 570 Will*

2 **prefer**, have a preference, like better, like best, would like, would rather, favour, fancy, incline, lean, have a bias, tend, might as well, might do worse, see fit, think fit, think it best to
▷ *784 Liking, 851 Approval*

3 **side with**, back, support, endorse, embrace, espouse, cast (*or* throw) in one's lot with, come out (*or* down) for, come out (*or* down) on one side, take sides, commit oneself, take the plunge, leap into, cross the Rubicon, burn one's bridges, burn one's boats, take for better or for worse, take for richer or for poorer, take in sickness and in health
▷ *574 Resolution, 662 Help, 823 Marriage*

4 **pick**, pick out, hand-pick, single out, pass, approve, recommend, put up, propose, nominate, second, appoint, commission, designate, delegate, detail, highlight, mark out, mark down, preselect, earmark, reserve, set aside, set apart, distinguish, identify, separate, isolate, abstract, excerpt, cull, anthologize, glean, winnow, sift, skim, skim off, cream, skim off the cream, pick the best, take one's pick, indulge one's fancy, discriminate, pick and choose
▷ *544 Identification, 703 Commission, 136 Separation, 481 Discrimination*

5 **vote**, choose by ballot, go to the polls, have a vote, have a voice, have a say, have the vote, be enfranchised, be on the electoral roll, cast a vote, register one's vote, cast one's ballot, be counted, raise one's hand, divide, vote for, vote in, elect, re-elect, return, vote out, vote down, deselect, reject, vote with one's feet, electioneer, canvass, accept a nomination, accept a candidacy (*or* candidature), run (US), stand, put to the vote, hold a referendum, poll, take a poll, take an opinion poll, measure public opinion, count votes, count ballots, count hands, count heads, count noses, count straws, hold an election, go to the country, appeal to the electorate, ask for a vote of confidence
▷ *581 Rejection, 12 Government and Politics*

NOUNS

6 **selection**, choice, choosing, decision, determination, making up one's mind, judgment, discretion, discrimination, picking and choosing, eclecticism, finickiness, fastidiousness, picking out, adoption, cooption, cooptation, nomination, appointment, commission, designation, right of choice, free will, freedom of choice, pick, variety, range, range of choice, list, shortlist, *embarras de richesses* (Fr), *embarras de choix* (Fr)
▷ *492 Judgment, 481 Discrimination, 570 Will, 710 Offer*

7 **preference**, predilection, partiality, inclination, leaning, tendency, prejudice, bias, favouritism, taste, liking, favour, fancy, preferability, desirability
▷ *784 Liking*

8 **choice**, possible choice, option, alternative, difficult choice, tough decision, dilemma, limited choice, limited options, only choice, Hobson's choice, no real alternative, no choice, zero option, nothing for it but, blind choice, blind date, unlucky choice, bad bargain, best option, better choice, greater good, lesser evil, lesser of two evils

9 **chosen thing**, pick, first choice, selection, assortment, pickings, gleanings, excerpts, anthology, the best, the cream, *crème de la crème* (Fr), the chosen, chosen people, elite
▷ *126 Superiority, 617 Worth*

10 **vote**, voice, cast vote, cumulative vote, transferable vote, majority vote, deciding vote, voice vote, positive vote, aye, yea, vote of confidence, negative vote, no, nay, vote of no confidence, blackball vote, blackballing, absentee vote, absentee ballot, mail-in vote (US), postal vote, card vote, ballot, secret ballot, open vote, show of hands, poll, opinion poll, public opinion poll, Gallup poll (Tm), MORI (Market and Opinion Research Institute) poll (Tm), straw poll, jury poll (US), direct vote, plebiscite, referendum, amendment referendum (US), *vox populi* (L)

11 **franchise**, right of representation, suffrage, universal suffrage, adult suffrage, manhood suffrage, women's suffrage, votes for women, suffragettism, democracy, democratic system, parliamentary system, congressional system (US), electoral system, electoral college (US), proportional representation, first-past-the-post system, counting hands, counting heads, counting noses

12 **election**, general election, national election, federal election (US), state election (US), by-election, local election, local-government election, indirect election, primary election (US), primary (US), direct primary (US), open primary (US), closed primary (US), polls, polling, voting, political campaign, ticket, mani-

festo, electioneering, whistle-stop tour, whistle-stopping, canvassing, stumping (US), doorstepping, hustings, candidacy (*or* candidature), polling day, polling place, polling station, polling booth, voting paper, ballot paper, ballot box, returns, vote counting, tabulation of ballots, evaluation of returns, voting machine, psephology, electoral roll, voting list, constituency, marginal constituency, electoral district, polling district, precinct (US), borough, pocket borough (Arch), rotten borough (Arch)

13 **electorate**, voters, voter, registered voter, absentee voter, constituent, elector (US), balloter, candidate, nominee, victorious candidate, president-elect (US), minister designate, losing candidate, also-ran, psephologist, suffragette, suffragist, poll watcher

ADJECTIVES

14 **selecting**, choosing, deciding, decisive, eclectic, optional, discretional, volitional, exercising choice, selective, particular, discriminating, discerning, showing preference, preferential, favouring, choosy (Inf), picky (Inf)
▶ *570 Will, 481 Discrimination, 851 Approval, 784 Liking*

15 **chosen**, selected, picked, sorted, assorted, seeded, well-chosen, worth choosing, to be jumped at, not to be sniffed at, select, choice, A-1, recherché, hand-picked, elite, elect, designate, elected, returned, adopted, deselected, on approval, preferable, better, desirable, advisable, preferred, special, favourite, fancy, pet, God's own, by appointment, not to be sneezed at (Inf)
▶ *784 Liking, 617 Worth*

16 **elective**, electoral, voting, enfranchised, vote-catching, electioneering, canvassing, psephological

ADVERBS

17 **selectively**, eclectically, optionally, by choice, by ballot, by referendum, alternatively, either...or, preferentially, preferably, rather, sooner, à la carte

581 Rejection

VERBS

1 **reject**, decline, turn down, not accept, say no to, refuse, draw the line at, rebuff, repulse, repel, spurn, dismiss out of hand, disallow, not approve, not pass, return, send back, look a gift horse in the mouth, not consider, pass over, ignore, disregard, not select, vote against, cast a negative vote, not vote for, deselect
▶ *711 Refusal, 852 Disapproval, 470 Negligence*

2 **discard**, throw away, scrap, ditch, throw aside, lay aside, set aside, renounce, give up, abandon, eliminate, get rid of, throw out, cast out, eject, jettison, expel, dismiss, oust, depose, supersede, junk (Inf), sling out (Inf), chuck out (Inf), kick out (Inf), boot out (Inf), kick downstairs (Inf)
▶ *349 Expulsion, 600 Nonuse*

3 **exclude**, except, count out, not count, exempt, blackball, cold-shoulder, turn one's back on, slight, snub, brush off, freeze out, scout (Arch), give a cold reception to, give a cool welcome to, make unwelcome, not cater for, not want, turn up one's nose at, sniff at, scorn, disdain, mock, deride, laugh at, ridicule, sneeze at (Inf)
▶ *147 Exclusion, 818 Discourtesy, 816 Unsociability, 799 Derision*

4 **revoke**, cancel, abrogate, negate, abnegate, repudiate, apostatize, recant, deny, disclaim, disavow
▶ *536 Negation, 578 Equivocation, 704 Cancellation*

NOUNS

5 **rejection**, declining, nonacceptance, refusal, nonapproval, disapproval, slight, snub, rebuff, repulse, spurn, kick, brush-off, cold shoulder, cold reception, cool welcome, more kicks than ha'pence , more bricks than bouquets, exclusion, exception, exemption, blackballing
▶ *147 Exclusion, 711 Refusal, 852 Disapproval, 816 Unsociability*

6 **discarding**, disuse, nonuse, abandonment, elimination, ejection, expulsion, dismissal, unemployment, disemployment (US), redundancy, defeat, electoral defeat, nonelection, deselection, lost election, forfeiture of deposit
▶ *600 Nonuse, 349 Expulsion, 683 Failure*

7 **abrogation**, cancellation, negation, abnegation, repudiation, apostasy, recantation, denial, disavowal
▶ *704 Cancellation, 536 Negation, 578 Equivocation*

8 **rejected thing**, reject, discard, unpopular cause, lost cause, failure, flop (Inf)
▶ *683 Failure*

9 **rejected person**, loser, born loser, defeated candidate, unsuccessful applicant, redundant worker, 4-F recruit (US), fired employee, spurned lover, ineligible athlete, no-hoper (Inf), wallflower (Inf)

ADJECTIVES

10 **rejected**, declined, turned down, not accepted, unchosen, unselected, ineligible, unqualified, unsuitable, unacceptable, unaccepted, unrequited, returned, sent back, unusable, unfit for human consumption, unfit for consideration, not be thought of, out of the question, unwanted, discarded, disused, thrown away, cast out, dismissed, redundant, excluded, snubbed

582   Predetermination

VERBS

1 **predetermine**, destine, predestine, predestinate, appoint, foreordain, preordain, decree, intend
▶ *571 Necessity, 199 Future Time, 588 Intention*

2 **premeditate**, preconceive, decide beforehand, resolve beforehand, plan, plan beforehand, preset, prearrange, arrange, contrive, agree beforehand, preconcert, ensure a result, contrive a result, pack a jury, prime a witness, stack the cards, load the dice, fix (Inf), set up (Inf), frame (Sl)
▶ *592 Plan, 152 Arrangement, 226 Cause, 540 Falsehood*

ADJECTIVES

3 **predetermined**, destined, predestined, fated, doomed, appointed, foreordained, preordained, ordained, decreed, on the cards (Inf), cut and dried (Inf)
▶ *571 Necessity, 199 Future Time*

4 **deliberate**, intentional, willed, premeditated, aforethought, prepense, with a motive, planned, preplanned, considered, measured, weighed, calculated, designed, prearranged, preset, pre-established, fixed, set, controlled, studied, advised, devised, contrived, packed, primed, stacked, loaded, put-up (Inf), set-up (Inf), framed (Inf)
▶ *588 Intention, 592 Plan, 152 Arrangement*

NOUNS

5 **predetermination**, predestination, foreordination, preordination, destiny, fate, doom, lot, karma, kismet, will, decree
▶ *571 Necessity, 570 Will*

6 **premeditation**, predeliberation, resolve, project, plan, intention, prearrangement, preparation, order of the day, order paper, agenda, plot, packed jury, primed witness, preconceived opinion, *parti pris* (Fr), closed mind, foregone conclusion, agreed result, ready-made verdict, closed book, open-and-shut case, frame-up (Sl), put-up job (Inf)
▶ *588 Intention, 594 Preparation, 592 Plan*

583   Improvisation

ADJECTIVES

1 **improvised**, makeshift, provisional, jury-rigged, inventive, ad hoc, impromptu, ad-lib, extemporaneous, extemporary, extempore, unrehearsed, unprepared, unpremeditated, unmediated, uncalculated, catch-as-catch-can (US), offhand, offhanded, off the cuff (Inf)

2 **spontaneous**, sudden, snap, spur-of-the-moment, unprompted, unmotivated, unprovoked, unforced, voluntary, willing, unguarded, incautious, rash, impetuous, impulsive, natural, instinctive, involuntary, automatic, kneejerk, intuitive, untaught, emotional
▶ *464 Intuition, 780 Rashness, 572 Willingness, 658 Naivety, 759 Feeling*

VERBS

3 **improvise**, make do, throw together, invent, devise, contrive, come up with, think up, dream up, ad-lib, extemporize, vamp, think on one's feet, act on impulse, act on the spur of the moment, come out with, blurt, say whatever comes into one's mind, say whatever pops into one's head, flash out with, rise to the occasion, have a sudden brainwave (Inf), jam (Inf)

NOUNS

4 **improvisation**, invention, ad hoc measures, extemporization, jam session, cadenza, ad-libbing, ad-lib, impromptu talk, unpremeditation, thinking on one's feet, offhandedness

5 **spontaneity**, involuntariness, reflex, automatic reflex, knee-jerk reaction, impulsiveness, impulse, blind impulse, instinct, intuition, hunch, sudden thought, idea, flash, inspiration, snap decision, spurt of activity, burst of confidence
▶ *464 Intuition, 471 Idea*

6 **improviser**, innovator, inventor, extemporizer, ad-libber, improvisatore, improvisatrice, creature of impulse, spontaneous person

ADVERBS

7 **extempore**, extemporaneously, impromptu, ad hoc, ad lib, spontaneously, suddenly, on the spur of the moment, involuntarily, instinctively, in an offhand manner, offhand, on the run, off the top of one's head, out of thin air, off the cuff (Inf)

584   Habit

Curious things, habits. People themselves never knew they had them. Agatha Christie.

Men's natures are alike; it is their habits that carry them far apart. Confucius.

NOUNS

1 **habit**, habitual action, force of habit, second nature, matter of course, custom, use, usage, wont, pattern, praxis, regularity, familiarity, inveteracy, confirmed habit, long habit, addiction, compulsion, bad habit, cacoethes, mania, obsession, fixation, complex
▶ *214 Regularity*

2 **tendency**, habitude, leaning, bent, propensity, proclivity, instinct, knack, trick, trait, idiosyncrasy, mannerism
▶ *234 Tendency*

3 **way**, ways, established ways, fixed ways, lifestyle, way of life, daily habit, constitutional, routine, run, round, daily round, routine work, repetitive job, groove, rut, tramlines,

beaten track, treadmill, grind (Inf), daily grind (Inf), the nine-to-five (Inf)

4 **custom**, usage, standard usage, established custom, standing custom, native custom, old custom, the old way, tradition, lore, folklore, social custom, social usage, mores, manners and customs, behaviour patterns, institution, ritual, rite, ceremony, observance, religious observance, religion, cult, cultus, trend, fashion, craze, the in thing (Inf)
▶ *219 Continuity, 188 Duration, 7 Religion, 796 Fashion*

5 **tradition**, consuetude, law, prescription, legal precedent, rules, rules and regulations, house rules, rules of business, convention, protocol, unwritten law, order of the day, formality, form, etiquette, manners, social manners, table manners, eating habits, conduct, behaviour, military conduct, military discipline, the done thing (Inf), spit and polish (Inf)
▶ *16 Law, 166 Rule, 652 Conduct, 813 Formality*

6 **procedure**, official procedure, standard procedure, recognized procedure, policy, usual policy, practice, standard practice, common practice, routine, system, drill, bureaucracy, red tape, beadledom, petty officialdom, conventionalism, conventionality, traditionalism, conservatism, old school, conformism, conformity
▶ *150 Order, 167 Conformity*

7 **habituation**, training, drilling, memorization, rote, indoctrination, brainwashing, inurement, institutionalization, hardening, seasoning, maturing, maturation, naturalization, acclimatization, adaptation, orientation, conditioning, association, reflex, conditioned reflex
▶ *511 Memory, 594 Preparation*

8 **creature of habit**, habitué, old fogy, conservative, old guard, traditionalist, conventionalist, hard-liner, regular, regular customer, frequent patron, frequenter, long-standing client, addict, drug addict, alcoholic, workaholic, devotee, fan, enthusiast, camp follower, stick-in-the-mud (Inf), dodo (Sl), groupie (Sl)
▶ *167 Conformity, 738 Purchase, 875 Drug-Taking, 874 Drunkenness*

ADJECTIVES

9 **habitual**, customary, accustomed, wonted, predictable, invariable, usual, regular, routine, everyday, daily, quotidian, weekly, monthly, annual, professional, occupational
▶ *214 Regularity, 212 Frequency, 225 Stability, 185 Time*

10 **familiar**, known, well-known, everyday, household, ordinary, common, commonplace, unexceptional, unoriginal, stock, trite, banal, hackneyed, clichéd, well-worn, trodden, beaten, current, prevalent, widespread, obtaining, universal, common or garden (Inf)
▶ *164 Generality*

11 **normal**, natural, in character, typical, stereotyped, conventional, orthodox, traditional, traditionary (US), traditive, ritual, time-honoured, old, old-fashioned, old-world, old-line (US), permanent, lasting
▶ *167 Conformity, 217 Permanence*

12 **established**, official, de rigueur, done, practised, approved, accepted, socially accepted, received, admitted, acknowledged, recognized, understood, accredited, instituted, institutionalized, hallowed by custom, in, fashionable, in fashion, in vogue, modish, in the mode, with it (Inf)
▶ *695 Compulsion, 851 Approval, 796 Fashion*

13 **fixed**, set, set in one's ways, staunch, true-blue, dyed-in-the-wool, ingrained, implanted, rooted, deep-rooted, deep-seated, imbued, permeated, soaked, dyed
▶ *103 Essence*

14 **habituated**, in the habit, used, accustomed, familiar, at home, conversant, *au fait* (Fr), practised, trained, tamed, broken in, acclimatized, naturalized, conditioned, inured, seasoned, hardened, confirmed, chronic, inveterate, addicted, given, dedicated, devoted, wedded, habitual, frequent, recurrent, constant, perpetual
▶ *594 Preparation, 501 Knowledge, 212 Frequency, 219 Continuity, 183 Repetition*

15 **habit-forming**, addictive, obsessive, haunting, besetting, clinging
▶ *586 Persuasion*

VERBS

16 **have a habit**, have the habit of, do regularly, be known to, have a tendency, go regularly, haunt, frequent, habituate (US), make a habit of, take up, go in for, never vary, observe routine, be in a rut, be stuck in a groove, tread the beaten path (*or* track), cling to custom, observe tradition

17 **become a habit**, become acceptable, catch on, grow on one, take hold of one, become part of one, stick, cling, adhere, settle, take root, be the rule, obtain, prevail, come into use, acquire the force of habit (*or* custom)

18 **habituate**, accustom, inure, season, harden, case-harden, teach, train, domesticate, tame, break in, naturalize, acclimatize, adapt, orient, orientate, implant, ingraft, imbue, indoctrinate, brainwash, condition, accustom oneself, get used to, get the feel of, get the knack of, warm up, get into one's stride, take to, take to like a duck to water, get into the way of, acquire the habit, learn a habit, develop a habit, cultivate a habit, fall into a habit, get into a habit, be slave to a habit, become addicted, catch oneself doing, keep one's hand

in, practise, get the hang of (Inf)

▶ *233 Influence*

ADVERBS

19 **habitually**, by force of habit, by tradition, by custom, customarily, wontedly, invariably, usually, regularly, with regularity, professionally, occupationally, as usual, as always, as is one's wont, systematically, mechanically, automatically, without thinking, in one's stride, traditionally, conventionally

585   Unaccustomedness

ADJECTIVES

1 **unaccustomed**, not used to, uncomfortable with, not in the habit of, nonobservant, unfamiliar, unwonted, unhabituated, untaught, untrained, uneducated, inexperienced, ignorant of, innocent, naive, new to, new, fresh, raw, callow, green, uninstructed, out of the habit, disaccustomed, rusty, unskilful, unseasoned, unripe, immature, undomesticated, untamed, unbroken, not broken, wild, still wet behind the ears (Inf)

▶ *502 Ignorance, 595 Lack of Preparation, 656 Unskilfulness, 658 Naivety, 206 Youth*

2 **not customary**, not done, out of the ordinary, not current, nonprevalent, unwonted, unpractised, not observed, unnecessary, not de rigueur, not in vogue, unfashionable, bad form, tactless, without manners, gauche, vulgar, out of step, out of fashion, antiquated, old-fashioned, old hat, stale, defunct, past, outgrown, discarded, disused, unconventional, nonconformist, unsanctified by custom, untraditional, unprecedented, unhackneyed, avant-garde, original, experimental, odd, strange, unusual, uncommon, way out (Inf), far out (Inf), non-U (Inf), out of time (Inf)

▶ *168 Nonconformity, 113 Diversity, 412 Tastelessness, 818 Discourtesy*

NOUNS

3 **unaccustomedness**, disusage, disuse, discontinuance, inexperience, unfamiliarity, unskilfulness, deterioration, staleness, lack of practice, rustiness, unconventionality, nonconformity

VERBS

4 **be unaccustomed**, slip, lapse, fall into disuse, grow rusty, deteriorate

5 **disaccustom**, wean from, cure, reform, break (*or* drop) a habit, give up, throw off, slough off, shed, kick (Inf)

ADVERBS

6 **unaccustomedly**, uncomfortably, ignorantly, innocently, naively, immaturely

7 **unskilfully**, inexpertly, incapably, inadequately, incompetently

8 **unusually**, uncommonly, oddly, strangely, unconventionally, eccentrically, originally, experimentally

586   Persuasion

They will conquer, but they will not convince.
Miguel de Unamuno y Jugo.

NOUNS

1 **persuasion**, persuasiveness, influence, clout (Inf), inducement, pressure, insistence, prompting, lobbying, salesmanship, sales pitch, sales talk, patter

2 **flattery**, cajolery, coaxing, teasing, wheedling, blandishment, honeyed words, side pressure, urging, incitement, encouragement, lecture, pleading, advocacy, solicitation, invitation, temptation, enticement, turn-on (Sl), soft soap (Sl)

3 **incentive**, lure, allure, allurement, seduction, seductiveness, tantalization, attractiveness, attraction, witchery, bewitchment, carrot, siren song, voice of the tempter, winning ways, fascination, charm, sex appeal, charisma, magnetism, it (Inf)

4 **exhortation**, pep talk (Inf), pep rally (US), rallying cry, clarion call, trumpet call

5 **propaganda**, promotion, self-promotion, publicity, advertising, pamphleteering, agitprop, consciousness-raising, indoctrination, hard selling, brainwashing

6 **advertising**, advertisement, sales promotion, promotional literature, direct mail, soft sell, hard sell, public relations (PR), publicity, Madison Avenue, flackery (US sl), ballyhoo (Sl), hype (Sl)

▶ *532 Publication*

7 **persuadability**, docility, tractability, teachableness, willingness, pliancy, pliability, softness, susceptibility, susceptivity, credulity, suggestibility, credulousness, impressibility, sensitivity, putty in one's hands (Inf)

8 **incentive**, inducement, stimulus, fillip, nudge, threat, prod, slap, spur, goad, whip, rod, crack of the whip, big stick, carrot, carrot and stick, sop, jam tomorrow (Inf)

9 **enticement**, lure, trap, decoy, decoy duck, bait, baited trap, greased palm, special offer, sale of the century, loss leader, come-on (Inf)

10 **bribe**, kickback, backhander, slush fund, offer of a lifetime, offer one cannot refuse, pork barrel (US sl)

11 **motive**, reason, cause, cause of action, rationale, reasoning, justification, grounds, motivation, driving force, impetus, mainspring, causation, intention, objective, aim, goal, aspiration, ambition, ideal, guiding principle, words to live by, guiding light, direction, calling, call, vocation, conscience, dictate of conscience, honour, duty, personal reasons, ul-

terior motive, impulse, spur of the moment
▶ *228 Motive, 226 Cause, 775 Hope, 847 Duty, 860 Selfishness, 583 Improvisation*

12 **persuader**, orator, rhetorician, advocate, pleader, coaxer, wheedler, salesman (*or* saleswoman), advertiser, ad man (*or* woman), promoter, propagandist, publicizer, publicist, publicity agent, public relations officer, PR man (*or* woman), vote-catcher (Inf), vote-snatcher (Sl), flak-catcher (Sl), spin doctor (Sl)
▶ *564 Speech, 532 Publication, 853 Flattery*

13 **tempter**, tantalizer, seducer, Romeo, rake, Casanova, temptress, seductress, Eve, vamp, femme fatale, Mata Hari, siren, Circe, Lorelei, Satan

14 **motivator**, mover, prime mover, manipulator, manager, agent, manoeuvrer, tactician, strategist, planner, instigator, prompter, suggester, hinter, inspirer, influence, counsellor, adviser, abettor, aider and abettor, agent provocateur, ringleader, firebrand, rabble-rouser, demagogue, seditionist, agitator, activist, lobbyist, lobbyer, lobby, pressure group, special-interest group, watchdog group, political association, ginger group, movers and shakers (Inf), wirepuller (US inf)
▶ *233 Influence, 592 Plan, 654 Advice, 662 Help, 653 Management*

VERBS

15 **persuade**, influence, advise, counsel, induce, pressure, lobby, insist, move, motivate, incline, dispose, prompt, instigate, bring about, cause, convince, win over, carry with one, carry one's point, prevail upon, talk into, urge, impel, push into, drive into, nag into, bully into, wear down, intimidate, browbeat, coerce, twist one's arm, compel, force, bring round, talk round, convert, indoctrinate, brainwash, bring to one's side, get in one's corner, bring over, make one of us, procure, enlist, engage, coax, wheedle, cajole, sweet-talk, blandish, turn someone's head, lay it on thick, conciliate, appease, pacify, take by storm (Inf), put the screws on (Sl)
▶ *233 Influence, 497 Belief, 220 Conversion, 853 Flattery, 677 Pacification*

16 **tempt**, lead into temptation, allure, lure, entice, seduce, hold out a carrot to, dangle before one's eyes, make one's mouth water, tantalize, tease, inveigle, ensnare, coax, wheedle, pander to, facilitate, make things easy for, clear the path for, grease the wheels, gild the pill, sugar the pill, sweeten the pot (Inf)
▶ *635 Trap, 660 Easiness*

17 **bribe**, offer a bribe, offer an inducement, hold out a carrot, give a sop to Cerberus, tip, reward, suborn, corrupt, buy off, square (Sl), pay under the table (Inf), offer a sweetener (Sl), grease the palm (Sl), oil (Sl), oil the hand (Sl)
▶ *710 Offer, 878 Reward*

18 **be persuaded**, yield, succumb, submit, give up, concede, agree, consent, believe, fall for, obey one's conscience, act on principle, come (*or* fall) under the influence, hear the call, feel the urge, buy (Inf), get it bad (Inf), catch the bug (Sl)
▶ *667 Agreement*

ADJECTIVES

19 **persuasive**, influential, impressive, convincing, cogent, hortatory, didactic, protreptic, directive, compelling, forceful, effective, telling, winning, inducing, incentive, motivating, encouraging, exciting, energizing, stimulating, tonic, challenging, rousing, inflaming, provocative, teasing, tantalizing, tempting, alluring, attractive, inviting, magnetic, fascinating, bewitching, hypnotic, mesmeric, charismatic, charming, sexy, irresistible, habit-forming, addictive
▶ *233 Influence, 497 Belief, 340 Attraction, 584 Habit*

20 **persuadable**, persuasible, credulous, receptive, open to suggestion, tractable, docile, inspired, motivated, goal-oriented, spurred on, incited, encouraged, egged on, spellbound, bewitched, induced, pressured

ADVERBS

21 **persuasively**, impressively, convincingly, cogently, forcefully, encouragingly, provocatively, temptingly, invitingly, irresistibly

587 Dissuasion

VERBS

1 **dissuade**, discourage, caution, warn, advise against, persuade against, convince to the contrary, talk out of, put off, argue against, confute, castigate, reprove, expostulate, remonstrate, cry out against, protest against
▶ *636 Warning, 476 Refutation, 852 Disapproval, 713 Protest*

2 **deter**, frighten off, frighten away, unnerve, rattle, shake, stagger, make one stop in one's tracks, give one pause, daunt, cow, intimidate, threaten, terrorize
▶ *777 Fear*

3 **deflect**, head off, steer one away from, turn one aside, wean away from, disaccustom, halt one's progress, ruin one's plans, hold back, keep back, restrain, crush, nip in the bud, stop, prevent
▶ *335 Deviation, 585 Unaccustomedness, 699 Restraint*

4 **put off**, disincline, disaffect, indispose, set against, turn against, repel, disgust, fill with distaste, render averse
▶ *785 Dislike*

5 **discourage**, dishearten, dispirit, depress, disillusion, disenchant, throw cold water on, dampen, extinguish, quench, squelch, cool, chill, damp the ardour, be a wet blanket, take the edge off, blunt, calm, quiet
▶ *770 Sorrow, 242 Moderation*

NOUNS

6 **dissuasion**, discouragement, no encouragement, contrary advice, caution, warning, reproof, admonition, expostulation, remonstrance, objection, protest, resistance, opposition, hindrance, setback, closed door, roadblock, red light, contraindication
▶ *636 Warning, 669 Resistance, 663 Opposition, 661 Hindrance*

7 **deterrence**, deterrent, disincentive, intimidation, terrorism, deflection, restraint, disinclination, disaffection, disheartenment, disenchantment, cold water, damper
▶ *777 Fear, 785 Dislike, 699 Restraint, 335 Deviation*

8 **cautionary person**, wet blanket, killjoy, spoilsport, party pooper (Sl)

ADJECTIVES

9 **dissuasive**, discouraging, contrary, contradictory, cautionary, warning, monitory, expostulatory, chilling, damping, disheartening, deterrent

10 **dissuaded**, discouraged, disenchanted, disillusioned, disheartened, dampened, reluctant, unwilling
▶ *573 Unwillingness*

ADVERBS

11 **dissuasively**, discouragingly, dishearteningly, as a deterrent

588   Intention

NOUNS

1 **intention**, intent, meaning, purpose, set purpose, settled purpose, motive, *mens rea* (L), criminal intent, good intention, benevolence, ulterior motive, axe to grind
▶ *520 Meaning, 228 Motive, 831 Benevolence, 832 Malevolence*

2 **intentionality**, deliberateness, calculation, calculated risk, determination, resolve, resolution, predetermination, premeditation
▶ *170 Calculation, 582 Predetermination, 574 Resolution*

3 **future intention**, prospect, view, purview, plan, proposal, design, project, enterprise, undertaking, pursuit, study, occupation, preoccupation, ambition, aspiration, hope, desire
▶ *199 Future Time, 782 Desire, 597 Undertaking*

4 **formulated intention**, decision, judgment, final decision, final word, ultimatum, threat, promise, engagement, bid, bid for, attempt
▶ *492 Judgment, 636 Warning, 714 Promise, 596 Attempt*

5 **final intention**, overall design, ultimate purpose, ultimate aim, teleology, final cause, God's purpose, eschatology, the four last things, the grand scheme, the big picture, *raison d'être* (Fr), trend, tendency, intentional bias, tendentiousness, be-all and end-all (Inf)
▶ *157 End, 226 Cause*

6 **objective**, final objective, end, end in view, destination, aim, object, goal, mark, target, stationary target, butt, quintain (Arch), moving target, target area, bull's-eye, finishing line, finishing tape, winning post, place of pilgrimage, Mecca, Lourdes, Canterbury, prey, quarry, game, prize, cup, trophy, silver cup, silver plate, crown, wreath, laurels, dream, lifelong dream, vision, heart's desire, Promised Land, land of milk and honey, El Dorado, Fountain of Youth, Shangri-la, Holy Grail, philosopher's stone, pot (*or* crock) of gold at the end of the rainbow
▶ *157 End, 344 Arrival, 590 Pursuit, 681 Trophy, 782 Desire*

VERBS

7 **intend**, mean, purpose, propose, have in mind, have in view, have an eye to, contemplate, think of, ponder, meditate, calculate, reckon on, plan, plan for, prepare for, look for, expect, foresee
▶ *592 Plan, 513 Expectation, 516 Foresight*

8 **resolve**, determine, determine to, mean to, have a mind to, really mean, have every intention, premeditate, predetermine, project, design, harbour a design, have a purpose, have a motive, undertake, engage, take on oneself, shoulder, promise, threaten
▶ *574 Resolution, 597 Undertaking, 714 Promise, 636 Warning*

9 **intend for**, destine for, predestine, mark down for, earmark, put aside for, hold for, keep for, reserve for, put on layaway (US)

10 **aim**, aim at, go for, try for, bid for, aspire to, dream of, strive after, work for, have designs on, set one's sights on, take aim, focus on, point at
▶ *596 Attempt, 332 Direction*

ADJECTIVES

11 **intending**, intent on, determined to, resolute, serious, serious-minded, seeking, out to, out for, with designs on, having in view, purposive, teleological, inclined, disposed, so minded, so inclined, prospective, would-be, hopeful, aspiring, ambitious, hellbent (Inf)
▶ *574 Resolution, 782 Desire*

12 **intended**, meant, for a purpose, for a reason, deliberate, intentional, voluntary, volitional, wilful, calculated, studied, planned, designed, purposed, purposeful, premeditated, aforethought, predetermined, determined, eschatological
▶ *592 Plan, 582 Predetermination, 570 Will*

ADVERBS

13 **intentionally**, deliberately, purposely, on purpose, by design, wittingly, knowingly, with full knowledge, with one's eyes open, pointedly, designedly, advisedly, voluntarily, wilfully, with meditation, with forethought, with malice aforethought, ruthlessly, in cold blood

14 **for**, for a purpose, in order to, with the intention of, with a view to, with an eye to, with the object of, in pursuance of, pursuant to

15 **according to plan**, as planned, as arranged, to design, to one's own design, to one's own specifications

589 Chance

NOUNS

1 **chance**, blind chance, randomness, random chance, whatever happens, unpredictability, fortuitousness, fortuity, indeterminacy, indetermination, uncertainty, unaccountability, inexplicability, casualness, coincidence, accident, contingency, hazard, risk, gamble, jeopardy
▶ *491 Uncertainty*

2 **luck**, blind luck, fortune, providence, wheel of fortune, lady luck, luck of the draw, whatever comes, destiny, fate, lot, one's lot, good luck, good fortune, luck on one's side, run of good luck, bad luck, ill fortune, tough luck, rotten luck, worst luck, run of bad luck, bit of luck, fluke, lucky shot, lucky strike, chance hit, chance meeting, chance encounter, chance discovery, serendipity, the way the ball bounces (Inf), the way the cookie crumbles (US inf), potluck (Inf), a good hand (Inf)
▶ *686 Prosperity, 687 Adversity, 514 Surprise, 496 Discovery*

3 **equal chance**, even chance, fifty-fifty, odds-on, toss-up, flip (*or* spin) of the coin, throw of the dice, turn of the card, spin of the wheel, random sample, game of chance, gambling, gaming, lottery, state lottery (US), raffle, draw, bingo, lucky dip, tombola, sweepstake, sweep, premium bond
▶ *122 Equality*

4 **fair chance**, decent chance, sporting chance, fighting chance, gambling chance, (distinct) possibility
▶ *486 Possibility*

5 **good chance**, best chance, main chance, favourable chance, opportunity, occasion, good odds, long odds, odds-on, probability, likelihood, small risk, safe bet, sure thing, certainty, dead cert (Inf)
▶ *210 Timeliness, 488 Probability, 490 Certainty*

6 **poor chance**, small chance, rare chance, half a chance, long shot, shot in the dark, chance

in a million, one in a hundred, improbability, impossibility, no chance (at all), snowball's chance in hell, fat chance (Sl)
▶ *489 Improbability, 487 Impossibility*

7 **calculation of chance**, probability, mathematical probability, the probabilities, theory of probabilities, aleatorics, statistics, stochastics, doctrine of chance, actuarial calculation, insurance, assurance, underwriting, risk-taking, speculation, gambling, bookmaking
▶ *633 Danger, 632 Safety, 479 Experiment, 52 Mathematics*

ADJECTIVES

8 **chance**, random, unpredictable, unforeseeable, fortuitous, indeterminable, incalculable, uncertain, stochastic, aleatoric, haphazard, hit-or-miss, sink-or-swim, catch-as-catch-can (US), casual, aleatory, serendipitous, accidental, adventitious, contingent, unexpected, unforeseen, noncausal, epiphenomenal, incidental, coincidental, lucky, fortunate, unlucky, unfortunate, risky, chancy (Inf), fluky (Inf), dicey (Inf), iffy (Inf)

9 **causeless**, groundless, uncaused, unmotivated, undesigned, unplanned, unpremeditated, unmeant, unintended, unintentional, inadvertent, unexplainable, unaccountable, inexplicable

VERBS

10 **chance**, happen, just happen, so happen, occur, turn up, pop up, crop up, fall to one's lot, befall, betide
▶ *196 Present Time*

11 **chance upon**, encounter by chance, encounter unexpectedly, meet by accident (*or* chance), run into, run across, come upon, light upon, hit upon, stumble upon, blunder upon, bump into (Inf)
▶ *496 Discovery*

12 **take a chance**, chance it, chance, chance one's arm, take a risk, risk it, risk, hazard, venture, go out on a limb, leave it to chance, leave it to fate, try one's luck, gamble, cast the die, speculate, bet, wager, have luck, be lucky, have a chance, have small chance
▶ *633 Danger*

ADVERBS

13 **by chance**, by accident, accidentally, inadvertently, unintentionally, casually, fortuitously, coincidentally, by coincidence, randomly, at random, haphazardly, unpredictably, unexpectedly, unaccountably, inexplicably, serendipitously, luckily, as (good) luck would have it, fortunately, unluckily, as ill luck would have it, unfortunately

14 **perchance**, perhaps, for all one knows, possibly, according to chance, as it may happen, as the case may be, as it may be, as it may chance, whatever happens, in any event

15 **good luck!**, lots of luck!, lucky dog!, bingo!,
hard luck!, better luck next time!, fat chance!

590 Pursuit

NOUNS

1 **pursuit**, pursuing, pursuance, going after,
seeking, looking for, search, quest, hunting,
tracking, trailing, stalking, spooring, chasing,
following, dogging, shadowing, manhunt,
dragnet, APB (all points bulletin) (US), persecution, witch-hunt, McCarthyism (US), kangaroo court, hounding, persistence, perseverance, prosecution, execution, effectuation,
tailing (Inf)
▶ *155 Sequence, 477 Question, 575 Perseverance,*
684 Completion

2 **chase**, pursuit, hot pursuit, run, paper chase,
steeplechase, race, racing, hunt, hunting,
hounding, casting, hue and cry, tally-ho, beat,
drive, battue, beating, shooting, gunning,
hunting, shooting, and fishing, blood sport,
fox hunt, stag hunt, elk hunt, pheasant shoot,
grouse shoot, duck shoot, turkey shoot, big-
game hunt, safari hunt, lion hunt, tiger hunt,
elephant hunt, bear hunt, boar hunt, pigsticking, stalking, deerstalking, hawking, falconry,
fowling, wildfowling, fishing, angling, fly fishing, coarse fishing, inshore fishing, offshore
fishing, freshwater fishing, trout fishing,
salmon fishing, sea fishing, deep-sea fishing,
game fishing, marlin fishing, whaling, ice fishing, beagling, coursing, ratting, trapping,
badger hunting, woodchuck hunting (US),
groundhog hunting (US), ferreting, rabbiting,
lamping, mole-catching, possuming (US),
catch
▶ *674 Contention, 721 Gain, 398 Killing*

3 **hunting and fishing equipment**, fishing
pole, fishing rod, fishing line, casting rod, rod
and line, rod and reel, rod and tackle, bait, fly,
fishing net, fish net, keepnet, dragnet, hunting rifle, gun, rifle, shotgun, fowling-piece,
trap
▶ *680 Weapon, 635 Trap*

4 **activity**, work, business, occupation, career,
leisure pursuit, hobby, pastime, interest, recreation
▶ *644 Work*

5 **pursuer**, seeker, searcher, researcher, quester,
search party member, vigilante committee
member, chaser, follower, dogger, shadow,
sleuth, tail (Inf)

6 **hunter**, tracker, trailer, stalker, huntsman,
huntress, Nimrod, Diana, whip, whipper-in,
beater, hounds, pack, field, hound, fox hound,
otterhound, bloodhound, gundog, athlete,
sportsman, sportswoman, marksman, markswoman, shot, good shot, gun, big-game

hunter, safari hunter, lion hunter, tiger
hunter, buffalo hunter, fox hunter, deerstalker, poacher, guddler, trapper, rat-catcher,
mole-catcher, bird-catcher, fowler, wildfowler,
falconer, hawker, fisherman, piscator, angler,
compleat angler, shrimper, oysterman,
trawler, trawlerman, whaler, headhunter, cannibal, man-eater, beast of prey, mouser, bird of
prey, hawk, falcon

7 **the hunted**, prey, quarry, game, victim, fugitive, escapee, deserter, missing person, lost
child, criminal, suspect on the lam(US sl)
▶ *638 Escape*

VERBS

8 **pursue**, go after, seek, look for, search for,
hunt for, quest after, cast about for, fish for,
dig for, organize a search party, organize a
vigilante committee, organize a dragnet,
be gunning for, send after, send for, send
out a search party, be in hot pursuit, conduct a witch-hunt, set up a kangaroo
court, persecute, oppress, harass, harry, chivy,
chevy
▶ *477 Question*

9 **follow**, track, trail, stalk, spoor, prowl after,
sneak after, walk as quiet as an Indian (US),
dog, shadow, sleuth, dog one's footsteps, dog
one's every step, stick like glue, follow the
scent, follow the trail, scent out, sniff out, run
to ground, discover, tail (Inf), sit on one's tail
(Inf)
▶ *155 Sequence, 496 Discovery*

10 **chase**, give chase, run after, whoop, halloo,
hark, cry on, raise the hunt, raise the hue and
cry, run down, ride down, rush at, charge at,
tilt at, ride full tilt at, leap at, jump at, grab
away, snatch at
▶ *670 Attack, 734 Taking*

11 **hunt**, go hunting, go big-game hunting, go
shooting, shoot, bag, follow the chase, ride to
hounds, go fishing, fish, fly-fish, angle, cast
one's net, trawl, whale, shrimp, ice fish, catch,
net, hook, reel in, guddle, trap, ensnare,
mouse, play cat and mouse, stalk, deer-stalk,
fowl, hawk, course, start game, start up, beat,
flush, lay traps, set snares, poach
▶ *635 Trap, 398 Killing*

12 **aim at**, be after, mark as one's prey, make
one's quarry, set one's course, steer for, woo,
court, throw oneself at, mob, swarm over,
strive for (or after), make it one's business to,
pursue one's goals, pursue one's ends, pursue
one's interest, set one's cap for (or at) (Inf),
look out for number one (Inf)
▶ *332 Direction, 588 Intention*

13 **follow up**, contact again, persist, persevere,
press on, progress, push one's way, elbow
one's way, force one's way, fight one's way
▶ *575 Perseverance, 336 Forward Motion*

14 **carry on**, continue, practise, conduct, pros-

ecute, execute, perform, undertake

▶ *640 Action, 597 Undertaking*

ADJECTIVES

15 **pursuing**, pursuant, seeking, searching, questing, in quest of, sent after, following, chasing, in pursuit, in hot pursuit, in full cry, on the trail, on one's scent, on one's tail (Inf)

16 **hunting**, shooting, fishing, piscatorial

17 **pursued**, sought, followed, chased, hounded, hunted

ADVERBS

18 **pursuant to**, in pursuance of, in search of, in quest of, on the lookout for, with a search party, on the trail, on the track, on the scent, after, in pursuit, in hot pursuit, hot on the trail, in full cry

INTERJECTIONS

19 **after him!**, stop thief!, follow that car!, shoot!, fire!, halloo!, view halloo!, yoicks!, tally-ho!, there she blows!, Geronimo!

591 Avoidance

VERBS

1 **avoid**, keep away from, keep from, stay away from, not go near, bypass, circumvent, steer clear, keep clear, stand clear, get out of the way, make way for, stand back, hold off, keep one's distance, keep at arm's length, give a wide berth to, shun, eschew, leave, let alone, have nothing to do with, keep out of, not touch with a bargepole, stand aloof, stand apart, keep oneself to oneself, have no hand in, play no part in, keep one's hands clean, turn away, turn aside, look the other way, turn a blind eye, ignore, cold-shoulder, snub, give the go-by, not give the time of day, cut (Inf)

▶ *335 Deviation, 263 Distance, 816 Unsociability, 581 Rejection*

2 **avert**, prevent, foil, obstruct, hinder

▶ *661 Hindrance*

3 **abstain**, forswear, deny oneself, do (*or* go) without, pass up, not indulge, not touch, refrain, forbear, spare, hold back, temper, moderate, pull one's punches, soften the blow, kick the habit (Inf), go on the wagon (Inf)

▶ *869 Self-Restraint, 873 Sobriety, 242 Moderation*

4 **shy**, shrink, flinch, blink, blench, fight shy, balk at, start aside, jib, refuse, give a miss, not try, not attempt, back away, back off, draw back, retreat, hang back, demur, drag one's feet, not push oneself forward, funk (Inf), turn tail (Sl)

▶ *777 Fear, 573 Unwillingness, 711 Refusal*

5 **shirk**, get out of, make excuses, malinger, pass the buck (Inf), cop out (Sl), skive (Sl), gold brick (US sl), scrimshank (Sl)

▶ *470 Negligence, 643 Inactivity*

6 **evade**, take evasive action, dodge, duck, deflect, ward off, parry, escape, elude, give one the slip, skulk, cower, hide, play hide-and-seek, send on a wild goose chase, lead one a dance, throw dust in one's eyes, throw off the scent, go on the lam (US sl)

▶ *671 Defence, 638 Escape, 531 Concealment*

7 **be evasive**, avoid the issue, duck the issue, sidestep, skirt round, talk round, equivocate, hedge, fence, fudge, prevaricate, procrastinate, delay, postpone, shelve, table, deny, disown, bury one's head in the sand, repress, suppress, ban, censor, beat about the bush (Inf), waffle (Inf), pussyfoot (Inf)

▶ *578 Equivocation, 209 Lateness, 536 Negation, 709 Veto*

8 **run away**, run off, escape, desert, play truant, jump bail, take French leave, go absent without leave (AWOL), abscond, elope, absent oneself, decamp, depart, leave, go, quit, shoot through (Aus), withdraw, retire, retreat, beat a retreat, turn one's back, make tracks, flee, fly, take flight, be off, make off, bolt, run, run for it, run for one's life, take to one's heels, show a clean pair of heels, make oneself scarce, scoot, part company, break away, slip the cable, shake the dust from one's feet, steal away, sneak off, slink off, shuffle off, creep off

9 **play truant**, truant, play hooky (*or* hookey) (US inf), do a bunk (Sl), flit (Inf), bug off (*or* out) (US sl), quit the scene (US sl), dust (US sl), bottle up and go (US sl), turn tail (Sl), slope off (*or* away), skive (Sl), mitch (Sl), cut (Inf), cut and run (Inf), scram (Inf), scat (Inf), skedaddle (Inf), beat it (Sl)

▶ *638 Escape, 254 Absence, 345 Departure, 337 Backward Motion, 648 Haste*

NOUNS

10 **avoidance**, bypassing, circumvention, averting, prevention, obstruction, hindrance, distance, safe distance, wide berth, shunning, aloofness, cold shoulder, snub

▶ *335 Deviation, 263 Distance, 816 Unsociability, 581 Rejection, 661 Hindrance*

11 **abstinence**, abstention, forswearing, self-denial, refraining, forbearance, temperance, moderation

▶ *869 Self-Restraint, 873 Sobriety, 242 Moderation*

12 **shyness**, shrinking, unwillingness, reluctance, flinching, blinking, blenching, jibbing, refusal, revulsion, recoil, retreat, withdrawal, retirement, neutrality, noninvolvement, nonintervention, isolationism, escapism

▶ *777 Fear, 573 Unwillingness, 711 Refusal, 331 Recoil, 783 Indifference*

13 **shirking**, inaction, apathy, inactivity, passivity, passing the buck (Inf), cop-out (Sl), skiving (Sl)

▶ *470 Negligence, 643 Inactivity*

14 **evasion**, evasive action, dodge, duck, deflection, parry, defence mechanism, defensive reaction, escape, elusiveness, skulking, cower-

ing, hide-and-seek, wild-goose chase, red herring

▶ *671 Defence, 638 Escape, 531 Concealment*

15 **evasiveness**, avoiding the issue, sidestep, equivocation, prevarication, procrastination, delaying action, noncooperation, denial, repression, suppression, waffle (Inf), pussyfooting (Inf)

▶ *578 Equivocation, 209 Lateness, 536 Negation, 709 Veto*

16 **desertion**, truancy, French leave, elopement, absence, departure, flight, hookey (*or* hooky) (US inf), flit (Inf)

▶ *638 Escape, 254 Absence, 345 Departure*

17 **avoider**, abstainer, nondrinker, teetotaller, dodger, sidestepper, evader, tax evader, coward, shrinker, quitter, shirker, slacker, idler, skulker, draft dodger, truant, deserter, apostate, renegade, absentee, runaway, teenage runaway, deserting husband, refugee, displaced person, escapee, escaper, fugitive, nonrealist, escapist, dreamer, visionary, ostrich, possum, welsher (Sl), couch potato (Sl), gold brick (US sl), gold bricker (US sl), scrimshanker (Sl), skiver (Sl), suspect on the lam (US sl)

▶ *873 Sobriety, 869 Self-Restraint, 779 Cowardice, 643 Inactivity, 638 Escape, 519 Imagination*

ADJECTIVES

18 **avoiding**, evasive, equivocal, elusive, slippery, hard to catch, untamed, wild, shy, flinching, blinking, blenching, shrinking, backward, reluctant, unwilling, noncooperative, noncommittal, unforthcoming, taciturn, passive, inert, inactive, not involved, apathetic, noncommitted, uncommitted, neutral, centrifugal, fugitive, escaped, runaway, hunted, hiding, skulking, cowering, hidden, latent, repressive, suppressive, preventive, censorial, defensive, on the defensive, fly-by-night (Inf), on the lam (US sl)

▶ *578 Equivocation, 777 Fear, 573 Unwillingness, 566 Taciturnity, 527 Latency*

19 **abstaining**, abstinent, ascetic, dry, on the wagon, shunning, going (*or* doing) without, temperate, moderate

20 **avoidable**, avertable, preventable, escapable, unsought, unattempted

ADVERBS

21 **away**, clear, aloof, apart, distantly, abstinently, temperately, moderately

22 **evasively**, equivocally, elusively, avoidably, avertably, preventably, preventively, obstructively

23 **shyly**, reluctantly, unwillingly, hesitantly, apathetically, passively

INTERJECTIONS

24 **hands off!**, keep off!, keep your distance!, run for it!, run for your life!, beware!, forbear!, beat it! (Sl), scram! (Sl)

592   Plan

NOUNS

1 **plan**, scheme, design, programme, project, proposal, proposition, suggestion, motion, amendment, resolution, intention, proposed action, proposed line of action, master plan, overall plan, corporate plan, management by objectives, financial plan, budget, national planning, five-year plan, schedule, schedule of events, timetable, agenda, order of the day, plan of the day, new business, old business, any other business (AOB)

▶ *588 Intention*

2 **policy**, procedure, system, strategy, plan of action, contingency plan, emergency plan, emergency procedure, course of action, working plan, company policy, tactics, preventive action, forethought, foresight, statesmanship, diplomacy, operational research, management review, way, approach, address, attack, steps, measures, countermeasures, actions, reactions, counteractions, stroke of policy, coup, coup d'état, *coup de main* (Fr), scenario, forecast, prediction, brochure, prospectus, manifesto, political party platform, platform, political plank, political party ticket, ticket, slate (US), political line, party line, mandate, formula, rule

▶ *516 Foresight, 327 Way, 602 Means, 640 Action, 517 Prediction, 166 Rule, 12 Government and Politics*

3 **expedient plan**, expedient, contrivance, resource, resort, last resort, *pis aller* (Fr), last-minute rescue, eleventh-hour rescue, winning card, trump card, card up one's sleeve, ace in the hole, recipe, nostrum, antidote, remedy, answer, loophole, way out, technicality, income-tax haven, flag of convenience, device, gimmick, trick, stratagem, artifice, ruse, dodge, evasion, ploy, shift, fiddle, swindle, knack, stunt, feat, *tour de force* (Fr), masterstroke, bold move, inspiration, brainwave, brainstorm (US), ingenious plan, happy thought, bright idea, right idea, idea, notion, invention, contraption, gadget, ad hoc measure, improvisation, makeshift, stopgap, wangle (Inf), sting (Sl), wheeze (Sl), gizmo (Sl)

▶ *602 Means, 630 Remedy, 638 Escape, 657 Cunning, 655 Skill, 471 Idea, 583 Improvisation*

4 **plot**, secret plan, scheme, intrigue, web of intrigue, web, cabal, conspiracy, inside job, insider trading, insider dealing, racket, game, manipulation, machination, wirepulling (US), string pulling, put-up, put-up job, secret influence, secrecy, latency, counterplot, countermine, frame-up (Sl), fit-up (Sl)

▶ *527 Latency, 529 Secrecy, 671 Defence*

5 **map**, plan, ground plan, floor plan, town plan, street map, road map, A to Z, atlas, scale

drawing, blueprint, layout, diagram, chart, flow chart
▶ *547 Representation*
6 **outline**, summary, skeleton, rough, rough-cast, sketch, model, pattern, pilot scheme, prototype, draft, first draft, proof, proof copy, revision, revise, revised copy
▶ *562 Summary*
7 **planning**, scheming, contrivance, organization, order, systematization, rationalization, centralization, headquarters, base, planning office, board room, committee room, back-room, operations room, drawing board
▶ *150 Order, 653 Management*
8 **planner**, organizer, manager, deviser, con-triver, framer, inventor, originator, hatcher, proposer, promoter, projector, founder, de-signer, architect, town-planner, backroom boy (*or* girl), mastermind, systematizer, systems analyst, strategist, tactician, manoeuvrer, dip-lomat, statesman, politician, Machiavelli, schemer, plotter, intriguer, intrigant, plot-spinner, cabal, conspirator, boffin (Inf), brains (Inf), wheeler-dealer (Inf), axe-grinder (Inf), go-getter (Inf)

VERBS
9 **plan**, scheme, design, contrive, organize, sys-tematize, methodize, rationalize, centralize, order, programme, propose, suggest, resolve, intend, project, aim, approach, approach a problem, confront a problem, attack a prob-lem, make (*or* draw up) a plan, conceive (*or* form) a plan
▶ *588 Intention, 150 Order*
10 **plan out**, draw up, draft, frame, shape, form, work out, map out, lay out, sketch, sketch out, chalk out, design, design a prototype, pro-gramme, draw up a programme, lay the foun-dation, lay the cornerstone, map out a course, mark out a course, shape a course, schedule, draw up a schedule, timetable, phase (US), adjust, revise, redo, recast, improve
▶ *306 Form, 547 Representation, 627 Improvement*
11 **invent**, create, concoct, hatch, formulate, think up, hit upon, fall on, discover, find a way, make shift, contrive, devise, engineer
▶ *496 Discovery, 519 Imagination*
12 **plan ahead**, prepare, arrange, prearrange, predetermine, think ahead, look ahead, calcu-late, budget, forecast, predict, foresee, envis-age, expect, follow a plan, have a policy, work to a schedule
▶ *594 Preparation, 152 Arrangement, 582 Predeter-mination, 517 Prediction, 516 Foresight, 513 Ex-pectation*
13 **plot**, scheme, have designs, be up to some-thing, conspire, intrigue, machinate, cabal, concoct, brew a plot, brew, hatch a plot, hatch, undermine, countermine, set a trap for, dig a pit for, trap, ensnare, work against,

manoeuvre, manipulate, wheel and deal (Inf), pull strings (Inf), pull wires (US inf), cook up (Inf), frame (Sl), fit up (Sl)
▶ *657 Cunning, 635 Trap, 233 Influence, 540 Falsehood*
ADJECTIVES
14 **planned**, intended, intentional, rational, meant, premeditated, contrived, designed, or-ganized, schematic, systematic, orderly, me-thodical, worked out, prepared, strategic, tac-tical, under discussion, under consideration, at the planning stage, on the drawing board, in draft, in proof, on the stocks, drawn up
15 **planning**, scheming, cunning, contriving, resourceful, ingenious, purposeful, up to something, involved, in deep, intriguing, plot-ting, conspiratorial, Machiavellian, wheeler-dealing (Inf)
ADVERBS
16 **as planned**, intentionally, purposefully, ac-cording to schedule, schematically, methodi-cally, systematically, strategically, tactically
17 **conspiratorially**, cunningly, intriguingly, resourcefully, ingeniously

593 Requirement

NOUNS
1 **requirement**, essential, *sine qua non* (L), ne-cessity, necessary, a must, desideratum, bare essentials, needs, necessities, necessaries, shopping list, order, indent, requisition, stipu-lation, specification, requisite, prerequisite, precondition, prior conditions, condition, proviso, provision, conditions, standards, re-quest, ultimatum, injunction, command
▶ *571 Necessity, 782 Desire, 716 Negotiation, 712 Request, 692 Command*
2 **need**, want, lack, insufficiency, shortage, shortfall, slippage, gap, lacuna, gap in the mar-ket, demand, consumer demand, call, call for, run on, sellers' market, consumption, con-sumer consumption, input, intake, balance due, what is owing, debt, claim
▶ *609 Insufficiency, 254 Absence, 358 Shortfall, 745 Debt, 740 Market*
3 **needfulness**, case of need, occasion, need for, necessity, essentiality, indispensability, desirability, necessitousness, neediness, want, pinch, poverty, poverty level, subsistence level, breadline, poverty trap, predicament, urgency, exigency, emergency, crisis, vital-ness, matter of life and death, obligation, duty, bare minimum, the least one can do, face-saving measures, Queer Street (Inf)
▶ *743 Poverty, 611 Importance, 571 Necessity*
ADJECTIVES
4 **required**, essential, necessary, needed, need-ful, vital, indispensable, not to be spared, com-pulsory, obligatory, requisite, prerequisite, de-

manded, ordered, requested, desired, wanted, in demand, called for, on call, earmarked, reserved, booked, on order, lacking, missing, absent

▶ *571 Necessity, 695 Compulsion, 712 Request, 782 Desire, 254 Absence, 609 Insufficiency*

5 **necessitous**, needy, in need, in want, poor, pinched, feeling the pinch, penniless, without a penny, bankrupt, destitute, on the breadline, at poverty level, below the poverty line, in the poverty trap, lacking, deprived of, needing, craving, longing for, hungry, starving, deprived, disadvantaged, bust (Inf), broke (Inf), dead (*or* stony) broke (Inf), stony (Inf), flat broke (Inf), in hock (US inf), down on one's uppers (Sl), skint (Sl), brassick (Sl)

▶ *743 Poverty, 609 Insufficiency, 782 Desire*

6 **demanding**, crying out for, calling for, imperative, urgent, exigent, exacting, crying, pressing, squeezing, pinching

VERBS

7 **require**, need, have need of, want, lack, not have, be without, stand in need of, feel the need for, have occasion for, have a vacancy for

▶ *254 Absence, 609 Insufficiency*

8 **miss**, long for, desire, desiderate, crave, need badly, ask for, call for, cry out for, clamour for, claim, put in a claim for, apply for

▶ *782 Desire*

9 **find necessary**, find indispensable, be unable to do without, must have, use, consume, take, use up

▶ *599 Use, 571 Necessity*

10 **necessitate**, render necessary, involve, create a need, oblige, compel, set requirements, make demands, demand, request, stipulate, dictate, order, send an order for, order by telephone, requisition, indent, reserve, book, earmark, set aside

▶ *712 Request, 692 Command, 695 Compulsion*

11 **be needy**, live in poverty, live on a pittance, live from hand to mouth, live on (*or* below) the breadline, be broke (Inf)

▶ *743 Poverty*

ADVERBS

12 **in need**, in want, necessarily, essentially, vitally, indispensably, *sine qua non* (L), of necessity, urgently, imperatively, in a pinch

594 Preparation

VERBS

1 **prepare**, make preparations, get ready, make ready, take steps, take measures, pioneer, pave the way, lead the way, show the way, go before, scout the territory, see the lay of the land, bridge, build a bridge, make contact, introduce, lead up to

▶ *154 Precedence*

2 **do the groundwork**, lay the foundations,

found, establish, provide the basis, prepare the ground, sow the seed, set the stage, predispose, incline, soften up, set to work on, address oneself to, begin, make basic plans, research, document, gather notes, outline, draft, sketch, make a rough sketch, cut out, block out, rough-hew, blueprint, plan, organize, plot, contrive, concert, prearrange, predetermine, improvise, rustle up (Inf)

▶ *156 Beginning, 592 Plan, 582 Predetermination*

3 **be prepared**, prepare for, forearm, guard against, insure, take precautions, save, put something aside, hoard supplies, prepare for a rainy day, anticipate, look for, wait for, expect

▶ *632 Safety, 513 Expectation, 756 Thrift, 606 Provision*

4 **prepare for action**, ready, make ready, finish one's preparations, have ready, set in order, put in readiness, mobilize, put on alert, make operational, commission, put in commission, put in working order, fix, adjust, focus, tune, tune up, wind, wind up, screw up, gear up, arrange, array, order, put together, assemble, count down, prepare for blastoff (US), prepare for takeoff, fasten (*or* buckle) one's seatbelt, prepare to dive, batten down the hatches, stow, stow away, pack, store, shuffle the cards, tee up, set the alarm, whet the knife, load the gun, prime, cock, raise steam, heat the boiler, stoke up, warm up, crank, crank up, rev up, get into gear, bring up to scratch (Inf), bring up to snuff (Inf), clear the decks (Inf)

▶ *629 Repair, 605 Store, 150 Order, 152 Arrangement*

5 **equip**, fit, fit out, outfit, furnish, provide, supply, kit out (*or* up), rig out, dress, arm, provide with arms, provide firepower, crew, man, provide with teeth (Inf)

▶ *606 Provision*

6 **brief**, inform, bring up to date, instruct, teach, educate, train, coach, groom, drill, exercise, rehearse, lick into shape (Inf)

▶ *528 Information, 6 Education*

7 **develop**, mature, mellow, ripen, bring to fruition, force, bring on, bring to a head, cook, stew, brew, gestate, hatch, incubate, breed, grow, farm, cultivate, fledge, nurse, nurture, raise, make, produce, concoct, elaborate, work out, carry through, cure, smoke, salt, dry, age, season, weather, temper, harden, inure, acclimatize

▶ *619 Perfection, 684 Completion, 45 Cookery, 243 Production, 245 Reproduction, 68 Agriculture, 373 Hardness, 584 Habit*

8 **prepare oneself**, ready oneself, get ready, compose oneself, brace oneself, study, educate oneself, brief oneself, do one's homework, serve an apprenticeship, train, exercise, rehearse, practise, limber up, warm up, gear one-

self up, gird up one's loins, roll up one's sleeves, flex one's muscles, buckle on one's armour, take sword in hand, shoulder arms, get ready for action, be prepared, stand ready, stand by, be on stand-by, be on call, hold oneself in readiness, order one's life, put one's house in order, psych oneself up (Sl), keep one's powder dry (Inf)

NOUNS

9 **preparation**, preparing, getting ready, making ready, taking steps, taking measures, pioneering, mobilization, battening down the hatches, tuning, priming, loading, cocking, planning, organization, prearrangement, premeditation, predetermination, consultation, preconsultation, forethought, anticipation, foresight, promotion, inauguration, flotation, launching
▶ *154 Precedence, 582 Predetermination, 654 Advice, 516 Foresight, 156 Beginning*

10 **preparations**, preliminaries, measures, steps, preliminary step, preliminary course, trial run, trial, experiment, practice, rehearsal, dress rehearsal, preparatory work, study, homework, spadework, groundwork, foundation, basis, framework, frame, scaffold, scaffolding, sketch, draft, rough sketch, first draft, rough, outline, plan, blueprint, original model, prototype, pilot scheme, arrangement, arrangements, savings, reserves, store, bottom drawer, nest egg
▶ *644 Work, 280 Base, 284 Support, 156 Beginning, 592 Plan, 152 Arrangement, 605 Store*

11 **fitting out**, provisioning, furnishing, provision, supply, appointment, commission, equipment, kit, gear, outfit, marshalling, array, armament, logistics

12 **briefing**, instruction, education, training, drill, exercise, practice, apprenticeship, novitiate, probationary period

13 **development**, maturation, ripening, seasoning, hardening, inurement, acclimatization, brewing, gestation, hatching, incubation, nursing, nurture, cultivation, tillage, sowing, planting, blooming, flowering, florescence, efflorescence, fruition, fructification, making, production, manufacture
▶ *245 Reproduction, 68 Agriculture, 684 Completion, 243 Production*

14 **preparedness**, readiness, maturity, ripeness, mellowness, puberty, nubility, fitness, prime condition, top condition, shipshape condition, peak, pitch of perfection
▶ *207 Age, 619 Perfection*

15 **preparer**, teacher, tutor, coach, trainer, drillmaster, drill sergeant, torchbearer, trailblazer, pioneer, bridge-builder, paver, paviour, loader, packer, stevedore, fitter, equipper, provisioner, provider, cultivator, grower, farmer, agriculturalist, ploughman, sower, planter, cook, brewer

ADJECTIVES

16 **preparatory**, preparative, preparing, preliminary, introductory, basic, elementary, provisional, stopgap, makeshift, precautionary
▶ *154 Precedence, 156 Beginning, 583 Improvisation, 222 Substitution, 632 Safety*

17 **developing**, maturing, cooking, stewing, brewing, marinating, brooding, hatching, incubating, in the embryonic stage, in embryo, in preparation, in progress, afoot, on foot, on the stocks, on the anvil, on the drawing board, in the offing, forthcoming, impending, being discussed, under consideration, at the committee stage, agitated for, mooted, planned, learning, under training, probationary, on probation
▶ *199 Future Time*

18 **prepared**, ready, alert, vigilant, made ready, readied, in readiness, at the ready, mobilized, standing by, on call, set, all set, ready to go, raring to go, teed up, keyed up, spoiling for, trained, fully trained, qualified, well-prepared, experienced, practised, well-rehearsed, organized, in practice, tuned, primed, on one's marks, briefed, instructed, tutored, warned, forewarned, forearmed, saddled, in the saddle, in harness, armed, in armour, fully armed, armed to the teeth, armed at all points, rigged, rigged out, equipped, furnished, fully furnished, well-appointed, groomed, accoutred, dressed, fully dressed, psyched up (Sl), in one's best bib and tucker (Inf), in full war-paint (Sl)
▶ *295 Dress*

19 **in hand**, in store, ready to hand, ready for use, ready for anything, fit for use, in working order, operational

20 **developed**, matured, ripened, mature, ripe, mellow, seasoned, weathered, hardened, veteran, adult, grown, grown up, full-grown, fledged, fully fledged (or full-fledged), blooming, flowering, in flower, florescent, fruiting, overripe, overmature, well-cooked, well-done, elaborate, wrought, highly wrought, overwrought, overdone, worked up, laboured, deep-laid, completed, perfected

21 **ready-made**, ready-mixed, cut-and-dried, ready to use, ready-to-wear, off the peg, ready-formed, prefabricated, ready-furnished, processed, convenience, oven-ready, ready-to-cook, precooked, ready-to-serve, instant, predigested
▶ *45 Cookery*

ADVERBS

22 **in preparation**, in hand, under way, under construction, on the stocks, under consideration, in anticipation, vigilantly, in readiness, readily, willingly

23 **preparatorily**, preparatively, preliminarily, introductorily, provisionally

595   Lack of Preparation

ADJECTIVES

1 **unprepared**, unready, not ready, backward, behind, behindhand, behind-time, late, slow, disorganized, unorganized, orderless, un-arranged, in all directions, at sixes and sevens, surprised, caught unawares, caught napping, taken off guard, on the wrong foot, unexpec-tant, unguarded, exposed, vulnerable, unbut-toned (Inf), with one's trousers (or pants) down (Inf)

▶ *209 Lateness, 151 Disorder, 514 Surprise*

2 **spontaneous**, ad hoc, extemporized, im-provised, impromptu, ad lib, unrehearsed, not memorized, in an offhand manner, on the spur of the moment, snap, uncontrived, un-studied, off the cuff (Inf), off the top of one's head (Inf)

▶ *583 Improvisation*

3 **without preparation**, unpremeditated, un-planned, without planning, poorly planned, inadequate, with little thought, catch-as-catch-can (US), careless, negligent, rushed, makeshift, jerry-built, temporary, hasty, rash, reckless, precipitant, precipitous, shiftless, im-provident, unthrifty, thoughtless, carefree, easygoing, happy-go-lucky, unworried, half-baked (Inf)

▶ *470 Negligence, 648 Haste, 780 Rashness, 757 Extravagance, 468 Inattention, 762 Joy*

4 **untrained**, scratch, untaught, untutored, ig-norant, uninstructed, undrilled, unexercised, unpractised, inexperienced, unskilled, ap-prentice, natural, simple, unsophisticated, art-less, in a natural state, uncultivated, unre-fined, unworked, unprocessed, untilled, fal-low, virgin, unused

▶ *502 Ignorance, 658 Naivety, 600 Nonuse, 656 Unskilfulness*

5 **immature**, ungrown, half-grown, unripe, unripened, green, underripe, half-ripe, un-mellowed, unseasoned, unblown, half-blown, unfledged, unlicked, callow, lacking maturity, nonadult, adolescent, young, juvenile, child-ish, childlike, puerile, boyish, girlish, undevel-oped, half-developed, underdeveloped, back-ward, retarded, unhatched, unborn, inchoate, embryonic, rudimentary, elementary, un-formed, half-formed, unfashioned, unhewn, unwrought, unworked, uncut, rough-hewn, rough, unpolished, unfinished, half-finished, raw, crude, imperfect, coarse, boorish, rude, savage, uncivilized, premature, before time, forward, precocious, forced, abortive, at half-cock, wet behind the ears (Inf)

▶ *206 Youth, 620 Imperfection, 685 Noncomple-tion, 818 Discourtesy, 208 Earliness*

6 **uncooked**, raw, red, pink, rare, bloody, underdone, half-cooked, half-baked, cold, un-warmed, unprepared, undressed, ungar-nished, indigestible, inedible, tough

▶ *378 Toughness, 45 Cookery*

7 **unequipped**, untrimmed, unrigged, dis-masted, dismantled, undressed, uncovered, unfurnished, half-furnished, ill-provided, de-ficient, incompetent, incapable, unqualified, disqualified, unfit

▶ *296 Undress, 294 Uncovering, 358 Shortfall, 609 Insufficiency*

NOUNS

8 **lack of preparation**, unpreparedness, un-readiness, backwardness, belatedness, late-ness, disorganization, lack of training, want of practice, rustiness, unfitness, incompetence, disqualification, unskilfulness, nonprepara-tion, unpremeditation, thoughtlessness, im-providence, nonprovision, neglect, negli-gence, rashness, hastiness, impetuousness, precipitance, rush, haste,

▶ *656 Unskilfulness, 470 Negligence, 780 Rashness, 648 Haste*

9 **spontaneity**, improvisation, extemporiza-tion, impromptu, snap answer, surprise, lack of expectation, potluck (Inf)

▶ *583 Improvisation, 514 Surprise*

10 **immaturity**, unripeness, greenness, youth, childishness, newness, undevelopment, under-development, rawness, crudeness, coarseness, imperfection, incompleteness, prematurity, forwardness, precocity

▶ *206 Youth, 201 Newness, 620 Imperfection, 685 Noncompletion, 208 Earliness*

11 **natural state**, native state, virgin soil, un-tilled ground, raw material, crude oil, unre-fined rubber, unpasteurized milk, rough dia-mond

VERBS

12 **be unprepared**, lack preparation, make no preparations, lack planning, have no plans, lie fallow, rust, want practice, need training, ex-temporize, improvise, live from day to day, let tomorrow take care of itself, go off at half-cock, take no precautions, drop one's guard, catch unawares, surprise

▶ *685 Noncompletion, 145 Incompleteness, 628 Deterioration, 583 Improvisation, 208 Earliness, 470 Negligence, 468 Inattention, 514 Surprise*

13 **improvise**, extemporize, ad lib, make it up as one goes along, talk off the top of one's head (Inf), wing it (Inf)

ADVERBS

14 **unreadily**, without preparation, un-preparedly, unpremeditatedly, thoughtlessly, unskilfully, improvidently, rashly, hastily, negligently, impetuously, headlong

15 **spontaneously**, surprisingly, extempore, impromptu, ad hoc, offhand, on the spur of the moment, off the cuff (Inf)

▶ *583 Improvisation*

16 **immaturely**, childishly, embryonically, prematurely, incompletely, imperfectly, crudely, coarsely

596 Attempt

VERBS

1 **attempt**, try, essay, seek, seek to, aim, aim to, make it one's aim, bid, offer, make a bid, make an attempt, make shift to, do something about, make the effort, not just stand there, not let the grass grow under one's feet, try one's hand at, have a go, give it a try, give it a go, give it a whirl (Inf), have a shot at (Inf), have a crack at (Inf), have a stab at (Inf)

▶ *588 Intention, 477 Question*

2 **try hard**, endeavour, struggle, strive, give it one's all, try and try again, do one's best, double (*or* redouble) one's efforts, go all out, exert oneself, work, labour, pull hard, push hard, strain, sweat, do one's damnedest (Inf), go flat out (Inf), give it one's best shot (Inf), go for broke (Inf)

▶ *644 Work, 574 Resolution*

3 **tackle**, take on, undertake, get down to, get to grips with, take the bull by the horns, take a chance, try one's luck, tempt providence, tempt fate, venture, speculate, gamble, attempt too much, bite off more than one can chew, have too much on one's plate, die in the attempt, chance one's arm (Inf)

▶ *597 Undertaking, 589 Chance, 683 Failure*

4 **test**, experiment, put out a feeler, dip a toe in the water, hold a finger to the wind, make a trial of, launch a trial balloon, launch a balloon d'essai, fly a kite

▶ *479 Experiment, 781 Caution*

NOUNS

5 **attempt**, try, essay, bid, move, step, gambit, endeavour, effort, struggle, strain, tackle, good try, stout try, brave try, valiant effort, best one can do, best effort, determined effort, set, dead set, half-hearted attempt, catch-as-catch can (US), first attempt, debut, final attempt, last try, swan song, last bid, last challenge, go (Inf), run (Inf), leap (Inf), shot (Inf), stab (Inf), jab (Inf), whirl (Inf), crack (Inf), whack (Inf), bash (Inf), best shot (Inf), one's level best (Inf), first go (Inf), last shot (Inf)

▶ *574 Resolution, 156 Beginning, 157 End*

6 **venture**, adventure, quest, speculation, trial (run), experiment, operation, exercise, undertaking, seeking, aiming, aim, goal, objective, intention, worthy aim, high endeavour, perfectionism

▶ *597 Undertaking, 588 Intention, 479 Experiment, 619 Perfection*

7 **attempter**, trier, essayer, bidder, volunteer, adventurer, adventurous person, tackler, tester, experimenter, researcher, searcher, quester, inquirer, striver, struggler, contestant, contender, fighter, challenger, idealist, perfectionist, lobbyist, activist, reformer, undertaker (US), contractor, entrepreneur

▶ *477 Question, 674 Contention, 627 Improvement, 619 Perfection*

ADJECTIVES

8 **attempting**, trying, essaying, seeking, striving, doing one's best, game, nothing daunted, daring, venturesome, ambitious, enterprising

9 **tentative**, experimental, trial, pilot, testing, searching, inquiring, probationary, on approval, on appro(Inf)

▶ *572 Willingness, 574 Resolution*

ADVERBS

10 **ambitiously**, out for (*or* to), as far as one can, with all one's might, valiantly, adventurously, experimentally, tentatively, speculatively, on the make (Inf)

INTERJECTIONS

11 **here goes!**, give it a (*or* your best) shot!, have a go!, go for it!, nothing ventured, nothing gained!

597 Undertaking

VERBS

1 **undertake**, engage in, devote oneself to, apply oneself to, address oneself to, get one's mind into, take up, go in for, venture on, do, tackle, confront, try, attempt, endeavour, go about, take in hand, turn (*or* put *or* set) one's hand to, set forward, set going, start, launch, initiate, begin, set about, embark on, launch into, plunge into, proceed to, fall to, set to, buckle to, get one's head down, put one's best foot forward, set one's shoulder to the wheel, set one's hand to the plough, get one's teeth into, come to grips with, take the bull by the horns, grasp the nettle, assume, take on, assume (*or* accept) responsibility, take charge of, direct, manage, execute, carry out, set up shop, have fish to fry, have irons in the fire, busy oneself, shoulder, take on one's shoulders, take upon oneself, assume an obligation, volunteer, agree, promise, contract, pledge, vow, engage, commit oneself, sign up, get involved, let oneself in for, take on too much, bite off more than one can chew, have too much on one's plate, have too many irons in the fire, show enterprise, pioneer, venture, adventure, dare, challenge, apprentice oneself, prepare onself, take a crack at (Inf), take a shot at (Inf), take a whack at (Inf), get down (US inf)

▶ *640 Action, 596 Attempt, 156 Beginning, 778 Courage, 653 Management, 684 Completion, 642 Activity, 847 Duty, 714 Promise, 572 Willingness, 633 Danger, 594 Preparation*

NOUNS

2 **undertaking**, engagement, venture, affair,

business, occupation, matter in hand, job, task, assignment, project, enterprise, campaign, mission, self-imposed task, labour of love, mission, pilgrimage, voluntary work, operation, exercise, programme, plan, design, planned event, big undertaking, a lot to ask, hard task, emprise (Arch), quest, adventure, search, inquiry, speculation, gambling, try, attempt, struggle, effort, endeavour, work, feat, tall order (Inf)

▶ *644 Work, 640 Action, 572 Willingness, 592 Plan, 659 Difficulty, 477 Question, 596 Attempt*

3 **contract**, agreement, signed agreement, gentlemen's (*or* gentleman's) agreement, promise, pledge, vow, assurance, guarantee, obligation, engagement, commitment

▶ *714 Promise*

4 **volunteer**, adventurer, speculator, innovator, pioneer, hard worker, workaholic, entrepreneur, enterprising businessman (*or* businesswoman), go-getter (Inf)

▶ *644 Work*

ADJECTIVES

5 **undertaken**, done, executed, incurred, assumed, self-imposed, assigned, promised, with obligations, contractual

6 **enterprising**, resourceful, innovative, pioneering, adventurous, venturesome, speculative, daring, courageous, go-ahead, progressive, opportunist, alive to opportunity, with an eye to the main chance, ambitious, responsible, managerial, taking on responsibility, shouldering responsibility

▶ *782 Desire, 778 Courage, 201 Newness*

7 **overambitious**, rash, overloaded, overextended, snowed under (Inf)

▶ *780 Rashness*

ADVERBS

8 **responsibly**, under obligation, contractually, as agreed

9 **enterprisingly**, innovatively, adventurously, ambitiously, progressively, courageously, daringly, as never before, overambitiously, rashly

598 Relinquishment

VERBS

1 **relinquish**, give up, surrender, drop, loosen one's grip, quit one's hold, unclench, let go of, release, loose, resign, abdicate, back down, lower one's sights, yield, waive, forgo, cede, transfer, hand over, assign, forfeit, lose, renounce, swear off, abnegate, recant, change one's mind, tergiversate, not proceed with, drop the idea, give up the idea, forget it, drop it, wean oneself, disaccustom, forswear, deny oneself, abstain, avoid, shed, slough, slough off, cast off, divest, doff, repudiate, discard, get rid of, tear up, shred, put through the shred-

der, jettison, throw away, scrap, stop using, lose interest, have other (*or* bigger) fish to fry, leave hold of (Inf), cough up (Inf), kick (the habit) (Inf), go cold turkey (Sl), junk (Inf), write off (Inf)

▶ *735 Giving Back, 727 Disposal, 806 Humility, 728 Transfer of Property, 722 Loss, 578 Equivocation, 512 Oblivion, 585 Unaccustomedness, 591 Avoidance, 296 Undress, 600 Nonuse, 783 Indifference*

2 **withdraw**, decline, remove one's name from, scratch, retire, abdicate, resign, stand down, drop out, throw in the sponge (*or* towel), throw up the game, throw in one's hand, give up, give in, submit, go, depart, leave, quit, vacate, evacuate, move out, abandon, forsake, run out on, leave stranded, desert, forsake one's duties, quit one's post, go absent without leave, go AWOL, play truant, strike, down tools, stop, cease, come out, walk out, secede, divide, schismatize, change allegiances, change sides, go over, sell out, apostatize, break off a relationship, break (it) off, end an affair, go back on one's word, jilt, abandon discussion, stop negotiations, waste no more time, pass on to the next, postpone, put off, shelve, table, invalidate, annul, void, cancel, abolish, abrogate, seek seclusion, turn one's back on the world, jack (*or* pack) it in (Sl), cut out (US sl), cop out (Sl), dump (Inf), chuck (Inf), play hooky (US inf), rat (Sl), throw over (Inf), ditch (Sl)

▶ *705 Resignation, 345 Departure, 254 Absence, 578 Equivocation, 209 Lateness, 704 Cancellation*

NOUNS

3 **relinquishment**, giving up, surrender, resignation, retirement, abdication, yielding, waiving, waiver, forgoing, transfer, handing over, cession, forfeit, abnegation, renunciation, recantation, abandonment, desertion, going, departure, leaving, evacuation, dereliction, defection, absence, truancy, withdrawal, secession, schism, strike, walk-out, lack of commitment, abstinence, avoidance, disuse, nonuse, discontinuance, desuetude, cancellation, abolition, annulment, abrogation, reclusion, seclusion, hooky (US inf), cop-out (Sl)

▶ *735 Giving Back, 727 Disposal, 728 Transfer of Property, 705 Resignation, 345 Departure, 254 Absence, 218 Cessation, 591 Avoidance, 600 Nonuse, 704 Cancellation, 816 Unsociability*

4 **deserter**, runaway, jilter, truant, dropout, hermit, castaway, striker, retiree (US), abdicator, abdicating monarch, abolitionist, abstainer, abnegator, recanter, yielder, defector, turncoat, cop-out (Sl), rat (Sl)

ADJECTIVES

5 **relinquished**, surrendered, dropped, waived, forgone, scrapped, jettisoned, cast-off, cast-

away, forsaken, apostatical, abandoned, derelict, deserted, stranded, jilted, cancelled, void, invalid, discontinued, abolished

▶ *727 Disposal, 728 Transfer of Property*

6 **apathetic**, indifferent, noncommittal, resigned, retired, withdrawn, aloof, absent, distant

▶ *783 Indifference, 705 Resignation, 643 Inactivity*

7 **on hold**, on a back burner, in abeyance, off the agenda, on the shelf, on the scrap heap, forsakenly, invalidly

8 **apathetically**, indifferently, resignedly, absently, distantly, apostatically, delinquently

INTERJECTIONS

9 **forget it!**, drop it!, let go!, quit!, all out!

599 Use

VERBS

1 **use**, make use of, put to use, utilize, employ, exercise, practise, put into practice, put into operation, take up, adopt, apply try out, try, bring to bear, administer, spend on, give to, devote to, consecrate to, dedicate to, assign to, allot, use up, exhaust, wear out, wear, go through, spend, expend, absorb, consume, waste, squander, handle, finger, touch, tread, follow, beat (a path), work, drive, manipulate, manoeuvre, operate, wield, ply, brandish, treat, overwork, tax, task, fatigue, prepare for use, work on, work up, mould, form

▶ *607 Waste, 407 Touch, 650 Fatigue, 306 Form, 584 Habit, 564 Speech*

2 **frequent**, be a (regular) customer of, shop at, use the services of, avail oneself of

▶ *738 Purchase*

3 **exploit**, exhaust the possibilities of, make the most of, use to the full (*or* fullest), maximize, milk, drain, extract, convert to use, convert, reuse, recycle, reclaim, get mileage out of, get the best out of, get one's money's worth, find useful, put to good use, turn to account, capitalize on, make capital out of, use to advantage, make hay of (US), profit by, take advantage of, make play with, play on, trade on, cash in on, play off, play off against, use people, make a tool (*or* handle) of, make a pawn of, make a cat's paw of, befool, make a fool of, abuse, misuse, run into the ground (Inf), make a patsy of (US sl)

▶ *355 Extraction, 613 Usefulness, 721 Gain, 539 Deception, 601 Misuse*

4 **resort to**, have recourse to, fall back on, rely on, run to, turn to, draw on, impose on, presume on, ask favours of, press into service, enlist in one's service, pick someone's brains

5 **dispose of**, have at one's disposal, control, command, have at one's command, call the tune, do what one likes with, assign, allot, allocate, apportion, requisition, call into play,

call in, set in motion, set in action, set going, deploy, motivate, ejoy, have the use of, have the usufruct, possess, consume, expend, use up, go through, make do with, make shift with, get by on, do what one can with, make the most (*or* best) of, spare, have to spare, call the shots (Sl)

▶ *731 Allocation, 586 Persuasion, 723 Possession*

NOUNS

6 **use**, usage, utilization, exploitation, employment, exercise, practice, operation, disposal, enjoyment, usufruct, possession, conversion to use, conversion, application, appliance, deployment, resort, recourse, control, management, mode of use, treatment, handling, normal use, good usage, proper treatment, carefulness, ill-treatment, hard usage, wrong use, misuse, abuse, effect of use, depreciation, wear, wear and tear, dilapidation, exhaustion, consumption, conspicuous consumption, waste, reuse, recycling, reclamation, usefulness, advantage, benefit, good, profit, service, serviceability, practicality, convertibility, applicability, utility, function, purpose, point, avail, functioning, power, long use, wont, habit, demand, need

▶ *584 Habit, 613 Usefulness, 723 Possession, 469 Carefulness, 601 Misuse, 628 Deterioration, 607 Waste, 593 Requirement*

7 **reused product**, recycled substance, blackboard, palimpsest, milk bottles, used car, second-hand clothes, reclaimed land

8 **user**, customer, shopper, client, driver, operator, consumer, owner, exploiter, abuser

▶ *738 Purchase*

ADJECTIVES

9 **used**, put to use, utilized, employed, exercised, in service, in use, occupied, in constant use, in everyday use, in practice, used up, exhausted, consumed, spent, worn, worn out, threadbare, shabby, down-at-heel, dilapidated, second-hand, previously owned, preowned, cast-off, reused, recycled, reclaimed, well-used, well-thumbed, dog-eared, wellworn, shopsoiled, beaten, well-trodden, wellknown, known, hackneyed, stale, pragmatic, practical, utilitarian, everyday, ordinary, convenient, makeshift, provisional, exploited, subservient, like putty in one's hands, instrumental, hand-me-down (Inf)

▶ *628 Deterioration, 613 Usefulness, 501 Knowledge, 615 Convenience*

10 **usable**, utilizable, employable, exploitable, convertible, applicable, available, at one's service, functioning, working, in operation, useful, profitable, advantageous, consumable, disposable, throwaway, takeaway, reusable, recyclale

▶ *613 Usefulness*

11 **usefully**, usably, practically, pragmatically, instrumentally, conveniently, profitably, advantageously, beneficially, powerfully, convertibly, reusably

600 Nonuse

ADJECTIVES
1 **unused**, not used, not utilized, not activated, out of order, out of service, inoperational, not available, absent, unusable, unemployable, useless, impractical, lacking application, unapplied, unconverted, nonconvertible, nonreturnable, undisposed of, in hand, in reserve, reserved, saved, stored, spare, extra, unspent, unconsumed, preserved, idle, fallow, untried, unessayed, unexercised, in abeyance, suspended, deferred, pigeonholed, left to rot, wasted, kaput (Inf), on the blink (Sl), on the fritz (US sl)
▶ 254 Absence, 614 Uselessness, 616 Inconvenience, 605 Store, 637 Preservation, 607 Waste
2 **new**, clean, pure, blank, fresh, unopened, untilled, virgin, unexploited, untapped, undeveloped, untrodden, unbeaten, untouched, unhandled, ungathered, unplucked, unharvested, unreaped
3 **not wanted**, unwanted, not required, unrequired, unneeded, unnecessary, unsold, unbought, remaindered, remaining, leftover, superfluous, redundant, otiose, vacant, free, dispensed with, waived, shunned, underused, unemployed, jobless, out of work, dismissed, discharged, laid off, redundant, superannuated, retired, resting, idle, inactive, fired (Inf), sacked (Inf)
▶ 783 Indifference, 643 Inactivity
4 **disused**, derelict, abandoned, discarded, castoff, jettisoned, scrapped, laid up, mothballed, out of commission, decommissioned, frozen, rusting, in limbo, neglected, done with, used up, run down, worn out, on the shelf, retired, out of use, supplanted, superseded, superannuated, discontinued, discredited, obsolete, old-fashioned, antiquated, archaic, junked (Inf), written off (Inf)
▶ 470 Negligence, 628 Deterioration
VERBS
5 **not use**, not utilize, have no use for, not activate, hold in abeyance, not touch, leave alone, abstain, forbear, hold off, do without, avoid, dispense with, waive, not proceed with, overlook, disregard, ignore, neglect, underuse, underutilize, waste, fail to take advantage of, keep, spare, save, reserve, store, have in reserve, keep in reserve, have on the side, keep in hand, keep stored away, not accept, decline, refuse, reject
▶ 591 Avoidance, 598 Relinquishment, 470 Negligence, 605 Store, 581 Rejection

6 **stop using**, disuse, turn off, leave off, ban, stop, cease, leave, lay up, put in mothballs, mothball, put out of commission, decommission, freeze, take apart, dismantle, be finished with, have done with, lay aside, put aside, set aside, put on the shelf, put in reserve, store away, stockpile, pack away, hang up, discard, dump, ditch, scrap, jettison, throw away, throw overboard, eject, slough, cast off, doff, take off, give up, relinquish, put in limbo, suspend, withdraw, cancel, abrogate, drop, supersede, replace, substitute, be unused, lie idle, lie fallow, deteriorate, squirrel away (Inf), sock away (US sl), junk (Inf), write off (Inf)
▶ 218 Cessation, 614 Uselessness, 628 Deterioration, 605 Store, 598 Relinquishment, 349 Expulsion, 296 Undress, 727 Disposal, 704 Cancellation, 222 Substitution
7 **stop work**, quit work, resign, retire, relinquish control, be dismissed, dismiss, discharge, lay off, pay off, make redundant, pension off, put out to grass, hang it up (US sl), hang up one's spikes (US sl), fire (Inf), sack (Inf)
▶ 644 Work, 705 Resignation, 349 Expulsion
NOUNS
8 **nonuse**, lack of use, abeyance, suspension, abstinence, forbearance, avoidance, neglect, negligence, underuse, underutilization, superfluity, unemployment, redundancy, reserve, store, storage
▶ 591 Avoidance, 470 Negligence, 605 Store, 581 Rejection
9 **newness**, cleanness, blankness, purity, freshness, virginity, mint condition
▶ 201 Newness, 206 Youth, 119 Originality
10 **disuse**, desuetude, dereliction, abandonment, rejection, limbo, inactivity, idleness, disposal, discarding, dumping, scrapping, dismissal, discharge, resignation, retirement, superannuation, obsolescence, obsoleteness
▶ 628 Deterioration, 705 Resignation, 349 Expulsion
11 **unused thing**, spare, extra, store, savings, stockpile, remainder, remains, reject, cast-off, discard
▶ 605 Store, 581 Rejection, 132 Remainder
ADVERBS
12 **out of use**, idly, out of operation, aside, unusably, uselessly, impractically, superfluously, redundantly, obsolescently, obsoletely
13 **newly**, cleanly, blankly, purely, freshly

601 Misuse

VERBS
1 **misuse**, abuse, use wrongly, misemploy, put to bad use, misdirect, divert, misappropriate, expropriate, embezzle, defraud, violate, des-

ecrate, defile, take in vain, profane, prostitute, pervert, distort, abuse the environment, pollute, spoil, make unclean, ill-use, ill-treat, maltreat, mistreat, molest, do violence to, harm, injure, manhandle, beat, batter, knock about, attack, force, strain, take advantage of, exploit, oppress, overwork, overtask, overtax, fatigue, work hard, wear out, impair, damage, misuse power, abuse power, misgovern, misrule, mismanage, maladminister, mishandle, bungle, misuse words, commit a malapropism, squander (away), fritter (away), waste, misapply, misjudge, overreact, use a sledgehammer to crack a nut, waste effort, overuse, overgraze, overfish, screw up (Inf), fuck up (Tab sl)

▶ *736 Stealing, 309 Distortion, 628 Deterioration, 618 Worthlessness, 622 Dirtiness, 241 Violence, 599 Use, 690 Severity, 656 Unskilfulness, 650 Fatigue, 607 Waste, 614 Uselessness, 854 Disparagement*

NOUNS

2 **misuse**, abuse, wrong use, misemployment, bad use, manipulation, misdirection, diversion, misappropriation, embezzlement, peculation, fraud, violation, desecration, profanation, defilement, impiety, prostitution, perversion, distortion, environmental abuse, pollution, mistreatment, molestation, maltreatment, ill-treatment, ill-use, violence, force, outrage, assault, battery, injury, harm, evil, exploitation, power abuse, oppression, misrule, mismanagement, maladministration, malpractice, mishandling, bungling, misuse of words, malapropism, solecism, barbarism, overuse, overgrazing, overcropping, overfishing, extravagance, waste, misapplication, misjudgment

▶ *736 Stealing, 309 Distortion, 628 Deterioration, 618 Worthlessness, 622 Dirtiness, 241 Violence, 599 Use, 690 Severity, 656 Unskilfulness, 607 Waste, 504 Error, 854 Disparagement*

3 **abuser**, child abuser, wife-beater, violent person, polluter, desecrator, dishonest politician, loudmouth (Inf), thug (Inf)

ADJECTIVES

4 **misused**, abused, misemployed, misdirected, diverted, misappropriated, violated, desecrated, defiled, perverted, distorted, polluted, spoilt, unclean, ill-treated, maltreated, beaten, battered, exploited, used, oppressed, mishandled, bungled, wasted

▶ *309 Distortion, 622 Dirtiness, 241 Violence, 599 Use, 607 Waste*

5 **abusive**, violent, harmful, injurious, forceful, offensive, damaging, evil, exploitative, oppressive, fraudulent, extravagant, wasteful, barbarous, solecistic, outrageous, impious, profane

ADVERBS

6 **abusively**, badly, wrongly, evilly, profanely, impiously, outrageously, pervertedly, distortedly, forcefully, offensively, violently, harmfully, injuriously, exploitatively, oppressively, fraudulently, extravagantly, wastefully, barbarously, solecistically

602 Means

NOUNS

1 **means**, way, manner, mode, method, methods, measure, measures, steps, course, ways and means, methods and resources, the wherewithal, the basics, power, capacity, ability, capability, strong hand, trumps, trump, trump card, ace, tool, instrument, vehicle, medium, agency, conveniences, facilities, appliances, tools, tools of the trade, tricks of the trade, bag of tricks, technology, new technology, high technology, high tech, knowledge, technique, knack, skill, process, approach, resort, recourse, expedient, device, contrivance, makeshift, ad hoc measure, substitute, let-out, means of escape, remedy, cure, desperate remedy, last resort, last hope, last gasp, last throw, alternative, choice, freedom of choice, know-how (Inf), lost shot (Inf)

▶ *327 Way, 235 Power, 603 Tool, 501 Knowledge, 655 Skill, 592 Plan, 638 Escape, 630 Remedy, 589 Chance, 580 Selection*

2 **supplies**, basic supplies, vital supplies, provisions, stock, material, materials, working materials, equipment, machinery, munitions, ammunition, resources, natural resources, raw material, nuts and bolts (Inf)

▶ *606 Provision, 603 Tool, 604 Materials*

3 **human resources**, labour resources, pool of labour, workforce, manpower, personnel, staff, workers

▶ *646 Worker*

4 **financial resources**, finances, funds, wealth, money, substance, liquidity, cash, cash flow, capital, start-up capital, investment capital, working capital, assets, stock in trade, premises, property, stocks and shares, stocks and bonds, investments, investment portfolio, revenue, income, receipts, credits, credit, overdraft, borrowing capacity, credit limit, line of credit, credit rating, creditworthiness, backing, support, sponsorship, subsidy, readies (Inf)

▶ *742 Wealth, 741 Money, 725 Property, 749 Receipt, 744 Credit, 284 Support*

5 **reserves**, reserve, store, something in reserve, backup, emergency funds, nest egg, stand-by, card up one's sleeve, two strings to one's bow, safeguard

▶ *605 Store, 632 Safety*

VERBS

6 **find means**, find a way, develop a method, provide the wherewithal, enable, facilitate, secure the basics, find, supply, furnish, provide, equip, buy supplies, fit out, make ready, prepare, hire personnel, staff, finance, fund, raise money, promote, sponsor, float, subsidize, have the means, be able, plan, contrive, think laterally, get by any means, beg, borrow, or steal, get by hook or (by) crook, get by fair means or foul, acquire

▶ *606 Provision, 594 Preparation, 235 Power, 592 Plan, 721 Gain*

ADVERBS

7 **by means of**, with, wherewith, by, by use of, using, through, with the aid of, by resorting to, with recourse to, by dint of, by hook or (by) crook, by fair means or foul, somehow

603 Tool

NOUNS

1 **tool**, implement, instrument, utensil, precision tool, machine tool, hand tool, garden tool, apparatus, appliance, machine, device, mechanical device, mechanical aid, contraption, gadget, contrivance, screwdriver, hammer, ram, drill, electric drill, perforator, punch, wrench, torque wrench, spanner, adjustable spanner, pipe wrench, Stillson (Tm), pliers, pincers, tweezers, nippers, chisel, wedge, edged tool, axe, knife, Stanley knife (Tm), saw, jigsaw, fretsaw, chain saw, rope, cable, peg, nail, tack, screw, nut, bolt, nuts and bolts, hanger, hook, support, prop, leverage, lever, jemmy, crowbar, handspike, jack, pivot, grip, lug, handle, helve, haft, shaft, tiller, helm, rudder, pulley, sheave, wheel, switch, stopcock, cock gunlock, trigger, pedal, pole, weapon, arm, arms, toolroom, tool shed, toolhouse (US), tools of the trade, tool-kit, do-it-yourself, bag of tricks, gizmo (US sl), doodah (Inf), thingumabob (Inf), thingummy (Inf), doohickey (US inf), whatsit (Inf), whatnot (Inf)

▶ *680 Weapon, 592 Plan, 136 Separation, 137 Connection, 284 Support*

2 **garden tool**, spade, shovel, trowel, fork, pitchfork, pickaxe, sickle, scythe, billhook, rake, hoe, cultivator, mattock, clough, dibber, riddle, roller, edging iron (*or* knife), pruning saw, hedge clipper (*or* trimmer), lopper, secateurs, shears, Rotavator (Tm), lawn mower, motor mower, Strimmer (Tm)

3 **prehistoric tool**, pebble hand-axe, flint chisel, bronze axe, iron sickle

4 **machine**, mechanical device, machinery, mechanism, works, clockwork, wheelwork, wheels within wheels, nuts and bolts, part, component, spring, mainspring, hairspring, cam, gear, gears, gearing, spur gear, spur wheel, bevel gear, clutch, synchromesh, automatic transmission, motor, engine, internal-combustion engine, lean-burn engine, rotary engine, Wankel engine, diesel engine, steam engine, turbine, generator, dynamo, dynamotor, servomechanism, servomotor, robot, automaton, computer

▶ *148 Component, 235 Power, 65 Computers, 33 Motor Racing*

5 **mechanics**, engineering, mechanical engineering, civil engineering, chemical engineering, electrical engineering, electronics, hydrodynamics, hydromechanics, hydraulics, cybernetics, automatic control, automation, computerization, robotics, artificial intelligence (AI), mechanical power, mechanical advantage, technics, technology, advanced technology, high technology, high tech, low technology, low tech, terotechnology

▶ *63 Engineering, 64 Electronics and Electrical Engineering, 65 Computers*

6 **equipment**, tools, utensils, furniture, appointments, fittings, fixtures, fixture, adjunct, upholstery, furnishing, trappings, accoutrement, dress, outfit, kit, gear, tackle, harness, paraphernalia, chattels, impedimenta, property, wares, stock-in-trade, merchandise

▶ *295 Dress, 725 Property*

7 **machinist**, operator, operative, driver, minder, machine-minder, engineer, technician, mechanician, mechanist, mechanic, fitter, tool-user, craftsman, artisan, manual worker, skilled worker

ADJECTIVES

8 **mechanical**, mechanized, mechanistic, motorized, technological, hydraulic, electronic, powered, power-driven, labour-saving, automatic, robotic, automated, computerized, computer-literate, machine-minded, tool-using, instrumental

VERBS

9 **use tools**, hammer, screw, ram, drill, punch, wrench, chisel, chop, saw, nail, tack, hook, lever, crowbar, shovel, rake, hoe, riddle, mow, mechanize

ADVERBS

10 **instrumentally**, mechanically, automatically, hydraulically, electronically, cybernetically, technologically

604 Materials

NOUNS

1 **materials**, raw materials, basic materials, resources, the essentials, the basics, means, elements, components, constituents, material, stuff, substance, matter, staple, stock, grain, grist, food, fodder, meat, fuel, oil, crude oil, petroleum, petrochemical, coal, anthracite,

hard coal, bituminous coal, soft coal, gas, natural gas, ore, mineral, uranium, yellow cake, metal ore, metal, pig iron, ingot, clay, adobe, china clay, potter's clay, gypsum, soil, sand, glass, plastic, synthetic resin, polymers, thermoplastic, celluloid, melamine formaldehyde, Formica (Tm), polyethylene, polythene, polypropylene, polystyrene, ABS, PVS (polyvinyl chloride), PTFE (polytetrafluoroethylene), fluorocarbon, acrylic, nylon, polyamide, thermoset, urea-formaldehyde, phenon formaldehyde, polyester, epoxy, polyurethane, latex, cellulose, fibreglass, carbon fibre, rope, yarn, filament, fibre, wool, cotton, silk, rayon, fabric, cloth, felt, textile, leather, hide, skin, rawhide, parchment, vellum, chamois, cowhide, sheephide, sheepskin, horsehide, goathide, goatskin, pighide, pigskin, doeskin, wood, timber, log, faggot, stick, rafter, board, beam, plank, planking, plywood, lath, stave

▶ *602 Means, 101 Reality, 45 Cookery, 410 Fuel, 442 Transparency, 67 Fabrics and Dyeing*

2 **building material**, building block, breeze block, brick, stone, marble, granite, ashlar, masonry, combined structure, bricks and mortar, lath and plaster, wattle and daub, roofing material, shingle, tile, slate, thatch, paving material, paving, paving stone, flag, flagstone, cobble, compo, composition, mortar, plaster, cement, Portland cement, concrete, reinforced concrete, ferroconcrete, prestressed concrete, hard core, gravel, Tarmac (Tm), asphalt, macadam, blacktop (US)

▶ *44 Ceramics, 293 Covering, 70 Transport*

3 **paper**, stationery, sheet, quire, ream, foolscap, imperial paper, A4 paper, writing paper, notepaper, typing paper, computer paper, wrapping paper, toilet paper, fibre paper, cotton paper, rag paper, rice paper, greaseproof paper, newsprint, cardboard, card, pasteboard, Bristol board, calendered paper, art paper, glossy paper, laminated paper, cartridge paper, India paper, Bible paper, tissue paper, tracing paper, carbon paper, crepe paper, wax paper, waterproof paper, Cellophane (Tm), papier-mâché, pulp, imperial wood pulp, cellulose fibre

4 **board**, millboard, strawboard, fibreboard, plasterboard, chipboard, hardboard

▶ *48 Literature*

605 Store

NOUNS

1 **store**, accumulation, hoard, mass, heap, load, stack, pile, stockpile, buildup, backlog, food mountain, butter mountain, wine lake, reservoir, bundle, bagful, packet, bucketful, amount, quantity, crop, harvest, vintage, mow, haystack, haycock, hayrick, stock, stock-in-trade, merchandise, property, assets, capi-

tal, holding, investment, fund, reserve fund, reserves, emergency reserves, something in reserve, something in hand, unexpended balance, savings, savings account, nest egg, deposit, treasure, buried treasure, cache, hiding-place, bottom drawer, trousseau, provision, pool, kitty, common fund, appeal fund, charity, community chest

▶ *161 Assembly, 120 Quantity, 721 Gain, 531 Concealment, 606 Provision, 740 Market*

2 **resource**, deposits, natural resource, natural deposit, quarry, mine, gold mine, coalmine, coalfield, coalbed, colliery, working, shaft, coalface, coal deposit, seam, stringer, lode, pipe, pipe vein, rich vein, vein, mineral deposit, gasfield, oilfield, well, oil well, gusher, fountain, fount, spring, source, bonanza (US), strike, discovery

▶ *226 Cause, 496 Discovery*

3 **supply**, constant supply, stream, tap, pipeline, artesian well, milch cow, the goose that lays the golden eggs, cornucopia, abundance, plenty, repertoire, range, collection, depleted supply, broken pipeline, scarcity

▶ *608 Sufficiency, 609 Insufficiency*

4 **storage**, stowage, gathering, garnering, accumulation, conservation, preservation, silage, ensilage, bottling, safe deposit, protection, stabling, warehousing, space, room, accommodation, storage space, shelf space, shelf room, cupboard space, cupboard room, boxroom, loft, attic, hold, bunker, basement, cellar, wine cellar, storeship, supply base, storehouse, storeroom, stockroom, warehouse, shed, stable, garage, depository, depot, entrepot, dock, wharf, magazine, arsenal, armoury, gunroom, treasure house, treasury, exchequer, strongroom, vault, gold vault, silver vault, coffer, moneybox, moneybag, till, money drawer, strongbox, safe, night safe, bank, blood bank, sperm bank, data bank, memory, store of memories, hive, honeycomb, granary, garner, barn, silo, water tower, reservoir, cistern, tank, petrol tank, gasholder, gasometer, battery, storage battery, dry battery, wet battery, petrol station, filling station, petrol pump, dump, tip, rubbish dump, refuse dump, trash dump (US), landfill, sump, drain, cesspool, septic tank, sewage works (*or* farm), pantry, larder, buttery, stillroom, chamber, cupboard, cabinet, shelf, chest of drawers, drawer, refrigerator, icebox (US), deepfreeze, freezer, portmanteau, suitcase, holdall, chest, trunk, packing case, box, container, receptacle, holder, quiver, fridge (Inf), fridge-freezer (Inf)

▶ *161 Assembly, 637 Preservation, 632 Safety, 248 Space, 258 Container, 256 Habitat, 65 Computers, 511 Memory, 622 Dirtiness*

5 **collection**, accumulation, set, complete set, archives, inventory, record, file, folder, bun-

dle, portfolio, stamp collection, coin collection, record collection, tape collection, video collection, book collection, archive, repository, museum, art museum, gallery, art gallery, library, yearbook, diary, almanac, farmer's almanac, encyclopedia, dictionary, thesaurus, zoo, menagerie, aquarium, waxworks, Madame Tussaud's (Tm), exhibition, exhibit, repertory, repertoire, bag of tricks (Inf)

▶ *161 Assembly, 545 Record, 200 Past Time, 48 Literature, 526 Display*

VERBS

6 **store**, amass, accumulate, heap, stack, pile up, load, stow, pack, bundle, stow away, pack away, put away, put in mothballs, mothball, lay up, fold up, roll up, store in the garage, store in the barn, stable, warehouse, garner, gather, bring together, harvest, reap, mow, pick, glean, stock, stock up, stock up one's cupboards, stock up one's larder, stock up one's freezer, lay in, bulk-buy, panic buy, board, stockpile, build up, build up one's stocks, increase, augment, store fuel, store coal, bunker, provision, provide, supply, take on, take in, fill, fill up, fuel, fuel up, top up, refill, refuel, replenish, save, keep, retain, hang on to, hold, put by, keep by, file, bottle, pickle, conserve, preserve, leave, set aside, put aside, lay away, lay by, keep back, keep in hand, reserve, fund, bank, deposit, invest, treasure, hive, bury, hide, conceal, secrete, cache, squirrel away, stash away, salt away, husband, economize, save up, make a nest egg, prepare for a rainy day, equip oneself, prepare oneself, put in the the bottom drawer, pool, put in the kitty, share, go together, communalize, sock away (US inf)

▶ *257 Contents, 68 Agriculture, 161 Assembly, 128 Increase, 606 Provision, 726 Retention, 637 Preservation, 531 Concealment, 756 Thrift, 594 Preparation*

ADJECTIVES

7 **stored**, amassed, accumulated, heaped, abundant, plentiful, stacked, piled up, loaded, stowed (away), packed (away), in store, in storage, in mothballs, laid up, hoarded, in deposit, in hand, held, saved, put aside, set aside, put by, kept by, in reserve, unused, unspent, unexpended, banked, funded, invested, available, in stock, spare, supernumerary, preserved, conserved, bottled, pickled

▶ *161 Assembly, 600 Nonuse, 637 Preservation*

606   Provision

NOUNS

1 **provision**, supplying, providing, furnishing, equipping, logistics, fitting out, outfitting, purveying, purveyance, catering, catered affair, service, delivery, distribution, self-service,

takeaway, procuring, pandering, feeding, entertainment, clothing, accommodation, bed and breakfast, bed and board, board and lodging, boarding house, boarding school, maintenance, support, assistance, lending, subsidy, subvention, equipment, stock, supply, food supply, water supply, constant supply, feed, pipeline, supply line, source, commissariat, provisioning, victualling, supplies, stores, reserves, rations, iron rations, K rations, food rations, food stamps (US), starvation rations, emergency rations, ration, helping, portion, share, reinforcement, replenishment, refill, filling-up, topping-up, plenitude, grist to the mill, fuel to the flame, yield, produce, product, return, increase, gain, conservation, resource management, economy, budgeting, budget, cash flow, possible need, preparation, precaution, measure, step

▶ *729 Giving, 662 Help, 605 Store, 45 Cookery, 326 Transfer, 724 Joint Possession, 144 Completeness, 243 Production, 721 Gain, 756 Thrift, 594 Preparation, 692 Command, 485 Qualification, 592 Plan*

2 **provisions**, food, provender, sustenance, foodstuffs, victuals, comestibles, eatables, drinkables, groceries, grub (Inf), nosh (Inf)

▶ *45 Cookery*

3 **provider**, supplier, donor, giver, creditor, lender, moneylender, bursar, purser, treasurer, waiter, waitress, steward, butler, commissary (US), quartermaster, storekeeper, victualler, sutler, provision merchant, ship chandler, drysalter, grocer, greengrocer, baker, poulterer, fishmonger, butcher, vintner, wine merchant, milkman, wholesaler, retailer, middleman, shopkeeper, wet nurse, feeder, procurer, panderer, pander, pimp, bawd

▶ *729 Giving, 732 Lending, 741 Money, 737 Trade, 877 Immorality*

4 **caterer**, private caterer, wedding caterer, purveyor, hotelier, hotelkeeper, hotel manager, restaurateur, head waiter, maître d'hôtel, innkeeper, host, publican, licensee, alewife, landlord, landlady, housekeeper, housewife, cook, chef, pastrycook, confectioner, mine host (Inf)

▶ *45 Cookery*

VERBS

5 **provision**, supply, provide, furnish, equip, purvey, cater, afford, offer, lend, contributes, give, endow, present, find, arm, man, staff, fit out, outfit, kit out (or up), fix up, prepare, make ready, get ready, maintain supply, keep supplied, yield, produce, bring in, bring in a supply, truck in (US), fly in, pump in, procure, pander, pimp, service, service an order, meet an order, meet a demand, sell, distribute, deliver, make deliveries, deliver the goods, hand out, hand round, serve, serve up, dish up, victual, feed, cook for, clothe, accommodate,

board, put up, maintain, keep, support, provide for, stock, keep a stock, budget, make provision, make due provision, provide for oneself, provision oneself, take on supplies, take in supplies, stock up, lay in a stock, store, stockpile, hoard, bunker, gather food, forage, fuel, coal, water, take on water, tap, draw, draw on, milk, extract, export, import, trade, dish out (Inf), do for (Inf), do for oneself (Inf)

▶ *729 Giving, 732 Lending, 594 Preparation, 243 Production, 739 Sale, 469 Carefulness, 605 Store, 355 Extraction, 737 Trade*

6 **replenish**, resupply, reinforce, fill, refill, fill up, top up, restock, revictual, refuel, reload, make up, make good, refresh, revitalize

▶ *144 Completeness*

ADJECTIVES

7 **provisioning**, supplying, providing, furnishing, equipping, catering, commissarial, self-service, takeaway, sufficing, all-sufficing, sufficient, available, available on request, in stock, on tap, on the menu

▶ *729 Giving, 608 Sufficiency*

8 **provisional**, supplied, provided, furnished, equipped, all found, all-in, well-appointed, catered, offered, given, staffed, prepared, ready, stocked, victualled

▶ *729 Giving, 594 Preparation*

607 Waste

VERBS

1 **waste**, squander, fritter (away), spend, spend money like water, overspend, run through, lavish, splurge, throw away, pour down the drain, dissipate, scatter, disperse, throw to the four winds, slop, spill, overwork, overcrop, overfish, overgraze, impoverish, milk dry, misuse, abuse, put to the wrong use, misapply, misspend, cast pearls before swine, not use, make no use of, waste effort, labour in vain, consume, eat, devour, gobble up, swallow, make a dent in, make inroads on, wade into, expend, lay out, take, use up, exhaust, deplete, drain, suck dry, empty, wear, wear away, wear out, erode, gnaw, damage, impair, pollute, be wasted, go to waste, suffer loss, waste away, emaciate, wither, wilt, shrivel, decay, decline, decrease, diminish, leak, ebb away, flow out, run low, dry up, melt, melt away, liquefy, evaporate, vaporize, run out, give out, burn, burn down, burn out, burn away, gut, deteriorate, run to seed, run to waste, go to ruin, go down the drain, go to pot, weaken, fade, wane, blow (Sl), blue (Sl), piss away (Tab sl)

▶ *757 Extravagance, 601 Misuse, 600 Nonuse, 614 Uselessness, 599 Use, 748 Expenditure, 628 Deterioration, 129 Decrease, 347 Exit, 387 Fluid, 388 Gas, 609 Insufficiency, 238 Weakness*

2 **lay waste**, devastate, ravage, ruin, destroy,

demolish, sabotage, vandalize, loot, plunder, sack, raze, despoil, pillage, kill, murder, wipe out, obliterate, nuke (Inf), trash (Inf)

▶ *244 Destruction, 736 Stealing, 398 Killing*

NOUNS

3 **waste**, wastage, wastefulness, squandering, frittering (away), extravagance, overspending, economy, thriftlessness, improvidence, useless expenditure, unnecessary expenditure, prodigality, lavishness, splurge, spree, spending, outlay, expense, expenditure, dissipation, dispersion, spillage, overwork, misuse, abuse, misapplication, consumption, inroads, using up, exhaustion, depletion, wear and tear, erosion, damage, wasting away, emaciation, atrophy, decay, decline, decrease, drainage, leakage, ebb, outflow, loss, melting, liquefaction, evaporation, vaporization, deterioration, (built-in) obsolescence, overproduction, superfluity

▶ *757 Extravagance, 748 Expenditure, 601 Misuse, 628 Deterioration, 129 Decrease, 347 Exit, 387 Fluid, 388 Gas, 238 Weakness, 610 Excess*

4 **destruction**, destructiveness, wilful destruction, vandalism, arson, sabotage, disaster area, scene of destruction, havoc, devastation, wreck, ruin, looting, pillage

▶ *244 Destruction, 736 Stealing*

5 **waste product**, litter, refuse, rubbish, trash (US), garbage, leftovers, scraps

▶ *614 Uselessness, 618 Worthlessness, 622 Dirtiness, 132 Remainder*

6 **waster**, big spender, last of the big spenders, squanderer, wastrel, spendthrift, prodigal

▶ *757 Extravagance, 748 Expenditure,*

7 **destroyer**, scourge, bane, polluter, vandal, arsonist, killer, murderer, Angel of Death

▶ *244 Destruction, 398 Killing*

ADJECTIVES

8 **wasteful**, extravagant, unnecessary, uneconomic, uneconomical, improvident, thriftless, prodigal, lavish, spendthrift, penny wise and pound foolish, time-consuming, energy-consuming

▶ *757 Extravagance, 748 Expenditure*

9 **waste**, superfluous, unwanted, unused, leftover, useless, worthless, throwaway

▶ *610 Excess, 614 Uselessness, 618 Worthlessness*

ADVERBS

10 **wastefully**, extravagantly, unnecessarily, uneconomically, improvidently, thriftlessly, prodigally, lavishly, superfluously, uselessly

11 **destructively**, damagingly, devastatingly, abusively

608 Sufficiency

ADJECTIVES

1 **sufficient**, enough, adequate, satisfactory, acceptable, sufficing, all-sufficing, complete,

self-sufficient, enough to go round, competent, equal, equal to, a match for, fitting, suitable, satisfying, contenting, measured, commensurate, up to the mark, just right, not too much, not too little, barely sufficient, only just enough, hand-to-mouth, makeshift, provisional, up to snuff (Inf), filling the bill (Inf)

▶ *606 Provision, 144 Completeness, 765 Satisfaction, 122 Equality, 222 Substitution, 609 Insufficiency*

2 **plentiful**, plenteous, ample, enough and to spare, more than enough, beyond expectations, superfluous, redundant, open-handed, generous, bountiful, lavish, liberal, extravagant, prodigal, wholesale, without stint, unsparing, unmeasured, endless, inexhaustible, bottomless, great, luxuriant, luxuriating, riotous, lush, rank, fat, fertile, prolific, profuse, abundant, copious, overflowing, superabundant, rich, opulent, affluent

▶ *610 Excess, 755 Generosity, 757 Extravagance, 246 Fertility, 742 Wealth*

3 **filled**, well-filled, full, full up, chock-ful, chock-a-block, flush, replete, sated, satiated, stuffed, glutted, bloated, ready to burst, satisfied, contented, content, well-provided, well-provisioned, well-stocked, well-furnished, rich in, teeming, crawling, overflowing, up to one's neck (*or* eyes) in, multitudinous, chocker (Austral inf), up to one's ass in (Tab sl)

▶ *144 Completeness, 765 Satisfaction, 606 Provision, 181 Multitude*

VERBS

4 **suffice**, be enough, prove adequate, prove acceptable, satisfy, content, do, answer, quench, just do, do and no more, work, get the job done, get one by, serve, serve as a makeshift, qualify, reach, make the grade, pass, pass muster, measure up to, meet requirements, withstand testing, do all that is possible, rise to the occasion, stand, stand up to, take the strain, support, do what is required, fulfil, carry out, fill, refill, replenish, fill up, top up, more than satisfy, sate, satiate, overeat, stuff oneself, glut oneself, gorge, have a bellyful, overdo it, provide for, make adequate provision, wash (Inf), fill the bill (Inf)

▶ *615 Convenience, 682 Success, 284 Support, 606 Provision*

5 **about**, be plentiful, proliferate, teem, swarm, bristle with, crawl with, exuberate, riot, luxuriate, grow in profusion, pour, flow, stream, shower, rain, snow, brim, overflow, flow with milk and honey, superabound, rain cats and dogs (Inf), roll in (Inf), wallow in (Inf), swim in (Inf), stink of (Sl)

▶ *181 Multitude, 610 Excess, 246 Fertility, 742 Wealth*

6 **have enough**, eat one's fill, drink one's fill, have had enough, have had more than

enough, have had it up to here, have had a bellyful, be fed up, afford, have the means

▶ *765 Satisfaction, 45 Cookery, 766 Dissatisfaction, 742 Wealth*

NOUNS

7 **sufficiency**, enough, adequacy, adequate amount, satisfaction, satisfactory amount, right amount, required number, quorum, right qualities, qualification, requirement, pass, pass marks, assets, competence, adequate income, living wage, enough to live on, enough to get by, enough to keep body and soul together, subsistence farming, autarky, self-sufficiency, exact amount, no surplus, minimum, bare minimum, no less, least one can do, minimum requirement, acceptability, the possible, all that is possible, all that could be desired, content, contentment, full measure, fulfilment, completion, repletion, one's fill, bellyful, satiety

▶ *765 Satisfaction, 486 Possibility, 684 Completion*

8 **plenty**, plentifulness, plenteousness, God's plenty, seven years of plenty, horn of plenty, cornucopia, abundance, proliferation, profusion, outpouring, shower, flood, spate, stream, great quantity, lots, galore, fullness, copiousness, amplitude, plenitude, affluence, riches, wealth, richness, fat, fat of the land, loaded table, groaning board, feast, banquet, orgy, riot, prodigality, extravagance, luxury, fertility, fecundity, productivity, productiveness, prolificacy, prolificness, luxuriance, lushness, rich harvest, vintage harvest, bumper crop, foison (Arch), rich vein, bonanza (US), bountiful supply, endless supply, more where it came from, more than enough, more that one can eat, too much, superabundance, glut, *embarras de richesses* (Fr), superfluity, excess, surplus, lashings(Inf), oodles (Inf), boo koos (US sl)

▶ *246 Fertility, 742 Wealth, 144 Completeness, 757 Extravagance, 610 Excess, 45 Cookery, 605 Store*

ADVERBS

9 **enough**, just enough, exactly enough, more than enough, sufficiently, adequately, satisfactorily, acceptably, tolerably, to the full, to one's heart's content, ad libitum, ad lib, on tap, on demand, abundantly, plentifully, plenteously, amply, inexhaustibly, interminably, endlessly, luxuriantly, prolifically, profusely, copiously, on the nose (Sl), flat out (Inf)

609 Insufficiency

ADJECTIVES

1 **insufficient**, not sufficient, inadequate, not enough, too little, too few, unsatisfactory, not satisfying, disappointing, unacceptable, in-

substantial, too small, limited, cramped, slender, meagre, skimpy, scanty, scant, sketchy, deficient, incomplete, lacking, light on, low on, wanting, found wanting, poor, inferior, incompetent, incapable, unequal to, not up to it, weak, weak as a kitten, weak as a baby, thin, watery, wersh (Scot), jejune, undernourished, underfed, niggardly, miserly, mean, stingy, parsimonious, not up to snuff (Inf), unable to hack it (US sl)

▶ *766 Dissatisfaction, 515 Disappointment, 145 Incompleteness, 127 Inferiority, 656 Unskilfulness, 238 Weakness, 102 Unreality, 758 Meanness*

2 **unprovided**, unsupplied, unfurnished, ill-furnished, ill-supplied, ill-equipped, absent, vacant, bare, empty, unstocked, unfilled, unreplenished, empty-handed, with empty pockets, unsuccessful, unsatisfied, discontented, unfulfilled, unprovided for, unaccommodated, insatiable, greedy, unsated, stinted, rationed, skimped, starved of, lacking, needing, hindered, hard up, scraping by, poor, undercapitalized, underfinanced, underpaid, underfunded, understaffed, undermanned, short-handed, under strength

▶ *254 Absence, 683 Failure, 766 Dissatisfaction, 782 Desire, 661 Hindrance, 743 Poverty*

3 **underfed**, undernourished, half-fed, half-starved, on short commons, hungry, hungry as a bear, famished, famine-stricken, unfed, starved, starving, voracious, ravenous, ravening, fasting, emaciated, macerated, thin, thin as a rail, lean, spare, skinny, skin and bone, wasting, anorexic, starveling, scurvy, scraggy, stunted

▶ *871 Fasting, 274 Thinness*

4 **scarce**, rare, infrequent, sparse, few, few and far between, short, in short supply, at a premium, hard to get, hard to come by, not to be had, not to be had at any price, not to be had for love or money, scarce (*or* rare) as hen's teeth, thin on the ground, unavailable, unobtainable, unprocurable, nonexistent, out of season, out of stock, sold out, out, off the market, out of print, off the menu, off

▶ *213 Infrequency, 182 Few*

VERBS

5 **be insufficient**, not suffice, not meet requirements, not meet expectations, cramp one's style, hinder, restrain, restrict, limit, lack, need, want, require, leave a gap, leave a lacuna, fail, disappoint, fall below, fall short, come short, default, run out, dry up, take half measures, tinker, fill in the gaps, paper over the cracks, nigger-rig (US tab sl)

▶ *620 Imperfection, 766 Dissatisfaction, 699 Restraint, 593 Requirement, 515 Disappointment, 358 Shortfall, 145 Incompleteness*

6 **be unsatisfied**, ask for more, beg for more,

come back, come again, take a second helping, still feel hungry, feel hungry, feel dissatisfied, feel cheated, increase one's demands, reject an offer, laugh at an offer, want, desire, desiderate, long for, yearn for, miss, feel unfulfilled, feel the lack, stand in need of, feel something is missing, need, require

▶ *782 Desire, 871 Fasting, 872 Gluttony, 766 Dissatisfaction, 581 Rejection, 593 Requirement*

7 **make insufficient**, demand too much, ask too much, expect too much, overtax, overextend, overwork, overcrop, overgraze, overfish, impoverish, damage, impair, exhaust, drain, deplete, run down, squander, waste, hold back, begrudge, grudge, stint, skimp, ration, put on half rations, put on short commons, deprive, disinherit, cut off without a penny, cut off without a dime (US), cut off with a shilling

▶ *607 Waste, 758 Meanness, 734 Taking*

NOUNS

8 **insufficiency**, inadequacy, not enough, too little, too few, nonsatisfaction, lack of satisfaction, disappointment, discontent, small amount, small quantity, little few, drop in the bucket, drop in the ocean, meagreness, skimpiness, scantiness, scantness, deficiency, deficit, shortfall, slippage, no quorum, not a full team, not a full deck, incompleteness, incompetence, inferiority, imperfection, defect, nonfulfilment, noncompletion, temporary substitute, makeshift, half measures, stopgap measures, tinkering, failure, weakness, bankruptcy, insolvency, bare subsistence, subsistence level, poverty level, stinginess, meanness, parsimony, low pay, pittance, dole, mite, minimum allowance, short allowance, short commons, iron rations, starvation rations, half rations, austerity, belt-tightening, Lenten fare, Spartan fare, starvation diet, bread and water, fast, fasting, asceticism, anorexia, anorexia nervosa, malnutrition, anaemia, vitamin deficiency

▶ *766 Dissatisfaction, 515 Disappointment, 182 Few, 358 Shortfall, 145 Incompleteness, 620 Imperfection, 685 Noncompletion, 747 Nonpayment, 743 Poverty, 758 Meanness, 871 Fasting*

9 **scarcity**, scarceness, paucity, dearth, shortage, leanness, seven lean years, drought, famine, starvation, infertility, unproductiveness, power cut, oil crisis, energy crisis, decrease, diminution, nothing (*or* none) to spare, short supply, sellers' market, bearish market, deprivation, poverty, lack, want, need, ebb, low water, shallowness, (a case of) the shorts (US sl)

▶ *182 Few, 247 Infertility, 129 Decrease, 743 Poverty, 593 Requirement, 278 Shallowness*

ADVERBS

10 **insufficiently**, inadequately, not enough,

less than somewhat, unsatisfactorily, disappointingly, unacceptably, insubstantially, skimpily, scantly, scantily, sketchily, poorly, incompetently, stingily, parsimoniously, scarcely, rarely, infrequently, sparsely, in default, failing, for want of, at a low ebb

610 Excess

NOUNS

1 **excess**, redundance, redundancy, overspill, overflow, inundation, flood, outflow, deluge, abundance, superabundance, glut, exuberance, luxuriance, riot, profusion, plenty, richness, *embarras de richesses* (Fr), bonanza (US), more than is fair, lion's share, most, main part, increase, upsurge, uprush, avalanche, spate, great quantity, too many, plethora, congestion, mob, crowd, overpopulation, saturation, supersaturation, saturation point, all the market can bear, plenitude, waste, excessiveness, nimiety, exorbitance, extreme, extremes, too much, exaggeration

▶ *608 Sufficiency, 347 Exit, 607 Waste, 605 Store, 144 Completeness, 128 Increase, 541 Exaggeration*

2 **overdoing it**, overstretching oneself, overextension, overexpression, too much on one's plate, too many irons in the fire, overactivity, overpoliteness, officiousness, excessive bureaucracy, red tape, overpraise, effusiveness, overoptimism, overestimation, overmeasure, overpayment, overweight, burden, load, overload, last straw, overindulgence, intemperance, immoderation, overeating, overfeeding, gluttony, overdrinking, drunkenness, engorgement, satiety, more than enough, one too many, bellyful, sufficiency, fat, fattiness, obesity, overdose, OD (Inf), overjolt (US sl), OJ (US sl)

▶ *642 Activity, 494 Overestimation, 369 Heaviness, 870 Self-Indulgence, 872 Gluttony, 874 Drunkenness, 608 Sufficiency, 259 Size*

3 **superfluity**, superfluousness, more than is needed, luxury, luxury article, luxury car, luxury hotel, luxury flat, luxuriousness, nonessential, extra, frill, perquisite, overfulfilment, overkill, duplication, supererogation, something over, something extra, lagniappe (US dial), bonus, spare cash, money to burn, margin, overlap, surplus, leftovers, overplus, surplusage, balance, remainder, spare, accessory, spare tyre, spare wheel, fifth wheel, excrescence, parasite, uselessness, inutility, expletive, pleonasm, rambling speech, padded text, circuitous writing, diffuseness, tautology, redundancy, inactivity, overemployment, overmanning, too much of a good thing, *embarras de richesses* (Fr), glut, oversupply, product dumping, inflation, surfeit, satiety, perk (Inf)

▶ *132 Remainder, 614 Uselessness, 553 Diffuseness, 643 Inactivity, 642 Activity*

VERBS

4 **be excessive**, have excess, overspill, overflow, brim over, well over, inundate, flood, engulf, flow out, flow, stream, deluge, overwhelm, burst its banks, burst at the seams, ooze at every pore, abound, superabound, luxuriate, riot, run riot, overproduce, overpopulate, bristle with, teem with, swarm with, crawl with, outnumber, meet one at every turn, extend, know no bounds, spread far and wide, reach to the far ends of the earth, reach to the four corners of the earth, overextend, overexpand, overstep, overlap, soak, saturate, drench, stuff, cram, fill, congest, choke, suffocate, oversatisfy, glut, cloy, satiate, sate, sicken, overfeed, gorge, overeat, overdrink, pamper oneself, overindulge oneself, overdose, overfulfil, oversubscribe, do more than enough, go overboard, oversell, flood the market, dump on the market, overstock, pile up, overdo, overplay, overact, overstep the mark, talk too much, pile it on, lay it on thick, lay it on with a trowel, exaggerate, overpraise, overload, overburden, bite off more than one can chew, have too much on one's plate, have too many irons in the fire, overcharge, surcharge, overspend, make a splash, lavish, lavish upon, overindulge, pamper, spoil, run one's mouth (US sl), roll in (Inf), wallow in (Inf), swim in (Inf), stink of (Sl), OD (Inf), overjolt (US sl), OJ (US sl), go over the top (Inf)

▶ *347 Exit, 608 Sufficiency, 246 Fertility, 181 Multitude, 144 Completeness, 357 Overstepping, 248 Space, 391 Moisture, 144 Completeness, 870 Self-Indulgence, 872 Gluttony, 541 Exaggeration, 755 Generosity, 757 Extravagance*

5 **be superfluous**, go begging (*or* a-begging), remain on one's hands, have on one's hands, do twice over, duplicate, carry coals to Newcastle, gild the lily, teach one's grandmother to suck eggs, labour the obvious, take a sledgehammer to crack a nut, flog a dead horse, exceed requirements, have no use

▶ *132 Remainder, 643 Inactivity, 614 Uselessness*

ADJECTIVES

6 **excessive**, redundant, overflowing, filled to overflowing, brimming over, running over, full, overfull, flooding, streaming, flowing, overwhelming, overwhelmed, saturated, supersaturated, drenched, soaked, abundant, superabundant, exuberant, luxuriant, riotous, profuse, plentiful, too many, one too many, plethoric, overpopulated, bristling, teeming, swarming, crawling, outnumbered, too much, overmuch, immoderate, exorbitant, extreme, inordinate, disproportionate, cloying, satiating, nauseating, sickening, cloyed, satiated,

sated, replete, overfed, gorged, crammed, stuffed, bloated, congested, ready to burst, bursting, overstretched, overburdened, overloaded, overcharged, exaggerated, overdone, overplayed, overacted, effusive, gushing, overpolite, overexcited, one over the eight (Sl), over the top (OTT) (Sl), over the moon (Inf)

▶ *608 Sufficiency, 181 Multitude, 541 Exaggeration, 391 Moisture, 788 Boredom, 870 Self-Indulgence, 872 Gluttony*

7 **superfluous**, supererogatory, excess, extra, spare, surplus, leftover, remaining, nonessential, luxury, unnecessary, needless, diffuse, rambling, circuitous, tautologous, tautological, otiose, pleonastic, redundant, overemployed, overmanned, overstaffed

▶ *132 Remainder, 614 Uselessness, 553 Diffuseness, 593 Requirement*

ADVERBS

8 **excessively**, redundantly, abundantly, immoderately, over and above, too much, overmuch, overly, unnecessarily, needlessly, beyond measure, to excess, in excess of requirements, superfluously, enough and to spare, above expectations

611 Importance

In heaven an angel is nobody in particular.
George Bernard Shaw.

Art and religion first; then philosophy; lastly science. That is the order of the great subjects of life, that's their order of importance. Muriel Spark.

NOUNS

1 **importance**, first importance, primacy, preeminence, priority, urgency, precedence, prominence, distinction, eminence, reputation, repute, paramountcy, supremacy, superiority, essentiality, irreplaceability, import, consequence, significance, weight, weightiness, gravity, seriousness, solemnity, materiality, materialness, substance, pith, moment, substantiality, interest, consideration, concern, business, matter, account, note, notability, noteworthiness, memorability, mark, influence, prestige, size, magnitude, greatness, degree, rank, rating, standing, status, high standing, high approval, value, worth, excellence, merit, use, usefulness, strategic importance, utility, power, stress, emphasis, insistence, affirmation

▶ *154 Precedence, 126 Superiority, 101 Reality, 259 Size, 121 Degree, 617 Worth, 613 Usefulness, 535 Affirmation, 233 Influence, 235 Power*

2 **important matter**, vital concern, grave affair, crucial moment, turning point, crisis, breath of life, matter of life and death, no joke, no laughing matter, key point, notable point, memorandum, reminder, news, big news, great news, exploit, deed, great doings, big deal, important occasion, landmark, milestone, red-letter day, big day, great day, special day, the crunch (Inf), be-all and end-all (Inf), nothing to sneeze at (Inf), not peanuts (Sl), not chickenfeed (Sl), heavy scene (Sl)

▶ *210 Timeliness, 511 Memory, 533 News, 640 Action, 812 Celebration*

3 **chief thing**, what matters, the thing, great thing, main thing, issue, supreme issue, crux of the matter, crux, main topic, fundamentals, basics, grass roots, bedrock, core, hard facts, reality, essential, *sine qua non* (L), requirement, priority, first priority, choice, first choice, highlight, main attraction, main feature, best part, cream, *crème de la crème* (Fr), pick, elite, gist, meaning, substance, essence, essential part, sum and substance, heart, heart of the matter, kernel, nucleus, nub, nitty-gritty (Inf), nuts and bolts (Inf), centre, hub, nexus, fulcrum, pivot, keynote, cornerstone, mainstay, linchpin, kingpin, head, spearhead, cardinal point, main point, salient point, half the battle, main part, chief hope, secret weapon, trump card, ace in the hole, big play, main chance, high spot (Inf)

▶ *101 Reality, 593 Requirement, 580 Selection, 520 Meaning, 103 Essence, 617 Worth, 291 Centre*

4 **bigwig**, important person, influential person, powerful person, personage, notable, notability, personality, captain of industry, magnate, mogul, tycoon, MD (managing director), lord of the manor, local worthy, pillar of the community, pillar of society, grandee, noble, aristocrat, member of the establishment, great man (*or* woman), top person, very important person, VIP, His (*or* Her) Highness, big name, high muck-a-muck, grand panjandrum, mandarin, leading light, master spirit, sage, kingpin, key person, expert, prima donna, star, lion, catch, great catch, favourite, uncrowned king (*or* queen), head, chief, leader, godfather, Big Brother, superior, superior person, the greatest, heavyweight (Inf), somebody (Inf), salt of the earth (Inf), top brass (Inf), brass hat (Inf), his (*or* her) nibs (Sl), biggie (US sl), big guy (US inf), big gun (Inf), big shot (Inf), big dooley (US sl), big noise (Sl), big wheel (Inf), big cheese (Inf), big enchilada (US inf), big fish (Inf), big but (Inf), big white Chief (Inf), big Chief (Inf), big Daddy (Inf), Mr Big (Inf), big-time operator (BTO) (Inf), wheeler-dealer (Inf), macher (US sl), big timer (Inf), big man (US sl), big man on campus (BMOC) (US inf), the man (US inf), Big John (US sl), first fiddle (Inf), superman (*or* superwoman) (Inf)

▶ *802 Aristocrat, 507 Wisdom, 655 Skill, 653 Management, 826 Endearment, 126 Superiority, 617 Worth, 233 Influence, 235 Power*

ADJECTIVES

5 **important**, primary, pre-eminent, urgent, imperative, prominent, distinct, eminent, weighty, grave, solemn, serious, pregnant, heavy, big, of consequence, consequential, significant, of importance, of weight, of concern, of consideration, considerable, worth considering, world-shattering, earth-shaking, momentous, critical, crucial, fateful, chief, cardinal, capital, staple, major, main, top, topmost, paramount, supreme, prime, foremost, leading, overriding, overruling, uppermost, most important, superior, essential, material, to the point, relevant, pivotal, central, basic, fundamental, bedrock, radical, going to the root, grass roots, worthwhile, to be taken seriously, not to be despised, not to be overlooked, valuable, necessary, vital, indispensable, irreplaceable, key, required, helpful, useful, telling, trenchant, meaningful, taking precedence, high-priority, high-level, top-level, summit, top-secret, secret, confidential, high, grand, noble, great, not to be sneezed at (Inf), hush-hush (Inf)

▶ 154 Precedence, 259 Size, 210 Timeliness, 126 Superiority, 107 Relatedness, 291 Centre, 617 Worth, 593 Requirement, 613 Usefulness, 520 Meaning, 279 Summit, 529 Secrecy

6 **notable**, noteworthy, remarkable, of mark, egregious (Arch), memorable, unforgettable, signal, first-rate, A1, gold-medal, silver-medal, bronze-medal, outstanding, sterling, excellent, superior, top-rank, top-ten, top-flight, ranking, high-ranking, prestigious, conspicuous, prominent, eminent, distinguished, exalted, august, dignified, imposing, leading, commanding, impressive, formidable, powerful, influential, newsworthy, front-page, eventful, stirring, breathtaking, shattering, monumental, world-shattering, seismic, earth-shaking, epoch-making

▶ 511 Memory, 126 Superiority, 617 Worth, 233 Influence, 235 Power

VERBS

7 **be important**, matter, bulk large, weigh, carry, carry weight, tell, count, make an impression, make someone sit up and notice, attract attention, cast a long shadow, influence, motivates, signify, represent, import, mean, concern, interest, affect, have priority, take precedence, precede, come before, come first, predominate, take the lead, command respect, take the limelight, deserve notice, make a stir, create a sensation, make it big, make waves (Inf), cut a figure (Inf), cut a dash (Inf)

▶ 233 Influence, 586 Persuasion, 467 Attention, 520 Meaning, 107 Relatedness, 126 Superiority, 154 Precedence, 849 Respect

8 **make important**, build up, give weight to, attach (or ascribe) importance to, seize on, fasten on, bring to the fore, place in the foreground, enhance, highlight, stress, emphasize, underline, labour, publicize, promote, advertise, put in bright lights, put in capital letters, headline, splash, bring to notice, bring to attention, put on the map, proclaim, announce, write in letters of gold, celebrate, lionize, honour, glorify, exalt, show respect, respect, value, esteem, regard, consider, take seriously, make a fuss about, make a stir, make much ado, make much of, put (or set) store by, think everything of, magnify, enlarge, exaggerate, overestimate, overrate

▶ 535 Affirmation, 532 Publication, 812 Celebration, 261 Expansion, 511 Exaggeration, 849 Respect, 494 Overestimation

ADVERBS

9 **importantly**, primarily, pre-eminently, urgently, prominently, eminently, seriously, consequentially, significantly, materially, considerably, critically, crucially, largely, mainly, in the main, above all, to crown all, supremely, par excellence (Fr), notably, remarkably, memorably

612   Unimportance

ADJECTIVES

1 **unimportant**, without importance, insignificant, immaterial, circumstantial, not related, not apropos, off the point, irrelevant, ineffectual, uninfluential, forgettable, inconsequential, of no consequence, of no great weight, insubstantial, inessential, nonessential, not vital, unnecessary, dispensable, expendable, small, little, slight, light, inconsiderable, negligible, forgivable, venial, nondescript, inappreciable, not worth considering, not worth worrying about, of little value, out of the running

▶ 108 Unrelatedness, 102 Unreality

2 **obscure**, disregarded, overlooked, neglected, not considered, beneath notice, beneath contempt, contemptible, good-for-nothing, wretched, miserable, measly, paltry, pitiful, pitiable, pathetic, impoverished, poor, mean, lowly, humble, sorry, scruffy, shabby, weak, powerless, impotent, puny, no-account (US inf), no-count (US inf)

▶ 470 Negligence, 850 Disrespect, 236 Powerlessness, 743 Poverty

3 **secondary**, minor, incidental, by-side, subsidiary, peripheral, low-level, of second rank

4 **trivial**, petty, trifling, nugatory, piffling, piddling, peddling (US), fiddling, niggling, technical, pettifogging, not serious, frivolous, puerile, childish, featherbrained, featherheaded, foolish, windy, airy, frothy, flimsy, insubstantial, superficial, shallow, not worthwhile, not

worth a thought, not worth a second thought, small, tiny, teeny, teeny-weeny, teensy-weensy, toy, token, nominal, symbolic, small-time, light-weight, cheap, low-priced, five-and-dime (US), twopenny, twopenny-halfpenny, inferior, bad, poor, poor quality, shoddy, jerry-built, tawdry, rubbishy, trashy, trumpery, catchpenny, pinchbeck, gimcrack, potboiling, pulp, worthless, valueless, useless, second-rate, third-rate, mediocre, commonplace, ordinary, usual, limited, parochial, parish-pump, uneventful, nit-picking (Inf), footling (Inf), grotty (Sl), dinky (US inf), rinky-dink (Sl), ricky-tick (US sl), two-bit (US sl), Mickey Mouse (Sl), no great shakes (Inf), one-horse (Inf), jerkwater (US sl)

▶ *508 Folly, 278 Shallowness, 754 Cheapness, 618 Worthlessness, 614 Uselessness*

NOUNS

5 **unimportance**, insignificance, immateriality, unrelatedness, irrelevance, irrelevancy, inconsequence, inessentiality, dispensability, expendability, lack of substance, insubstantiality, nothingness, nullity, vacancy, emptiness, secondariness

▶ *108 Unrelatedness, 102 Unreality*

6 **obscurity**, contemptibility, wretchedness, paltriness, meanness, weakness, powerlessness, impotence

▶ *850 Disrespect, 236 Powerlessness*

7 **triviality**, pettiness, lack of seriousness, frivolousness, frivolity, flippancy, snap of the fingers, superficiality, shallowness, smallness, cheapness, inferiority, worthlessness, uselessness, inutility, mediocrity

▶ *278 Shallowness, 754 Cheapness, 618 Worthlessness, 614 Uselessness*

8 **trifle**, insignificant matter, inessential, nonessential, triviality, technicality, detail, more detail, petty detail, details, trifles, minutiae, trivia, nothing, mere nothing, bagatelle, little bit, least bit, whit, jot, iota, tittle, trickle, dab, drop, drop in the bucket, drop in the ocean, damn, tinker's damn (*or* cuss), straw, rush, chaff, pin, button, feather, dust, cobweb, gossamer, tithe, fraction, small change, doit, cent (US), dime (US), twopence (*or* tuppence), fleabite, pinprick, scratch, child's play, nothing to it, taking candy from a baby, jest, joke, harmless joke, practical joke, farce, amusement, trifling fault, petty sin, venial sin, peccadillo, no matter, no great matter, accessory, secondary matter, sideshow, diversion, red herring, nothing of note, nothing in particular, matter of indifference, ordinary matter, nothing to boast of, nothing to write home about, nothing to speak of, nothing to worry about, not the end of the world, a mountain out of a molehill, a storm in a teacup, no great shakes (Inf), brass farthing (Inf), plugged nickel (US inf), bawbee (Scot inf),

peanuts (Sl), chickenfeed (Sl), small beer (Inf), small potatoes (US inf)

▶ *494 Overestimation, 660 Easiness, 506 Nonsense*

9 **bauble**, toy, plaything, small toy, rattle, trinket, novelty, gewgaw, geegaw (US), gimcrack, knick-knack (*or* nick-nack), bibelot, bric-a-brac, doodah, bagatelle, tinsel, trumpery, frippery, froth, foam, trash

▶ *754 Cheapness*

10 **nonentity**, nobody, unimportant person, obscure person, unknown, nonperson, man of straw, figurehead, cipher, zero, nothing, sleeping partner, fribbler, trifler, beachcomber, smatterer, jack of all trades and master of none, mediocrity, lightweight, small fry, small change, small game, other ranks, commonalty, inferior, subordinate, underling, understrapper, second fiddle, servant, puppet, pawn, pawn in the game, piece on the board, instrument, Cinderella, poor relation, weak person, pipsqueak, scorned person, object of scorn, scum, scum of the earth, trash (US), poor White trash (US), small beer (Inf), small potatoes (US inf), stooge (Sl), squirt (Inf), creep (Sl), wimp (Sl), twerp (*or* twirp) (Sl), squit (Sl), slum hustler (US sl)

▶ *803 Commoner, 697 Servant, 127 Inferiority, 850 Disrespect*

VERBS

11 **be unimportant**, not matter, weigh light upon, have no weight, carry no weight, not weigh, not count, count for nothing, have no clout, have no pull, make no impression, mean little, signify little, cut no ice (Inf)

▶ *506 Nonsense*

12 **think unimportant**, disregard, overlook, pass over, underrate, underestimate, pejorate, shrug off, snap one's fingers at, hold cheap

13 **make unimportant**, trivialize, belittle, degrade, denigrate, demote, relegate, reduce one's importance, deflate one's ego, trim (*or* cut) down to size, knock down a few rungs, humiliate, disparage, mock, scorn, put down (Inf)

▶ *806 Humility, 807 Insolence*

ADVERBS

14 **unimportantly**, insignificantly, circumstantially, irrelevantly, ineffectually, inconsequentially, unnecessarily, negligibly, secondarily, incidentally, trivially, superficially

INTERJECTIONS

15 **no matter!**, never mind!, so what!, too bad!, *tant pis* (Fr)!, who cares?, who gives a shit (*or* toss *or* fuck) (Tab sl)?

613 Usefulness

ADJECTIVES

1 **useful**, of use, handy, helpful, of help, of service, for everyday use, utilitarian, prag-

matic, practical, applied, functional, practicable, commodious, convenient, advisable, sensible, suitable, expedient, applicable, versatile, multipurpose, all-purpose, for all ages, of all work, adaptable, disposable, throwaway, ready, rough and ready, at hand, available, on call, ready for use, operative, up, on-line, on-stream, on tap (Inf)

▶ *662 Help, 599 Use, 615 Convenience*

2 **usable**, serviceable, fit (for), good (for), fit for use, approved for use, reusable, recyclable, employable, workable, good, valid, current

3 **instrumental**, subsidiary, subservient, able, competent, efficacious, effective, effectual, efficient, powerful, conducive, tending, adequate, sufficient

▶ *235 Power, 608 Sufficiency*

4 **profitable**, making a profit, remunerative, lucrative, paying, gainful, productive, fruitful, beneficial, advantageous, salutary, for one's benefit, to one's advantage, good, edifying, worthwhile, worth one's salt, worth one's keep, worth one's weight in gold, worth a mint, worth a million, valuable, invaluable, priceless

▶ *721 Gain, 243 Production, 617 Worth, 861 Good*

NOUNS

5 **usefulness**, use, purpose, point, utility, handiness, helpfulness, help, aid, service, avail, good stead, good, utilitarianism, practicality, application, functionalism, commodity, convenience, suitability, expediency, applicability, versatility, adaptability, readiness, availability, usage, utilization, employment

▶ *662 Help, 599 Use, 615 Convenience*

6 **usability**, serviceability, employability, workability, value, worth, merit, good, virtue, function, capacity

▶ *617 Worth, 861 Good*

7 **instrumentality**, ability, competence, efficacy, efficiency, power, potency, clout, influence, adequacy, sufficiency

▶ *235 Power, 608 Sufficiency*

8 **benefit**, advantage, gain, profit, profitability, return, earning capacity, productivity, productiveness, fruitfulness, general benefit, public benefit, public good, public utility, commonweal

▶ *721 Gain, 243 Production*

VERBS

9 **be useful**, come in handy, help, aid, advance, promote, prove helpful, avail, serve, do service, suit one's purpose, further one's purpose, have some use, perform a function, function, work, operate, perform do, answer, suffice, make oneself useful, subserve, serve one's turn, fill the bill (Inf)

▶ *662 Help, 599 Use, 608 Sufficiency*

10 **benefit**, advantage, be to one's advantage, serve one well, stand one in good stead, be-

stead (Arch), do good, bring results, bear fruit, profit, gain, pay, pay off

▶ *721 Gain, 617 Worth, 861 Good*

11 **find useful**, have a use for, find a use for, use, utilize, employ, make use of, take advantage of, turn to good account, capitalize on, make capital out of, profit by, gain from, reap the profit from, reap the benefit of, be the better for

▶ *721 Gain, 599 Use, 627 Improvement*

ADVERBS

12 **usefully**, handily, helpfully, practically, conveniently, usably, serviceably, efficiently, advantageously, profitably, *pro bono publico* (L), for the public good, *cui bono?* (L), to whose advantage?, for what purpose?

614 Uselessness

ADJECTIVES

1 **useless**, not useful, of no use, inutile, futile, unhelpful, unfit, unapt, inapt, unsuitable, inapplicable, inconvenient, inexpedient, impractical, impracticable, unworkable, unpractical, nonfunctional, functionless, ornamental, redundant, superfluous, extra, excessive, unnecessary, not needed, unneeded, unwanted, expendable, dispensable, disposable, throwaway, unusable, unserviceable, fit for nothing, good-for-nothing, unemployable, unqualified, unskilled, unskilful, unable, incompetent, inept, inefficient, ineffective, ineffectual, feckless, impotent, powerless, inadequate, nonfunctioning, inoperative, not working, out of order, down, broken down, worn out, spent, effete, *hors de combat* (Fr), no good, invalid, void, null, null and void, abrogated, obsolete, outmoded, old-fashioned, antiquated, worthless, valueless, rubbishy, trashy, unsaleable, not worth the paper it's written on, naff (Sl), no-go (US sl), screwed-up (Sl), fucked-up (Tab sl), dud (Inf), kaput (Inf), no bloody good (Sl), out of action (Inf), past it (Inf), over the hill (Inf), Mickey Mouse (Sl), crappy (Tab sl), shitty (Tab sl)

▶ *616 Inconvenience, 661 Hindrance, 557 Ornament, 610 Excess, 656 Unskilfulness, 236 Powerlessness, 704 Cancellation, 202 Oldness, 618 Worthlessness*

2 **futile**, purposeless, pointless, Sisyphean, hopeless, vain, in vain, idle, unavailing, abortive, unsuccessful, profitless, bootless, not worthwhile, offering no advantage, offering no benefit, unprofitable, not paying, loss-making, uneconomic, unproductive, fruitless, barren sterile, wasteful, ill-spent, wasted, squandered, time-wasting, effort-wasting, not worth the effort, unrewarding, unrewarded, thankless

▶ *722 Loss, 683 Failure, 607 Waste, 247 Infertility*

3 **uselessness**, lack of use, inutility, futility, unhelpfulness, disservice, unfitness, unaptness, inaptitude, unsuitability, inapplicability, inconvenience, inexpedience, inexpediency, impracticality, impracticability, unworkability, lack of function, redundancy, superfluousness, superfluity, expendability, dispensability, disposability, unserviceableness, unemployability, unskilfulness, lack of skill, inability, incompetence, ineptitude, inefficiency, ineffectiveness, inefficacy, ineffectualness, fecklessness, impotence, powerlessness, inadequacy, effeteness, worthlessness, unsaleability

▶ *616 Inconvenience, 661 Hindrance, 610 Excess, 656 Unskilfulness, 236 Powerlessness, 618 Worthlessness*

4 **futility**, purposelessness, lack of purpose, pointlessness, hopelessness, vanity, vanity of vanities, idleness, failure, loss, unprofitability, profitlessness, bootlessness, lack of advantage, lack of benefit, unproductiveness, fruitlessness, barrenness, sterility, waste, wastefulness, thanklessness

▶ *722 Loss, 683 Failure, 247 Infertility*

5 **waste of effort**, wasted effort, wasted labour, lost labour, waste of time, waste of breath, waste of space, false scent, red herring, wild-goose chase, fool's errand, fool's gold, labour of Sisyphus, Penelope's web, half measures, tinkering, futilitarianism, dead loss (Inf), blind alley (Inf), nigger-rigging (US sl)

▶ *607 Waste*

6 **refuse**, rubbish, trash (US), junk, litter, scrap, throwaway, disposable, castoff, reject, leftovers, leavings, scraps, lumber, stuff, spoilage, wastage, bilge, load of old rubbish, discarded matter, waste, waste product, mullock (Aus), wastepaper, scourings, offscourings, sweepings, shavings, chaff, husks, stubble, bran, seeds, cotton seeds, bits, crumbs, offal, carrion, debris, muck, dirt, dush, ash, cinder, clinker, dross, slag, scoria, scum, peel, apple peel, orange peel, banana skin, leaves, weeds, dead wood, old newspaper, tares, odds and ends, bits and pieces, rags and bones, old clothes, empty bottle, can, tin, compost, compost heap, dump, refuse dump, rubbish dump, rubbish pile, trash dump (US), rubbish heap, midden (Arch or Dial), landfill, tip, sump, drain, cesspool, septic tank, sewage works (or farm), dustheap, slag heap, dustbin

▶ *607 Waste, 132 Remainder, 622 Dirtiness*

VERBS

7 **be useless**, have no use, have no purpose, not help, hinder, achieve nothing, be in vain, have no chance, fail, not work, not function, not go, break down, fall by the wayside, go to waste, go (a-)begging

▶ *661 Hindrance, 683 Failure, 610 Excess*

8 **make useless**, disqualify, disable, render unfit, unfit, unman, disarm, unarm, render harmless, cripple, make lame, lame, dismantle, disassemble, undo, take to pieces, break up, break down, unmount, dismast, unrig, decommission, put of of commission, lay up, deactivate, make inactive, sabotage, put a spoke in one's wheel, obstruct, abrogate, withdraw from currency, devalue, cheapen, impair, deface, pollute, contaminate, destroy, obliterate, lay waste, make barren, sterilize, castrate, emasculate, exhaust, use up, overwork, overfish, take the sting out of (Inf), clip one's wings (Inf), let the air out of one's tyres (Inf), throw a wrench in one's plans (US inf), throw a spanner in the works (Inf), cramp one's style (Inf)

▶ *236 Powerlessness, 643 Inactivity, 704 Cancellation, 754 Cheapness, 244 Destruction, 546 Obliteration*

9 **waste effort**, labour the obvious, waste one's breath, waste (one's) time, go round in circles, accomplish nothing, get nowhere, labour in vain, sweat for nothing, attempt the impossible, tinker, leave unfinished, spin one's wheels (Inf), talk to a brick wall (Inf), beat one's head against a brick wall (Inf), rearrange the deckchairs on the Titanic (Inf), preach to the converted (Inf), carry coals to Newcastle (Inf), flog (or beat) a dead horse (Inf), beat the air (Inf), tilt at windmills (Inf), cry for the moon (Inf), search for the end of the rainbow (Inf), paper over the cracks (Inf), spoil the ship for a ha'p'orth of tar (Inf)

▶ *607 Waste, 487 Impossibility*

ADVERBS

10 **uselessly**, unhelpfully, inconveniently, impractically, incompetently, ineffectively, ineffectually, to no purpose, in vain, to no avail, unsuccessfully, unprofitably, on a wild-goose chase, until one is blue in the face, on a hiding to nothing (Inf)

615 Convenience

ADJECTIVES

1 **convenient**, handy, helpful, practical, pragmatic, practicable, usable, workable, effective, effectual, qualified, adapted to, cut out for, applicable, to the purpose, suitable, commodious, appropriate, fit, fitting, befitting, seemly, proper, right, expedient, expediential, advantageous, to one's advantage, beneficial, profitable, useful, prudent, politic, judicious, wise, advisable, commendable, desirable, worthwhile, acceptable, approved, owing, due, in loco, timely, well-timed, auspicious, opportune, seasonable, right up one's alley (Sl), right up one's street (Sl)

▶ *843 Right, 613 Usefulness, 210 Timeliness, 507 Wisdom, 851 Approval*

2 **nearby**, next door, accessible, available, ready, close, adjacent, neighbouring, touching, bordering on
▶ *264 Nearness, 267 Juxtaposition*

NOUNS
3 **convenience**, handiness, helpfulness, practicality, pragmatism, practicability, practicableness, usability, workability, qualification, adaptation, application, suitability, fitness, propriety, expedience, expediency, contrivance, utilitarianism, opportunism, rule of expediency, timeserving, profit, advantage, benefit, usefulness, utility, prudence, good policy, advisability, desirability, dueness, timeliness, auspiciousness, opportunity, proper time, right time, right time and place, high time (Inf), due time (Inf)
4 **nearness**, proximity, closeness, juxtaposition, adjacency, accessibility, availability
5 **convenience**, facilities, means, expedient, last resort, *pis aller* (Fr)

VERBS
6 **be convenient**, come in handy, come in useful, fit, befit, suit, suit the occasion, not come amiss, not go amiss, serve the time, expedite one's end, bring about, help, aid, promote, advance, forward, answer, have the desired effect, produce results, do, serve, prove itself, be better than nothing, succeed achieve one's aim, qualify for, correspond with, accord, profit, benefit, give an advantage, advantage, do good, hit the spot (Inf), wash (Inf), deliver the goods (Inf), fill the bill (Inf)
▶ *662 Help, 613 Usefulness, 608 Sufficiency, 682 Success, 116 Accord, 861 Good*

ADVERBS
7 **conveniently**, handily, practically, fittingly, expediently, opportunely, accessibly, within reach, in the right place at the right time, to fill (*or* fit) the bill (Inf)
8 **nearby**, close by, next to, at hand, in the vicinity (*or* neighbourhood), within reach, at one's fingertips, on the tip of one's tongue

616   Inconvenience

ADJECTIVES
1 **inconvenient**, discommodious, incommodious, disadvantageous, detrimental, hurtful, harmful, inexpedient, inadvisable, unadvisable, undesirable, uncommendable, not recommended, ill-advised, ill-considered, impolitic, imprudent, injudicious, unwise, inappropriate, unfitting, misapplied, malapropos, out of place, improper, unseemly, undue, not right, objectionable, offensive, wrong, unfit, unsuitable, ineligible, unqualified, inadmissible, unfortunate, unhappy, infelicitous, sad, inept, unapt, inopportune, unseasonable, untimely, ill-timed, poorly timed, wrongly

timed, disruptive, disrupting, disturbing, unsettling, useless, unprofitable, unhelpful, hindering, untoward, adverse, unprofessional, ill-contrived, ill-planned, awkward, clumsy, cumbersome, lumbering, hulking, unwieldy, burdensome, onerous, troublesome, bothersome, annoying, irritating, irksome, boring, tiresome, vexatious, tedious
▶ *852 Disapproval, 508 Folly, 844 Wrong, 211 Untimeliness, 614 Uselessness, 661 Hindrance, 153 Disturbance*
2 **distant**, remote, out of the way, innaccessible, unapproachable, unavailable
▶ *263 Distance*

NOUNS
3 **inconvenience**, disadvantage, drawback, detriment, hurt, harm, inexpedience, inexpediency, mixed blessing, Pyrrhic victory, two-edged sword, inadvisability, undesirability, bad policy, imprudence, inappropriateness, unfittingness, impropriety, lack of protocol, unseemliness, undueness, lack of planning, poor timing, wrongness, wrong, error, unfitness, unsuitability, inaptitude, inopportuneness, untimeliness, disruption, disturbance, disability, handicap, impediment, obstacle, hindrance, nuisance, bother, trouble, upset, discomfort, incommodiousness, pain, difficulty, annoyance, irritation, vexation, awkwardness, burden, cumbersomeness, troublesomeness, unwieldiness
▶ *844 Wrong, 211 Untimeliness, 614 Uselessness, 661 Hindrance, 153 Disturbance*
4 **distance**, remoteness, inaccessibility, unapproachability, unavailability

VERBS
5 **be inconvenient**, come amiss, go amiss, not do, not fit, not help, inconvenience, trouble, bother, disturb, disrupt, upset, put to inconvenience, put to trouble, discommode, incommode, put out, annoy, irritate, vex, irk, embarrass, hinder, obstruct, handicap, disadvantage, penalize, work against, militate against, hurt, harm, pester, make a nuisance of oneself, hassle (Inf)

ADVERBS
6 **inconveniently**, discommodiously, incommodiously, inexpediently, inadvisably, injudiciously, improperly, inopportunely, disruptively, uselessly, unhelpfully, awkwardly, clumsily, annoyingly, irritatingly, boringly, tediously, tiresomely, vexatiously

617   Worth

ADJECTIVES
1 **worthy**, praiseworthy, laudable, meritorious, deserving, admired, esteemed, respected, valued, admirable, estimable, creditable, approved, excellent, fine, braw (Scot), noble, ex-

emplary, worth imitating, good, good as gold, good as one's word, virtuous, above par, preferable, better, superior, very good, first-class, first-rate, first-string, capital, prime, quality, good quality, superfine, most desirable, rare, vintage, classic, outstanding, superlative, in a class by itself, all-star, all-American (US), topnotch, top-flight, of the first water, flawless, perfect, choice, select, picked, handpicked, exquisite, recherché, chosen, selected, tested, exclusive, restricted, pure, unmixed, famous, great, noteworthy, notable, eminent, distinguished, glorious, dazzling, splendid, splendiferous, brilliant, magnificent, marvellous, sensational, terrific, wonderful, superb, couleur de rose (Fr), grand, fantastic, fabulous, amazing, prodigious, gorgeous, lovely, heavenly, delicious, fab (Inf), super (Inf), superduper (Inf), superfly (US sl), super- (Inf), out of this world (Inf), dynamite (Sl), deadly (Sl), def (Sl), magic (Inf), way-out (Inf), radical (Sl), rad (US sl), way-rad (US sl), out of sight (Sl), ace (Inf), A1 (Inf), A-OK (Inf), alpha plus (Inf), stunning (Inf), famous (Inf), massive (US sl), (a) mean (Sl), bad (US sl), smashing (Inf), corking (Sl), spiffy (Sl), spiffing (Sl), topping (Sl), ripping (Sl), real George (US sl), George (US sl), swell (Sl), swellelegant (Sl), dandy (Inf), classy (Sl), neat (US sl), cool (Sl), hunky-dory (Inf), groovy (Sl), bully (Inf), brill (Sl), cosmic (Sl), wizard (Inf), boffo (US sl), bang-up (Inf), bangon (Inf), delish (Inf), scrumptious (Inf), juicy (Inf), plum (Inf), peachy (keen) (Inf), plummy (Inf), jammy (Sl), crackerjack (Sl), kopasetic (US sl), God's own (Inf), God's answer to (Inf)

▶ *861 Good, 863 Virtue, 126 Superiority, 619 Perfection, 845 Entitlement, 851 Approval*

2 **best**, very best, optimum, champion, grandchampion, winning, blue-ribbon, gold-medal, platinum (record), tiptop, nothing like it, first, first-class, first-rate, second to none, supreme, incomparable, unequalled, unbeaten, unbeatable, unmatched, matchless, unparalleled, peerless, unsurpassed, unsurpassable, perfect, record, record-breaking, world-beating, bestselling, chart-topping, number-one, crowning, principal, capital, cardinal, important, topnotch, top-hole, tops (Sl), ace (Inf), A1 (Inf), crack (Sl), a cut above (Inf), best-ever (Inf), all-time (Inf)

▶ *126 Superiority, 619 Perfection, 611 Importance*

3 **valuable**, of value, invaluable, inestimable, priceless, above price, beyond price, costly, expensive, rich, irreplaceable, unique, rare, precious, prized, valued, treasured, golden, worth its weight in gold, worth a king's ransom, worth a mint, worth a million, sterling, gilt-edged, blue-chip, sound, solid

▶ *753 Dearness, 751 Price*

4 **worthwhile**, profitable, useful, advantageous, beneficial, wholesome, healthy, salutary, sound, good (for), salubrious, refreshing, edifying, favourable, kind, propitious, harmless, hurtless, inoffensive, innocuous, innocent, like water off a duck's back

▶ *613 Usefulness, 721 Gain, 625 Hygiene, 865 Innocence*

5 **not bad**, tolerable, adequate, sufficient, fair, satisfactory, good enough, passable, respectable, standard, up to the mark, in good condition, in fair condition, nice, decent, pretty good, all right, unexceptionable, unobjectionable, indifferent, yes-and-no, middle-of-theroad, middling, fair to middling, neither good nor bad, mediocre, ordinary, average, median, sound, fresh, unspoiled, fifty-fifty (Inf), so-so (Inf), up to snuff (Inf), okay (Inf), OK (Inf), oke (Sl), okey-doke (*or* okey-dokey) (Sl)

▶ *124 Average, 608 Sufficiency*

NOUNS

6 **worth**, worthiness, praiseworthiness, merit, desert, admiration, esteem, respect, credit, value, price, cost, pricelessness, costliness, rarity, excellence, greatness, goodness, virtue, quality, good quality, classic quality, vintage, soundness, health, virtuosity, skill, forte, strong point, good point, redeeming feature, likable trait, claim to fame, title to fame, eminence, pre-eminence, supereminence, superiority, flawlessness, perfection, essence, distilled essence, quintessence, beneficence, benevolence, nobility, brilliance, magnificence, strong suit (Inf), long suit (Inf), best foot (Inf), best side (Inf)

▶ *861 Good, 863 Virtue, 126 Superiority, 619 Perfection, 611 Importance, 753 Dearness, 751 Price, 613 Usefulness*

7 **elite**, chosen few, chosen people, the elect, the saints, prime, flower, cream, crème de la crème (Fr), salt of the earth, pick, pick of the bunch, *corps d'elite* (Fr), SAS, Special Forces (US), best people, top people, meritocracy, meritocrat, aristocracy, aristocrat, gentry, nobility, upper class, charmed circle, top drawer, *haut monde* (Fr), jet set, Brahman (*or* Brahmin), Sloane Ranger (Brit), Valley Girl (US), choice bit, titbit, prime cut, *pièce de résistance* (Fr), plum, prize, trophy, crack troops (Sl), upper crust (Inf)

▶ *611 Importance, 126 Superiority, 681 Trophy*

8 **exceller**, nonpareil, nonesuch (Arch), champion, top seed, titleholder, world-beater, prizewinner, winner, victor, prodigy, gift child, genius, paragon, hero, star, film star, pop star, celebrity, idol, toast of the town, toast from coast to coast (US), beauty, charmer, wonder, wonder of the world, Miss Universe, Miss America, May Queen, homecoming queen (US), Admirable Crichton, grand fellow, one of

the best, one in a thousand, one in a million, treasure, perfect treasure, favourite, jewel, gem, gem of the first water, pearl pearl of price, ruby, diamond, gold, pure gold, refined gold, masterpiece, *chef-d'oeuvre* (Fr), *pièce de résistance* (Fr), collector's item, collector's piece, museum piece, record-breaker, bestseller, chart-topper, top of the pops, the greatest show on earth, best ever, best thing since sliced bread, best of its kind, *ne plus ultra* (L), last word (in), superhero (Inf), superman (*or* superwoman) (Inf), superjock (US inf), supermom (US inf), wonderwoman (Inf), the goods (Sl), winner (Inf), corker (Sl), humdinger (Sl), lollapalooza (US sl), wow (Sl), knockout (Inf), hit (Inf), smash hit (Inf), smasher (Inf), the tops (Sl), the greatest (Sl), bee's knees (Sl), cat's pyjamas (Sl), cat's whiskers (Sl), cat's meow (Sl), topnotcher (Inf), top banana (US sl), top brass (Inf), top dog (Sl), first-rater (Inf), cock of the walk (Inf)

▶ *619 Perfection, 826 Endearment, 611 Importance, 789 Beauty, 682 Success*

VERBS

9 **be worthy**, have merit, have quality, merit, deserve, qualify, stand the test, pass, pass muster, suffice, bear (*or* stand) comparison, contend, vie, rival, equal, equal the best, excel, surpass, transcend, overtop, take the prize, walk off with all the prizes, sweep the board

▶ *845 Entitlement, 126 Superiority, 122 Equality, 608 Sufficiency*

10 **do good**, benefit, have a good effect, improve, make better, edify, do a world of good, work wonders, be the making of, make a man of, help, favour, do a good turn, confer an obligation, put in one's debt, do no harm, cause no problems, not hurt, break no bones

ADVERBS

11 **worthily**, laudably, admirably, excellently, nobly, well, famously, greatly, notably, gloriously, splendidly, brilliantly, OK, all right, profitably, beneficially

INTERJECTIONS

12 **fantastic!**, great!, well done!, all right! (Inf)

618 Worthlessness

ADJECTIVES

1 **worthless**, valueless, of little value, unimportant, insignificant, paltry, useless, futile, not worth the effort, not worth a second thought, not worth powder and shot, not worth the paper it's written on, not worth a light, not worth a hill of beans (Inf), not worth a bean (*or* button) (Inf), not worth a piss in the snow (Tab sl), not worth a plugged nickel (US inf), not worth a bucket of warm spit (US inf), not worth a bumper (Aus inf)

▶ *612 Unimportance, 614 Uselessness*

2 **inferior**, no good, low-quality, low-grade, of poor quality, low-standard, faulty, flawed, imperfect, defective, substandard, badly made, shoddy, punk, tawdry, trashy, rubbishy, cheap, second-class, third-class, second-rate, third-rate, not good enough, unsatisfactory, bad, incompetent, inefficient, unskilled, clumsy, badly done, bungled, botched, mangled, spoiled, ruined, nowhere (US sl), crummy (Sl), pathetic (Inf), tacky (Inf), naff (Sl), junky (US sl), schlocky (US sl), crappy (Sl), ropy (*or* ropey) (Inf), klutzy (US sl)

▶ *127 Inferiority, 620 Imperfection, 766 Dissatisfaction, 656 Unskilfulness*

3 **bad**, nasty, obnoxious, noxious, noisome, objectionable, unpleasant, disagreeable, unlikable, not nice, horrible, horrid, evil, base, gross, black, utterly bad, irredeemable, as bad as (bad) can be, execrable, unspeakable, abominable, awful, horrific, horrendous, terrible, dreadful, perfectly dreadful, gruesome, grim, unendurable, intolerable, too bad, onerous, burdensome, tedious, fatiguing, annoying, distressing, vicious, villainous, wicked, heinous, depraved, immoral, accursed, sinful, dishonest, illegal, criminal, wrong, wrongful, unjust, ghastly (Inf), beastly (Inf), crooked (Inf)

▶ *764 Unpleasantness, 864 Wickedness, 862 Evil, 844 Wrong, 858 Improbity*

4 **poor**, mean, wretched, miserable, sad, woeful, melancholy, pitiful, pitiable, grievous, sore, lamentable, deplorable, abject, contemptible, despicable, disreputable, scruffy, shabby, mangy, sordid, sleazy, squalid, grubby, dirty, filthy, sickening, nauseating, nauseous, revolting, disgusting, loathsome, detestable, hateful, low, indecent, improper, coarse, vulgar, pornographic, obscene, X-rated, shocking, scandalous, reprehensible, disgraceful, unworthy, undeserving, discreditable, shameful, rotten, rotten to the core, decaying, decayed, decomposed, putrefying, putrid, rank, stinking, stinky (US), foul, noisome, fetid, corrupt, peccant, gone bad, off, not fresh, stale, mouldy, tainted, affected, unsound, disordered, morbid, diseased, infected, septic, poisoned, envenomed, incurable, irremediable, measly (Inf), lousy (Inf), grottty (Sl), sleazo (US sl), sleazoid (US sl), gungy (Inf), grungy (US sl), scrungy (Sl), gunky (US sl), manky (Sl), pukey (Sl), pukish (US sl), yucky (Sl), plaguy (*or* plaguey) (Inf)

▶ *743 Poverty, 758 Meanness, 628 Deterioration, 801 Disrepute, 622 Dirtiness, 624 Ill Health*

5 **harmful**, hurtful, injurious, damaging, deleterious, detrimental, prejudicial, disadvantageous, destructive, corrosive, wasting, consuming, pernicious, deadly, fatal, killing, virulent, disastrous, ruinous, calamitous, like the

end of the world, adverse, degenerative, noxious, noisome, malignant, unhealthy, unwholesome, infectious, insalubrious, contaminating, venomous, poisonous, toxic, miasmal, polluting, acid, radioactive, dangerous, unsafe, risky, evil, sinister, ominous, dire, dreadful, baleful, baneful, accursed, devilish, mischievous, spiteful, snide, vindictive, malign, malicious, malevolent, ill-disposed, malefic, mischief-making, puckish, impish, cruel, bloody, bloodthirsty, inhuman, violent, furious, rough, harsh, intolerant, persecuting, oppressive, monstrous, outrageous, bitchy (Inf), full of the devil (Inf), full of Old Nick (Inf)

▶ *244 Destruction, 398 Killing, 687 Adversity, 626 Lack of Hygiene, 633 Danger, 862 Evil, 832 Malevolence, 690 Severity*

6 **damnable**, damned, darned, blasted, confounded, bothersome, execrable, accursed, cursed, diabolic, diabolical, bloody (Sl), dad-blamed (US sl), dad-blasted (US inf), blinking (Inf), dratted (Inf), blankety-blank (Inf), bleeping (*or* blipping) (US inf), infernal (Inf), devilish (Inf), hellish (Inf)

NOUNS

7 **worthlessness**, lack of value, unimportance, insignificance, uselessness, futility

▶ *612 Unimportance, 614 Uselessness*

8 **inferiority**, poor quality, low quality, low grade, low standard, faultiness, fault, flaw, defect, imperfection, shoddiness, tawdriness, trashiness, trash, rubbish, cheapness, badness, incompetence, inefficiency, lack of skill, unskilfulness, clumsiness, bungle, botch, hiccup (Inf), glitch (Sl), blip (Sl), queeb (US sl), crumminess (Sl), tackiness (Inf), junk (Sl), schlock (US sl), crap (Sl), klutziness (US sl)

▶ *127 Inferiority, 620 Imperfection, 656 Unskilfulness*

9 **badness**, bad, nastiness, obnoxiousness, unpleasantness, horridness, evilness, evil, vileness, baseness, grossness, blackness, irredeemability, execrableness, abomination, awfulness, horror, dreadfulness, grimness, onerousness, tediousness, annoyance, distress, viciousness, villainousness, villainy, wickedness, heinousness, depravity, immorality, sinfulness, sin, vice, dishonesty, illegality, crime, wrong, wrongfulness, injustice, ghastliness (Inf), beastliness (Inf), crookedness (Inf)

▶ *764 Unpleasantness, 864 Wickedness, 862 Evil, 844 Wrong, 858 Improbity*

10 **poverty**, meanness, wretchedness, misery, sadness, woe, melancholy, pitifulness, abjectness, contemptibleness, despicableness, disreputability, scruffiness, shabbiness, sordidness, sleaziness, squalidness, squalor, grubbiness, dirtiness, dirt, filthiness, filth, sewer, lowness, indecency, impropriety, coarsenesss, vulgarity, pornography, obscenity, disgrace,

scandal, slur, unworthiness, shame, rottenness, decay, decomposition, putrefaction, putridness, rankness, stink, foulness, fetor, corruption, peccancy, staleness, mouldiness, taint, unsoundness, disorder, morbidity, disease, sickness, cancer, canker, blight, bane, plague, pestilence, scourge, infection, contamination, poison, venom, lousiness (Inf), grottiness (Sl), sleaze (Inf)

▶ *743 Poverty, 758 Meanness, 628 Deterioration, 801 Disrepute, 622 Dirtiness, 624 Ill Health*

11 **harmfulness**, harm, hurtfulness, hurt, injury, ill, damage, detriment, destruction, consumption, perniciousness, deadliness, virulence, disaster, ruin, calamity, the end of the world, adversity, noxiousness, malignancy, unhealthiness, insalubrity, venomousness, poisonousness, toxicity, miasma, pollution, danger, risk, balefulness, banefulness, mischievousness, mischief, spitefulness, spite, vindictiveness, malignity, malice, malevolence, hostility, unkindness, bitterness, rancour, gall, wormwood, suffering, anguish, angst, anxiety, agony, painfulness, pain, sting, ache, pang, cruelty, bloodthirstiness, inhumanity, violence, harshness, severity, intolerance, persecution, oppression, subjection, tyranny, harassment, sexual harassment, maltreatment, ill-treatment, abuse, sexual abuse, child abuse, molestation, child molestation, libel, slander, spell, curse, malediction, the evil eye, jinx, mojo, voodoo, voodoo doll, witchcraft, sorcery, black magic, bad omen, ill wind, evil star, poltergeist, gremlin, dog howling at night (US), hoodoo (Inf)

▶ *244 Destruction, 626 Lack of Hygiene, 406 Physical Pain, 832 Malevolence, 690 Severity*

12 **bad person**, bad character, bad influence, troublemaker, evildoer, evil genius, evil spirit, demon, devil, Satan, Hitler, Stalin, Simon Legree, wicked stepmother, bad fairy, wicked witch, snake in the grass (Inf)

VERBS

13 **be worthless**, have no value, do no good, be in vain, bungle, botch, do badly, make badly, spoil, ruin, hurt, injure, damage, impair, do one a mischief, scathe (Arch or Dial), rot, decay, pollute, contaminate, infect, corrupt, pervert, deprave, do evil, work evil, do wrong, torment, plague, vex, harass, trouble, land one in trouble, spite, thwart, queer one's pitch (Inf), do for (Inf)

▶ *614 Uselessness, 620 Imperfection, 656 Unskilfulness, 832 Malevolence*

14 **ill-treat**, mistreat, maltreat, mishandle, misuse, ill-use, burden, overburden, put upon, tyrannize, oppress, bear down on, tread on, trample (on), trample underfoot, crush, squash, victimize, harass, persecute, abuse, molest, prey upon, hold prisoner, hold as hos-

tage, wrong, aggrieve, distress, torment, torture, agonize, rack, crucify, force, outrage, violate, rape, wound, savage, maul, bite, scratch, tear, stab, pierce, strike, hit, slap, buffet, bruise, batter, spite, take out one's spite on, walk over, wipe one's feet on, wreak one's malice on, libel, slander, ruin, defeat, destroy, dump on (Sl)

▶ *601 Misuse, 406 Physical Pain*

ADVERBS

15 **worthlessly**, badly, ill, wrongly, amisss, nastily, unpleasantly, abominably, wickedly, awfully, cruelly, spitefully, in (*or* with) malice, disgracefully, shamefully, abjectly, contemptibly

619 Perfection

The pursuit of perfection, then, is the pursuit of sweetness and light…He who works for sweetness and light united, works to make reason and the will of God prevail. Matthew Arnold.

What's come to perfection perishes./ Things learned on earth, we shall practise in heaven./ Works done least rapidly, Art most cherishes. Robert Browning.

You would attain to the divine perfection,/ And yet not turn your back upon the world. Henry Wadsworth Longfellow.

Perfection has one grave defect; it is apt to be dull. W. Somerset Maugham.

Finality is death. Perfection is finality. Nothing is perfect. There are lumps in it. James Stephens.

ADJECTIVES

1 **perfect**, perfected, brought to perfection, finished, completed, fulfilled, polished, ripened, ripe, fully ripe, ready, matured, mature, fully mature, exact, just right, just so, ideal, best, flawless, unflawed, faultless, impeccable, infallible, indefectible, without defect, correct, precise, accurate, spot on, irreproachable, immaculate, without a stain, unstained, unspotted, spotless, unblemished, blemish-free, without blemish, unmarked, uncontaminated, untainted, pure, unmixed, unalloyed, blameless, exemplary, guiltless, innocent, impeccant, sinless, godly, saintly, sound, unbroken, uncracked, sound as a bell, right as right can be, right as rain, in perfect condition, undamaged, unmarred, unspoiled (*or* unspoilt), safe and sound, unhurt, unscathed, scatheless (Arch of Dial), unscarred, unscratched, no harm done, tight, airtight, vacuum-packed, watertight, seaworthy, intact, whole, entire, complete, absolute, utter, total, one hundred per cent, undiminished, un-

reduced, without loss, full, excellent, sublime, superb, dazzling, brilliant, masterly, expert, proficient, skilled, skilful, consummate, supreme, transcendent, unsurpassable, unequalled, unmatched, unrivalled, peerless, top, number-one, champion, at the peak of perfection, pattern, standard, model, archetypal, classic, classical, Augustan, in perfect health, in the pink, right as a trivet (Inf), A-OK (Inf), A1 (Inf)

▶ *134 Purity, 617 Worth, 126 Superiority, 865 Innocence, 655 Skill, 142 Whole, 144 Completeness, 623 Health*

2 **perfectionist**, purist, pedantic, precise, punctilious, meticulous, fastidious, scrupulous, particular, exacting, demanding, fussy

NOUNS

3 **perfection**, sheer perfection, perfectness, finish, completion, consummation, polish, ripeness, readiness, maturity, exactness, idealness, the ideal, flawlessness, faultlessness, impeccability, infallibility, indefectability, correctness, correctitude, preciseness, accuracy, irreproachability, immaculacy, immaculateness, spotlessness, purity, blamelessness, guiltlessness, innocence, impeccancy, soundness, perfect condition, wholeness, completeness, excellence, brilliance, mint condition, mastery, expertise, proficiency, skill, superiority, transcendence, essence, quintessence, peak, top, zenith, acme, summit, pinnacle, capstone, height (*or* pitch) of perfection, acme of perfection, peak of perfection, pattern, standard, model, archetype, paragon, *ne plus ultra* (L), ultimate, extreme, last word, crowning achievement, masterpiece, *chef-d'oeuvre* (Fr), flawless performance, ten out of ten, one hundred per cent

4 **perfectionist**, purist, pedant, stickler, perfecter, expert, master, expert mechanic, master painter, master thief, maestro, prima ballerina, *premier danseur* (*or* *première danseuse*) (Fr)

▶ *655 Skill*

VERBS

5 **perfect**, finish, complete, fulfil, realize, accomplish, achieve, execute, carry out, ripen, mature, bring to perfection, consummate, correct, rectify, improve, ameliorate, elaborate, polish, refine, put on the finishing touch, crown

6 **be perfect**, leave nothing to be desired, give a flawless performance, score ten out of ten, score one hundred per cent

ADVERBS

7 **perfectly**, flawlessly, faultlessly, impeccably, exactly, precisely, irreproachably, immaculately, spotlessly, excellently, consummately, to perfection, to just the right degree, to a turn, just as one would wish, verbatim, word for word, to the letter, literally

8 **completely**, wholly, entirely, absolutely, utterly, totally, quite, thoroughly, unequivocally, unambiguously, purely

620 Imperfection

ADJECTIVES

1 **imperfect**, flawed, faulty, defective, not perfect, not (quiet), right, less than perfect, capable of perfection, perfectible, fallible, peccable, irregular, uneven, good and bad, patchy, good in parts, like the curate's egg, unsteady, wobbly, shaky, rickety, weak, vulnerable, bungled, botched, damaged, broken, cracked, leaky, not airtight, not waterproof, unsound, soiled, shopsoiled, stained, spotted, marked, scratched, chipped, blemished, tainted, corked, stale, overripe, past its sell-by date, past its prime, bad, off, off-colour, not in the pink, below par, off form, off stride, unfit, unhealthy, not good enough, unsatisfactory, unacceptable, not up to expectations, not up to the mark, second-best, second-class, third-class, second-rate, third-rate, inferior, poor, unimpressive, worthless, flubbed (US inf), dodgy (Inf)
▶ 793 Blemish, 618 Worthlessness, 656n Unskilfulness, 238 Weakness, 628 Deterioration, 624 Ill Health, 127 Inferiority

2 **incomplete**, deficient, wanting, lacking, inadequate, insufficient, perfunctory, cursory, unthorough, careless, not entire, partial, fragmentary, unfilled, half-filled, unequipped, undermanned, short-staffed, short-handed, below strength, unfinished, half-finished, makeshift, jerry-built, rough and ready, provisional, raw, crude, untrained, scratch, immature, undeveloped, unpolished, unrefined, overwrought, overelaborated, overdone, exaggerated
▶ 145 Incompleteness, 468 Inattention, 609 Insufficiency, 358 Shortfall

3 **deformed**, distorted, warped, twisted, handicapped, disabled, blind, deaf, dumb, mute, deaf and dumb, deaf-mute, mutilated, maimed, armless, legless, lame, halt (Arch), crippled

4 **ordinary**, middling, average, median, everyday, commonplace, mediocre, much of a muchness, middle-of-the-road, moderate, unheroic, only passable, tolerable, bearable, better than nothing, so-so (Inf), wet (Inf)
▶ 124 Average

NOUNS

5 **imperfection**, imperfectness, faultiness, defectiveness, room for improvement, possibility of perfection, perfectibility, fallibility, peccability, erroneousness, error, peccadillo, bungle, botch, irregularity, unevenness, patchiness, curate's egg, adulteration, weakness, vulnerability, frailty, failure, damage, unsoundness, staleness, overripeness, unfitness, infirmity, ill health, inferiority, worthlessness, second class, third class, second rate, third rate, low standard, minimum requirement, passing grade, incompleteness, deficiency, want, lack, need, requirement, shortfall, inadequacy, insufficiency, perfunctoriness, cursoriness, lack of thoroughness, carelessness, underachievement, immaturity, unripeness, rawness, crudeness, undevelopment, underdevelopment, Third World, deformity, distortion, blindness, deafness, lameness
▶ 504 Error, 624 Ill Health, 127 Inferiority, 618 Worthlessness, 145 Incompleteness, 609 Insufficiency, 358 Shortfall, 309 Distortion

6 **imperfect item**, second, reject, misshape, shopsoiled item, not one's best, second best, poor effort, weak effort, inferior version, poor relation, missing link, incomplete set, broken set, makeshift, stopgap, *pis aller* (Fr), consolation, substitute

7 **defect**, fault, flaw, blemish, mark, taint, stain, blot, spot, smudge, scratch, chip, tear, mistake, error, rift, leak, loophole, crack, chink, lacuna, gap, deficiency, lack, limitation, shortfall, kink, quirk, idiosyncrasy, eccentricity, foible, failing, shortcoming, weakness, weak point, weak link in the chain, blind spot, soft spot, soft underbelly, tragic flaw, feet of clay, vulnerable point, chink in one's armour, Achilles' heel, soft heart, disability, handicap, disadvantage, difficulty, drawback, catch, snag, hindrance, obstacle, hang-up (Inf), fly in the ointment, loose screw (Inf)
▶ 793 Blemish, 504 Error, 265 Interval, 358 Shortfall, 510 Insanity, 661 Hindrance

8 **ordinariness**, averageness, mediocrity, nothing to speak of, nothing to write home about, nothing earthshattering (Inf), no great shakes (Inf)
▶ 124 Average

VERBS

9 **be imperfect**, have a fault, fall short, fall short of perfection, not live up to expectations, not impress, not bear inspection, not pass muster, fail, fail the test, not make the grade, dissatisfy, not suffice, barely pass, scrape through, have a chink in one's armour, show one's Achilles' heel, have feet of clay, have a crack, not hold water, leak
▶ 793 Blemish, 358 Shortfall, 609 Insufficiency, 766 Dissatisfaction

10 **leave imperfect**, finish halfway, leave unfinished, make a weak effort

ADVERBS

11 **imperfectly**, defectively, below par, irregularly, unevenly, incompletely, insufficiently, to a limited extent, barely, scarcely, almost, not quite, all but, with all its faults

621 Cleanness

NOUNS

1 **cleanness**, keeping clean, freedom from dirt, absence of dirt, immaculateness, spotlessness, freshness, dewiness, purity, whiteness, shine, polish, cleanliness, daintiness, fastidiousness, spit and polish (Inf)
▶ *446 Whiteness, 134 Purity*

2 **cleaning**, spring-cleaning, housecleaning (US), cleaning up, clearing up, tidying, washing-up, wiping up, mopping up, scrubbing, dusting, sweeping, vacuuming, hoovering, polishing, washing, laundry, dry-cleaning, washing out, flushing out, dialysis, cleansing, purification, purging, defecation, excretion, purgative, laxative, aperient, enema, freshening, ventilation, airing, deodorization, fumigation, desalination, decontamination, disinfestation, delousing, disinfection, sterilization, antisepsis, asepsis, chlorination, pasteurization, refining, distillation, clarification, filtration, percolation, hygiene, sanitation, drainage, plumbing, sewerage
▶ *622 Dirtiness, 353 Excretion, 625 Hygiene*

3 **religious cleansing**, purification, baptism, Asperges, sprinkling of water, lustration, purgation, Purgatory
▶ *10 Ritual*

4 **censorship**, expurgation, bowdlerization, blue-pencilling, editing, cleaning-up

5 **ablutions**, washing, wash, toilet, hygiene, oral hygiene, lavage, lavation (Fml), lick (and a promise), bathing, dipping, dip, plunge, rinsing, soaking, soaping, lathering, shampoo

6 **bath**, hot bath, hot tub, cold bath, bubble bath, steam bath, vapour bath, Turkish bath, sauna, Jacuzzi (Tm), sponge bath, blanket bath, foot bath, shower, hot shower, cold shower, douche, bath, bathtub (US), tub (US), hip bath, plunge bath, bidet, basin, washbasin, washbowl, washstand, basin and pitcher, basin and ewer, bathroom, washroom, baths, public baths, Turkish baths, thermae, sudatorium, swimming bath(s), swimming pool, natatorium

7 **washer**, washing machine, twin-tub, washer-drier, washtub, washboard, dolly (Dial), copper, boiler, laundrette, dishwasher, car wash

8 **laundry**, wash, washing, dirty clothes, dirty linen, dirty dishes, washing up

9 **cleaning agent**, cleansing agent, cleaner, cleanser, purifier, antiseptic, disinfectant, carbolic acid, phenol, bleach, freshener, air freshener, room freshener, deodorant, soda, washing soda, baking soda (US), detergent, washing powder, soap, scented soap, toilet soap, guest soap, soap flakes, soap powder, washing-up liquid, soap and water, water, hot water, shampoo, bubble bath, shower gel, cleansing cream, body lotion, hand lotion, face cream, cold cream, mouthwash, gargle, toothpaste, dentifrice, dental powder, abrasive, pumice, pumice stone, hearthstone, holystone, scouring powder, scouring pad, soap pad, polish, furniture polish, floor polish, shoe polish, boot polish, blacking, whiting, wax, varnish, whitewash, paint, graphite, black lead

10 **cleaning object**, broom, besom, mop, sponge, swab, scourer, strigil, dishcloth gourd, loofah, duster, feather duster, whisk, brush, scrubbing brush, shoe brush, clothes brush, lint remover, nailbrush, toothbrush, toothpick, dental floss, hairbrush, comb, pocket comb, dog brush, dustpan and brush, carpet sweeper, vacuum cleaner, Hoover (Tm), roadsweeper, snowplough, bin, dustbin, rubbish bin, litter bin, waste disposal unit, compactor, poop-scoop, doormat, boot-scraper, squeegee, squilgee, pipe cleaner, pull through, reamer, windscreen wiper, screen, sieve, riddle, strainer, filter, air filter, oil filter, fuel filter, water filter, blotter, eraser, rubber, rake, hoe, sprinkler, waterworks, sewer, drainpipe, waste pipe

11 **cleaning cloth**, duster, dishcloth, dishclout (Dial), dishrag (US), J-cloth (Tm), tea towel, chamois (leather), shammy (leather), leather, flannel, face flannel, facecloth, towel, bath towel, hand towel, handkerchief, paper handkerchief, tissue, Kleenex (Tm), toilet paper, toilet tissue, toilet roll, lavatory paper, apron, bib, (table) napkin, serviette, place mat, tablemat, doily (or doyley), tablecloth, mat, drugget, cover, chair cover, dust cover, dustsheet, bog roll (Sl), pinny (Inf)

12 **cleaner**, dry-cleaner, launderer, laundress, laundryman (or -woman), washerman, washwoman, washerwoman, dhobi, scrubber, swabber, washer-up, dishwasher, scullion (Arch), charwoman, charlady, housecleaner (US), housemaid, maid, domestic servant, domestic help, domestic, help, daily help, daily, home help, scavenger, street cleaner, sweeper, dustman, refuse collector, dustman, lavatory attendant, sanitary engineer, chimney sweep (or sweeper), window cleaner, bootblack, shoe-black, shoeshiner (US), shoeshine boy (US), barber, hairdresser, beautician, gleaner, picker, beachcomber, scavenger bird, crow, vulture, turkey buzzard, buzzard, char (Inf), Mrs Mop (Inf)

VERBS

13 **clean**, make clean, keep clean, remove the dirt, make immaculate, make fresh, freshen, freshen up, disinfect, phenolate, carbolize, spring-clean, clean up, clean out, clear, clear up, clear out, spruce, spruce up, groom, valet, make neat, neaten, tidy, make tidy, trim,

shave, wash, wash clean, wash up, wash off, wash out, wash down, wipe, wipe clean, wipe up, wipe off (*or* away), sponge, sponge off, mop, mop up, swab, scrub, scour, do the cleaning, dust, whisk, sweep, sweep up, beat, vacuum, hoover, brush, brush up, brush off, comb, polish, shine, buff, black, black lead, whiten, whitewash, bleach, launder, do the washing, do the laundry, starch, iron, dry-clean, erase, rub out, obliterate, strip, strip clean, pick clean, rake out, muck out, make a clean sweep, flush, flush out, sandblast, holy-stone, scrape, rub, dry, drip-dry, tumble-dry, wring, wring out, mangle

▶ *152 Arrangement, 446 Whiteness, 439 Light, 546 Obliteration*

14 **bathe**, take a bath, have a bath, dip, dunk, rinse, soak, steep, soap, lather, shampoo, shower, take a shower, have a shower, douche, sluice, swill (out), drench

▶ *389 Water, 391 Moisture*

15 **purify**, purge, censor, expurgate, bowdlerize, blue-pencil, edit out, clean up, sublimate, el-evate, cleanse, wash, lave (Arch), lustrate, pu-rify oneself, wash one's hands of, freshen, air, ventilate, fan, deodorize, fumigate, edulcor-ate, desalt, desalinate, desalinize, disinfect, de-contaminate, sterilize, antisepticize, chlori-nate, pasteurize, sanitize, free from impurities, depurate, refine, distil, clarify, rack, skim, scum, despumate, decarbonize, elutriate, de-cant, strain, filter, percolate, lixiviate, leach, sift, sieve, eliminate, sort out, weed out, flush out, dialyse, catheterize, clean out, wash out, drain

▶ *134 Purity, 625 Hygiene*

ADJECTIVES

16 **clean**, not dirty, dirt-free, unsoiled, unsullied, undefiled, virginal, untainted, unmuddied, untarnished, unstained, immaculate, spotless, stainless, blank, perfect, cleanly, dainty, nice, fastidious, fresh, dewy, pure, unmixed, un-adulterated, unpolluted, uncontaminated, hy-gienic, sanitary, sterile, aseptic, antiseptic, sa-lubrious, spruce, dapper, well-groomed, neat, tidy, spick-and-span, orderly, bright, shining, white, snowy, kosher, ritually clean, ritually prepared, untouched, clean as a whistle, fresh as a daisy, bright as a new pin, bright as silver, white as snow, natty (Inf)

▶ *446 Whiteness, 439 Light, 619 Perfection, 134 Purity, 625 Hygiene*

17 **cleaned**, freshened, disinfected, cleaned up, cleaned out, trimmed, shaven, washed, scrub-bed, scoured, swept, brushed, polished, whitened, bleached, laundered, starched, ironed, cleansed, purified, purged, expur-gated, decontaminated, sterilized, pasteurized, refined, distilled, filtered

18 **cleansing**, lustral, purificatory, disinfectant,

hygienic, sanitary, purgative, purgatory, cleaning, detergent, abstergent, ablutionary, balneal

ADVERBS

19 **cleanly**, spotlessly, hygienically, neatly, ti-dily

20 **clean**, altogether, wholly, entirely, totally, completely, utterly, absolutely, quite

622 Dirtiness

NOUNS

1 **dirtiness**, uncleanness, soiling, defilement, muckiness, grubbiness, griminess, filthiness, duskness, pollution, foulness, squalidity, squalidness, squalor, sleaziness, slumminess, untidiness, slovenliness, sluttishness, black-ness, dinginess, messiness, muddiness, slimi-ness, miriness, encrustation, turbidity, cloudi-ness, mustiness, mouldiness

▶ *858 Improbity*

2 **uncleanness**, unholiness, profanity, corrup-tion, impurity, coarseness, sepsis, infection, contamination, foulness, abomination, stink, stench, fetor, excretion, dirty habits, beastli-ness, wallowing, scruffiness, shabbiness, pe-diculosis, phthiriasis, rot, decomposition, pu-trefaction, putrescence, taint

▶ *626 Lack of Hygiene, 419 Stench, 353 Excretion*

3 **obscenity**, rudeness, indecency, ribaldry, smuttiness, scatology, pornography, dirty joke, dirty book, dirty magazine, dirty film, salaciousness, prurience, lewdness, lasciviious-ness, licentiousness, porn (Inf)

▶ *877 Immorality*

4 **dirt**, muck, grime, filth, stain, mark, patch, spot, blot, smudge, smear, mud, mire, quag-mire, bog, soil, earth, clay, loam, dung, ma-nure, ordure, faeces, excrement, stool, night soil, droppings, guano, mucus, nasal mucus, snot, pus, matter, dust, mote, smut, soot, smoke, grounds, grouts, dregs, lees, draff, sweepings, scourings, offscourings, shavings, leavings, leftovers, residue, residuum, sedi-ment, sedimentation, deposit, sludge, slime, ooze, goo, mullock (Aus), precipitate, fur, scum, froth, dross, scoria, ash, cinder, clinker, slag, castoff, castoff skin, exuviae, slough, dan-druff, scurf, scales, tartar, plaque, feculence, litter, rubbish, garbage (US), trash (US), refuse, rot, dry rot, wet rot, rust, mildew, mould, fungus, decay, carrion, offal, vermin, flea, nit, louse, cobweb, shit (Tab sl), crap (Tab sl), crud (Sl), gunk (Sl), grunge (US sl), gunge (Inf), yuck (Sl)

▶ *353 Excretion, 607 Waste*

5 **swill**, pigswill, slops, hogwash, bilge water, bilge, dishwater, ditchwater, stagnant water, dirty water, sewage, sewerage, drainage, wal-low, hog-wallow, slough, slosh

6 **dirty person**, chimney sweep, coalman, car mechanic, mud-wrestler, slut, sloven, slattern, drab (Arch), litterbug, litter lout, ragamuffin, urchin, street Arab, street urchin (US), scavenger, beachcomber, beggar, homeless person, vagrant, tramp, hobo (US), bog lady, beast, pig, wallower, obscene person, dirty old man, purveyor of filth, teller of dirty jokes, slammock (Arch sl), draggletail (Sl), mudlark (Sl), bum (US inf)

ADJECTIVES

7 **dirty**, not clean, unclean, uncleaned, soiled, defiled, mucky, grubby, grimy, filthy, dusty, sooty, smoky, polluted, unwashed, unwiped, unscrubbed, unscoured, unrinsed, unswept, littered, foul, fouled, befouled, squalid, sleazy, slummy, untidy, unkempt, bedraggled, frowzy, slatternly, slovenly, sluttish, black, dingy, unpolished, unburnished, tarnished, stained, spotted, smudged, besmirched, besmeared, messy, greasy, oily, muddy, slimy, miry, begrimed, clotted, caked, matted, encrusted, dirt-encrusted, mud-dried, thick, turbid, cloudy, murky, furred up, clogged, scummy, musty, mouldy, fusty, cobwebby

▶ 858 Improbity

8 **unclean**, unhallowed, unholy, profane, corrupt, impure, coarse, unrefined, unpurified, septic, festering, poisonous, toxic, unsterilized, nonsterile, insanitary, unhygienic, infectious, contaminated, insalubrious, unhealthy, offensive, foul, nasty, abominable, disgusting, repulsive, noisome, nauseous, nauseating, malodorous, stinking, stinky, fetid, uncleanly, unfastidious, beastly, hoggish, sordid, squalid, scruffy, shabby, scurfy, leprous, scabby, mangy, pediculous, crawling, faecal, dungy, stercoraceous, excremental, excrementitious, carious, rotting, rotted, tainted, flyblown, maggoty, carrion, grotty (Sl), manky (Sl), yuck (Sl), yucky (or yukky) (Sl), ponging (Inf), pongy (Inf), flea-bitten (Inf), lousy (Sl)

▶ 626 Lack of Hygiene, 419 Stench, 353 Excretion

9 **obscene**, dirty, filthy, rude, indecent, risque, ribald, smutty, scatological, pornographic, blue, adult, near the knuckle, salacious, prurient, lewd, lascivious, licentious, scabrous

▶ 877 Immorality

VERBS

10 **be dirty**, get dirty, collect dust, foul up, clog, rust, mildew, moulder, fester, have gangrene, gangrene, mortify, putrefy, decay, rot, go bad, go off, addle, grow rank, smell, stink, wallow, roll in the dirt (or mud)

11 **dirty**, make dirty, make unclean, soil, defile, foul, befoul, grime, begrime, cover with dust, stain, spot, patch, maculate (Arch), blot, sully, tarnish, blacken, untidy, make a mess (of), mess up, daub, smear, besmear, smirch, besmirch, smudge, blur, streak, grease, cake, clot, clog, muddy, bemire, beslime, roil, rile, draggle, bedraggle, drabble, spatter, bespatter, splash, slobber, slaver, poison, taint, corrupt, pollute, contaminate, infect, profane, desecrate, unhallow, much up (Inf)

ADVERBS

12 **dirtily**, grubbily, untidily, sluttishly, messily, mustily, uncleanly, coarsely, offensively, sordidly, obscenely, rudely, indecently, salaciously, pruriently, lewdly, lasciviously

623 Health

ADJECTIVES

1 **healthy**, fit, well, fine, sound, in health, in good health, bursting with health, fighting fit, eupeptic, fresh, thriving, flourishing, blooming, glowing, ruddy, rosy, rosy-cheeked, florid, hale, hearty, hale and hearty, bouncing, bonny, lusty, energetic, full of vitality, vigorous, of good constitution, never ill, strong, strong as a horse, strong as an ox, strapping, robust, hardy, sturdy, stalwart, fit and ready, in condition, in good condition, in good shape, in good heart, in peak condition, in tip-top condition, in A1 condition, in the pink, in fine fettle, on form, in fine form, in trim, in fine trim, in fine (or high) feather, feeling well, feeling fine, feeling good, feeling great, feeling like a million dollars (US), fit as a fiddle, sound in wind and limb, sound as a bell, fresh as a daisy, a picture of health, getting well, convalescent, on the mend, on the up-grade, on the up and up, on one's legs, up and about, cured, healed, restored to health, pretty good, not bad, in fair health, fair to middling, no worse, comfortable, holding one's own, as well as can be expected, safe and sound, unharmed, full of beans (Inf), full of steam (Inf), all steamed up (Inf), in good nick (Inf)

▶ 239 Vigour, 237 Strength, 630 Remedy, 629 Repair

2 **healthful**, health-giving, wholesome, good for one, nutritious, nourishing, tonic, bracing, invigorating, hygienic, sanitary, salubrious, salutary, beneficial

▶ 625 Hygiene

NOUNS

3 **health**, good health, glowing health, robust health, rude health, healthiness, fitness, well-being, physical well-being, soundness, trim, form, condition, good condition, tip-top condition, pink of condition, heartiness, constitution, good constitution, iron constitution, strength, vigour, health and strength, energy, vitality, robustness, bloom, ruddy complexion, rosiness, rosy cheeks, apple cheeks, eupepsia, haleness, *mens sana in corpore sano* (L), incorruption, incorruptibility, long life, lon-

gevity, ripe old age, shape, tone, fettle, state, healthy state, clean bill of health, goddess of health, Hygeia, recuperation, convalescence

▶ *239 Vigour, 237 Strength, 630 Remedy, 629 Repair*

4 **healthfulness**, wholesomeness, goodness, nutritiousness, hygiene, salubriousness, salubrity

▶ *625 Hygiene*

VERBS

5 **be healthy**, mind one's health, look after oneself, take care of oneself, feel well, feel fine, feel good, feel great, feel like a million dollars (US), have never felt better, look young, wear well, be well-preserved, bloom, thrive, flourish, have a clean bill of health, enjoy good health, brim with good health, be in the pink, keep (up) one's health, keep fit, keep well, keep body and soul together, keep on one's legs

6 **get healthy**, get well, recover, recover one's health, return to health, recuperate, feel (*or* look) like oneself again, get the colour back in one's cheeks, respond to treatment, mend, convalesce, become convalescent, get back on one's feet, take a fresh (*or* new) lease on (*or* of) life, become a new man (*or* woman), bounce back (Inf)

▶ *627 Improvement*

7 **make healthy**, make well, treat, cure, heal, revive, restore, restore to health, put the colour back in one's cheeks

▶ *630 Remedy, 629 Repair, 60 Medicine*

ADVERBS

8 **healthily**, heartily, healthfully, nutritiously, hygienically, salubriously

624 Ill Health

NOUNS

1 **ill health**, bad health, poor health, delicate health, failing health, unhealthiness, delicacy, weak constitution, lack of fitness, lack of strength, weakness, weakliness, infirmity, debility, diathesis, sickness, loss of condition, manginess, morbidity, illness, sickness, indisposition, cachexia, chronic illness, chronic complaint, allergy, hay fever, catarrh, chronic ill health, invalidism, valetudinarianism, hypochondria, nerves, neurosis, seediness (Inf)

▶ *238 Weakness, 650 Fatigue, 510 Insanity, 628 Deterioration*

2 **illness**, disease, disorder, sickness, ailment, indisposition, malady, distemper, affliction, complaint, disability, handicap, infirmity, weakness, condition, history of illness, bout of sickness, visitation, attack, acute attack, spasm, stroke, seizure, apoplexy, fit, shock, virus, poisoning, blood poisoning, food poisoning, metal poisoning, lead poisoning, com-

plication, terminal illness, terminal disease, fatal illness, coma, death, sickbed, deathbed, bug (Inf)

▶ *397 Death*

3 **symptom**, sign, sign of illness, indication, syndrome, rash, spots, sore, blister, discharge, congestion, breathing difficulty, hoarseness, sore throat, cough, lack of appetite, weight loss, weakness, fatigue, malaise, depression, numbness, diarrhoea, nausea, waves of nausea, queasiness, queasy stomach, vomiting, inflammation, swelling, lump, growth, tumour, carcinoma, temperature, high temperature, feverishness, fever, calenture, pyrexia, hyperpyrexia, hyperthermia, hyperthermy, delirium, ague, chill, hypothermia, shivers, shakes, spasm, pain, headache, splitting headache, migraine, dizziness, fainting, loss of consciousness, breakdown, collapse, unconsciousness, insensibility, prostration, stiffness, paralysis, bleeding, high blood pressure, hypertension, low blood pressure, hypotension

▶ *406 Physical Pain, 404 Insensibility, 650 Fatigue*

4 **disease**, notifiable disease, epidemic disease, endemic disease, congenital disease, infectious disease, contagious disease, communicable disease, tropical disease, deficiency disease, malnutrition, anorexia nervosa, bulimia nervosa, avitaminosis, kwashiorkor, beriberi, pellagra, rickets, scurvy, degenerative disease, debilitating disease, wasting disease, musuclar dystrophy, marasmus, atrophy, killer disease, AIDS (acquired immune deficiency syndrome), cancer, neoplastic disease, traumatic disease, trauma, organic disease, goitre, functional disease, circulatory disease, neurological disease, nervous disease, epilepsy, falling sickness, brain disease, mental disorder, musculoskeletal disease, cardiovascular disease, cardiopulmonary disease, heart disease, cardiac disease, coronary thrombosis, fibrosis, haematopoietic disease, endocrine disease, hyperthyroidism, diabetes, urogenital disease, venereal disease, sexually transmitted disease (STD), syphilis, gonorrhoea, herpes simplex, dermatological disease, skin cancer, respiratory disease, asthma, gastrointestinal disease, gastroenteritis, virus disease, influenza, lentivirus disease, retrovirus disease, leukaemia, bacterial disease, diarrhoea, waterborne disease, typhoid fever, febrile disease, febrile seizure, sweating sickness, hydrocele, dropsy, occupational disease, alcoholism, alcohol abuse, drug addiction, unknown disease, the crud (Sl)

▶ *510 Insanity*

5 **plague**, pest, scourge, bane, pestilence, infection, contagion, epidemic, pandemic, pneumonic plague, bubonic plague, Black Death

▶ *631 Blight*

6 **infection**, contagion, pollution, miasma, taint, infectiousness, contagiousness, toxicity, toxin, poisonousness, poisoning, poison, sepsis, purulence, suppuration, festering, gangrene, plague spot, trouble spot, hotbed, vector, host, carrier, germ-carrier, parasite, worm, toxocariasis, virus, lentivirus, retrovirus, HIV (human immunodeficiency virus), bacillus, bacterium, bacteria, germ, pathogen, blood poisoning, toxaemia, septicaemia, pyaemia, food poisoning, ptomaine poisoning, botulism, gastroenteritis, cholera, cold, common cold, influenza, diphtheria, pneumonia, viral pneumonia, infective hepatitis, tuberculosis (TB), consumption, measles, German measles, rubella, rubeola, roseola, whooping cough, pertussis, mumps, chickenpox, smallpox, variola, scarlet fever, scarlatina, fever, malarial fever, malaria, typhus, jail fever, trench fever, typhoid, paratyphoid, glandular fever, infectious mononucleosis, mono, poliomyelitis, polio, meningitis, ME (myalgic encephalomyelitis), encephalitis, encephalitis lethargica, sleeping sickness, tetanus, lockjaw, rabies, hydrophobia, flu (Inf), kissing disease (Inf)

▶ *626 Lack of Hygiene*

7 **tropical disease**, fever, malarial fever, malaria, ague, cholera, Asiatic cholera, yellow fever, blackwater fever, miliary fever, sweating sickness, breakbone fever, dengue, Lassa fever, green monkey disease, kala-azar, visceral leishmaniasis, trypanosomiasis, (South) American trypanosomiasis, Chagas' disease, (African) sleeping sickness, sleepy sickness, encephalitis lethargica, schistosomiasis, bilharziasis, ascariasis, ancylostomiasis, hookworm disease, trachoma, glaucoma, onchocerciasis, river blindness, framboesia, yaws, leprosy, dhobi itch, Hansen's disease, beriberi, kwashiorkor

8 **indigestion**, gastralgia, upset stomach, stomach ache, cramp, colic, gripes, acidity, hyperacidity, acidosis, heartburn, pyrosis, cardialgia, dyspepsia, liverishness, biliousness, nausea, vomiting, retching, stomach ulcer, peptic ulcer, gastric ulcer, duodenal ulcer, stomach cancer, bowel cancer, gastritis, enteritis, regional enteritis, Crohn's disease, colitis, duodenitis, dysentery, cholera, food poisoning, ptomaine poisoning, botulism, flatulence, flatus, gas, defecation, diarrhoea, constipation, stomach flu (Inf), bellyache (Inf), collywobbles (Sl), butterflies (Inf), wind (Inf), the trots (Inf), the runs (Inf), Montezuma's revenge (Sl), gyppy (*or* gippy tummy) (Sl)

▶ *353 Excretion, 349 Expulsion*

9 **respiratory disease**, cough, smoker's cough, cold, common cold, head cold, runny nose, watering eyes, catarrh, coryza, rhinitis, rhinorrhoea, sinusitis, influenza, sore throat, swollen adenoids, tonsillitis, pharyngitis, laryngitis, tracheitis, croup, bronchitis, asthma, emphysema, pleurisy, pneumonia, bronchopneumonia, legionnaire's disease, diphtheria, whooping cough, pertussis, lung cancer, asbestosis, silicosis, pneumoconiosis, anthracosis, black lung (disease), cystic fibrosis, tuberculosis (TB), pulmonary phthisis, consumption, flu (Inf), crying cold (Inf)

10 **cardiovascular disease**, heart disease, heart condition, heart trouble, bad heart, weak heart, coronary heart disease, rheumatic heart disease, cardiac disease, carditis, endocarditis, myocarditis, pericarditis, angina pectoris, angina, chest-pain, chest-spasm, breast-pang, brachycardia, tachycardia, galloping (*or* gallop) rhythm, palpitation, dyspnoea, vulvulitis, valvular lesion, mitral stenosis, cardiac hypertrophy, enlarged heart, athlete's heart, fatty degeneration of the heart, cardiac arrest, heart attack, heart failure, coronary thrombosis, coronary, myocardial infarction, stroke, blood pressure, high blood pressure, hypertension, low blood pressure, hypotension, vascular disease, atheroma, aneurysm (*or* aneurism), hardening of the arteries, arteriosclerosis, arteritis, phlebitis, varicose veins, thrombosis, clot, blood-clot, embolism, infarction

11 **blood disease**, anaemia, aplastic anaemia, haemolytic anaemia, anaemia, pernicious anaemia, sickle-cell anaemia, sickle-cell disease (US), leukaemia, lymphoma, Hodgkin's disease, haemophilia, bleeding, internal bleeding, haemorrhage, bleeder's disease (Inf)

12 **cancer**, neoplasm, growth, cancerous growth, primary growth, secondary growth, tumour, benign tumour, innocent tumour, malignant tumour, cancerous tumour, carcinoma, sarcoma, epithelioma, melanoma, skin cancer, breast cancer, throat cancer, lung cancer, stomach cancer, bone cancer, brain cancer, cervical cancer, prostate cancer, cancer of the pancreas, leukaemia, the big C (Inf)

13 **skin disease**, dermatitis, cutaneous disease, skin lesion, scabies, erythema, leucoderma, vitiligo, albinism, lupus, yaws, framboesia, leprosy, eczema, mange, miliaria, heat rash, prickly heat, erysipelas, St Anthony's fire, impetigo, herpes, herpes zoster, shingles, serpigo, ringworm, prurigo, pruritis, itch, dhobi itch, formication, urticaria, hives, nettle rash, rash, eruption, breaking out, athlete's foot, acne, spot, pimple, blackhead, pustule, cyst, blister, wart, verruca, swelling, blemish, macula, mole, freckle, birthmark, pockmark, variola, smallpox, chickenpox, cowpox, melanoma, skin cancer, tetter (Inf)

▶ *407 Touch, 793 Blemish, 316 Convexity*

14 **venereal disease**, VD, sexual disease, sexually transmitted disease (STD), social disease,

AIDS (acquired immune deficiency syndrome), AIDS-related complex, syphilis, gonorrhoea, NSU (nonspecific urethritis), herpes, herpes simplex, venereal ulcer, chancre, syphilitic sore, the French disease (Inf), (the) clap (Sl), (the) scrud (US sl), dose (Sl), crabs (Sl), lobstertails (US sl)

15 **ulcer**, ulceration, gathering, festering, purulence, inflammation, sore, abscess, boil, carbuncle, fistula, cyst, blain, chilblain, kibe (Arch), corn, hard corn, soft corn, swelling, gangrene, rot, decay, discharge, pus, matter

▶ *141 Disintegration*

16 **rheumatism**, rheumatics, rheumatic fever, muscular rheumatism, myalgia, fibrositis, tennis elbow, bursitis, frozen shoulder, prepatella bursitis, housemaid's knee, RSI (repetitive strain injury), arthritis, rheumatoid arthritis, gout, osteoarthritis, degenerative joint disease, lumbago, slipped disc, pulled muscle

17 **nervous disorder**, nervous breakdown, neuralgia, sciatica, neurilemma, seizure, paralysis, general paralysis, quadriplegia, tetraplegia, hemiplegia, diplegia, bilateral paralysis, paraplegia, atrophy, numbness, insensibility, partial paralysis, general paresis, paresis, palsy, cerebral palsy, tic, tic douloureux, trigeminal neuralgia, twitch, tremor, spasm, petit mal, grand mal, epilepsy, falling sickness, infantile paralysis, poliomyelitis, polio, spina bifida, paralysis agitans, Parkinson's disease, chorea, Huntingdon's chorea, St Vitus'(s) dance, multiple sclerosis (MS), disseminated sclerosis, muscular dystrophy, myasthenia gravis, myasthenia, motor neurone disease

▶ *404 Insensibility, 366 Agitation*

18 **veterinary disease**, mange, rabies, distemper, canine distemper, hard pad, equine distemper, strangles, BSE (bovine spongiform encephalopathy), mad-cow disease, scrapie, foot-and-mouth disease, hoof-and-mouth disease, swine fever, swinepox, variola porcina, myxomatosis, rinderpest, murrain, anthrax, blackleg, sheeprot, bloat, liver fluke, worms, megrims, staggers, glanders, farcy, sweeny, spavin, thrust, parrot fever, psittacosis

19 **sick person**, invalid, patient, hospital patient, nursing home patient, paediatric patient, geriatric patient, in-patient, out-patient, shut-in (US), sufferer, case, stretcher case, hospital case, mental case, chronic invalid, valetudinarian, hypochondriac, malingerer, martyr to ill health, weakling, consumptive, asthmatic, bronchitic, dyspeptic, diabetic, haemophiliac, bleeder, insomniac, neuropath, addict, drug addict, alcoholic, spastic, arthritic, paralytic, paraplegic, quadriplegic, hemiplegic, disabled person, cripple, (old) crock (Sl)

▶ *510 Insanity, 238 Weakness*

20 **pathology**, forensic pathology, diagnosis, prognosis, etiology, nosology, epidemiology, bacteriology, parasitology, therapy

▶ *60 Medicine, 630 Remedy*

ADJECTIVES

21 **unhealthy**, ill, unfit, unsound, sickly, infirm, decrepit, weakly, weak, tired, fatigued, exhausted, run down, delicate, of weak constitution, prone to sickness, liable to illness, chronically ill, chronically sick, always ill, invalid, valetudinarian, hypochondriac, mangy, undernourished, underfed, anorexic, malnourished, emaciated, sallow, wan, pale, white, pale as a ghost, white as a sheet, peaked, peaky, anaemic, colourless, jaundiced, yellow, bilious, green

▶ *238 Weakness, 650 Fatigue, 445 Colourlessness*

22 **sick**, ill, unwell, not well, not in good health, in bad health, in poor health, in poor condition, in poor shape, in a bad way, bad, poorly, peaky, below par, indisposed, out of sorts, off-colour, drooping, flagging, pining, languishing, wasting away, in a decline, squeamish, queer, queasy, nauseated, ailing, showing signs of, showing symptoms of, coming down with, off one's food, refusing to eat, feverish, headachy, confined, quarantined, shut in, bedridden, (flat) on one's back, prostrate, in bed, taking it easy, in hospital, hospitalized, on the sick list, invalided, seized, taken ill, taken bad, collapsed, comatose, in a coma, on the danger list, in intensive care, in ICU, not allowed visitors, serious, critical, chronic, incurable, terminal, inoperable, mortally ill, dying, near death, moribund, crummy (Sl), shitty (Tab sl), like death warmed up (Inf), in bad nick (Inf), out of kilter (Inf), under the weather (Inf), seedy (Inf), groggy (Inf), grotty (Sl), green around the gills (Inf), laid up (Inf)

23 **diseased**, infected, contaminated, tainted, affected, stricken, plague-stricken, distempered, disordered, pathological, pathogenic, morbid, morbific, peccant, insalubrious, unhygienic, iatrogenic, psychosomatic, vitiated, rotten, rotting, gangrenous, decaying, decomposed, infectious, contagious, poisonous, toxic, festering, purulent, degenerative, consumptive, phthistic, tuberculous, tubercular, diabetic, dropsical, hydrocephalic, hydrocephalous, anaemic, bloodless, leukaemic, haemophilic, arthritic, rheumatic, rheumatoid, rheumaticky, rickety, palsied, paralysed, paralytic, spastic, epileptic, leprous, carninomatous, carcinomatoid, cancerous, cankerous, oncogenic, oncogenous, carcinogenic, syphilitic, venereal, swollen, oedematous (or oedematose), gouty, bronchial, bronchitic, throaty, croupy, sniffly, snuffly, asthmatic, allergic, pyretic, febrile, fevered, feverish, delirious, shivering, aguish, sore, tender, painful, ulcerous, ulcerated, inflamed, rashy, spotty,

erysipelatous, spavined, mangy
▶ *141 Disintegration, 406 Physical Pain*

VERBS
24 be unhealthy, be ill, have poor health, ail, suffer, labour under, undergo treatment for, have a complaint, have an affliction, not feel well, feel ill, feel bad, feel rotten, come over all queer, complain of, feel sick, vomit, sicken, fall sick, fall ill, catch, catch an infection, contract a disease, go down with, break out in, have an attack, have a heart attack, have a stroke, collapse, faint, take to one's bed, go to hospital, be hospitalized, become a patient, become an in-patient, become an out-patient, go off sick, be invalided out, languish, pine, peak, droop, go into a decline, lose strength, weaken, grow weak, fail, flag, drop, sink, fade away, deteriorate, get worse, feel like hell (Sl), be laid up (Inf), waste away (Inf)
▶ *349 Expulsion, 628 Deterioration, 238 Weakness*

ADVERBS
25 unhealthily, weakly, chronically, morbidly, pathologically, in sickness, with suffering, in hospital, under the doctor, under doctor's orders, in the doctor's hands, under treatment, on the sick list

625 Hygiene

NOUNS
1 hygiene, sanitation, cleanliness, cleanness, asepsis, antisepsis, disinfection, sterilization, chlorination, pasteurization, preventive medicine, prophylaxis, prophylactic, quarantine, isolation, *cordon sanitaire* (Fr), protection, immunity, immunization, inoculation, vaccination, disease prevention, fumigation, decontamination, purification, sanatorium, health spa, spa, hot springs, thermae, health resort, health farm, health club (US), keeping healthy, keeping fit, exercise, sport, working-out, swimming, running, jogging, walking, constitutional, hygienics
▶ *621 Cleanness, 630 Remedy, 632 Safety, 60 Medicine*
2 salubrity, salubriousness, healthiness, health, state of health, well-being, fitness, healthfulness, wholesomeness, nutritiousness, good nutrition, healthy diet, health food, wholefood, smokeless area, no-smoking section, ventilation, fresh air, open air, sea air, outdoors, out-of-doors, good climate, congenial climate
▶ *623 Health, 390 Air*
3 hygienist, sanitarian, sanitary inspector, environmental health officer, health inspector, public-health inspector, sanitary engineer, medical officer, nutritionist, dietician (*or* dietitian), fresh-air fiend (Inf)

ADJECTIVES
4 hygienic, sanitary, disinfected, chlorinated, pasteurized, sterilized, sterile, clean, pure, aseptic, antiseptic, germ-free, sanative, prophylactic, immunizing, protective, remedial, salubrious, healthy, healthful, health-giving, ventilated, well-ventilated, refreshing, restorative, salutary, what the doctor ordered, beneficial, wholesome, nutritious, nourishing, high-fibre, low-fat, low-salt, body-building, noninjurious, harmless, benign, nonmalignant, uninfectious, noninfectious, innoxious, innocuous, immune, immunized, vaccinated, inoculated, protected, invulnerable
▶ *621 Cleanness, 630 Remedy, 629 Repair, 632 Safety, 623 Health*

VERBS
5 by hygienic, practise hygiene, prevent disease, keep fit, agree with one, do one good
6 make hygienic, sanitate, sanitize, disinfect, chlorinate, pasteurize, boil, sterilize, antisepticize, immunize, inoculate, vaccinate, quarantine, put in quarantine, isolate, ventilate, aerate, freshen, fumigate, decontaminate, purify, cleanse, clean, drain, dry, conserve, preserve
▶ *621 Cleanness, 134 Purity, 637 Preservation*

ADVERBS
7 hygienically, sanitarily, antiseptically, aseptically, salubriously, healthily, healthfully, wholesomely

626 Lack of Hygiene

NOUNS
1 lack of hygiene, uncleanliness, lack of sanitation, insanitariness, insanitation, dirty habits, verminousness, infestation, dirtiness, filth, squalor, uncleanness, insalubrity, unhealthiness, unwholesomeness, unhealthy conditions, unwholesome surroundings, condemned housing, slum, squalor, mephitis, poisonous fumes, unhealthy climate, bad air, pollution, miasma, greenhouse effect, smoke, smog, fog, radioactivity, fallout, deadliness, poisonousness, bane, infectiousness, contagiousness, sepsis, purulence, suppuration, decay, mould, stagnant water, bad drains, open sewer
▶ *622 Dirtiness, 631 Blight*
2 germ, bacterium, virus, microbe, contagium, microorganism, contagion, infection, bug (Inf), lergy (Inf)
▶ *624 Ill Health*
3 unhygienic person, dirty person, slovenly person, vector, slob (Inf), pig (Inf), sludgeball (US sl)
4 infectious person, ill person, sick person, invalid, convalescent, patient, case, carrier, symptomless carrier, germ-carrier, HIV-carrier,

syphilitic, gonorrhoeic

ADJECTIVES

5 **unhygienic**, unhealthy, detrimental to health, unwholesome, unsanitary, insanitary, insalubrious, verminous, dirty, filthy, unclean, squalid, sordid, bad, nasty, noxious, miasmal, dangerous, injurious, harmful, corrupting, polluting, deadly, poisonous, baneful (Arch), rat-infested, mosquito-infested, flea-bitten, flyblown, undrained, marshy, stagnant, foul, polluted, undrinkable, inedible, indigestible, unnutritious, unsound, not fresh, stale, bad, gone bad, off, gone off, rotten, decayed, mouldy, unventilated, windowless, airless, sealed off, musty, fusty, smoke-filled, smoky, humid, stuffy, muggy, fuggy, overheated, steaming, underheated, freezing

▶ *622 Dirtiness, 628 Deterioration, 323 Closure*

6 **contagious**, infectious, catching, catchable, communicable, infective, morbific, pathogenic, germ-carrying, zymotic, pestiferous, pestilent, plague-stricken, malarious, malarial, aguish, epidemic, pandemic, endemic, epizootic, enzootic, sporadic, unsterilized, nonsterile, infected, septic, contaminated, dirty

▶ *624 Ill Health, 622 Dirtiness*

7 **toxic**, poisonous, mephitic, pestilent, pestilential, germ-laden, venomous, envenomed, poisoned, steeped in poison, gathering, festering, septic, pussy, purulent, suppurating, lethal, deadly

▶ *398 Killing*

ADVERBS

8 **unhygienically**, uncleanly, insalubriously, unhealthily, unwholesomely, dirtily, filthily, squalidly, noxiously, venomously, poisonously, septically, pestilentially, morbidly, contagiously, infectiously

627 Improvement

He so improved the city that he justly boasted that he found it brick and left it marble.
Augustus.

VERBS

1 **improve**, make better, better, ameliorate, meliorate, reform, change for the better, make improvements, improve upon, polish, perfect, elaborate, enrich, enhance, improve out of all recognition, work miracles with, transform, transfigure, convert, redeem, rehabilitate, make, be the making of, have a good influence on, leaven, raise, uplift, regenerate, refine, upgrade, elevate, sublimate, purify, civilize, socialize, teach manners, mend, repair, straighten, straighten out, rectify, make healthy, restore, cure, recruit, revive, infuse new (or fresh) blood into, refresh, soften, lessen, alleviate, mitigate, palliate, moderate,

forward, further, advance, promote, market, hype, foster, encourage, bring to fruition, mature, profit from, make the most of, get the best out of, take advantage of, use, exploit, develop, open up, reclaim, till, weed, dress, water, cultivate, arrange, tidy, tidy up, make shipshape, make neat, neaten, spruce up, smarten up, freshen up, clean, clean up, do up, vamp up, shape up, tone up, touch up, patch up, fix up (US), rationalize, renovate, refurbish, recondition, renew, bring up to date, modernize, give a face-lift to, beautify, improve on nature, gild the lily, dress up, make up, titivate, prink, primp, embellish, adorn, ornament, decorate, add frills

▶ *617 Worth, 630 Remedy, 629 Repair, 216 Change, 220 Conversion, 233 Influence, 134 Purity, 651 Refreshment, 242 Moderation, 791 Beautification, 792 Decoration*

2 **get better**, grow better, improve, mend, take a turn for the better, turn the corner, pick up, rally, revive, recover, recuperate, get over the worst, pass the crisis, convalesce, make a comeback, feel like a new man (or woman), make progress, make headway, advance, develop, evolve, progress, mellow, ripen, mature, fructify, bear fruit, increase, rise, ascend, graduate, succeed, rise in the world, better oneself, be upwardly mobile, climb the ladder of success, make one's way, make out like a bandit (US), do well, prosper, mend one's ways, reform, turn over a new leaf, improve oneself, learn, study, learn by experience, take advantage of, make capital out of, cash in on, profit by, make the grade (Inf), make good (Inf), make it (Inf), make it big (Inf), go straight (Inf), straighten up and fly right (Inf)

▶ *623 Health, 128 Increase, 359 Ascent, 682 Success, 686 Prosperity*

3 **rectify**, put right, set right, remedy, make good, straighten, straighten out, adjust, repair, mend, patch, fix, correct, make corrections, make improvements, make clear, make concise, blue-pencil, proofread, remove errors, revise, redact, edit, copy-edit, subedit, amend, emend, alter, rewrite, redraft, retell, recast, remould, refashion, remodel, recreate, reform, reorganize, regularize, fine-tune, streamline, rationalize, review, re-examine

▶ *629 Repair, 630 Remedy*

4 **reconsider**, redo, take back to the drawing board, go back to square one, stop in time, stop and think, think again, think better of, have second thoughts, have cold feet (Inf)

NOUNS

5 **improvement**, betterment, amelioration, melioration, change for the better, turn for the better, sea change, transfiguration, transformation, conversion, redemption, rehabilitation, reform, reformation, radical reform,

penitence, new leaf, new resolution, good influence, the making of, polish, perfection, elaboration, enrichment, enhancement, rise, ascent, increase, lift, uplift, upturn, upswing, upward mobility, graduation, success, prosperity, self-improvement, regeneration, refinement, upgrading, elevation, sublimation, purification, cleansing, civilization, socialization, education, repair, rectification, remedy, restoration, cure, recruitment, revival, recovery, recuperation, convalescence, refreshment, alleviation, mitigation, palliation, moderation, furtherance, advancement, advance, onward march, progress, headway, progression, promotion, tidying, cleaning, rationalization, renovation, refurbishment, reconditioning, renewal, modernization, face-lift, beautification, titivation, adornment, embellishment, ornament, ornamentation, decoration, finishing touch, final touch, icing on the cake, last word, completion, perfectionism, fussiness, kick upstairs (Inf)

6 **rectification**, putting right, making good, straightening out, adjustment, repair, mending, correction, blue pencil, proofreading, revision, revise, revisal, recension, redaction, edition, editing, copy editing, subediting, amendment, emendation, alteration, reorganization, shake-up (Inf)

7 **reconsideration**, re-examination, review, further reflection

8 **better thing**, better choice, better idea, new idea, another idea, better thought, second thought, updated model, revised edition, new edition, updated version, improved version, corrected copy, corrected proof, sequel

9 **physical improvement**, exercise, aerobics, callisthenics, eurhythmics, jogging, yoga

10 **reformatory**, reform school, house of correction, youth custody centre, borstal, juvenile detention centre, juvenile home (US)

11 **reformism**, humanism, meliorism, perfectionism, idealism, Utopianism, millenarianism, chiliasm, liberalism, socialism, progressivism, gradualism, Fabianism, New Deal (US), radicalism, extremism, revolution, communism, Marxism, integration (US), social change, feminism, suffragism, suffragettism, antiracism, Black Consciousness, Black Power, antifascism, class war, prohibitionism, Prohibition (US), peace movement, Campaign for Nuclear Disarmament (CND), ecology, the environmental movement, Greenpeace, Friends of the Earth

▶ *833 Philanthropy*

12 **reformer**, reformist, humanist, meliorist, perfectionist, idealist, Utopian, millenarian, chiliast, visionary, liberal, egalitarian, Leveller, socialist, progressive, progressivist, progressionist, gradualist, Fabian, New Dealer (US), moderate, radical, extremist, revolutionary, communist, Marxist, Red, agitator, integrationist (US), antiracist, antifascist, social worker, philanthropist, feminist, suffragist, suffragette, prohibitionist, Prohibitionist (US), peace advocate, CND member, peacenik (US), ecologist, environmentalist, commie (Inf)

▶ *833 Philanthropy*

13 **reviser**, improver, repairer, restorer, mender, amender, emender, corrector, rewriter, editor, copy editor, subeditor, proofreader

▶ *532 Publication, 629 Repair*

ADJECTIVES

14 **improved**, better, superior, bettered, enhanced, touched up, beautified, reformed, transformed, revised, edited, rewritten, repaired, restored, renovated, modernized, better off, all the better for, recovering, recuperating, looking up, on the mend, rising, increasing, better advised, wiser

▶ *126 Superiority*

15 **improvable**, perfectible, ameliorable, meliorable, reformable, corrigible, curable

16 **improving**, advancing, ameliorative, meliorative, remedial, restorative, reformative, reformatory, reforming, reformist, progressive, radical, extreme, extremist, civilizing, cultural, idealistic, perfectionist, Utopian, millenarian, chiliastic, ecological, environmental

▶ *629 Repair*

ADVERBS

17 **better**, for the better, improvably, remedially, restoratively, progressively, radically, idealistically

628 Deterioration

VERBS

1 **deteriorate**, worsen, get worse, not improve, get no better, take a turn for the worse, go from bad to worse, go to the devil, go to rack and ruin, slip, slide, go downhill, lose ground, not maintain one's position, have seen better days, be a shadow of one's former self, fall, fall off, slump, decline, decrease, decelerate, slow down, wane, ebb, sink, fail, totter, droop, stoop, slip back, retrograde, retrogress, regress, revert, lapse, relapse, tergiversate, degenerate, let oneself go, take it easy, tread the primrose path, go to ruin, go to pieces, self-destruct, ruin oneself, go (*or* run) to seed, go (to the) bad, lose control, disintegrate, crumble, collapse, break down, come apart, fall apart, contract, shrink, wear out, age, grow old, become obsolete, lose value, depreciate, fade, wither, wilt, shrivel (up), wrinkle, perish, become dilapidated, fray, become threadbare, become shabby, weaken, lose health, sicken, fall ill, do worse, jump from the frying pan into the fire,

go farther and fare worse, go to pot (Inf), go to the dogs (Inf), hit the skids (Inf), flop (Inf)

▶ *129 Decrease, 360 Descent, 244 Destruction, 141 Disintegration, 262 Contraction, 207 Age, 238 Weakness, 624 Ill Health*

2 **decay**, decompose, rot, putrefy, moulder, mildew, grow moss, weather, rust, corrode, spoil, go bad, go off, go sour, become rancid, turn, stale, go stale, grow stale, lose taste, lose flavour, go flat, corrupt, rankle, fester, suppurate, go septic, gangrene, smell, stink, pong (Inf)

▶ *419 Stench*

3 **make worse**, worsen, deteriorate, make things worse, aggravate, exacerbate, irritate, embitter, adulterate, corrupt, sophisticate, alloy, debase, denature, infect, contaminate, taint, poison, envenom, ulcerate, canker, pollute, foul, dirty, make unclean, defile, desecrate, profane

▶ *768 Aggravation, 133 Mixture, 622 Dirtiness*

4 **impair**, damage, make inoperative (*or* inoperable), put out of action, deactivate, make inactive, dismantle, dismast, spoil, mar, maul, ruin, destroy, play havoc with, mess up, untidy, jumble, derange, disorganize, bungle, botch, touch, tinker, tamper, trifle with, meddle, wreck, vandalize, ravage, rape, plunder, waste, lay waste, scorch, overthrow, crush, crumble, pulverize, muck up (Sl), fuck up (Tab sl), bugger up (Tab sl), screw up (Sl), cock up (Sl), balls up (Tab sl), make a balls-up of (Tab sl), bollocks up (Tab sl), pull a boner (US sl), pull a bonehead play (US sl), monkey with (Inf), fool (around) with (Inf), screw around with (Sl), fuck (around) with (Tab sl)

▶ *643 Inactivity, 153 Disturbance, 656 Unskilfulness, 244 Destruction*

5 **hurt**, harm, injure, wound, weaken, damnify, scathe (Arch), not improve, do no good, waste one's efforts, kill with kindness, mutilate, maim, lame, cripple, hamstring, disable, scotch (Arch), pinion, clip the wings of, cramp, hamper, hinder, castrate, unman, undermine, mine, sap, demoralize, take the starch out of, take the wind out of someone's sails, shake, honeycomb, fret, bore, gnaw, gnaw at the roots, eat away, erode, corrode, rust, rot, decay, decompose, mildew, blight, blast, plague, overrun, invade, blacken, soil, stain, spot, blot, mark, blemish, deface, disfigure, scar, wrinkle, uglify, make ugly, dilapidate, fray, frazzle, wear out, reduce to rags, drain, deplete, exhaust, consume, use up, reduce, make small, trim back, cut back, shorten, truncate, dock, curtail, censor, cut out, expurgate, eviscerate, bowdlerize, cream (off), skim (off), asset strip, take the heart out of, put the skids under (*or* to) (Inf), cramp one's style (Inf), de-ball (Tab sl), beat (*or* whip)

with an ugly stick (US sl)

▶ *406 Physical Pain, 238 Weakness, 236 Powerlessness, 661 Hindrance, 793 Blemish, 790 Ugliness, 262 Contraction, 129 Decrease, 270 Shortness*

6 **pervert**, deform, warp, twist, distort, abuse, misuse, prostitute, deprave, debauch, ruin, vitiate, corrupt, subvert, lower, degrade, debase, abase, treat cruelly, brutalize, dehumanize, barbarize, denature, denaturalize, denationalize, detribalize, propagandize, brainwash, misteach, vulgarize, coarsen, make coarse, drag down to one's level, devalue, cheapen

▶ *309 Distortion, 601 Misuse, 877 Immorality, 864 Wickedness, 362 Lowering, 754 Cheapness*

NOUNS

7 **deterioration**, worsening, lack of improvement, lack of betterment, turn for the worse, losing ground, retrogradation, retrogression, regression, reversion to type, throwback, slipping back, backsliding, recidivism, lapse, relapse, tergiversation, setback, descent, downward course, primrose path, falling off, slump, downturn, downtrend, decline, depression, recession, decrease, depreciation, impoverishment, poverty, law of diminishing returns, bad money driving out good money, Gresham's law, exhaustion of supplies, Malthusianism, deceleration, slowing down, wane, ebb, twilight, fading, dimness, tragedy, misfortune, bad ending, the skids (Inf), the road to hell (Inf), going to hell in a basket (*or* handbasket) (Inf), bad news (Inf), bad scene (Sl)

▶ *129 Decrease, 360 Descent, 743 Poverty, 441 Dimness*

8 **perversion**, deformation, distortion, abuse, misuse, prostitution, depravation, depravity, immorality, degeneration, degeneracy, degenerateness, addiction, indulgence, drunkenness, intoxication, promiscuity, impureness, impurity, decadence, ruin, vitiation, corruption, subversion, degradation, debasement, abasement, brutalization, dehumanization, barbarism, vulgarization, coarsening, devaluation, cheapening

▶ *309 Distortion, 601 Misuse, 877 Immorality, 864 Wickedness, 754 Cheapness*

9 **dilapidation**, collapse, disintegration, breakdown, ruination, destruction, ruin, rack and ruin, lack of repair, disrepair, lack of maintenance, neglect, negligence, shabbiness, slum, backstreet, urban blight, inner-city ghetto, wreck, mere wreck, perfect wreck, physical wreck, rambling wreck (US), shadow of one's former self, wear and tear, erosion, corrosion, oxidization, rustiness, rust, moth and rust, rot, rottenness, decay, decomposition, putrefaction, gangrene, corruption, mould, mouldiness, mildew, blight, canker, cancer, discoloration, weathering, bleaching, patina, verdi-

gris, decrepitude, old age, senility, ravages of time, Father Time, one foot in the grave, hardening of the arteries, marasmus, atrophy, disease, illness, walking disaster (Inf), rat trap (US inf), fleapit (Inf), tired bones (Inf)

▶ *141 Disintegration, 244 Destruction, 470 Negligence, 207 Age, 624 Ill Health*

10 **impairment**, detriment, damage, spoiling, spoilage, waste, loss, ruination, devastation, havoc, demolition, destruction, attack, assault, insult, outrage, sabotage, terrorism, disorganization, derangement, aggravation, exacerbation, adulteration, sophistication, mixture, debasement, watering down, infection, contagion, contagious disease, contamination, poisoning, intoxication, autointoxication, autotoxaemia, ulceration, pollution, acid rain, dirtiness, uncleanness, defilement

▶ *244 Destruction, 670 Attack, 153 Disturbance, 768 Aggravation, 133 Mixture, 622 Dirtiness*

11 **hurt**, harm, mischief, injuriousness, injury, pain, sprain, strain, dislocation, pulled muscle, wound, mutilation, lameness, crippling, hobbling, disabling, disablement, weakening, weakness, demoralization, loss of morale, draining, depletion, exhaustion, nobbling (Sl)

▶ *406 Physical Pain, 238 Weakness, 236 Powerlessness*

ADJECTIVES

12 **deteriorated**, worsened, worse, getting worse, worse and worse, the worse for, gone from bad to worse, not improved, no better, exacerbated, aggravated, deteriorating, worsening, failing, going downhill, in a bad way, past one's best, decreasing, declining, in decline, on the decline, falling off, in recession, impoverished, poor, falling, slipping, sliding, nodding, tottering, senile, senescent, ageing (*or aging*), spoilt, bad, gone bad, gone off, off, rotten, corked, stale, flat, bland, tasteless, impaired, damaged, hurt, harmed, injured, ruined, destroyed, harmful, injurious, effete, worn out, exhausted, tired, overtired, drained, run-down, worthless, useless, descending, on the downgrade, on the downward path, downfallen (US), fallen by the wayside, weakened, undermined, honeycombed, sapped, shaken, faded, discoloured, decaying, decayed, decomposed, withered, sere (Arch), wasting away, ebbing, at low ebb, retrogressive, regressive, retrograde, unprogressive, unimproved, undeveloped, backward, old-fashioned, outdated, lapsed, relapsed, recidivist, tergiversating, degenerate, degenerative, depraved, corrupt, going to pot (Inf), past it (Inf), far gone (Inf), done in (Inf), done for (Inf), on the way out (Inf)

▶ *768 Aggravation, 743 Poverty, 412 Tastelessness, 650 Fatigue, 614 Uselessness, 618 Worthlessness, 360 Descent, 141 Disintegration, 129 Decrease*

13 **dilapidated**, in disrepair, the worse for wear, falling apart, falling to pieces, in ruins, in shreds, in bits and pieces, beyond repair, cracked, broken, leaking, battered, weatherbeaten, storm-tossed, decrepit, rickety, tottery, shaky, unsteady, not functioning, not working, out of order, not in proper condition, out of kilter, ruinous, ramshackle, derelict, tumbledown, run-down, on its last legs, about to go, exhausted, weakened, ruined, slummy, condemned, rat-infested, worn, well-worn, shopsoiled, frayed, shabby, tatty, unkempt, dingy, holey, in holes, in tatters, in rags, worn out, worn to a frazzle, worn to a fritter (US dial), worn to a shadow, worn to the threads, seedy, down-at-heel, down-and-out, rusty, mildewed, mouldering, moth-eaten, wormeaten, dog-eared, kaput (Inf), wonky (Inf), out of whack (US inf), on the fritz (US sl), fleabitten (Inf)

ADVERBS

14 **worse**, for the worse, down, downhill, down in the world, badly, poorly

629 Repair

VERBS

1 **repair**, do repairs, mend, patch up, fix, right, put right, set to rights, rectify, correct, straighten out, put in order, put into working order, get working, put back into operation, reactivate, remedy, amend, edit, emend, adjust, tune (up), overhaul, service, maintain, cobble, sole, resole, heel, retread, reface, cover, recover, resurface, thatch, line, reline, make good, splice, bind, bind up, tie, tie up, darn, patch, reupholster, stop, fill, fill in, plug, plug up, plug a hole, stop a gap, fill in the cracks, plaster, seal, paper over, caulk, pick up the pieces, piece together, glue together, reassemble, put back together, cannibalize, join

▶ *630 Remedy, 627 Improvement, 843 Right, 293 Covering, 292 Lining, 323 Closure, 135 Union*

2 **refurbish**, renovate, redecorate, repaint, repaper, recondition, revamp, refit, restore, renew, remodel, refashion, reform, retouch, touch up, freshen up, make over, change, smarten up, give a face-lift, improve, upgrade, modernize, do wonders with, gentrify, do up (Inf), fix up (US inf)

▶ *201 Newness, 621 Cleanness*

3 **restore**, return, replace, retrocede, repatriate, give back, hand back, put back, bring back, yield up, restitute, make amends, pay back, atone, recall, reappoint, reinstall, re-establish, reinstitute, reintroduce, relaunch, refound, rehabilitate, reconstitute, reformulate, reprogramme, reinforce, reconstruct, reform, reorganize, reorient, rebuild, re-erect, remake,

redo, make like new, return to mint condition, make as good as new, service, overhaul, valet, clean, make whole, reintegrate, redintegrate (Arch), replant, reclaim, reforest, reafforest, recycle, reprocess, revalidate, revive, rally, strengthen, replenish, fill up again, restock, reassemble, reconvene, bring together, redeem, ransom, rescue, save, salvage, deliver, release, free, liberate, cough up (Inf)

▶ 735 Giving Back, 840 Atonement, 623 Health, 237 Strength, 606 Provision, 161 Assembly, 639 Deliverance, 700 Liberation

4 **be restored**, recover, come round, come to, revive, pick up, rally, respond to treatment, pull through, get over, get well, get better, bounce back, convalesce, recuperate, regain one's strength, turn the corner, find one's feet again, pick oneself up, get up, weather the storm, survive, live through, sleep through, reawaken, live again, be reborn, be born again, come back to life, come to life again, cheat death, rise from the dead, rise like a phoenix from the ashes, return from the grave, return to the land of the living, reappear, take on a new lease of life, return to normal, get back to normal, go on as before, resume, start again, go back to square one, look like new, look in mint condition, look as good as new, undergo repairs, make a comeback (Inf), sleep off (Inf), snap out of it (Inf)

▶ 651 Refreshment, 623 Health, 627 Improvement, 156 Beginning

5 **revive**, revivify, revitalize, resuscitate, regenerate, recall to life, awaken, reawaken, resurrect, reanimate, rekindle, enliven, invigorate, reinvigorate, breathe fresh life into, give a new lease of life, restore vitality, rejuvenate, refresh, freshen, renew, recruit (Arch)

▶ 651 Refreshment

6 **cure**, heal, make well, cure of, break of, nurse, nurse through, treat, physic (Arch), medicate, prescribe medication, detoxify, use therapy, doctor, operate, bandage, put a plaster on, bind up one's wounds, work a cure, perform a miracle, snatch from the grave, restore to health, set up, set on one's feet again, set, knit together, cicatrize, heal over, form a scab, scab over, close, right itself, put itself right, heal itself, cure itself, work its own cure

▶ 630 Remedy, 627 Improvement, 623 Health

7 **resort**, go, head for, leave for, betake oneself, have recourse

NOUNS

8 **repair**, repairs, reparation, mending, patching up, fixing, putting right, rectification, correction, reactivation, remedy, amendment, editing, emendation, maintenance, running repairs, service, servicing, correcting faults, overhauling, overhaul, tuning, tune-up, adjustment, renovation, restoration, renewal, re-

conditioning, reintegration, redintegration (Arch), reassembling, do-it-yourself (DIY), making like new, putting in mint condition, making as good as new, mend, invisible mending, darn, darning, patch, patching, clout (Dial), cobbling, soling, resoling, heeling, resurfacing, splicing, binding, insertion, reinforcement, refit, new look, face-lift, beautification

▶ 630 Remedy, 627 Improvement, 791 Beautification

9 **restoration**, returning, giving back, replacement, putting back, retrocession, repatriation, restitution, redress, amends, reparation, reparations, atonement, finding again, getting back, retrieval, recovery, recall, reinvestment, reinstitution, reinstallation, reinstalment, rehabilitation, replanting, reafforestation, reforestation, reclamation, recycling, reprocessing, salvage, redemption, ransom, rescue, salvation, deliverance, re-establishment, reconstitution, reintroduction, relaunching, reformulation, re-erection, rebuilding, reformation, reprogramming, reconstruction, reorganization, readjustment, reorientation, remodelling, refashioning, reconversion, reaction, counter-reformation, counteraction, resumption, return to normal, derestriction, recruitment, reinforcement, strengthening, replenishment, provision

▶ 735 Giving Back, 840 Atonement, 639 Deliverance, 237 Strength, 606 Provision

10 **revival**, recovery, renewal, revivification, revitalization, revivescence, reawakening, resurgence, recurrence, comeback, return to fashion, turnabout, turnround, rally, fresh spurt, new energy, refreshment, new supply, recruitment, financial upturn, economic recovery, economic miracle, boom, prosperity, reactivation, reanimation, resuscitation, artificial respiration, rejuvenation, rejuvenescence, second childhood, second youth, second honeymoon, second spring, Indian summer, rebirth, renaissance (or renascence), new birth, second birth, palingenesis, regeneration, regeneracy, new life, new hope, second chance, resurrection, rising from the dead, recall from the grave, return to the land of the living, reappearance, resurrection day, the Resurrection, revivalism, evangelism

▶ 651 Refreshment, 686 Prosperity

11 **recuperation**, convalescence, recovery, healing, mending, cure, being cured, response to treatment, response to therapy, return to normal, rally, rallying, perking up, upturn, turn for the better, cicatrization, closing, scab formation, scabbing over, healing over, restoration to health, return to health, remedy, moderation, easing, relief, psychological cure, psychotherapy, catharsis, abreaction, curabil-

ity, curableness

▶ *623 Health, 627 Improvement, 630 Remedy, 767 Relief*

12 **repairer**, repairman, mender, fixer, handyman, renovator, painter, decorator, interior decorator, do-it-yourselfer (DIYer), mechanic, engineer, amender, emendator, editor, copy editor, subeditor, proofreader, rectifier, rebuilder, restorer, art restorer, refurbisher, darner, tailor, seamstress, patcher, cobbler, shoe-repairer, knife-grinder, tinker, plumber, electrician, salvager, salvor, doctor, surgeon, curer, healer, bone-setter, osteopath, chiropractor, plastic surgeon, psychiatrist, psychotherapist, psychoanalyst, hypnotist, reformist, reformer, faith healer

▶ *630 Remedy, 627 Improvement*

ADJECTIVES

13 **repaired**, mended, patched up, fixed, right, correct, restored, reconditioned, renovated, redecorated, remade, rebuilt, reconstructed, reconstituted, refurbished, re-equipped, refitted, redone, rectified, put right, reinforced, strengthened, improved, like new, in mint condition, as good as new, renewed, reborn, born again, redeemed, saved, resuscitated, revived, redivivus, renascent, resurgent, phoenix-like, like a phoenix from the ashes, reclaimed, recovered, salvaged, found

▶ *630 Remedy, 627 Improvement*

14 **repairable**, reparable, restorable, mendable, amendable, rectifiable, recoverable, retrievable, redeemable (*or* redemptible), curable, operable, treatable, medicable

15 **cured**, healed, returned to health, healthy, better, like new, as good as new, none the worse, convalescent, on the mend, back on one's feet, back to normal, oneself again, alive and kicking, in one's right mind

▶ *630 Remedy, 623 Health*

16 **restorative**, reparative, analeptic, reviving, recuperative, curative, sanative, healing, medicated, medicinal, remedial, redemptive (*or* redemptory)

▶ *630 Remedy, 651 Refreshment*

ADVERBS

17 **repairably**, reparably, recoverably, redeemably, remedially

630 Remedy

Cure the disease and kill the patient. Francis Bacon.

Well, now, there's a remedy for everything except death. Miguel de Cervantes.

Extreme remedies are most appropriate for extreme diseases. Hippocrates.

NOUNS

1 **remedy**, cure, antidote, help, aid, succour, relief, oil on troubled waters, moderator, remedial measure, corrective, correction, amendment, redress, amends, restitution, expiation, atonement, certain cure, recuperation, recovery, medicinal value, healing quality (*or* property), healing gift, sovereign remedy, specific remedy, specific, answer, solution, prescribed remedy, prescription, recipe, formula, quack remedy, nostrum, patent medicine, panacea, heal-all, cure-all, catholicon, elixir, *elixir vitae* (L), philosopher's stone

▶ *662 Help, 767 Relief, 242 Moderation, 627 Improvement, 629 Repair, 735 Giving Back, 840 Atonement, 478 Answer*

2 **medicine**, remedy, pharmaceutical, drug, prescription (drug), physic, materia medica, pharmacopoeia, pharmacognosy, herbal remedy, vegetable remedy, galenical, herb, medicinal herb, simple, balm, balsam, medication, medicament, over-the-counter medication, patent medicine, proprietary drug, generic drug, ethical drug, placebo, pill, bolus, tablet, tabloid, capsule, lozenge, pastille, draught, dose, drench, drip, injection, shot, jab (Inf), infusion, potion, elixir, decoction, preparation, mixture, powder, electuary, linctus, plaster, medicine chest, medicine cabinet, medicine bottle

▶ *62 Pharmacology, 875 Drug-Taking, 57 Chemistry*

3 **prophylactic**, preventive, preventative, contraception, sanitation, sanitary precaution, quarantine, isolation, *cordon sanitaire* (Fr), hygiene, prophylaxis, immunization, inoculation, vaccination, vaccine, triple vaccine, BCG, MMR (measles, mumps, rubella) vaccine, antimalarial pill, quinine, antisepsis, disinfection, sterilization, antiseptic, disinfectant, iodine, carbolic, boric acid, boracic acid, bactericide, germicide, insecticide, poison, fumigant, dentifrice, toothpaste, tooth powder, cleanser, mouthwash, gargle, fluoride, hydrogen peroxide, Mercurochrome (Tm)

▶ *591 Avoidance, 247 Infertility, 623 Health, 625 Hygiene, 631 Blight, 621 Cleanness*

4 **antidote**, countermeasure, antitoxin, counterpoison, counterirritant, antihistamine, antibody, monoclonal antibody, antiserum, mithridate, theriac, antipyretic, febrifuge, quinine, vermifuge, anthelmintic, antigen, interferon, antibiosis, antibiotic, immunosuppressant, antispasmodic, anticonvulsant, anticoagulant, sedative, muscle relaxant

▶ *231 Counteraction*

5 **analgesic**, painkiller, pain-reliever, anodyne, nepenthe, palliative, balm, salve, demulcent, arnica, aspirin, paracetamol, codeine, ibuprofen, meperidine, pethidine, nitrous oxide,

laughing gas, morphine, morphia, laudanum (Arch), anaesthetic, local anaesthetic, general anaesthetic, analgesia, pain relief, anaesthesia, local anaesthesia, general anaesthesia, acupuncture, hypnosis, mind over matter

▶ *406 Physical Pain*

6 **purgative**, purge, cathartic, laxative, aperient, castor oil, Epsom salts, health salts, senna pods, cascara, milk of magnesia, diuretic, expectorant, emetic, nauseant, antacid, ipecacuanha, carminative, digestive, liquorice, dill water, douche, enema

7 **tonic**, restorative, roborant, cordial, tonic water, reviver, refresher, stimulant, amphetamine, Benzedrine (Tm), caffeine, nicotine, alcohol, smelling salts, sal volatile, hartshorn, infusion, tisane, herb tea, ginseng, royal jelly, vitamin, iron, bracer (Inf), pick-me-up (Inf), pep pill (Inf)

▶ *239 Vigour, 651 Refreshment*

8 **drug**, wonder drug, miracle drug, synthetic drug, designer drug, antibiotic, sulpha drug, sulphonamide, penicillin, aureomycin, streptomycin, insulin, cortisone, hormone, steroid, progesterone, oestrogen, contraceptive pill, analgesic, aspirin, codeine, paracetamol, anaesthetic, tranquillizer, diazepam, Valium (Tm), antidepressant, sedative, barbiturate, sleeping pill, soporific, narcotic, dope, heroin, opium, cocaine, morphine, intoxicant, stimulant, drug-taking

▶ *247 Infertility, 404 Insensibility, 643 Inactivity, 62 Pharmacology, 875 Drug-Taking*

9 **balm**, balsam, oil, soothing syrup, emollient, moderator, salve, cerate, ointment, cream, face cream, moisturizer, cosmetic, petrolatum, petroleum jelly, Vaseline (Tm), lanolin, liniment, embrocation, lotion, wash, eyewash, collyrium

▶ *242 Moderation, 791 Beautification*

10 **surgical dressing**, dressing, lint, gauze, swab, bandage, fingerstall, sling, splint, cast, plaster of Paris, tourniquet, patch, application, external application, plaster, sticking plaster, Elastoplast (Tm), corn plaster, court plaster, mustard plaster, cataplasm, fomentation, poultice, compress, tampon, tent, roll, pledget, pessary, suppository, traumatic

11 **medical art**, therapeutics, healing, art of healing, gift of healing, healing touch, recuperation, medicine, clinical medicine, preventive medicine, medical advice, practice, medical practice, leechcraft (Arch), allopathy, homoeopathy, naturopathy, nature cure, acupuncture, alternative medicine, complementary medicine, holistic medicine, folk medicine, faith healing, laying on of hands, Christian Science

▶ *60 Medicine, 629 Repair, 624 Ill Health*

12 **surgery**, general surgery, brain surgery, heart surgery, cardiac surgery, open-heart surgery, bypass surgery, transplant surgery, grafting, plastic surgery, cosmetic surgery, rhinoplasty, prosthesis, prosthetics, surgical operation, operation, op (Inf), phlebotomy, venesection, bleeding, blood-letting, cupping, transfusion, perfusion, dialysis, transplant, graft, skin graft, renal (or kidney) graft, corneal graft, coronary bypass graft, cauterization, amputation, trephination, lobotomy, tonsillectomy, appendicectomy, colostomy, laparotomy, mastectomy, radical mastectomy, hysterectomy, vasectomy, dental surgery, bridging, drawing, extracting, stopping, filling, crowning, chiropody, podiatry, electrolysis

▶ *60 Medicine*

13 **therapy**, therapeutics, medical care, healing art, treatment, medical treatment, clinical treatment, nursing, bedside manner, first aid, aftercare, course, cure, faith cure, nature cure, cold-water cure, hydrotherapy, regimen, diet, dietary, chiropractic, bone-setting, manipulation, massage, orthopaedics, osteopathy, osteotherapy, hypnotherapy, hormone therapy, hormone replacement therapy (HRT), immunotherapy, chemotherapy, physiotherapy, occupational therapy, radiotherapy, phototherapy, heat treatment, electrotherapy, shock treatment, electroconvulsive therapy (ECT), mental treatment, clinical psychology, child psychology, psychotherapy, psychiatry, psychoanalysis, psychology, group therapy, behavioural therapy, aversion therapy, Gestalt therapy, primal (scream) therapy, acupuncture, acupressure, catheterization, intravenous injection, drip, drip-feed, fomentation, poulticing

▶ *459 Intellect*

14 **hospital**, infirmary, sanatorium, dispensary, clinic, nursing home, convalescent home, rest home, home for the dying, hospice, asylum, mental asylum, mental hospital, lazaretto (or lazaret or lazarette), lazar-house (or pesthouse), leper asylum, leper colony, hospital ship, HOPE, hospital train, MASH (mobile army surgical hospital) (US), stretcher, ambulance, ward, hospital ward, isolation ward, sick bay, sickroom, sickbed, hospital bed, ripple bed, tent, oxygen tent, iron lung, respirator, life-support system, heart-lung machine, kidney machine, scanner, body scanner, brain scanner, head scanner, CT (or CAT) scanner, MR scanner, dressing station, first-aid station, casualty station, operating room, operating theatre, operating table, consulting room, surgery, spa, hydro, watering place, pump room, baths, hot springs, thermae, solarium, sun lamp, sun bed

▶ *60 Medicine, 510 Insanity*

15 **healer**, therapeutist, doctor, physician, leech

(Arch), surgeon, dental surgeon, dentist, veterinary surgeon, veterinarian, vet, herbalist, herb doctor, faith healer, layer-on of hands, Christian Scientist, allopath, homeopath, naturopath, acupuncturist, hypnotist, hakim (*or* hakeem), flying doctor, witch doctor, medicine man, sorcerer, therapist, psychotherapist, psychiatrist, alienist (US), psychoanalyst, osteopath, bonesetter, chiropractor, masseur, masseuse, pedicurist, podiatrist, chiropodist, optician, oculist, orthoptist, nutritionist, dietician, nurse, Aesculapius, Hippocrates, the father of medicine, Galen, doc (*Inf*), quack (*Inf*), horse doctor (*Inf*), medic (*Inf*), medico (*Inf*), sawbones (*Sl*), headshrinker (*Sl*), shrink (*Sl*)

▶ *60 Medicine, 61 Psychology and Psychiatry*

16 **druggist**, pharmacist, apothecary, chemist, dispenser, posologist, pharmacologist, pharmacy

▶ *62 Pharmacology, 57 Chemistry*

ADJECTIVES

17 **remedial**, corrective, therapeutic, medicinal, analeptic, curative, first-aid, restorative, helpful, beneficial, healing, curing, hygienic, sanitary, salubrious, salutiferous, health-giving, specific, sovereign, panacean, all-healing, soothing, paregoric, balsamic, demulcent, emollient, palliative, lenitive, anodyne, analgesic, narcotic, hypnotic, anaesthetic, insensible, peptic, digestive, purging, cleansing, cathartic, emetic, vomitory, laxative, antidotal, counteracting, theriacal, prophylactic, preventive, preventative, disinfectant, antiseptic, antipyretic, febrifugal, tonic, stimulative, dietetic, alimentary, nutritive, nutritional

▶ *629 Repair, 617 Worth, 625 Hygiene, 242 Moderation, 404 Insensibility, 621 Cleanness, 231 Counteraction, 62 Pharmacology*

18 **medical**, pathological, Aesculapian, Hippocratic, Galenic, allopathic, homoeopathic, herbal, surgical, anaplastic, rhinoplastic, orthopaedic, orthotic, vulnerary, traumatic, obstetric, obstetrical, gynaecological, paediatric, geriatric, clinical, medicable, operable, curable

▶ *60 Medicine*

VERBS

19 **remedy**, correct, restore, fix, mend, put right, help, aid, succour, apply a remedy, treat, heal, cure, work a cure, palliate, alleviate, soothe, demulce, neutralize, relieve, ease

▶ *662 Help, 629 Repair, 767 Relief, 627 Improvement*

20 **doctor**, be a doctor, practise, have a practice, practise medicine, treat, prescribe, advise, attend, minister to, tend, nurse, give first aid, give the kiss of life, revive, hospitalize, put on the sick list, put to bed, physic, medicate, drench, dose, purge, inject, give a shot, dress, bind, swathe, bandage, put a plaster on, plaster, stop the bleeding, apply a tourniquet, staunch, poultice, foment, set, put in splints, drug, dope, anaesthetize, operate, use the knife, cut open, amputate, trepan, trephine, curette, cauterize, bleed, phlebotomize, transfuse, perfuse, massage, rub, manipulate, draw, extract, pull, stop, fill, crown, immunize, vaccinate, inoculate, sterilize, pasteurize, antisepticize, disinfect, sanitate

▶ *60 Medicine, 625 Hygiene*

ADVERBS

21 **remedially**, therapeutically, medicinally, medically, pathologically, surgically, clinically

631   Blight

NOUNS

1 **affliction**, evil, harm, curse, plague, infestation, pestilence, distress, pest, scourge, ruin, malady, disease, visitation, running sore, act of God, hand of God

2 **adversity**, woe, grief, misery, sorrow, trouble, cross to bear, cross, trial, bugbear, bugaboo, bogey (*or* bogy), *bête noire* (*Fr*)

3 **burden**, imposition, charge, duty, white elephant, albatross, albatross round one's neck, millstone, millstone round one's neck, thorn in one's flesh (*or* side)

4 **strain**, stress, fear, pressure, worry, anxiety, angst, torment, bitterness, sourness, acid, gall, wormwood

5 **pain**, hurt, agony, ache, pang, twinge, soreness, tenderness

6 **source of trouble**, Pandora's box, hornet's nest, pitfall, trap, viper, adder, serpent, snake, snake in the grass, bite, sting, serpent's tooth, thorn, briar, bur, barb, nettle, fly in the ointment, bitter cup

▶ *862 Evil, 624 Ill Health, 788 Boredom, 864 Wickedness, 687 Adversity, 770 Sorrow, 764 Unpleasantness, 828 Resentment; Anger, 777 Fear, 415 Sourness, 380 Sharpness, 635 Trap, 244 Destruction*

7 **poisoning**, poisonousness, toxicity, venomousness, blood poisoning, toxaemia, food poisoning, ptomaine poisoning, salmonella, salmonellosis, listeria, listeriosis, botulism, infection, contagion, virulence, germ, bacterium, bacillus, virus

8 **poison**, toxin, venom, carcinogen, hemlock, arsenic, arsenic oxide, prussic acid, hydrogen cyanide, sodium cyanide, cyanide, strychnine, rat poison, ratsbane, warfarin, insecticide, rotenone, weedkiller, Paraquat (Tm), carbon monoxide, exhaust fumes

9 **pollution**, pollutant, smoke, tar, smog, effluvium, mephitis, passive smoking, acid rain, sulphur dioxide, sulphuric acid, leaching, heavy-metal poisoning, greenhouse effect, greenhouse gas, carbon dioxide, ozone depletion, halon, CFC (chlorofluorocarbon), HCFC (hydrochlorofluorocarbon), contamination,

contaminant, dioxin, TCDD (tetrachlorodi-benzodioxin), BCP (polychlorinated biphen-yl), oxygen depletion, phosphates

10 **warfare**, chemical warfare, chemical wea-pon, asphixiant, tear gas, Mace (Tm), poison gas, war gas, chlorine, lewisite, mustard gas, phosgene, carbonyl chloride, VX, nerve gas, germ warfare, biological weapon, anthrax, defoliant, Agent Orange, nuclear weapon, fallout, radioactivity, strontium-90, pluto-nium

▶ *624 Ill Health, 626 Lack of Hygiene, 676 War*

11 **intoxicant**, drug, narcotic, cannabis, mari-juana, hashish, cocaine, heroin, opium, tran-quillizer, Valium (Tm), sleeping pill, sedative, nicotine, alcohol, caffeine, lethal dose, over-dose, toxicology, dope (Sl)

▶ *874 Drunkenness, 875 Drug-Taking*

12 **poisonous plant**, hemlock, deadly night-shade, belladonna, datura, henbane, wolfs-bane, monkshood, aconite, hellebore, nux vomica, upas tree, death cap, poison ivy

13 **oppressor**, tormentor, torturer, holy terror, tyrant, poisoner, murderer

▶ *690 Severity, 398 Killing*

VERBS

14 **afflict**, harm, curse, strike down, plague, in-fest, visit, blight, blast, wither, shrivel, decay, rot, mildew, mould, rust, mar, burden, strain, worry, pressurize, torment, bite, sting

15 **poison**, intoxicate, drug, pollute, taint, con-taminate, adulterate, infect, spoil, bespoil, be-smirch

▶ *141 Disintegration, 628 Deterioration, 624 Ill Health, 862 Evil, 244 Destruction, 515 Disap-pointment*

ADJECTIVES

16 **blighting**, blighted, rotting, rotten, decay-ing, decayed, mildewed, mouldy, baneful, pes-tilent, noisome, noxious, harmful, virulent, poisonous, venomous, toxic, malevolent, cursed, accursed, evil

▶ *862 Evil, 624 Ill Health, 141 Disintegration, 628 Deterioration*

ADVERBS

17 **banefully**, harmfully, virulently, malevo-lently

632 Safety

NOUNS

1 **safety**, safeness, security, protection, invul-nerability, impregnability, immunity, lack of danger, charmed life, lack of risk, harmless-ness, safety in numbers, safe place, safe dis-tance, wide berth, avoidance, regained safety, danger past, all clear, coast clear, storm blown over, safe job, secure position, permanent post. social security, welfare, welfare state, Medicaid (US), Medicare (US), National Health

Service, guarantee, warranty, warrant, cer-tainty, sense of security, assurance, confi-dence, faith, means of escape, back door, opt-out clause, escape clause, rescue, negotiated release, deliverance, nanny state (Inf), safety valve (Inf)

▶ *591 Avoidance, 2 Sociology, 490 Certainty, 638 Escape, 639 Deliverance*

2 **protection**, safeguard, precaution, security system, electronic surveillance, alarm system, burglar alarm, preventive measure, security check, vetting, positive vetting, Big Brother, surveillance, safe conduct, passport, pass, per-mit, escort, convoy, guard, armed force, de-fence, defences, sure defence, bulwark, bas-tion, tower of strength, moat, ditch, palisade, stockade, haven, sanctuary, asylum, refuge, safe house, shelter, battered women's shelter, homeless shelter, orphan's home, orphanage, care, keeping, custody, charge, safe hands, safekeeping, grasp, grip, embrace, ward, watch and ward (US), patronage, support, aid, spon-sorship, good offices, auspices, aegis, fatherly eye, tutelage, protectorate, guardianship, wardship, wardenship (US), custodianship, protective custody, surrogacy, anchor, sheet anchor, shield, breastplate, panoply, armour plate, armour, means of protection, deterrent, weapon, sanitary precaution, hygiene, im-munization, vaccination, inoculation, pro-phylaxis, contraception, *cordon sanitaire* (Fr), quarantine, isolation, segregation, seclusion, trade tariff, insurance, life insurance, life as-surance, fire insurance, car insurance, house-hold insurance, surety, buffer, cushion, screen, cover, umbrella, shelter, savings, sav-ings account, collateral, nest egg, something for a rainy day, provision, store

▶ *634 Refuge, 637 Preservation, 671 Defence, 662 Help, 469 Carefulness, 726 Retention, 301 Enclo-sure, 680 Weapon, 625 Hygiene, 781 Caution, 756 Thrift, 606 Provision*

3 **protector**, protectress, guardian, mentor, tutor, guardian angel, patron saint, tutelary god (*or* goddess), liege lord, feudal lord, pa-tron, patroness, benefactor, benefactress, fairy godmother, champion, knight in shining ar-mour, white knight, chaperon (*or* chaperone), governess, duenna, nurse, nursemaid, nanny, mammy (US), sitter, baby-sitter, child-minder, companion, keeper, defender, preserver, shep-herd, coastguard, lifeguard, life-saver, body-guard, minder, Secret Service (US), doorman, vigilante, Guardian Angels (US), Neighbour-hood Watch, conservator, custodian, curator, warden, warder, watcher, surveillant, lookout, watch, watchman, night watchman, guard, se-curity guard, security man (*or* woman), sentry, sentinel, garrison, picket, armed guard, van-guard, security forces, Home Guard, Territorial

Army, Territorial, militia, customs official, park keeper, gamekeeper, forester, (forest) ranger (US), firewatcher, fire fighter, fireman, police, policeman, policewoman, police officer, police constable, PC, WPC, police sergeant, detective, patrol, patrolman, riot policeman, sheriff, drug enforcement officer, vice squad member, private investigator, private detective, watchdog, guard dog, sniffer dog, police dog, Cerberus, Argus, strongarm man (Inf), bouncer (Inf), copper (Sl), cop (Sl), bobby (Inf), private eye (Inf), weekend warrior (US inf)

▶ *671 Defence, 637 Preservation*

4 **safety device**, means of safety, safeguard, protection, precautionary steps, precautions, alarm, burglar alarm, crowd control methods, crush barrier, police barrier, crash barrier, guardrail, railing, pilot (US), cowcatcher (US), mail, chainmail, armour, bulletproof vest, bulletproof car, bulletproof glass, shatterproof glass, toughened glass, fail-safe device, fail-safe system, deterrent, Star Wars, strategic defence initiative (SDI), respirator, oxygen tent, mask, gas mask, safety goggles, earmuffs, ear plugs, safety chain, dead man's handle (or pedal), safety catch, safety lock, bolt, dead bolt, deadlock, safety valve, safety pin, safety razor, safety match, lightning conductor, fuse, circuit breaker, earth, fire alarm, smoke alarm, fire extinguisher, fire blanket, sprinkler system, fire escape, fire door, fire wall, crash helmet, safety helmet, football helmet (US), protective clothing, seat belt, safety belt, safety harness, shoulder harness, air bag, ejector seat, escape hatch, means of escape, parachute, safety net, lifeboat, rubber dinghy, life raft, life buoy, lifeline, preserver, life belt, life vest (US), life jacket, buoyancy jacket, buoyancy aid, Mae West, water wings, breeches buoy, rope, plank, anchor, sheet anchor, kedge, grapnel, grappling iron, killick (or killock), drogue, lead, reins, brake, fetter, bar, lock, key, stopper, ballast, mole, breakwater, groyne, embankment, seawall, lighthouse, lightship, jury mast, jury rig, emergency part, spare part, spare, extra

▶ *671 Defence, 680 Weapon, 295 Dress, 323 Closure*

ADJECTIVES

5 **safe**, secure, protected, guarded, defended, not in danger, not at risk, assured, sure, certain, sound, safe and sound, safe as houses, snug, spared, preserved, intact, undamaged, unharmed, uninjured, unhurt, unscathed, with a whole skin, whole, garrisoned, well-defended, insured, covered, immunized, vaccinated, inoculated, disinfected, salubrious, hygienic, in safety, in security, under guard, on the safe side, on sure ground, on home

ground, on the home stretch, on terra firma, in harbour, in port, at anchor, above water, out of danger, out of the wood, out of harm's way, clear, in the clear, unaccused, unthreatened, unmolested, unexposed, under shelter, sheltered, shielded, screened, patronized, under the protection of, under the wing of, in safe hands, in safe keeping, held, in custody, behind bars, under lock and key, imprisoned, reliable, dependable, trustworthy, guaranteed, under warrant, warranted, benign, innocent, innocent as a lamb, tame, harmless, innocuous, unthreatening, not dangerous, without risk, risk-free, unhazardous, nonflammable, nontoxic, unpolluted, edible, eatable, drinkable, potable, good, home free (US sl), home and dry (Sl), home and hosed (Aus sl), in the clink (Sl), in the hoosegow (US sl)

▶ *637 Preservation, 490 Certainty, 625 Hygiene, 702 Prison, 857 Probity, 861 Good*

6 **invulnerable**, immune, impregnable, sacrosanct, inexpugnable, unassailable, unattackable, ungettable (or ungetable), unbreakable, unchallengeable, made in heaven, founded on a rock, built like a fortress, defensible, tenable, strong, proof, foolproof, fail-safe, mothproof, childproof, weatherproof, waterproof, showerproof, leakproof, rustproof, gasproof, fireproof, shatterproof, bulletproof, bombproof, armoured, steel-clad, panoplied, snug, tight, seaworthy, airworthy, shrink-wrapped, vacuum-packed, vacuum-sealed, hermetically sealed, freeze-dried, frozen

▶ *237 Strength*

7 **tutelary**, protective, custodial, guardian, surrogate, shepherdlike, watchful, vigilant, keeping, guarding, protecting, preserving, prophylactic, antiseptic, disinfectant, hygienic

▶ *637 Preservation, 469 Carefulness, 625 Hygiene*

VERBS

8 **be safe**, be out of danger, protect oneself, defend oneself, take precautions, play safe, be on the safe side, hedge one's bets, take no chances, demand assurances, seek safety, find safety, reach safety, come through, survive, save one's skin, keep a whole skin, live to fight another day, escape, run away, land on one's feet, keep one's head above water, weather the storm, ride it out, see it through, be saved by the bell, bear (or live) a charmed life, have nine lives, stay at home, be (or stay) under cover, have a roof over one's head, take refuge, hide, lie low, go underground, keep a safe distance, give a wide berth, shy away, avoid, save one's ass (Tab sl), save one's bacon, go on the lam (US sl), cut and run (Inf), do a runner (Inf), beat a retreat (Inf), skedaddle (Inf), shorten sail (Inf), run for port (Inf)

▶ *638 Escape, 591 Avoidance, 634 Refuge, 531 Concealment*

9 **protect**, safeguard, keep safe, guard, defend, spare, show mercy, support, champion, stand up for, vouch for, stand surety for, go bail for, cover up for, provide an alibi for, shield, harbour, rescue, save, deliver, patronize, grant (political) asylum, afford sanctuary, keep, conserve, preserve, treasure, hoard, store, lock away (*or* up), hide away, hide, conceal, put in a safe place, keep under cover, warehouse, garage, take in, house, shelter, imprison, keep in custody, keep behind bars, keep locked up, ward, watch over, care for, look after, mind, mother, take under one's wing, nurse, tend, foster, cherish, have charge of, take charge of, keep an eye on, monitor, chaperon (*or* chaperone), immunize, inoculate, vaccinate, pasteurize, chlorinate, fluoridate, fluorinate, disinfect, sanitate, sanitize, assure, give assurances, promise, give vows, warrant, guarantee, make certain, cushion, buffer, ensconce, enfold, embrace, envelop, cocoon, wrap, enclose, insulate, earth, cover, shroud, cloak, shade, screen, make safe, secure, fortify, strengthen, entrench, fence in, fence round, arm, armour, armour-plate, convoy, escort, shepherd, flank, garrison, mount guard, keep order, police, patrol, honcho (US sl), ride shotgun (US inf)
▶ 637 *Preservation*, 469 *Carefulness*, 835 *Pity*, 662 *Help*, 671 *Defence*, 639 *Deliverance*, 606 *Provision*, 531 *Concealment*, 625 *Hygiene*, 301 *Enclosure*, 490 *Certainty*, 237 *Strength*

ADVERBS

10 **safely**, securely, in safety, with impunity, without risk, out of danger, out of harm's way, under cover, in the lee of, under the aegis of, under lock and key, invulnerably, impregnably, protectively, watchfully, hygienically

633 Danger

Defend us from all perils and dangers of this night. The Book of Common Prayer.

Dangers by being despised grow great. Edmund Burke.

Believe me! The secret of reaping the greatest fruitfulness and the greatest enjoyment from life is to live dangerously! Friedrich Wilhelm Nietzsche.

ADJECTIVES

1 **dangerous**, perilous, treacherous, hazardous, risky, beset with perils, fraught with danger, unknown, uncertain, unlit, venturous, venturesome, difficult, chancy, tricky, snaggy, speculative, crucial, critical, serious, nasty, ugly, menacing, threatening, ominous, foreboding, alarming, frightening, at the boiling point, at the flash point, at stake, in question, inflammable, flammable, explosive, radioactive, toxic, poisonous, life-threatening, dead-

ly, harmful, unhealthy, infectious, unhygienic, sticky (Inf), dicey (Inf), dodgy (Inf), iffy (Inf), hairy (Sl), clutch (US inf)
▶ 777 *Fear*, 589 *Chance*, 491 *Uncertainty*, 626 *Lack of Hygiene*

2 **unsafe**, not safe, treacherous, untrustworthy, unreliable, doubtful, shaky, slippery, insecure, unsecure, unsound, precarious, unbalanced, unsteady, unstable, tottering, top-heavy, tumbledown, ramshackle, dilapidated, rickety, frail, falling to pieces, crumbling, condemned, jerry-built, shoddy, gimcrack, crazy, weak, built on sand, on shaky foundations, leaky, waterlogged, critical, delicate, ticklish, risky, heart-stopping, nerve-racking, touch and go, hanging by a thread, trembling in the balance, teetering on the edge, on the edge, on the brink, on the verge, last-second, last-minute, dicey, dicky (*or* dickey) (Inf)
▶ 491 *Uncertainty*, 628 *Deterioration*, 238 *Weakness*

3 **vulnerable**, unprotected, undefended, not secure, in danger, not immune, liable, susceptible, open to, wide open, exposed, naked, bare, uncovered, unarmoured, unfortified, expugnable, pregnable, helpless, at the whim of, at the mercy of, defenceless, unarmed, isolated, deserted, abandoned, stranded, left high and dry, out on a limb, unsupported, unshielded, shelterless, guideless, unattended, unguarded, unescorted, unshepherded, unflanked, unwarned, unaware, naive, not on guard, off one's guard, unprepared, unready
▶ 236 *Powerlessness*, 238 *Weakness*, 296 *Undress*, 486 *Possibility*, 595 *Lack of Preparation*

4 **endangered**, in danger, in peril, at risk, in jeopardy, in double jeopardy (US), slipping, drifting, on the rocks, in shallow water, on dangerous ground, on slippery ground, on thin ice, in a bad way, in a tight corner, in a bind, surrounded, trapped, at bay, cornered, with one's back to the wall, under siege, under fire, in the lion's den, thrown to the lions, on the razor's edge, in a catch-22 situation, caught both ways, between two fires, between two chairs, between the devil and the deep blue sea, between a rock and a hard place (US), between Scylla and Charybdis, on the run, not out of the wood, at the last stand, reduced to the last extremity, facing death, facing the firing squad, under sentence, condemned, with a noose round one's neck, awaiting execution, on death row (US), in a jam (Inf), in the soup (Inf), in the hot seat (Inf)

NOUNS

5 **danger**, peril, jeopardy, risk, hazard, dangerousness, perilousness, riskiness, hazardousness, treacherousness, treachery, dangerous situation, unhealthy situation, desperate situation, perilous state, parlous state (Arch),

shadow of death, jaws of death, lion's mouth, dragon's lair, dire straits, predicament, emergency, urgency, crisis, insecurity, unsoundness, ticklishness, ticklish business, precariousness, slipperiness, shakiness, unsteadiness, uncertainty, acute dilemma, razor's edge, black spot, deathtrap, snag, pitfall, trap, surprise attack, ambush, endangerment, imperilment, hazarding, venturesomeness, daring, overdaring, rashness, gambling, venture, risky venture, dangerous course, leap in the dark, throw of the dice, spin of the wheel, turn of a card, slippery slope, road to ruin, impending disaster, sword of Damocles, menace, threat, sense of danger, apprehension, anxiety, nervousness, fear, narrow escape, hairbreadth escape, near tragedy, near miss, near thing (Inf), close shave (Inf)

▶ *659 Difficulty, 491 Uncertainty, 635 Trap, 531 Concealment, 670 Attack, 597 Undertaking, 780 Rashness, 589 Chance, 777 Fear, 638 Escape*

6 **danger signal**, cause for alarm, night sounds, strange noise, gunshot, scream, sudden pain, snarling dog, ticking parcel, rocks ahead, breakers ahead, storm brewing, gathering storm, gathering clouds, thick fog, rising river, cloud on the horizon

▶ *636 Warning*

7 **vulnerability**, liability, susceptibility, nonimmunity, openness, exposure, nakedness, pregnability, helplessness, defencelessness, lack of protection, naivety, innocence, instability, insecurity, easy target, sitting target, exposed part, exposed flank, vulnerable point, undefended part, breach in the wall, chink in the armour, Achilles' heel, weakness, tender spot, soft spot, soft underbelly, unsoundness, failing, flaw, defect, imperfection, defect of character, human failing, feet of clay, tragic flaw, fatal flaw, sitting duck (or target) (Inf)

▶ *236 Powerlessness, 238 Weakness, 374 Softness, 620 Imperfection*

VERBS

8 **be in danger**, run the risk of, run into danger, enter the lion's den, put one's head in the lion's mouth, ride a tiger, walk into a trap, tread on dangerous ground, be on slippery ground, skate on thin ice, be out of one's depth, sail close (or near) to the wind, play with fire, feel the ground slip away, feel the ground give way, be up against it, have to run for it, hang by a thread, tremble in the balance, hover on the brink, teeter on the edge, totter, slip, slide, tumble, fall, get lost, wander away, stray, go astray, play with dynamite (Inf), sit on a powder keg (Inf), sleep on a volcano (Inf), lean on a broken reed (Inf)

▶ *360 Descent, 335 Deviation*

9 **face danger**, face death, take one's life in

one's hands, expose oneself, lay oneself open to, stand in the breach, risk, defy, look danger in the face, look down a gun barrel, face heavy odds, have the odds (stacked) against one, have the deck (or cards) stacked against one, have one's back to the wall, engage in a forlorn hope, challenge fate, tempt fate, tempt providence, court disaster, take a tiger by the tail, put one's head in the lion's mouth, play Russian roulette, dice with death, run the gauntlet, come under fire, venture, dare, hazard, gamble, take a chance, take a flier (US), stick one's neck out

▶ *668 Defiance, 778 Courage, 780 Rashness, 589 Chance*

10 **endanger**, expose to danger, put in danger, put at risk, put in jeopardy, put in double jeopardy (US), jeopardize, imperil, compromise, hazard, risk, stake, gamble, venture, drive headlong, run on the rocks, drive dangerously, drive recklessly, drive without due care and attention, put someone in fear of his (or her) life, threaten one's life, threaten danger, loom, forebode, bode ill, menace, intimidate, threaten, hold over one's head, run one hard, overtake, outdo

▶ *589 Chance, 777 Fear*

ADVERBS

11 **dangerously**, treacherously, perilously, hazardously, riskily, precariously, in the face of death, on the brink, naively, unawares, recklessly, rashly, ominously, threateningly, menacingly, vulnerably, helplessly, defencelessly

634   Refuge

NOUNS

1 **refuge**, sanctuary, asylum, retreat, safe retreat, safe place, place of safety, traffic island, pedestrian crossing, safety zone (US), zebra crossing, pelican crossing, resort, recourse, last resort, hole, foxhole, dugout, pit, bolt hole, trench, underground shelter, concrete shelter, (nuclear) bunker, blockhouse, bomb shelter, air-raid shelter, Anderson shelter, fallout (or nuclear) shelter, burrow, hide-out, hiding place, priest hole, cache, secret place, lap, bed, bedroom, hearth, home, private space, inviolable place, privacy, sanctum, chamber, monastery, nunnery, cloister, cell, hermitage, ivory tower, sanctum sanctorum, holy of holies, temple, ark, acropolis, citadel, wall, rampart, bulwark, parapet, battlement, fortification, bastion, stronghold, fortress, fastness, fort, keep, ward, rock, Rock of Gibraltar, Rock of Ages, pillar, tower, tower of strength, mainstay, buttress, prop, support, funk hole (Inf), hidy-hole (or hidey-hole) (Inf)

▶ *632 Safety, 531 Concealment, 256 Habitat, 671 Defence, 702 Prison, 284 Support*

2 **shelter**, cover, roof, roof over one's head, lee, lee wall, windbreak, hedge, wall, fence, camp, stockade, enclosure, raincoat, sou'wester, oilskin, umbrella, tarpaulin, canvas, shield, screen, fire screen, fireguard, wing, mudguard, bumper, windscreen, awning, shutter, window shade, blind, Venetian blind, curtain, lampshade, shade, suntan lotion, suntan oil, sun block, sunshade, parasol, sunglasses, eyeshade, sunhat, pith helmet, sun helmet, topee (*or* topi), goggles, snow suit, haven, harbour, port, harbourage, anchorage, quay, jetty, ghat, marina, dock, police protection, safe house, padded cell, asylum, mental hospital, halfway house, sheltered workshop (US), sheltered housing, almshouse, poorhouse, workhouse, children's home, orphanage, old people's home, retirement home, nursing home, hospice, home for the dying, charity, charitable institution, charitable foundation, welfare institution, social security, welfare state

▶ *638 Escape, 301 Enclosure, 632 Safety, 295 Dress*

3 **animal shelter**, dog's home, kennels, cat's home, cattery, animal home, (wild) bird sanctuary, (wild) animal sanctuary, hole, burrow, den, lair, earth, covert, warren, molehole, beaver lodge, snake pit, nest, bird nest, eyrie, mouse nest, fold, pen, pinfold, sheepfold, pound, sty, pigsty, barn, stall, stable, byre, coop, hutch, cage

▶ *256 Habitat*

VERBS

4 **shelter**, seek refuge, take refuge, seek sanctuary, claim sanctuary, seek asylum, ask for political asylum, seek shelter, seek safety, retreat, take to the woods, take to the hills, request aid, turn to, throw oneself in the arms of, clasp the knees of, kiss the hand of, hide behind the skirts of, shelter under the wing of, ask protection from, put up one's umbrella, pull the blankets over one's head, reach home, reach safety, make port, find shelter, lock oneself in, bolt the door, bar the entrance, let down the portcullis, raise the drawbridge, close the blinds, close the shutters, batten down the hatches, go on the lam (US sl)

635 Trap

NOUNS

1 **trap**, pitfall, pit, snare, gin, springe, trap door, trap for the unwary, danger, hazard, catch, snag, catch-22, pons asinorum, obstacle, stumbling block, booby trap, deathtrap, firetrap, mine, minefield, tank trap, dragon's teeth, trick, deception, ruse, subterfuge, artifice, stratagem, surprise, unexpected event, lying in wait, unexpected attack, ambush, sleeping dog, wolf in sheep's clothing, thin ice, quagmire, quicksand, marsh, sandbar,

sandbank, shoal, shoal water, breakers, shallows, shallow water, reef, sunken reef, coral reef, rock, ironbound coast, lee shore, steep, chasm, abyss, crevasse, precipice, rapids, white water, current, crosscurrent, undertow, vortex, maelstrom, whirlpool, eddy, rising water, incoming tide, tidal wave, flash flood, storm, squall, gale, hurricane, tornado, cyclone, twister (US), volcano, furnace, earthquake, dynamite, powder keg, time bomb, terrorist bomb, trouble spot, area of contamination, hotbed, source of trouble, Pandora's box, hornet's nest, bane

▶ *661 Hindrance, 539 Deception, 514 Surprise, 531 Concealment, 278 Shallowness, 680 Weapon, 633 Danger, 631 Blight*

2 **troublemaker**, mischief-maker, ill-wisher, wrecker, enemy, firebrand, revolutionary, terrorist, fundamentalist, *agent provocateur* (Fr), fifth columnist, agitator, dangerous person, criminal, outlaw, undesirable, delinquent, juvenile delinquent, ruffian, snake in the grass, fly in the ointment, viper in the bosom, nigger in the woodpile (Derog), hidden hand, communist threat, red menace, reds under the bed (Inf), fascist, neo-Nazi, skinhead, bovver (*or* bully) boy (Inf), yellow peril, avenger, revenger, Nemesis, stirrer (Inf), mixer (Inf), ugly customer (Inf), bad news (Sl), hooligan (Sl), thug (Inf), yob (Inf)

▶ *820 Enmity, 693 Disobedience, 233 Influence*

VERBS

3 **trap**, entrap, snare, ensnare, net, catch, catch out, catch unawares, surprise, take by surprise, lie in wait, ambush, trick, deceive, dupe, inveigle, cause trouble, make mischief

▶ *514 Surprise, 539 Deception*

636 Warning

NOUNS

1 **warning**, caution, caveat, example, warning example, advice, counsel, lesson, object lesson, notice, advance notice, notification, information, intelligence, news, word, word of warning, word in the ear, word to the wise, tip, tip-off, kick under the table, wink, pinch, nudge, hint, announcement, publication, public warning, storm warning, hurricane warning, final warning, final notice, final invoice, final demand, ultimatum, monition, admonition, admonishment, reprimand, deterrent, dissuasion, protest, expostulation, forewarning, foreboding, premonition, premonition of disaster, omen, bad omen, evil omen, portent, evil portent, prediction, augury, Mother Carey's chickens, storm(y) petrel, bird of ill omen, gathering clouds, gathering storm, rising river, cloud on the horizon, war cloud, conscience, voice of conscience, warn-

ing voice, note of warning, murmur of discontent, muttering, sign, symptom, indication, indicator, signal, signs of the times, knell, death knell, menace, danger, threat

▶ *654 Advice, 781 Caution, 528 Information, 533 News, 532 Publication, 692 Command, 852 Disapproval, 587 Dissuasion, 517 Prediction, 847 Duty, 766 Dissatisfaction, 544 Identification, 543 Sign, 633 Danger*

2 **danger signal**, alarm, warning alarm, warning sign, writing on the wall, beacon, light, shout, bell, whistle, horn, siren, blast, honk, toot, ring, gale warning, hurricane warning, storm signal, storm cone, alarum (Arch), hue and cry, alarm clock, alarm bell, security alarm, emergency buzzer, panic button, burglar alarm, fire alarm, fire bell, foghorn, fog signal, bell buoy, klaxon, car horn, bicycle bell, police whistle, church bell, curfew bell, tocsin, alert, red alert, beat of drum, tattoo, trumpet call, war cry, war whoop, war dance, battle cry, rallying cry, starter's gun, warning shot, shot across the bows, fiery cross (US), warning light, flashing light, red light, amber light, flare, warning flare, Very signal (*or* light), red flag, yellow flag, distress signal, SOS, mayday, distress flare, sign of alarm, wide eyes, open mouth, start, tremor, paleness, sweat, hair on end

▶ *543 Sign, 544 Identification, 633 Danger, 777 Fear*

3 **false alarm**, false alert, false warning, alarm test, cry of wolf, scare, hoax, bugbear, bugaboo, bogey (*or* bogy), *bête noire* (Fr), nightmare, bad dream, false pregnancy, blank cartridge, fool's gold, flash in the pan, canard, false report, false rumour, untruth

▶ *764 Unpleasantness, 539 Deception, 538 Untruth, 102 Unreality*

4 **warner**, cautioner, caveator, adviser, counsellor, admonisher, prophet, Ezekiel, Nostradamus, Cassandra, medicine man, witch doctor, shaman, diviner, scaremonger, alarmist, flagman, signaller, lighthouse-keeper, watchman, lookout, security guard, security man (*or* woman), watch, guard, picket, sentinel, sentry, scout, advanced guard, vanguard, rear sentry, rearguard, watchdog, protector, spy, informant, mole, rat (Sl), squealer (Sl)

▶ *654 Advice, 781 Caution, 528 Information, 517 Prediction, 632 Safety*

VERBS

5 **warn**, give fair warning, caution, issue a caveat, advise, counsel, give a word of warning, give a word in the ear, give a word to the wise, tip, tip off, kick under the table, wink, pinch, nudge, hint, drop a hint, give notice, notify, inform, apprise, issue a public warning, put on one's guard, alert, forewarn, forearm, prepare, spell danger, spell disaster, predict, augur, re-

mind, put one in mind, admonish, reprove, lour, menace, threaten, advise against, dissuade, remonstrate, protest, provoke action, cause panic

▶ *654 Advice, 781 Caution, 528 Information, 594 Preparation, 511 Memory, 852 Disapproval*

6 **be warned**, receive notice, beware, take heed, watch one's step, learn one's lesson, take someone's words to heart, profit by (the) example, profit by one's mistakes

7 **raise the alarm**, give the alarm, sound a warning, sound the alarm, sound the fire alarm, sound a siren, sound one's horn, honk, toot, blow the whistle, ring the bell, pull the emergency handle, press the emergency button, fire a warning flare, toll, knell, alert, arouse, scare, startle, frighten, alarm, cry, scream, raise a hue and cry, call out the troops, turn out the guard, call the police, dial 999, call a doctor, call an ambulance, call the fire brigade, call the emergency service, call the rescue service, call the AA (Automobile Association), call the RAC (Royal Automobile Club), give a false alarm, cry wolf, cry too soon, test the alarm system, cry blue murder (Inf)

▶ *514 Surprise, 777 Fear*

ADJECTIVES

8 **warning**, cautionary, exemplary, advisable, counsellable, instructive, informative, notifying, hinting, monitory, admonitory, protesting, symptomatic, prognostic, predicting, premonitory, boding, foreboding, ill-omened, ominous, presageful, menacing, minatory, threatening, deterrent, dissuasive, frightening

▶ *654 Advice, 781 Caution, 528 Information, 517 Prediction, 777 Fear*

9 **warned**, cautioned, advised, counselled, taught a lesson, cautious, wary, forewarned, forearmed, prepared, once bitten (Inf)

▶ *781 Caution, 594 Preparation*

INTERJECTIONS

10 **look out!**, beware!, careful!, watch out!, watch it!, take care!, mind your step!, mind the gap!, look where you're going!, cave!, (Sl), fore! (golf)

637 Preservation

NOUNS

1 **preservation**, protection, safekeeping, keeping alive, perpetuation, continuation, prolongation, conservation, conservancy, permanence, ecology, environmental movement, green movement, Greenpeace, Friends of the Earth, conservation area, protected area, (wild) bird sanctuary, (wild) animal sanctuary, game reserve, nature reserve, reservation, park, saving, salvation, redemption, deliverance, retention, keep, maintenance, support, provision,

self-preservation, selfishness, frugality, economy, thrift, saving up, insulation, heat retention, storage, keeping fresh, cold storage, freezing, deep-freezing, freeze-drying, refrigeration, boiling, pickling, marination, curing, smoking, dehydration, desiccation, drying, sun-drying, ultra heat treatment (UHT), canning, tinning, processing, packaging, packing, irradiation, sterilization, hygiene, preventive medicine, quarantine, *cordon sanitaire* (Fr), upkeep, service, servicing, valeting, cleansing, painting, varnishing, waterproofing, embalming, mummification, taxidermy

▶ *632 Safety, 217 Permanence, 396 Life, 639 Deliverance, 606 Provision, 860 Selfishness, 756 Thrift, 605 Store, 409 Cold, 392 Dryness, 625 Hygiene, 399 Burial*

2 **preserver**, preservative, formaldehyde, alcohol, camphor, mothball, amber, plastic, salt, brine, spice, pickle, marinade, aspic, pectin, jelly, ice, freezer, refrigerator, vacuum flask, Thermos (flask) (Tm), Dewar (flask), jar, pot, bottle, can, tin, paint, varnish, whitewash, creosote, rescue device, lifeline, life belt, life jacket, safety device, seat belt, safety belt, air bag, gas mask, incubator, respirator, iron lung, life support system, good-luck charm, charm, amulet, mascot, talisman, silo, cannery, canning factory, bottling plant, conservation campaign, preservation order, fridge (Inf)

▶ *632 Safety, 409 Cold, 45 Cookery*

3 **preserved thing**, protected building, registered historic building (US), listed building, protected species, endangered species, mummy, fossil, stuffed animal, frozen food, freeze-dried food, vacuum-packed food, long-life food, long-life milk, dehydrated food, dried food, dried milk, processed food, canned food, tinned food, preserves, jam, jelly, marmalade, conserve, pickles, bottled fruit

▶ *45 Cookery*

4 **preservationist**, conservationist, conservator, environmentalist, ecologist, green, Greenpeace member (*or* supporter), Friends of the Earth member (*or* supporter), lifeguard, lifesaver, saviour, rescuer, deliverer, embalmer, mummifier, bottler, canner, tinner, forester, (forest) ranger (US)

▶ *639 Deliverance*

VERBS

5 **preserve**, protect, guard, keep safe, keep alive, perpetuate, continue, prolong, uphold, defend, conserve, keep fresh, freeze, freeze-dry, keep on ice, refrigerate, irradiate, pickle, salt, souse, marinate, cure, smoke, kipper, dehydrate, dry, sun-dry, pot, bottle, can, tin, process, season, paint, varnish, whitewash, creosote, waterproof, embalm, mummify, stuff, maintain, service, keep up, keep running, keep in good repair, support, prop up,

shore up, bolster, sustain, feed, provision, provide, supply, keep going, safeguard, shelter, keep under cover, warehouse, garage, keep, store, reserve, save, save up, bottle up, withhold, nurse, mother, foster, tend, cherish, treasure, look after, hold, retain, not let go, grasp, hug, hide, spare, rescue, deliver

▶ *632 Safety, 396 Life, 409 Cold, 392 Dryness, 629 Repair, 284 Support, 605 Store, 606 Provision, 756 Thrift, 630 Remedy, 469 Carefulness, 726 Retention, 639 Deliverance*

ADJECTIVES

6 **preserving**, preservative, conserving, conservative, protecting, protective, prophylactic, preventive, preventative, salubrious, hygienic, redemptive, energy-saving, ecological, environment-friendly, environmental, conservational, green

7 **preserved**, well-preserved, kept, well-kept, alive, fresh, undecayed, intact, whole, perfect, dehydrated, desiccated, dried, sun-dried, freeze-dried, frozen, iced, on ice, in the freezer, in the refrigerator, pickled, marinated, salted, corned, soused, smoked, cured, canned, tinned, potted, bottled, mummified, embalmed, stuffed, laid up in lavender, mothballed, stored, conserved, protected, saved, safe, treasured, cherished

▶ *619 Perfection, 45 Cookery, 605 Store, 632 Safety*

ADVERBS

8 **preservatively**, conservatively, protectively, prophylactically, preventively, ecologically, environmentally

638 Escape

NOUNS

1 **escape**, breakout, getaway, get-out, jailbreak, freedom, decampment, flight, departure, withdrawal, retreat, hasty retreat, disappearance, disappearing trick, vanishing, vanishing into thin air, French leave, truancy, elopement, runaway wedding, elusion, evasion, avoidance, nonpayment, financial escape, tax avoidance, tax evasion, tax-dodging, tax shelter, tax haven, creative economy, black economy, moonlighting, narrow escape, hairbreadth escape, near miss, near thing, reprieve, overturned conviction, acquittal, release, setting free, liberation, immunity, impunity, exemption, escapology, escapism, rescue, deliverance, riddance, relief, hooky (US inf), flit (Inf), moonlight flit (Inf), close shave (Inf), close call (US inf), narrow squeak (Inf)

▶ *345 Departure, 337 Backward Motion, 458 Disappearance, 591 Avoidance, 747 Nonpayment, 633 Danger, 698 Freedom, 700 Liberation, 848 Exemption*

2 **means of escape**, exit, emergency exit, way out, egress, back door, trap door, escape hatch,

hidden panel, secret passage, backstairs, ladder, fire escape, drawbridge, vent, safety valve, camouflage, disguise, dodge, device, trick, contrivance, loophole, escape clause, technicality, let-out

▶ *347 Exit, 632 Safety, 592 Plan, 485 Qualification*

3 **escaper**, escapee, fugitive, runaway, fleer, retreater, eloper, truant, evader, tax evader, tax dodger, reprieved prisoner, released prisoner, escaped prisoner, jail-breaker, refugee, survivor, escapist, escapologist, Houdini

4 **leak**, leakage, air leakage, gas leakage, water loss, loss, emission, issue, seepage, discharge, outflow

▶ *347 Exit*

VERBS

5 **escape**, break out, get out, escape from jail, break out of prison, break loose, break one's chains, go over the wall, break away, get away, make a getaway, decamp, flee, fly, take flight, bolt, run away, abscond, depart, duck and run, make good one's escape, effect one's escape, get free, win freedom, find freedom, slip one's collar, slip one's lead (*or* leash), take to one's heels, retreat, beat a hasty retreat, disappear, vanish, vanish into thin air, make oneself scarce, sneak off, sneak out, steal away, go absent without leave (AWOL), take French leave, play truant, jump bail, elope, deliver oneself, save oneself, save one's skin, have a narrow escape, have a hairbreadth escape, escape by the skin of one's teeth, slip through someone's fingers, wiggle (*or* wriggle) out of, bluff one's way out, scrape through, slip through, break through, get a reprieve, have one's conviction overturned, secure an acquittal, receive immunity, secure exemption, go unpunished, go scot-free, get away with it, get off, get off on a technicality, get off lightly, survive, weather the storm, find relief, skip (US inf), vamoose (US sl), take it on the lam (US sl), do a bunk (*or* runner) (Inf), do a moonlight flit (Inf), play hooky (Inf), skive off (Inf), have a close shave (Inf), have a close call (US inf), have a narrow squeak (Inf), save one's bacon (Inf)

▶ *345 Departure, 458 Disappearance, 698 Freedom, 700 Liberation, 639 Deliverance, 591 Avoidance, 848 Exemption, 767 Relief*

6 **elude**, evade, avoid, dodge, miss, get rid of, rid oneself of, hide, lie low, stay underground, escape detection, give one the slip, shake off, throw off the trail, throw off the scent, give one a run for one's money, escape notice, avoid taxes, evade taxes, moonlight

▶ *591 Avoidance, 531 Concealment, 747 Nonpayment*

7 **leak**, leak away, leak air, leak gas, lose water, flow out, emerge, issue, seep out, gush, spurt

▶ *347 Exit*

ADJECTIVES

8 **escaping**, evasive, elusive, fugitive, runaway, truant, escaped, loose, free, scot-free, reprieved, acquitted, immune, exempt, relieved, emancipated, liberated, untied, unbound, unchained

▶ *698 Freedom, 700 Liberation*

ADVERBS

9 **fugitively**, in flight, in hiding, out of range (*or* sight), away, over the hills and far away, freely

639 Deliverance

VERBS

1 **deliver**, save, rescue, come to the rescue, throw a lifeline to, snatch from the jaws of death, save at the last second (*or* minute), rescue at the eleventh hour, save by the bell, extricate, unravel, untangle, extract, get out, unfasten, unloose, untie, unbind, unfetter, unchain, unburden, disburden, disencumber, rid of, save from, relieve, release, emancipate, liberate, free, declare free, set free, set at large, unlock, unbar, let out, let go, let off, get off, reprieve, acquit, exempt, excuse, dispense with, spare, redeem, ransom, bail out, buy off, purchase, salvage, retrieve, recover, bring back, restore

▶ *632 Safety, 767 Relief, 700 Liberation, 355 Extraction, 152 Arrangement, 136 Separation, 698 Freedom, 638 Escape, 848 Exemption, 729 Giving, 70 Transport*

NOUNS

2 **deliverance**, delivery, saving, life-saving, rescue, air-sea rescue, extrication, unravelling, untangling, extraction, disencumberment, riddance, good riddance, relief, release, emancipation, freedom, liberation, let-off, amnesty, discharge, reprieve, reprieval, acquittal, dispensation, excuse, exemption, escape, let-out, way out, salvation, redemption, ransom, bail, buying off, purchase, salvage, retrieval, recovery, restoration, day of grace, respite, delay, truce, standstill, cessation

▶ *767 Relief, 355 Extraction, 698 Freedom, 700 Liberation, 638 Escape, 218 Cessation*

3 **deliverer**, saviour, life-saver, rescuer, rescue team, air-sea rescue helicopter, lifeboat, lifeboatman, liberator, emancipator, redeemer, salvage company

▶ *632 Safety, 700 Liberation*

ADJECTIVES

4 **deliverable**, saveable, salvable, rescuable, extricable, redeemable, salvageable, fit for release, delivered, saved, rescued, liberated, free, saving, life-saving, saved by the bell

INTERJECTIONS

5 **to the rescue!**, man overboard!, all hands on deck!, all hands to the pump!, help!

6 **extricably**, redeemably, free, salvably

640 Action

Suit the action to the word, the word to the action; with this special observance, that you o'erstep not the modesty of nature. William Shakespeare.

So many worlds, so much to do,/ So little done, such things to be. Alfred, Lord Tennyson.

NOUNS

1 **action**, doing, happening, performance, execution, steps, measures, move, enactment, policy, transaction, commission, perpetration, dispatch, accomplishment, achievement, effectuation, completion, proceeding, process, procedure, routine, custom, praxis, practice, behaviour, conduct, movement, play, swing, motion, operation, functioning, working, interaction, evolution, agency, force, pressure, sway, control, influence, effect, power, work, labour, exertion, effort, attempt, endeavour, campaign, programme, crusade, battle, war, militancy, activism, activeness, activity, drama, occupation, business, manufacture, production, employment, use, implementation, putting into effect, administration, handling, management, direction, legal action, legal proceeding, lawsuit
▶ *592 Plan, 684 Completion, 584 Habit, 324 Motion, 233 Influence, 235 Power, 644 Work, 642 Activity, 243 Production, 599 Use, 596 Attempt, 653 Management, 676 War*

2 **deed**, act, overt act, action, exploit, feat, achievement, accomplishment, gesture, useless gesture, meaningless act, *beau geste* (Fr), good deed, bad deed, wrongdoing, criminal act, crime, foul play, stunt, *tour de force* (Fr), special effort, stroke of genius, pretence, dissimulation, posture, affectation, gesticulation, measure, step, move, policy, manoeuvre, evolution, tactics, sudden action, stroke, blow, coup, *coup de main* (Fr), *coup de grâce* (Fr), coup d'état, overthrow, job, task, work, operation, exercise, undertaking, proceeding, transaction, deal, doings, actions, dealings, affairs, handiwork, handicraft, workmanship, craftsmanship, skill, *pièce de résistance* (Fr), *chef-d'œuvre* (Fr), masterpiece, drama, play, scene, narrative
▶ *778 Courage, 592 Plan, 597 Undertaking, 539 Deception, 655 Skill, 560 Description, 51 Performing Arts*

3 **doer**, man (*or* woman) of action, self-starter, busy person, activist, political activist, lobbyist, active supporter, campaigner, crusader, militant, practical person, realist, finisher, achiever, high achiever, high-flier (*or* high-

flyer), hero, heroine, good role model, benefactor, brave person, practitioner, professional, expert, stunt man (*or* woman), player, performer, actor, actress, creative person, creative worker, artistic person, artist, executant, perpetrator, committer, offender, criminal, gangster, evildoer, malefactor, mover, mover and shaker (US), canvasser, controller, manipulator, motivator, operator, agent, contractor, undertaker, entrepreneur, executor, executive, chief executive, administrator, manager, general manager, managing director, director, hand, worker, manual worker, workman, operative, craftsman (*or* woman), handicraftsman (*or* woman), handicraft worker, artisan, go-getter (Inf), live wire (Inf), whiz kid (Inf), street-fighter (Inf), do-gooder (Inf)
▶ *642 Activity, 778 Courage, 655 Skill, 51 Performing Arts, 50 Painting and Sculpture, 832 Malevolence, 646 Worker, 653 Management*

VERBS

4 **act**, do, happen, perform, carry out, execute, take action, take steps, take measures, enact, legislate, commission, dispatch, accomplish, achieve, complete, carry through, get in on the act, be in on the action, take effect, come into operation, operate, function, militate for, militate against, act upon, sway, influence, manipulate, motivate, use tactics, twist, turn, manoeuvre, proceed, proceed with, get on with, push on with, get going, get cracking (Inf), move, do something, make an (*or* the) effort, lift a finger, raise a finger, try, attempt, tackle, take on, shoulder, undertake, do the deed, perpetrate, commit, do what is required (*or* needed), do the needful, take care of, implement, fulfil, put into practice, put into use, solemnize, observe, do great deeds, make history, win renown, become celebrated, become famous, acquire a reputation, practise, exercise, carry on, discharge, prosecute, pursue, wage, ply, ply one's trade, employ oneself, occupy oneself, busy oneself, do business, transact, deal, officiate, direct, be in charge, administer, administrate, manage, control, have to do with, deal with, work, labour, sweat, campaign, canvass, use, exploit, take advantage of, make the most of, intervene, come between, work for, strike a blow for, help, aid, have a hand in, be active in, take part in, play a part in, have a finger in (Inf), participate, interfere, deal in, get mixed up in, meddle, conduct oneself, indulge in, behave, play about, frolic about, lark around, skylark (Inf), fool around, stunt, perform a stunt, show off, pretend, feign, dissemble
▶ *230 Operation, 684 Completion, 233 Influence, 586 Persuasion, 657 Cunning, 597 Undertaking, 596 Attempt, 642 Activity*

5 **acting**, doing, happening, performing, enacting, working, at work, occupational, in action, red-handed, in operation, in harness, operative, up and doing, industrious, busy, active, interactive, creative, artistic, dramatic, militant, crusading, brave, heroic

▶ *642 Activity, 644 Work*

6 **effective**, forceful, powerful, productive, useful, direct, influential, functional, operational, procedural, professional, managerial, executive, administrative, tactical

▶ *644 Work, 227 Effect, 235 Power*

ADVERBS
7 **actively**, overtly, in the act, red-handed, in flagrante delicto, in the midst of, in the thick of, by enactment, by custom, with a stroke

8 **effectively**, forcefully, powerfully, productively, usefully, directly, influentially, functionally

641 Inaction

NOUNS
1 **inaction**, lack of action, nonaction, nothing happening, inertia, inertness, inability to act, impotence, refusal to act, failure to act, neglect, negligence, abstinence from action, abstention, refraining, avoidance, passive resistance, *laissez* (or *laisser*) *aller* (Fr), *laissez* (or *laisser*) *faire* (Fr), suspension, abeyance, dormancy, inactivity, nonuse, deadlock, stalemate, log jam (US), stop, standstill, lack of progress, bogging down, immobility, motionlessness, paralysis, impassivity, insensibility, passivity, apathy, stagnation, vegetation, doldrums, stillness, quiet, quietness, calm, calmness, tranquillity, quiescence, all the time in the world, time on one's hands, time to kill, idle hours, *dolce far niente* (It), leisure, rest, repose, relaxing, relaxation, lack of ambition, laziness, loafing, idleness, indolence, watching (or letting) the world go by, twiddling one's thumbs, unemployment, nonemployment, underemployment, joblessness, redundancy, no work, easy work, sinecure, Fabianism, Fabian policy, do-nothingism, delay, putting off till tomorrow, procrastination, noninterference, nonintervention, hands off, defeatism, hopelessness, no courage, cowardice, indifference, head in the sand

▶ *240 Inertness, 643 Inactivity, 649 Ease, 236 Powerlessness, 470 Negligence, 591 Avoidance, 600 Nonuse, 218 Cessation, 404 Insensibility, 325 Motionlessness, 209 Lateness, 783 Indifference, 779 Cowardice*

2 **nonacting person**, idler, idle rich, leisured classes, loafer, layabout, shirker, sleeper, dreamer, daydreamer, waverer, ditherer, hesitator, nihilist, solipsist, pessimist, fatalist, defeatist, non interventionist, abstainer, killjoy, wallflower, party-pooper (Inf), coward, chicken (Sl)

ADJECTIVES
3 **inactive**, nonactive, inert, unable to act, impotent, powerless, negligent, neglectful, abstaining, abstentious, suspended, in abeyance, dormant, inoperative, deadlocked, stalemated, at a standstill, stationary, immobile, motionless, still, calm, becalmed, tranquil, quiet, quiescent, stagnant, not stirring, hardly breathing, half-dead, half-gone, without a sign of life, gone, dead, extinct, benumbed, cold, frozen, paralysed, impassive, insensible, passive, apathetic, phlegmatic, dull, sluggish, leisured, leisurely, relaxed, lazy, indolent, idle, fallow, unoccupied, unemployed, without employment, underemployed, laid off, redundant, jobless, without a job, out of work, collecting unemployment (US), doing nothing, do-nothing, wait-and-see, unprogressive, ostrich-like, Fabian, refraining, delaying, procrastinating, cunctative, defeatist, cowardly, indifferent, neutral, hands-off, tolerant, unseeing, unhearing, blind, deaf, on the dole (Inf), signing on (Inf), collecting (US inf)

▶ *643 Inactivity, 240 Inertness, 236 Powerlessness, 470 Negligence, 397 Death, 325 Motionlessness, 404 Insensibility, 645 Leisure, 649 Ease, 209 Lateness, 783 Indifference, 779 Cowardice*

VERBS
4 **not act**, do nothing, fail to act, refuse to act, be inactive, be inert, suffer from inertia, refrain, avoid, abstain, pass up, stand by, look on, watch, have no ambition, loaf, idle, watch the world go by, let the world go by, watch and wait, wait and see, bide one's time, wait, sit tight, delay, procrastinate, put off (till tomorrow), defer, live and let live, let the good times roll, let things take their course, let things take care of themselves, leave alone, let alone, let sleeping dogs lie, let well (enough) alone, hold no brief for, wash one's hands of, keep out of, stay neutral, sit on the fence, tolerate, pretend not to see, disregard, ignore, let pass, not react, not move, not budge, not stir, not bat an eye (or eyelid), show no sign of life, not raise (or lift) a finger, stagnate, vegetate, rest on one's laurels, rest on one's oars, relax one's efforts, tread water, drift, glide, slide, coast, freewheel, abandon hope, have no hope, give up, despair, neglect, stay still, keep quiet, keep mum, sit back, relax, unwind, rest, repose, have no function, be redundant, be superfluous, be useless, have free time, have nothing to do, kill time, kick one's heels, twiddle one's thumbs, look out the window, sit on one's hands, stop, pause, desist, quit, cease, rust, gather dust, lie idle, lie fallow, stay on the shelf, stay packed away, have no life, be life-

less, lie dead, die, hang fire (US sl), pass the buck (Inf), turn a blind eye (Inf), turn a deaf ear (Inf), button (up) one's lip (*or* mouth) (Inf)

▶ *643 Inactivity, 240 Inertness, 209 Lateness, 783 Indifference, 649 Ease, 776 Hopelessness, 614 Uselessness, 645 Leisure, 218 Cessation, 397 Death*

ADVERBS

5 **without action**, without movement, with one's hands in one's pockets, with folded arms, inertly, powerlessly, negligently, impassively, apathetically, lazily, idly, indifferently, calmly, quietly, tranquilly, at rest

642 Activity

NOUNS

1 **activity**, action, activeness, movement, motion, life, stirring, stir, agitation, excitation, stimulation, ado, much ado, to-do, great doings, drama, commotion, racket, disturbance, row, quarrel, squabble, brawl, fray, tumult, turmoil, frenzy, whirl, maelstrom, vortex, midst of things, thick of things, thick of the action, kick (Sl), buzz (Sl), eye of the hurricane (*or* storm) (Inf)

▶ *640 Action, 324 Motion, 366 Agitation, 151 Disorder, 364 Rotation, 473 Argument*

2 **social activity**, group activity, interaction, person-to-person interaction, participation, active participation, volunteering, sociability, mingling, mixing, interest, special interest, active interest, hobby, pastime, pursuit, occupation, enterprise, undertaking, venture, a piece of the action (Inf)

▶ *815 Sociability, 724 Joint Possession, 645 Leisure, 644 Work, 597 Undertaking, 640 Action*

3 **nimbleness**, briskness, alacrity, promptitude, willingness, readiness, punctuality, quickness, speed, velocity, haste, dispatch, expedition, scramble, mad scramble, race, mad race, rat race, dash, mad dash, wild dash, burst, spurt, fit, spasm, overhaste, frantic haste, hurry, flurry, hurry-scurry, hustle, bustle, hustle and bustle, fuss, bother, fuss and bother, nuisance, botheration (Inf), hassle (Inf)

▶ *648 Haste, 208 Earliness, 572 Willingness*

4 **energy**, ceaseless energy, dynamic energy, dynamism, vigour, vigorousness, abandon, frenzy, vitality, vivacity, vivaciousness, life, liveliness, animation, spirit, high spirits, pep, eagerness, enthusiasm, ardour, fervour, vehemence, strong feeling, warm feeling, activation, motive, reason, cause, aggressiveness, enterprise, initiative, drive, push, ambition, go (Inf), get-up-and-go (Inf), moxie (US sl)

5 **activism**, political activism, militancy, militant scene, mass movement, popular movement, political movement, uprising, sedition

▶ *239 Vigour, 396 Life, 759 Feeling*

6 **business**, industry, call on one's time, imposition on one's time, press of business, pressure of work, pressure of deadlines, no sinecure, plenty to do, busyness, no break, no rest for the wicked, hive of activity, hive of industry, hive, beehive, high street, marketplace, workshop, hum of activity, hum, press, crush, jostling crowd, seething mob, hoi polloi, madding crowd (Arch), crush of shoppers, heavy traffic, a full plate (Inf), several (*or* many) irons in the fire (Inf)

▶ *644 Work, 647 Workshop*

7 **restlessness**, aimlessness, aimless activity, randomness, desultoriness, lack of concentration, inattention, dawdling, puttering (US), pottering, fiddling, fidgetiness, the fidgets, wanderlust, unrest, unease, unquietness, unquiet, jumpiness, nervousness, nerves, agitation, excitability, fever, fret, sleeplessness, insomnia, wakefulness, watchfulness, itchy feet (Inf)

▶ *468 Inattention, 469 Carefulness*

8 **assiduity**, application, concentration, intentness, attention, diligence, sedulity, industriousness, industry, hard work, laboriousness, monotonous work, drudgery, labour, determination, resolution, earnestness, *empressement* (Fr), tirelessness, indefatigability, perseverance, stamina, stickability (US), studiousness, painstaking, perfectionism, attention to detail, devotedness, wholeheartedness, gung-ho attitude, stick-to-itiveness (*or* stick-at-itiveness) (US inf)

▶ *467 Attention, 644 Work, 574 Resolution, 575 Perseverance*

9 **overactivity**, hyperactivity, overextension, overexpansion, overdiversification, overambition, oversupply, excess, redundancy, Parkinson's law, displacement activity, useless work, futile activity, wild-goose chase, chasing one's own tail, lost labour, wasted effort, useless exercise, hyperthyroidism, overexertion, petty officialdom, petty bureaucracy, red tape, officiousness, beadledom, meddlesomeness, interference, intrusiveness, interruption, meddling, interfering, sticking one's nose in, a finger in every pie, tampering, intrigue, conspiracy, secret plot, plot, song and dance (Inf)

▶ *610 Excess, 614 Uselessness, 366 Agitation, 592 Plan*

10 **busy person**, active person, fully occupied person, socially active person, jet-setter, socialite, energetic person, bustler, hustler, wheeler-dealer, someone in a hurry, fidget, hyperactive child, person of active habits, man (*or* woman) of action, activist, militant, doer, participator, volunteer, sharp fellow, sharpie (US inf), careerist, pusher, thruster, yuppie, enthusiast, zealot, fanatic, devotee, toiler, slogger, no

slouch, hard worker, tireless worker, fanatical worker, high-pressure worker, Stakhanovite, demon for work, glutton for work, workaholic, new broom, worker, factotum, handyman, jack of all trades, maid of all work, drudge, Trojan, live wire (Inf), dynamo (Inf), human dynamo (Inf), powerhouse (Inf), whiz kid (Inf), whiz (Inf), go-getter (Inf), buff (Inf), glutton for punishment (Inf), gofer (US sl), dogsbody (Inf), fag (Inf), slave (Inf), galley slave (Inf), horse (Inf), workhorse (Inf), willing horse (Inf), mule (Inf), beaver (Inf), ant (Inf), bee (Inf), busy bee (Inf), eager beaver (Inf)

▶ *577 Obstinacy, 646 Worker, 640 Action*

11 **meddler**, meddling person, prying person, busybody, interferer, intermeddler, dabbler, stirrer, troublemaker, officious person, inquisitive person, tamperer, intriguer, planner, adviser, nuisance, fuss-budget (US inf), fusspot (Inf), spoilsport (Inf), nosy parker (Inf), kibitzer (US inf), back-seat driver (Inf)

▶ *465 Curiosity, 592 Plan, 654 Advice*

VERBS

12 **be active**, act, do, wake up, rouse oneself, bestir oneself, rub the sleep from one's eyes, rise and shine, rise, get up, be up and doing, move, stir, agitate, squabble, start a row, run riot, rampage, have one's fling, roar, rage, bluster, blow, explode, burst, spurt, flow, surge, rush, dash, race, fly, run, move fast, hasten, hurry, scurry, scramble, have no time to lose, come and go, rush to and fro, hustle, bustle, fuss, bother, fret, fume, drum one's fingers, stamp with impatience, have other things to do, have other fish to fry (Inf), stir one's stumps (Inf), get the lead out (Inf), get one's ass in gear (Tab sl), kick up a shindy (Inf), raise the dust (Inf), go at it nineteen to the dozen (Inf)

▶ *640 Action, 324 Motion, 366 Agitation, 151 Disorder, 648 Haste, 241 Violence*

13 **be busy**, busy oneself, keep busy, prosper, thrive, hum, make progress, progress, keep moving, keep on the go, keep on, have several irons in the fire, have one's hands full, be rushed off one's feet, not have a moment to spare (*or* to call one's own), live in a whirl, join the rat race, go all ways at once, not know which way to turn, not know which way is up, waste effort, rise early, go to bed late, burn the midnight oil, burn the candle at both ends, make hay while the sun shines, not let the grass grow under one's feet, keep on keeping on (US inf), keep the pot boiling (Inf), have one's plate full (Inf), spread oneself thin (Inf), run round in circles (Inf), chase one's own tail (Inf)

▶ *336 Forward Motion, 682 Success, 614 Uselessness*

14 **push**, shove, thrust, drive, impel, elbow one's way, thrust oneself forward, assert oneself, seize the opportunity, take one's chance, take the bull by the horns, profit by, protest, demonstrate, defy, react, react sharply, show fight, be up in arms, not take it lying down, be willing, show willingness, jump to it, show zeal, burn with zeal, not sleep, wake, watch, be on one's toes, be alert, respond, anticipate

▶ *330 Impulsion, 239 Vigour, 713 Protest, 668 Defiance, 572 Willingness*

15 **try**, attempt, try hard, take pains, make an effort, exert oneself, strain oneself, do one's best, rise to the occasion, dispatch, make short work of, work wonders, concentrate, put one's mind to, buckle down, put one's shoulder to the wheel, put one's hand to the tiller, persist, persevere, beaver away, work, slave, slog, overwork, overdo it, make work, never stop, plug away (Inf), do one's damnedest (Sl), polish off (Inf), go the whole hog (Inf), make the sparks fly (Inf), make things hum (Inf)

▶ *596 Attempt, 467 Attention, 575 Perseverance, 644 Work*

16 **be sociable**, interact, mingle, circulate, mix, join in, participate actively, participate, volunteer, have an active interest, show interest, interest oneself in, get a piece of the action (Inf)

▶ *724 Joint Possession, 815 Sociability*

17 **meddle**, intermeddle, interpose, intervene, interfere, be officious, have a finger in every pie, not mind one's own business, pry, poke one's nose in, spy, put one's oar in, put one's two cents in (US), butt in, interrupt, intrude, pester, bother, dun, importune, annoy, irritate, trouble, harass, boss, boss around, bully, persecute, tyrannize, oppress, tinker, tamper, fiddle, touch, impair, hassle (Inf)

▶ *346 Entry, 465 Curiosity, 764 Unpleasantness, 690 Severity*

ADJECTIVES

18 **active**, interactive, sociable, activated, moving, going, running, working, operative, in action, incessant, unceasing, expeditious, businesslike, able, able-bodied, strong, quick, fast, speedy, brisk, spry, nimble, agile, smart, keen, gleg (Scot), light-footed, lightsome, tripping, vigorous, strenuous, energetic, forceful, dynamic, thrustful, thrusting, stirring, pushing, up-and-coming, enterprising, lively, sprightly, frisky, coltish, dashing, spirited, mettlesome, live, alive, alive and kicking, full of vitality, animated, vivacious, eager, ardent, fervent, perfervid, fierce, desperate, resolute, determined, enthusiastic, fanatical, zealous, prompt, instant, ready, willing, alert, on one's toes, awake, wakeful, watchful, careful, on the alert, vigilant, sleepless, restless, feverish, fretful, tossing, dancing, fidgety, nervous, nervy, jumpy, agitated, tense, fussy, like a cat on a hot tin roof, like a cat on hot bricks, like a long-tailed cat in a room full of rocking chairs

(US), like a hen on a hot griddle, frenzied, frenetic, frantic, manic, demonic, hyperactive, overactive, overwrought, excitable, involved, actively involved, deeply involved, *engagé* or *engagée* (Fr), aggressive, militant, up in arms, warlike, nippy (Inf), go-getting (Inf), full of beans (Inf), into (Inf), hyper (Inf)

▶ *324 Motion, 219 Continuity, 640 Action, 237 Strength, 648 Haste, 239 Vigour, 597 Undertaking, 759 Feeling, 574 Resolution, 572 Willingness, 469 Carefulness, 366 Agitation, 676 War*

19 **busy**, active, bustling, hustling, humming, hectic, lively, eventful, in full swing, coming and going, rushing to and fro, puttering (US), pottering, doing chores, up and doing, stirring, astir, afoot, on the move, on the go, employed, in harness, at work, at one's desk, engaged, occupied, fully occupied, fully engaged, hard at work, hard at it, slogging, overworked, overemployed, rushed off one's feet, up to one's eyes, up to one's ears, up to one's neck, working oneself into the grave, fussing like a hen with chickens, busy as a bee, busy as a beaver, on the trot (Inf), on the make (Inf), up to one's ass (Tab sl), up to one's neck (*or* eyes *or* elbows) (Inf)

20 **industrious**, sedulous, diligent, assiduous, studious, persevering, hard-working, workaholic, plodding, slogging, labouring, laborious, unflagging, unwearied, tireless, indefatigable, full of stamina, energetic, unsleeping, keeping long hours, burning the midnight oil, burning the candle at both ends, never-tiring, never-resting, never-slacking, never-sleeping, efficient, workmanlike, businesslike, professional, stick-to-itive (*or* stick-at-itive) (US inf)

▶ *575 Perseverance, 644 Work*

21 **meddling**, overbusy, officious, interfering, meddlesome, intrusive, nosy, prying, irritating, annoying, troublesome, tyrannical, intriguing, dabbling, fiddling, participating, taking part, in the business, pushy (Inf)

▶ *346 Entry, 465 Curiosity*

ADVERBS

22 **actively**, fast, nimbly, vigorously, forcefully, eagerly, enthusiastically, promptly, restlessly, busily, industriously, on the go, on one's toes, full tilt, on all cylinders, with haste, with might and main, for all one is worth, for dear life, as if one's life depended on it, like a bomb (Inf)

INTERJECTIONS

23 **rise and shine!** wakey wakey!, up you get! shake a leg! get going! get a move on! buckle down! get the lead out! (Sl)

643 Inactivity

ADJECTIVES

1 **inactive**, quiescent, still, quiet, motionless, immobile, stationary, static, sedentary, stag-

nant, inert, passive, extinct, lifeless, inanimate

▶ *641 Inaction, 240 Inertness, 325 Motionlessness, 422 Silence*

2 **not working** (*or* **operating**), unemployed, unengaged, laid off, redundant, on strike, out, out of work, between jobs, jobless, signing on (Inf), off work, off duty, resting, free, available, at a loose end, laid up, out of action, out of commission, off, at a standstill, broken down, unused, fallow, idle, disengaged, unoccupied, vacant, empty

3 **not participating**, lazy, idle, indolent, slothful, work-shy, bone idle, loafing, lolling, parasitic, slack, lax, slow, dilatory, dawdling, tardy, procrastinating, laggard, sluggish, lethargic, languid, dull, listless, torpid, apathetic, indifferent, uninterested, phlegmatic, impassive

4 **not awake**, somnolent, drowsy, dozy, sleepy, soporific, heavy-eyed, slumberous, nodding off, yawning, dozing, resting, dopey, half-asleep, drugged, sedated, narcotized, anaesthetized, hypnotized, sleeping, asleep, dormant, torpid, hibernating, aestivating, dreaming, fast asleep, sound asleep, dead to the world, unconscious, insensible, out cold, comatose, doped (Sl), flaked out (Sl)

NOUNS

5 **inactivity**, quiescence, stillness, quietness, quiet, silence, immobility, inaction, inertia, passivity, inertness, lull, suspension, cessation, extinction, lifelessness

6 **unemployment**, shutdown, lay-off, slump, recession, depression, redundancy

7 **idleness**, laziness, indolence, sloth, slothfulness, absenteeism, slowness, slow progress, dawdling, delay, procrastination, sluggishness, lethargy, languor, dullness, listlessness, torpor, apathy, indifference, phlegm, impassivity

8 **nonworker**, idler, shirker, slacker, dawdler, skiver, sluggard, *fainéant* (Fr), clock-watcher, passenger, dummy, sinecurist, sleeping partner, absentee landlord, *rentier* (Fr), idle rich, leisured classes, dreamer, lotus-eater, drifter, vagrant, tramp, hobo (US), beggar, drone, leech, parasite, layabout, *flâneur* (Fr), loafer, lounger, cadger, sponger, scrounger, freeloader (Inf), free-rider (US inf), couch potato (Inf), bum (Sl)

▶ *645 Leisure*

9 **sleep**, sleepiness, somnolence, doziness, drowsiness, heaviness, oscitancy, slumber, rest, repose, land of Nod, Morpheus, dreamland, sandman, heavy sleep, dormancy, hibernation, aestivation, unconsciousness, coma, stupor, trance, catalepsy, hypnosis, oblivion, insensibility, light sleep, nap, catnap, snooze, doze, siesta, forty winks (Inf), shut-eye (Inf), bye-byes (Inf), kip (Sl)

10 **soporific**, somnifacient, sleeping pill (*or* draught), nightcap, sedative, barbiturate, narcotic, opiate, poppy, opium, morphine, nepenthe, anaesthetic

11 **sleeper**, slumberer, dozer, drowser, hibernator, dormouse, Rip van Winkle, Sleeping Beauty, lie-abed (Inf), sleepyhead (Inf), Weary Willie (Inf)

VERBS

12 **be inactive**, stagnate, vegetate, do nothing, idle, laze, skive, loaf, lounge, cadge, sponge, slouch, mooch, kill time, kick one's heels (Inf), waste time, hang about, lie around, delay, procrastinate, hang fire, dawdle, drift

13 **sleep**, snooze, doze, drowse, yawn, nod off, nap, catnap, rest, slumber, sleep like a log (*or* top), lie dormant, hibernate, aestivate, kip (Sl), have forty winks (Inf), get one's head down (Inf)

14 **make inactive**, inactivate, dismantle, defuse, neutralize, extinguish, shut down, suspend, lay up, lay off, dismiss, fire, sack, sack, demobilize, immobilize, incapacitate, disable, deaden, drug, dope, sedate, narcotize, knock out, anaesthetize hypnotize

ADVERBS

15 **inactively**, motionlessly, statically, at a standstill, at rest, inertly, passively, lifelessly, inanimately

16 **impassively**, indifferently, apathetically, listlessly, dully, languidly, lethargically, sluggishly, slothfully, indolently, lazily

17 **sleepily**, somnolently, soporifically, dozily, dopily, drowsily, insensibly, unconsciously

644   Work

Whatsoever thy hand findeth to do, do it with thy might; for there is no work, nor device, nor knowledge, nor wisdom, in the grave, whither thou goest. Bible: Ecclesiastes.

There is dignity in work only when it is work freely accepted. Albert Camus.

When work is a pleasure, life is a joy! When work is a duty, life is slavery. Maxim Gorky.

Horny-handed sons of toil. Denis Kearney.

Work expands so as to fill the time available for its completion. Cyril Northcote Parkinson.

The only place where success comes before work is a dictionary. Vidal Sassoon.

Work banishes those three great evils, boredom, vice, and poverty. Voltaire.

NOUNS

1 **work**, labour, toil, industry, assigned work, assignment, easy work, labour of love, hard work, heavy work, uphill work, a long haul, warm work, exhausting work, punishing work, backbreaking work, spadework, donkeywork, legwork, manual work, manual labour, getting one's hands dirty, sweat of one's brow, sweat, everyday work, daily grind, housework, kitchen work, garden work, fieldwork, farmwork, school work, chores, travail, thankless task, drudgery, work without pay, slavery, grind, strain, swink (Arch), dreary routine, treadmill, grindstone, hack work, penal work, hard labour, breaking stones, penalty, forced labour, corvee, compulsion, fatigue, fatigue duty, spell of duty, duty, piecework, taskwork, take-home work, homework, outwork, journeywork, fag (Inf), shitwork (Tab sl)

2 **task**, chore, job, unpleasant job, operation, exercise, assignment, project, commission, deed, feat, trick, shift, stint, stretch, bout, spell of work, period of work, extra work, overtime, job of work, stroke of work, hand's turn, working life, working week, working day, man-hours

▶ *847 Duty, 640 Action, 187 Period, 597 Undertaking, 243 Production*

3 **job**, occupation, employment, profession, trade, métier, business, line of work, line of business, career, vocation, calling, mission, craft, racket (Sl), game (Sl)

4 **exertion**, effort, attempt, endeavour, struggle, straining, strain, stress, might and main, tug, squeeze, pull, push, stretch, rub, scrub, heave, lift, throw, drive, force, pressure, full pressure, maximum pressure, unbearable pressure, energy, applied energy, directed energy, power, manpower, horsepower, ergonomics, mighty effort, impressive effort, the hard way, muscle, muscle power, elbow grease, sweat of one's brow, pains, taking pains, operoseness, assidulty, elaboration, overwork, overexertion, overactivity, overdoing it, working oneself to death, battle, campaign, fray, ado, hassle, trouble, toil and trouble, busman's holiday (Inf)

▶ *596 Attempt, 235 Power, 642 Activity*

5 **exercise**, practice, regular practice, drill, training, the bar, preparation, warm-up, PE (physical education), PT (physical training), keep fit, keeping fit, running, jogging, cycling, walking, swimming, rowing, gymnastics, weightlifting, yoga, isometrics, eurhythmics, callisthenics, work-out, aerobics, athletics, games, sports, races, sport, pumping iron (Inf)

▶ *594 Preparation, 237 Strength, 642 Activity*

VERBS

6 **work**, labour, be busy, do easy work, do hard work, work at home, freelance, work in the field, toil, drudge, fag, grind, slog, peg away, moil (Dial), sweat, work up a sweat, work up a lather, clean, scrub, rub, lift, heave, pull, haul, tug, push, shove, dig, spade, do the work, soil one's hands, get one's hands dirty, spit on

one's palms, clock in (*or* on), punch in (US), begin, get down to it, set about, set to, take one's coat off, roll up one's sleeves, finish the job, quit work, clock out (*or* off), punch out (US), earn a wage, be a breadwinner, get on the gravy train (Inf), make short work of, make up for lost time, go slow, continue working, keep at it, plod, persevere, work hard, work all day, work all week, work a forty-hour week, do a nine-to-five (Inf), work overtime, work double time, do two jobs, work double, work shifts, work day shifts, work night shifts, shift, work all hours, work night and day, burn the midnight oil, burn the candle at both ends, slave, slave away, beaver away, work one's fingers to the bone, work like a galley slave, work like a horse, work like a Trojan, work oneself to death, work oneself into the grave, overdo it, overwork, make work, sweat blood (Inf), hump (Sl), ply the oar (Inf), moonlight (Inf)

▶ *156 Beginning, 575 Perseverance, 642 Activity, 640 Action, 230 Operation*

7 work for, serve, minister to, put to work, employ, task, tax, fatigue

▶ *662 Help, 650 Fatigue*

8 exert oneself, strive, strain, struggle, apply oneself, put one's best foot forward, make an effort, try, attempt, endeavour, travail, bestir oneself, spare no effort, do one's utmost, try one's best, put oneself out, trouble oneself, leave no stone unturned, turn every stone, use one's best endeavours, do all one can, go to any lengths, move heaven and earth, pull out all the stops, put one's heart and soul into it, put one's back into it, strain to the utmost, strain every nerve, use every muscle, give one's all, love one's job, have one's heart in one's work, force one's way, elbow one's way, drive through, wade through, persevere, hammer at, slog at, battle, campaign, take action, go all out (Inf), bend over backwards (Inf), sweat blood (Inf)

▶ *596 Attempt, 642 Activity, 572 Willingness, 575 Perseverance, 640 Action*

9 exercise, practise, drill, train, prepare, warm up, limber up, keep fit, run, jog, cycle, walk, swim, work out

ADJECTIVES

10 working, labouring, busy, industrious, employed, born to toil, horny-handed, drudging, sweating, grinding, slogging, hard-working, plodding, persevering, tireless, energetic, active, painstaking, thorough, attentive, diligent, assiduous, exercising, practising, gymnastic, athletic, on the go (Inf), hard at it (Inf)

▶ *642 Activity, 575 Perseverance, 467 Attention*

11 laborious, strenuous, full of labour, involving effort, requiring great effort, gruelling, punishing, unremitting, tiring, very tiring, exhausting, backbreaking, crushing, killing, toilsome,

troublesome, weary, wearisome, painful, burdensome, heroic, Herculean, arduous, hard, heavy, uphill, difficult, hard-fought, hard-won, thorough, painstaking, laboured, elaborate, detailed, fiddling, fussy, nit-picking (Inf)

▶ *659 Difficulty*

ADVERBS

12 laboriously, arduously, strenuously, energetically, lustily, heartily, the hard way, manually, by hand, by the sweat of one's brow, on the treadmill, with heart and soul, with might and main, with all one's might, on all cylinders, tooth and nail, hammer and tongs, for all one is worth, to one's utmost, on overtime, on double time

645 Leisure

The wisdom of a learned man cometh by opportunity of leisure: and he that hath little business shall become wise./ How can he get wisdom that holdeth the plough, and that glorieth in the goad, that driveth oxen, and is occupied in their labours, and whose talk is of bullocks? Bible: Ecclesiasticus.

If all the year were playing holidays, To sport would be as tedious as to work. William Shakespeare.

NOUNS

1 leisure, free time, spare time, spare hours, free moments, vacant moments, idle moments, odd moments, time to oneself, time for oneself, time one can call one's own, breathing space (*or* room), freedom, liberty, convenience, opportunity, time on one's hands, time to kill, no work, not enough work, sinecure, idleness, *dolce far niente* (It), inactivity, rest, repose, ease, relaxation, no hurry, time to spare, ample time, all the time in the world

▶ *643 Inactivity, 649 Ease*

2 time off, holiday, vacation, leave, day off, half-holiday, sabbatical, furlough, off duty, break, recess, time-out (US), respite, relief, peace, quiet, recreation, breather (Inf)

▶ *265 Interval*

3 unemployment, joblessness, redundancy, lay-off, no more work, dismissal, discharge, retirement, resignation, calling it quits, the sack (Inf), being fired (Inf)

▶ *705 Resignation*

VERBS

4 have leisure, have free time, have spare time, find time for, have plenty of time, have all the time in the world, have time on one's hand, be master of one's time, take one's ease, see no cause for haste, be in no hurry, take one's (own good) time, take time to smell the flowers (US), move slowly, spend, pass, while away, want something to do, find time hangs

heavy on one's hands, take a holiday, take a vacation (US), take a break, take time out (US), take leave, take a sabbatical, go on a furlough, rest, repose, resign, give up work, retire, go into retirement, take early retirement, get laid off, get the sack (Inf), get fired (Inf)

5 **dismiss**, discharge, lay off, make redundant, fire (Inf), sack (Inf)

ADJECTIVES

6 **leisure**, free, spare, unoccupied, recreational

7 **leisurely**, unhurried, slow, deliberate, relaxed, easy, labour-saving, idle, inactive, resting, reposeful, leisured, at leisure, unoccupied, free, available, disengaged, at a loose end, at ease, off duty, on holiday, on vacation, on leave, on furlough, on sabbatical, retired, in retirement, redundant, dismissed, discharged, laid off, unemployed, jobless, out of work, non-working, fired (Inf), sacked (Inf)

▶ *328 Slowness, 649 Ease, 643 Inactivity, 705 Resignation*

ADVERBS

8 **leisurely**, unhurriedly, conveniently, at one's convenience, at one's leisure, in one's own time, at any odd moment, in one's spare time

646 Worker

NOUNS

1 **worker**, employee, hand, operative, working man (*or* woman), voluntary worker, charity worker, volunteer, participator, social worker, philanthropist, independent worker, freelance, freelancer, self-employed person, housewife, hausfrau, chief cook and bottle-washer, toiler, moiler (Dial), drudge, hack, flunky (*or* flunkey), menial, factotum, handyman, wallah (*or* walla), servant, domestic, servant, domestic, butler, maid, cook, chauffeur, gardener, cleaner, charwoman, help, home help, hewer of wood and drawer of water, beast of burden, busy person, Stakhanovite, jack of all trades, maid of all work, professional person, businessman, businesswoman, career woman, executive, breadwinner, earner, salary earner, wage earner, trade unionist, intellectual, professor, teacher, brain worker, scientist, artist, artistic worker, writer, performer, player, actor, actress, dancer, ballet dancer, singer, opera singer, musician, orchestra conductor, orchestra director (US), executant, journalist, newsman (*or* woman), newscaster, anchor man (*or* woman), presenter, clerical worker, office worker, desk worker, white-collar worker, black-coat worker, secretary, executive assistant, personal assistant (PA), girl Friday, shop assistant, seller, artisan, workman, labourer, unskilled labourer, casual labourer, day labourer, agricultural labourer, farm worker, farm hand, farmer, pieceworker, manual worker, blue-collar worker, factory worker, factory hand, construction worker, excavator, road worker, roadman, ganger, plate-layer, docker, stevedore, packer, meatpacker, porter, coolie (*or* cooly), dustman, gofer (US inf), dogsbody (Inf), fag (Inf), slave (Inf), galley slave (Inf), beaver (Inf), bee (Inf), busy bee (Inf), ant (Inf), wage slave (Inf), boffin (Inf), navvy (Inf)

▶ *572 Willingness, 833 Philanthropy, 167 Conformity, 724 Joint Possession, 697 Servant, 642 Activity, 739 Sale, 621 Cleanness, 68 Agriculture, 163 Class*

2 **artisan**, artificer, skilled worker, master, proficient person, technician, semiskilled worker, tradesman, journeyman, apprentice, learner, craftsman (*or* -woman), handicraftsman (*or* -woman), potter, carpenter, joiner, carver, woodworker, cabinet-maker, turner, sawyer, cooper, wright, wheelwright, wainwright, coach-builder, shipwright, shipbuilder, boat-builder, builder, architect, master mason, mason, housebuilder, bricklayer, plasterer, tiler, thatcher, painter, decorator, metalworker, forger, smith, blacksmith, tinsmith, goldsmith, silversmith, gunsmith, locksmith, tinker, repairman, knife-grinder, miner, coal miner, collier, steelworker, foundryman, mechanic, automobile mechanic, car mechanic, aircraft mechanic, machinist, fitter, engineer, civil engineer, mining engineer, mechanical engineer, electrical engineer, radio engineer, television engineer, computer engineer, power-plant worker, gasman, plumber, welder, electrician, weaver, spinner, tailor, cutter, needlewoman, clothier, watchmaker, clockmaker, jeweller, glass-blower, chippie (Sl), mister fix-it (US inf), grease monkey (Inf)

3 **agent**, operator, doer, practitioner, perpetrator, minister, officer, functionary, instrument, tool, representative, rep, delegate, convention delegate, official, spokesman (*or* -woman), spokesperson, mediator, go-between, deputy, proxy, substitute, executor, executrix, executive, operative, administrator, manager, industrialist, manufacturer, producer, maker, wholesaler, middleman, merchant, dealer, broker, store owner, shop owner, employer

▶ *640 Action, 232 Instrumentality, 696 Master, 706 Delegate, 707 Deputy, 222 Substitution, 243 Production, 739 Sale, 737 Trade*

4 **personnel**, employees, workers, workpeople, staff, workforce, labour force, company, organization, team, gang, squad, crew, complement, cadre, nucleus, band, cast, dramatis personae, hands, men, women, payroll, labour, casual labour, labour pool, manpower, working classes, proletariat

▶ *161 Assembly, 51 Performing Arts, 163 Class*

5 **partner**, associate, co-worker, fellow worker, colleague, workmate, mate

▶ *662 Help, 664 Cooperation*

647 Workshop

NOUNS

1 **workshop**, workroom, workplace, place of work, working area, working space, laboratory, research laboratory, lab, studio, atelier, study, den, library, plant, installation, industrial estate, science park, works, factory, manufacturing plant, yard, sweatshop, mill, cotton mill, loom, sawmill, paper mill, foundry, metalworks, steelyard, steelworks, smelter, furnace, blast furnace, forge, smithy, stithy (Dial), power station, power plant, powerhouse (US), gasworks, waterworks, brickworks, quarry, mine, colliery, coalmine, pit, coalface, stannary, tin mine, mint, store, arsenal, armoury, dockyard, shipyard, slips, wharf, dock, barn, stable, construction site, building site, excavation site, refinery, distillery, brewery, malt house, malting, shop floor, bench, assembly line, production line, farm, dairy, creamery, stock farm, nursery, tree farm, sewing room, kitchen, laundry room, laundry, shop, office, main office, head office, branch office, subsidiary office, large office, executive office, small office, cubbyhole, bureau, business house, company headquarters, company, firm, offices, government offices, congressional offices (US), parliamentary offices, secretariat, industrial area, polluted area, industrial town, manufacturing town, hive of industry, activity, Rust Belt (US sl)

▶ *235 Power, 605 Store, 243 Production, 256 Habitat, 68 Agriculture, 642 Activity*

648 Haste

'Will you walk a little faster?' said a whiting to a snail,/ 'There's a porpoise close behind us, and he's treading on my tail.' Lewis Carroll.

In skating over thin ice, our safety is in our speed. Ralph Waldo Emerson.

For fools rush in where angels fear to tread. Alexander Pope.

If it were done when 'tis done, then 'twere well/ It were done quickly. William Shakespeare.

VERBS

1 **hasten**, speed up, accelerate, quicken, precipitate, hurry, rush, expedite, dispatch, urge, impel, propel, drive, stampede, spur, goad, whip, lash, flog, incite, hustle, hustle away, bundle out (*or* off), rush along, allow no time, push, press, push forward, brook no delay, railroad (Inf), breathe down someone's neck (Inf)

2 **make haste**, hasten, move fast, go fast, speed, rush, spurt, sprint, dash, bolt, race, fly, run, rush headlong, run helter-skelter, run pell-mell, go like a rocket, scurry, scuttle, scamper, decamp, hasten away, dash off, rush off, tear off, cut and run, make up for lost time, hurry, catch up, overtake, outrun, outstrip, whirl by, zoom past, make a forced march, accelerate, speed up, go faster, pick up the pace, hustle, bustle, fret, fume, fidget, rush to and fro, dart to and fro, have no time to spare, have no time to lose, ignore formalities, act without ceremony, brush aside, cut short the preliminaries, rush through, dash through, cut corners, rush one's fences, make short work of, bolt down one's meal, be pressed for time, work against time, work to a deadline, meet a deadline, be behind time, be late, miss one's deadline, work under pressure, think on one's feet, do at the last moment, lose no time, lose not a moment, make every second count, skedaddle (Inf), run like hell (Inf), run like the devil (Inf), fly like a bat out of hell (Sl), pick them up and lay them down (Inf), burn up the track (Inf), go into overdrive (Inf), make oneself scarce (Inf), make tracks (US inf), scat (Inf), show one's heels (Inf), make someone eat dust (Inf)

▶ *780 Rashness, 642 Activity, 209 Lateness, 345 Departure*

ADJECTIVES

3 **hasty**, done in haste, rushed, speedy, prompt, brisk, quick, presto, allegro, swift, rapid, fast, fleet, expeditious, impetuous, impulsive, precipitant, precipitate, headlong, overhasty, reckless, heedless, rash, hot-headed, feverish, impatient, all impatience, thoughtless, unthinking, ill-considered, ardent, fervent, rushing, scampering, pushing, shoving, elbowing, uncontrolled, boisterous, furious, violent, breathless, breakneck, without delay, urgent, immediate, in haste, in all haste, hotfoot, running, racing, hastening, speeding, in a hurry, in a rush, unable to wait, pressed for time, hard-pressed, driven, hurried, haphazard, slapdash, careless, negligent, cursory, perfunctory, superficial, fleeting, brief, rush, last-minute, rough-and-tumble, rough and ready, unprepared, forced, rushed into, stampeded, allowing no time, brooking no delay, pushed through, railroaded (Inf)

▶ *780 Rashness, 759 Feeling, 241 Violence, 470 Negligence, 595 Lack of Preparation*

NOUNS

4 **haste**, hurry, rush, speed, promptness, briskness, quickness, swiftness, rapidity, alacrity, celerity, expeditiousness, urge, impulsion, drive, stampede, push, spur, goad, whip, activity, scurry, hurry-scurry, hustle, bustle, hassle, flurry, whirl, scramble, flutter, fidget, fuss, agitation, distress, panic, last-minute rush, rush job, job due yesterday, nonpreparation, feverish haste, deadline, pressure, race against a deadline, race against time, no time to lose, lateness, urgency, immediacy, importance, expedition, dispatch, velocity, hastening, accel-

eration, dash, spurt, forced march, tearing hurry (Inf), flap (Inf), skedaddle (Inf)

▶ *642 Activity, 366 Agitation, 595 Lack of Preparation, 209 Lateness, 611 Importance*

5 **hastiness**, overhaste, precipitance, precipitateness, impetuosity, impetuousness, impulsiveness, recklessness, rashness, inability to wait, impatience, thoughtlessness, carelessness, negligence

ADVERBS

6 **hastily**, hurriedly, precipitantly, precipitately, helter-skelter, pell-mell, feverishly, posthaste, hotfoot, apace, quickly, swiftly, rapidly, fast, promptly, speedily, with all haste, like a rocket, like a bat out of hell, in a flash, before you can say Jack Robinson, at short notice, on the spur of the moment, immediately, without delay, straight away, right away, urgently, with urgency, under pressure, against the clock, by forced march, with not a moment to lose (*or* spare), pronto (Inf), like greased lightning (Inf), lickety-split (US inf), p.d.q. (pretty damned quick) (Sl), ASAP (as soon as possible) (Inf)

7 **rashly**, recklessly, impetuously, impulsively, impatiently, heedlessly, thoughtlessly, overhastily

▶ *780 Rashness*

INTERJECTIONS

8 **hurry up!**, faster!, quick!, be quick!, get a move on!, step on it!, at (*or* on) the double!, catch up!, speed up!, right now!, move it! (Sl)

649   Ease

NOUNS

1 **ease**, relaxation, repose, rest, rest from one's labours, inactivity, idleness, stillness, restfulness, comfort, well-being, content, contentment, eudemonia, peace, quiet, peace and quiet, tranquillity, serenity, quiescence, sleep, nap, catnap, sweet sleep, sweet dreams, happy dreams, refreshment, breathing space (*or* room), break, tea (*or* coffee) break, pause, respite, lull, recess, interval, interim, leave, holiday, vacation, furlough, time off, day off, sabbatical (year), leisure, free time, spare time, spare hours, day of rest, Sabbath, Lord's day, bank holiday, final rest, eternal peace, the peace that passeth all understanding, nirvana, death, let-up (Inf), breather (Inf), snooze (Inf), forty winks (Inf), shuteye (Inf)

▶ *643 Inactivity, 405 Physical Pleasure, 325 Motionlessness, 651 Refreshment, 218 Cessation, 185 Time, 645 Leisure, 767 Relief, 660 Easiness, 686 Prosperity*

VERBS

2 **take it easy**, take one's ease, relax, repose, rest, take a rest, have a rest, rest from one's labours, find peace and quiet, come to rest,

perch, roost, sit down, sit back, put one's feet up, recline, lie down, lie back, loll, lounge, laze, sprawl, couch, go to bed, bed down, go to sleep, sleep, doze, drowse, nap, take a nap, have a catnap, unwind, unbend, slow down, let up, slack off, forget one's problems, forget work, put on one's robe and slippers, rest and be thankful, rest on one's laurels, rest on one's oars, take time off (*or* out), take a holiday, go on vacation (US), go on leave, go on a furlough, kip down (Sl), catch some Zs (US sl), have forty winks (Inf), get some shuteye (Inf), snooze (Inf), take a breather (Inf), take five (Sl)

▶ *282 Horizontality, 362 Lowering, 643 Inactivity, 651 Refreshment, 325 Motionlessness, 660 Easiness*

3 **ease**, loosen, slacken, moderate, reduce, relieve, alleviate, comfort

▶ *767 Relief, 242 Moderation, 129 Decrease*

ADJECTIVES

4 **at ease**, easy, easeful, relaxed, relaxing, reposeful, resting, restful, robed, slippered, unbuttoned, in one's shirtsleeves, casual, carefree, laid-back, content, eudemonic, cushioned, pillowed, snug, comfortable, peaceful, quiet, still, quiescent, tranquil, leisured, idle, lazy, sluggish, slow, leisurely, unhurried, sabbatical, holiday, vacation, postprandial, after-dinner

▶ *765 Satisfaction, 405 Physical Pleasure, 325 Motionlessness, 645 Leisure*

5 **labour-saving**, back-saving, time-saving, restful, reposeful, easy on, thirst-quenching, like a breath of fresh air

ADVERBS

6 **with ease**, easily, at rest, restfully, reposefully, quietly, peacefully, casually, in a carefree manner, on leave, on holiday, on vacation, on sabbatical, on furlough

650   Fatigue

ADJECTIVES

1 **fatigued**, tired, weary, wearied, sleepy, drowsy, nodding, yawning, ready to rest, ready for bed, ready for sleep, half-awake, dozy, half-asleep, asleep on one's feet, fit to drop, dropping, exhausted, tired out, worn out, tired to death, dead tired, faint, spent, weak, drained, dull, stale, strained, overworked, overtired, overfatigued, overstrained, overwrought, burned out, weakened, enervated, fainting, swooning, flat, prostrate, more dead than alive, stiff, aching, sore, footsore, footweary, walked off one's feet, travel-weary, jet-lagged, wayworn, tired-looking, tired-eyed, heavy-eyed, heavy-lidded, hollow-eyed, haggard, worn, pale, drooping, flagging, languid, languorous, listless, lethargic, forever tired, still tired, unrefreshed, unrested, dopey (Inf), travelled out (Inf), dog-tired (Inf), dog-weary (Inf), dead to the world (Inf), out of it (Inf),

beat (Sl), dead beat (Sl), half-dead (Inf), done for (Inf), done in (Inf), done up (Inf), pooped (US sl), fagged (Inf), fagged out (Inf), knocked up (Inf), washed up (or out) (Inf), clapped out (Inf), tuckered out (US inf), worn to a frazzle (Inf), stupid with fatigue (Inf), all in (Inf), on one's last legs (Inf), bushed (Inf), whacked (Inf), knackered (Sl), flaked out (Inf), sacked out (Sl), flat out (Inf)

▶ *643 Inactivity, 238 Weakness*

2 **bored**, bored, tired, weary, jaded, satiated, sated, sick and tired of (Inf), sick of (Inf), fed up with (Inf), cheesed off (Inf), pissed (or fucked) off (Tab sl)

▶ *788 Boredom, 608 Sufficiency*

3 **panting**, puffing, blowing, puffing and blowing, out of breath, short of breath, breathless, gasping for breath, wheezing, snorting, winded, broken-winded

4 **fatiguing**, tiring, exhausting, laborious, tiresome, wearisome, wearying, wearing, gruelling, punishing, exacting, tough, demanding, physically demanding, irksome, vexatious, annoying, trying, tedious, boring, monotonous

VERBS

5 **be fatigued**, be tired, tire, become weary, flag, droop, languish, fail, sink, stagger, faint, swoon, feel dizzy, feel giddy, yawn, nod, drowse, sleep, succumb, drop, collapse, beg for sleep, cry out for rest, have no strength left, have nothing left to give, can do no more, tire oneself out, overdo it, overtax one's strength, overwork, overexert, ache in every muscle (or limb), gasp, pant, puff, blow, grunt, breathe heavily, get stale, need a rest, need a change, need a break, need a holiday, need a vacation (US), flake out (Inf), crack up (Inf), crock up (Sl), pack up (Inf)

▶ *238 Weakness, 643 Inactivity, 390 Air*

6 **fatigue**, exhaust, tire, tire out, tire to death, wear, wear out, weary, prostrate, double up, wind, work, drive, task, tax, strain, demand too much (of), make extra demands, overwork, overdrive, overtask, overtax, overburden, overload, overstrain, burn out, weaken, debilitate, enervate, drain, take it out of, distress, trouble, bother, harass, annoy, irritate, irk, vex, exasperate, jade, bore, bore to tears, put (or send) to sleep, keep from sleep, deprive of sleep, allow no rest, do up (Inf), do in (Inf), fag (Inf), fag out (Inf), whack (Inf), knock up (Inf), crock up (Sl)

NOUNS

7 **fatigue**, tiredness, weariness, sleepiness, drowsiness, exhaustion, lassitude, languor, listlessness, lethargy, dullness, staleness, jadedness, boredom, physical fatigue, aching muscles, mental fatigue, tired brain, mental and physical distress, limit of endurance, total exhaustion, collapse, prostration, strain, exertion, work, overtiredness, overexertion, over-work, overdoing it, shortness of breath, hard breathing, laboured breathing, panting, gasping, palpitations, heart pain, languishment, weakness, enervation, debilitation, faintness, fainting, faint, swoon, blackout, insensibility, loss of consciousness

▶ *644 Work, 238 Weakness, 404 Insensibility, 390 Air, 649 Ease*

ADVERBS

8 **tiredly**, wearily, sleepily, drowsily, weakly, listlessly, lethargically, dozily, dopily (Inf)

9 **tiringly**, exhaustingly, laboriously, wearisomely, annoyingly, tediously, monotonously

651 Refreshment

VERBS

1 **refresh**, freshen, freshen up, tidy, tidy up, spruce up, clean, clean up, air, ventilate, aerate, air-condition, provide more oxygen, open windows, fan, shade, cool, cool off, cool down, chill, refrigerate, brace, stimulate, exhilarate, invigorate, enliven, vitalize, animate, strengthen, fortify, give a second wind to, give renewed strength to, restore, renew, recruit, recreate, resuscitate, breathe new life into, revive, reanimate, reinvigorate, revitalize, rejuvenate, renovate, repair, ease, relieve, dispel, allow rest, give a break, feed, give food and drink, cheer, give a breather (Inf)

▶ *621 Cleanness, 390 Air, 409 Cold, 239 Vigour, 629 Repair, 767 Relief, 45 Cookery*

2 **be refreshed**, feel refreshed, refresh oneself, breathe deeply, draw breath, get one's breath back, regain (or recover) one's breath, get one's second wind, take a deep breath, take in oxygen, fill one's lungs, respire, clear one's head, come to, perk up, feel like a giant refreshed, feel like a new man (or woman), feel twice the man (or woman) one was, feel like a kid again, feel oneself again, be restored, recover, recuperate, revive, renew oneself, cool off, mop one's brow, stretch one's legs, take a break, take a recess, rest, have a rest, repose, sleep it off, have a change, have a change of pace, go on leave, clear the cobwebs out (Inf), snap out of it (Inf), come around (Inf), take a breather (Inf), take five (or ten) (Inf), sack out (Sl)

▶ *629 Repair, 649 Ease, 409 Cold*

ADJECTIVES

3 **refreshing**, bracing, stimulating, exhilarating, invigorating, fortifying, revitalizing, fresh, cool, cooling, cold, comforting, relieving, recreative, recreational, reviving, restorative, tonic

4 **refreshed**, freshened up, cool, cooled off, braced, stimulated, exhilarated, invigorated, enlivened, fortified, revitalized, recovered, revived, restored, like a giant refreshed, like a new man (or woman), twice the man (or

woman) one was, like a kid again, oneself again, rested, perked up, ready for more, ready for another round

NOUNS

5 **refreshment**, freshness, freshening up, tidiness, tidying up, cleanness, cleanliness, ventilation, aeration, respiration, shade, coolness, cooling off, cooling down, refrigeration, stimulation, exhilaration, invigoration, vitalization, animation, perking up, restoration, renewal, recruitment, recreation, R and R (rest and recreation), recovery, recuperation, resuscitation, new life, revival, reanimation, reinvigoration, revitalization, rejuvenation, renovation, repair, ease, relief, rest, repose

▶ 621 Cleanness, 390 Air, 409 Cold, 239 Vigour, 629 Repair, 767 Relief

6 **refresher**, reviver, restorative, stimulant, tonic, air, breath of air, breath of fresh air, breeze, cool breeze, oxygen, breath of oxygen, shower, cold shower, wash, wash and brush up, rest, repose, break, vacation, holiday, change of scene, recess, leave, lull

7 **refreshments**, refection, food, drink, sustenance, snack, pick-me-up (Inf), breather (Inf), quick one (Inf), one for the road (Inf), nineteenth hole (Inf)

ADVERBS

8 **refreshingly**, exhilaratingly, invigoratingly, freshly, coolly, restfully

652 Conduct

NOUNS

1 **conduct**, behaviour, deportment, bearing, personal bearing, comportment, carriage, posture, port, demeanour, mien, attitude, mental attitude, aspect, outlook, mood, opinion, feeling, look, look in one's eyes, appearance, tone, tone of voice, voice, delivery, motion, action, actions, gesticulation, gesture, mode of behaviour, manners, manner, style, fashion, guise, air, pose, affectation, role-playing, role model, example, democratic behaviour, gesture of equality, common touch, past behaviour, known attitudes, record, track record, history, study of conduct, psychology, behaviourism, reward of conduct, reciprocal manners, deserts, dueness, proposed conduct, intentions, good intentions, line of action, policy, course, race, walk, walk of life, vocation, career, observance, rule, rules, rules of life, the golden rule, rules of business, rules of the road (Inf)

▶ 457 Appearance, 564 Speech, 544 Identification, 797 Affectation, 497 Belief, 759 Feeling, 845 Entitlement, 592 Plan

2 **good conduct**, good behaviour, goodness, virtue, breeding, poise, dignity, presence, savoir-faire, etiquette, protocol, good manners, gracious manners, graciousness, courtesy, politeness, gentlemanly behaviour, ladylike behaviour

▶ 617 Worth, 861 Good, 863 Virtue, 817 Courtesy, 651 Refreshment

3 **well-behaved person**, well-mannered person, gentleman, lady, gracious host (or hostess), polite listener, good child, law-abiding citizen, saint, moralist

▶ 617 Worth, 861 Good, 863 Virtue, 817 Courtesy, 694 Obedience

4 **bad conduct**, misconduct, bad behaviour, misbehaviour, mischief, naughtiness, badness, vice, wickedness, ill-breeding, bad manners, ungraciousness, boorishness, rudeness, discourtesy, selfishness, vileness

▶ 818 Discourtesy, 693 Disobedience, 864 Wickedness, 862 Evil

5 **badly behaved person**, ill-mannered person, rude person, obnoxious person, boor, lout, cad, bounder, naughty child, criminal, egomaniac, immoralist, amoralist, inconsiderate driver, loud drunk, git (Sl), asshole (Tab sl)

▶ 618 Worthlessness, 862 Evil, 864 Wickedness, 818 Discourtesy, 693 Disobedience

6 **way of life**, lifestyle, ethos, morals, principles, ideals, customs, traditions, conventions, mores, praxis, modus vivendi (L), manners, habits

▶ 584 Habit, 7 Religion, 4 Philosophy

7 **way**, proven way, new way, method, method of operating, modus operandi (L), tried-and-true method, experimental method, practice, routine, procedure, routine procedure, process

▶ 327 Way

8 **treatment**, handling, manipulation, control, discipline, regulation, direction, management, administration, operation, organization, orchestration, masterminding, leadership, command, guidance, supervision, dealings, actions, transactions, affairs, deeds, gentle handling, tact, diplomacy, leniency, kid gloves, velvet glove, iron hand in a velvet glove, rough handling, severity, iron hand, boot, jackboot, kick in the pants (US), putting the boot in (Sl), kick in the ass (Tab sl)

▶ 332 Direction, 653 Management, 878 Reward, 879 Punishment, 691 Leniency, 690 Severity

9 **tactics**, strategy, campaign, plan, plan of campaign, plan of attack, game plan, logistics, programme, policy, line, party line, rules of the game, game rules, political science, politics, art of the possible, opportunism, realpolitik, diplomacy, statesmanship, governance, lifemanship, gamesmanship, cunning, brinkmanship, generalship, seamanship, skill, manoeuvres, manoeuvring, marching and countermarching, outflanking, jockeying, jockeying for position, wheeling and dealing, advantage, tactical advantage, built-in advantage, vantage ground, starting ahead of the game, stalling for time, playing for time,

delay, manoeuvre, move, gambit, deed, game, little game, tactic, stratagem, trick, shift, contrivance, one-upmanship (Inf)
▶ *592 Plan, 688 Authority, 657 Cunning, 655 Skill, 126 Superiority, 209 Lateness, 640 Action*

10 conductor, guide, leader, director, escort, usher, carrier, driver, pilot

VERBS

11 conduct oneself, behave, carry oneself, bear oneself, deport oneself, comport oneself, acquit oneself, act, do, set an example, provide a role model, gesture, gesticulate, posture, pose, affect, indulge in, play one's part, participate, pursue, follow a course, follow one's career, shape one's career, steer one's career, steer for, conduct one's affairs, busy oneself, paddle one's own canoe, be master of one's own ship, shift for oneself, employ tactics, manoeuvre, manipulate, mastermind, jockey, twist, turn, take advantage of, use
▶ *640 Action, 544 Identification, 797 Affectation, 642 Activity, 724 Joint Possession, 332 Direction, 698 Freedom*

12 behave well, behave oneself, behave, be good, keep out of mischief, conduct oneself properly, comport oneself well, lead a good life, set a good example, mind one's p's and q's, abide by the rules, play the game
▶ *617 Worth, 861 Good, 863 Virtue*

13 behave badly, misbehave, demean oneself, lead a bad life, set a bad example, break (all) the rules, deserve ill of, carry on (Inf), try it on (Inf), play up (Inf), have one's mind in the mud (US sl)
▶ *618 Worthlessness, 862 Evil, 864 Wickedness*

14 behave towards, treat, deal with, handle, do, see to, put on one's calendar, have in one's book, have on one's plate, have to do with, conduct, operate, carry on, run, direct, manage, cope with, manipulate, control, organize, orchestrate, mastermind, lead, do the necessary thing, do the needful (Inf), act, transact, enact, execute, dispatch, carry out, carry through, put into practice, put into effect, initiate, plan, work out, programme, work at, think through, work through, wade through, go through, read, study, research
▶ *640 Action, 653 Management, 684 Completion, 592 Plan, 644 Work*

15 conduct, guide, lead, direct, navigate, steer, pilot, escort, usher, carry, transmit, convey

ADJECTIVES

16 behaving, behavioural, behaviouristic, ethological, tactical, strategical, political, statesmanlike, governmental, businesslike

17 well-behaved, on one's best behaviour, well-bred, gentlemanly, ladylike, dignified, well-mannered, gracious, courteous, polite, good, ethical, virtuous, law-abiding
▶ *617 Worth, 861 Good, 863 Virtue, 817 Courtesy*

18 badly behaved, bad, ill-bred, mischievous, naughty, wicked, ill-mannered, ungracious, boorish, rude, discourteous, impolite, selfish, inconsiderate, obnoxious, playing up (Inf), bad news (Sl)
▶ *618 Worthlessness, 862 Evil, 864 Wickedness, 818 Discourtesy*

ADVERBS

19 well, in a gentlemanly (*or* ladylike) manner, properly, with propriety, politely, graciously, courteously, virtuously, ethically

20 badly, in an ungentlemanly (*or* unladylike) manner, wickedly, naughtily, ungraciously, rudely, discourteously, impolitely, selfishly, inconsiderately, obnoxiously

653 Management

VERBS

1 manage, administer, organize, orchestrate, mastermind, carry out goals, govern, rule, regulate, control, control results, supervise, supervise staff, watch over, superintend, motivate, direct, lead, oversee, have charge of, have in one's charge, manipulate, manoeuvre, pull the strings, influence, have the measure of, know, handle, conduct, run, carry on, minister, prescribe, caretake, invigilate, proctor (US), nurse, look after, take care of, hold the portfolio, hold the purse strings, hold the reins, keep order, police, legislate, pass laws, make legal, sway, have a way with, be the boss, have taped (Inf), call the shots (Inf)
▶ *233 Influence, 501 Knowledge, 469 Carefulness, 586 Persuasion, 688 Authority, 682 Success, 606 Provision*

2 direct, command, lead, be in charge, head, head up (Inf), boss, lead the way, pioneer, precede, come before, dictate, wear the trousers, hold power, hold office, hold (*or* have) a responsible position, have responsibility, have overall responsibility, assume command, assume responsibility, incur a duty, preside, take the chair, be in the chair, chair, captain, skipper, pilot, stroke, cox, steer, navigate, take the helm, hold the tiller, hold the reins, crack the whip, point, point to, show, show the way, indicate, advise, counsel, shepherd, guide, conduct, lead on, escort, accompany, channel, canalize, funnel, route, train, lead over, lead through, introduce, compere, host, act as a master of ceremonies, honcho (US sl), call the shots (Inf), emcee (Inf)
▶ *154 Precedence, 692 Command, 847 Duty, 332 Direction, 544 Identification, 654 Advice, 180 Accompaniment*

NOUNS

3 management, managing, administration, organization, orchestration, control, conduct, conduct of affairs, motivation, manipulation,

running, handling, managership, stewardship, proctorship, agency, commission,
power, authority, supervision, superintendence, overview, surveillance, care, charge, patronage, protection, art of management, tact,
man-management, human relations, public
relations, way with, judgment, skill, business
management, decision-making, work study,
management study, time and motion study,
operational research, cost-benefit analysis,
policy, home economics, household management, housekeeping, housewifery, husbandry,
economics, political economy, statesmanship,
statecraft, government, governance, regimen,
regime, regulation, legislation, lawmaking,
reins of government, reins, department, ministry, cabinet, inner cabinet, staff work, bureaucracy, civil service, secretariat, government office, workshop

▶ *703 Commission, 688 Authority, 469 Carefulness,
632 Safety, 655 Skill, 592 Plan, 647 Workshop*

4 **directorship**, direction, directing, responsibility, command, control, administrative
control, managerial control, supreme control,
dictatorship, leadership, premiership, chairmanship, captaincy (*or* captainship), superiority, guidance, steering, steerage, pilotage, steersmanship, helmsmanship

▶ *692 Command, 126 Superiority*

5 **guide**, controls, reins, helm, rudder, wheel,
tiller, joystick, pole star, lodestar, needle, magnetic needle, compass, binnacle, gyrocompass
(*or* gyro), automatic pilot (*or* autopilot *or*
gyropilot), navigational aid, direction-finding,
beam, radar, lighthouse, light ship, light vessel, foghorn, buoy, direction, remote control

6 **governing body**, controlling body, supervisory body, administration, quango, committee, steering committee, standing committee,
select committee, cabinet, inner cabinet, council, board, board of directors, directorate, directors, management, managers, executive, employers, bosses, staff, brass (Inf), top brass (Inf)

7 **council**, council board, round table, council
chamber, board room, court, tribunal, Privy
Council, Star Chamber, Curia Regis, Sanhedrin,
presidium, ecclesiastical council, Curia, consistory, vestry, cabinet, kitchen cabinet (US),
panel, board, advisory board, consultative
body, commission, Royal Commission, assembly, conference, conventicle, congregation,
ecclesia, conclave, convocation, synod, convention, congress, meeting, top-level meeting,
summit, durbar, diet, moot, folkmoot, comitia,
zemstvo, soviet, council of elders, elder statesmen, genro, federal council, League of Nations,
United Nations (UNO), Security Council, hearing, audience, sitting, session, think tank (Sl)

▶ *161 Assembly, 654 Advice, 7 Religion, 568 Conversation*

8 **British administrative council**, town
council, parish council, community council,
municipal council, county council, regional
council, district council

9 **US administrative council**, town council,
city council, mayor-council system, city commission, council-manager system, county
commission, county board, board of aldermen, aldermanic board

10 **legislative body**, legislative branch, legislative assembly, legislature, government, deliberative assembly, deliberative body, consultative assembly, division, quorum, senatus, senate, parliament, European Parliament, Dáil
Éireann (*or* Dáil), Seanad Éireann (*or* Seanad),
National Assembly, Chambre des Députés,
Bundesrat, Bundestag, States General, Storting, Folketing, Cortes, Majlis, Supreme Soviet

▶ *12 Government and Politics*

11 **British government**, Parliament, Mother of
Parliaments, Westminster, House of Commons, Lower House, Lower Chamber, House
of Lords, Upper House, Upper Chamber,
House of Peers, another place

12 **US government**, Congress, Capitol Hill, Sen-
ate, Upper House, Upper Chamber, House of
Representatives, House, Lower House, Lower
Chamber

13 **director**, manager, governor, controller, legislator, lawgiver, lawmaker, president, vice president, prime minister, premier, governor general, capitalist, VIP, employer, boss, master,
head, headman, chief, overseer, head of the
household, head of state, superior, principal
(US), headmaster (*or* mistress), superintendent
(US), moderator, dean, rector, chancellor, vice
chancellor, chair, chairperson, chairman (*or*
chairwoman), speaker, captain, skipper, stroke,
cox, mariner, steersman, helmsman, navigator,
pilot, guide, conductor, forerunner, precursor,
drill sergeant, trainer, academic adviser, director of studies, professor, teacher, tutor, instructor, mentor, adviser, political economist, kingmaker, wirepuller (US), animator, motivator,
hidden hand, influence, back-seat driver (Inf)

▶ *696 Master, 654 Advice, 126 Superiority, 524
Interpretation, 586 Persuasion, 233 Influence, 12
Government and Politics*

14 **leader**, charismatic leader, governor, Messiah, Mahdi, ayatollah, guru, maharajah, Senate majority leader (US), House majority
leader (US), leader of the House of Commons,
leader of the House of Lords, Senate minority
leader (US), House minority leader (US), leader
of the Opposition, floor leader, spearhead,
team captain, quarterback, centre forward,
shepherd, teamster, cowboy (*or* cowhand),
ranch foreman (US), drover, herdsman, bellwether, fugleman, pacemaker, pacesetter,
toastmaster, symposiarch, master of ceremo-

nies (MC), compere, ringmaster, high priest, mystagogue, chorus leader, choragus, coryphaeus, conductor, director (US), leader of the orchestra, first violin, precentor, drum major, drum majorette, cheerleader (US), ringleader, demagogue, rabble-rouser, agitator, captain, condottiere, autocrat, dictator, *Führer* (Ger), *Duce* (It)

▶ *696 Master, 693 Disobedience, 12 Government and Politics*

15 **manager**, manageress, person in responsibility, responsible person, person in charge, key person, VIP, kingpin, administrator, executive, chief executive officer (CEO), company director, managing director, store manager (*or* manageress), shop manager (*or* manageress), office manager, banker, bank official, bank manager, executor, doer, statesman (*or* stateswoman), politician, procurator, housekeeper, housewife, househusband, chatelaine, steward, farm manager, bailiff, reeve, agent, factor, consignee, superintendent, supervisor, inspector, overseer, foreman (*or* -woman), ganger, gaffer, charge hand, warden, matron, sister, charge nurse, nurse, senior nursing officer, protector, proctor, disciplinarian, party chairman, party manager, whip, party whip, majority whip (US), minority whip (US), chief whip, custodian, caretaker, curator, librarian, keeper, master of hounds, whipper-in, huntsman, circus manager, bigwig (Inf), big shot (Inf), big cheese (Sl), pol (US sl)

▶ *611 Importance, 640 Action, 706 Delegate, 632 Safety*

16 **official**, officer, office-holder, office bearer, Jack-in-office, tin god, marshal, steward, shop steward, representative, deputy, delegate, senator, Areopagite, Sanhedrist, Member of Parliament (MP), Parliamentarian, backbencher, peer, life peer, Lords Spiritual, Lords Temporal, member of Congress (US), Senator (US), Congressman (*or* Congresswoman) (US), Representative (US), government servant, public servant, civil servant, apparatchik, servant, officer of state, high official, vizier, grand vizier, cabinet minister, cabinet member (US), secretary, minister, undersecretary, junior minister, secretary-general, United Nations secretary-general, permanent secretary, bureaucrat, Eurocrat, European commissioner, European Parliament member, Euro-MP, MEP, mandarin, judicial officer, district officer, regional official, magistrate, justice of the peace (JP), commissioner, prefect, intendant, consul, proconsul, first secretary, counsellor, praetor, quaestor, aedile, ambassador, envoy, envoy extraordinary, special envoy, alderman, mayor, city manager (US), councillor, councilman (*or* councilwoman) (US), functionary, party official, petty official, administrative officer, clerk,

school prefect, monitor, jobsworth (Inf)

▶ *697 Servant, 696 Master, 688 Authority, 706 Delegate, 654 Advice, 92 Administrative Areas, 12 Government and Politics*

ADJECTIVES

17 **managerial**, administrative, executive, organizational, directorial, directing, leading, heading up, hegemonic, directional, guiding, steering, navigational, governing, controlling, political, official, bureaucratic, governmental, presidential, gubernatorial, legislative, judicial, economic, in charge, at the helm, holding the reins, in the driving seat, in the chair, authoritative, authoritarian, officious, dictatorial, despotic, tyrannical, supervisory, managing, nomothetic (*or* nomothetical), high-level, top-level, important

▶ *688 Authority, 611 Importance*

18 **parliamentary**, congressional, senatorial, legislative, deliberative, unicameral, bicameral, conciliar, convocational, ecclesiastical, synodal, canonical, decretal

ADVERBS

19 **managerially**, administratively, officially, politically, economically, authoritatively, in control, in charge, in command, at the helm, at the wheel, on the bridge, in the driving seat, in the saddle, in the chair, at the head, ex officio, on the cutting edge (US), with diplomacy, with statesmanship, in the hot seat (Inf)

654   Advice

Advice is seldom welcome; and those who want it the most always like it the least. Earl of Chesterfield.

One gives nothing so freely as advice. Duc de la Rochefoucauld.

No one wants advice – only corroboration. John Steinbeck.

It's queer how ready people always are with advice in any real or imaginary emergency, and no matter how many times experience has shown them to be wrong, they continue to set forth their opinions, as if they had received them from the Almighty! Annie Sullivan.

NOUNS

1 **advice**, word of advice, piece of advice, counsel, rede (Arch), tip, hint, word in the ear, word to the wise, words of wisdom, pearls of wisdom, wisdom, counselling, guidance, advising, therapy, didacticism, moralizing, moral injunction, prescription, precept, caution, warning, admonition, suggestion, recommendation, proposition, proposal, motion, supposition, submission, opinion, view, estimate, criticism, constructive criticism, briefing, instruction, information, notification, commu-

nication, intelligence, news, word, charge, charge to the jury, advice for, encouragement, advice against, deprecation

▶ *507 Wisdom, 630 Remedy, 492 Judgment, 636 Warning, 518 Supposition, 528 Information, 586 Persuasion, 587 Dissuasion*

2 **consultation**, taking counsel, seeking advice, deliberation, discussion, mutual consultation, heads together, tête-à-tête, parley, negotiation session, negotiations, conference, round table, meeting of minds, exchange of views, open exchange, reference, referment, council, huddle (Inf), powwow (Inf)

▶ *568 Conversation, 713 Protest, 653 Management*

3 **precept**, maxim, principle, moral, rule, moral rule, golden rule, guideline, moral guideline, guide, commandment, the Ten Commandments, the Twelve Tables, laws of Medes and the Persians, law, canon law, common law, unwritten law, custom, rule of custom, convention, practice, norm, habit and repute, advice, firm advice, admonition, warning, direction, instruction, general instruction, technicality, nice point, precedent, leading case, example, text, injunction, charge, command, commission, mission, mandate, order, written order, writ, warrant, rescript, decree, decretal, canon, judgment, prescript, prescription, remedy, ordinance, regulation, form, formula, formulary, rubric, recipe, receipt (US dial), statute, enactment, act, code, penal code, corpus juris, body of law, legislation, tenet, article, set of rules, constitution, party line, party ticket (US)

▶ *692 Command, 703 Commission, 492 Judgment, 166 Rule, 505 Maxim, 630 Remedy, 16 Law, 584 Habit, 529 Secrecy, 167 Conformity*

4 **adviser**, counsellor, guidance counsellor, consultant, professional consultant, management consultant, financial consultant, troubleshooter, expert, referee, independent referee, ombudsman, arbiter, arbitrator, judge, umpire, critic, estimator, prescriber, recommender, commender, advocate, mover, prompter, motivator, medical adviser, doctor, diagnostician, therapist, psychotherapist, psychiatrist, psychoanalyst, analyst, legal adviser, counsel, legal counsel, lawyer, attorney, solicitor, barrister, marriage adviser, marriage guidance counsellor, social worker, guide, cicerone, teacher, tutor, professor, priest, philosopher, mentor, confidant(e), friend, best friend, aide, helper, monitor, watchdog, admonisher, reminder, remembrancer (Arch), Nestor, Egeria, oracle, prophet, wise man, sage, committee of inquiry, public inquiry, governmental committee, congressional committee (US), parliamentary committee, select committee, consultative body, council, student council, emergency council, intrusive person, meddler, busybody, last word (Inf),

Dutch uncle (Inf), back-seat driver (Inf)

▶ *655 Skill, 492 Judgment, 586 Persuasion, 630 Remedy, 507 Wisdom, 642 Activity*

VERBS

5 **advise**, give advice, offer advice, counsel, give counsel, offer counsel, guide, criticize, moralize, command, dictate, enjoin, prescribe, advocate, recommend, commend, think best, suggest, propose, move, put to, submit, propound, press, urge, encourage, exhort, incite, advise against, dissuade, admonish, warn, caution, prompt, hint, teach, brief, instruct, tell, inform, notify, apprise, charge (a jury)

▶ *518 Supposition, 528 Information, 586 Persuasion, 587 Dissuasion, 636 Warning, 692 Command, 615 Convenience*

6 **consult**, seek advice, ask for advice, seek opinion, refer to, refer to arbitration, call in, call on, ask for a second opinion, hold a public inquiry, submit one's judgment to another's, confide in, have at one's elbow, accept advice, take advice, follow advice, listen to, learn from, take one's cue from, sit in council, sit in conclave, hold a consultation, deliberate, discuss, confer, huddle, hold a confidential discussion, meet with, swap ideas, iron out problems, negotiate, have a tête-à-tête with, put heads together, have a powwow with, hold a council of war, parley, sit round a table, compare notes

▶ *568 Conversation*

ADJECTIVES

7 **advising**, advisory, counselling, consultative, deliberative, hortatory, hortative, monitory, recommendatory, therapeutic, prescriptive, didactic, instructive, informative, moral, moralizing, persuasive, encouraging, dissuasive, admonitory, warning, cautionary

▶ *586 Persuasion, 587 Dissuasion, 636 Warning*

8 **advisable**, recommendable, recommended, prudent, wise, judicious, politic, sensible, practical, expedient

▶ *507 Wisdom, 615 Convenience*

ADVERBS

9 **advisably**, prudently, wisely, judiciously, hortatorily, hortatively, didactically, instructively, informatively, morally

655 Skill

NOUNS

1 **skill**, skilfulness, mental skill, manual skill, professional skill, technical skill, social skill, ability, proficiency, competence, efficiency, faculty, special faculty, capability, capacity, adroitness, dexterity, dexterousness, handiness, deftness, adeptness, address, ease, facility, grace, style, elegance, neatness, many-sidedness, all-round capacity, versatility, adaptability, amphibiousness, ambidexterity, ambidextrousness, flexibility, suppleness, touch,

grip, control, mastery, mastership, wizardry, virtuosity, excellence, prowess, expertise, expertness, professionalism, goodness, forte, strength, strong point, strong card, major suit, speciality, specialty (US), specialism, major subject (US), major (US), métier, accomplishment, attainment, acquirement, experience, knowledge, technical knowledge, practical knowledge, everyday knowledge, practical ability, technique, clever hands, deft fingers, craftsmanship, art, artistry, delicacy, fine workmanship, art that conceals art, execution, finish, perfection, ingenuity, resourcefulness, craft, craftiness, cunning, cleverness, sharpness, common sense, worldly wisdom, sophistication, sagacity, savoir-faire, finesse, tact, discretion, discrimination, gimmick, dodge, contrivance, trick, stratagem, tactics, skilful use, exploitation, use, nous (Sl)

▶ *558 Elegance, 660 Easiness, 235 Power, 617 Worth, 501 Knowledge, 619 Perfection, 657 Cunning, 507 Wisdom, 481 Discrimination, 592 Plan, 539 Deception, 652 Conduct, 599 Use*

2 **aptitude**, talent, natural talent, inborn aptitude, innate ability, inherent ability, feeling for, eye for, ear for, propensity, inclination, tendency, bent, natural bent, faculty, endowment, gift, flair, knack, turn, green fingers, genius, genius for, aptness, fitness, qualification, good head for (Inf), know-how (Inf)

▶ *234 Tendency*

3 **masterpiece**, work of art, great work of literature, creation of genius, creation, beauty, jewel, *chef-d'oeuvre* (Fr), *pièce de résistance* (Fr), masterwork, magnum opus, workmanlike job, stroke of genius, masterstroke, *coup-de-maître* (Fr), coup, exploit, feat, feat of skill, stunt, sporting feat, hat trick, act, deed, *tour de force* (Fr), brilliance, bravura, fireworks, ace, trump, clincher, exceller, *objet d'art* (Fr), curio, collectable, collector's piece (or item), classic, bestseller, hit (Inf), smash hit (Inf)

▶ *640 Action, 617 Worth*

4 **skilled person**, skilful person, proficient person, expert, adept, craftsman, craftswoman, do-it-yourselfer (US), DIY type, all-rounder, jack of all trades, handyman, admirable Crichton, paragon, Renaissance man, person of many parts, master, past master, graduate, intellectual, mastermind, sage, genius, wizard, gifted child, prodigy, maestro, virtuoso, bravura player, musician, first fiddle, prima donna, diva, prima ballerina, prizewinner, star, champion, world champion, Olympic champion, gold-medallist, silver-medallist, bronze-medallist, cordon bleu, blue-ribbon winner, titleholder, belt-holder, black belt, brown belt, dan, cup-holder, ace, exceller, top selection, picked man, capped player, lettered player (US), varsity player (US), first string, first-string

player, All-pro (US), All-American (US), star player, seeded player, seed, top seed, crack shot, dead shot, acrobat, gymnast, athlete, dab hand (Inf), dabster (Inf), white hope (Inf)

▶ *619 Perfection, 507 Wisdom, 786 Wonder, 617 Worth, 237 Strength*

5 **expert**, no novice, professional, practitioner, specialist, authority, doyen, learned person, intellectual, professor, teacher, scholar, pundit, guru, savant, polymath, scientist, veteran, old hand, old stager, old soldier, old dog, sea dog, practised hand, practised eye, knowing person, cunning fellow, slyboots, smart guy (US), fraud, trickster, sophisticate, member of the smart set, cosmopolitan, citizen of the world, man (*or* woman) of the world, man (*or* woman) about town, businessman, businesswoman, salesman (*or* saleswoman) of the month (*or* year), career woman, careerist, tactician, strategist, diplomatist, artist, artisan, craftsman, craftswoman, technician, skilled worker, experienced hand, right person for the job, key man, consultant, adviser, back-room boy, planner, connoisseur, cognoscente, fancier, pro (Inf), boffin (Inf), walking encyclopedia (Inf), brain (Inf), egghead (Inf), highbrow (Inf), wise guy (Inf), whiz kid (Inf), shellback (Inf), warhorse (Inf), smart customer (Inf), smart cookie (US inf), clever-clogs (Sl), sharp (Inf)

▶ *501 Knowledge, 657 Cunning, 646 Worker, 654 Advice, 592 Plan*

ADJECTIVES

6 **skilful**, skilled, able, proficient, competent, efficient, talented, gifted, good, good at, excellent, superb, topnotch, top-flight, top-level, apt, handy, adroit, dexterous, ambidextrous, deft, adept, slick, neat, agile, sure-footed, nimble, nimble-fingered, green-fingered, clever, quick, quick-witted, shrewd, cunning, crafty, smart, intelligent, politic, diplomatic, statesmanlike, wise, sagacious, many-sided, versatile, adaptable, flexible, ingenious, resourceful, ready, ready for anything, panurgic, sound, competitive, masterful, masterly, magisterial, expert, highly qualified, accomplished, finished, perfect, first-rate (Inf), A1 (Inf), ace (Inf), crack (Inf), wizard (Inf)

▶ *617 Worth, 507 Wisdom, 619 Perfection*

7 **gifted**, naturally gifted, talented, blessed with talent, of many parts, endowed, well-endowed, born for, suited for, cut out for

8 **expert**, skilled, experienced, tried, seasoned, veteran, versed in, *au fait* (Fr), instructed, practised, well-practised, well-prepared, trained, finished, passed, qualified, highly qualified, specialized, matured, proficient, competent, efficient, professional, businesslike, up on (Inf), well up on (Inf)

▶ *501 Knowledge, 594 Preparation*

9 **well-made**, expertly made, well-crafted, professional, workmanlike, shipshape, finished, stylish, elegant, sophisticated, happy, felicitous, artistic, artificial, Daedalian, cunning, clever, craftily contrived, deep-laid

▶ 558 Elegance

VERBS

10 **be skilful**, excel, do well, shine, have a flair for, have a knack for, have the knack, have a gift for, show a talent for, show aptitude, have the trick of, have (just) the right touch, have an eye for, have an ear for, have one's hand in, play one's cards well, not put a foot wrong, know what one is about, know just when to stop, use skilfully, exploit, take advantage of, squeeze the last ounce out of, make hay while the sun shines, profit by, live by one's wits, get around, know all the answers, have one's wits about one, be wise, exercise discretion, discriminate, know what's what (Inf), have a good head for (Inf)

▶ 617 Worth, 126 Superiority, 599 Use, 210 Timeliness, 507 Wisdom, 481 Discrimination

11 **be expert**, turn professional, know, know backwards, know forward and backward, know one's stuff, know the ropes, know all the ins and outs, have the knowledge, have experience, take in one's stride, display one's skill, demonstrate, play with, stunt, show off, have the know-how (Inf), know one's onions (Sl)

▶ 501 Knowledge, 811 Showiness, 6 Education

ADVERBS

12 **skilfully**, ably, adroitly, dexterously, proficiently, competently, efficiently, well, with skill, with aplomb, like an expert, like a master, handily, deftly, adeptly, neatly, stylishly, artistically, ingeniously, resourcefully, cleverly, shrewdly, intelligently, knowledgeably, expertly, professionally, scientifically, without fault, like a machine, naturally, swimmingly, in one's stride, as to the manner born

656 Unskilfulness

ADJECTIVES

1 **unskilful**, ungifted, untalented, talentless, unendowed, unaccomplished, unremarkable, unimpressive, unpromising, unversatile, disqualified, unfit, inept, unapt, unable, incapable, impotent, undependable, untrained, uninstructed, unenlightened, unequipped, incompetent, inefficient, ineffectual, unpractical, unadapted, unadaptable, like a fish out of water, unadventurous, unbusinesslike, unprofessional, unstatesmanlike, undiplomatic, impolitic, ill-considered, uninformed, stupid, silly, foolish, unwise, thoughtless, inattentive, undiscerning, wild, giddy, impulsive, scatterbrained, carefree, easy-going, happy-go-lucky, light-minded, feckless, futile, failed, unsuc-

cessful, unacclaimed, inadequate, insufficient, dumb (Inf), dim-witted (Inf), not up to scratch (Inf)

▶ 643 Inactivity, 666 Disagreement, 236 Powerlessness, 508 Folly, 468 Inattention, 683 Failure, 609 Insufficiency

2 **unskilled**, raw, green, unripe, undeveloped, young, callow, immature, inexperienced, uninitiated, wet behind the ears, in (or under) training, apprentice(d), half-skilled, semi-skilled, unseasoned, unprepared, unqualified, inexpert, scratch, ignorant, unversed, unconversant, untrained, uninstructed, uneducated, untaught, untutored, uneducable, unteachable, unfinished, nonprofessional, nonspecialist, lay, amateurish, amateur, self-taught, self-made, autodidactic, unscientific, unsound, charlatan, quack, quackish, specious, pretentious, affected, pickup (US inf), ham (Inf)

▶ 595 Lack of Preparation, 502 Ignorance, 797 Affectation

3 **clumsy**, awkward, gauche, gawky, gawkish, ungainly, uneasy, uncertain, boorish, churlish, discourteous, uncouth, unrefined, ill-mannered, rude, surly, stuttering, stammering, tactless, indiscreet, indiscriminating, bumbling, bungling, lubberly, maladroit, unhandy, all thumbs, left-handed, one-handed, heavy-handed, heavy-footed, unsteady, unbalanced, lumbering, hulking, gangling, stumbling, shambling, wobbly-legged, stiff, rusty, unused, on the shelf, unaccustomed, unhabituated, unpractised, out of practice, out of training, out of kilter, off one's timing, off one's stride, off form, out of touch, losing one's touch, losing one's feel, losing it, slipping, careless, hasty, haphazard, slapdash, negligent, slovenly, slatternly, fumbling, groping, tentative, experimental, ungraceful, graceless, inelegant, clownish, top-heavy, lopsided, unequal, cumbersome, ponderous, clumsily built, unmanageable, unsteerable, unwieldy, inexact, unadjusted, dribbling (US sl), babbling (US inf), out of sync (Inf), ham-handed (or ham-fisted) (Inf), cack-handed (Inf), butterfingered (Inf), rubber-legged (Inf)

▶ 818 Discourtesy, 564 Speech, 600 Nonuse, 585 Unaccustomedness, 470 Negligence, 479 Experiment, 559 Inelegance, 123 Inequality, 259 Size, 504 Error

4 **bungled**, badly done, botched, messed up, fouled-up, foozled, mismanaged, mishandled, maladministered, misapplied, botchy, messy, faulty, imperfect, misguided, ill-advised, ill-judged, ill-timed, unhappy, infelicitous, unplanned, unprepared, ill-contrived, ill-defined, ill-considered, ill-devised, ill-prepared, thrown together, cobbled together, crude, unpolished, rough and ready, inartistic, amateurish, amateur, jerry-built, home-made, do-it-yourself,

DIY, artless, slapdash, superficial, perfunctory, neglected, uncompleted, bodged (Inf), screwed up (Inf), fucked up (Tab sl), half-baked (Inf), half-assed (US sl)

▶ *620 Imperfection, 595 Lack of Preparation, 658 Naivety, 470 Negligence, 685 Noncompletion*

VERBS

5 **be unskilful**, lack skill, lack talent, not have the skills, not know how, not know, show one's ignorance, not have a clue, go the wrong way about it, start at the wrong end, do things backwards, do things halfway, do things by halves, not complete, not finish the job, tinker, paper over the cracks, burn one's fingers, put one's foot in it, catch a Tartar, reckon without one's host, not expect, mishandle, mismanage, maladminister, misconduct, misrule, misgovern, misapply, misuse, misdirect, blunder, err, make a mistake, miss one's cue, forget one's words, overact, underact, lose one's touch, lose one's feel, lose one's cunning, lose one's skill, lose it, go rusty, get out of practice, disaccustom, fail, face disaster, come unstuck, fluff one's lines (Inf), ham it up (Inf), come a cropper (Inf), lose out (Inf), lose one's nerve (Inf), lose one's head (Inf)

▶ *502 Ignorance, 685 Noncompletion, 514 Surprise, 504 Error, 512 Oblivion, 585 Unaccustomedness, 683 Failure, 777 Fear*

6 **act foolishly**, make a fool of oneself, make an ass of oneself, lose face, not know what one is about, not know one's own business, be one's own worst enemy, act in one's own worst interests, stand in one's own light, cut one's own throat, cut off one's nose to spite one's face, paint oneself into a corner, throw the baby out with the bath water, have egg on one's face, become an object lesson, quarrel with one's bread and butter, bite the hand that feeds one, kill the goose that lays the golden eggs, spoil the ship for a ha'porth of tar, bring one's house about one's ears, saw off the limb one sits on, shoot oneself in the foot, fall in one's own trap, knock one's head against a brick wall, put the cart before the horse, be penny-wise and pound-foolish, put all one's eggs in one basket, bite off more than one can chew, have too many irons in the fire, try to put a square peg in a round hole, put new wine into old bottles, blunder, labour in vain, attempt the impossible, go on a fool's errand, go on a wild goose chase, waste effort, lean on a broken reed, strain at a gnat and swallow a camel

▶ *506 Nonsense, 487 Impossibility, 614 Uselessness*

7 **be clumsy**, blunder, fumble, bumble, flounder, stumble, trip, trip over, not look where one is going, grope, lumber, hulk, get in the way, stand in the light, stutter, stammer, muff, fluff, foozle, pull, slice, mishit, misthrow,

overthrow, overshoot, overstep, play into the hands of, spill, slop, drop, drop a catch, drop a sitter, drop a pop-up, let fall, catch a crab, score an own goal, let the cat out of the bag, make a faux pas, put one's foot in one's mouth, put one's foot in it, get egg on one's face, do a bad job, do badly, bungle, botch, foul up, mess up, make a mess of, spoil, mar, blot, impair, meddle, miscarry, fail, bobble (US inf), boob, galumph, bodge (Inf), dribble (US sl), drop a brick (Inf), screw up (Inf), fuck up (Tab sl), cock up (Sl), balls up (Sl), blow (Sl), make a hash of (Inf), fool with (Inf)

▶ *468 Inattention, 479 Experiment, 357 Overstepping, 362 Lowering, 504 Error, 628 Deterioration, 642 Activity, 683 Failure*

NOUNS

8 **unskilfulness**, lack of skill, want of skill, lack of ability, lack of proficiency, lack of professionalism, amateurism, lack of talent, no gift for, ineptitude, ineptness, unaptness, inability, impotence, incompetence, inexpertness, inefficiency, ineffectuality, lack of practice, rustiness, nonuse, ignorance, inexperience, immaturity, rawness, greenness, unripeness, underdevelopment, incapacity, disqualification, unfitness, pretension, quackery, charlatanism, clumsiness, awkwardness, gaucherie, lubberliness, unhandiness, left-handedness, heavy-handedness, backwardness, slowness, unintelligence, booby prize, wooden spoon, cack-handedness (Inf), ham-handedness (or ham-fistedness) (Inf)

▶ *600 Nonuse, 595 Lack of Preparation, 502 Ignorance, 236 Powerlessness, 797 Affectation, 508 Folly*

9 **bungling**, botching, bumbling, tinkering, half-measures, pale imitation, travesty, noncompletion, bungle, botch, mess, shambles, foul-up, bad day, off day, one of those days, poor performance, poor show, bad job, unsatisfactory work, failure, flop, missed chance, untimeliness, dropped catch, fumble, foozle, muff, fluff, flub, miss, misfire, mishit, slice, misthrow, overthrow, own goal, mistake, error, thoughtlessness, inattention, tactlessness, indiscretion, infelicity, gaffe, faux pas, mishandling, mismanagement, misapplication, misuse, too many cooks, too many chiefs and not enough Indians, misrule, misgovernment, maladministration, misjudgment, misperception, misconduct, antics, much ado about nothing, wild-goose chase, wasted effort, lost labour, bobbling (US inf), dog's dinner (or breakfast) (Inf), pig's breakfast (Inf), pig's ear (Inf), cockup (Sl), balls-up (Sl), butterfingers (Inf)

▶ *685 Noncompletion, 683 Failure, 211 Untimeliness, 504 Error, 468 Inattention, 601 Misuse, 493 Misjudgment, 614 Uselessness*

10 **unskilled person**, learner, apprentice, trainee, student, probationer, beginner, novice, greenhorn, raw recruit, colt, rookie (Inf), dude (US), amateur, dabbler, tinker, bungler, failure, loser, bad learner, one's despair, incompetent, botcher, bumbler, blunderer, bungling idiot, marplot, mismanager, fumbler, muffer, muff, lump, hulk, lubber, lout, clumsy lout, oaf, clumsy oaf, bull in a china shop, dolt, ass, fool, booby, looby, clown, buffoon, joke, butt, bumpkin, country bumpkin, clod, scribbler, hack, dauber, bad hand, poor hand, bad shot, poor shot, no marksman, jack of all trades and master of none, landlubber, fairweather sailor, freshwater sailor, horse marine (US), ass in a lion's skin, jackdaw in peacock's feathers, imposter, quack, charlatan, mountebank, cowboy (Inf), nerd (Inf), wally (Inf), dipstick (Inf), ham (Inf), blunderbuss (Inf), boob (Sl), butterfingers (Inf), clumsy clot (Sl), swab (Sl), duffer (Inf), nitwit (Inf), nit (Inf), stooge (Sl), (big) galoot (US sl), bozo (US sl), jerk (Sl), stick (Inf), hick (US inf), rube (US sl), slob (Inf)

▶ *683 Failure, 508 Folly, 151 Disorder, 538 Untruth, 117 Disparity*

ADVERBS

11 **unskilfully**, ineptly, incompetently, inefficiently, unprofessionally, undiplomatically, foolishly, unsuccessfully, inexpertly, amateurishly, clumsily, awkwardly, carelessly, negligently, badly, imperfectly

657 Cunning

NOUNS

1 **cunning**, cunningness, slyness, wiliness, foxiness, artfulness, craftiness, craft, art, skill, lore, knowledge, resourcefulness, inventiveness, ingenuity, imagination, knack, guile, cleverness, smartness, sharpness, acuity, shrewdness, sophistication, intelligence, stealth, stealthiness, subtlety, latency, concealment, caution, wariness, suppleness, slipperiness, shiftiness, knavery, chicanery, chicane, trickery, imposture, foul play, finesse, jugglery, sleight, cheating, circumvention, deception, deceit, duplicity, sophistry, double-dealing, double-crossing, false political promises, chicken in every pot (US), forty acres and a mule (US), peace with honour, smoothness, flattery, beguilement, disguise, insincerity, hypocrisy, manoeuvring, evasion, temporizing, tactics, policy, diplomacy, Machiavellianism (or Machiavellism), realpolitik, jobbery, gerrymandering, improbity, sharp practice, underhanded (or underhand) deal, under-the-table deal, under-the-counter purchase, secret influence, backstage dealings, back-room influence, old boy network, gentleman's club, politics in a smoke-filled room (US), backdoor influence, intrigue,

plot, conspiracy, know-how (Inf), gamesmanship (Inf), cageyness (Inf), monkey business (Inf), wheeling and dealing (Inf)

▶ *655 Skill, 501 Knowledge, 519 Imagination, 527 Latency, 529 Secrecy, 858 Improbity, 539 Deception, 540 Falsehood, 853 Flattery, 652 Conduct, 233 Influence, 592 Plan, 474 Sophistry, 578 Equivocation*

2 **stratagem**, ruse, wile, art, artifice, device, resource, resort, ploy, shift, dodge, contrivance, expedient, machination, game, (dirty) little game, plot, subterfuge, evasion, excuse, pretext, white lie, lie, cheat, deception, sham, swindle, fraud, confidence trick, trick, old trick, bag of tricks, box of tricks, tricks of the trade, feint, catch, net, web, ambush, Greek gift, Trojan horse, political trick, stalking-horse, trial balloon, *ballon d'essai* (Fr), trap, ditch, pit, pitfall, Parthian shot, web of cunning, web of deceit, blind, smoke screen, dust thrown in the eyes, red herring, flag of convenience, thin end of the wedge, manoeuvre, move, tactic, tactics, wrinkle (Inf), scam (Sl), con (Inf), flimflam (Inf)

▶ *592 Plan, 538 Untruth, 539 Deception, 635 Trap, 652 Conduct*

3 **cunning person**, wily person, crafty fellow, slyboots, artful dodger, fast talker, sophist, casuist, logic-chopper, fox, Reynard, lurker, hider, serpent, snake, snake in the grass, troublemaker, fraud, dissembler, shammer, wolf in sheep's clothing, hypocrite, double-crosser, deceiver, forked tongue, liar, cheat, trickster, sharper, swindler, confidence trickster, knave (Arch), juggler, conjuror, flatterer, glib tongue, smooth talker, diplomat, diplomatist, self-serving politician, timeserver, Machiavelli, intriguer, conspirator, plotter, schemer, strategist, tactician, manoeuvrer, wirepuller (US), con man (Inf), flimflam man (Inf), sharp (Inf), fly-by-night(er) (Inf), smoothie (or smoothy) (Sl), wheeler-dealer (Inf)

▶ *531 Concealment, 635 Trap, 538 Untruth, 853 Flattery, 592 Plan, 586 Persuasion*

ADJECTIVES

4 **cunning**, sly, wily, foxy, artful, crafty, clever, skilful, knowledgeable, resourceful, inventive, ingenious, guileful, imaginative, disingenuous, subtle, serpentine, vulpine, feline, full of ruses, tricky, tricksy, devious, secret, stealthy, clandestine, underhand (or underhanded), under-the-table, under-the-counter, scheming, contriving, practising, plotting, planning, intriguing, conspiring, calculating, Machiavellian, arch, knowing, intelligent, smart, sharp, astute, shrewd, wise, acute, sophisticated, urbane, canny, pawky (Dial), too clever for, too clever by half, too smart for one's own good, up to everything, not to be caught napping, not born yesterday, experienced, reticent, re-

served, not to be drawn, cautious, wary, tactical, strategical, well-laid, well-planned, full of
snares, insidious, perfidious, shifty, slippery,
timeserving, temporizing, equivocal, sophistical, flattering, beguiling, hypocritical, insincere, deceitful, deceiving, rascally, crooked,
dishonest, knavish (Arch), slick (Inf), fly (Sl),
no flies on (Inf), cagey (Inf)
▶ *507 Wisdom, 529 Secrecy, 592 Plan, 655 Skill,
858 Improbity, 578 Equivocation, 539 Deception*

VERBS
5 **be cunning**, finesse, play the fox, shift,
dodge, manoeuvre, jockey, twist, turn, wriggle, hide, lie low, skulk, lurk, scheme, intrigue,
conspire, plot, plan, devise, contrive, wangle,
know a trick or two, fix the game, play a
dangerous game, spin a web, weave a plot,
confuse, muddy the waters, have method in
one's madness, have an ulterior motive, have
an axe to grind, play tricks with, monkey
about with, tinker, circumvent, gerrymander,
overreach, outsmart, outwit, outdo, be too
quick for, be too clever for, trick, cheat, swindle, defraud, double-cross, deceive, betray,
steal a march on, snatch from under one's
nose, coax, flatter, beguile, cajole, wheedle,
blarney, have the blarney, temporize, play for
time, juggle, ambush, waylay, dig a pit for,
undermine, bait the trap, get one's foot in the
door, create a catch-22 situation, match in
cunning, expose the trick, avoid the trap, see
the catch, have a card up one's sleeve, have a
shot in one's locker, know all the answers, live
by one's wits, fly by the seat of one's pants,
con (Inf), flimflam (Inf), sweet-talk (Inf), pull
a fast one (Inf), put one over (Inf), be one up
on (Inf), go one better (Inf), pip at the post (Sl)
▶ *314 Convolution, 527 Latency, 592 Plan, 539
Deception, 853 Flattery, 357 Overstepping, 531
Concealment, 586 Persuasion*

ADVERBS
6 **cunningly**, artfully, craftily, slyly, on the sly,
secretly, stealthily, shrewdly, astutely, tactically, strategically, deceitfully, guilefully, dishonestly, with a glib tongue

658 Naivety

ADJECTIVES
1 **naive**, naïf, artless, without art, simple, simple-minded, ingenuous, guileless, free from
guile, without artifice, without tricks, childlike, uncontrived, unstudied, uncomplicated,
unadorned, unvarnished, plain, homespun,
home-made, do-it-yourself, DIY, unskilled,
uncivilized, uncultured, unrefined, unpolished, native, natural, unartificial, in a state of
nature, primitive, wild, savage, untaught, self-
taught, uneducated, untutored, self-made, unguided, unlearned, unscientific, unprogres-

sive, backward, ignorant, Arcadian, young, innocent, unversed, uninitiated, born yesterday,
green, immature, inexperienced, unworldly,
unsophisticated, callow, wet behind the ears,
not dry behind the ears, not on guard, unsuspecting, unsuspicious, trusting, confiding,
credulous, gullible, unconstrained, uninhibited, unreserved, unaffected, undissembling,
spontaneous, candid, frank, open, straightforward, undesigning, truthful, veracious, single-
hearted, single, true, true-blue, loyal, honest,
sincere, honourable, aboveboard, out in the
open, on the up and up, blunt, outspoken,
free-spoken, transparent, undisguised, unpoetical, prosaic, no-nonsense, matter-of-fact,
down-to-earth, literal, literal-minded, accurate,
modest, shy, inarticulate, unassuming, unpretentious, unpretending, inartistic, Philistine,
unmusical, tone-deaf, uncouth, vulgar, hoydenish, ill-bred, on the level (Inf)
▶ *134 Purity, 556 Simplicity, 656 Unskilfulness,
502 Ignorance, 865 Innocence, 508 Folly, 583
Improvisation, 537 Truth, 857 Probity, 526 Display, 503 Accuracy, 810 Modesty, 795 Vulgarity*

NOUNS
2 **naivety**, artlessness, guilelessness, simplicity,
simple-mindedness, ingenuousness, freedom
from artifice, youth, innocence, greenness,
immaturity, inexperience, unworldliness, unsophistication, callowness, credulity, gullibility, plainness, unaffectedness, naturalness, ignorance, backwardness, uncivilized state,
primitiveness, savagery, darkness, barbarism,
nescience, indifference to art, candour, frankness, openness, straightforwardness, bluntness,
matter-of-factness, outspokenness, veracity,
truth, honesty, probity, sincerity, modesty,
unpretentiousness, Philistinism, imperfection, uncouthness, vulgarity, crudity, bad
taste
▶ *865 Innocence, 556 Simplicity, 537 Truth, 857
Probity, 502 Ignorance, 620 Imperfection, 795
Vulgarity*
3 **naive person**, unsophisticated person, ingenuous person, ingenue, Candide, child of
nature, savage, noble savage, *enfant terrible*
(Fr), lamb, babe in arms, child, youth, innocent, beginner, novice, greenhorn, rough diamond, simpleton, dolt, fool, ninny, dupe,
plain man, simple soul, pure heart, candid
speaker, Philistine, provincial, country cousin,
country dweller, rustic, yokel, clod, bumpkin,
country bumpkin, hillbilly (US), stick (Inf),
hick (US inf), rube (US sl), hayseed (US inf),
sucker (Inf)
▶ *865 Innocence, 508 Folly, 803 Commoner*

VERBS
4 **be naive**, live a simple life, live in a state of
nature, live in ignorance, know no better, be
wet behind the ears, eschew artifice, have no

guile, have no tricks, have no affectations, trust, confide, look one in the face, look one straight in the eyes, speak plainly, call a spade a spade, wear one's heart upon one's sleeve, say what is in one's mind, speak one's mind, not mince one's words, have no hang-ups (Inf)

▶ *865 Innocence, 556 Simplicity, 537 Truth*

ADVERBS

5 **naively**, artlessly, ingenuously, without guile, without artifice, innocently, credulously, gullibly, without pretensions, without affectation, frankly, candidly, openly, sincerely, straightforwardly, bluntly, matter-of-factly, with an open heart

659 Difficulty

NOUNS

1 **difficulty**, hardness, complexity, complication, intricacy, knottiness, technicality, abstruseness, convolution, reconditeness, obscurity, unintelligibility, effort, arduousness, laboriousness, strenuousness, strain, severity, toughness, ruggedness

▶ *151 Disorder, 551 Obscurity, 523 Unintelligibility, 644 Work, 690 Severity*

2 **awkwardness**, clumsiness, unwieldiness, lack of ease, lack of grace, lack of skill, ham-fistedness (Inf)

▶ *656 Unskilfulness*

3 **difficult task**, hard task, hard work, labour, toil, struggle, trial, tribulation, tough assignment, tough proposition, no easy task, tall order, large order (US), big undertaking, hard graft, hard row to hoe, tough lineup to buck (US), hard row of stumps (US), hard furrow to plough, hard pull (US), heavy sledding (US), hard going, rough going, rough ground, difficult terrain, rough terrain, hard road to travel, the hard way, uphill task, uphill struggle, herculean task, superhuman task, brutal task, handful (Inf), no picnic (Inf), backbreaker (Inf), ballbuster (US inf), bitch (Sl), bastard (Sl), bugger (Sl), sod (Sl), real bitch (Inf), real bastard (Inf), real bugger (Sl), real sod (Sl)

▶ *644 Work*

4 **problem**, worry, anxiety, quandary, dilemma, conundrum, brain-teaser, brain-twister, teaser, poser, nonplus, nodus, crux, maze, puzzle, perplexity, imbroglio, thorny problem, knotty problem, hard nut to crack, Gordian knot, can of worms, vexed question, headache (Inf)

▶ *523 Unintelligibility, 151 Disorder*

5 **predicament**, plight, situation, tangle, mess, muddle, tricky situation, tricky spot, ticklish spot, hot water, cleft stick, difficult position, nice predicament, fine mess, unholy mess, fine kettle of fish, pig in a poke, sorry plight, pretty pass, pretty pickle, no-win situation, catch-22 (situation), pickle (Inf), fix (Inf), jam (Inf), scrape (Inf), hobble (US inf), hole (Inf), spot (Inf), squeeze (Inf), clutch (US inf), bind (Inf), pinch (Inf), how-do-you-do (Inf), snarl (Inf), snarl-up (Inf), snafu (Sl)

6 **critical situation**, tight corner, tight spot, tight squeeze, nowhere to turn, desperate (*or* dire *or* parlous) straits, emergency, exigency, hard times, hard life, hardship, adversity, danger, slippery slope, quagmire, quicksand, swamp, morass, the crunch (Inf)

▶ *687 Adversity, 633 Danger*

7 **awkward situation**, awkward position, delicate situation, diplomatic incident, embarrassing situation, embarrassing position, financial embarrassment, bother, spot of bother, spot of trouble, bad patch, hard times, dispute, disagreement, tail in a gate (US inf), tit in the wringer (US tab), sticky wicket (Inf)

▶ *666 Disagreement*

8 **snag**, hitch, catch, drawback, pitfall, teething troubles, complication, aggravation, annoyance, inconvenience, obstacle, hurdle, obstruction, hindrance, impasse, stalemate, deadlock, standstill, logjam, halt, stop, stoppage, cul-de-sac, blind alley, dead end, blank wall, no-go area

▶ *661 Hindrance, 487 Impossibility*

9 **difficult person**, troublemaker, malcontent, problem child, (juvenile) delinquent, criminal, outlaw, disruptive pupil, fussy eater, all one can manage, thorn in one's flesh, *bête noire* (Fr), handful (Inf)

ADJECTIVES

10 **difficult**, hard, not easy, arduous, strenuous, laborious, toilsome, demanding, exacting, challenging, tough, heavy, hefty, onerous, burdensome, effortful, physically demanding, requiring effort, wearisome, backbreaking, gruelling, punishing, exhausting, fatiguing, uphill, oppressive, severe, formidable, superhuman, herculean, impossible, impracticable, easier said than done, steep (Inf), stiff (Inf)

▶ *644 Work, 650 Fatigue, 487 Impossibility*

11 **rough**, rugged, craggy, rough-going, heavy-going, impenetrable, impassable, unnavigable

12 **problematic**, puzzling, baffling, confusing, perplexing, troubling, obfuscating, demanding, exacting, challenging, tough, complex, complicated, intricate, delicate, convoluted, involved, confused, labyrinthine, skilled, specialized, technical, overspecialized, over-technical, abstruse, recondite, esoteric, impenetrable, obscure, unclear, unintelligible, illegible, indecipherable, garbled, jumbled, scrambled, jawbreaking, knotty (Inf), tricky (Inf), thorny (Inf), ticklish (Inf), sticky (Inf), hairy (Inf), pernickety (Inf), crabbed (Inf), cramped (Inf)

▶ *551 Obscurity, 151 Disorder, 523 Unintelligibility, 655 Skill*

13 **inconvenient**, awkward, troublesome, bothersome, irksome, vexatious, vexing, annoying, aggravating, exasperating, tedious, tiresome, boring, trying, worrying, worrisome, troubling, plaguey (Inf)
▶ *366 Agitation, 153 Disturbance, 788 Boredom*

14 **troublesome**, demanding, contrary, perverse, wayward, unmanageable, out of hand, beyond control, stubborn, obstinate, obdurate, headstrong, intractable, refractory, difficult to handle, ill-behaved, badly behaved, naughty, disobedient, disruptive, obstreperous, critical, overcritical, hypercritical, faultfinding, censorious, disapproving, grudging, discontented, hard to please, hard to satisfy, fussy, fastidious, finicky, particular, difficult to live with, bloody-minded (Inf), stroppy (Inf), moody (Inf), nit-picking (Inf), pedantic, pernickety (Inf)
▶ *577 Obstinacy, 652 Conduct, 852 Disapproval, 693 Disobedience*

15 **clumsy**, cumbersome, unwieldy, awkward, ungainly, hulking, ponderous, bulky, lumbering
▶ *259 Size*

16 **troubled**, beset, worried, anxious, perturbed, bothered, vexed, annoyed, puzzled, confused, baffled, perplexed, bewildered, mystified, nonplussed, inconvenienced, put out, harassed, plagued, distressed, embarrassed, in a predicament, in a mess, in a tangle, at a loss, at a standstill, at an impasse, deadlocked, at one's wits' end, at the end of one's tether, in a quandary, in a dilemma, between two stools, on the horns of a dilemma, between the devil and the deep blue sea, between Scylla and Charybdis, in trouble, in a tight spot, in a corner, snookered, behind the eight ball (US), on the spot, out of one's depth, in deep water, in hot water, in the soup, out on a limb, on a tightrope, in difficulties, stumped (Inf), stuck (Inf), in a scrape (Inf), in a jam (Inf), in a pickle (Inf), in a fix (Inf), up a tree (US inf), in Dutch (Sl), on Queer Street (Inf)
▶ *366 Agitation, 523 Unintelligibility*

VERBS

17 **be difficult**, present difficulties, present problems, pose problems, take some doing, require some effort, set one a problem, give one trouble, pester, hassle (Inf)

18 **find difficult**, struggle with, get all tangled up, get all snarled up, make heavy weather of, not see the wood for the trees

19 **have difficulty**, have trouble, struggle, flounder, be hard put (to), have one's work cut out, let oneself in for, labour under difficulties, labour under a disadvantage, have one hand tied behind one's back, do it the hard way, swim against the current, swim upstream, walk (*or* tread) on hot coals, come unstuck,

invite difficulties, make it hard on oneself
▶ *644 Work*

20 **be in difficulty**, have a problem, face difficulties, get into difficulties, run into trouble, get in a mess, strike a bad patch, hit hard times, have a hard time of it, feel the pinch, paint oneself into a corner, put oneself in a spot, tread carefully, pick one's way, tread on (*or* walk among) eggs (US), have one's hands full, bite off more than one can chew, have more than enough, be at a loss, be at one's wits' end, be at the end of one's tether, come to a standstill, have one's back to the wall, not know which way to turn, bear the brunt, go under, go to the wall, be out of one's depth, flounder, get one's ass in a bind (US tab sl)

21 **get into trouble**, get into hot water, be asking for trouble, fish in troubled waters, burn one's fingers, bring down on one's head (*or* around one's ears), cop it (Inf), catch it (Inf), catch a packet (Inf)

22 **cause trouble**, give trouble, irk, annoy, aggravate, exasperate, bedevil, try one's patience, lead one a merry dance, stir up a hornet's nest, have a tiger by the tail, have a wolf by the ears, open Pandora's box, raise the roof, raise the devil, raise Cain, raise (merry) hell, play (merry) hell, sow the wind and reap the whirlwind, raise hob (US inf), play hob (US inf)
▶ *652 Conduct, 768 Aggravation*

23 **cause difficulties**, trouble, raise difficulties, find problems, find fault, criticize, carp, disrupt, put out, disturb, worry, bother, perturb, baffle, perplex, nonplus, puzzle, mystify, confuse, bewilder, inconvenience, discommode, obstruct, hamper, hinder, embarrass, corner, box in, trap, snooker, put to a lot of trouble, make things awkward, make things (*or* matters) worse, complicate matters, put to it, give one a hard (*or* bad) time, make it tough for, put one's foot in it, force (*or* push *or* drive) to the wall, stump (Inf), tree (US inf), drop one in it (Sl)
▶ *153 Disturbance, 151 Disorder, 523 Unintelligibility, 661 Hindrance*

24 **create difficulties**, raise difficulties, make things difficult, criticize, carp, find fault, find problems
▶ *852 Disapproval*

ADVERBS

25 **difficultly**, hardly, ill, with difficulty, at a pinch, in spite of, in the teeth of, with much ado, the hard way, against the stream, against the wind, uphill

26 **arduously**, strenuously, laboriously, punishingly, formidably

27 **problematically**, intricately, delicately, obscurely, unintelligibly

28 **awkwardly**, clumsily, ponderously, unwieldily, unmanageably, inconveniently, annoyingly, tediously

29 **perversely**, waywardly, stubbornly, obstinately, disobediently, disruptively, critically,
censoriously, disapprovingly

660 Easiness

NOUNS

1 **easiness**, ease, facility, effortlessness, comfort, proficiency, competence, dexterity, fluency, ability, capability, talent, aptitude, skill,
skilfulness, speed, efficiency, readiness
▶ *655 Skill, 649 Ease*

2 **simplicity**, simpleness, plainness, uncomplicatedness, unambiguousness, preciseness, precision, comprehensibility, understandability,
clarity, intelligibility, lucidity, facileness, glibness, superficiality
▶ *556 Simplicity, 550 Clarity, 522 Intelligibility*

3 **wieldiness**, manageability, handiness, manoeuvrability, convenience, practicality, feasibility, practicableness, possibility, workability, flexibility, pliability, pliancy, adaptability

4 **ease of manner**, poise, nonchalance, polish,
insouciance, sang-froid, calmness, confidence
▶ *783 Indifference*

5 **smoothness**, freedom, lack of hindrance,
help, assistance
▶ *662 Help*

6 **easy thing**, simple twist of the wrist, soft
option, sinecure, plain sailing, easy ride, clear
course (US), clear coast (US), clear road,
smooth road, royal road, the high road, easy
meat, soft touch, sitting duck, easy target, no
trouble, a pleasure, cinch (Inf), snap (Inf), doddle (Inf), breeze (Inf), picnic (Inf), setup (US
inf), pie (US inf), velvet (US inf), pushover
(Inf), walkover (Inf), child's play (Inf), kid's
stuff (Inf), piece of cake (Inf), duck soup (US
inf), cushy number (Inf), dead cert (Sl), sure
thing (Inf), no sweat (Sl)

7 **easing**, facilitation, smoothing, expediting,
hastening, speeding, quickening, streamlining, simplifying, simplification, clarification
▶ *648 Haste*

8 **disentanglement**, disembarrassment, disinvolvement, extrication, disengagement,
freeing, clearing, disencumberment, uncluttering, disburdenment, unburdening, unscrambling, unsnarling
▶ *150 Order, 152 Arrangement*

ADJECTIVES

9 **easy**, facile, not difficult, not hard, undemanding, effortless, painless, light, moderate,
unburdensome, smooth, uncomplicated, simple, uninvolved, straightforward, plain, clear,
intelligible, elementary, glib, superficial, dead

easy, dead simple, easy as pie, easy as falling
off a log, nothing to it, simple as ABC, like
shooting fish in a barrel (US), like taking candy
from a baby (US), with the current (*or* tide),
with the crowd, downstream, downhill,
downhill all the way, no sooner said than
done, cushy (Inf), Mickey Mouse (Sl), easy as
winking (Inf), easy-peasy (Sl)
▶ *556 Simplicity, 550 Clarity, 522 Intelligibility*

10 **feasible**, practicable, workable, practical, possible, facilitating, helpful, useful, labour-
saving
▶ *486 Possibility, 662 Help, 613 Usefulness*

11 **made easy**, made easier, facilitated, simplified, user-friendly, accessible, comprehensive,
comprehensible, in plain English (*or* language)
(Inf)

12 **wieldy**, wieldable, manageable, manoeuvrable, tractable, flexible, pliable, pliant, malleable, ductile, yielding, handy, convenient,
foolproof, untroublesome, practical, adaptable, smooth-running, easy-running (US),
easy-flowing (US), frictionless, lubricated,
well-oiled, well-greased

13 **easygoing**, undemanding, lenient, tolerant,
permissive, indulgent, tractable, docile, relaxed, calm, serene, acquiescent, compliant,
submissive, biddable
▶ *691 Leniency, 673 Submission*

14 **relaxed**, comfortable, painfree, troublefree,
carefree, easy in one's mind, leisurely, unhurried, gentle
▶ *649 Ease, 328 Slowness*

VERBS

15 **be easy**, present no difficulties, give no trouble, make no demands, be one's for the asking,
be had for the asking, have a simple answer,
come out easily, be easy as pie

16 **make easy**, make easier, facilitate, ease, assist, aid, help, help on, help along, smooth,
grease, oil, lubricate, iron out, pave the way,
smooth the way, prepare the way, grease the
ways (US), soap the ways (US), grease the
wheels, clear, unclog, unblock, unjam, unbar,
free, loose, open up, clear the ground, clear the
way, make way for, not stand in the way of,
make all clear for (US), open the door to,
bridge the gap, allow, permit, enable, make
possible, promote, advance, further, forward,
hasten, speed, accelerate, expedite, pioneer,
give scope, make clear, explain, clarify, simplify, gloss, popularize, vulgarize, interpret,
translate
▶ *662 Help, 386 Lubrication, 708 Permission, 648
Haste, 550 Clarity, 556 Simplicity*

17 **do easily**, make light (*or* little) of, make light
work of, make short work of, think nothing of,
do with both eyes shut, do with one hand tied
behind one's back, do standing on one's head,
take in one's stride, take to like a duck to

water, be in one's element, be quite at home, have it easy, have it soft (US), have it all one's own way, have the game in one's hands, carry all before one, have it in the bag, hold all the trumps, freewheel, coast, coast home, sail home, breeze in, walk over the course (US), win in a walk (US), win hands down, win at a canter, have a walkover

▶ *682 Success*

18 **disentangle**, disembarrass, disinvolve, extricate, disengage, free, clear, disencumber, lighten, unload, unclutter, disburden, unburden, alleviate, obviate, cut free, untie, unravel, liberate, unscramble, unsnarl, untangle

▶ *150 Order, 152 Arrangement*

19 **go easily**, go smoothly, run smoothly, go (or run) like clockwork, work like a machine (US), work well, flow, glide, roll, slide, coast, freewheel, sweep, sail, go (or run) on oiled wheels

20 **take it easy**, swim with the stream, drift with the current, go with the tide, save oneself the trouble, take the easy way out, take the line of least resistance, look for a short cut, go easy, put one's feet up (Inf), cool it (Sl), easy does it (Inf)

▶ *649 Ease*

ADVERBS

21 **easily**, effortlessly, comfortably, facilely, simplistically, superficially, without difficulty, readily, simply, without ado, no problem, like nothing (US), just like that, at the flick of a switch, with one's eyes closed, with one hand tied behind one's back, hands down, freely, smoothly, without let or hindrance, without a hitch, like clockwork, swingingly (Inf), no sweat (Sl)

661 Hindrance

NOUNS

1 **hindrance**, hindering, impediment, encumbrance, let or hindrance (Fml), obstruction, obstructiveness, restriction, circumscription, restraint, retardation, control, curb, detention, detainment, limitation, friction, interruption, interference, interception, interposition, intervention, meddling, opposition, contrariness, unwillingness, refusal, interdiction, injunction, resistance, counteraction, countermeasure, obviation, determent, dissuasion, discouragement, frustration, foiling, prevention, repression, preclusion, prohibition, stopping, forestalling, hampering

▶ *669 Resistance, 302 Limit, 711 Refusal, 385 Friction, 149 Foreign Body, 663 Opposition, 573 Unwillingness, 231 Counteraction, 587 Dissuasion, 671 Defence, 218 Cessation*

2 **obstacle**, block, stumbling block, blockage, blockade, roadblock, lockout, log jam (US), stoppage, tollgate, strike, barrier, bar, picket line, embargo, intervention, impediment, turnstile, bottleneck, jam, traffic jam, contraflow, difficulty, deterrent, drawback, joker (US), inconvenience, bureaucracy, red tape, regulations, not plain sailing, hazard, hurdle, hitch, snag, drag, rub, catch, catch-22, vicious circle (or cycle), check, stay, arrest, sabotage, filibuster, delay, trouble, mishap, contretemps, accident, breakdown, flat tyre, puncture, technical hitch, technical problems, malfunction, computer malfunction, glitch, engine trouble, teething troubles, flaw, impasse, stalemate, deadlock, botch, mix-up, foul-up (US), hang-up (Inf), hiccup (Inf), bug (US inf), fly in the ointment (Inf), spanner in the works(Inf), spot of bother (Inf), cat among the pigeons (Inf), fox in the henhouse (Inf), nigger in the woodpile (Offensive), sabbing (Sl), cockup (Sl), screw-up (US sl), fuck-up (Tab sl)

▶ *328 Slowness, 70 Transport, 659 Difficulty, 247 Infertility, 616 Inconvenience, 12 Government and Politics, 65 Computers*

3 **barrier**, wall, brick wall, stone wall, fence, barbed wire, portcullis, sea wall, jetty, mole, breakwater, levee, dam, dike, bulwark, rampart, bunker, buffer, parapet, breastwork, earthwork, work, embankment, moat, ditch, weir, Iron Curtain, Bamboo Curtain, Berlin Wall, Hadrian's Wall, Great Wall of China, barrier method contraception, prophylaxis, condom, diaphragm, Dutch cap

▶ *323 Closure, 301 Enclosure, 671 Defence, 634 Refuge, 674 Contention*

4 **restraint**, curb, check, shackles, chains, ball and chain, tether, fetter, bond, tie, apron strings, knot, rein, leash, lead, brake, governor (of speed), wheel clamp, boot, Denver boot, doorstop, anchor

▶ *702 Prison, 701 Subjection*

5 **inhibition**, introversion, conservativeness, embarrassment, shyness, negativism, hanging back, foot-dragging (Inf)

▶ *573 Unwillingness, 290 Interior, 591 Avoidance, 816 Unsociability*

6 **burden**, inconvenience, handicap, encumbrance, debts, mortgage, dependents, family responsibilities, white elephant, overload, last straw, weight on one's shoulders, millstone round one's neck, albatross, dead weight, cross to bear, monkey on one's back (US sl)

▶ *369 Heaviness, 745 Debt*

7 **hinderer**, hindrance, interrupter, obstructer, obstructionist, negativist, introvert, impeder, marplot, filibuster (or filibusterer), staller, frustrator, killjoy, spoilsport, heckler, interferer, meddler, intruder, gate-crasher, damper, troublemaker, mischief-maker, gremlin, poltergeist, saboteur, snake in the grass, dog in the manger, interfering so-and-so (Inf), wet blanket (Inf), party-pooper (Inf)

VERBS

8 hinder, impede, encumber, obstruct, get in the way of, restrict, circumscribe, choke, stifle, restrain, disable, incapacitate, undermine, impair, control, curb, detain, hold back, hold one back, limit, retard, stall, cause friction, interrupt, interfere, intercept, upset, interpose, intervene, come between, meddle, bother, heckle, barrack, oppose, refuse, resist, counteract, devise countermeasures, obviate, deter, dissuade, discourage, frustrate, thwart, spike, foil, foul up, mix up, prevent, repress, preclude, prohibit, forbid, stop, stop one in the act, bring to a standstill, scotch, forestall, hamper, damper, stymie, cripple, hobble, drag one's feet, cut the ground from under one's feet, nip in the bud, throw cold water on, clip one's wings, take the wind out of one's sails, steal one's thunder, upset one's applecart, pull the rug from under one's feet, cramp someone's style (Inf), crimp (US inf), put a crimp in (US inf), spike someone's guns (Inf), snooker (Inf), hassle (Inf), crab one's act (*or* deal) (US inf), queer (Sl), louse up (Sl), snafu (US sl)

9 block, block up, blockade, throw up a roadblock, create an obstacle, create a barrier, wall, wall up, fence, dam, cut off, create a logjam (US), strike, picket, form a picket line, bar, lock out, embargo, intervene, impede, trip, trip up, cramp one's style, stand in the way of, get under one's feet, get in the way, bottleneck, cause a traffic jam, deter, use a condom, find a joker in the pack (US), inconvenience, snag, hit a snag, find oneself in a catch-22 situation, sabotage, filibuster, delay, stall, protract, play for time, cause trouble, have a mishap, have an accident, have a breakdown, have a flat, develop technical problems, malfunction, develop engine trouble, have teething troubles, reach an impasse, reach a stalemate, deadlock, have a hiccup (Inf), have a fly in the ointment (Inf), gum up (Inf), gum up the works (Inf), throw a spanner in the works (Inf), find a nigger in the woodpile (Offensive), have a cockup (Sl), sab (Sl)

10 restrain, curb, check, shackle, chain, tether, fetter, bind, tie one's hands, tie, rein, leash, brake, act as a brake, clamp a wheel, anchor

11 be inhibited, be introverted, have a conservative outlook, embarrass, shy, hang back, drag, drag one's feet (Inf)

12 burden, inconvenience, handicap, encumber, saddle with, have debts, mortgage one's house, have dependents to support, have family responsibilities, overload, have a weight on one's shoulders, have a millstone round one's neck, have an albatross round one's neck, have a cross to bear, have a monkey on one's back (US sl)

ADJECTIVES

13 hindering, hindered, impeding, impeded, held back, held up, unhelpful, uncooperative, unwilling, contrary, encumbering, encumbered, obstructive, restrictive, cramping, circumscriptive, limited, interfering, intrusive, interventional, intervening, meddling, deterrent, dissuasive, discouraging, off-putting, preventive, defensive, prophylactic, counteractive, repressive, preclusive, prohibitive, prohibiting, thwarting, more of a hindrance than a help

14 blocked, barred, in the way, walled in, fenced-in, up against a brick wall, with one's back to the wall, in a corner, restraining, restrained, anchored, curbed, shackled, chained, tethered, leashed, deterrent, interventional, inconvenient, bureaucratic, regulatory, hazardous, fraught with difficulties, not easy, accidental, malfunctioning, deadlocked, at a standstill, at an impasse, burdened, overburdened, heavy-laden, handicapped, saddled with, in debt, indebted, overloaded, backbreaking, lumbered with (Inf), in a fix (Inf), in a pickle (Inf), hairy (Sl)

15 inhibitive, introversive, conservative, embarrassing, embarrassed, shy, negative, footdragging (Inf)

ADVERBS

16 with delay, with much ado, without help, unhelpfully, without assistance, uncooperatively, unwillingly, contrarily, obstructively, restrictively, intrusively, in an intrusive manner, dissuasively, discouragingly, preventively, defensively, counteractively, repressively, preclusively, prohibitively

17 in the way, interventionally, inconveniently, bureaucratically, hazardously, with difficulty, the hard way, up against a brick wall, with one's back to the wall, in a corner, accidentally

18 inhibitively, with inhibitions, in an inhibited way, conservatively, embarrassingly, with embarrassment, shyly, negatively, in a negative manner

662 Help

NOUNS

1 help, aid, assistance, helping hand, hand, assist (US), springboard, instrument, means to an end, avail, use, benefit, advantage, improvement, following wind, fair wind, tail wind, leg-up (Inf)

▶ *602 Means, 599 Use, 627 Improvement*

2 support, moral support, succour, relief, comfort, ease, remedy, ministration, ministry, offices, good offices, kind offices, service, benefit, advice, counsel, guidance, constructive criticism, intercession, prayer, benediction,

lift, boost, good turn, good deed, favour, kindness, rescue, deliverance
▶ *767 Relief, 649 Ease, 630 Remedy, 654 Advice, 861 Good, 639 Deliverance*

3 **sustenance**, support, subsistence, sustainment, sustention, sustentation, maintenance, upkeep, livelihood, living, keep, daily bread, manna, provision, nourishment, nurture, mothering, care, tender loving care (TLC), sympathy
▶ *284 Support, 606 Provision*

4 **social assistance**, income support, public assistance (US), benefit, relief, welfare, welfare (*or* relief) payment, hand-out, charity, unemployment benefit, unemployment compensation (US), housing benefit, sickness benefit, disablement benefit, maternity benefit, maternity allowance, maternity grant, child benefit, family allowance, child allowance, family benefit, family credit, pension, retirement pension, state pension, old age pension, widow's pension, company pension, noncontributory benefit, maintenance, alimony, aliment (Scot), guaranteed annual income (US), national insurance, state insurance, health insurance, unemployment insurance, social security, public provision, state provision, social services, welfare services, National Health Service (NHS), welfare state, protection, self-support, self-improvement, independence, dole (Inf), the welfare (Inf)
▶ *2 Sociology, 632 Safety*

5 **medical assistance**, therapy, treatment, remedy, cure, medicine, first aid, self-help
▶ *60 Medicine, 629 Repair, 630 Remedy*

6 **financial assistance**, subsidy, subvention, grant, allowance, stipend, donation, contribution, endowment, settlement, bestowal, dowry, scholarship, bursary, fellowship, sponsorship, financial backing, funding, loan, advance, credit, monetary aid, economic aid
▶ *14 Finance, 746 Payment, 729 Giving, 732 Lending, 744 Credit*

7 **convenience**, facility, amenity, accommodation, appliance, aid, tool, labour-saving device, time-saving device, safeguard
▶ *660 Easiness, 615 Convenience, 603 Tool, 632 Safety*

8 **furtherance**, advancement, facilitation, expediting, forwarding, promotion, preferment, special (*or* preferential) treatment

9 **patronage**, fosterage, tutelage, auspices, aegis, championship, sponsorship, subsidization, seconding, advocacy, encouragement, backing, support, abetment, countenance
▶ *833 Philanthropy, 284 Support*

10 **helpfulness**, cooperation, collaboration, willingness, usefulness, utility, benevolence, kindness, goodwill, advantageousness, profitability
▶ *664 Cooperation, 572 Willingness, 613 Usefulness, 831 Benevolence, 721 Gain*

11 **helper**, assistant, assister, aid, aider, enabler, aide, mate, abettor, collaborator, colleague, partner, ally, attendant, adjutant, coadjutant, adjuvant, helping hand, facilitator, auxiliary, second, subordinate, deputy, lieutenant, backup, standby, henchman, right-hand man (*or* woman), man Friday, girl Friday, support, backing, backing group, backroom boys (*or* girls), second line, reinforcements, reserves, staff, workers, employees, hands, sidekick (Inf), gofer (Sl)
▶ *646 Worker*

12 **recipient**, beneficiary
▶ *730 Receiving*

13 **supporter**, mainstay, comfort, prop, succourer, tower of strength, friend in need, good neighbour, good Samaritan, ministering angel, carer, helpmate, helpmeet, friendly critic
▶ *819 Friendship, 861 Good*

14 **adviser**, mentor, guide, counsellor, minister, pastor, consultant, arbitrator, advocate, troubleshooter
▶ *654 Advice, 7 Religion, 678 Mediation*

15 **benefactor**, benefactress, well-wisher, philanthropist, patron, sponsor, promoter, backer, guardian angel, patron saint, tutelary, fairy godmother, genie, angel (Inf)
▶ *833 Philanthropy*

16 **home help**, housekeeper, help, daily help, daily, domestic help, domestic, cleaner, cleaning lady, charwoman, charlady, hired help, servant, Mrs Mop (Inf), char (Inf)
▶ *697 Servant*

VERBS

17 **help**, aid, assist, abet, aid and abet, help out, make oneself useful, be of assistance, be of help, do something, give a hand, lend (*or* bear) a hand, give (*or* render) assistance, give an assist (US), proffer aid, come to the aid (*or* assistance) of, rush (*or* fly) to the assistance of, go (*or* come) to the relief of, rescue, deliver, save, go for help
▶ *639 Deliverance, 613 Usefulness*

18 **receive help**, accept aid, collect unemployment, receive welfare payments, take charity

19 **support**, succour, comfort, hearten, give relief to, minister to, care for, tend, look after, nurse, alleviate, relieve, ease, remedy, treat, doctor, bolster, strengthen, reinforce, buttress, shore, shore up, prop, prop up, undergird, crutch, boost, lift, rally, revive, restore, give new life to
▶ *284 Support, 767 Relief, 649 Ease, 630 Remedy, 629 Repair*

20 **sustain**, support, maintain, keep, provide for, nourish, nurture, mother, hold someone's

hand, pamper, coddle, cosset, protect, sympathize

▶ *606 Provision, 632 Safety*

21 **be helpful**, benefit, advantage, do one good, do one a world of good, serve, avail, profit, gain

▶ *861 Good, 721 Gain, 613 Usefulness*

22 **improve**, better, ameliorate, enhance, do something for (*or* to), do a good turn, do a favour, give a leg-up, help a lame dog over a stile, help a lame duck, accommodate, oblige, indulge, favour, collaborate, cooperate, pitch in

▶ *627 Improvement, 847 Duty, 664 Cooperation*

23 **advise**, counsel, guide, countenance, encourage, uphold, support, subscribe to, cultivate, give (*or* lend *or* furnish) support, lend oneself, endorse, sanction, advocate, champion, argue for, hold a brief for, intercede, take by the hand, hold out a hand to, take under one's wing, patronize, sponsor, take up, propose, second, back, foster, take in hand, take in tow, plump for (Inf)

▶ *654 Advice, 284 Support, 678 Mediation*

24 **back**, back up, stand behind, stand back of (US), get in back of (US), get behind, stand by, stick by, take the part of, go to bat for (US), take up the cudgels for, stick up for, run interference for (US), side with, align with, associate oneself with, come down (*or* range oneself) on the side of, ally with

▶ *135 Union*

25 **serve**, attend, wait on, tend, look after, work for, labour on behalf of, cater for (*or* to), pander to, do for (Inf)

▶ *697 Servant, 646 Worker*

26 **be useful**, come in useful, not come (*or* go) amiss, fill a need, lend itself, augment, supplement, produce results

27 **find useful**, need, could (*or* can) do with, avail oneself of

▶ *613 Usefulness, 599 Use, 130 Addition, 571 Necessity*

28 **further**, advance, forward, promote, prefer, favour, advantage, facilitate, expedite, subserve, subvene, contribute to, make for, have a hand in, help along, boost, conduce to, ease (*or* smooth) the way, clear the track, grease the wheels, quicken, hasten, speed, lend wings to

▶ *336 Forward Motion, 660 Easiness, 648 Haste, 386 Lubrication*

29 **finance**, fund, sponsor, back, support, subsidize, subventionize, guarantee, endow, settle, bestow, donate, contribute to (*or* towards), pitch in, lend, loan, advance, set up, set (*or* put) on one's feet, provide the means, be the making of, help out, tide over, see through, bale (*or* bail) out, chip in (Inf)

▶ *14 Finance, 741 Money, 746 Payment, 732 Lending, 744 Credit, 729 Giving*

30 **helping**, aiding, assisting, adjuvant, serving, supporting, supplementing, of assistance, of service, of help, facilitative, facilitating, instrumental, promoting, favouring

▶ *284 Support, 660 Easiness, 336 Forward Motion*

31 **supplementary**, auxiliary, subsidiary, ancillary, accessory, subservient, on call, at one's service (*or* command), at one's beck and call

32 **supportive**, comforting, reassuring, succouring, morale-boosting, caring, tending, attending, ministering, ministrant, ministrative, encouraging, heartening, sustaining, fostering, nurturing

▶ *767 Relief*

33 **helpful**, assistant (Arch), useful, utilitarian, serviceable, convenient, handy, informative, practical, constructive, positive, furthering, promoting, contributory, conducive

▶ *613 Usefulness, 615 Convenience*

34 **beneficial**, good, salutary, advantageous, favourable, propitious, expedient, profitable, gainful, valuable, remedial, therapeutic

▶ *861 Good, 721 Gain, 630 Remedy, 617 Worth*

35 **benevolent**, kind, kindly, considerate, benign, sympathetic, friendly, neighbourly, cooperative, willing, accommodating, obliging, generous, charitable, beneficent, philanthropic, indulgent, well-disposed, favourably disposed, well-affected, well-meaning, well-meant, well-intentioned

▶ *831 Benevolence, 572 Willingness, 664 Cooperation, 833 Philanthropy*

36 **helpfully**, supportively, usefully, serviceably, conveniently, practically, constructively, positively, beneficially, to the good, advantageously, favourably, profitably, to advantage

37 **in aid of**, for the sake of, on behalf of, by the aid of, thanks to, under the auspices (*or* aegis) of, in the name of, in the service of

38 **benevolently**, kindly, considerately, sympathetically, cooperatively, willingly, obligingly, charitably

663 Opposition

…I have spent many years of my life in opposition and I rather like the role. Eleanor Roosevelt.

1 **opposition**, hostility, antagonism, antipathy, dislike, hate, hatred, aversion, repugnance, repugnancy, disapproval, disapprobation, unfriendliness, stiff opposition, resistance

▶ *785 Dislike, 822 Hate, 852 Disapproval, 669 Resistance*

2 **objection**, complaint, fuss, clamour, demurral, demur, remonstration, expostulation, pro-

test, dissent, dissidence, controversy, disputation, disagreement, argument, contradiction, contravention, challenge, impugnation, impugnment, rebuttal, refutation, controversion, denial, refusal, rejection, defiance

▶ *713 Protest, 500 Dissent, 666 Disagreement, 581 Rejection, 668 Defiance*

3 **conflict**, friction, disaccord, dissension, crosscurrent, undercurrent, collision, clashing, confrontation, strife, discord, rivalry, vying, competition, emulation, contention, fighting, fight, battle, war, warfare, attack, defence, bad blood, enmity

▶ *674 Contention, 670 Attack, 671 Defence, 820 Enmity, 676 War*

4 **uncooperativeness**, unhelpfulness, negativeness, negativity, unwillingness, nonacceptance, dissociation, noncooperation, obstructiveness, obstruction, prevention, footdragging, bloody-mindedness (Inf)

▶ *573 Unwillingness, 661 Hindrance*

5 **contrariness**, perverseness, perversity, oppugnancy, stubbornness, obstinacy, disobedience, fractiousness, refractoriness, recalcitrance, reaction

▶ *577 Obstinacy, 693 Disobedience*

6 **contrariety**, oppositeness, disagreement, difference, discrepancy, inconsistency, disparity, contrast, contradistinction, antithesis, polarity, contraposition

▶ *111 Oppositeness, 117 Disparity, 168 Nonconformity*

7 **countermeasure**, counterargument, counterproposal, countercheck, countermove, counterattack, counterwork, counteraction

▶ *231 Counteraction*

8 **the opposition**, the other side, opposing party, opposing force, opposite camp, the enemy, the field, all-comers, faction, minority (party *or* group), opposition party, crossbenches, Her Majesty's Loyal Opposition

▶ *12 Government and Politics, 665 Party*

9 **opposer**, oppositionist, objector, protester, dissenter, dissentient, dissident, agitator, heckler, disputant, litigant, plaintiff, defendant, radical, rebel, revolutionary, counterrevolutionary, resister, intransigent, die-hard, reactionary, conservative, true blue, obstructionist, filibusterer, obstructive, negativist, naysayer (US), gainsayer, anti (Inf), bitterender (US inf), last-ditcher (Inf)

▶ *536 Negation*

10 **competitor**, contestant, contender, player, rival, emulator, corrival

▶ *674 Contention*

11 **opponent**, adversary, antagonist, combatant, enemy, foe

▶ *679 Combatant, 820 Enmity*

VERBS

12 **oppose**, stand against, act against, go (*or* act) in opposition, traverse, protest against (*or* at *or*

about), fight against, strive against, resist

▶ *713 Protest, 669 Resistance*

13 **be contrary**, go against, work against, militate against, counter, run counter to, conflict with

▶ *111 Oppositeness*

14 **be against**, discountenance, disapprove of, disagree with, not support, vote against, object to, not hold with, not abide, not tolerate, not put up with, dissociate oneself from, not have anything to do with, set one's face (*or* oneself) against, reject, dislike, hate

▶ *852 Disapproval, 666 Disagreement, 581 Rejection, 785 Dislike, 822 Hate*

15 **object**, complain, demur, raise (*or* make) objections, make a fuss, gripe, grouse, moan, take exception, protest, remonstrate, expostulate, speak out, deprecate, dissent, express disapproval, assail, criticize, disagree, take issue, beg to differ, call into question, dispute, oppugn, contradict, contravene, belie, rebut, refute, negate, deny, controvert, gainsay, counter, retaliate, defend, defy, challenge, impugn, combat, fight, attack, litigate, kick (Inf)

▶ *713 Protest, 500 Dissent, 852 Disapproval, 666 Disagreement, 670 Attack, 671 Defence, 674 Contention, 668 Defiance*

16 **confront**, front, face, breast, stem, meet head-on, take on, conflict, clash, come into conflict, join battle, grapple with, contest with, contend, compete with (*or* against), vie with, rival, emulate, set against, pit against, match against

▶ *674 Contention*

17 **withstand**, stand firm (*or* fast), stand up to, hold one's own, breast the storm, stem the tide (*or* wind), hold out, resist, obstruct, make difficulties, hinder, check, block, bar, dig one's heels in, refuse to budge, stand one's ground, defy, disobey, refuse

▶ *669 Resistance, 699 Restraint, 661 Hindrance, 668 Defiance, 693 Disobedience*

18 **counteract**, antagonize, countervail, work against, act against, countercheck, counterattack, countermine, frustrate, cross, thwart, foil, prevent, counterbalance, match, offset, set off against, set in opposition, contrast, compare

▶ *231 Counteraction, 111 Oppositeness*

ADJECTIVES

19 **oppositional**, opposing, opposed, hostile, antagonistic, inimical, unfriendly, unfavourable, unpropitious, adverse, contrary, counteractive, counteracting, counter, cross, antipathetic(al), unsympathetic, averse, disapproving, alien, repugnant

▶ *820 Enmity, 231 Counteraction, 785 Dislike*

20 **discordant**, disagreeing, contentious, dissentient, dissenting, dissident, different, conflicting, clashing, adversarial, confronting, face to face, eyeball to eyeball, head-on,

challenging, defiant, rival, competitive, competing, contending, in opposition, at odds, at cross purposes, at variance, at issue, anti (Inf)
▶ *666 Disagreement, 500 Dissent, 674 Contention, 668 Defiance, 117 Disparity*

21 **contrary**, contrasting, contrasted, opposite, reverse, inconsistent, incompatible, contradictory, repugnant, antithetical, diametric(al), diametrically opposed, adversative, irreconcilable, polarized, con (Inf)
▶ *111 Oppositeness*

22 **uncooperative**, unhelpful, negative, noncooperative, unwilling, obstructive, hindering, contrary, perverse, oppugnant, stubborn, obstinate, disobedient, fractious, refractory, recalcitrant, reactionary, reactionist, conservative, true-blue, resistant, bloody-minded (Inf)
▶ *573 Unwillingness, 661 Hindrance, 577 Obstinacy, 669 Resistance, 693 Disobedience*

ADVERBS

23 **opposingly**, antagonistically, inimically, adversely, antipathetically, defiantly, competitively, contrastingly, contradictorily, antithetically, uncooperatively, perversely, unhelpfully, stubbornly

24 **in opposition**, on the other side, of the opposing party, of the opposite camp

25 **at odds**, at cross purposes, at variance, at issue, in confrontation, face to face, eyeball to eyeball, up in arms, at daggers drawn

26 **contrariwise**, against the tide (*or* stream *or* wind), counter, *au contraire* (Fr)

PREPOSITIONS

27 **opposed to**, in opposition to, in contrast to, in conflict with, against, versus, despite, in spite of, in the face of, counter to, at variance with, contrary to, agin (Inf)

664 Cooperation

NOUNS

1 **cooperation**, collaboration, coaction, concurrence, synergy, synergism, cooperativeness, assistance, support, backup, helpfulness, help
▶ *662 Help, 284 Support*

2 **fellowship**, comradeship, friendship, sodality, solidarity, togetherness, sympathy, fellow feeling, fraternalism, fraternity, sorority, clanship, freemasonry, community spirit, team spirit, morale, *esprit de corps* (Fr), concord, concordance, harmony, accord, consensus, concurrence, agreement, bipartisanship
▶ *819 Friendship, 116 Accord, 667 Agreement*

3 **mutual relationship**, correlation, interaction, symbiosis, sharing, participation, mutualism, mutualness, mutuality, reciprocity, interplay, mutual assistance, coadjuvancy, networking, aiding and abetting, logrolling (US),

compromise, concession, give and take, exchanging favours, backscratching (Inf)
▶ *109 Reciprocity, 717 Compromise, 815 Sociability*

4 **joint operation**, combined operation, common endeavour, joint effort (*or* venture), combined effort, concerted effort, communal effort, pulling together, joining of forces, pooling of resources, teamwork, working together, joint action, concerted action, collective action, united action, mass action, united front, cooperative enterprise, cooperative, collective, community, commune
▶ *135 Union, 640 Action, 644 Work, 724 Joint Possession, 13 Economics, 665 Party*

5 **joint control**, coagency, coadministration, comanagement, cochairmanship, co-directorship, partnership, copartnership, copartnery, codetermination, co-ownership, collegialism, federalism, federation, confederation, confederacy, cahoots (US inf)
▶ *653 Management*

6 **movement**, communalism, collectivism, socialism, communism, ecumenicalism (*or* ecumenicism)
▶ *12 Government and Politics, 7 Religion*

7 **association**, alliance, alignment, affiliation, combination, combine, cartel, consortium, union, unification, coalition, fusion, merging, merger, coalescence, coadunation, amalgamation, consolidation, incorporation, integration, hook-up (Inf), tie-up (Inf), tie-in (Inf)
▶ *135 Union, 665 Party*

8 **conferring**, conference, teleconferencing, consultation, connivance, collusion, complicity, conspiracy
▶ *592 Plan*

9 **team**, team mates, partners, co-workers, colleagues, associates, fellows, collaborators, coauthors, community, congregation, brotherhood, fraternity, confraternity, sisterhood, sorority, duet, duumvirate, trio, triumvirate, troika, quartet, quintet, sextet, septet, octet, nonet, league, federation, confederation
▶ *49 Music*

10 **cooperator**, helper, assistant, partner, coworker, ally, fellow, coadjutor, conspirator, collaborator, quisling

VERBS

11 **cooperate**, collaborate, concur, coact, help, assist, support, play ball (Inf)
▶ *662 Help, 284 Support*

12 **reciprocate**, respond, interrelate, interact, interplay, mesh, lend oneself, requite, repay, give and take, return the compliment, aid and abet, compromise
▶ *109 Reciprocity, 717 Compromise*

13 **work together**, act in concert, work as a team, pitch in, rally round, show willing, pull together, hang together, keep together, hold together, stand together, put heads together,

make common cause, unite efforts, sail (*or* row) in the same boat (US), stand shoulder to shoulder, stand or fall together, sink or swim together, contribute, join in, participate, share, throw in together (US inf)

▶ *644 Work, 572 Willingness, 815 Sociability*

14 **join with**, join up with, join hands with, go in with, do business with, get together with, team up with, ally (oneself) with, align (oneself) with, range (oneself) with, line up with, cast in one's lot with, join one's fortunes to, get together, band together, club together, gang together, join forces, pool resources, pool interests, merge with, go into partnership, go partners (Inf), gang up with (Inf), swing in with (US inf), stand in with (US inf), throw in with (US inf), string along with (Inf)

▶ *135 Union*

15 **concur**, go along with, harmonize, concert, collude, connive, conspire, be in cahoots (Inf)

▶ *116 Accord, 667 Agreement*

16 **join**, associate, ally, affiliate, combine, amalgamate, unite, fuse, merge, coalesce, consolidate, federate, confederate, hook up (Inf), tie up (Inf), tie in (Inf)

▶ *135 Union*

ADJECTIVES

17 **cooperative**, cooperating, cooperant, collaborative, coactive, coacting, concurrent, synergetic(al), synergistic(al), synergic(al), coadjutant, coadjuvant, symbiotic(al), helpful, obliging, willing, accommodating, supportive, contributory, participatory

▶ *662 Help, 284 Support, 572 Willingness, 673 Submission*

18 **joint**, shared, combined, collective, concerted, united, common, communal, pooled, mutual, reciprocal, correlational, interrelating, interactive, communalist(ic), collectivist(ic), communist, socialist, ecumenic(al)

▶ *724 Joint Possession, 109 Reciprocity*

19 **associating**, allied, affiliated, comradely, fraternal, friendly, concordant, harmonious, *en rapport* (Fr), concurring, commensal, uncompetitive, noncompetitive, conniving, collusive, conspiratorial, hand in glove, in cahoots (Inf)

▶ *135 Union, 116 Accord*

ADVERBS

20 **cooperatively**, cooperatingly, collaboratively, coactively, concurrently, synergistically, synergetically, jointly, together, collectively, combinedly, conjointly, concertedly, communally, harmoniously, concordantly, as one, with one accord, with one voice, unanimously, hand in glove, shoulder to shoulder, hand in hand, back to back, all for one, one for all

21 **in cooperation**, in collaboration, in conjunction, in concert, in tandem, in collusion, in league, in cahoots (Inf)

PREPOSITIONS

22 **with**, together with, jointly with, in cooperation with, in collaboration with, in conjunction with, in concert with, in association with

---

665 Party

NOUNS

1 **party**, group, body, band, company, set, bunch, gang, cabal, alliance, federation, mob, outfit, troupe, force, side, league, ring, camp, crew, team, squad, corps, troop, posse (US), coterie, clique, club, lodge, house, cadre, circle, inner circle, charmed circle, committee, working committee, council, congregation, sect, denomination, church, fellowship, fraternity, confraternity, fraternal order, fraternal society, brotherhood, sorority (US), sisterhood, guild, union, trade union, labour union (US), cooperative, society, cooperative society, secret society, order, association, partnership, institution, institute, establishment, enterprise, foundation, corporation, conglomerate, syndicate, consortium, cartel, monopoly, trust

▶ *107 Relatedness, 161 Assembly, 664 Cooperation, 148 Component*

2 **society**, social group, community, race, tribe, clan, family, nuclear family, extended family, class, social class, economic class, nation

▶ *815 Sociability, 163 Class*

3 **political grouping**, political party, Conservative Party, Labour Party, Social and Liberal Democrats, Democratic Party (US), Republican Party (US), GOP (Grand Old Party) (US), Green Party, Democratic Left, Socialist Worker's Party, Scottish National Party, Monster Raving Loony Party, Corrective Party, the right wing, the right, right of centre, the far right, the left wing, the left, the far left, left of centre, popular front, people's front, communist front, democracy, federalism, republicanism, liberalism, socialism, communism, coalition, alliance, federation, union, league, confederation, confederacy, cell, bloc, caucus, junta, splinter group, offshoot, faction, movement, grass-roots movement, breakaway movement, fringe group, far-out group, lunatic fringe, cabal, political machine, quango (quasiautonomous nongovernmental organization), the loony left (Sl), the rabid right (Sl)

▶ *12 Government and Politics*

4 **partisanship**, partisanism, partiality, factionalism, sectionalism, clannishness, cliquishness, exclusiveness, sectarianism, separatism, particularism

5 **member**, initiate, belonger, affiliate, insider, cardholder, card-carrier, associate, fellow, brother, sister, comrade, active member, honorary member, life member, member in good

standing, dues-paying member, club member, charter member member of the in-crowd (Inf)
▶ *346 Entry, 640 Action*

6 political party member, Conservative, Tory, Labourite, Liberal Democrat, Democrat (US), Republican (US), politician, politico (US), Green, activist, party member, party worker, party man, loyalist, stalwart, right-winger, rightist, true blue, liberal, moderate, independent, hardliner, left-winger, leftist, radical, socialist, communist, sectarian, comrade, lefty (Inf), Red (Inf), commie (Inf), wet (Inf), dry, pink (US inf), pinko (US sl)

7 social gathering, event, get-together, festive occasion, gala, reception, blowout (Inf), shindig, ceilidh, smoker, soirée, breakfast party, lunch (or luncheon) party, coffee party, tea party, dinner party, beanfeast, beano (Sl), supper party, drinks party, cocktail party, engagement party, stag party (or stag night), hen party (or hen night), wedding party, wedding breakfast, wedding reception, anniversary party, Christmas party, New Year party, Hallowe'en party, Thanksgiving party (US), bonfire party, fireworks party, house-warming, house-raising (US), launch party, garden party, tennis party, surprise party, costume party, fancy-dress party, pyjama party, slumber party, donation party, selling party, Tupperware party (Tm), lingerie party, wife-swapping party, orgy

ADJECTIVES

8 leagued, in league with, cliquish, cliquey, clubbish, clubbable, clubby, inner-circle, exclusive, congregational, sectarian, denominational, communal, fraternal, confraternal, brotherly, sisterly, cooperative, institutional, corporate, incorporated, syndicated, consortial, monopolistic

9 societal, racial, tribal, clannish, familial, federal, national

10 political, politicized, belonging to a party, party-minded, partisan, bipartisan, affiliated, associated, Conservative, Labour, Democratic (US), Republican (US), right-wing, rightist, true-blue, left-wing, leftist, popular, middle-of-the-road, liberal, independent, nonpartisan, green, radical, socialistic, communistic, factional, sectional, sectarian, separatist, particular, nationalistic, red (Inf), pink (US inf)

11 social, hospitable, congenial, gala, festive, celebratory

VERBS

12 be in league with, group together, band together, bunch together, gang together, team together, form a clique, form a club, club together, join the inner circle, work on a committee, fraternize, unionize, associate with, form a partnership, incorporate, syndicate, federate, collaborate, cooperate

13 be a member, become a member, take out membership, become affiliated, affiliate oneself to, subscribe to, hold membership, hold a card, carry a card, join, sign up, sign on, enlist, enrol, put one's name on the list, put one's name down, initiate, belong to, fit in, associate with, hold honorary membership in

14 be a party member, form a party, join a party, align oneself, side with, team up with, swell the ranks, sign on, get on the bandwagon, work for the party, canvass, solicit votes

15 politicize, democratize, federalize, liberalize, socialize, communize, form a coalition, ally, federate, confederate, unionize

16 host, give a party, throw (or toss) a party, have company, invite, extend an invitation, entertain, regale, fête, wine and dine

17 socialize, gather, party, make merry, rave (Inf), rage (Inf)

ADVERBS

18 cliquishly, exclusively, denominationally, communally, as one, fraternally, confraternally, with brotherhood, cooperatively, jointly, conjointly, in partnership, in association, societally, institutionally, as an institution, corporately, monopolistically, with a monopoly, racially, tribally, like a tribe, clannishly, like a clan, federally, nationally, politically, in a political way, liberally, independently, in a nonpartisan way, radically, socialistically, communistically

666 Disagreement

NOUNS

1 disagreement, difference of opinion, difference, argument, altercation, contention, contentiousness, dissension, dissent, dissidence, criticism, disaccord, discordance, disharmony, unharmoniousness, friction, noncooperation, hatred, unpleasantness, controversy, confrontation, difficulty, misunderstanding, disunity, breach of friendship, parting of the ways, estrangement, division, divisiveness, polarization, severance of cordial relations, incompatibility, irreconcilability, enmity, irascibility, provocativeness, cantankerousness, prickliness, quarrelsomeness, bickering, wrangling, hostility, bellicosity, combativeness, aggressiveness, belligerence, strife, fighting, infighting, clashing, area of disagreement, disputed area, theatre of war, sore point, ticklish issue, bone to pick, bone of contention, *casus belli* (L), house divided against itself, recall of ambassadors, uptightness (Inf)
▶ *500 Dissent, 113 Diversity, 434 Dissonance, 643 Inactivity, 136 Separation, 663 Opposition, 674 Contention*

2 argument, debate, polemic, quarrel, row,

dispute, spat, tiff, fuss, slanging match, discord, split, rift, breach, cleft, rupture, schism, struggle, scrimmage, squabble, wrangle, rumpus, tussle, scrap, brawl, fisticuffs, donnybrook, fracas, clash, conflict, open conflict, feud, blood feud, fight, battle, war, all-out war, storm in a teacup, tempest in a teapot (US), falling-out (Inf), hassle (Inf), flap (Inf), shindy (Inf), set-to (Inf), run-in (Inf), dust-up (Inf), ruckus (Inf), ruction (Inf), barney (Inf), argybargy (Inf), bobsy-die (NZ inf), knock-down-drag-out fight (Inf), rhubarb (US sl), rumble (US sl)

▶ *668 Defiance, 676 War*

3 **difference**, dissimilarity, nonconformity, deviation, divergence, variance, disparity, discord, discrepancy, incompatibility, incongruity, inequality, ambiguity, ambivalence, inconsistency, credibility gap, bad match, bad fit, misfitting, mismatching, misaligning, mistiming

▶ *123 Inequality, 309 Distortion, 117 Disparity, 168 Nonconformity, 211 Untimeliness*

4 **dissenter**, dissident, dissentient, protester, objector, disputer, critic, quarreller, troublemaker, intruder, gate-crasher, noncooperator, outsider, misfit, eccentric, crank, freak, laughing stock, wolf in sheep's clothing, ass in a lion's skin, odd man out, fish out of water, square peg in a round hole, scab, blackleg

▶ *799 Derision, 508 Folly, 539 Deception*

VERBS

5 **disagree**, differ, differ with, agree to differ, have differences with, hold opposite views, argue, altercate, not get along, contend, dissent, object to, not cooperate, have nothing to do with, hate, confront, quarrel, criticize, bicker, wrangle, misunderstand, divide, polarize, sever relations, part company with, come to a parting of the ways, split up with, break away from, provoke, show hostility, fight, clash, have an area of disagreement, have a bone to pick, fall out with (Inf), have a falling-out (Inf), not play ball (Inf), fight like cats and dogs

6 **argue**, debate, quarrel, row, dispute, spat (US), tiff, fuss, have a slanging match, split (up), rupture, struggle, squabble, wrangle, tussle, lock horns, go to court, scrap, brawl, engage in fisticuffs, have a donnybrook, clash, conflict, feud, fight, carry on a vendetta, battle, declare war, go to war, make all-out war, hassle (Inf), have a set-to (Inf), have a run-in (Inf), have a dust-up (Inf), kick up a row (*or* fuss) (Inf), kick up a shindy (Inf), kick up bobsy-die (NZ inf), have a knock-down-drag-out fight (Inf)

7 **pick a fight**, pick a quarrel, sow dissension, divide, provoke, set at odds, stir up trouble, make trouble, look for trouble, go looking for

trouble, look for a disagreement, spoil for a fight, challenge, intrude, gate-crash, pick a bone with, have a bone to pick, rub (up) the wrong way, have a chip on one's shoulder (Inf), go on the warpath (Inf)

8 **be different**, be at variance, vary, deviate, diverge, have a credibility gap, match poorly, fit badly, not fit in with, misfit, mismatch, misalign, mistime, go against the grain, march to a different drummer (Inf)

ADJECTIVES

9 **disagreeing**, differing, argumentative, polemic(al), contentious, dissenting, dissident, dissentient, discordant, disharmonious, unharmonious, noncooperative, hating, hateful, unpleasant, controversial, confrontational, disputing, quarrelsome, quarrelling, at odds with, at variance with, at loggerheads with, criticizing, bickering, wrangling, divisive, polarizing, schismatic, incompatible, irreconcilable, irascible, provocative, cantankerous, prickly, hostile, inimical, bellicose, combative, aggressive, militant, antagonistic, belligerent, fighting, squabbling, brawling, warring, at war, at strife, up in arms, like cats and dogs, at cross-purposes, knock-down-drag-out (Inf)

10 **different**, differing, dissimilar, deviating, divergent, variant, odd, alien, unsuitable, discordant, discrepant, incompatible, incongruous, unequal, ambiguous, ambivalent, inconsistent, misfit, mismatched, misaligned, mistimed, like a fish out of water, like a square peg in a round hole

ADVERBS

11 **in disagreement**, argumentatively, contentiously, dissentingly, discordantly, in defiance of, in contempt of, disharmoniously, without harmony, noncooperatively, without cooperation, despite, in spite of, hatefully, in a hateful manner, unpleasantly, controversially, in a controversial way, divisively, schismatically, incompatibly, at odds, irreconcilably, irascibly, provocatively, in order to provoke, cantankerously, hostilely, with hostility, inimically, bellicosely, combatively, aggressively, in an aggressive way, antagonistically, belligerently, like cats and dogs

12 **differently**, in a different way, dissimilarly, without similarity, divergently, unsuitably, discordantly, discrepantly, incompatibly, incongruously, unequally, ambiguously, ambivalently, in more than one way, inconsistently, without consistency, like a fish out of water, like a square peg in a round hole

667 Agreement

I am always of the opinion with the learned, if they speak first. William Congreve.

We seldom attribute common sense except to

those who agree with us. Duc de la Rochefoucauld.

Ah! don't say you agree with me. When people agree with me I always feel that I must be wrong. Oscar Wilde.

NOUNS

1 **agreement**, concord, concordance, accord, accordance, concurrence, approval, thumbs up, assent, consent, general consent, affirmation, affirmative, confirmation, blessing, approbation, permission, willingness, consensus, cooperation, working together, comity, acquiescence, acceptance, toleration, compliance, unity, unanimity, unison, understanding, mutual understanding, mutual support, attunement, congeniality, harmony, harmonization, sympathy, empathy, reciprocity, amity, cordiality, rapport, friendship, fellowship, fellow feeling, feeling of identity, likemindedness, kinship, family feeling, affinity, reconciliation, detente, *rapprochement* (Fr), coexistence, goodwill, peace, love and peace, honeymoon period, the OK (Inf), the nod (Inf), good vibrations (Sl), good vibes (Sl)

▶ *116 Accord, 499 Assent, 664 Cooperation, 433 Melody, 819 Friendship, 107 Relatedness, 675 Peace, 821 Love*

2 **contract**, pact, compact, covenant, settlement, gentleman's agreement, undertaking, transaction, bargain, obligation, promise, pledge, IOU, bond, sanction, international agreement, Treaty of Rome, concordat, treaty, peace treaty, surrender treaty, entente, entente cordiale, ratification, endorsement, authentication, seal, mark, stamp, indenture, title deed, deal (Inf)

▶ *715 Contract, 714 Promise, 745 Debt, 677 Pacification, 503 Accuracy*

3 **compatibility**, conformation, conformity, correspondence, congruity, consistency, uniformity, synchronization, timeliness, equality, parallelism, similarity, coinciding, good fit, perfect fit

▶ *167 Conformity, 112 Uniformity, 114 Similarity*

4 **suitability**, fitness, aptness, relevance, relevancy, pertinence, the very thing

5 **assenter**, cooperator, surrenderer, conformist, follower, yes man, sycophant, traditionalist, authenticator, endorser, ratifier, covenanter, pledger, contractor, contracting party, treaty-maker, peacemaker, sympathizer, perfect candidate, the right person for the job, the right man (*or* woman) in the right place

VERBS

6 **agree with**, agree, concur, approve, assent, consent, say yes to, give the thumbs up to, give the nod to, respond favourably, vote in the affirmative, affirm, confirm, bless, give one's blessing to, give permission, show willingness,

comply with, not oppose, not mind, have no objection to, accept, tolerate, concede, put up with, fall in with, arrive at a consensus, acquiesce, subscribe to, like the idea, welcome, unite, reach a unanimous decision, understand, support, echo, ditto, harmonize, sympathize, empathize, cooperate, reciprocate, act friendly, show friendship for, feel kinship for, see eye to eye, talk the same language, have an affinity for, reach an accord, work together, pull together, coexist, reconcile, have a honeymoon period, hit it off (Inf), give the OK (Inf), give the green light (Inf), rubber-stamp (Inf), have good vibrations (Sl), have good vibes (Sl), be on the same wavelength (Inf)

7 **contract**, sign a pact, sign (on the dotted line), make a compact, covenant, make terms, settle, reach a gentleman's agreement, undertake, transact, bargain, strike a bargain, obligate, promise, pledge, give one's IOU, sanction, reach an international agreement, sign a treaty, work towards peace, keep the peace, ratify, endorse, second, attest, authenticate, seal, mark, stamp, indenture, deal (Inf), make a deal (Inf), sign a deal (Inf), do a deal (Inf), shake on it (Inf)

8 **be compatible**, be uniform, conform, match, tally, correspond, synchronize, coincide, equal, run parallel, have conformity, maintain consistency

9 **be suitable**, be fit for, fit well, fit perfectly, have relevancy, have pertinence, find the very thing

ADJECTIVES

10 **agreeing**, agreed, agreeable, concordant, accordant, concurrent, concurring, approving, approved, voted in, carried, consenting, affirmative, confirmative, blessed, willing, acquiescent, acquiescing, accepting, compliant, united, unanimous, in unison, in chorus, with one voice, of one mind, unopposed, uncontradicted, unchallenged, undisputed, uncontested, uncontroversial, attuned, in tune, congenial, harmonious, in step, sympathetic, empathetic, *en rapport* (Fr), in rapport with, in keeping with, in accord with, reciprocal, cooperative, cordial, on good terms, cooperating, coexistent, coexisting, friendly, like-minded, of like mind, reconciliatory, reconcilable, peaceful, at peace

11 **contractual**, contracting, contracted, obligatory, promised, pledged, ratified, endorsed, authentic, signed (on the dotted line), signed, sealed, and delivered

12 **compatible**, conforming, corresponding, coinciding, congruent, congruous, consistent, matching, equal, uniform, synchronized, parallel, similar

13 **suitable**, fit, fitting, apt, appropriate, relevant, pertinent

ADVERBS

14 **agreeably**, with agreement, as agreed, concordantly, accordantly, concurrently, concurringly, approvingly, with approval, under official sanction, affirmatively, willingly, without hesitation, acquiescently, compliantly, as ordered, unanimously, with one voice, congenially, harmoniously, in harmony, sympathetically, with sympathy, empathetically, with empathy, eye to eye, reciprocally, cooperatively, with cooperation, cordially, congenially, on good terms, likemindedly, with a single mind, with one thought, reconcilably, peacefully, in a peaceful manner, on the same wavelength (Inf)

15 **contractually**, under contract, by a contract, obligatorily, as an obligation, authentically, with authenticity

16 **compatibly**, conformingly, to order, correspondingly, together, in the same way, at the same time, congruently, consistently, with consistency, equally, in equal portions, uniformly, similarly, in a similar way

17 **suitably**, aptly, in an apt way, appropriately, relevantly, with relevance, pertinently, in a pertinent way

668 Defiance

NOUNS

1 **defiance**, defying, audacity, nerve, impertinence, pertness, impudence, insolence, belligerence, courage, boldness, bold front, brave face, bravura, bravado, daringness, daring, presumption, temerity, self-assertion, assurance, self-assurance, arrogance, bluster, bumptiousness, shamelessness, contrariness, cockiness, brashness, brassiness, brazenness, rashness, effrontery, barefaced effrontery, provocativeness, sauce, sauciness, cheekiness, nerviness (US inf), (brass) neck (Inf), (barefaced) cheek (Inf), cussedness (Inf), chutzpah (US inf), lip (Sl), bottle (Inf)

▶ *807 Insolence, 778 Courage, 811 Showiness, 805 Pride, 780 Rashness*

2 **disobedience**, insubordination, resistance, opposition, dissent, disagreement, confrontation, challenge, rebelliousness, rebellion, refusal, contumacy, contemptuousness, contempt, derision, disdain, disregard

▶ *693 Disobedience, 663 Opposition, 500 Dissent, 666 Disagreement*

3 **act of defiance**, challenge, dare, threat, taunt, insult, rude remark, contumely, answering back, impudent talk, opposition rally, demonstration, sit-in, march, treason, insurrection, revolution, declaration of war, battle cry, rebel yell (US), backchat (Inf), back talk (US inf), sass (US inf)

▶ *850 Disrespect, 676 War*

4 **defiant person**, challenger, opponent, usurper, militant, protestor, rebel, leader of the opposition, demonstrator, marcher, activist, martyr, nonconformist, conscientious objector, devil's advocate, cheeky monkey (Inf), bigmouth (Sl)

VERBS

5 **defy**, challenge, oppose, protest, bid defiance to, hurl defiance at, flout, show insolence, show courage, face danger, dare, brave, bare one's teeth, fly in the face of, stand up to, withstand, refuse to bow to, call one's bluff, run the gauntlet, take one up on, present a bold front, present a brave face, outstare, brazen it out, presume, bluster, crow over, provoke, affront, have temerity, have (a) nerve, have barefaced cheek (Inf), have a cheek (Inf), cheek (Inf), cock a snook (Inf), have chutzpah (US inf), get on one's high horse (Inf), give someone some lip (Sl), sass (US inf)

6 **be insubordinate**, show contempt, scorn, spurn, slight, disregard, ignore, resist, refuse, confront, disobey, disagree, threaten, challenge, oppose, dissent, throw down the gauntlet, throw one's hat in the ring, dare, taunt, act insolent, snap one's fingers at, laugh in someone's face, insult, make a rude remark, answer back, play the devil's advocate, demonstrate, hold a demonstration, stage (or hold) a sit-in, march, rebel, usurp, declare war, give the battle cry, give a rebel yell (US)

ADJECTIVES

7 **defiant**, outspoken, assertive, emphatic, assured, self-assured, unabashed, audacious, bold, arrogant, presumptuous, stubborn, obstinate, stiff-necked, bumptious, offensive, impudent, impertinent, pert, insolent, insulting, contemptuous, disdainful, derisive, shameless, brash, bold as brass, brassy, brazen, courageous, daring, reckless, saucy, cocky, cheeky, nervy (US inf), sassy (US inf)

8 **defying**, challenging, disagreeing, disobedient, recalcitrant, refractory, obstinate, antagonistic, belligerent, bellicose, provocative, aggressive, rebellious, militant, warlike

ADVERBS

9 **defiantly**, assertively, emphatically, with emphasis, courageously, in a courageous way, in the face of, in the teeth of, assuredly, self-assuredly, unabashedly, audaciously, boldly, to one's face, daringly, as a dare, arrogantly, presumptuously, stubbornly, obstinately, bumptiously, offensively, impudently, impertinently, pertly, insolently, insultingly, contemptuously, disdainfully, derisively, shamelessly, without shame, without embarrassment, brashly, with a lot of nerve, brazenly, under the very nose of, courageously, recklessly, saucily, cockily, cheekily, nervily (US inf)

10 **in defiance**, challengingly, as a challenge, disobediently, obstinately, antagonistically, with antagonism, belligerently, in a belligerent way, bellicosely, provocatively, aggressively, rebelliously, in open rebellion, militantly, like a war

INTERJECTIONS

11 **how dare you!**, what cheek!

669 Resistance

NOUNS

1 **resistance**, refusal, unwillingness, noncooperation, uncooperativeness, opposition, objection, challenge, stand, brave front, refusal to work, strike, walkout, deprecation, protest, dissent, defiance, repulse, repulsion, repellence, rebuff, reluctance, renitency, negativeness

▶ *711 Refusal, 573 Unwillingness, 663 Opposition, 713 Protest, 668 Defiance, 341 Repulsion*

2 **obstinacy**, intractability, refractoriness, recalcitrance, stubbornness, obduracy, firmness, hardness, toughness, callousness, stiffness, starchiness, rigidity, inflexibility, inelasticity, not bending, not yielding

▶ *577 Obstinacy, 373 Hardness*

3 **resistance movement**, self-defence, withstanding, nonviolent resistance, passive resistance, civil disobedience, mutiny, uprising, insurgence, insurrection, revolution, revolt, guerrilla warfare, terrorism

▶ *671 Defence, 674 Contention, 668 Defiance, 676 War*

4 **desisting**, desistance, denial, self-denial, self-restraint, denying oneself, refusal, refusing oneself, refraining, abstaining, forbearance, forbearing, doing without, not touching

▶ *869 Self-Restraint*

5 **resister**, defender, repeller, opponent, opposer, revolutionary, freedom fighter, reactionary, terrorist, anarchist, die-hard, traditionalist, reactionary, conservative, hardliner, stick-in-the-mud, hard-head (US), refuser, conscientious objector, pacifist, refusenik, refrainer, abstainer, forbearer

▶ *12 Government and Politics*

VERBS

6 **resist**, offer resistance, withstand, endure, make a stand, stand against, put up a brave front, not give way, show reluctance, refuse, strike, walk out, come out, not cooperate, not be tempted by, oppose, object to, confront, contend with, obstruct, hinder, challenge, deprecate, protest, dissent, defy, refuse to bow down, repulse, repel, rebuff, hold off, keep at arm's length, keep at bay

7 **be obstinate**, stand firm, stand rigid, show no flexibility, not bend, not yield, stick to one's guns, dig in one's heels, refuse to budge

8 **revolt**, mutiny, rise up, not take it lying down, fight off, defend oneself

9 **desist**, deny oneself, refuse oneself, restrain from, refrain from, abstain from, forbear, do without, not touch

ADJECTIVES

10 **resistant**, resisting, renitent, withstanding, reluctant, negative, refusing, striking, unwilling, noncooperative, uncooperative, opposing, opposed, objecting, challenging, challenged, deprecative, deprecating, protesting, dissenting, defiant, rebuffing, repulsing, repellent, repelling, obstructive, hard-headed (US), hard-shell (US), hard-core, hard-nosed (Inf)

11 **obstinate**, intractable, refractory, recalcitrant, callous, hard, rigid, firm, standing firm, tough, stiff, starchy, stubborn, obdurate, inflexible, unbending, unyielding, unmalleable, die-hard, hardline, traditional, conservative

12 **resisting**, unsubmissive, up in arms, undefeated, unsubdued, unbowed, unquelled, unbeatable, invincible, bulletproof, self-defensive, revolutionary, rebellious, mutinous, insurgent, reactionary, terrorist, anarchist

13 **desisting**, denying, self-denying, refraining, abstaining, abstemious, forbearing

ADVERBS

14 **resistingly**, resistantly, reluctantly, negatively, unwillingly, noncooperatively, challengingly, deprecatingly, protestingly, under protest, dissentingly, repellently, obstinately, hard-headedly (US), intractably, traditionally, conservatively, callously, firmly, rigidly, toughly, stiffly, inflexibly, unbendingly, invincibly, defiantly, unsubmissively, mutinously, rebelliously

15 **abstemiously**, abstinently, forbearingly, with forbearance, through self-denial

INTERJECTIONS

16 **fight on!**, no surrender!, rise up!, resist!, we shall overcome!

670 Attack

VERBS

1 **attack**, launch an attack, break the peace, start a fight, take the offensive, assume the offensive, go (over) onto the offensive, go on the attack, engage, strike first, strike the first blow, fire the first shot, sound the charge, advance, advance against, march against, ride against, drive against, sail against, fly against, go over the top, bear down on, charge, charge against, rush, rush at, run at, dash at, gallop at, go full belt at, tilt at, ride full tilt at, go for, make a dead set at, drive, thrust, push, raid, foray, strike, pound, assault, blitz, bombard, assail, harry, hunt, ram, collide with, ambush, surprise

2 **fire**, fire on, open fire (on), fire at, level, draw a bead on, aim, find (*or* get) in the cross hairs, pull (*or* squeeze) the trigger, take a pot shot, pop at, snipe at, pick off, shoot, shoot at, let fly, volley, volley and thunder, rattle, blast, pour a broadside into, shoot down, bring down, torpedo, strafe, cannonade, shell, fusillade, pepper, rake, straddle, enfilade

3 **bomb**, throw bombs, drop bombs, carpet-bomb, drop the payload, hit the target, make the rubble bounce, blitz, nuke (Inf), lay eggs (Sl), plaster (Sl), prang (Sl)

4 **besiege**, lay siege to, starve out, surround, enclose, encircle, encroach, infringe, blockade, hem in, beset, beleaguer, invest

5 **strike**, hit, go for, set on, have a fling at, have a go at, pounce upon, fall upon, pitch into, sail into, launch out at, let fly at, lash out at, let someone have it, lay into, tear into, lace into, round on, strike at, raise one's hand against, grapple with, close with, fetch a blow, lay about one, swipe (at), flail, hammer, punch, butt, push, poke (at), kick, knock down, bring down, lay low, beat up, mug, attack tooth and nail, go berserk, run amok, savage, maul, jump (Inf), kick ass (US sl)

6 **stab**, make a pass at, have a cut at, lunge, thrust, thrust at, pierce, cut, slash, knife, spear, lance, bayonet, impale, run through, cut down

7 **stone**, throw a stone, heave a brick, lapidate, sling, pelt, shy, throw at, hurl at, chuck (Inf)

8 **counterattack**, fight back, retaliate, resist, oppose, rebel (against), confront, defy, challenge, take on, stand against, take a stand against, withstand, strike back at, return blow for blow, break out, sally, make a sortie
▶ *672 Retaliation, 669 Resistance, 668 Defiance*

9 **attack successfully**, break through, breach, take over, board, lay aboard, grapple, capture, storm, take by storm, carry, escalade, burst in, invade, incur upon, overrun, overcome, overmaster, overwhelm, overpower, ride down, run down, trample, beat, corner, bring to bay, go on the rampage, slaughter, kill, ravage, rape, terrorize, torture, wreak havoc, scorch, burn, lay waste
▶ *701 Subjection*

10 **criticize**, censure, cast aspersions on, inveigh against, disparage, denigrate, malign, decry, denounce, condemn, slander, defame, libel, berate, vituperate, abuse, vilify, revile, slur, smear
▶ *854 Disparagement, 852 Disapproval*

NOUNS

11 **attack**, assault, aggression, aggressiveness, pugnacity, hostility, intimidation, harassment, belligerence, combativeness, bellicosity

12 **military attack**, hostile attack, offensive, offensive operations, offensive campaign, strike, pre-emptive strike, onslaught, onset, charge, drive, push, thrust, rush, run, dead set, shock, surprise attack, raid, forray, find-and-destroy mission, surprise offensive, surprise blow, shock tactics, blitzkrieg, *coup de main* (Fr), land attack, armoured attack, ground-force attack, infantry assault, tank assault, pincer movement, flanking attack, enfilade, air attack, sea attack, boarding, combined attack, blind attack, night attack, camisado, concentrated attack, blitz, massed attack, relentless attack, day-and-night attack, bombardment, heavy bombardment, artillery bombardment, barrage, mortar attack, cannonade
▶ *676 War*

13 **air attack**, air strike, air raid, air campaign, aerial bombardment, bomb-dropping, bomb run, bombing, conventional bombing, strategic bombing, tactical bombing, precision bombing, dive-bombing, surgical air strike, saturation bombing, carpet bombing, indiscriminate bombing, kamikaze bombing, suicide bombing, high-level bombing, low-level bombing, missile strike, laser targeting, anti-aircraft fire, anti-aircraft artillery, triple-A, ack-ack, tracer flare, strafe

14 **siege**, blockade, encirclement, encroachment, infringement, inroad, investment, counterattack, counteroffensive, retaliation, rebellion, sally, sortie, break-out, breakthrough, taking by storm, storm, escalade, irruption, overstepping, overrunning, ingress, invasion, incursion, occupation, subjection, dragonnade, bloodbath, slaughter, devastation, laying waste, pillage, rape, havoc

15 **firing**, fire, shooting, musketry, gunnery, gunfire, broadside, shot across the bows, volley, salvo, burst, spray, machine-gun fire, strafe, rifle fire, fusillade, burst of fire, rapid fire, cross-fire, plunging fire, raking fire, sharpshooting, sniping
▶ *680 Weapon*

16 **terrorist attack**, terror tactics, hostage taking, kidnapping, assassination, bombing, letter bombing, mailbombing, car bombing, guerrilla attack, sniping, war of attrition

17 **personal attack**, physical attack, physical violence, mugging, armed robbery, assault and battery, grievous bodily harm (GBH), rape, date rape, indecent (*or* sexual) assault, foul play, stab in the back, injustice, verbal attack, criticism, censure, aspersion, disparagement, denigration, decrial, denunciation, slander, defamation, libel, calumny, abuse, vilification, revilement, slur, smear
▶ *241 Violence, 768 Aggravation, 854 Disparagement, 852 Disapproval*

18 **hit**, blow, punch, knock, swipe, kick, stab, jab, cut, cut and thrust, thrust, swordthrust, home-thrust, lunge, foin, pass, passado, quarte and

tierce, stabbing, knifing, bayonetting, impalement, goring, stoning, lapidation

19 **attacker**, assailant, aggressor, warrior, crusader, holy warrior, hawk, militant, attacking force, spearhead, strike force, storm trooper, fighter pilot, air ace, top gun, bomber, dive bomber, bombardier, sharpshooter, sniper, terrorist, guerrilla, besieger, blockader, raider, invader, stormer, escalader, mugger, rapist, murderer, assassin, killer

▶ 679 Combatant

20 **bout**, spell, spasm, fit, seizure, paroxysm, match, contest, fight, round

▶ 624 Ill Health

ADJECTIVES

21 **aggressive**, antagonistic, unfriendly, hostile, inimical, pugnacious, truculent, threatening, provocative, quarrelsome, contentious, disputatious, litigious

22 **militant**, militaristic, martial, belligerent, bellicose, combative, hawkish, warlike, warring, warmongering, sabre-rattling, offensive, on the offensive, spoiling for a fight, on the warpath, up in arms

▶ 676 War

23 **attacking**, assaulting, invading, storming, charging, boarding, fighting, striking, harrying, kicking, punching, flailing, cutting, slashing, destructive, violent, bloodthirsty, savage, brutal, brutish, cruel, barbarous, bloody, uncontrollable, overpowering, overwhelming, frenzied, raging, berserk

▶ 241 Violence

24 **counterattacking**, resisting, opposing, retaliatory, challenging, defiant, rebellious

▶ 669 Resistance, 663 Opposition

25 **critical**, censorious, disparaging, denigrating, maligning, decrying, denunciatory, defamatory, slanderous, libellous, vituperative, abusive

▶ 854 Disparagement, 827 Curse

ADVERBS

26 **aggresively**, forcefully, assertively, offensively, with hostility, on the offensive, on the attack, on the warpath, in combat

671 Defence

NOUNS

1 **defence**, defensive move, defensive tactic, the defensive, resistance, passive resistance, active resistance, parry, warding off, safeguarding, safekeeping, preserving, preservation

2 **safeguard**, protection, buffer, screen, rampart, bulwark, buffer, fender, bumper

3 **counter**, counterforce, counteraction, counterstroke

▶ 672 Retaliation

4 **defensiveness**, defence mechanism camouflage, protective colouring, elusiveness, shyness, nervousness

5 **self-defence**, boxing, martial arts, judo, karate, security, surveillance, burglar alarm, car alarm, personal alarm, rape alarm, whistle, Mace (Tm), guard dog

6 **protective clothing**, helmet, crash helmet, head guard, goggles, visor, body padding, shoulder pad, shin pad, gloves, gauntlets, protective belt, body belt, box, fireproof clothing, bulletproof vest, flak jacket, gas mask, breathing apparatus

7 **armour**, jousting armour, body armour, harness, full armour, panoply, mail, chain mail, chain armour, scale armour, fluted armour, splint armour, steel-plate armour, armour plate, breastplate, backplate, cuirass, lance rest, lorica, plastron, hauberk, habergeon, brigandine, coat of mail, corslet, helmet, helm, coif, gorget, casque, basinet, sallet, morion, siege cap, steel helmet, tin hat, bowl, skull, visor, beaver, shako, bearskin, busby, vambrace, brassard, cubitiere, elbow-cop, gauntlet, cuisse, greave, shield, buckler, scutum, target, pavis, mantelet, testudo

8 **military defences**, defensive line, fortified line, entrenchment, fixed position, fieldwork, redoubt, redan, lunette, breastwork, parados, contravallation, outwork, circumvallation, earthwork, embankment, mound, sandbag, moat, ditch, fosse, trench, dugout, foxhole, tripwire, trap, mine

9 **barrier**, barricade, blockade, boom, fence, wall, road block, stakes, pales, paling, abatis, palisade, stockade, zareba, defensive circle, circle of wagons, laager, entanglements, razor wire, electric fence, spike, caltrop, chevaux-defrise, Maginot Line, Siegfried Line, Hadrian's Wall, Antonine Wall, Great Wall of China

10 **shelter**, air-raid shelter, fallout shelter, concrete shelter, underground shelter, bunker, blockhouse, blackout, smokescreen

11 **fortification**, box fortification, triangle fortification, circumvallation, bulwark, rampart, wall, town wall, parapet, battlement, bailey, machicolation, embrasure, casemate, merlon, loophole, banquette, barbette, emplacement, gun emplacement, vallum, scarp, escarp, counterscarp, glacis, curtain, bastion, demibastion, ravelin, demilune, outwork, buttress, abutment, gabion, gabionade

12 **fort**, fortress, fortalice, rampart, stockade, earthwork, castle, keep, ward, barbican, tower, turret, battlements, curtain, bartizan, donjon, portcullis, drawbridge, moat, gate, gatehouse, postern, sally port, citadel, capitol, acropolis, refuge, Martello tower, pillbox, blockhouse, strong point, stronghold, fastness, laager, zareba

13 **defender**, champion, patron, aider, sup-

porter, henchman, angel (Inf), knight, knight errant, white knight, paladin

14 **guard**, bodyguard, lifeguard, watch, sentry, sentinel, vigilante, patrol, patrolman, patrolwoman, security guard, watchman, night watchman, night watch, doorman, bouncer (Sl), garrison, picket, armed guard, vanguard, rearguard, escort

15 **protector**, guardian, warden, warder, custodian, keeper, park keeper, gamekeeper, goalkeeper, wicketkeeper,

16 **rescuer**, deliverer, saviour

VERBS

17 **defend**, guard, protect, secure, keep, watch, safeguard, lock up, ward

18 **fence**, wall, hedge, moat, booby-trap, mine, circumscribe, enclose, barricade, palisade, block, obstruct

19 **buffer**, cushion, pad, shield, camouflage, curtain, cover, screen, cloak, conceal

20 **reinforce**, armour, fortify, strengthen, beef up (Inf)

21 **entrench**, dig in, make a stand, stand firm, stand in front, stand by, stand ready, garrison, man the fort, man the guns, man the defences, man the breach, man, plug the gap, stop the gap

22 **plead for**, hold a brief for, argue for, take up the cause of, protect the interests of, support, champion, vindicate, fight for, take up arms for, break a lance for, take up the cudgels for

23 **rescue**, come to the rescue, save, deliver

24 **parry**, counter, ripsote, fence, fend off, throw back, ward off, hold off, keep off, fight off, stave off, repulse, hold (or keep) at bay, keep at arm's length, avoid, turn, avert, deflect

25 **stall**, beat about the bush, quibble, vacillate, blow hot and cold, stonewall, block, obstruct, delay

26 **act on the defensive**, fight a defensive battle, take evasive action, play for a draw, stalemate,

27 **retaliate**, fight back, come back, show fight, show one's mettle, give a warm reception to, resist, repulse, repel, butt away

28 **survive**, withstand, escape, bear the brunt, hold one's own, fall back on, beat a strategic retreat, get out while the going is good, retire, turn back, scrape through, live to fight another day

ADJECTIVES

29 **defending**, defensive, on the defensive, on guard, resisting, extenuating, excusing, vindicating, challenged, protective, tutelary, responsible

30 **defended**, protected, secured, armoured, armour-plated, heavy-armed, mailed, mailclad, armour-clad, ironclad, panoplied, accoutred, prepared, harnessed (Arch), moated, palisaded, barricaded, walled, fortified, ma-

chicolated, castellated, battlemented, loopholed

31 **entrenched**, dug in, bombproof, bulletproof, invulnerable, unconquerable

ADVERBS

32 **defensively**, protectively, on the defensive, on guard, at bay, in defence, self-defensively, in self-defence

672 Retaliation

NOUNS

1 **retaliation**, reprisal, revenge, just revenge, vengeance, redress, desert, deserts, just deserts, dueness, justice, retribution, reparation, repayment, Nemesis, comeuppance (Inf), punishment, negative reaction, negative feedback, backlash, boomerang, counter, counterpunch, counterstroke, counteraction, counterblast, counterplot, countermine, counter suit, answering back, comeback, riposte, retort, rejoinder, returning good for evil, heaping coals of fire, reciprocation, talion, like for like, tit for tat, quid pro quo, measure for measure, blow for blow, an eye for an eye and a tooth for a tooth, a taste of one's own medicine, a Roland for an Oliver, a game at which two can play

2 **revenger**, avemger, vigilante, guerrilla, saboteur, member of the resistance, member of the underground

VERBS

3 **retaliate**, take reprisals, get satisfaction, exact compensation, recoup, repay, redress, redress the balance, inflict punishment, punish, revenge, make good, counter, riposte, parry, make a requital, pay one out, pay one back, shoot back, pay off old scores, wipe out a score, square the account, be quits, get even with, get one's own back, reciprocate, give and take, avenge, live by the golden rule, do unto others as you would be done by, return good for evil, heap coals of fire on one's head, fight fire with fire, return like for like, return the compliment, give as good as one got, pay one in his own coin, give a quid pro quo, return, retort, cap, answer back, answer, counter sue, counter charge, react, boomerang, recoil, round on, kick back, hit back, not take it lying down, resist, requite

4 **serve one right**, be rightly served, be one's own fault, make one's bed and lie in it, be taught a lesson, have had one's lesson, restitute, pay off, find one's match, meet one's match, get what one deserves, get one's deserts, get what was due, get what was coming, get a dose of one's own medicine, be hoisted with one's own petard, be chastised, be punished

ADJECTIVES

5 **retaliatory**, in retaliation, in reprisal, in self-

defence, retaliative, retributive, punitive, recriminatory, like for like, reciprocal, revengeful, vindictive, vengeful, rightly served

ADVERBS

6 **with vengeance**, by way of return, in requital, tit for tat

INTERJECTIONS

7 **revenge!**, it serves you right!, take that!, see how it feels!, put that in your pipe and smoke it!, the laugh's on you!

673   Submission

NOUNS

1 **submission**, submissiveness, appeasement, deference, obedience, tameness, submitting, succumbing, subservience, slavishness, servitude, collaboration, sell-out (Inf), consent, acquiescence, compliance, concession, assent, agreeing, nonresistance, passivity, passiveness, peace at any price, line of least resistance, resignation, fatalism, supineness, lethargy, apathy, cop-out (Sl), inactivity, surrender, yielding, giving way, giving in, giving up the fort, caving in (Inf), the white flag, capitulation, surrender, unconditional surrender, cession, abandonment, relinquishment, abdication, resignation, deference, abject loyalty, homage, bow, curtsy, humble submission, humility, kneeling, genuflection, kowtow, prostration, grovelling, obeisance, sexual submission, passive sex, masochism

2 **appeaser**, defeatist, quitter, pushover (Inf), mouse, doormat, wet (Inf), wimp (Sl), coward, sycophant, groveller, toady, brown-noser (US sl), brown-nose (US sl), Uriah Heep, Uncle Tom (Black derog sl), servant, menial, grunt (US sl), gofer (Sl), slave, masochist

VERBS

3 **submit**, yield, obey, give in, not resist, not insist, make no waves, keep quiet, pussyfoot (around) (Inf), defer to, bow to, accept, face reality, face the facts, resign oneself, be resigned, make a virtue of necessity, appease, collaborate with, sell out (Inf), yield with a good grace, admit defeat, yield the palm, play it low-key, take things easy, take the heat off (Inf), cool it (Sl), acquiesce, condone, buy (Sl), comply, consent, assent, relent, abide, overlook, ignore, disregard, allow, go along with, play along with, grant, concede, shrug one's shoulders, be indifferent, turn a blind eye toward, show apathy for, avoid responsibility for, cop out (Sl), withdraw, retreat, retire, hang it up (Inf), fade into the background, leave, step aside, make way for, turn back, not contest, let judgment go by default, pass up, pull out, be inactive, capitulate, surrender, be defeated, cease resistance, stop fighting, sue for peace, subdue oneself, call it a day, have no

fight left, have all the fight knocked out of one, give up, give way, cry quits, cry uncle (US sl), have had enough, abandon one's cause, relinquish, throw in the towel, hold up one's hands, show the white flag, ask for terms, haul down the flag, strike colours, ask for mercy, give oneself up, yield oneself, lay down one's arms, hand over one's sword, abdicate, renounce authority, resign, stand down

4 **succumb**, knuckle under, break under pressure, yield to the pressure, be out for the count, cave in (Inf), collapse, sag, wilt, tire, faint, drop, show no fight, take the line of least resistance, bow before the inevitable, bow before the storm, be swept aside, be submissive, submit, learn obedience, keep in one's place, know one's place, do homage, bow, curtsy, take it on the chin, swallow the pill, bite the bullet, apologize, eat humble pie, eat dirt, eat crow (US inf), be humble, take it, take it from one, take it lying down, pocket the insult, grin and bear it, bear, lump it (Inf), take one's lumps (Inf), suffer in patience, endure, digest, stomach, put up with, take the heat (Inf), suffer, bend, kneel, kowtow, toady, crouch, cringe, crawl, bow and scrape, stoop, grovel, lick the dust, lick the boots of, kiss the rod, brown-nose (Sl)

ADJECTIVES

5 **submitting**, surrendering, quiet, meek, humble, tame, docile, unresisting, nonresisting, law-abiding, peaceful, submissive, subservient, servile, menial, lowly, low, abject, obedient, slavish, unconcerned, fatalistic, resigned, subdued, acquiescent, concessionary, assenting, pliant, accommodating, malleable, biddable, tractable, amenable, agreeable, soft, weak-kneed, bending, crouching, crawling, cringing, lying down, supine, prostrate, bootlicking, bowing and scraping, kneeling, on bended knee, sycophantic, toadying, humble, masochistic

ADVERBS

6 **with humility**, humbly, meekly, obediently, without resistance

INTERJECTIONS

7 **I/we surrender!**, enough!, mercy!, uncle! (US sl)

674   Contention

NOUNS

1 **contention**, conflict, struggle, fight, clash, tussle, strife, military conflict, armed conflict, combat, war, warfare, fighting, battle, pitched battle, running battle, skirmish, engagement, encounter, firefight, dogfight, fight to the death, fight to the bitter end, fight to the last man, war to the knife, no prisoners taken, no holds barred, debate, dispute, dissent, dissen-

sion, controversy, polemics, paper warfare, ink-slinging, mudslinging, argument, quarrel, open quarrel, squabble, spat, hassle, wrangle, altercation, words, war of words, cold war, competition, rivalry, emulation, jealousy, competitiveness, gamesmanship, survival of the fittest, rat race, cutthroat competition, dog-eat-dog competition, sports, sport, team sports, field sports, games, athletic competition, athletics, gymnastics, stakes, bone of contention, root of dissension, area of disagreement, provocation, *casus belli* (L), dust-up (Inf), rhubarb (US sl), ding-dong battle (Inf), knock-down-drag-out fight (Inf)

▶ *676 War, 473 Argument, 117 Disparity*

2 **contest**, trial, trial of strength, test of endurance, workout, marathon, triathlon, pentathlon, decathlon, tug of war, tug of love, tussle, struggle, effort, essay, exertion, bitter struggle, needle match, grudge match, revenge match, equal contest, even match, close fight, nothing in it, close finish, photo finish, neck-and-neck finish, competition, open competition, free-for-all, pro-am, knockout competition, tournament, championship, prize competition, stakes, trophy, game, set, rubber, match, test match, friendly (match), fixture, event, concourse, rally, meeting, handicap, run-off, heat, quarterfinal, semifinal, final, Cup tie, Cup final, sporting event, track event, athletics meeting, sports day, games, Highland Games, Commonwealth Games, Olympic Games, Olympics, Summer Olympics, Winter Olympics, Special Olympics, sport, amusement, field day, Derby day, gymkhana, horse show, showjumping, rodeo, athletics, gymnastics, real sweat (US sl), ball-buster (US sl)

▶ *596 Attempt*

3 **stadium**, arena, show-ring, track, field, pitch, Wembley, Wimbledon, Lords, the Oval

4 **race**, racing, speed contest, speeding, running, races, foot race, flat race, sprint, dash, mile race, relay race, team race, road race, marathon, charity run, fun run, long-distance race, cross-country race, orienteering, downhill racing, slalom, obstacle race, hare and hounds race, sack race, egg and spoon race, pancake race, treasure hunt, horse racing, thoroughbred racing, the turf, sport of kings, the Classics, the Grand National, the Derby, the Oaks, the St Leger, harness racing, point-to-point, steeplechase, the Grand National, hurdles, fences, sticks, leap, jump, greyhound racing, dog racing, the dogs, pig racing, armadillo racing, tortoise racing, motor racing, Grand Prix racing, Formula One racing, IndyCar racing, Indianapolis 500, Mille Miglia, motor rally, Monte Carlo rally, drag racing, stockcar racing, speedway, dirt-track racing, autocross, rallycross, motorcycle rac-

ing, Isle of Man TT Races, motocross, cycle racing, Tour de France, cyclocross, boat racing, yacht racing, America's Cup, regatta, eights, Henley, Oxford-Cambridge boat race

5 **racecourse**, racetrack, track, Epsom, Ascot, Churchill Downs, Longchamp

6 **fight**, free fight, free-for-all, showdown, rough and tumble, roughhouse, horseplay, scuffle, brawl, broil, quarrel, row, rumpus, ruction, turmoil, upheaval, hubbub, brouhaha, affray, set-to, tussle, scrap, brush, scrum, scrummage, scrimmage, scramble, dogfight, melee, fracas, riot, uproar, gang warfare, street fight, fisticuffs, blows, hard knocks, give and take, blow for blow, tit for tat, cut and thrust, running fight, ding-dong fight, close fighting, hand-to-hand fighting, close grips, close quarters, infighting, hostilities, belligerency, blow-up, appeal to arms, war, warfare, state of war, holy war, war of attrition, deed of arms, feat of arms, passage of arms, combat, fray, clash, collision, conflict, military conflict, armed conflict, skirmish, skirmishing, engagement, encounter, military encounter, military action, battle, battle royal, pitched battle, stand-up fight, firefight, shoot-out, campaign, struggle, death struggle, death grapple, war to the knife, fight to the death, final battle, Armageddon, theomachy, gigantomachy, psychomachia, psychic combat, field of battle, battlefield, battleground, battlefront (US), killing fields, shindig (Sl), shindy (Sl), rumble (US sl), dust-up (Inf), punch-up (Inf)

▶ *473 Argument, 151 Disorder, 676 War*

7 **boxing**, pugilism, fighting, prizefighting, noble art of self-defence, shadow boxing, sparring, jabbing, punching, socking, slugging, pummelling, lambasting, fisticuffs, spar, clinch, infighting, boxing match, prizefight, fight, round, bout, the ring, the fancy (Arch), the canvas (Inf)

8 **wrestling**, Graeco-Roman wrestling, all-in wrestling, freestyle wrestling, catch-as-catch-can, no holds barred, catch, hold, wrestle, grapple, wrestling match, jujitsu, judo, karate, kung fu, aikido, tae kwon do, a grunt-and-groan match (US sl)

▶ *26 Combat Sports*

9 **duel**, duelling, duel to the death, affair of honour, pistols for two and coffee for one, seconds out, single combat, gladiatorial combat, one-on-one (US), head-to-head contest, hand-to-hand fight, nose-to-nose confrontation, close grips, close quarters, jousting, joust, tilting, tilt, tournament, tourney, fencing, swordplay, singlestick, quarterstaff, kendo, bullfight, tauromachy, bloodless bullfight, dogfight, cockfight, bullring, cockpit, boxing ring, field of battle, battlefield, lists, arena

▶ *28 Fencing*

10 contender, combatant, fighter, fighting man, soldier, warrior, battler, striver, struggler, tussler, gamecock, fighting cock, gladiator, bullfighter, boxer, prizefighter, pugilist, heavyweight, middleweight, lightweight, flyweight, puncher, wrestler, freestyle wrestler, duellist, fencer, swordsman, foilsman, challenger, contestant, player, participant, competitor, rival, emulator, opponent, adversary, runner-up, finalist, semifinalist, frontrunner, favourite, nap, odds-on favourite, the pick, the choice, seed, top seed, starter, also-ran, the field, all comers, racer, runner, miler, marathoner, sprinter, speeder, athlete, gymnast, jockey, debater, quarreller, mud-slinger, pothunter, candidate, applicant, hopeful, entrant, examinee, GI (US inf), Tommy (Inf), scrapper (US inf), slugger (US inf), Great White Hope (US inf), grappler (Sl), grunt-and-groaner (US sl)

▶ *679 Combatant, 473 Argument*

VERBS

11 contend, combat, battle, fight, tussle, wrestle, grapple, tackle, attempt, try, venture, essay, strive, struggle, try and try again, oppose, resist, withstand, struggle against, make a stand, put up a fight, argue for, stick out for, make a point (of), insist (on), emphasize, contest, compete, enter, enter for, challenge, take on, stake, wager, bet, play, play against, race, run a race, match oneself, vie with, emulate, rival, outrival, outdo, enter the lists, descend into the arena, take up the challenge, give it a try, pick up the gauntlet, close with, grapple with, engage with, lock horns with, strike at, cross swords with, couch one's lance (Arch), tilt with, joust with, break a lance with, slug it out with, try a fall, try conclusions with, have a bash (Inf), have a go at (Inf), stonewall (Inf), do a job on (Sl)

▶ *596 Attempt*

12 fight, have a fight, scuffle, row, scrimmage, scrap, set to, pitch into, go for, take on, engage, wade in, have at, sail into, assail, attack, open fire, square up to, put up one's fists, lay on, strike at, lay about one, join in the melee, come to blows, exchange blows, engage in fisticuffs, give hard knocks, give and take, give as good as one gets, box, spar, pummel, jostle, hit, punch, slap, strike, kick, scratch, bite, fall foul of, call out, answer for, give satisfaction, meet, encounter, have a brush with, scrap with, skirmish, exchange shots, fight a pitched battle, give battle, grapple, lock horns, come to grips, come to close quarters, duel, fence, cross swords, measure swords, use cold steel, cut and thrust, fight hand to hand, declare war, go to war, raise one's banner, combat, campaign, wage war, fight the good fight, shed blood, fight hard, shoot to kill, fight like devils (*or* fiends), fight it out, fight to the finish, fight to the last man, have a punch-up (Inf), mix it (up) (Sl), whip up on (US sl), give one a knuckle sandwich (Sl)

▶ *676 War, 151 Disorder, 241 Violence*

13 conflict, differ, disagree, dissent, dispute, join issue with, debate, quarrel, row, squabble, argue, affirm, aver, maintain

▶ *473 Argument, 117 Disparity, 535 Affirmation*

ADJECTIVES

14 contending, battling, fighting, grappling, struggling, competing, contesting, challenging, racing, rival, rivalling, vying, outdoing, surpassing, agonistic, athletic, sporting, starting, running, in the running, in with a chance

15 contentious, argumentative, quarrelsome, quarrelling, irritable, irascible, aggressive, combative, fight-hungry, spoiling for a fight, pugilistic, gladiatorial, pugnacious, bellicose, warmongering, warlike, hawkish, at loggerheads, at odds, at war, belligerent, warring, head-to-head, hand-to-hand, nose-to-nose, close, at close quarters, at close grips, at close range

▶ *676 War, 473 Argument*

16 competitive, keen, cutthroat, dog-eat-dog, keenly contested, ding-dong, close-run, cliffhanging, well-fought, fought to the finish, fought to the death

ADVERBS

17 contentiously, argumentatively, irritably, irascibly, aggressively, pugnaciously, belligerently

675 Peace

Peace I leave with you, my peace I give unto you: not as the world giveth, give I unto you. Let not your heart be troubled, neither let it be afraid. Bible: John.

Give peace in our time, O Lord. The Book of Common Prayer.

Don't tell me peace has broken out. Bertolt Brecht.

I believe it is peace for our time…peace with honour. Neville Chamberlain.

Nation shall speak peace unto nation. Montague John Rendall.

NOUNS

1 peace, freedom from war, peacetime, state of peace, peaceable kingdom, peace that passeth all understanding, quiet life, the line of least resistance, no hassle, peacefulness, peace and quiet, quiescence, rest, stillness, peace of mind, harmony, concord, piping times of peace, palmy days, golden times, bed of roses, lasting peace, universal peace, Pax Romana, Pax Britannica, Pax Americana, imposed

peace, law and order, order, truce, temporary truce, uneasy truce, lull in hostilities, cessation, end of war, end of hostilities, armistice, cease-fire, surrender, demobilization, military discharge (US), coexistence, armed neutrality, neutrality, nonalignment, nonaligned nations, noninvolvment, indifference, nonintervention, avoidance, peaceableness, nonaggression, cordial relations, amity, friendship, pacifism, pacification, peace at any price, mutually assured destruction, peace in our time, nonviolence, ahimsa, disarmament, nuclear disarmament, Campaign for Nuclear Disarmament (CND), ban-the-bomb movement, anti-war movement, anti-Vietnam War movement, peace movement, peace party, peace camp, peacemaking, irenics, irenic theology, peace offering, peace pipe, calumet, peace proposal, peace talks, peace treaty, peace agreement, nonaggression pact, disarmament treaty, arms limitation treaty, Strategic Arms Limitation Talks (SALT), Strategic Arms Reduction Talks (START), burying the hatchet, amnesty, pardon, forgiveness, no aggro (Sl), demob (Inf), civvy street (Sl)

▶ *677 Pacification, 678 Mediation, 422 Silence, 325 Motionlessness, 649 Ease, 591 Avoidance, 839 Forgiveness, 667 Agreement, 218 Cessation, 676 War, 783 Indifference, 242 Moderation, 819 Friendship, 116 Accord*

2 **symbol of peace**, dove, lamb, olive branch, flag of truce, white flag, peace sign, V-sign, peace pipe, Christ, angel, broken arrow (or lance), United Nations (UN), International Red Cross, Peace Corps

▶ *677 Pacification*

3 **pacifist**, pacifier, man (or woman) of peace, peacemaker, peacemonger, peace-lover, CND member, draft dodger (US), draft evader (US), draft protester (US), draft exile (US), draft-card burner (US), peacenik, dove, neutral, civilian, noncombatant, nonbelligerent, passive resister, conscientious objector, Quaker, peace negotiator, mediator, intermediary, peacekeeper, United Nations peacekeeping force, conchie (Inf)

▶ *677 Pacification, 678 Mediation*

4 **Nobel Peace Prize**, Willy Brandt, Mikhail Gorbachev, Dag Hammarskjöld, Martin Luther King, Henry Kissinger, Anwar Sadat and Menachem Begin, Andre Sakharov, Albert Schweitzer, Mother Teresa, Bishop Desmond Tutu, Lech Wałesa, Woodrow Wilson, Rigoberta Menchu, Aung San Suu Kyi, Dalai Lama

VERBS

5 **be at peace**, enjoy peace, stay at peace, observe neutrality, keep the peace, keep out of war, make love – not war, jaw, jaw – not war, war, avoid bloodshed, keep out of trouble, mean no harm, end hostilities, call a truce,

forget one's differences, bury the hatchet, smoke the peace pipe, beat swords into ploughshares, play it cool (Sl)

6 **make peace**, work for peace, ban the bomb, pacify, mediate, settle one's differences, halt the arms race, disarm, make the world a safer place, make the lion lie down with the lamb, surrender, sue for peace

▶ *677 Pacification, 678 Mediation*

ADJECTIVES

7 **peaceful**, quiet, quiet as a lamb, quiescent, tranquil, serene, still, calm, halcyon, piping, palmy, golden, bloodless, harmonious, peacelike, dovelike, harmless, inoffensive, innocent, mild, mild-mannered, easy-going, good-natured, agreeable, amiable, friendly, liberal, tolerant, uncompetitive, uncontentious, peaceable, law-abiding, peace-loving, pacific, unmilitary, unwarlike, unmilitant, nonaggressive, unaggressive, war-weary, pacifist, nonviolent, unresisting, passive, submissive, submitting, unarmed, noncombatant, civilian, neutral, nonaligned, peacemaking, conciliatory, placatory, irenic, without enemies, at peace (with the world), not at war, prewar, antebellum, postwar, postbellum, peacetime, in civvies (Sl), on civvy street (Sl)

▶ *422 Silence, 325 Motionlessness, 649 Ease, 677 Pacification, 678 Mediation, 667 Agreement, 116 Accord, 673 Submission, 819 Friendship, 676 War*

ADVERBS

8 **peacefully**, peaceably, pacifically, without violence, without fear, bloodlessly, safely, quietly, softly, tranquilly, serenely, in peace, in a peaceful way, at peace

INTERJECTIONS

9 **peace**! keep the peace! God's peace! peace be with you!

676 War

And ye shall hear of wars and rumours of wars: see that ye be not troubled: for all these things must come to pass, but the end is not yet./ For nation shall rise against nation, and kingdom against kingdom: and there shall be famines, and pestilences, and earthquakes, in divers places./ All these are the beginning of sorrows. Bible: Matthew.

Then said Jesus unto him, Put up again thy sword into his place: for all they that take the sword shall perish with the sword. Bible: Matthew.

C'est magnifique, mais ce n'est pas la guerre./ (It is magnificent, but it is not war.) Pierre Bosquet.

War is like love, it always finds a way. Bertolt Brecht.

War is the continuation of politics by other means. Karl von Clausewitz.

Older men declare war. But it is youth that must fight and die. Herbert Clark Hoover.

The first casualty when war comes is truth. Hiram Warren Johnson.

The Minstrel Boy to the war has gone,/ In the ranks of death you'll find him. Thomas Moore.

Don't fire until you see the whites of their eyes. William Prescott.

All Quiet on the Western Front. Erich Maria Remarque.

More than an end to war, we want an end to the beginnings of all wars. Franklin D. Roosevelt.

Cry 'Havoc!' and let slip the dogs of war. William Shakespeare.

I am tired and sick of war. Its glory is all moonshine…War is hell. General William Sherman.

They make a wilderness and call it peace. Tacitus.

You will be home before the leaves have fallen from the trees. Wilhelm II.

NOUNS

1 **war**, warfare, modern warfare, conflict, armed conflict, military conflict, military operation, intervention, armed intervention, arms, the sword, grim-visaged war, *horrida bella* (L), *ultima ratio regum* (L), fortunes of war, wager of battle, arbitrament of war, armed neutrality, defensive weapons, Fortress America, paper war, war of words, polemic, quarrel, war of nerves, sabre-rattling, gunboat diplomacy, superpower diplomacy, psychological warfare, intimidation, undeclared war, uneasy peace, cold war, half-war, doubtful war, phoney war, disguised war, economic war, trade war, Cod war, real war, hot war, civil war, brother war, internecine war, revolt, revolution, war of independence, ideological war, class war, war on want, war of liberation, holy war, religious war, crusade, jihad, aggressive war, war of conquest, war of expansion, imperialist war, limited war, war of containment, localized war, desert war, triphibious war, war on all fronts, all-out war, major war, general war, world war, First World War, Second World War, global war, total war, mother of all battles, war to end all wars, The Great War, Armageddon, blitzkrieg, blitz, atomic war, nuclear war, total destruction, pushbutton war, high-tech war, computer war, war of attrition, chemical warfare, truceless war, war to the knife, war to the end (*or* death), no prisoners taken, no holds barred

▶ *674 Contention, 670 Attack, 671 Defence, 777 Fear, 668 Defiance, 680 Weapon, 398 Killing*

2 **glory of war**, pomp and circumstance of war, panoply of war, triumphal procession, chivalry, shining armour, red coats, rows of nodding plumes, martial music, military band, drums, bugle, trumpet, bugle call, battle call, battle cry, battle yell, rallying cry, rebel yell (US), war cry, war whoop, war song, war dance

3 **gods and goddesses of war**, Mars, Ares, Odin, Wotan, Bellona, Athena, Eris, Fea, Indra, Kartikeya, Tyr

▶ *8 Divinity*

4 **belligerency**, militancy, hostilities, state of war, state of siege, resort to arms, declaration of war, outbreak of war, wartime, wartime conditions, time of war, the war years

5 **bellicosity**, war fever, love of war, warlike habits, military spirit, fighting spirit, pugnacity, pugnaciousness, combativeness, aggressiveness, aggression, hawkishness, Ramboism, sabre-rattling, militancy, militarism, military tradition, expansionism, war policy, patriotism, fervent patriotism, jingoism, chauvinism, my country right or wrong, might is right

▶ *674 Contention, 473 Argument, 666 Disagreement, 493 Misjudgment*

6 **art of war**, tactics of war, war strategy, war skills, grand strategy, warcraft, siegecraft, castrametation, fortification, military leadership, generalship, soldiership, seamanship, airmanship, military academy, Royal Military Academy, Sandhurst, Britannia Royal Naval College, war college, staff college, training drill, march, obstacle course, ballistics, gunnery, rifle practice, musketry practice, staffwork, logistics, planning, plan, plan of battle, battle plan, campaign plan, military evolutions, manoeuvres, tactics, strategy, war games, military experience, battlefield knowledge, knowledge of the enemy

▶ *592 Plan, 655 Skill, 501 Knowledge*

7 **war measures**, war policy, war footing, war readiness, war preparations, war effort, war work, arming, appeal to arms, call to arms, clarion call, call, rally, fiery cross, call-up, mobilization, recruitment, conscription, the draft (US), national service, military duty, enlisting, volunteering, joining up, doing one's duty for king (*or* queen) and country, rationing, blackout, civilian evacuation, victory gardens, censorship, propaganda, internment

▶ *543 Sign, 594 Preparation*

8 **warfare**, war, warring, waging war, making war, declaring war, open war, warpath, battles, skirmishes, sieges, bloodshed, deeds of blood, violence, fighting, campaigning, soldiering, active service, military service, infantry ser-

vice, naval service, air force service, serving one's country, bombing, bombardment, saturation bombing, strategic bombing, tactical bombing, carpet bombing, sea battles, sea bombardment, sea raiding, fleet blockade, blockading, besieging, investment, enclosure, artillery warfare, aerial warfare, naval warfare, submarine warfare, undersea warfare, amphibious warfare, chemical warfare, gas warfare, biological warfare, bacteriological warfare, germ warfare, atomic warfare, nuclear warfare, limited nuclear warfare, theatre nuclear warfare, tactical nuclear warfare, economic warfare, sanctions, economic sanctions, military sanctions, arms sanctions, blockade, attrition, scorched earth policy, psychological warfare, wartime propaganda, wartime censorship, offensive warfare, attack, defensive warfare, defence, Star Wars, Strategic Defense Initiative (SDI), mobile warfare, blitzkrieg, blitz, static warfare, trench warfare, desert warfare, mountain warfare, jungle warfare, bush-fighting, guerrilla warfare, sniping, campaign, expedition, mission, operation, operations, land operations, sea operations, naval operations, air operations, amphibious operations, combined operation, allied operation, joint operation, invasion, incursion, raid, word of command, order, military orders, battle orders, command, password, watchword

▶ *674 Contention, 679 Combatant, 680 Weapon, 670 Attack, 671 Defence*

9 **battle**, pitched battle, battle royal, armed conflict, action, fight, scrap, skirmish, brush, collision, clash, shoot-out, offensive, blitz, attack, defence, defensive battle, stand, engagement, infantry engagement, naval engagement, sea fight, air fight, dogfight, line of battle, order of battle

10 **battleground**, battlefield, field of battle, field of conflict, killing field, battle zone, war zone, theatre of war, combat zone, area of hostilities, front line, front, firing line, beachhead, bridgehead, sector, salient, bulge, pocket, field of blood, Aceldama (New Testament)

▶ *674 Contention, 670 Attack, 671 Defence*

11 **recruit**, conscript, draftee (US), volunteer, soldier, infantryman, navy man, seaman, marine, air force pilot, mercenary, veteran, legionnaire, old soldier, Chelsea Pensioner, GI (US inf), Tommy (Inf), tar (Inf), swabby (US sl), jarhead (US sl), fly-boy (US sl)

▶ *679 Combatant*

VERBS

12 **go to war**, declare war, resort to war (*or* arms), choose the military solution, open hostilities, call to arms, appeal to arms, take to arms, fly to arms, unleash the war dogs, unsheathe the sword, throw away the scabbard,

whet the sword, take up the cause, take up the cudgels, fight, rise, rebel, revolt, overthrow, display the flag, fly one's flag, raise one's banner, show the flag, show one's colours, set up one's standard, arm, militarize, mobilize, prepare for war, put on a war footing, rally, call up, call to the colours, rally round the flag, recruit, conscript, draft (US), commission, give a commission, join the army, join up, enlist, enrol, volunteer, take a commission, serve one's country, serve one's king (*or* queen), answer the call, get one's call-up papers, receive a letter from Uncle Sam (US), put on a uniform

▶ *674 Contention*

13 **be at war**, make war, wage war (against), engage in war (*or* hostilities), march to war, go on the warpath, war, war against, war upon, go on active service, ship out, shoulder a musket, smell powder, taste battle, flesh one's sword, open a campaign, campaign, soldier, take the field, take the offensive, invade, attack, raid, ambush, cut down, keep the field, hold one's ground, resist incursions, stand firm, defend, act on the defensive, counterattack, counter, manoeuvre, march, countermarch, blockade, cut off, beleaguer, besiege, starve out, invest, surround, shed blood, bloody, put to the sword, slaughter, mow down, slay, kill, ravage, rape, burn, scorch, lay waste, destroy, demolish, press the button, drop the bomb, nuke (Sl), kick ass (US sl)

▶ *674 Contention, 670 Attack, 671 Defence, 398 Killing, 244 Destruction*

14 **battle**, do battle, give battle, offer battle, accept battle, cross swords with, take issue with, contest, dispute, resist, make (*or* take) a stand, stand, take a position, choose one's ground, dig in, sound the charge, beat the drum, go over the top, charge, engage, provoke an engagement, confront, open fire, fire (at), shoot (at), stage a shoot-out, call for a show-down, join battle, meet on the battlefield, skirmish, brush with, contend, combat, fight it out, fight to the finish, fight to the last man, fight the good fight, fight, close the ranks, rally

▶ *674 Contention, 668 Defiance, 669 Resistance*

ADJECTIVES

15 **warring**, fighting, battling, campaigning, at war, waging war, engaged in war, on the warpath, in a state of war, belligerent, aggressive, bellicose, militant, mobilized, called, called-up, drafted (US), conscripted, armed, uniformed, in the army (*or* military), arrayed, embattled, up in arms, sword in hand, at the front, on active duty, in battle, on the offensive, attacking, on the defensive, defending, engaged, at grips, at loggerheads

▶ *674 Contention, 594 Preparation, 666 Disagreement, 670 Attack, 671 Defence*

16 **warlike**, militaristic, bellicose, hawkish, un-pacific, Ramboesque, militant, aggressive, belligerent, pugnacious, pugilistic, combative, gung-ho, war-loving, warmongering, bloodthirsty, battle-hungry, war-fevered, fierce, tough, cruel, ass-kicking (US sl)
▶ *241 Violence*

17 **military**, paramilitary, mercenary, martial, exercised in arms, bearing arms, veteran, battle-scarred, shell-shocked, knightly, chivalrous, soldierly, soldierlike, naval, operational, strategical, tactical

ADVERBS

18 **to war**, at arms, at the front, at sword's point, at the point of a bayonet, at the cannon's mouth, in the face of death, belligerently, militantly, militarily, militaristically

677   Pacification

NOUNS

1 **pacification**, pacifying, peacemaking, irenics, nonviolence, ahimsa, satyagraha, conciliation, propitiation, appeasement, peace at any price, peace in our time, mollification, moderation, reconciliation, reconcilement, improved relations, détente, rapprochement, accommodation, adjustment, agreement, compromise, composition of differences, mediation, arbitration, good offices, convention, entente, understanding, treaty, peace treaty, nonaggression pact, Strategic Arms Limitation Talks (SALT), SALT I Treaty, Strategic Arms Control Treaty (START), START 2, suspension of hostilities, truce, temporary truce, lull, cessation, armistice, cease-fire, burying the hatchet, imposed peace, forced reconciliation, compulsive cease-fire, moratorium, moratorium on nuclear testing, ban on testing, test ban, comprehensive test ban, disarmament, unilateral disarmament, defence cuts, arms cuts, arms reduction, arms control, reduction of nuclear stockpiles, destruction of weapons, de-escalation of the arms race, freedom from war, Campaign for Nuclear Disarmament (CND), ban-the-bomb movement, peace movement, anti-war movement, anti-Vietnam War movement, the peace process, demobilization, demob, disbanding, nuclear-free zone, peace camp
▶ *675 Peace, 678 Mediation, 242 Moderation, 717 Compromise, 667 Agreement, 715 Contract, 218 Cessation, 695 Compulsion*

2 **peace offering**, irenicon, dove of peace, olive branch, peace overture, peaceful approach, friendly approach, hand of friendship, outstretched hand, friendliness, flag of truce, white flag, peace pipe, calumet, wergild, blood money, compensation, reparation, atonement, restitution, fair offer, easy terms, plea for peace, amnesty, pardon, full pardon, mercy, forgiveness, leniency, clemency
▶ *675 Peace, 242 Moderation, 840 Atonement, 512 Oblivion, 839 Forgiveness*

3 **pacifist**, pacifier, conscientious objector, peace protester, passive resister, CND member, peacemaker, peace negotiator, negotiator, mediator, Sabine women
▶ *675 Peace, 678 Mediation*

VERBS

4 **pacify**, make peace, live in peace, enjoy peace, keep the peace, stay at peace, avoid war, avoid strife, impose peace, give peace to, halt the arms race, hold out the olive branch, hold out the peace pipe, hold out one's hand, return a soft answer, turn the other cheek, coo like a dove, conciliate, propitiate, disarm, reconcile, placate, appease, satisfy, content, make happy, make content, pour oil on troubled waters, put out the fire, douse the flames, allay, ease, alleviate, soothe, take the sting out of, tranquillize, mollify, assuage, calm down, cool one's temper, quell, subdue, smooth over, smooth one's ruffled feathers, compose, pour balm into (or on) one's wounds, restore, make well, heal, cure, restore peace, restore harmony, harmonize, win over, bring to terms, resolve problems, settle differences, accommodate, adjust, bridge over, bring together, mediate, show (tender) mercy, grant clemency, grant a truce, grant an armistice, grant peace, give terms
▶ *675 Peace, 242 Moderation, 629 Repair, 765 Satisfaction, 325 Motionlessness, 667 Agreement, 678 Mediation, 839 Forgiveness*

5 **make peace**, sue for peace, stop fighting, halt hostilities, call it quits, cry quits, break it up, bury the hatchet, let bygones be bygones, forgive and forget, forget grievances, pretend it never happened, make friends, shake hands, shake on it, make it up, kiss and make up, patch up a quarrel, come to an understanding, make a deal, get together, learn to live together, compose differences, compromise, meet halfway, agree, agree to differ, agree to disagree, disarm, lay down one's arms, put down one's gun, sheathe the sword, put up one's sword, beat swords into ploughshares, sign (or make or call) a truce, suspend hostilities, demilitarize, demobilize, smoke the peace pipe, leash the dogs of war, close the gates of Janus (Arch), cool it (Inf)
▶ *218 Cessation, 839 Forgiveness, 512 Oblivion, 717 Compromise, 667 Agreement, 715 Contract*

ADJECTIVES

6 **pacificatory**, pacifying, conciliatory, placatory, propitiatory, appeasing, irenic, irenical, peacemaking, peace-loving, dovelike, disarming, friendly, satisfying, calming, soothing,

emollient, lenitive, mediatory, negotiated, pacifiable, pacified, satisfied, happy, content
▶ *675 Peace, 242 Moderation, 678 Mediation*

ADVERBS

7 **pacifically**, peacefully, irenically, moderately, mediatorially, accommodatingly, leniently, mercifully, forgivingly, clemently, soothingly, balmily, agreeably, in agreement, together
▶ *116 Accord, 678 Mediation*

678 Mediation

VERBS

1 **mediate**, intermediate, negotiate, arbitrate, referee, umpire, judge, officiate, find agreement, settle differences, reconcile, conciliate, negotiate peace, pacify, propitiate, moderate, intercede, be a go-between, put oneself between, jump in the middle of, intervene, interpose, step in, bring together, bring to the table, act as a pander for, act as agent for, run messages for, offer one's intercession, proffer one's good offices, meddle, intermeddle, interfere, stick one's nose in (Inf)
▶ *492 Judgment, 654 Advice, 642 Activity, 677 Pacification, 242 Moderation, 298 Interface*

NOUNS

2 **mediation**, intermediation, negotiation, arbitration, give-and-take, coming-together, conciliation, reconciliation, diplomacy, gunboat diplomacy, statesmanship, judgment, umpirage, pacification, propitiation, moderation, intervention, interposition, intercession, stepping-in, troubleshooting, good offices, meddling, intermeddling
▶ *492 Judgment, 654 Advice, 677 Pacification, 242 Moderation, 642 Activity*

3 **mediator**, intermediary, intermediator, intercessor, interceder, negotiator, arbiter, arbitrator, referee, umpire, judge, diplomat, diplomatist, statesman, pacifier, propitiator, peacemaker, dove, appeaser, conciliator, moderator, moderating influence, troubleshooter, common friend, middleman, go-between, liaison, third party, matchmaker, marriage broker, pander, panderer, Pandarus, adviser, counsellor, marriage adviser, marriage counsellor, marriage guidance counsellor, Advisory Conciliation and Arbitration Service (ACAS), meddler
▶ *492 Judgment, 642 Activity, 242 Moderation, 298 Interface*

4 **representative**, rep, delegate, spokesman, spokeswoman, spokesperson, mouthpiece, agent, publicist, public relations officer, press agent, ombudsman, attorney, accountant, consultant, adviser, counsellor, pleader, propitiator, peacemaker
▶ *654 Advice, 707 Deputy*

5 **conference**, peace conference, parley, talks
▶ *568 Conversation*

ADJECTIVES

6 **mediatory**, mediatorial, arbitral, arbitrational, diplomatic, intercessory, intercessional, pacificatory, propitiatory, conciliatory, advisory
▶ *492 Judgment, 677 Pacification, 298 Interface, 654 Advice*

ADVERBS

7 **mediatorially**, mediately, intermediately, conciliatorily, diplomatically, judgmentally

679 Combatant

NOUNS

1 **combatant**, fighter, battler, struggler, contender, adversary, opponent, agonist, aggressor, assailant, assaulter, attacker, besieger, stormer, escalader, soldier, fighting man, belligerent, militarist, man-at-arms, storm trooper, shock trooper, warrior, brave, dueller, duellist, swordsman, sabreur, sword, good sword, blade (Arch), knight, knight errant, paladin, gunman, strong-arm man, assassin, killer, bully, hoodlum, rowdy, ruffian, neo-Nazi, National Front (NF) member, skinhead, Hell's Angel, thug, rough, tough, bravo, phansigar, fire-eater, swashbuckler, swaggerer, *miles gloriosus* (L), hit man (Sl), hooligan (Sl), bovver (or bully) boy (Sl)
▶ *674 Contention, 241 Violence, 670 Attack, 398 Killing*

2 **defender**, protector, policeman, bodyguard, Secret Service member (US), Home Guard, Guardian Angel (US), vigilante, minder (Sl), bouncer (Sl)
▶ *671 Defence*

3 **athlete**, sportsman, sportswoman, bullfighter, toreador, matador, picador, jouster, tilter, fencer, foilsman, gladiator, retiarius, fighter, prizefighter, boxer, pugilist, champion, bruiser, slogger, puncher, sparring partner, flyweight, bantamweight, featherweight, lightweight, welterweight, middleweight, cruiserweight, heavyweight, wrestler, Graeco-Roman wrestler, freestyle wrestler, sumo wrestler, grappler, jujitsuist, judoist, karate expert, champ (Inf), pug (Sl), grunt-and-groaner (US sl)

4 **fighting animal**, fighting dog, pit bull terrier, fighting bird, fighting cock, gamecock, fighting fish, bear and dog, badger and dog, snake and mongoose

5 **arguer**, reasoner, advocate, barrister, lawyer, litigant, quarreller, disputer, debater, wrangler, controversialist, troublemaker, firebrand, rabble-rouser
▶ *473 Argument, 666 Disagreement, 16 Law*

6 **militarist**, warmonger, hawk, militant,

hardliner, Dr. Strangelove, jingoist, chauvinist, imperialist, expansionist, crusader, militant Christian, warrior for God, conqueror, conquistador, Rajput, Ghazi, Kshatriya, Mameluke, samurai, professional soldier, Gurkha, sepoy, sowar, centurion, vexillary, mercenary, auxiliary, myrmidon, freelance, freelancer, soldier of fortune, adventurer, Hessian, condottiere, privateer, pirate, buccaneer, freebooter, marauder, raider, plunderer, robber

▶ *676 War, 736 Stealing*

7 **militarist nation**, nation in arms, martial race, Spartan race, warlike people

▶ *676 War*

8 **soldier**, serviceman, servicewoman, military man, fighting man, professional soldier, army man, warrior, hero, officer, standard-bearer, colours-bearer, ensign, redcoat, private soldier, private, common soldier, recruit, volunteer, conscript, enlisted man (US), draftee (US), pressed man, effective, Anzac, poilu, heavy-armed soldier, man-at-arms, hoplite, light-armed soldier, kern, bashi-bazouk, velites, tribal warrior, brave, skirmisher, sharpshooter, sniper, *franc-tireur* (Fr), shooter, long-term soldier, trooper, regular, campaigner, reservist, Guardsman (US), Territorial, Home Guardsman, militiaman, irregular, fencible, GI (US inf), rookie (Inf), tommy (Inf), Tommy Atkins (Inf), doughboy (US inf), weekend warrior (US inf)

9 **guerrilla**, freedom fighter, resistance fighter, underground fighter, partisan, terrorist, mosstrooper, raider, cateran, rapparee, fedayeen, Maquis, IRA member, PLO member

▶ *676 War, 674 Contention, 669 Resistance*

10 **woman soldier**, servicewoman, WRAC, WRAF, Wren (Inf), female warrior, heroine, battlemaid, Amazon, Boadicea, Joan of Arc, Valkyrie

11 **former soldier**, old soldier, old trooper, old campaigner, ex-serviceman, ex-servicewoman, veteran, vet (Inf), Chelsea pensioner, legionnaire, legionary, British Legion member

12 **ceremonial troops**, Guardsman, Grenadier Guard, Coldstream Guard, Scots Guard, Irish Guard, Welsh Guard, Life Guard, Horse Guard, Foot Guard, Swiss Guard, Praetorian Guard, colour guard, housecarl, janissary, protector

▶ *632 Safety*

13 **historical soldiery**, archer, bowman, crossbowman, arbalester, spearman, pikeman, halberdier, lancer, arquebusier, matchlockman, musketeer, fusilier, rifleman, pistoleer, carabineer, grenadier, cannoneer, miner

14 **armed forces**, military forces, services, fighting forces, combat troops, troops, combat-ready forces, allied forces, army, navy, air force, marines, coastguard, men, personnel, effectives, contingents, armament, armada, army of occupation, occupying force, occupation troops, garrison, *corps d'élite* (Fr), picked troops, crack troops, SAS (Special Air Service), Special Forces (US), shock troops, storm troops, Nazi SA (Sturmabteilung), Iraqi Republican Guards, spearhead, advance party, reconnaissance party, expeditionary force, striking force, flying column, assault troops, parachute troops, paratroops, commandoes, task force, raiding party, field army, line, front line, front-line troops, thin red line, first echelon, wing, van, vanguard, centre, main body, rear, rearguard, detachment, party, detail, patrol, night patrol, night watch, picket, sentry, sentinel, vedette, second echelon, base troops, base, staff, reserves, recruits, reinforcements, replacements, levy, general levy, draft (US), *arrière-ban* (Fr), mercenaries, auxiliaries, ceremonial troops, protector, Guards, household troops, Household Cavalry, guerrilla force, underground, resistance, Maquis, IRA (Irish Republican Army), PLO (Palestine Liberation Organization)

▶ *671 Defence, 669 Resistance, 632 Safety, 777 Fear*

15 **army**, professional army, standing army, regular army, volunteer army, conscript army, US Army, British Army, mercenary army, militia, Home Guard, Territorial Army (TA), Women's Royal Army Corps (WRAC), Queen Alexandra's Royal Army Nursing Corps (QARANC), Queen Alexandra's Royal Naval Nursing Service (QARNNS), British Army Reserve

16 **army unit**, corps, army corps, medical corps, division, armoured division, panzer division, brigade, heavy brigade, artillery brigade, light brigade, rifle brigade, battery, regiment, cavalry regiment, foot regiment, infantry, line infantry, light infantry, mountain infantry, squadron, troop, battalion, company, platoon, section, squad, detail, party, band, unit, group, detachment, army formation, array, line, column, file, rank, square, phalanx, legion, cohort, century, decury, maniple

17 **army person**, army officer field-marshal, general, lieutenant-general, major general, brigadier, colonel, lieutenant-colonel, major, captain, lieutenant, second lieutenant, cadet, warrant officer, noncommissioned officer, sergeant, corporal, lance-corporal, bombardier, enlisted person, private, common soldier, the ranks, rank and file, man-at-arms, cannon fodder, food for powder, gallant company, merry men, infantryman, foot soldier, foot, footslogger, peon, *chasseur* (Fr), Zouave, artilleryman, gunner, machine-gunner, bazookaman, sapper, pioneer

18 **army of people**, multitude, mass, host, horde, legion, mob
▶ *181 Multitude*

19 **cavalry**, yeomanry, heavy cavalry, light cavalry, sabres, horse, light horse, cavalry regiment, mounted troops, mounted rifles, mounted police, mounted infantry, horse artillery, warhorse, charger, destrier (Arch)

20 **cavalryman**, mounted soldier, mounted infantryman, horse soldier, horseman, rider, cavalier, trooper, man-at-arms, yeoman, knight, lancer, chivalry, sowar (India), uhlan (Poland), hussar, cuirassier, dragoon, light dragoon, heavy dragoon, Ironsides, Cossack, spahi (Turkey), rough-rider, cameleer

21 **armoured cavalry**, armoured division, armoured car, armoured personnel carrier, tank, Challenger, M1A1 (US), Leopard (Ger), Panzer (Ger), tank transporter

22 **navy**, fleet, fleet arm, admiralty, naval service, senior service, silent service, naval armament, sea power, gunboat diplomacy, sail, wooden walls, mothball fleet, Royal Navy (RN), Women's Royal Naval Service (WRNS), Royal Naval Reserve, Royal Naval Volunteer Reserve, merchant navy, merchant marine

23 **naval unit**, fleet, flotilla, squadron, little ships, convoy, armada, argosy, Fleet Air Arm

24 **warship**, war vessel, man-of-war, ship of the line, flag ship, command ship, flotilla leader, capital ship, aircraft carrier, battleship, dreadnought, cruiser, light cruiser, anti-submarine cruiser, armoured cruiser, battle cruiser, destroyer, guided-missile destroyer, destroyer escort, frigate, corvette, sloop, fast patrol boat, patrol boat, PT boat, gunboat, motor torpedo boat, torpedo boat, E-boat, submarine, nuclear submarine, U-boat, anti-submarine submarine, hunter-killer, submarine chaser, minelayer, minesweeper, fire ship, blockship, Q-ship, landing craft, amphibious ship, amphibian, duck, fleet auxiliary vessels, attack transport ship, attack cargo ship, fast transport ship, transport ship, troopship, tender, submarine tender, repair ship, store ship, depot ship, ammunition ship, supply ship, fuel ship, oil tanker, guard ship, hospital ship, icebreaker, ocean radar station ship, flattop (US inf)
▶ *74 Water Transport*

25 **historical naval ships**, war galley, bireme, trireme, quinquereme, galleon, galleass, three-decker, *Sovereign of the Seas, Victory,* turret ship, *Devastation,* ironclad, *Warrior, Monitor, Merrimack,* battleship, *Dreadnought,* raider, privateer, pirate ship

26 **naval mine**, torpedo, depth charge

27 **naval man**, navy man, naval officer, admiral of the fleet, admiral, vice admiral, rear-admiral, commodore, captain, command-er, lieutenant-commander, lieutenant, sub-lieutenant, midshipman, fleet chief petty officer, chief petty officer, petty officer, rating, able rating, ordinary rating, seaman, able seaman, ordinary seaman, sailor, bluejacket, mariner, buccaneer, pressed man, coastguardsman, submariner, naval airman, Seabee (US), woman sailor, Wren, Wave (US), Wran (Aus), powder monkey, powder boy, cabin boy, naval reservist, Royal Naval Reservist, Royal Naval Volunteer Reservist gob (US sl), swab (US sl), swabbie (US sl), limey (Sl), wavy navy (Sl)

28 **marines**, Royal Marines, Royal Marine Commandos, marine, leatherneck (US), jarhead (US), jolly (Inf)

29 **air force**, air arm, air corps, flying corps, air service, Fleet Air Arm, Royal Air Force (RAF), US Air Force (USAF), Women's Royal Air Force (WRAF), Royal Air Force Volunteer Reserve

30 **air force unit**, airborne division, air group, wing, squadron, flight

31 **military aircraft**, aircraft, plane, aeroplane, warplane, battle plane, bomber, fighter-bomber, heavy bomber, light bomber, jump jet, fighter, night fighter, interceptor, anti-submarine plane, ground-attack aircraft, interdictor, spy plane, AWACS (airborne warning and control system), patrol plane, scout, transport plane, troop carrier, flying boat, trainer, helicopter, helicopter gunship, zeppelin, captive balloon, observation balloon, barrage balloon, airship, tank-buster (Inf)
▶ *70 Transport, 390 Air*

32 **airman**, air force officer, marshal of the Royal Air Force, air chief marshal, air marshal, air vice-marshal, air commodore, group captain, wing commander, squadron leader, flight-lieutenant, flying officer, pilot officer, master aircrew, flight sergeant, flight sergeant aircrew, chief technician, sergeant aircrew, junior technician, senior aircraftman (*or* -woman), leading aircraftman (*or* -woman), air troops, parachute troops, paratrooper, ground staff, fighter pilot, bomber pilot, co-pilot, navigator, gunner, bombardier, observer, aircrew, para (Inf), Wingco (Inf)

ADJECTIVES

33 **combative**, aggressive, hostile, adversarial, opposing, inimical, agonistic, antagonistic, bellicose, belligerent, pugnacious, militant, militaristic, warlike, expansionistic, imperialistic, jingoistic, chauvinistic, hardline, crusading, buccaneering, piratical, bloodthirsty, rowdy, rough, tough, thuggish, trigger-happy (Inf), gung-ho (Inf)
▶ *17 Military Affairs, 670 Attack, 676 War*

34 **argumentative**, quarrelsome, litigious, controversial, troublemaking, rabble-rousing
▶ *473 Argument, 666 Disagreement*

35 **martial**, naval, gladiatorial, pugilistic, mercenary, auxiliary, soldierly, soldierlike, brave, heroic, armed, armoured, enlisted, drafted, conscripted, recruited, signed up (Inf)

VERBS

36 **combat**, make trouble, rabble-rouse, warmonger, crusade, break ceasefire, shatter the peace, declare war, wage a campaign, send (in) the marines, attack, assault, assail, storm, besiege, lay siege to

▶ *676 War, 670 Attack, 674 Contention*

37 **fight**, shoot, fire, pull the trigger, gun down, bomb, blast, plant mines, enter the lists, charge, strike, spear, lance, joust, tilt, fence, spar, put on one's boxing globes, box, punch, hit, wrestle, grapple

▶ *676 War, 17 Military Affairs*

38 **conquer**, win, subdue, quell, overcome, storm, take over, invade, maraud, raid, plunder, rob, kill, assassinate, massacre, terrorize

▶ *398 Killing, 734 Taking*

39 **defend**, protect, police, guard, resist, oppose, picket, protest

▶ *669 Resistance, 663 Opposition, 713 Protest, 671 Defence*

40 **argue**, contend, dispute, debate, disagree, quarrel, wrangle

▶ *473 Argument, 666 Disagreement*

ADVERBS

41 **aggressively**, inimically, agonistically, antagonistically, belligerently, pugnaciously, militantly, militaristically, imperialistically, jingoistically, chauvinistically, bloodthirstily, rowdily, argumentatively, litigiously, controversially

42 **martially**, pugilistically, bravely, heroically, at war, up in arms, under fire, under siege, on the front line, in the cannon's mouth, in the thick of the fray

680   Weapon

NOUNS

1 **weapon**, arm, deterrent, deadly weapon, defensive weapon, armour, plate, steel-plate armour, mail, chain mail, defence, offensive weapon, attack, air attack (or assault), air raid, artillery barrage, conventional weapon, nuclear weapon, theatre nuclear weapon, tactical nuclear weapon, nuclear deterrent, (nuclear) fallout, radioactivity, radioactive cloud, mushroom cloud, radiation, secret weapon, death ray, laser, natural weapon, teeth, fist, claws, nails

▶ *671 Defence, 670 Attack, 676 War, 631 Blight, 380 Sharpness*

2 **arms**, weapons, weaponry, side arms, small arms, armament, munitions, armaments, rocketry, missilery, gunnery, musketry, archery, bowmanship

3 **arms race**, defence, arms traffic, (nuclear) proliferation, arms trade, gun-running

▶ *671 Defence, 606 Provision*

4 **arsenal**, armoury, arms depot, ammunition ship, ammunition room, ammunition dump, ammunition chest, gunroom, gun rack, magazine, powder magazine, powder barrel, powder keg, powder flask, powder horn, caisson, ammunition box, bullet-pouch, cartridge belt, bandoleer, arrow-case, quiver, scabbard, sheath, holster, ammo dump (Inf)

▶ *605 Store, 258 Container*

5 **missile weapon**, missile, ballistic missile, intercontinental ballistic missile (ICBM), multiple independently targeted re-entry vehicle (MIRV), guided missile, surface-to-air missile (SAM), Cruise missile, Exocet (Tm), Scud (Inf), defensive missile, antimissile missile, antiballistic missile (ABM), Patriot, submarine, torpedo boat, torpedo, nuclear submarine, Polaris, Trident, Strategic Defense Initiative (SDI), Star Wars, antitank weapon, bazooka, rocket-launcher, rocket, shell, star shell, flare, gas shell, shrapnel, whiz-bang, V-1, V-2, bullet, pellet, rocket site, launching pad, silo

6 **historical missile weapon**, javelin, harpoon, dart, bola, lasso, boomerang, catapult, woomera (Aus), throwstick, arrow, barbed arrow, poisoned arrow, shaft, bolt, quarrel, arrowhead, barb, stone, brick, brickbat, fléchette, bow, longbow, crossbow, arbalest, ballista, mangonel, trebuchet, sling, blowpipe, ball, shot

▶ *338 Propulsion*

7 **blunt weapon**, blunt instrument, club, bludgeon, truncheon, cudgel, cosh, life preserver, blackjack (US), shillelagh (or shillala), lathi, mace, knobkerrie, knobstick, battering ram, ram, warhammer, hammer, staff, stave, stick, switch, quarterstaff, sandbag, knuckleduster, brass knuckles (US), bicycle chain, bottle, baseball bat

▶ *330 Impulsion*

8 **sharp weapon**, lance, javelin, jerid, harpoon, gaff, pike, assegai, partisan, bill, halberd, axe, battle-axe, poleaxe, tomahawk, hatchet, chopper, gisarme, sword, cold steel, naked steel, broadsword, two-edged sword, two-handed sword, cutlass, glaive (Arch), claymore, hanger, short sword, swordstick, cavalry sword, sabre, scimitar (or simitar), yataghan, falchion, blade, fine blade, trusty blade, bilbo, Toledo, rapier, tuck (Arch), fencing sword, foil, épée, bayonet, dagger, poniard, snickersnee (Arch), dirk, skean, sgian-dhu (or skean-dhu), dudgeon (Arch), misericord (or misericorde) (Arch), stylet, stiletto, machete, matchet, kukri, kris, parang, panga, knife, bowie knife, flick knife, pigsticker (US sl)

▶ *380 Sharpness*

9 **firearm**, gun, handgun (US), revolver, pistol, piece, automatic, semiautomatic, Colt (Tm), repeater, rifle, magazine rifle, repeating rifle, Winchester, fowling piece, sporting gun, shotgun, sawn-off shotgun, single-barrelled gun, double-barrelled gun, smoothbore, rifled bore, bore, calibre, carbine, breechloader, elephant gun, muzzle, trigger, lock, magazine, breech, butt, gunstock, sight, backsight, ramrod, six-shooter (US inf), rod (US sl), zipgun (US sl), Saturday night special (US sl), gat (US sl), shooting iron (US sl)

▶ *17 Military Affairs*

10 **historical gun**, arquebus, hackbut, hagbut, matchlock, wheel lock, flintlock, fusil, musket, Brown Bess, Blunderbuss, muzzleloader, chassepot, needlegun, Enfield rifle, duelling pistol, horse pistol, petronel, pistolet, cannon, brass cannon, horse artillery

11 **guns**, ordnance, cannonry, artillery, light artillery, heavy artillery, mountain artillery, galloping guns, battery, broadside, artillery park, gun park, piece, field piece, field gun, rifle, M-1 rifle (US), Garand rifle (US), siege gun, great gun, heavy gun, heavy metal, howitzer, trench-mortar, mine-thrower, *minenwerfer* (Ger), Minnie, trench gun, anti-aircraft gun, Bofers gun, anti-aircraft artillery, bazooka, assault gun, quick-firing gun, machine gun, pom-pom, M-60 machine gun, light machine gun, Bren gun, Sten gun, submachine gun, subgun, Thompson submachine gun (Tm), Tommy gun (Tm), uzi, kalashnikov, AK-47, gat, flamethrower, guncarriage, limber, caisson, gun emplacement

12 **historical guns**, bombard, falconet, swivel, basilisk, petard, carronade, culverin, mortar, cannon royal, seventy-four, Big Bertha, Whistling Dick (US), Gatling gun, mitrailleuse, pom-pom, Maxim gun, Lewis gun, Winchester

13 **ammunition**, live ammunition, live shot, round of ammunition, round, powder and shot, shot, small shot, buckshot, ball, bullet, expanding bullet, soft-nosed bullet, dumdum (bullet), rubber bullet, plastic bullet, baton round, projectile, missile, slug, pellet, shell, shrapnel, flak, ack-ack, wad, cartouche, cartridge, live cartridge, spent cartridge, dud, blank cartridge, blank, cartridge belt, cartridge clip, cartridge case, ammo (Inf)

14 **historical ammunition**, round shot, canister (shot), case shot, grapeshot, chain shot, mitraille, buckshot, ball, cannonball

▶ *338 Propulsion*

15 **explosive**, powder, gunpowder, propellant, saltpetre, high explosive, dynamite, gelignite, TNT (trinitrotoluene), nitroglycerine, lyddite, melinite, cordite, guncotton, plastic explosive, Semtex (Tm), cap, detonator, fuse, priming, charge, warhead, atomic warhead, fissionable material, fireworks

16 **bomb**, explosive device, shell, bombshell, grenade, hand grenade, Molotov cocktail, megaton bomb, atom bomb, A-bomb, nuclear bomb, hydrogen bomb, H-bomb, neutron bomb, enhanced radiation bomb, radioactivity, radiation, (nuclear) fallout, radioactive cloud, mushroom cloud, cluster bomb, fragmentation bomb, nailbomb, firebomb, incendiary bomb, napalm bomb, carcass, mine, landmine, magnetic mine, acoustic mine, limpet mine, letter bomb, mailbomb, car bomb, booby trap, infernal machine (Arch), depth charge, torpedo, tin fish, flying bomb, V-1, doodlebug, V-2, rocket bomb, time bomb, Greek fire, pineapple (Sl), blockbuster (Inf)

▶ *635 Trap*

681 Trophy

NOUNS

1 **trophy**, award, reward, prize, first prize, consolation prize, sports trophy, medal, gold medal, silver medal, bronze medal, military medal, war medal, *Croix de Guerre* (Fr), George Cross, Victoria Cross, campaign medal, medallion, plate, cup, loving cup, gold cup, silver cup, ribbon, blue ribbon, *cordon bleu* (Fr), military ribbon, figurine, statuette, wreath, chaplet, garland, palm, laurels, laurel wreath, crown, spurs, garter, decoration, military decoration, citation, military citation, honour, honours list, order of merit, order of chivalry, *Légion d'Honneur* (Fr), feather in one's cap, pot (Inf), gong (Sl), *victor ludorum* (L)

▶ *878 Reward, 804 Title*

2 **spoils**, spoils of war, booty, loot, plunder, pillage, winnings, scalp, head, shrunken head, swag (Sl)

3 **memento**, souvenir, keepsake, relic, token, token of remembrance, love token

▶ *511 Memory*

682 Success

One's religion is whatever he is most interested in, and yours is Success. J. M. Barrie.

Sweet Smell of Success. Ernest Lehman.

To succeed in the world, we do everything we can to appear successful. Duc de la Rochefoucauld.

The world continues to offer glittering prizes to those who have stout hearts and sharp swords. F. E. Smith.

There are no gains without pains. Adlai Stevenson.

NOUNS

1 **success**, achievement, accomplishment, attainment, feat, great success, triumphant success, runaway success, sweet smell of success, sensation, overnight sensation, breakthrough, mastery, ascendancy, fame and fortune, fame, famousness, success story, stardom, celebrity, name up in lights, name recognition, name, place in history, happiness, thriving, plenty, luxury, prosperity, fortune, wealth, riches, affluence, the big time (Inf), luck, lucky break, lucky stroke, beginner's luck, run of luck, favourable outcome, happy ending, fairy-tale ending, landing on one's feet, celebration, momentary success, flash in the pan, feather in one's cap, coming up roses (Inf), roaring success (Inf), howling success (Inf), hit (Inf), big hit (Inf), smash hit (Inf), smash (Inf), killing (Inf)

▶ *686 Prosperity, 126 Superiority, 592 Plan, 684 Completion, 812 Celebration, 742 Wealth*

2 **victory**, triumph, conquest, win, beating, whipping, thrashing, hiding, trouncing, runaway victory, crushing victory, landslide victory, knockout, winning by a mile, love game, overrunning, successful attack, taking by storm, rout, game, set, and match, extra-time victory, overtime victory (US), sudden-death victory, military victory, successful battle, defeat of the enemy, narrow victory, Pyrrhic victory, licking (Inf), pushover (Inf), walkover (Inf), piece of cake (Inf), KO (Sl), skunk (US sl)

▶ *655 Skill, 640 Action, 336 Forward Motion, 660 Easiness, 490 Certainty, 670 Attack, 244 Destruction*

3 **successful thing**, best seller, chart-topper, blockbuster, box-office success, rave reviews, number-one ranking (or rating), good move, checkmate, hole in one, ace, good shot, score, touchdown (TD) (soccer, American football), try (Rugby), goal, field goal (Basketball, American football), home run (Baseball), six (Cricket), hit (Baseball), bull's-eye, grand slam, triple crown, hat trick, championship, league championship, division championship, conference championship (US), exam success, sellout (Inf), box-office hit (Inf), number one (Inf), homer (US inf), KO (Sl), wow (Sl)

4 **successful person**, success, winner, hero, heroine, self-made man (or woman), achiever, high-flyer, superman, superwoman, man (or woman) of the year, record-breaker, star, star in the firmament, starlet, celebrity, top of the class, whiz kid, graduate, honour graduate, valedictorian (US), talk of the town, first-rater, VIP (very important person), man of the match, MVP (most valuable player) (US), *crème de la crème* (Fr), rising star, up-and-coming star, comer (Inf), sure-fire winner (Inf), hit (Inf), number one (Inf), the tops (Sl), wow (Sl), corker (Sl)

5 **victorious person**, victor, winner, conqueror, champion, reigning champion, Olympic champion, world champion, world-beater, titleholder, medallist, prizewinner, first-place finisher, first, victorious general, defeater, vanquisher, subjugator, subduer, sure winner, champ (Inf), shoo-in (US inf)

VERBS

6 **be successful**, succeed, have success, enjoy success, meet with success, score a success, make a success of, prosper, thrive, flourish, flower, blossom, accomplish, effect, achieve, compass, get results, show results, come off well, become a self-made man (or woman), do well, do oneself proud, pass, qualify, graduate, get on, get there, get ahead, get promoted, advance, progress, rise in the world, make good, make one's mark, gain one's goal, gain one's end, secure one's object, obtain one's objective, arrive, go over, earn a standing ovation, reap the harvest, reap the fruits, make money, get rich, break the bank, bring it off, bring off, pull it off, pull off, hit it off, hit it, carry off, work miracles, make the grade, do wonders, work wonders, not put a foot wrong, get lucky, win one's spurs, top the charts, write a bestseller, come off with flying colours, pull oneself up by one's bootstraps, work one's way up the ladder, have the world at one's feet, set the world on fire, ring the bell, hit the mark, make a go of (Inf), make a killing (Inf), hit the jackpot (Inf), make the big time (Inf), make a hit (Inf), bring home the bacon (Inf), make it (Inf), click (Sl), go great guns (Sl), go over big (Inf)

7 **overcome obstacles**, brush obstacles aside, overcome difficulties, sweep problems out of the way, manage, prevail, persevere, escape, surmount, get over the (or a) hump, get over a snag, avoid defeat, rise to the occasion, make headway against, muddle through, stem the tide, weather the storm, not know the meaning of failure, find a loophole, find a way out, find a way round, cut the Gordian knot, not know when one is beaten, come right in the end, turn out well, turn up trumps, land on one's feet, come up smiling, come up smelling like roses

▶ *661 Hindrance, 574 Resolution, 638 Escape*

8 **be effective**, be efficacious, work, go, do, answer the purpose, answer, show results, turn out well, do the job, do wonders, work like magic, act like a charm, pay dividends, pay off, bear fruit, come off (Inf), do the trick (Inf), ring the bell (Inf), fill the bill (Inf)

9 **be victorious**, be triumphant, triumph (over), conquer, win, win a victory, win by a landslide, win the game, win the match, beat, beat all comers, become champion, take the prize, take the cup, take the championship,

win the race, win the battle, achieve victory, claim a victory, win the last battle, force a surrender, defeat, defeat the enemy, vanquish, prevail, quell, subdue, carry the day, carry, take, storm, take by storm, sweep the boards, put down, crush, capture, subject, suppress, subjugate, win on points, win a (or the) point, win on moves, checkmate, check, put in check, wear the crown, wear the laurel wreath, wear the laurels, have the best of it, celebrate a victory, only just win, scrape through, scrape home, do for (Inf), win by a whisker (Inf), pip at the post (Sl)

10 **defeat heavily**, defeat easily, rout, put to flight, scatter, win hands down, win going away, romp home, storm home, win in straight sets, sweep the board, sweep, carry all before one, wipe out, break, bankrupt, drive to the wall, destroy, have it all one's way, walk off with, thrash, whip, trounce, overwhelm, crush, drub, give a drubbing, whitewash, trample underfoot, knock out, put out for the count, knock the stuffing out of, knock (or beat) the shit out of (Tab), flatten (Inf), lick (Inf), waltz away with (Inf), wipe the floor with (Inf), beat to a pulp (Inf), cook somone's goose (Inf), KO (Sl)

11 **overmaster**, beat, master, overpower, overcome, overthrow, overturn, override, outclass, outplay, outpoint, trump, carry a point, score a point, come off best, pass with flying colours, come through with flying colours, outflank, outmanoeuvre, break through

12 **succeed to**, succeed, inherit, come into, be left, take one's heritage

ADJECTIVES

13 **successful**, succeeding, winning, crowned with success, wealthy, prosperous, fruitful, thriving, flourishing, favourable, famous, renown, efficacious, effective, masterly, bestselling, chart-topping, best-ever, lucky, fortunate, never-failing, surefire, surefooted, certain, rising, on the up and up, crowning, sitting pretty (Inf), home and dry (Sl), home free (US sl)

14 **rewarding**, financially rewarding, profitable, lucrative, paying, gainful, remunerative, advantageous, worthwhile

15 **victorious**, winning, triumphant, triumphal, flushed with victory, match-winning, game-winning (US), prizewinning, the best, on top, top of the league, top of the division, world-beating, always victorious, ever-victorious, undefeated, unbeaten, unbowed, unvanquished, unbeatable, unconquerable, invincible, crushing, quelling, on top of the heap (Sl)

ADVERBS

16 **successfully**, victoriously, triumphantly, in triumph, with flying colours, prosperously,

rewardingly, fruitfully, profitably, lucratively, gainfully, advantageously, favourably, efficaciously, effectively, invincibly, luckily, fortunately, beyond all expectation, beyond one's fondest dreams, well, marvellously, swimmingly, to some purpose, to good purpose, with good results, with good effect

683 Failure

She knows there's no success like failure/ And that failure's no success at all. Bob Dylan.

Like a dull actor now/ I have forgot my part and I am out,/ Even to a full disgrace. William Shakespeare.

NOUNS

1 **failure**, nonfulfilment, lack of success, negative result, hopeless failure, fallibility, inability, inefficiency, ineffectiveness, weakness, unproductiveness, barrenness, nonperformance, noncompletion, discontinuation, dereliction, withdrawal, setback, error, mistake, mess, complete failure, collapse, debacle, fiasco, botch (or botch-up), bungle, bungling, blunder, omission, neglect, negligence, default, miss, near miss, vain attempt, futile effort, futility, frustration, disappointment, no luck, misfortune, uselessness, lost labour, no result, no answer, no progress, discontinuance, stoppage, shutdown, nonresumption, closure, stalling, stall, breakdown, dead stop, halt, fall, crash, decline, decline in health, failing health, deterioration, failing, ailing, downfall, comedown, letdown, shortage, shortfall, incapacity, insufficiency, insolvency, inability to pay, failure to pay, bankruptcy, ruin, nail in one's coffin, the pits (Sl)

▶ *687 Adversity, 685 Noncompletion, 504 Error, 238 Weakness, 661 Hindrance, 236 Powerlessness, 247 Infertility, 614 Uselessness, 656 Unskilfulness, 515 Disappointment, 218 Cessation, 360 Descent, 747 Nonpayment*

2 **defeat**, loss, collapse, reversal, retreat, total defeat, trashing, utter defeat, rout, beating, drubbing, hiding, thrashing, trouncing, subjugation, submission, deathblow, narrow defeat, final defeat, military defeat, lost battle, Waterloo, lost war, lost cause, losing move, fatal move, losing game, licking (Inf)

▶ *722 Loss, 244 Destruction, 673 Submission*

3 **personal fault**, foible, failing, weakness, weakness of the flesh, disloyalty, unfaithfulness, promiscuity, peccadillo, vice, mortal sin, sin

▶ *620 Imperfection, 870 Self-Indulgence*

4 **unsuccessful thing**, bankruptcy, bad idea, lost election, abortion, lost bet, wasted day, wild-goose chase, miscarriage, engine failure,

electrical fault, computer fault, mechanical malfunction, crop failure, damp squib, fauxpas, dud (Inf), nonstarter (Inf), washout (Inf), wipeout (Inf), flop (Inf), slip-up (Inf), boo-boo (Sl), boob (Sl), lemon (Sl), turkey (US sl), bomb (US sl)

5 **failing person**, failure, losing person, loser, defeated player, losing general, unsuccessful candidate, unsuccessful competitor, unsuccessful applicant, unsuccessful challenger, deposed champion, nonpaying person, nonpayer, debtor, insolvent, bankrupt, underachiever, slow learner, born loser, misfit, bungler, reject, second-rater, underling, underdog, unfortunate, victim, dupe, dropout (Inf), dud (Inf), hopeless case (Inf), also-ran (Inf), flop (Inf), nonstarter (Inf), washout (Inf), has-been (Inf), fly-by-night (Inf), no-hoper (Inf), patsy (US sl), lemon (Sl)

VERBS

6 **fail**, not succeed, lose out, come to nothing, get no results, not pass, do badly, make a bad move, blunder, bungle, collapse, discontinue, shut down, close up, wind up, come to the end of the line, bite the dust, spoil one's reputation, fail in one's duties, let someone down, disappoint, disillusion, dash someone's hopes, fall short, not come up to expectations, fall by the wayside, fall, miss the boat, miss an opportunity, miss, have bad luck, draw a blank, back the wrong horse, return empty-handed, tire, have fatigue, droop, sink, flag, fail in health, ail, decline, take a turn for the worse, make a loss, become insolvent, go bankrupt, go to the wall, go on the rocks, not make the grade (Inf), flop (Inf), fold (Inf), go bust (Inf), go to the dogs (Inf), slip up (Inf), fizzle out (Inf), not come off (Inf), come a cropper (Inf), not come up to scratch (Inf), not come up with the goods (Inf), drop a clanger (Inf), make a hash of (Inf), blot one's copybook (Inf), flunk (out) (US sl), plough (Sl), balls up (Sl), ball up (US sl), bollocks up (Tab sl), bollix up (US sl), poop (US sl), go belly up (US sl)

7 **be defeated**, suffer defeat, lose, lose the game, lose the match, lose the vote, lose the election, lose the battle, lose the war, retreat, run away, surrender, lose the race, come off second best, lose out, lose badly, lose hands down, take a beating, take a drubbing, come in last, fail to score, be eliminated, get the worse of it, concede defeat, lose by a whisker, just miss, get pipped at the post (Sl)

8 **miscarry**, abort, go wrong, go amiss, go awry, not go well, not come off, come to nothing, come to naught (Arch), come to grief, go by the board, end in futility, prove a fiasco, fall flat, go (or end) up in smoke

9 **malfunction**, not start, not work, stop running, stop, come to a dead stop, come to a halt,

fail, stall, misfire, jam, seize up, overheat, lose power, go wrong, break, fall to pieces, crash, conk out (Sl), go kaput (Sl)

ADJECTIVES

10 **failed**, failing, unsuccessful, ineffective, ineffectual, inefficacious, insufficient, unproductive, hopeless, insolvent, bankrupt, negligent, neglectful, unlucky, unfortunate, empty, miscarried, miscarrying, bungled, bungling, blundered, blundering, stillborn, abortive, aborted, shutdown, closed, weak, ailing, fruitless, bootless, profitless, useless, futile, of no effect, on the rocks, on one's beam-ends, washed up (US inf), dud (Inf), flunked (US sl), ploughed (Sl), kaput (Sl)

11 **defeated**, beaten, bested, lost, outmanoeuvred, outclassed, outmatched, outgunned, outplayed, outshone, outvoted, outwitted, thrashed, on the losing team (or side), out of the running, in retreat, put to flight, routed, captured, overthrown, knocked out, licked (Inf), among the also-rans (Inf), pipped (Sl), wiped out (Sl), KO'd (Sl)

ADVERBS

12 **unsuccessfully**, without success, to little purpose, to no purpose, in vain, fruitlessly, bootlessly, ineffectually, ineffectively, inefficaciously, insufficiently, unproductively, hopelessly, insolvently, negligently, neglectfully, unluckily, unfortunately, emptily, blunderingly, abortively, weakly, futilely, uselessly

684 Completion

NOUNS

1 **completion**, completeness, wholeness, entirety, totality, unity, fullness, fulfilment, exhaustiveness, thoroughness, complete cycle, fruition, ripeness, maturity, maturation, realization, achievement, crowning achievement, summit, success, attainment, accomplishment, *fait accompli* (Fr), work done, performance, readiness, *ne plus ultra* (L), carrying through (or out), execution, discharge, culmination, consummation, implementation, discharge of duty

▶ *144 Completeness, 279 Summit, 594 Preparation, 227 Effect, 640 Action, 682 Success*

2 **conclusion**, concluding, finish, finishing, termination, arrival, end, end of the matter, end of the affair, ending, wind-up, climax, payoff, close, finality, the end, finis, finale, epilogue, final story, last (or dying) words, final shot, final exam, final chapter, final curtain, last act, swan song, death, resolution, solution, denouement, upshot, result, end result, end product, finished product

▶ *344 Arrival, 157 End*

3 **elaboration**, finishing touch, final touch, last touch, crowning stroke, finishing stroke,

last stroke, *coup de grâce* (Fr), elaboration, capstone, finisher, icing on the cake, limit, last straw, breaking point, boiling point, finishing off, rounding off, winding up, mopping up (Inf), clincher (Inf)

▶ *619 Perfection, 467 Attention, 574 Resolution, 302 Limit*

VERBS

4 **complete**, make complete, consummate, fulfil, follow through, carry through, see through, see it through (to the end), follow up, drive home, clear up, tie up, come to fruition, mature, ripen, bring to a head, bring to a boil, reach the boiling point, come to a crisis, reach the limit, peak, reach its peak, reach the zenith, scale the heights, touch bottom, implement, carry out, execute, effect, enact, do, dispatch, discharge one's duty, discharge, put into effect, effectuate, realize, bring about, accomplish, achieve, achieve one's goal, compass, succeed, do thoroughly, exhaust, tie up all the loose ends, leave no loose ends, bring to a conclusion, leave no stone unturned, not do by halves, bring home the bacon (Inf), fill the bill (Inf), deliver the goods (Inf), mop up (Inf), go the whole hog (Sl)

5 **conclude**, culminate, terminate, arrive, end, come to its end, finish, finish off, switch off, wind up, close, bring to a close, bring to a (successful) conclusion, settle, find a resolution, find a solution, have a denouement, achieve a result, clinch the deal, clinch, have a payoff, have enough of, be through (*or* done) with, climax, reach a climax, have an orgasm, dispose of, get rid (*or* free) of, ring (*or* bring) down the curtain, die, polish off (Inf), get shot of (Inf), come (off) (Tab sl)

6 **elaborate**, perfect, crown, cap, top off, top out, put the icing on the cake, make complete, add the finishing touches, be the last straw (that broke the camel's back), give the *coup de grâce* (Fr)

ADJECTIVES

7 **completed**, completing, completive, complete, whole, entire, total, exhaustive, thorough, utter, perfect, perfected, perfective, well done, consummate, consummative, consummated, culminating, fulfilled, fulfilling, fully realized, thoroughgoing, comprehensive, unabridged, uncut, uncensored, intact, unbroken, full-blown, blooming, ripe, fully developed, full-grown, matured, maturing, mature, seasoned, mellow, highly wrought, elaborate, elaborated, polished, secured, accomplished, achieved, compassed, attained, effected, effectuated, implemented, executed, realized, discharged, disposed of, cleaned up, wrapped up, tied up, mopped up (Inf), in the bag (Sl)

8 **concluded**, concluding, conclusive, finished, finishing, finished up, terminated, ended, ending, finalized, wound up, done, crowned, crowning, last, final, ultimate, terminal, in the can

ADVERBS

9 **completely**, to completion, entirely, totally, utterly, wholly, fully, to the full, to the limit, to a turn, to a T, to the end, to a finish, exhaustively, thoroughly, elaborately, consummately, comprehensively, perfectly, maturely, ripely, to a frazzle (Inf)

685 Noncompletion

NOUNS

1 **noncompletion**, incompletion, incompleteness, nonfulfilment, nonachievement, nonaccomplishment, no success, failure, no performance, no execution, no result, drawn game, draw, tie, stalemate, deadlock, noncontinuation, non sequitur, going round in circles, failure to finish, procrastination, delay, incomplete work, unfinished task, shortfall, half measures, omission, missing part, missing link, never-ending story, lack, imperfection, superficiality, rough sketch, perfunctoriness, desultoriness, inattention, inattention to detail, neglect, negligence, oversight, loose ends, rough edges, underdevelopment, unripeness, immaturity, skimpiness, scantiness, scrappiness, sketchiness, sloppiness (Inf), a lick and a promise (Inf)

▶ *145 Incompleteness, 683 Failure, 470 Negligence, 609 Insufficiency, 358 Shortfall, 595 Lack of Preparation, 468 Inattention, 620 Imperfection*

2 **never-ending task**, a woman's work, painting the Forth Bridge, looking for a needle in a haystack, Penelope's web, Sisyphean labour

3 **quitter**, defeatist, idler, slacker, daydreamer, shirker, procrastinator, failure, nonpayer, dropout (Inf), fly-by-night (Inf)

ADJECTIVES

4 **uncompleted**, not complete, undone, not finished, unfinished, unperformed, unprocessed, unfulfilled, unconsummated, unrealized, unattained, unachieved, unaccomplished, not accomplished, unexecuted, never-ending, incomplete, imperfect, fragmentary, missing, short, truncated, left unfinished, neglected, not finalized, not cleared up, left hanging, left in the air, up in the air, unelaborated, not worked out, not thought through, unthorough, perfunctory, inattentive, neglectful, desultory, procrastinating, delaying, superficial, half-finished, half-done, half-begun, half-baked, underdone, underdeveloped, immature, unripe, lacking, skimpy, scanty, scrappy, sketchy, in outline, sloppy (Inf)

VERBS

5 **not complete**, not finish, leave undone,

leave unfinished, not fulfil, not achieve, not accomplish, fall short of one's goal, leave incomplete, leave hanging, leave in the air, neglect to finish, neglect, miss, truncate, not finalize, not clear up, half finish, half do, half begin, lack, sketch out, outline, do by halves, skimp, scrimp, scrape by, paper over the cracks, give up, not follow up, not follow through, fail to deliver, procrastinate, delay, postpone, put off (until tomorrow)

6 **drop out**, fall out, not complete, not stay the course, dip out of (Aus inf), do a bunk (Sl)

ADVERBS

7 **incompletely**, in the making, in preparation, in process of, in the air, under construction, perfunctorily, imperfectly, neglectfully, by halves, inattentively, superficially, skimpily, in outline form, immaturely, desultorily, sloppily (Inf)

686 Prosperity

NOUNS

1 **prosperity**, prosperousness, well-being, welfare, wealth, success, fame, fame and fortune, fortune, health and wealth, luxury, lap of luxury, comfort, ease, life of ease, the good life, having it good, thriving, security, plenty, economic prosperity, high standard of living, affluent society, affluence, boom, bull (or bullish) market, booming economy, expanding economy, roaring trade, prestige, glory, honour and glory, happiness, felicity, blessedness, blessings, milk and honey, fat of the land, fleshpots, bed of roses, life of Riley, place in the sun, weal (Arch), land-office business (US inf), living in clover (Inf), clover (Inf), Easy Street (Inf), lap of luxury (Inf)

▶ *682 Success, 742 Wealth, 762 Joy, 608 Sufficiency, 675 Peace, 405 Physical Pleasure*

2 **good fortune**, happy fortune, fortune, smiles of fortune, luck, good luck, piece of good luck, run of luck, streak of luck, winning streak, bonanza, lucky shot, lucky strike, luck of the draw, auspiciousness, favour, blessings, Midas touch, break (Inf), good break (Inf), lucky break (Inf), the breaks (Inf)

3 **time of plenty**, good times, golden days, golden age, golden time, halcyon days, palmy days, salad days, heyday, honeymoon period, easy times, holiday, summer, prime, youth, *Saturnia regna* (L), age of Aquarius

4 **prosperous person**, rich person, successful person, success, self-made man (or woman), man (or woman) of property, man (or woman) of means, man (or woman) of substance, person of repute, VIP (very important person), parvenu, nouveau riche, capitalist, plutocrat, tycoon, millionaire, multimillionaire, billionaire, the haves, the upwardly mobile, lucky

fellow, lucky devil, child of fortune, fortune's favourite, favourite of the gods, lucky dog (Inf), yuppie (Inf), Sloane Ranger (or Sloane) (Inf), fat cat (US sl)

VERBS

5 **be prosperous**, prosper, enjoy prosperity, do well, succeed, live well, get on well, get on swimmingly, fare well, make good, make one's mark, rise in the world, get on (or go up) in the world, have everything going one's way, do all right by oneself, get going, progress, advance, arrive, go far, thrive, flourish, blossom, flower, bloom, profit, make a profit, make one's fortune, make money, make a fortune, get rich, grow rich, strike it rich, feather one's nest, line one's pockets, get fat, grow fat, have a good time of it, strike it lucky, rise to fame, become famous, win fame, win glory, win fame and glory, have it easy, live a life of ease, live the life of Riley, live in the lap of luxury, bask in the sunshine, ride on the crest of a wave, live on the fat of the land, make it (Inf), have it made (Inf), make one's pile (Inf), be rolling in it (Inf), hit the big time (Inf), have a lucky break (Inf), live in clover (Inf), lie on velvet (Inf), live high on the hog (Inf), live on Easy Street (Inf)

6 **be fortunate**, be lucky, have luck, have all the luck, have a stroke of luck, have a lucky break, have a run of good luck, hit a streak of luck, strike it lucky, strike it rich, come into money, come into an inheritance, be on to a good thing, fall on one's feet, lead a charmed life, be born under a lucky star, be born with a silver spoon in one's mouth, strike oil (Inf), strike a rich vein (Inf), get a break (Inf), get on the gravy train (Sl)

7 **be auspicious**, bode well, promise well, augur well, favour, look kindly on, smile on, shine on, bless, shed blessings on

ADJECTIVES

8 **prosperous**, prospering, successful, thriving, flourishing, booming, doing well, well-to-do, well-off, rising, up-and-coming, on the up and up, upwardly mobile, up in the world, profiteering, famous, affluent, rich, opulent, wealthy, luxurious, in luxury, fat, comfortable, comfortably off, comfortably situated, cosy, at ease, bullish, fortunate, lucky, in luck, happy, felicitous, palmy, balmy, halcyon, golden, rosy, blissful, in bliss, blessed, favourable, promising, auspicious, propitious, cloudless, born with a silver spoon in one's mouth, born under a lucky star, on the make (Inf), in the money (Inf), well-heeled (Inf), rolling in it (Inf), high on the hog (Inf), in clover (Inf), on velvet (Inf), on Easy Street (Inf)

ADVERBS

9 **prosperously**, successfully, swimmingly, in the swim, famously, affluently, richly, opu-

lently, luxuriously, comfortably, in comfort, cosily, bullishly, fortunately, luckily, with luck, propitiously, happily, felicitously, blissfully, in a blissful manner, blessedly, favourably, promisingly, auspiciously, high on the hog (Inf), in clover (Inf), on velvet (Inf), on Easy Street (Inf)

INTERJECTIONS

10 **good luck!**, lots of luck!, bless you!, all the best!, live it up!, have a good time!, have fun!

687 Adversity

NOUNS

1 **adversity**, difficulty, opposition, struggle, trials, travail, hardship, hard life, adverse circumstances, decline, fall, comedown, trials and tribulations, troubles, pack of troubles, predicament, emergency, misadventure, mishap, casualty, accident, injury, hard blow, plight, misfortune, affliction, wretchedness, misery, bleakness, gloom and doom, pressure, suffering, sorrow, sadness, dejection, despondency, distress, worry, worries, cares, trouble ahead, threat, ill wind, gathering clouds, storm clouds, dark clouds, deterioration, humiliation, downfall, defeat, rebuff, unrequited love, lost love, lost game, lost match, lost battle, lost war, retreat, poor health, decline in health, setback, illness, terminal illness, cancer, pain, evil, death, bitter cup, cup of sorrows, bitter pill, bane, load, burden, cross to bear, coldness, cold wind, darkness, curse, infection, visitation, blight, scourge, plague, disaster, natural disaster, desolation, destitution, homelessness, ruin, calamity, catastrophe, the worst, hell (Inf), living hell (Inf), raw deal (Inf), downer (Sl), bad news (Sl), the pits (Sl)
► *659 Difficulty, 663 Opposition, 406 Physical Pain, 770 Sorrow, 683 Failure, 409 Cold, 440 Darkness, 628 Deterioration, 244 Destruction*

2 **economic adversity**, financial setback, financial reverse, financial disaster, financial ruin, mortgage arrears, rent arrears, negative equity, cash-flow problems, need, want, poverty, no money, lost fortune, lost inheritance, (personal) bankruptcy, stock market decline, bear market, slumping market, slump, recession, depression, unemployment
► *743 Poverty, 740 Market*

3 **bad fortune**, ill fortune, misfortune, frowns of fortune, bad luck, hard luck, no luck, no success, malign influence, evil star, hard fate, mischance, missed chance, rotten luck (Inf)
► *589 Chance*

4 **time of adversity**, time of sorrow, bad times, hard times, lean period, rough patch, tough time, bad patch, bad spell, winter of discontent, winter, cold day, gloomy day, rainy day

5 **person in adversity**, poor person, bankrupt, homeless person, destitute, poor wretch, sufferer, unfortunate, loser, born loser, underdog, weakling, lame duck, tramp, down-and-out, bag lady, poor risk, unlucky person, plaything of the gods, victim of fate, victim, dupe, scapegoat, prey, martyr, no-hoper (Inf), sad sack (US sl)

ADJECTIVES

6 **adverse**, contrary, conflicting, opposed, opposing, in opposition, hostile, antagonistic, troublesome, difficult, hard, bleak, cold, detrimental, dreadful, dire, inauspicious, ominous, unpropitious, unfavourable, bad, harmful, sinister, disadvantageous, disastrous, destructive, ruinous, tragic, doomed, unsuccessful, miserable, gloomy, not doing well, in trouble, in difficulties, up against it, in a bad way, in poor shape, in poor health, ill, unwell, on one's last legs, declining, on the wane, on the downgrade, on the slippery slope

7 **unprosperous**, badly off, in adverse circumstances, poor, penurious, impecunious, poverty-stricken, penniless, bankrupt, in dire straits, homeless, down-and-out, with one's back to the wall, on the road to ruin, on one's beam-ends, broke (Inf), flat broke (Inf), hard-up (Inf), stone-broke (Sl), stony-broke (Sl), stony (Sl), skint (Sl), belly up (US sl)

8 **unlucky**, not lucky, out of luck, down on one's luck, luckless, hapless, accident-prone, unfortunate, unblessed, ill-fated, ill-starred, star-crossed, accursed, under a cloud, born under an evil star, born under a bad sign, washed-up (Inf)

VERBS

9 **be in trouble**, have trouble, meet adversity, have a bad time, have a hard time of it, have difficulties, hit a bad patch, fall foul of, bear the brunt, bear more than one's share, not know which way to turn, fail, lose, lose the game, lose the match, lose the battle, lose the war, lose out on love, miscarry, endure hardship, fall on hard times, fall on bad days, have seen better days, have no luck, be unlucky, run out of luck, suffer misfortune, have a mishap, have an accident, sink, founder, decline, go down in the world, go downhill, slip, fall from grace, have a comedown, hit rock bottom, run aground, go on the rocks, go to rack and ruin, come to a bad end, come to grief, grieve, sorrow, regret, suffer humiliation, be ill, have an illness, suffer from poor health, suffer, feel pain, deteriorate, degenerate, go to pot, die, stew in one's own juice, go to the dogs (Inf), be on (*or* hit) the skids (Inf)

10 **need money**, have no money, have a financial setback, have a financial reverse, suffer a financial disaster, come to financial ruin, want, fall below the poverty line, lose one's

fortune, lose one's inheritance, have a cheque bounce, be overdrawn, go bankrupt, become insolvent, feel the pinch, feel the draught, have the wolf at one's door, go belly up (US sl)

11 **cause adversity**, cause grief, cause trouble, trouble, create a controversy, create problems, defeat, injure, oppress, sink, humiliate, make ill, burden, overburden, overload, weigh down, cause an accident, cause a death, bring bad luck, jinx, put the jinx on, put the evil eye on, put the skids under, voodoo (*or* hoodoo) (Inf), hex (US inf), put the (*or* a) whammy on (Sl), put the (*or* a) double whammy on (Sl)

ADVERBS

12 **in adversity**, adversely, in adverse circumstances, if worst comes to worst, from bad to worse, from the frying pan into the fire, sadly, unhappily, unfortunately, unluckily, as ill (*or* bad) luck would have it, conflictingly, contrarily, antagonistically, bleakly, unfavourably, detrimentally, dreadfully, grievously, inauspiciously, ominously, unpropitiously, harmfully, sinisterly, disastrously, tragically, accidentally, by accident, by mischance, by misadventure, unsuccessfully, miserably, poorly

INTERJECTIONS

13 **too bad!**, bad luck!, what rotten luck!, terrible!, dreadful!, alas!, woe is me! (Arch)

688 Authority

NOUNS

1 **authority**, power, control, command, leadership, direction, governance, domination, predominance, overbearance, dominance, ascendancy, hegemony, mastery, magistrality, superiority, supremacy, seniority, might, strength, potency, potence, absolute power, absolutism, legitimacy, legality, legal power, law, lawful authority, right, rightful authority, eminent domain, divine right, prerogative, royal prerogative, regality, royalty, nobility, constituted authority, derived authority, delegated authority, the upper hand, the whip hand, financial control, purse strings, indirect authority, hidden power, power behind the throne, stringpulling, wirepulling (US), manipulation, influence, pressure, patronage, puissance (Arch), clout (Inf)

▶ *235 Power, 126 Superiority, 741 Money*

2 **authoritativeness**, powerfulness, greatness, mightiness, masterfulness, lordliness, peremptoriness, imperativeness, imperiousness, majesty, self-assertion, confidence, knowledge

▶ *501 Knowledge, 490 Certainty*

3 **acquisition of power**, empowerment, election, selection, delegation, deputation, appointment, authorization, grant, succession, legitimate succession, accession, coronation, anointment, consecration, seizure of power, usurpation, coup d'état, coup, revolution, overthrowing, taking over

▶ *12 Government and Politics, 154 Precedence*

4 **governance**, reins of government, government, politics, administration, management, bureaucracy, red tape, civil service, officialism, beadledom, jurisdiction, direction, command, rule, sway, hold, grip, reign, sovereignty, suzerainty, dominion, officialdom, the government, the administration, the authorities, the Establishment, the ruling class (*or* classes), the system, the power structure, the powers that be, Big Brother, the top, the high command, the inner circle, the board, the directorship, higher-ups (Inf)

5 **position of authority**, office of power, high office, government post, federal post (US), seat of government, cabinet seat, governorship, mayoralty, consulate, proconsulate, prefecture, magistracy, headship, presidency, premiership, chairmanship, directorship, secretariat, superintendency, inspectorship, judgeship, police rank, military rank

▶ *16 Law, 679 Combatant*

6 **place of authority**, capital, palace, corridors of power, Whitehall, Downing Street, Number Ten, Parliament, Westminster, Washington (US), the White House (US), Congress (US), the Hill (US), the Capitol (US), Capitol Hill (US), classroom, courtroom, police station, prison, military base, military unit

7 **type of rule**, monarchy, constitutional monarchy, regnancy, regency, dynasty, aristocracy, plutocracy, meritocracy, oligarchy, tribalism, heteronomy, imperialism, colonialism, puppet government, caretaker government, representative government, majority rule, democracy, proportional representation, pluralism, republicanism, federalism, parliamentary government, constitutional government, egalitarianism, government of the people, by the people, for the people, self-government, rule of law, autonomy, home rule, theocracy, papal rule, ecclesiasticism, state control, collectivism, socialism, communism, Leninism, Marxism, Bolshevism, dictatorship of the proletariat, demagogy, demagoguery, despotism, benevolent despotism, authoritarianism, autocracy, autarchy, tyranny, dictatorship, totalitarianism, Fascism, Nazism, National Socialism, military government, martial law, police state, rule of terror, ochlocracy, mobocracy, mob rule, mob law, anarchy, syndicalism, anarcho-syndicalism, White supremacy, Black power

▶ *699 Restraint, 261 Expansion, 580 Selection, 698 Freedom, 690 Severity, 689 Anarchy*

8 **governmental organization**, body politic, regime, city, city state, state, county, district,

province, canton, territory, nation, country, realm, kingdom, duchy, dukedom, principality, palatinate, republic, empire, colony, dependency, protectorate, mandate, dominion, commonwealth, federation, confederation
▶ *249 Region*

9 **permission**, authorization, sanction, justification, testimonial, testimony, declaration, evidence, permit, warrant, licence, visa, credential, reference, avowal, say-so (Inf)
▶ *708 Permission, 483 Evidence*

10 **person of authority**, authority, leader, director, executive, manager, superior, head, chief, top man, patrician, ruler, autocrat, tyrant, dictator, despot, sovereign, monarch, king, queen, emperor, empress, pope, cardinal, primate, archbishop, bishop, dean, archdeacon, rabbi, president, prime minister, premier, minister of state, MP (Member of Parliament), MEP (Member of the European Parliament), Senator (US), Congressman (*or* -woman) (US), representative (US), cabinet member, governor, high commissioner, commissioner, military governor, seneschal, proconsul, consul general, consul, mayor, mayoress, judge, associate justice (US), chief justice of the United States (US), magistrate, sheriff, constable, marshal, justice of the peace, official, party official, chief whip, whip, party whip, Democratic whip (US), Republican whip (US), stringpuller, wirepuller (US), policeman, policewoman, military officer, commander-in-chief, commanding officer, commander, executive officer, educator, principal, headmaster, headmistress, chancellor, vice chancellor, provost, teacher, mentor, sage, wise man, guru, swami, exec (US inf), the Old Man (Inf), bobby (Inf), bluebottle (Inf), bigwig (Inf), big shot (Inf), big wheel (Inf), big cheese (Inf), top dog (Inf), boss (Inf), beak (Sl), head honcho (Sl), copper (Sl), cop (Sl), Smokey (US sl)
▶ *696 Master, 802 Aristocrat, 653 Management, 7 Religion*

11 **expert**, genius, intellectual, researcher, professor, don, scholar, scientist, historian, musical genius, maestro, virtuoso, master of the violin, specialist, connoisseur, past master, adept, practitioner, physician, consultant, guide, professional, old master, old hand, walking encyclopedia, lexicographer, pro (Inf), ace (Inf), dab hand (*or* dab) (Inf), highbrow (Inf), egghead (Inf), boffin (Inf)
▶ *459 Intellect, 49 Music, 45 Cookery, 50 Painting and Sculpture, 507 Wisdom, 501 Knowledge, 655 Skill*

ADJECTIVES

12 **authoritative**, official, definitive, ex officio, powerful, empowered, regal, royal, noble, controlling, commanding, holding the reins of government, leading, governing, ruling, reigning, on the throne, authoritarian, dominant, predominant, high-handed, overbearing, masterful, domineering, condescending, patronizing, imperative, imperious, arrogant, coercive, lordly, superior, supreme, senior, mighty, strong, potent, absolute, legitimate, legal, lawful, rightful, influential, preeminent, peremptory, overruling, self-assertive, confident, knowledgeable, puissant (Arch), bossy (Inf)

13 **elected**, selected, chosen, delegated, deputized, appointed, authorized, granted, successional, accessional

14 **governmental**, political, administrative, ministerial, managerial, bureaucratic, official, jurisdictional, sovereign, royal, regal, majestic, monarchal (*or* monarchial), kinglike, kingly, queenly, princely, aristocratic, imperial, oligarchic, plutocratic, suzerain, presidential, congressional, parliamentary, colonial, territorial, national, gubernatorial (US), democratic, popular, classless, republican, federal, constitutional, self-governing, autonomous, autarchic, independent, socialistic, communistic, Marxist, authoritarian, autocratic, tyrannical, dictatorial, totalitarian, Fascist, Nazi, patriarchal, matriarchal, anarchic

15 **true**, authentic, authenticated, official, legitimate, genuine, reliable, conclusive, certain, positive, sure

16 **authorized**, sanctioned, accredited, approved, allowed, permitted, licenced, warranted, chartered, made legal, legalized

17 **expert**, masterly, skilled, accomplished, professional, knowledgeable, intellectual

VERBS

18 **have authority**, have power, possess power, control, command, lead, direct, rule, govern, hold the reins of government, hold office, hold power, exercise power, wield authority, preside over, legislate, administer, manage, rule absolutely, hold sway, reign, reign supreme, sit on the throne, wear the crown, wield the sceptre, predominate, have the upper hand, have the whip hand, rule the roost, keep order, police, control the purse strings, pull strings, pull wires (US), manipulate, have under one's thumb, bend to one's will, influence, pressure, hold in the palm of one's hand (Inf), have over a barrel (Inf), have clout (Inf), have the say-so (Inf)

19 **be authoritarian**, dominate, domineer, discipline, drill, subjugate, dictate to, tyrannize, oppress, lord it over, play god, lay down the law, rule with an iron rod, hold all the aces, rule the roost, condescend, wear the trousers, wear the pants (US), crack the whip, call the shots, call the tune, ride roughshod over, lead by the nose, twist round one's little finger, boss (Inf), throw one's weight around (Inf)

20 **take authority**, assume authority, acquire authority, succeed, accede, mount the throne, take office, take command, assume command, take the helm, take over the reins (of government), gain the upper hand, get the whip hand, seize power, usurp power, lead a coup d'état), overthrow, take over

21 **grant authority**, delegate authority, give authority, empower, power, elect, select, delegate, deputize, appoint, authorize, legitimatize, coronate, anoint, consecrate, give permission, patronize, allow, permit, approve, grant, sanction, declare, accredit, license, charter, make legal, legalize

22 **be an authority on**, be an expert on, specialize in, have expertise, know, know all about, know the ropes, be well up on, know inside out, know back to front, know one's stuff (Inf), have the know how (Inf)

ADVERBS

23 **authoritatively**, with (or by) authority, with (or by) power, ex cathedra, in the name of, by warrant of, in (or by) virtue of one's authority, in authority, in charge, in control, officially, powerfully, in power, royally, on the throne, nobly, commandingly, in command, in the driving seat, at the wheel, at the helm, at the reins, in the saddle, high-handedly, dominantly, arrogantly, supremely, strongly, potently, absolutely, legitimately, legally, lawfully, rightfully, knowledgeably, confidently

24 **ministerially**, presidentially, congressionally, administratively, colonially, nationally, politically, in a political context, democratically, constitutionally, independently, socialistically, communistically

25 **authentically**, truly, offically, with official approval, legitimately, genuinely, reliably, conclusively, certainly, positively, surely

26 **expertly**, in an expert manner, masterly, skilfully, with skill, professionally, knowledgeably, intellectually

689   Anarchy

NOUNS

1 **anarchy**, lawlessness, disorder, breakdown of law and order, no authority, interregnum, power vacuum, powerlessness, impotence, disorganization, misgovernment, misrule, unrestraint, unruliness, disruption, irresponsibility, indiscipline, disobedience, insubordination, defiance of authority, arrogation, breakdown of government, chaos, turmoil, mob rule, mob law, lynch law, sedition, subversion, fifth column, revolution, rebellion, guerrilla tactics, the underground, usurpation, abdication, forced resignation, overthrow, coup d'état, coup, dethronement, mutiny, reign of terror, law of the jungle, every man for himself, dog-eat-dog

▶ *151 Disorder, 236 Powerlessness, 807 Insolence, 693 Disobedience*

2 **anarchism**, nihilism, antinomianism, syndicalism, anarcho-syndicalism, ochlocracy, mobocracy

▶ *720 Nonobservance*

3 **anarchist**, anarch (Arch), revolutionary, subversive, seditionary, rebel, mutineer, fifth columnist, terrorist, guerrilla, assassin, arrogator, antinomian, nihilist, syndicalist, ochlocrat, mobocrat

VERBS

4 **be anarchic**, be anarchistic, cause anarchy, cause disorder, defy authority, resist authority, reject authority, usurp authority, usurp, undermine, subvert, arrogate, resist control, disobey, not obey, act without authority, answer to no man, be a law unto oneself, take the law into one's own hands, please oneself, do as one pleases, indulge oneself, let oneself go, practise subversion, go underground, disrupt, revolt, rebel, mutiny, overthrow, depose, lead a coup d'état, lead a coup, topple a government, assassinate (a leader), unseat, dethrone, unthrone, uncrown, seize the crown, cause to abdicate, force to resign

5 **misgovern**, misrule, mismanage, exert no authority, become disorganized, reduce to chaos

ADJECTIVES

6 **anarchic**, anarchical, disorganized, ungoverned, lawless, unofficial, wildcat, disobedient, insubordinate, seditious, self-willed, wilful, headstrong, heady, rash, disorderly, confused, uncontrolled, undisciplined, unrestrained, unbridled, unreined, unaccountable, irresponsible, rampant, unruly, wild, riotous, chaotic, rebellious, revolutionary, mutinous, dog-eat-dog

7 **anarchistic**, nihilistic, antinomian, syndicalistic, ochlocratic, mobocratic

ADVERBS

8 **anarchically**, lawlessly, unofficially, disobediently, insubordinately, seditiously, without authority, wilfully, to please oneself, rashly, irresponsibly, wildly, chaotically, rebelliously, mutinously

690   Severity

NOUNS

1 **severity**, strictness, fastidiousness, pedantry, meticulousness, stringency, sternness, ruggedness, toughness, harshness, hardness, intolerance, no compromise, uncharitableness, rigorousness, rigour, fundamentalism, Draconian measures, rigidity, formality, orthodoxy, firmness, firm hand, strong hand, hard hand, firm control, tight rein, restraint, inflexibility, stub-

bornness, obstinacy, bigotry, regimentation, discipline, strict discipline, clampdown, martial law, letter of the law, authority, power, arbitrary power, no appeal, inclemency, lack of mercy, harsh treatment, asperity, callousness, pitilessness, inhumanity, cruelty, bullying, outrage, pound of flesh, tight ship (Inf)
▶ *373 Hardness, 688 Authority, 577 Obstinacy, 235 Power, 836 Pitilessness*

2 **suppression**, oppression, repression, subjugation, subjection, persecution, coercion, harassment, victimization, extortion, exploitation, Rachmanism, inquisition, censorship, expurgation, blue laws (US), Official Secrets Act, absolutism, authoritarianism, autocracy, totalitarianism, militarism, dictatorship, despotism, tyranny, Fascism, Nazism, Stalinism, brute force, naked force, show of force, iron rule, iron hand, mailed fist, jackboot, atrocity, torture, execution
▶ *701 Subjection, 699 Restraint, 877 Immorality, 844 Wrong, 864 Wickedness, 241 Violence, 879 Punishment*

3 **unadornment**, plainness, simplicity, austerity, asceticism, ascesis, restraint, self-restraint, self-denial, self-mortification, Spartanism, prudery, puritanism
▶ *372 Sparseness*

4 **strict person**, spartan, puritan, purist, pedant, stickler, bureaucrat, disciplinarian, martinet, petty tyrant, militarist, sergeant major, hanging judge, oppressive person, oppressor, Big Brother, authoritarian, despot, dictator, autocrat, inquisitor, persecutor, bully, hard master, taskmaster, taskmistress, slave-driver, bloodsucker, hardliner, hawk, dry (Inf), Dutch uncle (Inf)
▶ *696 Master*

VERBS

5 **be severe**, restrain, regiment, discipline, chastise, punish, wield power, exert authority, maintain firm control, keep a tight rein, take Draconian measures, get tough, deal harshly with, come down on, intimidate, frighten, take the heart out of, clamp down on, put a stop to, not tolerate, squeeze, crush, impose martial law, allow no appeal, give no quarter, offer no compromise, lack mercy, show no mercy, show no pity, shove around, boss around, wave the big stick, bully, bait, hassle, stick to the letter of the law, have one's pound of flesh, put one's foot down (Inf), run a tight ship (Inf)

6 **suppress**, oppress, repress, subjugate, subject, persecute, hunt down, coerce, harass, abuse, abuse one's authority, misgovern, misrule, mishandle, victimize, extort, exploit, enslave, censor, expurgate, tyrannize, use brute force, have a show of force, treat rough, ride roughshod over, stamp on, tread on, tread under

foot, walk over, pull no punches, torment, terrorize, rule with an iron hand, torture, commit an atrocity, execute, shed blood, put to the sword, get tough with (Inf), take off the gloves (Inf), put the screws on (Sl), put the frighteners on (Sl)

7 **be unadorned**, have simplicity, restrain oneself, show self-restraint, live a spartan life, be austere

ADJECTIVES

8 **severe**, strict, rigorous, harsh, hard, hard as nails, uncompromising, unbending, stubborn, obstinate, hard-headed (US), stern, rigid, firm, inflexible, uncharitable, Draconian, exacting, exact, pedantic, formal, orthodox, fundamental, fastidious, meticulous, stringent, censorious, censorial, regimented, disciplined, rugged, tough, hardhearted, intolerant, inquisitorial, bigoted, inclement, callous, pitiless, merciless, unsparing, unforgiving, inhumane, cruel, brutal, coercive, oppressive, repressive, exploitative, undemocratic, militaristic, authoritarian, totalitarian, despotic, dictatorial, autocratic, Fascist, tyrannical, domineering, dominating, high-handed, overbearing, heavy-handed, bossy (Inf)

9 **suppressed**, oppressed, repressed, subjugated, subjected, persecuted, coerced, harassed, censored, expurgated, exploited, victimized, tyrannized, tortured, executed

10 **unadorned**, plain, simple, purist, restrained, self-restrained, austere, ascetic, spartan, prudish, puritanical, strait-laced

ADVERBS

11 **severely**, strictly, under strict regulations, rigorously, harshly, stubbornly, obstinately, sternly, rigidly, firmly, inflexibly, stringently, uncharitably, exactingly, pedantically, formally, fundamentally, fastidiously, meticulously, uncompromisingly, without compromise, unsparingly, relentlessly, unrelentingly, intolerantly, callously, hardheartedly, inhumanely, cruelly, toughly, unyieldingly, mercilessly, brutally, high-handedly, in a high-handed manner, arbitrarily, heavy-handedly, with a heavy hand, with an iron hand, oppressively, repressively, dictatorially, autocratically, tyrannically

12 **plainly**, simply, without adornment, austerely, ascetically, prudishly, puritanically

691 Leniency

NOUNS

1 **leniency**, lenience, lenity, laxity, easiness, mildness, moderation, gentleness, softness, tenderness, patience, tolerance, toleration, forbearance, compassion, pity, mercifulness, mercy, quarter, forgiveness, pardon, amnesty, clemency, reasonableness, humanity, hu-

maneness, benevolence, kindness, kindliness, graciousness, charitableness, charity, magnanimity, generousness, favour, concession, sop, humouring, consideration, leave, allowance, permission, permissiveness, indulgence, *laissez faire* (Fr), spoiling, gratification, light rein, light hand, velvet glove, cotton-wool treatment (Inf), kidglove treatment, kid gloves

▶ *242 Moderation, 835 Pity, 839 Forgiveness, 831 Benevolence, 708 Permission*

2 **lenient person**, permissive parent, philanthropist, latitudinarian, liberal, bleeding-heart liberal (Inf), wet (Inf), old softy (Inf)

VERBS

3 **be lenient**, show leniency, go easy on, moderate, treat kindly, treat lightly, make no demands, make few demands, deal gently, handle tenderly, tolerate, forbear, not press, bear with, stretch a point, bend a rule, give quarter, have compassion, have pity, pity, show mercy, forgive, forget, pardon, spare, grant amnesty, favour, concede, humour, show consideration, allow, permit, indulge, oblige, gratify, spare the rod, handle with kid (*or* velvet) gloves, keep (*or* use) a light rein, use a light hand, pull one's punches (Inf), let off the hook (Sl)

ADJECTIVES

4 **lenient**, lax, easy, easy-going, mild, moderate, clement, gentle, soft, tender, patient, tolerant, forbearing, long-suffering, compassionate, pitying, merciful, forgiving, reasonable, considerate, humane, benevolent, kind, kindly, gracious, charitable, accepting, magnanimous, accommodating, generous, permissive, indulgent, spoiling, kid-glove, live-and-let-live

5 **given consideration**, given permission, allowed, permitted, granted amnesty, pardoned, forgiven, indulged, gratified, pitied, spoiled, spoiled rotten (Inf)

ADVERBS

6 **leniently**, easily, mildly, moderately, gently, softly, tenderly, patiently, with kid gloves, with a light rein, with a light hand, tolerantly, compassionately, mercifully, reasonably, considerately, humanely, benevolently, kindly, with kindness, graciously, in a gracious manner, charitably, magnanimously, accommodatingly, generously, permissively, indulgently, gratifyingly

692 Command

NOUNS

1 **command**, commandment, order, legal order, direct order, instruction, direction, ruling, rule, regulation, directive, word, sign, signal, law, act, enactment, legislation, manifesto, prescription, precept, charge, behest, dictate, ordinance, edict, fiat, canon, bull, encyclical, papal decree, decree, ukase, decree nisi, decree absolute, prescript, order of the day, marching orders, statement, pronouncement, proclamation, declaration, dictum, invitation, royal command, negative command, prohibition, proscription, counterorder, countermand, interdict, veto, ban, embargo

▶ *695 Compulsion, 535 Affirmation, 528 Information, 12 Government and Politics, 704 Cancellation, 709 Veto*

2 **demand**, claim, requisition, warning notice, final warning, red demand, final demand, ultimatum, legal order, tax demand, levy, warrant, bench warrant, warrant of arrest, search warrant, mittimus, writ, process, summons, writ of summons, subpoena, citation, habeas corpus, injunction, interdict, bidding, beck, call, beck and call, threat, extortion, blackmail

▶ *712 Request, 845 Entitlement*

3 **authority**, rule, control, government, power, sway, mastery, sovereignty, suzerainty, dominion, domination

4 **authorization**, commission, charge, written authority, permit, letters patent, patronage, appointment, mandate, electoral mandate, the go ahead (Inf)

▶ *688 Authority, 708 Permission, 703 Commission, 580 Selection*

5 **self-assurance**, self-confidence, presence, authority, look of power

6 **person in command**, head of state, chief executive, chief executive officer (CEO), president, prime minister, premier, chancellor, judge, policeman, jailer, process-server, summoner, commander, commander-in-chief, commanding officer (CO), commandant, general, lieutenant general, major general, brigadier, brigadier general (US), field marshal, air marshal, admiral, fleet admiral, admiral of the fleet

▶ *16 Law, 679 Combatant*

7 **overview**, survey, ball-park view, summary

8 **vantage point**, observation post, watchtower, crow's nest, bridge, cockpit

VERBS

9 **command**, issue a command, order, give an order, direct, instruct, rule, regulate, signal, enact, legislate, make law, lay down the law, issue a manifesto, promulgate, prescribe, give a direction, give a mandate, charge, call upon, dictate, decree, sign a decree, pass a decree, issue an edict, issue a statement, pronounce, pontificate, proclaim, declare, say so, invite, prohibit, proscribe, countermand, counterorder, interdict, veto, ban, impose a ban, embargo, impose an embargo

10 **demand**, make demands, ask for, call for, insist on, lay upon, require, impose, make obligatory, claim, make claims upon, requisi-

tion, order up, indent, issue a warning notice, give final notice, present with an ultimatum, take a strong line, demand tax payment, levy, exact, warrant, issue a warrant, subpoena, issue an injunction, interdict, threaten, extort, blackmail, put one's foot down (Inf)

11 **have authority over**, have power over, have sway over, rule over, rule, control, compel, impose, govern, dominate, dictate to, judge, pass judgment, give a ruling, show authority, have the look of power, call the shots (Sl), call the signals (US sl)

12 **be available to one**, have at one's command, have at one's disposal, have at one's beck and call

13 **authorize**, commission, charge, permit, appoint, mandate

ADJECTIVES

14 **commanding**, ordering, imperative, directive, compelling, ruling, regulatory, enacted, legislative, prescriptive, encyclical, papal, pontifical, authoritative, governmental, mandatory, obligatory, compulsory, dictatorial, prohibitive, proscriptive, injunctive, countermanded, interdicted, vetoed, banned, embargoed

15 **self-assured**, self-confident, controlling, domineering, superior, lordly, powerful, autocratic, imperious, high-handed, authorized, commissioned, appointed, mandated, bossy (Inf)

ADVERBS

16 **commandingly**, by command, at the word of command, by order, as ordered, as required, imperatively, compellingly, prescriptively, to order, authoritatively, governmentally, obligatorily, dictatorially, prohibitively, proscriptively, self-assuredly, self-confidently, with confidence, domineeringly, superiorly, powerfully, autocratically, imperiously, high-handedly

693 Disobedience

NOUNS

1 **disobedience**, noncompliance, noncooperation, uncooperativeness, nonconformity, nonobservance, undutifulness, unwillingness, opposition, recalcitrance, refractoriness, obstinacy, stubbornness, intractability, hindrance, obstruction, obstructionism, obstreperousness, indiscipline, restlessness, restiveness, wildness, delinquency, unruliness, dissension, defiance, defiance of orders, refusal to obey orders, violation of orders, disloyalty, perfidiousness, perfidy, unfaithfulness, faithlessness, defection, desertion, AWOL (absent without leave), tergiversation, insubordination, strike, mutinousness, mutineering, mutiny, civil disobedience, passive resistance, resistance, conscientious objection, religious disobedience, immorality, wickedness, sin, sinfulness, orneriness (US inf), misbehaviour, mischief-making, naughtiness, stroppiness (Inf), monkey tricks (Inf), monkey shines (US inf)

▶ *168 Nonconformity, 573 Unwillingness, 668 Defiance, 720 Nonobservance, 661 Hindrance, 663 Opposition, 366 Agitation, 244 Destruction, 151 Disorder, 241 Violence, 864 Wickedness*

2 **violation of the law**, infraction, infringement, transgression, felony, trespass, extortion, breach of the peace, civil disturbance, disorder, riot, street riot, rioting, street fight, gang warfare, tumult, turmoil, lawlessness, lawbreaking, criminality, crime, vandalism, robbery, murder, regicide, tyrannicide, homicide

▶ *858 Improbity, 736 Stealing, 398 Killing*

3 **subversion**, subversiveness, underground activities, sedition, seditiousness, conspiracy, intrigue, plot, cabal, faction, secret society, agit-prop, infiltration, spying, espionage, fifth columnism, fifth column, agitation, sabotage, terrorism, anarchy, treasonable activities, treason, high treason, lese-majesty

▶ *592 Plan, 669 Resistance*

4 **revolution**, rebellion, rebelliousness, revolt, sans-culottism, uprising, mutiny, mutinousness, coup d'état, coup, putsch, breakaway, schism, secession, sedition, insurrection, insurgence, insurgency, resistance movement, resistance, terrorism, guerrilla warfare, civil war, war

▶ *676 War*

5 **troublemaker**, mischief-maker, naughty child, scamp, pest, nuisance, rascal, scallywag, imp, handful, little monkey (Inf), pain in the neck (Inf), pain in the arse (Tab sl)

6 **nonconformist**, protestant, deviationist, radical, Jacobin, maverick, opponent, malcontent, Frondeur

7 **protester**, civil rights activist, suffragist, suffragette, women's libber, environmental activist, campaigner, demonstrator, marcher, dissident, recusant, recalcitrant, striker, picketer

8 **agitator**, *agent provocateur* (Fr), ringleader, rabble-rouser, soapbox orator, demagogue, firebrand

9 **criminal**, lawbreaker, robber, bandit, thief, burglar, house-breaker, murderer, assassin, extortionist, killer, rapist, sexual abuser, wife-batterer, gang member, gangster, Mafia member, Mafioso, petty criminal, mugger (Inf), hood (US sl), mobster (US sl), brawler, rowdy, ruffian, hoodlum (US), handful (Inf), bolshie (Inf), hooligan (Sl), bovver boy (Sl)

10 **seditionist**, seditionary, subversive, conspirator, Guy Fawkes, John Brown (US), traitor, collaborator, quisling, tergiversator, extremist, Black Panther (US), National Front

member, insurrectionist, insurgent, infiltrator, fifth columnist, anarchist, rioter, terrorist, Weatherman (US), IRA (Irish Republican Army) member, Provisional, Provo, guerrilla, urban guerrilla, partisan, saboteur, Luddite

11 **rebel**, secessionist, seceder, revolutionary, revolutionist, sans-culotte, revolter, mutineer, Contra, Bolshevist, Trotskyist, Red (Inf), commie (Inf), pinko (Inf), leftie (Inf)

12 **reactionary**, counter-revolutionary, conservative, monarchist, White Russian, counter-terrorist, nonstriker, strikebreaker, scab, blackleg

ADJECTIVES

13 **disobedient**, noncompliant, uncomplying, noncooperative, uncooperative, nonobservant, undutiful, unwilling, opposing, recalcitrant, obstinate, stubborn, intractable, obstructive, insubordinate, obstreperous, undisciplined, poorly disciplined, transgressing, restless, restive, wild, out of control, unmanageable, disobeying, misbehaved, mischiefmaking, naughty, delinquent, disorderly, riotous, tumultuous, unruly, dissenting, defiant, recusant, disloyal, perfidious, deserting, tergiversatory, mutinous, lawless, lawbreaking, criminal, immoral, wicked, sinning, ornery (US inf), bloody-minded (Inf)

14 **subversive**, seditious, conspiratorial, factional, anarchic, anarchical, treasonable, revolutionary, rebellious, in rebellion, mutinous, breakaway, schismatic, insurgent, insurrectional, insurrectionary

VERBS

15 **be disobedient**, disobey, not obey, not listen to, not heed, pay no attention to, ignore instructions, not do as one is told, refuse to cooperate, not cooperate, not comply with, not conform, oppose, hinder, obstruct, misbehave, make mischief, get into mischief, dissent, flout authority, show insubordination, defy, defy orders, refuse to obey orders, violate orders, defect, desert, go AWOL (absent without leave), tergiversate, strike, take industrial action, break the law, violate the law, commit a crime, infringe, transgress, breach the peace, trespass, riot, vandalize, rob, murder, sin, snap one's fingers at

16 **be subversive**, subvert, conspire, plot, betray, infiltrate, spy, agitate, sabotage, terrorize, create anarchy, lead a rebellion, uprise, rise in arms, mount the barricades, mutiny, secede, revolt, stage a revolt, rebel, fight, overthrow, lead a coup, kick over the traces

ADVERBS

17 **disobediently**, contrary to orders, unwillingly, obstinately, stubbornly, intractably, insubordinately, obstreperously, restlessly, restively, wildly, naughtily, delinquently, riotously, tumultuously, dissentingly, defiantly,

as a protest, disloyally, perfidiously, mutinously, lawlessly, criminally, immorally, without regard to morality, wickedly, in a wicked way

18 **subversively**, seditiously, conspiratorially, rebelliously, mutinously, schismatically

694 Obedience

NOUNS

1 **obedience**, compliance, complaisance, acquiescence, deference, obsequiousness, dutifulness, duty, abiding by the law, goodness, observance, conformity, willingness, readiness, nonresistance, meekness, submissiveness, submission, passivity, passiveness, yielding, docility, subservience, servility, slavishness, tractability, pliance, malleability, softness, tameness, inactivity

▶ *719 Observance, 847 Duty, 857 Probity, 167 Conformity, 572 Willingness, 677 Pacification, 675 Peace, 673 Submission, 808 Servility, 374 Softness, 643 Inactivity*

2 **loyalty**, fidelity, fealty, allegiance, service, faithfulness, good faith, good behaviour, devotion, constancy, comity, steadfastness, staunchness

3 **obeisance**, homage, worship, reverence, kneeling, humility, respect, courtesy, bow, curtsy, genuflection (*or* genuflexion), obsequy, salaam, prostration, grovelling, kowtow

4 **obedient person**, conformist, traditionalist, loyalist, loyal party member, law-abiding citizen, pillar of the community, soldier, well-behaved child, teacher's pet, henpecked husband, servant, slave, gofer (US sl)

▶ *697 Servant, 662 Help, 127 Inferiority*

VERBS

5 **obey**, comply, comply with, acquiesce, consent, assent, defer, defer to, yield to, do one's duty, show good faith, behave well, show devotion to, abide by the law, keep the law, observe the rules, follow the book, conform, not resist, obey orders, take orders, follow orders, follow like sheep, wait for the command, do as one is told, do the will of, carry out orders, discharge, perform, heed, mind, come to heel, toe the line, stay in line, submit, yield, bear allegiance, give allegiance to, go along with, follow the party line, serve, do service, put oneself at one's service, do one's bidding, come at one's call, wait upon, minister to, follow to the ends of the earth

6 **show obeisance to**, pay homage, offer homage, keep the faith, worship, kneel, show humility, show respect, pay tribute, show courtesy, bow, curtsy, bend, stoop, genuflect, salaam, prostrate oneself, grovel, scrape, kowtow

ADJECTIVES

7 **obedient**, compliant, complying, complaisant, acquiescent, deferential, obsequious, dutiful, duteous (Fml), conforming, law-abiding, observant, good, willing, ready, nonresisting, unresisting, meek, sheep-like, submitting, submissive, passive, yielding, docile, resigned, disciplined, well-behaved, well-trained, biddable, under control, at one's beck and call, at one's command, at one's pleasure, at one's disposal, subservient, servile, slavish, tractable, amenable, pliant, inactive, manageable, malleable, soft, tame, trained, regimented, under one's thumb, like putty in one's hands, like a puppet on a string, on a leash (or lead)

8 **loyal**, faithful, devoted, devoted to, dedicated to, sworn to, constant, steadfast, staunch, true, sycophantic, true-blue, leal (Scot)

9 **obeisant**, offering homage, worshipping, reverential, kneeling, humble, respectful, courteous

ADVERBS

10 **obediently**, in obedience to, compliantly, in compliance with, under orders, to order, as ordered, complaisantly, acquiescently, deferentially, obsequiously, dutifully, in conformity with, conformingly, observantly, willingly, readily, unresistingly, meekly, submissively, passively, docilely, subserviently, servilely, slavishly, tractably, pliantly, inactively, softly, tamely, loyally, faithfully, devotedly, steadfastly, staunchly, constantly, reverentially, respectfully, courteously

11 **yours to command**, at your command, at your orders, at your service, as you please, as you will

695 Compulsion

NOUNS

1 **compulsion**, compulsiveness, irresistibility, irresistible force, obsessiveness, obsessive need, obsession, preoccupation, need, urge, drive, essential, necessity, obligation, requirement, prerequisite, zero options, no choice, Hobson's choice, a must (Inf)
▶ *571 Necessity, 847 Duty*

2 **coercion**, pressure, order, command, mandate, forcing, force, legal force, enforcement, force majeure (Fml), main force, physical force, duress, restraint, constraint, intimidation, bullying, browbeating, threat, violence, brute force
▶ *701 Subjection, 692 Command, 235 Power, 699 Restraint, 241 Violence*

3 **coercive methods**, blackmail, extortion, bribery, carrot and stick, big stick, bludgeon, strong-arm tactics, arm-twisting, force-feeding, kidnapping, forced labour, labour camp, slavery, impressment, press gang, sanc-

tions, conscription, call-up, draft (US), penalty clause, fine, jail, torture
▶ *676 War, 690 Severity, 879 Punishment*

4 **coercive person**, forceful person, steamroller, bulldozer (Inf), bully, blackmailer, extortionist, briber, robber, kidnapper, hijacker, gunman, terrorist, torturer, mugger (Inf)

5 **compulsive person**, addict, monomaniac, compulsive eater, compulsive gambler, compulsive talker, compulsive liar, compulsive shopper, shoplifter, kleptomaniac, obsessive dieter, anorexic, alcoholic, smoker, workaholic, megalomaniac

VERBS

6 **compel**, coerce, urge, oblige, make, insist on, insist, make a point of, emphasize, not take no for an answer, pressure, bring pressure to bear upon, put pressure on, apply pressure, bear down on, press, put under duress, squeeze, impel, drive, force someone's hand, twist one's arm, leave no choice, leave no option, leave no escape, pin down, tie down, bind, constrain, restrain, hold back, oppress, necessitate, require, command, demand, dictate, mandate, order, regiment, discipline, impose, impose a duty, enforce, lean on (Inf)

7 **force**, intimidate, threaten, force upon, force to accept, force-feed, foist on, fob off on, take, take by force, requisition, commandeer, constrain, extort, blackmail, kidnap, hold to ransom, exact, wring from, drag from, use force against, bring legal force to bear, conscript, call up, draft (US), impress, dragoon, use physical force, inflict, bully, bully into, browbeat, steamroller, bludgeon, pressgang, use violence, ram down one's throat, stampede, take the gloves off (Inf), turn the heat on (Inf), strong-arm (Inf), bulldoze (Inf), railroad (Inf), put the screws on (Sl)

8 **be compelled**, be coerced, yield to pressure, have no choice, have no option, must, should, have to, cannot help but, cannot do otherwise, have got to, cannot be helped

ADJECTIVES

9 **compelling**, compulsive, coercive, irresistible, hypnotic, mesmeric, cogent, convincing, inspiring, influential, persuasive, involuntary, unavoidable, inevitable, necessary, of necessity, commanding, imperative, urgent, overriding, pressing, driving, high-pressure, oppressive, dictatorial, enforcing, binding, restraining, constraining, steamroller, steamrolling, forceful, forcible, violent, bludgeoning, strong-arm (Inf), bulldozing (Inf)

10 **compulsory**, mandatory, necessary, unavoidable, ineluctable, obligatory, required, requisite, prerequisite

ADVERBS

11 **compellingly**, compulsively, on compulsion, coercively, irresistibly, hypnotically, co-

gently, convincingly, influentially, persuasively, involuntarily, unavoidably, inevitably,
willy-nilly, necessarily, of necessity, perforce,
obligatorily, imperatively, urgently, oppressively, under pressure to, under pressure,
under duress, commandingly, violently, forcefully, forcibly, by force, by force majeure
(Fml), by main force, by force of arms, *vi et
armis* (L), at the sword's point, at the point of
a gun, at gunpoint, at knifepoint

696 Master

NOUNS

1 **master**, mistress, lord, lord and master, lord
paramount, overlord, liege lord, liege, nobleman, aristocrat, lady, dame, lord of the manor,
lady of the manor, master of the house, mistress of the house, man of the house, husband,
lady of the house, wife, sir, madam, matron,
mother superior, housemother, patriarch,
matriarch, dowager, elder, owner, property
owner, landowner, squire, laird (Scot), landlord, landlady, proprietor, governor, sahib,
bwana, seigneur, guvnor (or guv) (Inf)
▶ *401 Male, 402 Female, 804 Title, 802 Aristocrat,
723 Possession*

2 **sovereign**, crowned head, monarch, absolute
monarch, king, Rex, divine king, queen, Regina, Your Majesty, His (or Her) Highness,
Your Royal Highness, His (or Her) Royal Highness, queen mother, queen regent, prince,
crown prince, Prince of Wales, prince regent,
princess, crown princess, emperor, Caesar,
empress, rajah, rani (or ranee), Kaiser, Kaiserin,
tsar (or czar), tsarina (or czarina), Pharaoh,
shah, khan, mikado, Mogul, Great Mogul, maharajah, nabob, sultan, caliph, Dalai Lama
▶ *688 Authority, 611 Importance, 126 Superiority*

3 **leader**, head of state, chief of state, chief
executive, president, prime minister, premier,
chancellor, minister, minister of state, secretary, secretary of state, MP (Member of Parliament), MEP (Member of the European
Parliament), Senator (US), Congressman (or
-woman) (US), representative (US), cabinet
member, governor, governor general, lieutenant governor, high commissioner, commissioner, military governor, pasha, suzerain,
viceroy, proconsul, consul general, consul,
mayor, Lord Mayor, Lady Mayor, mayoress,
Supreme Court judge (US), judge, associate
justice (US), chief justice of the United States
(US), chief magistrate, magistrate, bailie (Scot),
bailiff (Brit), sheriff, constable, marshal, justice of the peace, justice, official, party official,
chief whip, whip, Democratic whip (US), Republican whip (US), officer, functionary, dignitary, person in office, person in authority,
ruler, potentate, protector, chief, chieftain,

headman, sheik, rajah, mandarin, Your Excellency (or Excellence), His (or Her) Excellency
(or Excellence)
▶ *12 Government and Politics*

4 **absolute ruler**, autocrat, *Führer* (Ger), *der
Führer* (Ger), Hitler, *duce* (It), tyrant, dictator,
despot, satrap, warlord, shogun, oppressor,
captor, martinet, Big Brother, tin god, petty
tyrant, jack-in-office, little Hitler (Inf), gauleiter (Inf)

5 **company leader**, company official, superior, senior, executive, director, chairman of
the board, board member, chair, chairman,
chairwoman, chairperson, manager, controller, capitalist, plutocrat, oligarch, tycoon, captain of industry, head, chief, employer, VIP
(very important person), doyen, doyenne,
cock of the walk, kingpin, bigwig (Inf), big gun
(Inf), big shot (Inf), big wheel (Inf), big cheese
(Inf), head honcho (Inf), top dog (Inf), kingfish (US inf), boss (Inf)
▶ *653 Management*

6 **religious leader**, pope, pontiff, cardinal,
dean, rabbi, guru, archbishop, bishop, provost, high priest, priest, ayatollah, imam, ecclesiastical governor
▶ *7 Religion*

7 **military leader**, military officer, commissioned officer, commander-in-chief, commanding officer, commander, commandant,
general, generalissimo, field marshal, air marshal, admiral, fleet admiral, admiral of the
fleet, executive officer, exec (US inf), the Old
Man (Inf), brass hat (Inf)
▶ *679 Combatant*

8 **the power structure**, the ruling class (or
classes), ruling party, the Establishment, the
authorities, officialdom, principalities and
powers, the powers that be, Big Brother, the
Government, Whitehall, Downing Street,
Westminster, Washington (US), the White
House (US), the Hill (US), Capitol Hill (US), the
Capitol (US), the Pentagon (US), the Kremlin,
the high command, the board, the directorship, the top, the corridors of power, the inner
circle, the in-group, the top brass (Inf), higher-
ups (Inf)

9 **educational leader**, scholar, pedagogue, intellectual, thinker, philosopher, sage, wise
man, mentor, guru, swami, trustee, regent
(US), instructor, college president (US), university president (US), chancellor, vice chancellor, provost, principal, dean, professor, don,
fellow, reader, lecturer, governor, head, master, headmaster, headmistress, head teacher,
head of department, head of sixth-form,
schoolmaster, schoolmistress, teacher, tutor,
housemaster, housemistress, schoolmarm
(Inf), highbrow (Inf), egghead (Inf), beak (Sl)
▶ *459 Intellect*

10 **expert**, grand master, master, champion, genius, musical genius, maestro, virtuoso, master of the violin, specialist, past master, adept, sailing master, master thief, practitioner, graduate, consultant, guide, professional, master carpenter, skilled worker, the right man for the job, old master, old hand, walking encyclopedia, champ (Inf), pro (Inf), ace (Inf), dab hand (or dab) (Inf)

11 **masterpiece**, masterwork, *chef-d'oeuvre* (Fr), *tour de force* (Fr), magnum opus, classic, treasure, work of art, thing of beauty and a joy forever, feat of creation, epic, perfection, *creme de la creme* (Fr)

▶ *50 Painting and Sculpture*

ADJECTIVES

12 **masterful**, magistral, lordly, noble, aristocratic, magisterial, majestic, matronly, patriarchal, matriarchal, elder, sovereign, crowned, absolute, divine, royal, head, chief, principal, main, major, great, leading, controlling, parliamentary, senatorial (US), congressional (US), autocratic, authoritarian, dominating, domineering, coercive, imperious, dictatorial, despotic, oppressive, executive, managerial, capitalistic, plutocratic, oligarchic, papal, pontifical, cardinal, rabbic, rabbinical, commissioned, commanding, able

13 **excellent**, expert, master, champion, specialist, professional, scholarly, intellectual, philosophical, masterly, skilled, skilful, adept, proficient, first-rate, supreme, consummate, polished, finished, competent, good at, experienced, qualified, ace (Inf), highbrow (Inf), bossy (Inf)

VERBS

14 **master**, rule, lead, govern, dictate, oppress, lord it over, conquer, vanquish, defeat, beat, overpower, overcome, crush, quell, subdue, subjugate, dominate, control, command, direct, manage, head, operate in the corridors of power, sit on the board, hold a directorship, reach the top, head an institution, head a school, teach, instruct, tutor, specialize, win, paint a masterpiece, create a treasure, boss (Inf)

15 **learn**, understand, comprehend, apprehend, grasp, acquire, become proficient, retain, remember, know how to, assimilate, learn a trade, work an apprenticeship, practise at, learn by heart, memorize, research into, specialize in, know all the answers, get the hang of (Inf), ace (US inf), bone up on (Sl)

ADVERBS

16 **masterfully**, nobly, in a noble manner, aristocratically, absolutely, royally, autocratically, dominatingly, domineeringly, imperiously, dictatorially, oppressively, in order to oppress, executively, managerially, excellently, expertly, with expertise, professionally, intellec-

tually, philosophically, skilfully, adeptly, proficiently, supremely, consummately, competently

697   Servant

NOUNS

1 **servant**, paid helper, help, retainer, household servant, domestic, worker, hired hand, farmhand, labourer, handyman, odd-job man, employee, assistant, subordinate, subaltern, attendant, servitor (Arch), orderly, factotum, general servant, humble servant, follower, henchman, liegeman, daily help (or daily), cleaning lady, occasional help, hired help, menial, underling, hireling, inferior, minion, flunky, lackey, drudge, mister fix-it (US inf)

▶ *662 Help, 646 Worker, 613 Usefulness, 127 Inferiority, 694 Obedience*

2 **public servant**, public official, civil servant, politician, public office holder

3 **attendant**, usher, server, maitre d'hotel (or maître d'hôtel), maître d' (US), maid, valet, butler, batman, hostess, airline hostess, airline attendant, flight attendant, cabin crew, head waiter, waiter, waitress, steward, wine steward, sommelier, stewardess, bus boy (US), carhop (US), barperson, barman, barmaid, bartender (US), barkeeper (US), barkeep (US), potboy, page, bellboy (US), bellhop (US), porter, redcap (US), skycap (US), caddie, cloakroom attendant, hatcheck girl (US), counterman (US), shop assistant, salesclerk (or clerk) (US), shoeblack, bootblack (US), shoeshine boy (US), caretaker, concierge, janitor, soda jerk (US sl)

▶ *642 Activity, 739 Sale*

4 **personal attendant**, personal servant, companion, confidante, nurse, nursemaid, au pair, governess, nanny, chaperon, driver, chauffeur, batman, bodyguard, henchman, tutor, barber, hairdresser, masseur, masseuse

5 **office assistant**, assistant, personal assistant (PA), executive assistant, secretary, clerk, right-hand man, man (or girl) Friday, office boy (or girl), errand boy (or girl), tea lady, copy aide (US), messenger, runner, courier, employee, office worker, staff member, peon, dogsbody (Inf), gofer (US sl)

▶ *653 Management*

6 **domestic servant**, domestic, steward, house steward, bailiff (Brit), housekeeper, chamberlain, butler, major-domo, cook, maid, maidservant, housemaid, parlourmaid, chambermaid, *femme de chambre* (Fr), upstairs maid, nursemaid, nurse, nanny, ayah (India), amah (China), girl, servant girl, wench (Arch), au pair, boy, house boy, live-in maid, handmaid, handmaiden, lady's maid, maid-in-waiting, lady-in-waiting, lord-in-waiting, lady of the bedchamber, lord of the bedchamber,

gentleman's gentleman, gentleman, man, manservant, serving man, serving maid, serving girl, kitchen maid, dishwasher, kitchen boy, laundry maid, cleaning woman, daily help (or daily), charwoman (or charlady), char (Inf), Mrs Mop (Inf), chauffeur, driver, gardener, footman, stableman, stableboy, groom, domestic drudge, skivvy, slavey (Inf)

▶ 621 Cleanness

7 **slave**, serf, slave-girl, bondservant, bondsman, bondmaid, thrall, vassal, galley slave, captive

VERBS

8 **serve**, be in service, do service, work for, care for, take care of, help, tend, look after, wait upon, attend upon, live in, make oneself useful, minister to, administer to, assist, do housework, do chores, clean for, accompany, follow, oblige, obey, pander to, wait on hand and foot, dance attendance upon, char (Inf), do for (Inf)

ADJECTIVES

9 **serving**, attending, attendant, in (domestic) service, working, in employment, in one's employ, on the staff, on the payroll, in one's pay, helping, ministering, aiding, waiting on, menial, obedient, subject, servile, at one's beck and call, unfree, in servitude, in slavery, in captivity, in bonds

ADVERBS

10 **obediently**, menially, servilely, in servitude, in slavery, in captivity

698 Freedom

So free we seem, so fettered fast we are! Robert Browning.

Liberty, too, must be limited in order to be possessed. Edmund Burke.

I know not what course others may take; but as for me, give me liberty or give me death. Patrick Henry.

The tree of liberty must be refreshed from time to time with the blood of patriots and tyrants. It is its natural manure. Thomas Jefferson.

It is true that liberty is precious – so precious that it must be rationed. Lenin.

Those who deny freedom to others, deserve it not for themselves. Abraham Lincoln.

The liberty of the individual must be thus far limited; he must not make himself a nuisance to other people. John Stuart Mill.

None can love freedom heartily, but good men; the rest love not freedom, but licence. John Milton.

Liberty is the right to do everything which the laws allow. Baron de Montesquieu.

My government will protect all liberties but one – the liberty to do away with other liberties. Gustavo Diaz Ordaz.

'O liberté! O liberté! Que de crimes on commet en ton nom!' / (Oh liberty! Oh liberty! What crimes are committed in thy name!) Madame Roland.

Man was born free and everywhere he is in chains. Jean Jacques Rousseau.

Man is condemned to be free. Jean-Paul Sartre.

I disapprove of what you say, but I will defend to the death your right to say it. Voltaire.

NOUNS

1 **freedom**, freedom of action, liberty, personal liberty, lack of confinement, freedom of movement, being at large, lack of restraint, unrestraint, noncoercion, nonintimidation, option, choice, freedom of choice, freedom of thought, prerogative, discretion, free will, own free will, own account, initiative, own initiative, personal initiative, own responsibility, own volition, liberation, women's liberation, gay liberation, licence, artistic licence, poetic licence, privilege, exemption, nonliability, exception, immunity, diplomatic immunity, discharge, release, deliverance, emancipation, Emancipation Proclamation (US), broadmindedness, open-mindedness, toleration, tolerance, liberalism, libertarianism, latitudinarianism, free thinking, liberated mind, Bohemianism, nonconformity, noninterference, nonintervention, *laissez faire* (Fr), free enterprise, free trade, free-trade area, free port, high seas, self-regulating market, open market, free market, capitalism, noninvolvement, seclusion, nonalignment, neutrality, isolationism, say-so (Inf), women's lib (Inf)

2 **free speech**, freedom of religion, freedom of the press, lack of censorship, academic freedom, the Four Freedoms, freedom of speech and expression, freedom of worship, freedom from want, freedom from fear (US), rights, the Bill of Rights (US), First Amendment, constitutional rights, legal rights, human rights, inalienable (or unalienable) rights, right to bear arms (US), equal rights, civil rights, civil liberties

3 **independence**, own authority, own way, being in control, self-determination, the Magna Carta (or Magna Carta), Declaration of Independence (US), Statue of Liberty (US), Liberty Bell (US), individualism, self-expression, individuality, self-reliance, self-sufficiency, independent means, private means, wealth, no allegiance, unmarried state, bachelorhood, maidenhood, franchisement, enfranchisement, citizenship, authority, statehood, na-

tionhood, national status, unilaterality, autonomy, autarky (*or* autarchy), self-rule, self-government, independent rule, home rule, states' rights (US)

4 **informality**, ease, familiarity, frankness, candidness, relaxation, friendliness, casualness, candour, openness, unconstraint

5 **scope**, free scope, full scope, play, free play, full play, full opportunity, wide range, free range, manoeuvrability, room, living room, *Lebensraum* (Ger), living space, elbowroom, wide berth, leverage, leeway, wide margin, latitude, clearance

6 **liberality**, carte blanche, blank cheque, free hand, laxness, laxity, licence, excess, excess of freedom, libertinism, immoderation, uninhibitedness, intemperance, incontinence, free love, illicit love, lack of discipline, unruliness, abandon, abandonment, no holds barred, free fight, licentiousness, wantonness, permissiveness, permissive society, nothing in one's way, one's own way, one's own devices, the run of, plenty of rope, enough rope to hang oneself, room to swing a cat, Liberty Hall (Inf), free-for-all (Inf)

7 **free person**, citizen, free citizen, freeman, freewoman, voter, burgher, burgess, bourgeois, freedman, freedwoman, ex-slave, no slave, ex-convict, released prisoner, escapee, free agent, freelancer (*or* freelance), free spirit, individualist, rugged individualist, independent, cross-bencher, mugwump, independent voter, undecided voter, floating voter, states' righter (US), isolationist, nonpartisan, neutral, moderate, liberal, free-trader, capitalist, women's libber (Inf), undecided (Inf), don't know (Inf), ex-con (Sl)

8 **free-thinker**, rationalist, humanist, atheist, nonbeliever, latitudinarian, libertarian, bohemian, hippie, libertine, eccentric, nonconformist, loner (Inf), lone wolf (Inf)

ADJECTIVES

9 **free**, freeborn, emancipated, liberated, franchised, enfranchised, authorized, constitutional, inalienable (*or* unalienable), national, unilateral, autonomous, self-governing, self-determining, self-ruling, autarkic (*or* autarchic), unconfined, unrestrained, unregulated, unhindered, unimpeded, unshackled, unfettered, unbridled, uncurbed, unbound, unchained, unmuzzled, unchecked, ungoverned, acquitted, on the loose, at large, escaped, discharged, released, freed, scot-free, privileged, exempt, nonliable, excepted, immune, noninvolved, secluded, nonaligned, nonpartisan, neutral, isolationist, noninterventional, free-trade, self-regulating, self-regulatory, open, capitalistic, broad-minded, open-minded, unbiased, unprejudiced, uninfluenceable, uninfluenced, cross-bench, undecided, floating,

moderate, just, tolerant, liberal, libertarian

10 **independent**, individual, self-employed, one's own boss, freelance, wildcat, free-minded, free-spirited, one's own man (*or* woman), maverick, individualistic, self-reliant, self-sufficient, self-contained, self-supporting, self-motivated, inner-directed, one's own master, unsubjected, unwedded (*or* unwed), unmarried, footloose, fancy-free, footloose and fancy-free, freewheeling, free as air, free as the wind, free as a bird, left to one's own devices, ungoverned, ungovernable, anarchic, uncontrolled, uncompelled, uninfluenced, unattached, detached, indifferent, free to choose, enjoying liberty, unconventional, breakaway, dissenting, free-thinking, rationalist, rationalistic, humanist, humanistic, atheistic(al), nonbelieving, latitudinarian, bohemian, nonconforming, eccentric, nonconformist, cowboy (Inf)

11 **ranging**, travelling, ranging freely, free-range, having full play, unconfined, untethered, unfettered, manoeuvrable

12 **unconditional**, unconditioned, unrestricted, unlimited, without strings, no strings attached, catch-as-catch-can (US), no holds barred, anything goes, absolute, discretionary, arbitrary, liberated, lax, excess, excessive, immoderate, loose, uninhibited, unbridled, intemperate, incontinent, unruly, abandoned, licentious, wanton, impure, permissive, wide-open (US inf), no catch (Inf), free-for-all (Inf)

13 **informal**, relaxed, casual, easy, easy-going, at ease, free and easy, at leisure, at home, out of harness, retired, familiar, frank, candid, open, self-expressive, free-speaking, plain-spoken, plain, uninhibited, unconstrained, spontaneous, willing, degage, unbuttoned (Inf)

VERBS

14 **be free**, go free, get free, sample freedom, breathe the air of freedom, escape, enjoy liberty, move freely, lack restraint, take French leave, have a free mind, speak freely, worship freely, publish freely, have artistic licence, have no censorship, teach freely, have freedom of choice, keep an open mind, have a liberated mind, tolerate, think freely, have free will, support human rights, support equal rights, support civil rights, support women's liberation, have a say-so (Inf)

15 **set free**, emancipate, manumit, enfranchise, franchise, liberate, release, let go, let off, excuse, grant immunity, give diplomatic immunity, exempt, except, loose, unchain, unfetter, unbind, untie, rescue, deliver, extricate, give scope, allow initiative, give one his head, allow full play, give the run of, give someone carte blanche, give someone a blank cheque, facilitate, give a free hand, give the freedom of,

give one leeway, give free rein to, allow enough rope, leave one to his own devices, leave to one's own choice, live and let live, keep hands off, not interfere, not tamper, not meddle, not butt in, let sleeping dogs lie, not cramp one's style (Inf)

16 **be independent**, have a will of one's own, go one's own way, have one's way, have (or do) it one's own way, use one's own initiative, fend for oneself, shift for oneself, become a free agent, freelance, stand alone, stand up for one's rights, stand on one's own two feet, stay in control, have the ball at one's feet, have authority, have self-reliance, have independent means, stay unmarried, ask no favours, call no man master, suit oneself, please oneself, do as one pleases, do as one chooses, do what one likes, vote independent, remain neutral, do one's own thing, follow one's bent, roam, stray, drift, drop out, paddle one's own canoe, act eccentric, live in a bohemian way, go it alone (Inf)

17 **be informal**, take it easy, feel at home, make oneself at home, feel free, feel at liberty, let one's hair down, show candour

18 **have scope**, have the run of, have the freedom of, range, have room to breathe, have play, have a free hand, have elbowroom, have one's head, have plenty of rope, have enough rope to hang oneself

19 **liberalize**, live immoderately, have a free hand, have carte blanche, have a blank cheque, lack restraint, let oneself go, let go, permit oneself, make bold to, take liberties, presume, make free with, cut loose, run wild, sow one's wild oats, have one's fling, let one's hair down, go too far, pull out all the stops, lack discipline, support free love, go all out (Inf), go flat out (Inf), let it all hang out (Sl)

ADVERBS

20 **freely**, free, with immunity, autonomously, independently, alone, by oneself, individually, individualistically, on one's own initiative, on one's own account, of one's own accord, of one's own volition, of one's own free will, at one's own discretion, on one's own responsibility, with self-reliance, with self-motivation, free-mindedly, broad-mindedly, open-mindedly, tolerantly, moderately, neutrally, justly, without affiliation, indifferently, with an indifferent attitude, rationalistically, atheistically, eccentrically, on one's own say-so (Inf), all on one's lonesome (Inf)

21 **excessively**, with excess, with full play, unconditionally, with no holds barred, with no strings attached, arbitrarily, immoderately, loosely, without control, without restraint, without stint, unreservedly, with abandon, intemperately, incontinently, licentiously, wantonly, impurely, permissively

22 **informally**, in an informal way, casually, easily, familiarly, frankly, candidly, with candour, freely, openly, plainly, spontaneously, willingly

699 Restraint

NOUNS

1 **restraint**, constraint, suppression, repression, strictness, coercion, hindrance, impediment, obstacle, stumbling block, retardation, deceleration, slowness, slowing down, stopping, prevention, control, strict control, curb, check, veto, ban, bar, blackball, prohibition, restriction, restraint, legal restraint, injunction, interdict, Official Secrets Act, D-notice, press laws, severity, discipline, penalty, fine, punishment, authority, duress, pressure, censorship, subdual, putting down, quelling, quashing, suppressant, squelching, smothering, stifling, throttling, crushing, smashing, crackdown, limitation, allotment, stipulation, qualification, requirement, limiting factor, limit, speed limit, limitations, retrenchment, constriction, squeeze, cuts, curtailment, circumscription, exclusive rights, exclusivity, copyright, circle, charmed circle, demarcation, restricted area, no-go area, off-limits area (US), cramping one's style (Inf)

▶ *701 Subjection, 262 Contraction, 218 Cessation, 709 Veto, 694 Obedience, 661 Hindrance, 688 Authority, 546 Obliteration, 528 Information, 532 Publication, 690 Severity, 879 Punishment, 147 Exclusion, 302 Limit*

2 **economic restraint**, economic pressure, rationing, ration, freeze, price freeze, pay freeze, price control, credit squeeze, rate-capping, restrictive practice, restraint of trade, monopoly, cartel, closed shop, intervention, interventionism, protectionism, price-fixing, protection racket, mercantilism, mercantile system tariff, protective tariff, tariff wall, embargo, Anti-Trust laws (US)

▶ *13 Economics, 14 Finance*

3 **self-restraint**, self-control, self-discipline, discipline, temperance, continence, abstinence, abstemiousness, asceticism, ascesis, spartanism, moderation, inhibition, introversion, formality, reserved nature, reserve, modesty, shyness, quietness, embarrassment, stiffness

▶ *869 Self-Restraint, 242 Moderation, 810 Modesty, 563 Voicelessness*

4 **detention**, quarantine, blockade, siege, starving out, guarding, care, custodianship, charge, ward, custody, protective custody, impoundment, restriction on movement, curfew, remand, refusal of bail, arrest, house arrest, sentence, incarceration, imprisonment, internment, confinement, solitary confine-

ment, captivity, kidnapping, bondage, slavery, servitude, durance (Arch), immurement (Arch), time (Inf), BOT (balance of time) (US sl), stretch (Sl), porridge (Sl), lag (Sl), bird (Sl)

▶ *670 Attack, 702 Prison*

5 **means of restraint**, diet, fast, ban, veto, damper, governor, drag, cramp, clamp, restraining hand, gag, muzzle, leash, lead, tether, hobble, reins, bridle, bit, halter, harness, collar, yoke, corset, girdle, straitjacket, fetters, bonds, irons, chains, shackles, ball and chain, handcuffs, manacles, trammels, bilboes, stocks, pillory, cuffs (Inf), bracelets (Sl)

6 **lawmaker**, legislator, judge, member of parliament (MP), District Attorney (DA), policeman (*or* policewoman), enforcer, censor, monopolist, protectionist, restrictionist, disciplinarian, dictator, tyrant, kidnapper, ascetic, Spartan, interventionalist, mercantilist, monetarist, warder, warden (US), jailer, prison guard, screw (Sl)

▶ *16 Law*

7 **charge**, ward, patient, shut-in, hostage, prisoner, jailbird, inmate, convict, con (Sl), old lag (Sl)

▶ *60 Medicine*

VERBS

8 **restrain**, constrain, suppress, repress, hold back, hold down, oppress, close down, coerce, hinder, impede, bottle up, clog up, retard, decelerate, slow, stop, put a stop to, vote down, veto, blackball, brake, put the brakes on, act as a brake, prevent, pull back, control, curb, check, hold in check, ban, bar, prohibit, restrict, put a damper on, damper, drag, cramp, clamp down on, clamp, issue an injunction, interdict, regulate, discipline, keep order, police, patrol, impose a fine, punish, pressure, censor, black out, subdue, put down, crack down, quell, quash, squelch, smother, stifle, throttle, crush, smash, allot, stipulate, require qualifications, list requirements, limit, enforce a speed limit, retrench, constrict, squeeze, cut, curtail, demarcate, draw the line, circumscribe, keep within bounds, stop from spreading, hem in, box in, hold at bay, localize, hold exclusive rights, copyright, join a charmed circle, exclude, keep out, rope out, sit on (Inf), put the lid on (Inf), cramp one's style (Inf)

9 **economize**, ration, freeze prices, control prices, freeze pay, squeeze credit, cap rates, restrain trade, monopolize, form a cartel, operate a closed shop, intervene, restrict supplies, restrict consumption, hold down inflation, protect, restrict imports, impose a tariff, impose an embargo

10 **restrain oneself**, show self-restraint, control oneself, demonstrate self-control, deny oneself, hold oneself back, hold back, diet, slim, fast, stay within one's limits, know when to

stop, keep calm, keep quiet, say nothing, abstain, take the pledge, live in a spartan way, live like a monk (*or* nun), take a cold bath (*or* shower), go on the wagon (Inf), keep one's wool (Inf), keep a stiff upper lip (Inf), keep one's shirt on (Inf), keep one's hair on (Inf), keep one's cool (Sl), stay cool (Sl), cool out (US sl)

11 **detain**, quarantine, put into quarantine, blockade, block, siege, besiege, starve out, guard, take custody of, protect, impound, restrict one's movement, impose a curfew, remand, refuse bail, arrest, make an arrest, put under arrest, take into custody, apprehend, seize, sentence, incarcerate, imprison, send to prison, throw in prison, take prisoner, intern, confine, keep under lock and key, keep behind bars, make captive, kidnap, take hostage, hold in captivity, hold incommunicado, hold, put in bondage, nab (Inf), collar (Inf), haul in (Inf), run in (Inf), serve time (Inf), serve a stretch (Sl), do porridge (Sl), lag (Sl), do bird (Sl), pinch (Sl), nick (Sl), send up the river (US sl), go to the big house (US sl)

12 **gag**, muzzle, silence, interdict, shout down, leash, lead, tether, hobble, rein in, keep a tight rein on, put a ball and chain on, harness, collar, yoke, girdle, straitjacket, fetter, bind, tie up (*or* down), tie hand and foot, tie, throw in irons, chain up (*or* down), chain, shackle, handcuff, manacle

ADJECTIVES

13 **restraining**, restrained, under restraint, constrained, kept under constraint, under the thumb, suppressive, suppressing, oppressive, suppressed, strict, coercive, slow, preventive, controllable, controlling, controlled, under control, under remission, strictly controlled, prohibitive, prohibited, conditional, restrictive, restricting, restricted, tied down, with strings attached, in check, injunctive, interdictive, severe, disciplined, punished, authoritative, pressurized, censorial, censorious, censoring, censored, banned, stifling, limiting, limited, required, constrictive, narrow, cramped, kept on a lead, circumscriptive, exclusive, copyrighted, rationed, frozen, rate-capped, monopolistic, interventional, protective, embargoed

14 **self-restrained**, temperate, self-disciplined, self-controlled, dieting, fasting, continent, abstinent, abstemious, ascetic, spartan, moderate, inhibiting, inhibited, introversive, formal, reserved, quiet, modest, shy, embarrassing, embarrassed, pent up, stiff, uptight (Inf), cool (Inf), ultracool (US sl)

15 **detained**, quarantined, shut-in, confined to bed, housebound, snowbound, fogbound, besieged, custodial, arrested, under arrest, under house arrest, sentenced, incarcerated, im-

prisoned, in custody, on remand, confined, captive, in captivity, kidnapped, enslaved, gagged, muzzled, in bonds, in irons, serving a sentence, doing time (Inf), doing porridge (Sl), up the river (US sl), in the big house (US sl)

ADVERBS

16 **under restraints**, strictly, coercively, slowly, preventively, controllably, with controls, under controls, prohibitively, conditionally, with conditions, restrictively, under restrictions, interdictively, severely, authoritatively, censorial, censoriously, circumscriptively, within limits, within bounds, exclusively, protectively, while confined to bed, while in captivity

17 **with self-restraint**, with self-control, with self-discipline, temperately, abstemiously, by abstaining, moderately, in moderation, formally, as a formality, modestly, with modesty, shyly, in a shy manner, embarrassingly, with embarrassment, to one's embarrassment, to one's chagrin, stiffly

700   Liberation

NOUNS

1 **liberation**, freedom, freeing, setting free, deliverance, delivery, release, disencumberment, emancipation, Emancipation Proclamation (US), manumission, unhanding, unbinding, unchaining, unshackling, unfettering, unknotting, unleashing, unbridling, unburdening, mental freedom, independent mind, liberated spirit, liberal thinking, loosing, unloosing, disengagement, decontrol, deregulation, liberalization, relaxation, discharge, dismissal, extrication, parole, bail, demobilization, disbanding, escape, rescue, redemption, pardoning, absolving, salvation, relief, reprieve, exemption, exemptibility, absolution, forgiveness of sins, forgiveness, acquittal, acquittance, quittance, quitclaim

▶ 698 Freedom, 639 Deliverance, 136 Separation, 507 Wisdom, 767 Relief, 848 Exemption, 704 Cancellation, 839 Forgiveness

2 **equal opportunity**, equal status, equal rights, ERA (Equal Rights Amendment) (US), civil rights, women's liberation, feminism, minority rights, animal liberation, animal-rights activism, gay liberation, women's lib (Inf)

▶ 481 Discrimination

3 **liberator**, emancipator, manumitter, deliverer, rescuer, absolver, redeemer, The Redeemer, saviour, The Saviour, escapee, parolee, animal-rights activist, ERA supporter (US), women's libber (Inf)

▶ 7 Religion

VERBS

4 **liberate**, free, set free, set at liberty, set at large, deliver, release, emancipate, manumit, disencumber, unhand, untie one's hands, unbind, unchain, unbolt, unlock, uncage, unshackle, unfetter, unknot, unleash, unbridle, unburden, give free rein, free mentally, have an independent mind, loose, loosen, unloose, unloosen, cast loose, let (or turn) loose, let out, let go of, let go free, disengage, decontrol, deregulate, liberalize, relax restrictions, lift controls, life a curfew, discharge, dismiss, extricate, parole, put on parole, bail, let out on bail, grant bail to, discharge, demobilize, disband, send home, release, escape, rescue, redeem, save, deliver, relieve, exempt, reprieve, acquit, pardon, absolve, pay off a debt, pay off a mortgage, go over the hill (Inf), go over the wall (Inf), go bail for (Inf), demob (Inf), let off the hook (Sl)

5 **be liberated**, achieve liberty, free oneself, gain one's freedom, go free, go scot-free, go at liberty, go AWOL (absent without leave), extricate oneself, break loose, eluctate, break out, break away, get away, get free, get off, get off scot-free, get out of, tear loose, get out, break (or burst) one's bonds, throw off the yoke, throw off, shake off, slip the collar, assert oneself, get the bit between one's teeth, stand on one's own two feet, fight for freedom, jump the wall, tunnel out, shake (US inf), shake free (US inf), go on the lam (US sl)

6 **treat equally**, grant equal rights to, grant equality to, enforce civil rights, enfranchise, abolish discrimination, end racial discrimination, end sexual discrimination, support women's liberation, end age discrimination, adopt affirmative action

ADJECTIVES

7 **liberated**, liberating, free, freed, emancipated, unshackled, unfettered, independent-minded, deregulated, liberalized, released, paroled, on parole, bailed, out on bail, redemptive, absolving, absolved, saved, rescued, exemptible, exempted, acquitted, scot-free

ADVERBS

8 **free**, scot-free, freely, with a free spirit, in a liberating atmosphere, carefree, without a care, without regulations, unshackled, unrestricted, unconfined, without chains, without discrimination, fairly, with equal chance

701   Subjection

NOUNS

1 **subjection**, subjugation, inferiority, inferior status, lower status, inferior rank, satellite status, subordination, subordinate position, subordinate role, subordinacy, junior rank, juniority, dependence, dependency, mutual dependence, symbiosis, wardship, tutelage, apprenticeship, obedience, subservience, servitude, servility, service, employment, employ,

allegiance, loss of rights, disenfranchisement, disfranchisement, loss of battle, defeat, loss of freedom, captivity, compulsory servitude, involuntary servitude, constraint, indentureship, bondage, enslavement, slavery, white slavery, peonage, feudalism, vassalage, thraldom, serfdom, villeinage

▶ *127 Inferiority, 664 Cooperation, 694 Obedience, 808 Servility, 847 Duty, 877 Immorality, 676 War, 683 Failure, 702 Prison*

2 **domination**, mastery, overpowering, overcoming, discipline, restraint, control, conquest, conquering, suppression, oppression, repression, intimidation, colonialism, tyranny

▶ *233 Influence, 688 Authority, 690 Severity, 12 Government and Politics*

3 **subordinate**, inferior, assistant, helper, apprentice, student, learner, servant, right-hand man, secretary, employee, staff member, conscript, substitute, underling, minion, tool, lackey, flunkey, sycophant, fag, low man on the totem pole (Inf), sidekick (Inf), gofer (US sl), grunt (US sl), stooge (Sl)

▶ *697 Servant*

4 **dependent**, child, foster child, orphan, junior, protégé, charge, ward, hanger-on, follower, satellite, parasite

▶ *206 Youth*

5 **subjected person**, loser, surrenderer, captive, hostage, prisoner, POW (prisoner of war), inmate, slave, white slave, liege, chattel, indentured servant, bondsman, bondwoman, bondslave, thrall, concubine, galley salve, serf, villein, peon, puppet

VERBS

6 **subject**, subjugate, subdue, make inferior, lower, humble, subordinate, hold down, keep down, give a subordinate role to, have at one's mercy, do what one likes with, humiliate, walk (all) over, walk on, sit on, regiment, tame, bring into line, bring to one's knees, bring to heel, bring low, keep under one's thumb, twist around one's little finger, keep at one's beck and call, lead by the nose, kick around, browbeat, henpeck, treat like dirt (under one's feet), exploit, treat like shit (Sl), trample on, tread on, make dependent, tutor, apprentice, employ, disenfranchise, disfranchise, reduce to servitude, take away one's freedom, rob of freedom, indenture, colonize, railroad (Inf), use as a doormat (Inf)

7 **defeat**, vanquish, capture, take prisoner, lead in triumph, lead captive, make a hostage of, constrain, dominate, overpower, overcome, master, prevail over, discipline, restrain, control, conquer, suppress, oppress, repress, intimidate, tyrannize

8 **be subject to**, be subjected to, have inferior rank, hold a subordinate position, depend on, have a mutual dependence, pay tribute to, pay homage to, grovel, eat out of one's hands, obey, bear allegiance to, owe loyalty to, serve, wait on, serve involuntarily, lose a battle, lose one's freedom, become a slave, become a hostage, fall into the clutches of, lose one's rights, serve as a doormat for (Inf)

ADJECTIVES

9 **subject**, subjecting, subjected, in subjection, in one's power, in one's control, in one's pocket, under one's thumb, like putty in one's hands, eating out of one's hands, subjugated, brought to one's knees, brought low, made to grovel, brought to heel, treated like dirt (under one's feet), treated like shit (Sl), led by the nose, kicked around, browbeaten, henpecked, inferior, lower, substitute, subordinate, under one's command, under the sway of, in the hands of, in the clutches of, like a puppet on a string, at one's feet, at one's beck and call, junior, dependent, tied to one's apron strings, at one's mercy, symbiotic(al), tutorial, apprenticed, subservient, obedient, servile, serving, employed, in the pay of, answering to, employable, captive, in captivity, taken prisoner, in bondage, in bonds, in chains, in harness, unfree, not independent, compulsory, involuntary, indentured, enslaving, enslaved, in slavery, reduced to slavery, sold into slavery, feudal

10 **dominating**, overpowering, overcoming, controlling, controllable, conquering, suppressive, suppressing, oppressive, oppressing, repressive, repressing, intimidating, colonial, tyrannical

ADVERBS

11 **under subjection**, while in one's power, under orders, at the beck and call of, dependently, subserviently, servilely, like a servant, in the pay of, in captivity, in slavery, involuntarily, against one's will

702 **Prison**

NOUNS

1 **prison**, jail (or gaol), county jail (US), city jail (US), jailhouse (US), (state) penitentiary (US), Sing Sing (US), women's penitentiary (US), federal prison (US), state prison (US), lockup, compound, pound, dungeon, oubliette, prison camp, concentration camp, Auschwitz, Buchenwald, labour camp, Gulag, prison colony, Devil's Island, prison farm (US), debtor's prison, maximum-security prison, Wormwood Scrubs, Dartmoor, Broadmoor, Alcatraz (US), minimum-security prison, house of detention, house of correction, correction facility (US), halfway house, reformatory, reform school, detention centre, borstal, young offender institution, youth custody centre, detention home (US), community home, ap-

proved school (Brit), military prison, guard-house, bring (US), stockade (US)

2 **the inside (Inf)**, borstal (Inf), pen (US inf), glasshouse (Inf), little school (US sl), nick (Sl), quod (Sl), clink (Sl), cooler (Sl), stir (Sl), slammer (Sl), sneezer (US sl), jug (Sl), can (Sl), bucket (Sl), tank (US sl), hoosegow (or hoosgow) (US sl), chokey (or choky) (Sl), poky (or pokey) (US sl), the big house (US sl), big school (US sl)

▶ *661 Hindrance*

3 **prison cell**, jail cell, solitary confinement, death cell, death row (US), solitary (Inf), bullpen (US inf), flowery (dell) (Sl), birdcage (Sl), icebox (US sl), the hole (Sl)

4 **prison sentence**, period of detention, life, time (Inf), BOT (balance of time) (US Black sl), stretch (Sl), fistful (Sl), handful (Sl), five fingers (Sl), both hands (Sl), the book (Sl), porridge (Sl), vacation (US sl), lag (Sl), bird (Sl)

5 **prisoner**, prisoner behind bars, POW (prisoner of war), prisoner of conscience, political prisoner, condemned prisoner, hostage, captive, convict, inmate, detainee, chain-gang member (US), government man (Aus arch), lifer (Inf), jailbird (or gaolbird), guest of His (or Her) Majesty (Inf), con (Sl), yardbird (US sl), rock crusher (US sl), zebra (US sl), old lag (Sl)

6 **prison officer**, prison governor, warder, warden (US), prison guard, keeper, correctional officer (US), custodian, jailer (or gaoler), turnkey, screw (Sl), the Man (US Black sl), horse (US sl)

7 **imprisonment**, confinement, solitary confinement, detention, detainment at His (or Her) Majesty's pleasure, detention in a young offender institution, internment, captivity, corrective training, durance (Arch), forced labour, immurement (Arch), solitary (Inf), porridge (Sl)

ADJECTIVES

8 **imprisoned**, in prison, under arrest, serving a sentence, captive, in captivity, on remand, in detention, detained, detained at His (or Her) Majesty's pleasure, confined, interned, incarcerated, restricted, locked up, under lock and key, behind bars, in solitary confinement, in solitary (Inf), doing time (Inf), in (Inf), inside (Inf), in the nick (Sl), in stir (Sl), in the cooler (Sl), on ice (Sl), buried (US sl), doing porridge (Sl), up the river (US sl), in the big house (US sl)

VERBS

9 **imprison**, take prisoner, jail, confine, intern, incarcerate, impound, lock up, put away, detain, detain at His (or Her) Majesty's pleasure, lock up and throw away the key, put in solitary confinement, immure (Arch), put in solitary (Inf), throw in the tank (US sl), throw in the cooler (Sl), jug (Sl), send up the river (US

sl), send up (US sl), send down (Sl), put in the big house (US sl)

10 **be in prison**, serve a sentence, join the chain gang (US), do time (Inf), enjoy His (or Her) Majesty's hospitality (Inf), land in the cooler (Sl), serve a stretch (Sl), do porridge (Sl), do bird (Sl), lag (Sl)

ADVERBS

11 **captively**, while in prison, under lock and key, on the inside (Inf)

703 Commission

NOUNS

1 **commission**, commissioning, delegation, devolution, devolvement, decentralization, representation, deputation, empowerment, federation, power to act, power, power of attorney, entrustment, entrusting, responsibility, assignment, assigning, appointment, patronage, accreditation, nomination, election, voting, ordination, ordainment, installation, instalment, instatement, induction, inauguration, investiture, enthronement, crowning, coronation

▶ *580 Selection, 222 Substitution, 235 Power, 16 Law, 12 Government and Politics, 7 Religion, 812 Celebration*

2 **engagement**, employment, enlistment, enrollment, conscription, recruitment, mission, errand, task, duty, job, office, activity, exercise, undertaking, function, quest

▶ *642 Activity, 597 Undertaking*

3 **authority**, written authority, delegated authority, vicarious authority, authorization, permission, warranty, warrant, charge, mandate, trust, permit, charter, writ, licence, brevet, diploma, proxy, passport

▶ *688 Authority, 708 Permission, 692 Command*

4 **council**, board, deputation, party, working party, group, delegation, committee, subcommittee, crew, establishment, agency, trusteeship, executorship, bureaucracy, public service, civil service, mission, embassy, legation, envoy, governorship, regentship, regency

5 **commissioner**, representative, official representative, elected representative, delegate, nominee, appointee, assignee, licensee, official, officer, bureaucrat, public servant, civil servant, envoy, ambassador, governor, regent, legate, diplomat, consul, attaché, functionary, emissary, plenipotentiary, deputy, messenger, missionary, agent, proxy, executor, trustee

▶ *706 Delegate*

VERBS

6 **commission**, commit, delegate, devolve, decentralize, appoint a representative, appoint, name, assign, accredit, deputize, depute, empower, grant power of attorney, entrust, trust with, patronize, consign, give responsibility,

put in one's hands, turn over to, give to, leave it to, nominate, elect, vote, ordain, install (*or* instal), instate, induct, inaugurate, invest, enthrone, crown, anoint

7 **engage**, employ, hire, enlist, enrol, conscript, recruit, post, send on an errand, go on a mission, quest after, undertake

8 **authorize**, give written authority, delegate authority, give permission, permit, warrant, charge, mandate, give a mandate, put in commission, charter, issue a writ, license, brevet, issue a diploma, earn a diploma, appoint a proxy, issue a passport

ADJECTIVES

9 **commissioned**, delegating, delegated, devolutionary, decentralized, representational, deputized, empowered, inaugural, responsible, assigned, appointed, accredited, nominated, authorized, vicarious, warranted, mandated, plenipotentiary, bureaucratic, ambassadorial, legationary, gubernatorial, offical, agential

10 **engaged**, employed, employable, functional, paid, mercenary

ADVERBS

11 **under commission**, by commission, responsibly, with responsibility, vicariously, by proxy, per pro, pp, *per procurationem* (L), *in loco parentis* (L), bureaucratically, like a bureaucracy, officially, with official approval, by delegated authority, under orders

704 Cancellation

NOUNS

1 **cancellation**, cancelling, nullification, annulment, repealing, repeal, reversion, discontinuation, discontinuance, waiver, suspension, setting aside, invalidation, disallowance, rescinding, rescindment, abjuration, abrogation, negation, revocation, reversal, recall, rejection, repudiation, amnesty, reprieve, abolition, abolition of sins, salvation, abolishment, elimination, write-off, censorship, deletion, removal, reneging, recantation, retraction, retractation, obliteration, defacement

▶ *221 Reversion, 536 Negation, 600 Nonuse, 7 Religion, 546 Obliteration*

2 **termination**, cessation, stoppage, discontinuance, nolle prosequi (Fml), resignation, honourable discharge, dismissal, discharge, expulsion, firing, redundancy, suspension, lay-off, furlough (US), services no longer required, cancellation of contract, recall, removal, ejection, dishonourable discharge, one's cards (Inf), the axe (Inf), the push (Inf), the bowler hat (Inf), golden handshake (Inf), the sack (Sl), the boot (Sl), the shove (Sl), the bounce (US sl), the bullet (Sl), the kiss off (US sl), the chop (Sl), walking papers (US sl),

marching orders (Inf), the old heave-ho (Sl), the elbow (Sl), the big E (Inf)

▶ *218 Cessation, 349 Expulsion*

3 **new beginning**, rebirth, reformation, renaissance, fresh start, clean sweep, tabula rasa, clean slate (Inf), new leaf (Inf)

▶ *201 Newness*

4 **cancelling out**, neutralizing, neutralization, making equal, equalizing, balance, equal weight, counterbalance, counterweight, sash weight, counterpoise, counterorder, countermand, counteraction, contradiction, refutation

5 **abrogator**, rescinder, revoker, reverser, rejecter, repudiator, repriever, reformer, new broom, abolitionist, reneger, recanter, retractor, defacer, contradicter, refuter, censor, British Board of Film Censors, Motion Picture Association of America

VERBS

6 **cancel**, nullify, make null and void, void, disallow, reject, negate, abolish, eliminate, suspend, call off, abandon, invalidate, withdraw, set aside, waiver, retract, renounce, abjure, quash, overrule, rescind, abrogate, repeal, reverse, recall, revoke, reprieve, offer amnesty to, renege, recant, repudiate, annul, annihilate, obliterate, destroy, delete, cut, erase, efface, write off, do away with, strike out, black out, blot out, cross out, censor, remove all signs of, remove, expunge, scribble out, scrub out, wipe out, deface, kill (Inf)

7 **terminate**, stop, dismiss, discontinue, cancel one's contract, resign, remove, bench (US), suspend, lay off, eject, discharge, give a dishonourable discharge to, cashier, dethrone, depose, divest, unfrock, strike off the register, oust, demote, fire (Inf), axe (Inf), give someone the axe (Inf), give someone the golden handshake (Inf), give someone the (old) heave-ho (Inf), sack (Sl), bump (Sl), kiss off (Sl), give someone the chop (Sl), get (*or* cop) the bullet (Sl), give someone their marching orders (Inf)

8 **be reborn**, have a new beginning, reform, have a fresh start, wipe the slate clean (Inf)

9 **cancel out**, cancel, eliminate each other, make neutral, neutralize, make equal, equalize, countervail, offset, weigh equally, weigh up against, counterbalance, counterweigh, balance, counterpoise, work both ways, cut both ways, work against, issue a counterorder, countermand, counteract, turn the tables on, contradict, refute

ADJECTIVES

10 **cancelled**, abrogated, stopped, annulled, nullified, null and void, voided, invalid, invalidated, killed, dead, repealed, revoked, rescinded, rescindable, set aside, recalled, negated, reprieved, terminated, abolished, laid

off, suspended, discharged, fired, reborn, reformative, reformed, censored, deleted, struck
out, struck off, wiped out, defaced, neutralized, equalized, balanced, counteracting,
counteractive, contrary, bowler-hatted (Inf),
fired (Inf), axed (Inf), sacked (Inf)

ADVERBS
11 **invalidly**, without validity, as a write-off, as
a retraction, as a counteraction, with equal
force, under censorship, with a dishonourable
discharge, like a new beginning, with a clean
slate (Inf), with a golden handshake (Inf)

705 Resignation

NOUNS
1 **resignation**, relinquishment, departure,
withdrawal, renouncement, renunciation,
surrender, quitting, quitting work, giving notice, handing in one's notice, calling it quits,
notice of resignation, forced resignation, voluntary resignation, retirement, retiral (Scot),
abdication, abandonment, throwing in the
towel (or sponge) (Inf)
▶ *345 Departure, 598 Relinquishment, 878 Reward,*
12 Government and Politics
2 **stoicism**, sanguinity, phlegm, indifference,
coldness
3 **resigner**, retiree, pensioner, abdicator, quitter, relinquisher, renouncer
4 **resignedness**, acceptance, reconciliation, acquiescence, coming to terms, resigned to one's
fate
VERBS
5 **resign**, offer (or tender) one's resignation,
hand in one's resignation, send in one's papers, give notice, quit work, quit, call it quits
(US), hand in one's notice, retire (from), go
into retirement, take early retirement, draw
one's social security benefits, draw one's pension, stand down, stand (or step) aside, abdicate, renounce the throne, give up the crown,
abandon, desert, leave one's post, leave, depart, withdraw, vacate, tear oneself away from,
drop, let go of, give up, resign under pressure,
forgo, renunciate, surrender, relinquish,
throw in the towel (or sponge) (Inf), chuck (in
or up) (Inf), jack (or pack) it in (Inf), take
someone's job and shove it (US sl)
6 **resign oneself**, accept, acquiesce, come to
terms with
ADJECTIVES
7 **resigning**, resigned, abdicating, abdicated,
retiring, retired, in retirement, past, former,
one-time, sometime, late, emeritus, on social
security benefits, on a pension, pensioned,
pensioned-off, forced out, outgoing, renunciatory
8 **resigned**, accepting, acquiescent, stoical,
sanguine, phlegmatic, indifferent

ADVERBS
9 **stoically**, sanguinely, phlegmatically, indifferently
10 **by resigning**, by retiring, in retirement, formerly, lately

706 Delegate

NOUNS
1 **delegate**, elected person, nominee, appointed person, appointee, envoy, emissary,
representative, elected representative, official
representative, political representative, member of Parliament (MP), Parliamentarian, Congressman (US), Congresswoman (US), Representative (US), Senator (US), minister, cabinet
member, diplomat (or diplomatist), diplomatic officer, ambassador, legate, high commissioner, commissioner, chargé d'affaires,
consul, negotiator, messenger, agent, middleman, intermediary, clerk, councillor, deputy,
depute (Scot), convention delegate, conference delegate, workshop delegate
▶ *12 Government and Politics, 707 Deputy*
2 **representative body**, delegation, legation,
diplomatic staff, diplomatic corps, corps diplomatique (CD), diplomatic service, foreign
service, consulate service, embassy, consulate,
mission, trade delegation, Parliament, Congress (US), Senate (US), council, town council,
county council, parish council, town meeting
(US), city council (US), board of aldermen,
aldermanic board, official body, negotiating
body, committee, forum, quorum, working
party, round table, panel, workshop, convention, conference, conclave
3 **delegation**, authorization, appointment,
nomination, assignment, election, delegation
of work, delegation of power, shared responsibility, decentralization, devolution, devolvement, job sharing, deputation, deputizing, deputing, assignment of work, consignation
▶ *326 Transfer*
VERBS
4 **delegate**, depute, deputize, assign, consign,
appoint, nominate, elect, authorize, commission, empower, entrust, spread the load, job-
share, share the work, devolve, decentralize,
transfer, turn over to
5 **represent**, act for, stand for, speak for, substitute for, represent the interests of, serve as a
representative, act as proxy for, attend a council meeting, attend a convention, attend a
conference, serve on a working party
▶ *707 Deputy*
ADJECTIVES
6 **delegated**, delegable, elected, nominated,
appointed, representative, Parliamentary,
Congressional (US), Senatorial (US), ministerial, diplomatic, ambassadorial, legatine,

legationary, consular, intermediary, deputy

7 **decentralized**, devolved, shared, deputized, deputed, assigned, consigned

ADVERBS

8 **representatively**, as a representative, in Parliament, in Congress (US), Congressionally (US), in the Senate (US), Senatorially (US), ministerially, diplomatically, with diplomacy, like an ambassador

707 Deputy

NOUNS

1 **deputy**, assistant, right-hand man, second-in-command, number two, aide, lieutenant, deputy prime minister, deputy chairman, deputy sheriff (US), viceregent, nuncio, vice president, vice chairman, vice chancellor, vice admiral, viceroy, vice consul, proconsul, propraetor (*or* propretor), vicar, vicar-general, executive assistant, helper, secretary, girl Friday, auxiliary, relief worker, temporary worker, spokesperson, spokesman, spokeswoman, public relations man (*or* woman), messenger, power behind the throne, temp (Inf), *éminence grise* (Fr)

▶ *662 Help, 653 Management, 586 Persuasion, 533 News*

2 **alternative**, alternate (US), surrogate, proxy, substitute, sub, scrub (US), replacement, locum (tenens), reserve, understudy, double, stand-in, backup, stunt man (*or* woman), twelfth man, twentieth man (Aus), ghost-writer, whipping boy, pinch hitter (US), red-shirt (US sl)

▶ *222 Substitution, 27 Cricket, 38 Soccer, 22 Baseball, 19 American Football*

3 **agent**, go-between, representative, delegate, intermediary, middleman, trustee, broker, literary agent, contact, negotiator, arbitrator, mediator, lawyer, solicitor, attorney, barrister, diplomat, diplomatic agent, emissary, envoy, minister, ambassador, minister plenipotentiary, commissioner, legate, attaché, consul, consular agent, vice consul, consul-general, brief (Sl), matchmaker, pander (*or* panderer), pimp

▶ *664 Cooperation, 706 Delegate, 298 Interface, 16 Law, 12 Government and Politics*

VERBS

4 **substitute for**, act for, act on behalf of, act instead of, do duty for, (temporarily) replace, appear for, negotiate for, replace, understudy, double for, back up, stand in for, stand in the stead of, ghostwrite (*or* ghost), act as proxy, pinch-hit for (US inf), front for (US)

5 **represent**, negotiate, arbitrate, mediate, assist, help, aid, speak for, act as a mouthpiece for, act as broker for, act as go-between for, hold in trust, manage the business of, manage

the interests of, manage

6 **deputize**, depute, commission, delegate, authorize, entrust, empower, charge, designate, appoint, nominate

ADJECTIVES

7 **deputizing**, deputative, representing, acting, standing in, stand-in, substituting, substitute, diplomatic, ambassadorial, plenipotentiary, consular, proconsular, ministerial, deputy, intermediary, provisional, temporary, imitative, imitation, ersatz, second-best

ADVERBS

8 **by proxy**, indirectly, in (*or* on) behalf of, *pro persona* (p.p.) (L), for, diplomatically, like a diplomat, ministerially, imitatively, in imitation of

708 Permission

NOUNS

1 **permission**, authorization, leave, approval, nod of approval, consent, implied consent, approbation, blessing, benevolence, clearance, security clearance, top-secret clearance, authority, legality, law, mandate, sanction, endorsement, confirmation, ratification, verification, corroboration, validation, tolerance, toleration, dispensation, exemption, non-liability, connivance, acquiescence, concession, licence, free hand, carte blanche, blank cheque, freedom, easiness, indulgence, leniency, permissiveness, laissez-faire attitude, unconstraint, promiscuity, free love, permissive society, the sixties, the green light, the thumbs-up, the go-ahead (Inf), the OK (Inf), the magic word (Inf), the Open Sesame (Inf), the nod (Inf), the all clear (Inf)

▶ *851 Approval, 831 Benevolence, 848 Exemption, 698 Freedom, 660 Easiness, 691 Leniency*

2 **permit**, written permission, grant, warrant, warranty, charter, patent, letters patent, certificate, credentials, diploma, testimonial, recommendation, reference, character reference, seal, signature (on the dotted line), endorsement, voucher, ticket, admission ticket, docket, chit, licence, fishing licence, driving licence, MOT (Ministry of Transport) certificate, release, waiver, nihil obstat (Fml), imprimatur, clearance papers, work permit, green card, pass, passport, visa, password, safe-conduct pass, *laissez passer* (Fr), leave, sick leave, leave of absence, furlough, holiday, vacation, sabbatical, parole, stamp, rubber stamp, mark, cross

▶ *483 Evidence, 823 Marriage, 20 Angling, 70 Transport, 12 Government and Politics, 645 Leisure*

VERBS

3 **permit**, give permission, allow, let, make possible, authorize, approve, clear, sanction, en-

dorse, confirm, ratify, verify, corroborate, validate, tolerate, exempt, connive, acquiesce, countenance, license, legitimize, legalize, make legal, decriminalize, lift the ban on, not stand in the way of, enable, empower, remove all obstacles, facilitate, say yes to, give the green light, give thumbs up, sign (on the dotted line), consent, bless, give one's blessing, give dispensation, make concessions, grant immunity, compromise, give the OK (Inf), give the all clear (Inf), give the go-ahead (Inf), give the nod (Inf), say the magic word (Inf)

4 **be permissive**, be lax, indulge, spoil, favour, pamper, adopt a laissez-faire attitude, give someone his (or her) head, give someone a free hand, bend the rules, stretch the point, not cramp someone's style, not stand in the way of, allow to have the run of, make it easy for, give someone a chance, allow someone to take liberties, let someone get away with it, relinquish authority, resign oneself to, give carte blanche to, give a blank cheque to, open the floodgates, let someone get away with murder (Inf)

5 **be permitted**, have permission, receive permission, have authorization, have clearance, have someone's blessing, have a free hand, take liberties, get away with it, have a blank cheque, get away with murder (Inf)

6 **ask permission**, beg permission, ask leave, beg leave, ask if one may, ask to be excused, request, petition, seek a favour, seek help, ask for someone's blessing

▶ *712 Request, 662 Help*

ADJECTIVES

7 **permitted**, allowed, authorized, warranted, sanctioned, licensed, legal, legalized, lawful, licit, decriminalized, chartered, patent, above board, legitimate, acceptable, worthwhile, approved, passed, unconditional, without strings, legit (Sl)

8 **permitting**, permissive, permissible, admissive, admissible, allowing, allowable, printable, sayable, unprohibitive, easy-going, tolerant, lenient, indulgent, *laissez faire* (Fr), loose, lax, easy come easy go, overindulgent, irresolute, unassertive, conniving

ADVERBS

9 **with permission**, under authorization, under licence, under warrant, under a charter, under a patent, legally, with legal protection, lawfully, legitimately, acceptably, unconditionally, without conditions, without strings, permissively, in a permissive fashion, permissibly, tolerantly, leniently, indulgently, loosely, laxly, with no questions asked, on the nod, irresolutely, unassertively, connivingly

709 Veto

NOUNS

1 **veto**, ban, embargo, injunction, interdiction, interdict, counterorder, countermand, check, curfew, thumbs down, turndown (US), red light, no, suspension, cancellation, denial, rejection, refusal, pocket veto (US), rebuff, abrogation, annulment, repealing, restriction, circumscription, exclusion, ostracism, debarment, forbidding, prohibition, taboo, repressive regime, repression, suppression, prevention, restraint, zoning law (US), obstruction, impediment, obstacle, interference, disallowance, abolition, prohibition of alcohol, temperance, Eighteenth Amendment (US), Volstead Act (US), unpermissibility, illicitness, illegality, illegitimacy, crackdown, excommunication

▶ *711 Refusal, 581 Rejection, 852 Disapproval, 147 Exclusion, 349 Expulsion, 704 Cancellation, 661 Hindrance*

2 **censorship**, proscription, deletion, blue pencil, classified document, secret document, top-secret document, restricted information, Official Secrets Act, news blackout, D-notice, banned book, the Index, *Index Librorum Prohibitorum* (L), film classification, R18 certificate, motion-picture rating (US), X-rated movie (US)

▶ *12 Government and Politics, 48 Literature, 457 Appearance, 529 Secrecy, 531 Concealment*

VERBS

3 **veto**, ban, impose a ban, embargo, interdict, counterorder, contermand, check, decide against, turn down, turn the thumbs down, give the thumbs down, withhold permission, refuse permission, deny, say no to, give the red light to, suspend, cancel, not tolerate, reject, refuse, rebuff, abrogate, annul, repeal, revoke, restrict, circumscribe, put out of bounds, make off-limits (US), exclude, shut the door on, ostracize, send to Coventry, blackball, debar, forbid, prohibit, disallow, prevent, obstruct, impede, inhibit, place an obstacle in someone's path, interfere, abolish, make illegal, outlaw, criminalize, put outside the law, crack down on, excommunicate

4 **censor**, proscribe, delete, blue-pencil, classify secret, make taboo, restrict, stop, repress, suppress, restrain, stifle, cancel, prohibit, ban a book, put on the Index, invoke the Official Secrets Act, issue a D-notice, black out, bleep out (US), classify a film, rate a movie (US), kill (Inf)

ADJECTIVES

5 **vetoed**, banned, embargoed, contraband, injunctive, interdictive, suspended, cancelled, null and void, denied, rejected, refused, blackballed, restrictive, forbidden, *verboten* (Ger),

impermissible, unauthorized, not allowed, circumscriptive, exclusive, prohibitive, prohibited, prohibiting, prohibitory, barred, out of bounds, off-limits (US), taboo, repressive, suppressive, preventive, preventative, obstructive, inhibiting, illicit, illegal, unlawful, illegitimate, excommunicated

6 **censored**, proscriptive, proscribed, deleted, blue-pencilled, blacked out, unprintable, bleeped out (US), unmentionable, unsayable, classified, secretive, secret, top-secret, restrictive, restricted, banned

ADVERBS

7 **by veto**, injunctively, under an injunction, interdictively, impermissibly, without permission, without authorization, circumscriptively, exclusively, prohibitively, repressively, in a repressive way, suppressively, preventively, in order to prevent, obstructively, illicitly, illegally, unlawfully, illegitimately

8 **under censorship**, proscriptively, with deletions, secretively, in a secret manner, restrictively, with restrictions

710 Offer

NOUNS

1 **offer**, proffer, proposal, invitation, proposition, bid, approach, offer one cannot refuse, come-on (Inf), freebie (US sl)

2 **tentative offer**, suggestion, presentation, submission, feeler, toe in the water, advance, overture, motion, chance, opening, opportunity, golden opportunity

3 **business offer**, merger, bid, takeover bid, buy-out, final offer, last word, ultimatum, firm price, asking price, fair offer, special offer, sale, special sale, bargain of the month

4 **illegal offer**, bribe, slush fund, blood money, pass (Inf), kickback (Inf), rake-off (Sl)

▶ *739 Sale, 714 Promise, 586 Persuasion, 340 Attraction, 228 Motive*

5 **offer of public service**, (political) candidature, solicitation of votes, bid for votes, request for support, offer to stand for Parliament, offer to run for Congress (US)

▶ *12 Government and Politics*

6 **offering**, sacrifice, martyrdom, gift, present, dedication, consecration, oblation, offertory, collection, votive offering, incense, peace offering, contribution, donation, subscription, propitiation, conciliation, appeasement, expiation, self-immolation, burnt offering, sacrificial offering, sacrificial lamb, hecatomb

▶ *397 Death, 7 Religion*

7 **martyr**, Christian martyr, Stephen, Sebastian, Catherine, willing sacrifice, human sacrifice, sacrificial lamb, suttee, proto-martyr

8 **volunteer**, voluntary worker, VSO (Voluntary Service Overseas), Peace Corps (US), char-

ity worker, unpaid worker, Good Samaritan, philanthropist, humanitarian, benefactor, contributor, altruist, social worker, community service worker, candy striper (US), public servant, candidate, missionary, do-gooder (Inf)

▶ *662 Help, 831 Benevolence, 833 Philanthropy*

VERBS

9 **offer**, proffer, propose, bid, approach, submit, suggest, put out a feeler, advance, make an overture, provide an opportunity, lay before, make an offer, make a fair offer, hold out, keep one's offer open, leave the door open, hold a special sale, offer for sale, put up for sale, invite offers, advertise, hand out a sample, auction, open bidding, hold out an incentive, lure, bait, spur, goad, persuade, induce, bribe, take a kickback (Inf), rake off (Sl)

10 **offer to buy**, attempt to buy, offer a fair price for, make an offer for, make a bid for, bid, negotiate, haggle

11 **volunteer**, do volunteer work, do charity work, do missionary work, work without pay, come forward, take on, lend a helping hand, act on one's own initiative, act without prompting, not wait to be asked, offer help, offer assistance, offer financial assistance, offer hospitality, provide, present, give, furnish, lend, loan, put into one's hands, lay at one's feet

12 **offer one's life**, sacrifice one's life, sacrifice oneself, become a martyr, die for a cause

13 **be a candidate**, offer oneself (for public office), stand as a candidate, run as a candidate (US), stand for office, run for office (US), enter the race, contest an office, solicit votes, bid for votes, request support

14 **offer reparation**, atone, make amends, apologize, offer one's apologies, beg one's pardon, propitiate, conciliate, appease, pacify, expiate, offer satisfaction, give satisfaction, make up for one's error

15 **offer worship**, celebrate mass, celebrate communion, administer the sacraments, minister, officiate, lead the worship, say the prayers, propitiate, appease, pacify

16 **make an offering**, offer a sacrifice, offer a gift, dedicate, consecrate, burn incense, make a peace offering, contribute, donate, subscribe, make a burnt offering, make a sacrificial offering, offer a sacrificial lamb

ADJECTIVES

17 **offered**, offering, inviting, propositional, bid, sale-price, persuasive, advertised, illegal, bribed, bribable, open to offers, on offer, on special offer, up for sale, for sale, cheap, reduced, up for auction, on auction, open for bid, requested, available, on the market, on hire, to let, for rent (US)

18 **voluntary**, unprompted, unforced, of one's

own free will, on one's own accord, off one's own bat, charity, unpaid, philanthropic, humanitarian, altruistic

19 **sacrificial**, sacrificed, martyred, consecrated, oblatory, oblational, contributory, donated, propitiatory, conciliatory, expiatory

ADVERBS

20 **persuasively**, in a persuasive manner, for sale, cheaply, with no strings attached, at no extra cost, illegally, voluntarily, for free, philanthropically, altruistically, like a Good Samaritan, sacrificially, as a sacrifice, conciliatorily

711 Refusal

NOUNS

1 **refusal**, refusal of consent, lack of consent, turning down, thumbs down, rejection, denial, repulsion, repulse, negative answer, negation, flat refusal, point-blank refusal, red light, noncompliance, resistance, retention, recalcitrance, unwillingness, nonwillingness, noncooperation, nonacceptance, denigration, refusal to work, strike, industrial action, lockout, sit-down strike (or sit-in), refusal to pay, nonpayment, default, tax evasion, creative accounting

▶ *581 Rejection, 341 Repulsion, 536 Negation, 726 Retention, 573 Unwillingness, 669 Resistance, 349 Expulsion, 591 Avoidance*

2 **dissent**, dissidence, lack of consent, contrary vote, a vote against, veto, disagreement, opposition, objection, discordance, refutation, repudiation, rebuttal, rebuff, contradiction, confutation, renunciation, confrontation, demonstration, civil disobedience, controversy, prohibition, counterorder, interdiction, interdict, ban, embargo, gainsaying (Arch), kick in the teeth (Sl)

▶ *668 Defiance, 663 Opposition, 713 Protest, 500 Dissent*

3 **abnegation**, relinquishment, self-restraint, self-sacrifice, self-renunciation, self-denial, denying oneself, refusing oneself

▶ *598 Relinquishment, 869 Self-Restraint*

4 **refuser**, refusenik, teetotaller, abstainer, tax evader, draft dodger (US), conscientious objector, deserter, truant, dissident, striker, scab, blackleg, gainsayer (Arch)

VERBS

5 **refuse**, reject, deny, say no, shake one's head, give the thumbs down to, show the red light to, repulse, repel, negate, not comply, resist, refuse permission, refuse flatly, refuse point-blank, retain, not cooperate, denigrate, not be willing to, not accept, decline, turn down, pass up, make one's excuses, send one's apologies, avoid, turn away, shy away from, shrink from, flinch at, balk at, jib at, keep away, not want

anything to do with, refuse to work, strike, go on strike, call a strike, lock out, have a sit-down strike, refuse to pay, default, evade taxes, turn one's back on, turn a deaf ear to, harden one's heart to, not buy (Sl), not wear (Sl)

6 **dissent**, withhold consent, withhold assent, express doubts, disagree, oppose, not allow, disallow, not stand for, reject, repudiate, rebuff, spurn, snub, object, refute, rebut, contradict, confute, nullify, renunciate, confront, withstand, not comply with, demonstrate against, cast a contrary vote, vote against, veto, prohibit, forbid, interdict, embargo, ban, gainsay (Arch), tell someone where to go (Inf), tell someone where to get off (Inf), kick someone in the teeth (Sl)

7 **refuse oneself**, deny oneself, deprive oneself of, renounce, forebear, demur, abstain, abstain from, go without, do without, live simply

ADJECTIVES

8 **refused**, refusing, noncooperative, uncooperative, unconsenting, uncompliant, noncompliant, noncomplying, resistant, resisting, negative, negating, recalcitrant, unwilling, nonwilling, nonaccepting, turned down, turned away, thrown out, ejected, excluded, withholding, withheld, kept back, not offered, retained, striking, strike-bound, sit-down, sit-in, given the thumbs down, given the red light, deaf to, not willing to hear of

9 **dissenting**, dissident, disagreeing, repudiating, demurring, opposing, opposite, adversarial, protesting, objecting to, discordant, refuting, denying, denied, disallowed, not allowed, not permitted, not granted, contradictory, contrary, contravening, confutative, renunciative, renunciatory, rejecting, rejected, rebuffed, revoking, revocatory, confrontational, controversial, prohibitionary, prohibited, prohibiting, interdictive, banned, embargoed

10 **abnegating**, abnegated, relinquishing, relinquished, self-sacrificing, self-renunciatory, self-denying

ADVERBS

11 **uncooperatively**, without a cooperative spirit, on no account, not at all, negatively, resistantly, resistingly, with resistance, unwillingly, dissentingly, dissidently, oppositely, discordantly, contradictorily, in contradiction, contrarily, controversially, in a controversial way, interdictively, no fear, not on your life (Inf), no chance (Inf), no way (Inf), not over one's dead body (Inf), not for all the tea in China (Inf), not on your nelly (Sl)

INTERJECTIONS

12 **no!**, no way!, a thousand times no!, never!, not likely!, impossible!, nothing doing!, far from it!, count me out!, over my dead body! (Inf), like hell! (Inf), nix (US inf)

712 Request

NOUNS

1 **request**, asking, entreaty, solemn entreaty, importunity, pressure, persuasion, insistence, urgency, urging, imploring, soliciting, accosting, invitation, application, appeal, bid, cry, desire, expressed desire, special request, favour, wish, want, petition, round robin, invocation, incantation, prayer, supplication, adjuration, *cri du coeur* (Fr), begging, beseeching, pestering, solicitation, suggestion, proposition, proposal, motion, approach, offer, requirement, claim, counterclaim, suit, courting, wooing

▶ *586 Persuasion, 782 Desire, 710 Offer, 593 Requirement*

2 **demand**, requisition, order, indent, summons, call, notice, claim, demand for payment, final demand, final notice, last time of asking, injunction, dunning, dun, command, ultimatum, forcible demand, demand backed by threats, threat, blackmail, exaction, extortion

▶ *692 Command, 845 Entitlement, 473 Argument, 695 Compulsion, 532 Publication*

3 **solicitation**, soliciting money, chain letter, mendicancy, begging, cadging, busking, fundraising, appealing, appeal, charity appeal, canvass, canvassing, charity events, charity show, charity ball, charity match, benefit game (US), (church) bazaar, benefit concert, Band-Aid, telethon, Children in Need Appeal, charity organization, OXFAM, United Way (US), charity funds, benefit gig (Inf), scrounging (Inf), sponging (Inf), bumming (US inf), panhandling (US inf), freeloading (Sl), mooching (Sl), the touch (Sl)

▶ *831 Benevolence, 733 Borrowing, 734 Taking*

4 **requester**, petitioner, appealer, lobbyist, supplicant, suppliant, appellant, solicitor, canvasser, charity worker, fund-raiser, claimant, counterclaimant, asker, blackmailer, extortionist, hustler, seeker, inquirer, questioner, borrower, customer, applicant, candidate, suitor, lover

5 **beggar**, cadger, busker, mendicant, mendicant friar, hanger-on, vagrant, freebooter, tramp, hobo (US), bum (US inf), scrounger (Inf), sponger (Inf), panhandler (US inf), freeloader (Sl), moocher (Sl), ligger (Sl)

VERBS

6 **request**, make a request, have a request to make, have a need for, lack, want, want to know, demand an answer, ask, ask for, ask for support, ask for one's blessing, ask if it is possible, ask a favour, ask leave, beg leave, ask permission, beg permission, ask to be excused, make a special request, go cap in hand, entreat, pressure, insist, urge, implore, solicit,

accost, hustle, invite, request the pleasure of one's company, apply for, appeal, bid, cry, desire, wish, petition, sign a petition, sign a round robin, invoke, incant, pray, pray for, address one's prayers to, kneel to, go down on one's knees to, supplicate, adjure, beg, beseech, cajole, coax, pester, tout, hawk, suggest, persuade, proposition, propose, move, approach, make overtures to, offer, apply, require, claim, counterclaim, issue a suit, court, woo, request one's hand in marriage, pop the question (Inf), go down on bended knee, bug (Inf)

7 **demand**, requisition, order, indent, summon, call, claim, press a claim, put in a claim, invoice, charge, bill, levy, tax, demand payment, make a final demand, receive a final notice, receive an injunction, dun, command, issue an ultimatum, threaten, demand with threats, blackmail, exact, extort, bleed someone (Inf), put the squeeze on someone (Inf), put the bite on someone (US and Aus sl)

8 **solicit money**, beg, cadge, hold out one's hand, go from door to door, pass around the hat, busk, raise funds, appeal, make a charity appeal, launch an appeal, canvass, hold a charity event, put the squeeze on, scrounge (Inf), sponge (Inf), bum (US inf), panhandle (US inf), freeload (Sl), mooch (Sl), put the touch on (Sl), tap (Inf)

ADJECTIVES

9 **requesting**, requested, asking, insistent, urgent, invitational, inviting, desired, petitioned, round-robin, invocational, incantational, adjuratory, entreating, beseeching, propositional, proposable, proposed, offered, required, courting, wooing

10 **demanding**, demanded, requisitionary, claiming, injunctive, forcible, threatening, threatened, blackmailing, blackmailed, extortive, extorting, extorted

11 **begging**, cadging, mendicant, fund-raising, chain-letter, scrounging (Inf), sponging (Inf), freeloading (Sl), mooching (Sl)

ADVERBS

12 **by request**, insistently, urgently, with urgency, entreatingly, by one's leave, with permission, beseechingly, forcibly, using force, with force

713 Protest

NOUNS

1 **protest**, opposition, objection, dissent, dissatisfaction, disagreement, disapproval, disapprobation, negation, negativity, contravention, hostility, discontent, recalcitrance, refractoriness, challenge, refusal to obey orders, refutation, noncooperation, noncompliance, disobedience, anger, defiance, recusance, mu-

tiny, refusal to pay, nonpayment, protestation, expostulation, deprecation, intercession, counteraction, warning, complaint, clamour, outcry, no, nay, denial, contradiction, repudiation, disclaimer, renunciation, disavowal, kicking against the pricks, gainsaying (Arch), kick (US inf), bitch (Inf), beef (Sl)

▶ *852 Disapproval, 666 Disagreement, 536 Negation, 711 Refusal, 573 Unwillingness, 693 Disobedience*

2 **disorder**, agitation, breach of the peace, lawlessness, anarchism, anarchy, insurgency, sedition, treason, high treason, riot, rioting, rebellion, revolt, mutiny, insurrection, uprising, coup d'état, putsch, terrorism, war, guerrilla war, civil war, assassination, regicide, tyrannicide

▶ *674 Contention, 668 Defiance*

3 **gesture of protest**, peaceful protest, strike, sit-down strike (*or* protest), go-slow, work to rule, hunger strike, boycott, picketing, demonstration, protest march, protest meeting, sit-in, work-in, raised fist, raised eyebrows, slow handclap, protest song, boo, hiss, groan, whistle, catcall, jeer, howl, raspberry, V-sign, squawk (Inf), the bird (Inf), the finger (US inf), Bronx cheer (US sl)

▶ *475 Demonstration*

4 **protester**, objector, conscientious objector, complainer, dissatisfied customer, grumbler, grouser, whiner, bellyacher, moaner, difficult character, mischief-maker, troublemaker, agitator, malcontent, ranter, rabble-rouser, dissident, dissentient, dissenter, critic, detractor, protestant, separatist, sectarian, dropout, nonconformist, hippie, rebel, demonstrator, striker, picketer, nonstriker, scab, blackleg, marcher, tub-thumper, counter-demonstrator, suffragette, suffragist, whinger (Inf), moaning Minnie (Inf)

5 **seditionist**, anarchist, nihilist, spy, counterspy, industrial spy, revolter, revolutionary, urban guerrilla, partisan, resistance fighter, freedom fighter, terrorist, IRA (Irish Republican Army) member

▶ *12 Government and Politics*

VERBS

6 **protest**, oppose, object, raise an objection, dissent, resist, show dissatisfaction, disagree with, disapprove of, show disapproval, deprecate, detract, contravene, show discontent, become agitated about, challenge, refuse to obey orders, not cooperate, not comply, disobey, become angry, raise one's fist, defy, mutiny, expostulate, intercede, counteract, warn, complain, clamour, say no, deny, contradict, repudiate, disclaim, renounce, disavow, speak out against, raise one's voice against, raise the roof over, kick against the pricks, gainsay (Arch), kick (US inf), bitch (Inf), beef (Sl)

7 **complain**, groan, grumble, grouse, whine, gripe, bellyache, moan, rant, boo, hiss, tut-tut, whistle, give a catcall, jeer, howl, give a raspberry, give the V-sign, squawk (Inf), whinge (Inf), cry (*or* scream) blue murder (Inf), cry (*or* scream) bloody murder (US inf), give someone the bird (Inf), give someone the finger (US inf), kick up a fuss about (Inf), give someone the Bronx cheer (US sl)

8 **cause mischief**, cause trouble, strike, come out on strike, go on strike (US), go slow, work to rule, stage a sit-down, take industrial action, go on hunger strike, boycott, picket, cause disorder, breach the peace, agitate against, demonstrate against, go on a protest march, hold a protest meeting, sit in, act lawlessly, cause anarchy, riot, rebel, revolt, mutiny, begin an insurrection, lead an uprising, pull off a coup d'état, lead a putsch, terrorize, belong to a terrorist organization, belong to the IRA (Irish Republican Army), use terrorist tactics, wage war, fight a guerrilla war, assassinate

ADJECTIVES

9 **protesting**, protestant, opposing, dissenting, dissatisfied, disapproving, negative, negating, hostile, critical, discontent, malcontent, discontented, unconsenting, deprecatory, recalcitrant, refractory, challenging, noncooperative, noncompliant, nonconformist, disobedient, angry, contrary, defiant, recusant, counteractive, denying, denied, contradictive, repudiated, clamorous, hissing, booing, jeering, bolshie (Inf), bloody-minded (Inf)

10 **lawbreaking**, lawless, anarchic(al), insubordinate, insurgent, mutinous, seditious, treasonous, riotous, rebellious, revolutionary, anarchist, nihilist, terrorist, guerrilla, counterrevolutionary, insurrectionary, assassinated, regicidal

ADVERBS

11 **disapprovingly**, without approval, in opposition, negatively, hostilely, with hostility, critically, in a critical way, deprecatorily, disobediently, angrily, with anger, contrarily, defiantly, in defiance of, in the face of, contradictively, in conflict with, lawlessly, insubordinately, mutinously, seditiously, rebelliously, in rebellion against

714 Promise

NOUNS

1 **promise**, solemn promise, commitment, voluntary commitment, pledge, vow, oath, one's word, testimony, swearing on the Bible, swearing, deposition, adjuration, statement under oath, affidavit, affirmation, firm date, delivery date, assurance, profession, promise-making, gentleman's agreement, unwritten agreement, covenant, bond, handshake, compact, con-

tract, mutual pledge, debt of honour, intention, declaration of intent, post (*or* put up) the banns, read (*or* publish) the banns, engagement, exchange of vows, betrothal, marriage contract

▶ *588 Intention, 537 Truth, 715 Contract, 535 Affirmation, 745 Debt, 733 Borrowing, 823 Marriage*

2 **guarantee**, security, written guarantee, warrant, warranty, promissory note, contract, insurance premium, IOU, voucher, pawn ticket, chit

▶ *718 Security*

3 **potential**, possibilities, capacity, capability, ability, good things to come, hope, good omen, favourable auspices, good prospects, bright prospects

▶ *483 Evidence, 497 Belief*

4 **promised land**, land of promise, land flowing with milk and honey, Canaan, Israel, El Dorado, end of the rainbow, pot of gold (at the end of the rainbow), Utopia, Erewhon, Shangri-la, Holy Grail, Sangreal, Goshen, Elysia, Elysian Fields, Fountain of Youth, eternal youth, eternal life, the millennium, Heaven, Valhalla (*or* Walhalla), the happy hunting ground

5 **promise-maker**, promiser, guarantor, party, surety, signatory, signer, cosignatory, co-signer, bondsman, obligor, swearer, attestor

6 **someone promised**, betrothed, fiancé, fiancée, affianced, engaged person, lucky man, bride-to-be, the intended (Inf)

VERBS

7 **promise**, make a promise, solemnly promise, pledge, confirm, assure, say yes to, say one will, proffer, affirm, give one's word (of honour), vow, commit oneself, swear, swear on (*or* under) oath, swear on the Holy Bible, swear on one's mother's life (*or* head), cross one's heart (and hope to die), testify, take responsibility for, pledge one's word, pledge oneself, pledge one's honour, enter into an agreement, give a firm date, undertake to, make a gentleman's agreement, shake on it, sign on the dotted line, covenant, contract, get engaged to, become engaged, become betrothed to, plight one's troth, exchange vows, espouse, ask for the hand of, accept a proposal, put up the banns, say "I do"

8 **guarantee**, warrant, certify, assure, answer for, vouch for, commit oneself, make it one's duty, take on, accept responsibility, accept obligation, accept liability, secure, insure, underwrite, stand bail for, go bond for, give a written guarantee, sign a promissory note, cosign a note, attest to, make a contract, promise to pay, give one's IOU, receive a voucher, receive a pawn ticket

9 **be auspicious**, be likely, promise well, augur well, hold out hopes for, build up hope, bid fair

10 **show potential**, show promise, have possibilities, hope, receive a good omen, have good prospects, have a bright future, get better, improve, develop, evolve, prove fruitful

11 **promise oneself**, have in mind, look forward to, have one's eye on, contemplate, think of, desire, want, set one's heart on, covet, have designs on

ADJECTIVES

12 **promised**, pledged, bound, committed, testimonial, sworn, on (*or* under) oath, on one's word, under hand and seal, adjuratory, votive, affirmative, assured, professed, engaged, betrothed, spoken for

13 **guaranteeing**, guaranteed, authenticating, authenticated, certified, assured, attested, certain, warranted, underwritten, signed, co-signed, securing, secured, pledging, pledged, committed, bound, obligated, promissory, contracted

14 **auspicious**, propitious, promising, full of promise, encouraging, hopeful, full of hope, potential, full of potential, possible, likely, fortunate, favourable, optimistic, good, bright, fair, golden, rosy, cloudless, clear

15 **future**, eventual, destined, fated, potential, prospective, to come, probable, possible, anticipated, looked for, hoped for, predicted, predictable, foreseeable, sure, certain

ADVERBS

16 **as promised**, as agreed, duly, upon one's word (of honour), on (*or* under) oath, under hand and seal, votively, assuredly, with assurance, certainly

17 **auspiciously**, propitiously, promisingly, full of promise, with promise, encouragingly, hopefully, full of hope, with hope, potentially, possibly, fortunately, favourably, optimistically, in an optimistic way, brightly, rosily, clearly

18 **potentially**, eventually, prospectively, probably, possibly, predictably, surely, certainly

715 Contract

NOUNS

1 **contract**, undertaking, assignment, engagement, obligation, commitment, promise, formal contract, mise (Fml), compact, arrangement, understanding, cooperation, accord, agreement, deal, mutual agreement, legal agreement, binding agreement, formal agreement, informal agreement, gentleman's agreement, pledge, exchanged vow, marriage contract, betrothal, matrimony, holy matrimony, nuptial bond, conjugal trust, wedlock, bond, union, alliance, partnership, covenant, pact, suicide pact, negotiation, bargain, bargaining,

bartering, give and take, mediation, settlement, ratification, completion, confirmation, consent, assent, seal, signet, signature, cosignature, countersignature, security, deed

▶ *597 Undertaking, 714 Promise, 664 Cooperation, 116 Accord, 823 Marriage, 716 Negotiation, 678 Mediation, 483 Evidence, 499 Assent, 718 Security*

2 **purchase contract**, building contract, service contract, rental contract, leasing contract, lease, employment contract, teaching contract, publishing contract, insurance policy, promissory note, IOU, debenture, debenture bond, mortgage deed, deed of trust

▶ *741 Money, 744 Credit, 745 Debt*

3 **alliance**, league, cartel, consortium, trust, *entente cordiale* (Fr), *entente* (Fr), Triple Entente, international agreement, arms-control agreement, SALT (Strategic Arms Limitation Talks), international pact, trade agreement, Treaty of Rome, convention, treaty, peace treaty, Treaty of Paris, Treaty of Versailles, nonaggression pact, concordat, mutual-defence treaty, NATO (North Atlantic Treaty Organization), SEATO (Southeast Asia Treaty Organization), GATT (General Agreement on Tariffs and Trade), Warsaw Pact

▶ *12 Government and Politics, 677 Pacification, 737 Trade*

4 **contractor**, contracting party, signatory, signer, cosigner, countersigner, the undersigned, endorser, ratifier, covenanter, consenting party, assenter, treaty-maker, peacemaker, mediator, negotiator, diplomat, arbitrator, jobber, entrepreneur, doer, operator, dealer, wheeler-dealer (Inf), fast operator (Inf)

VERBS

5 **contract**, enter into a contract, execute a contract, indent, make a compact, sign a pact, commit oneself, bind oneself, contract a marriage, marry, wed, sign (on the dotted line), cosign, countersign, seal, subscribe to, underwrite, endorse, ratify, attest, confirm, covenant, negotiate a treaty, sign a treaty, enter into an alliance, ally, join a consortium, league with, go into league with, form a cartel, bargain, strike a bargain, settle, negotiate, make terms, cooperate, give and take, barter, come to an agreement, come to terms, transfer, convey, deed (US), go into a partnership, form a partnership, work out a deal, conclude (*or* clinch) a deal (Inf), shake on a deal (Inf), close the deal (Inf), tie the knot (Inf), put out a contract on (Sl)

6 **catch**, get, come down with, become infected, break out with

ADJECTIVES

7 **contractual**, contracted, covenantal, covenanted, agreeable, agreed to, agreed, promised, sworn, consensual, assenting, negotiable,

negotiated, negotiating, treaty-making, bilateral, multilateral, signed (on the dotted line), cosigned, countersigned, signed sealed and delivered, under one's hand and seal, ratified, assigned, arranged, matrimonial, nuptial, conjugal, allied, united, conspiratorial

ADVERBS

8 **contractually**, as contracted for, according to the contract, covenantally, agreeably, as agreed upon (*or* to), as promised, according to the agreement, consensually, with consent, bilaterally, multilaterally, matrimonially, nuptially, conjugally, conspiratorially

716 Negotiation

NOUNS

1 **negotiation**, negotiations, mediation, arbitration, conciliation, compromising, compromise, exchange, discussions, bargaining, collective bargaining, hard bargaining, barter, bartering, horse trading, trade-off, haggling, wrangling, making terms, treaty-making, diplomacy, communication, intercommunication, dealing (Inf), an offer one can't refuse (Inf)

▶ *717 Compromise, 737 Trade, 534 Communications*

2 **basis for negotiations**, frame of reference, contract, terms, written terms, set of terms, conditions, part of the bargain, offer, provision, article, articles of agreement, requirement, qualification, clause, essential clause, *sine qua non* (L), escape clause, let-out clause, proviso, stipulation, concession, reservation, strings, small print

▶ *715 Contract, 710 Offer, 593 Requirement, 485 Qualification*

3 **discussion**, round-table discussion, conference, teleconference, bargaining session, debate, high-level talks, summit meeting, summit conference, summit, cabinet meeting, moot, teleconference, exchange of views, powwow (Inf), argy-bargy (Inf)

▶ *568 Conversation*

4 **negotiator**, mediator, intermediary, intercessor, go-between, diplomat (*or* diplomatist), ambassador, chargé d'affaires, matchmaker, link, broker, arbitrator, lawyer, solicitor, middleman, stockbroker, ACAS (Advisory Conciliation and Arbitration Service

▶ *12 Government and Politics, 16 Law*

VERBS

5 **negotiate**, mediate, arbitrate, seek agreement, seek accord, settle, conciliate, cooperate, compromise, exchange, exchange views, discuss, communicate, intercommunicate, bargain, do collective bargaining, do hard bargaining, barter, horse trade, trade off, trade, haggle, wrangle, come to terms, make terms,

make conditions, stipulate, make concessions, add strings, read the small print, use diplomacy, treat (Fml), make a treaty, hold a conference, attend a conference, have a summit meeting, hold a summit, confer, hold talks, get round the table, deliberate, have a discussion, put heads together, transact business, do business, do transactions, work at reaching an agreement, make overtures, test the ground, offer a solution, work out a formula, work something out, get something through, deal (Inf), make (or do) a deal (Inf), powwow (Inf), argy-bargy (Inf)

6 **make conditions**, impose conditions, make proposals, make a bid, make demands, stipulate, put in clauses, leave a loophole, add an escape clause, write in a let-out clause, leave the options open, hedge one's bets

7 **act as a go-between**, broker, matchmake, act as a middleman, act as a link, stand in for, replace, proxy

ADJECTIVES

8 **negotiated**, mediated, arbitrated, negotiable, practicable, practical, feasible, workable, pragmatic, transferable, conveyable, exchangeable, trade-off, subject to terms, conditional, provisional, provisory, stipulatory, concessionary, conciliatory, compromising, collective, haggling, wrangling, treaty-making, diplomatic, communicative, intercommunicative

ADVERBS

9 **feasibly**, pragmatically, conditionally, under certain conditions, provisionally, with provisions, conciliatorily, compromisingly, as a compromise, as a trade-off, collectively, diplomatically, in diplomatic language, like a diplomat, communicatively

717 Compromise

NOUNS

1 **compromise**, adaptation, adaptability, accommodation, sharing, cooperation, agreement, arrangement, working arrangement, practical compromise, modus vivendi, understanding, concession, mutual concession, give-and-take, adjustment, settlement, negotiation, negotiability, arbitration, middle way, middle course, middle ground, halfway, happy medium, balance, balancing act, central position, meeting halfway, splitting the difference, equal swap, trade-off, bargain, deal (Inf)

▶ *664 Cooperation, 116 Accord, 678 Mediation, 715 Contract, 124 Average, 737 Trade*

2 **half-measure**, stopgap measure, temporary substitute, second best

▶ *222 Substitution*

3 **irresolution**, hesitation, lack of resolution,

lack of conviction, lack of committal, lukewarmness, neutrality, desertion of principles, evasion of responsibility, dishonour, shame, cop-out (Sl)

▶ *576 Vacillation, 801 Disrepute*

VERBS

4 **compromise**, reach (or make) a compromise, meet halfway, adapt, accommodate, cooperate, make adjustments, adjust, readjust, negotiate, go to arbitration, arbitrate, make mutual concessions, concede, cede, give and take, average out, split the difference, agree to some of it, agree to half of it, strike a balance, stretch a point, play politics, go so far but no further, steer a middle course, strike an average, go half and half, have a foot in both camps, sit on the fence, take what's on offer, take the good with the bad, make the best of a bad job, make a virtue of necessity, make a deal (Inf), go fifty-fifty (Inf), go Dutch (Inf)

5 **be irresolute**, lack resolution, lack conviction, desert one's principles, evade one's responsibilities, duck responsibility (Inf), cop out (Sl)

ADJECTIVES

6 **compromising**, accommodating, adjusted, negotiable, adaptable, averaging out, averaged out, agreeing, agreed, arranged, conceding, give-and-take, settled, halfway, balancing, balanced, neither one thing nor the other

7 **half-measure**, stopgap, temporary, second-best

8 **irresolute**, noncommittal, lukewarm, neutral, evasive, discredited, dishonourable, dishonoured, damaging, cop-out (Sl)

ADVERBS

9 **compromisingly**, in equal measures, in equal parts, accommodatingly, in an accommodating manner, by negotiating, agreeably, under an agreement, under an arrangement, halfway, as a half-measure, in a temporary manner

10 **irresolutely**, without resolution, noncommittally, without commitment, lukewarmly, neutrally, evasively, in an evasive manner, dishonourably, without honour, as a cop-out (Sl)

718 Security

NOUNS

1 **protection**, safety, safeness, safekeeping, invulnerability, impregnability, immunity, secure position, asylum, sanctuary, shelter, refuge, cover, mainstay, anchor, support, hope, pillar of strength, defence, safeguard, shield, security system, alarm system, deterrent, sense of security, reliance, faith, confidence, courage, national insurance, health insurance, BUPA, Blue Cross (US), National Health Service (NHS), Medicare (US), unemployment

benefits, old-age security, social security, welfare, welfare state, retirement benefits, the dole (Inf)

▶ *632 Safety, 671 Defence, 781 Caution, 637 Preservation, 469 Carefulness, 778 Courage*

2 **promise**, pledge, word, word of honour, assurance, insurance, credit, honour, recognizance, warrant, warranty, guarantee, underwriting, certificate, bond, coupon, passport, visa, permit, authority, authorization, title deed, gilt-edged security, share, debenture, mortgage, deed, insurance policy, will, last will and testament, collateral, indemnity, covenant, receipt, IOU, counterfoil, stub, cheque stub, ticket stub, ticket, pawn ticket, docket, proof of purchase, acquittance, quittance, authentication, verification, endorsement, stamp, seal, signature

▶ *714 Promise, 715 Contract, 746 Payment, 483 Evidence, 545 Record*

3 **security officer**, protector, sentinel, sentry, watchman, night watchman, watch, warner, bodyguard, lifeguard, policeman, policewoman, police officer, police constable, special constable, highway patrolman (US), bobby (Inf), copper (Sl), cop (Sl), pig (Sl), Smokey (the bear) (US sl), bear (US sl), rozzer (Sl), flatfoot (Sl), Old Bill (or the Bill) (Sl), the fuzz (Sl), bizzy (Sl), ploddy (Sl)

4 **security forces**, national defence, armed forces, army, navy, air force, marines, police force, private security company, Securicor (Tm), Brinks (Tm) (US), Neighbourhood Watch

▶ *679 Combatant*

5 **safe**, safety deposit box, wall safe, lockbox, vault, bank vault

ADJECTIVES

6 **secure**, safe, sure, without risk, safe and sound, protective, protected, sheltered, invulnerable, impregnable, locked away, locked up, immune, safeguarded, shielded, deterrent, safe as houses (Inf), safe as the Bank of England (Inf)

7 **guaranteed**, warranted, under warranty, certified, authenticated, assured, certain, reliant, unshaken, gilt-edged, covered, insured, mortgaged, on mortgage, guaranteed, covenanted, pledged, promised, pawned, in hock (US sl), hocked (US sl)

8 **accomplished**, done, won, completed, sewn up (Inf), under one's belt (Inf), in the bag (Sl)

▶ *682 Success*

9 **fast**, fixed, sound, steadfast, stable, steady, immovable, irremovable

▶ *225 Stability, 135 Union*

VERBS

10 **secure**, make safe, protect, keep order, police, patrol, guard, safekeep, keep safe and sound, lock away, lock up, keep under lock and key,

offer refuge, offer shelter, anchor, support, defend, safeguard, shield, give a sense of security

11 **promise**, pledge, give one's word (of honour), give one's IOU, assure, insure, give personal recognizance, warrant, guarantee, act as guarantor, act as security, stand (or go) surety, stand (or go) bail, vouch for, endorse, seal, stamp, countersign, indemnify, underwrite, safeguard, make certain

12 **certify**, authenticate, cover, insure, mortgage, pledge, promise, verify, offer collateral, give security

13 **secure one's objective**, accomplish, reach one's goal, win through, win, succeed, complete, pull it off, bring it off, sew up (Inf), have under one's belt (Inf), have in the bag (Sl)

14 **make fast**, make firm, fortify, stabilize, steady, strengthen, fix to, secure to, nail down, screw down, make sound, make steadfast, make immovable

15 **reserve**, make a reservation, book, order, pay in advance, leave a deposit

▶ *545 Record*

ADVERBS

16 **surely**, safely, in a safe manner, without risk, safe and sound, protectively, invulnerably, impregnably, reliably, assuredly, verifiably, with assurance

17 **fastly**, fixedly, in a fixed position, soundly, steadfastly, immovably, without moving

719 Observance

NOUNS

1 **observance**, observation, compliance, recognition, adherence to, following, heeding, heed, regard, caring, care, keeping, acknowledgment, attention to, attending to, vigilance, diligence, proper observance, close observance, full observance, conscientiousness, conformity, conformance, accordance, regularity, dependability, reliability, accuracy, attachment, faithfulness, (good) faith, fidelity, loyalty, obedience, duty, respect, paying respect to, sense of responsibility, obeying the law, keeping on the right side of the law

▶ *467 Attention, 167 Conformity, 503 Accuracy, 694 Obedience, 847 Duty*

2 **religious observance**, ritual, ceremony, ceremonial, rite, liturgy, service, mass

▶ *7 Religion, 10 Ritual*

3 **performance**, practice, procedure, convention, custom, usage, routine, rule of business, discharge, execution, acquittal, carrying out, fulfilment, satisfaction, sufficiency

▶ *640 Action, 144 Completeness, 684 Completion, 608 Sufficiency*

VERBS

4 **observe**, comply with, recognize, adhere to, stick to, cling to, heed, regard, have regard for,

care, keep, follow, hold to (or by), abide by, acknowledge, give attention to, attend to, show diligence, keep the proper observance, keep a full observance, keep to the spirit of, conform to, keep (good) faith, show respect, pay respect to, pay homage to, have a sense of loyalty, have a sense of responsibility, obey the law

5 **observe religious ceremony**, observe a ritual, perform the rites, read a liturgy, say office, officiate, attend a service, celebrate mass, lead the worship, worship

6 **perform**, practise, observe a practice, follow a procedure, keep a routine, observe the rule of business, discharge, discharge one's responsibility (or function), execute, do, do one's duty, acquit, carry out, carry out to the letter, fulfil, fulfil one's role, meet, satisfy, suffice, make good, make good one's word (or promise), keep one's promise, redeem one's pledge, honour one's obligations

ADJECTIVES

7 **observant**, observing, heeding, heeded, heedful, watchful, regarding, regardful, attentive to, attentive, careful of, conscientious, diligent, meticulous, scrupulous, fastidious, punctual, punctilious, literal, pedantic, exact, accurate, reliable, responsible, dependable, dutiful, duteous, constant, compliant, conforming, conformable, obedient, adherent to, adhering to, sticking to, faithful, devout, religious, orthodox, traditional, conventional, loyal, true, honourable, as good as one's word

ADVERBS

8 **observantly**, with (proper) observance, heedfully, watchfully, while keeping watch, attentively, conscientiously, diligently, meticulously, scrupulously, fastidiously, punctually, punctiliously, literally, pedantically, exactly, to the letter, reliably, responsibly, dependably, dutifully, duteously, constantly, compliantly, conformingly, conformably, obediently, faithfully, devoutly, religiously, orthodoxly, traditionally, conventionally, loyally, truly, honourably

720 Nonobservance

NOUNS

1 **nonobservance**, inobservance, nonadherence, lack of ceremony, nonconformity, disconformity, nonconformance, noncompliance, noncooperation, rejection, indifference, inattention, avoidance, disregard, heedlessness, unmindfulness, obliviousness, oversight, overlooking, forgetfulness, carelessness, remissness, sloppiness (Inf), negligence, neglectfulness, neglect, laches (Fml), thoughtlessness, slight, casualness, procrastination, laxity, informality, superficiality, perfunctoriness,

breach, breach of promise, repudiation, breach of contract, breach of trust, disdain, discourtesy, breach of faith, bad faith, contempt

▶ *168 Nonconformity, 470 Negligence, 591 Avoidance, 581 Rejection, 850 Disrespect*

2 **nonperformance**, nonpractice, noncompletion, nonfulfilment, nonfeasance (Fml), dereliction of duty, undutifulness, omission, failure, default, shortcoming, insufficiency, defect

▶ *685 Noncompletion, 704 Cancellation, 643 Inactivity, 609 Insufficiency*

3 **disregard of orders**, noncompliance, insubordination, disobedience, disrespect, disloyalty, dissidence, mutinousness, mutiny, defection, desertion, treachery, treason

▶ *693 Disobedience, 713 Protest*

4 **infraction**, violation, breaking, infringement, unlawfulness, illegality, transgression, trespass, delinquency, contravention, offence, breach, breach of the peace, disorder, anarchy

▶ *858 Improbity, 241 Violence*

5 **nonobserver**, nonconformist, independent, nonpractising person, lapsed believer, nonbeliever, disbeliever, heathen, infidel, heretic, sceptic, atheist, agnostic, humanist, apostate, retractor, dissident, dissenter, nonstriker, strikebreaker, blackleg, scab, recalcitrant, angry young man, rebel, bohemian, beatnik, hippie, punk, long-haired weirdo (Sl)

6 **evader**, defaulter, tax evader, avoider, procrastinator, idler, slacker, shirker, dropout, truant, dodger, draft dodger (US), runaway, deserter, traitor, skiver (Sl)

VERBS

7 **not observe**, not adhere, not follow, not conform, stand out, not cooperate, not comply, not believe, disbelieve, reject, remain sceptical, disregard, avoid, ignore, have an oversight, overlook, pay no regard to, pay no heed to, pass over, skip, wink at, neglect, slight, procrastinate, repudiate, not accept, breach, break faith, break one's promise, break one's word, neglect one's vows, neglect one's obligations, dishonour one's pledge, renege on, go back on, back out, retract, dissent, not strike, rebel, live a bohemian life, do one's own thing (Inf), be oneself, let one's hair down (Inf), show disdain, snap one's fingers at, cock a snook

8 **not perform**, not practise, not complete, not fulfil, fail in responsibility, fail to fulfil one's duty, fail, prove unreliable, let someone down, omit, default, have a shortcoming, evade, avoid, elude, shirk, drop out, dodge, dodge the draft (US), run away, desert, skive off (Inf)

9 **disregard orders**, violate orders, not comply, disobey, defy, flout, flout authority, not do as one is told, show disrespect, show no

respect for, show disloyalty, fail in duty, mutiny, defect, desert, be absent without leave, go AWOL, show treachery, act treasonously

10 **violate the law**, break, infringe on, transgress, trespass, contravene, offend, ride roughshod over, trample on, trample underfoot, breach, breach the peace, lack order, cause anarchy, take the law into one's own hands

ADJECTIVES

11 **nonobservant**, inobservant, unobservant, nonadherent, lacking ceremony, nonconformant, nonconforming, noncompliant, nonconformist, independent, nonpractising, nonbelieving, disbelieving, rejecting, heretic(al), sceptic(al), atheist, atheistic(al), agnostic, unconverted, inattentive, unmindful, regardless, disregardful, disregarding, avoiding, heedless, thoughtless, oblivious, overlooking, overlooked, forgetful, careless, remissive, remiss, negligent, neglectful, casual, procrastinating, lax, unprofessional, informal, superficial, unthorough, perfunctory, repudiating, dissident, unconventional, bohemian, noncooperative, indifferent, disdainful, discourteous, contemptuous, sloppy (Inf)

12 **nonperforming**, nonpractising, nonfulfiling, undutiful, omissive, insufficient, failing, failed, defective, defaulting, defaulted, evading, dodging, truant, dropout, runaway, deserting, skiving (Sl)

13 **noncompliant**, insubordinate, disobedient, disrespectful, disloyal, unloyal, untrue, unfaithful, dissident, mutinous, defecting, deserting, absent without leave (AWOL), treacherous, treasonous

14 **violating**, violated, breaking, broken, infringing, infringed, unlawful, illegal, against the rules, transgressive, transgressing, transgressed, trespassing, delinquent, contravening, breaching, disorderly, anarchic(al)

ADVERBS

15 **inattentively**, heedlessly, unmindfully, obliviously, forgetfully, carelessly, thoughtlessly, casually, informally, superficially, insufficiently, negligently, defectively, sloppily (Inf)

16 **disobediently**, disloyally, discourteously, disrespectfully, heretically, sceptically, independently, anarchically, unlawfully, illegally, treacherously, mutinously

721 Gain

NOUNS

1 **gain**, gaining, getting, receiving, taking, winning, acquisition, acquirement, obtainment, attainment, attainability, advantage, unfair advantage, benefit, personal benefit, coming by, gathering in, bringing in, securement, procurement, procural, procurance, procuration,

earnings, makings, moneymaking, breadwinning, profitableness, profitmaking, profittaking, profitability, profitable transaction, lucrative deal, successful speculation, realization, gainfulness, remunerativeness, fundraising, profiteering, usury, greed, grist to the mill, getting hold of (Inf), pulling down (Inf), money-grubbing (Inf), raking (*or* coining) it in (Inf)

▶ *730 Receiving, 734 Taking, 741 Money, 860 Selfishness*

2 **augmentation**, increase, gain in value, appreciation, price increase, pay increase, rise, raise (US), increment, development, crescendo, growth, expansion, gaining weight, gaining height, broadening, widening, spreading, spread, escalation, inflation, dilation, advance, approach, headway, gaining ground, ground gained, improvement, improved mileage, performance gain, betterment, higher jump, faster race, further throw, longer endurance, gaining on, gaining time, overtaking, leaving behind

▶ *128 Increase, 739 Sale, 21 Athletics, 208 Earliness*

3 **acquisition**, collection, gathering, gleaning, bringing together, assembling, assemblage, accumulation, cumulation, amassment, accretion, catch, hoard, store, heap, stack, pile, stock, stockpile, mountain, pool, bunch (Inf), haul (Inf)

▶ *161 Assembly, 605 Store*

4 **earnings**, income, private income, corporate income, earned income, unearned income, advance earnings, advance, royalty, national income, GNP (gross national product), privy purse, revenue, wages, salary, pay, pay packet, pay cheque, money coming in, takings, makings, receipts, box-office receipts, gross receipts, net receipts, gross revenue, turnover, net revenue, return, gross return, net return, returns, proceeds, gate money, gate, winnings, pickings, gleanings, retirement pay, social security payments, pension, stipend, annuity, tontine, maintenance, alimony, palimony (US), fee, remuneration, take (US inf), take-in (US inf)

▶ *749 Receipt, 746 Payment, 12 Government and Politics, 823 Marriage*

5 **profit**, gain, gains, capital gains, clear profit, profits, gross profits, gross, net profits, net, emolument, interest, compound interest, simple interest, percentage, dividends, inheritance, bequest, legacy, endowment, dowry, grant, subsidy, compensation, honorarium, fellowship, scholarship, bursary (Scot), benefit, fringe benefit, extra, bonus, perquisite, perk, commission, expense account, allowance, pocket money, pin money, extra money, prosperity, wealth, pelf, lucre, filthy lucre, sav-

ings, spending money, money for a rainy day, reward, gratuity, tip, lagniappe (US), baksheesh, award, trophy, prize, jackpot, something for nothing, gift, free gift, giveaway (US), find, finding, discovery, trove, treasure-trove, buried treasure, piece of luck, windfall money, windfall profit, windfall, easy money, illegal gain, ill-gotten gains, theft, stealing, bribe, plunder, booty, spoils, spoils of war, plum (Inf), golden handshake (Inf), golden parachute (US inf), gettings (Inf), killing (Inf), clean up (US inf), rake-off (Sl), gravy (Sl), boodle (Sl), swag (Sl), freebie (US sl), exes (Brit inf)

▶ *125 Compensation, 686 Prosperity, 742 Wealth, 878 Reward, 729 Giving, 681 Trophy, 496 Discovery, 589 Chance, 660 Easiness, 736 Stealing*

6 **yield**, output, production, proceeds, produce, product, crop, vintage crop, bumper crop, cash crop, second crop, gleanings, harvest, fruit, vintage, vintage wine

▶ *243 Production, 68 Agriculture*

7 **gainer**, winner, moneymaker, breadwinner, wealthy person, rich person, billionaire, millionaire (*or* millionairess), parvenu (*or* parvenue), capitalist, tycoon, magnate, heir, heiress, beneficiary, procurer, earner, fund-raiser, profiteer, usurer, collector, gatherer, gleaner, hoarder, wage earner, wage worker (US), saver, thief, robber, briber, plunderer, moneyspinner (Inf), money-grubber (Inf), golddigger (Inf), fat cat (US sl)

8 **wealthy people**, the rich and famous, the well-to-do, the nouveaux riches, the jet set, the upper class, the upper crust (Inf), the wellheeled (Inf), glitterati (Inf), the haves (Inf), Sloanes (Inf)

VERBS

9 **gain**, get, win, have success, acquire, obtain, make one's own, appropriate, annex, attain, have an advantage, have an unfair advantage, benefit, receive a benefit, come by, gather in, bring in, secure, procure, earn, make, make money, profit, make a profit, realize, raise funds, collect funds, launch an appeal, beg, borrow, or steal, profiteer, lay hands on, get one's fingers on, get hold of (Inf), pull down (Inf), glom on to (US sl)

10 **augment**, increase, escalate, gain in value, appreciate, rise in price, receive a pay increase, receive a rise, receive a raise (US), reach a crescendo, grow, experience growth, gain height, develop, proliferate, mushroom, flower, expand, snowball, broaden, widen, spread, become larger, put on weight, gain weight, get fatter, inflate, dilate, advance, advance on, approach, get nearer, reach, get to, make headway, make rapid strides, cover the ground, gain ground, improve, perform better, jump higher, run faster, throw further, endure longer, gain on, gain time, recover lost

ground, overtake, leave behind

11 **acquire**, collect, gather together, gather in, have a bumper crop, glean, harvest, assemble, accumulate, cumulate, accrete, amass, save up, save, bring together, get together, scrape together (*or* up), round up, dig up, catch, hoard, store away, heap, stack, pile up, pile, stockpile, stock up, pool together, pool, bunch together (Inf), bunch (Inf), scare up (US inf)

12 **earn**, earn income, have a private income, earn a living, balance the books, have gainful employment, make money by, turn into money, get in advance, receive an advance, receive royalties, have regular wages, get paid, draw a salary, draw a pay cheque, credit to one's account, have money coming in, have wealth, draw retirement pay, receive social security payments, receive a pension, receive a stipend, receive maintenance, receive alimony (*or* aliment), receive palimony (US), keep the wolf from the door, turn an honest penny (Inf), bring home the bacon (Inf), earn a crust (Sl)

13 **be profitable**, be financially worthwhile, offer a good living, show a profit, pay, pay well, yield, produce, gross, bring in a return, pay interest, pay a dividend, accrue, roll in

14 **profit**, make a profit, make a net profit, take a profit, reap a profit, turn to profit, sell at a profit, capitalize on, make capital out of, have capital gains, cash in on, clear, make a good living, make a fortune, have the Midas touch, prosper, draw interest, take a percentage, earn a dividend, pay dividends, inherit, receive a bequest, receive a legacy, succeed to, come into money, fall heir to, compensate, study on a scholarship, receive a fringe benefit, receive a bonus, have an expense account, draw an allowance, have extra money, save, receive a tip, win an award, get a medal, win a trophy, win a prize, break the bank, win the pools, win the lottery, find the pot of gold, get something for nothing, receive a free gift, discover a treasure trove, come across, light upon, have a piece of luck, receive a windfall profit, steal, bribe, plunder, receive a golden handshake (Inf), make a killing (Inf), clean up (US inf), line one's pockets (Inf), make one's pile (Inf), laugh all the way to the bank (Inf), hit the jackpot (Inf), rake it in (Sl), rake off (Sl)

ADJECTIVES

15 **gainful**, beneficial, acquiring, acquired, obtainable, attainable, available, procurable, inheriting, inherited, beneficiary, compensatory, fund-raising, moneymaking, capitalistic, profitable, profitmaking, profit-taking, gross, net, on the credit side, gratuitous, giveaway (US), windfall, financially worthwhile, useful, paid, paying, well-paying, lucrative, remunerative, rewarding, money-spinning (Inf)

16 greedy, avaricious, acquisitive, grasping, plundering, grabby (US inf), money-grubbing (Inf), on the make (Inf), gold-digging (Inf)

17 well-off, well-to-do, in the black, comfortably off, doing fine, doing very nicely, solvent, well provided for, doing great, affluent, prosperous, rich, filthy rich, wealthy, worth millions, rich as Croesus, rich as King Midas, well-heeled (Inf), flush (Inf), rolling in it (Inf), loaded (Sl)

18 acquisitional, acquisitive, collective, accumulative, cumulative, mountainous, augmentative, augmented, expansive, gaining, ahead of time, widening, inflationary, improvable, improved

19 yielding, productive, fruitful, fertile, prolific, bumper, harvested

ADVERBS

20 gainfully, beneficially, for money (or profit or gain), advantageously, acquisitively, profitably, at a profit, gratuitously, lucratively, remuneratively, greedily, avariciously, affluently, prosperously, richly, wealthily, collectively, accumulatively, cumulatively, expansively, productively, fruitfully, fertilely, prolifically, in the black

722 Loss

'Tis better to have loved and lost than never to have lost at all. Samuel Butler.

What's lost upon the roundabouts we pulls up on the swings! Patrick Reginald Chalmers.

Where have all the flowers gone?/ Young girls picked them every one. Pete Seeger.

To lose one parent, Mr Worthing, may be regarded as a misfortune; to lose both looks like carelessness. Oscar Wilde.

NOUNS

1 loss, losing, misplacing, mislaying, taking away, decrease, decrement, subtraction, deprivation, privation, hopeless loss, dead loss, total loss, utter loss, irreparable loss, irretrievable loss, dispossession, eviction, expropriation, divestment, robbery, stripping, asset-stripping, detriment, disadvantage, setback, check, reverse, reversal, failure, defeat, penalty, forfeiture, forfeit, loss of freedom, loss of rights, disentitlement, disenfranchisement (or disfranchisement), disqualification, loss of consciousness, coma, death, bereavement, spiritual loss, perdition, sacrifice, denial, loss of weight, weight loss, dieting, slimming, fasting, weight-watching, figure-watching, anorexia, riddance, good riddance, nonrestoration, nonrecovery

▶ *129 Decrease, 131 Subtraction, 458 Disappearance, 254 Absence, 879 Punishment, 16 Law, 7 Religion, 60 Medicine, 45 Cookery, 734 Taking*

2 financial loss, loss of profit, lack of profit, loss of earnings, poor return, cut price, cut rate (US), loss leader, diminishing returns, losses, losings, operating at a loss, running at a loss, cost, expense, expenditure, not making ends meet, deficit, deficiency, insufficiency, shortfall, overspending, overdraft, debit, insolvency, bankruptcy, going to the wall, going belly-up (US sl)

▶ *741 Money, 752 Discount, 748 Expenditure, 744 Credit, 745 Debt, 743 Poverty*

3 waste, wastefulness, wastage, squandering, dissipation, misuse, losing battle, wasted effort, loss of interest, unproductiveness, fruitlessness, spilt milk, waste of breath, waste of time, vain labour, labour of Sisyphus, fool's errand, wild-goose chase

▶ *607 Waste, 614 Uselessness*

4 lessening, dwindling, falling off, waning, wasting away, fading out, dimming, wearing, wearing away, erosion, wear and tear, blood, sweat, and tears, exhaustion, depletion, shrinkage, depreciation, diminution, outflow, draining, drain, dribbling away, seeping away, leakage, haemorrhage, evaporation, impoverishment, deterioration

▶ *628 Deterioration*

5 destruction, denudation, spoiling, despoilment, spoliation, wilful destruction, sabotage, harm, injury, impairment, damage, ruin, ablation

▶ *244 Destruction*

6 loser, born loser, failure, reject, disqualified athlete, unsuccessful candidate, flounderer, black sheep, lost sheep, lost soul, damned soul, fallen angel, sinner, dissipated person, good-for-nothing, ne'er-do-well, scapegoat, victim, dupe, prey, bungler, incompetent, star-crossed lover, lame dog, lame duck, underdog, social outcast, down-and-out, wasteful person, waster, squanderer, polluter, overspender, defaulter, bankrupt, wallflower (Inf), no-hoper (Inf), no-good (US inf), flop (Inf), fall guy (US inf)

7 dieter, slimmer, weight watcher, Weight-watchers (Tm), anorexic, faster

8 lost thing, lost game, lost chance, lost opportunity, lost cause, lost election, lost labour, lost love, lost art, lost memory, lost time, lost hope, Lost Generation, lost tribes, lost ground, lost battle, lost war, lost life, lost youth, misspent youth

▶ *12 Government and Politics, 676 War*

VERBS

9 lose, suffer loss, incur loss, meet with a loss, have no more, not find, lose sight of, not be able to find, look in vain for, misplace, mislay, miss, lose track of, lose contact with, lose one's memory, forget, take away, decrease, subtract, consume, deprive, dispossess, evict, expropri-

ate, divest, rob, strip, asset-strip, have a set-back, have a reversal, fail, lose a chance, miss an opportunity, face defeat, lose out, lose the battle, lose the election, lose the day, lose the match, almost win, just lose, lose by a whisker, incur a penalty, forfeit, sacrifice, relinquish, lose one's freedom, become a prisoner, lose one's rights, become disenfranchised (*or* dis-franchised), face disqualification, face a total loss, die, lose weight, diet, slim, fast, starve oneself, refuse food, go on a hunger strike, become anorexic, lose consciousness, faint, collapse, say goodbye to, kiss goodbye (Sl), be pipped at the post (Sl)

10 **have a financial loss**, incur losses, sell at a loss, lose money, lose profits, lose earnings, have a poor return, cut prices, have diminish-ing returns, suffer a setback, have losses, oper-ate at a loss, run at a loss, throw good money after bad, make no profit, not make ends meet, run a deficit, fall short, have nothing to show for, overspend, pour money down the drain, overdraw, run up an overdraft, become insol-vent, face bankruptcy, go to the wall, go into the red (Inf), come to a sticky end (Inf), go broke (Inf), go bust (Inf), go belly-up (US sl)

11 **be wasteful**, waste, squander, dissipate, throw away, fritter away, pour down the drain, let slip through one's fingers, waste one's efforts, waste one's breath, waste one's time, labour in vain, draw a blank, go on a fool's errand, go on a wild-goose chase

12 **lessen**, dwindle, wane, fade out, dim, deplete, depreciate, diminish, deteriorate, waste away, wear, wear away, erode, drain, dribble away, leak, haemorrhage, seep away, evaporate, shrink, impoverish, become impoverished, undergo privation, lose the battle, lose interest in

13 **destroy**, misuse, despoil, spoliate, spoil, de-nude, destroy, wilfully destroy, sabotage, harm, injure, impair, damage, ruin, ablate

14 **go to waste**, come to nothing, come to naught, go (*or* run) to seed, go to pot, dissipate, scatter to the winds, throw out of the window, go to the dogs, go (*or* end) up in smoke, go down the drain (*or* tube *or* pan), go up the spout (Sl)

15 **lose someone**, give someone the slip, avoid, evade, elude, dodge, escape, outrun, outstrip, leave behind, shake off

ADJECTIVES

16 **losing**, lost, missing, gone missing, mis-placed, mislaid, astray, without, lacking, out of sight, out of view, lost from view, fallen by the wayside, nowhere to be found, long-lost, gone forever, gone for good, gone by the board, forgotten, out of mind, dead and bur-ied, lost at sea, sunk, irrecoverable, irretriev-able, incorrigible, irredeemable, hopeless, de-

priving, deprived, failing, failed, out of the window (Inf), squandered, depleted, stripped of, shorn of, bereft, spent, destroyed, ruined, irreclaimable, unsalvageable, the worse for wear, nonrecyclable, gone down the drain

17 **unprofitable**, profitless, non-profit-making, loss-leading, loss-making, cut-price, cut-rate (US), out-of-pocket, out, unsuccessful, defi-cient, insufficient, prodigal, wasteful, squan-dering, overspent, overextended, overdrawn, nonpaying, insolvent, impoverished, ruined, ruinous, bankrupt, poor, cash-poor, in the red (Inf), broke (Inf), bust (Inf), belly-up (US sl)

18 **at a loss**, out of place, off course, off familiar territory, lost in thought, disoriented, con-fused, bewildered, lost in amazement, aston-ished, dumbstruck, astray, floundering, out of one's element, out of one's depth, all at sea, like a fish out of water, like a square peg in a round hole, gobsmacked (Sl)

ADVERBS

19 **irrecoverably**, irretrievably, irredeemably, irreclaimably, hopelessly

20 **at a loss**, at a cut price, at a cut rate (US), out of pocket, unsuccessfully, deficiently, insuffi-ciently, prodigally, wastefully, in the red (Inf)

21 **out of place**, incongruously, anomalously, off course, off familiar territory, out of one's element, out of one's depth, out of sight, out of view, like a fish out of water, like a square peg in a round hole

723 Possession

NOUNS

1 **possession**, right of possession, possessor-ship, possessing, owning, ownership, propri-etorship, lawful possession, legal possession, rightful possession, enjoyment, property rights, proprietary rights, mineral rights, lord-ship, dominion, sovereignty, holding, hold, grasp, grip, retention, making one's own, claiming, laying claim to, taking, taking pos-session, appropriating, appropriation, control, marking one's territory, occupying, occu-pancy, occupation, hoisting one's flag over, landownership, landowning, landholding, land tenure, custody, title, original title, lease, leasehold, freehold, tenure, tenancy, tenantry, exclusive possession, sole possession, mo-nopoly, monopolization, cornering of the market, a corner on, engrossment, forestal-ment, sublease, squatting, squatterism, squatters' rights, claim, legal claim, heirship, heirdom, inheritance, heritage, patrimony, nine tenths of the law, nine points of the law, bird in the hand

▶ *734 Taking, 728 Transfer of Property, 845 Enti-tlement, 599 Use, 14 Finance, 13 Economics*

2 **legal terms**, pre-emption, prescription, fee

simple, seisin, de facto possession, de jure possession, uti possidetis, chose in possession, dominium
▶ *16 Law*

3 **medieval ownership**, villeinage, villeinhold, socage, free socage, burgage, frankalmoign, fee, fief, feud, feudality

4 **possession**, property, owned property, freehold, estate, landed estate, plantation, colony, dependency, protectorate, dominion, personal effects, belongings, accoutrements, appurtenances, chattel, bag and baggage, stuff, gear, things, all one's worldly goods and chattels, clothes off one's back
▶ *725 Property, 3 History*

5 **possessor**, owner, monopolizer, buyer, purchaser, holder, landowner, property owner, leaseholder, lessee, householder, occupant, occupier, owner-occupier, mortgagee, proprietor (*or* proprietress), landlord (*or* landlady), resident, tenant, sitting tenant, rent-payer, lodger, boarder, paying guest, guest, visitor, squatter, taker
▶ *255 Inhabitant, 344 Arrival*

6 **lord**, lord and master, overlord, master, mistress, lord (*or* lady) of the manor, squire, laird (Scot), thane, earldorman (Arch), man (*or* woman) of property, man (*or* woman) of substance
▶ *701 Subjection*

VERBS

7 **possess**, own, have in one's possession, have in hand, have in one's grip, have in one's grasp, command, have at one's command, have at one's disposal, buy, take up residence in, move into, take out a tenancy, take out a mortgage, become the proud owner of, have title to, have the deed for, have tenure of, have in one's name, have, have and hold, hold, number among one's possessions, call one's own, enjoy, occupy, dwell in, monopolize, have all to oneself, keep for oneself, have exclusive possession of, have exclusive rights to, forestall, engross, tie up, corner, get a corner on, corner the market, rent, let, claim, squat, squat on, claim squatter's rights, hog (Sl)

ADJECTIVES

8 **possessing**, possessed of, in possession, having possessions, possessory, owning, landowning, landed, property-owning, propertied, having, having and holding, holding, enjoying, proprietorial, occupying, squatting, exclusive, unshared, monopolistic

9 **possessed**, owned, owned by, in (*or* under) the ownership of, one's (very) own, in the possession of, in the hands of, in one's hands, in one's grasp, held, belonging to, in one's name, at one's disposal, at one's command, on hand, in store, in the bank, exclusive, unshared, monopolized by

ADVERBS

10 **possessively**, in the possession of, in one's name, at one's disposal, at one's command, monopolistically, exclusively

724 Joint Possession

NOUNS

1 **joint possession**, possession in common, having a part, having a share, joint tenancy, tenancy in common, joint ownership, common ownership, shared ownership, time sharing, time-share apartment, condominium (US), part ownership, partnership, copartnership, union, association, alliance, public corporation, public company, joint stock, common stock, common money, profit-sharing, dividend, share, joint bank account, pool, kitty, tontine, common supplies, store, common property, common land, common, public land, (public) park, cooperative system, public domain, nationalization, public ownership, state ownership, socialism, socialization, communism, communization, collectivism, collectivization, collective farm, collective, sharecropping (US), communal living, commune, community, communalization, kolkhoz, kibbutz, joint government, coalition, federation, confederation, commonwealth, commonweal, the Commonwealth of Nations, international organization, United Nations (UN), United Nations Organization (UNO), European Community (EC), Common Market, global village, cooperative, dependency, dominion, democracy, participatory democracy, town meeting
▶ *664 Cooperation, 146 Inclusion, 723 Possession, 725 Property, 741 Money, 605 Store, 746 Payment, 12 Government and Politics, 68 Agriculture*

2 **participation**, group participation, membership, affiliation, association, collaboration, cooperation, joint action, sympathy strike, companionship, fellowship, mutualism, inclusion, involvement, engagement, contribution, partaking, complicity, sharing, cosharing, shared feelings, fellow feeling, sympathy, empathy
▶ *759 Feeling*

3 **participant**, participator, partaker, sharer, co-tenant, fellow tenant, joint owner, timeshare owner, condominium owner (US), roommate, flatmate, apartment sharer (US), partner, copartner, shareholder, ally, confederate, associate, colleague, collaborator, accomplice, accessory, party, a party to, member, community member, commune member, communard, kibbutznik, socialist, communist, party member, union member, sympathizer, empathizer, sharecropper (US), sharefarmer (Aus)

VERBS

4 **have joint possession**, hold in common, share (in), take a share, share expenses, split the difference, go Dutch, have a stake in, co-operate, contribute, participate (in), become a member, join, associate oneself with (*or* to), take part in, enter into, partake of, involve oneself, have to do with, have a hand in, have a finger in (the pie), have a voice (*or* say) in, join in, be in on, communalize, socialize, communize, nationalize, internationalize, share and share alike, go shares (Inf), go halves (Inf), go fifty-fifty (Inf), go even-Stephen (Inf), have a piece of (Inf), get in on the act (Inf)

ADJECTIVES

5 **jointly possessing**, jointly possessed, joint, united, concerted, associate, corporate, profit-sharing, time-sharing, house-sharing, flat-sharing, apartment-sharing (US), cooperative, common, in common, communal, general, public, mutual, collective, socialistic, communistic, the people's, global, international, participating, participatory, participative, accessory, partaking, part of, involved (in), sympathetic, empathetic, in on, in the middle of, in the same boat, share and share alike

ADVERBS

6 **in common**, commonly, together, jointly, unitedly, cooperatively, in cooperation with, collectively, communally, socialistically, communistically, globally, throughout the world, internationally, on the international scene, sympathetically, empathetically

725 Property

NOUNS

1 **property**, possession, realty, real property, real estate (US), freehold, leasehold, estate, legal estate, *praedium* (L), title, right, copyright, patent, receipt, claim, rent-roll, domain, building, public property, common property, church property, benefice, living, holding, small holding, homestead, farm, cottage, bungalow, house, ranch, hacienda, chalet, villa, manor, mansion, flat, apartment, tenement, penthouse, plantation, castle, land, lands, acres, broad acres, acreage, tract, grounds, lot, plot, parcel, allotment, landed estate, landed property, common land, common, crown lands, political possession, territory, dependency, dominion

▶ *723 Possession, 724 Joint Possession, 728 Transfer of Property, 845 Entitlement, 7 Religion, 688 Authority, 12 Government and Politics*

2 **legal terms**, personalty, domain, demesne, chose, chose in possession, chose in action, messuage, tenement, tenure, hereditament, fee simple, fee tail, mortmain, dead hand, immovables, movables, jointure, entail, remainder, reversion, limitation

3 **historic property terms**, toft, allodium, feu, frankalmoign, fee, fief, feud, fiefdom, feudality, villeinage, villeinhold, socage, free socage, burgage, copyhold, seigneury, appanage

4 **possessions**, personal property, effects, personal effects, estate and effects, belongings, gear, stuff, things, material things, what one can call one's own, what one has to one's name, one's all, chattels (Fml), goods and chattels, worldly goods, trappings, temporalities, paraphernalia, accoutrements, appurtenances, duffel (*or* duffle) (US), accessories, appendages, impedimenta, luggage, baggage, bag and baggage, furniture, fixtures and fittings, bits and pieces

▶ *257 Contents*

5 **personal estate**, one's worth, what one is worth, net worth, circumstances, state, assessed valuation, assets, resources, collateral, valuables, one's money, one's fortune, wealth, inheritance, legacy, heirloom, funds, income, capital, revenue, means, substance, securities, stocks and shares, stocks and bonds, portfolio, tangible assets, tangibles, intangible assets, intangibles, fixed assets, frozen assets, liquid assets, net assets, current assets, stock, stock in trade, merchandise, wares, goods, contents, plant

▶ *742 Wealth, 602 Means, 729 Giving*

6 **marriage settlement**, dowry, dower, bride price, dot, portion, marriage portion, allotment, allowance, pin money, maintenance, alimony, aliment (Scot), palimony (US)

▶ *823 Marriage*

7 **property man** (*or* **woman**), dealer in real property, estate agent, real-estate agent (US), realtor (US), speculator, investor, stockholder, shareholder, developer, property owner, man (*or* woman) of property, man (*or* lady) of the house, lord (*or* lady) of the manor, freeholder, owner, landowner, holder, householder, leaseholder, lessee, tenant, sitting tenant

ADJECTIVES

8 **propertied**, proprietary, possessing, possessed, freehold, leasehold, copyhold, movable, immovable, real, allotted, territorial, landed, praedial, manorial, seignorial, feudal, feudatory, feodal, allodial, patrimonial, hereditary, heritable, testamentary, limited, assessed, collateral, secured, tangible, intangible, fixed, frozen, liquid, net, endowed, dowered, established, copyrighted, patented

VERBS

9 **own property**, possess, buy property, have an estate, occupy a freehold, rule a territory, own personal effects, have belongings, have to one's name, own assets, have resources, put up collateral, inherit, have substance, own stocks and shares (*or* bonds), have a portfolio, put in

possession, endow, dower, possess with, bless with, give, devise, bequeath, grant, allot, assign

ADVERBS

10 **proprietarily**, hereditarily, heritably, with a dowry, patrimonially, collaterally, territorially

726 Retention

NOUNS

1 **retention**, retainment, keeping, holding (on), grabbing, prehension, prehensility, adhesion, stickiness, viscidity, hanging on, clinging on (*or* to), tenaciousness, tenacity, persistence, handhold, foothold, footing, toehold, clutch, clamp, clinch, clench, grasp, hug, bear hug, embrace, clasp, cuddle, squeeze, compression, hold, firm hold, seizure, grip, tight grip, iron grip, grip of iron, grip of steel, vicelike grip, death grip, stranglehold, lock, headlock, hammerlock, fullnelson, half-nelson

▶ *284 Support, 407 Touch, 137 Connection, 138 Adhesion, 135 Union, 262 Contraction, 699 Restraint*

2 **detention**, suppression, repression, containment, envelopment, enclosing, pincer movement, keeping in, imprisoning, holding in, bottling up, plug, stop, stopper, cork, locking in, holding back, saving, cherishing, maintenance, preservation

▶ *661 Hindrance, 323 Closure, 531 Concealment, 711 Refusal, 826 Endearment, 637 Preservation, 605 Store*

3 **tools for gripping**, pliers, wrench, spanner, tongs, fire tongs, sugar tongs, tweezers, pincers, nippers, vice, clamp, grip, forceps, grapnel, grappling iron, hook, anchor, fastening, staple, stapler, glue, gum, paste, adhesive, clasp, clip, paperclip, tie clasp (*or* clip), finger, fingers, fist, clenched fist, hand, paw, claw, talon, fingernails, nails, tooth, teeth, fangs, tentacle, tendril, feeler, dukes (Sl), hooks (Sl), meathooks (Sl), mitts (Sl), bunch of fives (Sl)

▶ *603 Tool*

4 **wall**, stone wall, brick wall, retaining wall, bulwark, embankment, abutment, buttress, flying buttress, fence, picket fence, barbed wire, chicken wire

▶ *301 Enclosure*

5 **retentiveness**, retention, constipation, remembrance, good memory, photographic memory, recalling, recall, recollection, memorizing, memorization, not forgetting

▶ *511 Memory*

VERBS

6 **retain**, keep, hold (on to), take hold of, buttonhole, get a firm hold, maintain one's hold, hold tight (*or* fast), cleave to, not let go, grab, stick to, adhere (to), agglutinate, hang on (to),

staple, glue, gum, paste, fasten on, cling on (*or* to), show tenaciousness, have tenacity, have persistence, get a foothold, get one's footing, get a toehold, clutch, clamp, clinch, clench, grasp, hug, give a bear hug, embrace, grapple, clasp, cuddle, squeeze, compress, seize, grip, get a tight grip, have an iron grip, have a grip of iron, have a grip of steel, have a vicelike grip, get a stranglehold on, get a half-nelson on, have by the throat, throttle, strangle, lock, get a headlock on, tighten one's grip, fix one's teeth into, dig one's toes (*or* teeth *or* nails) into, never let go, hang on with all one's might, hang on for dear life, hold on like a bulldog, hold on like a snapping turtle (*or* snapper) (US), stick like a leech, gripe (Arch)

7 **detain**, suppress, repress, restrain, imprison, hold (*or* pin) down, get (*or* keep) a firm hold on, catch, steady, support, contain, draw the line, envelop, enclose, keep in, hold in, wall in, fence in, bottle up, plug, stop, cork, clog, constipate, lock in, keep secret, keep (*or* hold) back, hold up, keep to one side, keep to oneself, keep in one's own hands, keep in hand, keep, have in hand, hold on to, keep a tight hold (*or* rein) on, retain, withhold, refuse, monopolize, save, maintain, preserve, cherish, take to one's bosom, not part with, not dispose of, store

8 **remember**, have a good memory, have a photographic memory, not forget, recall, recollect, memorize, hold in one's mind

ADJECTIVES

9 **retentive**, retaining, tenacious, cohesive, adhesive, costive, constipated, clogged, indissoluble, firm, sticky, gluelike, gluey, gummy, prehensile, tightfisted, parsimonious, grasping, gripping, clinging, clasping, vicelike, strangling, throttling, restraining, gooey (Inf)

10 **retained**, stuck firm (*or* fast), fast, held, bound, glued, gummed, grasped, gripped, in the grip of, clasped, clutched, pinioned, pinned, stapled, strangled, detained, imprisoned, penned, kept in, held in, walled in, fenced-in, contained, circumscribed, saved, kept (back), withheld, refused, preserved

ADVERBS

11 **tenaciously**, with resolution, cohesively, adhesively, like glue, indissolubly, stickily, parsimoniously, with a tight fist, firmly, in a firm grip, like a vice, for keeps, to keep, for good, for good and all, forever, for always

727 Disposal

NOUNS

1 **disposal**, giving up, getting rid of, discarding, parting with, alienation, transfer, substitution, nonretention, letting go, releasing, release, dismissal, firing, sacking, freeing, liberation, liber-

ating, unfreezing, decontrol, dispensation, exemption, nonliability, dissolution, divorce, cession, abandonment, removal, clearance, ejection, riddance, dumping, scrapping, renunciation, relinquishment, forgoing, forswearing, swearing off, cancellation, abrogation, disuse, desuetude, availability, disposability, outflow, incontinence, excretion, marching orders (Inf), the boot (Sl), the chop (Sl)

▶ *598 Relinquishment, 349 Expulsion, 728 Transfer of Property, 222 Substitution, 704 Cancellation, 700 Liberation, 136 Separation*

2 **disposal of property**, sale, selling, selling off, putting on the market, clearance sale, closing-down sale, jumble sale, boot sale, car-boot sale, rummage sale (US), garage sale (US), bazaar, church bazaar, fair, auction, Dutch auction, saleableness, saleability, sale and lease back, disposability

▶ *739 Sale*

3 **disposable things**, junk, jumble, white elephant, castoff, flotsam, jetsam, flotsam and jetsam, rubbish, garbage (US), trash (US)

▶ *614 Uselessness*

4 **wastebin**, wastepaper basket, wastebasket, dustbin, garbage (or trash) can (US), rubbish bin, litter bin, bin, rubbish truck, dustcart (US), rubbish scow, skip, dredger, incinerator, waste disposer, waste disposal unit, drain, waste pipe, sewer

▶ *258 Container*

5 **wasteyard**, junkyard, dump, town (or city) dump, landfill site, scrapyard, dustheap (US), junk (or trash) pile, rubbish heap (or pile), refuse heap, compost heap, (kitchen) midden (Dial), cesspit, cesspool, septic tank, sewage farm (or works), nuclear reprocessing plant

6 **rubbish collector**, dustbin man (or woman), garbage man (or woman) (US), binman, dustman, litter picker, street sweeper, rag and bone man, junkman (US)

7 **toilet**, lavatory, water closet, WC, earth closet, outhouse (US), privy, latrine, head(s) (Naut), portable toilet, chemical toilet, commode, jakes (Dial), toilet bowl, pan, lavatory bowl (or pan), stool, chamber pot, bedpan, potty, urinal, Ladies, Gentlemen (or Gents), Men (US), Women (US), Men's (Rest) Room (US), Women's (Rest) Room (US), little boys' room, little girls' room, smallest room (in the house), public convenience, cloakroom, bathroom, rest room (US), washroom (US), comfort station (US), powder room, lounge, loo (Inf), bog (Sl), john (US sl), crapper (Sl), khazi (or kharzie) (Sl), thunderbox (Sl), thunderbowl (Sl), jerry (Inf), gazunder (Sl)

▶ *353 Excretion*

8 **sink**, kitchen sink, draining board, cistern, cesspit, cesspool, septic tank, septic (system) (Aus), sump, slough, soakaway, gutter, drain,

sewer, cloaca, main, dunghill, midden (Arch or Dial), tip, dump, refuse dump, rubbish dump, rubbish pile, trash dump (US), rubbish heap (Brit), landfill, compost-heap, compose, dustbin, coal cellar, Augean stables, pigsty, pigpen (US), den, slum, tenement building, tenement, shambles, abattoir, slaughterhouse, quarantine, quarantined house, quarantine flag, spittoon, cuspidor (US), coal hole (Inf)

▶ *607 Waste, 258 Container*

VERBS

9 **dispose of**, get rid of, not retain, dispense with, stop using, do without, get along without, spare, give up, let go, let loose of, release, waive, abandon, cede, yield, surrender, relinquish, part with, marry off, discard, throw away, cast off, eject, jettison, let out, leak, emit, cast away, cast overboard, scrap, dump, destroy, free, liberate, lift, lift restrictions, derestrict, raise an embargo, decontrol, deregulate, deration, substitute, replace, supersede, unhand, relax one's grip, release one's hold, unlock, unclinch, unclench, open, unbind, untie, disentangle, disunite, negate, dissolve, divorce, disinherit, turn one's back on, impoverish, cut off without a penny, cut off with a shilling, disown, maroon, cast out, renounce, abjure, forswear, swear off, disclaim, recant, cancel, revoke, abrogate, forgo, abandon one's stance, wash one's hands of, ditch (Sl)

10 **dismiss**, discharge, lay off, give notice (to quit), make redundant, fire, sack, give the sack to, ease out, edge out, elbow out, pension off, put out to grass, put out to pasture (US), kick out (Inf), boot out (Inf), give someone the (old) heave-ho (Inf), give someone their marching orders (Inf), drop (US sl), give someone the boot (Sl), give someone the chop (Sl)

11 **dispose of property**, sell property, sell, sell off, have a sale, put up for sale, put on the market, vend, peddle, hawk, push, auction, have an auction, put under the hammer, put on the block (US), sell to the highest bidder, sell over the counter, sell under the counter, sell on the black market, flog (Sl)

ADJECTIVES

12 **disposed (of)**, dispensed with, relinquished, released, not retained, not kept, got rid of, discarded, freed, liberated, abandoned, divorced, disowned, disinherited, forgone, forsworn

13 **dismissed**, discharged, fired, sacked, made redundant, under notice to quit, given notice to quit, laid off, given the sack, given one's marching orders (Inf), given the chop (Sl), given the boot (Sl)

14 **for sale**, available, saleable, to be disposed of, transferable, inheritable, sold off

15 unclaimed, remaining, left behind, unappropriated, unowned, unpossessed, derelict

ADVERBS

16 disposably, distributively, by letting go, by giving up, by auction, under the hammer, on the block (US), by sale, over the counter, under the counter, without an inheritance, without a penny

728 Transfer of Property

NOUNS

1 transfer of property, transfer, transference, change of ownership, transmission, transmittal, deeding, conveyancing, conveyance, consignment, delivery, handover, change of hands, changeover, lease, let, rental, hire, hire-purchase, buying, sale, trade, trade-off, barter, conversion, exchange, interchange, nationalization, privatization, takeover, takeover bid, substitution, delegation, devolution, settlement, settling, vesting, conferment, conferral, assignment, disposal, gift, dowry, disposition, bequeathal, bequest, heritability, succession, reversion, inheritance

▶ *727 Disposal, 223 Exchange, 222 Substitution, 737 Trade, 739 Sale, 742 Wealth, 729 Giving, 732 Lending, 12 Government and Politics*

2 person transferring property, conveyancer, seller, buyer, negotiator, lender, loaner, borrower, renter, hirer, pawnbroker

VERBS

3 transfer property, transfer ownership, transfer, convey, deliver, deed, deed over, confer ownership upon, put in possession, lease, lend, let, rent, hire, buy, sell, trade, make a trade-off, barter, convert, exchange, interchange, nationalize, privatize, consign, give delivery, hand over, cede, make over, sign over, sign away, change hands, change over, take over, make a takeover bid, substitute, delegate, devolve, settle, vest, confer, assign, dispose, make a disposition, make a bequest, bequeath, put in one's will, hand down, hand on, pass on, inherit

4 be transferred, change ownership, change hands, come into the hands of, pass from hand to hand, pass to another, devolve, pass on, descend

ADJECTIVES

5 transferring, transferred, transferable, exchangeable, negotiable, conveyed, conveyable, deeded over, made over, assigned, assignable, consignable, devisable, bequeathing, bequeathed, bequeathable, bestowable, giveable, inheritable

ADVERBS

6 by transfer, by conveyance, by deed, in exchange, under the terms of one's will, as a bequest

729 Giving

NOUNS

1 giving, donation, bestowal, charity, almsgiving, benevolence, benefaction, philanthropy, subvention, subsidization, generosity, generous giving, generous nature, liberality, largess, bounty, contributing, contribution, offering, tithing, subscription, prize-giving, presentation, presentment, awarding, service, commitment, labour of love, voluntary work, charity work, consignment, conveyance, imparting, impartation, delivery, supplying, transfer, provision, concession, surrender, surrendering, endowing, endowment, settlement, dowry, grant, granting, conferral, conferment, investment, investiture, enfeoffment (Fml), infeudation (Arch), bequeathal, leaving, will-making, will, testament, last will and testament, gifting, bribing

▶ *831 Benevolence, 833 Philanthropy, 755 Generosity, 741 Money, 823 Marriage, 725 Property, 728 Transfer Of Property, 16 Law*

2 gift, present, birthday present, anniversary present, Christmas present, Christmas box, box, souvenir, memento, keepsake, a little something, token, token of esteem, gift token, gift voucher, tip, fee, honorarium, incentive pay, subsidy, subvention, support, price support, tax benefit, tax write-off, grant, grant-in-aid, allowance, pocket money, stipend, allotment, aid, financial assistance, help, scholarship, fellowship, welfare, public welfare, relief, welfare payment, alimony, palimony (US), social security benefit, retirement benefit, annuity, pension, old-age insurance, bequest, legacy, inheritance, gratuity, baksheesh, cumshaw, *pourboire* (Fr), *Trinkgeld* (Ger), consideration, bribe, kickback, douceur, sensitive payment, slush fund, inducement, prize, reward, award, presentation, trophy, bonus, bonanza, something extra, lagniappe (US), perquisite, expense account, benefit, blessing, boon, grace, favour, free gift, giveaway (US), outright gift, ex gratia payment, piece of luck, windfall, (unsolicited) repayment, conscience money, payment, required giving, tribute, tax, income tax, transfer, handsel (Arch), fairing (Arch), golden handshake (Inf), perk (Inf), whip-round (Inf), palm oil (US sl), grease (Sl), gravy (Sl), freebie (US sl), backhander (Sl), hush money (Sl), cough syrup (Sl), rake-off (Sl), sweetener (Sl), schmear (US sl), eckies (*or* exes) (Sl)

▶ *662 Help, 746 Payment, 681 Trophy*

3 offering, dedication, consecration, votive offering, peace offering, thank offering, offertory, collection, sacrifice, self-sacrifice, oblation, Easter offering, Peter's pence (*or* Peter pence), tithe, widow's mite, mite box, contri-

bution, subscription, flag day, tag day (US), appeal, Red Cross, OXFAM, United Way (US), benefit, benefit match, charity game (US), benefit performance, Live Aid, alms, Maundy money, dole, food aid, food parcel, food stamp (US), meal ticket, free meal, bounty, manna, largess, donation, donative, hand-out, give-away (US)

▶ *755 Generosity*

4 **giver**, good giver, cheerful giver, generous giver, philanthropist, provider, benefactor, donator, donor, blood donor, organ donor, kidney donor, bestower, rewarder, tipper, briber, grantor, conferrer, awarder, imparter, presenter, prize-giver, settlor (Fml), testator (or testatrix) (Fml), legator (Fml), devisor (Fml), bequeather, subscriber, contributor, sacrificer, worshipper, tributary, tribute-payer, subject, almoner, almsgiver, saint, good Samaritan, kind person, helper, saviour, The Saviour, supporter, backer, financer, funder, patron (or patroness), distributor of largess, rich uncle, fairy godmother, Lady Bountiful, Santa Claus, Father Christmas, angel (Inf), sugar daddy (Sl)

▶ *572 Willingness, 755 Generosity*

VERBS

5 **give**, make a gift, make a present of, give a birthday present, give an anniversary gift, give a Christmas present, gift, give away, give free, not charge, treat, entertain, have a generous nature, pour out, lavish upon, shower upon, enrich, spare no expense, subscribe to, present, make a presentation, transmit, impart, convey, deliver, supply, consign, lend, render, provide, honour with, favour with, show favour, make time for, have time for, grant, vouchsafe, bestow upon, confer upon, award, accord, will, give by will, will to, make a will, draw up a will, execute a will, make a bequest, bequeath, leave, provide for, endow, dower, give a prize, tender, put into the hands of, lay at the feet of, transfer, turn over, hand over, give over, make over, give out, deal out, measure out, mete out, dole out, share out, share, share with, dispense, part with, come across with, accommodate with, delegate, allot, commission, dispatch, send, give up, cede, yield, entrust, vest, invest with, subsidize, pay, pay towards, finance, pay taxes, pay tribute, reward, offer a reward, dedicate, devote, consecrate, vow, give praise to, offer, offer up, sacrifice, give a gratuity, tip, cross one's palm (with silver), bribe, slip money to, stand (Inf), sweeten the kitty (Inf), put something in the pot (US inf), chip in (Inf), pay one's whack (Inf), dish out (Inf), shell out (Inf), fork out (or over or up) (Sl), kick in (US and Aus sl), grease the palm (Sl)

6 **give to charity**, philanthropize, donate,

tithe, contribute to, commit money, commit time, volunteer, give alms, bestow alms, give freely, give generously, open one's purse, put one's hand in one's pocket, pass round the hat, give the shirt off one's back, launch an appeal, help, help fund, help with money, do one's duty, pay one's share, commit oneself, participate, have a whip-round (Inf)

▶ *755 Generosity, 833 Philanthropy*

ADJECTIVES

7 **given**, giveable, bestowable, impartable, available, saleable, for sale, subventionary, bequeathed, willed, bequeathable, transferable, granted, accorded, bestowed, bonus, giveaway (US), given away, gratis, free (of charge), uncharged, for nothing, costing nothing, for the asking, voluntary, complimentary, courtesy, sacrificial, votive, oblatory, gratuitous, God-given, donative, contributory, tributary, testate (Fml), testamentary (Fml), testamental (Fml), endowed, subsidized, dowered, stipendiary, pensionary, insurable, taxable

8 **giving**, bestowing, imparting, granting, transferring, alms-giving, charitable, benevolent, philanthropic, generous, open-handed, bountiful, liberal

▶ *755 Generosity, 572 Willingness, 833 Philanthropy*

ADVERBS

9 **as a gift**, gratuitously, gratis, free (of charge), for free, without payment, on the house, on one, charitably, with charity, benevolently, generously, bountifully, liberally, sacrificially, votively, oblatorily

730 Receiving

NOUNS

1 **receiving**, recipience, reception, getting, taking, accepting, acceptance, acquisition, collection, collecting, collectorship, receivership, inheritance, heritage, patrimony, legacy, bequest, bequeathal, birthright, heirship, succession, line of succession, primogeniture, hereditament, heirloom

▶ *734 Taking, 723 Possession*

2 **something received**, gift, token, tribute, prize, trophy, money received, earnings, profits, income, salary, pay, take-home pay, revenue, net receipts, gross receipts, proceeds, receipts, returns, box-office returns, gate money, the gate, takings, credits, dividend, bursary, stipend, scholarship, fellowship, maintenance, annuity, tontine, fringe benefit, winnings, ill-gotten gains, allowance, pin money, pocket money, alimony, palimony (US), pension, compensation, bonus, commission, perquisite, perk (Inf)

▶ *729 Giving, 681 Trophy, 741 Money*

3 **acknowledgment of payment**, receipt of

custom, bill, voucher, ticket, counterfoil, stub (US), docket

4 **reception**, admitting, admission, admittance, greeting, welcoming, entertaining, welcoming ceremony, baptism, christening, confirmation, initiation, debut, reception room, reception, lobby, living area, living room, drawing room, sitting room
▶ *348 Admittance, 815 Sociability*

5 **recipient**, receiver, getter, taker, accepter, acceptor, receiver of stolen property, fence (Sl), buyer, purchaser, customer, acquirer, obtainer, procurer, holder, payee, endorsee, consignee, donee (Fml), grantee (Fml), trustee, allottee, lessee, licensee, earner, wage earner, pensioner, old age pensioner (OAP), annuitant, dependent, receiver of honours, scholarship winner, scholar, exhibitioner, fellowship winner, fellow, valedictorian (US), winner, prizewinner, message-receiver, addressee, reader, listener, hearer, viewer, spectator, beholder, audience, one at the receiving end, object of charity, charity case, beggar, sufferer, scapegoat, victim, butt, panhandler (US inf)
▶ *878 Reward, 767 Relief, 879 Punishment*

6 **beneficiary**, heir, heiress, legal heir, heritor (Fml), heir apparent (Fml), heir presumptive (Fml), heir-at-law (Fml), fiduciary heir (Fml), inheritor, inheritress (*or* inheritrix), successor, legatee (Fml), assignee (Fml), assign (Fml), devisee (Fml), coheir, joint heir, next in line
▶ *728 Transfer of Property*

7 **collector**, tax collector, customs officer, excise officer, exciseman, bill collector, debt collector, rent collector, *rentier* (Fr), bailiff, confiscator, sequestrator, receiver, official receiver, liquidator, administrative receiver
▶ *745 Debt*

8 **receiver**, radio receiver, radar receiver, telephone receiver, headset, headphones, earphones
▶ *534 Communications*

VERBS

9 **receive**, be given, have from, get, take, take in, take up, accept, acquire, gain, collect, obtain, secure, come by, come to hand, earn, have an income, gross, net, clear, bring in, take home, pocket, draw a pension, receive social security, inherit, become an heir (*or* heiress), receive a bequest, succeed to, come to one, come into, come in for, pass into one's hand, fall into one's hands, fall to one's lot, fall to one's share, step into the shoes of, take over, take off someone's hands, stick to one's fingers, acknowledge, receipt, give a receipt, credit, accept stolen property, fence (Sl)

10 **receive someone**, admit, greet, welcome, make welcome, shake hands with, hold out one's hand to, advance to meet, receive guests, usher in, entertain, host, act as host (*or* host-

ess), be at home to, open one's doors to, keep open house, receive into the church, baptize, christen, confirm
▶ *815 Sociability*

ADJECTIVES

11 **receiving**, recipient, receptive, taking, accepting, acceptant, wage-earning, salaried, paid, compensated, pensioned, pensioned-off, awarded, rewarded, given, allotted, on the receiving end

12 **receptive**, welcoming, open, open-minded, generous-hearted

13 **received**, accepted, taken, taken over, acquired, gained, collected, secured, inherited, admitted, taken in, heard, read, seen, acknowledged, well-received, welcomed, entertained, received into the church, baptized, christened, confirmed

14 **receivable**, takable, gettable, collectable, compensatory, compensative, pensionary, hereditary, primogenitary

ADVERBS

15 **receptively**, in a receptive way, as a wage-earner, hereditarily, with a warm welcome, as a new member, as a convert, with openness, with an open mind, in an open-minded way, with a generous heart, in a generous-hearted manner

731 Allocation

NOUNS

1 **allocation**, allotting, allotment, assignment, appointment, job allocation, job-sharing, apportionment, apportioning, appropriation, earmarking, tagging, setting aside, division, subdivision, partition, sharing, sharing out, distribution, parcelling out, doling out, dealing out, dispensing, dispensation, delimitation, demarcation, divvying up (US inf)
▶ *143 Part, 724 Joint Possession*

2 **portion**, share, fair share, dividend, allocation, allotment, lot, plot, strip of land, proportion, ratio, quota, dole, pittance, allowance, ration, dose, dosage, measure, dollop, helping, slice, slice of the cake, piece of the pie (US), piece of the action (Inf)
▶ *121 Degree, 302 Limit*

3 **allotted task**, assigned task, assigned job, chore, stint, shift, stretch, bout, period, spell of work
▶ *729 Giving*

VERBS

4 **allot**, allocate, apportion, appropriate, earmark, tag, demarcate, delimit, limit, divide, divide proportionately, split down the middle, prorate, divide up, subdivide, carve up, bisect, split, cut, share, share out, distribute, spread around, dispense, deal out, deal, portion out, dole out, parcel out, mete out, measure, ra-

tion, dose, divvy up (US inf), dish out (Inf)

5 **get one's allotment**, get one's (fair) share, get a share, take a share, take one's cut, be cut in, go shares (Inf), go halves (Inf), get a piece of the action (Inf)

6 **assign**, assign a task, assign a job, assign a part, assign a place, allot a billet, detail

ADJECTIVES

7 **allocated**, allotted, assigned, apportioned, divided, shared out, distributed, dividable, divisible

ADVERBS

8 **proportionately**, respectively, pro rata, per head, per capita, each according to his share

732 Lending

NOUNS

1 **lending**, loaning, giving temporarily, giving, lending money, moneylending, advancing, advance on salary, advance on royalties, advance, advancement, accommodation, grant, giving credit, lending at interest, lending on security, lending on collateral, usury, extortion, pawnbroking, loan-sharking (Inf), hocking (US sl), popping (Sl)
▶ *744 Credit, 48 Literature*

2 **loan**, unsecured loan, secured loan, collateral loan, long-term loan, short-term loan, student loan, instalment loan, bank loan, personal loan, business loan, international loan, foreign loan, lend-lease

3 **lender**, loaner, creditor, moneylender, moneybroker, banker, bank manager, loan officer (US), financier, usurer, loan shark, pawnbroker, mortgagee, mortgage holder, hire-purchase dealer, Shylock (Sl), uncle (Sl)

4 **lending institution**, financial institution, building society, friendly society, savings and loan association (US), credit company, credit-card company, American Express, VISA, finance company (*or* house), loan office (US), mortgage company, bank, credit union, *mont-de-piété* (Fr), IMP (International Monetary Fund), World Bank, European Bank, hock shop (US sl), pop shop (Sl), uncle's (Sl)

VERBS

5 **lend**, loan, give temporarily, give one a loan, negotiate a loan, float a loan (US), lend money, make an unsecured loan, make a secured loan, lend on security (*or* on collateral), give a long-term loan, give a short-term loan, advance, accommodate, grant, allow credit, give credit, lend at interest, practise usury, extort

ADJECTIVES

6 **loaned**, on loan, lent, lending, accommodative, secured, on collateral, unsecured, usurious, extortionate, on credit

ADVERBS

7 **on loan**, on security, on collateral, on (*or* in) advance, on credit

733 Borrowing

Be not made a beggar by banqueting upon borrowing, when thou hast nothing in thy purse: for thou shalt lie in wait for thine own life, and be talked on. Bible: Ecclesiasticus.

The human species, according to the best theory I can form of it, is composed of two distinct races, the men who borrow, and the men who lend. Charles Lamb.

Neither a borrower nor a lender be;/ For loan oft loses both itself and friend,/ And borrowing dulls the edge of husbandry./ William Shakespeare.

NOUNS

1 **borrowing**, request for money, money-raising, fund-raising, advance on salary, advance on royalties, advance, request for credit, loan application, loan transaction, loan agreement, buying on credit, repayment plan, taking out a loan, financing, mortgaging, pledging, pawning, begging, hocking (US sl), popping (Sl), touching (up) (Sl), hitting up (US sl)
▶ *712 Request, 732 Lending, 730 Receiving, 734 Taking*

2 **adoption**, adoptability, appropriation, assumption, using as one's own
▶ *599 Use*

3 **illegal borrowing**, unauthorized borrowing, infringement of copyright, plagiarism, bootlegging, parodying, copying, piracy, pirating, imitating, imitation, fake, pastiche (*or* pasticcio), stealing, autotheft, joyriding (Inf)
▶ *48 Literature, 49 Music, 539 Deception, 118 Imitation, 736 Stealing*

4 **credit**, credit account, credit facility, credit card, charge card, American Express (Tm), VISA (Tm), MasterCard (Tm), phonecard, instalment, buying, instalment plan (US), hire purchase (HP), plastic (Inf), tick (Inf), the never-never (Inf)
▶ *744 Credit, 738 Purchase*

5 **loan**, bank loan, personal loan, business loan, secured loan, mortgage, overdraft, debt, repayable amount, outstanding balance, IOU
▶ *745 Debt*

6 **borrower**, debtor, ower, fund-raiser, mortgagor (*or* mortgager), credit user, credit-card holder, pawner, pledger, sponger, cadger, plagiarist, pirate, imitator

VERBS

7 **borrow**, request money, raise money, take a salary advance, take an advance on royalties, request credit, make a loan application, sign a loan agreement, take out a loan, negotiate a loan, float a loan (US), secure a loan, secure a

personal loan, take out a business loan, provide collateral, finance a purchase, give one's IOU, mortgage one's house, take out a (second) mortgage, have an overdraft, pledge, pawn, beg, scrounge, cadge, sponge, touch someone (up) (Sl), hit someone up (US sl), bum (US sl), hock (US sl), pop (Sl)

8 **adopt**, appropriate, take on, avail oneself of, assume, use as one's own

9 **borrow illegally**, borrow without permission, borrow without authorization, infringe a copyright, plagiarize, bootleg, parody, sample, copy, pirate a record, pirate a video, imitate, fake, steal, steal one's stuff (Inf), joy-ride (Inf)

10 **buy on credit**, open a credit account, have a credit facility, use a credit card, get on credit, run up an account, run up a debt, incur liabilities, buy in instalments, buy on the instalment plan (US), buy on the HP, buy on the never-never (Inf), get on tick (Inf), get on the cuff (Inf)

ADJECTIVES

11 **borrowed**, loaned, mortgaged, secured, securing, money-raising, repayable, outstanding, credit-card, instalment, pawned, adopted, appropriated, infringed, plagiarized, copied, pirated, imitated, fake, ersatz, stolen, plastic (Inf)

12 **adoptive**, adopting, adopted, adoptable, appropriating, appropriated, appropriable, capable of being used

ADVERBS

13 **on loan**, as an advance, by credit, with a credit card, on one's credit account, in instalments

734 Taking

NOUNS

1 **taking**, capture, seizure, obtaining, snatching, grabbing, clutching, grasping, grasping nature, avarice, greed, rapacity, taking in, consumption, taking on, employment, engagement, taking in hand, taking hold, possession, taking possession, assuming ownership, inheritance, sexual possession, sexual assault, rape, ravishment, violation, deflowerment, taking over, takeover, takeover bid, buy-out, merger, appropriation, infringement of copyright, plagiarism, arrogation, annexation, colonization, subjection, subjugation, subduing, conquering, confiscation, nationalization, assumption, requisition, indention, indent, acquisition, usurpation, seizure of power, coup, coup d'état, getting, profit-taking, winning, cadging, bumming, scrounging (Inf), touching (up) (Sl), hitting up (US sl), mooching (Sl)

▶ *782 Desire, 48 Literature, 118 Imitation, 670 Attack, 832 Malevolence*

2 **taking back**, recovery, retrieval, recoupment, regaining, recapturing, recapture, reclaiming, taxing, tax-raising, levying, foreclosing, foreclosure, eviction, seizure, confiscation, dispossession, distraint, repossession, expropriation, disinheritance, deprivation, divestment, annexation, impounding, sequestration, withdrawing, withdrawing a statement, retracting, recanting, backtracking, U-turn, nabbing (Inf), nicking (Sl)

3 **taking away**, removal, eradication, deletion, erasure, blotting out, rubbing out, subtraction, extraction, deduction, cut, asset-stripping, taking out, borrowing, plagiarism, imitation, purloining, stealing, thieving, theft, raiding, raid, plundering, pillaging, marauding, sacking, sack, looting, despoiling, spoliation, grabbing, capturing, arresting, apprehending, making a prisoner, abduction, slavery, kidnapping, hijacking, skyjacking, piracy, taking money away, extorting, extortion, swindle, embezzlement, blackmail, deception, manipulation, pinch (Inf), protection racket (Inf), rip-off (Sl), shakedown (US sl), cop (Sl), nick (Sl), heist (US sl)

▶ *546 Obliteration, 676 War, 540 Falsehood, 16 Law, 877 Immorality*

4 **taking in**, hospitality, access, shelter, sanctuary, asylum, opening one's doors, granting a visa

▶ *831 Benevolence, 815 Sociability*

5 **takings**, take, catch, capture, tax, levy, ill-gotten gains, pickings, rich pickings, gleanings, revenue, receipts, proceeds, turnover, earnings, winnings, savings, spoils, spoils of war, booty, plunder, prize, haul (Inf), plum (Inf), swag (Sl), boodle (Sl), hot goods (Sl), hot property (Sl)

▶ *741 Money*

6 **taker**, usurper, seizer, remover, snatcher, bag-snatcher, grabber, cadger, appropriator, confiscator, sequestrator, receiver, expropriator, asset-stripper, infringer, plagiarist, bootlegger, taking by storm, spoiler, raider, pillager, marauder, sacker, ransacker, looter, despoiler, abductor, embezzler, robber, mugger, rapist, captor, kidnapper, hijacker, skyjacker, extortionist, extortioner, blackmailer, racketeer, greedy person, leech, parasite, vampire, locust, predator, vulture, wolf, shark, crook (Inf), shakedown artist (US sl)

VERBS

7 **take**, capture, seize, obtain, snatch, grab, clutch at, grasp, have a grasping nature, show greed, take in, accept, consume, take on, employ, engage, take in hand, inherit, take hold of, get hold of, lay one's hands on, stake one's claim to, possess, take possession of, squat, assume ownership of, take sexual possession of, assault sexually, rape, ravish, violate, de-

flower, takeover, buy out, merge, take for oneself, appropriate, infringe a copyright, plagiarize, annex, colonize, conquor, subject, subjugate, subdue, overrun, swarm over, earmark, confiscate, nationalize, communalize, assume, assume ownership, requisition, indent, acquire, usurp, seize power, lead a coup, get, take profits, win, bum, scrounge (Inf), touch up (Sl), hit up (US sl), mooch (Sl)

8 **take back**, recover, retrieve, recoup, recover one's costs, recover one's losses, recapture, regain, reclaim, tax, raise taxes, overtax, levy, foreclose, evict, seize, confiscate, dispossess, cut someone out of one's will, cut off without a penny, repossess, distrain, expropriate, disinherit, deprive, divest, annex, impound, sequester

9 **withdraw a statement**, retract, recant, backtrack, do a U-turn, eat one's words (Inf), eat humble pie (Inf)

10 **take away**, remove, eradicate, delete, erase, blot out, rub out, subtract, extract, deduct, take off, cut, mine, tap, milk, strip the assets of, take out, borrow, plagiarize, imitate, purloin, steal, thieve, pilfer, shoplift, help, oneself to, run away with, carry off, run off with, elope with, raid, plunder, pillage, sack, loot, despoil, grab, take into custody, take captive, capture, make a prisoner, trap, ensnare, hold, arrest, apprehend, run in, abduct, kidnap, take a hostage, enslave, shanghai, hijack, skyjack, take money away, extort, extort protection money, swindle, embezzle, fleece, blackmail, dupe, outwit, outsmart, deceive, manipulate, twist round one's little finger, fool, befool, make a fool of, take to the cleaners (Inf), take for a ride (Inf), run a protection racket (Inf), nab (Inf), pinch (Inf), nick (Sl), cop (Sl), rip off (Sl), shake down (US sl), heist (US sl)

11 **be hospitable**, take in, take on board, allow in, give access to, ask in, have round, give shelter to, shelter, give sanctuary to, give asylum to, grant a visa to, open one's doors to

ADJECTIVES

12 **taking**, avaricious, greedy, grasping, rapacious, predatory, possessive, acquisitive, acquiring, merged, takeover, inheriting, assaulted, raped, appropriated, requisitionary, acquisitional, retrievable, taxable, tax-raising, expropriatory, confiscatory, commandeering, annexed, deductive, asset-stripped, plundering, plundered, extortionate, deceptive, manipulative, thieving, rip-off (Sl)

ADVERBS

13 **avariciously**, with avarice, greedily, in a greedy fashion, graspingly, rapaciously, predatorily, like a predator, possessively, acquisitively, retrievably, deductively, extortionately, deceptively, with deception, manipulatively, in a manipulative way

735 Giving Back

NOUNS

1 **giving back**, returning, return, handing back, sending back, extradition, restitution, reversion, bringing back, repatriation, reinstatement, reappointment, reenthronement, reestablishment, restoration, restoring, recycling, recycled paper, retrocession, reinvestment, rehabilitation, replacement, redemption, atonement, deliverance, requital, ransom, rescue

▶ *639 Deliverance, 629 Repair*

2 **compensation**, repayment, recoupment, refund, reimbursement, indemnification, indemnity, doubl indemnity (US), damages, penalty, amends, making amends, making good, reparation, recompense, paying back, squaring, conscious money

▶ *746 Payment, 727 Disposal, 879 Punishment*

3 **returner**, compensator, restorer, reinstator, atoner, redeemer, The Redeemer, refunder, recycler

▶ *7 Religion*

VERBS

4 **give back**, return, hand back, send back, extradite, make restitution, bring back, repatriate, reinstate, reappoint, re-enthrone, restore one to favour, give back one's position, re-establish, restore, recycle, retrocede, reinvest, rehabilitate, replace, redeem, atone, deliver, requite, ransom, rescue

5 **compensate**, repay, refund, reimburse, give one's money back, indemnify, pay double indemnity (US), pay damages, make redress, make amends for, make good, render good, make reparations, recompense, square, pay back, pay back taxes, pay off a loan, pay conscious money

ADJECTIVES

6 **restoring**, restored, restitutive, restitutory, restorable, redemptive, redemptional, redeeming, redeemed, atoning, refunding, refunded, compensatory, indemnificatory, indemnifying, reparative, reparatory

ADVERBS

7 **redemptively**, in redemption, in recompense, in restitution, in compensation, in amends, in requital, in atonement, to atone for

736 Stealing

NOUNS

1 **stealing**, thieving, thievery, thievishness, theft, petty theft, grand theft, larceny, taking, pilfering, pilferage, filching, filch, petit (or petty) larceny, grand larceny, purloining, robbing, robbing the till, putting one's fingers in the till, robbery, bank robbery, train robbery, highway robbery, armed robbery, robbery

with violence, daylight robbery, assault and robbery, ram-raiding, mugging, purse-snatching, pickpocketing, burglarizing, burglary, aggrevated burglary, housebreaking, breaking and entering, unlawful entry, safe-breaking, safe-cracking, safe-blowing, hijacking, skyjacking, piracy, cattle raiding, cattle rustling, stock rustling, shoplifting, kleptomania, light-fingeredness, light fingers, poaching, borrowing, snatching, bag-snatching, scrumping (Dial), scrounging (Inf), lifting (Inf), pinching (Inf), sticky fingers (Inf), snitching (Sl), swiping (Sl), nicking (Sl), boosting (Sl), hustling (Sl), fiddling (Sl)

▶ *734 Taking, 670 Attack, 832 Malevolence*

2 **kidnapping**, abduction, false imprisonment, shanghaiing, impressment, crimping, dognapping (Inf)

3 **theft**, car theft, autotheft, robbery, train robbery, The Great Train Robbery, bank robbery, burglary, break-in, hold-up, grab, smash and grab raid, ram raid, job (Inf), steal (Inf), lift (Inf), snatch (Sl), heist (US sl), caper (US sl), stick-up (US sl), stick-up job (US sl), bag job (US sl), pinch (Sl)

4 **stolen goods**, ill-gotten gains, spoils, spoils of war, contraband, pillage, booty, loot, plunder, prize, pickings, rich pickings, stealings, gleanings, spoils of office, take (US inf), haul (Inf), steal (US inf), graft (Inf), swag (Sl), boodle (Sl), rip-off (Sl), hot goods (Sl), hot property (Sl)

5 **plundering**, plunder, pillaging, pillage, raiding, raid, foraging, foray, looting, looting and pillaging, sacking, sack, ransacking, privateering, buccaneering, brigandism, brigandage, banditry, outlawry, freebooting, despoliation, despoiling, despoilment, spoliation, depredation, grave-robbing, ravaging, raping, rape, gang rape, ravishment, date rape (US inf), body-snatching (Inf)

▶ *676 War, 877 Immorality*

6 **illegal borrowing**, unauthorized borrowing, misappropriation, infringement of copyright, plagiarism, plagiarizing, plagiary, literary theft, cheating, piracy, pirating, record piracy, video piracy, bootleg record, bootlegging, copying, imitating, imitation, fake, cribbing (Inf), lifting (Inf), joyriding (Inf), joyride (Inf)

▶ *48 Literature, 49 Music, 118 Imitation, 540 Falsehood*

7 **dishonesty**, cheating, deception, graft, embezzlement, misappropriation of funds, fraud, forgery, counterfeiting, extortion, blackmail, tax evasion, computer crime, swindle, confidence trick, confidence game (US), tricky business, shady business (Inf), protection racket (Inf), fiddle (Inf), flimflam (Inf), graft (Inf), con trick (Inf), con game (US inf), skin game

(Sl), scam (Sl), blag (Sl), sting (Sl), rip-off (Sl)

▶ *741 Money, 65 Computers*

8 **thief**, stealer, robber, Robin Hood, bank robber, Bonnie Parker and Clyde Barrow, train robber, Jesse James, highway robber, highwayman, Dick Turpin, bushranger (Aus), mugger, purloiner, taker, pickpocket, Artful Dodger, kleptomaniac, shoplifter, pilferer, filcher, petty thief, sneak thief, prowler, larcenist, bagsnatcher, burglar, cat burglar, housebreaker, safe-breaker, safe-cracker, cracksman, safeblower, picklock, hijacker, skyjacker, terrorist, kidnapper, abductor, shanghaier, crimp, chicken thief, cattle thief, cattle rustler (US), rustler (US), poacher, cutpurse (Arch), dognapper (Inf), lifter (Inf), scrounger (Inf), dip (Sl), cracksman (Sl), yegg (*or* yeggman) (US sl), peterman (Sl), booster (Sl)

9 **plunderer**, pillager, sacker, ransacker, brigand, bandit, raider, mosstrooper, marauder, slave-raider, buccaneer, Jean Lafitte, Blackbeard, privateer, corsair, freebooter, ravager, ravisher, rapist, spoiler, despoiler, depredator, wrecker, grave-robber, body-snatcher (Inf)

10 **infringer**, plagiarist, cheat, pirate, record pirate, video pirate, bootlegger, copier, imitator, cribber (Inf), joyrider (Inf)

11 **dishonest person**, criminal, confidence man, trickster, receiver of stolen property, cheat, liar, hypocrite, forger, counterfeiter, white-collar criminal, computer criminal, tax evader, creative accountant, defrauder, embezzler, swindler, sharper, shark, peculator, outlaw, thug, gangster, gang member, hoodlum (US), racketeer, gunman, hold-up man, flimflam man (Inf), diddler (Inf), crook (Inf), fiddler (Inf), con man (Inf), blagger (Sl), mob member (Sl), mobster (US sl), stick-up man (US sl), fence (Sl), ganef (US sl)

VERBS

12 **steal**, thieve, pilfer, filch, appropriate, purloin, rob, commit robbery, rob the till, put one's fingers in the till, borrow, let stick to one's fingers, make off with, sneak off with, walk off with, steal a car, rob a bank, rob a train, pull off a robbery in broad daylight, ram-raid, mug, hold someone up, snatch a purse, pick one's pockets, pickpocket, relieve one of, burglarize, burgle, commit burglary, break into a house, housebreak, make an unlawful entry, crack a safe, hijack, skyjack, rustle cattle, shoplift, poach, snatch, snatch a bag, scrounge (Inf), lift (Inf), pinch (Inf), snaffle (Inf), have sticky fingers (Inf), do a job (Inf), snitch (Sl), swipe (Sl), nick (Sl), stick someone up (US sl), knock off (Sl), boost (Sl), hustle (Sl), nobble (Sl), fiddle (Sl), heist (US sl)

13 **kidnap**, abduct, hold for ransom, shanghai, spirit away, carry off (*or* away), impress, crimp, dognap (Inf)

14 plunder, pillage, raid, prey upon, forage, foray, loot, loot and pillage, sack, ransack, free-boot, despoil, spoliate, depredate, rob a grave, ravage, rape, ravish

15 infringe, plagiarize, cheat, pirate, pirate a record, pirate a video, bootleg, copy, imitate, crib (Inf), lift (Inf), joyride (Inf)

16 act dishonest, evade taxes, defraud, deceive, bilk, dupe, embezzle, swindle, fleece, extort protection money, chisel (Sl), cook the books (Sl)

ADJECTIVES

17 stolen, purloined, pilfered, thieving, thiev-ish, light-fingered, burglarious, brigandish, kleptomaniac, larcenous, ill-gotten, kid-napped, kidnapping, hijacked, hijacking, sky-jacking, poaching, predatory, predacious, buccaneering, privateering, piratelike, raiding, plunderous, plundering, looting, pillaging, spolitory, marauding, foraging, ravaging, grave-robbing, body-snatching (Inf), sticky-fingered (Inf), hot (Sl), rip-off (Sl)

18 fraudulent, dishonest, cheating, cheated, de-ceptive, infringed, pirated, piratic(al), plagia-rized, misappropriated, unauthorized, black-mailed, blackmailing, swindled, crooked (Inf), scrounging (Inf), joyriding (Inf), fiddling (Sl), on the fiddle (Sl)

ADVERBS

19 thievishly, with light fingers, larcenously, with larceny in one's heart, predatorily, like a predator, fraudulently, dishonestly, in a dis-honest way, deceptively, with deception, pi-ratically, like a pirate, with sticky fingers (Inf)

737 Trade

VERBS

1 trade, exchange, make a fair exchange, bar-ter, truck, swap, do a swap, transact, deal, trade off, do business, merchandise, market, buy and sell, export and import, open a trade, drive a trade, sell, peddle, push, promote, traf-fic, buy cheap and sell dear, trade in, deal in, handle, traffic in, smuggle, operate on the black market, deal in the black market, rack-eteer, profiteer, turn over, turn over one's stock, nationalize, privatize, commercialize, put on a business footing, intervene, raise trade barriers, float, incorporate, trade with, do business with, deal with, have dealings with, open an account with, sell to, buy from, solicit business, go out for trade, profit, gain, make a profit, make a killing (Inf), turn ideas into profits, have an eye for (or to) business, look to one's profits, know the price of everything and the value of nothing, fence (Sl)

▶ *738 Purchase, 739 Sale, 223 Exchange*

2 speculate, venture, risk, gamble, invest, sink

one's capital in, put one's money to work, make one's money work for one, go on the stock exchange, play the stock market, play the futures market, deal in futures, dabble in shares, operate, bull, bear, stag, rig the market, manipulate market prices, do insider trading, make a killing (Inf), go bust (Inf)

3 bargain, negotiate, deal, haggle, chaffer, huckster, higgle, dicker, push up, beat down, offer, make an offer, tender, bid, make a bid, outbid, overbid, underbid, gazump, gazunder, make a takeover bid, propose a merger, initiate a (leveraged) buyout, resort to greenmail, act as white knight, pre-empt (a takeover), stickle, drive a (hard) bargain, state one's terms, ask for, charge, settle for, take, agree to, make (or do) a deal, shake hands on, shake on, sign on the dotted line, contract, stick out for (Inf), hold out for (Inf)

▶ *715 Contract*

NOUNS

4 trade, commerce, business, exchange, fair ex-change, trade-off, barter, truck, swap, ex-change of goods, payment in kind, transac-tion, commercial transaction, deal, business deal, trading, dealing, doing business, mer-chandising, buying and selling, trafficking, factorage, factorship, brokerage, agiotage, ar-bitrage, brokering, jobbing, stock-jobbing, share-pushing, profitmaking, traffic, drug traf-fic, prostitution, white slave traffic, slave trade, smuggling, black market, black econo-my, racketeering, profiteering

5 commercial trade, commercial intercourse, export and import, exporting and importing, visible trade, visible goods, visible earnings, visibles, invisible trade, invisible goods, invis-ible earnings, invisibles, foreign trade, interna-tional trade, home trade, domestic trade, pro-tection, protectionism, protective tariff, pro-tective duty, protective quota, customs bar-rier, tariff barrier, trade barrier, trade restric-tion, intervention, interventionism, free trade, open market, economic zone, free trade area, European Free Trade Association (EFTA), economic integration, European Community (EC), European Economic Community (EEC), Common Market, Euromarket, Organization of Petroleum-Exporting Countries (OPEC), General Agreement on Tariffs and Trade (GATT), capitalism, free enterprise, free econo-my, laissez faire, free-market economy, boom and bust, fluctuation, private sector, private enterprise, privatization, public sector, state enterprise, nationalization, chamber of com-merce, junior chamber of commerce (US), labor union (US), trade(s) union

▶ *740 Market*

6 business, venture, undertaking, enterprise, industry, profession, vocation, calling, craft,

métier, job, occupation, (line of) work

▶ *644 Work, 597 Undertaking*

7 **company**, firm, concern, corporation, private company, public company, incorporated company (Inc.) (US), limited company (Ltd), public limited company (plc)

8 **speculation**, gambling, investment, playing the stock market, insider trading, insider dealing

9 **bargaining**, negotiation, haggling, higgling, hard bargaining, horse-trading, tender, offer, bid, takeover, (leveraged) buyout, merger, greenmail, bargain, deal, agreement, contract, trade agreement, GATT (General Agreement on Tariffs and Trade)

10 **trader**, businessman, businesswoman, merchant, white knight, dealer, wholesaler, retailer, vendor, seller, marketer, buyer, purchaser, exporter, importer, merchandiser, distributor, broker, stockbroker, market maker, stock-jobber, jobber, speculator, negotiator, barterer, haggler, horse-trader, profiteer, racketeer, smuggler, fence (Sl)

▶ *738 Purchase, 739 Sale*

11 **chamber of commerce member**, junior chamber of commerce member (US), Jaycee (US), liveryman, guildsman, labor union member (US), trade(s) unionist, shop steward

12 **custom**, customer(s), clientele, client(s), patronage, patron(s)

ADJECTIVES

13 **mercantile**, merchant-like, trading, exchanging, swapping, commercialistic, capitalist, wholesale, retail, exchangeable, marketable, merchantable, saleable

14 **commercial**, economic, monetary, financial, fiscal

15 **profitable**, profitmaking, for profit, risky, speculative

16 **unprofitable**, non-profit-making, charitable, loss-making, unremunerative, break-even

17 **professional**, vocational, occupational, industrial

18 **contractual**, tendered, negotiated, leveraged

19 **corporate**, incorporated, limited, public, nationalized, private, privatized, merged

ADVERBS

20 **in trade**, in commerce, in business, in the marketplace, across the counter, under the counter

738 Purchase

VERBS

1 **purchase**, buy, get, obtain, come by, procure, acquire, acquire by purchase, make a purchase, complete a purchase, purchase by mail order, order, order through a catalogue, order by telephone, teleshop, buy on approval, buy on appro, buy cheaply, buy for a song, buy at

a cut price, make a find, make a good buy, get one's money's worth, make a bad buy, afford, pay for, buy outright, buy over the counter, buy on the spot, snap up, pay cash for, pay on the spot, buy on credit, buy on the instalment plan, buy on hire-purchase, buy on HP, buy on the never-never, buy on tick, buy on account, pay by credit (*or* charge) card, pay by cheque, buy in, hoard, buy up, buy up the shop, pre-empt, corner, make a corner in, corner the market, monopolize, engross (Arch), buy out, make a (leveraged) buyout, bargain, barter, bid, bid for, bid up, offer, make an offer, buy (oneself) in, buy a piece of, invest in, sink one's money in, buy shares, bull, stag, speculate, make a buy (Sl), be ripped-off (Sl)

▶ *730 Receiving, 746 Payment, 710 Offer, 733 Borrowing, 744 Credit*

2 **shop**, market, go shopping, shop till one drops, spend, expend, spend lavishly, be out of pocket, shop for, require, have a shopping list, hit the shops (Inf)

▶ *748 Expenditure, 757 Extravagance*

3 **buy back**, repurchase, redeem, ransom

4 **buy off**, bribe, square, suborn, corrupt, pay off

5 **defray**, pay for, bear the cost of, finance, bankroll (US inf)

NOUNS

6 **purchase**, buy, acquisition, purchases, shopping, good buy, bargain, good bargain, real bargain, find, one's money's worth, bad buy, rip-off (Sl)

7 **purchasing**, buying, outright purchase, on-the-spot purchase, cash purchase, deferred payment, credit (*or* charge) card purchase, purchase on account, purchase on credit, the instalment plan, hire purchase, the HP, the never-never, tick, buying up, takeover, (leveraged) buyout, management buyout, greenmail, pre-emption, cornering, forestalling, bid, takeover bid, offer, buy-back (US), first refusal, right of purchase

▶ *746 Payment, 710 Offer*

8 **shopping**, shopping spree, shopping by mail order, catalogue buying, teleshopping, spending, expenditure, requirement(s), shopping list

▶ *748 Expenditure*

9 **repurchase**, redemption, ransom

10 **bribery**, subornment, corruption

11 **custom**, patronage, demand, consumer demand

12 **purchaser**, buyer, customer, regular customer, loyal customer, patron, client, clientele, consumer, shopper, emptor, teleshopper, spender, credit-card holder, charge-card holder, bargain-hunter, bargainer, haggler, investor, speculator, share-buyer, bull, stag, vendee, transferee, consignee, offerer, bidder,

highest bidder, taker, acceptor, hoarder, pre-emptor, redeemer, ransomer, briber

ADJECTIVES

13 **bought**, purchased, paid for, charged, purchasable, emptional, worth buying, ransomed, redeemed, bribed, bribable

14 **buying**, purchasing, shopping, marketing, teleshopping, cash-and-carry, cash on delivery (COD), cut-price, for a song, bidding, bargaining, haggling, investing, speculative, bullish, pre-emptive, redemptive, acquisitive

▶ *753 Dearness, 754 Cheapness, 752 Discount*

ADVERBS

15 **cheaply**, inexpensively

16 **dearly**, expensively

17 **acquisitively**, pre-emptively, redemptively, profitably

INTERJECTIONS

18 **buyer beware!**, *caveat emptor!* (L)

739 Sale

VERBS

1 **sell**, vend, dispose of, transfer, convey, market, merchandise, put on sale, put up for sale, offer for sale, have for sale, have on offer, make a sale, deal, trade, barter, exchange, bring to market, unload on the market, unload, dump, get rid of, hawk, peddle, traffic in, push, promote, canvass, solicit, tout, cater to (or for), auction, auction off, put to auction, sell by auction, bring under the hammer, put to (or on) the block, sell to the highest bidder, knock down to, wholesale, retail, handle, carry, stock, deal in, sell over the counter, sell under the counter, sell on the black market, sell on the black economy, turn over one's stock, realize, encash, sell at a profit, make a profit, make a killing, gain, sell at a loss, sell at a sacrifice, lose money on, lose, undercut, have a price war, reduce, sell off, remainder, clear stock, hold (or have) a sale, hold a clearance sale, hold a going-out-of-business sale, hold a fire sale (US), sell up, sell out, wind up, sell again, resell, sell forward, sell short, flog (Sl)

▶ *737 Trade, 721 Gain, 722 Loss*

2 **be sold**, change hands, be on sale, come under the hammer, go to (or on) the block, fetch a good price, go for a good price, sell, have a buyer, have a market, meet a demand, be in demand, sell well, sell like hot cakes, sell out, boom, be a best-seller, sell badly, stay on the shelf, gather dust, flop (Inf)

NOUNS

3 **selling**, sale, vending, vendition, disposal, transfer, conveyance, transaction, deal, marketing, merchandising, distribution, sales coverage, promotion, advertisement, traffic, trade, trading, dealing, barter, exchange, trafficking, peddling, canvassing, soliciting, auction, wholesale, retail, sale of office, simony, private sale, exclusive sale, monopoly, oligopoly

▶ *737 Trade*

4 **sale**, sell-out, bargain sale, grand opening sale, sale of the century, spring sale, summer sale, autumn sale, winter sale, stock-taking sale, clearance sale, clearance, closing-down sale, going-out-of-business sale, fire sale (US), white sale, rummage sale, jumble sale, garage sale, car-boot sale, sale of work, charity sale, bazaar, church bazaar, charity bazaar, second-hand sale, junk sale, public sale, auction, art auction, sale by auction, roup (Dial), Dutch auction, vendue (US)

▶ *740 Market*

5 **sales**, good sales, boom, bad sales, recession, depression

▶ *686 Prosperity, 687 Adversity*

6 **salesmanship**, service, sales talk, pitch, sales patter, spiel, hard sell, soft sell, sales conference, sales forecasting

7 **market**, market research, consumer questionnaire, product testing, marketability, saleability, vendibility

8 **merchandise**, product, article, article for sale, vendible, article of commerce, line, range, repertoire, store, selling line, best-seller, loss-leader, staple, commodity, salable commodity, stock, stock-in-trade, supplies, wares, goods, goods on approval, goods on assignment, capital goods, shop goods, consumer goods, consumer durables, durables, perishable goods, perishables, canned goods, dry goods, white goods, sundries, freight, load, cargo

▶ *605 Store, 257 Contents*

9 **seller**, vendor, consignor, transferor, share-seller, bear, auctioneer

10 **salesman**, saleswoman, salesperson, salesgirl, shop assistant, shop girl, shopwalker, sales representative, representative, rep, agent, door-to-door salesman, sales force, traveller, commercial traveller, travelling salesman (or saleswoman), knight of the road (Inf)

11 **pedlar, peddler** (US), seller, rag-and-bone man (or ragman), junkman (or junk dealer) (US), street seller, street vendor, hawker, tinker, Gypsy, traveller, huckster, colporteur, bagman (Inf), chapman (Arch), cheap-jack (Inf), costermonger (or coster), barrow boy, market trader, stall-keeper, sutler (Arch)

12 **wholesaler**, marketer, merchandiser, merchant, wholesale merchant, business person, businessman, businesswoman, entrepreneur, merchant prince, merchant venturer, speculator, operator, monopolist, oligopolist, importer, exporter, dealer, middleman, broker, stockbroker, market maker, stock-jobber, jobber,

share-pusher, financier, company promoter, banker, lender, moneylender, moneychanger, foreign exchange dealer, cambist, procurer, trafficker, canvasser, tout, agent, estate agent, house agent, ticket agent, booking clerk, roundsman, milkman, fence (Sl)

13 **retailer**, middleman, regrater, shopkeeper, storekeeper, shop owner, store owner, dealer, merchant, trader, tradesman, monger, florist, milliner, tailor, shoe seller, fishmonger, ironmonger, mercer, haberdasher, grocer, groceryman (US), greengrocer, provision merchant, provisioner, butcher, baker, tobacconist, newsagent

14 **street trader**, street vendor, street seller, market trader, stall-keeper, stall-holder, barrow boy, costermonger, coster, sutler, vivandiere

ADJECTIVES

15 **saleable**, vendible, marketable, merchantable, available

16 **sold**, sold out, in demand, popular, sought after, called for

ADVERBS

17 **marketably**, saleably, commercially, profitably, speculatively, unprofitably

18 **on sale**, for sale, on the shelves, in the shops (*or* stores), in stock, on the market, up for sale, up for grabs, under the hammer, on the block (US)

740   Market

NOUNS

1 **market**, daily market, weekly market, weekend market, farmers' market, mart, open market, street market, bazaar, flea market, Petticoat Lane, Portobello Road, Orchard Street (US), produce market, vegetable market, flower market, Covent Garden, livestock market, meat market, Smithfield, fish market, Billingsgate, Fulton Street (US), auction room, Christie's, Sotheby's, saleroom, exchange, corn exchange, corn market, wheat pit, custom house, horse fair, goose fair

2 **fair**, world fair, international fair, trade fair, industries fair, show, trade show, motor show, boat show, exhibition, exposition, shop window

3 **sellers' market**, buyers' market, bear market, bull market, over-the-counter market, kerb market, black market, black economy, underground economy, grey market

▶ *737 Trade, 13 Economics, 14 Finance*

4 **free market**, free trade area, open market, European Free Trade Association (EFTA), Common Market, Euromarket, European Economic Community (EEC), European Community (EC), European Economic Area (EEA), single market, single European market, Organization of Petroleum-Exporting Countries

(OPEC), General Agreement on Tariffs and Trade (GATT), economic zone, economic integration, open-door policy

▶ *737 Trade*

5 **stock market**, Stock Exchange, securities market, unlisted securities market, commodity market, commodity exchange, change (Arch), bourse, Wall Street (US), the City, Third Market, Rialto, bucket shop, share shop

6 **marketplace**, market town, market cross, forum, agora

7 **emporium**, general market, covered market, arcade, Burlington Arcade, Trump Tower (US), shopping mall, mall, pedestrian precinct, shopping centre, trading centre, trading post, free port, entrepot, depot, warehouse, wharf, quay

▶ *605 Store*

8 **store**, shop, retail outlet, retailer's, department store, chain store, multiple store (*or* shop), boutique, bargain basement, corner shop, convenience store (US), 7-11 (US), mom and pop store (US), supermarket, superstore, hypermarket, cash and carry, business concern, family concern, concern, firm, establishment, trading company, trading house, house

▶ *647 Workshop*

9 **stall**, booth, stand, newsstand, kiosk, barrow, vending machine, counter, store window, shop window, window display

10 **bazaar**, sale of work, bring-and-buy sale, rummage sale, jumble sale, car-boot sale

741   Money

Money is like muck, not good except it be spread. Francis Bacon.

A feast is made for laughter, and wine maketh merry: but money answereth all things. Bible: Ecclesiastes.

For the love of money is the root of all evil: which while some coveted after, they have erred from the faith, and pierced themselves through with many sorrows. Bible: I Timothy.

For I don't care too much for money,/ For money can't buy me love. John Lennon.

Put money in thy purse. William Shakespeare.

Lack of money is the root of all evil. George Bernard Shaw.

NOUNS

1 **money**, legal tender, medium of exchange, specie, coinage, circulating medium, monetary unit, monetary denomination, currency, decimal currency, managed currency, fluctuating currency, hard currency, soft currency, sound currency, honest money, money of account, sterling, pound sterling, precious

metal, gold, ringing gold, clinking gold, silver, siller (Dial), bullion, coin, paper money, shell money, cowrie, wampum

2 **cash**, hard cash, spot cash, petty cash, ready money, pelf, mammon, lucre, filthy lucre, root of all evil, the ready (Inf), readies (Inf), shekels (Inf), dough (Sl), bread (Sl), dosh (Sl), lolly (Sl), jack (US sl), dib(s) (Sl), moolah (Sl), spondulix (*or* spondulicks) (Sl), coin (Inf), brass (Dial), loot (Sl), swag (Sl), boodle (Sl), rhino (Sl), poppy (Sl), wampum (US sl), gelt (Sl), green stuff (US sl), green (US sl), folding money (Inf), folding cabbage (*or* lettuce) (Sl), folding green (US sl), sugar (Sl), gravy (Sl), palm oil (US sl), palm grease (US sl)

3 **fortune**, wealth, riches, pile of money, heaps of money, stacks of money, mountain of money, mint of money, wads of money, bundle of money, millions, billions, crores, lakhs, scads of money (Inf), packet of money (Sl), big bucks (US sl), megabucks (Sl), cool million (Inf), zillions (Inf), century (Sl), ton (Sl), grand (Sl)

▶ *742 Wealth*

4 **change**, small change, coins, silver, pin money, allowance, pocket money, spending money, paltry sum, centime, sou, paisa, piastre, kopeck, chickenfeed (Sl), peanuts (Sl), coppers (Inf), nickles and dimes (US sl)

5 **sum**, sum of money, round sum, lump sum, figure, ballpark figure (Inf)

6 **funds**, cash supplies, monies, treasure, purse, store, provision, liquidity, hot money, liquid assets, money in the bank, account, bank account, current account, deposit account, savings account, higher interest rate account, bank annuities, wherewithal, means, ready money, capital, funds in hand, funds for investment, reserves, capital reserves, dollar reserves, gold reserves, reserve liability, balances, sterling balances, finances, exchequer, financial provision, cash flow, remittance, payment

7 **finance**, high finance, world of finance, financial world, financial circles, International Monetary Fund (IMF), World Bank, European Bank, International Finance Corporation (IFC), financial control, money power, dollar diplomacy, purse strings, power of the purse, almighty dollar, money dealings, cash transaction, money market, Euromarket, Eurodollar market, Eurocurrency market, Eurobond market, Eurodollar, ECU (European Currency Unit), hard ECU, green pound, foreign exchange market, stock market, exchange, stock exchange, Big Bang, exchange rate, floating exchange rate, free exchange rate, European Monetary System (EMS), ERM (exchange rate mechanism), exchange rate parity, parity, valuta, par, EC snake, exchange control, man-

aged currency, bank rate, prime lending rate (US), minimum lending rate, agio, agiotage, devaluation, depreciation, falling exchange rate, rising exchange rate, bimetallism, gold and silver standard, monometallism, gold standard, equalization fund, sinking fund, revolving fund, deficit finance, inflation, inflationary spiral, stagflation, stagnation, reflation, disinflation, deflation

▶ *14 Finance, 740 Market*

8 **American money**, American paper money, American coinage, penny, cent, one cent, nickel, five cents, 5c, dime, ten cents, 10c, quarter, twenty-five cents, 25c, half-dollar, fifty cents, 50c, dollar, silver dollar, Susan B. Anthony dollar, one-dollar bill, greenback, $1, two-dollar piece, American eagle bullion coin, eagle, five-dollar bill, $5, ten-dollar bill, $10, twenty-dollar bill, $20, fifty-dollar bill, $50, 100-dollar bill, $100, two bits (Sl), four bits (Sl), buck (Sl), smacker (Sl), fiver (Sl), tenner (Sl), sawbuck (Sl), C-note (Sl), one bill (Sl)

9 **British money**, British paper money, British coinage, decimal coinage, penny, new penny, 1p, twopence, 2p, five pence, 5p, ten pence, 10p, twenty pence, 20p, fifty pence, 50p, pound coin, pound note, £1, five-pound note, £5, ten-pound note, £10, twenty-pound note, £20, quid (Sl), nicker (Sl), smacker (Sl), oncer (Sl), sov (Sl), fiver (Sl), tenner (Sl), pony (Sl), monkey (Sl)

10 **former British money**, former British coinage, pre-decimal coinage, farthing, halfpenny, ha'penny, 1/2d, penny, old penny, threepenny bit, thrupenny bit, 3d, sixpence, 6d, shilling, 1s, two-shilling piece, florin, 2s, halfcrown, half-a-crown, two and six, two shillings and six pence, 2s 6d, 2/6, five shillings, crown, 5s, guinea, 21s, sovereign, gold sovereign, half sovereign, noble, groat, bawbee (Sl), tanner (Sl), bob (Sl), ship halfpenny, cartwheel penny (Inf), bun penny (Inf)

11 **national coins**, foreign coins, franc, new franc, mark, Deutschmark, pfennig, schilling, guilder, krona, krone, markka, drachma, lira, peseta, escudo, peso, cruzado, rupee, rouble, yuan, yen, won, kip, dinar, zloty, lek, riyal, dirham, rand, inti, naira

12 **ancient coins**, shekel, talent, denarius, obolus, soldo, ducat, sou, bezant, pistole, piece of eight

13 **coinage**, coins, minting, issue, specie, metallic currency, fractional currency, stamped coinage, minted coinage, gold coinage, silver coinage, electrum coinage, copper coinage, nickel coinage, billon coinage, bronze coinage, coin, piece, coin of the realm, coin collecting, numismatics, numismatology

14 **paper money**, note, bill (US), fiat money, fiduciary currency, assignat (Arch), banknote,

treasury note, bill of exchange, negotiable instrument, draft, order, money order, postal order, cheque, cashier's cheque, certified cheque, giro cheque, traveller's cheque, Eurocheque, letter of credit, certificate, debenture, promissory note, IOU, note of hand, commercial paper, coupon, warrant, scrip, scrip certificate, bond, bearer bond, corporate bond, convertible bond, zero coupon bond, US Savings Bond (US), Premium Savings Bond, premium bond, shinplaster (US inf)

15 **false money**, bad money, counterfeit money, base coin, forgery, forged note, flash note, kite, snide, rap (Arch), clipped coinage, demonetized coinage, withdrawn coinage, obsolete coinage, depreciated currency, devalued currency, bad check (US), rubber cheque, funny money (Inf), dud cheque (Inf)

▶ 747 Nonpayment

16 **bullion**, bar, gold bar, ingot, nugget, gold, solid gold, silver, solid silver, precious metal, yellow metal, platinum, electrum, billon, white gold, false gold, fool's gold

17 **financier**, money man, moneyer, minter, mint master, coiner, forger, money-dealer, moneychanger, cambist, moneylender, usurer, capitalist, tycoon, magnate, banker, treasurer, cashier, paymaster, bursar, purser, quaestor (Arch), coin collector, numismatist

18 **treasurer**, honorary treasurer, keeper of the purse, cashier, teller, payer, paymaster, bursar, almoner, purser, depositary, stakeholder, trustee, steward, consignee, bookkeeper, accountant, banker, financier, controller (or comptroller), Chancellor of the Exchequer, Secretary of the Treasury (US), Governor of the Bank of England, Chairman of the Federal Reserve System (US), mint master, minter, quaestor (in Ancient Rome)

19 **treasury**, treasure house, governmental funds, public money, public purse, exchequer, reserves, fund, store, counting house, custom house (or customs house), bursary, almonry (Arch), bank, Bank of England, Federal Reserve System (US), Old Lady of Threadneedle Street, commercial bank, financial company, financial house, savings bank, clearing bank, merchant bank, building society, savings and loan association (US), building and loan association (US), Post Office savings bank

20 **money store**, coffer, chest, box, treasure chest, depository, federal depository (US), Fort Knox (US), strongroom, strongbox, safe, wall safe, safe-deposit (or safety-deposit), safe-deposit box, cash box, moneybox, moneybag, piggy bank, money belt, pocket, wallet, billfold (US), change purse, handbag, purse (US), pocketbook (US), stocking, mattress

21 **till**, cash register, cash desk, slot machine, cash dispenser, automated teller machine (ATM), personal identification number (PIN)

▶ 605 Store, 258 Container

ADJECTIVES

22 **monetary**, pecuniary, financial, fiscal, numismatic, chrysological, budgetary, sumptuary, coined, stamped, minted, issued, nummular, nummary, fiduciary, gold-based, sterling-based, inflationary, deflationary, floating, clipped, devalued, depreciated, withdrawn, demonetized, decimal

23 **solvent**, sound, rich, wealthy

▶ 742 Wealth

VERBS

24 **monetize**, mint, coin, print, stamp, issue, circulate, counterfeit, forge, pass, utter, pass a bad check (US), kite a check (US inf), bounce a cheque (Inf)

25 **demonetize**, withdraw, withdraw from circulation, call in, debase, clip, devalue, depreciate, inflate

26 **bank**, deposit, draw, withdraw, cash, encash, realize, liquidate, cash a cheque, endorse a cheque, write a cheque, pay, change, exchange, get some kick (US sl)

27 **invest**, save, buy bonds, play the market

ADVERBS

28 **financially**, fiscally, numismatically, pecuniously, solvently, wealthily, in the money (Sl)

742 Wealth

ADJECTIVES

1 **wealthy**, rich, affluent, well-off, well-paid, prosperous, well-to-do, in the money, moneyed, propertied, worth a lot, worth a mint, worth millions, rolling in money, dripping with wealth, made of money, well-situated, well-provided for, well-endowed, well-housed, comfortably off, comfortable, in easy circumstances, doing nicely thank you, rich as Croesus, rich as Rockefeller, rich as Solomon, born with a silver spoon in one's mouth, born in (or to) the purple, blessed with this world's goods, stinking rich (Inf), filthy rich (Inf), disgustingly rich (Inf), rolling in it (Inf), rolling (Inf), dripping (Inf), loaded (Sl), flush (Inf), well-heeled (Inf), worth a bundle (Sl), worth a packet (Sl), lousy with money (Sl), in clover (Inf), in the chips (Sl), in the gravy (Sl), in the dough (US sl), in high (or tall) cotton (US sl), on Easy Street (Inf), quids in (Sl), raking it in (Inf)

▶ 686 Prosperity

2 **solvent**, financially stable, financially sound, sound, solid, taken care of, in the black, in funds, in cash, out of debt, credit-worthy, a good credit risk, able to pay, good for it, all straight (Brit Inf)

▶ 746 Payment, 744 Credit

3 opulent, luxurious, lavish, sumptuous, palatial, splendid, first-class, de luxe, expensive, dear, costly, richly furnished, elegantly upholstered, diamond-studded, gilded, glittering, plush (Inf), plushy (Inf), ritzy (Sl), glitzy (Sl), slap-up (Brit Inf)

▶ 811 Showiness

4 lush, fat, fertile, fecund, productive, prolific, abundant, plentiful, plenteous, bountiful, flowing with milk and honey

▶ 246 Fertility, 243 Production

NOUNS

5 wealth, richness, affluence, prosperity, financial power, fortune, handsome fortune, resources, substantial resources, limitless resources, capital, substantial capital, assets, liquid assets, means, income, high income, high tax bracket, surtax bracket, gain, gains, profit, profits, moneymaking, savings, investments, nest egg, savings account, investment account, large inheritance, generous endowment, estate, money, property, possessions, well-lined purse, bottomless purse, bonanza, mine, gold mine, cash cow, El Dorado, Golconda, pot of gold, end of the rainbow, purse of Fortunatus, philosopher's stone, golden goose, golden touch, Midas touch, nice little earner (Inf)

▶ 686 Prosperity, 721 Gain, 730 Receiving, 756 Thrift, 14 Finance

6 money, riches, lucre, filthy lucre, mammon, pelf, brass (Dial), cash, old money, new money, mint of money, pots of money, heaps of money, pile of money, mountain of money, wad of notes, riches of Solomon, tidy sum (Inf), king's ransom (Inf), bundle (Sl), packet (Sl), cool million (Inf), zillions (Inf), scads of money (Inf), megabucks (Sl), big bucks (US sl), tall money (US sl), long bread (US sl), long green (US sl)

▶ 741 Money

7 opulence, luxury, lavishness, sumptuousness, comfort, comfortable circumstances, ease, easy circumstances, the good life, good times, plenty, abundance, profusion, superfluity, bounty, cornucopia, fat of the land, fleshpots, plushness (Inf), easy street (Inf), life of Riley (Sl)

8 solvency, financial stability, financial soundness, soundness, solidity, substance, credit, credit-worthiness, fiscal competence, independence, self-sufficiency

▶ 744 Credit

9 plutocracy, timocracy, capitalism

10 wealthy person, rich person, millionaire, millionairess, multimillionaire, billionaire, moneymaker, big earner, tycoon, magnate, baron, self-made man (or woman), man (or woman) of means, Croesus, Midas, Dives, Plutus, Rockefeller, capitalist, plutocrat, yuppie, parvenu, heir, beneficiary, heir to a fortune, heiress, moneybags (Inf), money-spinner (Inf), fat cat (Sl), nabob (Inf)

11 the rich, the well-off, the well-to-do, the haves, the privileged, privileged class, moneyed class, propertied class, leisured class, the upper classes, the cream of society, the county set, the country club set (US), the well-heeled (Inf), the jet set, the glitterati, beau monde, beautiful people, jeunesse dorée (Fr), the new (or newly) rich, nouveaux riches, the upper crust (Inf)

VERBS

12 be rich, have wealth, have money, have money to burn, draw a large income, command capital, have the golden touch, turn all to gold, roll in money, drip with wealth, wallow in riches, have money coming out of one's ears (Inf), stink of money (Sl), rake (or coin) it in (Inf), sit on a goldmine (Inf), live on easy street (Inf), live the life of Riley (Sl)

13 get rich, prosper, make it, enrich oneself, make money, mint money, coin money, spin money, attract money, come into money, inherit, gain, make a profit, make one's fortune, make a fortune, make a mint, rake in the cash, feather one's nest, line one's pocket, strike it rich, hit the jackpot, win the pools, win the lottery (or sweepstake), have one's ship come in (or home), find the philosopher's stone, find one's El Dorado, find the pot of gold at the end of the rainbow, rake it in (Inf), make a killing (Sl), make a bundle (Sl), make a packet (Sl), make a pile (Sl), make a bomb (Sl), clean up (Sl)

▶ 686 Prosperity, 721 Gain, 730 Receiving

14 seek riches, chase fame and fortune, worship the almighty dollar (US), worship the golden calf, pay tribute to mammon

15 make rich, enrich, provide money, bequeath, endow, enhance, improve

ADVERBS

16 wealthily, richly, affluently, prosperously, well, comfortably, opulently, luxuriously, lavishly, in clover (Inf), on the gravy train (Sl), high on the hog (US sl)

743 Poverty

To be poor and independent is very nearly an impossibility. William Cobbett.

There's no scandal like rags, nor any crime so shameful as poverty. George Farquhar.

It is only the poor who are forbidden to beg. Anatole France.

Let not Ambition mock their useful toil,/ Their homely joys, and destiny obscure;/ Nor Grandeur hear with a disdainful smile,/ The short and simple annals of the poor. Thomas Gray.

I want there to be no peasant in my kingdom so poor that he is unable to have a chicken in his pot every Sunday. Henri IV.

Hard to train to accept being poor. Horace.

As for the virtuous poor, one can pity them, of course, but one cannot possibly admire them. Oscar Wilde.

ADJECTIVES

1 **poor**, impecunious, penniless, moneyless, penurious, poverty-stricken, badly off, poorly off, unprovided for, lowpaid, underpaid, underprivileged, deprived, needy, in need, indigent, wanting, in want, in distress, in reduced circumstances, straitened, hand-to-mouth, destitute, necessitous, on the breadline, below the poverty line, in the poverty trap, on the dole, on welfare (US), without prospects, with nothing to hope for, poor as dirt, poor as a church mouse, poor as Lazarus, poor as Job, poor as Mother Hubbard, unable to make both ends meet, unable to get by, unable to pay one's way, unable to keep the wolf from the door, not blessed with this world's goods, hard up (Inf)
▶ *747 Nonpayment, 659 Difficulty, 571 Necessity*

2 **insolvent**, indebted, in debt, owing, bankrupt, ruined, financially ruined, financially embarrassed, short, short of cash, short of funds, down to one's last penny, without a sou, without a cent (US), in the red, impoverished, pauperized, reduced to poverty (*or* beggary), broken, dispossessed, stripped, fleeced, robbed, disinherited, dowerless, portionless, in difficulties, not knowing which way to turn, up against it, broke (Inf), stonebroke (Sl), stony-broke (Sl), flat broke (Inf), flat (Inf), dead broke (Inf), skint (Sl), hard up (Inf), strapped (Sl), hurting (Inf), pinched (for money) (Inf), pushed (for money) (Inf), pressed (for money) (Inf), hard-pressed (Inf), hard put to it (Inf), put to one's shifts (Inf), on one's uppers (Inf), on one's beam-ends (Inf), on the rocks (Inf), in hock (US inf), in queer street (Inf), out of pocket (Inf), cleaned out (Sl), wiped out (US Inf), bust (Inf), busted (US Inf), without a bean (Sl), belly up (US sl)

3 **beggarly**, mendicant, down-and-out, on the street, homeless, shelterless, hungry, underfed, starving, barefoot, in rags, ragged, tattered, tatty, patched, threadbare, shabby, scruffy, down at heel (*or* the heels), out at (the) elbows, mean, seedy, squalid, dirty, slummy, dilapidated, gone to ruin, gone to pot, melted out (US sl)

4 **inadequate**, insufficient, deficient, lacking, scarce, meagre, scant, scanty, skimpy

NOUNS

5 **poverty**, poorness, impecuniousness, impecuniosity, pennilessness, penury, impoverishment, pauperism, deprivation, privation, hardship, need, neediness, necessitousness, necessity, dire necessity, indigence, want, lack, distress, difficulties, dire straits, reduced circumstances, straitened circumstance, hand-to-mouth existence, mere existence, destitution, low pay, low income, insufficient income, slender means, narrow means, meagre resources, subsistence level, breadline, poverty line, poverty trap, wolf at the door, Lady Poverty (Inf)
▶ *747 Nonpayment, 659 Difficulty, 571 Necessity*

6 **insolvency**, debt, indebtedness, dependence, unsoundness, financial unsoundness, fiscal incompetence, bankruptcy, ruin, financial ruin, financial collapse, financial embarrassment, loss of fortune, dispossession, disinheritance, hard times, bad times, depression, recession, slump, belt-tightening, shortage of cash, shortage of funds, insufficient funds, light pocket, empty purse, bare cupboard, empty larder, pinch (Inf), queer street (Inf), low water (Inf)

7 **beggary**, beggardom, beggarliness, mendicancy, homelessness, hunger, fasting, famine, raggedness, rags, tatters, shabbiness, scruffiness, meanness, seediness, squalor, dilapidation, slum, substandard housing, workhouse, poorhouse, rat trap (US Inf)
▶ *758 Meanness, 622 Dirtiness*

8 **renunciation of wealth**, voluntary poverty, vow of poverty, the Franciscan order, asceticism

9 **inadequacy**, insufficiency, deficiency, lack, shortage, dearth, scarcity, paucity, meagreness, scantness, scantiness, skimpiness

10 **poor person**, needy person, pauper, indigent, down-and-out, bankrupt, insolvent, broken man (*or* woman), beggar, mendicant, mendicant friar, lazar, Franciscan, Grey Friar, Poor Clare, Job, Lazarus, Cinderella, poor relation, vagrant, bag lady, tramp, hobo (US), homeless person, squatter, slum-dweller, ghetto resident, rag-picker, bum (Inf), freeloader (Inf)

11 **the poor**, the needy, the have-nots, the underprivileged, the underprivileged class, the disadvantaged, the deprived, Third World, the lower classes, the dregs of society, poor white, white trash, new (*or* newly) poor

VERBS

12 **be poor**, live poorly, live in poverty, need, want, lack, not have a penny, not have two halfpennies to rub together, earn little *or* nothing, live on a pittance, eke out a livelihood, scratch (out) a living, live from hand to mouth, watch the pennies, tighten one's belt, fall below the poverty line, be caught in the poverty trap, go on relief, go on welfare (US),

go on the dole, claim supplementary benefit, sign on (Inf), go on the parish, beg for one's bread, sing for one's supper, starve, have no prospects, feel the pinch (Inf), pinch pennies (Inf), pinch (Inf), have no more shots in one's locker (Inf)

13 **lose one's money**, lose everything, go to pot, go to ruin, go bankrupt, fall on hard times, decline in fortune, come down in the world, sell the family silver, go into debt, be deeply in debt, declare Chapter 11 (US), go broke (Inf), go bust (Inf), go busted (US inf), go to the wall (Sl), go belly up (US sl)

14 **impoverish**, make poor, reduce to poverty, beggar, pauperize, leave destitute, ruin, bankrupt, dispossess, disinherit, disendow, cut off with a shilling (Inf), deprive, strip, fleece, rob, take to the cleaners (Inf)

ADVERBS

15 **poorly**, impecuniously, penuriously, in need, in reduced circumstances, on the breadline, on the poverty line, in the poverty trap, on welfare (US), on the dole, on one's uppers, on the streets

16 **meanly**, shabbily, scruffily, seedily

17 **inadequately**, insufficiently, meagrely, scantly, scantily, skimpily

744 Credit

NOUNS

1 **credit**, customer credit, banker's credit, creditworthiness, sound proposition, good credit risk, credit rating, borrowing capacity, credit limit, line of credit, credit control, liquidity ratio, overdraft, the red, loan, mortgage, second mortgage, remortgage, debt, account, charge account, credit account, department store account, customer account, budget account, deferred payment, instalment plan, instalment buying, paying off (US), hire purchase (HP), score, tally, bill, accounts payable, unpaid bill, overdue account, outstanding balance, tick (Inf), the never-never (Inf)

▶ *732 Lending, 733 Borrowing, 745 Debt, 750 Accounts*

2 **credit card**, bank card, charge card, American Express (Tm), VISA (Tm), MasterCard (Tm), Access (Tm), Diners' Club (Tm), plastic money, plastic, phonecard, credit note, letter of credit

3 **deposit**, bank (*or* building society) deposit, current account deposit, savings account deposit, credit account, deposit account, the black, credits, balances, credit balance, righthand entry, receipts

▶ *749 Receipt*

4 **bank**, commercial bank, finance company, finance house, savings bank, building society, friendly society, credit union, credit bureau

(US), pawnshop, pawnbroker's

▶ *14 Finance*

5 **lender**, loan-maker, mortgagee, pledgee, pawnbroker, usurer, extortionist, lender of last resort, debt collector, (debt) collection agency, dun, loan shark (Inf)

6 **depositor**, investor, saver

7 **repute**, reputation, standing, prestige, trust, confidence, reliability, probity

▶ *857 Probity, 849 Respect, 497 Belief*

VERBS

8 **credit**, give (*or* furnish) credit, extend credit, lend, loan, grant a loan, grant, arrange a mortgage, sell on credit, await payment, seek payment, dun

▶ *732 Lending, 745 Debt*

9 **acquire credit**, take out credit, open a charge (*or* credit) account, have an account with, charge, charge to one's account, run up an account, run up a bill, defer payment, forgo repayment, buy on hire purchase (HP), buy on the instalment plan, buy on time (US), put on layaway (US), borrow, take out a loan, mortgage, overdraw, go into the red

▶ *733 Borrowing*

10 **deposit**, make a deposit, credit to one's account, place in one's account, place to one's credit, stay in the black

11 **recognize**, give recognition, ascribe, attribute, give credit where it's due

ADJECTIVES

12 **charged**, deferred, overdrawn, in the red

13 **in credit**, in the black, creditworthy

ADVERBS

14 **on credit**, on account, by deferred payment, by instalments, by hire purchase, on the cuff (Inf), on tick (Inf), on the never-never (Inf), on the slate (Inf)

15 **into the black**, out of the red, into the red, out of the black

745 Debt

NOUNS

1 **debt**, indebtedness, state of indebtedness, owing, liability, obligation, commitment, encumbrance, accountability, responsibility, secured debt, unsecured debt, debt of honour, good debt, bad debt, short-term debt, floating debt, promise to pay, something owing, what one owes, debts, bills, debit, charge, overdraft, the red, charge account, credit account, charge card, credit card, bank card

▶ *744 Credit*

2 **national debt**, national credit, government debt, federal debt (US), funded debt, trading deficit, trade gap, negative balance of payments, public sector borrowing, public sector borrowing requirement (PSBR)

3 **loan**, bank loan, business loan, capital gear-

age, leverage, personal loan, secured loan, guaranteed loan, mortgage, second mortgage, remortgage, guaranty, collateral security, unsecured loan, sum entrusted, loan capital, debt capital, loan repayment, mortgage repayment, lending, borrowing, prime (lending) rate (US), minimum lending rate, bill discounting rate

▶ *732 Lending, 733 Borrowing*

4 **interest**, premium, rate of interest, APR (annualized percentage rate), bank rate, simple interest, compound interest, high interest, excessive interest, usury, pound of flesh (Sl)

5 **amount owing**, unpaid amount, deficit, bill, account, tally, score, overdraft, balance to pay, accounts receivable, receivables, overdue amount, overdue payment, arrears, accumulated arrears, back pay, back rent, foreclosure, repossession, inability to pay, insufficient funds, defaulting, write-off, bad debt, bounced cheque, payment refused, frozen balance, blocked account, frozen assets

▶ *747 Nonpayment, 722 Loss*

6 **debtor**, credit buyer, cardholder, borrower, personal borrower, business borrower, loanee, loan applicant, guarantor, co-signer, obligor, drawee, mortgagor, pledgor, bad debtor, defaulter, nonpayer, bilker, insolvent, bankrupt

VERBS

7 **be in debt**, owe, owe money, borrow money, have to repay, have bills to pay, run up a bill, run up an account, run (*or* get) into debt, overspend, overdraw, go into the red, pay interest, accept a charge, get credit, have an account with, live on credit, buy on credit, buy on the instalment plan, buy on hire purchase, charge, charge to one's account, back another's credit, co-sign a loan, make oneself responsible, go bail for

▶ *744 Credit, 733 Borrowing*

8 **not pay**, default, reschedule one's debts, leave one's bills unpaid, cheat one's creditors, bilk, outrun the constable, welsh, levant, do a moonlight flit (Inf)

▶ *747 Nonpayment*

ADJECTIVES

9 **in debt**, indebted, pledged, bound, obliged, committed, encumbered, mortgaged, liable, responsible, accountable, answerable, beholden, borrowing, owing, unpaid, due, overdrawn, in the red, minus, in difficulties, in dire straits, deep in debt, burdened with debt, up to one's ears in debt, over one's head in debt, mortgaged to the hilt, in hock (US inf)

10 **unable to pay**, insolvent, nonpaying, defaulting, at the mercy of one's creditors, in the hands of the receiver, foreclosed, repossessed

ADVERBS

11 **insolvently**, in debt, in over one's head, in

the red, in arrears, on loan, on credit, on the slate (Inf), on tick (Inf), on the never-never (Inf), on the tab (Inf), in hock (Inf)

746 Payment

NOUNS

1 **payment**, paying, paying out, payout, disbursement, remittance, expenditure, outlay, paying for, meeting the cost, bearing the cost, defrayment, defrayal, defraying, paying off, payoff, discharge, written discharge, quittance, acquittance, release, satisfaction, full satisfaction, liquidation, clearance, settlement, full settlement, settlement on account, accounts receivable, receivables, receipt, receipted payment, receipt for payment, receipt in full, due payment, overdue payment, cash payment, ready cash, money, payment in kind, advance payment, first payment, partial payment, down payment, deposit, earnest money, earnest, handsel, instalment, premium, standing order, direct debit, deferred payment, charge-account payment, instalment-plan payment, hire-purchase payment, cash on delivery (COD), subscription, tribute, voluntary payment, donation, contribution, offering, appeal, collection, whip-round (Inf)

▶ *748 Expenditure, 749 Receipt*

2 **repayment**, reimbursement, refund, compensation, recompense, indemnity, restitution, payment-in-lieu, substitution, composition

3 **pay**, remuneration, salary, wage(s), stipend, emolument, honorarium, fee, commission, royalty, advance, payroll, payout, pay packet, pay slip, pay cheque, take-home pay, income, earnings, reward, tip, gratuity, pension, annuity, retirement pension, back pay, retroactive pay, redundancy pay, severance pay, payoff, ex-gratia payment, payment-in-lieu, overtime pay, golden handshake (Inf), golden parachute (Inf), golden handcuffs (Inf), golden hello (Inf)

▶ *878 Reward*

4 **grant**, grant-in-aid, subsidy, subvention, donation, contribution, subscription, tribute, damages, indemnity, penalty, tax, ransom, payoff, bribe, payola (US sl), sweetener (Sl)

5 **payer**, paymaster, bursar, purser, cashier, treasurer

VERBS

6 **pay**, pay out, disburse, remit, expend, spend, subscribe, make a payment, get a receipt, pay for, pay cash, pay by cheque, pay by cashier's check (US), pay by standing order (*or* direct debit), pay in kind, trade, negotiate a trade-off, barter, make a down payment, put down, pay in advance, put money up front, pay on sight, pay on call, pay on delivery, pay on demand,

pay on the dot, pay dearly, pay an exorbitant price, unloose the purse strings, open one's wallet (*or* purse), empty one's pocket, lay out (Inf), shell out (Inf), fork out (*or* over *or* up) (Sl), ante up (Inf), stump up (Inf), cough up (Inf), come across (Sl), do the needful (Inf), pay on the nail (Inf), pay through the nose (Inf)

▶ *748 Expenditure*

7 **pay off**, discharge, satisfy, redeem, meet, liquidate, clear, settle, settle an account, honour, honour a bill, clear (*or* square) accounts with, pay up, pay in full

8 **defray**, defray the cost, pay for, meet the cost, bear the cost, stand the cost, stand, treat, give, donate, contribute, fund, finance, put up money, pick up the bill (*or* tab), pay the piper, foot the bill (Inf), pay the freight (US sl)

9 **pay one's way**, pay one's share, share expenses, go Dutch, buy a round, stand a round

10 **pay back**, repay, reimburse, refund, compensate, recompense, indemnify, restitute

11 **remunerate**, pay wages, pay a salary, pay commission, distribute, reward, tip, bribe, dole out (Inf), dish out (Inf), tickle (*or* grease) one's palm (Sl), cross one's palm with silver (Inf), pay off (Inf), sweeten the pot (Inf), provide a sweetener (Sl)

▶ *878 Reward*

12 **be profitable**, yield a return, make money, benefit, avail, be worth the effort

▶ *721 Gain*

13 **retaliate**, avenge oneself, revenge oneself, reciprocate, requite, pay back, pay off, pay off old scores, take an eye for an eye, give tit for tat (Inf), settle a score (Inf), get even (Inf), get one's own back (Inf)

▶ *672 Retaliation*

14 **atone**, make amends, suffer, answer

ADJECTIVES

15 **paying**, disbursing, expending, spending

16 **paid**, paid in full, out of debt, liquidated, in the black, out of the red, owing nothing, debt-free, cleared, settled, discharged

17 **payable**, payable on demand, due, owed, owing, remittable, refundable, redeemable

18 **profitable**, worthwhile, advantageous, lucrative, remunerative, rewarding, money-making

19 **receiving pay**, earning, salaried, waged, wage-earning, hired, prepaid, paid in advance, post-paid

20 **paying in return**, compensatory, retributive, redemptive

ADVERBS

21 **cash down**, in advance, cash on delivery (COD), in instalments, by cheque, on demand, on the dot, on the nail (Inf)

747 Nonpayment

NOUNS

1 **nonpayment**, default, refusal to pay, avoiding financial obligations, tax avoidance, tax evasion, tax shelter, tax haven, creative accounting, black economy, embezzlement, defalcation, swindling, defrauding, improbity, protest (by creditor), repudiation of debts, forgiveness of debts, cancellation of debts, scam (Sl), fiddle (Inf)

▶ *858 Improbity, 591 Avoidance*

2 **stoppage**, deduction, moratorium, embargo, freeze, reduced payment, deferred payment, instalment plan, hire purchase

3 **bad payment**, bad cheque, dishonoured cheque, bogus cheque, dud cheque, bouncing cheque, protested bill, rubber cheque (Inf)

4 **depreciation**, devaluation, devalued currency, counterfeit money

▶ *741 Money, 14 Finance, 13 Economics*

5 **insolvency**, inability to pay, debt, insurmountable debt, unpayable debt, failure to meet one's obligations, nothing in the kitty, overdrawn account, overdraft, cash-flow crisis, financial crisis, crash, collapse, failure, bank failure, failure of credit, bankruptcy, ruin, financial ruin, bankruptcy court, bankruptcy proceedings, Chapter 11 (US)

▶ *745 Debt*

6 **nonpayer**, miser, Shylock, skinflint, defaulter, bankrupt, discharged bankrupt, undischarged bankrupt, debtor, insolvent debtor, embezzler, defalcator, defrauder, tax dodger, tax evader, tax exile, bilker, absconder, lame duck, welsher (Sl)

VERBS

7 **not pay**, default, refuse to pay, avoid financial obligations, practise tax evasion, evade taxes, divert, sequester, embezzle, defalcate, swindle, defraud, evade one's creditors, outrun the constable, bilk, welsh, levant, abscond, decamp, do a moonlight flit (Inf), fiddle one's income tax (Inf)

8 **stop payment**, withhold payment, freeze, block, refuse payment, disallow payment, bounce a cheque, dishonour a cheque, protest a bill, repudiate

9 **be unable to pay**, have no ready cash, get into debt, fall into arrears, get behindhand, become insolvent, have a cash-flow crisis, go bankrupt, go through the bankruptcy court, go to the wall, sink, fail, break, go bust, crash, collapse, wind up, go into liquidation, go belly-up (US sl)

▶ *745 Debt*

10 **forgive a debt**, cancel a debt, wipe the slate clean, discharge a bankrupt, write off

11 **be parsimonious**, keep one's wallet (*or* purse) shut, economize, scrimp, scrape and

save, make ends meet
▶ *756 Thrift, 758 Meanness*

12 devalue the currency, depreciate the currency, lower the official rate of exchange, go off the gold standard, demonetize
▶ *741 Money*

ADJECTIVES

13 nonpaying, miserly, mean, measly, skinflint, defaulting, behindhand, in arrears, unable to pay, insolvent, bankrupt, indebted, up to one's ears in debt, over one's head in debt, poor, beggared, ruined
▶ *745 Debt, 743 Poverty*

14 unpaid, unrewarded, unremunerated, uncompensated, unrecompensed, unpayable, irredeemable

ADVERBS

15 without paying, in arrears, in the red, in debt, insolvently, without a penny to one's name

INTERJECTIONS

16 can't pay! won't pay!

748   Expenditure

VERBS

1 expend, spend, disburse, pay, pay out, shop, buy, purchase, incur costs, incur expenses, invest, sink money, afford, meet the cost, run down one's account, use up one's credit, live on (*or* off) capital, dip into capital, draw on one's savings, dissave, disinvest, untie the purse-strings, empty one's pocket, open one's pocket, spare no expense, spend lavishly, splurge, overspend, be out of pocket, squander, fritter away, throw away, dissipate, go on a spending spree, shop till one drops, fling money around, throw money at, spend money like water, spend money as if it grows on trees, lay out (Inf), fork out (Inf), shell out (Inf), splash out (Inf), open the floodgates (Inf), do proud (Inf), blow (Sl), blow one's cash (Sl), blow a fortune (Sl), blow it (Sl), blue (Sl)
▶ *746 Payment, 738 Purchase, 757 Extravagance*

2 consume, use, use up, exhaust, deplete, go through, run through, get through, waste
▶ *607 Waste, 599 Use*

3 donate, give, give money, give to charity, contribute, support, back, finance, pay for, defray, bear the costs, treat, stand (Inf), bankroll (US inf)
▶ *755 Generosity, 729 Giving*

NOUNS

4 expenditure, spending, disbursement, payment, shopping, buying, buy, good buy, bad buy, purchase
▶ *746 Payment, 738 Purchase*

5 expense, expenses, expense account, miscellaneous expenses, out-of-pocket expenses, extras, outlay, investment, cost(s), cost of living,

monthly bills, outgoings, overheads, fee, charge, price, rate, tax
▶ *751 Price*

6 extravagance, prodigality, spending (*or* shopping) spree, spree, splurge, dissaving, disinvestment, run on savings, living off (*or* on) one's capital
▶ *757 Extravagance*

7 donation, giving, contribution, support, backing, finance, generosity, liberality
▶ *755 Generosity, 729 Giving*

8 spender, shopper, buyer, purchaser, investor

9 spendthrift, squanderer, wastrel, shopaholic (Inf)

ADJECTIVES

10 expending, spending, sumptuary, out-of-pocket, lighter in one's purse, generous, liberal

11 spendthrift, extravagant, profligate, prodigal, spending money like water, spending money as if it grows on trees, living on (*or* off) capital

12 expended, spent, disbursed, paid, paid out, invested, contributed, at one's expense, laid out (Inf), blown (Sl)

13 used, used up, exhausted, depleted

ADVERBS

14 generously, liberally, extravagantly, profligately, prodigally

749   Receipt

NOUNS

1 receipt, voucher, counterfoil, stub, proof of purchase, written acknowledgment of payment

2 money received, receipts, gross receipts, net receipts, box-office receipts, gate money, gate, revenue, sales revenue, proceeds, return(s), royalty, royalties, money coming in, incomings, credits, profits, gross profits, net profits, mesne profits, turnover, sales volume, interest, gain, capital gain, bonus, premium, tax, taxes, direct tax, indirect tax, sales tax (US), value-added tax (VAT), property tax, rates, dues, duty, customs, tariff, import levy, rent, rent-roll, takings (Inf), take (Inf)
▶ *730 Receiving, 721 Gain*

3 income, national income, business income, private income, privy purse, emolument, regular income, earnings, remuneration, salary, wages, pay, half pay, freelance pay, fees, pension, pension fund, retirement benefit (US), annuity, tontine, grant, allowance, personal allowance, spending money, pin money, pocket money, money for a rainy day, financial support, bursary, bursarship, scholarship, fellowship, work-study grant (US), maintenance, aliment, alimony, child support (US), palimony (Sl)
▶ *746 Payment, 878 Reward*

4 legacy, inheritance, dower, bequest, heritage, birthright, patrimony

5 winnings, prize, draw, lucky draw, raffle, lottery, lucky dip, cut, rake-off (Sl)

▶ *681 Trophy*

ADJECTIVES

6 received, paid, credited, gained, gotten, accepted, taken, receipted, acknowledged, acknowledged with thanks, inherited, bequeathed, hereditary, patrimonial, bursarial, granted, salaried, waged, profitable, gainful

VERBS

7 receive, get, gain, take, acquire, accept, admit, receipt, acknowledge, mark paid, earn, gross, net, come into, inherit, fall to one, accrue, pay, yield, credit, pay off (Inf)

▶ *730 Receiving*

ADVERBS

8 profitably, gainfully, in profit, in receipt, at a premium, remuneratively, with interest, patrimonially, supportively, financially

750 Accounts

NOUNS

1 accounts, accountancy, accounting, financial accounting, cost accounting, management accounting, financial records, book-keeping, commercial arithmetic, creative accounting, item, entry, double entry, single entry, credit, debit, account, profit-and-loss account, balance sheet, debit and credit, receipts and expenditures, payments and receipts, running account, current account, cash account, deposit account, savings account, suspense account, expense account

2 budgeting, budget, capital budget, materials budget, production budget, production cost budget, creditors budget, debtors budget, cash budget, zero-based budgeting, budget estimates

▶ *606 Provision*

3 accounting, reckoning, calculation, computation, enumeration, score, tally, audit, inspection of accounts, inspection of books

4 statement, statement of account, bank statement, bank reconciliation statement, account rendered, *compte rendu* (Fr), invoice, bill, waybill, manifest, account paid, account settled

5 account book, bankbook, passbook, chequebook, cash book, petty-cash book, daybook, journal, ledger, register, books, records, accounts code

▶ *545 Record*

6 accountant, chartered accountant (CA), cost accountant, book-keeper, store-keeper, cashier, paymaster, bursar, purser, treasurer, auditor, inspector of accounts, examiner of accounts, actuary, statistician

VERBS

7 account, keep accounts, keep the books, balance accounts, prepare a balance sheet, make up an account, cast an account, write up, write down, book, enter, journalize, post, carry over, carry forward, debit, credit, record, register, cost, value, estimate, prepare a cash-flow forecast, budget, prepare a budget, practise creative accounting, massage the accounts, falsify the accounts, defraud, garble, fudge, doctor, cook the accounts (*or* books) (Inf), fiddle (Inf)

8 audit, inspect accounts, examine the accounts, go through the books, take stock, check stock, inventory, catalogue, list

▶ *171 List*

9 settle accounts, square accounts, pay up, cough up (Inf), finalize accounts, wind up accounts, write off accounts, prepare a statement, present an account, invoice, bill, charge, surcharge, overcharge, undercharge

▶ *751 Price*

ADJECTIVES

10 accounting, book-keeping, reckoning, computing, calculating, accountable, fiscal, financial, economic, commercial, arithmetical, mathematical, statistical, actuarial, bursarial, budgetary, inventorial, itemized, creative

11 accounted, audited, balanced, tallied, registered, recorded, credited, debited, deposited, saved, received, spent, invoiced, billed, costed, settled, carried forward

ADVERBS

12 on account, on credit, on the bill, on the slate (Inf), on the tab (Inf)

13 financially, fiscally, economically, commercially, arithmetically, statistically, creatively, in debt, in credit, at a loss, at cost

751 Price

NOUNS

1 price, cost, charge, price charged, selling price, retail price, wholesale price, factory price, factory-gate price, market price, world price, quoted price, quotation, estimate, amount, figure, sum asked for, standard price, list price, current price, offer price, sale price, cut price, discount price, factory discount price, reduced price rate, price cut, price war, price control, fixed price, *prix fixe* (Fr), price range, price list, tariff, cheapness, dearness

▶ *739 Sale, 752 Discount, 754 Cheapness, 753 Dearness*

2 value, monetary value, face value, par value, fair value, scarcity value, exchange value, worth, money's worth, what it will fetch, valuation, assessment, premium, prize, bounty, reward

▶ *617 Worth*

3 **fee**, rate, going rate, rate for the job, service fee, piece rate, flat rate, high rate, ceiling, low rate, floor, basement price, commission, cut, refresher, charge, demand, dues, subscription, surcharge, supplement, extra, entrance fee, admission fee, cover charge (US), service charge, corkage, fare, flat fare, hire, rental, rent, ground rent, house rent, quitrent (Arch), overcharge, excessive charge, price-fixing, extortion, rip-off (Sl), rake-off (Sl)

4 **bill**, invoice, reckoning, statement

5 **cost**, buying price, purchase price, outlay, costs, expenses, expenditure, cost of living, cost-of-living index, inflation, damage (Inf)

▶ *748 Expenditure*

6 **business costs**, start-up costs, running costs, overheads, purchase (or rental) of premises, office supplies, postage, utilities, wages, wage bill, salary bill, legal costs, damages, transport charges, freight charges, freightage, wharfage, lighterage, salvage

7 **tax**, taxes, dues, taxation, direct tax, indirect tax, progressive tax, proportional tax, capitation tax, regressive tax, punitive tax, collective tax, income tax, corporate (or corporation) tax, company tax, excess profits tax, windfall profits tax, capital gains tax, capital levy, inheritance tax, death duty, estate duty, property tax, rates, community charge, poll tax, council tax, municipal tax (US), state tax (US), city (or town) tax (US), local tax, capital transfer tax, gift tax, ecclesiastical tax, Peter's pence, tithe, tenths, purchase tax, sales tax (US), VAT (value added tax), octroi, surtax, supertax, cess, tax system, tax office (or bureau), Inland Revenue, pay as you earn (PAYE), National Insurance, tax return, tax form, tax declaration, tax rate, tax table, tax computation, deduction, personal allowance, taxable income, tax demand, tax owed, tax payment, tax refund, rating, assessment, appraisement, valorization, rateable value, estimate

8 **levy**, duty, impost, toll, excise, customs, Customs and Excise, tariff, tonnage and poundage, charge, fine, penalty, imposition, exaction, aid, benevolence, tribute, blackmail, protection money, hush money, ransom, forced saving, involuntary saving

▶ *746 Payment*

9 **historical taxes**, Danegeld, stamp tax, salt tax, gabelle, window tax, scot and lot, feudal tax, scutage

10 **taxpayer**, ratepayer, tax assessor, tax collector, tax consultant

VERBS

11 **price**, fix the price of, set a price, quote a price, value, valuate, evaluate, appraise, rate, assess

12 **charge**, ask, demand, exact, levy, tax, put a tax on, tithe

13 **cost**, amount to, come to, sell for, fetch, bring (in), set one back (Sl)

ADJECTIVES

14 **priced**, valued, rated, assessed, worth, valued at

15 **chargeable**, rateable, taxable, dutiable, non-taxable, nondutiable, tax-free, tax-exempt, deductible, tax-deductible

ADVERBS

16 **at a price**, for the price of, to the amount of, to the tune of (Inf)

752   Discount

NOUNS

1 **discount**, reduction, price reduction, cut, decrease, decrement, something off, concession, allowance, margin, rebate, refund, drawback, tare, tare and tret (Arch), deduction, deferment, contango, backwardation, commission, percentage, poundage, agio, brokerage, one's cut, rake-off (Sl)

▶ *129 Decrease, 131 Subtraction*

2 **bargain**, special offer, loss leader, incentive, bargain price, special price, cut price, cut rate, basement price, bottom price, dumping, sale, bargain sale, grand opening sale, sale of the century, clearance sale, going-out-of-business sale, fire sale, rummage sale, garage sale, jumble sale, bring-and-buy sale, car-boot sale, knockdown price (Inf)

▶ *739 Sale, 754 Cheapness*

VERBS

3 **discount**, reduce, lower, reduce the price of, mark down, cut, slash, take something off, give a concession, allow a margin, rebate, refund, tare, deduct, subtract, take off, knock off, depreciate, cheapen, offer a bargain, offer a discount, allow a discount, dump, knock down (Inf)

4 **take a discount**, take one's commission (or cut), take one's percentage, let stick to one's finger, rake off (Sl)

5 **buy at a discount**, pick up cheap, get for a song, make a killing, buy wholesale, buy in bulk, buy in the sales, find a bargain, defer payment, make a deposit

ADJECTIVES

6 **discounted**, marked down, cut-price, cut-rate, bargain, cheap, rebated, shopworn (US), shop soiled

ADVERBS

7 **at a discount**, at cut price, at half price, at bargain prices, on special offer, below par, less than the going rate, less than the market rate, in the sale, in the bargain bin

753   Dearness

NOUNS

1 **high price**, dearness, expensiveness, costli-

ness, big price tag, fancy price, luxury price, up-market price, steep price (Inf), stiff price (Inf), pretty penny (Inf), ritzy price (Inf)

▶ *751 Price, 741 Money, 748 Expenditure, 746 Payment, 738 Purchase, 14 Finance, 13 Economics*

2 **unfair price**, overcharging, overpricing, excessive charge, surcharge, overcharge, exorbitance, exorbitant price, extortionate price, an arm and a leg (Inf), highway robbery (Inf), daylight robbery (Inf)

3 **inflationary price**, rising prices (*or* costs), climbing prices, soaring prices (*or* costs), spiralling prices, skyrocketing price, mounting costs, inflation, inflationary pressure, inflationary spiral, bullish tendency, bull market, sellers' market, prices going through the ceiling (*or* roof)

4 **extortion**, usury, profiteering, rack-rent, loan-sharking (Inf), gouging (US inf), rip-off (Sl)

▶ *740 Market, 734 Taking, 539 Deception, 610 Excess, 737 Trade, 736 Stealing*

5 **overcharger**, usurer, extortionist, shark, Shylock, rack-renter, loan shark (Inf), rip-off artist (Inf), con man (Inf)

▶ *733 Borrowing, 745 Debt, 736 Stealing*

6 **value**, worth, high value, great worth, valuableness, invaluableness, pricelessness, preciousness, scarcity value, rarity, rareness, dearth, scarcity

▶ *617 Worth, 213 Infrequency*

ADJECTIVES

7 **dear**, expensive, costly, high-priced, high-price, dear at the price, dear at any price, extravagant, fancy, luxury, up-market, exorbitant, excessive, overpriced, overcharging, overcharged, unreasonable, prohibitive, beyond one's means, not affordable, more than one can afford, more than one's pocket can stand, extortionate, inflationary, rising, climbing, soaring, spiralling, mounting, rocketing, high-cost, sky-high, bullish, bull, usurious, profiteering, pricey (*or* pricy) (Inf), ritzy (Sl), gouging (US inf), stiff (Inf), steep (Inf), skyrocketing (Inf), going through the roof (Inf), out-of-sight (US inf)

▶ *609 Insufficiency, 357 Overstepping, 610 Excess*

8 **valuable**, invaluable, high-value, priceless, beyond price, above price, inestimable, precious, too precious for words, at a premium, worth a pretty penny (Inf), worth a fortune, worth a king's ransom, worth its weight in gold, exclusive, rare, scarce, infrequent, like gold dust, not to be had for love or money

VERBS

9 **be dear**, cost a lot, cost one dear, cost a fortune, hurt one's pocket, make a hole in one's pocket, rise in price, appreciate, escalate, soar, mount, rocket, climb, go through the ceiling (*or* roof), run into money, harden, get

too dear, price itself out of the market, cost (Inf), cost a pretty penny (Inf), cost the earth (Inf), cost an arm and a leg (Inf), cost a packet (Sl), cost a bundle (Sl)

▶ *128 Increase, 13 Economics, 14 Finance, 751 Price, 617 Worth, 746 Payment*

10 **overcharge**, overprice, surcharge, sell dear, oversell, ask too much, rack-rent, profiteer, raise the price, put up prices, mark up, set the price tag too high, inflate, extort, fleece, swindle, do (Inf), commit highway robbery (Inf), commit daylight robbery (Inf), hold up (US inf), bleed (white) (Inf), gouge (US inf), con (Inf), rip off (Inf), burn (Sl), sting (Sl), soak (US sl), skin (Sl), clip (Sl), screw (Sl)

▶ *736 Stealing, 734 Taking, 539 Deception, 357 Overstepping, 610 Excess*

11 **overpay**, overspend, pay too much, pay more than it's worth, pay dearly, ruin oneself, be overdrawn, go into the red, raise the bid, bid up, pay a pretty penny (Inf), pay through the nose (Inf), be had (Inf), get ripped off (Sl)

▶ *610 Excess, 748 Expenditure, 757 Extravagance*

ADVERBS

12 **dearly**, dear, at great cost, at heavy cost, at great expense, at huge expense, expensively, grossly, extravagantly, outrageously, exorbitantly, excessively, extortionately, prohibitively, beyond one's means, more than one can afford, usuriously, stiffly (Inf), steeply (Inf), out of sight (US inf)

13 **valuably**, at great value, invaluably, inestimably, pricelessly, beyond worth, exclusively, rarely, scarcely, infrequently, preciously, at a premium

754 Cheapness

NOUNS

1 **cheapness**, inexpensiveness, reasonableness, reasonable charge, affordability, good value, value for money, money's worth, easy terms, popular price, sensible price, competitive price, sale price, reduced price, discount, budget price, economy price, bargain price, cut price, cut rate (US), price cut, markdown, knockdown price, slashed price, rock-bottom price, giveaway price, nominal price, peppercorn rent, low (*or* small) price tag, cheap rate, reduced rate, concessional rate

2 **declining prices**, fall, price fall, bear market, bearishness, buyers' market, sluggish market, deflation, slump, plunge, recession, depression, cooling off of the economy, devaluation, depreciation, Dutch auction, superfluity, redundance, oversupply, plenty, glut, drug on the market

▶ *738 Purchase, 741 Money, 752 Discount, 739 Sale, 14 Finance, 13 Economics, 748 Expenditure, 710 Offer, 751 Price*

3 **shoddiness**, cheapness, gaudiness, second-ratedness, inferiority, baseness, lowness, poorness, shabbiness, scruffiness, pettiness, paltriness, pokiness, meanness, commonness, vulgarity, kitsch, crumminess (Sl)
▶ *124 Average, 127 Inferiority, 758 Meanness, 811 Showiness, 795 Vulgarity*

4 **bargain**, good buy, good deal, special offer, two for the price of one, loss leader, sale goods, sale merchandise, *bon marché* (Fr), seconds, rejects, excursion fare, tourist fare, second-class fare, economy fare, off-season fare, off-peak fare, APEX (Advance Purchase Excursion), bucket-shop fare, cheap ticket, discount ticket, season ticket, bus pass, railcard, coachcard, travelcard, Interrail Card (Tm), half fare, stand-by fare, steal (US inf), snip (Inf), twofer (US inf)
▶ *740 Market, 716 Negotiation, 70 Transport*

5 **cheap item**, trifle, gewgaw, gimcrack, frippery, bauble, trinket, gaud, curio, knick-knack, kickshaw, bagatelle, brummagem, toy, plaything, novelty, bric-a-brac, tat, junk, jumble, white elephant
▶ *557 Ornament*

6 **absence of charge**, gift, free gift, giveaway (US), freesheet, complimentary gift, something for nothing, gratuitousness, gratuity, *gratuit* (Fr), free board, free lodging, free quarters, grace-and-favour flat, free drink, free lunch, free postage, Freepost (Tm), 0800 telephone number, Freefone (Tm), free admission, free entry, free seat, free ticket, guest ticket, complimentary ticket, pass, free pass, guest pass, complimentary pass, free port, free trade, free service, free delivery, volunteer work, voluntary work, charity, labour of love, perquisite, perk (Inf), free ride (Inf), freebie (US sl), Annie Oakley (US sl), paper (Sl)
▶ *747 Nonpayment, 755 Generosity, 729 Giving, 710 Offer*

7 **discounter**, street trader, wholesaler, cash and carry, warehouse, bucket shop, bargain basement, bargain bin, discount store, second-hand shop, junk shop, thrift shop, charity shop, flea market, jumble sale, rummage sale (US), car-boot sale, yard sale (US), garage sale, coupons, classified ads (Inf), small ads (Inf)
▶ *740 Market, 737 Trade*

8 **bargain hunter**, off-season traveller, passholder, gate-crasher, miser, penny-pincher, coupon-clipper (US), skinflint, scrooge, cheapjack (Inf), sponger (Inf), freeloader (Sl)
▶ *643 Inactivity, 734 Taking, 758 Meanness, 756 Thrift*

ADJECTIVES

9 **cheap**, inexpensive, unexpensive, uncostly, reasonable, sensible, manageable, affordable, within one's means, easy on the pocket, modest, moderate, bargain-basement, down-market, five-and-ten (US), dime-store (US), twopenny-halfpenny, good-value, low-budget, low-price(d), low, underpriced, catchpenny, brummagem, going cheap (*or* cheaply), going for a song, cheap at the price, cheap at half the price, (well) worth the money, sale, sale-price(d), off-season, off-peak, excursion, economy-class, tourist-class, second-class, third-class, bucket-shop, concessional, nominal, budget, economic(al), economy, economy-size, bargain, discount, half-price, cut-price, cut-rate (US), markdown, knockdown, marked down, reduced, reduced to clear, slashed, sacrificial, rock-bottom, giveaway, declining, falling, slumping, bearish, bear, devalued, depreciated, superfluous, redundant, oversupplied, a dime a dozen (US), dirt-cheap (Inf), cheap as dirt (Inf), cheapo (Inf), for peanuts (Sl)

10 **shoddy**, shabby, scruffy, base, low, mean, poor, paltry, poky, mangy, scummy, tacky, gaudy, tawdry, tatty, trashy, twopenny (*or* tuppenny), second-rate, inferior, low grade, low quality, useless, unsaleable, unsalable (US), unmarketable, valueless, worthless, shop-soiled, shopworn (US), unbought, unwanted, out of fashion, past its sell-by date, crummy (Sl), tinpot (Sl), two-bit (US sl), lousy (Sl), chintzy (US sl)
▶ *614 Uselessness, 618 Worthlessness*

11 **free of charge**, free, scot-free, free for the asking, for free, for nothing, without charge, not charged for, uncharged, unchargeable, gratis, given free, given away, given, giveaway, complimentary, on the house, courtesy, gratuitous, honorary, grace-and-favour, voluntary, unsalaried, unpaid, charity, eleemosynary, untaxed, tax-free, zero-rated, rent-free, post-paid, post-free, f.o.b. (free on board), buckshee (Sl)
▶ *747 Nonpayment*

VERBS

12 **be cheap**, cost next to nothing, go for a song, go dirt-cheap, fall in price, depreciate, decline, sag, fall, drift, slump, plunge, plummet
▶ *362 Lowering*

13 **make cheap**, cheapen, devalue, offer value for money, give someone his money's worth, lower the price, reduce the price, lower charges, trim, cut, mark down, slash, discount, offer easy terms, sacrifice, undercharge, undercut, undersell, let go for a song, flood the market, glut the market, dump, unload, depress the market, give away, knock the bottom out of the market (Inf), knock down (Inf)
▶ *362 Lowering, 608 Sufficiency*

14 **buy cheaply**, economize, shop around, find bargains, buy wholesale, buy in bulk, buy at factory prices, buy at cost, pick up for nothing, travel second-class, travel tourist-class, travel

off season, live within one's means, buy for nickles and dimes (US), haggle, beat down, buy dirt-cheap (Inf), sponge (off) (Inf), freeload (Sl)

▶ *740 Market, 737 Trade, 716 Negotiation, 756 Thrift*

ADVERBS

15 **cheaply**, cheap, inexpensively, unexpensively, reasonably, modestly, moderately, economically, nominally, at cost, wholesale, at a discount, *à bon marché* (Fr), for pennies, for nickels and dimes (US), for a (mere) song, for nothing, on the house, as a gift, on the cheap (Inf)

755 Generosity

ADJECTIVES

1 **generous**, liberal, open-handed, hospitable, giving, unstinting, ungrudging, beneficent, munificent, bountiful, bounteous, lavish, princely, handsome

2 **magnanimous**, charitable, benevolent, humanitarian, philanthropic

3 **abundant**, plentiful, ample, lavish, more than enough, copious, overflowing, profuse, superabundant

▶ *610 Excess*

4 **big**, roomy, large, capacious, spacious, commodious

NOUNS

5 **generosity**, liberality, open-handedness, beneficence, charity, bounty, bounteousness, munificence, hospitality

6 **magnanimity**, charitableness, benevolence, philanthropy

7 **gift**, contribution, subscription, donation, covenant, bonus, tip, hand-out, alms, baksheesh

▶ *741 Money, 746 Payment, 767 Relief*

8 **abundance**, plenty, plenteousness, profusion, superabundance

9 **generous person**, benefactor, backer, donor, donator, contributor, subscriber, philanthropist, humanitarian, good Samaritan, willing giver, Lady Bountiful, Father Christmas, Santa Claus, fairy godmother, angel (Inf)

VERBS

10 **be generous**, give generously, give freely, give away, keep open house, spare no expense, pay towards, give with both hands, tip well, splash out (Inf), cough up (Sl)

11 **give**, contribute, subscribe, donate, covenant, bequeath, endow, finance, fund, aid, support

▶ *284 Support*

ADVERBS

12 **generously**, liberally, freely, lavishly, copiously, amply, abundantly, plentifully, ungrudgingly, with open hands, with no expense spared

756 Thrift

I knew once a very covetous, sordid fellow, who used to say, 'Take care of the pence, for the pounds will take care of themselves.' Earl of Chesterfield.

...we owe something to extravagance, for thrift and adventure seldom go hand in hand. Jennie Jerome Churchill.

NOUNS

1 **thrift**, thriftiness, economy, good husbandry, good management, good housekeeping, carefulness, prudence, frugality, austerity, cheeseparing

▶ *758 Meanness*

2 **act of thrift**, economy drive, retrenchment, cutting back, cutback, budget, spending plan

3 **saver**, economizer, scrimper

ADJECTIVES

4 **thrifty**, economical, unlavish, unwasteful, conserving, saving, labour-saving, time-saving, money-saving, good with money, canny, careful, prudent, economizing, sparing, frugal, spartan, austere, meagre, scrimpy, cheeseparing

VERBS

5 **be thrifty**, make do, budget, live on a budget, live (*or* keep) within one's means, make both ends meet, conserve, husband, husband one's resources

6 **save**, economize, keep costs down, retrench, cut down, cut costs, cut back, cut corners, scrimp, scrape, cut one's coat according to one's cloth (Inf), tighten one's belt (Inf), batten down the hatches (Inf)

ADVERBS

7 **economically**, thriftily, prudently, frugally, with a sparing hand

757 Extravagance

ADJECTIVES

1 **extravagant**, wasteful, lavish, uneconomic, spendthrift, prodigal, profligate, thriftless, unthrifty, improvident, easy come easy go (Inf)

▶ *755 Generosity*

2 **unrestrained**, excessive, inordinate, immoderate, extreme, wild, exaggerated, hyperbolic, magnified, profuse, showy, ostentatious, preposterous, outrageous, fantastical

▶ *610 Excess, 128 Increase*

3 **costly**, high-priced, expensive, dear, overpriced, exorbitant, inflationary, sky-high, unaffordable, prohibitive, extortionate, steep (Inf), pricey (Inf), going through the roof (Inf)

NOUNS

4 **extravagance**, prodigality, lavishness, wastefulness, profligacy, conspicuous consumption, unthriftiness, squandering, im-

providence, spending spree

5 **unrestrainedness**, immoderation, exaggeration, hyperbole, profusion, superfluity, dissipation, extremes

6 **spendthrift**, prodigal, prodigal son, profligate, wastrel, squanderer, waster, big spender (Inf), spender (Inf), Mrs (*or* Mr) Spend Spend Spend (Inf)

VERBS

7 **waste**, squander, fritter, fritter away, misspend, dissipate, lavish, go through, use up, exhaust, pour down the drain (Inf), blow (Sl)

8 **overspend**, overdraw, live beyond one's means, throw money away, throw good money after bad, go on a spending spree, spend (money) like water, spend, spend, spend (Inf), splash out on (Inf), spend (money) like it's going out of style (*or* fashion) (Inf)

ADVERBS

9 **extravagantly**, wastefully, lavishly, uneconomically, excessively, inordinately, immoderately, inexhaustibly, to the full, no end (Inf)

758 Meanness

ADJECTIVES

1 **mean**, miserly, parsimonious, ungenerous, grudging, tight, tightfisted, close, close-fisted, near, money-grubbing, niggardly, penurious, penny-pinching, penny-wise, scrimping, cheeseparing, mingy, stingy, tight-arsed (Sl)
▶ *756 Thrift*

2 **unpleasant**, nasty, unkind, hurtful, spiteful, petty, small, small-minded, despicable, base, shabby, sordid, squalid, lowly, beastly (Inf)
▶ *127 Inferiority, 764 Unpleasantness*

NOUNS

3 **parsimony**, parsimoniousness, niggardliness, miserliness, ungenerousness, ungenerosity, tightness, tightfistedness, close-fistedness, cheeseparing, stinginess, minginess

4 **unpleasantness**, nastiness, hurtfulness, pettiness, spite, baseness, beastliness, shabbiness, lowliness, squalor

5 **miser**, niggard, skinflint, hoarder, money-grubber, Scrooge, penny-pincher, misanthrope, mean old stick (Inf), meanie (Inf), tight-wad (US sl), tight-arse (Sl)

6 **nasty person**, meanie (Inf), git (Inf)
▶ *764 Unpleasantness*

VERBS

7 **hoard**, save up, save, stint, scrimp, skimp, starve

8 **grudge**, begrudge, resent

ADVERBS

9 **meanly**, parsimoniously, ungenerously, niggardly, grudgingly, on a shoestring

759 Feeling

NOUNS

1 **feeling**, perception, sensation, sense, experience, aesthesia, awareness, consciousness, realization, understanding, knowledge, reaction
▶ *403 Sensation, 501 Knowledge*

2 **impression**, fancy, belief, idea, notion, shade of feeling, inkling, intimation, suggestion, hint, nuance, undercurrent, instinctive feeling, intuition, sixth sense, insight, extrasensory perception (ESP), clairvoyance, presentiment, divination, instinct, impulse, reflex, hunch, gut reaction (Inf), vibes (Sl)
▶ *464 Intuition, 11 Occultism*

3 **feelings**, sentiments, sensibilities, susceptibilities, affections, sympathies, finer feelings, attitudes, beliefs, opinion, view, viewpoint
▶ *760 Sensitivity*

4 **emotion**, mood, attitude, frame of mind, state of mind, strong feeling, passion, ardour, fervour, fire, heat, verve, ecstasy, rapture, zeal, intensity, vehemence, obsession, fanaticism, mania
▶ *610 Excess, 822 Hate, 762 Joy*

5 **good feeling**, fellow feeling, tender feeling, fondness, sympathy, empathy, identification, cordiality, warmth, friendliness, amicability, responsiveness, involvement, liking, love, devotion
▶ *760 Sensitivity, Love*

6 **bad feeling**, hard feelings, animosity, resentment, bitterness, ill will, offence, dislike, intolerance, spite, jealousy, grudge, envy, hatred, fury, rage, bad atmosphere, bad vibes (Sl)
▶ *785 Dislike, 841 Jealousy, 842 Envy*

7 **emotionalism**, emotionality, emotiveness, nostalgia, romanticism, sentimentality, overemotionalism, mawkishness, bathos, excitability, emotional instability
▶ *760 Sensitivity*

8 **seat of feelings**, deepest feelings, core of one's being, secret places, heart, bosom, soul, spirit, bottom of one's heart, cockles of one's heart, pit of one's stomach, bones, guts (Inf)

9 **feeling person**, sympathizer, friend, carer, sensitive person, emotional person, hot-head, wild boy, wild man, virago, shrew, spitfire
▶ *760 Sensitivity, 821 Love, 610 Excess*

ADJECTIVES

10 **feeling**, sensing, sentient, sensible, perceptive, aware, conscious, knowing, realizing, understanding, responsive, sensitive, impressionable, susceptible
▶ *760 Sensitivity, 403 Sensation*

11 **intuitive**, instinctive, impulsive, inspirational, clairvoyant, fey
▶ *11 Occultism*

12 **sensitive**, sympathetic, empathetic, feeling, caring, involved with, fond, cordial, friendly,

amicable, warm, warm-hearted, soft-hearted, tender, romantic, nostalgic, sentimental, bathetic, maudlin, mawkish, sloppy (Inf), emotional, overemotional, tearful, overcome, overwhelmed, overwrought, hypersensitive, highly strung

▶ *760 Sensitivity, 821 Love*

13 **passionate**, impassioned, intense, effusive, ardent, fervent, zealous, vehement, rapturous, ecstatic, fiery, heated, inflamed, excitable, impetuous, hot-headed, temperamental, touchy, volatile, mercurial, unstable, melodramatic, hysterical, obsessed, jealous, envious, fanatical, manic, raving, raging, over the top, OTT (Sl)

▶ *610 Excess, 822 Hate, 762 Joy, 841 Jealousy, 842 Envy*

14 **emotive**, affecting, touching, moving, deeply felt, heartfelt, overwhelming

VERBS

15 **feel**, experience, sense, perceive, be aware of, realize, understand, go through, live through, undergo

16 **feel in one's bones**, sense, intuit, feel instinctively, know by instinct, guess at, have a hunch about (Inf)

17 **feel deeply**, take to heart, show signs of emotion, get agitated about, go into ecstasies over, have hysterics, throw a tantrum, go mad, see red, run amok, explode, throw a wobbly (Inf), be a prima donna (Inf), be a little madam (Inf), have a nervous breakdown (Inf), throw a fit (Inf), hit the roof (Inf), freak out (Sl), go bananas (Sl)

▶ *464 Intuition*

18 **feel for**, empathize, relate to, enter into the spirit of, sympathize, commiserate, pity, be sorry for, grieve for, bleed for

▶ *760 Sensitivity, 835 Pity*

19 **believe**, think, opine, maintain, hold

▶ *497 Belief*

ADVERBS

20 **with feeling**, feelingly, affectingly, touchingly, warmly, with all one's heart, from the bottom of one's heart, passionately, ardently, fervently, intensely, zealously, vehemently, rapturously, ecstatically, hysterically

21 **emotionally**, sentimentally, mawkishly

760 Sensitivity

ADJECTIVES

1 **sensitive**, impressionable, suggestible, impressible, susceptible, affectible, receptive, responsive, perceptive, sentient, feeling, delicate, aware, empathetic, sympathetic, compassionate, caring, tender, tender-hearted, soft-hearted, emotional, sentimental

▶ *759 Feeling*

2 **oversensitive**, touchy, irritable, irascible,

thin-skinned, highly strung, temperamental, nervy, jumpy, like a cat on a hot tin roof

▶ *759 Feeling*

3 **sore**, painful, raw, tender, allergic, sensitized, ticklish, itchy, tingling

4 **accurate**, precise

▶ *503 Accuracy*

NOUNS

5 **sensitivity**, sensitiveness, sensibility, impressionability, suggestibility, impressibility, susceptibility, affectibility, receptivity, responsiveness, awareness, delicacy, finer feelings, tenderness, empathy, sympathy, commiseration, compassion, pity, sentimentality

▶ *759 Feeling, 403 Sensation*

6 **oversensitivity**, touchiness, irritability, irascibility, raw feelings, sore point

▶ *759 Feeling*

7 **soreness**, rawness, tenderness, ticklishness, allergy, itchiness, tingling

▶ *406 Physical Pain*

8 **sensitive person**, sympathizer, carer, counsellor, good listener, good Samaritan, new man

9 **oversensitive person**, bundle of nerves, neurotic, jitterbug, sensitive plant (*or* flower) (Inf), shrinking violet (Inf), mouse (Inf)

10 **accuracy**, pinpoint accuracy, precision, high fidelity, hi-fi, fine tuning

▶ *503 Accuracy*

VERBS

11 **be sensitive**, feel for, pity, sympathize, empathize, commiserate, show feelings, feel deeply, take to heart, be all heart, need kid-glove treatment (Inf)

ADVERBS

12 **sensitively**, feelingly, with feeling, perceptively, delicately, sympathetically, tenderly, caringly

13 **oversensitively**, emotionally, irritably, temperamentally

761 Insensitivity

Just as the meanest and most vicious deeds require spirit and talent, so even the greatest deeds require a certain insensitiveness which on other occasions is called stupidity. Georg Christoph Lichtenberg.

ADJECTIVES

1 **insensitive**, insensible, unsusceptible, immune, unresponsive, unimpressionable, unimpressible, unaffected, indifferent, apathetic, impassive, unfeeling, insensate, unemotional, frigid, cold, cold-hearted, cold-blooded, heartless, thick-skinned, impervious, proof against, rhino-hided, obtuse, blunt, tactless, unimaginative, callous, uncaring, tough, hard, hardened, blind, deaf, unaware, unconscious, im-

perceptive, impercipient, dull, thick (Inf)

2 **desensitized**, numb, frozen, paralysed, anaesthetized, dopey, groggy, torpid, sluggish, drugged, stupefied, comatose, unfeeling, unconscious, quiescent, inert, dead

▶ *404 Insensibility, 240 Inertness, 643 Inactivity*

NOUNS

3 **insensitiveness**, insensibility, unsusceptibility, unresponsiveness, indifference, apathy, impassivity, lack of feeling, coldness, coldheartedness, heartlessness, callousness, tactlessness, bluntness, hardness, unawareness, dullness, Philistinism

4 **desensitization**, narcotization, stupefaction, hypnosis, numbness, paralysis, stupor, torpor, sluggishness, grogginess, trance, coma, catalepsy, catatonia, narcosis, analgesia, anaesthesia, unconsciousness, stagnation, quiescence

▶ *404 Insensibility, 240 Inertness, 643 Inactivity*

5 **insensitive person**, ascetic, stoic, Philistine, bigot, hardnut (Inf), redneck (Inf), meathead (Inf), cold fish (Inf), iceberg (Inf), icicle (Inf), ice queen (Inf)

6 **desensitizing substance**, narcotic, anaesthetic, drug, soporific, painkiller, analgesic, sleeping draught, sleeping pill, nepenthes, tranquillizer, barbiturate, knock-out drops (Inf), Mickey Finn (Inf), downers (Sl), barbs (Sl), reds (Sl), red devils (Sl), dope (Sl), black bombers (Sl), green and blacks (Sl)

▶ *62 Pharmacology*

VERBS

7 **render insensitive**, desensitize, numb, benumb, paralyse, freeze, stupefy, anaesthetize, narcotize, drug, dope, hypnotize, deaden, blunt, concuss, knock out, knock senseless, brain (Inf)

▶ *404 Insensibility*

ADVERBS

8 **unfeelingly**, insensitively, in cold blood, indifferently, apathetically, unemotionally, coldly, heartlessly, bluntly, tactlessly, callously

762 Joy

NOUNS

1 **happiness**, contentment, euphoria, gladness, lightheartedness, cheerfulness, merriment, delight, pleasure, enjoyment, delectation, joy, joyfulness, joyousness, felicity, gaiety, glee, gleefulness, high spirits, *joie de vivre* (Fr), gusto, zest, exuberance, ebullience, transport, exaltation, exhilaration, rapture, ecstasy, bliss, enchantment, intoxication, delirium

▶ *769 Cheerfulness, 773 Rejoicing, 765 Satisfaction*

2 **fun**, entertainment, party, treat, holiday, celebration, merrymaking, revelry, honeymoon period, halcyon days, heaven, paradise, joy,

thrill, kick (Sl), buzz (Sl), lark (Sl), whizz (Sl), high (Sl)

▶ *812 Celebration*

3 **joyful person**, merrymaker, reveller, partygoer, groover (Inf), raver (Inf)

ADJECTIVES

4 **happy**, contented, euphoric, pleased, glad, gladsome, cheerful, joyful, joyous, full of joy, felicitous, gay, blithe, merry, delighted, exuberant, ebullient, blissful, starry-eyed, elated, overjoyed, thrilled, transported, ecstatic, celebratory, jubilant, captivated, enchanted, enraptured, delirious, intoxicated, beside oneself, beside oneself with joy, like a child with a new toy, pleased as Punch (Inf), happy as a sandboy (Inf), over the moon (Inf), on cloud nine (Inf), in seventh heaven (Inf), tickled pink (Inf), tickled to death (Inf), high as a kite (Sl), blissed out (Sl)

5 **delightful**, lovely, wonderful, marvellous, heavenly, enchanting, gorgeous, entrancing, charming, enthralling, captivating, Elysian (Fml), out of this world (Inf)

▶ *763 Pleasantness*

VERBS

6 **enjoy**, have fun, celebrate, relish, delight in, take pleasure in, have a good time, eat, drink, and be merry, kick up one's heels (Inf)

7 **show joy**, smile, grin, beam, laugh, chuckle, giggle, chortle, guffaw, crow, sing, purr, rejoice

8 **cause joy**, gladden, please, cheer, thrill, delight, charm, enchant, enrapture, enthral, captivate, intoxicate, send (Sl)

ADVERBS

9 **joyfully**, happily, gladly, cheerfully, with pleasure, merrily, gaily, gleefully

763 Pleasantness

ADJECTIVES

1 **pleasant**, pleasing, nice, enjoyable, pleasurable, agreeable, acceptable, gratifying, satisfying, tasteful, inviting, welcome, charming, appealing, sweet, lovely, delightful, idyllic, heavenly, divine, Elysian (Fml), sublime, blissful, out of this world (Inf)

2 **likable**, amiable, affable, friendly, cordial, compatible, congenial, genial, engaging, good-natured, easygoing, amusing, bright, sunny, attractive, kind, kindly, courteous, polite, well-mannered, chivalrous, civil, civilized

3 **comfortable**, soothing, relaxing, restful, dulcet, mellow, emollient, easy, cosy, snug, comfy (Inf)

4 **tasty**, palatable, appetizing, tempting, savoury, flavourful, mouthwatering, delicious, delectable, luscious, juicy, succulent

5 **pleasure-loving**, pleasure-seeking, hedonis-

tic, epicurean, gourmet, gourmand, voluptuous, self-indulgent

▶ *405 Physical Pleasure, 870 Self-Indulgence*

NOUNS

6 **pleasantness**, pleasurableness, niceness, agreeableness, charm, appeal, loveliness, delightfulness, heaven, bliss

7 **pleasure**, enjoyment, satisfaction, ease, comfort, luxury, creature comforts, hedonism, self-indulgence, epicureanism, voluptuousness, entertainment, amusement, diversion

8 **amiability**, affability, friendliness, cordiality, compatibility, congeniality, geniality, good company, attractiveness, kindliness, courtesy, chivalry, politeness, civility

9 **tastiness**, palatability, deliciousness, delectability, lusciousness

10 **pleasant thing**, treat, delicacy, luxury, holiday, honeymoon, pleasant remark, pleasantry, compliment, praise, tribute, honour, flattery

▶ *853 Flattery, 771 Humour*

11 **pleasant person**, charmer, delight, pleasure, joy

12 **pleasure-loving person**, hedonist, epicurean, voluptuary

VERBS

13 **give pleasure**, please, gratify, satisfy, comfort, soothe, agree with, charm, delight, brighten one's day

14 **like**, appreciate, delight in, enjoy, relish, savour

ADVERBS

15 **pleasantly**, agreeably, with pleasure, with good grace, cordially, genially, politely

764 Unpleasantness

ADJECTIVES

1 **unpleasant**, displeasing, unpleasing, disagreeable, unacceptable, rebarbative, uncomfortable, painful, discomfiting, discordant, unharmonious, trying, annoying, irksome, invidious, unwelcome, uninviting, disliked, distasteful, unpalatable, unsavoury, nasty, horrible, hateful, horrid, disgusting, offensive, odious, repulsive, loathsome, revolting, sickening, nauseating

▶ *822 Hate, 434 Dissonance, 341 Repulsion*

2 **objectionable**, awkward, unattractive, ungracious, discomforting, impolite, uncivil, discourteous, unchivalrous, unkind, uncouth, impertinent, rude, boorish, mean, cantankerous, obnoxious, quarrelsome, crabbed, crabby, quarrelling, aggressive, bellicose, beastly (Inf), bloody-minded (Inf), like a bear with a sore head (Inf)

▶ *768 Aggravation, 670 Attack, 473 Argument*

3 **unpalatable**, unappetizing, uneatable, inedible, acid, bitter, sour, rancid, off, turned

▶ *411 Taste, 415 Sourness*

4 **painful**, sore, tender, aching, smarting, stinging

▶ *406 Physical Pain*

NOUNS

5 **unpleasantness**, disagreeableness, pain, discomfort, discomfiture, affront, offence, umbrage, distastefulness, unpalatability, nastiness, offensiveness, repulsiveness

6 **objectionability**, awkwardness, unattractiveness, ungraciousness, impoliteness, incivility, discourtesy, unkindness, impertinence, rudeness, bad manners, boorishness, meanness, cantankerousness, aggressiveness, beastliness

7 **dissension**, disagreement, disharmony, bad feeling, friction, disunity, discord, discordance, aggravation, antagonism, squabbling, fighting, bickering

▶ *434 Dissonance, 768 Aggravation, 670 Attack*

8 **quarrel**, argument, difference of opinion, squabble, scuffle, clash, scrap, wrangle, brawl, fisticuffs, altercation, row, conflict, strife, chastisement, vendetta, feud, set-to (Inf), tiff (Inf), bother (Sl), stick (Sl), aggro (Sl), spot of bother (Sl)

9 **unpleasant person**, pest, nuisance, boor, oaf, lout, cad, shrew, troublemaker, mischief-maker, quarreller, wrangler, aggressor, fighter, hooligan, beast (Inf), pain (Inf), pain in the neck (Inf), pain in the arse (Tab sl), shit (Tab sl), shitbag (Tab sl)

VERBS

10 **displease**, put off, discomfit, discomfort, embarrass, enrage, offend, repel, appal, disgust, revolt, horrify, sicken, nauseate, stick in one's throat (Inf), get up one's nose (Inf)

11 **quarrel**, disagree, dissent, argue, nag, have differences with, take umbrage, insult, offend, take liberties with, squabble, wrangle, scrap, bicker, brawl, fight, cross swords with, clash, conflict, feud, wind up (Sl)

12 **be painful**, hurt, ache, throb, smart, sting

ADVERBS

13 **unpleasantly**, disagreeably, nastily, distastefully, offensively, repulsively, discourteously, aggressively

765 Satisfaction

Youth will be served, every dog has his day, and mine has been a fine one. George Henry Borrow.

The reward of a thing well done is to have done it. Ralph Waldo Emerson.

NOUNS

1 **satisfaction**, fulfilment, gratification, thankfulness, contentedness, contentment, content, peace of mind, serenity, equanimity, happiness, pleasure, enjoyment, comfort,

ease, satiation, satiety, self-satisfaction, smugness, complacency

▶ *762 Joy, 767 Relief, 405 Physical Pleasure, 763 Pleasantness*

2 **reparation**, recompense, compensation, atonement, amends, apology, indemnity, expiation, reconciliation, appeasement, propitiation

▶ *840 Atonement*

3 **satisfactoriness**, sufficiency, adequacy, tolerability

ADJECTIVES

4 **satisfied**, fulfilled, gratified, thankful, content, contented, serene, uncomplaining, without complaints, undemanding, secure, safe, happy, pleased, satiated, full, full-up, comfortable, self-satisfied, smug, complacent

5 **satisfying**, fulfilling, gratifying, pleasing, pacifying, comforting, satiating, filling, ample

6 **satisfactory**, sufficient, sufficing, enough, adequate, acceptable, passable, tolerable, all right, not bad, good enough, fair, so-so (Inf), OK (Inf)

VERBS

7 **be satisfied**, have nothing to complain about, have nothing to grumble about, be at ease, delight in, have one's heart's desire, have all one could ask for, purr (Inf), be like the cat that stole the cream (Inf), look like the cat that swallowed the canary (US inf)

8 **satisfy**, gratify, fulfil, content, please, indulge, satiate, sate, fill, quench, slake

9 **comfort**, pacify, placate, lull, appease, reassure, assure, convince, persuade, put someone's mind at rest, set at ease

10 **suffice**, serve, do, answer, settle, meet, meet the needs of

11 **recompense**, compensate, atone, make amends, apologize, indemnify, expiate, reconcile, appease, propitiate

ADVERBS

12 **satisfactorily**, adequately, enough

13 **with satisfaction**, thankfully, contentedly, serenely, happily

766   Dissatisfaction

NOUNS

1 **dissatisfaction**, displeasure, disgruntlement, discontent, discontentment, disappointment, disillusionment, consternation, disapprobation, disapproval, rejection, reprobation, censure, dislike, derision, deprecation, disgust, contempt, contemptuousness, scorn

2 **expression of dissatisfaction**, complaint, criticism, boo, hiss, whistle, snub, reprimand, remonstration, rebuke, reproof, black mark (Inf), gripe (Inf), rocket (Inf), telling off (Inf)

3 **dissatisfied person**, dissatisfied customer, reprover, complainer, grumbler, grouser, carper, moaner, whiner, bleater, spoilsport, malcontent, moper, sulker, brooder, angry young man, bellyacher (Inf), griper (Inf), whinger (Inf), kvetch (US sl)

ADJECTIVES

4 **dissatisfied**, displeased, disgruntled, discontented, discontent, malcontent, malcontented, sulking, sulky, brooding, disaffected, complaining, whingeing, disappointed, disillusioned, disapproving, unapproving, unimpressed, critical of, perjorative, disgusted, contemptuous, scornful, derisive, derisory

5 **unsatisfactory**, dissatisfactory, disappointing, disapproved of, unapproved, unpopular, rejected, substandard, not up to scratch (Inf)

VERBS

6 **dissatisfy**, displease, disappoint, disillusion, disgust, revolt, sicken

7 **be dissatisfied**, disapprove, not hold with, not think much of, dislike, resent, disfavour, criticize, find fault with, pick holes in, look askance at, tut-tut at, object to, cavil, grumble, grouse, carp, complain, whine, moan, sulk, brood, run down, belittle, deride, deprecate, deplore, reprove, rebuke, condemn, perjorate, reject, abhor, scorn, defame, revile, vilify, boo, hiss, whistle at, slate (Inf), bellyache (Inf), whinge (Inf), gripe (Inf), kvetch (US sl), slag off (Sl)

ADVERBS

8 **discontentedly**, disapprovingly, disgustedly, contemptuously, scornfully

767   Relief

NOUNS

1 **ease**, solace, comfort, consolation, alleviation, reassurance, relaxation, mollification, appeasement, mitigation, assuagement, abatement, remission, respite, lull, palliation, anaesthetization, tranquillization, sedation, a load off one's mind (*or* one's shoulders) (Inf)

2 **aid**, assistance, help, succour, support, helping hand, rescue, deliverance, liberation, release, emancipation, salvation, salvage

3 **reliever**, comforter, consoler, mollifier, remedy, cure, balm, palliative, anodyne, analgesic, painkiller, anaesthetic, tranquillizer, sedative, opiate, soporific, hypnotic, sleeping pill, sleeping draught, ray of sunshine (Inf), oil on troubled waters (Inf)

▶ *630 Remedy*

4 **charity**, alms, almsgiving, poor relief, benefaction, gift, donation, relief, aid, emergency aid, disaster relief, famine relief

5 **helper**, auxiliary, deputy, assistant, helpmate, helpmeet, aide, aide-de-camp, medic, paramedic, doctor, nurse, girl (*or* man) Friday, right-hand man (*or* woman), understudy, substitute, replacement, stand-in, locum, locum

tenens, reserve, stop-gap, back-up, supporter, twelfth man, good right arm (Inf)

6 **profile**, silhouette, delineation, lineament, outline, form, contour, elevation, emboss-ment, projection, relievo, bas-relief, low relief, basso rilievo, high relief, alto-relievo, mezzo relievo

ADJECTIVES

7 **relieved**, calmed, restored, refreshed, eased, comforted, soothed, consoled, reassured, mol-lified, appeased, relaxed, sedated, assuaged, cured

8 **relieving**, helping, helpful, refreshing, re-storative, comforting, consoling, reassuring, relaxing, easing, calming, soothing, balsamic, curative, remedial, assuaging, palliative, seda-tive, hypnotic

VERBS

9 **relieve**, ease, solace, comfort, pacify, soothe, calm, quiet, console, alleviate, reassure, allay, mollify, appease, mitigate, moderate, temper, assuage, abate, diminish, lessen, soften, relax, palliate, tranquillize, sedate, aneasthetize, take the sting out of (Inf)

10 **save**, rescue, throw a lifeline to, come to the rescue of, reprieve, deliver, free, set free, liber-ate, emancipate, release, rid

11 **assist**, help, aid, deputize for, stand in for, do duty for, substitute for, understudy for, step into the shoes of, take over from, replace, succeed

12 **relieve from duty**, dismiss, fire, let go, lay off, sack (Inf), axe (Inf), can (Sl)

13 **relieve oneself**, urinate, pee (Inf), take a pee (Inf), piddle (Inf), tinkle (Inf), go to the rest room (US inf), go to the men's (*or* women's) room (US inf), go to the little boys' (*or* little girls') room (US inf), use the bathroom (US inf), piss (Sl), go to the john (US sl), go to the bog (Sl), aim Archie at the Armitage (Sl), point Percy at the porcelain (Sl)

▶ *353 Excretion*

14 **take away**, confiscate, disencumber, se-questrate, commandeer, dispossess, snatch, steal, rob, mug, run away with (Inf), do out of (Inf)

ADVERBS

15 **comfortingly**, reassuringly, refreshingly, soothingly, helpfully

768 Aggravation

NOUNS

1 **aggravation**, exacerbation, worsening, de-terioration, intensification, heightening, deepening, magnification, augmentation, en-hancement, exaggeration

▶ *628 Deterioration, 128 Increase*

2 **annoyance**, exasperation, irritation, vexa-tion, provocation, anger

3 **nuisance**, bother, trouble, victimization, bul-lying, harassment, hassle (Inf), spot of bother (Inf), aggro (Sl), seeing to (Sl)

▶ *764 Unpleasantness, 670 Attack*

ADJECTIVES

4 **aggravated**, worsened, not improved, exac-erbated, intensified, heightened, deepened, increased, magnified, enhanced, enlarged

5 **aggravating**, annoying, irritating, exasper-ating, provoking, vexing, vexatious

VERBS

6 **aggravate**, make worse, worsen, exacerbate, inflame, intensify, heighten, deepen, increase, augment, magnify, enhance, exaggerate, bring to a head, rub it in (Inf), rub salt in the wound (Inf), rub one's nose in it (Inf)

7 **become aggravated**, get worse, worsen, build up, go from bad to worse, deteriorate, degenerate, decline

8 **annoy**, irritate, exasperate, goad, provoke, antagonize, anger, vex, tease, peeve, hassle (Inf)

ADVERBS

9 **from bad to worse**, out of the frying pan into the fire

10 **annoyingly**, irritatingly, vexatiously

769 Cheerfulness

ADJECTIVES

1 **cheerful**, cheery, happy, glad, joyful, in good spirits, radiant, sunny, smiling, grinning, beaming, laughing, genial, good-natured, good-humoured, optimistic, sociable, light-hearted, exhilarated, merry, jolly, jovial, con-vivial, genial, gay, funny, buoyant, carefree, jaunty, perky, vivacious, lively, animated, sparkling, high-spirited, in high spirits, bounc-ing, bouncy, chirpy, bonhomous, high (Sl), up (Sl)

▶ *762 Joy*

2 **cheering**, encouraging, heart-warming, re-viving, uplifting, amusing, diverting, enter-taining, wacky (Sl)

NOUNS

3 **cheerfulness**, cheer, cheeriness, happiness, joy, good spirits, sunniness, geniality, good humour, sociability, light-heartedness, exhila-ration, optimism, good cheer, jollity, joviality, conviviality, geniality, gaiety, levity, mirth, vivacity, jauntiness, liveliness, animation, high spirits, laughter, merriment, merry-making, fun

▶ *771 Humour*

4 **cheerful person**, optimist, life and soul of the party (Inf), ray of sunshine (Inf), smiler (Inf)

5 **cheer**, whoop, shout, yell, applause, clap, clapping

VERBS

6 **bring cheer**, cheer, gladden, cheer up, revive (the spirits of), brighten, lighten, hearten, enliven, uplift, animate, exhilarate, perk up (Inf), buck up (Inf), jolly along (Inf)

7 **be cheerful**, have fun, enjoy, smile, grin, beam, laugh, sparkle, grin and bear it, put on a brave face, look on the bright side

8 **cheer**, whoop, shout, yell, applaud, clap, hurrah, give three cheers, encourage, spur, spur on
▶ *812 Celebration*

ADVERBS

9 **cheerfully**, cheerily, with good cheer, with a cheerful heart, happily, gladly, joyfully, radiantly, light-heartedly, merrily, gaily, jauntily, perkily, buoyantly, with high spirits

770 Sorrow

Do you hear the children weeping, O my brothers,/ Ere the sorrow comes with years? Elizabeth Barrett Browning.

Adieu tristesse/ Bonjour tristesse/ Tu es inscrite dans les lignes du plafond./ (Farewell sadness/ Good day sadness/ You are written in the lines of the ceiling). Paul Éluard.

A moment of time may make us unhappy for ever. John Gay.

Art thou weary, art thou languid,/ Art thou sore distressed? John Mason Neale.

If you have tears, prepare to shed them now. William Shakespeare.

Down, thou climbing sorrow,/ Thy element's below. William Shakespeare.

'Tis held that sorrow makes us wise. Alfred, Lord Tennyson.

NOUNS

1 **sorrow**, sadness, regret, unhappiness, sorrowfulness, heartache, sadheartedness, downheartedness, heavyheartedness, wretchedness, misery, desolation, heartbreak, suffering, distress, anguish, languishment, agony, pain, torment, woe, grief, dolour, mourning, weeping and wailing and gnashing of teeth (Inf)
▶ *687 Adversity, 774 Lamentation*

2 **depression**, melancholy, malaise, droopiness, dreariness, joylessness, cheerlessness, low spirits, lowness, dejection, dejectedness, despondency, Slough of Despond, gloom, gloominess, the doldrums, dispiritedness, glumness, despair, black despair, death wish, the dumps (Inf), the blues (Inf)
▶ *776 Hopelessness*

3 **sad person**, sufferer, languisher, wretch, poor wretch, downer (Sl)

4 **depressing person**, depressive, melancholic, moper, whiner, whinger (Inf), complainer, Job's comforter, Jonah, killjoy, spoilsport (Inf), sourpuss (Inf), wet blanket (Inf), Eeyore (Inf), misery (Inf), miseryguts (Inf), bring-down (Sl)

ADJECTIVES

5 **sad**, unhappy, sorrowful, crestfallen, saddened, sadhearted, downhearted, heavyhearted, disheartened, distressed, miserable, wretched, forlorn, languishing, tormented, woebegone, tearful, doleful, dolorous, mournful, pining, heartbroken, broken-hearted, disconsolate, inconsolable, desolate, griefstricken, ululant, cut up (Inf)

6 **depressed**, melancholic, downcast, low, droopy, dreary, joyless, dejected, dispirited, despondent, in the doldrums, atrabilious, lugubrious, grey, lacklustre, listless, gloomy, morose, glum, dismal, long-faced, moody, moping, suicidal, out of sorts (Inf), down (Inf), down in the dumps (Inf), Eeyorish (Inf), bad (Inf), face like a tombstone (Inf), face like a wet weekend (Inf), blue (Inf), sunk (Inf), in the depths (Inf), in a black hole (Inf)

7 **distressing**, depressing, dispiriting, sorry, lamentable, heartbreaking, harrowing, painful, tragic, grievous

VERBS

8 **grieve**, sorrow, sadden, languish, mourn, pine, sigh, lament, cry, weep, sob, moan, howl, wail, ululate, eat one's heart out (Inf), be cut up (Inf)

9 **despair**, despond, lose heart, lose hope, give way, droop, mope, wilt, flag, brood, sulk, hit bottom (Inf), hit rock bottom (Inf), be a wet blanket (Inf)

10 **depress**, bring down, dishearten, dispirit, dampen, dampen the spirits of, put a wet blanket on (Inf), pour cold water on (Inf)

ADVERBS

11 **sadly,** sorrowfully, unhappily, miserably, mournfully, dolefully, with a sad heart, with tears in one's eyes

12 **joylessly**, gloomily, glumly, drearily, listlessly, dismally, lugubriously, with a long face

771 Humour

No mind is thoroughly well organized that is deficient in a sense of humour. Samuel Taylor Coleridge.

True wit is nature to advantage dress'd;/ What oft was thought, but ne'er so well express'd. Alexander Pope.

A jest's prosperity lies in the ear/ Of him that hears it, never in the tongue/ Of him that makes it. William Shakespeare.

It's hard to be funny when you have to be clean. Mae West.

NOUNS

1 **humorousness**, humour, funniness, wit, wittiness, jokiness, drollery, dryness, facetiousness, flippancy, pawkiness

2 **amusement**, entertainment, diversion, fun, merriment, mirth, laughter, enjoyment, hilarity

3 **wit**, ready wit, joking, jesting, joshing, teasing, kidding, clowning, buffoonery, quipping, wordplay, banter, badinage, repartee, dry wit, sarcasm, irony, gallows humour, black humour, sick humour, blue humour

4 **entertainment**, comedy, satire, parody, caricature, send-up, take-off, farce, lampoon, burlesque, slapstick, stand-up comedy, comedy routine, comedy skit, comedy hour, sitcom (situation comedy), musical comedy, cartoon, comic strip
▶ *51 Performing Arts*

5 **joke**, jest, jape, caper, practical joke, prank, trick, witticism, gag, pun, one-liner, wisecrack, quip, pleasantry, funny story, yarn, old chestnut, shaggy dog story, tall story, blue joke, *double entendre* (Fr), dirty story, belly laugh, a laugh (Inf), lark (Inf), leg-pull (Inf)
▶ *539 Deception*

6 **humorist**, wit, wag, joker, jester, tease, teaser, gagster, wisecracker, jokesmith, nimblewit (US), comic, comedian, stand-up comic (*or* comedian), alternative comedian, straight man, clown, buffoon, gag writer, ironist, satirist, lampooner, caricaturist, cartoonist, top banana (US sl), second banana (US sl)
▶ *51 Performing Arts*

7 **person who humours**, sycophant, toady, flatterer, bootlicker (Inf), brown-nose (US sl), creep (Inf)
▶ *853 Flattery, 808 Servility*

8 **temperament**, disposition, humour
▶ *103 Essence*

ADJECTIVES

9 **funny**, amusing, diverting, entertaining, laughable, risible, hilarious, uproarious, side-splitting, hysterical (Inf)

10 **humorous**, witty, funny, jocular, jocose, joking, slapstick, waggish, nimblewitted, quick-witted, smart, comic, droll, amusing, whimsical, quirky, zany, merry, pawky, dry, facetious, farcical, sarcastic, ironic, satirical, flippant, teasing, jokey (Inf), corny (Inf)

11 **humouring**, pleasing, placating, indulging, pampering, cossetting, spoiling, cajoling, flattering, sycophantic, servile, ingratiating, toadying, unctuous, oily, slimy (Inf), smarmy (Inf), bootlicking (Inf), brown-nosing (US sl)

12 **four humours**, phlegmatic, sanguine, choleric, melancholic

VERBS

13 **be humorous**, entertain, amuse, regale, divert, joke, crack a joke, josh, jest, banter, pun, quip, wisecrack, clown, play the fool, make fun of, poke fun at, play a joke on, pull someone's leg, tease, rag, twit, kid, rib, scoff, mock, satirize, parody, send up, take off, lampoon, caricature

14 **laugh**, giggle, snigger, snicker, titter, chuckle, chortle, guffaw, howl, roar, slap one's thighs, split one's sides, roll in the aisles, laugh like a drain, laugh till one cries, laugh one's head off, hoot (Inf)
▶ *762 Joy, 769 Cheerfulness, 773 Rejoicing*

15 **humour**, gratify, please, placate, indulge, pamper, cosset, spoil, cajole, flatter, patronize, condescend, smarm, cultivate, toady to, suck up to (Inf), butter up (Inf), bootlick (Inf), soft-soap (Inf), brown-nose (US sl)

ADVERBS

16 **humorously**, wittily, amusingly, funnily, laughably, hilariously, comically, drolly, whimsically, drily, facetiously, farcically, sarcastically, ironically, satirically

17 **jokingly**, as a joke, for fun, in fun, in sport, for sport, with tongue in cheek

772 Seriousness

ADJECTIVES

1 **solemn**, grave, serious, thoughtful, pensive, sedate, staid, sober, sober as a judge, stern, severe, unsmiling, straight-faced, grim, poker-faced, stony-faced, deadpan, humourless, sombre, dour, sullen, glum, long-faced, frowning
▶ *830 Sullenness, 805 Pride*

2 **earnest**, sincere, genuine, resolute, determined, purposeful, intent, dedicated, committed, eager, enthusiastic
▶ *572 Willingness*

3 **important**, significant, of consequence, serious, weighty, momentous, crucial, vital, life-and-death, critical, dangerous, ominous, perilous
▶ *611 Importance*

NOUNS

4 **solemnity**, gravity, gravitas, no laughing matter, no joke, straight face, thoughtfulness, staidness, sternness, severity, humourlessness, grimness, dourness, sullenness, gloom, long face

5 **earnestness**, sincerity, resolution, determination, dedication, commitment, eagerness, enthusiasm
▶ *572 Willingness*

6 **importance**, import, significance, consequence, weightiness, momentousness, moment, gravity, severity

7 **serious person**, heavyweight, intellectual, highbrow, egghead (Inf), sobersides (Inf)
▶ *459 Intellect*

VERBS

8 **be serious**, look serious, keep a straight face, compose one's features, keep from laughing, repress a smile, wipe the smile off one's face, pull (*or* make) a long face, frown, glare, glower

9 **take seriously**, be in earnest

ADVERBS

10 **solemnly**, gravely, seriously, soberly, with a straight face, thoughtfully, sternly, severely, sullenly, glumly

11 **earnestly**, sincerely, genuinely, really, actually, truly, honestly, in all seriousness

12 **indeed**, really, certainly, seriously, in all conscience, absolutely, definitely, unquestionably, undeniably

773 Rejoicing

NOUNS

1 **rejoicing**, celebrating, jubilation, exultation, triumph, happiness, joyfulness, joy, delight, jolliness, merriment, jollification, roistering, merrymaking, festivity, festivities, celebration, special day, holiday, festival, high days and holidays, anniversary, jubilee, party, revel, great day, feast, feast day, street party, banquet, field day, rave (Sl), beano (Sl)

▶ *812 Celebration, 762 Joy, 45 Cookery*

2 **fanfare**, salute, applause, ovation, cry, shout, yell, cheer, three cheers, hurrah, huzzah, hosanna, hallelujah, hallelujah chorus, hymn, praise, glory, thanksgiving, congratulation, congratulations

▶ *423 Loudness, 851 Approval, 7 Religion*

3 **laughter**, giggling, tittering, hilarity, laugh, giggle, titter, chortle, snigger, the giggles

▶ *771 Humour, 762 Joy*

4 **rejoicer**, celebrator, laugher, giggler, titterer, cackler, reveller, merrymaker, roisterer, raver (Sl)

VERBS

5 **rejoice**, celebrate, jubilate, exult, triumph, glory, leap for joy, make merry, have a party, roister, revel, carouse, feast, banquet, have a ball (Sl), make whoopee (Inf), paint the town red (Inf), go on a binge (Inf), rave (Sl), whoop it up (Inf), throw a party (Inf), have a knees-up (Inf)

▶ *812 Celebration, 762 Joy*

6 **fête**, lionize, sing the praises of, praise, honour, pay respects to, salute, kill the fatted calf for, give a hero's welcome to

▶ *851 Approval*

7 **dance**, skip, frolic, rollick, clap, applaud, cry, shout, yell, cheer, give thanks, congratulate

▶ *46 Dancing and Ballet, 423 Loudness, 851 Approval*

8 **laugh**, titter, giggle, chortle, get the giggles (Inf), split one's sides (Inf), fall about (Inf), roll in the aisles (Inf)

▶ *771 Humour*

ADJECTIVES

9 **rejoicing**, celebratory, jubilant, exultant, triumphant, glorious, ecstatic, euphoric, happy, joyful, cheery, merry, jolly, revelling, applauding, cheering, high (Sl)

▶ *812 Celebration, 762 Joy, 851 Approval*

10 **laughing**, giggling, tittering, laughable, comic, humorous, funny, hilarious, side-splitting (Inf)

▶ *771 Humour*

ADVERBS

11 **rejoicingly**, jubilantly, triumphantly, ecstatically, euphorically, joyfully, merrily

INTERJECTIONS

12 **hurrah!**, hip, hip, hurrah!, hooray!, hip, hip, hooray!, hosanna!, hallelujah!, yippee!

774 Lamentation

NOUNS

1 **lamentation**, lamenting, grieving, crying, weeping, wailing, weeping and wailing and gnashing of teeth, keening, mourning, wake, last rites, widow's weeds, sackcloth and ashes, dolefulness, tearfulness, sobbing, sadness, sorrow, sorrowfulness, mournfulness, plangency, wretchedness, woe

▶ *770 Sorrow, 399 Burial*

2 **lament**, lamentation, requiem, obsequies, dirge, elegy, swansong, threnody, coronach, knell, funeral oration, thanatopsis, last post, keen, howl, ululation, cry, moan, groan, sigh, complaint, sob story, tale of woe

▶ *49 Music, 770 Sorrow, 766 Dissatisfaction*

3 **lamenter**, griever, weeper, wailer, keener, mourner, elegist, threnodist, blubberer, crybaby, sniveller

ADJECTIVES

4 **lamenting**, grieving, crying, weeping, lachrymose, tearful, wailing, keening, mourning, mournful, miserable, doleful, wretched, woebegone, disconsolate, unhappy, sad, sorrowful, wet-eyed, red-eyed, plaintive, plangent, dirgelike, elegiac, threnodic, depressed, down (Sl)

5 **lamentable**, pitiful, tear-jerking, distressing, depressing, deplorable, regrettable

VERBS

6 **lament**, grieve, sorrow, mourn, mourn for, go into mourning for, elegize, threnodize, weep for, wail, keen, beat one's breast, bemoan, bewail, complain, deplore, regret, rue

▶ *770 Sorrow, 399 Burial, 766 Dissatisfaction*

7 **weep**, cry, sob, wail, shed tears over, weep over, cry one's eyes out, howl, ululate, sigh, snivel, blubber, blub (Sl)

ADVERBS

8 **mournfully**, tearfully, dolefully, sadly, plaintively, plangently, in mourning, in black, in sackcloth and ashes, at half-mast

775 Hope

Still nursing the unconquerable hope,/ Still clutching the inviolable shade. Matthew Arnold

While there is life, there's hope,' he cried;/ 'Then why such haste?' so groaned and died. John Gay.

After all, tomorrow is another day. Margaret Mitchell.

Hope springs eternal in the human breast;/ Man never is, but always to be blest. Alexander Pope.

NOUNS

1 **hope**, hoping, hopefulness, optimism, cheerfulness, buoyancy, positive thinking, bright side, silver lining, rose-coloured glasses (*or* spectacles), rose-tinted view, wishful thinking, false hope, hope and a prayer, faint hope, ray of hope, last hope
▶ *769 Cheerfulness*

2 **expectation**, expectations, anticipation, assumption, presumption, trust, confidence, faith, belief, conviction
▶ *513 Expectation, 497 Belief*

3 **aspiration**, ambition, dream, vision, high hopes, great expectations, aim, intention, wish, desire, longing, yearning, castles in the air, castles in Spain, pipe dream, fool's paradise, Utopia, Erewhon, promised land, cloud cuckoo land, dream world, fantasy
▶ *782 Desire, 102 Unreality*

4 **comfort**, cheer, reassurance, encouragement, support, security, promise, auspiciousness, propitiousness, prospects
▶ *714 Promise*

5 **hoper**, aspirant, hopeful, young hopeful, dreamer, optimist, idealist, Pollyanna, utopian

VERBS

6 **hope**, live in hope, hope against hope, hope and pray, hope to God, pin one's hopes on, count on, rely on, bank on, put one's trust in, trust, believe, feel confident, rest assured, assume, presume
▶ *497 Belief*

7 **aspire**, aim, dream, have high hopes, wish, desire, long, yearn, expect, look forward to, await, anticipate
▶ *782 Desire, 513 Expectation*

8 **be optimistic**, hope for the best, think positively, have faith, make the best of it, look on the bright side, look (*or* see) through rose-coloured glasses (*or* spectacles), not cross one's bridges before one comes to them, count one's chickens before they are hatched

9 **be hopeful**, cross one's fingers, keep one's fingers crossed, touch (*or* knock on) wood, take heart, cheer up, buck up, keep smiling, never say die, keep one's hopes (*or* spirits) up,

see light at the end of the tunnel

10 **inspire hope**, comfort, cheer, cheer up, reassure, encourage, raise one's hopes, promise, augur well, bid fair
▶ *769 Cheerfulness, 714 Promise, 517 Prediction, 486 Possibility*

ADJECTIVES

11 **hopeful**, hoping, full of hope, optimistic, sanguine, cheerful, buoyant, positive, starry-eyed, bullish (Inf), upbeat (Inf), up (Inf)
▶ *769 Cheerfulness*

12 **expectant**, expecting, anticipating, confident, assured
▶ *513 Expectation, 497 Belief*

13 **aspirant**, aspiring, ambitious, go-getting, dreaming, wishful, desirous, longing, yearning
▶ *782 Desire*

14 **cheering**, heartening, reassuring, encouraging, promising, auspicious, propitious, favourable, bright, sunny, golden, rosy, rose-coloured, rose-tinted
▶ *714 Promise*

ADVERBS

15 **hopefully**, with hope, optimistically, cheerfully, buoyantly, positively, confidently, expectantly, ambitiously, encouragingly, promisingly, auspiciously, propitiously

INTERJECTIONS

16 **never say die!,** nil desperandum!, where there's life, there's hope!

776 Hopelessness

NOUNS

1 **hopelessness**, lack of hope, no hope, loss of hope, despondency, alarm and despondency, discouragement, defeatism, scepticism, negativism, pessimism, cynicism, dejection, despair, black despair, desperation, melancholy, depression, doubt, self-doubt, gloom, gloominess, gloom and doom
▶ *770 Sorrow*

2 **hopeless situation**, lost cause, quandary, predicament, catch-22 (situation), bleak outlook, dashed hopes, disappointment, downer (Sl), write-off (Sl), let-down (Sl)
▶ *515 Disappointment, 659 Difficulty*

3 **hopeless person**, loser, born loser, failure, defeatist, negativist, pessimist, cynic, melancholic, moper, Cassandra, prophet of doom, Job's comforter, no-hoper (Inf), drag (Sl), hopeless case (Inf), goner (Sl), dead duck (Inf), Eeyore (Sl), drongo (Aus sl)
▶ *683 Failure*

ADJECTIVES

4 **hopeless**, without hope, forlorn, despondent, comfortless, cheerless, discouraged, defeated, defeatist, negative, sceptical, negativistic, pessimistic, cynical, dejected, downcast, despair-

ing, desperate, suicidal, desolate, disconsolate, melancholic, depressed, gloomy, down in the dumps (Inf), down at the mouth (Inf), in the doldrums (*or* depths) (Inf), down (Sl)
▶ *770 Sorrow*

5 **past hope**, terminal, incurable, inoperable, irremediable, irreparable, irrevocable, irreversible, incorrigible, irredeemable, irretrievable, beyond recall, lost, gone
▶ *397 Death*

6 **inauspicious**, unpropitious, ill-omened, ill-starred, doomed, ominous, black

7 **futile**, useless, worthless, pointless, vain, impossible
▶ *614 Uselessness, 618 Worthlessness, 487 Impossibility*

8 **bad**, poor, inferior, no good, without skill, incompetent, lamentable, awful, terrible, clumsy, inept, hopeless (Inf), pathetic (Inf), ham-fisted (Inf), cack-handed (Inf)
▶ *656 Unskilfulness*

VERBS

9 **be hopeless**, lack hope, lose hope, give up hope, give up, despair, doubt, lose heart, look on the black (*or* dark) side, think negatively, think the worst of, write off (Inf)
▶ *770 Sorrow*

10 **disappoint**, crush, shatter one's hopes, dash the cup from one's lips, drive to despair
                                                    515
Disappointment

ADVERBS

11 **hopelessly**, despondently, negatively, pessimistically, cynically, dejectedly, despairingly, desperately, gloomily, incurably, irredeemably

777   Fear

It is a miserable state of mind to have few things to desire and many things to fear. Francis Bacon.

For God hath not given us the spirit of fear; but of power, and of love, and of a sound mind. Bible: II Timothy.

There is no fear in love; but perfect love casteth out fear: because fear hath torment. He that feareth is not made perfect in love. Bible: I John.

Fear has many eyes and can see things underground. Miguel de Cervantes.

Like one, that on a lonesome road/ Doth walk in fear and dread,/ And having once turned round walks on,/ And turns no more his head;/ Because he knows, a frightful fiend/ Doth close behind him tread. Samuel Taylor Coleridge.

Let me assert my firm belief that the only thing

we have to fear is fear itself. Franklin D. Roosevelt.

Fear lent wings to his feet. Virgil.

NOUNS

1 **fear**, fright, terror, horror, horrification, affright (Arch), dread, awe, panic, phobia, aversion, mortal fear, fear and trembling, unholy terror, fit of terror, blind panic, icy fingers, cold sweat, blood running cold, hair standing on end, chattering teeth, knocking knees, funk (Inf), blue funk (Inf)

2 **fearfulness**, nervousness, timorousness, apprehension, apprehensiveness, anxiety, uneasiness, tension, trepidation, consternation, perturbation, alarm, unease, disquiet, dismay, foreboding, misgivings, qualms, agitation, nerves, palpitations, shivers, quaking, shaking, trembling, goose flesh, goose bumps, butterflies in the stomach, sinking stomach, stage fright, shivers up and down the spine, the jitters (Inf), the jumps (Inf), the willies (Inf), the jimjams (Inf), the collywobbles (Inf), the heebie-jeebies (Inf), a flat spin (Inf)
▶ *779 Cowardice*

3 **worry**, anxiety, uneasiness, angst, fretting, concern, care, solicitude
▶ *831 Benevolence, 833 Philanthropy*

4 **intimidation**, frightening, terrorism, terrorization, threatening, cowing, bullying, hectoring, demoralization, reign of terror, war of nerves, psychological warfare, Sword of Damocles
▶ *670 Attack, 768 Aggravation*

5 **frightener**, scarer, terrorist, bully, alarmist, scaremonger, doom merchant, spreader of alarm and despondency, bogeyman, bogey, spectre, ghost, bugbear, nightmare, bane, pet hate, *bête noire* (Fr)
▶ *670 Attack*

6 **frightened person**, chicken, mouse, rabbit, bag (*or* bundle) of nerves, nervous wreck, scarebaby (Inf), scaredy-cat (Inf)
▶ *779 Cowardice*

ADJECTIVES

7 **frightened**, afraid, scared, fearing, fear-stricken, terrified, terror-struck, horrified, horror-struck, aghast, petrified, panic-stricken, terrorized, intimidated, cowed, demoralized, affright (Arch), in fear and trembling, paralysed with fear, rigid with fear, rooted to the spot, frightened (*or* terrified *or* scared) out of one's wits, frightened (*or* scared) to death, white as a sheet, pale as a ghost, deadly pale, blanched, ashen-faced, in a cold sweat, frit (Inf), reduced to a jelly (Inf), in a funk (Inf), in a blue funk (Inf), scared stiff (Inf), scared shitless (Tab sl), shit scared (Tab sl)
▶ *779 Cowardice*

Phobias by Topic

anaemia - anaemophobia
bacteria - bacteriophobia
beards - pogonophobia
beating - mastigophobia
bed (going to bed) - clinophobia
bees - apiphobia
birds - ornithophobia
blood - haemaphobia (or haematophobia or haemophobia)
blushing - erythrophobia
body odour - bromidrosiphobia
bridges (crossing) - gephyrophobia
bullets - ballistophobia
cancer - cancerphobia (or cancerophobia or carcinophobia)
cats - ailurophobia
childbirth - tocophobia
children - paedophobia
Chinese - Sinophobia
cholera - cholerophobia
church - ecclesiophobia
clouds - nephophobia
coitus -coitophobia
cold - cheimaphobia (or cheimatophobia)
colour - chromophobia
comets - cometophobia
constipation - coprostasophobia
corpses -necrophobia
crowds - agoraphobia, demophobia
crystals - crystallophobia
dampness - hygrophobia
darkness - achluophobia, scotophobia
dawn -eosophobia
death - thanatophobia
demons -demonophobia
depth - bathophobia
diabetes - diabetophobia
dirt - mysophobia
disease - nephophobia, pathophobia
dogs - cynophobia
draughts - aerophobia
drink - potophobia
drugs - pharmacophobia
dust - koniophobia, amathophobia
electricity - electrophobia
enclosed places - claustrophobia
English - Anglophobia
everything - panphobia (or pantophobia)
eyes - ommataphobia
faeces - coprophobia
failure - kakorraphiaphobia
fatigue - kopophobia
fear - phobophobia
feathers - pteronophobia
fever - febriphobia
fire - pyrophobia
fish - ichthyophobia
floods - antlophobia
flowers - anthophobia
flutes - aulophobia
fog - homichlophobia
food - cibophobia, sitophobia
foreigners - xenophobia
freedom - eleutherophobia

French - Francophobia, Gallophobia
fur - doraphobia
Germans - Germanophobia, Teutonophobia
germs - spermophobia (or spermatophobia)
ghosts - phasmophobia
God - theophobia
gold - aurophobia
gravity - barophobia
hair - chaetophobia, trichophobia
hair disease - trichopathophobia
heart disease - cardiophobia
heat - thermophobia
heaven - uranophobia (or ouranophobia)
hell - hadephobia, stygiophobia
heredity - patroiophobia
high buildings - batophobia
high places - acrophobia, altophobia, batophobia, hypsophobia
home - ecophobia (or oecophobia or oikophobia)
horses - hippophobia
ice, frost - cryophobia
ideas - ideophobia
idleness - thaasophobia
imperfection - atelophobia
infinity - apeirophobia
injury - traumatophobia
inoculation - trypanophobia, vaccinophobia
insanity - lyssophobia, maniphobia
insects - entomophobia
insect stings - cnidophobia
itching - acarophobia
Japanese - Japanophobia
jealousy - zelophobia
Jews - Judeophobia
justice - dikephobia
lakes - limnophobia
lice - pediculophobia
light - photophobia
lightning - astraphobia (or astrapophobia)
loneliness - autophobia, monophobia, ermitophobia
machinery - mechanophobia
magic - rhabdophobia
marriage - gametophobia
men - androphobia
meningitis - meningitophobia
metal - metallophobia
mice - musophobia
microbes - bacillophobia, microbiophobia
mirrors - eisoptrophobia
mites - acarophobia
mobs - ochlophobia
money - chrometophobia
monsters - teratrophobia
motion - dromophobia, kinetophobia
music - musicophobia
names - onomatophobia
narrowness - anginophobia
needles - belonephobia
Negroes - Negrophobia
new things - neophobia

night - nyctophobia
open places - agoraphobia
pain -algophobia
parasites - parasitophobia
people - anthropophobia
philosophy - philosophobia
pins - enetophobia
places - topophobia
pleasure - hedonophobia
poison - toxiphobia (or toxophobia or toxicophobia)
politics - politicophobia
Pope - papaphobia
poverty - peniaphobia
precipices - cremnophobia
priests - hierophobia
punishment - poinephobia
rabies - hydrophobophobia
rectum - rectophobia
reptiles - batrachophobia, herpetophobia
responsibility - hypegiaphobia
ridicule - katagelophobia
rivers - potamophobia
robbers - harpaxophobia
ruin - atephobia
Russians - Russophobia
saints - hagiophobia
Satan - Satanophobia
scabies - scabiophobia
sea - thalassophobia
sex - erotophobia, genophobia
shadows - sciophobia
sharpness - acrophobia
shock - hormephobia
sin - hamartophobia, peccatiphobia
skin - dermatosiophobia
skin disease - dermatopathophobia
sleep - hypnophobia
slime - blennophobia, myxophobia
small things - microphobia
smell - olfactophobia, osmophobia, ophresiophobia
smothering - pnigophobia (or pnigerophobia)
snakes - ophiciophobia (or ophiophobia), snakephobia
snow - chionophobia
soiling - rypophobia
sound - acousticophobia
sourness - acerophobia (or acerbophobia)
speech - lalophobia (or laliophobia), glossophobia, phonophobia
speed - tachophobia
spiders - arachnephobia
spirits - pneumatophobia
standing - stasophobia
stars - siderophobia
stealing - kleptophobia
streets (crossing) - agyrophobia
string - linonophobia
sun - heliophobia
swallowing - phagophobia
symmetry - symmetrophobia
syphilis - syphilophobia
taste - geumatophobia
teeth - odontophobia
telephone - telephonophobia

thinking - phronemophobia
thirteen - triskaidekaphobia
thunder - brontophobia, tonitrophobia, keraunophobia
time (duration) - chronophobia
touch - haptophobia (or haphophobia), thixophobia
travel - hodophobia
trembling - tremophobia
trichinosis - trichinophobia

tuberculosis - tuberculophobia, phthisiophobia
tyrants - tyrannophobia
urine - urophobia
vehicles - ochophobia
venereal disease - venerophobia
void - kenophobia
vomiting - emetophobia
water - hydrophobia
waves - cymophobia

weakness - asthenophobia
wind - ancraophobia
women - gynephobia
words - logophobia
work - ergophobia
worms - vermiphobia, helminthophobia
writing - graphophobia
young girls - parthenophobia

Phobias by Name

acarophobia - itching
acarophobia - mites
acerophobia (or acerbophobia) - sourness
achluophobia - darkness
acousticophobia - sound
acrophobia - high places
acrophobia - sharpness
aerophobia - draughts
agoraphobia - crowds
agoraphobia - open places
agyrophobia - streets (crossing)
ailurophobia - cats
algophobia - pain
altophobia - high places
amathophobia - dust
anaemophobia - anaemia
ancraophobia - wind
androphobia - men
anginophobia - narrowness
Anglophobia - English
anthophobia - flowers
anthropophobia - people
antlophobia - floods
apeirophobia - infinity
apiphobia - bees
arachnephobia - spiders
asthenophobia - weakness
astraphobia (or astrapophobia) - lightning
atelophobia - imperfection
atephobia - ruin
aulophobia - flutes
aurophobia - gold
autophobia - loneliness
bacillophobia - microbes
bacteriophobia - bacteria
ballistophobia - bullets
barophobia - gravity
bathophobia - depth
batophobia - high buildings
batophobia - high places
batrachophobia - reptiles
belonephobia - needles
blennophobia - slime
bromidrosiphobia - body odour
brontophobia - thunder
cancerphobia (or cancerophobia or carcinophobia) - cancer
cardiophobia - heart disease
chaetophobia - hair
cheimaphobia (or cheimatophobia) - cold
chionophobia - snow
cholerophobia - cholera
chrometophobia - money

chromophobia - colour
chronophobia - time (duration)
cibophobia - food
claustrophobia - enclosed places
clinophobia - bed (going to bed)
cnidophobia - insect stings
coitophobia - coitus
cold cheimaphobia (or cheimatophobia)
cometophobia - comets
coprophobia - faeces
coprostasophobia - constipation
cremnophobia - precipices
cryophobia - ice, frost
crystallophobia - crystals
cymophobia - waves
cynophobia - dogs
demonophobia - demons
demophobia - crowds
dermatopathophobia - skin disease
dermatosiophobia - skin
diabetophobia - diabetes
dikephobia - justice
doraphobia - fur
dromophobia - motion
ecclesiophobia - church
ecophobia (or oecophobia or oikophobia) - home
eisoptrophobia - mirrors
electrophobia - electricity
eleutherophobia - freedom
emetophobia - vomiting
enetophobia - pins
entomophobia - insects
eosophobia - dawn
ergophobia - work
ermitophobia - loneliness
erotophobia - sex
erythrophobia - blushing
febriphobia - fever
Francophobia - French
Gallophobia - French
gametophobia - marriage
genophobia - sex
gephyrophobia - bridges (crossing)
Germanophobia - Germans
geumatophobia - taste
graphophobia - writing
gynephobia - women
hadephobia - hell
hagiophobia - saints
hamartophobia - sin
haptophobia (or haphophobia), thixophobia - touch
harpaxophobia - robbers

hedonophobia - pleasure
heliuphobia - sun
helminthophobia - worms
hemaphobia (or hematophobia or hemophobia) - blood
herpetophobia - reptiles
hierophobia - priests
hippophobia - horses
hodophobia - travel
homichlophobia - fog
hormephobia - shock
hydrophobia - water
hydrophobophobia - rabies
hygrophobia - dampness
hypegiaphobia - responsibility
hypnophobia - sleep
hypsophobia - high places
ichthyophobia - fish
ideophobia - ideas
Japanophobia - Japanese
Judeophobia - Jews
kakorraphiaphobia - failure
katagelophobia - ridicule
kenophobia - void
keraunophobia - thunder
kinetophobia - motion
kleptophobia - stealing
koniophobia -dust
kopophobia - fatigue
lalophobia (or laliophobia), glossophobia, phonophobia - speech
limnophobia - lakes
linonophobia - string
logophobia - words
lyssophobia - insanity
maniphobia - insanity
mastigophobia - beating
mechanophobia - machinery
meningitophobia - meningitis
metallophobia - metal
microbiophobia - microbes
microphobia - small things
monophobia - loneliness
musicophobia - music
musophobia - mice
mysophobia - dirt
myxophobia - slime
necrophobia -corpses
Negrophobia - Negroes
neophobia - new things
nephophobia - clouds
nephophobia - disease
nyctophobia - night
ochlophobia - mobs
ochophobia - vehicles

odontophobia - teeth
oecophobia - home
oikophobia - home
olfactophobia - smell
ommataphobia - eyes
onomatophobia - names
ophiciophobia (or ophiophobia),
    snakephobia - snakes
ophresiophobia - smell
ornithophobia - birds
osmophobia - smell
ouranophobia - heaven
paedophobia - children
panphobia (or pantophobia) -
    everything
papaphobia - Pope
parasitophobia - parasites
parthenophobia - young girls
pathophobia - disease
patroiophobia - heredity
peccatiphobia - sin
pediculophobia - lice
peniaphobia - poverty
phagophobia - swallowing
pharmacophobia - drugs
phasmophobia - ghosts
philosophobia - philosophy
phobophobia - fear
photophobia - light
phronemophobia - thinking

phthisiophobia - tuberculosis
pneumatophobia - spirits
pnigophobia (or pnigerophobia) -
    smothering
pogonophobia - beards
poinephobia - punishment
politicophobia - politics
potamophobia - rivers
potophobia - drink
pteronophobia - feathers
pyrophobia - fire
rectophobia - rectum
rhabdophobia - magic
Russophobia - Russians
rypophobia - soiling
Satanophobia - Satan
scabiophobia - scabies
sciophobia - shadows
scotophobia - darkness
siderophobia - stars
Sinophobia - Chinese
sitophobia - food
spermophobia (or spermatopho-
    bia) - germs
stasophobia - standing
stygiophobia - hell
symmetrophobia - symmetry
syphilophobia - syphilis
tachophobia - speed
telephonophobia - telephone

teratrophobia - monsters
Teutonophobia - Germans
thaasophobia - idleness
thalassophobia - sea
thanatophobia - death
theophobia - God
thermophobia - heat
tocophobia - childbirth
tonitrophobia - thunder
topophobia - places
toxiphobia (or toxophobia or
    toxicophobia) - poison
traumatophobia - injury
tremophobia - trembling
trichinophobia - trichinosis
trichopathophobia - hair disease
trichophobia - hair
triskaidekaphobia - thirteen
trypanophobia - inoculation
tuberculophobia - tuberculosis
tyrannophobia - tyrants
uranophobia (or ouranophobia) -
    heaven
urophobia - urine
vaccinophobia - inoculation
venerophobia - venereal disease
vermiphobia - worms
xenophobia - foreigners
zelophobia - jealousy

8 **fearful**, nervous, timorous, apprehensive, anxious, uneasy, alarmed, disquieted, agitated, jittery, jumpy, timid, tremulous, trembling, shaky, shaking, quaking, twitchy, tense, strained, highly strung, nervy, edge, panicky, distressed, on edge, on tenterhooks, on pins and needles, on a cliff edge, waiting for the bomb to drop, waiting for the other shoe to fall, with one's heart in one's mouth, afraid of one's shadow, shaking like a leaf (or jelly), uptight (Inf)

9 **worried**, troubled, concerned, solicitous, caring, anxious, fretting, harassed, plagued, haunted, tormented

10 **frightening**, fearsome, awesome, daunting, dismaying, formidable, menacing, intimidating, alarming, unnerving, startling, scaring, enervating, shocking, horrifying, terrifying, petrifying, terrible, frightful, fearful, dreadful, dire, grim, horrible, horrific, horrendous, ghastly, hideous, awful, appalling, hair-raising, scary (Inf), spooky (Inf)

VERBS

11 **be afraid**, be afraid of, be frightened (of), fear, dread, be in mortal dread (of), stand aghast, take fright, panic, show fear, tremble, shake, shiver, shudder, quiver, flinch, shrink, draw back, recoil, quail, blench, quake in one's boots (or shoes), shake like a leaf (or jelly), turn pale (or white or ashen), look as if one had seen a ghost, be paralysed with fear, jump out of one's skin, be petrified, freeze with horror, be rooted to the spot, feel one's blood (or bowels) turn to water, feel one's hair stand on end, shit oneself (or one's pants) (Sl)

12 **be fearful**, be nervous, shrink, start, flutter, palpitate, twitch, be on edge, have qualms, think twice, get cold feet, be all of a doodah (Inf), have kittens (Inf), funk (Inf)

13 **frighten**, scare, daunt, dismay, distress, alarm, fright (Arch), affright (Arch), menace, intimidate, cow, bully, terrorize, browbeat, bulldoze, unnerve, give someone a fright, enervate, make someone jump, shake, shock, stagger, startle, panic, horrify, appal, terrify, petrify, make someone's blood run cold, put the fear of God into, put the wind up (Inf), put the frighteners on (Inf), scare someone half to death (Inf), frighten (or scare) someone out of their wits (or to death) (Inf), scare the living daylights out of (Inf), scare the pants off (Sl), scare shitless (Sl)

14 **worry**, concern, trouble, harass, fret, plague, haunt, torment, be worried (about), fear for, be fearful for, be anxious for (or about), agonize over, bite (or chew) one's nails, sweat blood (Inf)

ADVERBS

15 **fearfully**, in fear of, nervously, timorously, timidly, tremulously, apprehensively, anxiously, uneasily, with fear and trembling, in mortal fear (or dread)

16 **frighteningly**, alarmingly, menacingly, horrifingly, frightfully, dreadfully, horribly, horrifically, hideously

778 Courage

NOUNS

1 **courage**, bravery, valour, valiance, courageousness, braveness, mettle, pluck, nerve, daring, audacity, audaciousness, boldness, hardiness, hardihood, fearlessness, dauntlessness, undauntedness, spirit, vim, nerves of steel, stout-heartedness, lion-heartedness, doughtiness, fighting spirit, backbone, grit, toughness, stamina, derring-do (Inf), bottle (Sl), guts (Inf), spunk (Sl), balls (Tab sl)
▶ *237 Strength*

2 **heroism**, chivalry, knightliness, gallantry, prowess, manliness, virility, stiff upper lip, aggressiveness, bellicosity
▶ *817 Courtesy, 857 Probity, 676 War*

3 **steadfastness**, confidence, self-reliance, fortitude, perseverance, endurance, tenacity, determination, resoluteness, intrepidity
▶ *575 Perseverance, 574 Resolution*

4 **adventurousness**, gameness, foolhardiness, rashness
▶ *780 Rashness*

5 **bold front**, bold façade, brave face, bravado, Dutch courage
▶ *457 Appearance*

6 **encouragement**, heartening, assurance, reassurance, incitement, exhortation, animation, bucking up (Inf)
▶ *228 Motive*

7 **courageous person**, brave person, brave (Arch), hero, heroine, knight, knight in shining armour, he-man, superman, superwoman, warrior, heart of oak, daredevil, stunt man (*or* woman), lion, tiger, bulldog, fighting cock
▶ *679 Combatant*

8 **courageous act**, act of courage, feat, feat of endurance, exploit, heroic exploit, deed, knightly deed, chivalry, prowess, derring-do, adventure, gallantry, heroics, *coup de grâce* (Fr)
▶ *640 Action*

ADJECTIVES

9 **courageous**, brave, heroic, gallant, valorous, valiant, mettlesome, mettled, plucky, daring, audacious, bold, hardy, fearless, dauntless, undaunted, spirited, stout-hearted, lion-hearted, unflinching, unshrinking, unshakable, unbowed, undismayed, indomitable, doughty, tough, bold as a lion, spunky (Sl), gutsy (Sl), ballsy (Sl)
▶ *237 Strength*

10 **chivalrous**, knightly, heroic, gallant, manly, soldierly
▶ *817 Courtesy, 857 Probity*

11 **militant**, aggressive, bellicose, martial, warlike
▶ *676 War*

12 **self-reliant**, confident, unafraid, unfearing, steadfast, persevering, tenacious, dogged, determined, resolute, intrepid
▶ *575 Perseverance, 574 Resolution*

13 **adventurous**, venturesome, game, foolhardy, rash, danger-loving
▶ *780 Rashness*

14 **encouraging**, heartening, assuring, reassuring

VERBS

15 **be courageous**, dare, venture, brave, face, confront, face (the) danger, face the odds, beard, defy, outface, look in the face (*or* eyes), stand up to, bell the cat, keep a stiff upper lip, brazen out, screw one's courage to the sticking place, take the plunge, take the bull by the horns, face the music, have the courage of one's convictions, court disaster, laugh at danger, show one's mettle, fight, win one's spurs, have a lot of bottle (Sl), have guts (Inf)
▶ *674 Contention, 668 Defiance, 597 Undertaking, 780 Rashness*

16 **take courage**, take heart, pluck up courage, dare, steel oneself, screw up one's courage, put on a brave face, grin and bear it, endure, persevere, keep one's chin up
▶ *575 Perseverance*

17 **give courage**, encourage, hearten, assure, reassure, embolden, inspirit, inspire, incite, exhort, animate
▶ *228 Motive*

ADVERBS

18 **courageously**, bravely, heroically, valiantly, audaciously, boldly, fearlessly, dauntlessly, steadfastly, tenaciously, defiantly, intrepidly, adventurously, rashly

779 Cowardice

NOUNS

1 **cowardice**, cowardliness, lack of courage, timidity, pusillanimity, chicken-heartedness, faint-heartedness, faint heart, dastardliness, cravenness, poltroonery, timorousness, fearfulness, abject fear, lack of spirit, lack of moral fibre, defeatism, desertion, cowering, overcaution, weakness, funk (Inf), blue funk (Inf), cold feet (Inf), yellow streak (Inf), white feather (Inf)
▶ *777 Fear, 776 Hopelessness, 781 Caution*

2 **coward**, dastard, craven, poltroon, deserter, milksop, milquetoast (US), rat (Inf), yellowbelly (Inf), chicken (Inf), rabbit (Inf), jellyfish (Inf), mouse (Inf), sissy (Inf), weed (Inf), wimp (Inf), baby (Inf), funk (Inf), scaredy-cat (Inf)
▶ *238 Weakness*

ADJECTIVES

3 **cowardly**, dastardly, craven, recreant (Arch), pusillanimous, timid, shy, spineless, soft,

namby-pamby, chicken-hearted, chicken-livered, lily-livered, faint-hearted, weak-kneed, timorous, wet, fearful, afraid, scared, frightened, rattled, daunted, cowed, unstaunch, unsteadfast, panicky, unheroic, defeatist, cowering, unable to say boo to a goose, chicken (Sl), gutless (Inf), sissy (Inf), windy (Sl), yellow (Inf), yellow-bellied (Sl)

▶ *777 Fear, 238 Weakness, 810 Modesty*

VERBS

4 **be a coward**, lack courage, lose one's nerve, back out, cower, quail, cringe, shrink, recoil, skulk, sneak, have no stomach for, show the white feather, retreat, desert, run away, turn tail, flee, beat a hasty retreat, scuttle, cut and run, live to fight another day, lose one's bottle (Sl), get cold feet (Inf), chicken out (Inf), funk (Inf), wet oneself (Inf), have no guts (Sl), do a bunk (Inf), throw a wobbly (*or* wobbler) (Sl)

▶ *777 Fear, 337 Backward Motion, 238 Weakness*

ADVERBS

5 **cravenly**, pusillanimously, timidly, spinelessly, chicken-heartedly, faint-heartedly, timorously, fearfully

780 Rashness

NOUNS

1 **rashness**, recklessness, hastiness, haste, impetuousness, impetuosity, overhaste, precipitancy, precipitateness, precipitance, imprudence, improvidence, indiscretion, inattention, negligence, carelessness, heedlessness, regardlessness, incautiousness, inconsideration, unwariness, irresponsibility, wildness, impulsiveness, capriciousness, frivolity, levity, flippancy, foolhardiness, folly, daring, audacity, audaciousness, temerity, presumption, overconfidence, overenthusiasm, impatience, hotheadedness, excitability, desperation, desperateness, adventurousness, brinkmanship, playing with fire, daredevilry

▶ *648 Haste, 778 Courage, 468 Inattention, 470 Negligence, 508 Folly*

2 **rash move**, risk, needless risk, dangerous game, leap in the dark, gamble

▶ *633 Danger, 589 Chance*

3 **rash person**, daredevil, hothead, madcap, brinkman, wild boy, desperado, hooligan, adventurer, gambler

ADJECTIVES

4 **rash**, reckless, hasty, impetuous, overhasty, precipitate, precipitant, headlong, breakneck, imprudent, improvident, injudicious, indiscreet, inconsiderate, ill-considered, ill-advised, thoughtless, inattentive, negligent, slapdash, hit-and-miss, careless, heedless, regardless, incautious, uncircumspect, unwary, irresponsible, wild, impulsive, capricious, frivo-lous, flippant, couldn't-care-less, devil-may-care, free-and-easy, happy-go-lucky, foolhardy, foolish, harebrained, hotheaded, madcap, daredevil, death-defying, danger-loving, risk-taking, adventurous, daring, bold, audacious, overconfident, overambitious, overenthusiastic, overzealous, impatient, desperate, do-or-die, trigger-happy (Inf), asking for trouble (Inf), asking for it (Sl), over-the-top (OTT) (Sl)

▶ *648 Haste, 778 Courage, 468 Inattention, 470 Negligence, 508 Folly, 633 Danger*

VERBS

5 **be rash**, rush into, rush one's fences, rush in where angels fear to tread, carry on regardless, ignore the consequences, gamble, take risks, play with fire, ride the tiger, bell the cat, throw caution to the wind, chance one's arm, stick one's neck out, drop one's guard, court danger (*or* disaster), tempt providence (*or* fate), count one's chickens before they are hatched, buy a pig in a poke, take a leap in the dark, ask for trouble (Inf), ask for it (Sl)

▶ *648 Haste, 633 Danger, 589 Chance*

ADVERBS

6 **rashly**, recklessly, hastily, impetuously, headlong, headfirst, carelessly, heedlessly, irresponsibly, wildly, impulsively, foolishly, overconfidently, impatiently

781 Caution

NOUNS

1 **caution**, cautiousness, carefulness, care, wariness, chariness, watchfulness, vigilance, alertness, heedfulness, heed, wisdom, prudence, circumspection, judiciousness, guardedness, scepticism, discretion, reticence, tentativeness, reluctance, slowness, hesitance, hesitancy, hesitation, deliberation, careful consideration, second thoughts, doubt, suspicion, self-preservation, self-protection, protection, providence, foresight, forethought, wait-and-see policy, waiting game, overcaution, overcautiousness

▶ *469 Carefulness, 507 Wisdom, 606 Provision, 516 Foresight, 461 Thought, 632 Safety, 718 Security, 328 Slowness, 467 Attention*

2 **insurance**, insurance policy, rainy day policy, nest egg, savings, warning, safeguard, safety first, precaution

▶ *636 Warning, 632 Safety, 756 Thrift, 328 Slowness*

3 **cautious person**, slow starter, hesitator, doubter

ADJECTIVES

4 **cautious**, careful, wary, chary, watchful, vigilant, alert, on one's guard, heedful, mindful, prudent, circumspect, sceptic, once bitten twice shy, suspicious, doubtful, tentative, re-

luctant, slow, hesitant, nervous, experimental, gingerly, anticipatory, provident, thrifty, economical, frugal, canny, guarded, secretive, conservative, discreet, reticent, politic, judicious, on the safe side, overcautious, unadventurous, cagey (Inf)
▶ *469 Carefulness, 507 Wisdom, 606 Provision, 461 Thought, 632 Safety, 328 Slowness, 467 Attention, 756 Thrift*

VERBS

5 **be cautious**, take care, hold back, hang back, count to ten, take one's time, take one step at a time, take it easy, take it slowly, tread warily, take tentative steps, feel one's way, proceed with caution, hedge, beat about the bush, take no risks, play safe, hedge one's bets, take pains, make sure, make certain, look twice, look before one leaps, watch one's step, safeguard oneself, beware, look out, keep a look out, keep tabs on, keep an eye on, see how the land lies, see how the wind blows, put a toe in the water, play it by ear, anticipate, take precautions, leave nothing to chance, cover oneself, take out insurance, count the cost, economize, save, hesitate, think twice, have second thoughts, doubt, suspect, pussyfoot (Inf)
▶ *469 Carefulness, 606 Provision, 632 Safety, 328 Slowness, 756 Thrift*

6 **caution**, warn, forewarn, advise
▶ *636 Warning, 654 Advice*

ADVERBS

7 **cautiously**, carefully, warily, watchfully, heedfully, prudently, circumspectly, tentatively, reluctantly, hesitantly, gingerly, providently, judiciously, sceptically, overcautiously

782 Desire

Sooner murder an infant in its cradle than nurse unacted desires. William Blake.

O, she is the antidote to desire. William Congreve.

There are two tragedies in life. One is to lose your heart's desire. The other is to gain it. George Bernard Shaw.

Desire is the very essence of man. Benedict Spinoza.

NOUNS

1 **desire**, wish, want, longing, craving, need, requirement, demand, will, urge, impulse, itch, eagerness, avidity, willingness, zeal, passion, ardour, aspiration, ambition, hope, covetousness, cupidity, greed, voracity, fascination, curiosity, inclination, leaning, penchant, predilection, preference, taste, appetancy, weakness, partiality, liking, fancy, fondness, love, lust, appetite, hunger, thirst,

yearning, yen (Inf), pining, hankering, wistfulness, nostalgia, homesickness
▶ *570 Will, 593 Requirement, 465 Curiosity, 234 Tendency, 572 Willingness, 784 Liking, 775 Hope, 872 Gluttony, 842 Envy*

2 **desirability**, expedience, suitability, advisability, meritoriousness, acceptability
▶ *615 Convenience*

3 **appetite**, keen appetite, hunger, hungriness, starvation, famine, empty stomach, thirst, thirstiness, dryness, dry throat
▶ *45 Cookery, 350 Eating, 871 Fasting, 874 Drunkenness*

4 **sexual desire**, carnal desire, concupiscence, lust, lechery, lecherousness, sexual appetite, sexual urge, libido, libidinousness, passion, ardour, sexuality, carnality, nymphomania, satyriasis, randiness (Inf), the hots (Sl), hot pants (Sl)
▶ *877 Immorality, 821 Love*

5 **object of desire**, desired object, one's heart's desire, desideratum, requirement, request, appeal, aim, objective, goal, catch, prize, trophy, lure, draw, attraction, ideal, the unattainable, forbidden fruit, the brass ring
▶ *712 Request, 588 Intention, 681 Trophy, 340 Attraction*

6 **desirer**, wisher, wanter, fancier, worshipper, devotee, aspirant, hoper, coveter, envier, lecher, lech (or letch), libertine, glutton, greedy pig (Inf)
▶ *872 Gluttony, 842 Envy*

ADJECTIVES

7 **desired**, wished for, wanted, needed, necessary, required, desirable, requested, longed for, yearned for, coveted, envied, enviable, in demand, popular, sought-after
▶ *593 Requirement, 571 Necessity, 712 Request, 842 Envy*

8 **desirable**, acceptable, welcome, pleasurable, pleasant, attractive, likable, appealing, inviting, tempting, appetizing, mouth-watering, admirable, creditable, laudable, praiseworthy, worthy, meritorious, deserving, worthwhile, good, beneficial, advantageous, profitable, expedient, convenient, suitable, fitting, apt, proper
▶ *763 Pleasantness, 617 Worth, 861 Good, 721 Gain, 615 Convenience*

9 **desirous**, desiring, wishful, wishing for, wanting, needing, demanding, longing for, coveting, craving, itching for, dying for, ardent, passionate, avid, eager, keen, partial to, fond, covetous, envious, gluttonous, voracious, greedy, acquisitive, possessive, insatiable, hoping, hopeful, aspiring, would-be, yearning, pining, wistful, nostalgic, homesick
▶ *842 Envy, 872 Gluttony, 775 Hope*

10 **hungry**, starving, starved, famished, raven-

ous, empty, half-starved, peckish, thirsty, dry, parched, dehydrated

11 **lustful**, libidinous, lecherous, lascivious, concupiscent, randy, hot for, sexually desirable, sexy, seductive, provocative, titillating, fanciable (Inf)
▶ *877 Immorality*

VERBS

12 **desire**, wish for, want, need, require, demand, cry out for, ask for, request, call, summon, welcome, long for, pray for, covet, envy, have one's eye on, set one's heart on, dream of, hope for, aspire to, aim for, set one's sights on, crave, itch for, hanker after, yearn for, pine for, miss, hunger for, thirst for, be dying for, pant for, lust after, prefer, favour, like, fancy
▶ *593 Requirement, 712 Request, 571 Necessity, 692 Command, 842 Envy, 784 Liking*

13 **like**, love, want, desire, woo, court, chase, run after, pursue, lust after, fancy (Inf), be turned on by (Sl), have the hots for (Sl)
▶ *821 Love, 590 Pursuit, 877 Immorality*

14 **be hungry**, hunger, starve, raven, be thirsty, thirst, lick one's lips, salivate

15 **cause desire**, awaken desire, fill with longing, tempt, tantalize, attract, allure, lure, draw, fill with desire, excite, titillate, stimulate, motivate, whet one's appetite, make one's mouth water, turn on (Sl)
▶ *340 Attraction*

16 **be desirable**, suit, befit, answer the problem, fit the bill, serve
▶ *613 Usefulness*

ADVERBS

17 **desirably**, acceptably, pleasantly, attractively, temptingly, appetizingly, meritoriously, beneficially, expediently, suitably

18 **desirously**, wishfully, avidly, eagerly, covetously, enviously, wistfully

19 **hungrily**, ravenously, thirstily

20 **lustfully**, libidinously, lecherously, lasciviously, sexily, seductively, provocatively

783 Indifference

But what is past my help is past my care.
Francis Beaumont.

At length the morn and cold indifference came.
Nicholas Rowe.

NOUNS

1 **indifference**, unconcern, lack of interest, apathy, disinterestedness, incuriosity, incuriousness, aloofness, detachment, dispassion, noninvolvement, inertia, inactivity, passiveness, passivity, ataraxia (*or* ataraxy), phlegmaticalness, (*or* phlegmaticness), phlegm, lethargy, listlessness, dispiritedness, spiritlessness, sluggishness, oscitation, inappetence, in-

appetency, lethargy, half-heartedness, perfunctoriness, inexcitability, calmness, lukewarmness, coldness, cold-heartedness, cold-bloodedness, coolness, want of zeal, want of excitement, nonchalance, insouciance, indifferentism, no desire for, lack of appetite, lackadaisicalness, insensibility, insensitivity, dullness, numbness, the blahs (US sl)
▶ *466 Lack of Curiosity, 787 Lack of Wonder, 643 Inactivity, 468 Inattention, 573 Unwillingness, 761 Insensitivity*

2 **carelessness**, disregard, inattention, laxity, heedlessness, negligence, neglect, recklessness, rashness, promiscuousness, amorality
▶ *470 Negligence, 780 Rashness, 482 Lack of Discrimination*

3 **impartiality**, indiscrimination, disinterest, objectivity, no prejudice, unbiased attitude, open mind, no preference, don't-care attitude, neutrality, middle way, moderation, justice, fairness
▶ *843 Right, 333 Middle Way, 242 Moderation*

4 **mediocrity**, averageness, ordinariness, tolerability, passableness
▶ *167 Conformity*

5 **insignificance**, unimportance, triviality, irrelevance, inconsequence, immateriality
▶ *612 Unimportance*

6 **indifferent person**, neutral, neutralist, moderate, middle-of-the-roader, fence-sitter, slacker, pococurante, laodicean, indifferentist, third party, impartial observer, cold fish, wet blanket (Inf)
▶ *641 Inaction*

ADJECTIVES

7 **indifferent**, disinterested, incurious, uninquisitive, uninterested, apathetic, detached, dispassionate, uninvolved, not involved, withdrawn, aloof, carefree, fancy-free, noncommittal, impersonal, matter-of-fact, unconcerned, uncaring, unresponsive, in one's shell, unaware, oblivious, insensible, blind to, deaf to, dead to, lost to, unconscious, comatose, inert, inactive, ataractic, listless, dispirited, spiritless, sluggish, inappetent, phlegmatic(al), lethargic, half-hearted, perfunctory, impassive, pococurante, blasé, easy-going, unsurprised, inexcitable, unimpressed, unaffected, unfeeling, untouched, unemotional, unmoved, unruffled, calm, lukewarm, cool, cold, cold-hearted, cold-blooded, frigid, frosty, unmoved, nonchalant, insouciant, unaffectionate, undesirous, passionless, lackadaisical, insensible, insensitive, thick-skinned, dull, deadpan, numb, benumbed, laid-back (Inf)

8 **careless**, disregarding, negligent, inattentive, lax, heedless, reckless, rash, devil-may-care, promiscuous, amoral

9 **impartial**, indiscriminate, disinterested, happy either way, don't-care, objective, unbiased, unprejudiced, open-minded, neutral, moderate, just, fair

10 **mediocre**, average, middling, ordinary, fair, unexceptional, unaspiring, tolerable, passable, all right, so-so (Inf), no great shakes (Inf)

▶ *124 Average*

11 **insignificant**, unimportant, trivial, irrelevant, inconsequential, immaterial, boring, blah (Sl)

VERBS

12 **be indifferent**, be incurious, mind one's own business, close one's eyes to, look the other way, disregard, dismiss, let go, not mind, care nothing for, not care, don't care, could not care less, not think twice about, not lose any sleep over, not have one's heart in it, have no taste for, not give a fig for, not care a straw about, not give a hoot, shrug off, detach oneself, withdraw, become aloof, show no concern for, take no interest, yawn, oscitate, fail to move, fail to act, not respond, not defend, not be affected by, remain unmoved, have a thick skin, have a heart of stone, harden, harden one's heart, not turn a hair, stay in one's shell, see nothing wonderful, not wonder, show no surprise, show no excitement, have no desires, have no passion, fall out of love, lose interest, cool off, become laid-back about (Inf), leave one cold (Inf), not give a damn (Sl)

13 **make indifferent**, lose someone's attention, fail to move, fail to inspire, make no impact upon, make insensitive, dull, blunt, desensitize, numb, benumb, deaden, bore, turn off (Inf)

14 **be careless**, disregard, act negligently, show poor attention, fail to heed, act recklessly, have no morals

15 **be impartial**, be objective, be unbiased, have no prejudice, be non-partisan, remain neutral about, not take sides, take neither side, sit on the fence

16 **be mediocre**, have no aspirations, get by, pass, not set the world on fire, sit and watch the world go by

ADVERBS

17 **indifferently**, disinterestedly, with no interest, incuriously, apathetically, aloofly, impersonally, matter-of-factly, uncaringly, unresponsively, obliviously, in oblivion, unconsciously, inertly, inactively, listlessly, dispiritedly, spiritlessly, sluggishly, phlegmatically, half-heartedly, unfeelingly, impassively, unemotionally, with dry eyes, with a straight face, deadpan, calmly, coolly, coldly, coldheartedly, cold-bloodedly, in cold blood, nonchalantly, insouciantly, dispassionately, insensibly, insensitively, numbly

18 **carelessly**, without a worry, inattentively,

negligently, heedlessly, recklessly, rashly, promiscuously, amorally, without morals

19 **impartially**, indiscriminately, objectively, open-mindedly, with an open mind, justly, fairly

20 **unexceptionally**, tolerably, middlingly, passably, fairly, insignificantly, without significance, unimportantly, trivially, irrelevantly, boringly, so-so (Inf)

INTERJECTIONS

21 **never mind!**, forget it!, what does it matter!, who cares?, so what?

784   Liking

NOUNS

1 **liking**, attachment, sentimental attachment, tender feeling, tenderness, fond feeling, fondness, affection, attraction, affinity, mutual affinity, friendship, friendliness, intimacy, empathy, sympathy, approval, favourable attitude, admiration, infatuation, titillation, fascination, temptation, allurement, devotion, loyal devotion, patriotism, adoration, love, mutual love, desire, passion, appetite, weakness, zest, wishing, longing, yearning, hankering

▶ *819 Friendship, 821 Love, 815 Sociability*

2 **inclination**, tendency, penchant, propensity, proclivity, preference, favour, predilection, predisposition, disposition, intention, partiality, prejudice, bias, leaning, selection, choice, readiness, willingness, eagerness, mind, cast of mind, turn, bent, aptitude

▶ *588 Intention, 580 Selection, 586 Persuasion, 582 Predetermination*

3 **likes**, hobby, fancy, caprice, whim, whimsy, phase, trend, craze, pleasure, relish, taste, mania, wish, craving, infatuation, soft spot, selection, choice, fad (Inf), crush (Inf), shine (Inf)

4 **likable person**, good person, kind person, helpful person, 861 Good Samaritan, rescuer, saviour, good acquaintance, close associate, friend, close friend, best friend, intimate friend, bosom friend, good neighbour, companion, confidant, confidante, dear one, dear, treasure, beloved one, darling, love, lover, childhood playmate, schoolmate, mate (Inf), pal (Inf), chum (Inf), buddy (US inf), bosom buddy (US inf), sidekick (Inf)

ADJECTIVES

5 **likable**, liked, favoured, admired, appreciated, popular, wished for, good, amicable, congenial, friendly, affectionate, appealing, fascinating, adorable, lovely, attractive, pleasing, endearing, captivating, infatuating, titillating, tempting, alluring, lovable, intimate

6 **liking**, admiring, fascinated, devoted, in-

clined towards, empathetic, sympathetic, tending, intending, turning, bending, leaning, predisposed, disposed, prejudiced, biased, favouring, favourable towards, preferrring, approving, partial to, wishing, hankering, longing, yearning, loving, infatuated, titillated, desirous, passionate, ready, willing, eager

VERBS

7 **like**, care for, have an affinity for, act in a friendly manner, show empathy, sympathize with, hold dear, cherish, appreciate, esteem, treasure, prize, think the world of, have high regard for, enjoy, delight in, adore, admire, relish, savour, have an attachment for, take a fancy to, take to, stay devoted to, feel fondness for, love, desire, have passion for, show a weakness for, wish, wish for oneself, set one's heart on, have designs, on, long, yearn, hanker after, be sweet on, be infatuated with, fancy (Inf), have a crush on (Inf)

8 **prefer**, want, have a preference for, have a propensity for, be inclined towards, approve, show approval for, favour, predispose oneself, lean towards, intend, select, choose, have a cast of mind, turn, bend, show aptitude for

9 **like to**, want to, wish to, love to, dearly love to, long to, choose to

ADVERBS

10 **with great liking**, with a likeable manner, popularly, amicably, congenially, affectionately, with affection, appealingly, fascinatingly, adorably, attractively, pleasingly, in a pleasing way, endearingly, captivatingly, infatuatingly, titillatingly, temptingly, lovably, intimately

11 **admiringly**, with great admiration, empathetically, sympathetically, in a sympathetic manner, favourably, approvingly, longingly, yearningly, lovingly, with love, desirously, passionately, in a passionate moment, readily, willingly, eagerly

785 Dislike

NOUNS

1 **dislike**, instinctive dislike, instant dislike, disapproval, disfavour, disaffection, aversion, prejudice, bias, ill feeling, distaste, disrelish, dissatisfaction, discontent, displeasure, avoidance, rejection, disinclination, no inclination for, no stomach for, reluctance, unwillingness, ill will, resentment, disagreement, dissent, antipathy, antagonism, enmity, animosity, bad blood, abhorrence, detestation, abomination, hatred, mutual hatred, common hatred, hate, loathing, hostility, repugnance, repulsion, disgust, horror, mortal horror, fear, phobia, xenophobia, claustrophobia, bitterness, sourness,

gall and wormwood, allergy (Inf)

▶ *852 Disapproval, 573 Unwillingness, 828 Resentment; Anger, 766 Dissatisfaction, 500 Dissent, 591 Avoidance, 581 Rejection, 764 Unpleasantness, 341 Repulsion, 822 Hate, 777 Fear*

2 **disliked thing**, object of dislike, pet aversion, pet hated, pet peeve, embarrassing situation, failure, defeat, dangerous encounter, danger

▶ *659 Difficulty, 683 Failure, 633 Danger*

3 **disliked person**, not one's type, rude person, mannerless brat, fault-finder, unfair opponent, ill-wisher, bad neighbour, antagonist, enemy, sworn enemy, *persona non grata* (L), *bête noire* (Fr), loudmouth (Inf)

▶ *816 Unsociability, 687 Adversity, 663 Opposition*

4 **sign of dislike**, shyness, drawing back, frown, scowl, shuddering, nausea, queasiness, heaving stomach, vomiting, cold sweat, creeping flesh

▶ *331 Recoil, 624 Ill Health*

VERBS

5 **dislike**, have no liking for, take a dislike to, not care for, have no inclination for, have no desire for, have no use for, have no stomach for, have no heart for, have no time for, not endure, prefer not to, disapprove, reject, object to, feel an aversion for, disfavour, disrelish, find not to one's taste, not like the look of, take a dim view of, have it in for, can't stand, can't bear, not be able to bear, take offence at, mind, demonstrate ill will, show resentment, resent, have a grudge against, disagree, dissent, antagonize, loathe, abhor, detest, despise, abominate, hate, share a common hatred, fear, feel fear, feel disgust, sicken at, feel sick at, want to vomit, mislike (Arch)

6 **react against**, vote against, not choose, avoid, recoil, shun, turn away, shrink from, look askance, make a face, sniff at, sneer at, yell at, grimace, shudder, vomit, fight, hit, attack, have one's knife in, turn up the nose (Inf)

7 **cause dislike**, repel, disgust, disincline, deter, frighten, go against the grain, rub the wrong way, annoy, antagonize, put one's back up, enrage, set against, set at odds, turn one against, make bad blood, excite hate, pall, pall on, jade, sate, disagree with, disagree, upset, put off, revolt, repel, offend, grate, jar, displease, torment, disgust, nauseate, sicken, make one sick, shock, scandalize, create a scandal, incur blame, get on one's nerves (Inf), stick in one's throat (Inf), get up one's nose (Inf), get one's goat (Sl), gross out (US sl)

ADJECTIVES

8 **disliking**, not liking, displeased, discontented, dissatisfied, disenchanted, disillusioned, without love, loveless, undesirous, unsympathetic, out of sympathy, disinclined,

loath, unwilling, reluctant, averse, not charmed, put off, disaffected, shy, avoiding, squeamish, queasy, disagreeing, dissenting, averse, resentful, fearful, unfriendly, hostile, antipathetic, antagonistic, bitter, inimical, repelled, not tolerating, prejudiced against, biased against, disapproving, disgusted, despising, abhorring, loathing, detesting, hating, hateful, fearing, fearful, sickened, sated, nauseous, nauseated, vomiting, sick of (Inf), sick and tired of (Inf), allergic (Inf)

9 **disliked**, dislikable, unlikable, unpopular, unappreciated, out of favour, disapproved, disfavoured, not one's sort, not to one's taste, uncared for, unwanted, avoided, undesired, undesirable, unprepossessing, unloved, unlovable, rejected, jilted, spurned, thrown over, unchosen, unwelcome, unrelished, distasteful, uncomforting, unconsoling, disagreeing, disagreeable, insufferable, not tolerated, intolerable, despised, loathsome, feared, fearsome, abhorred, abhorrent, disgusting, repulsive, repugnant, rebarbative, abominable, revolting, foul, stinking, unsavoury, nauseating, sickening, in one's bad book, not one's cup of tea (Inf), yucky (Sl)

ADVERBS

10 **discontentedly**, unsympathetically, unwillingly, under duress, reluctantly, with misgivings, shyly, aversely, resentfully

11 **disgustingly**, repulsively, repugnantly, rebarbatively

786 Wonder

Two things fill the mind with ever new and increasing wonder and awe, the more often and the more seriously reflection concentrates upon them: the starry heaven above me and the moral law within me. Immanuel Kant.

Philosophy is the product of wonder. A. N. Whitehead.

NOUNS

1 **wonder**, sense of wonder, state of wonder, breathless wonder, wonderment, awe, fascination, admiration, raptness, hero worship, love, lack of expectation, surprise, astonishment, astoundment, dumbfoundment, amazement, bafflement, bewilderment, puzzlement, sense of mystery, stupor, stupefaction, uncertainty, consternation, shock, fear

▶ *514 Surprise, 821 Love, 491 Uncertainty, 523 Unintelligibility*

2 **sign of wonderment**, exclamation, exclamation mark, shocked silence, silence, open mouth, popping eyes, eyes on stalks, cry of wonder, gasp of admiration, whistle

▶ *777 Fear*

3 **wonder-working**, miracle-working, magic,

sorcery, spellbinding, wonderful works, thaumatology, teratology, thaumaturgy, stroke of genius, feat, exploit, deed, transformation, *coup de théâtre* (Fr), dramaturgy

▶ *7 Religion, 655 Skill, 11 Occultism*

4 **wonder**, object of wonder, object of admiration, something incredible, eye-opener, quite something, one for the book, one in a thousand, phenomenon, best-seller, miracle, portent, omen, sign, marvel, masterpiece, masterstroke, *chef-d'oeuvre* (Fr), drama, sensation, cause célèbre, *annus mirabilis* (L), fantasy, cloud-cuckoo-land, Utopia, wonderland, fairyland, fantasy, theme park, Disneyland, spectacle, sight, Seven Wonders of the World, UFO (unidentified flying object)

▶ *519 Imagination*

5 **person of wonder**, amazing person, wonder, prodigy, child prodigy, infant prodigy, wonder boy (*or* girl), whiz kid, *wunderkind* (Ger), genius, man (*or* woman) of genius, ninedays wonder, miracle-worker, wizard, witch, fairy godmother, thaumaturge, sorcerer, hero, heroine, superman, superwoman, bionic man, wonder woman, paragon, curiosity, puzzle, enigma, idiot savant, oddity, freak, monster, monstrosity, *rara avis* (L), exceptional person, proficient person, millionaire, best-selling author, world champion, Olympic champion, star, idol, hit (Inf), knockout (Inf), stunner (Inf), wow (Inf)

▶ *514 Surprise*

ADJECTIVES

6 **wondering**, in wonderment, lost in wonder, astonished, astounded, amazed, lost in amazement, awed, awestruck, fascinated, admiring, impressed, surprised, inexpectant, marvelling, spellbound, rapt, unable to believe one's eyes (*or* senses), dazzled, blinded, dumbfounded, flabbergasted, shocked, scandalized, bowled over, thunderstruck, dazed, stupefied, bewildered, puzzled, aghast, fazed (US inf), gobsmacked (Sl)

7 **wide-eyed**, round-eyed, popeyed, with one's eyes starting out of one's head, with eyes on stalks, agog, all agog, open-mouthed, agape, gaping, dumb, struck dumb, dumbstruck, inarticulate, speechless, breathless, wordless, left without words, silenced, silent, transfixed, rooted to the spot

8 **wonderful**, to wonder at, wondrous, marvellous, miraculous, astounding, aweful, amazing, beguiling, fantastic, too good to be true, too bad to be true, imaginary, impossible, hardly possible, surprising, unexpected, improbable, unbelievable, incredible, inconceivable, unimaginable, indescribable, unutterable, unspeakable, ineffable, inexpressible, mind-boggling, mind-blowing, striking, overwhelming, awesome, awe-inspiring, breath-

taking, impressive, admirable, exquisite, excellent, record-breaking, best, rare, exceptional, extraordinary, unprecedented, unusual, remarkable, noteworthy, dramatic, sensational, shocking, scandalizing, exotic, outlandish, unheard of, strange, odd, very odd, outré, weird, weird and wonderful, bizarre, peculiar, unaccountable, mysterious, enigmatic, puzzling, shattering, bewildering, wonder-working, thaumaturgic, magic(al), like magic, monstrous, prodigous, phenomenal, stupendous, fearful, frightening, grotesque

VERBS

9 **wonder**, marvel, admire, whistle, hold one's breath, gasp, gasp with admiration, idolize, hero-worship, stare, gaze and gaze, goggle at, gawk, open one's eyes wide, rub one's eyes, not believe one's eyes (or ears), look aghast, gape, open one's mouth, have no words to express, not know what to say, stand in amazement, not expect, fear, become fazed by (US inf), gawp (Sl)

10 **be wonderful**, be marvellous, inspire awe, impress, surpass belief, stagger belief, boggle the mind, cause doubt, beggar all description, baffle description, spellbind, enchant, bewitch, dazzle, strike with admiration, turn one's head, excite love, strike dumb, stun, daze, stupefy, awe, electrify, impress, petrify, dumbfound, confound, astound, astonish, amaze, flabbergast, surprise, baffle, bewilder, boggle (the mind), puzzle, startle, shock, make one's eyes open, make one's head swim, make one sit up and take notice, take one's breath away, stagger, frighten, scandalize, faze (US inf), bowl over (Inf), blow one's mind (Sl)

11 **do wonders**, work wonders, work miracles, do magic, achieve marvels

12 **wonder whether**, speculate, conjecture, ponder, meditate, muse, think, question, query, suspect, have a suspicion, take a guess at, hazard a guess, ask oneself

▶ 477 Question, 491 Uncertainty

ADVERBS

13 **wonderfully**, wondrously, in wonder, marvellously, miraculously, fantastically, fabulously, stupendously, awesomely, mysteriously, weirdly, bizarrely, astonishingly, in astonishment, amazingly, in amazement, in awe, astoundingly, surprisingly, to one's surprise, to one's amazement, with gaping mouth, indescribably, ineffably, unspeakably, remarkably, splendidly, fearfully, strange to say, wonderful to relate, mirabile dictu (L), to the wonder of all

INTERJECTIONS

14 **wonderful!**, amazing!, incredible!, awesome!, smashing!, I don't believe it!, can you

beat that!, really!, what!, go on!, well I never!, blow me down!, did you ever!, gosh!, wow!, how about that!, bless my soul!, wonders will never cease!, goodness gracious!, whatever next!, never!, fab! (Inf), ace! (Inf), brill! (Inf), magic! (Inf), cool! (Inf), wicked! (Inf), holy cow! (Inf), holy mackerel! (Inf), holy Moses! (Inf), holy smoke! (Inf), holy shit! (Tab inf)

787 Lack of Wonder

NOUNS

1 **lack of wonder**, lack of amazement, lack of awe, refusal to be impressed, lack of admiration, irreverence, indifference, stony indifference, blankness, serenity, tranquillity, calmness, coolness, collectedness, composure, inexcitability, imperturbability, unimaginativeness, nonchalance, insouciance, disinterest, lack of interest, unconcern, dullness, impassivity, sanguinity, apathy, phlegmaticalness (or phlegmaticness), failure to arouse, lack of spirit, stiff upper lip, cold heart, cold blood, cool (Sl)

▶ 783 Indifference, 498 Disbelief, 325 Motionlessness, 513 Expectation, 761 Insensitivity

2 **predictability**, lack of surprise, unimpressiveness, customariness, ordinariness, commonness, straightforwardness, usualness, plainness

▶ 584 Habit, 488 Probability, 167 Conformity

ADJECTIVES

3 **unmoved**, uninspired, wonderless, unamazed, unawed, aweless, unimpressed, unimpressionable, unadmiring, irreverent, indifferent, blank, deaf to, blind to, dead to, serene, tranquil, calm, cool, collected, composed, unsurprised, unexcited, inexcitable, imperturbed, imperturbable, sanguine, unimaginative, nonchalant, insouciant, disinterested, uninterested, unconcerned, dull, taking for granted, impassive, apathetic, phlegmatic, blasé, unenthusiastic, unimaginative, unaroused, spiritless, cold-hearted, cold-blooded

4 **predictable**, unsurprising, not surprising, unimpressive, customary, ordinary, common, taken for granted, expected, straightforward, run-of-the-mill, nothing wonderful, usual, plain, plain as day, just as (or what) one thought, nothing to it, all in a day's work, nothing to wonder about, nothing to write home about

VERBS

5 **not wonder about**, accept, not turn a hair, see nothing remarkable, not admire, show irreverence, see through, lack amazement, lack awe, treat as routine, refuse to be impressed, not raise an eyebrow, not blink an eye, expect,

see it coming, know it all, show no excitement, take for granted, calm oneself, collect oneself, compose oneself, keep a stiff upper lip, have a cold heart, keep one's cool (Sl)

6 **understand**, have no questions (*or* doubts) about, know the score (Inf), be in the know (Inf), have seen it all before (Inf), catch on (Inf), twig (Inf), get wise to (Inf), wise up (US sl), suss out (Sl)

▶ *478 Answer*

7 **not cause wonder**, not interest, unimpress, impress no-one, provoke disbelief, uninspire, fail to amaze, fail to inspire, not arouse

8 **be predictable**, offer no surprises, appear straightforward, prove just as (*or* what) one thought, have nothing to it, turn out to be all in a day's work, turn out to be nothing to write home about

ADVERBS

9 **without wonder**, with no admiration, with irreverence, irreverently, indifferently, in an indifferent way, blankly, serenely, tranquilly, calmly, coolly, collectedly, imperturbably, unimaginatively, without imagination, nonchalantly, insouciantly, without concern, dully, impassively, apathetically, phlegmatically, unenthusiastically, inscrutably, coldheartedly, cold-bloodedly

10 **predictably**, unsurprisingly, with no surprises, unimpressively, customarily, ordinarily, usually, commonly, straightforwardly, all in a day's work, plainly

INTERJECTIONS

11 **naturally!,** of course!, quite so!, nothing to it!, big deal!, so what?, so?, why not?

788 Boredom

I wanted to be bored to death, as good a way to go as any. Peter De Vries.

Symmetry is tedious, and tedium is the very basis of mourning. Despair yawns. Victor Hugo.

Is not life a hundred times too short for us to bore ourselves? Friedrich Wilhelm Nietzsche.

NOUNS

1 **boredom**, boringness, tedium, tediousness, tiresomeness, ennui, dullness, dreariness, weariness, fatigue, irksomeness, slowness, inactivity, languor, longueur, thumb-twiddling, devil's tattoo, dissatisfaction, dislike, lack of enjoyment, flatness, tastelessness, insipidity, monotony, dull monotony, sameness, plainness, uniformity, lack of variation, humdrum, humdrumness, staleness, dryness, aridity, repetition, repetitiousness, repetitiveness, longwindedness, drawing out, prolixity, stodginess, stuffiness, heaviness, ponderousness, satiety, banality, triteness, prosaicness, prosi-

ness, commonplaceness, indifference, sullenness, lack of interest, melancholy, boring life, *taedium vitae* (L), world-weariness, *Weltschmerz* (Ger)

▶ *650 Fatigue, 643 Inactivity, 553 Diffuseness, 785 Dislike, 766 Dissatisfaction, 412 Tastelessness, 112 Uniformity, 167 Conformity, 556 Simplicity, 783 Indifference*

2 **boring thing**, boring situation, same old thing, broken record, time to kill, time on one's hands, leaden hours, bore, utter bore, no fun, too much of a good thing, twice-told tale, dull speech, unfunny joke, beaten track (*or* path), rut, no change of pace, no change of scenery, monotonous job, assembly-line work, boring work, dull work, chore, treadmill, grindstone, bromide, drag (Inf), bind (Inf), same old story (Inf), old chestnut (Inf), same damn thing (Sl), downer (Sl), bummer (US sl)

▶ *183 Repetition,*

3 **boring person**, bore, utter bore, egoist, egotist, long-winded speaker, humourless comedian, pest, buttonholer, killjoy, moper, bromide, Mrs Grundy, crashing bore, crasher (Inf), crusher (Inf), drag (Inf), drip (Inf), pain (Inf), pain in the neck (Inf), pain in the arse (Tab inf), misery (Inf), stick-in-the-mud (Inf), drag-ass (US tab inf), wet blanket (Inf), nerd (US sl), bummer (US sl), wanker (Sl), boring old fart (Tab sl)

▶ *860 Selfishness*

ADJECTIVES

4 **boring**, boresome (US), tedious, tiresome, tiring, uninteresting, dull, dreary, dreich (*or* dreigh) (Scot), drab, weary, wearisome, wearying, wearing, irksome, slow, inactive, languorous, time-killing, thumb-twiddling, disliked, unenjoyable, repeated, repetitious, repetitive, plain, flat, tasteless, insipid, cloying, satiating, too much, monotonous, uniform, unvarying, invariable, humdrum, pedestrian, suburban, prosaic, prosy, commonplace, stale, unfunny, humourless, soporific, sleep-inducing, unreadable, arid, dry, dry-as-dust, long-winded, overlong, drawn out, prolix, dragging, stodgy, stuffy, heavy, ponderous, leaden, banal, trite, indifferent, melancholy, world-weary, deadly (Inf), draggy (Sl), heavy (Sl), blah (Sl)

5 **bored**, afflicted with boredom, bored to death, bored to tears, tired, good and tired, tired to death, fatigued, drowsy, dreary, weary, wearied, world-weary, tired of living, jaded, sated, satiated, sick of, tired of, sick and tired of, dissatisfied, disinterested, sullen, twiddling one's thumbs, bored stiff (Inf), fed-up (Inf), cheesed off (Sl)

VERBS

6 **be boring**, be tedious, bore, bore to death, bore to tears, pall, tire, make one tired, send (*or*

put) one to sleep, make one yawn, dull, weary, fatigue, irk, dissatisfy, provide no enjoyment, repeat, lack variation, lack variety, draw out, go on forever, go on and on, drone on, never end, harp on, dwell upon, repeat oneself, sound like a broken record, play the same old tune, drag, move slowly, sate, satiate, jade, cloy, glut, cause dislike, lack interest, fail to interest, tell the same old story, buttonhole, talk too long, stay too long, outstay one's welcome, bore the pants off (Inf), bore stiff (Inf), pain (Inf), leave one cold (Inf), make one fed-up (Inf), cheese one off (Sl), give one a bellyful (Sl)

7 **suffer boredom**, lead a boring life, have a monotonous job, do boring work, do dull work, have (or keep) one's nose to the grindstone, do the same old thing, stay in a rut, have time to kill, have time on one's hands, twiddle one's thumbs, dislike, have no enjoyment from, grow weary of the world

ADVERBS

8 **boringly**, tediously, tiringly, uninterestingly, dully, drearily, drably, without excitement, without variety, on the beaten track, wearily, without a change of scenery, slowly, inactively, languorously, repeatedly, repetitiously, repetitively, to death, *ad nauseam* (L), flatly, tastelessly, insipidly, plainly, with no frills, monotonously, uniformly, without a change of pace, invariably, in the expected way, prosaically, stalely, soporifically, aridly, drily, long-windedly, stodgily, stuffily, heavily, ponderously, banally, tritely, indifferently, depressingly

789 Beauty

There is no excellent beauty that hath not some strangeness in the proportion. Francis Bacon.

Exuberance is Beauty. William Blake.

Beauty in distress is much the most affecting beauty. Edmund Burke.

She walks in beauty, like the night/ Of cloudless climes and starry skies;/ And all that's best of dark and bright/ Meet in her aspect and her eyes. Lord Byron.

Love built on beauty, soon as beauty, dies. John Donne.

Beauty in things exists in the mind which contemplates them. David Hume.

Beauty is altogether in the eye of the beholder. Margaret Wolfe Hungerford.

A thing of beauty is a joy for ever:/ Its loveliness increases; it will never/ Pass into nothingness; but still will keep/ A bower quiet for us, and a

sleep/ Full of sweet dreams, and health, and quiet breathing. John Keats.

'Beauty is truth, truth beauty,' – that is all/ Ye know on earth, and all ye need to know. John Keats.

Was this the face that launch'd a thousand ships/ And burnt the topless towers of Ilium?/ Christopher Marlowe.

Beauty itself doth of itself persuade/ The eyes of men without an orator. William Shakespeare.

For she was beautiful – her beauty made/ The bright world dim, and everything beside/ Seemed like the fleeting image of a shade. Percy Bysshe Shelley.

All changed, changed utterly:/ A terrible beauty is born. W. B. Yeats.

NOUNS

1 **gorgeousness**, brightness, brilliance, beauteousness, pulchritude, radiance, magnificence, fairness, loveliness, comeliness, prettiness, attractiveness, beauty, pulchritude, agreeableness, good looks, handsomenesss, shapeliness, grace, gracefulness, refinement, elegance, chic, splendour, exquisiteness, nobility, appeal, charm, glamour, delicacy, harmony, symmetry

2 **beautiful thing**, ornament, adornment, decoration, masterpiece, thing of beauty, *chef-d'oeuvre*, cynosure (or cynosura)

3 **attractive female**, beauty, masterpiece, belle, belle of the ball, raving beauty, dream, vision, pearl, pretty, jewel, treasure, dazzler, bobby dazzler, looker (Inf), beauty queen, smasher (Inf), lulu (Inf), pin-up girl, femme fatale, lovely

4 **attractive male**, dreamboat (Sl), hunk (Sl), dish (Inf), dream man, beau, charmer, looker, Adonis

ADJECTIVES

5 **beautiful**, beauteous, of beauty, lovely, lush (Sl), gorgeous, handsome, pretty, fine, good-looking, attractive, fair, bright, comely, shapely, bonny, cute, sweet, winsome, exquisite, glamorous, pulchritudinous, well-made, well-proportioned, gracile, well-built, manly, statuesque, Junoesque, aesthetically pleasing, aesthetic, tasteful, picturesque, scenic, ornamental

6 **personable**, appealing, enchanting, agreeable, charming, becoming presentable, tidy (Inf), trim, attractive, peachy, blooming, rosy, elegant, tasteful

VERBS

7 **be beautiful**, shine, dazzle, glow, sparkle

8 **beautify**, adorn, prettify, decorate, bejewel, transform, transfigure, primp (Inf), glamorize, tart up (Inf), titivate

790   Ugliness

NOUNS

1 **hideousness**, unsightliness, repulsiveness, gracelessness, homeliness, plainness, hideosity, deformity, contortedness, mutilation, defacement, disfigurement

2 **ugly person**, no beauty, no oil painting (Inf), no Adonis (Inf), back end of a bus (Inf), something the cat brought in (Inf), something the cat sicked up (Inf), dog's breakfast (Sl), fright (Inf), scarecrow, gargoyle, monster, horror, old witch, not one's type, paper-bag job (Sl)

3 **ugly place**, eyesore, blot on the landscape, carbuncle, blemish, slum

ADJECTIVES

4 **ugly**, plug ugly (Inf), hideous, repulsive, graceless, plain, homely, unsightly, unseemly, not fit to be seen, unshapely, deformed, contorted, mutilated, defaced, disfigured, unlovely, gross (Sl), unprepossessing, ill-favoured, monstrous, misshapen, misbegotten, gruesome, wan, grisly, graceless, inelegant, unaesthetic, unbecoming, unattractive, indelicate, uncouth, ungainly, distasteful, grotty (Sl), coarse, awkward

VERBS

5 **make ugly**, disfigure, deface, distort, deform, mutilate, blemish, mask, misshape, impair, spoil, scar

791   Beautification

NOUNS

1 **transfiguration**, transformation, improvement, refurbishment, restoration, rebuilding

2 **plastic surgery**, cosmetic surgery, facelift, nose job (Sl), nip and tuck (Inf)

3 **beauty treatment**, facial, face pack, toilet, toilette, manicure, pedicure, wash and brush up (Inf)

4 **cosmetics**, make-up, war paint (Sl), paint, greasepaint, slap (Sl), rouge, powder, eye make-up, blusher, lipstick, kohl, mascara, eyeliner, eye-shadow, nail polish, nail varnish

5 **make-up box**, paint box, toilet bag, wash bag, manicure set

6 **toiletries** , perfume, scent, toilet water, eau de toilette, eau de cologne, perfume oil, essential oil, smellies (Inf)

7 **hairdressing**, trichology, hair cutting, hair styling, hair colour, hair dyeing, barbering

8 **hair cut**, coiffure, trim, style, hairstyle, crop, cut and blow dry, hair-do, perm, beehive, Eton crop, bob, ponytail, plait, braids, fringe, chignon, dreadlocks, dreads (Inf), frizz, Afro, wet-look, curls, quiff, short-back-and-sides, mohican, skinhead, suedehead

9 **shave**, depilation, shaving

10 **wig**, false hair, toupé, rug (Sl)

11 **hairdressing salon**, hairdressers, barber shop, crimpers (Inf)

12 **beauty parlour**, beauty shop, beauty salon

13 **beautician**, beauty specialist, make-up artist, cosmetician, hairdresser, barber, trichologist, hair-stylist, crimper (Sl), coiffeur, coiffeuse, manicurist, pedicurist, plastic surgeon

▶ *792 Decoration*

ADJECTIVES

14 **beautified**, decorated, adorned, embellished, embroidered, trimmed, tricked out, decked out, improved, touched up, tarted up (Inf)

VERBS

15 **beautify**, prettily, glamorize, smarten up, spruce up, primp, prink, titivate

16 **make up**, doll up (Inf), paint, tart up (Inf), apply the war paint (Inf), perfume

17 **crimp**, coif, clop, curl

792   Decoration

NOUNS

1 **adornment**, garnish, ornamentation, ornateness, richness, enhancement, enrichment, embellishment

2 **pattern**, design, fancywork, detail, flourish, illustration, etching, tattooing, pokerwork, pyrography, filigree, gilding, gilt, gold leaf, scrollwork, illumination, lettering, moulding, beading, breadwork, fluting, ormolu, mosaic, needlework, embroidery, tapestry, cross-stitch, patchwork, appliqué, crochet, lacework, lace, broderie anglaise, smocking, crewel work

3 **honour**, decoration, medal, honours, title, spurs, badge, pips, stripes, star, gold star, garter, order, blue, gong (Sl)

4 **decorating**, painting and decorating, housepainting, wallpapering, interior decorating, interior design

5 **decorative articles**, trinkets, knick-knacks (Inf), gewgaws (Inf), spangles, sparklers, gandery, frippery, flounce, ruffle, frill, furbelow, fringe, ribbon, braid, feathers

6 **jewellery**, costume jewellery, baubles, necklace, bracelet, bangle, ear ring, ring, tiara, torque, badge, pin, brooch, tiepin, hatpin, anklet, medallion, nose-ring, stud, ear-cuff, chain

7 **decorator**, painter, illustrator, illuminator, embroiderer, crewelist, jeweller, gilder, scroll worker, pyrographer, lace maker, smocker

ADJECTIVES

8 **decorated**, ornamented, garnished, ornate, embellished, enriched, rich, enhanced, bejewelled, gilt, gilded, picked out, embroidered, trimmed, worked, inlaid, enamelled, patterned, over-decorated, decked out like a

Christmas tree (Inf), decorative, ornamental, fancy, pretty-pretty (Inf), nonfunctional, scenic, picturesque, baroque, rococo

9 **decorated**, knighted, honoured

VERBS

10 **decorate**, embellish, adorn, enhance, ornament, bejewel, bedeck, bedizen, array, garland, crown, illuminate, illustrate, emblazon, colour, embroider, chase, tool, engrave, festoon, emboss, trace, wreathe, paint, etch, smock

11 **paint and decorate**, wallpaper, refurbish, spruce up, give a face-lift to, smarten up, tart up (Inf)

12 **honour**, decorate, knight, wreathe

793   Blemish

NOUNS

1 **spot**, mark, scar, pockmark, welt, weal, flaw, defect, blot, imperfection, crud (Sl), disfigurement, distortion, defect, stigma, smudge, smear, stain, blotch, tarnish, speck

2 **pimple**, spot, pustule, boil, swelling, carbuncle, bubo, blackhead, whitehead, acne, zit (Sl)

3 **blot on the landscape**, eyesore, smur, carbuncle

ADJECTIVES

4 **blemished**, flawed, masked, defective, deformed, defaced, disfigured, imperfect, spoiled, spoilt, soiled, shop-soiled, damaged, polluted, cracked

5 **marked**, scarred, spotted, pitted, pockmarked, scabrous, scabrid

6 **seedy**, shabby, tatty, tacky, down-at-heel, moth-eaten, dog-eared

VERBS

7 **blemish**, flaw, crack, disfigure, deface, distort, deform, spot, smudge, smear, stain, soil, impair, spoil, mutilate, pustulate, misshape, impair, mar

794   Refinement

NOUNS

1 **elegance**, style, grace, taste, good taste, tastefulness, distinction, dignity, quality, polish, finish, culture, civility, good breeding, good manners, correctness, delicacy, beauty, courtesy, decency, seemliness, decorum, urbanity, propriety, sophistication, gracious living, connoisseurship

2 **subtlety**, distinction, delicacy

3 **etiquette**, custom, protocol, politeness, snobbery, the done thing (Inf), keeping up appearances (Inf)

4 **refined person**, connoisseur, aesthete, dilettante, man of taste, woman of taste, gentleman, gentlewoman

ADJECTIVES

5 **refined**, elegant, graceful, tasteful, dignified, polished, delicate, U(Inf), well-finished, well-bred, urbane, well-mannered, well-spoken, courteous, distingué, ladylike, gentlemanly, genteel, civilized, cosmopolitan, sophisticated, discriminating, fastidious, sensitive, artistic, aesthetic, appreciative, critical, refined

VERBS

6 **refine**, purify, distil

795   Vulgarity

The aristocratic pleasure of displeasing is not the only delight that bad taste can yield. One can love a certain kind of vulgarity for its own sake. Aldous Huxley.

NOUNS

1 **tastelessness**, no taste, bad taste, coarseness, gaudiness, showiness, glitz (Sl)

2 **tawdriness**, shoddiness, tackiness, cheapness

3 **grossness**, impropriety, unseemliness, ill-breeding, commonness, incivility, bad form, incorrectness, bad manners, boorishness, discourtesy, coarseness, crudeness, loutishness (Inf)

4 **inelegance**, uncouthness, solecism, putting one's foot in it

5 **vulgar person**, cad, bounder, slob, Philistine, Barbarian, boor, parvenu, nouveau riche, vulgarian, prole, pleb, savage, yokel, yob (Sl), lout (Inf), show off (Inf)

6 **vulgar herd**, the people, hoi polloi, the great unwashed (Inf), the proles, rank and file, rabble, riff-raff, scum, Tom, Dick, and Harry (Inf)

ADJECTIVES

7 **vulgar**, coarse, gross, cheap, ill-bred, infra dig, *infra dignitatem* (L), inelegant, ungentlemanly, unladylike, unfeminine, non-U (Inf), plebeian, plebby (Inf), loud, showy, meretricious, ostentatious, garish, Day-Glo (Tm), gandy, tawdry, glitzy

8 **discourteous**, boorish, uncouth, unseemly, unrefined, gauche, awkward, disorderly, unpolished, tasteless, unfashionable, uncultured, barbarian, parvenu, nouveau riche

9 **ribald**, bawdy, Rabelaisian, provocative, immoral, blue, unmentionable, unquotable, unprintable, filthy, obscene, smutty, barbarius, lewd, indecent, scatological, in the worst possible taste, in bad taste

VERBS

10 **vulgarize**, coarsen, cheapen, lower, lower the tone, commercialize

796 Fashion

One had as good be out of the world, as out of the fashion. Colley Cibber.

One week he's in polka dots, the next week he's in stripes./ Cos he's a dedicated follower of fashion. Ray Davies.

Fashions, after all, are only induced epidemics. George Bernard Shaw.

NOUNS
1 **fashion**, style, mode, vogue, look, new look, craze, set, rage, the latest, haute couture, high fashion, elegance, designer label
2 **fashionableness**, chic, stylishness, à la mode
3 **fashion business**, the rag trade (Sl), schmutter business (Sl)
4 **design**, mode, style, structure, set, mould, aspect, light, appearance, tendency, convention, protocol, form
5 **fashion model**, model, mannequin, fashion plate, clothes' horse, snappy dresser
6 **fashionable élite**, high society, café society, beautiful people (Inf), jet set (Sl), jet setter (Sl), Sloane Ranger (Sl)

ADJECTIVES
7 **fashionable**, smart, stylish, à la mode, snazzy, clothes' conscious, well-dressed, dressy, tasteful, classy, posh, glamorous, well-groomed, chic, dressed up to the nines (Inf), cool (Sl), with it (Sl), all the rage (Sl), crucial (Sl), hip (Sl), groovy (Sl)

VERBS
8 **fashion**, shape, produce, figure, turn, round, cut, style, tailor, cut out, create, model, chisel, carve, sculpt, hew, mould, cast, hammer out, forge, build, formulate, construct, knock into shape, shape

797 Affectation

NOUNS
1 **affectedness**, pretentiousness, artifice, histrionics, theatricality, euphuism, showmanship, euphemism, sanctimoniousness, sanctimony, irony, speciosity, speciarness, deceptiveness, puffery (Inf), exhibition, artifice, pretension, pretence, falsity, false display, posture, pose, airs and graces (Inf)
2 **pretender**, humbug (Inf), actor, bluffer, deceiver, poseur, poser (Sl), charlatan, attitudinizer, ironist, hypocrite, swank (Inf), exhibitionist, Tartuffe

ADJECTIVES
3 **affected**, precious, pretentious, mannered, chichi (Inf), self-conscious, conceited, artificial, unnatural, stilted, sanctimonious, stagey, euphemistic, showy, meretricious, theatrical, histrionic, puffed up, ironic, ironical, boastful,

swanky, mouthy (Sl), puffy (Inf), specious, tongue-in-cheek (Inf), all wind and water (Inf), all piss and wind (Sl), all mouth and trousers (Sl)

VERBS
4 **be affected**, affect, attitudinize, pose, put on airs, pretend, assume, posture, bluff, show off, play-act, play to the gallery, put on airs and graces, swank

798 Ridiculousness

NOUNS
1 **ludicrousness**, daftness, absurdity, laughableness, pricelesness, foolishness, comicality, drollery, eccentricity, clowning, buffoonery, whimsicality, zaniness, bizarreness, bathos, folly, senselessness, fatuity, fatuousness, muttiness (Inf)
2 **slapstick comedy**, farce, burlesque, knockabout (Inf), custard pie
3 **object of ridicule**, idiot, fool, clown, eccentric, buffoon, figure of fun, twit (Inf), nut (Inf)
4 **joke**, malapropism, spoonerism, piece of nonsense, drollery, clowning, howler, mistake, boob (Inf), boo-boo (Inf)

ADJECTIVES
5 **ridiculous**, preposterous, daft, nutty (Inf), laughable, priceless, absurd, asimine, foolish, funny, comical, clownish, droll, eccentric, bizarre, zany, humourous, witty, comic, farcical, slapstick, clownish, hilarious, rib-tickling (Inf), side-splitting (Inf), risible, fatuous, burlesque, knock-about, derisory, funny peculiar (Inf), funny ha-ha (Inf), rum (Inf)

VERBS
6 **be ridiculous**, play the fool, go from the sublime to the ridiculous, arse about (Sl)
7 **make one laugh**, have them rolling in the aisles, be funny, be hilarious, tickle one's fancy (Inf), set one off (Inf), give one the giggles (Inf)

799 Derision

NOUNS
1 **mockery**, derisiveness, banter, badinage, sarcasm, scoffing (Inf)
2 **act of derision**, satire, parody, caricature, cartoon, burlesque, lampoon, joke, denunciation, mockery, take off (Inf), piss-take (Sl), putdown (Sl)
3 **derider**, satirist, lampooner, lampoonist, joker, mimic, caricaturist, cartoonist
4 **laughing stock**, butt, figure of fun, stooge (Sl)

ADJECTIVES
5 **derisive**, ridiculing, satirical, sarcastic, sardonic, quizzical

VERBS
6 **deride**, laugh at, snigger about, poke fun at,

send up, mock, scoff at, jeer at, put down, make a mockery of, mock, pillary, satirize, lampoon, caricature, guy, denounce, debunk, deflate, take the piss (Inf)

800   Repute

NOUNS

1   **estimation**, reputation, report, good report, good reference, reference, regard, esteem, favour, good colour, cachet, approval, approbation, distinction, eminence, mark, prestige, credit, credibility, claim to fame (Inf), street credibility (Sl), street cred (Sl)

2   **person of repute**, man (or woman) of honour, pillar of the community, man (or woman) of high standing, optimate, emeritus, somebody, VIP, celebrity, star, megastar, notable, favourite, big shot (Sl), fat cat (Sl)

ADJECTIVES

3   **reputable**, of repute, creditworthy, creditable, respected, respectable, well thought of, highly thought of, honoured, honourable, emeritus, popular, in good odour with, favoured by, in favour with, distinguished, eminent, approved, renowned, famous, fabled, above board

4   **reputed**, alleged, supposed

VERBS

5   **have repute**, have a good reputation, be famous, be well thought of, be highly thought of, make a name for oneself

801   Disrepute

NOUNS

1   **disrespect**, bad name, shady past, notoriety, bad odour, bad light, infamy, ill-repute, disreputability, hatefulness, obnoxiousness, loathsomeness, unseemliness, disfavour, discredit, dishonour, slur, ignominy, degradation, disgrace, shame, scandal, skeleton in the cupboard (Inf)

2   **disreputable character**, rogue, rascal, scallywag, blackguard, undesirable, ugly customer, scoundrel, bad lot, bad egg, bad influence, black sheep, ne'er-do-well, cad, bounder, talk of the town, bad scene (Sl), shit (Sl), low-life (Sl)

3   **disreputable action**, foul play, dirty trick, skullduggery, fraud, sharp practice, con trick, con (Inf), hanky-panky (Inf), scam (Sl)

ADJECTIVES

4   **disreputable**, ignominious, degrading, notorious, infamous, nefarious, shady, questionable, scandalous, dishonourable, shameless, immoral, underhand, fraudulent, devious, suspicious, iffy (Sl), dodgy (Inf), not on the level (Inf),

VERBS

5   **bring into disrepute**, lose repute, shame,

fall from grace, fall from favour, disgrace oneself, lower oneself, demean oneself, degrade oneself, put to shame, bring shame upon, show oneself up, humiliate oneself, forfeit one's reputation, desecrate, defile, dishonour, discredit, cast a slur

802   Aristocrat

Like many of the upper class/ He liked the sound of broken glass. Hilaire Belloc.

Democracy means government by the uneducated, while aristocracy means government by the badly educated. G. K. Chesterton.

The Stately Homes of England/ How beautiful they stand,/ To prove the upper classes/ Have still the upper hand. Noël Coward.

If human beings could be propagated by cutting, like apple trees, aristocracy would be biologically sound. J. B. S. Haldane.

Kind hearts are more than coronets,/ And simple faith than Norman blood. Alfred, Lord Tennyson.

NOUNS

1   **nobleman**, noblewoman, noble, lord, lady, duke, duchess, marquis, marquess, marquise, marchioness, margrave, margravine, count, countess, earl, viscount, viscountess, baron, baronet, knight, gentleman, gentlewoman, grand duke, peer, life peer, titled person, blueblood, optimate, patrician, toff (Sl), upper-class twit (Sl), Lord Muck (Inf), Lady Muck (Inf), Sloane Ranger (Sl), nob (Sl), gent (Inf)

2   **aristocracy**, nobility, lordship, *ancien régime*, peerage, dukedom, earldom, viscounty, viscountcy, baronetcy, gentry, landed gentry, ruling class, upper classe, gentlefolk, élite, high society, beau monde, nobs (Sl), top set (Inf), jet set (Sl)

3   **nobleness**, nobility, kingliness, quality, virtue, distinction, lineage, pedigree, gentility, noble family, dynasty, good breeding, line, ancestory

ADJECTIVES

4   **aristocratic**, noble, blue blooded, thoroughbred, ennobled titled, high-class, upper-class, U (Sl), gentlemanly, ladylike, well-bred, ducal, lordly, princely, well-born, high-born, patrician, baronial, high-caste, classy (Inf), first-class, top-drawer (Inf), of good family

VERBS

5   **make noble**, ennoble, raise to the peerage, knight, kick upstairs (Inf)

803 Commoner

NOUNS

1 **plebeian**, pleb (Inf), man-in-the-street, regular guy, prole, proletarian, everyman, underling, Mr Nobody, common man, little man, bourgeois, yokel, peasant, rustic, bumpkin, country bumpkin, country cousin, hillbilly, hick (Sl), serf, villein, husbandman, churl

2 **the common people**, the commons, commonalty, the people, the masses, proletariat, plebeians, plebs, hoi-polloi, rank and file, grass-roots, lower orders, second-class citizens, working classes, bourgeoisie, vulgar herd, great unwashed, have nots, the world and his wife (Inf), Tom, Dick, and Harry (Inf)

ADJECTIVES

3 **common**, plebeian, provincial, of the people, titleless, low-down, second-class, low-born, low-caste, proletarian, plebby (Sl), of humble birth

4 **common**, parvenu, vulgar, uncultured, primitive, wild, savage, barbaric, infra dig, non-U (Sl)

804 Title

NOUNS

1 **right**, birthright, honour, knighthood, glorification, celebrity, renown, name, note, fame, glory, station, order, lionization, handle, dedication, commeration, conservation, sanctification, enthronement, knighting, ennoblement, exalting, canonization, beatification

2 **entitlement**, due, expectation, obligation, duty

3 **honours**, battle honours, accolade, favour, award, medal, ribbon, prize, gong (Sl)

4 **titleholder**, possessor, holder, owner, landowner, landlord, honoured, guest, knight, lord, lady

ADJECTIVES

5 **entitled**, worthy, deserving, meritorious, renowned, celebrated, sung, famous, fabled, illustrious

6 **worshipful**, honoured, right honourable, reverent, princely, lordly, majestic

VERBS

7 **be entitled to**, earn, deserve, be worthy of, claim, expect

805 Pride

Pride goeth before destruction, and an haughty spirit before a fall. Bible: Proverbs.

We are not ashamed of what we have done, because, when you have a great cause to fight for, the moment of greatest humiliation is the moment when the spirit is proudest. Christabel Pankhurst.

Of all the causes which conspire to blind/ Man's erring judgment, and misguide the mind,/ What the weak head with strongest bias rules,/ Is Pride, the never-failing vice of fools. Alexander Pope.

There is false modesty, but there is no false pride. Jules Renard.

NOUNS

1 **pride**, proudness, pridefulness, self-esteem, self-confidence, self-importance, self-regard, self-respect, *amour propre* (Fr), honour, courage, spirit

2 **unapproachability**, disdain, obstinacy, stiff-necked pride, stiff-neckedness, touchiness, self-sufficiency, independence

3 **conceit**, vanity, arrogance, insolence, haughtiness, self-admiration, overconfidence, overproudness, overweening pride, pretension, egotism, egoism, affectation, uppitiness, self-praise, snobbery, inverted snobbery, false pride, vainglory, purse-pride, overambitiousness, hubris

4 **prestige**, dignity, reputation, augustness, style, high-flier

5 **stateliness**, loftiness, proud bearing, nobility, condescension, hauteur

6 **majesty**, grandeur, grandiosity, venerability, sedateness, lordliness, princeliness, pomp, pomposity, pomp and circumstance, solemnity, gravity

7 **fulfilment**, satisfaction, enjoyment

8 **worthiness**, sobriety

9 **ostentation**, display, show

10 **boastfulness**, swank, side, big-headedness, puffed-out chest, self-glorification, bumptiousness

11 **prejudice**, contempt, class consciousness, class distinction, racial prejudice, racial class hatred, Paki-bashing, sexism, ageism, xenophobia, social discrimination, feminism, (male) chauvinism, white (or black) supremacy, segregation, apartheid, anti-semitism

12 **object of pride**, favourite, jewel in the crown, pick, pick of the bunch, source of pride, pride of place, pride and joy, boast

13 **proud person**, vain person, egoist, paragon, boaster, snob, parvenu, swank, swankpot, prima donna, Lord of Creation, swelled head, swollen head, true gentleman, grande dame, peacock, cock of the walk, swaggerer, bragger, braggart, blusterer, aristocrat, Lord (or Lady) Muck (Inf), his nibs (Inf), bighead (Inf), bigwig (Inf), toffeenose (Inf), *crach* (Welsh)

ADJECTIVES

14 **proud**, prideful, supercilious, self-important, self-confident, self-esteeming, self-regarding, spirited, high-spirited, courageous, proud-spirited, proud-looking, pleased as Punch, as proud as Lucifer, house-proud, proud as a pea-

cock, holier than thou, hoity-toity, high-hatted, pleased as a dog with two tails, honourable

15 **unapproachable**, disdainful, obstinate, starchy, erect, stiff, stiff-necked (or -backed), prickly, touchy, independent, self-sufficient, hardened, unbending, distant, aloof, standoffish

16 **oppressive**, overweening, overbearing, hubristic

17 **conceited**, vain, arrogant, pompous, insolent, brazen, unblushing, unabashed, condescending, haughty, self-admiring, affected, uppity, self-praising, snobbish, vainglorious, purse-proud, strutting, conceited, nose-in-the-air, snooty, on one's dignity, on one's high horse, inches taller, smug, pleased with oneself, like a cat that got the cream, stuck up (Inf), toffee-nosed (Inf)

18 **prestigious**, dignified, august, high-flying, stylish, commanding, patronizing, impressive, mighty, high-falutin(g) (Inf)

19 **stately**, lofty, condescending, aristocratic, noble, majestic, majesterial, imposing, grand, venerable, sedate, solemn, grave, sombre, worthy, august, pompous, high-and-mighty, high-minded, high-nosed, regal, lordly, princely, royal, kingly, queenly, statuesque, elevated, imperious, authoritative, high-handed

20 **fulfilled**, satisfied

21 **ostentatious**, showy, plumed, crested, fine, grand, fashionable, flaunting

22 **boastful**, puffed up, inflated, swollen, swollen-headed, big-headed, ungracious, strutting, swaggering, swanky, cocky, bumptious, self-glorifying, bursting (or bloated) with pride, elated, flushed with pride

23 **prejudiced**, contemptuous, class conscious, despising, undemocratic, xenophobic, racially prejudiced, anti-semitic, sexist, ageist, feminist, (male) chauvinist

VERBS

24 **be proud**, have one's pride, hold one's head (high), stand erect, stand up straight, hold oneself erect, refuse to stoop, look one in the face (or eye), have one's self-respect, stand on one's dignity

25 **be proud of**, take pride in, glory in, exult in

26 **be too proud**, give oneself airs, be vain, be on one's high horse, hold one's nose in the air, be too grand to, be stuck up, be snooty, think too much of oneself, be on an ego trip (Inf)

27 **be ostentatious**, show off, swank, swagger, strut

28 **disdain**, despise, condescend, patronize, think it beneath one, look down on, display hauteur, pull rank, overween, lord it over, queen it over, come it over, throw one's weight around

29 **feel pride**, swell with pride, take pride in,

preen oneself, congratulate oneself, boast, hug oneself, pat oneself on the back, flatter oneself, think a lot of oneself

30 **make proud**, do (someone) proud, gratify, elate, flush, turn (someone's) head

31 **save face**, save one's face, preserve one's dignity, preserve one's honour, preserve one's reputation, guard one's pride, be jealous of one's good name

ADVERBS

32 **proudly**, pridefully, self-confidently, self-reliantly, erectly, with head held high, with one's nose in the air, stiff-neckedly, egoistically, egotistically

33 **with dignity**, nobly, worthily, sedately, solemnly, soberly, gravely

34 **imposingly**, loftily, grandly, magisterially

35 **ostentatiously**, swankily, swaggeringly, showily

36 **majestically**, regally, royally, venerably, nobly, like a lord, en grand seigneur (Fr)

806 Humility

Blessed are the meek: for they shall inherit the earth. Bible: Matthew.

Humility is only doubt,/ And does the sun and moon blot out. William Blake.

It is difficult to be humble. Even if you aim at humility, there is no guarantee that when you have attained the state you will not be proud of the feat. Bonamy Dobrée.

ADJECTIVES

1 **humble**, meek, unpretentious, unassuming, modest, mouselike, harmless, inoffensive, not proud, undistinguished, unimportant, without airs, without side

2 **lowly**, low, poor, mean, small, low-born, plebeian, working-class

3 **humbled**, humiliated, embarrassed, mortified, deflated, wounded, shamed, scorned, abject, chagrined, crushed, hangdog, let down, set down, taken down a peg or two, cut down to size, put down, squashed, slapped in the face, debunked, slapped down, rebuked, disapproved, discomfited, defeated, reduced, diminished, dejected, degraded, deflated, lowered, brought down, laid low, bowed down, on one's knees, in the dust, ashamed, shamefaced, crestfallen, disconcerted, out of countenance, broken-spirited, dashed, abashed, sheepish, not proud of

4 **self-abasing**, self-effacing, deferent, self-submitting, diminished, self-abnegating, dispirited, self-doubting, self-deprecating, condescending, submitting

5 **submissive**, subservient, obedient, resigned, disinterested

6 **humiliating**, embarrassing, mortifying,

wounding, chastening, crushing

NOUNS

7 **humility**, humbleness, meekness, modesty, unpretentiousness, simplicity, undistinguished, unimportance

▶ *810 Modesty*

8 **lowliness**, lowlihood, poorness, meanness, smallness

▶ *127 Inferiority*

9 **humiliation**, embarrassment, mortification, come-down, descent, deflation, wounded (*or* humbled) pride, kenosis, hangdog look (*or* expression), hurt pride, injured pride, tail between the legs, offended dignity

10 **abasement**, debasement, degradation, letdown, setdown, putdown, climbdown, slap in the face, dump (Inf)

11 **self-abasement**, self-effacement, deference, self-submission, self-abnegation, diminishment, genuflection (*or* genuflexion)

12 **submissiveness**, subservience, obedience, resignation, disinterestedness

▶ *694 Obedience, 808 Servility*

13 **disrepute**, shame, disgrace, mortification, shamefacedness, shamefastness, shamefaced look

14 **rebuke**, retort, crushing reply, reprimand, chastening thought

15 **condescension**, condescendence, deigning, lowering oneself, stooping

16 **humble person**, mouse, shrinking violet, no boaster, Uriah Heep, sycophant, wimp (Inf)

VERBS

17 **humiliate**, humble, mortify, embarrass, put out, put out of countenance, chasten, disconcert, abash, make one feel small (*or* this high), teach one his place, rub one's nose in it, make one eat dirt, snub, cut, cut down to size, crush, squash, slight, sit on, send away with a flea in the ear

18 **condescend**, deign, stoop, lower oneself, demean oneself, unbend, patronize

19 **be humble**, have no sense of pride, play second fiddle, take a back seat, put others first

20 **submit**, crawl, eat humble pie, knuckle under, eat dirt, swallow one's pride, lick the dust, come on bended knee, grovel, come hat in hand, draw in one's horns, sing small, lower one's tone (*or* note), tuck one's tail, come down a peg or two

21 **humble oneself**, resign oneself, turn the other cheek, demean oneself, genuflect, bow, scrape, crawl, climb down, get down from one's high horse, put one's pride in one's pocket, deprecate oneself, set one's dignity aside, eat dirt (Inf)

22 **shame**, put to shame, disgrace, mortify, be rude, put a person's nose out of joint, make a fool of, put in the shade

23 **abase**, debase, crush, degrade, abash, reduce, diminish, demean, lower, bring low (*or* down), trip up, take down, set down, put down, dump (on), knock off one's perch, take down a peg (*or* two)

24 **be humiliated**, be put out of countenance, feel small, feel cheap, look foolish (*or* silly), sink through the floor, take shame, be ashamed, have a (very) red face, hang one's head (in shame), hide one's face, not dare to show one's face, not have a good word to say for oneself, drink the cup of humiliation, be cold-shouldered, get a slap in the face, be put in one's place

25 **deflate**, take the wind out of someone's sails, take the shine out of, take it out of, take the starch out of, put a person's nose out of joint, put a tuck in one's tail

26 **outdo**, outstare, frown down, daunt, get the better of, gain the upper (*or* whip) hand, triumph over, crow, gain ascendancy over

ADVERBS

27 **humbly**, meekly, modestly

28 **subserviently**, deferentially, with due deference, with bated breath, submissively, abjectly, on bended knee, on one's knees, on all fours, with one's tail between one's legs, with hat in hand

807 Insolence

NOUNS

1 **insolence**, procacity, effrontery, impudence, impertinence, rudeness, bumptiousness, contumely, incivility

2 **cheek**, face, mouth, sass, brass, brass neck, nerve, gall, crust, lip, chutzpah, brazenness

3 **audacity**, boldness, assurance, hubris, brazen face, hardened face, blatancy, flagrancy, presumptiousness, overweening

4 **arrogance**, loftiness, uppishness, uppitiness, pushiness, haughtiness, pride, tyranny, shamelessness

5 **bravado**, defiance, bluster, presumption

6 **contempt**, disdain, sneer, sneering, disparagement

7 **insult**, gesture, taunt, affront, snook, V-sign, throwaway manner

8 **rudeness**, disrespectfulness, contempt, derision, ridicule

9 **discourtesy**, petulance, defiance, answering back, backchat, back talk, rejoinder, raillery, banter, disrespectfulness

10 **impudence**, impertinence, flippancy, cockiness, cheek, cheekiness, freshness, brazenfacedness, brassiness

11 **sauciness**, disrespect, impertinence, pertness, impudence, freshness, sassiness

12 **impudent person**, upstart, young pup, whipper snapper, smart aleck, cheeky devil, brazen face, *chutzpadik* (Yid), swaggerer, smart

arse (Sl), minx, hussy, baggage, madame, beggar-on-horseback, Jack-in-office, tin god, braggart, blusterer, boaster, cockalorum, cock of the walk, smarty pants (Inf), wise guy (Inf), saucebox (Inf)

ADJECTIVES

13 **insolent**, impudent, malapert, impertinent, bumptious, contumelious, flip (Inf)

14 **cheeky**, brazen, mouthy, brassy, saucy, sassy, crusty, gally, nervy, smart-alecky (Inf), smart-arsed (Sl), wise-arsed (Sl)

15 **audacious**, bold, assured, brazen-faced, blatant, flagrant, precocious, obtrusive, familiar, unabashed

16 **arrogant**, lofty, haughty, uppish, uppity, pushy, proud, tyrannical, shameless, presumptuous, overweening

17 **contemptuous**, disdainful, sneering, cool, cold, disparaging, aweless

18 **insulting**, taunting, uncalled-for, gratuitous

19 **rude**, disrespectful, contemptuous, derisive, bluff, brash, barefaced

20 **discourteous**, petulant, defiant, backchatting, bantering, disrespectful

21 **impudent**, impertinent, pert, flippant, cocky, cheeky, fresh, brazen, brazen-faced, brassy, bold as brass, bold, unblushing, shameless

VERBS

22 **be rude**, have the cheek, have the audacity, make bold, make free with, have the gall, have the nerve, have the brass neck, dare, presume, take liberties, hold in contempt, forget one's place (*or* manners), get personal, get fresh (*or* smart) (Inf)

23 **be proud**, presume, put on airs, put one's nose in the air

24 **be vain**, brag, swagger, swank, swell, talk big, boast, brook no restraint

25 **answer back**, cheek, talk back, sass, backchat, provoke, retort, shout down, lip (Inf), give lip (Inf)

26 **oppress**, hector, bully, throw one's weight around, browbeat, grind down, trample on, ride roughshod over, treat with a high hand

27 **dare**, presume, take liberties, outface, brazen it out, brave it out, take a high tone, lord it, queen it, outlook, outface, lay down the law

28 **get above oneself**, presume, step out of line, lord it, come the high and mighty, forget one's place, confute, rise above one's station, throw one's weight around, be a law unto oneself, teach one's grandmother to suck eggs (Inf)

29 **ridicule**, express contempt, snort, sneer, jeer, cock a snook, snap one's fingers at, make a V sign, blow a raspberry, put one's tongue out, not give a fig, send to blazes, taunt, deride, despise, scorn, scoff, laugh in the face of, laugh out of court, guy

ADVERBS

30 **insolently**, impertinently, impudently, flippantly, bumptiously, pertly, precociously

31 **cheekily**, brazenly, cockily, saucily, sassily

32 **audaciously**, boldly, blatantly, flagrantly, precociously, obtrusively, brashly

33 **arrogantly**, presumptuously, loftily, haughtily, proudly, shamelessly, pushily

34 **contemptuously**, disdainfully, sneeringly, coolly, disparagingly

35 **rudely**, brashly, disrespectfully, derisively

36 **discourteously**, petulantly, disrespectfully

808 Servility

I am well aware that I am the 'umblest person going....My mother is likewise a very 'umble person. We live in a numble abode. Charles Dickens.

Wit that can creep, and pride that licks the dust. Alexander Pope.

Whenever he met a great man he grovelled before him, and my-lorded him as only a free-born Briton can do. William Makepeace Thackeray.

NOUNS

1 **servility**, slavishness, deference, compliance, pliancy, subservience, menialness, abjectness, submission, submissiveness, slavery, serfdom, helotism, peonage, lack of self-respect

2 **sycophancy**, obsequiousness, fawning, grovelling, toadying, sponging, parasitism, cringing, footlicking, bootlicking, backscratching, apple-polishing, handshaking, timeserving, obeisance, prostration, crawling, mealymouthing, bowing-and-scraping, ingratiation, truckling, bent back, ducking, bobbing, softsoaping, arse-licking (*or* kissing) (Sl), brown-nosing (Sl)

3 **sycophant**, toady, toad, toadeater, timeserver, creep, Uriah Heep, crawler, bootlicker, groveller, lickspit(tle), suck, mealy-mouth, assentor, yes-man, smoothie, lapdog, spaniel, poodle, jackal, creature, cat's-paw, dupe, stooge, footstool, doormat, instrument, tool, puppet, minion, lackie, courtier, faithful servant, man, slave, helot, serf, peon, kowtower, creeping Jesus (Inf), arse-licker (*or* -kisser) (Sl), brownie (Sl), brown-noser (Sl),

4 **sponger**, parasite, leech, sponge, barnacle, freeloader, deadbeat, gigolo, toy boy

5 **adherent**, hanger-on, follower, appendage, satellite, dangler, dependent, shadow, collaborator, retainer, servant, man

ADJECTIVES

6 **servile**, slavish, deferential, compliant, pliant, putty-like, supple, subservient, menial, abject, submissive, not free, dependent, under the thumb (Inf)

7 **sycophantic**, obsequious, flattering, fawning, grovelling, toadying, sponging, parasitic, cringing, footlicking, bootlicking, backscratching, apple-polishing, handshaking, timeserving, obeisant, prostrate, mealy-mouthed, crawling, ingratiating, truckling, soft-soaping, smarmy, whining, free-loading, cringing, cowering, snivelling, leechlike, beggarly, hangdog, on one's knees, on bended knee, bowed, stooping, kowtowing, bowing, scraping, crawling, sneaking, creepy, unctuous, soapy, oily, slimy, overattentive, arse-licking (*or* -kissing) (Sl), brown-nosing (Sl)

VERBS

8 **be servile**, lose (*or* forfeit) one's self-respect, let oneself be walked all over, act as a footstool, swallow insults, stoop, fall (all) over

9 **fawn**, toady, ingratiate oneself, insinuate oneself, flatter, truckle, crawl, grovel, curry favour, bootlick, lickspittle, lick the feet of, lick the shoes (*or* boots) of, suck up to, creep to, make up to, spaniel, soft-soap, pay court to, worm oneself into, lick the hem of one's garment, pay court to, play (*or* act) up to, handshake, polish the apple, get into the good graces of, get on the right side of, rub up the right way, lick the arse of (Sl), brown-nose (Sl)

10 **knuckle under**, demean oneself, cower, cringe, crouch, kneel, make obeisance, stoop, bend the knee, fall on one's knees, prostrate oneself, throw oneself at the feet of, defer to, tug one's forelock, bow, kowtow, bow and scrape, fetch and carry, bend, bob, duck, be the tool of, lick the dust, agree to anything

11 **pander to**, wait on (*or* upon), wait on hand and foot, cater for, fetch and carry, do service, serve, jump at the bidding of, do the dirty work of, stooge for, squire, dance attendance on, comply, fall at a person's feet, do the bidding of, run after

12 **beg**, beg for favours, wheedle, whine, beg for crumbs

13 **conform**, comply, serve the times, fall into line

14 **follow**, batten on, hang on, adhere to, jump on the bandwagon, run with the hare and hunt with the hounds, follow at heel, follow the crowd, go with the stream, swim with the tide, pin on to, latch on to, hang on the skirts (*or* sleeve) of

15 **sponge**, sponge on, feed on, live off, parasitize, fatten on, use, make use of, use as a meal ticket

ADVERBS

16 **with servility**, slavishly, subserviently, abjectly, menially, submissively, with cap in hand

17 **sycophantically**, obsequiously, ingratiatingly, fawningly grovellingly, on one's knees, creepily

18 **parasitically**, like a leech

809 Vanity

NOUNS

1 **vanity**, vainness, immodesty, overproudness, insubstantiality, vain pride, empty pride, conceit, conceitedness, self-importance, swollen headedness, big-headedness, megalomania

2 **self-satisfaction**, self-congratulation, self-assurance, smugness, self-approbation, self-content, complacency, self-sufficiency, solipsism

3 **cockiness**, perkiness, bumptiousness, pertness, aggressiveness, obtrusiveness, brashness, self-confidence, self-assertiveness, swank, airs and graces, pompousness

4 **self-admiration**, self-esteem, self-praise, self-applause, self-flattery, self-worship, self-love, self-endearment, *amour propre* (Fr), self-infatuation, narcissism, narcism, vaingloriousness

5 **self-interest**, selfishness, egotism, egoism, egoisticalness, egotisticalness, self-centredness, me-ism, Thatcher's children

6 **boastfulness**, pride, conceit, arrogance, side, showing off, exhibitionism, self-conceit, self-display, ostentation

7 **vain person**, egotist, show-off, swank, self-admirer, exhibitionist, peacock, turkey cock, Narcissus, braggart, know-all, know-it-all, big-head, toffeenose, swollen head, God's gift to women, Mr Clever, smarty pants (Inf), Miss Clever, pompous twit, stuffed shirt, empty head, fop, smart aleck (Inf), clever clogs (Inf), clever dick (Inf), wiseacre (Inf), wise guy (Inf), smart arse (Sl)

ADJECTIVES

8 **vain**, immodest, overproud, insubstantial, conceited, self-important, arrogant, stuck-up, snooty, big-headed, swollen-headed, megalomaniac

9 **self-satisfied**, self-congratulatory, self-assured, self-contented, complacent, contented, smug, self-sufficient

10 **self-admiring**, self-worshipping, self-loving, self-endearing, self-infatuated, narcissistic, self-glorifying, supercilious, vainglorious, smug, self-approving, stuck on oneself, impressed (*or* pleased) with oneself, all wrapped up in oneself

11 **cocky**, perky, pert, bumptious, pompous, aggressive, self-confident, self-assertive, swanky, pretentious, affected, foppish, obtrusive, full of oneself, overclever, too clever by half, too smart for one's own good

12 **self-interested**, selfish, egotistic(al), egoistic(al), egocentric, solipsistic, self-centred, self-styled

13 **boastful**, proud, prideful, arrogant, exhibitionistic, self-conceited, ostentatious, self-opinionated, stuck-up, too big for one's boots,

peacockish, know-it-all, overwise, wise in one's own conceit, dogmatic, opinionated, puffed up, blatant, swaggering, pompous, pretentious, putting on airs, affected, smart-alecky (Inf), smart-arsed (Sl)

14 **opinionated**, dogmatic, too big for one's boots

VERBS

15 **be vain**, have a high opinion of oneself, be stuck on oneself, be impressed with oneself, think a lot of oneself, flatter oneself, be puffed up, think one knows it all, fish for compliments, be pleased with oneself, be full of oneself, be wrapped up in oneself, set a high value on oneself, think oneself the cat's pyjamas (or whiskers), think oneself God Almighty, think oneself God's gift to mankind, think well of oneself, think one is it, have no self-doubt, love the sound of one's own voice, give oneself airs, get above oneself, give oneself a pat on the back

16 **show off**, feel pride, blow one's own trumpet, boast, hug oneself, swank, strut, put on airs, talk big, talk for effect, put on side, show one's paces, preen oneself, push oneself forward, go to one's head

17 **be affected**, dress up, doll up, play the fop, dandify, toot one's own horn

18 **make conceited**, fill with conceit, inflate, puff up with pride, turn one's head

ADVERBS

19 **vainly**, immodestly, conceitedly, vaingloriously, self-importantly

20 **smugly**, complacently, self-assuredly, self-congratulatory, self-sufficiently, self-contentedly

21 **cockily**, perkily, pertly, bumptiously, aggressively, self-confidently, self-assertively, obtrusively, swankily, pretentiously, affectedly, foppishly, superciliously

22 **selfishly**, egotistically, egocentrically, solipsistically

23 **boastfully**, proudly, arrogantly, conceitedly, ostentatiously

24 **pompously**, dogmatically

810 **Modesty**

She just wore/ Enough for modesty – no more. Robert Williams Buchanan.

Be modest! It is the kind of pride least likely to offend. Jules Renard.

Put off your shame with your clothes when you go in to your husband, and put it on again when you come out. Theano.

NOUNS

1 **modesty**, meekness, humility, unpretentiousness, unassumingness, unassuming nature, unostentatious, unobtrusiveness,

unboastfulness

▶ *806 Humility*

2 **blushing**, blush, flushing, flush, colouring, reddening, crimsoning, red face

3 **bashfulness**, coyness, prudishness, demureness, demurity, shamefacedness, shamefastness, skittishness, chastity, virtue

4 **shyness**, timidity, timidness, diffidence, self-consciousness, retiring, disposition, timorousness, embarrassment, stage fright

5 **self-deprecation**, self-effacement, distrust, undervaluing the self, self-doubt, lack of self-confidence, weak ego

6 **reserve**, restraint, reticence, constraint, backwardness, retiring disposition, reluctance

7 **modest person**, mouse, shrinking violet, doormat, stammerer, stutterer, blusher

ADJECTIVES

8 **modest**, meek, humble, unpretentious, unpretending, unassuming, unostentatious, unobtrusive, unboastful, unimposing, unimpressive, unaspiring

9 **blushing**, flushed, red, ruddy, reddening, crimsoning, nervous, awkward, shamefaced, sheepish

10 **bashful**, coy, prudish, shockable, demure, demuring, chaste, pure, shamefaced, confused, chaste, virtuous

11 **shy**, overshy, timid, diffident, self-conscious, retiring, timorous, embarrassed, frightened, mouselike, shrinking, unimportant, unsure of oneself, inarticulate, stammering

12 **self-deprecating**, self-effacing, self-doubting, unambitious, deprecating, self-distrustful

13 **reserved**, restrained, reticent, constrained, backward, retiring, reluctant, unseen, unheard, quiet

VERBS

14 **be modest**, deprecate oneself, show moderation, ration oneself, be temperate, not blow one's own trumpet, not push oneself forward, yield to others, play second fiddle, know one's place, not look for praise

15 **escape notice**, avoid, hide one's light under a bushel, take a back seat, keep a low profile, keep in (or merge into) the background, shun the limelight, hang back, shrink back, hesitate, crawl (or creep) into one's shell, be a back-room boy (or girl), blush unseen, shrink from public gaze, retire

16 **be self-conscious**, blush, flush, crimson, colour up, squirm, turn red, stammer, die of embarrassment, feel shame, die of shame

ADVERBS

17 **modestly**, quietly, demurely, meekly, humbly, unpretentiously, unobtrusively, without ceremony, without fuss (or frills), privately

18 **shyly**, timidly, bashfully, diffidently, timorously, chastely, virtuously, coyly, shame-

facedly, shamefastly, sheepishly, blushingly, with downcast eyes

811 Showiness

NOUNS

1 **showiness**, ostentation, ostentatiousness, demonstrativeness, pretension, pretentiousness, showmanship

2 **airs**, airs and graces, loftiness, high-and-mightiness, swank, delusions of grandeur, high-falutin(g) ways (Inf)

3 **dramatics**, histrionics, theatre, theatricality, sensationalism, camp

4 **flashiness**, gaudiness, loudness, extravagance, bombast, flamboyance, panache, dash, splash, splurge, garishness, glitter, tinsel, tawdriness, meretriciousness, colourfulness, dazzle, razamatazz

5 **pomposity**, pompousness, pontification, stuffiness, self-importance, grandiloquence, turgidity, bombast

6 **blatancy**, flagrancy, shamelessness, brazenness, luridness, extravagance, sensationalism, obtrusiveness, crudeness, self-importance, fuss

7 **pomp**, majesty, pageantry, parade, circumstance, state, stateliness, pride, formality, solemnity, stiffness, starchiness

8 **bravado**, machismo, heroics, back-slapping, bonhomie

9 **grandeur**, grandness, grandiosity, splendour, splendiferousness, magnificence, gorgeousness, resplendence, brilliance, glory, sumptuousness, lavishness, luxuriousness, elegance, elaborateness, luxury, ritziness, poshness, plushness, swankiness, Babylonian splendour

10 **exhibitionism**, showing off, vanity, boasting, flaunting, swaggering, strutting, swashbuckling, peacockry, window dressing, effect

▶ *809 Vanity*

11 **ritual**, drill, spit and polish, smartness, protocol, form, good form, right form, correctness

12 **magniloquence**, flourish, trumpet fanfare, fanfaronade, big drum

13 **ceremonial**, state occasion, function, red carpet, procession, Lord Mayor's show, marchpast, trooping the Colour, changing the guard, review, grand parade, fly-past, turnout

14 **show**, display, demonstration, manifestation, exhibition, parade, étalage, pageant, fête, gala, tournament, tattoo, spectacle, tableau, set piece, display, son et lumière, stunt, pyrotechnics, fireworks, carnival, Mardi Gras, waving plumes, fine feathers, stage show, play, act, scene, grand finale, concert, opera, ballet, gymnastics display, mime, circus, big top

15 **showman**, exhibitionist, swashbuckler, peacock, swank, grandstander, stuntman, ring-master, actor, actress, conductor, ballerina, opera singer, gymnast, clown, acrobat, tightrope walker, hot shot (Inf)

ADJECTIVES

16 **showy**, ostentatious, demonstrative, pretentious, shameless, window-dressing

17 **lofty**, high-and-mighty, deluded, prestigious, swanky (Inf), high-falutin(g) (Inf)

18 **dramatic**, histrionic, theatrical, sensational, daring, stagey, cosmetic

19 **flashy**, gaudy, loud, extravagant, flamboyant, exhibitionist, bombastic, garish, frothy, frilly, glittering, tinselly, tawdry, meretricious, colourful, dazzling, painted, tarted up, foppish, dressed to kill, rakish, gay, jaunty, sporty, snazzy (Inf), snappy (Inf)

20 **pompous**, stuffy, self-important, grandiloquent, bombastic, turgid, pontificating, windy, long-drawn-out

21 **blatant**, flagrant, shameless, brazen, lurid, extravagant, sensational, obtrusive, vulgar, crude, fussy, public, screaming, camp, over the top (OTT) (Inf)

22 **majestic**, stately, royal, proud, formal, princely, solemn, stiff, starchy, dignified, grand, fine, ceremonious, palatial

23 **brave**, heroic, macho, dashing, gallant

24 **grand**, grandiose, awe-inspiring, imposing, splendid, spectacular, scenic, magnificent, gorgeous, resplendent, brilliant, glorious, sumptuous, lavish, luxurious, elegant, elaborate, luxuriant, de luxe, superb, diamond-studded, costly, expensive, impressive, plush (Inf), swanky (Inf), ritzy (Inf), glitzy (Inf), posh (Inf)

25 **vain**, swaggering, swash-buckling, strutting, swanky (Inf)

26 **ritualistic**, smart, correct, formal, ceremonial, standing on ceremony, stickling, punctilious, celebratory

VERBS

27 **show**, exhibit, display, demonstrate, manifest, parade, present, perform, act, act the showman, window-dress, stage-manage, march, promenade, march past, fly past, sport, advertise

28 **flourish**, brandish, wave, wave banners, trumpet (forth), emblazon, dangle before the eyes, beat the big drum, proclaim, vaunt, flash

29 **show off**, play to the gallery, grab (*or* hog) the limelight, attract notice, put oneself forward, advertise oneself, dramatize oneself, fish for compliments, flaunt oneself, show one's paces, prance, promenade, swan around, peacock, strut, swagger, make a public exhibition of oneself, make people stare, do for effect, take centre stage, upstage, make oneself conspicuous, go over the top (go OTT) (Inf)

30 **put on airs**, give oneself airs, put (it) on, put up a front, put on side, look big, act the grand

seigneur dame, pontificate, exaggerate, swank, ritz it (Inf)

31 **put on a show**, make a show, cut a dash (*or* swath *or* figure), make a splash (*or* splurge), do for effect, observe the formalities, stand on ceremony, glitter, dazzle, sensationalize, camp up, talk for effect, paper over the cracks, shoot a line, pull out all the stops, step to the front, parade one's wares, go through one's paces

ADVERBS

32 **showily**, ostentatiously, demonstratively, pretentiously, shamelessly, with a trumpet flourish, with beat of drum, with flying colours

33 **loftily**, swankily, prestigiously

34 **dramatically**, histrionically, theatrically, sensationally, daringly, stagily, cosmetically

35 **flashily**, gaudily, loudly, extravagantly, flamboyantly, bombastically, garishly, glitteringly, meretriciously, colourfully, dazzlingly, foppishly, rakily, jauntily, sportily, snazzily (Inf), snappily (Inf)

36 **pompously**, stuffily, self-importantly, grandiloquently, turgidly, pontificatingly, windily, bombastically

37 **blantantly**, flagrantly, shamelessly, brazenly, luridly, extravagantly, sensationally, obtrusively, vulgarly, crudely, fussily, publicly, screamingly

38 **majestically**, stately, royally, proudly, formally, solemnly, stiffly, starchily, grandly, ceremoniously

39 **bravely**, heroically, gallantly

40 **grandly**, grandiosely, splendidly, magnificently, spectacularly, resplendently, brilliantly, gloriously, sumptuously, lavishly, luxuriously, elegantly, elaborately, luxuriantly, ritzily, glitzily, swankily, superbly, expensively

41 **vainly**, swaggeringly, swash-bucklingly, struttingly, swankily

42 **ritualistically**, correctly, formally, ceremonially, punctiliously

812 Celebration

NOUNS

1 **celebration**, celebrating, observance, festivity, festivities, festive occasion, fête, fiesta, festa, function, picnic, party, feast, banquet, beanfeast, rejoicing, revel, revelry, revels, carousal, orgy, debauch, drinking bout, dithyramb, *Oktoberfest* (Ger), Mardi Gras, saturnalia, performance, occasion, jubilation, jubilee, merrymaking, merriment, gaiety, jollity, jollification, conviviality, Whoopee, skylarking, holiday(-making), gala (affair), jamboree, high jinks, fair, carnival, binge (Inf), bender (Inf), blowout (Inf), do (Inf), bit of a do (Inf)

2 **commemoration**, memorialization, honouring, remembrance, memory, observance, ceremonial, solemnization, marking the occasion, jubilee, holiday, memorial service, remembrance service, anniversary

3 **ceremony**, ceremonial function, function, ritual, service, office, solemn observance, ritual observance, rite, liturgy, ovation, coronation, enthronement, triumph, rite of passage, bar mitzvah, convocation, graduation, inauguration, initiation, mummery

4 **reception**, hero's welcome, ticker-tape welcome, red-carpet treatment, reception committee, triumphal arch

5 **anniversary**, special day, day to remember, great day, gala day, flag day, feast day, fast day, field day, holy day, saint's day, high day, Armistice Day, Remembrance Sunday, poppy day, D-day, Fourth of July, Thanksgiving, Independence Day, Republic Day, Bastille Day, V-E Day, birthday, name-day, wedding anniversary, silver wedding, ruby wedding, golden wedding, diamond wedding, centenary, bicentenary, sesquicentenary, jubilee, silver jubilee, golden jubilee, diamond jubilee

6 **tribute**, testimonial, testimonial banquet (*or* dinner), toast, health, congratulation

7 **thanksgiving**, harvest home, Te Deum, thanks, hosannah, hallelujah

8 **salute**, salvo, fanfare, triumph, fanfare, fanfaronade, dressing ship, fly-past, march-past, drum roll, tattoo, flags, banners, waving, bunting, streamers, ticker tape, decorations, Chinese lanterns, illuminations, fireworks, bonfire

9 **rejoicing**, cheering, applause, ovation, standing ovation, flag-waving, mafficking

ADJECTIVES

10 **celebrative**, celebratory, festive, merry, gay, convivial, dithyrambic

11 **commemorative**, ceremonial, solemn, memorial, honourable

12 **ceremonial**, ritual, solemn, triumphal, crowning

13 **congratulatory**, welcoming, complimentary, auspicious

14 **centennial**, bicentennial, tricentennial, sesquicentennial

VERBS

15 **celebrate**, rejoice, revel, merrymake, fête, party, junket, felicitate, maffick

16 **commemorate**, honour, keep, mark, remember, memorialize, solemnize, observe, jubilate, jubilize, signalize, hallow, keep holy, perform, sanctify, mark the occasion, pay one's respects

17 **congratulate**, toast, drink the health of, drink to, raise (*or* fill) one's glass, praise, pay tribute to, sing the praises of, reward, drain a bumper, sing Happy Birthday

18 **salute**, welcome, cheer, applaud, roll out the

red carpet, kill the fatted calf, fête, chair, lionize, hang out the flags (*or* bunting), garland, throw a party, make much of, do one proud, carry shoulder high, mob, deck (*or* wreathe) with flowers, fling wide the gates, beat a tattoo, blow the trumpets, fire a salvo

19 **install**, enthrone, crown, inaugurate, launch, induct, initiate, instate, present, auspicate

20 **come out**, pass out, graduate

ADVERBS

21 **in honour of**, in memory of, in commemoration of, on the occasion of, in remembrance of

813   Formality

NOUNS

1 **formality**, form, formalness, state, stateliness, state occasion, dignity, ceremoniousness, stiffness, sedateness, staidness, starchiness, solemnity, solemness, royal we, etiquette, correct behaviour, protocol, the thing to do, doing the right thing, smartness, spit and polish, correctness, correctitude, fastidiousness, decorum, decorousness, stuffiness, stiff-neckedness, straitlacedness, hideboundness, preciseness, red carpet, conventionality, propriety, best behaviour, stylization, primness, rigidness, pomp, circumstance, pride, gravity, weightiness

2 **formalism**, ritualism, ceremonialism, pedantry, preciseness, precisionism, preciousness, preciosity, purism, punctiliousness, scrupulousness, conventionalism, conventionality, over-refinement, over-preciseness, goody-goodyism

3 **formal occasion**, ceremony, ceremonial, procedure, ritual, drill, practice, routine, drill attention, celebration, son et lumière, spectacle, set piece, tableau, scene, show, Lord Mayor's show, changing the guard, trooping the Colour, turnout, review, (grand) parade, march past, fly past, pageant, fête, gala, gala performance, tournament, tattoo, field day, red-letter day, rite, liturgy, religious ceremony, service, Christening, wedding, funeral, confirmation, baptism, coronation, rite of passage, convocation, graduation, inauguration, initiation, bar mitzvah

▶ 812 *Celebration*, 811 *Showiness*

4 **formal dress**, full dress, court dress, grand toilette, robes, regalia, finery, tails, black tie, white tie, white tie and tails, correct dress, uniform, formal attire, morning dress, evening dress, evening gown, ball gown, dinner jacket, dress suit, tuxedo, tux, lounge suit, long dress, cocktail dress, best bib and tucker, Sunday best, academic dress, cap and gown, subfusc, mourning black, widow's weeds, uniform, regimentals, livery, dress uniform, mess kit, battledress, fatigues, khaki, school uniform, vestments, clerical dress

5 **etiquette**, rules of conduct, social code, formalities, prescribed form, set form, social procedures, social graces, social conduct, social convention, social image, custom, good manners, politeness, *politesse* (Fr), natural politeness, civilities, comity, decencies, elegancies, mores, proprieties, decorum, good form, right form, protocol, diplomatic code, punctilio, point of etiquette, convention

ADJECTIVES

6 **formal**, formulary, formalistic, legalistic, pedantic, stately, dignified, ceremonious, ceremonial, stiff, refined, starchy, sedate, staid, stilted, rigid, solemn, royal, correct, smart, precise, conventional, ritual, procedural, standing on ceremony, official, stylized, prim, punctilious, precise, scrupulous, fastidious, precious, puristic, exact, meticulous, orderly, methodical, elegant, decorous, proud, grave, pompous, weighty

7 **dressed up**, formally dressed, uniformed, in full dress, black-tie, white-tie, in white tie and tails, in tails, dressed to kill, dressed fit to kill, in Sunday best, in one's best bib and tucker, in fine feathers, *en grande toilette* (Fr), chic, soignée, stylish, modish, fashionable, well turned out, dolled up, dressed (*or* dolled) up to the nines (Inf), spiffed (*or* fancied *or* slicked) up, glitzy (Inf), ritzy (Inf), right-on (Inf)

8 **ceremonious**, ceremonial, ritual, ritualistic, solemn, pompous, liturgic, stately

VERBS

9 **formalize**, ritualize, solemnize, conventionalize, stylize

10 **celebrate**, dignify

11 **be formal**, observe the formalities, stand on ceremony, do things by the book, follow protocol

ADVERBS

12 **formally**, in due form, in set form, pro forma, as a matter of form, precisely, smartly, officially, starchily, stiffly, stiltedly, rigidly, primly, solemnly, procedurally, conventionally, ritually, royally, correctly, ceremoniously

814   Informality

NOUNS

1 **informality**, informalness, lack of formality, lack of ceremony, unceremoniousness, lack of convention, unconventional, unofficial, indifference, nonconformity, casualness, offhandedness

2 **sociability**, affability, graciousness, cordiality, relaxedness, Bohemianism

3 **familiarity**, naturalness, simplicity, plainness, homeliness, homeyness, folksiness, the common touch, unaffectedness

4 **freedom**, licence, indulgence, toleration, free speech, free will, free thought, free-and-easiness, a free hand, leeway, margin, unconstraint, latitude, independence, freedom of action, laxity, permissiveness, relaxation, forbearance, ease, easygoingness, leave, looseness, irregularity, permissive society

5 **nonobservance**, nonadherence, breach of etiquette, bad form, gaffe, bad taste, bad manners, incorrectness, gaucherie

6 **informal dress**, casual dress, undress, mufti, casual clothes, leisure wear, slacks, jeans, tracksuits, shell suits, *déshabillé* (Fr), dishabille, dressing gown, loungewear, day dress, peignoir, bathrobe, robe, wrapper, housecoat, smoking jacket, slippers, shirtsleeves, civvies (Inf)

ADJECTIVES

7 **informal**, unceremonious, unconventional, unofficial, indifferent, nonconformist, casual, offhand, unstuffy, unaffected, unassuming

8 **sociable**, affable, gracious, cordial, relaxed, Bohemian

9 **familiar**, natural, simple, plain, homely, folksy, common, unaffected, *haymish* (Yid)

10 **free**, indulgent, tolerant, unconstrained, independent, lax, permissive, easygoing, free-and-easy, loose, irregular

VERBS

11 **not stand on ceremony**, let one's hair down, be oneself, be natural, relax, feel at home, make oneself at home, not insist, waive the rules, come as you are, be footloose and fancy free, go native, show no respect for

ADVERBS

12 **informally**, unceremoniously, without ceremony

13 **casually**, offhand, offhandedly, relaxedly, familiarly

14 **naturally**, simply, plainly

15 **unaffectedly**, unassumingly, unconstrainedly, unofficially, *en famille* (Fr)

815 Sociability

NOUNS

1 **sociability**, sociableness, socialness, sociality, social-mindedness, affability, amicability, amiability, friendliness, neighbourliness, gregariousness, kindness, warmth, fondness for company, fondness for society, geniality, congeniality, cordiality, conviviality, enjoyment, joviality, jollity, revelry, festivity, merriment, merrymaking, gaiety, cheer, good cheer, hospitality, companionability, compatibility, clubbishness, fraternization, participation, membership, cooperation, sharing, partaking, hobnobbing, conversation, intercourse, communicativeness, communication, intercommunication, communion, intercommunion,

social skills, social ability, social relations, social intercourse, social activity, group activity, association, consociation, affiliation, familiarity, intimacy, consorting, fratting (Inf)

▶ *664 Cooperation, 817 Courtesy, 769 Cheerfulness, 762 Joy, 755 Generosity, 568 Conversation, 534 Communications, 161 Assembly*

2 **social ambition**, ambition, social climbing, status-seeking, social success, popularity, social graces, good manners, *savoir-vivre* (Fr), refinement, breeding, courtesy, easy manner, *savoir-faire* (Fr), ability to mix, affability, conversableness, social demand, upward mobility, keeping up with the Joneses (Inf)

▶ *652 Conduct, 682 Success, 817 Courtesy*

3 **meeting**, appointment, engagement, rendezvous, assignation, date, double date, social gathering, social, social affair, gathering, at home, meeting one's friends, tête-à-tête, *conversazione* (It), soirée, coffee, coffee morning, tea, afternoon tea, high tea, reception, wedding reception, soiree, entertainment, seeing one's family, family reunion, class reunion, visiting, visit, formal visit, official visit, visitation, interview, calling, call, social call, courtesy call, frequenting, frequentation, stay, social round, round of visits, social whirl, mad round, calling card, tryst (Arch), get-together (Inf), dropping in (Inf), blind date (Inf), elevenses (Inf), dirty weekend (Inf)

4 **meeting place**, stadium, public hall, restaurant, salon, drawing room, love nest, pub

5 **party**, entertainment, festivity, feast, banquet, dinner, dinner party, supper party, tea party, house party, weekend party, at-home, open day, open house (US), house-warming, house-raising, barn-raising, surprise party, garden party, lawn party, *fête champêtre* (Fr), costume party, fancy-dress party, ball, hunt ball, masked ball, masquerade, masque (or mask), cocktail party, sherry party, beer party, drinks party, bottle party, drug party, smoker, mixed party, birthday party, coming-out party, coming-out, debut, presentation, wedding party, dance, barn dance, square dance (US), hoedown (dance) (US), disco, discotheque, barbecue, wienie roast (US), gala, (bit of a) do (Inf), knees-up (Inf), shindig (Inf), shindy (Inf), stag party (Inf), hen party (Inf), potluck dinner (Inf), hop (Inf), bop (Inf), rave (or rave-up) (Sl), blowout (Sl)

▶ *875 Drug-Taking, 46 Dancing and Ballet*

6 **social person**, convivial person, social butterfly, good host (or hostess), socialite, debutante, good neighbour, good fellow, charming fellow, conversationalist, friend, visitor, guest, welcome guest, one of the family, good company, good companion, *bon vivant* (Fr), playboy, man about town, social lion, habitué, clubman (or clubwoman), active member,

back-slapper, unwelcome guest, gate-crasher, parasite, mine host (Arch), pal (Inf), chum (Inf), mate (Inf), mixer (Inf), good mixer (Inf), joiner (Inf), life (and soul) of the party (Inf), raver (Sl)

▶ *826 Endearment*

7 human society, humanity, mankind, humankind, community, commune, public, social group, social circle, social set, one's set, social class, upper class, elite, high society, beau monde, gentry, nobility, aristocracy, middle class, working class, caste, peer group, one's group, one's gang, one's club, the crowd, family, one-parent family, family circle, home circle, friends and relations, friends and acquaintances

▶ *167 Conformity, 794 Refinement, 796 Fashion*

8 good company, company, comradeship, friendship, fellowship, good fellowship, fraternity, camaraderie, togetherness, bonhomie, cordiality, hospitality

9 welcome, welcoming, hearty welcome, cordial welcome, warm welcome, warmth, warm reception, smiling reception, greeting, handshake, handclasp (US), embrace, welcoming embrace, kiss, hug, peck on the cheek, back-slapping

10 social animal, ape, lion, bird, marmot, ant, bee, termite, wasp, dolphin, rook

▶ *77 Mammals, 78 Birds, 82 Insects and Arachnids*

VERBS

11 be sociable, be social, enjoy company, love company, entertain, invite, host, be hospitable, throw a party, act as host, act the host, act as hostess, act the hostess, have an open day, hold open house (US), welcome, bid welcome, make welcome, welcome with open arms, put out the welcome mat (US), hug, embrace, do the honours, preside, participate, mix with, mingle with, get together, join in, be a good mixer, know how to mix, get about (*or* around), go out, dine out, go to parties, fish for invitations, accept invitations, share, eat off the same platter, crack a bottle with, toast, drink to, pledge, love a party, go partying, gate-crash, go clubbing, go nightclubbing, go pubbing, go out on the town, go on a spree, kill the fatted calf, associate with, consort with, rub shoulders (*or* elbows) with (Inf), go Dutch (Inf), go shares (Inf), take potluck (Inf), go pub-crawling (Inf), paint the town red (Inf), keep up with the Joneses (Inf), freeload (Sl)

12 visit, call on, pay a visit, look up, see, stop off, stop over, make oneself welcome, make oneself at home, make oneself one of the family, unbend, relax, leave one's calling card, sojourn, stay, weekend, keep up with, be on visiting terms, winter, summer, drop in on (Inf), drop by (Inf)

13 fraternize, have friends, make friends (easi-

ly), hobnob, glad-hand, back-slap, have fun, introduce oneself, get along with, get on well with, keep company with, hang around with, walk hand in hand with, club together with, date, make a date, seek acquaintance, make acquaintance, live it up (Inf), hang out with (Inf), pal up with (Inf), gang up with (Inf), hook up with (Sl)

14 welcome, greet, shake hands with, embrace, kiss

ADJECTIVES

15 sociable, social, affable, social-minded, socially disposed, communal, collective, common, public, civic, companionable, amicable, amiable, affable, clubbish, clubby, communicative, friendly, fond of company, courteous, civil, urbane, easy, easy-going, free-and-easy, party-minded, cordial, genial, witty, amusing, charming, charismatic, extrovert, gregarious, outgoing, hearty, lively, hail-fellow-well-met, convivial, jolly, jovial, merry, cheerful, smiling, welcoming, warm, affectionate, hospitable, neighbourly, inviting, matey (Inf), pally (Inf)

16 popular, beloved, liked, sought after, welcome, ever-welcome, welcomed with open arms, socially accepted, accepted as one of the family, made to feel at home, socially successful, entertained, fêted, dined, wined and dined

17 festive, carnival-like, entertaining, fun, joyous, Christmassy

ADVERBS

18 sociably, socially, affably, amicably, amiably, convivially, family-oriented, *en famille* (Fr), genially, in friendship, in a friendly fashion, like friends, companionably, arm in arm, hand in hand, affectionately, with love, as lovers, communicatively, courteously, civilly, easily, cordially, hospitably, wittily, amusingly, in an amusing way, charmingly, with great charm, gregariously, heartily, with open arms, warmly, merrily, cheerfully, with good cheer, joyously, festively, entertainingly

816   Unsociability

NOUNS

1 unsociability, unsociableness, dissociability, dissociableness, unsocial habits, antisocial habits, ungregariousness, unclubability, uncongeniality, incompatibility, unfriendliness, unhappiness, sullenness, mopishness, moroseness, taciturnity, reticence, uncommunicativeness, standoffishness, haughtiness, lonely pride, reserve, aloofness, remoteness, detachment, indifference, apartness, distance, maintaining one's distance, reclusiveness, coolness, coldness, frigidity, chill, chilliness, iciness, frostiness, inhospitality, unreceptiveness, ungraciousness, discourtesy, avoidance,

withdrawal, refusal to mix, cutting someone off, privacy, keeping one's own company, keeping (oneself) to oneself, domesticity, homelife, seclusiveness, self-containment, retirement, singleness, celibacy, unapproachability, inaccessibility, exclusivity, privacy, private world, sending someone to Coventry, cutting someone dead (Inf)

▶ 591 Avoidance, 830 Sullenness, 566 Taciturnity, 805 Pride, 818 Discourtesy, 147 Exclusion

2 **shyness**, bashfulness, timidity, diffidence, modesty, introversion, anthropophobia, agoraphobia

▶ 810 Modesty

3 **separation**, seclusion, isolation, splendid isolation, solitariness, solitude, loneliness, exclusion, retreat, rejection, exile, banishment, deportation, expulsion, segregation, apartheid, blacklist, blackball, ostracism, sending one to Coventry, boycott, quarantine, concealment, purdah, Balkanization

▶ 136 Separation, 581 Rejection, 349 Expulsion, 531 Concealment

4 **place of confinement**, reserve, enclave, haven, reservation, American Indian reservation, homeland, Bantustan, ghetto, native quarter, prison, concentration camp, Dachau, prison camp, POW (prisoner of war) camp, jail (or gaol), penitentiary, penal institution, maximum-security prison, borstal, reformatory (or reform school), penal settlement, penal colony, Devil's Island, Siberia, pen (US inf)

▶ 256 Habitat, 702 Prison

5 **solitary place**, retreat, sanctuary, sanctum, den, study, cloister, cell, sequestered nook, ivory tower, private quarters, secret garden, backwater, back of beyond, back o'Bourke (Aus), desert island, hiding place, hide-out, godforsaken hole (Inf), hick town (US inf), Podunk (US inf), jerkwater town (US sl)

▶ 634 Refuge

6 **unsocial person**, solitary person, stay-at-home, recluse, hermit, anchorite, ascetic, Hieronymite, guellemin, cave-dweller, coenobite (or cenobite), santon, marabout, sannyasi, eremite, monk, outsider, not one of us, odd man out, oddity, eccentric, misfit, fish out of water, persona non grata (L), marooned person, castaway, Robinson Crusoe, loner (Inf), lone wolf (Inf), homebody (Inf), troglodyte (Inf), square peg (in a round hole) (Inf), iceberg (US sl)

▶ 149 Foreign Body, 104 Extraneousness

7 **outsider**, foreigner, expatriate, exile, evacuee, refugee, outcast, outcaste, untouchable, pariah, leper, reject, deported person, deportee, displaced person (DP), stateless person, flotsam, flotsam and jetsam, homeless person, trash (US), poor white trash (US), outlaw, bandit, prisoner, POW (prisoner of war), vagabond, orphan, waif, stray, foundling, expat (Inf)

▶ 2 Sociology

ADJECTIVES

8 **unsociable**, dissociable, dissocial, antisocial, ungregarious, uncompanionable, uncongenial, uncommunicative, reclusive, reticent, silent, sullen, mopy, morose, private, close, autistic, unforthcoming, unapproachable, withdrawn, in one's shell, domestic, seclusive, retiring, standoffish, aloof, haughty, remote, removed, distant, apart, detached, indifferent, Olympian, exclusive, self-sufficient, self-contained, inaccessible, forbidding, discourteous, impolite, uncivil, unmannerly, ungracious, rude, disrespectful, unfriendly, cool, cold, chilly, icy, frigid, frosty, unneighbourly, unwelcoming

9 **shy**, bashful, timid, taciturn, silent, introverted, afraid of the opposite sex, afraid of company

10 **lonely**, lonesome, alone, on one's own, solitary, isolated, secluded, stay-at-home, unpopular, friendless, boycotted, shunned, banned, frozen-out, prohibited, outlawed, desolate, lorn (Fml), forlorn, godforsaken, uninvited, deserted, avoided, rejected, ostracized, sent to Coventry, exiled, banished, deported, expelled, displaced, disbarred, confined, concealed, behind the veil, in purdah, single, celibate, unmarried, unwedded, separated, divorced, incompatible, not fit to live with, out of place, like a fish out of water, blanked (Inf), cold-shouldered (Inf), on one's tod (Sl)

11 **secluded**, private, isolated, quiet, off the beaten track, out of the way, remote, deserted, desolate, hidden, screened, cloistered, sequestered, unvisited, unexplored, uninhabited, unknown

VERBS

12 **be unsocial**, keep (oneself) to oneself, keep one's distance, shun company, stand aloof, seclude oneself, go into seclusion, retire, go into retirement, retire from the world, give up one's friends, give up one's social life, stay at home, shut oneself up, withdraw, see no one, bury oneself, creep into a corner, stay in one's shell, stew in one's own juice, abandon the world, take the veil, lead a cloistered life

13 **ignore**, not acknowledge, avoid, have nothing to do with, exclude, shun, ban, shut (or close) the door on, segregate, blacklist, blackball, treat as a leper, treat as an outsider, keep at arm's length, repel, act rude, snub, rebuff, frown on, turn one's back on, isolate, ostracize, freeze out, cut off, send to Coventry, shut out, reject, ban, boycott, prohibit, outlaw, turn out, displace, exile, banish, deport, expel, cast out, disbar, conceal, keep (in) private, keep in purdah, confine, shut up, quarantine,

seclude, sequester, imprison, jail (*or* gaol), cold-shoulder (Inf), cut someone dead (Inf), blank someone (out) (Inf)

ADVERBS

14 **unsocially**, antisocially, inhospitably, incompatibly, taciturnly, reticently, quietly, silently, without a word, sullenly, morosely, privately, in private, at home, domestically, aloofly, haughtily, with disdain, remotely, distantly, indifferently, inaccessibly, behind closed doors, exclusively, self-sufficiently, without assistance, forbiddingly, discourteously, impolitely, uncivilly, ungraciously, rudely, with rudeness, disrespectfully, coolly, coldly, icily, frigidly, shyly, in a shy manner, bashfully, timidly

817   Courtesy

NOUNS

1 **courtesy**, courteousness, common courtesy, politeness, civility, kindness, kindliness, amiability, sweetness, niceness, amenity, agreeableness, affability, comity, graciousness, humility, consideration, thoughtfulness, solicitousness, solicitude, decency, tact, tactfulness, discretion, charity, generosity, benevolence, help, friendliness, sociability, gallantry, chivalry, chivalrousness, courtliness, comity, noblesse oblige, graciousness, gracefulness, suavity, suaveness, blandness, social tact, smoothness, flattery, sweet talking, sweet tongue, soft tongue, honeyed tongue, fair words, soft words, easy temper, even temper, good humour, gentleness, mildness, mild manner, obligingness, the common touch, mansuetude (Arch), soft soap (Inf)

▶ *806 Humility, 831 Benevolence, 819 Friendship, 815 Sociability, 853 Flattery, 662 Help*

2 **good manners**, exquisite manners, mannerliness, etiquette, good behaviour, breeding, good breeding, good deportment, refinement, polish, culture, gentility, genteelness, sophistication, elegance, urbanity, savoir-vivre, savoir-faire, gentlemanliness, ladylikeness, formality, correctness, convention, protocol, custom, diplomacy

▶ *794 Refinement, 796 Fashion*

3 **courtesies**, social courtesies, civilities, urbanities, amenities, graces, gentilities, pleasantries, compliments (of the season), regards, best regards, best wishes, best respects, love, kind remembrances, elegances, dignities, respect, respectfulness, formalities, rites, rituals, ceremonies, invitation, presentation, welcome, introduction, reception, acknowledgment, compliment, toast, recognition, mark of recognition, valediction, fond farewell

▶ *826 Endearment, 467 Attention, 821 Love, 849 Respect, 811 Showiness, 345 Departure*

4 **deference**, obeisance, compliance, complaisance, condescension, oiliness, unctuousness, glibness, fulsomeness, sycophancy, ingratiation, doffing one's cap, touching one's cap, kissing someone's hand, bowing, nodding, kowtowing, salaaming, laying it on (Inf)

▶ *694 Obedience, 362 Lowering*

5 **sign of courtesy**, sign of politeness, act of kindness, salutation, salute, greeting, handshake, handclasp (US), hug, kiss, embrace, smile, wave, graceful gesture, bow, curtsy

6 **courteous person**, willing servant, sycophant, helpful neighbour, gallant, knight, chevalier, lady, gentleman, proper gentleman (*or* lady)

▶ *697 Servant, 802 Aristocrat*

ADJECTIVES

7 **courteous**, polite, civil, urbane, agreeable, affable, genial, amiable, gracious, humble, fair, considerate, thoughtful, solicitous, decent, tactful, discreet, generous, benevolent, charitable, accommodating, lenient, eventempered, gentle, mild, mild-mannered, good-humoured, obliging, amenable, sociable, friendly, kind, kindly, sweet, nice, welcoming, gallant, chivalrous, courtly, graceful, old-fashioned, old-world

8 **good-mannered**, well-behaved, well-bred, well-spoken, refined, cultured, cultivated, genteel, gentlemanly, ladylike, correct, urbane, polished, elegant, conventional, suave, bland, smooth, flattering, sweet-talking, softtongued, sweet-tongued, honey-tongued, formal, de rigueur, ceremonious, diplomatic, respectful

9 **deferential**, obeisant, compliant, condescending, complaisant, glib, fulsome, sycophantic, ingratiating, bowing, nodding, kowtowing, smug, oily, unctuous, buttery (Inf), soapy (Inf), slimy (Inf)

VERBS

10 **be courteous**, show courtesies, show kindness, give consideration, care, use tact, oblige, invite, receive, welcome, introduce, acknowledge, compliment, recognize, toast, drink to, give one's best regards, give one's best wishes, send one's respects, give respect, send one's regrets, express regrets, show love, love, flatter, have a sweet tongue, use soft words, possess an even temper, have a mild manner, not take offence, take in good part, remain good-humoured, have the common touch, soft-soap (Inf)

11 **have good manners**, mind one's manners, behave well, behave properly, remain on one's best behaviour, treat with politeness, observe etiquette, mind one's p's and q's, have good breeding, show refinement, act like a gentleman, act like a lady, observe protocol, follow custom, use diplomacy, not give offence

12 **greet**, welcome, welcome home, welcome with open arms, advance to meet, salute, hail, wave, smile, hug, squeeze, embrace, kiss, blow a kiss, say hello, bid good day, raise one's hat (*or* cap), shake hands, clasp hands (US), squeeze one's hand, pump one's hand, honour, fire a salute, parade, present arms, turn out, give a hero's welcome, crown, wreathe, garland, fête, celebrate

13 **defer to**, treat with deference, pay respects, pay homage, make obeisance, comply, condescend, ingratiate oneself, act sycophantic, bow, curtsy, bob, nod, duck, touch one's forelock, doff one's hat, touch one's cap, kiss someone's hand, kneel, kowtow, salaam, prostrate oneself, toady to, fawn on, lay it on (Inf)

ADVERBS

14 **courteously**, with courtesy, politely, in a polite manner, civilly, agreeably, affably, amiably, graciously, humbly, considerately, thoughtfully, solicitously, decently, tactfully, discreetly, generously, benevolently, charitably, accommodatingly, leniently, gently, mildly, good-humouredly, obligingly, amenably, sociably, kindly, with kindness, sweetly, nicely, gallantly, chivalrously, courtly, knightly, like a knight in shining armour, gracefully, with good grace, old-worldly

15 **genteelly**, correctly, urbanely, elegantly, conventionally, suavely, blandly, smoothly, politely, respectfully, considerately, thoughtfully, as a thoughtful gesture, generously, benevolently, solicitously, decently, tactfully, discretely, charitably, accommodatingly, formally, ceremoniously, diplomatically

16 **deferentially**, with deference, obeisantly, compliantly, condescendingly, complaisantly, glibly, fulsomely, sycophantically, ingratiatingly, unctuously

818 Discourtesy

NOUNS

1 **discourtesy**, discourteousness, impoliteness, unpoliteness, incivility, inurbanity, disagreeableness, ungraciousness, ungallantness, uncourtliness, ungentlemanliness, thoughtlessness, shortness, inconsiderateness, lack of consideration, unsolicitousness, tactlessness, insensitivity, inattention, sullenness, excessive frankness, bluntness, acerbity, sharpness, tartness, asperity, gruffness, bluffness, roughness, harshness, severity, brusqueness, ungentleness, unfriendliness, unpleasantness, surliness, crustiness, nastiness, anger, ridicule, derision, mockery, raillery, scoffing, jeering, beastliness (Inf)

▶ *850 Disrespect, 552 Conciseness, 468 Inattention, 830 Sullenness, 799 Derision, 690 Severity, 828 Resentment; Anger*

2 **bad manners**, shocking manners, no manners, lack of manners, unmannerliness, want of chivalry, lack of politeness, scant courtesy, rudeness, insolence, impudence, truculence, churlishness, impatience, interruption, vulgarity, offensiveness, coarseness, boorishness, caddishness, grossness, gross behaviour, crudeness, loutishness, ill-breeding, misconduct, bad behaviour, conduct unbecoming, cheek (Inf), sauce (Inf), lip (Sl)

▶ *807 Insolence, 766 Dissatisfaction, 829 Irascibility, 795 Vulgarity*

3 **act of discourtesy**, short answer, angry reply, rebuff, insult, jeer, snub, abuse, rude gesture, V-sign, sticking out one's tongue, black look, sour look, scowl, frown, bad language, bad words, rude words, dirty joke, cold shoulder (Inf)

4 **discourteous person**, rude person, insolent person, fault-finder, boor, lout, brute, yahoo, savage, barbarian, no shining knight, no gentleman, mannerless imp, curmudgeon, bear, grouser, sulker, grouch (Inf), crosspatch (Inf), loudmouth (Inf), pig (Inf), bellyacher (Sl), yob (*or* yobbo) (Sl), nerd (US sl), shithouse (Tab sl)

ADJECTIVES

5 **discourteous**, impolite, uncivil, disagreeable, inurbane, ungracious, ungallant, uncourtly, ungentlemanly, ungentlemanlike, unladylike, unfeminine, unpleasant, surly, sullen, crusty, nasty, unkind, thoughtless, offhanded, inconsiderate, unsolicitous, tactless, insensitive, inattentive, cavalier, abusive, vituperative, not anxious to please, unsmiling, grim, unneighbourly, unsociable, unfriendly, uncomplimentary, unflattering, disrespectful, familiar, gruff, blunt, over-blunt, over-frank, harsh, severe, ungentle, rough, rugged, brutal, brusque, curt, short, abrupt, impatient, discontented, peevish, testy, acerbic, sharp, sharp-tongued, tart, snappy, biting, growling, bearish, acrimonious, aggressive, beastly (Inf), cold-shoulder (Inf)

6 **bad-mannered**, ill-mannered, unmannerly, unchivalrous, badly behaved, rude, insolent, impudent, impertinent, saucy, churlish, truculent, abusive, cursing, obstreperous, forward, irascible, difficult, vulgar, offensive, injurious, coarse, boorish, caddish, gross, crude, loutish, ill-bred, unrefined, uncouth, uncultured, barbarian, savage, foul-mouthed, growling, grumbling, swearing, cheeky (Inf), sassy (US inf), lippy (US sl)

VERBS

7 **be discourteous**, not respect, ruffle feelings, show no regard for someone's feelings, abuse, affront, outrage, take liberties, make free with, make bold, treat rudely, have no manners, display bad manners, flout etiquette, cause offence, insult, know no better, refuse to say

thank you, refuse to say sorry, stare, ogle, gaze, ignore, interrupt, cut, snub, look right through, have no time for, turn one's back on, make unwelcome, show the door, behave badly, behave cheekily (Inf), cut dead (Inf), cold-shoulder (Inf), give someone lip (Sl)

▶ *349 Expulsion*

8 **get angry**, be sullen, pout, glower, lour (*or* lower), frown, scowl, growl, curse, swear, shout down, lose one's temper, rant, hit the roof, blow one's top (Inf), blow one's lid (*or* stack) (US inf)

ADVERBS

9 **discourteously**, without courteousness, impolitely, uncivilly, uncourtly, ungallantly, ungraciously, ungentlemanly, unlike a gentleman, charmlessly, without charm, disagreeably, unchivalrously, unpleasantly, in an unpleasant manner, sullenly, sulkily, nastily, unkindly, thoughtlessly, offhandedly, inconsiderately, tactlessly, insensitively, inattentively, abusively, vituperatively, grimly, unsociably, without warmth, impatiently, discontentedly, peevishly, gruffly, bluntly, harshly, severely, ungently, roughly, brutally, brusquely, curtly, abruptly, tartly, sharply, in a sharp tone, angrily, with (*or* in) anger, crossly, acrimoniously, aggressively

10 **rudely**, disrespectfully, without respect, insolently, impudently, impertinently, saucily, churlishly, abusively, with a volley of abuse, obstreperously, irascibly, vulgarly, offensively, in an offensive way, injuriously, coarsely, boorishly, like a boor, caddishly, loutishly, grossly, crudely, uncouthly, savagely, derisively, mockingly, scoffingly, jeeringly, cheekily (Inf), yobbishly (Sl), like a yob (Sl), like a nerd (US sl)

819 Friendship

Two are better than one; because they have a good reward for their labour./ For if they fall, the one will lift up his fellow: but woe to him that is alone when he falleth; for he hath not another to help him up. Bible: Ecclesiastes.

It is not so much our friends' help that helps us as the confident knowledge that they will help us. Epicurus.

These are called the pious frauds of friendship. Henry Fielding.

NOUNS

1 **friendship**, fellowship, companionship, amicableness, amicability, amiableness, amity, acquaintanceship, camaraderie, fraternization, comradeship, colleagueship, togetherness, solidarity, cooperation, concord, harmony, friendliness, making friends, sociability, neighbourliness, goodwill, benevolence, philanthropy, kindness, kindliness, hospitality, warmth, warm-heartedness, warmness, ar-

dency, love, cordiality, courtesy, regard, heartiness, bonhomie, geniality, brotherhood, fraternalism, fraternity, sodality, confraternity, brotherly interest, freemasonry, sorority, sisterhood, sisterly interest, partiality, prejudice, favouritism, partisanship, support, loyal support, mateyness (Inf), palliness (Inf), chuminess (Inf)

▶ *667 Agreement, 664 Cooperation, 815 Sociability, 831 Benevolence, 833 Philanthropy, 677 Pacification, 821 Love, 817 Courtesy, 401 Male, 402 Female*

2 **friendly relations**, compatibility, harmony, rapport, sympathy, understanding, good understanding, fellow feeling, community of interest, esprit de corps, mutual support, mutual respect, mutual regard, mutual good will, entente, entente cordiale, good terms, two minds with but a single thought, hands across the sea

3 **familiarity**, intimacy, fast friendship, close friendship, warm friendship, passionate friendship, closeness, nearness, inseparability, affinity, special affinity, devotion, devotedness, dedication, steadfastness, commitment, firmness, staunchness, constancy, trueness, triedness

▶ *694 Obedience, 7 Religion*

4 **act of friendship**, vow of loyalty, toast, handshake, handclasp (US), embrace, hug, kiss, peck on the cheek, rubbing noses, open arms, holding hands, dining together

5 **friend**, mutual friend, acquaintance, companion, fellow, fellow creature, colleague, comrade, shipmate, messmate, playmate, roommate, classmate, schoolmate, schoolfellow, amigo, friend in need (is a friend indeed), circle of friends, butty (Dial), crony (Inf), chum (Inf), pal (Inf), mate (Inf), my man (US Black inf), buddy (US inf), sidekick (Inf)

6 **close friend**, best friend, dear friend, intimate friend, childhood friend, lifelong friend, friend of the family, girlfriend, boyfriend, boon companion, intimate, confidant (*or* confidante), familiar, brother, sister, best man, bridesmaid, maid (*or* matron) of honour, alter ego, other self, shadow, stable companion, mutual friends, inseparables, birds of a feather, two peas in a pod, bosom pal (Inf), bosom buddy (US inf)

▶ *206 Youth, 823 Marriage*

7 **famous friendships**, Achilles and Patroclus, Castor and Pollux, Damon and Pythias, David and Jonathan, Nisus and Euryalus, Lewis Carroll and Alice, Wordsworth and Coleridge, Robinson Crusoe and Friday, John Smith and Pocahontas, Tom Sawyer and Huckleberry Finn, Don Quixote and Sancho Panza, the Three Musketeers, the Lone Ranger and Tonto

ADJECTIVES

8 **friendly**, friendlike, cordial, courteous, amicable, amiable, kindly, kind, peaceable, unhostile, sociable, affectionate, gracious, harmonious, pleasant, congenial, compatible, cooperative, agreeable, favourable, hospitable, demonstrative, effusive, back-slapping, ardent, warm, warm-hearted, well-meaning, genial, well-disposed, well-intended, generous, benevolent, philanthropic, companionable, fraternal, confraternal, brotherly, sisterly, neighbourly, welcoming, receptive, hearty, sympathetic, understanding, comradely, simpatico (Inf), matey (Inf), chummy (Inf), pally (Inf), palsy-walsy (Sl), buddy-buddy (Sl)

9 **friends with**, friendly with, acquainted, at home with, in favour, on good terms with, on a good footing, on the right side of, in the good graces of, in the good books of, regarded highly by, in (good) with (Inf)

10 **familiar**, on familiar terms, intimate, on intimate terms, close, near, inseparable, arm in arm, hand in hand, hand in glove, free and easy, on visiting terms, on a first-name basis, favourite, hail-fellow-well-met, thick (Inf), thick as thieves (Inf)

11 **devoted**, dedicated, supportive, loyal, true, tried-and-true, tested, faithful, steadfast, constant, committed, firm, fast, staunch, trustful, trustworthy

12 **favourable**, beneficial, helpful, promising, auspicious, propitious, advantageous, useful, profitable

VERBS

13 **befriend**, be friendly with, make friends, make friends with, win friends, cultivate friends, strike up a friendship, strike up an acquaintance, gain the friendship of, have friends, enjoy friendship with, fraternize with, hobnob with, have a wide acquaintance with, get to know, get acquainted, break the ice, make overtures, win friends, win friends and influence people, warm to, show benevolence, have dealings with, keep company with, go around with, become inseparable, stay on good terms, take up with (Inf), knock about with (Inf), get chummy with (Inf), get pally with (Inf), buddy up with (Inf), hit it off with (Inf), become as thick as thieves (Inf)

14 **seek the friendship of**, make friendly overtures to, extend the hand of friendship, seek the company of, make advances, court, pay court to, pay addresses to, woo, run after, date, take out, go out with, make up to (Inf), play up to (Inf), frat (Inf), cotton up (or on) to (US inf), shine up to (US inf), suck up to (Sl)

15 **be hospitable**, entertain friends, serve as host (or hostess), act as host (or hostess), entertain, greet, shake hands, clasp hands (US), welcome, welcome with open arms, embrace,

introduce, acquaint, present, make a toast, carve, serve, do the honours

16 **be favourable**, provide a benefit, help, promise, seem propitious, serve a use, profit

ADVERBS

17 **in friendship**, in a friendly way, in a friendly spirit, as friends, cordially, courteously, with a courteous manner, amicably, amiably, peaceably, sociably, affectionately, with affection, graciously, harmoniously, pleasantly, under pleasant circumstances, compatibly, cooperatively, agreeably, favourably, kindly, with kindness, hospitably, effusively, ardently, warmly, with warmth, warm-heartedly, with a warm heart, heartily, genially, generously, benevolently, fraternally, receptively, with open arms, sympathetically

18 **intimately**, in an intimate fashion, familiarly, closely, inseparably, arm in arm, hand in hand, hand in glove

19 **devotedly**, with devotion, supportively, in support, loyally, from loyalty, with loyalty, truly, faithfully, steadfastly, constantly, committedly, firmly, fastly, staunchly, trustfully, in (or with) good trust, trustworthily

20 **favourably**, beneficially, helpfully, with a helping hand, promisingly, with promise, auspiciously, propitiously, advantageously, usefully, profitably, in a profitable way

820 Enmity

NOUNS

1 **enmity**, hostility, aggression, unfriendliness, inimicality, uncordiality, coolness, iciness, coldness, chilliness, frostiness, unamiability, ungeniality, disaffinity, antipathy, animosity, abhorrence, animus, opposition, incompatibility, aggression, bellicosity, antagonism, repugnance, conflict, contention, collision, clash, clashing, friction, quarrelling, quarrelsomeness, dissension, belligerence, a bone to pick, hate, hatred, dislike, loathing, malice, malevolence, malignity, spite, spitefulness, despitefulness, virulence, venom, vitriol, intolerance, bigotry, prejudice, persecution, racism, colour bar, segregation, apartheid, anti-Semitism

▶ *816 Unsociability, 663 Opposition, 674 Contention, 409 Cold, 670 Attack, 822 Hate, 832 Malevolence*

2 **personal conflict**, strain, tension, envy, jealousy, the green-eyed monster, estrangement, alienation, separation, disloyalty, unfaithfulness, breach, breach of friendship, divorce

▶ *842 Envy*

3 **ill feeling**, ill will, acrimony, bitterness, rancour, sourness, soreness, resentment, hard feelings, bad blood, no love lost, grudge, peev-

ishness, aversion, abomination, odium, detestation, phobia

4 **act of hostility**, war, state of war, conflict, hostilities, vendetta, feud, blood feud, *casus belli* (L)

5 **hostile person**, misanthropist, misanthrope, misogynist, woman-hater, misandrist, man-hater, misogamist, enemy, sworn enemy, archenemy, no friend, foe, adversary, opponent, rival, competitor, contender, antagonist, traitor, public enemy (number one), combatant, aggressor, invader, tergiversator, troublemaker, ill-wisher, secret enemy, Trojan horse, viper in one's bosom, xenophobe, Anglophobe, Francophobe, anti-Semite, racist, bigot

ADJECTIVES

6 **hostile**, unfriendly, inimical, uncordial, cool, icy, cold, chilly, frosty, aloof, inhospitable, unsociable, antisocial, unsympathetic, unamiable, ungenial, discordant, strained, tense, unharmonious, ill-disposed, acrimonious, antipathetic, bitter, embittered, rancorous, sour, sore, resentful, grudging, peevish, envious, jealous, green-eyed, green (with envy), malevolent, malicious, malignant, full of hate, spiteful, virulent, venomous, vitriolic, acrid, caustic, baneful

7 **intolerant**, persecuting, oppressive, racist (*or* racialist), prejudiced, bigotted, xenophobic, Anglophobic, Francophobic, anti-Semitic

8 **estranged**, alienated, separated, irreconcilable, distant, disloyal, unfaithful, disaffected, not well inclined, at variance, divided, disunited, torn, on bad terms, not on speaking terms, in someone's bad books, in someone's black books, in bad odour with, on one's shitlist (Tab sl)

9 **aggressive**, antagonistic, repugnant, conflicting, contentious, clashing, opposing, opposed, quarrelsome, dissenting, belligerent, bellicose, at war with, militant, at daggers drawn, at loggerheads, at odds with, at each other's throats, at cross-purposes, at sixes and sevens

10 **hated**, hateful, disliked, loathed, scorned, abominated, detested, abhorred, abhorrent, odious

VERBS

11 **be hostile**, bear ill will, bear malice, bear a grudge, owe a grudge, hold it against, resent, grudge, take offence, take umbrage, harden one's heart, hate, detest, loathe, scorn, abhor, execrate, abominate, shudder at

12 **oppose**, oppress, persecute, hound, hunt down, clash, collide, conflict, quarrel, dissent, differ, fall out, come to blows, fight, feud, make war on, wage war, battle

13 **antagonize**, make enemies, set against, provoke, estrange, cause offence, irritate, infuriate, madden, divide, disunite, alienate, set at

each other's throats, aggravate, heat up, embitter, make bad blood, set at odds

ADVERBS

14 **hostilely**, with enmity, inimically, uncordially, coolly, coldly, frostily, unsympathetically, without sympathy, unkindly, inhospitably, unsociably, antisocially, unamiably, alone, ungenially, discordantly, unharmoniously, unfaithfully, disloyally, disaffectedly, bitterly, with bitterness, acrimoniously, rancorously, sourly, resentfully, grudgingly, peevishly, enviously, with envy, jealously, intolerantly, oppressively

15 **aggressively**, antagonistically, with antagonism, contentiously, hatefully, malevolently, spitefully, in a spiteful way, venomously, vitriolically, acridly, caustically, banefully

821 Love

NOUNS

1 **love**, affection, natural affection, sentiment, fondness, liking, like, attachment, devotion, parental love, filial love, maternal love, paternal love, adoration, worship, hero worship, admiration, fascination, idolization, idolatry, firm attachment, regard, popular regard, popularity, respect, brotherly love, Christian love, Christian charity, charity, Agape, spiritual love, Platonic love, friendship, loyalty, compatibility, fellow feeling, understanding, mutual understanding, mutual affection, mutual attraction, mutual love, love for one's country, patriotism, self-love, narcissism, egotism

▶ *759 Feeling, 784 Liking, 819 Friendship, 831 Benevolence, 760 Sensitivity, 849 Respect, 833 Philanthropy*

2 **romantic love**, ardour, ardency, fervour, ecstasy, transport, transport of love, light of love, infatuation, dawn of love, first love, young love, calf love, puppy love, fancy, passing fancy, love-hate relationship, fascination, enchantment, bewitchment, possessive love, possessiveness, jealousy, free love, true love, the real thing, faithful love, sexual love, lust, married love, conjugal love, uxoriousness, Cupid's string, Oedipus complex, Electra complex, crush (Inf), mush (Inf), shine (Inf), pash (Sl)

▶ *694 Obedience*

3 **lovingness**, amorousness, amativeness, affectionateness, tenderness, kindness, sentiment, sentimentality, sentimental attachment, demonstrativeness, feeling, tender feeling, susceptibility, emotion, romanticism, lovesickness, lovelornness

4 **lovability**, lovableness, loveliness, likability, amiability, agreeability, attractiveness, beauty, appeal, sweetness, charm, charms, endearment, adorability, desirability, sex appeal, sex-

iness, flirtatiousness, coquetry, enchantment, allurement, winsomeness, winning ways, gift of pleasing, pleasing qualities, endearing qualities

▶ *789 Beauty*

5 **desire**, lust, passion, yearning, longing, abnormal affection, itching, amorousness, aphrodisia, flames of love, flame, fire of love, lasciviousness, licentiousness, caprice, ecstasy, intimacy, bodily love, desires of the flesh, lovemaking, making love, sex, libido, sexual urge, sexual love, act of love, sex act, sexual intercourse, sexual relations, sexual union, pairing, connection, copula (Fml), coupling, copulation, coition, coitus, cohabitation, fornication, carnal knowledge, sleeping together, sleeping with, marital relations, marriage act, mating, consummation, sexiness, eroticism, erotomania, wantonness, libertinage, prurience, venery (Arch), fucking (Tab), sleeping around (Inf), diddling (Inf), randiness (Inf), horniness (Sl), making someone (Sl), making it with (Sl), nooky (Sl), screwing (Sl), bonking (Sl), rogering (Sl), balling (US tab sl), humping (Sl), rumpy-pumpy (Sl), having it off (Sl), getting one's leg over (Sl)

▶ *877 Immorality*

6 **courtship**, pursuit of love, pursuit of a loved one, courting, wooing, dating, suit, going together, going with, going out, taking out, walking out (Dial), flirtation, flirtatiousness, flirting, coquetry, coyness, dalliance, dallying, toying, sheep's eyes, coquettish glances, sly looks, ogle, side-glance, flattering, honeying, pressing one's suit, laying siege, gallantry, hoping for conquest, advances, addresses, billing and cooing, sighing, proposing, proposal, bestowal of love, favours, suing (Arch), going steady (Inf), getting pinned (US inf), come-hither look (Inf), necking (Inf), lollygagging (US inf), fooling around (Inf), making out (US inf), making whoopee (Inf), petting (Inf), smooching (Inf), smoodging (*or* smooging) (Aus and NZ inf), spooning (Sl), goo-goo eyes (Sl), poodle-faking (Sl)

▶ *826 Endearment*

7 **choice**, preference, sympathy, predilection, inclination, tendency

▶ *580 Selection*

8 **love affair**, romance, relationship, amour, liaison, intrigue, flirtation, seduction, illicit love, eternal triangle, *ménage à trois* (Fr), forbidden love, affair, affair of the heart, adultery, infidelity, unfaithfulness, cuckoldry, romantic tie, entanglement, amourette, flirtation, falling in love, course of love, something between them, the old, old story, betrothal, engagement, wedding bells, espousal (Arch), hanky-panky (Inf)

▶ *823 Marriage*

9 **lover**, wooer, suitor, pursuer, paramour, amorist, sweetheart, conquest, captive, admirer, adorer, follower, aficionado, fan, pop fan, hero-worshipper, date, girlfriend, lass, goddess, temptress, dangerous woman, *femme fatale* (Fr), flirt, coquette, fiancée, bride-to-be, old girl, old lady, mistress, the other woman, lady in amorata, jo (Scot), Amaryllis, Dulcinea, boyfriend, young man, beau, fiancé, escort, squire, cavalier, gallant, old man, gigolo, seducer, lecher, libertine, ladies' man, woman-chaser, skirt-chaser, heartbreaker, philanderer, womanizer, Casanova, Don Juan, Lothario, Romeo, swain (Arch), strumpet (Arch), gill (Arch), blind date (Inf), steady (Inf), girl (Inf), dream girl (Inf), dream man (Inf), heart-throb (Inf), catch (Inf), (old) flame (Inf), gold-digger (Inf), vamp (Inf), lady-killer (Inf), wolf (Inf), sheik (*or* sheikh) (Inf), dreamboat (Sl), bird (Sl), sweet potato (pie) (US Black sl), fella (US sl), man (*or* woman) on the make (Sl), make-out artist (US sl), masher (Sl), sugar daddy (Sl), teenybopper (Sl), groupie (Sl)

10 **lovers**, soul mates, mutual lovers, loving couple, engaged couple, turtledoves, star-crossed lovers, tragic loves, Romeo and Juliet, Daphnis and Chloe, David and Bathsheba, Antony and Cleopatra, Harlequin and Columbine, Benedick and Beatrice, Pyramus and Thisbe, Hero and Leander, Tristan and Isolde, Lancelot and Guinevere, Paris and Helen, Troilus and Cressida, Heloise and Abelard, Dante and Beatrice, Heathcliff and Cathy, Napoleon and Josephine, Lord Nelson and Lady Hamilton, King Edward and Wallis Simpson, Scarlett and Rhett, lovebirds (Inf)

11 **loved one**, love, true love, beloved, dearly beloved, beloved object, object of one's affections, light of one's life, dear love, well-beloved, valentine, soul mate, favoured suitor, favourite, preference, apple of one's eye, lucky man, man after one's own heart, kept woman, mistress, jewel in the crown, future, betrothed, bride-to-be, idol, matinée idol, pop star, hero, heroine, spoiled child, teacher's pet, family pet, cosset, blue-eyed boy (Inf), intended (Inf), bit on the side (Inf)

12 **nicknames for lovers**, love names, terms of endearment, love, lover, darling, dear, dear heart, precious, precious heart, cherub, angel, chickabiddy, lamb, honey (US), pet, poppet, sweetheart, sweetie (Inf), sweets (Inf), sweetkins (Inf), cookie (US inf), deary (*or* dearie) (Inf), honeybunch (US inf), lovey (Inf), sugar (US inf), petkins (Inf), snookums (Inf), honey child (US inf), lambkins (Inf), duck (*or* ducks) (Inf), ducky (Inf), hon (US sl), baby (Sl), baby doll (Sl), babe (US sl), chick (Sl), doll (Sl)

13 **abode of love**, love nest, bower, bower of bliss, boudoir, honeymoon suite, honeymoon

cottage, bridal suite, nuptial chamber, bridal bed, woman's quarters, gynaeceum, zenana, harem, seraglio

14 **communication of love**, loving words, sweet talk, soft words, honeyed words, sweet nothings, flattery, blandishments, pet names, pretty names, billing and cooing, loving looks, fond look, amorous glance, side-glance, ogle, languishing look, sheep's eyes, wink, coquettish smile, loving touch, cuddling, tickling, snuggling, hugging, embracing, nuzzling, squeezing, caressing, fondling, bundling, kissing, kiss, osculation, French kiss, smack, smack on the lips, lovebite, bearhug, poke, pat, love slap, pinch, nip, tickle, stroke, hug, embrace, squeeze, clasp, enfoldment, caress, cuddle, nuzzle, fondle, buss (Dial), petting (Inf), necking (Inf), smooching (Inf), smoodging (or smooging) (Aus and NZ inf), peck (Inf), peck on the cheek (Inf), nibble (Inf), (a bit of) slap and tickle (Inf), footsie (Inf), smacker (Sl), spooning (Sl), groping (Sl), grope (Sl), goose (Sl)

15 **love item**, love token, ribbon, pin, love letter, billet-doux, love poem, love sonnet, love song, serenade, love lyric, amorous ditty, caterwauling, valentine, aubade

16 **gods and goddesses of love**, Venus, Aphrodite, Astarte, Freya (or Freyja), Cupid, Eros, Amor, Kama

ADJECTIVES

17 **loving**, amorous, amative, affectionate, demonstrative, fond, attached, devoted, kind, friendly, amicable, sympathetic, charitable, agapistic, sentimental, faithful, loyal, uxorious, motherly, paternal, fraternal, platonic, charitable, Christian, brotherly, patriotic

18 **in love**, falling in love, head over heels in love, happily in love, blissfully in love, in love with, infatuated with, smitten (with), bitten, taken with, enamoured of, fond of, sweet on, keen on (or about), mad about, set on, attached to, engaged to, wedded to, caught, have a thing about (Inf), wild about (Inf), crazy about (Inf), nuts about (Sl), stuck on (Sl), sold on (Sl), (far) gone on (Sl), hipped on (US sl), hooked (Sl)

19 **enamoured**, attracted, charmed, becharmed, fervent, doting, devoted, gallant, enslaved, ensnared, enraptured, rapturous, infatuated, enchanted, captivated, fascinated, bewitched, besotted, mad, insane, crazed, lovesick, lovelorn, languishing, smitten, heartsmitten

20 **amorous**, amatory, romantic, sentimental, emotional, tender, soft, adoring, melting, flirtatious, flirty, coquettish, seductive, coy, passionate, lustful, ardent, yearning, longing, moping, mooning, desirous, lascivious, capricious, ecstatic, excited, erotic, sexy, sexual, alluring, erogenous, sexually enslaving, ensnaring, possessive, jealous, randy (Inf), horny (Sl)

21 **beloved**, loved, well-beloved, dearly loved, cherished, adored, esteemed, revered, preferred, fancied, favourite, chosen, pet, darling, dear, prized, treasured, dear to one's heart, after one's heart, admired, regarded, respected, well-liked, liked

22 **lovable**, loveworthy, lovesome, charming, endearing, adorable, appealing, interesting, intriguing, enchanting, captivating, beguiling, desirable, tempting, alluring, seductive, beautiful, lovely, winsome, sweet, winning, pleasing, engaging, graceful, angelic, seraphic, divine, kissable, cuddly, cuddlesome, caressable, huggable, popular, likable, congenial, compatible, to one's taste, to one's fancy, to one's mind

VERBS

23 **love**, dearly love, have love (only) for, love to distraction, adore, be sweet on, cherish, relish, treasure, hold dear, prize, value, esteem, have a high regard for, appreciate, like, desire, fancy, have a fancy for, have eyes for, go for, care for, have a soft spot for, have a weakness for, have a fondness for, hold in affection, make much of, revere, admire, idolize, worship, take pleasure in, delight in, take an interest in, feel for, think the world of, have a kind heart, have a kindness for, sympathize with

24 **be in love**, be sweet on, dote on, lose one's heart, have an infatuation, cling to, embrace, become enamoured with, fall for, yearn for, long for, become attached to, fall head over heels in love, burn (with love), sweat, faint, die of (or for) love, burn with love, burn with passion, flame with passion, warm to, take to, take a fancy to, take a liking to, have a mash on (Arch), be crazy about (Inf), have a crush on (Inf), take a shine to (Inf), cotton to (US inf), have it bad (Inf)

25 **be loved**, be courted, have many dates, become a favourite, steal every heart, break hearts, arouse, rouse, stir, excite, warm, heat up, inflame, draw interest, turn heads, turn on (Sl)

26 **court**, go courting, pay court to, woo, squire, escort, pursue, chase, press one's suit, bestow one's affections, lay siege to, set one's cap at (or for), lose one's heart, date, go out with, walk out with, have a date, make a date, make addresses, make advances, make passes, philander, tempt, tantalize, bait, lure, flirt, tease, trifle, dally, toy, draw on, lead on, coquet, vamp, make eyes, wink, ogle, whisper sweet nothings, sigh, serenade, run around, play around, declare one's love, offer one's heart to, sue (Arch), sweet-talk (Inf), give a come-hither look (Inf), go steady with (Inf), get pinned (US inf), pin (US inf), spoon (Sl), turn on (Sl)

27 **kiss**, blow a kiss, give a French kiss, smack, buss (Dial), osculate, bill and coo, pat the head, pat the cheek, pat the bottom, chuck under the

chin, caress, cuddle, bundle, squeeze, fold, enfold, embrace, embosom, press (*or* clasp) to one's bosom, throw one's arms around, take into one's arms, fold to one's heart, stroke, snuggle (up), nestle (up), nuzzle (up), fondle, drool over, slobber over, dandle, coddle, cosset, pet (Inf), neck (Inf), smooch (Inf), smoodge (*or* smooge) (Aus and NZ inf), fool around (Inf), play footsie (Inf), make out (US inf), make whoopee (Inf), lollygag (US inf), have a bit of slap and tickle (Inf), spoon (Sl)

28 **win the love of**, enamour, enchant, becharm, charm, beguile, captivate, fascinate, enrapture, enthral, hold in thrall, bewitch, allure, attract, make oneself attractive, appeal, endear oneself, ingratiate oneself, flatter, curry favour, worm oneself into the affections, carry away, sweep off one's feet, turn one's head, flutter someone's heart, dazzle, bedazzle, ensnare, win the affection of, win the love of, win the heart of, take the fancy of, make a conquest, catch, propose (marriage), become engaged, ask for one's hand, announce one's engagement, publish the banns, marry, honeymoon, plight one's troth (Arch), make (*or* score) a hit (Inf), bowl over (Inf), pop the question (Inf), lead to the altar (Inf)

29 **make love**, have sex, have intercourse, sleep with, sleep together, bestow one's favours, mate, couple, copulate, cohabit, fornicate, fuck (Tab), sleep around (Inf), diddle (Inf), have one's way with, make someone (Sl), make it with (Sl), have it off (with) (Sl), screw (Sl), ball (US tab sl)

ADVERBS

30 **lovingly**, with love, with all one's love, fondly, with fondness, affectionately, with affection, tenderly, dearly, amorously, adoringly, in an affectionate way, devotedly, charitably, with charity, faithfully, fervently, romantically, with romance, sentimentally, dotingly, emotionally, under an emotional strain, with great emotion, attractively, flirtatiously, coquettishly, seductively, jealously, passionately, ardently, madly, lustfully, with lust, in heat, lasciviously, sexily, lovably, charmingly, with great charm, endearingly, adorably, appealingly, excitedly, enchantingly, captivatingly, dazzlingly, desirably, temptingly, alluringly, tantalizingly, seductively, kindly, sympathetically, with a come-hither look (Inf)

---

822 Hate

We can scarcely hate any one that we know.
William Hazlitt.

Few people can be happy unless they hate some other person, nation or creed. Bertrand Russell.

NOUNS

1 **hate**, hatred, dislike, aversion, loathing, detestation, spleen, disfavour, displeasure, disaffection, disapproval, disapprobation, repugnance, revulsion, repulsion, disgust, abhorrence, abomination, antipathy, antagonism, animosity, enmity, hostility, odium, execration, spite, spitefulness, malice, malice aforethought, malevolence, malediction, malignity, bitterness, gall, rancour, acrimony, ill nature, ill feeling, ill will, ill wishes, bad wishes, sullenness, resentment, grudge, hard feelings, jealousy, envy, the green-eyed monster, venom, virulence, bad blood, bone to pick, baring one's fangs, despitefulness (Arch)

▶ *785 Dislike, 820 Enmity, 852 Disapproval, 666 Disagreement, 832 Malevolence, 830 Sullenness, 828 Resentment; Anger, 842 Envy*

2 **curse**, voodoo curse, spell, evil spell, evil eye, hex, pishogue, whammy (Sl), double whammy (Sl)

▶ *827 Curse*

3 **race (*or* racial) hatred**, racism (*or* racialism), colour prejudice, segregation, apartheid, prejudice, bigotry, anti-Semitism, racial phobia, xenophobia, Anglophobia, Francophobia

▶ *493 Misjudgment*

4 **hatefulness**, loathsomeness, obnoxiousness, despicability, contemptibility, unpopularity, alienation, estrangement, discredit, disrepute, black books, bad books, bad odour, beastliness (Inf), shitlist (Tab sl)

▶ *850 Disrespect, 801 Disrepute, 581 Rejection*

5 **anger**, burst of anger, wrath, rage, tears of rage, ire, fury, raging fury, temper, fit of temper, crossness, choler

6 **swearing**, cursing, profanity, shouting, foul mouth

7 **hated thing**, pet hate, pet aversion, abomination, anathema, bugbear, bitter pill, unwelcome necessity, embarrassing situation, phobia, fear, *bête noire* (Fr), filth, illness, injury, death, pet peeve (Inf)

▶ *777 Fear*

8 **hated person**, not one's type, menace, pest, devil, foe, enemy, sworn enemy, archenemy, tyrant, Hitler, Stalin, nobody's darling, shrew, virago, bane, heretic, blackleg, scab, public nuisance, public enemy, criminal, murderer, Dr Fell, dastard (Arch), cad (Inf), bastard (Inf), bad news (Sl), git (Sl), bitch (Derog sl)

▶ *663 Opposition, 679 Combatant*

9 **hater**, misanthrope, misanthropist, misogamist, misogynist, woman-hater, misandrist, man-hater, homophobe, bigot, racist (*or* racialist), anti-Semite, phobic, xenophobe, Anglophobe, Francophobe

▶ *834 Misanthropy*

ADJECTIVES

10 **hating**, hateful, full of hate, loathing, detest-

ing, abhorring, antipathetic, antagonistic, hostile, execrative, averse, spiteful, spleenful, vindictive, vicious, contemptuous, malicious, full of malice, malevolent, maledictive, malignant, rancorous, acrimonious, poisonous, bitter, sharp, ill-natured, set against, resentful, grudging, sour, sullen, jealous, envious, green-eyed, venomous, virulent

11 **racist** (*or* **racialist**), prejudiced, bigoted, anti-American, anti-Semitic, phobic, xenophobic, Anglophobic, Francophobic

12 **hated**, loathed, hateful, loathsome, not nice, detestable, disgusting, abhorrent, odious, obnoxious, despicable, contemptible, execrable, accursed, unlovable, invidious, unpopular, out of favour, discredited, disliked, unwelcome, unwanted, baneful, nasty, horrid, repugnant, revolting, repelling, abominable, disgusting, vile, repulsive, nauseous, nauseating, alien, strange, foreign, unloved, loveless, scorned, jilted, lovelorn, crossed in love, unvalued, unmissed, unlamented, unmourned, unchosen, spurned, condemned, in someone's bad books, in someone's black books, beastly (Inf), on someone's shitlist (Tab sl)

13 **angry**, wrathful, irate, furious, bad-tempered, in a bad temper, cross, choleric, implacable, profane, evil-speaking, cursing, swearing, foul-mouthed

VERBS

14 **hate**, dislike, have no love for, detest, utterly detest, loathe, find loathsome, abhor, execrate, hold in disgust, hold in contempt, despise, abominate, bear malice towards, take an aversion to, show displeasure, have hard feelings towards, disapprove, shudder at, turn away from, recoil at, shrink from, reject, spurn, refuse, not choose, object to, resent, bear a grudge, envy, disrelish, condemn, denounce, avoid, curse, have a bone to pick, bare one's fangs, have a down on (Inf), spit upon (Inf), have it in for (Inf), hate one's guts (Inf)

15 **curse**, cast a spell upon, give someone the evil eye, throw (*or* put) the whammy on (Sl), throw (*or* put) the double whammy on (Sl)

16 **cause hate**, excite hate, cause loathing, antagonize, aggravate, exacerbate, alienate, estrange, sour, envenom, embitter, poison, incense, enrage, disgust, repel, nauseate, make enemies, sow dissension, create bad blood, destroy good will, set by the ears, grate, jar, end up in someone's black books, mix it (Inf)

17 **anger**, have a burst of anger, rage, show ire, have a fit of temper, utter profanities, curse, swear, have a foul mouth, spit tacks (Aus sl)

ADVERBS

18 **hatefully**, in a hateful manner, loathingly, antipathetically, antagonistically, in an antagonistic way, hostilely, with hostility, execratively, aversely, spitefully, with spite, spleenfully, vindictively, viciously, contemptuously, with contempt, maliciously, with malice, malevolently, maledictively, malignantly, rancorously, acrimoniously, poisonously, bitterly, sharply, ill-naturedly, with an ill nature, resentfully, grudgingly, sourly, sullenly, jealously, enviously, venomously, virulently, obnoxiously, despicably, contemptibly, disreputably

823 Marriage

I married beneath me – all women do. Nancy Astor.

Happiness in marriage is entirely a matter of chance. Jane Austen.

Wives are young men's mistresses, companions for middle age, and old men's nurses. Francis Bacon.

He was reputed one of the wise men, that made answer to the question, when a man should marry? A young man not yet, an elder man not at all. Francis Bacon.

The majority of husbands remind me of an orangutang trying to play the violin. Honoré de Balzac.

Husbands, love your wives, and be not bitter against them. Bible: Colossians.

Let the husband render unto the wife due benevolence: and likewise also the wife unto the husband. Bible: I Corinthians.

But if they cannot contain, let them marry: for it is better to marry than to burn. Bible: I Corinthians.

Wherefore they are no more twain, but one flesh. What therefore God hath joined together, let not man put asunder. Bible: Matthew.

To have and to hold from this day forward, for better for worse, for richer for poorer, in sickness and in health, to love and to cherish, till death us do part. The Book of Common Prayer.

Marriage is distinctly and repeatedly excluded from heaven. Is this because it is thought likely to mar the general felicity? Samuel Butler.

Wedlock – the deep, deep peace of the double bed after the hurly-burly of the chaise-longue. Mrs Patrick Campbell.

The most happy marriage I can picture or imagine to myself would be the union of a deaf man to a blind woman. Samuel Taylor Coleridge.

SHARPER: Thus grief still treads upon the heels of pleasure:/ Marry'd in haste, we may repent at leisure./ SETTER: Some by experience find those

words mis-plac'd:/ At leisure marry'd, they repent in haste. William Congreve.

Every woman should marry – and no man. Benjamin Disraeli.

His designs were strictly honourable, as the phrase is; that is, to rob a lady of her fortune by way of marriage. Henry Fielding.

One fool at least in every married couple. Henry Fielding.

Then be not coy, but use your time;/ And while ye may, go marry:/ For having lost but once your prime,/ You may for ever tarry. Robert Herrick.

Marriage has many pains, but celibacy has no pleasures. Samuel Johnson.

I'm getting married in the morning!/ Ding dong! the bells are gonna chime./ Pull out the stopper!/ Let's have a whopper!/ But get me to the church on time! Alan Jay Lerner.

Strange to say what delight we married people have to see these poor fools decoyed into our condition. Samuel Pepys.

It doesn't much signify whom one marries, for one is sure to find next morning that it was someone else. Samuel Rogers.

For a light wife doth make a heavy husband. William Shakespeare.

Many a good hanging prevents a bad marriage. William Shakespeare.

My definition of marriage:....it resembles a pair of shears, so joined that they cannot be separated; often moving in opposite directions, yet always punishing anyone who comes between them. Sydney Smith.

Marriage is like life in this – that it is a field of battle, and not a bed of roses. Robert Louis Stevenson.

This I set down as a positive truth. A woman with fair opportunities and without a positive hump, may marry whom she likes. William Makepeace Thackeray.

Marriage is the only adventure open to the cowardly. Voltaire.

Marriage is a great instittition, but I'm not ready for an institution, yet. Mae West.

NOUNS

1 **marriage**, matrimony, holy matrimony, wedlock, holy wedlock, conjugality, union, sacrament of marriage, match, one flesh, alliance, married status, married state, wedded state, state of matrimony, conjugal bliss, nuptial bond, marriage tie, wedded bliss, weddedness, wifehood, husbandhood, spousehood, coverture (Fml), bridal bed, marriage bed, bridebed, cohabitation, living as man and wife, tying the knot (Inf), taking the plunge (Inf), getting hitched (Sl), shacking up (Sl)

▶ *135 Union, 7 Religion, 821 Love, 762 Joy*

2 **alliance**, merger, union, link, connection, consolidation, association, amalgamation, partnership, tie-up, hookup

▶ *135 Union*

3 **types of marriage**, monogamy, monogyny, monandry, polygamy, Mormonism, polygyny, polyandry, bigamy, digamy, deuterogamy, trigamy, second marriage, remarriage, morganatic marriage, marriage of convenience, *mariage de convenance* (Fr), love match, levirate, leviration, left-handed marriage, companionate marriage, trial marriage, common-law marriage, picture marriage, interfaith marriage, mixed marriage, intermarriage, interracial marriage, intercaste marriage, miscegenation, exogamy, endogamy, misalliance, mésalliance, spiritual marriage, free union, free love, compulsory marriage, arranged marriage, concubinage, homosexual marriage, lesbian marriage, marriage by proxy

4 **marriageability**, marriageableness, nubility, marriageable age, age of consent, ripeness, fitness for marriage, good match, proper match, suitable match, suitable party, eligible party, eligible bachelor

5 **wedding**, wedding ceremony, wedding service, white wedding, church wedding, nuptial Mass, nuptial benediction, marriage vows, nuptial vows, nuptials, hymenal rites, betrothal, spousal, civil wedding, civil ceremony, registry (*or* register) office wedding, court house wedding (US), marriage by the justice of the peace (US), solemn wedding, quiet wedding, elopement, Gretna Green wedding, Las Vegas wedding (US), forcible wedlock, espousal (Arch), tying the knot (Inf), shotgun wedding (Inf)

6 **general terms**, marriage licence, wedding announcement, wedding shower (US and Aus), wedding invitation, wedding rehearsal, wedding day, wedding morning, wedding bells, ring, wedding ring, wedding banns, wedding canopy, wedding march, wedding music, wedding song, marriage song, nuptial song, nuptial ode, hymeneal, prothalamium, epithalamium, marriage procession, wedding dress, wedding veil, saffron veil, saffron robe, wedding reception, bridal bouquet, wedding cake, wedding breakfast, marriage feast, marriage toast, wedding photographs, honeymoon, bridal chamber, honeymoon suite, bridal suite, marriage lines (Inf)

▶ *812 Celebration*

7 **bridal party**, bride, bridal attendant, brides-

maid, maid (*or* matron) of honour, young matron, attendant, flower girl, bridegroom, groom, best man, usher, page, pageboy, train-bearer

8 **spouse**, espouser, espoused, bride, blushing bride, war bride, bridegroom, groom, one's promised, one's betrothed, soul mate, helpmate, helpmeet, affinity, marriage partner, partner, faithful spouse, better half (Inf), GI bride (US inf)

9 **married couple**, the happy couple, bridal pair, newlyweds, honeymooners, man and wife, *vir et uxor* (L), one flesh, Mr and Mrs, Darby and Joan, Philemon and Baucis

10 **married man**, husband, househusband, consort, benedick, monogamist, monogynist, old man, lord and master, henpecked husband, injured husband, cuckold, second husband, much-married man, bigamist, polygamist, polygynist, Solomon, Mormon, Bluebeard, hubby (Inf), goodman (Arch)

11 **married woman**, wife, housewife, lady, good lady, old lady, matron, feme covert (Fml), second wife, wife in all but name, common-law wife, concubine, goodwife (Arch), goody (Arch), better half, missis (*or* missus) (Inf), trouble and strife (Inf), squaw (Inf), old dutch

12 **partner**, cohabitant, live-in lover, common-law wife (*or* husband)

13 **matchmaker**, marriage broker, *shadchan* (Yiddish), matrimonial agent, go-between, marriage adviser, marriage guidance counsellor, mediator, marriage bureau, dating agency, lonely hearts club, lonely hearts column, dating service, computer dating

▶ *678 Mediation*

14 **gods and goddesses of marriage**, Hymen, Hera, Juno, Teleia, Pronuba, Frigg

VERBS

15 **marry**, get married, wed, say "I do", couple, become one, affiance, publish the banns, contract matrimony, take a wife, ask for one's hand, take a husband, bestow one's hand upon, accept a proposal, take for better or for worse, quit the single state, elope, run away, cohabit, live together, live as man and wife, share one's bed and board, set up house together, honeymoon, go on honeymoon, consummate one's marriage, marry well, marry into money, make a good match, mismarry, make a bad match, marry in haste, repent at leisure, remarry, rewed, commit bigamy, intermarry, miscegenate, betroth (Arch), plight one's troth (Arch), espouse (Arch), wive (Arch), receive one's marriage lines (Inf), get spliced (Inf), tie the knot (Inf), take the plunge (Inf), make an honest woman of (Inf), lead to the altar (Inf), get hitched (Sl), hook up with (Sl)

16 **join in marriage**, join in holy wedlock, join, unite in holy wedlock, unite, celebrate a marriage, conduct the ceremony, conduct the wedding, read the wedding vows, read the wedding service, tie the wedding knot, tie the nuptial knot, make one, pronounce man and wife, give in marriage, give away, marry off, bestow in marriage

17 **matchmake**, make a match, match, mate, find a mate for, find a husband for, find a wife for, arrange a marriage

18 **live together**, cohabit, shack up with (Inf)

19 **merge**, unite, ally, link, connect, consolidate, associate, amalgamate, form a partnership, tie up with, hook up with

ADJECTIVES

20 **matrimonial**, marital, conjugal, connubial, nuptial, hymeneal, spousal, premarital, concubinal, concubinary, matronly, wifely, bridal, husbandly

21 **married**, wedded, united, espoused, partnered, joined, paired, coupled, mated, newlywed, matched, ill-matched, made man and wife, one, made one, one bone and one flesh, in double harness, remarried, hitched (Inf), spliced (Sl), hooked (Sl)

22 **marriageable**, nubile, eligible, suitable, fit for marriage, ripe for marriage, of (marriageable) age, betrothed, engaged, promised, affianced, plighted, spoken for

23 **monogamous**, bigamous, digamous, polygamous, polygynous, polyandrous, morganatic, miscegenetic

ADVERBS

24 **matrimonially**, in the way of marriage, in holy wedlock, like man and wife, maritally, conjugally, connubially, nuptially, in double harness, as one, monogamously, bigamously, with two wives, polygamously, morganatically

824   Divorce; Widowhood

NOUNS

1 **divorce**, divorcement, dissolution of marriage, divorce decree, decree nisi, decree absolute, annulment, decree of nullity, no marriage, breakdown of marriage, nonconsummation of marriage, broken marriage, broken home, marriage on the rocks, break-up, split-up, split, grass widowhood, grass widowerhood

▶ *136 Separation*

2 **separation**, legal separation, judicial separation, estrangement, living apart, desertion, impediment (Fml)

▶ *598 Relinquishment*

3 **divorce court**, divorce case, matrimonial cause, co-respondent, grounds for divorce, incompatibility, cruelty, mental cruelty, adul-

tery, divorce settlement, maintenance, alimony, custody of children, visiting rights

▶ *832 Malevolence, 877 Immorality, 741 Money*

4 **divorced person**, divorcer, divorced woman, divorcée, divorced man, divorcé, grass widow (*or* widower)

5 **widowhood**, widowerhood, weeds, widow's weeds, grass widowhood, grass widowerhood

▶ *397 Death, 295 Dress*

6 **surviving spouse**, survivor, widow, dowager, dowager queen, queen mother, war widow, grass widow, widow woman (Dial), merry widow, widower, grass widower, widowman (Dial), relic (Arch), golf widow (Inf), baseball widow (US inf)

VERBS

7 **divorce**, obtain a divorce, get divorced, dissolve one's marriage, separate, live separately, live apart, part, break up, split up, split, sever, come to a parting of the ways, unmarry, untie the knot, sue for divorce, file (suit) for divorce, grant a final decree, grant an annulment, grant a decree of nullity (Fml), annul a marriage, put asunder, put away, revert to the single state, revert to bachelorhood, regain one's freedom

8 **desert**, abandon, leave, walk out, come to a parting (of the ways)

9 **widow**, bereave, die before one's spouse, make a widow, make a widower, leave one's wife a widow, leave one's husband a widower

10 **be widowed**, outlive one's spouse, survive one's spouse, lose one's husband (*or* wife), mourn one's husband (*or* wife), put on widow's weeds

ADJECTIVES

11 **divorced**, dissolved, separated, legally separated, split, estranged, living apart, deserted, abandoned, on the rocks (Inf)

12 **widowed**, husbandless, widowered, wifeless, widowish, widowlike

ADVERBS

13 **without one's spouse**, without one's husband, without one's wife, by decree nisi (Fml), by decree absolute (Fml), by decree of nullity (Fml), by annulment, in estrangement, apart

825 Celibacy

NOUNS

1 **celibacy**, unmarried condition, unwed condition, singleness, single state, single blessedness, bachelorhood, spinsterhood, independence, misogamy, misogyny, misandry

▶ *698 Freedom, 834 Misanthropy*

2 **virginity**, chastity, continence, abstinence, life of abstinence, self-denial, lack of sex, maidenhood, maidenhead, purity

▶ *876 Morality*

3 **monasticism**, monastic order, celibate

order, holy orders, reclusive life, solitary state, Encratism, spiritual marriage, the veil

▶ *7 Religion*

4 **celibate person**, celibate, eunuch, religious celibate, Encratite, monk, monastic, priest, nun, bride of Christ, agamist, recluse, hermit, virgin, virgo intacta, vestal, vestal virgin, Virgin Mary, the Virgin, virtuous man, Galahad, virtuous woman, Lucretia, celibate goddess, Diana, Artemis

5 **single person**, single man (*or* woman), unmarried man (*or* woman), unwed man (*or* woman), unattached man (*or* woman), single, bachelor, confirmed bachelor, spinster (*or* spinstress), *femme sole* (Fml), debutant (*or* debutante), maiden, maiden lady, maid, single girl, bachelor girl, lone woman, maiden aunt, old maid, enemy of marriage, misogamist, misogynist, misandrist, (old) bach (Inf)

ADJECTIVES

6 **celibate**, celibatarian, unmarried, unwedded, unwed, single, sole (Fml), spouseless, wifeless, husbandless, unpartnered, unmated, mateless, spinsterly, spinsterish, spinsterlike, old-maidish, maiden, maidenly, bachelorly, bachelorlike, unwooed, unasked, unconsummated, independent, unattached, free, fancy-free, on the shelf, misogamic, misogynous, misandrous

▶ *683 Failure*

7 **virginal**, virgin, continent, abstinent, chaste, pure, innocent, maidenly, intact

8 **monastic**, monachal, monkish, nunnish, priestly, Encratite

VERBS

9 **be celibate**, practise celibacy, enforce celibacy on oneself, remain unmarried, stay single, live alone, have a bachelor's flat, have a bachelor's apartment (US), keep bachelor's hall, live in single blessedness, have no offers, receive no proposals, sit on the shelf, bach (it) (Inf)

10 **be continent**, be chaste, remain a virgin, abstain, stay pure, have no sex, forgo sex

11 **be monastic**, live like a monk, live like a nun, take the veil, take oneself to a nunnery, become a bride of Christ, take holy orders, live like a hermit

ADVERBS

12 **celibately**, singly, solitarily, by oneself, independently, freely, without obligations, virginally, continently, abstinently, chastely, purely, monastically, like a monk, like a nun

826 Endearment

NOUNS

1 **endearment**, affection, fondness, attachment, love, loving words, compliments, blandishments, flattery, sweet nothings, soft

words, honeyed words, pet name, pretty name, billing and cooing, kissing, kiss, osculation, French kiss, smack, lovebite, embrace, caress, hug, cuddle, squeeze, stroke, tickle, love slap, tap, pat, pinch, nip, fondling, bundling, smooching (Inf), smoodge (*or* smooge) (Aus and NZ inf), petting (Inf), necking (Inf), making out (US inf), making whoopee (Inf), lollygagging (US inf), fooling around (Inf), sweet-talk (Inf), peck (Inf), peck on the cheek (Inf), nibble (Inf), smacker (Sl), (a bit of) slap and tickle (Inf), footsie (Inf), spooning (Sl)

▶ *821 Love, 853 Flattery, 407 Touch*

2 **courtship**, courting, amorous pursuit, pursuit of a loved one, pursuit of love, dating, wooing, love-play, love suit, gallantry, addresses, advances, pass, dalliance, familiarity, going with, going together, going out, walking out (Dial), amourette, laying siege, pressing one's suit, hoping for conquest, bestowal of love, favours, flirtation, flirtatiousness, coquetry, philandering, fond look, amorous glance, side-glance, ogle, languishing look, sheep's eyes, proposal, offer of marriage, engagement, lovemaking (Arch), going steady (Inf), getting pinned (US inf), come-hither look (Inf), goo-goo eyes (Sl)

▶ *590 Pursuit, 435 Vision, 823 Marriage*

3 **love token**, ring, engagement ring, wedding ring, love letter, valentine, billet-doux, love poem, love sonnet, flowers, red roses, chocolates, candy, sweets

4 **terms of endearment**, darling, dear, dear heart, love, lover, sweetheart, pet, poppet, honey (US), precious, precious heart, cherub, angel, petal, chickabiddy, lamb, deary (*or* dearie) (Inf), lovey (Inf), cookie (US inf), sweetie (Inf), sweets (Inf), sweetkins (Inf), petkins (Inf), duck (*or* ducks) (Inf), ducky (Inf), lambkins (Inf), sugar (US inf), honeybun (US inf), honeybunch (US inf), honey child (US inf), hon (US sl), baby (Sl), baby doll (Sl), babe (US sl), chick (Sl), doll (Sl)

5 **courting person**, lover, girlfriend, boyfriend, sweetheart, wooer, beau, flirt, coquette, vamp, philanderer, pursuer, womanchaser, womanizer, skirt-chaser, ladies' man, heartbreaker, seducer, lecher, libertine, swain (Arch), heart-throb (Inf), gold-digger (Inf), lady-killer (Inf), wolf (Inf), man (*or* woman) on the make (Sl), make-out artist (US sl)

6 **object of endearment**, lover, teacher's pet, apple of one's eye, beloved parent, lovely child, spoiled darling, mother's darling, family pet, cosset, minion (Arch), blue-eyed boy (Inf)

VERBS

7 **show endearment for**, have affection for, attach oneself to, make much of, cherish, love, treasure, mother, smother, spoil, spoon-feed,

flatter, pamper, cosset, coddle, kill with kindness, pat on the head, chuck under the chin, brush the cheek, hug, embrace, clasp, hold in one's arms, hold tightly, press to one's bosom, fly into the arms of, cling, not let go, take in one's lap, cuddle (up), bundle (up), snuggle (up), nestle (up), nuzzle (up), kiss, give a French kiss, smack, osculate, blow a kiss, buss (Dial), pat, caress, squeeze, press, poke, pinch, goose, fondle, stroke, play with, be all over, tender (Arch), pet (Inf), paw (Inf), play footsie (Inf), neck (Inf), lollygag (US inf), make out (US inf), smooch (Inf), smoodge (*or* smooge) (Aus and NZ inf), snog (Sl)

8 **court**, go courting, pay court to, woo, pursue, chase, run after, set one's cap for (*or* at), wait on, pay attentions to, pay one's addresses to, pay suit to, press one's suit, make eyes at, cast eyes at, give the glad eye, make sheep's eyes, ogle, leer, eye, look one up and down, whisper sweet nothings, make overtures, make advances, flirt, trifle, dally, toy, play fast and loose, vamp, philander, become familiar, get fresh, make a pass, proposition, date, have a date, make a date, go out with, walk out with, hold hands, bill and coo, make love, propose, throw oneself at the feet of, offer one's heart, offer one's hand, ask for the hand of, plight one's troth, become engaged, announce one's engagement, publish the banns, sue (Arch), go steady with (Inf), get pinned (US inf), pin (US inf), pop the question (Inf), spoon (Sl)

ADJECTIVES

9 **endearing**, affectionate, demonstrative, sentimental, fond, loving, amorous, courting, wooing, pursuing, dating, familiar, flirtatious, flirty, coy, coquettish, toying, clinging, caressing, fondling, philandering, attached, engaged, pinned (US inf), sloppy (Inf), lovey-dovey (Inf)

ADVERBS

10 **endearingly**, affectionately, with affection, demonstratively, in a demonstrative way, sentimentally, fondly, lovingly, with love, in a loving manner, amorously, familiarly, on familiar terms, flirtatiously, coyly, coquettishly, with a coquettish look, caressingly

827 Curse

NOUNS

1 **curse**, curse word, oath, profanity, profanation, obscenity, vulgarity, scurrility, imprecation, dysphemism, naughty word, bad word, swearword, dirty word, four-letter word, expletive, invective, string of invectives, unrepeatable expression, ribaldry, bawdy verse, dirty joke, blue joke, dirty talk, filth, cursing, swearing, foul mouth, foul-mouthing, dirty mouth, billingsgate, scatology, blasphemy,

sacrilege, talking dirty, cuss (Inf), cuss word (Inf), no-no (Inf), tinker's damn (*or* cuss) (Sl), effing and blinding (Sl)

▶ *795 Vulgarity*

2 **offensive language**, bad language, indelicate language, unparliamentary language, colourful language, blue language, foul language, obscene language, profane language, strong language, vile language, dirty language, filthy language, Anglo-Saxon

3 **vilification**, vituperation, denunciation, fulmination, execration, revilement, scurrility, verbal abuse, volley of abuse, thundering, reproach, opprobrium, slander, libel, defamation, calumny, obloquy, threat, evil speaking, onslaught, attack, slanging match

▶ *856 Accusation, 852 Disapproval, 854 Disparagement, 850 Disrespect*

4 **malediction**, ill wishes, spell, voodoo spell, the evil eye, *maloccio* (It), curse, charm, jinx, imprecation, damnation, ban, excommunication, anathema, proscription, commination, malison (Arch), hex (US inf), whammy (Sl), double whammy (Sl)

▶ *832 Malevolence, 7 Religion, 11 Occultism*

VERBS

5 **curse**, use profanity, swear, curse and swear, talk filthy, talk dirty, tell dirty jokes, write bawdy poems, use bad language, use obscene language, use expletives, use billingsgate, scatologize, dysphemize, blaspheme, commit a sacrilege, take the Lord's name in vain, swear like a trooper, swear till one is blue in the face, make the air blue, cuss (Inf), eff and blind (Sl)

6 **vilify**, revile, denunciate, execrate, condemn, fulminate, rebuke, scold, chide, tongue-lash, abuse, heap abuse upon, pour vitriol upon, hurl a volley of abuse at, blackguard, accuse, reproach, vituperate, rail against, inveigh against, thunder, blast, damn and blast, slang, reproach, slander, libel, defame, call names, disgrace, threaten, attack, round upon, send to the devil, have a slanging match, give the rough edge of one's tongue to, send to blazes (Sl)

7 **wish ill**, put a spell on, put a curse on, call a curse down on, give the evil eye to, charm, put a jinx on, damn, curse up hill and down dale, imprecate, anathematize, ban, excommunicate, proscribe, curse with bell, book and candle, curse like hell (Inf), hex (US inf), put a hex on (US inf), throw (*or* put) a whammy on (Sl), throw (*or* put) a double whammy on (Sl)

ADJECTIVES

8 **cursing**, swearing, profane, obscene, vulgar, scurrilous, naughty, offensive, indelicate, blue, four-letter, Anglo-Saxon, invective, dirty, filthy, vile, indecent, ribald, bawdy, Rabelaisian, risque, raw (US), foul, foul-mouthed, foul-tongued, scatologic(al), dysphemistic, blasphemous, sacrilegious

9 **vituperative**, abusive, vitriolic, vilifying, reviling, denunciatory, denouncing, blasting, reproachful, ignominious, opprobrious, slanderous, libellous, defamatory, calumnious, attacking, threatening

10 **maledictive**, maledictory, imprecatory, damning, cursed, accursed, damned, wished on one, hexed, jinxed, under a spell, bewitched, unblest, execrative, under a ban, banned, excommunicated, proscribed, comminatory, hexed (US inf)

11 **miscellaneous euphemisms**, blessed, blamed (US), blankety-blank (Inf), confounded (Inf), dad-blamed (Inf), dad-blasted (Inf), dad-burned (Inf), doggone (US inf), deuced (Inf), darn (Inf), darned (Inf), goshdarn (Inf), goshdarned (Inf), dang (Inf), danged (Inf), durn (US dial), durned (US dial), ruddy (Inf), blasted (Sl), bloody (Sl), goldarn (US Sl), crikey (Sl), blazes (Sl), jeepers (creepers) (US sl)

ADVERBS

12 **swearingly**, profanely, obscenely, vulgarly, scurrilously, naughtily, offensively, with offence, indelicately, dirtily, vilely, indecently, in an indecent manner, ribaldly, bawdily, blasphemously, sacrilegiously

13 **vituperatively**, abusively, in an abusive manner, reproachfully, with reproach, slanderously, libellously, defamatorily, ignominiously, opprobriously

14 **damningly**, cursedly, as a curse, bewitchingly, by means of enchantment, while under a spell, execratively

INTERJECTIONS

15 **miscellaneous swearwords**, damn!, blast!, Christ!, Jesus Christ!, Christ Almighty!, Jesus wept!, bloody hell!, bugger it! (Tab), bugger off! (Tab), shit! (Tab), balls! (Tab), bollocks! (Tab), piss off! (Tab), fuck! (Tab), fuck it! (Tab), fuck me! (Tab), fuck off! (Tab), fuck you! (Tab), fucking hell! (Tab)

16 **euphemisms**, darn!, dang it!, gosh!, dadblast!, goshdarn!, the devil take it!, jeeperscreepers!, gee whiz!, gee whillikers! (US)

828 Resentment; Anger

NOUNS

1 **resentment**, bitterness, bitter resentment, burning resentment, resentfulness, rancour, rankling, acrimony, spleen, gall, acid, acidity, acidulousness, heart-burning, soreness, slow burn, grudge, malice, jealousy, envy, displeasure, dissatisfaction, disapproval, disapprobation, ill humour, animosity, hard feelings, ill feelings, irritation, vexation, discontent, annoyance, aggravation, exasperation, pique, peevishness, asperity, bone to pick

▶ *766 Dissatisfaction, 842 Envy, 366 Agitation, 764 Unpleasantness*

2 **offence**, umbrage, hurt, indignity, insult, affront, wrong, huff, dudgeon (Arch), high dudgeon (Arch), miff (Inf)

3 **cause of offence**, provocation, last straw, red rag to a bull, sore point, tender spot, dangerous subject, pinprick, raw nerve

4 **anger**, wrath, wrathfulness, rage, blind rage, furious rage, fury, blind fury, passion, ire, choler, aggression, belligerence, bellicosity, crossness, snappishness, sullenness, heat, vehemence, violence, fit of anger, fit of temper, tearing rage, outburst, tantrum, temper tantrum, paroxysm (of rage), convulsion, storm, scene, ferment, fret, tears of rage, explosion, going on the rampage, gnashing the teeth, stamping the foot, shouting, roaring, raging, tizzy (Inf), duck-fit (Inf), cat-fit (Inf), blow-up (Inf), flare-up (Inf), paddy (or paddywhack) (Inf), stew (Inf), wax (Inf), dander (US sl), conniption (fit) (US sl)

▶ 829 Irascibility, 832 Malevolence, 241 Violence, 423 Loudness

5 **quarrel**, argument, tiff, fight, box on the ear, rap on the knuckles, slap in the face, coming to blows, fisticuffs

▶ 666 Disagreement, 674 Contention

6 **sign of anger**, angry look, black look, frown, scowl, glower, glare, growl, snarl, bark, bite, snap

7 **gods and goddesses of anger**, the Furies, Allecto, Megaera, Tisiphone, the Eumenides, the Erinys, Ira, Nemesis

VERBS

8 **resent**, feel resentment, nurse resentment, feel offended, feel insulted, feel piqued, feel sore, feel discontented, bear malice, bear a grudge, have a bone to pick, find intolerable, not be able to bear, not be able to stomach, suffer, feel, smart under, take amiss, take exception to

9 **offend**, provoke, vex, annoy, aggravate, goad, sting, exasperate, irritate, antagonize, incense, arouse, inflame, nettle, fret, insult, affront, outrage, give umbrage, grieve, aggrieve, wound, hurt (the feelings), chafe, pique, huff, rile, rankle, ruffle, work up, get on one's nerves, get to one, bother, harass, pester, tease, bait, pinprick, torment, goad, sting, taunt, get one's back up, put one's fur up, put one's bristles up, ruffle the dignity, ruffle one's feathers, raise someone's hackles, step (or tread) on someone's toes, put someone's nose out of joint (Inf), stir the blood (Inf), stick in one's craw (or throat) (Inf), needle (Inf), miff (Inf), stir up (Inf), rub up the wrong way (Inf)

10 **be offended**, take offence, feel hurt, feel pique, take amiss, take ill, take in bad part, take to heart, mind, not take a joke, take umbrage, get huffy, get miffed (Inf), have one's nose out of joint (Inf)

11 **be angry**, rage, rave, rant, rant and rave, bluster, fulminate, burn, fume, seethe, simmer, smoke, smoulder, boil, glower, glare, frown, scowl, lour (or lower), look black, look like thunder, look daggers, snarl, growl, snap, create a scene, make a scene, weep with rage, quiver with rage, fret, chafe, storm, breathe fire, quarrel, have a tiff, fight, bite someone's head off, raise Cain, raise hell, raise the devil, raise the roof, throw a fit, have a (temper) tantrum, go berserk, rampage, foam at the mouth, shake with passion, stamp one's foot, paw the ground (Inf), champ (or chafe) at the bit (Inf), take on (Inf), carry on (Inf), kick up a row (Inf), kick up dirt (Inf), make a shindy (Inf), cut up rough (Inf), stew (Inf), sizzle (Inf), throw a cat-fit (Inf), throw a conniption fit (US inf), be pissed (off) (Tab sl), throw a conniption (US sl)

12 **become angry**, get angry, anger, lose one's temper, lose patience, get cross, get sore, fly into a rage, fly into a passion, explode, throw a tantrum, colour, redden, flush with anger, do a slow burn, ignite, kindle, take fire, forget oneself, lose control, get sore, bridle, bristle, raise one's hackles, get one's back up, get one's gorge up, get one's blood up, get mad (Inf), get one's Irish up (Inf), see red (Inf), get steamed up (Inf), get hot under the collar (Inf), flare up (Inf), reach boiling point (Inf), boil over (Inf), work up into a lather (Inf), work up into a sweat (Inf), work up into a stew (Inf), let fly (Inf), fly off the handle (Inf), hit (or go through) the roof (or ceiling) (Inf), blow one's top (Inf), blow one's lid (or stack) (US inf), become red (Inf), lose one's rag (Inf), have a haemorrhage (Inf), go off the deep end (Inf), out-Lear Lear (Inf), blow one's cool (Sl), blow a fuse (Sl), blow a gasket (Sl), go up the wall (Sl), go spare (Sl), flip one's lid (or wig) (Sl), get one's dander up (US sl), get one's monkey up (Sl), kick up shit (Tab sl)

13 **vent one's anger**, vent one's rancour, vent one's spleen, pour wrath onto, snap at, bite (or snap) one's head off, express one's feelings, take it out on (Inf), jump down one's throat (Inf)

14 **make angry**, make sore, aggravate, huff, put out, enrage, infuriate, madden, drive into a frenzy, work up into a passion, make one's blood boil, make one's gorge rise, make all hell break loose, disturb one's equanimity, ruffle one's temper, push too far, ulcerate, envenom, poison, set at loggerheads, set by the ear, make mad (Inf), brown off (Sl), drive up the wall (Sl), piss one off (Tab sl)

ADJECTIVES

15 **resentful**, offended, insulted, affronted, hurt, pained, put-out, indignant, reproachful, bitter, embittered, virulent, acrimonious,

sharp, acid, acidulous, splenetic, acerbic, caustic, irritated, vexed, wrought-up, discontented, disapproving, displeased, not amused, up in arms, provoked, riled, worked-up, annoyed, aggravated, exasperated, piqued, peeved, in a pet, nettled, stung, smarting, hurt, sore, grudging, malicious, jealous, envious, green with envy, full of hate, bileful, bilious, spiteful, ill-humoured, impatient, shirty (Sl)

16 **angry**, angered, irate, ireful, cross, aggressive, belligerent, bellicose, wrathful, furious, infuriated, choleric, indignant, livid, pale with anger, red with rage, red with anger, enraged, raging, incensed, fuming, flushed with rage, warm, boiling with rage, boiling, burning, smouldering, sulphurous, in a rage, in a huff, huffed, in a temper, beside oneself, crying with rage, frenzied, foaming at the mouth, foaming, rabid, berserk, fighting mad, hopping mad, hopping, mad as a hornet, mad as a wet hen, good and mad, speechless with rage, stuttering, gnashing, growling, snapping, dangerous, violent, fierce, savage, rampaging, roaring, in high dudgeon, rubbed (up) the wrong way, mad (Inf), apoplectic (Inf), sizzling (Inf), in a stew (Inf), in a paddy (Inf), seeing red (Inf), hot under the collar (Inf), ratty (Inf), waxy (Sl), browned off (Sl), het up (Sl), pissed off (Tab sl), PO'd (US sl)

ADVERBS

17 **resentfully**, with resentment, hurtfully, in a hurtful manner, indignantly, reproachfully, with reproach, virulently, acrimoniously, bitterly, with bitterness, sharply, acidly, caustically, irritatingly, discontentedly, annoyingly, aggravatingly, exasperatingly, maddeningly, grudgingly, maliciously, with malice, jealously, with a jealous heart, enviously, biliously, spitefully, disapprovingly, with one's nose out of joint (Inf)

18 **angrily**, in anger, irately, infuriatingly, crossly, wrathfully, furiously, with (or in) fury, indignantly, lividly, warmly, heatedly, sulphurously, in the heat of passion, in the height of passion, in the heat of the moment, in hot blood, rabidly, apoplectically (Inf), in a paddy (Inf), while seeing red (Inf), with one's dander up (US sl), with one's monkey up (Sl)

829 Irascibility

NOUNS

1 **irascibility**, irritability, impatience, temperamentalness, sharp temper, quick temper, fiery temper, short temper, bad temper, dangerous temper, thin skin, touchiness, tetchiness, prickliness, grumpiness, gruffness, readiness to take offence, quick passions, peevishness, pepperiness, testiness, petulance, querulousness, fretfulness, resentfulness, sullenness, shrewishness, vixenishness, fractiousness, crankiness, crossness, crabbedness, huffiness, cussedness, cantankerousness, churlishness, sharpness, tartness, acerbity, asperity, gall, bile, vinegar, sourness, acidity, acidness, shrewishness, waspishness, meanness, contentiousness, quarrelsomeness, disputatiousness, argumentativeness, belligerence, orneriness (US inf), grouchiness (Inf), crabbiness (Inf), bitchiness (Inf), short fuse

▶ *760 Sensitivity, 828 Resentment; Anger, 830 Sullenness, 780 Rashness, 816 Unsociability, 766 Dissatisfaction, 666 Disagreement*

2 **sign of irascibility**, bad temper, black look, frown, scowl, glare, grimace, glower, lour (or lower), growl, snarl, snap

3 **irascible person**, hothead, tartar, bear, bear with a sore head, crank (US), ugly customer, shrew, virago, vixen, termagant, fury, witch, tigress, spitfire, fishwife, nag, harridan, scold, grouch (Inf), grump (Inf), crosspatch (Inf), sorehead (US inf), cat (Inf), dragon (Inf), battle-axe (Inf), she-devil (Inf), bitch (Sl)

ADJECTIVES

4 **irascible**, irritable, impatient, nervous, jumpy, strained, fretful, oversensitive, touchy, tetchy, thin-skinned, petulant, peevish, querulous, testy, temperamental, highly-strung, short-tempered, short, huffy, annoyed, resentful, sullen, sore, riled, nettled, ill-humoured, snappish, snappy, bellicose, waspish, sharp-tongued, sharp, tart, acerbic, sour, acid, shrewish, vixenish, crusty, ornery, prickly, peppery, hot-blooded, hot-tempered, quick-tempered, short-tempered, easily roused, grumpy, gruff, cross, cantankerous, churlish, fractious, bilious, dyspeptic, contentious, quarrelsome, disputatious, argumentative, belligerent, angry, mean, bearish, like a bear with a sore head, grouchy (Inf), crotchety (Inf), cranky (US inf), crabby (Inf), uptight (Inf)

5 **showing irascibility**, frowning, scowling, glowering, louring (or lowering), pouting, grimacing, growling, snarling

VERBS

6 **be irascible**, strain, fret, rouse easily, have a short temper, have a temper, have a bad temper, have an uncontrollable temper, have a short fuse, have a bad liver, show impatience, become annoyed, resent, have a sharp tongue, turn sour, act like a vixen, quarrel, dispute, argue, get angry, turn against (or on), fly at, snap at, snap (or bite) one's head off, act like a bear, jump down someone's throat (Inf), act like a bitch (Sl)

7 **frown**, scowl, glower lour (or lower), pout, grimace, growl, snarl

8 **make irascible**, irritate, make impatient,

vex, annoy, bother, rile, nettle, rouse, test someone's patience, cause resentment, make angry, make uptight (Inf), peeve (Inf)

ADVERBS

9 **irascibly**, irritably, in an irritable mood, impatiently, without patience, petulantly, peevishly, querulously, temperamentally, resentfully, sullenly, ill-humouredly, waspishly, sharply, in a sharp tone, sourly, in a sour disposition, acidly, like a shrew, like a vixen, nervously, in a nervous state, fretfully, touchily, tetchily, grumpily, hot-bloodedly, gruffly, in a gruff manner, crossly, cantankerously, churlishly, biliously, contentiously, argumentatively, belligerently, angrily, with anger, meanly, with a frown, with a scowl, with a grimace, grouchily (Inf), crankily (Inf), like a bitch (Sl)

830 Sullenness

NOUNS

1 **sullenness**, sulkiness, surliness, glumness, moroseness, moodiness, mopiness, melancholy, atrabiliousness, dejection, grumpishness, whininess, ill humour, ill nature, unsociability, lack of communication, lack of talk, sourness, grimness, sternness, mumpishness (Arch)

▶ 816 Unsociability, 415 Sourness, 828 Resentment; Anger

2 **sign of sullenness**, sullen look, hangdog look, long face, pout, moue (Fr), sigh, moan, the blues, blue devils, the sulks, fit of the sulks, the sullens, the pouts, the mopes, the mumps (Arch), the dumps (Inf), the grumps (Inf), the mulligrubs (Inf)

3 **irritableness**, irritability, irascibility, discontent, dissatisfaction, petulance, temperament, ill temper, bad temper, shocking temper, touchiness, peevishness, grumpiness, gruffness, crossness, crankiness, cussedness, spitefulness, spleen, liver, bile, grouchiness (Inf), biliousness (Inf), bitchiness (Inf)

▶ 829 Irascibility, 766 Dissatisfaction, 818 Discourtesy

4 **sign of irritableness**, bad temper, scowl, frown, grimace, lour (or lower), glower, glare, wry face, black look, growl, snarl, snort, snap, mow (Arch), short fuse (Inf)

5 **sullen person**, sulker, grumbler, grouser, whiner, whinger, bear, bear with a sore head, hothead, witch, grouch (Inf), grump (Inf), crosspatch (Inf), sorehead (US inf), bellyacher (Sl), bitch (Sl)

ADJECTIVES

6 **sullen**, sulky, surly, serious, pouting, melancholy, melancholic, atrabilious, moody, morose, glum, grim, stern, dour, sour, gloomy, sombre, dismal, dark, black, dejected, de-

pressed, cheerless, ill-humoured, ill-natured, blue, saturnine

7 **irritable**, irascible, disagreeable, discontented, dissatisfied, smouldering, temperamental, bad-tempered, ill-tempered, surly, resentful, churlish, touchy, tetchy, testy, acid, tart, vinegary, grumpy, quarrelsome, cantankerous, curmudgeonly, out of humour, in a bad humour, out of temper, dyspeptic, bitter, peevish, petulant, shrewish, vixenish, cross, abrupt, brusque, gruff, frowning, unsmiling, louring (or lowering), glowering, scowling, grumbling, grousing, snarling, snapping, snappish, put out, mumpish (Arch), (down) in the dumps (Inf), bilious (Inf), grouchy (Inf), bitchy (Inf), cranky (US inf), bellyaching (Sl), beefing (Sl), shirty (Sl)

8 **overcast**, cloudy, louring (or lowering), glowering, dismal

▶ 55 Meteorology and Climatology

VERBS

9 **be sullen**, sulk, get oneself into a sulk, mope, brood, fret, pout, whine, whinge, have the blues, have a long face, make a lip, hang one's lip, moan, have the pip (Sl)

10 **make sullen**, deject, depress, sour, give someone the blues, put someone in a melancholy mood, pip (Sl), give someone the pip (Sl)

11 **be irritable**, glare, lour (or lower), glower, smoulder, look black, make a wry face, knit one's brows, frown, scowl, grimace, bare one's teeth, show one's fangs, growl, grouch, snarl, snap, spit, grumble, mutter, complain, grouse, carp, get out of bed on the wrong side (Inf), grouch (Inf), crab (Inf), bitch (Inf), bellyache (Sl), beef (Sl)

12 **make irritable**, irritate, annoy, acerbate, exacerbate, embitter, bitter, make bitter, envenom, put in a bad temper, put in a bad humour, discontent, dissatisfy, rub the wrong way

ADVERBS

13 **sullenly**, sulkily, seriously, in a serious mood, moodily, morosely, glumly, ill-humouredly, in an ill humour, grimly, sternly, dourly, sourly, gloomily, sombrely, dismally, darkly, blackly, under a black cloud, dejectedly, depressingly, in a fit of depression, cheerlessly, without cheer, saturninely

14 **irritably**, with irritation, irascibly, disagreeably, discontentedly, with bad grace, temperamentally, ill-naturedly, with an ill nature, resentfully, with resentment, churlishly, touchily, testily, acidly, with an acid tongue, tartly, grumpily, cantankerously, bitterly, crossly, peevishly, petulantly, abruptly, brusquely, gruffly, grouchily (Inf), crankily (Inf)

831 Benevolence

NOUNS

1 **benevolence**, benevolentness, benevolent disposition, kindness, kindliness, kind-heartedness, loving kindness, milk of human kindness, goodness, niceness, goodwill, benignity, cordiality, geniality, affability, helpfulness, kindly disposition, open-heartedness, heart of gold, amiability, sociability, bonhomie, friendship, good-naturedness, love, grace, grace of God, pity, mercy, goodness and mercy, forgiveness, compassion, tolerance, toleration, soft-heartedness, consideration, thoughtfulness, courteousness, attentiveness, mindfulness, decent feeling, fellow feeling, humaneness, humanity, humanitarianism, love of mankind, goodwill towards man, brotherly love, brotherliness, brotherhood of man

▶ *861 Good, 662 Help, 821 Love, 815 Sociability, 819 Friendship, 759 Feeling, 817 Courtesy, 835 Pity, 839 Forgiveness, 691 Leniency, 664 Cooperation*

2 **charity**, charitableness, hospitality, philanthropy, good works, Christian charity, generosity, generousness, bountifulness, liberality, patronage, magnanimity, altruism, unselfishness, selflessness, big-heartedness, open-handedness, Red Cross, OXFAM, Salvation Army, Amnesty International

▶ *833 Philanthropy, 755 Generosity, 729 Giving*

3 **welfare**, welfarism, welfare state, welfare work, social services, social security, social welfare, social work, public welfare, child welfare, community service, health care, unemployment benefits, retirement benefits, pension, socialism, liberalism, the dole (Inf)

4 **benevolent act**, kind act, helpful act, act of grace, kindness, kind deed, good deed, good turn, good work, mitzvah (Judaism), favour, courtesy, service, benefit, charitable act (*or* deed), rescue, relief, loan, alms, almsgiving, labour of love, offices, good offices

5 **benevolent person**, kind person, Good Samaritan, Christian, good neighbour, sympathizer, well-wisher, philanthropist, altruist, welfarist, humanitarian, man (*or* woman) of goodwill, welfare worker, social worker, patron, reformer, almsgiver, almoner, Mother Teresa, do-gooder (Inf), goody-goody (Inf), bleeding heart (Inf)

ADJECTIVES

6 **benevolent**, kind, kind-hearted, warm-hearted, good, nice, benign, helpful, amiable, sociable, friendly, affectionate, loving, considerate, decent, thoughtful, attentive, solicitous, courteous, mindful, condolent, sympathetic, empathetic, good-hearted, good-natured, good-humoured, cordial, genial, affable, well-meant, well-meaning, well-intentioned, tolerant, compassionate, open-hearted, humane, forgiving, indulgent, soft-hearted, lax, lenient, obliging, accommodating, neighbourly, fatherly, paternal, motherly, maternal, brotherly, fraternal, sisterly, cousinly, full of the milk of human kindness

7 **charitable**, beneficent, hospitable, philanthropic, Christian, generous, bountiful, magnanimous, altruistic, unselfish, big-hearted, open-handed, liberal, giving, alms-giving

VERBS

8 **be benevolent**, be kind, do a kindness, do a favour, do the offices, do right by, treat well, mean well, have the best intentions, love, make love not war, show consideration, show concern, have regard for, remember, understand, sympathize, empathize, comfort, relieve, mother, nurse, accommodate, indulge, tolerate, show mercy, forgive, return good for evil, do as one would be done by, practise the golden rule, have a heart of gold, have a generous heart, have a big heart, have one's heart in the right place, reform, oblige, respect, wish well, wish the best for, give one's blessing, support, encourage, look with a favourable eye

9 **be charitable**, give financial support, give freely, aid, provide aid, provide needed funds, raise money for, practise philanthropy, benefit, act like a Christian, patronize

ADVERBS

10 **benevolently**, kindly, kind-heartedly, with kindness, in kindness, out of kindness, tenderly, lovingly, with tender loving care, with love, while in love, benignly, helpfully, in a helpful manner, amiably, sociably, affectionately, considerately, decently, thoughtfully, attentively, solicitously, courteously, mindfully, condolently, compassionately, with compassion, by the grace of God, humanely, forgivingly, soft-heartedly, sympathetically, good-heartedly, with a good heart, good-naturedly, with a good nature, tolerantly, indulgently, obligingly, accommodatingly, paternally, like a father, maternally, like a mother, fraternally, like a brother

11 **charitably**, through charity, beneficently, hospitably, philanthropically, generously, bountifully, magnanimously, altruistically, unselfishly, big-heartedly, with a big heart, open-handedly, with open hands, liberally

832 Malevolence

NOUNS

1 **malevolence**, evilness, badness, ill will, bad will, ill nature, ill disposition, evil disposition, malignity, malignance, hate, hatred, hatefulness, loathing, blind fury, misanthropy, misandry, misogyny, lack of humanity, mal-

ice, maliciousness, malice aforethought, maleficence, evil intent, wickedness, devilry, devilishment, bad intention, worst intention, enmity, truculence, truculency, hostility, animosity, antagonism, meanness, nastiness, bad blood, cussedness (Inf), bloody-mindedness (Inf)

▶ 820 Enmity, 822 Hate, 864 Wickedness, 862 Evil, 836 Pitilessness

2 **cruelness**, cruelty, cruel conduct, inhumanity, inhumaneness, barbarism, barbarity, brutality, brutalness, brutishness, savagery, savageness, atrocity, bestiality, animality, viciousness, ferocity, ferociousness, violence, vandalism, sadism, sadistic cruelty, monstrousness, terrorism, heinousness, fiendishness, bloodthirstiness, bloodthirst, bloodlust, cannibalism

▶ 398 Killing, 633 Danger

3 **callousness**, callosity, unfeelingness, unnaturalness, hardness, hardheartedness, heartlessness, obduracy, obdurateness, heart of stone, stony-heartedness, heart of marble, heart of flint, coldness, cold-heartedness, coldbloodedness, gloating, gloating pleasure, unholy joy, Schadenfreude (Ger), harshness, roughness, severity, ruthlessness, sternness, grimness

4 **bitterness**, tartness, acrimony, asperity, resentment, acerbity, sourness, sharpness, sharp tongue, ill feeling, vengefulness, mordacity, mordancy, acidity, causticity, causticness, caustic reply, biting comment, spite, spitefulness, rancour, gall, spleen, bile, virulence, venom, venomousness, vitriol, vindictiveness, grudge, beastliness, waspishness, snideness, bitchiness (Inf), cattiness (Inf)

5 **intolerance**, persecution, intimidation, victimization, tyrannization, bullying, harassment, sexual harassment, racial harassment, racial hatred, racism, racialism

6 **inconsiderateness**, inconsideration, insensitivity, lack of care, lack of concern, thoughtlessness, heedlessness, unmindfulness, unhelpfulness, unobligingness, unkindness, unkindliness, unfriendliness, ungraciousness, uncharitableness, ungenerousness

7 **act of malevolence**, bad deed, bad turn, harm, disservice, ill service, ill turn, mischief, misfortune, crime, threat, menace, intimidation, blackmail, foul play, atrocity, brutal act, outrage, evil act, act of inhumanity, crime against humanity, cruel act, act of cruelty, reign of terror, bloodshed, torture, slaughter, murder, killing, mass murder, massacre, serial killing, homicide, genocide, fratricide, patricide, matricide, infanticide, abuse, physical abuse, verbal abuse, sexual abuse, child abuse, harm, hurt, grievous bodily harm (GBH), assault, sexual assault, rape, personal violence, ill-treatment, misuse, maltreatment

8 **malefactor**, bad person, evildoer, wrongdoer, malfeasant, miscreant, sinner, racist, vandal, larrikin (Aus), destroyer, nihilist, wrecker, spoiler, traitor, back-stabber, betrayer, double-crosser, Judas, villain, rogue, ruffian, scoundrel, caitiff, blackguard, bully, bullyboy, thug, phansigar, lout, punk, bruiser, criminal, offender, lawbreaker, felon, outlaw, desperado, gangster, hoodlum (US), sadist, torturer, molester, abuser, rapist, tyrant, Attila, vulture, hyena, predator, snake, viper, terrorist, anarchist, murderer, mass murderer, serial killer, homicidal maniac, killer, butcher, cutthroat, gunman, contract killer, assassin, hired assassin, baddie (Inf), bad egg (Inf), bad lot (Inf), terror (Inf), unholy terror (Inf), tough (Inf), rough (Inf), crook (Inf), mugger (Inf), con man (Inf), snake in the grass (Inf), Hun (Inf), hatchet man (Inf), hit man (Sl), crim (Sl), mobster (US sl), roughneck (Sl), yob (Sl), yobbo (Sl), skinhead (Sl), hood (US sl), hooligan (Sl), ugly customer (Sl), nasty piece of work (Sl)

9 **vixen**, hellcat, wildcat, tigress, shrew, virago, fury, siren, witch, hag, hell-hag (Sl), she-devil (Sl), bitch (Sl)

ADJECTIVES

10 **malevolent**, ill-willed, ill-intentioned, ill-wishing, ill-natured, ill-disposed, evil, evil-disposed, evil-minded, malignant, malign, meaning harm, pernicious, wicked, hating, full of hate, hateful, full of loathing, malicious, malefic, baleful, intolerant, persecuting, oppressive, tyrannical, intimidatory, menacing, harassing, racist

11 **cruel**, cruel-hearted, inhuman, inhumane, subhuman, dehumanized, atrocious, outrageous, barbaric, barbarous, brutal, brutish, savage, bestial, beastly, animal, vicious, ferocious, violent, sadistic, monstrous, terrorful, terroristic, heinous, bloodthirsty, bloody, cannibalistic, torturous, murderous, homicidal, fiendish, fiendlike, devilish, satanic, demoniac, demoniacal, diabolical, hellish, infernal, ghoulish

12 **callous**, calloused, unfeeling, unnatural, obdurate, hard, hard-hearted, hardened, hard of heart, heartless, cold, cold-hearted, cold of heart, cold-eyed, cold-blooded, steely, steely-eyed, stony, stony-hearted, flinty, flint-hearted, marble-hearted, harsh, rough, ungentle, severe, stern, grim, dour, gruff, rugged, tough, austere

13 **merciless**, pitiless, ruthless, revengeful, full of revenge, vengeful

14 **hostile**, truculent, antagonistic, mean, nasty, spiteful, despiteful, rancorous, splenetic, virulent, venomous, envenomed, poisonous, baneful, vitriolic, vindictive, beastly, snide,

waspish, viperish, bitter, bitter and twisted, tart, acrimonious, resentful, acerbic, sour, astringent, mordant, mordacious, sarcastic, acidic, acid, acrid, caustic, sharp, cutting, whipping, piercing, penetrating, biting, stinging, stabbing, cussed (Inf), bloody-minded (Inf), cattish (Inf), catty (Inf), bitchy (Inf)

15 **inconsiderate**, unthoughtful, thoughtless, insensitive, uncaring, unconcerned, unfeeling, unresponsive, unheedful, heedless, unmindful, unhelpful, unobliging, disobliging, unaccommodating, unsympathetic, unkind, unkindly, unfriendly, unamiable, sullen, ungenial, ungracious, uncordial, inhospitable, unchristian, unbenevolent, uncharitable, unphilanthropic, ungenerous

VERBS

16 **be malevolent**, bear malice, hate, show ill will, bear ill will, bear a grudge, cherish a grudge, loathe, spite, wreak one's spite, do one a bad turn, do one's worst, disoblige

17 **kill**, murder, slaughter, massacre, savage, thirst for blood, kill in cold blood

18 **torment**, attack, harm, hurt, injure, abuse, sexually abuse, rape, molest, maltreat, ill-treat, beat, tyrannize, oppress, persecute, intimidate, bully, harass, victimize, terrorize, torture, menace, hound, harry, threaten, frighten, scare, demand, blackmail, hold to ransom, use bully-boy tactics, beat up (Inf), bash (Inf), bullyrag (Inf), do over (Sl), bash up (Sl), cut up nasty (or ugly) (Sl), put the wind up (Sl), put the frighteners on (Sl), have it in for (Sl)

19 **be pitiless**, be merciless, have no mercy, exact revenge, take one's revenge

ADVERBS

20 **malevolently**, with evil intent, with the worst intentions, maliciously, with malice aforethought, spitefully, out of spite, in spite, unkindly, perniciously, with hate, wickedly, hatefully, with malice, cruelly, brutally, savagely, sadistically, callously, meanly, heartlessly, cold-heartedly, without mercy, without pity, truculently, acrimoniously, caustically, intolerantly, tyrannically, harshly, severely, inconsiderately, ungraciously

833 Philanthropy

NOUNS

1 **philanthropy**, philanthropism, humanitarianism, humaneness, humanity, welfarism, benevolence, charitableness, charity, welfare, altruism, dedication, helpfulness, kind-heartedness, kindness, compassion, brotherly love, goodwill, grace, beneficence, unselfishness, generosity, open-handedness, munificence, munificentness, bounty, liberality, do-gooding (Inf)

▶ *831 Benevolence, 835 Pity, 662 Help, 863 Virtue, 572 Willingness*

2 **public spiritedness**, public spirit, social conscience, social consciousness, citizenship, good citizenship, civism, utilitarianism, Benthamism, humanitarianism, universal benevolence, socialism, communism, reformism, urge to set the world to rights, greatest good of the greatest number

▶ *627 Improvement*

3 **philanthropist**, benefactor, benefactress, humanitarian, idealist, ideologist, altruist, visionary, utopian, utilitarian, Benthamite, internationalist, friend of the human race, welfare worker, social worker, community service worker, almoner, charity worker, voluntary worker, volunteer, aid worker, missionary, mission worker, helper, helping hand, aider, assister, befriender, succourer, Samaritan, Good Samaritan, kind person, good neighbour, do-gooder (Inf)

4 **welfare state**, social welfare, child welfare, social services, social security, poor relief, assistance, food stamps (US), benefit, unemployment benefit, the dole (Inf), income support, child support, nanny state (Inf)

5 **charity**, aid, good works, worthy cause, relief, disaster relief, gift, hand-out, donation, fund, flag day, charity event, fund-raiser, telethon, charitable foundation, Red Cross, community chest (or fund) (US), United Way (US), OXFAM, Save the Children

ADJECTIVES

6 **philanthropic**, philanthropical, humanitarian, benevolent, beneficent, humane, charitable, altruistic, aid-giving, aiding, alms-giving, generous, munificent, eleemosynary, kind, kind-hearted, kindly, compassionate, gracious, big-hearted, large-hearted, public spirited, civic, idealistic, enlightened, reforming, visionary, liberal, utilitarian, socialistic, communistic

VERBS

7 **be charitable**, philanthropize, show benevolence, have a social conscience, do good, do a good turn, do a good deed, help, benefit, render assistance, have one's heart in the right place

ADVERBS

8 **philanthropically**, benevolently, beneficently, humanely, from the heart, charitably, altruistically, for the public good, generously, munificently, kind-heartedly, compassionately, with compassion, with good will, idealistically, socialistically, communistically, *pro bono publico* (L)

834 Misanthropy

What though the spicy breezes/ Blow soft o'er Ceylon's isle;/ Though every prospect pleases,/ And only man is vile... Reginald Heber.

I love mankind – it's people I can't stand.
Charles M. Schultz.

NOUNS

1 **misanthropy**, misanthropism, hatred of mankind, distrust of mankind, misandry, misogyny, cynicism, unsociability, antisociability, unsociableness, antisocial attitude, antisocial behaviour, selfishness, egotism, egoism, inhumanity, malevolence

▶ *816 Unsociability, 766 Dissatisfaction, 860 Selfishness*

2 **misanthrope**, misanthropist, hater of mankind, mankind-hater, world-hater, hater of man, man-hater, misandrist, hater of women, woman-hater, misogynist, male chauvinist, antifeminist, sexist loner, solitary, unsocial person, cynic, egotist, egoist, Diogenes, Alceste, male chauvinist pig (Inf)

ADJECTIVES

3 **misanthropic**, antisocial, unsociable, inhuman, cynical, egoistic, egotistical, selfish, misandrous, man-hating, woman-hating, misogynous, sexist

VERBS

4 **become a misanthrope** (*or* **misanthropist**), lose faith in human nature, hate the world, hate mankind, hate men (*or* women), distrust people

ADVERBS

5 **misanthropically**, cynically, antisocially, inhumanly, with inhumanity, egotistically, in an egotistical manner, egoistically, selfishly, from a selfish standpoint

835 Pity

NOUNS

1 **pity**, sympathy, commiseration, condolence, feeling, fellow feeling, empathy, understanding, compassion, compassionateness, mercifulness, charity, humanity, kindness, benevolence, tenderness, gentleness, caring, softheartedness, warm-heartedness, tender-heartedness, soft heart, warm heart, tender heart, self-pity, tears of self-pity, tears for oneself, self-commiseration, self-compassion

▶ *831 Benevolence, 770 Sorrow, 691 Leniency*

2 **condolence**, condolences, sympathy, tears of sympathy, sympathy in grief, shared grief, mourning, sorrow, shared sorrow, shared suffering, comfort, balm, consolation, commiseration, remorse, compunction, regret, ruth (Arch), lament, wake, keen

3 **mercy**, compassion, grace, favour, quarter, forgiveness, mercifulness, forbearance, long-suffering, second chance, letting off, clemency, leniency, reprieve, relief, mitigation, pardon, acquittal

▶ *839 Forgiveness, 879 Punishment*

4 **pitying person**, sympathizer, commiserator, mourner, social reformer, bleeding heart (Inf)

5 **misfortune**, bad luck, disappointment, regret, a pity, a shame, a crying shame, a sin

ADJECTIVES

6 **pitying**, sympathetic, sympathizing, sorry for, comforting, consoling, commiserative, commiserating, condolent, understanding, compassionate, caring, tender, tender-hearted, gentle, kind, kind-hearted, soft, soft-hearted, warm-hearted, benevolent, gracious, generous, clement, yielding, lenient, forbearant, charitable, humane, human, merciful, full of mercy, forgiving, full of forgiveness

7 **pitiful**, pitiable, piteous, arousing pity, demanding pity, heart-rending, heart-breaking, pathetic, sad, distressing, grievous, touching, moving, tear-jerking, affecting, arousing compassion, ruthful (Arch), self-pitying, sorry for oneself

VERBS

8 **pity**, show pity, feel pity, have pity for, feel sorry for, feel sorrow for, feel for, take pity on, sympathize, sympathize with, empathize, empathize with, understand, show understanding, support

9 **sorrow**, grieve, grieve for, share grief, lament, condole with, commiserate, comfort, offer comfort, console, offer consolation, soothe, wipe away one's tears, weep with, weep for, bleed, bleed for, share one's sorrow, express sympathy for, express one's condolences, send one's condolences, pay one's respects

10 **show mercy**, have mercy on, have pity, take pity on, forgive, pardon, grant a pardon, absolve, reprieve, spare, forbear, give a second chance, give a last chance, relent, unbend, relax, give quarter, go easy on, give respite, be lenient, not be too hard on, put out of one's misery, give a break (Inf)

11 **excite pity**, move to compassion, melt, melt the heart, thaw, soften, move, touch, affect, reach, grieve, move to tears, disarm, appeal to one's better feelings

12 **ask for mercy**, plead for mercy, beg for mercy, ask for pity, plead with, cry for quarter, plead (*or* beg) for one's life, fall on one's knees, throw oneself upon another's mercy, plead (*or* beg) for forgiveness

ADVERBS

13 **pitifully**, pitiably, piteously, sympathetically, in sympathy, compassionately, with compassion, mercifully, with mercy, humanely, for humane reasons, tenderly, tender-heartedly, gently, kindly, kind-heartedly, in a kind-hearted way, warm-heartedly, in a warm-hearted manner, benevolently, graciously, generously, charitably

INTERJECTIONS

14 **have pity!**, have mercy!, have a heart!, take pity!, for pity's sake!, for mercy's sake!, for the love of God!

836 Pitilessness

NOUNS

1 **pitilessness**, lack of pity, without pity, unsympatheticness, uncompassionateness, intolerance, unfeelingness, mercilessness, unmercifulness, inclemency, ruthlessness, hardheartedness, heartlessness, hardness of heart, heart of stone, heart of flint, hardness, flintiness, callousness, inhumanity, cruelty, severity, remorselessness, unremorsefulness, unforgivingness, revengefulness, pound of flesh, short shrift

▶ 761 Insensitivity, 373 Hardness, 690 Severity, 832 Malevolence

2 **inflexibility**, implacability, unyieldingness, intractability, inexorableness, relentlessness

3 **pitiless person**, callous person, coldblooded killer, sadistic tyrant, hard case (Inf), loan shark (Inf)

ADJECTIVES

4 **pitiless**, unpitying, unpitiful, unfeeling, without feelings, unmoved, unresponsive, impassive, uncaring, obdurate, unsympathetic, unsympathizing, without compassion, heartless, hardhearted, cold, cold-hearted, stonyhearted, hard, hardened, harsh, severe, flinty, tough, callous, ruthless, cruel, soulless, brutal, cold-blooded, sadistic, barbarous, barbaric, remorseless, unremorseful, vengeful, revengeful, vindictive, unforgiving

5 **inflexible**, unbending, unrelenting, relentless, inexorable, implacable, unyielding, intractable

VERBS

6 **be pitiless**, have no pity, show no pity, have no mercy, show no mercy, show no sympathy, lack compassion, have no feelings, have no heart, show no leniency, give no quarter, insist on (or claim) one's pound of flesh, stand by (or on) the letter of the law, go by the rule book, show no flexibility, be unmoved, not be moved, turn a deaf ear, harden one's heart, not forgive, stop at nothing, let nothing stand in one's way, make short shrift of

ADVERBS

7 **pitilessly**, without pity, unsympathetically, mercilessly, unmercifully, unforgivingly, unyieldingly, heartlessly, unfeelingly, without feelings, without batting an eye (or eyelid), unresponsively, impassively, obdurately, coldly, cold-heartedly, without a twinge of conscience, harshly, severely, toughly, callously, cruelly, brutally, cold-bloodedly, in cold blood, sadistically, barbarously, remorselessly, vengefully, vindictively, unrelentingly, relentlessly

837 Gratitude

NOUNS

1 **gratitude**, gratefulness, thankfulness, appreciation, appreciativeness, obligation, sense (or feeling) of obligation, sense (or feeling) of indebtedness, awareness, mindfulness, cognizance

▶ 851 Approval, 812 Celebration, 228 Motive

2 **thanks**, thank you, grateful thanks, hearty thanks, sincere thanks, thanksgiving, Eucharist, blessing, benediction, Magnificat, Te Deum, prayer, prayer of thanks, paean, praise, hymn, grace, grace before meals

3 **recognition**, acknowledgment, credit, credit line, credits, by-line, thank-you letter, thank-you card (or note), bread-and-butter letter, thank offering, thank-you gift (or present), reward, tip, bonus, gratuity, token of one's gratitude, recognition of one's services, leaving present, retirement gift, parting gift, gold watch, vote of thanks, tribute, praise, testimonial, applause, round of applause, golden handshake (Inf)

▶ 878 Reward

ADJECTIVES

4 **grateful**, thankful, appreciative, pleased, gratified, pleased as punch, indebted, beholden, obliged, much obliged, under obligation, obligated, mindful of obligations, in one's debt, owing a favour

5 **thanking**, blessing, praising, crediting, giving credit, cognizant of, acknowledging

VERBS

6 **be grateful**, be thankful, feel (or have) an obligation, appreciate, express gratitude, thank, give thanks, express thanks, render thanks, return thanks, say thank you, receive with grateful thanks, receive with open arms, return a favour, show gratitude, show appreciation, reward, tip, give a bonus, acknowledge, express acknowledgments, pay tribute, praise, recognize, applaud, give a (big) hand, give three cheers, give credit, attribute

7 **give thanks**, say grace, bless, say a prayer of thanks, thank (or bless) one's lucky stars, count one's blessings, thank God, praise heaven, be thankful for small mercies

ADVERBS

8 **gratefully**, with gratitude, thankfully, with (special) thanks, appreciatively, to express appreciation(s), with a grateful heart, from a sense of obligation, in recognition of one's service(s), as a token of one's gratitude

INTERJECTIONS

9 **thank you!**, thank you very much!, bless you!, much obliged!, thank heaven!, thank God!, thank goodness!, heaven be praised!, Allah be praised!, gramercy! (Arch), thanks! (Inf), many thanks! (Inf), thanks a lot! (Inf), ta! (Inf), cheers! (Inf)

838   Ingratitude

And having looked to government for bread, on the very first scarcity they will turn and bite the hand that fed them. Edmund Burke.

Blow, blow, thou winter wind,/ Thou art not so unkind/ As man's ingratitude. William Shakespeare.

Ingratitude, thou marble-hearted fiend,/ More hideous when thou show'st thee in a child/ Than the sea-monster! William Shakespeare.

NOUNS

1   **ingratitude**, lack of gratitude, ungratefulness, thanklessness, unthankfulness, lack of appreciation, unappreciation, unappreciativeness, ungraciousness, thoughtlessness, discourteousness, forgetfulness, inconsiderateness, rudeness, selfishness, nonrecognition, nonacknowledgment, taking for granted, no thanks, no reward, lack of (due) credit, grudging thanks, half-hearted thanks, thankless task

▶ *818 Discourtesy, 761 Insensitivity*

2   **thankless person**, unappreciative person, ingrate (Arch), ungrateful wretch, ungrateful yob (Sl)

ADJECTIVES

3   **ungrateful**, unthankful, unappreciative, ungracious, discourteous, ill-mannered, bad-mannered, forgetful, thoughtless, inconsiderate, unmindful, heedless, rude, selfish

4   **unthanked**, unrewarded, unacknowledged, unrecognized, uncredited, unrequited, forgotten, neglected, ignored

5   **thankless**, unrewarding, · useless, fruitless, unprofitable, without thanks, without appreciation, without acknowledgment, without (due) credit

VERBS

6   **be ungrateful**, be unappreciative, fail to appreciate, see no reason to thank, give no credit, feel no obligation, be forgetful, forget, unrequite, be thoughtless, take for granted, be rude, begrudge, ignore, neglect, look a gift horse in the mouth, bite the hand that feeds one

ADVERBS

7   **ungratefully**, unappreciatively, without appreciation, ungraciously, discourteously, forgetfully, thoughtlessly, inconsiderately, heedlessly, rudely, selfishly, thanklessly, without thanks, without acknowledgment, without (due) credit, uselessly, fruitlessly, unprofitably

839   Forgiveness

Then said Jesus, Father, forgive them; for they know not what they do. And they parted his raiment, and cast lots. Bible: Luke.

The cut worm forgives the plough. William Blake.

To err is human, to forgive, divine. Alexander Pope.

NOUNS

1   **forgiveness**, pardon, full pardon, free pardon, amnesty, excuse, reprieve, sparing, indemnity, exemption, immunity, grace, dispensation, forgiveness of sin, absolution, remission, remission of sin, indulgence, shrift (Arch)

▶ *691 Leniency, 835 Pity, 7 Religion*

2   **forgivingness**, forgiving nature, mercifulness, clemency, compassion, kindness, benevolence, magnanimity, unresentfulness, unrevengefulness, placability, placableness, lenity, long-suffering, forbearance, patience, tolerance, indulgence, stoicism, overlooking, disregard

▶ *831 Benevolence*

3   **absolution**, acquittal, cancellation, discharge, release, deliverance, freeing, exoneration, condonation, exculpation, vindication, justification, reconciliation, conciliation, redemption, pacification, rehabilitation, atonement

▶ *855 Vindication, 677 Pacification*

ADJECTIVES

4   **forgiving**, pardoning, excusing, reprieving, sparing, absolving, shriving, exonerating, condoning, vindicating, justifying, reconciling, conciliatory, redeeming, pacifying, rehabilitating

5   **merciful**, compassionate, kind, clement, benevolent, magnanimous, unresentful, unrevengeful, unreproachful, placable, lenient, long-suffering, forbearing, patient, tolerant, indulgent, stoic

6   **forgiven**, pardoned, excused, granted amnesty, reprieved, spared, absolved, shriven, indulged, remitted, acquitted, cancelled, discharged, released, delivered, freed, let off, exonerated, condoned, exculpated, vindicated, justified, reconciled, redeemed, pacified, rehabilitated, atoned, restored, reinstated, taken back, let off the hook (Sl)

7   **forgivable**, pardonable, venial, excusable, easily excused

8   **overlooked**, disregarded, not held against one, blotted (out), wiped away, swept clean, removed from the record, erased from the record

VERBS

9   **forgive**, give (or grant) forgiveness, pardon, grant amnesty to, excuse, reprieve, spare, indemnify, exempt, grant immunity, forgive one's sins, absolve, grant absolution, shrive, forgive and forget, forget, reconcile, be reconciled, conciliate, redeem, make peace, shake hands, kiss and

make up, bury the hatchet, smoke the peace pipe, let bygones be bygones, dismiss from one's thoughts, think no more of, not give it another (*or* a second) thought, let it go, let it pass, charge to experience, come to an understanding, shake on it (Inf), make it up (Inf)

10 **absolve**, acquit, vindicate, cancel, discharge, release, deliver, free, set free, let off, let one off this time, exonerate, exculpate, remit, dismiss, clear one's name, clear, wipe the slate clean, sweep clean, blot out one's sins, start afresh, assoil (Arch), let one off the hook (Sl)

11 **condone**, overlook, disregard, connive, justify, give one the benefit of the doubt, wink at, close (*or* shut) one's eyes to, turn a blind eye to, ignore, let pass, pass over, let it go

12 **show mercy**, be merciful, show compassion, leave unavenged, turn the other cheek, return good for evil, pocket the affront, bear no malice, take no offence, take in good part, be lenient, be patient with, tolerate, show tolerance, endure, bear with, make allowances for, unbend, soften, relent, accept an apology, forbear (Arch), put up with (Inf)

13 **ask forgiveness**, plead (*or* beg) for forgiveness, beg pardon, offer apologies, ask (*or* beg) for mercy, ask for absolution

ADVERBS

14 **forgivingly**, with a forgiving heart, mercifully, compassionately, kindly, benevolently, magnanimously, patiently, with patience, tolerantly, indulgently, conciliatorily, venially, without bearing a grudge

840 Atonement

NOUNS

1 **atonement**, amends, making amends, satisfaction, expiation, reparation, rectification, redress, compensation, payment, repayment, indemnity, indemnification, reimbursement, restitution, requital, recompense, redemption, making right, making good, making up for, quittance, squaring, measure for measure, blood money, wergild, eye for an eye, propitiation, appeasement, conciliation, reconciliation, pacification, pouring oil on troubled waters, quits (Inf)

▶ 735 Giving Back, 677 Pacification, 717 Compromise

2 **apology**, abject apology, regrets, expression of regret, excuse, acknowledgment, acknowledgment of guilt, *mea culpa* (L), repentance, remorse, confession, penitence, penance, contrition, breast-beating, expiatory offering, offering, oblation, sacrifice, piaculum, burnt offering, peace offering, votive offering, penitential act, penitential exercise, mortification, flagellation, lustration, fasting, cleansing, purification, maceration, austerities, asceticism,

purgation, purgatory, sackcloth and ashes, hair shirt, bed of nails, shrift (Arch), Day of Atonement, Yom Kippur

▶ 867 Penitence, 7 Religion, 879 Punishment, 621 Cleanness

3 **atoner**, penitent, expiator, confessor, repenter, born-again Christian, faster, flagellant, scapegoat, whipping boy

ADJECTIVES

4 **atoning**, making amends, expiatory, reparatory, reparative, rectifying, redressing, compensatory, compensational, repaying, indemnificatory, restitutive, restitutory, restitutional, recompensing, righting, squaring, propitiatory, appeasing, satisfying, conciliatory, reconciliatory, pacifying, apologetic, apologetical, sorry, regretting, penitent, repentant, contrite, penitential, penitentiary, doing penance, lustral, lustrative, lustrational, purgative, purgatorial, cleansing, purifying, piacular, offering, oblatory, sacrificial

VERBS

5 **atone**, atone for, make amends for, satisfy, give satisfaction, expiate, propitiate, appease, conciliate, reconcile, pacify, repair, rectify, redress, compensate, pay back, pay the penalty, pay the forfeit, repay, indemnify, reimburse, requite, redeem, make right, make good, make up for, make matters up, square it, square things, clear the air, pour oil on troubled waters, pay one's dues (Inf), call it quits (Inf)

6 **apologize**, apologize to, make one's apologies, offer one's apologies, say one is sorry, express regret, express one's regrets, beg pardon, beg (*or* ask) forgiveness, come cap in hand, get down on one's knees, confess, go to confession, repent, express one's remorse, pray, offer, offer an oblation, offer sacrifice, sacrifice to, do penance, mortify oneself, mortify one's flesh, flagellate oneself, purify oneself, cleanse oneself of sin, cleanse oneself of guilt, fast, suffer purgatory, put on (*or* wear) sackcloth and ashes, don (*or* wear) a hair shirt, lie on a bed of nails, shrive oneself (Arch), put oneself through hell (Inf)

7 **be punished**, take one's punishment, swallow one's medicine, receive absolution, receive forgiveness, be saved, become a born-again Christian

ADVERBS

8 **penitently**, repentantly, in repentance, as penance, as atonement, to make amends, conciliatorily, apologetically, contritely, purgatively, purgatorially, sacrificially

841 Jealousy

For the ear of jealousy heareth all things: and the noise of murmurings is not hid. Bible: Wisdom.

O, beware, my lord, of jealousy;/ It is the green-ey'd monster which doth mock/ The meat it feeds on. William Shakespeare.

NOUNS

1 **jealousy**, jealousness, pangs of jealousy, enviousness, envy, covetousness, sexual jealousy, heartburning, heartburn, jaundice, jaundiced eye, jaundiced view, jaundiced look, green-eyed jealousy, sour grapes, resentment, hostility, possessiveness, rivalry, competition, competitiveness, competitive spirit, eternal triangle, crime of passion, green-eyed monster (Inf)

▶ *828 Resentment; Anger, 821 Love, 822 Hate, 674 Contention*

2 **distrust**, distrustfulness, mistrust, mistrustfulness, suspicion, suspiciousness, doubt, misdoubt, watchfulness, vigilance, possessiveness, solicitousness, anxiousness, apprehensiveness

▶ *498 Disbelief*

3 **rival**, rival in love, competitor, the other man, the other woman

ADJECTIVES

4 **jealous**, envious, covetous, devoured with jealousy, consumed with jealousy, eaten up with jealousy, obsessed with jealousy, jaundiced, jaundice-eyed, green, green-eyed, yellow, yellow-eyed, lynx-eyed, sour, resentful, possessive, overpossessive, hostile, invidious, rival, competitive, competing, emulative, emulous

5 **distrustful**, mistrustful, suspicious, doubtful, misdoubtful, watchful, vigilant, Argus-eyed, solicitous, anxious, apprehensive

VERBS

6 **be jealous**, envy, covet, view with jealousy, view with a jaundiced eye, suffer pangs of jealousy, have heartburn, eat one's heart out, resent, resent competition, brook no rival

7 **arouse jealousy**, make jealous, create resentment, give someone an inferiority complex, put someone's nose out of joint (Inf)

8 **distrust**, mistrust, be suspicious, be wary, doubt, misdoubt, be possessive, be overpossessive, strive to keep for oneself, not allow out of one's sight

ADVERBS

9 **jealously**, with a jealous heart, enviously, with envy, covetously, resentfully, possessively, in a possessive manner, hostilely, invidiously, competitively, emulously, distrustfully, mistrustfully, suspiciously, doubtfully, watchfully, vigilantly, solicitously, anxiously, apprehensively

842   Envy

NOUNS

1 **envy**, enviousness, covetousness, jealousy, desire, deadly sin of envy, resentment, resent-

fulness, grudgingness, grudge, ill will, spite, green-eyed monster (Inf)

▶ *841 Jealousy, 782 Desire, 766 Dissatisfaction, 828 Resentment; Anger*

ADJECTIVES

2 **envious**, envying, jealous, covetous, green-eyed, green with envy, envious-eyed, jaundiced, desirous, desiring, longing, resentful, grudging, begrudging, spiteful, malicious

VERBS

3 **be envious of**, envy, cast envious eyes, covet, desire, long for, hanker after, lust after, crave, resent, grudge, begrudge, turn green with envy

ADVERBS

4 **enviously**, with envy, jealously, with a jealous heart, covetously, longingly, desirously, resentfully, grudgingly, begrudgingly, spitefully, maliciously

843   Right

Right is more precious than peace. Woodrow Wilson.

NOUNS

1 **fairness**, rightness, justice, equity, equitableness, impartiality, equality, equalness, fairmindedness, fair play (*or* treatment), even handedness, square deal, even deal, lack of bias, even break (Inf), fair crack of the whip (Inf)

▶ *16 Law, 332 Direction*

2 **correctness**, accurateness, accuracy, authenticity, validity, legitimacy, truth, trueness, genuineness, veracity, precision, preciseness

▶ *503 Accuracy, 537 Truth*

3 **properness**, correctness, honesty, decency, propriety, seemliness, probity, integrity, honour, etiquette

▶ *861 Good, 876 Morality*

4 **righteousness**, virtue, virtuousness, uprightness, integrity, rectitude, uprightness, probity, godliness

▶ *863 Virtue, 857 Probity, 861 Good, 7 Religion, 8 Divinity*

5 **righting wrong**, reform, reformation, rectification, correction

▶ *216 Change, 12 Government and Politics*

6 **right**, entitlement, due, desert, claim, prerogative

▶ *845 Entitlement*

ADJECTIVES

7 **right**, fair, just, equitable, equal, impartial, fair-minded, open-minded, square, unbiased, disinterested, even-handed, objective, neutral, unprejudiced

8 **correct**, accurate, true, authentic, genuine, valid, legitimate, veracious, unerring, precise, exact, dead-right (Inf), spot on (Inf), bang on

(Inf), on the button (Inf)

9 **in the right**, justified, justifiable, excusable, forgivable, unimpeachable, unchallengeable, rightful, deserved, due, entitled

10 **moral**, moralistic, ethical, high-principled, righteous, virtuous, godly, clean, pure, honest, honourable, truthful, upright, upstanding, straight, straightforward, blameless

11 **right-minded**, decent, law-abiding, sporting, sportsmanlike, on the side of the angels, squeaky clean (Inf)

12 **all right**, fine, fit, well, healthy, in good health, balanced, all there (Inf), in the pink (Inf), up to par (Inf), OK (Inf)

VERBS

13 **be right**, be in the right, have right on one's side, be within one's rights, have grounds for, be justified, deserve, merit, have a claim to, be entitled to

14 **be fair**, see justice done, see fair play, do the right thing, play the game, hear both sides, arbitrate, give the Devil his due

15 **put right**, set right, set to rights, right a wrong, rectify, redress, reform, mend, fix, repair, compensate for, make reparation for, sort out

ADVERBS

16 **right**, rightly, rightfully, deservedly

17 **by rights**, by right, properly, justly, in fairness

18 **properly**, correctly, as is fitting, as is befitting, aptly, befittingly, fittingly, satisfactorily, suitably

19 **equally**, fairly, justly, impartially, without bias, without distinction, without fear or favour

20 **correctly**, aright, accurately, truly, precisely, genuinely, bang, squarely

21 **in the right**, within one's rights

844 Wrong

NOUNS

1 **unfairness**, wrongness, injustice, inequity, discrimination, bias, one-sidedness, unevenness, favouritism, partiality, prejudice, partisanship

▶ 493 Misjudgment, 481 Discrimination

2 **incorrectness**, falseness, error, mistake, untruthfulness, inaccuracy, fallaciousness, erroneousness, unsoundness, invalidity, mistakenness

▶ 504 Error, 538 Untruth

3 **impropriety**, unseemliness, indecorousness, vulgarity, vulgarness, bad taste

▶ 862 Evil, 858 Improbity, 877 Immorality, 412 Tastelessness, 795 Vulgarity

4 **abnormality**, irregularity, oddity, oddness, queerness, aberrance, aberration, perversion

▶ 215 Irregularity, 168 Nonconformity

5 **unrighteousness**, sinfulness, wickedness, badness, evilness

▶ 862 Evil, 877 Immorality, 864 Wickedness

6 **unlawfulness**, lawlessness, illegality, illegitimacy, illicitness, infraction, violation, delinquency, criminality, foul play

7 **sense of wrong**, complaint, grouse, grievance, injury, wrong, injustice, tort, foul, foul play, raw deal (Inf), gripe (Inf)

8 **wrongdoing**, wrong, sin, vice, guilty act, bad deed, evil deed, misdeed, abomination, crime, felony, misdemeanour, offence, misdoing, transgression, trespass, infraction, infringement, injury, harm, hurt, abuse, error, mistake, mischief

▶ 504 Error, 652 Conduct

9 **dishonour**, disgrace, scandal, shame, crying shame, slur, stain, stigma, blot, blot on one's copybook (Inf)

10 **wrongdoer**, sinner, offender, culprit, criminal, felon, lawbreaker, delinquent, juvenile delinquent, trespasser, transgressor, infractor, miscreant, villain, malefactor, crook (Inf), crim (Sl)

ADJECTIVES

11 **wrong**, wrongful, unjust, unfair, inequitable, biased, prejudiced, racially prejudiced, discriminatory, favouring, partial, partisan, uneven, unbalanced, weighted, one-sided, leaning to one side, unsportsmanlike, not playing the game, not cricket (Inf), below the belt (Inf), out of line (Inf)

▶ 493 Misjudgment

12 **incorrect**, not right, inaccurate, imprecise, false, untrue, untruthful, fallacious, unsound, invalid, erroneous, mistaken, misinformed, at fault, off course, off beam, off target, off base (US), wide of the mark

▶ 504 Error, 538 Untruth

13 **improper**, incorrect, unsuitable, unfit, unfitting, unbefitting, inappropriate, inapt, incongruous, indecorous, unseemly, unbecoming, undesirable, vulgar, tasteless, not done (Inf), not the done thing (Inf), not the thing (Inf)

▶ 412 Tastelessness, 795 Vulgarity

14 **abnormal**, irregular, odd, queer, aberrant, perverted, deviant, unsound, unhinged, wrong in the head (Inf)

▶ 215 Irregularity, 168 Nonconformity, 510 Insanity

15 **immoral**, amoral, corrupt, unprincipled, unethical, dishonest, dishonourable, disgraceful, shameful, shamefaced, shameless, scandalous, infamous, sacrilegious

▶ 877 Immorality, 858 Improbity

16 **in the wrong**, guilty, at fault, blameworthy, to be blamed, culpable, sinful, unrighteous, bad, wicked, evil, vicious, abominable, unlawful, lawless, illegal, illegitimate, illicit, criminal, felonious, delinquent, transgressive, infringing, viola-

tive, offensive, abusive, injurious, hurtful, harmful, mischievous, crooked (Inf)
▶ *866 Guilt*
17 **unforgivable**, unpardonable, unjustifiable, inexcusable, reprehensible, objectionable
18 **gone wrong**, not working, broken down, out of commission, out of order, in need of repair, awry, askew, defective, malfunctioning, on the blink (Inf), conked out (Inf), kaput (Inf), buggered up (Sl)

VERBS
19 **be wrong**, make a mistake, give the wrong answer, blunder, slip up (Inf), make a bloomer (Inf)
▶ *504 Error*
20 **wrong**, hurt, harm, injure, offend, abuse, maltreat, ill-treat, ill-use, oppress, malign, defame
▶ *854 Disparagement*
21 **do wrong**, break the law, break (*or* not play by) the rules, commit a crime, commit an offence, offend, trespass, transgress, infringe, violate, cheat, not play the game, commit a foul, hit below the belt (Inf)
22 **discriminate**, discriminate against, be biased, show partiality, show favouritism, favour, lean towards, lean to one side
▶ *493 Misjudgment*
23 **sin**, fall from grace, err, go astray, stray from the straight and narrow, go to the bad, go to the dogs (Inf)
▶ *862 Evil, 864 Wickedness*
24 **go wrong**, break down, go out of commission, be out of order, fail, malfunction, conk out (Inf), go on the blink (Sl), go phut (Inf), go kaput (Inf)

ADVERBS
25 **wrongly**, wrongfully, unjustly, unfairly
26 **wrong**, incorrectly, inaccurately, imprecisely, falsely, untruthfully, erroneously, mistakenly
27 **improperly**, unsuitably, inappropriately, indecorously
28 **immorally**, dishonestly, sinfully, wickedly, unlawfully, illicitly

845   Entitlement

NOUNS
1 **entitlement**, entitledness, dueness, merit, deservingness, deservedness, expectation
2 **due**, one's due, merits, deserts, deservings, what one deserves, what one merits, what one has coming, reward, due reward, credit, acknowledgment, recognition, cognizance, tribute, thanks, compensation, punishment, due punishment, just deserts, just retribution, comeuppance (Inf)
▶ *878 Reward, 851 Approval, 837 Gratitude, 125 Compensation, 879 Punishment*

3 **prerogative**, right, privilege, power, authority, legal right, title, claim, demand, birthright, rights of man, human rights, civil rights, constitutional rights, women's rights, gay rights, animal rights, Bill of Rights, Constitution, Magna Carta
4 **duty**, responsibility, obligation, accountability
▶ *847 Duty*
5 **dues**, fees, payment, levy, contribution
▶ *746 Payment, 745 Debt*
6 **bond**, security, title deed, patent, copyright, contract, covenant, guarantee, warranty, warrant, licence, permit, charter, franchise, grant, qualification, authority
▶ *715 Contract, 708 Permission*
7 **beneficiary**, heir, heiress, heir apparent, heir-at-law, inheritor, next in line, claimant, owner
▶ *723 Possession, 728 Transfer of Property*

ADJECTIVES
8 **entitled**, warranted, justified, qualified, worthy, just, rightful, legitimate, lawful, legal, licit, inviolable, inalienable, admitted, permitted, allowed, sanctioned
▶ *708 Permission*
9 **meritorious**, meriting, deserving, worthy, worthy of
10 **due**, deserved, well-deserved, richly-deserved, merited, well-merited, earned, well-earned, coming to one
11 **entitled to**, due, with a right to, having the right, claiming the right, standing up for one's rights
12 **owed**, owing, unpaid, unsettled, in arrears, outstanding, payable, chargeable, redeemable, coming, coming to
▶ *746 Payment, 747 Nonpayment, 745 Debt*
13 **fit**, fitting, right, rightful, proper, as it should be, appropriate, condign
▶ *843 Right*

VERBS
14 **be entitled**, have the right, warrant, justify, expect, have coming, have a right to, have a title to, have a claim to, have a rightful claim to, claim, claim as one's right, lay claim to, stake a claim to, exercise one's prerogative, exercise divine right, demand, demand one's rights, stand up for one's rights, insist on one's rights
▶ *712 Request*
15 **merit**, deserve, richly deserve, rate, earn, reap the fruits (of), get one's (just) deserts, have only oneself to blame, be in line for (Inf), have it coming (Inf), get one's comeuppance (Inf), serve one right (Inf)
▶ *878 Reward, 879 Punishment*
16 **entitle**, allow, permit, establish a right, give one the right, patent, copyright, enable, empower, enfranchise, license, warrant,

authorize, qualify
▶ *708 Permission*
17 **credit**, acknowledge, recognize, attribute, give credit where credit is due, give every man (*or* woman) his (*or* her) due, confer a title, confer an honour, hand it to one (Inf)
▶ *851 Approval*
18 **be due**, fall due, mature, come of age (Inf)
▶ *745 Debt, 747 Nonpayment*
19 **pay**, discharge, redeem, clear one's debts, honour, meet an obligation
▶ *746 Payment*

ADVERBS
20 **duly**, rightfully, by right, by divine right, legally, by law, as is one's right, as is one's due
21 **deservedly**, justly, justifiably, meritoriously

846 Lack of Entitlement

NOUNS
1 **lack of entitlement**, nonentitlement, absence of right, no right, absence of claim (*or* title), lack of claim (*or* title)
2 **disentitlement**, loss of right, disfranchisement, disenfranchisement, dispossession, expropriation, deprivation, forfeiture, disqualification, disestablishment, unfrocking, deposal, dethronement, denaturalization, deportation, expulsion
▶ *722 Loss, 349 Expulsion*
3 **arrogation**, presumption, assumption, usurpation, appropriation, seizure, violation, invasion, trespass, encroachment, infringement, illegal occupation
▶ *734 Taking*
4 **presumptuousness**, familiarity, undue liberty, impertinence, licentiousness
▶ *357 Overstepping*
5 **undueness**, unwarrantedness, undeservedness, gratuitousness, unfittingness, unworthiness, demerit
6 **excessiveness**, immoderateness, overpayment, too much
▶ *610 Excess*
7 **usurper**, arrogator, pretender, imposter, invader, trespasser, illegal occupier, illegal occupant, squatter

ADJECTIVES
8 **unentitled**, without title, without rights, unauthorized, unsanctioned, unlicensed, unqualified, unempowered, unfranchised, unchartered, unconstitutional, unlawful, illicit, illegal, illegitimate, unrightful, invalid, false, counterfeit, bogus, spurious, fictitious
▶ *709 Veto, 540 Falsehood*
9 **presumptive**, presumptuous, usurpative, violative, arrogative, familiar, impertinent
10 **undue**, unwarranted, unjustified, unnecessary, gratuitous, excessive, immoderate, unexpected, uncalled-for, unlooked-for, unde-

served, unmerited, unearned
▶ *610 Excess, 844 Wrong*
11 **undeserving**, unworthy, unmeriting, unmeritorious, non-meritorious
▶ *618 Worthlessness*
12 **disentitled**, disfranchised, disenfranchised, dispossessed, deprived, disqualified, disestablished, unfrocked, deposed, dethroned, denaturalized, deported, expelled, criminalized, banned, forbidden, prohibited, vetoed, censored

VERBS
13 **not be entitled**, have no right, have no claim to, have no title to, not have a leg to stand on (Inf)
14 **arrogate**, assume, take upon oneself, usurp, appropriate, seize, steal, violate, encroach, infringe, invade, trespass, break in, occupy illegally, squat
▶ *734 Taking, 736 Stealing*
15 **presume**, take liberties, make free, make bold, abuse one's rights, abuse a privilege, overstep, overstep the mark, go too far, give an inch and take a mile, be impertinent
▶ *357 Overstepping*
16 **disentitle**, disfranchise, disenfranchise, dispossess, expropriate, deprive, forfeit, disqualify, disestablish, unfrock, depose, dethrone, uncrown, denaturalize, deport, expel
▶ *349 Expulsion, 722 Loss*
17 **criminalize**, illegalize, make illegal, ban, forbid, prohibit, veto, censor

ADVERBS
18 **unduly**, unnecessarily, gratuitously, excessively, presumptuously, impertinently
19 **unrightfully**, unlawfully, illicitly, illegally, illegitimately

847 Duty

Do your duty and leave the rest to the Gods.
Pierre Corneille.

England expects every man will do his duty.
Lord Nelson.

When a stupid man is doing something he is ashamed of, he always declares that it is his duty. George Bernard Shaw.

NOUNS
1 **duty**, one's duty, the right thing, the proper thing, bounden duty, obligation, imposition, onus, burden, charge, assignment, responsibility, responsibleness, liability, accountability, accountableness, answerability
2 **task**, function, work, service, line of duty, office, station, profession, business, place, calling, engagement, commission, mission, assignment, fatigue, shift, watch
▶ *644 Work*
3 **allegiance**, loyalty, fealty, homage, devo-

tion, dedication, deference, respect, reverence, obedience, compliance, comity, submission, docility

▶ *694 Obedience, 849 Respect, 673 Submission*

4 **sense of duty**, dutifulness, duteousness, devotion (*or* dedication) to duty, moral obligation, moral imperative, call of duty, moral sense, claims of conscience, conscience, inner voice, still small voice, stern daughter of the voice of God, willingness

▶ *876 Morality, 572 Willingness*

5 **discharge of duty**, performance, acquittal, observance

6 **ethics**, rules, regulations, maxim, precept, morals, rule of conduct, code of conduct, code of duty, code of honour, unwritten code, professional code, Hippocratic oath, Ten Commandments, Decalogue

▶ *166 Rule, 505 Maxim*

7 **commitment**, promise, pledge, vow, oath, word, word of honour, contract, engagement, obligation, tie, bond, covenant, assurance, understanding, gentleman's agreement

▶ *714 Promise, 715 Contract*

ADJECTIVES

8 **dutiful**, duteous, conscientious, scrupulous, punctilious, ethical, moral, principled, virtuous, honourable, decent, upright

▶ *876 Morality, 863 Virtue, 857 Probity, 861 Good*

9 **loyal**, devoted, dedicated, deferential, respectful, reverential, obedient, compliant, submissive, docile, tractable, amenable, willing

▶ *849 Respect, 694 Obedience, 673 Submission, 572 Willingness*

10 **liable**, accountable, answerable, responsible

11 **duty-bound**, bound, bound by duty, obligated, obliged, beholden, tied, committed, engaged, pledged, sworn, saddled

12 **obligatory**, mandatory, compulsory, *de rigueur* (Fr), binding, incumbent on, inescapable, unavoidable, unconditional, categorical, peremptory, imperative

▶ *695 Compulsion*

13 **on duty**, on call, at work

VERBS

14 **be the duty of**, fall to, fall to the lot of, rest with, rest on the shoulders of, devolve upon, belong to, pertain to, lie at the door of, be up to, behove, become, befit, must, should, ought to, had better, had best

▶ *695 Compulsion*

15 **be liable**, answer for, account for, stand responsible for, incur a duty, incur a responsibility, make it one's duty, take on the responsibility, accept the responsibility, take upon one's shoulders, make oneself liable, commit oneself, engage oneself, pledge oneself

16 **do one's duty**, discharge one's duty, carry out (*or* perform) one's duty, fulfil one's duty,

do what one has to do, shoulder one's responsibilities, obey, acquit, do the needful, do what is necessary, do what is expected, do one's bit, act (*or* play) one's part, stay at one's post, go down with one's ship, (lie back and) think of England (Inf)

▶ *694 Obedience*

17 **impose a duty**, oblige, put under an obligation, obligate, bind, saddle with, make incumbent, tie, commit, engage, pledge, require, order, command, decree, call upon, enjoin, expect, expect it of, look to

▶ *593 Requirement, 692 Command*

ADVERBS

18 **on duty**, in the line of duty, dutifully, duteously, ethically, morally, loyally, respectfully, accountably, responsibly

848 Exemption

NOUNS

1 **exemption**, immunity, impunity, nonliability, nonresponsibility, dispensation, special treatment, privilege, exception, exclusion, diplomatic immunity

▶ *147 Exclusion*

2 **acquittal**, absolution, pardon, exoneration, excuse, discharge, release, liberation, freedom, liberty, independence

▶ *839 Forgiveness, 700 Liberation, 698 Freedom*

3 **self-exemption**, self-certification, escapism, evasion of responsibility, dereliction of duty, washing one's hands (Inf), passing the buck (Inf)

4 **licence**, permission, permit, certificate of exemption, charter, franchise, patent, privilege, leave, compassionate leave, leave of absence, aegrotat

▶ *708 Permission*

ADJECTIVES

5 **exempt**, exempted, immune, not subject to, nonliable, not liable, not responsible, unaccountable, not accountable, not answerable, unanswerable, privileged, excepted, excluded, shielded, protected, unpunishable

▶ *632 Safety, 147 Exclusion*

6 **acquitted**, absolved, pardoned, exonerated, excused, let off, spared, clear, free, freed from blame, discharged, released, liberated, off the hook (Inf)

▶ *839 Forgiveness*

7 **independent**, free, unrestricted, unbound, unconstrained, uncontrolled

8 **tax-free**, duty-free, post-free, zero-rated

VERBS

9 **exempt**, exclude, except, leave out, set apart, privilege, grant immunity, grant impunity

▶ *147 Exclusion*

10 **acquit**, exonerate, exculpate, absolve, grant absolution, pardon, excuse, let off, let off scot-

free, spare, show mercy, forgive, grant amnesty to, dismiss, discharge, release, liberate, free, set free, set at liberty, let go

▶ *839 Forgiveness, 700 Liberation*

11 **be exempt**, have no liability, have no responsibility, enjoy immunity, enjoy diplomatic immunity

12 **exempt oneself**, excuse oneself, go on leave, take compassionate leave, escape, evade one's responsibilities, fail in one's duty, admit no responsibility, evade liability, shift (*or* transfer) the responsibility, shift the blame, pass the buck (Inf), shrug off (Inf), wash one's hands of (Inf), get off scot-free (Inf), get away with it (Inf), get away with murder (Inf)

ADVERBS

13 **with impunity**, freely, tax-free, duty-free, unaccountably, unanswerably, unrestrainedly

849 Respect

Let them hate, so long as they fear. Lucius Accius.

We owe respect to the living; to the dead we owe only truth. Voltaire.

NOUNS

1 **respect**, regard, esteem, consideration, attention, honour, favour, approbation, approval, appreciation, repute, recognition, good opinion, high opinion, high standing, prestige, authority

▶ *851 Approval, 688 Authority*

2 **admiration**, adoration, breathless adoration, adulation, worship, hero-worship, idolization, veneration, awe, reverence, homage, fealty, obeisance, great respect, high regard

▶ *786 Wonder*

3 **respectfulness**, due respect, deference, humbleness, humility, devotion, loyalty, courtesy, comity, polite regard, attentions

▶ *806 Humility, 817 Courtesy, 694 Obedience*

4 **mark of respect**, show of respect, salute, nod, inclination, bend, bending, bow, bowing and scraping, scrape, stooping, curtsy, bob, bending the knee, genuflection (*or* genuflexion), kneeling, prostration, kissing the hem, salaam, kowtow, obeisance

5 **presenting arms**, standing at (*or* to) attention, dipping the colours, guard of honour, parade of honour, flypast, red carpet, ticker-tape parade (*or* reception)

6 **greeting**, welcome, salutation, salute, obeisance, obsequy

7 **respects**, regards, kind regards, kindest regards, greetings, salutations, compliments, devoirs, good wishes, best wishes

ADJECTIVES

8 **respectful**, regardful, considerate, attentive, honorific, ceremonious, appreciative

9 **showing respect**, deferential, courteous, polite, gracious, dutiful, obeisant, humble, knowing one's place, conscious of one's place, submissive, submitting, compliant, obsequious, servile, ingratiating, fawning, kowtowing, bootlicking (Inf)

▶ *817 Courtesy, 847 Duty, 806 Humility, 808 Servility*

10 **reverent**, reverential, venerative, venerational, admiring, adoring, worshipping, worshipful, adulatory, deifying, hero-worshipping, idolizing, awestruck, awestricken, in awe, wondering

11 **in a respectful stance**, standing, on one's feet, upstanding, rising, kneeling, on bended knee, on one's knees, prostrate, saluting, cap in hand, bare-headed, forelock-tugging, nodding, bending, bowing, curtsying, bobbing, bowing and scraping, stooping

12 **respected**, held in respect, well respected, highly regarded, esteemed, honoured, revered, reverenced, admired, well thought of, highly thought of, highly considered, appreciated, valued, prized, time-honoured, prestigious

▶ *851 Approval*

13 **respectable**, reputable, upright, worthy, venerable, estimable, praiseworthy, laudable

▶ *617 Worth*

14 **awe-inspiring**, imposing, impressive, important, authoritative, august, sage, wise

▶ *611 Importance, 688 Authority, 507 Wisdom*

VERBS

15 **respect**, regard, esteem, entertain respect for, think well of, think highly of, regard highly, hold in high regard, hold in high esteem, have (*or* hold) a high opinion of, look up to, rank high (*or* highly), hold dear, value, admire, prize, treasure, favour, appreciate, set store by (Inf)

▶ *617 Worth, 851 Approval*

16 **revere**, reverence, hold in reverence, venerate, honour, admire, adore, cherish, think the world of, look up to, worship, lionize, hero-worship, put on a pedestal, worship the ground one walks on, idolize, idolatrize, deify, apotheosize

17 **praise**, exalt, extol, acclaim, glorify, laud, sing the praises of

18 **show respect**, pay respect, accord respect to, defer to, heed, obey, consider, do (*or* pay) homage, pay one's respects, pay tribute to, acknowledge, do the honours, carry shoulder high

▶ *694 Obedience*

19 **take off one's hat to**, uncover one's head, doff one's cap to, tug one's forelock, rise, stand, rise to one's feet, be upstanding, nod, incline the head, bow one's head, bow, bow and scrape, bow down, bend, stoop, salaam,

curtsy, bob, bob down, genuflect, bend the knee, kneel, get down on one's knees, fall on one's knees, fall down before, fall at the feet of, prostrate oneself, kiss the hem of one's garment, kiss the ring of, make obeisance, grovel, kowtow

▶ *808 Servility, 806 Humility*

20 **salute**, present arms, fire a salute, turn out the guard, roll out the red carpet, put out the bunting, raise the flag, greet, welcome, address

21 **command respect**, compel respect, inspire respect, impose, impress, rank high, stand high, awe, overawe, overwhelm

▶ *611 Importance*

ADVERBS

22 **respectfully**, with due respect, with all respect, with all due respect, deferentially, courteously, politely, graciously, reverentially, reverently, worshipfully, humbly, obsequiously

23 **saving your grace**, saving your reverence, excusing the liberty

850   Disrespect

NOUNS

1 **disrespect**, disrespectfulness, lack of respect, want of respect, rudeness, discourtesy, impoliteness, unmannerliness, incivility, impertinence, impudence, insolence, irreverence, lack of veneration, blasphemy, scurrility, defamation, obloquy, opprobrium

▶ *818 Discourtesy, 807 Insolence, 854 Disparagement*

2 **disesteem**, undervaluation, underestimation, disregard, neglect, dishonour, disrepute, disfavour, disapprobation, disapproval

▶ *495 Underestimation, 470 Negligence, 852 Disapproval*

3 **contempt**, contemptuousness, scorn, scornfulness, disdain, disdainfulness, superciliousness, superiority, loftiness, contumely, despite, low opinion, low esteem

4 **ridicule**, mockery, derision, sarcasm, irony, satire, imitation, impersonation, burlesque, caricature, lampoon, parody, take-off (Inf), send-up (Inf)

▶ *799 Derision, 118 Imitation*

5 **insult**, aspersion, affront, snub, slight, rebuff, repulse, spurn, spurning, cold shoulder, slap in the face, backhanded compliment, left-handed compliment, cut, cutting remark, unkindest cut of all, put-down, the go-by (Inf)

6 **taunt**, jeer, mock, scoff, jibe (*or* gibe), dig, barb, sneer, snort, sniff, hiss, boo, catcall, hoot, raspberry, brickbat, banter, chaff, teasing, barracking (Inf), the bird (Inf), Bronx cheer (US sl)

▶ *852 Disapproval*

7 **sign of disrespect**, rude gesture, snook, V-

sign, two-fingered salute, Harvey Smith salute, mooning

8 **indignity**, humiliation, degradation, mortification, chagrin, embarrassment, loss of face, egg on one's face (Inf)

▶ *806 Humility, 810 Modesty*

9 **butt**, dupe, target, victim, game, fair game, easy mark, Aunt Sally, fall guy, fool, everybody's fool, jest, joke, figure of fun, laughing stock, monkey, stooge (Sl), mug (Sl)

ADJECTIVES

10 **disrespectful**, wanting in respect, irreverent, irreverential, blasphemous, scurrilous, rude, discourteous, impolite, unmannered, uncivil, impertinent, cheeky, saucy, pert, impudent, insolent, insubordinate, brazen, brazen-faced, bold, audacious, forward, familiar, sassy (US inf), fresh (Inf)

▶ *818 Discourtesy, 807 Insolence*

11 **insulting**, abusive, offensive, pejorative, defamatory, opprobrious, contumacious, outrageous, snubbing, slighting, rebuffing, repulsing, spurning, backhanded, left-handed, cutting

▶ *854 Disparagement*

12 **disregardful**, neglectful, negligent, dishonourable, disreputable, contemptible, despicable, worthless, shameful, base, low

▶ *470 Negligence, 618 Worthlessness, 801 Disrepute*

13 **contemptuous**, scornful, disdainful, pejorative, supercilious, lofty, haughty, arrogant, snobbish, snooty, contumelious, snotty (Inf)

14 **ridiculing**, mocking, derisive, derisory, sarcastic, ironic, satirical, imitating, burlesque, caricatural, parodic

▶ *799 Derision, 118 Imitation*

15 **taunting**, jeering, mocking, flouting, scoffing, scorning, jibing (*or* gibing), sneering, hissing, booing, catcalling, hooting, bantering, chaffing, teasing, barracking (Inf)

16 **humiliating**, degrading, mortifying, embarrassing

▶ *806 Humility, 810 Modesty*

17 **unrespected**, disrespected, unrevered, unreverenced, unvenerated, held in low esteem, trivialized, of no value, of no account

▶ *618 Worthlessness*

18 **undervalued**, underestimated, underrated, disparaged, belittled, denigrated, ignored, disregarded, unregarded, neglected

▶ *495 Underestimation, 470 Negligence*

VERBS

19 **disrespect**, have no respect for, have no regard for, have a low opinion of, hold in low esteem, hold in contempt, have no time for, rank low, hold cheap, underrate, underestimate, undervalue, perjorate, misprize

▶ *495 Underestimation*

20 **scorn**, disdain, despise, asperse, look down

on, hold in contempt, disparage, belittle, trivialize, denigrate, depreciate, run down, defame, look down one's nose at (Inf)

▶ *854 Disparagement*

21 **disregard**, ignore, neglect, dishonour, disgrace, shame, put to shame, drag in the mud

▶ *470 Negligence*

22 **show disrespect**, show no respect, be rude, lack courtesy, turn one's back on, tread on someone's toes, ride roughshod over, brush aside, shove aside, elbow aside, crowd, jostle, remain seated, keep one's hat on

▶ *818 Discourtesy, 807 Insolence*

23 **insult**, offend, affront, snub, slight, rebuff, repulse, spurn, give the cold shoulder, cold shoulder, cut dead, put down, slap in the face, add insult to injury, give the go-by (Inf), dump on (Sl)

24 **ridicule**, mock, deride, make fun of, satirize, imitate, caricature, make a laughing stock of, poke fun at, tease, send up (Inf), take off (Inf), pan (Sl), roast (Sl), rag (Sl), pull one's leg (Inf)

▶ *799 Derision*

25 **taunt**, jeer, mock, scoff, jibe (*or* gibe) at, dig at, sneer, snort, sniff, hiss, boo, catcall, hoot, blow a raspberry, heckle, rail at, laugh at, call names, twit, guy, give one the bird (Inf), barrack (Inf)

▶ *852 Disapproval*

26 **cock a snook**, thumb one's nose at, stick out one's tongue at, make faces at, spit at, moon

27 **desecrate**, despoil, defile, profane, commit sacrilege, cheapen, lower, degrade, humiliate, treat like dirt, treat like shit (Tab sl)

ADVERBS

28 **disrespectfully**, irreverently, rudely, discourteously, impertinently, impudently, insolently, sassily (US inf)

29 **mockingly**, derisively, sarcastically, satirically

30 **contemptuously**, scornfully, disdainfully, superciliously

851 Approval

NOUNS

1 **approval**, approbation, satisfaction, acceptance, adoption, sanction, countenance, blessing, agreement, formal agreement, permission, authorization, assent, consent, acquiescence, vote, imprimatur, endorsement, mandate, support, backing, advocacy, championship, patronage, recommendation, licence, rubber stamp, stamp of approval, seal of approval, nod of approval, nod, wink, OK (*or* okay) (Inf), go-ahead (Inf), thumbs up (Inf), green light (Inf)

▶ *765 Satisfaction, 667 Agreement, 499 Assent, 708 Permission, 662 Help, 664 Cooperation*

2 **admiration**, respect, regard, esteem, credit, acknowledgment, recognition, appreciation, gratitude, honour, favour, good opinion, good books, good graces, popularity, prestige, liking, affection, love

▶ *849 Respect, 784 Liking, 821 Love*

3 **praise**, honour, laud, laudation, glory, glorification, extolment, exaltation, overpraise, overestimation, flattery, compliments, adulation, idolatry, deification, apotheosis, lionization, hero worship

▶ *494 Overestimation, 853 Flattery*

4 **compliment**, complimentary remark, praise, word of praise, congratulation, felicitation, pat on the back, good word, commendation, citation, honourable mention, accolade, kudos, glowing terms, eulogy, encomium, panegyric, tribute, favourable review, rave review, good notice, good press, bouquet, paean

5 **acclaim**, acclamation, plaudit, applause, round of applause, thunderous applause, clap, handclap, clapping, handclapping, hand, big hand, ovation, standing ovation, cheers, three cheers, cheering, huzzah (US), whistling, stamping, curtain call, encore

6 **recommendation**, testimonial, reference, character reference, credential, letter of introduction

7 **advocate**, champion, supporter, backer, patron, sponsor, recommender, favourable critic

8 **admirer**, supporter, follower, fan, supporters' club, fan club, hero-worshipper, rooter (Inf), groupie (Sl)

9 **praiser**, commender, laudator, eulogist, eulogizer, panegyrist, extoller

10 **applauder**, clapper, claqueur, claque, cheerer, cheerleader

VERBS

11 **approve**, approve of, hold with, like, think well of, think highly of, think the best of, have no fault to find, find no fault, admire, respect, regard highly, hold in high regard, esteem, value, prize

▶ *784 Liking, 849 Respect, 617 Worth*

12 **accept**, pass, adopt, sanction, countenance, give one's blessing, agree, grant permission, authorize, ratify, assent, give one's assent, consent, give one's consent, acquiesce, condone, endorse, license, give the stamp (*or* seal *or* nod) of approval, rubber-stamp, nod, wink, tip the wink (Inf), OK (*or* okay) (Inf), give the OK (*or* okay) (Inf), give the go-ahead (Inf), give the thumbs up (Inf), give the green light (Inf)

▶ *667 Agreement, 499 Assent, 708 Permission*

13 **support**, back, lend one's backing to, uphold, advocate, champion, recommend, favour, commend, speak well of, speak highly of, speak up for, put in a good word for, give a reference for, act as referee for

14 **praise**, laud, glorify, honour, exalt, extol, magnify, overpraise, overestimate, flatter,

compliment, adulate, idolize, deify, apotheosize, lionize, hero-worship

▶ *494 Overestimation, 853 Flattery*

15 compliment, pay a compliment, praise, congratulate, pat on the back, give a bouquet (*or* posy), take one's hat off to, doff one's hat to, hand it to, commend, eulogize, panegyrize, pay tribute to, sing the praises of, sound the praises of, wax lyrical, trumpet, praise to the skies, cry up, boost, puff, puff up, hype, hype up, rave about (Inf)

16 acclaim, hail, applaud, clap, clap one's hands, give a big hand, give a standing ovation, cheer, give three cheers, huzzah (US), whistle, stamp, shout for more, encore, shout bravo, roar one's approval, bring the house down, raise the roof, throw flowers, root for (Inf)

17 meet with approval, meet with approbation, win praise, find favour, gain credit, satisfy, pass, pass muster, pass the test, come up to scratch, gain one's spurs

▶ *682 Success, 765 Satisfaction*

ADJECTIVES

18 approving, satisfied, content, appreciatory, appreciative, grateful, approbatory, respectful, well-inclined, favourable, complimentary, commendatory, laudatory, admiring, eulogistic, encomiastic, panegyric, acclamatory, fulsome, overpraising, overappreciative, uncritical, undiscriminating, flattering, adulatory, idolatrous, lionizing, hero-worshipping

▶ *765 Satisfaction, 837 Gratitude, 784 Liking, 853 Flattery*

19 supporting, supportive, backing, advocating, championing, recommending, in favour, for, pro

▶ *662 Help*

20 acclamatory, applauding, clapping, cheering

21 praiseworthy, laudable, commendable, worthy, estimable, creditable, admirable, unimpeachable, meritorious, deserving, well-deserving

▶ *617 Worth, 845 Entitlement*

22 approvable, satisfactory, acceptable, passable, permissible, worthwhile

23 approved, passed, tested, accepted, supported, backed, endorsed, favoured, recommended

24 admired, respected, well thought of, popular, in demand, in good odour, in high esteem

▶ *849 Respect*

ADVERBS

25 approvingly, admiringly, with compliments, with praise

26 approvably, satisfactorily, acceptably, passably, to approval, to satisfaction

INTERJECTIONS

27 bravo!, encore!, more!, *bis*! (Fr) well done!, congratulations!, hear hear!, hurrah!

852   Disapproval

NOUNS

1 disapproval, disapprobation, dissatisfaction, discontent, discontentment, discontentedness, unhappiness, displeasure, disfavour, disgruntlement, indignation, distaste, dislike, unpopularity

▶ *766 Dissatisfaction, 770 Sorrow, 785 Dislike*

2 disrespect, disesteem, disrepute, contempt, despite, low opinion, poor opinion, low esteem (*or* estimation), dim view

▶ *850 Disrespect, 801 Disrepute*

3 nonacceptance, rejection, refusal, ostracism, cold shoulder, sending to Coventry, blackballing, ban, bar, boycott, veto, negative veto, thumbs down (Inf), red light (Inf)

▶ *581 Rejection, 711 Refusal, 709 Veto, 536 Negation, 147 Exclusion*

4 disagreement, dissension, opposition, hostility, objection, complaint, exception, contradiction, cavil

▶ *666 Disagreement, 500 Dissent, 663 Opposition, 473 Argument*

5 criticism, hostile criticism, critical remarks, critical review, unfavourable review, bad press, bad notice, dispraise, brickbat, rap, flak (Inf), slating (Inf), panning (Inf), knock (Inf), slam (Sl)

▶ *854 Disparagement*

6 fault-finding, carping, cavilling, pettifoggery, captiousness, hairsplitting, niggling, quibbling, fastidiousness, fussing, pestering, nagging, henpecking, overcriticalness, hypercriticism, hypercriticalness, censoriousness, crabbing (Inf), nit-picking (Inf)

7 blame, censure, reprobation, recrimination, complaint, charge, accusation, condemnation, denunciation, denouncement, impeachment, castigation, chastisement, reproof, reprehension, reprimand, rebuke, reproach, stricture, upbraiding, scolding, chiding, admonishment, admonition, warning, lesson, lecture, sermon, set-down, taking to task, hauling (*or* raking) over the coals, home truths, piece of one's mind, rap over the knuckles, black mark, telling-off (Inf), ticking-off (Inf), talking-to (Inf), flea in one's ear (Inf), earful (Inf), wigging (Sl), carpeting (Inf), dressing-down (Inf), rocket (Sl)

▶ *856 Accusation, 879 Punishment, 636 Warning*

8 berating, railing, abuse, tirade, diatribe, onslaught, attack, verbal attack, harsh words, rough edge of one's tongue, tongue-lashing, laying into, pitching into, lambasting, vituperation, execration, revilement, vilification, skinning alive (Inf), roasting (Inf)

▶ *670 Attack, 822 Hate*

9 show of disapproval, display of disapproval, slow handclap, hiss, hissing, boo, cat-

call, raspberry, taunt, jeer, sneer, derision, ridicule, protest, clamour, outcry

▶ *850 Disrespect, 799 Derision, 713 Protest*

10 **disapproving look**, dirty look, black look, reproving look (*or* glance), raised eyebrow, glare, silent reproach, frown, scowl

11 **disapprover**, objector, opposer, opponent, attacker, prude, puritan, censor, censurer, castigator

12 **critic**, criticizer, fault-finder, pettifogger, quibbler, knocker (Inf), nit-picker (Inf)

13 **pessimist**, misery, killjoy, moaner, grouser, wet blanket (Inf), spoilsport (Inf), grouch (Inf), sourpuss (Inf)

▶ *776 Hopelessness, 770 Sorrow*

VERBS

14 **disapprove**, disapprove of, not approve, express disapproval, express disapprobation, disfavour, view with disfavour, take a dim view of, dislike, not admire, have a low (*or* poor) opinion of, think little of, hold in low esteem (*or* estimation), hold in contempt, have no respect for, have no regard for, think ill of, discountenance, look down on, frown on, look down one's nose at, turn up one's nose at

▶ *785 Dislike, 850 Disrespect*

15 **withhold approval**, say no to, not hear of, turn down, reject, refuse, exclude, ostracize, cold shoulder, give the cold shoulder, send to Coventry, black, blacklist, blackball, ban, bar, boycott, veto, disallow, prohibit, give the thumbs down (Inf), turn thumbs down on (Inf), give the red light (Inf)

▶ *581 Rejection, 711 Refusal, 709 Veto, 147 Exclusion*

16 **disagree**, oppose, object to, remonstrate, complain, show hostility, set oneself against, set one's face against

▶ *663 Opposition, 666 Disagreement*

17 **criticize**, fault, deplore, deprecate, depreciate, decry, denigrate, disparage, dispraise, belittle, cry down, run down, tear apart, hand out brickbats, snipe at, rap, knock (Inf), slate (Inf), pan (Inf), slam (Inf)

▶ *854 Disparagement*

18 **find fault**, carp, carp at, cavil, derogate, split hairs, niggle, quibble, pick holes, pick to pieces, pester, nag, henpeck, crab (Inf), bug (Inf), hassle (Inf), nit-pick (Inf)

19 **blame**, hold responsible, accuse, charge, reprobate, recriminate, condemn, denunciate, denounce, impeach, incriminate

▶ *856 Accusation*

20 **censure**, castigate, chastise, reprove, reprehend, reprimand, rebuke, reproach, upbraid, scold, chide, admonish, warn, lecture, deliver a sermon (*or* lesson), set down, take to task, haul (*or* rake) over the coals, give a piece of one's mind, rap over the knuckles, give a black mark, call to account, dress down (Inf), give

a dressing-down (Inf), tell off (Inf), tick off (Inf), give an earful (Inf), give a wigging (Sl), carpet (Inf), come down on like a ton of bricks (Inf)

▶ *879 Punishment, 636 Warning*

21 **berate**, rail, rail (*or* rage) against, assail, attack, abuse, give the rough edge of one's tongue, lash, tongue-lash, lay into, pitch into, lambast (*or* lambaste), read the riot act, throw the book at, give one what for (Inf), bawl out (Inf), skin alive (Inf), give a roasting (Inf)

22 **vituperate**, execrate, revile, pour vitriol, curse, vilify, blacken, defame

▶ *822 Hate, 854 Disparagement*

23 **show disapproval**, tut-tut, frown, scowl, raise one's eyebrows, hiss, boo, catcall, jeer, heckle, shout down, throw mud, throw stones, pelt with rotten eggs, deride, ridicule, mob, lynch

▶ *850 Disrespect, 799 Derision*

24 **be open to criticism**, get a bad press, meet with disapproval, get a bad name, take the blame, take the rap (Sl), carry the can (Sl)

ADJECTIVES

25 **disapproving**, unapproving, disapprobatory, dissatisfied, discontented, unhappy, disappointed, displeased, disgruntled, indignant, disrespectful

▶ *766 Dissatisfaction, 770 Sorrow, 785 Dislike, 850 Disrespect*

26 **disagreeing**, dissenting, opposing, hostile, contradicting, contradictory, against, agin, objecting, protesting

▶ *666 Disagreement, 500 Dissent*

27 **critical**, dispraising, abusive, execratory, vituperative, disparaging, deprecatory, damaging, defamatory, unfavourable, poor, uncomplimentary

▶ *854 Disparagement*

28 **fault-finding**, captious, carping, cavilling, pettifogging, hairsplitting, nagging, niggling, quibbling, fastidious, overcritical, hypercritical, ultracritical, censorious, crabbing (Inf), nit-picking (Inf)

29 **blaming**, blameful, accusatory, accusing, judgmental, damning, condemning, condemnatory, denunciatory, recriminative

▶ *856 Accusation*

30 **censuring**, castigatory, chastising, reprimanding, rebuking, reproaching, reproachful, upbraiding, chiding, scolding, admonitory, stern

31 **disapproved**, unapproved, rejected, refused, unaccepted, opposed, excluded, ostracized, blacked, blacklisted, blackballed, banned, barred, boycotted, vetoed

▶ *581 Rejection, 711 Refusal, 709 Veto, 147 Exclusion*

32 **unsatisfactory**, unacceptable, unpraiseworthy, uncommendable, not to be recom-

mended, found wanting, not good enough, inadequate, insufficient

▶ 609 Insufficiency, 766 Dissatisfaction

33 **criticized**, dispraised, uncommended, run down, given a bad press, panned (Inf), slated (Inf)

34 **censured**, castigated, chastised, reprimanded, rebuked, reproached, upbraided, scolded, admonished, lambasted, berated, assailed, attacked, abused, given the rough edge of one's tongue, laid into, skinned alive (Inf)

▶ 670 Attack

35 **hissed**, booed, taunted, jeered, sneered at, derided, ridiculed

36 **blameworthy**, blamable, to blame, responsible, culpable, criminal, guilty, open to criticism, reprehensible, objectionable, impeachable

ADVERBS

37 **disapprovingly**, critically, censoriously, reproachfully

853 Flattery

It is happy for you that you possess the talent of flattering with delicacy. May I ask whether these pleasing attentions proceed from the impulse of the moment, or are the result of previous study? Jane Austen.

Every woman is infallibly to be gained by every sort of flattery, and every man by one sort or other. Earl of Chesterfield.

Be advised that all flatterers live at the expense of those who listen to them. Jean de La Fontaine.

NOUNS

1 **flattery**, adulation, compliments, praise, overpraise, excessive praise, overlaudation, overcommendation, hagiography, panegyric, hype, insincere praise, insincerity, hypocrisy, eyewash (Inf)

▶ 851 Approval, 826 Endearment, 539 Deception, 541 Exaggeration

2 **blarney**, honeyed words, honeyed phrases, salve, sweet talk (Inf), soft soap (Inf), flannel (Inf), bunkum (Inf)

3 **cajolery**, wheedling, inveiglement, blandishments, ingratiation, getting round (Inf)

▶ 586 Persuasion

4 **unctuousness**, unctuosity, oiliness, smarm, smarminess, sliminess

5 **sycophancy**, servility, toadyism, fawning, bootlicking, backscratching, arse licking (Tab sl)

6 **flatterer**, adulator, charmer, smooth talker, cajoler, wheedler, inveigler

7 **sycophant**, obligor, toady, fawner, yes-man, bootlicker, backscratcher, Uriah Heep, crawler (Sl), creep (Sl), hanger-on (Inf), arse licker (Tab sl), brown-nose (Sl)

VERBS

8 **flatter**, adulate, compliment, praise, overpraise, overlaud, overcommend, overesteem, overestimate, hype, puff, overdo it (Inf), lay it on (Inf), lay it on thick (Inf), lay it on with a trowel (Inf)

▶ 851 Approval, 826 Endearment, 541 Exaggeration, 494 Overestimation, 791 Beautification

9 **blarney**, sugar, charm, smarm, oil, oil the tongue, flatter to deceive, sweet-talk, soft-soap (Inf), butter (Inf), butter up (Inf), soften up (Inf), flannel (Inf)

10 **cajole**, wheedle, inveigle, blandish, coax, court, ingratiate oneself, curry favour, suck up to (Inf), make up to (Inf), get round (Inf)

11 **be sycophantic**, insinuate oneself, toady, fawn, fawn on, creep, crawl, bootlick, backscratch, arse-lick (Tab sl), brown-nose (Sl)

▶ 808 Servility

ADJECTIVES

12 **flattering**, adulatory, complimentary, laudatory, praising, insincere, hypocritical, tongue-in-cheek

▶ 851 Approval, 539 Deception, 791 Beautification

13 **honeyed**, sugary, saccharine, saccharine sweet, blarneying, honey-tongued, smooth-tongued, smooth-spoken, buttery (Inf), sweet-talking (Inf), soft-soaping (Inf)

14 **cajoling**, wheedling, inveigling, blandishing, coaxing, ingratiating

15 **unctuous**, oily, smarmy, slimy, greasy

16 **sycophantic**, servile, obsequious, toadyish, fawning, creeping, crawling, bootlicking, backscratching, arse-licking (Tab sl)

▶ 808 Servility

ADVERBS

17 **flatteringly**, with honeyed words, unctuously, smarmily, sycophantically, obsequiously

854 Disparagement

NOUNS

1 **disparagement**, deprecation, depreciation, decrial, detraction, derogation, denigration, belittlement, slighting, crying down, underestimation, understatement, faint praise, lukewarm support, fault-finding, nit-picking (Inf), running down (Inf), putting down (Inf)

▶ 495 Underestimation

2 **criticism**, hostile criticism, critical remarks, bad review, bad press, brickbat (Inf), flak (Inf), knocking (Inf), panning (Inf), slating (Inf), slam (Inf), hatchet job (Inf)

▶ 852 Disapproval

3 **defamation**, obloquy, defamation of character, character assassination, slander, libel, traducement, calumny, obloquy, smear campaign, muckraking, mudslinging, scandal, gossip, malicious gossip, backbiting

▶ 670 Attack, 548 Misrepresentation

4 aspersion, insinuation, innuendo, slur, smear, disparaging remark, defamatory remark, slighting remark, poison-pen letter
▶ *538 Untruth, 856 Accusation, 801 Disrepute*

5 scorn, contempt, disdain, derision, revilement, vilification, abuse, insult, degradation, debasement, scurrility, defilement, blackening, tarnishing
▶ *799 Derision*

6 ridicule, lampoon, satire, pasquinade, burlesque, skit, squib, caricature, send-up (Inf), takeoff (Inf)
▶ *850 Disrespect*

7 disparager, depreciator, decrier, detractor, derogator, belittler, critic, hostile critic, hatchet man (Inf), knocker (Inf)

8 defamer, slanderer, libeller, muckraker, mudslinger, backbiter, smircher, smearer, gossiper, gossip, scandalmonger, gossip columnist

9 ridiculer, lampooner, lampoonist, satirist, caricaturist, mocker

VERBS

10 disparage, deprecate, depreciate, decry, detract, derogate, denigrate, belittle, slight, cry down, minimize, play down, underestimate, underrate, undervalue, understate, run down (Inf), put down (Inf), do down (Inf), sell short (Inf)
▶ *495 Underestimation, 362 Lowering*

11 criticize, find fault, dispraise, put down, knock (Inf), pan (Inf), slate (Inf), slam (Inf), pull to pieces (Inf), tear to shreds (Inf), nit-pick (Inf), slag off (Sl)
▶ *852 Disapproval*

12 defame, slander, libel, traduce, calumniate, malign, damage, compromise, discredit, dishonour, bring into disrepute, blacken, tarnish, sully, soil, smear, besmear, smirch, besmirch, bespatter, drag through the gutter, drag through the mud, throw mud, sling mud, muckrake, backbite, stab in the back, badmouth (US sl)
▶ *801 Disrepute*

13 vilify, revile, abuse, degrade, debase, defile, asperse, cast aspersions on, insinuate, slur, cast a slur on, whisper, gossip, talk about, talk about behind one's back, speak ill of

14 ridicule, lampoon, satirize, caricature, make fun of, poke fun at, mock, guy, scoff, sneer, deride, scorn, send up (Inf), take off (Inf)
▶ *850 Disrespect, 799 Derision*

ADJECTIVES

15 disparaging, deprecatory, depreciatory, decrying, detractory, derogatory, pejorative, denigratory, belittling, slighting, minimizing, critical, knocking (Inf), nit-picking (Inf)
▶ *852 Disapproval*

16 defamatory, slanderous, libellous, calumnious, calumniatory, scandalous, scurrilous,

abusive, insulting, aspersive, insinuating, gossiping, whispering, mudslinging, smearing, besmirching, blackening, tarnishing, damaging, injurious, destructive, venomous, caustic, bitter, back-biting, snide, catty (Inf), bitchy (Inf)
▶ *801 Disrepute*

17 scornful, contemptuous, contumelious, sarcastic, ridiculing, mocking, scoffing, sneering, derisive
▶ *799 Derision, 850 Disrespect*

ADVERBS

18 disparagingly, derogatorily, pejoratively, slightingly, critically, slanderously, libellously, scornfully, contemptuously, derisively

855 Vindication

NOUNS

1 vindication, exoneration, exculpation, compurgation (Fml), absolution, remission, remittal, acquittal, verdict of acquittal, verdict of innocence, verdict of not guilty, quashing of the charge, discharge, dismissal, release, pardon, clearance, clearing from guilt, clearing of one's name, purging, purgation, reinstatement, restitution, restoration, rehabilitation, triumph of justice, assertion of truth, the OK (Inf), the green light (Inf)
▶ *16 Law, 492 Judgment, 865 Innocence*

2 defence, legal defence, successful defence, reply for the defence, rebuttal, refutation, rejoinder, retort, recrimination, *tu quoque* (L), counterargument, argument, plea, justification, explanation, grounds, good grounds, truth, reason, good reason, excuse, good excuse, alibi, cause, just cause, supportive evidence, corroboration, partial excuse, extenuation, extenuating circumstances, mitigation, mitigating circumstances, palliation, qualification, allowance, out (US)
▶ *671 Defence, 478 Answer, 503 Accuracy, 537 Truth, 485 Qualification*

3 cover-up, whitewash, whitewashing, cop-out (Inf)

4 revenge, vengeance, reprisal, requital, retribution, fitting retribution, punishment, just punishment, poetic justice
▶ *672 Retaliation, 879 Punishment*

5 vindicator, justifier, defender, pleader, advocate, proponent, apologist, excuser, champion, palliator, whitewasher

6 avenger, vindicator, retaliator, punisher, Nemesis

VERBS

7 vindicate, exonerate, exculpate, absolve, remit, grant remission, allow for, make allowances for, excuse, pardon, clear, put in the clear, clear one's name, free from blame, withdraw the charge, acquit, discharge, dismiss,

release, liberate, free, set free, purge, reinstate, restore, rehabilitate, make good, assert the truth, do justice to, set right, give the OK to (Inf), give the green light to (Inf)

8 **justify**, defend, make a legal defence, rebut the charge, rebut, refute, rejoin, retort, recriminate, argue, argue for, plead, plead one's own cause, attest to, warrant, explain, show good grounds, prove the truth of, prove, demonstrate, corroborate, substantiate, give supportive evidence, give a good reason, furnish a good excuse, make excuses for, alibi, speak up for, champion, uphold, stand up for, extenuate, mitigate, palliate, soften, ease, qualify, find an out (US), stick up for (Inf)

9 **cover up**, whitewash, cop out

10 **avenge**, revenge, requite, give fitting retribution, punish

ADJECTIVES

11 **vindicatory**, vindicating, exculpatory, exculpating, exonerative, exonerating, justifying, defensive, defending, argumentative, refuting, rejoining, retorting, rebutting, explanatory, excusatory, excusing, supportive, corroborative, apologetic, extenuating, extenuatory, mitigative, mitigating, qualifying, palliative, remissive, justifying

12 **innocent**, not guilty, acquitted, dismissed, discharged, released, pardoned, cleared, restored, rehabilitated

13 **vindicable**, justifiable, defensible, arguable, refutable, rebuttable, warrantable, admissible, allowable, reasonable, explainable, excusable, having an excuse, pardonable, remissible, forgivable, condonable, venial, exemptible, dispensable

14 **vindictive**, vengeful, revengeful, avenging, requiting, retributive, unforgiving, spiteful, venomous, malicious, malevolent, punitive, punishing

ADVERBS

15 **in vindication**, justifyingly, defensively, argumentatively, in explanation, as an excuse, supportively, in support, apologetically, extenuatingly, with qualifications, palliatively, remissively, justifyingly, with justification, forgivably, venially

16 **vindictively**, vengefully, revengefully, retributively, unforgivably, spitefully, in a spiteful manner, venomously, maliciously, with malice, malevolently, punitively, punishingly, as punishment

856   Accusation

I do not know the method of drawing up an indictment against an whole people. Edmund Burke.

J'accuse./ (I accuse.) Émile Zola.

NOUNS

1 **accusation**, complaint, accusing, bringing of charges, charge, countercharge, blame, insinuation, implication, reproach, denunciation, denouncement, allegation, imputation, suit, lawsuit, plaint, action, litigation, citation, summons, arrest, booking, prosecution, impeachment, indictment, true bill (US), gravamen, incrimination, recrimination, count, case, court case, case for the prosecution, evidence

▶ 852 Disapproval, 854 Disparagement, 668 Defiance, 473 Argument, 483 Evidence

2 **false accusation**, false charge, false evidence, fake confession, perjured testimony, perjury, libel, slander, calumny, scandal, defamation, trumped-up charge, misrepresentation, plant (Inf), cooked-up charge (Inf), put-up job (Inf), put-up (Inf), frame-up (Sl), frame (Sl)

3 **accuser**, denouncer, incriminator, charger, petitioner, plaintiff, complainant, claimant, litigant, appellant, petitioner, party to a suit, witness for the prosecution, hostile witness, indicter, prosecutor, public prosecutor, district attorney (US), impeacher, false witness, perjurer, libeller, libellant, informer, whistleblower (Inf), stool pigeon (Inf), stoolie (Inf), grass (Sl), supergrass (Sl), nark (Sl), squealer (Sl), fink (US sl), snitcher (Sl), snitch (Sl), canary (Sl)

4 **accused person**, the accused, defendant, respondent, correspondent, culprit, suspect, prisoner, guilty party, marked man

VERBS

5 **accuse**, complain, bring charges, charge with, charge, countercharge, blame, lay the blame on, insinuate, implicate, impute, reproach, denunciate, denounce, allegate, sue, bring a charge, file charges, bring a lawsuit, bring (an) action, bring a case, bring litigation, litigate, serve a citation, serve a summons, summon, serve with a writ, cite, prosecute, impeach, indict, swear (or bring) an indictment, inculpate, incriminate, recriminate, arrest, arraign, book, hold a court case, put on trial, hold a trial, try, send before the judge, send before the beak (Sl), put in the dock, bring evidence against, witness, bear witness, lodge a complaint, inform against (or on), point the finger at, throw the book at (Inf), haul up (Inf), blow the whistle (Inf), stool (US inf), put the finger on (US inf), blow the gaff (Sl), grass (Sl), nark (Sl), squeal (Sl), fink (US sl), snitch (Sl), sing (US sl)

6 **accuse falsely**, give false evidence, bear false witness, fake the evidence, fake a confession, commit perjury, perjure oneself, libel, slander, defame, misrepresent, calumniate, trump up a charge, plant evidence, frame (Sl), cook up a charge (Inf), cook the evidence (Sl)

7 **be accused**, stand accused, help (or assist) the

police with their inquiries, receive a summons, have charges brought against one, await trial, go on trial, stand before the judge, stand in the dock, defend oneself, offer a defence

ADJECTIVES

8 **accusatory**, accusing, accused, imputative, charged, up on a charge, countercharged, blamed, implicated, pointing to, denunciatory, denunciated, denounced, alleging, alleged, under suspicion, litigious, cited, summoned, arrested, booked, awaiting trial, liable to prosecution, prosecuted, impeachable, impeached, indictable, indicted, incriminatory, incriminated, recriminatory, recriminated, hauled up (Inf)

9 **perjurious**, perjured, libellous, libelled, slanderous, slandered, defamatory, defamed, misrepresented, calumnious, trumped-up, planted (Inf), cooked-up (Inf), put-up (Inf), framed (Sl)

ADVERBS

10 **accusingly**, in accusation, allegedly, before the judge, litigiously, perjuriously, libellously, slanderously, defamatorily, in a frame-up (Sl)

857 Probity

NOUNS

1 **probity**, honourableness, honour, goodness, integrity, respectability, decency, incorruptibility, principles, high principles, ethics, morality, morals, moral fibre, high ideals, high-mindedness, uprightness, nobleness, good character, repute, trustworthiness, trustiness, reliability, dependability, honesty, truthfulness, truth, candidness, candour, frankness, openness, veracity, plainness, straightforwardness, sincerity, scrupulousness, scruples, fastidiousness, carefulness, conscientiousness, meticulousness, soundness, sense of duty, sense of responsibility, impartiality, fairness, equity, justice, clean hands, clear conscience, conscience, good faith, bona fides (Fml), faithfulness, fidelity, constancy, steadfastness, trueness, loyalty, devotion, chivalry

▶ *876 Morality, 861 Good, 719 Observance, 469 Carefulness, 537 Truth, 556 Simplicity, 503 Accuracy, 694 Obedience*

2 **purity**, sanctity, faith, virtue, virginity, innocence, righteousness, godliness, holiness, rectitude, pure heart

▶ *621 Cleanness, 7 Religion, 863 Virtue, 865 Innocence*

3 **honourable person**, honest person, man (or woman) of honour, man of his word, woman of her word, good person, perfect gentleman, Galahad, true lady, fair fighter, good loser, sportsman, sportswoman, knight in shining armour, champion of lost causes, salt of the

earth, good sort (Inf), brick (Inf), square (or straight) shooter (US inf), good sport (Inf)

ADJECTIVES

4 **honourable**, respectable, decent, good, reputable, incorruptible, high-minded, principled, fastidious, high-principled, ethical, moral, upright, upstanding, noble, trustworthy, trusty, sure, reliable, dependable, as good as one's word, responsible, dutiful, honest, true, truthful, candid, frank, open, above board, on the up and up, law-abiding, veracious, plain, plain-spoken, straightforward, sincere, undeceitful, undeceptive, scrupulous, careful, meticulous, conscientious, sound, impartial, fair, fair-dealing, straight, equitable, bona fide, just, faithful, constant, steadfast, loyal, true-blue, true to the core, devoted, chivalrous, gentlemanly, sportsmanlike, sporting, on the level (Inf), fair and square (Inf), square (Inf), straight-up (Sl)

5 **pure**, undefiled, sanctified, saintly, pious, religious, godly, virtuous, virginal, innocent, righteous, pure as the driven snow

VERBS

6 **be honourable**, act honourably, preserve one's honour, behave well, behave like a gentleman, act like a lady, live like a Christian, fear God, keep (the) faith, have virtue, have decency, act morally, deal fairly, play by the rules, stick to the rules, go by the book, shoot straight, guard one's reputation, keep one's promise, keep one's word, speak truthfully, speak (or tell) the truth, stick to the truth, tell the whole truth and nothing but the truth, tell the truth and shame the devil, speak plainly, tell it like it is, call a spade a spade, put (or lay) one's cards on the table, show respect, show a sense of duty, keep steadfast, level with (Inf), give it straight (Inf), keep to the straight and narrow (Inf)

ADVERBS

7 **honourably**, respectably, decently, well, reputably, high-mindedly, ethically, morally, nobly, reliably, dependably, responsibly, dutifully, honestly, truly, truthfully, to tell the truth, in truth, with truth, candidly, frankly, openly, veraciously, plainly, in plain words, in plain English, straight from the shoulder, not to mince words, without equivocation, unequivocally, sincerely, scrupulously, sedulously, carefully, meticulously, conscientiously, in all conscience, impartially, fairly, squarely, in (or with) good faith, justly, faithfully, constantly, steadfastly, loyally, devotedly, chivalrously, sportingly, straight up (Sl)

8 **purely**, with pure intentions, piously, religiously, virtuously, innocently, in all innocence, righteously

858 Improbity

NOUNS

1 **improbity**, dishonour, dishonesty, disrepute, shame, worthlessness, good-for-nothingness, evilness, wickedness, badness, villainy, villainousness, corruption, depravity, venality, turpitude, moral turpitude, knavery, lack of integrity, disrespect, disgrace, debasement, baseness, indecency, immorality, lack of morals, lack of principles, lack of conscience, unscrupulousness, deviousness, opportunism, unfairness, partiality, bias, prejudice, injustice, insincerity, hypocrisy, disingenuousness, untruthfulness, falsehood, lie, foul play, contrivance, chicanery, trickery, trick, dirty trick, not playing the game, crookedness (Inf), hitting below the belt (Inf)

▶ 844 Wrong, 864 Wickedness, 578 Equivocation, 538 Untruth, 540 Falsehood, 693 Disobedience, 539 Deception, 657 Cunning

2 **faithlessness**, unfaithfulness, bad faith, infidelity, perfidy, perfidiousness, deceit, falseness, falsity, breach of faith, broken word, broken promise, breach of promise, unreliability, untrustworthiness, undependability, wavering loyalty, sitting on the fence, disloyalty, disobedience, duplicity, double-dealing, double-crossing, U-turn, volte-face, tergiversation, defection, desertion, betrayal, treachery, Judas kiss, stab in the back, treason, high treason, sedition, rebellion, running with the hare and hunting with the hounds, sellout (Inf)

3 **criminality**, crime, lawbreaking, felony, racketeering, fraudulency, fraudulence, fraud, thieving, thievishness, light fingers, embezzlement, bribery, tax evasion, graft, sharp practice, swindle, confidence trick, confidence game (US), underhand dealings, dirty dealings, racket, skulduggery (Inf), shadiness (Inf), crookedness (Inf), fishy transaction (Inf), fiddle (Inf), con trick (Inf), con game (US inf), scam (Sl)

▶ 844 Wrong, 736 Stealing, 877 Immorality

4 **dishonourable person**, dishonest person, man (or woman) of dishonour, scoundrel, good-for-nothing, bad influence, rascal, rogue, knave, villain, fraud, double-dealer, double-crosser, traitor, Judas, criminal, gangster, racketeer, lawbreaker, embezzler, felon, snake in the grass, slippery customer (Inf), shady character (Inf), two-timer (Inf), con man (Inf), shyster (US inf), crook (Inf), spiv (Sl), mobster (US sl)

ADJECTIVES

5 **dishonourable**, dishonest, disreputable, shameful, worthless, good-for-nothing, evil, wicked, bad, villainous, nefarious, corrupt, corruptible, unprincipled, unethical, bribable, depraved, venal, disrespectful, disgraceful, ignoble, contemptible, debased, base, indecent, immoral, unscrupulous, ungentlemanly, unsportsmanlike, rotten, devious, up to something, up to no good, opportunistic, scheming, unfair, biased, prejudiced, unjust, insincere, hypocritical, disingenuous, uncandid, untruthful, lying, tricky, foxy, vulpine, slippery, wrangling (Inf), shady (Inf), crooked (Inf), low-down (Inf), not cricket (Inf), on the fiddle (Inf)

6 **faithless**, unfaithful, perfidious, deceitful, false, two-faced, untrustworthy, not to be trusted, unreliable, undependable, questionable, shaky, disloyal, disobedient, double-dealing, double-crossing, duplicitous, deserting, betraying, treacherous, treasonous, seditious, rebellious

7 **criminal**, lawbreaking, felonious, fraudulent, underhanded, thieving, light-fingered, embezzling, swindling, bribing, not straight, shady (Inf), crooked (Inf), fishy (Inf), bent (Sl)

VERBS

8 **be dishonourable**, be dishonest, lack honesty, have no morals, forget one's principles, yield to temptation, live by one's wits, evade, shift the blame, falsify, perjure oneself, tell lies, lie, prevaricate, pull the wool over someone's eyes, shed crocodile tears, bend the rules (Inf), pass the buck (Inf), wangle (Inf), finagle (Inf), smell fishy (Inf), do the dirty on (Inf), play dirty pool (US sl)

9 **prove false**, dissemble, deceive, double-cross, break one's word, break faith, go back on one's promises, let down one's side, let down, turn against, forsake, betray, stab in the back, go over to the enemy, collaborate, run with the hare and hunt with the hounds, bite the hand that feeds one, sell out (Inf), two-time (Inf), sell down the river (Inf)

10 **be criminal**, lead a life of crime, smuggle, defraud, cheat, rob, embezzle, racketeer, fence, swindle, steal, thieve, pilfer, shoplift, fiddle (Inf), do someone out of (Inf), cook the books (Inf), scam (Sl)

ADVERBS

11 **dishonourably**, without honour, dishonestly, without regard for honesty, shamefully, like a thief in the night, worthlessly, wickedly, badly, corruptly, unethically, by fair means or foul, disrespectfully, disgracefully, ignobly, indecently, immorally, unscrupulously, deviously, mala fide, unfairly, naughtily, insincerely, hypocritically, uncandidly, untruthfully, faithlessly, unfaithfully, deceitfully, falsely, unreliably, shakily, disloyally, disobediently, treacherously, seditiously, rebelliously, criminally, fraudulently, underhandedly, shadily (Inf)

859 Disinterestedness

NOUNS

1 **disinterestedness**, disinterest, indifference, detachment, ataraxia, impartiality, lack of bias, lack of prejudice, objectivity, equitableness, fairness, fair-mindedness, open-mindedness, justice, neutrality, nonalignment, noninvolvement, lack of emotion, self-control, self-restraint, dispassion, stoicism, keeping a stiff upper lip, keeping cool (Sl)
▶ *843 Right, 857 Probity, 869 Self-Restraint*

2 **unselfishness**, selflessness, altruism, considerateness, consideration, thought for others, kindness, compassion, sympathy, pity, humility, modesty, self-denial, self-effacement, self-abnegation, self-sacrifice, martyrdom, idealism, high-mindedness, honesty, honourableness, sublimity, loftiness, magnanimity, nobleness, munificence, benevolence, charity, generosity, open-handedness, big-heartedness

3 **impartial person**, judge, jury member, arbitrator, moderator, referee, umpire
▶ *817 Courtesy, 806 Humility, 835 Pity, 831 Benevolence, 833 Philanthropy, 729 Giving*

ADJECTIVES

4 **disinterested**, indifferent, detached, impersonal, impartial, unbiased, unprejudiced, objective, equitable, nonpartisan, fair, fairminded, open-minded, open, just, neutral, nonaligned, uninvolved, not bothered, self-controlled, dispassionate, stoical (*or* stoic), cool (Sl)

5 **unselfish**, selfless, altruistic, considerate, kind, compassionate, sympathetic, humble, modest, self-abnegating, self-sacrificing, self-denying, self-effacing, ready to die for, martyred, idealistic, high-minded, honest, honourable, sublime, lofty, magnanimous, noble, munificent, benevolent, charitable, generous, open-handed, big-hearted

VERBS

6 **be disinterested**, show (*or* take) no interest in, show indifference towards, lack bias, lack prejudice, keep an open mind, open one's mind to, do the fair thing, lack emotion, demonstrate self-control, keep a stiff upper lip, mind one's own business, live and let live, keep cool (Sl)

7 **be unselfish**, think of others first, put oneself last, sacrifice oneself, make a sacrifice, sacrifice, rise above oneself, do the right thing by, show compassion for, sympathize with, pity, give generously, have a big heart, take a back seat (Inf), bend (*or* lean) over backwards (Inf)

ADVERBS

8 **disinterestedly**, indifferently, impersonally, impartially, objectively, without bias, without prejudice, equitably, fairly, open-mindedly, with an open mind, openly, justly, neutrally,

dispassionately, stoically, with a stiff upper lip, coolly (Sl)

9 **unselfishly**, selflessly, altruistically, with others in mind, for the sake of others, considerately, kindly, compassionately, sympathetically, humbly, in a humble manner, modestly, with modesty, idealistically, high-mindedly, honestly, honourably, sublimely, loftily, magnanimously, nobly, with noble intentions, munificently, benevolently, charitably, generously, open-handedly, big-heartedly

860 Selfishness

It's 'Damn you, Jack – I'm all right!' with you chaps. David Bone.

NOUNS

1 **selfishness**, self-interest, self-concern, self-pity, self-preservation, self-consideration, self-indulgence, self-pleasing, self-serving, self-seeking, personal desires, personal aims, possessiveness, keeping for oneself, covetousness, jealousy, envy, avarice, acquisitiveness, mundaneness, worldliness, materialism, greed, ambition, careerism, opportunism, individualism, stinginess, miserliness, niggardliness, littleness, meanness, mean-mindedness, mean-spiritedness, parsimony, charity that begins at home, every man for himself (Inf), looking after number one (Inf)
▶ *870 Self-Indulgence, 723 Possession, 726 Retention, 841 Jealousy, 842 Envy, 782 Desire, 758 Meanness*

2 **egoism**, egotism, ego, conceit, vanity, self-love, self-devotion, self-absorption, narcissism, self-centredness, no thought for others, egocentrism, egocentricity, ego-centredness, self-praise, ego trip (Inf)
▶ *809 Vanity*

3 **selfish person**, egoist, egotist, egomaniac, narcissist, self-seeker, self-pleaser, self-server, opportunist, monopolist, dog in the manger, money-grubber (Inf), hog (Inf), road hog (Inf)

ADJECTIVES

4 **selfish**, self-concerned, self-indulgent, self-interested, self-seeking, possessive, covetous, jealous, envious, avaricious, acquisitive, materialistic, worldly, ambitious, greedy, monopolistic, opportunistic, individualistic, ungenerous, uncharitable, stingy, miserly, niggardly, mean, mean-minded, mean-spirited, parsimonious, cold-hearted, on the make (Inf), money-grubbing (Inf)

5 **egoistic**, egoistical, egotistic, egotistical, conceited, vain, narcissistic, self-loving, self-absorbed, self-centred, egocentric, ego-centred, wrapped up in oneself (Inf), concerned with number one (Inf), stuck on oneself (Sl)

VERBS

6 **be selfish**, indulge oneself, spoil oneself, please oneself, put oneself first, think only of oneself, pursue one's interests, advance one's own interests, sacrifice the interests of others, have personal motives, have ambition, covet, envy, acquire, monopolize, possess, keep for oneself, hang onto, feather one's nest, have an axe to grind, hog (Sl)

7 **be egoistic**, be egotistic, love oneself, have no thought for others, praise oneself, brag, take an ego trip (Inf), take care of (*or* look after) number one (Inf)

ADVERBS

8 **selfishly**, only for oneself, for one's own sake, self-indulgently, possessively, covetously, jealously, enviously, avariciously, acquisitively, materialistically, ambitiously, for profit, from personal motives, for private ends, greedily, individualistically, ungenerously, uncharitably, stingily, meanly, parsimoniously, coldheartedly, on the make (Inf)

9 **egoistically**, egotistically, conceitedly, self-lovingly, vainly, with self-love, egocentrically, with no thought for others, as an ego trip (Inf)

861   Good

ADJECTIVES

1 **good**, excellent, first-rate, first-class, superior, better, superb, splendid, great, famous, fine, superfine, exquisite, high-class, wonderful, magnificent, terrific, impressive, meritorious, praiseworthy, admirable, worthy, valuable, profitable, sound, healthy, salubrious, salutary, favourable, propitious, heaven-sent, auspicious, lucky, suitable, appropriate, apt, right, fabulous (Inf), fine and dandy (Inf), super (Inf), crackerjack (Inf), topnotch (Inf), A-OK (*or* A-okay) (US inf), dandy (Inf), jim-dandy (US inf), smashing (Inf), cool (US inf), hunky-dory (US inf), wizard (Inf), top-hole (Inf), brill (Inf), fab (Inf), radical (Sl), rad (Inf), swell (Sl), spiffy (Sl), corking (Sl), crack (Sl), copacetic (*or* kopasetic) (US sl), bad (Sl), wicked (Sl), deadly (Sl)

▶ *126 Superiority, 686 Prosperity, 742 Wealth, 617 Worth, 623 Health*

2 **best**, very best, best ever, top, essential, quintessential, choice, elite, unequalled, nonpareil, peerless, matchless, record-breaking, class A, perfect, flawless, supreme, superlative

▶ *619 Perfection*

3 **kind**, goodly, nice, gracious, fair, virtuous, righteous, moral, honest, honourable, benevolent, beneficent, helpful, good-natured, friendly, well-wishing, thoughtful, generous

▶ *863 Virtue, 664 Cooperation, 857 Probity, 831 Benevolence, 729 Giving*

4 **well-behaved**, well-mannered, obedient, compliant, docile, willing, biddable, dutiful

▶ *673 Submission*

5 **proficient**, efficient, competent, accomplished, expert, handy, skilled, skilful, deft, versatile, dexterous, adroit, talented, gifted, masterful, masterly, wicked (Sl)

▶ *655 Skill*

6 **beneficial**, useful, advantageous, worthwhile, profitable, improving, bettering, edifying, beatific

▶ *613 Usefulness, 721 Gain, 627 Improvement*

7 **large**, goodly, ample, substantial, large-size(d), ample-size(d), adequate-size(d), sufficient-size(d)

▶ *259 Size*

NOUNS

8 **good**, goodness, excellence, first class, quality, good quality, superiority, superbness, splendidness, greatness, fame, wonderfulness, magnificence, merit, worth, worthiness, praiseworthiness, value, soundness, healthiness, favourableness, propitiousness, auspiciousness, suitableness, appropriateness, aptness, rightness

9 **the best**, the very best, the best ever, tops, essence, quintessence, choice, pick, elite, cream, cream of the crop, flower, paragon, nonpareil, gem of the first water, jewel in the crown, top marks, class A, superlative, perfection, flawlessness, supremacy

10 **kindness**, kindliness, goodliness, niceness, graciousness, fairness, virtue, virtuousness, righteousness, rectitude, morality, honesty, honourableness, benevolence, beneficence, thoughtfulness, helpfulness, grace, good-naturedness, friendliness, well-wishing, generosity, kind act, good turn

11 **good behaviour**, good manners, obedience, compliance, docility, willingness, biddability, dutifulness

12 **proficiency**, efficiency, competence, accomplishment, expertise, skilfulness, deftness, versatility, dexterousness, adroitness, handiness, ability, talent, gift, masterfulness, masterliness

13 **benefit**, well-being, welfare, public weal, common good, interest, behalf, happiness, blessing, benediction, betterment, improvement, advantage, worthwhileness, profitability, prosperity, boon, gift, profit, gain, usefulness, use, advantage, edification

14 **largeness**, goodliness, ampleness, substantiality, large size, ample size, adequate size, sufficient size

15 **good person**, saint, priest, nun, monk, Good Samaritan, altruist, philanthropist, friend, good neighbour, well-wisher, helper, rescuer, white knight

16 **superior person**, star, superstar, champion, superman, superwoman, prodigy, genius, wonder, virtuoso, paragon, high achiever, ace,

high flyer, *crème de la crème* (Fr), pick of the bunch, nonesuch (*or* nonsuch), *übermensch* (Ger), first-rater, number one, numero uno (Inf), topnotcher (Inf), whiz kid (Inf), whiz (Inf), the cat's pyjamas (*or* whiskers) (Sl)

17 good thing, the very thing, just the thing, good luck, (good) fortune, favour, blessing, halcyon days, happy ending, treasure, gem, jewel, dream, pride and joy, pride, prize, find, winner, godsend, windfall, masterstroke, *tour de force* (Fr), *chef-d'oeuvre* (Fr), work of art, masterpiece, collector's item, record-breaker, best seller, hit (Inf), smash (Inf), smash hit (Inf), dandy (Inf), jim-dandy (US inf), crackerjack (Inf), peach (Inf), plum (Inf), knockout (Inf), humdinger (Sl), corker (Sl), doozy (US sl), killer (Sl), killer-diller (US sl), dilly (US sl), beaut (US and Aus sl), lollapalooza (US sl)

VERBS

18 be good, behave well, obey, comply, conform, show respect, bear allegiance to, pay homage to

19 be good at, do well at, master, excel, qualify for, pass, transcend, have the knack, have a gift for, show skill for, perform skilfully, exploit, play one's cards right

20 do good, help, serve, benefit, avail, make better, do a world of good, do someone a favour, bless, better, improve, advance, profit, bring prosperity

21 do well, thrive, flourish, prosper, succeed, improve, get better, make a profit, gain, turn to good account, make money, get rich, be on top of the world, be on the crest of a wave

ADVERBS

22 well, impressively, admirably, excellently, superbly, splendidly, famously, fabulously, exquisitely, wonderfully, magnificently, perfectly, peerlessly

23 nicely, friendlily, helpfully, benevolently, beneficently, generously, good-naturedly, honestly, morally

24 obediently, willingly, compliantly, dutifully, docilely

25 skilfully, expertly, dexterously, adroitly, giftedly, masterfully, competently

26 usefully, beneficially, advantageously, profitably

INTERJECTIONS

27 great!, super! (Inf), rad! (Inf), brill! (Inf), fab! (Inf), bad! (Sl)

862 Evil

NOUNS

1 evil, evilness, badness, wickedness, meanness, wrongness, wrong, sin, improbity, malevolence, maleficence, malignity, malice, viciousness, hatefulness, injustice, untruthfulness, unkindness, ill will, vindictiveness, revengeful-

ness, mischievousness, mischief, devilry, obnoxiousness, offensiveness, iniquity, vice, immorality, corruption, defilement, depravity, foulness, vileness, nastiness, noxiousness, wretchedness, rottenness, worthlessness, terribleness, dreadfulness, horribleness, awfulness, atrociousness, deadliness, beastliness (Inf)

▶ *844 Wrong, 858 Improbity, 538 Untruth, 832 Malevolence*

2 affliction, trouble, troubles, adversity, plague, blight, ruin, destruction, mental affliction, unease, annoyance, angst, depression, mental illness, suffering, distress, misery, grief, sorrow, woe, bodily harm, harmfulness, harm, abuse, hurtfulness, hurt, discomfort, malaise, painfulness, pain, sickness, illness, unhealthiness, sore, running sore, malignancy (*or* malignance) malignity, casualty, accident, damage, injury, wound, tragedy, calamity, disaster, catastrophe, fiasco, sad ending, fatality, mortal blow, deathblow, death, vale of tears

▶ *687 Adversity, 659 Difficulty, 631 Blight, 244 Destruction, 406 Physical Pain, 770 Sorrow, 397 Death*

3 bad luck, misfortune, ill fortune, adversity, inauspiciousness, ominousness, unfavourableness, slings and arrows (of misfortune), ill wind, evil star

▶ *517 Prediction*

4 evil power, bad influence, malign influence, bad spell, evil spell, the evil eye, malediction, curse, jinx, voodoo, bad karma, whammy (Sl), double whammy (Sl), hex (US inf), hoodoo (Inf)

5 evil thing, evil plight, evil wish, bane, pornography, poison, pollution, pollutant, crime, murder, foul play, skeleton in the cupboard, Pandora's box

▶ *16 Law, 398 Killing*

6 evil person, bad influence, bane, evil genius, evildoer, wrongdoer, malefactor, troublemaker, mischief-maker, villain, blackguard, scoundrel, bully, holy terror, terrorist, traitor, criminal, robber, kidnapper, pervert, child abuser, pornographer, rapist, killer, serial killer, murderer, mass murderer, homicidal maniac, assassin, cutthroat, poisoner, gang member, mafioso, evil ruler, Hitler, Stalin, devil, Satan, the Evil One, snake in the grass, Old Nick (Inf), baddie (*or* baddy) (Inf), crook (Inf), mobster (US sl)

▶ *7 Religion*

ADJECTIVES

7 evil, bad, wicked, mean, wrong, sinful, sinister, nefarious, malevolent, maleficent, malignant, malicious, vicious, diabolic(al), demonic(al), ungodly, hateful, unkind, untruthful, prejudicial, vindictive, revengeful, mischievous, obnoxious, offensive, odious, iniquitous, immoral, corrupt, defiled, blighted,

depraved, foul, vile, nasty, wretched, deplorable, rotten, worthless, terrible, dreadful, horrible, awful, atrocious, despicable, detestable, contemptible, reprehensible, deadly, beastly (Inf), lousy (Sl)

8 **afflicted**, troubled, plagued, depressed, distressed, miserable, grievous, grief-stricken, sorrowful, woeful, sad, hurt, in pain, sick, ill, unhealthy, sore, damaged, injured, wounded, tragic

9 **detrimental**, damaging, destructive, deleterious, harmful, injurious, hurtful, distressing, troublous, baleful, baneful, pernicious, noxious, toxic, corruptive, corrosive, malignant, catastrophic, dire, mortal, deadly

10 **inauspicious**, unfavourable, unfortunate, unlucky, adverse, ominous, accursed, jinxed, voodooed, hoodooed (Inf), hexed (US inf)

VERBS

11 **be evil**, do evil, work evil, do wrong, do wrong by, wrong, do mischief to, do ill, not tell the truth, trouble, get into trouble, distress, aggrieve, afflict, plague, harass, persecute, threaten, menace, mistreat, maltreat, abuse, molest, defile, violate, despoil, lay a hand on, befoul, torment, condemn, hurt, harm, corrupt, pervert, damage, impair, blight, pollute, wreak havoc on, poison, injure, wound, destroy, doom, kill, curse, jinx, hex (US inf), put the (or a) whammy on (Sl), put the (or a) double whammy on (Sl)

ADVERBS

12 **evilly**, badly, ill, wickedly, wrongly, wrong, all wrong, sinfully, sinisterly, nefariously, malevolently, maliciously, with malice, viciously, diabolically, hatefully, with hate, unkindly, prejudicially, with prejudice, untruthfully, vindictively, in a vindictive way, revengefully, for revenge, mischievously, obnoxiously, offensively, odiously, immorally, corruptly, deplorably, terribly, dreadfully, horribly, awfully, atrociously, detestably, reprehensibly

13 **destructively**, in a destructive manner, depressingly, distressingly, miserably, grievously, sorrowfully, to one's sorrow, woefully, sadly, balefully, harmfully, hurtfully, perniciously, with malice, deleteriously, painfully, accidentally, tragically, disastrously, fatally, with fatal results, mortally

14 **inauspiciously**, ominously, as a bad omen, unfavourably, unfortunately, without good fortune, unluckily, adversely

INTERJECTIONS

15 **bad luck!**, terrible!, horrible!, that's awful!, woe is me!, jinxed again!, a plague on you!

863   Virtue

Virtue is like a rich stone, best plain set. Francis Bacon.

To be able to practise five things everywhere under heaven constitutes perfect virtue…gravity, generosity of soul, sincerity, earnestness, and kindness. Confucius.

The greatest offence against virtue is to speak ill of it. William Hazlitt.

Most men admire/ Virtue, who follow not her lore. John Milton.

NOUNS

1 **virtue**, virtuousness, righteousness, probity, goodness, good behaviour, virtuous conduct, Christian conduct, moral goodness, moral rectitude, rectitude, morality, moral strength, moral tone, spirituality, saintliness, sanctity, godliness, holiness, perfection, nobleness, magnanimity, philanthropy, benevolence, generosity, altruism, unselfishness, disinterestedness, idealism, uprightness, irreproachability, guiltlessness, blamelessness, stainlessness, uncorruptness, sinlessness, innocence, honour, personal honour, integrity, decency, chivalry, properness, good conscience, clear conscience, the straight and narrow (path)

▶ *843 Right, 857 Probity, 876 Morality, 7 Religion, 619 Perfection, 831 Benevolence, 865 Innocence*

2 **virtues**, morals, mores, ethics, principles, high principles, ideals, cardinal virtues, moral virtues, theological virtues, moral laws, faith, hope, charity, love, natural virtues, prudence, justice, temperance, soberness, self-control, character, chastity, purity, virginity, fortitude, honesty, duty, obedience, grace, saving grace, qualities, fine qualities, saving qualities, heroic qualities

▶ *869 Self-Restraint, 847 Duty*

3 **worth**, worthiness, excellence, credit, merit, desert

▶ *617 Worth, 851 Approval*

4 **virtuous person**, good person, honest person, saint, angel, priest, nun, monk, paragon, paragon of virtue, altruist, virgin, martyr, white knight, knight in shining armour, Good Samaritan, good example, goody-goody (Inf)

ADJECTIVES

5 **virtuous**, righteous, good, good as gold, Christian, moral, spiritual, saintly, saintlike, seraphic, angelic, sanctified, godly, holy, perfect, unerring, noble, magnanimous, philanthropic, benevolent, generous, altruistic, unselfish, disinterested, idealistic, upright, irreproachable, above reproach, impeccable, above temptation, guiltless, blameless, stainless, spotless, without blemish, immaculate, uncorrupt, uncorrupted, sinless, innocent, honourable, decent, chivalrous, proper, on the side of the angels, pure as driven snow

6 **ethical**, principled, high-principled, faithful, charitable, loving, prudent, just, honest, duti-

ful, obedient, temperate, self-controlled, sober, chaste, pure, virginal

7 **worthy**, praiseworthy, commendable, excellent, meritorious, exemplary

VERBS

8 **be virtuous**, be good, do good, love good, do no evil, hate evil, hear no evil, see no evil, speak no evil, behave, stay on one's good (or best) behaviour, practise virtue, have all the virtues, resist temptation, rise above temptation, control one's passions, control oneself, fight the good fight, keep straight, go straight, follow one's conscience, keep to (or on) the straight and narrow path, follow the straight and narrow, walk humbly with one's God, shame the devil, discharge one's obligations, do one's duty, set a good example, be a shining light, have saving grace

ADVERBS

9 **virtuously**, righteously, innocently, in all innocence, goodly, with good intentions, morally, spiritually, angelically, perfectly, nobly, for noble reasons, magnanimously, benevolently, generously, altruistically, for the benefit of others, unselfishly, idealistically, uprightly, irreproachably, impeccably, guiltlessly, without guilt, blamelessly, without blame, stainlessly, immaculately, sinlessly, without sin, honourably, decently, chivalrously, properly

10 **ethically**, faithfully, charitably, lovingly, with a loving heart, prudently, justly, honestly, with honesty, dutifully, obediently, temperately, soberly, chastely, purely, virginally

11 **worthily**, commendably, excellently, in an excellent manner, meritoriously

864 Wickedness

NOUNS

1 **wickedness**, badness, sinfulness, sin, evil, cruelty, brutality, wrong, improbity, iniquity, flagitiousness, unrighteousness, wrongdoing, evildoing, bad behaviour, misbehaviour, wicked ways, bad ways, bad conduct, bad character, disrepute, fallen nature, recidivism, backsliding, deterioration, naughtiness, disobedience, dishonesty, wicked deed, peccability, transgression, trespass, delinquency, criminality, corruption, vitiation, loss of innocence, shamelessness, vileness, baseness, heinousness, viciousness, cruelness, hellishness, malevolence, hardness of heart, villainy, knavery, roguery, enormity, inhumanity, infamy, flagrancy, outrage, abomination, atrocity

▶ *862 Evil, 844 Wrong, 858 Improbity, 801 Disrepute, 628 Deterioration, 693 Disobedience, 618 Worthlessness, 832 Malevolence*

2 **vice**, immorality, amorality, amoralism, no morals, loose morals, unvirtuousness, impur-

ity, indecency, lust, vulgarity, carnality, debauchery, degeneration, degeneracy, profligacy, depravity, turpitude, moral turpitude, degradation, perversion

▶ *877 Immorality*

3 **venial sin**, small fault, flaw, fatal flaw, imperfection, shortcoming, failing, frailty, human frailty, foible, weakness, human weakness, moral weakness, weakness of the flesh, weak point, laxity, lack of principle, infirmity, fault, defect, demerit, deficiency, limitation, indecorum, impropriety, indiscretion, unseemliness, bad taste, peccadillo, slight transgression, minor offence

▶ *238 Weakness*

4 **sin**, original sin, capital sin, mortal sin, deadly sin

5 **seven deadly sins**, pride, covetousness, lust, anger, gluttony, envy, sloth

6 **religious sin**, impiety, ungodliness, blasphemy, sacrilege, desecration, profaneness, idolatry, devilry, devil worship, Satanism, diabolism, witchcraft, sorcery, the Old Adam, devil, Satan, Mephistopheles

▶ *805 Pride, 842 Envy, 7 Religion*

7 **criminality**, criminal act, criminal offence, guilty act, guilt, foul play, illegality, unlawful act, lawbreaking, crime, misdemeanour, white-collar crime, shoplifting, delinquency, juvenile delinquency, felony, drug peddling, robbery, rape, assault, assault and battery, murder, capital crime, deadly crime, hanging offence, career of crime, criminal world, underworld, gangland, organized crime, the syndicate (US), the Mafia, Cosa Nostra, Black Hand, the rackets (Inf), the mob (Sl)

▶ *866 Guilt, 875 Drug-Taking, 398 Killing, 670 Attack*

8 **wicked place**, den of iniquity, den of vice, brothel, house of prostitution, opium den, gambling den, road to hell, hell, Hades (Inf), robbers' lair (Inf), cathouse (US sl)

9 **wicked person**, wrongdoer, evildoer, transgressor, sinner, lost soul, lost sheep, prodigal son, black sheep, outcast, undesirable, troublemaker, good-for-nothing, ne'er-do-well, scamp, rake, knave, rogue, rascal, scoundrel, rapscallion, reprobate, wastrel, profligate, degenerate, lecher, pervert, child abuser, paedophile, fallen woman, fallen angel, demimonde, hussy, whore, streetwalker, call girl, pimp, nasty type, thug, bully, tyrant, fiend, brute, savage, sadist, ogre, monster, demon, ghoul, Satanist, devil worshipper, devil, devil incarnate, miscreant, renegade, recreant, blasphemer, idolater, profaner, traitor, betrayer, quisling, Judas, snake, snake in the grass, swine, swindler, villain, blackguard, criminal, lawbreaker, malefactor, outlaw, desperado, culprit, offender, felon, cheat, thief, robber,

rapist, drug peddler, hoodlum (US), gangster, racketeer, hired killer, killer, murderer, assassin, terrorist, the wicked, the bad, scum of the earth, dregs of society
▶ *862 Evil, 877 Immorality*

10 **bad person**, ugly customer (Inf), bad egg (Inf), baddie (Inf), bad lot (Inf), rotten apple (Inf), crook (Inf), bastard (Inf), rat (Inf), skunk (Inf), polecat (US inf), bitch (Sl), stinker (Sl), rotter (Sl), wrong'un (Sl), lowlife (Sl), son of a bitch (s.o.b.) (US sl), hooker (US sl), hood (Sl), hooligan (Sl), hit man (Sl), tea leaf (Sl), mobster (US sl), bounder (Sl), gross-out (US sl), bad news (Sl), louse (Sl)

ADJECTIVES

11 **wicked**, bad, sinful, full of sin, sinning, evil, evildoing, wrong, wrongdoing, erring, iniquitous, nefarious, flagitious, unrighteous, badly behaved, misbehaved, misbehaving, improper, disreputable, disgraceful, fallen, knavish, roguish, rascally, slipping, sliding, backsliding, recidivous, deteriorating, naughty, disobedient, dishonest, transgressing, trespassing, delinquent, criminal, corrupt, rotten, rotten to the core, shameless, unprincipled, worthless, unscrupulous, conscienceless, despicable, reprehensible, vile, base, foul, beastly, heinous, vicious, cruel, brutal, brutalized, hellish, maleficent, malevolent, hardhearted, hardened, callous, villainous, miscreant, inhuman, infamous, flagrant, outrageous, abominable, atrocious, hopeless, incorrigible, irreclaimable, unredeemed, irredeemable, unforgivable, unexcusable, inexcusable, unpardonable, irremissible, inexpiable, unatonable
▶ *862 Evil*

12 **immoral**, steeped in vice, vicious, unvirtuous, virtueless, ruined, scarlet, without morals, unchaste, impure, indecent, obscene, gross, shocking, outrageous, lustful, vulgar, carnal, debauched, degenerate, profligate, depraved, degraded, perverse, perverted, amoral
▶ *877 Immorality*

13 **venial**, vulnerable, not above temptation, easily tempted, not perfect, imperfect, failing, frail, infirm, feeble, weak, morally weak, lax, having a weaker side, having one's foibles, having a touch of human frailty, human, only human, too human, defective, deficient, indecorous, indiscreet, unseemly, flagrant, scandalous, scandalizing

14 **impious**, irreligious, ungodly, godless, godforsaken, blasphemous, sacrilegious, profane, accursed, damned, reprobate, not in a state of grace, infernal, devilish, diabolical, satanic, fiendish, Mephistophelian

15 **criminal**, offensive, culpable, accusable, blameworthy, guilty, foul, illegal, unlawful, lawbreaking, delinquent, felonious
▶ *844 Wrong*

VERBS

16 **be wicked**, do wrong, err, make a mistake, slip, trip, stumble, fall, fall from grace, stray, have one's foibles, have one's weak side, misbehave, sin, commit sin, transgress, trespass, offend, shock, scoff at virtue, become corrupt, go to the bad, fall into evil ways, shame oneself, disgrace oneself, ruin one's name, sow one's (wild) oats, kick over the traces, have an affair, lapse, relapse, backslide, deviate from the path of virtue, stray from (*or* leave) the straight and narrow, blot one's copybook (Inf), go to the dogs (Inf), carry on (Inf), gross someone out (US sl)

17 **make wicked**, set a bad example, mislead, lead astray, teach wickedness, tempt, pervert, corrupt, distort, demoralize, brutalize, seduce, shame, dehumanize, diabolize

ADVERBS

18 **wickedly**, badly, sinfully, evilly, with evil intentions, wrongly, iniquitously, disreputably, to one's discredit, disgracefully, disobediently, dishonestly, corruptly, unscrupulously, vilely, viciously, cruelly, without regard to feelings, brutally, malevolently, flagrantly, scandalously, hard-heartedly, callously, inhumanly, incorrigibly, irredeemably, inexcusably, unpardonably

19 **vulnerably**, imperfectly, indecorously, indiscreetly

20 **immorally**, without morals, amorally, indecently, obscenely, in an obscene manner, lustfully, vulgarly, carnally, degenerately, mortally, impiously, irreligiously, blasphemously, sacrilegiously, profanely, devilishly, diabolically, satanically, fiendishly

21 **criminally**, offensively, with offence, culpably, guiltily, illegally, unlawfully, delinquently, feloniously

865 Innocence

NOUNS

1 **innocence**, innocentness, virtue, goodness, morality, uprightness, probity, purity, virginity, chastity, purity of heart, saintliness, state of grace, perfection, immaculacy, cleanness, cleanliness, spotlessness, stainlessness, whiteness, incorruption, incorruptibility, incorruptedness, sinlessness, freedom from sin, guiltlessness, inculpability, clear conscience, clean hands, faultlessness, impeccability, blamelessness, freedom from blame, unblameworthiness, irreproachability, nothing to confess, nothing to declare, innocent intentions, pure motives, inoffensiveness, harmlessness, playfulness
▶ *863 Virtue, 876 Morality, 857 Probity, 621 Cleanness, 7 Religion*

2 **legal innocence**, verdict of innocence, find-

ing of innocence, acquittal, exoneration, exculpation, absolution
▶ *16 Law*

3 **naivety**, ingenuousness, guilelessness, artlessness, unsophistication, inexperience, immaturity, callowness, greenness, unworldliness, naturalness, simplicity, credulousness, childhood, days of innocence, golden age, prelapsarian innocence, salad days
▶ *658 Naivety, 502 Ignorance, 206 Youth*

4 **innocent person**, innocent party, innocent, beginner, ingenue, virgin, newcomer, greenhorn, tenderfoot, infant, child, good person, saint, lamb, dove, angel (Inf), goody-goody (Inf), babe (Inf), newborn babe (Inf), babe in arms (Inf)

ADJECTIVES

5 **innocent**, virtuous, good, upright, pure, virginal, chaste, pure of heart, saintly, perfect, angelic, immaculate, unblemished, untainted, stainless, spotless, unspotted, unsullied, undefiled, unsoiled, clean, pristine, white, sinless, free from sin, prelapsarian, untouched by evil, faultless, impeccable, unerring, blameless, unblamable, unblameworthy, irreprehensible, inculpable, reproachless, irreproachable, above suspicion, not guilty, guiltless, cleared, in the clear, with clean hands, clean-handed, uncorrupt, uncorruptible, uncorrupted, incorrupt, incorruptible, innocent as a lamb, lamblike, innocent as a dove, dovelike, gentle, inoffensive, harmless, innocuous, safe, playful, holier than thou, goody-goody (Inf), clean (Sl)

6 **declared innocent**, found innocent, found not guilty, cleared, acquitted, exonerated, exculpated, absolved

7 **naive**, ingenuous, guileless, artless, unsophisticated, credulous, inexperienced, immature, callow, green, unworldly, natural, simple, knowing no wrong, knowing no better, prelapsarian, childlike, innocent as a child, innocent as a newborn babe (Inf)

VERBS

8 **be innocent**, have no guilt, stand above suspicion, wrong no-one, have clean hands, have a clear conscience, have nothing to be ashamed of, have nothing to hide, have nothing to declare, have nothing to confess, live in a state of grace, not fall from grace, mean no harm, have the best intentions, salve one's conscience, look as if butter would not melt in one's mouth

9 **declare innocent**, find innocent, find not guilty, clear, acquit, exonerate, exculpate, absolve

10 **be naive**, have no guile, lack sophistication, lack experience, lack maturity, know no wrong, know no better, have the innocence of a child, have the innocence of a newborn babe (Inf)

ADVERBS

11 **innocently**, in all innocence, with clean hands, with a clear conscience, with an easy conscience, virtuously, uprightly, purely, with pure intentions, virginally, chastely, perfectly, to perfection, in a perfect way, angelically, immaculately, spotlessly, faultlessly, impeccably, unerringly, guiltlessly, with no guilt, blamelessly, irreproachably, inoffensively, harmlessly, in a harmless way, innocuously, with the best (of) intentions, unknowingly, unconsciously, unawares, playfully

12 **naively**, ingenuously, guilelessly, artlessly, without affectation, credulously, immaturely, naturally, simply, like an innocent child, with the innocence of a newborn babe (Inf)

866 Guilt

NOUNS

1 **guilt**, guiltiness, culpability, liability, one's fault, blood guilt, red-handedness, delinquency, illegality, criminality, implication, complicity, aiding and abetting, responsibility, reproach, reproachfulness, censure, blame, peccancy, inculpation, reprehensibility, blameworthiness, impeachability, indictability, accusation of guilt, accusation, conviction of guilt, conviction
▶ *864 Wickedness, 530 Disclosure, 16 Law, 856 Accusation, Conviction*

2 **signs of guilt**, burden of guilt, onus of guilt, guilt complex, guilty feelings, guilty conscience, bad conscience, twinge of conscience, qualms, remorse, shame, contrition, regret, self-reproach, self-accusation, penitence, guilty behaviour, blush, stammer, embarrassment, dirty hands, bloody hands, red hands
▶ *867 Penitence*

3 **sin**, sinfulness, sinning, deadly sin, venial sin, original sin, vice, iniquity, wickedness, guilty act, wrongdoing, misconduct, misdoing, misdeed, misbehaviour, lapse, slip, faux pas, blunder, mistake, fault, failure, dereliction of duty, injury, wrong, sin of omission, negligence, culpable omission, unprofessional conduct, indiscretion, impropriety, peccadillo, naughtiness, wicked deed, transgression, trespass, injustice, illegality, tort (Fml), delict (Scot fml), crime, criminal offence, offence, misdemeanour, white-collar crime, malpractice, felony, atrocity, outrage, enormity
▶ *844 Wrong, 504 Error, 470 Negligence, 832 Malevolence*

4 **guilty person**, guilty party, offender, culprit, wrongdoer, reprobate, recidivist, malefactor, delinquent, accomplice, criminal, confessed criminal, convicted criminal, felon, convict, prisoner, prison inmate, jailbird (or gaolbird), old lag (Sl)

ADJECTIVES

5 **guilty**, blood-guilty, responsible, reprehensible, reprehensive, censurable, inexcusable, without excuse, unjustifiable, unpardonable, unforgivable, reproachable, reproachful, reprovable, in the wrong, at fault, to blame, on one's head, culpable, inculpated, caught in the act, caught red-handed, caught with one's trousers down, caught with one's pants down (US), caught with one's hand in the till, impeachable, chargeable, accusable, blameworthy, blameful, blamed, implicated, censured, peccant, condemned, convicted, found guilty, proved guilty

6 **appearing guilty**, looking guilty, shamefaced, shameful, ashamed, sheepish, blushing, stammering, hangdog, red-handed, feeling guilty, contrite, conscience-stricken, remorseful, regretful, sorry

7 **sinful**, wicked, illegal, criminal, trespassing, transgressing, heinous, mortal, deadly, murderous

VERBS

8 **be guilty**, be at fault, have no excuse, have no alibi, have nothing to say for oneself, get caught in the act, get caught red-handed, get caught with one's trousers down, get caught with one's pants down (US), get caught with one's hand in the till, have crimes to answer for, have blood on one's hands, acknowledge one's guilt, acknowledge one's sins, bear the blame, plead guilty, confess, stand condemned

9 **appear guilty**, look guilty, seem guilty, look ashamed, look embarrassed, look sheepish, blush, stammer, feel guilty, have a bad conscience, accuse oneself, torture oneself, punish oneself, wear a hair shirt, look like the cat that swallowed the canary (or that got the cream)

10 **sin**, trespass, transgress, commit a crime, commit a white-collar crime, commit a misdemeanour, commit a felony, rob, steal, kidnap, murder, assassinate

ADVERBS

11 **guiltily**, reprehensibly, reprehensively, inexcusably, without excuse, unjustifiably, unpardonably, unforgivably, reproachfully, with reproach, blamefully, criminally, red-handed, red-handedly, in the (very) act, in flagrante delicto (Fml), shamefacedly, shamefully, ashamedly, sheepishly, blushingly, contritely, remorsefully, regretfully, sorrily, with sorrow, with a guilty conscience

867 Penitence

NOUNS

1 **penitence**, repentance, contrition, remorsefulness, remorse, self-remorse, self-reproach, regretfulness, regret, regrets, regretting, sorriness, shamefulness, shame, scruples, qualms, soul-searching, compunction, guilt, guilt feelings, self-accusation, self-condemnation, hair shirt, guilty conscience, bad conscience, uneasy conscience, twinge of conscience, pangs of conscience, pangs, pricking of conscience, voice of one's conscience, weight on one's mind, confession, humble confession, recantation, apology, apologies, heartfelt apology, humble apology, abject apology, grudging apology, deathbed repentance, deathbed confession, reformation, conversion, change of heart

▶ 530 Disclosure, 866 Guilt, 774 Lamentation, 7 Religion, 220 Conversion, 627 Improvement

2 **type of penance**, atonement, reparation, mortification, mortification of the flesh, breast-beating, sackcloth and ashes, wearing a sackcloth, wearing a hair shirt, flagellation, self-flagellation, self-scourging, prostration, self-punishment, self-humiliation, purification, purgation

▶ 840 Atonement, 673 Submission, 806 Humility

3 **penitent person**, penitent, confessor, flagellant, ascetic, prodigal son, prodigal returned, contrite sinner, born-again Christian, reformed character, reformed prostitute, magdalen (Fml), sadder but wiser man (or woman)

VERBS

4 **be penitent**, do penance, repent, feel contrite, feel remorse, blame oneself, reprove oneself, accuse oneself, reproach oneself, search one's soul, rue the day, wish undone, regret, have regrets, express regrets, feel sorry, say one is sorry, apologize, feel shame, hang one's head in shame, show compunction, feel guilty, have guilt feelings, blame oneself, accuse oneself, condemn oneself, bewail one's sins, confess one's sins, confess, go to confession, acknowledge one's sins, acknowledge one's faults, recant one's errors, recant, think again, have second thoughts, think better of, learn one's lesson, learn from (bitter) experience, see the error of one's ways, see the light, reform, make a fresh start, turn from sin, return to the straight and narrow, become a born-again Christian, turn over a new leaf, wipe the slate clean

5 **do penance**, atone, atone for, make amends, salve one's conscience, mortify one's flesh, beat one's breast, repent in sackcloth and ashes, wear a sackcloth, wear a hair shirt, flagellate oneself, scourge oneself, prostrate oneself, punish oneself, humiliate oneself

ADJECTIVES

6 **penitent**, repentant, repenting, contrite, remorseful, full of remorse, remorsing, regretful, full of regrets, regretting, lamenting, sorry, apologetic, sorrowful, ashamed, shameful, shamefaced, rueful, self-reproachful, self-reproaching, self-accusing, self-condemning,

compunctious, guilty, full of guilt, conscience-stricken, conscience-smitten, pricked by conscience, plagued by conscience, confessing, confessed, reformed, regenerate, reclaimed, converted, born-again

7 **penitential**, penitentiary, doing penance, atoning, atoned, self-punishing, humiliating, humiliated

ADVERBS

8 **penitently**, repentantly, with repentance, contritely, remorsefully, regretfully, with regret, apologetically, to apologize, sorrowfully, ruefully, shamefully, shamefacedly, in self-reproach, self-accusingly, compunctiously, guiltily, with a guilty conscience, penitentially, like a penitent, in sackcloth and ashes, humiliatingly, to make a fresh start

INTERJECTIONS

9 **sorry!**, I confess!, I'm guilty!, *mea culpa*! (L), I repent!

4 **unatoned**, unrepented, unregretted, unapologized for

VERBS

5 **be impenitent**, remain unrepentant, not reform, have no regrets, have no remorse, have no conscience, feel nothing, remain obstinate, refuse to recant, make no confession, not confess, offer no apologies, want no forgiveness, feel no remorse, harden one's heart, steel oneself, indurate, refuse to see the error of one's ways

ADVERBS

6 **impenitently**, unregretfully, with no regrets, without regret, unremorsefully, remorselessly, with no remorse, without remorse, without compunction, unashamedly, shamelessly, unblushingly, cold-heartedly, hard-heartedly, without any qualms, without any scruples, without looking back, without seeing the error of one's ways

868 Impenitence

NOUNS

1 **impenitence**, impenitentness, nonrepentance, lack of contrition, refusal to recant, lack of confession, incorrigibility, obstinacy, stubbornness, obduracy, hardness, hardness of heart, cold-heartedness, hard-heartedness, heart of stone, callousness, induration, remorselessness, pitilessness, shamelessness, seared conscience, no apologies, no regrets, no remorse, no going back

▶ *577 Obstinacy, 373 Hardness, 836 Pitilessness, 575 Perseverance*

2 **impenitent person**, cold-hearted person, hard-hearted person, hardened sinner, inveterate sinner, dyed-in-the-wool sinner, shameless hussy, brazen hussy, callous murderer, lost cause, hopeless case, hard case (Sl)

▶ *832 Malevolence, 864 Wickedness*

ADJECTIVES

3 **impenitent**, unrepentant, unrepenting, incorrigible, inveterate, obdurate, obstinate, brazen, shameless, unreformed, unregretting, not sorry, unsorry, unapologetic, uncontrite, unmoved, unashamed, unblushing, unremorseful, without remorse, remorseless, having no remorse, unsorrowful, having no sorrow, unregretful, without regrets, having no regrets, regretless, unregretting, without a pang of regret, without compunction, without a conscience, conscienceless, cold-hearted, heartless, hard-hearted, hardened, hard, callous, indurative, untouched, hopeless, lost, irreclaimable, irredeemable, not redeemable, not redeemed, unredeemed, unreconciled, unreformed, unregenerated, unchastened, unrecanting, unshriven, not confessing, rotten to the core, dyed-in-the-wool

869 Self-Restraint

NOUNS

1 **self-restraint**, self-control, self-discipline, self-denial, self-abnegation, self-mastery, restraint, constraint, restriction, repression, avoidance, eschewal, forbearance, renunciation, relinquishment, refrainment, abstaining, abstinence, abstention, abstemiousness, sexual abstinence, ascesis, celibacy, chastity, purity, puritanism, continence, temperance, temperateness, soberness, sobriety, total abstinence, teetotalism, prohibition, Rechabitism, Volstead Act (US), Eighteenth Amendment (US), Woman's Christian Temperance Union (WCTU), Church of England Temperance Society, diet, dieting, Weightwatchers, vegetarianism, veganism, fast, fasting, Lenten fare, fish day, asceticism, Spartanism, frugality, parsimony, economy, simple life, plain living, plainness, self-sufficiency, passing up (Inf)

▶ *591 Avoidance, 859 Disinterestedness, 598 Relinquishment, 876 Morality, 272 Narrowness, 45 Cookery, 871 Fasting, 756 Thrift, 758 Meanness*

2 **moderation**, moderateness, prudence, reasonableness, nothing in excess, middle way, happy medium, golden mean

▶ *242 Moderation*

3 **calmness**, composure, lack of emotion, Stoicism, keeping a stiff upper lip, sang-froid

▶ *404 Insensibility, 661 Hindrance*

4 **self-restrained person**, sober person, (total) abstainer, teetotaller, Rechabite, prohibitionist, nonsmoker, vegetarian, vegan, ascetic, dieter, faster, puritan, Spartan, sobersides, dry (US inf), tight-arse (*or* tight-ass) (Tab sl)

VERBS

5 **be self-restrained**, restrain oneself, control

oneself, exercise self-control, discipline one-self, restrict oneself, limit oneself, deny one-self, do without, never touch, constrain one-self, ration oneself, refrain, abstain, repress, retard, hold back, rein in, avoid excess, avoid, eschew, forbear, renounce, relinquish, put a stop to, swear off, give up, forgo, ban, curb, brake, veto, know when to stop, know when one has had enough, temper, drink in moder-ation, shun alcohol, prohibit drinking, re-nounce drinking, take (*or* sign) the pledge, diet, go on a diet, lose weight, control one's appetite, eat sparingly, eat in moderation, eat to live, not live to eat, half starve, starve, fast, control one's lusts, repress one's desires, mor-tify the flesh, economize, live plainly, live simply, live frugally, tighten one's belt, pass up (Inf), go dry (US inf), go on the wagon (Inf)

6 **moderate**, do nothing in excess, keep within bounds, circumscribe, confine, observe a limit, keep to the middle way, keep a happy medium, keep the golden mean

7 **be calm**, have composure, lack emotion, keep a stiff upper lip

ADJECTIVES

8 **self-restrained**, self-controlled, self-disciplined, self-denying, restrictive, restricted, strict, repressive, repressed, prohibited, renunciative, relinquished, restrained, anal-retentive, re-fraining, forbearing, abstaining, abstemious, abstinent, sexually abstinent, celibate, con-tinent, chaste, pure, puritanic(al), temperate, tempered, not excessive, not overdoing it, sober, teetotal, sworn off, dieting, vegetarian, vegan, fasting, Lenten, ascetic, plain, Spartan, frugal, economical, parsimonious, stinting, sparing, costive, self-sufficient, on the wagon (Inf), dry (US inf), strait-laced (Inf), uptight (Inf), tight-arsed (*or* tight-assed) (Tab sl)

9 **moderate**, prudent, reasonable, measured, within bounds, circumscribed, confined, within reasonable limits, limiting, limited, under control

10 **calm**, composed, lacking emotion, Stoic, keeping a stiff upper lip

ADVERBS

11 **with self-restraint**, with self-control, re-strictively, strictly, repressively, forbearingly, abstemiously, chastely, purely, puritanically, temperately, teetotally, without excess, with-out overdoing it, ascetically, plainly, frugally, economically, parsimoniously, stintingly, sparingly, self-sufficiently

12 **moderately**, with moderation, prudently, with prudence, reasonably, within reason, within bounds, within reasonable limits, under control

13 **calmly**, without emotion, stoically, with a stiff upper lip

870 Self-Indulgence

NOUNS

1 **self-indulgence**, self-gratification, pleasure seeking, hedonism, sybaritism, epicureanism, luxury, sensuality, voluptuousness, carnality
▶ *405 Physical Pleasure*

2 **dissipation**, riotous living, fast living, high living, free living, dissoluteness, licentious-ness, debauchery, profligacy, carousal, orgy, saturnalia

3 **overindulgence**, immoderation, uncontrol, unrestraint, abandon, indiscipline, inordi-nateness, inordinancy, overdoing, excess, ex-cessiveness, incontinence, concupiscence, in-temperance, drunkenness, crapulence, addic-tion, overeating, greed, gluttony, gourmandiz-ing, extravagance, wastefulness, prodigality
▶ *874 Drunkenness, 610 Excess, 757 Extravagance, 872 Gluttony*

4 **self-absorption**, self-obsession, self-devotion, self-worship, self-love, narcissism, vanity, self-centredness, egoism, selfishness, I'm all right Jack (Inf)
▶ *860 Selfishness*

5 **self-indulgent person**, pleasure-seeker, free-liver, high-liver, fast-liver, hedonist, syba-rite, epicure, *bon vivant* (Fr), gourmet, gour-mand, glutton, toper, voluptuary, sensualist, debauchee, narcissist, egoist

ADJECTIVES

6 **self-indulgent**, self-gratifying, pleasure-seeking, pleasure-bound, hedonistic, sybaritic, epicurean, sensual, voluptuous, carnal

7 **dissipated**, dissipating, dissolute, riotous, fast-living, high-living, free-living, licentious, debauched, debauching, profligate

8 **overindulgent**, immoderate, uncontrolled, unrestrained, undisciplined, ill-disciplined, abandoned, inordinate, excessive, inconti-nent, concupiscent, intemperate, drunk, crapulent, addicted, greedy, gluttonous, gour-mandizing, extravagant, wasteful, prodigal

9 **self-absorbed**, self-obsessed, self-devoted, self-worshipping, self-loving, narcissistic, vain, self-centred, egotistic, selfish

VERBS

10 **indulge oneself**, indulge in, luxuriate in, wallow in, deny oneself nothing, put oneself first, look after number one

11 **overindulge**, overdo, waste, squander, dissi-pate, gorge, debauch, carouse, not know when to stop, burn the candle at both ends, sow one's wild oats, have a fling (Inf), go on a bender (Inf), binge (Inf)

ADVERBS

12 **self-indulgently**, intemperately, inconti-nently, immoderately, excessively, in (*or* to) excess, beyond all bounds

871 Fasting

NOUNS

1 **fasting**, fast, abstinence from food, abstinence, abstemiousness, austerity, atrophy, religious fasting, Lenten fare, Quadragesimal fare, dieting, diet, prescribed diet, health diet, crash diet, starvation diet, slimming diet, liquid diet, weight loss, lean cuisine, slimming, reducing, weight-watching, Weightwatchers, losing weight, counting calories, anorexia (nervosa)

2 **short rations**, military rations, K rations (US), iron rations, short commons, asceticism, Spartan fare, prison fare, diet of bread and water, hunger striking, bare subsistence, bare cupboard, insufficient diet, hunger, famishment, starvation

▶ *218 Cessation, 869 Self-Restraint, 609 Insufficiency, 624 Ill Health*

3 **fast day**, fast, *jour maigre* (Fr), day of abstinence, meatless day, fish day, Lent, Friday, Good Friday, Yom Kippur, Tishah b'Av, Ramadan

▶ *7 Religion*

4 **fasting person**, faster, dieter, hunger striker, anorexic, ascetic, weight watcher, calorie counter

VERBS

5 **fast**, abstain from eating, abstain, eat nothing, having nothing to eat, live on air, go hungry, hunger, clem (*or* clam) (Brit dial), go without food, go without, avoid food, have an empty stomach, suffer from anorexia (nervosa), give up eating, refuse food, go on a hunger strike, eat sparingly, eat no meat, keep Lent, keep a Spartan regimen, live on bread and water, live on rations, eat less, control one's appetite, lose weight, take off weight, join Weightwatchers, diet, go on a diet, go on a crash diet, go on a starvation diet, go on a liquid diet, slim, reduce, count calories, half starve, starve, famish, die for food, tighten one's belt, make a little go a long way

ADJECTIVES

6 **fasting**, abstinent, abstemious, not eating, anorexic, without food, off food, unfed, going without, with an empty stomach, empty, keeping one's fast, keeping Lent, Lenten, Quadragesimal, keeping a Spartan regimen, Spartan, on a diet, slimming, reducing, on a crash diet, austere, ascetic, on a starvation diet, on a liquid diet, on meagre rations, on (a) hunger strike, on bread and water, underfed, poorly fed, half-starved, starving, starved, famishing, famished, ravenous, clemmed (*or* clammed) (Brit dial), hungry, dying for food, wasting away, thin, anorexic, hungry enough to eat a horse

ADVERBS

7 **abstemiously**, in a Spartan manner, on bread and water, without food, ravenously, hungrily, to near starvation

872 Gluttony

NOUNS

1 **gluttony**, greediness, greed, overeating, self-indulgence, overindulgence, overindulging, intemperance, insatiability, voraciousness, voracity, ravenousness, rapacity, edaciousness, edacity, polyphagia, hedonism, concupiscence, big appetite, wolfishness, piggishness (Inf), hoggishness (Inf), bingeing (Inf)

▶ *350 Eating, 782 Desire, 870 Self-Indulgence*

2 **epicurism**, epicureanism, gourmandise, gourmandism, gastronomy

3 **act of gluttony**, banquet, feast, bacchanalia, Lucullan banquet, clambake (US), feeding frenzy (Inf), spread (Inf), food orgy (Inf), beano (Sl), beanfeast (Inf), blowout (Sl), pigout (US sl), nosh-up (Sl)

4 **glutton**, greedy person, good eater, big eater, hearty eater, heavy eater, guzzler, gorger, trencherman, trencherwoman, omnivore, bacchanal, Lucullus, gourmet, gourmand, gormandizer, gastronome, epicure, epicurean, *bon vivant* (Fr), cormorant, wolf, binger (Inf), foodie (Inf), gobbler (Inf), pig (Inf), greedy pig (Inf), porker (Inf), hog (Inf), hyena (Inf), locust (Inf), bottomless pit (Inf), human garbage can (US sl), gannet (Sl), greedy guts (Sl)

VERBS

5 **be greedy**, gluttonize, gormandize, hedonize, overeat, self-indulge, overindulge, indulge one's appetite, indulge oneself, have a big appetite, love food, love to eat, live to eat, eat up, set to, wipe the plate clean, devour, bolt, guzzle, gobble, gulp, snap up, wolf, make a pig (*or* hog) of oneself, fill oneself, stuff oneself, stuff, cram, glut oneself, glut, gorge, engorge, have eyes bigger than one's stomach, eat like a horse, eat one's head off, eat out of house and home, tuck into (Inf), binge (Inf), go on a binge (Inf), graze (Inf), pig out (US sl)

ADJECTIVES

6 **gluttonous**, greedy, insatiable, never full, intemperate, hedonistic, self-indulgent, overeating, overindulgent, voracious, ravenous, rapacious, well-nourished, edacious, polyphagous, epicurean, gastronomic, omnivorous, devouring, all-devouring, stuffing, stuffed, cramming, bolting, gobbling, gulping, glutting, gluttonizing, gorging, gorged, overgorging, overgorged, engorged, guzzling, wolfing, wolfish, esurient, piggish (Inf), hoggish (Inf), bingeing (Inf)

ADVERBS

7 **gluttonously**, greedily, with pure greed, self-

indulgently, hungrily, with one bite, at a gulp, voraciously, ravenously, out of house and home, gastronomically, edaciously, like a horse, wolfishly, like a wolf, piggishly (Inf), like a pig (Inf), hoggishly (Inf), like a hog (Inf)

873 Sobriety

ADJECTIVES

1 **sober**, not drunk, unintoxicated, clear-headed, with a clear head, without a hangover, sobered up, abstinent, abstemious, temperate, teetotal (TT), strictly teetotal, prohibitionist, nondrinking, off drink, off the hard stuff, on soft drinks, water-drinking, tea-drinking, sober as a judge, stone-cold sober (Inf), unfuddled (Inf), on the (water) wagon (Inf), not indulging (Inf), dry (Inf), off the bottle (Inf), drying out (Sl)
▶ *869 Self-Restraint, 591 Avoidance, 242 Moderation*

2 **nonalcoholic**, alcohol-free, unfermented, soft

VERBS

3 **be sober**, stay sober, keep (*or* have) a clear head, not drink, abstain, avoid alcohol, keep off liquor, stay away from the hard stuff, never touch a drop, never let liquor pass one's lips, drink water, prefer soft drinks, drink moderately, drink sociably, hold one's liquor, carry one's liquor, not imbibe (Inf), not indulge (Inf)

4 **give up alcohol**, give up drinking, become teetotal, become a teetotaller, come off (drink), kick the habit, turn prohibitionist, sign the pledge, join the Band of Hope, go dry (Sl), go on the (water) wagon (Inf)

5 **sober up**, clear one's head, sleep it off, get rid of a hangover, detoxify, get the fumes out of one's brain (Inf), dry out (Sl)

NOUNS

6 **sobriety**, soberness, abstinence, abstemiousness, temperance, teetotalism, water-drinking, tea-drinking, state of sobriety, unintoxicated state, clear head, no hangover, unfuddled brain (Inf)
▶ *869 Self-Restraint, 591 Avoidance, 242 Moderation*

7 **prohibition**, Prohibition (US), the Volstead Prohibition Act (US), the 18th Amendment (US), the noble experiment (US), dry county (US), dry state (US)

8 **sober person**, nondrinker, nonalcoholic, nonaddict, moderate drinker, social drinker, water-drinker, tea-drinker, abstainer, teetotaller, strict teetotaller, prohibitionist, Rechabite, temperance society, Woman's Christian Temperance 135 Union, Alcoholics Anonymous (AA), the Betty Ford Clinic, the Band of Hope

ADVERBS

9 **soberly**, with sobriety, abstemiously, temperately, with a clear head

874 Drunkenness

For when the wine is in, the wit is out. Thomas Becon.

Others mocking said, These men are full of new wine. Bible: Acts.

Wine is a mocker, strong drink is raging: and whosoever is deceived thereby is not wise. Bible: Proverbs.

ADJECTIVES

1 **drunk**, inebriated, intoxicated, ebriate, ebriated, ebriose, under the influence (of alcohol), having had (a drop) too much, having had one too many, in liquor, the worse for liquor, comfortably drunk, gloriously drunk, roaring drunk, fighting drunk, pot-valiant, drunk and disorderly, drunken, drunk as a lord, drunk as a fiddler, drunk as a fiddler's bitch, drunk as a skunk (US), drunk as an owl, drunk as David's sow, fou as a coot (Scot), fou as a wulk (Scot), tight (Sl), in one's cups (Inf), half-seas over (Sl), three (*or* four) sheets in (*or* to) the wind (Sl), one over the eight (Sl), boozed up (Sl), ginned up (Sl), liquored up (Sl), lit up (Sl), flushed (Inf), merry (Inf), happy (Inf), high (Inf), elevated (Inf), exhilarated (Inf), tanked up (Sl), bevvied up (Dial), pissed (Sl), Brahms (and Liszt) (Sl), pissed as a newt (Sl), well-oiled (Sl), well-lubricated (Sl), pickled (Sl), potted (Sl), canned (Sl), bottled (Sl), stewed (Sl), fried (Sl), pixilated (Sl), ratted (Sl), rat-faced (Sl), rat-arsed (Sl)

2 **slightly drunk**, tipsy, maudlin, tearful, tired and emotional, muzzy, glazed, glassy-eyed, pie-eyed, seeing double, woozy, dizzy, giddy, reeling, staggering, hiccupping, tiddly (Sl), squiffy (Sl), half-cut (Sl), half-bagged (Sl), half-shot (Sl), fuddled (Inf), muddled (Inf), flustered (Inf), boozy (Sl)

3 **dead drunk**, in a drunken stupor, stupefied, stinking drunk (Sl), stinko (Sl), blind drunk (Sl), blind (Sl), blotto (Sl), stoned (Sl), smashed (Sl), sloshed (Sl), sozzled (Sl), soused (Sl), soaked (Sl), juiced (Sl), lushed (US sl), loaded (US sl), plastered (Sl), bagged (Sl), blasted (Sl), plowed under (US sl), plotzed (US sl), legless (Sl), arseholed (Tab sl), shitfaced (US tab sl), paralytic (Inf), gone (Inf), shot (Sl), blitzed (Sl), bombed (out of one's mind) (Sl), zonked (out) (Sl), zonkers (Sl), zonko (Sl), wiped out (Sl), teed (Sl), twisted (US sl), stiff (Sl), out (of it) (Inf), out cold (Inf), under the table (Inf), dead to the world (Inf)

4 **crapulous**, crapulent, hung over, with a hangover, with a sick headache, with a thick

head, with a fuzzy tongue, dizzy, giddy, sick

5 **drunken**, inebriate, intemperate, habitually drunk, never sober, alcoholic, dipsomaniac(al), with a drink problem, addicted to alcohol, a slave to drink, given to drink, on the bottle, sottish, sodden, gin-sodden, beery, vinous, smelling of drink, stinking of liquor, fond of a drink, thirsty, bibulous, bibbing, wine-bibbing, tippling, toping, swilling, swigging, guzzling, hard-drinking, carousing, wassailing, red-nosed, bloodshot, gouty, liverish, boozy (Sl), boozing (Inf), pub-crawling (Inf)

6 **intoxicating**, intoxicant, inebriating, inebriative, inebriant, temulent, stimulant, exhilarating, exciting, going to the head, heady, winy, vinous, beery, spiritous, alcoholic, hard, potent, strong, double-strength, proof, overproof, straight, neat, unmixed, undiluted, addictive, habit-forming

VERBS

7 **be drunk**, have had (a drop) too much, have had one too many, not hold one's liquor, hiccup, slur one's words, stutter, stammer, see double, see pink elephants, not walk straight, lurch, stagger, reel, succumb, pass out

8 **get drunk**, have (a drop) too much, have one too many, drink, drink deep, drink hard, drink like a fish, tipple, tope, guzzle, swig, swill, quaff, crack a bottle, hit the bottle, go on a spree, carouse, wassail, sacrifice to Bacchus, booze (Sl), souse (Sl), soak (Sl), lush (US sl), bib (Arch sl), fuddle (Inf), liquor up (Sl), tank up (Sl), bend one's elbow (Inf), knock back a few (Inf), chug-a-lug (US sl), have one over the eight (Sl), go on a blind (Inf), go on a bender (Inf), go on the fuddle (Inf), go on a pub-crawl (Inf), pub-crawl (Inf), drown one's sorrows (Inf), commune with the spirits (Inf)

9 **be intoxicating**, inebriate, make drunk, stupefy, stimulate, exhilarate, elevate, excite, go to one's head, make one's head swim, fuddle (Inf), befuddle (Inf), put one under the table (Inf)

NOUNS

10 **drunkenness**, inebriation, intoxication, inebriety, insobriety, ebriety, ebriosity, tipsiness, drunken (or alcoholic) stupor, influence of alcohol, stimulation, exhilaration, elevation, excitation, Dutch courage, hiccup, hiccupping, slurred speech, thick speech, stuttering, stammering, seeing double, wooziness, dizziness, staggering, reeling, blackout, befuddlement (Inf), blind staggers (Sl)

11 **drinking**, excessive drinking, hard drinking, getting drunk, intemperance, bibulousness, wine-bibbing, tippling, swilling, weakness for liquor, fondness for the bottle, sottishness, beeriness, vinousness, soaking (Sl)

12 **alcohol**, drink, alcoholic drink, liquor, alcoholic liquor, intoxicating liquor, hard drink, strong drink, Dutch courage, potations, libations, grog, wine, beer, spirits, water of life, John Barleycorn, cocktail, tall (or long) drink, bootleg liquor, home brew, booze (Inf), juice (Sl), vino (Inf), plonk (Inf), hooch (Sl), moonshine (Sl), rotgut (Sl), gnat's piss (Sl)

13 **drink**, beverage, potation, compotation, libation, libation to Bacchus, flowing bowl, cup that cheers, tipple, bevvy (Dial), nip, dram, drop, finger, snort, round, round of drinks, snifter (Inf), one for the road (Inf), hair of the dog (that bit one) (Inf), one over the eight (Sl)

▶ *351 Drinking*

14 **drinking bout**, binge, spree, orgy of drinking, bacchanalia, revel, jag (Sl), lush (Sl), blind (Sl), bender (Inf), pub-crawl (Brit Inf)

15 **crapulence**, crapulousness, hangover, morning after (the night before), (sick) headache, thick head, fuzzy tongue, dizziness, giddiness, sickness

16 **alcoholism**, alcoholic addiction, alcohol abuse, dipsomania, drink problem, tremors, delirium tremens, cirrhosis of the liver, red nose, DT's (Inf), jimjams (Sl), the horrors (Inf), heebie-jeebies (Sl), pink elephants (Sl), grog-blossom (Sl)

17 **drunkard**, drunk, inebriate, intoxicated person, habitual drunkard, sot, alcoholic, dipsomaniac, slave to drink, pathological drunk, drinker, hard drinker, problem drinker, secret drinker, social drinker, bibber, wine-bibber, tippler, swiller, toper, tosspot, thirsty soul, devotee of Bacchus, bacchanal, bacchant, maenad, Silenus, carouser, reveller, boozer (Inf), soaker (Sl), (old) soak (Sl), souse (Sl), sponge (Sl), juice head (Sl), wineskin (Sl), froth-blower (Sl), pub-crawler (Inf), alehead (Sl), pisshead (Sl), piss-artist (Sl)

ADVERBS

18 **drunkenly**, under the influence, tipsily, in a drunken stupor, crapulously, crapulently

875 Drug-Taking

NOUNS

1 **drug-taking**, drug addiction, drug abuse, drug dependence, habit, smoking, sniffing, glue-sniffing, injecting, snorting (Sl), freebasing (Sl), hitting up (Sl), shooting up (Sl), skin-popping (Sl), mainlining (Sl), pill-popping (Sl), chasing the dragon (Sl), belly habit (US sl), banging (Sl), blowing (Sl), cocktailing (US sl), buzz (Sl), trip (Sl), acid trip (Sl), bad trip (Sl), tracks (Sl), trackmarks (Sl), whore scars (US sl), quill (US sl), shooting gallery (Sl)

2 **drug pushing**, drug peddling, drug trafficking, possessing narcotics, carrying (Inf), holding (Inf)

3 **withdrawal**, withdrawal symptoms, with-

drawal sickness, cold turkey (Sl), bogue (US sl)

4 **drug taker**, drug user, drug addict, druggie (Sl), junkie (Sl), dope fiend (Inf), drug scorer (Sl), greasy junkie (US sl), DA (Inf), freak (Sl), head (Sl), acid-head (Sl), hophead (Sl), chippy (US sl), coke-head (Sl), mainliner (Sl), hype (Sl), jones (US sl), scag jones (US sl)

5 **drug pusher**, pusher, drug peddler, drug dealer, connection, candy man (US sl), reefer man (Sl), viper (US sl)

6 **drug**, drugs, dope, narcotic, narcotics, fix, hard drug, soft drug, designer drug, ecstasy, cannabis, marijuana, hashish, cocaine, heroin, methadone, barbiturate, morphine, opium, amphetamine, stimulant, excitant, hallucinogen, LSD (lysergic acid diethylamide), PCP (phencyclidine), STP, mescaline, peyote, joint (Sl), the joint (Sl), reefer (Sl), stick (Sl), hit (Sl), bang (Sl), spliff (Sl), roach (Sl), shot (Inf), snort (Sl), blockbuster (US sl), dime's worth (US sl), hash (Inf), Mary Ann (Sl), Mary Jane (Sl), Mary Warner (Sl), OZ (Sl), mooter (Sl), muggles (US sl), birdwood (US sl), tea (Sl), grass (Sl), weed (Sl), rope (Sl), panatella (Sl), black gunion (US sl), ganja (Sl), hemp (Sl), kef (Sl), pot (Sl), Acapulco gold (Sl), gage (or gauge) (US sl), gangster (US sl), gungeon (US sl), Jamaican ganga (US sl), coke (Sl), snow (Sl), crack (Sl), crack cocaine (Sl), C (Sl), C and H (Sl), C and M (Sl), white stuff (Sl), speedball (Sl), Peruvian marching powder (US sl), rock (Sl), dynamite (US sl), dyno (Sl), girl (Sl), horse (Sl), junk (Sl), smack (Sl), H (Sl), scag (or skag) (Sl), boy (Sl), brown sugar (Sl), hot shot (US sl), black tar (Sl), candy (Sl), needle candy (Sl), nose candy (Sl), gumball (Sl), Mexican mud (US sl), tootsie roll (US sl), peanut butter (Sl), dogfood (Sl), downer (Sl), barb (Inf), yellow jacket (Sl), morph (Inf), M (Sl), black stuff (US sl), brown stuff (Sl), blue velvet (US sl), pep pill (Inf), dex (Sl), dexie (Sl), dexo (Sl), upper (Sl), speed (Sl), green dragon (Sl), green hornet (Sl), purple heart (Sl), black beauty (US sl), acid (Sl), blue cheer (Sl), purple haze (US sl), yellow (Sl), yellow sunshine (Sl), orange (US sl), orange sunshine (US sl), angel dust (Sl), magic mushroom (Sl)

ADJECTIVES

7 **drugged**, doped, incapacitated, insensible, high (Inf), stoned (Sl), zonked (out) (Sl), zonkers (Sl), zonko (Sl), spaced out (Sl), freaked out (Sl), floating (Sl), loaded (US sl), turned on (Sl), bogue (Sl)

8 **addicted**, drug-dependent, hooked (Sl)

9 **addictive**, narcotic, psychedelic, hallucinogenic, mind-blowing (Sl)

VERBS

10 **drug oneself**, take drugs, smoke, inject oneself, possess narcotics, traffic in drugs, have withdrawal symptoms, snort (Sl), chase the

dragon (Sl), drop (Sl), drop acid (Sl), freebase (Sl), shoot up (Inf), shoot gravy (US sl), mainline (Sl), hot-shot (US sl), cook up (Sl), turn on (Sl), trip out (Sl), take a trip (Sl), blow one's mind (Sl), freak out (Sl), bang (Sl), blow (Sl), blow smoke (Sl), blow gage (or gauge) (US sl), carry (Inf), hold (Inf), dry out (Sl), go cold turkey (Sl)

ADVERBS

11 **in a trance**, insensibly, dopily (Inf), narcotically, psychedelically, habitually, dependently

876   Morality

No morality can be founded on authority, even if the authority were divine. A. J. Ayer.

Morality's not practical. Morality's a gesture. A complicated gesture learnt from books. Robert Bolt.

What is moral is what you feel good after, and what is immoral is what you feel bad after. Ernest Hemingway.

Morality which is based on ideas, or on an ideal, is an unmitigated evil. D. H. Lawrence.

We know no spectacle so ridiculous as the British public in one of its periodical fits of morality. Lord Macaulay.

Victorian values...were the values when our country became great. Margaret Thatcher.

NOUNS

1 **morality**, moralness, moral climate, moral standards, morals, ethics, ethicalness, principles, standards, ideals, beliefs, scruples, behaviour, conduct, ethos, attitudes, customs, mores, habits, manners
▶ *584 Habit, 4 Philosophy, 7 Religion*

2 **good morals**, integrity, propriety, probity, decency, goodness, virtue, honour, honesty, nobility, rectitude, uprightness, righteousness, right, sense of right and wrong, conscience, voice of conscience, justice, fairness, fair play, good taste, spirituality, piousness, saintliness, Moral Rearmament
▶ *863 Virtue, 843 Right, 794 Refinement, 857 Probity, 7 Religion*

3 **moral purity**, purity, faultlessness, perfection, sinlessness, sainthood, immaculacy, immaculateness, Immaculate Conception, innocence, modesty, bashfulness, coyness, pudency, shame, chastity, abstinence, continence, celibacy, Encratism, temperance, coldness, frigidity, virginity, maidenhood, maidenhead, cherry (Tab sl)
▶ *619 Perfection, 865 Innocence, 810 Modesty, 825 Celibacy*

4 **self-righteousness**,   narrow-mindedness,

mealy-mouthedness, prudery, prudishness, Grundyism, priggishness, primness, smugness, sanctimony, sanctimoniousness, pietism, puritanism, gravity, graveness, seriousness, sternness, Sunday-opening laws, blue laws (US), Prohibition (US), censorship, expurgation, bowdlerization, euphemism, genteelism, affectation, shockability, squeamishness, overmodesty, false modesty, false shame, *mauvaise honte* (Fr)

▶ *690 Severity, 797 Affectation*

5 **pure person**, virtuous person, virgin, maiden, vestal, vestal virgin, virgo intacta, Sir Galahad, the Virgin Mary, celibate, Encratite, religious celibate, monk, nun, saint

▶ *7 Religion, 825 Celibacy*

6 **moralist**, puritan, Victorian, prig, prude, prohibitionist, teetotaller, guardian of morality, censor, watchdog, Watch Committee, Moral Majority, Mrs Grundy, Mrs Mary Whitehouse, Carry Nation (US), wowser (Aus and NZ sl)

7 **moral**, lesson, teaching, message, point, precept, homily, maxim, apophthegm, adage, proverb, saying, saw, epigram, motto

ADJECTIVES

8 **moral**, ethical, principled, high-minded, good, decent, honourable, honest, noble, upright, righteous, virtuous, right-minded, right, proper, just, fair, scrupulous, saintly

9 **pure**, faultless, perfect, sinless, immaculate, spotless, purified, refined, snowy, white, pure as the driven snow, innocent, modest, bashful, blushing, coy, shy, chaste, undefiled, unfallen, virgin, virginal, vestal, maidenly, untouched, unwedded, celibate, continent, temperate, Platonic, sublimated, sexless, cold, frigid

10 **moralistic**, moralizing, self-righteous, narrow-minded, mealy-mouthed, prudish, priggish, prim, old-maidish, smug, sanctimonious, holier-than-thou, pietistic, pious, puritan, Victorian, strait-laced, grave, serious, severe, stern, censorious, censored, edifying, clean, printable, publishable, quotable, repeatable, mentionable, expurgated, bowdlerized, euphemistic, genteel, affected, overmodest, overdelicate, squeamish, shockable

VERBS

11 **be moral**, do no wrong, fight the good fight, follow (*or* keep on) the straight and narrow, abstain, wait, forgo sex, practise abstinence, remain celibate, remain a virgin, remain pure

12 **moralize**, sermonize, preach, pontificate, lecture, harangue, hold forth, go on about, point a moral, have the right moral attitude

ADVERBS

13 **morally**, ethically, ideally, purely, sanctimoniously, piously, moralistically

877 Immorality

NOUNS

1 **immorality**, moral badness, bad morals, lack of morals, amorality, lack of principles, unscrupulousness, unethicalness, moral delinquency, moral turpitude, badness, wickedness, vice, viciousness, evil nature, evil, wrong, wrongdoing, criminality, dishonesty

▶ *858 Improbity, 864 Wickedness, 844 Wrong, 736 Stealing, 538 Untruth, 539 Deception, 540 Falsehood, 846 Lack of Entitlement, 862 Evil, 868 Impenitence, 866 Guilt, 504 Error, 850 Disrespect, 689 Anarchy*

2 **indecency**, salaciousness, prurience, impure thoughts, lewdness, filthiness, defilement, uncleanness, indelicacy, bad taste, coarseness, vulgarity, grossness, nastiness, ribaldry, bawdiness, bawdry (Arch), loose talk, filthy talk, blue joke, dirty joke, dirty story, naughty story, smoking-room story, double entendre, filth, dirt, smut, obscenity, corruption, depravity, sexually explicit literature, obscene literature, adult literature, dirty books, erotic literature, erotica, facetiae, pornography, porn (Inf), soft-core pornography, soft porn (Inf), page 3 girl, girlie magazine, men's magazine, *Playboy, Lady Chatterley's Lover*, X-rated movie (*or* film) (US), blue movie (*or* film), voyeurism, sexploitation, hard-core pornography, hard porn (Inf), child pornography, video nasty, skin flick (Sl), snuff movie (*or* film) (Sl)

3 **sexual immorality**, unchastity, promiscuity, wantonness, incontinence, easy virtue, lightness, shamelessness, immodesty, laxity, loose morals, no morals, morals of an alley cat, amorality, permissive society, free love, wife swapping, sexual delinquency, roving eye, libido, lust, lecherousness, lickerishness (Arch), concupiscence, carnality, sexuality, eroticism (*or* erotism), fleshliness, the flesh, sexual indulgence, sexiness, lasciviousness, salaciousness, lubricity, dissoluteness, decadence, degeneracy, profligacy, dissipation, debauchery, depravity, licentiousness, sexual licence, libertinism (*or* libertinage), seduction, defloration, venery, lechery, satyriasis, priapism, nymphomania, fornication, whorishness, harlotry, womanizing, whoring, running around, bed hopping (Inf), fooling around (Inf), sleeping around (Inf), screwing around (Sl), wenching (Arch)

▶ *405 Physical Pleasure, 870 Self-Indulgence, 809 Vanity*

4 **illicit love**, forbidden love, guilty love, unlawful desires, forbidden fruit, unlawful carnal knowledge, adultery, criminal conversation, unfaithfulness, infidelity, marital infidelity, extramarital relations, eternal triangle, liaison, intrigue, amour, irregular union, ménage à

trois, concubinage, cuckolding, cuckoldry, cheating (Inf), a bit on the side (Inf)

▶ *821 Love, 823 Marriage, 693 Disobedience*

5 **prostitution**, vice, vice squad, soliciting, importuning, kerb crawling, streetwalking, harlot's trade, harlotry, whoredom, oldest profession, Mrs Warren's profession, pimping, pandering, procuring, living on immoral earnings, brothel-keeping, white slave trade (*or* traffic)

6 **brothel**, bordello, bagnio, whorehouse, bawdy-house (Arch), disorderly house, house of ill repute (*or* ill-fame), massage parlour, red-light district, cathouse (US sl), knocking shop (Sl), juke house (US sl)

7 **sexual assault**, sexual offence, sexual perversion, sexual deviancy, incest, buggery, sodomy, bestiality, sadism, sado-masochism, s and m (Inf), sexual abuse, child abuse, pederasty, indecent assault, rape, ravishment, violation, gang rape, date rape, gangbang (Tab sl), the train (*or* the choochoo) (US sl), gross indecency, indecent exposure, exposing oneself, flashing (Inf), mooning (US sl)

▶ *670 Attack, 822 Hate, 676 War*

8 **immoral man**, adulterer, rake, rakehell (Arch), Casanova, Don Juan, libertine, lecher, degenerate, debauchee, roué, satyr, dirty old man, womanizer, philanderer, playboy, gigolo, pimp, pander, procurer, hustler (US), male prostitute, catamite, rent boy

9 **immoral woman**, fallen woman, adulteress, loose woman, scarlet woman, nymphomaniac, nympho (Inf), strumpet, trollop, slut, whore, harlot, courtesan, concubine, kept woman, prostitute, streetwalker, call girl, brothel keeper, madam, tart (Inf), hooker (US sl), Cyprian (Arch)

10 **sex offender**, sex fiend, sex criminal, rapist, sadist, child abuser (*or* molester), pederast, pervert, pornographer, flasher (Inf)

ADJECTIVES

11 **immoral**, amoral, unethical, unprincipled, unscrupulous, bad, wicked, wrong, morally wrong, evil, criminal, illegal, dishonest

12 **indecent**, salacious, prurient, lewd, lubricious, indelicate, improper, suggestive, provocative, risqué, titillating, arousing, erotic, naughty, blue, coarse, crude, vulgar, ribald, strong, racy, louche, bawdy, Rabelaisian, unwholesome, insalubrious, defiling, corrupting, depraving, impure, unclean, dirty, smutty, filthy, scrofulous, scabrous, scatological, stinking, rank, offensive, shocking, obscene, pornographic, uncensored, unexpurgated, unmentionable, unquotable, unprintable, fruity (Inf), near the knuckle (Inf), near the bone (Inf)

13 **unchaste**, unvirtuous, of easy virtue, wanton, light, loose, frail, fallen, seduced, prostituted, fast, naughty, immodest, unblushing, shameless, flaunting, brazen, amoral, promiscuous, sex-mad, man-mad, man-crazy, nymphoma-

niac, scarlet, whorish, tarty, meretricious (Arch), on the game (Sl)

14 **lecherous**, carnal, fleshly, voluptuous, libidinous, lustful, lickerish (Arch), concupiscent, incontinent, Paphian, sexy, hot, rampant, rutting, ruttish, oversexed, sex-mad, sex-crazy, woman-mad, woman-crazy, priapic, lewd, lascivious, licentious, libertine, wild, rakish, amoral, adulterous, unfaithful, dissolute, dissipated, profligate, whoremongering, debauched, depraved, vicious, turned on (Sl), horny (US sl), randy (Inf), goatish (Arch)

15 **unlawful**, abnormal, incestuous, sadistic, sado-masochistic, perverted, bestial, animalistic

VERBS

16 **do wrong**, err, sin, go wrong, stray, go astray, fall, lapse, sink, degenerate, go to the bad, go to rack and ruin, go to the dogs (Inf), go to pot (Inf)

17 **be sexually immoral**, have no morals, have the morals of an alley cat, break the marriage vow, commit adultery, keep a mistress, see another woman (*or* man), cuckold, fornicate, womanize, philander, whore (around), sleep around (Inf), screw around (Sl), lech (around) (Inf), have the hots for (Sl), cheat (Inf), put the horns on (Inf), have a bit on the side (Inf)

18 **prostitute**, solicit, importune, streetwalk, pimp, pander, procure, live on immoral earnings, be on the game (Inf), hook (US sl), hustle (US sl)

19 **corrupt**, debase, demoralize, lead astray, ruin, wreck, disgrace, shame, dishonour, defile, smirch, sully, soil, debauch, deprave, vitiate, pervert

20 **seduce**, take advantage of, have one's way with, take one's pleasure with, deflower, ravish, rape, force, violate, sexually assault, indecently assault, abuse, sexually abuse, interfere with

ADVERBS

21 **immorally**, indecently, suggestively, salaciously, immodestly, without shame

878   Reward

NOUNS

1 **reward**, financial reward, remuneration, recompense, deserved reward, deserts, just deserts, justice, guerdon, meed (Arch), satisfaction, job satisfaction, personal reward, recognition, public recognition, due recognition, credit, due credit, acknowledgment, thanks, gratitude, favour, tribute, deserved tribute, proof of regard, acclaim, acclamation, bouquet, praise, honour, honours, decoration, title, honorary degree, honorary title, letters after one's name, peerage, Birthday Honours, New Year Honours

▶ *837 Gratitude, 851 Approval, 804 Title, 792 Decoration, 845 Entitlement, 879 Punishment, 765 Satisfaction*

2 **prize**, award, crown, trophy, cup, pot, shield,

certificate, medal, kewpie doll (US), consolation prize, second prize, runner-up prize, booby prize, wooden spoon, cash prize, prize money, jackpot, kitty, Nobel Prize, Pulitzer Prize (US), Booker Prize, Academy Award (US), Oscar (US), Emmy (US), BAFTA Award, Man/Woman of the Year, Olympic Gold (or Silver or Bronze) Medal, America's Cup, Blue Riband, blue ribbon

▶ *681 Trophy*

3 **grant**, aid, assistance, subsidy, subvention, fellowship, scholarship, stipend, exhibition, bursary, bursarship, allowance

4 **reward for service**, remuneration, fee, retainer, honorarium, emolument, payment, payment in kind, payoff, pension, retirement pension, pay, wage, wages, salary, basic salary, take-home pay, compensation (US), severance pay, redundancy money, income, earnings, wage (or salary) scale, (pay) rise, raise (US), increment, overtime pay, commission, bonus, incentive, inducement, enticement, offer, tempting offer, bait, lure, perquisite, fringe benefits, hidden income, expense account, perk (Inf), golden hello (Inf), golden handcuffs (Inf), golden handshake (Inf), golden parachute (Inf)

▶ *746 Payment, 710 Offer*

5 **turnover**, return, profitable return, gain, profit, gross profit, net profit, pre-tax profit, profit after tax, profit margin, margin of profit, bottom line

▶ *721 Gain*

6 **compensation**, indemnification, indemnity, satisfaction, consideration, solatium, damages, quid pro quo, requital, retaliation, reparation, amends, restitution, comeuppance (Inf)

▶ *672 Retaliation, 735 Giving Back*

7 **bounty**, premium, gift, gratuity, baksheesh, tip, *douceur* (Fr), *pourboire* (Fr), *trinkgeld* (Ger)

▶ *729 Giving*

8 **secret money**, laundered money, slush fund, smart money, protection money, blackmail, kickback, bribe, rake-off (Sl), payoff (Inf), sweetener (Sl), hush money (Sl)

VERBS

9 **reward**, offer (or give) a reward, remunerate, recompense, give financial reward, give a deserved reward, guerdon, satisfy, give job satisfaction, give personal reward, recognize, credit, acknowledge, thank, show one's gratitude, pay tribute, pat on the back, acclaim, praise, hand out bouquets, award, present, offer (or give) a prize, honour, decorate, bestow a medal, bestow an honorary degree, honour with a title

▶ *837 Gratitude, 851 Approval, 804 Title, 792 Decoration, 800 Repute*

10 **grant**, aid, assist, subsidize, award a fellowship, give a scholarship

11 **pay**, remunerate, give, tip, tip well, bribe, offer

a bribe, pay off, repay, pay back, give what is due, pay back in his (or her) own coin, retaliate, settle up, compensate, indemnify, requite, make reparation, make amends, restitute, pay under the table (Inf), offer a sweetener (Sl), grease the palm (Sl), make it worth one's while (Inf)

▶ *746 Payment, 729 Giving, 672 Retaliation, 735 Giving Back*

12 **be rewarded**, get a reward, gain a reward, have one's reward, get one's deserts, receive one's due, get what is coming to one, get job satisfaction, win a prize, get a medal, receive an honorary degree, receive a title, get one's comeuppance (Inf)

▶ *845 Entitlement*

13 **get paid**, draw a salary, earn an income, have a gainful occupation, accept payment, accept a gratification, take a bribe, have one's palm greased (Sl), receive a sweetener (Sl)

▶ *730 Receiving*

14 **gain**, reap, reap a profit, reap the fruits

▶ *721 Gain*

ADJECTIVES

15 **rewarding**, financially rewarding, satisfying, paying, profitable, moneymaking, lucrative, remunerative, gainful

▶ *721 Gain, 746 Payment*

16 **rewarded**, recognized, credited, acknowledged, acclaimed, praised

17 **compensatory**, indemnificatory, reparatory, retributive, retaliatory

▶ *125 Compensation*

18 **giving**, generous, open-handed, liberal, offering

▶ *729 Giving, 755 Generosity, 710 Offer*

ADVERBS

19 **rewardingly**, satisfyingly, as a reward, as a prize, for one's service, in compensation

20 **profitably**, lucratively, remuneratively, gainfully

879 Punishment

When thou tillest the ground, it shall not henceforth yield unto thee her strength; a fugitive and a vagabond shalt thou be in the earth./ And Cain said unto the Lord, My punishment is greater than I can bear. Bible: Genesis.

There is no peace, saith the Lord, unto the wicked. Bible: Isaiah.

Love is a boy, by poets styl'd,/ Then spare the rod, and spoil the child. Samuel Butler.

Punishment is not for revenge, but to lessen crime and reform the criminal. Elizabeth Fry.

My object all sublime/ I shall achieve in time –/ To let the punishment fit the crime –/ The punishment fit the crime. W. S. Gilbert.

VERBS

1 **punish**, inflict punishment (upon), discipline, take disciplinary action, give (or teach) a lesson, chastise, chasten, correct, administer correction, castigate, admonish, reprimand, reprove, rebuke, chide, scold, tell off, dust down, take to task, rap across the knuckles, smack on the wrist, have one's head for, hurt, inflict pain (upon), afflict, inflict, visit, impose, persecute, victimize, make an example of, shame, pillory, put in the stocks, tar and feather, toss in a blanket, duck, masthead, keelhaul, picket, spread-eagle, imprison, jail, incarcerate, intern, lock up, transport, condemn to the galleys, demote, degrade, downgrade, unfrock, reduce to the ranks, suspend, expel, send down, cashier, drum out, ban, proscribe, banish, exile, deport, ostracize, blackball, outlaw, put in the corner, send out of the room, put in detention, keep in, give lines, confiscate, take away, sequestrate, deprive, forfeit, fine, amerce, mulct, bind over, strafe (Sl), have (or call) on the carpet (Inf), dress down (Inf), give a dressing-down (Inf), put away (Inf), send down (or up) (Inf), send to Coventry (Inf), gate (Sl), ground (US sl)
▶ *690 Severity, 702 Prison*

2 **penalize**, come down on, come down hard on, come down on like a ton of bricks, impose a penalty, exact a penalty, condemn, sentence, execute (or carry out) a sentence, execute justice, exact retribution, settle, fix, bring to book, give what was coming to him (or her), retaliate, settle with, get even with, pay back, avenge, revenge oneself, throw the book at (Inf), give what for (Inf), give his (or her) comeuppance (Inf)
▶ *672 Retaliation*

3 **hit**, strike, smack, slap, slap on the wrist, lambaste, paddle, slipper, put across one's knee, cuff, clout, box someone's ears, clip on (or round) the ear, rap over the knuckles, drub, trounce, beat, beat black and blue, beat the living daylights out of, belt, strap, leather, larrup (Dial), wallop, welt, tan, tan one's hide, cane, birch, switch, whack, thwack, thrash, flog, whip, horsewhip, lash, lay on the lash, scourge, give stripes, give strokes, give the cat, flay, flay one's back, lay one's back open, flail, flagellate, bastinado, cudgel, belabour, fustigate (Arch), give a hiding (Inf), hide (Inf), lather (Inf), dust (off) (Inf)

4 **torture**, put to torture, torment, inflict pain, give the third degree, thumbscrew, rack, put on the rack, break on the wheel, press, apply *peine forte et dure* (Fr), mutilate, kneecap, persecute, martyr, martyrize, work over, give the works (Sl)
▶ *406 Physical Pain*

5 **execute**, put to death, punish with death, condemn, condemn to death, sentence to death, kill, lynch, electrocute, send to the chair, hang, hang by the neck, string up, send to the gallows, send to the scaffold, gibbet, hang, draw, and quarter, gas, put in the gas chamber, give a lethal injection, shoot, put in front of a firing squad, stand against a wall, guillotine, behead, cut off one's head, decapitate, decollate, send to the block, strangle, garrotte, bow-string, burn, burn alive, burn at the stake, send to the stake, flay, flay alive, stone, stone to death, lapidate, dismember, tear limb from limb, impale, crucify, hold mass executions, commit genocide, purge, massacre, decimate, slaughter, murder, butcher (Sl), send to the hot seat (US sl), stretch one's neck (Sl), necklace (S Afr sl), give one a necklace (S Afr sl)
▶ *398 Killing*

6 **be punished**, suffer punishment, take the consequences, have it coming to one, get what one was asking for, get one's deserts, regret it, smart for it, hold one's hand out, pay the ultimate price, pay for it with one's head, die the death, come to execution, lay one's head on the block, come to the gallows, get one's comeuppance (Inf), be for the high jump (Inf), catch it (Inf), catch (or get) it in the neck (Inf), take the rap (Sl), stand the racket (Sl), face the music (Inf), take one's medicine (Inf), take one's gruel (Inf), take a ride to Tyburn (Arch inf), kick the air (Sl), dance upon nothing (Sl), swing (Sl)

NOUNS

7 **punishment**, penalization, discipline, disciplinary action, chastisement, chastening, chiding, correction, lesson, castigation, admonition, reprimand, reproof, rebuke, scolding, telling off, dusting down, rap across the knuckles, smack on the wrist, persecution, victimization, example, shame, tarring and feathering, tossing in a blanket, ducking, keelhauling, walking the plank, detention, house arrest, imprisonment, incarceration, confinement, internment, prison (or jail) sentence, debt to society, penal servitude, hard labour, chain gang, labour camp, penal colony, Gulag, transportation, galleys, demotion, degrading, downgrading, unfrocking, suspension, expulsion, banishment, exile, deportation, ostracism, blackballing, outlawing, proscription, banning, keeping in, lines, confiscation, sequestration, escheat, deprivation, expropriation, forfeit, forfeiture, fine, fining, court fine, amercement, mulct, deodand, binding over, dressing-down (Inf), high jump (Inf), chewing out (Inf), kicking ass (US sl), sending to Coventry (Inf), gating (Sl), grounding (US sl)
▶ *690 Severity, 702 Prison*

8 **penalty**, official punishment, legal punishment, prescribed punishment, pains and pen-

alties, condemnation, sentence, sentencing, execution of sentence, execution of justice, exaction of penalty, liability, legal liability, legal obligation, legal debt, dueness, court award, damages, costs, compensation, restoration, restitution, payment, court payment, compulsory payment, compensatory payment, ransom

9 **retribution**, just retribution, fitting retribution, Nemesis, deserts, just deserts, meet reward (Arch), justice, poetic justice, divine justice, retributive justice, doom, doomsday, judgment, day of judgment, day of reckoning, reckoning, what is coming to one, retaliation, reprisal, requital, repayment, revenge, getting even, what for (Inf), comeuppance (Inf), hell (or the devil) to pay (Sl)

▶ *672 Retaliation*

10 **affliction**, infliction, visitation, imposition, trial, task, punishing experience, dose, hard dose, pill, bitter pill, hard (or tough) row (to hoe), hard lines, adversity, suffering, damage, loss, injury

▶ *687 Adversity*

11 **penance**, self-punishment, atonement, self-mortification, self-discipline, asceticism, hara-kiri, seppuki, felo de se, suicide

12 **corporal punishment**, chastisement of the flesh, bodily chastisement, hitting, striking, spanking, smacking, slapping, paddling, drubbing, trouncing, beating, caning, birching, thrashing, thrashing of a lifetime, flogging, whipping, horsewhipping, scourging, flagellation, running the gauntlet, hit, spank, smack, slap, slap on the wrist, rap, rap over the knuckles, box on the ear, clip on (or round) the ear, blow, buffet, cuff, clout, stroke, stripe, torture, third degree, racking, breaking on the wheel, hanging by the wrists, strappado, bastinado, death by a thousand cuts, hiding (Inf), dusting (Inf)

▶ *406 Physical Pain*

13 **capital punishment**, execution, legalized killing, judicial murder, extreme penalty, death sentence, death penalty, death warrant, traitor's death, electrocution, hanging, hanging, drawing, and quartering, gas, poison, injection, shooting, guillotining, beheading, decapitation, decollation, strangulation, garrotte, stoning, lapidation, impalement, crucifixion, flaying alive, burning, burning at the stake, auto-da-fé, drowning, noyade, massacre, mass murder, mass execution, purge, genocide, the Holocaust, Final Solution, slaughter, martyrdom, martyrization, persecution to the death, illegal execution, lynching, lynch law

▶ *398 Killing*

14 **instrument of punishment**, pillory, stocks, ducking stool, cucking stool, stool of repentance, cutty stool (Scot), corner, dunce's cap, open hand, hairbrush, belt, strap, tawse (Scot), thong, quirt, lash, whip, horsewhip, cowhide, sjambok (S Afr), knout, scourge, cat-o'-nine-tails, cat, rope's end, whipping post, ruler, ferule, stick, birch, birch-rod, switch, big stick, rattan, cane, rod, cudgel, cosh, club, rubber hose, bicycle chain, sandbag, chain, irons, bilboes, fetters, cell, jail, prison, prison house

▶ *702 Prison, 699 Restraint*

15 **instrument of torture**, rack, thumbscrew, iron boot, pilliwinks, triangle, wheel, treadmill, tightened headband, weights, *peine forte et dure* (Fr), spiked device, Iron Maiden, *Fass* (Ger), crushing device, Scavenger's Daughter, torture chamber, the Inquisition, the Star Chamber

16 **instrument of execution**, electric chair, the chair, hanging rope, rope, noose, halter, hempen collar, drop, scaffold, gallows, gibbet, gas, gas chamber, hemlock, poison, lethal injection, bullet, firing squad, wall, axe, headsman's axe, block, guillotine, maiden (Scot), garrotte, bowstring, cross, stake, condemned cell, death chamber, lethal chamber, death house (US), death row (US), the hot seat (Sl), Tyburn tree (Sl), necklace (S Afr sl)

17 **punisher**, discipliner, chastiser, chastener, corrector, castigator, persecutor, tyrant, vindicator, revenger, avenger, retaliator, sentencer, justiciary, magistrate, judge, caner, whipper, flogger, flagellator, scourger, torturer, inquisitor, witch-hunter, executioner, high executioner, hangman, Jack Ketch (Arch), hanging judge (US), headsman, garrotter, bowstringer, lyncher, hit man, assassin, murderer, hatchet man (Sl)

18 **penology**, penal code, penologist

ADJECTIVES

19 **punitive**, punitory, punishing, penalizing, penal, penological, capital, corporal, disciplinary, corrective, correctional, instructive, castigatory, admonitory, vindictive, retributive, revengeful, retaliatory

20 **punished**, disciplined, castigated, imprisoned, in confinement, under house arrest, fined, beaten, tortured, executed, gated (Sl), grounded (US sl)

21 **punishing**, hard, arduous, strenuous, exhausting, gruelling, laborious, backbreaking, demanding, taxing, torturous, painful

22 **punishable**, liable, amerceable, mulctable, deserving punishment, condemned, awaiting execution

ADVERBS

23 **punitively**, penally, penologically, vindictively, retributively, punishingly, punishably

INTERJECTIONS

24 **string him up!**, lynch him!, hang 'em high!, off with his head!, throw the book at him! (Inf), heads will roll! (Inf)

INDEX

Note that all figures refer to category numbers.
A full explanation of the use of the index is given on page xi in **How to Use the Thesaurus**.

A

A 2.7 *social stratification*
A1 29.5 *golf ball*, 126.14 *best*,
611.6 *notable*, 617.1 *worthy*,
617.2 *best*, 619.1 *perfect*, 655.6
skilful
A-1 580.15 *chosen*
A4 paper 604.3 *paper*
aa 54.25 *eruption*
Aaah-te-huti 8 Deities
Aachen 93 Cities
Aalborg 93 Cities
aardvark 77 Placental Mammals, 77.6 *insect-eating mammal*
aardwolf 77 Placental Mammals
Aaron's rod 84 Flowers and Flowering Plants
abacist 170.6 *calculator*
aback 36.20 *offshore*
abacus 43 Architectural Decoration, 43.9 *miscellaneous architectural features*, 52.67 *calculator*, 65.3, 170.5 *computer*, 279.3 *architectural summit*
Abadan 93 Cities
Abaddon 8.7 *devil*, 8.11 *heaven*
abaft 36.20 *offshore*
abalone 81 Molluscs
abampere 75 Scientific and Technical Units
abandon 132.8 *leave*, 136.13 *diverge*, 147.7 *exclude*, 254.19
leave empty, 345.2 *withdraw*,
581.2 *discard*, 598.2 *withdraw*,
642.4 *energy*, 698.6 *liberality*,
704.6 *cancel*, 705.5 *resign*,
727.9 *dispose of*, 824.8 *desert*,
870.3 *overindulgence*
abandon discussion 598.2 *withdraw*
abandoned 132.9 *remaining*,
136.17 *unjoined*, 174.16 *alone*,
254.14 *unoccupied*, 598.5 *relinquished*, 600.4 *disused*, 633.3
vulnerable, 698.12 *unconditional*, 727.12 *disposed*, 824.11
divorced, 870.8 *overindulgent*
abandon hope 641.4 *not act*
abandonment 218.1 *cessation*,
345.7 *departure*, 581.6 *discarding*, 598.3 *relinquishment*,
600.10 *disuse*, 673.1 *submission*, 698.6 *liberality*, 705.1 *resignation*, 727.1 *disposal*
abandon one's cause 673.3 *submit*
abandon one's stance 727.9 *dispose of*
abandon the world 816.12 *be unsocial*
abase 806, 362.4 *debase*, 628.6
pervert
abasement 806, 127.1 *inferiority*, 628.8 *perversion*
abash 806.17 *humiliate*, 806.23
abase
abashed 806.3 *humbled*
abate 121.6 *change gradually*,
129.4 *decrease*, 242.4 *moderate*,
360.9 *descend*, 767.9 *relieve*
abatement 129.1 *decrease*, 242.1
moderation, 767.1 *ease*
abating 129.6 *decreasing*
abatis 671.9 *barrier*

abattoir 398.15 *slaughterhouse*,
727.8 *sink*
a battuta 49 Musical Terms
abbacomes 7.7 *monk*
abbacy 7.9 *priesthood*
abbess 7.7 *monk*
Abbeville 93 Cities
abbey 10.11 *place of worship*
abbot 7.7 *monk*
abbreviate 129.5 *make smaller*,
131.3 *subtract*, 262.5 *make
smaller*, 270.10 *shorten*, 299.5
outline, 543.13 *punctuate*,
552.4 *be concise*, 562.8 *summarize*
abbreviated 131.7 *reduced*,
145.4 *incomplete*, 262.7
smaller, 270.8 *shortened*, 299.6
outlined, 543.17 *punctuated*,
552.3 *concise*, 562.7 *shortened*
abbreviation 129.1 *decrease*,
131.1 *subtraction*, 262.1 *contraction*, 270.2 *shortening*,
270.3 *shortened version*, 299.1
outline, 552.1 *conciseness*,
562.2 *outline*
abbreviator 562.5 *summarizer*
ABC 5.14 *alphabet*, 65.3 *computer*, 528.5 *reference book*,
534.24 *television broadcasting*
abcoulomb 75 Scientific and
Technical Units
ABC powder 62 Medication
abdicate 598.1 *relinquish*, 598.2
withdraw, 673.5 *submit*, 705.5
resign
abdicated 705.7 *resigning*
abdicating 705.7 *resigning*
abdicating monarch 598.4 *deserter*
abdication 598.3 *relinquishment*,
673.1 *submission*, 689.1 *anarchy*, 705.1 *resignation*
abdicator 598.4 *deserter*, 705.3
resigner
Abdiel 8.6 *angel*
abdomen 258.18 *stomach*, 290.4
insides
abdominable 618.3 *bad*
abdominal 290.10 *visceral*
abdominal protector 31.1 *hockey*
abdominous 259.16 *fat*
abducent 341
abduct 734.10 *take away*,
736.13 *kidnap*
abduction 734.3 *taking away*,
736.2 *kidnapping*
abductive 341.9 *abducent*
abductor 734.6 *taker*, 736.8 *thief*
abeam 36.10 *sailing*, 36.20 *offshore*
abecedarian 6.7 *learner*
Abecedarianism 7 Christian
Movements
abecedarium 6.14 *school book*
Abel 52 Scientists, 52 Scientists
Abelard 52 Philosophers
Abelian group 52 Named Concepts
Abelianism 7 Christian Movements
Aberdare 93 Cities
Aberdeen 77 Breeds of Dogs,
93 Cities, 93.4 *British cities*
Aberdeen Angus 68 Breeds of
Cattle
Aberdonian 255.9 *British inhabitant*
Abergavenny 93 Cities

aberrance 215.2 *unusualness*,
844.4 *abnormality*
aberrancy 335.13 *deviation*,
504.7 *errancy*
aberrant 168.17 *abnormal*,
215.5 *unusual*, 335.20 *deviant*,
343.6 *divergent*, 504.16 *errant*,
844.14 *abnormal*
aberrantly 343.16 *divergently*
aberrate 343.10 *diverge*
aberration 56.31 *lens element*,
168.6 *deviation*, 215.2 *unusualness*, 252.1 *displacement*,
335.13 *deviation*, 343.1 *divergence*, 468.1 *inattention*, 510.1
insanity, 844.4 *abnormality*
aberrational 335.20 *deviant*
Aberystwyth 93 Cities
abet 226.12 *determine*, 228.10
manipulate, 284.14 *give moral
support*, 662.17 *help*
abetment 284.6 *moral support*,
662.9 *patronage*
abettor 226.8 *contributor*,
586.14 *motivator*, 662.11 *helper*
abeyance 283.6 *interruption*,
325.1 *motionlessness*, 527.6 *latency*, 600.8 *nonuse*, 641.1 *inaction*
abeyant 283.9 *interrupted*, 325.5
sedentary
abfarad 75 Scientific and Technical Units
Abhayagiri 10.13 *shrine*
abhenry 75 Scientific and Technical Units
abhiseka 10.7 *non-Christian ritual*
abhor 766.7 *be dissatisfied*,
785.5 *dislike*, 820.11 *be hostile*,
822.14 *hate*
abhorred 785.9 *disliked*, 820.10
hated
abhorrence 573.13 *dissociation*,
785.1 *dislike*, 820.1 *enmity*,
822.1 *hate*
abhorrent 341.8 *repulsive*, 785.9
disliked, 820.10, 822.12 *hated*
abhorrently 341.11 *repulsively*
abhorring 785.8 *disliking*,
822.10 *hating*
abidance 167.2 *compliance*,
217.1 *permanence*
abide 188.6 *last*, 217.5 *be permanent*, 219.4 *protract*, 284.12
bear, 325.8 *be motionless*,
396.17 *dwell*, 673.5 *submit*
abide by 167.8 *comply*, 572.13
be willing, 719.4 *observe*
abide by the law 16.67 *follow
the law*, 694.5 *obey*
abide by the rules 652.12 *behave well*
abide in 255.14, 256.17 *inhabit*
abiding 99.12, 188.8 *lasting*,
217.7 *permanent*, 256.14 *inhabiting*
abiding by the law 694.1 *obedience*
abidingly 217.9 *permanently*
Abilene 93 Cities
ability 235, 485, 233 *influence*,
234.3 *aptitude*, 485.1 *qualification*, 486.2 *possibleness*, 567.3
skill, 602.1 *means*, 613.7 *instrumentality*, 655.1 *skill*, 660.1
easiness, 714.3 *potential*,
861.12 *proficiency*

ability to mix 815.2 *social ambition*
ability to sense 403
abiogenesis 245.3 *propagation*
abirritant 62.7 *ointment*
a bit 121.11 *to a degree*, 143.12
partly, 185.3 *duration*
a bit on the side 877.4 *illicit love*
abject 618.4 *poor*, 673.5 *submitting*, 806.3 *humbled*, 808.6 *servile*
abject apology 840.2 *apology*,
867.1 *penitence*
abject fear 779.1 *cowardice*
abject loyalty 673.1 *submission*
abjectly 618.15 *worthlessly*,
806.28 *subserviently*, 808.16
with servility
abjectness 618.10 *poverty*, 808.1
servility
abjuration 484.2 *reversal*, 536.4
renunciation, 578.8 *recantation*,
704.1 *cancellation*
abjuratory 536.11 *negative*
abjure 484.8 *reverse*, 536.9 *renounce*, 578.4 *recant*, 704.6 *cancel*, 727.9 *dispose of*
abjured 484.6 *countered*
Abkhaz 5 Languages and
Groups of Languages
ablate 722.13 *destroy*
ablation 385.2 *wearing away*,
722.5 *destruction*
ablative 5.31 *case*, 385.10 *frictional*
ablative absolute 5.35 *part of
speech*
ablaut 5.36 *accent*
ablaze 408.10 *on fire*, 439.16
bright
able 74.11 *nautical*, 122.9 *adequate*, 235.13 *powerful*, 306.12
on form, 407.10 *handed*, 485.9
qualified, 486.5 *possible*, 507.6
intelligent, 613.3 *instrumental*,
642.18 *active*, 655.6 *skilful*,
696.12 *masterful*
able-bodied 74.11 *nautical*,
142.8 *sound*, 642.18 *active*
able-bodied seaman 74.7 *nautical person*
ableness 485.1 *qualification*
ablepsia 436.1 *blindness*
able rating 679.27 *naval man*
able seaman 74.7 *nautical person*, 679.27 *naval man*
able to pay 742.2 *solvent*
able to speak 564.19 *speaking*
ablution 10.5 *Christian rite*,
389.11 *wash*
ablutionary 134.15 *purifying*,
621.18 *cleansing*
ablutions 621
ably 485.17 *capably*, 655.12
skilfully
Abnaki 5 Languages and
Groups of Languages
abnegate 476.9 *deny*, 484.8 *reverse*, 536.7 *be negative*, 581.4
revoke, 598.1 *relinquish*
abnegated 484.6 *countered*,
711.10 *abnegating*
abnegating 711, 476.7 *refuting*
abnegation 711, 476.2 *denial*,
484.2 *reversal*, 536.1 *negation*,
581.7 *abrogation*, 598.3 *relinquishment*
abnegative 536.11 *negative*

abnegator 476.5 *refuter*, 598.4 *deserter*

abnormal 168, 844, 113.5 *diverse*, 117.8 *contradictory*, 215.5 *unusual*, 510.11 *insane*, 510.13 *mentally ill*, 514.8 *surprising*, 523.5 *strange*, 877.15 *unlawful*

abnormal affection 821.5 *desire*

abnormality 844, 113.1 *diversity*, 117.2 *contradiction*, 168.6 *deviation*, 215.2 *unusualness*, 510.1 *insanity*

abnormally 113.10 *diversely*, 117.15 *dissimilarly*, 168.21 *unconformably*, 215.9 *unusually*, 510.17 *insanely*

abnormal psychology 61.1 *psychology*

Abo 91 Names for Inhabitants

abodah 10.4 *public worship*

abode 256.1 *habitat*, 256.2 *environment*, 567.5 *place of residence*

abode of love 821

Abode of Love 7 Christian Movements

abode of mammals 77

abohm 75 Scientific and Technical Units

abolish 244.8 *destroy*, 598.2 *withdraw*, 704.6 *cancel*, 709.3 *veto*

abolish discrimination 700.6 *treat equally*

abolished 598.5 *relinquished*, 704.10 *cancelled*

abolishment 244.1 *destruction*, 704.1 *cancellation*

abolition 244.1 *destruction*, 598.3 *relinquishment*, 704.1 *cancellation*, 709.1 *veto*

abolitionist 598.4 *deserter*, 704.5 *abrogator*

abolition of sins 704.1 *cancellation*

A-bomb 680.16 *bomb*

abominable 622.8 *unclean*, 785.9 *disliked*, 822.12 *hated*, 844.16 *in the wrong*, 864.11 *wicked*

abominable snowman 76.7 *legendary beast*, 95.3 *mountaineer*, 529.6 *natural mystery*

abominably 618.15 *worthlessly*

abominate 785.5 *dislike*, 820.11 *be hostile*, 822.14 *hate*

abominated 820.10 *hated*

abomination 618.9 *badness*, 622.2 *uncleanness*, 785.1 *dislike*, 820.3 *ill feeling*, 822.1 *hate*, 822.7 *hated thing*, 844.8 *wrong-doing*, 864.1 *wickedness*

a bone to pick 820.1 *enmity*

aboriginal 1.13 *racial*, 3.15 *historic*, 156.31 *prime*, 208.15 *precursory*, 226.13 *causal*, 255.12 *native*

aboriginally 3.24 *historically*, 208.19 *primevally*

aborigine 1.6 *race*, 208.4 *early comer*, 255.1 *inhabitant*

Aborigine 5 Languages and Groups of Languages, 208.4 *early comer*

aborigines 400.3 *uncivilized human*

Aborigines 1 Peoples, 200.6 *people of the past*

abort 65, 100.14 *cause not to exist*, 157.16 *cease*, 244.11 *ruin*, 247.7 *be infertile*, 683.8 *miscarry*

aborted 683.10 *failed*

abortifacient 62.4 *drug type*, 62.17 *stimulating*

abortion 247.1 *infertility*, 683.4 *unsuccessful thing*

abortive 247.6 *having no effect*, 515.11 *disappointing*, 595.5 *immature*, 614.2 *futile*, 683.10 *failed*

abortively 683.12 *unsuccessfully*

abound 610.4 *be excessive*

about 608, 36.20 *offshore*, 52.87 *mathematically*, 120.6 *quantitative*, 120.7 *quantita-*

tively, 124.11 *on average*, 264.6 *near*, 297.8 *round*

about-face 337.9 *turn round*, 337.13 *about-turn*, 484.2 *reversal*

about gone 397.18 *dying*

about this big 259.13 *this size*

about this size 259.13 *this size*

about to 234.5 *tending to*

about to give birth 245.16 *reproductive*

about to go 628.13 *dilapidated*

about-turn 337, 221.1 *reversion*, 335.11, 337.9 *turn round*, 578.6 *equivocation*

above 51.15 *stage*, 95.11 *on the mountain*, 126.12 *superior*, 154.11 *prior*, 275.19 *high*, 293.42 *inclusively*

above all 126.17 *supremely*, 611.9 *importantly*

above and below 293.42 *inclusively*

above average 126.12 *superior*, 126.16 *superiorly*

above board 537.18 *truthful*, 658.1 *naive*, 708.7 *permitted*, 800.3 *reputable*, 857.4 *honourable*

above expectations 610.8 *excessively*

above ground 396.12 *alive*

above-mentioned 154.11 *prior*

above one's head 236.14 *powerlessly*, 275.19 *high*

above par 126.15 *superiorly*, 617.1 *worthy*

above price 617.3, 753.8 *valuable*

above reproach 863.5 *virtuous*

above stairs 275.19 *high*

above suspicion 865.5 *innocent*

above temptation 863.5 *virtuous*

above the horizon 437.1 *visible*

above the law 16

above water 632.5 *safe*

abracadabra 11.5 *spell*, 521.1 *lack of meaning*

abrade 385, 296.15 *make nude*, 384.26 *grate*

abraded 54.59 *weathered*

Abrahamites 7 Christian Movements

Abraham's bosom 397.14 *the spiritual world*

abrase 385.13 *abrade*

abrasion 54.35 *weathering*, 56.10 *force*, 278.4 *shallow thing*, 384.4 *pulverization*, 385.2 *wearing away*, 406.3 *injury*

abrasive 384, 385.10 *frictional*, 546.4 *eraser*, 621.9 *cleaning agent*

abrasively 385, 384.30 *flakily*

abraxas 11.5 *spell*

abreaction 61.3 *psychiatric treatment*, 629.11 *recuperation*

abreast 122.8 *on equal terms*, 122.12 *equally*, 285.7 *in parallel*

abreast of the times 336.17 *forward*

a breath of fresh air 417.1 *odourlessness*

a brick short of a load 460.6 *unintelligent*

abridge 5.46 *translate*, 129.5 *make smaller*, 131.3 *subtract*, 262.5 *make smaller*, 270.10 *shorten*, 299.5 *outline*, 552.4 *be concise*, 562.8 *summarize*

abridged 5.40 *translated*, 131.7 *reduced*, 145.4 *incomplete*, 262.7 *smaller*, 270.8 *shortened*, 299.6 *outlined*, 552.3 *concise*, 562.7 *shortened*

abridger 562.5 *summarizer*

abridgment 5.12 *translation*, 129.1 *decrease*, 131.1 *subtraction*, 262.1 *contraction*, 270.2 *shortening*, 270.3 *shortened version*, 299.1 *outline*, 552.1 *conciseness*, 562.2 *outline*

abroad 149, 104.18 *extraneously*, 263.10 *distantly*, 390.24 *out-of-doors*

abrogate 16.77 *annul*, 16.78 *ac-*

quit, 157.16 *cease*, 231.3 *counteract*, 236.7 *remove power from*, 244.8 *destroy*, 476.8 *refute*, 484.8 *reverse*, 536.9 *renounce*, 546.1 *obliterate*, 578.4 *recant*, 581.4 *revoke*, 598.2 *withdraw*, 600.6 *stop using*, 614.8 *make useless*, 704.6 *cancel*, 709.3 *veto*, 727.9 *dispose of*

abrogated 16.57 *null*, 240.6 *suspended*, 484.6 *countered*, 614.1 *useless*, 704.10 *cancelled*

abrogation 581, 157.2 *cessation*, 231.1 *counteraction*, 476.1 *refutation*, 484.2 *reversal*, 536.4 *renunciation*, 546.3 *obliteration*, 578.8 *recantation*, 598.3 *relinquishment*, 704.1 *cancellation*, 709.1 *veto*, 727.1 *disposal*

abrogative 536.11 *negative*

abrogator 704, 476.5 *refuter*

abrupt 270, 241.6 *violent*, 381.2 *outspoken*, 818.5 *discourteous*, 830.7 *irritable*

abruptly 241.10 *violently*, 270.12 *short*, 381.12 *bluntly*, 425.10 *explosively*, 818.9 *discourteously*, 830.14 *irritably*

abruptness 270, 381.6 *outspokenness*

ABS 604.1 *materials*

ABS brake 71 Motor Vehicle Parts

abscess 624.15 *ulcer*

abscise 83.22 *be dormant*

abscisic acid 58.17 *plant hormone*

abscissa 52.33 *coordinates*, 268.4 *size*

abscission 83.6 *leaf*, 136.3 *separateness*, 296.6 *peeling*

abscond 254, 345.3 *quit*, 591.8 *run away*, 638.5 *escape*, 747.7 *not pay*

absconded 254.9 *away*

absconder 747.6 *nonpayer*

abseil 34.3 *climbing technique*, 34.9 *mountaineer*, 360.9 *descend*

abseil down 34.9 *mountaineer*

abseiling down 34.3 *climbing technique*

absence 100, 254, 438.4 *invisibility*, 458.4 *disappearance*, 591.16 *desertion*, 598.3 *relinquishment*

Absence 254

absence of charge 754

absence of claim 846.1 *lack of entitlement*

absence of dirt 621.1 *cleanness*

absence of intellect 460.1 *lack of intellect*

absence of meaning 521.1 *lack of meaning*

absence of power 236.1 *powerlessness*

absence of right 846.1 *lack of entitlement*

absent 254, 100.9 *nonexistent*, 147.11 *excluded*, 458.7 *disappeared*, 593.4 *required*, 598.6 *apathetic*, 600.1 *unused*, 609.2 *unprovided*

absentation 254.4 *absenteeism*

absentee 254, 254.11 *truant*, 591.17 *avoider*

absentee ballot 580.10 *vote*

absenteeism 254, 643.7 *idleness*

absentee landlord 643.8 *nonworker*

absentee vote 580.10 *vote*

absentee voter 580.13 *electorate*

absently 172, 254, 460.11 *unintelligently*, 598.8 *apathetically*

absent-minded 468, 136.17 *unjoined*, 462.8 *thoughtless*, 512.9 *blank*

absent-mindedly 136.22 *in isolation*, 512.16 *obliviously*

absent-mindedness 468, 462.1 *lack of thought*, 512.2 *blankness*, 546.5 *forgetfulness*

absent-minded professor 468.6 *inattentive person*, 512.7 *forgetful person*

absent oneself 254, 345.3 *quit*, 458.2 *depart*, 591.8 *run away*

absent without leave 720.13 *noncompliant*

absinthe 351.7 *alcoholic drink*

absolute 8.13 *divine*, 144.7 *complete*, 490.1 *certain*, 535.16 *definite*, 537.21 *accurate*, 619.1 *perfect*, 688.12 *authoritative*, 696.12 *masterful*, 698.12 *unconditional*

absolute age 54.41 *geological time*

absolute ceiling 73.5 *flight*

absolute command 12.3 *governance*

absolute frequency 52.58 *frequency distribution*

absolute humidity 55.6 *weather data*, 391.3 *humidity*

absolute idealism 368.5 *idealism*

absolute likeness 537.12 *true to life*

absolutely 8.19 *divinely*, 142.11 *wholly*, 144.9 *completely*, 490.23 *certainly*, 499.9 *yes*, 535.23 *affirmatively*, 619.8 *completely*, 621.20 *clean*, 688.23 *authoritatively*, 696.16 *masterfully*, 772.12 *indeed*

absolutely it 119.2 *original*

absolutely not 100.15 *not at all*, 536.16 *no*

absolute magnitude 53.13 *luminosity*

absolute monarch 696.2 *sovereign*

absoluteness 134.8 *simplicity*, 490.9 *certainty*, 535.8 *definiteness*, 537.8 *accuracy*

absolute pitch 49.21 *tone*, 420.1 *hearing*

absolute power 688.1 *authority*

absolute rate theory 57.14 *chemical reaction*

absolute realism 537.12 *true to life*

absolute ruler 696

absolute scale 75.3 *scale*

absolute unit 75.2 *unit system*

absolute value 52.6 *complex number*, 52.50 *scalar quantity*

absolute zero 56.38 *thermodynamics*, 172.1 *zero*, 409.2 *freezing*

absolution 839, 16.42 *acquittal*, 512.6 *amnesty*, 700.1 *liberation*, 839.1 *forgiveness*, 848.2 *acquittal*, 855.1 *vindication*, 865.2 *legal innocence*

absolutism 688.1 *authority*, 690.2 *suppression*

absolve 839, 10.18 *perform rites*, 16.78 *acquit*, 700.4 *liberate*, 835.10 *show mercy*, 839.9 *forgive*, 848.10 *acquit*, 855.7 *vindicate*, 865.9 *declare innocent*

absolved 16.63 *acquitted*, 700.7 *liberated*, 839.6 *forgiven*, 848.6 *acquitted*, 865.6 *declared innocent*

absolver 700.3 *liberator*

absolving 700.1 *liberation*, 700.7 *liberated*, 839.4 *forgiving*

absorb 57, 348, 392, 53.37 *observe*, 130.6 *add*, 140.5 *combine*, 290.15 *keep inside*, 350.21 *eat*, 599.1 *use*

absorbed 57, 4.17 *thoughtful*, 6.18 *educated*, 110.12 *same*, 140.7 *combined*, 461.9 *concentrating*, 512.8 *oblivious*

absorbed dose 56.70 *radioactivity*

absorbency 348.5 *absorption*

absorbent 348, 348.6 *sponge*, 392.15 *dryer*

absorption 348, 6.8 *learning*, 55.9 *atmospheric process*, 56.15 *wave property*, 56.68 *emission*, 57.20 *surface chemistry*, 59.5 *physiology*, 67.6 *dye*, 140.1 *combination*, 350.1 *eating*, 512.1 *oblivion*

absorption indicator 57.18 *gravimetric analysis*

absorption medium 53.8 *interstellar medium*

absorption spectrum 56.68 *emission*

absorptive 348.17 *absorbent*
absquatulate 345.4 *hurry off*
abstain 591, 573.9 *not cooperate,* 598.1 *relinquish,* 600.5 *not use,* 641.4 *not act,* 699.10 *restrain oneself,* 711.7 *refuse oneself,* 825.10 *be continent,* 869.5 *be self- restrained,* 871.5 *fast,* 873.3 *be sober,* 876.11 *be moral*
abstainer 573.16 *reluctant person,* 591.17 *avoider,* 598.4 *deserter,* 641.2 *nonacting person,* 669.5 *resister,* 711.4 *refuser,* 873.8 *sober person*
abstain from 669.9 *desist,* 711.7 *refuse oneself*
abstain from eating 871.5 *fast*
abstaining 591, 641.3 *inactive,* 669.4, 669.13 *desisting,* 869.1 *self-restraint,* 869.8 *self-restrained*
abstemious 669.13 *desisting,* 699.14, 869.8 *self-restrained,* 871.6 *fasting,* 873.1 *sober*
abstemiously 669, 871, 699.17, 869.11 *with self-restraint,* 873.9 *soberly*
abstemiousness 699.3, 869.1 *self-restraint,* 871.1 *fasting,* 873.6 *sobriety*
abstention 573.13 *dissociation,* 591.1 *abstinence,* 641.1 *inaction,* 869.1 *self-restraint*
abstentious 641.3 *inactive*
abstergent 621.18 *cleansing*
abstinence 591, 598.3 *relinquishment,* 600.8 *nonuse,* 699.3 *self-restraint,* 825.2 *virginity,* 869.1 *self-restraint,* 871.1 *fasting,* 873.6 *sobriety,* 876.3 *moral purity*
abstinence from action 641.1 *inaction*
abstinence from food 871.1 *fasting*
abstinent 591.19 *abstaining,* 699.14 *self-restrained,* 825.7 *virginal,* 869.8 *self-restrained,* 871.6 *fasting,* 873.1 *sober*
abstinently 591.21 *away,* 669.15 *abstemiously,* 825.12 *celibately*
Abstinents 7 Christian Movements
abstract 4.13 *of philosophy,* 50.29 *realist,* 52.69 *theoretic,* 66.4 *portrait,* 102.10 *theoretical,* 131.3 *subtract,* 131.6 *subtractive,* 164.8 *generalization,* 164.20 *generalized,* 270.3 *shortened version,* 270.10 *shorten,* 299.1, 299.5 *outline,* 368.11 *internal,* 471.10 *theoretical,* 518.8 *supposed,* 519.12 *imaginary,* 547.13 *representational,* 551.2 *obscure,* 552.4 *be concise,* 560.13 *representing,* 562.1 *summary,* 562.8 *summarize,* 580.4 *pick*
abstract algebra 52.23 *algebra*
abstract art 50 Western Art Styles and Movements
abstracted 131.5 *subtracted,* 136.17 *unjoined,* 270.8 *shortened,* 335.25 *wandering,* 462.8 *thoughtless,* 512.8 *oblivious*
abstractedly 471.20 *theoretically,* 512.16 *obliviously*
abstractedness 335.16 *wandering,* 461.4 *deliberation,* 512.1 *oblivion,* 519.6 *reverie*
abstract expression 50 Western Art Styles and Movements
abstraction 52.65 *theory,* 61.13 *depression,* 131.1 *subtraction,* 164.8 *generalization,* 471.1 *idea,* 519.6 *reverie,* 551.1 *obscurity*
Abstraction-Création 50 Schools and Groups of Artists
abstractly 4.25 *theoretically,* 50.30 *pictorially,* 136.22 *in isolation,* 368.14 *subjectively,* 471.20 *theoretically*
abstract sculptor 50.17 *sculptor*
abstract sculpture 50.12 *sculpture*
abstract thought 4.4 *philosophi-*

cal investigation, 461.4 *deliberation*
abstruse 523.4 *difficult,* 529.11 *mysterious,* 551.2 *obscure,* 659.12 *problematic*
abstrusely 551.4 *obscurely*
abstruseness 443.8, 551.1 *obscurity,* 659.1 *difficulty*
absurd 117.8 *contradictory,* 487.1 *impossible,* 506.5 *nonsensical,* 508.5 *foolish,* 519.11 *fantastical,* 520.6 *meaningful,* 521.10 *meaningless,* 798.5 *ridiculous*
absurdism 48 Literary Groups and Movements
absurdity 487.5 *impossibility,* 506.1 *nonsense,* 508.1 *folly,* 519.4 *ideality,* 520.4 *type of meaning,* 521.1 *lack of meaning,* 521.4 *senseless talk,* 798.1 *ludicrousness*
absurdly 117.15 *dissimilarly,* 487.11 *impossibly,* 506.9 *nonsensically,* 508.8 *foolishly*
Abu al-Wafa 52 Scientists
Abu Dhabi 93 Cities
Abuja 93 Cities
a bunch of fives 179.1 *five*
abundance 755, 132.4 *surplus,* 181.3 *profuseness,* 246.1 *fertility,* 273.6 *denseness,* 553.1 *diffuseness,* 605.3 *supply,* 608.8 *plenty,* 610.1 *excess,* 742.7 *opulence*
abundant 755, 181.9 *ample,* 246.5 *fertile,* 273.2 *dense,* 553.3 *diffuse,* 605.7 *stored,* 608.2 *plentiful,* 610.6 *excessive,* 742.4 *lush*
abundantly 132.11 *residually,* 246.8 *fruitfully,* 553.7 *diffusely,* 608.9 *enough,* 610.8 *excessively,* 755.12 *generously*
abuse 241.8 *use violence,* 599.3 *exploit,* 599.6 *use,* 601.1, 601.2 *misuse,* 607.1, 607.3 *waste,* 618.11 *harmfulness,* 618.14 *illtreat,* 628.6 *pervert,* 628.8 *perversion,* 670.10 *criticize,* 670.16 *terrorist attack,* 690.6 *suppress,* 818.3 *act of discourtesy,* 818.7 *be discourteous,* 827.6 *vilify,* 832.7 *act of malevolence,* 832.18 *torment,* 844.8 *wrongdoing,* 844.20 *wrong,* 852.8 *berating,* 852.21 *berate,* 854.5 *scorn,* 854.13 *vilify,* 862.2 *affliction,* 862.11 *be evil,* 877.20 *seduce*
abuse a privilege 846.15 *presume*
abused 601.4 *misused,* 852.34 *censured*
abuse of language 504.11 *grammatical error,* 525.2 *misinterpretation*
abuse of terms 504.11 *grammatical error*
abuse one's authority 690.6 *suppress*
abuse one's rights 846.15 *presume*
abuse power 601.1 *misuse*
abuser 601, 599.8 *user,* 832.8 *malefactor*
abuse the environment 601.1 *misuse*
abusive 601, 670.25 *critical,* 818.5 *discourteous,* 818.6 *badmannered,* 827.9 *vituperative,* 844.16 *in the wrong,* 850.11 *insulting,* 852.27 *critical,* 854.16 *defamatory*
abusive language 31.3 *ice hockey*
abusively 601, 607.11 *destructively,* 818.9 *discourteously,* 818.10 *rudely,* 827.13 *vituperatively*
abut 407, 43.19 *decorate,* 267.3 *juxtapose,* 284.11 *support,* 298.4 *interface*
abutment 43.8 *column,* 63.21 *bridge,* 63.27 *superstructure,* 267.1 *juxtaposition,* 284.1 *support,* 284.2 *supporting part,* 298.1 *interface,* 671.11 *fortification,* 726.4 *wall*
abut on 298.4 *interface*

abuttal 267.1 *juxtaposition*
abutting 43.17 *structured,* 267.5 *juxtaposed,* 298.6 *interfacial,* 407.9 *touching*
abvolt 75 Scientific and Technical Units
abwatt 75 Scientific and Technical Units
Abydos 10.13 *shrine*
a bygone age 200.1 *past time*
abysmal 8.16 *devilish,* 277.8 *deep*
abyss 8.11 *heaven,* 265.3 *gulf,* 277.4 *deep thing,* 317.2 *concave land,* 635.1 *trap*
abyssal 54.51, 97.7 *oceanic,* 277.8 *deep*
abyssal hill 54.16 *ocean floor*
abyssal plain 54.16 *ocean floor*
Abyssinian 77 Breeds of Cats
Abyssinian Church 7 Christian Movements
AC 185.29 *one day,* 390.7 *ventilator*
acacia 84 Flowers and Flowering Plants, **85** Trees and Shrubs
Acacianism 7 Christian Movements
academia 501
academic 43 Architectural Styles, 4.10 *philosophic,* 4.12 *sage,* 4.13 *of philosophy,* 4.19 *learned,* 6.4 *educator,* 6.16 *educational,* 6.18 *educated,* 459.8 *intellectual person,* 461.7 *thinker,* 463.5 *reasoner,* 501.6 *knowledgeable person,* 501.9 *literate,* 507.4 *intellectual,* 518.4 *theorist,* 518.7 *suppositional*
academic adviser 653.13 *director*
academically 4.25 *theoretically,* 6.26 *studiously,* 501.15 *knowledgeably*
academicals 295.3 *formal dress*
academic dress 295.3, 813.4 *formal dress*
academic freedom 698.2 *free speech*
academician 50.16 *artist,* 459.8 *intellectual person*
academic journal 187.7 *periodical,* 532.5 *journal*
academic psychology 61.1 *psychology*
academic researcher 518.4 *theorist*
academic robe 295.3 *formal dress*
academic year 187.4 *period of activity*
Academy 6.12 *educational institution*
Academy Award 878.2 *prize*
Acanthocephala 81.6 *worm*
acanthocephalan 81.6 *worm*
acanthoid 380.2 *spiked*
acanthus 380.2 *spiked*
acanthus 43 Architectural Decoration, **84** Flowers and Flowering Plants
Acapulco 93 Cities
Acapulco gold 875.6 *drug*
acarid 82.2 *arachnid,* 82.11 *arachnidan*
acaroid 82.11 *arachnidan*
acaroid gum 85 Tree Products, 395.10 *resin*
acarological 82.15 *arachnological*
acarologist 82.9 *arachnologist*
acarology 82.7 *study*
acarophobia 777 Phobias by Name, **777** Phobias by Name
ACAS 716.4 *negotiator*
Acca Larentia 8 Deities
accede 116.21 *be in accord,* 167.8 *comply,* 499.5 *assent to,* 688.20 *take authority*
accedence 116.1 *accord*
accede to 195.11 *follow in office*
accede to the throne 12.12 *take authority*
accelerando 49 Musical Terms, 329.12 *swiftly*
accelerate 329, 21.6 *race,* 128.5 *make bigger,* 330.1 *impel,* 336.8 *further,* 648.1 *hasten,* 648.2 *make haste,* 660.16 *make easy*

accelerated 128.7 *increased,* 329.3 *accelerating*
accelerating 329
acceleration 329, 21.1 *track events,* 56.8 *time,* 128.1 *increase,* 648.4 *haste*
acceleration due to gravity 56.8 *time*
acceleration path 21.2 *field events*
accelerator 71 Motor Vehicle Parts, 56.94 *particle accelerator,* 57.15 *catalysis*
accelerometer 268.8 *meter,* 329.8 *speed*
accent 5, 5.26 *dialect,* 48.9 *metre,* 235.1 *power,* 543.7 *punctuation,* 543.13 *punctuate,* 554.1 *emphasis,* 554.6 *emphasize,* 564.3 *mode of speech*
accented 543.17 *punctuated,* 564.18 *phonetic*
accentor 78 Birds
accentual 48.20 *metrical*
accentual metre 48.9 *metre*
accentual-syllabic metre 48.9 *metre*
accentuate 526.3 *reveal,* 554.6 *emphasize*
accentuated 526.14 *manifest,* 554.4 *emphasized*
accentuation 5.30 *syntax,* 48.9 *metre,* 526.10 *manifestation,* 554.1 *emphasis,* 564.6 *phonetics*
accept 851, 348.9 *welcome,* 482.12 *be fair,* 490.20 *be certain,* 497.7 *believe,* 499.5 *assent to,* 572.13 *be willing,* 580.1 *select,* 667.6 *agree with,* 673.3 *submit,* 705.6 *resign oneself,* 730.9 *receive,* 734.7 *take,* 749.7 *receive,* 787.5 *not wonder about*
acceptability 348.3 *introduction,* 485.1 *qualification,* 608.7 *sufficiency,* 782.2 *desirability*
acceptable 116.20 *agreeable,* 284.10 *supportable,* 348.14 *admissive,* 485.9 *qualified,* 608.1 *sufficient,* 615.1 *convenient,* 708.7 *permitted,* 763.1 *pleasant,* 765.6 *satisfactory,* 782.8 *desirable,* 851.22 *approvable*
acceptably 485.17 *capably,* 608.9 *enough,* 708.9 *with permission,* 782.17 *desirably,* 851.26 *approvably*
accept a candidacy 580.5 *vote*
accept a charge 745.7 *be in debt*
accept advice 654.6 *consult*
accept a gratification 878.13 *get paid*
accept aid 662.18 *receive help*
accept an apology 839.12 *show mercy*
acceptance 116.1 *accord,* 348.1 *admittance,* 490.10 *conviction,* 497.3 *believing,* 499.1 *assent,* 667.1 *agreement,* 705.4 *resignedness,* 730.1 *receiving,* 851.1 *approval*
accept a nomination 580.5 *vote*
acceptant 730.11 *receiving*
accept a proposal 714.7 *promise,* 823.15 *marry*
accept battle 676.14 *battle*
accepted 116.10 *in accord,* 124.1 *average,* 164.19 *prevailing,* 497.14 *believed,* 584.12 *established,* 730.13, 749.6 *received,* 851.23 *approved*
accepted as one of the family 815.16 *popular*
accepted meaning 520.4 *type of meaning*
accepted reading 524.1 *interpretation*
accepter 730.5 *recipient*
accepting 116.10 *in accord,* 490.2 *convinced,* 667.10 *agreeing,* 691.4 *lenient,* 705.8 *resigned,* 730.1, 730.11 *receiving*
accept invitations 815.11 *be sociable*
accept liability 714.8 *guarantee*
accept obligation 714.8 *guarantee*
accept on faith 497.7 *believe*
acceptor 57.11 *chemical bond,*

730.5 *recipient*, 738.12 *purchaser*
acceptor impurity 56.44, 64.4 *semiconductor*
accept payment 878.13 *get paid*
accept responsibility 714.8 *guarantee*
accept stolen property 730.9 *receive*
accept the Lord 7.19 *be religious*
accept the responsibility 847.15 *be liable*
access 356, 65.17 *computing term*, 65.19 *abort*, 322.19 *open up*, 327.2 *route*, 346.1 *entry*, 346.4 *right of entry*, 346.5 *entrance*, 348.2 *receptivity*, 366.8 *spasm*, 734.4 *taking in*
Access 744.2 *credit card*
accessibility 253.4 *availability*, 264.1 *nearness*, 486.2 *possibleness*, 615.4 *nearness*
accessible 327, 253.10 *available*, 264.5 *near*, 322.13 *opened up*, 344.20 *attainable*, 348.15 *receptive*, 486.5 *possible*, 615.2 *nearby*, 660.11 *made easy*
accessibly 322.25 *obviously*, 615.7 *conveniently*
accession 195, 130.1 *addition*, 344.17 *achievement*, 688.3 *acquisition of power*
accessional 688.13 *elected*
accessories 295, 136.7 *separates*, 725.4 *possessions*
accessory 34.8 *mountaineering*, 130.1 *addition*, 180.4 *concomitant*, 180.17 *accompanying*, 226.8 *contributor*, 610.3 *superfluity*, 612.8 *trifle*, 662.31 *supplementary*, 724.3 *participant*, 724.5 *jointly possessing*
accessory cord 34.4 *climbing equipment*
access road 137.5 *road*
acciaccatura 49.16 *musical note*
accident 211.4 *mishap*, 229.3 *coincidence*, 589.1 *chance*, 661.2 *obstacle*, 687.1 *adversity*, 862.2 *affliction*
accidental 211, 49.16 *musical note*, 229.6 *motiveless*, 489.3 *unexpected*, 589.8 *chance*, 661.14 *blocked*
accidental death 397.5 *ways of dying*
accidental discovery 229.3 *coincidence*, 496.6 *discovery*
accidental killing 398, 398.1 *killing*
accidentally 211.17 *mistakenly*, 229.8, 589.13 *by chance*, 661.17 *in the way*, 687.12 *in adversity*, 862.13 *destructively*
accident neurosis 61.10 *neurosis*
accident prevention 15.2 *industrial negotiations*
accident-prone 687.8 *unlucky*
Accius 48 Dramatists
acclaim 851, 851, 9.7 *worship*, 849.17 *praise*, 878.1, 878.9 *reward*
acclaimed 878.16 *rewarded*
acclamation 431.3 *cry of praise*, 851.5 *acclaim*, 878.1 *reward*
acclamatory 851, 851.18 *approving*
acclimate 203.7 *season*
acclimatization 167.3 *pliancy*, 584.7 *habituation*, 594.13 *development*
acclimatize 167.10 *assimilate*, 203.7 *season*, 584.18 *habituate*, 594.7 *develop*
acclimatized 584.14 *habituated*
acclivity 275.2 *heights*, 360.6 *slide*
accolade 43 Architectural Decoration, 804.3 *honours*, 851.4 *compliment*
accommodate 122.11 *equalize*, 146.4 *include*, 167.9 *make conform*, 332.8 *orient*, 348.9 *welcome*, 377.10 *be adaptable*, 606.5 *provision*, 662.22 *improve*, 677.4 *pacify*, 717.4 *com-*

promise, 732.5 *lend*, 831.8 *be benevolent*
accommodate oneself 167.8 *comply*
accommodate with 729.5 *give*
accommodating 116.10 *in accord*, 146.7 *including*, 167.13 *compliant*, 377.7 *adaptive*, 662.35 *benevolent*, 664.17 *cooperative*, 673.5 *submitting*, 691.4 *lenient*, 717.6 *compromising*, 817.7 *courteous*, 831.6 *benevolent*
accommodatingly 377.12 *adaptably*, 677.7 *pacifically*, 691.6 *leniently*, 717.9 *compromisingly*, 817.14 *courteously*, 817.15 *genteelly*, 831.10 *benevolently*
accommodation 116.1 *accord*, 146.1 *inclusion*, 167.3 *pliancy*, 248.5 *reserved space*, 256.1 *habitat*, 259.1 *size*, 332.3 *orientation*, 377.2 *adaptability*, 605.4 *storage*, 606.1 *provision*, 662.7 *convenience*, 677.1 *pacification*, 717.1 *compromise*, 732.1 *lending*
accommodation ladder 74 Parts of a Ship, 359.9 *ladder*
accommodative 732.6 *loaned*
accompanied 180, 107.4 *related*, 135.12 *united*
accompanier 180
accompaniment 180, 49.15 *composition*, 107.1 *relatedness*, 198.1 *same time*, 253.2 *omnipresence*
Accompaniment 180
accompanist 180.6 *accompanier*
accompany 180, 135.8 *unite*, 198.6 *be simultaneous*, 433.9 *set to music*, 653.2 *direct*, 697.8 *serve*
accompanying 180, 198.9 *simultaneous*, 253.8 *attendant*
accomplice 724.3 *participant*, 866.4 *guilty person*
accomplish 142.10, 144.4 *complete*, 227.5 *show an effect*, 243.10 *produce*, 319.6 *notch up*, 344.9 *achieve*, 619.5 *perfect*, 640.4 *act*, 682.6 *be successful*, 684.4 *complete*, 718.13 *secure one's objective*
accomplished 718, 4.19 *learned*, 6.19 *knowledgeable*, 144.7 *complete*, 655.6 *skilful*, 684.7 *completed*, 688.17 *expert*, 861.5 *proficient*
accomplishment 144.3 *completion*, 243.1 *production*, 344.17 *achievement*, 501.2 *information*, 640.1 *action*, 640.2 *deed*, 655.1 *skill*, 682.1 *success*, 684.1 *completion*, 861.12 *proficiency*
accomplishments 501.3 *learning*
accomplish nothing 614.9 *waste effort*
accord 116, 107.8 *be proportionate to*, 112.3 *agreement*, 114.10 *be similar*, 116.21 *be in accord*, 135.2 *agreement*, 150.20 *harmonize*, 167.1 *conformity*, 167.7 *conform*, 433.8 *harmonize*, 499.1 *assent*, 520.10 *mean*, 615.6 *be convenient*, 664.2 *fellowship*, 667.1 *agreement*, 715.1 *contract*, 729.5 *give*
Accord 116
accordance 110.2 *equivalence*, 114.1 *similarity*, 116.1 *accord*, 167.1 *conformity*, 667.1 *agreement*, 719.1 *observance*
accordant 110.13 *equivalent*, 116.10 *in accord*, 167.12 *conforming*, 667.10 *agreeing*
accordantly 667.14 *agreeably*
accorded 729.7 *given*
accordingly 116, 106.15 *under the circumstances*, 227.12 *with the effect of*
according to chance 229.8 *by chance*, 589.14 *perchance*
according to circumstances 106.15 *under the circumstances*
according to law 16.44 *legal*, 16.81 *legally*, 214.17 *orderly*

according to order 214.17 *orderly*
according to plan 588, 150.25 *in order*
according to rule 167, 150.17 *disciplined*, 214.17 *orderly*
according to schedule 592.16 *as planned*
according to the agreement 715.8 *contractually*
according to the book 520.13 *meaningfully*
according to the contract 715.8 *contractually*
according to the rules 166.19 *to rule*
according to tradition 214.17 *orderly*
accordion 49 Musical Instruments
accordion pleat 320.2 *pleat*
accord respect to 849.18 *show respect*
accord with 122.10 *be equal*
accost 567.9 *approach*, 712.6 *request*
accosting 712.1 *request*
accouchement 245.7 *obstetrics*
account 750, 3.5 *chronicle*, 170.12 *check*, 171.4 *bill*, 528.2 *communication*, 545.1 *record*, 560.1 *description*, 560.3 *narration*, 611.1 *importance*, 741.6 *funds*, 744.1 *credit*, 745.5 *amount owing*, 750.1 *accounts*
accountability 475.5 *demonstrability*, 478.9 *answerability*, 513.2 *expectations*, 745.1 *debt*, 845.4, 847.1 *duty*
accountable 478.16 *answerable*, 745.9 *in debt*, 750.10 *accounting*, 847.10 *liable*
accountableness 847.1 *duty*
accountably 475.22 *demonstrably*, 478.27 *answerably*, 847.18 *on duty*
accountancy 545.8 *registration*, 750.1 *accounts*
accountant 750, 170.7 *mathematician*, 545.9 *recorder*, 678.4 *representative*, 741.18 *treasurer*
account book 750, 545.6 *record book*
account books 171.4 *bill*
accounted 750
accounted for 196.8 *available*
account for 4.21 *rationalize*, 847.15 *be liable*
accounting 750, 750, 14.1 *finance*, 170.3 *count*, 750.1 *accounts*
account paid 750.4 *statement*
account rendered 750.4 *statement*
accounts 750, 545.8 *registration*
Accounts 750
accounts code 750.5 *account book*
account settled 750.4 *statement*
accounts payable 744.1 *credit*
accounts receivable 745.5 *amount owing*, 746.1 *payment*
accoutre 295.32 *dress*, 295.35 *make clothing*
accoutred 594.18 *prepared*, 671.30 *defended*
accoutrement 295.1 *dress*, 603.6 *equipment*
accoutrements 130.3 *additional item*, 295.25 *accessories*, 723.4 *possession*, 725.4 *possessions*
Accra 93 Cities
accredit 116.28 *consent*, 688.21 *grant authority*, 703.6 *commission*
accreditation 703.1 *commission*
accredited 116.17 *consenting*, 497.14 *believed*, 584.12 *established*, 688.16 *authorized*, 703.9 *commissioned*
accrete 130.6 *add*, 721.11 *acquire*
accretion 128.1 *increase*, 130.1 *addition*, 721.3 *acquisition*
accretionary 130.8 *additional*
accretive 130.8 *additional*
accrual 128.1 *increase*, 130.1 *addition*
accrue 130.6 *add*, 227.8 *grow*,

721.13 *be profitable*, 749.7 *receive*
accrue to 128.5 *make bigger*
accumbency 282.1 *horizontality*
accumbent 282.10 *lying*
accumulate 128.4 *increase*, 135.8 *unite*, 161.37 *assemble*, 605.6 *store*, 721.11 *acquire*
accumulated 161.47 *collected*, 605.7 *stored*
accumulated arrears 745.5 *amount owing*
accumulation 128.1 *increase*, 161.25 *assemblage*, 605.1 *store*, 605.4 *storage*, 605.5 *collection*, 721.3 *acquisition*
accumulative 721.18 *acquisitional*
accumulatively 721.20 *gainfully*
accumulator 64.29 *power source*, 161.35 *collector*, 235.7 *electrical power*
accuracy 503, 537, 760, 52.8 *number system*, 56.83 *sensitivity*, 150.6 *methodicalness*, 490.9 *certainty*, 550.1 *clarity*, 619.3 *perfection*, 719.1 *observance*, 843.2 *correctness*
Accuracy 503
accuracy event 20.1 *angling*
accurate 503, 537, 760, 150.14 *well-ordered*, 490.1 *certain*, 492.9 *judicious*, 550.3 *clear*, 619.1 *perfect*, 658.1 *naive*, 719.7 *observant*, 843.8 *correct*
accurately 503, 537, 550.4 *clearly*, 843.20 *correctly*
accurateness 843.2 *correctness*
accurate person 503
accurate thing 503
accursed 618.3 *bad*, 618.5 *harmful*, 618.6 *damnable*, 631.16 *blighting*, 687.8 *unlucky*, 822.12 *hated*, 827.10 *maledictive*, 862.10 *inauspicious*, 864.14 *impious*
accusable 16.47 *liable to law*, 16.54 *litigated*, 16.58 *unjust*, 864.15 *criminal*, 866.5 *guilty*
accusation 856, 16.5 *litigation*, 852.7 *blame*, 866.1 *guilt*
Accusation 856
accusation of guilt 866.1 *guilt*
accusative 5.31 *case*
accusatory 856, 852.29 *blaming*
accuse 856, 16.70 *litigate*, 528.13 *inform on*, 530.7 *betray*, 827.6 *vilify*, 852.19 *blame*
accused 16.8 *litigant*, 856.8 *accusatory*
accused person 856, 16.8 *litigant*
accuse falsely 856
accuse oneself 866.9 *appear guilty*, 867.4, 867.4 *be penitent*
accuser 856, 16.8 *litigant*, 528.10 *informer*
accusing 16.53 *litigating*, 852.29 *blaming*, 866.1 *accusation*, 856.8 *accusatory*
accusingly 856
accustom 203.7 *season*, 584.18 *habituate*
accustomed 124.1 *average*, 164.21 *common*, 166.10 *customary*, 203.15 *seasoned*, 584.9 *habitual*, 584.14 *habituated*
accustom oneself 584.18 *habituate*
AC/DC 176.10 *two-sided*
ace 29.3 *golf shots*, 29.7 *golf*, 40.2 *tennis strokes*, 42.3 *card game terms*, 126.6 *paragon*, 174.1 *one*, 264.2 *short distance*, 485.8 *qualified person*, 602.1 *means*, 617.1 *worthy*, 617.2 *best*, 655.3 *masterpiece*, 655.4 *skilled person*, 655.6 *skilful*, 682.3 *successful thing*, 688.11, 696.10 *expert*, 696.13 *excellent*, 696.15 *learn*, 786.14 *wonderful*, 861.16 *superior person*
ACE 65.3 *computer*
ace in the hole 126.3, 300.4 *advantage*, 592.3 *expedient plan*, 611.3 *chief thing*

Aceldama 398.6 *ritual killing*, 676.10 *battleground*
acellular 59.23 *cellular*
ACE mixture 62 Medication
acer 85 Trees and Shrubs
acerbate 830.12 *make irritable*
acerbic 380.5 *mentally sharp*, 415.5 *acid*, 818.5 *discourteous*, 828.15 *resentful*, 829.4 *irascible*, 832.14 *hostile*
acerbity 415.1 *sourness*, 818.1 *discourtesy*, 829.1 *irascibility*, 832.4 *bitterness*
acerophobia 777 Phobias by Name
acetal 57 Types of Compounds
acetaldehyde 57 Common Chemical Compounds
acetamide 57 Common Chemical Compounds
acetanilide 62 Medication, **62** Medication
acetate 67 Synthetic Fibres and Fabrics
acetate rayon 67 Synthetic Fibres and Fabrics
acetazolamide 62 Medication
acetic 58 Common Fatty Acids
acetic acid 57 Common Chemical Compounds, 415.3 *sour thing*
acetohexamide 62 Medication
acetone 57 Common Chemical Compounds
acetylate 57.26 *react*
acetylation 57 Types of Chemical Reaction
acetylcysteine 62 Medication
acetylene 57 Common Chemical Compounds
acetylene lamp 439.5 *incandescent light*
a.c. generator 64.30 *generator*
Achaeans 1 Peoples
a chance in a million 489.4 *improbability*
ache 406.1 *pain*, 406.9 *feel pain*, 406.10 *be painful*, 618.11 *harmfulness*, 631.5 *pain*, 764.12 *be painful*
ache in every muscle 650.5 *be fatigued*
achene 86.2 *botanical fruit*
Achernar 53 Named Stars
aches and pains 406.1 *pain*
Acheson process 57 Named Reactions
achievable 101.9 *realizable*, 344.20 *attainable*, 486.5 *possible*
achieve 344, 142.10, 144.4 *complete*, 157.15 *end*, 227.5 *show an effect*, 232.4 *be an instrument*, 243.10 *produce*, 319.6 *notch up*, 619.5 *perfect*, 640.4 *act*, 682.6 *be successful*, 684.4 *complete*
achieve a result 684.5 *conclude*
achieved 144.7 *complete*, 684.7 *completed*
achieve liberty 700.5 *be liberated*
achieve marvels 786.11 *do wonders*
achievement 344, 144.3 *completion*, 227.1 *effect*, 232.1 *instrumentality*, 243.1 *production*, 336.12 *advance*, 544.8 *heraldic device*, 640.1 *action*, 640.2 *deed*, 682.1 *success*, 684.1 *completion*
achieve nothing 614.7 *be useless*
achieve one's goal 684.4 *complete*
achiever 640.3 *doer*, 682.4 *successful person*
achieve victory 682.9 *be victorious*
Achilles 53 Minor Planets
Achilles and Patroclus 819.7 *famous friendships*
Achilles' heel 238.1 *weakness*, 620.7 *defect*, 633.7 *vulnerability*
Achinese 5 Languages and Groups of Languages
aching 406.1 *pain*, 406.5 *painful*, 406.7 *feeling pain*, 650.1 *fatigued*, 764.4 *painful*

aching all over 406.7 *feeling pain*
achingly 406.13 *painfully*
aching muscles 650.7 *fatigue*
achluophobia 777 Phobias by Name
achondrite 53.20 *meteor*
achromatic 445.7 *colourless*, 446.2 *whitened*, 447.2 *dark*
achromatically 445.9 *colourlessly*, 446.14 *whitely*
achromatic hue 446.8 *whitener*
achromaticity 445.1 *colourlessness*
achromatic lens 56.29 *optical element*
achromatism 445.1 *colourlessness*, 446.7 *whiteness*
achromatize 445.6 *decolour*
acicular 380.1 *sharp*
aciculate 380.1 *sharp*
acid 57, 57, 415, 244.7 *agent of destruction*, 411.7 *tasty*, 618.5 *harmful*, 631.4 *strain*, 764.3 *unpalatable*, 828.1 *resentment*, 828.15 *resentful*, 829.4 - *irascible*, 830.7 *irritable*, 832.14 *hostile*, 875.6 *drug*
acid anhydride 57 Types of Compounds
acid–base catalysis 57.15 *catalysis*
acid dye 67.6 *dye*
acid-head 875.4 *drug taker*
acid house 49.9 *popular music*
acid-house party 161.10 *dance*
acidic 57.36, 415.5 *acid*, 832.14 *hostile*
acidify 57.26 *react*, 415.8 *sour*
acidimeter 268.8 *meter*
acidimetric 268.16 *micrometric*
acidimetry 268.2 *micrometry*
acidity 415.1 *sourness*, 624.8 *indigestion*, 828.1 *resentment*, 829.1 *irascibility*, 832.4 *bitterness*
acid jazz 49.8 *jazz*
acid kiln 44.6 *ceramic workshop*
acidly 828.17 *resentfully*, 829.9 *irascibly*, 830.14 *irritably*
acidness 829.1 *irascibility*
acidosis 624.8 *indigestion*
acid rain 55.26 *raininess*, 415.3 *sour thing*, 628.10 *impairment*, 631.9 *pollution*
acid rock 49.9 *popular music*, 54.30 *igneous rock*
acid salt 57.10 *salt*
acid stop 66.12 *development*
acid taste 411.1 *taste*
acid test 479.1 *experiment*
acid trip 875.1 *drug-taking*
acidulated 415.5 *acid*
acidulous 415.5 *acid*, 828.15 *resentful*
acidulousness 415.1 *sourness*, 828.1 *resentment*
ACK 65.14 *data transfer*
ack-ack 670.13 *air attack*, 680.13 *ammunition*
ackee 86 Fruits
acknowledge 478.17 *answer*, 499.4 *assent*, 530.8 *admit*, 534.31 *correspond*, 719.4 *observe*, 730.9, 749.7 *receive*, 817.10 *be courteous*, 837.6 *be grateful*, 845.17 *credit*, 849.18 *show respect*, 878.9 *reward*
acknowledged 478.11 *answering*, 530.10 *disclosed*, 584.12 *established*, 730.13, 749.6 *received*, 878.16 *rewarded*
acknowledged with thanks 749.6 *received*
acknowledge one's faults 867.4 *be penitent*
acknowledge one's guilt 866.8 *be guilty*
acknowledge one's sins 866.8 *be guilty*, 867.4 *be penitent*
acknowledging 837.5 *thanking*
acknowledgment 478, 65.14 *data transfer*, 499.1 *assent*, 530.2 *divulgence*, 719.1 *observance*, 817.3 *courtesies*, 837.3 *recognition*, 840.2 *apology*, 845.2 *due*, 851.2 *admiration*, 878.1 *reward*

acknowledgment of guilt 840.2 *apology*
acknowledgment of payment 730
aclinic line 54.45 *magnetic pole*
acme 126.4 *summit*, 275.2 *heights*, 279.1 *summit*, 619.3 *perfection*
Acmeism 48 Literary Groups and Movements
acme of perfection 619.3 *perfection*
acne 375.7 *rough thing*, 624.13 *skin disease*, 793.2 *pimple*
A.C. Nielsen ratings 532.2 *mass media*
acoelomate 81.16 *invertebrate*
acolyte 7.3 *religious person*, 7.8 *priest*, 284.8 *supporter*
Aconcagua 95 Mountains, 95.6 *other major mountains and ranges*
aconite 62 Medication, **84** Flowers and Flowering Plants, 58.19 *alkaloid*, 631.12 *poisonous plant*
acorn 86 Nuts
acorn academy 510.8 *mental hospital*
acorn barnacle 81.4 *arthropod*
a corner on 723.1 *possession*
acorns 350.8 *animal food*
acorn worm 81.2 *protochordate*, 81.6 *worm*
acouchi 77 Placental Mammals
a couple 175.1 *plurality*
acoustic 56.98 *physical*, 420.11 *aural*
acoustically 56.100 *physically*
acoustic coupler 65.7 *peripheral*, 65.14 *data transfer*
acoustic guitar 49 Musical Instruments
acoustic mine 680.16 *bomb*
acousticophobia 777 Phobias by Name
acoustic phonetics 564.6 *phonetics*
acoustics 56.2 *classical physics*, 420.1 *hearing*
acoustic wave 56.14 *sound wave*, 365.5 *wave*
acquaint 6.22 *educate*, 528.11 *inform*, 819.15 *be hospitable*
acquaintance 501.1 *knowledge*, 528.1 *information*, 819.5 *friend*
acquaintanceship 819.1 *friendship*
acquainted 819.9 *friends with*
acquainted with 501.8 *knowledgeable*
acquaint oneself 501.13 *get to know*
acquest 132.5 *estate*
acquiesce 116.21 *be in accord*, 167.8 *comply*, 499.5 *assent to*, 572.13 *be willing*, 667.6 *agree with*, 673.3 *submit*, 694.5 *obey*, 705.6 *resign oneself*, 708.3 *permit*, 851.12 *accept*
acquiescence 572, 116.1 *accord*, 167.2 *compliance*, 499.1 *assent*, 667.1 *agreement*, 673.1 *submission*, 694.1 *obedience*, 705.4 *resignedness*, 708.1 *permission*, 851.1 *approval*
acquiescent 116.10 *in accord*, 167.13 *compliant*, 499.6 *assenting*, 572.3 *amenable*, 660.13 *easygoing*, 667.10 *agreeing*, 673.5 *submitting*, 694.7 *obedient*, 705.8 *resigned*
acquiescently 499.8 *unanimously*, 667.14 *agreeably*, 694.10 *obediently*
acquiescing 116.10 *in accord*, 667.10 *agreeing*
acquire 721, 496.2 *detect*, 602.6 *find means*, 696.15 *learn*, 721.9 *gain*, 730.9 *receive*, 734.7 *take*, 738.1 *purchase*, 749.7 *receive*, 860.6 *be selfish*
acquire a reputation 640.4 *act*
acquire authority 688.20 *take authority*
acquire by purchase 738.1 *purchase*
acquire credit 744

acquired 721.15 *gainful*, 730.13 *received*
acquired knowledge 501.3 *learning*
acquire knowledge 6.23 *learn*
acquirement 655.1 *skill*, 721.1 *gain*
acquirements 501.3 *learning*
acquirer 730.5 *recipient*
acquire the force of habit 584.17 *become a habit*
acquire the habit 584.18 *habituate*
acquiring 721.15 *gainful*, 734.12 *taking*
acquisition 721, 496.7 *detection*, 721.1 *gain*, 730.1 *receiving*, 734.1 *taking*, 738.6 *purchase*
acquisitional 721, 734.12 *taking*
acquisition of knowledge 6.8 *learning*
acquisition of power 688
acquisitive 721.16 *greedy*, 721.18 *acquisitional*, 734.12 *taking*, 738.14 *buying*, 782.9 *desirous*, 860.4 *selfish*
acquisitively 738, 721.20 *gainfully*, 734.13 *avariciously*, 860.8 *selfishly*
acquisitiveness 860.1 *selfishness*
acquit 16, 848, 492.11 *judge*, 639.1 *deliver*, 700.4 *liberate*, 719.6 *perform*, 839.10 *absolve*, 847.16 *do one's duty*, 855.7 *vindicate*, 865.9 *declare innocent*
acquit oneself 652.11 *conduct oneself*
acquittal 16, 848, 16.7 *legal trial*, 492.2 *verdict*, 638.1 *escape*, 639.2 *deliverance*, 700.1 *liberation*, 719.3 *performance*, 835.3 *mercy*, 839.3 *absolution*, 847.5 *discharge of duty*, 855.1 *vindication*, 865.2 *legal innocence*
acquittance 700.1 *liberation*, 718.2 *promise*, 746.1 *payment*
acquitted 16, 848, 638.8 *escaping*, 698.9 *free*, 700.7 *liberated*, 839.6 *forgiven*, 855.12 *innocent*, 865.6 *declared innocent*
acraniate 81.16 *invertebrate*
acre 75 General Units
acreage 68.11 *farmland*, 249.12 *plot*, 725.1 *property*
acre-foot 75 General Units
acre-inch 75 General Units
acres 725.1 *property*
acrid 415.5 *acid*, 820.6, 832.14 *hostile*
acridine dye 67.6 *dye*
acridity 415.2 *unpalatability*
acridly 820.15 *aggressively*
Acrilan 67 Synthetic Fibres and Fabrics
acrimonious 818.5 *discourteous*, 820.6 *hostile*, 822.10 *hating*, 828.15 *resentful*, 832.14 *hostile*
acrimoniously 818.9 *discourteously*, 820.14 *hostilely*, 822.18 *hatefully*, 828.17 *resentfully*, 832.20 *malevolently*
acrimony 820.3 *ill feeling*, 822.1 *hate*, 828.1 *resentment*, 832.4 *bitterness*
acrobat 51.29 *circus performer*, 237.5 *athlete*, 655.4 *skilled person*, 811.15 *showman*
acrobatic 18.5 *sporting*, 41.12 *ski*, 374.2 *pliant*
acrobatically 41.17 *on a ski run*, 374.17 *softly*
acrobatic jump 41.1 *skiing*
acrobatic skiing 41.1 *skiing*
acromegaly 259.4 *gigantism*
acronym 5.13 *letter*
acronymic 5.41 *lettered*
acronymous 5.41 *lettered*
acrophobia 777 Phobias by Name, **777** Phobias by Name
acropolis 243.8 *construction*, 634.1 *refuge*, 671.12 *fort*
Acropolis 43 Noted Buildings
acrospire 83.9 *seed*
across 271.8 *breadthwise*, 286.8 *obliquely*, 356.14 *by the way*

across the board 112.14 *equanimously*, 124.1 *average*
across-the-board 142.6 *whole*, 146.7 *including*, 164.15 *general*
across the counter 737.20 *in trade*
across the line 357.17 *ahead*
across the sea 97.11 *nautically*
acrostic 5.13 *letter*, 5.41 *lettered*, 529.4 *brain-teaser*
acroter 43 Architectural Decoration
Acrux 53 Named Stars
a crying shame 835.5 *misfortune*
acrylic 58 Common Fatty Acids, 67 Synthetic Fibres and Fabrics, 50.8 *painting*, 604.1 *materials*
acrylic paints 444.5 *paint*
act 51, 547, 640, 3.14 *historicalness*, 51.6 *scene*, 51.27 *entertainer*, 166.1 *rule*, 227.5 *show an effect*, 230.7 *be operational*, 232.4 *be an instrument*, 457.13 *occur*, 492.2 *verdict*, 526.1 *display*, 538.24 *pretend*, 540.12 *facade*, 540.20 *pretend*, 540.24 *mask*, 640.2 *deed*, 642.12 *be active*, 652.11 *conduct oneself*, 652.14 *behave towards*, 654.3 *precept*, 655.3 *masterpiece*, 692.1 *command*, 811.14, 811.27 *show*
act according to the book 537.32 *be literal*
act against 663.12 *oppose*, 663.18 *counteract*
act aimlessly 521.7 *mean nothing*
act as a brake 661.10, 699.8 *restrain*
act as a foil to 109.8 *interrelate*
act as a footstool 808.8 *be servile*
act as a freight carrier 70.4 *transport*
act as agent for 678.1 *mediate*
act as a go-between 716
act as a link 716.7 *act as a go-between*
act as a magnet 467.13 *attract attention*
act as a master of ceremonies 653.2 *direct*
act as a middleman 716.7 *act as a go-between*
act as a mouthpiece for 707.5 *represent*
act as a pander for 678.1 *mediate*
act as a white knight 13.11 *deal*
act as broker for 707.5 *represent*
act as deputy for 222.4 *be a substitute*
act as go-between for 707.5 *represent*
act as guarantor 718.11 *promise*
act as guide 524.8 *interpret*
act as host 730.10 *receive someone*, 815.11 *be sociable*, 819.15 *be hospitable*
act as hostess 815.11 *be sociable*
act as interpreter 524.12 *translate*
act as proxy 707.4 *substitute for*
act as proxy for 706.5 *represent*
act as referee 851.13 *support*
act as security 718.11 *promise*
act as spokesman for 524.13 *interpret news*
act as white knight 737.3 *bargain*
act curtain 51.17 *stage set*
act decisively 535.21 *be assertive*
act dishonest 736
act drop 51.17 *stage set*
act dumb 531.12 *be silent*
act eccentric 698.16 *be independent*
act erratic 215.7 *be unusual*
act foolishly 656
act for 222.4 *be a substitute*, 547.12 *stand for*, 706.5 *represent*, 707.4 *substitute for*
act forcefully 535.21 *be assertive*
act for pander 158.19 *mediate*
act friendly 667.6 *agree with*
ACTH 58 Hormones
act honourably 857.6 *be honourable*
act in 457.13 *occur*

act in a friendly manner 784.7 *like*
act in concert 664.13 *work together*
acting 51, 547, 640, 12.10 *governing*, 222.7 *substitute*, 538.9 *hypocrisy*, 538.18 *pretentious*, 540.7 *pretence*, 540.30 *pretending*, 707.7 *deputizing*
acting according to the book 537.11 *pedantry*
acting area 51.15 *stage*
acting as a law unto oneself 16.62 *above the law*
actinium 57 Chemical Elements
actinoid 57.6 *chemical element*
actinolite 54 Minerals
actinometer 268.8 *meter*
actinometric 268.16 *micrometric*
actinometry 268.2 *micrometry*
actinomycin 62 Medication, 89.6 *fungal antibiotic*
act in one's own worst interests 656.6 *act foolishly*
act insolent 668.6 *be insubordinate*
act instead of 707.4 *substitute for*
action 640, 15.4 *industrial dispute*, 16.5 *litigation*, 48.3 *aspect of fiction*, 51.7 *dramaturgy*, 226.6 *undertaking*, 227.1 *effect*, 230.1 *operation*, 324.2 *momentum*, 640.2 *deed*, 642.1 *activity*, 652.1 *conduct*, 676.9 *battle*, 856.1 *accusation*
Action 640
actionable 16.47 *liable to law*, 16.54 *litigated*, 16.58 *unjust*
action art 50 Western Art Styles and Movements
action painter 50.16 *artist*
action painting 50 Western Art Styles and Movements, 50.2, 50.8 *painting*
actions 592.2 *policy*, 640.2 *deed*, 652.1 *conduct*, 652.8 *treatment*
action sequence 66.4 *portrait*
action shot 66.4 *portrait*
activate 156, 230, 57.26 *react*, 216.8 *cause change*, 233.8 *influence*, 239.3 *invigorate*, 403.13 *arouse sensation*
activated 57.39 *catalytic*, 642.18 *active*
activated complex 57.14 *chemical reaction*
activation 216.1 *change*, 642.4 *energy*
activation energy 57.14 *chemical reaction*
activator 216.5 *changer*
active 642, 5.32 *voice*, 230.10 *operational*, 233.11 *influential*, 239.4 *vigorous*, 324.16 *moving*, 396.13 *lively*, 640.5 *acting*, 642.19 *busy*, 644.10 *working*
active galaxy 53.7 *galaxy*
active interest 642.2 *social activity*
active list 171.6 *list of names*
actively 640, 642, 230.13 *operationally*, 324.18 *in motion*
actively involved 642.18 *active*
active member 665.5 *member*, 815.6 *social person*
activeness 640.1 *action*, 642.1 *activity*
active participation 642.2 *social activity*
active person 642.10 *busy person*
active power 64.26 *electrical energy*
active principle 62.5 *prescription*
active resistance 671.1 *defence*
active-ride 33.11 *racing*
active service 676.8 *warfare*
active site 58.11 *enzyme*
active sun 53.15 *sun*
active supporter 640.3 *doer*
active suspension system 33.6 *motor racing terms*
active treatment 60.8 *treatment*
active volcano 54.24 *volcanic activity*
activism 642, 51.8 *theatre movements*, 640.1 *action*
activist 51, 586.14 *motivator*,

596.7 *attempter*, 640.3 *doer*, 642.10 *busy person*, 665.6 *political party member*, 668.4 *defiant person*
activity 590, 642, 42.8 *pastime*, 56.70 *radioactivity*, 239.1 *vigour*, 324.2 *momentum*, 640.1 *action*, 647.1 *workshop*, 648.4 *haste*, 703.2 *engagement*
Activity 642
act lawlessly 713.8 *cause mischief*
act like a bear 829.6 *be irascible*
act like a bitch 829.6 *be irascible*
act like a charm 682.8 *be effective*
act like a Christian 831.9 *be charitable*
act like a gentleman 817.11 *have good manners*
act like a lady 817.11 *have good manners*, 857.6 *be honourable*
act like a tonic 239.3 *invigorate*
act like a vixen 829.6 *be irascible*
act Machiavellian 538.25 *be dishonest*
act morally 857.6 *be honourable*
act negligently 783.14 *be careless*
act odd 215.7 *be unusual*
act of courage 778.8 *courageous act*
act of cruelty 832.7 *act of malevolence*
act of defiance 668
act of derision 799
act of discourtesy 818
act of dying 397.1 *death*
act of folly 508
act of friendship 819
act of gluttony 872
act of God 244.4 *ruin*, 490.16 *inevitability*, 571.6 *necessitarianism*, 631.1 *affliction*
act of grace 831.4 *benevolent act*
act of hostility 820
act of inhumanity 832.7 *act of malevolence*
act of kindness 817.5 *sign of courtesy*
act of love 821.5 *desire*
act of malevolence 832
act of smelling 416.2 *sense of smell*
act of thrift 756
Acton 4 Philosophers
act on behalf of 478.23 *answer for*, 707.4 *substitute for*
act one's part 847.16 *do one's duty*
act on impulse 583.3 *improvise*
act on one's own initiative 710.11 *volunteer*
act on principle 586.18 *be persuaded*
act on the defensive 671, 676.13 *be at war*
act on the spur of the moment 583.3 *improvise*
actor 51, 224.8 *person who changes costume*, 547.5 *performer*, 640.3 *doer*, 646.1 *worker*, 797.2 *pretender*, 811.15 *showman*
actor manager 51.25 *producer*
actor-manager 51.22 *actor*
a.c. transmission 64.33 *power distribution*
act recklessly 783.14 *be careless*
actress 51.22 *actor*, 224.8 *person who changes costume*, 547.5 *performer*, 640.3 *doer*, 646.1 *worker*, 811.15 *showman*
act rough 378.10 *be tough*
act rude 816.13 *ignore*
act sanctimoniously 540.18 *be hypocritical*
act sycophantic 817.13 *defer to*
act the fool 506.8 *fool*
act the goat 506.8 *fool*, 508.7 *play the fool*
act the grand seigneur dame 811.30 *put on airs*
act the host 815.11 *be sociable*
act the hostess 815.11 *be sociable*
act the part of 547.10 *act*
act the showman 811.27 *show*
act together 140.6 *come together*

act treasonously 720.9 *disregard orders*
actual 3.19 *chronicled*, 99.13, 101.6 *real*, 196.6, 253.7 *present*, 490.1 *certain*, 537.16 *existing*
actuality 196, 3.14 *historicalness*, 99.4 *demonstrable existence*, 101.1 *reality*, 253.1 *presence*, 490.9 *certainty*, 537.2 *reality*
actualization 99.8 *creation*
actualize 99.20 *bring into being*, 101.11 *make real*, 537.28 *bring into existence*
actualized 99.15 *created*
actually 3.25 *reportedly*, 99.22, 101.13 *really*, 253.14 *in person*, 490.23 *certainly*, 537.35 *truly*, 772.11 *earnestly*
actual thing 110.1 *sameness*
actuarial 170.13 *calculative*, 750.10 *accounting*
actuarial calculation 589.7 *calculation of chance*
actuary 170.7 *mathematician*, 268.9 *measurer*, 750.6 *accountant*
actuate 228.9 *motivate*, 230.8 *activate*, 233.8 *influence*, 324.14 *set in motion*, 330.1 *impel*
actuation 324.1 *motion*, 324.2 *momentum*
act upon 228.9 *motivate*, 230.9 *take action*, 640.4 *act*
act vulgar 412.9 *have bad taste*
act without authority 689.4 *be anarchic*
act without ceremony 648.2 *make haste*
act without prompting 710.11 *volunteer*
act without thinking 462.12 *lack thought*
ACU 65.12 *electronic office*
acuity 237.2 *healthiness*, 277.3 *profundity*, 380.13 *mental sharpness*, 459.4 *cleverness*, 503.1 *accuracy*, 554.1 *emphasis*, 657.1 *cunning*
acumen 6.11 *refinement*, 380.13 *mental sharpness*, 459.2 *ways of thinking*, 481.2 *judiciousness*, 507.1 *wisdom*
acuminate 380.1 *sharp*, 380.14 *be sharp*
acumination 380.6 *sharpness*
acuminous 380.5 *mentally sharp*
acupressure 60.2 *natural medicine*, 630.13 *therapy*
acupuncture 60.2 *natural medicine*, 60.9 *surgery*, 404.4 *anaesthetic*, 630.5 *analgesic*, 630.11 *medical art*, 630.13 *therapy*
acupuncturist 60.12, 630.15 *healer*
a cut above 617.2 *best*
acutance 66.8 *composition*
acute 5.36 *accent*, 237.11 *strong in spirit*, 241.6 *violent*, 277.11 *wise*, 300.10 *advantaged*, 380.5 *mentally sharp*, 406.5 *painful*, 430.9 *shrill*, 459.10 *intelligent*, 657.4 *cunning*
acute accent 543.7 *punctuation*
acute angle 52.39, 310.1 *angle*
acute-angled 310.9 *angled*
acute-angled triangle 52.43 *triangle*
acute attack 624.2 *illness*
acute dilemma 633.5 *danger*
acutely 237, 300.12 *at an advantage*, 380.18 *sharply*, 459.15 *intelligently*
acuteness 380.13 *mental sharpness*, 459.4 *cleverness*
acute note 430.3 *shrillness*
acyclic 57.35 *combined*
acyclic compound 57.7 *chemical compound*
acylate 57.26 *react*
acylation 57 Types of Chemical Reaction
acylglycerol 58.7 *fat*
acyl halide 57 Types of Compounds

ad 528.4 *mass communication,* 532.9 *advertisement*
AD 185.29 *one day*
Ada 65 Programming Languages
Adad 8 Deities, **8** Deities
adage 5.21 *catchword,* 505.1 *maxim,* 876.7 *moral*
adagietto 49 Musical Terms
adagio 49 Musical Terms, 49.19 *tempo,* 328.16 *slowly*
Adam 401.2 *male*
adamant 373.2 *tough,* 373.7 *hard substance,* 570.7 *iron-willed,* 574.3 *strong-willed,* 577.3 *unyielding*
adamantine 577.5 *obstinacy*
Adamawa 5 Languages and Groups of Languages
Adam Hepplewhite 47.7 *furniture style*
adamic 202.12 *olden*
Adamite 400.7 *person*
Adamites 7 Christian Movements
Adamov 48 Dramatists
Adams 48 Writers, **52** Scientists
Adam's ale 389.1 *water*
Adam's apple 86.5 *figurative usage,* 564.5 *organ of speech*
Adam's-needle 84 Flowers and Flowering Plants, 380.8 *sharp-pointed thing*
Adam's Peak 10.13 *shrine*
Adam's wine 389.1 *water*
adapt 152, 49.35 *compose,* 167.8 *comply,* 216.7 *be changed,* 216.8 *cause change,* 332.8 *orient* , 374.16 *yield,* 377.10 *be adaptable,* 485.15 *modify,* 524.12 *translate,* 584.1 *habituate,* 717.4 *compromise*
adaptability 377, 167.3 *pliancy,* 228.6 *suggestibility,* 374.12 *gentleness,* 613.5 *usefulness,* 655.1 *skill,* 660.3 *wieldiness,* 717.1 *compromise*
adaptable 167.11 *conformable,* 228.13 *suggestible,* 374.2 *pliant,* 374.7 *impressionable,* 377.7 *adaptive,* 613.1 *useful,* 655.6 *skilful,* 660.12 *wieldy,* 717.6 *compromising*
adaptably 167, 377
adaptation 49.15 *composition,* 152.9 *musical arrangement,* 167.3 *pliancy,* 216.1 *change,* 332.3 *orientation,* 485.5 *modification,* 524.4 *translation,* 584.7 *habituation,* 615.3 *convenience,* 717.1 *compromise*
adapted 377.7 *adaptive,* 485.11 *modified*
adapted for speed 329.1 *swift*
adapted to 615.1 *convenient*
adapted to drought 392
adapter 216.5 *changer*
adapt for the stage 51.36 *dramatize*
adapting 374.7 *impressionable,* 377.7 *adaptive*
adaption 167.3 *pliancy*
adaptive 377, 167.11 *conformable*
adapt oneself 167.8 *comply*
add 52, 130, 170, 57.26 *react,* 120.8 *quantify,* 169.10 *number,* 219.3 *continue,* 354.1 *insert,* 525.1 *misinterpret*
add a meaning 525.1 *misinterpret*
add an escape clause 716.6 *make conditions*
addax 77 Placental Mammals
add commentary 524.10 *annotate*
added 107.4 *related,* 120.6 *quantitative,* 130.8 *additional,* 146.8 *included,* 201.14 *renewed,* 354.12 *inserted*
added attraction 228.5 *positive stimulus*
added contribution 128.1 *increase*
added extra 130.4 *extra*
addend 52.15 *addition*
addendum 130.1 *addition,* 130.3 *additional item,* 155.8 *addition*

adder 79 Reptiles, 631.6 *source of trouble*
adder's-tongue 88 Ferns
add explanation 524.10 *annotate*
add frills 627.1 *improve*
add fuel to 128.5 *make bigger*
add fuel to the flames 241.9 *make violent*
addict 584.8 *creature of habit,* 624.19 *sick person,* 695.5 *compulsive person*
addicted 875, 584.14 *habituated,* 870.8 *overindulgent*
addicted to alcohol 874.5 *drunken*
addiction 611.15 *compulsion,* 584.1 *habit,* 628.8 *perversion,* 870.3 *overindulgence*
addictive 875, 233.12 *appealing,* 584.15 *habit-forming,* 586.19 *persuasive,* 874.6 *intoxicating*
adding 130.1 *addition,* 170.3 *count*
adding machine 52.67 *calculator,* 65.3, 170.5 *computer*
adding-up 130.2 *mathematical addition*
add insult to injury 850.23 *insult*
Addis Ababa 93 Cities
Addison 48 Writers
additament 130.3 *additional item*
addition 52, 130, 155, 57.14 *chemical reaction,* 107.1 *relatedness,* 120.2 *certain amount,* 123.1 *inequality,* 128.1 *increase,* 130.3 *additional item,* 143.7 *piece,* 170.1 *calculation,* 201.5 *fresh start,* 219.2 *protraction,* 261.1 *growth,* 354.8 *insertion,* 525.2 *misinterpretation*
Addition 130
additional 130, 155, 128.6 *increasing,* 201.14 *renewed,* 219.5 *continual,* 222.7 *substitute*
additional comment 524.2 *annotation*
additional item 130
additionally 130, 128.8 *increasingly,* 219.7 *continually,* 222.9 *instead,* 261.10 *largely*
additional part 130.3 *additional item*
additional power 235.1 *power*
addition polymer 57.21 *polymer*
additive 57.38 *reactive,* 130.3 *additional item,* 130.8 *additional,* 146.2 *thing included*
additive colour 444.4 *pigment*
additive process 56.28 *colour*
addle 151.22 *discompose,* 460.10 *bemuse,* 622.10 *be dirty*
addled 247.6 *having no effect*
add nothing 122.11 *equalize*
add on 201.20 *make new*
add-on 130.3 *additional item,* 155.8 *addition*
add one's share 130.6 *add*
add one's support 130.7 *support*
add one's two penn'orth 130.6 *add*
add-ons 136.7 *separates*
address 567, 567, 65.17 *computing term,* 65.19 *abort,* 250.2 *exact location,* 326.13 *post,* 534.3 *correspondence,* 534.31 *correspond,* 564.7 *utterance,* 564.8 *speech,* 564.9 *art of public speaking,* 564.14 *speak to,* 567.3 *skill,* 567.10 *send,* 592.2 *policy,* 655.1 *skill,* 849.20 *salute*
Address 567
address book 171.3 *dictionary,* 545.6 *record book*
addressee 255.3 *householder,* 478.10 *answerer,* 730.5 *recipient*
addresses 821.6, 826.2 *courtship*
addressing 560.7 *nomenclature*
addressing the ball 29.3 *golf shots*
address of welcome 567.2 *salutation*
address oneself to 567, 594.2 *do the groundwork,* 597.1 *undertake*
address one's prayers to 712.6 *request*
address the general public 522.5 *simplify*

address the question 107.7 *relate to*
add taste to 411.10 *make taste*
add the finishing touches 684.6 *elaborate*
add to 128.5 *make bigger,* 130.6 *add,* 135.8 *unite,* 146.6 *subsume,* 261.5 *make bigger,* 319.6 *notch up*
adduce 106.11 *circumstantiate,* 526.3 *reveal*
adduced 526.13 *displayed*
adducent 340.8 *attracting*
adduct 340.11 *attract*
adduction 340.2 *pulling power*
adductive 340.8 *attracting*
add up 52.91, 130.6 *add,* 170.9 *add,* 522.4 *be intelligible*
add up to 142.9 *be whole,* 170.10 *total,* 520.10 *mean*
add up to the same thing 122.11 *equalize*
add value 130.6 *add*
add water 140.5 *combine,* 389.30 *dilute,* 391.13 *moisten*
Adelaide 93 Cities
Aden 93 Cities
adenkum 49 Musical Instruments
adenography 382.8 *science of structure*
adenoidectomy 60 Surgical Operations
adenology 382.8 *science of structure*
adenosine 59.12 *molecular biology*
adeps 395.8 *fat*
adept 11.12 *occultist,* 655.4 *skilled person,* 655.6 *skilful,* 688.11, 696.10 *expert,* 696.13 *excellent*
adeptly 655.12 *skilfully,* 696.16 *masterfully*
adeptness 655.1 *skill*
adequacy 124.6 *mediocrity,* 485.1 *qualification,* 608.7 *sufficiency,* 613.7 *instrumentality,* 765.3 *satisfactoriness*
adequate 122, 124.3 *mediocre,* 144.7 *complete,* 235.13 *powerful,* 608.1 *sufficient,* 613.3 *instrumental,* 617.5 *not bad,* 765.6 *satisfactory*
adequate amount 608.7 *sufficiency*
adequate income 608.7 *sufficiency*
adequately 235.18 *powerfully,* 608.9 *enough,* 765.12 *satisfactorily*
adequate size 861.14 *largeness*
adequate-size 861.7 *large*
adesnine 58.10 *nucleoside*
Adhara 53 Named Stars
adhere 138, 135.8 *unite,* 137.13 *intercommunicate,* 138.8 *be tenacious,* 225.6 *be stable,* 394.10 *stick,* 574.10 *insist,* 584.17 *become a habit,* 726.6 *retain*
adherence 138.2 *tenacity*
adherence to 719.1 *observance*
adherence to the law 16.28 *legality*
adherence to the letter of the law 16.28 *legality*
adherent 138, 808, 9.5 *worshipper,* 138.5 *follower,* 138.9 *adhesive,* 155.14 *follower,* 284.8 *supporter*
adherent to 719.7 *observant*
adhere to 4.22 *propound a philosophy,* 130.7 *support,* 719.4 *observe,* 808.14 *follow*
adhering 135.15 *tied*
adhering to 719.7 *observant*
adhesion 138, 137.1 *connection,* 339.4 *friction,* 340.2 *pulling power,* 726.1 *retention*
Adhesion 138
adhesive 138, 138, 394, 135.12 *united,* 137.14 *connective,* 394.8 *viscous,* 726.3 *tools for gripping,* 726.9 *retentive*
adhesive label 544.3 *means of identification*
adhesively 135.16 *as one,*

137.17 *in connection with,* 339.16 *magnetically,* 340.13 *attractionally,* 394.12 *viscously,* 726.11 *tenaciously*
adhesiveness 138.1 *adhesion,* 394.1 *viscosity*
adhesive tape 137.6 *line,* 138.3 *adhesive,* 293.6 *medical covering*
ad hoc 583.1 *improvised,* 583.7 *extempore,* 595.2 *spontaneous,* 595.15 *spontaneously*
ad hoc measure 592.3 *expedient plan,* 602.1 *means*
ad hoc measures 583.4 *improvisation*
adiabatic 55.43 *atmospheric*
adiabatic change 56.39 *expansion*
adiabatic cooling 55.9 *atmospheric process*
adiabatic lapse rate 55.9 *atmospheric process*
adiabatic process 55.9 *atmospheric process*
Adiaphorism 7 Christian Movements
Adibuddhism 7 Non-Christian Religions
adieu 345.9 *parting,* 345.14 *goodbye*
a different kettle of fish 115.2 *unlikeness*
Adige 96 Rivers
a dime a dozen 754.9 *cheap*
ad infinitum 184.10 *infinitely,* 269.11 *lengthily*
adipocere 141.1 *disintegration,* 395.8 *fat*
adipose 259.16 *fat,* 386.10, 395.11 *oily*
adiposis 395.1 *oiliness*
adiposity 259.5 *fatness,* 395.1 *oiliness*
Adirondack 95 Mountains
Adirondack 95 Mountains 95.4 *US mountains*
a distinction without a difference 122.2 *equilibrium*
adit 327.2 *route,* 346.5 *entrance*
Aditi 8 Deities
Aditya 8 Deities
adjacency 267.1 *juxtaposition,* 298.1 *interface,* 615.4 *nearness*
adjacent 52.43 *triangle,* 267.5 *juxtaposed,* 298.6 *interfacial,* 407.9 *touching,* 615.2 *nearby*
adjacently 267.7 *beside,* 298.7 *interfacially*
adjectival 5.44 *grammatical*
adjectival phrase 5.23 *phrase*
adjective 5.35 *part of speech,* 130.3 *additional item*
adjoin 267.3 *juxtapose,* 298.4 *interface,* 407.12 *abut*
adjoined 130.8 *additional*
adjoining 264.5 *near,* 267.5 *juxtaposed,* 298.6 *interfacial,* 407.9 *touching*
adjoining section 298.1 *interface*
adjourn 209.8 *delay,* 218.9 *pause,* 283.12 *interrupt*
adjourned 209.10 *held up,* 218.10 *finished,* 283.9 *interrupted*
adjournment 209.3 *delayed action,* 283.6 *interruption*
adjudge 16.76, 492.11 *judge*
adjudicate 16.71 *try a case,* 16.76 *judge,* 166.13 *rule,* 492.11 *judge*
adjudication 492.1 *judgment,* 492.2 *verdict*
adjudicator 492.5 *judge*
adjunct 107.1 *relatedness,* 130.3 *additional item,* 130.8 *additional,* 155.8 *addition,* 180.4 *concomitant,* 603.6 *equipment*
adjunctive 130.8 *additional,* 135.14 *conjunctive*
adjunctly 130.10 *additionally*
adjuration 535.3 *vow,* 712.1 *request,* 714.1 *promise*
adjuratory 712.9 *requesting,* 714.12 *promised*
adjure 535.18 *vow,* 712.6 *request*
adjust 116.24 *harmonize,* 122.11 *equalize,* 125.5 *counterbalance,* 152.14 *rearrange,*

167.8 *comply,* 167.9 *make conform,* 214.10 *make regular,* 216.7 *be changed,* 216.8 *cause change,* 242.4 *moderate,* 259.18 *measure,* 295.35 *make clothing,* 332.8 *orient ,* 377.10 *be adaptable,* 485.15 *modify,* 537.31 *be accurate,* 592.10 *plan out,* 594.4 *prepare for action,* 627.3 *rectify,* 629.1 *repair,* 677.4 *pacify,* 717.4 *compromise*

adjustability 377.2 *adaptability*

adjustable 167.11 *conformable,* 377.7 *adaptive*

adjustable spanner 603.1 *tool*

adjusted 116.13 *harmonious,* 125.10 *counterbalancing,* 152.23 *rearranged,* 377.7 *adaptive,* 485.11 *modified,* 717.6 *compromising*

adjusting 377.7 *adaptive*

adjustment 116.4 *harmony,* 122.3 *equalization,* 125.2 *counterbalance,* 167.3 *pliancy,* 216.1 *change,* 242.1 *moderation,* 332.3 *orientation,* 485.5 *modification,* 627.6 *rectification,* 629.8 *repair,* 677.1 *pacification,* 717.1 *compromise*

adjust the clock 185

adjust the hands of the clock 192.14 *keep time*

adjutant 662.11 *helper*

adjutant stork 78 Birds

adjuvant 662.11 *helper,* 662.30 *helping*

Adler 61.29 *psychologist*

Adlerian 61.33 *Freudian*

Adlerian psychology 61.1 *psychology*

ad lib 49 Musical Terms, 51.33 *overact,* 570.17 *at will,* 583.7 *extempore,* 595.2 *spontaneous,* 595.13 *improvise,* 608.9 *enough*

ad-lib 583.1 *improvised,* 583.3 *improvise,* 583.4 *improvisation*

ad-libber 583.6 *improviser*

ad-libbing 583.4 *improvisation*

ad libitum 570.17 *at will,* 608.9 *enough*

Admadiya 7 Non-Christian Religions

ad man 586.12 *persuader*

admeasure 268.10 *measure*

admeasured 268.13 *measured*

admeasurement 268.1 *measurement*

administer 62, 92, 60.19 *practise medicine,* 166.16 *direct,* 599.1 *use,* 640.4 *act,* 653.1 *manage,* 688.18 *have authority*

administer an oath 535.18 *vow*

administer correction 879.1 *punish*

administer justice 16.69 *have jurisdiction over,* 16.76 *judge*

administer the sacraments 710.15 *offer worship*

administer to 697.8 *serve*

administrate 640.4 *act*

administration 62, 12.1 *government,* 166.8 *authority,* 640.1 *action,* 652.8 *treatment,* 653.3 *management,* 653.6 *governing body,* 688.4 *governance*

administrational 16.48 *jurisdictional*

administration of justice 16.2 *jurisdiction*

administrative 92, 12.9 *governmental,* 16.48 *jurisdictional,* 166.9 *legal,* 640.6 *effective,* 653.17 *managerial,* 688.14 *governmental*

administrative area 92

Administrative Areas 92

administrative centre 92.5 *administrative headquarters*

administrative control 653.4 *directorship*

administrative headquarters 92

administratively 92, 12.14 *politically,* 16.86 *jurisdictionally,* 653.19 *managerially,* 688.24 *ministerially*

administrative officer 653.16 *official*

administrative receiver 730.7 *collector*

administrative unit 17.4 *military organization*

administrator 230.5 *operator,* 640.3 *doer,* 646.3 *agent,* 653.15 *manager*

admirable 617.1 *worthy,* 782.8 *desirable,* 786.8 *wonderful,* 851.21 *praiseworthy,* 861.1 *good*

Admirable Crichton 617.8 *exceller,* 655.4 *skilled person*

admirably 617.11 *worthily,* 861.22 *well*

admiral 74.7 *nautical person,* 679.27 *naval man,* 692.6 *person in command,* 696.7 *military leader*

Admiral 17 British Military Ranks, **17** US Military Ranks

Admiral of the Fleet 17 British Military Ranks, 74.7 *nautical person,* 679.27 *naval man,* 692.6 *person in command,* 696.7 *military leader*

admiralty 679.22 *navy*

Admiralty chart 74.5 *navigation,* 97.5 *oceanography*

Admiralty Division 16.20 *British court*

admiralty metal 57 Alloys

admiration 849, 851, 617.6 *worth,* 784.1 *liking,* 786.1 *wonder,* 821.1 *love*

admire 9.8 *idolatrize,* 784.7 *like,* 786.9 *wonder,* 821.23 *love,* 849.15 *respect,* 849.16 *revere,* 851.11 *approve*

admired 851, 9.11 *worshipped,* 617.1 *worthy,* 784.5 *likable,* 821.21 *beloved,* 849.12 *respected*

admirer 851, 9.5 *worshipper,* 284.8 *supporter,* 821.9 *lover*

admiring 514.7 *amazed,* 784.6 *liking,* 786.6 *wondering,* 849.10 *reverent,* 851.18 *approving*

admiringly 784, 851.25 *approvingly*

admissibility 146.1 *inclusion,* 348.3 *introduction,* 486.2 *possibleness*

admissible 146.8 *included,* 348.14 *admissive,* 486.5 *possible,* 708.8 *permitting,* 855.13 *vindicable*

admission 535, 146.1 *inclusion,* 346.1 *entry,* 346.4 *right of entry,* 348.1 *admittance,* 483.5 *legal evidence,* 499.1 *assent,* 530.2 *divulgence ,* 730.4 *reception*

admission fee 751.3 *fee*

admission ticket 708.2 *permit*

admissive 348, 708.8 *permitting*

admissory 348.14 *admissive*

admit 348, 530, 535, 146.4 *include,* 346.14 *enrol,* 354.7 *install,* 499.4 *assent,* 730.10 *receive someone,* 749.7 *receive*

admit defeat 218.6 *cease,* 673.3 *submit*

admit no responsibility 848.12 *exempt oneself*

admit of 146.4 *include*

admittance 348, 146.1 *inclusion,* 346.4 *right of entry,* 730.4 *reception*

Admittance 348

admitted 146.8 *included,* 530.10 *disclosed,* 535.11 *stated,* 584.12 *established,* 730.13 *received,* 845.8 *entitled*

admitting 730.4 *reception*

admix 133.8 *mix*

admixture 133, 130.1 *addition,* 133.1 *mixture*

admonish 636.5 *warn,* 654.5 *advise,* 852.20 *censure,* 879.1 *punish*

admonished 852.34 *censured*

admonisher 636.4 *warner,* 654.4 *adviser*

admonishment 636.1 *warning,* 852.7 *blame*

admonition 587.6 *dissuasion,* 636.1 *warning,* 654.1 *advice,*

654.3 *precept,* 852.7 *blame,* 879.7 *punishment*

admonitory 636.8 *warning,* 654.7 *advising,* 852.30 *censuring,* 879.19 *punitive*

adnate 89.10 *of fungi*

ad nauseam 183.23 *repeatedly,* 553.7 *diffusely*

adnexed 89.10 *of fungi*

ado 151.9 *disorder,* 153.5 *commotion,* 642.1 *activity,* 644.4 *exertion*

adobe 44.2 *raw material,* 44.9 *industrial ceramics,* 293.8 *wall covering,* 604.1 *materials*

adolescence 206.1 *youth,* 245.4 *development,* 396.5 *life cycle*

adolescent 206.6 *young person,* 206.11 *young,* 400.7 *person,* 595.5 *immature*

Adonai 8.3 *God*

Adonis 53 Minor Planets, 340.6 *charmer,* 401.4 *boyfriend,* 789.4 *attractive male*

Adonism 7 Non-Christian Religions

adopt 733, 348.9 *welcome,* 580.1 *select,* 599.1 *use,* 851.12 *accept*

adoptability 733.2 *adoption*

adoptable 733.12 *adoptive*

adopt affirmative action 700.6 *treat equally*

adopt a laissez-faire attitude 708.4 *be permissive*

adopted 580.15 *chosen,* 733.11 *borrowed,* 733.12 *adoptive*

adopting 733.12 *adoptive*

adoption 733, 580.6 *selection,* 851.1 *approval*

Adoptionism 7 Christian Movements

adoptive 733

adorability 821.4 *lovability*

adorable 784.5 *likable,* 821.22 *lovable*

adorably 784.10 *with great liking,* 821.30 *lovingly*

adoration 7.2 *religiousness,* 9.1 *worship,* 10.3 *rite of worship,* 784.1 *liking,* 821.1 *love,* 849.2 *admiration*

adorational 9.9 *worshipful*

adore 7.19 *be religious,* 9.7 *worship,* 10.19 *offer worship,* 784.7 *like,* 821.23 *love,* 849.16 *revere*

adored 9.11 *worshipped,* 821.21 *beloved*

adorer 9.5 *worshipper,* 821.9 *lover*

adoring 9.9 *worshipful,* 821.20 *amorous,* 849.10 *reverent*

adoringly 9.12 *worshipfully,* 821.30 *lovingly*

adorn 557.5 *ornament,* 627.1 *improve,* 792.8 *beautify,* 792.10 *decorate*

adorned 557.4 *ornate,* 791.14 *beautified*

adornment 792, 557.1 *ornament,* 627.5 *improvement,* 789.2 *beautiful thing*

Adorno 4 Philosophers

adown 360.19 *down*

ADP 58.22 *bioenergetics*

Adrammelech 8 Deities

adrenal 352.5 *of a secretion*

adrenal gland 352 Endocrine Glands

adrenalin 58 Hormones

Adriatic 97 Oceans and Seas

adrift 36.10 *sailing,* 36.20 *offshore,* 98.13 *continentally,* 136.17 *unjoined,* 136.22 *in isolation,* 162.25 *sprawled,* 335.27 *astray*

adroit 655.6 *skilful,* 861.5 *proficient*

adroitly 655.12 *skilfully,* 861.25 *skillfully*

adroitness 567.3, 655.1 *skill,* 861.12 *proficiency*

adscititious 130.8 *additional*

adsorb 57.29, 348.13 *absorb*

adsorbed 57.43 *absorbed*

adsorbent 348.6 *sponge,* 348.17 *absorbent*

adsorption 57.5 *process,* 57.20 *surface chemistry,* 348.5 *absorption*

Adsullata 8 Deities

adularia 54 Gemstones

adulate 8.17 *deify,* 9.7 *worship,* 851.14 *praise,* 853.8 *flatter*

adulated 8.15 *deified*

adulation 8.9 *deification,* 9.1 *worship,* 849.2 *admiration,* 851.3 *praise,* 853.1 *flattery*

adulator 853.6 *flatterer*

adulatory 849.10 *reverent,* 851.18 *approving,* 853.12 *flattering*

adult 207, 207.7 *older person,* 400.7 *person,* 594.20 *developed,* 622.9 *obscene*

adult education 6.2 *educational system*

adult-education centre 6.12 *educational institution*

adulterate 133.8 *mix,* 216.8 *cause change,* 233.9 *change,* 238.7 *weaken,* 362.4 *debase,* 372.6 *make sparse,* 389.30, 412.8 *dilute,* 540.21 *be fraudulent,* 628.3 *make worse,* 631.15 *poison*

adulterated 133.12 *mixed,* 372.2 *rarefied,* 389.22 *diluted,* 412.5 *tasteless*

adulteration 133.1 *mixture,* 216.1 *change,* 238.1 *weakness,* 372.4 *rarefaction,* 389.5 *dilution,* 412.1 *tastelessness,* 540.8 *fraud,* 620.5 *imperfection,* 628.10 *impairment*

adulterer 224.6 *fickle person,* 548.3 *deceiver,* 576.15 *indecisive person,* 877.8 *immoral man*

adulteress 877.9 *immoral woman*

adulterous 538.20 *unfaithful,* 576.2 *changeable,* 877.14 *lecherous*

adultery 821.8 *love affair,* 824.3 *divorce court,* 877.4 *illicit love*

adult fiction 532.6 *book publishing*

adulthood 207, 245.4 *development,* 396.5 *life cycle*

adult literature 877.2 *indecency*

adultness 207.2 *adulthood*

adult suffrage 580.11 *franchise*

adumbrate 440.14 *make dark,* 518.6 *propound,* 560.14 *describe*

adumbration 527.10 *quietness*

advance 336, 6.22 *educate,* 128.1, 128.4 *increase,* 143.2 *particular,* 201.16 *avant-garde,* 219.3 *continue,* 226.12 *determine,* 232.4 *be an instrument,* 324.3 *motion towards,* 324.13 *be in motion,* 324.17 *directional,* 324.19 *go,* 336.1 *go forward,* 336.8 *further,* 336.10 *forward motion,* 338.21 *move forward,* 342.2 *approach,* 344.10 *arrival,* 518.6 *propound,* 543.6 *word,* 613.9 *be useful,* 615.6 *be convenient,* 627.1 *improve,* 627.2 *get better,* 627.5 *improvement,* 660.16 *make easy,* 662.6 *financial assistance,* 662.28 *further,* 662.29 *finance,* 670.1 *attack,* 682.6 *be successful,* 686.5 *be prosperous,* 710.2 *tentative offer,* 710.9 *offer,* 721.2 *augmentation,* 721.4 *earnings,* 721.10 *augment,* 732.1 *lending,* 732.5 *lend,* 733.1 *borrowing,* 746.3 *pay,* 861.20 *do good*

advance against 670.1 *attack*

advance agent 51.25 *producer*

advance by leaps and bounds 336.9 *maintain progress*

advance camp 34.1 *mountaineering*

advanced 6.20 *refined,* 194.10 *prior,* 201.10 *new,* 201.16 *avant-garde,* 208.12 *early,* 336.17 *forward*

advanced gas-cooled reactor 56.73 *nuclear reactor,* 235.8, 410.7 *nuclear power*

advanced guard 636.4 *warner*

advanced hour 209.2 *late hour*

advanced in years 202.11 *old,* 207.14 *aged*
Advanced level 485 Educational Qualifications
Advanced Ordinary level 485 Educational Qualifications
advanced stage 208.3 *early stage*
Advanced Supplementary level 485 Educational Qualifications
advanced technology 603.5 *mechanics*
advanced thinker 201.9 *modern person*
advanced years 207.5 *old age*
advance earnings 721.4 *earnings*
advance guard 201.6 *avant-garde,* 303.1 *front*
advance man 51.25 *producer,* 208.4 *early comer*
advancement 6.1 *education,* 60.9 *surgery,* 128.1 *increase,* 232.1 *instrumentality,* 336.12 *advance,* 627.5 *improvement,* 662.8 *furtherance,* 732.1 *lending*
advance notice 517.3 *plan,* 636.1 *warning*
advance on 721.10 *augment*
advance one's own interests 860.6 *be selfish*
advance on royalties 732.1 *lending,* 733.1 *borrowing*
advance on salary 732.1 *lending,* 733.1 *borrowing*
advance party 679.14 *armed forces*
advance payment 746.1 *payment*
advances 567.2 *salutation,* 821.6, 826.2 *courtship*
advance to meet 730.10 *receive someone,* 817.12 *greet*
advance to the rear 337.2, 337.11 *retreat*
advancing 342, 232.6 *instrumental,* 324.17 *directional,* 336.17 *forward,* 344.19 *approaching,* 627.16 *improving,* 732.1 *lending*
advantage 126, 300, 38.2 *football play,* 40.4 *tennis terms,* 194.5 *gift of priority,* 233 *influence,* 599.6 *use,* 613.8, 613.10 *benefit,* 615.3 *convenience,* 615.6 *be convenient,* 652.9 *tactics,* 662.1 *help,* 662.21 *be helpful,* 662.28 *further,* 721.1 *gain,* 861.13, 861.13 *benefit*
advantaged 300
advantageous 599.10 *usable,* 613.4 *profitable,* 615.1 *convenient,* 617.4 *worthwhile,* 662.34 *beneficial,* 682.14 *rewarding,* 746.18 *profitable,* 782.8 *desirable,* 819.12 *favourable,* 861.6 *beneficial*
advantageously 126.16 *superiorly,* 599.11, 613.12 *usefully,* 662.36 *helpfully,* 682.16 *successfully,* 721.20 *gainfully,* 819.20 *favourably,* 861.26 *usefully*
advantageousness 662.10 *helpfulness*
advection 55.9 *atmospheric process*
advection fog 55.33 *fog*
advection frost 55.36 *frost*
advective 55.43 *atmospheric*
advent 199.6 *future event,* 344.10 *arrival,* 457.1 *appearance*
Advent 10.16 *religious festival*
Adventism 7 Christian Movements
Adventist 7.5 *Christian*
adventitious 104.8 *intruder,* 106.7 *circumstantial,* 130.8 *additional,* 229.6 *motiveless,* 589.8 *chance*
adventitious bud 83.8 *bud*
adventitiously 104.18 *extraneously,* 106.16 *relatively,* 229.8 *by chance*
adventitious root 83.7 *root*
Advent season 203.1 *season*
adventure 491.15 *unreliability,* 596.6 *venture,* 597.1 *undertake,* 597.2 *undertaking,* 778.8 *courageous act*

adventurer 224.7 *person who moves around,* 465.3 *curious person,* 508.4 *rash person,* 596.7 *attempter,* 597.4 *volunteer,* 679.6 *militarist,* 780.3 *rash person*
adventure story 48.2, 560.5 *fiction*
adventurous 229, 778, 465.5 *curious,* 597.6 *enterprising,* 780.4 *rash*
adventurously 465.8 *curiously,* 596.10 *ambitiously,* 597.9 *enterprisingly,* 778.18 *courageously*
adventurousness 778, 780.1 *rashness*
adventurous person 596.7 *attempter*
adverb 5.35 *part of speech,* 130.3 *additional item*
adverbial 5.44 *grammatical*
adverbially 5.52 *grammatically*
adverbial phrase 5.23 *phrase*
adversaria 545.3 *notes*
adversarial 663.20 *discordant,* 679.33 *combative,* 711.9 *dissenting*
adversary 663.11 *opponent,* 674.10 *contender,* 679.1 *combatant,* 820.5 *hostile person*
adversative 663.21 *contrary*
adverse 687, 136.18 *disagreeable,* 244.14 *destructive,* 517.15 *presageful,* 573.2 *refusing,* 616.1 *inconvenient,* 618.5 *harmful,* 663.19 *oppositional,* 862.10 *inauspicious*
adverse circumstances 687.1 *adversity*
adversely 136.23 *disagreeably,* 663.23 *opposingly,* 687.12 *in adversity,* 862.14 *inauspiciously*
adversity 631, 687, 618.11 *harmfulness,* 659.6 *critical situation,* 862.2 *affliction,* 862.3 *bad luck,* 879.10 *affliction*
Adversity 687
advert 528.4 *mass communication,* 532.9 *advertisement*
advertise 517.11 *predict,* 526.2 *display something,* 526.3 *reveal,* 532.16 *publicize,* 534.30 *communicate,* 611.8 *make important,* 710.9 *offer,* 811.27 *show*
advertised 526.13 *displayed,* 534.34 *communicated,* 710.17 *offered*
advertise for 532.16 *publicize*
advertisement 532, 526.8 *showplace,* 528.4 *mass communication,* 586.6 *advertising,* 739.3 *selling*
advertisement curtain 51.17 *stage set*
advertise oneself 811.29 *show off*
advertiser 228.7 *motivator,* 526.12 *displayer,* 528.9 *informant,* 532.10 *publicizer,* 586.12 *persuader*
advertising 586, 228.2 *inducement,* 526.10 *manifestation,* 586.5 *propaganda*
advertising account executive 532.10 *publicizer*
advertising agent 532.10 *publicizer*
advertorial 532.9 *advertisement*
advice 528, 654, 6.1 *education,* 228.2 *inducement,* 636.1 *warning,* 654.3 *precept,* 662.2 *support*
Advice 654
advice against 654.1 *advice*
advice column 532.3 *journalism*
advice for 654.1 *advice*
advisability 615.3 *convenience,* 782.2 *desirability*
advisable 654, 580.15 *chosen,* 613.1 *useful,* 615.1 *convenient,* 636.8 *warning*
advisably 654, 4.29 *wisely*
advise 654, 662, 6.22 *educate,* 60.19 *practise medicine,* 228.9 *motivate,* 518.6 *propound,* 528.11 *inform,* 586.15 *persuade,* 630.20 *doctor,* 636.5 *warn,* 653.2 *direct,* 781.6 *caution*

advise against 587.1 *dissuade,* 636.5 *warn,* 654.5 *advise*
advised 528.18 *informed,* 582.4 *deliberate,* 636.9 *warned*
advisedly 4.29 *wisely,* 6.25 *educationally,* 588.13 *intentionally*
adviser 654, 662, 4.12 *sage,* 6.4 *educator,* 228.7 *motivator,* 492.5 *judge,* 528.9 *informant,* 528.10 *informer,* 586.14 *motivator,* 485.8 *qualified person,* 636.4 *warner,* 653.13 *director,* 655.5 *expert,* 678.3 *mediator,* 678.4 *representative*
advising 654, 654.1 *advice*
advisory 6.16 *educational,* 528.16 *informative,* 568.13 *discussing,* 654.7 *advising,* 678.6 *mediatory*
advisory board 653.7 *council*
Advisory Conciliation and Arbitration Services 13.8 *industrial relations*
Advisory Conciliation and Arbitration Service 15.4 *industrial dispute,* 678.3 *mediator*
advocaat 351.7 *alcoholic drink*
advocacy 228.2 *inducement,* 284.6 *moral support,* 586.2 *flattery,* 662.9 *patronage,* 851.1 *approval*
advocate 851, 16.13 *lawyer,* 16.70 *litigate,* 228.9 *motivate,* 284.8 *supporter,* 284.14 *give moral support,* 535.9 *affirmer,* 564.10 *speaker,* 586.12 *persuader,* 654.4 *adviser,* 654.5 *advise,* 662.14 *adviser,* 662.23 *advise,* 679.5 *arguer,* 851.13 *support,* 855.5 *vindicator*
advocating 851.19 *supporting*
advocatory 284.9 *supportive*
Adygei 5 Languages and Groups of Languages
adze 34.4 *climbing equipment,* 380.9 *sharp-edged thing,* 47.11 *woodworking tool,* 380.9 *sharp-edged thing*
adzuki bean 45 Vegetables
aechmea 84 Flowers and Flowering Plants
AED 65 Programming Languages
aedes 82 Insects
aedile 653.16 *official*
a-effect 51.7 *dramaturgy*
Aegean 7 Non-Christian Religions, **97** Oceans and Seas, 400.4 *civilized human*
Aegir 8 Deities
aegis 632.2 *protection,* 662.9 *patronage*
aegrotat 848.4 *licence*
Aelfric 48 Writers
aeolian 55.47 *windy*
aeolian harp 49 Musical Instruments
Aeolian mode 49.20 *key*
aeon 185.4 *term,* 185.5 *indefinite period,* 187.2 *time period,* 190.2 *a long time*
aeonian 190.9 *agelong*
aeons 188.5 *long duration*
Aepyornis 78 Birds, 78.8 *extinct bird*
aerage 390.6 *ventilation*
aerate 388, 390, 370.10 *lighten,* 390.23 *whisk,* 625.6 *make hygienic,* 651.1 *refresh*
aerated 370.3 *lightening,* 388.21 *gassy,* 390.18 *bubbly*
aerating 370.3 *lightening*
aeration 390, 370.6 *lightening,* 388.10 *vaporization,* 390.6 *ventilation,* 651.5 *refreshment*
aerator 390.7 *ventilator*
aerial 390, 41.1 *skiing,* 41.12 *ski,* 50.24 *pictorial,* 275.9 *high,* 388.17, 390.12 *airy,* 534.17 *antenna*
aerial bombardment 670.13 *air attack*
aerial perspective 50.4 *treatment*
aerial photography 66.1 *photography*

aerial reconnaissance 73.1 *aviation*
aerial root 83.7 *root*
aerial warfare 676.8 *warfare*
aerie 78.14 *nest*
aeriferous 390.12 *airy*
aerification 388.10 *vaporization*
aeriform 390.12 *airy*
aerify 388.26, 390.20 *aerate*
aerily 388
aeriness 388
aeriolate 89.10 *of fungi*
aeroball 18 Sporting Activities
aeroballistics 73.2 *aeronautics*
aerobatics 18 Sporting Activities, 73.1 *aviation*
aerobe 59.3 *organism*
aerobic 59.22 *physiological*
aerobic respiration 58.24 *respiration,* 59.6 *cell biology*
aerobics 42 Hobbies and Pastimes, 46.1 *dancing,* 324.11 *bodily movement,* 627.9 *physical improvement,* 644.5 *exercise*
aerodontalgia 388.6 *aerogastria*
aerodrome 73.4 *airport,* 344.15 *destination*
aerodynamic 56.98 *physical,* 388.22 *aerostatic*
aerodynamically 56.100 *physically,* 388.29 *aerostatically*
aerodynamic brake 73 Aircraft Parts
aerodynamics 56.2 *classical physics,* 388.12 *aerostatics*
aerodyne 73 Types of Aircraft
aero engine 73 Aircraft Parts, 63.11 *engine*
aerofoil 225.3 *stabilizer*
aerogastria 388
aerogenesis 388.6 *aerogastria*
aerogram 534.3 *correspondence*
aerolite 53.20 *meteor*
aerology 55.1 *meteorology*
aerometer 268.8 *meter,* 371.3 *relative density,* 388.15 *vaporimeter*
aerometric 268.16 *micrometric*
aerometry 268.2 *micrometry*
aeronaut 360.8 *descender*
aeronautical engineering 63.1 *engineering,* 63.3 *mechanical engineering,* 73.2 *aeronautics*
aeronautics 73
aeroneurosis 388.6 *aerogastria*
aero-optics 73.2 *aeronautics*
aeropause 73.5 *flight*
aerophagia 388.6 *aerogastria*
aerophobia 777 Phobias by Name
aerophone 49.25 *musical instrument*
aeroplane 70.5 *transportable,* 73.8 *aircraft,* 679.31 *military aircraft*
aeroplane cloth 73 Aircraft Parts
aerosol 57.3 *phase,* 62.10 *inhalant,* 388.11 *vaporizer,* 389.12 *sprinkler*
aerosol spray 388.11 *vaporizer*
aerospace 248.2 *empty space*
aerosphere 390
aerostatic 388
aerostatically 388
aerostatics 388
aerostructure 73 Aircraft Parts
aerothermodynamics 73.2 *aeronautics*
aery 388.17, 390.12 *airy*
Aeschylean tragedy 51.9 *tragedy*
Aeschylus 48 Dramatists
Aesculapian 630.18 *medical*
Aesculapius 8 Deities, 630.15 *healer*
Aeshma 8.7 *devil*
Aesma 8.6 *angel*
aesthesia 407.1 *touch,* 759.1 *feeling*
aesthesis 407.1 *touch*
aesthete 403.4 *someone or something that feels,* 794.4 *refined person*
aesthetic 4.11 *follower of a doctrine,* 4.14 *of a philosophy,* 50.26 *artistic,* 403.7 *susceptible,* 789.5 *beautiful,* 794.5 *refined*
aesthetically 50.31 *artistically*

aesthetically pleasing 789.5 *beautiful*
aestheticism 50 Western Art Styles and Movements, 4.7 *school of thought*
Aesthetic movement 48 Literary Groups and Movements
aesthetics 4.6 *branch of philosophy*
aestival 203.11 *summer*
aestivate 643.13 *sleep*
aestivating 527.1 *latent*, 643.4 *not awake*
aestivation 203.3 *summer*, 527.6 *latency*, 643.9 *sleep*
aetiology 60.3 *medical specialty*
AEW 73.6 *flight control*
afar 263.10 *distantly*
a far cry from 115.4 *dissimilar*
Afars 1 Peoples
AFC 19.1 *football*
a few 175.1 *plurality*, 182.1, 182.5 *few*
a few sandwiches short of a picnic 145.2 *omission*
affability 763.8 *amiability*, 814.2, 815.1 *sociability*, 815.2 *social ambition*, 817.1 *courtesy*, 831.1 *benevolence*
affable 763.2 *likable*, 814.8, 815.15 *sociable*, 815.15 *sociable*, 817.7 *courteous*, 831.6 *benevolent*
affably 815.18 *sociably*, 817.14 *courteously*
affair 230.3 *business*, 472.3 *matter of interest*, 597.2 *undertaking*, 821.8 *love affair*
affair of honour 674.9 *duel*
affair of the heart 821.8 *love affair*
affairs 640.2 *deed*, 652.8 *treatment*
affect 107.7 *relate to*, 216.8 *cause change*, 227.5 *show an effect*, 233.8 *influence*, 234.4 *tend*, 538.24, 540.20 *pretend*, 611.7 *be important*, 652.11 *conduct oneself*, 797.4 *be affected*, 835.11 *excite pity*
affectation 557, 495.1 *underestimation*, 518.1 *supposition*, 538.8, 540.7 *pretence*, 549.1 *style*, 549.3 *inelegance*, 640.2 *deed*, 652.3 *conduct*, 805.3 *conceit*, 876.4 *self-righteousness*
Affectation 797
affected 797, 357.13 *exaggerated*, 538.18 *pretentious*, 557.4 *ornate*, 559.9 *inelegant*, 618.4 *poor*, 624.23 *diseased*, 656.2 *unskilled*, 805.17 *conceited*, 809.11 *cocky*, 809.13 *boastful*, 876.10 *moralistic*
affectedly 495.6 *pessimistically*, 538.27 *pretentiously*, 809.21 *cockily*
affectedness 797
affectibility 760.5 *sensitivity*
affectible 760.1 *sensitive*
affecting 233.12 *appealing*, 540.30 *pretending*, 759.14 *emotive*, 835.7 *pitiful*
affectingly 759.20 *with feeling*
affection 475.2 *demonstrativeness*, 784.1 *liking*, 821.1 *love*, 826.1 *endearment*, 851.2 *admiration*
affectionate 475.10 *demonstrative*, 784.5 *likable*, 815.15 *sociable*, 819.8 *friendly*, 821.17 *loving*, 826.9 *endearing*, 831.6 *benevolent*
affectionately 475.21 *demonstratively*, 784.10 *with great liking*, 815.18 *sociably*, 819.17 *in friendship*, 821.30 *lovingly*, 826.10 *endearingly*, 831.10 *benevolently*
affectionateness 821.3 *lovingness*
affections 759.3 *feelings*
affective psychosis 61.11 *psychosis*
affenpinscher 77 Breeds of Dogs
affettuoso 49 Musical Terms
affiance 823.15 *marry*

affianced 714.6 *someone promised*, 823.22 *marriageable*
affidavit 16.5 *litigation*, 483.5 *legal evidence*, 535.3 *vow*, 545.2 *certificate*, 714.1 *promise*
affiliate 116.22 *form an alliance*, 664.16 *join*, 665.5 *member*
affiliated 107.4 *related*, 116.11 *allied*, 664.19 *associating*, 665.10 *political*
affiliate oneself to 665.13 *be a member*
affiliation 107.1 *relatedness*, 116.2 *alliance*, 664.7 *association*, 724.2 *participation*, 815.1 *sociability*
affine transformation 52.48 *transformation*
affinity 107.1 *relatedness*, 114.1 *similarity*, 116.1 *accord*, 234.2 *attitude*, 340.1 *attraction*, 667.1 *agreement*, 784.1 *liking*, 819.3 *familiarity*, 823.8 *spouse*
affirm 535, 16.68 *legislate*, 116.28 *consent*, 473.15 *state*, 475.17 *prove*, 480.3 *testify*, 483.11 *give evidence*, 490.21 *make certain*, 497.7 *believe*, 499.4 *assent*, 518.5 *suppose*, 520.10 *mean*, 530.8 *admit*, 564.11 *speak*, 667.6 *agree with*, 674.13 *conflict*, 714.7 *promise*
affirmance 535.1 *affirmation*
affirmant 535.9 *affirmer*
affirmation 535, 16.5 *litigation*, 16.31 *legislation*, 52.63 *mathematical logic*, 116.7 *consent*, 473.3 *line of argument*, 475.4 *proof*, 480.4 *verification*, 490.13 *confirmation*, 499.1 *assent*, 526.10 *manifestation*, 530.2 *divulgence* , 554.1 *emphasis*, 564.7 *utterance*, 611.1 *importance*, 667.1 *agreement*, 714.1 *promise*
Affirmation 535
affirmative 535, 116.17 *consenting*, 499.2 *yes*, 499.6 *assenting*, 499.9 *yes*, 520.6 *meaningful*, 554.3 *emphatic*, 667.1 *agreement*, 667.10 *agreeing*, 714.12 *promised*
affirmative action 122.3 *equalization*
affirmatively 535, 116.39 *with consent*, 499.8 *unanimously*, 667.14 *agreeably*
affirmativeness 490.13 *confirmation*
affirmatory 535.10 *affirmative*
affirmed 473.11 *logical*, 475.19 *proven*, 480.10 *verified*, 535.11 *stated*
affirmer 535
affirming 116.17 *consenting*, 535.10 *affirmative*
affirmingly 116.39 *with consent*
affirm the contrary 536.8 *rebut*
affix 5.35 *part of speech*, 130.3 *additional item*, 130.6 *add*, 135.10 *link*
affixing 5.39 *of language*
affixing language 5.10 *language type*
affix to 138.7 *cause to adhere*
affixture 130.1 *addition*
afflatus 48.13 *poetic genius*, 519.2 *inspiration*
afflict 631, 862.11 *be evil*, 879.1 *punish*
afflicted 862, 406.7 *feeling pain*
afflicted with boredom 788.5 *bored*
affliction 631, 862, 879, 406.1 *pain*, 624.2 *illness*, 687.1 *adversity*
affluence 96.6 *river flow*, 346.2 *influx*, 608.8 *plenty*, 682.1 *success*, 686.1 *prosperity*, 742.5 *wealth*
affluent 96.1 *river*, 96.10 *fluvial*, 608.2 *plentiful*, 686.8 *prosperous*, 721.17 *well-off*, 742.1 *wealthy*
affluently 96.13 *fluently*, 686.9 *prosperously*, 721.20 *gainfully*, 742.16 *wealthily*

affluent society 686.1 *prosperity*
afflux 96.6 *river flow*, 346.2 *influx*
affluxion 346.2 *influx*
afford 116.30 *grant*, 606.5 *provision*, 608.6 *have enough*, 738.1 *purchase*, 748.1 *expend*
affordability 754.1 *cheapness*
affordable 754.9 *cheap*
afforded 116.19 *granted*
afford sanctuary 632.9 *protect*
afforestation 85.5 *forestry*
afforested 85.16 *wooded*
affray 151.9 *disorder*, 473.1 *argument*, 674.6 *fight*
affrettando 49 Musical Terms
affriction 385.1 *friction*
affright 777.1 *fear*, 777.7 *frightened*, 777.13 *frighten*
affront 668.5 *defy*, 764.5 *unpleasantness*, 807.7 *insult*, 818.7 *be discourteous*, 828.2 *offence*, 828.9 *offend*, 850.5, 850.23 *insult*
affronted 828.15 *resentful*
affusion 10.5 *Christian rite*, 389.8 *watering*, 391.5 *sprinkle*
afghan 293.5 *body covering*, 295.25 *accessories*
Afghan 5 Languages and Groups of Languages
Afghan hound 77 Breeds of Dogs
Afghanistan 91 Countries
aficionado 9.5 *worshipper*, 821.9 *lover*
afield 263.10 *distantly*
a finger in every pie 642.9 *overactivity*
aflame 439.16 *bright*
a flat spin 777.2 *fearfulness*
AFL-CIO 15.3 *organized labour*
afloat 74.11 *nautical*, 74.12 *nautically*, 96.11 *flooded*, 97.11 *nautically*
afoot 472.13 *problematically*, 594.17 *developing*, 642.19 *busy*
afore 194.11 *before*
aforementioned 154.11 *prior*
aforenamed 154.11 *prior*
aforesaid 154.11 *prior*
aforethought 582.4 *deliberate*, 588.12 *intended*
aforetime 3.24 *historically*, 200.22 *in the past*
a fortiori 4.16 *dialectical*
afp test 245.7 *obstetrics*
afraid 777.7 *frightened*, 779.3 *cowardly*
afraid of company 816.9 *shy*
afraid of one's shadow 777.8 *fearful*
afraid of the opposite sex 816.9 *shy*
A-frame 284.2 *supporting part*, 310.1 *angle*
A-framed 310.7 *angular*
a free hand 814.4 *freedom*
afreet 8.7 *devil*
afresh 183.24, 201.22 *again*
Africa 98.1 *continent*, 408.8 *hot place*
African 5 Languages and Groups of Languages, 68 Breeds of Fowl, 5.11 *family of languages*
African-American 1.6 *race*
Africander 68 Breeds of Cattle
African elephant 77 Placental Mammals
Africanism 5.26 *dialect*
Africanize 220.12 *naturalize*
Africanized 220.17 *naturalized*
African Methodism 7 Christian Movements
African Orthodox Church 7 Christian Movements
African tribal art 50 Non-Western Art
African violet 84 Flowers and Flowering Plants
Afrikaans 5 Languages and Groups of Languages
Afrikaners 1 Peoples
Afro 791.8 *hair cut*
Afro-American 1.6 *race*, 1.13 *racial*
Afro-Asiatic 5 Languages and

Groups of Languages, 5.11 *family of languages*
Afro-Caribbean 1.6 *race*, 1.13 *racial*
Afro-Cuban 49.8 *jazz*
aft 36.10 *sailing*, 304.9 *in the rear*
after 155, 199, 204.4 *afternoon*, 304.9 *in the rear*, 590.18 *pursuant to*
after a fashion 327.16 *how*
after ages 199.1 *future time*
after a while 209.17 *later*
after back rest 36.8 *punting*
afterbirth 245.7 *obstetrics*
afterburner 73 Aircraft Parts
aftercare 60.8 *treatment*, 630.13 *therapy*
afterdamp 388.3 *miasma*
after dark 205.7 *evening*
after death 397, 325.10 *motionlessly*, 397.23 *fatally*
after deck 74 Parts of a Ship
after-dinner 45.56 *culinary*, 649.4 *at ease*
after-dinner speaker 564.10 *speaker*
after-dinner speech 564.8 *speech*
aftereffect 130.3 *additional item*, 132.1 *remainder*, 155.6 *aftermath*, 227.1 *effect*
afterglow 132.1 *remainder*, 155.6 *aftermath*
aftergrowth 246.1 *fertility*
after him! 590
after-image 457.4 *something that appears*, 547.6 *image*
afterlife 368.1 *nonmaterial world*, 396.5 *life cycle*, 397.14 *the spiritual world*, 492.4 *judgment day*
after life's fitful fever 325.10 *motionlessly*
aftermath 155, 159.4 *repercussion*, 195.9 *sequel*, 227.1 *effect*, 246.1 *fertility*
aftermost 304.9 *in the rear*
afternoon 204, 204, 205.6, 205.7 *evening*
afternoons 110.20 *regularly*
afternoon tea 204.4 *afternoon*, 205.4 *evening thing*, 350.12 *meal*, 815.3 *meeting*
after one's heart 821.21 *beloved*
afterpains 406.2 *painful condition*
afterpart 36.3 *parts of a sailing boat*, 304.1 *rear*
afterpiece 51.6 *scene*, 155.8 *addition*, 304.1 *rear*
afterquarters 304.1 *rear*
afters 45.9 *dish*, 350.14 *mouthful*, 414.3 *dessert*
aftershaft 78.11 *plumage*
after-shave 418.2 *fragrant thing*
aftershock 54.22 *seismic activity*
after-shove 36.8 *punting*
aftertaste 155.6 *aftermath*, 411.1 *taste*
after this fashion 327.16 *how*
afterthought 155, 209.3 *delayed action*, 304.1 *rear*, 547.6 *image*, 578.6 *equivocation*
after thoughts 484.2 *reversal*
afterwards 155.28, 199.15 *after*
afterword 155.8 *addition*, 195.9 *sequel*, 304.1 *rear*
aft mast 36.3 *parts of a sailing boat*
a full plate 642.6 *business*
Aga 45.5 *cooker*
again 183, 201, 110.18 *identically*, 176.19 *twice*
again and again 183.23 *repeatedly*, 212.1 *frequently*
against 111.6 *oppositely*, 117.16 *disagreeably*, 231.5 *counter*, 341.12 *defensively*, 663.27 *opposed to*, 852.26 *disagreeing*
against nature 117.8 *contradictory*
against one's nature 117.8 *contradictory*
against one's will 573.17 *unwillingly*, 701.11 *under subjection*
against the clock 648.6 *hastily*
against-the-clock competition 32.9 *jumping*

against the grain 117.8 *contradictory*, 337.29 *in reverse*, 375.14 *roughly*, 573.17 *unwillingly*
against the law 16.55 *illegal*, 16.82 *illegally*, 16.89 *guiltily*
against the nap 375.14 *roughly*
against the rules 168.15 *irregular*, 720.14 *violating*
against the stream 659.25 *difficultly*
against the tide 663.26 *contrariwise*
against the wind 332.11 *in all directions*, 659.25 *difficultly*
agama 79 *Reptiles*
Agama 7.12 *religious text*
a game at which two can play 672.1 *retaliation*
agamist 825.4 *celibate person*
agapanthus 84 *Flowers and Flowering Plants*
agape 10.16 *religious festival*, 322.12 *open*, 786.7 *wide-eyed*
Agape 821.1 *love*
Agapemonites 7 *Christian Movements*
agapistic 821.17 *loving*
agar 58.4 *polysaccharide*, 90.5 *algal product*, 393.9 *jelly*
agaric 89 *Fungi*
agarics 89.3 *fungi*
Agartala 93 *Cities*
Agassi 18 *Sporting Personalities*
Agassiz 52 *Scientists*
Agassou 8 *Deities*
agate 54 *Gemstones*, 456.5 *variegated thing*
agateware 44.1 *ceramics*
agave 84 *Flowers and Flowering Plants*
age 207, 207, 185.5 *indefinite period*, 187.2 *time period*, 190.2 *a long time*, 202.1 *oldness*, 202.17 *grow old*, 220.8 *be transformed*, 594.7 *develop*, 628.1 *deteriorate*
Age 207
aged 207, 202.11 *old*, 396.12 *alive*, 448.2 *grey-haired*
Agee 48 *Writers*
age group 2.6 *social group*, 161.18 *generation*, 198.5 *contemporary*
ageing 207, 628.12 *deteriorated*
ageism 481.4 *social discrimination*, 493.3 *injustice*, 805.11 *prejudice*
ageist 207.15 *age-related*, 481.7 *bigot*, 481.10 *discriminatory*, 493.8 *unjust*, 805.23 *prejudiced*
ageless 186.5 *timeless*
agelessness 186
agelong 190
Agence France Presse 528.8 *source of information*, 533.7 *press agency*
agency 232.1 *instrumentality*, 232.2 *instrument*, 547.8 *representative*, 602.1 *means*, 640.1 *action*, 653.3 *management*, 703.4 *council*
agenda 171.5 *list of appointments*, 257.5 *divisions*, 472.2 *issue*, 582.6 *premeditation*, 592.1 *plan*
ageneric 165.17 *exceptional*
agent 646, 707, 51.25 *producer*, 127.6 *inferior*, 135.7 *joiner*, 158.9 *middleman*, 216.5 *changer*, 222.2 *substitute person*, 226.4 *contributing factor*, 226.8 *contributor*, 230.5 *operator*, 232.3 *assistant*, 496.12 *discoverer*, 532.12 *publisher*, 547.8 *representative*, 586.14 *motivator*, 640.3 *doer*, 653.15 *manager*, 678.4 *representative*, 703.5 *commissioner*, 706.1 *delegate*, 739.10 *salesman*, 739.12 *wholesaler*
agential 232.7 *causal*, 703.9 *commissioned*
agent of destruction 244
Agent Orange 547.7 *agent of destruction*, 631.10 *warfare*
agent provocateur 586.14 *motivator*

age of Aquarius 686.3 *time of plenty*
age of consent 823.4 *marriageability*
Age of Enlightenment 200.5 *historical period*
age of puberty 206.1 *youth*
Age of Reason 3.10 *past age*, 200.5 *historical period*
age-old 202.12 *olden*
age-related 207
ages 185.5 *indefinite period*, 188.5 *long duration*
ages ago 200.22 *in the past*, 202.19 *anciently*
age set 1.5 *anthropological concept*
agglomerate 138.6 *adhere*, 161.37 *assemble*, 161.48 *cumulate*
agglomeration 138.1 *adhesion*, 140.3 *assembly*, 161.25 *assemblage*
agglutinate 130.6 *add*, 138.7 *cause to adhere*, 726.6 *retain*
agglutination 130.1 *addition*, 135.1 *union*, 138.1 *adhesion*
agglutinative 5.39 *of language*, 130.8 *additional*
agglutinative language 5.10 *language type*
aggrandize 128.5 *make bigger*, 261.5 *make bigger*, 541.8 *enlarge*
aggrandized 541.13 *enlarged*
aggrandizement 128.1 *increase*, 261.1 *growth*, 541.2 *enlargement*
aggravate 768, 128.5 *make bigger*, 241.9 *make violent*, 541.7 *exaggerate*, 628.3 *make worse*, 659.22 *cause trouble*, 820.13 *antagonize*, 822.16 *cause hate*, 828.9 *offend*, 828.14 *make angry*
aggravated 768, 541.12 *exaggerated*, 628.12 *deteriorated*, 828.15 *resentful*
aggravating 768, 659.13 *inconvenient*
aggravatingly 828.17 *resentfully*
aggravation 768, 128.1 *increase*, 541.1 *exaggeration*, 628.10 *impairment*, 659.8 *snag*, 764.7 *dissension*, 828.1 *resentment*
Aggravation 768
aggregate 52.15 *addition*, 52.91 *add*, 120.4 *total*, 140.3 *assembly*, 140.5 *combine*, 149.9 *assembled*, 142.2 *whole thing*, 161.37 *assemble*, 161.48 *cumulate*, 169.4 *mathematical result*, 170.10 *total*, 371.4 *solid body*
aggregated 140.9 *assembled*
aggregate fruit 86.2 *botanical fruit*
aggregation 140.3 *assembly*, 161.25 *assemblage*
aggression 237.1 *strength*, 241.1 *violence*, 670.11 *attack*, 676.5 *bellicosity*, 820.1 *enmity*, 828.4 *anger*
aggressive 670, 820, 17.8 *military*, 237.11 *strong in spirit*, 239.4 *vigorous*, 241.6 *violent*, 642.18 *active*, 666.9 *disagreeing*, 668.8 *defying*, 674.15 *contentious*, 676.15 *warring*, 676.16 *warlike*, 679.33 *combative*, 764.2 *objectionable*, 778.11 *militant*, 809.11 *cocky*, 818.5 *discourteous*, 828.16 *angry*
aggressively 670, 679, 820, 237.14 *strongly*, 666.11 *in disagreement*, 668.10 *in defiance*, 674.17 *contentiously*, 764.13 *unpleasantly*, 809.21 *cockily*, 818.9 *discourteously*
aggressiveness 237.1 *strength*, 642.4 *energy*, 666.1 *disagreement*, 670.11 *attack*, 676.5 *bellicosity*, 764.6 *objectionability*, 778.2 *heroism*, 809.3 *cockiness*
aggressive war 676.1 *war*
aggressor 500.5 *dissenter*, 670.19 *attacker*, 679.1 *combatant*, 764.9 *unpleasant person*, 820.5 *hostile person*

aggrevated burglary 736.1 *stealing*
aggrieve 618.14 *ill-treat*, 828.9 *offend*, 862.11 *be evil*
aggro 151.9 *disorder*, 764.8 *quarrel*, 768.3 *nuisance*
aghast 777.7 *frightened*, 786.6 *wondering*
Aghorapanthi 7 *Non-Christian Religions*
agile 329.1 *swift*, 642.18 *active*, 655.6 *skilful*
agilely 329.14 *swiftly*
agility 329.8 *speed*
agin 663.27 *opposed to*, 852.26 *disagreeing*
agio 14.1, 741.7 *finance*, 752.1 *discount*
agiotage 14.1 *finance*, 737.4 *trade*, 741.7 *finance*
agitate 366, 153.7 *disturb*, 365.9 *vibrate*, 403.13 *arouse sensation*, 475.19 *protest*, 642.12 *be active*, 693.16 *be subversive*
agitate against 231.3 *counteract*, 713.8 *cause mischief*
agitated 366, 153.12 *disturbed*, 241.6 *violent*, 324.16 *moving*, 375.4 *bumpy*, 403.7 *susceptible*, 642.18 *active*, 777.8 *fearful*
agitated depression 61.13 *depression*
agitated for 594.17 *developing*
agitatedly 366
agitating 324.17 *directional*, 365.14 *vibrating*, 475.14 *demonstrating*
agitation 366, 153.1 *disturbance*, 224.2 *irresolution*, 241.1 *violence*, 324.2 *momentum*, 324.5 *circuition*, 365.2 *vibration*, 403.1 *sensation*, 642.1 *activity*, 642.7 *restlessness*, 648.4 *haste*, 693.3 *subversion*, 713.2 *disorder*, 777.2 *fearfulness*
Agitation 366
agitato 49 *Musical Terms*
agitator 366, 693, 151.11 *troublemaker*, 228.7 *motivator*, 241.4 *violent person or animal*, 475.8 *protester*, 500.5 *dissenter*, 586.14 *motivator*, 627.12 *reformer*, 635.2 *troublemaker*, 653.14 *leader*, 663.9 *opposer*, 713.4 *protester*
agitprop 228.2 *inducement*, 586.5 *propaganda*, 693.3 *subversion*
Aglaia 8 *Deities*
aglow 439.15 *lucent*
agnate 107.4 *related*
Agnesi 52 *Scientists*, 52 *Named Concepts*
Agni 8 *Deities*
Agnoetae 7 *Christian Movements*
agnolotti 45 *Types of Pasta*
agnomen 560.8 *name*
agnostic 4.11 *follower of a doctrine*, 4.14 *of a philosophy*, 333.3 *moderate person*, 477.9 *questioner*, 477.15 *sceptical*, 491.1 *uncertain*, 491.17 *uncertain person*, 498.5 *disbeliever*, 498.6 *disbelieving*, 536.6 *negativist*, 536.11 *negative*, 720.5 *nonobserver*, 720.11 *nonobservant*
agnostically 477.23 *questioningly*
agnosticism 4.7 *school of thought*, 477.6 *uncertainty*, 491.10 *suspicion*, 498.4 *unbelief*, 536.2 *rejection*
Agnus Dei 10.9 *prayer*
ago 3.24 *historically*, 200.22 *in the past*
agog 786.7 *wide-eyed*
agogics 564.6 *phonetics*
agonic line 54.45 *magnetic pole*
agonist 679.1 *combatant*
agonistic 18.5 *sporting*, 674.14 *contending*, 679.33 *combative*
agonistically 679.41 *aggressively*
Agonizants 7 *Christian Movements*

agonize 406.9 *feel pain*, 618.14 *ill-treat*
agonized 406.7 *feeling pain*
agonize over 777.14 *worry*
agonizing 406.5 *painful*
agony 406.1 *pain*, 618.11 *harmfulness*, 631.5 *pain*, 770.1 *sorrow*
agony aunt 532.11 *newspaper man*, 560.10 *descriptive writer*
agony column 532.3 *journalism*
a good credit risk 742.2 *solvent*
a good few 181.6 *many*
a good hand 589.2 *luck*
a good many 181.6 *many*
a good time 405.4 *pleasurable things*
agora 740.6 *marketplace*
agoraphobia 777 *Phobias by Name*, 777 *Phobias by Name*, 816.2 *shyness*
Agostini 18 *Sporting Personalities*
agouti 77 *Placental Mammals*
Agra 93 *Cities*
agrarian 68.19 *agricultural*
agrarianism 68.1 *agriculture*
a greater number 175.1 *plurality*
agree 112, 135, 110.7 *be the same*, 114.10 *be similar*, 116.21 *be in accord*, 116.28 *consent*, 140.6 *come together*, 152.17 *come to an arrangement*, 167.7 *conform*, 167.8 *comply*, 433.8 *harmonize*, 478.21 *answer to*, 499.4 *assent*, 572.13 *be willing*, 586.18 *be persuaded*, 597.1 *undertake*, 667.6 *agree with*, 677.5 *make peace*, 851.12 *accept*
agreeability 821.4 *lovability*
agreeable 116, 135, 110.13 *equivalent*, 167.13 *compliant*, 405.6 *pleasant*, 572.1 *willing*, 667.10 *agreeing*, 673.5 *submitting*, 675.7 *peaceful*, 715.7 *contractual*, 763.1 *pleasant*, 789.6 *personable*, 817.7 *courteous*, 819.8 *friendly*
agreeableness 763.6 *pleasantness*, 789.1 *gorgeousness*, 817.1 *courtesy*
agreeably 135, 667, 110.18 *identically*, 116.33 *harmoniously*, 478.26 *correspondingly*, 572.16 *willingly*, 677.7 *pacifically*, 715.8 *contractually*, 717.9 *compromisingly*, 763.15 *pleasantly*, 817.14 *courteously*, 819.17 *in friendship*
agree beforehand 582.2 *premeditate*
agreed 499, 107.5 *interrelated*, 110.12 *same*, 112.7 *agreeing*, 116.10 *in accord*, 116.17 *consenting*, 135.13 *agreeable*, 667.10 *agreeing*, 715.7 *contractual*, 717.6 *compromising*
agreed result 582.6 *premeditation*
agreed to 715.7 *contractual*
agreeing 112, 667, 110.13 *equivalent*, 116.10 *in accord*, 116.17 *consenting*, 167.12 *conforming*, 433.7 *harmonious*, 444.11 *colourful*, 478.15 *correspondent*, 499.6 *assenting*, 673.1 *submission*, 717.6 *compromising*
agree in meaning 520.10 *mean*
agree in principle 499.4 *assent*
agreement 112, 135, 152, 667, 5.30 *syntax*, 107.1 *relatedness*, 110.1 *sameness*, 110.2 *equivalence*, 114.1 *similarity*, 116.1 *accord*, 116.7 *consent*, 140.2 *cooperation*, 167.1 *conformity*, 478.8 *correspondence*, 499.1 *assent*, 597.3 *contract*, 664.2 *fellowship*, 677.1 *pacification*, 715.1 *contract*, 717.1 *compromise*, 737.9 *bargaining*, 851.1 *approval*
Agreement 667
agree on a verdict 16.76 *judge*
agree to 737.3 *bargain*
agree to anything 808.10 *knuckle under*
agree to differ 500.8 *dissent*,

666.5 *disagree*, **677.5** *make peace*
agree to disagree 677.5 *make peace*
agree to half of it 717.4 *compromise*
agree to some of it 717.4 *compromise*
agree with 667, 122.10 *be equal*, 499.4 *assent*, 763.13 *give pleasure*
agree with one 625.5 *by hygienic*
agrestic 68.19 *agricultural*
agribusiness 68.1 *agriculture*
Agricola 52 Scientists
agricultural 68, 243.11 *productive*
agricultural dance 46.4 *historic dancing*
agricultural engineering 63.1 *engineering*
agriculturalist 68.15 *agriculturist*, 594.15 *preparer*
agricultural labourer 646.1 *worker*
agriculturally 68
agricultural meteorology 55.1 *meteorology*
agricultural sale 68.1 *agriculture*
agricultural science 68.1 *agriculture*
agriculture 68, 243.2 *manufacture*
Agriculture 68
agriculturist 68
Agrigento 93 Cities
agrimony 84 Flowers and Flowering Plants
Agrionia 10.16 *religious festival*
Agrippa 29.5 *golf ball*
agrobiological 68.19 *agricultural*
agrobiologist 68.15 *agriculturist*, 83.12 *plant scientist*
agrobiology 68.1 *agriculture*, 83.10 *plant science*
agrochemicals 68.14 *pest control*
agrocybe 89 Fungi
agroecological 68.19 *agricultural*
agroecologist 68.15 *agriculturist*
agroecology 68.1 *agriculture*
agroforestry 68.1 *agriculture*, 85.5 *forestry*
agrogeologist 68.15 *agriculturist*
agrogeology 68.1 *agriculture*
agrological 68.19 *agricultural*
agrologist 68.15 *agriculturist*
agrology 68.1 *agriculture*
agromania 510.4 *delusion*
agronomic 68.19 *agricultural*
agronomics 68.1 *agriculture*
agronomist 68.15 *agriculturist*
agronomy 68.1 *agriculture*
agroscience 68.1 *agriculture*
aground 225.9 *stable*, 344.22 *on arrival*
a grunt-and-groan match 674.8 *wrestling*
ague 366.7 *shake*, 624.3 *symptom*, 624.7 *tropical disease*
aguey 366.18 *shaky*
aguish 624.23 *diseased*, 626.6 *contagious*
agyrophobia 777 Phobias by Name
AH 185.29 *one day*
aha 471.25 *got it*
a handful 175.1 *plurality*
ahead 357, 126.12 *superior*, 154.21 *first*, 199.11 *future*, 263.10 *distantly*, 300.10 *advantaged*, 303.11 *in front*, 336.19 *forward*
ahead of its time 208.17 *early*
ahead of oneself 208.17 *early*
ahead of one's time 193.5 *too early*, 193.7 *out of chronological order*, 208.16 *premature*, 208.20 *prematurely*
ahead of schedule 208.12, 208.17 *early*
ahead of the times 197.2 *occurring at a different time*
ahead of time 193.5 *too early*, 193.7 *out of chronological order*, 208.12, 208.17 *early*, 721.18 *acquisitional*
Ahi 8 Deities

ahimsa 4.7 *school of thought*, 675.1 *peace*, 677.1 *pacification*
Ahmadiya 7 Non-Christian Religions
Ahmedabad 93 Cities
A horizon 54.36 *soil*
Ahriman 8.7 *devil*
Ahsonnulti 8 Deities
a-hull 36.20 *offshore*
a hundred and one 181.7 *myriad*
Ahura Mazda 8.3 *God*
ai 77 Placental Mammals
aid 767, 34.8 *mountaineering*, 226.12 *determine*, 232.1 *instrumentality*, 232.4 *be an instrument*, 284.6 *moral support*, 284.14 *give moral support*, 336.8 *further*, 361.3 *promote*, 361.7 *lift*, 572.14 *cooperate*, 613.5 *usefulness*, 613.9 *be useful*, 615.6 *be convenient*, 630.1, 630.19 *remedy*, 632.2 *protection*, 640.4 *act*, 660.16 *make easy*, 662.1 *help*, 662.7 *convenience*, 662.11 *helper*, 662.17 *help*, 707.5 *represent*, 729.2 *gift*, 751.8 *levy*, 755.11 *give*, 767.4 *charity*, 767.11 *assist*, 831.9 *be charitable*, 833.5 *charity*, 878.3, 878.10 *grant*
AID 245.3 *propagation*
aid and abet 228.10 *manipulate*, 662.17 *help*, 664.12 *reciprocate*
aid climbing 34.1 *mountaineering*
aide 232.3 *assistant*, 284.8 *supporter*, 654.4 *adviser*, 662.11 *helper*, 707.1 *deputy*, 767.5 *helper*
aide-de-camp 767.5 *helper*
aider 226.8 *contributor*, 662.11 *helper*, 671.13 *defender*, 833.3 *philanthropist*
aider and abettor 228.7, 586.14 *motivator*
aid for poor sight 436
aid-giving 833.6 *philanthropic*
aiding 232.6 *instrumental*, 662.30 *helping*, 697.9 *serving*, 833.6 *philanthropic*
aiding and abetting 664.3 *mutual relationship*, 866.1 *guilt*
AIDS 244.7 *agent of destruction*, 624.4 *disease*, 624.14 *venereal disease*
AIDS-related complex 624.14 *venereal disease*
aid worker 572.11 *willing worker*, 833.3 *philanthropist*
aiguillette 544.4 *insignia*
AIH 245.3 *propagation*
aikido 18 Sporting Activities, **26**, 26.1 *combat sports*, 26.15, 674.8 *wrestling*
aikido grade 26.10 *aikido*
aikido technique 26.10 *aikido*
aikido throws 26.10 *aikido*
ail 624.24 *be unhealthy*, 683.6 *fail*
ailanthus 85 Trees and Shrubs
aileron 73 Aircraft Parts, 122.4 *equilizer*, 225.3 *stabilizer*
ailing 624.22 *sick*, 683.1 *failure*, 683.10 *failed*
ailment 624.2 *illness*
ailurophobia 777 Phobias by Name
aim 157, **471**, **588**, 226.5 *reason*, 228.1 *motive*, 332.1 *direction*, 332.6 *direct*, 332.7 *take a direction*, 471.4 *purpose*, 520.5 *point*, 520.12 *intend*, 586.11 *motive*, 588.6 *objective*, 592.9 *plan*, 596.1 *attempt*, 596.6 *venture*, 670.2 *fire*, 775.3 *aspiration*, 775.7 *aspire*, 782.5 *object of desire*
aim a blow 330.3 *hit*
aim Archie at the Armitage 767.13 *relieve oneself*
aim at 590, 37.7 *shoot*, 332.7 *take a direction*, 588.10 *aim*
aimed 332.14 *directed*, 471.12 *purposive*
aim for 782.12 *probe*
aim for the lowest common denominator 522.5 *simplify*
aim high 471.18 *aim*

aiming 25.9 *bowls*, 471.12 *purposive*, 596.6 *venture*
aiming at 234.5 *tending to*
aiming for the lowest common denominator 522.2 *simple*
aiming point 25.2 *grip*
aimless 521, 229.6 *motiveless*, 553.4 *circumlocutory*
aimless activity 642.7 *restlessness*
aimlessly 229.8 *by chance*, 521.13 *meaninglessly*
aimlessness 521, **521**, 229.1 *lack of motive*, 553.2 *circumlocution*, 642.7 *restlessness*
aim to 596.1 *attempt*
aim too high 357.1 *overstep*
aim well 537.31 *be accurate*
Ain 96 Rivers
ain't it the truth 537.40 *right*
Ainu 1 Peoples, **5** Languages and Groups of Languages, **7** Non-Christian Religions
aïoli 45.15 *sauce*
air 390, 49.13 *melody*, 55.8 *atmosphere*, 70.1 *transport*, 70.5 *transportable*, 370.7 *light thing*, 372.5, 388.1 *gas*, 390.20 *aerate*, 392.2 *drip-dry*, 396.3 *life requirements*, 416.1 *odour*, 433.1 *melody*, 442.8 *transparent thing*, 457.3 *external appearance*, 475.15 *demonstrate*, 526.1 *display*, 530.6 *divulge*, 532.13 *make public*, 621.15 *purify*, 651.1 *refresh*, 651.6 *refresher*, 652.1 *conduct*
Air 390
air ace 670.19 *attacker*
air arm 679.29 *air force*
air attack 670, 670.12 *military attack*, 680.1 *weapon*
air bag 71 Motor Vehicle Parts, 632.4 *safety device*, 637.2 *preserver*
air ball 23.4 *playing terms*
air balloon 388.13 *gas balloon*, 390.10 *air bubble*
airbase 73.4 *airport*
air bladder 80.5 *fish anatomy*, 90.3 *plant body*, 388.13 *gas balloon*, 390.10 *air bubble*
airborne 359.23 *rising*
airborne division 17.4 *military organization*, 679.30 *air force unit*
airborne particles 384.5 *powder*
air brake 73 Aircraft Parts
airbrush 50.11 *artist's materials*
airbrush painting 50.8 *painting*
air bubble 390
air campaign 670.13 *air attack*
air cargo 73.1 *aviation*
air-cargo 70.5 *transportable*
air chief marshal 679.32 *airman*
Air Chief Marshal 17 British Military Ranks
air commodore 679.32 *airman*
Air Commodore 17 British Military Ranks
air-condition 390.20 *aerate*, 409.12 *make cold*, 651.1 *refresh*
air-conditioned 390.17 *ventilated*, 409.9 *heat-resistant*
air conditioner 390.7 *ventilator*, 409.4 *cooler*
air conditioning 390.6 *ventilation*
air-conditioning 409.4 *cooler*
air-cool 390.20 *aerate*
air-cooled 390.17 *ventilated*, 409.9 *heat-resistant*
air cooler 390.7 *ventilator*
air cooling 390.6 *ventilation*
air corps 679.29 *air force*
air corridor 73.1 *aviation*, 327.13 *flight path*
aircraft 73, 679.31 *military aircraft*
aircraft carrier 679.24 *warship*
aircraft design 73.2 *aeronautics*
aircraft division 17.4 *military organization*
aircraft mechanic 646.2 *artisan*
aircraft personnel 73
aircraftsman 73.3 *aircraft personnel*
aircrew 73.3 *aircraft personnel*, 679.32 *airman*

air current 55.10 *air movement*, 390.4 *air flow*
air dam 73 Aircraft Parts
air density 55.6 *weather data*
air division 17.4 *military organization*
air-dried 392.8 *baked*
airdrop 73.1 *aviation*
air-dry 392.17 *dry*
air-drying 392.13 *drying*
Aire 96 Rivers
aired 392.8 *baked*, 532.19 *published*
Airedale terrier 77 Breeds of Dogs
air express 326.2 *transportation*
air-express 326.13 *post*
airfield 73.4 *airport*
air fight 676.9 *battle*
air filter 390.7 *ventilator*, 621.10 *cleaning object*
air-filter 417.2 *deodorant*
air flow 390
airflow 55.10 *air movement*
air flow 73.7 *miscellaneous aviation terms*, 390.8 *respiration*
air force 679, 17.2 *the military*
airforce 17.8 *military*
air force 161.14 *force*, 679.14 *armed forces*, 718.4 *security forces*
Air Force Academy 17.3 *military training*
air-force blue 454.1 *blue*
Air Force Cross 17 British Military Medals and Decorations, **17** US Military Medals and Decorations
Air Force Medal 17 British Military Medals and Decorations
air force officer 679.32 *airman*
air force pilot 676.11 *recruit*
air force service 676.8 *warfare*
air force staff 17.5 *military staff*
air force uniform 544.5 *uniform*
air force unit 679
airframe 73 Aircraft Parts
air freight 73.1 *aviation*, 326.2 *transportation*
air freshener 621.9 *cleaning agent*
air-freshener 134.3 *purifier*, 417.2 *deodorant*
air frost 55.36 *frost*
air group 679.30 *air force unit*
air gun 425.3 *banger*
airgun shooting 18 Sporting Activities
airhole 322.5 *hole*
air hostess 73.3 *aircraft personnel*
airily 390, 368.13 *metaphysically*, 372.7 *sparsely*
airiness 390, 370.5 *lightness*, 372.3 *sparseness*
airing 134.2 *purification*, 390.6 *ventilation*, 392.13 *drying*, 621.2 *cleaning*
air intake 73 Aircraft Parts
airlane 327.13 *flight path*, 356.2 *passing along*
air-layer 245.13 *propagate*
air leakage 638.4 *leak*
airless 325.4 *motionless*, 626.5 *unhygienic*
airlessness 325.2 *repose*
air letter 534.3 *correspondence*
airlift 73.1 *aviation*, 326.2 *transportation*, 326.12 *transport*
airlike 390.12 *airy*
airline attendant 697.3 *attendant*
airline hostess 697.3 *attendant*
airline pilot 73.3 *aircraft personnel*
airliner 73.8 *aircraft*
airline ticket 544.3 *means of identification*
air mail 73.1 *aviation*, 326.13 *post*, 534.2 *postal communication*, 534.31 *correspond*
air-mail letter 534.3 *correspondence*
air-mail stamp 534.3 *correspondence*
airman 679
airmanship 676.6 *art of war*
air marshal 679.32 *airman*, 692.6 *person in command*, 696.7 *military leader*

Air Marshal 17 British Military Ranks
air mass 55.10 *air movement*
Air Medal 17 US Military Medals and Decorations
air mile 75 General Units
air miss 73.7 *miscellaneous aviation terms*
air movement 55, 55.6 *weather data*
airometer 388.15 *vaporimeter*
air operations 676.8 *warfare*
air passage 390.7 *ventilator*
air-pistol shooting 37.1 *target shooting*
airplane 73.8 *aircraft*
air plant 83.2 *plant*
air pocket 73.7 *miscellaneous aviation terms,* 375.9 *broken water,* 390.10 *air bubble*
air point 34.5 *rock face*
air pollution 384.5 *powder,* 419.2 *something that makes an unpleasant smell*
airport 73, 218.4 *stopping place,* 291.4 *centre of activity,* 344.15 *destination,* 345.10 *place of departure*
airport engineering 63.17 *civil engineering*
airport police 16.14 *police*
air pressure 55.6 *weather data*
Air Pump 53 The Constellations
air-purifier 417.2 *deodorant*
air racing 18 Sporting Activities
air raid 670.13 *air attack,* 680.1 *weapon*
airraid shelter 671.10 *shelter*
air-raid shelter 378.7 *tough thing,* 634.1 *refuge*
air-raid siren 543.4 *signal*
air-raid warden 543.8 *signer*
air rifle 425.3 *banger*
air-rifle shooting 37.1 *target shooting*
air route 34.1 *mountaineering,* 73.1 *aviation,* 327.13 *flight path*
airs 811
airs and graces 797.1 *affectedness,* 809.3 *cockiness,* 811.2 *airs*
air scoop 73 Aircraft Parts
airscrew 364.6 *rotator*
air-sea rescue 639.2 *deliverance*
air-sea rescue helicopter 639.3 *deliverer*
air service 679.29 *air force*
airship 388.13 *gas balloon,* 679.31 *military aircraft*
airsick 349.30 *vomiting*
airsickness 73.7 *miscellaneous aviation terms*
airside 73.4 *airport*
airspace 248.2 *empty space,* 248.6 *available space,* 249.3 *regional boundary,* 390.1 *air*
airspeed 73.5 *flight,* 329.8 *speed*
air squadron 140.3 *assembly*
air station 73.4 *airport*
air stream 55.10 *air movement*
air strike 670.13 *air attack*
airstrip 73.4 *airport,* 327.13 *flight path*
air temperature 55.6 *weather data*
air terminal 218.4 *stopping place,* 344.15 *destination*
airtight 323.12 *closed,* 619.1 *perfect*
air-traffic control 73.6 *flight control*
air-traffic controller 73.3 *aircraft personnel,* 356.7 *traffic controller*
air transport 73.1 *aviation,* 326.5 *means of transport*
air travel 73.1 *aviation,* 324.2 *momentum*
air troops 679.32 *airman*
air vice-marshal 679.32 *airman*
Air Vice-Marshal 17 British Military Ranks
airworthy 70.5 *transportable,* 326.17 *transferable,* 632.6 *invulnerable*
airy 388, 390, 11.18 *spiritual,* 102.8 *unreal,* 248.13 *spacious,* 275.9 *high,* 368.8 *nonmaterial,* 370.2 *insubstantial,* 372.1 *sparse,* 612.4 *trivial*

Airy 52 Scientists
airy-fairy 372.1 *sparse,* 519.11 *fantastical*
aisle 10.12 *church,* 322.7 *passageway,* 327.2 *route,* 327.7 *urcade,* 327.11 *channel*
Aisne 96 Rivers
ait 98.2 *island*
aitiou 45.53 *African dish*
Aitken 53 Lunar Features
Aix-en-Provence 93 Cities
Aiyanar 8 Deities
Aizen myo-o 8 Deities
ajar 322.12 *open*
Ajivika 7 Non-Christian Religions
Ajmer 93 Cities
AK-47 680.11 *guns*
Aka-kanet 8 Deities
Akali 7 Non-Christian Religions
Akan 5 Languages and Groups of Languages
Akhal Teke 32 Breeds of Horse and Pony
akin 114.7 *similar,* 146.8 *included*
akin to 107.4 *related*
Akkadian 5 Languages and Groups of Languages
akrasia 4.9 *philosophical problem*
Akron 93 Cities
Akshobhya 8.3 *God*
Akycha 8 Deities
Alabama 92 American States, **96** Rivers, 96.3 *US rivers*
alabaster 376.8 *smooth thing,* 446.1 *white,* 446.9 *white thing*
alacritous 208.12 *early,* 329.1 *swift,* 572.2 *eager*
alacrity 208.1 *earliness,* 329.10 *quickness of mind,* 572.7 *eagerness,* 642.3 *nimbleness,* 648.4 *haste*
alanine 58 Amino Acids
alarm 153.7 *disturb,* 238.7 *weaken,* 423.1 *loudness,* 423.4 *sound maker,* 543.4 *signal,* 632.4 *safety device,* 636.2 *danger signal,* 636.7 *raise the alarm,* 777.2 *fearfulness,* 777.13 *frighten*
alarm and despondency 776.1 *hopelessness*
alarm bell 543.4 *signal,* 636.2 *danger signal*
alarm clock 191 Timepieces and Timers, 192.6 *clock,* 420.8 *something heard,* 543.4 *signal,* 636.2 *danger signal*
alarmed 153.12 *disturbed,* 777.8 *fearful*
alarming 153.17 *disturbing,* 633.1 *dangerous,* 777.10 *frightening*
alarmingly 153.18 *disturbingly,* 777.16 *frighteningly*
alarmist 543.8 *signer,* 636.4 *warner,* 777.5 *frightener*
alarm system 632.2, 718.1 *protection*
alarm test 636.3 *false alarm*
alarum 543.4 *signal,* 636.2 *danger signal*
alarums and excursions 51.6 *scene*
Alaska 92 American States
Alaska–Hawaii Daylight Time 185.9 *time zone*
Alaska–Hawaii Standard Time 185.9 *time zone*
Alaskan malamute 77 Breeds of Dogs
Alaskan oil 410.6 *oil*
Ala-Tau 68 Breeds of Cattle
a laugh 771.5 *joke*
alb 7.11 *vestment*
alba 48.7 *poem*
albacore 80 Fishes
Albania 91 Countries
Albanian 5 Languages and Groups of Languages
Albany 93 Cities
albatross 78 Birds, 29.2 *golfing terms,* 78.3 *water bird,* 631.3, 661.6 *burden*
albatross round one's neck 631.3 *burden*

albedo 53.16 *planet*
Albee 48 Dramatists
Alberich 260.4 *little person*
Albert 94 Lakes, **191** Timepieces and Timers, 94.5 *other major lakes*
Alberta 92 Canadian Provinces and Territories
Alberti 48 Poets
Albert Schweitzer 675.4 *Nobel Peace Prize*
albescence 446.7 *whiteness*
albescent 446.1 *white*
Albigensianism 7 Christian Movements
albinic 1.13 *racial*
albiniotic 1.13 *racial*
albinism 445.2 *paleness,* 446.7 *whiteness,* 624.13 *skin disease*
albinistic 1.13 *racial,* 446.1 *white*
albino 439.21 *light,* 445.8 *drained of colour*
Albino 32 Breeds of Horse and Pony
albinoism 445.2 *paleness,* 446.7 *whiteness*
albinotic 445.8 *drained of colour,* 446.1 *white*
Albion ware 44 Types of Ceramics
Albireo 53 Named Stars
albite 54 Minerals
alboka 49 Musical Instruments
Al Borak 32.1 *horse*
album 511.4 *reminder,* 545.6 *record book,* 562.3 *compendium*
albumen 58.9 *protein,* 393.10, 394.5 *mucus*
albumin 58.9 *protein*
Albuquerque 93 Cities
alburum 85.3 *timber*
Alcaeus 48 Poets
Alcaics 48.10 *verse form*
Alcaid 53 Named Stars
Alcatraz 702.1 *prison*
Alceste 834.2 *misanthrope*
alchemic 11.15 *witchlike*
alchemical 57.31 *chemical*
alchemist 11.12 *occultist,* 57.2 *chemist,* 133.7 *person who mixes,* 216.6, 224.4 *editor,* 529.7 *esotericism*
alchemistic 11.15 *witchlike*
alchemize 220.9 *transform*
alchemy 11.1 *occultism,* 11.3 *witchcraft,* 57.1 *chemistry,* 220.1 *conversion,* 529.7 *esotericism*
Alcmaeon 4 Philosophers
alcohol 57 Types of Compounds, **57** Common Chemical Compounds, **874,** 351.7 *alcoholic drink,* 630.7 *tonic,* 631.11 *intoxicant,* 637.2 *preserver*
alcohol abuse 624.4 *disease,* 874.16 *alcoholism*
alcohol-free 873.2 *nonalcoholic*
alcoholic 351.17 *drinkable,* 584.8 *creature of habit,* 624.19 *sick person,* 695.5 *compulsive person,* 874.5 *drunken,* 874.6 *intoxicating,* 874.17 *drunkard*
alcoholic addiction 874.16 *alcoholism*
alcoholic drink 351, 874.12 *alcohol*
alcoholic liquor 874.12 *alcohol*
alcoholic psychosis 61.11, 510.5 *psychosis*
Alcoholics Anonymous 873.8 *sober person*
alcoholism 874, 351.1 *drinking,* 624.4 *disease*
alcoholometer 268.8 *meter*
alcohol thermometer 56.89 *thermometer*
Alcor 53 Named Stars
Alcora ware 44 Types of Ceramics
Alcott 48 Writers
alcove 258.2 *compartment,* 317.3 *cavity*
Alcyone 53 Named Stars
aldaric acid 58.3 *carbohydrate*
Aldebaran 53 Named Stars

aldehyde 57 Types of Compounds
al dente 45.56 *culinary*
alder 85 Trees and Shrubs
alderfly 82 Insects
alderman 653.16 *official*
aldermanic board 16.2 *jurisdiction,* 653.9 *US administrative council,* 706.2 *representative body*
Alderney 98 Islands
Aldington 48 Writers
Aldiss 48 Writers
aldoheptose 58.3 *carbohydrate*
aldohexose 57 Types of Compounds, 58.3 *carbohydrate*
aldol 57 Types of Compounds
aldonic acid 58.3 *carbohydrate*
aldooctose 58.3 *carbohydrate*
aldopentose 57 Types of Compounds, 58.3 *carbohydrate*
aldose 57 Types of Compounds, 58.3 *carbohydrate*
aldosterone 58 Hormones
aldotetrose 58.3 *carbohydrate*
aldotriose 58.3 *carbohydrate*
Aldrich 48 Writers
aldrin 68.14 *pest control*
ale 351.7 *alcoholic drink*
aleatoric 108.7 *illogical,* 229.6 *motiveless,* 491.8 *capricious,* 589.8 *chance*
aleatorics 589.7 *calculation of chance*
aleatory 229.6 *motiveless,* 589.8 *chance*
alehead 351.12 *drinker,* 874 17 *drunkard*
Alekhine 18 Sporting Personalities
Alemannic 5 Languages and Groups of Languages
alembic 57 Laboratory Apparatus, 220.4 *medium of conversion*
Alen 93 Cities
alenu 10.9 *prayer*
Aleppo 93 Cities
alerce 85 Trees and Shrubs
alert 380.5 *mentally sharp,* 459.10 *intelligent,* 467.7 *watchful,* 469.9 *careful,* 507.6 *intelligent,* 528.18 *informed,* 543.12 *signal,* 594.18 *prepared,* 636.2 *danger signal,* 636.5 *warn,* 636.7 *raise the alarm,* 642.18 *active,* 781.4 *cautious*
alertly 380.18 *sharply,* 459.15 *intelligently,* 467.15 *attentively,* 469.12 *carefully*
alertness 380.13 *mental sharpness,* 459.4 *cleverness,* 467.2 *close attention,* 469.3 *circumspection,* 781.1 *caution*
Aleut 1 Peoples, **5** Languages and Groups of Languages
alevin 80.3 *young fish*
alewife 80 Fishes, 606.4 *caterer*
Alexander of Hales 4 Philosophers
Alexandria 93 Cities
Alexandrine 48.9 *metre*
alexandrite 54 Gemstones
Alfa 534 Phonetic Alphabet
alfalfa 84 Flowers and Flowering Plants, 68.12 *crop,* 350.8 *animal food*
alfar 11.11 *ghost*
al-Farabi 4 Philosophers
al fine 49 Musical Terms
alfresco 289.7 *outside,* 289.15 *externally,* 390.16 *open-air,* 390.26 *out-of-doors*
Alfvén 52 Scientists
alga 90, 83.4 *lower plant,* 88.3 *moss*
algae 90, 396.9 *classifications of life*
Algae and Lichens 90
Algahom Naum 8 Deities
algal 90
algal bloom 90.1 *alga*
algal constituent 90.6 *lichen*
algal pigment 90.3 *plant body*
algal product 90
algebra 52, 52.1 *mathematics,* 170.1 *calculation*

algebraic 52.68, 170.15 *mathematical*
algebraically 170.16 *mathematically*
algebraic expression 52
algebraic geometry 52.34 *geometry*
algebraic number 52.6 *complex number*, 169.2 *kind of number*
algebraic operation 52.14 *operation*
algebraic topology 52.47 *topology*
algebraist 52.2, 170.7 *mathematician*
algebra of propositions 52.23 *algebra*
Algeiba 53 Named Stars
Algenib 53 Named Stars
Algeria 91 Countries
alghaita 49 Musical Instruments
al-Ghazālī 4 Philosophers
algicide 398.14 *plant killer*
algid 409.8 *cold*
algidity 409.2 *freezing*
Algiers 93 Cities
algin 90.5 *algal product*
alginate 90.5 *algal product*
algoid 90.7 *algal*
Algol 53 Named Stars, **65** Programming Languages
algological 90.7 *algal*
algologically 90, 83.25 *botanically*
algologist 83.12 *plant scientist*, 90.2 *algae*
algology 59.1 *life science*, 83.10 *plant science*, 90.2 *algae*
Algol variable 53.12 *variable star*
algometer 268.8 *meter*
algometry 268.2 *micrometry*
Algonquian 5 Languages and Groups of Languages
Algonquin 1 Peoples, **5** Languages and Groups of Languages, **7** Non-Christian Religions
algophobia 777 Phobias by Name
algorithm 52, 65.17 *computing term*, 170.1 *calculation*, 327.1 *way*
algorithmic 169.8 *odd*, 170.15 *mathematical*
Algren 48 Writers
Ali 18 Sporting Personalities
alias 529.8 *anonymity*, 531.7 *concealer*, 560.8 *name*
alibi 855.2 *defence*, 855.8 *justify*
Alicante 93 Cities
Alice Springs 93 Cities
Alicia Markova 46.14 *famous ballet dancers*
a lick and a promise 685.1 *non-completion*
alicyclic 57.7 *chemical compound*, 57.35 *combined*
alidade 63.17 *civil engineering*, 268.8 *meter*
alien 11.11 *ghost*, 11.18 *spiritual*, 53.34 *SETI* , 83.15 *wild*, 104.6 *outsider*, 104.10 *foreign*, 108.3 *unconnected person*, 108.6 *unrelated*, 117.6 *misfit*, 117.7 *disparate*, 117.11 *unfit*, 136.17 *unjoined*, 147.5 *excluded person*, 149.4 *foreigner*, 149.5 *extraterrestrial*, 149.11 *foreign*, 149.12 *extraterrestrial*, 201.8 *new arrival*, 289.10 *extraneous*, 663.19 *oppositional*, 666.10 *different*, 822.12 *hated*
alienage 104.2 *foreignness*
alienate 136.11 *divide*, 820.13 *antagonize*, 822.16 *cause hate*
alienated 510.11 *insane*, 820.8 *estranged*
alienation 61.13 *depression*, 61.19 *defence mechanism*, 220.2 *evolution*, 727.1 *disposal*, 820.2 *personal conflict*, 822.4 *hatefulness*
alienation effect 51.7 *dramaturgy*
alien encounter 11.10 *psychic phenomenon*
alienism 104.2 *foreignness*
alienist 61.30 *psychiatrist*, 630.15 *healer*

alienness 149.3 *foreignness*
alif 5.36 *accent*
a life sentence 188.5 *long duration*
a lifetime 188.5 *long duration*
alight 325.8 *be motionless*, 344.4 *land*, 360.9 *descend*, 362.8 *sit*, 408.10 *on fire*, 439.16 *bright*
alight upon 360.12 *drop*
align 52, 112.10 *conform*, 116.26 *make uniform*, 150.18 *order*, 152.12 *arrange*, 159.16 *arrange consecutively*, 167.9 *make conform*, 285.6 *correlate*
aligned 112.6 *conforming*, 152.20 *arranged*, 285.4 *correlated*, 332.11 *directed*
aligned wheels 285.2 *parallel thing*
alignment 152.1 *arrangement*, 285.1 *parallelism*, 332.3 *orientation*, 664.7 *association*
align oneself 665.14 *be a party member*
align one's march 332.7 *take a direction*
align with 662.24 *back*, 664.14 *join with*
alike 110.14 *lookalike*, 110.18 *identically*, 112.5 *uniform*, 114.7 *similar*, 482.5 *vague*
alikeness 114.1 *similarity*
aliment 350.7 *food*, 350.25 *provide food*, 662.4 *social assistance*, 725.6 *marriage settlement*, 749.3 *income*
alimental 350.27 *edible*
alimentary 59.22 *physiological*, 322.15 *providing passage*, 350.27 *edible*, 630.17 *remedial*
alimentary canal 322.7 *passageway*
alimentation 350.7 *food*
alimony 284.7 *financial support*, 662.4 *social assistance*, 721.4 *earnings*, 725.6 *marriage settlement*, 729.2 *gift*, 730.2 *something received*, 749.3 *income*, 824.3 *divorce court*
A-line 295.31 *styled*
A-line skirt 295.6 *skirt*
Alioth 53 Named Stars
aliphatic 57.7 *chemical compound*, 57.35 *combined*
aliquant 143.1 *part*
aliquot 143.1 *part*, 143.11 *partial*, 169.9 *fractional*
aliquot part 52.18 *division*
a little 121.11 *to a degree*, 143.12 *partly*, 182.1, 182.5 *few*
a little at a time 121.10 *by degrees*, 143.12 *partly*
a little something 729.2 *gift*
alive 396, 59.21 *living*, 637.7 *preserved*, 642.18 *active*
alive and kicking 396.12 *alive*, 629.15 *cured*, 642.18 *active*
alive to 403.5 *sensible*
alive to opportunity 597.6 *enterprising*
alive with 144.8 *full*
alizarin 450.6 *red pigment*
alizarin crimson 450.6 *red pigment*
alizarin dye 67.6 *dye*
alkahest 387.9 *solvent*
Alkaid 53 Named Stars
alkali 57.9 *base*
alkali feldspar 54.34 *mineral*
alkali metal 57.6 *chemical element*
alkalimeter 268.8 *meter*
alkalimetric 268.16 *micrometric*
alkalimetry 268.2 *micrometry*
alkaline 57.36 *acid*
alkaline battery 64.29 *power source*
alkaline-earth element 57.6 *chemical element*
alkaloid 57 Types of Compounds, **58**, 62.4 *drug type*
alkane 57 Types of Compounds
alkanet 84 Flowers and Flowering Plants
Alka Seltzer 62 Medication
alkene 57 Types of Compounds
al-Khwarizmi 52 Scientists

alkie 351.12 *drinker*
Al-Kindi 4 Philosophers
alkoxide 57 Types of Compounds
alkylating agent 62.4 *drug type*
alkyl halide 57 Types of Compounds
alkyne 57 Types of Compounds, **57** Types of Compounds
all 142, 120.4 *total*, 120.6 *quantitative*, 142.6 *whole*, 164.10 *everyone*
alla caccia 49 Musical Terms
alla cappella 49 Musical Terms
all agog 786.7 *wide-eyed*
Allah 8.3 *God*
Allahabad 93 Cities
Allah be praised 837.9 *thank you*
all along 185.26 *all the time*
allamanda 84 Flowers and Flowering Plants
all-American 237.5 *athlete*, 617.1 *worthy*
All-American 19.2 *football player*, 22.2 *baseball player*, 23.2 *basketball player*, 655.4 *skilled person*
all and sundry 113.6 *assorted*, 164.10 *everyone*
all and then some 161.20 *crowd*, 164.10 *everyone*
allanite 54 Minerals
allantoic 59.26 *developmental*
allantois 59.15 *developmental biology*
all anyhow 151.28 *anyhow*
allargando 49 Musical Terms, 328.17 *in slow motion*
all around 144.9 *completely*, 248.16 *extensively*, 293.42 *inclusively*
all-around 30.11 *gymnastic*, 113.5 *diverse*
All-Around Champion 32.12 *rodeo*
All-Around Cow Horse 32.12 *rodeo*
all around the houses 314.8 *circularly*
Allat 8 Deities
all at sea 123.7 *unequally*, 722.18 *at a loss*
Allatu 8 Deities
allay 242.4 *moderate*, 376.13 *smooth over*, 677.4 *pacify*, 767.9 *relieve*
all but 142.13 *on the whole*, 143.5 *largest part*, 264.7 *nearly*, 620.11 *imperfectly*
all but the kitchen sink 143.5 *largest part*
all by oneself 174.21 *alone*
all clear 453.15 *green light*, 632.1 *safety*
all-clear siren 543.4 *signal*
all colours of the rainbow 113.2 *assortment*
all-comers 663.8 *the opposition*, 674.10 *contender*
all-comprehending 164.15 *general*
all concerned 400.7 *person*
all-consuming 244.14 *destructive*, 574.2 *tenacious*
all-covering 164.15 *general*
all-devouring 872.6 *gluttonous*
all ears 420.11 *aural*, 467.8 *diligent*
Allecto 828.7 *gods and goddesses of anger*
allegate 856.5 *accuse*
allegation 535.1 *affirmation*, 564.7 *utterance*, 856.1 *accusation*
allege 483.11 *give evidence*, 535.17 *affirm*, 564.11 *speak*
alleged 497.14 *believed*, 518.8 *supposed*, 535.11 *stated*, 800.4 *reputed*, 856.8 *accusatory*
allegedly 102.19 *apparently*, 497.16 *believably*, 518.10 *supposedly*, 535.23 *affirmatively*, 856.10 *accusingly*
Allegheny 95 Mountains
Allegheny Mountains 95.4 *US mountains*
allegiance 847, 694.2 *loyalty*, 701.1 *subjection*
alleging 856.8 *accusatory*

allegorical 48.17 *fictional*, 109.6 *correlative*, 520.6 *meaningful*, 527.5 *mysterious*
allegorically 109.11 *correlatively*
allegorical meaning 520.4 *type of meaning*
allegorist 48.14 *author*
allegorization 524.1 *interpretation*
allegory 109.3 *correlation*, 114.1 *similarity*, 473.4 *gist*, 527.6 *latency*, 527.11 *mysteriousness*, 560.3 *narration*
allegretto 49 Musical Terms
allegro 49 Musical Terms, 329.14 *swiftly*, 648.3 *hasty*
allele 59.13 *genetic material*
alleluia 431.3 *cry of praise*
Alleluia 10.8 *hymn*
allemande 46.4 *historic dancing*
all-embracing 142.6 *whole*, 144.7 *complete*, 146.7 *including*, 164.15 *general*, 482.4 *wholesale*
all-encompassing 164.15 *general*
All-England Championships 40.1 *tennis*
All England Women's Hockey Association 31.1 *hockey*
allergic 403.7 *susceptible*, 624.23 *diseased*, 760.3 *sore*, 785.8 *disliking*
allergy 403.2 *ability to sense*, 624.1 *ill health*, 760.7 *soreness*, 785.1 *dislike*
allerome 59.14 *chromosome*
Allervale pottery 44 Types of Ceramics
alleviate 129.5 *make smaller*, 131.3 *subtract*, 242.4 *moderate*, 370.10 *lighten*, 376.13 *smooth over*, 405.10 *comfort*, 627.1 *improve*, 630.19 *remedy*, 649.3 *ease*, 660.18 *disentangle*, 662.19 *support*, 677.4 *pacify*, 767.9 *relieve*
alleviating 370.3 *lightening*
alleviation 131.1 *subtraction*, 242.1 *moderation*, 370.6 *lightening*, 627.5 *improvement*, 767.1 *ease*
alleviative 242.2 *moderator*, 242.8 *moderating*, 370.3 *lightening*
alley 18.2 *sportsground*, 327.3 *road*, 327.11 *channel*
alley cat 133.5 *hybrid*
alley-oop! 359
alleyway 327.3 *road*
all fingers and thumbs 559.7 *graceless*
all-flying tail 73 Aircraft Parts
all for one, one for all 664.20 *cooperatively*
all found 606.8 *provisional*
all fours 42 Card Games
all gone 172.6 *zero*
all Greek 502.3 *unknown thing*
All Hallows' Day 10.15 *holy day*
all hands 164.10 *everyone*
all hands on deck 639.5 *to the rescue*
all hands to the pump 639.5 *to the rescue*
all-healing 630.17 *remedial*
all hell let loose 151.5 *confusion*, 151.9 *disorder*, 423.2 *outcry*
alliance 116, 715, 823, 107.1 *relatedness*, 135.1 *union*, 140.2 *cooperation*, 664.7 *association*, 665.1 *party*, 665.3 *political grouping*, 715.1 *contract*, 724.1 *joint possession*, 823.1 *marriage*
alliance of states 400.11 *nation*
allied 116, 107.4 *related*, 114.7 *similar*, 140.8 *cooperative*, 664.19 *associating*, 715.7 *contractual*
Allied Artists Association 50 Schools and Groups of Artists
allied forces 679.14 *armed forces*
allied operation 676.8 *warfare*
Allier 96 Rivers
alligator 79 Reptiles, 79.5 *crocodilian*
alligator pear 86 Fruits
all impatience 648.3 *hasty*

all in 236.12 *impotent*, 650.1 *fatigued*
all-in 26.15 *wrestling*, 144.7 *complete*, 146.7 *including*, 606.8 *provisional*
all in a day's work 787.4 *predictable*, 787.10 *predictably*
all in all 124.11 *on average*, 142.13 *on the whole*, 144.9 *completely*, 164.31 *overall*
all-inclusive 142.6 *whole*, 144.7 *complete*, 146.7 *including*, 164.15 *general*, 482.4 *wholesale*
Allingham 48 Writers
all-in wrestling 26.5, 674.8 *wrestling*
alliterate 114.12 *imitate*, 116.24 *harmonize*, 183.22 *resound*
alliterating 183.15 *reverberatory*
alliteration 48.12 *poetic language*, 116.4 *harmony*, 183.6 *reverberation*, 557.1 *ornament*
alliterative 48.20 *metrical*, 114.7 *similar*, 116.13 *harmonious*, 183.15 *reverberatory*, 557.4 *ornate*
alliteratively 114.14 *comparably*
Alliterative Revival 48 Literary Groups and Movements
alliterative verse 48.10 *verse form*
allium 84 Flowers and Flowering Plants
all-knowing 8.13 *divine*, 501.8 *knowledgeable*
all mixed up together 482.14 *indiscriminately*
all mouth 565.6 *effusive*
all mouth and trousers 797.3 *affected*
all my eye 538.4 *lie*
all my own work 119.1 *originality*
allocate 120.8 *quantify*, 124.10 *make average*, 152.12 *arrange*, 599.5 *dispose of*, 731.4 *allot*
allocated 731
allocation 731, 731.2 *portion*
Allocation 731
allocation of work 15.2 *industrial negotiations*
allocution 10.9 *prayer*, 567.1 *address*
allodial 725.8 *propertied*
allodium 725.3 *historic property terms*
all of 120.7 *quantitatively*
all of a flutter 366.16 *restless*
all of a piece 116.14 *conforming*, 134.16 *simple*, 142.6 *whole*
all of a sudden 270.12 *short*
all of a tizz 366.16 *restless*
all of a twitter 366.28 *shakily*
all off 157.22 *cancelled*
allogamy 133.1 *mixture*
all one 110.12 *same*, 122.8 *on equal terms*
all one can manage 659.9 *difficult person*
all one's worldly goods and chattels 723.4 *possession*
all on one's lonesome 698.20 *freely*
allonym 560.8 *name*
allopath 630.15 *healer*
allopathic 60.22, 630.18 *medical*
allopathic medicine 60.1 *medicine*
allopathy 60.8 *treatment*, 630.11 *medical art*
allophane 54 Minerals
allopolyploidy 59.14 *chromosome*
allopurinol 62 Medication
allosaur 79 Fossil Reptiles
allot 731, 120.8 *quantify*, 268.11 *measure out*, 302.7 *limit*, 599.1 *use*, 599.5 *dispose of*, 699.8 *restrain*, 725.9 *own property*, 729.5 *give*
allot a billet 731.6 *assign*
allotheism 9.2 *idolatry*
allotheist 9.6 *idolater*
allotheistic 9.10 *idolatrous*
allotment 69.2 *garden*, 143.7 *piece*, 249.12 *plot*, 302.2 *limiting factor*, 699.1 *restraint*, 725.1 *property*, 725.6 *marriage settlement*, 729.2 *gift*, 731.1 *allocation*, 731.2 *portion*
allotropic 113.6 *assorted*

allotropy 113.2 *assortment*
allotted 725.8 *propertied*, 730.11 *receiving*, 731.7 *allocated*
allotted days 396.5 *life cycle*
allotted span 185.3 *duration*, 207.5 *old age*, 396.5 *life cycle*
allotted task 731
allotting 731.1 *allocation*
allottee 730.5 *recipient*
all out 239.6 *with vigour*, 329.14 *swiftly*, 574.2 *tenacious*, 598.9 *forget it*
all-out 144.7 *complete*, 329.1 *swift*
all-out war 666.2 *argument*, 676.1 *war*
all over 100.11 *no more*, 151.28 *anyhow*, 157.21 *ended*, 248.16 *extensively*
all-over 253.7 *present*
all over again 201.22 *again*
all over and done with 100.11 *no more*
all over bar the shouting 157.21 *ended*
all over hell 248.16 *extensively*
all over the lot 162.25 *sprawled*
all over the map 248.16 *extensively*
all over the place 113.11 *irregularly*, 151.28 *anyhow*
all over the shop 151.28 *anyhow*, 248.16 *extensively*
allow 16.65 *make legal*, 116.29 *permit*, 131.3 *subtract*, 146.4 *include*, 485.15 *modify*, 486.7 *make possible*, 499.4 *assent*, 530.8 *admit*, 660.16 *make easy*, 673.3 *submit*, 688.21 *grant authority*, 691.3 *be lenient*, 708.3 *permit*, 845.16 *entitle*
allowable 16.44 *legal*, 708.8 *permitting*, 855.13 *vindicable*
allow access 348.7 *admit*
allowance 116.8 *permit*, 125.2 *counterbalance*, 131.2 *subtracted item*, 146.1 *inclusion*, 284.7 *financial support*, 485.5 *modification*, 662.6 *financial assistance*, 691.1 *leniency*, 721.5 *profit*, 725.6 *marriage settlement*, 729.2 *gift*, 730.2 *something received*, 731.2 *portion*, 741.4 *change*, 749.3 *income*, 752.1 *discount*, 855.2 *defence*, 878.3 *grant*
allow credit 732.5 *lend*
allowed 116.18 *permitting*, 146.8 *included*, 485.10, 688.16 *authorized*, 691.5 *given consideration*, 708.7 *permitted*, 845.8 *entitled*
allowed in 346.15 *entering*
allow enough rope 698.15 *set free*
allow for 146.4 *include*, 855.7 *vindicate*
allow full play 698.15 *set free*
allow in 348.7 *admit*, 734.11 *be hospitable*
allowing 106.15 *under the circumstances*, 116.18 *permitting*, 146.7 *including*, 708.8 *permitting*
allowing no delay 191
allowing no time 648.3 *hasty*
allow initiative 698.15 *set free*
allow no appeal 690.5 *be severe*
allow no rest 650.6 *fatigue*
allow no time 648.1 *hasten*
allow one's mind to wander 468.12 *be inattentive*
allow rest 651.1 *refresh*
allow someone to take liberties 708.4 *be permissive*
allow the occasion to go by 211.6 *lose one's chance*
allow to have the run of 708.4 *be permissive*
alloy 57.7 *chemical compound*, 57.30 *extract*, 133.2 *mixed thing*, 133.8 *mix*, 140.4 *compound*, 628.3 *make worse*

alloyed 57.45 *metallurgical*, 133.12 *mixed*
alloy extractive metallurgy 57.23 *metallurgy*
alloy steel 57 Alloys
all-pervading 133.12 *mixed*, 164.15 *general*, 233.13 *dominant*
all-pervasive 253.7 *present*
all piss and wind 797.3 *affected*
Allport-Vernon draw-a-person test 61.5 *psychological test*
Allport-Vernon study of values 61.5 *psychological test*
all-powerful 8.13 *divine*
all-presence 253.2 *omnipresence*
all-present 253.7 *present*
All-pro 655.4 *skilled person*
All-Pro 19.2 *football player*, 23.2 *basketball player*
all-purpose 613.1 *useful*
all-red 26.15 *wrestling*
all right 843, 617.5 *not bad*, 617.11 *worthily*, 617.12 *fantastic*, 765.6 *satisfactory*, 783.10 *mediocre*
all round 144.9 *completely*, 297.8 *round*, 332.11 *in all directions*
all-round 113.5 *diverse*
all-round capacity 655.1 *skill*
all rounder 27.4 *team*, 175.5 *pluralist*, 237.5 *athlete*, 655.4 *skilled person*
all-round gymnast 30.9 *gymnasts*
all-round player 237.5 *athlete*
all round the globe 248.16 *extensively*
All Saints' Day 10.15 *holy day*
all seats taken 144.8 *full*
all-seeing 8.13 *divine*
all set 594.18 *prepared*
all shapes and sizes 113.2 *assortment*
all shipshape and Bristol fashion 150.13 *orderly*
all sorts 133.3 *miscellany*
all sorts and conditions 113.2 *assortment*
All Souls' Day 10.15 *holy day*
allspice 45 Herbs and Spices, 413.5 *herbs*
all square match 29.2 *golfing terms*
all-star 51.39 *stagestruck*, 617.1 *worthy*
All-Star 22.2 *baseball player*
All-Star Game 22.1 *baseball*
all steamed up 623.1 *healthy*
all straight 742.2 *solvent*
all-sufficing 606.7 *provisioning*, 608.1 *sufficient*
All's Well That Ends Well 48 Shakespeare's plays
all talk and no action 236.2 *futile effort*
all-terrain vehicle 68.10 *farm tool*
all that could be desired 608.7 *sufficiency*
all that goes with it 130.3 *additional item*
all that is left 132.1 *remainder*
all that is possible 608.7 *sufficiency*
all the best 686.10 *good luck*
all the better for 627.14 *improved*
all the market can bear 610.1 *excess*
all the more 126.17 *supremely*, 128.8 *increasingly*
all the perfumes of Arabia 418.2 *fragrant thing*
all the rage 201.16 *avant-garde*, 796.7 *fashionable*
all there 144.7 *complete*, 457.7 *appearing*, 507.6 *intelligent*, 509.4 *sane*, 843.12 *all right*
all the same 110.12 *same*, 122.8 *on equal terms*
all the time 185, 212.1 *frequently*, 219.7 *continually*
all the time in the world 641.1 *inaction*, 645.1 *leisure*
all the trimmings 130.3 *additional item*
all the way 144.9 *completely*

all the way across 271.8 *breadthwise*
all the world 142.4 *all*
all the world and his wife 161.20 *crowd*, 164.10 *everyone*
all things being equal 124.11 *on average*, 471.23 *ideally*
all things considered 124.11 *on average*, 142.13 *on the whole*, 164.31 *overall*, 488.11 *probably*, 492.14 *considering*
all through 185.26 *all the time*, 327.17 *via*
all through the night 205.7 *evening*
all thumbs 656.3 *clumsy*
all-time 617.2 *best*
all-time low 127.5 *inferior state*
all together 116.31 *in accord*, 135.16 *as one*, 142.12 *one and all*, 161.51, 180.21 *together*, 198.12 *simultaneously*
all told 144.9 *completely*
allude 518.6 *propound*, 527.14 *imply*
allude to 520.10 *mean*, 564.11 *speak*
all up 157.21 *ended*
allure 340.4 *allurement*, 340.12 *lure*, 586.3 *incentive*, 586.16 *tempt*, 782.15 *cause desire*, 821.28 *win the love of*
allurement 340, 228.2 *inducement*, 586.3 *incentive*, 784.1 *liking*, 821.4 *lovability*
alluring 228.11 *motivational*, 340.9 *attractive*, 586.19 *persuasive*, 784.5 *likable*, 821.20 *amorous*, 821.22 *lovable*
alluringly 228.14 *influentially*, 821.30 *lovingly*
allusion 551.1 *obscurity*
allusive 518.7 *suppositional*, 520.6 *meaningful*, 527.4 *unsaid*, 551.2 *obscure*
allusively 551.4 *obscurely*
allusory 527.4 *unsaid*
alluvial 54.52 *coastal*, 98.11 *continental*
alluvial deposit 54.27 *sediment*
alluvial plain 98.6 *lowland*
alluvion 326.10 *transferred thing*
alluvium 54.36 *soil*, 96.6 *river flow*, 132.2 *residue*, 326.10 *transferred thing*
all wind and water 797.3 *affected*
all wool and a yard wide 537.6 *authenticity*
all wrapped up in oneself 809.10 *self-admiring*
all wrong 504.17 *mistaken*, 862.12 *evilly*
ally 91.3 *dominion*, 116.22 *form an alliance*, 137.3 *associate*, 140.6 *come together*, 284.8 *supporter*, 499.3 *assenter*, 535.9 *affirmer*, 662.11 *helper*, 664.10 *cooperator*, 664.16 *join*, 665.15 *politicize*, 715.5 *contract*, 724.3 *participant*, 823.19 *merge*
allylestrenol 62 Medication
ally with 662.24 *back*, 664.14 *join with*
Alma-Ata 93 Cities
Almach 53 Named Stars
almanac 171.3 *dictionary*, 517.3 *plan*, 528.5 *reference book*, 605.5 *collection*
almandine 54 Gemstones
almightily 8.19 *divinely*
almightiness 8.2 *divine attribute*
almighty 8.13 *divine*, 235.13 *powerful*, 259.15 *big*
almighty dollar 741.7 *finance*
Almighty God 8.3 *God*
Almohades 7 Non-Christian Religions
almond 85 Trees and Shrubs, **86** Nuts
almoner 7.8 *priest*, 729.4 *giver*, 741.18 *treasurer*, 831.5 *benevolent person*, 833.3 *philanthropist*
almonry 741.19 *treasury*
Almoravides 7 Non-Christian Religions
almost 52.87 *mathematically*,

142.13 *on the whole*, 264.7 *nearly*, 620.11 *imperfectly*
almost all 143.5 *largest part*
almost always 164.30 *usually*
almost entirely 103.13 *in essence*
almost none 182.1 *few*
almost the same way 114.14 *comparably*
almost unheard-of 213.2 *infrequent*
almost win 722.9 *lose*
alms 729.3 *offering*, 755.7 *gift*, 767.4 *charity*, 831.4 *benevolent act*
almsgiver 729.4 *giver*, 831.5 *benevolent person*
almsgiving 10.3 *rite of worship*, 729.1 *giving*, 767.4 *charity*, 831.4 *benevolent act*
alms-giving 729.8 *giving*, 831.7 *charitable*, 833.6 *philanthropic*
almshouse 634.2 *shelter*
Alnico 57 Alloys
a load off one's mind 767.1 *ease*
aloes 62 Medication, 415.3 *sour thing*
aloft 36.10 *sailing*, 36.20 *offshore*, 95.11 *on the mountain*, 275.19 *high*, 361.13 *highly*
Alogi 7 Christian Movements
aloha 344.12 *reception*
Alombrados 7 Christian Movements
alone 174, **174**, 136.17 *unjoined*, 139.11 *aloofly*, 174.15 *solo*, 698.20 *freely*, 816.10 *lonely*, 820.14 *hostilely*
aloneness 174
along 269.12 *longitudinally*, 336.19 *forward*
a long haul 644.1 *work*
alongside 267.7 *beside*, 285.7 *in parallel*, 305.10 *laterally*
a long stretch 188.5 *long duration*
along these lines 327.16 *how*
a long time 190, 188.5 *long duration*
a long time ago 3.24 *historically*
a long way away 263.10 *distantly*
a long way off 263.10 *distantly*
along with 130.10 *additionally*, 180.24 *with*
aloof 139, 136.22 *in isolation*, 168.16 *solitary*, 174.16 *alone*, 263.9 *reserved*, 263.10 *distantly*, 466.4 *uninterested*, 531.16 *silent*, 591.21 *away*, 598.6 *apathetic*, 783.7 *indifferent*, 805.15 *unapproachable*, 816.8 *unsociable*, 820.6 *hostile*
aloofly 139, 263.11 *reservedly*, 783.17 *indifferently*, 816.14 *unsocially*
aloofness 139, 174.5 *aloneness*, 263.1 *distance*, 263.4 *reserve*, 591.10 *avoidance*, 783.1 *indifference*, 816.1 *unsociability*
alopecia 294.6, 296.5 *baldness*, 296.7 *depilation*
a lot 181.2 *multitude*
a lot to ask 597.2 *undertaking*
aloud 423, 420.17 *aurally*
aloxiprin 62 Medication
alp 95.1, 275.3 *mountain*
alpaca 67 Natural Fabrics, **77** Placental Mammals, 288.4 *textile*
alpenstock 284.3 *body support*
alpestrine 95.7, 275.13 *mountainous*
Alpha and Omega 8.3 *God*, 142.4 *all*
alphabet 5
alphabetic 5.41 *lettered*
alphabetical 150.12 *hierarchical*
alphabetically 5.48 *linguistically*, 150.25 *in order*, 171.13 *inventorially*
alphabetical order 150.3 *hierarchy*
alphabetization 152.5 *categorization*
alphabetize 5.47 *word*, 152.15 *categorize*
alphabetized 152.24 *categorized*
Alpha Centauri 53 Named Stars

Alpha Crucis 53 Named Stars
alpha decay 56.70 *radioactivity*
alpha emitter 56.70 *radioactivity*
alpha-fetoprotein test 245.7 obstetrics
alpha-helix 58.9 *protein*
alpha-naphthol test 58.5 *sugar test*
alphanumeric character 65.10 *character*
alpha particle 56.70 *radioactivity*
alpha plus 617.1 *worthy*
alpha rays 56.70 *radioactivity*
Alphard 53 Named Stars
alpha rhythm 214.2 *cycle*
alpha-sorting 152.5 *categorization*
alpha test 61.6 *intelligence test*
alpha to omega 146.9 *inclusively*
alpha wave 214.2 *cycle*
Alpher 52 Scientists
Alpheratz 53 Named Stars
Alphonsus 53 Lunar Features
alphorn 49 Musical Instruments
alpigene 95.7 *mountainous*
alpine 41.12 *ski*, 69.9 *garden plant*, 69.19 *ornamental*, 95.7, 275.13 *mountainous*
Alpine 1.13 *racial*
alpine chain 54.21 *mountain building*
alpine climbing 18 Sporting Activities
Alpine Club 34.6 *mountaineering association*
Alpine Club of Canada 34.6 *mountaineering association*
Alpine combined event 18 Sporting Activities
alpine garden 69.2 *garden*
alpine glacier 54.38 *glacier*
alpine race 41.3 *ski racing*
alpine racing 41.3 *ski racing*
alpine ski 41.5 *ski equipment*, 41.14 *ski*
alpine skiing 41.1 *skiing*
Alpine skiing 18 Sporting Activities
Alpine type 1.6 *race*
Alpine Valley 53 Rills and Valleys
alpinism 34.1 *mountaineering*, 359.6 *mounting*
alpinist 34.7 *mountaineer*, 359.11 *ascender*
Alpinist 95.3 *mountaineer*
alprenolol 62 Medication
Alps 53 Mountains, **95** Mountains, 95.6 *other major mountains and ranges*, 275.4 *mountain range*
already 200.23 *before now*
alright 124.3 *mediocre*
alright? 344.23 *hello*
Alsatian 77 Breeds of Dogs
al segno 49 Musical Terms
alsike 84 Flowers and Flowering Plants
also 130.10 *additionally*
also-ran 32.7 *horseracing*, 127.6 *inferior*, 195.8 *follower*, 580.13 *electorate*, 674.10 *contender*, 683.5 *failing person*
Altai 95 Mountains
Altaic 5 Languages and Groups of Languages
Altair 53 Named Stars
Altai Scarp 53 Mountains
altar 10.12 *church*
Altar 53 The Constellations
altarpiece 50.8 *painting*
altazimuth mounting 53.25 *mounting*
alter 131.4 *take off*, 201.20 *make new*, 216.7 *be changed*, 216.8 *cause change*, 220.7 *convert into*, 485.15 *modify*, 627.3 *rectify*
alterability 113.1 *diversity*
alterable 201.15 *renewable*, 216.11 *changeable*, 220.15 *convertible*, 224.13 *changeable*
alterably 216.15, 224.15 *changeably*
alteration 201.5 *fresh start*, 216.1 *change*, 220.1 *conversion*, 485.5 *modification*, 627.6 *rectification*

alteration of plan 578.6 *equivocation*
altercate 473.13 *argue*, 666.5 *disagree*
altercation 473.1 *argument*, 500.1 *dissent*, 666.1 *disagreement*, 674.1 *contention*, 764.8 *quarrel*
altered 201.14 *renewed*, 216.12 *changed*, 485.11 *modified*
alter ego 109.2 *interconnection*, 110.3 *lookalike*, 114.5 *counterpart*, 116.5 *conformity*, 165.11 *identity*, 819.6 *close friend*
alterer 216.6 *editor*
alter from one's course 335.1 *deviate*
altering 131.1 *subtraction*, 220.14 *converting*
alternate 155, 109.4 *reciprocal*, 109.7 *reciprocate*, 155.16 *alternating*, 160.8 *discontinuous*, 195.12 *succeeding*, 214.7 *be regular*, 214.11 *regular*, 216.10 *exchange*, 222.2 *substitute person*, 222.7 *substitute*, 224.11 *be changeable*, 293.21 *substitution*, 293.34 *cover for*, 365.8 *oscillate*, 365.13 *oscillating*, 707.2 *alternative*
alternate angles 52.39 *angle*
alternate breathing 39.2 *swimming technique*
alternately 155.27 *in sequence*, 214.15 *regularly*
alternating 155, 109.4 *reciprocal*, 160.8 *discontinuous*, 214.11 *regular*, 224.13 *changeable*, 365.13 *oscillating*
alternating current 56.51, 64.9 *electric current*, 214.5 *regular thing*, 235.7 *electrical power*
alternating personality 61.8 *disordered personality*, 61.16 *dissociation*
alternating voltage 64.10 *electric potential*
alternation 52.63 *mathematical logic*, 107.2 *interrelatedness*, 109.1 *interchange*, 155.2 *series*, 214.1 *regularity*, 216.4 *exchange*, 222.1 *substitution*, 224.1 *changeableness*, 365.1 *oscillation*
alternative 707, 109.4 *reciprocal*, 214.11 *regular*, 222.1 *substitution*, 222.7 *substitute*, 293.21 *substitution*, 293.40 *substitutive*, 365.13 *oscillating*, 580.8 *choice*, 602.1 *means*
alternative choice 222.1 *substitution*
alternative comedian 771.6 *humorist*
alternative comedy 51.10 *comedy*
alternative hypothesis 52.54 *hypothesis testing*
alternatively 293, 109.10 *reciprocally*, 214.15 *regularly*, 222.9 *instead*, 224.15 *changeably*, 580.17 *selectively*
alternative medicine 60.2 *natural medicine*, 630.11 *medical art*
alternative practitioner 60.12 *healer*
Alternative Prayer Book 10.10 *religious manual*
alternative reading 524.1 *interpretation*
alternative route 356.2 *passing along*
alternative theatre 51.1 *drama*
alternator 71 Motor Vehicle Parts, 64.30 *generator*, 235.6 *source of energy*
Alter-Réal 32 Breeds of Horse and Pony
althaea 84 Flowers and Flowering Plants
although 231.5 *counter*, 518.11 *supposing*
Althusser 4 Philosophers
altimeter 73 Aircraft Parts, **56**, 268.8 *meter*, 275.5 *height measure*
altimetric 275, 268.16 *micrometric*

altimetry 268.2 *micrometry*, 275.5 *height measure*
altitude 52.37 *line*, 52.43 *triangle*, 53.5 *celestial sphere*, 56.7 *space*, 120.1 *quantity*, 121.1 *degree*, 126.1 *superiority*, 251.1 *situation*, 268.4 *size*, 275.1 *height*
altitudinal 275.9 *high*
altitudinous 95.7 *mountainous*, 275.9 *high*
alto 49.32 *instrumental*, 433.5 *melodist*
alto clef 49.17 *notation*
altocumuliform 55.49 *cloudy*
altocumulous 55.49 *cloudy*
altocumulus 55.18 *cloud*
altogether 124.11 *on average*, 135.16 *as one*, 142.12 *one and all*, 142.13 *on the whole*, 144.9 *completely*, 621.20 *clean*
altohorn 49 Musical Instruments
alto-relievo 767.6 *profile*
altostratous 55.49 *cloudy*
altostratus 55.18 *cloud*
altricial 78.24 *newly hatched*
altruism 4.7 *school of thought*, 831.2 *charity*, 833.1 *philanthropy*, 859.2 *unselfishness*, 863.1 *virtue*
altruist 4.11 *follower of a doctrine*, 710.8 *volunteer*, 831.5 *benevolent person*, 833.3 *philanthropist*, 861.15 *good person*, 863.4 *virtuous person*
altruistic 4.14 *of a philosophy*, 710.18 *voluntary*, 831.7 *charitable*, 833.6 *philanthropic*, 859.5 *unselfish*, 863.5 *virtuous*
altruistically 710.20 *persuasively*, 831.11 *charitably*, 833.8 *philanthropically*, 859.9 *unselfishly*, 863.9 *virtuously*
ALU 65.5 *processor*
aludel 57 Laboratory Apparatus
alula 78.11 *plumage*
alum 57 Common Chemical Compounds, 57.10 *salt*
alumina 57 Common Chemical Compounds
aluminate 57 Types of Compounds
aluminiferous 57.34 *elemental*
aluminium 57 Chemical Elements, 43.4 *building material*, 64.3 *electricity*, 373.7 *hard substance*
aluminium alloy 63.25 *construction material*, 74.4 *shipbuilding*
aluminium bronze 57 Alloys
aluminium coating 56.29 *optical element*
aluminium foil 45.6 *kitchen equipment*, 293.4 *wrapping*
aluminous 57.34 *elemental*
alumna 6.7 *learner*
alumnus 6.7 *learner*
alunite 54 Minerals
Alvarez 52 Scientists
alveolar palate 564.5 *organ of speech*
alveolate 89.10 *of fungi*
alveoli 390.8 *respiration*
always 110.20 *regularly*, 112.13 *uniformly*, 116.35 *consistently*, 185.26 *all the time*, 186.8 *ever*, 217.9 *permanently*, 219.7 *continually*
always ill 624.21 *unhealthy*
always the bridesmaid but never the bride 195.7 *subordinate*
always the same 110.17 *regular*
always victorious 682.15 *victorious*
Alzheimer's disease 236.4 *disability*, 510.3 *mental deterioration*
a.m. 192.18 *horologically*, 204.1 *morning*
Amagat's experiments 56 Named Laws
amah 697.6 *domestic servant*
amain 329.14 *swiftly*
Amalekites 1 Peoples
amalgam 57 Alloys, 57.7 *chemi-*

cal compound, 133.2 mixed
thing, 140.4 compound
amalgamate 133.8 mix, 140.5
combine, 148.10 compose,
407.12 abut, 664.16 join,
823.19 merge
amalgamated 133.12 mixed,
140.9 assembled
amalgamation 133.1 mixture,
140.1 combination, 664.7 association, 823.2 alliance
Amalricianism 7 Christian Movements
amandine 45 Herbs and Spices
amanita 89 Fungi
a man of his word 225.5 stable
person
amantadine 62 Medication
amanuensis 232.3 assistant,
545.9 recorder
amaranth 455.2 purple pigment
amaranthine 455.6 purple
amaranthus 84 Flowers and
Flowering Plants
amarelle 86 Fruits
Amarillo 93 Cities
amaryllis 84 Flowers and Flowering Plants
Amaryllis 821.9 lover
amass 135.8 unite, 161.37 assemble, 605.6 store, 721.11 acquire
amassed 161.47 collected, 605.7
stored
amassment 721.3 acquisition
a match for 608.1 sufficient
Amaterasu-omikami 8 Deities
amateur 26.14 combat, 201.8
new arrival, 201.12 immature,
502.5 ignorant person, 502.7
semi-skilled, 656.2 unskilled,
656.4 bungled, 656.10 unskilled
person
amateur athlete 21.3, 237.5 athlete
**Amateur Athletic Union of the
United States** 30.4 gymnastic organization
amateur boxer 26.4 boxer
amateur dramatics 42 Hobbies
and Pastimes, 51.1 drama
amateurish 201.12 immature,
502.7 semi-skilled, 656.2 unskilled, 656.4 bungled
amateurishly 201.24 immaturely,
656.11 unskilfully
amateurishness 502.2 half-
knowledge
amateurism 502.2 half-knowledge, 656.8 unskilfulness
amateur radio 534.20 radio
broadcasting
amateur radio operator 534.29
broadcaster
amateur rowing 36.4 rowing
Amateur Swimming Association
39.5 swimming association
amateur theatricals 51.1 drama
amateur wrestler 26.6 wrestler
amateur wrestling 26.5 wrestling
amathophobia 777 Phobias by
Name
amative 821.17 loving
amativeness 821.3 lovingness
amatory 821.20 amorous
amaurosis 436.1 blindness
amaurotic 436.8 blind
amaze 514, 498.9 cause disbelief, 515.6 disappoint, 786.10 be
wonderful
amazed 514, 786.6 wondering
amazement 514, 498.3 incredulity, 786.1 wonder
amazing 514.8 surprising, 617.1
worthy, 786.8, 786.14 wonderful
amazingly 514.13 surprisingly,
786.13 wonderfully
amazing person 786.5 person of
wonder
amazon 237.6 muscleman,
259.10 big person
Amazon 96 Rivers, 96.5 other
major rivers, 241.4 violent person or animal, 275.7 tall person,
402.2 female, 679.10 woman
soldier
Amazon ant 82 Insects

Amazon Basin 408.8 hot place
amazonian 237.9 physically
strong
Amazonian 275.12 tall, 402.15
female
amazonite 54 Gemstones
Amazon lily 84 Flowers and
Flowering Plants
ambage 334.2 detour, 553.2 circumlocution
ambages 363.2 circuitousness
ambagious 334.7 circuitous,
363.9 orbital, 553.4 circumlocutory
ambarvalia 10.7 non-Christian
ritual
ambassador 547.8 representative,
653.16 official, 703.5 commissioner, 706.1 delegate, 707.3
agent, 716.4 negotiator
ambassadorial 703.9 commissioned, 706.6 delegated, 707.7
deputizing
ambatch 85 Trees and Shrubs
amber 54 Gemstones, 200.10
fossilization, 395.10 resin,
449.1 brown, 451.1 orange,
451.3 orange thing, 452.1 yellow, 452.8 yellow thing, 517.6
good-luck sign, 637.2 preserver
ambergris 418.3 incense
amberjack 80 Fishes
amber light 439.6 electric light,
451.3 orange thing, 543.4 signal, 636.2 danger signal
ambidexterity 176.3 duality,
538.7, 540.2 duplicity, 655.1
skill
ambidextrous 176.10 two-sided,
407.10 handed, 538.17, 540.26
duplicitous, 655.6 skilful
ambidextrously 538.28 dishonestly
ambidextrousness 655.1 skill
ambience 50.4 treatment, 297.3
atmosphere
ambient 297.6 atmospheric
ambient light 66.15 lighting
ambiguity 117.1 disparity, 176.3
duality, 443.8 obscurity, 477.7
questionableness, 491.14 indeterminacy, 504.11 grammatical
error, 520.3 comprehension,
523.11 unintelligibility, 538.8
pretence, 551.1 obscurity, 578.5
equivocalness, 666.3 difference
ambiguous 314, 117.7 disparate, 176.11 double-edged,
443.4 inscrutable, 477.14 questionable, 491.6 indeterminate,
520.6 meaningful, 523.4 difficult, 538.15 lying, 551.2 obscure, 578.10 equivocal, 666.10
different
ambiguously 117.15 dissimilarly,
314.8 circularly, 443.13
opaquely, 477.24 questionably,
491.25 indeterminately, 520.13
meaningfully, 538.27 pretentiously, 551.4 obscurely, 578.12
equivocally, 666.12 differently
ambiguousness 520.3 comprehension
ambiguous passage 520.3 comprehension
ambit 233.7 sphere of influence,
249.14 sphere, 313.2 circle,
315.6 round, 334.1 circuit,
363.3 orbit
ambition 228.1 motive, 513.2 expectations, 586.11 motive,
588.3 future intention, 642.4 energy, 775.3 aspiration, 782.1 desire, 815.2 social ambition,
860.1 selfishness
ambitious 588.11 intending,
596.8 attempting, 597.6 enterprising, 775.13 aspirant, 860.4
selfish
ambitiously 596, 597.9 enterprisingly, 775.15 hopefully,
860.8 selfishly
ambivalence 61.12 stress, 117.1
disparity, 176.3 duality, 491.11
irresoluteness, 538.8 pretence,
540.11 evasion, 578.5 equivocalness, 666.3 difference

ambivalent 117.7 disparate,
176.11 double-edged, 491.2 irresolute, 538.15 lying, 540.34
evasive, 578.10 equivocal,
666.10 different
ambivalently 117.15 dissimilarly,
538.27 pretentiously, 578.12
equivocally, 666.12 differently
ambiversion 61.7 personality type
ambivert 61.7 personality type
amble 324.12 gait, 324.15 walk,
328.1 move slowly, 328.10 slow
motion
ambler 32.4 saddle horse
ambling 328.4 slow
amblygonite 54 Minerals
amblyopia 436.2 poor sight
amblyopic 436.9 weak-sighted
amboyna 85 Trees and Shrubs
ambrosia 350.7 food, 405.4 pleasurable things, 414.2 sweetener
ambrosia beetle 82 Insects
ambrosial 405.6 pleasant, 411.7
tasty, 414.6 sweet, 418.4 fragrant
Ambrosian chant 10.8 hymn
Ambrosianism 7 Christian Movements
ambulance 71 Motor Vehicles,
630.14 hospital
ambulance chaser 463.6 arguer
ambulanceman 60.17 paramedic
ambulance siren 543.4 signal
ambulant 324.16 moving
ambulatory 43.9 miscellaneous architectural features, 43.10
church architecture, 327.7 arcade
ambush 514, 527.8 concealment, 531.3 covering up,
539.13, 539.33 snare, 633.5
danger, 635.1, 635.3 trap,
657.2 stratagem, 657.5 be cunning, 670.1 attack, 676.13 be at
war
ambushed 514.6 surprised,
539.42 trapped
ameliorable 627.15 improvable
ameliorate 216.8 cause change,
376.13 smooth over, 619.5 perfect, 627.1, 662.22 improve
amelioration 6.1 education,
216.1 change, 627.5 improvement
ameliorative 216.11 changeable,
627.16 improving
amen 499.2, 499.9 yes
amenability 572.8 acquiescence
amenable 572, 673.5 submitting, 694.7 obedient, 817.7 courteous, 847.9 loyal
amenable to law 16.47 liable to
law
amenably 817.14 courteously
amend 216.8 cause change,
524.8 interpret, 627.3 rectify,
629.1 repair
amendable 125.8 compensable,
629.14 repairable
amendatory 125.9 compensatory
amended 216.12 changed,
524.15 interpreted
amender 125.3 compensator,
224.4 editor, 627.13 reviser,
629.12 repairer
amending 125.9 compensatory
amendment 125.1 compensation,
216.1 change, 524.1 interpretation, 592.1 plan, 627.6 rectification, 629.8 repair, 630.1 remedy
amendment referendum 580.10
vote
amends 125.1 compensation,
629.9 restoration, 630.1 remedy,
735.2 compensation, 765.2 reparation, 840.1 atonement, 878.6
compensation
amenities 817.3 courtesies
amenity 405.4 pleasurable
things, 662.7 convenience,
817.1 courtesy
amenity tree 85.1 tree
amenorrhoea 353.11 menstruation
ament 84.4 flower head
Amenti 8.11 heaven
amentia 510.2 subnormality

amen to that 499.9 yes
amerce 879.1 punish
amerceable 879.22 punishable
amercement 879.7 punishment
America 91.7 United States , 98.1
continent
American 5 Languages and
Groups of Languages, **43** Architectural Styles, **78** Birds,
255.10 US inhabitant
Americana 91.7 United States
**American Abstract Artists' Group
50** Schools and Groups of Art-
ists
American accent 5.26 dialect
American Alpine Club 34.6 moun-
taineering association
American art glass 44.1 ceramics
American Ballet 46.12 ballet com-
panies
American Birkebeiner 41.2 cross-
country skiing
American Canoe Association 36.6
canoeing
American Casting Association
20.1 angling
American cities 93
American cocker spaniel 77
Breeds of Dogs
American coinage 741.8 Ameri-
can money
American eagle 91.7 United States
American eagle bullion coin
741.8 American money
American elk 37.5 game
American Express 732.4 lending
institution, 733.4 credit, 744.2
credit card
**American Federation of Labor and
Congress of Industrial Organiza-
tions** 13.8 industrial relations
American football 18 Sporting
Activities
American Football 19
American game fish 20
American household china 44.1
ceramics
American Indian 208.4 early
comer
American Indian reservation
816.4 place of confinement
American Indians 200.6 people of
the past
Americanism 5.26 dialect, 91.7
United States
Americanization 91.7 United
States
Americanize 91.18 exert sover-
eignty, 220.12 naturalize
Americanized 220.17 naturalized
American League 22.1 baseball
American money 741
American Motorcycle Association
33.7 racing governing body
American Orthodox Church 7
Christian Movements
American paper money 741.8
American money
American pocket billiards 24.6
pool
American quarter horse 32
Breeds of Horse and Pony
American Rowing Association
36.4 rowing
American saddle 32.14 horse-ri-
ding terms
American saddle horse 32
Breeds of Horse and Pony
American Shetland pony 32
Breeds of Horse and Pony
American Sign Language 421.1
deafness
American spread eagle 544.6 na-
tional emblem
American stroke 36.4 rowing
American thoroughbred 32
Breeds of Horse and Pony
American Triple Crown 32.7
horseracing
American twist service 40.2 ten-
nis strokes
American water spaniel 37.6
sporting dog
America's Cup 674 4 race, 878.2
prize
America's national sport 22.1
baseball

americium 57 Chemical Elements
Amerindian 1.6 race, **1.13** racial
Amesha Spentas 8.6 angel
amethocaine 62 Medication
amethyst 54 Gemstones, **455.3** purple thing
amethystine 455.6 purple
Amhara 1 Peoples
Amharic 5 Languages and Groups of Languages
amiability 763, **815.1** sociability, **817.1** courtesy, **821.4** lovability, **831.1** benevolence
amiable 675.7 peaceful, **763.2** likable, **815.15** sociable, **817.7** courteous, **819.8** friendly, **831.6** benevolent
amiableness 819.1 friendship
amiably 815.18 sociably, **817.14** courteously, **819.17** in friendship, **831.10** benevolently
amicability 759.5 good feeling, **815.1** sociability, **819.1** friendship
amicable 116.10 in accord, **759.12** sensitive, **784.5** likable, **815.15** sociable, **819.8** friendly, **821.17** loving
amicableness 819.1 friendship
amicably 784.10 with great liking, **815.18** sociably, **819.17** in friendship
amice 7.11 vestment
Amici 52 Scientists
amicus curiae 233.4 indirect influence
amid 158.20 in the middle
Amida 8.3 God
amide 57 Types of Compounds
amidships 36.3 parts of a sailing boat, **158.21** midway
amidst 133.14 in the midst, **158.20** in the middle
A Midsummer Night's Dream 48 Shakespeare's plays
Amiens 93 Cities
amigo 819.5 friend
a mile long 269.1 long
a mile off 115.4 dissimilar
amiloride 62 Medication
amimation 50.9 drawing
amine 57 Types of Compounds
amino acid 57 Types of Compounds, **58**, **350.11** food content
amino-acid residue 58.8 amino acid
amino-acid sequence 59.12 molecular biology
aminophylline 62 Medication, **62** Medication
a minute or two 189.3 short duration
Amirini 8 Deities
Amis 48 Writers, **48** Writers
Amish 7 Christian Movements
amiss 117.11 unsuitably, **151.18** muddled, **358.7** short, **358.10** not enough, **504.22** wrongly, **618.15** worthlessly
Amitayus 8 Deities
amitosis 59.10 cell division
amitriptyline 62 Medication
amity 667.1 agreement, **675.1** peace, **819.1** friendship
Amman 93 Cities
ammeter 56, **64.23** electrical instrument, **268.8** meter
ammine 57.7 chemical compound
ammo 680.13 ammunition
ammo dump 680.4 arsenal
Ammon 8 Deities
ammonia 57 Common Chemical Compounds, **419.2** something that makes an unpleasant smell
ammoniacal 419.3 stinking
ammonia clock 191 Timepieces and Timers
ammonite 81 Molluscs, **54.43** fossil, **200.10** fossilization, **202.8** prehistoric animal, **314.3** convoluted thing
Ammonite 7 Non-Christian Religions

ammonium salts 246.3 fertilizer
ammunition 680, **37.3** hunting equipment, **602.2** supplies
ammunition box 258.6 box, **680.4** arsenal
ammunition case 293.13 casing
ammunition chest 680.4 arsenal
ammunition dump 680.4 arsenal
ammunition room 680.4 arsenal
ammunition round 37.3 hunting equipment
ammunition ship 679.24 warship, **680.4** arsenal
amnesia 61.14 trance, **462.5** mental block, **512.2** blankness, **546.5** forgetfulness
amnesiac 512.7 forgetful person
amnesic 512.9 blank
amnesty 512, **546.3** obliteration, **639.2** deliverance, **675.1** peace, **677.2** peace offering, **691.1** leniency, **704.1** cancellation, **839.1** forgiveness
Amnesty International 831.2 charity
amniocentesis 60.7 diagnosis, **245.7** obstetrics
amnion 59.15 developmental biology
amniotic 59.26 developmental
amniotic fluid 245.7 obstetrics
amniotic sac 245.7 obstetrics
amniotomy 60 Surgical Operations
amobarbital 62 Medication
amodiaquine 62 Medication
amoeba 260.2 little thing, **307.2** shapeless thing
amoebiasis 81.12 protozoal disease
amoebic 81.23 protozoan, **260.7** little
amoebic dysentery 81.12 protozoal disease
amoeboid 81.23 protozoan, **260.7** little
amoeboid protozoan 81.9 protozoan
among 133.14 in the midst, **158.20** in the middle
among many 133.14 in the midst
among others 133.14 in the midst
among other things 133.14 in the midst
amongst 158.20 in the middle
among the also-rans 683.11 defeated
among those remaining 132.12 with a remainder
Amon-ra 8 Deities
a month of Sundays 188.5 long duration
Amor 8 Deities, **53** Minor Planets, **821.16** gods and goddesses of love
amoral 783.8 careless, **844.15**, **864.12** immoral, **877.11** immoral, **877.13** unchaste, **877.14** lecherous
amoralism 864.2 vice
amoralist 652.5 badly behaved person
amorality 151.8 lawlessness, **151.11** troublemaker, **783.2** carelessness, **864.2** vice, **877.1** immorality, **877.3** sexual immorality
amorally 783.18 carelessly, **864.20** immorally
amorist 821.9 lover
Amorite 7 Non-Christian Religions
Amorites 1 Peoples
amoroso 49 Musical Terms
amorous 821, **821.17** loving, **826.9** endearing
amorous ditty 821.15 love item
amorous glance 821.14 communication of love, **826.2** courtship
amorously 821.30 lovingly, **826.10** endearingly
amorousness 821.3 lovingness, **821.5** desire
amorous pursuit 826.2 courtship
amorphism 307.1 shapelessness
amorphous 57.33 crystalline, **307.5** shapeless, **491.6** indeter-

minate, **523.4** difficult, **551.2** obscure, **555.1** unemphatic
amorphously 57.46 chemically, **307.6** shapelessly, **491.25** indeterminately
amorphous mineral 54.34 mineral
amorphousness 307.1 shapelessness, **491.14** indeterminacy, **551.1** obscurity
amorphous substance 57.4 crystal
amount 120.1 quantity, **121.1** degree, **169.4** mathematical result, **268.4** size, **490.18** particularity, **605.1** store, **751.1** price
a mountain out of a molehill 612.8 trifle
amount of substance 56.9 mass
amount outstanding 132.3 difference
amount owing 745
amount to 142.9 be whole, **169.11**, **170.10** total, **751.13** cost
amour 821.8 love affair, **877.4** illicit love
amourette 821.8 love affair, **826.2** courtship
amp 235.5 unit of work, **420.9** audio device, **423.4** sound maker
AMP 58.22 bioenergetics
amperage 235.5 unit of work
ampere 75 SI Units, **75** Scientific and Technical Units, **235.5** unit of work
Ampère 52 Scientists
ampere-hour 75 Scientific and Technical Units
Ampère–Laplace law 56 Named Laws
Ampère's law 56 Named Laws
ampere-turn 75 Scientific and Technical Units
amphetamine 62 Medication, **630.7** tonic, **875.6** drug
Amphibia 79.7 amphibian
amphibian 71 Motor Vehicles, **73** Types of Aircraft, **79**, **79**, **74.11** nautical, **76.4** type of animal, **679.24** warship
amphibians 396.5 classifications of life
amphibious 74.11 nautical
amphibious force squadron 17.4 military organization
amphibious landing craft 74 Ships and Boats
amphibiously 74.12 nautically
amphibiousness 655.1 skill
amphibious operations 676.8 warfare
amphibious ship 679.24 warship
amphibious warfare 676.8 warfare
amphibole 54.34 mineral
amphibology 578.5 equivocalness
amphibolous 578.10 equivocal
amphibolously 578.12 equivocally
amphibrach 48.9 metre
amphigoric 521.10 meaningless
amphigory 506.1 nonsense, **521.1** lack of meaning
amphimacer 48.9 metre
Amphineura 81.5 mollusc
amphineuran 81.5 mollusc
amphioxus 81.2 protochordate
amphipod 81.4 arthropod
amphisbaena 79 Reptiles
amphitheatre 34.5 rock face, **51.14** theatre, **435.9** viewpoint
Amphitrite 97.4 sea god
amphora 44.8 ceramic object, **258.11** vessel
amphoteric 57.36 acid
amphoteric compound 57.9 base
amphotericin 62 Medication
ampicillin 62 Medication
ample 181, **120.6** quantitative, **248.13** spacious, **259.15** big, **271.1** broad, **273.1** thick, **608.2** plentiful, **755.3** abundant, **765.5** satisfying, **861.7** large
ampleness 259.2 bigness, **271.4** breadth, **861.14** largeness
ample size 861.14 largeness
ample-size 861.7 large
ample time 645.1 leisure
amplifiable 261.9 enlargeable

amplification 64.15 circuit function, **128.1** increase, **261.1** growth, **420.9** audio device, **522.10** simplicity, **524.4** translation, **541.2** enlargement, **553.1** diffuseness
amplified 261.7 bigger, **534.34** communicated, **541.13** enlarged, **553.3** diffuse
amplifier 56.18 source of sound, **56.55** circuit, **64.21** rectifier, **420.9** audio device, **423.4** sound maker, **534.18** radio
amplify 64.35 conduct, **128.5** make bigger, **235.12** generate power, **261.5** make bigger, **261.6** become bigger, **524.12** translate, **534.30** communicate, **541.8** enlarge, **553.5** be diffuse
amplifying 560.11 descriptive
amplitude 56.16 waveform, **120.1** quantity, **121.1** degree, **248.6** available space, **259.1** size, **271.4** breadth, **365.5** wave, **553.1** diffuseness, **608.8** plenty
amplitude modulation 212.6 radio frequency, **534.14** radio transmission
amplitudinous 248.13 spacious
amply 120.7 quantitatively, **248.15** spaciously, **259.20** largely, **608.9** enough, **755.12** generously
ampulla 44.8 ceramic object
amputate 60.20 practise surgery, **131.4** take off, **136.10** set apart, **630.20** doctor
amputation 60.9 surgery, **131.1** subtraction, **136.3** separateness, **630.12** surgery
amrita 350.7 food
Amritsar 93 Cities
Amsterdam 93 Cities
Amtrak 72.10 miscellaneous
AM transmitter 534.16 transmitter
amu 75 Scientific and Technical Units
Amu Darya 96 Rivers
amulet 10.14 sacred object, **11.6** talisman, **637.2** preserver
Amundsen 97 Oceans and Seas
Amur 96 Rivers
amuse 405.9 give pleasure, **771.13** be humorous
amusement 771, **42.8** pastime, **612.8** trifle, **674.2** contest, **763.7** pleasure
amusing 42.9 recreational, **763.2** likable, **769.2** cheering, **771.9** funny, **771.10** humorous, **815.15** sociable
amusingly 771.16 humorously, **815.18** sociably
a must 593.1 requirement, **695.1** compulsion
amygdalectomy 61.3 psychiatric treatment
amylaceous 393.18 pulpy
amylase 58.11 enzyme
amyl nitrite 62 Medication
amylobarbitone 62 Medication
amyloid 89.10 of fungi
amylopectin 58.4 polysaccharide
amylose 58.4 polysaccharide
Amyraldianism 7 Christian Movements
anabaena 90 Algae
Anabaptism 7 Christian Movements
anabasis 359.6 mounting
anabatic 36.10 sailing, **359.23** rising
anabatic wind 36.1 sailing, **55.12** wind
anabolic 58.26 biochemical, **59.22** physiological, **62.17** stimulating
anabolically 58.27 biochemically
anabolic steroid 21.5 competition, **58.16** hormone, **62.4** drug type
anabolism 58.21 metabolism, **59.5** physiology
anabranch 96.1 river
anachronism 211, **193.1** wrong time, **197.1** different time
anachronistic 211, **193.4**

mistimed, 197.2 *occurring at a different time,* 200.19 *antiquarian*
anachronistically 211, 193.7 *out of chronological order*
anacoluthia 504.11 *grammatical error*
anaconda 79 Reptiles, 79.3 *snake*
Anacreon 48 Poets
Anacreontics 48.10 *verse form*
anacrusis 48.9 *metre*
anaemia 777 Phobias by Topic, 238.3 *poor health,* 445.2 *paleness,* 609.8 *insufficiency,* 624.11, 624.11 *blood disease*
anaemic 238.10 *ill,* 445.8 *drained of colour,* 624.21 *unhealthy,* 624.23 *diseased*
anaemophobia 777 Phobias by Name
anaepest 48.9 *metre*
anaerobe 59.3 *organism*
anaerobic 59.22 *physiological*
anaerobic respiration 58.24 *respiration,* 59.6 *cell biology*
anaesthesia 60.9 *surgery,* 404.1 *lack of feeling,* 630.5 *analgesic,* 761.4 *desensitization*
anaesthesiologist 60.13 *medical specialist*
anaesthesiology 60.3 *medical specialty*
anaesthetic 404, 404, 62.4 *drug type,* 62.14 *counteracting,* 242.2 *moderator,* 630.5 *analgesic,* 630.8 *drug,* 630.17 *remedial,* 643.10 *soporific,* 761.6 *desensitizing substance,* 767.3 *reliever*
anaesthetics 60.3 *medical specialty*
anaesthetist 60.13 *medical specialist,* 60.17 *paramedic*
anaesthetization 761.1 *ease*
anaesthetize 404, 60.20 *practise surgery,* 242.4 *moderate,* 460.10 *bemuse,* 630.20 *doctor,* 761.7 *render insensitive*
anaesthetized 404, 643.4 *not awake,* 761.2 *desensitized*
anaesthetize hypnotize 643.14 *make inactive*
anagalactic nebula 53.7 *galaxy*
an age 188.5 *long duration*
anaglyph 50.13 *relief-carving*
anaglyptic 50.25 *sculptural*
anaglyptics 50.13 *relief-carving*
anaglyptography 50.13 *relief-carving*
anagnosis 48.3 *aspect of fiction*
anagnorisis 530.1 *disclosure*
anagoge 527.11 *mysteriousness*
anagogic 11.14 *occult*
anagogical 527.5 *mysterious*
anagogics 11.1 *occultism*
anagram 5.13 *letter,* 529.4 *brainteaser*
anagrammatic 5.41 *lettered,* 578.10 *equivocal*
anagrammatically 5.48 *linguistically*
anagrammatism 5.13 *letter*
Anaheim 93 Cities
Anahita 8 Deities, 8.5 *deity*
anal 304.4 *rear,* 322.15 *providing passage*
anal canal 322.7 *passageway*
analcite 54 Minerals
analeptic 62.4 *drug type,* 62.17 *stimulating,* 629.16 *restorative,* 630.17 *remedial*
anal fin 80.5 *fish anatomy*
analgesia 404.1 *lack of feeling,* 406.4 *pain-relief,* 630.5 *analgesic,* 761.4 *desensitization*
analgesic 630, 62.4 *drug type,* 62.14 *counteracting,* 242.2 *moderator,* 242.8 *moderating,* 404.4, 404.9 *anaesthetic,* 630.8 *drug,* 630.17 *remedial,* 761.6 *desensitizing substance,* 767.3 *reliever*
anally 322.27 *cavernously*
analog 110.2 *equivalence*
analog dial 192.8 *face*
analogical 116.14 *conforming*
analogous 107.5 *interrelated,*

109.6 *correlative,* 110.13 *equivalent,* 114.7 *similar,* 116.14 *conforming*
analogously 107.10 *relevantly,* 109.11 *correlatively,* 110.18 *identically,* 114.14 *comparably*
analogousness 116.5 *conformity*
analogue 109.3 *correlation,* 110.2 *equivalence*
analogue clock 191 Timepieces and Timers, 56.87 *clock*
analogue watch 192.7 *watch*
analogy 4.8 *philosophical term,* 107.1 *relatedness,* 109.3 *correlation,* 110.2 *equivalence,* 114.1 *similarity,* 116.5 *conformity,* 222.3 *substitute thing*
anal-retentive 869.8 *self-restrained*
analyse 4.20 *philosophize,* 4.23 *discuss philosophically,* 52.89 *theorize,* 57.27 *synthesize,* 61.38 *psychologize,* 136.11 *divide,* 141.4 *deconstruct,* 152.15 *categorize,* 163.14 *sort,* 463.11 *reason,* 477.17 *question,* 479.11 *experiment,* 481.12 *discriminate,* 524.8 *interpret,* 544.10 *identify,* 568.11 *confer*
analysed 152.24 *categorized,* 477.16 *questioned*
analyser 65.8 *software*
analysis 57, 4.4 *philosophical investigation,* 52.1 *mathematics,* 52.30 *calculus,* 57.1 *chemistry,* 61.3 *psychiatric treatment,* 136.1 *separation,* 141.2 *deconstruction,* 152.5 *categorization,* 170.1 *calculation,* 463.2 *reasoning,* 477.2 *questioning,* 479.1 *experiment,* 510.9 *treatment,* 524.1 *interpretation,* 544.1 *identification,* 568.6 *interview*
analysis of variance 52.55 *statistical methods*
analysis situs 52.47 *topology*
analyst 4.10 *philosopher,* 57.2 *chemist,* 61.29 *psychologist,* 61.30 *psychiatrist,* 477.9 *questioner,* 479.5 *experimenter,* 654.4 *adviser*
analytic 57, 4.16 *dialectical,* 5.38 *linguistic,* 5.39 *of language,* 50.29 *realist,* 52.68 *mathematical,* 52.69 *theoretic,* 57.31 *chemical,* 152.26 *diagrammatic,* 477.12 *questioning,* 479.8 *experimental*
analytical 170.15 *mathematical,* 463.8 *rational*
analytical chemist 57.2 *chemist*
analytical chemistry 57.1 *chemistry*
analytical cubism 50 Western Art Styles and Movements
Analytical Engine 65.3 *computer*
analytical journalism 533.3 *reporting*
analytically 4.24 *philosophically,* 5.48 *linguistically,* 52.87 *mathematically,* 57.46 *chemically,* 141.7 *to pieces,* 152.28 *in place,* 477.23 *questioningly,* 479.14 *experimentally,* 481.16 *judiciously*
analytical philosophy 4.6 *branch of philosophy*
analytic geometry 52.34 *geometry*
analytic language 5.10 *language type*
analytic psychology 61.1 *psychology*
anamnesis 10.9 *prayer,* 511.1 *memory*
anamorphosis 548.1 *misrepresentation*
ananas 86 Fruits
Ananias 538.11, 539.16 *liar*
Ananke 8 Deities
anapaestic 48.20 *metrical*
anaphase 59.10 *cell division*
anaphora 48.12 *poetic language,* 183.1 *repetition,* 426.7 *repeated word*
anaplastic 630.18 *medical*
anarch 689.3 *anarchist*
anarchic 689, 4.14 *of a philoso-*

phy, 12.9 *governmental,* 16.61 *lawless,* 104.11 *separate,* 151.20 *disorderly,* 168.12 *nonconformist,* 688.14 *governmental,* 693.14 *subversive,* 698.10 *independent,* 713.10 *law-breaking,* 720.14 *violating*
anarchical 689.6 *anarchic,* 693.14 *subversive*
anarchically 689, 16.84 *lawlessly,* 151.29 *riotously,* 720.16 *disobediently*
anarchism 689, 4.7 *school of thought,* 713.2 *disorder*
anarchist 689, 4.11 *follower of a doctrine,* 12.6 *political party,* 104.5 *nonconformist,* 117.6 *misfit,* 151.11 *troublemaker,* 168.8 *dissenter,* 241.4 *violent person or animal,* 244.6 *destroyer,* 669.5 *resister,* 669.12 *resisting,* 693.10, 713.5 *seditionist,* 713.10 *law-breaking,* 832.8 *malefactor*
anarchistic 689, 104.11 *separate,* 244.14 *destructive*
anarcho-syndicalism 4.7 *school of thought,* 688.7 *type of rule,* 689.2 *anarchism*
anarcho-syndicalist 4.11 *follower of a doctrine,* 4.14 *of a philosophy,* 12.6 *political party*
anarchy 689, 12.1 *government,* 16.41, 151.8 *lawlessness,* 151.9 *disorder,* 688.7 *type of rule,* 693.3 *subversion,* 713.2 *disorder,* 720.4 *infraction*
Anarchy 689
an arm and a leg 753.2 *unfair price*
anastomosis 135.1 *union*
anatase 54 Minerals
anathema 822.7 *hated thing,* 827.4 *malediction*
anathematize 827.7 *wish ill*
Anatolian 5 Languages and Groups of Languages, 5.11 *family of languages*
Anatolic 5.11 *family of languages*
anatomic 382.12 *organic*
anatomical 1.11 *anthropological,* 59.20 *biological*
anatomically 59.29 *biologically,* 382.18 *structurally*
anatomist 382, 59.19 *life scientist*
anatomization 141.2 *deconstruction*
anatomize 106.11 *circumstantiate,* 136.11 *divide*
anatomy 59, 48.4 *non-fiction,* 59.1 *life science,* 306.6 *nature,* 382.3 *form,* 382.8 *science of structure*
anatriptic 385.10 *frictional*
Anaxagoras 4 Philosophers
Anaximander 4 Philosophers
Anaximenes 4 Philosophers
ancestor 154.9 *predecessor,* 194.6 *person having priority,* 208.4 *early comer,* 226.7 *Prime Mover*
ancestors 202.2 *old people,* 397.13 *the dead*
ancestor worship 9.2 *idolatry*
Ancestor Worship 7 Non-Christian Religions
ancestor worshipper 9.6 *idolater*
ancestor-worshipping 9.10 *idolatrous*
ancestry 802.3 *nobleness*
ancestral 3.15 *historic,* 200.19 *antiquarian,* 202.12 *olden,* 208.15 *precursory*
ancestral hall 256.4 *official residence*
ancestrally 3.24 *historically,* 202.21 *archaically,* 208.19 *primevally*
ancestry 163.8 *genealogy*
anchor 34.4 *climbing equipment,* 135.10 *link,* 137.9 *yoke,* 137.12 *bind,* 280.4 *base,* 632.2 *protection,* 632.4 *safety device,* 661.4 *restraint,* 661.10 *restrain,* 718.1 *protection,* 718.10 *secure,* 726.3 *tools for gripping*

anchorage 634.2 *shelter*
Anchorage 93 Cities
anchor bait 20.7 *angle*
anchor chain 137.7 *tackle*
anchored 225.10 *stabilized,* 661.14 *blocked*
anchoretic 7.15 *religious*
anchorite 7.7 *monk,* 139.4 *individualist,* 168.9 *hermit,* 174.8 *loner,* 816.6 *unsocial person*
anchor light 439.6 *electric light*
anchorman 528.9 *informant,* 533.4 *journalist,* 534.29 *broadcaster*
anchor man 646.1 *worker*
anchor ring 52.45 *curved surface*
anchor space 24.4 *carom*
anchorwoman 534.29 *broadcaster*
anchovy 80 Fishes
anchovy pear 86 Fruits
anchusa 84 Flowers and Flowering Plants
ancien régime 3.8 *past time*
ancient 3.15 *historic,* 5.39 *of language,* 200.17 *past,* 202.12 *olden,* 207.14 *aged,* 208.14 *primeval,* 396.12 *alive*
ancient and modern 111.2 *opposites*
Ancient and Mystical Order of Poahtun 7 Non-Christian Religions
ancient coins 741
Ancient Egyptian text 7.12 *religious text*
ancient flint 200.7 *thing of the past*
Ancient Greek 5 Languages and Groups of Languages
ancient Greeks 200.6 *people of the past*
ancient history 3.8 *past time,* 208.3 *early stage*
ancient language 5
ancient lineage 200.12 *genealogy*
anciently 202, 208.19 *primevally*
ancient man 400.3 *uncivilized human*
ancient manuscript 202.5 *old thing*
Ancient Mariner 74.7 *nautical person*
ancient monument 3.11 *relic,* 200.7 *thing of the past,* 202.5 *old thing,* 243.8 *construction,* 545.11 *monument*
ancientness 202.3 *antiquity*
ancient people 202
ancient Romans 200.6 *people of the past*
ancient ruin 200.7 *thing of the past*
ancient ruins 244.4 *ruin*
Ancients 50 Schools and Groups of Artists
ancient tale 202.6 *tradition*
ancient times 3.9 *distant past,* 3.10 *past age,* 200.1 *past time,* 202.3 *antiquity*
ancient wisdom 1.8, 202.6 *tradition*
ancient woodland 85.4 *trees*
ancillary 127.15 *subordinate,* 284.9 *supportive,* 662.31 *supplementary*
ancon 43.9 *miscellaneous architectural features*
Ancona 68 Breeds of Fowl
ancraophobia 777 Phobias by Name
ancylostomiasis 624.7 *tropical disease*
and 130.10 *additionally*
and a jump 366.29 *jerkily*
and all 142.12 *one and all*
Andalusian 32 Breeds of Horse and Pony, **68** Breeds of Cattle, **68** Breeds of Fowl
andalusite 54 Minerals, **54** Gemstones
Andaman 97 Oceans and Seas
Andamanese 1 Peoples, **7** Non-Christian Religions
andante 49.19 *tempo,* 328.16 *slowly*
Andean 275.13 *mountainous*
Andersen 48 Writers

Anderson 48 Writers, **52** Scientists

Anderson shelter 634.1 *refuge*

Andes 95 Mountains, **275.4** *mountain range*

andesine 54 Minerals

andesite 54 Common Rocks

Andes Mountains 95.6 *other major mountains and ranges*

Andjeti 8 Deities

and others 175.12 *et cetera*

andradite 54 Minerals, **54** Gemstones

Andre Agassi 40.7 *famous tennis players*

Andre Sakharov 675.4 *Nobel Peace Prize*

Andrews' experiments 56 Named Laws

Andrić 48 Writers

androecium 84.3 *flower part*

androgen 58 Hormones, 58.16 *hormone*, 62.4 *drug type*

androgyny 402.1 *female sex*

android 400.8 *humanlike machine*, 404.5 *unfeeling person*

Andromeda 53 Galaxies, **53** The Constellations, **53** The Constellations

androphobia 777 Phobias by Name

androsterone 58 Hormones

and so 106.15 *under the circumstances*, 227.12 *with the effect of*

and so forth 130.10 *additionally*, 146.9 *inclusively*

and so on 130.10 *additionally*, 146.9 *inclusively*, 175.12 *et cetera*

and the fish of the sea 76.1 *animals*

and the gatepost 529.15 *in secret*

and then some 144.10 *fully*

and there 227.12 *with the effect of*

and the rest 175.12 *et cetera*

and Villages 93

aneasthetize 767.9 *relieve*

anecdotage 207.5 *old age*

anecdote 511.2 *retrospect*, 560.3 *narration*

anecdotist 560.10 *descriptive writer*

anechoic chamber 56.21 *architectural acoustics*

Aneirin 48 Poets

anemogram 55.6 *weather data*

anemograph 55.7 *weather instruments*

anemographic 55.42 *barometric*

anemological 55.47 *windy*

anemology 55.1 *meteorology*

anemometer 55.7 *weather instruments*, 268.8 *meter*, 329.8 *speed*

anemometric 55.42 *barometric*, 268.16 *micrometric*

anemometry 268.2 *micrometry*

anemone 84 Flowers and Flowering Plants

anemone fish 80 Fishes

aneroid 34.8 *mountaineering*

aneroid barometer 34.4 *climbing equipment*, 55.7 *weather instruments*, 56.88 *barometer*

an eternity 188.5 *long duration*

aneurysm 624.10 *cardiovascular disease*

anew 183.24, 201.22 *again*

an exception in favour of 147.1 *exclusion*

an eye for an eye 109.1 *interchange*, 122.1 *equality*, 125.2 *counterbalance*

an eye for an eye and a tooth for a tooth 672.1 *retaliation*

anfractuosity 314.1 *convolution*

Angara 96 Rivers

angel 8, 51.25 *producer*, 134.5 *pure person*, 284.8 *supporter*, 662.15 *benefactor*, 671.13 *defender*, 675.2 *symbol of peace*, 729.4 *giver*, 755.9 *generous person*, 821.12 *nicknames for lovers*, 824.4 *terms of endearment*, 863.4 *virtuous person*, 865.4 *innocent person*

angel cake 45.36 *cake*

angel chimes 49 Musical Instruments

angel dust 875.6 *drug*

angelfish 80 Fishes

angelhood 8.6 *angel*

angelic 8.14 *heavenly*, 134.12 *morally pure*, 821.22 *lovable*, 863.5 *virtuous*, 865.5 *innocent*

angelica 45 Herbs and Spices, 413.5 *herbs*

angelical 8.14 *heavenly*

angelically 8.19 *divinely*, 134.18, 863.9 *virtuously*, 865.11 *innocently*

angelic host 8.6 *angel*

angelization 8.9 *deification*

angelize 8.17 *deify*

angelized 8.15 *deified*

Angeln 68 Breeds of Cattle

Angel of Death 8.6 *angel*, 397.2 *death personified*, 607.7 *destroyer*

angel of light 8.6 *angel*

angel of love 8.6 *angel*

angel of mercy 60.16 *nurse*

angelology 7.13 *theology*

angelophany 8.8 *divine manifestation*

Angelou 48 Poets

Angelus 10.9 *prayer*

Angelus bell 543.4 *signal*

anger 822, 822, 828, 241.9 *make violent*, 713.1 *protest*, 768.2 *annoyance*, 768.8 *annoy*, 818.1 *discourtesy*, 828.12 *become angry*, 864.5 *seven deadly sins*

angered 828.16 *angry*

Angkar Wat 10.13 *shrine*

angina 406.2 *painful condition*, 624.10 *cardiovascular disease*

angina pectoris 406.2 *painful condition*, 624.10 *cardiovascular disease*

anginophobia 777 Phobias by Name

angiogram 60.7 *diagnosis*

angiography 60.7 *diagnosis*, 382.8 *science of structure*

angiology 382.8 *science of structure*

angioplasty 60 Surgical Operations

angiosperm 83.3 *seed plant*, 84.2 *flowering plant*

Angiospermae 83.3 *seed plant*

angiotensin 58 Hormones

Anglais 32.13 *breeding*

angle 20, 52, 310, 310, 56.7 *space*, 80.15 *fish*, 310.6 *motive*, 398.22 *kill animals*, 457.3 *external appearance*, 472.1 *topic*, 497.1 *belief*, 590.11 *hunt*

Angle 310

angle bracket 137.4 *means of connection*

angle brackets 52.25 *algebraic expression*

angled 310, 52.80 *linear*, 472.7 *focused*

angled figure 310

angled toward 310.10 *biased*

angle harp 49 Musical Instruments

angle iron 310.1 *angle*

angle of bank 73.7 *miscellaneous aviation terms*

angle of depression 52.39 *angle*

angle of elevation 52.39 *angle*

angle off 286.6 *be oblique*

angle of incidence 73.7 *miscellaneous aviation terms*

angle of view 66.17 *lens*

Anglepoise 439.6 *electric light*

angler 20, 80.10 *fisher*, 590.6 *hunter*

anglerfish 80 Fishes

Angles 1 Peoples, 200.6 *people of the past*

anglesite 54 Minerals, **57** Common Metal Ores

angle subtended 52.39 *angle*

Anglican 7.5 *Christian*, 7.16 *denominational*

Anglican Communion 7 Christian Movements

Anglicism 5.26 *dialect*, 91.9 *England*

Anglicization 91.9 *England*

Anglicize 91.18 *exert sovereignty*, 220.12 *naturalize*

Anglicized 220.17 *naturalized*

angling 20, 20, 80.7 *fishing*, 590.2 *chase*

Angling 20

Anglo 91 Names for Inhabitants

Anglo-African 1.6 *race*, 1.13 *racial*

Anglo-American 1.6 *race*

Anglo-Arab 32 Breeds of Horse and Pony

Anglo-Australian Observatory 53.23 *observatory*

Anglo-Australian Telescope 53.24 *telescope*

Anglo-Catholic 7.5 *Christian*

Anglo-Catholicism 7 Christian Movements

Anglo-French 5 Languages and Groups of Languages

Anglo-Indian 1.6 *race*, 1.13 *racial*

Anglo-Irish 5 Languages and Groups of Languages

Anglo-Kabardin 32 Breeds of Horse and Pony

Anglo-Norman 5 Languages and Groups of Languages, **32** Breeds of Horse and Pony

Anglo-Persian 32 Breeds of Horse and Pony

Anglophile 91.9 *England*

Anglophobe 91.9 *England*, 820.5 *hostile person*, 822.9 *hater*

Anglophobia 777 Phobias by Name, 822.3 *race hatred*

Anglophobic 820.7 *intolerant*, 822.11 *racist*

Anglophone 564.19 *speaking*

Anglo-Saxon 5 Languages and Groups of Languages, **7** Non-Christian Religions, 5.19 *swearword*, 827.2 *offensive language*, 827.8 *cursing*

Anglo-Saxon art 50 Western Art Styles and Movements

Anglo-Saxons 1 Peoples

Angola 91 Countries

angora 288.4 *textile*

angostura bitters 351.8 *mixed drink*

Angostura bitters 415.3 *sour thing*

Angpetu Wi 8 Deities

Angra Mainyu 8.7 *devil*

angrily 828, 713.11 *disapprovingly*, 818.9 *discourteously*, 829.9 *irascibly*

angry 822, 828, 97.7 *oceanic*, 241.6 *violent*, 713.9 *protesting*, 829.4 *irascible*

angry look 828.6 *sign of anger*

angry reply 818.3 *act of discourtesy*

angry sea 97.3 *wave*

angry young man 168.8, 500.5 *dissenter*, 720.5 *nonobserver*, 766.3 *dissatisfied person*

Angry Young Men 48 Literary Groups and Movements, 51.8 *theatre movements*

angst 618.11 *harmfulness*, 631.4 *strain*, 777.3 *worry*, 862.2 *affliction*

angstrom 75 Scientific and Technical Units

anguilliform 80.13 *fishlike*

anguine 79.12 *snakelike*

anguish 406.1 *pain*, 618.11 *harmfulness*, 770.1 *sorrow*

anguished 406.7 *feeling pain*

angular 310, 52.80 *linear*, 324.17 *directional*

angular acceleration 56.8 *time*

angular deformation 63.16 *deformation*

angular direction 52.39 *angle*

angular distance 52.39 *angle*

angular frequency 56.8 *time*

angular measure 74.5 *navigation*

angular measurement 310, 52.39 *angle*

angular momentum 56.9 *mass*, 235.4 *energy*

angular motion 324.5 *circuition*, 364.1 *rotation*

angular resolution 53.28 *resolution*

angular velocity 56.8 *time*

Angus 8 Deities

angustifoliate 272.4 *narrow-leaved*

angustirostrate 272.4 *narrow-leaved*

angwantibo 77 Placental Mammals

anhedral 73.7 *miscellaneous aviation terms*

Anhur 8 Deities

anhydrate 392.17 *dry*

anhydration 392.13 *drying*

anhydride 57.10 *salt*

anhydrite 54 Minerals

anhydrous 57.36 *acid*, 392.1 *dry*

anhydrously 392.24 *drily*

anhydrous salt 57.10 *salt*

anile 207.14 *aged*, 510.11 *insane*

anileridine 62 Medication

aniline 444.4 *pigment*

aniline dye 67.6 *dye*

anility 207.5 *old age*

anima 11.7 *spirit*, 61.21 *psyche*, 290.5 *inner nature*

animal 76, 59.3 *organism*, 59.21 *living*, 76.14 *animalian*, 460.8 *nonhuman*, 832.11 *cruel*

animal anatomy 76.9 *animal science*

animal behaviour 61.1 *psychology*, 76.9 *animal science*

animal biochemistry 76.9 *animal science*

animal breeding 68.3 *livestock farming*, 76.8 *animal welfare*

animal call 432.1 *animal cry*

animal cell 59.7 *cell*

animal charge 544.8 *heraldic device*

animal conservation 76.8 *animal welfare*

animal costume 295.5 *fancy dress*

animal covering 293

animal cry 432

Animal Cry 432

animalcular 76.15 *of animals*, 260.7 *little*

animalcule 59.3 *organism*, 76.4 *type of animal*, 260.2 *little thing*

animal dance 46.4 *historic dancing*

animal doctor 60.15 *veterinarian*

animal ecologist 76.11 *zoologist*

animal ecology 59.18 *ecology*, 76.9 *animal science*

animal fat 395.8 *fat*

animal-fearing 76

animal feedstuff 68

animal food 350

animal health 68.3 *livestock farming*, 76.8 *animal welfare*

animal home 634.3 *animal shelter*

animal husbandry 68.3 *livestock farming*, 243.2 *manufacture*

Animalia 76.1 *animals*

animalian 76

animalic 76.14 *animalian*

animalism 76.12 *zoophilism*

animalistic 76.14 *animalian*, 877.15 *unlawful*

animality 76.12 *zoophilism*, 460.4 *nonhuman existence*, 832.2 *cruelness*

animal killer 398

animal killing 398

animal kingdom 76.1 *animals*

animal liberation 76.8 *animal welfare*, 700.2 *equal opportunity*

Animal Liberation Front 76.8 *animal welfare*

animal liberationist 76.10 *animal welfarist*

animal life 76.1 *animals*, 396.1 *life*

animal-like 76.14 *animalian*

animal lover 76.10 *animal welfarist*

animal-loving 76

animal magnetism 340.4 *allurement*

animal nutrition 68.3 *livestock farming*

animal oil 395.7 *oil*

animal painter 50.16 *artist*

animal painting 50.10 *art subject*

animal pathology 76.9 *animal science*

animal physiologist 76.11 *zoologist*

animal physiology 76.9 *animal science*

animal production 68.3 *livestock farming*

animal products 243.7 *produce*

animal protection 76.8 *animal welfare*

animal psychology 61.1 *psychology*, 76.9 *animal science*

animal rights 845.3 *prerogative*

animal-rights activism 700.2 *equal opportunity*

animal-rights activist 76.10 *animal welfarist*, 700.3 *liberator*

animal rights movement 76.8 *animal welfare*

animals 76, 396.9 *classifications of life*

animal science(s 76

Animals (General) 76

animal shelter 634

animal spirits 396.1 *life*

animal starch 58.4 *polysaccharide*

animal suicide 398.9 *animal killing*

animal taxonomist 76.11 *zoologist*

animal taxonomy 76.9 *animal science*

animal transport 71

animal welfare 76, 60.5 *veterinary medicine*

animal welfarist 76

animal worship 9.2 *idolatry*

animal worshipper 9.6 *idolater*

animal-worshipping 9.10 *idolatrous*

animate 59.21 *living*, 228.9 *motivate*, 235.11 *give power*, 237.8 *strengthen*, 330.1 *impel*, 396.12 *alive*, 403.13 *arouse sensation*, 471.16 *inspire*, 651.1 *refresh*, 769.6 *bring cheer*, 778.17 *give courage*

animated 228.12 *motivated*, 235.15 *full of energy*, 239.4 *vigorous*, 396.13 *lively*, 642.18 *active*, 769.1 *cheerful*

animated cartoon 50.9 *drawing*

animatedly 396.22 *vitally*

animate existence 396.1 *life*

animation 235.3 *vitality*, 239.1 *vigour*, 396.1 *life*, 642.4 *energy*, 651.5 *refreshment*, 769.3 *cheerfulness*, 778.6 *encouragement*

animatism 9.2 *idolatry*, 368.3 *spiritual world*

animatist 9.6 *idolater*

animatistic 9.10 *idolatrous*

animato 49 *Musical Terms*

animator 50.16 *artist*, 653.13 *director*

animé 85 *Tree Products*

animism 4.7 *school of thought*, 9.2 *idolatry*, 11.1 *occultism*, 368.3 *spiritual world*

animist 4.11 *follower of a doctrine*, 9.6 *idolater*, 368.7 *believer in a nonmaterial world*, 368.9 *parapsychological*

animistic 4.14 *of a philosophy*, 9.10 *idolatrous*, 368.9 *parapsychological*

animistic spirit 8.5 *deity*

animosity 111.3 *opposition*, 759.6 *bad feeling*, 785.1 *dislike*, 820.1 *enmity*, 822.1 *hate*, 828.1 *resentment*, 832.1 *malevolence*

animus 11.7 *spirit*, 61.21 *psyche*, 290.5 *inner nature*, 820.1 *enmity*

Aningan 8 *Deities*

anion 56.66 *ion*, 64.5 *electrolytic conduction*

anise 45 *Herbs and Spices*

aniseed 413.5 *herbs*

anisogamy 90.4 *reproductive body*

Anit 8 *Deities*

Ankara 93 *Cities*, 93.6 *other cities*

ankerite 54 *Minerals*

ankh 11.6 *talisman*

ankle 135.5 *joint*

ankle-biter 156.15 *baby*, 206.9 *child*

anklebone 382 *Bones*

ankle-deep 277.8 *deep*, 278.1 *shallow*

ankle-high 276.5 *low*

ankle-length 269.1 *long*

ankle socks 295.20 *legwear*

anklet 313.3 *circular thing*, 792.6 *jewellery*

anklets 295.20 *legwear*

anklung 49 *Musical Instruments*

Ankole 68 *Breeds of Cattle*

ankus 380.8 *sharp-pointed thing*

ankylosaur 79 *Fossil Reptiles*

annabergite 54 *Minerals*

annalist 48.14 *author*, 185.14 *time keeper*, 192.13 *chronicler*, 545.9 *recorder*, 560.10 *descriptive writer*

annalistic 185.25 *of known date*, 192.17 *timekeeping*

annalistically 192.18 *horologically*

annals 3.5 *chronicle*, 48.4 *nonfiction*, 545.1 *record*, 560.3 *narration*

Annamese 5 *Languages and Groups of Languages*

Annan 96 *Rivers*

Anna Pavlova 46.14 *famous ballet dancers*

Annapolis 93 *Cities*

Annapurna 95 *Mountains*, 95.6 *other major mountains and ranges*

Ann Arbor 93 *Cities*

annatto 85 *Tree Products*

anneal 57.30 *extract*, 203.7 *season*, 373.9 *harden*, 378.11 *make tough*

annealed 373.3 *hardened*, 378.2 *toughened*

annelid 81.20 *wormlike*

Annelida 81.6 *worm*

annelidan 81.20 *wormlike*

annelid worm 81 *Worms*, 81.6 *worm*

annellini 45 *Types of Pasta*

annex 130.6 *add*, 135.10 *link*, 721.9 *gain*, 734.7 *take*, 734.8 *take back*

annexation 130.1 *addition*, 734.1 *taking*, 734.2 *taking back*

annexe 130.3 *additional item*

annexed 130.8 *additional*, 734.12 *taking*

Annie Oakley 22.4 *pitching terms*, 754.6 *absence of charge*

annihilate 172, 100.14 *cause not to exist*, 157.17 *kill*, 244.8 *destroy*, 398.18 *slaughter*, 458.3 *cause to disappear*, 546.1 *obliterate*, 704.6 *cancel*

annihilated 157, 100.11 *no more*, 546.6 *obliterated*

annihilating 244.14 *destructive*

annihilation 157, 100.8 *extinction*, 244.1 *destruction*, 398.4 *slaughter*, 458.5 *disguise*, 512.5 *death*, 546.3 *obliteration*

Annihilationism 7 *Christian Movements*

annihilationist 244.6 *destroyer*

anniversary 214, 214, 812, 185.11 *date*, 511.5 *day to remember*, 773.1 *rejoicing*, 812.2 *commemoration*

anniversary party 665.7 *social gathering*

anniversary present 729.2 *gift*

annotate 524, 544.10 *identify*, 561.4 *dissertate*

annotated 524.15 *interpreted*

annotation 524, 130.3 *additional item*, 561.1 *dissertation*

annotations 545.3 *notes*

annotative 524, 561.5 *expository*

annotator 524.6 *interpreter*, 561.3 *dissertator*

announce 517.11 *predict*, 528.12 *communicate*, 530.6 *divulge*, 532.14 *proclaim*, 534.30 *communicate*, 535.17 *affirm*, 543.12 *signal*, 611.8 *make important*

announced 532.19 *published*,

534.34 *communicated*, 535.11 *stated*

announcement 517.3 *plan*, 528.2 *communication*, 530.2 *divulgence* , 532.1 *publication*, 532.9 *advertisement*, 535.2 *statement*, 543.6 *word*, 636.1 *warning*

announce one's engagement 821.28 *win the love of*, 826.8 *court*

announcer 154.8 *precursor*, 528.9 *informant*, 530.4 *discloser*, 532.10 *publicizer*, 534.29 *broadcaster*, 535.9 *affirmer*, 543.8 *signer*, 564.10 *speaker*

announce with a flourish of trumpets 532.14 *proclaim*

announcing 543.16 *signalling*

annoy 768, 153.7 *disturb*, 616.5 *be inconvenient*, 642.17 *meddle*, 650.6 *fatigue*, 659.22 *cause trouble*, 785.7 *cause dislike*, 828.9 *offend*, 829.8 *make irascible*, 830.12 *make irritable*

annoyance 768, 153.1 *disturbance*, 616.3 *inconvenience*, 618.9 *badness*, 659.8 *snag*, 828.1 *resentment*, 862.2 *affliction*

annoyed 153.12 *disturbed*, 659.16 *troubled*, 828.15 *resentful*, 829.4 *irascible*

annoying 153.17 *disturbing*, 616.1 *inconvenient*, 618.3 *bad*, 642.21 *meddling*, 650.4 *fatiguing*, 659.13 *inconvenient*, 764.1 *unpleasant*, 768.5 *aggravating*

annoyingly 768, 153 18 *disturbingly*, 616.6 *inconveniently*, 650.9 *tiringly*, 659.28 *awkwardly*, 828.17 *resentfully*

annual 69.9 *garden plant*, 69.17 *botanical*, 83.2 *plant*, 83.14 *of plants*, 84.2 *flowering plant*, 110.17 *regular*, 185.22 *periodic*, 187.7, 187.8 *periodical*, 214.12 *cyclic*, 214.13 *anniversary*, 532.5 *journal*, 584.9 *habitual*

annual company get-together 350.13 *feast*

annual dinner 350.13 *feast*

annually 69.20 *horticulturally*, 83.24 *herbaceously*, 110.20 *regularly*, 185.30 *chronologically*, 187.13 *for specified periods*, 214.16 *cyclically*

annually celebrated day 214

annual occurrence 214.3 *anniversary*

annual period 203.1 *season*

annual report 528.3 *document*, 545.1 *record*

annual return 528.3 *document*

annual ring 85.3 *timber*

annual vacation 214.5 *regular thing*

annuitant 730.5 *recipient*

annuity 721.4 *earnings*, 729.2 *gift*, 730.2 *something received*, 746.3 *pay*, 749.3 *income*

annul 16, 100.14 *cause not to exist*, 157.16 *cease*, 231.3 *counteract*, 244.8 *destroy*, 476.8 *refute*, 484.7 *counter*, 536.9 *renounce*, 546.1 *obliterate*, 598.2 *withdraw*, 704.6 *cancel*, 709.3 *veto*

annul a marriage 824.7 *divorce*

annular 52.81 *curvilinear*, 313.5 *circular*

annularity 313.1 *circularity*

annularly 313.8 *circularly*

annulate 313.5 *circular*

annulation 313.2 *circle*

annulet 43 *Architectural Decoration*, 544.8 *heraldic device*

annulled 16.57 *null*, 484.6 *countered*, 536.12 *rejected*, 704.10 *cancelled*

annulment 157.2 *cessation*, 476.1 *refutation*, 484.1 *counterevidence*, 536.4 *renunciation*, 546.3 *obliteration*, 598.3 *relinquishment*, 704.1 *cancellation*, 709.1 *veto*, 824.1 *divorce*

annulus 52.42 *circle*, 89.4 *fungal body*, 313.2 *circle*

annunciate 535.17 *affirm*

annunciated 535.11 *stated*

annunciation 8.8 *divine manifestation*, 50.10 *art subject*, 535.2 *statement*

annunciative 535.10 *affirmative*

annunciatory 535.10 *affirmative*

Annwn 8.11 *heaven*

anoa 77 *Placental Mammals*

a nobody 102.5 *insubstantial person*

anode 56.43 *electrical conduction*, 57.19 *electrochemistry*, 64.5 *electrolytic conduction*, 64.20 *electron tube*, 235.7 *electrical power*

anode sludge 57.19 *electrochemistry*

anodic 57.42 *electrochemical*

anodyne 62.4 *drug type*, 62.16 *soothing*, 242.2 *moderator*, 242.8 *moderating*, 630.5 *analgesic*, 630.17 *remedial*, 767.3 *reliever*

an offer one can't refuse 716.1 *negotiation*

anoint 386, 395, 7.21 *ordain*, 10.18 *perform rites*, 62.19 *administer*, 688.21 *grant authority*, 703.6 *commission*

anointed 395.12 *unguent*

anointing the sick 10.5 *Christian rite*

anointment 386, 395, 688.3 *acquisition of power*

anole 79 *Reptiles*

anomalous 117.8 *contradictory*, 168.17 *abnormal*, 215.5 *unusual*

anomalously 117.15 *dissimilarly*, 215.9 *unusually*, 722.21 *out of place*

anomalousness 168.6 *deviation*, 215.2 *unusualness*

anomaly 117.2 *contradiction*, 165.6 *exception*, 168.6 *deviation*

anomer 57.13 *structure*

anomeric 57.37 *structural*

anomerism 57.13 *structure*

Anomoianism 7 *Christian Movements*

anon 208.17 *early*

anon. 502.4 *unknown person*

Anon. 529.8 *anonymity*

anonymity 529, 172.5 *nonentity*, 502.3 *unknown thing*, 527.6 *latency*, 531.3 *covering up*

anonymous 502.8 *unknown*, 529.11 *mysterious*, 531.15 *disguised*

anonymously 172.12 *absently*, 529.15 *in secret*

anonymous person 502.4 *unknown person*

anopheles 82 *Insects*

Anoplura 82 *Orders of Insects*

anopluran 82.10 *insectan*

anorak 41.5 *ski equipment*, 295.11 *jacket*

anorexia 238.3 *poor health*, 274.8 *emaciation*, 350.3 *delicate eating*, 609.8 *insufficiency*, 722.1 *loss*, 871.1 *fasting*

anorexia nervosa 61.15 *compulsion*, 238.3 *poor health*, 274.8 *emaciation*, 350.3 *delicate eating*, 609.8 *insufficiency*, 624.4 *disease*

anorexic 238.10 *ill*, 274.2 *emaciated*, 274.9 *thin person*, 350.18 *eater*, 609.3 *underfed*, 624.21 *unhealthy*, 695.5 *compulsive person*, 722.7 *dieter*, 871.4 *fasting person*, 871.6, 871.6 *fasting*

anorthite 54 *Minerals*

anorthosite 54 *Common Rocks*

anosmia 417.1 *odourlessness*

another 130.8, 155.19 *additional*, 195.12 *succeeding*

A. N. Other 502.4 *unknown person*

another edition 114.5 *counterpart*

another idea 627.8 *better thing*

another matter 115.2 *unlikeness*

another place 653.11 *British government*

another story 115.2 *unlikeness*

another time 197, 197.1 *different time*
another world 368.1 *nonmaterial world*
a nothing 102.5 *insubstantial person*
Anouilh 48 Dramatists
Anpao 8 Deities
Anquet 8 Deities
Ansafone 420.9 *audio device*
Anselm 4 Philosophers
anseriform 78.23 *avian*
anserine 78.23 *avian*, 506.5 *nonsensical*, 508.5 *foolish*
Anshan 93 Cities
Anshar 8 Deities
answer 478, 478, 4.21 *rationalize*, 4.23 *discuss philosophically*, 109.9 *correlate*, 110.7 *be the same*, 221.5, 221.9 *reply*, 226.5 *reason*, 331.2 *respond*, 473.5 *plea*, 473.16 *plead*, 476.3, 476.10 *countercharge*, 478.2 *acknowledgment*, 478.4 *reaction*, 478.5 *counterstatement*, 478.6 *solution*, 478.7 *numerical result*, 484.1 *counterevidence*, 484.7 *counter*, 524.1 *interpretation*, 534.31 *correspond*, 564.7 *utterance*, 564.11 *speak*, 592.3 *expedient plan*, 608.4 *suffice*, 613.9 *be useful*, 615.6 *be convenient*, 630.1 *remedy*, 672.3 *retaliate*, 682.8 *be effective*, 746.14 *atone*, 765.10 *suffice*
Answer 478
answerability 478, 847.1 *duty*
answerable 478, 226.13 *causal*, 745.9 *in debt*, 847.10 *liable*
answerableness 478.8 *correspondence*
answerably 478, 226.14 *causally*, 478.26 *correspondingly*
answer back 478, 807, 223.5 *exchange*, 331.2 *respond*, 476.10 *countercharge*, 668.6 *be insubordinate*, 672.3 *retaliate*
answer book 6.14 *school book*
answered 221.11 *reversed*
answerer 478
answer for 478, 674.12 *fight*, 714.8 *guarantee*, 847.15 *be liable*
answering 478, 476.7 *refuting*, 484.5 *countering*
answering back 668.3 *act of defiance*, 672.1 *retaliation*, 807.9 *discourtesy*
answering machine 420.9 *audio device*, 534.9 *telephone*, 545.10 *recording instrument*
answering service 420.9 *audio device*
answering to 701.9 *subject*
answerphone 420.9 *audio device*
answer the call 676.12 *go to war*
answer the call of nature 353.15 *excrete*
answer the problem 782.16 *be desirable*
answer the purpose 682.8 *be effective*
answer to 478, 107.7 *relate to*
answer to no man 689.4 *be anarchic*
ant 82 Insects, 82.1 *insect*, 82.4 *social insect*, 642.10 *busy person*, 646.1 *worker*, 815.10 *social animal*
anta 43.9 *miscellaneous architectural features*
Antabuse 62 Medication
antacid 62.4 *drug type*, 62.14 *counteracting*, 630.6 *purgative*
antagonism 111.3 *opposition*, 117.4 *disagreement*, 231.1 *counteraction*, 663.1 *opposition*, 764.7 *dissension*, 785.1 *dislike*, 820.1 *enmity*, 822.1 *hate*, 832.1 *malevolence*
antagonist 51.21 *role*, 62.5 *prescription*, 663.11 *opponent*, 785.3 *disliked person*, 820.5 *hostile person*
antagonistic 51.37 *dramatic*, 111.5 *opposing*, 117.10 *disagreeing*, 231.4 *counteracting*, 473.9

hostile, 663.19 *oppositional*, 666.9 *disagreeing*, 668.8 *defying*, 670.21 *aggressive*, 679.33 *combative*, 687.6 *adverse*, 785.8 *disliking*, 820.9 *aggressive*, 822.10 *hating*, 832.14 *hostile*
antagonistically 51.42 *dramatically*, 111.7 *disapprovingly*, 117.16 *disagreeably*, 231.5 *counter*, 473.17 *argumentatively*, 663.23 *opposingly*, 666.11 *in disagreement*, 668.10 *in defiance*, 679.41 *aggressively*, 687.12 *in adversity*, 820.15 *aggressively*, 822.18 *hatefully*
antagonize 820, 111.9 *oppose*, 117.14 *disagree*, 231.3, 663.18 *counteract*, 768.8 *annoy*, 785.5 *dislike*, 785.7 *cause dislike*, 822.16 *cause hate*, 828.9 *offend*
antagonized 111.5 *opposing*
antagonizing 111.5 *opposing*
Antananarivo 93 Cities
antarctic 332.13 *directional*
Antarctic 97 Oceans and Seas, 409.6 Arctic
Antarctica 231.1 *continent*
Antarctic waste 247.1 *infertility*
Antares 53 Named Stars
antazoline 62 Medication
ant bear 77 Placental Mammals, 77.6 *insect-eating mammal*
antbird 78 Birds
ante 42.3 *card game terms*, 303.10 *be in front*
An Teallach 95 Mountains
anteater 77 Placental Mammals, 77.6 *insect-eating mammal*
anteating 77.26 *insectivorous*
antebellum 202.12 *olden*, 675.7 *peaceful*
antecede 154.15 *precede*, 194.8 *be before*
antecedence 154.1 *precedence*, 194.1 *priority*
antecedency 154.1 *precedence*
antecedent 4.8 *philosophical term*, 154.4 *precedent*, 154.10 *preceding*, 194.6 *person having priority*, 200.19 *antiquarian*
antechamber 303.1 *front*
antedate 154.15 *precede*, 193.3 *mistime*, 194.8 *be before*
antedated 193.5 *too early*
antediluvian 3.15 *historic*, 202.12 *olden*, 202.15 *primal*
antefix 43 Architectural Decoration
antelope 77 Placental Mammals, 37.5 *game*, 329.12 *swift animal*, 544.8 *heraldic device*
antemeridian 204.5 *morning*
ante meridiem 204.8 *in the morning*
antenatal 245.16 *reproductive*
antenatal clinic 60.10 *hospital*
antenna 534, 53.26 *radio telescope*, 143.4 *component*, 318.3 *protuberance*, 403.4 *someone or something that feels*, 407.7 *sense organ*
anteposition 154.1 *precedence*
antepost betting 32.7 *horseracing*
anterior 154.10 *preceding*, 303.6 *front*
anteriority 154.1 *precedence*, 194.1 *priority*
anteroom 256.7 *room*, 303.1 *front*
ante up 746.6 *pay*
Anthat 8 Deities
antheap 82.4 *social insect*
anthelion 55.22 *sun*
anthelmintic 62.4 *drug type*, 62.14 *counteracting*, 630.4 *antidote*
anthem 10.8 *hymn*, 49.5 *sacred music*, 433.2 *song*
anthemic 10.21 *ritualistic*
anthemion 43 Architectural Decoration
anther 84.3 *flower part*, 143.6 *branch*, 245.8 *organs of reproduction*
antheridium 88.2 *fern plant*, 88.4

moss plant, 90.4 *reproductive body*
antherozoid 90.4 *reproductive body*
anthesis 84.5 *flowering*
Anthesteria 10.16 *religious festival*
anthill 82.4 *social insect*, 256.13 *lair*
anthocyanin 58.18 *pigment*
anthologize 562.9 *compile*, 580.4 *pick*
anthology 133.3 *miscellany*, 140.3 *assembly*, 161.30 *compilation*, 562.3 *compendium*, 580.9 *chosen thing*
anthophobia 777 Phobias by Name
Anthozoa 81.7 *coelenterate*
anthozoan 81.7 *coelenterate*
anthracite 410.5 *coal*, 604.1 *materials*
anthracosis 624.9 *respiratory disease*
anthrax 624.18 *veterinary disease*, 631.10 *warfare*
anthrometry 1.10 *measurement*
anthropocentric 400.12 *human*
anthropogenesis 400.5 *study of mankind*
anthropogenic 1.11 *anthropological*
anthropogeny 1.1 *anthropology*
anthropogeographer 1.3 *anthropologist*
anthropogeographic 1.11 *anthropological*
anthropogeographical 1.11 *anthropological*
anthropogeographically 1.16 *anthropologically*
anthropogeography 1.1 *anthropology*
anthropographical 1.11 *anthropological*
anthropographically 1.16 *anthropologically*
anthropography 1.1 *anthropology*, 400.5 *study of mankind*
anthropoid 77.34 *primate*, 400.12 *human*
anthropoid ape 400.3 *uncivilized human*
anthropoid apes 77.16 *primate*
anthropoids 77.16 *primate*
anthropolatrous 9.9 *worshipful*
anthropolatry 9.2 *idolatry*
anthropological 1, 400.12 *human*
anthropological concept 1
anthropological linguistics 5.1 *linguistics*
anthropologically 1, 400.15 *humanly*
anthropologist 1, 400.6 *studier of mankind*
anthropology 1, 396.7 *studies of life*, 400.5 *study of mankind*
Anthropology 1
anthropometric 1.11 *anthropological*, 268.16 *micrometric*
anthropometrical 1.11 *anthropological*
anthropometrically 1.16 *anthropologically*
anthropometrist 1.3 *anthropologist*
anthropometry 1.1 *anthropology*, 268.2 *micrometry*, 400.5 *study of mankind*
anthropomorphic 9.10 *idolatrous*, 400.12 *human*
anthropomorphism 9.2 *idolatry*, 400.5 *study of mankind*
anthropomorphist 9.6 *idolater*
anthropomorphize 9.8 *idolatrize*, 400.14 *make human*
anthropophagite 350.18 *eater*
anthropophagy 300.5 *eating habit*
anthropophobia 777 Phobias by Name, 816.2 *shyness*
anthroposcopic 1.11 *anthropological*
anthroposophical 11.16 *psychic*
anthroposophist 11.12 *occultist*
anthroposophy 11.1 *occultism*, 400.5 *study of mankind*

anthropotomy 382.8 *science of structure*
anthroscopy 1.10 *measurement*
anthrozoan 81.21 *coelenterate*
anthurium 84 Flowers and Flowering Plants
anti 663.9 *opposer*, 663.20 *discordant*
anti-aircraft artillery 670.13 *air attack*, 680.11 *guns*
anti-aircraft fire 670.13 *air attack*
anti-aircraft gun 680.11 *guns*
anti-American 822.11 *racist*
antibacterial 62.14 *counteracting*
antiballistic missile 680.5 *missile weapon*
antibiosis 630.4 *antidote*
antibiotic 62.4 *drug type*, 62.14 *counteracting*, 630.4 *antidote*, 630.8 *drug*
antibody 387.4 *blood*, 630.4 *antidote*
antibonding orbital 57.12 *valence*
anticathexis 61.28 *cathexis*
anticholinergic 62.14 *counteracting*
anticholinergic drug 62.4 *drug type*
Antichrist 8.7 *devil*
anticipant 513.4 *expectant person*, 513.5 *expecting*, 516.6 *foreseeing*
anticipate 193.3 *mistime*, 194.8 *be before*, 194.9 *do before*, 199.10 *expect*, 208.7 *be early*, 208.9 *prepare*, 435.16 *visualize*, 488.10 *think likely*, 513.8 *expect*, 516.1 *foresee*, 594.3 *be prepared*, 642.14 *push*, 775.7 *aspire*, 781.5 *be cautious*
anticipated 199.13 *foreseen*, 488.6 *probable*, 513.7 *expected*, 714.15 *future*
anticipating 513.5 *expecting*, 775.12 *expectant*
anticipation 193.1 *wrong time*, 199.4 *looking to the future*, 208.5 *prematurity*, 435.4 *visualization*, 488.1 *probability*, 513.1 *expectation*, 516.3 *foresight*, 594.9 *preparation*, 775.2 *expectation*
anticipative 208.16 *premature*, 513.5 *expecting*
anticipatively 208.20 *prematurely*, 513.12 *expectantly*
anticipatorily 208.20 *prematurely*, 513.12 *expectantly*
anticipatory 208.16 *premature*, 513.5 *expecting*, 516.6 *foreseeing*, 781.4 *cautious*
anticlastic surface 52.38 *surface*
anticlimax 514.2 *amazement*, 515.2 *bad outcome*, 555.2 *lack of emphasis*
anticline 54.20 *earth movement*, 320.1 *fold*
anticlockwise 332.10 *clockwise*, 337.25 *reversed*, 337.29 *in reverse*, 364.13 *round*
anticoagulant 62.4 *drug type*, 62.14 *counteracting*, 630.4 *antidote*
anticoagulent 387.9 *solvent*, 387.20 *liquefying*
anticodon 59.13 *genetic material*
anticonvulsant 62.4 *drug type*, 630.4 *antidote*
antics 506.3 *tomfoolery*, 656.9 *bungling*
anticyclone 55.11 *weather system*, 325.2 *repose*
anticyclonic 55.44 *frontal*
antidazzle mirror 71 Motor Vehicle Parts
antidepressant 62.4 *drug type*, 62.14 *counteracting*, 630.8 *drug*
antidiuretic hormone 58 Hormones
antidotal 62.14 *counteracting*, 125.10 *counterbalancing*, 231.4 *counteracting*, 478.14 *solved*, 630.17 *remedial*
antidotally 231.5 *counter*
antidote 630, 11.6 *talisman*, 62.4 *drug type*, 125.2 *counterbalance*, 231.2 *counteracting thing*,

478.6 *solution*, **592.3** *expedient plan*, **630.1** *remedy*
antielectron 56.77 *elementary particle*
antiemetic 62.4 *drug type*, **62.14** *counteracting*
antifascism 627.11 *reformism*
antifascist 627.12 *reformer*
antifebrile 62.4 *drug type*
antifeminist 834.2 *misanthrope*
antiferromagnetism 56.59 *ferromagnetism*
antifreeze 408.3 *heater*
antifriction 386.4, **395.5** *lubricant*
anti-friction 41.12 *ski*
anti-friction pad 41.5 *ski equipment*
antifungal 62.14 *counteracting*
antifungal agent 89
antifungal drug 62.4 *drug type*
antigen 387.4 *blood*, **630.4** *antidote*
antigravity 341.5 *repulsion*, **361.6** *raising*
Antigua and Barbuda 91 Countries
antihero 51.21 *role*
antihistamine 62.4 *drug type*, **630.4** *antidote*
antihydrotic 62.4 *drug type*, **62.14** *counteracting*
anti-icer 73 Aircraft Parts
anti-inflammatory 62.4 *drug type*, **62.14** *counteracting*
antilock brake 71 Motor Vehicle Parts
antilog 169.6 *power*
antilogarithm 52.19 *logarithm*, **169.6** *power*
antilogy 474.2 *sophism*
antimacassar 293.12 *protective covering*
antimalarial 62.14 *counteracting*
antimalarial drug 62.4 *drug type*
antimalarial pill 630.1 *prophylactic*
antimasque 51.2 *play*
antimetabolite 62.4 *drug type*
antimissile missile 680.5 *missile weapon*
antimitotic 62.14 *counteracting*
antimonic 57.34 *elemental*
antimonous 57.34 *elemental*
antimony 57 Chemical Elements
antimycotic 62.4 *drug type*, **62.14** *counteracting*, **89.7** *antifungal agent*
antineutron 56.77 *elementary particle*
antinode 56.12, **365.5** *wave*
antinomian 16.61 *lawless*, **689.3** *anarchist*, **689.7** *anarchistic*
antinomianism 16.41 *lawlessness*, **689.2** *anarchism*
antinomic 117.8 *contradictory*
antinomically 117.15 *dissimilarly*
antinomy 16.4 *bad law*, **117.2** *contradiction*
antinovel 48.2 *fiction*
Antiope 534.25 *broadcast material*
Antipaedobaptism 7 Christian Movements
antiparallel 285.3 *parallel*
antiparticle 56.77 *elementary particle*
antipasto 45.12 *hors d'oeuvre*, **45.47** *Italian dish*
antipathetic 111.5 *opposing*, **117.10** *disagreeing*, **136.18** *disagreeable*, **231.4** *counteracting*, **341.8** *repulsive*, **573.2** *refusing*, **663.19** *oppositional*, **785.8** *disliking*, **820.6** *hostile*, **822.10** *hating*
antipathetically 136.23 *disagreeably*, **231.5** *counter*, **341.11** *repulsively*, **663.23** *opposingly*, **822.18** *hatefully*
antipathy 111.3 *opposition*, **231.1** *counteraction*, **663.1** *opposition*, **785.1** *dislike*, **820.1** *enmity*, **822.1** *hate*
anti-perspirant 417.2 *deodorant*
antiphon 10.8 *hymn*, **478.4** *reaction*

antiphonal 155.16 *alternating*, **331.9**, **478.12** *reactive*
antiphonal chant 478.4 *reaction*
antipodal 52.81 *curvilinear*, **111.4** *opposite*
antipodal points 111.1 *oppositeness*
antipodean 249.16 *regional*, **263.8** *distant*
antipodes 111.1 *oppositeness*, **263.3** *distant place*
Antipodes 249.7 *regions of the world*
anti-private language argument 4.9 *philosophical problem*
antiproton 56.77 *elementary particle*
antipruritic 62.4 *drug type*, **62.14** *counteracting*
antipsychiatry 61.2 *psychiatry*
antipsychotic 62.14 *counteracting*
antipsychotic drug 62.4 *drug type*
antipyretic 62.4 *drug type*, **62.14** *counteracting*, **630.4** *antidote*, **630.17** *remedial*
antiquarian 200, 200, 202, **202.12** *olden*, **545.9** *recorder*
antiquarianism 200, 202, **3.12** *historicism*
antiquarianize 3, 200.15 *look back*
antiquark 56.77 *elementary particle*
antiquary 200.11, **202.9** *antiquarian*
antiquated 3.15 *historic*, **200.19** *antiquarian*, **202.12** *olden*, **585.2** *not customary*, **600.4** *disused*, **614.1** *useless*
antique 3.11 *relic*, **200.7** *thing of the past*, **202.5** *old thing*, **202.12** *olden*, **526.7** *showpiece*
antique collector 202.9 *antiquarian*
antique costume 295.5 *fancy dress*
antiqued 202.12 *olden*
antique dealer 202.9 *antiquarian*
antiques fair 526.6 *display*
antique show 526.6 *display*
antiquity 202, **3.9** *distant past*, **3.11** *relic*, **200.1** *past time*
antiracism 627.11 *reformism*
antiracist 627.12 *reformer*
anti-realism 4.7 *school of thought*
anti-realist 4.11 *follower of a doctrine*, **4.14** *of a philosophy*
antireflection coating 56.29 *optical element*
anti-roll bar 71 Motor Vehicle Parts
antirrhinum 84 Flowers and Flowering Plants
antiscorbutic 62.14 *counteracting*
anti-semite 481.7 *bigot*
anti-Semite 820.5 *hostile person*, **822.9** *hater*
anti-semitic 481.10 *discriminatory*, **805.23** *prejudiced*
anti-Semitic 493.8 *unjust*, **820.7** *intolerant*, **822.11** *racist*
anti-semitism 481.4 *social discrimination*, **805.11** *prejudice*
anti-Semitism 493.3 *injustice*, **820.1** *enmity*, **822.3** *race hatred*
antisepsis 134.2 *purification*, **621.2** *cleaning*, **625.1** *hygiene*, **630.3** *prophylactic*
antiseptic 62.4 *drug type*, **62.14** *counteracting*, **134.14** *purified*, **621.9** *cleaning agent*, **621.16** *clean*, **625.4** *hygienic*, **630.3** *prophylactic*, **630.17** *remedial*, **632.7** *tutelary*
antiseptically 134.19 *purely*, **625.7** *hygienically*
antisepticize 621.15 *purify*, **625.6** *make hygienic*, **630.20** *doctor*
antiserum 62.4 *drug type*, **630.4** *antidote*
antisociability 834.1 *misanthropy*
antisocial 139.9 *aloof*, **168.16** *solitary*, **566.1** *taciturn*, **816.8** *unsociable*, **820.6** *hostile*, **834.3** *misanthropic*

antisocial attitude 834.1 *misanthropy*
antisocial behaviour 834.1 *misanthropy*
antisocial habits 816.1 *unsociability*
antisocially 816.14 *unsociably*, **820.14** *hostilely*, **834.5** *misanthropically*
antisocial personality 61.8 *disordered personality*
antispasmodic 62.4 *drug type*, **62.14** *counteracting*, **630.4** *antidote*
antispastic 62.4 *drug type*, **62.14** *counteracting*
Antisthenes 4 Philosophers
antistrophe 48.8 *part of poem*, **478.4** *reaction*
anti-submarine cruiser 679.24 *warship*
anti-submarine plane 679.31 *military aircraft*
anti-submarine submarine 679.24 *warship*
antisymmetric relation 52.63 *mathematical logic*
antitank weapon 680.5 *missile weapon*
anti-theft device 71 Motor Vehicle Parts
antithesis 4.5 *philosophical argument*, **4.8** *philosophical term*, **111.1** *oppositeness*, **287.1** *inversion*, **478.4** *reaction*, **536.3** *rebuttal*, **557.1** *ornament*, **663.6** *contrariety*
antithetic 111.4 *opposite*
antithetical 478.12 *reactive*, **557.4** *ornate*, **663.21** *contrary*
antithetically 111.6 *oppositely*, **478.24** *in answer*, **663.23** *opposingly*
antithrombin 62.4 *drug type*
antitoxin 231.2 *counteracting thing*, **630.4** *antidote*
antitrade winds 55.17 *wind system*
anti-transmit-receive switch 534.28 *radar*
Anti-Trust laws 699.2 *economic restraint*
antitussive 62.4 *drug type*, **62.14** *counteracting*
antivenene 62.4 *drug type*
antivenin 231.2 *counteracting thing*
antivenom 231.2 *counteracting thing*
anti-Vietnam War movement 675.1 *peace*, **677.1** *pacification*
antiviral 62.14 *counteracting*
antiviral drug 62.4 *drug type*
antivivisectionist 76.10 *animal welfarist*
anti-war movement 675.1 *peace*, **677.1** *pacification*
antler 380.8 *sharp-pointed thing*
Antlia 53 The Constellations
antlion 82 Insects, **82.5** *larva*
antlophobia 777 Phobias by Name
Antonian 7 Members of Religious Orders
Antonine Wall 298.1 *interface*, **671.9** *barrier*
antonomasia 48.12 *poetic language*, **560.7** *nomenclature*
Antony and Cleopatra 48 Shakespeare's plays, **821.10** *lovers*
antonym 5.17 *word*, **520.4** *type of meaning*
antonymous 5.42 *worded*, **520.6** *meaningful*
antrectomy 60 Surgical Operations
Antrim 92 Counties, **93** Cities
antrostomy 60 Surgical Operations
Antwerp 93 Cities
Antwerp blue 454.5 *blueness*
Antwerp Mannerists 50 Schools and Groups of Artists
Anu 8 Deities, **8** Deities
Anubis 8 Deities
a number 175.1 *plurality*

Anungite 8 Deities
anuran 79.7, **79.13** *amphibian*
anus 304.2 *rear end*, **322.4** *body orifice*, **347.7** *outlet*
anvil 382 Bones, **220.4** *medium of conversion*, **420.5** *internal ear*
anvil cloud 55.18 *cloud*
Anwar Sadat and Menachem Begin 675.4 *Nobel Peace Prize*
anxiety 61.12 *stress*, **153.1** *disturbance*, **510.6** *mental breakdown*, **513.1** *expectation*, **618.11** *harmfulness*, **631.4** *strain*, **633.5** *danger*, **659.4** *problem*, **777.2** *fearfulness*, **777.3** *worry*
anxiety equivalent 61.12 *stress*
anxiety hysteria 61.12 *stress*
anxiety neurosis 61.10 *neurosis*
anxiety reaction 61.10 *neurosis*
anxiety state 61.12 *stress*
anxious 153.12 *disturbed*, **513.5** *expecting*, **659.16** *troubled*, **777.8** *fearful*, **777.9** *worried*, **841.5** *distrustful*
anxiously 153.19 *distractedly*, **513.12** *expectantly*, **777.15** *fearfully*, **841.9** *jealously*
anxiousness 841.2 *distrust*
any 164, **120.6** *quantitative*, **142.6** *whole*
anybody 164.12 *any*
anybody's guess 477.6 *uncertainty*, **502.3** *unknown thing*
any day 185.27 *at what time*
anyhow 151, **327.16** *how*
any old thing 482.8 *indiscriminateness*
any old way 470.7 *negligently*
anyone 164.12 *any*
anyone's guess 491.9 *uncertainty*
any other business 472.2 *issue*, **592.1** *plan*
anything 164.12 *any*
anything but 536.17 *never*
anything goes 698.12 *unconditional*
anytime 185.27 *at what time*
any time 197.3 *another time*
any time but this 197.1 *different time*
any Tom, Dick, or Harry 502.4 *unknown person*
anyway 327.16 *how*
anywhere 253.15 *here*
anywise 327.16 *how*
Anzac 679.8 *soldier*
A-OK 537.21 *accurate*, **617.1** *worthy*, **619.1** *perfect*, **861.1** *good*
AOR 49.9 *popular music*
Aorangi 92 New Zealand Regions and Territories
aorist 5.34 *tense*
aoudad 77 Placental Mammals
apace 329.14 *swiftly*, **648.6** *hastily*
Apache 1 Peoples, **5** Languages and Groups of Languages
Apadana 7.12 *religious text*
apart 136, 136, 265, **104.11** *separate*, **104.18** *extraneously*, **108.6** *unrelated*, **136.22** *in isolation*, **174.16** *alone*, **174.22** *one by one*, **263.8** *distant*, **263.10** *distantly*, **343.16** *divergently*, **347.18** *forth*, **355.21**, **591.21** *away*, **816.8** *unsociable*, **824.13** *without one's spouse*
apart from 130.10 *additionally*, **147.12** *exclusively*
apartheid 104.3 *separateness*, **136.2** *setting apart*, **147.4** *exclusiveness*, **481.4** *social discrimination*, **493.3** *injustice*, **805.11** *prejudice*, **816.3** *separation*, **820.1** *enmity*, **822.3** *race hatred*
apartment 256.5 *house*, **725.1** *property*
apartment block 256
apartment building 63.20 *building*, **243.8** *construction*
apartment sharer 724.3 *participant*
apartment-sharing 724.5 *jointly possessing*
apartness 174.5 *aloneness*, **816.1** *unsociability*
a party to 724.3 *participant*

apathetic 598, 240.5 *inert,*
325.5 *sedentary,* 328.5 *unhur-*
ried, 404.6 *unfeeling,* 466.4 *un-*
interested, 468.7 *inattentive,*
573.3 *cautious,* 576.4 *unsteady,*
591.18 *avoiding,* 641.3 *inactive,*
643.3 *not participating,* 761.1
insensitive, 783.7 *indifferent,*
787.3 *unmoved*
apathetically 598, 240.7 *inertly,*
325.10 *motionlessly,* 466.8 *dis-*
interestedly, 468.14 *inatten-*
tively, 591.23 *shyly,* 641.5 *with-*
out action, 643.16 *impassively,*
761.8 *unfeelingly,* 783.17 *indif-*
ferently, 787.9 *without wonder*
apathy 576, 61.13 *depression,*
240.1 *inertness,* 325.1 *motion-*
lessness, 404.1 *lack of feeling,*
466.2 *lack of interest,* 468.1 *in-*
attention, 573.13 *dissociation,*
591.13 *shirking,* 641.1 *inaction,*
643.7 *idleness,* 673.1 *submis-*
sion, 761.3 *insensitiveness,*
783.1 *indifference,* 787.1 *lack of*
wonder
apatite 54 Minerals
apatosaur 79 Fossil Reptiles
Apaturia 10.16 *religious festival*
Apaya 8.11 *heaven*
APB 590.1 *pursuit*
ape 77 Placental Mammals,
110.9 *duplicate,* 114.12 *imitate,*
118.7 *imitator,* 118.9 *imitate,*
510.11 *insane,* 815.10 *social an-*
imal
aped 114.8 *simulated*
apeirophobia 777 Phobias by
Name
apellative 560.8 *name*
apeman 202.7 *ancient people,*
400.3 *uncivilized human*
Apennine 95 Mountains
Apennines 53 Mountains
Apep 8 Deities
aperient 62.4 *drug type,* 62.17
stimulating, 134.4 *purgative,*
349.28 *propellant,* 353.25 *fae-*
cal, 621.2 *cleaning,* 630.6 *purga-*
tive
apéritif 154.5 *preface,* 351.7 *alco-*
holic drink, 411.3 *appetizer*
aperture 53.28 *resolution,* 66.18
exposure time, 265.2 *crack,*
322.1 *opening*
aperture priority 66.18 *exposure*
time
aperture setting 66.18 *exposure*
time
aperture stop 56.32 *optical in-*
strument
aperture synthesis 53.26 *radio*
telescope
apery 118.3 *mockery*
apes 77.16 *primate*
Apet 8 Deities
apex 33.6 *motor racing terms,*
52.39 *angle,* 275.2 *heights,*
279.1 *summit*
APEX 754.4 *bargain*
Apfelstrudel 45.46 *German dish*
aphaeresis 270.2 *shortening*
aphanitic texture 54.28 *rock*
aphasia 61.14 *trance,* 563.3
speech defect
aphasic 422.3 *silent,* 563.12 *in-*
articulate
aphelion 53.21 *orbit*
apheresis 562.2 *outline*
aphid 82 Insects, 69.12 *pests*
and diseases, 82.3 *pest*
aphonia 61.14 *trance,* 422.4 *si-*
lence, 563.1 *voicelessness*
aphonic 422.3 *silent,* 563.9 *voice-*
less
aphorism 4.1 *philosophy,* 505.1
maxim, 537.4 *truism,* 552.2 *out-*
line
aphoristic 505.2 *proverbial,*
537.17 *truistic,* 552.3 *concise*
aphoristically 505.4 *proverbially*
aphorize 505, 4.22 *propound a*
philosophy
aphrenia 61.12 *subnormality*
aphrodisia 821.5 *desire*
aphrodisiac 405.4 *pleasurable*
things

Aphrodite 8 Deities, 821.16 *gods*
and goddesses of love
a piacere 49 Musical Terms
apiarian 82.14 *entomological*
apiarist 82.8 *entomologist*
apiary 82.4 *social insect*
apical 279.5 *top*
apical bud 83.8 *bud*
apicectomy 60 Surgical Operations
a picture of health 623.1 *healthy*
apiece 165.32 *severally*
a piece of the action 642.2 *social*
activity
aping 114.1 *similarity,* 118.12
imitative
apiphobia 777 Phobias by Name
apish 118.12 *imitative*
apishly 118.14 *imitatively*
Apisirahts 8 Deities
a pity 835.5 *misfortune*
APL 65 Programming Languages
a place for everything and every-
thing in its place 150.5 *orderli-*
ness
a plague on you 862.15 *bad luck*
aplanospore 90.4 *reproductive*
body
aplastic anaemia 624.11 *blood*
disease
a pleasure 660.6 *easy thing*
aplenty 181.13 *numerously*
aplite 54 Common Rocks
aplomb 4.3 *detachment,* 225.2
determination, 574.16 *fortitude*
apoandrous 84.12 *of flowers*
apocalypse 157.5 *fate,* 244.4
ruin, 457.4 *something that ap-*
pears, 517.1 *prediction,* 530.1
disclosure
apocalyptic 157.20 *ending,*
244.4 *destructive,* 457.7 *ap-*
pearing, 517.13 *predicting,*
530.12 *revelatory*
apocarpous 86.9 *of a fruit*
apocope 270.2 *shortening,* 552.1
conciseness, 562.2 *outline*
apocrine 352.4 *secretory*
apocrine secretion 352.1 *secretion*
Apocrypha 7.12 *religious text*
apocryphal 491.5 *uncertified,*
540.28 *spurious*
Apoda 79.7 *amphibian*
apodal 79.11 *reptilian*
apodan 79.7, 79.13 *amphibian*
apodasis 5.23 *phrase*
apodeictic 4.16 *dialectical,* 475.9
demonstrated, 522.2 *simple,*
526.13 *displayed,* 550.3 *clear*
apoenzyme 58.11 *enzyme*
apogee 53.35 *rocketry,* 279.1
summit
apolitical 116.20 *agreeable*
Apollinaire 48 Poets
Apollinarianism 7 Christian
Movements
Apollo 8 Deities, **8** Deities, **53**
Minor Planets, 48.13 *poetic ge-*
nius, 53.31 *space travel*
Apollonius 53 Mountains
Apollonius of Perga 52 Scientists
Apollonius of Rhodes 48 Poets
Apollonius' theorem 52 Named
Concepts
Apollyon 8.7 *devil*
apologetic 473, 484.5 *counter-*
ing, 840.4 *atoning,* 855.11 *vin-*
dicatory, 867.6 *penitent*
apologetical 840.4 *atoning*
apologetically 473, 484.9 *to the*
contrary, 840.8 *penitently,*
855.15 *in vindication,* 867.8
penitently
apologetics 7.13 *theology,* 463.3
debate
apologies 867.1 *penitence*
apologist 463.5 *reasoner,* 855.5
vindicator
apologize 840, 473.16 *plead,*
484.7 *counter,* 578.4 *recant,*
673.4 *succumb,* 710.14 *offer rep-*
aration, 765.11 *recompense,*
867.4 *be penitent*
apologize to 840.6 *apologize*
apology 840, 48.4 *non-fiction,*
473.5 *plea,* 484.1 *counterevid-*

ence, 578.8 *recantation,* 765.2
reparation, 867.1 *penitence*
apomorphine 62 Medication
a poor thing but my own 119.1
originality
apopetalous 84.12 *of flowers*
apophthegm 505.1 *maxim,*
876.7 *moral*
apophyge 43 Architectural Decoration
apophyllite 54 Minerals
apoplectic 1.15 *physical,* 828.16
angry
apoplectically 828.18 *angrily*
apoplectic build 1.9 *physical type*
apoplexy 236.4 *disability,* 366.8
spasm, 624.2 *illness*
aporetic 4.16 *dialectical*
aposepalous 84.12 *of flowers*
apostasize 484.8 *reverse,* 536.9
renounce
apostasy 578, 221.1 *reversion,*
476.2 *denial,* 484.2 *reversal,*
536.2 *rejection,* 581.7 *abrogation*
apostate 168.8 *dissenter,* 220.6
convert, 484.4 *tergiversator,*
498.5 *disbeliever,* 536.6 *negativ-*
ist, 578.9 *equivocator,* 578.11
equivocating, 591.17 *avoider,*
720.5 *nonobserver*
apostatic 484.5 *countering*
apostatical 598.5 *relinquished*
apostatically 598.8 *apathetically*
apostatize 578, 220.10 *be con-*
verted, 498.8 *disbelieve,* 576.9
change sides, 581.4 *revoke,*
598.2 *withdraw*
a posteriori 4.16 *dialectical*
apostle 138.5, 155.14 *follower,*
220.5 *converter*
Apostolic Brethren 7 Christian
Movements
apostrophe 5.36 *accent,* 48.12
poetic language, 543.7 *punctua-*
tion, 567.1 *address,* 569.1 *solilo-*
quy
apostrophic 569.5 *soliloquizing*
apostrophize 564.14 *speak to,*
567.7 *address,* 569.3 *soliloquize*
apostrophized 543.17 *punctuated*
apothecaries' measure 268.5
measuring system
apothecaries' weight 75.1 *unit,*
268.5 *measuring system,* 369.9
avoirdupois weight
apothecary 630.16 *druggist*
apotheosis 8.9 *deification,* 361.7
lift, 851.3 *praise*
apotheosize 8.17 *deify,* 9.8
idolatrize, 361.3 *promote,*
849.16 *revere,* 851.14 *praise*
apotheosized 361.12 *exalted*
apozem 387.10 *solution*
appal 341.4 *be repulsive,* 764.10
displease, 777.13 *frighten*
Appalachian 95 Mountains
Appalachian Mountains 95.4 *US*
mountains
appalling 341.8 *repulsive,*
777.10 *frightening*
Appaloosa 32 Breeds of Horse
and Pony
appanage 130.1 *addition,* 725.3
historic property terms
apparat 12.3 *governance*
apparatchik 653.16 *official*
apparatus 232.2 *instrument,*
603.1 *tool*
apparatus criticus 524.2 *annota-*
tion
apparel 295.1, 295.32 *dress*
apparelled 295.29 *dressed*
apparent 289, 322.13 *opened*
up, 435.23, 437.1 *visible,* 457.7
appearing, 475.12 *demonstrable,*
483.9 *evident,* 488.6 *probable,*
513.7 *expected,* 526.13 *dis-*
played, 526.14 *manifest,*
540.30 *pretending*
apparently 102, 457, 289.15 *ex-*
ternally, 322.25 *obviously,*
435.25, 437.11 *visibly,* 483.15
evidently, 488.11 *probably,*
496.16 *originally,* 526.16 *mani-*
festly, 528.19 *reportedly,* 540.37
spuriously

apparent magnitude 53.13 *lumi-*
nosity
apparentness 289.3 *appearance,*
442.10 *openness,* 540.7 *pretence*
apparent power 64.26 *electrical*
energy
apparent wind 36.1 *sailing*
apparition 8.8 *divine manifesta-*
tion, 11.11 *ghost,* 253.6 *ghostly*
presence, 435.5 *imagination,*
457.4 *something that appears,*
519.5 *fantasy,* 526.10 *manifes-*
tation
apparitor 16.10 *law officer*
appeal 16.7 *legal trial,* 27.19 *dis-*
miss, 233.8 *influence,* 340.4 *al-*
lurement, 340.11 *attract,*
477.17 *question,* 484.1 *coun-*
terevidence, 484.7 *counter,*
536.3 *rebuttal,* 536.8 *rebut,*
567.2 *salutation,* 712.1 *request,*
712.3 *solicitation,* 712.6 *re-*
quest, 712.8 *solicit money,*
729.3 *offering,* 746.1 *payment,*
763.6 *pleasantness,* 782.5 *object*
of desire, 789.1 *gorgeousness,*
821.4 *lovability,* 821.28 *win the*
love of
appealed 536.12 *rejected*
appealer 712.4 *requester*
appeal fund 605.1 *store*
appealing 233, 340.9 *attractive,*
712.3 *solicitation,* 763.1 *pleas-*
ant, 782.8 *desirable,* 784.5 *lik-*
able, 789.6 *personable,* 821.22
lovable
appealingly 340.14 *attractively,*
784.10 *with great liking,* 821.30
lovingly
appeal to 567, 228.9 *motivate,*
564.14 *speak to*
appeal to arms 674.6 *fight,*
676.7 *war measures,* 676.12 *go*
to war
appeal to law 16.70 *litigate*
appeal to one's better feelings
835.11 *excite pity*
appeal to the electorate 580.5
vote
appear 437, 457, 475, 51.32
act, 156.27 *emerge,* 253.11 *be*
present, 253.12 *attend,* 289.13
appear outwardly, 344.1 *arrive,*
347.10 *emerge,* 435.19 *be vis-*
ible, 457.12 *become visible,*
496.5 *be discovered,* 526.4 *show*
oneself, 530.9 *be disclosed,*
540.24 *mask*
appearance 289, 457, 8.8 *di-*
vine manifestation, 102.2 *illu-*
sion, 105.1 *state,* 156.2 *cre-*
ation, 253.2 *omnipresence,*
306.6 *nature,* 344.10 *arrival,*
346.1 *entry,* 483.3 *evidentness,*
519.4 *ideality,* 526.10 *manifes-*
tation, 540.12 *facade,* 652.1
conduct, 796.4 *design*
Appearance 457
appearance of truth 537.12 *true*
to life
appear for 478.23 *answer for,*
707.4 *substitute for*
appear guilty 866
appear in 457.13 *occur*
appear in court 457.13 *occur*
appearing 457, 344.18 *arriving,*
457.1 *appearance,* 526.14 *mani-*
fest
appearing before the judge
16.53 *litigating*
appearing guilty 866
appearing in court 16.53 *litigat-*
ing
appearing true 537.25 *lifelike*
appear in the shops 457.13 *occur*
appear like 457.11 *appear*
appear on a chat show 477.19 *be*
questioned
appear on film 457.13 *occur*
appear on stage 457.13 *occur*
appear outwardly 289
appear straightforward 787.8 *be*
predictable
appear to be 457.11 *appear*
appease 9.7 *worship,* 242.4 *mod-*
erate, 374.16 *yield,* 376.13
smooth over, 405.10 *comfort,*

586.15 *persuade*, 673.3 *submit*, 677.4 *pacify*, 710.14 *offer reparation*, 710.15 *offer worship*, 765.9 *comfort*, 765.11 *recompense*, 767.9 *relieve*, 840.5 *atone*
appeased 767.7 *relieved*
appeasement 9.1 *worship*, 374.12 *gentleness*, 673.1 *submission*, 677.1 *pacification*, 710.6 *offering*, 765.2 *reparation*, 767.1 *ease*, 840.1 *atonement*
appeaser 673, 678.3 *mediator*
appeasing 374.7 *impressionable*, 677.6 *pacificatory*, 840.4 *atoning*
appellant 16.8 *litigant*, 712.4 *requester*, 856.3 *accuser*
appellate 16.49 *judicatory*
appellate court 16.19 *lawcourt*
appellation 560.7 *nomenclature*, 560.8 *name*
append 130.6 *add*
appendage 130.1 *addition*, 143.4 *component*, 180.4 *concomitant*, 808.5 *adherent*
appendages 725.4 *possessions*
appendant 155.19 *additional*
appendectomy 60 Surgical Operations, 630.12 *surgery*
appendicostomy 60 Surgical Operations
appendicular skeleton 382.7 *skeleton*
appendix 107.1 *relatedness*, 130.3 *additional item*, 155.8 *addition*, 157.10 *ending*, 304.1 *rear*, 524.2 *annotation*
apperceive 459.12 *think*
apperception 459.1 *mind*
apperceptionism 61.1 *psychology*
appertain 107.7 *relate to*, 116.27 *fit*
appertaining 116.16 *fitting*
appertain to 146.5 *be included*
appetency 782.1 *desire*
appetite 350, 782, 411.5 *taster*, 782.1 *desire*, 784.1 *liking*
appetizer 411, 45.12 *hors d'oeuvre*, 143.2 *particular*, 154.5 *preface*, 350.14 *mouthful*
appetizing 350.27 *edible*, 411.7 *tasty*, 413.9 *piquant*, 763.4 *tasty*, 782.8 *desirable*
appetizingly 782.17 *desirably*
appinite 54 Common Rocks
applaud 9.7 *worship*, 543.11 *gesture*, 769.8 *cheer*, 773.7 *dance*, 812.18 *salute*, 837.6 *be grateful*, 851.16 *acclaim*
applauder 851
applauding 773.9 *rejoicing*, 851.20 *acclamatory*
applause 51.6 *scene*, 431.3 *cry of praise*, 543.3 *gesture*, 769.5 *cheer*, 773.2 *fanfare*, 812.9 *rejoicing*, 837.3 *recognition*, 851.5 *acclaim*
apple 85 Trees and Shrubs, **86** Fruits, 22.3 *baseball equipment*, 23.3 *basketball equipment*
apple aphid 69.12 *pests and diseases*
apple blossom 84.1 *flower*
apple blossom weevil 69.12 *pests and diseases*
apple box 85 Trees and Shrubs
apple cheeks 450.7 *red thing*, 623.3 *health*
apple corer 355.9 *extractor*
apple fritter 45.36 *cake*
apple juice 351.6 *soft drink*
apple-knocker 255.5 *countryman*
apple of discord 86.5 *figurative usage*
apple of one's eye 86.5 *figurative usage*, 821.11 *loved one*, 826.6 *object of endearment*
apple peel 614.6 *refuse*
apple pie 45.36 *cake*, 414.3 *dessert*
apple-pie order 150.5 *orderliness*
apple polisher 86.5 *figurative usage*
apple-polishing 808.2 *sycophancy*, 808.7 *sycophantic*
apples 86.5 *figurative usage*

apple sauce 45.15 *sauce*, 86.5 *figurative usage*
apple sawfly 69.12 *pests and diseases*
Appleton layer 390.3 *atmospheric layers*
appliance 232.2 *instrument*, 599.6 *use*, 603.1 *tool*, 662.7 *convenience*
appliances 602.1 *means*
applicability 485.1 *qualification*, 599.6 *use*, 613.5 *usefulness*
applicable 232.6 *instrumental*, 599.10 *usable*, 613.1 *useful*, 615.1 *convenient*
applicant 674.10 *contender*, 712.4 *requester*
application 65, 232.1 *instrumentality*, 467.3 *carefulness*, 520.4 *type of meaning*, 524.1 *interpretation*, 575.2 *commitment*, 599.6 *use*, 613.5 *usefulness*, 615.3 *convenience*, 630.10 *surgical dressing*, 642.8 *assiduity*, 712.1 *request*
applications program 65.8 *software*
applied 56.99 *theoretical*, 232.8 *practical*, 613.1 *useful*
applied arts 50.1 *art*
applied energy 644.4 *exertion*
applied linguistics 5.1 *linguistics*
applied load 63.14 *load*
applied mathematics 52
applied physics 56.4 *experimental physics*, 367.6 *natural science*
applied psychology 61.1 *psychology*
applied science 501.5 *science*
applied sociology 2.1 *sociology*
appliqué 42 Hobbies and Pastimes, 792.2 *pattern*
apply 62.19 *administer*, 107.7 *relate to*, 485.14 *be qualified*, 712.6 *request*
apply a remedy 630.19 *remedy*
apply a tourniquet 630.20 *doctor*
apply for 593.8 *miss*, 712.6 *request*
applying pressure 407.2 *touching*
apply oneself 644.8 *exert oneself*
apply oneself to 567.12 *address oneself to*, 597.1 *undertake*
apply one's mind 461.13 *concentrate*
apply peine forte et dure 879.4 *torture*
apply pressure 695.6 *compel*
apply the match 156.20 *activate*
apply the war paint 791.16 *make up*
apply to 107.7 *relate to*, 567.8 *appeal to*
apply try out 599.1 *use*
appoggiatura 49.16 *musical note*
appoint 7.21 *ordain*, 580.4 *pick*, 582.1 *predetermine*, 688.21 *grant authority*, 692.13 *authorize*, 703.6 *commission*, 706.4 *delegate*, 707.6 *deputize*
appoint a proxy 703.8 *authorize*
appoint a representative 703.6 *commission*
appointed 251.6 *situated*, 582.3 *predetermined*, 688.13 *elected*, 692.15 *self-assured*, 703.9 *commissioned*, 706.6 *delegated*
appointed day 185.11 *date*
appointed person 706.1 *delegate*
appointee 703.5 *commissioner*, 706.1 *delegate*
appointment 7.9 *priesthood*, 161.8 *rendezvous*, 580.6 *selection*, 594.11 *fitting out*, 688.3 *acquisition of power*, 692.4 *authorization*, 703.1 *commission*, 706.3 *delegation*, 731.1 *allocation*, 815.3 *meeting*
appointments 603.6 *equipment*
appointments calendar 516.4 *prudence*, 517.3 *plan*
Appomattox 93 Cities
apportion 120.8 *quantify*, 136.11 *divide*, 143.10 *part*, 268.11 *measure out*, 599.5 *dispose of*, 731.4 *allot*
apportioned 731.7 *allocated*

apportioning 731.1 *allocation*
apportionment 731.1 *allocation*
appose 267.3 *juxtapose*
apposite 107.4 *related*, 116.16 *fitting*
appositely 107.10 *relevantly*, 116.38 *fittingly*
appositeness 107.1 *relatedness*, 485.1 *qualification*
apposition 5.30 *syntax*, 267.1 *juxtaposition*
appraisable 268.14 *measurable*
appraisal 268.1 *measurement*, 481.1 *discrimination*, 492.1 *judgment*
appraise 268.10 *measure*, 492.12 *estimate*, 751.11 *price*
appraisement 268.1 *measurement*, 751.7 *tax*
appraiser 268.9 *measurer*, 492.5 *judge*
appreciate 128.4 *increase*, 411.9 *taste*, 501.11 *know*, 721.10 *augment*, 753.9 *be dear*, 763.14, 784.7 *like*, 821.23 *love*, 837.6 *be grateful*, 849.15 *respect*
appreciated 784.5 *likable*, 849.12 *respected*
appreciation 128.1 *increase*, 481.2 *judiciousness*, 492.1 *judgment*, 721.2 *augmentation*, 837.1 *gratitude*, 849.1 *respect*, 851.2 *admiration*
appreciative 481.9 *discriminating*, 492.8 *judging*, 794.5 *refined*, 837.4 *grateful*, 849.8 *respectful*, 851.18 *approving*
appreciatively 481.16 *judiciously*, 837.8 *gratefully*
appreciativeness 837.1 *gratitude*
appreciatory 851.18 *approving*
apprehend 4.21 *rationalize*, 471.14 *have an idea*, 501.11 *know*, 513.8 *expect*, 522.6 *understand*, 696.15 *learn*, 699.11 *detain*, 734.10 *take away*
apprehending 734.3 *taking away*
apprehensibility 522.9 *intelligibility*
apprehensible 522.1 *intelligible*
apprehension 16.6 *legal process*, 471.1 *idea*, 501.1 *knowledge*, 513.1 *expectation*, 522.12 *understanding*, 633.5 *danger*, 777.2 *fearfulness*
apprehensive 513.5 *expecting*, 777.8 *fearful*, 841.5 *distrustful*
apprehensively 513.12 *expectantly*, 777.15 *fearfully*, 841.9 *jealously*
apprehensiveness 513.1 *expectation*, 777.2 *fearfulness*, 841.2 *distrust*
apprentice 6.7 *learner*, 149.7 *newcomer*, 156.14 *beginner*, 201.12 *immature*, 595.4 *untrained*, 646.2 *artisan*, 656.2 *unskilled*, 656.10 *unskilled person*, 701.3 *subordinate*, 701.6 *subject*
apprentice chef 45.2 *cook*
apprenticed 701.9 *subject*
apprentice oneself 597.1 *undertake*
apprenticeship 206.1 *youth*, 594.12 *briefing*, 701.1 *subjection*
apprise 6.22 *educate*, 528.11 *inform*, 636.5 *warn*, 854.5 *advise*
approach 342, 344, 567, 567, 21.2 *field events*, 29.1 *golf*, 52.94 *order*, 73.5 *flight*, 199.7 *be in the future*, 234.4 *tend*, 264.1 *nearness*, 264.9 *near*, 324.3 *motion towards*, 327.1 *way*, 327.2 *route*, 327.14 *find one's way*, 342.9 *converge*, 344.10 *arrival*, 346.5 *entrance*, 356.4 *access*, 549.1 *style*, 592.2 *policy*, 592.9 *plan*, 602.1 *means*, 710.1, 710.9 *offer*, 712.1, 712.6 *request*, 721.2 *augmentation*, 721.10 *augment*
approachability 486.2 *possibleness*
approachable 344.20 *attainable*, 486.5 *possible*
approach a problem 592.9 *plan*
approaches 264.3 *near place*

approaching 344, 199.11 *future*, 264.5 *near*, 342.8 *advancing*
approaching shot 29.3 *golf shots*
approach light 439.6 *electric light*
approach of time 199.6 *future event*
approbation 499.1 *assent*, 667.1 *agreement*, 708.1 *permission*, 800.1 *estimation*, 849.1 *respect*, 851.1 *approval*
approbatory 851.18 *approving*
appropriable 733.12 *adoptive*
appropriate 122.9 *adequate*, 203.14 *seasonable*, 210.6 *timely*, 210.9 *opportunely*, 485.9 *qualified*, 615.1 *convenient*, 667.13 *suitable*, 721.9 *gain*, 731.4 *allot*, 733.8 *adopt*, 734.7 *take*, 736.12 *steal*, 845.13 *fit*, 846.14 *arrogate*, 861.1 *good*
appropriated 733.11 *borrowed*, 733.12 *adoptive*, 734.12 *taking*
appropriately 116.38 *fittingly*, 485.17 *capably*, 667.17 *suitably*
appropriateness 210.1 *timeliness*, 485.1 *qualification*, 861.8 *good*
appropriating 723.1 *possession*, 733.12 *adoptive*
appropriation 723.1 *possession*, 731.1 *allocation*, 733.2 *adoption*, 734.1 *taking*, 846.3 *arrogation*
appropriation of land 301.1 *enclosure*
appropriator 734.6 *taker*
approvable 851
approvably 851
approval 851, 116.7 *consent*, 284.6 *moral support*, 453.15 *green light*, 499.1 *assent*, 667.1 *agreement*, 708.1 *permission*, 784.1 *liking*, 800.1 *estimation*, 849.1 *respect*
Approval 851
approve 851, 116.28 *consent*, 499.4 *assent*, 580.4 *pick*, 667.6 *agree with*, 688.21 *grant authority*, 708.3 *permit*, 784.8 *prefer*
approved 851, 116.17 *consenting*, 584.12 *established*, 615.1 *convenient*, 617.1 *worthy*, 667.10 *agreeing*, 688.16 *authorized*, 708.7 *permitted*, 800.3 *reputable*
approved for use 613.2 *usable*
approved school 702.1 *prison*
approved strike 15.4 *industrial dispute*
approve of 284.14 *give moral support*, 492.11 *judge*, 851.11 *approve*
approving 851, 116.17 *consenting*, 492.8 *judging*, 499.6 *assenting*, 667.10 *agreeing*, 784.6 *liking*
approvingly 851, 116.39 *with consent*, 492.13 *judicially*, 667.14 *agreeably*, 784.11 *admiringly*
approximate 52.93 *equate*, 114.7 *similar*, 120.6 *quantitative*, 164.20 *generalized*, 264.5 *near*, 375.5 *unfinished*, 375.13 *be unfinished*
approximately 52.87 *mathematically*, 114.14 *comparably*, 120.7 *quantitatively*, 164.29 *generally*, 264.7 *nearly*, 375.15 *incompletely*, 504.22 *wrongly*
approximately equal to 52.88 *equal to*
approximateness 375.10 *rough idea*
approximate to 114.11 *make similar*
approximating 114.7 *similar*, 264.5 *near*
approximation 52.66 *proof*, 114.1 *similarity*, 170.1 *calculation*, 264.1 *nearness*, 268.1 *measurement*, 504.2 *inaccuracy*
appulse 264.1 *nearness*
appurtenance 130.1 *addition*, 146.2 *thing included*, 180.4 *concomitant*

appurtenances 723.4 *possession*, 725.4 *possessions*
appurtenant 146.8 *included*, 148.8 *belonging*
APR 745.4 *interest*
apricate 392.19 *bake*
apricot 86 *Fruits*, 451.1 *orange*, 451.3 *orange thing*
April fool 539.22 *dupe*
April fool hoax 539.11 *hoax*
April Fools' Day 214.6 *annually celebrated day*
April shower 224.3 *changeable thing*
April showers 55.25 *rain*
a priori 4.16 *dialectical*
a priori knowledge 4.9 *philosophical problem*
apriorism 4.7 *school of thought*
apriorist 4.11 *follower of a doctrine*
apron 7.11 *vestment*, 51.15 *stage*, 73.4 *airport*, 295.25 *accessories*, 621.11 *cleaning cloth*
apron stage 51.15 *stage*
apron strings 661.4 *restraint*
apropos 210.6 *timely*, 210.9 *opportunely*
apse 43.10 *church architecture*
apt 6.17 *educatable*, 122.9 *adequate*, 210.6 *timely*, 478.15 *correspondent*, 485.9 *qualified*, 486.5 *possible*, 488.6 *probable*, 537.21 *accurate*, 558.3 *elegant*, 655.6 *skilful*, 667.13 *suitable*, 782.8 *desirable*, 861.1 *good*
APT 72.10 *miscellaneous*
apterium 78.17 *plumage*
apteryx 78 *Birds*
aptitude 234, 655, 6.10 *educatability*, 165.7 *special skill*, 235.2 *ability*, 459.4 *cleverness*, 485.1 *qualification*, 486.2 *possibleness*, 501.2 *information*, 507.2 *intelligence*, 660.1 *easiness*, 784.2 *inclination*
aptitude test 61.5 *psychological test*
aptly 6.26 *studiously*, 116.38 *fittingly*, 210.9 *opportunely*, 478.26 *correspondingly*, 485.17 *capably*, 558.5 *elegantly*, 667.17 *suitably*, 843.18 *properly*
aptness 6.10 *educatability*, 210.1 *timeliness*, 478.8 *correspondence*, 485.1 *qualification*, 537.8 *accuracy*, 558.1 *elegance*, 655.2 *aptitude*, 667.7 *suitability*, 861.8 *good*
apt to 234.5 *tending to*
Apu-hau 8 *Deities*
Apuleius 48 *Writers*
Apu-matangi 8 *Deities*
Apus 53 *The Constellations*
aquaculture 97.5 *oceanography*
aquamarine 54 *Gemstones*, 453.1 *green*, 453.11 *green thing*, 454.1 *blue*, 454.6 *blue thing*
aquaplaning 71.21 *miscellaneous motoring terms*
aquarelle 50.8 *painting*
aquarellist 50.16 *artist*
aquarist 80.12 *ichthyologist*
aquarium 80.6 *study of fish*, 161.31 *exhibition*, 256.12 *stall*, 605.5 *collection*
aquarium fish 80.2 *fish*
Aquarius 53 *The Constellations*, 53 *Zodiac Constellations*, 326.7 *transferor*
aquatic 74.11 *nautical*, 76.15 *of animals*, 83.2 *plant*, 83.14 *of plants*, 389.21 *watery*
aquatic animal 76
aquatint 50.7 *picture*, 50.15 *engraving*, 50.22 *engrave*
aquatinter 50.18 *engraver*
aquavit 351.7 *alcoholic drink*
aqueduct 63.21, 327.9 *bridge*
aqueous 389.21 *watery*
aqueous humour 435.2 *eye*
aquicultural 69.16 *horticultural*
aquiculture 69.5 *gardening*, 389.18 *hydrography*
aquifer 54.9 *groundwater*
Aquila 53 *The Constellations*

aquilegia 84 *Flowers and Flowering Plants*
aquiline 78.23 *avian*
Aquinas 4 *Philosophers*
Ara 53 *The Constellations*
Arab 32 *Breeds of Horse and Pony*
arabesque 41.7 *ice-dancing*, 46.9 *ballet steps*, 288.2 *braid*
arabesque penchée 46.9 *ballet steps*
arabesques 557.1 *ornament*
Arabian 97 *Oceans and Seas*, 98 *Deserts*
Arabic 5 *Languages and Groups of Languages*, 5.41 *lettered*
Arabic alphabet 5.41 *alphabet*
Arabic numeral 52.9 *numeral*, 169.1 *number*
arabinan 58.4 *polysaccharide*
arabinose 58 *Common Sugars*
Arabist 200.11 *antiquarian*
arable 68.11 *farmland*, 68.20 *farmable*
arable farm 68.6 *farm*
arable farmer 68.15 *agriculturist*
arable farming 68, 68.1 *agriculture*
arable land 68.11 *farmland*
Arabs 1 *Peoples*
arachnephobia 777 *Phobias by Name*
arachnid 82, 81.4 *arthropod*
Arachnida 81.4 *arthropod*, 82.2 *arachnid*
arachnidan 82, 81.18 *arthropodous*
arachnoid 81.18 *arthropodous*, 82.11 *arachnidan*
arachnological 82, 81.18 *arthropodous*
arachnologist 82, 81.15 *invertebrate zoologist*
arachnology 81.14 *invertebrate zoology*, 82.7 *study*
Arafura 97 *Oceans and Seas*
Aragadro's hypothesis 56 *Named Laws*
Arago 52 *Scientists*
Aragon 48 *Poets*
aragonite 54 *Minerals*
Aral 97 *Oceans and Seas*
Aral Sea 94.5 *other major lakes*
Aralu 8.11 *heaven*
Aramaic 5 *Languages and Groups of Languages*
Aranda 5 *Languages and Groups of Languages*
Aran sweater 295.13 *sweater*
Aranyaka 7.12 *religious text*
Arapaho 1 *Peoples*, 5 *Languages and Groups of Languages*
Ararat 95 *Mountains*, 95.6 *other major mountains and ranges*
araroba 85 *Tree Products*
Arat Duzzakh 8.11 *heaven*
Araucana 68 *Breeds of Fowl*
Araucanian 5 *Languages and Groups of Languages*, 7 *Non-Christian Religions*
Araucanians 1 *Peoples*
araucaria 85 *Trees and Shrubs*
Arawakan 5 *Languages and Groups of Languages*
Arawaks 1 *Peoples*, 200.6 *people of the past*
arbalest 680.6 *historical missile weapon*
arbalester 679.13 *historical soldiery*
arbiter 16.23 *judge*, 242.2 *moderator*, 492.5 *judge*, 654.4 *adviser*, 678.3 *mediator*
arbitrage 737.4 *trade*
arbitral 678.6 *mediatory*
arbitrament of war 676.1 *war*
arbitrarily 16.85 *summarily*, 229.8 *by chance*, 579.6 *capriciously*, 690.11 *severely*, 698.21 *excessively*
arbitrariness 108.1 *unrelatedness*, 229.1 *lack of motive*, 579.2 *caprice*
arbitrary 108.7 *illogical*, 229.6 *motiveless*, 570.9 *autocratic*,

577.2 *refractory*, 579.1 *capricious*, 698.12 *unconditional*
arbitrary power 690.1 *severity*
arbitrate 15.12 *have an industrial dispute*, 158.19 *mediate*, 242.4 *moderate*, 492.11 *judge*, 678.1 *mediate*, 707.5 *represent*, 717.4 *compromise*, 843.14 *be fair*
arbitrated 15.10 *unionized*, 716.8 *negotiated*
arbitrating 15.10 *unionized*
arbitration 15.4 *industrial dispute*, 158.6 *middle ground*, 492.1 *judgment*, 677.1 *pacification*, 678.2 *mediation*, 716.1 *negotiation*, 717.1 *compromise*
arbitrational 678.6 *mediatory*
arbitration award 15.4 *industrial dispute*
arbitration court 15.4 *industrial dispute*
arbitration of interests 15.4 *industrial dispute*
arbitration of rights 15.4 *industrial dispute*
arbitration tribunal 15.4 *industrial dispute*
arbitrator 15.6 *employer*, 16.23 *judge*, 26.8 *karate*, 158.9 *middleman*, 242.2 *moderator*, 333.3 *moderate person*, 492.5 *judge*, 654.4, 662.14 *adviser*, 678.3 *mediator*, 707.3 *agent*, 715.4 *contractor*, 716.4 *negotiator*, 859.3 *impartial person*
arboraceous 85.14 *treelike*
arboreal 69.16 *horticultural*, 76.15 *of animals*, 85.14 *treelike*, 343.9 *branched*
arboreous 85.16 *wooded*
arborescence 343.4 *branching*
arborescent 85.14 *treelike*, 343.9 *branched*
arboretum 69.2 *garden*, 85.4 *trees*
arborical 69.16 *horticultural*
arboricultural 85, 69.16 *horticultural*
arboriculturally 85
arboriculture 69.1 *horticulture*, 83.10 *plant science*, 85.5 *forestry*
arboriculturist 69.13 *horticulturist*, 85.8 *forester*
arboriform 343.9 *branched*
arborist 85.8 *forester*
arborization 343.4 *branching*
arbor vitae 85 *Trees and Shrubs*
arbour 69.3 *ornamental garden*, 85.4 *trees*
Arbroath smokey 45.16 *fish dish*
arbutus 85 *Trees and Shrubs*
arc 51.18 *stage lighting*, 52.37 *line*, 52.42 *circle*, 56.46, 64.6 *electric discharge*, 143.1 *part*, 311.2 *bend*, 311.6 *curve*, 313.2 *circle*, 313.4 *parts of a circle*, 316.2 *bulge*, 316.3 *dome*
arcade 327, 43.9 *miscellaneous architectural features*, 740.7 *emporium*
arcade game 65.18 *computer game*
Arcadia 519.8 *dreamland*
Arcadian 658.1 *naive*
arcane 11.14 *occult*, 440.11 *benighted*, 443.4 *inscrutable*, 523.1 *unintelligible*, 527.2 *concealed*, 529.11 *mysterious*, 551.2 *obscure*
arcanely 11.25 *occultly*
arcaneness 523.11 *unintelligibility*
arcanum 11.2 *the occult*, 529.7 *esotericism*
arc discharge 56.46, 64.6 *electric discharge*
arch 43, 43.19 *decorate*, 63.27 *superstructure*, 126.12 *superior*, 137.4 *means of connection*, 311.2 *bend*, 311.6 *curve*, 316.3 *dome*, 316.5 *be convex*, 322.7 *passageway*, 413.10 *stimulating*, 657.4 *cunning*
Archaean 54 *Geological Time Intervals*
archaeological 3

archaeological anthropologist 1.4 *palaeoanthropologist*
archaeological anthropology 1.2 *palaeoanthropology*
archaeological dig 200.8 *excavation*
archaeologist 3, 200.11, 202.9 *antiquarian*, 317.4 *digger*, 496.12 *discoverer*, 545.9 *recorder*
archaeologize 200.16 *excavate*
archaeology 3, 200.9, 202.4 *antiquarianism*, 496.7 *detection*
Archaeopteryx 78 *Birds*, 78.8 *extinct bird*
archaic 3.15 *historic*, 5.42 *worded*, 197.2 *occurring at a different time*, 202.12 *olden*, 600.4 *disused*
archaically 202, 3.24 *historically*, 5.50 *lexically*
Archaic art 50 *Western Art Styles and Movements*
archaicism 48.12 *poetic language*
archaic speech 5.9 *ancient language*
archaism 3.11 *relic*, 3.12 *historicism*, 5.9 *ancient language*, 197.1 *different time*, 202.4 *antiquarianism*, 202.5 *old thing*
archaist 202.9 *antiquarian*
archaistic 202.12 *olden*
archaize 3.21 *antiquarianize*, 200.15 *look back*, 221.6 *reverse*
archangel 8.6 *angel*
archangelic 8.14 *heavenly*
archangelship 8.6 *angel*
archbishop 7.8 *priest*, 126.5 *superior*, 688.10 *person of authority*, 696.6 *religious leader*
archbishopric 249.5 *state*
arch bridge 63.21 *bridge*
arch dam 63.23 *dam*
archdeacon 688.10 *person of authority*
archdeaconry 7.10 *priestly dwelling*
archdiocese 7.9 *priesthood*, 249.5 *state*
Arch Druid 7.8 *priest*
Arch Druidess 7.8 *priest*
archduchy 12.5 *political organization*, 91.3 *dominion*
archdukedom 91.3 *dominion*
arched 43, 311.4 *curved*, 316.4 *convex*, 327.15 *accessible*
arched bridge 327.9 *bridge*
archegonium 88.2 *fern plant*, 88.4 *moss plant*
archenemy 820.5 *hostile person*, 822.8 *hated person*
archer 338, 679.13 *historical soldiery*
Archer 53 *The Constellations*
archer fish 80 *Fishes*
archer's bow 311.3 *curved things*
archery 338.6 *shooting*, 680.2 *arms*
archetypal 1.14 *societal*, 119.4 *original*, 547.13 *representational*, 619.1 *perfect*
archetypal image 61.24 *symbolism*
archetypally 1.18 *societally*, 471.24 *ideologically*
archetypal myth 1.8 *tradition*
archetype 1.8 *tradition*, 61.24 *symbolism*, 103.3 *quintessence*, 119.2 *original*, 471.6 *ideal*, 619.3 *perfection*
archetypical 103.8 *quintessential*, 471.13 *ideal*
Archfiend 8.7 *devil*
archiform 311.4 *curved*
Archimedes 52 *Scientists*, 53 *Lunar Features*
Archimedes' principle 56 *Named Laws*
Archimedes' screw 364.6 *rotator*, 389.13 *irrigator*
Archimedes spiral 52.40 *curve*
archine 75 *Some Foreign Units*
arching 311.1 *curvature*
archipelagic 98.11 *continental*
archipelago 98.2 *island*
architect 43, 156.16 *originator*, 243.9 *producer*, 592.8 *planner*, 646.2 *artisan*

architect-designed 243.12 *produced*
architectonic 43.11 *architectural*, 63.32 *structural*, 243.11 *productive*, 382.11 *structural*
architectonically 43.20 *architecturally*, 63.33, 382.18 *structurally*
architectonics 43.1 *architecture*, 382.1 *structure*
architectural 43, 63.32, 382.11 *structural*
architectural acoustics 56
architectural artist 50.16 *artist*
architectural design 43.1 *architecture*
architectural engineer 43.2 *architect*
architectural engineering 43.1 *architecture*, 63.17 *civil engineering*
architecturally 43, 63.33, 382.18 *structurally*
architecturally designed 43.11 - *architectural*
architecturally engineered 43.11 *architectural*
architectural monstrosity 43.3 *building*
architectural photography 66.1 *photography*
architectural sculptor 50.17 *sculptor*
architectural sculpture 50.12 *sculpture*
architectural summit 279
architectural tile 44.9 *industrial ceramics*
architecture 43, 48.3 *aspect of fiction*, 65.4 *computer part*, 243.2 *manufacture*, 382.1 *structure*, 382.3 *form*
Architecture 43
architrave 43 Architectural Decoration, 279.3 *architectural summit*
architypal 527.1 *latent*
archival 3.19 *chronicled*
archive 3.5 *chronicle*, 65.17 *computing term*, 65.19 *abort*, 605.5 *collection*
archives 545.1 *record*, 605.5 *collection*
archivist 3.3 *historian*, 545.9 *recorder*
archness 413.4 *stimulation*
archtraitor 539.21 *traitor*
archway 346.6 *means of entry*
Archytas 4 Philosophers
arciform 311.4 *curved*
arc lamp 439.7 *lantern*
arc light 55.18 *stage lighting*
arctic 55.55 *cool*, 332.13 *directional*
Arctic 97 Oceans and Seas, **409**, 409.8 *cold*
arctic char 20.4 *American game fish*
Arctic Circle 409.6 *Arctic*
arctic conditions 409.7 *cold weather*
Arctic fox 77 Placental Mammals
Arctic hare 77 Placental Mammals
Arctic tern 78 Birds
Arctic waste 247.1 *infertility*
Arcturus 53 Named Stars
arcuate 43.13 *arched*, 52.81 *curvilinear*, 316.5 *be convex*
arcuated 43.13 *arched*, 43.17 *structured*, 316.4 *convex*
arcuation 43.5 *arch*
ardeb 75 Some Foreign Units
Arden 48 Dramatists
ardency 819.1 *friendship*, 821.2 *romantic love*
Ardennes 32 Breeds of Horse and Pony
ardent 7.15 *religious*, 241.6 *violent*, 408.12 *warm-hearted*, 554.3 *emphatic*, 642.18 *active*, 648.3 *hasty*, 759.13 *passionate*, 782.9 *desirous*, 819.8 *friendly*, 821.20 *amorous*
ardently 7.23 *religiously*, 408.17 *warmly*, 554.7 *emphatically*,

759.20 *with feeling*, 819.17 *in friendship*, 821.30 *lovingly*
ardour 554.1 *emphasis*, 572.7 *eagerness*, 574.13 *concentration*, 642.4 *energy*, 759.9 *emotion*, 782.1 *desire*, 782.4 *sexual desire*, 821.2 *romantic love*
ardour of the chase 572.7 *eagerness*
arduous 644.11 *laborious*, 659.10 *difficult*, 879.21 *punishing*
arduously 659, 644.12 *laboriously*
arduousness 659.1 *difficulty*
are 75 General Units
area 6.3 *subject*, 52.35 *space*, 52.38 *surface*, 56.7 *space*, 92.1 *administrative area*, 120.1 *quantity*, 143.1 *part*, 165.8 *specialization*, 248.1 *space*, 248.7 *range*, 249.1 *region*, 249.13 *locality*, 259.1 *size*, 297.1 *surroundings*, 472.4 *sphere*
area code 534.11 *dialling*
areal 249.16 *regional*
a real honey 402.9 *woman considered as a sex object*
areal linguistics 5.1 *linguistics*
area of contamination 635.1 *trap*
area of disagreement 666.1 *disagreement*, 674.1 *contention*
area of high pressure 55.11 *weather system*
area of hostilities 676.10 *battleground*
area of influence 233.7 *sphere of influence*
area of low pressure 55.11 *weather system*
arear 337.28 *backward*
area rug 293.9 *floor covering*
areca 86 Nuts
arena 18.2 *sportsground*, 51.14 *theatre*, 249.14 *sphere*, 297.1 *surroundings*, 398.15 *slaughterhouse*, 435.9 *viewpoint*, 674.3 *trap*, 674.9 *duel*
arenaceous 384.18 *grainy*
arenarious 384.18 *grainy*
arena theatre 51.14 *theatre*
Arend–Roland 53 Comets
Arendt 4 Philosophers
arenose 384.18 *grainy*
Areopagite 653.16 *official*
Areopagus 16.18 *tribunal*
Arequipa 93 Cities
Ares 8 Deities, 676.3 *god of war*
arête 34.5 *rock face*, 275.4 *mountain range*, 380.8 *sharp-pointed thing*
argali 77 Placental Mammals
Argand diagram 52 Named Concepts
argent 446.1 *white*, 544.8 *heraldic device*, 544.13 *heraldic*
argental 54.1 *white*
argentic 57.34 *elemental*
argentiferous 57.34 *elemental*
Argentina 91 Countries
argentine 446.1 *white*
Argentine tango 41.7 *ice-dancing*
argentite 54 Minerals, **57** Common Metal Ores
argentous 57.34 *elemental*
arghul 49 Musical Instruments
Argie 91 Names for Inhabitants
argil 44.2 *raw material*
argillaceous 37.4 *compressible*
argillite 54 Common Rocks
arginine 58 Amino Acids
argon 57 Chemical Elements
argonaut 81 Molluscs, 74.7 *nautical person*
argosy 679.23 *naval unit*
argot 5.3 *spoken language*, 5.20 *jargon word*, 5.26 *dialect*, 165.10 *specialized language*
argotic 5.42 *worded*
arguable 473, 16.54 *litigated*, 477.14 *questionable*, 855.13 *vindicable*
arguably 473, 477.24 *questionably*
argue 473, **666**, **679**, 4.23 *discuss philosophically*, 16.70 *litigate*, 111.9 *oppose*, 117.14,

434.11 *disagree*, 463.13 *debate*, 472.10 *focus on*, 473.15 *state*, 473.16 *plead*, 478.18 *answer back*, 518.6 *propound*, 561.4 *dissertate*, 576.8 *balance*, 666.5 *disagree*, 674.13 *conflict*, 764.11 *quarrel*, 829.6 *be irascible*, 855.8 *justify*
argue against 476.9 *deny*, 587.1 *dissuade*
argue all round the houses 474.13 *quibble*
argued 16.54 *litigated*
argue down 476.8 *refute*
argue for 662.23 *advise*, 671.22 *plead for*, 674.11 *contend*, 855.8 *justify*
argue into a corner 476.8 *refute*
argue one's case 16.70 *litigate*
arguer 463, 473, 679, 117.6 *misfit*
argue the hind legs off a donkey 474.13 *quibble*
argue the toss 473.14 *discuss*
argue with 476.9 *deny*, 500.8 *dissent*
arguing 473, 16.53 *litigating*, 500.7 *dissenting*
argument 473, **666**, 4.5 *philosophical argument*, 48.3 *aspect of fiction*, 52.6 *complex number*, 52.29 *mathematical function*, 52.64 *reasoning*, 111.3 *opposition*, 117.4 *disagreement*, 151.9 *disorder*, 434.6 *disagreement*, 463.3 *debate*, 472.1 *topic*, 473.4 *gist*, 473.5 *pleu*, 477.2 *questioning*, 478.5 *counterstatement*, 518.1 *supposition*, 561.1 *dissertation*, 663.2 *objection*, 666.1 *disagreement*, 674.1 *contention*, 764.8, 828.5 *quarrel*, 855.2 *defence*
Argument 473
argument ad hominem 4.8 *philosophical term*
argument a fortiori 4.8 *philosophical term*
argument a posteriori 4.8 *philosophical term*
argument a priori 4.8 *philosophical term*
argumentation 117.4 *disagreement*, 463.3 *debate*, 473.2 *logical argument*
argumentative 463, **473**, **679**, 16.53 *litigating*, 117.10 *disagreeing*, 478.13 *retaliatory*, 666.9 *disagreeing*, 674.15 *contentious*, 829.4 *irascible*, 855.11 *vindicatory*
argumentatively 473, 4.24 *philosophically*, 111.7 *disapprovingly*, 117.16 *disagreeably*, 478.24 *in answer*, 666.11 *in disagreement*, 674.17 *contentiously*, 679.41 *aggressively*, 829.9 *irascibly*, 855.15 *in vindication*
argumentativeness 829.1 *irascibility*
argumentative type 473.6 *arguer*
argument from first principles 4.8 *philosophical term*
arguments 16.7 *legal trial*
Argus 435.2 *eye*, 632.3 *protector*
Argus-eyed 435.21 *seeing*, 841.5 *distrustful*
argy-bargy 151.9 *disorder*, 473.1, 666.2 *argument*, 716.3 *discussion*, 716.4 *negotiator*
argyles 295.20 *legwear*
aria 49.4 *opera*, 49.13, 433.1 *melody*
Ariane 53.35 *rocketry*
Arianism 7 Christian Movements
Arica movement 61.3 *psychiatric treatment*
arid 247.3 *birth control*, 392.1 *dry*, 392.6 *desert*, 412.5 *tasteless*, 788.4 *boring*
Aridaeus 53 Rills and Valleys
arid climate 55.38 *climate*
aridity 247.1 *infertility*, 392.11 *dryness*, 412.1 *tastelessness*, 788.1 *boredom*

aridly 392.24 *drily*, 412.10 *without taste*, 788.8 *boringly*
aridness 247.1 *infertility*, 392.11 *dryness*
Ariel 329.13 *swift person*
Aries 53 The Constellations, **53** Zodiac Constellations
aright 843.20 *correctly*
Arikara 1 Peoples
Ariosto 48 Poets
arise 361, 99.18 *come to be*, 155.25 *result*, 156.27 *emerge*, 227.9 *take effect*, 281.5 *be vertical*, 347.10 *emerge*, 359.13 *ascend*, 457.12 *become visible*
arise from 227.7 *follow from*
arising 347.15 *outgoing*, 457.1 *appearance*, 457.7 *appearing*
arising from 227.10 *caused*
Aristarchus 53 Lunar Features
Aristarchus of Samos 52 Scientists
Aristillus 53 Lunar Features
Aristippus 4 Philosophers
aristocracy 802, 12.1 *government*, 126.7 *the best people*, 400.9 *group*, 617.7 *elite*, 688.7 *type of rule*, 815.7 *human society*
aristocrat 400.10 *member of society*, 611.4 *bigwig*, 617.7 *elite*, 696.1 *master*, 805.13 *proud person*
Aristocrat 802
aristocratic 802, 12.9, 688.14 *governmental*, 696.12 *masterful*, 805.19 *stately*
aristocratically 696.16 *masterfully*
Aristophanean comedy 51.10 *comedy*
Aristophanes 48 Dramatists
aristos 126.7 *the best people*
Aristotelian 4.11 *follower of a doctrine*, 4.14 *of a philosophy*
Aristotelianism 4.7 *school of thought*
Aristotelian philosophy 4.7 *school of thought*
Aristotle 4 Philosophers
Arita ware 44 Types of Ceramics
arithmetic 52.1 *mathematics*, 52.68 *mathematical*, 130.2 *mathematical addition*
arithmetical 169.8 *odd*, 170.15 *mathematical*, 750.10 *accounting*
arithmetically 169.12 *numerically*, 170.16 *mathematically*, 750.13 *financially*
arithmetician 52.2, 170.7 *mathematician*
arithmetic mean 52.60 *parameter*
arithmetic operation 52.14 *operation*
arithmetic operator 52.13 *mathematical symbol*
arithmetic progression 52.20 *sequence*, 336.10 *forward motion*
arithmetic series 52.20 *sequence*
arithmomancy 11.9 *divination*
Arizona 92 American States
ark 74 Ships and Boats, 10.14 *sacred object*, 634.1 *refuge*
Arkansas 92 American States, **96** Rivers
ark shell 81 Molluscs
Arkwright 52 Scientists
Arlington 93 Cities
arm 74 Rigging, 53.7 *galaxy*, 143.4 *component*, 235.11 *give power*, 295.24 *part of garment*, 543.5 *indicator*, 594.5 *equip*, 603.1 *tool*, 606.5 *provision*, 632.9 *protect*, 676.12 *go to war*, 680.1 *weapon*
armada 679.14 *armed forces*, 679.23 *naval unit*
armadillo 77 Placental Mammals
armadillo racing 674.4 *race*
Armageddon 674.6 *fight*, 676.1 *war*
Armagh 92 Counties, **93** Cities
armament 594.11 *fitting out*, 679.14 *armed forces*, 680.2 *arms*
armaments 680.2 *arms*

armature 50.14 *sculptor's materials*, 64.30 *generator*
armband 39.3 *survival swimming*, 295.25 *accessories*
armchair 47.2 *chair*, 374.11 *soft thing*, 518.7 *suppositional*
armchair critic 4.10 *philosopher*, 518.4 *theorist*
armchair detective 518.4 *theorist*
armchair quarterback 518.4 *theorist*
armchair strategist 518.4 *theorist*
Armco 33.6 *motor racing terms*
armed 235.14 *operative*, 237.13 *strengthened*, 594.18 *prepared*, 676.15 *warring*, 679.35 *martial*
armed at all points 594.18 *prepared*
armed conflict 674.1 *contention*, 674.6 *fight*, 676.1 *war*, 676.9 *battle*
armed force 161.14 *force*, 632.2 *protection*
armed forces 679, 718.4 *security forces*
armed guard 632.3 *protector*, 671.14 *guard*
armed intervention 676.1 *war*
armed neutrality 675.1 *peace*, 676.1 *war*
armed robbery 670.16 *terrorist attack*, 736.1 *stealing*
armed to the teeth 594.18 *prepared*
Armenia 91 Countries
Armenian 5 Languages and Groups of Languages, 5.11 *family of languages*
Armenians 1 Peoples
armful 120.3 *container*
arm-guard 31.3 *ice hockey*
armhole 295.24 *part of garment*
arm in arm 135.12 *united*, 180.22 *hand in hand*, 815.18 *sociably*, 819.10 *familiar*, 819.18 *intimately*
arm-in-arm 264.5 *near*
arming 676.7 *war measures*
Arminianism 7 Christian Movements
armistice 218.3 *pause*, 675.1 *peace*, 677.1 *pacification*
Armistice Day 812.5 *anniversary*
armless 143.11 *partial*, 145.4 *incomplete*, 620.3 *deformed*
armlet 295.25 *accessories*
arm of the sea 98.9 *inlet*
arm of the service 17.2 *the military*
armorial 544.13 *heraldic*
armorial bearings 544.8 *heraldic device*
armory 544.8 *heraldic device*
armour 671, 293.12 *protective covering*, 293.30 *protect*, 295.5 *fancy dress*, 373.7 *hard substance*, 632.2 *protection*, 632.4 *safety device*, 632.9 *protect*, 671.20 *reinforce*, 680.1 *weapon*
armour-clad 671.30 *defended*
armoured 373.3 *hardened*, 574.4 *undaunted*, 632.6 *invulnerable*, 671.30 *defended*, 679.35 *martial*
armoured attack 670.12 *military attack*
armoured car 71 Motor Vehicles, 679.21 *armoured cavalry*
armoured cavalry 679
armoured corps 17.4 *military organization*
armoured cruiser 679.24 *warship*
armoured division 17.4 *military organization*, 679.16 *army unit*, 679.21 *armoured cavalry*
armoured personnel carrier 679.21 *armoured cavalry*
armour plate 632.2 *protection*, 671.7 *armour*
armour-plate 632.9 *protect*
armour-plated 373.3 *hardened*, 671.30 *defended*
armoury 605.4 *storage*, 647.1 *workshop*, 680.4 *arsenal*
arm-pad 31.5 *lacrosse*
armpits 419.2 *something that makes an unpleasant smell*
arms 680, 17.1 *military affairs*,

544.8 *heraldic device*, 603.1 *tool*, 676.1 *war*
arms akimbo 543.3 *gesture*
arms control 677.1 *pacification*
arms-control agreement 715.3 *alliance*
arms cuts 677.1 *pacification*
arms depot 680.4 *arsenal*
arms limitation treaty 675.1 *peace*
arms race 680
arms reduction 677.1 *pacification*
arms sanctions 676.8 *warfare*
arms trade 680.3 *arms race*
arms traffic 680.3 *arms race*
arm stroke 39.2 *swimming technique*
arm-twisting 695.3 *coercive methods*
army 679, 17.2 *the military*, 82.4 *social insect*, 140.3 *assembly*, 161.14 *force*, 161.23 *flock*, 181.4 *throng*, 679.14 *armed forces*, 718.4 *security forces*
Army Alpha test 61.6 *intelligence test*
army ant 82 Insects, 82.4 *social insect*
Army Beta test 61.6 *intelligence test*
Army Commendation Medal 17 US Military Medals and Decorations
army corps 17.4 *military organization*, 679.16 *army unit*
army formation 679.16 *army unit*
Army General Classification Test 61.6 *intelligence test*
army man 679.8 *soldier*
army officer field-marshal 679.17 *army person*
army of occupation 679.14 *armed forces*
army of people 679
army person 679
army rule 12.1 *government*
army service corps 17.4 *military organization*
army staff 17.5 *military staff*
army uniform 544.5 *uniform*
army unit 679
army worm 82 Insects, 82.5 *larva*
Arnaknagsak 8 Deities
Arnauld 4 Philosophers
Arne 49 Musicians and Composers
Arnewood International Double AA 68 Breeds of Fowl
Arnewood International Treble CCC 68 Breeds of Fowl
Arnhem 93 Cities
arnica 630.5 *analgesic*
Arno 96 Rivers
Arnold 49 Musicians and Composers
A road 71.2, 137.5 *road*, 327.3 *road*
a Roland for an Oliver 672.1 *retaliation*
a roll in the hay 135.4 *sexual union*
aroma 165.3 *characteristic*, 413.1 *piquancy*, 416.1 *odour*, 418.1 *fragrance*
aromatherapeutic 418.4 *fragrant*
aromatherapist 60.12 *healer*, 418.1 *fragrance*
aromatherapy 60.2 *natural medicine*, 418.1 *fragrance*
aromatic 57.7 *chemical compound*, 57.35 *combined*, 413.9 *piquant*, 416.5 *odorous*, 418.4 *fragrant*
aromatically 413.15 *piquantly*, 416.10 *odorously*, 418.7 *fragrantly*
aromaticity 416.1 *odour*
aromatization 57.14 *chemical reaction*
aromatize 416.9 *impart odour to*, 418.6 *perfume*
arondissement 92.3 *other*
aronha-kodesh 10.14 *sacred object*
around 251.11 *geographically*, 256.20 *environmentally*, 264.6 *near*, 293.42 *inclusively*, 327.17

via, 332.11 *in all directions*, 364.13 *round*
around and about 264.6 *near*
arousal 355.5 *drawing out*, 405.1 *physical pleasure*
arouse 228.9 *motivate*, 355.15 *draw out*, 403.13 *arouse sensation*, 405.9 *give pleasure*, 636.7 *raise the alarm*, 821.25 *be loved*, 828.9 *offend*
aroused 405.7 *pleased*
arouse jealousy 841
arouse no echoes 428.9 *be non-resonant*
arouse sensation 403
arousing 355.18 *extractive*, 877.12 *indecent*
arousing compassion 835.7 *pitiful*
arousing pity 835.7 *pitiful*
Arpanet 65.15 *network*
arpanetta 49 Musical Instruments
arpeggio 49.16 *musical note*, 159.2 *consecution*
arpent 75 Some Foreign Units
arquebus 680.10 *historical gun*
arquebusade 62.7 *ointment*
arquebusier 679.13 *historical soldiery*
Arrabal 48 Dramatists
arrack 351.7 *alcoholic drink*
arraign 16.70 *litigate*, 856.5 *accuse*
arraignment 16.5 *litigation*
arrange 116, 152, 49.35 *compose*, 50.23 *design*, 150.18 *order*, 152.16 *adapt*, 163.14 *sort*, 216.8 *cause change*, 243.10 *produce*, 306.7 *form*, 382.14 *structure*, 582.2 *premeditate*, 592.12 *plan ahead*, 594.4 *prepare for action*, 627.1 *improve*
arrange a fatal accident 398.17 *murder*
arrange a marriage 823.17 *matchmake*
arrange a mortgage 744.8 *credit*
arrange consecutively 159
arranged 116, 152, 150.10 *ordered*, 195.12 *succeeding*, 715.7 *contractual*, 717.6 *compromising*
arranged marriage 823.3 *types of marriage*
arrange for 152.18 *make arrangements*
arrange in 146.6 *subsume*
arrange in a circle 313.7 *make circular*
arrange in layers 266.10 *layer*
arrange in succession 159.16 *arrange consecutively*
arrangement 116, 152, 49.15 *composition*, 50.4 *treatment*, 150.1 *order*, 152.2 *array*, 152.10 *agreement*, 195.1 *succession*, 306.1 *form*, 382.1 *structure*, 433.3 *melodiousness*, 557.1 *ornament*, 594.10 *preparations*, 715.1 *contract*, 717.1 *compromise*
Arrangement 152
arrangements 152, 594.10 *preparations*
arranger 49.24 *musician*
arranging 152.1 *arrangement*
arrant 526.14 *manifest*
array 152, 53.26 *radio telescope*, 150.1, 150.18 *order*, 152.12 *arrange*, 159.16 *arrange consecutively*, 181.4 *throng*, 248.7 *range*, 248.21 *space*, 295.1 *dress*, 295.33 *dress up*, 526.6 *display*, 594.4 *prepare for action*, 594.11 *fitting out*, 679.16 *army unit*, 792.10 *decorate*
arrayed 150.10 *ordered*, 152.20 *arranged*, 295.29 *dressed*, 676.15 *warring*
arraying 152.1 *arrangement*
arrear 358.6 *shortcoming*, 358.9 *behind*
arrearage 358.6 *shortcoming*
arrears 145.1 *incompleteness*, 145.2 *omission*, 358.6 *shortcoming*, 745.5 *amount owing*
arrest 16.6 *legal process*, 218.8

cause to cease, 283.12 *interrupt*, 328.3 *slow down*, 328.12 *hesitation*, 661.2 *obstacle*, 699.4 *detention*, 699.11 *detain*, 734.10 *take away*, 856.1 *accusation*, 856.5 *accuse*
arrested 328.7 *delayed*, 699.15 *detained*, 856.8 *accusatory*
arrested development 61.17 *fixation*
arrester 73 Aircraft Parts
arresting 734.3 *taking away*
arrête 54.7 *landform*
Arrhenius 52 Scientists
Arrhenius equation 57 Named Reactions
arrhythmia 365.2 *vibration*
arridge 41.10 *curling*
arrival 344, 156.2 *creation*, 324.3 *motion towards*, 346.1 *entry*, 346.7 *entrant*, 457.1 *appearance*, 684.2 *conclusion*
Arrival 344
arrival at the winning post 344.15 *destination*
arrive 344, 156.27 *emerge*, 346.9 *enter*, 457.12 *become visible*, 682.6 *be successful*, 684.5 *conclude*, 686.5 *be prosperous*
arrive ahead of schedule 208.7 *be early*
arrive ahead of time 208.7 *be early*
arrive at 344.2 *reach*
arrive at a consensus 667.6 *agree with*
arrive at the wrong time 211.5 *take untimely action*
arrive early 208.7 *be early*, 211.5 *take untimely action*
arrive first 208.7 *be early*
arrive last 209.6 *be late*
arrive late 193.2 *be untimely*, 209.6 *be late*, 211.5 *take untimely action*
arriving 344, 457.7 *appearing*
arroba 75 Some Foreign Units
arrogance 807, 303.5 *boldness*, 494.1 *overestimation*, 668.1 *defiance*, 805.3 *conceit*, 809.6 *boastfulness*
arrogant 303, 807, 494.5 *overestimating*, 668.7 *defiant*, 688.12 *authoritative*, 805.17 *conceited*, 809.13 *boastful*, 850.13 *contemptuous*
arrogantly 807, 494.7 *overoptimistically*, 668.9 *defiantly*, 688.23 *authoritatively*, 809.23 *boastfully*
arrogate 846, 689.4 *be anarchic*
arrogation 846, 16.41 *lawlessness*, 357.9 *excessiveness*, 689.1 *anarchy*, 734.1 *taking*
arrogative 846.9 *presumptive*
arrogator 689.3 *anarchist*, 846.7 *usurper*
arrow 42.6 *darts*, 319.2 *notched thing*, 329.11 *swift thing*, 338.8 *missile*, 338.10 *ball*, 380.8 *sharp-pointed thing*, 543.5 *indicator*, 680.6 *historical missile weapon*
Arrow 53 The Constellations
arrow-case 680.4 *arsenal*
arrowhead 200.7 *thing of the past*, 380.8 *sharp-pointed thing*, 680.6 *historical missile weapon*
arrow-like 380.1 *sharp*
arrow of time 185.1 *time*
arrow-poison frog 79 Amphibians
arrowroot 84 Flowers and Flowering Plants
arrow worm 81 Worms, 81.6 *worm*
arroyo 96.1 *river*
arse 304.2 *rear end*, 322.4 *body orifice*
arse about 798.6 *be ridiculous*
arsehole 322.4 *body orifice*
arseholed 874.3 *dead drunk*
arse-lick 467.14 *be solicitous*, 853.11 *be sycophantic*
arse licker 853.7 *sycophant*
arse-licker 499.3 *assenter*, 808.3 *sycophant*

arse licking 853.5 *sycophancy*
arse-licking 808.2 *sycophancy*,
808.7, 853.16 *sycophantic*
arsenal 680, 605.4 *storage*,
647.1 *workshop*
arsenic 57 Chemical Elements,
57.34 *elemental*, 631.8 *poison*
arsenic oxide 631.8 *poison*
arsenious 57.34 *elemental*
arsenopyrite 54 Minerals, **57
Common Metal Ores**
arsenous 57.34 *elemental*
arse over tit 287.4 *inversely*
arson 244.3 *destructiveness*,
408.6 *fire*, 607.4 *destruction*
arsonist 241.4 *violent person or
animal*, 244.6 *destroyer*, 408.7
fireman, 607.7 *destroyer*
arsy-versy 151.18 *muddled*,
151.28 *anyhow*, 287.2 *inverted*,
287.4 *inversely*
art 50, 50.5 *artistry*, 243.1 *production*, 474.3 *cunning*, 567.3,
655.1 *skill*, 657.1 *cunning*,
657.2 *stratagem*
art auction 739.4 *sale*
art brut 50 Western Art Styles
and Movements
art college 6.12 *educational institution*
Art Deco 43 Architectural
Styles, **50** Western Art Styles
and Movements
artefact 3.11 *relic*, 200.7 *thing of
the past*, 202.5 *old thing*, 243.3
product, 367.5 *object*
Artemis 8 Deities, 53.17 *moon*,
338.16 *archer*, 825.4 *celibate
person*
Artemonism 7 Christian Movements
arte povera 50 Western Art
Styles and Movements
art equipment 444.5 *paint*
arterial 322.15 *providing passage*,
327.15 *accessible*
arterial blood 387.4 *blood*
arterially 322.27 *cavernously*
arterial road 137.5, 327.3 *road*
arterial street 327.3 *road*
arteriectomy 60 Surgical Operations
arteriography 60.7 *diagnosis*
arterioplasty 60 Surgical Operations
arteriosclerosis 373.6 *solidification*, 624.10 *cardiovascular disease*
arteriotomy 60 Surgical Operations
arteritis 624.10 *cardiovascular
disease*
artery 322.7 *passageway*, 327.3
road, 396.3 *life requirements*
artesian basin 54.9 *groundwater*
artesian spring 54.9 *groundwater*
artesian well 605.3 *supply*
art form 306.3 *kind*
artful 474.8 *cunning*, 539.34 *deceiving*, 540.29 *deceitful*, 657.4
cunning
artful dodge 539.8 *trick*
artful dodger 657.3 *cunning person*
Artful Dodger 736.8 *thief*
artfully 474.15 *hypocritically*,
657.6 *cunningly*
artfulness 474.3 *cunning*, 539.1
deception, 540.5 *deceitfulness*,
657.1 *cunning*
art gallery 605.5 *collection*
arthrectomy 60 Surgical Operations
arthritic 624.19 *sick person*,
624.23 *diseased*
arthritis 406.2 *painful condition*,
624.16 *rheumatism*
arthrodire 80.4 *fossil fish*
arthroplasty 60 Surgical Operations
arthropod 81, 76.4 *type of animal*
Arthropoda 81.4 *arthropod*
arthropodial 81.18 *arthropodous*
arthropod-like invertebrate 81.4
arthropod
arthropodous 81

arthrotomy 60 Surgical Operations
Arthur Ashe 40.7 *famous tennis
players*
article 561, 5.35 *part of speech*,
143.2 *particular*, 174.1 *one*,
243.3 *product*, 243.5 *work of
art*, 367.5 *object*, 654.3 *precept*,
716.2 *basis for negotiations*,
739.8 *merchandise*
article for sale 739.8 *merchandise*
article of clothing 295.1 *dress*
article of commerce 739.8 *merchandise*
article of virtu 50.6 *work of art*
articles of agreement 716.2 *basis
for negotiations*
articles of faith 497.2 *religious belief*
articulacy 522.10 *simplicity*,
564.2 *power of speech*
articulate 5.45 *use language*,
43.19 *decorate*, 135.10 *link*,
522.2 *simple*, 522.5 *simplify*,
564.19 *speaking*
articulated 43.17 *structured*,
135.12 *united*, 564.16 *speech*
articulated lorry 71 Motor Vehicles
articulated vehicle 71.20 *truck*
articulately 522.13 *intelligibly*,
564.21 *orally*
articulateness 522.10 *simplicity*,
564.2 *power of speech*
articulate sound 564.7 *utterance*
articulation 564, 43.9 *miscellaneous architectural features*,
135.3 *unification*
articulator 564.5 *organ of speech*
articulatory phonetics 564.6 *phonetics*
artifact 102.7 *artificiality*
artifice 474.3 *cunning*, 538.9 *hypocrisy*, 539.7 *tricking*, 539.8
trick, 540.5 *deceitfulness*, 592.3
expedient plan, 635.1 *trap*,
657.2 *stratagem*, 797.1, 797.1
affectedness
artificer 243.9 *producer*, 646.2 *artisan*
artificial 5.39 *of language*, 20.8
angling, 34.8 *mountaineering*,
41.12 *ski*, 102.12 *not the real
thing*, 114.8 *simulated*, 118.13
imitation, 243.12 *produced*,
538.14 *unreal*, 538.18 *pretentious*, 539.37 *hypocritical*,
539.39 *imitative*, 540.28 *spurious*, 540.29 *deceitful*, 540.33
fake, 558.3 *elegant*, 559.9 *inelegant*, 655.9 *well-made*, 797.3 *affected*
artificial colouring 444.4 *pigment*
artificial dye 444.4 *pigment*
artificial eye 436.3 *aid for poor
sight*
artificial fertilizer 246.3 *fertilizer*
artificial fly 20
artificial fly-fishing 20.1 *angling*
artificial grass 19.4 *stadium*
artificial horizon 73 Aircraft Parts
artificial insemination 68.3 *livestock farming*, 245.3 *propagation*
artificial intelligence 4.9 *philosophical problem*, 603.5 *mechanics*
artificial intelligence (AI 65
artificiality 102, 538.2 *unrealness*, 538.8 *pretence*, 539.3 *hypocrisy*, 540.4 *spuriousness*,
558.1 *elegance*
artificial lake 94.1 *lake*
artificial language 5
artificial light 66.15 *lighting*,
439.5 *incandescent light*
artificial limb 222.3 *substitute
thing*
artificial lure 20.2 *artificial fly*
artificially 20.9 *on the water*,
41.17 *on a ski run*, 114.14 *comparably*, 118.14 *imitatively*,
538.27 *pretentiously*, 538.28 *dishonestly*, 540.37 *spuriously*,
558.5 *elegantly*
artificial magnet 340.3 *magnet*
artificial memory 511
artificial minnow 20.2 *artificial fly*

artificial respiration 39.3 *survival
swimming*, 629.10 *revival*
artificial route 34.1 *mountaineering*
artificial satellite 53.32 *satellite*
artificial silk 67 Synthetic Fibres
and Fabrics
artificial slope 41.1 *skiing*
artificial sweetener 350.11 *food
content*, 414.2 *sweetener*
artificial turf 376.8 *smooth thing*
artillery 338.6 *shooting*, 423.1
loudness, 680.11 *guns*
artillery barrage 680.1 *weapon*
artillery bombardment 670.12
military attack
artillery brigade 17.4 *military organization*, 679.16 *army unit*
artillery commander 17.5 *military
staff*
artillery man 338.15 *shooter*
artilleryman 679.17 *army person*
artillery park 680.11 *guns*
artillery shell 293.13 *casing*
artillery warfare 676.8 *warfare*
artiness 50.5 *artistry*
art informel 50 Western Art
Styles and Movements
Artio 8 Deities
artiodactyl 77.15 *hoofed mammal*, 77.33 *ungulate*
Artiodactyla 77.15 *hoofed mammal*
artiodactylous 77.33 *ungulate*
artisan 646, 50.16 *artist*, 243.9
producer, 603.7 *machinist*,
640.3 *doer*, 646.1 *worker*, 655.5
expert
artisanship 50.5 *artistry*
artist 50, 51.27 *entertainer*,
243.9 *producer*, 519.9 *visionary*,
545.9 *recorder*, 547.4 *person
who makes a representation*,
640.3 *doer*, 646.1 *worker*, 655.5
expert
artist colours 444.5 *paint*
artiste 49.24 *musician*, 51.27 *entertainer*
artistic 50, 30.11 *gymnastic*,
407.10 *handed*, 547.13 *representational*, 558.3 *elegant*, 560.13
representing, 640.5 *acting*,
655.9 *well-made*, 794.5 *refined*
artistically 50, 558.5 *elegantly*,
655.12 *skilfully*
artistically done 558.3 *elegant*
artistic creation 50.6 *work of art*
artistic flair 50.5 *artistry*
artistic gymnastics 30.1 *gymnastics*
artistic invention 50.5 *artistry*
artistic licence 698.1 *freedom*
artistic movement 201.2 *trendiness*
artistic person 640.3 *doer*
artistic production 50.6 *work of
art*
artistic quality 50.5 *artistry*
artistic skill 50.5 *artistry*
artistic structure 382
artistic taste 50.5 *artistry*
artistic temperament 50.5 *artistry*
artistic worker 646.1 *worker*
artistique technique 50.5 *artistry*
artistry 50, 519.1 *imagination*,
655.1 *skill*
artist's materials 50
artless 322.16 *open*, 453.3 *raw*,
537.18 *truthful*, 556.3 *natural*,
559.9 *inelegant*, 595.4 *untrained*, 656.4 *bungled*, 658.1,
865.7 *naive*
artlessly 322.26 *openly*, 658.5,
865.12 *naively*
artlessness 322.9 *openness*,
502.1 *ignorance*, 537.5 *truthfulness*, 556.6 *naturalness*, 658.2,
865.3 *naivety*
art museum 50.11 *artist's materials*, 605.5 *collection*
Art Nouveau 43 Architectural
Styles, **50** Western Art Styles
and Movements, 47.7 *furniture
style*
art object 50.6 *work of art*
art of healing 630.11 *medical art*

art of management 653.3 *management*
art of public speaking 564
art of the Indus valley 50 Non-
Western Art
art of the possible 652.9 *tactics*
art of war 676, 17.1 *military affairs*
art paper 50.11 *artist's materials*,
604.3 *paper*
art pottery 44.1 *ceramics*
art project 472.5 *educational
topic*
art restorer 629.12 *repairer*
art review 524.3 *criticism*
art room 6.15 *schoolroom*
arts 6.3 *subject*
arts and crafts 50.1 *art*
arts and crafts movement 50
Western Art Styles and Movements
art show 526.6 *display*
arts of design 50.1 *art*
art subject 50
art supplies 444.5 *paint*
artsy-craftiness 50.5 *artistry*
artsy-fartsiness 50.5 *artistry*
art that conceals art 655.1 *skill*
artwork 50.6 *work of art*, 547.2
reproduction
arty 50.26 *artistic*
arty-craftiness 50.5 *artistry*
arty-crafty 50.26 *artistic*
arty-farty 50.26 *artistic*
arum lily 84 Flowers and Flowering Plants
Arundel 93 Cities
Aruru 8 Deities
Aryan 5 Languages and Groups
of Languages, 1.6 *race*, 1.13 *racial*, 5.11 *family of languages*
Aryanism 481.4 *social discrimination*, 493.3 *injustice*
Aryans 1 Peoples
Arya Samaj 7 Non-Christian Religions
Arzachel 53 Lunar Features
as 198, 114.13 *similarly*,
327.16 *how*
as a bad omen 862.14 *inauspiciously*
as a bequest 728.6 *by transfer*
as a challenge 668.10 *in defiance*
as a compromise 716.9 *feasibly*
as a con 474.15 *hypocritically*
as a consequence 155.29 *consequently*, 227.12 *with the effect of*
as a convert 730.15 *receptively*
as a cop-out 717.10 *irresolutely*
as a counteraction 704.11 *invalidly*
as a curse 827.14 *damningly*
as a dare 668.9 *defiantly*
as a defence 473.20 *apologetically*, 476.11 *in reply*
as a deterrent 587.11 *dissuasively*
asafoetida 419.2 *something that
makes an unpleasant smell*
as a formality 699.17 *with self-restraint*
as a general rule 124.11 *on average*
as a gift 729, 754.15 *cheaply*
as a gloss 474.15 *hypocritically*
as agreed 597.8 *responsibly*,
667.14 *agreeably*, 714.16 *as
promised*
as agreed upon 116.39 *with consent*, 715.8 *contractually*
as a group 142.12 *one and all*
as a half-measure 717.9 *compromisingly*
as a joke 771.17 *jokingly*
as a lagniappe 130.10 *additionally*
as always 167.18 *as usual*,
584.19 *habitually*
as a matter of course 124.11 *on
average*, 164.30 *usually*, 167.18
as usual
as a matter of fact 99.22 *really*,
537.35 *truly*
as a matter of form 813.12 *formally*
as an academic exercise 518.10
supposedly
as an advance 733.13 *on loan*

as an alternative 222.9 *instead,* 252.20 *out of place*
as an amateur 26.16 *professionally*
as an answer 476.11 *in reply*
as an approximation 124.11 *on average*
as an ego trip 860.9 *egoistically*
as a new member 730.15 *receptively*
as an example 475.22 *demonstrably*
as an excuse 855.15 *in vindication*
as an individual 108.12 *irrelevantly*
as an institution 665.18 *cliquishly*
as an obligation 667.15 *contractually*
ASA number 66.10 *graininess*
ASAP 191.9 *in the shortest possible time,* 329.14 *swiftly*
A.S.A.P. 648.6 *hastily*
asapao 45.51 *West Indian dish*
as a preliminary 154.22 *in anticipation*
as a prelude 154.22 *in anticipation*
as a prize 878.19 *rewardingly*
as a protest 693.17 *disobediently*
as a replacement 478.27 *answerably*
as a representative 706.8 *representatively*
as a result 155.29 *consequently,* 227.12 *with the effect of*
as a retraction 704.11 *invalidly*
as a reward 878.19 *rewardingly*
Asari 8 Deities
as arranged 116.39 *with consent,* 588.15 *according to plan*
as a rule 166, 116.37 *conventionally,* 124.11 *on average,* 142.13 *on the whole,* 164.30 *usually*
as a sacrifice 710.20 *persuasively*
as ... as can be 144.10 *fully*
as a sign 543.18 *indicatively*
as ... as possible 144.10 *fully*
as a start 156.40 *first*
as a symbol 543.18 *indicatively,* 544.14 *identifiably*
as a team 142.12 *one and all*
as a temptation 228.14 *influentially*
as a thoughtful gesture 817.15 *genteelly*
as a tip 130.10 *additionally*
as a token of one's gratitude 837.8 *gratefully*
as atonement 840.8 *penitently*
as a trade-off 716.9 *feasibly*
as a unit 142.12 *one and all*
as a wage-earner 730.15 *receptively*
as a whole 124.11 *on average,* 142.12 *one and all,* 164.31 *over-all*
as a write-off 704.11 *invalidly*
Asaya-Gigagei 8 Deities
as bad as can be 618.3 *bad*
as bad luck would have it 229.9 *luckily*
as before 167.18 *as usual,* 217.9 *permanently*
asbestos 54 Minerals
asbestosis 624.9 *respiratory disease*
as broad as long 122.6 *equal*
as can be 259.20 *largely*
ascariasis 81.11 *helminthic disease,* 624.7 *tropical disease*
Ascaris 81 Worms
ascend 359, 8.17 *deify,* 34.9 *mountaineer,* 235.10 *be powerful,* 275.16 *rise,* 324.13 *be in motion,* 370.9 *be light,* 627.2 *get better*
ascendancy 12.3 *governance,* 126.1 *superiority,* 233.3 *personal influence,* 235.1 *power,* 682.1 *success,* 688.1 *authority*
ascendant 126.12 *superior,* 359.23 *rising*
ascender 359, 34.4 *climbing equipment,* 34.7 *mountaineer*
ascending 359, 34.3 *climbing*

technique, 95.7 *mountainous,* 275.9 *high,* 324.7 *ascending motion,* 324.17 *directional*
ascending motion 324
ascending order 150.3 *hierarchy,* 159.2 *consecution,* 312.7 *straight line*
ascend the throne 12.12 *take authority*
ascension 359.1 *ascent*
ascensional 359.23 *rising*
Ascension Day 10.15 *holy day*
ascent 359, 34.3 *climbing technique,* 324.7 *ascending motion,* 336.12 *advance,* 345.8 *start,* 361.6 *raising,* 370.5 *lightness,* 627.5 *improvement*
Ascent 359
ascentive 359.23 *rising*
ascertain 6.23 *learn,* 101.12 *establish reality,* 475.17 *prove,* 479.11 *experiment,* 480.2 *prove,* 490.21 *make certain,* 496.3 *find out,* 537.30 *prove true*
ascertained 475.13 *proven,* 490.1 *certain,* 537.20 *proved*
ascertaining 496.8 *finding out*
ascertainment 475.4 *proof,* 479.3 *experimentation,* 480.5 *proof,* 490.13, 537.7 *confirmation*
ascesis 556.4 *simplicity,* 690.3 *unadornment,* 699.3, 869.1 *self-restraint*
ascetic 7.7 *monk,* 7.15 *religious,* 9.9 *worshipful,* 139.4 *individualist,* 168.9 *hermit,* 174.8 *loner,* 556.1 *simple,* 591.19 *abstaining,* 690.10 *unadorned,* 699.6 *law-maker,* 699.14 *self-restrained,* 761.5 *insensitive person,* 816.6 *unsocial person,* 867.3 *penitent person,* 869.4 *self-restrained person,* 869.8 *self-restrained,* 871.4 *fasting person,* 871.6 *fasting*
ascetically 9.12 *worshipfully,* 690.12 *plainly,* 869.11 *with self-restraint*
asceticism 9.1 *worship,* 556.4 *simplicity,* 609.8 *insufficiency,* 690.3 *unadornment,* 699.3 *self-restraint,* 743.8 *renunciation of wealth,* 840.2 *apology,* 869.1 *self-restraint,* 871.2 *short rations,* 879.11 *penance*
as changeable as a weathercock 576.2 *changeable*
aschelminth 81.6 *worm*
ascidian 81.2 *protochordate*
ASCII 65.10 *character*
as clear as crystal 442.1 *transparent*
as clear as day 437.2 *clear,* 522.2 *simple*
as clear as mud 551.2 *obscure*
Asclepius 8 Deities
ascocarp 89.4 *fungal body*
ascogenous 89.10 *of fungi*
ascomycetes 89 Fungi, 89.3 *fungi*
Ascomycotina 89.3 *fungi*
as contracted for 116.39 *with consent,* 715.8 *contractually*
ascospore 89.4 *fungal body*
ascot 295.14 *neckwear*
Ascot 674.5 *racecourse*
ascribe 744.11 *recognize*
ascribe a meaning to 524.8 *interpret*
ascus 89.4 *fungal body*
ASDE 73.6 *flight control*
as deep as a well 277.8 *deep*
as deep as hell 277.8 *deep*
as deep as the ocean 277.8 *deep*
asdic 420.9 *audio device*
as dull as ditchwater 412.5 *tasteless*
a sec 191.3 *instant*
a second or two 189.3 *short duration*
Aseel 68 Breeds of Fowl
aseity 99.7 *self-existence*
asepsis 621.2 *cleaning,* 625.1 *hygiene*

aseptic 134.14 *purified,* 621.16 *clean,* 625.4 *hygienic*
aseptically 134.19 *purely,* 625.7 *hygienically*
as ever 217.9 *permanently*
as every schoolboy knows 501.15 *knowledgeably*
as evidence 483, 475.22 *demonstrably*
as expected 488.11 *probably*
as far as one can 596.10 *ambitiously*
as far as one can tell 142.13 *on the whole*
as far as one is concerned 165.29 *personally*
as far as one knows 501.15 *knowledgeably*
as far as possible 463.15 *reasonably*
as far as the eye can see 263.10 *distantly*
as fast as one's legs would carry one 329.14 *swiftly*
as follows 195
as freight 70.6 *commercially*
as friends 817.19 *in friendship*
as God 8.19 *divinely*
as God is my witness! 535
as good as 110.16 *equal,* 122.12 *equally,* 142.13 *on the whole,* 264.7 *nearly*
as good as new 629.13 *repaired,* 629.15 *cured*
as good as one's word 312.5 *honourable,* 719.7 *observant,* 857.4 *honourable*
as good luck would have it 229.9 *luckily*
ash 85 Trees and Shrubs, 54.25 *eruption,* 384.5 *powder,* 393.13 *mud,* 408.6 *fire,* 614.6 *refuse,* 622.4 *dirt*
a shame 835.5 *misfortune*
ashamed 806.3 *humbled,* 866.6 *appearing guilty,* 867.6 *penitent*
ashamedly 866.11 *guiltily*
Ashanti 1 Peoples
ash-blond 446.3 *white-haired,* 452.3 *yellow-haired*
Ashcan school 50 Schools and Groups of Artists
ashen 85.15 *woody,* 397.21 *deathly,* 445.8 *drained of colour,* 446.4 *pale,* 448.1 *grey*
ashen-faced 777.7 *frightened*
ashen-hued 445.8 *drained of colour*
Asheratian 8 Deities
ashes 132.2 *residue,* 397.11 *dead person,* 448.5 *grey thing*
ash-grey 448.1 *grey*
as high as a kite 275.19 *high*
as high as a steeple 275.9 *high*
a ship that passes in the night 189.2 *transient thing*
Ashirat 8 Deities
ashi-waza 26.7 *judo*
Ashkenazim 1 Non-Christian Religions
ashlar 43.9 *miscellaneous architectural features,* 604.2 *building material*
ashore 98.11, 98.11 *continental,* 98.13 *continentally,* 344.22 *on arrival*
a short time ago 201.21 *newly*
a short while 185.3 *duration*
ashram 7.10 *priestly dwelling*
ashtry 413.7 *tobacco*
Ashur 8 Deities
Ashushu-Namir 8 Deities
Ash Wednesday 10.15 *holy day*
ashy 445.8 *drained of colour,* 446.4 *pale,* 448.1 *grey*
Asia 98.1 *continent*
Asian 1.6 *race,* 1.13 *racial*
Asian pear 86 Fruits
Asiatic cholera 624.7 *tropical disease*
aside 51.20 *acting,* 263.10 *distantly,* 335.13 *deviation,* 424.7, 428.10 *faintly,* 527.10 *quietness,* 528.7 *advice,* 563.4 *whispering,* 564.7 *utterance,* 569.1 *soliloquy,* 600.12 *out of use*

as if 114.13 *similarly,* 518.11 *supposing*
as if one's life depended on it 642.22 *actively*
as ill luck would have it 589.13 *by chance,* 687.12 *in adversity*
asimine 798.5 *ridiculous*
Asimov 48 Writers
a sin 835.5 *misfortune*
as in a mirror 114.13 *similarly*
asinine 77.33 *ungulate,* 506.5 *nonsensical,* 508.5 *foolish*
asininity 508.1 *folly*
as intended 520.13 *meaningfully*
as is 217.9 *permanently*
as is befitting 843.18 *properly*
as is fitting 843.18 *properly*
as is one's due 845.20 *duly*
as is one's right 845.20 *duly*
as is one's wont 166.18 *as a rule,* 584.19 *habitually*
as I stand here 535.26 *as God is my witness*
as it happened 106.15 *under the circumstances*
as it happens 99.22 *really,* 116.36 *accordingly,* 472.12 *topically*
as it is 105.9 *conditionally,* 106.15 *under the circumstances*
as it is said 528.19 *reportedly*
as it may be 589.14 *perchance*
as it may chance 589.14 *perchance*
as it may happen 106.15 *under the circumstances,* 589.14 *perchance*
as it reads 537.38 *literally*
as it should be 845.13 *fit*
as it stands 105.9 *conditionally,* 251.12 *circumstantially*
as it turns out 106.15 *under the circumstances,* 478.25 *conclusively*
as it were 114.13 *similarly,* 518.10 *supposedly*
ask 4.20 *philosophize,* 477.17 *question,* 712.6 *request,* 751.12 *charge*
ask a favour 712.6 *request*
askance 286.8 *obliquely*
asked 477.16 *questioned*
asker 4.10 *philosopher,* 477.9 *questioner,* 712.4 *requester*
askew 310, 123.3 *unequal,* 151.18 *muddled,* 286.4 *oblique,* 286.8 *obliquely,* 309.6 *distorted,* 844.18 *gone wrong*
ask favours of 599.4 *resort to*
ask for 593.8 *miss,* 692.10 *demand,* 712.6 *request,* 737.3 *bargain,* 782.12 *desire*
ask for absolution 839.13 *ask forgiveness*
ask for advice 654.6 *consult*
ask for a second opinion 654.6 *consult*
ask for a vote of confidence 580.5 *vote*
ask forgiveness 839
ask for it 780.5 *be rash*
ask for mercy 835, 673.3 *submit,* 839.13 *ask forgiveness*
ask for more 350.22 *eat well,* 609.6 *be unsatisfied*
ask for one's blessing 712.6 *request*
ask for one's hand 821.28 *win the love of,* 823.15 *marry*
ask for pity 835.12 *ask for mercy*
ask for political asylum 634.4 *shelter*
ask for seconds 350.22 *eat well*
ask for someone's blessing 708.6 *ask permission*
ask for someone's hand in marriage 477.22 *pop the question*
ask for support 712.6 *request*
ask for terms 673.3 *submit*
ask for the hand of 714.7 *promise,* 826.8 *court*
ask for trouble 508.6 *be foolish,* 780.5 *be rash*
ask if it is possible 712.6 *request*
ask if one may 708.6 *ask permission*
ask in 734.11 *be hospitable*

asking 4.4 *philosophical investigation,* 712.1 *request,* 712.9 *requesting*
asking for it 780.4 *rash*
asking for trouble 780.4 *rash*
asking price 710.3 *business offer*
ask leave 708.6 *ask permission,* 712.6 *request*
ask no favours 698.16 *be independent*
ask oneself 786.12 *wonder whether*
ask permission 708, 712.6 *request*
ask protection from 634.4 *shelter*
ask to be excused 708.6 *ask permission,* 712.6 *request*
ask to be tried 16.72 *stand trial*
ask to marry 477.22 *pop the question*
ask too much 609.7 *make insufficient,* 753.10 *overcharge*
aslant 310.12 *askew*
a slave to drink 874.5 *drunken*
asleep 404.8 *unconscious,* 643.4 *not awake*
asleep in Jesus 397.19 *dead*
asleep on one's feet 650.1 *fatigued*
as likely as not 488.11 *probably*
as long as one's arm 269.1 *long*
as lovers 815.18 *sociably*
as luck would have it 210.9 *opportunely,* 229.9 *luckily,* 589.13 *by chance*
Asmara 93 Cities
as matters stand 106.15 *under the circumstances*
as meant 520.13 *meaningfully*
Asmodeus 8.7 *devil*
as much again 176.19 *twice*
as much as 120.7 *quantitatively*
as much as to say 122.12 *equally*
as near as makes no difference 264.6 *near*
as never before 479.15 *inventively,* 597.9 *enterprisingly*
as new 201.21 *newly*
Aso 95 Mountains
as often as not 212.1 *frequently*
as often as one likes 212.1 *frequently*
as old as Adam 202.12 *olden*
as old as Methuselah 202.12 *olden*
as old as the hills 202.12 *olden*
as old as time 202.12 *olden*
as one 135, 116.31 *in accord,* 140.10 *in combination,* 161.51 *together,* 174.23 *wholly,* 198.13 *synchronously,* 499.8 *unanimously,* 664.20 *cooperatively,* 665.18 *cliquishly,* 823.24 *matrimonially*
as one goes 326.18 *in transit*
as one man 198.13 *synchronously*
as one pleases 570.17 *at will*
as one sees it 471.24 *ideologically*
as one thinks fit 570.17 *at will*
as ordered 667.14 *agreeably,* 692.16 *commandingly,* 694.10 *obediently*
asp 79 Reptiles, 79.3 *snake*
asparagine 58 Amino Acids
asparagus 45 Vegetables
asparagus beetle 69.12 *pests and diseases*
asparagus fern 88.1 *fern*
asparagus soup 45.13 *soup*
aspartame 414.2 *sweetener*
aspartic acid 58 Amino Acids
aspect 106, 305, 105.1 *state,* 148.1 *component,* 251.1 *situation,* 289.3 *appearance,* 306.6 *nature,* 310.5 *viewpoint,* 435.7 *view,* 457.3 *external appearance,* 652.1 *conduct,* 796.4 *design*
Aspect experiment 56.80 *quantum theory*
aspect of fiction 48
aspectual 457
aspen 85 Trees and Shrubs, 366.6 *shaking,* 366.15 *agitated*
as penance 840.8 *penitently*

aspergation 389.8 *watering*
asperge 389.33, 391.5 *sprinkle*
asperger 10.14 *sacred object*
Asperges 10.5 *Christian rite,* 134.2 *purification,* 621.3 *religious cleansing*
aspergillosis 89.5 *fungal association*
aspergillum 10.14 *sacred object,* 389.12 *sprinkler*
aspergillus 89 Fungi
asperity 373.8 *mental hardness,* 554.1 *emphasis,* 690.1 *severity,* 818.1 *discourtesy,* 828.1 *resentment,* 829.1 *irascibility,* 832.4 *bitterness*
asperse 10.18 *perform rites,* 850.20 *scorn,* 854.13 *vilify*
aspersion 854, 10.5 *Christian rite,* 389.8 *watering,* 391.5 *sprinkle,* 670.16 *terrorist attack,* 850.5 *insult*
aspersive 854.16 *defamatory*
as per usual 124.11 *on average*
asphalt 63.25 *construction material,* 293.11 *paving,* 327.4 *road surface,* 376.8 *smooth thing,* 395.10 *resin,* 604.2 *building material*
asphaltic 395.14 *resinous*
asphixiant 631.10 *warfare*
asphodel 84 Flowers and Flowering Plants
asphyxiant 398.23 *deadly*
asphyxiate 398.17 *murder*
asphyxiating 419.3 *stinking*
asphyxiation 398.2 *murder*
aspic 45.7 *basic ingredient,* 393.9 *jelly,* 637.2 *preserver*
aspidistra 84 Flowers and Flowering Plants
aspirant 775, 775.5 *hoper,* 782.6 *desirer*
aspirate 5.16 *spoken letter,* 348.12 *draw in,* 355.14 *suck,* 564.18 *phonetic*
aspirated 564.18 *phonetic*
aspiration 775, 157.14 *aim,* 228.1 *motive,* 348.4 *intake,* 355.4 *sucking,* 513.2 *expectations,* 586.11 *motive,* 588.3 *future intention,* 782.1 *desire*
aspirator 57 Laboratory Apparatus, 355.9 *extractor*
aspire 775, 275.15 *be high,* 359.13 *ascend,* 471.18 *aim*
aspire to 588.10 *aim,* 782.12 *desire*
aspirin 62 Medication, **62** Medication, 630.5 *analgesic,* 630.8 *drug*
aspiring 201.12 *immature,* 275.9 *high,* 588.11 *intending,* 775.13 *aspirant,* 782.9 *desirous*
aspiringly 201.24 *immaturely*
as plain as the nose on one's face 475.20 *manifestly,* 522.2 *simple*
as planned 592, 588.15 *according to plan*
a spoonful of sugar 414.2 *sweetener*
asportation 326.2 *transportation*
as promised 714, 116.39 *with consent,* 715.8 *contractually*
as proof 475.22 *demonstrably*
as proud as Lucifer 805.14 *proud*
as punishment 855.16 *vindictively*
as quick as a flash 191.8 *immediately*
as quick as lightning 191.8 *immediately*
as regards 107.10 *relevantly*
as reported 533.15 *journalistically*
as required 692.16 *commandingly*
as rumour has it 518.10 *supposedly*
ass 77 Placental Mammals, 326.6 *beast of burden,* 508.3 *foolish person,* 656.10 *unskilled person*
assai 49 Musical Terms, **86** Fruits
assail 330.8 *club,* 663.15 *object,*

670.1 *attack,* 674.12 *fight,* 679.36 *combat,* 852.21 *berate*
assailant 670.19 *attacker,* 679.1 *combatant*
assailed 852.34 *censured*
Assam 351.3 *tea*
Assam-Burmese 5.11 *family of languages*
Assamese 5 Languages and Groups of Languages
assassin 241.4 *violent person or animal,* 244.6 *destroyer,* 398.11 *murderer,* 670.19 *attacker,* 679.1 *combatant,* 689.3 *anarchist,* 693.9 *criminal,* 832.8 *malefactor,* 862.6 *evil person,* 864.9 *wicked person,* 879.17 *punisher*
assassinate 398.17 *murder,* 679.38 *conquer,* 689.4 *be anarchic,* 713.8 *cause mischief,* 866.10 *sin*
assassinated 713.10 *law-breaking*
assassination 398.2 *murder,* 670.16 *terrorist attack,* 713.2 *disorder*
assassin bug 82 Insects
Assateague 32 Breeds of Horse and Pony
assault 16.39 *crime,* 241.3 *instance of violence,* 241.8 *use violence,* 330.12 *collision,* 601.2 *misuse,* 628.10 *impairment,* 670.1, 670.11 *attack,* 679.36 *combat,* 832.7 *act of malevolence,* 864.7 *criminality*
assault and battery 330.12 *collision,* 670.16 *terrorist attack,* 864.7 *criminality*
assault and robbery 736.1 *stealing*
assaulted 734.12 *taking*
assaulter 679.1 *combatant*
assault gun 680.11 *guns*
assaulting 670.23 *attacking*
assault sexually 734.7 *take*
assault troops 679.14 *armed forces*
assay 268.10 *measure,* 479.1, 479.11 *experiment*
assayer 479.5 *experimenter*
ass backwards 287.4 *inversely*
assegai 85 Trees and Shrubs, 680.8 *sharp weapon*
assemblage 161, 50.12 *sculpture,* 135.3 *unification,* 140.3 *assembly,* 152.2 *array,* 161.1 *assembly,* 161.33 *putting together,* 721.3 *acquisition*
assemblage of birds 78
assemblage of mammals 77
assemble 161, 382, 135.8 *unite,* 140.5 *combine,* 148.13 *make,* 243.10 *produce,* 257.8 *embody,* 342.10 *come together,* 344.8 *meet,* 543.6 *word,* 594.4 *prepare for action,* 721.11 *acquire*
assembled 140, 161, 135.12 *united,* 371.6 *dense*
assembler 161
assembling 721.3 *acquisition*
assembly 140, 161, 10.17 *worshipper,* 135.1 *union,* 161.3 *meeting,* 161.33 *putting together,* 243.2 *manufacture,* 342.4 *meeting place,* 568.4 *conference,* 653.7 *council*
Assembly 161
assembly hall 6.15 *schoolroom*
assembly language 5.8 *artificial language*
assembly line 110.6 *regularity,* 159.6 *continuum,* 161.33 *putting together,* 243.2 *manufacture,* 647.1 *workshop*
assembly-line work 788.2 *boring thing*
assembly of materials 243.1 *production*
assent 499, 499, 116.7, 116.28 *consent,* 530.8 *admit,* 572.13 *be willing,* 667.1 *agreement,* 667.6 *agree with,* 673.1 *submission,* 673.3 *submit,* 694.5 *obey,* 715.1 *contract,* 851.1 *approval,* 851.12 *accept*

Assent 499
assentatious 116.17 *consenting*
assented 518.8 *supposed*
assenter 499, 667, 715.4 *contractor*
assenters 499.3 *assenter*
assentient 116.17 *consenting*
assenting 499, 116.17 *consenting,* 572.1 *willing,* 673.5 *submitting,* 715.7 *contractual*
assentingly 116.39 *with consent*
assentor 808.3 *sycophant*
assent to 499
assert 4.22 *propound a philosophy,* 480.3 *testify,* 483.11 *give evidence,* 518.5 *suppose,* 520.10 *mean,* 535.17 *affirm,* 535.21 *be assertive,* 564.11 *speak*
asserted 473.11 *logical,* 535.11 *stated*
asserter 535.9 *affirmer*
assertion 4.1 *philosophy,* 16.5 *litigation,* 52.63 *mathematical logic,* 473.3 *line of argument,* 535.1 *affirmation,* 564.7 *utterance*
assertion of truth 855.1 *vindication*
assertion sign 4.8 *philosophical term*
assertive 535, 237.11 *strong in spirit,* 490.2 *convinced,* 535.10 *affirmative,* 668.7 *defiant*
assertively 237.14 *strongly,* 490.24 *with certainty,* 535.23 *affirmatively,* 668.9 *defiantly,* 670.26 *aggresively*
assertiveness 535, 237.1 *strength,* 490.10 *conviction*
assertiveness training 61.3 *psychiatric treatment*
assert oneself 475.18 *appear,* 490.20 *be certain,* 570.15 *impose one's will,* 642.14 *push,* 700.5 *be liberated*
assert onself 526.4 *show oneself*
assertory 535.10 *affirmative,* 535.14 *assertive*
assert the truth 855.7 *vindicate*
assess 268.10 *measure,* 492.12 *estimate,* 751.11 *price*
assessable 268.14 *measurable*
assessed 268.13 *measured,* 725.8 *propertied,* 751.14 *priced*
assessed valuation 725.5 *personal estate*
assessment 170.1 *calculation,* 268.1 *measurement,* 492.1 *judgment,* 751.2 *value,* 751.7 *tax*
assessor 16.23 *judge,* 268.9 *measurer,* 492.5 *judge*
assets 13.7 *corporation,* 602.4 *financial resources,* 605.1 *store,* 608.7 *sufficiency,* 725.5 *personal estate,* 742.5 *wealth*
asset strip 628.5 *hurt*
asset-strip 722.9 *lose*
asset-stripped 734.12 *taking*
asset-stripper 734.6 *taker*
asset-stripping 722.1 *loss,* 734.3 *taking away*
asseverate 535.17 *affirm*
asseverated 535.11 *stated*
asseveration 535.1 *affirmation*
asshole 508.3 *foolish person,* 652.5 *badly behaved person*
assibilate 429.4 *hiss*
assibilation 429.1 *hiss*
assidously 212.1 *frequently*
assiduity 642, 212.4 *frequency,* 469.1 *carefulness,* 575.2 *commitment,* 644.4 *exertion*
assiduous 212.3 *frequent,* 467.8 *diligent,* 469.9 *careful,* 575.10 *persevering,* 642.20 *industrious,* 644.10 *working*
assiduously 106.19 *meticulously,* 467.15 *attentively*
assiduousness 212.4 *frequency,* 467.3 *carefulness,* 575.2 *commitment*
assign 731, 163.13 *class,* 165.24 *specify,* 326.11 *transfer,* 326.14 *bring back,* 598.1 *relinquish,* 599.5 *dispose of,* 703.6 *commission,* 706.4 *delegate,* 725.9 *own property,* 728.3

transfer property, 730.6 *beneficiary*
assignable 728.5 *transferring*
assign a date to 185.17 *date*
assign a job 731.6 *assign*
assign a part 731.6 *assign*
assign a place 731.6 *assign*
assignat 741.14 *paper money*
assign a task 731.6 *assign*
assignation 161.8 *rendezvous,* 815.3 *meeting*
assigned 597.5 *undertaken,* 703.9 *commissioned,* 706.7 *decentralized,* 715.7 *contractual,* 728.5 *transferring,* 731.7 *allocated*
assigned job 731.3 *allotted task*
assigned task 731.3 *allotted task*
assigned work 644.1 *work*
assignee 703.5 *commissioner,* 730.6 *beneficiary*
assigning 703.1 *commission*
assignment 597.2 *undertaking,* 644.1 *work,* 644.2 *task,* 703.1 *commission,* 706.3 *delegation,* 715.1 *contract,* 728.1 *transfer of property,* 731.1 *allocation,* 847.1 *duty,* 847.2 *task*
assignment of work 706.3 *delegation*
assign to 599.1 *use*
assimilate 167, 103.12 *embody,* 110.8 *make the same,* 114.11 *make similar,* 116.26 *make uniform,* 140.5 *combine,* 220.8 *be transformed,* 220.12 *naturalize,* 348.13 *absorb,* 696.15 *learn*
assimilated 110.12 *same,* 220.13 *converted,* 220.17 *naturalized*
assimilation 5.30 *syntax,* 110.1 *sameness,* 114.1 *similarity,* 140.1 *combination,* 167.3 *pliancy,* 220.2 *evolution,* 348.5 *absorption*
Assimilationism 7 *Non-Christian Religions*
assimilative 348.17 *absorbent*
as simple as pie 522.2 *simple*
ass in a lion's skin 335.12 *cheat,* 539.15 *deceiver,* 656.10 *unskilled person,* 666.4 *dissenter*
Assiniboine 1 *Peoples,* **5** *Languages and Groups of Languages,* **96** *Rivers*
assist 767, 31.3 *ice hockey,* 31.9 *play hockey,* 232.4 *be an instrument,* 284.14 *give moral support,* 572.14 *cooperate,* 660.16 *make easy,* 662.1, 662.17 *help,* 664.11 *cooperate,* 697.8 *serve,* 707.5 *represent,* 878.10 *grant*
assistance 232.1 *instrumentality,* 284.6 *moral support,* 606.1 *provision,* 660.5 *smoothness,* 662.1 *help,* 664.1 *cooperation,* 762.2 *aid,* 833.1 *welfare state,* 878.3 *grant*
assistant 232, 127.6 *inferior,* 195.7 *subordinate,* 284.8 *supporter,* 662.11 *helper,* 662.33 *helpful,* 664.10 *cooperator,* 697.1 *servant,* 697.5 *office assistant,* 701.3 *subordinate,* 707.1 *deputy,* 767.5 *helper*
assistant coach 19.2 *football player,* 23.2 *basketball player*
assisted 31.8 *hockey*
assister 662.11 *helper,* 833.3 *philanthropist*
assisting 31.3 *ice hockey,* 31.8 *hockey,* 232.6 *instrumental,* 662.30 *helping*
assize 16.7 *legal trial,* 16.26 *jury*
assize judge 16.25 *British judge,* 492.6 *justice*
assizes 16.19 *lawcourt,* 16.20 *British court,* 492.3 *place of judgment*
assize sessions 492.3 *place of judgment*
ass-kicking 676.16 *warlike*
associate 137, 107.7 *relate to,* 135.8 *unite,* 137.13 *intercommunicate,* 140.6 *come together,*

148.5 *member,* 180.11 *companion,* 646.5 *partner,* 664.16 *join,* 665.5 *member,* 724.3 *participant,* 724.5 *jointly possessing,* 823.19 *merge*
associated 180, 107.4 *related,* 107.5 *interrelated,* 116.11 *allied,* 135.12 *united,* 137.14 *connective,* 140.8 *cooperative,* 253.8 *attendant,* 665.10 *political*
Associated Press 528.8 *source of information,* 533.7 *press agency*
associate justice 492.6 *justice,* 688.10 *person of authority,* 696.3 *leader*
associate justice of the Supreme Court 16.9 *lawmaker,* 16.24 *US judge*
Associate of Arts 485 *Educational Qualifications*
associate oneself with 662.24 *back,* 724.4 *have joint possession*
associates 664.9 *team*
associate with 116.22 *form an alliance,* 135.8 *unite,* 180.14 *keep company with,* 665.12 *be in league with,* 665.13 *be a member,* 815.11 *be sociable*
associating 664
association 137, 161, 664, 52.61 *correlation,* 61.27 *association of ideas,* 107.1 *relatedness,* 107.2 *interrelatedness,* 116.2 *alliance,* 133.1 *mixture,* 133.2 *mixed thing,* 135.1 *union,* 140.2 *cooperation,* 140.3 *assembly,* 180.1 *accompaniment,* 253.2 *omnipresence,* 396.1 *life,* 584.7 *habituation,* 665.1 *party,* 724.1 *joint possession,* 724.2 *participation,* 815.1 *sociability,* 823.2 *alliance*
association bargaining 15.1 **industrial relations**
association by contiguity 61.27 *association of ideas*
association by sound 61.27 *association of ideas*
Association Football,football 38.1 *soccer*
associationism 61.1 *psychology*
association of ideas 61, 518.2 *basis of supposition*
association psychology 61.1 *psychology*
association test 61.5 *psychological test*
associative 140.9 *assembled,* 340.8 *attracting*
associative law 52 *Theorems and Laws*
associatively 140.10 *in combination*
associative operation 52.14 *operation*
assoil 839.10 *absolve*
assonance 48.12 *poetic language,* 116.4 *harmony,* 183.6 *reverberation,* 426.7 *repeated word,* 557.1 *ornament*
assonant 48.20 *metrical,* 114.7 *similar,* 116.13 *harmonious,* 183.15 *reverberatory,* 433.7 *harmonious*
assonate 49.34, 116.24 *harmonize*
as soon as 198.15 *as*
as soon as possible 208.17 *early*
assort 152.15 *categorize,* 163.14 *sort*
assorted 113, 152.24 *categorized,* 482.3 *indiscriminate,* 580.15 *chosen*
assortment 113, 133.3, 161.32 *miscellany,* 580.9 *chosen thing*
as stated 528.19 *reportedly,* 533.15 *journalistically*
assuage 242.4 *moderate,* 325.9 *make motionless,* 374.14 *ease,* 376.13 *smooth over,* 677.4 *pacify,* 767.9 *relieve*
assuaged 767.7 *relieved*
assuagement 242.1 *moderation,* 767.1 *ease*
assuage one's hunger 242.5 *moderate one's hunger*

assuage one's thirst 242.5 *moderate one's hunger*
assuaging 242.8 *moderating,* 767.8 *relieving*
as substitute 293.43 *alternatively*
assumable 518.8 *supposed*
assume 4.22 *propound a philosophy,* 52.89 *theorize,* 195.11 *follow in office,* 463.14 *premise,* 471.17 *theorize,* 497.8 *be of the opinion,* 513.9 *predict,* 518.5 *suppose,* 540.20 *pretend,* 597.1 *undertake,* 733.8 *adopt,* 734.7 *take,* 775.6 *hope,* 797.4 *be affected,* 846.14 *arrogate*
assume an obligation 597.1 *undertake*
assume authority 12.12, 688.20 *take authority*
assume command 12.12 *take authority,* 653.2 *direct,* 688.20 *take authority*
assumed 52.77 *given,* 102.10 *theoretical,* 303.7 *outward,* 471.10 *theoretical,* 518.8 *supposed,* 597.5 *undertaken*
assumed name 529.8 *anonymity,* 560.8 *name*
assume office 195.11 *follow in office*
assume ownership 734.7 *take*
assume ownership of 734.7 *take*
assume responsibility 207.18 *mature,* 597.1 *undertake,* 653.2 *direct*
assume the character of 220.8 *be transformed*
assume the guise of 540.20 *pretend*
assume the mantle 195.11 *follow in office*
assume the nature of 220.8 *be transformed*
assume the offensive 670.1 *attack*
assume the role of 547.10 *act*
assume the shape of 220.8 *be transformed*
assuming 106.15 *under the circumstances*
assuming ownership 734.1 *taking*
assuming that 518.11 *supposing*
assumption 4.1 *philosophy,* 8.9 *deification,* 102.4 *theorization,* 195.4 *accession,* 359.1 *ascent,* 361.7 *lift,* 463.4 *explanation,* 471.1 *idea,* 513.1 *expectation,* 518.1 *supposition,* 733.2 *adoption,* 734.1 *taking,* 775.2 *expectation,* 846.3 *arrogation*
Assumption 10.15 *holy day*
Assumptionism 7 *Christian Movements*
assumption of office 195.4 *accession*
assumptive 463.10 *causal,* 518.7 *suppositional*
assumptively 4.25 *theoretically*
assurance 303, 480.4 *verification,* 490.10 *conviction,* 490.13 *confirmation,* 490.14 *guarantee,* 497.3 *believing,* 513.1 *expectation,* 535.3 *vow,* 535.4 *confirmation,* 535.6 *assertiveness,* 589.7 *calculation of chance,* 597.3 *contract,* 632.1 *safety,* 668.1 *defiance,* 714.1, 718.2 *promise,* 778.6 *encouragement,* 807.3 *audacity,* 847.7 *commitment*
assure 480.1 *verify,* 497.9 *make someone believe,* 535.18 *vow,* 535.19 *confirm,* 535.21 *be assertive,* 632.9 *protect,* 714.7 *promise,* 714.8 *guarantee,* 718.11 *promise,* 765.9 *comfort,* 778.17 *give courage*
assured 303, 480.10 *verified,* 490.2 *convinced,* 490.4 *guaranteed,* 497.11 *believing,* 535.12 *vowed,* 535.13 *supported,* 535.14 *assertive,* 632.5 *safe,* 668.7 *defiant,* 714.12 *promised,* 714.13 *guaranteeing,* 718.7 *guaranteed,* 775.12 *expectant,* 807.15 *audacious*
assuredly 480, 490.24 *with cer-*

tainty, 535.23 *affirmatively,* 535.24 *truthfully,* 668.9 *defiantly,* 714.16 *as promised,* 718.16 *surely*
assuredness 490.10 *conviction*
assurer 535.9 *affirmer*
assuring 480.9 *verificatory,* 778.14 *encouraging*
Assyrian 5 *Languages and Groups of Languages,* **7** *Non-Christian Religions,* 400.4 *civilized human*
Assyrian art 50 *Non-Western Art*
Assyriological 3.17 *archaeological*
Assyriologist 1.4 *palaeoanthropologist,* 3.4 *archaeologist,* 200.11 *antiquarian*
Assyriology 1.2 *palaeoanthropology,* 3.2 *archaeology*
as tall as a maypole 275.12 *tall*
A star 53.13 *luminosity*
Astarte 8 *Deities,* 821.16 *gods and goddesses of love*
astatine 57 *Chemical Elements*
aster 84 *Flowers and Flowering Plants,* 59.10 *cell division*
asterisk 10.14 *sacred object,* 543.7 *punctuation,* 543.13 *punctuate*
asterism 543.7 *punctuation*
astern 36.20 *offshore,* 337.28 *backward*
asteroid 53.16 *planet,* 81.3 *echinoderm,* 81.17 *echinodermal,* 363.4 *orbiting body*
asteroidal 53.36 *astronomical*
asteroid belt 53.16 *planet*
as the case may be 106.15 *under the circumstances,* 229.8 *by chance,* 589.14 *perchance*
as the crow flies 312.1, 312.12 *straight,* 332.9 *directly*
as the fancy takes one 579.6 *capriciously*
as the matter stands 105.9 *conditionally,* 116.36 *accordingly*
as the mood takes one 579.6 *capriciously*
asthenia 238.3 *poor health*
asthenic 238.10 *ill*
asthenophobia 777 *Phobias by Name*
asthenosphere 54.18 *earth's crust*
as the saying goes 505.4 *proverbially*
as the story goes 528.19 *reportedly*
as the winds blow 106.15 *under the circumstances*
as they say 4.25 *theoretically,* 505.4 *proverbially*
as things are 105.9 *conditionally*
as things may fall 106.15 *under the circumstances*
as things stand 106.15 *under the circumstances*
asthma 624.4 *disease,* 624.9 *respiratory disease*
asthmatic 429.6 *hissing,* 624.19 *sick person,* 624.23 *diseased*
asthmatically 429.8 *sibilantly*
as though 518.11 *supposing*
astiamnu 10.3 *rite of worship*
astigmatic 436.9 *weak-sighted*
astigmatism 53.25 *mounting,* 56.31 *lens element,* 436.2 *poor sight*
astilbe 84 *Flowers and Flowering Plants*
astir 324.18 *in motion,* 642.19 *busy*
as to 107.10 *relevantly*
Aston 52 *Scientists*
a stone's throw away 264.6 *near*
astonish 514.11 *amaze,* 786.10 *be wonderful*
astonished 514.7 *amazed,* 722.18 *at a loss,* 786.6 *wondering*
astonishing 514.8 *surprising*
astonishingly 786.13 *wonderfully*
astonishment 514.2 *amazement,* 786.1 *wonder*
a storm in a teacup 612.8 *trifle*

as to the manner born 655.12 *skilfully*
astound 514.11 *amaze*, 786.10 *be wonderful*
astounded 514.7 *amazed*, 786.6 *wondering*
astounding 514.8 *surprising*, 786.8 *wonderful*
astoundingly 514.13 *surprisingly*, 786.13 *wonderfully*
astoundment 514.2 *amazement*, 786.1 *wonder*
Astra 534.7 *satellite communication*
Astraea 53 Minor Planets
astragal 43 Architectural Decoration
astragalus 382 Bones
astrakhan 67 Natural Fabrics
Astrakhan 93 Cities
astral 11.18 *spiritual*, 53.36 *astronomical*, 368.9 *parapsychological*
astral body 11.7 *spirit*, 368.3 *spiritual world*
astral plane 11.2 *the occult*, 368.3 *spiritual world*
astral-project 11.24 *experience psychic phenomena*
astral projection 11.1 *occultism*
astraphobia 777 Phobias by Name
astray 335, 162.25 *sprawled*, 263.10 *distantly*, 335.21 *indirect*, 358.10 *not enough*, 722.16 *losing*, 722.18 *at a loss*
astriction 135.3 *unification*
astringence 262.1 *contraction*
astringency 262.1 *contraction*, 415.1 *sourness*
astringent 62.4 *drug type*, 62.17 *stimulating*, 135.14 *conjunctive*, 262.4 *contractor*, 262.8 *contracting*, 371.6 *dense*, 832.14 *hostile*
astrobiology 53.1 *astronomy*, 59.1 *life science*
astrobotany 53.1 *astronomy*
astrochemical 57.31 *chemical*
astrochemist 57.2 *chemist*
astrochemistry 53.1 *astronomy*, 57.1 *chemistry*
astrocompass 73 Aircraft Parts, 74.5 *navigation*
astrodiagnosis 11.9 *divination*
astrodome 73 Aircraft Parts
astrodynamics 53.1 *astronomy*
astrogeology 53.1 *astronomy*, 54.1 *earth science*
astrolabe 268.6 *measuring instrument*
astrolable 53.23 *observatory*
astrologer 11.13 *diviner*, 199.5 *predictor*, 226.8 *contributor*, 516.5 *predictor*, 517.9 *forecaster*
astrological 11.17 *divinatory*
astrological angle 310.4 *angular measurement*
astrological influence 226.4 *contributing factor*
astrologically 11.25 *occultly*
astrology 11.1 *occultism*, 11.9 *divination*, 199.4 *looking to the future*, 233.2 *occult influence*, 516.3 *foresight*, 517.2 *divination*
astromancer 11.13 *diviner*
astromancy 11.9 *divination*
astrometric 268.16 *micrometric*
astrometry 53.1 *astronomy*, 268.2 *micrometry*
astronaut 53.31 *space travel*, 248.10 *spaceman*
astronautic 53.36 *astronomical*
astronautics 53
astronavigation 74.5 *navigation*
astronavigator 248.10 *spaceman*
astronomer 53
astronomer royal 53.2 *astronomer*
astronomical 53, 184.2 *immeasurable*, 259.15 *big*
astronomical almanac 528.5 *reference book*
astronomical clock 191 Timepieces and Timers
astronomical distance 263.1 *distance*

astronomically 53, 184.11 *immeasurably*
astronomical number 169.3 *large number*
astronomical observatory 53.23 *observatory*
astronomical satellite 53.32 *satellite*
astronomical telescope 53.24 *telescope*
astronomical time 192.3 *chronology*
astronomical unit 75 Scientific and Technical Units, 53
astronomy 53
Astronomy 53
astrophotography 53.1 *astronomy*, 66.1 *photography*
astrophysical 53.36 *astronomical*
astrophysically 53.39 *astronomically*
astrophysicist 53.2 *astronomer*
astrophysics 53.1 *astronomy*, 56.4 *experimental physics*
Astroturf 19.4 *stadium*, 376.8 *smooth thing*, 376.11 *smooth*
astute 6.20 *refined*, 277.11 *wise*, 380.5 *mentally sharp*, 459.10 *intelligent*, 501.8 *knowledgeable*, 507.6 *intelligent*, 657.4 *cunning*
astutely 380.18 *sharply*, 459.15, 507.10 *intelligently*, 657.6 *cunningly*
astuteness 277.3 *profundity*, 380.13 *mental sharpness*, 459.4 *cleverness*, 507.1 *wisdom*
astylar 43.9 *miscellaneous architectural features*
asunder 136.16, 136.21 *apart*, 263.8 *distant*, 263.10 *distantly*, 355.21 *away*
as understood 520.13 *meaningfully*
Asura 8 Deities, 8 Deities
as usual 167, 217.9 *permanently*, 488.11 *probably*, 584.19 *habitually*
asvamedha 10.3 *rite of worship*
Asvin 8 Deities
Aswan 93 Cities
as well 130.10 *additionally*
as well as 146.9 *inclusively*
as well as can be expected 623.1 *healthy*
as wide as a barn door 271.1 *broad*
as wide as a truck 271.1 *broad*
as yet 200.23 *before now*
asylum 348.2 *receptivity*, 531.2 *hiding place*, 630.14 *hospital*, 632.2 *protection*, 634.1 *refuge*, 634.2 *shelter*, 718.1 *protection*, 734.4 *taking in*
asymmetric 52.79 *spatial*, 57.37 *structural*, 117.7 *disparate*, 215.4 *irregular*, 309.6 *distorted*
asymmetrical 108.8 *distorted*, 115.4 *dissimilar*, 123.3 *unequal*, 215.4 *irregular*
asymmetrically 309, 108.13 *disproportionately*, 117.15 *dissimilarly*, 123.7 *unequally*, 215.8 *irregularly*
asymmetric bars 18 Sporting Activities
asymmetric centre 57.13 *structure*
asymmetric relation 52.63 *mathematical logic*
asymmetry 108.4 *distortion*, 115.2 *unlikeness*, 117.1 *disparity*, 123.1 *inequality*, 215.1 *irregularity*, 309.1 *distortion*
asymptote 52.37 *line*, 342.5 *focus*
asymptotic 52.80 *linear*, 342.7 *convergent*
asynchronism 197.1 *different time*
asynchronous 197.2 *occurring at a different time*
asynchronously 197.3 *another time*
asynchronous motor 64.31 *electric motor*
asyndeton 5.30 *syntax*
As You Like It 48 Shakespeare's plays

as you please 694.11 *yours to command*
as you were 221.13 *reversibly*
as you will 694.11 *yours to command*
Atacama 98 Deserts
at a crucial point 106.17 *difficultly*
at a crucial time 106.17 *difficultly*
atactic 57.44 *polymeric*
atactic polymer 57.21 *polymer*
at a cut price 722.20 *at a loss*
at a cut rate 722.20 *at a loss*
at a disadvantage 123.3 *unequal*, 123.7 *unequally*
at a discount 752, 131.8 *by subtraction*, 754.15 *cheaply*
at a distance 263.10 *distantly*
at a funeral pace 328.17 *in slow motion*
at a glance 435.25 *visibly*, 496.16 *originally*
at a good pace 21.7 *fast*
at a good slip 329.14 *swiftly*
at a guess 124.11 *on average*, 518.10 *supposedly*
at a gulp 872.7 *gluttonously*
at a halt 325.10 *motionlessly*
at a late hour 209
at a later date 155.28 *after*
at a later time 209.17 *later*
at all 327.16 *how*
at all costs 574.17 *resolutely*
at a loose end 643.2 *not working*, 645.7 *leisurely*
at a loss 722, 722, 659.16 *troubled*, 750.13 *financially*
at a loss for words 491.3 *confused*
at a low ebb 127.19 *inferiorly*, 362.18 *lowering*, 362.24 *down*, 609.10 *insufficiently*
at a lower price 129.8 *decreasingly*
at a lower rate 129.8 *decreasingly*
at an advanced age 207.14 *aged*, 207.16 *maturely*
at an advantage 300, 123.3 *unequal*, 123.7 *unequally*
at an angle 52.80 *linear*, 286.8 *obliquely*, 310.12 *askew*
at anchor 225.9 *stable*, 325.4 *motionless*, 632.5 *safe*
at an early time 208.17 *early*
at an end 157.21 *ended*, 218.10 *finished*
at an impasse 659.16 *troubled*, 661.14 *blocked*
at any odd moment 645.7 *leisurely*
at any price 574.17 *resolutely*
at any rate 327.16 *how*
at a pinch 659.25 *difficultly*
at a premium 609.4 *scarce*, 749.8 *profitably*, 753.8 *valuable*, 753.13 *valuably*
at a price 751
at a profit 721.20 *gainfully*
Ataquchu 8 Deities
ataractic 783.7 *indifferent*
at a rate of knots 329.14 *swiftly*
ataraxia 4.3 *detachment*, 325.2 *repose*, 512.1 *oblivion*, 783.1 *indifference*
ataraxy 859.1 *disinterestedness*
at arms 676.18 *to war*
at arm's length 263.10 *distantly*
at a slow pace 328.17 *in slow motion*
at a snail's pace 328.17 *in slow motion*
at a stand 325.10 *motionlessly*
at a standstill 217.9 *permanently*, 641.3 *inactive*, 643.2 *not working*, 643.15 *inactively*, 659.16 *troubled*, 661.14 *blocked*
a taste of one's own medicine 672.1 *retaliation*
at a stroke 244.16 *destructively*
at a tangent 335.28 *indirectly*
atavism 221.1 *reversion*
atavistic 3.15 *historic*, 221.10 *regressive*
atavistically 221.13 *reversibly*
ataxia 236.4 *disability*
ATB 71.12 *bicycle*

at bargain prices 752.7 *at a discount*
at bay 633.4 *endangered*, 671.32 *defensively*
at best 471.23 *ideally*
at bottom 103.14 *at heart*
at break of day 204.8 *in the morning*
at close grips 674.15 *contentious*
at close quarters 264.6 *near*, 674.15 *contentious*
at close range 264.6 *near*, 674.15 *contentious*
at cockcrow 204.8 *in the morning*
at cost 750.13 *financially*, 754.15 *cheaply*
at cross purposes 473.7 *arguing*, 473.17 *argumentatively*, 663.20 *discordant*, 663.25 *at odds*
at cross-purposes 117.10 *disagreeing*, 151.28 *anyhow*, 666.9 *disagreeing*, 820.9 *aggressive*
at cut price 752.7 *at a discount*
at daggers drawn 663.25 *at odds*, 820.9 *aggressive*
at dawn 204.8 *in the morning*
at daybreak 204.8 *in the morning*
at death's door 397.18 *dying*
at different times 115.7 *dissimilarly*
Ate 8 Deities
at each other's throats 473.9 *hostile*, 473.17 *argumentatively*, 820.9 *aggressive*
at ease 649, 405.7 *pleased*, 645.7 *leisurely*, 686.8 *prosperous*, 698.13 *informal*
atelier 50.11 *artist's materials*, 647.1 *workshop*
atelophobia 777 Phobias by Name
Aten 8 Minor Planets
atephobia 777 Phobias by Name
at express speed 329.14 *swiftly*
at face value 457.15 *apparently*
at fault 504.17 *mistaken*, 844.12 *incorrect*, 844.16 *in the wrong*, 866.5 *guilty*
at first 156.40 *first*
at first blush 457.15 *apparently*, 526.16 *manifestly*
at first hearing 420.17 *aurally*
at first light 204.8 *in the morning*, 439.30 *lightly*
at first sight 435.24 *visually*, 457.15 *apparently*, 496.16 *originally*
at fixed intervals 214.15 *regularly*
at fixed periods 214.15 *regularly*
at full blast 329.14 *swiftly*
at full pitch 423.6 *loud*
at full power 410.12 *powerfully*
at full speed 329.14 *swiftly*
at full steam 410.12 *powerfully*
at full stretch 144.10 *fully*
at full throttle 329.14 *swiftly*
at full tilt 239.6 *with vigour*, 329.14 *swiftly*
at great cost 753.12 *dearly*
at great expense 753.12 *dearly*
at great intervals 182.6 *sparse*
at great length 553.7 *diffusely*
at great value 753.13 *valuably*
at grips 676.15 *warring*
at gunpoint 241.10 *violently*, 695.11 *compellingly*
Athabasca 94 Lakes, 96 Rivers, 94.5 *other major lakes*
at half-cock 595.5 *immature*
at half-mast 362.24 *down*, 774.8 *mournfully*
at half price 752.7 *at a discount*
at half speed 242.9 *moderately*
at half-speed 328.17 *in slow motion*
at hand 196.8 *available*, 199.11 *future*, 208.13 *imminent*, 253.10 *available*, 264.5, 264.6 *near*, 407.8 *touchable*, 613.1 *useful*, 615.8 *nearby*
Athapascan 1 Peoples, 5 Languages and Groups of Languages
Atharvaveda 7.12 *religious text*
at heart 103

at heavy cost 753.12 *dearly*
atheism 491.10 *suspicion*, 498.4 *unbelief*, 536.2 *rejection*
atheist 498.5 *disbeliever*, 536.6 *negativist*, 573.16 *reluctant person*, 698.8 *free-thinker*, 720.5 *nonobserver*, 720.11 *nonobservant*
atheistic 498.6 *disbelieving*, 536.11 *negative*, 573.5 *reluctant*, 698.10 *independent*, 720.11 *nonobservant*
atheistically 536.15 *negatively*, 698.20 *freely*
Athena 676.3 *god of war*
Athenagoras 4 Philosophers
Athene 8 Deities
Athens 93 Cities, 12.5 *political organization*, 93.6 *other cities*
atheroma 624.10 *cardiovascular disease*
atherosclerosis 373.6 *solidification*
athirst 392.2 *thirsty*
athlete 21, **237, 679**, 18.3 *sportsman*, 590.6 *hunter*, 655.4 *skilled person*, 674.10 *contender*
athlete's foot 89.5 *fungal association*, 624.13 *skin disease*
athlete's heart 624.10 *cardiovascular disease*
athletic 18.5 *sporting*, 237.9 *physically strong*, 374.2 *pliant*, 378.4 *powerful*, 644.10 *working*, 674.14 *contending*
athletically 374.17 *softly*, 378.13 *powerfully*
athletic belt 284.5 *supporting garment*
athletic build 378.8 *physical strength*
athletic competition 674.1 *contention*
athleticism 237.1 *strength*
athletics 21.6 *track*, 324.11 *bodily movement*, 644.5 *exercise*, 674.1 *contention*, 674.2 *contest*
Athletics 21
athletics meeting 674.2 *contest*
athletics track 327.6 *path*
athletic support 21.4 *sports equipment*, 284.5 *supporting garment*
at home 253, 253.9 *resident*, 256.14 *inhabiting*, 584.14 *habituated*, 698.13 *informal*, 815.3 *meeting*, 816.14 *unsocially*
at-home 161.9 *social gathering*, 815.5 *party*
at home with 6.19 *knowledgeable*, 819.9 *friends with*
Athos 95 Mountains
a thousand and one 181.7 *myriad*
a thousand times no 536.16, 711.12 *no*
at huge expense 753.12 *dearly*
athwart 36.20 *offshore*, 271.8 *breadthwise*
atilt 286.4 *oblique*
at infrequent intervals 213.1 *infrequently*
at intervals 160.17 *discontinuously*, 265.8 *apart*
at issue 473.18 *arguably*, 477.14 *questionable*, 663.20 *discordant*, 663.25 *at odds*
at journey's end 344.22 *on arrival*
at just the wrong time 211.15 *at the wrong time*
at knifepoint 241.10 *violently*, 695.11 *compellingly*
Atlanta 93 Cities, 93.2 *American cities*
atlantes 43 Architectural Decoration, 50.12 *sculpture*
Atlantic 97 Oceans and Seas
Atlantic City 93 Cities
Atlantic Daylight Time 185.9 *time zone*
Atlantic salmon 20.4 *American game fish*, 45.17 *freshwater fish*
Atlantic Standard Time 185.9 *time zone*
Atlantis 53.30 *spacecraft*, 519.8

dreamland, 529.6 *natural mystery*
atlantosaur 79 Fossil Reptiles
at large 139.11 *aloofly*, 698.9 *free*
atlas 43 Architectural Decoration, 6.14 *school book*, 171.3 *dictionary*, 299.4, 547.7 *map*, 592.5 *map*
Atlas 95 Mountains, 237.6 *muscleman*, 259.10 *big person*
ATLAS 65.3 *computer*
Atlas Mountains 95.6 *other major mountains and ranges*
at last 157.26 *finally*, 209.16 *at a late hour*, 323.17 *finally*
at law 16.87 *in litigation*
at law with 16.53 *litigating*
at leisure 645.7 *leisurely*, 698.13 *informal*
at length 269.11 *lengthily*, 553.7 *diffusely*
at loggerheads 117.10 *disagreeing*, 473.7 *arguing*, 473.17 *argumentatively*, 674.15 *contentious*, 676.15 *warring*, 820.9 *aggressive*
at loggerheads with 666.9 *disagreeing*
at long last 157.26 *finally*, 209.16 *at a late hour*
at low ebb 129.8 *decreasingly*, 628.12 *deteriorated*
ATM 65.12 *electronic office*
atman 11.7 *spirit*
Atman 8.3 *God*
at maximum speed 33.12 *in a race*
at midnight 440.15 *darkly*
atmometer 268.8 *meter*
atmometry 268.2 *micrometry*
atmosphere 75 Scientific and Technical Units, **55, 297**, 48.3 *aspect of fiction*, 50.4 *treatment*, 50.24 *pictorial*, 54.5 *earth*, 233 *influence*, 251.2 *circumstances*, 266.5 *layered thing*, 372.5, 388.1 *gas*, 390.1 *air*
atmospheric 55, 297, 390, 54.50 *terrestrial*, 251.8 *circumstantial*, 388.17 *airy*
atmospheric air 388.1 *gas*
atmospherically 50.31 *artistically*, 388.28 *aerily*, 390.25 *airily*
atmospheric circulation 55.10 *air movement*
atmospheric dissonance 434
atmospheric dust 55.8 *atmosphere*
atmospheric electricity 56.42 *electricity*
atmospheric layer 55.8 *atmosphere*
atmospheric layers 390
atmospheric model 56.6 *law*
atmospheric physics 55.1 *meteorology*
atmospheric pressure 56.10 *force*
atmospheric process 55
atmospherics 366.13 *tempest*, 534.19 *radio reception*
atmospheric water vapour 55.8 *atmosphere*
Atmu 8 Deities
at night 205.7 *evening*
at nightfall 440.15 *darkly*
at no extra cost 710.20 *persuasively*
at no time 100.16 *not ever*, 186.9 *never*
at odds 663, 117.10 *disagreeing*, 473.7 *arguing*, 473.17 *argumentatively*, 500.7 *dissenting*, 663.20 *discordant*, 666.11 *in disagreement*, 674.15 *contentious*
at odds with 666.9 *disagreeing*, 820.9 *aggressive*
at odd times 187.14 *for short periods*
atoll 54.16 *ocean floor*, 98.2 *island*
atom 56, 148.3 *unit*, 173.3 *fragment*, 174.1 *one*, 260.2 *little thing*, 367.4 *matter*
atom bomb 680.16 *bomb*
atomic 56.98 *physical*, 143.11

partial, 148.7 *modular*, 174.11 *one*, 235.17 *powered*, 260.7 *little*
atomically 148.14 *constituently*, 260.9 *microscopically*
atomic bomb 235.8 *nuclear power*
atomic clock 191 Timepieces and Timers, 56.87, 192.6 *clock*, 503.3 *accurate thing*
atomic energy 56.72 *nuclear fission*, 235.4 *energy*
atomic-force microscope 56.85 *microscope*
atomic mass 75 Scientific and Technical Units, 56.69 *isotope*
atomic mass constant 56.69 *isotope*
atomic mass unit 75 Scientific and Technical Units
atomic number 56.69 *isotope*
atomic orbital 56.65 *atom*
atomic physics 56.3 *modern physics*, 367.6 *natural science*
atomic pile 56.73 *nuclear reactor*, 235.8 *nuclear power*
atomic power 235.4 *energy*, 235.8 *nuclear power*
atomic structure 56.65 *atom*
atomic war 676.1 *war*
atomic warfare 676.8 *warfare*
atomic warhead 680.15 *explosive*
atomic weight 56.69 *isotope*, 369.9 *avoirdupois weight*
atomism 4.7 *school of thought*
atomist 4.11 *follower of a doctrine*, 367.3 *materialist*
atomistic 4.14 *of a philosophy*
atomization 139.1 *nonadhesion*, 141.2 *deconstruction*, 384.4 *pulverization*, 388.10 *vaporization*
atomize 106.11 *circumstantiate*, 141.4 *deconstruct*, 244.9 *demolish*, 384.23 *pulverize*, 388.25 *gasify*, 388.26 *aerate*, 389.33 *sprinkle*
atomizer 62.10 *inhalant*, 384.11 *pulverizer*, 388.11 *vaporizer*, 389.12 *sprinkler*, 418.2 *fragrant thing*
atom smasher 235.8 *nuclear power*
atom smashing 56.72 *nuclear fission*
atom-smashing 141.2 *deconstruction*
Aton 8 Deities
atonable 125.8 *compensable*
atonal 434.9 *unmelodious*
atonality 434
atonally 434.12 *dissonantly*
at once 191.8 *immediately*
atone 746, 840, 9.7 *worship*
at one 116.10 *in accord*
atone 125.4 *compensate*, 629.3 *restore*, 710.14 *offer reparation*, 735.4 *give back*, 765.11 *recompense*, 867.5 *do penance*
at one another's throats 117.10 *disagreeing*
atoned 125.7 *compensated*, 839.6 *forgiven*, 867.7 *penitential*
at one fell swoop 241.10 *violently*
atone for 840.5 *atone*, 867.5 *do penance*
at one go 159.19 *continuously*
atonement 840, 9.1 *worship*, 125.1 *compensation*, 125.2 *counterbalance*, 629.9 *restoration*, 630.1 *remedy*, 677.2 *peace offering*, 735.1 *giving back*, 765.2 *reparation*, 839.3 *absolution*, 867.2 *type of penance*, 879.11 *penance*
Atonement 840
atoner 840, 735.3 *returner*
at one remove 335.28 *indirectly*
at one's beck and call 662.31 *supplementary*, 694.7 *obedient*, 697.9 *serving*, 701.9 *subject*
at one's command 694.7 *obedient*, 723.9 *possessed*, 723.10 *possessively*
at one's convenience 645.7 *leisurely*
at one's desk 642.19 *busy*
at one's disposal 694.7 *obedient*, 723.9 *possessed*, 723.10 *possessively*

at one's elbow 264.6 *near*
at one's expense 748.12 *expended*
at one's feet 264.6 *near*, 701.9 *subject*
at one's fingertips 253.10 *available*, 264.5, 264.6 *near*, 615.8 *nearby*
at one's last gasp 397.18 *dying*
at one's leisure 209.15 *late*, 645.7 *leisurely*
at one's lowest ebb 127.19 *inferiorly*
at one's mercy 701.9 *subject*
at one's own discretion 698.20 *freely*
at one's own sweet will 579.6 *capriciously*
at one's pleasure 570.17 *at will*, 694.7 *obedient*
at one's service 599.10 *usable*, 662.31 *supplementary*
at one's side 264.6 *near*
at one's top speed 329.14 *swiftly*
at one's wits' end 659.16 *troubled*
at one time 198.13 *synchronously*
atoning 840, 735.6 *restoring*, 867.7 *penitential*
atop 95.11 *on the mountain*
at opposite extremes 111.6 *oppositely*
A to Z 299.4, 547.7 *map*, 592.5 *map*
ATP 58.22 *bioenergetics*
at par 122.8 *on equal terms*
ATP cycle 58.22 *bioenergetics*
at peace 667.10 *agreeing*, 675.7 *peaceful*, 675.8 *peacefully*
at poverty level 593.5 *necessitous*
at present 196
atrabilious 770.6 *depressed*, 830.6 *sullen*
atrabiliousness 830.1 *sullenness*
at random 133.14 *in the midst*, 151.27 *in disorder*, 215.8 *irregularly*, 229.8, 589.13 *by chance*
at regular intervals 214.15 *regularly*
at rest 225.9 *stable*, 240.7 *inertly*, 325.6 *quiescent*, 641.5 *without action*, 643.15 *inactively*, 649.6 *with ease*
at right angles 281.12 *perpendicularly*
at risk 633.4 *endangered*
atrocious 832.11 *cruel*, 862.7 *evil*, 864.11 *wicked*
atrociously 862.12 *evilly*
atrociousness 862.1 *evil*
atrocity 241.3 *instance of violence*, 690.2 *suppression*, 832.2 *cruelness*, 832.7 *act of malevolence*, 864.1 *wickedness*, 866.3 *sin*
at rock bottom 277.16 *deep*, 362.24 *down*
atrophy 129.1, 129.4 *decrease*, 236.4 *disability*, 262.1 *contraction*, 274.8 *emaciation*, 607.3 *waste*, 624.4 *disease*, 624.17 *nervous disorder*, 628.9 *dilapidation*, 871.1 *fasting*
atropine 58.19 *alkaloid*
Atropos 8 Deities
at sea 74.11 *nautical*, 74.12, 97.11 *nautically*
at sea level 276.7 *lowland*
at short notice 208.18 *soon*, 648.6 *hastily*
at sight 435.24 *visually*, 457.15 *apparently*
at sixes and sevens 113.11 *irregularly*, 151.18 *muddled*, 151.28 *anyhow*, 595.1 *unprepared*, 820.9 *aggressive*
at specified times 214.15 *regularly*
at stake 633.1 *dangerous*
at stated times 214.15 *regularly*
at strife 666.9 *disagreeing*
at such a late hour 209.16 *at a late hour*
at sunrise 204.8 *in the morning*
at sunup 204.8 *in the morning*
at sword's point 676.18 *to war*
atta 384.8 *meal*

attacca 49 Musical Terms
attach 130.6 add, 135.10 link, 137.11 connect, 407.12 abut
attaché 703.5 commissioner, 707.3 agent
attaché case 258.9 baggage
attached 107.4 related, 130.8 additional, 135.15 tied, 137.15 connected, 138.10 tenacious, 821.17 loving, 826.9 endearing
attached to 821.18 in love
attach importance to 611.8 make important
attachment 107.1 relatedness, 130.1 addition, 130.3 additional item, 137.1 connection, 138.1 adhesion, 138.2 tenacity, 719.1 observance, 784.1 liking, 821.1 love, 826.1 endearment
attach oneself to 138.8 be tenacious, 180.16 attend, 826.7 show endearment
attack 670, 670, 28.3 fencing movements, 28.5 fence, 35.5 play rugby, 241.3 instance of violence, 330.2 collide, 330.8 club, 330.12, 330.12 collision, 346.3 inroad, 346.10 invade, 359.6 mounting, 366.8 spasm, 564.4 articulation, 567.4 approach, 592.2 policy, 601.1 misuse, 624.2 illness, 628.10 impairment, 663.3 conflict, 663.15 object, 674.12 fight, 676.8 warfare, 676.9 battle, 676.13 be at war, 679.36 combat, 680.1 weapon, 785.6 react against, 827.3 vilification, 827.6 vilify, 832.18 torment, 852.8 berating, 852.21 berate
Attack 670
attack a problem 592.9 plan
attack cargo ship 679.24 warship
attacked 852.34 censured
attacker 670, 35.4 rugby player, 346.8 intruder, 679.1 combatant, 852.11 disapprover
attacking 670, 28.6 fencing, 31.8 hockey, 346.16 invasive, 676.15 warring, 827.9 vituperative
attacking force 670.19 attacker
attacking stroke 27.9 stroke
attacking zone 31.3 ice hockey
attack of nerves 510.6 mental breakdown
attack player 31.6 lacrosse player
attack successfully 670.9
attack tooth and nail 670.5 strike
attack transport ship 679.24 warship
attain 344.9 achieve, 721.9 gain
attainability 721.1 gain
attainable 344, 101.9 realizable, 407.8 touchable, 486.5 possible, 721.15 gainful
attainder 16.43 conviction
attained 684.7 completed
attain majority 207.18 mature
attainment 144.3 completion, 344.17 achievement, 655.1 skill, 682.1 success, 684.1 completion, 721.1 gain
attainments 501.3 learning
attainment targets 501.3 learning
attaint 16.79, 16.79 convict
Attar 8 Deities
attar of roses 84.8 flower product
attempt 596, 596, 226.6 undertaking, 243.1 production, 479.13 invent, 588.4 formulated intention, 597.1 undertake, 597.2 undertaking, 640.1 action, 640.4 act, 642.15 try, 644.4 exertion, 644.8 exert oneself, 674.11 contend
Attempt 596
attempted suicide 398.7 suicide
attempter 596
attempting 596
attempt the impossible 487, 614.9 waste effort, 656.6 act foolishly
attempt to buy 710.10 offer to buy
attempt too much 596.3 tackle
attend 180, 253, 60.19 practise

medicine, 420.15 hear, 457.11 appear, 467.10 be attentive, 630.20 doctor, 662.25 serve
attend a conference 706.5 represent, 716.4 negotiator
attend a convention 706.5 represent
attend a council meeting 706.5 represent
attendance 180, 253.2 omnipresence, 457.2 being in view, 467.5 solicitude
attendant 180, 253, 697, 155.14 follower, 180.4 concomitant, 180.17 accompanying, 284.8 supporter, 662.11 helper, 697.1 servant, 697.9 serving, 823.7 bridal party
attend a service 719.5 observe religious ceremony
attend classes 6.23 learn
attended 180.20 accompanied
attendee 253.5 someone present
attender 253.5 someone present
attending 180.17 accompanying, 284.9, 662.32 supportive, 697.9 serving
attending regularly 212.5 frequenting
attending to 719.1 observance
attend regularly 212.8 frequent
attend to 469.11 care for, 719.4 observe
attend upon 697.8 serve
attention 467, 420.1 hearing, 469.1 carefulness, 554.2 seriousness, 575.2 commitment, 642.8 assiduity, 849.1 respect
Attention 467
attentions 849.3 respectfulness
attention to 719.1 observance
attention to detail 467.2 close attention, 469.4 fastidiousness, 503.1 accuracy, 642.8 assiduity
attention to details 537.8 accuracy
attention to fact 503.2 correctness
attentive 4.17 thoughtful, 420.11 aural, 467.7 watchful, 467.9 solicitous, 469.9 careful, 501.8 knowledgeable, 644.10 working, 719.7 observant, 831.6 benevolent, 849.8 respectful
attentively 467, 4.28 thoughtfully, 420.17 aurally, 719.8 observantly, 831.10 benevolently
attentiveness 467.1 attention, 469.1 carefulness, 831.1 benevolence
attentive person 467
attentive to 719.7 observant
attenuate 162.14 dilute, 272.3 tapered, 272.10 narrow, 274.5 thinned, 274.16 make thin, 372.2 rarefied, 372.6 make sparse
attenuated 272.3 tapered, 274.5 thinned, 372.2 rarefied
attenuation 56.15 wave property, 162.3 dilution, 272.9 narrowing, 274.12 thinning, 372.4 rarefaction, 384.4 pulverization
Atter 8 Deities
attest 101.12 establish reality, 116.28 consent, 473.15 state, 475.17 prove, 480.3 testify, 483.11 give evidence, 535.17 affirm, 535.19 confirm, 537.30 prove true, 667.7, 715.5 contract
attestable 475.12 demonstrable
attestant 480.7 verifier, 483.7 person who gives evidence, 535.9 affirmer
attestation 116.7 consent, 473.3 line of argument, 475.4 proof, 480.4 verification, 535.1 affirmation, 535.4, 537.7 confirmation
attested 473.11 logical, 475.13 proven, 480.10 verified, 483.8 evidential, 535.11 stated, 535.13 supported, 537.20 proved, 714.13 guaranteeing
attestor 714.5 promise-maker
attest to 714.8 guarantee, 855.8 justify
at that hour 192.18 horologically

at that moment 185.27 at what time
at that rate 106.15 under the circumstances, 116.36 accordingly
at that time 192.18 horologically
at the bar 16.86 jurisdictionally
at the beck and call of 701.11 under subjection
at the beginning 156.38 in the beginning
at the boiling point 633.1 dangerous
at the bottom 276.10 low
at the bottom of 226.13 causal
at the breast 206.11 young, 206.14 youthfully
at the cannon's mouth 676.18 to war
at the committee stage 594.17 developing
at the core 103.14 at heart, 291.10 centrally
at the crack of dawn 204.8 in the morning
at the dawning of the day 204.8 in the morning
at the dawn of time 200.22 in the past
at the door 344.22 on arrival
at the double 648.8 hurry up
at the drop of a hat 208.18 soon, 572.17 spontaneously, 579.6 capriciously
at the earliest 208.17 early
at the eleventh hour 209.16 at a late hour, 210.11 in time
at the end 155.30 behind, 218.11 finally, 304.9 in the rear
at the end of one's tether 659.16 troubled
at the end of the day 157.26 finally
at the expense of 222.9 instead
at the extreme 300.11 marginally
at the finish 218.11 finally
at the first 156.38 in the beginning
at the first opportunity 208.17 early
at the flash point 633.1 dangerous
at the flick of a switch 660.21 easily
at the foot 276.10 low
at the front 676.15 warring, 676.18 to war
at the hands of 232.9 instrumentally
at the head 653.19 managerially
at the heart of 291.10 centrally
at the height of one's powers 235.13 powerful
at the helm 74.11 nautical, 74.12 nautically, 653.17 managerial, 653.19 managerially, 688.23 authoritatively
at the highest level 279.8 on top
at the last minute 209.16 at a late hour, 210.11 in time
at the last stand 633.4 endangered
at the limit 300.11 marginally
at the lowest point 277.16 deep
at the mercy of 633.3 vulnerable
at the mercy of one's creditors 745.10 unable to pay
at the moment 99.22 now
at the moment of 198.15 as
at the peak 126.17 supremely
at the peak of perfection 619.1 perfect
at the Pearly Gates 397.19 dead
at the planning stage 592.14 planned
at the point of a bayonet 676.18 to war
at the point of a gun 695.11 compellingly
at the point of a sword 241.10 violently
at the point of death 397.18 dying
at the ready 594.18 prepared
at the reins 688.23 authoritatively
at the right time 199.14 in the future

at the same rate 122.12 equally
at the same time 110.18 identically, 114.14 comparably, 130.10 additionally, 198.12 simultaneously, 667.16 compatibly
at the summit 279.8 on top
at the sword's point 695.11 compellingly
at the three-mile limit 302.6 furthest
at the time 185.27 at what time
at the top 275.19 high, 279.8 on top
at the top of one's voice 423.6 loud, 423.9 loudly, 431.20 vociferously
at the top of the ladder 279.8 on top
at the top of the scale 126.17 supremely
at the very start 156.38 in the beginning
at the wheel 74.12 nautically, 653.19 managerially, 688.23 authoritatively
at the whim of 633.3 vulnerable
at the word of command 692.16 commandingly
at the wrong time 211
at the zenith 126.17 supremely
at this hour 192.18 horologically
at this moment 185.27 at what time, 196.9 at present
at this moment in time 185.27 at what time, 196.9 at present
at this point 250.12 where
at this time 192.18 horologically, 196.9 at present
attic 43.9 miscellaneous architectural features, 256.7 room, 275.8 high thing, 531.2 hiding place, 605.4 storage
Attic 558.3 elegant
Atticism 558.1 elegance
Attila 832.8 malefactor
attire 295.1, 295.32 dress
attired 295.29 dressed
attire oneself 295.34 wear
Attis 8 Deities
attitude 234, 4.1 philosophy, 7.1 religion, 46.9 ballet steps, 105.4 state of mind, 106.1 circumstances, 306.6 nature, 461.6 idea, 497.1 belief, 518.1 supposition, 652.1 conduct, 759.4 emotion
attitudes 759.3 feelings, 876.1 morality
attitudinize 538.24, 540.20 pretend, 797.4 be affected
attitudinizer 797.2 pretender
attitudinizing 538.8, 540.7 pretence, 540.30 pretending
atto 75 SI Units
attolent 361.11 raised
attorney 16.13 lawyer, 654.4 adviser, 678.4 representative, 707.3 agent
attorney-at-law 16.13 lawyer
Attorney General 16.11 British law officer, 16.12 US law officer
attract 340, 228.9 motivate, 339.15 pull towards, 782.15 cause desire, 821.28 win the love of
attractance 340.1 attraction
attractancy 340.1 attraction
attract attention 467, 526.5 be visible, 611.7 be important
attracted 228.12 motivated, 821.19 enamoured
attracting 340, 339.8 tractional
attraction 340, 5.30 syntax, 228.2 inducement, 233 influence, 234.2 attitude, 235.4 energy, 339.5 magnetism, 437.6 visible thing, 586.3 incentive, 782.5 object of desire, 784.1 liking
Attraction 340
attractionally 340
attractive 340, 228.11 motivational, 233.12 appealing, 235.15 full of energy, 339.10 magnetic, 405.6 pleasant, 457.10 aspectual, 586.19 per-

suasive, 763.2 likable, 782.8 desirable, 784.5 likable, 789.5 beautiful, 789.6 personable
attractive female 789
attractively 340, 339.16 magnetically, 340.13 attractionally, 782.17 desirably, 784.10 with great liking, 821.30 lovingly
attractive male 789
attractiveness 228.2 inducement, 340.1 attraction, 586.3 incentive, 763.8 amiability, 789.1 gorgeousness, 821.4 lovability
attractivity 340.1 attraction
attract money 742.13 get rich
attract notice 526.5 be visible, 543.11 gesture, 811.29 show off
attributable to 227.10 caused
attribute 103.4 nature, 165.3 characteristic, 180.4 concomitant, 235.2, 485.2 ability, 744.11 recognize, 837.6 be grateful, 845.17 credit
attributed to 227.10 caused
attribution 226.1 cause
attributive 5.44 grammatical
attributively 5.52 grammatically, 227.12 with the effect of
attrition 129.1 decrease, 384.4 pulverization, 385.2 wearing away, 676.8 warfare
attritive 385.10 frictional
attritus 384.5 powder
attune 49.34, 116.24 harmonize, 125.5 counterbalance, 433.8 harmonize, 485.15 modify
attuned 49.30 harmonic, 116.13 harmonious, 125.10 counterbalancing, 433.7 harmonious, 485.11 modified, 667.10 agreeing
attunement 49.13 melody, 116.4 harmony, 125.2 counterbalance, 433.3 melodiousness, 485.5 modification, 667.1 agreement
atumpan 49 Musical Instruments
ATU tape 65.7 peripheral
at variance 117.10, 434.8 disagreeing, 663.20 discordant, 663.25 at odds, 820.8 estranged
at variance with 663.27 opposed to, 666.9 disagreeing
at war 117.10 disagreeing, 473.9 hostile, 473.17 argumentatively, 666.9 disagreeing, 674.15 contentious, 676.15 warring, 679.42 martially
at war with 820.9 aggressive
at what place? 477.25 what?
at what time 185
at what time? 477.25 what?
at will 570
Atwood 48 Writers
at work 640.5 acting, 642.19 busy, 847.13 on duty
at your command 694.11 yours to command
at your orders 694.11 yours to command
at your service 694.11 yours to command
atypical 115.4 dissimilar
aubade 48.7 poem, 433.2 song, 821.15 love item
Aube 96 Rivers
Auber 49 Musicians and Composers
aubergine 45 Vegetables, 440.3 dark colour, 455.3 purple thing, 455.6 purple
aubergine and tomato pie 45.34 vegetarian dish
aubergine roll 45.34 vegetarian dish
Aubrac 68 Breeds of Cattle
Aubrey 48 Writers
aubrietia 84 Flowers and Flowering Plants
auburn 449.1 brown, 450.3 red-haired
AUC 185.29 one day
Auckland 92 New Zealand Regions and Territories, **93** Cities
auction 710.9 offer, 727.2 disposal of property, 727.11 dispose

of property, 739.1 sell, 739.3 selling, 739.4 sale
auction bridge 42 Card Games
auctioneer 739.9 seller
auction off 739.1 sell
auction room 740.1 market
audacious 807, 668.7 defiant, 778.9 courageous, 780.4 rash, 850.10 disrespectful
audaciously 807, 668.9 defiantly, 778.18 courageously
audaciousness 778.1 courage, 780.1 rashness
audacity 807, 303.5 boldness, 668.1 defiance, 778.1 courage, 780.1 rashness
Auden 48 Poets
audibility 423, 56.17 sound, 420.1 hearing
audible 19.8 huddle, 403.8 sensate, 423.7 heard, 522.1 intelligible
audibly 420.17 aurally, 423.10 aloud
audience 51.31 theatregoer, 140.3 assembly, 253.5 someone present, 346.7 entrant, 420.2 hearer, 435.11 observer, 532.2 mass media, 568.6 interview, 653.7 council, 730.5 recipient
audience participation 534.25 broadcast material
audience survey 532.2 mass media
audient 420.11 aural
audile 420.11 aural
audio 420.9 audio device, 420.11 aural
audio amplifier 64.21 rectifier
audio cassette 534.26 recording
audio device 420
audiofrequency 56.19 sound propagation
audiofrequency amplifier 534.18 radio
audiological 420.13 otological
audiologist 420.6 otology
audiology 420.6 otology
audiometer 268.8 meter, 420.6 otology
audiometric 268.16 micrometric
audiometry 268.2 micrometry
audiophile 420.2 hearer
audio signal 534.21 television
audiovisual 420.11 aural
audiovisually 420.17 aurally
audit 750, 170.12 check, 750.3 accounting
audited 750.11 accounted
audition 51.12 production, 420.1 hearing, 477.3 questionnaire, 479.2 rehearsal, 479.12 rehearse, 568.6 interview
auditive 420.11 aural
auditor 420.2 hearer, 750.6 accountant
auditorium 51, 420, 6.15 schoolroom, 51.14 theatre, 56.21 architectural acoustics, 63.20 building, 526.8 showplace
auditory 420.11 aural
auditory ossicle 420.5 internal ear
auditory range 420.1 hearing
Audubon 52 Scientists
au fait 528.18 informed
Augean stables 727.8 sink
augend 52.15 addition
auger 63.29 construction equipment, 322.2 opener, 380.8 sharp-pointed thing
auger shell 81 Molluscs
aught 172.2 nothing
augite 54 Minerals
augment 721, 121.6 change gradually, 128.5 make bigger, 130.3 additional item, 130.6 add, 261.5 make bigger, 261.6 become bigger, 336.8 further, 605.6 store, 662.26 be useful, 768.6 aggravate
augmentation 721, 128.1 increase, 130.1 addition, 130.3 additional item, 261.1 growth, 768.1 aggravation
augmentative 5.35 part of speech, 5.44 grammatical, 128.6 increas-

ing, 261.9 enlargeable, 721.18 acquisitional
augmented 128.7 increased, 261.7 bigger, 721.18 acquisitional
augmenter 261.4 enlarger
augmentor 261.4 enlarger
au gratin 45.56 culinary
Augsburg 93 Cities
augur 7.8 priest, 11.13 diviner, 199.5 predictor, 199.9 look ahead, 516.1 foresee, 516.5 predictor, 517.9 forecaster, 517.11 predict, 520.12 intend, 636.5 warn
augural 11.17 divinatory, 517.15 presageful
augur well 517.11 predict, 686.7, 714.9 be auspicious, 775.10 inspire hope
augury 11.9 divination, 513.4 expectant person, 516.3 foresight, 517.2 divination, 517.5 omen, 636.1 warning
august 611.6 notable, 805.18 prestigious, 805.19 stately, 849.14 awe-inspiring
Augusta 93 Cities, 29.1 golf
Augustan 48.19 narrative, 558.3 elegant, 619.1 perfect
Augustans 48 Literary Groups and Movements
Augustine of Hippo 4 Philosophers
Augustinian 7 Members of Religious Orders, 4.11 follower of a doctrine, 4.14 of a philosophy
Augustinian philosophy 4.7 school of thought
augustness 805.4 prestige
auk 78 Birds, 78.3 water bird
auklet 78 Birds
auld lang syne 3.8, 200.1 past time
auloi 49 Musical Instruments
aulophobia 777 Phobias by Name
au naturel 45.56 culinary
Aung San Suu Kyi 675.4 Nobel Peace Prize
aunt 402.12 woman in the family
auntie 402.12 woman in the family
Auntie 534.20 radio broadcasting
Aunt Sally 850.9 butt
au pair 223.4 person who exchanges, 223.8 in exchange, 697.4 personal attendant, 697.6 domestic servant
aura 11.10 psychic phenomenon, 297.3 atmosphere, 416.4 reputation
aural 420, 297.6 atmospheric
aural cavity 322.4 body orifice
aurally 420
aureate 452.1 yellow
aureate diction 48.12 poetic language
aureole 439.12 highlight
aureomycin 630.8 drug
auric 57.34 elemental
auricle 87.3 grass plant
auricula 84 Flowers and Flowering Plants
auricular 420.11 aural, 420.12 eared
auricularly 420.17 aurally
auriculate 420.12 eared
auriferous 57.34 elemental
auriform 420.12 eared
Auriga 53 The Constellations
auriscope 60.7 diagnosis, 420.6 otology
aurist 60.13 medical specialist, 420.6 otology
aurochs 77 Placental Mammals
aurophobia 777 Phobias by Name
aurora 54, 13.10 planet
Aurora 8 Deities, **93** Cities, 204.1 morning
aurora australis 54.46 aurora, 439.4 natural light
aurora borealis 54.46 aurora, 439.4 natural light
auroral 204.5 morning
auroral display 54.46 aurora

aurorally 204.8 in the morning
aurous 57.34 elemental
Auschwitz 398.15 slaughterhouse, 702.1 prison
auscultate 420.15 hear
auscultation 420.1 hearing
auscultator 420.9 audio device
auscultatorily 420.17 aurally
auspex 11.13 diviner, 517.9 forecaster
auspicate 119.7 originate, 156.23 inaugurate, 812.19 install
auspication 201.4 beginning
auspice 517.5 omen
auspices 632.2 protection, 662.9 patronage
auspicial 517.15 presageful
auspicious 714, 106.9 comfortable, 210.6 timely, 517.15 presageful, 615.1 convenient, 686.8 prosperous, 775.14 cheering, 812.13 congratulatory, 819.12 favourable, 861.1 good
auspiciously 714, 106.18 comfortably, 210.9 opportunely, 517.16 predictively, 686.9 prosperously, 775.15 hopefully, 819.20 favourably
auspicious moment 210.1 timeliness
auspiciousness 210.1 timeliness, 615.3 convenience, 686.2 good fortune, 775.4 comfort, 861.8 good
Aussie 91 Names for Inhabitants
Austen 48 Writers
Auster 55.15 wind direction
austere 542.14 simple, 550.3 clear, 556.1 simple, 690.10 unadorned, 756.4 thrifty, 832.12 callous, 871.6 fasting
austerely 542.24 simply, 690.12 plainly
austereness 542.4 simplicity
austerities 840.2 apology
austerity 542.4 simplicity, 550.1 clarity, 556.4 simplicity, 609.8 insufficiency, 690.3 unadornment, 756.1 thrift, 871.1 fasting
austerity lunch 350.12 meal
Austin 4 Philosophers, **4** Philosophers, **93** Cities
Austin Friar 7 Members of Religious Orders
austral 332.13 directional
Australasia 98.1 continent
Australasian 1.6 race, 1.13 racial
Australia 91 Countries, **98** Islands
Australia Day 214.6 annually celebrated day
Australian 5 Languages and Groups of Languages, **98** Deserts
Australian crawl 39.1 swimming
Australian GP at Adelaide 33.2 Formula 1 race
Australian Illawarra Shorthorn 68 Breeds of Cattle
Australian pony 32 Breeds of Horse and Pony
Australian rules football 18 Sporting Activities
Australian terrier 77 Breeds of Dogs
Australids 53 Meteor Showers
Australopithecus 202.7 ancient people
Australorp 68 Breeds of Fowl
Austria 91 Countries
Austrian neutrality 400.11 nation
Austric 5.11 family of languages
Austro-Asiatic 5 Languages and Groups of Languages
Austronesian 5 Languages and Groups of Languages, 5.11 family of languages
autarchic 12.9, 688.14 governmental
autarchy 12.1 government, 688.7 type of rule
autarkic 698.9 free
autarky 608.7 sufficiency, 698.3 independence
autecology 59.18 ecology

auteur 51.25 *producer*
authentic 119, 537, 3.19 *chronicled,* 16.51 *legitimate,* 99.13 *real,* 101.7 *realistic,* 480.8 *verifiable,* 483.8 *evidential,* 667.11 *contractual,* 688.15 *true,* 843.8 *correct*
authentically 537, 688, 480.11 *verifiably,* 483.14 *as evidence,* 535.23 *affirmatively,* 667.15 *contractually*
authenticate 101.12 *establish reality,* 116.28 *consent,* 480.1 *verify,* 483.12 *prove,* 490.21 *make certain,* 499.4 *assent,* 535.19 *confirm,* 537.30 *prove true,* 544.10 *identify,* 667.7 *contract,* 718.12 *certify*
authenticated 480.10 *verified,* 535.13 *supported,* 537.20 *proved,* 544.12 *identified,* 688.15 *true,* 714.13 *guaranteeing,* 718.7 *guaranteed*
authenticating 714.13 *guaranteeing*
authentication 480.4 *verification,* 535.4, 537.7 *confirmation,* 544.1 *identification,* 667.2 *contract,* 718.2 *promise*
authenticator 535.9 *affirmer,* 667.5 *assenter*
authenticity 537, 16.30 *legitimacy,* 99.4 *demonstrable existence,* 101.3 *realism,* 119.1 *originality,* 843.2 *correctness*
author 48, 5.2 *linguist,* 226.7 *Prime Mover,* 226.9 *be the cause of,* 243.9 *producer,* 243.10 *produce,* 496.12 *discoverer,* 532.12 *publisher,* 560.10 *descriptive writer,* 561.3 *dissertator*
authoritarian 570.9 *autocratic,* 653.17 *managerial,* 688.12 *authoritative,* 688.14 *governmental,* 690.4 *strict person,* 690.8 *severe,* 696.12 *masterful*
authoritarianism 688.7 *type of rule,* 690.2 *suppression*
authoritative 688, 6.16 *educational,* 121.8 *ranked,* 126.13 *dominant,* 165.21 *specialized,* 166.12 *ruling,* 233.11 *influential,* 235.13 *powerful,* 303.8 *assured,* 490.1 *certain,* 497.14 *believed,* 537.24 *pedantic,* 653.17 *managerial,* 692.14 *commanding,* 699.13 *restraining,* 805.19 *stately,* 849.14 *awe-inspiring*
authoritatively 688, 4.29 *wisely,* 6.25 *educationally,* 121.9 *differentially,* 126.16 *superiorly,* 233.14 *influentially,* 235.18 *powerfully,* 653.19 *managerially,* 692.16 *commandingly,* 699.16 *under restraints*
authoritativeness 688, 490.9 *certainty,* 537.11 *pedantry*
authority 166, 688, 692, 703, 4.12 *sage,* 6.4 *educator,* 16.2 *jurisdiction,* 16.29 *legalization,* 116.7 *consent,* 121.2 *rank,* 126.2 *leadership,* 165.14 *specialist,* 233 *influence,* 233.3 *personal influence,* 235.1 *power,* 303.4 *assurance,* 483.6 *documentation,* 501.6 *knowledgeable person,* 528.8 *source of information,* 537.11 *pedantry,* 653.3 *management,* 655.5 *expert,* 688.10 *person of authority,* 690.1 *severity,* 692.5 *self-assurance,* 698.3 *independence,* 699.1 *restraint,* 708.1 *permission,* 718.2 *promise,* 845.3 *prerogative,* 845.6 *bond,* 849.1 *respect*
Authority 688
authorization 692, 16.29 *legalization,* 116.7 *consent,* 126.2 *leadership,* 485.3 *qualifications,* 485.4 *permission,* 545.2 *certificate,* 688.3 *acquisition of power,* 688.9 *permission,* 703.3 *authority,* 706.3 *delegation,* 708.1 *permission,* 718.2 *promise,* 851.1 *approval*
authorize 692, 703, 16.65 *make legal,* 116.28 *consent,* 235.11

give power, 485.13 *qualify,* 499.4 *assent,* 688.21 *grant authority,* 706.4 *delegate,* 707.6 *deputize,* 708.3 *permit,* 845.16 *entitle,* 851.12 *accept*
authorized 485, 688, 16.44 *legal,* 16.50 *law-abiding,* 116.17 *consenting,* 688.13 *elected,* 692.15 *self-assured,* 698.9 *free,* 703.9 *commissioned,* 708.7 *permitted*
Authorized Version 7.12 *religious text*
authorizing 116.17 *consenting*
authorship 226.1 *cause,* 243.1 *production*
autism 61.19 *defence mechanism,* 510.2 *subnormality*
autistic 460.7 *intellectually subnormal,* 816.8 *unsociable*
auto 71.16 *car*
autobahn 71.2 *road*
autobiographer 48.14 *author,* 545.9 *recorder*
autobiographical 3.19 *chronicled,* 48.19, 560.12 *narrative*
autobiographically 3.25 *reportedly*
autobiographical novel 48.2 *fiction*
autobiography 3.6 *biography,* 48.4 *non-fiction,* 396.11 *life story,* 511.2 *retrospect,* 545.1 *record,* 560.4 *factual account*
autocade 71.21 *miscellaneous motoring terms*
autocatalysis 57.15 *catalysis*
autocatalytic 57.39 *catalytic*
autochthon 255.1 *inhabitant*
autochthonous 255.12 *native*
autocracy 12.1 *government,* 688.7 *type of rule,* 690.2 *suppression*
autocrat 653.14 *leader,* 688.10 *person of authority,* 690.4 *strict person,* 696.4 *absolute ruler*
autocratic 570, 688.14 *governmental,* 690.8 *severe,* 692.15 *self-assured,* 696.12 *masterful*
autocratically 690.11 *severely,* 692.16 *commandingly,* 696.16 *masterfully*
autocross 18 Sporting Activities, 33.1 *motor racing,* 674.4 *race*
autocycle 71.13 *motorcycle*
Auto-Cycle Union 33.7 *racing governing body*
auto-da-fé 398.5 *execution,* 879.13 *capital punishment*
autodidact 6.7 *learner*
autodidactic 6.17 *educatable,* 656.2 *unskilled*
autodidactics 6.2 *educational system*
autodidactism 501.3 *learning*
autoexposure 66.18 *exposure time*
autofocus 66.18 *exposure time*
autogenesis 245.3 *propagation*
autogiro 73 Types of Aircraft
autograph 119.2 *original,* 543.1 *sign,* 543.9 *use signs,* 544.3 *means of identification,* 544.11 *identify oneself,* 545.4 *inscription,* 560.8 *name*
autographer 543.8 *signer*
autograph hunting 42 Hobbies and Pastimes
autogyro 364.6 *rotator*
autoharp 49 Musical Instruments
autohypnosis 61.3 *psychiatric treatment*
autohypnotic 11.15 *witchlike*
autohypnotism 11.1 *occultism*
autointoxication 628.10 *impairment*
auto-loading 37.8 *shooting*
auto-loading rifle 37.3 *hunting equipment*
Autolycus 53 Lunar Features
automat 350.15 *eating place*
automate 15.11 *conduct industrial relations,* 110.8 *make the same,* 112.10 *conform,* 243.10 *produce*
automated 15.9 *negotiated,* 110.17 *regular,* 112.6 *conform-*

ing, 232.8 *practical,* 235.15 *full of energy,* 243.11 *productive,* 603.8 *mechanical*
automated teller machine 741.21 *till*
automatic 71 Motor Vehicles, 112.6 *conforming,* 232.8 *practical,* 462.9, 464.8 *instinctive,* 571.13 *involuntary,* 583.2 *spontaneous,* 603.8 *mechanical,* 680.9 *firearm*
automatically 112.13 *uniformly,* 232.9 *instrumentally,* 464.11 *intuitively,* 584.19 *habitually,* 603.10 *instrumentally*
automatic buoy 55.5 *weather station*
automatic camera 66.16 *camera*
automatic choke 71 Motor Vehicle Parts
automatic control 603.5 *mechanics*
automatic direction finder 74.5 *navigation*
automatic exchange 534.12 *public telephone system*
automatic pilot 73 Aircraft Parts, 653.5 *guide*
automatic pin-setter 25.4 *bowling*
automatic reaction 464.4 *instinct*
automatic reflex 583.5 *spontaneity*
automatic response 331.6 *response*
automatic transmission 71 Motor Vehicle Parts, 603.4 *machine*
automatic writing 11.1 *occultism*
automation 13.6 *economic factors,* 15.2 *industrial negotiations,* 110.6 *regularity,* 112.2 *conformity,* 232.1 *instrumentality,* 235.9 *electronics,* 243.2 *manufacture,* 603.5 *mechanics*
automatism 11.1 *occultism*
automatist 11.12 *occultist*
Automatistes 50 Schools and Groups of Artists
automative 110.17 *regular*
automaton 183.8 *creature of habit,* 400.8 *humanlike machine,* 547.6 *image,* 603.4 *machine*
autometamorphism 54.32 *metamorphism*
automobile 71 Motor Vehicles, 33.11 *racing,* 71.16 *car,* 326.5 *means of transport*
automobile mechanic 646.2 *artisan*
automobile race 33.1 *motor racing*
automobile racer 33.8 *driver*
automobile rally 33.1 *motor racing*
automobile trial 33.1 *motor racing*
automobilia 71.21 *miscellaneous motoring terms*
automotive 324.16 *moving*
automotive engine 63.11 *engine*
automotive engineering 63.1 *engineering,* 63.3 *mechanical engineering,* 71.21 *miscellaneous motoring terms*
automotively 324.18 *in motion*
autonomic 571.13 *involuntary*
autonomous 12.9 *governmental,* 570.10 *free,* 688.14 *governmental,* 698.9 *free*
autonomously 698.20 *freely*
autonomy 12.1 *government,* 12.3 *governance,* 570.4 *free will,* 688.7 *type of rule,* 698.3 *independence*
autophobia 777 Phobias by Name
autopista 71.2 *road*
autopolyploidy 59.14 *chromosome*
autopsy 60.7 *diagnosis,* 397.8 *after death,* 399.7 *inquest*
auto race 33.9 *race*
auto racing 33.1 *motor racing*
autorickshaw 71 Motor Vehicles, /1.13 *motorcycle*
autoroute 71.2 *road*
autosome 59.14 *chromosome*
autospore 90.4 *reproductive body*

autostrada 71.2 *road*
autosuggestion 61.3 *psychiatric treatment,* 519.6 *reverie*
autotheft 733.3 *illegal borrowing,* 736.3 *theft*
autotoxaemia 628.10 *impairment*
autumn 203, 203, 214.5 *regular thing*
autumnal 55.46 *seasonal,* 203.12 *autumn*
autumnal equinox 10.15 *holy day,* 53.5 *celestial sphere,* 203.4 *autumn*
autumnally 203.18 *seasonally*
autumn colours 449.5 *brown thing*
autumn crocus 84 Flowers and Flowering Plants
autumnlike 203.12 *autumn*
autumn of one's life 207.5 *old age*
autumn sale 739.4 *sale*
autumn wood 85.3 *timber*
autunite 54 Minerals
auxiliaries 130.4 *extra,* 679.14 *armed forces*
auxiliary 127.15 *subordinate,* 130.5 *extra person,* 130.8 *additional,* 284.8 *supporter,* 284.9 *supportive,* 662.11 *helper,* 662.31 *supplementary,* 679.6 *militarist,* 679.35 *martial,* 707.1 *deputy,* 767.5 *helper*
auxiliary fleet 17.4 *military organization*
auxiliary forces 130.4 *extra*
auxiliary memory 65.6 *memory*
auxiliary power unit 73 Aircraft Parts
auxin 58.17 *plant hormone*
Auxois 32 Breeds of Horse and Pony
Avadana 7.12 *religious text*
avadavat 78 Birds
avail 599.6 *use,* 613.5 *usefulness,* 613.9 *be useful,* 662.1 *help,* 662.21 *be helpful,* 746.12 *be profitable,* 861.20 *do good*
availability 253, 437.3 *visibility,* 486.2 *possibleness,* 613.5 *usefulness,* 615.4 *nearness,* 727.1 *disposal*
available 196, 253, 254.14 *unoccupied,* 322.13 *opened up,* 437.1 *visible,* 486.5 *possible,* 599.10 *usable,* 605.7 *stored,* 606.7 *provisioning,* 613.1 *useful,* 615.2 *nearby,* 643.2 *not working,* 645.7 *leisurely,* 710.17 *offered,* 721.15 *gainful,* 727.14 *for sale,* 729.7 *given,* 739.15 *saleable*
available man 401.5 *single man*
available on request 606.7 *provisioning*
available post 322.10 *opportunity*
available space 248
available to all 522.2 *simple*
availably 322.25 *obviously*
avail nothing 236.6 *be powerless*
avail oneself of 599.2 *frequent,* 662.27 *find useful,* 733.8 *adopt*
avalanche 34.2 *climbing dangers,* 54.26 *mass movement,* 55.30 *snow,* 244.7 *agent of destruction,* 360.3 *downflow,* 360.13 *drip,* 409.5 *ice,* 610.1 *excess*
avant-garde 201, 201, 49.33 *jazz,* 119.5 *novel,* 154.8 *precursor,* 154.14 *preparatory,* 194.10 *prior,* 197.2 *occurring at a different time,* 303.1 *front,* 479.4 *originality,* 479.9 *original,* 585.2 *not customary*
avant-garde artist 201.9 *modern person*
avant-garde jazz 49.8 *jazz*
avant-gardism 154.3 *preparation*
avant-gardist 154.8 *precursor,* 201.9 *modern person*
Avar 5 Languages and Groups of Languages
avarice 734.1 *taking,* 860.1 *selfishness*
avaricious 721.16 *greedy,* 734.12 *taking,* 860.4 *selfish*
avariciously 734, 721.20 *gainfully,* 860.8 *selfishly*

avast! 36
avatar 8.8 *divine manifestation*, 526.10 *manifestation*
Ave 10.9 *prayer*
Avebury 10.13 *shrine*
Avelignese 32 Breeds of Horse and Pony
Ave Maria 10.9 *prayer*
avemger 672.2 *revenger*
avenge 855, 125.5 *counterbalance*, 672.3 *retaliate*, 879.2 *penalize*
avenged 125.7 *compensated*
avenge oneself 746.13 *retaliate*
avenger 855, 635.2 *troublemaker*, 879.17 *punisher*
avenging 125.10 *counterbalancing*, 855.14 *vindictive*
avenging angel 244.7 *agent of destruction*
avens 84 Flowers and Flowering Plants
aventurine 54 Gemstones
avenue 327.3 *road*, 347.6 *way out*
aver 480.3 *testify*, 535.17 *affirm*, 564.11 *speak*, 674.13 *conflict*
average 124, 124, 158, 164, 52.60 *parameter*, 120.5 *numbers*, 120.6 *quantitative*, 124.2 *medium*, 124.3 *mediocre*, 124.5 *medium*, 158.3, 158.13 *median*, 158.15 *middling*, 164.21 *common*, 167.15 *everyday*, 242.1 *moderation*, 242.6 *moderate*, 259.14 *medium*, 284.10 *supportable*, 291.6 *central*, 333.1 *middle way*, 482.5 *vague*, 617.5 *not bad*, 620.4 *ordinary*, 783.10 *mediocre*
Average 124
averaged out 717.6 *compromising*
average life 396.5 *life cycle*
averageness 164, 124.4 *average*, 124.6 *mediocrity*, 620.8 *ordinariness*, 783.4 *mediocrity*
average out 124.10 *make average*, 482.11 *not discriminate*, 717.4 *compromise*
average person 124, 400.7 *person*
averages 170.2 *statistics*
average-size 259.14 *medium*
average value 52.60 *parameter*
averaging out 717.6 *compromising*
averment 16.5 *litigation*, 480.4 *verification*, 535.1 *affirmation*, 564.7 *utterance*
Avernal 8.16 *devilish*
Avernus 8.11 *heaven*
averred 480.10 *verified*, 535.11 *stated*
Averroes 4.5 Philosophers
Averroism 4.7 *school of thought*
Averroist 4.11 *follower of a doctrine*, 4.14 *of a philosophy*
averse 573.1 *unwilling*, 663.19 *oppositional*, 785.8, 785.8 *disliking*, 822.10 *hating*
aversely 785.10 *discontentedly*, 822.18 *hatefully*
averseness 573.13 *dissociation*
aversion 573.13 *dissociation*, 663.1 *opposition*, 777.1 *fear*, 785.1 *dislike*, 820.3 *ill feeling*, 822.1 *hate*
aversion therapy 61.3 *psychiatric treatment*, 630.13 *therapy*
avert 591, 335.7 *misdirect*, 335.8 *sidestep*, 671.24 *parry*
avertable 591.20 *avoidable*
avertably 591.22 *evasively*
averting 591.10 *avoidance*
avert one's gaze 436.16 *be blind to*
Avery 52 Scientists
Aves 78.1 *birds*
Avesta 7.12 *religious text*
Avestan 5 Languages and Groups of Languages
avian 78
avian anatomy 78
aviary 68.7 *farm building*, 78.19 *ornithology*, 161.31 *exhibition*, 256.12 *stall*

aviation 73
Aviation 73
aviation beacon 439.6 *electric light*
aviation fuel 410.6 *oil*
aviation meteorology 55.1 *meteorology*
aviator 73.3 *aircraft personnel*
Avicenna 4 Philosophers
avici 8.11 *heaven*
avicultural 78.25 *ornithological*
aviculture 78.19 *ornithology*
aviculturist 78.21 *ornithologist*
avid 782.9 *desirous*
avidity 782.1 *desire*
avidly 782.18 *desirously*
avifauna 78.1 *birds*
Avignon 93 Cities
avionics 73.2 *aeronautics*
avitaminosis 624.4 *disease*
avocado 86 Fruits, 453.1 *green*, 453.9 *greenstuff*
avocado pear 45 Vegetables
avocet 78 Birds, 78.3 *water bird*
Avogadro 52 Scientists
Avogadro constant 56.97 *fundamental constant*
avoid 591, 305.8 *move sideways*, 331.2 *respond*, 334.4 *detour*, 335.8, 335.8 *sidestep*, 337.6 *shrink back*, 470.6 *be neglectful*, 531.11 *conceal oneself*, 576.6 *hesitate*, 578.1 *be equivocal*, 598.1 *relinquish*, 600.5 *not use*, 632.8 *be safe*, 638.6 *elude*, 641.4 *not act*, 671.24 *parry*, 711.5 *refuse*, 720.7 *not observe*, 720.8 *not perform*, 722.15 *lose someone*, 785.6 *react against*, 810.15 *escape notice*, 816.13 *ignore*, 822.14 *hate*, 869.5 *be self-restrained*
avoidable 591
avoidably 591.22 *evasively*
avoid alcohol 873.3 *be sober*
avoidance 591, 61.19 *defence mechanism*, 136.2 *setting apart*, 331.6 *response*, 470.2 *indifference*, 598.3 *relinquishment*, 600.8 *nonuse*, 632.1 *safety*, 638.1 *escape*, 641.1 *inaction*, 675.1 *peace*, 720.1 *nonobservance*, 785.1 *dislike*, 816.1 *unsociability*, 869.1 *self-restraint*
Avoidance 591
avoidance conditioning 61.20 *conditioning*
avoid a parry 28.5 *fence*
avoid bloodshed 675.5 *be at peace*
avoid both Scylla and Charybdis 333.7 *be halfway*
avoid defeat 682.7 *overcome obstacles*
avoided 785.9 *disliked*, 816.10 *lonely*
avoider 591, 519.9 *visionary*, 720.6 *evader*
avoid excess 869.5 *be self-restrained*
avoid financial obligations 747.7 *not pay*
avoid food 871.5 *fast*
avoid gobbledegook 522.5 *simplify*
avoiding 591, 470.5 *indifferent*, 720.11 *nonobservant*, 785.8 *disliking*
avoiding financial obligations 747.1 *nonpayment*
avoiding the issue 591.15 *evasiveness*
avoid notice 527.13 *hide*
avoid recognition 527.13 *hide*
avoid responsibility for 673.3 *submit*
avoid strife 677.4 *pacify*
avoid taxes 638.6 *elude*
avoid the issue 108.10 *be unrelated*, 474.13 *quibble*, 591.7 *be evasive*
avoid the trap 657.5 *be cunning*
avoid war 677.4 *pacify*
avoirdupois 268.12 *metrical*
avoirdupois weight 369, 75.1 *unit*, 268.5 *measuring system*

Avon 92 Counties, 96 Rivers, 96.4 British rivers
a vote against 711.2 *dissent*
avouch 535.20 *admit*
avouched 480.10 *verified*, 535.11 *stated*
avouchment 480.4 *verification*, 535.5 *admission*
avow 480.3 *testify*, 530.8, 535.20 *admit*
avowal 480.4 *verification*, 530.2 *divulgence*, 535.5 *admission*, 688.9 *permission*
avowed 480.10 *verified*, 530.10 *disclosed*, 535.11 *stated*
avowedly 102.19 *apparently*, 535.23 *affirmatively*
avulse 355.11 *extract*
avulsion 355.1 *extraction*
AWACS 679.31 *military aircraft*
Awahili 8 Deities
Awahokshu 8 Deities
await 199.10 *expect*, 209.7, 513.10 *wait*, 775.7 *aspire*
await discovery 527.13 *hide*
awaited 199.13 *foreseen*
awaiting discovery 527.2 *concealed*
awaiting execution 633.4 *endangered*, 879.22 *punishable*
awaiting trial 856.8 *accusatory*
await payment 744.8 *credit*
await trial 856.7 *be accused*
awake 403, 403.6 *conscious*, 642.18 *active*
awake late 209.6 *be late*
awaken 226, 629.5 *revive*
awaken desire 782.15 *cause desire*
awake the echoes 423.8 *be loud*
awake to life immortal 397.15 *die*
award 492.2 *verdict*, 492.11 *judge*, 681.1 *trophy*, 721.5 *profit*, 729.2 *gift*, 729.5 *give*, 804.3 *honours*, 878.2 *prize*, 878.9 *reward*
award a fellowship 878.10 *grant*
awarded 730.11 *receiving*
awarder 729.4 *giver*
awarding 729.1 *giving*
aware 403.5 *sensible*, 435.21 *seeing*, 471.11 *ideational*, 501.8 *knowledgeable*, 528.18 *informed*, 759.10 *feeling*, 760.1 *sensitive*
awareness 403.1 *sensation*, 435.4 *visualization*, 459.1 *mind*, 471.1 *idea*, 501.1 *knowledge*, 759.1 *feeling*, 760.5 *sensitivity*, 837.1 *gratitude*
aware of 403.5 *sensible*
awash 96.11 *flooded*, 389.23 *wet*, 389.24 *flooded*
Awassi 68 Breeds of Sheep
away 254, 254, 355, 591, 136.22 *in isolation*, 263.8 *distant*, 263.10 *distantly*, 347.18 *forth*, 349.33 *go away*, 458.7 *disappeared*, 458.8 *fleetingly*, 487.3 *hopeless*, 638.9 *fugitively*
away from 104.18 *extraneously*
away from home 254.10 *nonresident*
away side 305.5 *team*
away with the fairies 404.8 *unconscious*
away with you 349.33 *go away*
awe 9.1 *worship*, 777.1 *fear*, 786.1 *wonder*, 786.10 *be wonderful*, 849.2 *admiration*, 849.21 *command respect*
Awe 94 Lakes
awed 514.7 *amazed*, 786.6 *wondering*
aweful 786.8 *wonderful*
aweigh 36.10 *sailing*
awe-inspiring 849, 786.8 *wonderful*, 811.24 *grand*
aweless 787.3 *unmoved*, 807.17 *contemptuous*
awesome 777.10 *frightening*, 786.8, 786.14 *wonderful*
awesomely 786.13 *wonderfully*
awestricken 849.10 *reverent*
awestruck 514.7 *amazed*, 786.6 *wondering*, 849.10 *reverent*

awful 422.3 *silent*, 618.3, 776.8 *bad*, 777.10 *frightening*, 862.7 *evil*
awfully 618.15 *worthlessly*, 862.12 *evilly*
awfulness 618.9 *badness*, 862.1 *evil*
awful silence 422.4 *silence*
a while 185.3 *duration*, 185.5 *indefinite period*
a while ago 200.22 *in the past*
a while back 200.22 *in the past*
Awhiowhio 8 Deities
awkward 106.8 *difficult*, 206.12 *immature*, 211.10 *untimely*, 453.3 *raw*, 502.6 *ignorant*, 559.7 *graceless*, 577.1 *obstinate*, 616.1 *inconvenient*, 656.3 *clumsy*, 659.13 *inconvenient*, 659.15 *clumsy*, 764.2 *objectionable*, 790.4 *ugly*, 795.8 *discourteous*, 810.9 *blushing*
awkward age 206.1 *youth*
awkwardly 659, 106.17 *difficultly*, 206.15 *immaturely*, 211.15 *at the wrong time*, 559.11 *inelegantly*, 616.6 *inconveniently*, 656.11 *unskilfully*
awkwardness 659, 206.3 *immaturity*, 211.1 *untimeliness*, 502.1 *ignorance*, 559.1 *inelegance*, 616.3 *inconvenience*, 656.8 *unskilfulness*, 764.6 *objectionability*
awkward occurrence 211.1 *untimeliness*
awkward position 659.7 *awkward situation*
awkward question 477.4 *difficult question*
awkward situation 659, 106.4 *difficult circumstances*
awl 322.2 *opener*, 380.8 *sharp-pointed thing*
awn 87.3 *grass plant*, 375.7 *rough thing*, 380.8 *sharp-pointed thing*
awned 380.2 *spiked*
awning 293.7 *overhead covering*, 293.12 *protective covering*, 440.6 *shade*, 634.2 *shelter*
AWOL 254.4 *absenteeism*, 254.11 *truant*, 693.1 *disobedience*
a woman's work 685.2 *never-ending task*
Awonawilona 8 Deities
awry 123.3 *unequal*, 151.18 *muddled*, 504.22 *wrongly*, 844.18 *gone wrong*
axe 34.4 *climbing equipment*, 85.7 *timber production*, 244.8 *destroy*, 270.10 *shorten*, 322.2 *opener*, 349.2 *dismiss*, 380.9 *sharp-edged thing*, 380.16 *use a sharp tool*, 398.5 *execution*, 603.1 *tool*, 680.8 *sharp weapon*, 704.7 *terminate*, 767.12 *relieve from duty*, 879.16 *instrument of execution*
axe-breaker 85 Trees and Shrubs
axed 704.10 *cancelled*
axe-grinder 592.8 *planner*
axe kick 26.9 *tae kwon do*
axel jump 41.6 *ice-skating*
axel lift 41.6 *ice-skating*
axeltree 85.12 *figurative usage*
axeman 398.12 *executioner*
axe murderer 398.11 *murderer*
axe to grind 588.1 *intention*
axial 83.17 *of stems*, 291.6 *central*, 324.17 *directional*, 332.14 *directed*
axial motion 324.5 *circuition*, 364.1 *rotation*
axial ray 56.31 *lens element*
axial skeleton 382.7 *skeleton*
axil 83.5 *stem*
axillary 83.17 *of stems*
axillary bud 83.8 *bud*
axing 349.18 *dismissal*
axinite 54 Minerals
axiological 4.14 *of a philosophy*
axiologically 4.24 *philosophically*

axiologist 4.11 *follower of a doctrine*
axiology 4.6 *branch of philosophy*
axiom 4.1 *philosophy*, 4.8 *philosophical term*, 52.65 *theory*, 56.6 *law*, 166.4 *guide*, 505.1 *maxim*, 537.4 *truism*
axiomatic 52.69 *theoretic*, 505.2 *proverbial*, 537.17 *truistic*
axiomatically 505.4 *proverbially*
axiomatic set theory 4.6 *branch of philosophy*
axiomatic drawing 547.2 *reproduction*
axis 52.32 *graph*, 83.5 *stem*, 291.1 *centre*, 364.4 *vortex*
axis deer 77 *Placental Mammals*
axis of symmetry 308.2 *symmetry operation*
axle 71 *Motor Vehicle Parts*, **364**, 41.9 *bobsledding* , 63.8 *machine element*
axlebar 364.4 *vortex*
axlebox 364.4 *vortex*
axle load 369.9 *avoirdupois weight*
axle shaft 364.4 *vortex*
axle spindle 364.4 *vortex*
axle-true 364.4 *vortex*
Axminster 67.3 *fabric*
axolotl 79 *Amphibians*, 79.8 *young amphibian*
ayah 697.6 *domestic servant*
ayatollah 7.8 *priest*, 653.14 *leader*, 696.6 *religious leader*
Ayckbourn 48 *Dramatists*
aye 499.2 *yes*, 580.10 *vote*
aye-aye 77 *Placental Mammals*, 499.9 *yes*
Ayer 4 *Philosophers*
Ayers Rock 10.13 *shrine*
Aylesbury 68 *Breeds of Fowl*, **93** *Cities*
Aylesbury duck 45.44 *British dish*
Aymara 1 *Peoples*, 5 *Languages and Groups of Languages*
ayn 5.36 *accent*
Ayr 93 *Cities*
Ayrshire 68 *Breeds of Cattle*
Ayurvedic medicine 60.2 *natural medicine*
A–Z 528.5 *reference book*
azalea 84 *Flowers and Flowering Plants*
azan 10.4 *public worship*
Azande 1 *Peoples*
azapetine 62 *Medication*
azathioprine 62 *Medication*
Azazil 8.7 *devil*
Azerbaijan 91 *Countries*
Azerbaijani 5 *Languages and Groups of Languages*
Azidahaka 8.7 *devil*
azide 57 *Types of Compounds*
azimuth 53.5 *celestial sphere*, 268.4 *size*, 282.2 *horizontal surface*, 332.3 *orientation*
azine 57 *Types of Compounds*
azo compound 57 *Types of Compounds*
azo dye 67.6 *dye*
Azores high 55.11 *weather system*
Azorín 48 *Writers*
Azov 97 *Oceans and Seas*
Azrael 8.6 *angel*, 397.2 *death personified*
Aztec 1 *Peoples*, 5 *Languages and Groups of Languages*, 7 *Non-Christian Religions*, 400.4 *civilized human*
Aztec art 50 *Non-Western Art*
Aztecs 200.6 *people of the past*
Aztec two-step 353.2 *defecation*
azure 454.1 *blue*, 454.5 *blueness*, 454.9 *blue*, 544.8 *heraldic device*, 544.13 *heraldic*
azurite 54 *Minerals*
Az-Zargu 93 *Cities*

B

B 65 Programming Languages, 2.7 *social stratification*
ba 110.3 *lookalike*
baa 432.1 *animal cry*, 432.4 *cry*
Baal 8 *Deities*, 9.3 *idol*
Baalat 8 *Deities*
Baal Shamain 8 *Deities*
Baalwen 68 *Breeds of Sheep*
babaco 86 *Fruits*
babassu 85 *Trees and Shrubs*
Babbage 52 *Scientists*, 65 *Programming Languages*
Babbar 8 *Deities*
Babbitt 49 *Musicians and Composers*, 124.8 *middle classes*, 167.6 *conformist*
babbitt metal 57 *Alloys*
Babbittry 158.8 *middle class*, 167.4 *conventionalism*
babble 5.5 *nonstandard language*, 96.7 *flow*, 424.1 *faintness*, 424.5 *sound faint*, 426.3, 426.10 *rattle*, 521.5 *empty talk*, 521.9 *talk nonsense*, 523.7 *be unintelligible*, 563.14 *have difficulty speaking*, 565.3 *talk*, 565.7 *be talkative*
babbler 78 *Birds*, 565.4 *talker*
babbling 523.11 *unintelligibility*, 563.3 *speech defect*, 563.12 *inarticulate*, 565.5 *talkative*, 656.3 *clumsy*
babbling brook 96.1 *river*
Babcock-Levy test 61.6 *intelligence test*
babe 206.8 *young woman*, 206.9 *child*, 402.9 *woman considered as a sex object*, 539.22 *dupe*, 821.12 *nicknames for lovers*, 826.4 *terms of endearment*, 865.4 *innocent person*
babe in arms 156.15 *baby*, 206.9 *child*, 539.22 *dupe*, 658.3 *naive person*, 865.4 *innocent person*
babe-in-arms 238.4 *weakling*
babe in the woods 539.22 *dupe*
babel 133.3 *miscellany*
Babel 5.5 *nonstandard language*, 434.2 *dissonant noise*, 521.4 *senseless talk*
babesiosis 81.12 *protozoal disease*
babirusa 77 *Placental Mammals*
Babism 7 *Non-Christian Religions*
baboon 77 *Placental Mammals*
babu 401.3 *male title of address*
baby 156, 156.32 *embryonic*, 165.8 *specialization*, 206.8 *young woman*, 206.11 *young*, 238.4 *weakling*, 243.7 *produce*, 245.6 *progeny*, 260.2 *little thing*, 260.7 *little*, 400.7 *person*, 402.9 *woman considered as a sex object*, 779.2 *coward*, 821.12 *nicknames for lovers*, 826.4 *terms of endearment*
baby boom 246.2 *productiveness*
baby buggy 71.8 *baby carriage*
baby carriage 71
baby clothes 295.23 *children's clothes*
baby doll 821.12 *nicknames for lovers*, 826.4 *terms of endearment*
baby doll pyjamas 295.22 *nightwear*
baby food 350.7 *food*
babygro 295.23 *children's clothes*
babyhood 156.4 *conception*, 206.1 *youth*, 236.3 *helplessness*
babyish 206.11 *young*
Babylonian 5 *Languages and Groups of Languages*, 7 *Non-Christian Religions*, 400.4 *civilized human*
Babylonian art 50 *Non-Western Art*

Babylonians 1 *Peoples*, 200.6 *people of the past*
Babylonian splendour 811.9 *grandeur*
baby-mind 469.11 *care for*
baby-minder 469.8 *watchful person*
baby-minding 469.5 *watchfulness*
baby's bottom 376.8 *smooth thing*
baby's-breath 84 *Flowers and Flowering Plants*
baby-sit 469.11 *care for*
baby-sitter 469.8 *watchful person*, 632.3 *protector*
baby-sitting 469.5 *watchfulness*
baby talk 5.5 *nonstandard language*
baby tooth 380.11 *tooth*
baby walker 71.8 *baby carriage*
Bacab 8 *Deities*
Bacardi 351.7 *alcoholic drink*
baccalaureate 485.3 *qualifications*
baccarat 42 *Card Games*
bacchanal 350.18 *eater*, 872.4 *glutton*, 874.17 *drunkard*
bacchanalia 350.13 *feast*, 872.3 *act of gluttony*, 874.14 *drinking bout*
bacchant 350.18 *eater*, 874.17 *drunkard*
Bacchus 8 *Deities*
baccy 413.7 *tobacco*
bach 825.9 *be celibate*
Bach 49 *Musicians and Composers*
bachelor 174.7 *single person*, 401.5 *single man*, 825.5 *single person*
bachelor girl 174.7 *single person*, 402.5 *single girl*, 825.5 *single person*
bachelorhood 698.3 *independence*, 825.1 *celibacy*
bachelorlike 825.6 *celibate*
bachelorly 825.6 *celibate*
Bachelor of Arts 485 *Educational Qualifications*
Bachelor of Divinity 485 *Educational Qualifications*
Bachelor of Education 485 *Educational Qualifications*
Bachelor of Laws 485 *Educational Qualifications*
Bachelor of Medicine 485 *Educational Qualifications*
Bachelor of Music 485 *Educational Qualifications*
Bachelor of Science 485 *Educational Qualifications*
bachelor's-button 84 *Flowers and Flowering Plants*
bacillary 272.2 *fine*
bacilliform 272.2 *fine*
bacillophobia 777 *Phobias by Name*
bacillus 59.3 *organism*, 260.2 *little thing*, 624.6 *infection*, 631.7 *poisoning*
back 662, 31.2 *hockey player*, 55.58 *blow*, 74.9 *navigate*, 111.1 *oppositeness*, 116.28 *consent*, 155.10, 155.20 *rear*, 157.25 *hindmost*, 224.11 *be changeable*, 284.13 *support financially*, 284.14 *give moral support*, 292.3 *line*, 304.2 *rear end*, 304.4 *rear*, 305.9 *side with*, 324.13 *be in motion*, 324.17 *directional*, 335.1 *deviate*, 337.3 *reverse*, 359.15 *mount*, 373.9 *harden*, 535.19 *confirm*, 580.3 *side with*, 662.23 *advise*, 662.29 *finance*, 748.3 *donate*, 851.13 *support*
backache 406.2 *painful condition*
back and fill 74.9 *navigate*, 365.8 *oscillate*
back and foot 34.3 *climbing technique*
back-and-foot 34.8 *mountaineering*
back and forth 216.15 *changeably*, 223.8 *in exchange*, 224.15 *changeably*, 365.18 *to and fro*
back-and-forth 365.13 *oscillating*

back and front 30.5 *horizontal bar*
back and knee 34.3 *climbing technique*
back-and-knee 34.8 *mountaineering*
back another's credit 745.7 *be in debt*
back a sail 36.15 *sail*
back away 373.3 *reverse*, 573.7 *refuse*, 576.6 *hesitate*, 591.4 *shy*
back bacon 45.30 *bacon*
back beat 49.19 *tempo*
backbencher 12.8 *politician*, 127.6 *inferior*, 653.16 *official*
backbend 30.8 *floor exercises*
backbite 854.12 *defame*
backbiter 854.8 *defamer*
backbiting 854.3 *defamation*, 854.16 *defamatory*
backboard 23.3 *basketball equipment*, 25.1 *green bowling*
backbone 382 *Bones*, 103.2 *essential content*, 237.1 *strength*, 284.2 *supporting part*, 291.1 *centre*, 373.7 *hard substance*, 574.16 *fortitude*, 575.4 *stamina*, 778.1 *courage*
backbone of steel 574.16 *fortitude*
back boundary line 40.12 *badminton terms*
backbreaker 659.3 *difficult task*
backbreaking 644.11 *laborious*, 659.10 *difficult*, 661.14 *blocked*, 879.21 *punishing*
backbreaking work 644.1 *work*
backchat 478.1 *answer*, 478.18 *answer back*, 568.2 *chat*, 668.3 *act of defiance*, 807.9 *discourtesy*, 807.25 *answer back*
backchatting 478.11 *answering*, 807.20 *discourteous*
backcheck 31.3 *ice hockey*, 31.9 *play hockey*
backchecked 31.8 *hockey*
backchecker 31.4 *ice hockey player*
backchecking 31.3 *ice hockey*, 31.8 *hockey*
backcloth 51.17 *stage set*
back country 248.3 *geographical space*
back-country 249.6 *regions*, 249.18 *local*
back court 23.1 *basketball*
back crawl 39.1 *swimming*
back door 304.1 *rear*, 327.2 *route*, 346.6 *means of entry* , 347.6 *way out*, 632.1 *safety*, 638.2 *means of escape*
backdoor influence 657.1 *cunning*
back down 221.6 *reverse*, 337.2 *retreat*, 578.4 *recant*, 598.1 *relinquish*
backdrop 51.17 *stage set*, 297.1 *surroundings*
backed 116.17 *consenting*, 373.3 *hardened*, 535.13 *supported*, 851.23 *approved*
back e.m.f. 64.10 *electric potential*
back e.m.f. ground 56.52 *electric potential*
back end 203.4 *autumn*, 304.1 *rear*
back end of a bus 790.2 *ugly person*
backer 14.3 *stockbroker*, 51.25 *producer*, 284.8 *supporter*, 535.9 *affirmer*, 662.15 *benefactor*, 729.4 *giver*, 755.9 *generous person*, 851.7 *advocate*
backest 25.9 *bowls*
backest bowl 25.2 *grip*
backfill 63.28 *substructure*
backfire 221.1 *reversion*, 221.6 *reverse*, 231.1 *counteraction*, 231.3 *counteract*, 331.1, 331.4 *recoil*, 425.1, 425.5 *bang*
backfired 221.11 *reversed*
backfiring 331.8 *recoiling*
back floating 39.1 *swimming*
backflow 96.6 *river flow*
backflowing 324.4 *backward motion*, 324.17 *directional*
back formation 5.17 *word*

back-formed 5.42 *worded*
backgammon 42 *Board Games*
background 3.5 *chronicle,* 6.11 *re-finement,* 48.3 *aspect of,* 106.1 *circumstances,* 106.7 *cir-cumstantial,* 180.4 *concomitant,* 180.17 *accompanying,* 251.2 *cir-cumstances,* 263.3 *distant place,* 297.1 *surroundings,* 297.4 *sur-rounding,* 304.1 *rear,* 485.3 *qualifications*
background murmur 426.2 *hum-ming*
backhand 25.9 *bowls,* 31.8 *hockey,* 40.14 *forehand,* 286.5 *devious,* 330.14 *sporting hit*
backhand drive 40.2 *tennis strokes*
backhanded 286.5 *devious,* 334.7 *circuitous,* 538.17 *duplici-tous,* 578.10 *equivocal,* 850.11 *insulting*
backhanded compliment 538.7 *duplicity,* 850.5 *insult*
backhandedly 334.8 *circuitously,* 538.26 *untruthfully*
backhandedness 286.3 *devious-ness*
backhander 586.10 *bribe,* 729.2 *gift*
backhand grip 25.2 *grip*
backhand shot 25.2 *grip,* 31.3 *ice hockey*
backhand volley 40.2 *tennis strokes*
backhoe 63.29 *construction equipment*
back home 344.22 *on arrival*
backhouse 353.13 *lavatory*
backing 55.15 *wind direction,* 66.11 *emulsion,* 284.6 *moral support,* 284.7 *financial support,* 292.1 *lining,* 324.4 *backward motion,* 337.12 *reversal,* 373.5 *hardness,* 535.4 *confirmation,* 602.4 *financial resources,* 662.9 *patronage,* 662.11 *helper,* 748.7 *donation,* 851.1 *approval,* 851.19 *supporting*
backing band 180.6 *accompanier*
backing down 221.1 *reversion*
backing group 662.11 *helper*
backing store 65.6 *memory,* 65.7 *peripheral*
backing up 284.1 *support,* 337.12 *reversal*
backing-up 535.4 *confirmation*
backing vocalist 49.23 *singer*
backing vocalists 180.6 *accompanier*
back into a corner 337.2 *retreat*
back judge 19.2 *football player*
back kick 26.9 *tae kwon do*
back kitchen 256.7 *room*
backlash 159.4 *repercussion,* 221.1 *reversion,* 231.1 *counterac-tion,* 331.1, 331.4 *recoil,* 478.4 *reaction,* 672.1 *retaliation*
back-layout 21.6 *track*
back-layout style 21.2 *field-events*
backless dress 295.7 *frock*
backlighting 66.15 *lighting*
back line 41.10 *curling*
backlog 605.1 *store*
back matter 155.8 *addition,* 157.10 *ending,* 304.1 *rear*
back o'Bourke 263.3 *distant place,* 816.5 *solitary place*
back of beyond 248.3 *geographi-cal space,* 249.6 *regions,* 302.3 *furthest point,* 816.5 *solitary place*
back off 337.3 *reverse,* 591.4 *shy*
back on one's feet 629.15 *cured*
back out 337.2 *retreat,* 578.2 *equivocate,* 720.7 *not observe,* 779.4 *be a coward*
back out of 337.2 *retreat*
backpack 71.5 *pack,* 258.9 *bag-gage,* 326.10 *transferred thing*
back part 304.1 *rear*
back pass 38.2 *football play*
back passage 304.2 *rear end*
back pay 745.5 *amount owing,* 746.3 *pay*

back-pedal 328.3 *slow down,* 337.3 *reverse,* 484.8 *reverse,* 578.4 *recant*
back-pedalling 484.2 *reversal,* 578.6 *equivocation,* 578.11 *equivocating*
backplate 671.7 *armour*
back rent 745.5 *amount owing*
back rest 284.4 *rest*
back rib 45.23 *beef*
backroom 527.2 *concealed,* 592.7 *planning*
back-room boy 471.9 *person of ideas* 592.8 *planner,* 655.5 *ex-pert*
back-room boys 438.5 *invisible thing,* 662.11 *helper*
back-room influence 657.1 *cun-ning*
back rope 34.3 *climbing tech-nique*
back row 35.4 *rugby player*
back-saving 649.5 *labour-saving*
backscratch 853.11 *be sycophan-tic*
backscratcher 499.3 *assenter,* 853.7 *sycophant*
backscratching 664.3 *mutual rela-tionship,* 808.2 *sycophancy,* 808.7 *sycophantic,* 853.5 *syco-phancy,* 853.16 *sycophantic*
back seat 127.1 *inferiority*
back-seat driver 642.11 *meddler,* 653.13 *director,* 654.4 *adviser*
backset 337.18 *setback*
backsettler 255.5 *countryman*
back-shove 36.8 *punting*
backside 304.2 *rear end*
back side 305.2 *surface*
backsight 435.10 *visual aid,* 680.9 *firearm*
back slang 5.18 *slang*
back-slap 815.13 *fraternize*
back-slapper 815.6 *social person*
back-slapping 811.8 *bravado,* 815.9 *welcome,* 819.8 *friendly*
backslide 221.6 *reverse,* 337.1 *go backward,* 864.16 *be wicked*
backslider 337, 220.6 *convert,* 578.9 *equivocator*
backsliding 337, 221.1 *rever-sion,* 337.23 *receding,* 628.7 *de-terioration,* 864.1 *wickedness,* 864.11 *wicked*
backspin 29.3 *golf shots*
back-stabber 832.8 *malefactor*
backstage 51.15 *stage,* 51.41 *onstage,* 304.1 *rear,* 438.3 *pri-vate,* 438.9 *invisibly*
backstage dealings 657.1 *cun-ning*
backstage manipulator 527
backstairs 359.7 *means of as-cent,* 638.2 *means of escape*
back stalls 51.16 *auditorium*
backstay 74 Rigging, 36.3 *parts of a sailing boat*
back stream 96.6 *river flow*
backstreet 628.9 *dilapidation*
backstroke 39.1 *swimming,* 330.14 *sporting hit*
back surfaced 56.29 *optical ele-ment*
backswimmer 82 Insects
backswing 29.3 *golf shots*
back talk 478.1 *answer,* 668.3 *act of defiance,* 807.9 *discourtesy*
back the wrong horse 504.18 *be in error,* 683.6 *fail*
back to back 111.6 *oppositely,* 664.20 *cooperatively*
back-to-back 256.5 *house,* 256.16 *manorial*
back to front 221.13 *reversibly*
back-to-front 287.2 *inverted*
back to normal 629.15 *cured*
back tooth 380.11 *tooth*
back to sail 36.20 *offshore*
back to sail inside the boom 36.20 *offshore*
back to the beginning 221.13 *re-versibly*
back to where one started 337.28 *backward*
backtrack 337.3 *reverse,* 337.13 *about-turn,* 484.8 *reverse,* 734.9 *withdraw a statement*

backtracking 324.17 *directional,* 337.13 *about-turn,* 484.2 *rever-sal,* 734.2 *taking back*
backtrail 337.3 *reverse*
back trail 337.13 *about-turn*
backup 25.5 *bowling delivery,* 25.10 *bowling,* 65.17 *computing term,* 65.19 *abort*
back up 101.12 *establish reality,* 116.28 *consent*
backup 130.5 *extra person,* 155.13 *replacement,* 284.8 *sup-porter*
back up 284.11 *support,* 284.14 *give moral support*
backup 293.21 *substitution*
back up 293.34 *cover for,* 324.13 *be in motion,* 337.3 *reverse*
backup 337.12 *reversal*
back up 483.12 *prove,* 535.19 *confirm*
backup 602.5 *reserves,* 662.11 *helper*
back up 662.24 *back*
backup 664.1 *cooperation,* 707.2 *alternative*
back up 707.4 *substitute for*
back-up 293.40 *substitutive,* 767.5 *helper*
back-view 457.3 *external appear-ance*
back wall 40.8 *squash*
backward 337, 30.11 *gymnastic,* 39.11 *swimming,* 304.9 *in the rear,* 324.17 *directional,* 328.7 *delayed,* 460.5 *lacking intellect,* 460.7 *intellectually subnormal,* 502.6 *ignorant,* 573.3 *cautious,* 591.18 *avoiding,* 595.1 *unpre-pared,* 595.5 *immature,* 628.12 *deteriorated,* 658.1 *naive,* 810.13 *reserved*
backward and forward 365.18 *to and fro*
backwardation 752.1 *discount*
backward dislocate circle 30.7 *stationary rings*
backward dive 39.6 *diving*
backward-looking 200.21 *retro-spective,* 337.24 *retroactive*
backward motion 324, 337
Backward Motion 337
backwardness 460.1 *lack of intel-lect,* 502.1 *ignorance,* 510.2 *sub-normality,* 573.13 *dissociation,* 595.8 *lack of preparation,* 656.8 *unskilfulness,* 658.2 *naivety,* 810.6 *reserve*
backward peoples 400.3 *uncivi-lized human*
backward(s 337
backwards 30.12 *competitively,* 287.4 *inversely*
backwards and forwards 223.8 *in exchange*
backward somersault 30.5 *hori-zontal bar,* 30.8 *floor exercises*
backward step 337.10 *backward motion*
backward swing 30.5 *horizontal bar*
backward uprise 30.7 *stationary rings*
backward upstart 30.7 *stationary rings*
backwash 73 Aircraft Parts, 96.6 *river flow,* 227.2 *visible ef-fect*
backwater 94.2 *small lake,* 96.2 *channel,* 98.9 *inlet,* 249.6 *re-gions*
back water 328.3 *slow down,* 337.3 *reverse*
backwater 816.5 *solitary place*
backwood bowl 25.2 *grip*
backwoods 249.6 *regions*
back-woods 249.18 *local*
backwoodsman 255.5 *country-man*
back yard 249.13 *locality*
backyard 301.2 *enclosed place*
bacon 45, 45.11 *sandwich*
Bacon 4 Philosophers, **4** Phi-losophers
baconer 68.8 *livestock*
Baconian 4.11 *follower of a doc-trine,* 4.14 *of a philosophy*

bacon joint 45.30 *bacon*
bacteria 777 Phobias by Topic, 396.9 *classifications of life,* 624.6 *infection*
bacterial 59.21 *living,* 260.7 *little*
bacterial cell 59.7 *cell*
bacterial disease 624.4 *disease*
bactericide 62.4 *drug type,* 630.3 *prophylactic*
bacteriocidal 62.14 *counteracting*
bacteriological virological 59.20 *biological*
bacteriological warfare 676.8 *war-fare*
bacteriologist 59.19 *life scientist,* 60.13 *medical specialist*
bacteriology 59.1 *life science,* 60.3 *medical specialty,* 624.20 *pathology*
bacteriophage 59.3 *organism*
bacteriophobia 777 Phobias by Name
bacteriostatic 62.4 *drug type,* 62.14 *counteracting*
bacterium 59.3 *organism,* 260.2 *little thing,* 624.6 *infection,* 626.2 *germ,* 631.7 *poisoning*
Bactrian camel 77 Placental Mammals
bad 618, 776, 16.60 *offending,* 127.14 *poor,* 141.5 *disinte-grated,* 415.6 *unpalatable,* 538.13 *untrue,* 612.4 *trivial,* 617.1 *worthy,* 618.2 *inferior,* 618.9 *badness,* 620.1 *imperfect,* 624.22 *sick,* 626.5, 626.5 *un-hygienic,* 628.12 *deteriorated,* 652.18 *badly behaved,* 687.6 *ad-verse,* 770.6 *depressed,* 844.16 *in the wrong,* 858.5 *dishonour-able,* 861.1 *good,* 861.27 *great super,* 862.7 *evil,* 864.11 *wicked,* 877.11 *immoral*
bad air 626.1 *lack of hygiene*
bad apple 216.6 *editor*
bad art 548.1 *misrepresentation*
bad atmosphere 759.6 *bad feeling*
bad bargain 580.8 *choice*
bad behaviour 652.4 *bad con-duct,* 818.2 *bad manners,* 864.1 *wickedness*
bad blood 663.3 *conflict,* 785.1 *dislike,* 820.3 *ill feeling,* 822.1 *hate,* 832.1 *malevolence*
bad books 822.4 *hatefulness*
bad breath 419.2 *something that makes an unpleasant smell*
bad buy 738.6 *purchase,* 748.4 *expenditure*
bad character 618.12 *bad person,* 864.1 *wickedness*
bad check 741.15 *false money*
bad cheque 747.3 *bad payment*
bad condition 105.5 *physical state*
bad conduct 652, 864.1 *wicked-ness*
bad connection 108.5 *misconnec-tion*
bad conscience 866.2 *signs of guilt,* 867.1 *penitence*
bad day 656.9 *bungling*
bad debt 745.1 *debt,* 745.5 *amount owing*
bad debtor 745.6 *debtor*
bad deed 640.2 *deed,* 832.7 *act of malevolence,* 844.8 *wrong-doing*
baddeleyite 54 Minerals
badderlocks 90 Algae
baddie 832.8 *malefactor,* 862.6 *evil person,* 864.10 *bad person*
bad drains 419.2 *something that makes an unpleasant smell,* 626.1 *lack of hygiene*
bad dream 519.5 *fantasy,* 636.3 *false alarm*
bad ear 420.1 *hearing*
bad egg 419.2 *something that makes an unpleasant smell,* 801.2 *disreputable character,* 832.8 *malefactor,* 864.10 *bad person*
Baden-Baden 93 Cities
bad ending 628.7 *deterioration*

bad estimation 538.1 *untruth*
bad fairy 618.12 *bad person*
bad faith 538.10 *dishonesty*, 540.1 *falsehood*, 720.1 *nonobservance*, 858.2 *faithlessness*
bad feeling 759, 764.7 *dissension*
bad fit 117.2 *contradiction*, 666.3 *difference*
bad form 585.2 *not customary*, 795.3 *grossness*, 814.5 *nonobservance*
bad fortune 687
badge 437.6 *visible thing*, 544.3 *means of identification*, 544.4 *insignia*, 544.8 *heraldic device*, 792.3 *honour*, 792.6 *jewellery*
badge of merit 544.4 *insignia*
badge of office 544.4 *insignia*
badge of rank 544.4 *insignia*
badge of sovereignty 544.4 *insignia*
badger 77 Placental Mammals
badger and dog 679.4 *fighting animal*
badger hunting 590.2 *chase*
bad grammar 5.29 *grammar*, 504.11 *grammatical error*, 559.4 *inelegance of speech*
bad guy 51.21 *role*
bad habit 584.1 *habit*
bad hand 656.10 *unskilled person*
bad health 624.1 *ill health*
bad heart 624.10 *cardiovascular disease*
bad humour 105.4 *state of mind*
bad-humoured 105.8 *in a state of*
bad-humouredly 105.9 *conditionally*
bad idea 683.4 *unsuccessful thing*
badinage 771.3 *wit*, 799.1 *mockery*
bad influence 216.6 *editor*, 618.12 *bad person*, 801.2 *disreputable character*, 858.4 *dishonourable person*, 862.4 *evil power*, 862.6 *evil person*
bad intention 832.1 *malevolence*
bad job 656.9 *bungling*
bad judgment 16.4 *bad law*
bad karma 862.4 *evil power*
badlands 392.14 *desert*
bad language 559.4 *inelegance of speech*, 818.3 *act of discourtesy*, 827.2 *offensive language*
bad law 16
bad learner 656.10 *unskilled person*
bad light 439.10 *window*, 440.1 *darkness*, 441.1 *dimness*, 801.1 *disrespect*
bad likeness 115.3 *disguise*, 547.1 *representation*, 548.1 *misrepresentation*
bad lot 801.2 *disreputable character*, 832.8 *malefactor*, 864.10 *bad person*
bad luck 862
bad luck! 862
bad luck 211.3 *lost chance*, 229.2 *chance*, 515.2 *bad outcome*, 589.2 *luck*, 687.3 *bad fortune*, 835.5 *misfortune*
bad-luck sign 517
badly 127, 652, 504.22 *wrongly*, 538.26 *untruthfully*, 601.6 *abusively*, 618.15 *worthlessly*, 628.14 *worse*, 656.11 *unskilfully*, 858.11 *dishonourably*, 862.12 *evilly*, 864.18 *wickedly*
badly behaved 652, 659.14 *troublesome*, 818.6 *bad-mannered*, 864.11 *wicked*
badly behaved person 652
badly done 618.2 *inferior*, 656.4 *bungled*
badly dressed 559.10 *ugly*
badly lit 440.8 *dark*
badly made 618.2 *inferior*
badly matched 117.8 *contradictory*
badly off 687.7 *unprosperous*, 743.1 *poor*
badly served 515.9 *disappointed*
badly timed 211.10 *untimely*

bad-mannered 818, 838.3 *ungrateful*
bad manners 818, 652.4 *bad conduct*, 764.6 *objectionability*, 795.3 *grossness*, 814.5 *nonobservance*
bad match 117.2 *contradiction*, 666.3 *difference*
badminton 18 Sporting Activities, **40**
Badminton 32.11 *eventing*, 40
badminton court 40.11 *badminton equipment*
badminton equipment 40
badminton terms 40
bad money 741.15 *false money*
bad money driving out good money 628.7 *deterioration*
bad morals 877.1 *immorality*
bad-mouth 854.12 *defame*
bad move 504.1 *mistake*
bad name 801.1 *disrespect*
bad neighbour 785.3 *disliked person*
badness 618, 127.4 *poor quality*, 618.8 *inferiority*, 652.4 *bad conduct*, 832.1 *malevolence*, 844.5 *unrighteousness*, 858.1 *improbity*, 862.1 *evil*, 864.1 *wickedness*, 877.1 *immorality*
bad news 515.2 *bad outcome*, 628.7 *deterioration*, 635.2 *troublemaker*, 652.18 *badly behaved*, 687.1 *adversity*, 822.8 *hated person*, 864.10 *bad person*
bad nose 417.1 *odourlessness*
bad notice 852.5 *criticism*
bad odour 416.4 *reputation*, 419.1 *stench*, 801.1 *disrespect*, 822.4 *hatefulness*
bad omen 517.5 *omen*, 618.11 *harmfulness*, 636.1 *warning*
bad outcome 515
bad patch 659.7 *awkward situation*, 687.4 *time of adversity*
bad payment 747
bad person 618, 864, 832.8 *malefactor*
bad policy 616.3 *inconvenience*
bad press 852.5, 854.2 *criticism*
bad result 515.2 *bad outcome*
bad review 524.3, 854.2 *criticism*
Badrinath 10.13 *shrine*
bad sailor 74.7 *nautical person*
bad sales 739.5 *sales*
bad scene 628.7 *deterioration*, 801.2 *disreputable character*
bad shot 656.10 *unskilled person*
bad spell 687.4 *time of adversity*, 862.4 *evil power*
bad spirits 105.4 *state of mind*
bad taste 412, 117.5 *unfitness*, 127.4 *poor quality*, 411.2 *taste of life*, 482.6 *lack of discrimination*, 559.2 *impropriety*, 559.3 *ugliness*, 658.2 *naivety*, 795.1 *tastelessness*, 814.5 *nonobservance*, 844.3 *impropriety*, 864.3 *venial sin*, 877.2 *indecency*
bad temper 829.1 *irascibility*, 829.2 *sign of irascibility*, 830.3 *irritableness*, 830.4 *sign of irritableness*
bad-tempered 822.13 *angry*, 830.7 *irritable*
bad time 211.1 *untimeliness*
bad time of the month 211.1 *untimeliness*
bad times 687.4 *time of adversity*, 743.6 *insolvency*
bad timing 211.1 *untimeliness*
bad trip 875.1 *drug-taking*
bad turn 832.7 *act of malevolence*
bad use 601.2 *misuse*
bad vibes 759.6 *bad feeling*
bad visibility 438.4 *invisibility*
bad ways 864.1 *wickedness*
bad weather 34.2 *climbing dangers*, 241.5 *violent weather*
bad will 832.1 *malevolence*
bad wishes 822.1 *hate*
bad word 5.19 *swearword*, 827.1 *curse*
bad words 818.3 *act of discourtesy*
Baedeker 528.5 *reference book*
bael 86 Fruits

Baer 52 Scientists
Baffin 98 Islands
baffle 421.3 *inaudibility*, 421.10 *muffle*, 443.12 *obscure*, 460.10 *bemuse*, 491.20 *make uncertain*, 515.7 *thwart*, 523.7 *be unintelligible*, 529.13 *mystify*, 659.23 *cause difficulties*, 786.10 *be wonderful*
baffled 491.3 *confused*, 515.9 *disappointed*, 523.6 *confused*, 659.16 *troubled*
baffle description 786.10 *be wonderful*
bafflement 491.12 *confusion*, 498.3 *incredulity*, 515.1 *disappointment*, 523.11 *unintelligibility*, 786.1 *wonder*
baffling 443.4 *inscrutable*, 491.3 *confused*, 523.4 *difficult*, 659.12 *problematic*
baffling attitude 523.12 *unintelligible thing*
baffy 29.4 *golf club*
BAFTA Award 878.2 *prize*
bag 258, 120.3 *container*, 165.8 *specialization*, 590.11 *hunt*
bag and baggage 723.4 *possessions*, 725.4 *possessions*
bagatelle 612.8 *trifle*, 612.9 *bauble*, 754.5 *cheap item*
bagel 45.39 *loaf*
bagful 605.1 *store*
baggage 258, 70.2 *thing transported*, 206.8 *young woman*, 326.10 *transferred thing*, 402.9 *woman considered as a sex object*, 725.4 *possessions*, 807.12 *impudent person*
baggage car 72.6 *rolling stock*
bagged 258.20 *containing*, 874.3 *dead drunk*
baggily 139.10 *noncohesively*, 259.20 *largely*
bagginess 139.1 *nonadhesion*, 259.2 *bigness*, 271.4 *breadth*
baggy 139.8 *nonadhesive*, 259.15 *big*, 271.1 *broad*, 295.31 *styled*
Baghdad 93 Cities
bag job 736.3 *theft*
bag lady 168.7 *nonconformist*, 687.5 *person in adversity*, 743.10 *poor person*
bag limit 37.2 *hunting*
bagman 739.11 *pedlar*
bagmuck 638.13 *fertilizer*
bagnio 877.6 *brothel*
bag of bones 274.9 *thin person*
bag of nerves 777.6 *frightened person*
bag of tricks 539.7 *tricking*, 539.8 *trick*, 602.1 *means*, 603.1 *tool*, 605.5 *collection*, 657.2 *stratagem*
bag of waters 245.7 *obstetrics*
bagpipe 49 Musical Instruments
bags 181.3 *profuseness*, 295.9 **trousers**
bag-snatcher 734.6 *taker*, 736.8 *thief*
bag-snatching 736.1 *stealing*
bag trolley 71.7 *handcart*
baguette 43 Architectural Decoration, 45.39 *loaf*
baguio 55.16 *wind vortex*
bagwig 295.15 *headgear*
bagworm 82.5 *larva*
bagworm moth 82 Insects
Baha'i 7.6 *non-Christian*
Bahaism 7 Non-Christian Religions
Bahamas 91 Countries
Bahasa Indonesia 5 Languages and Groups of Languages
Bahir 7.12 *religious text*
Bahrain 91 Countries
Baikal 94 Lakes
bail 16.6 *legal process*, 27.5 *wicket*, 326.15 *take away*, 639.2 *deliverance*, 700.1 *liberation*, 700.4 *liberate*
bailed 700.7 *liberated*
bailey 671.11 *fortification*

Bailey bridge 63.21, 327.9 *bridge*
bailie 696.3 *leader*
bailiff 16.10 *law officer*, 68.16 *farm worker*, 653.15 *manager*, 696.3 *leader*, 697.6 *domestic servant*, 730.7 *collector*
bailiwick 16.2 *jurisdiction*, 233.7 *sphere of influence*, 249.5 *state*, 249.14 *sphere*, 256.2 *environment*
Bailly 53 Lunar Features
bail out 639.1 *deliver*
Baily 52 Scientists
bain marie 45.8 *cooking technique*
bain-marie 258.15 *pot*
Baird 52 Scientists
bairn 206.9 *child*
bait 20.1 *angling*, 228.5 *positive stimulus*, 340.5, 340.12 *lure*, 539.13, 539.33 *snare*, 586.9 *enticement*, 590.3 *hunting and fishing equipment*, 690.5 *be severe*, 710.9 *offer*, 821.26 *court*, 828.9 *offend*, 878.4 *reward for service*
bait a hook 539.33 *snare*
bait a trap 539.33 *snare*
bait casting 20.1 *angling*
baited 20.8 *angling*, 539.42 *trapped*
baited trap 539.13 *snare*, 586.9 *enticement*
bait fishing 20.1 *angling*
baiting 20.8 *angling*
bait the hook 20.7 *angle*
bait the trap 657.5 *be cunning*
baize 67 Natural Fabrics, 24.1 *billiards*
bake 392, 44.11 *make ceramics*, 45.55 *cook*, 373.9 *harden*, 408.14 *be hot*
bakeapple 86 Fruits
baked 392, 408.13 *heated*
baked brick 373.7 *hard substance*
bakehouse 45.3 *kitchen*
Bakelite 57.21 *polymer*, 395.10 *resin*
baker 45.2 *cook*, 133.7 *person who mixes*, 350.20 *food provider*, 606.3 *provider*, 739.13 *retailer*
Baker 49 Musicians and Composers
baker's 350.17 *food shop*
baker's dozen 179.7 *double figures*
bakery 45.3 *kitchen*, 350.17 *food shop*
Bakewell tart 45.36 *cake*
Bakhtyari 5 Peoples
baking 45.1 *cookery*, 45.8 *cooking technique*
baking hot 408.9 *hot*
baking powder 45.7 *basic ingredient*, 370.8 *leavening*
baking sheet 45.6 *kitchen equipment*
baking soda 57 Common Chemical Compounds, 621.9 *cleaning agent*
baklava 45.52 *Greek dish*
baksheesh 228.5 *positive stimulus*, 721.5 *profit*, 729.2, 755.7 *gift*, 878.7 *bounty*
Baku 93 Cities
Bala 93 Cities, **94** Lakes, 94.4 *British lakes*
balaclava helmet 295.15 *headgear*
balalaika 49 Musical Instruments
balance 57 Laboratory Apparatus, **576,** 4.3 *detachment*, 30.5 *horizontal bar*, 30.8 *floor exercises*, 30.10 *compete in gymnastics*, 34.8 *mountaineering*, 36.4 *rowing*, 36.16 *row*, 46.3 *ballroom dance steps*, 50.4 *treatment*, 50.23 *design*, 56.86 *weighing instrument*, 107.8 *be proportionate to*, 109.1 *interchange*, 109.7 *reciprocate*, 110.5 *equality*, 110.8 *make the same*, 110.10 *be equal*, 112.9 *be uniform*, 116.4 *harmony*, 116.24 *harmonize*, 122.2 *equilibrium*,

122.11 *equalize*, 124.5 *medium*, 124.10 *make average*, 125.2, 125.5 *counterbalance*, 143.1 *part*, 144.1 *completeness*, 158.3 *median*, 158.16 *place in the middle*, 159.7 *stability*, 170.12 *check*, 214.4 *orderliness*, 214.10 *make regular*, 225.1 *stability*, 225.7 *make stable*, 268.7 *standard*, 285.1 *parallelism*, 285.6 *correlate*, 308.1 *symmetry*, 308.6 *symmetrize*, 325.1 *motionlessness*, 333.2 *middle of the road*, 333.7 *be halfway*, 369.10 *scales*, 369.12 *be heavy*, 382.9 *artistic structure*, 558.1 *elegance*, 610.3 *superfluity*, 704.4 *cancelling out*, 704.9 *cancel out*, 717.1 *compromise*
Balance 53 The Constellations
balance accounts 750.7 *account*
balance beam 30.6 *pommel horse*
balance carried forward 132.3 *difference*
balance climbing 34.1 *mountaineering*
balanced 36.11 *rowing*, 110.16 *equal*, 116.13 *harmonious*, 122.6 *equal*, 124.2 *medium*, 150.10 *ordered*, 158.13 *median*, 214.14 *orderly*, 225.10 *stabilized*, 242.6 *moderate*, 285.4 *correlated*, 308.4 *symmetrical*, 325.4 *motionless*, 507.5 *wise*, 509.5 *rational*, 558.3 *elegant*, 704.10 *cancelled*, 717.6 *compromising*, 750.11 *accounted*, 843.12 *all right*
balanced diet 350.6 *nutrition*
balanced line 19.7 *offence*
balanced mind 509.1 *sanity*
balance due 593.2 *need*
balance movement 30.7 *stationary rings*
balance of form 308.1 *symmetry*
balance of mind disturbed 510.1 *insanity*
balance of payments 13.5 *international trade*, 13.6 *economic factors*
balance of power 122.2 *equilibrium*
balance of terror 122.2 *equilibrium*
balance of trade 13.5 *international trade*
balance out 124.10 *make average*
balances 741.6 *funds*, 744.3 *deposit*
balance sheet 13.7 *corporation*, 750.1 *accounts*
balance the books 170.12 *check*, 721.12 *earn*
balance to pay 745.5 *amount owing*
balance wheel 364.6 *rotator*
balancing 30.11 *gymnastic*, 36.11 *rowing*, 109.4 *reciprocal*, 122.3 *equalization*, 125.10 *counterbalancing*, 231.4 *counteracting*, 717.6 *compromising*
balancing act 578.5 *equivocalness*, 717.1 *compromise*
balancing exercises 30.1 *gymnastics*
balas 54 Gemstones
balata 85 Trees and Shrubs
Balaton 94 Lakes
balbriggan 67 Natural Fabrics
Balchin 48 Writers
balcony 43.9 *miscellaneous architectural features*, 51.16 *auditorium*, 51.31 *theatregoer*, 256.7 *room*, 283.5 *projecting object*, 318.2 *projection*
bald 78 Birds, **294**, 296.13 *hairless*, 376.1 *smooth*, 537.18 *truthful*, 556.1 *simple*
bald as a billiard ball 294.10 *bald*, 296.13 *hairless*
bald as a coot 296.13 *hairless*
bald as an egg 294.10 *bald*, 296.13 *hairless*
bald cypress 85 Trees and Shrubs
Balder 8 Deities

balderdash 506.1 *nonsense*, 521.4 *senseless talk*
bald head 294.6 *baldness*
baldhead 296.5 *baldness*
bald head 376.8 *smooth thing*
baldheaded 296.13 *hairless*
baldly 296.17 *nakedly*, 556.8 *simply*
baldness **294**, **296**, 537.5 *truthfulness*, 556.4 *simplicity*
baldpate 296.5 *baldness*
bald-pated 296.13 *hairless*
baldpatedness 296.5 *baldness*
bald person 296.5 *baldness*
baldric 295.25 *accessories*
bald top 296.5 *baldness*
Baldwin 48 Writers
baldy 296.5 *baldness*
bale 68.9 *animal feedstuff*, 68.17 *farm*, 161.27 *bundle*, 161.38 *group*, 369.6 *displacement*
Balearic 32 Breeds of Horse and Pony
bale carrier 68.10 *farm tool*
bale-carting 68.5 *cultivation*
baled 161.49 *grouped*
baleen 377.3 *elastic thing*
bale-fire 439.8 *fire*
baleful 618.5 *harmful*, 832.10 *malevolent*, 862.9 *detrimental*
balefully 862.13 *destructively*
balefulness 618.11 *harmfulness*
bale out 347.10 *emerge*, 662.29 *finance*
baler 68.10 *farm tool*
bale sledge 68.10 *farm tool*
bale wrapper 68.10 *farm tool*
Bali 8 Deities, **98** Islands
Balinese 5 Languages and Groups of Languages
Bali pony 32 Breeds of Horse and Pony
balk 22.4 *pitching terms*, 22.7 *play baseball*, 515.2 *bad outcome*, 515.7 *thwart*, 573.8 *hold back*, 576.6 *hesitate*
Balkan 95 Mountains
Balkanization 816.3 *separation*
Balkanize 12.11 *govern*
balk at 591.4 *shy*, 711.5 *refuse*
balked 515.9 *disappointed*
Balkhash 94 Lakes, 94.5 *other major lakes*
balking 573.12 *opposition*
ball **338**, 22.4 *pitching terms*, 27.7 *bat*, 46.1 *dancing*, 135.11 *make love*, 161.10 *dance*, 315.3 *round thing*, 315.11 *make round*, 338.8 *missile*, 680.6 *historical missile weapon*, 680.13 *ammunition*, 680.14 *historical ammunition*, 815.5 *party*, 821.29 *make love*
Balla 93 Cities
ballad 48.7 *poem*, 560.3 *narration*
ballade 48.7 *poem*, 48.10 *verse form*
balladeer 48.14 *author*, 49.24 *musician*, 433.5 *melodist*
ballad maker 48.14 *author*
ballad monger 48.14 *author*
ballad opera 51.3 *musical drama*
balladry 48.6 *poetry*
ball and chain 402.12 *woman in the family*, 661.4 *restraint*, 699.5 *means of restraint*
ball-and-claw leg 47.3 *chair leg*
ball-and-socket joint 135.5 *joint*
ballast 36.3 *parts of a sailing boat*, 72.3 *rail*, 122.4 *equilizer*, 125.2 *counterbalance*, 225.3 *stabilizer*, 369.8 *displacement*, 369.10 *scales*, 369.14 *make heavy*, 632.4 *safety device*
ballasting 369.10 *scales*
ball bearing 63.8 *machine element*, 364.4 *vortex*
ball boy 40.6 *tennis player*
ball-breaker 402.9 *woman considered as a sex object*
ballbuster 659.3 *difficult task*
ball-buster 674.2 *contest*
ball-carrier 35.4 *rugby player*

ball clay 44.2 *raw material*
ball-control offence 23.4 *playing terms*
ballerina 46.13 *ballet dancer*, 51.28 *dancer*, 811.15 *showman*
Ballesteros 18 Sporting Personalities
ballet 46, 41.12 *ski*, 51.3 *musical drama*, 243.5 *work of art*, 526.9 *production*, 811.14 *show*
ballet companies 46
ballet costume 295.5 *fancy dress*
ballet dancer 46, 51.28 *dancer*, 646.1 *worker*
ballet dancing 46.1 *dancing*, 46.8 *ballet*
balletgoer 51.31 *theatregoer*
balletic 51.37 *dramatic*
ballet music 49.7 *dance music*
balletomane 51.31 *theatregoer*
Ballet Rambert 46.12 *ballet companies*
ballet school 6.12 *educational institution*
ballet shoes 295.19 *footwear*
ballet-skiing 41.1 *skiing*
ballet skirt 295.6 *skirt*
ballet steps 46
ball game 42.1 *game*, 251.2 *circumstances*
ballgown 295.7 *frock*
ball gown 813.4 *formal dress*
balling 135.4 *sexual union*, 821.5 *desire*
ball in touch 35.3 *rugby play*
ballista 680.6 *historical missile weapon*
ballistic 338.18 *projectile*
ballistically 338.34 *forward*
ballistic missile 338.8 *missile*, 680.5 *missile weapon*
ballistics 338.6 *shooting*, 676.6 *art of war*
ballistophobia 777 Phobias by Name
ball lightning 55.21 *thunderstorm*
ball milling 44.5 *ceramic process*
ball of fire 336.16 *progressive person*
ballong 46.9 *ballet steps*
balloon 73.8 *aircraft*, 258.19 *inflatable*, 261.3 *enlarged thing*, 261.6 *become bigger*, 315.3 *round thing*, 370.7 *light thing*, 390.10 *air bubble*
ballooning 18 Sporting Activities
balloon out 315.11 *make round*, 316.5 *be convex*
ballot 580.10 *vote*
ballot box 580.12 *election*
ballot-box stuffing 539.10 *fraud*
balloter 580.13 *electorate*
ballot paper 580.12 *election*
ballot-rigged 539.35 *deceptive*
ballot rigging 539.10 *fraud*
ballpark figure 741.5 *sum*
ball-park view 692.7 *overview*
ball return 25.4 *bowling*
ballroom 46.6 *famous dancers*
ballroom dance 46.2 *dance*
ballroom dance steps 46
ballroom dancing 46.1 *dancing*
ballroom music 49.7 *dance music*
balls 239.1 *vigour*, 245.8 *organs of reproduction*, 316.2 *bulge*, 506.1, 538.6 *nonsense*, 540.13 *nonsense*, 778.1 *courage*, 827.15 *miscellaneous swear-words*
ballsed-up 151.19 *mixed-up*
balls up 504.19 *make a mistake*, 628.4 *impair*, 656.7 *be clumsy*, 683.6 *fail*
balls-up 151.6 *mix-up*, 151.23 *confuse*, 504.10, 559.6 *blunder*, 656.9 *bungling*
ballsy 778.9 *courageous*
ball the jack 329.5 *run like a shot*
ball up 315.11 *make round*, 683.6 *fail*
ballyhoo 423.2 *outcry*, 532.7 *publicity*, 532.16 *publicize*, 541.1 *exaggeration*, 541.7 *exaggerate*, 586.6 *advertising*
ballyhooed 541.12 *exaggerated*
Ballymena 93 Cities

Ballymurphy 93 Cities
balm **630**, 62.7 *ointment*, 242.2 *moderator*, 386.5, 395.6 *ointment*, 413.5 *herbs*, 418.1 *fragrance*, 630.2 *medicine*, 630.5 *analgesic*, 767.3 *reliever*, 835.2 *condolence*
Balmer series 56 Named Laws
balmily 677.7 *pacifically*
balminess 418.1 *fragrance*
balm of Gilead 62 Medication, **85** Tree Products, 242.2 *moderator*
balmoral 295.15 *headgear*
Balmoral 256.4 *official residence*, 295.18 *underwear*
balmy 55.50, 408.11 *warm*, 418.4 *fragrant*, 686.8 *prosperous*
balneal 621.18 *cleansing*
balneation 389.11 *wash*
baloney 474.2 *sophism*, 521.5 *empty talk*, 521.14, 538.6 *nonsense*, 540.13 *nonsense*
balsa 85 Trees and Shrubs, 379.3 *brittle thing*
balsam 62 Medication, **85** Tree Products, 45.7 *basic ingredient*, 62.7, 386.5 *ointment*, 630.2 *medicine*, 630.9 *balm*
balsam fir 85 Trees and Shrubs
balsamic 62.16 *soothing*, 630.17 *remedial*, 767.8 *relieving*
balsam poplar 85 Trees and Shrubs
Balt 91 Names for Inhabitants
balthazar 258.14 *bottle*
balti 45.54 *other dishes*
Baltic 5 Languages and Groups of Languages, **97** Oceans and Seas, 5.11 *family of languages*
Baltimore 93 Cities
Baltimore oriole 78 Birds
Balto-Slavic 5.11 *family of languages*
Baluchi 5 Languages and Groups of Languages
Baluchitherium 77 Placental Mammals
balustrade 284.2 *supporting part*, 301.3 *enclosing thing*
Balzac 48 Writers
Bamako 93 Cities
Bambara 5 Languages and Groups of Languages
Bamboccianati 50 Schools and Groups of Artists
bamboo 87 Grasses
bamboo curtain 87.7 *figurative usage*
Bamboo Curtain 147.3 *exclusion zone*, 298.1 *interface*, 661.3 *barrier*
bamboo pole 20.3 *fishing tackle*
bamboo rat 77 Placental Mammals
bamboo shoot 83.9 *seed*
bamboo shoots 45 Vegetables
bamboo worm 81 Worms
bamboozle 531.9 *disguise*, 539.28 *trick*, 565.9 *out-talk*
bamboozlement 539.7 *tricking*
bamboozler 539.15 *deceiver*
ban 16.35 *illegality*, 16.75 *make illegal*, 136.10 *set apart*, 147.1 *exclusion*, 147.7 *exclude*, 302.2 *limiting factor*, 302.7 *limit*, 349.4 *ostracize*, 487.8 *make impossible*, 529.12 *keep secret*, 532.1 *publication*, 591.7 *be evasive*, 600.6 *stop using*, 692.1, 692.9 *command*, 699.1 *restraint*, 699.5 *means of restraint*, 699.8 *restrain*, 709.1, 709.3 *veto*, 711.2, 711.6 *dissent*, 816.13, 816.13 *ignore*, 827.4 *malediction*, 827.7 *wish ill*, 846.17 *criminalize*, 852.3 *nonacceptance*, 852.15 *withhold approval*, 869.5 *be self-restrained*, 879.1 *punish*
Bana 48 Writers
ban a book 709.4 *censor*
Banach space 52 Named Concepts
banak 85 Trees and Shrubs

banal 124.3 *mediocre*, 412.5 *tasteless*, 505.2 *proverbial*, 521.10 *meaningless*, 584.10 *familiar*, 788.4 *boring*
banality 412.1 *tastelessness*, 505.1 *maxim*, 788.1 *boredom*
banally 788.8 *boringly*
banana 86 Fruits, 452.8 *yellow thing*
Banana bender 86.5 *figurative usage*
banana boat 74 Ships and Boats
banana bond 57.11 *chemical bond*
banana drum 49 Musical Instruments
banana-nut bread 45.38 *bread*
banana republic 12.5 *political organization*, 86.5 *figurative usage*
bananas 510.11 *insane*
banana skin 86.5 *figurative usage*, 504.10 *blunder*, 614.6 *refuse*
banana split 45.35 *dessert*
band 43 Architectural Decoration, **137**, 40.3 *tennis equipment*, 49.26 *musical group*, 116.2 *alliance*, 137.4 *means of connection*, 137.6 *line*, 140.3 *assembly*, 161.11 *group*, 161.12 *team*, 163.5 *social class*, 266.1 *layer*, 269.5 *piece*, 272.8 *narrow thing*, 295.14 *neckwear*, 313.3 *circular thing*, 456.3 *striping*, 456.11 *variegate*, 534.14 *radio transmission*, 646.4 *personnel*, 665.1 *party*, 679.16 *army unit*
Banda 97 Oceans and Seas
bandage 135.10 *link*, 137.6 *line*, 137.11 *connect*, 222.3 *substitute thing*, 284.3 *body support*, 293.6 *medical covering*, 293.25 *wrap*, 301.4 *wrapper*, 301.6 *wrap*, 323.2 *stopper*, 323.8 *stop*, 629.6 *cure*, 630.10 *surgical dressing*, 630.20 *doctor*
bandaged 293.37 *protected*, 323.13 *stopped*
bandaging 293.6 *medical covering*
Band-Aid 138.3 *adhesive*, 222.3 *substitute thing*, 712.3 *solicitation*
bandanna 295.14 *neckwear*
bandeau 544.8 *heraldic device*
banded 456.9 *striped*
banderole 544.7 Architectural Decoration, 544.7 *flag*
bandicoot 77 Marsupials
bandit 693.9 *criminal*, 736.9 *plunderer*, 816.7 *outsider*
banditry 736.5 *plundering*
bandleader 192.11 *person keeping time*
bandmaster 49.24 *musician*
band of cloud 55.20 *cloud appearance*
bandoleer 34.4 *climbing equipment*, 137.10 *band*, 295.25 *accessories*, 680.4 *arsenal*
bandoura 49 Musical Instruments
band-pass filter 64.22 *transformer*
band printer 65.7 *peripheral*
band rate 65.17 *computing term*
band saw 47.11 *woodworking tool*, 63.9 *machine tool*, 85.7 *timber production*
band spectrum 56.68 *emission*
bandstand 51.15 *stage*
band-stop filter 64.22 *transformer*
band together 161, 140.6 *come together*, 664.14 *join with*, 665.12 *be in league with*
Bandung 93 Cities
bandurria 49 Musical Instruments
bandwidth 534.14 *radio transmission*
bandy 18 Sporting Activities
bandy about 532.13 *make public*
bandy words 474.13 *quibble*
bandy words with 223.5 *exchange*
bane 607.7 *destroyer*, 618.10 *poverty*, 624.5 *plague*, 626.1 *lack of hygiene*, 635.1 *trap*,

687.1 *adversity*, 777.5 *frightener*, 822.8 *hated person*, 862.5 *evil thing*, 862.6 *evil person*
baneful 244.14 *destructive*, 618.5 *harmful*, 626.5 *unhygienic*, 631.16 *blighting*, 820.6 *hostile*, 822.12 *hated*, 832.14 *hostile*, 862.9 *detrimental*
banefully 631, 820.15 *aggressively*
banefulness 618.11 *harmfulness*
Banff 93 Cities
bang 425, 425, 330.2 *collide*, 330.3 *hit*, 330.13 *blow*, 423.1 *loudness*, 423.8 *be loud*, 425.10 *explosively*, 843.20 *correctly*, 875.6 *drug*, 875.10 *drug oneself*
Bangalore 93 Cities
banger 425, 45.29 *sausage*, 71.16 *car*, 439.8 *fire*
banger racing 33.1 *motor racing*
bangers and mash 45.44 *British dish*
banging 425, 423.2 *outcry*, 875.1 *drug-taking*
Bangkok 93 Cities
Bangladesh 91 Countries
bangle 792.6 *jewellery*
bang on 843.8 *correct*
bang-on 503.5, 537.21 *accurate*, 617.1 *worthy*
Bangor 93 Cities, **93** Cities
bangtail 32.1 *horse*
bang up 323.10 *enclose*
bang-up 617.1 *worthy*
bang up-to-date 196.6 *present*, 201.10 *new*
Bangus 68 Breeds of Cattle
Bangweulu 94 Lakes
banish 136.10 *set apart*, 147.8 *eject*, 252.16 *replace*, 349.4 *ostracize*, 816.13 *ignore*, 879.1 *punish*
banished 252.10 *replaced*, 816.10 *lonely*
banishment 147.2 *ejection*, 252.3 *replacement*, 349.19 *ostracism*, 816.3 *separation*, 879.7 *punishment*
banjo 49 Musical Instruments
banjolele 49 Musical Instruments
bank 741, 744, 25.1 *green bowling*, 42.10 *play*, 73.5 *flight*, 161.26 *mass*, 161.37 *assemble*, 223.2 *place of exchange*, 275.4 *mountain range*, 278.4 *shallow thing*, 286.1 *obliqueness*, 286.6 *be oblique*, 300.1 *edge*, 310.11 *angle*, 605.4 *storage*, 605.5 *store*, 732.4 *lending institution*, 741.19 *treasury*
bank account 14.4 *personal finance*, 741.6 *funds*
bank-account number 544.3 *means of identification*
bank annuities 741.6 *funds*
bankbook 750.5 *account book*
bank card 744.2 *credit card*, 745.1 *debt*
bank deposit 744.3 *deposit*
bank down the fires 242.4 *moderate*
banked 33.11 *racing*, 605.7 *stored*
banked circuit 33.6 *motor racing terms*
banker 42 Card Games, 14.3 *stockbroker*, 42.3 *card game terms*, 223.4 *person who exchanges*, 653.15 *manager*, 732.3 *lender*, 739.12 *wholesaler*, 741.17 *financier*, 741.18 *treasurer*
banker's credit 744.1 *credit*
banker's draft 223.3 *something in exchange*
bank failure 747.5 *insolvency*
bank holiday 214.5 *regular thing*, 649.1 *ease*
banking 14.1 *finance*, 73.5 *flight*
bank loan 732.2, 733.5 *loan*, 745.3 *loan*
bank manager 653.15 *manager*, 732.3 *lender*
banknote 741.14 *paper money*

bank of cloud 55.20 *cloud appearance*
Bank of England 741.19 *treasury*
bank official 653.15 *manager*
bank of snow 55.30 *snow*
bank on 497.7 *believe*, 513.9 *predict*, 775.6 *hope*
bank rate 14.1, 741.7 *finance*, 745.4 *interest*
bank reconciliation statement 750.4 *statement*
bank robber 16.40 *lawbreaker*, 736.8 *thief*
bank robbery 736.1 *stealing*, 736.3 *theft*
bankroll 13.11 *deal*, 284.13 *support financially*, 738.5 *defray*, 748.3 *donate*
bankrupt 244.8 *destroy*, 244.15 *destroyed*, 320.6 *closed*, 593.5 *necessitous*, 682.10 *defeat heavily*, 683.5 *failing person*, 683.10 *failed*, 687.5 *person in adversity*, 687.7 *unprosperous*, 722.6 *loser*, 722.17 *unprofitable*, 743.2 *insolvent*, 743.10 *poor person*, 743.11 *impoverish*, 745.6 *debtor*, 747.6 *nonpayer*, 747.13 *nonpaying*
bankruptcy 244.4 *ruin*, 320.4 *closure*, 609.8 *insufficiency*, 683.1 *failure*, 683.4 *unsuccessful thing*, 722.2 *financial loss*, 743.6, 747.5 *insolvency*
bankruptcy court 747.5 *insolvency*
bankruptcy proceedings 747.5 *insolvency*
Banks 52 Scientists, **98** Islands
bank shot 23.4 *playing terms*, 24.2 *billiards play*
banksia 85 Trees and Shrubs
bank statement 750.4 *statement*
bank up 161.37 *assemble*
bank vault 531.2 *hiding place*, 718.5 *safe*
banned 16.55 *illegal*, 147.11 *excluded*, 487.4 *forbidden*, 692.14 *commanding*, 699.13 *restraining*, 709.5 *vetoed*, 709.6 *censored*, 711.9 *dissenting*, 816.10 *lonely*, 827.10 *maledictive*, 846.12 *disentitled*, 852.31 *disapproved*
banned book 709.2 *censorship*
banner 126.15 *excellent*, 532.9 *advertisement*, 543.1 *sign*, 544.7 *flag*
bannerette 544.7 *flag*
banner head 533.12 *headline*
banner headline 532.3 *journalism*
bannerol 544.7 *flag*
banners 812.8 *salute*
banning 349.19 *ostracism*, 879.7 *punishment*
Bannister 18 Sporting Personalities
bannock 45.39 *loaf*
Bannock 1 Peoples
Bannockburn 93 Cities
banquet 350.13 *feast*, 350.24 *have a meal*, 350.30 *provide food*, 405.4 *pleasurable things*, 608.8 *plenty*, 773.1 *rejoicing*, 773.5 *rejoice*, 812.1 *celebration*, 815.5 *party*, 872.3 *act of gluttony*
banqueter 350.18 *eater*
banquet hall 350.4 *eating place*
banqueting 350.4 *eating meals*
banqueting hall 350.15 *eating place*
banquette 671.11 *fortification*
banshee 76.7 *legendary beast*
bantam 260.4 *little person*, 260.7 *little*, 270.5 *short person*
bantamweight 26.3 *boxing weight divisions*, 26.4 *boxer*, 26.14 *combat*, 369.7 *weighing*, 370.1 *light*, 679.3 *athlete*
banteng 77 Placental Mammals
banter 506.3 *tomfoolery*, 568.2 *chat*, 771.3 *wit*, 771.13 *be humorous*, 799.1 *mockery*, 807.9 *discourtesy*, 850.6 *taunt*
bantering 807.20 *discourteous*, 850.15 *taunting*

ban the bomb 675.6 *make peace*
ban-the-bomb movement 675.1 *peace*, 677.1 *pacification*
Bantu 1 Peoples, **5** Languages and Groups of Languages, **7** Non-Christian Religions, 5.11 *family of languages*
Bantustan 816.4 *place of confinement*
banty 270.5 *short person*
banyan 85 Trees and Shrubs
Banyan tree 10.14 *sacred object*
baobab 85 Trees and Shrubs
bap 45.39 *loaf*
Bapedi 68 Breeds of Cattle
baptising 560.7 *nomenclature*
baptism 10.5 *Christian rite*, 156.8 *enrolment*, 348.3 *introduction*, 354.10 *immersion*, 389.15 *holy water*, 560.7 *nomenclature*, 621.3 *religious cleansing*, 730.4 *reception*, 813.3 *formal occasion*
Baptism 7 Christian Movements
baptismal 10.21 *ritualistic*, 154.13 *precursory*, 156.36, 348.16 *introductory*
baptismal name 560.8 *name*
baptism of fire 156.8 *enrolment*
Baptist 7.5 *Christian*
baptize 7.20 *preach*, 10.18 *perform rites*, 156.25 *enrol*, 348.10 *introduce*, 354.4 *immerse*, 730.10 *receive someone*
baptized 156.37 *enrolled*, 354.14 *immersed*, 730.13 *received*
baptizer 5.2 *linguist*
Baqqarah 1 Peoples
bar 75 General Units, 16.18 *tribunal*, 16.27 *courtroom*, 16.79 *convict*, 49.17 *notation*, 54.11 *coast*, 121.3 *gradation*, 131.8 *by subtraction*, 136.10 *set apart*, 137.8 *fastening*, 143.7 *piece*, 147.1 *exclusion*, 147.7 *exclude*, 147.12 *exclusively*, 269.5 *piece*, 278.4 *shallow thing*, 323.1 *closure*, 323.3 *restrainer*, 323.7 *close*, 323.8 *stop*, 456.3 *striping*, 456.11 *variegate*, 487.8 *make impossible*, 544.4 *insignia*, 544.8 *heraldic device*, 632.4 *safety device*, 661.2 *obstacle*, 661.9 *block*, 663.17 *withstand*, 699.1 *restraint*, 699.8 *restrain*, 741.16 *bullion*, 852.3 *nonacceptance*, 852.15 *withhold approval*
Baraim 10.16 *religious festival*
Baraka 48 Poets, **48** Dramatists
barb 375.7 *rough thing*, 380.8 *sharp-pointed thing*, 380.15 *make sharp*, 631.6 *source of trouble*, 680.6 *historical missile weapon*, 850.6 *taunt*, 875.6 *drug*
Barb 32 Breeds of Horse and Pony
Barbados 91 Countries, **98** Islands
barbarian 104.10 *foreign*, 149.4 *foreigner*, 149.11 *foreign*, 241.4 *violent person or animal*, 244.6 *destroyer*, 482.9 *undiscriminating person*, 795.8 *discourteous person*, 818.6 *bad-mannered*
Barbarian 795.5 *vulgar person*
barbarians 400.3 *uncivilized human*
barbaric 104.10 *foreign*, 559.8 *indecorous*, 803.4 *common*, 832.11 *cruel*, 836.4 *pitiless*
barbarism 5.5 *nonstandard language*, 504.11 *grammatical error*, 601.2 *misuse*, 628.8 *perversion*, 658.2 *naivety*, 832.2 *cruelness*
barbarity 241.2 *physical violence*, 832.2 *cruelness*
barbarius 795.9 *ribald*
barbarize 628.6 *pervert*
barbarous 5.42 *worded*, 241.6 *violent*, 559.8 *indecorous*, 601.5 *abusive*, 670.23 *attacking*, 832.11 *cruel*, 836.4 *pitiless*
barbarously 601.6 *abusively*, 836.7 *pitilessly*
Barbary 32 Breeds of Horse and Pony

Barbary ape 77 Placental Mammals

barbastelle 77 Placental Mammals

barbecue 45.5 *cooker*, 45.55 *cook*, 69.3 *ornamental garden*, 350.13 *feast*, 815.5 *party*

barbecue cook 45.2 *cook*

barbecued 45.56 *culinary*

barbecued spare ribs 45.43 *US dish*

barbecue pit 408.4 *burner*

barbecue sandwich 45.11 *sandwich*

barbecue sauce 45.15 *sauce*, 413.2 *seasoning*

barbecuing 45.8 *cooking technique*

barbed 375, 380.2 *spiked*

barbed arrow 680.6 *historical missile weapon*

barbed wire 68.11 *farmland*, 375.7 *rough thing*, 380.8 *sharp-pointed thing*, 661.3 *barrier*, 726.4 *wall*

barbel 80 Fishes, 20.5 *British game fish*

barbellate 375.3 *barbed*

barber 294.7 *shedder*, 621.12 *cleaner*, 697.1 *personal attendant*, 791.13 *beautician*

barber hauler 36.3 *parts of a sailing boat*

barbering 791.7 *hairdressing*

Barber paradox 4.9 *philosophical problem*

barberry 86 Fruits

barber shop 791.11 *hairdressing salon*

barber's striped pole 544.3 *means of identification*

barbet 78 Birds

barbette 671.11 *fortification*

barbican 275.6 *tall thing*, 671.12 *fort*

Barbican 93.5 *London*

barbicel 78.17 *plumage*

barbie 69.3 *ornamental garden*

Barbirolli 49 Musicians and Composers

barbitone 62 Medication, **62** Medication, **62** Medication

barbiturate 62.4 *drug type*, 242.2 *moderator*, 404.4 *anaesthetic*, 630.8 *drug*, 643.10 *soporific*, 761.6 *desensitizing substance*, 875.6 *drug*

Barbizon school 50 Schools and Groups of Artists

Barbour 295.12 *coat*

BARB ratings 532.2 *mass media*

barbs 761.6 *desensitizing substance*

barbule 78.17 *plumage*

Barbusse 48 Writers

barbwire 380.8 *sharp-pointed thing*

barcarolle 433.2 *song*

Barcelona 93 Cities

barchan 54.37 *dune*

bar chart 52.32 *graph*, 152.8 *chart*

Barclayism 7 Christian Movements

bar code 456.5 *variegated thing*

bar-code reader 65.7 *peripheral*

bard 45.55 *cook*, 48.14 *author*, 49.24 *musician*

Bardeen 52 Scientists

bare 134.17 *direct*, 247.3 *birth control*, 254.13 *vacant*, 294.8 *uncovered*, 294.11 *uncover*, 296.9 *undressed*, 296.14 *undress*, 322.13 *opened up*, 392.6 *desert*, 526.15 *open*, 530.5 *disclose*, 542.14 *simple*, 556.1 *simple*, 609.2 *unprovided*, 633.3 *vulnerable*

bare-ass 294.8 *uncovered*, 296.9 *undressed*

bare as the back of one's hand 296.13 *hairless*

barebacked 296.11 *exposed*

bareback rider 32.15 *horse person*, 51.29 *circus performer*, 237.5 *athlete*

bareback riding 32.6 *horsemanship*

bareback-riding 32.12 *rodeo*

bare-bollock 294.8 *uncovered*, 296.9 *undressed*

bare bones 299.1 *outline*

bare-bottomed 294.8 *uncovered*

barebreasted 296.11 *exposed*

barechested 296.11 *exposed*

bare-chested 294.8 *uncovered*

bare cupboard 350.10 *scarcity*, 743.6 *insolvency*, 871.2 *short rations*

bared 296.9 *undressed*

bare essentials 143.5 *largest part*, 299.1 *outline*, 593.1 *requirement*

barefaced 526.15 *open*, 807.19 *rude*

barefaced effrontery 668.1 *defiance*

barefaced lie 538.4 *lie*

barefaced lying 538.3, 540.6 *lying*

bare feet 424.3 *faint-sounding thing*

barefoot 294.8 *uncovered*, 296.10 *in dishabille*, 296.11 *exposed*, 743.3 *beggarly*

bare head 296.5 *baldness*

bareheaded 294.8 *uncovered*, 296.10 *in dishabille*

bare-headed 849.11 *in a respectful stance*

barelegged 296.10 *in dishabille*, 296.11 *exposed*

bare-legged 294.8 *uncovered*

barely 182.11 *sparsely*, 272.11 *narrowly*, 296.17 *nakedly*, 620.11 *imperfectly*

barely audible 424.4 *faint*

barely heard 424.4 *faint*

barely move 328.1 *move slowly*, 328.2 *hesitate*

barely pass 620.9 *be imperfect*

barely sufficient 608.1 *sufficient*

bare minimum 593.3 *needfulness*, 608.7 *sufficiency*

Barenboim 49 Musicians and Composers

barenecked 296.11 *exposed*

bareness 254.3 *emptiness*, 294.1 *uncovering*, 296.1 *undress*, 296.2 *nudity*, 542.4, 556.4 *simplicity*

Barents 97 Oceans and Seas

bare one's breast to 530.8 *admit*

bare one's fangs 822.14 *hate*

bare one's teeth 668.5 *defy*, 830.11 *be irritable*

bare subsistence 609.8 *insufficiency*, 871.2 *short rations*

bare supposition 518.3 *conjecture*

barf 349.15 *vomit*

Barfoed's test 58.5 *sugar test*

bargain 737, 752, 754, 116.3 *arrangement*, 116.23 *arrange*, 158.19 *mediate*, 568.11 *confer*, 667.2, 667.7 *contract*, 715.1, 715.5 *contract*, 717.1 *compromise*, 737.9 *bargaining*, 738.1, 738.6 *purchase*, 752.6 *discounted*, 754.9 *cheap*

bargain basement 740.8 *store*, 754.7 *discounter*

bargain-basement 754.9 *cheap*

bargain bin 754.7 *discounter*

bargainer 738.12 *purchaser*

bargain for 513.9 *predict*

bargain hunter 754

bargain-hunter 738.12 *purchaser*

bargaining 737, 116.12 *arranged*, 568.5 *talks*, 715.1 *contract*, 716.1 *negotiation*, 738.14 *buying*

bargaining session 716.3 *discussion*

bargain of the month 710.3 *business offer*

bargain price 752.2 *bargain*, 754.1 *cheapness*

bargain sale 739.4 *sale*, 752.2 *bargain*

barge 74 Ships and Boats, 74.3 *vessel*, 326.12 *transport*

bargee 74.8 *boatman*

barge in 346.10 *invade*, 357.5 *transgress*

barge in on 160.16 *interrupt*

bargeman 74.8 *boatman*

bar graph 52.32 *graph*, 299.1 *outline*

baring 296.1 *undress*

baring one's fangs 822.1 *hate*

baritone 49.32 *instrumental*, 427.3 *deepness*

barium 57 Chemical Elements

barium enema 60.7 *diagnosis*

barium meal 60.7 *diagnosis*

bark 85.3 *timber*, 266.3 *coat*, 293.13 *casing*, 385.13 *abrade*, 432.1 *animal cry*, 432.4 *cry*, 564.13 *speak in a particular way*, 828.6 *sign of anger*

bark beetle 82 Insects

barkeep 697.3 *attendant*

barkeeper 697.3 *attendant*

barker 51.29 *circus performer*, 431.9 *crier*, 526.12 *displayer*, 532.10 *publicizer*

Barker 48 Dramatists

Barkhausen 52 Scientists

Barkhausen effect 56 Named Laws

barking 432.1 *animal cry*

barking deer 77 Placental Mammals

barking mad 510.11 *insane*

bark rubbing 42 Hobbies and Pastimes

bark up the wrong tree 504.18 *be in error*

barley 87 Grasses, 68.12 *crop*, 350.8 *animal food*

barley baron 68.15 *agriculturist*

barley beef 68.8 *livestock*

barleycorn 75 General Units, 87.4 *cereal grass*

barleycorn lead 20.3 *fishing tackle*

barley straw 68.9 *animal feedstuff*

barley sugar 45.41 *sweet*

barley water 351.6 *soft drink*

barm 370.8 *leavening*

bar magnet 56.60, 340.3 *magnet*

barmaid 697.3 *attendant*

barman 697.3 *attendant*

barm cake 45.39 *loaf*

bar mitzvah 10.7 *non-Christian ritual*, 812.3 *ceremony*, 813.3 *formal occasion*

barmy 508.5 *foolish*, 510.11 *insane*

barn 75 Scientific and Technical Units, 68.7 *farm building*, 256.12 *stall*, 605.4 *storage*, 634.3 *animal shelter*, 647.1 *workshop*

Barnabite 7 Members of Religious Orders

barnacle 81.4 *arthropod*, 138.4 *adherent*, 808.3 *sycophant*

barnacle goose 78 Birds

Barnard 52 Scientists

Barnard's Star 53 Named Stars

barn dance 46.1 *dancing*, 46.4 *historic dancing*, 161.10 *dance*, 815.5 *party*

Barnevelder 68 Breeds of Fowl

barney 473.1, 666.2 *argument*

barn owl 78 Birds, 78.5 *bird of prey*

barn-raising 815.5 *party*

Barnsley 93 Cities

barnstorm 51.33 *overact*

barnstormer 51.22 *actor*

barnstorming 51.20 *acting*

barnyard 68.7 *farm building*

bar of justice 16.18 *tribunal*

barograph 55.7 *weather instruments*

barographic 55.42 *barometric*

barometer 56, 55.7 *weather instruments*, 268.8 *meter*, 543.5 *indicator*

barometric 55, 268.16 *micrometric*

barometry 268.2 *micrometry*

baron 742.10 *wealthy person*, 802.1 *nobleman*

baronet 802.1 *nobleman*

baronetcy 802.2 *aristocracy*

baronial 802.4 *aristocratic*

Baron Münchhausen 538.11, 539.16 *liar*, 541.6 *exaggerator*

barony 92.3 *other*

barophobia 777 Phobias by Name

baroque 43 Architectural Styles, **50** Western Art Styles and Movements, 47.7 *furniture style*, 50.26 *artistic*, 792.8 *decorated*

Baroque 50.29 *realist*

baroque costume 295.5 *fancy dress*

barostat 73 Aircraft Parts

Barotse 1 Peoples, **5** Languages and Groups of Languages

barouche 71 Carriages and Carts

barperson 697.3 *attendant*

barque 74 Sailing Ships and Boats

barquentine 74 Sailing Ships and Boats

barrack 661.8 *hinder*, 850.25 *taunt*

barracking 850.6 *taunt*, 850.15 *taunting*

barrack-room lawyer 463.6 *arguer*

barracks 17.1 *military affairs*

barracuda 80 Fishes, 20.4 *American game fish*

barrage 32.9 *jumping*, 63.23 *dam*, 63.24 *water system*, 670.12 *military attack*

barrage balloon 361.10 *elevator*, 679.31 *military aircraft*

barramunda 80 Fishes

Barranquilla 93 Cities

barred 147.11 *excluded*, 323.12 *closed*, 456.9 *striped*, 487.4 *forbidden*, 661.14 *blocked*, 709.5 *vetoed*, 852.31 *disapproved*

barred spiral galaxy 53.7 *galaxy*

barred-window boys 61.30, 510.10 *psychiatrist*

barrel 75 General Units, 120.3 *container*, 258.11 *vessel*

barrel along 329.4 *be swift*

barrel chair 47.2 *chair*

barrel-chested 273.1 *thick*

barrel drum 49 Musical Instruments

barrelling 329.1 *swift*, 329.8 *speed*

barrel organ 49 Musical Instruments

barrel printer 65.7 *peripheral*

barrel-racing 32.12 *rodeo*

barrel roll 73.5 *flight*

barrels 181.3 *profuseness*

barrel scale 369.10 *scales*

barrel vault 43.7 *vault*

barren 236.13 *unsexed*, 247.3 *birth control*, 254.13 *vacant*, 392.6 *desert*

barren cow 68.8 *livestock*

barren land 392.14 *desert*

barrenness 236.1 *powerlessness*, 247.1 *infertility*, 254.3 *emptiness*, 614.4 *futility*, 683.1 *failure*

barren sterile 614.2 *futile*

barren waste 247.1 *infertility*

barrette 137.8 *fastening*

barricade 136.6 *boundary*, 147.3 *exclusion zone*, 671.9 *barrier*, 671.18 *fence*

barricaded 671.30 *defended*

Barrie 48 Dramatists

barrier 661, 671, 21.1 *track events*, 72.8 *railway station*, 136.6 *boundary*, 147.3 *exclusion zone*, 231.1 *counteraction*, 301.3 *enclosing thing*, 323.1 *closure*, 487.7, 661.2 *obstacle*

barrier board 31.3 *ice hockey*

barrier contraceptive 247.3 *birth control*

barrier cream 55.22 *sun*

barrier island 54.11 *coast*

barrier method contraception 661.3 *barrier*

barrier reef 54.11 *coast*

barring 131.8 *by subtraction*, 147.12 *exclusively*

Barrington 18 Sporting Personalities

barrio 93.7 *city district*

barrister 16.13 *lawyer*, 473.6 *arguer*, 477.9 *questioner*, 654.4 *adviser*, 679.5 *arguer*, 707.3 *agent*
barrister's wig 295.15 *headgear*
Barrosã 68 Breeds of Cattle
barrow 3.11 *relic*, 66.8 *livestock*, 71.7 *handcart*, 200.7 *thing of the past*, 258.10 *cart*, 275.3 *mountain*, 316.3 *dome*, 399.6 *grave*, 545.11 *monument*, 740.9 *stall*
barrow boy 739.11 *pedlar*, 739.14 *street trader*
barry 544.13 *heraldic*
Barry 93 Cities
bar sinister 544.8 *heraldic device*
barspoon 20.2 *artificial fly*
bar stool 47.2 *chair*
bartender 133.7 *person who mixes*, 697.3 *attendant*
barter 13.11 *deal*, 109.1 *interchange*, 109.7 *reciprocate*, 122.3 *equalization*, 216.4, 216.10 *exchange*, 223.1, 223.5 *exchange*, 326.1, 326.11 *transfer*, 715.5 *contract*, 716.1 *negotiation*, 728.1 *transfer of property*, 728.3 *transfer property*, 737.1, 737.4 *trade*, 738.1 *purchase*, 739.1 *sell*, 739.3 *selling*, 746.6 *pay*
bartered 109.4 *reciprocal*, 223.7 *exchanged*
barterer 13.9 *economist*, 737.10 *trader*
bartering 109.1 *interchange*, 715.1 *contract*, 716.1 *negotiation*
Barth 48 Writers
bar the entrance 634.4 *shelter*
Barthes 48 Writers
Bartholin's gland 352 Exocrine Glands
bartizan 671.12 *fort*
Bartók 49 Musicians and Composers
barton 68.7 *farm building*
barye 75 Scientific and Technical Units
baryon 56.77 *elementary particle*
barytes 54 Minerals
baryton 49 Musical Instruments
basal 280.3 *base*, 284.9 *supportive*
basal body 59.8 *cell organ*
basalt 54 Common Rocks
basaltic 54.57 *chalky*
basaltware 44.1 *ceramics*
bascule bridge 63.21 *bridge*
base 57, 280, 280, 280, 17.1 *military affairs*, 43.9 *miscellaneous architectural features*, 52.8 *number system*, 52.19 *logarithm*, 52.43 *triangle*, 64.19 *transistor*, 127.5 *inferior state*, 127.16 *ordinary*, 226.3 *rudiment*, 250.1 *location*, 250.9 *locate*, 256.2 *environment*, 256.3 *home*, 276.4 *low thing*, 284.2 *supporting part*, 345.10 *place of departure*, 544.8 *heraldic device*, 592.7 *planning*, 618.3 *bad*, 679.14 *armed forces*, 754.10 *shoddy*, 758.2 *unpleasant*, 850.12 *disregardful*, 858.5 *dishonourable*, 864.11 *wicked*
Base 280
baseball 18 Sporting Activities, **22,** 22.3 *baseball equipment*
Baseball 22
baseball bat 22.3 *baseball equipment*, 330.15 *ram*, 680.7 *blunt weapon*
baseball cap 295.15 *headgear*
baseball equipment 22
baseball field 22.1 *baseball*
baseball game 22.1 *baseball*
baseball pass 23.4 *playing terms*
baseball player 22, 237.5 *athlete*
baseball season 203.1 *season*
baseball shoes 22.3 *baseball equipment*
baseball sign 543.3 *gesture*
baseball stadium 22.1 *baseball*
baseball uniform 22.3 *baseball equipment*, 545.4 *uniform*
baseball widow 824.6 *surviving spouse*

baseboard 280.2 *foot*
base camp 34.1 *mountaineering*
base coin 741.15 *false money*
based 251.8 *circumstantial*, 472.7 *focused*
base electrode 64.19 *transistor*
Basel 93 Cities
baseless 474.7 *sophistic*
baseline 40.4 *tennis terms*
basely 127
basement 256.7 *room*, 276.4 *low thing*, 280.2 *foot*, 284.2 *supporting part*, 353.13 *lavatory*, 605.4 *storage*
basement price 751.3 *fee*, 752.2 *bargain*
baseness 127.1 *inferiority*, 618.9 *badness*, 754.3 *shoddiness*, 758.4 *unpleasantness*, 858.1 *improbity*, 864.1 *wickedness*
basenji 77 Breeds of Dogs
base on balls 22.4 *pitching terms*
baseplate 280.2 *foot*
base runner 22.2 *baseball player*
base troops 679.14 *armed forces*
base unit 75.2 *unit system*
bash 161.9 *social gathering*, 330.2 *collide*, 330.3 *hit*, 330.13 *blow*, 596.5 *attempt*, 832.18 *torment*
bashful 810, 573.3 *cautious*, 816.9 *shy*, 876.9 *pure*
bashfully 810.18 *shyly*, 816.14 *unsocially*
bashfulness 810, 573.13 *dissociation*, 816.2 *shyness*, 876.3 *moral purity*
bashi-bazouk 679.8 *soldier*
bashing 330.12 *collision*
Bashkir 1 Peoples, **5** Languages and Groups of Languages
Bashkirsky 32 Breeds of Horse and Pony
bash off 245.9 *reproduce*
bash out 243.10 *produce*, 245.9 *reproduce*
bash up 832.18 *torment*
basic 52.70 *universal*, 57.36 *acid*, 99.11, 103.6 *intrinsic*, 134.16 *simple*, 154.13 *precursory*, 156.35 *rudimentary*, 226.13 *causal*, 280.3 *base*, 472.7 *focused*, 556.1 *simple*, 594.10 *preparatory*, 611.5 *important*
Basic 65 Programming Languages
basically 280, 52.87 *mathematically*, 99.22 *really*, 103.14 *at heart*, 156.42 *principally*, 226.14 *causally*, 472.14 *thematically*, 556.8 *simply*
basic dye 67.6 *dye*
basic English 5.4 *parent language*
basichromatin 59.9 *cell nucleus*
basic ingredient 45
basic materials 148.3 *unit*, 367.4 *matter*, 604.1 *materials*
basic palette 444.5 *paint*
basic rock 54.30 *igneous rock*
basics 101.5 *realities*, 156.7 *rudiments*, 226.3 *rudiment*, 611.3 *chief thing*
basic salary 878.4 *reward for service*
basic salt 57.10 *salt*
basic slag 68.13 *fertilizer*
basic substance 367.4 *matter*
basic supplies 602.2 *supplies*
basic swing 41.4 *skiing technique*
basic truth 537.4 *truism*
basidiocarp 89.4 *fungal body*
basidiomycetes 89.3 *fungi*
Basidiomycotina 89.3 *fungi*
basidiospore 89.4 *fungal body*
basidium 89.4 *fungal body*
basil 45 Herbs and Spices, 413.5 *herbs*
basilar 280.3 *base*
basilary 280.3 *base*
Basildeanism 7 Christian Movements
basilica 10.11 *place of worship*, 43.10 *church architecture*

basilisk 79 Reptiles, 76.7 *legendary beast*, 79.2 *lizard*, 79.3 *snake*, 435.2 *eye*, 680.12 *historical guns*
basin 53.17 *moon*, 54.7 *landform*, 258.12 *bath*, 277.4 *deep thing*, 317.3 *cavity*, 621.6 *bath*
basin and ewer 621.6 *bath*
basin and pitcher 621.6 *bath*
basinet 671.7 *armour*
basis 103.2 *essential content*, 226.3 *rudiment*, 226.5 *reason*, 251.2 *circumstances*, 280.1 *base*, 463.4 *explanation*, 472.1 *topic*, 594.10 *preparations*
basis for belief 483.1 *evidence*
basis for negotiations 716
basis of supposition 518
basitracin 62 Medication
bask 161 Collective Names for Birds and Animals, 405.8 *feel pleasure*, 408.16 *feel hot*
basket 258, 23.3 *basketball equipment*, 41.5 *ski equipment*, 120.3 *container*
basket arch 43.5 *arch*
basketball 18 Sporting Activities, **23,** 23.3 *basketball equipment*, 377.3 *elastic thing*
Basketball 23
basketball arena 23.1 *basketball*
basketball equipment 23
basketball game 23.1 *basketball*
basketball gym 23.1 *basketball*
basketball gymnasium 23.1 *basketball*
Basketball Hall of Fame 23.1 *basketball*
basketball player 23, 275.7 *tall person*
basketball season 203.1 *season*
basketcase 168.10 *eccentric*
basketry 42 Hobbies and Pastimes
bask in 405.8 *feel pleasure*
basking shark 80 Fishes
bask in the sunshine 686.5 *be prosperous*
Basque 1 Peoples, **5** Languages and Groups of Languages
Basra 93 Cities
bas relief 43 Architectural Decoration
bas-relief 50.13 *relief-carving*, 767.6 *profile*
bass 80 Fishes, 45.17 *freshwater fish*, 49.32 *instrumental*, 420.10 *sound quality*, 427.3 *deepness*, 433.5 *melodist*
bassanello 49 Musical Instruments
bass baritone 427.3 *deepness*
bass clef 49.17 *notation*, 49.20 *key*
bass drum 49 Musical Instruments
Bassenthwaite 94 Lakes, 94.4 *British lakes*
basset horn 49 Musical Instruments
basset hound 77 Breeds of Dogs
bass guitar 49 Musical Instruments
bass horn 49 Musical Instruments
bassinet 258.7 *basket*
bass note 427.3 *deepness*
basso 427.3 *deepness*
basso continuo 433.3 *melodiousness*
Basso-juan 8 Deities
bassonore 49 Musical Instruments
bassoon 49 Musical Instruments
basso profondo 427.3 *deepness*
basso rilievo 767.6 *profile*
basswood 85 Trees and Shrubs
bast 137.6 *line*
Bast 8 Deities
bastard 659.3 *difficult task*, 822.8 *hated person*, 864.10 *bad person*
bastardize 16.75 *make illegal*
bastard-trench 69.15 *cultivate*
bastard wing 78.17 *plumage*

baste 45.55 *cook*, 135.10 *link*, 330.5 *beat*, 395.18 *anoint*
basted 395
Bastille Day 214.6 *annually celebrated day*, 812.5 *anniversary*
bastinado 879.3 *hit*, 879.12 *corporal punishment*
basting 137.8 *fastening*
bastion 632.2 *protection*, 634.1 *refuge*, 671.11 *fortification*
bastnaesite 54 Minerals
Basuto 32 Breeds of Horse and Pony
bat 77 Placental Mammals, **27, 27, 330, 338,** 22.3 *baseball equipment*, 76.6 *flying animal*, 329.8 *speed*, 330.3 *hit*, 330.15 *ram*, 407.11 *touch*, 436.4 *blind people*
bata 49 Musical Instruments
Batak 32 Breeds of Horse and Pony
Batan 5 Languages and Groups of Languages
batch 120.2 *certain amount*, 161.24 *brace*, 161.25 *assemblage*, 161.27 *bundle*, 161.38 *group*
batch processing 65.17 *computing term*
bate 381.10 *blunt*
bat ears 420.4 *ear*
bateau 74 Ships and Boats
bated 381.1 *blunt*, 424.4 *faint*
bated breath 424.1 *faintness*, 428.4 *faint sound*
bateleur 78 Birds
Bates 48 Writers, **52** Scientists
Bateson 52 Scientists
batfish 80 Fishes
bath 258, 621, 354.10 *immersion*, 389.11 *wash*, 531.6 *privacy*, 621.6 *bath*
Bath 93 Cities
Bath bun 45.36 *cake*
Bath chap 45.31 *offal*
bathe 621, 389.34 *hose*
bathed 389.23 *wet*
bathed in sweat 353.28 *sweaty*
bathers 39.8 *swimwear*, 295.21 *beachwear*
bathetic 759.12 *sensitive*
bathing 10.7 *non-Christian ritual*, 39.11 *swimming*, 389.11 *wash*, 621.5 *ablutions*
bathing cap 39.8 *swimwear*
bathing suit 39.8 *swimwear*, 295.21 *beachwear*
bathmat 293.9 *floor covering*
bath oil 418.2 *fragrant thing*
batholith 54.28 *rock*, 54.30 *igneous rock*
bathometer 268.8 *meter*, 277.4 *deep thing*
bathometric 268.16 *micrometric*, 277.13 *bathymetric*
bathometry 268.2 *micrometry*, 277.6 *bathymetry*
bathophobia 777 Phobias by Name
bathos 759.7 *emotionalism*, 798.1 *ludicrousness*
bathrobe 295.4 *informal dress*, 295.16 *robe*, 296.4 *dishabille*, 814.6 *informal dress*
bathroom 256.7 *room*, 353.13 *lavatory*, 621.6 *bath*, 727.7 *toilet*
bathroom scales 369.10 *scales*
baths 621.6 *bath*, 630.14 *hospital*
bath sponge 81.8 *sponge*
bath towel 621.11 *cleaning cloth*
bathtub 258.12, 621.6 *bath*
bathyal 277.12 *under*
bathymal 54.51 *oceanic*
bathymetric 277, 54.49 *geophysical*, 97.8 *oceanographic*, 268.16 *micrometric*
bathymetrically 54.66 *geographically*, 97.12 *oceanographically*
bathymetry 277, 54.17 *ocean research vessel*, 97.5 *oceanography*, 268.2 *micrometry*
bathypelagic 277.12 *under*
bathyscaph 54.17 *ocean research vessel*, 97.5 *oceanography*, 277.4 *deep thing*

bathysphere 54.17 *ocean research vessel*, 97.5 *oceanography*, 277.4 *deep thing*, 360.8 *descender*
bathythermograph 97.5 *oceanography*
batik 42 Hobbies and Pastimes, 50.1 *art*, 67.7 *dyeing*
bat in a run 22.7 *play baseball*
batiste 67 Natural Fabrics
Bat Kol 8.8 *divine manifestation*
batman 295.28 *valet*, 697.3 *attendant*, 697.4 *personal attendant*
Batman and Robin 237.6 *muscleman*
bat mitzvah 10.7 *non-Christian ritual*
baton 21.1 *track events*, 21.6 *track*, 544.4 *insignia*, 544.8 *heraldic device*
baton change 21.1 *track events*
baton changing 21.1 *track events*
Baton Rouge 93 Cities
baton round 680.13 *ammunition*
batophobia 777 Phobias by Name, **777** Phobias by Name
bat out of hell 329.12 *swift animal*
batrachian 79.7, 79.13 *amphibian*
batrachophobia 777 Phobias by Name
bats 510.11 *insane*
bats in the belfry 510.1 *insanity*
batsman 27.4 *team*
Battak 5 Languages and Groups of Languages
battalion 17.4 *military organization*, 161.14 *force*, 679.16 *army unit*
battalion commander 17.5 *military staff*
battement 46.10 *positions at the barre*
batten 51.17 *stage set*, 137.8 *fastening*, 137.12 *bind*
batten down 225.7 *make stable*, 323.7 *close*
batten down the hatches 323.7 *close*, 594.4 *prepare for action*, 634.4 *shelter*, 756.6 *save*
battened 137.16 *bound*
battening down the hatches 594.9 *preparation*
batten on 350.22 *eat well*, 808.14 *follow*
battens 36.3 *parts of a sailing boat*, 51.18 *stage lighting*
batter 22.2 *baseball player*, 27.4 *team*, 126.8 *be superior*, 244.9 *demolish*, 330.5 *beat*, 393.8 *pulp*, 406.11 *inflict pain*, 601.1 *misuse*, 618.14 *ill-treat*
battercake 45.39 *loaf*
battered 601.4 *misused*, 628.13 *dilapidated*
battered women's shelter 632.2 *protection*
batterie 46.9 *ballet steps*
battering ram 244.7 *agent of destruction*, 330.15 *ram*, 680.7 *blunt weapon*
batter's box 22.1 *baseball*
Battersea Power Station 43 Noted Buildings
batter's helmet 22.3 *baseball equipment*
battery 17.4 *military organization*, 56.43 *electrical conduction*, 57.19 *electrochemistry*, 64.5 *electrolytic conduction*, 64.29 *power source*, 235.7 *electrical power*, 256.12 *stall*, 410.4 *electricity*, 601.2 *misuse*, 605.4 *storage*, 679.16 *army unit*, 680.11 *guns*
battery charger 64.29 *power source*
battery hen 68.8 *livestock*
battery house 68.7 *farm building*
battery of tests 60.7 *diagnosis*
battery radio 534.18 *radio*
battiness 510.1 *insanity*
batting 27.12 *cricketing*
batting average 22.5 *batting terms*

batting champion 22.2 *baseball player*
batting coach 22.2 *baseball player*
batting crease 27.5 *wicket*
batting hit 330.11 *sporting hit*
batting side 27.4 *team*
batting terms 22
battle 676, 676, 398.4 *slaughter*, 640.1 *action*, 644.4 *exertion*, 644.8 *exert oneself*, 663.3 *conflict*, 666.2 *argument*, 666.6 *argue*, 674.1 *contention*, 674.6 *fight*, 674.11 *contend*, 820.12 *oppose*
battle-axe 680.8 *sharp weapon*, 829.3 *irascible person*
battle call 676.2 *glory of war*
battle cruiser 679.24 *warship*
battle cry 431.1 *cry*, 543.6 *word*, 636.2 *danger signal*, 668.3 *act of defiance*, 676.2 *glory of war*
battledore 40.10 *badminton*
battledress 295.3, 813.4 *formal dress*
battle fatigue 61.10 *neurosis*
battlefield 398.15 *slaughterhouse*, 674.6 *fight*, 674.9 *duel*, 676.10 *battleground*
battlefield knowledge 676.6 *art of war*
battlefront 298.1 *interface*, 303.1 *front*, 674.6 *fight*
battleground 676, 398.15 *slaughterhouse*, 674.6 *fight*
battleground theatre of war 303.1 *front*
battle group 17.4 *military organization*
battle honours 804.3 *honours*
battle-hungry 676.16 *warlike*
battlemaid 671.10 *woman soldier*
battlement 634.1 *refuge*, 671.11 *fortification*
battlemented 671.30 *defended*
battlements 319.2 *notched thing*, 671.12 *fort*
battle orders 676.8 *warfare*
battle painting 50.10 *art subject*
battle plan 676.6 *art of war*
battle plane 679.31 *military aircraft*
battler 674.10 *contender*, 679.1 *combatant*
battle royal 674.6 *fight*, 676.9 *battle*
battles 676.8 *warfare*
battle-scarred 676.17 *military*
battle scene 51.6 *scene*
battleship 74 Ships and Boats, 679.24 *warship*, 679.25 *historical naval ships*
battle yell 676.2 *glory of war*
battle zone 676.10 *battleground*
battling 674.14 *contending*, 676.15 *warring*
battue 398.4 *slaughter*, 590.2 *chase*
batty 510.11 *insane*
bauble 612, 754.5 *cheap item*
baubles 792.6 *jewellery*
baud 75 Scientific and Technical Units
Baudelaire 48 Poets
baud rate 65.17 *computing term*
Baudrillard 4 Philosophers
Bauhaus 43 Architectural Styles, **50** Schools and Groups of Artists, 47.7 *furniture style*
baulk 24.5 *snooker*
baulk cushion 24.3 *English billiards*
baulk line 24.3 *English billiards*, 24.5 *snooker*
baulk-line 24.4 *carom*, 24.9 *billiard*
baulk-line game 24.4 *carom*
baulk-line spot 24.3 *English billiards*
baulk spot 24.5 *snooker*
Baum 48 Writers
Baumgarten 4 Philosophers
bauxite 57 Common Metal Ores
Bavarian Warmblood 32 Breeds of Horse and Pony
bavette 45 Types of Pasta
bawbee 612.8 *trifle*, 741.10 *former British money*

bawd 606.3 *provider*
bawdily 827.12 *swearingly*
bawdiness 877.2 *indecency*
bawdry 877.2 *indecency*
bawdy 454.4 *indecent*, 795.9 *ribald*, 827.8 *cursing*, 877.12 *indecent*
bawdyhouse 877.6 *brothel*
bawdy verse 827.1 *curse*
bawl 431.1 *cry*, 431.6 *cry of pain*, 431.10 *cry out*, 431.13 *cry*, 564.12 *speak loudly*
bawler 431.9 *crier*
bawling 423.2 *outcry*
bawl out 431.14 *hiss*, 852.21 *berate*
Bax 49 Musicians and Composers
bay 73 Aircraft Parts, **85** Trees and Shrubs, 32.1 *horse*, 72.8 *railway station*, 98.9 *inlet*, 258.2 *compartment*, 432.4 *cry*, 449.1 *brown*
Bayard 32.1 *horse*
bay at the moon 432.4 *cry*
bayberry 85 Trees and Shrubs, **86** Fruits
Bayerd–Alpert gauge 57.20 *surface chemistry*
Bayes's theorem 52 Named Concepts
Bayeux 93 Cities
baying 432.8 *hunting*, 432.1 *animal cry*
Baykal 94.5 *other major lakes*
Bayle 4 Philosophers
bay leaf 43 Architectural Decoration
bayleaf 45 Herbs and Spices
bay leaf 413.5 *herbs*
bayo coyote 32.1 *horse*
Bay of Bengal 98.9 *inlet*
Bay of Biscay 98.9 *inlet*
Bay of Plenty 92 New Zealand Regions and Territories
Bayon 10.13 *shrine*
bayonet 322.2 *opener*, 322.20 *hole*, 380.8 *sharp-pointed thing*, 380.16 *use a sharp tool*, 398.17 *murder*, 670.6 *stab*, 680.8 *sharp weapon*
bayoneted 322.14 *holed*
bayonet-fence 28.5 *fence*
bayonet fencing 28.1 *fencing*
bayonetting 670.18 *hit*
Bayonne 93 Cities
bayou 94.2 *small lake*, 96.1 *river*, 98.3 *marsh*, 98.9 *inlet*
bay rum tree 85 Trees and Shrubs
bays 544.4 *insignia*
bay window 258.18 *stomach*
baywood 85 Trees and Shrubs
bazaar 740, 727.2 *disposal of property*, 739.4 *sale*, 740.1 *market*
bazooka 680.5 *missile weapon*, 680.11 *guns*
bazookaman 679.17 *army person*
BBC 534.20 *radio broadcasting*
BBC1 534.24 *television broadcasting*
BBC2 534.24 *television broadcasting*
BBC English 5.6 *official language*
BBC Radio 534.20 *radio broadcasting*
BBC's BRD Daily Survey of Listening 532.2 *mass media*
BBC Television 534.24 *television broadcasting*
BBC World Service 534.20 *radio broadcasting*
BC 185.29 *one day*
BCE 185.29 *one day*
BCG 630.3 *prophylactic*
BCP 631.9 *pollution*
BCPL 65 Programming Languages
be 99.17 *exist*, 196.5 *be present*, 251.9 *be situated*, 253.11 *be present*, 396.16 *live*, 457.11 *appear*
be a back-room boy 810.15 *escape notice*
be a best-seller 739.2 *be sold*

be able 235.10 *be powerful*, 602.6 *find means*
be able to take it or leave it 466.6 *be incurious*
be a botanist 83.23 *study plants*
be about right 124.9 *be average*
be about to 199.8 *intend*
be a breadwinner 644.6 *work*
be absent 254, 172.8 *not exist*
be absent without leave 720.9 *disregard orders*
be a candidate 710
be accurate 503, 537
be accused 856
beach 39.7 *swimming pool*, 54.11, 98.4 *coast*, 300.1 *edge*, 300.8 *edging*, 322.8 *open space*, 344.4 *land*
beach buggy 71 Motor Vehicles
beach-casting 20.1 *angling*
beachcomber 161.35 *collector*, 612.10 *nonentity*, 621.12 *cleaner*, 622.6 *dirty person*
beachcombing 42 Hobbies and Pastimes
beach grass 87 Grasses
beachhead 676.10 *battleground*
Beach-la-Mar 5 Languages and Groups of Languages
beach plum 86 Fruits
beach robe 295.21 *beachwear*
beach umbrella 440.6 *shade*
beachwear 295
beacon 439.6 *electric light*, 439.8 *fire*, 543.4 *signal*, 636.2 *danger signal*
beacon fire 408.6 *fire*, 543.4 *signal*
be a coward 779
be active 642
be active in 640.4 *act*
be a customer of 599.2 *frequent*
bead 43 Architectural Decoration, 315.3 *round thing*
be adaptable 377
be a different time 197
beading 792.2 *pattern*
be adjacent 298.4 *interface*
beadle 7.8 *priest*, 16.10 *law officer*
Beadle 52 Scientists
beadledom 12.3 *governance*, 584.6 *procedure*, 642.9 *overactivity*, 688.4 *governance*
be admitted 346.9 *enter*
be a doctor 630.20 *doctor*
beadroll 10.14 *sacred object*
beadsman 7.7 *monk*
beads of sweat 353.8 *sweat*
be affected 797, 809
be afflicted 406.9 *feel pain*
be a fly on the wall 528.15 *be informed*
be a founder member 156.23 *inaugurate*
be afraid 777
be afraid of 777.11 *be afraid*
be after 590.12 *aim at*
be against 663
be agitated 366
beagle 77 Breeds of Dogs
beagler 398.13 *animal killer*
beagling 18 Sporting Activities, 37.2 *hunting*, 77.23 *mammal hunting*, 590.2 *chase*
be agnostic 536.7 *be negative*
be a go-between 678.1 *mediate*
be a good mixer 815.11 *be sociable*
be ahead 126.11 *get ahead*, 300.7 *have an advantage*
be ahead of 303.10 *be in front*
be a hypocrite 539
beak 43 Architectural Decoration, 43.9 *miscellaneous architectural features*, 78.16 *avian anatomy*, 318.3 *protuberance*, 416.2 *sense of smell*, 688.10 *person of authority*, 696.9 *educational leader*
beaked 318.5 *protuberant*
beaker 57 Laboratory Apparatus, 258.13 *drinking vessel*
beaky 318.5 *protuberant*
be a law unto oneself 689.4 *be anarchic*, 807.28 *get above oneself*

be alert 642.14 *push*
be a little madam 759.17 *feel deeply*
be alive 396.16 *live*
be alive to 403.11 *sense*
be-all and end-all 126.1 *superiority*, 142.4 *all*, 588.5 *final intention*, 611.2 *important matter*
be all ears 420.15 *hear*
be all eyes 435.13 *look*
be all heart 760.11 *be sensitive*
be all of a doodah 777.12 *be fearful*
be all over 826.7 *show endearment for*
be all present and correct 253.12 *attend*
be all the rage 233.10 *be a prevailing influence*
be alongside **305**
be aloof **139**
be always the same 217.5 *be permanent*
beam **18** Sporting Activities, 30.6 *pommel horse*, 36.3 *parts of a sailing boat*, 47.12 *wood*, 63.27 *superstructure*, 137.4 *means of connection*, 225.3 *stabilizer*, 271.4 *breadth*, 284.2 *supporting part*, 439.1 *light*, 439.2 *quality of light*, 439.25 *light up*, 604.1 *materials*, 653.5 *guide*, 762.7 *show joy*, 769.7 *be cheerful*
be a martyr 406.9 *feel pain*
be ambiguous **314**, 578.1 *be equivocal*
be ambivalent 538.24 *pretend*, 540.23 *evade*
beam bridge 63.21 *bridge*
beamed 47.16 *joined*
be a member **665**
beamer 27.8 *delivery*
beaming 439.15 *lucent*, 769.1 *cheerful*
beam reaching 36.1 *sailing*
beamy 271.1 *broad*
bean **45** Vegetables, 69.11 *vegetable*
be anarchic **689**
be anarchistic 689.4 *be anarchic*
be an architect **43**
be an authority on **688**
bean curd 45.21 *meat substitute*
beanery 350.15 *eating place*
be an expert on 688.22 *be an authority on*
beanfeast 161.9 *social gathering*, 350.13 *feast*, 405.4 *pleasurable things*, 665.7 *social gathering*, 812.1 *celebration*, 872.3 *act of gluttony*
be angry **828**, 366.21 *be agitated*
beanie 295.15 *headgear*, 295.23 *children's clothes*
be an instrument **232**
beano 161.9 *social gathering*, 350.13 *feast*, 665.7 *social gathering*, 773.1 *rejoicing*, 872.3 *act of gluttony*
be a nobody 124.9 *be average*
be an open sesame to 226.11 *inaugurate*
beanpole 69.6 *garden tool*, 259.11 *tall person*, 274.9 *thin person*, 275.7 *tall person*
beans 68.12 *crop*
beansprout **45** Vegetables
bean tree **85** Trees and Shrubs
be anxious for 777.14 *worry*
be a party member **665**
be apathetic 404.11 *be unfeeling*
be a pedant 537.32 *be literal*
be a prevailing influence **233**
be a prima donna 759.17 *feel deeply*
bear **77** Placental Mammals, **284**, 14.3 *stockbroker*, 14.5 *invest*, 14.6 *financial*, 37.5 *game*, 156.26, 243.10 *produce*, 245.10 *reproduce oneself*, 246.6 *be fertile*, 284.11 *support*, 326.12 *transport*, 330.1 *impel*, 332.7 *take a direction*, 499.5 *assent to*, 673.4 *succumb*, 718.3 *security officer*, 737.2 *speculate*, 739.9

seller, 754.9 *cheap*, 818.4 *discourteous person*, 829.3 *irascible person*, 830.5 *sullen person*
Bear **94** Lakes, 94.3 *US lakes*
bearable 284.10 *supportable*, 620.4 *ordinary*
bear a charmed life 632.8 *be safe*
bear a date 192.15 *chronologize*
bear a grudge 820.11 *be hostile*, 822.14 *hate*, 828.8 *resent*, 832.16 *be malevolent*
bear allegiance 694.5 *obey*
bear allegiance to 701.8 *be subject to*, 861.18 *be good*
bear and dog 679.4 *fighting animal*
bear and ragged staff 544.8 *heraldic device*
bear-baiting 77.23 *mammal hunting*
bearberry **86** Fruits
bear comparison 617.9 *be worthy*
beard 295.5 *fancy dress*, 375.7 *rough thing*, 380.8 *sharp-pointed thing*, 778.15 *be courageous*
bearded 375.3 *barbed*
bearded lizard **79** Reptiles
bearded tit **78** Birds
bearded vulture **78** Birds
beard grass **87** Grasses
beardless 206.11 *young*, 296.13 *hairless*
beardlessness 296.5 *baldness*
bear down 36.15 *sail*
bear down on **362**, 574.9 *undertake*, 618.14 *ill-treat*, 670.1 *attack*, 695.6 *compel*
beards **777** Phobias by Topic
beard worm **81** Worms, 81.6 *worm*
be a regular customer of 212.8 *frequent*
bearer 71.5 *pack*, 326.7 *transferor*
bearer bond 741.14 *paper money*
bear false witness 538.21 *lie*, 856.6 *accuse falsely*
bear for 332.7 *take a direction*
bear fruit 86.10 *fruit*, 227.8 *grow*, 245.11 *have young*, 613.10 *benefit*, 627.2 *get better*, 682.8 *be effective*
bear garden 133.3 *miscellany*, 151.5 *confusion*
bear hard upon 369.14 *make heavy*
bear hug 726.1 *retention*
bearhug 821.14 *communication of love*
bear hunt 37.2 *hunting*, 590.2 *chase*
bear hunting 37.2 *hunting*
bear ill will 820.11 *be hostile*, 832.16 *be malevolent*
bearing **332**, 52.39 *angle*, 63.8 *machine element*, 63.27 *superstructure*, 107.1 *relatedness*, 163.9 *distinction*, 324.12 *gait*, 332.1 *direction*, 364.4 *vortex*, 457.3 *external appearance*, 488.2 *tendency*, 520.1 *meaning*, 544.8 *heraldic device*, 652.1 *conduct*
bearing arms 676.17 *military*
bearing in mind 511.8 *remembering*
bearing metal **57** Alloys
bearing off 36.1 *sailing*
bearing out 475.4 *proof*
bearing plate 63.27 *superstructure*
bearings 52.39 *angle*, 74.5 *navigation*, 250.2 *exact location*, 251.1 *situation*, 332.1 *direction*, 332.3 *orientation*
bearing the cost 746.1 *payment*
bear in mind 511.11 *memorize*
bear interest 130.6 *add*
bearish 77.28 *carnivorous*, 360.16 *descending*, 754.9 *cheap*, 818.5 *discourteous*, 829.4 *irascible*
bearish market 609.9 *scarcity*
bearishness 754.2 *declining prices*
bearlike 77.28 *carnivorous*

bear malice 820.11 *be hostile*, 828.8 *resent*, 832.16 *be malevolent*
bear malice towards 822.14 *hate*
bear market 13.6 *economic factors*, 14.2 *stock exchange*, 129.3 *decreasing thing*, 687.2 *economic adversity*, 740.3 *sellers' market*, 754.2 *declining prices*
bear more than one's share 687.9 *be in trouble*
béarnaise sauce 45.15 *sauce*
bear no malice 839.12 *show mercy*
bear no resemblance 115.5 *be dissimilar*
bear off 36.15 *sail*, 286.6 *be oblique*, 335.1 *deviate*
bear oneself 652.11 *conduct oneself*
be around 297.7 *surround*
bear out 101.12 *establish reality*, 475.17, 480.2 *prove*
bear resemblance 114.10 *be similar*
bears **161** Collective Names by Animal
bearskin 671.7 *armour*
bear the blame 866.8 *be guilty*
bear the brunt 659.20 *be in difficulty*, 671.28 *survive*, 687.9 *be in trouble*
bear the cost 746.8 *defray*
bear the cost of 738.5 *defray*
bear the costs 748.3 *donate*
bear the marks of 543.10 *signify*
bear the palm 126.8 *be superior*
bear the stamp of 227.7 *follow from*, 543.10 *signify*
bear up 237.7 *be strong*
bear upon 107.7 *relate to*, 230.9 *take action*, 233.8 *influence*, 330.1 *impel*
bear up to 332.7 *take a direction*
bear with 691.3 *be lenient*, 839.12 *show mercy*
bear with a sore head 829.3 *irascible person*, 830.5 *sullen person*
bear witness 535.18 *vow*, 856.5 *accuse*
bear witness to 483.11 *give evidence*, 543.10 *signify*
Beas **96** Rivers
be a shadow of one's former self 628.1 *deteriorate*
be ashamed 806.24 *be humiliated*
be a shining light 863.8 *be virtuous*
be asking for trouble 659.21 *get into trouble*
be as like as two peas in a pod 110.7 *be the same*
be assertive **535**
beast 76.2 *animal*, 127.6 *inferior*, 241.4 *violent person or animal*, 622.6 *dirty person*, 764.9 *unpleasant person*
beast fable 48.2 *fiction*
beastlike 76.14 *animalian*
beastliness 618.9 *badness*, 622.2 *uncleanness*, 758.4 *unpleasantness*, 764.6 *objectionability*, 818.1 *discourtesy*, 822.4 *hatefulness*, 832.4 *bitterness*, 862.1 *evil*
beastly 76.14 *animalian*, 618.3 *bad*, 622.8 *unclean*, 758.2 *unpleasant*, 764.2 *objectionable*, 818.5 *discourteous*, 822.12 *hated*, 832.11 *cruel*, 832.14 *hostile*, 862.7 *evil*, 864.11 *wicked*
beast of burden **326**, 32.1 *horse*, 76.3 *domesticated animal*, 646.1 *worker*
beast of prey 37.5 *game*, 398.13 *animal killer*, 590.6 *hunter*
be a storm in a teacup 541.7 *exaggerate*
beasts 68.8 *livestock*
beasts of the field 127.6 *inferior*
be a substitute **222**
be a surprise 514.11 *amaze*
beat **330**, **366**, **384**, 28.3 *fencing movements*, 36.15 *sail*, 37.7 *shoot*, 45.55 *cook*, 48.9 *metre*, 49.19 *tempo*, 49.38 *sound*,

126.8 *be superior*, 168.13 *unconventional*, 183.6 *reverberation*, 183.22 *resound*, 185.12 *musical time*, 214.1 *regularity*, 214.2 *cycle*, 214.5 *regular thing*, 236.12 *impotent*, 249.13 *locality*, 250.1 *location*, 327.2 *route*, 334.1 *circuit*, 356.1 *passage*, 363.3 *orbit*, 365.2 *vibration*, 365.5 *wave*, 365.9 *vibrate*, 366.22 *agitate*, 366.24 *shake*, 390.23 *whisk*, 406.11 *inflict pain*, 426.1 *drumming*, 426.8 *drum*, 433.3 *melodiousness*
be at 457.11 *appear*
beat 590.2 *chase*, 590.11 *hunt*, 599.1 *use*, 601.1 *misuse*, 621.13 *clean*, 650.1 *fatigued*, 670.9 *attack successfully*, 682.9 *be victorious*, 682.11 *overmaster*, 696.14 *master*, 832.18 *torment*, 879.3 *hit*
beat about the bush 104.13 *be extraneous*, 334.4, 363.8 *detour*, 474.13 *quibble*, 531.13 *equivocate*, 553.6 *be circuitous*, 578.1 *be equivocal*, 591.7 *be evasive*, 671.25 *stall*, 781.5 *be cautious*
beat a hasty retreat 638.5 *escape*, 779.4 *be a coward*
beat all comers 682.9 *be victorious*
be at a loss 659.20 *be in difficulty*
beat a retreat 345.2 *withdraw*, 543.12 *signal*, 591.8 *run away*, 632.8 *be safe*
beat around the bush 104.13 *be extraneous*
beat a strategic retreat 671.28 *survive*
beat a tattoo 426.8 *drum*, 812.18 *salute*
beat black and blue 879.3 *hit*
beat black-and-blue 406.11 *inflict pain*
beat down 244.9 *demolish*, 737.3 *bargain*, 754.14 *buy cheaply*
be at ease 765.7 *be satisfied*
beaten 45.56 *culinary*, 127.18 *outclassed*, 327.15 *accessible*, 584.10 *familiar*, 599.9 *used*, 601.4 *misused*, 683.11 *defeated*, 879.20 *punished*
beaten flat 282.9 *flattened*
beaten track 327.2 *route*, 584.3 *way*, 788.2 *boring thing*
beater 37.4 *hunter*, 45.6 *kitchen equipment*, 133.6 *mixer*, 366.14 *agitator*, 590.6 *hunter*
be at fault 866.8 *be guilty*
beat flat 282.7 *make horizontal*
Beat Generation **48** Literary Groups and Movements
beat hollow 357.3 *exceed*
be at home to 730.10 *receive someone*
beatific 861.6 *beneficial*
beatification 8.9 *deification*, 361.7 *lift*, 804.1 *right*
beatified 8.15 *deified*, 361.12 *exalted*
beatified soul 8.10 *deified person*
beatify 8.17 *deify*, 361.3 *promote*
beating **777** Phobias by Topic, 36.1 *sailing*, 37.2 *hunting*, 183.15 *reverberatory*, 214.11 *regular*, 330.12 *collision*, 365.2 *vibration*, 365.14 *vibrating*, 366.10 *beat*, 384.4 *pulverization*, 426.1, 426.15 *drumming*, 590.2 *chase*, 682.2 *victory*, 683.2 *defeat*, 879.12 *corporal punishment*
beating about the bush 474.4 *quibbling*, 553.2 *circumlocution*
beating heart 396.1 *life*
beating up 85.6 *tree management*
beat it 345.4 *hurry off*, 345.15 *go*, 349.33 *go away*, 591.9 *play truant*, 591.24 *hands off*
beatnik 104.5 *nonconformist*, 117.6 *misfit*, 168.7 *nonconformist*, 770.5 *nonobserver*
be at odds 434.11 *disagree*
be at odds with 500.8 *dissent*

beat of drum 636.2 *danger signal*
beat off 341.3 *fend off*
be at one 116.21 *be in accord,* 433.8 *harmonize*
beat one's breast 774.6 *lament,* 867.6 *do penance*
beat one's head against a brick wall 614.9 *waste effort*
be at one's wits' end 659.20 *be in difficulty*
be at peace 675
beat poet 48.14 *author*
be a trendsetter 228.9 *motivate*
be at sea 523.9 *find unintelligible*
beat someone hollow 126.8 *be superior*
beat swords into ploughshares 675.5 *be at peace,* 677.5 *make peace*
be attentive 467
beat the air 614.9 *waste effort*
beat the big drum 532.14 *proclaim,* 811.28 *flourish*
be at the bottom of 290.13 *be interior*
be at the brink 300.5 *border*
beat the drum 543.12 *signal,* 676.14 *battle*
be at the end of one's tether 659.20 *be in difficulty*
beat the living daylights out of 879.3 *hit*
beat the record 126.8 *be superior*
be at the station 344.8 *meet*
beat time 185.16 *time,* 192.16 *measure time,* 214.7 *be regular,* 365.9 *vibrate*
beat to a pulp 682.10 *defeat heavily*
beat to death 398.17 *murder*
beat to windward 74.9 *navigate*
beat up 241.8 *use violence,* 330.5 *beat,* 366.22 *agitate,* 393.24 *pulp,* 406.11 *inflict pain,* 670.5 *strike,* 832.18 *torment*
be at variance 666.8 *be different*
be at war 676
beat with an ugly stick 628.5 *hurt*
beau 401.4 *boyfriend,* 789.4 *attractive male,* 821.9 *lover,* 826.5 *courting person*
Beau 295.27 *model*
Beau Brummel 295.27 *model*
Beaufort 45 Cheeses, 97 Oceans and Seas
Beaufort scale 55.13 *wind strength*
beaujolais 351.9 *wine*
Beaumarchais 48 Dramatists
beau monde 742.11 *the rich,* 802.2 *aristocracy,* 815.7 *human society*
Beaumont 48 Dramatists
be auspicious 686, 714
be austere 690.7 *be unadorned*
beaut 861.17 *good thing*
beauteous 789.5 *beautiful*
beauteousness 789.1 *gorgeousness*
be authoritarian 688
beautician 791, 385.8 *masseur,* 621.12 *cleaner*
beautification 627.5 *improvement,* 629.8 *repair*
Beautification 791
beautified 791, 557.4 *ornate,* 627.14 *improved*
beautiful 789, 308.5 *even,* 457.10 *aspectual,* 558.3 *elegant,* 821.22 *lovable*
beautiful handwriting 522.10 *simplicity*
beautifully 558.5 *elegantly*
beautifully handwritten 522.2 *simple*
beautiful people 201.6 *avant-garde,* 742.11 *the rich,* 796.6 *fashionable élite*
beautiful thing 789
beautify 789, 791, 295.33 *dress up,* 557.5 *ornament,* 627.1 *improve*
beauty 56.78 *quantum,* 308.3 *evenness,* 457.3 *external appearance,* 558.1 *elegance,* 617.8 *exceller,* 655.3 *masterpiece,* 789.1

gorgeousness, 789.3 *attractive female,* 794.1 *elegance,* 821.4 *lovability*
Beauty 789
beauty and the beast 111.2 *opposites*
beauty parlour 791
beauty queen 789.3 *attractive female*
beauty salon 791.12 *beauty parlour*
beauty shop 791.12 *beauty parlour*
beauty specialist 791.13 *beautician*
beauty treatment 791
beauty unadorned 542.4 *simplicity*
Beauvoir 4 Philosophers, 48 Writers
beaux-arts 43 Architectural Styles
be available to one 692
be avenged 125.6 *be compensated*
beaver 77 Placental Mammals, 295.15 *headgear,* 642.10 *busy person,* 646.1 *worker,* 671.7 *armour*
be average 124
beaver away 642.15 *try,* 644.6 *work*
beaver lodge 634.3 *animal shelter*
beaver pelt 293.14 *animal covering*
beaverskin 295.15 *headgear*
be awarded a free kick 19.17 *kick*
be aware 403.11 *sense*
be aware of 403.11 *sense,* 435.16 *visualize,* 759.15 *feel*
be a waste of time 487.9 *be impossible*
be a wet blanket 587.5 *discourage,* 770.9 *despair*
be beautiful 789
bebeeru 85 Trees and Shrubs
be before 194
be behind 304.6 *be in the rear*
be behindhand 209.6 *be late*
be behind time 648.2 *make haste*
be believed 497
be benevolent 831
be bent on 570.13 *intend*
be beside 267.3 *juxtapose*
be better than nothing 615.6 *be convenient*
be beyond one's reach 523.7 *be unintelligible*
be biased 123.6 *be unjust,* 234.4 *tend,* 844.22 *discriminate*
be big 259
be bitten by the bug 228.8 *be motivated*
be blind 436
be blind to 436.7
bebop 46.2 *dance,* 49.8 *jazz*
bebopper 46.5 *dancer*
be boring 788
be born 396, 99.18 *come to be,* 156.27 *emerge,* 245.11 *have young*
be born again 220.10 *be converted,* 629.4 *be restored*
be born under a lucky star 686.6 *be fortunate*
be born with a silver spoon in one's mouth 686.6 *be fortunate*
be bound to happen 488.8 *be probable*
be brief 562
be brittle 379
be broad 271
be broad-minded 271
be broke 593.11 *be needy*
be brought 344
be brought to bed of 245.10 *reproduce oneself*
be brushed off 22.7 *play baseball*
be busy 211, 642, 644.6 *work*
be called out 60.19 *practise medicine*
be calm 869
becalm 325.9 *make motionless*
becalmed 325.4 *motionless,* 641.3 *inactive*
be capable of 235.10 *be powerful*

be capricious 579
be careful 469
be careless 783
be cast away 74.10 *sail*
be caught in the poverty trap 743.12 *be poor*
be caught short 353.16 *defecate*
because 226.14 *causally*
because of 227.12 *with the effect of*
be cautious 781, 469.10 *be careful,* 516.2 *show prudence*
be celibate 825
be central to 103.10 *be essential*
be certain 490
béchamel sauce 45.15 *sauce*
be changeable 224
be changed 216, 220.8 *be transformed*
be charitable 831, 833
becharm 821.28 *win the love of*
becharmed 821.19 *enamoured*
Becharof 94 Lakes
be chaste 825.10 *be continent*
be chastised 672.4 *serve one right*
be cheap 754
bêche-de-mer 81.3 *echinoderm*
be cheerful 769
be childless 247.7 *be infertile*
be circuitous 553
beck 96.1 *river,* 692.2 *demand*
beck and call 692.2 *demand*
becket knot 74 Knots
Beckett 48 Writers, 48 Dramatists
Beckmann thermometer 57 Laboratory Apparatus, 57 Named Reactions
beckon 543.11 *gesture*
beckoning look 543.3 *gesture*
be clairvoyant 516.1 *foresee*
beclamide 62 Medication
beclomethasone 62 Medication
becloud 441.10 *make dim,* 531.9 *disguise*
be clumsy 656
be coerced 695.8 *be compelled*
be cold 409
be cold-shouldered 806.24 *be humiliated*
become 99.18 *come to be,* 220.7 *convert into,* 847.14 *be the duty of*
become a born-again Christian 840.7 *be punished,* 867.4 *be penitent*
become a bride of Christ 825.11 *be monastic*
become acceptable 584.17 *become a habit*
become addicted 584.18 *habituate*
become adult 144.5 *be complete*
become a factor 107.7 *relate to*
become a favourite 821.25 *be loved*
become affiliated 665.13 *be a member*
become a free agent 698.16 *be independent*
become aggravated 768
become agitated about 713.6 *protest*
become a habit 584
become a hostage 701.8 *be subject to*
become airborne 359.19 *take off*
become a karate expert 26.13 *do martial arts*
become alive to 528.15 *be informed*
become aloof 783.12 *be indifferent*
become a martyr 710.12 *offer one's life*
become a member 665.13 *be a member,* 724.4 *have joint possession*
become a misanthrope 834
become a nation 91
become a new man 578.2 *equivocate,* 623.6 *get healthy*
become angry 828, 713.6 *protest*
become an heir 730.9 *receive*
become an in-patient 624.24 *be unhealthy*

become annoyed 829.6 *be irascible*
become an object lesson 656.6 *act foolishly*
become anorexic 129.5 *make smaller,* 722.9 *lose*
become an out-patient 624.24 *be unhealthy*
become a patient 624.24 *be unhealthy*
become apparent 522.4 *be intelligible*
become a prisoner 722.9 *lose*
become a self-made man 682.6 *be successful*
become a slave 701.8 *be subject to*
become as thick as thieves 819.13 *befriend*
become a teetotaller 873.4 *give up alcohol*
become attached to 821.24 *be in love*
become available 457.13 *occur*
become aware of 6.23 *learn*
become betrothed to 714.7 *promise*
become bigger 261
become black-and-blue 407.13 *be touched by*
become celebrated 640.4 *act*
become champion 682.9 *be victorious*
become choppy 97.10 *billow*
become cold 409
become complete 144.5 *be complete*
become convalescent 623.6 *get healthy*
become corrupt 864.16 *be wicked*
become dark 440
become different 216.7 *be changed*
become dilapidated 628.1 *deteriorate*
become dim 441.9 *be dim*
become disenfranchised 722.9 *lose*
become disorganized 689.5 *misgovern*
become dry 392.17 *dry*
become enamoured with 821.24 *be in love*
become endangered 129.4 *decrease*
become enemies 136.11 *divide*
become engaged 714.7 *promise,* 821.28 *win the love of,* 826.8 *court*
become entangled with 133.10
become extinct 129.4 *decrease,* 157.19 *expire,* 200.14 *pass,* 397.15 *die,* 458.1 *disappear*
become familiar 826.8 *court*
become famous 532, 640.4 *act,* 686.5 *be prosperous*
become fazed by 786.9 *wonder*
become green 453.17 *green*
become grey 441.9 *be dim*
become grown-up 144.5 *be complete*
become impoverished 722.12 *lessen*
become inaudible 424.5 *sound faint*
become independent 91.17 *become a nation*
become inextricably linked with 133.10 *become mixed*
become infected 715.6 *catch*
become inferior 127
become insane 510
become inseparable 819.13 *befriend*
become insolvent 683.6 *fail,* 687.10 *need money,* 722.10 *have a financial loss,* 747.9 *be unable to pay*
become invisible 438, 129.4 *decrease,* 458.1 *disappear*
become involved with 133.10 *become mixed,* 146.5 *be included*
become irrelevant 108.10 *be unrelated*
become known 530.9 *be disclosed*

become known from coast to coast be sold 532.18 *become famous*
become laid-back about 783.12 *be indifferent*
become larger 128.4 *increase,* 261.6 *become bigger,* 721.10 *augment*
become law 227.9 *take effect*
become long in the tooth 207.17 *age*
become mixed 133
become new 201
become obsolete 202.17 *grow old,* 458.1 *disappear,* 628.1 *deteriorate*
become one 174, 823.15 *marry*
become opaque 443.10 *be opaque*
become overweight 261.6 *become bigger*
become part of one 584.17 *become a habit*
become possessed of 195.11 *follow in office*
become proficient 696.15 *learn*
become public knowledge 530.9 *be disclosed,* 532.17 *be published*
become rancid 628.2 *decay*
become red 828.12 *become angry*
become redundant 15.11 *conduct industrial relations*
become runny 139.6 *come unstuck*
become sane 509.6 *be sane*
become scarce 129.4 *decrease*
become self-governing 91.17 *become a nation*
become shabby 628.1 *deteriorate*
become silent 422.1 *be silent*
become smaller 262
become solid 371.8 *be dense*
become stranded on an island 98.12 *be marooned*
become stronger 237.7 *be strong*
become stuck in a quagmire 98.12 *be marooned*
become tainted with 133.10 *become mixed*
become teetotal 873.4 *give up alcohol*
become the proud owner of 723.7 *possess*
become thick 371.8 *be dense*
become thin 274
become threadbare 628.1 *deteriorate*
become too old to cut the mustard 207.17 *age*
become transparent 442.11 *be transparent*
become turbulent 97.10 *billow*
become unconscious 236.6 *be powerless*
become unsociable 139.7 *be aloof*
become visible 457, 437.9 *appear*
become weary 650.5 *be fatigued*
be comfortable 106
becoming 220.14 *converting*
becoming dim 441.3 *dimming*
becoming law 16.31 *legislation*
becoming presentable 789.6 *personable*
be compatible 667, 298.5 *cooperate*
be compelled 571, 695
be compensated 125
be complete 144
be composed of 148.11 *consist of*
be concave 317
be concerned with 472.10 *focus on*
be concise 552
be consecutive 159
be consequent upon 195.10 *succeed*
be consistent 116.25 *conform*
be conspicuous 318.8 *protrude,* 544.11 *identify oneself*
be conspicuous by one's absence 254.15 *be absent*
be contemporary 198.6 *be simultaneous*
be contiguous 298.4 *interface*
be continent 825
be continuous 159.14 *continue*
be contrary 663

be convenient 615
be conventional 116.25 *conform*
be converted 220, 7.19 *be religious,* 216.7 *be changed*
be convex 316
be convinced 490.20 *be certain*
be cornered 571.16 *be compelled*
be counted 580.5 *vote*
be courageous 778
be courted 821.25 *be loved*
be courteous 817
becquerel 75 SI Units, 75 Scientific and Technical Units
Becquerel 52 Scientists
be crazy about 821.24 *be in love*
be crestfallen 515
be criminal 858
be cunning 657
be curious 465
be cut in 731.5 *get one's allotment*
be cut up 770.8 *grieve*
be cyclic 214
bed 777 Phobias by Topic, **47,** 54.31 *sedimentary rock,* 68.18 *practise livestock farming,* 69.3 *ornamental garden,* 135.11 *make love,* 218.5 *resting place,* 266.1 *layer,* 280.1 *base,* 282.3 *flat thing,* 284.4 *rest,* 325.3 *resting place,* 634.1 *refuge*
be damp 391.15 *be moist*
bed and board 256.10 *hotel,* 606.1 *provision*
bed and breakfast 256.10 *hotel,* 606.1 *provision*
be dark 440
be dated 185.17 *date,* 192.15 *chronologize*
bedazzle 436.15 *blind,* 439.24 *light,* 460.10 *bemuse,* 821.28 *win the love of*
bedazzling 436.11 *blinding*
bedbug 82 Insects, 82.3 *pest*
bed canopy 293.10 *bed covering*
bedchamber 256.7 *room*
bedclothes 293.10 *bed covering*
bed cover 293.10 *bed covering*
bed covering 293
bedding 54.31 *sedimentary rock,* 266.1 *layer,* 293.10 *bed covering*
bedding out 69.5 *gardening*
bedding plane 282.3 *flat thing*
bedding-plane 148.9 *earth's crust*
bedding plant 69.9 *garden plant*
Beddoes 48 Poets
bed down 649.2 *take it easy*
be dead 397.15 *die*
be deaf 421
be dear 753
be deceitful 540
be deceived 539
bedeck 295.33 *dress up,* 792.10 *decorate*
bedecked 295.29 *dressed*
be deeply in debt 743.13 *lose one's money*
be defeated 683, 673.3 *submit*
be definite 535.22 *emphasize*
be delivered 344.7 *be brought*
be dense 371
be dependent upon 127.10 *follow*
be derived from 227.7 *follow from*
be desirable 782
be destroyed 244
bedevil 8.18 *devilize,* 11.21 *bewitch,* 244.11 *ruin,* 523.7 *be unintelligible,* 659.22 *cause trouble*
bedevilled 11.19 *bewitched*
bedevilment 11.3 *witchcraft*
be devoted to 9.7 *worship*
bedewed 391.10 *misty*
Bedford 93 Cities
Bedfordshire 92 Counties
bedgown 295.22 *nightwear*
bed hopping 877.3 *sexual immorality*
be different 666, 104.17 *not conform*
be difficult 659
be diffuse 553
bedight 295.30 *dressed up*
be dim 441
bedim 441.10 *make dim,* 445.6 *decolour,* 531.9 *disguise*
bed in 354.5 *inset*

be dirty 622
be disappointed 515
be disclosed 530
be discourteous 818
be discovered 496
be dishonest 515, 538, 539.23 *deceive,* 858.8 *be dishonourable*
be dishonourable 858
be disinterested 859
be disjoined 343.12 *separate*
be dismissed 347, 600.7 *stop work*
be disobedient 693
be disordered 151
be disorderly 151
be disparate 117
be dispersed 162
be disposed 234.4 *tend*
be disposed to 4.22 *propound a philosophy*
be dissatisfied 766
be dissimilar 115
be distant 263
be diverse 113
bedizen 295.33 *dress up,* 792.10 *decorate*
bedizened 295.30 *dressed up*
bedizenment 295.5 *fancy dress*
bed jacket 295.4 *informal dress,* 295.16 *robe,* 295.22 *nightwear*
bedlam 151.5 *confusion,* 153.5 *commotion,* 423.2 *outcry,* 434.2 *dissonant noise*
Bedlam 510.8 *mental hospital*
bed linen 293.10 *bed covering*
Bedlington terrier 77 Breeds of Dogs
bed of nails 840.2 *apology*
bed of roses 84.9 *figurative usage,* 405.5 *idealized pleasure,* 418.2 *fragrant thing,* 675.1 *peace,* 1069.1 *prosperity*
be done with 157.15 *end*
be dormant 83
Bedouin 1 Peoples
bed out 69.15 *cultivate,* 354.6 *plant*
bedpan 353.14, 727.7 *toilet*
bedraggle 151.24 *make disordered,* 622.11 *dirty*
bedraggled 151.15 *untidy,* 622.7 *dirty*
bedridden 325.5 *sedentary,* 624.22 *sick*
be driving at 520.10 *mean*
bedrock 54.27 *sediment,* 134.8 *simplicity,* 225.4 *stable thing,* 226.3 *rudiment,* 276.4 *low thing,* 280.1 *base,* 284.2 *supporting part,* 611.3 *chief thing,* 611.5 *important*
bedroom 256.7 *room,* 531.6 *privacy,* 634.1 *refuge*
bedroom couch 218.5 *resting place*
bedroom farce 51.10 *comedy*
bedroom suburb 93.8 *suburb*
be drunk 874
bedsheet 293.10 *bed covering*
bedside lamp 439.6 *electric light*
bedside manner 630.13 *therapy*
bedside table 47.4 *table*
bedsit 256.5 *house*
bedsocks 295.22 *nightwear*
bedspread 293.10 *bed covering*
bedspring 377.5 *spring*
bedstead 47.6 *bed*
bedstraw 84 Flowers and Flowering Plants
bedtime 205.2 *night*
be due 845
be due to 227.7 *follow from*
be duped 515.4 *be disappointed*
bed-wetting 353.3 *urination*
be dying for 782.12 *desire*
bee 82 Insects, 82.1 *insect,* 82.4 *social insect,* 642.10 *busy person,* 646.1 *worker,* 815.10 *social animal*
be early 208
be easy 660
be easy about 466.6 *be incurious*
be easy as pie 660.15 *be easy*
Beeb 534.20 *radio broadcasting*
be eccentric 215.7 *be unusual*
beech 85 Trees and Shrubs

Beecham 49 Musicians and Composers
beechen 85.15 *woody*
beech fern 88 Ferns
beech mast 85.4 *trees*
beechmast 350.8 *animal food*
beechnut 86 Nuts
be economical with the truth 309.12 *distort the truth,* 489.7 *be improbable,* 538.21 *lie*
bee-eater 78 Birds
beef 45.20 *meat,* 369.4 *heaviness,* 713.1, 713.6 *protest,* 830.11 *be irritable*
Beefalo 68 Breeds of Cattle
beefburger 45.20 *meat*
beefcake 66.4 *portrait,* 237.6 *muscleman,* 401.4 *boyfriend*
beef: chuck 45
beef congee 45.48 *Chinese dish*
beef farm 68.6 *farm*
beef farmer 68.15 *agriculturist*
beef farming 68.3 *livestock farming*
be effective 682
be efficacious 682.8 *be effective*
beefiness 237.1 *strength,* 259.6 *squatness,* 369.4 *heaviness*
beefing 830.7 *irritable*
bee fly 82 Insects
beef mountain 68.2 *Common Agricultural Policy*
beef: neck 45
beef ranch 68.6 *farm*
beef road 71.2 *road*
beef sausage 45.29 *sausage*
Beef Shorthorn 68 Breeds of Cattle
beefsteak fungus 89 Fungi
beef tomato 45 Vegetables
be up 128.5 *make bigger,* 237.8 *strengthen,* 671.20 *reinforce*
beefwood 85 Trees and Shrubs
beefy 237.9 *physically strong,* 259.17 *stocky,* 369.1 *heavy*
be egoistic 860
be egotistic 860.7 *be egoistic*
beehive 82.4 *social insect,* 256.13 *lair,* 316.3 *dome,* 642.6 *business,* 791.8 *hair cut*
Beehive 53 Clusters
beehive kiln 44.6 *ceramic workshop*
beehive shelf 57 Laboratory Apparatus
beehive tomb 200.7 *thing of the past,* 399.6 *grave*
bee in the bonnet 579.3 *whim*
beekeeper 82.8 *entomologist*
bee keeping 42 Hobbies and Pastimes
beekeeping 82.7 *study*
be elastic 377
be elegant 558
be eliminated 683.7 *be defeated*
beeline 312.7 *straight line,* 332.2 *bearing,* 333.1 *middle way*
be elsewhere 468.12 *be inattentive*
Beelzebub 8.7 *devil*
be emaciated 274
be enfranchised 580.5 *vote*
be engaged 211.7 *be busy*
be engraved on one's memory 511.15 *be remembered*
be enough 124.9 *be average,* 608.4 *suffice*
be entitled 845
be entitled to 804, 843.13 *be right*
be envious of 842
be equal 110, 122
be equal to 122.10 *be equal*
be equivocal 578
beer 351.7 *alcoholic drink,* 874.12 *alcohol*
beer barrel 258.11 *vessel*
beer belly 259.8 *fat*
Beerbohm 48 Writers
beer bottle 258.14 *bottle*
beer bread 45.38 *bread*
beer garden 69.2 *garden*
beer glass 258.13 *drinking vessel*
beer gut 258.18 *stomach,* 316.2 *bulge*
beeriness 874.11 *drinking*

beer making 42 Hobbies and Pastimes
beer party 815.5 *party*
Beersheba 93 Cities
beery 874.5 *drunken*, 874.6 *intoxicating*
bees 161 Collective Names by Animal, **777** Phobias by Topic
bee's knees 617.8 *exceller*
be essential 103
beestings 77.2 *mammalian characteristic*, 351.5 *milk*
beeswax 82.4 *social insect*, 386.13 *lubricate*, 394.2 *adhesive*, 395.18 *anoint*
beet 45 Vegetables
be eternal 190, 184.9 *be infinite*
beet harvester 68.10 *farm tool*
Beethoven 49 Musicians and Composers
beetle 82 Insects, 69.12 *pests and diseases*, 82.1 *insect*, 275.15 *be high*, 283.11 *project*, 393.15 *pulper*
beetle-browed 283.8 *projecting*
beetle-crushers 295.19 *footwear*
beetle off 345.4 *hurry off*
beetling 275.9 *high*, 283.8 *projecting*
beet planter 68.10 *farm tool*
beetroot 45 Vegetables, 450.7 *red thing*, 455.3 *purple thing*
beetroot-red 450.1 *red*
beet sugar 414.2 *sweetener*
be evasive 591
be everywhere 253.11 *be present*
be evil 862
be exalted 318.9 *be prominent*
be excessive 610
be excluded 147
be exclusive 302.7 *limit*
be exempt 848
be expert 655
be exterior 289
be external 104
be extinguished 440.13 *become dark*
be extraneous 104
be extravagant 541
be fair 482, 843
befall 229.5 *happen by chance*, 589.10 *chance*
be false 539, 540, 309.12 *distort the truth*
be famous 800.5 *have repute*
Befana 11.11 *ghost*
be fast 193.3 *mistime*, 208.7 *be early*
be fatigued 650
be favourable 819
be fearful 777
be fearful for 777.14 *worry*
be fed up 608.6 *have enough*
be fertile 246
be feverish 408.16 *feel hot*
be fictitious 172.8 *not exist*
be financially worthwhile 721.13 *be profitable*
be finished with 600.6 *stop using*
be fired 218.7 *stop working*
be first 194.8 *be before*, 303.10 *be in front*
befit 615.6 *be convenient*, 782.16 *be desirable*, 847.14 *be the duty of*
be fit for 235.10 *be powerful*, 667.9 *be suitable*
befit the occasion 210.4 *be timely*
befit the time 210.4 *be timely*
befitting 116.16 *fitting*, 210.6 *timely*, 615.1 *convenient*
befittingly 116.38 *fittingly*, 210.9 *opportunely*, 843.18 *properly*
be fleeting 189.4 *be transient*
befog 55.64 *fog*, 441.10 *make dim*, 531.9 *disguise*
befool 515.7 *thwart*, 539.28 *trick*, 599.3 *exploit*, 734.10 *take away*
befooling 539.36 *deceived*
befooling 539.7 *tricking*
be foolish 508
be footloose and fancy free 814.11 *not stand on ceremony*

before 154, 194, 202.20 *formerly*, 253.16 *on the spot*, 303.11 *in front*
before all 526.16 *manifestly*
before everything 156.40 *first*
before God 526.16 *manifestly*
beforehand 154.20, 194.11 *before*, 208.16 *premature*, 208.20 *prematurely*
be foreign 104, 149
before long 208.18 *soon*
beforementioned 154.11 *prior*
before now 200, 3.24 *historically*, 194.11 *before*, 202.20 *formerly*
before one 526.16 *manifestly*
before one could say Jack Robinson 329.14 *swiftly*
before one knows it 191.8 *immediately*
before one's eyes 253.10 *available*, 435.23 *visible*
before one's very eyes 253.16 *on the spot*
before the bar 492.10 *judged*
before the bench 16.81 *legally*
before the committee 472.13 *problematically*
before the Flood 3.15 *historic*
before the house 472.13 *problematically*
before the ink was dry 208.17 *early*
before the judge 16.87 *in litigation*, 856.10 *accusingly*
before the mast 74.12 *nautically*
before then 194.11 *before*
before the wind 332.11 *in all directions*
before time 208.17 *early*, 595.5 *immature*
before you can say Jack Robinson 191.8 *immediately*, 648.6 *hastily*
be forgetful 512, 838.6 *be ungrateful*
be forgotten 512
be formal 306, 813
be for the high jump 879.6 *be punished*
be fortunate 686
befoul 622.11 *dirty*, 862.11 *be evil*
be found 99.17 *exist*, 344.1 *arrive*
be found at 212.8 *frequent*
be found wanting 358.1 *fall short*
be fragile 379.4 *be brittle*
be fragrant 418
be fraudulent 539, 540
be free 698
be frequent 212
befriend 819, 180.14 *keep company with*
befriender 833.3 *philanthropist*
be friendly with 819.13 *befriend*
be frightened 777.11 *be afraid*
be fruitful 86.10 *fruit*
befuddle 151.22 *discompose*, 460.10 *bemuse*, 874.9 *be intoxicating*
befuddlement 874.10 *drunkenness*
be full 144.5 *be complete*
be full of baloney 538.23 *talk nonsense*
be full of blarney 540.18 *be hypocritical*
be full of bullshit 538.23 *talk nonsense*
be full of crap 538.23 *talk nonsense*
be full of hokum 538.23 *talk nonsense*
be full of oneself 809.15 *be vain*
be full of piss and vinegar 239.2 *be full of vigour*
be full of vigour 239
be funny 798.7 *make one laugh*
beg 808
beg 602.6 *find means*
beg 712.6 *request*, 712.8 *solicit money*, 733.7 *borrow*
beg, borrow, or steal 721.9 *gain*
be generous 755
beget 226.9 *be the cause of*, 243.10 *produce*, 245.13 *propagate*, 396.19 *give birth to*

begetter 226.7 *Prime Mover*, 243.9 *producer*, 245.5 *propagator*
be getting at 520.10 *mean*
beg for crumbs 808.12 *beg*
beg for favours 808.12 *beg*
beg forgiveness 840.6 *apologize*
beg for mercy 835.12 *ask for mercy*
beg for more 609.6 *be unsatisfied*
beg for one's bread 743.12 *be poor*
beg for sleep 650.5 *be fatigued*
beggar 712, 622.6 *dirty person*, 643.8 *nonworker*, 730.5 *recipient*, 743.10 *poor person*, 743.14 *impoverish*
beggar all description 786.10 *be wonderful*
beggardom 743.7 *beggary*
beggared 747.13 *nonpaying*
beggarliness 127.2 *deficiency*, 743.7 *beggary*
beggarly 743, 808.7 *sycophantic*
beggar my neighbour 42 Card Games
beggar-on-horseback 807.12 *impudent person*
beggary 743
begging 712, 712.1 *request*, 712.3 *solicitation*, 733.1 *borrowing*
begin 156, 201, 322, 119.7 *originate*, 145.5 *be incomplete*, 226.11 *inaugurate*, 228.9 *motivate*, 396.18 *be born*, 457.12 *become visible*, 594.2 *do the groundwork*, 597.1 *undertake*, 644.6 *work*
begin again 156, 183.20 *renew*, 201.17 *become new*, 221.7 *restore*
begin an insurrection 713.8 *cause mischief*
begin from 227.7 *follow from*
beginner 156, 6.7 *learner*, 26.8 *karate*, 201.8 *new arrival*, 346.7 *entrant*, 539.22 *dupe*, 656.10 *unskilled person*, 658.3 *naive person*, 865.4 *innocent person*
beginner's luck 682.1 *success*
beginning 156, 156, 201, 322, 322, 119.1 *originality*, 208.3 *early stage*, 303.1 *front*, 344.10 *arrival*, 457.1 *appearance*, 457.7 *appearing*
Beginning 156
beginning again 183.4 *return*
beginning of the end 157.9 *close*
beginning of time 4.9 *philosophical problem*
beginnings 226.3 *rudiment*
begin to understand 522.6 *understand*
be given 730.9 *receive*
beg leave 708.6 *ask permission*, 712.6 *request*
Begochiddi 8 Deities
begone 345.15 *go*, 349.33 *go away*
be gone 397.15 *die*
beg one's pardon 710.14 *offer reparation*
begonia 84 Flowers and Flowering Plants
be good 861, 652.12 *behave well*, 863.8 *be virtuous*
be good at 861
begotten 243.12 *produced*, 396.15 *born*
be governed 12
beg pardon 839.13 *ask forgiveness*, 840.6 *apologize*
beg permission 708.6 *ask permission*, 712.6 *request*
be grateful 837
be greedy 872
be Greek to 521.8 *not understand*
begrime 622.11 *dirty*
begrimed 622.7 *dirty*
be grounded in 6.24 *know*
begrudge 573.10 *grudge*, 609.7 *make insufficient*, 758.8 *grudge*, 838.6 *be ungrateful*, 842.3 *be envious of*
begrudging 842.2 *envious*
begrudgingly 842.4 *enviously*
beg the question 474.13 *quibble*

beg to differ 500.8 *dissent*, 663.15 *object*
beguile 539.27 *be false*, 657.5 *be cunning*, 821.28 *win the love of*
beguilement 657.1 *cunning*
beguiler 539.15 *deceiver*
beguiling 657.4 *cunning*, 786.8 *wonderful*, 821.22 *lovable*
be guilty 866
beguine 46.2 *dance*
Beguines 7 Christian Movements
begun 145.4 *incomplete*
be gunning for 590.8 *pursue*
be had 539.24 *be deceived*, 753.11 *overpay*
be had for the asking 660.15 *be easy*
behalf 861.13 *benefit*
be half-baked 208.10 *hasten*
be halfway 333
Behan 48 Dramatists
be hard on 481.14 *discriminate against*
be hard put 659.19 *have difficulty*
behave 640.4 *act*, 652.11 *conduct oneself*, 652.12 *behave well*, 863.8 *be virtuous*
behave badly 652, 818.7 *be discourteous*
behave cheekily 818.7 *be discourteous*
behave like a gentleman 857.6 *be honourable*
behave oneself 652.12 *behave well*
behave properly 817.11 *have good manners*
behave towards 652
behave well 652, 306.8 *be formal*, 694.5 *obey*, 817.11 *have good manners*, 857.6 *be honourable*, 861.18 *be good*
behaving 652
behaviour 306.5 *formality*, 327.1 *way*, 584.5 *tradition*, 640.1 *action*, 652.1 *conduct*, 876.1 *morality*
behavioural 2.12 *sociological*, 306.11 *formal*, 652.16 *behaving*
behaviourally 2.16 *sociologically*
behavioural pattern 2.3 *social environment*
behavioural psychology 61.1 *psychology*
behavioural science 1.1 *anthropology*, 2.1 *sociology*
behavioural scientist 1.3 *anthropologist*
behavioural therapy 630.13 *therapy*
behaviourism 4.7 *school of thought*, 61.1 *psychology*, 652.1 *conduct*
behaviourist 4.11 *follower of a doctrine*, 4.14 *of a philosophy*
behaviouristic 652.16 *behaving*
behaviourist zoographer 76.11 *zoologist*
behaviour modification 61.3 *psychiatric treatment*
behaviour patterns 584.4 *custom*
behaviour therapist 61.30 *psychiatrist*
behaviour therapy 61.3 *psychiatric treatment*
behead 131.4 *take off*, 136.10 *set apart*, 270.10 *shorten*, 398.19, 879.5 *execute*
be head and shoulders above the rest 163.15 *be in a class of one's own*
beheaded 131.7 *reduced*, 270.8 *shortened*
beheading 131.1 *subtraction*, 136.3 *separateness*, 270.2 *shortening*, 398.5 *execution*, 879.13 *capital punishment*
be healthy 623
be heard 420
be heavy 369
be helpful 662
behemoth 76.7 *legendary beast*, 259.9 *big thing*
be here 253.11 *be present*

be here for good 217.5 *be permanent*

be here for the duration 217.5 *be permanent*

be here to stay 217.5 *be permanent*

behest 692.1 *command*

be high 275

be highly thought of 800.5 *have repute*

be hilarious 798.7 *make one laugh*

behind 155, 358, 263.10 *distantly*, 304.1 *rear*, 304.2 *rear end*, 304.9 *in the rear*, 328.7 *delayed*, 595.1 *unprepared*

behind bars 632.5 *safe*, 702.8 *imprisoned*

behind closed doors 529.15 *in secret*, 531.18 *privately*, 816.14 *unsocially*

behindhand 209.9, 209.15 *late*, 358.9 *behind*, 595.1 *unprepared*, 747.13 *nonpaying*

behind one's back 254.20 *absently*, 529.16 *stealthily*

behind schedule 209.9, 209.15 *late*

behind someone's back 474.15 *hypocritically*

behind-the-back pass 23.4 *playing terms*

behind the eight ball 659.16 *troubled*

behind the scenes 51.41 *onstage*, 226.13 *causal*, 226.14 *causally*, 304.9 *in the rear*, 438.3 *private*, 438.9 *invisibly*, 527.2 *concealed*

behind the times 193.6 *too late*, 193.7 *out of chronological order*, 197.2 *occurring at a different time*, 200.19 *antiquarian*

behind the veil 397.19 *dead*, 816.10 *lonely*

behind time 193.6 *too late*, 193.7 *out of chronological order*, 209.9, 209.15 *late*

behind-time 595.1 *unprepared*

be history 200.13 *be past*

be hit by a pitched ball 22.7 *play baseball*

be hoist with one's own petard 672.4 *serve one right*

behold 435.12 *see*

beholden 478.16 *answerable*, 745.9 *in debt*, 837.4 *grateful*, 847.11 *duty-bound*

beholder 253.5 *someone present*, 435.11 *observer*, 730.5 *recipient*

be holier than the Pope 540.18 *be hypocritical*

be holier than thou 540.18 *be hypocritical*

be honourable 857

be hopeful 775

be hopeless 776

be horizontal 282

be hospitable 734, 819, 815.11 *be sociable*

be hospitalized 624.24 *be unhealthy*

be hostile 820

be hot 408

behove 847.14 *be the duty of*

be humble 806, 673.4 *succumb*

be humiliated 806

be humorous 771

be hungry 782

be hypocritical 540, 538.24 *pretend*

be identical 110.7 *be the same*

be identified 544.11 *identify oneself*

beige 446.1 *white*, 449.1 *brown*, 452.1 *yellow*

be ignorant 502

Beijing 93 Cities, 93.6 *other cities*

be ill 238.6 *be weak*, 624.24 *be unhealthy*, 687.9 *be in trouble*

be illegal 16

be impartial 783

be impassive 404.11 *be unfeeling*

be impenitent 868

be imperfect 620

be impertinent 846.15 *presume*

be implicated in 146.5 *be included*

be important 611

be impossible 487

be impotent 236.6 *be powerless*

be impressed with oneself 809.15 *be vain*

be improbable 489

be in 164.28 *prevail*

be in a catch-22 situation 106.13 *get into difficulties*

be in accord 116

be in accordance 116.21 *be in accord*

be in a class of one's own 163, 165.25 *excel*

be in action 230.7 *be operational*

be inactive 643, 641.4 *not act*, 673.3 *submit*

be in a predicament 105

be in a rut 584.16 *have a habit*

be in a state of 105

be inattentive 468, 335.4 *lose track of*, 468.13 *be thoughtless*

be in at the beginning 156.23 *inaugurate*

be in at the death 344.2 *reach*

be in-between 333.7 *be halfway*

be in bloom 84.13 *flower*

be in cahoots 116.22 *form an alliance*, 664.15 *concur*

be in charge 12.11 *govern*, 640.4 *act*, 653.2 *direct*

be inclined towards 784.8 *prefer*

be included 146

be incomplete 145

be in conflict 434.11 *disagree*

be inconsiderate 462

be inconvenient 616

be incurious 466, 783.12 *be indifferent*

be in danger 633

be in debt 745

be in demand 739.2 *be sold*

be independent 168, 698, 104.17 *not conform*

be indifferent 783, 673.3 *submit*

be in difficulty 659

be induced 228.8 *be motivated*

be in earnest 772.9 *take seriously*

be in error 504

be inert 240, 641.4 *not act*

be infatuated with 784.7 *like*

be infected 228.8 *be motivated*

be inferior 127

be infertile 247

be infinite 184

be in flower 84.13 *flower*

be in force 230.7 *be operational*

be informal 698

be informed 528, 6.24 *know*, 522.6 *understand*

be in front 303

being 59.3 *organism*, 99.1 *existence*, 99.2 *thing*, 99.10 *existing*, 165.13 *person*, 253.1 *presence*, 396.1 *life*, 400.7 *person*, 457.2 *being in view*

being ahead 126.3 *advantage*

being alive 396.1 *life*

being a regular customer 212.5 *frequenting*

being at large 698.1 *freedom*

being cured 629.11 *recuperation*

being discussed 594.17 *developing*

being fired 645.3 *unemployment*

being hit by a pitched ball 22.5 *batting terms*

being in control 698.3 *independence*

being in view 457

being there 457.2 *being in view*

be in harmony 116.21 *be in accord*, 433.8 *harmonize*

be inhibited 661, 302.7 *limit*

be in hot pursuit 590.8 *pursue*

be in league with 665, 135.8 *unite*

be in line for 845.15 *merit*

be in love 821

be in mortal dread 777.11 *be afraid*

be in motion 324, 336.1 *go forward*

be in no hurry 645.4 *have leisure*

be in on 724.4 *have joint possession*

be in one's element 660.17 *do easily*

be in on the action 640.4 *act*

be in on the ground floor 156.23 *inaugurate*

be in order 150, 214.7 *be regular*

be in play 230.7 *be operational*

be in power 12.11 *govern*, 166.16 *direct*

be in prison 702

be in residence 253.13 *reside*

be insane 510.14 *become insane*

be in service 697.8 *serve*

be insincere 540.18 *be hypocritical*

be instinctive 464

be instructed 6.23 *learn*

be instrumental 232.4 *be an instrument*

be insubordinate 668

be insufficient 609

be intelligent 459, 507

be intelligible 522

be intentionally walked 22.7 *play baseball*

be interior 290

be in the chair 653.2 *direct*

be in the dark 502.9 *be ignorant*

be in the driver's seat 233.10 *be a prevailing influence*

be in the future 199

be in the know 528.15 *be informed*, 787.6 *understand*

be in the limelight 526.5 *be visible*

be in the middle 333

be in the news 532.18 *become famous*

be in the past 200.13 *be past*

be in the pink 623.5 *be healthy*

be in the rear 304

be in the right 843.13 *be right*

be in the right place at the right time 322.23 *find an opening*

be in the running 488.8 *be probable*

be in the shotgun 19.15 *play offence*

be in the vanguard 303.10 *be in front*, 496.4 *invent*

be into 165.27 *specialize*

be in touch 534.30 *communicate*

be in touch with 420.15 *hear*

be intoxicating 874

be in trouble 687

be introverted 661.11 *be inhibited*

be intuitive 464

be in turmoil 366.21 *be agitated*

be in two minds about 491.19 *hesitate*

be in unison 433.8 *harmonize*

be in vain 614.7 *be useless*, 618.13 *be worthless*

be invalided out 624.24 *be unhealthy*

be in working order 150.23 *be in order*

be irascible 829

be irregular 215

be irrelevant 104.13 *be extraneous*

be irresolute 224, 576, 717, 491.19 *hesitate*

be irritable 830, 403.11 *sense*

be irritated 403.11 *sense*

Beirut 93 Cities

be itchy 403.11 *sense*

be jealous 841

be jealous of one's good name 805.31 *save face*

bejewel 789.8 *beautify*, 792.10 *decorate*

bejewelled 792.8 *decorated*

be justified 843.13 *be right*

be just the job 116.27 *fit*, 478.22 *be the answer*

be just the thing 116.27 *fit*

be kept waiting 209.7 *wait*

be kind 374, 831.8 *be benevolent*

be knowledgeable 277.15 *be profound*

be known to 584.16 *have a habit*

bel 75 Scientific and Technical Units

belabour 183.18 *harp*, 879.3 *hit*

be lacking 145.5 *be incomplete*

belah 85 Trees and Shrubs

be laid off 218.7 *stop working*

be laid up 624.24 *be unhealthy*

Belarus 91 Countries

be last 304.6 *be in the rear*

be late 209, 211.5 *take untimely action*, 648.2 *make haste*

belated 209.9 *late*

belatedly 209.15 *late*

belatedness 209.1 *lateness*, 595.8 *lack of preparation*

be latent 527

be lawless 16

be lax 708.4 *be permissive*

belay 34.8 *mountaineering*, 34.9 *mountaineer*, 36.21 *avast*, 135.10 *link*

belay anchor 34.4 *climbing equipment*

belay brake 34.4 *climbing equipment*

belay braking 34.3 *climbing technique*

belayed 34.8 *mountaineering*

belaying 34.3 *climbing technique*, 34.8 *mountaineering*

bel canto 49.4 *opera*

belch 349, 349, 388, 425, 425, 430.2 *hoarseness*, 430.5 *sound hoarse*

belching 349.24 *belch*, 349.31 *eructative*

beleaguer 670.4 *besiege*, 676.13 *be at war*

be led astray 515.4 *be disappointed*

be led to believe 497.7 *believe*

be left 132, 682.12 *succeed to*

be left over 132.7 *be left*

be legal 16

belemnite 81 Molluscs

be lenient 691, 835.10, 839.12 *show mercy*

Belet 8 Deities

be level pegging 198.8 *run equally*

Belfast 93 Cities, 93.4 *British cities*

belfry 275.6 *tall thing*

Belgian 68 Breeds of Fowl, 68 Breeds of Fowl

Belgian Ardennes 32 Breeds of Horse and Pony

Belgian Blue 68 Breeds of Cattle

Belgian GP at Spa Francorchamps 33.2 *Formula 1 race*

Belgian Heavy Draught 32 Breeds of Horse and Pony

Belgians 1 Peoples

Belgian shepherd dog 77 Breeds of Dogs

Belgium 91 Countries

Belgrade 93 Cities, 93.6 *other cities*

Belgravia 93.5 *London*

be liable 847

Belial 8.7 *devil*

be liberated 700

belie 102.16 *delude*, 476.8 *refute*, 536.8 *rebut*, 639.26 *be a hypocrite*, 548.4 *misrepresent*, 663.15 *object*

belief 497, 7.1 *religion*, 461.6 *idea*, 490.10 *conviction*, 492.1 *judgment*, 513.1 *expectation*, 759.2 *impression*, 775.2 *expectation*

Belief 497

beliefs 471.5 *ideology*, 759.3 *feelings*, 876.1 *morality*

belief system 2.4 *social organization*, 4.2 *philosophical system*, 7.1 *religion*

belie one's expectations 515.6 *disappoint*

believability 497

believable 497, 486.5 *possible*, 488.7 *plausible*

believably 497, 486.11 *potentially*

believe 497, 759, 7.19 *be religious*, 466.5 *not ask*, 471.17 *theorize*, 490.20 *be certain*, 492.12

estimate, 513.9 predict, 518.5 suppose, 586.18 be persuaded, 775.6 hope
believed 497
believe in 4.22 propound a philosophy
believer 497, 7.3 religious person, 155.14 follower, 490.11 opinionist
believer in a nonmaterial world 368
believing 497, 497, 7.15 religious, 490.2 convinced
believingly 497
be lifeless 641.4 not act
be light 370
be like 114.10 be similar, 116.25 conform
be likely 714.9 be auspicious
be like putty in someone's hands 236.6 be powerless
be like the cat that stole the cream 765.7 be satisfied
Belili 8 Deities
be limiting 300.5 border
be linked with 180.13 accompany
be lippy 478.18 answer back
Belisha beacon 71.3 carriageway, 356.5 crossing point, 439.6 electric light, 543.4 signal
be listened to 233.8 influence
Belit 8 Deities
be literal 537
be little 260
belittle 129.5 make smaller, 495.3 underestimate, 542.21 detract from, 612.13 make unimportant, 766.7 be dissatisfied, 850.20 scorn, 852.17 criticize, 854.10 disparage
belittled 129.6 decreasing, 850.18 undervalued
belittlement 129.1 decrease, 542.2 detraction, 854.1 disparagement
belittler 854.7 disparager
belittling 854.15 disparaging
Belize 91 Countries
bell 26.2 boxing, 192.10 signal, 423.4 sound maker, 427.4 sources of resonance, 432.4 cry, 534.10 telephone call, 543.4 signal, 636.2 danger signal
Bell 52 Scientists
belladonna 84 Flowers and Flowering Plants, 631.12 poisonous plant
belladonna lily 84 Flowers and Flowering Plants
Bellatrix 53 Named Stars
bell, book, and candle 11.6 talisman
bell-bottomed 271.1 broad
bell-bottoms 295.9 trousers
bellboy 326.7 transferor , 697.3 attendant
bell bronze 57 Alloys
bell buoy 636.2 danger signal
bell cittern 49 Musical Instruments
belle 789.3 attractive female
Belleek ware 44 Types of Ceramics
belle of the ball 789.3 attractive female
belles-lettres 48.1 literature
belletrist 48.15 literary person
belletristic 48.16 literary
bellflower 84 Flowers and Flowering Plants
bellhop 697.3 attendant
bellicose 17.8 military, 237.11 strong in spirit, 241.6 violent, 473.9 hostile, 500.7 dissenting, 666.9 disagreeing, 668.8 defying, 670.22 militant, 674.15 contentious, 676.15 warring, 676.16 warlike, 679.33 combative, 764.2 objectionable, 778.11 militant, 820.9 aggressive, 828.16 angry, 829.4 irascible
bellicosely 666.11 in disagreement, 668.10 in defiance
bellicosity 676, 237.1 strength, 666.1 disagreement, 670.11 attack, 778.2 heroism, 820.1 enmity, 828.4 anger

belligerence 666.1 disagreement, 668.1 defiance, 670.11 attack, 820.1 enmity, 828.4 anger, 829.1 irascibility
belligerency 676, 674.6 fight
belligerent 17.8 military, 473.9 hostile, 666.9 disagreeing, 668.8 defying, 670.22 militant, 674.15 contentious, 676.15 warring, 676.16 warlike, 679.1 combatant, 679.33 combative, 820.9 aggressive, 828.16 angry, 829.4 irascible
belligerently 473.17 argumentatively, 666.11 in disagreement, 668.10 in defiance, 674.17 contentiously, 676.18 to war, 679.41 aggressively, 829.9 irascibly
belling 432.1 animal cry
Bellingshausen 97 Oceans and Seas
Bellini 49 Musicians and Composers
bell metal 57 Alloys
Belloc 48 Poets
Bellona 8 Deities, 676.3 god of war
bellow 423.8 be loud, 431.1 cry, 431.10 cry out, 432.4 cry, 554.6 emphasize
Bellow 48 Writers
bellowing 423.6 loud, 431.16 vociferous, 432.1 animal cry, 432.7 ululant
bell-ringer 543.8 signer
bell ringing 49.6 campanology, 427.2 ringing
bell-ringing 543.16 signalling
bell rope 283.3 suspended object
bells 49 Musical Instruments, 423.1 loudness
bell shape 315.5 cone
bell-shaped 315.9 round
Bell's inequality 56.80 quantum theory
bell the cat 574.8 brace oneself, 778.15 be courageous, 780.5 be rash
bell tower 275.6 tall thing
bellwether 653.14 leader
belly 45.24 pork , 258.18 stomach, 261.6 become bigger, 290.4 insides, 350.16 eating utensil
bellyache 406.2 painful condition, 624.8 indigestion, 713.7 complain, 766.7 be dissatisfied, 830.11 be irritable
bellyacher 713.4 protester, 766.3 dissatisfied person, 818.4 discourteous person, 830.5 sullen person
bellyaching 830.7 irritable
bellyband 137.10 band
belly button 291.2 central thing
belly dance 46.2 dance
belly dancer 51.28 dancer
belly flop 39.10 dive, 360.12 drop
belly-flop 360.5 dive
bellyful 144.2 fullness, 608.7 sufficiency, 610.2 overdoing it
belly habit 875.1 drug-taking
belly landing 73.5 flight
belly laugh 771.5 joke
belly pork 45.30 bacon
belly to belly 111.6 oppositely
belly up 236.12 impotent, 687.7 unprosperous, 743.2 insolvent
belly-up 722.17 unprofitable
Belmont y García 18 Sporting Personalities
Belmont Stakes 32.7 horseracing
be located 251.9 be situated
belonephobia 777 Phobias by Name
be long 269
belong 116.27 fit, 146.5 be included
belonger 665.5 member
belonging 148, 116.16 fitting, 146.8 included, 180.17 accompanying
belongings 227.2 visible effect, 723.4 possession, 725.4 possessions
belonging to 723.9 possessed

belonging to a party 665.10 political
belonging to the past 200.19 antiquarian
belong to 107.7 relate to, 146.5 be included, 148.12 be one of, 665.13 be a member, 847.14 be the duty of
belong to a class 107.9 have a relative position
belong to a school of thought 4.22 propound a philosophy
belong to a terrorist organization 713.8 cause mischief
belong to the IRA 713.8 cause mischief
belong to the past 202.16 be old
belong with 180.13 accompany
be lost 523.9 find unintelligible
be lost and gone 200.13 be past
be loud 423
beloved 821
be loved 821
beloved 815.16 popular, 821.11 loved one
beloved object 821.11 loved one
beloved one 784.4 likable person
beloved parent 826.6 object of endearment
be low 276
below 8.20 devilishly, 51.15 stage, 127.19 inferiorly, 155.30 behind, 276.10 low, 293.42 inclusively
below ground 399.10 buried
below par 123.3 unequal, 238.10 ill, 238.13 insufficient, 620.1 imperfect, 620.11 imperfectly, 624.22 sick, 752.7 at a discount
below sea level 276.7 lowland
below standard 127.19 inferiorly
below strength 620.2 incomplete
below the belt 26.16 professionally, 844.11 wrong
below the horizon 438.1 invisible, 458.8 fleetingly
below the mark 127.19 inferiorly, 358.10 not enough
below the poverty line 593.5 necessitous, 743.1 poor
below the salt 127.12 inferior
below the surface 458.8 fleetingly, 527.1 latent
below zero 55.55 cool
Bel Paese 45 Cheeses
Belsen 398.15 slaughterhouse
belt 63.8 machine element, 137.10 band, 249.1 region, 266.1 layer, 295.25 accessories, 313.3 circular thing, 330.13 hit, 330.13 blow, 390.3 atmospheric layers, 879.3 hit, 879.14 instrument of punishment
Beltane 10.16 religious festival
Belted Galloway 68 Breeds of Cattle
Belted Welsh 68 Breeds of Cattle
belter 49.23 singer
belt-holder 655.4 skilled person
belt loader 63.29 construction equipment
belt of cloud 55.20 cloud appearance
belt of rain 55.25 rain
belt out 49.39 sing, 431.15 sing out
belt printer 65.7 peripheral
belt sander 47.11 woodworking tool
Beltsville 68 Breeds of Fowl
belt-tightening 609.8 insufficiency, 743.6 insolvency
beltway 327.3 road, 334.2 detour
be lucky 589.12 take a chance, 686.6 be fortunate
beluga 80 Fishes
Beluga caviar 45.16 fish dish
belvedere 69.3 ornamental garden, 256.7 room, 435.9 viewpoint
be made of the right stuff 235.10 be powerful
be made redundant 218.7 stop working

be made up of 146.4 include, 148.11 consist of
be magnetic 340.11 attract
be malevolent 832
be marooned 98
be marvellous 786.10 be wonderful
be master of one's own ship 652.11 conduct oneself
be master of one's time 645.4 have leisure
be material 367
Bemba 1 Peoples, **5** Languages and Groups of Languages
be mealy-mouthed 538.24 pretend
be mediocre 783
be mentally sharp 380
be merciful 839.12 show mercy
be merciless 832.19 be pitiless
bemire 621.11 dirty
bemist 55.64 fog
be mixed up 133
be mixed up in 146.5 be included
bemoan 397.17 bury, 774.6 lament
be moderate 242, 124.9 be average
be modern 196.5 be present
be modest 810
be moist 391
be monastic 825
be monotonous 112
be moral 876
be more important 194.8 be before
be more than a match for 237.7 be strong
be motionless 325
be motivated 228
bemuse 460
be my guest 490.26 certainly
ben 85 Trees and Shrubs, 95.1, 275.3 mountain
be naive 658, 865
Benares 10.13 shrine
be natural 814.11 not stand on ceremony
bench 16.18 tribunal, 16.23 judge, 16.27 courtroom, 47.2 chair, 69.3 ornamental garden, 275.4 mountain range, 647.1 workshop, 704.7 terminate
Benchley 48 Writers
benchmark 65.17 computing term, 103.2 essential content
bench mark 250.2 exact location, 268.7 standard, 543.5 indicator
bench of judges 16.18 tribunal
bench seat 71 Motor Vehicle Parts
bench warrant 692.2 demand
bend 74 Knots, **311,** 20.3 fishing tackle, 33.6 motor racing terms, 35.5 play rugby, 63.31 load, 71.3 carriageway, 228.9 motivate, 234.4 tend, 276.8 be low, 286.1 obliqueness, 286.6 be oblique, 307.3 make shapeless, 310.1, 310.11 angle, 311.6 curve, 320.1, 320.7 fold, 335.5 twist, 335.12 deflect, 335.14 deviating course, 362.8 sit, 362.9 bow, 362.16 courtesy, 363.7 ring, 374.13 soften, 544.8 heraldic device, 673.4 succumb, 694.6 show obeisance to, 784.8 prefer, 808.10 knuckle under, 849.4 mark of respect, 849.19 take off one's hat to
bendability 374.8 softness
bendable 374.2 pliant
bend a rule 691.3 be lenient
benday 440.2 darkening
bend backward 362.7 lean
bender 812.1 celebration, 874.14 drinking bout
bend forks 11.24 experience psychic phenomena
bend forward 362.7 lean
bending 63.16 deformation, 286.4 oblique, 311.1 curvature, 335.21 indirect, 673.5 submitting, 784.6 liking, 849.4 mark of respect, 849.11 in a respectful stance

bending moment 63.15 *strength of materials*
bending the knee 849.4 *mark of respect*
bend in the road 311.3 *curved things*
bend one's elbow 874.8 *get drunk*
bend over 362.7 *lean*
bend over backwards 572.13 *be willing,* 644.8 *exert oneself,* 859.7 *be unselfish*
bendrofluazide 62 Medication
bend sinister 544.8 *heraldic device*
bend the knee 808.10 *knuckle under,* 849.19 *take off one's hat to*
bend the law 16.73 *be illegal*
bend the rules 708.4 *be permissive,* 858.8 *be dishonourable*
bend the truth 286.7 *deviate*
bend to one's will 688.18 *have authority*
be near 264
beneath 127.19 *inferiorly,* 276.10 *low*
beneath contempt 612.2 *obscure*
beneath notice 612.2 *obscure*
beneath the sod 399.12 *funereally*
Benedicite 10.8 *hymn*
benedick 823.10 *married man*
Benedick and Beatrice 821.10 *lovers*
Benedict Arnold 539.21 *traitor,* 540.15 *false person*
Benedictine 7 Members of Religious Orders
benediction 10.3 *rite of worship,* 10.9 *prayer,* 662.2 *support,* 837.2 *thanks,* 861.13 *benefit*
Benedict's test 58.5 *sugar test*
be needy 593
benefaction 729.1 *giving,* 767.4 *charity*
benefactor 662, 284.8 *supporter,* 632.3 *protector,* 640.3 *doer,* 710.8 *volunteer,* 729.4 *giver,* 755.9 *generous person,* 833.3 *philanthropist*
benefactress 632.3 *protector,* 662.15 *benefactor,* 833.3 *philanthropist*
benefice 725.1 *property*
beneficence 617.6 *worth,* 755.5 *generosity,* 833.1 *philanthropy,* 861.10 *kindness*
beneficent 662.35 *benevolent,* 755.1 *generous,* 831.7 *charitable,* 833.6 *philanthropic,* 861.3 *kind*
beneficently 831.11 *charitably,* 833.8 *philanthropically,* 861.23 *nicely*
beneficial 662, 861, 613.4 *profitable,* 615.1 *convenient,* 617.4 *worthwhile,* 623.2 *healthful,* 625.4 *hygienic,* 630.17 *remedial,* 721.15 *gainful,* 782.8 *desirable,* 819.12 *favourable*
beneficially 599.11 *usefully,* 617.11 *worthily,* 662.36 *helpfully,* 721.20 *gainfully,* 782.17 *desirably,* 819.20 *favourably,* 861.26 *usefully*
beneficiary 730, 845, 155.12, 195.5 *successor,* 513.4 *expectant person,* 662.12 *recipient,* 721.7 *gainer,* 721.15 *gainful,* 742.10 *wealthy person*
benefit 613, 613, 861, 51.11 *theatrical performance,* 130.4 *extra,* 599.6 *use,* 615.3 *convenience,* 615.6 *be convenient,* 617.10 *do good,* 662.1 *help,* 662.2 *support,* 662.4 *social assistance,* 662.21 *be helpful,* 721.1 *gain,* 721.5 *profit,* 721.9 *gain,* 729.2 *gift,* 729.3 *offering,* 746.12 *be profitable,* 831.4 *benevolent act,* 831.9 *be charitable,* 833.4 *welfare state,* 833.7 *be charitable,* 861.20 *do good*
benefit concert 712.3 *solicitation*
benefit game /12.3 *solicitation*
benefit gig 712.3 *solicitation*
benefit match 729.3 *offering*

benefit of the doubt 16.42 *acquittal*
benefit performance 51.11 *theatrical performance,* 729.3 *offering*
benefits 15.2 *industrial negotiations,* 228.5 *positive stimulus*
be negative 536
be neglectful 470
be neither fish nor fowl 158.18 *stand in the middle*
be neither one thing nor the other 158.18 *stand in the middle*
Benelux 13.5 *international trade*
be nervous 777.12 *be fearful*
Benét 48 Writers, 48 Poets
be neutral about 466.6 *be incurious*
benevolence 831, 572.9 *goodwill,* 588.1 *intention,* 617.6 *worth,* 662.10 *helpfulness,* 691.1 *leniency,* 708.1 *permission,* 729.1 *giving,* 751.8 *levy,* 755.6 *magnanimity,* 817.1 *courtesy,* 819.1 *friendship,* 835.1 *pity,* 839.2 *forgivingness,* 859.2 *unselfishness,* 861.10 *kindness,* 863.1 *virtue*
Benevolence 831
benevolent 662, 831, 284.9 *supportive,* 572.4 *helpful,* 691.4 *lenient,* 729.8 *giving,* 755.2 *magnanimous,* 817.7 *courteous,* 819.8 *friendly,* 833.6 *philanthropic,* 835.6 *pitying,* 839.5 *merciful,* 859.5 *unselfish,* 861.3 *kind,* 863.5 *virtuous*
benevolent act 831
benevolent despotism 12.1 *government,* 688.7 *type of rule*
benevolent disposition 831.1 *benevolence*
benevolently 662, 831, 691.6 *leniently,* 729.9 *as a gift,* 817.14 *courteously,* 817.15 *genteelly,* 819.17 *in friendship,* 833.8 *philanthropically,* 835.13 *pitifully,* 839.14 *forgivingly,* 859.9 *unselfishly,* 861.23 *nicely,* 863.9 *virtuously*
benevolentness 831.1 *benevolence*
benevolent person 831
be next to 267.3 *juxtapose,* 305.7 *be alongside*
Bengali 5 Languages and Groups of Languages
Bengalis 1 Peoples
Bengal light 439.8 *fire*
Benghazi 93 Cities
benighted 440, 205.6 *evening,* 436.12 *blind to*
benightedness 436.7 *figurative blindness*
benign 625.4 *hygienic,* 632.5 *safe,* 662.35, 831.6 *benevolent*
benignity 831.1 *benevolence*
benignly 831.10 *benevolently*
benign tumour 624.12 *cancer*
Benin 91 Countries
Benin bronzes 50 Non-Western Art
Beninese 7 Non-Christian Religions
benison 10.9 *prayer*
Ben Lomond 95.5 *British mountains*
Bennett 48 Writers, 48 Dramatists, 49 Musicians and Composers, 53 Comets
Ben Nevis 95.5 *British mountains,* 275.3 *mountain*
Benoit de Sainte-Maure 48 Poets
be no more 157.18 *come to an end,* 397.15 *die*
be non-partisan 783.15 *be impartial*
be nonresonant 428
be nonsense 506
benorylate 62 Medication, 62 Medication
be not all there 460.9 *lack intellect*
be nothing 536
be now 196.5 *be present*
bent 87 Grasses, 16.59 *stolen,* 16.60 *offending,* 234.2 *attitude,* 310.7 *angular,* 311.4 *curved,*

320.5 *folded,* 332.2 *bearing,* 362.23 *sedentary,* 485.2 *ability,* 527.5 *mysterious,* 584.2 *tendency,* 655.2 *aptitude,* 784.2 *inclination,* 858.7 *criminal*
bent back 808.2 *sycophancy*
bent bond 57.11 *chemical bond*
bent double 362.23 *sedentary*
Benten 8 Deities
bent grass 29.1 *golf*
benthal 277.12 *under*
Bentham 4 Philosophers
Benthamism 4.7 *school of thought,* 833.2 *public spiritedness*
Benthamite 4.11 *follower of a doctrine,* 4.14 *of a philosophy,* 833.3 *philanthropist*
benthazine penicillin 62 Medication
benthic 54.51 *oceanic,* 76.15 *of animals,* 97.7 *oceanic,* 277.12 *under*
benthonic 277.12 *under*
benthos 76.5 *aquatic animal,* 97.1 *sea,* 277.4 *deep thing*
benthoscope 277.4 *deep thing*
Bentley 48 Writers
bent upon 574.1 *resolute*
bentwood chair 47.2 *chair*
Benue-Congo 5 Languages and Groups of Languages
be null and void 100.12 *not exist,* 536.10 *be nothing*
benumb 236.8 *overpower,* 404.12 *anaesthetize,* 409.12 *make cold,* 761.7 *render insensitive,* 783.13 *make indifferent*
benumbed 641.3 *inactive,* 783.7 *indifferent*
Benz 52 Scientists
benzalkonium 62 Medication
Benzedrine 630.7 *tonic*
benzelthonium 62 Medication
benzene hexachloride 69.8 *weedkiller*
benzhexol 62 Medication
benzocaine 62 Medication
benzodiazepine 62 Medication
benzoic acid 62 Medication
benzoin 85 Tree Products
benzoylate 57.26 *react*
benzoylation 57 Types of Chemical Reaction
Benzozia 8 Deities
benzyl penicillin 62 Medication
be objective 783.15 *be impartial*
be oblique 286, 335.8 *sidestep,* 360.14 *slide*
be oblivious 404.11 *be unfeeling*
be obstinate 577, 669
be obvious 437.8 *be visible*
be of assistance 662.17 *help*
be off 345.5 *set out,* 349.33 *go away,* 591.8 *run away*
be offended 828
be officious 642.17 *meddle*
be offside 19.18 *be penalized*
be of help 662.17 *help*
be of no avail 236.6 *be powerless*
be of no help 236.6 *be powerless*
be often seen at 212.8 *frequent*
be of the opinion 497, 4.22 *propound a philosophy*
be of two minds 576.7 *be irresolute*
be of unsound mind 460.9 *lack intellect*
be old 202
be on 353.22 *menstruate*
be on a collision course 342.9 *converge*
be on a different wavelength 523.9 *find unintelligible*
be on a high 403.12 *awake*
be on an ego trip 805.26 *be too proud*
be on call 513.10 *wait,* 594.8 *prepare oneself*
be one 174
be on edge 777.12 *be fearful*
be one in the eye for 514.11 *amaze*
be one of 148, 146.5 *be included*
be oneself 720.7 *not observe,* 814.11 *not stand on ceremony*

be one's for the asking 660.15 *be easy*
be one's own fault 672.4 *serve one right*
be one's own man 570.14 *follow one's own will*
be one's own worst enemy 656.6 *act foolishly*
be one up on 657.5 *be cunning*
be on fire 408.15 *burn*
be on guard 28.5 *fence*
be on hand 253.12 *attend*
be on one's high horse 805.26 *be too proud*
be on one's toes 642.14 *push*
be on one's way 345.5 *set out*
be on sale 739.2 *be sold*
be on slippery ground 633.8 *be in danger*
be on stand-by 513.10 *wait,* 594.8 *prepare oneself*
be on tenterhooks 403.12 *awake*
be on the ball 403.12 *awake*
be on the beach 300.5 *border*
be on the cards 488.8 *be probable*
be on the crest of a wave 861.21 *do well*
be on the electoral roll 580.5 *vote*
be on the game 877.18 *prostitute*
be on the run 531.11 *conceal oneself*
be on the safe side 632.8 *be safe*
be on the same wavelength 667.6 *agree with*
be on the sideline 300.5 *border*
be on the skids 687.9 *be in trouble*
be on the special team 19.17 *kick*
be on the threshold 344.3 *approach*
be on the track 33
be on the waiting list for 513.10 *wait*
be on to 522.6 *understand*
be on to a good thing 686.6 *be fortunate*
be on top of the world 861.21 *do well*
be on trial 16.72 *stand trial*
be on visiting terms 815.12 *visit*
be opaque 443
be open 322, 537.29 *be truthful*
be open to criticism 852
be operational 230
be opposite 111, 536.8 *rebut*
be optimistic 775
be ostentatious 805
be out for the count 673.4 *succumb*
be out in front 194.8 *be before*
be out of danger 632.8 *be safe*
be out-of-doors 289.12 *be outside*
be out of one's depth 523.9 *find unintelligible,* 633.8 *be in danger,* 659.20 *be in difficulty*
be out of one's mind 460.9 *lack intellect*
be out of order 844.24 *go wrong*
be out of place 149.15 *be foreign*
be out of pocket 738.2 *shop,* 748.1 *expend*
be outside 289
be over 157.18 *come to an end,* 200.13 *be past*
be over and done with 200.13 *be past*
be overdrawn 687.10 *need money,* 753.11 *overpay*
be overpossessive 841.8 *distrust*
be painful 406, 764
be paralysed with fear 777.11 *be afraid*
be parsimonious 747
be part and parcel of 103.10 *be essential*
be partisan 305.9 *side with*
be part of 146.5 *be included,* 148.12 *be one of*
be past 200
be patient with 839.12 *show mercy*
be penalized 19
be penitent 867
be penny-wise and pound-foolish 656.6 *act foolishly*
be perfect 619
be periodical 187

be permanent **217**, 190.5 *be eternal*
be permissive **708**
be permitted **708**
be persuaded **586**
be pessimistic 536.7 *be negative*
be petrified 777.11 *be afraid*
be pipped at the post 722.9 *lose*
be piquant **413**
be pissed 828.11 *be angry*
be pitiless **832, 836**
be pleased with oneself 809.15 *be vain*
be plentiful 608.5 *about*
be pointed 380.14 *be sharp*
be poor **743**
be possessed by the spirit 7.19 *be religious*
be possessive 841.8 *distrust*
be possible **486**
be powerful **235**
be powerless **236**
be predictable **787**
be prejudiced 123.6 *be unjust*
be prepared **594**, 516.1 *foresee*, 594.8 *prepare oneself*
be present **196, 253**, 344.1 *arrive*, 457.11 *appear*
be present at 253.12 *attend*
be pressed for time 648.2 *make haste*
be prevalent 233.10 *be a prevailing influence*
be probable **488**
be proficient in 6.24 *know*
be profitable **721, 746**, 128.4 *increase*
be profound **277**
be prominent **318**
be proportionate to **107**
be prosperous **686**
be proud **805, 807**
be proud of **805**
be published **532**, 457.13 *occur*
be puffed up 809.15 *be vain*
be punished **840, 879**, 672.4 *serve one right*
be pure **134**
be pushed against the wall 571.16 *be compelled*
be put in one's place 806.24 *be humiliated*
be put out of countenance 806.24 *be humiliated*
be put to death 397.16 *meet one's fate*
be qualified **485**
bequeath **570**, 132.8 *leave*, 326.14 *bring back*, 725.9 *own property*, 728.3 *transfer property*, 729.5 *give*, 742.15 *make rich*, 755.11 *give*
bequeathable 728.5 *transferring*, 729.7 *given*
bequeathal 728.1 *transfer of property*, 729.1 *giving*, 730.1 *receiving*
bequeathed 728.5 *transferring*, 729.7 *given*, 749.6 *received*
bequeather 729.4 *giver*
bequeathing 728.5 *transferring*
bequest 132.5 *estate*, 326.10 *transferred thing*, 570.5 *will*, 721.5 *profit*, 728.1 *transfer of property*, 729.2 *gift*, 730.1 *receiving*, 749.4 *legacy*
be questioned **477**
be quick 648.8 *hurry up*
be quiet 218.6 *cease*, 422.1 *be silent*
be quite at home 660.17 *do easily*
be quits 672.3 *retaliate*
berakah 10.9 *prayer*
be rash **780**
berate **852**, 670.10 *criticize*
berated 852.34 *censured*
berating **852**
Beratron 56.94 *particle accelerator*
Berber **5** Languages and Groups of Languages
berceuse 433.2 *song*
Berdyaev **4** Philosophers
be ready 572.13 *be willing*
be ready and waiting 208.7 *be early*
be real **101**

be reasonable **463**
bereave 824.9 *widow*
bereavement 722.1 *loss*
be reborn **704**, 396.16 *live*, 629.4 *be restored*
be received 344.2 *reach*
be recognizable **522**
be recognized 233.8 *influence*
be reconciled 116.21 *be in accord*, 839.9 *forgive*
be redundant 641.4 *not act*
be reflected 427.9 *resonate*
be refreshed **651**
bereft 132.9 *remaining*, 722.16 *losing*
bereft of life 397.19 *dead*
be regular **110, 214**
be rejuvenated 220.8 *be transformed*
be relieved 22.7 *play baseball*
be religious **7**
be remembered **511**
be repeated **183**, 427.9 *resonate*
be repulsive **341**
be resigned 673.3 *submit*
be resolute **574**
be responsible 478.23 *answer for*
be responsible for 232.4 *be an instrument*
be restored **629**, 651.2 *be refreshed*
beret 295.15 *headgear*
be rewarded **878**
berg 54.39 *iceberg*
Berg **49** Musicians and Composers
bergamot **45** Herbs and Spices, **86** Fruits
Bergen **93** Cities
bergenia **84** Flowers and Flowering Plants
Bergius **52** Scientists
Bergmann's rule 1.10 *measurement*
bergschrund 34.5 *rock face*
Bergson **4** Philosophers
Bergsonian 4.11 *follower of a doctrine*, 4.14 *of a philosophy*
Bergsonism 4.7 *school of thought*
berg wind **55** Winds
beriberi 58.14 *vitamin deficiency disease*, 350.10 *scarcity*, 624.4 *disease*, 624.7 *tropical disease*
be rich **742**
be ridiculous **798**
be rife 233.10 *be a prevailing influence*
be right **843**
be rightly served 672.4 *serve one right*
Bering **97** Oceans and Seas
Bering Daylight Time 185.9 *time zone*
Bering Standard Time 185.9 *time zone*
be ripped-off 738.1 *purchase*
berk 502.5 *ignorant person*
Berkeley **4** Philosophers, **93** Cities
Berkelian 4.11 *follower of a doctrine*, 4.14 *of a philosophy*
Berkelianism 4.7 *school of thought*
berkelium **57** Chemical Elements
Berkshire **68** Breeds of Pig, **92** Counties
Berlin **4** Philosophers, **93** Cities, 93.6 *other cities*
Berlin Wall 136.6 *boundary*, 298.1 *interface*, 661.3 *barrier*
Berlin ware **44** Types of Ceramics
Berlioz **49** Musicians and Composers
berm 327.6 *path*
Bermejo **96** Rivers
Bermuda **98** Islands
Bermuda grass **87** Grasses
Bermudan 36.10 *sailing*
Bermudan rig 36.3 *parts of a sailing boat*
Bermudan-rigged 36.10 *sailing*
Bermuda Race 36.1 *sailing*
Bermuda rig **74** Sails
Bermuda shorts 295.9 **trousers**

Bermuda Triangle 529.6 *natural mystery*
Bern **93** Cities
Bernadine **7** Members of Religious Orders
Bernard of Chartres **4** Philosophers
Bernese Alps **95** Mountains
Bernese mountain dog **77** Breeds of Dogs
Bernhard **48** Writers
Bernice's Hair **53** The Constellations
Bernina **95** Mountains
Bernouilli effect **56** Named Laws
Bernoulli trial **52** Named Concepts
Bernreuter personality inventory 61.5 *psychological test*
Bernstein **49** Musicians and Composers
be rolling in it 686.5 *be prosperous*
be rooted to the spot 777.11 *be afraid*
be rough **375**
Berouth **8** Deities
berry 86.2 *botanical fruit*, 243.7 *produce*
berserk 241.6 *violent*, 510.12 *manic*, 670.23 *attacking*, 828.16 *angry*
berserker 244.6 *destroyer*
berth **74** Parts of a Ship, 47.6 *bed*, 248.5 *reserved space*, 251.4 *employment*, 344.4 *land*, 344.16 *stopover*
bertha collar 295.14 *neckwear*
berthage 248.5 *reserved space*
Berthelot **52** Scientists
Berthollet **52** Scientists
be rude **807**, 806.22 *shame*, 838.6 *be ungrateful*, 850.22 *show disrespect*
be rushed off one's feet 642.13 *be busy*
Berwick-on-Tweed **93** Cities
beryl **54** Minerals, 453.11 *green thing*, 454.6 *blue thing*
beryllium **57** Chemical Elements
Berzelius **52** Scientists
Bes **8** Deities
be sacked 218.7 *stop working*
be safe **632**
be sane **509**
be satisfied **765**
be saved 7.19 *be religious*, 220.10 *be converted*, 840.7 *be punished*
be saved by the bell 632.8 *be safe*
be seated 362.8 *sit*
beseech 10.20 *pray*, 712.6 *request*
beseeching 712.1 *request*, 712.9 *requesting*
beseechingly 712.12 *by request*
be seen 437.8 *be visible*, 526.4 *show oneself*
be self-conscious **810**
be selfish **860**
be self-restrained **869**
be sensitive **760**, 403.11 *sense*, 407.13 *be touched by*
be serious **772**
be servile **808**
beset 357.11 *overrun*, 659.16 *troubled*, 670.4 *besiege*
besetting 584.15 *habit-forming*
beset with perils 633.1 *dangerous*
be severe **690**
be sexually immoral **877**
be shallow **278**
be sharp **380**
be shrill **430**
be sick 349.15 *vomit*
be sick at heart 515.5 *be crestfallen*
be sick with disappointment 515.5 *be crestfallen*
beside **267**, 130.10 *additionally*
be side by side 267.3 *juxtapose*
beside oneself 762.4 *happy*, 828.16 *angry*
beside oneself with joy 762.4 *happy*

besides 130.10 *additionally*
beside the point 104.18 *extraneously*, 108.7 *illogical*, 108.12 *irrelevantly*, 358.10 *not enough*
besiege **670**, 676.13 *be at war*, 679.36 *combat*, 699.11 *detain*
besieged 699.15 *detained*
besieger 147.5 *excluded person*, 670.19 *attacker*, 679.1 *combatant*
besieging 676.8 *warfare*
be silent **422, 531**, 218.6 *cease*, 563.13 *be voiceless*
be similar **114**
be simple **556**
be simultaneous **198**
be situated **251**
be six feet under 397.15 *die*
be skilful **655**
be slave to a habit 584.18 *habituate*
beslime 622.11 *dirty*
be slow 193.3 *mistime*, 209.6 *be late*
be small 260.6 *be little*
besmear 622.11 *dirty*, 854.12 *defame*
besmeared 622.7 *dirty*
be smiled on by fate 106.14 *be comfortable*
besmirch 622.11 *dirty*, 631.15 *poison*, 854.12 *defame*
besmirched 622.7 *dirty*
besmirching 854.16 *defamatory*
be snooty 805.26 *be too proud*
be snowed in 409.11 *become cold*
be snowed under 409.11 *become cold*
be so 105.6 *be in a state of*
be sober **873**
be sociable **642, 815**
be social 815.11 *be sociable*
be so cold one's toes drop off 409.11 *become cold*
be soggy 391.15 *be moist*
be sold **739**
be solicitous **467**
besom 41.10 *curling*, 621.10 *cleaning object*
be sorry for 759.18 *feel for*
besotted 821.19 *enamoured*
be sour 415.8 *sour*
be spared 396.16 *live*
bespatter 389.33 *sprinkle*, 622.11 *dirty*, 854.12 *defame*
bespeak 520.10 *mean*
bespeak performance 51.11 *theatrical performance*
bespeckle 133.8 *mix*
bespectacled **435**
bespoil 631.15 *poison*
bespoke 165.20 *personalized*, 295.31 *styled*
bespoke clothes 295.1 *dress*
besprinkle 133.8 *mix*
Bessel functions **52** Named Concepts
Bessemer **52** Scientists
best **126, 617, 861**, 126.8 *be superior*, 619.1 *perfect*, 786.8 *wonderful*
be stable **225**
best-ball match 29.1 *golf*
best behaviour 813.1 *formality*
best bet 488.4 *chance*
best bib and tucker 295.1 *dress*, 813.4 *formal dress*
best bit 143.5 *largest part*
best chance 210.2 *opportunity*, 229.2 *chance*, 486.3 *strong possibility*, 589.5 *good chance*
best clothes 295.1 *dress*
bestead 613.10 *benefit*
bested 127.18 *outclassed*, 683.11 *defeated*
best effort 596.5 *attempt*
best end of neck 45.26 *lamb*
best ever 126.14 *best*, 617.8 *exceller*, 861.2 *best*
best-ever 617.2 *best*, 682.13 *successful*
best foot 617.6 *worth*
best forgotten 512.11 *forgotten*
best friend 180.11 *companion*, 233.5 *influential person*, 654.4 *adviser*, 784.4 *likable person*, 819.6 *close friend*

bestial 76.14 *animalian*, 241.6 *violent*, 832.11 *cruel*, 877.15 *unlawful*
bestiality 76.12 *zoophilism*, 241.2 *physical violence*, 832.2 *cruelness*, 877.7 *sexual assault*
bestiary 76.7 *legendary beast*
bestir oneself 642.12 *be active*, 644.8 *exert oneself*
best man 819.6 *close friend*, 823.7 *bridal party*
best of its kind 617.8 *exceller*
best one can do 596.5 *attempt*
best option 580.8 *choice*
bestow 116.30 *grant*, 662.29 *finance*
bestowable 728.5 *transferring*, 729.7 *given*
bestowal 116.9 *grant*, 662.6 *financial assistance*, 729.1 *giving*
bestow alms 729.6 *give to charity*
bestowal of love 821.6, 826.2 *courtship*
bestow a medal 878.9 *reward*
bestow an honorary degree 878.9 *reward*
bestowed 116.19 *granted*, 729.7 *given*
bestower 729.4 *giver*
bestowing 729.8 *giving*
bestow in marriage 823.16 *join in marriage*
bestow one's affections 821.26 *court*
bestow one's favours 821.29 *make love*
bestow one's hand upon 823.15 *marry*
bestow upon 729.5 *give*
best part 143.5 *largest part*, 611.3 *chief thing*
best people 617.7 *elite*
bestraddle 359.15 *mount*
be straight 312
best regards 817.3 *courtesies*
best respects 817.3 *courtesies*
bestride 135.10 *link*, 233.10 *be a prevailing influence*, 271.10 *span*, 275.15 *be high*, 356.11 *cross*, 359.15 *mount*
be strident 430
be strong 237
best room 256.7 *room*
be struck by 471.14 *have an idea*
be struck dumb 422.1 *be silent*, 563.14 *have difficulty speaking*
best seller 682.3 *successful thing*, 861.17 *good thing*
best-seller 532.6 *book publishing*, 560.5 *fiction*, 617.8 *exceller*, 655.3 *masterpiece*, 739.8 *merchandise*, 786.4 *wonder*
best-selling 617.2 *best*, 682.13 *successful*
best-selling author 786.5 *person of wonder*
best shot 596.5 *attempt*
best side 617.6 *worth*
best thing since sliced bread 617.8 *exceller*
be stubborn 373
be stuck in a groove 584.16 *have a habit*
be stuck on oneself 809.15 *be vain*
be stuck up 805.26 *be too proud*
be stumped 502.9 *be ignorant*
be stupid 460.9 *lack intellect*
best wishes 817.3 *courtesies*, 849.7 *respects*
be stylish 558.4 *be elegant*
be subjected to 701.8 *be subject to*
be subject to 701, 227.7 *follow from*
be submissive 673.4 *succumb*
be subsequent to 195.10 *succeed*
be subversive 693
be successful 682, 344.9 *achieve*
be suitable 667
be sullen 830, 818.8 *get angry*
be superfluous 610, 641.4 *not act*
be superior 126, 154.16 *take precedence*
be surprised 514
be suspicious 841.8 *distrust*

be sweet on 784.7 *like*, 821.23 *love*, 821.24 *be in love*
be swept aside 673.4 *succumb*
be swift 329
be sycophantic 853
bet 32.7 *horseracing*, 229.4 *chance*, 589.12 *take a chance*, 674.11 *contend*
beta blocker 62.4 *drug type*
Beta Centauri 53 Named Stars
be taciturn 566
Beta Crucis 53 Named Stars
beta decay 56.70 *radioactivity*
beta emitter 56.70 *radioactivity*
beta function 52.29 *mathematical function*
be taken 397.15 *die*
be taken aback 514.12 *be surprised*
be taken in 466.5 *not ask*
betake oneself 629.7 *resort*
be talkative 565
betamethasone 62 Medication
beta minus 124.6 *mediocrity*
beta particle 56.70 *radioactivity*
beta rays 56.70 *radioactivity*
be tasteless 412
beta test 61.6 *intelligence test*
betatron 56.94 *particle accelerator*
be taught 6.23 *learn*
be taught a lesson 672.4 *serve one right*
be tedious 788.6 *be boring*
Betelgeuse 53 Named Stars
betel nut 86 Nuts
betel palm 85 Trees and Shrubs
be temperate 810.14 *be modest*
be tenacious 138
bethanidine 62 Medication
be thankful 837.6 *be grateful*
be thankful for small mercies 837.7 *give thanks*
Bethe 52 Scientists
be the answer 478
be the author of 226.9 *be the cause of*
be the better for 613.11 *find useful*
be the boss 653.1 *manage*
be the case 537.27 *be true*
be the cause of 226
be the centre of attention 467.13 *attract attention*
be the duty of 847
be the field general 19.15 *play offence*
be the in thing 164.28 *prevail*
Bethel 10.13 *shrine*
be the last straw 684.6 *elaborate*
be the making of 617.10 *do good*, 627.1 *improve*, 662.29 *finance*
be the norm 124.9 *be average*
be the rage 164.28 *prevail*
be there 99.17 *exist*, 253.11 *be present*, 457.11 *appear*
be there in person 253.12 *attend*
be the result of 227.7 *follow from*
be the rule 164, 164.28 *prevail*, 584.17 *become a habit*
be the same 110
be the same as ever 217.5 *be permanent*
be the sport of wind and waves 366.25 *pitch*
be the tool of 808.10 *knuckle under*
be thirsty 392.18 *thirst*, 782.14 *be hungry*
Bethlehem 93 Cities, 93 Cities, 10.13 *shrine*
be thoughtless 468, 838.6 *be ungrateful*
be thrifty 756
be through with 684.5 *conclude*
be thrown out 22.7 *play baseball*
betide 589.10 *chance*
be timely 210
betimes 208.17 *early*
be tired 650.5 *be fatigued*
Betjeman 48 Poets
be to come 199.7 *be in the future*
be together 433.8 *harmonize*
betoken 473.15 *state*, 517.11 *predict*, 520.10 *mean*, 543.10 *signify*
be told 522.6 *understand*

be told by a little bird 528.15 *be informed*
bet on 488.10 *think likely*
bet one's bottom dollar on 488.10 *think likely*
be too clever for 657.5 *be cunning*
be too early 193.2 *be untimely*
be too good to be true 494.4 *overestimate*
be too grand to 805.26 *be too proud*
be to one's advantage 613.10 *benefit*
be too proud 805
be too quick for 657.5 *be cunning*
be touched by 407
be tough 378
Betpak-Dala 98 Deserts
be trained 485.14 *be qualified*
be transferred 728
be transformed 220
be transient 189
be transparent 442
betray 530, 483.13 *turn Queen's evidence*, 484.8 *reverse*, 491.21 *change*, 496.2 *detect*, 515.8 *be dishonest*, 526.3 *reveal*, 528.13 *inform on*, 539.27 *be false*, 578.3 *apostatize*, 657.5 *be cunning*, 693.16 *be subversive*, 858.9 *prove false*
betrayal 496.7 *detection*, 530.2 *divulgence*, 539.4 *false-heartedness*, 578.7 *apostasy*, 858.2 *faithlessness*
betrayed 515.10 *deceived*
betrayed hopes 515.1 *disappointment*
betrayer 528.10 *informer*, 530.4 *discloser*, 539.21 *traitor*, 540.15 *false person*, 578.9 *equivocator*, 832.8 *malefactor*, 864.9 *wicked person*
betraying 539.38 *treacherous*, 543.14 *signifying*, 858.6 *faithless*
betray one's hopes 515.6 *disappoint*
betray one's trust 515.8 *be dishonest*
be trendy 201
be triumphant 682.9 *be victorious*
betroth 823.15 *marry*
betrothal 714.1 *promise*, 715.1 *contract*, 821.8 *love affair*, 823.5 *wedding*
betrothed 135.12 *united*, 714.6 *someone promised*, 714.12 *promised*, 821.11 *loved one*, 823.22 *marriageable*
be true 537, 99.17 *exist*
be truthful 537
better 627, 32.15 *horse person*, 126.8 *be superior*, 126.12 *superior*, 142.8 *sound*, 216.8 *cause change*, 216.11 *changeable*, 336.8 *further*, 580.15 *chosen*, 617.1 *worthy*, 627.1 *improve*, 627.14 *improved*, 629.15 *cured*, 662.22 *improve*, 861.1 *good*, 861.20 *do good*
better advised 627.14 *improved*
better choice 580.8 *choice*, 627.8 *better thing*
better days 199.3 *future condition*
bettered 627.14 *improved*
better element 143.1 *part*
better half 114.5 *counterpart*, 180.12 *partner*, 823.8 *spouse*, 823.11 *married woman*
better idea 627.8 *better thing*
bettering 6.16 *educational*, 861.6 *beneficial*
better luck next time 589.15 *good luck*
betterment 6.1 *education*, 216.1 *change*, 336.15, 627.5 *improvement*, 722.2 *augmentation*, 861.13 *benefit*
better off 627.14 *improved*
better oneself 216.7 *be changed*, 627.2 *get better*
better than nothing 620.4 *ordinary*
better thing 627

better thought 627.8 *better thing*
better thoughts 155.7 *afterthought*, 578.6 *equivocation*
better time 197.1 *different time*
betting 32.7 *horseracing*
bettong 77 Placental Mammals
betty 45.35 *dessert*
be turned into 220.7 *convert into*
be turned on by 782.13 *like*
between 158.20 *in the middle*
between a rock and a hard place 158.22 *half and half*, 576.16 *irresolutely*, 633.4 *endangered*
between jobs 643.2 *not working*
between races 133.14 *in the midst*
between Scylla and Charybdis 158.22 *half and half*, 576.16 *irresolutely*, 633.4 *endangered*, 659.16 *troubled*
between the devil and the deep blue sea 158.22 *half and half*, 576.16 *irresolutely*, 633.4 *endangered*, 659.16 *troubled*
between the lines 527.4 *unsaid*
between the teeth 424.7 *faintly*
between times 185
between two chairs 633.4 *endangered*
between two fires 633.4 *endangered*
between two stools 659.16 *troubled*
between whiles 185.26 *all the time*, 189.9 *for the time being*
between you 529.15 *in secret*
betwixt and between 124.12 *mediumly*, 158.22 *half and half*
be two-faced 578.2 *equivocate*
Beulah 8 Deities
Beulah Speckled Face 68 Breeds of Sheep
be unable to do without 593.9 *find necessary*
be unable to pay 747
be unable to see something under one's nose 436.14 *be blind*
be unable to see straight 436.14 *be blind*
be unable to see the wood for the trees 436.14 *be blind*, 493.10 *misjudge*
be unaccustomed 585
be unadorned 690
be unappreciative 838.6 *be ungrateful*
be unbiased 271.12 *be broad-minded*, 783.15 *be impartial*
be uncertain 491
be unclear 307.3 *make shapeless*
be unconcerned 108
be undecided 522.6 *understand*
be undemocratic 123.6 *be unjust*
be under authority 12.13 *be governed*
be under cover 632.8 *be safe*
be under the impression 497.8 *be of the opinion*
be unequal 123
be unexplained 523
be unfaithful 576.9 *change sides*
be unfeeling 404
be unfinished 375
be unforgotten 511.15 *be remembered*
be ungrateful 838
be unhealthy 624
be unheard 421
be uniform 112, 116.25 *conform*, 667.8 *be compatible*
be unimportant 612
be unintelligible 523
be unjust 123, 493
be unlike 115.5 *be dissimilar*
be unlucky 211.6 *lose one's chance*, 687.9 *be in trouble*
be unmasked 496.5 *be discovered*
be unmoved 836.6 *be pitiless*
be unprepared 595
be unrelated 108
be unsatisfied 609
be unselfish 859
be unskilful 656
be unsocial 816
be untimely 193
be untruthful 538.21 *lie*

be unused 600.6 *stop using*
be unusual 215
be unwilling 573
be up against it 633.8 *be in danger*
be up and doing 239.2 *be full of vigour*, 642.12 *be active*
be up in arms 642.14 *push*
be up on 6.24 *know*
be up shit creek 105.7 *be in a predicament*
be upstanding 281.5 *be vertical*, 361.5 *arise*, 849.19 *take off one's hat to*
be up to 847.14 *be the duty of*
be up to something 592.13 *plot*
be upwardly mobile 627.2 *get better*
be upwind of 417.6 *have no smell*
be useful 613, 662, 232.4 *be an instrument*
be useless 614, 641.4 *not act*
be vague 307.3 *make shapeless*
be vain 807, 809, 805.26 *be too proud*
bevel 47.10 *carpenter's term*, 310.2 *obliquity*, 310.11 *angle*
bevel bearing 364.4 *vortex*
bevel gear 63.7 *gear*, 603.4 *machine*
bevelled 286.4, 310.8 *oblique*
bevelled edge 286.2 *oblique line*
bevel square 310.4 *angular measurement*
beverage 351.2 *drink*, 387.1 *fluid*, 874.13 *drink*
be verballed 16.80 *convict oneself*
Beverley 93 Cities
Beverly Hills 93 Cities
be vertical 281, 361.5 *arise*
be victorious 682
be vigilant 469.10 *be careful*
be violent 241
be virtuous 863
be visible 435, 437, 526
be voiceless 563
bevvied up 874.1 *drunk*
bevvy 874.13 *drink*
bevy 161 Collective Names for Birds and Animals, 77.21 *assemblage of mammals*, 161.11 *group*, 181.4 *group*
bewail 774.6 *lament*
bewail one's sins 867.4 *be penitent*
be walked 22.7 *play baseball*
be wanting 145.5 *be incomplete*
beware 591.24 *hands off*, 636.6 *be warned*, 636.10 *look out*, 781.5 *be cautious*
be warned 636
be wary 841.8 *distrust*
be wasted 607.1 *waste*
be wasteful 722
be weak 238
bewegt 49 Musical Terms
be well-preserved 623.5 *be healthy*
be well thought of 800.5 *have repute*
be well up on 688.22 *be an authority on*
be wet behind the ears 658.4 *be naive*
bewhiskered 375.3 *barbed*
be whole 142
be wicked 864
be widowed 824
bewig 295.35 *make clothing*
bewigged 295.29 *dressed*
bewilder 133.9 *mix up*, 460.10 *bemuse*, 491.20 *make uncertain*, 523.7 *be unintelligible*, 529.13 *mystify*, 659.23 *cause difficulties*, 786.10 *be wonderful*
bewildered 133.13 *mixed-up*, 491.3, 523.6 *confused*, 659.16 *troubled*, 722.18 *at a loss*, 786.6 *wondering*
bewildering 491.3 *confused*, 529.11 *mysterious*, 786.8 *wonderful*
bewilderingly 491.24 *confusingly*
bewilderment 491.12 *confusion*, 498.3 *incredulity*, 786.1 *wonder*
be willing 572, 642.14 *push*

be wise 507, 277.15 *be profound*, 655.10 *be skilful*
bewitch 11, 228.10 *manipulate*, 786.10 *be wonderful*, 821.28 *win the love of*
bewitched 11, 220.13 *converted*, 228.12 *motivated*, 586.20 *persuadable*, 821.19 *enamoured*, 827.10 *maledictive*
bewitcher 11.4 *witch*
bewitchery 11.3 *witchcraft*
bewitching 11.15 *witchlike*, 228.11 *motivational*, 586.19 *persuasive*
bewitchingly 228.14 *influentially*, 827.14 *damningly*
bewitchment 220.1 *conversion*, 228.2 *inducement*, 586.3 *incentive*, 821.2 *romantic love*
be within one's rights 843.13 *be right*
be with it 522.6 *understand*
be with one 522.6 *understand*
be without 593.7 *require*
be wonderful 786
be worried 777.14 *worry*
be worthless 618
be worthy 617
be worthy of 804.7 *be entitled to*
be wrapped up in oneself 809.15 *be vain*
be wrong 844
be years old 207.17 *age*
beyond all bounds 870.12 *self-indulgently*
beyond all expectation 682.16 *successfully*
beyond all reason 241.10 *violently*
beyond belief 487.2 *unbelievable*, 489.2 *questionable*, 498.7 *disbelieved*
beyond compare 126.14 *best*
beyond comprehension 184.2 *immeasurable*
beyond control 659.14 *troublesome*
beyond count 181.13 *numerously*
beyond criticism 126.14 *best*
beyond expectations 608.2 *plentiful*
beyond measure 181.8 *numberless*, 181.13 *numerously*, 610.8 *excessively*
beyond mortal ken 397.19 *dead*
beyond one 236.14 *powerlessly*, 523.4 *difficult*
beyond one's comprehension 523.4 *difficult*
beyond one's fondest dreams 682.16 *successfully*
beyond one's means 753.7 *dear*, 753.12 *dearly*
beyond one's power 236.14 *powerlessly*
beyond price 617.3, 753.8 *valuable*
beyond question 480.12 *assuredly*
beyond reach 263.10 *distantly*
beyond recall 512.11 *forgotten*, 776.5 *past hope*
beyond reckoning 184.2 *immeasurable*
beyond repair 628.13 *dilapidated*
beyond seas 97.11 *nautically*, 149.19 *abroad*
beyond the bounds of possibility 487.1 *impossible*
beyond the frontiers of knowledge 502.8 *unknown*
beyond the grave 397.19 *dead*
beyond the pale 147.11 *excluded*, 559.8 *indecorous*
beyond time 186
beyond worth 753.13 *valuably*
be young 206
bezant 43 Architectural Decoration, 741.12 *ancient coins*
bezel 71 Motor Vehicle Parts, 310.2 *obliquity*
bezique 42 Card Games
B-feature 243.5 *work of art*
Bhagavad-Gita 7.12 *religious text*
Bhairava 8 Deities
bhaji 45.49 *Indian dish*
bhakti 9.1 *worship*

bhangra 49.10 *world music*
Bhaskhara II 52 Scientists
Bhavachakra 396.8 *theories of life*
bhaya 49 Musical Instruments
bhikku 7.7 *monk*
bhikkunis 7.7 *monk*
bhikshu 7.3 *religious person*
bhindi 45 Vegetables
Bhopal 93 Cities
B horizon 54.36 *soil*
Bhubaneswar 93 Cities
bhuna 45.49 *Indian dish*
Bhutan 91 Countries
Bhutia 32 Breeds of Horse and Pony
B-lame 8 Deities
biannual 176.10 *two-sided*, 185.22 *periodic*, 187.8 *periodical*, 214.12 *cyclic*
biannually 185.30 *chronologically*, 187.13 *for specified periods*, 214.16 *cyclically*
Biarritz 93 Cities
bias 493, 25.1 *green bowling*, 52.57 *population*, 64.10 *electric potential*, 123.2 *injustice*, 228.10 *manipulate*, 233.8 *influence*, 234.2 *attitude*, 286.1 *obliqueness*, 309.1 *distortion*, 309.9 *distort*, 310.5 *viewpoint*, 335.6 *distort*, 335.13 *deviation*, 420.10 *sound quality*, 481.3 *prejudice*, 481.13 *prejudge*, 490.10 *conviction*, 493.3 *injustice*, 504.6 *fallibility*, 577.7 *opinionatedness*, 580.7 *preference*, 784.2 *inclination*, 785.1 *dislike*, 844.1 *unfairness*, 858.1 *improbity*
biased 310, 123.4 *unjust*, 234.5 *tending to*, 335.23 *oblique*, 481.10 *discriminatory*, 490.2 *convinced*, 493.8 *unjust*, 504.17 *mistaken*, 548.6 *misrepresented*, 784.6 *liking*, 844.11 *wrong*, 858.5 *dishonourable*
biased against 785.8 *disliking*
biased sample 52.57 *population*
bias slope 310.2 *obliquity*
bias voltage 64.10 *electric potential*
biathlon 18 Sporting Activities, 41.1 *skiing*, 41.2 *cross-country skiing*, 41.12 *ski*, 176.2 *double*
biathlon race 41.2 *cross-country skiing*
biathlon relay race 41.2 *cross-country skiing*
bib 295.23 *children's clothes*, 295.24 *part of garment*, 621.11 *cleaning cloth*, 874.8 *get drunk*
bibb 74 Rigging
bibber 351.12 *drinker*, 874.17 *drunkard*
bibbing 874.5 *drunken*
bibelot 612.9 *bauble*
Bible 7.12 *religious text*, 220.4 *medium of conversion*, 517.10 *cards*
Bible bash 7.20 *preach*
Bible-basher 7.5 *Christian*
Bible-bashing 7.2 *religiousness*, 7.15 *religious*
Bible oath 535.3 *vow*
Bible paper 604.3 *paper*
bible regal 49 Musical Instruments
Bible school 6.12 *educational institution*
Bible-worship 7.2 *religiousness*
Bible-worshipping 7.15 *religious*
Biblical 537.15 *true*
Biblical Aramaic 5 Languages and Groups of Languages
Biblical interpretation 5.12 *translation*
Biblical proverb 5.21 *catchword*
Biblical strong men 237.6 *muscleman*
Biblical truth 537.3 *the truth*
Biblicism 7 Christian Movements
bibliography 6.14 *school book*, 171.2 *table*
bibliolater 7.4 *religionist*, 9.6 *idolater*
bibliolatrous 9.10 *idolatrous*

bibliolatry 7.2 *religiousness*, 9.2 *idolatry*
bibliomancy 517.2 *divination*
bibliophagic 6.18 *educated*
bibliophile 459.8 *intellectual person*
bibulous 348.17 *absorbent*, 351.16 *drinking*, 874.5 *drunken*
bibulousness 874.11 *drinking*
bicameral 176.10 *two-sided*, 653.18 *parliamentary*
bicarbonate 57 Types of Compounds
bicarbonate of soda 57 Common Chemical Compounds, 62 Medication, 45.7 *basic ingredient*
bicarpellary 86.9 *of a fruit*
bice 454.5 *blueness*
bice-green 453.1 *green*
bicentenary 179.9 *treble figures*, 214.3, 214.13 *anniversary*, 511.5 *day to remember*, 812.5 *anniversary*
bicentennial 179.9 *treble figures*, 812.14 *centennial*
bicentennially 214.16 *cyclically*
biceps 237.1 *strength*, 316.2 *bulge*
bichir 80 Fishes
bicitrabin 49 Musical Instruments
bicker 117.4 *disagreement*, 117.14 *disagree*, 366.26 *flicker*, 473.13 *argue*, 666.5 *disagree*, 764.11 *quarrel*
bickering 117.4 *disagreement*, 117.10 *disagreeing*, 473.1 *argument*, 473.7 *arguing*, 666.1 *disagreement*, 666.9 *disagreeing*, 764.7 *dissension*
bicolour 456.6 *variegated*
biconditional 4.8 *philosophical term*
biconvex lens 56.29 *optical element*
bicuspid 380.11 *tooth*
bicycle 71, 176.2 *double*, 326.5 *means of transport*
bicycle bell 636.2 *danger signal*
bicycle chain 71.11 *bicycle part*, 330.16 *weapons*, 680.7 *blunt weapon*, 879.14 *instrument of punishment*
bicycle clips 71.11 *bicycle part*
bicycle courier 71.14 *cyclist*
bicycle-made-for-two 71.12 *bicycle*
bicycle part 71
bicycle path 327.6 *path*
bicycle pump 71.11 *bicycle part*
bicycle rickshaw 71.12 *bicycle*
bicycle tube 388.13 *gas balloon*
bicyclist 71.14 *cyclist*
bid 42.3 *card game terms*, 42.10 *play*, 479.1 *experiment*, 588.4 *formulated intention*, 596.1, 596.5 *attempt*, 710.1 *offer*, 710.3 *business offer*, 710.9 *offer*, 710.10 *offer to buy*, 710.17 *offered*, 712.1, 712.6 *request*, 737.3 *bargain*, 737.9 *bargaining*, 738.1 *purchase*, 738.7 *purchasing*
biddability 86.11 *good behaviour*
biddable 572.3 *amenable*, 660.13 *easygoing*, 673.5 *submitting*, 694.7 *obedient*, 861.4 *well-behaved*
bid defiance to 668.5 *defy*
bidder 14.3 *stockbroker*, 596.7 *attempter*, 738.12 *purchaser*
bidding 692.2 *demand*, 738.14 *buying*
bidding prayer 10.9 *prayer*
biddings 10.6 *Eucharist*
bide one's time 209.8 *delay*, 513.10 *wait*, 641.4 *not act*
bidet 258.12 *bath*, 389.11 *wash*, 621.6 *bath*
bid fair 234.4 *tend*, 517.11 *predict*, 714.9 *be auspicious*, 775.10 *inspire hope*
bid fair to 488.8 *be probable*
bid farewell 345.6 *part*

bid for 14.5 *invest*, 588.4 *formulated intention*, 588.10 *aim*, 738.1 *purchase*
bid for votes 710.5 *offer of public service*, 710.13 *be a candidate*
bid goodbye 345.6 *part*
bid good day 817.12 *greet*
bid price 14.2 *stock exchange*
bid up 738.1 *purchase*, 753.11 *overpay*
bid welcome 815.11 *be sociable*
Biedermeier 50 Western Art Styles and Movements, 47.7 *furniture style*
Biela 53 Comets
biennial 69.9 *garden plant*, 69.17 *botanical*, 83.2 *plant*, 83.14 *of plants*, 84.2 *flowering plant*, 176.10 *two-sided*, 185.22 *periodic*, 187.8 *periodical*, 214.12 *cyclic*
biennially 69.20 *horticulturally*, 83.24 *herbaceously*, 187.13 *for specified periods*, 214.16 *cyclically*
bier 71.6 *litter*, 399.4 *funeral objects*
Bierce 48 Writers
biff 330.3 *hit*, 330.13 *blow*
biflagellate 90.7 *algal*
bifocal 176.10 *two-sided*
bifocals 56.29 *optical element*, 435.10 *visual aid*
bifold 176.9 *two*
biforked 343.9 *branched*
biforking 343.4 *branching*
biform 176.10 *two-sided*
Bifrost 327.9 *bridge*
bifurcate 136.13 *diverge*, 176.10 *two-sided*, 176.16 *halve*, 310.7 *angular*, 343.9 *branched*, 343.14 *branch*
bifurcated 176.13 *half*
bifurcation 176.7 *halving*, 343.4 *branching*
big 259, 755, 611.5 *important*
bigamist 823.10 *married man*
bigamous 823.23 *monogamous*
bigamously 823.24 *matrimonially*
bigamy 823.3 *types of marriage*
big appetite 872.1 *gluttony*
Big Apple 249.10 *urban area*
big as a house 273.1 *thick*
big baby 238.4 *weakling*
big-bale silage 68.9 *animal feedstuff*
big bang 53.4 *cosmological model*, 208.3 *early stage*
Big Bang 14.2 *stock exchange*, 741.7 *finance*
big-bang theory 99.8 *creation*
big-bellied 259.16 *fat*
big-bottomed 259.16 *fat*
big boys 126.7 *the best people*
Big Brother 233.6 *group influence*, 611.4 *bigwig*, 632.2 *protection*, 688.4 *governance*, 690.4 *strict person*, 696.4 *absolute ruler*, 696.8 *the power structure*
big bucks 181.2 *multitude*, 741.3 *fortune*, 742.6 *money*
big bud mite 69.12 *pests and diseases*
big but 611.4 *bigwig*
big cat 77.10 *cat*
big cheese 126.5 *superior*, 233.5 *influential person*, 611.4 *bigwig*, 653.15 *manager*, 688.10 *person of authority*, 696.5 *company leader*
big Chief 611.4 *bigwig*
big Daddy 611.4 *bigwig*
big day 611.2 *important matter*
big deal 494.2 *overestimate*, 611.2 *important matter*
Big Dick 179.6 *ten*
big dooley 611.4 *bigwig*
big drum 811.12 *magniloquence*
big-eared 420.12 *eared*
big earner 742.10 *wealthy person*
big-ears 465.4 *meddler*
big eater 350.18 *eater*, 872.4 *glutton*
big enchilada 126.5 *superior*, 611.4 *bigwig*

big fish 611.4 *bigwig*
big fish in a small pond 126.5 *superior*
bigfoot 529.6 *natural mystery*
Bigfoot 76.7 *legendary beast*, 95.3 *mountaineer*
big freeze 55.32 *freeze*
big game 37.5 *game*, 76.1 *animals*
big-game 37.8 *shooting*
big-game fisherman 20.6 *angler*
big-game fishing 18 Sporting Activities, 20.1 *angling*, 80.7 *fishing*
big-game hunt 590.2 *chase*
big-game hunter 37.4, 77.24 *hunter*, 590.6 *hunter*
big-game hunting 37.2 *hunting*, 77.23 *mammal hunting*
bigger 261
bigger and better 128.6 *increasing*, 128.8 *increasingly*
bigger and bigger 128.8 *increasingly*
biggest slice of the cake 143.5 *largest part*
biggie 611.4 *bigwig*
big gun 126.5 *superior*, 611.4 *bigwig*, 696.5 *company leader*
big guy 611.4 *bigwig*
big hand 851.5 *acclaim*
bighead 805.13 *proud person*
big head 809.7 *vain person*
big-headed 805.22 *boastful*, 809.8 *vain*
big-headedness 805.10 *boastfulness*, 809.1 *vanity*
big-hearted 831.7 *charitable*, 833.6 *philanthropic*, 859.5 *unselfish*
big-heartedly 831.11 *charitably*, 859.9 *unselfishly*
big-heartedness 831.2 *charity*, 859.2 *unselfishness*
big hit 682.1 *success*
bighorn 77 Placental Mammals
Bighorn Mountains 95.4 *US mountains*
bight 98.9 *inlet*
Bight of Benin 98.9 *inlet*
big jobs 353.5 *faeces*
Big John 611.4 *bigwig*
big letter 5.15 *type style*
Big Mac 45.11 *sandwich*
big man 611.4 *bigwig*
big man on campus 611.4 *bigwig*
bigmouth 564.10 *speaker*, 565.1 *talkativeness*, 565.4 *talker*, 668.4 *defiant person*
big-mouthed 423.6 *loud*, 528.16 *informative*, 565.6 *effusive*
big name 611.4 *bigwig*
bigness 259
big news 611.2 *important matter*
big noise 126.5 *superior*, 233.5 *influential person*, 611.4 *bigwig*
bigoli 45 Types of Pasta
bigot 481, 7.4 *religionist*, 490.11 *opinionist*, 493.5 *misjudging person*, 577.8 *obstinate person*, 761.5 *insensitive person*, 820.5 *hostile person*, 822.9 *hater*
bigoted 7.15 *religious*, 481.10 *discriminatory*, 490.2 *convinced*, 493.8 *unjust*, 577.4 *set*, 690.8 *severe*, 822.11 *racist*
bigotry 7.2 *religiousness*, 481.3 *prejudice*, 490.10 *conviction*, 493.3 *injustice*, 577.7 *opinionatedness*, 690.1 *severity*, 820.1 *enmity*, 822.3 *race hatred*
bigotted 820.7 *intolerant*
big person 259
big play 611.3 *chief thing*
big price tag 753.1 *high price*
big school 702.2 *the inside*
big shot 233.5 *influential person*, 611.4 *bigwig*, 653.15 *manager*, 688.10 *person of authority*, 696.5 *company leader*, 800.2 *person of repute*
big smoke 249.10 *urban area*
big spender 607.6 *waster*, 757.6 *spendthrift*

big stick 228.4 *negative stimulus*, 586.8 *incentive*, 695.3 *coercive methods*, 879.14 *instrument of punishment*
big thing 259
big-time operator 611.4 *bigwig*
big timer 611.4 *bigwig*
big toe 407.7 *sense organ*
big top 51.14 *theatre*, 293.7 *overhead covering*, 811.14 *show*
big tree 85 Trees and Shrubs
big undertaking 597.2 *undertaking*, 659.3 *difficult task*
bi-guy 401.10 *bisexual*
big wave 375.9 *broken water*
big wheel 233.5 *influential person*, 611.4 *bigwig*, 688.10 *person of authority*, 696.5 *company leader*
big white Chief 611.4 *bigwig*
bigwig 611, 126.5 *superior*, 233.5 *influential person*, 653.15 *manager*, 688.10 *person of authority*, 696.5 *company leader*, 805.13 *proud person*
big with 245.16 *reproductive*, 246.5 *fertile*
big with fate 517.15 *presageful*
Bihari 5 Languages and Groups of Languages
bijou 260.7 *little*
bike 71.12 *bicycle*, 71.13 *motorcycle*
biked 70.5 *transportable*
biker 71.14 *cyclist*
bike rider 71.14 *cyclist*
bikie 71.14 *cyclist*
biking 70.5 *transportable*
bikini 39.8 *swimwear*, 295.21 *beachwear*
bikini-clad 296.10 *in dishabille*
Bikol 5 Languages and Groups of Languages
Bil 8 Deities
bilateral 109.5 *interconnected*, 176.10 *two-sided*, 305.6 *side*, 715.7 *contractual*
bilaterally 109.10 *reciprocally*, 715.8 *contractually*
bilateral paralysis 624.17 *nervous disorder*
bilateral symmetry 308.1 *symmetry*, 308.2 *symmetry operation*
Bilbao 93 Cities
bilberry 86 Fruits
bilbo 680.8 *sharp weapon*
bilboes 699.5 *means of restraint*, 879.14 *instrument of punishment*
Bilderdijk 48 Writers
bile 352.2 *secreted substance*, 415.2 *unpalatability*, 415.4 *spleen*, 829.1 *irascibility*, 830.3 *irritableness*, 832.4 *bitterness*
Bile 8 Deities
bile acid 58.6 *lipid*
bileful 828.15 *resentful*
bile pigment 58.18 *pigment*
bilge 74 Parts of a Ship, 36.3 *parts of a sailing boat*, 132.2 *residue*, 280.2 *foot*, 506.1 *nonsense*, 521.4 *senseless talk*, 614.6 *refuse*, 622.5 *swill*
bilge water 622.5 *swill*
bilharziasis 624.7 *tropical disease*
bilingual 5.2 *linguist*, 5.38 *linguistic*, 176.10 *two-sided*, 524.17 *translational*, 564.19 *speaking*
bilingual dictionary 5.28 *dictionary*
bilingualism 5.1 *linguistics*, 176.3 *duality*
bilingually 5.48 *linguistically*
bilingual text 524.4 *translation*
bilious 415.7 *splenetic*, 452.4 *yellow-faced*, 453.6 *sick*, 624.21 *unhealthy*, 828.15 *resentful*, 829.4 *irascible*, 830.7 *irritable*
biliously 828.17 *resentfully*, 829.9 *irascibly*
biliousness 415.4 *spleen*, 452.6 *yellowness*, 624.8 *indigestion*, 830.3 *irritableness*
bilirubin 58.18 *pigment*
biliverdin 58.18 *pigment*

bilk 515.7 *thwart*, 539.30 *be fraudulent*, 736.16 *act dishonest*, 745.8, 747.7 *not pay*
bilked 515.9 *disappointed*
bilker 539.17 *cheat*, 745.6 *debtor*, 747.6 *nonpayer*
bill 171, 751, 51.6 *scene*, 51.11 *theatrical performance*, 51.36 *dramatize*, 78.16 *avian anatomy*, 98.5 *peninsula*, 169.4 *mathematical result*, 171.8 *list*, 526.8 *showplace*, 532.9 *advertisement*, 532.16 *publicize*, 544.3 *means of identification*, 545.1 *record*, 680.8 *sharp weapon*, 712.7 *demand*, 730.3 *acknowledgment of payment*, 741.14 *paper money*, 744.1 *credit*, 745.5 *amount owing*, 750.4 *statement*, 750.9 *settle accounts*
billabong 96.1 *river*
bill and coo 821.27 *kiss*, 826.8 *court*
billboard 532.9 *advertisement*
bill collector 730.7 *collector*
bill discounting rate 745.3 *loan*
billed 750.11 *accounted*
billet 43 Architectural Decoration, 17.1 *military affairs*, 218.5 *resting place*, 250.9 *locate*, 251.4 *employment*, 256.1 *habitat*, 344.16 *stopover*
Billetdoux 48 Dramatists
billet-doux 821.15 *love item*, 826.3 *love token*
billeted 256.14 *inhabiting*
billfold 741.20 *money store*
billhook 85.7 *timber production*, 380.9 *sharp-edged thing*, 603.2 *garden tool*
billiard 24
billiard ball 376.8 *smooth thing*
billiard cloth 24.1 *billiards*
billiard cue 330.15 *ram*
billiards 24
Billiards 24
billiards club 24.1 *billiards*
billiards game 42.1 *game*
billiards play 24
billiards player 24
billiard spot 24.3 *English billiards*, 24.5 *snooker*
billiard table 24.1 *billiards*, 282.3 *flat thing*, 376.8 *smooth thing*
Billie Jean King 40.7 *famous tennis players*
billing and cooing 821.6 *courtship*, 821.14 *communication of love*, 826.1 *endearment*
billingsgate 5.19 *swearword*, 827.1 *curse*
Billingsgate 740.1 *market*
billion 169.3 *large number*, 179.11 *million*, 181.7 *myriad*
billionaire 179.11 *million*, 686.4 *prosperous person*, 721.7 *gainer*, 742.10 *wealthy person*
billions 181.2 *multitude*, 741.3 *fortune*
billionth 173.4 *less than one*, 179.22 *millionth*
bill of exchange 223.3 *something in exchange*, 741.14 *paper money*
bill of fare 171.4 *bill*
bill of lading 171.4 *bill*, 544.3 *means of identification*
bill of mortality 397.12 *death count*
Bill of Rights 845.3 *prerogative*
billon 133.2 *mixed thing*, 741.16 *bullion*
billon coinage 741.13 *coinage*
billow 97, 97.3 *wave*, 316.5 *be convex*
billowing 97.7 *oceanic*, 316.1 *convexity*, 316.4 *convex*
billowy cloud 55.20 *cloud appearance*
bill poster 532.10 *publicizer*
bills 745.1 *debt*
bill sticker 532.10 *publicizer*
Bill Tilden 40.7 *famous tennis players*

billy goat 68.8 *livestock*, 77.17 *male mammal*, 401.16 *male animal*, 419.2 *something that makes an unpleasant smell*
Biloxi 93 Cities
bimbo 502.5 *ignorant person*
Bimbo-gami 8 Deities
bimetallism 14.1, 741.7 *finance*
bimodal distribution 52.59 *probability distribution*
bimolecular 57.38 *reactive*
bimolecular reaction 57.14 *chemical reaction*
bimonthly 214.12 *cyclic*, 214.16 *cyclically*
bin 49 Musical Instruments, 120.3 *container*, 258.11 *vessel*, 349.13 *throw away*, 510.8 *mental hospital*, 621.10 *cleaning object*, 727.4 *wastebin*
binary 52.71 *numerical*, 57.35 *combined*, 176.9 *two*
binary code 65.10 *character*
binary compound 57.7 *chemical compound*
binary digit 52.9 *numeral*
binary notation 52.8 *number system*
binary number 52.8 *number system*
binary star 53.9 *constellation*
binary system 52.8 *number system*, 169.1 *number*
bind 137, 28.3 *fencing movements*, 35.5 *play rugby*, 135.10 *link*, 137.11 *connect*, 161.38 *group*, 225.7 *make stable*, 293.25 *wrap*, 300.5 *border*, 301.6 *wrap*, 323.11 *restrain*, 371.9 *make dense*, 485.16 *specify*, 629.1 *repair*, 630.20 *doctor*, 659.5 *predicament*, 661.10 *restrain*, 695.6 *compel*, 699.12 *gag*, 788.2 *boring thing*, 847.17 *impose a duty*
binder 68.10 *farm tool*, 137.6 *line*, 293.4 *wrapping*
binding 41.5 *ski equipment*, 137.6 *line*, 293.4 *wrapping*, 371.7 *condensed*, 571.10 *obligatory*, 629.8 *repair*, 695.9 *compelling*, 847.12 *obligatory*
binding agreement 715.1 *contract*
binding energy 56.65 *atom*, 235.4 *energy*
binding over 879.7 *punishment*
binding twine 137.6 *line*
bind oneself 715.5 *contract*
bind over 879.1 *punish*
bind up 629.1 *repair*
bind up one's wounds 629.6 *cure*
bindweed 84 Flowers and Flowering Plants
bin end 157.8 *tail*
bin ends 143.8 *bits and pieces*
Binet test 61.6 *intelligence test*
binge 350.2 *appetite*, 350.22 *eat well*, 812.1 *celebration*, 870.11 *overindulge*, 872.5 *be greedy*, 874.14 *drinking bout*
bingeing 350.2 *appetite*, 872.1 *gluttony*, 872.6 *gluttonous*
binger 872.4 *glutton*
binghi 91 Names for Inhabitants
bingo 229.2 *chance*, 589.3 *equal chance*, 589.15 *good luck*
biniou 49 Musical Instruments
binman 727.6 *rubbish collector*
binnacle 74.5 *navigation*, 653.5 *guide*
binned 258.20 *containing*
binocular 176.10 *two-sided*, 435.20 *visual*
binoculars 37.3 *hunting equipment*, 56.32 *optical instrument*, 176.2 *double*, 435.10 *visual aid*
binomial 52.25 *algebraic expression*, 52.76 *functional*
binomial distribution 52.59 *probability distribution*
binomial expression 52.25 *algebraic expression*
binomial nomenclature 59.17 *taxonomy*
binomial series 52.20 *sequence*

binomial theorem 52 Theorems and Laws
bint 402.9 *woman considered as a sex object*
binturong 77 Placental Mammals
bioaeronautics 73.2 *aeronautics*
bioastronautics 53.29 *astronautics*
Bío-Bío 96 Rivers
biochemical 58, 57.31 *chemical*, 59.20 *biological*
biochemical genetics 59.11 *genetics*
biochemically 58, 59.29 *biologically*
biochemical taxonomy 58.1 *biochemistry*
biochemist 58, 59.19 *life scientist*
biochemistry 58, 57.1 *chemistry*, 59.1 *life science*, 59.6 *cell biology*, 60.3 *medical specialty*
Biochemistry 58
biocytin 58.12 *coenzyme*
biodegradable 136.19 *separable*, 141.5 *disintegrated*, 189.7 *impermanent*
biodynamic farming 68.1 *agriculture*
bioecology 59.1 *life science*
bioelectricity 56.42 *electricity*
bioenergetic 58.26 *biochemical*
bioenergetics 58, 58.1 *biochemistry*, 61.3 *psychiatric treatment*
bioengineering 63.1 *engineering*
biofeedback 11.10 *psychic phenomenon*, 61.3 *psychiatric treatment*
biogenesis 245.3 *propagation*
biogenetic 396.14 *biotic*
biogenetical 396.14 *biotic*
biogenetics 59.1 *life science*
biographer 3.3 *historian*, 48.14 *author*, 545.9 *recorder*, 560.10 *descriptive writer*
biographical 3.19 *chronicled*, 48.19, 560.12 *narrative*
biographical dictionary 5.28 *dictionary*
biographically 3.25 *reportedly*
biographical record 3.6 *biography*, 545.1 *record*
biographical sketch 48.4 *non-fiction*
biography 3, 48.4 *non-fiction*, 396.11 *life story*, 545.1 *record*, 560.4 *factual account*
biologic 396.14 *biotic*
biological 59, 396.14 *biotic*
biological anthropology 1.1 *anthropology*
biological classification 59.17 *taxonomy*
biological clock 187.5 *recurrent period*, 192.6 *clock*, 396.4 *biological function*
biological coloration 444.1 *colour*
biological death 397.1 *death*
biological function 396
biologically 59, 396.22 *vitally*
biological molecule 59.12 *molecular biology*
biological science 59.1 *life science*
biological shield 56.73 *nuclear reactor*
biological warfare 676.8 *warfare*
biological weapon 631.10 *warfare*
biologist 59.19 *life scientist*
biology 59.1 *life science*, 367.6 *natural science*, 396.7 *studies of life*
bioluminescence 56.24 *light emission*
biomass 410.8 *renewable energy*
biomedicine 60.3 *medical specialty*
biometric 59.20 *biological*, 268.16 *micrometric*
biometrics 1.10 *measurement*, 268.2 *micrometry*
biometrist 59.19 *life scientist*
biometry 59.1 *life science*, 268.2 *micrometry*, 396.5 *life cycle*
biomolecular 58.26 *biochemical*
biomolecule 58.1 *biochemistry*
bionic 59.20 *biological*, 400.12 *human*

bionic man 400.8 *humanlike machine*, 786.5 *person of wonder*
bionics 59.1 *life science*
bionic woman 400.8 *humanlike machine*
bionomic 59.20 *biological*
bionomics 59.1 *life science*
biophysical 59.20 *biological*
biophysicist 59.19 *life scientist*
biophysics 56.4 *experimental physics*, 59.1 *life science*
bioplasm 59.7 *cell*, 396.2 *living matter*
bioplasma 11.10 *psychic phenomenon*
bioplast 396.2 *living matter*
bioplastic 396.14 *biotic*
biopsy 60.7 *diagnosis*
biorhythm 187.5 *recurrent period*, 214.2 *cycle*
biorhythmic 214.12 *cyclic*
biosphere 54.5 *earth*, 59.2 *living world*, 390.2 *aerosphere*
biosynthesis 57.16 *synthesis*, 58.1 *biochemistry*
biosynthetic 58.26 *biochemical*
biosynthetically 58.27 *biochemically*
biosystematic 59.28 *taxonomic*
biosystematics 59.17 *taxonomy*
biota 59.2 *living world*
biotechnological 59.20 *biological*
biotechnology 57.16 *synthesis*, 58.1 *biochemistry*, 59.1 *life science*, 59.12 *molecular biology*
biotic 396, 59.21 *living*
biotical 396.14 *biotic*
biotically 396.22 *vitally*
biotic potential 246.2 *productiveness*
biotin 58.13 *vitamin*
biotite 54 Minerals
Biot–Savart law 56 Named Laws
biotype 59.11 *genetics*
bipartisan 116.20 *agreeable*, 665.10 *political*
bipartisanship 664.2 *fellowship*
bipartite 136.15 *separate*, 176.10 *two-sided*
bipartition 176.7 *halving*
biped 76.4 *type of animal*, 176.2 *double*, 176.10 *two-sided*
bipedal 76.15 *of animals*, 176.10 *two-sided*
biperiden 62 Medication
bipinnate 83.18 *of leaves*
biplane 176.2 *double*
BIPM 75.4 *standard*
bipod 176.2 *double*
bipolar transistor 64.19 *transistor*
biquintile 310.4 *angular measurement*
birch 85 Trees and Shrubs, 879.3 *hit*, 879.14 *instrument of punishment*
birchbark 36.12 *canoeing*
birchbark canoe 36.6 *canoeing*
birching 879.12 *corporal punishment*
birch-rod 879.14 *instrument of punishment*
bird 40.11 *badminton equipment*, 76.4 *type of animal*, 76.6 *flying animal*, 206.8 *young woman*, 402.9 *woman considered as a sex object*, 431.7 *cry of disapproval*, 699.4 *detention*, 702.4 *prison sentence*, 815.10 *social animal*, 821.9 *lover*
birdbanding 78.19 *ornithology*
birdbath 69.3 *ornamental garden*
bird box 78.14 *nest*
birdbox 78.19 *ornithology*
birdbrain 460.3 *unintelligent person*, 508.3 *foolish person*
bird-brained 508.5 *foolish*
birdcage 78.19 *ornithology*
bird cage 256.12 *stall*
birdcage 702.3 *prison cell*
birdcall 78.18 *birdsong*
bird call 432.2 *bird song*
bird-catcher 590.6 *hunter*
birder 78.21 *ornithologist*
bird food 350.8 *animal food*
bird god 78.9 *fabulous bird*
birdhouse 78.14 *nest*, 78.19 *ornithology*, 256.12 *stall*

birdie 29.2 *golfing terms*, 78.1 *birds*
bird in the hand 723.1 *possession*
birdlife 78.1 *birds*
birdlike 78.23 *avian*
birdlime 138.3, 394.2 *adhesive*, 539.13, 539.33 *snare*
bird nest 634.3 *animal shelter*
bird of ill omen 517.7 *bad-luck sign*, 636.1 *warning*
bird of paradise 78 Birds
Bird of Paradise 53 The Constellations
bird-of-paradise flower 84 Flowers and Flowering Plants
bird of passage 78.1 *birds*, 189.2 *transient thing*
bird of peace 78.1 *birds*
bird of prey 78, 398.13 *animal killer*, 590.6 *hunter*
bird reserve 78.19 *ornithology*
birds 777 Phobias by Topic, **78** Birds
Birds 78
bird sanctuary 78.19 *ornithology*
bird scarer 49 Musical Instruments, 68.14 *pest control*
birdseed 83.9 *seed*, 350.8 *animal food*
bird's-eye 164.15 *general*
bird's-eye view 50.10 *art subject*, 142.3 *whole situation*, 164.7 *global view*, 435.9 *viewpoint*, 562.1 *summary*
birdsmouth joint 47.10 *carpenter's term*
birdsnest 41.14 *ski*
bird's-nest fern 88 Ferns
bird's-nest fungus 89 Fungi
birdsnesting 41.1 *skiing*
bird's-nesting 78.20 *bird sport*
bird's nest orchid 84 Flowers and Flowering Plants
bird's nest soup 45.13 *soup*
birds of a feather 110.1 *sameness*, 114.6 *couple*, 116.5 *conformity*, 138.1 *adhesion*, 819.6 *close friend*
birdsong 78
bird song 432
bird spider 82 Arachnids
bird sport 78
bird strike 73.7 *miscellaneous aviation terms*
bird table 69.3 *ornamental garden*
birdwatcher 78.21 *ornithologist*, 435.11 *observer*
birdwatching 42 Hobbies and Pastimes, 78.19 *ornithology*
birdwood 875.6 *drug*
birdy 78.23 *avian*
birefringence 56.27 *polarized light*
bireme 679.25 *historical naval ships*
biretta 7.11 *vestment*, 295.15 *headgear*
Birkhoff 52 Scientists
Birman 77 Breeds of Cats
Birmingham 93 Cities, **93** Cities, 93.4 *British cities*
Birmingham accent 5.26 *dialect*
birth 99.8 *creation*, 156.4 *conception*, 163.8 *genealogy*, 201.4 *beginning*, 245.3 *propagation*, 322.11 *beginning*, 396.4 *biological function*, 396.5 *life cycle*, 457.1 *appearance*
birth certificate 544.3 *means of identification*, 545.2 *certificate*
birth chart 11.9 *divination*
birth control 247
birthday 185.11 *date*, 214.6 *annually celebrated day*, 812.5 *anniversary*
birthday cake 45.36 *cake*
Birthday Honours 878.1 *reward*
birthday party 815.5 *party*
birthday present 729.2 *gift*
birthday suit 294.3 *nakedness*, 296.2 *nudity*
birthmark 149.2 *impurity*, 456.4 *maculation*, 544.3 *means of identification*, 624.13 *skin disease*
birth pangs 245.7 *obstetrics*

birthplace 91.6 *native land,* 226.2 *source,* 256.3 *home*
birth rate 245.3 *propagation*
birthright 194.4 *claim to priority,* 730.1 *receiving,* 749.4 *legacy,* 804.1 *right,* 845.3 *prerogative*
births, marriages, and deaths 528.4 *mass communication*
biryani 45.49 *Indian dish*
bis 49 Musical Terms, 183.24 *again*
bisacodyl 62 Medication
bisbigliando 49 Musical Terms
biscuit 45.39, 45.39 *loaf,* 350.7 *food,* 45.49 *loaf,* 350.7
biscuit barrel 45.4 *kitchen container*
biscuit firing 44.5 *ceramic process*
biscuit ware 44.1 *ceramics*
bise 55 Winds
bisect 52.97 *align,* 124.10 *make average,* 136.11 *divide,* 143.10 *part,* 158.17 *average,* 176.16 *halve,* 731.4 *allot*
bisected 176.13 *half*
bisection 158.4 *midline,* 176.7 *halving*
bisection search 65.17 *computing term*
bisector 52.37 *line,* 122.7 *dividing line,* 176.8 *half*
bisexual **401,** 176.10 *two-sided,* 245.15 *reproductive,* 402.10 *homosexual*
bisexuality 176.3 *duality*
Bishamon 8 Deities
bishop 7.8 *priest,* 42.4 *chess terms,* 126.5 *superior,* 688.10 *person of authority,* 696.6 *religious leader*
Bishop Desmond Tutu 675.4 *Nobel Peace Prize*
bishopdom 7.9 *priesthood*
bishopric 7.9 *priesthood,* 249.5 *state*
bishop's palace 7.10 *priestly dwelling*
bishop's purple 455.1 *purpleness*
bishop's weed 84 Flowers and Flowering Plants
Bismarck 93 Cities
Bismarck brown 449.4 *brown pigment*
bismuth 57 Chemical Elements
bismuthic 57.34 *elemental*
bismuthinite 54 Minerals
bismuthous 57.34 *elemental*
bismuthyl 57.34 *elemental*
bison 77 Placental Mammals, **161** Collective Names by Animal
bisque 29.3 *golf shots,* 45.13 *soup*
bissextile 214.12 *cyclic*
bistable circuit 74.13 *circuit*
bistort 84 Flowers and Flowering Plants
bistoury 380.10 *knife*
bistre 449.4 *brown pigment*
bistro 350.15 *eating place*
bisulphan 62 Medication
bisymmetric 308.4 *symmetrical*
bit **75** Scientific and Technical Units, 32.14 *horse-riding terms,* 51.21 *role,* 52.9 *numeral,* 65.17 *computing term,* 143.7 *piece,* 146.2 *thing included,* 148.2 *piece,* 173.3 *fragment,* 174.2 *item,* 260.3 *little piece,* 322.2 *opener,* 699.5 *means of restraint*
bit by bit 121.10 *by degrees,* 136.20 *separately,* 143.12 *partly,* 165.32 *severally,* 328.16 *slowly*
bitch 77.9 *dog,* 77.18 *female mammal,* 402.8 *nasty woman,* 402.14 *female animal,* 659.3 *difficult task,* 713.1, 713.6 *protest,* 822.8 *hated person,* 829.3 *irascible person,* 830.5 *sullen person,* 830.11 *be irritable,* 832.9 *vixen,* 864.10 *bad person*
bitchiness 829.1 *irascibility,* 830.3 *irritableness,* 832.4 *bitterness*

bitchy 618.5 *harmful,* 830.7 *irritable,* 832.14 *hostile,* 854.16 *defamatory*
bite 20.1 *angling,* 50.22 *engrave,* 82.16 *infest,* 136.9 *separate,* 143.7 *piece,* 350.14 *mouthful,* 350.21 *eat,* 380.14 *be sharp,* 406.3 *injury,* 406.10 *be painful,* 406.11 *inflict pain,* 413.1 *piquancy,* 413.13 *be piquant,* 543.11 *gesture,* 554.1 *emphasis,* 618.14 *ill-treat,* 631.6 *source of trouble,* 631.14 *afflict,* 674.12 *fight,* 828.6 *sign of anger*
bite into 136.9 *separate,* 346.11 *infiltrate*
biteless 381.4 *toothless*
bite off more than one can chew 596.3 *tackle,* 597.1 *undertake,* 610.4 *be excessive,* 656.6 *act foolishly,* 659.20 *be in difficulty*
bite one's head off 828.13 *vent one's anger*
bite one's nails 777.14 *worry*
bite someone's head off 828.11 *be angry*
bite the bullet 406.9 *feel pain,* 574.8 *brace oneself,* 673.4 *succumb*
bite the dust 244.13 *be destroyed,* 360.11 *trip,* 397.15 *die,* 683.6 *fail*
bite the hand that feeds one 656.6 *act foolishly,* 838.6 *be ungrateful,* 858.9 *prove false*
bite through 136.9 *separate*
bite to eat 350.12 *meal*
biting 55 47 *windy,* 237 12 *strong to the senses,* 300.10 *advantaged,* 350.1 *eating,* 406.5 *painful,* 409.8 *cold,* 413.9 *piquant,* 415.5 *acid,* 818.5 *discourteous,* 832.14 *hostile*
biting comment 832.4 *bitterness*
bit map 65.17 *computing term*
BITNET 65.15 *network*
bit of a do 812.1 *celebration*
bit of fluff 402.9 *woman considered as a sex object*
bit of luck 589.2 *luck*
bit of skirt 402.9 *woman considered as a sex object*
bit on the side 130.4 *extra,* 821.11 *loved one*
bit part 51.21 *role*
bit player 51.22 *actor*
bits 132.1 *remainder,* 614.6 *refuse*
bits and bobs 132.2 *residue,* 133.3 *miscellany,* 143.8 *bits and pieces,* 161.32 *miscellany*
bits and pieces **143,** 132.2 *residue,* 133.3, 161.32 *miscellany,* 614.6 *refuse,* 725.4 *possessions*
bitsy 260.7 *little*
bitt 74 Rigging, **74** Parts of a Ship
bitten 821.18 *in love*
bitter 55.47 *windy,* 351.7 *alcoholic drink,* 409.8 *cold,* 411.7 *tasty,* 413.9 *piquant,* 415.5 *acid,* 415.7 *splenetic,* 764.3 *unpalatable,* 785.8 *disliking,* 820.6 *hostile,* 822.10 *hating,* 828.15 *resentful,* 830.7 *irritable,* 830.12 *make irritable,* 832.14 *hostile,* 854.16 *defamatory*
bitter and twisted 832.14 *hostile*
bitter comedy 51.10 *comedy*
bitter cup 631.6 *source of trouble,* 687.1 *adversity*
bitter disappointment 515.1 *disappointment*
bitter end 157.8 *tail*
bitter-ender 577.8 *obstinate person,* 663.9 *opposer*
bitter lemon 351.6 *soft drink*
bitterly 409.13 *coldly,* 411.11 *tastily,* 413.15 *piquantly,* 415.10 *sourly,* 820.14 *hostilely,* 822.18 *hatefully,* 828.17 *resentfully,* 830.14 *irritably*
bitterly cold 55.55 *cool*
bittern 78 Birds, 78.3 *water bird*
bitterness **832,** 411.4 *flavour,* 413.1 *piquancy,* 415.1 *sourness,* 415.2 *unpalatability,* 415.4

spleen, 618.11 *harmfulness,* 631.4 *strain,* 759.6 *bad feeling,* 785.1 *dislike,* 820.3 *ill feeling,* 822.1 *hate,* 828.1 *resentment*
bitternut 86 Nuts
Bitter pattern 85 Named Laws
bitter pill 687.1 *adversity,* 822.7 *hated thing,* 879.10 *affliction*
bitter pit 69.12 *pests and diseases*
bitter resentment 828.1 *resentment*
bitters 415.3 *sour thing*
bitter struggle 674.2 *contest*
bittersweet **84** Flowers and Flowering Plants, 414.6 *sweet*
bitter taste 411.1 *taste,* 411.2 *taste of life*
bittiness 145.1 *incompleteness*
bitts 36.3 *parts of a sailing boat*
bitty 143.11 *partial,* 145.4 *incomplete,* 160.8 *discontinuous*
bitumen 63.25 *construction material,* 327.4 *road surface,* 395.10 *resin*
bituminous 395.14 *resinous,* 410.10 *powered*
bituminous coal 410.5 *coal,* 604.1 *materials*
biuret test 58.9 *protein*
bivalence 4.8 *philosophical term*
bivalent 57.35 *combined*
bivalve 76.5 *aquatic animal,* 81.5 *mollusc,* 81.19 *molluscan,* 176.2 *double*
bivalve bell 49 Musical Instruments
Bivalvia or Lamellibranchia 81.5 *mollusc*
bivalvular 81.19 *molluscan*
bivouac 34.1 *mountaineering,* 34.9 *mountaineer,* 256.18 *take up residence,* 325.3 *resting place*
biwa 49 Musical Instruments
biweekly 214.12 *cyclic,* 214.16 *cyclically,* 532.5 *journal*
bizarre 117.9 *nonconforming,* 168.14 *eccentric,* 487.2 *unbelievable,* 519.11 *fantastical,* 523.5 *strange,* 786.8 *wonderful,* 798.5 *ridiculous*
bizarrely 786.13 *wonderfully*
bizarreness 168.4 *unusualness,* 798.1 *ludicrousness*
Bizet 49 Musicians and Composers
bizzy 16.17 *police officer,* 718.3 *security officer*
Bjerknes 52 Scientists
Björn Borg 40.7 *famous tennis players*
blab 528.13 *inform on ,* 530.7 *betray,* 565.3 *talk,* 565.7 *be talkative*
blabber 528.10 *informer,* 565.3 *talk,* 565.4 *talker,* 565.7 *be talkative*
blabberer 530.4 *discloser*
blabbermouth 530.4 *discloser,* 564.10 *speaker,* 565.4 *talker*
blabbing 565.6 *effusive*
black **447,** 26.15 *wrestling,* 32.1 *horse,* 41.12 *ski,* 295.3 *formal dress,* 351.17 *drinkable,* 399.11 *funeral,* 440.3 *dark colour,* 440.4 *dark thing,* 440.8 *dark,* 440.10 *dark-coloured,* 443.1 *opaque,* 444.13 *soft-hued,* 447.11 *blacken,* 618.3 *bad,* 621.13 *clean,* 622.7 *dirty,* 776.6 *inauspicious,* 830.6 *sullen,* 852.15 *withhold approval*
Black 52 Scientists, 52 Scientists, **95** Mountains, **97** Oceans and Seas, 1.13 *racial,* 447.2 *dark*
black-and-blue 406.7 *feeling pain,* 447.3 *blackened,* 454.2 *bluish,* 455.7 *livid*
Black and Tan 447.9 *black thing*
black and white 66.3 *photograph,* 111.2 *opposites,* 447.7 *blackness*
black-and-white 50.9 *drawing,* 439.12 *highlight,* 456.8 *checked*
black-and-white drawing 445.3 *pen-and-ink sketch*
black-and-white film 66.9 *film*

black-and-white photograph 445.3 *pen-and-ink sketch*
black-and-white photography 66.1 *photography*
black-and-white print 445.3 *pen-and-ink sketch*
black-and-white television 534.21 *television ,* 534.22 *television set*
black Angus 447.9 *black thing*
black armband 544.5 *uniform*
black art 11.3 *witchcraft,* 447.10 *figurative usage*
black as a tinker's pot 447.1 *black*
black as coal 447.1 *black*
black as hell 447.1 *black*
black as ink 440.10 *dark-coloured,* 447.1 *black*
black as jet 447.1 *black*
black as midnight 447.1 *black*
black as my hat 447.1 *black*
black as night 440.10 *dark-coloured,* 447.1 *black*
black as pitch 447.1 *black*
black as soot 447.1 *black*
black as thunder 447.1 *black*
black ball 24.5 *snooker*
blackball 136.10 *set apart,* 147.1 *exclusion,* 147.7 *exclude,* 349.4 *ostracize,* 447.10 *figurative usage,* 447.11 *blacken,* 581.3 *exclude,* 699.1 *restraint,* 699.8 *restrain,* 709.3 *veto,* 816.3 *separation,* 816.13 *ignore,* 852.15 *withhold approval,* 879.1 *punish*
blackballed 147.11 *excluded,* 709.5 *vetoed,* 852 31 *disapproved*
blackballing 349.19 *ostracism,* 580.10 *vote,* 581.5 *rejection,* 852.3 *nonacceptance,* 879.7 *punishment*
blackball vote 580.10 *vote*
black bass 80 Fishes, 447.9 *black thing*
black bean 85 Trees and Shrubs
black bean aphid 69.12 *pests and diseases*
black beans 68.12 *crop*
black bean soup 45.50 *Central American dish*
black bear 77 Placental Mammals, 447.9 *black thing*
Blackbeard 736.9 *plunderer*
black beauty 875.6 *drug*
Black Beauty 32.1 *horse*
black beetle 82 Insects
black belt 26.7 *judo,* 68.11 *farmland,* 447.9 *black thing,* 695.4 *skilled person*
black bent 87 Grasses
blackberry 86 Fruits, 447.9 *black thing*
blackberry cobbler 45.36 *cake*
blackberry lily 84 Flowers and Flowering Plants
Black Bess 32.1 *horse*
blackbird 78 Birds, 447.9 *black thing*
blackboard 447.9 *black thing,* 599.7 *reused product*
black body 56.40 *heating effect*
black-body radiation 56.40 *heating effect*
black bombers 761.6 *desensitizing substance*
black book 447.10 *figurative usage*
black books 822.4 *hatefulness*
blackbottom 45.36 *cake*
black bottom 46.2 *dance,* 447.10 *figurative usage*
black box 73 Aircraft Parts, 447.10 *figurative usage,* 545.10 *recording instrument*
black bread 45.38 *bread*
blackbuck 77 Placental Mammals
Blackburn 93 Cities
blackcap 78 Birds
black cap 16.43 *conviction*
black cat 11.6, 11.6 *talisman,* 517.6 *good-luck sign*
black caviar 45.16 *fish dish*
black-coat worker 646.1 *worker*
blackcock 78.10 *male bird*

thoughtless, 502.6 *ignorant*, 523.1 *unintelligible*, 543.7 *punctuation*, 600.2 *new*, 621.16 *clean*, 680.13 *ammunition*, 787.3 *unmoved*
blank an end 41.16 *bobsled*
blank cartridge 636.3 *false alarm*, 680.13 *ammunition*
blank cheque 698.6 *liberality*, 708.1 *permission*
blanked 816.10 *lonely*
blanket 146.7 *including*, 164.15 *general*, 244.8 *destroy*, 266.3 *coat*, 293.10 *bed covering*, 293.24 *coat*, 408.3 *heater*, 482.4 *wholesale*, 531.8 *conceal*
blanket bath 621.6 *bath*
blanket coverage 146.1 *inclusion*, 164.3 *nonspecificness*, 293.19 *inclusion*, 528.4 *mass communication*
blanketing 293.1 *covering*
blanket of snow 55.30 *snow*
blankety-blank 618.6 *damnable*, 827.11 *miscellaneous euphemisms*
blankly 112.15 *monotonously*, 254.20 *absently*, 322.26 *openly*, 445.9 *colourlessly*, 512.16 *obliviously*, 523.13 *unintelligibly*, 600.13 *newly*, 787.9 *without wonder*
blank mind 462.1 *lack of thought*
blankness 512, 112.2 *conformity*, 254.3 *emptiness*, 462.1 *lack of thought*, 502.1 *ignorance*, 523.11 *unintelligibility*, 600.9 *newness*, 787.1 *lack of wonder*
blank out 438.8 *make invisible*, 462.12 *lack thought*
blank paper 254.3 *emptiness*
blank slate 254.3 *emptiness*
blank someone 816.13 *ignore*
blank spot 462.5 *mental block*
blank verse 48.10 *verse form*, 48.11 *rhyme*
blank wall 438.6 *that which makes invisible*, 659.8 *snag*
blatantly 811
Blantyre-Limbe 93 Cities
blare 423.1 *loudness*, 423.8 *be loud*, 427.2 *ringing*, 427.10 *ring*, 430.1 *stridency* , 430.4 *be strident*, 564.12 *speak loudly*
blaring 423.6 *loud*, 430.7 *strident*
blarney 853, 853, 506.6 *talk nonsense*, 521.5 *empty talk*, 521.9 *talk nonsense*, 540.3 *hypocrisy*, 564.2 *power of speech*, 564.9 *art of public speaking*, 657.5 *be cunning*
Blarney 93 Cities
blarneying 853.13 *honeyed*
Blasco Ibáñez 48 Writers
blasé 783.7 *indifferent*, 787.3 *unmoved*
blaspheme 5.45 *use language*, 827.5 *curse*
blasphemer 864.9 *wicked person*
blasphemous 5.39 *of language*, 827.8 *cursing*, 850.10 *disrespectful*, 864.14 *impious*
blasphemously 5.49 *colloquially*, 827.12 *swearingly*, 864.20 *immorally*
blasphemy 827.1 *curse*, 850.1 *disrespect*, 864.6 *religious sin*
blast 55.14 *windiness*, 63.30 *engineer*, 241.3 *instance of violence*, 244.9 *demolish*, 338.28 *shoot*, 390.4 *air flow*, 390.22 *blow*, 423.1 *loudness*, 423.8 *be loud*, 425.1, 425.5 *bang*, 430.1 *stridency* , 430.4 *be strident*, 532.14 *proclaim*, 628.5 *hurt*, 631.14 *afflict*, 636.2 *danger signal*, 670.2 *fire*, 679.37 *fight*, 827.6 *vilify*, 827.15 *miscellaneous swearwords*
blast away 156.18 *make a beginning*
blasted 247.3 *birth control*, 618.6 *damnable*, 827.11 *miscellaneous euphemisms*, 874.3 *dead drunk*

blast furnace 57.23 *metallurgy*, 647.1 *workshop*
blasting 827.9 *vituperative*
blasting powder 244.7 *agent of destruction*
blast neurosis 61.10 *neurosis*
blastocyst 59.15 *developmental biology*
blast off 156.18 *make a beginning*, 327.13 *flight path*, 327.14 *find one's way*, 345.8 *start*, 156.11 *starting point*
blastomere 59.15 *developmental biology*
blastomycosis 89.5 *fungal association*
blast out 431.10 *cry out*
blastula 59.15 *developmental biology*
blastulation 59.15 *developmental biology*
blatancy 811, 437.4 *clarity*, 526.10 *manifestation*, 807.3 *audacity*
blatant 811, 437.2 *clear*, 526.14 *manifest*, 532.20 *well-known*, 807.15 *audacious*, 809.13 *boastful*
blatantly 437.11 *visibly*, 532.22 *publicly*, 807.32 *audaciously*
blather 521.9 *talk nonsense*
Blaue Reiter 50 Schools and Groups of Artists
Blaue Vier 50 Schools and Groups of Artists
blaze 55.61 *shine*, 408.6 *fire*, 408.15 *burn*, 439.8 *fire*, 439.25 *light up*, 532.14 *proclaim*, 543.9 *use signs*, 544.10 *identify*
blaze abroad 532.14 *proclaim*
blaze a trail 154.18 *forerun*, 156.21 *pioneer*
blaze of publicity 532.7 *publicity*
blazer 295.4 *informal dress*, 295.11 *jacket*
blazes 827.11 *miscellaneous euphemisms*
blazing 439.16 *bright*
blazon 532.14 *proclaim*, 543.10 *signify*, 544.8 *heraldic device*, 544.10 *identify*
blazoned 544.13 *heraldic*
blazonry 544.8 *heraldic device*
bleach 439, 67.6 *dye*, 67.15 *treat*, 392.19 *bake*, 445.4 *colour remover*, 445.5 *lose colour*, 445.6 *decolour*, 446.13 *whiten*, 621.9 *cleaning agent*, 621.13 *clean*
bleached 67.11 *treated*, 392.8 *baked*, 439.21 *light*, 445.7 *colourless*, 446.12 *whitened*, 621.17 *cleaned*
bleacher 445.4 *colour remover*
bleachers 22.1 *baseball*, 435.9 *viewpoint*
bleaching 67.8 *fabric treatment*, 392.13 *drying*, 439.3 *lightening*, 445.1 *colourlessness*, 628.9 *dilapidation*
bleaching powder 57 Common Chemical Compounds, 445.4 *colour remover*
bleak 80 Fishes, 55.55 *cool*, 247.3 *birth control*, 409.8 *cold*, 410.6 *adverse*
bleakly 687.12 *in adversity*
bleakness 687.1 *adversity*
bleak outlook 776.2 *hopeless situation*
blear 441.6 *murky*, 441.10 *make dim*
bleared 438.2 *difficult to see*, 441.6 *murky*
blearily 441.12 *dimly*
bleariness 436.2 *poor sight*, 441.2 *murk*
bleary 436.9 *weak-sighted*, 438.2 *difficult to see*, 441.6 *murky*
bleary-eyed 436.9 *weak-sighted*
bleat 432.4 *cry*
bleater 766.3 *dissatisfied person*
bleating 432.1 *animal cry*

bleed 353, 349.14 *let out*, 353.22 *menstruate*, 355.14 *suck*, 387.25 *flow*, 389.32, 391.16 *seep*, 630.20 *doctor*, 753.10 *overcharge*, 835.9 *sorrow*
bleeder 624.19 *sick person*
bleeder's disease 624.11 *blood disease*
bleed for 759.18 *feel for*, 835.9 *sorrow*
bleeding 353, 353, 349.22 *disgorgement*, 355.4 *sucking*, 387.18 *bloody*, 406.7 *feeling pain*, 624.3 *symptom*, 624.11 *blood disease*, 630.12 *surgery*
bleeding heart 84 Flowers and Flowering Plants, 835.6 *benevolent person*, 835.4 *pitying person*
bleeding-heart liberal 691.2 *lenient person*
bleeding tooth 81 Molluscs
bleed someone 712.7 *demand*
bleed to death 397.16 *meet one's fate*
bleep 430.3 *shrillness*, 534.18 *radio*, 534.30 *communicate*, 543.4 *signal*
bleeped out 709.6 *censored*
bleeper 420.9 *audio device*, 430.3 *shrillness*, 543.4 *signal*
bleeping 430.9 *shrill*, 543.16 *signalling*, 618.6 *damnable*
bleep out 709.4 *censor*
blemish 793, 127.2 *deficiency*, 149.2 *impurity*, 309.3 *deformity*, 309.11 *deform*, 358.6 *shortcoming*, 435.7 *view*, 544.3 *means of identification*, 620.7 *defect*, 624.3 *skin disease*, 628.5 *hurt*, 790.3 *ugly place*, 790.5 *make ugly*
Blemish 793
blemished 793, 145.4 *incomplete*, 309.7 *deformed*, 358.8 *defective*, 456.10 *mottled*, 620.1 *imperfect*
blemish-free 619.1 *perfect*
blench 331.2 *respond*, 439.28 *bleach*, 446.13 *whiten*, 573.7 *refuse*, 591.4 *shy*, 777.11 *be afraid*
blenching 591.12 *shyness*, 591.18 *avoiding*
blend 45.55 *cook*, 113.8 *be diverse*, 116.4 *harmony*, 116.24 *harmonize*, 133.2 *mixed thing*, 133.8 *mix*, 133.10 *become mixed*, 140.1 *combination*, 140.4 *compound*, 140.5 *combine*, 174.19 *become one*, 243.10 *produce*, 298.2 *interaction*, 298.5 *cooperate*, 387.22 *make fluid*, 393.24 *pulp*
blended 116.13 *harmonious*, 133.12 *mixed*, 140.7 *combined*, 298.6 *interfacial*
blender 45.6 *kitchen equipment*, 133.6 *mixer*, 387.11 *liquidizer*, 393.15 *pulper*
blending 133.1 *mixture*, 140.1 *combination*, 393.5 *pulping*
blend into the background 438.7 *become invisible*, 458.1 *disappear*
blend with the crowd 124.9 *be average*
Blenheim 86 Fruits
Blenheim Palace 43 Noted Buildings
Blenheim spaniel 77 Breeds of Dogs
blennophobia 777 Phobias by Name
blenny 80 Fishes
bleomycin 62 Medication
blepharoplast 90.3 *plant body*
blepharoplasty 60 Surgical Operations
blesbok 77 Placental Mammals
bless 8.17 *deify*, 10.18 *perform rites*, 116.28 *consent*, 667.6 *agree with*, 686.7 *be auspicious*, 708.3 *permit*, 837.7 *give thanks*, 861.20 *do good*
blessed 8.13 *divine*, 9.11 *worshipped*, 667.10 *agreeing*, 686.8 *prosperous*, 827.11 *miscellaneous euphemisms*

blessedly 686.9 *prosperously*
blessedness 8.1 *divinity*, 686.1 *prosperity*
blessed state 8.1 *divinity*
blessed with stamina 378.4 *powerful*
blessed with talent 655.7 *gifted*
blessed with this world's goods 742.1 *wealthy*
blessing 10.3 *rite of worship*, 10.6 *Eucharist*, 10.9 *prayer*, 116.7 *consent*, 667.1 *agreement*, 708.1 *permission*, 729.2 *gift*, 837.2 *thanks*, 837.5 *thanking*, 851.1 *approval*, 861.13 *benefit*, 861.17 *good thing*
blessings 686.1 *prosperity*, 686.2 *good fortune*
bless my soul 786.14 *wonderful*
bless with 725.9 *own property*
bless you 686.10 *good luck*, 837.9 *thank you*
blether 521.5 *empty talk*
blether on 553.5 *be diffuse*
blewit 45.33 *vegetable*
blewits 89 Fungi
blight 69.12 *pests and diseases*, 85.10 *tree disease*, 89.1 *fungus*, 244.7 *agent of destruction*, 618.10 *poverty*, 628.5 *hurt*, 628.9 *dilapidation*, 631.14 *afflict*, 687.1 *adversity*, 862.2 *affliction*, 862.11 *be evil*
Blight 631
blighted 69.17 *botanical*, 89.9 *fungal*, 93.14 *urban*, 631.16 *blighting*, 862.7 *evil*
blighted area 93.7 *city district*
blighted hopes 515.1 *disappointment*
blighted neighbourhood 93.7 *city district*
blighting 631
blight one's hopes 515.6 *disappoint*
blimp 73.8 *aircraft*, 259.12 *fat person*, 577.8 *obstinate person*
blimpish 577.4 *set*
blind 436, 436, 29.1 *golf*, 34.8 *mountaineering*, 293.12 *protective covering*, 404.6 *unfeeling*, 436.6 *blinder*, 438.6 *that which makes invisible*, 439.24 *light*, 440.6 *shade*, 440.11 *benighted*, 443.7 *opaque thing*, 512.8 *oblivious*, 539.8 *trick*, 577.4 *set*, 620.3 *deformed*, 634.2 *shelter*, 641.3 *inactive*, 657.2 *stratagem*, 761.1 *insensitive*, 874.3 *dead drunk*, 874.14 *drinking bout*
blind alley 323.4 *closed place*, 327.3 *road*, 614.5 *waste of effort*, 659.8 *snag*
blind as a bat 436.8 *blind*
blind as a mole 436.8 *blind*
blind attack 670.12 *military attack*
blind chance 589.1 *chance*
blind choice 580.8 *choice*
blind corner 438.5 *invisible thing*
blind date 502.4 *unknown person*, 580.8 *choice*, 815.3 *meeting*, 821.9 *lover*
blind drunk 874.3 *dead drunk*
blinded 436, 577.4 *set*, 786.6 *wondering*
blinder 436
blind eye 436.7 *figurative blindness*
blind faith 466.1 *incuriousness*, 497.3 *believing*
blindfish 80 Fishes
blind flying 436.7 *figurative blindness*
blindfold 436.6 *blinder*, 436.10 *blinded*, 436.15 *blind*, 436.17 *blindly*, 440.6 *shade*, 440.14 *make dark*, 531.9 *disguise*
blind fury 828.4 *anger*, 832.1 *malevolence*
blind impulse 583.5 *spontaneity*
blinding 436, 55.53 *rainy*, 439.16 *bright*
blindingly 436
blind luck 589.2 *luck*
blindly 436

blind man's buff 42 Children's Games and Party Games, 438.5 invisible thing
blind move 34.3 climbing technique
blindness 436, 238.3 poor health, 440.1 darkness, 440.7 spiritual darkness, 577.7 opinionatedness, 620.5 imperfection
Blindness 436
blind oneself 481.13 prejudge
blind panic 777.1 fear
blind people 436
blind poker 42 Card Games
blind rage 828.4 anger
blind register 436.3 aid for poor sight
blind side 436.7 figurative blindness, 577.7 opinionatedness
blind snake 79 Reptiles
blind spot 435.2 eye, 436.7 figurative blindness, 438.5 invisible thing, 462.5 mental block, 620.7 defect
blind staggers 874.10 drunkenness
blindstorey 43.10 church architecture
blind to 436, 783.7 indifferent, 787.3 unmoved
blindworm 79 Reptiles
blini 45.12 hors d'oeuvre
blink 331.2 respond, 436.14 be blind, 439.25 light up, 591.4 shy
blink at 436.16 be blind to
blink comparator 53.27 imaging
blinker 71 Motor Vehicle Parts, 436.15 blind, 543.5 indicator
blinkered 436.10 blinded, 436.12 blind to, 481.10 discriminatory, 577.4 set
blinkers 32.14 horse-riding terms, 436.6 blinder
blinking 436.2 poor sight, 436.9 weak-sighted, 439.15 lucent, 591.12 shyness, 591.18 avoiding, 618.6 damnable
blip 618.8 inferiority
bliss 405.1 physical pleasure, 762.1 happiness, 763.6 pleasantness
Bliss 49 Musicians and Composers
bliss body 11.7 spirit
blissed out 762.4 happy
blissful 405.6 pleasant, 686.8 prosperous, 762.4 happy, 763.1 pleasant
blissfully 405.11 pleasingly, 686.9 prosperously
blissfully in love 821.18 in love
blister 73 Aircraft Parts, 258.19 inflatable, 316.2 bulge, 408.5 hot weather, 408.16 feel hot, 624.3 symptom, 624.13 skin disease
blister beetle 82 Insects
blistered 375.2 coarse, 406.7 feeling pain
blistering 55.51 hot, 408.11 warm
blister pack 442.8 transparent thing
blithe 762.4 happy
blithering 521.10 meaningless
blitz 19.11 defensive huddle, 19.16 play defence, 244.5 havoc, 244.9 demolish, 423.1 loudness, 670.1 attack, 670.3 bomb, 670.12 military attack, 676.1 war, 676.8 warfare, 676.9 battle
blitzed 874.3 dead drunk
blitzkrieg 670.12 military attack, 676.1 war, 676.8 warfare
blitz the media 512.6 publicize
blizzard 55.30, 55.63 snow, 241.5 violent weather, 409.5 ice, 443.7 opaque thing
bloat 161 Collective Names for Birds and Animals, 144.6 fill, 261.1 growth, 261.5 make bigger, 261.6 become bigger, 624.18 veterinary disease
bloated 128.7 increased, 259.16 fat, 261.7 bigger, 350.26 eating, 608.3 filled, 610.6 excessive

bloatedness 259.5 fatness, 261.1 growth
bloater 45.16 fish dish, 80.8 food fish
bloating 261.1 growth
blob 172.1 zero, 307.2 shapeless thing
bloc 12.6 political party, 140.3 assembly, 665.3 political grouping
Bloch 49 Musicians and Composers
Bloch wall 56 Named Laws
block 661, 19.9 play, 19.15 play offence, 23.4 playing terms, 23.6 play basketball, 25.9 bowls, 26.2 boxing, 26.9 tae kwon do, 26.11 do a combat sport, 26.13 do martial arts, 27.9 stroke, 27.17 bat, 34.5 rock face, 35.5 play rugby, 36.3 parts of a sailing boat, 50.15 engraving, 51.35 rehearse, 61.19 defence mechanism, 65.17 computing term, 93.7 city district, 143.7 piece, 209.3 delayed action, 209.8 delay, 218.8 cause to cease, 231.1 counteraction, 231.3 counteract, 249.12 plot, 259.7 mass, 323.1 closure, 323.8 stop, 371.4 solid body, 487.7 obstacle, 487.8 make impossible, 661.2 obstacle, 663.17 withstand, 671.18 fence, 671.25 stall, 699.11 detain, 747.8 stop payment, 879.16 instrument of execution
blockade 323.1 closure, 323.8 stop, 661.2 obstacle, 661.9 block, 670.4 besiege, 670.14 siege, 671.9 barrier, 676.8 warfare, 676.13 be at war, 699.4 detention, 699.11 detain
blockader 670.19 attacker
blockading 676.8 warfare
blockage 61.19 defence mechanism, 209.3 delayed action, 218.2 stop, 323.1 closure, 661.2 obstacle
block an attack 28.5 fence
block and tackle 63.6 simple machine, 361.9 lifter
blockboard 47.12 wood
blockbuster 48.2 fiction, 244.7 agent of destruction, 560.5 fiction, 680.16 bomb, 682.3 successful thing, 875.6 drug
blocked 661, 61.37 subconscious, 209.10 held up, 323.13 stopped, 487.4 forbidden
blocked account 745.5 amount owing
blocked nose 417.1 odourlessness
blocked up 323.13 stopped
blocker 19.7 offence, 23.2 basketball player, 35.4 rugby player
block fault 54.20 earth movement
blockhead 460.3 unintelligent person, 502.5 ignorant person, 508.3 foolish person
blockheaded 460.6 unintelligent
blockhouse 634.1 refuge, 671.10 shelter, 671.12 fort
blocking 23.4 playing terms, 26.2 boxing, 26.14 combat, 26.15 wrestling, 51.12 production, 61.19 defence mechanism, 209.12 delaying
blocking high 55.11 weather system
blocking kick 26.9 tae kwon do
blocking techniques 26.9 tae kwon do
blocking with wrist and hand 26.9 tae kwon do
blockish 404.6 unfeeling
block of flats 63.20 building, 243.8 construction
block out 299.5 outline, 306.7 form, 546.2 forget, 547.11 paint, 594.2 do the groundwork
block out light 440.14 make dark
block-print 50.7 picture
blocks 21.4 sports equipment
blockship 679.24 warship
block shot 25.2 grip
block up 323.8 stop, 661.9 block

Bloemfontein 93 Cities
Blok 48 Poets
bloke 401.2 male
blond 439.21 light, 446.3 white-haired, 452.3 yellow-haired, 452.6 yellowness
blonde 439.21 light
Blonde d'Aquitaine 68 Breeds of Cattle
Blondel 4 Philosophers
blondness 439.14 light colour
blood 777 Phobias by Topic, **387,** 156.25 enrol, 163.8 genealogy, 387.3 body fluid, 450.7 red thing
blood and thunder 51.7 dramaturgy
blood bank 387.4 blood, 605.4 storage
bloodbath 241.3 instance of violence, 398.4 slaughter, 670.14 siege
blood brother 114.5 counterpart
blood cell 59.7 cell, 387.4 blood
blood clot 323.2 stopper, 371.4 solid body, 387.4 blood
blood-clot 624.10 cardiovascular disease
blood count 387.4 blood
blood disease 624
blood donor 729.4 giver
blooded horse 32.13 breeding
blood feud 666.2 argument, 820.4 act of hostility
blood fluke 81 Worms, 81.6 worm, 81.10 parasite
blood group 387.4 blood
blood guilt 866.1 guilt
blood-guilty 866.5 guilty
blood heat 408.1 heat
blood-horse 32.2 thoroughbred
bloodhound 77 Breeds of Dogs, 416.2 sense of smell, 590.6 hunter
bloodily 353.33 scatologically
bloodiness 387.5 fluidity
blood kin 137.3 associate
blood knot 74 Knots
bloodless 238.10 ill, 445.8 drained of colour, 624.23 diseased, 675.7 peaceful
bloodless bullfight 674.9 duel
bloodlessly 675.8 peacefully
bloodlessness 445.2 paleness
blood-letting 241.2 physical violence, 349.22 disgorgement, 355.4 sucking, 398.1 killing, 630.12 surgery
bloodline 159.3 line
blood-line 32.13 breeding
bloodlust 241.2 physical violence, 832.2 cruelness
bloodmobile 71 Motor Vehicles, 387.4 blood
blood money 125.1 compensation, 677.2 peace offering, 710.4 illegal offer, 840.1 atonement
blood of the grape 351.9 wine
blood picture 387.4 blood
blood plasma 387.4 blood
blood platelet 387.4 blood
blood poisoning 624.2 illness, 624.6 infection, 631.7 poisoning
blood pressure 387.4 blood, 624.10 cardiovascular disease
blood pudding 45.29 sausage
blood-red 450.1 red
blood relationship 107.1 relatedness
blood running cold 777.1 fear
blood sample 60.7 diagnosis
blood sausage 45.29 sausage
blood serum 387.4 blood
bloodshed 676.8 warfare, 832.7 act of malevolence
blood-shedding 398.1 killing
bloodshot 436.9 weak-sighted, 450.4 bloody, 874.5 drunken
bloodshot eyes 436.2 poor sight
blood-soaked 353.30 bleeding
blood sport 18.4 sporting activity, 590.2 chase
blood sports 398.9 animal killing
bloodstained 398.24 murderous
blood-stained 450.4 bloody
bloodstock 32.2 thoroughbred

bloodstone 54 Gemstones, 517.6 good-luck sign
bloodstream 387.4 blood
blood substitute 387.4 blood
bloodsucker 76.4 type of animal, 81.10 parasite, 82.3 pest, 690.4 strict person
bloodsucking 76.15 of animals
blood, sweat, and tears 722.4 lessening
blood test 60.7 diagnosis, 479.1 experiment
bloodthirst 832.2 cruelness
bloodthirstily 398.25 lethally, 679.41 aggressively
bloodthirstiness 241.2 physical violence, 618.11 harmfulness, 832.2 cruelness
bloodthirsty 241.6 violent, 398.24 murderous, 618.5 harmful, 670.23 attacking, 676.16 warlike, 679.33 combative, 832.11 cruel
blood transfusion 387.4 blood
bloodworm 82 Insects, 82.5 larva
bloody 387, 450, 241.6 violent, 353.21 bleed, 353.30 bleeding, 398.24 murderous, 406.11 inflict pain, 595.6 uncooked, 618.5 harmful, 618.6 damnable, 670.23 attacking, 676.13 be at war, 827.11 miscellaneous euphemisms, 832.11 cruel
bloody flux 353.2 defecation
bloody hands 866.2 signs of guilt
bloody hell 827.15 miscellaneous swearwords
Bloody Mary 351.8 mixed drink
bloody-minded 570.8 wilful, 577.1 obstinate, 659.14 troublesome, 663.22 uncooperative, 693.13 disobedient, 713.9 protesting, 764.2 objectionable, 832.14 hostile
bloody-mindedness 570.3 wilfulness, 577.5 obstinacy, 663.4 uncooperativeness, 832.1 malevolence
bloody nose 406.3 injury
bloom 84.1, 84.13 flower, 85.19, 206.18 grow, 207.18 mature, 245.11 have young, 246.6 be fertile, 261.6 become bigger, 266.3 coat, 384.1 powderiness, 450.5 redness, 623.3 health, 623.5 be healthy, 686.5 be prosperous
bloomed lens 56.29 optical element
bloomer 45.39 loaf, 84.2 flowering plant, 493.2 mistake, 504.10 blunder, 508.2 act of folly, 559.6 blunder
bloomers 295.9 **trousers**, 295.18 underwear
blooming 84.5, 84.11 flowering, 206.13 maturing, 261.1 growth, 261.8 growing, 450.2 red-faced, 453.4 fresh, 457.1 appearance, 594.13 development, 594.20 developed, 623.1 healthy, 684.7 completed, 789.6 personable
bloom of youth 206.1 youth
Bloomsbury group 48 Literary Groups and Movements, **50** Schools and Groups of Artists
bloomy 84.10 floral
blooper 493.2 mistake, 504.10 blunder, 508.2 act of folly
blossom 84.1, 84.13 flower, 128.4 increase, 227.3 growth, 227.8 grow, 243.7 produce, 246.6 be fertile, 261.6 become bigger, 682.6 be successful, 686.5 be prosperous
blossoming 84.5, 84.11 flowering, 227.11 growing, 261.1 growth, 261.8 growing
blossom time 203.2 spring
blot 133.4 admixture, 293.31 hide, 348.13, 392.20 absorb, 435.7 view, 447.11 blacken, 456.11 variegate, 546.1 obliterate, 620.7 defect, 622.4 dirt, 622.11 dirty, 628.5 hurt, 656.7 be clumsy, 793.1 spot, 844.9 dishonour

blotch 456.4 *maculation*, 793.1 *spot*
blot one's copybook 683.6 *fail*, 864.16 *be wicked*
blot on one's copybook 844.9 *dishonour*
blot on the landscape 793, 790.3 *ugly place*
blot out 147.8 *eject*, 244.8 *destroy*, 293.31 *hide*, 458.3 *cause to disappear*, 546.1 *obliterate*, 704.6 *cancel*, 734.10 *take away*
blot out light 440.14 *make dark*
blot out one's sins 839.10 *absolve*
blotted 839.8 *overlooked*
blotted out 531.14 *concealed*
blotter 348.6 *sponge*, 392.15 *dryer* , 621.10 *cleaning object*
blotting 348.5 *absorption*, 348.17 *absorbent*, 392.13 *drying*
blotting out 293.1 *covering*, 734.3 *taking away*
blotting paper 348.6 *sponge*, 392.15 *dryer*
blotto 874.3 *dead drunk*
blot up 348.13, 392.20 *absorb*
blouse 295.8 *shirt*, 295.35 *make clothing*
bloused 295.31 *styled*
blouson 295.4 *informal dress*
blow 55, 330, 390, 49.38 *sound*, 55.14 *windiness*, 84.1 *flower*, 84.5 *flowering*, 84.13 *flower*, 306.7 *form*, 349.11 *void*, 349.14 *let out*, 349.33 *go away*, 407.3 *press*, 424.5 *sound faint*, 514.3 *shock*, 515.2 *bad outcome*, 528.13 *inform on* , 607.1 *waste*, 640.2 *deed*, 642.12 *be active*, 650.5 *be fatigued*, 656.7 *be clumsy*, 670.18 *hit*, 748.1 *expend*, 757.7 *waste*, 875.10 *drug oneself*, 879.12 *corporal punishment*
blow a fortune 748.1 *expend*
blow a fuse 828.12 *become angry*
blow a gale 55.59 *storm*
blow a gasket 828.12 *become angry*
blow a gut 431.11 *laugh*
blow a hurricane 55.59 *storm*
blow a kiss 817.12 *greet*, 821.27 *kiss*, 826.7 *show endearment for*
blow a raspberry 349.16 *belch*, 429.5 *catcall*, 543.11 *gesture*, 807.29 *ridicule*, 850.25 *taunt*
blow away 244.8 *destroy*, 244.9 *demolish*, 338.28 *shoot*
blow-by-blow account 553.1 *diffuseness*
blow down 244.9 *demolish*, 362.6 *throw down*
blower 390.7 *ventilator*, 534.9 *telephone*
blowfish 80 Fishes
blowfly 82 Insects
blow for blow 107.2 *interrelatedness*, 109.1 *interchange*, 223.1 *exchange*, 672.1 *retaliation*, 674.6 *fight*
blow-for-blow 109.4 *reciprocal*
blow gage 875.10 *drug oneself*
blowhole 322.5 *hole*, 347.7 *outlet*
blow hot and cold 216.7 *be changed*, 224.12 *be irresolute*, 576.6 *hesitate*, 579.5 *be capricious*, 671.25 *stall*
blow in 344.1 *arrive*
blowing 84.5 *flowering*, 650.3 *panting*, 875.1 *drug-taking*
blowing away 398.2 *murder*
blowing hot and cold 576.12 *inconstancy*
blowing one's own trumpet 494.1 *overestimation*
blowing up 261.1 *growth*, 541.2 *enlargement*
blow it 211.6 *lose one's chance*, 748.1 *expend*
blow me down 786.14 *wonderful*
blown 306.9 *formed*, 748.12 *expended*
blown up 361.11 *raised*
blown-up 261.7 *bigger*, 390.14 *aerial*, 541.12 *exaggerated*, 541.13 *enlarged*

blow off 349.16 *belch*
blow one's cash 748.1 *expend*
blow one's chance 211.6 *lose one's chance*
blow one's cool 828.12 *become angry*
blow one's lid 818.8 *get angry*, 828.12 *become angry*
blow one's mind 786.10 *be wonderful*, 875.10 *drug oneself*
blow one's nose 353.20 *salivate*
blow one's own trumpet 809.16 *show off*
blow one's top 818.8 *get angry*, 828.12 *become angry*
blow on the ears 330.13 *blow*
blow on the embers 241.9 *make violent*
blow open 241.8 *use violence*
blow out 244.8 *destroy*, 347.11 *run out*, 349.11 *void*, 349.14 *let out*, 440.14 *make dark*
blowout 349.22 *disgorgement*, 350.13 *feast*, 425.1 *bang*, 665.7 *social gathering*, 812.1 *celebration*, 815.5 *party*, 872.3 *act of gluttony*
blow out one's brains 398.21 *commit suicide*
blow out the brains of 398.17 *murder*
blow over 218.6 *cease*, 362.6 *throw down*
blowpipe 57 Laboratory Apparatus, 338.9 *firearm*, 680.6 *historical missile weapon*
blows 674.6 *fight*
blow smoke 875.10 *drug oneself*
blow someone's cover 530.7 *betray*
blow the gaff 528.13 *inform on* , 530.6 *divulge*, 856.5 *accuse*
blow the lid off 528.13 *inform on* , 530.6 *divulge*
blow the roof off 423.8 *be loud*
blow the trumpets 812.18 *salute*
blow the whistle 636.7 *raise the alarm*, 856.5 *accuse*
blow the whistle on 528.13 *inform on* , 530.7 *betray*
blow to bits 244.9 *demolish*
blow to kingdom come 244.9 *demolish*
blow to pieces 136.9 *separate*
blowtorch 408.6 *fire*
blow to smithereens 244.9 *demolish*
blow up 338, 55.58 *blow*, 66.21 *photograph*, 128.5 *make bigger*, 136.9 *separate*, 141.3 *disintegrate*, 244.9 *demolish*, 261.5 *make bigger*, 359.17 *spring up*, 361.2 *send up*, 425.5 *bang*, 530.9 *be disclosed*, 541.8 *enlarge*, 541.10 *boast*, 547.9 *represent*
blow-up 66.12 *development*, 241.3 *instance of violence*, 674.6 *fight*, 828.4 *anger*
blowy 55.47 *windy*, 390.15 *breezy*
blowzy 450.2 *red-faced*
blub 431.13 *cry*, 774.7 *weep*
blubber 259.8 *fat*, 273.5 *thickness*, 395.8 *fat*, 431.13 *cry*, 774.7 *weep*
blubberer 774.3 *lamenter*
blubbering 431.18 *crying*
blubbery 386.10, 395.11 *oily*
blubbing 431.18 *crying*
bludgeon 680.7 *blunt weapon*, 695.3 *coercive methods*, 695.7 *force*
bludgeoning 695.9 *compelling*
blue 45 Cheeses, 89 Fungi, **454**, **454**, 31.8 *hockey*, 41.12 *ski*, 49.33 *jazz*, 56.28, 56.28 *colour*, 454.3 *depressed*, 454.4 *indecent*, 607.1 *waste*, 622.9 *obscene*, 748.1 *expend*, 770.6 *depressed*, 792.3 *honour*, 795.9 *ribald*, 827.8 *cursing*, 830.6 *sullen*, 877.12 *indecent*
Blue 95 Mountains
Blue Albian 68 Breeds of Cattle
blue and red 455.1 *purpleness*

blue and white ware 44.1 *ceramics*
blue around the gills 454.2 *bluish*
blue baby 454.8 *bluishness*
blue ball 24.5 *snooker*
blue ball clay 44.2 *raw material*
blue balls 454.7 *figurative usage*
Bluebeard 454.6 *blue thing*, 823.10 *married man*
bluebell 84 Flowers and Flowering Plants, 454.6 *blue thing*
blueberry 86 Fruits, 454.6 *blue thing*
blueberry muffin 45.39 *loaf*
blueberry pancake 45.39 *loaf*
bluebill 78 Birds, 454.6 *blue thing*
bluebird 78 Birds, 454.6 *blue thing*
blue-black 447.1 *black*, 447.8 *black pigment*
blue blood 454.7 *figurative usage*
blueblood 802.1 *nobleman*
blue blooded 802.4 *aristocratic*
bluebonnet 454.6 *blue thing*
bluebook 454.6 *blue thing*
bluebottle 688.10 *person of authority*
blue Burmese 77 Breeds of Cats
blue cheer 454.6 *blue thing*, 875.6 *drug*
blue cheese 45 Cheeses, 454.6 *blue thing*
blue chip 454.7 *figurative usage*
blue-chip 126.15 *excellent*, 617.3 *valuable*
blue-collar 15.10 *unionized*
blue-collar union 15.3 *organized labour*
blue-collar worker 15.7 *employee*, 400.10 *member of society*, 454.7 *figurative usage*, 646.1 *worker*
blue colour 454.5 *blueness*
blue crab 454.6 *blue thing*
blue cream 77 Breeds of Cats
Blue Cross 60.1 *medicine*, 454.6 *blue thing*, 718.1 *protection*
blue devils 454.7 *figurative usage*, 830.2 *sign of sullenness*
blue dye 444.4 *pigment*, 454.5 *blueness*
Blue Ensign 544.7 *flag*
blue-eyed boy 401.2 *male*, 454.7 *figurative usage*, 821.11 *loved one*, 826.6 *object of endearment*
Bluefaced Leicester 68 Breeds of Sheep
blue film 296.3 *pornography*, 454.7 *figurative usage*
bluefish 80 Fishes, 20.4 *American game fish*, 454.6 *blue thing*
blue flu 454.7 *figurative usage*
blue fox 77 Placental Mammals, 454.6 *blue thing*
blue funk 454.7 *figurative usage*, 777.1 *fear*, 779.1 *cowardice*
bluegill 454.6 *blue thing*
bluegrass 87 Grasses, 49.11 *folk music*, 454.6 *blue thing*, 454.7 *figurative usage*
blue-green 453.1 *green*
blue-green algae 90.2 *algae*
blue-grey 448.1 *grey*
blue gum 85 Trees and Shrubs
blue humour 771.3 *wit*
blue in the face 454.2 *bluish*
bluejacket 454.7 *figurative usage*, 679.27 *naval man*
blue jay 454.6 *blue thing*
bluejeans 295.9 *trousers*, 454.6 *blue thing*
blue joke 771.5 *joke*, 827.1 *curse*, 877.2 *indecency*
blue language 454.7 *figurative usage*, 827.2 *offensive language*
blue law 454.7 *figurative usage*
blue laws 690.2 *suppression*, 876.4 *self-righteousness*
blue line 31.3 *ice hockey*
blue marlin 20.4 *American game fish*
blue moon 454.7 *figurative usage*
Blue Mosque 43 Noted Buildings, 10.13 *shrine*
blue mould 454.6 *blue thing*

Blue Mountains 454.6 *blue thing*
blue movie 877.2 *indecency*
blue murder 454.7 *figurative usage*
blueness 454
Blueness 454
Blue Nile 454.6 *blue thing*
blue note 49.8 *jazz*, 454.7 *figurative usage*
Blue Nun 7 Members of Religious Orders
blue ointment 62 Medication
blue pencil 454.6 *blue thing*, 454.7 *figurative usage*, 546.3 *obliteration*, 627.6 *rectification*, 709.2 *censorship*
blue-pencil 454, 131.3 *subtract*, 134.10 *purify*, 147.8 *eject*, 242.4 *moderate*, 546.1 *obliterate*, 621.15 *purify*, 627.3 *rectify*, 709.4 *censor*
blue-pencilled 709.6 *censored*
blue-pencilling 621.4 *censorship*
blue peter 454.6 *blue thing*, 544.7 *flag*
blue pigment 454.5 *blueness*
blue-plate special 454.7 *figurative usage*
bluepoint 45.19 *shellfish*
blue-pointed Siamese 77 Breeds of Cats
bluepoint oyster 454.6 *blue thing*
blueprint 119.2 *original*, 119.7 *originate*, 299.1, 299.5 *outline*, 306.2 *prototype*, 454.6 *blue thing*, 454.7 *figurative usage*, 547.2 *reproduction*, 562.2 *outline*, 592.5 *map*, 594.2 *do the groundwork*, 594.10 *preparations*
blue racer 454.6 *blue thing*
Blue Riband 878.2 *prize*
blue ribbon 454.6 *blue thing*, 544.4 *insignia*, 681.1 *trophy*, 878.2 *prize*
blue-ribbon 617.2 *best*
blue-ribbon winner 655.4 *skilled person*
Blue Ridge 95 Mountains
Blue Ridge Mountains 454.6 *blue thing*
blue run 41.1 *skiing*
blues 46.2 *dance*, 49.8 *jazz*, 295.3 *formal dress*, 454.7 *figurative usage*
blue shark 80 Fishes, 20.5 *British game fish*
Blue Shield 60.1 *medicine*
blueshift 53.21 *orbit*
blue sky 55.22 *sun*, 390.1 *air*
blue-sky 518.7 *suppositional*
blue-sky law 454.7 *figurative usage*
bluesman 49.24 *musician*
blue spruce 85 Trees and Shrubs
Blue Stilton 45 Cheeses
bluestocking 6.7 *learner*, 454.7 *figurative usage*, 459.8 *intellectual person*, 501.6 *knowledgeable person*
bluestone 454.6 *blue thing*
blue streak 329.8 *speed*, 454.7 *figurative usage*
blue thing 454
bluetit 78 Birds, 454.6 *blue thing*
bluets 84 Flowers and Flowering Plants
blue velvet 454.6 *blue thing*, 875.6 *drug*
blue Vinney 45 Cheeses
blue vitriol 57 Common Chemical Compounds
blue water 97.1 *sea*
blue whale 77 Placental Mammals, 454.6 *blue thing*
blue with cold 409.8 *cold*, 454.2 *bluish*
bluff 241.6 *violent*, 275.3 *mountain*, 281.3 *vertical thing*, 381.2 *outspoken*, 474.12 *deceive*, 502.2 *half-knowledge*, 538.8 *pretence*, 538.12 *cheat*, 538.24 *pretend*, 539.8 *trick*, 539.11 *hoax*, 539.15 *deceiver*, 539.28 *trick*, 539.31 *hoax*, 540.12 *facade*, 540.24 *mask*, 797.4 *be affected*, 807.19 *rude*
bluffed 539.36 *deceived*

bluffer 502.5 *ignorant person*, 538.12 *cheat*, 539.15 *deceiver*, 797.2 *pretender*

bluffing 538.8 *pretence*, 538.18 *pretentious*, 539.7 *tricking*, 540.12 *facade*, 540.30 *pretending*

bluffness 381.6 *outspokenness*, 818.1 *discourtesy*

bluff one's way out 638.5 *escape*

bluish 454

bluishness 454

Blunden 48 *Poets*

blunder 504, 559, 211.3 *lost chance*, 211.8 *make a mistake*, 335.4 *lose track of*, 366.25 *pitch*, 468.5 *inattentive act*, 493.2 *mistake*, 493.10 *misjudge*, 504.19 *make a mistake*, 508.2 *act of folly*, 525.1 *misinterpret*, 525.2 *misinterpretation*, 656.5 *be unskilful*, 656.6 *act foolishly*, 656.7 *be clumsy*, 683.1 *failure*, 683.6 *fail*, 844.19 *be wrong*, 866.3 *sin*

blunderbuss 338.9 *firearm*, 656.10 *unskilled person*, 680.10 *historical gun*

blundered 683.10 *failed*

blunderer 656.10 *unskilled person*

blundering 211.13 *mistaken*, 683.10 *failed*

blunderingly 211.17 *mistakenly*, 683.12 *unsuccessfully*

blunder into 229.5 *happen by chance*

blunder upon 589.11 *chance upon*

blunge 44.11 *make ceramics*

blunged 44.10 *ceramic*

blunger 44.6 *ceramic workshop*

blunging 44.5 *ceramic process*, 44.10 *ceramic*

blunt 381, 381, 242.4 *moderate*, 322.16 *open*, 376.2 *uniform*, 404.12 *anaesthetize*, 460.10 *bemuse*, 526.15 *open*, 535.14 *assertive*, 537.18 *truthful*, 556.3 *natural*, 587.5 *discourage*, 658.1 *naive*, 761.1 *insensitive*, 761.7 *render insensitive*, 783.13 *make indifferent*, 818.5 *discourteous*

blunted 381.1 *blunt*

blunt edge 381.9 *blunt instrument*

blunt-edged 381.1 *blunt*

blunt-ended 381.1 *blunt*

blunt instrument 381, 398.2 *murder*, 680.7 *blunt weapon*

bluntish 381.1 *blunt*

bluntly 381, 322.26 *openly*, 376.14 *smoothly*, 404.13 *insensibly*, 535.25 *explicitly*, 537.36 *truthfully*, 556.8 *simply*, 658.5 *naively*, 761.8 *unfeelingly*, 818.9 *discourteously*

bluntness 381, 322.9 *openness*, 535.6 *assertiveness*, 537.5 *truthfulness*, 556.6 *naturalness*, 658.2 *naivety*, 761.3 *insensitiveness*, 818.1 *discourtesy*

Bluntness 381

blunt-nosed 381.1 *blunt*

blunt-pointed 381.1 *blunt*

blunt weapon 680

blur 124.9 *be average*, 307.3 *make shapeless*, 436.15 *blind*, 438.7 *become invisible*, 438.8 *make invisible*, 441.2 *murk*, 441.10 *make dim*, 555.4 *de-emphasize*, 622.11 *dirty*

blurb 532.9 *advertisement*

blurb writer 532.10 *publicizer*

blurred 102.8 *unreal*, 307.5 *shapeless*, 438.2 *difficult to see*, 441.6 *murky*, 443.2 *shady*

blurred vission 436.2 *poor sight*

blurriness 307.1 *shapelessness*, 441.2 *murk*

blurry 436.9 *weak-sighted*, 438.2 *difficult to see*, 441.6 *murky*

blurt 583.3 *improvise*

blurt out 530.7 *betray*, 564.11 *speak*

blush 408.1 *heat*, 408.16 *feel hot*, 444.9 *complexion*, 444.16 *make up*, 450.5 *redness*, 450.9 *redden*, 543.3 *gesture*, 810.2 *blushing*, 810.16 *be self-conscious*, 866.2 *signs of guilt*, 866.9 *appear guilty*

blusher 89 *Fungi*, 444.9 *complexion*, 450.6 *red pigment*, 791.4 *cosmetics*, 810.7 *modest person*

blushing 777 *Phobias by Topic*, 810, 810, 408.12 *warmhearted*, 450.2 *red-faced*, 866.6 *appearing guilty*, 876.9 *pure*

blushing bride 823.8 *spouse*

blushingly 450.10 *ruddily*, 810.18 *shyly*, 866.11 *guiltily*

blush unseen 810.15 *escape notice*

bluster 55.58 *blow*, 236.2 *futile effort*, 241.1 *violence*, 241.7 *be violent*, 366.4 *fuss*, 642.12 *be active*, 668.1 *defiance*, 668.5 *defy*, 807.5 *bravado*, 828.11 *be angry*

blusterer 541.6 *exaggerator*, 805.13 *proud person*, 807.12 *impudent person*

blustering 241.6 *violent*

blustery 55.47 *windy*, 241.6 *violent*

Blu-tack 138.3 *adhesive*

Blyton 48 *Writers*

B-movie 127.7 *inferior thing*, 243.5 *work of art*

BMX 71.12 *bicycle*

BO 353.8 *sweat*

boa 79 *Reptiles*, 79.3 *snake*, 295.14 *neckwear*

boa constrictor 79 *Reptiles*

Boadicea 241.4 *violent person or animal*, 679.10 *woman soldier*

boar 77 *Placental Mammals*, 68.8 *livestock*, 77.17 *male mammal*, 401.16 *male animal*

board 74 *Parts of a Ship*, 604, 16.18 *tribunal*, 31.9 *play hockey*, 36.7 *windsurfing*, 40.8 *squash*, 42.4 *chess terms*, 42.6 *darts*, 47.4 *table*, 47.12 *wood*, 47.17 *carpenter*, 51.15 *stage*, 161.7 *committee*, 255.14 *inhabit*, 256.18 *take up residence*, 293.28 *face*, 345.5 *set out*, 346.9 *enter*, 350.24 *have a meal*, 350.25 *provide food*, 359.15 *mount*, 373.7 *hard substance*, 604.1 *materials*, 605.6 *store*, 606.5 *provision*, 653.6 *governing body*, 653.7 *council*, 670.9 *attack successfully*, 703.4 *council*

board and lodging 256.10 *hotel*, 606.1 *provision*

boarded 31.8 *hockey*, 47.16 *joined*

boarder 255.3 *householder*, 350.18 *eater*, 723.5 *possessor*

board foot 75 *General Units*

board game 42.1 *game*

boarding 31.3 *ice hockey*, 31.8 *hockey*, 47.12 *wood*, 47.16 *joined*, 293.8 *wall covering*, 345.8 *start*, 670.12 *military attack*, 670.23 *attacking*

boarding card 73.7 *miscellaneous aviation terms*

boarding house 256.10 *hotel*, 606.1 *provision*

boarding school 6.12 *educational institution*, 606.1 *provision*

board measure 75.1 *unit*

board meeting 161.6 *sitting*

board member 696.5 *company leader*

board of aldermen 16.2 *jurisdiction*, 653.9 *US administrative council*, 706.2 *representative body*

board of directors 653.6 *governing body*

board of governors 6.5 *educationalist*

Board of Trade Unit 75 *Scientific and Technical Units*

board room 592.7 *planning*, 653.7 *council*

board rule 75 *General Units*

boardsurf 36.18 *windsurf*

boardsurfer 36.9 *sailor*

boardsurfing 36.7, 36.13 *windsurfing*

board zither 49 *Musical Instruments*

boar hunt 590.2 *chase*

boar hunting 77.23 *mammal hunting*

boast 541, 146.4 *include*, 541.4 *bombast*, 557.5 *ornament*, 805.12 *object of pride*, 805.29 *feel pride*, 807.24 *be vain*, 809.16 *show off*

boaster 541.6 *exaggerator*, 805.13 *proud person*, 807.12 *impudent person*

boastful 805, 809, 797.3 *affected*

boastfully 809

boastfulness 805, 809

boasting 541.4 *bombast*, 541.15 *bombastic*, 557.2 *affectation*, 811.10 *exhibitionism*

boat 74.3 *vessel*, 326.12 *transport*

boatbill 78 *Birds*

boat-builder 646.2 *artisan*

boat deck 74 *Parts of a Ship*

boatel 74 *Ships and Boats*

boater 295.15 *headgear*

boathouse 256.7 *room*

boating 74.1 *water travel*, 74.11 *nautical*

boatload 257.2 *load*

boatman 74, 326.7 *transferor*

boat racing 674.4 *race*

boat show 526.6 *display*, 740.2 *fair*

boatswain 74.7 *nautical person*

boat trip 74.1 *water travel*

bob 26.2 *boxing*, 26.11 *do a combat sport*, 39.9 *swim*, 41.9 *bobsledding* , 270.10 *shorten*, 339.3 *jerk*, 362.9 *bow*, 362.16 *courtesy*, 365.7 *oscillator*, 365.11 *rock*, 366.9, 366.23 *jolt*, 741.10 *former British money*, 791.8 *hair cut*, 808.10 *knuckle under*, 817.13 *defer to*, 849.4 *mark of respect*, 849.19 *take off one's hat to*

bob and weave 224.12 *be irresolute*

bob and wheel 48.8 *part of poem*

bobbed 270.8 *shortened*

bobber 20.3 *fishing tackle*

bobbery 366.2 *tumult*

bobbin 20.3 *fishing tackle*, 67.4 *weaving*, 364.6 *rotator*

bobbing 26.2 *boxing*, 26.14 *combat*, 39.1 *swimming*, 366.9 *jolt*, 808.2 *sycophancy*, 849.11 *in a respectful stance*

bobbing and weaving 224.2 *irresolution*

bobble 656.7 *be clumsy*

bobble hat 295.15 *headgear*

bobbling 656.9 *bungling*

bobby 16.17 *police officer*, 632.3 *protector*, 688.10 *person of authority*, 718.3 *security officer*

bobby dazzler 789.3 *attractive female*

bobby pin 137.8 *fastening*

bobby socks 295.20 *legwear*

bobcat 77 *Placental Mammals*

bob down 849.19 *take off one's hat to*

Bob Major 49.6 *campanology*

bobolink 78 *Birds*

bobrun 41.9 *bobsledding*

bobsled 41, 41.9 *bobsledding* , 71.10 *sled*

bobsled captain 41.11 *skier*

bobsledder 41.11 *skier*

bobsledding 41

bobsleigh racing 18 *Sporting Activities*

bobsy-die 666.2 *argument*

bob up 344.1 *arrive*, 359.17 *spring up*

bob up and down 46.15 *dance*, 365.11 *rock*

bobwhite 78 *Birds*

bocage 85.4 *trees*

Boccaccio 48 *Writers*, 48 *Poets*

bod 400.7 *person*

bodacious 574.2 *tenacious*

bode 517.11 *predict*

bode ill 843.10 *endanger*

Boden 93 *Cities*

bode well 234.4 *tend*, 686.7 *be auspicious*

bodge 656.7 *be clumsy*

bodged 656.4 *bungled*

Bodhisattva 8.3 *God*

bodhisattva 7.3 *religious person*

bodhran 49 *Musical Instruments*

bodice 295.24 *part of garment*

bodice ripper 48.2 *fiction*, 532.6 *book publishing*

bodiless 368.8 *nonmaterial*

bodiliness 367.1 *material world*

bodily 142.12 *one and all*, 241.10 *violently*, 253.14 *in person*, 290.10 *visceral*, 367.7 *material*

bodily assumption 361.7 *lift*

bodily chastisement 879.12 *corporal punishment*

bodily harm 862.2 *affliction*

bodily love 821.5 *desire*

bodily movement 324

bodily organs 290.4 *insides*

bodily presence 253.1 *presence*

Bodin 4 *Philosophers*

boding 636.8 *warning*

bodkin 322.2 *opener*, 380.8, 380.8 *sharp-pointed thing*

body 59.3 *organism*, 99.2 *thing*, 120.1 *quantity*, 132.1 *remainder*, 161.7 *committee*, 161.11 *group*, 273.5 *thickness*, 295.18 *underwear*, 306.6 *nature*, 367.4 *matter*, 367.5 *object*, 382.3 *form*, 397.11 *dead person*, 400.7 *person*, 457.3 *external appearance*, 665.1 *party*

body and blood of Christ 10.6 *Eucharist*

body and soul 142.11 *wholly*, 144.9 *completely*

body armour 671.7 *armour*

body art 50 *Western Art Styles and Movements*

body belt 671.6 *protective clothing*

body blow 330.13 *blow*, 330.14 *sporting hit*

bodybuilder 237.6 *muscleman*

body-building 350.27 *edible*, 625.4 *hygienic*

body-centred 57.33 *crystalline*

body-centred-cubic crystal 57.4 *crystal*

bodycheck 31.9 *play hockey*

bodychecked 31.8 *hockey*

bodychecking 31.3 *ice hockey*, 31.5 *lacrosse*, 31.8 *hockey*

body clock 192.6 *clock*

body cord 28.2 *fencing equipment*

body covering 293

body fluid 387

bodyguard 180.7 *attendant*, 469.8 *watchful person*, 632.3 *protector*, 671.14 *guard*, 679.2 *defender*, 697.4 *personal attendant*, 718.3 *security officer*

body harness 34.4 *climbing equipment*

body heat 408.1 *heat*

body language 5.5 *nonstandard language*, 457.3 *external appearance*, 543.3 *gesture*

bodyline bowling 27.8 *delivery*

body lotion 418.2 *fragrant thing*, 621.9 *cleaning agent*

body louse 82 *Insects*, 82.3 *pest*

body odour 777 *Phobias by Topic*, 419.2 *something that makes an unpleasant smell*

body of law 16.1 *the law*, 654.3 *precept*

body orifice 322

body padding 671.6 *protective clothing*

body politic 12.5 *political organization*, 91.1 *country*, 400.11 *nation*, 688.8 *governmental organization*

bodypop 46.15 *dance*
body popping 46.1 *dancing*
body scan 60.7 *diagnosis*
body scanner 630.14 *hospital*
body shirt 295.8 *shirt*
body shop 71.21 *miscellaneous motoring terms*
body slam 26.5 *wrestling*
body slip 44.3 *glaze*
body-snatcher 736.9 *plunderer*
body-snatching 736.5 *plundering*, 736.17 *stolen*
body stocking 295.18 *underwear*
body support 284
body type 457.3 *external appearance*
body wave 54.23 *seismic wave*
body weight 369.4 *heaviness*
bodywork 71 *Motor Vehicle Parts*, 382.4 *framework*
Boehmite 54 *Minerals*
Boer War 17 *Major Wars*
Boethius 4 *Philosophers*
Boethusian 7 *Non-Christian Religions*
boeuf bourguignon 45.45 *French dish*
Bofers gun 680.11 *guns*
boffin 4.12 *sage*, 459.8 *intellectual person*, 471.9 *person of ideas*, 485.8 *qualified person*, 501.6 *knowledgeable person*, 518.4 *theorist*, 592.8 *planner*, 646.1 *worker*, 655.5, 688.11 *expert*
boffo 617.1 *worthy*
bog 98.3 *marsh*, 256.7 *room*, 353.13 *lavatory*, 374.11 *soft thing*, 391.8 *marsh*, 622.4 *dirt*, 727.7 *toilet*
bogey 29.2 *golfing terms*, 519.5 *fantasy*, 631.2 *adversity*, 636.3 *false alarm*, 777.5 *frightener*
bogeyman 777.5 *frightener*
bogged down 209.10 *held up*
bogginess 391 374.10 *compressibility*
bogging down 641.1 *inaction*
boggle 477.21 *confuse*, 514.11 *amaze*, 576.5 *vacillate*, 786.10 *be wonderful*
boggle at 573.6 *be unwilling*
boggle one's mind 515.6 *disappoint*
boggle the mind 786.10 *be wonderful*
boggling 576.1 *vacillating*
boggy 98.11 *continental*, 374.4 *compressible*, 391.11 *marshy*
bog hair grass 87 *Grasses*
bogie 72.7 *train*
bog lady 622.6 *dirty person*
bog moss 88.3 *moss*
bog off 345.15 *go*
Bogomils 7 *Christian Movements*
Bogotá 93 *Cities*
bog roll 621.11 *cleaning cloth*
bogtrotter 91 *Names for Inhabitants*
bogue 875.3 *withdrawal*, 875.7 *drugged*
bogus 102.12 *not the real thing*, 474.10 *hypocritical*, 538.14 *unreal*, 539.39 *imitative*, 540.28 *spurious*, 540.33 *fake*, 846.8 *unentitled*
bogus cheque 747.3 *bad payment*
bogusly 538.28 *dishonestly*, 540.36 *falsely*
bogusness 538.2 *unrealness*, 540.4 *spuriousness*
bohemian 104.5 *nonconformist*, 117.6 *misfit*, 139.4 *individualist*, 500.5 *dissenter*, 698.8 *freethinker*, 698.10 *independent*, 720.5 *nonobserver*, 720.11 *nonobservant*
Bohemian 5 *Languages and Groups of Languages*, 50.29 *realist*, 168.7 *nonconformist*, 168.13 *unconventional*, 335.19 *deviant person*, 814.8 *sociable*
Bohemian art 50 *Western Art Styles and Movements*

Bohemianism 168.3 *nonconformism*, 698.1 *freedom*, 814.2 *sociability*
Bohr 52 *Scientists*
Bohr atom 56 *Named Laws*
Bohr radius 56.97 *fundamental constant*
bohunk 91 *Names for Inhabitants*
Boiardo 48 *Poets*
boil 45.55 *cook*, 316.2 *bulge*, 366.3 *turbulence*, 366.21 *be agitated*, 408.14 *be hot*, 624.15 *ulcer*, 625.6 *make hygienic*, 793.2 *pimple*, 828.11 *be angry*
boil away 162.14 *dilute*
boil down 262.5 *make smaller*, 262.6 *become smaller*, 270.10 *shorten*, 273.7 *thicken*, 299.5 *outline*, 562.8 *summarize*
boil down to 520.10 *mean*
boiled 45.56 *culinary*, 408.13 *heated*
boiled away 162.27 *dilute*
boiled cabbage 419.2 *something that makes an unpleasant smell*
boiled-down 262.7 *smaller*, 273.2 *dense*
boiled fish 45.16 *fish dish*
boiled ham 45.30 *bacon*
boiled sweet 45.41 *sweet*, 414.4 *confectionery*
boiler 68.8 *livestock*, 72.5 *locomotive part*, 258.15 *pot*, 408.3 *heater*, 621.7 *washer*
boilermaker 410.9 *power-worker*
boiler room 74 *Parts of a Ship*, 408.8 *hot place*, 539.7 *tricking*
boiler suit 295.10 *suit*
boiling 45.8 *cooking technique*, 55.51 *hot*, 56.37 *temperature*, 57.3 *phase*, 241.6 *violent*, 366.3 *turbulence*, 366.17 *turbulent*, 408.9 *hot*, 637.1 *preservation*, 828.16 *angry*
boiling away 162.3 *dilution*
boiling point 56.37 *temperature*, 408.1 *heat*, 684.3 *elaboration*
boiling tube 57 *Laboratory Apparatus*
boiling-water reactor 56.73 *nuclear reactor*, 410.7 *nuclear power*
boiling with rage 828.16 *angry*
boil over 366.21 *be agitated*, 828.12 *become angry*
Boise 93 *Cities*
boisterous 151.20 *disorderly*, 241.6 *violent*, 423.6 *loud*, 648.3 *hasty*
boisterously 151.29 *riotously*, 151.8 *lawlessness*, 241.1 *violence*
boisterousness 151.8 *lawlessness*, 241.1 *violence*
bok choy 45 *Vegetables*
Bokhara 32 *Breeds of Horse and Pony*
Bokmål 5 *Languages and Groups of Languages*
bola 680.6 *historical missile weapon*
bold 5.41 *lettered*, 34.8 *mountaineering*, 237.12 *strong to the senses*, 303.9 *arrogant*, 526.14 *manifest*, 526.15 *open*, 554.3 *emphatic*, 668.7 *defiant*, 778.9 *courageous*, 780.4 *rash*, 807.15 *audacious*, 807.21 *impudent*, 850.10 *disrespectful*
bold as a lion 778.9 *courageous*
bold as brass 668.7 *defiant*, 807.21 *impudent*
bold climbing 34.1 *mountaineering*
bold façade 778.5 *bold front*
bold front 778, 668.1 *defiance*
bold imagination 519.1 *imagination*
boldly 237.14 *strongly*, 526.17 *frankly*, 668.9 *defiantly*, 778.18 *courageously*, 807.32 *audaciously*
bold move 592.3 *expedient plan*
boldness 303, 554.1 *emphasis*, 668.1 *defiance*, 778.1 *courage*, 807.3 *audacity*
bold relief 437.6 *visible thing*, 437.7 *that which makes visible*

bold type 5.15 *type style*
bole 85.2 *tree part*, 143.6 *branch*, 315.4 *cylinder*
bolero 46.4 *historic dancing*, 295.11 *jacket*
boletus 89 *Fungi*, 45.33 *vegetable*
bolide 53.20 *meteor*
Bolivia 91 *Countries*
Böll 48 *Writers*
bollard 74 *Parts of a Ship*, 34.5 *rock face*, 137.8 *fastening*
bollix up 151.23 *confuse*, 683.6 *fail*
bollocks 245.8 *organs of reproduction*, 316.2 *bulge*, 506.1, 521.14 *nonsense*, 827.15 *miscellaneous swearwords*
bollocks up 628.4 *impair*, 683.6 *fail*
boll weevil 82 *Insects*, 82.3 *pest*
Bologna 93 *Cities*
bologna sausage 45.29 *sausage*
bolognese sauce 45.15 *sauce*
Bolognese school 50 *Western Art Styles and Movements*
bolometer 56.92 *light meter*, 268.8 *meter*
bolometric 268.16 *micrometric*
bolometry 268.2 *micrometry*
boloney 45.29 *sausage*
bolopunch 330.14 *sporting hit*
Bolsheviks 12.6 *political party*
Bolshevism 12.1 *government*, 688.7 *type of rule*
Bolshevist 693.11 *rebel*
bolshie 693.9 *criminal*, 713.9 *protesting*
Bolshoi Ballet 46.12 *ballet companies*
bolster 43.9 *miscellaneous architectural features*, 284.4 *rest*, 284.11 *support*, 637.5 *preserve*, 662.19 *support*
bolt 34.4 *climbing equipment*, 34.8 *mountaineering*, 63.27 *superstructure*, 135.10 *link*, 137.8 *fastening*, 137.11 *connect*, 137.12 *bind*, 161.27 *bundle*, 269.5 *piece*, 323.3 *restrainer*, 323.7 *close*, 329.6 *accelerate*, 338.8 *missile*, 345.4 *hurry off*, 350.22 *eat well*, 591.8 *run away*, 603.1 *tool*, 632.4 *safety device*, 638.5 *escape*, 648.2 *make haste*, 680.6 *historical missile weapon*, 872.5 *be greedy*
Bolt 48 *Dramatists*
bolt-action rifle 37.3 *hunting equipment*
bolt down one's meal 648.2 *make haste*
bolted 137.16 *bound*, 323.12 *closed*
bolt from the blue 514.3 *shock*
bolt hole 531.2 *hiding place*, 634.1 *refuge*
bolting 350.2 *appetite*, 872.6 *gluttonous*
bolt of lightning 55.21 *thunderstorm*
bolt rope 36.3 *parts of a sailing boat*
bolt route 34.1 *mountaineering*
bolt the door 634.4 *shelter*
bolt upright 281.8 *vertical*, 281.11 *vertically*
Boltzmann 52 *Scientists*
Boltzmann constant 56 *Named Laws*, 56.97 *fundamental constant*
bolus 350.14 *mouthful*, 630.2 *medicine*
Bolyai 52 *Scientists*
bomb 670, 680, 19.9 *play*, 51.11 *theatrical performance*, 71.16 *car*, 244.7 *agent of destruction*, 244.9 *demolish*, 398.17 *murder*, 425.3 *banger*, 679.37 *fight*, 683.4 *unsuccessful thing*
bombard 244.9 *demolish*, 338.28 *shoot*, 670.1 *attack*, 680.12 *historical guns*
bombarde 49 *Musical Instruments*

bombardier 71.10 *sled*, 670.19 *attacker*, 679.17 *army person*, 679.32 *airman*
bombardier beetle 82 *Insects*
bombardment 338.7 *shot*, 423.1 *loudness*, 670.12 *military attack*, 676.8 *warfare*
bombardon 49 *Musical Instruments*
bombast 541, 506.1 *nonsense*, 541.10 *boast*, 557.2 *affectation*, 559.4 *inelegance of speech*, 811.4 *flashiness*, 811.5 *pomposity*
bombastic 541, 357.13 *exaggerated*, 553.3 *diffuse*, 557.4 *ornate*, 564.20 *eloquent*, 811.19 *flashy*, 811.20 *pompous*
bombastically 541.16 *exaggeratedly*, 553.7 *diffusely*, 557.6 *ornately*, 811.35 *flashily*, 811.36 *pompously*
Bombay 93 *Cities*
Bombay duck 80 *Fishes*, 45.18 *sea fish*
bombay mix 45.49 *Indian dish*
bomb-disposal expert 469.6 *careful person*
bomb-dropping 670.13 *air attack*
bombed 874.3 *dead drunk*
bomber 73 *Types of Aircraft*, 398.11 *murderer*, 670.19 *attacker*, 679.31 *military aircraft*
bomber jacket 295.11 *jacket*
bomber pilot 679.32 *airman*
bombinate 426.9 *hum*, 432.6 *buzz*
bombination 426.2 *humming*, 432.3 *insect noise*
bombing 670.13 *air attack*, 670.16 *terrorist attack*, 676.8 *warfare*
bombproof 378.1 *tough*, 378.11 *make tough*, 632.6 *invulnerable*, 671.31 *entrenched*
bomb run 670.13 *air attack*
bombshell 514.3 *shock*, 680.16 *bomb*
bomb shelter 531.2 *hiding place*, 634.1 *refuge*
bombsight 73 *Aircraft Parts*
Bön 7 *Non-Christian Religions*
bona fide 119.6, 537.19 *authentic*, 857.4 *honourable*
bona fideness 537.6 *authenticity*
bona fides 857.1 *probity*
bonanza 605.2 *resource*, 608.8 *plenty*, 610.1 *excess*, 686.2 *good fortune*, 729.2 *gift*, 742.5 *wealth*
Bonar Bridge 93 *Cities*
bonbon 45.41 *sweet*, 414.4 *confectionery*
bond 845, 57.26 *react*, 63.26 *masonry*, 107.1 *relatedness*, 116.3 *arrangement*, 135.1 *union*, 135.5 *joint*, 137.4 *means of connection*, 137.11 *connect*, 140.6 *come together*, 661.4 *restraint*, 667.2 *contract*, 714.1 *promise*, 715.1 *contract*, 718.2 *promise*, 741.14 *paper money*, 847.7 *commitment*
Bond 48 *Dramatists*
bondage 699.4 *detention*, 701.1 *subjection*
bond angle 57.11 *chemical bond*
bonded 107.4 *related*, 116.11 *allied*, 135.15 *tied*, 137.15 *connected*, 138.9 *adhesive*
bond energy 57.11 *chemical bond*
Bondi 52 *Scientists*
bonding 135.1 *union*, 138.1 *adhesion*
bonding agent 137.4 *means of connection*
bonding orbital 57.12 *valence*
bondmaid 697.7 *slave*
bonds 699.5 *means of restraint*
bondservant 697.7 *slave*
bondslave 701.5 *subjected person*
bondsman 697.7 *slave*, 701.5 *subjected person*, 714.5 *promise-maker*
bond strength 57.11 *chemical bond*
bondwoman 701.5 *subjected person*

bone 45.55 *cook*, 349.11 *void*, 371.4 *solid body*, 373.7 *hard substance*, 382.7 *skeleton*
bone ash 44.2 *raw material*
bone cancer 624.12 *cancer*
bone-carving 50.12 *sculpture*
bone cell 59.7 *cell*
bone china 44.1 *ceramics*
boned 373.2 *tough*
bone-dry 392.3 *dried-up*
bonefish 80 *Fishes*, 20.4 *American game fish*
boneheaded 273.3 *thick-witted*
bone idle 643.3 *not participating*
boneless rump roast 45.23 *beef*
bonemeal 68.13, 246.3 *fertilizer*
bone of contention 472.2 *issue*, 477.4 *difficult question*, 666.1 *disagreement*, 674.1 *contention*
boner 504.10 *blunder*
bones 132.1 *remainder*, 759.8 *seat of feelings*
bonesetter 60.12 *healer*, 407.5 *toucher*, 630.15 *healer*
bone-setter 629.12 *repairer*
bone-setting 630.13 *therapy*
boneshaker 71.12 *bicycle*
bone to pick 666.1 *disagreement*, 822.1 *hate*, 828.1 *resentment*
bone turquoise 54 *Gemstones*
bone up 6.23 *learn*
bone up on 696.15 *learn*
bone urn 399.4 *funeral objects*
boneyard 399.5 *cemetery*
bonfire 408.6, 439.8 *fire*, 812.8 *salute*
bonfire party 665.7 *social gathering*
bong 34.4 *climbing equipment*
bongo 77 *Placental Mammals*
bongo drums 49 *Musical Instruments*
bonhomie 811.8 *bravado*, 815.8 *good company*, 819.1 *friendship*, 831.1 *benevolence*
Bonhomin 7 *Members of Religious Orders*
bonhomous 769.1 *cheerful*
boniness 274.7 *thinness*, 274.8 *emaciation*
Bonington 18 *Sporting Personalities*
bonito 80 *Fishes*, 20.4 *American game fish*
bonk 245.14 *have sex*, 330.3 *hit*, 330.13 *blow*
bonkers 510.11 *insane*
bonking 135.4 *sexual union*, 821.5 *desire*
Bonn 93 *Cities*
bonnang 49 *Musical Instruments*
bonnet 71 *Motor Vehicle Parts*, 295.15 *headgear*
Bonnet 52 *Scientists*
bonneted 295.29 *dressed*
Bonnie Parker and Clyde Barrow 736.8 *thief*
Bonnin and Morris porcelain 44 *Types of Ceramics*
bonny 259.16 *fat*, 623.1 *healthy*, 789.5 *beautiful*
bonnyclabber 393.8 *pulp*
Bonosianism 7 *Christian Movements*
bonsai 69.2 *garden*
bonsai tree 85.1 *tree*
bonspiel 41.10 *curling*
bontebok 77 *Placental Mammals*
bonus 130.4 *extra*, 132.4 *surplus*, 228.5 *positive stimulus*, 610.3 *superfluity*, 721.5 *profit*, 729.2 *gift*, 729.7 *given*, 730.2 *something received*, 749.2 *money received*, 755.7 *gift*, 837.3 *recognition*, 878.4 *reward for service*
bonuses 15.2 *industrial negotiations*
bon voyage 345.14 *goodbye*
bony 274.1 *thin*, 373.1 *hard*, 382.13 *skeletal*
bony fish 80.2 *fish*
bonze 7.7 *monk*

boo 429.2, 429.5 *catcall*, 431.7 *cry of disapproval*, 431.14 *hiss*, 543.3, 543.11 *gesture*, 713.3 *gesture of protest*, 713.7 *complain*, 766.2 *expression of dissatisfaction*, 766.7 *be dissatisfied*, 850.6, 850.25 *taunt*, 852.9 *show of disapproval*, 852.23 *show disapproval*
boob 211.3 *lost chance*, 211.8 *make a mistake*, 493.2 *mistake*, 504.10 *blunder*, 504.19 *make a mistake*, 656.7 *be clumsy*, 656.10 *unskilled person*, 683.4 *unsuccessful thing*, 798.4 *joke*
boo-boo 211.3 *lost chance*, 493.2 *mistake*, 504.10 *blunder*, 683.4 *unsuccessful thing*, 798.4 *joke*
boobs 316.2 *bulge*
boob tube 534.22 *television set*
booby 78 *Birds*, 510.7 *insane person*, 656.10 *unskilled person*
booby hutch 510.8 *mental hospital*
booby prize 656.8 *unskilfulness*, 878.2 *prize*
booby trap 539.13 *snare*, 635.1 *trap*, 680.16 *bomb*
booby-trap 671.18 *fence*
boodle 721.5 *profit*, 734.5 *takings*, 736.4 *stolen goods*, 741.2 *cash*
booed 852.35 *hissed*
boogerboo 531.7 *concealer*
boogie-woogie 49.8 *jazz*
boohoo 431.6 *cry of pain*
boo-hurrah theory 4.7 *school of thought*
booing 429.7 *catcalling*, 431.19 *hissing*, 713.9 *protesting*, 850.15 *taunting*
book 48.8 *part of poem*, 51.2 *play*, 171.8 *list*, 208.9 *prepare*, 243.5 *work of art*, 532.6 *book publishing*, 545.15 *register*, 593.10 *necessitate*, 718.15 *reserve*, 750.7 *account*, 856.5 *accuse*
bookbinder 293.17 *coverer*, 532.12 *publisher*
book binding 42 *Hobbies and Pastimes*
bookcase 47.5, 258.3 *cabinet*
book club 532.6 *book publishing*
book collection 605.5 *collection*
book cover 293.4 *wrapping*
booked 593.4 *required*, 856.8 *accusatory*
Booker Prize 532.6 *book publishing*, 878.2 *prize*
book fair 532.6 *book publishing*
bookie 32.15 *horse person*
book illustration 547.2 *reproduction*
book in advance 208.9 *prepare*
booking 51.13 *engagement*, 545.8 *registration*, 856.1 *accusation*
booking agent 51.25 *producer*
booking clerk 739.12 *wholesaler*
booking office 72.8 *railway station*
bookish 4.19 *learned*, 6.18 *educated*
bookishly 6.26 *studiously*
bookishness 6.9 *learnedness*, 501.3 *learning*
bookkeeper 170.7 *mathematician*, 545.9 *recorder*, 741.18 *treasurer*
book-keeper 750.6 *accountant*
bookkeeping 545.8 *registration*
book-keeping 750.1 *accounts*, 750.10 *accounting*
booklearning 501.3 *learning*
book list 171.2 *table*
booklouse 82 *Insects*
bookmaker 32.15 *horse person*
bookmaking 589.7 *calculation of chance*
bookman 459.8 *intellectual person*
bookmobile 71 *Motor Vehicles*
Book of Common Prayer 10.10 *religious manual*

book of hours 10.10 *religious manual*
Book of Mormon 7.12 *religious text*
Book of the Dead 7.12 *religious text*
book of words 51.2 *play*
boo koos 608.8 *plenty*
bookperson 532.12 *publisher*
bookplate 544.3 *means of identification*
book publisher 532.12 *publisher*
book publishing 532
book review 524.3 *criticism*, 532.6 *book publishing*
book reviewer 48.15 *literary person*
books 171.4 *bill*, 750.5 *account book*
bookseller 532.12 *publisher*
bookselling 532.6 *book publishing*
book serialization 532.6 *book publishing*
bookshelf 47.5, 258.3 *cabinet*
bookshop 532.6 *book publishing*
book trade 532.6 *book publishing*
book-wise 6.18 *educated*
bookworm 82 *Insects*, 6.7 *learner*, 81.6 *worm*, 82.3 *pest*, 459.8 *intellectual person*
Boole 52 *Scientists*
Boolean algebra 52 *Named Concepts*, 52.23 *algebra*
boolhipper 295.11 *jacket*
boom 74 *Rigging*, 13.2 *economy*, 36.3 *parts of a sailing boat*, 36.7 *windsurfing*, 63.27 *superstructure*, 128.2 *spread*, 128.4 *increase*, 246.2 *productiveness*, 246.6 *be fertile*, 423.1 *loudness*, 423.8 *be loud*, 425.1, 425.5 *bang*, 426.8 *drum*, 427.9 *resonate*, 564.12 *speak loudly*, 629.10 *revival*, 671.9 *barrier*, 686.1 *prosperity*, 739.2 *be sold*, 739.5 *sales*
boom and bust 365.1 *oscillation*, 737.5 *commercial trade*
boom box 420.9 *audio device*, 534.18 *radio*
boom/bust cycle 13.2 *economy*
boomerang 221.6 *reverse*, 231.3 *counteract*, 331.1, 331.4 *recoil*, 672.1 *retaliation*, 672.3 *retaliate*, 680.6 *historical missile weapon*
boomerang effect 221.1 *reversion*, 231.1 *counteraction*
booming 246.5 *fertile*, 423.6 *loud*, 425.8 *banging*, 426.1 *drumming*, 427.3 *deepness*, 427.8 *deep*, 431.16 *vociferous*, 686.8 *prosperous*
booming economy 246.2 *productiveness*, 686.1 *prosperity*
boom off 74.9 *navigate*
boom preventer 36.3 *parts of a sailing boat*
boomps-a-daisy 46.2 *dance*
boomslang 79 *Reptiles*
boom town 93.9 *town*, 249.11 *settlement*
boom vang 36.3 *parts of a sailing boat*
boon 729.2 *gift*, 861.13 *benefit*
boon companion 819.6 *close friend*
boondocks 249.6 *regions*
boonies 249.6 *regions*
boor 460.3 *unintelligent person*, 652.5 *badly behaved person*, 764.9 *unpleasant person*, 795.5 *vulgar person*, 818.4 *discourteous person*
boorish 460.6 *unintelligent*, 559.8 *indecorous*, 595.5 *immature*, 652.18 *badly behaved*, 656.3 *clumsy*, 764.2 *objectionable*, 795.8 *discourteous*, 818.6 *bad-mannered*
boorishly 818.10 *rudely*
boorishness 460.2 *unintelligence*, 559.2 *impropriety*, 652.4 *bad conduct*, 764.6 *objectionability*, 795.3 *grossness*, 818.2 *bad manners*

boost 128.2 *spread*, 128.5 *make bigger*, 237.8 *strengthen*, 239.3 *invigorate*, 361.1 *raise*, 361.7 *lift*, 532.16 *publicize*, 662.2, 662.19 *support*, 662.28 *further*, 736.12 *steal*, 851.15 *compliment*
booster 53.35 *rocketry*, 338.11 *propeller*, 534.18 *radio*, 736.8 *thief*
booster station 534.20 *radio broadcasting*, 534.24 *television broadcasting*
boosting 736.1 *stealing*
boot 71 *Motor Vehicle Parts*, 27.6 *pad*, 41.5 *ski equipment*, 65.19 *abort*, 156.20 *activate*, 252.17 *relegate*, 258.10 *cart*, 330.7 *kick*, 330.13 *blow*, 652.8 *treatment*, 661.4 *restraint*
boot-axe 34.8 *mountaineering*
boot-axe belay 34.3 *climbing technique*
bootblack 621.12 *cleaner*, 697.3 *attendant*
booted 295.29 *dressed*
Booted 68 *Breeds of Fowl*
booted out 252.11 *relegated*
bootees 295.23 *children's clothes*
booter 295.26 *fashion designer*
Boötes 53 *The Constellations*
booth 51.14 *theatre*, 256.8 *shelter*, 258.2 *compartment*, 740.9 *stall*
booting out 349.17 *expulsion*
bootlace 137.6 *line*
bootlace fungus 89 *Fungi*
bootlace worm 81 *Worms*
bootleg 19.9 *play*, 19.15 *play offence*, 118.2 *copy*, 538.14 *unreal*, 540.10 *fake*, 733.9 *borrow illegally*, 736.15 *infringe*
bootleg copy 114.2 *copy*
bootlegger 118.8 *copier*, 734.6 *taker*, 736.10 *infringer*
bootlegging 733.3, 736.6 *illegal borrowing*
bootleg liquor 874.12 *alcohol*
bootleg record 736.6 *illegal borrowing*
bootless 614.2 *futile*, 683.10 *failed*
bootlessly 358.11 *in vain*, 683.12 *unsuccessfully*
bootlessness 614.4 *futility*
bootlick 771.15 *humour*, 808.9 *fawn*, 853.11 *be sycophantic*
bootlicker 771.7 *person who humours*, 808.3, 853.7 *sycophant*
bootlicking 673.5 *submitting*, 771.11 *humouring*, 808.2 *sycophancy*, 808.7 *sycophantic*, 849.9 *showing respect*, 853.5 *sycophancy*, 853.16 *sycophantic*
bootmaker 295.26 *fashion designer*
bootmaking 295.2 *dressing*
boot out 252.16 *replace*, 341.2 *eject*, 349.1 *expel*, 349.2 *dismiss*, 581.2 *discard*, 727.10 *dismiss*
boot-out 252.4 *relegation*
boot out on one's ear 252.16 *replace*
boot polish 621.9 *cleaning agent*
boots 38.1 *soccer*, 295.19 *footwear*
boot sale 727.2 *disposal of property*
boot-scraper 621.10 *cleaning object*
bootstrap 65.17 *computing term*, 65.19 *abort*
booty 681.2 *spoils*, 721.5 *profit*, 734.5 *takings*, 736.4 *stolen goods*
booze 351.7 *alcoholic drink*, 351.13 *drink*, 874.8 *get drunk*, 874.12 *alcohol*
boozed up 874.1 *drunk*
boozer 256.10 *hotel*, 351.12 *drinker*, 874.17 *drunkard*
boozing 351.16 *drinking*, 874.5 *drunken*
boozy 874.2 *slightly drunk*, 874.5 *drunken*

bop 46.1 *dancing*, 46.2, 46.15 *dance*, 49.8 *jazz*, 161.10 *dance*, 330.3 *hit*, 815.5 *party*
bora 55 Winds
boracic acid 57 Common Chemical Compounds, **62** Medication, 630.3 *prophylactic*
boracite 54 Minerals
borage 45 Herbs and Spices, 413.5 *herbs*
Boran 68 Breeds of Cattle
borane 57 Types of Compounds
borate 57 Types of Compounds
borax 54 Minerals, **62** Medication
Bordeaux 93 Cities, 351.9 *wine*
Bordeaux mixture 69.8 *weedkiller*
bordelaise sauce 45.15 *sauce*
bordello 877.6 *brothel*
border 300, 51.17 *stage set*, 69.3 *ornamental garden*, 130.3 *additional item*, 136.6 *boundary*, 157.7 *limit*, 267.1 *juxtaposition*, 267.3 *juxtapose*, 289.1 *exterior*, 289.11 *be exterior*, 297.7 *surround*, 298.4 *interface*, 299.3, 300.1 *edge*, 300.2 *edging*, 300.6 *edge*, 302.6 *furthest*, 407.12 *abut*
border ballad 49.11 *folk music*
Border collie 77 Breeds of Dogs
bordered 300.8 *edging*
bordering 157.24 *limiting*, 267.1 *juxtaposition*, 267.5 *juxtaposed*, 302.6 *furthest*, 407.9 *touching*
bordering on 615.2 *nearby*
borderland 249.6 *regions*, 267.1 *juxtaposition*
Border Leicester 68 Breeds of Sheep
borderline 477.14 *questionable*, 491.6 *indeterminate*
borderline case 491.11 *irresoluteness*
border on 298.4 *interface*
borders 249.6 *regions*
Borders 92 Counties, 249.9 *regions of Britain*
Border terrier 77 Breeds of Dogs
Bordet 52 Scientists
bordure 544.8 *heraldic device*
bore 47.17 *carpenter*, 96.2 *channel*, 112.12 *be monotonous*, 271.4 *breadth*, 317.7 *make concave*, 322.1 *opening*, 322.20 *hole*, 360.15 *tunnel*, 380.16 *use a sharp tool* , 412.7 *be tasteless*, 553.5 *be diffuse*, 565.8 *talk too much*, 628.5 *hurt*, 650.6 *fatigue*, 680.9 *firearm*, 783.13 *make indifferent*, 788.2 *boring thing*, 788.3 *boring person*, 788.6 *be boring*
boreal 55.47 *windy*, 55.55 *cool*, 332.13 *directional*
Boreas 55.15 *wind direction*, 409.7 *cold weather*
bored 650, 788, 322.14 *holed*, 466.4 *uninterested*, 650.2 *bored*
boredom 788, 112.4 *monotony*, 412.1 *tastelessness*, 466.2 *lack of interest*, 555.2 *lack of emphasis*, 556.4 *simplicity*, 650.7 *fatigue*
Boredom 788
bored stiff 788.5 *bored*
bored to death 788.5 *bored*
bored to tears 788.5 *bored*
bored tunnel 63.22 *tunnel*
borehole 317.2 *concave land*, 322.5 *hole*
bore in 346.11 *infiltrate*
bore into 317.7 *make concave*
borer 82 Insects, 47.11 *woodworking tool*, 82.3 *pest*, 317.4 *digger*, 380.8 *sharp-pointed thing*
Boreray 68 Breeds of Sheep
boresome 788.4 *boring*
bore stiff 788.6 *be boring*
bore the pants off 788.6 *be boring*
bore to death 788.6 *be boring*
bore to tears 650.6 *fatigue*, 788.6 *be boring*
Borg 18 Sporting Personalities
Borges 48 Writers
boric acid 630.3 *prophylactic*
boride 57 Types of Compounds

boring 788, 112.8, 183.13 *monotonous*, 360.7 *tunnelling*, 412.5 *tasteless*, 553.3 *diffuse*, 555.1 *unemphatic*, 556.1 *simple*, 616.1 *inconvenient*, 650.4 *fatiguing*, 659.13 *inconvenient*, 783.11 *insignificant*
boring life 788.1 *boredom*
boringly 788, 616.6 *inconveniently*, 783.20 *unexceptionally*
boring machine 47.11 *woodworking tool*, 63.9 *machine tool*
boringness 788.1 *boredom*
boring old fart 788.3 *boring person*
boring person 788
boring situation 788.2 *boring thing*
boring thing 788
boring work 788.2 *boring thing*
Boris Becker 40.7 *famous tennis players*
Bormanus 8 Deities
born 396, 243.12 *produced*
Born 52 Scientists
born again 220.16 *influenced*, 629.13 *repaired*
born-again 497.11 *believing*, 867.6 *penitent*
born-again Christian 7.5 *Christian*, 497.5 *believer*, 840.3 *atoner*, 867.3 *penitent person*
born alive 396.15 *born*
born dead 397.19 *dead*
Borneo 98 Islands
borneol 85 Tree Products
borne out 475.13 *proven*
born for 655.7 *gifted*
Born–Haber cycle 57 Named Reactions
born in the purple 742.1 *wealthy*
bornite 54 Minerals
born leader 225.5 *stable person*
born loser 581.9 *rejected person*, 683.5 *failing person*, 687.5 *person in adversity*, 722.6 *loser*, 776.3 *hopeless person*
born of 227.10 *caused*
born to the purple 455.4 *figurative usage*
born to toil 644.10 *working*
born under a bad sign 687.8 *unlucky*
born under a lucky star 686.8 *prosperous*
born under an evil star 687.8 *unlucky*
born with a silver spoon in one's mouth 686.8 *prosperous*, 742.1 *wealthy*
born yesterday 658.1 *naive*
Borodin 49 Musicians and Composers
boron 57 Chemical Elements
boron hydride 57 Types of Compounds
borosilicate 57 Types of Compounds
borough 92.1 *administrative area*, 92.4 *community*, 93.9 *town*, 249.5 *state*, 580.12 *election*
Borrelly 53 Comets
borrow 733, 52.91 *add*, 118.10 *copy*, 734.10 *take away*, 736.12 *steal*, 744.9 *acquire credit*
Borrow 48 Writers
borrowed 733
borrowed plumes 539.12 *disguise*
borrowed word 5.17 *word*
borrower 733, 712.4 *requester*, 728.2 *person transferring property*, 745.6 *debtor*
borrow from 227.7 *follow from*
borrow illegally 733
borrowing 733, 41.10 *curling*, 734.3 *taking away*, 736.1 *stealing*, 745.3 *loan*, 745.9 *in debt*
Borrowing 733
borrowing capacity 602.4 *financial resources*, 744.1 *credit*
borrow money 745.7 *be in debt*
borrow without authorization 733.9 *borrow illegally*
borrow without permission 733.9 *borrow illegally*
borscht 45.13 *soup*

borscht belt 51.13 *engagement*
borstal 323.4 *closed place*, 627.10 *reformatory*, 702.1 *prison*, 702.2 *the inside* , 816.4 *place of confinement*
Borvo 8 Deities
borzoi 77 Breeds of Dogs
bo-san 7.7 *monk*
Bosanquet 4 Philosophers
Bosch 52 Scientists
Bosch process 57 Named Reactions
Bosci 7 Christian Movements
Bose 52 Scientists
Bose–Einstein statistics 56 Named Laws
bosey 539.9 *sleight of hand*
bosh 474.2 *sophism*, 506.1 *nonsense*, 521.4 *senseless talk*, 538.6, 540.13 *nonsense*
bosie 27.8 *delivery*
bosk 85.4 *trees*
bosket 85.4 *trees*
bosky 85.16 *wooded*
Bosnia-Hercegovina 91 Countries
Bosnian 32 Breeds of Horse and Pony
Bosnians 1 Peoples
bosom 295.24 *part of garment*, 316.2 *bulge*, 759.8 *seat of feelings*
bosom buddy 784.4 *likable person*, 819.6 *close friend*
bosom friend 784.4 *likable person*
bosom pal 819.6 *close friend*
bosomy 359.16 *fat*
boson 56.77 *elementary particle*
boss 43 Architectural Decoration, 15.6 *employer*, 31.7 *hurling*, 43.19 *decorate*, 50.13 *relief-carving*, 126.5 *superior*, 316.2 *bulge*, 375.12 *make rough*, 642.17 *meddle*, 653.2 *direct*, 653.13 *director*, 688.10 *person of authority*, 688.19 *be authoritarian*, 696.5 *company leader*, 696.14 *master*
bossanova 46.2 *dance*
boss around 642.17 *meddle*, 690.5 *be severe*
bossed 43.17 *structured*
bosses 653.6 *governing body*
boss-eyed 436.9 *weak-sighted*
bossy 688.12 *authoritative*, 690.8 *severe*, 692.15 *self-assured*, 696.13 *excellent*
Boston 42 Card Games, **93** Cities, 93.2 *American cities*
Boston accent 5.26 *dialect*
Boston bag 258.9 *baggage*
Boston brown bread 45.38 *bread*
Boston cream pie 45.36 *cake*
Boston fern 88 Ferns
Boston rocker 47.2 *chair*
Boston terrier 77 Breeds of Dogs
Boston two-step 46.2 *dance*
bosun's chair 36.3 *parts of a sailing boat*
bosun's mate 74.7 *nautical person*
Boswell 48 Writers
bot 407.3 *press*
BOT 699.4 *detention*, 702.4 *prison sentence*
botanic 83.20 *botanical*
botanical 69, 83, 59.20 *biological*
botanical fruit 86
botanical garden 69.2 *garden*
botanically 83, 59.29 *biologically*, 69.20 *horticulturally*
botanic garden 69.2 *garden*, 83.11 *herbarium*
botanist 59.19 *life scientist*, 83.12 *plant scientist*
botanize 83.23 *study plants*
botany 59.1 *life science*, 83.10 *plant science*, 396.7 *studies of life*
botch 151.23 *confuse*, 548.1 *misrepresentation*, 548.4 *misrepresent*, 618.8 *inferiority*, 618.11 *be worthless*, 620.5 *imperfection*, 628.4 *impair*, 656.7 *be clumsy*, 656.9 *bungling*, 661.2 *obstacle*, 683.1 *failure*

botched 618.2 *inferior*, 620.1 *imperfect*, 656.4 *bungled*
botcher 656.10 *unskilled person*
botching 656.9 *bungling*
botch up 504.19 *make a mistake*
botch-up 504.10 *blunder*
botchy 656.4 *bungled*
bot fly 82 Insects
both 176.9 *two*
bother 151.9 *disorder*, 153.1 *disturbance*, 153.5 *commotion*, 153.7 *disturb*, 366.4 *fuss*, 462.7 *inconsiderate person*, 462.13 *be inconsiderate*, 616.3 *inconvenience*, 616.5 *be inconvenient*, 642.3 *nimbleness*, 642.12 *be active*, 642.17 *meddle*, 650.6 *fatigue*, 659.7 *awkward situation*, 659.23 *cause difficulties*, 661.8 *hinder*, 764.8 *quarrel*, 768.3 *nuisance*, 828.9.9 *offend*, 829.8 *make irascible*
botheration 642.3 *nimbleness*
bothered 153.12 *disturbed*, 659.16 *troubled*
bothering 462.10 *inconsiderate*
bothersome 153.17 *disturbing*, 616.1 *inconvenient*, 618.6 *damnable*, 659.13 *inconvenient*
both hands 702.4 *prison sentence*
bothy 256.8 *shelter*
bo tree 85 Trees and Shrubs
Bo tree 10.14 *sacred object*, 85.13 *tree mythology*
botrytis 89 Fungi, 69.12 *pests and diseases*
Botswana 91 Countries
bottle 258, 120.3 *container*, 258.21 *put* **in a container**, 303.5 *boldness*, 351.10 *drink container*, 574.16 *fortitude*, 575.4 *stamina*, 605.6 *store*, 637.2 *preserver*, 637.5 *preserve*, 668.1 *defiance*, 680.7 *blunt weapon*, 778.1 *courage*
bottlebrush 85 Trees and Shrubs
bottled 258.20 *containing*, 605.7 *stored*, 637.7 *preserved*, 874.1 *drunk*
bottled beer 351.7 *alcoholic drink*
bottled fruit 45.42 *preserve*, 637.3 *preserved thing*
bottled water 389.2 *drinking water*
bottleful 351.2 *drink*
bottle garden 69.2 *garden*
bottle glass 44.1 *ceramics*, 442.9 *glass*
bottle green 453.1 *green*
bottle kiln 44.6 *ceramic workshop*
bottleneck 262.3 *contracted thing*, 272.6 *narrow place*, 342.6 *narrowing*, 661.2 *obstacle*, 661.9 *block*
bottlenose 77 Placental Mammals
bottle-opener 322.2 *opener*
bottle party 815.5 *party*
bottler 637.4 *preservationist*
bottle tree 85 Trees and Shrubs
bottle up 290.15 *keep inside*, 302.7 *limit*, 531.8 *conceal*, 637.5 *preserve*, 699.8 *restrain*, 726.7 *detain*
bottle up and go 591.9 *play truant*
bottling 258.20 *containing*, 605.4 *storage*
bottling plant 637.2 *preserver*
bottling up 726.2 *detention*
bottom 20.8 *angling*, 127.5 *inferior state*, 276.4 *low thing*, 276.6 *lower*, 277.10 *deeper*, 280.1, 280.3 *base*, 302.2 *limiting factor*, 304.2 *rear end*
bottom cushion 24.5 *snooker*
bottom dollar 157.8 *tail*
bottom drawer 47.5 *cabinet*, 594.10 *preparations*, 605.1 *store*
bottom gear 33.6 *motor racing terms*
bottoming out 129.2 *decline*, 262.1 *contraction*
bottom land 98.6 *lowland*
bottomless 184.1 *infinite*, 277.8 *deep*, 608.2 *plentiful*
bottomlessness 277.1 *depth*

bottomless pit 8.11 *heaven,* 184.4 *infinity,* 277.4 *deep thing,* 872.4 *glutton*
bottomless purse 742.5 *wealth*
bottom line 101.5 *realities,* 103.2 *essential content,* 878.5 *turnover*
bottommost 127.12 *inferior,* 276.6 *lower,* 280.3 *base*
bottom of one's heart 759.8 *seat of feelings*
bottom of the barrel 157.8 *tail*
bottom of the bill 51.6 *scene*
bottom of the inning 22.1 *baseball*
bottom of the sea 277.4 *deep thing*
bottom out 129.4 *decrease,* 262.6 *become smaller,* 276.8 *be low*
bottom patting 543.3 *gesture*
bottom pinching 543.3 *gesture*
bottom pocket 24.3 *English billiards,* 24.5 *snooker*
bottom price 752.2 *bargain*
bottom side 305.2 *surface*
bottoms up 351.18 *cheers*
bottom turn 36.1 *sailing*
bottom-up 287.2 *inverted*
botulism 624.6 *infection,* 624.8 *indigestion,* 631.7 *poisoning*
Botvinnik 18 Sporting Personalities
bouclé 375.2 *coarse,* 375.7 *rough thing*
boudoir 256.7 *room,* 531.6 *privacy,* 821.13 *abode of love*
boudoir dress 295.16 *robe*
bouffant 295.31 *styled*
Bougainville 98 Islands
bougainvillea 84 Flowers and Flowering Plants
bough 85.2 *tree part,* 143.6 *branch*
bought 738
bought-in 68.21 *domesticated*
bouillabaisse 45.13 *soup*
bouillon 45.13 *soup*
Boulanger 49 Musicians and Composers
boulder 54.27 *sediment,* 373.7 *hard substance*
Boulder 93 Cities
boulder clay 54.38 *glacier*
bouldering 34.1 *mountaineering,* 34.8 *mountaineering*
boules 18 Sporting Activities
boulevard 327.3 *road*
boulle 47.7 *furniture style,* 47.9 *decorative woodwork*
Boulogne 93 Cities
Boulonnais 32 Breeds of Horse and Pony
Boult 49 Musicians and Composers
bounce 27.8 *delivery,* 27.18 *bowl,* 331.1, 331.4 *recoil,* 349.1 *expel,* 359.5, 359.18 *jump,* 365.11 *rock,* 366.9 *jolt,* 366.21 *be agitated,* 366.23 *jolt,* 377.1 *elasticity,* 377.8 *be elastic*
bounce a cheque 741.24 *monetize,* 747.8 *stop payment*
bounce back 331.1, 337.7 *recoil,* 377.10 *be adaptable,* 478.4 *reaction,* 478.19 *react,* 623.6 *get healthy,* 629.4 *be restored*
bounce-back 331.4 *recoil*
bounced cheque 745.5 *amount owing*
bounced light 66.15 *lighting*
bounce pass 23.4 *playing terms*
bouncer 27.8 *delivery,* 237.6 *muscleman,* 349.26 *ejector,* 632.3 *protector,* 671.14 *guard,* 679.2 *defender*
bounce up 336.8 *further*
bouncily 377.11 *elastically*
bounciness 377.1 *elasticity*
bouncing 239.5 *invigorating,* 331.8 *recoiling,* 359.24 *leaping,* 377.6 *elastic,* 623.1 *healthy,* 769.1 *cheerful*
bouncing baby 206.9 *child*
bouncing billy 29.5 *golf ball*
bouncing cheque 747.3 *bad payment*

bouncy 239.5 *invigorating,* 366.17 *turbulent,* 377.6 *elastic,* 769.1 *cheerful*
bound 137, 21.6 *jump,* 52.21 *set,* 107.4 *related,* 135.15 *tied,* 137.15 *connected,* 293.37 *protected,* 329.4 *be swift,* 329.9 *acceleration,* 331.1, 331.4 *recoil,* 359.5, 359.18 *jump,* 485.12 *conditional,* 714.12 *promised,* 714.13 *guaranteeing,* 726.10 *retained,* 745.9 *in debt,* 847.11 *duty-bound*
boundary 136, 25.1 *green bowling,* 27.10 *score,* 52.37 *line,* 157.7 *limit,* 157.24 *limiting,* 249.3 *regional boundary,* 300.1 *edge,* 302.3 *furthest point,* 302.6 *furthest*
boundary condition 485.7 *condition*
boundary marker 302
Boundary Peak 95 Mountains
boundary stone 302.4 *boundary marker*
bound back 331.1 *recoil*
bound by duty 847.11 *dutybound*
bounded volume 52.41 *geometric figure*
bounden duty 847.1 *duty*
bounder 22.5 *batting terms,* 401.7 *libertine,* 652.5 *badly behaved person,* 795.5 *vulgar person,* 801.2 *disreputable character,* 864.10 *bad person*
bound for 332.14 *directed*
bound forward 329.6 *accelerate*
bounding 21.2 *field events,* 331.8 *recoiling,* 359.24 *leaping,* 485.6 *specification*
bounding main 97.1 *sea*
boundless 53.36 *astronomical,* 181.8 *numberless,* 184.1 *infinite,* 248.12 *extensive*
boundlessly 53.39 *astronomically,* 184.10 *infinitely*
boundlessness 184.4 *infinity*
bounds 249.3 *regional boundary,* 300.1 *edge,* 485.6 *specification*
bounteous 246.5 *fertile,* 755.1 *generous*
bounteousness 755.5 *generosity*
bountiful 246.5 *fertile,* 608.2 *plentiful,* 729.8 *giving,* 742.4 *lush,* 755.1 *generous,* 831.7 *charitable*
bountifully 729.9 *as a gift,* 831.11 *charitably*
bountifulness 831.2 *charity*
bountiful supply 608.8 *plenty*
bounty 878, 246.1 *fertility,* 729.1 *giving,* 729.3 *offering,* 742.7 *opulence,* 751.2 *value,* 755.5 *generosity,* 831.1 *philanthropy*
bouquet 84.1 *flower,* 161.29 *bunch,* 416.1 *odour,* 418.1 *fragrance,* 418.2 *fragrant thing,* 851.4 *compliment,* 878.1 *reward*
bouquet garni 133.4 *admixture*
Bourbaki 52 Scientists
bourbon 351.7 *alcoholic drink*
Bourbon Red 68 Breeds of Fowl
bourbon whiskey 351.7 *alcoholic drink*
bourgeois 124.8 *middle classes,* 167.6, 167.14 *conformist,* 400.10 *member of society,* 698.7 *free person,* 803.1 *plebeian*
bourgeois ethic 167.4 *conventionalism*
bourgeoisie 124.8 *middle classes,* 158.8 *middle class,* 400.9 *group,* 803.2 *the common people*
Bourges Cathedral 43 Noted Buildings
bourguignonne 45.15 *sauce*
Bourignianism 7 Christian Movements
bourn 96.1 *river,* 344.15 *destination*
Bournemouth 93 Cities
bourrée 46.9 *ballet steps*
bourse 740.5 *stock market*
Bourse 223.2 *place of exchange*
Boursin 45 Cheeses

bout 670, 18.1 *sport,* 42.2 *contest,* 187.4 *period of activity,* 644.2 *task,* 674.7 *boxing,* 731.3 *allotted task*
boutade 579.3 *whim*
boutique 740.8 *store*
bout of sickness 624.2 *illness*
boutonniere 84.1 *flower*
Bouvier des Flandres 77 Breeds of Dogs
bouzouki 49 Musical Instruments
Bovet 52 Scientists
bovid 77.15 *hoofed mammal,* 77.33 *ungulate*
Bovidae 77.15 *hoofed mammal*
bovine 77.15 *hoofed mammal,* 77.33 *ungulate*
bovine somatotrophin 58 Hormones
bovver boy 241.4 *violent person or animal,* 635.2 *troublemaker,* 679.1 *combatant,* 693.9 *criminal*
bow 74 Knots, 74 Parts of a Ship, 362, 10.19 *offer worship,* 36.3 *parts of a sailing boat,* 36.6 *canoeing,* 36.9 *sailor,* 36.11 *rowing,* 36.12 *canoeing,* 43.9 *miscellaneous architectural features,* 49.38 *sound,* 276.8 *be low,* 311.6 *curve,* 316.5 *be convex,* 338.9 *firearm,* 362.16 *courtesy,* 673.1 *submission,* 673.4 *succumb,* 680.6 *historical missile weapon,* 694.3 *obeisance,* 694.6 *show obeisance to,* 806.21 *humble oneself,* 808.10 *knuckle under,* 817.5 *sign of courtesy,* 817.13 *defer to,* 849.4 *mark of respect,* 849.19 *take off one's hat to*
bow and arrow 244.7 *agent of destruction*
bow and scrape 673.4 *succumb,* 808.10 *knuckle under,* 849.19 *take off one's hat to*
bow before the inevitable 673.4 *succumb*
bow before the storm 673.4 *succumb*
bowdlerization 131.1 *subtraction,* 134.1 *purity,* 147.2 *ejection,* 621.4 *censorship,* 876.4 *self-righteousness*
bowdlerize 131.3 *subtract,* 134.10 *purify,* 147.8 *eject,* 216.8 *cause change,* 621.15 *purify,* 628.5 *hurt*
bowdlerized 876.10 *moralistic*
bowdlerizer 116.6 *editor*
bow down 360.12 *drop,* 362.9 *bow,* 849.19 *take off one's hat to*
bowed 311.4 *curved,* 808.7 *sycophantic*
bowed down 806.3 *humbled*
bowed out 316.4 *convex*
bowel cancer 624.8 *indigestion*
bowel movement 353.2 *defecation*
bowels 257.3 *insides,* 350.16 *eating utensil*
bowels of the earth 277.4 *deep thing*
Bowen 48 Writers, 52 Scientists
bower 69.3 *ornamental garden,* 85.4 *trees,* 821.13 *abode of love*
Bower 52 Scientists
bowerbird 78 Birds
bower of bliss 821.13 *abode of love*
bowfin 80 Fishes
bow harp 49 Musical Instruments
bowie knife 380.10 *knife,* 680.8 *sharp weapon*
bowing 808.7 *sycophantic,* 817.4 *deference,* 817.9 *deferential,* 849.11 *in a respectful stance*
bowing and scraping 362.15 *debasement,* 673.5 *submitting,* 849.4 *mark of respect,* 849.11 *in a respectful stance*
bowing-and-scraping 808.2 *sycophancy*
bowknot 74 Knots

bowl 25, 25, 27, 19.4 *stadium,* 25.1 *green bowling,* 27.19 *dismiss,* 44.8 *ceramic object,* 120.3 *container,* 258.12 *bath,* 258.16 *crockery,* 315.6 *round,* 317.3 *cavity,* 338.5 *throw,* 338.10 *ball,* 338.22 *roll,* 350.16 *eating utensil,* 351.10 *drink container,* 364.9 *roll,* 671.7 *armour*
bowl a bosey 539.29 *juggle*
bowl a googly 539.29 *juggle*
bowl a hook ball 25.8 *bowl*
bowl a hoop 338.22 *roll*
bowl along 329.4 *be swift,* 376.12 *go smoothly*
bowl a wrong'un 539.29 *juggle*
bowled over 514.7 *amazed,* 786.6 *wondering*
bowler 25, 27.4 *team,* 295.15 *headgear,* 338.14 *thrower*
bowler-hatted 704.10 *cancelled*
Bowles 48 Writers
bowl game 19.1 *football*
bowline 74 Knots, 36.7 *windsurfing,* 137.7 *tackle*
bowline on the bight 74 Knots
bowling 18 Sporting Activities, 25, 25, 27, 25.1 *green bowling,* 27.11 *dismissal,* 27.12 *cricketing,* 364.2 *turning,* 364.11 *rotating*
Bowling 25
bowling alley 376.8 *smooth thing*
bowling along 329.8 *speed*
bowling bag 25.4 *bowling*
bowling ball 25.4 *bowling*
bowling delivery 25
bowling green 25.1 *green bowling,* 282.3 *flat thing,* 376.8 *smooth thing,* 433.8 *greenness*
bowling lane 25.4 *bowling*
bowling pin 25.4 *bowling*
bowling rink 25.1 *green bowling*
bowling shoes 25.4 *bowling*
bowling side 25.1 *green bowling*
bowl lyre 49 Musical Instruments
bowl over 236.8 *overpower,* 362.3 *bring down,* 514.11 *amaze,* 786.10 *be wonderful,* 821.28 *win the love of*
bow low 362.9 *bow*
bowls 25, 25.1 *green bowling*
bowl-shaped 317.5 *concave*
bowls match 25.1 *green bowling*
bowls player 25
bowl wide 335.2 *divert*
bowman 338.16 *archer,* 679.13 *historical soldiery*
bowmanship 680.2 *arms*
bow one's head 849.19 *take off one's hat to*
bow out 254.16 *absent oneself,* 345.2 *withdraw,* 349.7 *exit*
bowsaw 85.7 *timber production*
bowser 71 Motor Vehicles
bowshot 264.2 *short distance,* 338.7 *shot*
bow side 36.4 *rowing*
bowsprit 303.1 *front*
Bow Street runner 16.11 *British law officer*
bowstring 879.16 *instrument of execution*
bow-string 879.5 *execute*
bowstringer 879.17 *punisher*
bow stroke 36.6 *canoeing*
bow tie 295.3 *formal dress,* 295.14 *neckwear*
bow to 127.9 *yield to,* 673.3 *submit*
bow to fate 571.16 *be compelled*
bow wave 56.14 *sound wave*
bow-wow 77.9 *dog*
bow-wow theory 5.37 *linguistic theory*
box 85 Trees and Shrubs, **258,** 26.11 *do a combat sport,* 27.6 *pad,* 36.8 *punting,* 51.16 *auditorium,* 68.7 *farm building,* 120.3 *container,* 136.2 *setting apart,* 258.2 *compartment,* 293.4 *wrapping,* 293.13 *casing,* 293.25 *wrap,* 330.3 *hit,* 330.9 *fight,* 330.13 *blow,* 354.5 *inset,* 413.7 *tobacco,* 605.4 *storage,* 671.6

protective clothing, 674.12, 679.37 *fight,* 729.2 *gift,* 741.20 *money store*
box a round 26.11 *do a combat sport*
box Brownie 66.16 *camera*
box canyon 265.3 *gulf*
boxcar 179.7 *double figures*
box chair 47.2 *chair*
box chronometer 191 Time-pieces and Timers
boxed 258.20 *containing,* 293.37 *protected*
box elder 85 Trees and Shrubs
boxer 77 Breeds of Dogs, **26,** 237.5 *athlete,* 674.10 *contender,* 679.3 *athlete*
boxer shorts 295.18 *underwear*
boxes 51.31 *theatregoer*
boxfile 125.6 *box*
boxfish 80 Fishes
box fortification 671.11 *fortification*
box-girder bridge 63.21 *bridge*
box in 659.23 *cause difficulties,* 699.8 *restrain*
boxing 18 Sporting Activities, **26, 674,** 26.1 *combat sports,* 330.12 *collision,* 671.5 *self-defence*
boxing association 26.2 *boxing*
boxing blow 330.14 *sporting hit*
Boxing Day 214.6 *annually celebrated day*
boxing glove 330.16 *weapons*
boxing gloves 26.2 *boxing*
boxing match 26.2, 674.7 *boxing*
boxing punch 26.2 *boxing*
boxing purse 26.2 *boxing*
boxing ring 26.2 *boxing,* 674.9 *duel*
boxing rules 26.2 *boxing*
boxing scorecard 26.2 *boxing*
boxing shorts 26.2 *boxing*
boxing technique 26.2 *boxing*
boxing weight 369.7 *weighing*
boxing weight divisions 26
box junction 71.3 *carriageway*
box lyre 49 Musical Instruments
box off 147.7 *exclude*
box office 51.16 *auditorium*
box-office hit 51.11 *theatrical performance,* 682.3 *successful thing*
box-office receipts 721.4 *earnings,* 749.2 *money received*
box-office returns 730.2 *something received*
box-office staff 51.26 *stagehand*
box-office success 682.3 *successful thing*
box of tricks 657.2 *stratagem*
box on the ear 828.5 *quarrel,* 879.12 *corporal punishment*
box pleat 320.2 *pleat*
box room 256.7 *room*
boxroom 65.4 *storage*
box seat 51.16 *auditorium*
box set 51.17 *stage set*
box someone's ears 330.3 *hit,* 879.3 *hit*
box spring 377.5 *spring*
box springs 284.4 *rest*
box the compass 332.8 *orient ,* 337.7 *recoil*
box turtle 79 Reptiles
box up 257.6 *contain,* 258.21 *put* **in a container**
boy 206.7 *young man,* 206.9 *child,* 400.7 *person,* 401.2 *male,* 401.3 *male title of address,* 401.4 *boyfriend,* 401.13 *man in the family,* 697.6 *domestic servant,* 875.6 *drug*
boycott 15.4 *industrial dispute,* 15.12 *have an industrial dispute,* 136.2 *setting apart,* 136.10 *set apart,* 147.1 *exclusion,* 147.7 *exclude,* 447.11 *blacken,* 475.6 *mass demonstration,* 475.19 *protest,* 713.3 *gesture of protest,* 713.8 *cause mischief,* 816.3 *separation,* 816.13 *ignore,* 852.3 *nonacceptance,* 852.15 *withhold approval*

boycotted 15.10 *unionized,* 816.10 *lonely,* 852.31 *disapproved*
boycotting 15.10 *unionized,* 475.14 *demonstrating*
boyfriend 401, 180.12 *partner,* 819.4 *close friend,* 821.9 *lover,* 826.5 *courting person*
boyhood 206.1 *youth*
boyish 206.11 *young,* 274.1 *thin,* 595.5 *immature*
boyish figure 274.7 *thinness*
boyishly 206.14 *youthfully*
boyishness 206.2 *youthfulness*
Boyle 52 Scientists
Boyle's law 56 Named Laws
boylike 206.11 *young*
boy next door 124.7 *average person*
boyo 401.3 *male title of address*
Boy Scout uniform 544.5 *uniform*
boysenberry 86 Fruits, 133.5 *hybrid*
Boy's experiment 56 Named Laws
boys in the back-room 226.8 *contributor,* 527.9 *backstage manipulator*
bozo 401.2 *male,* 656.10 *unskilled person*
bra 284.5 *supporting garment,* 295.18 *underwear*
Bra 93 Languages
Brabant 32 Breeds of Horse and Pony
Brabham 18 Sporting Personalities
bra burner 402.11 *liberated woman*
brace 161, 49.17 *notation,* 137.4 *means of connection,* 137.8 *fastening,* 176.1 *two,* 237.8 *strengthen,* 284.2 *supporting part,* 284.11 *support,* 373.9 *harden,* 651.1 *refresh*
brace and bit 322.2 *opener*
braced 237.13 *strengthened,* 373.3 *hardened,* 651.4 *refreshed*
bracelet 313.3 *circular thing,* 792.6 *jewellery*
bracelets 137.8 *fastening,* 699.5 *means of restraint*
brace oneself 574, 594.8 *prepare oneself*
bracer 630.7 *tonic*
braces 52.25 *algebraic expression,* 137.8 *fastening,* 283.4 *hanger,* 295.18 *underwear,* 543.7 *punctuation*
brachiopod 81.5 *mollusc*
Brachiopoda 81.5 *mollusc*
brachiosaur 79 Fossil Reptiles
brachycardia 624.10 *cardiovascular disease*
brachylogous 552.3 *concise*
brachylogy 552.1 *conciseness*
bracing 55.45 *fine,* 239.5 *invigorating,* 409.8 *cold,* 623.2 *healthful,* 651.3 *refreshing*
bracken 88 Ferns, 88.1 *fern*
bracket 41.6 *ice-skating,* 89.4 *fungal body,* 107.7 *relate to,* 135.5 *joint,* 135.8 *unite,* 137.4 *means of connection,* 137.11 *connect,* 152.6 *category,* 163.2 *class,* 176.14 *pair,* 284.2 *supporting part,* 284.11 *support*
bracket clock 192.6 *clock*
bracketed 137.15 *connected,* 176.9 *two*
bracketed with 114.7 *similar*
bracket fungi 89.3 *fungi*
bracket fungus 89 Fungi
bracketing 66.13 *framing*
brackets 52.25 *algebraic expression,* 543.7 *punctuation*
bracket together 107.7 *relate to,* 135.8 *unite,* 140.5 *combine*
brackish 415.6 *unpalatable*
brackishness 415.2 *unpalatability*
bract 83.6 *leaf,* 84.3 *flower part*
bracteole 83.6 *leaf*
brad 137.8 *fastening*
Bradbury 48 Writers, **48** Writers
Bradford 93 Cities
Bradley 4 Philosophers

Bradman 18 Sporting Personalities
Bradshaw 528.5 *reference book*
bradykinin 58.8 *amino acid*
brae 95.1, 275.3 *mountain*
Braemar 93 Cities
brag 42 Card Games, 541.6 *exaggerator,* 541.10 *boast,* 807.24 *be vain,* 860.7 *be egoistic*
Bragg 52 Scientists
braggadocio 541.6 *exaggerator*
braggart 462.7 *inconsiderate person,* 541.6 *exaggerator,* 805.13 *proud person,* 807.12 *impudent person,* 809.7 *vain person*
bragger 805.13 *proud person*
bragging 541.4 *bombast,* 541.15 *bombastic*
Bragg's law 56 Named Laws, 57.4 *crystal*
Bragi 8 Deities
Brahe 52 Scientists
Brahma 8 Deities, **68** Breeds of Fowl
Brahmahood 8.1 *divinity*
Brahman 68 Breeds of Cattle, 7.8 *priest,* 617.7 *elite*
Brahmanism 7 Non-Christian Religions, 7.9 *priesthood*
Brahmaputra 96 Rivers
Brahms 49 Musicians and Composers, 874.1 *drunk*
Brahui 5 Languages and Groups of Languages
braid 288, 67.2 *spinning,* 67.13 *spin,* 96.7 *flow,* 133.8 *mix,* 135.10 *link,* 137.6 *line,* 137.11 *connect,* 288.8 *interweave,* 314.3 *convoluted thing,* 314.6 *convolute,* 375.7 *rough thing,* 375.12 *make rough,* 792.5 *decorative articles*
braided 67.9 *spun,* 133.12 *mixed,* 135.15 *tied,* 137.15 *connected,* 288.6 *interwoven,* 314.4 *convolutional*
braided fibre 67.1 *fibre*
braided line 20.1 *angling*
braided river 96.1 *river*
braided rug 293.9 *floor covering*
braiding 67.2 *spinning,* 288.1 *interweaving*
braids 791.8 *hair cut*
brail 135.8 *unite*
Braille 436.3 *aid for poor sight*
brain 459, 398.17 *murder,* 404.12 *anaesthetize,* 459.3 *intelligence,* 501.4 *intellect,* 507.2 *intelligence,* 655.5 *expert,* 761.7 *render insensitive*
brainbox 459.8 *intellectual person,* 461.7 *thinker,* 501.6 *knowledgeable person,* 507.4 *intellectual*
brain cancer 624.12 *cancer*
brainchild 243.4 *mental product,* 471.3 *plan,* 519.4 *ideality*
brain-creation 519.4 *ideality*
brain damage 460.1 *lack of intellect,* 510.3 *mental deterioration*
brain-damaged 460.5 *lacking intellect,* 460.7 *intellectually subnormal*
brain-dead 464.4 *uninterested*
brain death 397.1 *death*
brain disease 510.3 *mental deterioration,* 624.4 *disease*
brain disorder 510.3 *mental deterioration*
brain fungus 89 Fungi
brainily 6.26 *studiously*
braininess 459.4 *cleverness*
brainless 460.5 *lacking intellect,* 508.5 *foolish*
brainlessly 460.11 *unintelligently,* 508.8 *foolishly*
brainlessness 460.1 *lack of intellect*
brains 45.31 *offal,* 459.3 *intelligence,* 459.4 *cleverness,* 501.4 *intellect,* 507.2 *intelligence,* 592.8 *planner*
brain scanner 630.14 *hospital*
brainstorm 461.6 *idea,* 462.5 *mental block,* 471.3 *plan,* 510.6 *mental breakdown,* 579.3 *whim,* 592.3 *expedient plan*

brain surgeon 60.13 *medical specialist*
brain surgery 60.9, 630.12 *surgery*
brain-teaser 529, 477.4 *difficult question,* 659.4 *problem*
brain-twister 529.4 *brain-teaser,* 659.4 *problem*
brainwash 167.10 *assimilate,* 220.11 *persuade,* 233.8 *influence,* 309.12 *distort the truth,* 497.9 *make someone believe,* 584.18 *habituate,* 586.15 *persuade,* 628.6 *pervert*
brainwashed 220.13 *converted,* 220.16 *influenced*
brainwashing 220.3 *persuasion,* 309.4 *distortion of the truth,* 584.7 *habituation,* 586.5 *propaganda*
brainwave 228.1 *motive,* 243.4 *mental product,* 461.6 *idea,* 471.3 *plan,* 507.2 *intelligence,* 592.3 *expedient plan*
brainwork 4.4 *philosophical investigation,* 6.8 *learning,* 461.2 *intellectual exercise*
brain worker 646.1 *worker*
brainy 4.19 *learned,* 6.18 *educated,* 459.10 *intelligent,* 501.8 *knowledgeable,* 507.6 *intelligent*
braise 45.55 *cook,* 408.14 *be hot*
braised 45.56 *culinary*
brake 71 Carriages and Carts, **71** Motor Vehicle Parts, 41.5 *ski equipment,* 41.9 *bobsledding* , 71.11 *bicycle part,* 85.4 *trees,* 88.1 *fern,* 218.6 *cease,* 242.2 *moderator,* 302.2 *limiting factor,* 302.7 *limit,* 325.8 *be motionless,* 328.3 *slow down,* 328.9 *deceleration,* 632.4 *safety device,* 661.4 *restraint,* 661.10, 699.8 *restrain,* 869.5 *be self-restrained*
brake block 71.11 *bicycle part*
brake drum 71 Motor Vehicle Parts
brake-fade 71.21 *miscellaneous motoring terms*
brake light 71 Motor Vehicle Parts, 439.6 *electric light*
braky 85.16 *wooded*
bramble 138.4 *adherent,* 380.8 *sharp-pointed thing*
brambling 78 Birds
brambly 380.2 *spiked*
Bramley 86 Fruits
bran 45.40 *breakfast cereal,* 68.9 *animal feedstuff,* 87.4 *cereal grass,* 132.2 *residue,* 384.8 *meal,* 614.6 *refuse*
branch 143, 343, 6.3 *subject,* 7.1 *religion,* 52.1 *mathematics,* 65.17 *computing term,* 65.19 *abort,* 83.5 *stem,* 85.2 *tree part,* 90.3 *plant body,* 96.1 *river,* 137.4 *means of connection,* 148.2 *piece,* 163.2 *class,* 163.3 *kingdom,* 176.8 *half,* 176.16 *halve,* 261.6 *become bigger,* 335.1 *deviate,* 343.5 *fork,* 472.4 *sphere*
branched 343, 83.14 *of plants,* 176.13 *half*
branching 343, 85.14 *treelike,* 137.4 *means of connection,* 162.5 *divergence,* 162.24 *divergent,* 176.7 *halving,* 261.1 *growth,* 261.8 *growing,* 335.24 *diverging,* 343.9 *branched*
branching off 335.13 *deviation*
branching out 162.5 *divergence,* 343.4 *branching*
branchiopod 81.4 *arthropod*
branchiuran 81.4 *arthropod*
branchlet 90.3 *plant body*
branchlike 343.9 *branched*
branch line 72.2 *track,* 327.10 *railway*
branch off 343.14 *branch*
branch office 647.1 *workshop*
branch of philosophy 4
branch of the service 17.2 *the military*

branch out 85.19 *grow*, 113.8 *be diverse*, 162.10 *diverge*, 261.6 *become bigger*, 335.1 *deviate*
branchwood 85.3 *timber*
brand 68.18 *practise livestock farming*, 163.4 *type*, 163.13 *class*, 165.3 *characteristic*, 165.22 *characterize*, 408.15 *burn*, 410.2 *lighter*, 439.7 *lantern*, 543.1 *sign*, 544.3 *means of identification*, 544.10 *identify*
branded 544.12 *identified*
Brandenburg 32 Breeds of Horse and Pony, **93** Cities
branding iron 408.3 *heater*
brandish 365.12 *wave*, 366.22 *agitate*, 475.15 *demonstrate*, 526.1 *display*, 599.1 *use*, 811.28 *flourish*
brandished 526.13 *displayed*
brandishing 365.4 *rock*
brand name 62.3 *drug*, 544.3 *means of identification*
brand new 201.10 *new*
brand spanking new 201.10 *new*
brandy Alexander 351.8 *mixed drink*
brandy and soda 351.8 *mixed drink*
brandy balloon 258.13 *drinking vessel*
brandy snifter 258.13 *drinking vessel*
bran flakes 45.40 *breakfast cereal*
branniness 384.3 *graininess*
branny 384.17 *mealy*
brash 668.7 *defiant*, 807.19 *rude*
brashing 85.6 *tree management*
brashly 668.9 *defiantly*, 807.32 *audaciously*, 807.35 *rudely*
brashness 668.1 *defiance*, 809.3 *cockiness*
brashy 143.11 *partial*
Brasilia 93 Cities
brass 57 Alloys, 49.25 *musical instrument*, 133.2 *mixed thing*, 399.4 *funeral objects*, 427.2 *ringing*, 430.1 *stridency* , 451.3 *orange thing*, 653.6 *governing body*, 741.2 *cash*, 742.6 *money*, 807.2 *cheek*
brassard 544.4 *insignia*, 671.7 *armour*
brass band 49.26 *musical group*, 140.3 *assembly*
brass cannon 680.10 *historical gun*
brasserie 350.15 *eating place*
brass farthing 612.8 *trifle*
brass hat 126.5 *superior*, 233.5 *influential person*, 611.4 *bigwig*, 696.7 *military leader*
brass horn 423.4 *sound maker*
brassica 45.33, 69.11 *vegetable*
brassicaceous 83.16 *taxonomic*
brassick 593.5 *necessitous*
brassie 29.4 *golf club*
brassiere 284.5 *supporting garment*, 295.18 *underwear*
brassiness 303.5 *boldness*, 423.1 *loudness*, 430.1 *stridency* , 668.1 *defiance*, 807.10 *impudence*
brass inlay 47.9 *decorative woodwork*
brass knuckles 330.16 *weapons*, 680.7 *blunt weapon*
brass-monkey weather 55.31 *coldness*, 409.7 *cold weather*
brass neck 303.5 *boldness*, 807.2 *cheek*
brass on shell 47.9 *decorative woodwork*
brass plate 544.3 *means of identification*
brass rubbing 42 Hobbies and Pastimes, 50.7 *picture*
brass tacks 99.5 *fact*
brassy 423.6 *loud*, 430.7 *strident*, 451.1 *orange*, 557.4 *ornate*, 668.7 *defiant*, 807.14 *cheeky*, 807.21 *impudent*
brat 206.9 *child*
Bratislava 93 Cities
Bratwurst 45.46 *German dish*
braunite 54 Minerals

bravado 807, 811, 668.1 *defiance*, 778.5 *bold front*
brave 811, 237.11 *strong in spirit*, 640.5 *acting*, 668.5 *defy*, 679.1 *combatant*, 679.8 *soldier*, 679.35 *martial*, 778.7 *courageous person*, 778.9 *courageous*, 778.15 *be courageous*
brave face 668.1 *defiance*, 778.5 *bold front*
brave front 669.1 *resistance*
brave it out 807.27 *dare*
bravely 811, 237.14 *strongly*, 679.42 *martially*, 778.18 *courageously*
braveness 778.1 *courage*
brave person 640.3 *doer*, 778.7 *courageous person*
bravery 237.1 *strength*, 778.1 *courage*
brave try 596.5 *attempt*
bravo! 851
bravo 241.4 *violent person or animal*, 398.11 *murderer*, 431.3 *cry of praise*, 679.1 *combatant*
Bravo 534 Phonetic Alphabet
bravura 655.3 *masterpiece*, 668.1 *defiance*
bravura player 655.4 *skilled person*
braw 617.1 *worthy*
brawl 151.9 *disorder*, 473.1 *argument*, 473.13 *argue*, 500.1 *dissent*, 642.1 *activity*, 666.2 *argument*, 666.6 *argue*, 674.6 *fight*, 764.8, 764.11 *quarrel*
brawler 693.9 *criminal*
brawling 473.9 *hostile*, 666.9 *disagreeing*
brawn 45.31 *offal*, 237.1 *strength*, 369.4 *heaviness*, 378.8 *physical strength*
brawniness 259.6 *squatness*
brawny 237.9 *physically strong*, 259.17 *stocky*, 378.4 *powerful*
bray 384.23 *pulverize*, 384.27 *beat*, 423.1 *loudness*, 423.8 *be loud*, 430.1 *stridency* , 430.4 *be strident*, 432.4 *cry*
braying 423.6 *loud*, 430.7 *strident*
braze 135.10 *link*, 138.7 *cause to adhere*
brazen 303.9 *arrogant*, 430.7 *strident*, 526.15 *open*, 668.7 *defiant*, 805.17 *conceited*, 807.14 *cheeky*, 807.21 *impudent*, 811.21 *blatant*, 850.10 *disrespectful*, 868.3 *impenitent*, 877.13 *unchaste*
brazen face 807.3 *audacity*, 807.12 *impudent person*
brazen-faced 807.15 *audacious*, 807.21 *impudent*, 850.10 *disrespectful*
brazen-facedness 807.10 *impudence*
brazen hussy 868.2 *impenitent person*
brazen it out 577.9 *be obstinate*, 668.5 *defy*, 807.27 *dare*
brazenly 668.9 *defiantly*, 807.31 *cheekily*, 811.37 *blatantly*
brazen-mouthed 423.6 *loud*
brazenness 303.5 *boldness*, 668.1 *defiance*, 807.2 *cheek*, 811.6 *blatancy*
brazen out 778.15 *be courageous*
brazier 258.15 *pot*, 408.6 *fire*
brazil 86 Nuts
Brazil 91 Countries
Brazilian GP at Interlagos 33.2 Formula 1 race
Brazzaville 93 Cities
breach 16.38 *lawbreaking*, 117.4 *disagreement*, 117.14 *disagree*, 136.3 *separateness*, 160.4 *interruption*, 265.2, 265.5 *crack*, 322.1 *opening*, 322.18 *open*, 357.5 *transgress*, 357.8 *transgression*, 500.4 *faction*, 666.2 *argument*, 670.9 *attack successfully*, 720.1 *nonobservance*, 720.4 *infraction*, 720.7 *not observe*, 720.10 *violate the law*, 820.2 *personal conflict*
breached 322.12 *open*

breaching 16.60 *offending*, 720.14 *violating*
breach in the wall 633.7 *vulnerability*
breach of contract 720.1 *nonobservance*
breach of etiquette 814.5 *nonobservance*
breach of faith 720.1 *nonobservance*, 858.2 *faithlessness*
breach of friendship 666.1 *disagreement*, 820.2 *personal conflict*
breach of promise 538.4 *lie*, 720.1 *nonobservance*, 858.2 *faithlessness*
breach of the peace 151.9 *disorder*, 153.5 *commotion*, 693.2 *violation of the law*, 713.2 *disorder*, 720.4 *infraction*
breach of trust 720.1 *nonobservance*
breach the peace 693.15 *be disobedient*, 713.8 *cause mischief*, 720.10 *violate the law*
bread 45, 20.1 *angling*, 350.7 *food*, 396.3 *life requirements*, 741.2 *cash*
bread-and-butter letter 837.3 *recognition*
bread-and-butter pudding 45.35 *dessert*
bread-and-cheese lunch 350.12 *meal*
bread and circuses 405.2 *good time*
bread and milk 412.3 *tasteless items*
bread and water 412.3 *tasteless items*, 609.8 *insufficiency*
bread-and-water diet 350.10 *scarcity*
bread and wine 10.6 *Eucharist*
bread basket 258.7 *basket*, 258.18 *stomach*
bread bin 45.4 *kitchen container*
breadfruit 86 Fruits
bread knife 380.10 *knife*
breadline 593.3 *needfulness*, 743.5 *poverty*
bread mould 89 Fungi
breadnut 86 Nuts
bread sauce 45.15 *sauce*
bread stick 45.39 *loaf*
breadth 271, 52.37 *line*, 56.7 *space*, 120.1 *quantity*, 121.1 *degree*, 248.1 *space*, 259.1, 268.4 *size*, 273.5 *thickness*
Breadth 271
breadth of vision 507.1 *wisdom*
breadthways 271.8 *breadth wise*
breadthwise 271
bread tin 258.15 *pot*
breadwinner 15.7 *employee*, 646.1 *worker*, 721.7 *gainer*
breadwinning 721.1 *gain*
breadwork 792.2 *pattern*
break 24.1 *billiards*, 24.3 *English billiards*, 24.8 *play billiards*, 51.6 *scene*, 55.60 *cloud*, 97.10 *billow*, 100.4 *emptiness*, 136.3 *separateness*, 136.9 *separate*, 143.10 *part*, 145.2 *omission*, 160.3 *interval*, 160.4 *interruption*, 160.14 *disconnect*, 185.6 *interval*, 187.1 *period*, 210.2 *opportunity*, 215.6 *be irregular*, 216.1 *change*, 218.3, 218.9 *pause*, 238.6 *be weak*, 241.8 *use violence*, 244.9 *demolish*, 248.8 *intervening space*, 248.21 *space*, 254.5 *leave of absence*, 265.2, 265.5 *crack*, 322.1 *opening*, 322.10 *opportunity*, 322.18 *open*, 335.15 *deviating motion*, 375.12 *make rough*, 379.4 *be brittle*, 439.26 *grow light*, 530.9 *be disclosed*, 533.13 *report*, 645.2 *time off*, 649.1 *ease*, 651.6 *refresher*, 682.10 *defeat heavily*, 683.9 *malfunction*, 686.2 *good fortune*, 720.10 *violate the law*, 747.9 *be unable to pay*
breakability 379.2 *brittleness*

breakable 41.12 *ski*, 136.19 *separable*, 238.8 *weak*, 379.1 *brittle*
breakable crust 41.1 *skiing*
breakableness 379.2 *brittleness*
breakage 136.1 *separation*, 145.2 *omission*
break a habit 585.5 *disaccustom*
break a lance for 671.22 *plead for*
break a lance with 674.11 *contend*
break a law 168.20 *infringe a law*
break and enter 346.10 *invade*
break an egg 41.16 *bobsled*
break apart 379.4 *be brittle*
break a story 532.15 *publish*
break away 136.13 *diverge*, 168.19 *be independent*, 591.8 *run away*, 638.5 *escape*, 700.5 *be liberated*
breakaway 500.7 *dissenting*, 693.4 *revolution*, 693.14 *subversive*, 698.10 *independent*
break away from 500.8 *dissent*, 666.5 *disagree*
breakaway group 500.6 *dissenters*
breakaway movement 665.3 *political grouping*
break ball 24.6 *pool*
breakbone fever 624.7 *tropical disease*
break bounds 168.19 *be independent*, 357.5 *transgress*
break bread 350.24 *have a meal*
break camp 345.3 *quit*
break ceasefire 679.36 *combat*
break cover 347.10 *emerge*
break crop 68.12 *crop*
breakdance 46.15 *dance*
breakdancing 46.1 *dancing*
breakdown 61.10 *neurosis*, 136.1 *separation*, 141.2 *deconstruction*, 218.2 *stop*, 236.4 *disability*, 244.4 *ruin*, 624.3 *symptom*, 628.1 *deteriorate*
break down 136.9 *separate*, 141.3 *disintegrate*, 141.4 *deconstruct*, 218.6 *cease*, 244.9 *demolish*, 358.1 *fall short*, 358.3 *fall through*, 379.4 *be brittle*, 614.7 *be useless*, 614.8 *make useless*
breakdown 628.9 *dilapidation*, 661.2 *obstacle*, 683.1 *failure*, 844.24 *go wrong*
breakdown in negotiations 15.4 *industrial dispute*
breakdown of government 689.1 *anarchy*
breakdown of law and order 16.41 *lawlessness*, 689.1 *anarchy*
breakdown of marriage 824.1 *divorce*
breakdown van 71 Motor Vehicles
breakdown voltage 56.48 *insulation*
breaker 22.4 *pitching terms*, 32.15 *horse person*, 54.14 *wave*, 68.10 *farm tool*, 97.3 *wave*
breakers 635.1 *trap*
breakers ahead 633.6 *danger signal*
break even 110.10, 122.10 *be equal*
break-even 737.16 *unprofitable*
break faith 720.7 *not observe*, 858.9 *prove false*
breakfast 204.2 *morning thing*, 350.12 *meal*, 350.24 *have a meal*
breakfast cereal 45
breakfast in bed 350.4 *eating meals*
breakfasting 350.4 *eating meals*
breakfast party 665.7 *social gathering*
breakfast roll 45.39 *loaf*
breakfast room 256.7 *room*
break forth 347.10 *emerge*, 530.9 *be disclosed*
break glass 380.15 *make sharp*
break hearts 821.25 *be loved*
break in 32.16 *ride*, 241.8 *use violence*, 346.10 *invade*, 584.18 *habituate*, 846.14 *arrogate*

break-in 736.3 *theft*
breaking 97.7 *oceanic*, 379.1 *brittle*, 379.2 *brittleness*, 563.10 *low-voiced*, 720.4 *infraction*, 720.14 *violating*
breaking and entering 346.3 *inroad*, 736.1 *stealing*
breaking away 168.2 *dissent*
breaking news 533.1 *news*, 533.9 *news story*
breaking of bread 10.6 *Eucharist*
breaking off 218.2 *stop*
breaking off of negotiations 218.2 *stop*
breaking of the waters 245.7 *obstetrics*
breaking on the wheel 879.12 *corporal punishment*
breaking out 624.13 *skin disease*
breaking point 684.3 *elaboration*
breaking stones 644.1 *work*
breaking surface 359.1 *ascent*
breaking the law 16.60 *offending*
breaking up 244.2 *destroying*
breaking violation 24.6 *pool*
breaking voice 563.2 *inarticulation*
breaking wind 349.24 *belch*, 419.2 *something that makes an unpleasant smell*
break in on 153.10 *disrupt*
break into a house 736.12 *steal*
break into factions 117.14 *disagree*
break into song 49.39 *sing*
break in two 136.9 *separate*
break in upon 211.5 *take untimely action*
break it to 530.6 *divulge*
break it up 218.12 *stop*, 677.5 *make peace*
break loose 638.5 *escape*, 700.5 *be liberated*
breakneck 329.1 *swift*, 648.3 *hasty*, 780.4 *rash*
breakneck speed 329.8 *speed*
break new ground 156.21 *pioneer*
break no bones 617.10 *do good*
break of 629.6 *cure*
break of day 156.2 *creation*, 204.1 *morning*
break off 160.12 *discontinue*, 218.6 *cease*, 218.8 *cause to cease*, 379.4 *be brittle*, 598.2 *withdraw*
breakoff 218.1 *cessation*
break off a relationship 598.2 *withdraw*
break off negotiations 218.6 *cease*
break one's bonds 700.5 *be liberated*
break one's chain of thought 160.16 *interrupt*
break one's chains 638.5 *escape*
break one's fast 350.24 *have a meal*
break one's journey 344.6 *stop at*
break one's neck 397.16 *meet one's fate*
break one's promise 538.21 *lie*, 720.7 *not observe*
break one's word 538.21 *lie*, 720.7 *not observe*, 858.9 *prove false*
break on the wheel 879.4 *torture*
break open 241.8 *use violence*
break-out 31.8 *hockey*, 638.1 *escape*, 670.14 *siege*
break out 241.7 *be violent*, 347.1 *exit*, 347.10 *emerge*, 638.5 *escape*, 670.8 *counterattack*, 700.5 *be liberated*
break out in 624.24 *be unhealthy*
break out in a sweat 353.19 *sweat*
break out of prison 638.5 *escape*
breakout play 31.3 *ice hockey*
break out with 715.6 *catch*
break shot 24.4 *carom*
break step 168.19 *be independent*
break the back of 336.2 *start*
break the bank 682.6 *be successful*, 721.14 *profit*
break the connection 160.14 *disconnect*
break the fall of 242.4 *moderate*

break the habit 168.19 *be independent*
break the ice 156.21 *pioneer*, 819.13 *befriend*
break the law 16.73 *be illegal*, 693.15 *be disobedient*, 844.21 *do wrong*
break the link 136.9 *separate*
break the marriage vow 877.17 *be sexually immoral*
break the mould 168.19 *be independent*
break the news 528.12 *communicate*, 530.6 *divulge*
break the peace 241.7 *be violent*, 670.1 *attack*
break the rules 168.20 *infringe a law*, 652.13 *behave badly*, 844.21 *do wrong*
break the seal 530.5 *disclose*
break the silence 423.8 *be loud*
break the skin 320.20 *hole*
break the sound barrier 329.4 *be swift*
break the speed limit 329.4 *be swift*
break the wax 530.5 *disclose*
breakthrough 154.3 *preparation*, 670.14 *siege*, 682.1 *success*
break through 346.11 *infiltrate*, 638.5 *escape*, 670.9 *attack successfully*, 682.11 *overmaster*
break through the clouds 530.9 *be disclosed*
break under pressure 673.4 *succumb*
breakup 136.1 *separation*, 141.1 *disintegration*
break up 136.9 *separate*, 141.3 *disintegrate*, 141.4 *deconstruct*, 143.10 *part*, 151.21 *disorder*, 162.9 *be dispersed*, 162.11 *explode*, 244.9 *demolish*, 244.13 *be destroyed*, 265.4 *space*, 384.28 *come to dust*, 614.8 *make useless*, 824.7 *divorce*
break-up 162.5 *divergence*, 244.4 *ruin*, 379.2 *brittleness*, 824.1 *divorce*
breakwater 63.24 *water system*, 318.2 *projection*, 632.4 *safety device*, 661.3 *barrier*
break water 74.10 *sail*, 359.17 *spring up*
break wind 349.16 *belch*, 419.5 *stink*, 425.7 *belch*
break with custom 168.19 *be independent*
break with the past 216.1 *change*, 216.7 *be changed*, 512.13 *forget*
bream 80 *Fishes*, 20.5 *British game fish*
Bream 49 *Musicians and Composers*
breast 352 *Exocrine Glands*, 45.26, 45.27 *lamb* , 45.28 *poultry*, 316.2 *bulge*, 359.14 *climb*, 663.16 *confront*
breast-beating 840.2 *apology*, 867.2 *type of penance*
breastbone 382 *Bones*
breast cancer 624.12 *cancer*
breast-fed 351.16 *drinking*
breast-feed 77.36 *lactate*, 350.25 *provide food*
breast line 36.3 *parts of a sailing boat*
breast milk 351.5 *milk*
breast-pang 624.10 *cardiovascular disease*
breastplate 632.2 *protection*, 671.7 *armour*
breaststroke 39.1 *swimming*
breast the storm 663.17 *withstand*
breast the tape 344.2 *reach*
breastwork 661.3 *barrier*, 671.8 *military defences*
breath 388.2 *exhalation*, 416.1 *odour*, 424.1 *faintness*
breath control 39.2 *swimming technique*
breathe 99.17 *exist*, 253.11 *be present*, 349.14 *let out*, 390.21 *respire*, 396.16 *live*, 416.7 *smell*, 424.5, 428.8 *sound faint*,

528.14 *tip*, 530.6 *divulge*, 564.13 *speak in a particular way*
breathe deeply 651.2 *be refreshed*
breathe down someone's neck 648.1 *hasten*
breathe down the neck of 264.10 *stay near*
breathe fire 828.11 *be angry*
breathe fresh life into 629.5 *revive*
breathe heavily 650.5 *be fatigued*
breathe in 348.12 *draw in*, 390.21 *respire*, 416.7 *smell*
breathe life into 396.19 *give birth to*
breathe new life into 651.1 *refresh*
breathe of 520.10 *mean*
breathe one's last 397.15 *die*
breathe out 347.12 *leak*, 390.21 *respire*
breather 185.6 *interval*, 187.1 *period*, 218.3 *pause*, 645.2 *time off*, 649.1 *ease*, 651.7 *refreshments*
breathe regularly 214.7 *be regular*
breathe the air of freedom 698.14 *be free*
breath-freshener 417.2 *deodorant*
breathing 114.9 *lifelike*, 214.5 *regular thing*, 390.8 *respiration*, 390.19 *respiratory*, 396.4 *biological function*, 396.12 *alive*
breathing apparatus 671.6 *protective clothing*
breathing difficulty 624.3 *symptom*
breathing in 348.4 *intake*
breathing space 185.6 *interval*, 218.3 *pause*, 648.6 *available space*, 645.1 *leisure*, 649.1 *ease*
breathless 366.16 *restless*, 397.19 *dead*, 648.3 *hasty*, 650.3 *panting*, 786.7 *wide-eyed*
breathless adoration 849.2 *admiration*
breathless wonder 786.1 *wonder*
breath of air 651.6 *refresher*
breath of fresh air 651.6 *refresher*
breath of life 396.3 *life requirements*, 611.2 *important matter*
breath of one's nostrils 396.3 *life requirements*
breath of oxygen 651.6 *refresher*
breath of wind 55.14 *windiness*
breath-sweetener 417.2 *deodorant*
breathtaking 611.6 *notable*, 786.8 *wonderful*
breath-taking 403.9 *exciting*
breccia 54 *Common Rocks*, **54** Common Rocks, 54.31 *sedimentary rock*, 384.9 *grit*
breccial 384.18 *grainy*
brecciate 384.23 *pulverize*
brecciated 384.18 *grainy*
brecciation 384.4 *pulverization*
Brecht 48 *Dramatists*
Brecknock Hill Cheviot 68 Breeds of Sheep
Brecon 93 *Cities*
Brecon Beacons 95 Mountains, 95.5 *British mountains*
Brecon Buff 68 Breeds of Fowl
bred 304, 68.21 *domesticated*, 243.12 *produced*
bred horse 32.13 *breeding*
bred in the bone 140.7 *combined*
bred-in-the-bone 103.6 *intrinsic*
bred into 140.7 *combined*
breech 680.9 *firearm*
breeches 295.9 *trousers*
Breeches Bible 7.12 *religious text*
breeches buoy 632.4 *safety device*
breeches part 51.21 *role*
breechloader 680.9 *firearm*
breech presentation 245.7 *obstetrics*
breed 68.18 *practise livestock farming*, 69.15 *cultivate*, 103.4 *nature*, 128.4 *increase*, 128.5 *make bigger*, 156.26 *produce*, 163.8 *genealogy*, 243.10 *produce*, 245.13 *propagate*, 261.6

become bigger, 304.8 *nurture*, 396.19 *give birth to*, 560.6 *sort*, 594.7 *develop*
breeder 32.15 *horse person*, 68.15 *agriculturist*
breeder reactor 56.73 *nuclear reactor*
breeding 6.11 *refinement*, 163.9 *distinction*, 245.3 *propagation*, 245.16 *reproductive*, 261.1 *growth*, 652.2 *good conduct*, 815.2 *social ambition*, 817.2 *good manners*
breeding ground 226.2 *source*
breed with 135.11 *make love*
breeks 295.9 *trousers*
breeze 55.12 *wind*, 55.13 *wind strength*, 374.11 *soft thing*, 390.4 *air flow*, 477.5 *easy question*, 651.6 *refresher*, 660.6 *easy thing*
breeze block 43.4 *building material*, 63.26 *masonry*, 604.2 *building material*
breeze in 660.17 *do easily*
breeziness 55.14 *windiness*
breezy 390, 55.47 *windy*, 409.8 *cold*
Bremen 93 *Cities*
Bren gun 680.11 *guns*
Brentano 4 Philosophers, **48** Writers
brent goose 78 *Birds*
Brenton 48 Dramatists
Bresse 68 Breeds of Fowl
Brest 93 *Cities*, **93** Cities
Breton 5 Languages and Groups of Languages, **32** Breeds of Horse and Pony, **48** Poets
Breton Heavy Draught 32 Breeds of Horse and Pony
Bretons 1 Peoples
breve 5.36 *accent*, 49.17 *notation*, 543.7 *punctuation*
brevet 703.3 *authority*, 703.8 *authorize*
breviary 10.10 *religious manual*
brevity 189.1 *transience*, 270.1 *shortness*, 552.1 *conciseness*, 562.4 *summariness*, 566.4 *taciturnity*
brew 55.59 *storm*, 133.2 *mixed thing*, 133.8 *mix*, 261.6 *become bigger*, 592.13 *plot*, 594.7 *develop*
brew a plot 592.13 *plot*
brewer 594.15 *preparer*
brewers' 89 Fungi
brewers' grains 68.9 *animal feedstuff*
brewers' yeast 68.9 *animal feedstuff*
brewery 647.1 *workshop*
brewing 243.1 *production*, 261.8 *growing*, 389.10 *steeping*, 594.13 *development*, 594.17 *developing*
brewis 45.40 *breakfast cereal*
Brewster 52 Scientists
Brewster angle 36 Named Laws
Breydon 94 Lakes
Breydon Water 94.4 *British lakes*
briar 84 Flowers and Flowering Plants, 631.6 *source of trouble*
briard 77 Breeds of Dogs
bribable 710.17 *offered*, 738.13 *bought*, 858.5 *dishonourable*
bribe 586, 586, 228.5 *positive stimulus*, 710.4 *illegal offer*, 710.9 *offer*, 721.5, 721.14 *profit*, 729.2 *gift*, 729.5 *give*, 738.4 *buy off*, 746.4 *grant*, 746.11 *remunerate*, 878.8 *secret money*, 878.11 *pay*
bribed 710.17 *offered*, 738.13 *bought*
briber 695.4 *coercive person*, 721.7 *gainer*, 729.4 *giver*, 738.12 *purchaser*
bribery 695.3 *coercive methods*, 858.3 *criminality*
bribing 729.1 *giving*, 858.7 *criminal*
bric-a-brac 612.9 *bauble*, 754.5 *cheap item*

brick 43.4 *building material,* 43.18 *be an architect,* 44.9 *industrial ceramics,* 44.11 *make ceramics,* 63.25 *construction material,* 63.26 *masonry,* 293.28 *face,* 327.4 *road surface,* 373.7 *hard substance,* 450.7 *red thing,* 604.2 *building material,* 680.6 *historical missile weapon,* 857.3 *honourable person*
brickbat 338.8 *missile,* 680.6 *historical missile weapon,* 850.6 *taunt,* 852.5, 854.2 *criticism*
bricked 293.36 *covered*
brick house 373.7 *hard substance*
bricking 44.10 *ceramic*
brick kiln 44.6 *ceramic workshop*
bricklayer 293.17 *coverer,* 646.2 *artisan*
bricklaying 63.26 *masonry*
brick-red 450.1 *red*
bricks 293.8 *wall covering*
bricks and mortar 243.8 *construction,* 604.2 *building material*
brick wall 373.7 *hard substance,* 438.6 *that which makes invisible,* 443.7 *opaque thing,* 661.3 *barrier,* 726.4 *wall*
brickwork 43.4 *building material,* 63.26 *masonry,* 243.8 *construction,* 382.2 *fabric*
brickworks 647.1 *workshop*
bridal 823.20 *matrimonial*
bridal attendant 823.7 *bridal party*
bridal bed 821.13 *abode of love,* 823.1 *marriage*
bridal bouquet 823.6 *general terms*
bridal chamber 823.6 *general terms*
bridal outfit 295.1 *dress*
bridal pair 823.9 *married couple*
bridal party 823
bridal suite 821.13 *abode of love,* 823.6 *general terms*
bridal wreath 84 Flowers and Flowering Plants
bride 402.4 *girlfriend,* 823.7 *bridal party,* 823.8 *spouse*
bridebed 823.1 *marriage*
bridegroom 401.4 *boyfriend,* 823.7 *bridal party,* 823.8 *spouse*
bride of Christ 825.4 *celibate person*
bride price 725.6 *marriage settlement*
bridesmaid 819.6 *close friend,* 823.7 *bridal party*
bride-to-be 114.6 *someone promised,* 821.9 *lover,* 821.11 *loved one*
bridge 42 Card Games, **74** Parts of a Ship, **63, 327,** 34.9 *mountaineer,* 51.15 *stage,* 56.90 *ammeter,* 63.19 *structure,* 64.13 *circuit,* 65.15 *network,* 96.2 *channel,* 135.10 *link,* 137.5 *road,* 137.11 *connect,* 232.4 *be an instrument,* 272.6 *narrow place,* 293.26 *overlie,* 326.2 *transportation,* 356.5 *crossing point,* 356.11 *cross,* 435.9 *viewpoint,* 594.1 *prepare,* 692.8 *vantage point*
bridge a river 327.14 *find one's way*
bridgeboard 359.10 *step*
bridge-builder 594.15 *preparer*
bridged 137.15 *connected,* 327.15 *accessible*
bridgehead 676.10 *battleground*
Bridgend 93 Cities
bridge over 677.4 *pacify*
bridge roll 45.39 *loaf*
bridges 777 Phobias by Topic
Bridges 48 Poets
bridge the gap 660.16 *make easy*
bridging 34.3 *climbing technique,* 630.12 *surgery*
Bridgman 52 Scientists
bridle 32.14 *horse-riding terms,* 68.18 *practise livestock farming,* 699.5 *means of restraint,* 828.12 *become angry*

bridle path 327.6 *path,* 356.4 *access*
Brie 45 Cheeses
brief 594, 6.22 *educate,* 16.13 *lawyer,* 189.6 *transient,* 270.7 *short,* 299.6 *outlined,* 475.16 *explain,* 501.14 *cause to know,* 528.11 *inform,* 552.3 *concise,* 562.6 *summary,* 648.3 *hasty,* 654.5 *advise,* 707.3 *agent*
briefcase 258.9 *baggage*
brief counsel 16.70 *litigate*
brief description 560, 299.1 *outline*
briefed 6.19, 501.8 *knowledgeable,* 528.18 *informed,* 594.18 *prepared*
brief encounter 189.2 *transient thing*
brief impression 299.1 *outline*
briefing 594, 475.3 *explanation,* 528.2 *communication,* 654.1 *advice*
briefly 189.8 *transiently,* 270.12 *short,* 552.5 *concisely,* 562.11 *summarily*
briefness 270.1 *shortness,* 552.1 *conciseness,* 562.4 *summariness*
brief oneself 594.8 *prepare oneself*
briefs 295.18 *underwear*
brief sketch 552.2 *outline*
brief span 189.3 *short duration*
brier 138.4 *adherent,* 380.8 *sharp-pointed thing,*
briery 380.2 *spiked*
brig 74 Sailing Ships and Boats, **74** Parts of a Ship
brigade 17.4 *military organization,* 140.3 *assembly,* 140.6 *come together,* 161.14 *force,* 679.16 *army unit*
brigade commander 17.5 *military staff*
brigadier 679.17 *army person,* 692.6 *person in command*
Brigadier 17 British Military Ranks
brigadier general 692.6 *person in command*
Brigadier General 17 US Military Ranks
brigand 736.9 *plunderer*
brigandage 736.5 *plundering*
brigandine 671.7 *armour*
brigandish 736.17 *stolen*
brigandism 736.5 *plundering*
Briganta 8 Deities
brigantine 74 Sailing Ships and Boats
Briggs 52 Scientists
Briggsian logarithms 52 Named Concepts
bright 439, 6.17 *educatable,* 55.45 *fine,* 134.14 *purified,* 237.12 *strong to the senses,* 329.2 *mentally quick,* 380.5 *mentally sharp,* 437.2 *clear,* 439.18 *lit,* 439.22 *enlightened,* 444.11 *colourful,* 446.6 *light,* 459.10, 507.6 *intelligent,* 621.16 *clean,* 714.14 *auspicious,* 763.2 *likable,* 775.14 *cheering,* 789.5 *beautiful*
bright and early 208.12, 208.17 *early*
bright as a new pin 134.14 *purified,* 621.16 *clean*
bright as silver 621.16 *clean*
bright blue 454.1 *blue*
brighten 55.61 *shine,* 439.24 *light,* 439.26 *grow light,* 442.12 *make transparent,* 444.15 *colour,* 769.6 *bring cheer*
brightened 439.18 *lit*
brightening 439.3 *lightening,* 439.15 *lucent*
brighten one's day 763.13 *give pleasure*
brighter 55.45 *fine*
bright idea 228.1 *motive,* 471.3 *plan,* 507.2 *intelligence,* 592.3 *expedient plan*
bright light 439.2 *quality of light*

brightly 6.26 *studiously,* 237.15 *acutely,* 380.18 *sharply,* 439.30 *lightly,* 444.18 *colourfully,* 714.17 *auspiciously*
bright nebula 53.8 *interstellar medium*
brightness 6.10 *educatability,* 56.23 *light,* 329.10 *quickness of mind,* 380.13 *mental sharpness,* 437.4 *clarity,* 439.1 *light,* 439.2 *quality of light,* 446.12 *light,* 459.4 *cleverness,* 507.2 *intelligence,* 534.22 *television set,* 789.1 *gorgeousness*
Brighton 93 Cities
Brighton Belle 72.10 *miscellaneous*
bright prospects 714.3 *potential*
bright red 450.1 *red*
bright side 305.4 *aspect,* 775.1 *hope*
bright spark 501.6 *knowledgeable person,* 507.4 *intellectual*
bright yellow 452.1 *yellow*
bright young thing 201.9 *modern person*
Brigit 8 Deities
Brigittine 7 Members of Religious Orders
Brihaspati 8 Deities
brill 80 Fishes, 45.18 *sea fish,* 617.1 *worthy,* 786.14 *wonderful,* 861.1 *good,* 861.27 *great super*
brillant 49 Musical Terms
Brillat Savarin 45 Cheeses
Brillat-Savarin 48 Writers
brilliance 437.4 *clarity,* 439.1 *light,* 439.2 *quality of light,* 444.3 *hue,* 459.4 *cleverness,* 507.2 *intelligence,* 617.6 *worth,* 619.3 *perfection,* 655.3 *masterpiece,* 789.1 *gorgeousness,* 811.9 *grandeur*
brilliant 237.12 *strong to the senses,* 437.2 *clear,* 439.16 *bright,* 439.22 *enlightened,* 444.11 *colourful,* 459.10, 507.6 *intelligent,* 617.1 *worthy,* 619.1 *perfect,* 811.24 *grand*
brilliantine 386.6 *pomade,* 395.6 *ointment*
brilliantly 237.15 *acutely,* 439.30 *lightly,* 444.18 *colourfully,* 507.10 *intelligently,* 617.11 *worthily,* 811.40 *grandly*
brim 181.11 *crowd,* 300.1 *edge,* 608.5 *about*
brimful 144.8 *full*
brimmer 144.2 *fullness*
brimming 144.2 *fullness,* 144.8 *full,* 357.11 *overrun*
brimming over 610.6 *excessive*
brim over 357.1 *overstep,* 610.4 *be excessive*
brimstone 452.8 *yellow thing*
brimstone butterfly 82 Insects
brim with 144.5 *be complete*
brim with good health 623.5 *be healthy*
Brindisi 93 Cities
brindle 456.4 *maculation,* 456.11 *variegate*
brindled 456.10 *mottled*
Brindley 52 Scientists
brindling 456.4 *maculation*
brine 97.1 *sea,* 389.1 *water,* 389.31 *steep,* 637.2 *preserver*
brine shrimp 81.4 *arthropod*
bring 326.14 *bring back,* 702.1 *prison,* 751.13 *cost*
bring about 226.9 *be the cause of,* 228.9 *motivate,* 243.10 *produce,* 520.12, 570.13 *intend,* 586.15 *persuade,* 615.6 *be convenient,* 684.4 *complete*
bring a case 856.5 *accuse*
bring a charge 856.5 *accuse*
bring action 856.5 *accuse*
bring a lawsuit 16.70 *litigate,* 856.5 *accuse*
bring alive 537.34 *render*
bring-and-buy sale 740.10 *bazaar,* 752.2 *bargain*
bring a suit 16.70 *litigate*
bring a verdict 492.11 *judge*

bring back 326, 511.13 *remind,* 629.3 *restore,* 639.1 *deliver,* 735.4 *give back*
bring bad luck 687.11 *cause adversity*
bring before the court 16.70 *litigate*
bring charges 856.5 *accuse*
bring cheer 769
bring destruction 244.10 *lay waste*
bring down 362, 670.2 *fire,* 670.5 *strike,* 770.10 *depress*
bring-down 770.4 *depressing person*
bring down on one's head 659.21 *get into trouble*
bring down to earth 515.6 *disappoint,* 542.21 *detract from*
bring down to the grave 398.16 *kill*
bring evidence against 856.5 *accuse*
bring forth 245.10 *reproduce oneself,* 355.15 *draw out,* 526.3 *reveal*
bring forward 336.8 *further,* 526.1 *display*
bring home the bacon 682.6 *be successful,* 684.4 *complete,* 721.12 *earn*
bring home the charge 16.79 *convict*
bring in 348.7 *admit,* 348.10 *introduce,* 354.1 *insert,* 606.5 *provision,* 721.9 *gain,* 730.9 *receive*
bring in an unfavourable verdict 16.79 *convict*
bring in a return 721.13 *be profitable*
bring in a supply 606.5 *provision*
bring in a verdict 16.71 *try a case,* 16.76 *judge*
bringing back 735.1 *giving back*
bringing down to earth 515.2 *bad outcome*
bringing forth 355.5 *drawing out*
bringing in 348.3 *introduction,* 721.1 *gain*
bringing legal action against 16.53 *litigating*
bringing of charges 856.1 *accusation*
bringing together 135.3 *unification,* 140.1 *combination,* 161.1 *assembly,* 721.3 *acquisition*
bringing to light 526.10 *manifestation*
bringing up the rear 155.30 *behind*
bring in new blood 216.8 *cause change*
bring into action 230.8 *activate*
bring into being 99, 156.26 *produce,* 226.9 *be the cause of,* 243.10 *produce,* 245.13 *propagate,* 306.7 *form*
bring into contact 267.3 *juxtapose*
bring into disrepute 801, 854.12 *defame*
bring into effect 230.8 *activate,* 232.4 *be an instrument*
bring into existence 537, 243.10 *produce,* 245.13 *propagate*
bring into focus 291.9 *centre,* 342.11 *focus*
bring into force 230.8 *activate*
bring into line 112.10 *conform,* 166.14 *regulate,* 167.9 *make conform,* 701.6 *subject*
bring into operation 230.8 *activate*
bring into play 230.8 *activate*
bring into the open 289.14 *externalize,* 530.5 *disclose,* 532.13 *make public*
bring into the wind 74.9 *navigate*
bring into the world 156.26 *produce,* 226.9 *be the cause of,* 243.10 *produce,* 245.13 *propagate*
bring in tow 180.15 *escort*

bring it off 682.6 *be successful*, 718.13 *secure one's objective*
bring legal action 16.70 *litigate*
bring legal force to bear 695.7 *force*
bring litigation 856.5 *accuse*
bring low 701.6 *subject*, 806.23 *abase*
bring near 264.9 *near*
bring off 226.9 *be the cause of*, 682.6 *be successful*
bring on 226.10 *awaken*, 228.9 *motivate*, 336.8 *further*, 594.7 *develop*
bring one's house about one's ears 656.6 *act foolishly*
bring order out of chaos 214.10 *make regular*
bring out 226.10 *awaken*, 243.10 *produce*, 289.14 *externalize*, 475.15 *demonstrate*, 526.3 *reveal*, 532.15 *publish*
bring over 228.9 *motivate*, 586.15 *persuade*
bring pressure to bear 228.10 *manipulate*
bring pressure to bear on 330.1 *impel*
bring pressure to bear upon 695.6 *compel*
bring prosperity 861.20 *do good*
bring results 613.10 *benefit*
bring round 242.4 *moderate*, 396.19 *give birth to*, 586.15 *persuade*
bring shame upon 801.4 *disreputable*
bring someone round 228.9 *motivate*
bring the house down 423.8 *be loud*, 851.16 *acclaim*
bring to 128.5 *make bigger*, 130.6 *add*
bring to a boil 684.4 *complete*
bring to a close 684.5 *conclude*
bring to a conclusion 684.4 *complete*, 684.5 *conclude*
bring to a head 128.5 *make bigger*, 142.10 *complete*, 594.7 *develop*, 684.4 *complete*, 768.6 *aggravate*
bring to an end 157.16 *cease*, 189.5 *make transient*, 218.8 *cause to cease*
bring to a standstill 218.8 *cause to cease*, 325.9 *make motionless*, 661.8 *hinder*
bring to attention 611.8 *make important*
bring to bay 670.9 *attack successfully*
bring to bear 599.1 *use*
bring to bear upon 107.7 *relate to*
bring to birth 245.10 *reproduce oneself*
bring to book 879.2 *penalize*
bring to fruition 594.7 *develop*, 627.1 *improve*
bring together 135.8 *unite*, 140.5 *combine*, 161.37 *assemble*, 324.14 *set in motion*, 371.9 *make dense*, 605.6 *store*, 629.3 *restore*, 677.4 *pacify*, 678.1 *mediate*, 721.11 *acquire*
bring to heel 701.6 *subject*
bring to justice 16.70 *litigate*
bring to life 396.19 *give birth to*, 560.15 *recount*
bring to light 355.15 *draw out*, 435.18, 437.10 *make visible*, 496.2 *detect*, 526.3 *reveal*, 530.5 *disclose*
bring to market 739.1 *sell*
bring to mind 114.10 *be similar*, 511.13 *remind*
bring to notice 526.1 *display*, 526.3 *reveal*, 611.8 *make important*
bring to one's knees 701.6 *subject*
bring to one's side 228.9 *motivate*, 586.15 *persuade*
bring to pass 226.9 *be the cause of*
bring to perfection 619.5 *perfect*
bring to public notice 532.13 *make public*

bring to rest 74.10 *sail*
bring to ruin 244.11 *ruin*
bring to terms 677.4 *pacify*
bring to the bar 16.70 *litigate*
bring to the boil 128.5 *make bigger*
bring to the fore 611.8 *make important*
bring to the table 678.1 *mediate*
bring to trial 16.70 *litigate*
bring under the hammer 739.1 *sell*
bring up 6.22 *educate*, 36.15 *sail*, 243.10 *produce*, 245.13 *propagate*, 349.15 *vomit*, 526.3 *reveal*, 532.13 *make public*
bring up children 304.8 *nurture*
bring up for debate 518.6 *propound*
bring up the rear **155**, 195.10 *succeed*, 304.6 *be in the rear*
bring up to date 201.20 *make new*, 594.6 *brief*, 627.1 *improve*
bring up to scratch 594.4 *prepare for action*
bring up to snuff 594.4 *prepare for action*
bring within the law 16.65 *make legal*
brink 264.2 *short distance*, 300.1 *edge*, 302.3 *furthest point*
brinkman 780.3 *rash person*
brinkmanship 652.9 *tactics*, 780.1 *rashness*
Brinks 718.4 *security forces*
Brin process 57 Named Reactions
Brinsers 7 Christian Movements
briny 97.7 *oceanic*
brioche 45.39 *loaf*
briquette 410.5 *coal*
Brisbane 93 Cities
brisé volé 46.9 *ballet steps*
brisk 55.45 *fine*, 55.47 *windy*, 239.4 *vigorous*, 241.6 *violent*, 329.2 *mentally quick*, 552.3 *concise*, 554.3 *emphatic*, 642.18 *active*, 648.3 *hasty*
brisket 45.22, 45.23 *beef*
briskly 552.5 *concisely*
briskness 329.8 *speed*, 552.1 *conciseness*, 642.3 *nimbleness*, 648.4 *haste*
brisk wind 55.14 *windiness*
brisling 80 Fishes, 80.8 *food fish*
bristle 77.2 *mammalian characteristic*, 181.11 *crowd*, 281.6 *make vertical*, 375.7 *rough thing*, 375.11 *be rough*, 380.14 *be sharp-pointed thing*, 380.14 *be sharp*, 828.12 *become angry*
bristlecone pine 85 Trees and Shrubs
bristled 375.3 *barbed*
bristle grass 87 Grasses
bristletail 82 Insects
bristle up 375.11 *be rough*
bristle with 380.14 *be sharp*, 608.5 *about*, 610.4 *be excessive*
bristle worm 81 Worms, 81.6 *worm*
bristliness 375.6 *roughness*, 380.6 *sharpness*
bristling 45.18 *sea fish*, 161.50 *crowded*, 375.3 *barbed*, 380.2 *spiked*, 610.6 *excessive*
bristly 375.3 *barbed*, 380.2 *spiked*
Bristol 93 Cities
Bristol board 604.3 *paper*
Bristolian 255.9 *British inhabitant*
Brit 91.8 *Great Britain*, 255.9 *British inhabitant*
Britain 91.8 *Great Britain*
Britannia 91.8 *Great Britain*
Britannia Cup 36.5 *Henley trophies*
Britannia metal 57 Alloys, 539.6 *imitation*
Britannia Royal Naval College 676.6 *art of war*
britches 295.9 *trousers*
Briticism 5.26 *dialect*, 91.8 *Great Britain*

British 5 Languages and Groups of Languages
British accent 5.26 *dialect*
British administrative council 653
British Amateur Gymnastics Association 30.4 *gymnastic organization*
British Army 679.15 *army*
British Army Reserve 679.15 *army*
British Bleu du Maine 68 Breeds of Sheep
British blue 77 Breeds of Cats
British Board of Film Censors 704.5 *abrogator*
British Boxing Board of Control 26.2 *boxing*
British bulldog 91.8 *Great Britain*
British Canoe Union 36.6 *canoeing*
British Charolais 68 Breeds of Sheep
British cities 93
British coinage 741.9 *British money*
British Colombia 92 Canadian Provinces and Territories
British Commonwealth 91.2 *union of nations*
British court 16
British dish 45
British Empire 91.3 *dominion*
British Friesland 68 Breeds of Sheep
British game fish 20
British government 653, 12.4 *governing body*
British GP at Silverstone 33.2 *Formula 1 race*
British inhabitant 255
Britishism 91.8 *Great Britain*
British judge 16
British lakes 94
British law officer 16
British Legion member 679.11 *former soldier*
British lion and unicorn 544.6 *national emblem*
British Lop 68 Breeds of Pig
British military academies 17.3 *military training*
British Milksheep 68 Breeds of Sheep
British money 741
British Mountaineering Council 34.6 *mountaineering association*
British mountains 95
British Museum 43 Noted Buildings
British Oldenburg 68 Breeds of Sheep
British paper money 741.9 *British money*
British police 16
British Racing Drivers' Club 33.7 *racing governing body*
British Rail 72.10 *miscellaneous*
British rivers 96
British Saddleback 68 Breeds of Pig
British Schools Canoeing Association 36.6 *canoeing*
British Ski Federation 41.1 *skiing*
British Summer Time 185.9 *time zone*
British Texel 68 Breeds of Sheep
British thermal unit 75 Scientific and Technical Units
British warm 408.3 *heater*
British weather 215.3 *irregular thing*
British White 68 Breeds of Cattle
Briton 91.8 *Great Britain*, 255.9 *British inhabitant*
Britons 1 Peoples
Brittany spaniel 37.6 *sporting dog*
Britten 49 Musicians and Composers
brittle 379, 189.7 *impermanent*, 238.8 *weak*
brittle as glass 379.1 *brittle*
brittleness 379, 384.2 *crumbliness*
Brittleness 379
brittle star 81.3 *echinoderm*
brittle thing 379
britzka 71 Carriages and Carts
Brno 93 Cities

broach 156.18 *make a beginning*, 226.11 *inaugurate*, 355.14 *suck*, 380.8 *sharp pointed thing*
broaching 355.4 *sucking*
broaching machine 63.9 *machine tool*
broach to 36.15 *sail*
broad 271, 271, 94.1 *lake*, 164.15 *general*, 164.20 *generalized*, 248.13 *spacious*, 259.15 *big*, 273.1 *thick*, 402.9 *woman considered as a sex object*, 482.4 *wholesale*, 491.6 *indeterminate*
B road 71.2, 327.3 *road*
broad accent 564.3 *mode of speech*
broad acres 725.1 *property*
broad-backed 271.2 *broad-shaped*
broad-based 146.7 *including*, 164.15 *general*, 271.2 *broad-shaped*
broad-beamed 271.2 *broad-shaped*
broad bean 45 Vegetables
broadbill 78 Birds, 271.5 *broad thing*
broad-billed 271.2 *broad-shaped*
broad-bottomed 271.2 *broad-shaped*
broad-breasted 271.2 *broad-shaped*
Broad-Breasted Bronze 68 Breeds of Fowl
Broad-Breasted White 68 Breeds of Fowl
broad-brimmed 271.2 *broad-shaped*
broad canvas 164.3 *nonspecificness*
broadcast 164, 68.17 *farm*, 162.1 *dispersion*, 162.16 *distribute*, 162.22 *distributed*, 271.1 *broad*, 362.6 *throw down*, 420.11 *aural*, 420.16 *be heard*, 526.2 *display something*, 528.2 *communication*, 528.12 *communicate*, 530.2 *divulgence* , 530.6 *divulge*, 532.1 *publication*, 532.13 *make public*, 532.19 *published*, 533.13 *report*, 534.30 *communicate*, 534.34 *communicated*, 564.8 *speech*
broadcast drama 51.2 *play*
broadcaster 534, 528.9 *informant*, 530.4 *discloser*, 564.10 *speaker*
broadcasting 162.1 *dispersion*, 528.4 *mass communication*, 532.1 *publication*, 532.2 *mass media*, 534.1 *communications*
broadcasting authority 534.20 *radio broadcasting*, 534.24 *television broadcasting*
broadcasting device 420.9 *audio device*
broadcasting station 534.20 *radio broadcasting*, 534.24 *television broadcasting*
broadcast journalist 533.4 *journalist*
broadcast material 534
broadcast television 534.21 *television*
broad-chested 271.2 *broad-shaped*
Broad Church 7 Christian Movements, 164.2 *catholicity*
broadcloth 67.3 *fabric*, 271.5 *broad* **thing**, 288.4 *textile*
broad comedy 51.10 *comedy*
broaden 164, 271, 128.4 *increase*, 128.5, 261.5 *make bigger*, 261.6 *become bigger*, 721.10 *augment*
broadened 261.7 *bigger*
broadener 261.4 *enlarger*
broadening 128.1 *increase*, 261.1 *growth*, 261.8 *growing*, 721.2 *augmentation*
broadening the mind 6.8 *learning*
broaden the mind 6.23 *learn*
broad-faced 271.2 *broad-shaped*
broad gauge 72.3 *rail*, 271.5 *broad thing*
broad-gauge 271.1 *broad*
broad-gauged 271.1 *broad*

broad-headed 271.2 broad-shaped
broad in the beam 259.16 fat, 271.2 broad-shaped
broad jump 21.2 field events
broad jumper 21.3 athlete
broad jumping 21.2 field events
broadleaf 85.1 tree, 271.5 broad thing
broad-leaved 271.2 broad-shaped
broadleaved tree 85.1 tree
broad-lipped 271.2 broad-shaped
broadloom 67.3 fabric, 271.1 broad
broadloom carpet 293.9 floor covering
broadly 271, 124.11 on average, 164.29 generally, 261.10 largely, 263.10 distantly, 491.25 indeterminately
broadly speaking 124.11 on average, 164.29 generally
broad-minded 271, 482.2 impartial, 507.5 wise, 698.9 free
broad-mindedly 698.20 freely
broad-mindedness 271, 482.7 impartiality, 698.1 freedom
Broadmoor 702.1 prison
broadness 164.3 nonspecificness, 259.2 bigness, 271.4 breadth, 491.14 indeterminacy
broad-nosed 271.2 broad-shaped
broad reaching 36.1 sailing
Broads 249.9 regions of Britain
broad-shaped 271
broadsheet 532.3 journalism, 532.4 newspaper, 533.5 mass communication
broad-shouldered 271.2 broad-shaped
broadside 271.8 breadthwise, 670.15 firing, 680.11 guns
broadside-on 36.20 offshore
broad spectrum 164.3 nonspecificness
broad-spectrum drug 62.3 drug
broadsword 271.5 broad thing, 380.10 knife, 680.8 sharp weapon
broad-tailed 271.2 broad-shaped
broad-toothed 271.2 broad-shaped
Broadway 49.12 Tin Pan Alley, 51.1 drama, 51.4 show business
Broadway costume 295.5 fancy dress
Broadway melody 433.1 melody
Broadway musical 51.3 musical drama
broadways 271.8 breadthwise
broad-winged 271.2 broad-shaped
broadwise 271.8 breadthwise
broagh 5.26 dialect
Brobdingnagian 259.10 big person, 259.15 big
brocade 67 Natural Fabrics
brocatelle 67 Natural Fabrics
broccoli 45 Vegetables, 453.9 greenstuff
Broch 48 Writers
brochette 137.8 fastening
brochure 532.9 advertisement, 562.2 outline, 592.2 policy
Brocken 95 Mountains
Brocken Spectre 95.3 mountaineer
broderie anglaise 792.2 pattern
Brodsky 48 Poets
brogue 5.26 dialect, 564.3 mode of speech
brogues 295.19 footwear
broil 674.6 fight
broiler 68.8 livestock
broiler house 68.7 farm building
broiling 45.8 cooking technique
broke 593.5 necessitous, 687.7 unprosperous, 722.17 unprofitable, 743.2 insolvent
broken 136.16 apart, 143.11 partial, 145.4 incomplete, 160.8 discontinuous, 215.4 irregular, 236.10 powerless, 238.9 dilapidated, 244.15 destroyed, 265.7 cracked, 322.12 open, 358.8 defective, 375.2 coarse, 379.1 brittle, 406.6 injured, 487.3 hope-

less, 620.1 imperfect, 628.13 dilapidated, 720.14 violating, 743.2 insolvent
broken arrow 675.2 symbol of peace
broken bone 406.3 injury
broken chord 49.16 musical note
broken clock 240.3 inert thing
broken cloud 55.19 cloud cover
broken down 68.20 farmable, 141.5 disintegrated, 236.10 powerless, 614.1 useless, 643.2 not working , 844.18 gone wrong
broken-down 238.9 dilapidated
broken English 5.26 dialect
broken glass 375.7 rough thing, 380.9 sharp-edged thing
broken ground 375.8 rough ground
broken-hearted 770.5 sad
broken home 824.1 divorce
broken in 68.21 domesticated, 584.14 habituated
broken jaw 406.3 injury
brokenly 136.21 apart, 160.18 disconnectedly, 375.14 roughly
broken man 743.10 poor person
broken marriage 824.1 divorce
broken mirror 517.7 bad-luck sign
brokenness 160.1 discontinuity, 215.1 irregularity, 375.6 roughness
broken off 160.10 interrupted
broken pipeline 605.3 supply
broken promise 538.4 lie, 576.11 vacillation, 858.2 faithlessness
broken record 788.2 boring thing
broken reed 87.7 figurative usage, 102.5 insubstantial person, 236.5 powerless person, 238.4 weakling
broken resolve 576.11 vacillation
broken rhyme 48.11 rhyme
broken set 620.6 imperfect item
broken silence 423.3 audibility
broken-spirited 806.3 humbled
broken state 145.1 incompleteness
broken thread 160
broken train of thought 160.7 broken thread
broken up 136.15 separate, 139.8 nonadhesive, 244.15 destroyed
broken-up 162.20 separated
broken water 375, 97.3 wave
broken-winded 650.3 panting
broken word 538.4 lie, 858.2 faithlessness
broker 14.3 stockbroker, 158.9 middleman, 646.3, 707.3 agent, 716.4 negotiator, 716.7 act as a go-between, 737.10 trader, 739.12 wholesaler
brokerage 737.4 trade, 752.1 discount
brokering 737.4 trade
brolly 293.12 protective covering
brome 87 Grasses
bromeliaceous 83.16 taxonomic
bromic 57.34 elemental
bromide 62 Medication, 62.4 drug type, 242.2 moderator, 505.1 maxim, 788.2 boring thing, 788.3 boring person
bromide paper 66.9 film
bromidrosiphobia 777 Phobias by Name
brominate 57.26 react
brominated 57.34 elemental
bromination 57 Types of Chemical Reaction
bromine 57 Chemical Elements
bromodiphenylhydraine 62 Medication
bromoform 57 Common Chemical Compounds
bromopheniramine 62 Medication
Bromo Seltzer 62 Medication
bromous 57.34 elemental
bronchial 390.19 respiratory, 624.23 diseased
bronchiole 390.8 respiration
bronchitic 624.19 sick person, 624.23 diseased

bronchitis 413.8 smoking, 624.9 respiratory disease
bronchoconstrictor 62.4 drug type
bronchodilator 62.4 drug type
bronchopneumonia 624.9 respiratory disease
bronchoscope 60.7 diagnosis
bronchoscopy 60.7 diagnosis
bronchus 390.8 respiration
bronco 32.1 horse, 32.4 saddle horse
broncobuster 68.16 farm worker
bronco-buster 32.15 horse person
Bronsen–Metcalf 53 Comets
Brontë 48 Writers, 48 Writers, 48 Writers
brontophobia 777 Phobias by Name
brontosaur 79 Fossil Reptiles
brontosaurus 202.8 prehistoric animal
Brontotherium 77 Placental Mammals
Bronx cheer 429.2 catcall, 431.7 cry of disapproval, 543.3 gesture, 713.3 gesture of protest, 850.6 taunt
bronze 57 Alloys, 21.6 track, 50.12 sculpture, 50.14 sculptor's materials, 133.2 mixed thing, 449.1, 449.7 brown, 451.1 orange
Bronze Age 3.10 past age, 200.4 prehistoric age
Bronze-Age 202.15 primal
Bronze Age man 202.7 ancient people
bronze axe 603.3 prehistoric tool
bronze coinage 741.13 coinage
bronzed 449.2 browned
bronze medal 21.5 competition, 30.1 gymnastics, 544.4 insignia, 681.1 trophy
bronze-medal 611.6 notable
bronze medallist 21.3 athlete, 237.5 athlete, 655.4 skilled person
Bronze Star 17 US Military Medals and Decorations
bronzing 408.5 hot weather
brooch 137.8 fastening, 792.6 jewellery
brood 161 Collective Names for Birds and Animals, 4.20 philosophize, 78.12 young bird, 78.26 nest, 161.24 brace, 181.4 throng, 206.4 young animal, 766.7 be dissatisfied, 770.9 despair, 830.9 be sullen
brooder 766.3 dissatisfied person
broodily 4.28 thoughtfully
brooding 4.17 thoughtful, 594.17 developing, 766.4 dissatisfied
brood mare 32.1 horse
broody 245.16 reproductive
brook 96.1 river, 284.12 bear
Brooke 48 Poets
brooking no delay 648.3 hasty
brooking no denial 535.14 assertive
brookite 54 Minerals
brooklet 96.1 river
Brooklyn 93 Cities, 93.3 New York
Brooklyn accent 5.26 dialect
brook no delay 648.1 hasten
brook no denial 535.21 be assertive, 577.9 be obstinate
brook no restraint 807.24 be vain
brook no rival 841.6 be jealous
brook trout 80 Fishes, 20.4 American game fish
broom 84 Flowers and Flowering Plants, 621.10 cleaning object
broomcorn 87 Grasses
Broome 18 Sporting Personalities
broomrape 84 Flowers and Flowering Plants
broomstick 274.9 thin person
brose 45.40 breakfast cereal
broth 45.13 soup, 133.2 mixed thing
brothel 877, 864.8 wicked place
brothel creepers 295.19 footwear

brothel keeper 877.9 immoral woman
brothel-keeping 877.5 prostitution
brother 7.7 monk, 116.5 conformity, 122.5 equal, 146.3 person included, 198.5 contemporary, 401.13 man in the family, 665.5 member, 819.6 close friend
brotherhood 135.2 agreement, 161.15 association, 400.9 group, 664.9 team, 665.1 party, 819.1 friendship
brotherhood of man 831.1 benevolence
Brotherhood of Ruralists 50 Schools and Groups of Artists
brotherliness 831.1 benevolence
brotherly 665.8 leagued, 819.8 friendly, 821.17 loving, 831.6 benevolent
brotherly interest 819.1 friendship
brotherly love 821.1 love, 831.1 benevolence, 833.1 philanthropy
brother under the skin 114.5 counterpart
brother war 676.1 war
brotulid 80 Fishes
Brough 18 Sporting Personalities
brougham 71 Carriages and Carts
brought before the court 16.54 litigated
brought down 806.3 humbled
brought face to face 526.13 displayed
brought forth 526.13 displayed
brought in 149.14 imported
brought low 701.9 subject
brought to attention 526.13 displayed
brought to heel 701.9 subject
brought to one's knees 701.9 subject
brought to one's notice 526.13 displayed
brought to perfection 619.1 perfect
brought to public notice 526.13 displayed
brought up 243.12 produced
brought within the law 16.44 legal
brouhaha 153.5 commotion, 241.3 instance of violence, 366.2 tumult, 674.6 fight
Brouwer 52 Scientists
brow 279.1 summit, 318.3 protuberance, 457.3 external appearance
browbeat 228.10 manipulate, 586.15 persuade, 695.7 force, 701.6 subject, 777.13 frighten, 807.26 oppress
browbeaten 701.9 subject
browbeating 695.2 coercion
brown 449, 449, 45.55 cook, 392.6 desert, 408.16 feel hot
Brown 52 Scientists
brown algae 90.2 algae, 449.5 brown thing
brown as a berry 449.2 browned
brown as a nut 449.2 browned
brown-bagger 449.6 figurative usage
brown ball 24.5 snooker
brown bear 77 Placental Mammals, 449.5 brown thing
brown belt 26.7 judo, 449.5 brown thing, 655.4 skilled person
Brown Bess 680.10 historical gun
brown betty 45.35 dessert, 449.5 brown thing
brown-black 447.1 black
brown bread 45.38 bread, 449.5 brown thing
brown Burmese 77 Breeds of Cats
brown coal 200.10 fossilization, 410.5 coal, 449.5 brown thing
brown colour 449.3 brownness
brown dye 449.4 brown pigment
Browne 48 Writers
browned 449, 45.56 culinary

browned off 828.16 *angry*
brown fat 449.5 *brown thing*
brown glass 44.1 *ceramics*
brown goods 243.7 *produce*
brown-grey 448.1 *grey*
Brownian 324.17 *directional*
Brownian movement 57 Named Reactions, 324.5 *circuition*
brownie 11.11 *ghost*, 260.4 *little person*, 270.5 *short person*, 414.3 *dessert*, 449.5 *brown thing*, 449.6 *figurative usage*, 808.3 *sycophant*
Brownie Girl Scout 449.6 *figurative usage*
Brownie Guide 449.6 *figurative usage*
Brownie point 449.6 *figurative usage*
brownies 45.36 *cake*
browning 408.5 *hot weather*
Browning 48 Poets
brownish-red 450.1 *red*
brownish-yellow 452.1 *yellow*
Brownism 7 Christian Movements
Brown, Jones, and Robinson 124.7 *average person*
brown-lung disease 449.5 *brown thing*
brown madder 450.6 *red pigment*
brownness 449
Brownness 449
brown nose 467.14 *be solicitous*
brown-nose 673.2 *appeaser*, 673.4 *succumb*, 771.7 *person who humours*, 771.15 *humour*, 808.9 *fawn*, 853.7 *sycophant*, 853.11 *be sycophantic*
brown-noser 449.6 *figurative usage*, 499.3 *assenter*, 673.2 *appeaser*, 808.3 *sycophant*
brown-nosing 771.11 *humouring*, 808.2 *sycophancy*, 808.7 *sycophantic*
brown off 828.14 *make angry*
brownout 64.34 *power supply*, 410.4 *electricity*
brown-out 449.6 *figurative usage*
Brown Owl 449.6 *figurative usage*
brown paper bag 449.5 *brown thing*
Brown personality inventory 61.5 *psychological test*
brown pigment 449
brown pigmentation 449.3 *brownness*
brown recluse spider 449.5 *brown thing*
brown rice 449.5 *brown thing*
brown rot 89 Fungi, 69.12 *pests and diseases*, 449.5 *brown thing*
brown sauce 45.15 *sauce*
Brown Shirt 449.6 *figurative usage*
Brownshirts 12.6 *political party*
brownstone 43.4 *building material*, 449.5 *brown thing*
brown study 449.6 *figurative usage*, 461.3 *thoughtfulness*, 462.6 *daydream*, 519.6 *reverie*
brown stuff 449.6 *figurative usage*, 875.6 *drug*
brown sugar 45.7 *basic ingredient*, 414.2 *sweetener*, 449.5 *brown thing*, 875.6 *drug*
Brown Swiss 68 Breeds of Cattle
Brown Swiss cattle 449.5 *brown thing*
brown tabby 77 Breeds of Cats
brown-tail moth 449.5 *brown thing*
brown thing 449
brown-trousers 449.6 *figurative usage*
brown trout 80 Fishes, 45.17 *freshwater fish*, 449.5 *brown thing*
browse 77.37 *graze*, 87.11 *eat grass*, 350.21 *eat*
browser 76.4 *type of animal*, 87.6 *grass-eater*
browsing 87.10 *grass-eating*
Bruch 49 Musicians and Composers
Brücke 50 Schools and Groups of Artists

Bruckner 49 Musicians and Composers
Bruges 93 Cities
Brugglers 7 Christian Movements
bruise 353.10 *bleeding*, 384.27 *beat*, 406.3 *injury*, 406.11 *inflict pain*, 407.13 *be touched by*, 447.9 *black thing*, 455.5 *lividness*, 455.9 *empurple*, 618.14 *illtreat*
bruised 406.6 *injured*, 454.2 *bluish*, 455.7 *livid*
bruiser 237.6 *muscleman*, 679.3 *athlete*, 832.8 *malefactor*
bruising 353.10 *bleeding*, 454.8 *bluishness*, 455.5 *lividness*
bruit 532.13 *make public*
bruit abroad 532.13 *make public*
brumal 203.13 *winter*
brumby 32.1 *horse*
Brumby 32 Breeds of Horse and Pony
brume 55.34 *mist*
brummagem 754.5 *cheap item*, 754.9 *cheap*
Brummie 255.9 *British inhabitant*
brunch 350.12 *meal*, 350.24 *have a meal*
Brunei 91 Countries
Brunel 52 Scientists
brunette 440.3 *dark colour*, 440.10 *dark-coloured*, 447.4 *black-haired*, 449.2 *browned*, 449.3 *brownness*
Brunner's gland 352 Exocrine Glands
Bruno 4 Philosophers, **18** Sporting Personalities
Brunswick 93 Cities
brunt 330.2 *collide*, 330.13 *blow*
brush 50.19 *paint*, 67.14 *weave*, 85.4 *trees*, 249.6 *regions*, 267.2 *meeting*, 267.4 *meet*, 330.6 *tap*, 330.13 *blow*, 376.9 *smoother*, 385.12 *rub*, 392.15 *dryer*, 392.20 *absorb*, 407.3 *press*, 407.11 *touch*, 407.12 *abut*, 621.10 *cleaning object*, 621.13 *clean*, 674.6 *fight*, 676.9 *battle*
brush aside 648.2 *make haste*, 850.22 *show disrespect*
brushed 67.10 *woven*, 376.1 *smooth*, 621.17 *cleaned*
brushing 267.6 *meeting*
brushing off the batter 22.4 *pitching terms*
brush obstacles aside 682.7 *overcome obstacles*
brush off 341.1 *repel*, 349.4 *ostracize*, 546.1 *obliterate*, 581.3 *exclude*, 621.13 *clean*
brush-off 22.4 *pitching terms*, 341.6 *repulse*, 581.1 *rejection*
brush off the batter 22.7 *play baseball*
brush the cheek 826.7 *show endearment for*
brush turkey 78 Birds
brush up 6.23 *learn*, 511.13 *remind*, 621.13 *clean*
brush with 676.14 *battle*
brushwood 85.3 *timber*, 410.2 *lighter*
brushwork 50.4 *treatment*
brusque 241.6 *violent*, 270.9 *abrupt*, 552.3 *concise*, 562.6 *summary*, 566.3 *sparing with words*, 818.5 *discourteous*, 830.7 *irritable*
brusquely 552.5 *concisely*, 562.11 *summarily*, 818.9 *discourteously*, 830.14 *irritably*
brusqueness 270.6 *abruptness*, 552.1 *conciseness*, 562.4 *summariness*, 566.4 *taciturnity*, 818.1 *discourtesy*
Brussels 93 Cities
Brussels sprout 45 Vegetables
brutal 76.14 *animalian*, 241.6 *violent*, 378.4 *powerful*, 398.24 *murderous*, 406.8 *inflicting pain*, 670.23 *attacking*, 690.8 *severe*, 818.5 *discourteous*, 832.11 *cruel*, 836.4 *pitiless*, 864.11 *wicked*

brutal act 832.7 *act of malevolence*
brutalist 43 Architectural Styles
brutality 241.2 *physical violence*, 378.8 *physical strength*, 832.2 *cruelness*, 864.1 *wickedness*
brutalization 628.8 *perversion*
brutalize 378.10 *be tough*, 628.6 *pervert*, 864.17 *make wicked*
brutalized 864.11 *wicked*
brutally 378.13 *powerfully*, 690.11 *severely*, 818.9 *discourteously*, 832.20 *malevolently*, 836.7 *pitilessly*, 864.18 *wickedly*
brutal murder 398.2 *murder*
brutalness 832.2 *cruelness*
brutal task 659.3 *difficult task*
brute 76.2 *animal*, 241.4 *violent person or animal*, 460.8 *nonhuman*, 818.4 *discourteous person*, 864.9 *wicked person*
brute creation 460.4 *nonhuman existence*
brute force 235.1 *power*, 237.1 *strength*, 241.2 *physical violence*, 378.8 *physical strength*, 690.2 *suppression*, 695.2 *coercion*
brute instinct 460.4 *nonhuman existence*
brute matter 367.4 *matter*
brute strength 235.1 *power*, 237.1 *strength*
brutish 76.14 *animalian*, 670.23 *attacking*, 832.11 *cruel*
brutishness 832.2 *cruelness*
Brutus 539.21 *traitor*
Bryant 48 Poets
bryological 88.6 *mosslike*
bryologist 83.12 *plant scientist*, 88.4 *moss thing*
bryology 59.1 *life science*, 83.10 *plant science*, 88.4 *moss plant*
bryony 84 Flowers and Flowering Plants
Bryophyta 83.4 *lower plant*
bryophyte 83.4 *lower plant*, 88.3 *moss*, 88.6 *mosslike*
bryophytes 396.9 *classifications of life*
bryophytic 88.6 *mosslike*
bryopsid 88.3 *moss*
Bryopsida 88.3 *moss*
Bryozoa 81.7 *coelenterate*
bryozoan 81.7 *coelenterate*
Brythonic 5 Languages and Groups of Languages
BSE 624.18 *veterinary disease*
B setting 66.18 *exposure time*
BSI 75.4 *standard*
B star 53.13 *luminosity*
BTU 408.2 *heat measurement*
bubble 390, 41.1 *skiing*, 96.7 *flow*, 258.19 *inflatable*, 261.3 *enlarged thing*, 315.3 *round thing*, 316.2 *bulge*, 366.21 *be agitated*, 370.7 *light thing*, 379.3 *brittle thing*, 539.3 *hypocrisy*
bubble and squeak 45.44 *British dish*, 133.2 *mixed thing*
bubble bath 621.6 *bath*, 621.9 *cleaning agent*
bubble car 71 Motor Vehicles
bubble gum 377.3 *elastic thing*, 394.2 *adhesive*
bubble-jet printer 65.7 *peripheral*
bubble memory 66.6 *memory*
bubble pack 442.8 *transparent thing*
bubblewrap 301.4 *wrapper*
bubbliness 370.5 *lightness*
bubbling 370.2 *insubstantial*
bubbly 390, 351.9 *wine*, 370.2 *insubstantial*, 388.21 *gassy*
bubby-jock 78.10 *male bird*
bubo 316.2 *bulge*, 793.2 *pimple*
bubonic plague 244.7 *agent of destruction*, 624.5 *plague*
bucatini 45 Types of Pasta
buccal gland 352 Exocrine Glands
buccaneer 74.7 *nautical person*, 679.6 *militarist*, 736.7 *plunderer*
buccaneering 679.33 *combative*, 736.5 *plundering*
buccanneer 679.27 *naval man*
buccannering 736.17 *stolen*

buccina 49 Musical Instruments
Bucephalus 32.3 *warhorse*
Buchan 48 Writers
Buchanan 4 Philosophers
Buchanites 7 Christian Movements
Bucharest 93 Cities
Buchenwald 702.1 *prison*
Büchner 48 Dramatists
buck 91 Names for Inhabitants, 77.17 *male mammal*, 401.7 *libertine*, 401.16 *male animal*, 741.8 *American money*
Buck 48 Writers
buckaroo 32.15 *horse person*, 68.16 *farm worker*
buckboard 71 Carriages and Carts
bucket 75 Scientific and Technical Units, 41.1 *skiing*, 120.3 *container*, 258.11 *vessel*, 326.15 *take away*, 702.2 *the inside*
bucket down 55.62 *rain*
bucketful 605.1 *store*
bucket seat 71 Motor Vehicle Parts, **73** Aircraft Parts, 47.2 *chair*
bucket shop 740.5 *stock market*, 754.7 *discounter*
bucket-shop 754.9 *cheap*
bucket-shop fare 754.4 *bargain*
Buckingham 93 Cities
Buckingham Palace 43 Noted Buildings, 256.4 *official residence*
Buckinghamshire 92 Counties
bucking up 778.6 *encouragement*
buckle 135.10 *link*, 137.8 *fastening*, 137.11 *connect*, 320.7 *fold*
buckled 137.15 *connected*
buckle down 642.15 *try*
buckled shoes 295.19 *footwear*
buckle on one's armour 594.8 *prepare oneself*
buckler 671.7 *armour*
buckler fern 88 Ferns
buckle to 574.9 *undertake*, 597.1 *undertake*
buckling 320.1 *fold*
buck naked 296.9 *undressed*
Büchner funnel 57 Laboratory Apparatus
buckrake 68.10 *farm tool*
buckram 67 Natural Fabrics
Bucks fizz 351.8 *mixed drink*
buckshee 754.11 *free of charge*
buckshot 680.13 *ammunition*, 680.14 *historical ammunition*
buckskin 293.14 *animal covering*
buckskins 295.9 *trousers*
buck the trend 168.19 *be independent*
bucktooth 380.11 *tooth*
buck up 769.6 *bring cheer*, 775.9 *be hopeful*
buckwheat 87 Grasses
buclizine 62 Medication, **62** Medication
bucolic 48.7 *poem*, 48.19 *narrative*, 68.19 *agricultural*
bucolically 68.22 *agriculturally*
bud 83, 69.15 *cultivate*, 83.21 *vegetate*, 84.13 *flower*, 128.4 *increase*, 156.3 *source*, 156.26 *produce*, 206.18 *grow*, 226.3 *rudiment*, 227.3 *growth*, 227.8 *grow*, 245.13 *propagate*, 261.6 *become bigger*, 316.2 *bulge*, 354.6 *plant*, 401.3 *male title of address*
Budapest 93 Cities, 93.6 *other cities*
Buddha 8.3 *God*
Buddhahood 8.1 *divinity*
Buddhic body 11.7 *spirit*
Buddhism 4.7 *school of thought*
Buddhist 4.11 *follower of a doctrine*, 4.14 *of a philosophy*, 7.6 *non-Christian*, 7.16 *denominational*
Buddhist text 7.12 *religious text*
Buddhology 7.13 *theology*
budding 69.5 *gardening*, 83.8 *bud*, 156.32 *embryonic*, 201.12 *immature*, 206.13 *maturing*, 227.11 *growing*, 261.1 *growth*, 261.8 *growing*

buddleia 84 Flowers and Flowering Plants

buddy 180.11 *companion,* **401.3** *male title of address,* **784.4** *likable person,* **819.5** *friend*

buddy-buddy 819.8 *friendly*

buddy up with 819.13 *befriend*

budge 324.13 *be in motion*

Budge 18 Sporting Personalities

budgerigar 78 Birds, 78.7 *cagebird*

budget 13.7 *corporation,* **14.1** *finance,* **592.1** *plan,* **592.12** *plan ahead,* **606.1, 606.5** *provision,* **750.2** *budgeting,* **750.7** *account,* **754.9** *cheap,* **756.2** *act of thrift,* **756.5** *be thrifty*

budget account 744.1 *credit*

budgetary 13.13 *economic,* **741.22** *monetary,* **750.10** *accounting*

budgetary control 13.7 *corporation*

budget deficit 13.13 *economic statistics,* 13.7 *corporation*

budget estimates 750.2 *budgeting*

budgeting 750, 606.1 *provision*

budget price 754.1 *cheapness*

budget surplus 13.7 *corporation*

budgie 78.7 *cagebird*

budstick 69.5 *gardening*

budtime 203.2 *spring*

Budyonny 32 Breeds of Horse and Pony

Bueno 18 Sporting Personalities

Buenos Aires 93 Cities

buff 51.31 *theatregoer,* **376.11** *smooth,* **385.12** *rub,* **449.1** *brown,* **452.1** *yellow,* **621.13** *clean,* **642.10** *busy person*

buffalo 77 Placental Mammals, **161** Collective Names by Animal

Buffalo 93 Cities

buffalo chips 353.5 *faeces*

buffalo fish 80 Fishes

buffalo gnat 82 Insects

buffalo grass 87 Grasses

buffalo hunter 590.6 *hunter*

buffer 671, 65.6 *memory,* 72.3 *rail,* 91.1 *national,* 242.2 *moderator,* 376.9 *smoother,* 632.2 *protection,* 632.9 *protect,* 661.3 *barrier,* 671.2, 671.2 *safeguard*

buffer state 12.5 *political organization,* 91.3 *dominion,* 267.1 *juxtaposition*

buffet 55.58 *blow,* 330.3 *hit,* 330.13 *blow,* 350.12 *meal,* 350.15 *eating place,* 618.14 *illtreat,* 879.12 *corporal punishment*

buffeting 73.5 *flight*

buffing 385.5 *polishing*

buffing wheel 364.6 *rotator*

buffo 49 Musical Terms

Buffon 52 Scientists

buffoon 506, 51.21 *role,* 51.30 *clown,* 656.10 *unskilled person,* 771.6 *humorist,* 798.3 *object of ridicule*

buffoonery 506.3 *tomfoolery,* 771.3 *wit,* 798.1 *ludicrousness*

bug 82 Insects, 65.17 *computing term,* 82.3 *pest,* 153.7 *disturb,* 420.9 *audio device,* 420.15 *hear,* 504.14 *computer error,* 545.10 *recording instrument,* 624.2 *illness,* 626.2 *germ,* 661.2 *obstacle,* 712.6 *request,* 852.18 *find fault*

Bug 96 Rivers

bugaboo 631.2 *adversity,* 636.3 *false alarm*

bugbear 631.2 *adversity,* 636.3 *false alarm,* 777.5 *frightener,* 822.7 *hated thing*

bugged 153.12 *disturbed,* 420.11 *aural*

bugger 400.7 *person,* 659.3 *difficult task*

bugger all 172.2 *nothing*

buggered 236.10 *powerless,* 244.15 *destroyed*

buggered up 844.18 *gone wrong*

bugger it 827.15 *miscellaneous swearwords*

bugger off 345.1 *depart,* 345.15 *go,* 349.33 *go away,* 827.15 *miscellaneous swearwords*

bugger up 628.4 *impair*

buggery 877.7 *sexual assault*

Buggins's turn 195.1 *succession*

buggy 71 Carriages and Carts, **71** Motor Vehicles, 71.16 *car,* 82.12 *verminous*

bughouse 510.8 *mental hospital*

bug hunter 82.8 *entomologist*

Bugi 5 Languages and Groups of Languages

bugia 10.14 *sacred object*

bug-infested 69.17 *botanical*

bugle 49 Musical Instruments, 318.3 *protuberance,* 423.4 *sound maker,* 423.8 *be loud,* 676.2 *glory of war*

bugle call 49.22 *phrase,* 676.2 *glory of war*

bugle-call 543.6 *word*

bugle corps 17.4 *military organization*

bugler 543.8 *signer*

bugloss 84 Flowers and Flowering Plants

bug off 349.33 *go away,* 591.9 *play truant*

build 1.9 *physical type,* 43.18 *be an architect,* 63.30 *engineer,* 148.13 *make,* 243.10 *produce,* 257.8 *embody,* 261.5 *make bigger,* 261.6 *become bigger,* 275.18 *erect,* 280.4 *base,* 281.6 *make vertical,* 306.6 *nature,* 306.7 *form,* 361.1 *raise,* 382.2 *fabric,* 382.3 *form,* 382.16 *construct,* 796.8 *fashion*

build a breakwater 96.9 *stop the flow*

build a bridge 594.1 *prepare*

build a tree house 85.18 *manage trees*

build buildings 43.18 *be an architect*

build castles in Spain 519.15 *fantasize*

build castles in the air 102.15 *idealize,* 468.12 *be inattentive,* 471.15 *imagine,* 489.7 *be improbable,* 519.15 *fantasize*

build castles in the sand 519.15 *fantasize*

builder 43.2 *architect,* 243.9 *producer,* 646.2 *artisan*

builder's knot 74 Knots

build houses 43.18 *be an architect*

build in 47.18 *work wood,* 301.5 *enclose*

building 43, 63, 63.19 *structure,* 243.2 *manufacture,* 243.8 *construction,* 261.1 *growth,* 281.2 *making vertical,* 382.5 *structuring,* 382.6 *construction,* 725.1 *property*

building and loan association 741.19 *treasury*

building block 43.4 *building material,* 148.3 *unit,* 367.4 *matter,* 604.2 *building material*

building blocks 103.1 *essence,* 226.3 *rudiment*

building brick 148.3 *unit*

building contract 715.2 *purchase contract*

building design 43.1 *architecture*

building material 43, 604, 63.25 *construction material*

building site 647.1 *workshop*

building society 732.4 *lending institution,* 741.19 *treasury,* 744.4 *bank*

building society account 14.4 *personal finance*

building stone 43.4 *building material,* 63.26 *masonry*

building style 43.1 *architecture*

build on a firm foundation 225.7 *make stable*

build on a rock 225.7 *make stable*

build up 121.6 *change gradually,* 128.5 *make bigger,* 144.4 *complete,* 148.13 *make,* 161.37 *as-*

build up *semble,* 237.8 *strengthen,* 261.5 *make bigger,* 261.6 *become bigger,* 532.16 *publicize*

buildup 605.1 *store*

build up 605.6 *store,* 611.8 *make important,* 768.7 *become aggravated*

build-up 128.1 *increase,* 261.1 *growth*

build up hope 714.9 *be auspicious*

build up hopes 517.11 *predict*

build up one's stocks 605.6 *store*

build Utopias 519.15 *fantasize*

built-in 47.14 *wooden,* 103.7 *integral,* 146.8 *included,* 148.7 *modular,* 301.7 *enclosed*

built-in advantage 652.9 *tactics*

built-in cupboard 47.1 *furniture,* 258.3 *cabinet*

built-in furniture 47.1 *furniture*

built like a fortress 632.6 *invulnerable*

built on sand 224.13 *changeable,* 633.2 *unsafe*

built on weak foundations 224.13 *changeable*

built-up 256.15 *environmental,* 261.7 *bigger*

built-up area 93.8 *suburb,* 249.10 *urban area*

buisine 49 Musical Instruments

Bulawayo 93 Cities

bulb 69.9 *garden plant,* 83.5 *stem,* 84.2 *flowering plant,* 226.3 *rudiment,* 315.3 *round thing,* 439.6 *electric light*

bulbous 83.14 *of plants,* 89.10 *of fungi,* 261.8 *growing,* 315.9 *round,* 316.4 *convex*

bulbously 261.10 *largely,* 315.13 *roundly,* 316.6 *convexly*

bulbousness 261.1 *growth,* 316.1 *convexity*

bulbul 78 Birds

Bulgaria 91 Countries

Bulgarian 5 Languages and Groups of Languages

Bulgars 1 Peoples

bulge 316, 34.5 *rock face,* 126.3 *advantage,* 128.4 *increase,* 144.5 *be complete,* 261.3 *enlarged thing,* 261.6 *become bigger,* 316.5 *be convex,* 676.10 *battleground*

bulginess 316.1 *convexity*

bulging 128.1 *increase,* 144.8 *full,* 261.1 *growth,* 261.8 *growing,* 316.1 *convexity,* 316.4 *convex*

bulgingly 316.6 *convexly*

bulgy 316.4 *convex*

bulimarexia 350.2 *appetite*

bulimia 350.2 *appetite*

bulimia nervosa 61.15 *compulsion,* 350.2 *appetite,* 624.4 *disease*

bulimic 350.18 *eater,* 350.26 *eating*

bulk 120.1 *quantity,* 143.5 *largest part,* 175.3 *majority,* 259.1 *size,* 259.19 *be big,* 273.5 *thickness,* 350.7 *food,* 350.11 *food content,* 369.4 *heaviness,* 371.1 *density*

bulk-buy 605.6 *store*

bulk carrier 74 Ships and Boats

bulkhead 73 Aircraft Parts, **74** Parts of a Ship, 36.3 *parts of a sailing boat,* 63.19 *structure*

bulkiness 259.2 *bigness,* 273.5 *thickness,* 369.4 *heaviness*

bulk large 611.7 *be important*

bulk memory 65.6 *memory*

bulk strain 63.14 *load*

bulk tank 68.10 *farm tool*

bulky 259.15 *big,* 273.1 *thick,* 369.1 *heavy,* 659.15 *clumsy*

bull 14.3 *stockbroker,* 14.5 *invest,* 14.6 *financial,* 16.17 *police officer,* 42.6 *darts,* 68.8 *livestock,* 77.17 *male mammal,* 291.2 *central thing,* 309.4 *distortion of the truth,* 401.16 *male animal,* 504.11 *grammatical error,* 506.1 *nonsense,* 521.4

senseless talk, 521.14, 538.6 *nonsense,* 540.13 *nonsense,* 692.1 *command,* 737.2 *speculate,* 738.1 *purchase,* 738.12 *purchaser,* 753.7 *dear*

Bull 53 The Constellations

bullace 86 Fruits

bull beef 68.8 *livestock*

bull-calf 401.16 *male animal*

bulldog 77 Breeds of Dogs, 778.7 *courageous person*

bulldog breed 574.16 *fortitude*

bulldog courage 575.4 *stamina*

bull-dogging 32.12 *rodeo*

bulldog tenacity 577.6 *determination*

bulldoze 244.9 *demolish,* 330.2 *collide,* 570.15 *impose one's will,* 695.7 *force,* 777.13 *frighten*

bulldozer 71 Motor Vehicles, 63.29 *construction equipment,* 244.7 *agent of destruction,* 282.4 *flattener,* 330.15 *ram,* 376.9 *smoother,* 384.11 *pulverizer,* 695.4 *coercive person*

bulldozing 330.12 *collision,* 695.9 *compelling*

bulldyke 402.10 *homosexual*

bullet 329.11 *swift thing,* 338.8 *missile,* 680.5 *missile weapon,* 680.13 *ammunition,* 879.16 *instrument of execution*

bulletin 55.4 *weather forecast,* 187.7 *periodical,* 528.2 *communication,* 532.1 *publication*

bulletin board 65.12 *electronic office,* 526.8 *showplace*

bullet-pouch 680.4 *arsenal*

bulletproof 378.1 *tough,* 378.11 *make tough,* 632.6 *invulnerable,* 669.12 *resisting,* 671.31 *entrenched*

bulletproof car 632.4 *safety device*

bulletproof glass 293.12 *protective covering,* 373.7 *hard substance,* 378.7 *tough thing,* 442.9 *glass,* 632.4 *safety device*

bulletproof vest 378.7 *tough thing,* 632.4 *safety device,* 671.6 *protective clothing*

bullets 777 Phobias by Topic

Bullet Train 72.10 *miscellaneous*

bulletwood 85 Trees and Shrubs

bullfight 674.9 *duel*

bullfighter 398.13 *animal killer,* 674.10 *contender,* 679.3 *athlete*

bullfighting 18 Sporting Activities, 77.23 *mammal hunting,* 398.9 *animal killing*

bullfinch 78 Birds

bullfrog 79 Amphibians

bullhead 80 Fishes

bull-headed 138.10 *tenacious,* 570.8 *wilful,* 577.1 *obstinate*

bull-headedness 138.2 *tenacity,* 577.5 *obstinacy*

bullhorn 420.9 *audio device,* 532.1 *publication*

bull in a china shop 656.10 *unskilled person*

bulling 330.12 *collision*

bullion 741, 741.1 *money*

bullish 77.33 *ungulate,* 359.23 *rising,* 686.8 *prosperous,* 738.14 *buying,* 753.7 *dear,* 775.11 *hopeful*

bullishly 686.9 *prosperously*

bullish tendency 753.3 *inflationary price*

bull kelp 90 Algae

bull-like 77.33 *ungulate*

bull market 13.6 *economic factors,* 14.2 *stock exchange,* 128.3 *increasing thing,* 686.1 *prosperity,* 740.3 *sellers' market,* 753.3 *inflationary price*

bull mastiff 77 Breeds of Dogs

bull-necked 273.1 *thick*

bullock 68.8 *livestock,* 401.16 *male animal*

bullocks 161 Collective Names by Animal

bullpen 22.1 *baseball,* 702.3 *prison cell*

bull-riding 32.12 *rodeo*

bullring 398.15 *slaughterhouse,* 674.9 *duel*

bullroarer 49 Musical Instruments, 423.4 *sound maker*

Bulls Blood 351.9 *wine*

bull's eye 74 Parts of a Ship

bull's-eye 74 Rigging, 158.2 *core,* 291.2 *central thing,* 503.3 *accurate thing,* 588.6 *objective,* 682.3 *successful thing*

bullshit 309.4 *distortion of the truth,* 309.12 *distort the truth,* 474.2 *sophism,* 474.12 *deceive,* 506.1 *nonsense,* 506.6 *talk nonsense,* 521.4 *senseless talk,* 521.9 *talk nonsense,* 521.14, 538.6 *nonsense,* 538.23 *talk nonsense,* 540.13 *nonsense*

bullshitter 309.5 *defacer,* 538.11, 539.16 *liar,* 541.6 *exaggerator*

bullshitting 309.8 *exaggerated,* 538.15 *lying*

bull snake 79 Reptiles

bull terrier 77 Breeds of Dogs

bully 228.10 *manipulate,* 237.6 *muscleman,* 241.4 *violent person or animal,* 378.10 *be tough,* 570.15 *impose one's will,* 617.1 *worthy,* 642.17 *meddle,* 679.1 *combatant,* 690.4 *strict person,* 690.5 *be severe,* 695.4 *coercive person,* 695.7 *force,* 777.5 *frightener,* 777.13 *frighten,* 807.26 *oppress,* 832.8 *malefactor,* 832.18 *torment,* 862.6 *evil person,* 864.9 *wicked person*

bullyboy 237.6 *muscleman,* 241.4 *violent person or animal,* 832.8 *malefactor*

bullying 398.4 *powerful,* 378.8 *physical strength,* 690.1 *severity,* 695.2 *coercion,* 768.3 *nuisance,* 777.4 *intimidation,* 832.5 *intolerance*

bully into 586.15 *persuade,* 695.7 *force*

bully off 156.18 *make a beginning,* 338.33 *start*

bully-off 156.11 *starting point*

bullyrag 832.18 *torment*

bulrush 87 Grasses

bulwark 284.2 *supporting part,* 284.11 *support,* 632.2 *protection,* 634.1 *refuge,* 661.3 *barrier,* 671.2 *safeguard,* 671.11 *fortification,* 726.4 *wall*

bulwarks 74 Parts of a Ship, 36.3 *parts of a sailing boat*

bum 304.2 *rear end,* 622.6 *dirty person,* 643.8 *nonworker,* 712.5 *beggar,* 712.8 *solicit money,* 733.7 *borrow,* 734.7 *take,* 743.10 *poor person*

bum bag 258.8 *bag*

bumbass 49 Musical Instruments

bumbershoot 293.12 *protective covering*

bumble 656.7 *be clumsy*

bumblebee 82 Insects

bumbledom 12.3 *governance,* 16.2 *jurisdiction*

bumbler 656.10 *unskilled person*

bumbling 656.3 *clumsy,* 656.9 *bungling*

bumboat 74 Ships and Boats

bumfreezer 295.11 *jacket*

bummer 515.2 *bad outcome,* 788.2 *boring thing,* 788.3 *boring person*

bumming 712.3 *solicitation,* 734.1 *taking*

bump 41.1 *skiing,* 215.1 *irregularity,* 215.6 *be irregular,* 316.2 *bulge,* 318.3 *protuberance,* 330.2 *collide,* 330.12 *collision,* 366.9, 366.23 *jolt,* 375.11 *be rough,* 406.3 *injury,* 406.11 *inflict pain,* 407.3 *press,* 407.12 *abut,* 424.1 *faintness,* 424.5 *sound faint,* 428.5 *dull sound,* 701.7 *terminate*

bumpa 49 Musical Instruments

bump and run 19.11 *defensive huddle,* 19.16 *play defence*

bumper 71 Motor Vehicle Parts, 24.6 *pool,* 36.7 *windsurfing,* 144.2 *fullness,* 181.9 *ample,* 259.15 *big,* 351.2 *drink,* 634.2 *shelter,* 671.2 *safeguard,* 721.19 *yielding*

bumper car 71 Motor Vehicles

bumper crop 608.8 *plenty,* 721.6 *yield*

bumper pool 24.6 *pool*

bumpers 295.19 *footwear*

bumper to bumper 159.20 *in a line,* 267.7 *beside*

bumper-to-bumper 264.5 *near,* 267.5 *juxtaposed,* 327.15 *accessible*

bumph 12.3 *governance,* 528.3 *document*

bumpily 113.10 *diversely,* 215.8 *irregularly,* 375.14 *roughly*

bumpiness 113.1 *diversity,* 160.1 *discontinuity,* 366.3 *turbulence,* 375.6 *roughness*

bumping 215.1 *irregularity,* 215.4 *irregular*

bumping off 398.2 *murder*

bumping race 36.4 *rowing*

bump into 229.5 *happen by chance,* 330.2 *collide,* 344.8 *meet,* 407.12 *abut,* 589.11 *chance upon*

bumpkin 460.3 *unintelligent person,* 656.10 *unskilled person,* 658.3 *naive person,* 803.1 *plebeian*

bump off 398.17 *murder*

bump start 71.21 *miscellaneous motoring terms*

bumptious 668.7 *defiant,* 805.22 *boastful,* 807.13 *insolent,* 809.11 *cocky*

bumptiously 668.9 *defiantly,* 807.30 *insolently,* 809.21 *cockily*

bumptiousness 668.1 *defiance,* 805.10 *boastfulness,* 807.1 *insolence,* 809.3 *cockiness*

bump up 128.5 *make bigger,* 239.3 *invigorate*

bumpy 375, 113.5 *diverse,* 160.8 *discontinuous,* 215.4 *irregular,* 318.5 *protuberant,* 366.17 *turbulent*

bumpy face 375.7 *rough thing*

bum steer 539.5 *falseness*

bun 45.39 *loaf*

Buna 377.4 *rubber*

bunch 161, 116.2 *alliance,* 120.2 *certain amount,* 138.6 *adhere,* 161.11 *group,* 161.27 *bundle,* 161.38 *group,* 161.39 *come together,* 181.4 *throng,* 665.1 *party,* 721.3 *acquisition,* 721.11 *acquire*

bunched 120.6 *quantitative,* 161.49 *grouped*

bunch grass 87 Grasses

bunch light 51.18 *stage lighting*

bunch of fives 726.3 *tools for gripping*

bunch of flowers 418.2 *fragrant thing*

bunch together 138.6 *adhere,* 665.12 *be in league with,* 721.11 *acquire*

bunch up 138.6 *adhere*

bunco 539.8 *trick*

bunco artist 539.17 *cheat*

bunco steerer 539.17 *cheat*

Bundesrat 653.10 *legislative body*

Bundestag 653.10 *legislative body*

bundle 161, 161.38 *group,* 258.5 *packet,* 258.8 *bag,* 258.21 *put in a container,* 338.33 *start,* 605.1 *store,* 605.5 *collection,* 605.6 *store,* 742.6 *money,* 821.27 *kiss,* 826.7 *show endearment for*

bundle away 349.6 *send away*

bundled 161.49 *grouped,* 258.20 *containing*

bundle off 338.33 *start,* 349.6 *send away*

bundle of joy 206.9 *child*

bundle of money 741.3 *fortune*

bundle of nerves 760.9 *oversensitive person*

bundle out 648.1 *hasten*

bundling 821.14 *communication of love,* 826.1 *endearment*

bunfight 161.9 *social gathering*

bun fight 350.13 *feast*

bung 293.2, 293.23 *cover,* 323.2 *stopper,* 323.8 *stop,* 338.23 *throw*

bungalow 256.5 *house,* 276.4 *low thing,* 725.1 *property*

bunged up 323.13 *stopped*

bungee jump 283.10 *suspend*

bungee rope 377.3 *elastic thing*

bungle 151.23 *confuse,* 211.3 *lost chance,* 211.8 *make a mistake,* 493.10 *misjudge,* 504.10 *blunder,* 504.19 *make a mistake,* 601.1 *misuse,* 618.8 *inferiority,* 618.13 *be worthless,* 620.5 *imperfection,* 628.4 *impair,* 656.7 *be clumsy,* 656.9 *bungling,* 683.1 *failure,* 683.6 *fail*

bungled 656, 601.4 *misused,* 618.2 *inferior,* 620.1 *imperfect,* 683.10 *failed*

bungler 493.5 *misjudging person,* 502.5 *ignorant person,* 656.10 *unskilled person,* 683.5 *failing person,* 722.6 *loser*

bungling 656, 211.13 *mistaken,* 493.2 *mistake,* 601.2 *misuse,* 656.3 *clumsy,* 683.1 *failure,* 683.10 *failed*

bungling idiot 656.10 *unskilled person*

bung up 323.8 *stop*

Bunin 48 Poets

bunion 316.2 *bulge*

bunji jumping 18 Sporting Activities

bunk 254.4 *absenteeism,* 521.5 *empty talk,* 521.14, 538.6 *nonsense,* 540.13 *nonsense*

bunk bed 47.6 *bed*

bunker 29.1 *golf,* 41.10 *curling,* 256.7 *room,* 605.4 *storage,* 605.6 *store,* 606.5 *provision,* 661.3 *barrier,* 671.10 *shelter*

bunker shot 29.3 *golf shots*

bunk off 254.18 *abscond*

bunkum 474.2 *sophism,* 506.1 *nonsense,* 521.5 *empty talk,* 538.6, 540.13 *nonsense,* 853.2 *blarney*

bunny hop 46.2 *dance*

bun penny 741.10 *former British money*

Bunsen 52 Scientists

Bunsen burner 57 Laboratory Apparatus, 408.6 *fire*

Bunsen cell 56 Named Laws, 57.19 *electrochemistry*

bunt 89 Fungi, 22.5 *batting terms,* 22.7 *play baseball,* 330.14 *sporting hit,* 337.29 *in reverse,* 338.21 *move forward*

bunting 67 Natural Fabrics, **78** Birds, 73.5 *flight,* 78.6 *songbird,* 544.7 *flag,* 812.8 *salute*

bunya 85 Trees and Shrubs

Bunyan 48 Writers

buoy 74.5 *navigation,* 370.10 *lighten,* 543.5 *indicator,* 653.5 *guide*

buoyance 377.2 *adaptability*

buoyancy 39.1 *swimming,* 56.10 *force,* 235.4 *energy,* 370.5 *lightness,* 372.3 *sparseness,* 390.9 *airiness,* 775.1 *hope*

buoyancy aid 632.4 *safety device*

buoyancy jacket 632.4 *safety device*

buoyant 39.11 *swimming,* 74.11 *nautical,* 359.23 *rising,* 370.2 *insubstantial,* 372.1 *sparse,* 377.7 *adaptive,* 390.14 *aerial,* 769.1 *cheerful,* 775.11 *hopeful*

buoyantly 769.9 *cheerfully,* 775.15 *hopefully*

buoyed up 370.2 *insubstantial*

buoy up 284.14 *give moral support,* 361.1 *raise,* 370.10 *lighten*

BUPA 60.1 *medicine,* 718.1 *protection*

buphenine 62 Medication

bupivacaine 62 Medication

bur 138.4 *adherent,* 631.6 *source of trouble*

buran 55 Winds

Burbank 52 Scientists

Burberry 295.12 *coat*

Burbidge 52 Scientists

burble 96.7 *flow,* 424.1 *faintness,* 424.5 *sound faint*

burbot 80 Fishes

bur-chisel 50.15 *engraving*

burden 161, 661, 661, 48.8 *part of poem,* 130.1 *addition,* 130.6 *add,* 257.2 *load,* 259.1 *size,* 369.8 *weighing down,* 369.14 *make heavy,* 426.6 *musical repetition,* 610.2 *overdoing it,* 616.3 *inconvenience,* 618.14 *ill-treat,* 631.14 *afflict,* 687.1 *adversity,* 687.11 *cause adversity,* 847.1 *duty*

burdened 257.11 *loaded,* 369.3 *ponderous,* 661.14 *blocked*

burdened with age 207.14 *aged,* 207.16 *maturely*

burdened with debt 745.9 *in debt*

burdening 369.8 *weighing down*

burden of guilt 866.2 *signs of guilt*

burdensome 257.11 *loaded,* 369.3 *ponderous,* 616.1 *inconvenient,* 616.3 *bad,* 644.11 *laborious,* 659.10 *difficult*

burdensomely 369

burdensomeness 369.8 *weighing down*

burden with 130.6 *add*

burdock 84 Flowers and Flowering Plants

Bure 96 Rivers

bureau 16.2 *jurisdiction,* 47.4 *table,* 258.3 *cabinet,* 647.1 *workshop*

bureaucracy 12.1 *government,* 12.3 *governance,* 584.6 *procedure,* 653.3 *management,* 661.2 *obstacle,* 688.4 *governance,* 703.4 *council*

bureaucrat 209.5 *delayer,* 653.16 *official,* 690.4 *strict person,* 703.5 *commissioner*

bureaucratic 2.12 *sociological,* 12.9 *governmental,* 653.17 *managerial,* 661.14 *blocked,* 688.14 *governmental,* 703.9 *commissioned*

bureaucratically 2.16 *sociologically,* 12.14 *politically,* 661.17 *in the way,* 703.11 *under commission*

bureau de change 223.2 *place of exchange*

burette 57 Laboratory Apparatus

burg 93.9 *town,* 249.10 *urban area*

burgage 723.3 *medieval ownership,* 725.3 *historic property terms*

burgee 36.3 *parts of a sailing boat,* 544.7 *flag*

burgeon 83.8 *bud,* 83.21 *vegetate,* 89.12 *mushroom,* 128.4 *increase,* 206.18 *grow,* 245.12 *multiply,* 246.6 *be fertile,* 261.6 *become bigger*

burgeoning 206.13 *maturing,* 261.1 *growth,* 261.8 *growing*

Bürger 48 Poets

burgess 93.11 *urbanite,* 255.4 *townsman,* 698.7 *free person*

Burgess 48 Writers

burgh 93.9 *town*

burgher 93.11 *urbanite,* 124.8 *middle classes,* 167.6 *conformist,* 255.4 *townsman,* 698.7 *free person*

burgherdom 124.8 *middle classes,* 158.8 *middle class*

Burghley 32.11 *eventing*

burglar 16.40 *lawbreaker,* 147.5 *excluded person,* 346.8 *intruder,* 693.9 *criminal,* 736.8 *thief*

burglar alarm 231.2 *counteracting thing*, 543.4 *signal*, 632.2 *protection*, 632.4 *safety device*, 636.2 *danger signal*, 671.5 *self-defence*
burglarious 736.17 *stolen*
burglarize 736.12 *steal*
burglarizing 736.1 *stealing*
burglar-proof 323.12 *closed*
burglary 16.39 *crime*, 346.3 *inroad*, 736.1 *stealing*, 736.3 *theft*
burgle 346.10 *invade*, 736.12 *steal*
Burgundian school 50 Western Art Styles and Movements
burgundy 351.9 *wine*, 450.7 *red thing*
burial 399, 277.1 *depth*, 354.10 *immersion*, 399.11 *funeral*, 458.5 *disguise*, 546.3 *obliteration*
Burial 399
burial at sea 354.10 *immersion*, 399.1 *burial*
burial chamber 200.7 *thing of the past*, 399.6 *grave*
burial clothes 399.4 *funeral objects*
burial customs 399.1 *burial*
burial ground 325.3 *resting place*, 399.5 *cemetery*
burial mound 3.11 *relic*
burial of the dead 10.5 *Christian rite*
burial place 399.5 *cemetery*
burial service 399.2 *funeral*
Buriash 8 Deities
Buridan 4 Philosophers
buried 399, 277.12 *under*, 354.14 *immersed*, 397.19 *dead*, 438.1 *invisible*, 458.7 *disappeared*, 546.6 *obliterated*, 702.8 *imprisoned*
buried treasure 605.1 *store*, 721.5 *profit*
burin 47.11 *woodworking tool*, 50.14 *sculptor's materials*, 50.15 *engraving*, 380.8 *sharp-pointed thing*
burka 295.16 *robe*
burke 398.17 *murder*
Burkina Faso 91 Countries
burl 85.2 *tree part*, 371.4 *solid body*
burlap 67 Natural Fabrics
burlesque 51.2 *play*, 51.4 *show business*, 51.5 *show*, 51.10 *comedy*, 51.38 *tragic*, 118.3 *mockery*, 118.9 *imitate*, 309.4 *distortion of the truth*, 506.3 *tomfoolery*, 525.1 *misinterpret*, 525.2 *misinterpretation*, 541.1 *exaggeration*, 541.7 *exaggerate*, 548.1 *misrepresentation*, 548.4 *misrepresent*, 771.4 *entertainment*, 798.2 *slapstick comedy*, 798.5 *ridiculous*, 799.2 *act of derision*, 850.4 *ridicule*, 850.14 *ridiculing*, 854.6 *ridicule*
burlesqued 309.8 *exaggerated*
burlesque house 51.14 *theatre*
burlesque queen 51.27 *entertainer*
burlesque show 51.5 *show*
burlesque theatre 51.14 *theatre*
burletta 51.10 *comedy*
burliness 237.1 *strength*, 259.6 *squatness*
Burlington Arcade 740.7 *emporium*
burly 237.9 *physically strong*, 259.17 *stocky*, 378.4 *powerful*
Burma 91 Countries
Burma pony 32 Breeds of Horse and Pony
Burmese 1 Peoples, **5** Languages and Groups of Languages, **77** Breeds of Cats
Burmese cat 449.5 *brown thing*
burn 408, 53.35 *rocketry*, 55.61 *shine*, 96.1 *river*, 244.12 *consume*, 392.19 *bake*, 398.17 *murder*, 398.20 *kill ritually*, 406.3 *injury*, 406.10 *be painful*, 406.11 *inflict pain*, 408.1 *heat*, 408.16 *feel hot*, 439.25 *light up*, 447.11 *blacken*, 449.7 *brown*,

539.30 *be fraudulent*, 607.1 *waste*, 670.9 *attack successfully*, 676.13 *be at war*, 753.10 *overcharge*, 821.24 *be in love*, 828.11 *be angry*, 879.5 *execute*
burn a cross 543.9 *use signs*
burn alive 398.17 *murder*, 398.19, 879.5 *execute*
burn a stone 41.16 *bobsled*
burn at the stake 408.15 *burn*, 879.5 *execute*
burn away 607.1 *waste*
burn coal 410.11 *fuel*
burn down 408.15 *burn*, 607.1 *waste*
burned out 650.1 *fatigued*
burner 408
Burnett 48 Writers
Burney 48 Writers, **49** Musicians and Composers
burn gas 410.11 *fuel*
burn in 544.10 *identify*
burn incense 418.6 *perfume*, 710.16 *make an offering*
burning 56.35 *heat*, 191.6 *allowing no delay*, 406.5 *painful*, 408.10 *on fire*, 408.12 *warm-hearted*, 439.15 *lucent*, 539.7 *tricking*, 828.16 *angry*, 879.13 *capital punishment*
burning alive 398.5 *execution*
burning at the stake 879.13 *capital punishment*
burning glass 410.2 *lighter*
burning in hell 16.64 *convicted*
burning question 477.4 *difficult question*
burning resentment 828.1 *resentment*
burning rubber 329.8 *speed*
burning the candle at both ends 642.20 *industrious*
burning the midnight oil 642.20 *industrious*
burnish 376.10 *polish*, 376.11 *smooth*, 385.12 *rub*, 439.27 *glaze*
burnished 376.4 *polished*, 439.17 *lustrous*
burnisher 376.9 *smoother*
burnishing 385.5 *polishing*
burn one's boats 574.8 *brace oneself*, 580.3 *side with*
burn one's bridges 574.8 *brace oneself*, 580.3 *side with*
burn one's fingers 656.5 *be unskilful*, 659.21 *get into trouble*
burn on the pyre 399.8 *bury*
burn out 202.17 *grow old*, 238.3 *poor health*, 408.15 *burn*, 607.1 *waste*, 650.6 *fatigue*
burn rubber 329.4 *be swift*
Burns 48 Poets
Burns stanza 48.10 *verse form*
burnt 45.56 *culinary*, 392.8 *baked*, 408.13 *heated*
burnt almond 449.5 *brown thing*
burnt cork 447.8 *black pigment*
burnt down 408.13 *heated*
burnt end 25.2 *grip*
burn the candle at both ends 209.6 *be late*, 642.13 *be busy*, 644.6 *work*, 870.11 *overindulge*
burn the guy 214.9 *commemorate*
burn the midnight oil 209.6 *be late*, 642.13 *be busy*, 644.6 *work*
burn to a cinder 408.15 *burn*
burnt offering 710.6 *offering*, 840.2 *apology*
burn to the ground 408.15 *burn*, 546.1 *obliterate*
burnt out 238.11 *weakened*, 408.13 *heated*
burnt sienna 449.4 *brown pigment*
burnt to a cinder 408.10 *on fire*
burnt to a crisp 45.56 *culinary*, 408.10 *on fire*
burnt umber 449.4 *brown pigment*
burn up 244.12 *consume*, 408.15 *burn*
burn-up 329.8 *speed*
burn up the miles 329.4 *be swift*
burn up the track 648.2 *make haste*
burn with love 821.24 *be in love*

burn with passion 821.24 *be in love*
burn with zeal 642.14 *push*
burp 349.16, 388.5 *belch*, 425.4, 425.7 *belch*
burr 5.26 *dialect*, 85.2 *tree part*, 375.7 *rough thing*, 380.8 *sharp-pointed thing*, 564.3 *mode of speech*
burrawang nut 86 Nuts
burring 5.39 *of language*
burrito 45.50 *Central American dish*
burro 326.6 *beast of burden*
Burroughs 48 Writers, **48** Writers
burrow 77.20 *abode of mammals*, 256.13 *lair*, 256.18 *take up residence*, 317.2 *concave land*, 317.7 *make concave*, 322.20 *hole*, 360.15 *tunnel*, 527.13 *hide*, 634.1 *refuge*, 634.3 *animal shelter*
burrowed 322.14 *holed*
burrower 317.4 *digger*
burrowing 360.7 *tunnelling*
burrowing owl 78 Birds
bursar 606.3 *provider*, 741.17 *financier*, 741.18 *treasurer*, 746.5 *payer*, 750.6 *accountant*
bursarial 749.6 *received*, 750.10 *accounting*
bursarship 749.3 *income*, 878.3 *grant*
bursary 662.6 *financial assistance*, 721.5 *profit*, 730.2 *something received*, 741.19 *treasury*, 749.3 *income*, 878.3 *grant*
bursitis 624.16 *rheumatism*
burst 162.11 *explode*, 181.11 *crowd*, 241.3 *instance of violence*, 329.9 *acceleration*, 379.1 *brittle*, 379.4 *be brittle*, 423.1 *loudness*, 423.8 *be loud*, 425.1, 425.5 *bang*, 642.3 *nimbleness*, 642.12 *be active*, 670.15 *firing*
burst ahead 329.6 *accelerate*
burst at the seams 610.4 *be excessive*
burst forth 156.27 *emerge*
burst in 241.7 *be violent*, 241.8 *use violence*, 346.10 *invade*, 670.9 *attack successfully*
bursting 241.6 *violent*, 379.1 *brittle*, 425.8 *banging*, 610.6 *excessive*
bursting at the seams 144.8 *full*
bursting open 241.3 *instance of violence*
bursting with health 623.1 *healthy*
bursting with pride 805.22 *boastful*
burst into flames 408.15 *burn*
burst its banks 610.4 *be excessive*
burst like a balloon 189.4 *be transient*
burst like a bubble 189.4 *be transient*
burst of anger 822.5 *anger*
burst of confidence 583.5 *spontaneity*
burst of energy 329.9 *acceleration*
burst of fire 670.15 *firing*
burst of sound 423.1 *loudness*
burst of speed 329.9 *acceleration*
burst on the ear 425.5 *bang*
burst open 322.18 *open*
burst out 241.7 *be violent*, 347.10 *emerge*
burst someone's bubble 189.5 *make transient*
burst the bubble 515.6 *disappoint*
burst the eardrums 421.9 *deafen*
burst upon 344.5 *get in*
burst with energy 239.2 *be full of vigour*
burst with health 239.2 *be full of vigour*
burton 74 Rigging
Burundi 91 Countries
bury 161 Collective Names for Birds and Animals, **397, 399,** 277.14 *deepen*, 323.10 *enclose*, 354.4 *immerse*, 438.8 *make in-*

visible, 458.3 *cause to disappear*, 531.8 *conceal*, 546.1 *obliterate*, 605.6 *store*
bury alive 398.17 *murder*
bury a stone 41.16 *bobsled*
Buryat 5 Languages and Groups of Languages
burying 82 Insects, 399.1 *burial*
burying the hatchet 675.1 *peace*, 677.1 *pacification*
bury oneself 816.12 *be unsocial*
bury oneself in 354.4 *immerse*
bury one's head in the sand 591.7 *be evasive*
bury one's talents 247.7 *be infertile*
bury the hatchet 512.15 *forgive*, 675.5 *be at peace*, 677.5 *make peace*, 839.9 *forgive*
bus 71 Motor Vehicles, **71,** 64.27 *wire*, 65.15 *network*, 70.4 *transport*, 326.5 *means of transport*, 326.12 *transport*
bus boy 326.7 *transferor* , 697.3 *attendant*
busby 295.15 *headgear*, 671.7 *armour*
Busby 18 Sporting Personalities
bus driver 326.7 *transferor*
bush 63.8 *machine element*, 83.2 *plant*, 85.1 *tree*, 249.6 *regions*
bushbaby 77 Placental Mammals
bushbuck 77 Placental Mammals
bush cricket 82 Insects
bushed 650.1 *fatigued*
bushel 75 General Units, 295.35 *make clothing*
busheller 295.26 *fashion designer*
bush-fighting 676.8 *warfare*
bushing 364.4 *vortex*
bush knife 380.10 *knife*
bush lot 85.4 *trees*
bushman 255.5 *countryman*
Bushman 5 Languages and Groups of Languages, 5.11 *family of languages*
bushmaster 79 Reptiles
bushmen 400.3 *uncivilized human*
Bushmen 1 Peoples
bush metal 57 Alloys
bushranger 736.8 *thief*
bushtit 78 Birds
bush track 32.7 *horseracing*
bush tree 69.10 *fruit tree*
bush wren 78 Birds
bushy 69.17 *botanical*, 85.14 *treelike*, 371.6 *dense*, 375.3 *barbed*
busily 642.22 *actively*
business 230, 642, 737, 51.7 *dramaturgy*, 51.20 *acting*, 93.14 *urban*, 243.2 *manufacture*, 472.3 *matter of interest*, 472.4 *sphere*, 590.4 *activity*, 597.2 *undertaking*, 611.1 *importance*, 640.1 *action*, 644.3 *job*, 737.4 *trade*, 847.2 *task*
business affairs 13.7 *corporation*
business associate 137.3 *associate*
business association 13.7 *corporation*
business borrower 745.6 *debtor*
business card 544.3 *means of identification*
business cards 223.3 *something in exchange*
business concern 740.8 *store*
business costs 751
business cycle 13.6 *economic factors*
business deal 737.4 *trade*
business district 93.7 *city district*
business executive 243.9 *producer*
business failure 320.4 *closure*
business house 647.1 *workshop*
business income 749.3 *income*
business language 5.7 *international language*
business law 16.1 *the law*

businesslike 101.8 *practical,* 150.14 *well-ordered,* 485.9 *qualified,* 642.18 *active,* 642.20 *industrious,* 652.16 *behaving,* 655.8 *expert*
business loan 732.2, 733.5 *loan,* 745.3 *loan*
business magazine 532.5 *journal*
businessman 13.9 *economist,* 243.9 *producer,* 646.1 *worker,* 655.5 *expert,* 737.10 *trader,* 739.12 *wholesaler*
business management 653.3 *management*
business manager 51.25 *producer*
business meeting 161.6 *sitting*
business offer 710
business on hand 472.2 *issue*
business person 739.12 *wholesaler*
business school 6.12 *educational institution*
business suit 295.10 *suit,* 440.4 *dark thing*
businesswoman 243.9 *producer,* 646.1 *worker,* 655.5 *expert,* 737.10 *trader,* 739.12 *wholesaler*
business zone 93.7 *city district*
busk 712.8 *solicit money*
busker 49.24 *musician,* 51.27 *entertainer,* 712.5 *beggar*
buskin 51.9 *tragedy,* 295.5 *fancy dress*
buskined 51.38 *tragic*
busking 712.3 *solicitation*
buskins 295.19 *footwear*
busload 257.2 *load*
busman's holiday 644.4 *exertion*
bus pass 754.4 *bargain*
buss 821.14 *communication of love,* 821.7 *kiss,* 826.7 *show endearment for*
bussed 70.5 *transportable*
bussing 70.5 *transportable,* 71.15 *motor transport*
bus station 218.4 *stopping place,* 345.10 *place of departure*
bus stop 218.4 *stopping place,* 345.10 *place of departure*
Bussumanus 8 Deities
bust 50.12 *sculpture,* 244.15 *destroyed,* 316.2 *bulge,* 320.4 *closure,* 349.3 *disbar,* 545.11 *monument,* 547.6 *image,* 593.5 *necessitous,* 722.17 *unprofitable,* 743.2 *insolvent*
bustard 78 Birds
busted 320.6 *closed,* 743.2 *insolvent*
buster 401.3 *male title of address*
bus ticket 544.3 *means of identification*
bustier 295.8 *shirt*
bustiness 259.5 *fatness*
bust in on 211.5 *take untimely action*
bustle 295.18 *underwear,* 324.2 *momentum,* 366.2 *tumult,* 366.4 *fuss,* 366.21 *be agitated,* 642.3 *nimbleness,* 642.12 *be active,* 648.2 *make haste,* 648.4 *haste*
bustler 336.16 *progressive person,* 642.10 *busy person*
bustling 324.16 *moving,* 642.19 *busy*
busty 259.16 *fat*
busy 211, 642, 233.11 *influential,* 327.15 *accessible,* 640.5 *acting,* 644.10 *working*
busy as a beaver 642.19 *busy*
busy as a bee 642.19 *busy*
busy bee 642.10 *busy person,* 646.1 *worker*
busybody 465.4, 642.11 *meddler,* 654.4 *adviser*
busy Lizzie 84 Flowers and Flowering Plants
busyness 161 Collective Names for Birds and Animals, 642.6 *business*
busy oneself 597.1 *undertake,* 640.4 *act,* 642.13 *be busy,* 652.11 *conduct oneself*

busy person 642, 640.3 *doer,* 646.1 *worker*
busy signal 534.11 *dialling*
butacaine 62 Medication
butadiene 57 Common Chemical Compounds
butane 410.3 *gas*
butch 401.17 *male,* 402.10 *homosexual,* 402.15 *female*
butcher 241.4 *violent person or animal,* 244.9 *demolish,* 350.17 *food shop,* 350.20 *food provider,* 398.10 *killer,* 398.18 *slaughter,* 606.3 *provider,* 739.13 *retailer,* 832.8 *malefactor,* 879.5 *execute*
butcherbird 78 Birds
butcher's 350.17 *food shop,* 435.6 *look*
butcher's broom 85 Trees and Shrubs
butchery 398.4 *slaughter*
butler 606.3 *provider,* 646.1 *worker,* 697.3 *attendant,* 697.6 *domestic servant*
Butler 48 Writers, 48 Poets
butobarbitone 62 Medication
Butsuden 10.13 *shrine*
butt 75 General Units, **850,** 26.2 *boxing,* 26.11 *do a combat sport,* 132.1 *remainder,* 157.8 *tail,* 267.3 *juxtapose,* 304.2 *rear end,* 330.1 *impel,* 330.2 *collide,* 330.13 *blow,* 337.29 *in reverse,* 338.21 *move forward,* 413.7 *tobacco,* 493.6 *misjudged person,* 588.6 *objective,* 616.10 *unskilled person,* 670.5 *strike,* 680.9 *firearm,* 730.5 *recipient,* 799.4 *laughing stock*
Butt 49 Musicians and Composers
butt away 671.26 *act on the defensive*
butte 275.3 *mountain*
Butte 93 Cities
butt end 132.1 *remainder,* 157.8 *tail*
butt-end 31.9 *play hockey*
butt-ended 31.8 *hockey*
butt-ending 31.3 *ice hockey,* 31.8 *hockey*
butter 45.7 *basic ingredient,* 243.7 *produce,* 374.11 *soft thing,* 376.11 *smooth,* 386.13 *lubricate,* 393.8 *pulp,* 395.8 *fat,* 395.18 *anoint,* 452.8 *yellow thing,* 853.9 *blarney*
butter bean 45 Vegetables
butter chicken 45.49 *Indian dish*
buttercup 84 Flowers and Flowering Plants, 452.8 *yellow thing*
buttercup family 83.3 *seed plant*
butterfingered 656.3 *clumsy*
butterfingers 656.9 *bungling,* 656.10 *unskilled person*
butterfish 80 Fishes
butterflies 366.1 *agitation,* 624.8 *indigestion*
butterflies in the stomach 777.2 *fearfulness*
butterfly 39.1 *swimming,* 76.6 *flying animal,* 82.1 *insect,* 576.15 *indecisive person,* 579.4 *capricious person*
butterfly collecting 42 Hobbies and Pastimes
butterfly diagram 53.15 *sun*
butterfly fish 80 Fishes
butteriness 393.4 *pulpiness,* 395.1 *oiliness*
butter knife 350.16 *eating utensil*
Buttermere 94 Lakes, 94.4 British lakes
buttermilk 387.2 *juice,* 395.8 *fat*
buttermilk biscuit 45.39 *loaf*
buttermilk pancake 45.39 *loaf*
buttermilk sky 55.20 *cloud appearance,* 456.5 *variegated thing*
butter mountain 68.2 *Common Agricultural Policy ,* 246.2 *productiveness,* 605.1 *store*
butternut 85 Trees and Shrubs, **86** Nuts
butternut pumpkin 45 Vegetables

butterscotch 45.41 *sweet,* 449.5 *brown thing*
butter up 395.18 *anoint,* 771.15 *humour,* 853.9 *blarney*
butterwort 84 Flowers and Flowering Plants
buttery 45.3 *kitchen,* 376.4 *polished,* 386.10 *oily,* 393.18 *pulpy,* 395.11 *oily,* 605.4 *storage,* 817.9 *deferential,* 853.13 *honeyed*
butt guide 20.3 *fishing tackle*
butt in 160.16 *interrupt,* 211.5 *take untimely action,* 346.10 *invade,* 478.18 *answer back,* 642.17 *meddle*
butting 26.2 *boxing,* 330.12 *collision*
butt in on 153.10 *disrupt*
butt into 344.8 *meet*
buttocks 304.2 *rear end*
button 36.4 *rowing,* 41.1 *skiing,* 41.10 *curling,* 135.10 *link,* 137.8 *fastening,* 137.11 *connect,* 295.24 *part of garment,* 316.2 *bulge,* 323.7 *close,* 612.8 *trifle*
buttonball 85 Trees and Shrubs
button-down collar 295.14 *neckwear*
buttoned 137.15 *connected,* 323.12 *closed*
buttoned up 323.12 *closed*
buttoned-up 295.31 *styled,* 531.17 *noncommittal*
buttonhole 84.1 *flower,* 137.8 *fastening,* 322.5 *hole,* 407.11 *touch,* 418.2 *fragrant thing,* 565.8 *talk too much,* 567.9 *approach,* 726.6 *retain,* 788.6 *be boring*
buttonholer 788.3 *boring person*
button mushroom 45.33 *vegetable,* 89.2 *mushroom*
button one's lip 563.13 *be voiceless,* 641.4 *not act*
button quail 78 Birds
button-through 295.31 *styled*
button up 135.10 *link,* 295.34 *wear,* 323.7 *close*
buttonwood 85 Trees and Shrubs
buttress 34.5 *rock face,* 43.18 *column,* 43.19 *decorate,* 63.27 *superstructure,* 225.3, 225.3 *stabilizer,* 225.7 *make stable,* 237.8 *strengthen,* 283.5 *projecting object,* 284.1 *support,* 284.2 *supporting part,* 284.11 *support,* 373.9 *harden,* 535.19 *confirm,* 634.1 *refuge,* 662.19 *support,* 671.11 *fortification,* 726.4 *wall*
buttress dam 63.23 *dam*
buttressed 43.16 *columned,* 237.13 *strengthened,* 373.3 *hardened,* 535.13 *supported*
buttressing 535.4 *confirmation*
buttress root 83.7 *root*
butt rot 85.10 *tree disease*
butty 45.11 *sandwich,* 819.5 *friend*
Butyl 377.4 *rubber*
butyraceous 386.10, 395.11 *oily*
butyric 58 Common Fatty Acids, 395.11 *oily*
buxom 259.16 *fat,* 273.1 *thick*
buxomly 259.20 *largely*
buxomness 259.5 *fatness,* 273.5 *thickness*
Buxton blue 45 Cheeses
buy 497.7 *believe,* 586.18 *be persuaded,* 673.3 *submit,* 723.7 *possess,* 728.3 *transfer property,* 738.1, 738.6 *purchase,* 748.1 *expend,* 748.4 *expenditure*
buy and sell 737.1 *trade*
buy a piece of 738.1 *purchase*
buy a pig in a poke 508.6 *be foolish,* 539.24 *be deceived,* 780.5 *be rash*
buy a return-trip ticket 221.8 *return*
buy a round 746.9 *pay one's way*
buy at a cut price 738.1 *purchase*
buy at a discount 752
buy at cost 754.14 *buy cheaply*

buy at factory prices 754.14 *buy cheaply*
buy back 738
buy-back 738.7 *purchasing*
buy bonds 741.27 *invest*
buy cheap and sell dear 737.1 *trade*
buy cheaply 754, 738.1 *purchase*
buy dirt-cheap 754.14 *buy cheaply*
buyer 13.9 *economist,* 723.5 *possessor,* 728.2 *person transferring property,* 730.5 *recipient,* 737.10 *trader,* 738.12 *purchaser,* 748.8 *spender*
buyer beware! 738
buyers' market 13.6 *economic factors,* 740.3 *sellers' market,* 754.2 *declining prices*
buy for a song 738.1 *purchase*
buy for nickles and dimes 754.14 *buy cheaply*
buy from 737.1 *trade*
buy in 738.1, 738.1 *purchase*
buy in bulk 752.5 *buy at a discount,* 754.14 *buy cheaply*
buying 738, 728.1 *transfer of property,* 733.4 *credit,* 738.7 *purchasing,* 748.4 *expenditure*
buying and selling 737.4 *trade*
buying off 639.2 *deliverance*
buying on credit 733.1 *borrowing*
buying price 751.5 *cost*
buying up 738.7 *purchasing*
buy in instalments 733.10 *buy on credit*
buy in the sales 752.5 *buy at a discount*
buy it 397.15 *die*
buy off 738, 586.17 *bribe,* 639.1 *deliver*
buy on account 738.1 *purchase*
buy on appro 738.1 *purchase*
buy on approval 738.1 *purchase*
buy on credit 733, 738.1 *purchase,* 745.7 *be in debt*
buy on hire purchase 738.1 *purchase,* 744.9 *acquire credit,* 745.7 *be in debt*
buy on HP 738.1 *purchase*
buy on the HP 733.10 *buy on credit*
buy on the instalment plan 733.10 *buy on credit,* 738.1 *purchase,* 744.9 *acquire credit,* 745.7 *be in debt*
buy on the never-never 733.10 *buy on credit,* 738.1 *purchase*
buy on the spot 738.1 *purchase*
buy on tick 738.1 *purchase*
buy on time 744.9 *acquire credit*
buy out 734.7 *take,* 738.1 *purchase*
buy-out 13.7 *corporation,* 230.2 *joint operation,* 710.3 *business offer,* 734.1 *taking*
buy outright 738.1 *purchase*
buy over the counter 738.1 *purchase*
buy property 725.9 *own property*
buy shares 14.5 *invest,* 738.1 *purchase*
buy supplies 602.6 *find means*
buy the farm 397.15 *die*
buy time 209.8 *delay*
buy up 738.1 *purchase*
buy up the shop 738.1 *purchase*
buy wholesale 752.5 *buy at a discount,* 754.14 *buy cheaply*
buzz 432, 82.16 *infest,* 181.11 *crowd,* 403.3 *stimulus,* 424.1 *faintness,* 424.5 *sound faint,* 426.2 *humming,* 426.9 *hum,* 427.9 *resonate,* 534.10 *telephone call,* 642.1 *activity,* 762.2 *fun,* 875.1 *drug-taking*
buzz about 532.13 *make public,* 532.17 *be published*
buzzard 78 Birds, 78.5 *bird of prey,* 621.12 *cleaner*
buzz disk 49 Musical Instruments
buzzer 423.4 *sound maker*
buzzing 426.2, 426.16 *humming,* 427.1 *resonance,* 427.6 *resonant,* 432.3 *insect noise,* 432.9 *humming*

buzz off 345.1 *depart*, 345.15 *go*, 349.33 *go away*
buzz word 5.21 *catchword*, 426.7 *repeated word*
BVD's 295.18 *underwear*
bwana 696.1 *master*
by 227.10 *caused*, 232.9 *instrumentally*, 327.17 *via*, 396.15 *born*, 602.7 *by means of*
by abstaining 699.17 *with self-restraint*
by accident 229.8 *by chance*, 489.9 *unexpectedly*, 489.11 *luckily*, 589.13 *by chance*, 687.12 *in adversity*
by a classic route 34.10 *on a climb*
by a contract 667.15 *contractually*
by aeroplane 70.6 *commercially*
by a gondola lift 41.17 *on a ski run*
by a hair's-breadth 264.6 *near*, 272.11 *narrowly*
by air 70.6 *commercially*
by all means 490.26 *certainly*
by an artificial route 34.10 *on a climb*
by and by 199.14 *in the future*, 208.18 *soon*
by-and-by 199.1 *future time*
by and large 103.13 *in essence*, 124.11 *on average*, 142.13 *on the whole*, 271.7 *broadly*
by annulment 824.13 *without one's spouse*
by any means 327.16 *how*, 486.9 *possibly*
by appointment 580.15 *chosen*
by artificial light 439.30 *lightly*
by a side door 363.12 *circuitously*
by auction 727.16 *disposably*
by authority 12.14 *politically*
by a whisker 264.6 *near*, 272.11 *narrowly*
by ballot 580.17 *selectively*
by birth 537.19 *authentic*
by bursting 379.6 *by cracking*
by bus 70.6 *commercially*
by casting 20.9 *on the water*
by catches 160.18 *disconnectedly*
by chance 229, 589, 151.27 *in disorder*, 486.9 *possibly*, 489.11 *luckily*
by cheque 746.21 *cash down*
by chipping 379.6 *by cracking*
by choice 580.17 *selectively*
by coincidence 589.13 *by chance*
by command 692.16 *commandingly*
by commission 703.11 *under commission*
by comparison 121.9 *differentially*
by compulsion 237.15 *acutely*
by consensus 116.31 *in accord*
by conveyance 728.6 *by transfer*
by counterattacking 28.7 *on guard*
by cracking 379
by credit 733.13 *on loan*
by custom 214.17 *orderly*, 584.19 *habitually*, 640.7 *actively*
by day 439.30 *lightly*
by daylight 439.30 *lightly*
by decree absolute 824.13 *without one's spouse*
by decree nisi 824.13 *without one's spouse*
by decree of nullity 824.13 *without one's spouse*
by deed 728.6 *by transfer*
by deferred payment 744.14 *on credit*
by deflection 26.16 *professionally*
by degrees 121, 143.12 *partly*, 160.17 *discontinuously*, 328.16 *slowly*
by delegated authority 703.11 *under commission*
by design 43.20 *architecturally*, 306.13 *formatively*, 588.13 *intentionally*
by dint of 235.18 *powerfully*, 602.7 *by means of*

by divine right 8.19 *divinely*, 845.20 *duly*
by dribbling 31.10 *on the field*
by dribs and drabs 579.6 *capriciously*
bye 27.10 *score*, 345.14 *goodbye*
by ear 420.17 *aurally*, 436.17 *blindly*
by easy stages 328.16 *slowly*
bye-bye 345.14 *goodbye*
bye-byes 643.9 *sleep*
bye holes 29.2 *golfing terms*
by-election 580.12 *election*
Byelorussia 91 Countries
Byelorussian 5 Languages and Groups of Languages
Byelun 8 Deities
by enactment 640.7 *actively*
by expanding 372.7 *sparsely*
by express 326.18 *in transit*
by eye 435.24 *visually*
by fair means or foul 327.16 *how*, 602.7 *by means of*, 858.11 *dishonourably*
by far 126.17 *supremely*
by feel 436.17 *blindly*
by feinting 26.16 *professionally*
by fits 160.17 *discontinuously*
by fits and starts 143.12 *partly*, 151.27 *in disorder*, 160.18 *disconnectedly*, 187.14 *for short periods*, 215.8 *irregularly*, 366.29 *jerkily*, 579.6 *capriciously*
by force 235.18 *powerfully*, 237.14 *strongly*, 241.10 *violently*, 695.11 *compellingly*
by forced march 648.6 *hastily*
by force majeure 695.11 *compellingly*
by force of arms 235.18 *powerfully*, 695.11 *compellingly*
by force of circumstances 571.19 *necessarily*
by force of habit 584.19 *habitually*
by giving up 727.16 *disposably*
by God's will 8.19 *divinely*
bygone 3.18 *in the past*, 200.18 *over*
bygone days 3.8, 200.1 *past time*
bygones 3.8 *past time*
by guess and God 479.14 *experimentally*
by halves 145.6, 685.7 *incompletely*
by hand 44.12 *ornamentally*, 326.18 *in transit*, 407.17 *manually*, 644.12 *laboriously*
by heart 511.16 *memorably*
by hire purchase 744.14 *on credit*
by hit and miss 479.14 *experimentally*
by hook or crook 327.16 *how*, 602.7 *by means of*
by hygienic 625
by inches 121.10 *by degrees*
by instalments 744.14 *on credit*
by instinct 464.11 *intuitively*
by intuition 464.11 *intuitively*
by itself 174.21 *alone*
by jerks 160.18 *disconnectedly*
by law 12.14 *politically*, 16.81 *legally*, 845.20 *duly*
bylaw 16.3 *law*, 166.1 *rule*
by leaps and bounds 181.13 *numerously*, 329.14 *swiftly*, 336.20 *in progress*
by letting go 727.16 *disposably*
by-line 533.12 *headline*, 837.3 *recognition*
by lorry 70.6 *commercially*
by main force 695.11 *compellingly*
by means of 602, 232.9 *instrumentally*
by means of enchantment 827.14 *damningly*
by misadventure 687.12 *in adversity*
by mischance 687.12 *in adversity*
by mistake 504.21 *erroneously*
by motorway 70.6 *commercially*
by negotiating 717.9 *compromisingly*
by night 205.7 *evening*, 440.15 *darkly*
by no means 100.15 *not at all*

by offering resistance 373.12 *toughly*
by oneself 174.21 *alone*, 698.20 *freely*, 825.12 *celibately*
by one's leave 712.12 *by request*
by order 16.81 *legally*, 692.16 *commandingly*
by parrying 28.7 *on guard*
bypass 137.5 *road*, 313.2, 313.6 *circle*, 327.2 *route*, 327.14 *find one's way*, 334.2, 334.4 *detour*, 335.14 *deviating course*, 363.5 *ringroad*, 363.8 *detour*, 591.1 *avoid*
bypassing 591.10 *avoidance*
bypass ratio 73 Aircraft Parts
bypass surgery 60.9, 630.12 *surgery*
bypath 335.14 *deviating course*
by-path 327.6 *path*
by pipeline 70.6 *commercially*
byplay 51.20 *acting*
by-product 57.16 *synthesis*, 130.4 *extra*, 155.6 *aftermath*, 227.1 *effect*, 243.3 *product*
by proxy 707, 172.12 *absently*, 222.9 *instead*, 703.11 *under commission*
by rail 70.6 *commercially*, 326.18 *in transit*
Byrd 49 Musicians and Composers
byre 68.7 *farm building*, 256.12 *stall*, 634.3 *animal shelter*
by reason of 226.14 *causally*
by referendum 580.17 *selectively*
by remittance 326.18 *in transit*
by request 712
by resigning 705
by resorting to 602.7 *by means of*
by retiring 705.10 *by resigning*
Byrgius 53 Rills and Valleys
by right 16.44 *legal*, 16.81 *legally*, 843.17 *by rights*, 845.20 *duly*
by rights 843
by road 70.6 *commercially*
Byron 48 Poets
by rote 511.16 *memorably*
by rule of thumb 479.14 *experimentally*
by sale 727.16 *disposably*
by scooping 31.10 *on the field*
by sea 70.6 *commercially*, 97.11 *nautically*
by shattering 379.6 *by cracking*
by sheer force 237.14 *strongly*
by ship 70.6 *commercially*
by-side 612.3 *secondary*
by sight 435.24 *visually*
by skips 160.18 *disconnectedly*
by snatches 366.29 *jerkily*
by some means 327.16 *how*
by someone's leave 116.39 *with consent*
by special delivery 326.18 *in transit*
by stages 121.10 *by degrees*, 150.25 *in order*
bystander 253.5 *someone present*, 264.4 *neighbour*, 435.11 *observer*, 480.7 *verifier*, 483.7 *person who gives evidence*
by storm 241.10 *violently*
by subtraction 131
by swimming 39
by tanker 70.6 *commercially*
byte 75 Scientific and Technical Units, 65.17 *computing term*
by telephone 420.17 *aurally*
by the agency of 222.9 *instead*
by the aid of 662.37 *in aid of*
by the back door 529.16 *stealthily*
by the book 7.23 *religiously*, 150.27 *methodically*, 166.19 *to rule*, 167.19 *according to rule*, 503.8 *accurately*, 537.38 *literally*
by-the-by 354.12 *inserted*
by the clock 192.18 *horologically*
by the dawn's early light 204.8 *in the morning*
by the good offices of 232.9 *instrumentally*
by the grace of God 831.10 *benevolently*

by the hand of 232.9 *instrumentally*
by the head 36.20 *offshore*
by the lee 36.20 *offshore*
by the numbers 167.19 *according to rule*
by the same token 106.15 *under the circumstances*, 114.13 *similarly*, 116.34 *uniformly*, 122.12 *equally*
by the side door 334.8 *circuitously*
by the skin of one's teeth 264.6 *near*, 272.11 *narrowly*
by the stern 36.20 *offshore*
by the sweat of one's brow 644.12 *laboriously*
by the way 356, 108.12 *irrelevantly*
by this token 543.18 *indicatively*
by touch 436.17 *blindly*
by tradition 584.19 *habitually*
by train 70.6 *commercially*
by transfer 728, 326.18 *in transit*
by trial and error 479.14 *experimentally*
by trolling 20.9 *on the water*
by turns 109.10 *reciprocally*, 214.15 *regularly*, 223.8 *in exchange*
by use of 602.7 *by means of*
by veto 709
by virtue of 232.9 *instrumentally*, 235.18 *powerfully*
by warrant of 12.14 *politically*, 688.23 *authoritatively*
by water 70.6 *commercially*, 97.11 *nautically*
byway 327.3 *road*
by way of 232.9 *instrumentally*, 327.17 *via*, 356.14 *by the way*
by way of return 672.6 *with vengeance*
byword 505.1 *maxim*
by word of mouth 528.19 *reportedly*, 564.21 *orally*
Byzantine 43 Architectural Styles, 50.29 *realist*, 202.14 *historic*
Byzantine art 50 Western Art Styles and Movements

C

C 65 Programming Languages, 875.6 *drug*
C₁ 2.7 *social stratification*, 124.8 *middle classes*
C₂ 2.7 *social stratification*, 124.8 *middle classes*
cab 71 Carriages and Carts, 71
cabal 140.2 *cooperation*, 161.16 *party*, 527.6 *latency*, 529.2 *secretiveness*, 592.4 *plot*, 592.8 *planner*, 592.13 *plot*, 665.1 *party*, 665.3 *political grouping*, 693.3 *subversion*
cabalistic 161.49 *grouped*, 529.10 *secretive*, 551.2 *obscure*
cabaret 51.3 *musical drama*, 51.5 *show*, 51.14 *theatre*
cabbage 45 Vegetables, 68.12 *crop*, 240.2 *inert person*, 453.9 *greenstuff*
cabbage aphid 69.12 *pests and diseases*
cabbage fly 69.12 *pests and diseases*
cabbage lettuce 45 Vegetables
cabbage palm 85 Trees and Shrubs
cabbage patch 69.2 *garden*
cabbage root fly 82 Insects
cabbage rose 84 Flowers and Flowering Plants
cabbage tree 85 Trees and Shrubs
cabbage white 69.12 *pests and diseases*
cabbage white butterfly 82 Insects

cabbala 11.1 *occultism*, 11.2 *the occult*, 527.11 *mysteriousness*, 529.7 *esotericism*
cabbalism 11.1 *occultism*, 529.7 *esotericism*
cabbalist 11.12 *occultist*
cabbalistic 11.14 *occult*, 140.8 *cooperative*, 527.5, 529.11 *mysterious*
cabbalistically 11.25 *occultly*, 140.10 *in combination*
caber 338.10 *ball*
cabernet sauvignon 351.9 *wine*
caber tossing 18 Sporting Activities
cabin 73 Aircraft Parts, 74 Parts of a Ship, 256.5 *house*
cabin boy 74.7 *nautical person*, 679.27 *naval man*
cabin crew 697.3 *attendant*
cabin cruiser 74 Ships and Boats
cabinet 47, 258, 161.7 *committee*, 605.4 *storage*, 653.3 *management*, 653.6 *governing body*, 653.7 *council*
cabinet-maker 47.13 *carpenter*, 646.2 *artisan*
cabinet-making 47.1 *furniture*, 47.8 *woodwork*, 85.5 *forestry*
cabinet meeting 716.3 *discussion*
cabinet member 12.8 *politician*, 653.16 *official*, 688.10 *person of authority*, 696.3 *leader*, 706.1 *delegate*
cabinet minister 12.8 *politician*, 653.16 *official*
cabinet painting 50.8 *painting*
cabinet seat 688.5 *position of authority*
cabinet shop 47.1 *furniture*
cabin lift 41.1 *skiing*
cable 74 Rigging, 75 General Units, 41.9 *bobsledding* , 137.6 *line*, 235.7 *electrical power*, 528.2 *communication*, 534.6 *telecommunication*, 534.8 *data transmission*, 534.31 *correspond*, 603.1 *tool*
cable brake 71.11 *bicycle part*
cable car 41.1 *skiing*, 72.1 *railway*, 359.8 *lift*
cablecast 532.13 *make public*
cablecasting 532.2 *mass media*
cablegram 528.2 *communication*, 534.8 *data transmission*
cable railway 72.1 *railway*, 327.10 *railway*, 327.12 *cableway*
cable release 66.18 *exposure time*
cable ship 74 Ships and Boats
cable-stayed bridge 63.21 *bridge*
cable stitch 67.5 *knitting*
cable television 532.2 *mass media*, 534.21 *television* , 534.24 *television broadcasting*
CableText 534.25 *broadcast material*
cable-vision 532.2 *mass media*
cableway 327, 63.29 *construction equipment*
caboose 72.6 *rolling stock*
cabriole 46.9 *ballet steps*
cabriole leg 47.3 *chair leg*
cabriolet 71 Carriages and Carts
ca-ca 353.5 *faeces*, 353.16 *defecate*
cacao 85 Trees and Shrubs
cachalot 77 Placental Mammals
cache 65.6 *memory*, 293.15 *shelter*, 531.2 *hiding place*, 605.1, 605.6 *store*, 634.1 *refuge*
cachet 62.6 *pill*, 165.3 *characteristic*, 318.1 *prominence*, 544.3 *means of identification*, 800.1 *estimation*
cachexia 624.1 *ill health*
cachinnate 423.8 *be loud*, 431.11 *laugh*
cachinnation 423.1 *loudness*, 431.2 *cry of joy*
cachou 417.2 *deodorant*, 418.2 *fragrant thing*
cack-handed 559.7 *graceless*, 656.3 *clumsy*, 776.8 *bad*
cack-handedness 559.1 *inelegance*, 656.8 *unskilfulness*

cackle 432.5 *sing*, 564.13 *speak in a particular way*
cackler 773.4 *rejoicer*
cacoepy 564.3 *mode of speech*
cacoethes 584.1 *habit*
cacographic 5.42 *worded*
cacography 5.27 *spelling*
cacological 559.9 *inelegant*
cacology 504.11 *grammatical error*, 559.4 *inelegance of speech*
cacomistle 77 Placental Mammals
cacophonous 423.6 *loud*, 430.7 *strident*, 434.7 *dissonant*, 559.9 *inelegant*
cacophonously 434.12 *dissonantly*
cacophony 151.5 *confusion*, 423.1 *loudness*, 430.1 *stridency*, 434.2 *dissonant noise*
Cactoblastis 82 Insects
cactus 84 Flowers and Flowering Plants, 83.2 *plant*, 380.8 *sharp-pointed thing*
cactus moth 82 Insects
cad 401.7 *libertine*, 652.5 *badly behaved person*, 764.9 *unpleasant person*, 795.5 *vulgar person*, 801.2 *disreputable character*, 822.8 *hated person*
CAD 63.1 *engineering*, 65.1 *computing*
cadaster 171.6 *list of names*
cadastral 171.12 *inventorial*
cadaver 397.11 *dead person*
cadaverous 274.2 *emaciated*, 397.18 *dying*, 397.21 *deathly*, 445.8 *drained of colour*
cadaverousness 274.8 *emaciation*, 397.1 *death*
caddie 29.6 *golfer*, 697.3 *attendant*
caddis fly 82 Insects, 82.1 *insect*
caddish 818.6 *bad-mannered*
caddishly 818.10 *rudely*
caddishness 818.2 *bad manners*
caddis worm 82.5 *larva*
Caddo 1 Peoples
Caddoan 5 Languages and Groups of Languages
caddy 258.6 *box*, 326.7 *transferor*
cade 85 Trees and Shrubs
cadence 49.13 *melody*, 360.2 *sinkage*, 433.3 *melodiousness*, 564.6 *phonetics*
cadenza 49.16 *musical note*, 583.4 *improvisation*
Cader Idris 95 Mountains, 95.5 *British mountains*
cadet 679.17 *army person*
Cadet 17 British Military Ranks, 17 British Military Ranks, 17 US Military Ranks
cadge 643.12 *be inactive*, 712.8 *solicit money*, 733.7 *borrow*
cadger 643.8 *nonworker*, 712.5 *beggar*, 733.6 *borrower*, 734.6 *taker*
cadging 712.3 *solicitation*, 712.11 *begging*, 734.1 *taking*
Cádiz 93 Cities
cadmium 57 Chemical Elements
cadmium lemon 452.7 *yellow pigment*
cadmium orange 451.2 *orangeness*
cadmium red 450.6 *red pigment*
cadmium scarlet 450.6 *red pigment*
cadmium yellow 452.7 *yellow pigment*
cadre 382.4 *framework*, 646.4 *personnel*, 665.1 *party*
caducity 238.3 *poor health*
CAE 63.1 *engineering*
caecilian 79 Amphibians, 79.7 *amphibian*
caecostomy 60 Surgical Operations
Caedmon 48 Poets
Caelum 53 The Constellations
Caen 93 Cities
caenurus 81.13 *invertebrate larva*
Caernarfon 93 Cities
Caerphilly 45 Cheeses
Caesar 696.2 *sovereign*
Caesarian 245.7 *obstetrics*

Caesarian section 245.7 *obstetrics*
Caesar salad 45.14 *salad*
caesious 454.2 *bluish*
caesium 57 Chemical Elements
caesium clock 192.6 *clock*
Caesium clock 191 Timepieces and Timers
caesiumX clock 56.87 *clock*
caesura 160, 48.9 *metre*, 136.5 *separator*, 218.3 *pause*, 265.1 *interval*
café 350.15 *eating place*
café-au-lait 449.1 *brown*
café society 796.6 *fashionable élite*
cafeteria 256.7 *room*, 350.15 *eating place*
caffeine 58.19 *alkaloid*, 630.7 *tonic*, 631.11 *intoxicant*
caftan 295.16 *robe*
cage 77.20 *abode of mammals*, 136.2 *setting apart*, 256.12 *stall*, 258.2 *compartment*, 258.21 *put in a container*, 323.4 *closed place*, 323.10 *enclose*, 634.3 *animal shelter*
Cage 49 Musicians and Composers
cagebird 78
caged 258.20 *containing*
cage rotor 64.31 *electric motor*
cagey 531.17 *noncommittal*, 566.3 *sparing with words*, 657.4 *cunning*, 781.4 *cautious*
cageyness 657.1 *cunning*
cagoule 295.11 *jacket*
cahoots 664.5 *joint control*
CAI 65.1 *computing*
Cain 398.11 *murderer*
caïque 74 Ships and Boats, 74 Sailing Ships and Boats
cairn 399.6 *grave*, 543.5 *indicator*, 545.11 *monument*
cairngorm 54 Gemstones
Cairngorm 95 Mountains
Cairngorm Mountains 95.5 *British mountains*
Cairn terrier 77 Breeds of Dogs
Cairo 93 Cities, 93.6 *other cities*
caisson 63.28 *substructure*, 680.4 *arsenal*, 680.11 *guns*
caitiff 832.8 *malefactor*
cajole 853, 228.9 *motivate*, 586.15 *persuade*, 657.5 *be cunning*, 712.6 *request*, 771.15 *humour*
cajoler 853.6 *flatterer*
cajolery 853, 228.2 *inducement*, 586.2 *flattery*
cajoling 853, 771.11 *humouring*
Cajun cabin 94.7 *lake dwelling*
Cajun dialect 5.26 *dialect*
cajuput 85 Tree Products
cake 45, 45.35 *dessert*, 259.7 *mass*, 371.4 *solid body*, 371.8 *be dense*, 414.3 *dessert*, 622.11 *dirty*
cake candle 439.5 *incandescent light*
caked 371.7 *condensed*, 622.7 *dirty*
cakes and ale 350.7 *food*
cake tin 45.4 *kitchen container*, 45.6 *kitchen equipment*, 258.15 *pot*
cakewalk 46.2 *dance*
CAL 65.1 *computing*
calabash 85 Trees and Shrubs, 258.14 *bottle*
calabrese 45 Vegetables
Calabrese 32 Breeds of Horse and Pony
Calais 93 Cities
calalou 45.51 *West Indian dish*
calamari 45.18 *sea fish*, 45.52 *Greek dish*
calamite 88.1 *fern*
calamitous 211.14 *accidental*, 618.5 *harmful*
calamitously 211.17 *mistakenly*
calamity 211.4 *mishap*, 244.4 *ruin*, 618.11 *harmfulness*, 687.1 *adversity*, 862.2 *affliction*
calamondin 86 Fruits
calando 49 Musical Terms
calash 71 Carriages and Carts
calaverite 54 Minerals

calcancus 382 Bones
calcareous 54.57 *chalky*, 81.22 *spongelike*, 384.16 *powdery*
calcareous clay 44.2 *raw material*
calceolaria 84 Flowers and Flowering Plants
calciferous 57.34 *elemental*
calcification 373.6 *solidification*
calcified 373.3 *hardened*
calcify 57.26 *react*, 373.10 *solidify*
calcimine 446.8 *whitener*, 446.13 *whiten*
calcination 57 Types of Chemical Reaction
calcine 57.26 *react*, 408.15 *burn*
calcite 54 Minerals
calcitonin 58 Hormones
calcium 57 Chemical Elements, 58.15 *essential element*, 350.11 *food content*
calculable 170, 52.73 *numerable*, 268.14 *measurable*
calculably 170.16 *mathematically*
calculate 170, 4.21 *rationalize*, 52.90 *enumerate*, 121.5 *measure*, 130.6 *add*, 268.10 *measure*, 492.12 *estimate*, 513.9 *predict*, 588.7 *intend*, 592.12 *plan ahead*
calculated 234.5 *tending to*, 268.15, 582.4 *deliberate*, 588.12 *intended*
calculated deception 539.1 *deception*
calculated risk 588.2 *intentionality*
calculated to 234.5 *tending to*
calculate one's position 250.11 *find*
calculating 170.3 *count*, 170.13 *calculative*, 507.6 *intelligent*, 539.34 *deceiving*, 657.4 *cunning*, 750.10 *accounting*
calculating machine 65.3 *computer*
calculation 170, 4.4 *philosophical investigation*, 52.1 *mathematics*, 52.12 *numeration*, 130.2 *mathematical addition*, 268.1 *measurement*, 492.1 *judgment*, 588.2 *intentionality*, 750.3 *accounting*
Calculation 170
calculation of chance 589
calculative 170
calculator 52, 170, 65.3, 170.5 *computer*
calculus 52, 52.1 *mathematics*, 170.1 *calculation*
calculus of variations 52.30 *calculus*
Calcutta 93 Cities, 93.6 *other cities*
Calcutta Cup 35.2 *championship*
caldera 54.24 *volcanic activity*
Calderón de la Barca 48 Dramatists
Caldwell 48 Writers
Caledonia 91.11 *Scotland*
Caledonian 91.11 *Scotland*
calefacient 408.9 *hot*
calembour 578.5 *equivocalness*
calendar 171.5 *list of appointments*, 185.13 *timer*, 185.17 *date*, 192.2 *timetable*, 192.3 *chronology*, 192.15 *chronologize*, 214.5 *regular thing*, 545.6 *record book*
calendar clock 191 Timepieces and Timers
calendarist 185.14 *time keeper*
calendar-maker 185.14 *time keeper*, 192.12 *chronologist*
calendar-making 192.1 *timekeeping*
calendar month 185.4 *term*
calendar of events 516.4 *prudence*, 517.3 *plan*
calender 376.11 *smooth*
calendered paper 604.3 *paper*
calendrical 185.25 *of known date*, 192.17 *timekeeping*
calendrist 192.12 *chronologist*
Calends 185.11 *date*
calendula 84 Flowers and Flowering Plants

calenture 624.3 *sympton*
calescence 408.1 *heat*
calf 54.39 *iceberg*, 68.8 *livesto* 77.19 *young mammal*, 206.4 *young animal*, 293.14 *animal covering*
calf horse 32.12 *rodeo*
calf love 821.2 *romantic love*
calf-roping 32.12 *rodeo*
calf's head 45.31 *offal*
calf's liver 45.31 *offal*
Calgary 93 Cities
Cali 93 Cities
calibrate 121.5, 268.10 *measure*
calibrated 121.7 *gradational*, 268.13 *measured*
calibrated scale 268.6 *measuring instrument*
calibration 56.83 *sensitivity*, 121.3 *gradation*, 268.1 *measurement*
calibrator 369.10 *scales*
calibre 121.1 *degree*, 259.1 *size*, 271.4 *breadth*, 680.9 *firearm*
caliche 57 Common Chemical Compounds
calico 67 Natural Fabrics
calico cat 456.5 *variegated thing*
calidarium 408.8 *hot place*
California 92 American States
California lilac 84 Flowers and Flowering Plants
californium 57 Chemical Elements
caliper brake 71.11 *bicycle part*
caliph 696.2 *sovereign*
calisaya 85 Tree Products
Calixtines 7 Christian Movements
call 7.21 *ordain*, 42.10 *play*, 49.22 *phrase*, 228.1 *motive*, 346.9 *enter*, 420.9 *audio device*, 423.1 *loudness*, 423.8 *be loud*, 431.1 *cry*, 431.10 *cry out*, 432.4 *cry*, 528.12 *communicate*, 534.10 *telephone call*, 534.32 *telephone*, 543.6 *word*, 543.12 *signal*, 586.11 *motive*, 593.2 *need*, 676.1 *war measures*, 692.2, 712.2 *demand*, 712.7 *demand*, 782.12 *desire*, 815.3 *meeting*
call a ball 24.8 *play billiards*
call a curse down on 827.7 *wish ill*
call a doctor 636.7 *raise the alarm*
call a draw 19.15 *play offence*
call a halt 157.16 *cease*, 218.8 *cause to cease*
calla lily 84 Flowers and Flowering Plants
call a meeting 161.42 *call together*
call an ambulance 636.7 *raise the alarm*
call an audible 19.15 *play offence*
Callao 93 Cities
call a pocket 24.8 *play billiards*
Callas 49 Musicians and Composers
call a spade a spade 537.29 *be truthful*, 556.7 *be simple*, 658.4 *be naive*, 857.6 *be honourable*
call a strike 15.12 *have an industrial dispute*, 218.7 *stop working*, 711.5 *refuse*
call a truce 218.9 *pause*, 325.9 *make motionless*, 675.5 *be at peace*
call attention to 554.6 *emphasize*, 564.11 *speak*
call box 534.9 *telephone*
callboy 51.26 *stagehand*
called 24.9 *billiard*, 676.15 *warring*
called ball 24.6 *pool*
called by God 397.19 *dead*
called for 593.4 *required*, 739.16 *sold*
called off 157.22 *cancelled*
called pocket 24.6 *pool*
called strike 15.4 *industrial dispute*
called to one's eternal rest 397.19 *dead*
called up 161.46 *assembled*

called-up 676.15 *warring*
Callendar and Barnes' experiment 56 Named Laws
caller 346.7 *entrant*, 534.13 *telephoner*
call evidence 16.70 *litigate*
call for 326.14 *bring back*, 513.11 *demand*, 591.14 *necessitate*, 593.2 *need*, 593.8 *miss*, 692.10 *demand*
call for a fair catch 19.17 *kick*
call for a relief pitcher 22.7 *play baseball*
call for a show-down 676.14 *battle*
call for help 543.12 *signal*
call forth 228.9 *motivate*
call girl 402.7 *prostitute*, 864.9 *wicked person*, 877.9 *immoral woman*
call heads or tails 229.4 *chance*
calligraphic 50.24 *pictorial*
calligraphy 42 Hobbies and Pastimes, 50.1 *art*, 547.2 *reproduction*
Callimachus 48 Poets
call in 161.43 *herd*, 346.9 *enter*, 348.9 *welcome*, 599.5 *dispose of*, 654.6 *consult*, 741.25 *demonetize*
calling 37.2 *hunting*, 228.1 *motive*, 543.16 *signalling*, 560.7 *nomenclature*, 586.11 *motive*, 644.3 *job*, 737.6 *business*, 815.3 *meeting*, 847.2 *task*
calling card 815.3 *meeting*
calling for 593.6 *demanding*
calling forth 355.5 *drawing out*
calling it quits 645.3 *unemployment*, 705.1 *resignation*
calling the ball 24.6 *pool*
calling the pocket 24.6 *pool*
call in the receiver 218.7 *stop working*
call into being 156.22 *invent*
call into play 599.5 *dispose of*
call into question 477.20 *doubt*, 498.9 *cause disbelief*, 536.8 *rebut*, 663.15 *object*
calliope 49 Musical Instruments
callipers 56.84 *altimeter*, 268.6 *measuring instrument*
callisthenics 30.8 *floor exercises*, 627.9 *physical improvement*, 644.5 *exercise*
call it a day 160.12 *discontinue*, 218.6 *cease*, 673.3 *submit*
call it quits 160.12 *discontinue*, 218.6 *cease*, 677.5 *make peace*, 705.5 *resign*, 840.5 *atone*
call letters 534.20 *radio broadcasting*, 544.3 *means of identification*
call madam 567.11 *title*
call names 827.6 *vilify*, 850.25 *taunt*
call no man master 698.16 *be independent*
call of duty 847.4 *sense of duty*
call off 218.8 *cause to cease*, 704.6 *cancel*
call of nature 353.3 *urination*
call on 654.6 *consult*, 815.12 *visit*
call one's bluff 668.5 *defy*
call one's own 723.7 *possess*
call on one's time 642.6 *business*
callosity 832.3 *callousness*
callous 832, 273.4 *thick-skinned*, 373.1 *hard*, 373.3 *hardened*, 373.4 *mentally hard*, 378.5 *mentally tough*, 669.11 *obstinate*, 690.8 *severe*, 761.1 *insensitive*, 836.4 *pitiless*, 864.11 *wicked*, 868.3 *impenitent*
calloused 373.3 *hardened*, 832.12 *callous*
callously 373.13 *inflexibly*, 378.14 *single-mindedly*, 669.14 *resistingly*, 690.11 *severely*, 761.8 *unfeelingly*, 832.20 *malevolently*, 836.7 *pitilessly*, 864.18 *wickedly*
callous murderer 868.2 *impenitent person*

callousness 832, 373.8 *mental hardness*, 378.9 *mental toughness*, 404.3 *heedlessness*, 669.2 *obstinacy*, 690.1 *severity*, 761.3 *insensitiveness*, 836.1 *pitilessness*, 868.1 *impenitence*
callous person 836.3 *pitiless person*
call out 15.12 *have an industrial dispute*, 431.10 *cry out*, 674.12 *fight*
call-out 60.6 *health care*
call out the troops 636.7 *raise the alarm*
callow 201.12, 206.12 *immature*, 453.3 *raw*, 585.1 *unaccustomed*, 595.5 *immature*, 656.2 *unskilled*, 658.1, 865.7 *naive*
callowness 201.3, 206.3 *immaturity*, 658.2, 865.3 *naivety*
call sign 534.20 *radio broadcasting*, 544.3 *means of identification*
call signals 19.15 *play offence*
call sir 567.11 *title*
call the AA 636.7 *raise the alarm*
call the emergency service 636.7 *raise the alarm*
call the fire brigade 636.7 *raise the alarm*
call the plays 19.15 *play offence*
call the police 636.7 *raise the alarm*
call the RAC 636.7 *raise the alarm*
call the rescue service 636.7 *raise the alarm*
call the roll 170.11 *number*
call the shots 599.5 *dispose of*, 653.1 *manage*, 653.2 *direct*, 688.19 *be authoritarian*, 692.11 *have authority over*
call the signals 692.11 *have authority over*
call the tune 228.10 *manipulate*, 599.5 *dispose of*, 688.19 *be authoritarian*
call time-out 218.9 *pause*
call to 567.9 *approach*
call to account 852.20 *censure*
call to arms 543.6 *word*, 676.7 *war measures*, 676.12 *go to war*
call together 161
call to mind 3.22 *remember*, 114.10 *be similar*, 511.12 *remember*, 519.14 *imagine*
call to prayer 10.4 *public worship*, 543.6 *word*, 543.12 *signal*
call to the colours 676.12 *go to war*
call up 161.42 *call together*, 355.15 *draw out*, 511.12 *remember*, 519.14 *imagine*, 528.12 *communicate*, 676.12 *go to war*, 695.7 *force*
call-up 161.1 *assembly*, 676.7 *war measures*, 695.3 *coercive methods*
call upon 692.9 *command*, 847.17 *impose a duty*
call up spirits 11.22 *conjure*
callus 373.7 *hard substance*
call witnesses 16.71 *try a case*
calm 869, 4.18 *detached*, 55.13 *wind strength*, 55.45 *fine*, 150.8 *harmony*, 150.16 *harmonious*, 150.22 *pacify*, 225.1 *stability*, 225.9 *stable*, 242.4, 242.6 *moderate*, 325.2 *repose*, 325.6 *quiescent*, 325.9 *make motionless*, 376.3 *soothing*, 376.7 *smoothness*, 376.13 *smooth over*, 422.3 *silent*, 422.4 *silence*, 462.1 *lack of thought*, 587.5 *discourage*, 641.1 *inaction*, 641.3 *inactive*, 660.13 *easygoing*, 675.7 *peaceful*, 767.9 *relieve*, 783.7 *indifferent*, 783.3 *unmoved*
calm as a mill pond 325.6 *quiescent*, 376.5 *smooth as a peach*
calmative 62.15 *sedative*, 242.8 *moderating*
calm before the storm 325.2 *repose*
calm down 242.3 *be moderate*, 677.4 *pacify*
calmed 767.7 *relieved*

calming 242.1 *moderation*, 242.8 *moderating*, 677.6 *pacificatory*, 767.8 *relieving*
calming influence 242.2 *moderator*
calmly 869, 4.27 *stoically*, 225.12 *stably*, 242.9 *moderately*, 325.10 *motionlessly*, 376.15 *soothingly*, 422.5 *silently*, 641.5 *without action*, 783.17 *indifferently*, 787.9 *without wonder*
calmness 869, 4.3 *detachment*, 242.1 *moderation*, 325.2 *repose*, 376.7 *smoothness*, 641.1 *inaction*, 660.4 *ease of manner*, 783.1 *indifference*, 787.1 *lack of wonder*
calm oneself 787.5 *not wonder about*
calm water 376.8 *smooth thing*
calomel 57 Common Chemical Compounds, **62** Medication, **62** Medication
Calor gas 410.3 *gas*
calorie 75 Scientific and Technical Units, 235.5 *unit of work*, 408.2 *heat measurement*
Calorie 75 Scientific and Technical Units
calorie-controlled diet 350.6 *nutrition*
calorie counter 350.6 *nutrition*, 871.4 *fasting person*
calorie-counter 274.9 *thin person*
calorie-counting 274.3 *slimming*, 274.10 *diet*
calories 350.11 *food content*
calorific 56.98 *physical*, 350.27 *edible*, 408.9 *hot*
calorifically 56.100 *physically*, 350.29 *edibly*
calorific value 408.2 *heat measurement*
calorimeter 56.89 *thermometer*, 268.8 *meter*, 408.2 *heat measurement*
calorimetric 268.16 *micrometric*
calorimetry 268.2 *micrometry*
calorochromic 444.14 *chromolithographic*
calotte 43 Architectural Decoration, 7.11 *vestment*
caloyer 7.7 *monk*
calque 5.17 *word*
caltrop 380.8 *sharp-pointed thing*, 671.9 *barrier*
calumet 675.1 *peace*, 677.2 *peace offering*
calumniate 854.12 *defame*, 856.6 *accuse falsely*
calumniatory 854.16 *defamatory*
calumnious 827.9 *vituperative*, 854.16 *defamatory*, 856.9 *perjurious*
calumny 670.16 *terrorist attack*, 827.3 *vilification*, 854.3 *defamation*, 856.2 *false accusation*
calve 68.18 *practise livestock farming*, 77.35 *give birth*, 245.11 *have young*
Calvin 52 Scientists
Calvin cycle 58.23 *photosynthesis*
Calvinism 7 Christian Movements
Calvinist 7.5 *Christian*
Calvino 48 Writers
calvities 296.5 *baldness*
calypso 49.10 *world music*, 433.2 *song*
Calypso 97.4 *sea god*
calypso orchid 84 Flowers and Flowering Plants
calyptra 83.7 *root*, 88.4 *moss plant*
calyx 84.3 *flower part*, 143.6 *branch*
cam 63.8 *machine element*, 603.4 *machine*
Cam 96 Rivers, 96.4 *British rivers*
CAM 65.1 *computing*
Camaldolese Monk 7 Members of Religious Orders
camaraderie 815.8 *good company*, 819.1 *friendship*
Camargue 32 Breeds of Horse and Pony

Camaxtli 8 Deities
Camazotz 8 Deities
camber 71.3 *carriageway*, 123.1 *inequality*, 286.1 *obliqueness*, 286.6 *be oblique*, 310.11 *angle*, 311.2 *bend*, 316.1 *convexity*, 316.5 *be convex*
cambered 311.4 *curved*
camber inducer 36.7 *windsurfing*
Camberwell beauty 82 Insects
cambist 739.12 *wholesaler*, 741.17 *financier*
cambium 83.5 *stem*
Cambodia 91 Countries
Cambrian 54 Geological Time Intervals, **95** Mountains
Cambrian Mountains 95.5 *British mountains*
Cambrian period 200.3 *geological period*
cambric 67 Natural Fabrics
Cambridge 68 Breeds of Sheep, **93** Cities, **93** Cities
Cambridge blue 454.1 *blue*
Cambridge Bronze 68 Breeds of Fowl
Cambridge Diet 350.6 *nutrition*
Cambridge Platonism 4.7 *school of thought*
Cambridge Platonist 4.11 *follower of a doctrine*
Cambridge roll 68.10 *farm tool*
Cambridgeshire 92 Counties
camcorder 66.14 *cine film*, 66.16 *camera*, 114.3 *copier*, 118.6 *phototocopier*, 534.26 *recording*, 545.10 *recording instrument*
Camden 93 Cities
Camden Town Group 50 Schools and Groups of Artists
camel 77 Placental Mammals, 326.6 *beast of burden*
cameleer 679.20 *cavalryman*
camel hair 67 Natural Fabrics
camelid 77.15 *hoofed mammal*, 77.33 *ungulate*
Camelidae 77.15 *hoofed mammal*
camellia 84 Flowers and Flowering Plants
camel-like 77.33 *ungulate*
camel litter 71.6 *litter*
camelopard 77 Placental Mammals, 77.15 *hoofed mammal*
Camelopardalis 53 The Constellations
camel's milk 351.5 *milk*
camel spin 41.6 *ice-skating*
Camembert 45 Cheeses
cameo 50.13 *relief-carving*, 51.21 *role*, 560.2 *brief description*
cameo glass 44.1 *ceramics*
camera 66, 56.32 *optical instrument*, 114.3 *copier*, 118.6 *photocopier*, 435.8 *reflection*, 545.10 *recording instrument*
camera lens 56.30 *lens system*
camera lucida 50.11 *artist's materials*
cameraman 545.9 *recorder*
camera obscura 50.11 *artist's materials*, 66.16 *camera*
camera-shy 66.22 *photographic*
Cameronianism 7 Christian Movements
Cameroon 91 Countries
camiknickers 295.18 *underwear*
camisado 670.12 *military attack*
camisole 295.18 *underwear*
camming 34.8 *mountaineering*
camming device 34.4 *climbing equipment*
Camões 48 Poets
camomile 45 Herbs and Spices, **84** Flowers and Flowering Plants, 413.5 *herbs*
camomile tea 84.8 *flower product*, 351.3 *tea*
camouflage 118, 114.12 *imitate*, 115.3 *disguise*, 115.6 *differentiate*, 118.2 *copy*, 293.16 *disguise*, 293.31 *hide*, 295.5 *fancy dress*, 436.6 *blinder*, 436.15 *blind*, 438.6 *that which makes invisible*, 458.3 *cause to disappear*, 458.5 *disguise*, 474.11 *practise sophistry*, 531.3 *cover-*

ing up, 531.9, 539.12 *disguise*, 539.32 *disguise*, 540.3 *hypocrisy*, 540.18 *be hypocritical*, 638.2 *means of escape*, 671.19 *buffer*
camouflaged 293.37 *protected*, 436.13 *hidden*, 438.3 *private*, 458.7 *disappeared*, 529.11 *mysterious*, 531.15, 539.41 *disguised*
camouflager 293.17 *coverer*
camp 17.1 *military affairs*, 34.1 *mountaineering*, 34.9 *mountaineer*, 51.10 *comedy*, 256.18 *take up residence*, 305.5 *team*, 634.2 *shelter*, 665.1 *party*, 811.3 *dramatics*, 811.21 *blatant*
campagna 87.2 *grassland*
campaign 17.1 *military affairs*, 597.2 *undertaking*, 640.1 *action*, 640.4 *act*, 644.4 *exertion*, 644.8 *exert oneself*, 652.9 *tactics*, 674.6, 674.12 *fight*, 676.8 *warfare*, 676.13 *be at war*
campaigner 640.3 *doer*, 679.8 *soldier*
Campaign for Nuclear Disarmament 627.11 *reformism*, 675.1 *peace*, 677.1 *pacification*
campaigning 676.8 *warfare*, 676.15 *warring*
campaign medal 681.1 *trophy*
Campaign Medal 17 US Military Medals and Decorations
campaign plan 676.6 *art of war*
Campanella 4 Philosophers
campanile 275.6 *tall thing*
campanology 49, 423.1 *loudness*, 427.2 *ringing*
campanula 84 Flowers and Flowering Plants
camp bed 47.6 *bed*
Campbell 48 Poets, **48** Poets
camp chair 47.2 *chair*
camp-drafting 32.12 *rodeo*
camper 71 Motor Vehicles, 256.9 *mobile home*
campervan 256.9 *mobile home*
campestral 98.11 *continental*
campfire 408.6 *fire*
camp follower 127.6 *inferior*, 180.9, 195.8 *follower*, 584.8 *creature of habit*
camp followers 155.14 *follower*
camphor 85 Tree Products, 58.20 *terpene*, 418.3 *incense*, 637.2 *preserver*
camphorated 418.4 *fragrant*
camphor tree 85 Trees and Shrubs
Campine 68 Breeds of Fowl
camping it up 51.20 *acting*
campion 45 Herbs and Spices, **84** Flowers and Flowering Plants
Campion 49 Musicians and Composers
campo 87.2 *grassland*
Campolino 32 Breeds of Horse and Pony
campos 98.6 *lowland*
camp up 811.31 *put on a show*
campus 6.15 *schoolroom*
campus novel 48.2 *fiction*
camshaft 71 Motor Vehicle Parts
Camus 48 Writers
camwood 85 Trees and Shrubs
can 120.3 *container*, 258.6 *box*, 258.21 *put in a container*, 323.4 *closed place*, 351.2 *drink*, 351.10 *drink container*, 353.13 *lavatory*, 614.6 *refuse*, 637.2 *preserver*, 637.5 *preserve*, 702.2 *the inside* , 767.12 *relieve from duty*
Canaan 714.4 *promised land*
Canaanite 5 Languages and Groups of Languages, **7** Non-Christian Religions
Canaanitic 5 Languages and Groups of Languages
Canada 91 Countries
Canada Day 214.6 *annually celebrated day*
Canada goose 78 Birds
Canadian 96 Rivers, 36.12 *canoeing*
Canadian 5-pin bowling 18 Sporting Activities

Canadian bacon 45.30 *bacon*
Canadian canoe 36.6 *canoeing*
Canadian canoe racing 18 Sporting Activities
Canadian Charbray 68 Breeds of Cattle
Canadian Coureur des Bois 41.2 *cross-country skiing*
Canadian Curling Association 41.10 *curling*
Canadian Cutting Horse 32 Breeds of Horse and Pony
Canadian football 18 Sporting Activities
Canadian GP at Montreal 33.2 *Formula 1 race*
Canadian maple leaf 544.6 *national emblem*
Canadian Pacific 72.10 *miscellaneous*
Canadian Ski Association 41.1 *skiing*
canal 63.24 *water system*, 70.5 *transportable*, 74.2 *waterway*, 74.11 *nautical*, 96.1 *river*, 137.4 *means of connection*, 317.2 *concave land*, 321.1, 321.6 *furrow*, 327.11 *channel*
canal boat 74 Ships and Boats, 74.3 *vessel*
canal bridge 63.21 *bridge*
canalize 653.2 *direct*
canal travel 74.1 *water travel*
canapé 45.12 *hors d'oeuvre*
canard 73 Types of Aircraft, 538.5 *half-truth*, 540.8 *fraud*, 540.9 *falsification*, 636.3 *false alarm*
canari 45.53 *African dish*
canary 78 Birds, 78.7 *cagebird*, 433.5 *melodist*, 856.3 *accuser*
canary grass 87 Grasses
canary-yellow 452.1 *yellow*
can a shot 23.6 *play basketball*
canasta 42 Card Games
canasta pack 42.3 *card game terms*
Canberra 93 Cities
cancan 46.2 *dance*
cancan dancer 46.5 *dancer*, 51.28 *dancer*
cancel 704, 16.77 *annul*, 52.92 *manipulate*, 100.14 *cause not to exist*, 131.3 *subtract*, 147.8 *eject*, 157.16 *cease*, 218.8 *cause to cease*, 231.3 *counteract*, 244.8 *destroy*, 458.3 *cause to disappear*, 536.9 *renounce*, 546.1 *obliterate*, 581.4 *revoke*, 598.2 *withdraw*, 600.6 *stop using*, 704.9 *cancel out*, 709.3 *veto*, 709.4 *censor*, 727.9 *dispose of*, 839.10 *absolve*
cancel a debt 747.10 *forgive a debt*
cancellation 704, 52.24 *evaluation*, 125.2 *counterbalance*, 147.2 *ejection*, 157.2 *cessation*, 231.1 *counteraction*, 458.5 *disguise*, 536.4 *renunciation*, 546.3 *obliteration*, 581.7 *abrogation*, 598.3 *relinquishment*, 709.1 *veto*, 727.1 *disposal*, 839.3 *absolution*
Cancellation 704
cancellation of contract 704.2 *termination*
cancellation of debts 747.1 *nonpayment*
cancelled 157, 704, 487.4 *forbidden*, 536.12 *rejected*, 546.6 *obliterated*, 598.5 *relinquished*, 709.5 *vetoed*, 839.6 *forgiven*
cancelled out 125.10 *counterbalancing*
cancelling 704.1 *cancellation*
cancelling out 704
cancel one's contract 704.7 *terminate*
cancel out 704, 122.11 *equalize*, 125.5 *counterbalance*, 231.3 *counteract*
cancer 777 Phobias by Topic, **624,** 227.3 *growth*, 527.7 *latent things*, 618.10 *poverty*, 624.4 *disease*, 628.9 *dilapidation*, 687.1 *adversity*

Cancer 53 The Constellations, **53** Zodiac Constellations
cancer of the pancreas 624.12 *cancer*
cancerous 624.23 *diseased*
cancerous growth 624.12 *cancer*
cancerous tumour 624.12 *cancer*
cancerphobia 777 Phobias by Name
cancer stick 413.7 *tobacco*
candela 75 SI Units, **75** Scientific and Technical Units
candelabra 439.5 *incandescent light*
candelabrum 439.5 *incandescent light*
candent 408.9 *hot*
candescence 439.1 *light*
candescent 439.15 *lucent*
C and H 875.6 *drug*
candicidin 62 Medication
candid 271.3 *broad-minded*, 312.5 *honourable*, 322.16 *open*, 381.2 *outspoken*, 442.4 *easily seen through*, 475.10 *demonstrative*, 526.15 *open*, 528.16 *informative*, 530.11 *disclosing*, 537.18 *truthful*, 556.3 *natural*, 565.6 *effusive*, 658.1 *naive*, 698.13 *informal*, 857.4 *honourable*
candida 89 Fungi
candidacy 580.12 *election*
candidate 477.10 *person questioned*, 580.13 *electorate*, 674.10 *contender*, 710.8 *volunteer*, 712.4 *requester*
Candide 658.3 *naive person*
candidiasis 89.5 *fungal association*
candidly 322.26 *openly*, 381.12 *bluntly*, 475.21 *demonstratively*, 526.17 *frankly*, 530.13 *openly*, 537.36 *truthfully*, 556.8 *simply*, 565.11 *effusively*, 658.5 *naively*, 698.22 *informally*, 857.7 *honourably*
candidness 381.6 *outspokenness*, 556.6 *naturalness*, 698.4 *informality*, 857.1 *probity*
candid speaker 658.3 *naive person*
candied 414.6 *sweet*
candied fruit 414.2 *sweetener*
candle 75 Scientific and Technical Units, 10.14 *sacred object*, 439.5 *incandescent light*
candleberry 85 Trees and Shrubs
candlefish 80 Fishes
candleholder 439.5 *incandescent light*
candlelight 56.23 *light*, 439.5 *incandescent light*
candlelit 439.18 *lit*
candlemaking 42 Hobbies and Pastimes
Candlemas 10.15 *holy day*
candlenut 86 Nuts
candlepins 25.4 *bowling*
Candle problem 61.5 *psychological test*
candlestick 439.5 *incandescent light*
candlewood 85 Trees and Shrubs
C and M 875.6 *drug*
can do no more 650.5 *be fatigued*
candour 312.8 *directness*, 322.9 *openness*, 475.2 *demonstrativeness*, 526.11, 530.3 *openness*, 537.5 *truthfulness*, 556.6 *naturalness*, 565.2 *effusiveness*, 658.2 *naivety*, 698.4 *informality*, 857.1 *probity*
candy 373.10 *solidify*, 414.4 *confectionery*, 414.8 *sweeten*, 826.3 *love token*, 875.6 *drug*
candyfloss 414.4 *confectionery*
candy man 875.5 *drug pusher*
candy striper 710.8 *volunteer*
candytuft 84 Flowers and Flowering Plants
cane 87 Grasses, 28.1 *fencing*, 87.3 *grass plant*, 284.3 *body support*, 330.5 *beat*, 879.3 *hit*, 879.14 *instrument of punishment*
Canea 93 Cities

cane chair 47.2 *chair*
canella 85 Tree Products
canephorae 43 Architectural Decoration
caner 879.17 *punisher*
cane rat 77 Placental Mammals
canescence 446.7 *whiteness*, 448.4 *greyness*
canescent 446.3 *white-haired*, 448.1 *grey*
cane sugar 414.2 *sweetener*
Canes Venatici 53 The Constellations
canework 42 Hobbies and Pastimes
canid 77.8 *flesh-eating mammal*
Canidae 77.8 *flesh-eating mammal*
canine 77.8 *flesh-eating mammal*, 77.9 *dog*, 77.28 *carnivorous*, 380.11 *tooth*
canine distemper 624.18 *veterinary disease*
caning 879.12 *corporal punishment*
Canis Major 53 The Constellations
Canis Minor 53 The Constellations
canistel 86 Fruits
canister 258.6 *box*, 680.14 *historical ammunition*
can it 218.12 *stop*, 422.2 *silence*, 422.6 *hush sh silence quiet shut up that's enough peace soft mum's the word whist*
canker 69.12 *pests and diseases*, 85.10 *tree disease*, 89.1 *fungus*, 618.10 *poverty*, 628.3 *make worse*, 628.9 *dilapidation*
cankered 89.9 *fungal*
cankerous 624.23 *diseased*
canna 84 Flowers and Flowering Plants
cannabis 631.11 *intoxicant*, 875.6 *drug*
canned 258.20 *containing*, 637.7 *preserved*, 874.1 *drunk*
canned food 637.3 *preserved thing*
canned goods 739.8 *merchandise*
cannel coal 410.5 *coal*
cannelloni 45 Types of Pasta
canner 637.4 *preservationist*
cannery 637.2 *preserver*
Cannes 93 Cities
cannibal 350.18 *eater*, 398.10 *killer*, 590.6 *hunter*
cannibalism 10.7 *non-Christian ritual*, 350.5 *eating habit*, 832.2 *crueIness*
cannibalistic 10.21 *ritualistic*, 350.26 *eating*, 398.24 *murderous*, 832.11 *cruel*
cannibalistically 350.28 *carnivorously*
cannibalize 136.9 *separate*, 629.1 *repair*
cannikin 258.13 *drinking vessel*
canniness 459.4 *cleverness*
canning 258.20 *containing*, 637.1 *preservation*
canning factory 637.2 *preserver*
Cannizzaro 52 Scientists
Cannizzaro reaction 57 Named Reactions
Cannock Chase Cardy 68 Breeds of Sheep
cannon 24.2 *billiards play*, 24.3 *English billiards*, 24.8 *play billiards*, 244.7 *agent of destruction*, 330.12 *collision*, 331.1, 331.4 *recoil*, 338.8 *missile*, 680.10 *historical gun*
cannonade 338.7 *shot*, 338.28 *shoot*, 670.2 *fire*, 670.12 *military attack*
cannonball 39.10 *dive*, 329.11 *swift thing*, 338.8 *missile*, 680.14 *historical ammunition*
cannon bone 382 Bones
cannoneer 338.15 *shooter*, 679.13 *historical soldiery*
cannon fodder 679.17 *army person*
cannon into 330.2 *collide*
cannon royal 680.12 *historical guns*

cannonry 680.11 *guns*
cannot 236.6 *be powerless*
cannot be helped 695.8 *be compelled*
cannot do otherwise 695.8 *be compelled*
cannot help but 695.8 *be compelled*
canny 507.6 *intelligent*, 657.4 *cunning*, 756.4 *thrifty*, 781.4 *cautious*
canoe 74 Ships and Boats, **36**, 36.12 *canoeing*
canoe association 36.6 *canoeing*
canoeing 36, 36
canoeist 74.8 *boatman*
canoe over rapids 36.17 *canoe*
canoe poling 36.8 *punting*
canoe polo 18 Sporting Activities
canoe race 36.6 *canoeing*
canoe racing 36.6 *canoeing*
canoe sailing 18 Sporting Activities
canoe slalom racing 18 Sporting Activities
canoe sprint racing 18 Sporting Activities
canoe techniques 36.6 *canoeing*
canoe trophy 36.6 *canoeing*
canoewood 85 Trees and Shrubs
can of worms 659.4 *problem*
canon 166, 4.1 *philosophy*, 7.8 *priest*, 7.12 *religious text*, 10.10 *religious manual*, 16.3 *law*, 118.1 *imitation*, 166.4 *guide*, 268.7 *standard*, 426.6 *musical repetition*, 492.2 *verdict*, 497.2 *religious belief*, 654.3 *precept*, 692.1 *command*
canoness 7.7 *monk*
canonical 6.21 *curricular*, 7.17 *priestly*, 7.18 *theological*, 52.70 *universal*, 653.18 *parliamentary*
canonical hour 10.4 *public worship*
canonically 6.25 *educationally*, 7.23 *religiously*
canonicals 7.11 *vestment*, 295.3 *formal dress*
canonical writings 7.12 *religious text*
canonist 7.14 *theologian*
canonization 8.9 *deification*, 361.7 *lift*, 804.1 *right*
canonize 8.17 *deify*, 361.3 *promote*
canonized 8.15 *deified*, 361.12 *exalted*
canonized person 8.10 *deified person*
canon law 16.1 *the law*, 654.3 *precept*
can opener 45.6 *kitchen equipment*
canopic urn 399.4 *funeral objects*
canopied 47.14 *wooden*
canopied bed 47.6 *bed*
Canopus 53 Named Stars
canopy 73 Aircraft Parts, 293.7 *overhead covering*, 293.27 *roof*
canorous 433.6 *melodious*
cans 420.9 *audio device*
cant 5.20 *jargon word*, 5.42 *worded*, 5.45 *use language*, 25.2 *grip*, 286.1 *obliqueness*, 286.6 *be oblique*, 310.2 *obliquity*, 310.11 *angle*, 540.3 *hypocrisy*, 540.18 *be hypocritical*, 564.1 *faculty of speech*
cantabile 49 Musical Terms
Cantabrian 95 Mountains
cantaloupe 86 Fruits
cantankerous 473.8 *argumentative*, 500.7 *dissenting*, 666.9 *disagreeing*, 764.2 *objectionable*, 829.4 *irascible*, 830.7 *irritable*
cantankerously 666.11 *in disagreement*, 829.9 *irascibly*, 830.14 *irritably*
cantankerousness 666.1 *disagreement*, 764.6 *objectionability*, 829.1 *irascibility*
cantata 10.8 *hymn*, 49.5 *sacred music*
can't bear 785.5 *dislike*

canteen 256.7 *room*, 350.15 *eating place*, 351.10 *drink container*
canter 32.16 *ride*, 324.12 *gait*, 329.4 *be swift*, 329.9 *acceleration*, 539.19 *hypocrite*
canterbury 47.5 *cabinet*
Canterbury 92 New Zealand Regions and Territories, **93** Cities, 93.4 *British cities*, 588.6 *objective*
Canterbury bell 84 Flowers and Flowering Plants
Canterbury hoe 69.6 *garden tool*
cantering 329.1 *swift*
canticle 10.8 *hymn*, 49.5 *sacred music*
cantide 433.2 *song*
cantilena 49 Musical Terms
cantilever 73 Aircraft Parts, 43.9 *miscellaneous architectural features*, 43.19 *decorate*, 63.27 *superstructure*, 283.5 *projecting object*, 382.4 *framework*
cantilever brake 71.11 *bicycle part*
cantilever bridge 63.21, 327.9 *bridge*
canting 5.42 *worded*, 7.15 *religious*, 123.3 *unequal*
canticle 10.8 *hymn*, 49.5 *sacred music*
canto 48.8 *part of poem*, 143.2 *particular*, 433.1 *melody*
canton 92.3 *other*, 249.5 *state*, 544.7 *flag*, 544.8 *heraldic device*, 688.8 *governmental organization*
Canton 93 Cities, **93** Cities
Canton crepe 67 Natural Fabrics
Cantonese 5 Languages and Groups of Languages
cantor 7.8 *priest*
Cantor 52 Scientists
Cantor set 52 Named Concepts
can't pay! won't pay! **747**
can't stand 785.5 *dislike*
cantus 433.1 *melody*
cantus firmus 433.1 *melody*, 433.3 *melodiousness*
Canuck 91 Names for Inhabitants
canvas 67 Natural Fabrics, **74** Sails, 30.8 *floor exercises*, 50.8 *painting*, 293.7 *overhead covering*, 634.2 *shelter*
canvasback 78 Birds
canvass 473.16 *plead*, 477.17 *question*, 568.11 *confer*, 580.5 *vote*, 640.4 *act*, 665.14 *be a party member*, 712.3 *solicitation*, 712.8 *solicit money*, 739.1 *sell*
canvassed 477.16 *questioned*
canvasser 12.6 *political party*, 477.9 *questioner*, 640.3 *doer*, 712.4 *requester*, 739.12 *wholesaler*
canvas shoes 295.19 *footwear*
canvassing 580.12 *election*, 580.16 *elective*, 712.3 *solicitation*, 739.3 *selling*
canyon 54.7 *landform*, 98.8 *valley*, 265.3 *gulf*, 317.2 *concave land*, 375.8 *rough ground*
can you beat that 786.14 *wonderful*
Caodaism 7 Non-Christian Religions
caoutchouc 377.4 *rubber*
cap 22.3 *baseball equipment*, 27.6 *pad*, 29.4 *golf club*, 43.8 *column*, 88.4 *moss plant*, 89.4 *fungal body*, 126.8 *be superior*, 144.4 *complete*, 157.15 *end*, 279.2 *head*, 279.7 *top*, 293.2, 293.23 *cover*, 295.15 *headgear*, 295.32 *dress*, 323.2 *stopper*, 323.8 *stop*, 410.2 *lighter*, 672.3 *retaliate*, 680.15 *explosive*, 684.6 *elaborate*
cap. 5.15 *type style*
capability 233 *influence*, 235.2 *ability*, 485.1 *qualification*, 485.2 *ability*, 602.1 *means*, 655.1 *skill*, 660.1 *easiness*, 714.3 *potential*
Capablanca y Graupera 18 Sporting Personalities

capable 122.9 *adequate*, 235.13 *powerful*, 306.12 *on form*, 485.9 *qualified*, 486.5 *possible*
capableness 485.1 *qualification*
capable of being used 733.12 *adoptive*
capable of life 396.12 *alive*
capable of perfection 620.1 *imperfect*
capably 485
capacious 248.13 *spacious*, 259.15, 755.4 *big*
capaciously 248.15 *spaciously*, 259.20 *largely*
capaciousness 248.4 *spaciousness*, 259.2 *bigness*
capacitance 56.53, 64.12 *resistance*, 235.7 *electrical power*
capacitive 64.36 *electronic*
capacitor 56.55 *circuit*, 64.17 *resistor*
capacity 52.35 *space*, 64.12 *resistance*, 120.1 *quantity*, 144.2 *fullness*, 146.1 *inclusion*, 235.2 *ability*, 248.1 *space*, 248.5 *reserved space*, 259.1, 268.4 *size*, 485.2 *ability*, 486.2 *possibleness*, 602.1 *means*, 613.6 *usability*, 655.1 *skill*, 714.3 *potential*
capacity for life 396.5 *life cycle*
cap and bells 51.10 *comedy*, 51.30 *clown*, 295.5 *fancy dress*
cap and gown 295.3 *formal dress*, 544.5 *uniform*, 813.4 *formal dress*
caparison 295.1 *dress*
cape 98.5 *peninsula*, 295.25 *accessories*, 318.2 *projection*
Cape Breton 98 Islands
Cape buffalo 77 Placental Mammals
Cape cart 71 Carriages and Carts
Cape Coloured 133.5 *hybrid*
Cape doctor 55 Winds
Cape Horn 98.5 *peninsula*
capelin 80 Fishes
Capella 53 Named Stars
capelli 45 Types of Pasta
capellini 45 Types of Pasta
Cape of Good Hope 98.5 *peninsula*
caper 45 Herbs and Spices, 46.15 *dance*, 413.5 *herbs*, 736.3 *theft*, 771.5 *joke*
capercaillie 78 Birds
capers 506.3 *tomfoolery*
Cape Town 93 Cities
Cape Verde 93 Countries
capillarity 340.2 *pulling power*
capillary attraction 340.2 *pulling power*
capillary tube 57 Laboratory Apparatus
cap in hand 849.11 *in a respectful stance*
capital 5.15 *type style*, 5.41 *lettered*, 13.6 *economic factors*, 43.8 *column*, 92.5 *administrative headquarters*, 93.1 *city*, 126.14 *best*, 279.3 *architectural summit*, 279.5 *top*, 291.4 *centre of activity*, 398.23 *deadly*, 602.4 *financial resources*, 605.1 *store*, 611.5 *important*, 617.1 *worthy*, 617.2 *best*, 688.6 *place of authority*, 725.5 *personal estate*, 741.6 *funds*, 742.5 *wealth*, 879.19 *punitive*
capital accumulation 13.4 *economic development*
capital budget 750.2 *budgeting*
capital city 249.10 *urban area*, 291.4 *centre of activity*
capital crime 16.39 *crime*, 864.7 *criminality*
capital gain 749.2 *money received*
capital gains 721.5 *profit*
capital gains tax 751.7 *tax*
capital gearage 745.3 *loan*
capital goods 13.2 *economy*, 739.8 *merchandise*
capital investment 13.4 *economic development*

capitalism 4.7 *school of thought*, 13.6 *economic factors*, 698.1 *freedom*, 737.5 *commercial trade*, 742.9 *plutocracy*

capitalist 4.11 *follower of a doctrine*, 4.14 *of a philosophy*, 14.3 *stockbroker*, 653.13 *director*, 686.4 *prosperous person*, 696.5 *company leader*, 698.7 *free person*, 721.7 *gainer*, 737.13 *mercantile*, 741.17 *financier*, 742.10 *wealthy person*

capitalist country 91.1 *country*

capitalistic 696.12 *masterful*, 698.9 *free*, 721.15 *gainful*

capitalize on 210.5 *take the opportunity*, 599.3 *exploit*, 613.11 *find useful*, 721.14 *profit*

cap it all 126.8 *be superior*

capital letter 5.15 *type style*

capital levy 751.7 *tax*

capital murder 398.2 *murder*

capital punishment 879, 397.4 *death sentence*, 398.5 *execution*

capital reserves 741.6 *funds*

capital ship 679.24 *warship*

capital sin 864.4 *sin*

capital transfer tax 751.7 *tax*

capitation tax 751.7 *tax*

capitol 671.12 *fort*

Capitol Hill 12.4 *governing body*, 653.12 *US government*, 688.6 *place of authority*, 696.8 *the power structure*

capitulate 673.3 *submit*

capitulation 116.1 *accord*, 673.1 *submission*

capitulum 84.4 *flower head*

capnomancer 11.13 *diviner*

capomancy 11.9 *divination*

cap of darkness 11.6 *talisman*

capon 68.8 *livestock*, 401.12 *eunuch*, 401.16 *male animal*

caponize 131.4 *take off*

caponized 236.13 *unsexed*

capote 295.25 *accessories*

Capote 48 *Writers*

capped 279.6 *topped*, 293.36 *covered*, 295.29 *dressed*, 323.13 *stopped*

capped player 655.4 *skilled person*

cappelletti 45 *Types of Pasta*

capping 60.4 *dentistry*, 126.12 *superior*, 157.20 *ending*

cap rates 699.9 *economize*

capreomycin 62 *Medication*

capric 58 *Common Fatty Acids*

caprice 579, 215.1 *irregularity*, 216.2 *change of mind*, 224.2 *irresolution*, 519.4 *ideality*, 578.6 *equivocation*, 579.3 *whim*, 784.3 *likes*, 821.5 *desire*

Caprice 579

capricious 491, 579, 215.4 *irregular*, 216.11 *changeable*, 224.14 *irresolute*, 576.2 *changeable*, 578.11 *equivocating*, 780.4 *rash*, 821.20 *amorous*

capriciously 491, 579, 215.8 *irregularly*, 216.15, 224.15 *changeably*

capriciousness 491, 215.1 *irregularity*, 216.2 *change of mind*, 224.2 *irresolution*, 576.12 *inconstancy*, 579.2 *caprice*, 780.1 *rashness*

capricious person 579

Capricornids 53 *Meteor Showers*

Capricornus 53 *The Constellations*, **53** *Zodiac Constellations*

caprine 77.33 *ungulate*

Capri pants 295.9 *trousers*

caproic 58 *Common Fatty Acids*

caprylic 58 *Common Fatty Acids*

capsicum 45 *Herbs and Spices*, **45** *Vegetables*

capsid 82 *Insects*

capsize 74.10 *sail*, 123.5 *be unequal*, 287.3 *invert*, 360.11 *trip*, 362.7 *lean*

capsized 287.2 *inverted*

capsizing 287.1 *inversion*, 287.2 *inverted*

---

capstan 74 *Parts of a Ship*, 361.9 *lifter*, 364.6 *rotator*

capstan lathe 63.9 *machine tool*

capstone 43 *Architectural Decoration*, 34.5 *rock face*, 279.3 *architectural summit*, 619.3 *perfection*, 684.3 *elaboration*

capsule 62.6 *pill*, 86.2 *botanical fruit*, 270.3 *shortened version*, 293.13 *casing*, 630.2 *medicine*

capsulization 270.2 *shortening*

capsulize 270.10 *shorten*

capsulized 270.8 *shortened*

capsulotomy 60 *Surgical Operations*

captain 19.2 *football player*, 23.2 *basketball player*, 36.9 *sailor*, 36.15 *sail*, 38.3 *football player*, 73.3 *aircraft personnel*, 74.7 *nautical person*, 126.5 *superior*, 126.10 *lead*, 653.2 *direct*, 653.13 *director*, 653.14 *leader*, 679.17 *army person*, 679.27 *naval man*

Captain 17 *British Military Ranks*, **17** *British Military Ranks*, **17** *US Military Ranks*, **17** *US Military Ranks*

Captain Ahab 74.7 *nautical person*

Captain America 237.6 *muscleman*

captaincy 126.2 *leadership*, 653.4 *directorship*

Captain Hicks 179.2 *six*

captain of industry 611.4 *bigwig*, 696.5 *company leader*

captain's chair 47.2 *chair*

caption 560.2 *brief description*

captious 474.9 *quibbling*, 579.1 *capricious*, 852.28 *fault-finding*

captiously 474.14 *sophistically*

captiousness 474.4 *quibbling*, 852.6 *fault-finding*

captivate 228.9 *motivate*, 340.12 *lure*, 762.8 *cause joy*, 821.28 *win the love of*

captivated 762.4 *happy*, 821.19 *enamoured*

captivating 340.9 *attractive*, 762.5 *delightful*, 784.5 *likable*, 821.22 *lovable*

captivatingly 784.10 *with great liking*, 821.30 *lovingly*

captive 697.7 *slave*, 699.15 *detained*, 701.5 *subjected person*, 701.9 *subject*, 702.5 *prisoner*, 702.8 *imprisoned*, 821.9 *lover*

captive balloon 679.31 *military aircraft*

captively 702

captive nation 91.3 *dominion*

captivity 699.4 *detention*, 701.1 *subjection*, 702.7 *imprisonment*

captor 696.4 *absolute ruler*, 734.6 *taker*

capture 514.10 *ambush*, 519.14 *imagine*, 547.9 *represent*, 670.9 *attack successfully*, 682.9 *be victorious*, 701.7 *defeat*, 734.1 *taking*, 734.5 *takings*, 734.7 *take*, 734.10 *take away*

capture an expression 560.14 *describe*

captured 683.11 *defeated*

capture on film 545.13 *record*

capturing 734.3 *taking away*

capuche 7.11 *vestment*

Capuchin 7 *Members of Religious Orders*

capuchin monkey 77 *Placental Mammals*

capulin 86 *Fruits*

capybara 77 *Placental Mammals*

car 71 *Motor Vehicles*, **71**, 72.6 *rolling stock*, 326.5 *means of transport*

carabineer 338.15 *shooter*, 679.13 *historical soldiery*

caracal 77 *Placental Mammals*

caracara 78 *Birds*

Caracas 93 *Cities*

caracole 32.10 *dressage*

carafe 258.14 *bottle*

car alarm 543.4 *signal*, 671.5 *self-defence*

carambola 86 *Fruits*

---

caramel 45.41 *sweet*, 449.5 *brown thing*

carapace 293.14 *animal covering*, 382.7 *skeleton*

carat 75 *General Units*, 369.9 *avoirdupois weight*

caravan 159.8 *procession*, 256.9 *mobile home*

caravel 74 *Sailing Ships and Boats*

caraway seeds 45 *Herbs and Spices*, 413.5 *herbs*

carbachol 62 *Medication*

carbamazepine 62 *Medication*

carbenicillin 62 *Medication*

carbide 57 *Types of Compounds*

carbimazole 62 *Medication*

carbine 680.9 *firearm*

carbinoxamine 62 *Medication*

carbocyclic 57.35 *combined*

carbohydrate 57 *Types of Compounds*, **58**

carbohydrate diet 350.6 *nutrition*

carbohydrates 350.11 *food content*

carbolic 630.3 *prophylactic*

carbolic acid 57 *Common Chemical Compounds*, 134.3 *purifier*, 621.9 *cleaning agent*

carbolic soap 395.8 *fat*

carbolize 621.13 *clean*

car bomb 539.13 *snare*, 680.16 *bomb*

car bombing 670.16 *terrorist attack*

carbomycin 62 *Medication*

carbon 57 *Chemical Elements*, 58.15 *essential element*

carbon-14 dating 54.42 *dating*

carbonaceous 410.10 *powered*

carbonaceous chondrite 53.20 *meteor*

carbonate 57 *Types of Compounds*, 57.26 *react*, 388.26 *aerate*

carbonated 388.21 *gassy*

carbonated water 351.6 *soft drink*, 389.2 *drinking water*

carbonation 57 *Types of Chemical Reaction*

carbon copy 110.4 *duplicate*, 118.2 *copy*, 118.5 *duplicate*, 545.5 *copy*, 547.2 *reproduction*

carbon-copy 176.5 *twin*, 183.7 *replica*

carbon dating 188.5 *dating*

carbon dioxide 57 *Common Chemical Compounds*, 631.9 *pollution*

carbon dioxide laser 56.26 *laser*

carbon fibre 63.25 *construction material*, 604.1 *materials*

carbonic 57.34 *elemental*

carboniferous 57.34 *elemental*, 410.10 *powered*

Carboniferous 54 *Geological Time Intervals*

Carboniferous period 200.3 *geological period*

carbonize 408.15 *burn*

carbon monoxide 57 *Common Chemical Compounds*, 631.8 *poison*

car bonnet 293.12 *protective covering*

carbon paper 604.3 *paper*

carbon steel 57 *Alloys*

carbon tetrachloride 57 *Common Chemical Compounds*

carbonyl 57 *Types of Compounds*

carbonyl chloride 631.10 *warfare*

car-boot sale 727.2 *disposal of property*, 739.4 *sale*, 740.10 *bazaar*, 752.2 *bargain*, 754.7 *discounter*

carborundum 57 *Common Chemical Compounds*

Carborundum 380.12 *sharpener*

carboxylic acid 57 *Types of Compounds*, 57.8 *acid*, 58.7 *fat*

carbromal 62 *Medication*

---

carbuncle 54 *Gemstones*, 43.3 *building*, 316.2 *bulge*, 624.15 *ulcer*, 790.3 *ugly place*, 793.2 *pimple*, 793.3 *blot on the landscape*

carburation 33.6 *motor racing terms*

carburettor 71 *Motor Vehicle Parts*

carburization 57 *Types of Chemical Reaction*

carburize 57.26 *react*

carcajou 77 *Placental Mammals*

carcass 397.11 *dead person*, 680.16 *bomb*

carcerulus 86.2 *botanical fruit*

carcinogen 631.8 *poison*

carcinogenic 624.23 *diseased*

carcinoma 227.3 *growth*, 624.3 *symptom*, 624.12 *cancer*

carcinomatoid 624.23 *diseased*

card 74.5 *navigation*, 168.10 *eccentric*, 326.10 *transferred thing*, 376.9 *smoother*, 401.2 *male*, 544.3 *means of identification*, 545.6 *record book*, 604.3 *paper*

cardamom 45 *Herbs and Spices*

Cardano 52 *Scientists*

cardboard 548.6 *misrepresented*, 604.3 *paper*

cardboard box 258.6 *box*

card-carrier 665.5 *member*

carded 376.1 *smooth*

card game 42.1 *game*, 42.3 *card game terms*

card game terms 42

cardholder 346.7 *entrant*, 665.5 *member*, 745.6 *debtor*

cardiac 60.22 *medical*, 290.10 *visceral*

cardiac arrest 624.10 *cardiovascular disease*

cardiac disease 624.4 *disease*, 624.10 *cardiovascular disease*

cardiac glycoside 58.3 *carbohydrate*

cardiac hypertrophy 624.10 *cardiovascular disease*

cardiac surgery 630.12 *surgery*

cardialgia 624.8 *indigestion*

cardie 295.11 *jacket*, 295.13 *sweater*

Cardiff 93 *Cities*, 93.4 *British cities*

cardigan 295.11 *jacket*, 295.13 *sweater*

Cardigan 93 *Cities*

cardinal 78 *Birds*, 7.8 *priest*, 52.7 *natural number*, 52.75 *equal*, 126.5 *superior*, 126.14 *best*, 169.8 *odd*, 450.7 *red thing*, 611.5 *important*, 617.2 *best*, 688.10 *person of authority*, 696.6 *religious leader*, 696.12 *masterful*

cardinal flower 84 *Flowers and Flowering Plants*

cardinal number 52.7 *natural number*, 169.2 *kind of number*

cardinal point 332.4 *compass point*, 611.3 *chief thing*

cardinal red 450.1 *red*

cardinal's cap 544.5 *uniform*

cardinal's hat 7.11 *vestment*

cardinalship 7.9 *priesthood*

cardinal virtues 863.2 *virtues*

card index 171.2 *table*

cardioid 52.40 *curve*

cardiologist 60.13 *medical specialist*

cardiology 60.3 *medical specialty*

cardiomyotomy 60 *Surgical Operations*

cardiophobia 777 *Phobias by Name*

cardiopulmonary disease 624.4 *disease*

cardiovascular 290.10 *visceral*

cardiovascular disease 624, 624.4 *disease*

carditis 624.10 *cardiovascular disease*

cardoon 45 *Vegetables*

cardphone 534.9 *telephone*

card punch 65.7 *peripheral*

cards 517, 42.3 *card game terms*

carrot fly 69.12 *pests and diseases*
carrot-top 450.7 *red thing*
carroty 450.3 *red-haired*, 451.1 *orange*
carry 29.3 *golf shots*, 52.91 *add*, 70.4 *transport*, 130.6 *add*, 245.10 *reproduce oneself*, 263.7 *reach*, 284.11 *support*, 284.14 *give moral support*, 326.2 *transportation*, 326.12 *transport*, 420.16 *be heard*, 611.7 *be important*, 652.15 *conduct*, 670.9 *attack successfully*, 682.9 *be victorious*, 739.1 *sell*, 875.10 *drug oneself*
carry a card 665.13 *be a member*
carry across 356.11 *cross*
carry a date 185.17 *date*, 192.15 *chronologize*
carryall 71 Carriages and Carts, **71** Motor Vehicles, 258.8 *bag*, 258.9 *baggage*
carry all before one 660.17 *do easily*, 682.10 *defeat heavily*
carry a point 682.11 *overmaster*
carry a protest sign 543.9 *use signs*
carry a suggestion 527.14 *imply*
carry away 244.9 *demolish*, 821.28 *win the love of*
carry clout 233.8 *influence*
carry coals to Newcastle 610.5 *be superfluous*, 614.9 *waste effort*
carry conviction 537.33 *seem lifelike*
carrycot 71.8 *baby carriage*
carry forward 750.7 *account*
carrying 31.8 *hockey*, 420.14 *hearable*, 423.6 *loud*, 427.6 *resonant*, 875.2 *drug pushing*
carrying force 230.12 *operative*
carrying out 719.3 *performance*
carrying the puck 31.3 *ice hockey*
carrying through 684.1 *completion*
carrying too far 541.3 *extravagance*
carry into effect 232.4 *be an instrument*
Carry Nation 876.6 *moralist*
carry no weight 612.11 *be unimportant*
carry off 326.15 *take away*, 682.6 *be successful*, 734.10 *take away*, 736.13 *kidnap*
carry off the laurels 126.8 *be superior*
carry on 590, 159.14 *continue*, 219.4 *protract*, 219.8 *go on*, 396.16 *live*, 575.7 *maintain*, 640.4 *act*, 652.13 *behave badly*, 652.14 *behave towards*, 653.1 *manage*, 828.11 *be angry*, 864.16 *be wicked*
carry on a conversation 568.9 *converse*
carry on a vendetta 666.6 *argue*
carry on bag 258.9 *baggage*
carry one's bat 219.4 *protract*
carry oneself 652.11 *conduct oneself*
carry one's liquor 873.3 *be sober*
carry one's point 228.9 *motivate*, 586.15 *persuade*
carry on regardless 780.5 *be rash*
carry on the line 245.13 *propagate*
carry out 144.4 *complete*, 232.4 *be an instrument*, 243.10 *produce*, 597.1 *undertake*, 608.4 *suffice*, 619.5 *perfect*, 640.4 *act*, 652.14 *behave towards*, 684.4 *complete*, 719.6 *perform*
carry out goals 653.1 *manage*
carry out one's duty 847.16 *do one's duty*
carry out orders 694.5 *obey*
carry out to the full 144.4 *complete*
carry out to the letter 144.4 *complete*, 719.6 *perform*
carry over 130.6 *add*, 750.7 *account*
carry-over 130.3 *additional item*, 132.3 *difference*
carry sail 74.9 *navigate*

carry shoulder high 812.18 *salute*, 849.18 *show respect*
carry the can 852.24 *be open to criticism*
carry the day 126.8 *be superior*, 682.9 *be victorious*
carry the puck 31.9 *play hockey*
carry through 142.10, 144.4 *complete*, 232.4 *be an instrument*, 574.6 *be resolute*, 575.9 *endure*, 594.7 *develop*, 640.4 *act*, 652.14 *behave towards*, 684.4 *complete*
carry to 263.7 *reach*
carry too far 541.9 *be extravagant*
carry weight 233.8 *influence*, 369.12 *be heavy*, 611.7 *be important*
carry with one 228.9 *motivate*, 586.15 *persuade*
carsick 349.30 *vomiting*
carsickness 71.21 *miscellaneous motoring terms*
car silencer 293.12 *protective covering*, 424.2 *sound reducer*
Carson 48 Writers, **93** Cities
cart 71 Carriages and Carts, **258**, 70.4 *transport*, 71.7 *handcart*, 71.20 *truck*, 326.12 *transport*
cartage 70.1 *transport*, 326.2 *transportation*
Cartagena 93 Cities
cart away 326.15 *take away*
carte 171.4 *bill*
carte blanche 698.6 *liberality*, 708.1 *permission*
cartel 13.6 *economic factors*, 116.2 *alliance*, 302.2 *limiting factor*, 664.7 *association*, 665.1 *party*, 699.2 *economic restraint*, 715.3 *alliance*
car telephone 534.9 *telephone*
carter 326.7 *transferor*
Cartesian 4.11 *follower of a doctrine*, 4.14 *of a philosophy*
Cartesian coordinates 52 Named Concepts, 52.33 *coordinates*
Cartesianism 4.7 *school of thought*
Cartesian space 52.35 *space*
cart grease 386.4 *lubricant*
Carthaginian 7 Non-Christian Religions
car theft 736.3 *theft*
car thief 16.40 *lawbreaker*
carthorse 32.2 *thoroughbred*, 71.9 *animal transport*
Carthusian 7 Members of Religious Orders, **32** Breeds of Horse and Pony
cartilage 371.4 *solid body*, 373.7 *hard substance*, 378.7 *tough thing*, 382.7 *skeleton*
cartilaginous 373.1, 378.3 *hard*
cartilaginous fish 80.2 *fish*
carting 70.1 *transport*
cartogram 547.7 *map*
cartographer 268.9 *measurer*, 547.4 *person who makes a representation*
cartographic 268.12 *metrical*
cartographical 250.8 *locational*
cartographically 250.13 *topographically*, 268.17 *measurably*
cartography 250.5 *topography*, 268.1 *measurement*, 299.4, 547.7 *map*
cartomancy 517.2 *divination*
carton 120.3 *container*, 258.6 *box*, 413.7 *tobacco*
cartoon 50.9 *drawing*, 50.20 *draw*, 299.1 *outline*, 547.2 *reproduction*, 771.4 *entertainment*, 799.2 *act of derision*
cartoonist 50.16 *artist*, 547.4 *person who makes a representation*, 771.6 *humorist*, 799.3 *derider*
cartouche 43 Architectural Decoration, 680.13 *ammunition*
car transporter 71 Motor Vehicles
cartridge 65.7 *peripheral*, 66.9 *film*, 680.13 *ammunition*
cartridge belt 680.4 *arsenal*, 680.13 *ammunition*
cartridge case 680.13 *ammunition*

cartridge clip 680.13 *ammunition*
cartridge paper 604.3 *paper*
cartulary 545.6 *record book*
cartwheel 30.8 *floor exercises*, 287.1 *inversion*, 287.3 *invert*, 364.6 *rotator*
cartwheel penny 741.10 *former British money*
Cartwright 52 Scientists
Caruso 49 Musicians and Composers
carve 47.18 *work wood*, 50.21 *sculpt*, 136.9 *separate*, 243.10 *produce*, 306.7 *form*, 380.16 *use a sharp tool*, 545.14 *inscribe*, 547.11 *paint*, 796.8 *fashion*, 819.15 *be hospitable*
carved 41.12 *ski*, 47.15 *woodcrafted*, 50.28 *sculpted*, 306.9 *formed*
carved turn 41.4 *skiing technique*
carvel-built 36.10 *sailing*
carvel-built hull 36.3 *parts of a sailing boat*
carve letters 5.47 *word*
carve one's way 336.7 *make one's way*
carver 47.13 *carpenter*, 50.17 *sculptor*, 380.10 *knife*, 646.2 *artisan*
Carver 52 Scientists
carver chair 47.2 *chair*
carvery 350.15 *eating place*
carve up 136.9 *separate*, 406.11 *inflict pain*, 731.4 *allot*
carving 47.8 *woodwork*, 50.12 *sculpture*
carving knife 350.16 *eating utensil*, 380.10 *knife*
carvone 58.20 *terpene*
car wash 621.7 *washer*
Cary 48 Writers
caryatid 43 Architectural Decoration, 50.12 *sculpture*, 284.2 *supporting part*
caryopsis 86.2 *botanical fruit*
casaba 86 Fruits
Casablanca 93 Cities
Casals 49 Musicians and Composers
Casa Milá 43 Noted Buildings
Casanova 340.6 *charmer*, 401.7 *libertine*, 539.15 *deceiver*, 540.15 *false person*, 586.13 *tempter*, 821.9 *lover*, 877.8 *immoral man*
cascade 96.2 *channel*, 96.7 *flow*, 360.3 *downflow*, 360.13 *drip*
Cascade Range 95.4 *US mountains*
cascara 62 Medication, **85** Tree Products, 630.6 *purgative*
case 5, 5.30 *syntax*, 16.5 *litigation*, 43.9 *miscellaneous architectural features*, 60.18 *patient*, 106.2 *occurrence*, 120.3 *container*, 168.10 *eccentric*, 226.6 *undertaking*, 251.2 *circumstances*, 258.6 *box*, 293.13 *casing*, 293.25 *wrap*, 354.5 *inset*, 472.2 *issue*, 473.3 *line of argument*, 624.19 *sick person*, 626.4 *infectious person*, 856.1 *accusation*
case dismissed 16.42 *acquittal*
case for decision 16.5 *litigation*
case for the prosecution 856.1 *accusation*
case grammar 5.29 *grammar*
case-harden 57.30 *extract*, 237.8 *strengthen*, 373.9 *harden*, 378.11 *make tough*, 584.18 *habituate*
case-hardened 373.3 *hardened*, 373.4 *mentally hard*, 378.2 *toughened*, 378.5 *mentally tough*, 577.3 *unyielding*
case history 3.5 *chronicle*, 60.6 *health care*, 483.6 *documentation*, 545.1 *record*, 560.1 *description*
casein 58.9 *protein*
case law 16.7 *legal trial*
casemate 671.11 *fortification*
casement 43.9 *miscellaneous architectural features*, 382.4 *framework*

case notes 3.5 *chronicle*
case of need 593.3 *needfulness*
case record 16.7 *legal trial*
case shot 680.14 *historical ammunition*
cash 741, 223.3 *something in exchange*, 228.5 *positive stimulus*, 602.4 *financial resources*, 741.26 *bank*, 742.6 *money*
cash account 750.1 *accounts*
cash a cheque 741.26 *bank*
cash and carry 740.8 *store*, 754.7 *discounter*
cash-and-carry 738.14 *buying*
cashbook 545.6 *record book*
cash book 750.5 *account book*
cash box 741.20 *money store*
cash budget 750.2 *budgeting*
cash cow 742.5 *wealth*
cash crop 68.12 *crop*, 721.6 *yield*
cash desk 741.21 *till*
cash dispenser 741.21 *till*
cash down 746
cashew 86 Nuts
cash flow 602.4 *financial resources*, 606.1 *provision*, 741.6 *funds*
cash-flow crisis 747.5 *insolvency*
cash-flow problems 687.2 *economic adversity*
cashier 349.3 *disbar*, 362.4 *debase*, 704.7 *terminate*, 741.17 *financier*, 741.18 *treasurer*, 746.5 *payer*, 750.6 *accountant*, 879.1 *punish*
cashiering 349.18 *dismissal*
cashier's cheque 741.14 *paper money*
Cashinahua 1 Peoples
cash in on 210.5 *take the opportunity*, 599.3 *exploit*, 627.2 *get better*, 721.14 *profit*
cash in one's chips 397.15 *die*
cashmere 67 Natural Fabrics, 288.4 *textile*
cashmere sweater 295.13 *sweater*
cash on delivery 534.2 *postal communication*, 738.14 *buying*, 746.1 *payment*, 746.21 *cash down*
cash payment 746.1 *payment*
cash-poor 722.17 *unprofitable*
cash prize 878.2 *prize*
cash purchase 738.7 *purchasing*
cash register 52.67 *calculator*, 170.5 *computer*, 545.10 *recording instrument*, 741.21 *till*
cash supplies 741.6 *funds*
cash transaction 14.1, 741.7 *finance*
casing 293, 293.1 *covering*
cask 258.11 *vessel*
casket 258.6 *box*, 399.4 *funeral objects*
Caslon type 5.15 *type style*
Caspian 32 Breeds of Horse and Pony, **97** Oceans and Seas
Caspian Sea 94.5 *other major lakes*
casque 671.7 *armour*
Cassandra 516.5 *predictor*, 517.8 *oracle*, 636.4 *warner*, 776.3 *hopeless person*
cassation 484.2 *reversal*
cassava 45 Vegetables
Cassegrain telescope 53.24 *telescope*
casserole 45.6 *kitchen equipment*, 45.32 *meat dish*, 45.55 *cook*, 258.15 *pot*
casseroling 45.8 *cooking technique*
cassette 65.7 *peripheral*, 66.9 *film*, 420.9 *audio device*, 545.7 *recording*
cassette recorder 420.9 *audio device*, 545.10 *recording instrument*
cassette tape 545.7 *recording*
cassia 85 Trees and Shrubs, 413.5 *herbs*
cassia bark 85 Tree Products
cassimere 67 Natural Fabrics
Cassiopeia 53 The Constellations, **53** The Constellations
Cassirer 4 Philosophers
cassis 351.7 *alcoholic drink*

catboat 74 Ships and Boats, **74** Sailing Ships and Boats
catbrier 84 Flowers and Flowering Plants
cat burglar 736.8 *thief*
catcall 429, 429, 423.8 *be loud,* 430.3 *shrillness,* 430.6 *be shrill,* 431.7 *cry of disapproval,* 431.14 *hiss,* 543.3 *gesture,* 713.3 *gesture of protest,* 850.6, 850.25 *taunt,* 852.9 *show of disapproval,* 852.23 *show disapproval*
catcalling 429, 850.15 *taunting*
catch 42 Children's Games and Party Games, **715,** 19.12 *special team,* 20.1 *angling,* 27.11 *dismissal,* 27.19 *dismiss,* 35.3 *rugby play,* 36.4 *rowing,* 36.16 *row,* 80.7 *fishing,* 135.5 *joint,* 137.8 *fastening,* 218.8 *cause to cease,* 323.3 *restrainer,* 325.9 *make motionless,* 385.15 *grind,* 407.11 *touch,* 420.15 *hear,* 477.4 *difficult question,* 496.2 *detect,* 496.7 *detection,* 539.8, 539.28 *trick,* 539.33 *snare,* 547.9 *represent,* 590.2 *chase,* 590.11 *hunt,* 611.4 *bigwig,* 620.7 *defect,* 624.24 *be unhealthy,* 635.1, 635.3 *trap,* 657.2 *stratagem,* 659.8 *snag,* 661.2 *obstacle,* 674.8 *wrestling,* 721.3 *acquisition,* 721.11 *acquire,* 726.7 *detain,* 734.5 *takings,* 782.5 *object of desire,* 821.9 *lover,* 821.28 *win the love of*
catch-22 106.4 *difficult circumstances,* 477.4 *difficult question,* 635.1 *trap,* 659.5 *predicament,* 661.2 *obstacle,* 776.2 *hopeless situation*
catchable 626.6 *contagious*
catch a crab 36.16 *row,* 656.7 *be clumsy*
catch a fly 22.7 *play baseball*
catch a glimpse of 435.12 *see,* 496.1 *discover*
catch a likeness 547.9 *represent,* 560.14 *describe*
catch-all 164.3 *nonspecificness*
catch an infection 624.24 *be unhealthy*
catch a packet 659.21 *get into trouble*
catch-as-catch can 596.5 *attempt*
catch-as-catch-can 26.15 *wrestling,* 583.1 *improvised,* 589.8 *chance,* 595.3 *without preparation,* 674.8 *wrestling,* 698.12 *unconditional*
catch-as-catch-can wrestling 26.5 *wrestling*
catch at 572.13 *be willing*
catch a Tartar 656.5 *be unskilful*
catch a whiff of 416.7 *smell*
catch cold 409.10 *be cold*
catch crop 68.12 *crop*
catcher 22.2 *baseball player*
catcher's box 22.1 *baseball*
catcher's glove 22.3 *baseball equipment*
catcher's mask 22.3 *baseball equipment*
catcher's mitt 22.3 *baseball equipment*
catcher's sign 22.4 *pitching terms*
catch exactly 547.9 *represent*
catch fire 408.15 *burn*
catch fish 20.7 *angle*
catch in a run-down 22.7 *play baseball*
catching 233.12 *appealing,* 496.7 *detection,* 626.6 *contagious*
catching a crab 36.4 *rowing*
catching glove 31.3 *ice hockey*
catching the eye 526.14 *manifest*
catch in the act 496.2 *detect*
catch it 659.21 *get into trouble,* 879.6 *be punished*
catch it in the neck 879.6 *be punished*
catchment area 54.8 *drainage*
catch napping 208.9 *prepare,* 514.9 *surprise*
catch off-guard 514.9 *surprise*

catch on 233.10 *be a prevailing influence,* 496.3 *find out,* 501.11 *know,* 522.6 *understand,* 584.17 *become a habit,* 787.6 *understand*
catch one's death 397.16 *meet one's fate*
catch oneself doing 584.18 *habituate*
catch one's eye 318.8 *protrude*
catch out 514.9 *surprise,* 635.3 *trap*
catchpenny 612.4 *trivial,* 754.9 *cheap*
catchphrase 5.21 *catchword,* 426.7 *repeated word,* 505.1 *maxim*
catch points 72.3 *rail*
catchpoll 16.11 *British law officer*
catch red-handed 496.2 *detect,* 514.9 *surprise*
catch sight of 435.12 *see*
catch some Zs 649.2 *take it easy*
catch the bug 228.8 *be motivated,* 586.18 *be persuaded*
catch the drift of 522.6 *understand*
catch the eye 435.19 *be visible*
catch the eye of 467.13 *attract attention*
catch the wind 487.10 *attempt the impossible*
catch unawares 514.9 *surprise,* 595.12 *be unprepared,* 635.3 *trap*
catch up 329.6 *accelerate,* 648.2 *make haste,* 648.8 *hurry up*
catch-waist 41.13 *ice-skating*
catch-waist camel spin 41.6 *ice-skating*
catch with one's pants down 514.9 *surprise*
catchword 5, 426.7 *repeated word,* 505.1 *maxim,* 543.6 *word*
catchy 49.30 *harmonic,* 433.6 *melodious*
cat-cracking reforming 57.22 *industrial chemistry*
catechism 477.3 *questionnaire,* 497.2 *religious belief*
catechismic 477.13 *problematic*
catechization 6.1 *education*
catechize 477.17 *question*
catecholamine 58.16 *hormone*
catechu 85 Tree Products
catechumen 7.3 *religious person,* 220.6 *convert*
categorial 152, 148.6 *component,* 150.11 *grouped,* 163.10 *classificatory,* 535.16 *definite,* 554.3 *emphatic,* 847.12 *obligatory*
categorial imperative 4.9 *philosophical problem*
categorially 4.24 *philosophically,* 163.16 *taxonomically,* 535.23 *affirmatively*
categorialness 535.8 *definiteness*
categorial proposition 4.8 *philosophical term*
categorization 152, 150.2 *grouping,* 163.1 *classification,* 544.1 *identification*
categorize 152, 150.19 *systematize,* 163.13 *class,* 544.10 *identify*
categorize as 146.6 *subsume*
categorized 152, 150.11 *grouped,* 163.12 *classed,* 544.12 *identified*
category 152, 105.1 *state,* 124.4 *average,* 143.1 *part,* 148.2 *piece,* 150.4 *position,* 163.2 *class*
category mistake 4.9 *philosophical problem*
catenary 52.40 *curve,* 159.9 *consecutive,* 360.2 *sinkage*
catenary arch 43.5 *arch*
catenate 159.15 *concatenate*
catenation 159.2 *consecution*
cater 350.25 *provide food,* 606.5 *provision*
cateran 679.9 *guerrilla*
cater-cornered 286.4 *oblique,* 286.8 *obliquely*
catered 606.8 *provisional*
catered affair 606.1 *provision*

caterer 606, 45.2 *cook,* 350.20 *food provider*
cater for 662.25 *serve,* 808.11 *pander to*
catering 45.1 *cookery,* 606.1 *provision,* 606.7 *provisioning*
caterpillar 71 Motor Vehicles, 69.12 *pests and diseases,* 81.6 *worm,* 82.5 *larva,* 206.4 *young animal*
cater to 739.1 *sell*
caterwaul 423.8 *be loud,* 431.1 *cry,* 431.10 *cry out,* 432.4 *cry*
caterwauling 434.2 *dissonant noise,* 821.15 *love item*
catfish 80 Fishes, 45.17 *freshwater fish*
cat-fit 828.4 *anger*
cat flea 82 Insects, 82.3 *pest*
cat food 350.8 *animal food*
Catharism 7 Christian Movements
catharsis 48.3 *aspect of fiction,* 51.9 *tragedy,* 61.3 *psychiatric treatment,* 349.21 *removal,* 353.2 *defecation,* 629.11 *recuperation*
cathartic 51.38 *tragic,* 62.4 *drug type,* 62.17 *stimulating,* 134.4 *purgative,* 349.29 *expulsive,* 353.25 *faecal,* 630.6 *purgative,* 630.17 *remedial*
cathartically 349.32 *expulsively*
cathead 74 Parts of a Ship
cathectic energy 61.28 *cathexis*
cathection 61.28 *cathexis*
cathedral 10.11 *place of worship,* 243.8 *construction*
cathedral city 93.4 *British cities,* 249.10 *urban area*
Catherine 710.7 *martyr*
Catherine wheel 364.6 *rotator,* 439.8 *fire*
catheterization 630.13 *therapy*
catheterize 134.10, 621.15 *purify*
cathexis 61
cathode 56.43 *electrical conduction,* 57.19 *electrochemistry,* 64.5 *electrolytic conduction,* 64.20 *electron tube,* 235.7 *electrical power*
cathode-ray tube 235.7 *electrical power,* 534.21 *television*
cathodic 57.42 *electrochemical*
cat hole 74 Parts of a Ship
catholic 164.15 *general,* 482.1 *undiscriminating,* 482.4 *wholesale*
Catholic 7.5 *Christian*
catholicism 164.2 *catholicity*
Catholicism 7 Christian Movements
catholicity 164, 271.4 *breadth,* 482.6 *lack of discrimination*
catholicize 164.23 *generalize*
catholicon 62.3 *drug,* 630.1 *remedy*
Catholic Roman 7.16 *denominational*
catholic tastes 482.6 *lack of discrimination*
cathouse 864.8 *wicked place,* 877.6 *brothel*
cation 56.66 *ion,* 64.5 *electrolytic conduction*
catkin 84.4 *flower head*
catlike 77.28 *carnivorous*
cat lover 76.10 *animal welfarist*
catmint 84 Flowers and Flowering Plants
catnap 643.9, 643.13 *sleep,* 649.1 *ease*
cat-nap 404.2 *unconsciousness*
cat-o'-nine-tails 879.14 *instrument of punishment*
cats 161 Collective Names by Animal, **777** Phobias by Topic
cat's concert 434.2 *dissonant noise*
cat's cradle 288.2 *braid*
Catseye 543.5 *indicator*
cat's eye 435.8 *reflection*
cat's-eye 54 Gemstones
cat's home 634.3 *animal shelter*
cat show 526.6 *display*
cat's meow 617.8 *exceller*
cat's nine lives 396.5 *life cycle*

cat's-paw 74 Knots, 232.3 *assistant,* 539.22 *dupe,* 808.3 *sycophant*
cat's pyjamas 617.8 *exceller*
cat's-tail 87 Grasses
catsuit 295.10 *suit*
catsup 45.15 *sauce*
cat's whisker 534.18 *radio*
cat's whiskers 617.8 *exceller*
Cattell's Infant Intelligence Scale 61.6 *intelligence test*
cattery 256.12 *stall,* 634.3 *animal shelter*
cattiness 832.4 *bitterness*
cattish 77.28 *carnivorous,* 832.14 *hostile*
cattle 77 Placental Mammals, **161** Collective Names by Animal, 68.8 *livestock*
cattle breeder 68.15 *agriculturist*
cattle cake 350.8 *animal food*
cattleman 68.15 *agriculturist*
cattle raiding 736.1 *stealing*
cattle ranch 68.6 *farm*
cattle rustler 736.8 *thief*
cattle rustling 736.1 *stealing*
cattle thief 736.8 *thief*
cat-train 71.10 *sled*
catty 77.28 *carnivorous,* 832.14 *hostile,* 854.16 *defamatory*
Catullus 48 Poets
catwalk 63.21, 327.9 *bridge*
Cauac 8 Deities
Caucasian 5 Languages and Groups of Languages, 1.6 *race,* 1.13 *racial,* 446.1 *white*
Caucasoid 1.13 *racial*
Caucasoid race 1.6 *race*
Caucasus 53 Mountains, **95** Mountains, 95.6 *other major mountains and ranges,* 275.4 *mountain range*
Cauchy 52 Scientists
Cauchy Fault 53 Rills and Valleys
Cauchy sequence 52 Named Concepts
caucus 161.5 *conference,* 665.3 *political grouping*
caudal 304.4 *rear*
caudal fin 80.5 *fish anatomy*
caudate 79.7, 79.13 *amphibian*
caudex 83.5 *stem*
caudle 351.7 *alcoholic drink*
caught 821.18 *in love*
caught both ways 633.4 *endangered*
caught in the act 866.5 *guilty*
caught napping 514.6 *surprised,* 595.1 *unprepared*
caught red-handed 866.5 *guilty*
caught unawares 514.6 *surprised,* 595.1 *unprepared*
caught with one's hand in the till 866.5 *guilty*
caught with one's pants down 866.5 *guilty*
caught with one's trousers down 866.5 *guilty*
caul 245.7 *obstetrics*
cauldron 220.4 *medium of conversion,* 258.15 *pot*
caulid 83.5 *stem*
cauliflower 45 Vegetables
cauliflower cheese 45.34 *vegetarian dish*
cauliflower ear 420.4 *ear*
cauliflower-eared 420.12 *eared*
cauline 83.17 *of stems*
caulis 83.5 *stem*
caulk 629.1 *repair*
causal 226, 232, 463, 159.10 *repercussive,* 233.11 *influential,* 473.12 *apologetic*
causal body 11.7 *spirit*
causality 56, 159.4 *repercussion,* 226.1 *cause*
causal law 56.81 *causality*
causally 226, 233.14 *influentially,* 473.20 *apologetically*
causal relationship 518.2 *basis of supposition*
causal theory of perception 4.9 *philosophical problem*
causation 226.1 *cause,* 586.11 *motive*
causative 226.13 *causal*

causatively 226.14 *causally*
cause 226, 16.5 *litigation,* 99.20 *bring into being,* 156.23 *inaugurate,* 216.8 *cause change,* 226.9 *be the cause of,* 228.1 *motive,* 228.9 *motivate,* 230.3 *business,* 230.9 *take action,* 232.1 *instrumentality,* 232.4 *be an instrument,* 233 *influence,* 243.10 *produce,* 463.4 *explanation,* 473.5 *plea,* 520.12, 570.13 *intend,* 571.14 *necessitate,* 586.11 *motive,* 586.15 *persuade,* 642.4 *energy,* 855.2 *defence*
Cause 226
cause a death 687.11 *cause adversity*
cause adversity 687
cause an accident 687.11 *cause adversity*
cause anarchy 689.4 *be anarchic,* 713.8 *cause mischief,* 720.10 *violate the law*
cause and effect 56.81 *causality,* 159.4 *repercussion*
cause a sensation 403.13 *arouse sensation*
cause a shambles 244.10 *lay waste*
cause a traffic jam 661.9 *block*
cause célèbre 786.4 *wonder*
cause change 216
cause chaos 141.4 *deconstruct,* 307.4 *disorder*
caused 227, 155.18 *consequent,* 228.12 *motivated,* 473.12 *apologetic*
caused by 227.10 *caused*
cause desire 782
cause difficulties 659
cause disbelief 498
cause discontent 515.7 *thwart*
cause dislike 785, 788.6 *be boring*
cause disorder 689.4 *be anarchic,* 713.8 *cause mischief*
cause doubt 523.7 *be unintelligible,* 786.10 *be wonderful*
cause for alarm 633.6 *danger signal*
cause friction 661.8 *hinder*
cause grief 687.11 *cause adversity*
cause hate 822
cause joy 762
causeless 589
cause list 16.7 *legal trial*
cause loathing 822.16 *cause hate*
cause mischief 713
cause no problems 617.10 *do good*
cause not to exist 100
cause of action 586.11 *motive*
cause offence 818.7 *be discourteous,* 820.13 *antagonize*
cause of offence 828
cause opposition 231.3 *counteract*
cause panic 636.5 *warn*
cause resentment 829.8 *make irascible*
causerie 568.2 *chat*
cause the downfall of 244.9 *demolish*
cause to abdicate 689.4 *be anarchic*
cause to adhere 138
cause to cease 218
cause to disappear 458
cause to flow 96
cause to know 501
cause trouble 659, 635.3 *trap,* 661.9 *block,* 687.11 *cause adversity,* 713.8 *cause mischief*
causeway 63.21 *bridge,* 137.5, 327.3 *road*
causey 327.4 *road surface*
causing death 398.1 *killing*
caustic 56.31 *lens element,* 62.4 *drug type,* 408.10 *on fire,* 820.6 *hostile,* 828.15 *resentful,* 832.14 *hostile,* 854.16 *defamatory*
caustically 820.15 *aggressively,* 828.17 *resentfully,* 832.20 *malevolently*
causticity 832.4 *bitterness*
causticness 832.4 *bitterness*
caustic reply 832.4 *bitterness*

cauterization 630.12 *surgery*
cauterize 408.15 *burn,* 630.20 *doctor*
cauterizing 408.9 *hot*
caution 781, 781, 328.12 *hesitation,* 469.1 *carefulness,* 491.10 *suspicion,* 516.4 *prudence,* 517.5 *omen,* 528.7 *advice,* 587.1 *dissuade,* 587.6 *dissuasion,* 636.1 *warning,* 636.5 *warn,* 654.1 *advice,* 654.5 *advise,* 657.1 *cunning*
Caution 781
cautionary 517.13 *predicting,* 528.16 *informative,* 587.9 *dissuasive,* 636.8 *warning,* 654.7 *advising*
cautionary person 587
cautionary tale 560.3 *narration*
cautioned 636.9 *warned*
cautioner 636.4 *warner*
caution light 543.4 *signal*
cautious 573, 781, 312.4 *traditional,* 328.6 *hesitant,* 516.6 *foreseeing,* 566.3 *sparing with words,* 636.9 *warned,* 657.4 *cunning*
cautiously 781, 328.16 *slowly,* 469.12 *carefully,* 516.8 *foresightedly*
cautiousness 328.12 *hesitation,* 781.1 *caution*
cautious person 781
Cauvery 96 Rivers
Cavafy 48 Poets
cavalcade 159.8 *procession*
Cavalcanti 48 Poets
cavalier 32.15 *horse person,* 180.7 *attendant,* 679.20 *cavalryman,* 818.5 *discourteous,* 821.9 *lover*
Cavalier Poets 48 Literary Groups and Movements
cavalry 679
cavalry commander 17.5 *military staff*
cavalry horse 32.3 *warhorse*
cavalryman 679, 32.15 *horse person*
cavalry regiment 32.15 *horse person,* 679.16 *army unit,* 679.19 *cavalry*
cavalry sword 680.8 *sharp weapon*
Cavan 92 Counties, **93** Cities
cavatate 36.18 *windsurf*
cavatation 36.7 *windsurfing*
cavatina 433.2 *song*
cave 34.5 *rock face,* 256.13 *lair,* 290.1 *interior,* 317.2 *concave land,* 322.5 *hole,* 360.10 *droop,* 636.10 *look out*
caveat 636.1 *warning*
caveator 636.4 *warner*
cave dweller 202.7 *ancient people,* 400.3 *uncivilized human*
cave-dweller 200.6 *people of the past,* 816.6 *unsocial person*
cave fish 80 Fishes
cave in 136.9 *separate,* 262.6 *become smaller,* 317.6 *be concave,* 320.10 *close,* 360.10 *droop,* 673.4 *succumb*
cave-in 262.1 *contraction*
caveman 200.6 *people of the past,* 202.7 *ancient people,* 241.4 *violent person or animal,* 400.3 *uncivilized human,* 401.6 *macho man*
Cavendish 52 Scientists
Cavendish's experiment 56 Named Laws
cave painting 50 Non-Western Art, 3.11 *relic,* 50.8 *painting*
cavern 317.2 *concave land,* 322.5 *hole*
cavernous 248.13 *spacious,* 277.8 *deep,* 317.5 *concave,* 322.11 *holed*
cavernously 322, 317.8 *concavely*
cavernousness 277.1 *depth*
cavesson 32.14 *horse-riding terms*
cavetto 43 Architectural Decoration
caviar 45.16 *fish dish,* 80.9 *fish product*

cavicorn 77.33 *ungulate*
cavil 473.14 *discuss,* 474.2 *sophism,* 474.13 *quibble,* 766.7 *be dissatisfied,* 852.4 *disagreement,* 852.18 *find fault*
caviller 474.6 *sophist,* 500.5 *dissenter*
cavilling 474.4, 474.9 *quibbling,* 852.6, 852.28 *fault-finding*
caving 18 Sporting Activities, 360.7 *tunnelling*
caving in 673.1 *submission*
cavity 317, 265.2 *crack,* 277.4 *deep thing,* 322.1 *opening,* 362.14 *depression*
cavort 46.15 *dance*
cavy 77 Placental Mammals
caw 430.2 *hoarseness,* 430.5 *sound hoarse,* 432.2 *bird song,* 432.5 *sing*
cawing 430.8 *hoarse*
cay 98.2 *island*
cayenne 413.5 *herbs*
cayenne pepper 45 Herbs and Spices
Cayley 52 Scientists, **52** Scientists
cayman 79 Reptiles, 79.5 *crocodilian*
Cayuga 5 Languages and Groups of Languages, **68** Breeds of Fowl
cayuse 32.1 *horse*
CBL 65.1 *computing*
CB radio 534.20 *radio broadcasting*
CBS 534.24 *television broadcasting*
C clef 49.20 *key*
CD 545.7 *recording*
CD-ROM 65.6 *memory,* 65.7 *peripheral*
CdS meter 66.18 *exposure time*
CE 185.29 *one day*
ceanothus 84 Flowers and Flowering Plants
cease 157, 218, 160.2 *cessation,* 160.12 *discontinue,* 323.9 *close down,* 325.8 *be motionless,* 458.1 *disappear,* 598.2 *withdraw,* 600.6 *stop using,* 641.4 *not act*
ceased 160.9 *discontinued*
ceasefire 218.3 *pause*
cease fire 218.9 *pause*
cease-fire 209.3 *delayed action,* 675.1 *peace,* 677.1 *pacification*
ceaseless 159.11 *continuous,* 183.14 *recurrent,* 184.3 *eternal,* 190.10 *continuing forever*
ceaseless energy 642.4 *energy*
ceaselessly 159.19 *continuously,* 575.14 *continually*
ceaselessness 159.5 *continuity,* 575.3 *constancy*
cease publication 458.1 *disappear*
cease resistance 673.3 *submit*
cease to be 397.15 *die,* 458.1 *disappear*
cease to exist 100, 458.1 *disappear*
cease to live 397.15 *die*
cease to see 438.7 *become invisible*
cease trading 218.7 *stop working*
cease work 345.2 *withdraw*
ceasing 157.2, 160.2 *cessation,* 218.1 *cessation*
Cebú 98 Islands
cecropia moth 82 Insects
cedar 85 Trees and Shrubs
cedar of Lebanon 85 Trees and Shrubs
Cedar Rapids 93 Cities
cede 598.1 *relinquish,* 717.4 *compromise,* 727.9 *dispose of,* 728.3 *transfer property,* 729.5 *give*
cede to 127.9 *yield to*
cedilla 5.36 *accent,* 543.7 *punctuation*
Ceefax 534.25 *broadcast material*
ceil 227.9 *roof*
ceilidh 46.1 *dancing,* 161.10 *dance,* 665.7 *social gathering*

ceiling 73.5 *flight,* 120.2 *certain amount,* 275.8 *high thing,* 279.3 *architectural summit,* 282.3 *flat thing,* 293.7 *overhead covering,* 302.2 *limiting factor,* 751.3 *fee*
ceiling light 439.6 *electric light*
ceiling plaster 293.7 *overhead covering*
ceiling rose 439.6 *electric light*
Cela 48 Writers
celadon 453.1 *green*
celadonite 453.10 *green pigment*
Celan 48 Poets
celandine 84 Flowers and Flowering Plants
Celanese 67 Synthetic Fibres and Fabrics
cele 400.7 *person*
celebrant 9.5, 10.17 *worshipper*
celebrate 812, 813, 9.7 *worship,* 10.18 *perform rites,* 10.19 *offer worship,* 511.14 *commemorate,* 611.8 *make important,* 762.6 *enjoy,* 773.5 *rejoice,* 817.12 *greet*
celebrate a birthday 214.9 *commemorate*
celebrate a marriage 823.16 *join in marriage*
celebrate an anniversary 214.9 *commemorate*
celebrate a victory 682.9 *be victorious*
celebrate Christmas 203.6 *spend the season,* 214.9 *commemorate*
celebrate communion 710.15 *offer worship*
celebrated 501.10 *known,* 532.20 *well-known,* 804.5 *entitled*
celebrate mass 710.15 *offer worship,* 719.5 *observe religious ceremony*
celebrate the yuletide 203.6 *spend the season*
celebrating 773.1 *rejoicing,* 812.1 *celebration*
celebration 812, 9.1 *worship,* 10.3 *rite of worship,* 10.16 *religious festival,* 161.9 *social gathering,* 682.1 *success,* 762.2 *fun,* 773.1 *rejoicing,* 813.3 *formal occasion*
Celebration 812
celebrative 812
celebrator 773.4 *rejoicer*
celebratory 10.21 *ritualistic,* 511.10 *memorial,* 665.11 *social,* 762.4 *happy,* 773.9 *rejoicing,* 811.26 *ritualistic,* 812.10 *celebrative*
celebrity 9.4 *idolized person,* 126.6 *paragon,* 400.7 *person,* 617.8 *exceller,* 682.1 *success,* 682.4 *successful person,* 800.2 *person of repute,* 804.1 *right*
celeriac 45 Vegetables
celerity 329.8 *speed,* 648.4 *haste*
celery 45 Vegetables
celery fly 69.12 *pests and diseases*
celery pine 85 Trees and Shrubs
celery salt 45 Herbs and Spices
celery soup 45.13 *soup*
celeste 49 Musical Instruments
celestial 8.6 *angel,* 8.14 *heavenly,* 53.36 *astronomical,* 368.8 *nonmaterial*
celestial body 53.10 *star*
celestial equator 53.5 *celestial sphere*
celestial latitude 53.5 *celestial sphere*
celestial longitude 53.5 *celestial sphere*
celestially 8.19 *divinely,* 53.39 *astronomically,* 368.13 *metaphysically*
celestial mechanics 53.1 *astronomy*
celestial navigation 74.5 *navigation*
celestial poles 53.5 *celestial sphere*
celestial sphere 53
celestite 54 Minerals

cephalin 58.6 *lipid*
Cephalochordata 81.2 *protochordate*
cephalochordate 81.2 *protochordate*, 81.16 *invertebrate*
cephaloglycin 62 *Medication*
cephalometer 268.8 *meter*
cephalometric 268.16 *micrometric*
cephalometry 268.2 *micrometry*
cephalopod 76.5 *aquatic animal*, 81.5 *mollusc*
Cephalopoda 81.5 *mollusc*
cephalopodan 81.19 *molluscan*
cephalopodic 81.19 *molluscan*
cephalopodous 81.19 *molluscan*
cephaloridine 62 *Medication*
cephalosporin 62 *Medication*
cephalothin sodium 62 *Medication*
Cepheids 53 *Meteor Showers*
Cepheid variable 53.12 *variable star*
Cepheus 53 *The Constellations*, 53 *The Constellations*
ceramic 44, 50.25 *sculptural*, 57.7 *chemical compound*
ceramic capacitor 64.17 *resistor*
ceramic decoration 44.1 *ceramics*
ceramic object 44
ceramic process 44
ceramics 44, 50.1 *art*
Ceramics 44
ceramic tiles 293.8 *wall covering*
ceramic ware 44.1 *ceramics*
ceramic workshop 44
ceramist 44.7 *potter*
cerargyrite 54 *Minerals*
cerate 630.9 *balm*
cerated 395.11 *oily*
Cerberus 76.7 *legendary beast*, 632.3 *protector*
cercaria 81.13 *invertebrate larva*
Cerdonianism 7 *Christian Movements*
cereal 69.16 *horticultural*, 83.2 *plant*, 87.4 *cereal grass*
cereal bowl 258.16 *crockery*
cereal crop 68.12 *crop*
cereal grass 87, 87.1 *grass*
cereals 83.3 *seed plant*
cerebral 459.9 *mental*, 461.8 *thoughtful*, 471.11 *ideational*
cerebral death 397.1 *death*
cerebrally 459.14 *mentally*
cerebral palsy 624.17 *nervous disorder*
cerebrate 461.12 *think*
cerebration 461.1 *thought*
cerebroside 58.6 *lipid*
cerebrum 459.7 *brain*
cerecloth 399.4 *funeral objects*
cerements 399.4 *funeral objects*
ceremonial 811, 812, 10.1 *ritual*, 10.21 *ritualistic*, 306.11 *formal*, 719.2 *religious observance*, 811.26 *ritualistic*, 812.2 *commemoration*, 812.11 *commemorative*, 813.3 *formal occasion*, 813.6 *formal*, 813.8 *ceremonious*
ceremonial attire 7.11 *vestment*
ceremonial function 812.3 *ceremony*
ceremonialism 10.2 *ritualism*, 813.2 *formalism*
ceremonially 306.14 *conventionally*, 811.42 *ritualistically*
ceremonial troops 679, 679.14 *armed forces*
ceremonies 817.3 *courtesies*
ceremonious 813, 811.22 *majestic*, 813.6 *formal*, 817.8 *good-mannered*, 849.8 *respectful*
ceremoniously 811.38 *majestically*, 813.12 *formally*, 817.15 *genteelly*
ceremoniousness 813.1 *formality*
ceremony 812, 10.1 *ritual*, 306.5 *formality*, 526.10 *manifestation*, 584.4 *custom*, 719.2 *religious observance*, 813.3 *formal occasion*
cereous 395.11 *oily*
Ceres 8 *Deities*, 53 *Minor Planets*, 246.4 *fertility cult*
ceresin 395.8 *fat*
ceric 57.34 *elemental*
Ceridwen 8 *Deities*

cerise 450.1 *red*
cerium 57 *Chemical Elements*
Cermait 8 *Deities*
CERN 235.8 *nuclear power*
cerography 50.15 *engraving*
ceroplastic 50.25 *sculptural*
ceroplastics 50.12 *sculpture*
cerous 57.34 *elemental*
cerrusite 57 *Common Metal Ores*
certain 490, 120.6 *quantitative*, 175.6 *plural*, 199.12 *predictable*, 225.11 *determined*, 475.12 *demonstrable*, 480.10 *verified*, 483.8 *evidential*, 490.2 *convinced*, 497.11 *believing*, 501.10 *known*, 513.5 *expecting*, 513.7 *expected*, 522.1 *intelligible*, 526.14 *manifest*, 554.3 *emphatic*, 571.12 *inevitable*, 632.5 *safe*, 682.13 *successful*, 688.15 *true*, 714.13 *guaranteeing*, 714.15 *future*, 718.7 *guaranteed*
certain amount 120
certain cure 630.1 *remedy*
certainly 101, 490, 475.22 *demonstrably*, 480.12 *assuredly*, 483.14 *as evidence*, 490.25 *inevitably*, 537.37 *authentically*, 571.19 *necessarily*, 688.25 *authentically*, 714.16 *as promised*, 714.18 *potentially*, 772.12 *indeed*
certainly not 536.16 *no*
certainness 490.10 *conviction*
certain proportion 143.1 *part*
certainty 490, 32.7 *horseracing*, 52.62 *probability*, 475.5 *demonstrability*, 483.2 *proof*, 490.10 *conviction*, 490.16 *inevitability*, 497.1 *belief*, 513.1 *expectation*, 516.3 *foresight*, 522.9 *intelligibility*, 535.8 *definiteness*, 571.5 *inevitability*, 589.5 *good chance*, 632.1 *safety*
Certainty 490
certifiable 480.8 *verifiable*, 510.11 *insane*
certifiably 480.11 *verifiably*
certificate 545, 116.8 *permit*, 485.3 *qualifications*, 528.3 *document*, 544.3 *means of identification*, 708.2 *permit*, 718.2 *promise*, 741.14 *paper money*, 878.2 *prize*
certificated 116.18 *permitting*
certificate of exemption 848.4 *licence*
Certificate of Prevocational Education 485 *Educational Qualifications*
Certificate of Secondary Education 485 *Educational Qualifications*
Certificate of the Business and Technician Education Council 485 *Educational Qualifications*
certification 116.7 *consent*, 480.4 *verification*, 485.3 *qualifications*, 490.9 *yes*, 535.1 *affirmation*, 535.4, 537.7 *confirmation*
certified 480.10 *verified*, 485.10 *authorized*, 490.1 *certain*, 510.13 *mentally ill*, 535.13 *supported*, 537.20 *proved*, 714.13 *guaranteeing*, 718.7 *guaranteed*
certified cheque 741.14 *paper money*
certifier 535.9 *affirmer*
certify 510, 718, 101.12 *establish reality*, 116.28 *consent*, 480.1 *verify*, 483.12 *prove*, 485.13 *qualify*, 490.21 *make certain*, 528.11 *inform*, 535.17 *affirm*, 535.19 *confirm*, 537.30 *prove true*, 714.8 *guarantee*
certiorari 16.6 *legal process*
certitude 490.10 *conviction*
Certosina work 47.9 *decorative woodwork*
cerulean 454.1 *blue*
cerulean blue 454.5 *blueness*
cerussite 54 *Minerals*
Cervantes 48 *Writers*
cervical 245.16 *reproductive*
cervical cancer 624.12 *cancer*

cervical smear 60.7 *diagnosis*
cervid 77.15 *hoofed mammal*, 77.33 *ungulate*
Cervidae 77.15 *hoofed mammal*
cervine 77.33 *ungulate*
cervix 245.8 *organs of reproduction*
České Budějovice 93 *Cities*
cespitose 89.10 *of fungi*
cess 751.7 *tax*
cessation 157, 160, 218, 323.1 *closure*, 325.1 *motionlessness*, 458.4 *disappearance*, 546.3 *obliteration*, 639.2 *deliverance*, 643.5 *inactivity*, 675.1 *peace*, 677.1 *pacification*, 704.2 *termination*
Cessation 218
cession 598.3 *relinquishment*, 673.1 *submission*, 727.1 *disposal*
cesspit 419.2 *something that makes an unpleasant smell*, 727.5 *wasteyard*, 727.8 *sink*
cesspool 419.2 *something that makes an unpleasant smell*, 605.4 *storage*, 614.6 *refuse*, 727.5 *wasteyard*, 727.8 *sink*
Cestoda 81 *Worms*, 81.6 *worm*
cestode 81.6 *worm*
cestoid 81.20 *wormlike*
Cetacea 77.11 *marine mammal*
cetacean 77, 76.5 *aquatic animal*, 77.11 *marine mammal*
cetaceous 77.29 *cetacean*
cetrimide 62 *Medication*
Cetus 53 *The Constellations*
Cévennes 95 *Mountains*
Ceylon moss 90 *Algae*
Ceylon tea 351.3 *tea*
CFC 55.8 *atmosphere*, 388.11 *vaporizer*, 631.9 *pollution*
C grade 124.6 *mediocrity*
chabazite 54 *Minerals*
chablis 351.9 *wine*
cha-cha-cha 46.2 *dance*
Chacmool 8 *Deities*
chaconne 433.3 *melodiousness*
Chad 91 *Countries*, 94 *Lakes*, 94.5 *other major lakes*
Chadic 5 *Languages and Groups of Languages*
chador 438.6 *that which makes invisible*
Chadwick 52 *Scientists*
chaetognath 81.6 *worm*
Chaetognatha 81.6 *worm*
chaetophobia 777 *Phobias by Name*
chafe 385.3 *grinding*, 385.15 *grind*, 406.9 *feel pain*, 408.14 *be hot*, 828.9 *offend*, 828.11 *be angry*
chafer 82 *Insects*, 82.3 *pest*
chaff 87.4 *cereal grass*, 132.2 *residue*, 293.13 *casing*, 612.8 *trifle*, 614.6 *refuse*, 850.6 *taunt*
chaffer 737.3 *bargain*
chaffinch 78 *Birds*
chaffing 850.15 *taunting*
chafing 385.3 *grinding*, 385.11 *rough*
Chagas' disease 624.7 *tropical disease*
chagrin 515.1 *disappointment*, 850.8 *indignity*
chagrined 515.9 *disappointed*, 806.3 *humbled*
Chahuru 8 *Deities*
chain 71 *Motor Vehicle Parts*, 75 *General Units*, 57.21 *polymer*, 95.1 *mountain*, 137.4 *means of connection*, 137.7 *tackle*, 137.12 *bind*, 155.2 *series*, 159.2 *consecution*, 159.15 *concatenate*, 195.1 *succession*, 268.6 *measuring instrument*, 275.4 *mountain range*, 323.3 *restrainer*, 323.11, 661.10 *restrain*, 699.12 *gag*, 792.6 *jewellery*, 879.14 *instrument of punishment*
Chain 52 *Scientists*
chain armour 671.7 *armour*
chained 137.16 *bound*, 225.10 *stabilized*, 661.14 *blocked*

chain gang 19.2 *football player*, 879.7 *punishment*
chain-gang member 702.5 *prisoner*
chainguard 71.11 *bicycle part*
chain harrows 68.10 *farm tool*
chaining 159.2 *consecution*
chain letter 712.3 *solicitation*
chain-letter 712.11 *begging*
chain locker 74 *Parts of a Ship*
chainmail 632.4 *safety device*
chain mail 671.7 *armour*, 680.1 *weapon*
chain of office 544.4 *insignia*
chainplates 36.3 *parts of a sailing boat*
chain printer 65.7 *peripheral*
chain reaction 56.72 *nuclear fission*, 57.14 *chemical reaction*, 159.4 *repercussion*, 235.8 *nuclear power*
chains 19.4 *stadium*, 661.4 *restraint*, 699.5 *means of restraint*
chain saw 85.7 *timber production*, 603.1 *tool*
chain saw mortiser 47.11 *woodworking tool*
chain shot 680.14 *historical ammunition*
chain-smoke 413.14 *smoke*
chain-smoking 413.8 *smoking*
chain store 740.8 *store*
chain together 135.10 *link*
chain up 699.12 *gag*
chair 47, 6.6 *instructorship*, 242.4 *moderate*, 284.4 *rest*, 361.3 *promote*, 492.3 *place of judgment*, 653.2 *direct*, 653.13 *director*, 696.5 *company leader*, 812.18 *salute*
chair cover 293.12 *protective covering*, 621.11 *cleaning cloth*
chair leg 47
chair lift 41.1 *skiing*, 327.12 *cableway*, 359.8 *lift*, 361.10 *elevator*
chairman 233.5 *influential person*, 653.13 *director*, 696.5 *company leader*
chairman of the board 696.5 *company leader*
Chairman of the Federal Reserve System 741.18 *treasurer*
chairmanship 653.4 *directorship*, 688.5 *position of authority*
chair of Saint Peter 10.14 *sacred object*
chairperson 242.2 *moderator*, 653.13 *director*, 696.5 *company leader*
chair socket 20.1 *angling*
chairwoman 696.5 *company leader*
chaise 71 *Carriages and Carts*
chaise longue 47.2 *chair*, 47.6 *bed*
Chaitanya Vaishnava 7 *Non-Christian Religions*
chakay 49 *Musical Instruments*
chalaza 78.15 *eggs*
chalcanthite 54 *Minerals*
chalcedony 54 *Gemstones*
chalcocite 54 *Minerals*, 57 *Common Metal Ores*
chalcography 50.15 *engraving*
Chalcolithic 202.15 *primal*
Chalcolithic period 200.4 *prehistoric age*
chalconide 57.6 *chemical element*
chalcopyrite 54 *Minerals*, 57 *Common Metal Ores*
Chaldean 7 *Non-Christian Religions*
Chaldee 5 *Languages and Groups of Languages*
chalet 256.5 *house*, 725.1 *property*
chalice 10.14 *sacred object*, 258.13 *drinking vessel*
chalk 54 *Common Rocks*, 24.1 *billiards*, 34.4 *climbing equipment*, 50.11 *artist's materials*, 50.20 *draw*, 384.5 *powder*, 446.9 *white thing*, 544.10 *identify*
chalk and cheese 111.2 *opposites*
chalk a stick 24.8 *play billiards*

chalk bag 34.4 *climbing equipment*
chalkily 446.14 *whitely*
chalkiness 384.1 *powderiness*, 446.7 *whiteness*
chalklike 384.16 *powdery*
chalk mark 25.2 *grip*
chalk out 543.9 *use signs*, 592.10 *plan out*
chalk up 544.10 *identify*
chalky 54, 384.16 *powdery*, 446.1 *white*
challenge 4.4 *philosophical investigation*, 4.20 *philosophize*, 117.4 *disagreement*, 117.14 *disagree*, 228.9 *motivate*, 303.10 *be in front*, 473.2 *logical argument*, 473.14 *discuss*, 477.1 *question*, 477.2 *questioning*, 477.21 *confuse*, 498.8 *disbelieve*, 536.3 *rebuttal*, 536.8 *rebut*, 597.1 *undertake*, 663.2 *objection*, 663.15 *object*, 666.7 *pick a fight*, 668.2 *disobedience*, 668.3 *act of defiance*, 668.5 *defy*, 668.6 *be insubordinate*, 669.1 *resistance*, 669.6 *resist*, 670.8 *counterattack*, 674.11 *contend*, 713.1, 713.9 *protest*
challenged 228.12 *motivated*, 472.8 *problematic*, 477.16 *questioned*, 536.12 *rejected*, 669.10 *resistant*, 671.29 *defending*
challenge fate 633.9 *face danger*
challenger 18.3 *sportsman* , 26.4 *boxer*, 237.5 *athlete*, 536.6 *negativist*, 596.7 *attempter*, 668.4 *defiant person*, 674.10 *contender*
Challenger 53.30 *spacecraft*, 679.21 *armoured cavalry*
challenging 117.10 *disagreeing*, 228.11 *motivational*, 472.8 *problematic*, 473.10 *arguable*, 477.13 *problematic*, 536.13 *rebutting*, 586.19 *persuasive*, 659.10 *difficult*, 659.12 *problematic*, 663.20 *discordant*, 668.8 *defying*, 669.10 *resistant*, 670.24 *counterattacking*, 674.14 *contending*, 713.9 *protesting*
challengingly 472.13 *problematically*, 477.24 *questionably*, 536.15 *negatively*, 668.10 *in defiance*, 669.14 *resistingly*
challis 67 *Natural Fabrics*
chalone 352.2 *secreted substance*
chalukah 10.3 *rite of worship*
chalumeau 49 *Musical Instruments*
Cham 5 *Languages and Groups of Languages*
chamber 256.7 *room*, 353.14 *toilet*, 605.4 *storage*, 634.1 *refuge*
chamber group 49.26 *musical group*
chamberlain 697.6 *domestic servant*
Chamberlain 52 *Scientists*
chambermaid 697.6 *domestic servant*
chamber music 49.3 *classical music*
chamber of commerce 13.7 *corporation*, 737.5 *commercial trade*
chamber of commerce member 737, 13.9 *economist*
chamber orchestra 49.26 *musical group*, 140.3 *assembly*
chamber pot 258.15 *pot*, 353.14, 727.7 *toilet*
chambray 67 *Natural Fabrics*
chambré 408.9 *hot*
Chambre des Députés 653.10 *legislative body*
chameleon 79 *Reptiles*, 79.2 *lizard*, 224.3 *changeable thing*, 456.5 *variegated thing*, 576.15 *indecisive person*
Chameleon 53 *The Constellations*, **53** *The Constellations*
chameleonic 456.6 *variegated*
chamois 77 *Placental Mammals*, 299.14 *animal covering*, 376.9 *smoother*, 604.1 *materials*, 621.11 *cleaning cloth*

Chamorro 5 *Languages and Groups of Languages*
champ 26.4 *boxer*, 350.21 *eat*, 679.3 *athlete*, 682.5 *victorious person*, 696.10 *expert*
champac 85 *Trees and Shrubs*
champagne 351.9 *wine*, 452.1 *yellow*
champagne flute 258.13 *drinking vessel*
champaign 87.2 *grassland*
Champaign 93 *Cities*
champ at the bit 828.11 *be angry*
champers 351.9 *wine*
champerty 16.39 *crime*
champignon 45.33 *vegetable*
champing 350.1 *eating*
champing at the bit 572.2 *eager*
champion 21.3 *athlete*, 26.4 *boxer*, 26.14 *combat*, 126.6 *paragon*, 126.14 *best*, 237.5 *athlete*, 284.8 *supporter*, 284.14 *give moral support*, 535.9 *affirmer*, 617.2 *best*, 617.8 *exceller*, 619.1 *perfect*, 632.3 *protector*, 632.9 *protect*, 655.4 *skilled person*, 662.23 *advise*, 671.13 *defender*, 671.22 *plead for*, 679.3 *athlete*, 682.5 *victorious person*, 696.10 *expert*, 696.13 *excellent*, 851.7 *advocate*, 851.13 *support*, 855.5 *vindicator*, 855.8 *justify*, 861.16 *superior person*
Champion 32.1 *horse*
championing 851.19 *supporting*
champion of lost causes 857.3 *honourable person*
championship 35, 284.6 *moral support*, 662.9 *patronage*, 674.2 *contest*, 682.3 *successful thing*, 851.1 *approval*
championship fight 26.2 *boxing*
Champlain 94 *Lakes*
champlevé 44 *Types of Ceramics*
Chamuel 8.6 *angel*
chance 229, 229, 488, 589, 589, 589, 52.62 *probability*, 210.2 *opportunity*, 224.3 *changeable thing*, 229.6 *motiveless*, 322.10 *opportunity*, 477.20 *doubt*, 479.13 *invent*, 486.1 *possibility*, 488.1 *probability*, 489.3 *unexpected*, 489.5 *unexpectedness*, 491.16 *capriciousness*, 491.22 *risk*, 589.12 *take a chance*, 710.2 *tentative offer*
Chance 589
chanced 479.10 *tested*
chance discovery 229.3 *coincidence*, 589.2 *luck*
chance encounter 229.3 *coincidence*, 589.2 *luck*
chance happening 229.3 *coincidence*
chance hit 229.3 *coincidence*, 589.2 *luck*
chance in a million 589.6 *poor chance*
chance it 229.4 *chance*, 589.12 *take a chance*
chancel 10.12 *church*, 43.10 *church architecture*
chancellor 6.4 *educator*, 653.13 *director*, 688.10 *person of authority*, 692.6 *person in command*, 696.3 *leader*, 696.9 *educational leader*
chancellor governor general 12.7 *governor*
Chancellor of the Exchequer 741.18 *treasurer*
chance meal 350.12 *meal*
chance meeting 229.3 *coincidence*, 589.2 *luck*
chance one's arm 229.4 *chance*, 589.12 *take a chance*, 596.3 *tackle*, 780.5 *be rash*
Chancery Division 16.20 *British court*
chance upon 589, 229.5 *happen by chance*, 250.11 *find*
chancing upon 250.3 *locating*
chancre 624.14 *venereal disease*

chancy 229.6 *motiveless*, 477.14 *questionable*, 479.9 *original*, 491.8 *capricious*, 589.8 *chance*, 633.1 *dangerous*
chandelier 283.3 *suspended object*
chandelle 73.5 *flight*
Chandigarh 93 *Cities*
Chandler 48 *Writers*
Chandrasekhar 52 *Scientists*
Chanel No. 5 418.2 *fragrant thing*
chang 49 *Musical Instruments*
Changchun 93 *Cities*
change 216, 233, 491, 741, 41.13 *ice-skating*, 49.6 *campanology*, 109.1 *interchange*, 109.7 *reciprocate*, 115.6 *differentiate*, 123.5 *be unequal*, 201.5 *fresh start*, 201.20 *make new*, 215.1 *irregularity*, 215.6 *be irregular*, 216.7 *be changed*, 220.1 *conversion*, 222.1 *substitution*, 222.6 *give a substitute*, 223.1 *exchange*, 223.3 *something in exchange*, 224.11 *be changeable*, 295.34 *wear*, 296.14 *undress*, 324.13 *be in motion*, 324.15 *walk*, 485.5 *modification*, 485.15 *modify*, 579.5 *be capricious*, 629.2 *refurbish*, 740.5 *stock market*, 741.26 *bank*
Change 216
changeability 113.1 *diversity*, 224.1 *changeableness*, 579.2 *caprice*
changeable 216, 224, 576, 55.46 *seasonal*, 113.5 *diverse*, 215.4 *irregular*, 220.15 *convertible*, 223.6 *in exchange*, 456.6 *variegated*, 491.8, 579.1 *capricious*
changeableness 224, 215.1 *irregularity*, 220.1 *conversion*, 366.3 *turbulence*, 491.16 *capriciousness*, 576.12 *inconstancy*, 579.2 *caprice*
Changeableness 224
changeable person 224
changeable thing 224
changeably 216, 224, 113.10 *diversely*, 215.8 *irregularly*, 223.8 *in exchange*, 491.27 *capriciously*
change address 250.10 *settle*
change allegiances 598.2 *withdraw*
change back 216.8 *cause change*, 221.7 *restore*
change bowler 27.4 *team*
change countenance 445.5 *lose colour*
change course 74.9 *navigate*, 216.7 *be changed*, 335.2 *divert*
changed 216, 109.4 *reciprocal*, 201.14 *renewed*, 220.13 *converted*, 222.8 *substituted*, 223.7 *exchanged*, 485.11 *modified*
changed beyond recognition 220.13 *converted*
changed grip 30.5 *horizontal bar*
change direction 343, 216.7 *be changed*, 324.13 *be in motion*, 335.1 *deviate*
change directions 215.6 *be irregular*
changed meaning 520.4 *type of meaning*
change down 33.10 *be on the track*
changed person 220.6 *convert*
change for 222.6 *give a substitute*
change for better or for worse 233.9 *change*
change for the better 216.1 *change*, 216.7 *be changed*, 216.8 *cause change*, 627.1 *improve*, 627.5 *improvement*
change for the worse 216.1 *change*, 216.7 *be changed*, 216.8 *cause change*
change front 578.2 *equivocate*
changeful 106.7 *circumstantial*, 215.4 *irregular*, 216.11, 224.13 *changeable*
changefully 106.16 *relatively*
changefulness 224.1 *changeableness*
change gradually 121

change hands 728.3 *transfer property*, 728.4 *be transferred*, 739.2 *be sold*
change into 220.7 *convert into*
changeless 186, 110.17 *regular*, 183.13 *monotonous*, 217.7 *permanent*, 225.9 *stable*
changelessly 110.20 *regularly*, 217.9 *permanently*
changelessness 110.6 *regularity*, 186.1 *timelessness*, 217.1 *permanence*, 225.1 *stability*
changeling 11.11 *ghost*, 222.2 *substitute person*, 224.10 *person who is exchanged*
change loop 41.6 *ice-skating*
changement 46.9 *ballet steps*
change money 223.5 *exchange*
change of allegiance 578.7 *apostasy*
change of belief 216.2 *change of mind*
change of clothes 216.4 *exchange*
change of course 216.1 *change*
change of direction 216.1 *change*, 578.6 *equivocation*
change of hands 728.1 *transfer of property*
change of heart 216.2 *change of mind*, 867.1 *penitence*
change of life 207.4 *middle age*, 247.1 *infertility*
change of mind 216, 578.6 *equivocation*, 579.3 *whim*
change of mood 578.6 *equivocation*
change of opinion 216.2 *change of mind*
change of ownership 728.1 *transfer of property*
change-of-pace 22.4 *pitching terms*
change of place 216.1 *change*
change of position 216.1 *change*, 324.1 *motion*
change of purpose 578.6 *equivocation*
change of scene 651.6 *refresher*
change of scenery 216.1 *change*
change of stance 216.2 *change of mind*
change one's address 324.15 *walk*
change one's allegiance 578.3 *apostatize*
change one's belief 216.7 *be changed*
change one's clothes 216.10 *exchange*, 295.34 *wear*, 296.14 *undress*
change one's colours 578.3 *apostatize*
change one's expression 216.7 *be changed*
change one's heart 216.7 *be changed*
change one's mind 216.7 *be changed*, 224.12 *be irresolute*, 484.8 *reverse*, 536.9 *renounce*, 576.6 *hesitate*, 578.2 *equivocate*, 598.1 *relinquish*
change one's opinion 216.7 *be changed*
change one's stance 216.7 *be changed*
change one's tune 216.7 *be changed*, 484.8 *reverse*, 578.2 *equivocate*
change one's ways 220.10 *converted*
changeover 21.1 *track events*, 195.4 *accession*, 728.1 *transfer of property*
change over 728.3 *transfer property*
change ownership 728.4 *be transferred*
change place 324.13 *be in motion*
change places 216.7 *be changed*, 223.5 *exchange*
change position 216.7 *be changed*, 324.13 *be in motion*
change purse 741.20 *money store*
changer 216
change ringing 49.6 *campanology*

charlatanism 474.5 *hypocrisy,* 502.2 *half-knowledge,* 540.4 *spuriousness,* 656.8 *unskilfulness*
charlatanistic 540.28 *spurious*
charlatanry 540.4 *spuriousness*
Charles' law 56 Named Laws
Charleston 93 Cities, 46.2, 46.15 *dance*
Charley 32.8 *hunting*
Charlie 534 Phonetic Alphabet
charlock 84 Flowers and Flowering Plants
charlotte 45.35 *dessert*
Charlotte 93 Cities
charlotte russe 45.35 *dessert*
Charlottetown 93 Cities
Charlton 18 Sporting Personalities
charm 161 Collective Names for Birds and Animals, 10.14 *sacred object,* 11.5 *spell,* 11.6 *talisman,* 11.21 *bewitch,* 56.78 *quantum,* 78.13 *assemblage of birds,* 228.2 *inducement,* 228.5 *positive stimulus,* 228.9 *motivate,* 233.2 *occult influence,* 340.4 *allurement,* 340.5 *lure,* 340.11 *attract,* 376.13 *smooth over,* 405.9 *give pleasure,* 474.12 *deceive,* 549.2 *stylishness,* 586.3 *incentive,* 637.2 *preserver,* 762.8 *cause joy,* 763.6 *pleasantness,* 763.13 *give pleasure,* 789.1 *gorgeousness,* 821.4 *lovability,* 821.28 *win the love of,* 827.4 *malediction,* 827.7 *wish ill,* 853.9 *blarney*
charmed 11.19 *bewitched,* 228.12 *motivated,* 821.19 *enamoured*
charmed circle 617.7 *elite,* 665.1 *party,* 699.1 *restraint*
charmed life 632.1 *safety*
charmer 340, 11.4 *witch,* 474.6 *sophist,* 617.8 *exceller,* 763.11 *pleasant person,* 789.4 *attractive male,* 853.6 *flatterer*
charming 11.15 *witchlike,* 228.11 *motivational,* 233.12 *appealing,* 340.9 *attractive,* 405.6 *pleasant,* 586.19 *persuasive,* 762.5 *delightful,* 763.1 *pleasant,* 789.6 *personable,* 815.15 *sociable,* 821.22 *lovable*
charming fellow 815.6 *social person*
charmingly 228.14, 233.14 *influentially,* 340.14 *attractively,* 815.18 *sociably,* 821.30 *lovingly*
charmlessly 818.9 *discourteously*
charms 821.4 *lovability*
charnel house 397.8 *after death,* 399.1 *burial*
Charollais Half-bred 32 Breeds of Horse and Pony, **68** Breeds of Cattle
Charon 74.8 *boatman*
Charpentier 49 Musicians and Composers
charred 447.3 *blackened,* 449.2 *browned*
Charro 32 Breeds of Horse and Pony
Charron 4 Philosophers
chart 152, 49.18 *written music,* 52.32 *graph,* 54.65 *map,* 74.5 *navigation,* 74.9 *navigate,* 171.1, 171.8 *list,* 250.2 *exact location,* 257.5 *divisions,* 299.1, 299.5 *outline,* 547.2 *reproduction,* 547.7 *map,* 547.11 *paint,* 592.5 *map*
chart-busting 126.14 *best*
charted 171.11 *listed,* 257.12 *itemized*
charter 16.1 *the law,* 116.8, 116.29 *permit,* 166.2 *canon,* 545.2 *certificate,* 688.21 *grant authority,* 703.3 *authority,* 703.8 *authorize,* 708.2 *permit,* 845.6 *bond,* 848.4 *licence*
chartered 116.18 *permitting,* 688.16 *authorized,* 708.7 *permitted*
chartered accountant 750.6 *accountant*
chartered engineer 63.2 *engineer*

Charteris 48 Writers
charter member 665.5 *member*
charting 152.3 *organization,* 171.7 *listing*
chart recorder 268.8 *meter*
Chartres 93 Cities
Chartres Cathedral 43 Noted Buildings
chartreuse 452.1 *yellow,* 453.1 *green*
chart room 74 Parts of a Ship
charts 49.9 *popular music*
chart-topper 126.6 *paragon,* 617.8 *exceller,* 682.3 *successful thing*
chart-topping 126.14, 617.2 *best,* 682.13 *successful*
charwoman 621.12 *cleaner,* 646.1 *worker,* 662.16 *home help,* 697.6 *domestic servant*
chary 573.3, 781.4 *cautious*
charybdis 364.4 *vortex*
Charybdis 96.6 *river flow*
Chasca 8 Deities
chase 590, 590, 40.5 *real tennis,* 50.22 *engrave,* 77.23 *mammal hunting,* 326.14 *bring back,* 329.4 *be swift,* 398.9 *animal killing,* 782.13 *like,* 792.10 *decorate,* 821.26, 826.8 *court*
chase after 326.14 *bring back*
chased 590.17 *pursued*
chase fame and fortune 742.14 *seek riches*
chase off 341.1 *repel*
chase one's own tail 364.8 *rotate,* 642.13 *be busy*
chase one's tail 334.3 *circuit,* 363.6 *orbit*
chase out 349.7 *drive out*
chaser 50.18 *engraver,* 51.6 *scene,* 590.5 *pursuer*
chase the dragon 875.10 *drug oneself*
chasing 50.13 *relief-carving,* 50.15 *engraving,* 590.1 *pursuit,* 590.15 *pursuing*
chasing one's own tail 642.9 *overactivity*
chasing the dragon 875.1 *drug-taking*
chasm 136.3 *separateness,* 265.3 *gulf,* 277.4 *deep thing,* 322.1 *opening,* 635.1 *trap*
chassé 46.3 *ballroom dance steps,* 46.9 *ballet steps*
chassepot 680.10 *historical gun*
chassis 71 Motor Vehicle Parts, **73** Aircraft Parts, 280.2 *foot,* 284.2 *supporting part,* 382.4 *framework*
chaste 134.12 *morally pure,* 174.17 *single,* 446.5 *pure,* 556.1 *simple,* 810.10, 810.10 *bashful,* 825.7 *virginal,* 863.6 *ethical,* 865.5 *innocent,* 869.8 *self-restrained,* 876.9 *pure*
chastely 134.18 *virtuously,* 810.18 *shyly,* 825.12 *celibately,* 863.10 *ethically,* 865.11 *innocently,* 869.11 *with self-restraint*
chasten 242.4 *moderate,* 806.17 *humiliate,* 879.1 *punish*
chastened 242.6 *moderate*
chastener 879.17 *punisher*
chastening 806.6 *humiliating,* 879.7 *punishment*
chastening thought 806.14 *rebuke*
chaste tree 85 Trees and Shrubs
chastise 690.5 *be severe,* 852.20 *censure,* 879.1 *punish*
chastised 852.34 *censured*
chastisement 764.8 *quarrel,* 852.7 *blame,* 879.7 *punishment*
chastisement of the flesh 879.12 *corporal punishment*
chastiser 879.17 *punisher*
chastising 852.30 *censuring*
chastity 134.1 *purity,* 174.6 *singleness,* 446.11 *purity,* 556.4 *simplicity,* 810.3 *bashfulness,* 825.2 *virginity,* 863.2 *virtues,* 865.1 *innocence,* 869.1 *self-restraint,* 876.3 *moral purity*
chasuble 7.11 *vestment*

chat 78 Birds, **568, 568,** 564.1 *faculty of speech,* 565.3 *talk,* 565.7 *be talkative,* 568.1 *conversation*
château 256.4 *official residence*
chateaubriand 45.45 *French dish*
Chateaubriand 48 Writers
chatelaine 653.15 *manager*
chat line 534.12 *public telephone system*
chatoyancy 456.1 *variegation*
chatoyant 54 Gemstones, 456.7 *iridescent*
chat show 534.25 *broadcast material*
chat show guest 477.10 *person questioned*
chat show host 51.27 *entertainer,* 477.9 *questioner*
Chattanooga 93 Cities
chattel 701.5 *subjected person,* 723.4 *possession*
chattels 603.6 *equipment,* 725.4 *possessions*
chatter 426.3, 426.10 *rattle,* 432.5 *sing,* 564.1 *faculty of speech,* 565.3 *talk,* 565.7 *be talkative,* 568.10 *chat*
chatterbox 565.4 *talker*
chatterer 568, 478.10 *answerer,* 564.10 *speaker,* 565.4 *talker*
chattering 161 Collective Names for Birds and Animals, 426.17 *rattling,* 432.3 *bird song,* 432.8 *singing,* 565.3 *talk,* 565.5 *talkative*
chattering teeth 777.1 *fear*
Chatterton 48 Poets
chattily 432.10 *howlingly,* 565.11 *effusively*
chattiness 565.1 *talkativeness*
chatting 568.12 *conversing*
chatty 528.16 *informative,* 530.11 *disclosing,* 565.6 *effusive,* 568.14 *conversational*
Chaucer 48 Poets
Chaucerian stanza 48.10 *verse form*
chaudfroid 45.15 *sauce*
chauffeur 326.7 *transferor,* 646.1 *worker,* 697.4 *personal attendant,* 697.6 *domestic servant*
chauffeur's uniform 544.5 *uniform*
chaulmoogra 85 Trees and Shrubs
Chausson 49 Musicians and Composers
chauvinism 91.4 *nationalism,* 400.11 *nation,* 481.4 *social discrimination,* 493.3 *injustice,* 541.4 *bombast,* 676.5 *bellicosity*
chauvinist 481.7 *bigot,* 481.10 *discriminatory,* 493.5 *misjudging person,* 679.6 *militarist*
chauvinistic 91.16 *national,* 493.8 *unjust,* 679.33 *combative*
chauvinistically 91.19 *nationally,* 481.17 *prejudicially,* 493.14 *unjustly,* 679.41 *aggressively*
chayote 45 Vegetables, **86** Fruits
Chazar 7 Non-Christian Religions
cheap 754, 127.14 *poor,* 495.5 *underestimated,* 612.4 *trivial,* 618.2 *inferior,* 710.17 *offered,* 752.6 *discounted,* 754.15 *cheaply,* 795.7 *vulgar*
cheap as dirt 754.9 *cheap*
cheap at half the price 754.9 *cheap*
cheap at the price 754.9 *cheap*
cheapen 614.8 *make useless,* 628.6 *pervert,* 752.3 *discount,* 754.13 *make cheap,* 795.10 *vulgarize,* 850.27 *desecrate*
cheapening 628.8 *perversion*
cheap item 754
cheap-jack 739.11 *pedlar,* 754.8 *bargain hunter*
cheaply 738, 754, 127.21 *badly,* 710.20 *persuasively*
cheapness 754, 127.4 *poor quality,* 612.7 *triviality,* 618.8 *inferiority,* 751.1 *price,* 754.3 *shoddiness*
Cheapness 754

cheapo 754.9 *cheap*
cheap rate 754.1 *cheapness*
cheap ticket 754.4 *bargain*
cheat 13, 538, 539, 34.9 *mountaineer,* 474.12 *deceive,* 515.8 *be dishonest,* 538.10 *dishonesty,* 538.25 *be dishonest,* 539.10 *fraud,* 539.15 *deceiver,* 539.30 *be fraudulent,* 540.15 *false person,* 540.21 *be fraudulent,* 548.3 *deceiver,* 657.2 *stratagem,* 657.3 *cunning person,* 657.5 *be cunning,* 736.10 *infringer,* 736.11 *dishonest person,* 736.15 *infringe,* 844.21 *do wrong,* 858.10 *be criminal,* 864.9 *wicked person,* 877.17 *be sexually immoral*
cheat death 396.16 *live,* 629.4 *be restored*
cheated 515.10 *deceived,* 538.16 *misinformed,* 539.36 *deceived,* 736.18 *fraudulent*
cheater 539.17 *cheat*
cheating 34.3 *climbing technique,* 515.12 *deceptive,* 538.8 *pretence,* 538.19 *dishonest,* 538.20 *unfaithful,* 539.10 *fraud,* 539.34 *deceiving,* 540.8 *fraud,* 540.31 *fraudulent,* 657.1 *cunning,* 736.6 *illegal borrowing,* 736.7 *dishonesty,* 736.18 *fraudulent,* 877.4 *illicit love*
cheatingly 538.28 *dishonestly*
cheat on 539.30 *be fraudulent*
cheat one's creditors 745.8 *not pay*
check 170, 456, 31.3 *ice hockey,* 31.9 *play hockey,* 42.4 *chess terms,* 116.7 *consent,* 116.27 *fit,* 116.28 *consent,* 218.2 *stop,* 218.8 *cause to cease,* 231.1 *counteraction,* 231.3 *counteract,* 242.1 *moderation,* 242.4 *moderate,* 265.2, 265.5 *crack,* 268.7 *standard,* 302.2 *limiting factor,* 302.7 *limit,* 325.8 *be motionless,* 328.3 *slow down,* 328.12 *hesitation,* 456.11 *variegate,* 469.11 *care for,* 477.17 *question,* 479.1, 479.11 *experiment,* 480.1 *verify,* 480.4 *verification,* 485.6 *specification,* 485.16 *specify,* 490.21 *make certain,* 492.12 *estimate,* 544.10 *identify,* 545.1 *record,* 661.2 *obstacle,* 661.4 *restraint,* 661.10 *restrain,* 663.17 *withstand,* 682.9 *be victorious,* 699.1 *restraint,* 699.8 *restrain,* 709.1, 709.3 *veto,* 722.1 *loss*
checked 456, 31.8 *hockey,* 116.17 *consenting,* 328.7 *delayed,* 479.10 *tested,* 480.10 *verified,* 485.12 *conditional*
checkers 42 Board Games
check in 344.5 *get in*
checking 31.3 *ice hockey,* 31.8 *hockey,* 480.9 *verificatory*
check list 171.1 *list*
checklist 257.5 *divisions,* 477.3 *questionnaire*
checkmate 42.4 *chess terms,* 218.2 *stop,* 218.8 *cause to cease,* 682.3 *successful thing,* 682.9 *be victorious*
check off 136.10 *set apart,* 544.10 *identify*
check one's course 332.8 *orient*
check out 345.2 *withdraw,* 479.11 *experiment,* 492.12 *estimate*
checkpoint 302.4 *boundary marker,* 356.5 *crossing point*
check stock 750.8 *audit*
check-up 60.6 *health care*
Cheddar 45 Cheeses
cheek 807, 303.5 *boldness,* 305.1 *side,* 457.3 *external appearance,* 668.5 *defy,* 807.10 *impudence,* 807.25 *answer back,* 818.2 *bad manners*
cheekbone 382 Bones, 457.3 *external appearance*
cheek by jowl 116.32 *in alliance,* 180.22 *hand in hand,* 267.7 *beside*

cheek-by-jowl 138.9 *adhesive*, 138.11 *cohesively*, 264.5 *near*, 267.5 *juxtaposed*

cheekily 807, 668.9 *defiantly*, 818.10 *rudely*

cheekiness 668.1 *defiance*, 807.10 *impudence*

cheeks 304.2 *rear end*

cheek wall 43.9 *miscellaneous architectural features*

cheeky 807, 668.7 *defiant*, 807.21 *impudent*, 818.6 *bad-mannered*, 850.10 *disrespectful*

cheeky devil 807.12 *impudent person*

cheeky monkey 668.4 *defiant person*

cheep 78.18 *birdsong*, 78.28 *sing*, 432.2 *bird song*, 432.5 *sing*

cheer 431, 769, 769, 350.7 *food*, 405.9 *give pleasure*, 431.3 *cry of praise*, 543.3 *gesture*, 651.1 *refresh*, 762.8 *cause joy*, 769.3 *cheerfulness*, 769.6 *bring cheer*, 773.2 *fanfare*, 773.7 *dance*, 775.4 *comfort*, 775.10 *inspire hope*, 812.18 *salute*, 815.1 *sociability*, 851.16 *acclaim*

cheerer 431.9 *crier*, 851.10 *applauder*

cheer for 431.12 *cheer*

cheerful 769, 762.4 *happy*, 775.11 *hopeful*, 815.15 *sociable*

cheerful compliance 572.6 *willingness*

cheerful giver 729.4 *giver*

cheerfully 769, 572.16 *willingly*, 762.9 *joyfully*, 775.15 *hopefully*, 815.18 *sociably*

cheerfulness 769, 762.1 *happiness*, 775.1 *hope*

Cheerfulness 769

cheerful person 769

cheerily 769.9 *cheerfully*

cheeriness 769.3 *cheerfulness*

cheering 431, 769, 775, 773.9, 812.9 *rejoicing*, 851.5 *acclaim*, 851.20 *acclamatory*

cheerio 345.14 *goodbye*

cheerleader 19.14 *miscellaneous terms*, 431.9 *crier*, 653.14 *leader*, 851.10 *applauder*

cheerless 440.11 *benighted*, 776.4 *hopeless*, 830.6 *sullen*

cheerlessly 830.13 *sullenly*

cheerlessness 770.2 *depression*

cheer on 228.9 *motivate*, 239.3 *invigorate*

cheers! 351

cheers 345.14 *goodbye*, 837.9 *thank you*, 851.5 *acclaim*

cheer up 517.11 *predict*, 769.6 *bring cheer*, 775.9 *be hopeful*, 775.10 *inspire hope*

cheery 769.1 *cheerful*, 773.9 *rejoicing*

cheese 45.9 *dish*, 243.7 *produce*

cheese and biscuits 45.35 *dessert*

cheese board 45.35 *dessert*

cheeseburger 45.11 *sandwich*

cheesecake 45.36 *cake*, 66.4 *portrait*, 402.9 *woman considered as a sex object*, 414.3 *dessert*

cheesecloth 67 Natural Fabrics, 288.4 *textile*

cheese dip 45.15 *sauce*

cheesed off 650.2, 788.5 *bored*

cheese grater 384.13 *grater*

cheese it 349.33 *go away*

cheese one off 788.6 *be boring*

cheeseparing 756.1 *thrift*, 756.4 *thrifty*, 758.1 *mean*, 758.3 *parsimony*

cheese pastry 45.37 *pastry*

cheese sandwich 45.11 *sandwich*

cheese sauce 45.15 *sauce*

cheese straws 45.10 *snack*

cheetah 77 Placental Mammals, 329.12 *swift animal*

chef 45.2 *cook*, 133.7 *person who mixes*, 350.20 *food provider*, 606.4 *caterer*

chef's salad 45.14 *salad*, 45.43 *US dish*

chef's special 165.9 *special*

cheimaphobia 777 Phobias by Name

Chekhov 48 Dramatists

chela 7.7 *monk*

chelate 57.7 *chemical compound*

chelicerate 81.18 *arthropodous*

chelonian 79, 79.11 *reptilian*

chelonid 79.4 *chelonian*

Chelsea bun 45.36 *cake*

Chelsea Pensioner 676.11 *recruit*

Chelsea pensioner 679.11 *former soldier*

Chelsea porcelain 44 Types of Ceramics

Cheltenham 93 Cities

chemiatrist 57.2 *chemist*

chemical 57

chemical bond 57

chemical change 220.1 *conversion*

chemical compound 57

chemical dye 67.6 *dye*

chemical element 57, 367.4 *matter*

chemical energy 56.11, 235.4 *energy*

chemical engineer 57.2 *chemist*

chemical engineering 57.1 *chemistry*, 57.22 *industrial chemistry*, 63.1 *engineering*, 603.5 *mechanics*

chemical fertilizer 246.3 *fertilizer*

chemical formula 57.13 *structure*

chemically 57

chemical messenger 58.16 *hormone*

chemical physics 56.4 *experimental physics*, 57.1 *chemistry*

chemical porcelain 44.9 *industrial ceramics*

chemical reaction 57

chemical toilet 353.13 *lavatory*, 727.7 *toilet*

chemical warfare 631.10 *warfare*, 676.1 *war*, 676.8 *warfare*

chemical weapon 631.10 *warfare*

chemical weathering 54.35 *weathering*

chemin de fer 42 Card Games

chemise 295.18 *underwear*

chemisette 295.14 *neckwear*

chemisorb 57.29, 348.13 *absorb*

chemisorbed 57.43 *absorbed*

chemisorption 57.20 *surface chemistry*, 348.5 *absorption*

chemisorptive 348.17 *absorbent*

chemist 57, 62.2 *pharmacologist*, 133.7 *person who mixes*, 136.8 *person who separates*, 216.6, 224.4 *editor*, 367.3 *materialist*, 630.16 *druggist*

chemistry 57, 220.1 *conversion*, 367.6 *natural science*

Chemistry 57

chemosphere 390.3 *atmospheric layers*

chemotherapy 60.8 *treatment*, 62.1 *pharmacology*, 630.13 *therapy*

chempaduk 86 Fruits

chemurgy 57.1 *chemistry*

Chenab 92 Rivers

chengcheng 49 Musical Instruments

Chengdu 93 Cities

Chénier 48 Poets

chenille 67 Natural Fabrics, 288.4 *textile*

chenopodiaceous 83.16 *taxonomic*

cheongsam 295.7 *frock*

cheque 223.3 *something in exchange*, 741.14 *paper money*

chequebook 545.6 *record book*, 750.5 *account book*

chequebook journalism 533.4 *journalist*

chequebook journalist 528.9 *informant*, 533.11 *newspaper man*

chequer 113.8 *be diverse*, 447.7 *blackness*, 456.2 *check*, 456.11 *variegate*

chequered 113.5 *diverse*, 113.6 *assorted*, 456.8 *checked*

chequered career 113.3 *diverse thing*

chequered flag 33.6 *motor racing terms*

cheque stub 545.1 *record*, 718.2 *promise*

Cherbourg 93 Cities

Cheremiss 5 Languages and Groups of Languages

Cherenkov 52 Scientists

cherimoya 86 Fruits

cherish 632.9 *protect*, 637.5 *preserve*, 726.7 *detain*, 784.7 *like*, 821.23 *love*, 826.7 *show endearment for*, 849.16 *revere*

cherish a grudge 832.16 *be malevolent*

cherished 637.7 *preserved*, 821.21 *beloved*

cherishing 726.2 *detention*

Chernobyl 93 Cities, 56.75 *nuclear accident*, 410.7 *nuclear power*, 531.5 *evasion*

Chernovtsy 93 Cities

Cherokee 1 Peoples, 5 Languages and Groups of Languages

Cherokee alphabet 5.14 *alphabet*

cheroot 413.7 *tobacco*

cherry 86 Fruits, 86.5 *figurative usage*, 450.1 *red*, 450.7 *red thing*, 876.3 *moral purity*

cherry blossom 84.1 *flower*

cherry lips 450.7 *red thing*

cherry picker 86.5 *figurative usage*

cherry plum 86 Fruits

cherry-red 450.1 *red*

cherry stoner 355.9 *extractor*

cherry tomato 45 Vegetables

chersonese 98.5 *peninsula*

chert 54 Common Rocks

cherub 8.6 *angel*, 821.12 *nicknames for lovers*, 826.4 *terms of endearment*

cherubic 7.15 *religious*, 8.14 *heavenly*

cherubically 8.19 *divinely*

cherubicon 10.8 *hymn*

chervil 45 Herbs and Spices, 45 Vegetables, 413.5 *herbs*

Chesapeake Bay 98.9 *inlet*

Chesapeake Bay retriever 37.6 *sporting dog*

Cheshire 45 Cheeses, 92 Counties

chesil 54.27 *sediment*

chess 42 Board Games

chessboard 456.5 *variegated thing*

chessman 42.4 *chess terms*

chess pie 45.36 *cake*

chess piece 42.4 *chess terms*

chess terms 42

chest 47.5, 258.3 *cabinet*, 258.6 *box*, 605.4 *storage*, 741.20 *money store*

Chester 93 Cities

chesterfield 47.2 *chair*, 295.12 *coat*

Chesterfield 93 Cities

Chesterton 48 Writers

Chester White 68 Breeds of Pig

chest-high 275.12 *tall*

chestnut 85 Trees and Shrubs, 86 Nuts, 32.1 *horse*, 449.1 *brown*, 450.3 *red-haired*

chestnut brown 77 Breeds of Cats

chest of drawers 47.5, 258.3 *cabinet*, 605.4 *storage*

chest-pain 624.10 *cardiovascular disease*

chest protector 28.2 *fencing equipment*, 31.3 *ice hockey*

chest protectors 22.3 *baseball equipment*

chest-spasm 624.10 *cardiovascular disease*

chest X-ray 60.7 *diagnosis*

cheval-de-frise 380.8 *sharp-pointed thing*

cheval glass 435.8 *reflection*

chevalier 817.6 *courteous person*

chevaux-de-frise 671.9 *barrier*

chevet 43.10 *church architecture*

cheviot 67 Natural Fabrics

Cheviot 68 Breeds of Sheep, 95 Mountains

Cheviot Hills 95.5 *British mountains*

chèvre 45 Cheeses

chevron 43 Architectural Decoration, 310.1 *angle*, 544.4 *insignia*, 544.8 *heraldic device*

chevrotain 77 Placental Mammals

chew 350.21 *eat*, 374.13 *soften*, 380.14 *be sharp*

Chewa 5 Languages and Groups of Languages

chewiness 378.6 *toughness*

chewing 350.1 *eating*

chewing gum 138.4 *adherent*, 377.3 *elastic thing*, 394.2 *adhesive*

chewing out 879.7 *punishment*

chewing the cud 350.5 *eating habit*

chewing tobacoo 413.7 *tobacco*

chew the cud 77.37 *graze*, 87.11 *eat grass*, 350.21 *eat*

chew the fat 568.9 *converse*

chew the scenery 541.7 *exaggerate*

chew up 350.21 *eat*

chew up the scenery 51.33 *overact*

chewy 378.3 *hard*

Cheyenne 1 Peoples, 5 Languages and Groups of Languages, 93 Cities

Cheyenne Frontier Days 32.12 *rodeo*

Chia 8 Deities

Chianina 68 Breeds of Cattle

chianti 351.9 *wine*

Chianti 95 Mountains

chiaroscuro 439.12 *highlight*, 447.7 *blackness*

chiasmus 48.12 *poetic language*, 308.1 *symmetry*

chiastic 308.4 *symmetrical*

Chibcha 1 Peoples

Chibchan 5 Languages and Groups of Languages

chic 163.9 *distinction*, 295.30 *dressed up*, 549.2 *stylishness*, 549.7 *stylish*, 789.1 *gorgeousness*, 796.2 *fashionableness*, 796.7 *fashionable*, 813.7 *dressed up*

Chicago 93 Cities, 93.2 *American cities*

chicane 33.6 *motor racing terms*, 71.3 *carriageway*, 539.7 *tricking*, 539.28 *trick*, 657.1 *cunning*

chicanery 474.5 *hypocrisy*, 539.7 *tricking*, 657.1 *cunning*, 676.9 *improbity*

Chichester 93 Cities

Chichewa 5 Languages and Groups of Languages

chichi 797.3 *affected*

chick 68.8 *livestock*, 78.12 *young bird*, 206.4 *young animal*, 206.8 *young woman*, 402.9 *woman considered as a sex object*, 821.12 *nicknames for lovers*, 826.4 *terms of endearment*

chickabiddy 821.12 *nicknames for lovers*, 826.4 *terms of endearment*

chickadee 78 Birds

chickaree 77 Placental Mammals

Chickasaw 1 Peoples, 5 Languages and Groups of Languages

chicken 45.20 *meat*, 68.8 *livestock*, 238.4 *weakling*, 238.12 *weak-willed*, 452.5 *cowardly*, 544.4 *insignia*, 641.2 *nonacting person*, 777.6 *frightened person*, 779.2 *coward*, 779.3 *cowardly*

chicken coop 256.12 *stall*

chicken farm 68.6 *farm*

chicken farming 68.3 *livestock farming*

chicken feed 350.8 *animal food*

chickenfeed 612.8 *trifle*, 741.4 *change*

chicken-hearted 238.12 *weak-willed*, 452.5, 779.3 *cowardly*

chicken-heartedly 779.5 *cravenly*

chicken-heartedness 779.1 *cowardice*

chicken house 68.7 *farm building*

chicken-in-a-basket circuit 51.13 *engagement*
chicken in every pot 657.1 *cunning*
chicken liver 45.31 *offal*
chicken-livered 779.3 *cowardly*
chicken out 779.4 *be a coward*
chickenpox 624.6 *infection*, 624.13 *skin disease*
chicken run 68.7 *farm building*
chickens 161 Collective Names by Animal
chicken sandwich 45.11 *sandwich*
chicken soup 45.13 *soup*
chicken thief 736.8 *thief*
chicken tikka masala 45.49 *Indian dish*
chicken wire 726.4 *wall*
chick pea 45 Vegetables, 45.33 *vegetable*
chickweed 84 Flowers and Flowering Plants
chicle 85 Tree Products, 394.2 *adhesive*
chicle gum 394.2 *adhesive*
chicly 295.36 *dressily*
chicory 45 Herbs and Spices, 45 Vegetables
chide 827.6 *vilify*, 852.20 *censure*, 879.1 *punish*
chiding 852.7 *blame*, 852.30 *censuring*, 879.7 *punishment*
chief 126.5 *superior*, 126.14 *best*, 154.12 *primary*, 194.6 *person having priority*, 279.5 *top*, 291.5 *focus*, 291.8 *focal*, 544.8 *heraldic device*, 611.4 *bigwig*, 611.5 *important*, 653.13 *director*, 688.10 *person of authority*, 696.3 *leader*, 696.5 *company leader*, 696.12 *masterful*
chief constable 16.17 *police officer*
chief cook and bottle-washer 646.1 *worker*
chief executive 640.3 *doer*, 692.6 *person in command*, 696.3 *leader*
chief executive officer 126.5 *superior*, 653.13 *manager*, 692.6 *person in command*
chief hope 611.3 *chief thing*
chief justice 16.23 *judge*, 492.6 *justice*
Chief Justice of the United States 16.9 *lawmaker*, 16.24 *US judge*
chief justice of the United States 688.10 *person of authority*, 696.3 *leader*
chiefly 103.13 *in essence*, 124.11 *on average*, 126.16 *superiorly*, 156.42 *principally*, 166.18 *as a rule*
chief magistrate 696.3 *leader*
chief meaning 520.4 *type of meaning*
Chief of Naval Operations 17 US Military Ranks
chief of police 16.17 *police officer*
chief of staff 17.5 *military staff*
Chief of Staff 17 US Military Ranks
chief of state 696.3 *leader*
chief part 51.21 *role*, 143.5 *largest part*
chief petty officer 679.27 *naval man*
chief rabbi 7.8 *priest*
chieftain 696.3 *leader*
chieftaincy 91.3 *dominion*
chief technician 679.32 *airman*
chief thing 611
chief whip 12.8 *politician*, 653.15 *manager*, 688.10 *person of authority*, 696.3 *leader*
Chiemsee 94 Lakes
chiffchaff 78 Birds
chifferi 45 Types of Pasta
chifferoni 45 Types of Pasta
chiffon 67 Natural Fabrics, 288.4 *textile*, 442.8 *transparent thing*
chigetai 77 Placental Mammals
chigger 82 Arachnids, 82.3 *pest*
chignon 791.8 *hair cut*
chigoe 82 Insects, 82.3 *pest*
chihuahua 77 Breeds of Dogs
Chihuahuan 98 Deserts

chilblain 409.3 *chill*, 624.15 *ulcer*
child 206, 155.11 *progeny*, 243.7 *produce*, 245.6 *progeny*, 400.7 *person*, 658.3 *naive person*, 701.4 *dependent*, 865.4 *innocent person*
child abuse 241.2 *physical violence*, 618.11 *harmfulness*, 832.7 *act of malevolence*, 877.7 *sexual assault*
child abuser 601.3 *abuser*, 862.6 *evil person*, 864.9 *wicked person*, 877.10 *sex offender*
child allowance 662.4 *social assistance*
child-bearing 402.15 *female*
childbed 247.3 *obstetrics*
child benefit 662.4 *social assistance*
childbirth 777 Phobias by Topic, 245.3 *propagation*, 245.7 *obstetrics*
child-health clinic 60.10 *hospital*
childhood 156.4 *conception*, 206.1 *youth*, 396.5 *life cycle*, 865.3 *naivety*
childhood friend 819.6 *close friend*
childhood playmate 784.4 *likable person*
childish 5.39 *of language*, 206.11 *young*, 460.6 *unintelligent*, 508.5 *foolish*, 595.5 *immature*, 612.4 *trivial*
childish language 5.5 *nonstandard language*
childishly 206.14 *youthfully*, 460.11 *unintelligently*, 595.16 *immaturely*
childishness 206.2 *youthfulness*, 460.2 *unintelligence*, 508.1 *folly*, 595.10 *immaturity*
childless 247.3 *birth control*
childlessness 247.1 *infertility*
childlike 206.11 *young*, 460.6 *unintelligent*, 595.5 *immature*, 658.1, 865.7 *naive*
child-minder 632.3 *protector*
child molestation 618.11 *harmfulness*
child of fortune 686.4 *prosperous person*
child of God 7.3 *religious person*
child of nature 658.3 *naive person*
child pornography 877.2 *indecency*
child prodigy 786.5 *person of wonder*
childproof 632.6 *invulnerable*
child psychologist 61.29 *psychologist*
child psychology 61.1 *psychology*, 630.13 *therapy*
children 777 Phobias by Topic, 155.11 *progeny*, 206.10 *the young*
Children in Need Appeal 712.3 *solicitation*
children's book 532.6 *book publishing*
children's clothes 295
children's court 16.19 *lawcourt*
children's dentist 60.14 *dentist*
children's dictionary 5.28 *dictionary*
children's game 42.1 *game*
children's home 634.2 *shelter*
children's hospital 60.10 *hospital*
children's nurse 60.16 *nurse*
children's swimming pool 39.7 *swimming pool*
child's play 477.5 *easy question*, 612.8 *trifle*, 660.6 *easy thing*
child support 284.7 *financial support*, 749.3 *income*, 833.4 *welfare state*
child welfare 831.3 *welfare*, 833.4 *welfare state*
Chile 91 Countries
Chile saltpetre 54 Minerals, 57 Common Chemical Compounds
chiliad 179.10 *thousand*, 187.2 *time period*
chiliasm 627.11 *reformism*
Chiliasm 7 Christian Movements

chiliast 627.12 *reformer*
chiliastic 627.16 *improving*
chill 409, 55.31 *coldness*, 55.55 *cool*, 409.1 *coldness*, 409.8 *cold*, 409.12 *make cold*, 587.5 *discourage*, 624.3 *symptom*, 651.1 *refresh*, 816.1 *unsociability*
CHILL 65 Programming Languages
chilladas 45.34 *vegetarian dish*
chill cupboard 409.4 *cooler*
chilled 409.8 *cold*
chilled counter 409.4 *cooler*
chilled to the bone 409.8 *cold*
chilled to the marrow 409.8 *cold*
chiller 409.4 *cooler*
chill factor 55.6 *weather data*, 409.7 *cold weather*
chilli 45 Herbs and Spices, 413.5 *herbs*
chilli con carne 45.50 *Central American dish*
chilliness 55.31, 409.1 *coldness*, 816.1 *unsociability*, 820.1 *enmity*
chilling 409.9 *heat-resistant*, 587.9 *dissuasive*
chill in the air 55.31 *coldness*
chilly 55.55 *cool*, 409.8 *cold*, 816.8 *unsociable*, 820.6 *hostile*
chilopod 81.4 *arthropod*
Chilopoda 81.4 *arthropod*
Chiltern 95 Mountains
Chimborazo 95 Mountains
chime 49 Musical Instruments, 49.13 *melody*, 116.4 *harmony*, 116.24 *harmonize*, 426.12 *ring*, 427.2 *ringing*, 427.10 *ring*, 433.3 *melodiousness*
chime bar 49 Musical Instruments
chime in 160.16 *interrupt*, 433.8 *harmonize*
chime in with 499.4 *assent*
chimera 80 Fishes, 76.7 *legendary beast*, 102.2 *illusion*, 435.5 *imagination*, 457.4 *something that appears*, 519.5 *fantasy*
chimerical 102.9 *illusory*, 457.9 *ostensible*, 519.12 *imaginary*, 539.40 *illusory*
chimes 423.1 *loudness*, 427.4 *sources of resonance*
chiming 116.4 *harmony*, 116.13 *harmonious*, 183.15 *reverberatory*, 426.5 *ringing*, 426.18 *pealing*, 427.7 *ringing*, 433.6 *melodious*
chimney 34.5 *rock face*, 34.9 *mountaineer*, 98.8 *valley*, 265.3 *gulf*, 275.6 *tall thing*, 322.7 *passageway*, 408.6 *fire*
chimney corner 408.6 *fire*
chimneying 34.3 *climbing technique*
chimneystack 322.7 *passageway*
chimney sweep 621.12 *cleaner*, 622.6 *dirty person*
chimpanzee 77 Placental Mammals
Chimú 1 Peoples
chin 457.3 *external appearance*
Chin 5 Languages and Groups of Languages
ch'in 49 Musical Instruments
china 44.1 *ceramics*, 238.5 *weak thing*, 243.7 *produce*, 258.16 *crockery*
China 91 Countries, 97 Oceans and Seas
chinaberry 85 Trees and Shrubs, 86 Fruits
china cabinet 47.5 *cabinet*
china clay 44.2 *raw material*, 604.1 *materials*
china decorator 44.7 *potter*
china doll 547.6 *image*
China grass 87 Grasses
China ink 447.8 *black pigment*
chinaman 27.8 *delivery*
china painter 44.7 *potter*
china plumbing ware 44.9 *industrial ceramics*
china stone 44.2 *raw material*
China syndrome 244.4 *ruin*
China tea 351.3 *tea*
Chinatown 93.3 *New York*

chinaware 44.1 *ceramics*, 258.16 *crockery*
chinch bug 82 Insects
chinchilla 67 Natural Fabrics, 77 Breeds of Cats, 77 Placental Mammals, 293.14 *animal covering*
Chincoteague 32 Breeds of Horse and Pony
chine 98.8 *valley*, 275.4 *mountain range*
Chinese 1 Peoples, 5 Languages and Groups of Languages, 68 Breeds of Fowl, 777 Phobias by Topic, 400.4 *civilized human*
Chinese cabbage 45 Vegetables
Chinese calligraphy 50 Non-Western Art
Chinese character 5.13 *letter*
Chinese checkers 42 Board Games
Chinese dish 45
Chinese gooseberry 86 Fruits
Chinese lantern 439.7 *lantern*
Chinese lantern plant 84 Flowers and Flowering Plants
Chinese lanterns 812.8 *salute*
Chinese leaves 45 Vegetables
Chinese mushroom 45.33 *vegetable*
Chinese New Year 10.16 *religious festival*
Chinese puzzle 529.4 *brain-teaser*
Chinese remainder theorem 52 Named Concepts
Chinese-Siamese 5.11 *family of languages*
Chinese water deer 77 Placental Mammals
Chinese whisper 420.8 *something heard*
Chinese whispers 42 Children's Games and Party Games
Chinese white 446.8 *whitener*
Chinese wood block 49 Musical Instruments
Ching 44 Types of Ceramics
Ch'ing dynasty art 50 Non-Western Art
chink 265.2 *crack*, 272.6 *narrow place*, 321.1, 321.6 *furrow*, 424.1 *faintness*, 424.5 *sound faint*, 427.2 *ringing*, 427.10 *ring*, 620.7 *defect*
Chink 91 Names for Inhabitants
chink in one's armour 620.7 *defect*
chink in the armour 633.7 *vulnerability*
chinky 321.4 *furrowed*
chino 67 Natural Fabrics
chinoiserie 47.1 *furniture*, 47.7 *furniture style*
chinook 55 Winds
Chinook 1 Peoples, 5 Languages and Groups of Languages
Chinook Jargon 5 Languages and Groups of Languages
chinook salmon 20.4 *American game fish*
Chinook salmon 80 Fishes
chinquapin 86 Nuts
chintz 67 Natural Fabrics, 288.4 *textile*
chintzy 754.10 *shoddy*
chinwag 564.1 *faculty of speech*, 565.3 *talk*, 568.2 *chat*
chionophobia 777 Phobias by Name
Chios 68 Breeds of Sheep
chip 29.3 *golf shots*, 29.7 *golf*, 38.4 *play soccer*, 50.21 *sculpt*, 64.13 *circuit*, 65.17 *computing term*, 136.9 *separate*, 143.7 *piece*, 173.3 *fragment*, 260.2 *little thing*, 266.4 *slice*, 379.4 *be brittle*, 384.24 *crumble*, 544.3 *means of identification*, 620.7 *defect*
chip a stone 41.16 *bobsled*
chipboard 47.12 *wood*, 604.4 *board*
chip in 160.16 *interrupt*, 662.29 *finance*, 729.5 *give*
chip log 329.8 *speed*
chipmunk 77 Placental Mammals

chip off 379.4 *be brittle*
chip off the old block 110.3 *lookalike*, 114.5 *counterpart*
chipolata 45.29 *sausage*
chipped 379.1 *brittle*, 620.1 *imperfect*
Chippendale 47.7 *furniture style*
chipper 85.7 *timber production*
Chippewa 1 Peoples
chippie 47.13 *carpenter*, 646.2 *artisan*
chipping 379.1 *brittle*
chippings 293.11 *paving*
chipping sparrow 78 Birds
chip-proof 378.1 *tough*
chippy 350.15 *eating place*, 875.4 *drug taker*
chiquetaille 45.51 *West Indian dish*
chiral 57.37 *structural*
chiral centre 57.13 *structure*
chirality 57.13 *structure*
chirognomy 11.9 *divination*
chiromancer 11.13 *diviner*
chiromancy 11.9, 517.2 *divination*
Chiron 53 Minor Planets
chiropodist 60.17 *paramedic*, 630.15 *healer*
chiropody 60.6 *health care*, 630.12 *surgery*
chiropractic 60.2 *natural medicine*, 60.8 *treatment*, 407.2 *touching*, 630.13 *therapy*
chiropractor 60.12 *healer*, 407.5 *toucher*, 629.12 *repairer*, 630.15 *healer*
Chiroptera 77.7 *flying mammal*
chiropteran 77, 77.7 *flying mammal*
chirp 78.18 *birdsong*, 78.28, 432.5 *sing*
chirping 432.2 *bird song*
chirpy 769.1 *cheerful*
chirr 432.5 *sing*
chirrup 78.18 *birdsong*, 78.28, 432.5 *sing*
chirruping 432.2 *bird song*
chiru 77 Placental Mammals
chisel 47.11 *woodworking tool*, 47.17 *carpenter*, 50.14 *sculptor's materials*, 50.15 *engraving*, 50.21 *sculpt*, 243.10 *produce*, 306.7 *form*, 380.9 *sharp-edged thing*, 380.16 *use a sharp tool* , 603.1 *tool*, 603.9 *use tools*, 736.16 *act dishonest*, 796.8 *fashion*
Chisel 53 The Constellations
chiseller 539.17 *cheat*
chisel plough 68.10 *farm tool*
chi-square distribution 52.59 *probability distribution*
chit 260.4 *little person*, 483.6 *documentation*, 544.3 *means of identification*, 708.2 *permit*, 714.2 *guarantee*
chital 77 Placental Mammals
chitarra 45 Types of Pasta
chitarra battente 49 Musical Instruments
chitarrone 49 Musical Instruments
chit-chat 568.2 *chat*
Chitimacha 1 Peoples
chitin 58.4 *polysaccharide*, 59.7 *cell*
chit of a girl 206.8 *young woman*
chiton 81 Molluscs, 295.16 *robe*
chitterlings 45.31 *offal*
chitty 544.3 *means of identification*
chiuso 49 Musical Terms
chivalrous 778, 401.17 *male*, 676.17 *military*, 763.2 *likable*, 817.7 *courteous*, 857.4 *honourable*, 863.5 *virtuous*
chivalrously 817.14 *courteously*, 857.7 *honourably*, 863.9 *virtuously*
chivalrousness 817.1 *courtesy*
chivalry 32.15 *horse person*, 676.2 *glory of war*, 679.20 *cavalryman*, 763.8 *amiability*,

778.2 *heroism*, 778.8 *courageous act*, 817.1 *courtesy*, 857.1 *probity*, 863.1 *virtue*
chives 45 Herbs and Spices, 413.5 *herbs*
chivy 77.23 *mammal hunting*, 590.8 *pursue*
chivy along 329.7 *hurry someone up*
chloral 57 Common Chemical Compounds, **62** Medication
chloral hydrate 57 Common Chemical Compounds, **62** Medication
chlorambucil 62 Medication
chloramine 62 Medication
chloramphenical 89.6 *fungal antibiotic*
chloramphenicol 62 Medication
chlorate 57 Types of Compounds
chlorazepate potassium 62 Medication
chlorbutanol 62 Medication
chlorcyclizine 62 Medication
chlordantoin 62 Medication
chlordiazepoxide 62 Medication, **62** Medication
chlorella 90 Algae
chlorhexadol 62 Medication
chlorhexidine 62 Medication
chloric 57.34 *elemental*
chloride 57 Types of Compounds
chloride of lime 445.4 *colour remover*
chlorinate 57.26 *react*, 134.10, 621.15 *purify*, 625.6 *make hygienic*, 632.9 *protect*
chlorinated 57.34 *elemental*, 625.4 *hygienic*
chlorinated lime 445.4 *colour remover*
chlorination 57 Types of Chemical Reaction, 621.2 *cleaning*, 625.1 *hygiene*
chlorine 57 Chemical Elements, 58.15 *essential element*, 631.10 *warfare*
chlorite 54 Minerals, **57** Types of Compounds
chlormethiazole 62 Medication
chlormezanone 62 Medication, **62** Medication
chlorocresol 62 Medication
chlorofluorocarbon 57 Types of Compounds
chloroform 57 Common Chemical Compounds, **62** Medication
chlorooxylenol 62 Medication
chlorophyll 58.18 *pigment*, 90.3 *plant body*, 453.10 *green pigment*
chlorophyll b 58.23 *photosynthesis*
Chlorophyta 90.2 *algae*
chlorophyte 90.2 *algae*
chloroplast 59.8 *cell organ*
chloroprene rubber 57.21 *polymer*
chloropyrilene 62 Medication
chlorosis 69.12 *pests and diseases*
chlorothiazide 62 Medication
chlorotrianisene 62 Medication
chlorous 57.34 *elemental*
chlorpheniramine 62 Medication
chlorphenoxamine 62 Medication
chlorphentermine 62 Medication
chlorpromazine 62 Medication
chlorpropamide 62 Medication
chlorprothixene 62 Medication
chlortetracycline 62 Medication
chlorthalidone 62 Medication
Chnoumis 8 Deities
chock 34.4 *climbing equipment*, 323.1 *closure*
chock-a-block 144.8 *full*, 161.50 *crowded*, 273.2 *dense*, 608.3 *filled*
chocker 608.3 *filled*
chock-ful 608.3 *filled*
chock-full 144.8 *full*
chockstone 34.5 *rock face*
chocolate 45.41 *sweet*, 414.4 *confectionery*, 449.1 *brown*, 449.5 *brown thing*

chocolate bar 45.41 *sweet*
chocolate cake 45.36 *cake*, 414.3 *dessert*
chocolate gateau 45.36 *cake*
chocolate milk 351.5 *milk*
chocolate mousse 414.3 *dessert*
chocolate-point 449.5 *brown thing*
chocolate-pointed Siamese 77 Breeds of Cats
chocolates 826.3 *love token*
Choctaw 1 Peoples, **5** Languages and Groups of Languages
chohan 7.2 *religiousness*
choice 580, 821, 136.2 *setting apart*, 147.10 *excluding*, 492.1 *judgment*, 570.1 *will*, 580.6 *selection*, 580.15 *chosen*, 602.1 *means*, 611.3 *chief thing*, 617.1 *worthy*, 698.1 *freedom*, 784.2 *inclination*, 784.3 *likes*, 861.2 *best*, 861.9 *the best*
choice bit 617.7 *elite*
choice meat 401.4 *boyfriend*
choice of expression 5.24 *phrasing*
choice of words 5.24 *phrasing*, 549.4 *literary style*
choir 10.12 *church*, 116.4 *harmony*, 140.3 *assembly*
choir invisible 8.6 *angel*
choir master 49.24 *musician*
choir school 6.12 *educational institution*
choirstall 10.12 *church*
choir stall 47.2 *chair*
choke 26.5 *wrestling*, 26.12 *wrestle*, 64.17 *resistor*, 236.8 *overpower*, 323.2 *stopper*, 323.8 *stop*, 398.17 *murder*, 430.5 *sound hoarse*, 610.4 *be excessive*, 661.8 *hinder*
chokeberry 86 Fruits
chokecherry 86 Fruits
choked 323.13 *stopped*, 563.11 *speechless*
chokedamp 388.3 *miasma*
choked up 323.13 *stopped*
choker 295.14 *neckwear*, 313.3 *circular thing*
chokey 702.2 *the inside*
choking 26.5 *wrestling*
choko 86 Fruits
cholagogic 352.6 *inducing secretion*
cholecystectomy 60 Surgical Operations
cholecystenterostomy 60 Surgical Operations
cholecystoduodenostomy 60 Surgical Operations
cholecystogastrostomy 60 Surgical Operations
cholecystokinin 58 Hormones
cholecystotomy 60 Surgical Operations
choledochotomy 60 Surgical Operations
choler 822.5, 828.4 *anger*
cholera 777 Phobias by Topic, 244.7 *agent of destruction*, 624.6 *infection*, 624.7 *tropical disease*, 624.8 *indigestion*
choleretic 62.4 *drug type*, 62.17 *stimulating*
choleric 61.7 *personality type*, 473.8 *argumentative*, 771.12 *four humours*, 822.13, 828.16 *angry*
cholerophobia 777 Phobias by Name
cholesterol 58.6 *lipid*, 350.11 *food content*
choline 58.13 *vitamin*
choline salicylate 62 Medication
choline theophyllinate 62 Medication
chomp 350.21 *eat*
chomping 350.1 *eating*
Chomsky 4 Philosophers
Chomskyan 4.11 *follower of a doctrine*, 4.14 *of a philosophy*
Chondrichthyes 80.2 *fish*
chondriosome 59.8 *cell organ*
chondrite 53.20 *meteor*
chondroblast 382.7 *skeleton*

Chongquig 93 Cities
choo choo 72.4 *locomotive*
choose 570, 481.12 *discriminate*, 580.1 *select*, 784.8 *prefer*
choose an alternative 222.5 *take a substitute*
choose by ballot 580.5 *vote*
choose one's ground 676.14 *battle*
choose one's words carefully 549.9 *style*
choose the military solution 676.12 *go to war*
choose to 784.9 *like to*
choosing 580.6 *selection*, 580.14 *selecting*
choosy 481.9 *discriminating*, 580.14 *selecting*
chop 45.55 *cook*, 136.9 *separate*, 143.7 *piece*, 362.2 *flatten*, 380.16 *use a sharp tool*, 603.9 *use tools*
chop and change 216.8 *cause change*, 224.12 *be irresolute*, 579.5 *be capricious*
chop down 362.2 *flatten*
chophouse 350.15 *eating place*
Chopin 49 Musicians and Composers
choplogic 473.14 *discuss*, 474.11 *practise sophistry*, 504.4 *faulty reasoning*
chop off 131.4 *take off*
chopped 45.56 *culinary*, 131.7 *reduced*
chopper 71.12 *bicycle*, 73.8 *aircraft*, 245.8 *organs of reproduction*, 380.10 *knife*, 680.8 *sharp weapon*
choppily 375.14 *roughly*
choppiness 97.3 *wave*, 160.1 *discontinuity*, 215.1 *irregularity*, 366.3 *turbulence*, 375.6 *roughness*
chopping 131.1 *subtraction*
chopping and changing 224.2 *irresolution*
chopping board 45.6 *kitchen equipment*
choppy 97.7 *oceanic*, 160.8 *discontinuous*, 215.4 *irregular*, 366.17 *turbulent*, 375.4 *bumpy*
choppy sea 97.3 *wave*, 321.3 *furrowed thing*, 375.9 *broken water*
chopsticks 350.16 *eating utensil*
chop suey 45.48 *Chinese dish*
chop the air 543.11 *gesture*
choragus 653.14 *leader*
choral 49.32 *instrumental*, 51.37 *dramatic*, 116.13 *harmonious*
chorale 49.5 *sacred music*, 433.2 *song*
chorally 51.42 *dramatically*, 116.33 *harmoniously*
choral music 49.3 *classical music*
chord 49.16 *musical note*, 52.37 *line*, 52.42 *circle*, 140.2 *cooperation*, 313.4 *parts of a circle*
Chordata 81.2 *protochordate*
chordate 76.4 *type of animal*, 76.15 *of animals*, 81.2 *protochordate*
chordophone 49.25 *musical instrument*
chore 644.2 *task*, 731.3 *allotted task*, 788.2 *boring thing*
chorea 366.7 *shake*, 624.17 *nervous disorder*
choreal 366.19 *convulsive*
choreic 366.19 *convulsive*
choreograph 46.15 *dance*, 152.16 *adapt*
choreographer 46.5 *dancer*, 51.24 *dramatist*, 51.25 *producer*
choreographic 51.37 *dramatic*
choreographically 51.42 *dramatically*
choreography 46.1 *dancing*, 46.8 *ballet*, 51.7 *dramaturgy*, 152.9 *musical arrangement*, 382.9 *artistic structure*
chores 644.1 *work*
choriamb 48.9 *metre*
choric ode 48.7 *poem*
chorion 59.15 *developmental biology*
chorionic 59.26 *developmental*

chorionic gonadotrophin 58 Hormones
chorionic villus sampling 60.7 *diagnosis*
chorister 433.5 *melodist*
C horizon 54.36 *soil*
chorography 250.5 *topography*
Chorten 10.13 *shrine*
chortle 431.2 *cry of joy*, **431.11** *laugh*, 762.7 *show joy*, 771.14 *laugh*, 773.3 *laughter*, 773.8 *laugh*
chorus 48.8 *part of poem*, 49.39 *sing*, 51.6 *scene*, 51.21 *role*, 51.23 *cast*, 116.4 *harmony*, 140.3 *assembly*, 155.8 *addition*, 198.7 *synchronize*, 426.6 *musical repetition*, 426.13 *trill*, 431.8 *musical cry*, 431.15 *sing out*, 433.1 *melody*, 564.10 *speaker*
chorus boy 51.27 *entertainer*
chorus girl 51.27 *entertainer*, 51.28 *dancer*
chorus leader 653.14 *leader*
chorus master 49.24 *musician*
chose 725.2 *legal terms*
chose in action 725.2 *legal terms*
chose in possession 723.2, 725.2 *legal terms*
chosen 580, 126.15 *excellent*, 513.7 *expected*, 617.1 *worthy*, 688.13 *elected*, 821.21 *beloved*
chosen few 126.7 *the best people*, 617.7 *elite*
chosen people 580.9 *chosen thing*, 617.7 *elite*
chosen thing 580
chough 78 Birds
choughs 161 Collective Names by Animal
choux pastry 45.37 *pastry*
chow 77 Breeds of Dogs, 350.7 *food*
chowder 45.13 *soup*
chow down 45.58 *grub's on*
chow mein 45.48 *Chinese dish*
chrestomathy 133.3, 161.32 *miscellany*, 562.3 *compendium*
Chrétien de Troyes 48 Poets
Chris Evert 40.7 *famous tennis players*
chrism 10.18 *perform rites*, 386.5 *ointment*, 395.4 *anointment*
Chrism 10.5 *Christian rite*
chrismal 10.14 *sacred object*, 10.21 *ritualistic*, 386.11, 395.12 *unguent*
chrismation 386.3, 395.4 *anointment*
chrismatory 386.11 *unguent*, 395.4 *anointment*, 395.12 *unguent*
Christ 8.4 *God the Son*, 675.2 *symbol of peace*, 827.15 *miscellaneous swearwords*
Christ Almighty 827.15 *miscellaneous swearwords*
Christchurch 93 Cities
christen 10.18 *perform rites*, 156.25 *enrol*, 730.10 *receive someone*
christened 156.37 *enrolled*, 730.13 *received*
christener 5.2 *linguist*
christening 10.5 *Christian rite*, 74.4 *shipbuilding*, 156.8 *enrolment*, 389.15 *holy water*, 560.7 *nomenclature*, 730.4 *reception*
Christening 813.3 *formal occasion*
Christian 43 Architectural Styles, **7**, 7.16 *denominational*, 134.12 *morally pure*, 821.17 *loving*, 831.5 *benevolent person*, 831.7 *charitable*, 863.5 *virtuous*
Christian Broadcasting Network 534.25 *broadcast material*
Christian charity 821.1 *love*, 831.2 *charity*
Christian conduct 863.1 *virtue*
Christian Democratic Party 12.6 *political party*
Christian Democratic Union 12.6 *political party*
christiania 41.4 *skiing technique*
Christianize 7.20 *preach*
Christian love 821.1 *love*

Christian martyr 710.7 *martyr*
Christian name 560.8 *name*
Christian rite 10
Christian Science 7 Christian Movements, 630.11 *medical art*
Christian Scientist 7.5 *Christian*, 630.15 *healer*
Christian text 7.12 *religious text*
christie 41.4 *skiing technique*
Christie 48 Writers
Christie's 740.1 *market*
Christlike 8.13 *divine*
Christly 8.13 *divine*
Christmas 10.16 *religious festival*, 203.5 *winter*, 214.6 *annually celebrated day*
Christmas box 729.2 *gift*
Christmas cactus 84 Flowers and Flowering Plants
Christmas cake 45.36 *cake*
Christmas carol 433.2 *song*
Christmas dinner 45.30 *feast*
Christmas party 665.7 *social gathering*
Christmas present 729.2 *gift*
Christmas pudding 45.35 *dessert*
Christmas rose 84 Flowers and Flowering Plants
Christmassy 815.17 *festive*
Christmas time 203.5 *winter*
Christmas tree 85.1 *tree*
Christmas tree lights 439.6 *electric light*
Christological 7.18 *theological*
Christology 7.13 *theology*
Christophany 8.8 *divine manifestation*
chroma 444.3 *hue*
chromascope 444.8 *chromatics*
chromate 57 Types of Compounds
chromatic 444.10 *coloured*
chromatic aberration 53.25 *mounting*, 56.31 *lens element*, 444.1 *colour*
chromatic colour 444.1 *colour*
chromaticism 444.1 *colour*
chromaticity 444.3 *hue*
chromaticity chart 444.8 *chromatics*
chromaticity diagram 444.8 *chromatics*
chromatic painter 444.6 *painter*
chromatic painting 444.7 *colour painting*
chromatics 444
chromatic scale 49.20 *key*
chromatid 59.14 *chromosome*
chromatin 59.9 *cell nucleus*, 59.14 *chromosome*
chromatin strands 59.9 *cell nucleus*
chromatism 444.1 *colour*
chromatist 444.6 *painter*
chromatogram 57.17 *analysis*
chromatographic 57.41 *analytic*
chromatography 57.5 *process*, 57.17 *analysis*
chromatography paper 348.6 *sponge*
chromatolithographic 444.14 *chromolithographic*
chromatology 444.8 *chromatics*
chromatophore 59.8 *cell organ*
chrome alum 57 Common Chemical Compounds
chromel 57 Alloys
chrome steel 57 Alloys
chrometophobia 777 Phobias by Name
chrome yellow 452.7 *yellow pigment*
chromic 57.34 *elemental*
chromite 54 Minerals, **57** Common Metal Ores, 54.34 *mineral*
chromium 57 Chemical Elements, 58.15 *essential element*
chromogenic film 66.9 *film*
chromolithographer 444.6 *painter*
chromolithographic 444
chromolithography 444.7 *colour painting*
chromomere 59.14 *chromosome*
chromonema 59.14 *chromosome*
chromophobia 777 Phobias by Name
chromophore 67.6 *dye*

chromoplast 59.8 *cell organ*
chromosomal 59.25 *genetic*
chromosome 59, 59.11 *genetics*, 59.14 *chromosome*
chromosome mutation 59.14 *chromosome*
chromosome number 59.14 *chromosome*
chromosphere 53.15 *sun*
chromotrope 67.6 *dye*
chromous 57.34 *elemental*
chromyl 57.34 *elemental*
chronic 185.21 *lasting through time*, 406.5 *painful*, 577.3 *unyielding*, 584.14 *habituated*, 624.22 *sick*
chronically 624.25 *unhealthily*
chronically ill 624.21 *unhealthy*
chronically sick 624.21 *unhealthy*
chronic complaint 624.1 *ill health*
chronic ill health 624.1 *ill health*
chronic illness 624.1 *ill health*
chronic invalid 624.19 *sick person*
chronicle 3, 3, 48.4 *non-fiction*, 171.8 *list*, 192.15 *chronologize*, 545.1, 545.13 *record*, 560.3 *narration*, 560.15 *recount*
chronicled 3, 545.16 *recorded*
chronicler 192, 48.14 *author*, 185.14 *time keeper*, 545.9 *recorder*, 560.10 *descriptive writer*
chronogram 185.13 *timer*, 192.8 *face*
chronogrammatic 185.25 *of known date*, 192.17 *timekeeping*
chronograph 185.13 *timer*, 192.9 *hourglass*
chronographer 185.14 *time keeper*, 192.12 *chronologist*
chronographic 185.25 *of known date*, 192.17 *timekeeping*
chronographically 192.18 *horologically*
chronography 185.7 *time measurement*, 192.3 *chronology*
chronologer 192.12 *chronologist*
chronologic 192.17 *timekeeping*
chronological 159.9 *consecutive*, 185.25 *of known date*, 192.17 *timekeeping*
chronological error 193.1 *wrong time*, 197.1 *different time*, 211.2 *anachronism*
chronologically 185, 159.18 *consecutively*, 192.18 *horologically*
chronological order 159.2 *consecution*
chronologist 192, 185.14 *time keeper*
chronologize 192, 185.17 *date*
chronology 192, 185.7 *time measurement*
chronometer 56.87 *clock*, 74.5 *navigation*, 185.13 *timer*, 192.5 *timekeeper*, 268.8 *meter*
chronometric 185.25 *of known date*, 192.17 *timekeeping*, 268.16 *micrometric*
chronometry 185, 268.2 *micrometry*
chronon 75 Scientific and Technical Units, 185.1 *time*
chronophobia 777 Phobias by Name
chronoscope 192.9 *hourglass*
chronoscopy 185.10 *chronometry*
chronostratigraphic unit 54.41 *geological time*
chrysalid 82.13 *immature*
chrysalis 59.15 *developmental biology*, 82.5 *larva*, 206.4 *young animal*, 226.3 *rudiment*, 293.14 *animal covering*
chrysanthemum 84 Flowers and Flowering Plants
chrysoberyl 54 Minerals, **54** Gemstones
chrysolite 54 Gemstones, 54.34 *mineral*
Chrysophyta 90.2 *algae*
chrysophyte 90.2 *algae*
chrysoprase 54 Gemstones, 453.11 *green thing*
chrysotile 54 Minerals
Chryssipus 4 Philosophers
chthonian 8.16 *devilish*

chthonic 8.16 *devilish*
chub 80 Fishes, 20.5 *British game fish*
chubbiness 259.5 *fatness*, 273.5 *thickness*, 315.2 *round body*
chubby 259.16 *fat*, 273.1 *thick*, 315.10 *well-rounded*
chubby-cheeked 259.16 *fat*
chubby-faced 259.16 *fat*
chuck 19.18 *be penalized*, 45.22, 45.23 *beef*, 330.6 *tap*, 330.13 *blow*, 338.5, 338.23 *throw*, 350.7 *food*, 598.2 *withdraw*, 670.7 *stone*, 705.5 *resign*
chucker 338.14 *thrower*
chucker out 349.26 *ejector*
chucker-out 237.6 *muscleman*
chuckhole 393.14 *puddle*
chucking 19.13 *penalty*, 338.3 *throwing*
chuck it 218.12 *stop*
chuckle 431.2 *cry of joy*, 431.11 *laugh*, 432.5 *sing*, 762.7 *show joy*, 771.14 *laugh*
chuckling 431.17 *cheering*
chuck out 244.8 *destroy*, 349.1 *expel*, 581.2 *discard*
chuck under the chin 821.27 *kiss*, 826.7 *show endearment for*
chuck up 349.15 *vomit*
chuck-wagon cook 45.2 *cook*
chuckwalla 79 Reptiles
chuff chuff 72.4 *locomotive*
chuffed 405.7 *pleased*
chuffer 72.4 *locomotive*
chug 324.15 *walk*, 351.13 *drink*, 426.10 *rattle*
chug-a-lug 351.18 *cheers*, 874.8 *get drunk*
chughole 393.14 *puddle*
chug on 328.1 *move slowly*
Chukchi 1 Peoples, **5** Languages and Groups of Languages
chukka boots 295.19 *footwear*
chukker 315.6 *round*
chum 20.1 *angling*, 401.3 *male title of address*, 784.4 *likable person*, 815.6 *social person*, 819.5 *friend*
chuminess 819.1 *friendship*
chummy 819.8 *friendly*
chump 45.26 *lamb*
chump chops 45.26 *lamb*
Chumphon 93 Cities
chunder 349.15 *vomit*
chunk 120.2 *certain amount*, 132.1 *remainder*, 143.7 *piece*, 259.7 *mass*, 338.5 *throw*, 371.4 *solid body*
chunkiness 259.6 *squatness*, 273.5 *thickness*
chunky 259.17 *stocky*, 273.1 *thick*, 369.1 *heavy*
Chunnel 327.8 *tunnel*
Chuntokyo 7 Non-Christian Religions
church 777 Phobias by Topic, **10**, 2.8 *human institution*, 7.1 *religion*, 10.11 *place of worship*, 63.20 *building*, 220.4 *medium of conversion*, 243.8 *construction*, 665.1 *party*
church architecture 43
church bazaar 727.2 *disposal of property*, 739.4 *sale*
church bell 427.4 *sources of resonance*, 543.4 *signal*, 543.6 *word*, 636.2 *danger signal*
church book 10.10 *religious manual*
church candle 439.5 *incandescent light*
churchgoer 9.5, 10.17 *worshipper*, 497.5 *believer*
churchgoing 7.15 *religious*
church government 12.1 *government*
Churchill 48 Dramatists, **96** Rivers
Churchill Downs 674.5 *racecourse*
churchiness 7.2 *religiousness*
churchly 7.17 *priestly*
churchman 7.8 *priest*
church member 497.5 *believer*
church music 49.5 *sacred music*
Church of England 7 Christian Movements

Church of England Temperance Society 869.1 *self-restraint*

Church of Ireland 7 Christian Movements

Church of Scotland 7 Christian Movements

Church of the Madeleine 43 Noted Buildings

church parable 49.5 *sacred music*

church property 725.1 *property*

church service 10.4 *public worship*

churchwarden 7.8 *priest*, 413.7 *tobacco*

church wedding 823.5 *wedding*

churchy 7.15 *religious*

churchyard 399.5 *cemetery*

churl 803.1 *plebeian*

churlish 559.8 *indecorous*, 656.3 *clumsy*, 818.6 *bad-mannered*, 829.4 *irascible*, 830.7 *irritable*

churlishly 818.10 *rudely*, 829.9 *irascibly*, 830.14 *irritably*

churlishness 559.2 *impropriety*, 818.2 *bad manners*, 829.1 *irascibility*

churn 68.10 *farm tool*, 133.6 *mixer*, 366.3 *turbulence*, 366.14 *agitator*, 366.22 *agitate*, 393.25 *thicken*

churn out 183.18 *harp*, 243.10 *produce*, 245.9 *reproduce*

churn up 366.22 *agitate*

churrigueresque 43 Architectural Styles

chute 96.2 *channel*, 347.7 *outlet*, 360.3 *downflow*, 376.8 *smooth thing*

chutney 45.42 *preserve*, 413.2 *seasoning*

chutzpah 303.5 *boldness*, 535.6 *assertiveness*, 668.1 *defiance*, 807.2 *cheek*

Chuvash 5 Languages and Groups of Languages

chyle 387.3 *body fluid*

chylifaction 387.7 *juiciness*

chylifactive 387.16 *rheumy*

chylifactory 387.16 *rheumy*

chylific 387.16 *rheumy*

chylification 387.7 *juiciness*

chypre 418.3 *incense*

CIA 529.2 *secretiveness*

cibophobia 777 Phobias by Name

ciborium 10.14 *sacred object*, 293.7 *overhead covering*

cicada 82 Insects

cicatrix 309.3 *deformity*

cicatrization 629.11 *recuperation*

cicatrize 309.11 *deform*, 629.6 *cure*

Cicero 4 Philosophers

cicerone 654.4 *adviser*

Ciceronian 558.3 *elegant*

cichlid 80 Fishes

cig 413.7 *tobacco*

cigar 315.4 *cylinder*, 413.7 *tobacco*

cigarette 413.7 *tobacco*

cigarette butt 132.1 *remainder*

cigarette case 258.6 *box*, 413.7 *tobacco*

cigarette end 132.1 *remainder*, 413.7 *tobacco*

cigarette lighter 410.2 *lighter*, 413.7 *tobacco*

cigarette machine 413.7 *tobacco*

cigarette paper 413.7 *tobacco*

cigarette smoke 419.2 *something that makes an unpleasant smell*

cigarillo 413.7 *tobacco*

ciggie 413.7 *tobacco*

Cihuacoatl 8 Deities

Ciliata 81.9 *protozoan*

ciliate 81.9 *protozoan*, 81.23 *protozoa*

ciliate protozoan 81.9 *protozoan*

cilium 59.8 *cell organ*

CIM 65.1 *computing*

cimbalom 49 Musical Instruments

Cimmerian 440.8 *dark*, 551.2 *obscure*

cinch 137.10 *band*, 477.5 *easy question*, 490.12 *something certain*, 539.22 *dupe*, 660.6 *easy thing*

cinchocaine 62 Medication

cinchona 85 Tree Products

Cincinatti 93 Cities

cincture 295.25 *accessories*

cinder 614.6 *refuse*, 622.4 *dirt*

Cinderella 612.10 *nonentity*, 743.10 *poor person*

cinders 132.2 *residue*, 408.6 *fire*

cine camera 66.14 *cine film*, 66.16 *camera*, 435.8 *reflection*

cine film 66

cinema 51.14 *theatre*, 435.9 *viewpoint*, 526.9 *production*

Cinemascope 271.5 *broad thing*

cinema ticket 544.3 *means of identification*

cinematography 66.1 *photography*

cinema vérité 101.3 *realism*

cine photography 66.1 *photography*

Cinerama 271.5 *broad thing*

cineraria 84 Flowers and Flowering Plants

cinerarium 399.5 *cemetery*

cinerary 399.11 *funeral*

cinerary urn 399.4 *funeral objects*

cinereous 448.1 *grey*

cingulectomy 60 Surgical Operations, 61.3 *psychiatric treatment*

cingulum 7.11 *vestment*

cinnabar 54 Minerals, **57** Common Chemical Compounds, **57 Common Metal Ores**, 450.6 *red pigment*

cinnabar moth 82 Insects

cinnamon 45 Herbs and Spices, 413.5 *herbs*, 449.5 *brown thing*

cinnamon bear 77 Placental Mammals

cinnamon roll 45.36 *cake*

cinnamon toast 45.38 *bread*

cinque 179.1 *five*

cinquecento 43 Architectural Styles

cinquefoil 43 Architectural Decoration, **84** Flowers and Flowering Plants, 179.1 *five*, 544.8 *heraldic device*

Cintzotl 8 Deities

cipactli 49 Musical Instruments

cipher 11.2 *the occult*, 169.1 *number*, 170.8 *calculate*, 172.1 *zero*, 523.12 *unintelligible thing*, 524.12 *translate*, 529.4 *brain-teaser*, 529.14 *make mysterious*, 543.1 *sign*, 612.10 *nonentity*

cipher clerk 524.6 *interpreter*

ciphered 5.40 *translated*

ciphering 170.3 *count*

circadian rhythm 187.5 *recurrent period*, 214.2 *cycle*

Circassian 5 Languages and Groups of Languages

Circe 11.4 *witch*, 340.6 *charmer*, 586.13 *tempter*

Circean 11.15 *witchlike*

Circinus 53 The Constellations

circle 52, 313, 313, 21.2 *field events*, 51.16 *auditorium*, 51.31 *theatregoer*, 52.97 *align*, 159.6 *continuum*, 161.11 *group*, 161.19 *clique*, 214.8 *be cyclic*, 297.7 *surround*, 305.5 *team*, 311.2 *bend*, 311.6 *curve*, 315.3 *round thing*, 315.12 *move round*, 334.1 *circuit*, 334.3 *circuit*, 363.3 *orbit*, 363.7 *ring*, 364.8 *rotate*, 435.9 *viewpoint*, 665.1 *party*, 699.1 *restraint*

circle of friends 819.5 *friend*

circle of least confusion 56.31 *lens element*

circle of wagons 671.9 *barrier*

circle theatre 51.14 *theatre*

circle upon itself 314.6 *convolute*

circlewise 363.12 *circuitously*

circling 214.12 *cyclic*, 334.1 *circuit*, 363.1 *orbital motion*, 363.11 *orbiting*, 364.12 *rotary*

circling upon itself 314.1 *convolution*

circuit 56, 64, 334, 334, 32.9 *jumping*, 32.11 *eventing*, 33.6 *motor racing terms*, 51.13 *engagement*, 142.3 *whole situation*, 214.2 *cycle*, 235.7 *electrical power*, 249.13 *locality*, 311.2 *bend*, 313.2 *circle*, 315.3 *round thing*, 315.6 *round*, 327.2 *route*, 363.3, 363.6 *orbit*, 364.8 *rotate*

Circuit 334

circuit breaker 64.28 *plug*, 632.4 *safety device*

circuit court 16.21 *US court*, 492.3 *place of judgment*

circuit court of appeals 16.21 *US court*

circuit design 64.13 *circuit*

circuit diagram 64.13 *circuit*

circuit element 64, 56.55 *circuit*

circuit function 64

circuition 324, 334.2 *detour*, 363.2 *circuitousness*

circuit judge 16.24 *US judge*

circuitous 334, 286.5 *devious*, 324.17 *directional*, 335.25 *wandering*, 363.9 *orbital*, 553.4 *circumlocutory*, 610.7 *superfluous*

circuitously 334, 363, 553, 286.9 *deviously*, 311.7 *curvedly*, 313.8, 314.8 *circularly*, 324.18 *in motion*

circuitousness 363, 286.3 *deviousness*, 334.2 *detour*, 335.16 *wandering*

circuitous route 313.2 *circle*, 334.2 *detour*

circuitous writing 553.2 *circumlocution*, 610.3 *superfluity*

circuitry 64.13 *circuit*, 334.2 *detour*, 363.2 *circuitousness*

circular 313, 334, 363, 52.81 *curvilinear*, 164.3 *nonspecificness*, 214.12 *cyclic*, 311.4 *curved*, 474.7 *sophistic*, 528.4 *mass communication*, 532.9 *advertisement*

circular argument 337.17 *resilience*, 474.2 *sophism*, 504.4 *faulty reasoning*

circular decimal 52.18 *division*

circular function 52.52 *trigonometric function*

circularity 313, 311.1 *curvature*, 363.1 *orbital motion*, 474.1 *sophistry*

Circularity 313

circularize 313.7 *make circular*, 532.15 *publish*

circularized 532.19 *published*

circularly 313, 314, 214.16 *cyclically*, 311.7 *curvedly*, 474.14 *sophistically*

circularly polarized light 56.27 *polarized light*

circular mil 75 Scientific and Technical Units

circular motion 56.8 *time*

circularness 311.1 *curvature*

circular path 313.2 *circle*

circular polarization 56.15 *wave property*

circular return 214.2 *cycle*

circular road 313.2 *circle*

circular saw 47.11 *woodworking tool*, 63.9 *machine tool*, 85.7 *timber production*, 364.6 *rotator*

circular thing 313

circular triangle 52.43 *triangle*

circulate 162.16 *distribute*, 313.6 *circle*, 315.12 *move round*, 334.3 *circuit*, 356.9 *proceed*, 363.6 *orbit*, 364.8 *rotate*, 532.13 *make public*, 532.17 *be published*, 533.13 *report*, 642.16 *be sociable*, 741.24 *monetize*

circulated 162.22 *distributed*

circulating 334.6 *circular*, 532.19 *published*

circulating medium 741.1 *money*

circulation 162.1 *dispersion*, 334.1 *circuit*, 356.2 *passing along*, 363.1 *orbital motion*, 363.2 *circuitousness*, 364.1 *rotation*, 387.4 *blood*, 532.1 *publication*

circulation pattern 54.13 *ocean current*

circulatory 313.5, 334.6 *circular*, 363.9 *orbital*, 364.12 *rotary*

circulatory disease 624.4 *disease*

circumambience 297.2 *encirclement*, 334.2 *detour*, 363.1 *orbital motion*

circumambient 297.5 *surrounded*, 334.6 *circular*, 363.9 *orbital*

circumambulate 313.6 *circle*, 315.12 *move round*, 334.3 *circuit*, 363.7 *ring*

circumambulation 10.7 *non-Christian ritual*, 315.6 *round*, 363.1 *orbital motion*

circumambulatory 334.6 *circular*

circumbendibus 327.2 *route*, 334.2 *detour*, 335.16 *wandering*, 363.2 *circuitousness*

circumcircle 52.42 *circle*

circumcise 131.4 *take off*

circumcision 10.7 *non-Christian ritual*, 131.1 *subtraction*, 136.3 *separateness*

circumference 52.37 *line*, 52.42 *circle*, 104.4 *externality*, 248.1 *space*, 259.1 *size*, 263.3 *distant place*, 289.1 *exterior*, 299.3 *edge*, 313.2 *circle*, 313.4 *parts of a circle*, 327.2 *route*, 334.1 *circuit*, 364.1 *rotation*

circumferential 313.5 *circular*

circumferentially 313.8 *circularly*

circumflex 5.36 *accent*, 543.7 *punctuation*

circumflex angle 310.1 *angle*

circumflexion 363.1 *orbital motion*

circumfluent 334.6 *circular*

circumfusion 162.4 *sprinkling*

circumgyratory 364.12 *rotary*

circumlocute 286.7 *deviate*, 363.8 *detour*

circumlocution 553, 5.24 *phrasing*, 286.3 *deviousness*, 327.2 *route*, 334.2 *detour*, 335.16 *wandering*, 363.2 *circuitousness*, 525.2 *misinterpretation*, 557.2 *affectation*, 578.5 *equivocalness*

circumlocutory 553, 5.43 *phrasal*, 286.5 *devious*, 314.4 *convolutional*, 334.7 *circuitous*, 363.9 *orbital*, 557.4 *ornate*, 578.10 *equivocal*

circummigrate 334.3 *circuit*, 363.7 *ring*

circummigration 334.2 *detour*, 363.1 *orbital motion*

circumnavigable 334.6 *circular*, 363.9 *orbital*

circumnavigate 74.9 *navigate*, 313.6 *circle*, 315.12 *move round*, 334.3 *circuit*, 363.7 *ring*

circumnavigation 74.1 *water travel*, 315.6 *round*, 324.5 *circuition*, 334.2 *detour*, 363.1 *orbital motion*

circumnavigator 74.7 *nautical person*

circumnavigatory 334.6 *circular*

circumnutate 364.8 *rotate*

circumnutation 364.1 *rotation*

circumpolar star 53.10 *star*

circumrotation 364.1 *rotation*

circumrotatory 364.12 *rotary*

circumscribability 262.2 *contractibility*

circumscribable 262.9 *contractible*

circumscribe 52.97 *align*, 136.11 *divide*, 147.7 *exclude*, 262.5 *make smaller*, 272.10 *narrow*, 301.6 *wrap*, 302.7 *limit*, 354.5 *inset*, 485.16 *specify*, 560.17 *describe a circle*, 661.8 *hinder*, 671.18 *fence*, 699.8 *restrain*, 709.3 *veto*, 869.6 *moderate*

circumscribed 262.7 *smaller*, 272.1 *narrow*, 297.5 *surrounded*, 485.12 *conditional*, 726.10 *retained*, 869.9 *moderate*

circumscribed figure 52.41 *geometric figure*

circumscription 147.1 *exclusion*, 262.1 *contraction*, 299.3 *edge*, 301.1 *enclosure* , 302.1 *limita-*

tion, 485.6 *specification*, 661.1 *hindrance*, 699.1 *restraint*, 709.1 *veto*

circumscriptive 262.8 *contracting*, 299.6 *outlined*, 661.13 *hindering*, 699.13 *restraining*, 709.5 *vetoed*

circumscriptively 699.16 *under restraints*, 709.7 *by veto*

circumspect 328.5 *unhurried*, 459.11 *thoughtful*, 467.7 *watchful*, 469.9 *careful*, 507.5 *wise*, 516.6 *foreseeing*, 781.4 *cautious*

circumspection 469, 272.5 *narrowness*, 328.8 *slowness*, 459.6 *thoughtfulness*, 467.3 *carefulness*, 516.4 *prudence*, 781.1 *caution*

circumspectly 328.16 *slowly*, 467.15 *attentively*, 781.7 *cautiously*

circumstance 121.2 *rank*, 811.7 *pomp*, 813.1 *formality*

circumstances 106, 251, 105.1 *state*, 233 *influence*, 725.5 *personal estate*

Circumstances 106

circumstances beyond one's control 571.6 *necessitarianism*

circumstantial 106, 251, 480.9 *verificatory*, 483.8 *evidential*, 612.1 *unimportant*

circumstantial evidence 16.7 *legal trial*, 483.5 *legal evidence*

circumstantiality 553.1 *diffuseness*

circumstantially 251, 106.15 *under the circumstances*, 480.11 *verifiably*, 483.14 *as evidence*, 612.14 *unimportantly*

circumstantiate 106, 475.17, 480.2 *prove*, 483.12 *prove*

circumstantiation 480.5 *proof*

circumvallation 301.1 *enclosure*, 671.8 *military defences*, 671.11 *fortification*

circumvent 334.3 *circuit*, 363.7 *ring*, 539.23 *deceive*, 539.28 *trick*, 591.1 *avoid*, 657.5 *be cunning*

circumvention 539.1 *deception*, 539.7 *tricking*, 591.10 *avoidance*, 657.1 *cunning*

circumvent the law 16.73 *be illegal*

circumvolute 364.8 *rotate*

circumvolution 314.1 *convolution*, 364.1 *rotation*

circumvolve 364.8 *rotate*

circus 51.5 *show*, 51.14 *theatre*, 133.3 *miscellany*, 327.5 *road*, 811.14 *show*

circus animal 76.3 *domesticated animal*

circus artist 51.29 *circus performer*

circus horse 32.1 *horse*

circus manager 653.15 *manager*

circus performer 51, 237.5 *athlete*

circus troupe 51.23 *cast*

cirque 54.7 *landform*, 98.8 *valley*, 277.4 *deep thing*

cirque glacier 54.38 *glacier*

cirrhosis of the liver 874.16 *alcoholism*

cirriform 55.49 *cloudy*

cirripede 81.4 *arthropod*

cirrocumuliform 55.49 *cloudy*

cirrocumulous 55.49 *cloudy*

cirrocumulus 55.18 *cloud*

cirrose 55.49 *cloudy*

cirrostratous 55.49 *cloudy*

cirrostratus 55.18 *cloud*

cirrus 55.18 *cloud*

CIS 91.2 *union of nations*

cisco 80 Fishes

CIS-COBOL 65 Programming Languages

cissoid 52.40 *curve*

cist 399.4 *funeral objects*

Cistercian 7 Members of Religious Orders

cistern 258.11 *vessel*, 389.16 *water carrier*, 605.4 *storage*, 727.8 *sink*

cisternum 59.8 *cell organ*

cis–trans isomer 57.13 *structure*

citadel 634.1 *refuge*, 671.12 *fort*

Citallinicue 8 Deities

citation 16.6 *legal process*, 107.2 *interrelatedness*, 143.2 *particular*, 526.8 *showplace*, 681.1 *trophy*, 692.2 *demand*, 851.4 *compliment*, 856.1 *accusation*

cite 16.70 *litigate*, 106.11 *circumstantiate*, 165.24 *specify*, 183.17 *iterate*, 476.16 *explain*, 526.3 *reveal*, 564.11 *speak*, 856.5 *accuse*

cited 183.10 *iterated*, 526.13 *displayed*, 856.8 *accusatory*

Cities, Towns, and Villages 93

citified 93.14 *urban*

citify 93.15 *urbanize*

citizen 91.13 *native*, 146.3 *person included*, 255.4 *townsman*, 255.8 *national*, 400.10 *member of society*, 698.7 *free person*

citizen by adoption 255.8 *national*

citizen of the world 91.15 *internationalist*, 255.8 *national*, 655.5 *expert*

citizenry 255.2 *inhabitants*, 400.9 *group*

citizen's army 17.2 *the military*

citizens band 212.6 *radio frequency*

Citizens' Band 534.16 *transmitter*

Citizens' Band radio 420.9 *audio device*

Citizen's Band radio 534.20 *radio broadcasting*

citizenship 698.3 *independence*, 833.2 *public spiritedness*

Citlaltépetl 95 Mountains

citric 58 Common Fatty Acids, 86.7 *fruitlike*

citric acid 57 Common Chemical Compounds

citric acid cycle 58.24 *respiration*

citriculture 69.1 *horticulture*

citrine 54 Gemstones, 86.7 *fruitlike*, 452.1 *yellow*

citron 86 Fruits, 452.1 *yellow*, 452.8 *yellow thing*

citronella 87 Grasses

citrous 86.7 *fruitlike*

citrulline 58 Amino Acids

citrus 86.7 *fruitlike*

citrus belt 68.11 *farmland*

citrus fruit 69.10 *fruit tree*, 86.1 *fruits*, 86.2 *botanical fruit*

cittern 49 Musical Instruments

city 93, 12.5 *political organization*, 92.4 *community*, 93.14 *urban*, 249.10 *urban area*, 688.8 *governmental organization*

city centre 93.7 *city district*, 249.10 *urban area*

city commission 653.9 *US administrative council*

city council 16.2 *jurisdiction*, 653.9 *US administrative council*, 706.2 *representative body*

city district 93

city dweller 93.11 *urbanite*

city-dweller 255.4 *townsman*

city editor 532.11 *newspaper man*

city farm 68.6 *farm*

city father 93.11 *urbanite*

city hall 93.13 *municipal building*

city hospital 60.10 *hospital*

city jail 702.1 *prison*

city magistrate 16.23 *judge*

city manager 16.10 *law officer*, 93.11 *urbanite*, 653.16 *official*

city map 299.4, 547.7 *map*

city of the dead 399.5 *cemetery*

city person 255.4 *townsman*

city police 16.16 *US police*

cityscape 435.7 *view*

city slicker 93.11 *urbanite*, 255.4 *townsman*

city state 400.11 *nation*, 688.8 *governmental organization*

city-state 12.5 *political organization*

city tax 751.7 *tax*

civet 77 Placental Mammals, 418.3 *incense*

civic 12.9 *governmental*, 93.14 *urban*, 400.13 *national*, 815.15 *sociable*, 833.6 *philanthropic*

civically 93.16 *municipally*

civic architecture 43.1 *architecture*

civic centre 291.4 *centre of activity*

civic garden 69.2 *garden*

civics 6.3 *subject*

civil 12.9 *governmental*, 93.14 *urban*, 290.8 *internal*, 400.13 *national*, 763.2 *likable*, 815.15 *sociable*, 817.7 *courteous*

civil affairs 12.2 *politics*

civil architect 43.2 *architect*

civil architecture 43.1 *architecture*

civil ceremony 823.5 *wedding*

civil code 16.1 *the law*

civil court 16.19 *lawcourt*, 492.3 *place of judgment*

civil disobedience 669.3 *resistance movement*, 693.1 *disobedience*, 711.2 *dissent*

civil disturbance 693.2 *violation of the law*

civil engineer 63, 63.2 *engineer*, 646.2 *artisan*

civil engineering 63, 63.1 *engineering*, 243.2 *manufacture*, 603.5 *mechanics*

civilian 675.3 *pacifist*, 675.7 *peaceful*

civilian evacuation 676.7 *war measures*

civilian targets 398.15 *slaughterhouse*

civilities 813.5 *etiquette*, 817.3 *courtesies*

civility 763.8 *amiability*, 794.1 *elegance*, 817.1 *courtesy*

civilization 6.1 *education*, 48.1 *literature*, 400.4 *civilized human*, 501.3 *learning*, 627.5 *improvement*

civilize 2.15 *socialize*, 6.22 *educate*, 400.14 *make human*, 627.1 *improve*

civilized 6.20 *refined*, 400.12 *human*, 763.2 *likable*, 794.5 *refined*

civilized human 400

civilized humanity 400.4 *civilized human*

civilizing 627.16 *improving*

civil law 16.1 *the law*

civil liberties 698.2 *free speech*

civil list 171.6 *list of names*

civilly 43.20 *architecturally*, 815.18 *sociably*, 817.14 *courteously*

civil rights 698.2 *free speech*, 700.2 *equal opportunity*, 845.3 *prerogative*

civil servant 653.16 *official*, 697.2 *public servant*, 703.5 *commissioner*

civil service 12.3 *governance*, 653.3 *management*, 688.4 *governance*, 703.4 *council*

civil society 400.1 *nation*

civil state 400.11 *nation*

civil time 192.3 *chronology*

civil war 676.1 *war*, 693.4 *revolution*, 713.2 *disorder*

civil wedding 823.5 *wedding*

civil wrong 16.39 *crime*

civism 833.2 *public spiritedness*

civvies 295.4, 814.6 *informal dress*

civvy street 675.1 *peace*

clabber 393.8 *pulp*, 393.25, 394.11 *thicken*

clabbered 393.20 *thick*

clabbering 394.1 *viscosity*

clack 426.3, 426.10 *rattle*, 432.5 *sing*

clad 293.28 *face*, 295.29 *dressed*, 295.32 *dress*

cladding 293.8 *wall covering*

clade 59.17 *taxonomy*

cladism 59.17 *taxonomy*

cladist 59.19 *life scientist*

cladistic 59.28 *taxonomic*

cladistics 59.17 *taxonomy*

cladode 83.6 *leaf*

claim 15.4 *industrial dispute*, 16.5 *litigation*, 16.70 *litigate*, 249.12 *plot*, 355.6 *extorsion*, 355.16 *extort*, 473.3 *line of argument*, 473.5 *plea*, 473.15 *state*,

473.16 *plead*, 593.2 *need*, 593.8 *miss*, 692.2, 692.10 *demand*, 712.1 *request*, 712.2 *demand*, 712.6 *request*, 712.7 *demand*, 723.1 *possession*, 723.7 *possess*, 725.1 *property*, 804.7 *be entitled to*, 843.6 *right*, 845.3 *prerogative*, 845.14 *be entitled*

claimant 712.4 *requester*, 845.7 *beneficiary*, 856.3 *accuser*

claim as one's right 845.14 *be entitled*

claim a victory 682.9 *be victorious*

claimed 16.54 *litigated*, 473.11 *logical*

claiming 16.53 *litigating*, 712.10 *demanding*, 723.1 *possession*

claiming the right 845.11 *entitled to*

claim sanctuary 634.4 *shelter*

claims of conscience 847.4 *sense of duty*

claim squatter's rights 723.7 *possess*

claim supplementary benefit 743.12 *be poor*

claim to fame 165.8 *specialization*, 617.6 *worth*, 800.1 *estimation*

claim to priority 194

clairaudience 11.8 *psychic power*

clairaudient 11.13 *diviner*, 11.17 *divinatory*

clairsentience 11.8 *psychic power*

clairsentient 11.13 *diviner*, 11.17 *divinatory*

clairvoyance 8.8 *divine manifestation*, 11.8 *psychic power*, 11.9 *divination*, 368.4 *parapsychology*, 403.1 *sensation*, 435.5 *imagination*, 464.2 *precognition*, 517.2 *divination*, 759.2 *impression*

clairvoyancy 516.3 *foresight*

clairvoyant 11.13 *diviner*, 11.17 *divinatory*, 368.7 *believer in a nonmaterial world*, 368.9 *parapsychological*, 435.11 *observer*, 464.5 *intuitive person*, 464.7 *precognitive*, 516.5 *predictor*, 516.6 *foreseeing*, 517.8 *oracle*, 517.13 *predicting*, 759.11 *intuitive*

clairvoyantly 11.25 *occultly*, 368.13 *metaphysically*, 516.8 *foresightedly*

Claisen condensation 57 Named Reactions

clam 81 Molluscs, 566.7 *taciturn person*

clamant 423.6 *loud*

clambake 350.13 *feast*, 872.3 *act of gluttony*

clamber 359.6 *mounting*, 359.14 *climb*

clamber up 359.14 *climb*

clam chowder 45.13 *soup*, 45.43 *US dish*

clamlike 81.19 *molluscan*, 531.17 *noncommittal*

clammed up 422.3 *silent*

clammily 353.33 *scatologically*, 391.17 *moistly*

clamminess 391.3 *humidity*, 394.1 *viscosity*

clammy 353.28 *sweaty*, 391.9 *moist*, 394.8 *viscous*

clamorous 423.6 *loud*, 430.7 *strident*, 431.16 *vociferous*, 713.9 *protesting*

clamorously 431.20 *vociferously*

clamour 133.3 *miscellany*, 153.5 *commotion*, 423.2 *outcry*, 430.1 *stridency*, 431.1 *cry*, 434.2 *dissonant noise*, 663.2 *objection*, 713.1, 713.6 *protest*, 852.9 *show of disapproval*

clamour for 593.8 *miss*

clamp 57 Laboratory Apparatus, **74** Rigging, 135.10 *link*, 137.8 *fastening*, 137.12 *bind*, 242.2 *moderator*, 242.4 *moderate*, 262.4 *contractor*, 262.5 *make smaller*, 323.3 *restrainer*, 699.5 *means of restraint*, 699.8 *restrain*, 726.1 *retention*, 726.3 *tools for gripping*, 726.6 *retain*

clamp a wheel 661.10 *restrain*

clampdown 531.4 *silence*, 690.1 *severity*
clamp down on 150.22 *pacify*, 242.4 *moderate*, 244.8 *destroy*, 690.5 *be severe*, 699.8 *restrain*
clamped 137.16 *bound*
clamping 262.1 *contraction*
clamshell 73 Aircraft Parts, 63.29 *construction equipment*
clam shell 293.14 *animal covering*
clam up 422.1 *be silent*, 529.12 *keep secret*
clan 1.7 *society*, 137.3 *associate*, 161.17 *family*, 163.8 *genealogy*, 255.2 *inhabitants*, 400.9 *group*, 665.2 *society*
Clan 29.5 *golf ball*
clandestine 438.3 *private*, 527.5 *mysterious*, 529.10 *secretive*, 657.4 *cunning*
clandestineness 527.6 *latency*, 529.2 *secretiveness*
clang 423.1 *loudness*, 423.8 *be loud*, 426.12 *ring*, 427.2 *ringing*, 427.10 *ring*
clang association 61.27 *association of ideas*
clanger 71.11 *bicycle part*, 493.2 *mistake*, 504.10, 559.6 *blunder*
clanging 427.7 *ringing*
clangorous 423.6 *loud*
clangour 423.1 *loudness*, 427.2 *ringing*
clank 430.5 *sound hoarse*
clanking 430.8 *hoarse*
clannish 147.10 *excluding*, 500.7 *dissenting*, 665.9 *societal*
clannishly 665.18 *cliquishly*
clannishness 665.4 *partisanship*
clanship 664.2 *fellowship*
clan system 12.1 *government*
clap 423.1 *loudness*, 423.8 *be loud*, 425.2, 425.6 *crack*, 543.11 *gesture*, 769.5, 769.8 *cheer*, 773.7 *dance*, 851.5, 851.16 *acclaim*
clapboard 47.12 *wood*, 293.8 *wall covering*
clapboard house 266.5 *layered thing*
clap eyes on 435.12 *see*
clap of thunder 55.21 *thunderstorm*, 425.1 *bang*
clap one's hands 851.16 *acclaim*
clapped out 236.12 *impotent*, 650.1 *fatigued*
clapper 427.4 *sources of resonance*, 851.10 *applauder*
clapper bell 49 Musical Instruments
clappers 49 Musical Instruments
clapping 543.3 *gesture*, 543.15 *gestural*, 769.5 *cheer*, 851.5 *acclaim*, 851.20 *acclamatory*
clap someone on the back 543.11 *gesture*
claptrap 506.1 *nonsense*, 521.5 *empty talk*, 538.6, 540.13 *nonsense*
claque 851.10 *applauder*
claqueur 851.10 *applauder*
Clare 48 Poets, 92 Counties, 93 Cities
clarence 71 Carriages and Carts
Clarenceux 544.9 *herald*
claret 351.9 *wine*, 387.4 *blood*, 450.7 *red thing*
claret cup 351.7 *alcoholic drink*
clarification 439.13 *enlightenment*, 475.3 *explanation*, 480.5 *proof*, 524.1 *interpretation*, 621.2 *cleaning*, 660.7 *easing*
clarified 134.13 *pure*, 439.22 *enlightened*, 442.1 *transparent*, 475.11 *explanatory*, 524.15 *interpreted*
clarifier 5.2 *linguist*, 475.7 *demonstrator*, 524.6 *interpreter*
clarify 439, 550, 4.21 *rationalize*, 134.10 *purify*, 387.24 *melt*, 437.10 *make visible*, 442.12 *make transparent*, 475.16 *explain*, 480.2 *prove*, 522.5 *simplify*, 524.8 *interpret*, 621.15 *purify*, 660.16 *make easy*

clarifying 524.14 *interpretive*
clarinet 49 Musical Instruments
clarinet d'amore 49 Musical Instruments
clarion call 423.1 *loudness*, 586.4 *exhortation*, 676.7 *war measures*
clarity 437, 550, 56.23 *light*, 134.1 *purity*, 312.8 *directness*, 318.4 *conspicuousness*, 439.13 *enlightenment*, 442.5 *transparency*, 520.3 *comprehension*, 522.10, 556.4 *simplicity*, 558.1 *elegance*, 660.2 *simplicity*
Clarity 550
Clark 94 Lakes
Clark cell 56 Named Laws
clarkia 84 Flowers and Flowering Plants
clash 49.38 *sound*, 117.4 *disagreement*, 117.14 *disagree*, 231.1 *counteraction*, 231.3 *counteract*, 241.3 *instance of violence*, 330.2 *collide*, 389.33 *sprinkle*, 407.12 *abut*, 423.2 *outcry*, 423.8 *be loud*, 425.1, 425.5 *bang*, 430.4 *be strident*, 434.6 *disagreement*, 434.10 *lack harmony*, 434.11 *disagree*, 473.1 *argument*, 473.13 *argue*, 500.1, 500.8 *dissent*, 663.16 *confront*, 666.2 *argument*, 666.5 *disagree*, 666.6 *argue*, 674.1 *contention*, 674.6 *fight*, 676.9 *battle*, 764.8, 764.11 *quarrel*, 820.1 *enmity*, 820.12 *oppose*
clashing 117.4 *disagreement*, 117.10 *disagreeing*, 231.4 *counteracting*, 434.1 *dissonance*, 434.7 *dissonant*, 444.12 *gaudy*, 473.7 *arguing*, 663.3 *conflict*, 663.20 *discordant*, 666.1 *disagreement*, 820.1 *enmity*, 820.9 *aggressive*
clasp 135.5 *joint*, 135.10 *link*, 137.8 *fastening*, 137.12 *bind*, 138.6 *adhere*, 320.3 *enfoldment*, 320.9 *enfold*, 323.3 *restrainer*, 726.1 *retention*, 726.3 *tools for gripping*, 726.6 *retain*, 821.14 *communication of love*, 826.7 *show endearment for*
clasped 137.16 *bound*, 726.10 *retained*
clasp hands 817.12 *greet*, 819.15 *be hospitable*
clasping 726.9 *retentive*
clasp knife 380.10 *knife*
clasp someone's shoulder 543.11 *gesture*
clasp the knees of 634.4 *shelter*
class 163, 163, 52.21 *set*, 59.17 *taxonomy*, 105.1 *state*, 107.3 *relative position*, 121.2 *rank*, 121.5 *measure*, 124.4 *average*, 143.1 *part*, 148.2 *piece*, 150.4 *position*, 150.19 *systematize*, 152.6 *category*, 152.15 *categorize*, 161.17 *family*, 163.3 *kingdom*, 163.6 *students*, 163.7 *lecture*, 198.5 *contemporary*, 400.9 *group*, 665.2 *society*
Class 163
class A 861.2 *best*, 861.9 *the best*
class boundary 2.7 *social stratification*
class conflict 2.7 *social stratification*
class conscious 805.23 *prejudiced*
class consciousness 805.11 *prejudice*
class discrimination 481.4 *social discrimination*
class distinction 805.11 *prejudice*
classed 163, 105.8 *in a state of*, 107.6 *ranked*
classed with 146.8 *included*
classic 124.1 *average*, 126.15 *excellent*, 202.12 *olden*, 295.31 *styled*, 556.1 *simple*, 558.2 *stylist*, 558.3 *elegant*, 617.1 *worthy*, 619.1 *perfect*, 655.3, 696.11 *masterpiece*
classic abseil 34.3 *climbing technique*

classical 43 Architectural Styles, 5.39 *of language*, 6.21 *curricular*, 48.16 *literary*, 50.29 *realist*, 56.98 *physical*, 202.12 *olden*, 202.14 *historic*, 558.3 *elegant*, 619.1 *perfect*
Classical 3.15 *historic*
Classical Age 3.10 *past age*, 200.5 *historical period*
classical author 549.5, 558.2 *stylist*
classical ballet 46.8 *ballet*
classical ballets 46
classical conditioning 61.20 *conditioning*
classical costume 295.5 *fancy dress*
classical dancer 46.5 *dancer*
classical genetics 59.11 *genetics*
Classical Greek art 50 Western Art Styles and Movements
classical guitar 49 Musical Instruments
classical language 5.9 *ancient language*
classically 56.100 *physically*, 202.21 *anachronically*
classical mathematics 52.1 *mathematics*
classical mechanics 56.2 *classical physics*
classical music 49
classical physics 56
classical riding 32.6 *horsemanship*
classical taxonomy 59.17 *taxonomy*
classical tragedy 51.9 *tragedy*
classicism 50 Western Art Styles and Movements, 200.9, 202.4 *antiquarianism*, 558.1 *elegance*
Classicism 48 Literary Groups and Movements
classicist 5.2 *linguist*, 200.11, 202.9 *antiquarian*, 558.2 *stylist*
classic murder 398.2 *murder*
classic quality 617.6 *worth*
classic route 34.1 *mountaineering*
classification 163, 107.3 *relative position*, 121.3 *gradation*, 150.2 *grouping*, 152.5 *categorization*, 171.7 *listing*, 544.1 *identification*, 560.7 *nomenclature*
classificational 163.10 *classificatory*
classifications of life 396
classificatory 163, 150.11 *grouped*, 152.25 *categorical*, 171.11 *listed*
classified 107.6 *ranked*, 121.7 *gradational*, 150.11 *grouped*, 152.24 *categorized*, 163.12 *classed*, 527.2 *concealed*, 529.9 *secret*, 544.12 *identified*, 709.6 *censored*
classified ad 528.4 *mass communication*, 532.9 *advertisement*
classified ads 754.7 *discounter*
classified advertisement 532.9 *advertisement*
classified document 527.8 *concealment*, 709.2 *censorship*
classified information 528.3 *document*, 529.1 *secrecy*, 531.4 *silence*
classified with 146.8 *included*
classify 121.5 *measure*, 150.19 *systematize*, 152.15 *categorize*, 163.13 *class*, 171.8 *list*, 257.9 *itemize*, 529.12 *keep secret*, 544.10 *identify*
classify a film 709.4 *censor*
classify as 146.6 *subsume*
classifying 544.1 *identification*
classify secret 709.4 *censor*
classism 481.4 *social discrimination*
classist 481.10 *discriminatory*
classless 12.9, 688.14 *governmental*
classmate 6.7 *learner*, 180.11 *companion*, 198.5 *contemporary*, 819.5 *friend*
class notes 299.1 *outline*
class of 198.5 *contemporary*

class prejudice 481.4 *social discrimination*
class-prejudiced 493.8 *unjust*
class project 472.5 *educational topic*
class reunion 815.3 *meeting*
class ring 544.5 *uniform*
classroom 6.15 *schoolroom*, 688.6 *place of authority*
class structure 2.7 *social stratification*
class war 481.4 *social discrimination*, 627.11 *reformism*, 676.1 *war*
class with 146.6 *subsume*
classy 617.1 *worthy*, 796.7 *fashionable*, 802.4 *aristocratic*
clastic 54.56 *petrographic*
clastic rock 54.31 *sedimentary rock*
clathrate 57.7 *chemical compound*
clatter 133.3 *miscellany*, 423.2 *outcry*, 423.8 *be loud*, 425.6 *crack*, 426.3, 426.10 *rattle*
clattering 426.17 *rattling*
Claude glass 50.11 *artist's materials*
Claudel 48 Dramatists
Claude tint 452.7 *yellow pigment*
Claudian 48 Poets
clausal 5.43 *phrasal*
clause 5.23 *phrase*, 143.2 *particular*, 716.2 *basis for negotiations*
Clausius 52 Scientists
claustrophobia 777 Phobias by Name, 785.1 *dislike*
claustrophobic 301.7 *enclosed*
claustrophobically 301.8 *confinedly*
clave 49 Musical Instruments
clavichord 49 Musical Instruments
clavicle 382 Bones
clavicor 49 Musical Instruments
clavicytherium 49 Musical Instruments
claviorgan 49 Musical Instruments
Clavius 53 Lunar Features
claw 137.9 *yoke*, 380.8 *sharp-pointed thing*, 380.16 *use a sharp tool*, 406.11 *inflict pain*, 407.7 *sense organ*, 726.3 *tools for gripping*
clawback 131.2 *subtracted item*
claw bell 49 Musical Instruments
claw chisel 50.14 *sculptor's materials*
clawed 77.28 *carnivorous*
clawed frog 79 Amphibians
claw-hammer coat 295.11 *jacket*
claw one's way up 359.14 *climb*
claw ring 36.3 *parts of a sailing boat*
claws 680.1 *weapon*
claw skyward 359.19 *take off*
clay 44.2 *raw material*, 54.27 *sediment*, 54.36 *soil*, 63.26 *masonry*, 138.3 *adhesive*, 371.4 *solid body*, 393.13 *mud*, 604.1 *materials*, 622.4 *dirt*
Clay 18 Sporting Personalities
clayey 54.58 *earthy*, 374.4 *compressible*
clay mineral 54.34 *mineral*
claymore 680.8 *sharp weapon*
clay pigeon shooting 18 Sporting Activities, 37.1 *target shooting*
clay pipe 413.7 *tobacco*
clay sculpture 50.12 *sculpture*
claystone 54 Common Rocks
clayware 44.1 *ceramics*
clean 621, 621, 621, 34.8 *mountaineering*, 34.9 *mountaineer*, 134.10 *purify*, 134.13 *pure*, 134.14 *purified*, 144.9 *completely*, 150.13 *orderly*, 150.21 *tidy*, 201.12 *immature*, 201.24 *immaturely*, 254.13 *vacant*, 376.11 *smooth*, 390.20 *aerate*, 417.3 *odourless*, 417.5 *deodorize*, 442.12 *make transparent*, 446.5 *pure*, 446.13 *whiten*, 556.1 *simple*, 600.2 *new*, 625.4 *hygienic*, 625.6 *make hygienic*,

627.1 *improve,* 629.3 *restore,*
644.6 *work,* 651.1 *refresh,*
843.10 *moral,* 865.5, 865.5 *innocent,* 876.10 *moralistic*
clean as a new pin 201.12 *immature*
clean as a whistle 621.16 *clean*
clean bill of health 623.3 *health*
clean climbing 34.1 *mountaineering*
clean dry air 55.8 *atmosphere*
cleaned 621, 134.14 *purified*
cleaned out 621.17 *cleaned,*
743.2 *insolvent*
cleaned up 621.17 *cleaned,*
684.7 *completed*
cleaner 621, 134.3 *purifier,*
621.9 *cleaning agent,* 646.1
worker, 662.16 *home help*
clean for 697.8 *serve*
clean forget 512.13 *forget*
clean-handed 865.5 *innocent*
clean hands 857.1 *probity,* 865.1
innocence
cleaning 621, 34.3 *climbing technique,* 34.8 *mountaineering,*
67.8 *fabric treatment,* 134.2 *purification,* 621.18 *cleansing,*
627.5 *improvement*
cleaning agent 621
cleaning cloth 621
cleaning lady 662.16 *home help,*
697.1 *servant*
cleaning object 621
cleaning out 349.21 *removal*
cleaning up 621.2 *cleaning*
cleaning-up 621.4 *censorship*
cleaning woman 697.6 *domestic*
servant
cleanliness 134.1 *purity,* 201.3
immaturity, 556.4 *simplicity,*
621.1 *cleanness,* 625.1 *hygiene,*
651.5 *refreshment,* 865.1 *innocence*
cleanly 621, 134.13 *pure,*
134.19 *purely,* 201.24 *immaturely,* 380.19 *suddenly,*
417.7 *odourlessly,* 600.13
newly, 621.16 *clean*
cleanness 621, 134.1 *purity,*
150.5 *orderliness,* 201.3 *immaturity,* 417.1 *odourlessness,*
442.5 *transparency,* 446.11 *purity,* 556.4 *simplicity,* 600.9
newness, 625.1 *hygiene,* 651.5
refreshment, 865.1 *innocence*
Cleanness 621
clean one's plate 350.22 *eat well*
clean out 134.10 *purify,* 349.11
void, 621.13 *clean,* 621.15 *purify*
cleanse 134.10 *purify,* 417.5
deodorize, 442.12 *make transparent,* 621.15 *purify,* 625.6 *make*
hygienic
cleansed 134.13 *pure,* 134.14 *purified,* 621.17 *cleaned*
cleanse oneself of guilt 840.6
apologize
cleanse oneself of sin 840.6 *apologize*
cleanser 134.3 *purifier,* 386.6 *pomade,* 546.4 *eraser,* 621.9 *cleaning agent,* 630.3 *prophylactic*
clean-shaven 294.9 *shed,* 296.13
hairless, 591.1 *smooth*
clean sheet 254.3 *emptiness*
cleansing 389, 621, 10.5 *Christian rite,* 10.7 *non-Christian ritual,* 134.2 *purification,* 134.15
purifying, 389.11 *wash,* 417.4
deodorizing, 621.2 *cleaning,*
627.5 *improvement,* 630.17 *remedial,* 637.1 *preservation,*
840.2 *apology,* 840.4 *atoning*
cleansing agent 134.3 *purifier,*
621.9 *cleaning agent*
cleansing cream 134.3 *purifier,*
621.9 *cleaning agent*
clean slate 201.5 *fresh start,*
254.3 *emptiness,* 546.4 *eraser,*
704.3 *new beginning*
clean sweep 704.3 *new beginning*
Cleanthes 4 *Philosophers*

clean up 150.22 *pacify,* 152.19
tidy, 621.13 *clean,* 621.15 *purify,* 627.1 *improve,* 651.1 *refresh*
clean up 721.5 *profit,* 721.14
profit, 742.13 *get rich*
clean-up man 22.2 *baseball player*
clear 437, 550, 16.63 *acquitted,*
16.78 *acquit,* 55.45 *fine,* 55.61
shine, 85.18 *manage trees,* 94.9
lakelike, 116.73 *permit,* 134.10
purify, 134.13 *pure,* 237.10 *potent,* 254.13 *vacant,* 263.10 *distantly,* 265.4 *space,* 275.15 *be*
high, 312.2 *straightforward,*
322.13 *opened up,* 322.19 *open*
up, 359.14 *climb,* 433.6 *melodious,* 435.23, 437.1 *visible,*
439.19 *sunny,* 442.1 *transparent,* 475.9 *demonstrated,* 520.6
meaningful, 522.2 *simple,*
526.15 *open,* 528.16 *informative,* 530.10 *disclosed,* 556.1
simple, 558.3 *elegant,* 591.21
away, 621.13 *clean,* 632.5 *safe,*
660.9 *easy,* 660.16 *make easy,*
660.18 *disentangle,* 708.3 *permit,* 714.14 *auspicious,* 721.14
profit, 730.9 *receive,* 746.7 *pay*
off, 839.10 *absolve,* 848.6 *acquitted,* 855.7 *vindicate,* 865.9
declare innocent
Clear 65 Programming Languages
clear accounts with 746.7 *pay off*
clear across 271.8 *breadthwise*
clearage 349.21 *removal*
clear-air turbulence 73.7 *miscellaneous aviation terms*
clearance 16.42 *acquittal,* 21.2
field events, 35.6 *rugger,* 116.8
permit, 134.2 *purification,*
248.6 *available space,* 265.1 *interval,* 349.21 *removal,* 353.2
defecation, 356.6 *passport,*
698.5 *scope,* 708.1 *permission,*
727.1 *disposal,* 739.4 *sale,*
746.1 *payment,* 855.1 *vindication*
clearance kick 35.3 *rugby play*
clearance papers 356.6 *passport,*
708.2 *permit*
clearance sale 727.2 *disposal of*
property, 739.4 *sale,* 752.2 *bargain*
clear as a bell 433.6 *melodious*
clear as air 442.1 *transparent*
clear as daylight 526.14 *manifest*
clear as mud 438.2 *difficult to*
see, 441.6 *murky,* 443.4 *inscrutable,* 523.4 *difficult*
clear away 349.11 *void*
clear bulb 439.6 *electric light*
clear coast 660.6 *easy thing*
clear conscience 857.1 *probity,*
863.1 *virtue,* 865.1 *innocence*
clear course 660.6 *easy thing*
clear-cut 237.10 *potent,* 318.7
conspicuous, 435.23 *visible,*
437.2 *clear,* 475.12 *demonstrable,* 522.1 *intelligible,* 550.3
clear
cleared 16.63 *acquitted,* 116.18
permitting, 746.16 *paid,*
855.12, 865.5 *innocent,* 865.6
declared innocent
cleared up 152.27 *tidied,* 475.11
explanatory, 478.14 *solved*
clear-eyed 435.21 *seeing*
clear field 210.2 *opportunity*
clear glass 439.10 *window,*
442.9 *glass*
clear head 873.6 *sobriety*
clear-headed 4.15 *rational,*
507.6 *intelligent,* 509.5 *rational,* 873.1 *sober*
clear image 547.6 *image*
clearing 68.11 *farmland,* 85.4
trees, 84.3 *geographical space,*
322.8 *open space,* 349.21 *removal,* 660.8 *disentanglement*
clearing bank 741.19 *treasury*
clearing from guilt 855.1 *vindication*
clearing of one's name 855.1 *vindication*

clearing up 478.6 *solution,* 621.2
cleaning
clearly 550, 94.10 *limnologically,* 322.25 *obviously,* 435.25,
437.11 *visibly,* 442.13 *transparently,* 457.15 *apparently,*
475.20 *manifestly,* 520.13
meaningfully, 522.13 *intelligibly,* 556.8 *simply,* 558.5 *elegantly,* 714.17 *auspiciously*
clearly printed 522.2 *simple*
clearly visible 318.7 *conspicuous*
clear message 520.3 *comprehension*
clearness 134.1 *purity,* 318.4
conspicuousness, 437.4 *clarity,*
442.5 *transparency,* 522.10 *simplicity,* 550.1 *clarity*
clear off 345.1 *depart,* 345.15 *go,*
349.11 *void,* 349.33 *go away*
clear one's debts 845.19 *pay*
clear one's head 651.2 *be refreshed,* 873.5 *sober up*
clear one's name 839.10 *absolve,*
855.7 *vindicate*
clear one's throat 353.20 *salivate,* 430.5 *sound hoarse*
clear out 134.11 *simplify,*
345.15 *go,* 349.11 *void,* 349.33
go away, 621.13 *clean*
clear pool 94.2 *small lake*
clear printing 522.10 *simplicity*
clear profit 721.5 *profit*
clear road 660.6 *easy thing*
clear round 32.9 *jumping*
clear run 210.2 *opportunity*
clear shot 40.12 *badminton terms*
clear-sighted 435.21 *seeing*
clear sky 55.22 *sun*
clear soup 45.13 *soup*
clear space 248.3 *geographical*
space
clear stock 739.1 *sell*
clear the air 417.5 *deodorize,*
840.5 *atone*
clear the cobwebs out 651.2 *be*
refreshed
clear the crossbar 21.6 *jump*
clear the decks 152.19 *tidy,*
349.11 *void,* 594.4 *prepare for*
action
clear the ground 356.10 *enter,*
660.16 *make easy*
clear the path for 586.16 *tempt*
clear the track 662.28 *further*
clear the water 36.16 *row*
clear the way 660.16 *make easy*
clear the way for 486.7 *make possible*
clear thinking 459.5 *common*
sense
clear to anyone 522.2 *simple*
clear up 4.21 *rationalize,* 152.19
tidy, 478.20 *solve,* 480.2 *prove,*
490.21 *make certain,* 522.5 *simplify,* 621.13 *clean,* 684.4 *complete*
clear varnish 442.8 *transparent*
thing
clear view 210.2 *opportunity*
clear visibility 318.4 *conspicuousness*
clearway 71.2 *road,* 73.4 *airport,*
327.2 *road,* 356.2 *passing along*
clearwing moth 82 *Insects*
cleat 74 *Parts of a Ship,* 36.3
parts of a sailing boat, 36.7
windsurfing, 137.8 *fastening*
cleated 34.8 *mountaineering*
cleated boots 34.4 *climbing*
equipment
cleavage 54.20 *earth movement,*
54.28 *rock,* 59.15 *developmental*
biology, 136.3 *separateness*
cleave 54.64 *fold,* 136.9 *separate,* 176.16 *halve,* 265.5 *crack,*
322.18 *open,* 380.16 *use a*
sharp tool
cleaver 380.10 *knife*
cleavers 84 *Flowers and Flowering Plants*
cleave to 138.6 *adhere,* 726.6 *retain*
cleave to the line 332.7 *take a direction*
cleek 29.4 *golf club*
clef 49.17 *notation,* 49.20 *key*

cleft 136.3 *separateness,* 136.16
apart, 176.13 *half,* 265.2 *crack,*
265.7 *cracked,* 319.1 *notch,*
322.1 *opening,* 322.12 *open,*
666.2 *argument*
cleft palate 309.3 *deformity*
cleft stick 491.11 *irresoluteness,*
659.5 *predicament*
Cleland 48 Writers
clem 871.5 *fast*
clematis 84 Flowers and Flowering Plants, 455.3 *purple thing*
clemency 677.2 *peace offering,*
691.1 *leniency,* 835.3 *mercy,*
839.2 *forgivingness*
clement 408.11 *warm,* 691.4 *lenient,* 835.6 *pitying,* 839.5 *merciful*
Clementi 49 Musicians and
Composers
clementine 86 Fruits, 133.5 *hybrid,* 451.3 *orange thing*
clemently 677.7 *pacifically*
clemizole 52 Medication
clemmed 871.6 *fasting*
clench 262.5 *make smaller,*
726.1 *retention,* 726.6 *retain*
clenched 262.7 *smaller*
clenched fist 543.3 *gesture,*
726.3 *tools for gripping*
clenched jaw 543.3 *gesture,*
574.16 *fortitude*
clenched teeth 543.3 *gesture,*
574.16 *fortitude*
clenching 262.1 *contraction*
clench one's fist 543.11 *gesture*
clench one's jaw 543.11 *gesture*
clench one's teeth 422.1 *be silent,* 543.11 *gesture,* 574.8
brace oneself
Cleomedes 53 Lunar Features
Cleopatra's Needle 275.6 *tall*
thing
clepsydra 192.6 *clock*
clepystra 191 Timepieces and
Timers
clerestory 10.12 *church,* 43.10
church architecture, 275.8 *high*
thing
clergyman 7.8 *priest*
clergywoman 7.8 *priest*
cleric 7.8 *priest*
clerical 7.17 *priestly*
clerical collar 7.11 *vestment,*
295.14 *neckwear*
clerical dress 295.3, 813.4 *formal dress*
clerical error 504.12 *typing error*
clerical garb 295.3 *formal dress*
clerical hat 295.15 *headgear*
clericalism 7.9 *priesthood,* 12.1
government
clerical robe 295.16 *robe*
clericals 7.11 *vestment*
clerical worker 646.1 *worker*
clerihew 48.7 *poem,* 552.2 *outline*
clerk 545.9 *recorder,* 653.16 *official,* 697.5 *office assistant,*
706.1 *delegate*
clerk in holy orders 7.8 *priest*
clerk of the court 16.10 *law officer*
cleveite 54 Minerals
Cleveland 92 Counties, 93 Cities
Cleveland Bay 32 Breeds of
Horse and Pony
clever 6.17 *educatable,* 6.18 *educated,* 380.5 *mentally sharp,*
459.10 *intelligent,* 501.8 *knowledgeable,* 507.6 *intelligent,*
519.10 *imaginative,* 655.6 *skilful,* 655.9 *well-made,* 657.4 *cunning*
clever-clever 507.6 *intelligent*
clever clogs 459.8 *intellectual*
person, 501.6 *knowledgeable person,* 809.7 *vain person*
clever-clogs 655.5 *expert*
clever dick 501.6 *knowledgeable*
person, 507.4 *intellectual,* 809.7
vain person
clever hands 655.1 *skill*
cleverly 6.26 *studiously,* 380.18
sharply, 459.15, 507.10 *intelligently,* 655.12 *skilfully*

cleverness 459, 6.10 *educatability*, 380.13 *mental sharpness*, 501.3 *learning*, 507.2 *intelligence*, 567.3, 651.1 *skill*, 657.1 *cunning*

clew 36.3 *parts of a sailing boat*, 36.7 *windsurfing*, 36.10 *sailing*

clew gybe 36.1 *sailing*, 36.15 *sail*

clew line 137.7 *tackle*

clew tack 36.1 *sailing*, 36.15 *sail*

clianthus 84 Flowers and Flowering Plants

cliché 5.21 *catchword*, 5.42 *worded*, 112.2 *conformity*, 164.8 *generalization*, 183.3 *repetitiveness*, 426.7 *repeated word*, 505.1 *maxim*, 521.1 *lack of meaning*, 555.2 *lack of emphasis*

clichéd 5.42 *worded*, 183.13 *monotonous*, 505.2 *proverbial*, 521.10 *meaningless*, 555.1 *unemphatic*, 584.10 *familiar*

cliché-ridden 183.13 *monotonous*, 555.1 *unemphatic*

click 424.1 *faintness*, 424.5 *sound faint*, 425.2, 425.6 *crack*, 682.6 *be successful*

click beetle 82 Insects

clicking 425.9 *crackling*, 426.17 *rattling*

client 13.9 *economist*, 60.18 *patient*, 599.8 *user*, 737.12 *custom*, 738.12 *purchaser*

client-centred therapy 61.3 *psychiatric treatment*

clientele 13.9 *economist*, 737.12 *custom*, 738.12 *purchaser*

cliff 54.11 *coast*, 275.3 *mountain*, 281.3 *vertical thing*, 318.2 *projection*

cliffbrake 88 Ferns

cliffhanger 48.2 *fiction*, 122.2 *equilibrium*

cliffhanging 674.16 *competitive*

climacteric 207.4 *middle age*, 207.13 *middle-aged*

climacterically 207.16 *maturely*

climactic 279.5 *top*

climate 55, 233.1 *influence*, 234.1 *tendency*, 251.2 *circumstances*

climate modification 55.40 *climatic change*

climate of opinion 234.1 *tendency*, 497.1 *belief*

climatic 55.41 *meteorologic*, 251.8 *circumstantial*

climatically 55.65 *meteorologically*

climatic change 55

climatic trend 55.40 *climatic change*

climatic variation 55.40 *climatic change*

climatic zone 55

climatological 54.49 *geophysical*, 55.41 *meteorologic*

climatologically 55.65 *meteorologically*

climatologist 54.4 *geophysicist*, 55.2 *meteorologist*

climatology 54.2 *geophysics*, 55.1 *meteorology*

climax 51.6 *scene*, 59.18 *ecology*, 126.4 *summit*, 126.8 *be superior*, 128.1 *increase*, 128.5 *make bigger*, 142.10 *complete*, 144.5 *be complete*, 157.10 *ending*, 279.1 *summit*, 279.7 *top*, 366.8 *spasm*, 405.1 *physical pleasure*, 405.8 *feel pleasure*, 684.2 *conclusion*, 684.5 *conclude*

climb 359, 34.1 *mountaineering*, 41.14 *ski*, 73.5 *flight*, 95.1 *mountain*, 95.10 *climb a mountain*, 128.2 *spread*, 128.4 *increase*, 275.2 *heights*, 275.16 *rise*, 324.13 *be in motion*, 336.3 *press on*, 336.7 *make one's way*, 359.6 *mounting*, 359.13 *ascend*, 753.9 *be dear*

climbable 359.25 *ladder-like*

climb a hill 34.9 *mountaineer*

climb a mountain 95, 34.9 *mountaineer*

climb down 360.9 *descend*

climbdown 806.10 *abasement*

climb down 806.21 *humble oneself*

climbed 34.8 *mountaineering*

climber 34.7 *mountaineer*, 69.9 *garden plant*, 83.2 *plant*, 359.11 *ascender*

climb hand over fist 359.14 *climb*

climbing 34.1, 34.8 *mountaineering*, 41.4 *skiing technique*, 41.12 *ski*, 83.14 *of plants*, 324.7 *ascending motion*, 324.17 *directional*, 359.6 *mounting*, 359.22 *ascending*, 753.7 *dear*

climbing boots 34.4 *climbing equipment*

climbing club 34.6 *mountaineering association*

climbing dangers 34

climbing equipment 34

climbing expedition 34.1 *mountaineering*

climbing gear 34.4 *climbing equipment*

climbing mountains 34.1 *mountaineering*

climbing perch 80 Fishes

climbing plant 69.9 *garden plant*

climbing prices 753.3 *inflationary price*

climbing technique 34

climbing the pole 36.8 *punting*

climb into the saddle 359.15 *mount*

climb on 359.15 *mount*

climb on the bandwagon 112.10 *conform*, 118.11 *emulate*

climb over 359.14 *climb*

climb the ladder of success 627.2 *get better*

climb the pole 36.19 *punt*

clinch 74 Rigging, 28.3 *fencing movements*, 28.5 *fence*, 101.12 *establish reality*, 135.8 *unite*, 135.10 *link*, 138.6 *adhere*, 475.17 *prove*, 674.7 *boxing*, 684.5 *conclude*, 726.1 *retention*, 726.6 *retain*

clincher 157.13 *ender*, 476.1 *refutation*, 655.3 *masterpiece*, 684.3 *elaboration*

clinch the deal 684.5 *conclude*

clindamycin 62 Medication

cling 378.10 *be tough*, 575.8 *hold out*, 584.17 *become a habit*, 826.7 *show endearment for*

clinger 138.5 *follower*

clingfilm 293.4 *wrapping*, 301.4 *wrapper*, 442.8 *transparent thing*

Clingfilm 45.6 *kitchen equipment*

clingfish 80 Fishes

clinging 138.9 *adhesive*, 272.1 *narrow*, 378.3 *hard*, 378.6 *toughness*, 584.15 *habit-forming*, 726.9 *retentive*, 826.9 *endearing*

clinging on 726.1 *retention*

clinging vine 138.4 *adherent*, 138.5 *follower*

cling like ivy 138.6 *adhere*

cling on 726.6 *retain*

clingstone 86 Fruits

cling to 138.6 *adhere*, 138.8 *be tenacious*, 264.10 *stay near*, 719.4 *observe*, 821.24 *be in love*

cling to custom 577.9 *be obstinate*, 584.16 *have a habit*

clingy 138.10 *tenacious*

clinic 60.10, 630.14 *hospital*

clinical 60.22 *medical*, 367.7 *material*, 542.14 *simple*, 630.18 *medical*

clinical death 397.1 *death*

clinical depression 61.13 *depression*, 510.6 *mental breakdown*

clinical dextran 387.4 *blood*

clinically 60.26 *medically*, 367.9 *materially*, 630.21 *remedially*

clinical medicine 60.3 *medical specialty*, 630.11 *medical art*

clinicalness 542.4 *simplicity*

clinical psychologist 61.29 *psychologist*, 61.30 *psychiatrist*

clinical psychology 61.1 *psychology*, 630.13 *therapy*

clinical thermometer 56.89 *thermometer*, 408.2 *heat measurement*

clinical treatment 60.8 *treatment*, 630.13 *therapy*

clinician 60.13 *medical specialist*, 61.29 *psychologist*

clink 323.4 *closed place*, 424.1 *faintness*, 424.5 *sound faint*, 427.2 *ringing*, 427.10 *ring*, 430.5 *sound hoarse*, 702.2 *the inside*

clinker 127.7 *inferior thing*, 353.5 *faeces*, 408.6 *fire*, 434.3 *musical dissonance*, 614.6 *refuse*, 622.4 *dirt*

clinker-built 36.10 *sailing*

clinker-built hull 36.3 *parts of a sailing boat*

clinking 430.8 *hoarse*

clinking gold 741.1 *money*

clinometer 617.17 *civil engineering*, 268.8 *meter*

clinometric 268.16 *micrometric*

clinometry 268.2 *micrometry*

clinophobia 777 Phobias by Name

clinopyroxene 54.34 *mineral*

clip 19.18 *be penalized*, 33.10 *be on the track*, 129.5 *make smaller*, 135.9 *joint*, 135.10 *link*, 136.10 *set apart*, 137.8 *fastening*, 137.11 *connect*, 262.5 *make smaller*, 270.10 *shorten*, 324.12 *gait*, 380.16 *use a sharp tool* , 544.7 *flag*, 552.4 *be concise*, 726.3 *tools for gripping*, 741.25 *demonetize*, 753.10 *overcharge*

clip one's wings 614.8 *make useless*, 661.8 *hinder*

clip on the ear 879.3 *hit*, 879.12 *corporal punishment*

clipped 5.42 *worded*, 262.7 *smaller*, 270.8 *shortened*, 552.3 *concise*, 562.7 *shortened*, 741.22 *monetary*

clipped accent 5.26 *dialect*

clipped coinage 741.15 *false money*

clipped speech 552.1 *conciseness*

clipped word 5.17 *word*

clipper 74 Sailing Ships and Boats, 329.11 *swift thing*

clippers 380.9 *sharp-edged thing*

clipping 19.13 *penalty*, 33.6 *motor racing terms*, 262.1 *contraction*, 270.2 *shortening*

clippings 132.2 *residue*, 143.8 *bits and pieces*

clip round the ear 330.3 *hit*

clip the apex 33.10 *be on the track*

clip the wings 328.3 *slow down*

clip the wings of 628.5 *hurt*

clip to 130.6 *add*

clip watch 192.7 *watch*

clique 161, 147.4 *exclusiveness*, 163.5 *social class*, 400.9 *group*, 665.1 *party*

cliquey 147.10 *excluding*, 665.8 *leagued*

cliquish 147.10 *excluding*, 665.8 *leagued*

cliquishly 665

cliquishness 665.4 *partisanship*

clitoral 245.16 *reproductive*

clitoridectomy 60 Surgical Operations, 10.7 *non-Christian ritual*

clitoris 245.8 *organs of reproduction*

clitter-clatter 426.3 *rattle*

cloaca 63.22 *tunnel*, 322.4 *body orifice*, 727.8 *sink*

cloak 7.11 *vestment*, 11.20 *occult*, 293.5 *body covering*, 293.31 *hide*, 295.25 *accessories*, 295.32 *dress*, 436.6 *blinder*, 438.8 *make invisible*, 531.8 *conceal*, 539.12, 539.32 *disguise*, 632.9 *protect*, 671.19 *buffer*

cloak-and-dagger 529.10 *secretive*

cloaked 293.37 *protected*, 295.29 *dressed*, 539.41 *disguised*

cloaked in secrecy 527.2 *concealed*

cloaking 293.1 *covering*

cloakroom 256.7 *room*, 727.7 *toilet*

cloakroom attendant 697.3 *attendant*

cloakroom ticket 544.3 *means of identification*

clobber 126.8 *be superior*, 241.8 *use violence*, 244.11 *ruin*, 295.1 *dress*, 330.3 *hit*

cloche 69.4 *nursery*, 295.15 *headgear*

clock 56, 192, 65.17 *computing term*, 185.13 *timer*, 185.16 *time*, 192.14 *keep time*, 303.2 *face*, 543.5 *indicator*

Clock 53 The Constellations

clock case 44.8 *ceramic object*

clockface 192.8 *face*

clock in 185.19 *clock on*, 192.16 *measure time*, 344.5 *get in*, 644.6 *work*

clockmaker 185.14 *time keeper*, 192.12 *chronologist*, 646.2 *artisan*

clockmaking 185.10 *chronometry*, 192.4 *horology*

clock off 185.19 *clock on*

clock on 185

clock out 192.16 *measure time*, 345.2 *withdraw*, 644.6 *work*

clock radio 191 Timepieces and Timers, 192.6 *clock*, 420.8 *something heard*, 534.18 *radio*

clock rate 65.17 *computing term*

clock speed 121.5 *measure*

clock that stops 517.7 *bad-luck sign*

clock time 185.7 *time measurement*, 192.3 *chronology*

clockwatch 185.19 *clock on*

clock watcher 185.14 *time keeper*

clock-watcher 643.8 *nonworker*

clockwise 332, 364.13 *round*

clockwork 110.17, 214.11 *regular*, 603.4 *machine*

clockwork precision 503.1 *accuracy*

clockwork regularity 110.6, 214.1 *regularity*

clod 143.7 *piece*, 255.5 *countryman*, 259.7 *mass*, 371.4 *solid body*, 460.3 *unintelligent person*, 656.10 *unskilled person*, 658.3 *naive person*

clodhoppers 295.19 *footwear*

clofibrate 62 Medication

clog 323.8 *stop*, 622.10 *be dirty*, 622.11 *dirty*, 726.7 *detain*

clog dance 46.2 *dance*

clog dancer 46.5 *dancer*

clog dancing 46.1 *dancing*

clogged 323.13 *stopped*, 622.7 *dirty*, 726.9 *retentive*

clogged up 323.13 *stopped*

clogs 295.19 *footwear*

clog up 323.8 *stop*, 699.8 *restrain*

cloisonné 44 Types of Ceramics

cloisonnism 50 Western Art Styles and Movements

cloister 7.10 *priestly dwelling*, 10.12 *church*, 301.2 *enclosed place*, 301.5 *enclose*, 327.7 *arcade*, 634.1 *refuge*, 816.5 *solitary place*

cloistered 301.7 *enclosed*, 816.11 *secluded*

cloisteredly 301.8 *confinedly*

clomipramine 62 Medication

clonazepam 62 Medication

clone 110.3 *lookalike*, 110.8 *make the same*, 114.2 *copy*, 114.5 *counterpart*, 114.12 *imitate*, 116.5 *conformity*, 118.2, 118.10 *copy*, 175.9 *pluralize*, 176.5 *twin*, 176.15 *double*, 245.2 *print*, 245.9 *reproduce*, 457.5 *impression*

cloned 110.14 *lookalike*, 176.12 *double*

clonidine 62 Medication

cloning 176.4 *doubling*

cloning vector 59.12 *molecular biology*

Clonmel 93 Cities

clop 330.7 *kick*, 330.13 *blow*, 791.17 *crimp*

clopamide 62 Medication

clorexolone 62 Medication
clorindole 62 Medication
close 157, 320, 323, 55.52
humid, 114.7 *similar,* 135.10
link, 135.15 *tied,* 138.9 *adhesive,* 144.3 *completion,* 144.4
complete, 144.5 *be complete,*
147.10 *excluding,* 157.1,
157.15 *end,* 161.50 *crowded,*
195.12 *succeeding,* 218.7 *stop
working,* 253.10 *available,*
264.5, 264.6 *near,* 267.5 *juxtaposed,* 272.1 *narrow,* 301.2 *enclosed place,* 301.5 *enclose,*
327.3 *road,* 342.9 *converge,*
371.6 *dense,* 371.7 *condensed,*
391.9 *moist,* 408.11 *warm,*
458.1 *disappear,* 529.10 *secretive,* 531.17 *noncommittal,*
537.24 *pedantic,* 615.2 *nearby,*
629.6 *cure,* 674.15 *contentious,*
684.2 *conclusion,* 684.5 *conclude,* 758.1 *mean,* 816.8 *unsociable,* 819.10 *familiar*
close associate 784.4 *likable person*
close at hand 199.11 *future,*
264.6 *near*
close attention 467
close binary 53.9 *constellation*
close by 196.8 *available,* 264.6
near, 615.8 *nearby*
close call 638.1 *escape*
closed 320, 323, 15.10 *unionized,* 37.8 *shooting,* 41.12 *ski,*
144.7 *complete,* 147.10 *excluding,* 218.10 *finished,* 527.2 *concealed,* 529.9 *secret,* 683.10
failed
closed book 502.3 *unknown
thing,* 582.6 *premeditation*
closed circuit 64.13 *circuit,* 235.7
electrical power
closed-circuit television 534.21
television
closed couplet 48.8 *part of poem*
closed door 147.1 *exclusion,*
587.6 *dissuasion*
closed down 323
closed-face 20.8 *angling*
closed-face reel 20.3 *fishing
tackle*
closed figure 52.41 *geometric figure*
closed gate 41.3 *ski racing*
closed in 323.15 *enclosed*
closed-in 301.7 *enclosed*
closed-in person 323
closed lips 527.10 *quietness*
closed mind 493.3 *injustice,*
577.7 *opinionatedness,* 582.6
premeditation
closed order 531.6 *privacy*
close down 323, 157.16 *cease*
closedown 218.2 *stop*
close down 218.7 *stop working,*
218.8 *cause to cease,* 320.10
close, 458.1 *disappear,* 699.8 *restrain*
close-down 320.4 *closure,* 320.6
closed, 323.1 *closure*
closed place 323
closed primary 580.12 *election*
closed season 37.2 *hunting*
closed session 529.1 *secrecy*
closed shop 13.8 *industrial relations,* 15.3 *organized labour,*
15.5 *labour law,* 147.4 *exclusiveness,* 302.2 *limiting factor,*
699.2 *economic restraint*
closed surface 52.38 *surface,*
52.45 *curved surface*
closed universe 53.4 *cosmological model*
closed up 323.14 *closed down*
closed-up 262.7 *smaller*
close fight 674.2 *contest*
close fighting 674.6 *fight*
close finish 344.15 *destination,*
674.2 *contest*
close-fisted 758.1 *mean*
close-fistedness 758.3 *parsimony*
close-fitting 138.9 *adhesive,*
272.1 *narrow*
close friend 819, 784.4 *likable
person*
close friendship 819.3 *familiarity*

close grips 674.6 *fight,* 674.9
duel
close-haul 36.15 *sail*
close hauled 332.11 *in all directions*
close-hauled 36.10 *sailing*
close hauling 36.1 *sailing*
close imitation 114.2 *copy*
close in 301.5 *enclose,* 342.9 *converge*
close-knit 147.10 *excluding,*
371.6 *dense*
close likeness 114.1 *similarity*
closely 114.14 *comparably,*
116.31 *in accord,* 135.18 *inextricably,* 138.11 *cohesively,* 264.6
near, 272.11 *narrowly,* 819.18
intimately
closeness 191, 114.1 *similarity,*
116.1 *accord,* 135.1 *union,*
264.1 *nearness,* 267.1 *juxtaposition,* 272.5 *narrowness,* 273.6
denseness, 371.1 *density,* 391.3
humidity, 531.4 *silence,* 537.11
pedantry, 615.4 *nearness,* 819.3
familiarity
close observance 467.2 *close attention,* 719.1 *observance*
close of day 205.1 *evening*
close of play 157.11 *finality*
close one's ears 421.8 *be deaf*
close one's eyes 397.15 *die*
close one's eyes to 783.12 *be indifferent,* 839.11 *condone*
close one's mind 481.13 *prejudge*
close packed 57.33 *crystalline*
close-packed 135.15 *tied,* 138.9
adhesive, 371.6 *dense*
close-passing 35.3 *rugby play*
close quarters 264.2 *short distance,* 674.6 *fight,* 674.9 *duel*
closer 264.5 *near*
close range 264.2 *short distance*
close ranks 138.6 *adhere*
close reaching 36.1 *sailing*
close-run 264.5 *near,* 674.16
competitive
close season 203.1 *season,*
218.3 *pause*
close-set 135.15 *tied*
close shave 633.5 *danger,* 638.1
escape
closest 253.10 *available,* 264.5
near
closestool 353.14 *toilet*
closet 531.2 *hiding place*
closet drama 51.2 *play*
close-textured 371.6 *dense*
close the blinds 634.4 *shelter*
close the circle 334.3 *circuit*
close the deal 715.5 *contract*
close the eyes 399.8 *bury*
close the gates of Janus 677.5
make peace
close the pleadings 16.71 *try a
case*
close the proceedings 16.71 *try a
case*
close the ranks 676.14 *battle*
close the shutters 440.14 *make
dark,* 634.4 *shelter*
close to the wind 332.11 *in all
directions*
close union 135.1 *union*
close up 262.5 *make smaller,*
262.6 *become smaller,* 264.9
near, 323.7 *close,* 323.9 *close
down,* 342.9 *converge,* 683.6 *fail*
close-up 66.4 *portrait*
close with 138.6 *adhere,* 342.9
converge, 670.5 *strike,* 674.11
contend
close-woven 371.6 *dense,* 383.9
smooth
closing 157.20 *ending,* 218.1 *cessation,* 320.4, 323.1 *closure,*
629.11 *recuperation*
closing down 218.2 *stop,* 323.1
closure
closing-down sale 727.2 *disposal
of property,* 739.4 *sale*
closing in 28.3 *fencing movements,* 301.1 *enclosure*
closing stages 157.9 *close*
closing the grave 399.2 *funeral*
closing time 157.11 *finality*

closing up 262.1 *contraction,*
323.1 *closure*
closure 320, 323, 52.21 *set,*
218.2 *stop,* 218.8 *cause to
cease,* 683.1 *failure*
Closure 323
closure of debate 218.2 *stop*
clot 273.7 *thicken,* 371.4 *solid
body,* 371.8 *be dense,* 387.4
blood, 393.10 *mucus,* 393.25
thicken, 622.11 *dirty,* 624.10
cardiovascular disease
cloth 7.11 *vestment,* 51.17 *stage
set,* 67.3 *fabric,* 67.10 *woven,*
243.7 *produce,* 288.4, 383.5 *textile,* 604.1 *materials*
cloth cap 295.15 *headgear*
clothe 295.32 *dress,* 606.5 *provision*
clothed 295.29 *dressed*
clothe oneself 295.34 *wear*
clothes 295.1 *dress,* 457.3 *external appearance*
clothes basket 258.7 *basket*
clothes brush 621.10 *cleaning object*
clothes' conscious 796.7 *fashionable*
clothes-conscious 295.30 *dressed
up*
clothes-dryer 392.15 *dryer*
clotheshorse 114.4 *person who
copies,* 283.4 *hanger,* 295.27
model, 392.15 *dryer*
clothes' horse 796.5 *fashion
model*
clothes label 544.3 *means of
identification*
clothesless 296.9 *undressed*
clothesline 283.4 *hanger*
clothes marking 544.3 *means of
identification*
clothes moth 82 Insects
clothes off one's back 723.4 *possession*
clothes peg 283.4 *hanger*
clothier 295.26 *fashion designer,*
646.2 *artisan*
clothing 295.1 *dress,* 457.3 *external appearance,* 606.1 *provision*
Clotho 8 Deities
cloth of gold 439.2 *quality of
light*
clotrimazole 62 Medication
clotted 273.2 *dense,* 371.7 *condensed,* 393.20 *thick,* 622.7 *dirty*
clotting 371.7 *condensed,* 393.6
thickening
cloture 218.2 *stop,* 218.8 *cause
to cease*
cloud 55, 55, 181.4 *throng,*
293.2 *cover,* 293.31 *hide,* 388.4
water vapour, 389.3 *wateriness,*
391.2 *mistiness,* 440.4 *dark
thing,* 441.10 *make dim,* 443.7
opaque thing, 443.11 *make
opaque,* 456.11 *variegate,* 531.9
disguise
cloud appearance 55
cloud base 55.18 *cloud*
cloudburst 55.25 *rain,* 241.5 *violent weather*
cloud-capped 55.49 *cloudy,* 95.7
mountainous, 275.9 *high*
cloud-capped peak 95.1 *mountain*
cloud cover 55
cloud-covered 55.49 *cloudy*
cloud-crossed 55.49 *cloudy*
cloud cuckoo land 775.3 *aspiration*
cloud-cuckoo land 519.8 *dreamland*
cloud-cuckoo-land 786.4 *wonder*
clouded 440.11 *benighted,* 441.7
dimmed, 443.2 *shady*
clouded leopard 77 Placental
Mammals
cloud-flecked 55.49 *cloudy*
cloud forest 85.4 *trees*
cloudily 55.65 *meteorologically,*
441.12 *dimly,* 443.13 *opaquely,*
448.9 *greyly*
cloudiness 55.19 *cloud cover,*
441.2 *murk,* 443.6 *opaqueness,*
448.7 *dullness,* 551.1 *obscurity,*
622.1 *dirtiness*

clouding over 441.3 *dimming*
cloud-laden 55.49 *cloudy*
cloudless 55.45 *fine,* 392.5 *rainless,* 439.19 *sunny,* 442.1 *transparent,* 686.8 *prosperous,*
714.14 *auspicious*
cloudlessness 442.5 *transparency*
cloudless sky 55.22 *sun*
cloud nine 279.1 *summit*
cloud of words 553.1 *diffuseness*
cloud on the horizon 633.6 *danger signal,* 636.1 *warning*
cloud over 55.60 *cloud,* 440.13
become dark, 441.9 *be dim,*
443.10 *be opaque*
clouds 777 Phobias by Topic
cloudscape 50.10 *art subject,*
66.4 *portrait*
cloud-seeding 55.26 *raininess*
cloud street 55.20 *cloud appearance*
cloud the issue 108.10 *be unrelated*
cloud-topped 55.49 *cloudy,*
275.9 *high*
cloud tower 55.20 *cloud appearance*
cloudy 55, 388.19 *smoky,*
391.10 *misty,* 440.8 *dark,*
441.5 *dim,* 441.6 *murky,* 443.2
shady, 448.3 *dull,* 456.10 *mottled,* 519.12 *imaginary,* 551.2
obscure, 622.7 *dirty,* 830.8 *overcast*
clough 98.8 *valley,* 265.3 *gulf,*
603.2 *garden tool*
clout 126.1 *superiority,* 233 *influence,* 318.1 *prominence,* 330.3
hit, 330.13 *blow,* 586.1 *persuasion,* 613.7 *instrumentality,*
629.8 *repair,* 688.1 *authority,*
879.3 *hit,* 879.12 *corporal punishment*
clove 413.5 *herbs*
clove hitch 74 Knots
cloven 136.16 *apart,* 176.13
half, 265.7 *cracked*
cloven-hoofed 77.33 *ungulate*
clove pink 84 Flowers and Flowering Plants
clover 84 Flowers and Flowering Plants, 68.12 *crop,* 350.8
animal food, 686.1 *prosperity*
clover honey 414.2 *sweetener*
cloverleaf 71.3 *carriageway,*
137.5 *road,* 288.5 *crossroads*
clover leaf 327.3 *road,* 356.5
crossing point
cloves 45 Herbs and Spices,
418.2 *fragrant thing*
clowder 161 Collective Names
for Birds and Animals
clown 51, 51.29 *circus performer,* 506.4 *buffoon,* 506.8
fool, 656.10 *unskilled person,*
771.6 *humorist,* 771.13 *be humorous,* 798.3 *object of ridicule,*
811.15 *showman*
clown around 508.7 *play the fool*
clown face 51.19 *stage requisite*
clowning 506.3 *tomfoolery,*
771.3 *wit,* 798.1 *ludicrousness,*
798.4 *joke*
clownish 559.7 *graceless,* 656.3
clumsy, 798.5, 798.5 *ridiculous*
cloxacillin sodium 62 Medication
cloy 610.4 *be excessive,* 788.6 *be
boring*
cloyed 610.6 *excessive*
cloying 414.1 *sweetness,* 414.6
sweet, 610.6 *excessive,* 788.4
boring
club 74 Rigging, **330,** 42.3 *card
game terms,* 51.14 *theatre,*
140.3 *assembly,* 161.15 *association,* 665.1 *party,* 680.7 *blunt
weapon,* 879.14 *instrument of
punishment*
clubbable 665.8 *leagued*
clubbish 665.8 *leagued,* 815.15
sociable
clubbishness 815.1 *sociability*
clubby 665.8 *leagued,* 815.15 *sociable*
club chair 47.2 *chair*
club circuit 51.13 *engagement*
club foot 74 Rigging

clubfoot 309.3 *deformity*
clubfooted 309.7 *deformed*
club fungi 89.3 *fungi*
clubhaul 74.10 *sail*
clubman 815.6 *social person*
club member 665.5 *member*
clubmoss 88.1 *fern*
Club of Paris 13.5 *international trade*
club root 69.12 *pests and diseases*
clubs 42 Card Games
club sandwich 45.11 *sandwich*, 266.5 *layered thing*
club tie 544.5 *uniform*
club together 180.14 *keep company with*, 664.14 *join with*, 665.12 *be in league with*
club together with 815.13 *fraternize*
cluck 432.2 *bird song*, 432.5 *sing*
clue 439.13 *enlightenment*, 471.2 *theory*, 483.4 *indication*, 518.2 *basis of supposition*, 524.1 *interpretation*, 543.1 *sign*
Cluedo 42 Board Games
clued up 403.5 *sensible*, 528.18 *informed*
clued-up 6.19 *knowledgeable*
clueless 502.6 *ignorant*
clue up 528.11 *inform*
clumber spaniel 77 Breeds of Dogs
clump 87.2 *grassland*, 161.27 *bundle*, 161.38 *group*, 259.7 *mass*, 330.7 *kick*, 330.13 *blow*, 371.4 *solid body*
clumped 161.49 *grouped*
clumsily 117.17 *unsuitably*, 407.15 *insensitively*, 559.11 *inelegantly*, 616.6 *inconveniently*, 656.11 *unskilfully*, 659.28 *awkwardly*
clumsily built 656.3 *clumsy*
clumsiness 404.1 *lack of feeling*, 559.1 *inelegance*, 559.4 *inelegance of speech*, 618.8 *inferiority*, 656.8 *unskilfulness*, 659.2 *awkwardness*
clumsy 656, 659, 117.11 *unfit*, 328.4 *slow*, 404.6 *unfeeling*, 407.10 *handed*, 549.8 *inelegant*, 559.7 *graceless*, 616.1 *inconvenient*, 618.2 *inferior*, 776.8 *bad*
clumsy clot 656.10 *unskilled person*
clumsy construction 559.4 *inelegance of speech*
clumsy lout 656.10 *unskilled person*
clumsy oaf 656.10 *unskilled person*
Clun Forest 68 Breeds of Sheep
Cluniac 7 Members of Religious Orders
clunk 424.1 *faintness*, 424.5 *sound faint*, 425.6 *crack*, 428.5 *dull sound*, 428.9 *be nonresonant*
Cluny 93 Cities
clupeoid 80.13 *fishlike*
cluricaune 11.11 *ghost*
cluster 161, 53.7 *galaxy*, 161.27 *bundle*, 161.38 *group*, 161.39 *come together*, 259.7 *mass*, 342.10 *come together*, 371.4 *solid body*
cluster analysis 52.55 *statistical methods*
cluster bomb 680.16 *bomb*
clustered 161.49 *grouped*
clutch 71 Motor Vehicle Parts, 78.12 *young bird*, 78.15 *eggs*, 161.24 *brace*, 206.4 *young animal*, 407.11 *touch*, 603.4 *machine*, 633.1 *dangerous*, 659.5 *predicament*, 726.1 *retention*, 726.6 *retain*
clutch at 734.7 *take*
clutch bag 258.8 *bag*
clutched 726.10 *retained*
clutches 12.3 *governance*
clutching 407.2 *touching*, 734.1 *taking*
clutch-slip 33.6 *motor racing terms*, 33.10 *be on the track*
Clutha 96 Rivers
clutter 151.4 *litter*, 181.4 *throng*
cluttered 181.10 *crowded*

Clwyd 92 Counties, **96** Rivers, 96.4 British rivers
Clyde 96 Rivers, 96.4 British rivers
Clydesdale 32 Breeds of Horse and Pony
clyster 354.11 *thing inserted*, 389.11 *wash*
Clywedog 94 Lakes
CMI 65.1 *computing*
CND member 627.12 *reformer*, 675.3, 677.3 *pacifist*
Cnidaria 81.7 *coelenterate*
cnidarian 81.7 *coelenterate*
cnidophobia 777 Phobias by Name
CNN 534.24 *television broadcasting*
C-note 741.8 *American money*
CoA 58.12 *coenzyme*
coach 71 Carriages and Carts, **71** Motor Vehicles, 6.4 *educator*, 6.22 *educate*, 19.2 *football player*, 21.3 *athlete*, 23.2 *basketball player*, 71.19 *bus*, 167.10 *assimilate*, 501.14 *cause to know*, 594.6 *brief*, 594.15 *preparer*
coach-builder 47.13 *carpenter*, 646.2 *artisan*
coach building 71.21 *miscellaneous motoring terms*
coachcard 754.4 *bargain*
coached 6.19 *knowledgeable*
coach horse 32.2 *thoroughbred*, 326.6 *beast of burden*
coaching 6.1 *education*
coachwood 85 Trees and Shrubs
coact 116.22 *form an alliance*, 664.11 *cooperate*
coacting 664.17 *cooperative*
coaction 664.1 *cooperation*
coactive 116.11 *allied*, 664.17 *cooperative*
coactively 664.20 *cooperatively*
coadjutant 662.11 *helper*, 664.17 *cooperative*
coadjutor 664.10 *cooperator*
coadjuvancy 664.3 *mutual relationship*
coadjuvant 664.17 *cooperative*
coadministration 664.5 *joint control*
coadunation 664.7 *association*
coagency 140.2 *cooperation*, 180.1 *accompaniment*, 664.5 *joint control*
coagent 140.8 *cooperator*
coagulate 138.6 *adhere*, 273.7 *thicken*, 371.8 *be dense*, 393.25 *thicken*
coagulated 138.9 *adhesive*, 273.2 *dense*, 371.7 *condensed*, 393.20 *thick*
coagulating 135.14 *conjunctive*, 371.7 *condensed*
coagulation 135.1 *union*, 273.6 *denseness*, 371.2 *concentration*, 393.6 *thickening*
coagulum 371.4 *solid body*
coal 54 Common Rocks, **410**, 54.43 *fossil*, 200.10 *fossilization*, 235.6 *source of energy*, 338.13, 410.1 *fuel*, 410.3 *gas*, 447.9 *black thing*, 604.1 *materials*, 606.5 *provision*
coalbed 605.2 *resource*
coal-bed 410.5 *coal*
coal bin 410.5 *coal*
coal-black 447.1 *black*
coal box 410.5 *coal*
coal bunker 410.5 *coal*
coal-burning 408.13 *heated*
coal cellar 410.5 *coal*, 727.8 *sink*
coal deposit 605.2 *resource*
coal dust 384.5 *powder*, 410.5 *coal*
coalesce 110.7 *be the same*, 110.8 *make the same*, 135.8 *unite*, 140.5 *combine*, 664.16 *join*
coalesced 110.12 *same*
coalescence 110.1 *sameness*, 135.1 *union*, 140.1 *combination*, 371.1 *density*, 664.7 *association*

coalescent 110.12 *same*, 135.12 *united*, 140.7 *combined*
coalface 410.5 *coal*, 605.2 *resource*, 647.1 *workshop*
coalfield 410.5 *coal*, 605.2 *resource*
coal fire 408.6 *fire*
coal-fired 408.13 *heated*, 410.10 *powered*
coalfish 45.18 *sea fish*
coal hole 256.7 *room*, 410.5 *coal*, 727.8 *sink*
coalition 12.6 *political party*, 116.2 *alliance*, 135.1 *union*, 664.7 *association*, 665.3 *political grouping*, 724.1 *joint possession*
coalman 622.6 *dirty person*
coal measures 200.10 *fossilization*
Coal Measures 410.5 *coal*
coal merchant 410.9 *power-worker*
coal mine 266.5 *layered thing*, 317.2 *concave land*
coalmine 410.5 *coal*, 605.2 *resource*, 647.1 *workshop*
coal miner 410.9 *power-worker*, 646.2 *artisan*
coal oil 395.9 *petroleum*, 410.6 *oil*
Coalport 44 Types of Ceramics
Coalsack 53 Nebulae, 53.8 *interstellar medium*
coal scuttle 258.11 *vessel*, 410.5 *coal*
coal tit 78 Birds
coaly 410.10 *powered*
coarctate 262.7 *smaller*
coarctation 262.1 *contraction*
coarse 375, 412, 20.8 *angling*, 67.10 *woven*, 273.4 *thick-skinned*, 383.8 *rough*, 454.4 *indecent*, 482.1 *undiscriminating*, 559.8 *indecorous*, 595.5 *immature*, 618.4 *poor*, 622.8 *unclean*, 790.4 *ugly*, 795.7 *vulgar*, 818.6 *bad-mannered*, 877.12 *indecent*
coarse cloth 375.6 *roughness*
coarse fish 45.17 *freshwater fish*
coarse fishing 18 Sporting Activities, 20.1 *angling*, 80.7 *fishing*, 590.2 *chase*
coarse grain 66.10 *graininess*, 375.6 *roughness*
coarse-grained 375.2 *coarse*, 383.8 *rough*
coarse-grained texture 54.28 *rock*
coarsely 273.9 *thick*, 375.14 *roughly*, 383.15 *texturally*, 412.11 *tastelessly*, 482.13 *unselectively*, 559.11 *inelegantly*, 595.16 *immaturely*, 622.12 *dirtily*, 818.10 *rudely*
coarsen 383, 273.8 *fatten*, 375.12 *make rough*, 628.6 *pervert*, 795.10 *vulgarize*
coarseness 375.6 *roughness*, 412.4 *bad taste*, 559.2 *impropriety*, 595.10 *immaturity*, 618.10 *poverty*, 622.2 *uncleanness*, 795.1 *tastelessness*, 818.2 *bad manners*, 877.2 *indecency*
coarsening 628.8 *perversion*
coarse pottery 44.1 *ceramics*
coarse-woven 383.8 *rough*
coast 54, 98, 300.1 *edge*, 324.15 *walk*, 325.8 *be motionless*, 360.6, 360.14 *slide*, 376.12 *go smoothly*, 641.4 *not act*, 660.17 *do easily*, 660.19 *go easily*
Coast 95 Mountains
coastal 54, 98.11 *continental*, 300.8 *edging*
coastal dune 54.37 *dune*
coastal engineering 63.17 *civil engineering*
coastal fog 55.33 *fog*
coastal plain 54.7 *landform*, 98.4 *coast*
coastal station 55.5 *weather station*
coastal waters 54.12 *ocean*
coast clear 632.1 *safety*
coastguard 632.3 *protector*, 679.14 *armed forces*

coastguardsman 74.7 *nautical person*, 679.27 *naval man*
coast home 660.17 *do easily*
coasting 74.11 *nautical*, 360.18 *falling*
coastland 98.4 *coast*
coastline 54.11, 98.4 *coast*, 299.3 *edge*
coat 266, 293, 295, 50.19 *paint*, 130.6 *add*, 266.10 *layer*, 292.3 *line*, 293.3 *coating*, 293.5 *body covering*, 376.11 *smooth*, 443.11 *make opaque*, 444.15 *colour*
coated 266, 67.11 *treated*, 443.1 *opaque*
coated lens 56.29 *optical element*
coatee 295.23 *children's clothes*
coat hanger 283.4 *hanger*, 295.27 *model*
coati 77 Placental Mammals
coating 293, 266.3 *coat*, 289.1 *exterior*, 292.1 *lining*, 293.1 *covering*
Coatlicue 8 Deities
coat of arms 544.8 *heraldic device*
coat of mail 671.7 *armour*
coat-of-mail shell 81 Molluscs
coat of many colours 113.3 *diverse thing*
coat-tail 283.3 *suspended object*, 295.24 *part of garment*
coauthors 664.9 *team*
coax 228.9 *motivate*, 340.12 *lure*, 586.15 *persuade*, 586.16 *tempt*, 657.5 *be cunning*, 712.6 *request*, 853.10 *cajole*
coaxed 228.12 *motivated*
coaxer 228.7 *motivator*, 586.12 *persuader*
coaxial cable 64.27 *wire*, 534.6 *telecommunication*
coaxing 228.2 *inducement*, 586.2 *flattery*, 853.14 *cajoling*
cob 86 Nuts, 32.1 *horse*, 32.5 *pony*, 45.39 *loaf*, 78.10 *male bird*, 87.4 *cereal grass*
cobalt 57 Chemical Elements, 56.59 *ferromagnetism*, 58.15 *essential element*
cobalt blue 454.1 *blue*, 454.5 *blueness*
cobaltic 57.34 *elemental*
cobaltite 54 Minerals
cobaltous 57.34 *elemental*
cobalt violet 455.2 *purple pigment*
cobble 293.11 *paving*, 293.29 *surface*, 295.35 *make clothing*, 604.2 *building material*, 629.1 *repair*
cobbled 327.15 *accessible*
cobbled together 656.4 *bungled*
cobbler 295.26 *fashion designer*, 629.12 *repairer*
cobblers 506.1 *nonsense*
cobblestone 293.11 *paving*, 327.4 *road surface*
cobble together 243.10 *produce*
cobbling 295.2 *dressing*, 629.8 *repair*
cobia 80 Fishes
Cobol 65 Programming Languages
cobra 79 Reptiles, 79.3 *snake*
Cobra 50 Schools and Groups of Artists
cobweb 82.6 *spinner*, 238.5 *weak thing*, 370.7 *light thing*, 539.13 *snare*, 612.8 *trifle*, 622.4 *dirt*
cobwebbed 539.42 *trapped*
cobwebby 370.2 *insubstantial*, 622.7 *dirty*
cobwebs of antiquity 202.3 *antiquity*
cobza 49 Musical Instruments
Coca-Cola 351.6 *soft drink*, 414.5 *sweet drink*
cocaine 62 Medication, 58.19 *alkaloid*, 404.4 *anaesthetic*, 630.8 *drug*, 631.11 *intoxicant*, 875.6 *drug*
coccidioidomycosis 89.5 *fungal association*
coccidiosis 81.12 *protozoal disease*
coccus 59.3 *organism*

coccyx 382 Bones
Cochabamba 93 Cities
cochairmanship 664.5 *joint control*
Cochin 68 Breeds of Fowl
cochineal 444.4 *pigment*, 450.6 *red pigment*
cochlea 314.3 *convoluted thing*, 420.5 *internal ear*
cochlear nerve 420.5 *internal ear*
cochleate 314.4 *convolutional*
Cocidius 8 Deities
cock 68.8 *livestock*, 78.10 *male bird*, 245.8 *organs of reproduction*, 338.32 *load*, 401.3 *male title of address*, 401.16 *male animal*, 594.4 *prepare for action*
cockade 544.4 *insignia*
cock-a-doodle-doo 78.18 *birdsong*, 432.8 *bird song*
Cockaigne 519.8 *dreamland*
cock-a-leekie 45.13 *soup*, 45.44 *British dish*
cockalorum 807.12 *impudent person*
cock-and-bull 540.32 *falsified*
cock-and-bull story 665.7 *distortion of the truth*, 538.4 *lie*
cock and hen 179.6 *ten*
cock a snook 850, 543.11 *gesture*, 668.5 *defy*, 720.7 *not observe*, 807.29 *ridicule*
cockatiel 78 Birds
cockatoo 78 Birds, 78.7 *cagebird*
cockatrice 76.7 *legendary beast*, 78.9 *fabulous bird*, 79.3 *snake*, 544.8 *heraldic device*
cockchafer 82 Insects, 82.3 *pest*
Cockcroft 52 Scientists
cockcrow 204.1 *morning*
cocked hat 295.15 *headgear*
cocked up 281.9 *unbowed*
cockee 41.10 *curling*
cockerel 78.10 *male bird*, 401.16 *male animal*
cocker spaniel 77 Breeds of Dogs
cockeye 436.2 *poor sight*
cockeyed 151.18 *muddled*, 309.6 *distorted*, 436.9 *weak-sighted*
cockfight 674.9 *duel*
cock-fighting 78.20 *bird sport*
cock gunlock 603.1 *tool*
cockily 809, 668.9 *defiantly*, 807.31 *cheekily*
cockiness 809, 668.1 *defiance*, 807.10 *impudence*
cocking 594.9 *preparation*
cockle 81 Molluscs, 45.19 *shellfish*
cockleboat 74 Ships and Boats
cocklebur 84 Flowers and Flowering Plants
cockleshell 74 Ships and Boats
cockles of one's heart 759.8 *seat of feelings*
cockloft 275.8 *high thing*
cockney 255.9 *British inhabitant*
cockney accent 5.26 *dialect*
cockney rhyming slang 5.18 *slang*
cock of the walk 126.5 *superior*, 617.8 *exceller*, 696.5 *company leader*, 805.13 *proud person*, 807.12 *impudent person*
cockpit 73 Aircraft Parts, 36.3 *parts of a sailing boat*, 36.6 *canoeing*, 674.9 *duel*, 692.8 *vantage point*
cockroach 82 Insects, 82.1 *insect*, 82.3 *pest*
cock-robin 78.10 *male bird*
Cockroft–Walton accelerator 56 Named Laws
cockscomb 84 Flowers and Flowering Plants
cocksfoot 87 Grasses, 68.12 *crop*
cockshy 33.5 *throw*
cocksman 401.6 *macho man*
cock-sparrow 78.10 *male bird*
cockspur 85 Trees and Shrubs, 87 Grasses, 380.8 *sharp-pointed thing*
cocksure 490.2 *convinced*
cocksureness 490.10 *conviction*
cocktail 133.2 *mixed thing*, 140.4 *compound*, 351.2 *drink*, 351.8 *mixed drink*, 874.12 *alcohol*

cocktail dress 295.7 *frock*, 813.4 *formal dress*
cocktail drums 49 Musical Instruments
cocktailing 875.1 *drug-taking*
cocktail party 665.7 *social gathering*, 815.5 *party*
cocktail sausage 45.29 *sausage*
cocktail shaker 133.6 *mixer*
cock the float 20.7 *angle*
cock up 151.23 *confuse*, 281.6 *make vertical*, 504.19 *make a mistake*, 559.6 *blunder*, 628.4 *impair*, 656.7 *be clumsy*
cockup 656.9 *bungling*, 661.2 *obstacle*
cock-up 151.6 *mix-up*, 504.10 *blunder*
cocky 809, 668.7 *defiant*, 805.22 *boastful*, 807.21 *impudent*
cocoa 351.5 *milk*, 414.5 *sweet drink*
coco de mer 85 Trees and Shrubs, 86 Nuts
coconscious 61.21 *psyche*, 61.37 *subconscious*
coconut 86 Fruits, 86 Nuts, 378.7 *tough thing*
coconut meal 68.9 *animal feedstuff*
coconut milk 351.6 *soft drink*
coconut palm 85 Trees and Shrubs
coconut pie 45.36 *cake*
cocoon 82.5 *larva*, 82.6 *spinner*, 206.4 *young animal*, 226.3 *rudiment*, 258.21 *put in a container*, 293.14 *animal covering*, 632.9 *protect*
cocooned 258.20 *containing*
cocooning 258.20 *containing*
cocotte 45.6 *kitchen equipment*
co-counselling 61.3 *psychiatric treatment*
Cocteau 48 Writers, 48 Poets
cocuswood 85 Trees and Shrubs
cod 80 Fishes, 45.18 *sea fish*, 80.8 *food fish*
COD 534.2 *postal communication*
coda 49 Musical Terms, 49.13 *melody*, 130.3 *additional item*, 155.8 *addition*, 157.10 *ending*, 195.9 *sequel*, 304.1 *rear*
coddle 45.55 *cook*, 405.10 *comfort*, 662.20 *sustain*, 821.27 *kiss*, 826.7 *show endearment for*
coddled 45.56 *culinary*, 405.7 *pleased*
coddling 45.8 *cooking technique*
code 4.2 *philosophical system*, 5.5 *nonstandard language*, 11.2 *the occult*, 65.10 *character*, 165.10 *specialized language*, 166.2 *canon*, 257.5 *divisions*, 523.12 *unintelligible thing*, 527.8 *concealment*, 529.4 *brain-teaser*, 529.14 *make mysterious*, 543.1 *sign*, 543.9 *use signs*, 564.1 *faculty of speech*, 654.3 *precept*
code-breaker 524.6 *interpreter*
codec 65.14 *data transfer*
code cracking 524.1 *interpretation*
coded 257.12 *itemized*, 524.15 *interpreted*, 527.2 *concealed*, 531.15 *disguised*
codeine 62 Medication, 630.5 *analgesic*, 630.8 *drug*
code name 529.8 *anonymity*, 531.7 *concealer*
code of conduct 4.2 *philosophical system*, 847.6 *ethics*
code of duty 847.6 *ethics*
code of honour 847.6 *ethics*
code of practice 4.2 *philosophical system*
coder 529.4 *brain-teaser*
codetermination 664.5 *joint control*
codetta 49 Musical Terms
codicil 130.3 *additional item*, 155.8 *addition*, 570.5 *will*
codification 16.1 *the law*, 16.31 *legislation*, 150.2 *grouping*, 152.5 *categorization*

codified 16.46 *legislated*, 150.11 *grouped*, 152.24 *categorized*, 531.15 *disguised*
codified law 16.1 *the law*
codify 16.68 *legislate*, 150.19 *systematize*, 152.15 *categorize*, 163.14 *sort*
codirectorship 664.5 *joint control*
codlike 80.13 *fishlike*
codling moth 82 Insects, 69.12 *pests and diseases*
cod-liver oil 80.9 *fish product*
codomain 52.29 *mathematical function*
codon 59.13 *genetic material*
codpiece 295.24 *part of garment*, 295.25 *accessories*
Cod war 676.1 *war*
coefficient 52.25 *algebraic expression*
coefficient of friction 385.1 *friction*
coelacanth 80 Fishes, 80.4 *fossil fish*
coelenterate 81, 81, 76.5 *aquatic animal*
coelomate 81.16 *invertebrate*
coenobial 90.7 *algal*
coenobite 816.6 *unsocial person*
coenobium 90.4 *reproductive body*
coenocyte 59.7 *cell*
coenocytic 59.23 *cellular*
coenzyme 58, 58.11 *enzyme*
coequal 110.16, 122.5 *equal*, 122.6 *equal*
coequality 110.5, 122.1 *equality*
coequally 110.19, 122.12 *equally*
coerce 571.15 *compel*, 586.15 *persuade*, 690.6 *suppress*, 695.6 *compel*, 699.8 *restrain*
coerced 690.9 *suppressed*
coercion 695, 571.3 *lack of choice*, 690.2 *suppression*, 699.1 *restraint*
coercive 688.12 *authoritative*, 690.8 *severe*, 695.9 *compelling*, 696.12 *masterful*, 699.13 *restraining*
coercively 695.11 *compellingly*, 699.16 *under restraints*
coercive methods 695
coercive person 695
coeternal 198.9 *simultaneous*
coeternally 198.12 *simultaneously*
coeval 198.5 *contemporary*, 198.9 *simultaneous*
coevality 198.1 *same time*
coevally 198.12 *simultaneously*
coexist 99.17 *exist*, 198.6 *be simultaneous*, 667.6 *agree with*
coexistence 99.1 *existence*, 180.1 *accompaniment*, 198.1 *same time*, 667.1 *agreement*, 675.1 *peace*
coexistent 99.10 *existing*, 180.18 *concurrent*, 198.9 *simultaneous*, 667.10 *agreeing*
coexisting 180.18 *concurrent*, 198.9 *simultaneous*, 667.10 *agreeing*
co-existing 116.11 *allied*
coextend 285.5 *parallel*
coextension 285.1 *parallelism*
coextensive 122.6 *equal*, 285.3 *parallel*
coextensively 122.13 *equitably*, 285.7 *in parallel*
cofactor 58.11 *enzyme*
co-favourite 32.7 *horseracing*
C of E 7.16 *denominational*
coffee 351, 449.1 *brown*, 449.5 *brown thing*, 815.3 *meeting*
coffee bar 350.15 *eating place*, 351.11 *drink provider*
coffee cake 45.36 *cake*
coffee-coloured 449.1 *brown*
coffeecup 258.13 *drinking vessel*
coffee cup 351.10 *drink container*
coffee estate 68.6 *farm*
coffee grinder 36.3 *parts of a sailing boat*, 45.6 *kitchen equipment*, 384.11 *pulverizer*
coffee grounds 393.13 *mud*
coffee house 350.15 *eating place*
coffee jar 258.11 *vessel*
coffee maker 258.15 *pot*

coffee morning 815.3 *meeting*
coffee nut 86 Nuts
coffee party 665.7 *social gathering*
coffee plantation 68.6 *farm*
coffee planter 68.15 *agriculturist*
coffeepot 258.15 *pot*
coffee stall 350.15 *eating place*
coffee table 47.4 *table*, 276.4 *low thing*
coffee-table book 532.6 *book publishing*
coffee tree 85 Trees and Shrubs
coffee urn 258.15 *pot*
coffer 43.19 *decorate*, 258.6 *box*, 605.4 *storage*, 741.20 *money store*
cofferdam 63.28 *substructure*
coffer dam 147.3 *exclusion zone*
coffin 258.6 *box*, 397.8 *after death*, 399.4 *funeral objects*, 399.8 *bury*
coffin lead 20.3 *fishing tackle*
coffin nail 413.7 *tobacco*
cog 47.17 *carpenter*, 319.2 *notched thing*, 319.5 *notch*, 364.6 *rotator*, 380.8 *sharp-pointed thing*
cogency 235.1 *power*, 237.3 *intensity*, 537.11 *pedantry*
cogent 4.16 *dialectical*, 235.13 *powerful*, 237.10 *potent*, 537.24 *pedantic*, 554.3 *emphatic*, 586.19 *persuasive*, 695.9 *compelling*
cogently 235.18 *powerfully*, 586.21 *persuasively*, 695.11 *compellingly*
cogged 47.16 *joined*, 319.4 *notched*
cogging 47.10 *carpenter's term*, 47.16 *joined*
cog in the wheel 148.5 *member*
cogitate 4.20 *philosophize*, 243.10 *produce*, 461.12 *think*
cogitate upon 243.10 *produce*
cogitatingly 4.28 *thoughtfully*
cogitation 4.4 *philosophical investigation*, 243.1 *production*, 461.1 *thought*
cogitative 4.17 *thoughtful*
cognate 5.17 *word*, 5.42 *worded*, 107.4 *related*
cognate word 5.17 *word*
cognition 459.1 *mind*, 461.1 *thought*, 501.1 *knowledge*
cognitive 461.8 *thoughtful*
cognitively 501.15 *knowledgeably*
cognitive psychology 61.1 *psychology*
cognizability 522.11 *recognizability*
cognizable 16.47 *liable to law*, 16.58 *unjust*
cognizance 16.2 *jurisdiction*, 501.1 *knowledge*, 837.1 *gratitude*, 845.2 *due*
cognizant 6.19, 501.8 *knowledgeable*
cognizant of 837.5 *thanking*
cognize 459.12 *think*
cognomen 560.8 *name*
cognoscente 655.5 *expert*
cog railway 72.1 *railway*, 327.10 *railway*
cog rattle 49 Musical Instruments
cogwheel 364.6 *rotator*
cohabit 135.11 *make love*, 180.14 *keep company with*, 821.29 *make love*, 823.15 *marry*, 823.18 *live together*
cohabitant 180.12, 823.12 *partner*
cohabitation 180.1 *accompaniment*, 180.3 *companionship*, 821.5 *desire*, 823.1 *marriage*
cohabitee 180.12 *partner*
cohabiting 180.18 *concurrent*
coheir 730.6 *beneficiary*
cohere 116.25 *conform*, 135.8 *unite*, 137.13 *intercommunicate*, 138.6 *adhere*, 174.19 *become one*, 219.3 *continue*, 371.8 *be dense*

coherence 116.5 *conformity*, 135.1 *union*, 138.1 *adhesion*, 150.7 *method*, 174.3 *oneness*, 371.1 *density*, 378.6 *toughness*, 509.2 *rationality*, 522.9 *intelligibility*, 550.1 *clarity*
coherent 116.14 *conforming*, 137.14 *connective*, 138.9 *adhesive*, 150.14 *well-ordered*, 378.3 *hard*, 509.5 *rational*, 522.1 *intelligible*, 550.3 *clear*
coherent light 439.1 *light*
coherently 138.11 *cohesively*, 378.12 *toughly*, 509.7 *sanely*, 522.13 *intelligibly*, 550.4 *clearly*
coherent radiation 56.26 *laser*
coherent units 75.2 *unit system*
cohesion 135.1 *union*, 137.1 -*connection*, 138.1 *adhesion*, 219.1 *continuity*, 340.2 *pulling power*, 371.1 *density*, 378.6 *toughness*
cohesive 135.15 *united*, 135.15 *tied*, 137.14 *connective*, 138.9 *adhesive*, 219.5 *continual*, 371.6 *dense*, 378.3 *hard*, 726.9 *retentive*
cohesively 138, 135.16 *as one*, 137.17 *in connection with*, 371.10 *densely*, 378.12 *toughly*, 726.11 *tenaciously*
cohesively inductively 340.13 *attractionally*
cohesiveness 138.1 *adhesion*, 378.6 *toughness*
cohesive strength 63.15 *strength of materials*
Cohn 52 Scientists
cohort 161.18 *generation*, 679.16 *army unit*
coif 295.15 *headgear*, 671.7 *armour*, 791.17 *crimp*
coiffeur 791.13 *beautician*
coiffeuse 791.13 *beautician*
coiffure 791.8 *hair cut*
coign of vantage 126.3 *advantage*
coil 314, 56.60 *magnet*, 247.3 *birth control*, 269.5 *piece*, 311.2 *bend*, 311.6 *curve*, 314.6 *convolute*, 320.1, 320.7 *fold*, 363.1 *orbital motion*
coiled 311.4 *curved*, 314.4 *convolutional*, 363.10 *circular*, 377.6 *elastic*
coiling 377.6 *elastic*
coil magnet 340.3 *magnet*
coil spring 377.5 *spring*
coil up 315.11 *make round*
Coimbra 93 Cities
coin 314 49 *miscellaneous architectural features*, 156.22 *invent*, 243.10 *produce*, 306.7 *form*, 519.14 *imagine*, 741.1 *money*, 741.2 *cash*, 741.13 *coinage*, 741.24 *monetize*
coinage 741, 5.17 *word*, 156.5 *invention*, 741.1 *money*
coinage metal 57 Alloys, 57.6 *chemical element*
coinage of the brain 519.4 *ideality*
coin a phrase 505.3 *aphorize*
coin a word 5.45 *use language*
coincide 110.7 *be the same*, 114.10 *be similar*, 116.24 *harmonize*, 180.13 *accompany*, 198.6 *be simultaneous*, 520.10 *mean*, 667.8 *be compatible*
coincidence 229, 48.3 *aspect of fiction*, 108.1 *unrelatedness*, 110.2 *equivalence*, 116.4 *harmony*, 140.1 *combination*, 180.2 *synchronism*, 198.1 *same time*, 589.1 *chance*
coincident 116.13 *harmonious*, 122.6 *equal*, 140.8 *cooperative*, 180.18 *concurrent*, 198.9 *simultaneous*
coincidental 108.7 *illogical*, 110.13 *equivalent*, 198.9 *simultaneous*, 229.6 *motiveless*, 589.8 *chance*
coincidentally 108.12 *irrelevantly*, 110.18 *identically*, 122.13 *equitably*, 140.10 *in*

combination, 198.12 *simultaneously*, 229.8, 589.13 *by chance*
coincide with 122.10 *be equal*
coinciding 116.13 *harmonious*, 180.18 *concurrent*, 667.3 *compatibility*, 667.12 *compatible*
coin collecting 42 Hobbies and Pastimes, 741.13 *coinage*
coin collection 605.5 *collection*
coin collector 161.35 *collector*, 741.17 *financier*
coined 741.22 *monetary*
coiner 741.17 *financier*
coin money 742.13 *get rich*
coin of the realm 741.13 *coinage*
coins 741.4 *change*, 741.13 *coinage*
coin-toss 19.14 *miscellaneous terms*
Cointreau 351.7 *alcoholic drink*
coital 135.14 *conjunctive*
coition 135.4 *sexual union*, 245.3 *propagation*, 396.4 *biological function*, 821.5 *desire*
coitophobia 777 Phobias by Name
coitus 777 Phobias by Topic, 135.4 *sexual union*, 821.5 *desire*
coitus interruptus 135.4 *sexual union*, 247.3 *birth control*
coke 408.6 *fire*, 410.5 *coal*, 875.6 *drug*
Coke 351.6 *soft drink*
coke-head 875.4 *drug taker*
col 137.4 *means of connection*, 265.3 *gulf*, 275.4 *mountain range*, 317.2 *concave land*
cola 86 Nuts, 351.6 *soft drink*
colander 45.6 *kitchen equipment*, 322.6 *porous thing*
colascione 49 Musical Instruments
Colbred 68 Breeds of Sheep
Colby 45 Cheeses
col canto 49 Musical Terms
Colchester 93 Cities
colchicine 62 Medication, 58.19 *alkaloid*
colcynth 62 Medication, **62** Medication
cold 777 Phobias by Topic, **777** Phobias by Name, **409,** 55.31 *coldness*, 55.47 *windy*, 55.55 *cool*, 56.35 *heat*, 263.9 *reserved*, 397.19 *dead*, 595.6 *uncooked*, 624.6 *infection*, 624.9 *respiratory disease*, 641.3 *inactive*, 651.3 *refreshing*, 687.6 *adverse*, 761.1 *insensitive*, 783.7 *indifferent*, 807.17 *contemptuous*, 816.8 *unsociable*, 820.6 *hostile*, 832.12 *callous*, 836.4 *pitiless*, 876.9 *pure*
Cold 409
cold air 55.10 *air movement*
cold as charity 409.8 *cold*
cold as marble 409.8 *cold*
cold as the grave 409.8 *cold*
cold bath 621.6 *bath*
cold blood 787.1 *lack of wonder*
cold-blooded 79.11 *reptilian*, 80.13 *fishlike*, 398.24 *murderous*, 404.6 *unfeeling*, 761.1 *insensitive*, 783.7 *indifferent*, 787.3 *unmoved*, 832.12 *callous*, 836.4 *pitiless*
cold-blooded animal 79.1 *reptile*
cold-blooded killer 836.3 *pitiless person*
cold-bloodedly 783.17 *indifferently*, 787.9 *without wonder*, 836.7 *pitilessly*
cold-blooded murderer 398.11 *murderer*
cold-bloodedness 783.1 *indifference*, 832.3 *callousness*
cold body 56.35 *heat*
cold climate 55.38 *climate*
coldcock 330.3 *hit*
cold cream 134.3 *purifier*, 386.6 *pomade*, 395.6 *ointment*, 621.9 *cleaning agent*
cold cuts 45.12 *hors d'oeuvre*
cold day 687.4 *time of adversity*
cold enough to freeze the balls off a brass monkey 409.8 *cold*

colder 55.55 *cool*
cold-eyed 832.12 *callous*
cold feet 779.1 *cowardice*
cold fingers of death 397.1 *death*
cold fish 761.5 *insensitive person*, 783.6 *indifferent person*
cold frame 69.4 *nursery*
cold front 55.10 *air movement*, 409.7 *cold weather*
cold fusion 56.72 *nuclear fission*
cold heart 787.1 *lack of wonder*
cold-hearted 761.1 *insensitive*, 783.7 *indifferent*, 787.3 *unmoved*, 832.12 *callous*, 836.4 *pitiless*, 860.4 *selfish*, 868.3 *impenitent*
cold-heartedly 783.17 *indifferently*, 787.9 *without wonder*, 832.20 *malevolently*, 836.7 *pitilessly*, 860.8 *selfishly*, 868.6 *impenitently*
cold-heartedness 761.3 *insensitiveness*, 783.1 *indifference*, 832.3 *callousness*, 868.1 *impenitence*
cold-hearted person 868.2 *impenitent person*
cold in the nose 417.1 *odourlessness*
coldish 55.55 *cool*
coldly 409, 55.65 *meteorologically*, 263.11 *reservedly*, 325.10 *motionlessly*, 761.8 *unfeelingly*, 783.17 *indifferently*, 816.14 *unsocially*, 820.14 *hostilely*, 836.7 *pitilessly*
cold meat party 397.8 *after death*, 399.2 *funeral*
coldness 55, 409, 263.4 *reserve*, 687.1 *adversity*, 705.2 *stoicism*, 761.3 *insensitiveness*, 783.1 *indifference*, 816.1 *unsociability*, 820.1 *enmity*, 832.3 *callousness*, 876.3 *moral purity*
cold occlusion 55.10 *air movement*
cold of heart 832.12 *callous*
cold reception 581.5 *rejection*
cold rubber 377.4 *rubber*
cold season 409.7 *cold weather*
cold shivers 366.7 *shake*
cold shoulder 341.6 *repulse*, 468.1 *inattention*, 581.5 *rejection*, 591.10 *avoidance*, 818.3 *act of discourtesy*, 850.5, 850.23 *insult*, 852.3 *nonacceptance*, 852.15 *withhold approval*
cold-shoulder 147.7 *exclude*, 341.1 *repel*, 468.13 *be thoughtless*, 581.3 *exclude*, 591.1 *avoid*, 816.13 *ignore*, 818.5 *discourteous*, 818.7 *be discourteous*
cold-shouldered 816.10 *lonely*
cold shower 621.6 *bath*, 651.6 *refresher*
cold snap 55.31 *coldness*, 409.7 *cold weather*
cold spell 409.7 *cold weather*
cold steel 680.8 *sharp weapon*
cold storage 637.1 *preservation*
cold store 45.4 *kitchen container*
Coldstream 93 Cities
Coldstream Guard 679.12 *ceremonial troops*
cold substance 56.35 *heat*
cold sweat 353.8 *sweat*, 777.1 *fear*, 785.4 *sign of dislike*
cold turkey 875.3 *withdrawal*
cold war 674.1 *contention*, 676.1 *war*
cold water 587.7 *deterrence*
cold-water cure 630.13 *therapy*
cold wave 55.31 *coldness*
cold weather 409, 55.31 *coldness*
cold wind 687.1 *adversity*
colectomy 60 Surgical Operations
colemanite 54 Minerals
coleopter 73 Types of Aircraft
Coleoptera 82 Orders of Insects
coleopteran 82.10 *insectan*
coleoptile 83.9 *seed*
coleorhiza 83.9 *seed*
Coleraine 93 Cities
Coleridge 48 Poets
Coleridge-Taylor 49 Musicians and Composers

coleslaw 45.14 *salad*
Colette 48 Writers
coleus 84 Flowers and Flowering Plants
coley 45.18 *sea fish*
colic 406.2 *painful condition*, 624.8 *indigestion*
Coliseum 243.8 *construction*
colistin 62 Medication
colitis 624.8 *indigestion*
collaborate 116.22 *form an alliance*, 140.6 *come together*, 284.14 *give moral support*, 572.14 *cooperate*, 578.3 *apostatize*, 662.22 *improve*, 664.11 *cooperate*, 665.12 *be in league with*, 858.9 *prove false*
collaborate with 673.3 *submit*
collaborating 116.11 *allied*, 499.6 *assenting*
collaboration 116.2 *alliance*, 140.2 *cooperation*, 284.6 *moral support*, 572.9 *goodwill*, 578.7 *apostasy*, 662.10 *helpfulness*, 664.1 *cooperation*, 673.1 *submission*, 724.2 *participation*
collaborationist 539.20 *plotter*, 578.9 *equivocator*
collaborative 116.11 *allied*, 284.9 *supportive*, 572.4 *helpful*, 664.17 *cooperative*
collaboratively 664.20 *cooperatively*
collaborator 284.8 *supporter*, 499.3 *assenter*, 539.20 *plotter*, 578.9 *equivocator*, 662.11 *helper*, 664.10 *cooperator*, 693.10 *seditionist*, 724.3 *participant*, 808.5 *adherent*
collaborators 664.9 *team*
collage 42 Hobbies and Pastimes, 50.7 *picture*, 140.2 *cooperation*, 161.33 *putting together*, 456.5 *variegated thing*
collagen 58.9 *protein*
collapse 129.2 *decline*, 129.4 *decrease*, 141.1 *disintegration*, 141.3 *disintegrate*, 218.7 *stop working*, 236.4 *disability*, 236.6 *be powerless*, 244.4 *ruin*, 262.1 *contraction*, 262.5 *make smaller*, 262.6 *become smaller*, 317.6 *be concave*, 320.4 *closure*, 320.10 *close*, 358.3 *fall through*, 360.4 *fall*, 360.10 *droop*, 624.3 *symptom*, 624.5 *be unhealthy*, 628.1 *deteriorate*, 628.9 *dilapidation*, 650.5 *be fatigued*, 650.7 *fatigue*, 673.4 *succumb*, 683.1 *failure*, 683.2 *defeat*, 683.6 *fail*, 722.9 *lose*, 747.5 *insolvency*, 747.9 *be unable to pay*
collapse breccia 384.9 *grit*
collapsed 262.7 *smaller*, 624.22 *sick*
collapsibility 262.2 *contractibility*
collapsible 262.9 *contractible*
collapsing 35.6 *rugger*, 262.8 *contracting*, 360.16 *descending*
collapsing scrum 35.3 *rugby play*
collar 36.4 *rowing*, 85.2 *tree part*, 137.9 *yoke*, 137.10 *band*, 295.14 *neckwear*, 295.24 *part of garment*, 313.3 *circular thing*, 407.11 *touch*, 699.5 *means of restraint*, 699.11 *detain*, 699.12 *gag*
collarbone 382 Bones
collard 45 Vegetables
collaring 44.5 *ceramic process*
collar stud 137.8 *fastening*
collate 480.1 *verify*
collated 480.10 *verified*
collateral 130.8 *additional*, 180.17 *accompanying*, 305.6 *side*, 632.2 *protection*, 718.2 *promise*, 725.5 *personal estate*, 725.8 *propertied*
collateral evidence 483.5 *legal evidence*
collateral loan 732.2 *loan*
collaterally 130.10 *additionally*, 285.7 *in parallel*, 725.10 *proprietarily*
collateral security 745.3 *loan*

collation 350.12 *meal*, 480.4 *verification*
collative 480.9 *verificatory*
colleague 148.5 *member*, 180.11 *companion*, 284.8 *supporter*, 400.10 *member of society*, 646.5 *partner*, 662.11 *helper*, 724.3 *participant*, 819.5 *friend*
colleagues 664.9 *team*
colleagueship 819.1 *friendship*
collect 10.9 *prayer*, 135.8 *unite*, 140.5 *combine*, 161.37 *assemble*, 721.11 *acquire*, 730.9 *receive*
collectable 526.7 *showpiece*, 655.3 *masterpiece*, 730.14 *receivable*
collectanea 161.32 *miscellany*
collect call 534.10 *telephone call*
collect dust 622.10 *be dirty*
collected 161, 4.18 *detached*, 135.12 *united*, 140.9 *assembled*, 562.7 *shortened*, 730.13 *received*, 787.3 *unmoved*
collectedly 787.9 *without wonder*
collectedness 787.1 *lack of wonder*
collect funds 721.9 *gain*
collecting 42 Hobbies and Pastimes, 161.1 *assembly*, 641.3 *inactive*, 730.1 *receiving*
collecting unemployment 641.3 *inactive*
collecting yard 68.7 *farm building*
collection 605, 133.3 *miscellany*, 135.1 *union*, 135.3 *unification*, 140.3, 161.1 *assembly*, 161.25 *assemblage*, 161.30 *compilation*, 161.31 *exhibition*, 526.6 *display*, 562.3 *compendium*, 605.3 *supply*, 710.6 *offering*, 721.3 *acquisition*, 729.3 *offering*, 730.1 *receiving*, 746.1 *payment*
collective 2.13 *communal*, 15.8 *industrial*, 140.9 *assembled*, 161.48 *cumulate*, 664.4 *joint operation*, 664.18 *joint*, 716.8 *negotiated*, 721.18 *acquisitional*, 724.1 *joint possession*, 724.5 *jointly possessing*, 815.15 *sociable*
collective action 664.4 *joint operation*
collective adaptation 2.5 *society*
collective agreement 15.1 *industrial relations*
collective bargaining 716.1 *negotiation*
collective creation 51.2 *play*
collective farm 68.6 *farm*, 724.1 *joint possession*
collectively 2.16 *sociologically*, 15.13 *industrially*, 140.10 *in combination*, 142.12 *one and all*, 161.51, 180.21 *together*, 664.20 *cooperatively*, 716.9 *feasibly*, 721.20 *gainfully*, 724.6 *in common*
collective memory 511.1 *memory*
collective noun 5.35 *part of speech*
collective tax 751.7 *tax*
collective unconscious 1.8 *tradition*, 61.21 *psyche*
collectivism 4.7 *school of thought*, 12.1 *government*, 664.6 *movement*, 688.7 *type of rule*, 724.1 *joint possession*
collectivist 4.11 *follower of a doctrine*, 664.18 *joint*
collectivistic 4.14 *of a philosophy*
collectivity 2.5 *society*
collectivization 724.1 *joint possession*
collect on delivery 534.2 *postal communication*
collect oneself 787.5 *not wonder about*
collector 161, 730, 64.19 *transistor*, 721.7 *gainer*
collector electrode 64.19 *transistor*
collectorship 730.1 *receiving*
collector's item 617.8 *exceller*, 861.17 *good thing*

collector's piece 526.7 *showpiece*, 617.8 *exceller*, 655.3 *masterpiece*
collect plants 83.23 *study plants*
Collects 10.6 *Eucharist*
collect together 161.39 *come together*, 562.9 *compile*
collect unemployment 662.18 *receive help*
colleen 402.2 *female*
college 6.12 *educational institution*, 6.13 *university*, 243.8 *construction*
college baseball 22.1 *baseball*
college basketball 23.1 *basketball*
college days 206.1 *youth*
college dictionary 5.28 *dictionary*
college football 19.1 *football*
College of Arms 544.9 *herald*
College of Heralds 544.9 *herald*
college president 696.9 *educational leader*
college radio 534.20 *radio broadcasting*
collegialism 664.5 *joint control*
collegiate 6.21 *curricular*, 19.19 *varsity*
col legno 49 Musical Terms
Collembola 82 Orders of Insects
collembolan 82.10 *insectan*
collide 74.9 *navigate*, 407.12 *abut*, 820.12 *oppose*
collider 56.94 *particle accelerator*
collide with 344.8 *meet*, 670.1 *attack*
colliding 407.9 *touching*
collie 77 Breeds of Dogs
collier 74 Ships and Boats, 646.2 *artisan*
colliery 317.2 *concave land*, 605.2 *resource*, 647.1 *workshop*
colligate 161.44 *put together*
colligation 161.1 *assembly*
colligative 57.32 *solid*
colligative property 57.3 *phase*
collimate 285.5 *parallel*, 332.7 *take a direction*
collimation 33.25 *mounting*, 285.1 *parallelism*, 332.3 *orientation*
collinear 52.80 *linear*
Collingwood 4 Philosophers
collins 351.8 *mixed drink*
Collins 48 Writers
colliquation 387.5 *fluidity*
colliquative 387.20 *liquefying*
colliquefaction 387.8 *fluidification*
collision 330, 56.71 *nuclear reaction*, 342.1 *convergence*, 385.2 *wearing away*, 663.3 *conflict*, 674.6 *fight*, 676.9 *battle*, 820.1 *enmity*
collision course 264.1 *nearness*, 342.2 *approach*
collision theory 57.14 *chemical reaction*
collocated 5.43 *phrasal*
collocating 5.43 *phrasal*
collocation 5.23 *phrase*, 161.1 *assembly*
collocutor 568.7 *conversationalist*
collodion 394.4 *emulsion*
colloid 57.3 *phase*, 133.2 *mixed thing*, 393.1 *semiliquid*, 394.4 *emulsion*
colloidal 133.12 *mixed*, 138.9 *adhesive*, 393.16 *semiliquid*, 394.8 *viscous*
colloidality 393.6 *thickening*, 394.1 *viscosity*
colloidally 57.46 *chemically*
colloidal solution 57.3 *phase*
colloider 393.11 *thickener*
collop 143.7 *piece*, 266.4 *slice*
colloquial 5.39 *of language*, 568.14 *conversational*
colloquialism 5.3 *spoken language*
colloquialize 5.45 *use language*
colloquially 5, 568.15 *conversationally*
colloquial speech 564.1 *faculty of speech*
colloquist 568.7 *conversationalist*
colloquium 568.4 *conference*
colloquize 4.23 *discuss philosophically*

colloquy 4.5 *philosophical argument*, 564.1 *faculty of speech*, 568.1 *conversation*
collotype 547.2 *reproduction*
collude 116.22 *form an alliance*, 539.28 *trick*, 540.22 *falsify*, 664.15 *concur*
colluding 116.11 *allied*, 539.34 *deceiving*
collusion 116.2 *alliance*, 539.7 *tricking*, 540.9 *falsification*, 664.8 *conferring*
collusive 540.29 *deceitful*, 664.19 *associating*
colly 522.6 *understand*
collybia 89 Fungi
collyrium 62.4 *drug type*, 386.6 *pomade*, 395.6 *ointment*, 630.9 *balm*
collywobbles 366.1 *agitation*, 624.8 *indigestion*
colobus 77 Placental Mammals
cologne 418.2 *fragrant thing*
Cologne 93 Cities
Cologne Cathedral 43 Noted Buildings
Cologne school 50 Western Art Styles and Movements
Colombia 91 Countries
Colombo 93 Cities
colon 290.4 *insides*, 322.7 *passageway*, 543.7 *punctuation*
colonel 679.17 *army person*
Colonel 17 British Military Ranks, 17 US Military Ranks
Colonel Blimp 577.8 *obstinate person*
colonial 43 Architectural Styles, 43.12 *structural*, 47.7 *furniture style*, 76.15 *of animals*, 90.7 *algal*, 91.16 *national*, 149.6, 149.13 *immigrant*, 208.15 *precursory*, 249.17 *national*, 255.7 *settler*, 255.13 *resident*, 688.14 *governmental*, 701.10 *dominating*
Colonial 202.14 *historic*
Colonial bed 47.6 *bed*
colonial home 43.3 *building*
colonialism 12.3 *governance*, 91.3 *dominion*, 400.11 *nation*, 688.7 *type of rule*, 701.2 *domination*
colonialist 91.14 *nationalist*
colonially 90.9 *algologically*, 91.19 *nationally*, 208.19 *primevally*, 249.20 *nationally*, 688.24 *ministerially*
colonic 290.10 *visceral*, 322.15 *providing passage*
colonist 208.4 *early comer*, 255.7 *settler*, 346.7 *entrant*, 347.8 *outgoer*
colonization 734.1 *taking*
colonize 91.18 *exert sovereignty*, 208.8 *precede*, 255.15 *settle*, 256.17 *inhabit*, 346.14 *enrol*, 701.6 *subject*, 734.7 *take*
colonized 255.13 *resident*
colonizer 255.7 *settler*
colonnade 43.8 *column*, 159.2 *consecution*, 312.7 *straight line*, 327.7 *arcade*
colony 12.5 *political organization*, 91.3 *dominion*, 161.23 *flock*, 181.4 *throng*, 249.4 *territorial division*, 255.2 *inhabitants*, 688.8 *governmental organization*, 723.4 *possession*
colophon 304.1 *rear*, 544.3 *means of identification*
Colorado 92 American States, **96** Rivers, **98** Deserts, 96.3 *US rivers*
Colorado beetle 69.12 *pests and diseases*
Colorado potato beetle 82 Insects
colorant 444.4 *pigment*
coloration 444.1 *colour*
colorific 444.10 *coloured*
colorimeter 56.92 *light meter*, 268.8 *meter*, 444.8 *chromatics*
colorimetric 268.16 *micrometric*, 444.14 *chromolithographic*
colorimetry 268.2 *micrometry*, 444.8 *chromatics*

colossal 43 Architectural Styles, 259.15 *big*, 275.12 *tall*
Colosseum 43 Noted Buildings, 243.8 *construction*
colossus 259.10 *big person*, 259.11, 275.7 *tall person*
colostomy 60 Surgical Operations, 630.12 *surgery*
colostrum 77.2 *mammalian characteristic*, 351.5 *milk*, 352.2 *secreted substance*, 387.3 *body fluid*
colour 777 Phobias by Topic, **56**, **444**, **444**, 1.6 *race*, 50.4 *treatment*, 50.19 *paint*, 133.4 *admixture*, 133.8 *mix*, 163.4 *type*, 233.8 *influence*, 447.7 *blackness*, 450.9 *redden*, 485.15 *modify*, 534.22 *television set*, 540.12 *facade*, 540.24 *mask*, 544.1 *identification*, 548.4 *misrepresent*, 557.1 *ornament*, 792.10 *decorate*, 828.12 *become angry*
Colour 444
colourable 444.10 *coloured*
colourant 67.6 *dye*
colour balance 66.8 *composition*
colour-balancing filter 66.20 *filter*
colour bar 147.4 *exclusiveness*, 820.1 *enmity*
colour-blind 436.9 *weak-sighted*, 482.1 *undiscriminating*
colour-blindness 436.2 *poor sight*, 444.1 *colour*
colourcast 444
colour cast 66.8 *composition*
colourcast 444.2 *colourfulness*
colour chart 444.2 *colourfulness*
colour circle 444.2 *colourfulness*
colour code 444.2 *colourfulness*
colour-coordinated 295.31 *styled*
colour coordination 444.2 *colourfulness*
colour coordinator 444.6 *painter*
colour-correcting filter 66.20 *filter*
colour decoration 557.1 *ornament*
colour design 557.1 *ornament*
colour disk 444.2 *colourfulness*
coloured 444, 50.27 *painted*, 67.11 *treated*, 133.12 *mixed*, 540.35 *disguised*, 557.4 *ornate*
coloured chalk 444.5 *paint*
coloured crayon 444.5 *paint*
coloured glaze 44.3 *glaze*
coloured paper 444.5 *paint*
coloured pencil 444.5 *paint*
colour falsely 540.24 *mask*
colourfast 444.10 *coloured*
colourfastness 444.4 *pigment*
colour-field painter 444.6 *painter*
colour-field painting 444.7 *colour painting*
colour film 66.9 *film*, 444.7 *colour painting*
colour filter 51.18 *stage lighting*, 444.7 *colour painting*
colourful 444, 456.6 *variegated*, 811.19 *flashy*
colourful language 827.2 *offensive language*
colourfully 444, 811.35 *flashily*
colourfulness 444, 811.4 *flashiness*
colour guard 679.12 *ceremonial troops*
colour harmony 444.2 *colourfulness*
colour highly 541.7 *exaggerate*
colour hologram 66.5 *stereoscopic image*
colour in 444.15 *colour*
colouring 50.2 *painting*, 67.7 *dyeing*, 133.4 *admixture*, 444.1 *colour*, 444.4 *pigment*, 520.1 *meaning*, 540.12 *facade*, 544.1 *identification*, 548.1 *misrepresentation*, 810.2 *blushing*
colouring matter 444.4 *pigment*
colouring the truth 525.2 *misinterpretation*
colourist 50.16 *artist*, 444.6 *painter*
colouristically 444.18 *colourfully*
colourization 444.7 *colour painting*

colourize 50.19 *paint*, 444.15 *colour*

colourized 444.10 *coloured*

colourizing 50.2 *painting*

colourless **445**, 439.21 *light*, 442.1 *transparent*, 446.2 *whitened*, 555.1 *unemphatic*, 624.21 *unhealthy*

colourlessly **445**, 555.3 *unemphatically*

colourlessness **445**, 439.14 *light colour*, 442.5 *transparency*, 446.7 *whiteness*

Colourlessness 445

colour negative 66.12 *development*, 444.7 *colour painting*

colour painting 444

colour perception 444.1 *colour*

colour photo 66.3 *photograph*

colour photographer 444.6 *painter*

colour photography 56.28 *colour*, 66.1 *photography*, 444.7 *colour painting*

colourpoint 77 *Breeds of Cats*

colour prejudice 822.3 *race hatred*

colour-prejudiced 493.8 *unjust*

colour print 50.7 *picture*, 66.12 *development*, 444.15 *colour*

colour printer 65.7 *peripheral*

colour printing 56.28 *colour*, 444.7 *colour painting*

colour prints 444.7 *colour painting*

colour processing 66.12 *development*

colour quality 444.3 *hue*

colour remover 445

colour reproduction 444.7 *colour painting*

colours 24.5 *snooker*, 295.5 *fancy dress*, 544.7 *flag*

colours-bearer 679.8 *soldier*

colour scheme 444.2 *colourfulness*

colour slides 444.7 *colour painting*

colour supplement 532.4 *newspaper*, 533.5 *mass communication*

colour television 56.28 *colour*, 534.21 *television* , 534.22 *television set*

colour temperature 66.15 *lighting*, 444.3 *hue*

colour theory 444.8 *chromatics*

colour transparencies 444.7 *colour painting*

colour up 450.9 *redden*, 810.16 *be self-conscious*

colour vision 56.23 *light*, 444.1 *colour*

colourwash 444.4 *pigment*, 444.15 *colour*

colour wheel 51.18 *stage lighting*, 444.2 *colourfulness*

colpoperineoplasty 60 *Surgical Operations*

colporteur 739.11 *pedlar*

colposcope 60.7 *diagnosis*

colposcopy 60.7 *diagnosis*

colpotomy 60 *Surgical Operations*

colt 32.1 *horse*, 77.17 *male mammal*, 77.19 *young mammal*, 206.4 *young animal*, 401.16 *male animal*, 656.10 *unskilled person*

Colt 680.9 *firearm*

colter 380.7 *sharp-edged thing*

coltish 642.18 *active*

coltsfoot 84 *Flowers and Flowering Plants*

colubriform 79.12 *snakelike*

colubrine 79.12 *snakelike*

colugo 77 *Placental Mammals*

Colum 48 *Poets*

Columba 53 *The Constellations*

columbarium 78.19 *ornithology*, 399.5 *cemetery*

Columbia 68 *Breeds of Sheep*, **93** *Cities*, **96** *Rivers*, 53.30 *spacecraft*, 91.7 *United States* , 96.3 *US rivers*

columbic 57.34 *elemental*

columbiform 78.23 *avian*

columbine 84 *Flowers and Flowering Plants*, 78.23 *avian*

Columbine 51.21 *role*, 51.30 *clown*

columbite 54 *Minerals*

columbous 57.34 *elemental*

Columbus 93 *Cities*

column 43, 17.4 *military organization*, 52.22 *matrix*, 63.27 *superstructure*, 159.8 *procession*, 275.6 *tall thing*, 281.3 *vertical thing*, 284.2 *supporting part*, 315.4 *cylinder*, 533.9 *news story*, 545.11 *monument*, 561.2 *article*, 679.16 *army unit*

columnar 43.16 *columned*

columnated 43.16 *columned*

column chromatography 57.17 *analysis*

columned 43

columniation 43.8 *column*

column inch 75 *General Units*

columnist 524.7 *news interpreter*, 528.9 *informant*, 532.11 *newspaper man*, 533.4 *journalist*, 545.9 *recorder*, 560.10 *descriptive writer*

Colwyn Bay 93 *Cities*

coly 78 *Birds*

coma 53.19 *comet*, 53.25 *mounting*, 56.31 *lens element*, 236.4 *disability*, 325.1 *motionlessness*, 404.2 *unconsciousness*, 512.1 *oblivion*, 624.2 *illness*, 643.9 *sleep*, 722.1 *loss*, 761.4 *desensitization*

Coma Berenices 53 *The Constellations*

COMAL 65 *Programming Languages*

comanagement 664.5 *joint control*

Comanche 1 *Peoples*, **5** *Languages and Groups of Languages*

Comaneci 18 *Sporting Personalities*

Comas Solá 53 *Comets*

comatose 236.12 *impotent*, 404.8 *unconscious*, 624.22 *sick*, 643.4 *not awake*, 761.2 *desensitized*, 783.7 *indifferent*

comatose patient 240.2 *inert person*

comb 68.18 *practise livestock farming*, 97.10 *billow*, 275.4 *mountain range*, 376.9 *smoother*, 376.11 *smooth*, 380.8 *sharp-pointed thing*, 380.16 *use a sharp tool* , 621.10 *cleaning object*, 621.13 *clean*

combat 26, 679, 663.15 *object*, 674.1 *contention*, 674.6 *fight*, 674.11 *contend*, 674.12 *fight*, 676.14 *battle*

combatant 679, 17.9 *enlisted*, 398.10 *killer*, 663.11 *opponent*, 674.10 *contender*, 820.5 *hostile person*

Combatant 679

combat boots 295.19 *footwear*

combative 679, 17.8 *military*, 26.14 *combat*, 666.9 *disagreeing*, 670.22 *militant*, 674.15 *contentious*, 676.16 *warlike*

combatively 666.11 *in disagreement*

combativeness 666.1 *disagreement*, 670.11 *attack*, 676.5 *bellicosity*

combative sport 26.1 *combat sports*

combat neurosis 61.10 *neurosis*

combat-ready forces 679.14 *armed forces*

combat sports 26

Combat Sports 26

combat team 17.4 *military organization*

combat troops 679.14 *armed forces*

combat zone 676.10 *battleground*

combe 317.2 *concave land*

combed 376.1 *smooth*

comber 97.3 *wave*

combination 140, 52.21 *set*, 71.13 *motorcycle*, 107.1 *relatedness*, 133.1 *mixture*, 133.2

mixed thing, 135.1 *union*, 161.1 *assembly*, 180.1 *accompaniment*, 664.7 *association*

Combination 140

combination lock 137.8 *fastening*

combination obstacle 32.9 *jumping*

combinations 295.18 *underwear*

combinative 140.7 *combined*

combinatory 140.7 *combined*

combine 140, 68.10 *farm tool*, 133.8 *mix*, 135.8 *unite*, 140.3 *assembly*, 161.44 *put together*, 174.19 *become one*, 243.10 *produce*, 664.7 *association*, 664.16 *join*

combined 57, 140, 30.11 *gymnastic*, 107.4 *related*, 116.11 *allied*, 133.12 *mixed*, 135.12 *united*, 146.8 *included*, 161.48 *cumulate*, 180.19 *associated*, 664.18 *joint*

combined attack 670.12 *military attack*

combined effort 664.4 *joint operation*

combinedly 664.20 *cooperatively*

combined movement 30.8 *floor exercises*

combined operation 664.4 *joint operation*, 676.8 *warfare*

combined structure 604.2 *building material*

combined tactics 34.3 *climbing technique*

combine harvester 68.10 *farm tool*

combine in 148.10 *compose*

combine with 116.22 *form an alliance*, 130.7 *support*

combine with gas 388.27 *give off*

combings 132.2 *residue*

combining 116.11 *allied*, 140.1 *combination*

comb jelly 81.7 *coelenterate*

comblike 380.4 *toothed*

combo 116.2 *alliance*, 133.2 *mixed thing*

comb out 312.10 *straighten*

combustibility 408.6 *fire*

combustible 408.10 *on fire*, 410.10 *powered*

combustibly 410.12 *powerfully*

combustion 56.35 *heat*, 408.6 *fire*

come 344.1 *arrive*, 457.12 *become visible*, 684.5 *conclude*

come about 99.18 *come to be*, 227.9 *take effect*, 337.9 *turn round*

come a cropper 656.5 *be unskilful*, 683.6 *fail*

come across 250.11 *find*, 496.1 *discover*, 721.14 *profit*, 746.6 *pay*

come across with 729.5 *give*

come adrift 139.6 *come unstuck*

come after 155.21 *follow in sequence*, 159.13 *be consecutive*, 195.10 *succeed*

come again 214.8 *be cyclic*, 609.6 *be unsatisfied*

come again and again 183.21 *be repeated*

come alive 522.4 *be intelligible*, 537.33 *seem lifelike*

come along 336.1 *go forward*

come amiss 616.5 *be inconvenient*

come and get it 45.58 *grub's on*

come and go 214.7 *be regular*, 221.8 *return*, 365.8 *oscillate*, 642.12 *be active*

come apart 136.9 *separate*, 141.3 *disintegrate*, 151.25 *be disordered*, 162.11 *explode*, 628.1 *deteriorate*

come apart at the seams 238.6 *be weak*

come around 651.2 *be refreshed*

come as a revelation 530.9 *be disclosed*

come as no surprise 488.8 *be probable*

come as you are 814.11 *not stand on ceremony*

come at one's call 694.5 *obey*

come at the right time 210.4 *be timely*

comeback 109.1 *interchange*, 183.4 *return*, 476.3 *countercharge*, 478.1 *answer*, 484.1 *counterevidence*, 629.10 *revival*, 672.1 *retaliation*

come back 183.20 *renew*, 478.17 *answer*, 511.15 *be remembered*, 609.6 *be unsatisfied*, 671.26 *act on the defensive*

come back at 331.2 *respond*

come back to life 629.4 *be restored*

come back to where one started 337.7 *recoil*

come before 16.72 *stand trial*, 154.15 *precede*, 194.8 *be before*, 348.8 *show in*, 517.11 *predict*, 611.7 *be important*, 653.2 *direct*

come between 136, 158.19 *mediate*, 640.4 *act*, 661.8 *hinder*

come by 721.9 *gain*, 730.9 *receive*, 738.1 *purchase*

come cap in hand 840.6 *apologize*

come clean 530.8 *admit*

comedian 51.22 *actor*, 51.24 *dramatist*, 51.27 *entertainer*, 506.4 *buffoon*, 771.6 *humorist*

comedienne 51.22 *actor*, 51.27 *entertainer*

comedown 360.1 *descent*, 360.4 *fall*, 515.2 *bad outcome*, 683.1 *failure*, 687.1 *adversity*

come down 55.62 *rain*, 129.4 *decrease*, 360.9 *descend*

come-down 806.9 *humiliation*

come down a peg 360.10 *droop*

come down a peg or two 806.20 *submit*

come down cats and dogs 389.29 *water*

come down hard on 879.2 *penalize*

come down in buckets 55.62 *rain*

come down in the world 743.13 *lose one's money*

come down like a ton of bricks 237.7 *be strong*

come down off the fence 226.12 *determine*

come down on 360.12 *drop*, 690.5 *be severe*, 879.2 *penalize*

come down on like a ton of bricks 852.20 *censure*, 879.2 *penalize*

come down on one side or the other 226.12 *determine*

come down on the side of 662.24 *back*

come down with 715.6 *catch*

comedy 51, 771.4 *entertainment*

comedy actor 51.22 *actor*

comedy actress 51.22 *actor*

comedy hour 771.4 *entertainment*

comedy of character 51.10 *comedy*

comedy of humours 51.10 *comedy*

comedy of ideas 51.10 *comedy*

comedy of intrigue 51.10 *comedy*

comedy of manners 51.10 *comedy*

comedy of morals 51.10 *comedy*

comedy of situation 51.10 *comedy*

comedy routine 771.4 *entertainment*

comedy skit 771.4 *entertainment*

come eyeball to eyeball 526.4 *show oneself*

come face to face 526.4 *show oneself*

come first 21.6 *compete in athletics*, 126.10 *lead*, 611.7 *be important*

come forth 156.27 *emerge*, 457.12 *become visible*, 475.18 *appear*, 526.4 *show oneself*

come forward 303.10 *be in front*, 457.12 *become visible*, 710.11 *volunteer*

come from another country 104.14 *be foreign*

come from without 104.16 *be external*

come full circle 334.3 *circuit*, 363.6 *orbit*

come hat in hand 806.20 *submit*

come hell or high water 574.17 *resolutely*

come-hither look 435.6 *look*, 543.3 *gesture*, 821.6, 826.2 *courtship*

come home 344.4 *land*

come in 344.5 *get in*, 346.9 *enter*

come in for 730.9 *receive*

come in force 237.7 *be strong*

come in front 357.3 *exceed*

come in handy 613.9 *be useful*, 615.6 *be convenient*

come in last 683.7 *be defeated*

come in like a lion 241.7 *be violent*

come in sight 457.12 *become visible*

come in the wake of 155.21 *follow in sequence*

come into 195.11 *follow in office*, 682.12 *succeed to*, 730.9, 749.7 *receive*

come into an inheritance 686.6 *be fortunate*

come into being 156.27 *emerge*

come into conflict 463.16 *confront*

come into contact 267.3 *juxtapose*, 344.8 *meet*, 407.12 *abut*

come into effect 227.9 *take effect*, 230.7 *be operational*

come into existence 156.27 *emerge*, 396.18 *be born*

come into focus 437.9 *appear*

come into money 686.6 *be fortunate*, 721.14 *profit*, 742.13 *get rich*

come into operation 230.7 *be operational*, 640.3 *act*

come into ownership of 195.11 *follow in office*

come into possession of 195.11 *follow in office*

come into power 235.10 *be powerful*

come into the hands of 728.4 *be transferred*

come into the picture 457.12 *become visible*

come into the world 156.27 *emerge*, 396.18 *be born*

come into use 584.17 *become a habit*

come into view 435.19 *be visible*

come in useful 615.6 *be convenient*, 662.26 *be useful*

come it over 805.28 *disdain*

come last 155.26 *bring up the rear*, 195.10 *succeed*

comeliness 789.1 *gorgeousness*

comely 789.5 *beautiful*

come near 264.9 *near*

come next 155.21 *follow in sequence*, 195.10 *succeed*

come of 227.7 *follow from*

come of age 207.18 *mature*, 845.18 *be due*

come off 139.6 *come unstuck*, 227.9 *take effect*, 682.8 *be effective*, 873.4 *give up alcohol*

come off best 682.11 *overmaster*

come off it 218.12 *stop*

come off on 138.6 *adhere*

come off second best 683.7 *be defeated*

come off well 682.6 *be successful*

come off with flying colours 682.6 *be successful*

come on 105.6 *be in a state of*, 336.5 *develop*, 353.22 *menstruate*

come-on 228.5 *positive stimulus*, 340.4 *allurement*, 586.9 *enticement*, 710.1 *offer*

come on bended knee 806.20 *submit*

come on like gangbusters 532.14 *proclaim*

come-on man 539.18 *decoy*

come on the scene 457.12 *become visible*

come on the stage 457.13 *occur*

come out 812, 105.6 *be in a state of*, 156.27, 347.10 *emerge*, 457.12 *become visible*, 457.13 *occur*, 530.9 *be disclosed*, 532.17 *be published*, 598.2 *withdraw*, 669.6 *resist*

come out easily 660.15 *be easy*

come out for 580.3 *side with*

come out from the woodwork 437.9 *appear*

come out in the open 347.10 *emerge*

come out in the wash 445.5 *lose colour*

come out into the open 526.4 *show oneself*

come out of 227.7 *follow from*

come out of the blue 514.11 *amaze*

come out on one side 580.3 *side with*

come out on strike 218.7 *stop working*, 713.8 *cause mischief*

come out the other side 356.8 *pass*

come out with 526.3 *reveal*, 530.6 *divulge*, 583.3 *improvise*

come over 522.4 *be intelligible*

come over all queer 624.24 *be unhealthy*

come over the horizon 437.9 *appear*, 457.12 *become visible*

comer 346.7 *entrant*, 682.4 *successful person*

come rain or shine 574.17 *resolutely*

come right in the end 682.7 *overcome obstacles*

come round 396.16 *live*, 629.4 *be restored*

come round again 187.10 *be periodical*, 214.8 *be cyclic*, 457.13 *occur*

come short 609.5 *be insufficient*

come short of 127.8 *be inferior*

come soon 199.7 *be in the future*

comestible 350.27 *edible*, 411.7 *tasty*

comestibles 350.7 *food*, 606.2 *provisions*

comet 53, 213.4 *rare things*, 214.5 *regular thing*, 439.4 *natural light*

cometary 53.36 *astronomical*

cometary nucleus 53.19 *comet*

come the high and mighty 807.28 *get above oneself*

come through 105.6 *be in a state of*, 396.16 *live*, 632.8 *be safe*

come through loud and clear 522.4 *be intelligible*

come through with flying colours 682.11 *overmaster*

come to 142.9 *be whole*, 169.11, 170.10 *total*, 220.7 *convert into*, 263.7, 344.2 *reach*, 396.16 *live*, 629.4 *be restored*, 651.2 *be refreshed*, 751.13 *cost*

come to a bad end 687.9 *be in trouble*

come to a close 144.5 *be complete*

come to a crisis 684.4 *complete*

come to a crossroads 106.12 *come to a juncture*, 327.14 *find one's way*

come to a dead stop 683.9 *malfunction*

come to a focus 342.11 *focus*

come to a halt 218.6 *cease*, 325.8 *be motionless*, 683.9 *malfunction*

come to a head 353.18 *fester*

come to a junction 288.9 *cross*

come to a juncture 106

come to an agreement 140.6 *come together*, 152.17 *come to an arrangement*, 715.5 *contract*

come to an arrangement 152

come to anchor 36.15 *sail*

come to an end 157, 144.5 *be complete*, 218.6 *cease*, 244.13 *be destroyed*

come to an understanding 677.5 *make peace*, 839.9 *forgive*

come to an untimely end 397.16 *meet one's fate*

come to a parting 824.8 *desert*

come to a parting of the ways 666.5 *disagree*, 824.7 *divorce*

come to a point 291.9 *centre*

come to a standstill 218.6 *cease*, 325.8 *be motionless*, 659.20 *be in difficulty*

come to a sticky end 157.19 *expire*, 244.13 *be destroyed*, 722.10 *have a financial loss*

come to a stop 218.6 *cease*

come to bat 22.7 *play baseball*

come to be 99, 156.27 *emerge*

come to blows 117.14 *disagree*, 674.12 *fight*, 820.12 *oppose*

come to close quarters 674.12 *fight*

come to dust 384, 189.4 *be transient*, 397.15 *die*

come to execution 879.6 *be punished*

come to financial ruin 687.10 *need money*

come to fruition 684.4 *complete*

come together 140, 141, 342, 135.8 *unite*, 407.12 *abut*

come to grief 683.8 *miscarry*, 687.9 *be in trouble*

come to grips 674.12 *fight*

come to grips with 597.1 *undertake*

come to hand 344.7 *be brought*, 407.12 *abut*, 730.9 *receive*

come to heel 694.5 *obey*

come to its end 684.5 *conclude*

come to journey's end 325.8 *be motionless*

come to know 528.15 *be informed*

come to life 396.16 *live*

come to life again 629.4 *be restored*

come to light 435.19 *be visible*, 437.9 *appear*, 457.12 *become visible*, 496.5 *be discovered*, 526.5 *be visible*, 530.9 *be disclosed*

come to maturity 207.18 *mature*

come to mind 471.14 *have an idea*

come to naught 247.7 *be infertile*, 358.3 *fall through*, 683.8 *miscarry*, 722.14 *go to waste*

come to nothing 247.7 *be infertile*, 683.6 *fail*, 683.8 *miscarry*, 722.14 *go to waste*

come to often 212.8 *frequent*

come to one 471.14 *have an idea*, 730.9 *receive*

come to one's journey's end 344.2 *reach*

come to one's senses 403.12 *awake*, 509.6 *be sane*

come to pass 155.25 *result*, 227.9 *take effect*

come to pieces 136.9 *separate*, 141.3 *disintegrate*

come to rest 325.8 *be motionless*, 344.2 *reach*, 649.2 *take it easy*

come to stay 217.5 *be permanent*

come to terms 152.17 *come to an arrangement*, 715.5 *contract*

come to terms with 705.6 *resign oneself*

come to the aid of 662.17 *help*

come to the end of the line 327.14 *find one's way*, 683.6 *fail*

come to the end of the road 157.18 *come to an end*

come to the front 126.8 *be superior*, 303.10 *be in front*

come to the gallows 879.6 *be punished*

come to the point 107.7 *relate to*, 165.23 *particularize*, 342.11 *focus*, 552.4 *be concise*, 556.7 *be simple*, 562.10 *be brief*

come to the point of no return 106.12 *come to a juncture*

come to the rescue 639.1 *deliver*, 671.23 *rescue*

come to the rescue of 767.10 *save*

come to the same thing 110.10 *be equal*, 122.11 *equalize*

come to the surface 437.9 *appear*, 457.12 *become visible*

come to understand 522.6 *understand*

comets 777 *Phobias by Topic*

come under fire 633.9 *face danger*

come under the hammer 739.2 *be sold*

come under the influence 586.18 *be persuaded*

come under the influence of 228.8 *be motivated*

come undone 136.9 *separate*, 139.6 *come unstuck*

come unstuck 139, 136.9 *separate*, 151.25 *be disordered*, 162.11 *explode*, 656.5 *be unskilful*, 659.19 *have difficulty*

come up 457.12 *become visible*

come up for more 575.9 *endure*

come up for trial 16.72 *stand trial*

come upon 229.5 *happen by chance*, 344.2 *reach*, 344.8 *meet*, 496.1 *discover*, 589.11 *chance upon*

comeuppance 672.1 *retaliation*, 845.2 *due*, 878.6 *compensation*, 879.9 *retribution*

come up short 515.4 *be disappointed*

come up smelling like roses 682.7 *overcome obstacles*

come up smiling 682.7 *overcome obstacles*

come up to 122.10 *be equal*

come up to scratch 851.17 *meet with approval*

come up with 156.22 *invent*, 583.3 *improvise*

come what may 571.19 *necessarily*, 574.17 *resolutely*

come with 180.13 *accompany*

come with a blinding flash 530.9 *be disclosed*

come within earshot 420.16 *be heard*

come within the law 16.66 *be legal*

comfit 45.41 *sweet*, 414.4 *confectionery*

comfort 405, 765, 775, 106.5 *comfortable circumstances*, 242.4 *moderate*, 405.1 *physical pleasure*, 649.1, 649.3 *ease*, 660.1 *easiness*, 662.2 *support*, 662.13 *supporter*, 662.19 *support*, 686.1 *prosperity*, 742.7 *opulence*, 763.7 *pleasure*, 763.13 *give pleasure*, 765.1 *satisfaction*, 767.1 *case*, 767.9 *relieve*, 775.10 *inspire hope*, 831.8 *be benevolent*, 835.2 *condolence*, 835.9 *sorrow*

comfortable 106, 763, 405.6 *pleasant*, 405.7 *pleased*, 623.1 *healthy*, 649.4 *at ease*, 660.14 *relaxed*, 686.8 *prosperous*, 742.1 *wealthy*, 765.4 *satisfied*

comfortable circumstances 106, 742.7 *opulence*

comfortably 106, 405.11 *pleasingly*, 660.21 *easily*, 686.9 *prosperously*, 742.16 *wealthily*

comfortably drunk 874.1 *drunk*

comfortably off 686.8 *prosperous*, 721.17 *well-off*, 742.1 *wealthy*

comfort blanket 405.4 *pleasurable things*

comforted 767.7 *relieved*

comforter 293.5 *body covering*, 293.10 *bed covering*, 295.14 *neckwear*, 405.4 *pleasurable things*, 767.3 *reliever*

comforting 242.8 *moderating*, 405.6 *pleasant*, 651.3 *refreshing*, 662.32 *supportive*, 765.5 *satisfying*, 767.8 *relieving*, 835.6 *pitying*

comfortingly 767

comfortless 776.4 *hopeless*

comfort station 256.7 *room*, 353.13 *lavatory*, 727.7 *toilet*

comfrey 45 *Herbs and Spices*

comfy 763.3 *comfortable*

comic 48.19 *narrative*, 50.9 *drawing*, 51.27 *entertainer*, 51.38 *tragic*, 506.5 *nonsensical*, 532.5 *journal*, 771.6 *humorist*, 771.10 *humorous*, 773.10 *laughing*, 798.5 *ridiculous*

comical 798.5 *ridiculous*

comicality 798.1 *ludicrousness*
comically 51.42 *dramatically,* 771.16 *humorously*
comic business 51.10 *comedy*
comic magazine 532.5 *journal*
comic muse 51.10 *comedy*
comic opera 51.3 *musical drama*
comic poet 48.14 *author,* 51.24 *dramatist*
comic poetry 48.6 *poetry*
comic relief 48.3 *aspect of fiction,* 51.10 *comedy,* 51.21 *role*
comic strip 50.9 *drawing,* 532.5 *journal,* 771.4 *entertainment*
comic-strip artist 50.16 *artist*
coming 199.6 *future event,* 199.11 *future,* 344.10 *arrival,* 344.19 *approaching,* 457.1 *appearance,* 457.7 *appearing,* 845.12 *owed*
coming across 250.3 *locating*
coming after 155.1 *sequence*
coming alive 537.25 *lifelike*
coming and going 365.1 *oscillation,* 642.19 *busy*
coming apart at the seams 244.15 *destroyed*
coming ashore 344.11 *landing*
coming back 344.13 *return*
coming before 154.1 *precedence*
coming by 721.1 *gain*
coming down in buckets 55.53 *rainy*
coming down with 624.22 *sick*
coming events 199.3 *future condition*
coming from 227.10 *caused*
coming from without 104.4 *externality*
coming into being 99.8 *creation,* 457.1 *appearance,* 457.7 *appearing*
coming into sight 457.7 *appearing*
coming into view 457.1 *appearance,* 457.7 *appearing*
coming later 209.12 *delaying*
coming man 336.16 *progressive person*
coming on the scene 457.7 *appearing*
coming out 156.9 *premiere,* 347.1 *exit,* 347.15 *outgoing*
coming-out 815.5 *party*
coming out of one's ears 144.8 *full*
coming-out party 815.5 *party*
comings and goings 221.4 *return*
coming through loud and clear 522.1 *intelligible*
coming to 845.12 *owed*
coming to blows 828.5 *quarrel*
coming together 135.1 *union,* 161.1 *assembly,* 342.1 *convergence*
coming-together 678.2 *mediation*
coming to often 212.5 *frequenting*
coming to one 845.10 *due*
coming to terms 705.4 *resignedness*
coming to the point 342.5 *focus*
coming up roses 682.1 *success*
comitia 653.7 *council*
comity 362.16 *courtesy,* 667.1 *agreement,* 694.2 *loyalty,* 813.5 *etiquette,* 817.1, 817.1 *courtesy,* 847.3 *allegiance,* 849.3 *respectfulness*
comity of nations 400.9 *group*
comma 136.5 *separator,* 343.7 *punctuation*
command 692, 692, 6.24 *know,* 12.3 *governance,* 12.11 *govern,* 65.17 *computing term,* 95.9 *tower,* 126.2 *leadership,* 166.8 *authority,* 166.16 *direct,* 275.15 *be high,* 543.6 *word,* 543.12 *signal,* 570.15 *impose one's will,* 593.1 *requirement,* 599.5 *dispose of,* 652.8 *treatment,* 653.2 *direct,* 653.4 *directorship,* 654.3 *precept,* 654.5 *advise,* 676.8 *warfare,* 688.1 *authority,* 688.4 *governance,* 688.18 *have authority,* 695.2 *coercion,* 695.6 *compel,* 696.14 *master,* 712.2, 712.7 *demand,* 723.7 *possess,* 847.17 *impose a duty*

Command 692
commandant 692.6 *person in command,* 696.7 *military leader*
command capital 742.12 *be rich*
commandeer 695.7 *force,* 767.14 *take away*
commandeering 734.12 *taking*
commander 17.5 *military staff,* 126.5 *superior,* 543.8 *signer,* 679.27 *naval man,* 688.10 *person of authority,* 692.6 *person in command,* 696.7 *military leader*
Commander 17 US Military Ranks
commander-in-chief 688.10 *person of authority,* 692.6 *person in command,* 696.7 *military leader*
command influence 233.8 *influence*
commanding 692, 12.10 *governing,* 166.12 *ruling,* 233.11 *influential,* 497.13 *believable,* 543.16 *signalling,* 611.6 *notable,* 688.12 *authoritative,* 695.9 *compelling,* 696.12 *masterful,* 805.18 *prestigious*
commanding lead 126.3 *advantage*
commandingly 692, 233.14 *influentially,* 688.23 *authoritatively,* 695.11 *compellingly*
commanding officer 17.5 *military staff,* 688.10 *person of authority,* 692.6 *person in command,* 696.7 *military leader*
commandment 166.1 *rule,* 654.3 *precept,* 692.1 *command*
commandos 679.14 *armed forces*
command of idiom 549.4 *literary style*
command of language 549.4 *literary style,* 564.2 *power of speech*
command of the air 17.1 *military affairs*
command of the sea 17.1 *military affairs*
commando unit 17.4 *military organization*
command performance 51.11 *theatrical performance*
command respect 849, 611.7 *be important*
command ship 679.24 *warship*
commedia dell'arte 51.2 *play*
commemorate 214, 511, 812
commemoration 812, 214.3 *anniversary,* 511.3 *memento*
commemorative 812, 214.13 *anniversary,* 511.10 *memorial*
commemoratively 214.16 *cyclically,* 511.16 *memorably*
commence 156.17, 201.19 *begin,* 322.24 *begin*
commencement 156.1, 201.4 *beginning,* 322.11 *beginning*
commencing 156.29, 322.17 *beginning*
commencing move 156.12 *first move*
commend 654.5 *advise,* 851.13 *support,* 851.15 *compliment*
commendable 615.1 *convenient,* 851.21 *praiseworthy,* 863.7 *worthy*
commendably 863.11 *worthily*
commendation 851.4 *compliment*
commendatory 851.18 *approving*
commender 654.4 *adviser,* 851.9 *praiser*
commensal 59.18 *ecology,* 76.4 *type of animal,* 76.15 *of animals,* 664.19 *associating*
commensalism 59.18 *ecology*
commensurable 52.74 *divisible,* 114.7 *similar*
commensurate 107.5 *interrelated,* 116.14 *conforming,* 122.6 *equal,* 608.1 *sufficient*
commensurately 107.10 *relevantly*
comment 492.1 *judgment,* 524.2 *annotation,* 561.1 *dissertation,* 564.7 *utterance*
commentarial 524.16 *annotative*
commentary 48.4 *non-fiction,* 524.2 *annotation,* 561.1 *dissertation*

commentate 561.4 *dissertate*
commentator 492.5 *judge,* 524.6 *interpreter,* 524.7 *news interpreter,* 534.29 *broadcaster,* 561.3 *dissertator*
commented on 524.15 *interpreted*
comment on 4.23 *discuss philosophically,* 492.12 *estimate,* 524.8 *interpret,* 524.10 *annotate,* 524.13 *interpret news,* 561.4 *dissertate*
commeration 804.1 *right*
commerce 13.5 *international trade,* 135.1 *union,* 137.2 *association,* 737.4 *trade*
commercial 737, 13.13 *economic,* 70.5 *transportable,* 532.9 *advertisement,* 534.25 *broadcast material,* 750.10 *accounting*
commercial arithmetic 750.1 *accounts*
commercial art 50.1 *art*
commercial artist 50.16 *artist*
commercial bank 741.19 *treasury,* 744.4 *bank*
commercial break 534.25 *broadcast material*
commercial building 63.20 *building*
commercial city 93.1 *city*
commercial gain 93.1 *city*
commercial intercourse 737.5 *commercial trade*
commercialistic 13.13 *economic,* 737.13 *mercantile*
commercialize 13.10 *trade with,* 737.1 *trade,* 795.10 *vulgarize*
commercial law 16.1 *the law*
commercial listing 532.9 *advertisement*
commercially 70, 13.14 *economically,* 739.17 *marketably,* 750.13 *financially*
commercial paper 741.14 *paper money*
commercial radio 534.20 *radio broadcasting*
commercial television 534.24 *television broadcasting*
commercial trade 737
commercial transaction 737.4 *trade*
commercial transport 70.1 *transport*
commercial traveller 739.10 *salesman*
commie 12.6 *political party,* 627.12 *reformer,* 665.6 *political party member,* 693.11 *rebel*
commination 827.4 *malediction*
comminatory 10.21 *ritualistic,* 827.10 *maledictive*
commingle 133.8 *mix,* 140.5 *combine*
comminute 384.23 *pulverize*
comminuted 384.19 *pulverized*
comminution 384.4 *pulverization*
comminutor 384.11 *pulverizer*
commis chef 45.2 *cook*
commiserate 759.18 *feel for,* 760.11 *be sensitive,* 835.9 *sorrow*
commiserating 835.6 *pitying*
commiseration 760.5 *sensitivity,* 835.1 *pity,* 835.2 *condolence*
commiserative 835.6 *pitying*
commiserator 835.4 *pitying person*
commissarial 606.7 *provisioning*
commissariat 350.7 *food,* 350.17 *food shop,* 606.1 *provision*
commissary 350.17 *food shop,* 606.3 *provider*
commission 703, 156.23 *inaugurate,* 161.7 *committee,* 580.4 *pick,* 580.6 *selection,* 594.4 *prepare for action,* 594.11 *fitting out,* 640.1 *action,* 640.4 *act,* 644.2 *task,* 653.3 *management,* 653.7 *council,* 654.3 *precept,* 676.12 *go to war,* 692.4 *authorization,* 692.13 *authorize,* 706.4 *delegate,* 707.6 *deputize,* 721.5 *profit,* 729.5 *give,* 730.2 *something received,* 746.3 *pay,* 751.3 *fee,* 752.1 *discount,* 847.2 *task,* 878.4 *reward for service*

Commission 703
commissionaire 323.5 *person who closes*
commissioned 703, 17.9 *enlisted,* 692.15 *self-assured,* 696.12 *masterful*
commissioned officer 696.7 *military leader*
commissioner 703, 653.16 *official,* 688.10 *person of authority,* 696.3 *leader,* 706.1 *delegate,* 707.3 *agent*
commissioner of police 16.17 *police officer*
commissioning 703.1 *commission*
commission of the peace 16.2 *jurisdiction,* 16.18 *tribunal*
commit 326.14 *bring back,* 510.16 *certify,* 535.18 *vow,* 640.4 *act,* 703.6 *commission,* 847.17 *impose a duty*
commit a crime 16.73 *be illegal,* 693.15 *be disobedient,* 844.21 *do wrong,* 866.10 *sin*
commit adultery 576.9 *change sides,* 877.17 *be sexually immoral*
commit a felony 866.10 *sin*
commit a foul 844.21 *do wrong*
commit a malapropism 601.1 *misuse*
commit a misdemeanour 866.10 *sin*
commit an atrocity 690.6 *suppress*
commit an offence 844.21 *do wrong*
commit a sacrilege 827.5 *curse*
commit a white-collar crime 866.10 *sin*
commit bigamy 823.15 *marry*
commit burglary 736.12 *steal*
commit crime 168.20 *infringe a law*
commit daylight robbery 753.10 *overcharge*
commit euthanasia 397.16 *meet one's fate*
commit for trial 16.71 *try a case,* 492.11 *judge*
commit genocide 398.18 *slaughter,* 879.5 *execute*
commit hara-kiri 398.21 *commit suicide*
commit highway robbery 753.10 *overcharge*
commitment 575, 847, 535.3 *vow,* 574.13 *concentration,* 597.3 *contract,* 714.1 *promise,* 715.1 *contract,* 729.1 *giving,* 745.1 *debt,* 772.5 *earnestness,* 819.3 *familiarity*
commit money 729.6 *give to charity*
commit murder 398.17 *murder*
commit oneself 535.18 *vow,* 574.9 *undertake,* 580.3 *side with,* 597.1 *undertake,* 714.7 *promise,* 714.8 *guarantee,* 715.5 *contract,* 729.6 *give to charity,* 847.15 *be liable*
commit perjury 856.6 *accuse falsely*
commit robbery 736.12 *steal*
commit sacrilege 850.27 *desecrate*
commit sin 864.16 *be wicked*
commit suicide 398, 157.19 *expire,* 397.16 *meet one's fate*
commit suttee 398.21 *commit suicide*
committal 16.6 *legal process*
committed 535.12 *vowed,* 574.2 *tenacious,* 714.12 *promised,* 714.13 *guaranteeing,* 745.9 *in debt,* 772.2 *earnest,* 819.11 *devoted,* 847.11 *duty-bound*
committedly 819.19 *devotedly*
committed to memory 511.9 *memorized*
committee 161, 653.6 *governing body,* 665.1 *party,* 703.4 *council,* 706.2 *representative body*
committee boat 36.2 *sailing boat*
committee of inquiry 654.4 *adviser*
committee room 592.7 *planning*
committee rule 12.1 *government*
committer 640.3 *doer*

commit time 729.6 *give to charity*
committing move 34.3 *climbing technique*
commit to memory 511.11 *memorize*
commit to writing 545.14 *inscribe*
commit unsportsmanlike conduct 19.18 *be penalized*
commix 133.8 *mix*
commixture 133.1 *mixture*
commode 47.5, 258.3 *cabinet*, 353.14, 727.7 *toilet*
commodious 248.13 *spacious*, 613.1 *useful*, 615.1 *convenient*, 755.4 *big*
commodity 13.6 *economic factors*, 243.7 *produce*, 367.5 *object*, 613.5 *usefulness*, 739.8 *merchandise*
commodity exchange 740.5 *stock market*
commodity market 740.5 *stock market*
commodore 679.27 *naval man*
Commodore 17 British Military Ranks
common 164, 803, 803, 5.39 *of language*, 87.2 *grassland*, 124.1 *average*, 124.7 *average person*, 127.16 *ordinary*, 164.19 *prevailing*, 167.15 *everyday*, 212.3 *frequent*, 298.6 *interfacial*, 453.8 *greenness*, 501.10 *known*, 549.8 *inelegant*, 556.1 *simple*, 559.10 *ugly*, 584.10 *familiar*, 664.18 *joint*, 724.1 *joint possession*, 724.5 *jointly possessing*, 725.1 *property*, 787.4 *predictable*, 814.9 *familiar*, 815.15 *sociable*
Common Agricultural Policy 68
commonality 124.4 *average*, 164.5 *averageness*
commonalty 400.9 *group*, 612.10 *nonentity*, 803.2 *the common people*
common as muck 559.10 *ugly*
common border 298.1 *interface*
common boundary 298.1 *interface*
common carrier 326.7 *transferor*
common chord 49.16 *musical note*
common cold 409.3 *chill*, 624.6 *infection*, 624.9 *respiratory disease*
common courtesy 817.1 *courtesy*
common denominator 52.18 *division*
common endeavour 664.4 *joint operation*
commoner 124.7 *average person*, 400.10 *member of society*
Commoner 803
common feature 114.1 *similarity*
common folk 124.7 *average person*
common fraction 52.18 *division*, 169.5 *ratio*, 173.1 *fraction*
common friend 678.3 *mediator*
common fund 605.1 *store*
common good 861.13 *benefit*
common grave 399.6 *grave*
common ground 298.2 *interaction*
common hatred 785.1 *dislike*
common informer 16.8 *litigant*
common jury 16.26 *jury*
common knowledge 501.2 *information*, 532.7 *publicity*
common land 724.1 *joint possession*, 725.1 *property*
common law 1.8 *tradition*, 16.1 *the law*, 202.6 *tradition*, 654.3 *precept*
common-law marriage 823.3 *types of marriage*
common-law spouse 180.12 *partner*
common-law wife 823.11 *married woman*, 823.12 *partner*
Common Lisp 65 Programming Languages
common logarithm 52.19 *logarithm*, 169.6 *power*
commonly 124.11 *on average*, 127.20 *insignificantly*, 164.32 *universally*, 166.18 *as a rule*, 212.1 *frequently*, 298.7 *interfaci-*

ally, 482.14 *indiscriminately*, 724.6 *in common*, 787.10 *predictably*
common man 164.9 *everyman*, 400.7 *person*, 803.1 *plebeian*
Common Market 724.1 *joint possession*, 737.5 *commercial trade*, 740.4 *free market*
common money 724.1 *joint possession*
commonness 124.4 *average*, 164.5 *averageness*, 212.4 *frequency*, 549.3 *inelegance*, 556.4 *simplicity*, 559.3 *ugliness*, 754.3 *shoddiness*, 787.2 *predictability*, 795.3 *grossness*
common noun 5.35 *part of speech*
common occurrence 212.4 *frequency*
common or garden 124.1 *average*, 164.22 *commonplace*, 167.15 *everyday*, 584.10 *familiar*
common-or-garden 556.1 *simple*
common or garden variety 124.4 *average*
common ownership 724.1 *joint possession*
common people 164.11 *general public*, 400.9 *group*
common persons 400.9 *group*
commonplace 164, 5.42 *worded*, 116.15 *conventional*, 124.3 *mediocre*, 167.15 *everyday*, 505.1 *maxim*, 505.2 *proverbial*, 521.1 *lack of meaning*, 521.10 *meaningless*, 555.1 *unemphatic*, 555.2 *lack of emphasis*, 556.1 *simple*, 584.10 *familiar*, 612.4 *trivial*, 620.4 *ordinary*, 788.4 *boring*
commonplace book 545.6 *record book*
commonplaceness 788.1 *boredom*
commonplace saying 5.21 *catchword*
common practice 584.6 *procedure*
common property 724.1 *joint possession*, 725.1 *property*
common room 6.15 *schoolroom*
common run 164.6 *average*
common salt 57 Common Chemical Compounds
common sense 459, 4.3 *detachment*, 507.2 *intelligence*, 509.2 *rationality*, 655.1 *skill*
common-sensical 4.15 *rational*, 509.5 *rational*
common soldier 679.8 *soldier*, 679.17 *army person*
common speech 5.3 *spoken language*, 556.4 *simplicity*
common stock 724.1 *joint possession*
common supplies 724.1 *joint possession*
common touch 652.1 *conduct*
common type 164.9 *everyman*
common-variety 556.1 *simple*
commonweal 91.2 *union of nations*, 613.8 *benefit*
commonweal 724.1 *joint possession*
commonwealth 12.5 *political organization*, 91.2 *union of nations*, 249.4 *territorial division*, 400.11 *nation*, 688.8 *governmental organization*, 724.1 *joint possession*
Commonwealth Games 21.5 *competition*, 674.2 *contest*
Commonwealth of Nations 400.11 *nation*
commotion 153, 151.9 *disorder*, 241.3 *instance of violence*, 366.2 *tumult*, 541.1 *exaggeration*, 642.1 *activity*
communal 2, 1.14 *societal*, 2.12 *sociological*, 93.14 *urban*, 116.11 *allied*, 164.19 *prevailing*, 255.1 *inhabited*, 400.13 *national*, 664 18 *joint*, 665.8 *leagued*, 724.5 *jointly possessing*, 815.15 *sociable*
communal eating 350.4 *eating meals*

communal effort 664.4 *joint operation*
communalism 664.6 *movement*
communalist 664.18 *joint*
communalization 724.1 *joint possession*
communalize 605.6 *store*, 724.4 *have joint possession*, 734.7 *take*
communal living 724.1 *joint possession*
communally 1.18 *societally*, 2.16 *sociologically*, 10.23 *ritually*, 16.86 *jurisdictionally*, 93.16 *municipally*, 116.31 *in accord*, 664.20 *cooperatively*, 665.18 *cliquishly*, 724.6 *in common*
communard 724.3 *participant*
commune 10.18, 10.18 *perform rites*, 92.3 *other*, 255.2 *inhabitants*, 568.9 *converse*, 664.4 *joint operation*, 724.1 *joint possession*, 815.7 *human society*
commune member 724.3 *participant*
commune with God 9.7 *worship*
commune with the spirits 874.8 *get drunk*
communicable 534, 326.17 *transferable*, 626.6 *contagious*
communicable disease 624.4 *disease*
communicably 326.18 *in transit*
communicant 7.5 *Christian*, 9.5, 10.17 *worshipper*, 497.5 *believer*
communicate 528, 534, 2.15 *socialize*, 5.45 *use language*, 6.22 *educate*, 135.10 *link*, 137.13 *intercommunicate*, 520.10 *mean*, 530.6 *divulge*, 532.13 *make public*, 543.12 *signal*, 560.15 *recount*, 564.11 *speak*, 568.9 *converse*
communicated 534, 532.19 *published*
communicated insanity 510.4 *delusion*
communicate with 534.30 *communicate*
communicate with aliens 11.24 *experience psychic phenomena*
communicating 327.15 *accessible*, 534.33 *communicational*
communication 528, 2.14 *socioeconomic*, 135.1 *union*, 137.2 *association*, 326 3 *transmission*, 530.2 *divulgence* , 532.2 *mass media*, 568.1 *conversation*, 654.1 *advice*, 716.1 *negotiation*, 815.1 *sociability*
communicational 534
communication cord 137.6 *line*
communication network 137.2 *association*
communication of love 821
communications 534
Communications 534
communications channel 534.6 *telecommunication*
communications engineering 534.6 *telecommunication*
communication service 17.4 *military organization*
communications line 534.6 *telecommunication*
communications link 534.6 *telecommunication*
communications medium 534.1 *communications*
communications network 135.1 *union*, 534.6 *telecommunication*
communications satellite 53.32 *satellite*, 534.7 *satellite communication*
communications system 534.6 *telecommunication*
communications technology 534.6 *telecommunication*
communicative 2.14 *socioeconomic*, 6.16 *educational*, 137.14 *connective*, 528.16 *informative*, 530.11 *disclosing*, 565.6 *effusive*, 568.12 *conversing*, 716.8 *negotiated*, 815.15 *sociable*
communicatively 2.16 *sociologically*, 565.11 *effusively*, 568.15 *conversationally*, 716.9 *feasibly*, 815.18 *sociably*

communicativeness 565.2 *effusiveness*, 815.1 *sociability*
communicator 135.7 *joiner*, 528.9 *informant*, 530.4 *discloser*, 543.8 *signer*, 564.10 *speaker*
communion 116.1 *accord*, 568.1 *conversation*, 815.1 *sociability*
Communion 10.6 *Eucharist*
communion with God 7.2 *religiousness*, 9.1 *worship*
communiqué 528.2 *communication*, 532.1 *publication*
communism 4.7 *school of thought*, 12.1 *government*, 112.4 *monotony*, 400.11 *nation*, 627.11 *reformism*, 664.6 *movement*, 665.3 *political grouping*, 688.7 *type of rule*, 724.1 *joint possession*, 833.2 *public spiritedness*
communist 4.11 *follower of a doctrine*, 4.14 *of a philosophy*, 91.16 *national*, 627.12 *reformer*, 664.18 *joint*, 665.6 *political party member*, 724.3 *participant*
Communist 12.9 *governmental*, 450.8 *figurative usage*
communist bloc 12.5 *political organization*
communist country 91.1 *country*
communist front 665.3 *political grouping*
communistic 12.9 *governmental*, 91.16, 400.13 *national*, 665.10 *political*, 688.14 *governmental*, 724.5 *jointly possessing*, 833.6 *philanthropic*
communistically 91.19 *nationally*, 665.18 *cliquishly*, 688.24 *ministerially*, 724.6 *in common*, 833.8 *philanthropically*
communistic state 400.11 *nation*
Communists 12.6 *political party*
communist threat 635.2 *troublemaker*
community 92, 1.7 *society*, 2.4, 2.4 *social organization*, 2.5 *society*, 59.18 *ecology*, 92.1 *administrative area*, 93.1 *city*, 93.9 *town*, 93.14 *urban*, 116.2 *alliance*, 143.1 *part*, 161.17 *family*, 164.19 *prevailing*, 180.3 *companionship*, 255.2 *inhabitants*, 400.9 *group*, 664.4 *joint operation*, 664.9 *team*, 665.2 *society*, 724.1 *joint possession*, 815.7 *human society*
community at large 400.9 *group*
community centre 93.13 *municipal building*
community charge 751.7 *tax*
community chest 605.1 *store*, 833.5 *charity*
community college 6.12 *educational institution*
community council 16.2 *jurisdiction*, 653.8 *British administrative council*
community drama 51.2 *play*
community home 702.1 *prison*
community hospital 60.10 *hospital*
community medicine 60.1 *medicine*, 60.6 *health care*
community member 724.3 *participant*
community of interest 819.2 *friendly relations*
community of nations 400.9 *group*
community physician 60.11 *doctor*
community planning 63.17 *civil engineering*
community police 16.15 *British police*
community relations 2.5 *society*
community service 2.10 *social services*, 831.3 *welfare*
community service worker 710.8 *volunteer*, 833.3 *philanthropist*
community spirit 664.2 *fellowship*
community study 2.2 *sociological research*
community theatre 51.8 *theatre movements*
community-wide 2.12 *sociological*

community work 572.10 *voluntary work*
communization 724.1 *joint possession*
communize 91.17 *become a nation,* 665.15 *politicize,* 724.4 *have joint possession*
commutability 216.4 *exchange*
commutable 216.14 *exchangeable*
commutation 222.1 *substitution,* 223.1 *exchange*
commutative 223.6 *in exchange*
commutative law 52 *Theorems and Laws*
commutatively 223.8 *in exchange*
commutative operation 52.14 *operation*
commutator 64.31 *electric motor,* 235.6 *source of energy*
commute 2.15 *socialize,* 70.4 *transport,* 93.15 *urbanize,* 214.7 *be regular,* 216.8 *cause change,* 216.10 *exchange,* 221.4, 221.8 *return,* 222.5 *take a substitute,* 223.5 *exchange*
commuter 93.11 *urbanite,* 124.8 *middle classes,* 255.4 *townsman*
commuter belt 124.8 *middle classes*
commuting 70.1 *transport,* 70.5 *transportable,* 221.4 *return*
Como 94 *Lakes*
Comoros 91 Countries
comp 532.12 *publisher*
compact 41.12 *ski,* 116.3 *arrangement,* 135.8 *unite,* 138.9 *adhesive,* 152.10 *agreement,* 260.7 *little,* 262.5 *make smaller,* 362.7 *smaller,* 371.6 *dense,* 371.9 *make dense,* 552.3 *concise,* 552.4 *be concise,* 562.6 *summary,* 667.2 *contract,* 714.1 *promise,* 715.1 *contract*
compactability 262.2 *contractibility*
compactable 262.9 *contractible*
compact camera 66.16 *camera*
compact dictionary 5.28 *dictionary*
compact disc 420.9 *audio device*
compact disk 364.6 *rotator*
compacted 262.7 *smaller,* 562.7 *shortened*
compactedness 262.1 *contraction*
compacter 262.4 *contractor*
compaction 135.1 *union,* 138.1 *adhesion,* 262.1 *contraction*
compactly 138.11 *cohesively,* 371.10 *densely,* 552.5 *concisely*
compactness 135.1 *union,* 260.1 *littleness,* 371.1 *density,* 552.1 *conciseness,* 562.4 *summariness*
compactor 63.29 *construction equipment,* 621.10 *cleaning object*
compact ski 41.5 *ski equipment*
companion 180, 114.5 *counterpart,* 122.5 *equal,* 359.7 *means of ascent,* 632.3 *protector,* 697.4 *personal attendant,* 784.4 *likable person,* 819.5 *friend*
companionability 815.1 *sociability*
companionable 255.8 *attendant,* 815.15 *sociable,* 819.8 *friendly*
companionably 815.18 *sociably*
companionate marriage 823.3 *types of marriage*
companion ladder 74 Parts of a Ship, 359.9 *ladder*
companionless 174.16 *alone*
companionship 180, 253.2 *omnipresence,* 724.2 *participation,* 819.1 *friendship*
companionway 74 Parts of a Ship, 36.3 *parts of a sailing boat,* 359.7 *means of ascent*
company 737, 13.7 *corporation,* 17.4 *military organization,* 51.23 *cast,* 140.3 *assembly,* 146.3 *person included,* 161.11 *group,* 161.12 *team,* 180.3 *companionship,* 253.2 *omnipresence,* 646.4 *personnel,* 647.1 *workshop,* 665.1 *party,* 679.16 *army unit,* 815.8 *good company*
company canteen 350.15 *eating place*

company commander 17.5 *military staff*
company director 653.15 *manager*
company grade officer 17.5 *military staff*
company headquarters 647.1 *workshop*
company leader 696
company man 167.6 *conformist*
company official 696.5 *company leader*
company pension 662.4 *social assistance*
company policy 592.2 *policy*
company promoter 739.12 *wholesaler*
company report 545.1 *record*
company spokesman 524.7 *news interpreter*
company tax 751.7 *tax*
company-wide bargaining 15.1 *industrial relations*
comparability 107.2 *interrelatedness,* 109.3 *correlation,* 114.1 *similarity*
comparable 107.5 *interrelated,* 109.6 *correlative,* 114.7 *similar,* 121.7 *gradational*
comparably 114, 107.10 *relevantly,* 109.11 *correlatively,* 121.9 *differentially*
comparative 5.38 *linguistic,* 5.44 *grammatical,* 121.7 *gradational*
comparative anatomist 76.11 *zoologist*
comparative anatomy 59.4 *anatomy,* 76.9 *animal science*
comparative grammar 5.1 *linguistics,* 5.30 *syntax*
comparative historical linguistics 5.1 *linguistics*
comparative linguistics 5.1 *linguistics*
comparatively 2.16 *sociologically,* 5.48 *linguistically,* 5.52 *grammatically,* 107.10 *relevantly,* 121.9 *differentially*
comparative macrosociology 2.1 *sociology*
comparative psychology 61.1 *psychology*
comparative sociology 2.1 *sociology*
compare 107.8 *be proportionate to,* 109.9 *correlate,* 114.10 *be similar,* 114.11 *make similar,* 121.5 *measure,* 663.18 *counteract*
compare and contrast 481.12 *discriminate*
compare notes 654.6 *consult*
compare with 114.11 *make similar*
comparison 107.1 *relatedness,* 109.3 *correlation,* 121.3 *gradation,* 295.13 *dress up,* 526.10 *manifestation*
compartment 258, 136.2 *setting apart,* 143.1 *part,* 152.6 *category,* 163.2 *class*
compartmental 143.11 *partial*
compartmentalization 141.2 *deconstruction,* 152.5 *categorization*
compartmentalize 136.11 *divide,* 141.4 *deconstruct,* 143.10 *part,* 152.15 *categorize*
compartmentalized 143.11 *partial,* 152.24 *categorized*
compartmentation 141.2 *deconstruction*
compass 34.4 *climbing equipment,* 52.49 *geometric construction,* 56.84 *altimeter,* 74.5 *navigation,* 121.1 *degree,* 170.5 *computer,* 235.2 *ability,* 248.7 *range,* 332.3 *orientation,* 363.7 *ring,* 543.5 *indicator,* 653.5 *guide,* 682.6 *be successful,* 684.4 *complete*
compass bearing 332.2 *bearing*
compass card 74.5 *navigation,* 332.3 *orientation*
compass direction 250.2 *exact location,* 332.2 *bearing*
compassed 684.7 *completed*

compasses 52.49 *geometric construction*
Compasses 53 The Constellations
compassion 469.2 *consideration,* 691.1 *leniency,* 760.5 *sensitivity,* 831.1 *benevolence,* 833.1 *philanthropy,* 835.1 *pity,* 835.3 *mercy,* 839.2 *forgivingness,* 859.2 *unselfishness*
compassionate 374.6 *softhearted,* 691.4 *lenient,* 760.1 *sensitive,* 831.6 *benevolent,* 833.6 *philanthropic,* 835.6 *pitying,* 839.5 *merciful,* 859.5 *unselfish*
compassionate leave 254.5 *leave of absence,* 848.4 *licence*
compassionately 374.18 *softheartedly,* 691.6 *leniently,* 831.10 *benevolently,* 833.8 *philanthropically,* 835.13 *pitifully,* 839.14 *forgivingly,* 859.9 *unselfishly*
compassionateness 835.1 *pity*
compass needle 543.5 *indicator*
compass point 332
compass reading 74.5 *navigation*
compass rose 332.3 *orientation*
compatibilist 4.11 *follower of a doctrine,* 4.14 *of a philosophy*
compatibility 667, 52.64 *reasoning,* 65.17 *computing term,* 116.1 *accord,* 167.1 *conformity,* 298.2 *interaction,* 763.8 *amiability,* 815.1 *sociability,* 819.2 *friendly relations,* 821.1 *love*
compatible 667, 52.86 *logical,* 116.10 *in accord,* 167.12 *conforming,* 298.6 *interactional,* 763.2 *likable,* 819.8 *friendly,* 821.22 *lovable*
compatibly 667, 116.31 *in accord,* 167.17 *conformingly,* 298.7 *interfacially,* 819.17 *in friendship*
compatriot 255.8 *national*
compeer 122.5 *equal,* 198.5 *contemporary*
compeers 161.18 *generation*
compel 571, 695, 226.10 *awaken,* 228.10 *manipulate,* 233.10 *be a prevailing influence,* 235.10 *be powerful,* 330.1 *impel,* 586.15 *persuade,* 593.10 *necessitate,* 692.11 *have authority over*
compelling 695, 226.13 *causal,* 226.14 *causally,* 228.11 *motivational,* 233.12 *appealing,* 235.13 *powerful,* 237.10 *potent,* 554.3 *emphatic,* 586.19 *persuasive,* 692.14 *commanding*
compellingly 695, 228.14 *influentially,* 235.18 *powerfully,* 237.15 *acutely,* 692.16 *commandingly*
compel respect 849.21 *command respect*
compendious 270.7 *short,* 552.3 *concise,* 562.6 *summary*
compendiously 552.5 *concisely*
compendiousness 270.1 *shortness,* 552.1 *conciseness,* 562.4 *summariness*
compendium 562, 140.3 *assembly,* 152.7 *catalogue,* 161.30 *compilation,* 171.5 *list of appointments,* 262.3 *contracted thing,* 270.3 *shortened version,* 552.2 *outline*
compensable 125
compensate 125, 735, 109.7 *reciprocate,* 122.11 *equalize,* 125.5 *counterbalance,* 221.7 *restore,* 223.5 *exchange,* 721.14 *profit,* 746.10 *pay back,* 765.11 *recompense,* 840.5 *atone,* 878.11 *pay*
compensated 125, 222.8 *substituted,* 223.7 *exchanged,* 730.11 *receiving*
compensate for 222.6 *give a substitute,* 231.3 *counteract,* 843.15 *put right*
compensating 125.9 *compensatory,* 125.10 *counterbalancing*

compensation 125, 735, 878, 41.12 *ski,* 61.19 *defence mechanism,* 109.1 *interchange,* 122.3 *equalization,* 125.2 *counterbalance,* 144.2 *fullness,* 221.2 *restoration,* 222.1 *substitution,* 223.1 *exchange,* 231.1 *counteraction,* 677.2 *peace offering,* 721.5 *profit,* 730.2 *something received,* 746.2 *repayment,* 765.2 *reparation,* 840.1 *atonement,* 845.2 *due,* 878.4 *reward for service,* 879.8 *penalty*
Compensation 125
compensational 125.9 *compensatory,* 840.4 *atoning*
compensation neurosis 61.10 *neurosis*
compensation technique 41.4 *skiing technique*
compensative 125.9 *compensatory,* 730.14 *receivable*
compensator 125, 735.3 *returner*
compensatory 125, 878, 109.4 *reciprocal,* 221.10 *regressive,* 223.6 *in exchange,* 231.4 *counteracting,* 721.15 *gainful,* 730.14 *receivable,* 735.6 *restoring,* 746.20 *paying in return,* 840.4 *atoning*
compensatory payment 879.8 *penalty*
compere 534.29 *broadcaster,* 653.2 *direct,* 653.14 *leader*
compete 18.6 *participate,* 42.10 *play,* 674.11 *contend*
compete in athletics 25
compete in gymnastics 30
competence 16.2 *jurisdiction,* 235.2 *ability,* 485.1 *qualification,* 608.7 *sufficiency,* 613.7 *instrumentality,* 655.1 *skill,* 660.1 *easiness,* 861.12 *proficiency*
competent 16.50 *law-abiding,* 122.9 *adequate,* 235.13 *powerful,* 485.9 *qualified,* 501.8 *knowledgeable,* 608.1 *sufficient,* 613.3 *instrumental,* 655.6 *skilful,* 655.8 *expert,* 696.13 *excellent,* 861.5 *proficient*
competently 235.18 *powerfully,* 485.17 *capably,* 655.12 *skilfully,* 696.16 *masterfully,* 861.25 *skillfully*
compete with 663.16 *confront*
competing 663.20 *discordant,* 674.14 *contending,* 841.4 *jealous*
competition 21, 13.6 *economic factors,* 42.2 *contest,* 59.18 *ecology,* 663.3 *conflict,* 674.1 *contention,* 674.2 *contest,* 841.1 *jealousy*
competition aikido 26.10 *aikido*
competition judo 26.7 *judo*
competitive 674, 18.5 *sporting,* 26.15 *wrestling,* 30.11 *gymnastic,* 39.11 *swimming,* 42.9 *recreational,* 655.6 *skilful,* 663.20 *discordant,* 841.4 *jealous*
competitive canoeing 36.6 *canoeing*
competitive casting 20.1 *angling*
competitive diving 39.6 *diving*
competitive diving marks 39.6 *diving*
competitive fishing 20.1 *angling*
competitive gymnast 30.9 *gymnasts*
competitive gymnastics 30.1 *gymnastics*
competitive ice-dancing 41.7 *ice-dancing*
competitive ice-skating 41.6 *ice-skating*
competitive lugeing 41.9 *bobsledding*
competitively 30, 20.9 *on the water,* 26.16 *professionally,* 39.12 *by swimming,* 663.23 *opposingly,* 841.9 *jealously*
competitiveness 674.1 *contention,* 841.1 *jealousy*
competitive price 754.1 *cheapness*
competitive punting 36.8 *punting*
competitive rowing 36.4 *rowing*
competitive sailing 36.1 *sailing*

competitive scoring 41.7 *ice-dancing*
competitive skiing 41.1 *skiing*
competitive spirit 841.1 *jealousy*
competitive swimmer 39.4 *swimmer*
competitive swimming 39.1 *swimming*
competitive tae kwon do 26.9 *tae kwon do*
competitor 663, 21.3 *athlete*, 26.9 *tae kwon do*, 122.5 *equal*, 346.7 *entrant*, 674.10 *contender*, 820.5 *hostile person*, 841.3 *rival*
compilation 161, 562.3 *compendium*
compile 562, 65.19 *abort*, 148.13 *make*, 161.44 *put together*
compiled language 65.9 *programming language*
compiler 65.8 *software*
complacency 466.2 *lack of interest*, 765.1 *satisfaction*, 809.2 *self-satisfaction*
complacent 466.4 *uninterested*, 765.4 *satisfied*, 809.9 *self-satisfied*
complacently 466.8 *disinterestedly*, 809.20 *smugly*
complain 713, 15.12 *have an industrial dispute*, 500.9 *refuse*, 663.15 *object*, 713.6 *protest*, 766.7 *be dissatisfied*, 774.6 *lament*, 830.11 *be irritable*, 852.16 *disagree*, 856.5 *accuse*
complain about 475.19 *protest*
complainant 856.3 *accuser*
complainer 713.4 *protester*, 766.3 *dissatisfied person*, 770.4 *depressing person*
complaining 766.4 *dissatisfied*
complain of 624.24 *be unhealthy*
complaint 15.4 *industrial dispute*, 48.7 *poem*, 500.2 *disapproval*, 624.2 *illness*, 663.2 *objection*, 713.1 *protest*, 766.2 *expression of dissatisfaction*, 774.2 *lament*, 844.7 *sense of wrong*, 852.4 *disagreement*, 852.7 *blame*, 856.1 *accusation*
complaisance 694.1 *obedience*, 817.4 *deference*
complaisant 167.13 *compliant*, 374.6 *softhearted*, 694.7 *obedient*, 817.9 *deferential*
complaisantly 167.16 *obligingly*, 374.18 *softheartedly*, 694.10 *obediently*, 817.16 *deferentially*
compleat 144.7 *complete*
compleat angler 20.6 *angler*, 590.6 *hunter*
complement 5.35 *part of speech*, 52.21 *set*, 59.14 *chromosome*, 109.2 *interconnection*, 109.8 *interrelate*, 116.5 *conformity*, 116.25 *conform*, 130.1 *addition*, 144.2 *fullness*, 144.4 *complete*, 146.1 *inclusion*, 146.3 *person included*, 161.12 *team*, 180.13 *accompany*, 646.4 *personnel*
complemental 109.5 *interconnected*
complementally 109.10 *reciprocally*
complementarity 107.2 *interrelatedness*
complementary 5.44 *grammatical*, 107.5 *interrelated*, 109.5 *interconnected*, 116.14 *conforming*, 130.8 *additional*, 144.7 *complete*, 180.17 *accompanying*, 223.6 *in exchange*
complementary angle 52.39 *angle*
complementary colour 444.1 *colour*
complementary colours 56.28 *colour*
complementary medicine 60.2 *natural medicine*, 630.11 *medical art*
complete 142, 144, 144, 684, 52.86 *logical*, 130.6 *add*, 142.6 *whole*, 157.15 *end*, 157.21 *ended*, 174.13 *whole*, 218.10

finished, 227.5 *show an effect*, 323.9 *close down*, 575.9 *endure*, 608.1 *sufficient*, 619.1, 619.5 *perfect*, 640.4 *act*, 684.7 *completed*, 718.13 *secure one's objective*
complete a circuit 315.12 *move round*
complete a purchase 738.1 *purchase*
complete blank 502.3 *unknown thing*
complete cycle 684.1 *completion*
completed 684, 200.18 *over*, 323.14 *closed down*, 594.20 *developed*, 619.1 *perfect*, 718.8 *accomplished*
complete failure 683.1 *failure*
complete idiot 460.3 *unintelligent person*
complete list 142.5 *unit*
completely 144, 619, 684, 142.11, 174.23 *wholly*, 323.17 *finally*, 621.20 *clean*
completely past 200.18 *over*
completeness 144, 52.64 *reasoning*, 142.1 *whole*, 619.3 *perfection*, 684.1 *completion*
Completeness 144
complete pass 19.9 *play*
complete set 142.5 *unit*, 146.1 *inclusion*, 605.5 *collection*
complete works 142.2 *whole thing*
completing 144.3 *completion*, 157.20 *ending*, 684.7 *completed*
completion 144, 684, 155.9 *conclusion*, 157.1 *end*, 227.1 *effect*, 323.1 *closure*, 608.7 *sufficiency*, 619.3 *perfection*, 627.5 *improvement*, 640.1 *action*, 715.1 *contract*
Completion 684
completive 157.20 *ending*, 684.7 *completed*
complex 52, 61, 57.7 *chemical compound*, 57.35 *combined*, 133.12 *mixed*, 142.2 *whole thing*, 314.5 *ambiguous*, 382.6 *construction*, 510.4 *delusion*, 523.4 *difficult*, 529.11 *mysterious*, 551.2 *obscure*, 584.1 *habit*, 659.12 *problematic*
complex analysis 52.30 *calculus*
complex conjugate 52.6 *complex number*
complex fraction 52.18 *division*
complexion 444, 103.4 *nature*, 105.1 *state*, 163.4 *type*, 457.3 *external appearance*
complexity 133.1 *mixture*, 133.3 *miscellany*, 529.3 *mystification*, 551.1 *obscurity*, 659.1 *difficulty*
complex lipid 58.6 *lipid*
complexly 133.14 *in the midst*, 314.8 *circularly*
complex number 52, 169.2 *kind of number*
complex sugar 58.3 *carbohydrate*
compliance 167, 116.1 *accord*, 228.6 *suggestibility*, 374.12 *gentleness*, 377.2 *adaptability*, 499.1 *assent*, 572.8 *acquiescence*, 667.1 *agreement*, 673.1 *submission*, 694.1 *obedience*, 719.1 *observance*, 808.1 *servility*, 817.4 *deference*, 847.3 *allegiance*, 861.11 *good behaviour*
compliant 167, 116.10 *in accord*, 228.13 *suggestible*, 377.7 *adaptive*, 499.6 *assenting*, 572.3 *amenable*, 660.13 *easygoing*, 667.10 *agreeing*, 694.7 *obedient*, 719.7 *observant*, 808.6 *servile*, 817.9 *deferential*, 847.9 *loyal*, 849.9 *showing respect*, 861.4 *well-behaved*
compliantly 167.16 *adaptably*, 228.14 *influentially*, 374.18 *softheartedly*, 377.12 *adaptably*, 499.8 *unanimously*, 667.14 *agreeably*, 694.10 *obediently*, 719.8 *observantly*, 817.16 *deferentially*, 861.24 *obediently*
complicate 314.7 *be ambiguous*, 523.8 *make unintelligible*, 551.3 *make obscure*

complicated 133.12 *mixed*, 314.5 *ambiguous*, 523.4 *difficult*, 659.12 *problematic*
complicatedly 133.14 *in the midst*
complicate matters 659.23 *cause difficulties*
complication 48.3 *aspect of fiction*, 133.1 *mixture*, 624.2 *illness*, 659.1 *difficulty*, 659.8 *snag*
complicity 664.8 *conferring*, 724.2 *participation*, 866.1 *guilt*
compliment 851, 851, 763.10 *pleasant thing*, 817.3 *courtesies*, 817.10 *be courteous*, 851.14 *praise*, 853.8 *flatter*
complimentary 5.43 *phrasal*, 729.7 *given*, 754.11 *free of charge*, 812.13 *congratulatory*, 851.18 *approving*, 853.12 *flattering*
complimentary gift 754.6 *absence of charge*
complimentary pass 754.6 *absence of charge*
complimentary phrase 5.24 *phrasing*
complimentary remark 851.4 *compliment*
complimentary ticket 754.6 *absence of charge*
compliments 5.24 *phrasing*, 817.3 *courtesies*, 826.1 *endearment*, 849.7 *respects*, 851.3 *praise*, 853.1 *flattery*
compline 10.4 *public worship*
comply 167, 116.21 *be in accord*, 306.8 *be formal*, 374.16 *yield*, 377.10 *be adaptable*, 499.5 *assent to*, 572.13 *be willing*, 673.3 *submit*, 694.5 *obey*, 808.11 *pander to*, 808.13 *conform*, 817.13 *defer to*, 861.18 *be good*
complying 116.10 *in accord*, 374.7 *impressionable*, 374.12 *gentleness*, 377.7 *adaptive*, 694.7 *obedient*
comply with 167.8 *comply*, 667.6 *agree with*, 694.5 *obey*, 719.4 *observe*
compo 604.2 *building material*
component 143, 148, 148, 52.50 *scalar quantity*, 64.16 *circuit element*, 103.7 *integral*, 130.3 *additional item*, 146.2 *thing included*, 146.8 *included*, 257.10 *containing*, 367.4 *matter*, 603.4 *machine*
Component 148
component part 146.2 *thing included*
components 148, 257.1 *contents*, 604.1 *materials*
componium 49 Musical Instruments
comportment 652.1 *conduct*
comport oneself 652.11 *conduct oneself*
comport oneself well 652.12 *behave well*
compose 49, 148, 48.21, 48.21 *write*, 50.23 *design*, 99.20 *bring into being*, 140.5 *combine*, 144.4 *complete*, 146.4 *include*, 148.13 *make*, 150.18 *order*, 152.12 *arrange*, 152.16 *adapt*, 161.44 *put together*, 243.10 *produce*, 257.8 *embody*, 382.15 *shape*, 519.14 *imagine*, 677.4 *pacify*, 727.8 *sink*
compose an epic 48.21 *write*
composed 49, 4.18 *detached*, 140.7 *combined*, 150.10 *ordered*, 242.6 *moderate*, 257.10 *containing*, 303.8 *assured*, 306.9 *formed*, 325.6 *quiescent*, 787.3 *unmoved*, 869.10 *calm*
compose differences 677.5 *make peace*
composedly 4.27 *stoically*
composed of 146.7 *including*
compose oneself 594.8 *prepare oneself*, 787.5 *not wonder about*
compose one's features 772.8 *be serious*
composer 49.24 *musician*, 119.3 *originator*, 243.9 *producer*

composer and lyricist 135.7 *joiner*
composing 148, 49.2 *music making*, 146.1 *inclusion*
composite 28.6 *fencing*, 52.74 *divisible*, 63.25 *construction material*, 83.16 *taxonomic*, 133.12 *mixed*, 135.12 *united*, 140.4 *compound*, 175.7 *various*
Composite 43.16 *columned*
composite attack 28.3 *fencing movements*
composite fruit 86.2 *botanical fruit*
composite function 52.29 *mathematical function*
compositeness 175.2 *multiplicity*
composite number 52.5 *number*
Composite order 43.8 *column*
composite parry 28.3 *fencing movements*
composite volcano 54.24 *volcanic activity*
composition 49, 66, 49.2 *music making*, 50.2 *painting*, 50.4 *treatment*, 50.6 *work of art*, 52.29 *mathematical function*, 103.4 *nature*, 133.1 *mixture*, 133.2 *mixed thing*, 135.3 *unification*, 140.1 *combination*, 146.1 *inclusion*, 150.1 *order*, 152.1 *arrangement*, 152.2 *array*, 161.30 *compilation*, 243.1 *production*, 243.5 *work of art*, 257.1 *contents*, 306.1 *form*, 306.4 *forming*, 382.3 *form*, 382.9 *artistic structure*, 561.1 *dissertation*, 604.2 *building material*, 746.2 *repayment*
composition of differences 677.1 *pacification*
compositor 532.12 *publisher*
compost 68.13, 69.7 *fertilizer*, 69.15 *cultivate*, 141.1 *disintegration*, 246.3 *fertilizer*, 246.7 *make fertile*, 614.6 *refuse*
compostable 141.5 *disintegrated*
composted 141.5 *disintegrated*
compost heap 69.4 *nursery*, 614.6 *refuse*, 727.5 *wasteyard*, 727.8 *sink*
composting 69.5 *gardening*
composure 4.3 *detachment*, 242.1 *moderation*, 303.4 *assurance*, 306.1 *form*, 325.2 *repose*, 787.1 *lack of wonder*, 869.3 *calmness*
compotation 874.13 *drink*
compote 45.35 *dessert*
compound 140, 52.74 *divisible*, 57.7 *chemical compound*, 83.18 *of leaves*, 133.2 *mixed thing*, 133.8 *mix*, 140.5 *combine*, 148.13 *make*, 243.3 *product*, 301.2 *enclosed place*, 702.1 *prison*
compound epithet 48.12 *poetic language*
compound fertilizer 68.13 *fertilizer*
compound fraction 52.18 *division*, 169.5 *ratio*, 173.1 *fraction*
compound interest 128.3 *increasing thing*, 721.5 *profit*, 745.4 *interest*
compound lens 56.30 *lens system*
compound microscope 56.85 *microscope*
compound unit 75.2 *unit system*
comprecation 10.9 *prayer*
comprehend 4.21 *rationalize*, 146.4 *include*, 501.11 *know*, 522.6 *understand*, 696.15 *learn*
comprehensibility 522.9 *intelligibility*, 550.1 *clarity*, 660.2 *simplicity*
comprehensible 134.16 *simple*, 520.6 *meaningful*, 522.1 *intelligible*, 550.3 *clear*, 660.11 *made easy*
comprehensibly 522.13 *intelligibly*, 550.4 *clearly*
comprehension 520, 146.1, 293.19 *inclusion*, 459.13 *enlightenment*, 459.3 *intelligence*, 471.1 *idea*, 501.1 *knowledge*, 507.1 *wisdom*, 522.12 *understanding*

comprehensive 142.6 *whole,* 144.7 *complete,* 146.7 *including,* 164.15 *general,* 259.15 *big,* 293.39 *inclusive,* 482.4 *wholesale,* 660.11 *made easy,* 684.7 *completed*

comprehensive insurance policy 293.19 *inclusion*

comprehensively 142.12 *one and all,* 146.9 *inclusively,* 277.17 *profoundly,* 293.42 *inclusively,* 684.9 *completely*

comprehensiveness 142.1 *whole,* 144.1 *completeness,* 146.1 *inclusion,* 164.1 *generality,* 259.2 *bigness*

comprehensive school 6.12 *educational institution*

comprehensive test ban 677.1 *pacification*

compress 129.5 *make smaller,* 135.8 *unite,* 262.5 *make smaller,* 270.10 *shorten,* 272.10 *narrow,* 273.7 *thicken,* 371.9 *make dense,* 552.4 *be concise,* 630.10 *surgical dressing,* 726.6 *retain*

compressed 262.7 *smaller,* 270.8 *shortened,* 272.1 *narrow,* 552.3 *concise*

compressibility 374, 56.39 *expansion,* 262.2 *contractibility,* 372.3 *sparseness*

compressible 374, 262.9 *contractible,* 372.1 *sparse*

compression 41.1 *skiing,* 41.12 *ski,* 56.39 *expansion,* 63.14 *load,* 63.16 *deformation,* 129.1 *decrease,* 235.4 *energy,* 262.1 *contraction,* 270.2 *shortening,* 552.1 *conciseness,* 562.2 *outline,* 726.1 *retention*

compression turn 41.4 *skiing technique*

compression wood 85.3 *timber*

compressive 262.8 *contracting*

compressive strengh 237.1 *strength*

compressor 262.4 *contractor,* 371.5 *condenser*

comprisal 146.1 *inclusion*

comprise 103.12 *embody,* 135.8 *unite,* 142.9 *be whole,* 146.4 *include,* 148.10 *compose,* 148.11 *consist of,* 293.32 *include*

comprising 146.1 *inclusion,* 146.7 *including,* 148.9 *composing*

compromise 576, 717, 717, 109.1 *interchange,* 109.7 *reciprocate,* 116.1 *accord,* 116.23 *arrange,* 152.17 *come to an arrangement,* 158.6 *middle ground,* 158.17 *average,* 158.19 *mediate,* 222.1 *substitution,* 222.5 *take a substitute,* 232.2 *instrument,* 232.4 *be an instrument,* 242.1 *moderation,* 242.3 *be moderate,* 333.2 *middle of the road,* 333.7 *be halfway,* 633.10 *endanger,* 664.3 *mutual relationship,* 664.12 *reciprocate,* 677.1 *pacification,* 677.5 *make peace,* 708.3 *permit,* 716.1 *negotiation,* 854.12 *defame*

Compromise 717

compromiser 576.15 *indecisive person*

compromising 717, 109.4 *reciprocal,* 116.10 *in accord,* 716.1 *negotiation,* 716.8 *negotiated*

compromisingly 717, 109.10 *reciprocally,* 716.9 *feasibly*

Comptometer 170.5 *computer*

Compton 18 Sporting Personalities, **52** Scientists

Compton-Burnett 48 Writers

Compton effect 56 Named Laws

compulsion 61, 695, 226.1 *cause,* 228.1 *motive,* 237.2 *healthiness,* 330.11 *impulsion,* 510.4 *delusion,* 571.3 *lack of choice,* 571.8 *involuntariness,* 574.14 *tenacity,* 584.1 *habit,* 644.1 *work*

Compulsion 695

compulsion complex 61.18 *complex*

compulsion neurosis 61.10 *neurosis*

compulsive 235.13 *powerful,* 695.9 *compelling*

compulsive cease-fire 677.1 *pacification*

compulsive eater 695.5 *compulsive person*

compulsive eating 350.2 *appetite*

compulsive gambler 695.5 *compulsive person*

compulsive liar 695.5 *compulsive person*

compulsively 235.18 *powerfully,* 237.15 *acutely,* 695.11 *compellingly*

compulsiveness 695.1 *compulsion*

compulsive person 695

compulsive shopper 695.5 *compulsive person*

compulsive talker 695.5 *compulsive person*

compulsory 695, 41.13 *ice-skating,* 103.5 *essential,* 166.9 *legal,* 571.10 *obligatory,* 571.13 *involuntary,* 593.4 *required,* 692.14 *commanding,* 701.9 *subject,* 847.12 *obligatory*

compulsory arbitration 15.4 *industrial dispute*

compulsory dancing 41.7 *ice-dancing*

compulsory figure 41.6 *ice-skating*

compulsory marriage 823.3 *types of marriage*

compulsory payment 879.8 *penalty*

compulsory service 17.1 *military affairs*

compulsory servitude 701.1 *subjection*

compunction 835.2 *condolence,* 867.1 *penitence*

compunctious 867.6 *penitent*

compunctiously 867.8 *penitently*

compurgation 16.42 *acquittal,* 855.1 *vindication*

computable 52.73 *numerable,* 170.14 *calculable,* 268.14 *measurable*

computably 170.16 *mathematically*

computation 4.4 *philosophical investigation,* 52.1 *mathematics,* 52.12 *numeration,* 130.2 *mathematical addition,* 170.1 *calculation,* 170.4 *computing,* 268.1 *measurement,* 750.3 *accounting*

computational 170.13 *calculative*

computational linguistics 5.1 *linguistics*

computative 170.13 *calculative*

compute 4.21 *rationalize,* 52.90 *enumerate,* 130.6 *add,* 170.8 *calculate,* 235.12 *generate power,* 268.10 *measure*

computed value 56.83 *sensitivity*

computer 65, 170, 52.67, 170.6 *calculator,* 603.4 *machine*

computer crime 736.7 *dishonesty*

computer criminal 736.11 *dishonest person*

computer dating 823.13 *matchmaker*

computer electronics 64.1 *electronics*

computer engineer 646.2 *artisan*

computer error 504

computer fault 683.4 *unsuccessful thing*

computer file 152.7 *catalogue*

computer game 65, 42.1 *game*

computerization 15.2 *industrial negotiations,* 112.2 *conformity,* 232.1 *instrumentality,* 235.9 *electronics,* 243.2 *manufacture,* 603.5 *mechanics*

computerize 15.11 *conduct industrial relations,* 112.10 *conform,* 243.10 *produce*

computerized 15.9 *negotiated,* 112.6 *conforming,* 232.8 *practical,* 243.11 *productive,* 603.8 *mechanical*

computerized information 528.6 *information technology*

computer language 5.8 *artificial language*

computer listing 152.7 *catalogue,* 171.2 *table*

computer-literate 603.8 *mechanical*

computer malfunction 661.2 *obstacle*

computer memory 511.6 *artificial memory*

computer network 135.1 *union*

computer networking 534.6 *telecommunication*

computer operator 170.6 *calculator,* 230.5 *operator,* 545.9 *recorder*

computer paper 604.3 *paper*

computer part 65

computer printer 114.3 *copier,* 118.6 *photocopier*

computer programmer 170.6 *calculator*

Computers 65

computer science 65.1 *computing*

computerspeak 564.1 *faculty of speech*

computer tape 545.6 *record book*

computer technology 170.4 *computing*

computer war 676.1 *war*

computing 65, 170, 170.13 *calculative,* 235.9 *electronics,* 750.10 *accounting*

computing term 65

comrade 12.6 *political party,* 122.5 *equal,* 180.11 *companion,* 400.10 *member of society,* 401.3 *male title of address,* 665.5 *member,* 665.6 *political party member,* 819.5 *friend*

comradely 664.19 *associating,* 819.8 *friendly*

comradeship 664.2 *fellowship,* 815.8 *good company,* 819.1 *friendship*

Comsat 534.7 *satellite communication*

Comtois 32 Breeds of Horse and Pony

con 6.23 *learn,* 13.12 *cheat,* 51.35 *rehearse,* 474.12 *deceive,* 501.13 *get to know,* 515.8 *be dishonest,* 538.10 *dishonesty,* 539.8 *trick,* 539.10 *fraud,* 539.28 *trick,* 539.30 *be fraudulent,* 540.8 *fraud,* 540.21 *be fraudulent,* 657.2 *stratagem,* 657.5 *be cunning,* 663.21 *contrary,* 699.7 *charge,* 702.5 *prisoner,* 753.10 *overcharge,* 801.3 *disreputable action*

con artist 539.17 *cheat*

conation 570.1 *will*

conative 570.6 *willed*

con brio 49 Musical Terms, 239.6 *with vigour*

concatenate 159, 135.10 *link*

concatenation 135.1 *union,* 159.2 *consecution*

concave 317, 52.81 *curvilinear,* 311.4 *curved*

concave land 317

concave lens 56.29 *optical element*

concavely 317, 311.7 *curvedly*

concave mirror 56.29 *optical element*

concave surface 52.38 *surface*

concavity 317, 52.38 *surface,* 311.1 *curvature,* 362.14 *depression*

Concavity 317

conceal 531, 115.6 *differentiate,* 257.6 *contain,* 290.15 *keep inside,* 293.31 *hide,* 438.8 *make invisible,* 458.3 *cause to disappear,* 527.13 *hide,* 529.12 *keep secret,* 538.24 *pretend,* 539.32 *disguise,* 540.18 *be hypocritical,* 546.1 *obliterate,* 605.6 *store,* 632.9 *protect,* 671.19 *buffer,* 816.13 *ignore*

concealed 527, 531, 293.37 *protected,* 438.3 *private,* 458.7 *disappeared,* 529.11 *mysterious,* 539.41 *disguised,* 546.6 *obliterated,* 816.10 *lonely*

concealed crevasse 34.2 *climbing dangers*

concealer 531

concealment 527, 531, 115.3 *disguise,* 293.15 *shelter,* 438.4 *invisibility,* 458.5 *disguise,* 538.8 *pretence,* 539.12 *disguise,* 540.3 *hypocrisy,* 546.3 *obliteration,* 578.5 *equivocalness,* 657.1 *cunning,* 816.3 *separation*

Concealment 531

conceal oneself 531

concede 116.21 *be in accord,* 228.8 *be motivated,* 499.4 *assent,* 530.8 *admit,* 586.18 *be persuaded,* 667.6 *agree with,* 673.3 *submit,* 691.3 *be lenient,* 717.4 *compromise*

concede a hole 29.7 *golf*

concede defeat 683.7 *be defeated*

conceded hole 29.2 *golfing terms*

concede the victory to 127.9 *yield to*

conceding 116.10 *in accord,* 717.6 *compromising*

conceit 805, 48.12 *poetic language,* 494.1 *overestimation,* 508.1 *folly,* 518.1 *supposition,* 519.4 *ideality,* 809.1 *vanity,* 809.6 *boastfulness,* 860.2 *egoism*

conceited 805, 797.3 *affected,* 805.17 *conceited,* 809.8 *vain,* 860.5 *egoistic*

conceitedly 809.19 *vainly,* 809.23 *boastfully,* 860.9 *egoistically*

conceitedness 809.1 *vanity*

conceivability 486.2 *possibleness*

conceivable 486.5 *possible,* 519.13 *imaginable*

conceivableness 486.2 *possibleness*

conceivably 486.11 *potentially*

conceive 119.7 *originate,* 156.22 *invent,* 243.10 *produce,* 245.10 *reproduce oneself,* 246.6 *be fertile,* 396.19 *give birth to,* 471.15 *imagine,* 501.11 *know,* 518.5 *suppose,* 519.14 *imagine,* 522.7 *recognize*

conceive a plan 592.9 *plan*

conceived 471.11 *ideational*

conceive of 461.16 *have an idea*

concentralization 342.11 *focus*

concentralize 342.11 *focus*

concentrate 461, 57.25 *solidify,* 57.30 *extract,* 103.3 *quintessence,* 128.5 *make bigger,* 135.8 *unite,* 262.5 *make smaller,* 262.6 *become smaller,* 291.9 *centre,* 342.10 *come together,* 342.11 *focus,* 355.8 *extract,* 355.17 *obtain an extract,* 371.9 *make dense,* 420.15 *hear,* 642.15 *try*

concentrated 4.17 *thoughtful,* 57.32 *solid,* 138.9 *adhesive,* 237.12 *strong to the senses,* 262.7 *smaller,* 291.7 *centralized,* 371.7 *condensed,* 574.1 *resolute*

concentrated attack 670.12 *military attack*

concentratedness 135.1 *union*

concentrated solution 57.3 *phase*

concentrate on 291.9 *centre,* 472.10 *focus on*

concentrate sprayer 389.12 *sprinkler*

concentrating 461, 4.17 *thoughtful*

concentration 371, 574, 4.4 *philosophical investigation,* 115.1 *increase,* 135.1 *union,* 138.1 *adhesion,* 165.8 *specialization,* 237.3 *intensity,* 262.1 *contraction,* 291.3 *centrality,* 342.1 *convergence,* 355.7 *obtaining an extract,* 461.3 *thoughtfulness,* 467.3 *carefulness,* 575.2 *commitment,* 642.8 *assiduity*

concentration camp 702.1 *prison*, 816.4 *place of confinement*
concentration cell 57.19 *electrochemistry*
concentrative 135.14 *conjunctive*
concentre 342.11 *focus*
concentric 52.81 *curvilinear*, 285.3 *parallel*, 291.7 *centralized*
concentric circles 52.42 *circle*
concentricity 285.1 *parallelism*, 291.3 *centrality*
Concepción 93 Cities
concept 4.1 *philosophy*, 461.6, 471.1 *idea*, 519.4 *ideality*
conceptacle 90.4 *reproductive body*
conception 156, 156.5 *invention*, 243.1 *production*, 245.3 *propagation*, 396.4 *biological function*, 459.1 *mind*, 461.6, 471.1 *idea*, 519.4 *ideality*
conceptional 156.33 *inventive*
conceptive 4.13 *of philosophy*, 156.33 *inventive*, 459.9 *mental*
conceptual 4.13 *of philosophy*, 459.9 *mental*, 471.10 *speculative*, 471.10 *theoretical*, 519.12 *imaginary*
conceptual art 50 Western Art Styles and Movements
conceptualism 4.7 *school of thought*
conceptualist 4.11 *follower of a doctrine*
conceptualistic 4.14 *of a philosophy*
conceptualization 471.8, 519.1 *imagination*
conceptualize 4.20 *philosophize*, 102.14 *theorize*, 459.12 *think*, 471.15, 519.14 *imagine*
conceptualized 471.11 *ideational*
conceptually 4.25 *theoretically*, 50.31 *artistically*, 119.8 *originally*, 459.14 *mentally*, 471.20 *theoretically*
conceptual thought 4.4 *philosophical investigation*
concern 146.1 *inclusion*, 153.7 *disturb*, 467.1 *attention*, 472.1 *topic*, 472.2 *issue*, 472.4 *sphere*, 611.1 *importance*, 611.7 *be important*, 737.7 *company*, 740.8 *store*, 777.3, 777.14 *worry*
concerned 153.12 *disturbed*, 467.9 *solicitous*, 777.9 *worried*
concerned with 472.7 *focused*
concerned with number one 860.5 *egoistic*
concerning 107.10 *relevantly*
concert 49.13 *melody*, 49.27 *performance*, 116.1 *accord*, 116.24 *harmonize*, 135.2 *agreement*, 526.9 *production*, 594.2 *do the groundwork*, 664.15 *concur*, 811.14 *show*
concerted 116.10 *in accord*, 664.18 *joint*, 724.5 *jointly possessing*
concerted action 664.4 *joint operation*
concerted effort 664.4 *joint operation*
concertedly 116.31 *in accord*, 664.20 *cooperatively*
concert hall 49, 51.14 *theatre*, 420.3 *auditorium*
concerto 243.5 *work of art*
concert pitch 49.21 *tone*
concession 116.1 *accord*, 664.3 *mutual relationship*, 673.1 *submission*, 691.1 *leniency*, 708.1 *permission*, 716.2 *basis for negotiations*, 717.1 *compromise*, 729.1 *giving*, 752.1 *discount*
concessional rate 754.1 *cheapness*
concessionary 673.5 *submitting*, 716.8 *negotiated*
concessive 116.10 *in accord*
conch 81 Molluscs, 43.10 *church architecture*, 293.14 *animal covering*
concha 43.9 *miscellaneous architectural features*
conchie 675.3 *pacifist*
conchiglie 45 Types of Pasta

conchigliette 45 Types of Pasta
conchological 81.19 *molluscan*
conchologist 81.15 *invertebrate zoologist*
conchology 81.14 *invertebrate zoology*
concierge 323.5 *person who closes*, 697.3 *attendant*
conciliar 653.18 *parliamentary*
conciliate 586.15 *persuade*, 677.4 *pacify*, 678.1 *mediate*, 710.14 *offer reparation*, 839.9 *forgive*, 840.5 *atone*
conciliation 15.4 *industrial dispute*, 677.1 *pacification*, 678.2 *mediation*, 710.6 *offering*, 716.1 *negotiation*, 839.3 *absolution*, 840.1 *atonement*
conciliator 15.6 *employer*, 678.3 *mediator*
conciliatorily 15.13 *industrially*, 678.7 *mediatorially*, 710.20 *persuasively*, 716.9 *feasibly*, 839.14 *forgivingly*, 840.8 *penitently*
conciliatory 15.10 *unionized*, 116.10 *in accord*, 675.7 *peaceful*, 677.6 *pacificatory*, 678.6 *mediatory*, 710.19 *sacrificial*, 716.8 *negotiated*, 839.4 *forgiving*, 840.4 *atoning*
concise 552, 270.7 *short*, 562.6 *summary*, 566.3 *sparing with words*
concise dictionary 5.28 *dictionary*
concisely 552, 270.12 *short*, 522.13 *intelligibly*, 562.11 *summarily*
concisely styled 552.3 *concise*
conciseness 552, 270.1 *shortness*, 562.4 *summariness*, 566.6 *guarded speech*
Conciseness 552
concise style 552.1 *conciseness*
concise version 562.2 *outline*
conclave 161.5, 568.4 *conference*, 653.7 *council*, 706.2 *representative body*
conclude 684, 4.22 *propound a philosophy*, 52.89 *theorize*, 144.4 *complete*, 157.15 *end*, 218.6 *cease*, 227.5 *show an effect*, 323.9 *close down*, 461.16 *have an idea*, 478.20 *solve*, 492.11 *judge*, 518.5 *suppose*, 535.17 *affirm*, 574.7 *resolve*
conclude a deal 715.5 *contract*
concluded 684, 144.7 *complete*, 157.21 *ended*, 478.14 *solved*
concluding 157.20 *ending*, 684.2 *conclusion*, 684.8 *concluded*
conclusion 155, 684, 4.1 *philosophy*, 52.64 *reasoning*, 130.3 *additional item*, 144.3 *completion*, 155.8 *addition*, 157.1 *end*, 195.9 *sequel*, 218.2 *stop*, 227.1 *effect*, 323.1 *closure*, 461.6 *idea*, 478.6 *solution*, 492.2 *verdict*, 535.2 *statement*
conclusive 157.20 *ending*, 475.12 *demonstrable*, 535.10 *affirmative*, 684.8 *concluded*, 688.15 *true*
conclusive argument 476.1 *refutation*
conclusively 157, 478, 476.11 *in reply*, 535.23 *affirmatively*, 688.25 *authentically*
concoct 102.17 *fabricate*, 243.10 *produce*, 309.12 *distort the truth*, 382.16 *construct*, 519.14 *imagine*, 538.21 *lie*, 540.22 *falsify*, 592.11 *invent*, 592.13 *plot*, 594.7 *develop*
concocted 538.13 *untrue*, 540.32 *falsified*
concoction 133.2 *mixed thing*, 243.1 *production*, 243.3 *product*, 351.2 *drink*, 538.1 *untruth*, 540.9 *falsification*
concomitance 116.4 *harmony*, 180.1 *accompaniment*, 198.1 *same time*

concomitant 180, 116.13 *harmonious*, 180.17 *accompanying*, 198.9 *simultaneous*, 253.8 *attendant*
concomitantly 198.12 *simultaneously*
concomitant with 198.12 *simultaneously*
concord 49.13 *melody*, 116.1 *accord*, 116.21 *be in accord*, 135.2 *agreement*, 140.2 *cooperation*, 144.1 *completeness*, 150.8 *harmony*, 433.3 *melodiousness*, 664.2 *fellowship*, 667.1 *agreement*, 675.1 *peace*, 819.1 *friendship*
Concord 86 Fruits, **93** Cities
concordance 5.28 *dictionary*, 110.2 *equivalence*, 116.1 *accord*, 499.1 *assent*, 664.2 *fellowship*, 667.1 *agreement*
concordant 110.13 *equivalent*, 116.10 *in accord*, 135.13 *agreeable*, 150.16 *harmonious*, 167.12 *conforming*, 433.7 *harmonious*, 499.6 *assenting*, 664.19 *associating*, 667.10 *agreeing*
concordantly 110.18 *identically*, 135.17 *agreeably*, 664.20 *cooperatively*, 667.14 *agreeably*
concordat 667.2 *contract*, 715.3 *alliance*
concourse 10.17 *worshipper*, 96.6 *river flow*, 116.1 *accord*, 135.1 *union*, 161.3 *meeting*, 342.1 *convergence*, 674.2 *contest*
concrescence 135.1 *union*
concrete 43.4 *building material*, 44.9 *industrial ceramics*, 44.11 *make ceramics*, 49.32 *instrumental*, 50.29 *realist*, 63.25 *construction material*, 99.11 *intrinsic*, 138.9 *adhesive*, 280.1 *base*, 293.11 *paving*, 293.29 *surface*, 306.9 *formed*, 327.4 *road surface*, 367.7 *material*, 371.4 *solid body*, 371.6 *dense*, 373.7 *hard substance*, 407.8 *touchable*, 437.1 *visible*, 604.2 *building material*
concrete art 50 Western Art Styles and Movements
concrete block 373.7 *hard substance*
concrete bridge 63.21 *bridge*
concrete dam 63.23 *dam*
concretely 50.30 *pictorially*, 138.11 *cohesively*, 306.13 *formatively*, 367.9 *materially*, 371.10 *densely*
concreteness 367.1 *material world*, 371.1 *density*, 407.1 *touch*
concrete poetry 48.6 *poetry*
concrete shelter 634.1 *refuge*, 671.10 *shelter*
concrete slab 63.27 *superstructure*
concretion 135.1 *union*, 371.2 *concentration*, 371.4 *solid body*
concretive 135.12 *united*
concretization 371.2 *concentration*
concubinage 823.3 *types of marriage*, 877.4 *illicit love*
concubinal 823.20 *matrimonial*
concubinary 823.20 *matrimonial*
concubine 701.5 *subjected person*, 823.11 *married woman*, 877.9 *immoral woman*
concupiscence 782.4 *sexual desire*, 870.3 *overindulgence*, 872.1 *gluttony*, 877.3 *sexual immorality*
concupiscent 782.11 *lustful*, 870.8 *overindulgent*, 877.14 *lecherous*
concur 664, 116.21 *be in accord*, 135.9 *agree*, 140.6 *come together*, 167.7 *conform*, 180.13 *accompany*, 198.6 *be simultaneous*, 499.4 *assent*, 664.11 *cooperate*, 667.6 *agree with*
concurrence 116.1 *accord*, 135.1 *union*, 135.2 *agreement*, 140.1 *combination*, 140.2 *cooperation*, 167.1 *conformity*, 180.2 *synchronism*, 198.1 *same time*,

concurrent 180, 116.10 *in accord*, 140.8 *cooperative*, 198.9 *simultaneous*, 342.7 *convergent*, 664.17 *cooperative*, 667.10 *agreeing*
concurrently 180, 140.10 *in combination*, 198.12 *simultaneously*, 342.12 *convergently*, 664.20 *cooperatively*, 667.14 *agreeably*
concurrent with 198.12 *simultaneously*
concurring 180.18 *concurrent*, 499.6 *assenting*, 664.19 *associating*, 667.10 *agreeing*
concurringly 667.14 *agreeably*
concuss 330.2 *collide*, 330.8 *club*, 404.12 *anaesthetize*, 761.7 *render insensitive*
concussed 404.8 *unconscious*
concussion 330.12 *collision*
condemn 8.18 *devilize*, 16.79 *convict*, 398.19 *execute*, 492.11 *judge*, 670.10 *criticize*, 766.7 *be dissatisfied*, 822.14 *hate*, 827.6 *vilify*, 852.19 *blame*, 862.11 *be evil*, 879.2 *penalize*, 879.5 *execute*
condemnation 16.7 *legal trial*, 16.43 *conviction*, 492.2 *verdict*, 852.7 *blame*, 879.8 *penalty*
condemnatory 492.8 *judging*, 852.29 *blaming*
condemned 16.64 *convicted*, 628.13 *dilapidated*, 633.2 *unsafe*, 633.4 *endangered*, 822.12 *hated*, 866.5 *guilty*, 879.22 *punishable*
condemned cell 16.43 *conviction*, 879.16 *instrument of execution*
condemned housing 626.1 *lack of hygiene*
condemned man 397.10 *dying person*
condemned prisoner 702.5 *prisoner*
condemned to death 397.18 *dying*
condemned to die 397.18 *dying*
condemning 852.29 *blaming*
condemn oneself 867.4 *be penitent*
condemn to death 398.19, 879.5 *execute*
condemn to the galleys 879.1 *punish*
condensability 262.2 *contractibility*
condensable 262.9 *contractible*
condensation 55.9 *atmospheric process*, 57.3 *phase*, 57.14 *chemical reaction*, 128.1 *increase*, 131.1 *subtraction*, 135.1 *union*, 138.1 *adhesion*, 262.1 *contraction*, 273.6 *denseness*, 299.1 *outline*, 355.7 *obtaining an extract*, 371.2 *concentration*, 387.1 *fluid*, 389.3 *wateriness*, 441.2 *murk*, 552.2 *outline*
condensation nuclei 55.8 *atmosphere*
condensation polymer 57.21 *polymer*
condensation trail 543.1 *sign*
condense 57.25 *solidify*, 57.26 *react*, 128.5 *make bigger*, 129.5 *make smaller*, 131.3 *subtract*, 135.8 *unite*, 138.6 *adhere*, 262.5 *make smaller*, 262.6 *become smaller*, 270.10 *shorten*, 273.7 *thicken*, 299.5 *outline*, 355.17 *obtain an extract*, 371.8 *be dense*, 373.10 *solidify*, 552.4 *be concise*, 562.8 *summarize*
condensed 371, 55.43 *atmospheric*, 57.32 *solid*, 131.7 *reduced*, 138.9 *adhesive*, 262.7 *smaller*, 270.8 *shortened*, 273.2 *dense*, 552.3 *concise*
condensed milk 351.5 *milk*
condenser 57 Laboratory Apparatus, **371**, 56.30 *lens system*, 64.17 *resistor*, 262.4 *contractor*, 388.11 *vaporizer*

condensing 135.14 *conjunctive*
condescend 806, 688.19 *be authoritarian*, 771.15 *humour*, 805.28 *disdain*, 817.13 *defer to*
condescendence 806.15 *condescension*
condescending 688.12 *authoritative*, 805.17 *conceited*, 805.19 *stately*, 806.4 *self-abasing*, 817.9 *deferential*
condescendingly 817.16 *deferentially*
condescension 806, 805.5 *stateliness*, 817.4 *deference*
condign 845.13 *fit*
Condillac 4 *Philosophers*
condiment 133.4 *admixture*, 413.2 *seasoning*
condiments 180.5 *side dish*
condition 485, 52.64 *reasoning*, 61.38 *psychologize*, 105.1 *state*, 106.1 *circumstances*, 166.4 *guide*, 251.2 *circumstances*, 306.6 *nature*, 518.1 *supposition*, 584.18 *habituate*, 593.1 *requirement*, 623.3 *health*, 624.2 *illness*
conditional 485, 4.8 *philosophical term*, 5.34 *tense*, 52.26 *equality*, 52.63 *mathematical logic*, 52.86 *logical*, 105.8 *in a state of*, 106.7 *circumstantial*, 699.13 *restraining*, 716.8 *negotiated*
conditionally 105, 106.16 *relatively*, 485.18 *with qualification*, 699.16 *under restraints*, 716.9 *feasibly*
conditional phrase 5.23 *phrase*
conditional probability 52.62 *probability*
conditioned 485.11 *modified*, 584.14 *habituated*
conditioned reflex 61.20 *conditioning*, 331.6 *response*, 462.3 *instinct*, 584.7 *habituation*
conditioner 68.10 *farm tool*
conditioning 61, 61.3 *psychiatric treatment*, 584.7 *habituation*
conditions 55.3 *weather*, 106.1 *circumstances*, 165.4 *specifications*, 485.6 *specification*, 518.1 *supposition*, 593.1 *requirement*, 716.2 *basis for negotiations*
conditions of employment 15.2 *industrial negotiations*
condolence 835, 835.1 *pity*
condolences 835.2 *condolence*
condolent 831.6 *benevolent*, 835.6 *pitying*
condolently 831.10 *benevolently*
condole with 835.9 *sorrow*
condom 231.2 *counteracting thing*, 247.3 *birth control*, 377.3 *elastic thing*, 661.3 *barrier*
condominium 12.3 *governance*, 256.6 *apartment block*, 724.1 *joint possession*
condominium owner 724.3 *participant*
condonable 855.13 *vindicable*
condonation 839.3 *absolution*
condone 839, 673.3 *submit*, 851.12 *accept*
condoned 839.6 *forgiven*
condoning 839.4 *forgiving*
condor 78 *Birds*, 78.5 *bird of prey*
condordance 49.13 *melody*
condottiere 653.14 *leader*, 679.6 *militarist*
conduce 234.8 *further*
conduce to 234.4 *tend*, 662.28 *further*
conducive 613.3 *instrumental*, 662.33 *helpful*
conducive to 234.5 *tending to*
conduct 49, 64, 652, 652, 180.15 *escort*, 306.5 *formality*, 326.11 *transfer*, 327.1 *way*, 332.6 *direct*, 584.5 *tradition*, 590.14 *carry on*, 640.1 *action*, 652.14 *behave towards*, 653.1 *manage*, 653.2 *direct*, 653.3 *management*, 876.1 *morality*
Conduct 652
conduct a dig 200.16 *excavate*
conductance 56.53, 64.12 *resistance*

conduct an experiment 479.11 *experiment*
conduct an inquiry into 477.17 *question*
conduct a sea survey 97.9 *sail the high seas*
conduct a trial 16.76 *judge*
conduct a witch-hunt 590.8 *pursue*
conducted 180.20 *accompanied*
conduct industrial relations 15
conducting medium 56.43 *electrical conduction*, 64.3 *electricity*
conductiometric titration 57.18 *gravimetric analysis*
conduction 56.36 *heat flow*, 64.3 *electricity*, 235.7 *electrical power*, 326.3 *transmission*
conductional 326.17 *transferable*
conduction band 56.44 *semiconductor*
conduction current 56.51 *electric current*
conduction of electricity 56.43 *electrical conduction*
conductive 326.17 *transferable*
conductively 326.18 *in transit*
conductivity 56.43 *electrical conduction*, 56.53 *resistance*, 64.3 *electricity*, 64.12 *resistance*, 235.7 *electrical power*
conduct of affairs 653.3 *management*
conduct one's affairs 652.11 *conduct oneself*
conduct oneself 652, 640.4 *act*
conduct oneself properly 652.12 *behave well*
conductor 652, 49.24 *musician*, 56.43 *electrical conduction*, 64.3 *electricity*, 72.9 *railway worker*, 180.8 *usher*, 192.11 *person keeping time*, 230.5 *operator*, 235.7 *electrical power*, 653.13 *director*, 653.14 *leader*, 811.15 *showman*
conduct the ceremony 823.16 *join in marriage*
conduct the wedding 823.16 *join in marriage*
conduct unbecoming 818.2 *bad manners*
conduit 321.1 *furrow*, 322.7 *passageway*, 327.11 *channel*, 346.5 *entrance*, 347.7 *outlet*, 389.13 *irrigator*
cone 315, 52.45 *curved surface*, 85.2 *tree part*, 272.8 *narrow thing*, 435.2 *eye*
cone-bearing 83.16 *taxonomic*
coneflower 84 *Flowers and Flowering Plants*
cone-shaped 52.83 *spherical*, 272.3 *tapered*
cone shell 81 *Molluscs*
Conestoga wagon 71 *Carriages and Carts*
cone worm 81 *Worms*
confab 568.2 *chat*
confabulate 540.22 *falsify*, 568.9 *converse*
confabulated 540.32 *falsified*
confabulation 540.9 *falsification*, 568.2 *chat*
confabulator 568.7 *conversationalist*
confabulatory 568.12 *conversing*
confection 62.5 *prescription*, 133.2 *mixed thing*, 243.3 *product*
confectionary 45.41 *sweet*, 350.17 *food shop*
confectioner 350.20 *food provider*, 606.4 *caterer*
confectioner's shop 414.4 *confectionery*
confectionery 414
confederacy 140.2 *cooperation*, 664.5 *joint control*, 665.3 *political grouping*
confederate 140.6 *come together*, 140.8 *cooperative*, 664.16 *join*, 665.15 *politicize*, 724.3 *participant*
Confederate flag 544.7 *flag*
confederation 12.5 *political organization*, 91.2 *union of nations*, 140.2 *cooperation*, 664.5 *joint*

control, 664.9 *team*, 665.3 *political grouping*, 688.8 *governmental organization*, 724.1 *joint possession*
Confederation of British Industry 15.1 *industrial relations*
confer 568, 116.30 *grant*, 570.16 *bequeath*, 654.6 *consult*, 716.4 *negotiator*, 728.3 *transfer property*
confer an honour 845.17 *credit*
confer an obligation 617.10 *do good*
confer a title 845.17 *credit*
conference 161, 568, 678, 532.7 *publicity*, 653.7 *council*, 654.2 *consultation*, 664.8 *conferring*, 706.2 *representative body*, 716.3 *discussion*
Conference 86 *Fruits*
conference call 534.10 *telephone call*
conference championship 682.3 *successful thing*
conference delegate 706.1 *delegate*
conferential 568.13 *discussing*
confer holy orders on 7.21 *ordain*
conferment 7.9 *priesthood*, 116.9 *grant*, 728.1 *transfer of property*, 729.1 *giving*
confer ownership upon 728.3 *transfer property*
conferral 116.9 *grant*, 728.1 *transfer of property*, 729.1 *giving*
conferred 116.19 *granted*
conferrer 729.4 *giver*
conferring 664, 568.13 *discussing*
confer upon 729.5 *give*
conferva 90 *Algae*
conferval 90.7 *algal*
confervoid 90.7 *algal*
confess 10.18 *perform rites*, 16.80 *convict oneself*, 497.7 *believe*, 499.4 *assent*, 530.8, 535.20 *admit*, 840.6 *apologize*, 866.8 *be guilty*, 867.4 *be penitent*
confessed 530.10 *disclosed*, 535.11 *stated*, 867.6 *penitent*
confessed criminal 866.4 *guilty person*
confessing 16.64 *convicted*, 867.6 *penitent*
confession 9.1 *worship*, 10.3 *rite of worship*, 10.5 *Christian rite*, 483.5 *legal evidence*, 499.1 *assent*, 530.2 *divulgence*, 535.5 *admission*, 840.2 *apology*, 867.1 *penitence*
confessional 10.12 *church*, 16.18 *tribunal*
confessional poetry 48.6 *poetry*
confessions 48.4 *non-fiction*, 560.4 *factual account*
confess one's sins 867.4 *be penitent*
confessor 7.8 *priest*, 530.4 *discloser*, 535.9 *affirmer*, 840.3 *atoner*, 867.3 *penitent person*
confess the truth 537.29 *be truthful*
confetti 456.5 *variegated thing*
confidant 529.1 *secrecy*, 654.4 *adviser*, 784.4 *likable person*, 819.6 *close friend*
confidante 51.21 *role*, 697.4 *personal attendant*, 784.4 *likable person*
confide 528.11 *inform*, 530.6 *divulge*, 658.4 *be naive*
confide in 497.7 *believe*, 654.6 *consult*
confidence 207.3 *maturity*, 303.4 *assurance*, 490.10 *conviction*, 497.3 *believing*, 513.1 *expectation*, 529.1 *secrecy*, 632.1 *safety*, 660.4 *ease of manner*, 688.2 *authoritativeness*, 718.1 *protection*, 744.7 *repute*, 775.2 *expectation*, 778.3 *steadfastness*
confidence game 736.7 *dishonesty*, 858.3 *criminality*
confidence level 52.60 *parameter*
confidence limits 52.60 *parameter*

confidence man 539.17 *cheat*, 540.15 *false person*, 736.11 *dishonest person*
confidence trick 538.10 *dishonesty*, 539.8 *trick*, 540.8 *fraud*, 657.2 *stratagem*, 736.7 *dishonesty*, 858.3 *criminality*
confidence trickster 548.3 *deceiver*, 657.3 *cunning person*
confident 490.2 *convinced*, 497.11 *believing*, 513.5 *expecting*, 535.14 *assertive*, 688.12 *authoritative*, 775.12 *expectant*, 778.12 *self-reliant*
confidential 529.9 *secret*, 611.5 *important*
confidential information 529.1 *secrecy*
confidentiality 529.1 *secrecy*, 531.4 *silence*
confidentially 529.15 *in secret*
confidently 490.24 *with certainty*, 497.15 *believingly*, 513.12 *expectantly*, 688.23 *authoritatively*, 775.15 *hopefully*
confiding 658.1 *naive*
configuration 52.41 *geometric figure*, 61.26 *gestalt*, 165.3 *characteristic*, 306.1, 382.3 *form*
configurational 306.9 *formed*
configurationally 306.13 *formatively*
configurationism 61.1 *psychology*
configurative 306.9 *formed*
configure 52.96 *represent*
confine 272.10 *narrow*, 290.15 *keep inside*, 300.5 *border*, 301.2 *enclosed place*, 301.5 *enclose*, 302.7 *limit*, 323.10 *enclose*, 485.16 *specify*, 531.8 *conceal*, 699.11 *detain*, 702.9 *imprison*, 816.13 *ignore*, 869.6 *moderate*
confined 249.18 *local*, 272.1 *narrow*, 301.7 *enclosed*, 302.5 *limited*, 323.15 *enclosed*, 485.12 *conditional*, 624.22 *sick*, 699.15 *detained*, 702.8 *imprisoned*, 816.10 *lonely*, 869.6 *moderate*
confinedly 301
confined space 272.6 *narrow place*
confined to bed 699.15 *detained*
confinement 245.7 *obstetrics*, 272.5 *narrowness*, 290.2 *inside*, 396.4 *biological function*, 485.6 *specification*, 699.4 *detention*, 702.7 *imprisonment*, 879.7 *punishment*
confines 249.3 *regional boundary*, 264.3 *near place*, 297.1 *surroundings*, 300.1 *edge*
confirm 535, 10.18 *perform rites*, 16.68 *legislate*, 101.12 *establish reality*, 116.28 *consent*, 225.7 *make stable*, 237.8 *strengthen*, 475.17 *prove*, 478.17 *answer*, 479.11 *experiment*, 480.1 *verify*, 483.12 *prove*, 490.21 *make certain*, 499.4 *assent*, 537.30 *prove true*, 667.6 *agree with*, 708.3 *permit*, 714.7 *promise*, 715.5 *contract*, 730.10 *receive someone*
confirmability 475.5 *demonstrability*
confirmable 475.12 *demonstrable*
confirmation 490, 535, 537, 10.5 *Christian rite*, 16.31 *legislation*, 475.4 *proof*, 478.2 *acknowledgment*, 480.4 *verification*, 480.6 *evidence*, 483.2 *proof*, 499.1 *assent*, 667.1 *agreement*, 708.1 *permission*, 715.1 *contract*, 730.4 *reception*, 813.3 *formal occasion*
Confirmation name 560.8 *name*
confirmative 499.6 *assenting*, 667.10 *agreeing*
confirmed 116.17 *consenting*, 475.13 *proven*, 478.11 *answering*, 480.10 *verified*, 483.8 *evidential*, 535.13 *supported*, 537.20 *proved*, 584.14 *habituated*, 730.13 *received*
confirmed bachelor 825.5 *single person*
confirmed habit 584.1 *habit*
confirmed liar 538.11, 539.16 *liar*

confirming 116.17 *consenting,* 480.9 *verificatory*

confiscate 734.7 *take,* 734.8 *take back,* 767.14 *take away,* 879.1 *punish*

confiscation 734.1 *taking,* 734.2 *taking back,* 879.7 *punishment*

confiscator 730.7 *collector,* 734.6 *taker*

confiscatory 734.12 *taking*

conflab 568.2 *chat*

conflagration 408.6, 439.8 *fire*

conflate 524.8 *interpret*

conflated 524.15 *interpreted*

conflation 140.1 *combination,* 524.1 *interpretation*

conflict 663, 674, 61.12 *stress,* 111.3 *opposition,* 115.5 *be dissimilar,* 117.4 *disagreement,* 117.14 *disagree,* 231.1 *counteraction,* 434.6 *disagreement,* 434.11 *disagree,* 473.1 *argument,* 473.13 *argue,* 500.1, 500.8 *dissent,* 663.16 *confront,* 666.2 *argument,* 666.6 *argue,* 674.1 *contention,* 674.6 *fight,* 676.1 *war,* 764.8, 764.11 *quarrel,* 820.1 *enmity,* 820.4 *act of hostility,* 820.12 *oppose*

conflicting 117.10 *disagreeing,* 231.4 *counteracting,* 434.8 *disagreeing,* 473.9 *hostile,* 500.7 *dissenting,* 663.20 *discordant,* 687.6 *adverse,* 820.9 *aggressive*

conflictingly 231.5 *counter,* 687.12 *in adversity*

conflict in meaning 520.10 *mean*

conflict of opinion 117.4 *disagreement*

conflict with 231.3 *counteract,* 663.13 *be contrary*

confluence 96.1 *river,* 96.6 *river flow,* 116.1 *accord,* 135.1 *union,* 161.1 *assembly,* 291.3 *centrality,* 342.1 *convergence,* 407.6 *contiguity*

confluent 96.1 *river,* 96.10 *fluvial,* 116.10 *in accord,* 161.48 *cumulate,* 291.7 *centralized,* 342.7 *convergent*

confluently 342.12 *convergently*

confluent stream 96.1 *river*

conflux 96.6 *river flow,* 342.1 *convergence*

confocal 52.81 *curvilinear,* 342.7 *convergent*

conform 112, 116, 167, 808, 110.11 *be regular,* 124.9 *be average,* 167.9 *make conform,* 306.8 *be formal,* 433.8 *harmonize,* 478.21 *answer to,* 499.5 *assent to,* 667.8 *be compatible,* 694.5 *obey,* 861.18 *be good*

conformable 167, 116.14 *conforming,* 306.9 *formed,* 719.7 *observant*

conformably 167.16 *adaptably,* 306.13 *formatively,* 719.8 *observantly*

conformance 110.6 *regularity,* 116.5, 167.1 *conformity,* 719.1 *observance*

conformation 32.13 *breeding,* 116.5, 167.1 *conformity,* 306.1, 382.3 *form,* 667.3 *compatibility*

conformational 57.37 *structural*

conformer 167.6 *conformist,* 497.5 *believer*

conforming 112, 116, 167, 110.17 *regular,* 478.15 *correspondent,* 667.12 *compatible,* 694.7 *obedient,* 719.7 *observant*

conformingly 167, 478.26 *correspondingly,* 667.16 *compatibly,* 694.10 *obediently,* 719.8 *observantly*

conformism 167.4 *conventionalism,* 584.6 *procedure*

conformist 167, 167, 7.5 *Christian,* 497.5 *believer,* 497.11 *believing,* 499.3, 667.5 *assenter,* 694.4 *obedient person*

conformity 112, 116, 167, 110.6 *regularity,* 114.1 *similarity,* 118.1 *imitation,* 124.4 *average,* 308.3 *evenness,* 478.8

correspondence, 584.6 *procedure,* 667.3 *compatibility,* 694.1 *obedience,* 719.1 *observance*

Conformity 167

conform to 167.7 *conform,* 719.4 *observe*

conform to facts 537.27 *be true*

confound 133.9 *mix up,* 460.10 *bemuse,* 476.8 *refute,* 482.11 *not discriminate,* 491.20 *make uncertain,* 515.7 *thwart,* 523.7 *be unintelligible,* 551.3 *make obscure,* 786.10 *be wonderful*

confounded 133.13 *mixed-up,* 491.3 *confused,* 515.9 *disappointed,* 523.6 *confused,* 618.6 *damnable,* 827.11 *miscellaneous euphemisms*

confounding 476.1 *refutation,* 476.7 *refuting*

confoundment 491.12 *confusion*

confraternal 665.8 *leagued,* 819.8 *friendly*

confraternally 665.18 *cliquishly*

confraternity 664.9 *team,* 665.1 *party,* 819.1 *friendship*

confrication 385.1 *friction*

confront 663, 111.8 *be opposite,* 111.9 *oppose,* 117.14 *disagree,* 267.4 *meet,* 298.4 *interface,* 303.10 *be in front,* 330.2 *collide,* 526.4 *show oneself,* 597.1 *undertake,* 666.5 *disagree,* 668.6 *be insubordinate,* 669.6 *resist,* 670.8 *counterattack,* 676.14 *battle,* 711.6 *dissent,* 778.15 *be courageous*

confront a problem 592.9 *plan*

confrontation 111.3 *opposition,* 117.4 *disagreement,* 267.2 *meeting,* 342.2 *approach,* 526.10 *manifestation,* 663.3 *conflict,* 666.1 *disagreement,* 668.2 *disobedience,* 711.2 *dissent*

confrontational 111.5 *opposing,* 117.10 *disagreeing,* 298.6 *interfacial,* 666.9 *disagreeing,* 711.9 *dissenting*

confrontationally 111.7 *disapprovingly*

confrontation therapy 61.3 *psychiatric treatment*

confronted 111.5 *opposing,* 526.13 *displayed*

confronter 298.3 *interfacer*

confronting 111.4 *opposite,* 111.5 *opposing,* 117.10 *disagreeing,* 663.20 *discordant*

confrontment 111.1 *oppositeness*

Confucian 4.11 *follower of a doctrine,* 4.14 *of a philosophy*

Confucianism 7 *Non-Christian Religions,* 4.7 *school of thought*

Confucian text 7.12 *religious text*

Confucius 4 *Philosophers*

con fuoco 49 *Musical Terms*

confuse 151, 477, 133.9 *mix up,* 151.22 *discompose,* 153.8 *disarrange,* 460.10 *bemuse,* 491.20 *make uncertain,* 510.15 *make insane,* 521.8 *not understand,* 523.7 *be unintelligible,* 523.8 *make unintelligible,* 529.13 *mystify,* 531.9 *disguise,* 551.3 *make obscure,* 657.5 *be cunning,* 659.23 *cause difficulties*

confused 151, 491, 523, 133.12 *mixed,* 133.13 *mixed-up,* 151.18 *muddled,* 153.12 *disturbed,* 153.13 *disarranged,* 160.8 *discontinuous,* 366.15 *agitated,* 460.7 *intellectually subnormal,* 477.13 *problematic,* 482.3 *indiscriminate,* 515.9 *disappointed,* 520.6 *meaningful,* 551.2 *obscure,* 659.12 *problematic,* 659.16 *troubled,* 689.6 *anarchic,* 722.18 *at a loss,* 810.10 *bashful*

confusedly 151.27 *in disorder*

confused message 520.3 *comprehension*

confusing 477.13 *problematic,* 523.4 *difficult,* 529.11 *mysterious,* 659.12 *problematic*

confusingly 491, 153.18 *disturbingly*

confusion 151, 491, 133.1 *mixture,* 133.3 *miscellany,* 139.1 *nonadhesion,* 151.1 *disorder,* 153.2 *disarrangement,* 160.1 *discontinuity,* 244.5 *havoc,* 366.2 *tumult,* 477.1 *question,* 482.8 *indiscriminateness,* 510.3 *mental deterioration,* 523.11 *unintelligibility,* 551.1 *obscurity*

confusion of tongues 5.5 *nonstandard language*

confutability 476.4 *refutability*

confutable 476.6 *refutable*

confutably 476.12 *refutably*

confutation 16.7 *legal trial,* 221.5 *reply,* 476.2 *denial,* 484.1 *counterevidence,* 711.2 *dissent*

confutative 476.7 *refuting,* 484.5 *countering,* 711.9 *dissenting*

confute 221.9 *reply,* 476.8 *refute,* 477.20 *doubt,* 478.18 *answer back,* 484.7 *counter,* 500.8 *dissent,* 587.1 *dissuade,* 711.6 *dissent,* 807.28 *get above oneself*

confuted 484.6 *countered*

confuter 476.5 *refuter*

confuting 476.7 *refuting*

conga 46.2 *dance*

conga line 46.2 *dance*

con game 736.7 *dishonesty,* 858.3 *criminality*

congé 43 Architectural Decoration, 345.9 *parting,* 349.18 *dismissal*

congeal 273.7 *thicken,* 371.8 *be dense,* 393.25 *thicken,* 409.11 *become cold*

congealed 138.9 *adhesive,* 273.2 *dense,* 371.7 *condensed*

congealing 371.7 *condensed*

congealment 138.1 *adhesion,* 273.6 *denseness,* 371.2 *concentration*

congeneric 146.8 *included*

congenerous 146.8 *included*

congenial 116.10 *in accord,* 405.6 *pleasant,* 665.11 *social,* 667.10 *agreeing,* 763.2, 784.5 *likable,* 819.8 *friendly,* 821.22 *lovable*

congenial climate 625.2 *salubrity*

congeniality 667.1 *agreement,* 763.8 *amiability,* 815.1 *sociability*

congenially 667.14, 667.14 *agreeably,* 784.10 *with great liking*

congenital disease 624.4 *disease*

conger eel 80 Fishes, 20.5 *British game fish*

congeries 161.25 *assemblage*

congest 323.8 *stop,* 610.4 *be excessive*

congested 144.8 *full,* 161.50, 181.10 *crowded,* 323.13 *stopped,* 610.6 *excessive*

congestion 323.1 *closure,* 610.1 *excess,* 624.3 *symptom*

congius 75 Some Foreign Units

conglomerate 54 Common Rocks, 138.6 *adhere,* 140.3 *assembly,* 140.9 *assembled,* 161.48 *cumulate,* 371.4 *solid body,* 371.8 *be dense,* 665.1 *party*

conglomerated 133.12 *mixed*

conglomeration 133.1 *mixture,* 133.3 *miscellany,* 138.1 *adhesion,* 140.3 *assembly,* 161.25 *assemblage*

conglutinate 138.7 *cause to adhere*

conglutination 138.1 *adhesion*

Congo 91 Countries, **96** Rivers, 96.5 *other major rivers*

congo eel 79 Amphibians

congratulate 812, 773.7 *dance,* 851.15 *compliment*

congratulate oneself 805.29 *feel pride*

congratulation 773.2 *fanfare,* 812.6 *tribute,* 851.4 *compliment*

congratulations 773.2 *fanfare,* 851.27 *bravo*

congratulatory 812

congregate 140.5 *combine,* 161.39 *come together,* 161.46 *assembled,* 181.11 *crowd,* 342.10 *come together,* 344.8 *meet,* 346.12 *flood in*

congregated 140.9, 161.46 *assembled*

congregation 10.17 *worshipper,* 140.3, 161.1 *assembly,* 161.5 *conference,* 181.4 *throng,* 342.4 *meeting place,* 420.2 *hearer,* 653.7 *council,* 664.9 *team,* 665.1 *party*

congregational 10.22 *worshipping,* 140.9 *assembled,* 161.49 *grouped,* 665.8 *leagued*

Congregationalism 7 Christian Movements

Congregationalist 7.5 *Christian*

congregationally 10.23 *ritually,* 140.10 *in combination*

congress 10.17 *worshipper,* 135.1 *union,* 161.5 *conference,* 342.4 *meeting place,* 568.4 *conference,* 653.7 *council*

Congress 12.4 *governing body,* 653.12 *US government,* 688.6 *place of authority,* 706.2 *representative body*

congressional 92.6 *administrative,* 161.49 *grouped,* 653.18 *parliamentary,* 688.14 *governmental,* 696.12 *masterful*

Congressional 706.6 *delegated*

congressional committee 654.4 *adviser*

Congressional Cup 36.1 *sailing*

congressional district 92.1 *administrative area,* 249.5 *state*

congressionally 688.24 *ministerially*

Congressionally 706.8 *representatively*

Congressional Medal of Honor 544.4 *insignia*

congressional offices 647.1 *workshop*

Congressional Record 545.1 *record*

congressional system 580.11 *franchise*

Congressman 12.8 *politician,* 653.16 *official,* 688.10 *person of authority,* 696.3 *leader,* 706.1 *delegate*

Congresswoman 706.1 *delegate*

Congreve 48 Dramatists

congruence 52.48 *transformation,* 110.2 *equivalence,* 116.5 *conformity,* 308.1 *symmetry,* 478.8 *correspondence*

congruent 110.13 *equivalent,* 116.14 *conforming,* 122.6 *equal,* 167.12 *conforming,* 308.4 *symmetrical,* 478.15 *correspondent,* 667.12 *compatible*

congruently 110.18 *identically,* 122.13 *equitably,* 342.12 *convergently,* 478.26 *correspondingly,* 667.16 *compatibly*

congruent triangles 52.43 *triangle*

congruity 116.5, 167.1 *conformity,* 308.1 *symmetry,* 667.3 *compatibility*

congruous 116.14, 167.12 *conforming,* 667.12 *compatible*

congruously 167.17 *conformingly*

conic 315.9 *round,* 380.1 *sharp*

conical 52.83 *spherical,* 272.3 *tapered,* 315.9 *round,* 342.7 *convergent*

conical flask 57 Laboratory Apparatus

conically 315.13 *roundly*

conic projection 547.7 *map*

conic section 52.42 *circle*

conidium 89.4 *fungal body*

conifer 85.1 *tree*

coniferous 83.16 *taxonomic,* 85.14 *treelike*

coniferous forest 85.4 *trees*

coniferous tree 85.1 *tree*

coniine 58.19 *alkaloid*

Coniston 94 Lakes

Coniston Water 94.4 *British lakes*

conjecturability 518.2 *basis of supposition*

conjectural 4.13 *of philosophy,* 106.7 *circumstantial,* 461.10 *speculative,* 471.10 *theoretical,* 477.15 *sceptical,* 479.8 *experimental,* 491.1 *uncertain,* 518.7 *suppositional*
conjecturally 106.16 *relatively,* 471.20 *theoretically,* 477.24 *questionably,* 479.14 *experimentally,* 491.23 *uncertainly,* 518.10 *supposedly*
conjecture 518, 4.1 *philosophy,* 4.20 *philosophize,* 52.65 *theory,* 102.4 *theorization,* 102.14 *theorize,* 461.6 *idea,* 461.16 *have an idea,* 471.2 *theory,* 471.17 *theorize,* 477.6 *uncertainty,* 477.20 *doubt,* 479.3 *experimentation,* 479.11 *experiment,* 491.10 *suspicion,* 491.18 *be uncertain,* 492.1 *judgment,* 492.12 *estimate,* 497.1 *belief,* 518.5 *suppose,* 786.12 *wonder whether*
conjectured 518.8 *supposed*
conjoin 116.22 *form an alliance,* 116.24 *harmonize,* 130.6 *add,* 135.8 *unite,* 137.11 *connect,* 140.5 *combine,* 407.12 *abut*
conjoined 135.12 *united,* 140.7 *combined*
conjoint 116.11 *allied,* 116.13 *harmonious,* 135.12 *united,* 140.7 *combined*
conjointly 130.10 *additionally,* 135.16 *as one,* 664.20 *cooperatively,* 665.18 *cliquishly*
conjoint therapy 61.3 *psychiatric treatment*
conjugal 715.7 *contractual,* 823.20 *matrimonial*
conjugal bliss 823.1 *marriage*
conjugality 823.1 *marriage*
conjugal love 821.2 *romantic love*
conjugally 715.8 *contractually,* 823.24 *matrimonially*
conjugal trust 715.1 *contract*
conjugate 140.5 *combine,* 140.7 *combined*
conjugate angles 52.39 *angle*
conjugated protein 58.9 *protein*
conjugation 5.30 *syntax*
conjunction 4.8 *philosophical term,* 5.30 *syntax,* 5.35 *part of speech,* 52.63 *mathematical logic,* 53.16 *planet,* 116.4 *harmony,* 135.1 *union,* 135.5 *joint,* 137.1 *connection,* 140.1 *combination,* 140.2 *cooperation,* 180.1 *accompaniment,* 180.2 *synchronism,* 264.1 *nearness,* 407.6 *contiguity*
conjunction-reduction 5.30 *syntax*
conjunctiva 435.2 *eye*
conjunctive 135, 5.44 *grammatical,* 130.8 *additional,* 137.14 *connective,* 140.8 *cooperative*
conjunctively 5.52 *grammatically,* 135.16 *as one,* 137.17 *in connection with*
conjunctivitis 436.2 *poor sight*
conjuncture 106.2 *occurrence*
conjural 11.15 *witchlike*
conjuration 11.5 *spell,* 539.9 *sleight of hand*
conjure 11, 216.8 *cause change,* 539.29 *juggle*
conjured 539.40 *illusory*
conjure into 220.9 *transform*
conjurement 11.5 *spell*
conjurer 216.6 *editor*
conjure up 11.22 *conjure,* 102.13, 435.17 *imagine,* 471.15 *imagine,* 511.12 *remember,* 519.14 *imagine*
conjure up a vision 519.14 *imagine*
conjuring 102.3 *delusion,* 539.9 *sleight of hand*
conjuror 51.27 *entertainer,* 657.3 *cunning person*
conk 89.4 *fungal body,* 318.3 *protuberance,* 416.2 *sense of smell*
conked out 844.18 *gone wrong*
conker 86 *Nuts*
conk out 397.15 *die,* 683.9 *malfunction,* 844.24 *go wrong*

con man 474.6 *sophist,* 539.17 *cheat,* 540.15 *false person,* 548.3 *deceiver,* 657.3 *cunning person,* 736.11 *dishonest person,* 753.5 *overcharger,* 832.8 *malefactor,* 858.4 *dishonourable person*
Connacht 92 Counties
connatural 114.7 *similar*
connect 137, 64.35 *conduct,* 107.7 *relate to,* 135.10 *link,* 140.5 *combine,* 159.15 *concatenate,* 161.44 *put together,* 219.3 *continue,* 267.3 *juxtapose,* 407.12 *abut,* 823.19 *merge*
connected 137, 107.4 *related,* 114.7 *similar,* 116.11 *allied,* 135.12 *united,* 140.7 *combined,* 161.48 *cumulate,* 219.5 *continual,* 327.15 *accessible*
connectedness 107.1 *relatedness,* 138.1 *adhesion,* 219.1 *continuity*
Connecticut 92 American States, **96** Rivers
connecting 267.5 *juxtaposed,* 327.15 *accessible,* 407.9 *touching*
connecting rod 71 Motor Vehicle Parts
connection 137, 107.1 *relatedness,* 135.1 *union,* 138.1 *adhesion,* 161.33 *putting together,* 219.1 *continuity,* 267.1 *juxtaposition,* 407.6 *contiguity,* 420.9 *audio device,* 821.5 *desire,* 823.2 *alliance,* 875.5 *drug pusher*
Connection 137
connections 42 Card Games
connective 137, 135.14 *conjunctive,* 137.4 *means of connection,* 138.9 *adhesive*
connectively 135.16 *as one,* 137.17 *in connection with*
connective tissue 137.6 *line*
connect together 148.13 *make*
connect up 159.15 *concatenate*
connect with 135.10 *link*
conned 515.10 *deceived*
Connemara 32 Breeds of Horse and Pony, **93** Cities
conning 6.8 *learning,* 539.7 *tricking,* 539.34 *deceiving*
conning tower 435.9 *viewpoint*
conniption 828.4 *anger*
connivance 539.7 *tricking,* 664.8 *conferring,* 708.1 *permission*
connive 539.28 *trick,* 664.15 *concur,* 708.3 *permit,* 839.11 *condone*
connivent 342.8 *advancing*
conniving 539.34 *deceiving,* 664.19 *associating,* 708.8 *permitting*
connivingly 708.9 *with permission*
connoisseur 165.14 *specialist,* 350.18 *eater,* 405.3 *pleasure-seeker,* 411.5 *taster,* 481.6 *discriminating person,* 485.8 *qualified person,* 492.5 *judge,* 655.5, 688.11 *expert,* 794.4 *refined person*
connoisseurship 6.11 *refinement,* 50.5 *artistry,* 481.2 *judiciousness,* 794.1 *elegance*
Connors 18 Sporting Personalities
connotation 520.1 *meaning,* 520.4 *type of meaning,* 524.1 *interpretation,* 527.10 *quietness,* 543.1 *sign*
connotative 520.6 *meaningful,* 543.14 *signifying*
connote 520.10 *mean,* 527.14 *imply,* 543.10 *signify*
connubial 823.20 *matrimonial*
connubially 823.24 *matrimonially*
conquer 679, 682.9 *be victorious,* 696.14 *master,* 701.7 *defeat*
conquer a mountain 95.10 *climb a mountain*
conquering 701.10 *dominating,* 734.1 *taking*
conqueror 679.6 *militarist,* 682.5 *victorious person*

conquest 682.2 *victory,* 701.2 *domination,* 821.9 *lover*
conquistador 679.6 *militarist*
conquor 734.7 *take*
conquoring 701.2 *domination*
Conrad 48 Writers
consanguine 107.4 *related*
consanguinely 107.10 *relevantly*
consanguineous 107.4 *related*
consanguineously 107.10 *relevantly*
consanguinity 1.5 *anthropological concept,* 107.1 *relatedness*
conscience 586.11 *motive,* 636.1 *warning,* 847.4 *sense of duty,* 857.1 *probity,* 876.2 *good morals*
conscience money 729.2 *gift*
conscience-smitten 867.6 *penitent*
conscience-stricken 866.6 *appearing guilty,* 867.6 *penitent*
conscientious 719.7 *observant,* 847.8 *dutiful,* 857.4 *honourable*
conscientiously 719.8 *observantly,* 857.7 *honourably*
conscientious objection 693.1 *disobedience*
conscientious objector 498.5 *disbeliever,* 500.5 *dissenter,* 668.4 *defiant person,* 669.5 *resister,* 675.3, 677.3 *pacifist,* 711.4 *refuser,* 713.4 *protester*
conscious 403, 368.11 *internal,* 396.12 *alive,* 501.8 *knowledgeable,* 759.10 *feeling*
consciously 11.25 *occultly,* 368.14 *subjectively,* 501.15 *knowledgeably*
conscious mind 61.21 *psyche*
conscious money 735.2 *compensation*
consciousness 368.6 *internal world,* 403.1 *sensation,* 459.1 *mind,* 501.1 *knowledge,* 759.1 *feeling*
consciousness raising 61.3 *psychiatric treatment*
consciousness-raising 586.5 *propaganda*
conscious of one's place 849.9 *showing respect*
conscious self 61.21 *psyche*
conscript 17.10 *enlist,* 676.11 *recruit,* 676.12 *go to war,* 679.8 *soldier,* 695.7 *force,* 701.3 *subordinate,* 703.7 *engage*
conscriptless 679.15 *army*
conscripted 17.9 *enlisted,* 676.15 *warring,* 679.35 *martial*
conscripting 17.1 *military affairs*
conscription 17.1 *military affairs,* 676.7 *war measures,* 695.3 *coercive methods,* 703.2 *engagement*
consecrate 7.21 *ordain,* 8.17 *deify,* 688.21 *grant authority,* 710.16 *make an offering,* 729.5 *give*
consecrated 8.15 *deified,* 10.21 *ritualistic,* 710.19 *sacrificial*
consecrated elements 10.6 *Eucharist*
consecrate to 599.1 *use*
consecration 8.9 *deification,* 10.6 *Eucharist,* 688.3 *acquisition of power,* 710.6, 729.3 *offering*
consecution 159, 155.1 *sequence*
consecutive 159, 155.15 *sequential,* 195.12 *succeeding,* 212.3 *frequent*
consecutively 159, 155.27 *in sequence,* 195.14 *in succession,* 212.1 *frequently*
consecutiveness 159, 155.1 *sequence,* 212.4 *frequency*
Consecutiveness 159
consensual 715.7 *contractual*
consensually 715.8 *contractually*
consensus 112.3 *agreement,* 116.1 *accord,* 499.1 *assent,* 664.2 *fellowship,* 667.1 *agreement*
consent 116, 116, 167.8 *comply,* 453.15 *green light,* 499.1 *assent,* 572.6 *willingness,* 572.13

be willing, 586.18 *be persuaded,* 667.1 *agreement,* 667.6 *agree with,* 673.1 *submission,* 673.3 *submit,* 694.5 *obey,* 708.1 *permission,* 708.3 *permit,* 715.1 *contract,* 851.1 *approval,* 851.12 *accept*
consentaneity 116.1 *accord*
consentaneous 116.10 *in accord,* 116.17 *consenting*
consenter 499.3 *assenter*
consentient 116.10 *in accord,* 116.17 *consenting*
consenting 116, 116.10 *in accord,* 499.6 *assenting,* 572.1 *willing,* 667.10 *agreeing*
consentingly 116.39 *with consent*
consenting party 715.4 *contractor*
consent to 499.4 *assent*
consequence 155, 157.12 *end result,* 159.4 *repercussion,* 195.9 *sequel,* 227.1 *effect,* 243.3 *product,* 611.1, 772.6 *importance*
consequences 42 Children's Games and Party Games
consequent 155, 195.12 *succeeding,* 227.10 *caused*
consequential 155.18 *consequent,* 159.10 *repercussive,* 227.10 *caused,* 520.7 *significant,* 611.5 *important*
consequentialism 4.7 *school of thought*
consequentialist 4.11 *follower of a doctrine,* 4.14 *of a philosophy*
consequentially 227.12 *with the effect of,* 611.9 *importantly*
consequently 155, 106.15 *under the circumstances,* 116.36 *accordingly,* 227.12 *with the effect of*
consequent upon 227.10 *caused*
conservancy 217.1 *permanence,* 637.1 *preservation*
conservation 59.18 *ecology,* 85.5 *forestry,* 136.2 *setting apart,* 217.1 *permanence,* 605.4 *storage,* 606.1 *provision,* 637.1 *preservation,* 804.1 *right*
conservational 637.6 *preserving*
conservation area 637.1 *preservation*
conservation campaign 637.2 *preserver*
conservationism 453.16 *green politics*
conservationist 217, 76.10 *animal welfarist,* 453.7 *environmental,* 637.4 *preservationist*
conservation of charge 56.50 *electric charge*
conservation of energy 56.11 *energy*
conservation of mass 56.9 *mass*
conservation of mass and energy 56.11 *energy*
conservatism 217, 167.4 *conventionalism,* 584.6 *procedure*
conservative 217, 116.15 *conventional,* 167.14 *conformist,* 217.3 *conservative person,* 312.4 *traditional,* 312.9 *straight person,* 495.4 *underestimating,* 542.12 *understated,* 577.4 *set,* 577.8 *obstinate person,* 584.8 *creature of habit,* 637.6 *preserving,* 661.15 *inhibitive,* 663.9 *opposer,* 663.22 *uncooperative,* 669.5 *resister,* 669.11 *obstinate,* 693.12 *reactionary,* 781.4 *cautious*
Conservative 7.16 *denominational,* 12.9 *governmental,* 217.3 *conservative person,* 665.6 *political party member,* 665.10 *political*
conservative attitude 217.2 *conservatism*
conservative estimate 495.1 *underestimation,* 542.1 *understatement*
Conservative Judaism 7 Non-Christian Religions

conservatively 217, 495.6 *pessimistically*, 542.23 *unobtrusively*, 637.8 *preservatively*, 661.18 *inhibitively*, 669.14 *resistingly*
conservativeness 542.1 *understatement*, 661.5 *inhibition*
Conservative Party 12.6 *political party*, 665.3 *political grouping*
conservative person 217
conservative politics 217.2 *conservatism*
conservative treatment 60.8 *treatment*
conservator 217.4 *conservationist*, 632.3 *protector*, 637.4 *preservationist*
conservatory 6.12 *educational institution*, 69.4 *nursery*, 256.7 *room*, 408.8 *hot place*, 442.8 *transparent thing*
conserve 45.42 *preserve*, 136.10 *set apart*, 217.6 *make permanent*, 414.2 *sweetener*, 605.6 *store*, 625.6 *make hygienic*, 632.9 *protect*, 637.3 *preserved thing*, 637.5 *preserve*, 756.5 *be thrifty*
conserved 217.7 *permanent*, 605.7 *stored*, 637.7 *preserved*
conserving 637.6 *preserving*, 756.4 *thrifty*
consider 4.20 *philosophize*, 4.22 *propound a philosophy*, 435.16 *visualize*, 461.12 *think*, 467.10 *be attentive*, 473.14 *discuss*, 492.12 *estimate*, 497.8 *be of the opinion*, 611.8 *make important*, 849.18 *show respect*
considerable 181.6 *many*, 259.15 *big*, 369.1 *heavy*, 611.5 *important*
considerably 259.20 *largely*, 611.9 *importantly*
considerate 461.8 *thoughtful*, 467.9 *solicitous*, 662.35 *benevolent*, 691.4 *lenient*, 817.7 *courteous*, 831.6 *benevolent*, 849.8 *respectful*, 859.5 *unselfish*
considerately 662.38 *benevolently*, 691.6 *leniently*, 817.14 *courteously*, 817.15 *genteelly*, 831.10 *benevolently*, 859.9 *unselfishly*
considerateness 859.2 *unselfishness*
consideration 469, 4.4 *philosophical investigation*, 223.1 *exchange*, 435.4 *visualization*, 459.6, 461.3 *thoughtfulness*, 467.1 *attention*, 467.5 *solicitude*, 473.2 *logical argument*, 473.5 *plea*, 492.1 *judgment*, 568.6 *interview*, 611.1 *importance*, 691.1 *leniency*, 729.2 *gift*, 817.1 *courtesy*, 831.1 *benevolence*, 849.1 *respect*, 859.2 *unselfishness*, 878.6 *compensation*
considered 582.4 *deliberate*
considering 492, 146.7 *including*
consider the pros and cons 568.11 *confer*
consign 70.4 *transport*, 326.11 *transfer*, 326.12 *transport*, 567.10 *send*, 703.6 *commission*, 706.4 *delegate*, 728.3 *transfer property*, 729.5 *give*
consignable 326.17 *transferable*, 728.5 *transferring*
consignation 706.3 *delegation*
consigned 70.5 *transportable*, 706.7 *decentralized*
consignee 70.3 *transporter*, 653.15 *manager*, 730.5 *recipient*, 738.12 *purchaser*, 741.18 *treasurer*
consignment 70.2 *thing transported*, 326.10 *transferred thing*, 728.1 *transfer of property*, 729.1 *giving*
consignor 739.9 *seller*
consign to earth 399.8 *bury*
consign to oblivion 512.13 *forget*
consistency 52.64 *reasoning*, 110.6 *regularity*, 112.1 *uniformity*, 116.5 *conformity*, 166.7 *uniformity*, 167.1 *conformity*, 214.4 *orderliness*, 225.1 *stability*, 308.3 *evenness*, 371.1 *density*, 383.1 *texture*, 407.1 *touch*, 667.3 *compatibility*
consistent 52.86 *logical*, 110.17 *regular*, 112.5 *uniform*, 116.14 *conforming*, 166.11 *uniform*, 167.12 *conforming*, 214.11 *regular*, 214.14 *orderly*, 225.9 *stable*, 308.5 *even*, 371.6 *dense*, 667.12 *compatible*
consistently 116, 112.13 *uniformly*, 167.17 *conformingly*, 214.15 *regularly*, 214.17 *orderly*, 225.12 *stably*, 667.16 *compatibly*
consist in 148.12 *be one of*
consisting of 146.7 *including*
consist of 148, 146.4 *include*
consistory 653.7 *council*
consociation 815.1 *sociability*
consolation 620.6 *imperfect item*, 767.1 *ease*, 835.2 *condolence*
consolation prize 681.1 *trophy*, 878.2 *prize*
console 43 Architectural Decoration, 65.7 *peripheral*, 767.9 *relieve*, 835.9 *sorrow*
consoled 767.7 *relieved*
consoler 767.3 *reliever*
console table 47.4 *table*
consolidate 54.62 *lithify*, 135.8 *unite*, 138.6 *adhere*, 140.5 *combine*, 371.8 *be dense*, 562.9 *compile*, 664.16 *join*, 823.19 *merge*
consolidated 54.56 *petrographic*, 282.9 *flattened*, 371.7 *condensed*
consolidated snow 55.30 *snow*
consolidation 54.29 *petrogenesis*, 135.1 *union*, 138.1 *adhesion*, 371.2 *concentration*, 664.7 *association*, 823.2 *alliance*
consoling 767.8 *relieving*, 835.6 *pitying*
consol system 74.5 *navigation*
consommé 45.13 *soup*
consonance 48.11 *rhyme*, 48.12 *poetic language*, 116.4 *harmony*, 433.3 *melodiousness*
consonancy 116.4 *harmony*
consonant 5.16 *spoken letter*, 116.13 *harmonious*, 167.12 *conforming*, 433.7 *harmonious*
consonantal 5.41 *lettered*
consort 180.12 *partner*, 823.10 *married man*
consortial 665.8 *leagued*
consorting 815.1 *sociability*
consortium 116.2 *alliance*, 140.3 *assembly*, 664.7 *association*, 665.1 *party*, 715.3 *alliance*
consortship 180.3 *companionship*
consort with 180.14 *keep company with*, 815.11 *be sociable*
conspectus 142.3 *whole situation*, 270.3 *shortened version*, 562.1 *summary*
conspicuous 318, 435.23, 437.1 *visible*, 457.7 *appearing*, 526.14 *manifest*, 611.6 *notable*
conspicuous consumption 599.6 *use*, 757.4 *extravagance*
Conspicuous Gallantry Medal 17 British Military Medals and Decorations
conspicuously 318.10 *protuberantly*, 435.25, 437.11 *visibly*, 526.16 *manifestly*
conspicuousness 318, 437.3 *visibility*, 526.10 *manifestation*
conspiracy 116.2 *alliance*, 140.2 *cooperation*, 529.2 *secretiveness*, 539.7 *tricking*, 592.4 *plot*, 642.9 *overactivity*, 657.1 *cunning*, 664.8 *conferring*, 693.3 *subversion*
conspirational 529.10 *secretive*
conspirator 531.7 *concealer*, 539.20 *plotter*, 592.8 *planner*, 657.3 *cunning person*, 664.10 *cooperator*, 693.10 *seditionist*
conspiratorial 116.11 *allied*, 140.8 *cooperative*, 539.35 *deceptive*, 592.15 *planning*, 664.19 *associating*, 693.14 *subversive*, 715.7 *contractual*
conspiratorially 592, 116.32 *in alliance*, 140.10 *in combination*, 529.16 *stealthily*, 693.18 *subversively*, 715.8 *contractually*
conspire 116.22 *form an alliance*, 140.6 *come together*, 539.28 *trick*, 592.13 *plot*, 657.5 *be cunning*, 664.15 *concur*, 693.16 *be subversive*
conspirer 539.20 *plotter*
conspire with 305.9 *side with*
conspiring 116.11 *allied*, 657.4 *cunning*
constable 16.17 *police officer*, 688.10 *person of authority*, 696.3 *leader*
constabulary 16.14 *police*
Constan 93 Cities
constance 214.4 *orderliness*
Constance 94 Lakes
constancy 575, 110.6 *regularity*, 112.1 *uniformity*, 116.5 *conformity*, 159.5 *continuity*, 166.7 *uniformity*, 188.4 *long-lastingness*, 212.4 *frequency*, 214.4 *orderliness*, 217.1 *permanence*, 219.1 *continuity*, 225.1 *stability*, 537.9 *uniformity*, 574.15 *will*, 694.2 *loyalty*, 819.3 *familiarity*, 857.1 *probity*
constant 52.25 *algebraic expression*, 52.77 *given*, 110.17 *regular*, 112.5 *uniform*, 116.14 *conforming*, 159.11 *continuous*, 166.11 *uniform*, 169.1 *number*, 183.14 *recurrent*, 184.3 *eternal*, 185.21 *lasting through time*, 190.10 *continuing forever*, 212.3 *frequent*, 214.11 *regular*, 214.14 *orderly*, 217.7 *permanent*, 219.5 *continual*, 225.4 *stable thing*, 225.9 *stable*, 444.10 *coloured*, 537.22 *uniform*, 574.5, 575.11 *steady*, 584.14 *habituated*, 694.8 *loyal*, 719.7 *observant*, 819.11 *devoted*, 857.4 *honourable*
constantan 57 Alloys
constant companion 180.12 *partner*
constant flow 159.5 *continuity*
Constantine 18 Sporting Personalities, **93** Cities
constantly 110.20 *regularly*, 112.13 *uniformly*, 116.35 *consistently*, 159.19 *continuously*, 184.12 *eternally*, 212.1 *frequently*, 214.15 *regularly*, 214.17 *orderly*, 217.9 *permanently*, 219.7 *continually*, 225.12 *stably*, 694.10 *obediently*, 719.8 *observantly*, 819.19 *devotedly*, 857.7 *honourably*
constant supply 605.3 *supply*, 606.1 *provision*
constellation 53, 161.28 *cluster*
consternation 766.1 *dissatisfaction*, 777.2 *fearfulness*, 786.1 *wonder*
constipate 323.8 *stop*, 371.8 *be dense*, 726.7 *detain*
constipated 323.13 *stopped*, 371.7 *condensed*, 726.9 *retentive*
constipating 371.7 *condensed*
constipation 777 Phobias by Topic, 323.1 *closure*, 353.2 *defecation*, 371.2 *concentration*, 624.8 *indigestion*, 726.5 *retentiveness*
constituency 92.1 *administrative area*, 249.5 *state*, 580.12 *election*
constituent 92.6 *administrative*, 103.7 *integral*, 143.4 *component*, 146.2 *thing included*, 146.8 *included*, 148.1, 148.6 *component*, 257.10 *containing*, 367.4 *matter*, 580.13 *electorate*
constituently 148
constituents 257.1 *contents*, 604.1 *materials*
constitute 103.12 *embody*, 146.4 *include*, 148.10 *compose*, 243.10 *produce*, 257.8 *embody*
constituted 257.10 *containing*
constituted authority 688.1 *authority*
constituting 146.1 *inclusion*, 148.9 *composing*
constitution 12.5 *political organization*, 16.1 *the law*, 103.4 *nature*, 146.1 *inclusion*, 166.2 *canon*, 257.1 *contents*, 382.3 *form*, 383.1 *texture*, 623.3 *health*, 654.3 *precept*
Constitution 845.3 *prerogative*
constitutional 12.9 *governmental*, 16.46 *legislated*, 103.8 *quintessential*, 290.11 *intrinsic*, 584.3 *way*, 625.1 *hygiene*, 688.14 *governmental*, 698.9 *free*
constitutional anthropology 1.10 *measurement*
constitutional government 12.1 *government*, 688.7 *type of rule*
constitutional history 3.1 *history*
constitutionalism 12.1 *government*, 16.31 *legislation*
constitutionality 16.31 *legislation*
constitutional law 16.1 *the law*
constitutionally 12.14 *politically*, 688.24 *ministerially*
constitutional monarchy 12.1 *government*, 688.7 *type of rule*
constitutional psychology 61.1 *psychology*
constitutional rights 698.2 *free speech*, 845.3 *prerogative*
constrain 242.4 *moderate*, 302.7 *limit*, 542.22 *play down*, 695.6 *compel*, 695.7 *force*, 699.8 *restrain*, 701.7 *defeat*
constrained 542.15 *reserved*, 542.19 *downplayed*, 699.13 *restraining*, 810.13 *reserved*
constraining 695.9 *compelling*
constrain oneself 869.5 *be self-restrained*
constraint 302.1 *limitation*, 542.5 *reserve*, 542.9 *down-playing*, 571.3 *lack of choice*, 695.2 *coercion*, 699.1 *restraint*, 701.1 *subjection*, 810.6 *reserve*, 869.1 *self-restraint*
constrict 135.8 *unite*, 242.4 *moderate*, 262.5 *make smaller*, 272.10 *narrow*, 323.8 *stop*, 699.8 *restrain*
constricted 262.7 *smaller*, 272.1 *narrow*, 323.13 *stopped*
constricting 262.8 *contracting*
constriction 262.1 *contraction*, 272.5 *narrowness*, 323.1 *closure*, 371.2 *concentration*, 699.1 *restraint*
constrictive 262.8 *contracting*, 371.6 *dense*, 699.13 *restraining*
constrictively 371.10 *densely*
constrictor 79 Reptiles, 79.3 *snake*, 262.4 *contractor*
constringe 262.5 *make smaller*
constringency 262.1 *contraction*
constringent 262.8 *contracting*
construct 382, 43.18 *be an architect*, 52.96 *represent*, 63.30 *engineer*, 144.4 *complete*, 148.13 *make*, 161.44 *put together*, 243.10 *produce*, 275.18 *erect*, 306.7 *form*, 382.6 *construction*, 471.1 *idea*, 796.8 *fashion*
constructed 306.9 *formed*
construction 243, 382, 52.49 *geometric construction*, 63.17 *civil engineering*, 63.19 *structure*, 146.1 *inclusion*, 161.33 *putting together*, 243.2 *manufacture*, 306.1 *form*, 306.4 *forming*, 518.3 *conjecture*, 520.4 *type of meaning*, 524.1 *interpretation*
constructional 63.32, 382.11 *structural*
constructionally 43.20 *architecturally*, 63.33, 382.18 *structurally*
construction engineering 63.17 *civil engineering*
construction equipment 63
constructionism 382.9 *artistic structure*
construction material 63
construction site 617.1 *workshop*
construction worker 646.1 *worker*
constructive 243.11 *productive*, 483.8 *evidential*, 524.14 *interpretive*, 662.33 *helpful*

constructive criticism 492.1 *judgment*, 654.1 *advice*, 662.2 *support*
constructively 148.14 *constituently*, 306.13 *formatively*, 662.36 *helpfully*
constructivism 50 *Western Art Styles and Movements*, 51.8 *theatre movements*
constructivist 50.29 *realist*, 51.40 *activist*
constructor 243.9 *producer*
construe 4.21 *rationalize*, 524.8 *interpret*
construing 5.30 *syntax*
consubstantial 110.12 *same*
consubstantiality 110.1 *sameness*
consubstantially 110.18 *identically*
consubstantiate 110.8 *make the same*
consubstantiation 10.6 *Eucharist*, 110.1 *sameness*
consuetude 584.5 *tradition*
consul 653.16 *official*, 688.10 *person of authority*, 696.3 *leader*, 703.5 *commissioner*, 706.1 *delegate*, 707.3 *agent*
consular 706.6 *delegated*, 707.7 *deputizing*
consular agent 707.3 *agent*
consulate 256.4 *official residence*, 688.5 *position of authority*, 706.2 *representative body*
consulate service 706.2 *representative body*
consul general 688.10 *person of authority*, 696.3 *leader*
consul-general 707.3 *agent*
consult 654, 60.19 *practise medicine*, 568.11 *confer*
consultant 4.12 *sage*, 60.11 *doctor*, 60.13 *medical specialist*, 165.14 *specialist*, 485.8 *qualified person*, 517.9 *forecaster*, 654.4 *adviser*, 655.5 *expert*, 662.14 *adviser*, 678.4 *representative*, 688.11, 696.10 *expert*
consultation 654, 568.4 *conference*, 594.9 *preparation*, 664.8 *conferring*
consultative 568.13 *discussing*, 654.7 *advising*
consultative assembly 653.10 *legislative body*
consultative body 653.7 *council*, 654.4 *adviser*
consultatory 568.13 *discussing*
consulting room 60.10, 630.14 *hospital*
consult the Ouija board 516.1 *foresee*
consumable 350.27 *edible*, 599.10 *usable*
consumably 350.29 *edibly*
consumate liar 539.16 *liar*
consume 244, 748, 141.3 *disintegrate*, 236.7 *remove power from*, 350.21 *eat*, 593.9 *find necessary*, 599.1 *use*, 599.5 *dispose of*, 607.1 *waste*, 628.5 *hurt*, 722.9 *lose*, 734.7 *take*
consumed 599.9 *used*
consumed with jealousy 841.4 *jealous*
consumer 13.9 *economist*, 59.18 *ecology*, 350.18 *eater*, 599.8 *user*, 738.12 *purchaser*
consumer confidence 13.6 *economic factors*
consumer consumption 593.2 *need*
consumer demand 593.2 *need*, 738.11 *custom*
consumer durables 739.8 *merchandise*
consumer goods 13.2 *economy*, 739.8 *merchandise*
consumer questionnaire 739.7 *market*
consuming 244.14 *destructive*, 350.1 *eating*, 618.5 *harmful*
consummate 103.8 *quintessential*, 144.7 *complete*, 157.15 *end*, 279.5 *top*, 619.1, 619.5 *perfect*, 684.4 *complete*, 684.7 *completed*, 696.13 *excellent*

consummate a marriage 135.11 *make love*
consummated 684.7 *completed*
consummate liar 538.11 *liar*
consummately 619.7 *perfectly*, 684.9 *completely*, 696.16 *masterfully*
consummate one's marriage 823.15 *marry*
consummation 135.4 *sexual union*, 144.1 *completeness*, 144.3 *completion*, 619.3 *perfection*, 684.1 *completion*, 821.5 *desire*
consummative 157.20 *ending*, 684.7 *completed*
consummatory 157.20 *ending*
consumption 129.1 *decrease*, 262.1 *contraction*, 348.4 *intake*, 350.1 *eating*, 593.2 *need*, 599.6 *use*, 607.3 *waste*, 618.11 *harmfulness*, 624.6 *infection*, 624.9 *respiratory disease*, 734.1 *taking*
consumptive 262.7 *smaller*, 624.19 *sick person*, 624.23 *diseased*
contact 2.15 *socialize*, 135.1 *union*, 135.10 *link*, 137.3 *associate*, 137.13 *intercommunicate*, 267.1 *juxtaposition*, 298.4 *interface*, 326.3 *transmission*, 407.11 *touch*, 407.12 *abut*, 528.10 *informer*, 707.3 *agent*
contact again 590.13 *follow up*
contact herbicide 68.14 *pest control*
contact insecticide 68.14 *pest control*
contact lenses 56.29 *optical element*, 435.10, 435.10 *visual aid*
contact metamorphism 54.32 *metamorphism*
contact print 66.12 *development*, 110.4 *duplicate*
contacts 435.10 *visual aid*
contact sport 18.4 *sporting activity*
contagion 133.1 *mixture*, 233 *influence*, 326.3 *transmission*, 624.5 *plague*, 624.6 *infection*, 626.2 *germ*, 628.10 *impairment*, 631.7 *poisoning*
contagious 626, 233.12 *appealing*, 326.17 *transferable*, 624.23 *diseased*
contagious disease 326.10 *transferred thing*, 624.4 *disease*, 628.10 *impairment*
contagiously 133.14 *in the midst*, 233.14 *influentially*, 326.18 *in transit*, 626.8 *unhygienically*
contagiousness 624.6 *infection*, 626.1 *lack of hygiene*
contagium 626.2 *germ*
contain 257, 146.4 *include*, 148.11 *consist of*, 248.20 *extend*, 290.15 *keep inside*, 293.32 *include*, 297.7 *surround*, 301.6 *wrap*, 302.7 *limit*, 323.7 *close*, 472.10 *focus on*, 726.7 *detain*
contained 258.20 *containing*, 726.10 *retained*
container 258, 70.2 *thing transported*, 70.5 *transportable*, 301.4 *wrapper*, 326.10 *transferred thing*, 605.4 *storage*
Container 258
containerful 120
containerization 70.1 *transport*
containerize 257.6 *contain*, 258.21 *put in a container*
containerload 257.2 *load*
containing 257, 258, 146.7 *including*, 148.9 *composing*, 257.11 *loaded*
containment 146.1 *inclusion*, 302.1 *limitation*, 726.2 *detention*
contaminant 147.6 *thing excluded*, 149.2 *impurity*, 631.9 *pollution*
contaminate 82.16 *infest*, 133.8 *mix*, 133.10 *become mixed*, 233.9 *change*, 326.11 *transfer*,

614.8 *make useless*, 618.13 *be worthless*, 622.11 *dirty*, 628.3 *make worse*, 631.15 *poison*
contaminated 415.6 *unpalatable*, 622.8 *unclean*, 624.23 *diseased*, 626.6 *contagious*
contaminating 618.5 *harmful*
contamination 133.1 *mixture*, 326.3 *transmission*, 618.10 *poverty*, 622.2 *uncleanness*, 628.10 *impairment*, 631.9 *pollution*
contaminator 326.9 *disease carrier*
contango 752.1 *discount*
contemplate 4.20 *philosophize*, 6.23 *learn*, 9.7 *worship*, 435.16 *visualize*, 461.13 *concentrate*, 513.8 *expect*, 520.10 *mean*, 588.7 *intend*, 714.11 *promise oneself*
contemplated 513.7 *expected*
contemplation 4.4 *philosophical investigation*, 6.8 *learning*, 9.1 *worship*, 325.2 *repose*, 435.4 *visualization*, 461.3 *thoughtfulness*, 513.1 *expectation*
contemplative 4.17 *thoughtful*, 6.18 *educated*, 9.9 *worshipful*, 325.6 *quiescent*, 461.9 *concentrating*, 497.5 *believer*
contemplatively 4.28 *thoughtfully*, 6.26 *studiously*, 9.12 *worshipfully*, 461.18 *thoughtfully*
contemporaneity 180.2 *synchronism*, 198.1 *same time*, 201.1 *newness*
contemporaneous 180.18 *concurrent*, 196.6 *present*, 198.9 *simultaneous*
contemporaneously 180.23 *concurrently*, 198.12 *simultaneously*
contemporaneousness 198.1 *same time*
contemporarily 198.12 *simultaneously*, 201.21 *newly*
contemporariness 198.1 *same time*
contemporary 198, 180.18 *concurrent*, 196.6 *present*, 198.9 *simultaneous*, 201.10 *new*, 472.6 *topical*
contemporary life 196.2 *the present day*
contempt 807, 850, 668.2 *disobedience*, 720.1 *nonobservance*, 766.1 *dissatisfaction*, 805.11 *prejudice*, 807.8 *rudeness*, 852.2 *disrespect*, 854.5 *scorn*
contemptibility 612.6 *obscurity*, 822.4 *hatefulness*
contemptible 612.2 *obscure*, 618.4 *poor*, 822.12 *hated*, 850.12 *disregardful*, 858.5 *dishonourable*, 862.7 *evil*
contemptibleness 618.10 *poverty*
contemptibly 618.15 *worthlessly*, 822.18 *hatefully*
contemptuous 807, 850, 668.7 *defiant*, 720.11 *nonobservant*, 766.4 *dissatisfied*, 805.23 *prejudiced*, 807.19 *rude*, 822.10 *hating*, 854.17 *scornful*
contemptuously 807, 850, 668.9 *defiantly*, 766.8 *discontentedly*, 822.18 *hatefully*, 854.18 *disparagingly*
contemptuousness 668.2 *disobedience*, 766.1 *dissatisfaction*, 850.3 *contempt*
contend 674, 4.23 *discuss philosophically*, 21.6 *compete in athletics*, 346.14 *enrol*, 472.11 *raise the point*, 617.9 *be worthy*, 663.16 *confront*, 666.5 *disagree*, 676.14 *battle*, 679.40 *argue*
contend against 111.9 *oppose*
contender 674, 18.3 *sportsman*, 237.5 *athlete*, 346.7 *entrant*, 596.7 *attempter*, 663.10 *competitor*, 679.1 *combatant*, 820.5 *hostile person*
contending 674, 663.20 *discordant*
contend with 669.6 *resist*
content 148.1 *component*, 257.1 *contents*, 259.1 *size*, 382.2 *fabric*, 405.7 *pleased*, 405.10 *com-*

fort, 572.1 *willing*, 608.3 *filled*, 608.4 *suffice*, 608.7 *sufficiency*, 649.1 *ease*, 649.4 *at ease*, 677.4 *pacify*, 677.6 *pacificatory*, 765.1 *satisfaction*, 765.4 *satisfied*, 765.8 *satisfy*, 851.18 *approving*
contented 405.7 *pleased*, 608.3 *filled*, 762.4 *happy*, 765.4 *satisfied*, 809.9 *self-satisfied*
contentedly 765.13 *with satisfaction*
contentedness 765.1 *satisfaction*
contenting 608.1 *sufficient*
contention 674, 111.3 *opposition*, 473.3 *line of argument*, 476.2 *denial*, 663.3 *conflict*, 666.1 *disagreement*, 820.1 *enmity*
Contention 674
contentious 674, 16.52 *legalistic*, 111.5 *opposing*, 473.10 *arguable*, 500.7 *dissenting*, 663.20 *discordant*, 666.9 *disagreeing*, 670.21, 820.9 *aggressive*, 829.4 *irascible*
contentiously 674, 111.7 *disapprovingly*, 500.10 *dissentiently*, 666.11 *in disagreement*, 820.15 *aggressively*, 829.9 *irascibly*
contentiousness 666.1 *disagreement*, 829.1 *irascibility*
contentment 405.1 *physical pleasure*, 608.7 *sufficiency*, 649.1 *ease*, 762.1 *happiness*, 765.1 *satisfaction*
contents 257, 70.2 *thing transported*, 146.2 *thing included*, 171.2 *table*, 290.4 *insides*, 472.1 *topic*, 520.1 *meaning*, 725.5 *personal estate*
Contents 257
contermand 709.3 *veto*
conterminous 267.5 *juxtaposed*
contest 42, 674, 4.23 *discuss philosophically*, 16.5 *litigation*, 18.1 *sport*, 21.6 *compete in athletics*, 473.13 *argue*, 477.20 *doubt*, 491.18 *be uncertain*, 536.8 *rebut*, 670.20 *bout*, 674.11 *contend*, 676.14 *battle*
contestability 491.9 *uncertainty*
contestable 491.1 *uncertain*
contest an office 710.13 *be a candidate*
contestant 596.7 *attempter*, 663.10 *competitor*, 674.10 *contender*
contest at law 16.70 *litigate*
contested 16.54 *litigated*, 536.12 *rejected*
contesting 16.53 *litigating*, 536.3 *rebuttal*, 674.14 *contending*
contest with 663.16 *confront*
context 106.1 *circumstances*, 180.4 *concomitant*, 251.2 *circumstances*, 520.1 *meaning*, 520.4 *type of meaning*
contextual 106.7 *circumstantial*, 180.17 *accompanying*, 251.8 *circumstantial*
contextualism 4.7 *school of thought*
contextualist 4.11 *follower of a doctrine*, 4.14 *of a philosophy*
contextually 106.16 *relatively*, 251.12 *circumstantially*
contexture 382.2 *fabric*, 383.1 *texture*
contiguity 407, 135.1 *union*, 191.2 *closeness*, 267.1 *juxtaposition*, 298.1 *interface*
contiguous 264.5 *near*, 267.5 *juxtaposed*, 298.6 *interfacial*, 407.9 *touching*
contiguously 267.7 *beside*, 298.7 *interfacially*
contiguousness 135.1 *union*, 267.1 *juxtaposition*
continence 699.3 *self-restraint*, 825.2 *virginity*, 869.1 *self-restraint*, 876.3 *moral purity*
continent 54, 98, 249.1 *region*, 353.26 *urinary*, 699.14 *self-restrained*, 825.7 *virginal*, 869.8 *self-restrained*, 876.9 *pure*

continental **98**, 54.50 *terrestrial*, 104.10 *foreign*, 249.16 *regional*, 290.9 *inland*
continental breakfast 350.12 *meal*
continental climate 55.38 *climate*
continental crust 54.18 *earth's crust*
continental divide 54.8 *drainage*
Continental Divide 275.4 *mountain range*
continental drift 54.6 *continent*, 54.19 *plate tectonics*
continental glacier 54.38 *glacier*
continental ice sheet 54.38 *glacier*
continental island 98.2 *island*
continentally **98**, 54.66, 249.19 *geographically*
continental margin 54.6 *continent*, 54.11 *ocean floor*
continental quilt 293.10 *bed covering*, 374.11 *soft thing*
continental rise 54.16 *ocean floor*
continental shelf 54.6 *continent*, 54.16 *ocean floor*, 98.4 *coast*, 249.3 *regional boundary*
continental slope 54.16 *ocean floor*
continental zone 55.39 *climatic zone*
continently 825.12 *celibately*
contingency 52.64 *reasoning*, 106.1, 251.2 *circumstances*, 486.1 *possibility*, 513.2 *expectations*, 589.1 *chance*
contingency plan 516.4 *prudence*, 517.3 *plan*, 592.2 *policy*
contingent 52.86 *logical*, 106.7 *circumstantial*, 227.10 *caused*, 251.8 *circumstantial*, 485.12 *conditional*, 589.8 *chance*
contingently 105.9 *conditionally*, 106.16 *relatively*, 227.12 *with the effect of*, 251.12 *circumstantially*, 485.18 *with qualification*
contingents 679.14 *armed forces*
contingent truth 4.8 *philosophical term*
contingent upon 227.10 *caused*
continual **219**, 99.12 *lasting*, 159.11 *continuous*, 183.14 *recurrent*, 184.3 *eternal*, 188.8 *lasting*, 212.3 *frequent*, 214.14 *orderly*, 324.17 *directional*, 575.11 *steady*
continually **219**, **575**, 116.35 *consistently*, 159.19 *continuously*, 183.23 *repeatedly*, 188.12 *everlastingly*, 212.1 *frequently*, 214.17 *orderly*
continual movement 324.10 *regular movement*
continualness 159.5 *continuity*
continuance 99.6 *continuing existence*, 159.5 *continuity*, 186.3 *immutability*, 217.1 *permanence*, 219.1 *continuity*, 575.3 *constancy*
continuation 130.1 *addition*, 155.3 *continuity*, 155.4 *sequel*, 185.3 *duration*, 188.3 *continuity*, 195.1 *succession*, 195.9 *sequel*, 219.1 *continuity*, 293.22 *progression*, 304.1 *rear*, 637.1 *preservation*
continue 159, 219, 99.19 *continue to be*, 112.9 *be uniform*, 132.7 *be left*, 184.9 *be infinite*, 188.7 *go on*, 190.7 *make permanent*, 212.7 *be frequent*, 217.5 *be permanent*, 219.4 *protract*, 269.10 *lengthen*, 293.35 *progress*, 396.16 *live*, 575.7 *maintain*, 590.14 *carry on*, 637.5 *preserve*
continued 304.4 *rear*
continued fraction 52.18 *division*
continue forever 190.5 *be eternal*
continue on 293.35 *progress*
continue the same 110.11 *be regular*
continue the same way 112.12 *be monotonous*
continue to be **99**
continue working 644.6 *work*

continuing 112.5 *uniform*, 145.4 *incomplete*, 188.8 *lasting*, 217.7 *permanent*, 219.5 *continual*, 293.22 *progression*, 336.18 *ongoing*
continuing existence **99**
continuing forever **190**
continuingly 112.13 *uniformly*
continuing on 293.22 *progression*
continuity **155, 159, 188, 219**, 48.3 *aspect of fiction*, 112.1 *uniformity*, 116.5 *conformity*, 138.1 *adhesion*, 186.3 *immutability*, 190.1 *eternity*, 212.4 *frequency*, 214.4 *orderliness*, 217.1 *permanence*, 267.1 *juxtaposition*
Continuity **219**
continuity girl 298.3 *interfacer*
continuity of germ plasm 59.16 *evolution*
continuity person 135.7 *joiner*
continuo 433.3 *melodiousness*
continuous **159, 312**, 52.70 *universal*, 57.32 *solid*, 99.12 *lasting*, 112.5 *uniform*, 116.14 *conforming*, 138.9 *adhesive*, 155.15 *sequential*, 183.14 *recurrent*, 184.3 *eternal*, 186.5 *timeless*, 188.8 *lasting*, 190.10 *continuing forever*, 217.7 *permanent*, 219.5 *continual*, 267.5 *juxtaposed*, 293.41 *progressing*, 324.17 *directional*
continuous beam 63.27 *superstructure*
continuous distortion 52.47 *topology*
continuous distribution 52.59 *probability distribution*
continuous function 52.29 *mathematical function*
continuously **159**, 52.87 *mathematically*, 112.13 *uniformly*, 116.35 *consistently*, 188.12 *everlastingly*, 217.9 *permanently*, 219.7 *continually*, 267.7 *beside*
continuous motion 159.6 *continuum*
continuousness 112.1 *uniformity*, 159.5, 188.3 *continuity*, 214.4 *orderliness*, 219.1 *continuity*
continuous phase 57.3 *phase*
continuous spectrum 56.68 *emission*
continuous-wave radar 534.28 *radar*
continuum **159**, 248.9 *fourth dimension*
contort 309.9 *distort*, 309.10 *make faces*
contorted 314.5 *ambiguous*, 790.4 *ugly*
contortedly 309.13 *asymmetrically*
contortedness 790.1 *hideousness*
contortion 309.1 *distortion*, 309.2 *facial distortion*
contortionist 52.19 *circus performer*, 537.5 *athlete*
contour 52.37 *line*, 299.1 *outline*, 299.2 *shadow*, 306.1 *form*, 457.3 *external appearance*, 767.6 *profile*
contour feather 78.17 *plumage*
contour line 299.1 *outline*
Contra 693.11 *rebel*
contraband 16.36 *stolen property*, 16.59 *stolen*, 709.5 *vetoed*, 736.4 *stolen goods*
contrabass 49 *Musical Instruments*
contrabassoon 49 *Musical Instruments*
contraception 247.3 *birth control*, 630.3 *prophylactic*, 632.2 *protection*
contraceptive 231.2 *counteracting thing*, 231.4 *counteracting*, 247.3 *birth control*
contraceptive injection 247.3 *birth control*
contraceptive pill 247.3 *birth control*, 630.8 *drug*
contraceptive sponge 247.3 *birth control*

contract **597, 667, 667, 715, 715**, 42.3 *card game terms*, 116.3 *arrangement*, 116.23 *arrange*, 129.4 *decrease*, 129.5 *make smaller*, 152.10 *agreement*, 262.5 *make smaller*, 262.6 *become smaller*, 272.10 *narrow*, 299.5 *outline*, 323.8 *stop*, 371.8 *be dense*, 552.4 *be concise*, 562.8 *summarize*, 597.1 *undertake*, 628.1 *deteriorate*, 714.1 *promise*, 714.2 *guarantee*, 714.7 *promise*, 716.2 *basis for negotiations*, 737.3 *bargain*, 737.9 *bargaining*, 845.6 *bond*, 847.7 *commitment*
Contract **715**
contract a disease 624.24 *be unhealthy*
contract a marriage 715.5 *contract*
contract bridge 42 Card Games
contracted 15.8 *industrial*, 260.7 *little*, 262.7 *smaller*, 272.1 *narrow*, 552.3 *concise*, 562.7 *shortened*, 667.11 *contractual*, 714.13 *guaranteeing*, 715.7 *contractual*
contracted thing 262
contractibility 262
contractible 262
contractile 262.9 *contractible*
contractility 262.2 *contractibility*
contracting 262, 15.8 *industrial*, 667.11 *contractual*
contracting party 667.5 *assenter*, 715.4 *contractor*
contraction 262, 129.1 *decrease*, 135.3 *unification*, 272.9 *narrowing*, 299.1 *outline*, 323.1 *closure*, 360.1 *descent*, 552.1 *conciseness*, 562.2 *outline*
Contraction 262
contractional 262.8 *contracting*
contractions 245.7 *obstetrics*
contractive 262.8 *contracting*
contract killer 398.11 *murderer*, 832.8 *malefactor*
contract matrimony 823.15 *marry*
contract murder 398.2 *murder*
contract of employment 15.1 *industrial relations*
contractor 262, **715**, 63.18 *civil engineer*, 243.9 *producer*, 596.7 *attempter*, 640.3 *doer*, 667.5 *assenter*
contract theory of morality 4.9 *philosophical problem*
contractual **667, 715, 737**, 15.8 *industrial*, 116.12 *arranged*, 597.5 *undertaken*
contractually **667, 715**, 15.13 *industrially*, 597.8 *responsibly*
contractual obligations 15.2 *industrial negotiations*
contradict 4.23 *discuss philosophically*, 111.8 *be opposite*, 111.9 *oppose*, 117.14 *disagree*, 473.13 *argue*, 476.9 *deny*, 478.18 *answer back*, 484.7 *counter*, 500.9 *refuse*, 520.10 *mean*, 536.8 *rebut*, 663.15 *object*, 704.9 *cancel out*, 711.6 *dissent*, 713.6 *protest*
contradicter 704.5 *abrogator*
contradicting 536.13 *rebutting*, 852.26 *disagreeing*
contradiction **117**, 52.64 *reasoning*, 111.1 *oppositeness*, 343.1 *divergence*, 476.2 *denial*, 478.5 *counterstatement*, 484.1 *counterevidence*, 536.3 *rebuttal*, 663.2 *objection*, 704.4 *cancelling out*, 711.2 *dissent*, 713.1 *protest*, 852.4 *disagreement*
contradiction in terms 474.2 *sophism*
contradictive 536.11 *negative*, 713.9 *protesting*
contradictively 713.11 *disapprovingly*
contradict oneself 117.12 *be disparate*, 474.11 *practise sophistry*, 484.8 *reverse*

contradictorily 117.16 *disagreeably*, 536.15 *negatively*, 663.23 *opposingly*, 711.11 *uncooperatively*
contradictory **117**, 52.86 *logical*, 343.6 *divergent*, 474.7 *sophistic*, 476.7 *refuting*, 484.5 *countering*, 536.11 *negative*, 587.9 *dissuasive*, 663.21 *contrary*, 711.9 *dissenting*, 852.26 *disagreeing*
contradictory law 16.4 *bad law*
contradictory meaning 520.4 *type of meaning*
contradistinction 663.6 *contrariety*
contraflow 661.2 *obstacle*
contraindicate 484.7 *counter*
contraindication 484.1 *counterevidence*, 587.6 *dissuasion*
contralto 427.3 *deepness*, 433.5 *melodist*
contrapose 111.8 *be opposite*, 125.5 *counterbalance*
contraposed 125.10 *counterbalancing*
contraposing 125.10 *counterbalancing*
contraposition 111.1 *oppositeness*, 125.2 *counterbalance*, 663.6 *contrariety*
contrapositive 111.4 *opposite*
contraption 232.2 *instrument*, 592.3 *expedient plan*, 603.1 *tool*
contrapuntal 49.32 *instrumental*, 116.13 *harmonious*
contrapuntal music 49.3 *classical music*
contraremonstrance 484.1 *counterevidence*
contraremonstrate 484.7 *counter*
contraries 111.1 *oppositeness*
contrariety **663**, 111.1 *oppositeness*, 117.2 *contradiction*, 168.2 *dissent*, 343.1 *divergence*, 578.5 *equivocalness*
contrarily 111.6 *oppositely*, 117.16 *disagreeably*, 231.5 *counter*, 473.18 *arguably*, 484.9 *to the contrary*, 536.15 *negatively*, 661.16 *with delay*, 687.12 *in adversity*, 711.11 *uncooperatively*, 713.11 *disapprovingly*
contrariness **663**, 111.1 *oppositeness*, 536.3 *rebuttal*, 661.1 *hindrance*, 668.1 *defiance*
contrariwise **663**, 109.10 *reciprocally*, 111.4 *opposite*, 111.6 *oppositely*, 287.4 *inversely*
contrary **663**, 111.4 *opposite*, 117.8 *contradictory*, 168.12 *nonconformist*, 231.4 *countering*, 287.1 *inversion*, 434.8 *disagreeing*, 473.8 *argumentative*, 476.7 *refuting*, 484.5 *countering*, 520.6 *meaningful*, 536.3 *rebuttal*, 536.11 *negative*, 577.2 *refractory*, 579.1 *capricious*, 587.9 *dissuasive*, 659.14 *troublesome*, 661.13 *hindering*, 663.19 *oppositional*, 663.22 *uncooperative*, 687.6 *adverse*, 704.10 *cancelled*, 711.9 *dissenting*, 713.9 *protesting*
contrary advice 587.6 *dissuasion*
contrary assertion 536.3 *rebuttal*
contrary to 231.5 *counter*, 663.27 *opposed to*
contrary to expectation 489.9 *unexpectedly*
contrary-to-fact 540.32 *falsified*
contrary to law 16.55 *illegal*, 16.82 *illegally*
contrary to orders 693.17 *disobediently*
contrary to reason 487.1 *impossible*
contrary vote 711.2 *dissent*
contrast 56.23 *light*, 66.8 *composition*, 107.2 *interrelatedness*, 107.7 *relate to*, 111.1 *oppositeness*, 111.8 *be opposite*, 113.1 *diversity*, 113.8 *be diverse*, 115.1 *dissimilarity*, 115.2 *unlikeness*, 115.5 *be dissimilar*, 117.1 *disparity*, 117.12 *be disparate*,

168.1 *nonconformity*, 534.22 *television set*, 663.6 *contrariety*, 663.18 *counteract*
contrasted 663.21 *contrary*
contrasting 111.4 *opposite*, 113.5 *diverse*, 115.4 *dissimilar*, 117.7 *disparate*, 168.11 *nonconforming*, 663.21 *contrary*
contrastingly 115.7 *dissimilarly*, 663.23 *opposingly*
contrastive linguistics 5.1 *linguistics*
contrastively 111.6 *oppositely*
contravallation 671.8 *military defences*
contravene 231.3 *counteract*, 476.9 *deny*, 536.8 *rebut*, 663.15 *object*, 713.6 *protest*, 720.10 *violate the law*
contravened 536.12 *rejected*
contravening 231.4 *counteracting*, 476.7 *refuting*, 711.9 *dissenting*, 720.14 *violating*
contravention 16.38 *lawbreaking*, 231.1 *counteraction*, 476.2 *denial*, 536.3 *rebuttal*, 663.2 *objection*, 713.1 *protest*, 720.4 *infraction*
contredanse 46.4 *historic dancing*
contretemps 211.4 *mishap*, 661.2 *obstacle*
contribute 148.10 *compose*, 234.4 *tend*, 284.13 *support financially*, 664.13 *work together*, 710.16 *make an offering*, 724.4 *have joint possession*, 746.8 *defray*, 748.3 *donate*, 755.11 *give*
contributed 748.12 *expended*
contributes 606.5 *provision*
contribute to 128.5 *make bigger*, 130.6 *add*, 226.12 *determine*, 336.8, 662.28 *further*, 662.29 *finance*, 729.6 *give to charity*
contributing 116.11 *allied*, 233.11 *influential*, 729.1 *giving*
contributing factor 226
contribution 130.3 *additional item*, 226.4 *contributing factor*, 234.1 *tendency*, 284.7 *financial support*, 564.7 *utterance*, 662.6 *financial assistance*, 710.6 *offering*, 724.2 *participation*, 729.1 *giving*, 729.3 *offering*, 746.1 *payment*, 746.4 *grant*, 748.7 *donation*, 755.7 *gift*, 845.5 *dues*
contributor 226, 561.3 *dissertator*, 710.8 *volunteer*, 729.4 *giver*, 755.9 *generous person*
contributory 130.8 *additional*, 233.11 *influential*, 284.9 *supportive*, 662.33 *helpful*, 664.17 *cooperative*, 710.19 *sacrificial*, 729.7 *given*
contributory cause 226.4 *contributing factor*
con trick 736.7 *dishonesty*, 801.3 *disreputable action*, 858.3 *criminality*
contrite 840.4 *atoning*, 866.6 *appearing guilty*, 867.6 *penitent*
contritely 840.8 *penitently*, 866.11 *guiltily*, 867.8 *penitently*
contrite sinner 867.3 *penitent person*
contrition 840.2 *apology*, 866.2 *signs of guilt*, 867.1 *penitence*
contriturate 384.23 *pulverize*
contrivance 48.3 *aspect of fiction*, 232.2 *instrument*, 474.2 *sophism*, 478.6 *solution*, 496.9 *invention*, 539.8 *trick*, 592.3 *expedient plan*, 592.7 *planning*, 602.1 *means*, 603.1 *tool*, 615.3 *convenience*, 638.2 *means of escape*, 652.9 *tactics*, 655.1 *skill*, 657.2 *stratagem*, 858.1 *improbity*
contrive 152.18 *make arrangements*, 226.10 *awaken*, 474.11 *practise sophistry*, 478.20 *solve*, 496.4 *invent*, 539.28 *trick*, 582.2 *premeditate*, 583.3 *improvise*, 592.9 *plan*, 592.11 *invent*, 594.2 *do the groundwork*, 602.6 *find means*, 657.5 *be cunning*
contrive a result 582.2 *premeditate*

contrived 474.7 *sophistic*, 478.14 *solved*, 519.12 *imaginary*, 539.35 *deceptive*, 582.4 *deliberate*, 592.14 *planned*
contriver 592.8 *planner*
contriving 539.34 *deceiving*, 592.15 *planning*, 657.4 *cunning*
control 4.3 *detachment*, 12.3 *governance*, 12.11 *govern*, 126.2 *leadership*, 150.9 *discipline*, 150.22 *pacify*, 166.8 *authority*, 166.16 *direct*, 232.4 *be an instrument*, 233.3 *personal influence*, 233.10 *be a prevailing influence*, 235.1 *power*, 235.10 *be powerful*, 242.1 *moderation*, 242.4 *moderate*, 302.1 *limitation*, 302.7 *limit*, 479.2 *rehearsal*, 485.6 *specification*, 485.16 *specify*, 599.5 *dispose of*, 599.6 *use*, 640.1 *action*, 640.4 *act*, 652.8 *treatment*, 652.14 *behave towards*, 653.1 *manage*, 653.3 *management*, 653.4 *directorship*, 655.1 *skill*, 661.1 *hindrance*, 661.8 *hinder*, 688.1 *authority*, 688.18 *have authority*, 692.3 *authority*, 692.11 *have authority over*, 696.14 *master*, 699.1 *restraint*, 699.8 *restrain*, 701.2 *domination*, 701.7 *defeat*, 723.1 *possession*
control character 65.10 *character*
control column 73 *Aircraft Parts*
controllable 699.13 *restraining*, 701.10 *dominating*
controllably 699.16 *under restraints*
controlled 4.18 *detached*, 25.9 *bowls*, 61.37 *subconscious*, 150.17 *disciplined*, 242.6 *moderate*, 485.12 *conditional*, 582.4 *deliberate*, 699.13 *restraining*
controlled access highway 327.3 *road*
controlled association 61.27 *association of ideas*
controlled-association test 61.5 *psychological test*
controlled blur 66.13 *framing*
controlled nuclear fusion 56.72 *nuclear fission*
controlled shot 25.2 *grip*
controller 12.7 *governor*, 65.17 *computing term*, 242.2 *moderator*, 640.3 *doer*, 653.13 *director*, 696.5 *company leader*, 741.18 *treasurer*
controlling 12.10 *governing*, 166.12 *ruling*, 653.17 *managerial*, 688.12 *authoritative*, 692.15 *self-assured*, 696.12 *masterful*, 699.13 *restraining*, 701.10 *dominating*
controlling body 653.6 *governing body*
control one's appetite 869.5 *be self-restrained*, 871.5 *fast*
control oneself 134.9 *be pure*, 699.10 *restrain oneself*, 863.8 *be virtuous*, 869.5 *be self-restrained*
control one's lusts 869.5 *be self-restrained*
control one's passions 863.8 *be virtuous*
control prices 699.9 *economize*
control results 653.1 *manage*
control rods 56.73 *nuclear reactor*
controls 534.22 *television set*, 653.5 *guide*
control stick 73 *Aircraft Parts*
control surface 73 *Aircraft Parts*
control the purse strings 688.18 *have authority*
control tower 73.4 *airport*
controversial 113.7 *dissenting*, 117.10 *disagreeing*, 473.10 *arguable*, 477.4 *questionable*, 491.1 *uncertain*, 666.9 *disagreeing*, 679.34 *argumentative*, 711.9 *dissenting*
controversialist 473.6, 679.5 *arguer*
controversially 117.16 *disagreeably*, 473.18 *arguably*, 477.24 *questionably*, 491.23 *uncer-*

tainly, 666.11 *in disagreement*, 679.41 *aggressively*, 711.11 *uncooperatively*
controversion 663.2 *objection*
controversy 113.4 *dissension*, 117.4 *disagreement*, 473.1 *argument*, 477.4 *difficult question*, 500.1 *dissent*, 663.2 *objection*, 666.1 *disagreement*, 674.1 *contention*, 711.2 *dissent*
controvert 476.9 *deny*, 491.18 *be uncertain*, 536.8 *rebut*, 663.15 *object*
controvertibility 491.9 *uncertainty*
controvertible 491.1 *uncertain*
contumacious 151.20 *disorderly*, 168.12 *nonconformist*, 577.2 *refractory*, 850.11 *insulting*
contumacy 577.5 *obstinacy*, 668.2 *disobedience*
contumelious 807.13 *insolent*, 850.13 *contemptuous*, 854.17 *scornful*
contumely 168.2 *dissent*, 668.3 *act of defiance*, 807.1 *insolence*, 850.3 *contempt*
conturbation 366.1 *agitation*
contuse 406.11 *inflict pain*
contusion 384.4 *pulverization*, 406.3 *injury*
conundrum 477.4 *difficult question*, 523.12 *unintelligible thing*, 529.4 *brain-teaser*, 578.5 *equivocalness*, 659.4 *problem*
conurbation 93.1 *city*
convalesce 237.7 *be strong*, 623.6 *get healthy*, 627.2 *get better*, 629.4 *be restored*
convalescence 237.4 *strengthening*, 623.3 *health*, 627.5 *improvement*, 629.11 *recuperation*
convalescent 623.1 *healthy*, 626.4 *infectious person*, 629.15 *cured*
convalescent home 60.10, 630.14 *hospital*
convalescing 237.4 *strengthening*
convect 326.11 *transfer*
convection 55.9 *atmospheric process*, 56.36 *heat flow*, 326.3 *transmission*
convection cell 55.10 *air movement*
convection heater 408.3 *heater*
convective 55.43 *atmospheric*
convene 161.42 *call together*
convened 161.46 *assembled*
convener 15.7 *employee*, 161.34 *assembler*
convenience 615, 615, 662, 191.7 *prepared for immediate use*, 210.1 *timeliness*, 253.4 *availability*, 264.1 *nearness*, 353.13 *lavatory*, 594.21 *readymade*, 613.5 *usefulness*, 645.1 *leisure*, 660.3 *wieldiness*
Convenience 615
convenience food 350.7 *food*
conveniences 602.1 *means*
convenience store 740.8 *store*
convenient 615, 203.14 *seasonable*, 210.6 *timely*, 253.10 *available*, 264.5 *near*, 599.9 *used*, 613.1 *useful*, 660.12 *wieldy*, 662.33 *helpful*, 782.8 *desirable*
conveniently 615, 210.9 *opportunely*, 599.11, 613.12 *usefully*, 645.7 *leisurely*, 662.36 *helpfully*
convent 7.10 *priestly dwelling*, 301.2 *enclosed place*, 531.6 *privacy*
conventicle 10.11 *place of worship*, 653.7 *council*
convention 116, 167, 10.1 *ritual*, 116.3 *arrangement*, 161.5 *conference*, 166.6 *custom*, 306.5 *formality*, 555.2 *lack of emphasis*, 568.4 *conference*, 584.5 *tradition*, 653.7 *council*, 654.3 *precept*, 677.1 *pacification*, 706.2 *representative body*, 715.3 *alliance*, 719.3 *performance*, 796.4 *design*, 813.5 *etiquette*, 817.2 *good manners*
conventional 116, 124.1 *average*, 164.21 *common*, 166.10 *customary*, 167.14 *conformist*,

306.11 *formal*, 312.4 *traditional*, 555.1 *unemphatic*, 584.11 *normal*, 719.7 *observant*, 813.6 *formal*, 817.8 *good-mannered*
conventional bombing 670.13 *air attack*
conventionalism 167, 584.6 *procedure*, 813.2 *formalism*
conventionalist 167.6 *conformist*, 584.8 *creature of habit*
conventionality 124.4 *average*, 584.6 *procedure*, 813.1 *formality*, 813.2 *formalism*
conventionalize 116.26 *make uniform*, 120.10 *make average*, 813.9 *formalize*
conventionally 116, 306, 167.19 *according to rule*, 555.3 *unemphatically*, 584.19 *habitually*, 719.8 *observantly*, 813.12 *formally*, 817.15 *genteelly*
conventional medicine 60.1 *medicine*
conventional representation 547.1 *representation*
conventional symbol 543.1 *sign*
conventional weapon 680.1 *weapon*
convention delegate 646.3 *agent*, 706.1 *delegate*
conventions 652.6 *way of life*
convent school 6.12 *educational institution*
conventual 7.7 *monk*, 301.7 *enclosed*
converge 342, 52.97 *align*, 96.7 *flow*, 135.8 *unite*, 140.5 *combine*, 264.9 *near*, 272.10 *narrow*, 291.9 *centre*, 330.2 *collide*, 380.14 *be sharp*, 407.12 *abut*
convergence 342, 96.6 *river flow*, 135.1 *union*, 161.1 *assembly*, 264.1 *nearness*, 272.9 *narrowing*, 291.3 *centrality*, 330.12 *collision*, 407.6 *contiguity*
Convergence 342
convergence zone 54.19 *plate tectonics*
convergent 342, 52.80 *linear*, 96.10 *fluvial*, 161.48 *cumulate*, 264.5 *near*, 272.3 *tapered*, 291.7 *centralized*, 340.10 *magnetic*, 380.1 *sharp*
convergent evolution 59.16 *evolution*
convergently 342, 96.13 *fluently*
convergent series 52.20 *sequence*
convergent strabismus 436.2 *poor sight*
convergent view 342
converge on 291.9 *centre*
converging 264.5 *near*, 291.7 *centralized*, 342.1 *convergence*, 342.7 *convergent*
converging lens 56.29 *optical element*
converging line 342.5 *focus*
converging lines 52.37 *line*
conversableness 815.2 *social ambition*
conversant 584.14 *habituated*
conversant with 6.19, 501.8 *knowledgeable*
conversation 568, 4.5 *philosophical argument*, 420.8 *something heard*, 564.1 *faculty of speech*, 815.1 *sociability*
Conversation 568
conversational 568, 5.39 *of language*, 565.6 *effusive*
conversationalism 5.3 *spoken language*
conversationalist 568, 478.10 *answerer*, 564.10 *speaker*, 815.6 *social person*
conversationally 568, 5.49 *colloquially*, 478.24 *in answer*
conversation piece 50.10 *art subject*
conversation poem 48.7 *poem*
converse 568, 52.64 *reasoning*, 52.86 *logical*, 111.1 *oppositeness*, 111.4 *opposite*, 287.1 *inversion*, 478.19 *react*, 568.1 *conversation*

conversely 111.6 *oppositely*, 287.4 *inversely*
converser 568.7 *conversationalist*
converse with 567.9 *approach*
conversing 568
conversion 220, 19.6 *scoring*, 216.2 *change of mind*, 216.3 *transformation*, 223.1 *exchange*, 578.7 *apostasy*, 599.6 *use*, 627.5 *improvement*, 728.1 *transfer of property*, 867.1 *penitence*
Conversion 220
conversion goal 35.3 *rugby play*
conversion hysteria 61.12 *stress*
conversion neurosis 61.10 *neurosis*
conversion to use 599.6 *use*
convert 220, 7.3 *religious person*, 7.19 *be religious*, 7.20 *preach*, 19.15 *play offence*, 115.6 *differentiate*, 216.7 *be changed*, 216.8 *cause change*, 220.11 *persuade*, 223.5 *exchange*, 497.5 *believer*, 497.9 *make someone believe*, 586.15 *persuade*, 599.3 *exploit*, 627.1 *improve*, 728.3 *transfer property*
convert a try 35.5 *play rugby*
converted 220, 25.10 *bowling*, 35.6 *rugger*, 220.16 *influenced*, 223.7 *exchanged*, 497.11 *believing*, 867.6 *penitent*
converted split 25.5 *bowling delivery*
converter 220, 44.6 *ceramic workshop*, 64.34 *power supply*, 216.5 *changer*
convertibility 220.1 *conversion*, 599.6 *use*
convertible 71 Motor Vehicles, 220, 47.14 *wooden*, 71.16 *car*, 122.6 *equal*, 223.6 *in exchange*, 599.10 *usable*
convertible bond 741.14 *paper money*
convertible sofa 47.6 *bed*
convertibly 220, 599.11 *usefully*
converting 220, 220.1 *conversion*
convert into 220, 220.9 *transform*, 223.5 *exchange*
convertiplane 73 Types of Aircraft
convertive 216.13 *transformative*
convert to use 599.3 *exploit*
convex 316, 52.81 *curvilinear*, 311.4 *curved*, 315.9 *round*
convexity 316, 52.38 *surface*, 311.1 *curvature*, 315.1 *roundness*
Convexity 316
convex lens 56.29 *optical element*
convexly 316, 311.7 *curvedly*, 315.13 *roundly*
convex mirror 56.29 *optical element*
convexness 316.1 *convexity*
convex surface 52.38 *surface*
convey 70.4 *transport*, 324.14 *set in motion*, 326.12 *transport*, 356.11 *cross*, 520.10 *mean*, 528.12 *communicate*, 564.11 *speak*, 652.15 *conduct*, 715.5 *contract*, 728.3 *transfer property*, 729.5 *give*, 739.1 *sell*
conveyable 326.17 *transferable*, 716.8 *negotiated*, 728.5 *transferring*
convey a meaning 520.10 *mean*
convey a message 520.10 *mean*
conveyance 326.2 *transportation*, 326.5 *means of transport*, 728.1 *transfer of property*, 729.1 *giving*, 739.3 *selling*
conveyancer 326.7 *transferor* , 728.2 *person transferring property*
conveyancing 728.1 *transfer of property*
convey an idea 520.10 *mean*
conveyed 728.5 *transferring*
conveyor 63.29 *construction equipment*, 70.3 *transporter*, 326.7 *transferor* , 361.10 *elevator*
conveyor belt 112.2 *conformity*, 159.6 *continuum*, 243.2 *manufacture*, 326.5 *means of transport*

convict 16, 16.40 *lawbreaker*, 699.7 *charge*, 702.5 *prisoner*, 866.4 *guilty person*
convicted 16, 866.5 *guilty*
convicted criminal 866.4 *guilty person*
conviction 16, 490, 7.1 *religion*, 497.1 *belief*, 775.2 *expectation*, 866.1 *guilt*
conviction of guilt 866.1 *guilt*
convict oneself 16
convince 7.20 *preach*, 228.9 *motivate*, 490.21 *make certain*, 497.9 *make someone believe*, 554.6 *emphasize*, 586.15 *persuade*, 765.9 *comfort*
convinced 490, 497.11 *believing*
convinced person 490.11 *opinionist*
convince oneself 518.5 *suppose*
convince to the contrary 587.1 *dissuade*
convincing 228.11 *motivational*, 237.10 *potent*, 497.13 *believable*, 554.3 *emphatic*, 560.11 *descriptive*, 586.19 *persuasive*, 695.9 *compelling*
convincingly 228.14 *influentially*, 237.15 *acutely*, 497.16 *believably*, 586.21 *persuasively*, 695.11 *compellingly*
convivial 405.6 *pleasant*, 769.1 *cheerful*, 812.10 *celebrative*, 815.15 *sociable*
conviviality 405.1 *physical pleasure*, 769.3 *cheerfulness*, 812.1 *celebration*, 815.1 *sociability*
convivially 815.18 *sociably*
convivial person 815.6 *social person*
convocation 161.5 *conference*, 653.7 *council*, 812.3 *ceremony*, 813.3 *formal occasion*
convocational 653.18 *parliamentary*
convoke 161.42 *call together*
convolute 314
convoluted 151.16 *confused*, 286.4 *oblique*, 314.4 *convolutional*, 551.2 *obscure*, 557.4 *ornate*, 659.12 *problematic*
convolutedness 314.1 *convolution*
convoluted thing 314
convolution 314, 52.31 *differentiation*, 170.1 *calculation*, 286.1 *obliqueness*, 551.1, 551.1 *obscurity*, 557.2 *affectation*, 659.1 *difficulty*
Convolution 314
convolutional 314
convolve 314.6 *convolute*
convolvulus 84 Flowers and Flowering Plants
convoy 180.1 *accompaniment*, 180.15 *escort*, 632.2 *protection*, 632.9 *protect*, 679.23 *naval unit*
convulse 153.7 *disturb*, 366.21 *be agitated*, 406.11 *inflict pain*
convulsed 151.17 *discomposed*, 153.12 *disturbed*, 406.7 *feeling pain*
convulsion 153.1 *disturbance*, 241.3 *instance of violence*, 366.8 *spasm*, 406.1 *pain*, 510.3 *mental deterioration*, 828.4 *anger*
convulsive 366, 241.6 *violent*
convulsively 366.29 *jerkily*
convulsive therapy 61.3 *psychiatric treatment*
Conwy 96 Rivers, 96.4 *British rivers*
cony 77 Placental Mammals
coo 432.2 *bird song*, 432.5 *sing*, 564.13 *speak in a particular way*
co-occurrence 180.2 *synchronism*
cook 45, 45, 133.7 *person who mixes*, 350.20 *food provider*, 408.14 *be hot*, 594.7 *develop*, 594.15 *preparer*, 606.4 *caterer*, 646.1 *worker*, 697.6 *domestic servant*
Cook 95 Mountains
cookbook 45.1 *cookery*, 532.6 *book publishing*
cooked 45.56 *culinary*
cooked-up 856.9 *perjurious*

cooked-up charge 856.2 *false accusation*
cooker 45, 56.35 *heat*, 408.4 *burner*
cooker hood 417.2 *deodorant*
cookery 42 Hobbies and Pastimes, 45
Cookery 45
cookery book 45.1 *cookery*, 532.6 *book publishing*
cook for 350.25 *provide food*, 606.5 *provision*
cookhouse 45.3 *kitchen*
cookie 45.2 *cook*, 45.39 *loaf*, 821.12 *nicknames for lovers*, 826.4 *terms of endearment*
cooking 45.1 *cookery*, 594.17 *developing*
cooking equipment 34.4 *climbing equipment*
cooking pot 45.6 *kitchen equipment*, 258.15 *pot*
cooking salt 45.7 *basic ingredient*
cooking smells 419.2 *something that makes an unpleasant smell*
cooking technique 45
cooking utensil 45.6 *kitchen equipment*
Cook Islands 92 New Zealand Regions and Territories
cookout 350.13 *feast*
cook's helper 45.2 *cook*
cook's knife 380.10 *knife*
cook somone's goose 682.10 *defeat heavily*
cook the accounts 750.7 *account*
cook the books 13.12 *cheat*, 539.30 *be fraudulent*, 540.22 *falsify*, 736.16 *act dishonest*, 858.10 *be criminal*
cook the evidence 856.6 *accuse falsely*
cook up 102.17 *fabricate*, 592.13 *plot*, 875.10 *drug oneself*
cook up a charge 856.6 *accuse falsely*
cool 55, 4.3 *detachment*, 4.18 *detached*, 49.33 *jazz*, 225.11 *determined*, 235.12 *generate power*, 242.4, 242.6 *moderate*
cool 242.6 *moderate*
cool 263.9 *reserved*, 325.6 *quiescent*, 409.8 *cold*, 466.4 *uninterested*, 587.5 *discourage*, 617.1 *worthy*, 651.1 *refresh*, 651.3 *refreshing*, 651.4 *refreshed*, 699.14 *self-restrained*, 783.7 *indifferent*, 786.14 *wonderful*, 787.1 *lack of wonder*, 787.3 *unmoved*, 796.7 *fashionable*, 807.17 *contemptuous*, 816.8 *unsociable*, 820.6 *hostile*, 859.4 *disinterested*, 861.1 *good*
coolabah 85 Trees and Shrubs
coolant 56.73 *nuclear reactor*, 63.9 *machine tool*, 235.8 *nuclear power*, 409.4 *cooler*
cool as a cucumber 325.6 *quiescent*
cool bag 258.8 *bag*, 409.4 *cooler*
cool box 258.6 *box*, 409.4 *cooler*
cool breeze 651.6 *refresher*
cool climate 55.38 *climate*
cool down 150.22 *pacify*, 409.11 *become cold*, 651.1 *refresh*
cooled 390.17 *ventilated*
cooled off 651.4 *refreshed*
cooler 409, 55.55 *cool*, 323.4 *closed place*, 702.2 *the inside*
cool-headed 4.18 *detached*
cool-headedness 4.3 *detachment*
coolhouse 69.4 *nursery*
cool hue 444.3 *hue*
coolie 326.7 *transferor* , 646.1 *worker*
coolie hat 295.15 *headgear*
coo like a dove 677.4 *pacify*
cooling 55.47 *windy*, 409.1 *coldness*, 409.9 *heat-resistant*, 651.3 *refreshing*
cooling down 651.5 *refreshment*
cooling fluid 63.9 *machine tool*
coolingly 55.65 *meteorologically*
cooling off 651.5 *refreshment*
cooling off of the economy 754.2 *declining prices*

cooling-off period 209.3 *delayed action*, 218.3 *pause*, 283.6 *interruption*
cooling system 56.35 *heat*
cooling tower 409.4 *cooler*
coolish 409.8 *cold*
cool it 218.12 *stop*, 325.8 *be motionless*, 325.11 *stop*, 374.14 *ease*, 660.20 *take it easy*, 673.3 *submit*, 677.5 *make peace*
cool jazz 49.8 *jazz*
coolly 4.27 *stoically*, 225.13 *determinedly*, 263.11 *reservedly*, 409.13 *coldly*, 651.8 *refreshingly*, 783.17 *indifferently*, 787.9 *without wonder*, 807.34 *contemptuously*, 816.14 *unsocially*, 820.14 *hostilely*, 859.8 *disinterestedly*
cool million 741.3 *fortune*, 742.6 *money*
coolness 4.3 *detachment*, 55.31 *coldness*, 225.2 *determination*, 242.1 *moderation*, 263.4 *reserve*, 409.1 *coldness*, 651.5 *refreshment*, 783.1 *indifference*, 787.1 *lack of wonder*, 816.1 *unsociability*, 820.1 *enmity*
cool off 150.22 *pacify*, 218.9 *pause*, 409.11 *become cold*, 651.1 *refresh*, 651.2 *be refreshed*, 783.12 *be indifferent*
cool one's heels 209.7 *wait*
cool one's temper 677.4 *pacify*
cool out 374.14 *ease*, 699.10 *restrain oneself*
cool welcome 581.5 *rejection*
coomb 98.8 *valley*
coombe 277.4 *deep thing*
coon 91 Names for Inhabitants
cooncan 42 Card Games
coonhound 77 Breeds of Dogs
coonskin hat 295.15 *headgear*
coop 68.7 *farm building*, 256.12 *stall*, 323.4 *closed place*, 323.10 *enclose*, 634.3 *animal shelter*
cooper 47.13 *carpenter*, 646.2 *artisan*
Cooper 48 Writers, 96 Rivers
cooperant 664.17 *cooperative*
cooperate 298, 572, 664, 109.8 *interrelate*, 140.6 *come together*, 223.5 *exchange*, 232.4 *be an instrument*, 284.14 *give moral support*, 662.22 *improve*, 665.12 *be in league with*, 667.6 *agree with*, 715.5 *contract*, 717.4 *compromise*, 724.4 *have joint possession*
cooperating 664.17 *cooperative*, 667.10 *agreeing*
cooperatingly 664.20 *cooperatively*
cooperation 140, 664, 109.2 *interconnection*, 223.1 *exchange*, 230.2 *joint operation*, 232.1 *instrumentality*, 284.6 *moral support*, 298.2 *interaction*, 572.9 *goodwill*, 662.10 *helpfulness*, 667.1 *agreement*, 715.1 *contract*, 717.1 *compromise*, 724.2 *participation*, 815.1 *sociability*, 819.1 *friendship*
Cooperation 664
cooperative 140, 664, 13.6 *economic factors*, 109.5 *interconnected*, 135.12 *united*, 232.6 *instrumental*, 284.9 *supportive*, 298.6 *interfacial*, 499.6 *assenting*, 572.4 *helpful*, 662.35 *benevolent*, 664.4 *joint operation*, 665.1 *party*, 665.8 *leagued*, 667.10 *agreeing*, 724.1 *joint possession*, 724.5 *jointly possessing*, 819.8 *friendly*
cooperative enterprise 664.4 *joint operation*
cooperative hospital 60.10 *hospital*
cooperative living 396.1 *life*
cooperatively 664, 109.10 *reciprocally*, 135.16 *as one*, 140.10 *in combination*, 232.9 *instrumentally*, 298.7 *interfacially*, 662.38 *benevolently*, 665.18

cliquishly, 667.14 agreeably, 724.6 in common, 819.17 in friendship
cooperativeness 664.1 cooperation
cooperative society 665.1 party
cooperative system 724.1 joint possession
cooperator 664, 284.8 supporter, 667.5 assenter
coopt 580.1 select
cooptation 580.6 selection
cooption 580.6 selection
coordinate 5.44 grammatical, 57.26 react, 114.5 counterpart, 116.24 harmonize, 122.6 equal, 122.7 dividing line, 122.11 equalize, 152.13 organize, 308.4 symmetrical, 308.6 symmetrize, 485.15 modify
coordinate bond 57.11 chemical bond
coordinate clause 143.2 particular
coordinate conjunction 5.35 part of speech
coordinated 116.13 harmonious, 485.11 modified
coordinate geometry 52.34 geometry
coordinateness 308.1 symmetry
coordinates 52, 52.36 point, 56.7 space, 136.7 separates, 250.2 exact location, 268.4 size, 295.10 suit
coordinate system 52.33 coordinates
coordination 116.4 harmony, 150.7 method, 152.3 organization, 230.2 joint operation, 485.5 modification
coordination complex 57.7 chemical compound
coordination compound 57.7 chemical compound
coot 78 Birds, 78.3 water bird
cootie 82 Insects, 82.3 pest
co-ownership 664.5 joint control
cop 16.17 police officer, 407.11 touch, 632.3 protector, 688.10 person of authority, 718.3 security officer, 734.3 taking away, 734.10 take away
copacetic 861.1 good
copalm 85 Tree Products
copartner 724.3 participant
copartnership 664.5 joint control, 724.1 joint possession
copartnery 664.5 joint control
cope 7.11 vestment, 279.3 architectural summit
Copenhagen 93 Cities, 32.3 warhorse
Copenhagen interpretation 56.80 quantum theory
copepod 81.4 arthropod
Copernican universe 53.4 cosmological model
Copernicus 52 Scientists, **53** Lunar Features
copestone 279.3 architectural summit
cope with 122.10 be equal, 652.14 behave towards
copied 50.27 painted, 110.15 duplicate, 112.6 conforming, 114.8 simulated, 118.13 imitation, 176.12 double, 245.15 reproduced, 539.39 imitative, 540.31 fraudulent, 545.16 recorded, 733.11 borrowed
copier 114, 118, 118.6 photocopier, 736.10 infringer
copilot 73.3 aircraft personnel, 679.32 airman
coping 279.3 architectural summit
coping stone 43 Architectural Decoration, 279.3 architectural summit
copious 181.9 ample, 246.5 fertile, 553.3 diffuse, 608.2 plentiful, 755.3 abundant
copiously 553.7 diffusely, 608.9 enough, 755.12 generously
copiousness 553.1 diffuseness, 608.8 plenty

cop it 397.15 die, 659.21 get into trouble
coplanar 52.79 spatial
Copland 49 Musicians and Composers
copolymer 57.21 polymer
copolymeric 57.44 polymeric
cop out 591.5 shirk, 598.2 withdraw, 673.3 submit, 717.5 be irresolute, 855.9 cover up
cop-out 591.13 shirking, 598.3 relinquishment, 598.4 deserter, 673.1 submission, 717.3 irresolution, 717.8 irresolute, 855.3 cover-up
Coppelia 46.11 classical ballets
copper 57 Chemical Elements, 16.17 police officer, 58.15 essential element, 64.3 electricity, 408.3 heater, 449.1 brown, 451.3 orange thing, 621.7 washer, 632.3 protector, 688.10 person of authority, 718.3 security officer
copper coinage 741.13 coinage
copper-coloured 449.1 brown
copper engraving 50.15 engraving
copperhead 79 Reptiles
Coppermine 96 Rivers
copper plate 50.15 engraving
copperplate 293.3 coating, 293.24 coat
copperplated 293.36 covered
copper/pyrites 57 Common Metal Ores
coppers 741.4 change
copper's nark 528.10 informer
coppery 449.1 brown, 451.1 orange
coppice 85.1 tree, 85.4 trees, 85.18 manage trees
coppicing 85.6 tree management
copremesis 353.2 defecation
coprinus 89 Fungi
coprolalia 5.19 swearword
coprolite 54 Minerals, 54.43 fossil, 353.5 faeces
coprolith 353.5 faeces
coprophilous 89.10 of fungi
coprophobia 777 Phobias by Name
coprostasophobia 777 Phobias by Name
cops and robbers 111.2 opposites
copse 85.4 trees
copsy 85.16 wooded
copter 73.8 aircraft
Coptic 5 Languages and Groups of Languages
copula 5.35 part of speech, 135.5 joint, 137.4 means of connection, 821.5 desire
copular 5.44 grammatical
copulate 135.11 make love, 140.6 come together, 245.14 have sex, 821.29 make love
copulation 135.4 sexual union, 245.3 propagation, 396.4 biological function, 821.5 desire
copulative 135.14 conjunctive
copulatively 135.16 as one
copulatory 135.14 conjunctive
copy 114, 118, 118, 533, 545, 50.7 picture, 50.20 draw, 65.19 abort, 110.4 copy, 110.9 duplicate, 112.2 conformity, 112.10 conform, 114.5 counterpart, 114.12 imitate, 115.3 disguise, 167.8 comply, 176.5 twin, 176.15 double, 183.7 replica, 183.16 repeat, 245.2 print, 245.9 reproduce, 326.16 translate, 457.5 impression, 457.11 appear, 540.10 fake, 540.21 be fraudulent, 544.3 means of identification, 545.13 record, 547.1 representation, 547.9 represent, 733.9 borrow illegally, 736.15 infringe
copy after 118.9 imitate
copy aide 697.5 office assistant
copybook 6.14 school book, 166.10 customary
copycat 114.4 person who copies, 118.13 imitation, 167.6 conformist, 183.8 creature of habit
copy desk 533.8 newsroom

copy-edit 524.8 interpret, 532.15 publish, 627.3 rectify
copy editing 627.6 rectification
copy editor 524.6 interpreter, 532.11 newspaper man, 532.12 publisher, 627.13 reviser, 629.12 repairer
copyhold 725.3 historic property terms, 725.8 propertied
copying 50.3 drawing, 114.1 similarity, 118.1 imitation, 183.1 repetition, 245.1 reproduction, 326.4 translation, 733.3, 736.6 illegal borrowing
copyist 50.16 artist, 114.4 person who copies, 118.8 copier, 547.4 person who makes a representation
copy nature 537.34 render
copyright 119.7 originate, 302.2 limiting factor, 302.7 limit, 544.3 means of identification, 699.1 restraint, 699.8 restrain, 725.1 property, 845.6 bond, 845.16 entitle
copyrighted 119.6 authentic, 302.5 limited, 699.13 restraining, 725.8 propertied
copyrighted work 119.2 original
copywriter 532.10 publicizer
CoQ 58.12 coenzyme
coq au vin 45.43 French dish
coquet 579.5 be capricious, 821.26 court
coquetry 579.3 whim, 821.4 lovability, 821.6, 826.2 courtship
coquette 578.9 equivocator, 579.4 capricious person, 821.9 lover, 826.5 courting person
coquettish 579.1 capricious, 821.20 amorous, 826.9 endearing
coquettish glances 821.6 courtship
coquettishly 821.30 lovingly, 826.10 endearingly
coquettishness 579.2 caprice
coquettish smile 821.14 communication of love
coquilla nut 86 Nuts
coquito 85 Trees and Shrubs
coracle 74 Ships and Boats
coral 76.5 aquatic animal, 450.1 red
Coral 97 Oceans and Seas
CORAL 65 Programming Languages
coral island 98.2 island
coralline 81.21 coelenterate
coralloid 81.21 coelenterate
coral-pink 450.1 red
coral reef 98.2 island, 278.4 shallow thing, 635.1 trap
coral snake 79 Reptiles
coral tree 85 Trees and Shrubs
cor anglais 49 Musical Instruments
corbel 43.9 miscellaneous architectural features
corbel arch 43.5 arch
Cor Caroli 53 Named Stars
cord 67 Natural Fabrics, **75** General Units, 64.27 wire, 85.3 timber, 137.6 line, 235.7 electrical power
cordage 85.3 timber, 137.7 tackle
cordate 83.18 of leaves
cordectomy 60 Surgical Operations
cordgrass 87 Grasses
cordial 413, 351.6 soft drink, 351.7 alcoholic drink, 408.12 warm-hearted, 414.5 sweet drink, 572.10 willing, 630.7 tonic, 667.10 agreeing, 759.12 sensitive, 763.2 likable, 814.8, 815.15 sociable, 819.8 friendly, 831.6 benevolent

cordially 667.14 agreeably, 763.15 pleasantly, 815.18 sociably, 819.17 in friendship
cordial relations 675.1 peace
cordial welcome 815.9 welcome
cordierite 54 Minerals
cordille 95.1 mountain, 275.4 mountain range
Cordillera 53 Mountains
cordite 338.13 fuel, 680.15 explosive
cordless 64.36 electronic
cordless appliance 64.27 wire
cordless telephone 534.9 telephone
Cordoba 93 Cities
Córdoba 93 Cities
cordon 43 Architectural Decoration, 43.9 miscellaneous architectural features, 69.10 fruit tree
cordon bleu 655.4 skilled person
cordon bleu chef 45.2 cook
cordotomy 60 Surgical Operations
cords 295.9 trousers
corduroy 67 Natural Fabrics, 288.4 textile, 375.7 rough thing
corduroy material 321.3 furrowed thing
corduroy road 327.3 road
cordwainer 295.26 fashion designer
cordwood 47.12 wood, 85.3 timber
core 158, 158, 54.18 earth's crust, 56.73 nuclear reactor, 103.2 essential content, 257.3 insides, 290.2 inside, 290.5 inner nature, 291.1 centre, 410.7 nuclear power, 520.1 meaning, 611.3 chief thing
core curriculum 6.3 subject
Corelli 48 Writers, **49** Musicians and Composers
core of one's being 759.8 seat of feelings
co-respondent 130.5 extra person, 824.3 divorce court
core store 65.6 memory
Corfu 98 Islands
corgi 77 Breeds of Dogs
coriaceous 378.3 hard
coriander 45 Herbs and Spices, 413.5 herbs
Corinth 93 Cities
Corinthian 43 Architectural Styles, 43.16 columned
Corinthian order 43.8 column
Coriolanus 48 Shakespeare's plays
Coriolis force 55.9 atmospheric process
Corius method 57 Named Reactions
cork 20.3 fishing tackle, 85.3 timber, 293.2, 293.23 cover, 323.2 stopper, 323.8 stop, 370.7 light thing, 424.2 sound reducer, 726.2 detention, 726.7 detain
Cork 92 Counties, **93** Cities
corkage 751.3 fee
corked 293.36 covered, 323.13 stopped, 415.6 unpalatable, 620.1 imperfect, 628.12 deteriorated
corker 617.8 exceller, 682.4 successful person, 861.17 good thing
corking 617.1 worthy, 861.1 good
cork oak 85 Trees and Shrubs
corkscrew 314.2 coil, 314.6 convolute, 322.2 opener, 355.10 excavator
cork-tip 413.7, 413.11 tobacco
corkwood 85 Trees and Shrubs
corky 392.5 dried-up
Corlay 32 Breeds of Horse and Pony
corm 69.9 garden plant, 83.5 stem, 84.2 flowering plant
cormorant 78 Birds, 78.3 water bird, 872.4 glutton
cormous 83.14 of plants
corn 87 Grasses, 68.12 crop, 316.2 bulge, 350.8 animal food, 351.7 alcoholic drink, 373.7 hard substance, 624.15 ulcer
corn belt 68.11 farmland

corn borer 82 Insects, 82.3 pest
corn bread 45.38 bread, 45.43 US dish
corn chafer 82 Insects, 82.3 pest
corncob 87.4 cereal grass
corncockle 84 Flowers and Flowering Plants
corncrake 78 Birds
corn drill 68.10 farm tool
cornea 435.2 eye
corneal graft 630.12 surgery
corned 637.7 preserved
Corneille 48 Dramatists
cornel 85 Trees and Shrubs
cornemuse 49 Musical Instruments
corneous 373.1 hard
corner 26.2 boxing, 26.5 wrestling, 31.1 hockey, 33.6 motor racing terms, 34.5 rock face, 35.6 rugger, 38.5 soccer, 41.14 ski, 52.39 angle, 71.3 carriageway, 106.4 difficult circumstances, 310.1 angle, 335.14 deviating course, 659.23 cause difficulties, 670.9 attack successfully, 723.7 possess, 738.1 purchase, 879.14 instrument of punishment
corner area 38.1 soccer
cornerback 19.10 defence
corner cupboard 47.5 cabinet
cornered 310.7 angular, 633.4 endangered
corner flag 35.1 rugger, 38.1 soccer
cornering 41.4 skiing technique, 71.21 miscellaneous motoring terms, 363.2 circuitousness, 738.7 purchasing
cornering of the market 723.1 possession
corner judge 26.7 judo
corner kick 38.2 football play
cornerman 33.8 driver
corner shop 740.8 store
cornerstone 103.2 essential content, 225.4 stable thing, 284.2 supporting part, 611.3 chief thing
corner the market 13.10 trade with, 723.7 possess, 738.1 purchase
cornet 49 Musical Instruments, 315.5 cone
cornetfish 80 Fishes
cornett 49 Musical Instruments
corn exchange 740.1 market
cornfield 68.11 farmland
cornflakes 45.40 breakfast cereal
cornflour 45.7 basic ingredient, 393.11 thickener
cornflower 84 Flowers and Flowering Plants, 454.6 blue thing
corn god 8.5 deity
cornhusk 293.13 casing
cornice 43 Architectural Decoration, 43.19 decorate, 279.3 architectural summit
corniced 43.17 structured
corniculate 380.4 toothed
Cornish 5 Languages and Groups of Languages
Cornish accent 5.26 dialect
Cornish cream 395.8 fat
Cornish rex 77 Breeds of Cats
Cornish stone 44.2 raw material
corn liquor 351.7 alcoholic drink
corn market 740.1 market
cornmeal 45.7 basic ingredient
corn on the cob 45 Vegetables
cornopean 49 Musical Instruments
corn pone 45.38 bread
corn poppy 84 Flowers and Flowering Plants
CORN rule 57.13 structure
corn smut 89 Fungi
cornu 49 Musical Instruments
cornucopia 246.1 fertility, 350.9 plenty, 605.3 supply, 608.8 plenty, 742.7 opulence
cornute 380.4 toothed
Cornwall 92 Counties
corn whisky 351.7 alcoholic drink
corny 771.10 humorous
corolla 84.3 flower part

corollary 5.25 inscription, 52.65 theory, 130.3 additional item, 180.4 concomitant, 227.1 effect, 492.1 judgment
corona 43 Architectural Decoration, 53.15, 55.22 sun, 313.3 circular thing, 413.7 tobacco, 439.12 highlight
Corona Australis 53 The Constellations
Corona Borealis 53 The Constellations
coronach 774.2 lament
corona discharge 64.6 electric discharge
coronary 624.10 cardiovascular disease
coronary bypass graft 630.12 surgery
coronary heart disease 624.10 cardiovascular disease
coronary thrombosis 624.4 disease, 624.10 cardiovascular disease
coronate 688.21 grant authority
coronation 688.3 acquisition of power, 703.1 commission, 812.3 ceremony, 813.3 formal occasion
coroner 16.23 judge, 397.9 person dealing with the dead, 477.9 questioner, 492.6 justice
coroner's court 16.19 lawcourt, 492.3 place of judgment
coroner's jury 492.7 jury
coronet 295.15 headgear, 313.3 circular thing, 544.8 heraldic device
corpora allata 352 Endocrine Glands
corpora cardiaca 352 Endocrine Glands
corporal 367.7 material, 679.17 army person, 879.19 punitive
corporality 367.1 material world
corporally 367.9 materially
corporal punishment 879, 330.12 collision
corporate 77.16.11 allied, 135.12 united, 665.8 leagued, 724.5 jointly possessing
corporate bond 741.14 paper money
corporate income 721.4 earnings
corporately 116.32 in alliance, 142.12 one and all, 665.18 cliquishly
corporate plan 592.1 plan
corporate sector 13.2 economy
corporate tax 751.7 tax
corporation 3, 16.2 jurisdiction, 140.3 assembly, 259.8 fat, 367.2 materialization, 665.1 party, 737.7 company
corporative state 12.5 political organization
corporeal 101.6 real, 367.7 material
corporeality 101.1 reality, 367.1 material world
corporealize 367.8 be material
corporeity 367.1 material world
corposant 439.9 firefly
corps 161.12 team, 161.14 force, 665.1 party, 679.16 army unit
corps commander 17.5 military staff
corps de ballet 46.13 ballet dancer
corps diplomatique 706.2 representative body
corpse 132.1 remainder, 397.11 dead person
corpse candle 439.9 firefly
corpselike 274.2 emaciated
corpse-like 397.21 deathly
corpses 777 Phobias by Topic
corpulence 259.5 fatness, 273.5 thickness, 315.2 round body, 369.4 heaviness
corpulent 259.16 fat, 273.1 thick, 315.10 well-rounded, 369.1 heavy
corpus 142.2 whole thing, 161.30 compilation, 367.4 matter, 562.3 compendium
Corpus Christi 93 Cities

corpuscle 59.7 cell, 260.2 little thing
corpuscular 260.7 little
corpus juris 16.1 the law, 654.3 precept
Corpus Juris Canonici 16.1 the law
Corpus Juris Civilis 16.1 the law
corpus luteum 352 Endocrine Glands
corradiate 342.11 focus
corral 68.7 farm building, 68.18 practise livestock farming, 77.20 abode of mammals, 161.43 herd, 301.2 enclosed place, 301.5 enclose, 323.4 closed place, 323.10 enclose
corralling 161.2 herding
correct 503, 843, 5.39 of language, 52.86 logical, 125.5 counterbalance, 150.13 orderly, 150.21 tidy, 167.10 assimilate, 167.14 conformist, 242.4 moderate, 528.11 inform, 537.21 accurate, 537.31 be accurate, 558.3 elegant, 619.1, 619.5 perfect, 627.3 rectify, 629.1 repair, 629.13 repaired, 630.19 remedy, 811.26 ritualistic, 813.6 formal, 817.8 good-mannered, 879.1 punish
correct behaviour 813.1 formality
correct dress 295.3, 813.4 formal dress
corrected 125.10 counterbalancing
corrected copy 627.8 better thing
corrected proof 627.8 better thing
correct English 5.29 grammar
correct for 52.93 equate
correcting 125.10 counterbalancing
correcting faults 629.8 repair
correction 125.2 counterbalance, 242.1 moderation, 627.6 rectification, 629.8 repair, 630.1 remedy, 843.5 righting wrong, 879.7 punishment
correctional 2.13 communal, 879.19 punitive
correctional institution 2.8 human institution
correctional officer 702.6 prison officer
correction facility 702.1 prison
correction fluid 438.6 that which makes invisible, 546.4 eraser
correctitude 619.3 perfection, 813.1 formality
corrective 125.10 counterbalancing, 231.4 counteracting, 630.1 remedy, 630.17 remedial, 879.19 punitive
correctively 125.11 in compensation, 231.5 counter
Corrective Party 665.3 political grouping
corrective training 702.7 imprisonment
correctly 843, 5.52 grammatically, 30.12 competitively, 503.8, 537.39 accurately, 811.42 ritualistically, 813.12 formally, 817.15 genteelly, 843.18 properly
correctness 503, 843, 30.1 gymnastics, 52.64 reasoning, 150.5 orderliness, 537.8 accuracy, 619.3 perfection, 794.1 elegance, 811.11 ritual, 813.1 formality, 817.2 good manners, 843.3 properness
corrector 224.4 editor, 627.13 reviser, 879.17 punisher
correct speech 5.6 official language
correct style 5.29 grammar
correlate 109, 285, 52.93 equate, 107.8 be proportionate to, 116.25 conform, 223.5 exchange, 308.6 symmetrize, 478.21 answer to
correlated 285, 107.5 interrelated, 109.6 correlative, 116.14 conforming
correlating 109.6 correlative

correlation 52, 109, 107.1 relatedness, 107.2 interrelatedness, 116.5 conformity, 223.1 exchange, 285.1 parallelism, 308.1 symmetry, 478.8 correspondence, 664.3 mutual relationship
correlational 109.6 correlative, 308.4 symmetrical, 664.18 joint
correlation coefficient 52.61 correlation
correlative 109, 116.14 conforming, 180.18 concurrent, 285.4 correlated, 478.15 correspondent
correlatively 109, 223.8 in exchange, 478.26 correspondingly
correlativity 109.3 correlation
Correns 52 Scientists
correspond 285, 109.9 correlate, 110.7 be the same, 114.10 be similar, 116.25, 167.7 conform, 285.6 correlate, 433.8 harmonize, 478.21 answer to, 560.15 recount, 667.8 be compatible
correspondence 478, 534, 107.1 relatedness, 109.3 correlation, 110.2 equivalence, 112.2 conformity, 114.1 similarity, 116.5 conformity, 122.1 equality, 167.1 conformity, 285.1 parallelism, 308.1 symmetry, 528.4 mass communication, 534.1 communications, 545.1 record, 667.3 compatibility
correspondence column 532.3 journalism
correspondence course 6.2 educational system
correspondent 478, 534, 109.6 correlative, 112.6 conforming, 114.5 counterpart, 116.14 conforming, 122.6 equal, 285.4 correlated, 308.4 symmetrical, 478.10 answerer, 528.9 informant, 532.11 newspaper man, 533.4 journalist, 560.10 descriptive writer, 856.4 accused person
correspondently 110.18 identically
corresponding 107.5 interrelated, 109.6 correlative, 110.13 equivalent, 112.6 conforming, 114.7 similar, 116.14 conforming, 122.6 equal, 167.12 conforming, 285.4 correlated, 308.4 symmetrical, 433.7 harmonious, 478.15 correspondent, 667.12 compatible
correspondingly 478, 107.10 relevantly, 109.11 correlatively, 110.18 identically, 112.13 uniformly, 114.13 similarly, 114.14 comparably, 122.12 equally, 308.7 symmetrically, 667.16 compatibly
correspond to 107.8 be proportionate to, 112.10 conform, 122.10 be equal
correspond with 534.31 correspond, 615.6 be convenient
corridor 249.6 regions, 256.7 room, 272.6 narrow place, 322.7 passageway, 327.2 route
corridors of power 688.6 place of authority
corrie 98.8 valley, 277.4 deep thing
Corriedale 68 Breeds of Sheep
corrigendum 504.12 typing error
corrigible 627.15 improvable
corrival 663.10 competitor
corroborate 101.12 establish reality, 284.14 give moral support, 475.17, 480.2 prove, 483.12 prove, 499.4 assent, 535.19 confirm, 537.30 prove true, 544.10 identify, 708.3 permit, 855.8 justify
corroborated 475.13 proven, 535.13 supported, 537.20 proved, 544.12 identified
corroboration 284.6 moral support, 475.4, 480.5 proof, 483.2 proof, 499.1 assent, 535.4, 537.7 confirmation, 544.1 identification, 708.1 permission, 855.2 defence

corroborative 284.9 *supportive*, 475.13 *proven*, 480.9 *verificatory*, 483.8 *evidential*, 855.11 *vindicatory*
corroboratively 480.11 *verifiably*
corroborator 284.8 *supporter*, 535.9 *affirmer*
corroboree 46.4 *historic dancing*
corrode 129.4 *decrease*, 131.3 *subtract*, 141.3 *disintegrate*, 385.14 *erode*, 628.2 *decay*, 628.5 *hurt*
corroded 131.7 *reduced*, 141.5 *disintegrated*
corroding 141.6 *disintegrating*
corrosion 63.16 *deformation*, 131.1 *subtraction*, 141.1 *disintegration*, 244.7 *agent of destruction*, 385.2 *wearing away*, 628.9 *dilapidation*
corrosive 129.7 *descrescent*, 244.7 *agent of destruction*, 618.5 *harmful*, 862.9 *detrimental*
corrosively 131.9 *decreasingly*, 141.8 *destructively*
corrugate 314.6 *convolute*, 320.8 *pleat*, 321.6 *furrow*, 375.12 *make rough*
corrugated 314.4 *convolutional*, 320.5 *folded*, 321.4 *furrowed*, 375.1 *rough*, 375.2 *coarse*
corrugated iron 321.3 *furrowed thing*, 375.7 *rough thing*
corrugated paper 321.3 *furrowed thing*
corrugation 314.2 *coil*, 320.2 *pleat*, 321.1 *furrow*, 375.6 *roughness*
corrupt 877, 16.60 *offending*, 141.3 *disintegrate*, 586.17 *bribe*, 618.4 *poor*, 618.13 *be worthless*, 622.8 *unclean*, 622.11 *dirty*, 628.2 *decay*, 628.3 *make worse*, 628.6 *pervert*, 628.12 *deteriorated*, 738.4 *buy off*, 844.15 *immoral*, 858.5 *dishonourable*, 862.7 *evil*, 862.11 *be evil*, 864.11 *wicked*, 864.17 *make wicked*
corrupted 5.42 *worded*, 141.5 *disintegrated*
corruptible 858.5 *dishonourable*
corrupting 626.5 *unhygienic*, 877.12 *indecent*
corruption 5.5 *nonstandard language*, 16.39 *crime*, 141.1 *disintegration*, 419.2 *something that makes an unpleasant smell*, 618.10 *poverty*, 622.2 *uncleanness*, 628.8 *perversion*, 628.9 *dilapidation*, 738.10 *bribery*, 858.1 *improbity*, 862.1 *evil*, 864.1 *wickedness*, 877.2 *indecency*
corruptive 862.9 *detrimental*
corruptly 858.11 *dishonourably*, 862.12 *evilly*, 864.18 *wickedly*
corsage 295.24 *part of garment*, 418.2 *fragrant thing*
corsair 74 Sailing Ships and Boats, 736.9 *plunderer*
corset 262.4 *contractor*, 284.5 *supporting garment*, 295.18 *underwear*, 699.5 *means of restraint*
Corsica 98 Islands
Corsican pony 32 Breeds of Horse and Pony
corslet 671.7 *armour*
cortege 180.10 *attendance*, 399.2 *funeral*
cortège 155.14 *follower*, 159.8 *procession*
Cortes 653.10 *legislative body*
cortex 83.5 *stem*, 289.1 *exterior*, 293.14 *animal covering*
corticoid 58 Hormones
corticolous 90.8 *lichenoid*
corticosteroid 58.16 *hormone*, 62.4 *drug type*
corticosterone 58 Hormones
corticotrophin 58 Hormones
cortinarius 89 Fungi
cortisol 58 Hormones
cortisone 58 Hormones, 62 Medication, 630.8 *drug*

corundum 54 Minerals, **54** Gemstones, **57** Common Chemical Compounds
coruscate 439.25 *light up*
coruscating 439.16 *bright*
coruscation 439.2 *quality of light*
corvee 644.1 *work*
corvette 74 Sailing Ships and Boats, 679.24 *warship*
corvine 78.23 *avian*
Corvus 53 The Constellations
corydalis 84 Flowers and Flowering Plants
corymb 84.4 *flower head*
corymbose 84.12 *of flowers*
coryphaeus 653.14 *leader*
coryphée 51.28 *dancer*
coryza 409.3 *chill*, 624.9 *respiratory disease*
Cosa Nostra 864.7 *criminality*
cosecant 52.52 *trigonometric function*
cosh 330.8 *club*, 330.16 *weapons*, 680.7 *blunt weapon*, 879.14 *instrument of punishment*
co-sharing 122.6 *equal*, 724.2 *participation*
cosidou 45.53 *African dish*
cosign 715.5 *contract*
co-sign a loan 715.4 *be in debt*
cosign a note 714.8 *guarantee*
cosignatory 714.5 *promise-maker*
cosignature 715.1 *contract*
cosigned 714.13 *guaranteeing*, 715.7 *contractual*
cosigner 714.5 *promise-maker*, 715.4 *contractor*
co-signer 745.6 *debtor*
cosily 405.11 *pleasingly*, 686.9 *prosperously*
cosine 52.52 *trigonometric function*
cosine rule 52.51 *trigonometry*
cosiness 260.1 *littleness*, 405.1 *physical pleasure*
cos lettuce 45 Vegetables
cosmetic 630.9 *balm*, 811.18 *dramatic*
cosmetically 811.34 *dramatically*
cosmetician 791.13 *beautician*
cosmetics 791, 118.4 *camouflage*, 384.5 *powder*, 444.9 *complexion*
cosmetic surgery 115.3 *disguise*, 630.12 *surgery*, 791.2 *plastic surgery*
cosmic 11.16 *psychic*, 53.36 *astronomical*, 149.12 *extraterrestrial*, 164.16 *universal*, 617.1 *worthy*
cosmically 53.39 *astronomically*, 149.18 *extraneously*, 164.32 *universally*
cosmic background 53.4 *cosmological model*
cosmic being 11.11 *ghost*, 104.6 *outsider*, 149.5 *extraterrestrial*
cosmic consciousness 11.8 *psychic power*
cosmic dust 53.8 *interstellar medium*, 384.5 *powder*
cosmic rays 53.8 *interstellar medium*, 56.70 *radioactivity*
cosmic vibration 11.10 *psychic phenomenon*
cosmochemist 53.2 *astronomer*
cosmochemistry 53.1 *astronomy*
cosmogenist 53.2 *astronomer*
cosmogeny 53.1 *astronomy*
cosmoid scale 80.5 *fish anatomy*
cosmological 53.36 *astronomical*
cosmologically 53.39 *astronomically*
cosmological model 53, 56.6 *law*
cosmologist 4.10 *philosopher*, 53.2 *astronomer*
cosmology 4.6 *branch of philosophy*, 53.1 *astronomy*, 56.4 *experimental physics*
cosmonaut 53.31 *space travel*, 248.10 *spaceman*
cosmonautics 53.29 *astronautics*
cosmopolitan 91.15 *internationalist*, 164.15 *general*, 164.16 *universal*, 400.13 *national*, 655.5 *expert*, 794.5 *refined*

cosmopolitanism 91.5 *internationalism*, 164.1 *generality*
cosmos 84 Flowers and Flowering Plants, 53.3 *universe*, 101.2 *real world*, 142.2 *whole thing*
Cossack 32.15 *horse person*, 679.20 *cavalryman*
Cossack dance 46.4 *historic dancing*
Cossacks 1 Peoples
cosset 405.10 *comfort*, 662.20 *sustain*, 771.15 *humour*, 821.11 *loved one*, 821.27 *kiss*, 826.6 *object of endearment*, 826.7 *show endearment for*
cosseted 405.7 *pleased*
cossetting 771.11 *humouring*
cost 751, 751, 268.10 *measure*, 617.6 *worth*, 722.2 *financial loss*, 748.5 *expense*, 750.7 *account*, 751.1 *price*, 753.9 *be dear*
costa 382 Bones
Costa Brava 98.4 *coast*
cost a bundle 753.9 *be dear*
cost accountant 750.6 *accountant*
cost accounting 750.1 *accounts*
Costa del Sol 98.4 *coast*
cost a fortune 753.9 *be dear*
cost a lot 753.9 *be dear*
cost an arm and a leg 753.9 *be dear*
cost a packet 753.9 *be dear*
cost a pretty penny 753.9 *be dear*
co-star 51.32 *act*
costard 86 Fruits
Costa Rica 91 Countries
cost-benefit analysis 653.3 *management*
costed 750.11 *accounted*
coster 739.14 *street trader*
costermonger 739.11 *pedlar*, 739.14 *street trader*
coster's barrow 71.7 *handcart*
costing nothing 729.7 *given*
costive 323.13 *stopped*, 371.7 *condensed*, 726.9 *retentive*, 869.8 *self-restrained*
costively 323.16 *impermeably*, 371.10 *densely*
costliness 617.6 *worth*, 753.1 *high price*
costly 757, 617.3 *valuable*, 742.3 *opulent*, 753.7 *dear*, 811.24 *grand*
cost next to nothing 754.12 *be cheap*
cost of living 13.3 *economic statistics*, 748.5 *expense*, 751.5 *cost*
cost-of-living 15.9 *negotiated*
cost-of-living adjustment 15.2 *industrial negotiations*
cost-of-living index 751.5 *cost*
cost one dear 753.9 *be dear*
costs 13.7 *corporation*, 125.1 *compensation*, 751.5 *cost*, 879.8 *penalty*
cost the earth 753.9 *be dear*
costume 51.19 *stage requisite*, 295.5 *fancy dress*, 295.10 *suit*, 295.32 *dress*, 295.35 *make clothing*
costume ball 46.1 *dancing*
costumed 295.29 *dressed*
costume designer 51.25 *producer*, 295.26 *fashion designer*
costume drama 534.25 *broadcast material*
costume jewellery 792.6 *jewellery*
costume party 531.3 *covering up*, 665.7 *social gathering*, 815.5 *party*
costumier 295.26 *fashion designer*
cosy 260.7 *little*, 405.6 *pleasant*, 405.7 *pleased*, 686.8 *prosperous*, 763.3 *comfortable*
cosy chat 568.2 *chat*
cot 47.6 *bed*
cotangent 52.52 *trigonometric function*
co-tenant 724.3 *participant*
coterie 161.19 *clique*, 163.5 *social class*, 305.5 *team*, 665.1 *party*
coterminous 267.5 *juxtaposed*
cothurnus 51.9 *tragedy*, 295.5 *fancy dress*

cotillion 46.1 *dancing*, 46.4 *historic dancing*
Cotopaxi 95 Mountains
co-trimoxazole 62 Medication
Cotswold 68 Breeds of Sheep, **95** Mountains
Cotswolds 95.5 *British mountains*
Cotswold stone 43.4 *building material*
cottage 43.3 *building*, 256.5 *house*, 725.1 *property*
cottage cheese 45 Cheeses
cottage hospital 60.10 *hospital*
cottage loaf 45.39 *loaf*
cottage pie 45.44 *British dish*
cottager 255.5 *countryman*
cotter pin 137.8 *fastening*
cotton 67 Natural Fabrics, 67.12 *natural*, 68.12 *crop*, 288.4 *textile*, 604.1 *materials*
cotton belt 68.11 *farmland*
Cotton Bowl 19.1 *football*
cotton grass 87 Grasses
cotton jersey 288.4 *textile*
cotton mill 647.1 *workshop*
cottonmouth 79 Reptiles
cotton paper 604.3 *paper*
cottonseed 83.9 *seed*
cottonseed cake 68.9 *animal feedstuff*
cotton seeds 614.6 *refuse*
cotton stainer 82 Insects
cottontail 77 Placental Mammals
cotton to 821.24 *be in love*
cotton up to 819.14 *seek the friendship of*
cottonwood 85 Trees and Shrubs
cotton wool 374.11 *soft thing*
cotton-wool treatment 691.1 *leniency*
cottony 383.9 *smooth*
cottony cloud 55.20 *cloud appearance*
cotyledon 83.6 *leaf*, 83.9 *seed*
cotylosaur 79 Fossil Reptiles
couch 87 Grasses, 47.2 *chair*, 77.20 *abode of mammals*, 276.8 *be low*, 284.4 *rest*, 362.3 *bring down*, 362.8 *sit*, 549.9 *style*, 649.2 *take it easy*
couchant 276.5 *low*, 282.10 *lying*, 544.13 *heraldic*
couch one's lance 674.11 *contend*
couch potato 325.7 *sedentary person*, 591.17 *avoider*, 643.8 *nonworker*
cougar 77 Placental Mammals
cough 353.9 *saliva*, 353.20 *salivate*, 430.2 *hoarseness*, 430.5 *sound hoarse*, 624.3 *symptom*, 624.9 *respiratory disease*
cough drop 424.2 *sound reducer*
coughing 353.9 *saliva*, 353.29 *salivating*
cough linctus 133.2 *mixed thing*
cough mixture 133.2 *mixed thing*
cough syrup 729.2 *gift*
cough up 125.4 *compensate*, 353.20 *salivate*, 598.1 *relinquish*, 629.3 *restore*, 746.6 *pay*, 750.9 *settle accounts*, 755.10 *be generous*
could be 486.8 *be possible*
could do with 662.27 *find useful*
could not care less 466.6 *be incurious*, 783.12 *be indifferent*
couldn't-care-less 508.5 *foolish*, 780.4 *rash*
coulee 265.3 *gulf*
couleur de rose 617.1 *worthy*
couloir 34.5 *rock face*, 41.1 *skiing*, 98.8 *valley*, 265.3 *gulf*
coulomb 75 SI Units, **75** Scientific and Technical Units
Coulomb 52 Scientists
Coulomb's law 56 Named Laws
coulometer 268.8 *meter*
coulometric 268.16 *micrometric*
coulometry 268.2 *micrometry*
coulter 330.9 *sharp-edged thing*
coumarone resin 395.10 *resin*
council 653, 703, 16.2 *jurisdiction*, 16.18 *tribunal*, 161.5 *conference*, 161.7 *committee*, 568.4 *conference*, 653.6 *governing*

body, 654.2 *consultation*, 654.4
adviser, 665.1 *party*, 706.2 *representative body*
council board 653.7 *council*
council chamber 653.7 *council*
Council for Mutual Economic Assistance 13.5 *international trade*
councillor 15.7 *employee*, 653.16
official, 706.1 *delegate*
councilman 653.16 *official*
council-manager system 653.9
US administrative council
council of elders 653.7 *council*
council of war 568.4 *conference*
council tax 751.7 *tax*
counsel 16.13 *lawyer*, 61.38 *psychologize*, 228.9 *motivate*,
586.15 *persuade*, 636.1 *warning*, 636.5 *warn*, 653.2 *direct*,
654.1 *advice*, 654.4 *adviser*,
654.5 *advise*, 662.2 *support*,
662.23 *advise*
counsellable 636.8 *warning*
counselled 636.9 *warned*
counselling 61.3 *psychiatric treatment*, 510.9 *treatment*, 654.1
advice, 654.4 *advising*
counsellor 4.12 *sage*, 15.6 *employer*, 61.30 *psychiatrist*, 158.9
middleman, 228.7 *motivator*,
492.5 *judge*, 586.14 *motivator*,
636.4 *warner*, 653.16 *official*,
654.4, 662.14 *adviser*, 678.3
mediator, 678.4 *representative*,
760.8 *sensitive person*
count **170**, 26.2 *boxing*, 52.12
numeration, 52.90 *enumerate*,
120.4 *total*, 120.8 *quantify*,
130.6 *add*, 146.4 *include*,
169.10 *number*, 170.8 *calculate*,
170.11 *number*, 185.16 *time*,
268.10 *measure*, 611.7 *be important*, 802.1 *nobleman*, 856.1
accusation
countable 52.73 *numerable*,
170.14 *calculable*
count as 222.5 *take a substitute*
count ballots 580.5 *vote*
count calories 871.5 *fast*
count down 594.4 *prepare for action*
counted 120.6 *quantitative*
counted person 400.7 *person*
countenance 284.12 *bear*, 303.2
face, 457.3 *external appearance*,
662.9 *patronage*, 662.23 *advise*,
708.3 *permit*, 851.1 *approval*,
851.12 *accept*
counter **74** *Parts of a Ship*, **231**,
484, 671, 36.8 *punting*, 41.6
ice-skating, 65.17 *computing
term*, 111.6 *oppositely*, 117.14
disagree, 125.10 *counterbalancing*, 170.6 *calculator*, 185.13
timer, 231.1 *counteraction*,
231.3 *counteract*, 231.4 *counteracting*, 337.25 *reversed*, 476.10
countercharge, 536.8 *rebut*,
544.3 *means of identification*,
663.13 *be contrary*, 663.15 *object*, 663.19 *oppositional*,
663.26 *contrariwise*, 671.24
parry, 672.1 *retaliation*, 672.3
retaliate, 676.13 *be at war*,
740.9 *stall*
counteraccusation 476.3 *countercharge*, 484.1 *counterevidence*
counteraccuse 484.7 *counter*
counteract **231**, **663**, 109.7
reciprocate, 111.8 *be opposite*,
125.5 *counterbalance*, 221.6 *reverse*, 227.5 *show an effect*,
244.8 *destroy*, 331.2 *respond*,
661.8 *hinder*, 704.9 *cancel out*,
713.6 *protest*
counteracted 125.10 *counterbalancing*
counteracting **62**, **231**, 109.4 *reciprocal*, 125.10 *counterbalancing*, 630.17 *remedial*, 663.19 *oppositional*, 704.10 *cancelled*
counteracting thing **231**
counteraction **231**, 109.1 *interchange*, 111.3 *opposition*, 122.3
equalization, 125.2 *counterbalance*, 221.1 *reversion*, 227.1 *effect*, 337.16 *countermotion*,

476.3 *countercharge*, 629.9 *restoration*, 661.1 *hindrance*, 663.7
countermeasure, 671.3 *counter*,
672.1 *retaliation*, 704.4 *cancelling out*, 713.1 *protest*
Counteraction 231
counteractions 592.2 *policy*
counteractive 109.4 *reciprocal*,
125.10 *counterbalancing*, 231.4
counteracting, 476.7 *refuting*,
484.5 *countering*, 661.13 *hindering*, 663.19 *oppositional*,
704.10 *cancelled*, 713.9 *protesting*
counteractively 125.11 *in compensation*, 231.5 *counter*, 484.9
to the contrary, 661.16 *with
delay*
counterargument 16.7 *legal trial*,
476.3 *countercharge*, 663.7
countermeasure, 855.2 *defence*
counterattack 670, 28.3 *fencing
movements*, 28.5 *fence*, 231.1
counteraction, 341.7 *deflection*,
663.7 *countermeasure*, 663.18
counteract, 670.14 *siege*, 676.13
be at war
counterattacking 670, 28.6 *fencing*
counterbalance 125, **125**,
122.11 *equalize*, 225.3 *stabilizer*, 231.1 *counteraction*, 231.3
counteract, 233.9 *change*, 308.1
symmetry, 308.6 *symmetrize*,
369.10 *scales*, 663.18 *counteract*, 704.4 *cancelling out*, 704.9
cancel out
counterbalanced 125.10 *counterbalancing*, 308.4 *symmetrical*
counterbalancing 125
counterblast 125.5 *counterbalance*, 231.1 *counteraction*,
476.3, 476.10 *countercharge*,
478.5 *counterstatement*, 478.18
answer back, 484.1 *counterevidence*, 484.7 *counter*, 672.1 *retaliation*
counterblasted 478.13 *retaliatory*
countercathexis 61.28 *cathexis*
counterchange 109.7 *reciprocate*
countercharge 476, **476**, 478.5
counterstatement, 478.18 *answer back*, 484.1 *counterevidence*, 484.7 *counter* 672.3 *retaliate* 856.1 *accusation*, 856.5 *accuse*
countercharged 478.13 *retaliatory*, 856.8 *accusatory*
countercharm 231.1 *counteraction*
countercheck 663.7 *countermeasure*, 663.18 *counteract*
counter claim 16.5 *litigation*
counterclaim 476.3, 476.10 *countercharge*, 484.1 *counterevidence*, 484.7 *counter*, 712.1,
712.6 *request*
counterclaimant 484, 712.4 *requester*
counterclockwise 332.10 *clockwise*, 337.25 *reversed*, 337.29 *in
reverse*, 364.13 *round*
counterconditioning 61.20 *conditioning*
counterculture 500.3 *dissentience*
countercurrent 96.6 *river flow*
counterdemand 484.1 *counterevidence*, 484.7 *counter*
counter-demonstrator 713.4 *protester*
countered 484, 28.6 *fencing*
counterevidence 484, 480.6 *evidence*, 483.5 *legal evidence*
Counterevidence 484
counterexample 4.8 *philosophical
term*
counterfactual 4.8 *philosophical
term*
counterfactual history 3.1 *history*
counterfeit 102.12 *not the real
thing*, 114.8 *simulated*, 114.12
imitate, 115.3 *disguise*, 118.2,
118.10 *copy*, 118.13 *imitation*,
474.10 *hypocritical*, 538.14 *unreal*, 538.22 *make unreal*,
538.25 *be dishonest*, 539.30 *be
fraudulent*, 539.39 *imitative*,
540.10 *fake*, 540.21 *be fraudu-*

lent, 540.22 *falsify*, 540.31
fraudulent, 540.32 *falsified*,
540.33 *fake*, 741.24 *monetize*,
846.8 *unentitled*
counterfeited 540.28 *spurious*
counterfeiter 114.4 *person who
copies*, 118.8 *copier*, 538.12,
539.17 *cheat*, 540.15 *false person*, 547.4 *person who makes a
representation*, 736.11 *dishonest
person*
counterfeiting 539.10 *fraud*,
540.4 *spuriousness*, 540.8 *fraud*,
540.9 *falsification*, 736.7 *dishonesty*
counterfeit money 741.15 *false
money*, 747.4 *depreciation*
counterfeitness 538.2 *unrealness*,
538.10 *dishonesty*
counterfeit note 540.14 *false
thing*
counterflow 96.6 *river flow*
counterflux 96.6 *river flow*
counterfoil 545.1 *record*, 718.2
promise, 730.3 *acknowledgement
of payment*, 749.1 *receipt*
counterforce 671.3 *counter*
counterglow 439.4 *natural light*
countering 484, 28.6 *fencing*,
536.3 *rebuttal*, 536.13 *rebutting*
counterintelligence 231.1 *counteraction*, 529.2 *secretiveness*
counterintuitive 487.2 *unbelievable*
counterinvestment 61.28 *cathexis*
counterirritant 62.4 *drug type*,
62.14 *counteracting*, 231.1 *counteraction*, 630.4 *antidote*
counterman 697.3 *attendant*
countermand 484.1 *counterevidence*, 484.7 *counter*, 536.4 *renunciation*, 536.9 *renounce*,
692.1, 692.9 *command*, 704.4
cancelling out, 704.9 *cancel out*,
709.1 *veto*
countermanded 536.12 *rejected*,
692.14 *commanding*
countermarch 337.3 *reverse*,
676.13 *be at war*
countermarching 337.16 *countermotion*
countermeasure 663, 125.2,
125.5 *counterbalance*, 231.1
counteraction, 630.4 *antidote*,
661.1 *hindrance*
countermeasures 592.2 *policy*
countermine 592.4, 592.13 *plot*,
663.18 *counteract*, 672.1 *retaliation*
countermotion 337
countermove 231.1 *counteraction*, 663.7 *countermeasure*
countermovement 337.16 *countermotion*
counteroffensive 231.1 *counteraction*, 670.14 *siege*
counterorder 484.1 *counterevidence*, 484.7 *counter*, 692.1,
692.9 *command*, 704.4 *cancelling out*, 709.1, 709.3 *veto*,
711.2 *dissent*
counterpane 293.10 *bed covering*
counter parry 28.3 *fencing movements*
counterpart 114, 109.2 *interconnection*, 109.16 *conformity*,
122.5 *equal*, 176.5 *twin*
counterplot 592.4 *plot*, 672.1 *retaliation*
counterpoint 48.9 *metre*, 49.19
tempo, 116.4 *harmony*, 140.2
cooperation, 287.1 *inversion*,
433.3 *melodiousness*
counterpoint rhythm 49.19 *tempo*
counterpoise 116.24 *harmonize*,
122.2 *equilibrium*, 122.4
equilizer, 122.11 *equalize*,
125.2, 125.5 *counterbalance*,
231.1 *counteraction*, 231.3 *counteract*, 369.10 *scales*, 369.12 *be
heavy*, 704.4 *cancelling out*,
704.9 *cancel out*
counterpoised 125.10 *counterbalancing*
counterpoison 630.4 *antidote*
counterpole 111.1 *oppositeness*
counterpose 125.5 *counterbalance*

counterposed 125.10 *counterbalancing*
counterposing 125.10 *counterbalancing*
counterpressure 231.1 *counteraction*
counterproposal 663.7 *countermeasure*
counterpunch 231.1 *counteraction*, 672.1 *retaliation*
counter-reformation 221.1 *reversion*, 629.9 *restoration*
counterreply 484.1 *counterevidence*, 484.7 *counter*
counterrevisionist *history* 3.1 *history*
counter-revolution 221.1 *reversion*
counter-revolutionary 663.9 *opposer*, 693.12 *reactionary*,
713.10 *law-breaking*
counter-riposte 28.3 *fencing
movements*
counter scale 369.10 *scales*
counterscarp 671.11 *fortification*
countersign 480.1 *verify*, 483.12
prove, 499.4 *assent*, 543.1 *sign*,
543.9 *use signs*, 544.3 *means of
identification*, 544.11 *identify
oneself*, 715.5 *contract*, 718.11
promise
countersignature 715.1 *contract*
countersigned 499.7 *agreed*,
715.7 *contractual*
countersigner 715.4 *contractor*
counterspell 231.1 *counteraction*
counterspy 224.6 *fickle person*,
713.5 *seditionist*
counterstaining 59.6 *cell biology*
counterstate 478.18 *answer back*,
484.7 *counter*
counterstated 478.13 *retaliatory*
counterstatement 478, 476.3
countercharge, 484.1 *counterevidence*
counterstrike 109.7 *reciprocate*
counterstroke 109.1 *interchange*,
341.7 *deflection*, 671.3 *counter*,
672.1 *retaliation*
counter sue 672.3 *retaliate*
counter suit 672.1 *retaliation*
counterterrorist 693.12 *reactionary*
counter to 231.5 *counter*, 663.27
opposed to
countervail 122.11 *equalize*,
125.5 *counterbalance*, 231.3,
663.18 *counteract*, 704.9 *cancel
out*
countervailing 125.10 *counterbalancing*
counterweigh 125.5 *counterbalance*, 369.12 *be heavy*, 704.9
cancel out
counterweighing 125.10 *counterbalancing*
counterweight 122.4 *equilizer*,
125.2 *counterbalance*, 225.3 *stabilizer*, 231.1 *counteraction*,
704.4 *cancelling out*
counterweighted 125.10 *counterbalancing*
counterword 5.21 *catchword*
counterwork 663.7 *countermeasure*
countess 802.1 *nobleman*
count for nothing 612.11 *be unimportant*
count hands 170.11 *number*,
580.5 *vote*
count heads 170.11 *number*,
580.5 *vote*
counting 52.12 *numeration*,
146.7 *including*, 170.3 *count*
counting calories 871.1 *fasting*
counting hands 580.11 *franchise*
counting heads 580.11 *franchise*
counting house 741.19 *treasury*
counting noses 580.11 *franchise*
counting system 52.8 *number system*
counting-up 130.2 *mathematical
addition*
countless 181.8 *numberless*,
184.2 *immeasurable*
**countless as the hairs on one's
head** 181.8 *numberless*

countless as the stars 181.8 *numberless*
countlessly 181.13 *numerously*
countlessness 181.1 *multiplicity*, 184.5 *immeasurability*
count me out 711.12 *no*
count noses 170.11 *number*, 580.5 *vote*
count on 488.10 *think likely*, 497.7 *believe*, 513.9 *predict*, 775.6 *hope*
count one's beads 10.20 *pray*
count one's blessings 837.7 *give thanks*
count one's chickens before they are hatched 513.9 *predict*, 775.8 *be optimistic*, 780.5 *be rash*
count out 147.7, 147.7 *exclude*, 581.3 *exclude*
Countries 91
countrification 93.1 *city*
countrified 93.14 *urban*
countrify 93.15 *urbanize*
country 91, 12.5 *political organization*, 32.8 *hunting*, 49.33 *jazz*, 93.14 *urban*, 249.4 *territorial division*, 249.5 *state*, 249.6 *regions*, 400.11 *nation*, 688.8 *governmental organization*
country and western 49.11 *folk music*
country bumpkin 93.12 *rural dweller*, 255.5 *countryman*, 656.10 *unskilled person*, 658.3 *naive person*, 803.1 *plebeian*
country cottage 43.3 *building*
country cousin 255.5 *countryman*, 658.3 *naive person*, 803.1 *plebeian*
country dance 46.4 *historic dancing*
country dancing 46.1 *dancing*
country dweller 658.3 *naive person*
country-dweller 255.5 *countryman*
country gentleman 255.5 *countryman*
countryman 255, 91.13 *native*, 93.12 *rural dweller*
country music 49.11 *folk music*
country of origin 91.6 *native land*, 249.4 *territorial division*
country road 327.3 *road*
country rock 49.9 *popular music*
country route 363.5 *ringroad*
countryside 249.6 *regions*
country town 93.1 *city*, 93.9 *town*
country village 93.10 *village*
countrywide 164.16 *universal*
country-wide circulation 532.7 *publicity*
countrywoman 255.5 *countryman*
count straws 580.5 *vote*
count the calories 274.14 *become thin*, 350.23 *taste*
count the cost 781.5 *be cautious*
count the hours 185.19 *clock on*, 192.16 *measure time*
count the minutes 192.16 *measure time*
count to ten 781.5 *be cautious*
count up 130.6 *add*, 170.11 *number*
count votes 580.5 *vote*
count with 146.6 *subsume*
county 12.5 *political organization*, 92.1 *administrative area*, 93.14 *urban*, 143.1 *part*, 688.8 *governmental organization*
county board 16.2 *jurisdiction*, 653.9 *US administrative council*
county building 93.13 *municipal building*
county commission 16.2 *jurisdiction*, 653.9 *US administrative council*
county council 16.2 *jurisdiction*, 653.8 *British administrative council*, 706.2 *representative body*
county court 16.19 *lawcourt*
county courthouse 93.13 *municipal building*
county court judge 16.23 *judge*, 492.6 *justice*

county cricket 27.1 *cricket match*
county hospital 60.10 *hospital*
county jail 702.1 *prison*
county map 547.7 *map*
county seat 92.5 *administrative headquarters*, 93.2 *American cities*, 93.9 *town*
county sheriff 16.16 *US police*
county town 92.5 *administrative headquarters*, 93.4 *British cities*, 93.9 *town*, 249.11 *settlement*
coup 24.2 *billiards play*, 216.1 *change*, 252.3 *replacement*, 592.2 *policy*, 640.2 *deed*, 655.3 *masterpiece*, 688.3 *acquisition of power*, 689.1 *anarchy*, 693.4 *revolution*, 734.1 *taking*
coup de grâce 157.13 *ender*
coup d'état 16.41 *lawlessness*, 592.2 *policy*, 640.2 *deed*, 688.3 *acquisition of power*, 689.1 *anarchy*, 693.4 *revolution*, 713.2 *disorder*, 734.1 *taking*
coupé 71 Carriages and Carts, **71** Motor Vehicles, 71.16 *car*
Couperin 49 Musicians and Composers
couple 114, 56.10 *force*, 107.7 *relate to*, 135.8 *unite*, 135.11 *make love*, 137.11 *connect*, 140.6 *come together*, 176.1 *two*, 176.14 *pair*, 180.14 *keep company with*, 182.1 *few*, 407.12 *abut*, 821.29 *make love*, 823.15 *marry*
coupled 137.15 *connected*, 176.9 *two*, 180.19 *associated*, 823.21 *married*
coupled column 43.8 *column*
coupled with 130.10 *additionally*, 180.24 *with*
coupler 137.9 *yoke*
couplet 48.8 *part of poem*, 176.2 *double*
couple up 176.14 *pair*
coupling 63.8 *machine element*, 72.7 *train*, 135.4 *sexual union*, 137.1 *connection*, 137.9 *yoke*, 821.5 *desire*
coupling circuit 64.13 *circuit*
coupon 718.2 *promise*, 741.14 *paper money*
coupon-clipper 754.8 *bargain hunter*
coupons 754.7 *discounter*
courage 778, 237.1 *strength*, 574.16 *fortitude*, 575.4 *stamina*, 668.1 *defiance*, 718.1 *protection*, 805.1 *pride*
Courage 778
courageous 778, 237.11 *strong in spirit*, 597.6 *enterprising*, 668.7 *defiant*, 805.14 *proud*
courageous act 778
courageously 778, 237.14 *strongly*, 597.9 *enterprisingly*, 668.9, 668.9 *defiantly*
courageousness 778.1 *courage*
courageous person 778
courante 46.4 *historic dancing*
courbaril 85 Trees and Shrubs
coure 85 *river flow*
courgette 45 Vegetables
courier 32.15 *horse person*, 70.3 *transporter*, 326.8 *messenger*, 329.13 *swift person*, 534.4 *postal worker*, 697.5 *office assistant*
course 74 Sails, **336**, 6.3 *subject*, 18.2 *sportsground*, 32.9 *jumping*, 32.11 *riverring*, 36.1 *sailing*, 45.9 *dish*, 62.5 *prescription*, 96.7 *flow*, 155.2 *series*, 159.2 *consecution*, 185.3, 188.1 *duration*, 192.2 *timetable*, 195.1 *succession*, 230.1 *operation*, 234.1 *tendency*, 266.1 *layer*, 324.2 *momentum*, 327.2 *route*, 332.2 *bearing*, 350.6 *nutrition*, 350.14 *mouthful*, 356.2 *passing along*, 472.4 *sphere*, 472.5 *educational topic*, 590.11 *hunt*, 602.1 *means*, 630.13 *therapy*, 602.1 *conduct*
course of action 230.1 *operation*, 592.2 *policy*
course of law 16.6 *legal process*

course of love 821.8 *love affair*
course of time 185.3, 188.1 *duration*
courser 78 Birds, 32.2 *thoroughbred*, 32.3 *warhorse*, 329.12 *swift animal*, 329.13 *swift person*
courses 353.11 *menstruation*
coursing 18 Sporting Activities, 96.10 *fluvial*, 590.2 *chase*
court 821, 826, 16.19 *lawcourt*, 18.2 *sportsground*, 40.5 *real tennis*, 180.10 *attendance*, 322.8 *open space*, 327.3 *road*, 467.14 *be solicitous*, 567.2 *salutation*, 590.12 *aim at*, 653.7 *council*, 712.6 *request*, 782.13 *like*, 819.14 *seek the friendship of*, 853.10 *cajole*
court appearance 457.2 *being in view*
courtaut 49 Musical Instruments
court award 879.8 *penalty*
court card 42.3 *card game terms*
court case 856.1 *accusation*
court costs 16.43 *conviction*
court dance 46.4, 46.4 *historic dancing*
court danger 780.5 *be rash*
court disaster 633.9 *face danger*, 778.15 *be courageous*
court dress 295.3, 813.4 *formal dress*
courteous 817, 362.21 *degraded*, 467.9 *solicitous*, 652.17 *well-behaved*, 694.9 *obeisant*, 763.2 *likable*, 794.5 *refined*, 815.15 *sociable*, 819.8 *friendly*, 831.6 *benevolent*, 849.9 *showing respect*
courteous act 362.16 *courtesy*
courteously 362, 817, 652.19 *well*, 694.10 *obediently*, 815.18 *sociably*, 819.17 *in friendship*, 831.10 *benevolently*, 849.22 *respectfully*
courteousness 817.1 *courtesy*, 831.1 *benevolence*
courteous person 817
courtesan 405.3 *pleasure-seeker*, 877.9 *immoral woman*
courtesies 817
courtesy 362, 817, 467.5 *solicitude*, 652.2 *good conduct*, 694.3 *free of charge*, 763.8 *amiability*, 794.1 *elegance*, 815.2 *social ambition*, 819.1 *friendship*, 831.4 *benevolent act*, 849.3 *respectfulness*
Courtesy 817
courtesy call 815.3 *meeting*
courtesy light 71 Motor Vehicle Parts, 439.6 *electric light*
court fine 879.7 *punishment*
court handball 18 Sporting Activities
courthouse 16.27 *courtroom*, 93.13 *municipal building*
court house wedding 823.5 *wedding*
courtier 808.3 *sycophant*
courting 712.1 *request*, 712.9 *requesting*, 821.6, 826.2 *courtship*, 826.9 *endearing*
courting person 826
courtliness 817.1 *courtesy*
courtly 558.3 *elegant*, 817.7 *courteous*, 817.14 *courteously*
court martial 17.6 *military law*, 492.3 *place of judgment*
court-martial 16.19 *lawcourt*
Court of Appeal 16.20 *British court*, 492.3 *place of judgment*
court of appeals 16.21 *US court*
Court of Arches 16.22 *ecclesiastical court*
court of chancery 16.21 *US court*
court of claims 16.21 *US court*
court of common pleas 16.21 *US court*
Court of Common Pleas 16.20 *British court*
court of conscience 16.18 *tribunal*
court of equity 16.19 *lawcourt*

Court of Exchequer 16.20 *British court*
court officer 16.10 *law officer*
court of justice 16.19 *lawcourt*
court of law 16.7 *legal trial*, 16.19 *lawcourt*, 492.3 *place of judgment*
court of oyer and terminer 16.20 *British court*, 16.21 *US court*
court of record 16.19 *lawcourt*
court of session 16.19 *lawcourt*
Court of Session 16.20 *British court*
court payment 879.8 *penalty*
court plaster 630.10 *surgical dressing*
courtroom 16, 492.3 *place of judgment*, 688.6 *place of authority*
court sessions 16.7 *legal trial*
courtship 821, 826
courtship dance 46.4 *historic dancing*
court shoes 295.19 *footwear*
court sitting 16.7 *legal trial*
courtyard 301.2 *enclosed place*, 323.4 *closed place*
couscous 45.54 *other dishes*
Coushatla 1 Peoples
Cousin 4 Philosophers
cousinly 831.6 *benevolent*
couture 295.2 *dressing*
couturier 295.26 *fashion designer*
couvade 10.7 *non-Christian ritual*
covalent 57.35 *combined*
covalent bond 57.11 *chemical bond*
covalent compound 57.7 *chemical compound*
covalently 57.46 *chemically*
covariance 52.60 *parameter*
covariation 107.2 *interrelatedness*
cove 43 Architectural Decoration, 98.9 *inlet*, 317.2 *concave land*, 401.2 *male*
coven 11.3 *witchcraft*
covenant 116.3 *arrangement*, 116.23 *arrange*, 152.10 *agreement*, 166.1 *rule*, 667.2, 667.7 *contract*, 714.1, 714.7 *promise*, 715.1, 715.5 *contract*, 718.2 *promise*, 755.7 *gift*, 755.11 *give*, 845.6 *bond*, 847.7 *commitment*
covenantal 116.12 *arranged*, 715.7 *contractual*
covenantally 715.8 *contractually*
covenanted 116.12 *arranged*, 715.7 *contractual*, 718.7 *guaranteed*
covenanter 667.5 *assenter*, 715.4 *contractor*
Covenanters 7 Christian Movements
Covent Garden 740.1 *market*
Coventry 93 Cities
cover 293, 293, 27.4 *team*, 35.3 *rugby play*, 135.11 *make love*, 144.6 *fill*, 146.4 *include*, 148.11 *consist of*, 224.4 *be a substitute*, 248.20 *extend*, 258.5 *packet*, 258.21 *put in a container*, 266.10 *layer*, 279.7 *top*, 289.11 *be exterior*, 293.1 *covering*, 293.10 *bed covering*, 293.15 *shelter*, 295.32 *dress*, 323.2 *stopper*, 323.7 *close*, 354.5 *inset*, 436.6 *blinder*, 438.8 *make invisible*, 440.6 *shade*, 440.14 *make dark*, 443.11 *make opaque*, 524.13 *interpret news*, 531.8 *conceal*, 532.15 *publish*, 533.13 *report*, 546.1 *obliterate*, 546.3 *obliteration*, 560.15 *recount*, 621.11 *cleaning cloth*, 629.1 *repair*, 632.2 *protection*, 632.9 *protect*, 634.2 *shelter*, 671.19 *buffer*, 718.1 *protection*, 718.12 *certify*
cover a blade 36.16 *row*
coverage 146.1 *inclusion*, 248.7 *range*, 259.1 *size*, 293.1 *covering*, 532.3 *journalism*, 532.7 *publicity*, 533.3 *reporting*
coveralls 295.10 *suit*
cover charge 751.3 *fee*
cover crop 68.12 *crop*
cover defence 35.3 *rugby play*

covered 293, 258.20 *containing*, 279.6 *topped*, 289.6 *exterior*, 438.3 *private*, 443.1 *opaque*, 531.14 *concealed*, 546.6 *obliterated*, 632.5 *safe*, 718.7 *guaranteed*

covered market 740.7 *emporium*

covered over 293.36 *covered*

covered pit 527.7 *latent things*

covered up 293.36 *covered*

covered wagon 71 Carriages and Carts

covered way 327.7 *arcade*

covered yard 68.7 *farm building*

coverer 293

cover for 293, 222.4 *be a substitute*

cover ground 336.3 *press on*

covering 293, 293, 146.7 *including*, 258.20 *containing*, 266.3 *coat*, 289.1 *exterior*, 295.2 *dressing*, 323.2 *stopper*, 436.6 *blinder*, 457.3 *external appearance*

Covering 293

covering over 293.1 *covering*

covering up 531, 293.1 *covering*, 539.34 *deceiving*, 546.3 *obliteration*

coverlet 291.10 *bed covering*

cover oneself 781.5 *be cautious*

cover one's tracks 531.11 *conceal oneself*

cover point 31.6 *lacrosse player*

covert 11.14 *occult*, 77.20 *abode of mammals*, 78.13 *assemblage of birds*, 78.14 *nest*, 78.17 *plumage*, 85.4 *trees*, 256.13 *lair*, 293.15 *shelter*, 438.3 *private*, 527.2 *concealed*, 529.10 *secretive*, 531.15 *disguised*, 634.3 *animal shelter*

cover the ground 721.10 *augment*

covertly 527.15 *latently*

covertness 529.2 *secretiveness*

coverture 823.1 *marriage*

cover up 855, 293.31 *hide*, 529.12 *keep secret*, 531.8 *conceal*, 546.1 *obliterate*

cover-up 855, 531.5 *evasion*

cover up for 632.9 *protect*

cover with dust 622.11 *dirty*

covet 714.11 *promise oneself*, 782.12 *desire*, 841.6 *be jealous*, 842.3 *be envious of*, 860.6 *be selfish*

coveted 782.7 *desired*

coveter 782.6 *desirer*

coveting 782.9 *desirous*

covetous 453.5 *green-eyed*, 782.9 *desirous*, 841.4 *jealous*, 842.2 *envious*, 860.4 *selfish*

covetously 782.18 *desirously*, 841.9 *jealously*, 842.4 *enviously*, 860.8 *selfishly*

covetousness 453.14 *green-eyed monster*, 782.1 *desire*, 841.1 *jealousy*, 842.1 *envy*, 860.1 *selfishness*, 864.5 *seven deadly sins*

covey 161 Collective Names for Birds and Animals, 78.13 *assemblage of birds*, 181.4 *throng*

covin 539.7 *tricking*

cow 77 Placental Mammals, 68.8 *livestock*, 77.18 *female mammal*, 402.14 *female animal*, 587.2 *deter*, 777.13 *frighten*

coward 779, 238.4 *weakling*, 591.17 *avoider*, 641.2 *nonacting person*, 673.2 *appeaser*

cowardice 779, 238.2 *indecisiveness*, 576.13 *timidity*, 641.1 *inaction*

Cowardice 779

cowardliness 238.2 *indecisiveness*, 779.1 *cowardice*

cowardly 452, 779, 238.12 *weak-willed*, 238.14 *weakly*, 576.3 *timid*, 641.3 *inactive*

cowbell 49 Musical Instruments, 427.4 *sources of resonance*

cowbird 78 Birds

cowboy 32.15 *horse person*, 68.16 *farm worker*, 539.17 *cheat*, 653.14 *leader*, 656.10 *unskilled person*, 698.10 *independent*

cowboy boots 295.19 *footwear*

cowboy hat 295.15 *headgear*

cowboys and Indians 42 Children's Games and Party Games, 111.2 *opposites*

cowcatcher 632.4 *safety device*

cow chips 353.5 *faeces*

Cowdrey 18 Sporting Personalities

cow dung 246.3 *fertilizer*

cowed 777.7 *frightened*, 779.3 *cowardly*

cower 362.9 *bow*, 591.6 *evade*, 779.4 *be a coward*, 808.10 *knuckle under*

cowering 591.14 *evasion*, 591.18 *avoiding*, 779.1 *cowardice*, 779.3 *cowardly*, 808.7 *sycophantic*

Cowes 93 Cities

Cowes regatta 36.1 *sailing*

cow flops 353.5 *faeces*

cowgirl 32.15 *horse person*, 68.16 *farm worker*

cowhand 68.16 *farm worker*

cowheel 45.31 *offal*

cowherd 68.16 *farm worker*

cowhide 604.1 *materials*, 879.14 *instrument of punishment*

cow horse 32.12 *rodeo*

cowhouse 256.12 *stall*

cowing 777.4 *intimidation*

cowish 77.33 *ungulate*

cowl 71 Motor Vehicle Parts, 293.5 *body covering*, 293.31 *hide*, 295.15 *headgear*

Cowley 48 Poets

cowlick 77.33 *ungulate*

cowling 73 Aircraft Parts, 41.9 *bobsledding*

cowman 68.16 *farm worker*

cowork 116.22 *form an alliance*

co-worker 146.3 *person included*, 148.5 *member*, 180.11 *companion*, 230.5 *operator*, 400.10 *member of society*, 646.5 *partner*, 646.10 *cooperator*

co-workers 664.9 *team*

cow parsley 84 Flowers and Flowering Plants

cow pats 353.5 *faeces*

cowpea 84 Flowers and Flowering Plants

cow-pea soup 45.43 *US dish*

Cowper 48 Poets

Cowper's gland 352 Exocrine Glands

cow pony 32.4 *saddle horse*

cowpox 624.13 *skin disease*

cowpuncher 32.15 *horse person*, 68.16 *farm worker*

cowrie 81 Molluscs, 741.1 *money*

cowshed 68.7 *farm building*, 256.12 *stall*

cowslip 84 Flowers and Flowering Plants, 452.8 *yellow thing*

cow's milk 351.5 *milk*

cow's tail 34.4 *climbing equipment*

cow's udder 45.31 *offal*

cow tree 85 Trees and Shrubs

cox 36.16 *row*, 653.2 *direct*, 653.13 *director*

coxcomb 51.10 *comedy*, 295.15 *headgear*

coxed 36.11 *rowing*

coxed fours 36.4 *rowing*

coxed pairs 36.4 *rowing*

Cox's Orange Pippin 86 Fruits

coxswain 36.9 *sailor*, 74.7 *nautical person*

coxswainless 36.11 *rowing*

coxswainless fours 36.4 *rowing*

coxswainless pairs 36.4 *rowing*

coy 134.12 *morally pure*, 810.10 *bashful*, 821.20 *amorous*, 826.9 *endearing*, 876.9 *pure*

coyly 134.18 *virtuously*, 810.18 *shyly*, 826.10 *endearingly*

coyness 134.1 *purity*, 810.3 *bashfulness*, 821.6 *courtship*, 876.3 *moral purity*

coyote 77 Placental Mammals

coypu 77 Placental Mammals

cozen 538.25 *be dishonest*

cozenage 538.10 *dishonesty*

cozener 538.12, 539.17 *cheat*

CP/M 65.8 *software*

CPL 65 Programming Languages

C-plus 65 Programming Languages

CPU 65.5 *processor*

CR 65.10 *character*

crab 82 Insects, 45.19 *shellfish*, 73.5 *flight*, 74.9 *navigate*, 81.4 *arthropod*, 82.3 *pest*, 361.9 *lifter*, 830.11 *be irritable*, 852.18 *find fault*

Crab 53 The Constellations

crab apple 86 Fruits, 415.3 *sour thing*

Crabbe 48 Poets

crabbed 415.7 *splenetic*, 523.1 *unintelligible*, 551.2 *obscure*, 659.12 *problematic*, 764.2 *objectionable*

crabbedness 415.4 *spleen*, 829.1 *irascibility*

crabber 74 Ships and Boats

crabbiness 829.1 *irascibility*

crabbing 852.6, 852.28 *fault-finding*

crabby 415.7 *splenetic*, 764.2 *objectionable*, 829.4 *irascible*

crabeater seal 77 Placental Mammals

crab grass 87 Grasses

crablike 81.18 *arthropodous*

crab louse 82.3 *pest*

Crab nebula 53.8 *interstellar medium*

Crab Nebula 53 Nebulae

crab one's act 661.8 *hinder*

crabs 624.14 *venereal disease*

crabwalk 335.15 *deviating motion*

crabwood 85 Trees and Shrubs

crack 265, 265, 425, 425, 34.5 *rock face*, 136.3 *separateness*, 136.9 *separate*, 160.4 *interruption*, 264.9 *narrow place*, 322.1 *opening*, 322.18 *open*, 375.8 *rough ground*, 375.11 *be rough*, 375.12 *make rough*, 379.4 *be brittle*, 456.3 *striping*, 456.11 *variegate*, 479.1 *experiment*, 506.2 *solecism*, 524.9 *decipher*, 564.7 *utterance*, 568.2 *chat*, 596.5 *attempt*, 617.2 *best*, 620.7 *defect*, 655.6 *skilful*, 793.7 *blemish*, 861.1 *good*, 875.6 *drug*

crackable 379.1 *brittle*

crack a bottle 351.13 *drink*, 874.8 *get drunk*

crack a bottle with 815.11 *be sociable*

crack a code 524.9 *decipher*

crack a joke 771.13 *be humorous*

crack a safe 736.12 *steal*

crackback block 19.13 *penalty*

crack-brained 510.11 *insane*

crack cocaine 875.6 *drug*

crackdown 699.1 *restraint*, 709.1 *veto*

crack down 699.8 *restrain*

crack down on 709.3 *veto*

cracked 265, 322.12 *open*, 375.2 *coarse*, 379.1 *brittle*, 430.8 *hoarse*, 434.9 *unmelodious*, 510.11 *insane*, 524.15 *interpreted*, 563.10 *low-voiced*, 620.1 *imperfect*, 628.13 *dilapidated*, 793.4 *blemished*

cracked glass 456.5 *variegated thing*

cracked ice 409.5 *ice*

cracked voice 430.2 *hoarseness*

cracker 45.39 *loaf*, 255.5 *countryman*, 425.3 *banger*

crackerjack 617.1 *worthy*, 861.1 *good*, 861.17 *good thing*

crackers 510.11 *insane*

cracking 57.22 *industrial chemistry*, 379.1 *brittle*, 379.2 *brittleness*, 410.6 *oil*

crack jokes 506.6 *talk nonsense*

crackle 44.1 *ceramics*, 44.3 *glaze*, 408.15 *burn*, 425.2, 425.6 *crack*, 428.4 *faint sound*, 428.8 *sound faint*, 456.3 *striping*

crackled 379.1 *brittle*

crackling 425, 425.2 *crack*

crackling biscuit 45.43 *US dish*

crack of dawn 204.1 *morning*

crack of doom 157.5 *fate*, 244.4 *ruin*, 397.4 *death sentence*

crack off 379.4 *be brittle*

crack of the whip 228.4 *negative stimulus*, 586.8 *incentive*

crack one's throat 431.10 *cry out*

crack one's voice 423.8 *be loud*, 430.5 *sound hoarse*

crackpot 168.10 *eccentric*, 510.7 *insane person*

crack shot 338.15 *shooter*, 655.4 *skilled person*

cracksman 736.8, 736.8 *thief*

crack the cipher 524.9 *decipher*

crack the whip 512.3 *direct*, 688.19 *be authoritarian*

crack troops 617.7 *elite*, 679.14 *armed forces*

crackup 379.2 *brittleness*

crack up 650.5 *be fatigued*

crack-up 244.4 *ruin*, 510.6 *mental breakdown*

Cracow 93 Cities

cradle 47.6 *bed*, 91.6 *native land*, 156.3 *source*, 156.4 *conception*, 226.2 *source*, 256.3 *home*, 284.4 *rest*, 365.7 *oscillator*

cradle song 433.2 *song*

craft 50.1 *art*, 74.3 *vessel*, 165.8 *specialization*, 243.10 *produce*, 539.1 *deception*, 644.3 *job*, 655.1 *skill*, 657.1 *cunning*, 737.6 *business*

craftily 474.15 *hypocritically*, 657.6 *cunningly*

craftily contrived 655.9 *well-made*

craftiness 474.3 *cunning*, 507.1 *wisdom*, 539.1 *deception*, 655.1 *skill*, 657.1 *cunning*

craft knife 380.10 *knife*

crafts fair 526.6 *display*

craft show 526.6 *display*

craftsman 50.16 *artist*, 243.9 *producer*, 603.7 *machinist*, 640.3 *doer*, 646.2 *artisan*, 655.4 *skilled person*, 655.5 *expert*

craftsman-built 243.12 *produced*

craftsmanship 50.5 *artistry*, 243.1 *production*, 501.3 *learning*, 640.2 *deed*, 655.1 *skill*

craftswoman 243.9 *producer*, 655.4 *skilled person*, 655.5 *expert*

craft union 15.3 *organized labour*

craftworker 243.9 *producer*

crafty 474.8 *cunning*, 507.6 *intelligent*, 539.34 *deceiving*, 540.29 *deceitful*, 655.6 *skilful*, 657.4 *cunning*

crafty fellow 657.3 *cunning person*

crag 34.5 *rock face*, 95.1, 275.3 *mountain*, 281.3 *vertical thing*, 380.8 *sharp-pointed thing*

cragged 375.2 *coarse*

cragginess 373.5 *hardness*, 375.6 *roughness*

craggy 375.2 *coarse*, 380.4 *toothed*, 659.11 *rough*

cragsman 34.7 *mountaineer*, 359.11 *ascender*

crake 78 Birds, 78.3 *water bird*

cram 6.23 *learn*, 144.6 *fill*, 161.40 *crowd*, 257.7 *stuff*, 262.5 *make smaller*, 371.9 *make dense*, 610.4 *be excessive*, 872.5 *be greedy*

crambo 42 Children's Games and Party Games

cram-full 144.8 *full*

cram in 346.12 *flood in*, 354.3 *impact*

crammed 144.8 *full*, 161.50 *crowded*, 257.11 *loaded*, 610.6 *excessive*

crammer 6.4 *educator*

cramming 6.8 *learning*, 872.6 *gluttonous*
cramoisy 450.1 *red*
cramp 137.8 *fastening*, 262.5 *make smaller*, 272.10 *narrow*, 366.8 *spasm*, 406.1 *pain*, 406.10 *be painful*, 624.8 *indigestion*, 628.5 *hurt*, 699.5 *means of restraint*, 699.8 *restrain*
cramp ball 89 Fungi
cramped 260.7 *little*, 262.7 *smaller*, 272.1 *narrow*, 302.5 *limited*, 323.1 *unintelligible*, 609.1 *insufficient*, 659.12 *problematic*, 699.13 *restraining*
cramping 262.1 *contraction*, 262.8 *contracting*, 406.5 *painful*, 661.13 *hindering*
cramping one's style 699.1 *restraint*
crampit 41.10 *curling*
cramp one's style 609.5 *be insufficient*, 614.8 *make useless*, 628.5 *hurt*, 661.9 *block*, 699.8 *restrain*
crampons 34.4 *climbing equipment*
cramp someone's style 661.8 *hinder*
cranberry 86 Fruits
cranberry sauce 45.15 *sauce*, 413.2 *seasoning*
crane 78 Birds, 63.29 *construction equipment*, 78.3 *water bird*, 269.9 *be long*, 275.6 *tall thing*, 283.4 *hanger*, 361.9 *lifter*
Crane 48 Writers, 53 The Constellations
cranefly 82 Insects, 82.1 *insect*
crane one's neck 269.9 *be long*, 337.9 *turn round*
cranesbill 84 Flowers and Flowering Plants
Craniata 81.2 *protochordate*
craniate 81.2 *protochordate*
craniologer 1.3 *anthropologist*
craniological 1.11 *anthropological*
craniologically 1.16 *anthropologically*
craniologist 400.6 *studier of mankind*
craniology 1.1 *anthropology*, 400.5 *study of mankind*
craniometer 268.8 *meter*
craniometric 1.11 *anthropological*, 268.16 *micrometric*
craniometrical 1.11 *anthropological*
craniometrically 1.16 *anthropologically*
craniometrist 1.3 *anthropologist*
craniometry 1.1 *anthropology*, 1.10 *measurement*, 268.2 *micrometry*, 400.5 *study of mankind*
craniotomy 60 Surgical Operations
cranium 382 Bones
crank 71 Motor Vehicle Parts, 63.8 *machine element*, 63.11 *engine*, 71.11 *bicycle part*, 104.5 *nonconformist*, 168.8 *dissenter*, 335.19 *deviant person*, 364.9 *roll*, 510.7 *insane person*, 519.9 *visionary*, 579.4 *capricious person*, 594.4 *prepare for action*, 666.4 *dissenter*, 829.3 *irascible person*
crankcase 71 Motor Vehicle Parts
crankily 829.9 *irascibly*, 830.14 *irritably*
crankiness 510.1 *insanity*, 579.2 *caprice*, 829.1 *irascibility*, 830.3 *irritableness*
cranking over 33.6 *motor racing terms*
crank over 33.10 *be on the track*
crankshaft 63.11 *engine*
crank up 594.4 *prepare for action*
cranky 510.11 *insane*, 829.4 *irascible*, 830.7 *irritable*
crannog 94.7 *lake dwelling*
cranny 258.2 *compartment*, 265.2 *crack*, 317.3 *cavity*, 531.2 *hiding place*

crap 353.5 *faeces*, 353.16 *defecate*, 506.1 *nonsense*, 521.4 *senseless talk*, 521.14, 538.6 *nonsense*, 540.13 *nonsense*, 618.8 *inferiority*, 622.4 *dirt*
crapper 353.13 *lavatory*, 727.7 *toilet*
crappie 80 Fishes
crappily 353.33 *scatologically*
crappy 127.14 *poor*, 614.1 *useless*, 618.2 *inferior*
craps 42.5 *dice*
crapulence 874, 870.3 *overindulgence*
crapulent 870.8 *overindulgent*, 874.4 *crapulous*
crapulently 874.18 *drunkenly*
crapulous 874
crapulously 874.18 *drunkenly*
crapulousness 874.15 *crapulence*
crash 67 Natural Fabrics, **161** Collective Names for Birds and Animals, 65.17 *computing term*, 65.19 *abort*, 97.10 *billow*, 129.3 *decreasing thing*, 241.3 *instance of violence*, 244.4 *ruin*, 256.18 *take up residence*, 330.2 *collide*, 330.12 *collision*, 360.4 *fall*, 360.5 *dive*, 360.10 *droop*, 360.11 *trip*, 360.12 *drop*, 379.4 *be brittle*, 407.12 *abut*, 423.2 *outcry*, 423.8 *be loud*, 425.1, 425.5 *bang*, 434.10 *lack harmony*, 683.1 *failure*, 683.9 *malfunction*, 747.5 *insolvency*, 747.9 *be unable to pay*
Crashaw 48 Poets
crash barrier 71.21 *miscellaneous motoring terms*, 632.4 *safety device*
crash diet 350.6 *nutrition*, 871.1 *fasting*
crash-dieting 274.10 *diet*
crash-dive 73.5 *flight*
crash down 255.15 *settle*
crasher 788.3 *boring person*
crash helmet 295.15 *headgear*, 632.4 *safety device*, 671.6 *protective clothing*
crash in 241.7 *be violent*
crashing 360.16 *descending*, 407.9 *touching*, 423.6 *loud*, 425.8 *banging*
crashing bore 788.3 *boring person*
crash into 330.2 *collide*
crashland 360.12 *drop*
crash landing 73.5 *flight*
crash-landing 360.5 *dive*
crash pad 256.1 *habitat*
crash wagon 71 Motor Vehicles
crashworthiness 71.21 *miscellaneous motoring terms*
crass 412.6 *coarse*
crassly 412.11 *tastelessly*
crassness 412.4 *bad taste*
crate 71.16 *car*, 120.3 *container*, 258.6 *box*, 293.13 *casing*, 293.25 *wrap*
crated 293.37 *protected*
crater 53.17 *moon*, 54.24 *volcanic activity*, 277.4 *deep thing*, 317.2 *concave land*
Crater 53 The Constellations
crate up 258.21 *put in a container*
cravat 137.6 *line*, 295.14 *neckwear*
cravattine 45 Types of Pasta
crave 593.8 *miss*, 782.12 *desire*, 842.3 *be envious of*
craven 452.5 *cowardly*, 779.2 *coward*, 779.3 *cowardly*
cravenly 779
cravenness 779.1 *cowardice*
craving 61.15 *compulsion*, 350.2 *appetite*, 510.4 *delusion*, 593.5 *necessitous*, 782.1 *desire*, 782.9 *desirous*, 784.3 *likes*
crawdad 45.19 *shellfish*
crawfish 45.19 *shellfish*, 81.4 *arthropod*, 337.3 *reverse*
crawl 39.1 *swimming*, 79.15 *live as a reptile*, 79.15 *live as an amphibian*, 161.40, 181.11 *crowd*, 276.8 *be low*, 328.1 *move slowly*, 328.10 *slow motion*, 467.14 *be solicitous*, 578.4 *re-

cant, 673.4 *succumb*, 806.20 *submit*, 806.21 *humble oneself*, 808.9 *fawn*, 853.11 *be sycophantic*
crawler 808.3, 853.7 *sycophant*
crawler lane 71.3 *carriageway*
crawler tractor 71 Motor Vehicles
crawling 161.50 *crowded*, 328.4 *slow*, 334.19 *radio reception*, 608.3 *filled*, 610.6 *excessive*, 622.8 *unclean*, 673.5 *submitting*, 808.2 *sycophancy*, 808.7, 808.7 *sycophantic*, 853.16 *sycophantic*
crawlingly 328.17 *in slow motion*
crawling with 144.8 *full*
crawl into one's shell 810.15 *escape notice*
crawl out of the woodwork 457.12 *become visible*
crawl with 82.16 *infest*, 608.5 *about*, 610.4 *be excessive*
Cray 65.3 *computer*
crayfish 45.19 *shellfish*, 81.4 *arthropod*
crayon 50.9 *drawing*, 50.11 *artist's materials*, 444.15 *colour*
craze 61.15 *compulsion*, 379.4 *be brittle*, 456.3 *striping*, 456.11 *variegate*, 510.4 *delusion*, 579.3 *whim*, 584.4 *custom*, 784.3 *likes*, 796.1 *fashion*
crazed 241.6 *violent*, 821.19 *enamoured*
crazily 153.19 *distractedly*, 510.17 *insanely*
craziness 508.1 *folly*, 510.1 *insanity*
crazing 44.3 *glaze*
crazy 379.1 *brittle*, 506.5 *nonsensical*, 508.5 *foolish*, 510.11 *insane*, 579.1 *capricious*, 633.2 *unsafe*
crazy about 821.18 *in love*
crazy idea 461.6 *idea*
crazy paving 69.3 *ornamental garden*, 113.3 *diverse thing*, 293.11 *paving*, 456.5 *variegated thing*
creak 424.1 *faintness*, 424.5 *sound faint*, 430.3 *shrillness*, 430.6 *be shrill*
creakiness 430.3 *shrillness*
creaking 430.9 *shrill*
creaking door 430.3 *shrillness*
creaky 238.8 *weak*, 430.9 *shrill*
cream 77 Breeds of Cats, 62.7 *ointment*, 126.7 *the best people*, 243.7 *produce*, 351.5 *milk*, 386.5 *ointment*, 386.14 *anoint*, 393.8 *pulp*, 395.6 *ointment*, 395.8 *fat*, 395.18 *anoint*, 439.14 *light colour*, 580.4 *pick*, 611.3 *chief thing*, 617.7 *elite*, 628.5 *hurt*, 630.9 *balm*, 861.9 *the best*
cream cheese 45 Cheeses
cream-coloured 439.21 *light*, 452.1 *yellow*
creamcracker 45.39 *loaf*
creamer 133.6 *mixer*
creamery 647.1 *workshop*
creamily 395.20 *oilily*, 446.14 *whitely*, 452.11 *yellowly*
creaminess 393.4 *pulpiness*, 395.1 *oiliness*, 446.7 *whiteness*
cream-maker 133.6 *mixer*
cream off 355.17 *obtain an extract*
cream of the crop 126.7 *the best people*, 861.9 *the best*
cream sherry 351.9 *wine*
cream soda 351.6, 351.6 *soft drink*, 414.5 *sweet drink*
cream soup 45.13 *soup*
cream tea 350.12 *meal*
creamware 44.1 *ceramics*
creamy 393.8 *pulp*, 395.11 *oily*, 444.13 *soft-hued*, 446.1 *white*, 452.1 *yellow*
crease 27.5 *wicket*, 135.5 *joint*, 151.24 *make disordered*, 320.2, 320.8 *pleat*, 321.2, 321.7 *wrinkle*, 375.12 *make rough*
creased 320.5 *folded*, 321.5 *wrinkly*

crease-resistant 67.11 *treated*
creasy 320.5 *folded*
create 50.23 *design*, 99.20 *bring into being*, 119.7 *originate*, 156.22 *invent*, 226.9 *be the cause of*, 243.10 *produce*, 306.7 *form*, 382.15 *shape*, 471.15 *imagine*, 479.13, 496.4 *invent*, 519.14 *imagine*, 592.11 *invent*, 796.8 *fashion*
create a barrier 661.9 *block*
create a catch-22 situation 657.5 *be cunning*
create a controversy 687.11 *cause adversity*
create a log jam 209.8 *delay*, 661.9 *block*
create anarchy 693.16 *be subversive*
create a need 593.10 *necessitate*
create an obstacle 661.9 *block*
create an opening for oneself 210.5 *take the opportunity*
create a scandal 785.7 *cause dislike*
create a scene 828.11 *be angry*
create a sensation 611.7 *be important*
create a treasure 696.14 *master*
create a vacuum 372.6 *make sparse*
create bad blood 822.16 *cause hate*
created 99, 243.12 *produced*, 306.9 *formed*, 519.12 *imaginary*
create difficulties 659
create life 396.19 *give birth to*
create nonrepresentational art 548.4 *misrepresent*
create problems 687.11 *cause adversity*
create resentment 841.7 *arouse jealousy*
creatine phosphate 58.22 *bioenergetics*
creating a part 51.20 *acting*
creating a role 51.20 *acting*
creation 99, 156, 119.1 *originality*, 156.5 *invention*, 208.3 *early stage*, 226.1 *cause*, 243.1 *production*, 243.3 *product*, 295.1 *dress*, 306.4 *forming*, 382.3 *form*, 382.5 *structuring*, 396.8 *theories of life*, 496.9 *invention*, 655.3 *masterpiece*
creation of genius 655.3 *masterpiece*
creative 119.4 *original*, 156.33 *inventive*, 226.13 *causal*, 243.11 *productive*, 246.5 *fertile*, 306.9 *formed*, 309.8 *exaggerated*, 471.11 *ideational*, 479.9 *original*, 519.10 *imaginative*, 640.5 *acting*, 750.10 *accounting*
creative accountant 736.11 *dishonest person*
creative accounting 711.1 *refusal*, 747.1 *nonpayment*, 750.1 *accounts*
creative artist 135.7 *joiner*, 243.9 *producer*, 471.9 *person of ideas*, 479.5 *experimenter*
creative composition 560.5 *fiction*
creative economy 638.1 *escape*
creative exercise 519.4 *ideality*
creative force 519.1 *imagination*
creative imagination 48.13 *poetic genius*
creative impulse 243.1 *production*
creatively 50.31 *artistically*, 119.8 *originally*, 226.14 *causally*, 243.13 *productively*, 246.8 *fruitfully*, 306.13 *formatively*, 461.18 *thoughtfully*, 471.22 *imaginatively*, 479.15 *inventively*, 519.17 *imaginatively*, 750.13 *financially*
creativeness 119.1 *originality*, 519.1 *imagination*
creative person 640.3 *doer*
creative thought 461, 519.1 *imagination*
creative urge 243.1 *production*
creative work 519.1 *imagination*
creative worker 519.9 *visionary*, 640.3 *doer*

creative writer 119.3 *originator*, 560.10 *descriptive writer*
creative writing 519.4 *ideality*, 560.5 *fiction*
creativity 119.1 *originality*, 471.8 *imagination*, 479.4 *originality*, 519.1 *imagination*
creator 119.3, 156.16 *originator*, 243.9 *producer*, 471.9 *person of ideas*, 479.5 *experimenter*
creature 59.3 *organism*, 76.2 *animal*, 232.3 *assistant*, 243.3 *product*, 400.7 *person*, 808.3 *sycophant*
creature comforts 350.7 *food*, 405.4 *pleasurable things*, 763.7 *pleasure*
creaturely 400.12 *human*
creature of habit 183, 584
creature of impulse 583.6 *improviser*
crecelle 49 *Musical Instruments*
crèche 6.12 *educational institution*
cred 105.1 *state*, 105.8 *in a state of*
credence 490.10 *conviction*, 497.3 *believing*
credential 480.6 *evidence*, 483.6 *documentation*, 545.2 *certificate*, 688.9 *permission*, 851.6 *recommendation*
credentials 485.3 *qualifications*, 544.3 *means of identification*, 708.2 *permit*
credibility 486.2 *possibleness*, 488.3 *plausibility*, 497.4 *believability*, 800.1 *estimation*
credibility gap 117.1 *disparity*, 666.3 *difference*
credible 486.5 *possible*, 488.7 *plausible*, 497.13 *believable*
credibly 486.11 *potentially*, 497.16 *believably*
credit 733, 744, 744, 845, 132.3 *difference*, 233.3 *personal influence*, 490.20 *be certain*, 497.3 *believing*, 497.7 *believe*, 602.4 *financial resources*, 617.6 *worth*, 662.9 *financial assistance*, 718.2 *promise*, 730.9 *receive*, 742.8 *solvency*, 749.7 *receive*, 750.1 *accounts*, 750.7 *account*, 800.1 *estimation*, 837.3 *recognition*, 845.2 *due*, 851.2 *admiration*, 863.3 *worth*, 878.1, 878.9 *reward*
Credit 744
creditable 497.13 *believable*, 617.1 *worthy*, 782.8 *desirable*, 800.3 *reputable*, 851.21 *praiseworthy*
credit account 733.4, 744.1 *credit*, 744.3 *deposit*, 745.1 *debt*
credit balance 744.3 *deposit*
credit bureau 744.4 *bank*
credit buyer 745.6 *debtor*
credit card 744, 56.64 *magnetic recording*, 733.4 *credit*, 745.1 *debt*
credit-card 733.11 *borrowed*
credit-card company 732.4 *lending institution*
credit-card holder 733.6 *borrower*, 738.12 *purchaser*
credit-card number 544.3 *means of identification*
credit card purchase 738.7 *purchasing*
credit company 732.4 *lending institution*
credit control 744.1 *credit*
credited 749.6 *received*, 750.11 *accounted*, 878.16 *rewarded*
credit facility 733.4 *credit*
crediting 837.5 *thanking*
credit limit 602.4 *financial resources*, 744.1 *credit*
credit line 837.3 *recognition*
credit note 744.2 *credit card*
creditor 606.3 *provider*, 732.3 *lender*
creditors budget 750.2 *budgeting*
credit rating 602.4 *financial resources*, 744.1 *credit*

credits 171.6 *list of names*, 602.4 *financial resources*, 730.2 *something received*, 744.3 *deposit*, 749.2 *money received*, 837.3 *recognition*
credit squeeze 699.2 *economic restraint*
credit to one's account 721.12 *earn*, 744.10 *deposit*
credit union 732.4 *lending institution*, 744.4 *bank*
credit user 733.6 *borrower*
creditworthiness 602.4 *financial resources*, 742.8 *solvency*, 744.1 *credit*
creditworthy 742.2 *solvent*, 744.13 *in credit*, 800.3 *reputable*
credo 4.2 *philosophical system*, 7.1 *religion*, 10.6 *Eucharist*, 471.5 *ideology*, 497.2 *religious belief*
Credo 10.9 *prayer*
credulity 466.1 *incuriousness*, 497.3 *believing*, 586.7 *persuadability*, 658.2 *naivety*
credulous 453.3 *raw*, 466.3 *incurious*, 497.11 *believing*, 497.12 *gullible*, 586.20 *persuadable*, 658.1, 865.7 *naive*
credulously 466.7 *incuriously*, 497.15 *believingly*, 658.5, 865.12 *naively*
credulousness 466.1 *incuriousness*, 497.3 *believing*, 586.7 *persuadability*, 865.3 *naivety*
Cree 1 *Peoples*, **5** *Languages and Groups of Languages*
creed 4.2 *philosophical system*, 7.1 *religion*, 10.6 *Eucharist*, 471.5 *ideology*, 497.2 *religious belief*, 535.2 *statement*
creedal 497.14 *believed*, 535.10 *affirmative*
creek 96.1 *river*
Creek 1 *Peoples*, **5** *Languages and Groups of Languages*
creel 258.7 *basket*
Creeley 48 *Poets*
creep 54.26 *mass movement*, 63.16 *deformation*, 79.15 *live as a reptile*, 79.16 *live as an amphibian*, 276.8 *be low*, 324.12 *gait*, 328.1 *move slowly*, 328.10 *slow motion*, 375.11 *be rough*, 527.13 *hide*, 531.11 *conceal oneself*, 612.10 *nonentity*, 771.7 *person who humours*, 808.3, 853.7 *sycophant*, 853.11 *be sycophantic*
creeper 78 *Birds*, 69.9 *garden plant*
creepers 295.23 *children's clothes*
creepily 376.16 *suavely*, 808.17 *sycophantically*
creep in 346.11 *infiltrate*
creeping 79.21 *reptilian*, 83.14 *of plants*, 328.4 *slow*, 328.10 *slow motion*, 534.19 *radio reception*, 853.16 *sycophantic*
creeping bent 87 *Grasses*
creeping flesh 375.7 *rough thing*, 785.4 *sign of dislike*
creeping Jenny 84 *Flowers and Flowering Plants*
creeping Jesus 7.5 *Christian*, 808.3 *sycophant*
creepingly 328.17 *in slow motion*
creeping thing 76.2 *animal*
creep into a corner 816.12 *be unsocial*
creep off 591.8 *run away*
creep to 808.9 *fawn*
creep up on 514.10 *ambush*
creep up to 376.13 *smooth over*
creepy 11.18 *spiritual*, 376.6 *smooth-mannered*, 808.7 *sycophantic*
creepy-crawly 82.1 *insect*, 328.14 *slow creature*
cremate 399.8 *bury*, 408.15 *burn*
cremated 399.10 *buried*
cremation 399.1 *burial*
crematorial 399.11 *funeral*
crematorium 397.8 *after death*, 399.1 *burial*, 399.2 *funeral*, 408.6 *fire*
crematory 399.11 *funeral*

crème caramel 45.35 *dessert*
crème de la crème 617.7 *elite*
crème de menthe 351.7 *alcoholic drink*
crème fraîche 393.8 *pulp*
cremnophobia 777 *Phobias by Name*
cremocarp 86.2 *botanical fruit*
crenate 83.18 *of leaves*, 319.4 *notched*, 375.12 *make rough*
crenated 319.4 *notched*
crenately 319.7 *jaggedly*
crenation 319.1 *notch*
crenature 319.1 *notch*
crenel 319.1 *notch*
crenellate 300.6 *edge*, 319.5 *notch*
crenellation 300.2 *edging*
crenulation 319.1 *notch*
creodont 77 *Placental Mammals*
creole 5.10 *language type*
Creole 133.5 *hybrid*
creophagous 350.26 *eating*
creophagously 350.28 *carnivorously*
creophagy 350.5 *eating habit*
creosote 293.3 *coating*, 293.24 *coat*, 637.2 *preserver*, 637.5 *preserve*
crepe 67 *Natural Fabrics*, 447.9 *black thing*, 544.5 *uniform*
crêpe 45.39 *loaf*
crepe de Chine 67 *Natural Fabrics*
crêpe pan 45.6 *kitchen equipment*
crepe paper 604.3 *paper*
crêperie 350.15 *eating place*
crepe rubber 377.4 *rubber*
crepe-soled shoes 295.19 *footwear*
crêpes suzette 45.45 *French dish*
crepitant 425.9 *crackling*
crepitate 425.6 *crack*
crepitation 425.2 *crack*
crepuscular 205.6 *evening*, 441.5 *dim*
Crepuscular school 48 *Literary Groups and Movements*
Crescas 4 *Philosophers*
crescendo 121.6 *change gradually*, 128.2 *spread*, 128.4 *increase*, 261.1 *growth*, 261.6 *become bigger*, 423.1 *loudness*, 423.6 *loud*, 423.9 *loudly*, 721.2 *augmentation*
crescent 26.15 *wrestling*, 52.42 *circle*, 128.6 *increasing*, 261.8 *growing*, 311.2 *bend*, 313.4 *parts of a circle*, 327.3 *road*, 543.1 *sign*, 544.8 *heraldic device*
crescent dune 54.37 *dune*
crescentic 311.4 *curved*
crescent kick 26.9 *tae kwon do*
crescent moon 53.17 *moon*
crescent-shaped 52.81 *curvilinear*
cresol 57 *Types of Compounds*, **62** *Medication*
cress 45 *Vegetables*
crest 78.17 *plumage*, 95.1 *mountain*, 126.4 *summit*, 275.4 *mountain range*, 279.1 *summit*, 365.5 *wave*, 544.8 *heraldic device*
Cresta Run at St. Moritz 41.9 *bobsledding*
crested 279.6 *topped*, 544.13 *heraldic*, 805.21 *ostentatious*
Crested 68 *Breeds of Fowl*
crested tit 78 *Birds*
crestfallen 515.9 *disappointed*, 770.5 *sad*, 806.3 *humbled*
crest of the wave 126.4, 279.1 *summit*
Cretaceous 54 *Geological Time Intervals*
Cretaceous period 200.3 *geological period*
Crete 98 *Islands*
cretic 48.9 *metre*
cretin 460.3 *unintelligent person*, 508.3 *foolish person*, 510.7 *insane person*
cretinism 510.2 *subnormality*
cretinous 460.5 *lacking intellect*, 460.7 *intellectually subnormal*
cretonne 67 *Natural Fabrics*

Creutzfeld-Jacob disease 510.3 *mental deterioration*
crevasse 34.5 *rock face*, 54.38 *glacier*, 98.8 *valley*, 160.4 *interruption*, 265.3 *gulf*, 277.4 *deep thing*, 317.2 *concave land*, 635.1 *trap*
crevassed 34.8 *mountaineering*
Creve-coeur 68 *Breeds of Fowl*
crevice 265.2 *crack*, 322.1 *opening*
creviced 322.12 *open*
crew 36.15 *sail*, 68.16 *farm worker*, 73.3 *aircraft personnel*, 74.9 *navigate*, 116.2 *alliance*, 146.3 *person included*, 161.12 *team*, 161.13 *workforce*, 230.9 *take action*, 594.5 *equip*, 646.4 *personnel*, 665.1 *party*, 703.4 *council*
crew cut 270.4 *short thing*
Crewe 93 *Cities*
crewelist 792.7 *decorator*
crewel work 792.2 *pattern*
crewman 36.9 *sailor*
crew member 146.3 *person included*
crew-neck 295.13 *sweater*
crew socks 295.20 *legwear*
crib 6.14 *school book*, 47.6 *bed*, 118.2, 118.10 *copy*, 256.1 *habitat*, 284.4 *rest*, 524.4 *translation*, 736.15 *infringe*
cribbage 42 *Card Games*
cribber 736.10 *infringer*
cribbing 736.6 *illegal borrowing*
cribriform 322.14 *holed*
crick 96.1 *river*
Crick 52 *Scientists*
cricket 18 *Sporting Activities*, **82** *Insects*
Cricket 27
cricket ball 338.10 *ball*
cricketer 27.4 *team*, 237.5 *athlete*
cricketing 27
cricket match 27
cricket season 203.1 *season*
crick in the neck 406.2 *painful condition*
crier 431, 154.8 *precursor*, 532.10 *publicizer*
crikey 827.11 *miscellaneous euphemisms*
crim 832.8 *malefactor*, 844.10 *wrongdoer*
crime 16, 504.8 *moral error*, 618.9 *badness*, 640.2 *deed*, 693.2 *violation of the law*, 832.7 *act of malevolence*, 844.8 *wrong-doing*, 858.3 *criminality*, 862.5 *evil thing*, 864.7 *criminality*, 866.3 *sin*
crime against humanity 832.7 *act of malevolence*
Crimean War 17 *Major Wars*
crime fiction 560.5 *fiction*
crime of passion 398.2 *murder*, 841.1 *jealousy*
crime story 48.2 *fiction*
crime wave 16.41 *lawlessness*
crime writer 48.14 *author*, 560.10 *descriptive writer*
criminal 693, 858, 864, 16.40 *lawbreaker*, 16.60 *offending*, 127.15 *subordinate*, 335.19 *deviant person*, 477.15 *sceptical*, 590.7 *the hunted*, 618.3 *bad*, 635.2 *troublemaker*, 640.3 *doer*, 652.5 *badly behaved person*, 659.9 *difficult person*, 693.13 *disobedient*, 736.11 *dishonest person*, 822.8 *hated person*, 832.8 *malefactor*, 844.10 *wrongdoer*, 844.16 *in the wrong*, 852.36 *blameworthy*, 858.4 *dishonourable person*, 862.6 *evil person*, 864.9 *wicked person*, 864.11 *wicked*, 866.4 *guilty person*, 866.7 *sinful*, 877.11 *immoral*
criminal act 640.2 *deed*, 864.7 *criminality*
criminal activity 16.39 *crime*
criminal classes 127.6 *inferior*
criminal conversation 877.4 *illicit love*

criminal court 16.19 *lawcourt,* 492.3 *place of judgment*
criminal insanity 510.1 *insanity*
criminal intent 588.1 *intention*
criminal investigation 477.2 *questioning*
criminality 858, 864, 16.38 *lawbreaking,* 16.39 *crime,* 693.2 *violation of the law,* 844.6 *unlawfulness,* 864.1 *wickedness,* 866.1 *guilt,* 877.1 *immorality*
criminalize 846, 16.75 *make illegal,* 709.3 *veto*
criminalized 846.12 *disentitled*
criminal law 16.1 *the law*
criminally 864, 16.82 *illegally,* 693.17 *disobediently,* 858.11 *dishonourably,* 866.11 *guiltily*
criminal offence 16.39 *crime,* 864.7 *criminality,* 866.3 *sin*
criminal psychology 61.1 *psychology*
criminal record 545.1 *record*
criminal statistics 16.37 *criminology*
criminal world 864.7 *criminality*
criminologist 16.37 *criminology*
criminology 16
crimp 791, 320.2, 320.8 *pleat,* 539.17 *cheat,* 661.8 *hinder,* 736.8 *thief,* 736.13 *kidnap*
crimper 791.11 *beautician*
crimpers 791.11 *hairdressing salon*
crimping 736.2 *kidnapping*
Crimplene 67 Synthetic Fibres and Fabrics
crimson 450.1 *red,* 450.9 *redden,* 810.16 *be self-conscious*
crimsoning 810.2, 810.9 *blushing*
crimson lake 450.6 *red pigment*
cringe 331.2 *respond,* 331.6 *response,* 362.9 *bow,* 578.4 *recant,* 673.4 *succumb,* 779.4 *be a coward,* 808.10 *knuckle under*
cringing 673.5 *submitting,* 808.2 *sycophancy,* 808.7, 808.7 *sycophantic*
crinkle 69.12 *pests and diseases,* 320.2, 320.8 *pleat,* 321.2, 321.7 *wrinkle,* 375.12 *make rough*
crinkled 321.5 *wrinkly,* 375.1 *rough*
crinkly 321.5 *wrinkly,* 375.1 *rough*
crinkum-crankum 519.4 *ideality*
crinoid 81.3 *echinoderm*
crinoidal 81.17 *echinodermal*
crinoline 67 Natural Fabrics, 295.6 *skirt,* 295.18 *underwear*
Criollo 32 Breeds of Horse and Pony
Crioulu Braziliero 32 Breeds of Horse and Pony
cripple 236.8 *overpower,* 238.7 *weaken,* 614.8 *make useless,* 624.19 *sick person,* 628.5 *hurt,* 661.8 *hinder*
crippled 236.12 *impotent,* 238.10 *ill,* 620.3 *deformed*
crippling 628.11 *hurt*
crisis 106.4 *difficult circumstances,* 121.4 *interval,* 210.3 *critical time,* 221.3 *turning point,* 477.4 *difficult question,* 593.3 *needfulness,* 611.2 *important matter,* 633.5 *danger*
crisis point 172.4 *zero level,* 221.3 *turning point*
crisis theology 7.13 *theology*
crisp 55.45 *fine,* 373.9 *harden,* 379.1 *brittle,* 384.20 *crumbly,* 552.3 *concise*
crispbread 45.39 *loaf*
crispily 379.5 *fragilely*
crispiness 379.2 *brittleness*
crisply 552.5 *concisely,* 562.11 *summarily*
crispness 379.2 *brittleness,* 552.1 *conciseness*
crisps 45.10 *snack*
crispy 379.1 *brittle*
crisscross 288.1 *interweaving,* 288.6 *interwoven,* 288.8 *interweave*
cristobalite 54 Minerals

criterion 52.65 *theory,* 56.6 *law,* 124.4 *average,* 154.4 *precedent,* 166.4 *guide,* 268.7 *standard*
critic 852, 51.31 *theatregoer,* 136.8 *person who separates,* 481.6 *discriminating person,* 492.5 *judge,* 500.5 *dissenter,* 518.4 *theorist,* 524.6 *interpreter,* 532.11 *newspaper man,* 533.4 *journalist,* 561.3 *dissertator,* 654.4 *adviser,* 666.4 *dissenter,* 713.4 *protester,* 854.7 *disparager*
critical 210, 670, 852, 6.20 *refined,* 16.49 *judicatory,* 48.16 *literary,* 106.8 *difficult,* 230.12 *operative,* 481.9 *discriminating,* 492.8 *judging,* 524.16 *annotative,* 561.5 *expository,* 611.5 *important,* 624.22 *sick,* 633.1 *dangerous,* 633.2 *unsafe,* 659.14 *troublesome,* 713.9 *protesting,* 772.3 *important,* 794.5 *refined,* 854.15 *disparaging*
critical edition 524.1 *interpretation*
critical juncture 210.3 *critical time*
critically 210, 106.17 *difficultly,* 230.13 *operationally,* 481.16 *judiciously,* 492.13 *judicially,* 535.25 *explicitly,* 611.9 *importantly,* 659.29 *perversely,* 713.11, 852.37 *disapprovingly,* 854.18 *disparagingly*
critical mass 56.72 *nuclear fission*
critical moment 106, 210.3 *critical time*
critical of 766.4 *dissatisfied*
critical power 524.3 *criticism*
critical remarks 852.5, 854.2 *criticism*
critical review 852.5 *criticism*
critical situation 659
critical state 56.38 *thermodynamics*
critical success 51.11 *theatrical performance*
critical temperature 56.38 *thermodynamics*
critical time 210
criticism 524, 852, 854, 48.4 *non-fiction,* 481.2 *judiciousness,* 492.1 *judgment,* 524.5 *science of interpretation,* 561.2 *article,* 654.1 *advice,* 666.1 *disagreement,* 670.16 *terrorist attack,* 766.2 *expression of dissatisfaction*
criticize 524, 670, 852, 854, 4.23 *discuss philosophically,* 481.14 *discriminate against,* 492.11 *judge,* 492.12 *estimate,* 561.4 *dissertate,* 654.5 *advise,* 659.23 *cause difficulties,* 659.24 *create difficulties,* 663.15 *object,* 666.5 *disagree,* 766.7 *be dissatisfied*
criticized 852
criticizer 852.12 *critic*
criticizing 492.8 *judging,* 666.9 *disagreeing*
critic's gift 524.3 *criticism*
critique 48.4 *non-fiction,* 492.1 *judgment,* 524.3 *criticism,* 524.11 *criticize,* 561.2 *article*
critter 76.2 *animal*
Croad Langshan 68 Breeds of Fowl
croak 79.16 *live as an amphibian,* 397.15 *die,* 430.2 *hoarseness,* 430.5 *sound hoarse,* 432.2 *bird song,* 432.4 *cry*
croaker 80 Fishes
croakily 432.10 *howlingly*
croakiness 563.2 *inarticulation*
croaking 430.8 *hoarse,* 563.10 *low-voiced*
croaky 430.8 *hoarse*
Croatia 91 Countries
Croatians 1 Peoples
croc 79.5 *crocodilian*
Croce 4 Philosophers
crocein 67.6 *dye*
crochet 42 Hobbies and Pastimes, 135.10 *link,* 288.2 *braid,* 288.8 *interweave,* 792.2 *pattern*
crocidolite 54 Minerals
crock 44.8 *ceramic object*

crockery 258, 44.1 *ceramics*
crocket 43 Architectural Decoration
crock up 650.5 *be fatigued,* 650.6 *fatigue*
crocodile 79 Reptiles, 79.5 *crocodilian,* 159.8 *procession,* 269.5 *piece*
crocodile bird 78 Birds
crocodiles 161 Collective Names by Animal
crocodile tears 538.9, 540.3 *hypocrisy*
Crocodilia 79.1 *reptile*
crocodilian 79, 79.11 *reptilian*
crocoite 54 Minerals
crocus 84 Flowers and Flowering Plants, 452.8 *yellow thing*
Croesus 742.10 *wealthy person*
croft 68.6 *farm*
crofter 68.15 *agriculturist,* 255.5 *countryman*
Crohn's disease 624.8 *indigestion*
croissant 45.39 *loaf*
Cro-Magnon man 200.6 *people of the past,* 202.7 *ancient people,* 400.3 *uncivilized human*
crombie 295.12 *coat*
cromlech 3.11 *relic,* 10.13 *shrine,* 200.7 *thing of the past,* 399.6 *grave,* 545.11 *monument*
Crommelin 53 Comets
cromolyn sodium 62 Medication
Crompton 52 Scientists
Cronin 48 Writers
Cronos 8 Deities
crony 819.5 *friend*
crook 7.11 *vestment,* 16.40 *lawbreaker,* 286.6 *be oblique,* 335.5 *twist,* 539.17 *cheat,* 734.6 *taker,* 736.11 *dishonest person,* 832.8 *malefactor,* 844.10 *wrongdoer,* 858.4 *dishonourable person,* 862.6 *evil person,* 864.10 *bad person*
crooked 16.60 *offending,* 286.4 *oblique,* 309.6 *distorted,* 335.21 *indirect,* 527.5 *mysterious,* 540.31 *fraudulent,* 618.3 *bad,* 657.4 *cunning,* 736.18 *fraudulent,* 844.16 *in the wrong,* 858.5 *dishonourable,* 858.7 *criminal*
crookedly 309.13 *asymmetrically*
crookedness 16.38 *lawbreaking,* 286.1 *obliqueness,* 309.1 *distortion,* 540.8 *fraud,* 618.9 *badness,* 858.1 *improbity,* 858.3 *criminality*
crooked teeth 215.3 *irregular thing*
Crookes 52 Scientists
crook horn 49 Musical Instruments
croon 49.39 *sing,* 424.5, 428.8 *sound faint,* 433.10 *sing*
crooner 49.23 *singer,* 433.5 *melodist*
crop 68, 68.17 *farm,* 69.15 *cultivate,* 78.16 *avian anatomy,* 86.1 *fruits,* 87.11 *eat grass,* 161.27 *bundle,* 227.3 *growth,* 243.7 *produce,* 270.10 *shorten,* 350.16 *eating utensil,* 350.21 *eat,* 605.1 *store,* 721.6 *yield,* 791.8 *hair cut*
crop circle 11.10 *psychic phenomenon*
crop circles 529.6 *natural mystery*
crop dusting 73.1 *aviation*
crop-eared 420.12 *eared*
crop failure 683.4 *unsuccessful thing*
crop-full 144.8 *full*
crop husbandry 68.4 *arable farming,* 83.10 *plant science*
cropped 68.20 *farmable,* 145.4 *incomplete,* 270.8 *shortened*
cropping 66.13 *framing,* 350.5 *eating habit*
crop rotation 68.4 *arable farming*
crop-spraying 68.5 *cultivation*
crop top 295.18 *underwear*
crop up 156.27 *emerge,* 183.21 *be repeated,* 227.9 *take effect,* 229.5 *happen by chance,* 437.9 *appear,* 457.12 *become visible,* 589.10 *chance*

crop up all over the place 245.12 *multiply*
croquet 18 Sporting Activities
crore 179.11 *million*
crores 741.3 *fortune*
crosier 7.11 *vestment*
cross 288, 356, 357, 10.14 *sacred object,* 30.7 *stationary rings,* 30.11 *gymnastic,* 133.5 *hybrid,* 133.8 *mix,* 231.3 *counteract,* 271.10 *span,* 399.4 *funeral objects,* 473.8 *argumentative,* 536.8 *rebut,* 543.1 *sign,* 543.13 *punctuate,* 544.4 *insignia,* 544.8 *heraldic device,* 631.2 *adversity,* 663.18 *counteract,* 663.19 *oppositional,* 708.2 *permit,* 822.13, 828.16 *angry,* 829.4 *irascible,* 830.7 *irritable,* 879.16 *instrument of execution*
cross a land bridge 98.12 *be marooned*
cross an isthmus 98.12 *be marooned*
cross-appeal 536.3 *rebuttal,* 536.8 *rebut*
cross-appealed 536.12 *rejected*
crossbar 19.4 *stadium,* 21.2 *field event,* 31.7 *hurling,* 35.1 *rugger,* 38.1 *soccer,* 71.11 *bicycle part,* 284.2 *supporting part*
crossbar exchange 534.12 *public telephone system*
crossbeam 225.3 *stabilizer,* 271.5 *broad thing,* 284.2 *supporting part*
cross-bench 698.9 *free*
cross-bencher 698.7 *free person*
cross-benches 663.8 *the opposition*
crossbill 78 Birds
cross block 19.9 *play,* 19.15 *play offence*
crossbow 244.7 *agent of destruction,* 338.9 *firearm,* 680.6 *historical missile weapon*
cross bow archery 18 Sporting Activities
crossbowman 679.13 *historical soldiery*
cross-bred 68.21 *domesticated,* 133.12 *mixed*
crossbreed 133.8 *mix*
cross-breed 77.9 *dog,* 133.5 *hybrid*
cross-breeding 133.1 *mixture*
cross-Channel 39.11 *swimming*
cross-Channel swimming 39.1 *swimming*
crosscheck 31.9 *play hockey,* 480.1 *verify,* 480.4 *verification*
crosschecked 31.8 *hockey*
cross-checked 480.10 *verified*
crosschecking 31.3 *ice hockey,* 31.8 *hockey*
cross-checking 480.9 *verificatory*
cross-communication 135.1 *union*
cross-connection 135.1 *union*
cross-country 18 Sporting Activities, 21.6 *track,* 32.11 *eventing,* 32.17 *equine,* 41.12 *ski,* 332.14 *directed*
cross-country championships 41.2 *cross-country skiing*
cross-country equipment 41.2 *cross-country skiing*
cross-country race 674.4 *race*
cross-country racing 21.1 *track events*
cross-country runner 21.3 *athlete*
cross-country running 18 Sporting Activities
cross-country ski 41.5 *ski equipment*
cross-country skiing 41, 41.1 *skiing*
cross-country technique 41.2 *cross-country skiing*
crosscurrent 96.6 *river flow,* 111.3 *opposition,* 231.2 *counteracting thing,* 390.4 *air flow,* 635.1 *trap,* 663.3 *conflict*
crosscut 47.17 *carpenter*
crosscut saw 47.11 *woodworking tool*
cross-dresser 401.11 *transsexual*
crosse 31.5 *lacrosse*

crossed 133.12 *mixed*, 536.12 *rejected*
crossed fingers 540.3 *hypocrisy*
Crossed Friar 7 Members of Religious Orders
crossed in love 822.12 *hated*
crossed legs 543.3 *gesture*
crossed-loop goniometer 74.5 *navigation*
crossed out 546.6 *obliterated*
cross-examination 16.7 *legal trial*, 477.2 *questioning*
cross-examine 16.71 *try a case*, 477.18 *interrogate*
cross-examined 477.16 *questioned*
cross-examiner 477.9 *questioner*, 568.7 *conversationalist*
cross-eye 436.9 *poor sight*
cross-eyed 436.9 *weak-sighted*
cross-fertilize 133.8 *mix*
crossfire 231.2 *counteracting thing*
cross-fire 670.15 *firing*
crossflow 96.6 *river flow*
cross-foot spin 41.6 *ice-skating*
cross-grained 375.2 *coarse*, 577.2 *refractory*
cross hairs 435.10 *visual aid*
cross handstand 30.7 *stationary rings*
cross hang 30.7 *stationary rings*
cross-hatch 50.20 *draw*, 440.14 *make dark*
cross-hatching 440.2 *darkening*
crosshead 74 Rigging
crossing 288, 327, 357, 43.10 *church architecture*, 71.3 *carriageway*, 72.2 *track*, 74.1 *water travel*, 74.2 *waterway*, 288.5 *crossroads*, 342.4 *meeting place*, 343.4 *branching*, 356.1 *passage*, 356.5 *crossing point*, 356.12 *passing*, 536.3 *rebuttal*
crossing out 546.3 *obliteration*
crossing over 59.10 *cell division*
crossing-over 357.7 *crossing*
crossing point 356
crossing the bar 397.1 *death*
crossing the picket lines 15.4 *industrial dispute*
crossing the Styx 397.1 *death*
crossjack 74 Rigging
cross linking 57.21 *polymer*
crossly 473.11 *argumentatively*, 818.9 *discourteously*, 828.18 *angrily*, 829.9 *irascibly*, 830.14 *irritably*
cross-multiplication 52.24 *evaluation*
cross multiply 52.91 *add*
cross my heart and hope to die 535.26 *as God is my witness*
crossness 822.5, 828.4 *anger*, 829.1 *irascibility*, 830.3 *irritableness*
cross one's bows 74.9 *navigate*
cross oneself 10.19 *offer worship*
cross one's fingers 540.18 *be hypocritical*, 775.9 *be hopeful*
cross one's heart 535.18 *vow*, 714.7 *promise*
cross one's legs 543.11 *gesture*
cross one's mind 471.14 *have an idea*
cross one's palm 729.5 *give*
cross one's palm with silver 746.11 *remunerate*
cross one's Rubicon 106.12 *come to a juncture*
crossopterygian 80.2 *fish*, 80.4 *fossil fish*
cross out 131.3 *subtract*, 147.8 *eject*, 543.13 *punctuate*, 546.1 *obliterate*, 704.6 *cancel*
crossover 36.14 *running*, 39.11 *swimming*, 72.3 *rail*
cross over 356.11, 357.2 *cross*, 578.3 *apostatize*
crossover kick 39.2 *swimming technique*
crossover recovery 36.8 *punting*
crosspatch 415.4 *spleen*, 818.4 *discourteous person*, 829.3 *irascible person*, 830.5 *sullen person*
cross-pollination 84.6 *pollination*

cross product 52.50 *scalar quantity*
cross purposes 493.1 *misjudgment*
cross-question 477.18 *interrogate*
cross-questioned 477.16 *questioned*
cross-questioning 477.2 *questioning*
cross-refer 107.7 *relate to*
cross-reference 107.1 *relatedness*, 107.2 *interrelatedness*
cross-referenced 543.17 *punctuated*
cross-reference mark 543.7 *punctuation*
cross-referred 107.5 *interrelated*
crossroads 288, 71.3 *carriageway*, 93.10 *village*, 106.3 *critical moment*, 135.6 *point of union*, 327.3 *road*, 343.4 *branching*, 356.5 *crossing point*
crossroad sign 543.5 *indicator*
cross section 52.41 *geometric figure*, 56.71 *nuclear reaction*
cross-section 547.8 *representative*
cross-stitch 792.2 *pattern*
cross swords 117.14 *disagree*, 330.2 *collide*, 434.11 *disagree*, 674.12 *fight*
cross swords with 674.11 *contend*, 676.14 *battle*, 764.11 *quarrel*
cross talk 65.17 *computing term*
crosstalk 534.19 *radio reception*
cross the bar 397.15 *die*
cross the border 357.2 *cross*
cross the floor 576.9 *change sides*, 578.3 *apostatize*
cross the picket lines 15.12 *have an industrial dispute*
cross the Rubicon 357.2 *cross*, 574.8 *brace oneself*, 580.3 *side with*
cross the street 327.14 *find one's way*
cross the Styx 397.15 *die*
cross the threshold 346.9 *enter*
cross through 546.1 *obliterate*
cross to bear 631.2 *adversity*, 661.6 *burden*, 687.1 *adversity*
cross tree 85.12 *figurative usage*
cross-tree 36.3 *parts of a sailing boat*
cross-ventilation 390.6 *ventilation*
crossways 271.8 *breadthwise*
crosswind 55.15 *wind direction*
crosswise 271.8 *breadthwise*, 286.4 *oblique*, 286.8 *obliquely*
crossword 529.4 *brain-teaser*
crosswords 42 Hobbies and Pastimes
crotals 49 Musical Instruments
crotamiton 62 Medication
crotch 295.24 *part of garment*
crotched 24.9 *billiard*
crotchet 49.17 *notation*, 579.3 *whim*
crotchety 577.2 *refractory*, 579.1 *capricious*, 829.4 *irascible*
croton 85 Trees and Shrubs
croton bug 82 Insects
crotonic 58 Common Fatty Acids
crouch 276.8 *be low*, 362.8 *sit*, 362.16 *courtesy*, 673.4 *succumb*, 808.10 *knuckle under*
Crouch 96 Rivers
crouched 276.5 *low*
crouching 276.5 *low*, 362.23 *sedentary*, 673.5 *submitting*
crouch ware 44.1 *ceramics*
croup 30.6 *pommel horse*, 624.9 *respiratory disease*
croupy 624.23 *diseased*
crouton 45.38 *bread*
crow 78 Birds, 78.6 *songbird*, 432.5 *sing*, 447.9 *black thing*, 564.13 *speak in a particular way*, 621.12 *cleaner*, 762.7 *show joy*, 806.26 *outdo*
Crow 1 Peoples, **5** Languages and Groups of Languages, **53** The Constellations
crowbar 355.10 *excavator*, 603.1 *tool*, 603.9 *use tools*
crowberry 86 Fruits

crowd 161, 161, 181, 135.1 *union*, 161.11 *group*, 181.4 *throng*, 273.7 *thicken*, 371.9 *make dense*, 610.1 *excess*, 850.22 *show disrespect*
crowd control methods 632.4 *safety device*
crowd 161, 181, 144.8 *full*, 212.3 *frequent*, 273.2 *dense*, 327.15 *accessible*
crowdedly 212.1 *frequently*
crowdedness 212.4 *frequency*
crowd in 346.12 *flood in*, 354.3 *impact*
crowds 777 Phobias by Topic
crowd together 262.6 *become smaller*
crowfoot 74 Rigging, **84** Flowers and Flowering Plants
crowing cock 204.2 *morning thing*
crowlike 78.23 *avian*
crown 43 Architectural Decoration, 42.10 *play*, 43.19 *decorate*, 60.21 *practise dentistry*, 85.2 *tree part*, 130.6 *add*, 144.4 *complete*, 156.25 *enrol*, 157.15 *end*, 279.2 *head*, 279.7 *top*, 293.23 *cover*, 295.15 *headgear*, 313.3 *circular thing*, 330.8 *club*, 361.3 *promote*, 380.11 *tooth*, 544.4 *insignia*, 544.8 *heraldic device*, 588.6 *objective*, 619.5 *perfect*, 630.20 *doctor*, 681.1 *trophy*, 684.6 *elaborate*, 703.6 *commission*, 741.10 *former British money*, 792.10 *decorate*, 812.19 *install*, 817.12 *greet*, 878.2 *prize*
Crown Attorney 16.10 *law officer*
Crown Counsel 16.11 *British law officer*
crown court 16.20 *British court*, 492.3 *place of judgment*
crown court judge 16.25 *British judge*, 492.1 *justice*
Crown Derby porcelain 44 Types of Ceramics
crowned 43.17 *structured*, 279.6 *topped*, 684.8 *concluded*, 696.12 *masterful*
crowned head 696.2 *sovereign*
crowned with success 682.13 *successful*
crown gall 69.12 *pests and diseases*, 85.10 *tree disease*
crown glass 442.9 *glass*
crown-green 25.9 *bowls*
crown-green bowls 18 Sporting Activities, 25.1 *green bowling*
crowning 60.4 *dentistry*, 126.14 *best*, 144.7 *complete*, 157.20 *ending*, 279.5 *top*, 617.2 *best*, 630.12 *surgery*, 682.13 *successful*, 684.8 *concluded*, 703.1 *commission*, 812.12 *ceremonial*
crowning achievement 243.6 *great work*, 619.3 *perfection*, 684.1 *completion*
crowning glory 157.10 *ending*
crowning stroke 684.3 *elaboration*
crown lands 725.1 *property*
crown of thorns 84 Flowers and Flowering Plants
crown-of-thorns 81.3 *echinoderm*
crownpiece 279.2 *head*
crown prince 696.2 *sovereign*
crown princess 696.2 *sovereign*
Crown Prosecution Service 16.11 *British law officer*
crown rot 69.12 *pests and diseases*
crown wheel 364.6 *rotator*
crow over 668.5 *defy*
crows 161 Collective Names by Animal
crow's-foot 321.2 *wrinkle*
crow's nest 74 Parts of a Ship, 435.9 *viewpoint*, 692.8 *vantage point*
crow's-nest 275.8 *high thing*
CRT 64.20 *electron tube*
crucial 103.5 *essential*, 106.8 *difficult*, 210.7 *critical*, 226.13 *causal*, 230.12 *operative*, 291.8 *focal*, 477.13 *problematic*, 611.5 *important*, 633.1 *dangerous*, 772.3 *important*, 796.7 *fashionable*

crucially 106.17 *difficultly*, 210.10 *critically*, 226.14 *causally*, 230.13 *operationally*, 611.9 *importantly*
crucial moment 210.3 *critical time*, 221.3 *turning point*, 611.2 *important matter*
crucial point 221.3 *turning point*
crucial time 210.3 *critical time*
crucible 57 Laboratory Apparatus, 133.6 *mixer*, 220.4 *medium of conversion*, 408.3 *heater*
cruciferous 83.16 *taxonomic*
crucifix 10.14 *sacred object*, 11.6 *talisman*
crucifixion 50.10 *art subject*, 397.4 *death sentence*, 398.6 *ritual killing*, 879.13 *capital punishment*
cruciform 52.40 *curve*
crucify 398.20 *kill ritually*, 406.11 *inflict pain*, 618.14 *illtreat*, 879.5 *execute*
crud 622.4 *dirt*, 793.1 *spot*
crude 145.4 *incomplete*, 375.5 *unfinished*, 395.9 *petroleum*, 410.6 *oil*, 412.6 *coarse*, 444.12 *gaudy*, 559.8 *indecorous*, 595.5 *immature*, 620.2 *incomplete*, 656.4 *bungled*, 811.21 *blatant*, 818.6 *bad-mannered*, 877.12 *indecent*
crude data 52.57 *population*
crude estimate 518.3 *conjecture*
crudely 145.6, 375.15 *incompletely*, 412.11 *tastelessly*, 595.16 *immaturely*, 811.37 *blatantly*, 818.10 *rudely*
crudeness 375.10 *rough idea*, 412.4 *bad taste*, 559.2 *impropriety*, 595.10 *immaturity*, 620.5 *imperfection*, 811.6 *blatancy*, 818.2 *bad manners*
crude oil 395.9 *petroleum*, 410.6 *oil*, 595.11 *natural state*, 604.1 *materials*
crude rubber 377.4 *rubber*
crudity 658.2 *naivety*
cruel 832, 241.6 *violent*, 398.24 *murderous*, 406.8 *inflicting pain*, 618.5 *harmful*, 670.23 *attacking*, 676.16 *warlike*, 690.8 *severe*, 836.4 *pitiless*, 864.11 *wicked*
cruel act 832.7 *act of malevolence*
cruel conduct 832.2 *cruelness*
cruel-hearted 832.11 *cruel*
cruelly 618.15 *worthlessly*, 690.11 *severely*, 832.20 *malevolently*, 836.7 *pitilessly*, 864.18 *wickedly*
cruelness 832, 864.1 *wickedness*
cruel side 305.4 *aspect*
cruelty 618.11 *harmfulness*, 690.1 *severity*, 824.3 *divorce court*, 832.2 *cruelness*, 836.1 *pitilessness*, 864.1 *wickedness*
cruet 10.14 *sacred object*
cruise 324.15 *walk*
cruise control 71 Motor Vehicle Parts
Cruise missile 680.5 *missile weapon*
cruiser 74 Ships and Boats, 36.2 *sailing boat*, 679.24 *warship*
cruiser division 17.4 *military organization*
cruiser racing 36.1 *sailing*
cruiserweight 26.3 *boxing weight divisions*, 26.4 *boxer*, 26.14 *combat*, 369.7 *weighing*, 679.3 *athlete*
cruising 36.10 *sailing*, 36.12 *canoeing*, 74.1 *water travel*, 74.11 *nautical*, 538.20 *unfaithful*
cruising canoe 36.6 *canoeing*
cruising hook 36.6 *canoeing*
cruising stroke 36.6 *canoeing*
cruising yacht 36.2 *sailing boat*
crumb 384, 45.38 *bread*, 143.7 *piece*, 173.3 *fragment*, 260.3 *little piece*, 384.2 *crumble*
crumble 384, 45.35 *dessert*, 136.9 *separate*, 141.3 *disintegrate*, 202.17 *grow old*, 238.6 *be*

weak, 244.13 *be destroyed,* 379.4 *be brittle,* 384.6 *crumb,* 628.1 *deteriorate,* 628.4 *impair*
crumble away 189.4 *be transient,* 244.13 *be destroyed*
crumbled 379.1 *brittle,* 384.20 *crumbly*
crumble into dust 202.17 *grow old,* 384.28 *come to dust*
crumble to dust 244.13 *be destroyed*
crumblies 202.2 *old people*
crumbliness 384, 139.1 *nonadhesion,* 379.2 *brittleness*
crumbling 141.6 *disintegrating,* 202.12 *olden,* 244.15 *destroyed,* 379.1 *brittle,* 379.2 *brittleness,* 384.4 *pulverization,* 384.20 *crumbly,* 633.2 *unsafe*
crumbly 384, 139.8 *nonadhesive,* 143.11 *partial,* 207.7 *older person,* 379.1 *brittle*
crumbs 127.7 *inferior thing,* 132.2 *residue,* 614.6 *refuse*
crumhorn 49 Musical Instruments
crumminess 618.8 *inferiority,* 754.3 *shoddiness*
crummy 127.14 *poor,* 618.2 *inferior,* 624.22 *sick,* 754.10 *shoddy*
crump 330.2 *collide*
crumpet 45.39 *loaf,* 402.9 *woman considered as a sex object*
crumple 151.24 *make disordered,* 320.2, 320.8 *pleat,* 375.12 *make rough*
crumpled 151.15 *untidy,* 375.1 *rough*
crumple up 244.13 *be destroyed*
crumply 375.1 *rough*
crunch 101.5 *realities,* 136.9 *separate,* 330.2 *collide,* 330.12 *collision,* 350.21 *eat,* 384.27 *beat,* 407.12 *abut,* 430.5 *sound hoarse*
crunchie 91 Names for Inhabitants
crusade 7.20 *preach,* 640.1 *action,* 676.1 *war,* 679.36 *combat*
crusader 7.4 *religionist,* 640.3 *doer,* 670.19 *attacker,* 679.6 *militarist*
crusading 7.2 *religiousness,* 7.15 *religious,* 640.5 *acting,* 679.33 *combative*
cruse 44.8 *ceramic object*
crush 68.10 *farm tool,* 161.21 *scrum,* 181.4 *throng,* 181.11 *crowd,* 244.9 *demolish,* 262.1 *contraction,* 262.5 *make smaller,* 362.2 *flatten,* 379.4 *be brittle,* 384.27 *beat,* 476.8 *refute,* 587.3 *deflect,* 618.14 *illtreat,* 628.4 *impair,* 642.6 *business,* 682.9 *be victorious,* 682.10 *defeat heavily,* 690.5 *be severe,* 696.14 *master,* 699.8 *restrain,* 776.10 *disappoint,* 784.3 *likes,* 806.17 *humiliate,* 806.23 *abase,* 821.2 *romantic love*
crushability 262.2 *contractility,* 379.2 *brittleness*
crushable 262.9 *contractible,* 379.1 *brittle*
crush barrier 632.4 *safety device*
crushed 181.10 *crowded,* 244.15 *destroyed,* 262.7 *smaller,* 379.1 *brittle,* 384.10 *pulverized,* 515.9 *disappointed,* 806.3 *humbled*
crusher 157.13 *ender,* 262.4 *contractor,* 384.11 *pulverizer,* 788.3 *boring person*
crushing 244.2 *destroying,* 262.1 *contraction,* 262.8 *contracting,* 379.1 *brittle,* 384.4 *pulverization,* 644.11 *laborious,* 682.15 *victorious,* 699.1 *restraint,* 806.6 *humiliating*
crushing blow 244.4 *ruin*
crushing device 879.15 *instrument of torture*
crushing reply 806.14 *rebuke*
crushing victory 682.2 *victory*
crush note 49.16 *musical note*
crush of shoppers 642.6 *business*
crush one's hopes 515.6 *disappoint*
crush to pieces 244.9 *demolish*

crust 45.38 *bread,* 54.18 *earth's crust,* 143.7 *piece,* 289.1 *exterior,* 293.2 *cover,* 371.8 *be dense,* 373.7 *hard substance,* 807.2 *cheek*
Crustacea 81.4 *arthropod*
crustacean 81.4 *arthropod,* 81.18 *arthropodous*
crustaceous 81.18 *arthropodous*
crustal 54.53 *solid-earth*
crustal movement 54.20 *earth movement*
crusted 289.6 *exterior,* 373.3 *hardened*
crusted port 351.9 *wine*
crustily 373.12 *toughly*
crustiness 818.1 *discourtesy*
crustose 90.8 *lichenoid*
crustose lichen 90.6 *lichen*
crusty 289.6 *exterior,* 373.1 *hard,* 807.14 *cheeky,* 818.5 *discourteous,* 829.4 *irascible*
crutch 85.2 *tree part,* 284.3 *body support,* 662.19 *support*
Crutched Friar 7 Members of Religious Orders
crux 103.2 *essential content,* 210.3 *critical time,* 477.4 *difficult question,* 611.3 *chief thing,* 659.4 *problem*
Crux 53 The Constellations
crux of the matter 611.3 *chief thing*
Cruyff 18 Sporting Personalities
cruzado 741.11 *national coins*
crwth 49 Musical Instruments
cry 431, 431, 432, 32.8 *hunting,* 352.7 *secrete,* 389.32 *seep,* 423.2 *outcry,* 423.8 *be loud,* 473.5 *plea,* 532.14 *proclaim,* 543.6 *word,* 543.12 *signal,* 564.12 *speak loudly,* 636.7 *raise the alarm,* 712.1, 712.6 *request,* 770.8 *grieve,* 773.2 *fanfare,* 773.7 *dance,* 774.2 *lament,* 774.7 *weep*
cryalite 57 Common Chemical Compounds
crybaby 238.4 *weakling,* 403.4 *someone or something that feels,* 774.3 *lamenter*
cry bloody murder 713.7 *complain*
cry blue murder 636.7 *raise the alarm,* 713.7 *complain*
cry crocodile tears 538.24 *pretend*
cry down 852.17 *criticize,* 854.10 *disparage*
cry for help 543.6 *word*
cry for quarter 835.12 *ask for mercy*
cry for the moon 487.10 *attempt the impossible,* 614.9 *waste effort*
cry havoc 398.26 *no quarter*
cry Hughie 349.15 *vomit*
crying 431, 352.1 *secretion,* 352.4 *secretory,* 423.6 *loud,* 431.6 *cry of pain,* 532.20 *well-known,* 593.6 *demanding,* 774.1 *lamentation,* 774.4 *lamenting*
crying cold 624.9 *respiratory disease*
crying down 854.1 *disparagement*
crying out for 593.6 *demanding*
crying shame 844.9 *dishonour*
crying with rage 828.16 *angry*
cryobiological 59.20 *biological*
cryobiologist 59.19 *life scientist*
cryobiology 59.1 *life science*
cry of disapproval 431
cry of greeting 431
cry of joy 431
cry of pain 431
cry of praise 431
cry of the chase 431.5 *hunting cry*
cry of wolf 636.3 *false alarm*
cry of wonder 786.2 *sign of wonderment*
cryogen 409.4 *cooler*
cryogenic 56.98 *physical,* 409.9 *heat-resistant*
cryogenically 56.100 *physically*
cryogenic memory 65.6 *memory*

cryogenic pump 57.20 *surface chemistry*
cryogenics 56.3 *modern physics,* 409.4 *cooler*
cryohydrate 57.7 *chemical compound*
cryolite 54 Minerals
cryometer 268.8 *meter*
cryometry 268.2 *micrometry*
cry on 590.10 *chase*
cry one's eyes out 774.7 *weep*
cryonic 409.9 *heat-resistant*
cryonics 409.4 *cooler*
cryophobia 777 Phobias by Name
cryostat 409.4 *cooler*
cryosurgery 409.4 *cooler*
cry out 431
cry out against 587.1 *dissuade*
cry out for 358.1 *fall short,* 593.8 *miss,* 782.12 *desire*
cry out for rest 650.5 *be fatigued*
crypt 10.12 *church,* 277.4 *deep thing,* 399.6 *grave*
cryptanalysis 524.5 *science of interpretation*
cryptanalyst 524.6 *interpreter*
cryptic 11.14 *occult,* 440.11 *benighted,* 443.4 *inscrutable,* 491.3 *confused,* 523.1 *unintelligible,* 527.5, 529.11 *mysterious,* 531.15 *disguised,* 551.2 *obscure*
cryptically 443.13 *opaquely,* 523.13 *unintelligibly,* 551.4 *obscurely*
cryptogam 83.4 *lower plant*
cryptogamic 83.16 *taxonomic*
cryptogram 529.4 *brain-teaser*
cryptographer 524.6 *interpreter,* 529.4 *brain-teaser*
cryptographic 527.2 *concealed,* 531.15 *disguised*
cryptography 524.5 *science of interpretation,* 527.8 *concealment,* 529.4 *brain-teaser*
cryptologist 524.6 *interpreter*
cryptology 524.5 *science of interpretation*
cryptomeria 85 Trees and Shrubs
cry quits 673.3 *submit,* 677.5 *make peace*
cry sob 406.12 *express pain*
crystal 57, 371.4 *solid body,* 379.3 *brittle thing,* 442.1 *transparent,* 442.9 *glass*
crystal ball 11.9 *divination,* 442.8 *transparent thing,* 517.10 *cards*
crystal-ball gazing 199.4 *looking to the future*
crystal boundary 57.4 *crystal*
crystal-clear 437.2 *clear,* 442.1 *transparent,* 522.2 *simple,* 526.15 *open*
crystal-controlled oscillator 64.21 *rectifier*
crystal-gaze 11.23 *divine,* 435.17 *imagine*
crystal gazer 11.13 *diviner,* 199.5, 516.5 *predictor*
crystal-gazer 368.7 *believer in a nonmaterial world,* 435.11 *observer,* 517.9 *forecaster*
crystal-gazing 11.9 *divination,* 199.4 *looking to the future,* 435.5 *imagination,* 516.3 *foresight,* 517.2 *divination*
crystal glass 442.9 *glass*
crystalline 57, 371.7 *condensed,* 373.1 *hard,* 442.1 *transparent*
crystalline mineral 54.34 *mineral*
crystalline texture 54.28 *rock*
crystallinity 442.5 *transparency*
crystallite 57.4 *crystal*
crystallization 54.29 *petrogenesis,* 57.4 *crystal,* 57.5 *process,* 220.1 *conversion,* 371.2 *concentration,* 373.6 *solidification*
crystallize 44.11 *make ceramics,* 54.62 *lithify,* 57.25 *solidify,* 220.7 *convert into,* 371.8 *be dense,* 373.10 *solidify,* 442.11 *be transparent,* 442.12 *make transparent*
crystallized 44.10 *ceramic,* 57.33 *crystalline,* 371.7 *condensed,* 373.3 *hardened,* 414.6 *sweet*

crystallized fruit 45.41 *sweet*
crystallized glass 44.9 *industrial ceramics*
crystallized rose petals 84.8 *flower product*
crystallize out 57.25 *solidify*
crystallizing 220.14 *converting*
crystallographer 57.2 *chemist*
crystallographic 56.98 *physical,* 57.31 *chemical*
crystallographically 56.100 *physically*
crystallography 56.3 *modern physics,* 57.1 *chemistry,* 57.4 *crystal*
crystalloid 57.33 *crystalline*
crystallophobia 777 Phobias by Name
crystal oscillator 64.21 *rectifier*
Crystal Palace 43 Noted Buildings
crystals 777 Phobias by Topic
crystal set 534.18 *radio*
crystal system 57.4 *crystal*
crystal vision 11.8 *psychic power*
cry too soon 636.7 *raise the alarm*
cry uncle 673.3 *submit*
cry up 851.15 *compliment*
cry wolf 540.22 *falsify,* 636.7 *raise the alarm*
C-shape 36.14 *punting*
C-shape shove 36.8 *punting*
Ctenophora 81.7 *coelenterate*
ctenophoran 81.21 *coelenterate*
ctenophore 81.7 *coelenterate*
CT scan 60.7 *diagnosis*
CT scanner 630.14 *hospital*
CU 65.5 *processor*
cub 77.19 *young mammal,* 77.35 *give birth,* 206.4 *young animal,* 206.7 *young man,* 245.11 *have young*
Cuba 91 Countries, 98 Islands
cubage 259.1 *size*
Cuban heels 295.19 *footwear*
cubature 259.1 *size*
cubby 258.2 *compartment*
cubbyhole 258.2 *compartment,* 260.5 *little space,* 531.2 *hiding place,* 647.1 *workshop*
cube 52.17 *multiplication,* 52.46 *polyhedron,* 52.91 *add,* 128.5 *make bigger,* 170.9 *add,* 177.1 *three,* 177.10 *triple*
cubed 177.7 *three*
cube root 52.17 *multiplication,* 169.6 *power*
cubic 52, 52.76 *functional,* 57.33 *crystalline,* 248.11 *spatial,* 268.12 *metrical*
cubic close packed 57.33 *crystalline*
cubic close packing 57.4 *crystal*
cubic crystal 57.4 *crystal*
cubic equation 52.27 *equation*
cubicle 68.7 *farm building,* 258.2 *compartment*
cubic measure 75.1 *unit*
cubiform 52.84 *cubic*
cubism 50 Western Art Styles and Movements
cubist 50.29 *realist*
cubitiere 671.7 *armour*
cuboid 382 Bones, 52.46 *polyhedron,* 52.84 *cubic*
cub reporter 533.4 *journalist*
cucking stool 879.14 *instrument of punishment*
cuckold 823.10 *married man,* 877.17 *be sexually immoral*
cuckolding 877.4 *illicit love*
cuckoldry 821.8 *love affair,* 877.4 *illicit love*
cuckoo 78 Birds, 255.6 *illegal occupant,* 349.26 *ejector,* 432.2 *bird song,* 510.11 *insane*
cuckoo clock 191 Timepieces and Timers, 192.6 *clock*
cuckoo in the nest 104.8 *intruder,* 108.2 *unrelated thing,* 149.10 *intruder,* 349.26 *ejector*
cuckoo-like 78.23 *avian*
cuckooprint 84 Flowers and Flowering Plants
cuckoo-shrike 78 Birds

cuckoo-spit insect **82** Insects
cuculiform 78.23 *avian*
cucumber **45** Vegetables
cucumber sandwich 45.11 *sandwich*
cucumber tree **85** Trees and Shrubs
cud-chewer 77.15 *hoofed mammal*
cud-chewing 77.33 *ungulate*
cuddle 405.9 *give pleasure*, 405.10 *comfort*, 726.1 *retention*, 726.6 *retain*, 821.14 *communication of love*, 821.27 *kiss*, 826.1 *endearment*, 826.7 *show endearment for*
cuddlesome 405.6 *pleasant*, 821.22 *lovable*
cuddling 821.14 *communication of love*
cuddly 405.6 *pleasant*, 821.22 *lovable*
cuddy 326.6 *beast of burden*
cudgel 330.8 *club*, 330.16 *weapons*, 680.7 *blunt weapon*, 879.3 *hit*, 879.14 *instrument of punishment*
cudgerie **85** Trees and Shrubs
Cudworth **4** Philosophers
cue 24.3 *English billiards*, 24.9 *billiard*, 51.20 *acting*, 51.36 *dramatize*, 330.15 *ram*, 511.4 *reminder*, 543.1 *sign*
cue ball 24.3 *English billiards*, 24.5 *snooker*
cue rest 24.1 *billiards*
cue stick 24.1 *billiards*
cuff 295.24 *part of garment*, 330.13 *blow*, 879.3 *hit*, 879.12 *corporal punishment*
cufflink 137.8 *fastening*
cuffs 699.5 *means of restraint*
cuirass 671.7 *armour*
cuirassier 679.20 *cavalryman*
cuisine 45.1 *cookery*
cuisinier 45.2 *cook*
cuisse 671.7 *armour*
Culbertson **18** Sporting Personalities
Culdee **7** Members of Religious Orders
cul-de-sac 323.4 *closed place*, 327.3 *road*, 659.8 *snag*
culex **82** Insects
culinarily **45**
culinary **45**
culinary herb 69.11 *vegetable*, 83.2 *plant*
culinary masterpiece 45.9 *dish*
cull 37.7 *shoot*, 42.3 *card game terms*, 131.3 *subtract*, 398.9 *animal killing*, 398.22 *kill animals*, 580.4 *pick*
culled 37.8 *shooting*
culling 37.2 *hunting*
culm 87.3 *grass plant*
culminate 126.8 *be superior*, 128.5 *make bigger*, 142.10 *complete*, 144.5 *be complete*, 157.15 *end*, 227.5 *show an effect*, 275.16 *rise*, 279.7 *top*, 359.13 *ascend*, 684.5 *conclude*
culminating 144.7 *complete*, 157.20 *ending*, 279.5 *top*, 684.7 *completed*
culmination 128.1 *increase*, 144.1 *completeness*, 144.3 *completion*, 157.10 *ending*, 227.1 *effect*, 279.1 *summit*, 359.6 *mounting*, 684.1 *completion*
culminative 157.20 *ending*
culottes 295.6 *skirt*
culpability 16.38 *lawbreaking*, 504.7 *errancy*, 866.1 *guilt*
culpable 16.60 *offending*, 504.16 *errant*, 844.16 *in the wrong*, 852.36 *blameworthy*, 864.15 *criminal*, 866.5 *guilty*
culpable omission 866.3 *sin*
culpably 16.89 *guiltily*, 864.21 *criminally*
Culpeper **52** Scientists
culprit 16.40 *lawbreaker*, 844.10 *wrongdoer*, 856.4 *accused person*, 864.9 *wicked person*, 866.4 *guilty person*

cult 7.1 *religion*, 9.2 *idolatry*, 9.10 *idolatrous*, 10.2 *ritualism*, 497.2 *religious belief*, 584.4 *custom*
cultish 9.10 *idolatrous*
cultism 9.2 *idolatry*, 10.2 *ritualism*
cultist 9.6 *idolater*, 9.10 *idolatrous*
cultivable 68.20 *farmable*
cultivar 59.17 *taxonomy*, 69.5 *gardening*
cultivate 69, 6.22 *educate*, 68.17 *farm*, 69.14 *practise horticulture*, 226.9 *be the cause of*, 243.10 *produce*, 594.7 *develop*, 627.1 *improve*, 662.23 *advise*, 771.15 *humour*
cultivate a habit 584.18 *habituate*
cultivated 6.20 *refined*, 69.19 *ornamental*, 83.15 *wild*, 411.8 *tasteful*, 501.9 *literate*, 558.3 *elegant*, 817.8 *good-mannered*
cultivated land 68.11 *farmland*
cultivated mushroom 89.2 *mushroom*
cultivated plant 83.2 *plant*
cultivate friends 819.13 *befriend*
cultivation **68**, 6.1 *education*, 6.11 *refinement*, 226.1 *cause*, 411.2 *taste of life*, 501.3 *learning*, 594.13 *development*
cultivator 68.10 *farm tool*, 68.15 *agriculturist*, 69.6 *garden tool*, 243.9 *producer*, 245.5 *propagator*, 594.15 *preparer*, 603.2 *garden tool*
cultrate 380.3 *sharp-edged*
cultural 1.14 *societal*, 627.16 *improving*
cultural anthropology 1.1 *anthropology*
cultural commentator 48.15 *literary person*
cultural ecology 2.1 *sociology*
culturally 1.18 *societally*, 2.16 *sociologically*
culture 1.7 *society*, 48.1 *literature*, 68.5 *cultivation*, 400.4 *civilized human*, 501.3 *learning*, 558.1, 794.1 *elegance*, 817.2 *good manners*
cultured 4.19 *learned*, 6.20 *refined*, 69.19 *ornamental*, 114.8 *simulated*, 118.13 *imitation*, 501.9 *literate*, 539.39 *imitative*, 817.8 *good-mannered*
cultured pearl 539.6 *imitation*
cultus 584.4 *custom*
culumet 413.7 *tobacco*
culverin 680.12 *historical guns*
culvert 63.22 *tunnel*, 327.11 *channel*
Cumans **1** Peoples
cumber 369.14 *make heavy*
Cumberland **4** Philosophers
Cumberland sausage 45.29 *sausage*
cumbersome 369.3 *ponderous*, 559.7 *graceless*, 616.1 *inconvenient*, 656.3, 659.15 *clumsy*
cumbersomely 369.17 *burdensomely*
cumbersomeness 259.2 *bigness*, 369.8 *weighing down*, 616.3 *inconvenience*
cumbrance 369.8 *weighing down*
Cumbria **92** Counties
Cumbrian **95** Mountains
Cumbrian Mountains 95.5 *British mountains*
cumbrous 369.3 *ponderous*
cumbrously 369.17 *burdensomely*
cumbrousness 559.4 *inelegance of speech*
cumin **45** Herbs and Spices, 413.5 *herbs*
cummerbund 137.10 *band*, 295.3 *formal dress*, 313.3 *circular thing*
cummings **48** Poets
cumshaw 729.2 *gift*
cumulate **161**, 721.11 *acquire*
cumulation 721.3 *acquisition*
cumulative 128.6 *increasing*, 130.8 *additional*, 721.18 *acquisitional*

cumulative distribution function 52.59 *probability distribution*
cumulative effect 128.1 *increase*
cumulative evidence 483.5 *legal evidence*
cumulatively 128.8 *increasingly*, 130.10 *additionally*, 721.20 *gainfully*
cumulativeness 128.1 *increase*
cumulative vote 580.10 *vote*
cumuliform 55.49 *cloudy*
cumulonimbiform 55.49 *cloudy*
cumulonimbus 55.18 *cloud*
cumulous 55.49 *cloudy*
cumulus 55.18 *cloud*
cunctative 641.3 *inactive*
cuneal 5.41 *lettered*
cuneate 310.9 *angled*
cuneiform 5.13 *letter*, 5.41 *lettered*, 310.9 *angled*
cuniform 43.17 *structured*
cuniform church 43.10 *church architecture*
cunning **474, 474, 657, 657**, 507.1 *wisdom*, 507.6 *intelligent*, 538.19 *dishonest*, 539.1 *deception*, 539.34 *deceiving*, 540.5 *deceitfulness*, 540.29 *deceitful*, 592.15 *planning*, 652.9 *tactics*, 655.1 *skill*, 655.6 *skilful*, 655.9 *well-made*
Cunning **657**
cunning fellow 655.5 *expert*
Cunningham 36.10 *sailing*
Cunningham hole 36.3 *parts of a sailing boat*
Cunningham tackle 36.3 *parts of a sailing boat*
cunningly 474.15 *hypocritically*, 538.28 *dishonestly*, 592.17 *conspiratorially*
cunningness 657.1 *cunning*
cunning person **657**
cunning plan 471.3 *plan*
cunt 245.8 *organs of reproduction*, 402.9 *woman considered as a sex object*
cup **75** General Units, 29.2 *golfing terms*, 41.10 *curling*, 44.8 *ceramic object*, 120.3 *container*, 258.13 *drinking vessel*, 317.3 *cavity*, 351.2 *drink*, 351.7 *alcoholic drink*, 351.10 *drink container*, 355.14 *suck*, 545.11 *monument*, 588.6 *objective*, 681.1 *trophy*, 878.2 *prize*
Cup **53** The Constellations
cup anemometer 55.7 *weather instruments*
cupbearer 326.7 *transferor*
cupboard 47.5, 258.3 *cabinet*, 605.4 *storage*
cupboard love 540.3 *hypocrisy*
cupboard room 605.4 *storage*
cupboard space 605.4 *storage*
cupcake 45.36 *cake*, 402.9 *woman considered as a sex object*
Cup final 674.2 *contest*
cupful 351.2 *drink*
cup fungi 89.3 *fungi*
cup-holder 126.6 *paragon*, 655.4 *skilled person*
Cupid **8** Deities, 821.16 *gods and goddesses of love*
Cupid's string 821.2 *romantic love*
cupidity 782.1 *desire*
cup of sorrows 687.1 *adversity*
cup of tea 165.8 *specialization*, 351.2 *drink*
cupola 43.9 *miscellaneous architectural features*, 275.8 *high thing*, 293.7 *overhead covering*, 316.3 *dome*
cuppa 351.2 *drink*
cupping 349.22 *disgorgement*, 355.4 *sucking*, 630.12 *surgery*
Cupra **8** Deities
cupreous 449.1 *brown*
cupressus **85** Trees and Shrubs
cupric 57.34 *elemental*
cupriferous 57.34 *elemental*
cuprite **54** Minerals
cupronickel **57** Alloys
cuprous 57.34 *elemental*
cup-shaped 317.5 *concave*
cup that cheers 874.13 *drink*

Cup tie 674.2 *contest*
cur 77.9 *dog*, 133.5 *hybrid*
Cura **98** Islands
curability 629.11 *recuperation*
curable 627.15 *improvable*, 629.14 *repairable*, 630.18 *medical*
curableness 629.11 *recuperation*
curacy 7.9 *priesthood*
curassow **78** Birds
curate 7.8 *priest*
curate's egg 620.5 *imperfection*
curative 60.25 *therapeutic*, 629.16 *restorative*, 630.17 *remedial*, 767.8 *relieving*
curative dance 46.4 *historic dancing*
curator 632.3 *protector*, 653.15 *manager*
curb 242.4 *moderate*, 302.2 *limiting factor*, 302.7 *limit*, 328.3 *slow down*, 328.9 *deceleration*, 661.1 *hindrance*, 661.4 *restraint*, 661.8 *hinder*, 661.10 *restrain*, 699.1 *restraint*, 699.8 *be self-restrained*, 869.5 *be self-restrained*
curbed 485.12 *conditional*, 661.14 *blocked*
curd 371.4 *solid body*, 393.8 *pulp*
curd cheese **45** Cheeses
curdle 371.8 *be dense*, 393.25 *thicken*, 415.8 *sour*
curdled 141.5 *disintegrated*, 371.7 *condensed*, 393.20 *thick*, 415.6 *unpalatable*
curdler 393.11 *thickener*
curdling 393.6 *thickening*
cure **629**, 60.19 *practise medicine*, 231.2 *counteracting thing*, 231.3 *counteract*, 392.17 *dry*, 413.12 *season*, 585.5 *disaccustom*, 594.7 *develop*, 602.1 *means*, 623.7 *make healthy*, 627.1 *improve*, 627.5 *improvement*, 629.11 *recuperation*, 630.1 *remedy*, 630.13 *therapy*, 630.19 *remedy*, 637.5 *preserve*, 662.5 *medical assistance*, 677.4 *pacify*, 767.3 *reliever*
cure-all 62.3 *drug*, 630.1 *remedy*
cured **629**, 413.9 *piquant*, 623.1 *healthy*, 637.7 *preserved*, 767.7 *relieved*
cured fish 45.16 *fish dish*
cure itself 629.6 *cure*
cure of 629.6 *cure*
curer 629.12 *repairer*
curette 349.11 *void*, 630.20 *doctor*
curfew 302.2 *limiting factor*, 699.4 *detention*, 709.1 *veto*
curfew bell 636.2 *danger signal*
Curia 16.22 *ecclesiastical court*, 653.7 *council*
curial 16.49 *judicatory*
Curia Regis 653.7 *council*
curie 75 *Scientific and Technical Units*
Curie **52** Scientists
Curie's law **56** Named Laws
Curie–Weiss law **56** Named Laws
curing 413, 45.8 *cooking technique*, 630.17 *remedial*, 637.1 *preservation*
curio 526.7 *showpiece*, 655.3 *masterpiece*, 754.5 *cheap item*
curiosity **465, 477**, 6.10 *educatability*, 168.4 *unusualness*, 782.1 *desire*, 786.5 *person of wonder*
Curiosity **465**
curious **465**, 6.17 *educatable*, 165.16 *characteristic*, 168.14 *eccentric*, 467.7 *watchful*, 472.8 *problematic*, 477.12 *questioning*
curiously **465**, 472.13 *problematically*, 477.23 *questioningly*
curiousness 465.1 *curiosity*
curious person **465**
curium **57** Chemical Elements
curl 41.10 *curling*, 52.50 *scalar quantity*, 311.2 *bend*, 311.6 *curve*, 314.2 *coil*, 314.6 *convolute*, 791.17 *crimp*
curled 311.4 *curved*
curled-up 262.7 *smaller*

curler 338.14 *thrower*
curlers 137.8 *fastening*
curlew 78 Birds, 78.3 *water bird*
curlicue 314.2 *coil*
curliness 311.1 *curvature*
curling 18 Sporting Activities, **41**
curling association 41.10 *curling*
curling broom 41.10 *curling*
curling championship 41.10 *curling*
curling ice 41.10 *curling*
curling match 41.10 *curling*
curling player 41.11 *skier*
curling rink 41.10 *curling*
curling stone 41.10 *curling*, 338.10 *ball*
curling technique 41.10 *curling*
curling tee 41.10 *curling*
curl one's lip 543.11 *gesture*
curl pass 19.9 *play*
curls 791.8 *hair cut*
curl up 262.6 *become smaller*
curl up and die 397.15 *die*
curl upwards 359.13 *ascend*
curly 375.3 *barbed*
curly kale 45 Vegetables
curmudgeon 818.4 *discourteous person*
curmudgeonly 830.7 *irritable*
currach 74 Ships and Boats
Curraleiro 32 Breeds of Horse and Pony
currant 86 Fruits, 45.42 *preserve*
currant bun 45.39 *loaf*
currawong 78 Birds
currency 196.4 *up-to-dateness*, 201.1 *newness*, 532.7 *publicity*, 741.1 *money*
current 56.51, 64.9 *electric current*, 96.6 *river flow*, 99.10 *existing*, 124.1 *average*, 196.6 *present*, 201.10 *new*, 234.1 *tendency*, 324.2 *momentum*, 336.11 *course*, 472.6 *topical*, 532.19 *published*, 584.10 *familiar*, 613.2 *usable*, 635.1 *trap*
current account 741.6 *funds*, 750.1 *accounts*
current account deposit 744.3 *deposit*
current affairs 533.1 *news*
current assets 725.5 *personal estate*
current density 56.51, 64.9 *electric current*
current electricity 56.42, 64.3 *electricity*
currently 99.23 *now*, 201.21 *newly*, 472.12 *topically*
current of air 390.4 *air flow*
current price 751.1 *price*
current transformer 64.22 *transformer*
curricle 71 Carriages and Carts
curricular 6
curriculum 6.3 *subject*, 171.5 *list of appointments*, 192.2 *timetable*
curriculum vitae 48.4 *non-fiction*, 545.1 *record*, 560.4 *factual account*
curried 45.56 *culinary*
curry 45 Herbs and Spices, 32.16 *ride*, 45.49 *Indian dish*, 45.55 *cook*, 385.12 *rub*, 413.2 *seasoning*, 413.12 *season*
Curry 18 Sporting Personalities
currycomb 32.14 *horse-riding terms*, 385.12 *rub*
curry favour 808.9 *fawn*, 821.28 *win the love of*, 853.10 *cajole*
curry powder 413.2 *seasoning*
curse 822, 822, 827, 827, 5.45 *use language*, 8.18 *devilize*, 10.18 *perform rites*, 11.21 *bewitch*, 16.79 *convict*, 233.2 *occult influence*, 431.7 *cry of disapproval*, 431.14 *hiss*, 618.11 *harmfulness*, 631.1 *affliction*, 631.14 *afflict*, 687.1 *adversity*, 818.8 *get angry*, 822.14 *hate*, 822.17 *anger*, 827.4 *malediction*, 852.22 *vituperate*, 862.4 *evil power*, 862.11 *be evil*
Curse 827
curse and swear 827.5 *curse*

cursed 10.21 *ritualistic*, 11.19 *bewitched*, 618.6 *damnable*, 631.16 *blighting*, 827.10 *maledictive*
cursedly 827.14 *damningly*
curse like hell 827.7 *wish ill*
curse up hill and down dale 827.7 *wish ill*
curse with bell 827.7 *wish ill*
curse word 827.1 *curse*
cursing 827, 431.19 *hissing*, 559.4 *inelegance of speech*, 818.6 *bad-mannered*, 822.6 *swearing*, 822.13 *angry*, 827.1 *curse*
cursive 5.41 *lettered*
cursive type 5.15 *type style*
cursor 65.17 *computing term*, 543.5 *indicator*
cursorily 278.8 *shallowly*, 470.7 *negligently*
cursoriness 278.3 *shallowness*, 358.5 *shortfall*, 375.10 *rough idea*, 620.5 *imperfection*
cursory 278.2 *superficial*, 358.8 *defective*, 375.5 *unfinished*, 482.1 *undiscriminating*, 620.2 *incomplete*, 648.3 *hasty*
curt 270.7 *short*, 270.9 *abrupt*, 381.2 *outspoken*, 552.3 *concise*, 562.6 *summary*, 566.3 *sparing with words*, 818.5 *discourteous*
curtail 129.5 *make smaller*, 131.4 *take off*, 136.10 *set apart*, 189.5 *make transient*, 262.5 *make smaller*, 270.10 *shorten*, 302.7 *limit*, 542.22 *play down*, 628.5 *hurt*, 699.8 *restrain*
curtailed 131.7 *reduced*, 145.4 *incomplete*, 262.7 *smaller*, 270.8 *shortened*, 302.5 *limited*, 542.19 *downplayed*
curtailment 129.1 *decrease*, 131.1 *subtraction*, 136.3 *separateness*, 262.1 *contraction*, 270.2 *shortening*, 302.2 *limiting factor*, 542.9 *down-playing*, 699.1 *restraint*
curtain 51.6 *scene*, 51.17 *stage set*, 136.6 *boundary*, 147.3 *exclusion zone*, 283.3 *suspended object*, 293.8 *wall covering*, 293.28 *face*, 436.6 *blinder*, 438.6 *that which makes invisible*, 440.6 *shade*, 443.7 *opaque thing*, 531.8 *conceal*, 634.2 *shelter*, 671.11 *fortification*, 671.12 *fort*, 671.19 *buffer*
curtain call 51.6 *scene*, 183.5 *repeat*, 851.5 *acclaim*
curtain-lifter 51.2 *play*, 51.6 *scene*
curtain-music 51.6 *scene*
curtain off 147.7 *exclude*
curtain raiser 154.5 *preface*, 156.9 *premiere*
curtain-raiser 51.2 *play*, 51.6 *scene*
curtain rise 156.9 *premiere*
curtain rod 283.4 *hanger*
curtains 157.3 *death*, 360.4 *fall*, 397.1 *death*
curtain wall 43.9 *miscellaneous architectural features*
curtal 49 Musical Instruments, 270.8 *shortened*
curtate 270.8 *shortened*
Curtiss 52 Scientists
curtly 270.12 *short*, 381.12 *bluntly*, 552.5 *concisely*, 818.9 *discourteously*
curtness 270.1 *shortness*, 270.6 *abruptness*, 381.6 *outspokenness*, 552.1 *conciseness*, 566.4 *taciturnity*
curtsy 362.9 *bow*, 362.16 *courtesy*, 673.1 *submission*, 673.4 *succumb*, 694.3 *obeisance*, 694.6 *show obeisance to*, 817.5 *sign of courtesy*, 817.13 *defer to*, 849.4 *mark of respect*, 849.19 *take off one's hat to*
curtsying 849.11 *in a respectful stance*
curvaceous 311.5, 315.10 *well-rounded*
curvaceously 311.7 *curvedly*, 315.13 *roundly*

curvaceousness 315.2 *round body*
curvature 311, 52.37 *line*, 52.38 *surface*, 286.1 *obliqueness*, 335.13 *deviation*
curve 52, 311, 25.5 *bowling delivery*, 52.32 *graph*, 52.37 *line*, 52.97 *align*, 143.1 *part*, 286.6 *be oblique*, 313.2 *circle*, 316.5 *be convex*, 335.1 *deviate*, 335.5 *twist*, 335.14 *deviating course*, 338.5 *throw*, 363.7 *ring*, 539.9 *sleight of hand*
Curve 311
curve ball 22.4 *pitching terms*
curveball 539.9 *sleight of hand*
curved 311, 25.10 *bowing*, 52.81 *curvilineal*, 363.10 *circular*, 376.2 *uniform*
curved inwards 317.5 *concave*
curved line 52.37 *line*
curvedly 311
curvedness 313.1 *circularity*
curved surface 52, 52.38 *surface*
curved things 311
curve inwards 317.6 *be concave*
curve putt 29.3 *golf shots*
curve running 21.1 *track events*
curvet 32.10 *dressage*
curviform 311.4 *curved*
curvilinear 52, 311.4 *curved*
curvilinearity 311.1 *curvature*
curvilinearly 311.7 *curvedly*
curving 311.4 *curved*, 335.21 *indirect*, 381.1 *blunt*
curving inwards 317.1 *concavity*
curvy 311.5 *well-rounded*
Curwen 49 Musicians and Composers
cuscus 77 Marsupials
cusec 75 Scientific and Technical Units
cushion 24.1 *billiards*, 242.2 *moderator*, 242.4 *moderate*, 374.11 *soft thing*, 374.13 *soften*, 405.4 *pleasurable things*, 632.2 *protection*, 632.9 *protect*, 671.19 *buffer*
cushion cover 293.12 *protective covering*
cushioned 649.4 *at ease*
cushion of air 390.10 *air bubble*
cushiony 374.4 *compressible*
Cushitic 5 Languages and Groups of Languages
cushy 405.6 *pleasant*, 660.9 *easy*
cushy number 660.6 *easy thing*
cusp 43 Architectural Decoration, 52.39 *angle*, 157.7 *limit*, 279.1 *summit*, 380.7 *sharp point*
cusped 380.4 *toothed*
cuspidate 380.4 *toothed*
cuspidor 727.8 *sink*
cuss 827.1, 827.5 *curse*
cussed 832.14 *hostile*
cussedness 577.5 *obstinacy*, 668.1 *defiance*, 829.1 *irascibility*, 830.3 *irritableness*, 832.1 *malevolence*
cuss word 827.1 *curse*
custard 45.35, 414.3 *dessert*
custard apple 86 Fruits
custard pie 798.2 *slapstick comedy*
Custer's Last Stand 398.4 *slaughter*
custodial 632.7 *tutelary*, 699.15 *detained*
custodian 632.3 *protector*, 653.15 *manager*, 671.15 *protector*, 702.6 *prison officer*
custodianship 632.2 *protection*, 699.4 *detention*
custody 632.2 *protection*, 699.4 *detention*, 723.1 *possession*
custody of children 824.3 *divorce court*
custom 166, 584, 737, 738, 1.8 *tradition*, 10.1 *ritual*, 116.6 *convention*, 150.7 *method*, 167.5 *convention*, 202.6 *tradition*, 214.4 *orderliness*, 306.5 *formality*, 513.3 *the expected thing*, 584.1 *habit*, 640.1 *action*, 654.3 *precept*, 719.3 *performance*, 794.3, 813.5 *etiquette*, 817.2 *good manners*

custom and practice 15.1 *industrial relations*
customarily 1.18 *societally*, 116.37 *conventionally*, 166.18 *as a rule*, 214.17 *orderly*, 584.19 *habitually*, 787.10 *predictably*
customariness 787.2 *predictability*
customary 166, 1.14 *societal*, 116.15 *conventional*, 124.1 *average*, 150.15 *habitual*, 164.21 *common*, 214.14 *orderly*, 306.11 *formal*, 584.9 *habitual*, 787.4 *predictable*
custom board 36.7 *windsurfing*
custom-build 243.10 *produce*
custom-built 165.20 *personalized*, 243.12 *produced*, 306.10 *prototypical*
customer 13.9 *economist*, 400.7 *person*, 599.8 *user*, 712.4 *requester*, 730.5 *recipient*, 737.12 *custom*, 738.12 *purchaser*
customer account 744.1 *credit*
customer credit 744.1 *credit*
custom house 740.1 *market*, 741.19 *treasury*
customize 243.10 *produce*
custom-made 295.31 *styled*
custom-make 295.35 *make clothing*
customs 36.7 *windsurfing*, 652.6 *way of life*, 749.2 *money received*, 751.8 *levy*, 876.1 *morality*
Customs and Excise 751.8 *levy*
customs barrier 13.6 *economic factors*, 147.3 *exclusion zone*, 737.5 *commercial trade*
customs officer 730.7 *collector*
customs official 632.3 *protector*
cut 23.6 *play basketball*, 27.9 *stroke*, 27.17 *bat*, 27.18 *bowl*, 42.3 *card game terms*, 42.10 *play*, 45.55 *cook*, 47.8 *woodwork*, 47.17 *carpenter*, 50.21 *sculpt*, 67.10 *woven*, 68.17 *farm*, 69.15 *cultivate*, 69.19 *ornamental*, 74.2 *waterway*, 87.12 *manage grassland*, 96.1 *river*, 129.5 *make smaller*, 131.1 *subtraction*, 131.2 *subtracted item*, 131.3 *subtract*, 136.9, 136.15 *separate*, 143.7 *piece*, 160.4 *interruption*, 160.14 *disconnect*, 165.3 *characteristic*, 254.4 *absenteeism*, 254.18 *abscond*, 265.2, 265.5 *crack*, 265.7 *cracked*, 266.4 *slice*, 270.2 *shortening*, 270.8 *shortened*, 270.10 *shorten*, 306.6 *nature*, 306.7 *form*, 319.1 *notch*, 319.4 *notched*, 319.5 *notch*, 321.1, 321.6 *furrow*, 322.1 *opening*, 322.12, 322.18 *open*, 330.3 *hit*, 330.5 *beat*, 330.10 *bat*, 330.13 *blow*, 330.14 *sporting hit*, 338.26 *bat*, 341.1 *repel*, 341.6 *repulse*, 345.4 *hurry off*, 349.4 *ostracize*, 372.2 *rarefied*, 372.6 *make sparse*, 376.11 *smooth*, 380.14 *be sharp*, 380.16 *use a sharp tool*, 389.30 *dilute*, 406.3 *injury*, 406.6 *injured*, 406.11 *inflict pain*, 457.3 *external appearance*, 545.14 *inscribe*, 547.11 *paint*, 552.3 *concise*, 552.4 *be concise*, 562.2 *shortened*, 591.1 *avoid*, 591.9 *play truant*, 670.6 *stab*, 670.18 *hit*, 699.8 *restrain*, 704.6 *cancel*, 731.4 *allot*, 734.3 *taking away*, 734.10 *take away*, 749.5 *winnings*, 751.3 *fee*, 752.1, 752.3 *discount*, 754.13 *make cheap*, 796.8 *fashion*, 806.17 *humiliate*, 818.7 *be discourteous*, 850.5 *insult*
cut above 126.12 *superior*
cut a corner 270.11 *short-cut*
cut across 270.11 *short-cut*
cut a dash 611.7 *be important*, 811.31 *put on a show*
cut a figure 611.7 *be important*

cut a long story short 299.5 *outline*, 552.4 *be concise*, 562.10 *be brief*

cut and blow dry 791.8 *hair cut*

cut-and-cover tunnel 63.22 *tunnel*

cut and dried 582.3 *predetermined*

cut-and-dried 594.21 *readymade*

cut and run 329.4 *be swift*, 345.4 *hurry off*, 591.9 *play truant*, 632.8 *be safe*, 648.2 *make haste*, 779.4 *be a coward*

cut and thrust 330.9 *fight*, 330.12 *collision*, 670.18 *hit*, 674.6, 674.12 *fight*

cut and try 479.1 *experiment*

cutaneous disease 624.13 *skin disease*

cut a tooth 380.14 *be sharp*

cutaway 295.11 *jacket*

cutback 19.9 *play*, 19.15 *play of fence*, 129.1 *decrease*, 131.2 *subtracted item*, 270.2 *shortening*, 756.2 *act of thrift*

cut back 121.6 *change gradually*, 129.5 *make smaller*, 182.8 *reduce*, 270.10 *shorten*, 542.21 *detract from*, 628.5 *hurt*, 756.6 *save*

cut-back 542.18 *deflated*

cut both ways 578.1 *be equivocal*, 704.9 *cancel out*

cut corners 648.2 *make haste*, 756.6 *save*

cut costs 756.6 *save*

cut dead 818.7 *be discourteous*, 850.23 *insult*

cut down 129.5 *make smaller*, 244.9 *demolish*, 270.10 *shorten*, 362.2 *flatten*, 398.18 *slaughter*, 542.21 *detract from*, 670.6 *stab*, 676.13 *be at war*, 756.6 *save*

cut-down 542.18 *deflated*

cut down to size 167.9 *make conform*, 542.21 *detract from*, 806.3 *humbled*, 806.17 *humiliate*

cute 789.5 *beautiful*

cut flowers 84.1 *flower*

cut free 660.15 *disentangle*

cut-grass 87 Grasses

cuticle 278.4 *shallow thing*, 289.1 *exterior*, 293.14 *animal covering*

cuticular 289.6 *exterior*, 293.38 *covering*

cut in 160.16 *interrupt*

cut in half 158.17 *average*

cut into 346.11 *infiltrate*

cut it out 218.12 *stop*

cutlass 380.10 *knife*, 680.8 *sharp weapon*

cutlass fish 80 Fishes

cutlet 143.7 *piece*

cut loose 136.13 *diverge*, 698.19 *liberalize*

cut no ice 236.6 *be powerless*, 612.11 *be unimportant*

cut off 131.4 *take off*, 136.10 *set apart*, 160.12 *discontinue*, 189.5 *make transient*, 218.8 *cause to cease*, 244.11 *ruin*, 270.10 *shorten*, 357.15 *out of reach*, 398.16 *kill*, 552.4 *be concise*, 661.9 *block*, 676.13 *be at war*, 816.13 *ignore*

cut off one's head 879.5 *execute*

cut off one's nose to spite one's face 656.6 *act foolishly*

cut off with a shilling 609.7 *make insufficient*, 727.9 *dispose of*, 743.14 *impoverish*

cut off without a dime 609.7 *make insufficient*

cut off without a penny 609.7 *make insufficient*, 727.9 *dispose of*, 734.8 *take back*

cut of one's jib 306.6 *nature*

cut one's coat according to one's cloth 756.6 *save*

cut one's own throat 656.6 *act foolishly*

cut one's throat 398.21 *commit suicide*

cut open 322.12, 322.18 *open*, 630.20 *doctor*

cut out 306.7 *form*, 355.13 *dig out*, 594.2 *do the groundwork*, 598.2 *withdraw*, 628.5 *hurt*, 796.8 *fashion*

cut-out 440.2 *darkening*

cut out for 116.16 *fitting*, 485.9 *qualified*, 615.1 *convenient*, 655.7 *gifted*

cutout switch 323.2 *stopper*

cutover 28.3 *fencing movements*, 28.6 *fencing*

cut price 722.2 *financial loss*, 751.1 *price*, 752.2 *bargain*, 754.1 *cheapness*

cut-price 131.7 *reduced*, 722.17 *unprofitable*, 738.14 *buying*, 752.6 *discounted*, 754.9 *cheap*

cut prices 131.3 *subtract*, 722.10 *have a financial loss*

cut rate 722.2 *financial loss*, 752.2 *bargain*, 754.1 *cheapness*

cut-rate 131.7 *reduced*, 722.17 *unprofitable*, 752.6 *discounted*, 754.9 *cheap*

cuts 699.1 *restraint*

cut short 160.12 *discontinue*, 218.8 *cause to cease*, 244.11 *ruin*, 270.8 *shortened*, 270.10 *shorten*, 552.4 *be concise*, 562.7 *shortened*, 562.8 *summarize*, 563.15 *strike dumb*

cut short the preliminaries 648.2 *make haste*

cut someone dead 816.13 *ignore*

cut someone off in his prime 218.8 *cause to cease*

cut someone out of one's will 734.8 *take back*

cutter 74 Ships and Boats, 74 Sailing Ships and Boats, 27.8 *delivery*, 36.2 *sailing boat*, 68.8 *livestock*, 295.26 *fashion designer*, 380.9 *sharp-edged thing*, 380.11 *tooth*, 562.5 *summarizer*, 646.2 *artisan*

cut the cackle 422.6 *hush sh silence quiet shut up that's enough peace soft mum's the word whist*, 552.4 *be concise*

cut the first turf 156.24 *open*

cut the Gordian knot 682.7 *overcome obstacles*

cut the ground from under one's feet 661.8 *hinder*

cut the knot 136.9 *separate*

cut the lawn 380.16 *use a sharp tool*

cut the ribbon 156.24 *open*

cut the throat of 398.18 *slaughter*

cut the ties that bind 136.9 *separate*

cutthroat 244.14 *destructive*, 398.11 *murderer*, 674.16 *competitive*, 832.8 *malefactor*, 862.6 *evil person*

cutthroat competition 674.1 *contention*

cut through 136.9 *separate*, 270.11 *short-cut*

cut timber 85.18 *manage trees*

cutting 69.5 *gardening*, 69.9 *garden plant*, 72.2 *track*, 131.1 *subtraction*, 136.3 *separateness*, 270.2 *shortening*, 317.2 *concave land*, 327.10 *railway*, 380.3 *sharp-edged*, 545.1 *record*, 554.3 *emphatic*, 670.23 *attacking*, 832.14 *hostile*, 850.11 *insulting*

cutting away 136.3 *separateness*

cutting back 69.5 *gardening*, 131.1 *subtraction*, 542.10 *deflation*, 756.2 *act of thrift*

cutting down 542.10 *deflation*

cutting down to size 542.9 *downplaying*

cutting edge 300, 380.7 *sharp point*

cutting fluid 63.9 *machine tool*

cutting horse 32.4 *saddle horse*

cutting off 131.1 *subtraction*

cutting out 355.3 *digging out*

cutting remark 850.5 *insult*

cuttings 562.3 *compendium*

cutting someone dead 816.1 *unsociability*

cutting someone off 816.1 *unsociability*

cutting the ribbon 156.9 *premiere*

cutting torch 50.14 *sculptor's materials*

cuttlefish 81 Molluscs, 76.5 *aquatic animal*

cut to pieces 136.16 *apart*, 244.9 *demolish*, 398.18 *slaughter*

cut to ribbons 398.18 *slaughter*

cut to the quick 406.11 *inflict pain*

cutty stool 879.14 *instrument of punishment*

cut up 136.11 *divide*, 136.16 *apart*, 143.10 *part*, 770.5 *sad*

cut up nasty 832.18 *torment*

cut up rough 151.26 *be disorderly*, 828.11 *be angry*

cutworm 82 Insects, 69.12 *pests and diseases*, 82.3 *pest*, 82.5 *larva*

Cuvier 52 Scientists

Cuzco 93 Cities

CV 483.6 *documentation*, 562.1 *summary*

c.v. 3.6 *biography*

Cwellyn 94 Lakes

cwm 54.7 *landform*, 98.8 *valley*, 265.3 *gulf*, 277.4 *deep thing*

Cwmbran 93 Cities

cyan 56.28 *colour*, 454.1 *blue*, 454.5 *blueness*

cyanamide 57 Common Chemical Compounds

cyanic 454.1 *blue*

cyanide 57 Types of Compounds, 57 Common Chemical Compounds, 631.8 *poison*

cyanite 54 Minerals

cyanobacteria 90.2 *algae*

cyanogen 57 Common Chemical Compounds

Cyanophyta 90.2 *algae*

cyanosed 454.2 *bluish*

cyanosis 454.8 *bluishness*

cyanotic 454.2 *bluish*

Cybele 8 Deities, 8 Deities

cybernetically 603.10 *instrumentally*

cybernetics 59.1 *life science*, 65.1 *computing*, 65.16 *artificial intelligence*, 603.5 *mechanics*

cyborg 400.8 *humanlike machine*

cycad 88.1 *fern*

cycad fern 88.1 *fern*

Cycladic art 50 Non-Western Art

cyclamate 414.2 *sweetener*

cyclamen 450.1 *red*

cyclandelate 62 Medication

cycle 75 Scientific and Technical Units, 214, 71.12 *bicycle*, 155.2 *series*, 159.6 *continuum*, 183.4 *return*, 185.4 *term*, 187.5 *recurrent period*, 195.1 *succession*, 212.4 *frequency*, 214.8 *be cyclic*, 313.2 *circle*, 334.1, 334.3 *circuit*, 363.3 *orbit*, 364.1 *rotation*, 644.9 *exercise*

cycle racing 18 Sporting Activities, 674.4 *race*

cycle round 214.8 *be cyclic*

cycles per second 212.6 *radio frequency*

cyclic 52, 214, 57.35 *combined*, 57.38 *reactive*, 185.22 *periodic*, 187.8 *periodical*, 212.3 *frequent*, 313.5 *circular*, 364.12 *rotary*

cyclical 159, 155.16 *alternating*, 183.14 *recurrent*, 212.3 *frequent*, 214.12 *cyclic*, 363.10 *circular*, 364.12 *rotary*

cyclically 214, 212.1 *frequently*, 313.8 *circularly*

cyclic compound 57.7 *chemical compound*

cycling 71.1 *road transport*, 356.2 *passing along*, 644.5 *exercise*

cycling shorts 295.9 *trousers*

cyclist 71

cyclization 57.14 *chemical reaction*

cyclize 57.26 *react*

cyclizine 62 Medication

cyclobarbitone 62 Medication

cyclocross 674.4 *race*

cyclogiro 73 Types of Aircraft

cyclohexane 57 Common Chemical Compounds

cycloid 52.40 *curve*, 61.8 *disordered personality*

cycloid personality 61.8 *disordered personality*

cycloid psychosis 61.11 *psychosis*

cyclometer 268.8 *meter*, 329.8 *speed*

cyclomethycaine 62 Medication

cyclometry 268.2 *micrometry*

cyclone 55.11 *weather system*, 55.16 *wind vortex*, 241.5 *violent weather*, 364.4 *vortex*, 375.9 *broken water*, 635.1 *trap*

cyclonic 55.44 *frontal*, 55.48 *stormy*, 364.12 *rotary*

Cyclopean 43 Architectural Styles, 259.15 *big*

cyclopentamine 62 Medication

cyclopenthiazide 62 Medication

cyclopentolate 62 Medication

cyclophosphamide 62 Medication

cyclopropane 62 Medication

cyclops 76.7 *legendary beast*, 81.4 *arthropod*

Cyclops 259.10 *big person*

cyclorama 51.17 *stage set*

cycloserine 62 Medication

cyclosilicate 54.34 *mineral*

cyclostome 80.2 *fish*

cyclothyme 61.8 *disordered personality*

cyclothymia 61.8 *disordered personality*, 61.11, 510.5 *psychosis*

cyclothymic personality 61.8 *disordered personality*

cyclotron 56.94 *particle accelerator*, 235.8 *nuclear power*

cygnet 78.12 *young bird*, 206.4 *young animal*

Cygnids 53 Meteor Showers

Cygnus 53 The Constellations

Cyhiraeth 8 Deities

cylcamen 84 Flowers and Flowering Plants

cylinder 71 Motor Vehicle Parts, 315, 52.45 *curved surface*, 63.11 *engine*

cylinder head 71 Motor Vehicle Parts

cylinder mower 69.6 *garden tool*

cylindrical 52.83 *spherical*, 315.9 *round*

cylindrical coordinates 52.33 *coordinates*

cylindrical drums 49 Musical Instruments

cylindricality 315.1 *roundness*

cylindrical lens 56.29 *optical element*

cylindrically 315.13 *roundly*

cyma 43 Architectural Decoration

cyma recta 43 Architectural Decoration

cyma reversa 43 Architectural Decoration

cymatium 43 Architectural Decoration, 279.3 *architectural summit*

cymbals 49 Musical Instruments

Cymbeline 48 Shakespeare's plays

cymbidium 84 Flowers and Flowering Plants

cyme 84.4 *flower head*

cymophane 456.5 *variegated thing*

cymophobia 777 Phobias by Name

cymose 84.12 *of flowers*

cymose inflorescence 84.4 *flower head*

Cymric 5 Languages and Groups of Languages

Cynewulf 48 Poets

D

cynic 495.2 *pessimist*, 776.3 *hopeless person*, 834.2 *misanthrope*
Cynic 4.11 *follower of a doctrine*, 4.14 *of a philosophy*
cynical 378.5 *mentally tough*, 776.4 *hopeless*, 834.3 *misanthropic*
cynically 378.14 *single-mindedly*, 495.6 *pessimistically*, 776.11 *hopelessly*, 834.5 *misanthropically*
cynicalness 378.9 *mental toughness*
cynicism 4.7 *school of thought*, 495.1 *underestimation*, 776.1 *hopelessness*, 834.1 *misanthropy*
cynophobia 777 Phobias by Name
cynosural 291.8 *focal*
cynosure 291.5 *focus*, 340.7 *centre of attraction*, 437.6 *visible thing*, 543.5 *indicator*, 789.2 *beautiful thing*
Cynthia 53.17 *moon*
cyperaceous 83.16 *taxonomic*
cypher 52.10 *zero*
cypress 85 Trees and Shrubs
cypress pine 85 Trees and Shrubs
Cyprian 877.9 *immoral woman*
cyprinoid 80.13 *fishlike*
cyproheptadine 62 Medication
cyproterone 62 Medication
Cyprus 91 Countries, **98** Islands
cypsela 86.2 *botanical fruit*
Cyrano de Bergerac 48 Writers, **48** Dramatists
Cyrenaic 4.11 *follower of a doctrine*, 4.14 *of a philosophy*
Cyrillas 53 Lunar Features
Cyrillic 5.41 *lettered*
Cyrillic alphabet 5.14 *alphabet*
cyst 90.4 *reproductive body*, 316.2 *bulge*, 624.13 *skin disease*, 624.15 *ulcer*
cystectomy 60 Surgical Operations
cysteine 58 Amino Acids
cysticercus 81.13 *invertebrate larva*
cystic fibrosis 624.9 *respiratory disease*
cystine 58.8 *amino acid*
cystoplasty 60 Surgical Operations
cystoscope 60.7 *diagnosis*
cystoscopy 60.7 *diagnosis*
cystostomy 60 Surgical Operations
cystotomy 60 Surgical Operations
cytarabine 62 Medication
cythara anglica 49 Musical Instruments
cytochemistry 59.6 *cell biology*
cytogenetics 59.11 *genetics*
cytokinesis 59.10 *cell division*
cytokinin 58.17 *plant hormone*
cytological 59.20 *biological*
cytologically 59.29 *biologically*
cytological test 59.6 *cell biology*
cytologist 59.19 *life scientist*
cytology 59.1 *life science*, 59.6 *cell biology*
cytoplasm 59.7 *cell*
cytoplasmic 59.23 *cellular*
cytosine 58.10 *nucleoside*, 59.12 *molecular biology*
cytosome 59.7 *cell*
cytotaxonomy 59.17 *taxonomy*
cytotoxic 62.14 *counteracting*
cytotoxic drug 62.4 *drug type*
czardas 46.4 *historic dancing*
Czarnobog 8 Deities
Czech 5 Languages and Groups of Languages
Czechoslovak 5 Languages and Groups of Languages
Czech Republic 91 Countries
Czechs 1 Peoples

D 2.7 *social stratification*
DA 875.4 *drug taker*
dab 80 Fishes, 45.18 *sea fish*, 330.6 *tap*, 330.13 *blow*, 407.3 *press*, 407.11 *touch*, 612.8 *trifle*
dabble 391.14 *sprinkle*
dabble in 502.10 *know little*
dabble in occultism 368.12 *enter a nonmaterial world*
dabble in shares 737.2 *speculate*
dabble in sorcery 216.8 *cause change*
dabbler 502.5 *ignorant person*, 576.15 *indecisive person*, 642.11 *meddler*, 656.10 *unskilled person*
dabbling 502.2 *half-knowledge*, 642.21 *meddling*
dabbling duck 78.3 *water bird*
dabchick 78 Birds
dab hand 655.4 *skilled person*, 688.11, 696.10 *expert*
Da-bog 8 Deities
dabster 655.4 *skilled person*
da capo 49 Musical Terms, 183.24 *again*
dace 80 Fishes
Dachau 398.15 *slaughterhouse*, 816.4 *place of confinement*
dachshund 77 Breeds of Dogs, 276.4 *low thing*
Dacron 67 Synthetic Fibres and Fabrics
dacryocystorhinostomy 60 Surgical Operations
dactyl 48.9 *metre*
dactylic 48.20 *metrical*
dactylic hexameter 48.9 *metre*
dactylographic 543.15 *gestural*
dactylography 544.3 *means of identification*
dactylology 421.1 *deafness*, 543.3 *gesture*
dad 401.13 *man in the family*
Dada 50 Western Art Styles and Movements
da-daiko 49 Musical Instruments
Dadaism 48 Literary Groups and Movements
Dadaist 50.29 *realist*
dad-blamed 618.6 *damnable*, 827.11 *miscellaneous euphemisms*
dad-blast 827.16 *euphemisms*
dad-blasted 618.6 *damnable*, 827.11 *miscellaneous euphemisms*
dad-burned 827.11 *miscellaneous euphemisms*
daddy 401.13 *man in the family*
daddy longlegs 82 Insects, **82** Arachnids, 82.1 *insect*
dado 43.9 *miscellaneous architectural features*, 280.2 *foot*
Dadu Panthis 7 Non-Christian Religions
Daedalian 655.9 *well-made*
daemon 8.5 *deity*
daffodil 84 Flowers and Flowering Plants, 452.8 *yellow thing*
Dafla 5 Languages and Groups of Languages
daft 460.6 *unintelligent*, 508.5 *foolish*, 510.11 *insane*, 798.5 *ridiculous*
daft as a brush 510.11 *insane*
daftness 508.1 *folly*, 798.1 *ludicrousness*
Dafydd ap Gwilym 48 Poets
Dagan 8 Deities
Dagda 8 Deities
dagger 244.7 *agent of destruction*, 380.8 *sharp-pointed thing*, 543.7 *punctuation*, 680.8 *sharp weapon*
daggerboard 74 Parts of a Ship, 36.3 *parts of a sailing boat*, 36.7 *windsurfing*
Dag Hammarskjöld 675.4 *Nobel Peace Prize*
dago 91 Names for Inhabitants

dagoba 10.13 *shrine*
Dagon 8 Deities
Daguerre 52 Scientists
daguerreotype 66.3 *photograph*
Dagwood sandwich 45.11 *sandwich*
dah 534.8 *data transmission*
Dahl 48 Writers
dahlia 84 Flowers and Flowering Plants
daibyoshi 49 Musical Instruments
Daikoku 8 Deities
Dáil Éireann 12.4 *governing body*, 653.10 *legislative body*
daily 110.17 *regular*, 110.20 *regularly*, 185.22 *periodic*, 187.8 *periodical*, 187.13 *for specified periods*, 212.1 *frequently*, 214.12 *cyclic*, 214.16 *cyclically*, 532.4 *newspaper*, 532.5 *journal*, 584.9 *habitual*, 621.12 *cleaner*, 662.16 *home help*
daily beat 112.4 *monotony*
daily bread 350.7 *food*, 396.3 *life requirements*, 662.3 *sustenance*
daily grind 183.3 *repetitiveness*, 584.3 *way*, 644.1 *work*
daily habit 584.3 *way*
daily help 621.12 *cleaner*, 662.16 *home help*, 697.1 *servant*, 697.6 *domestic servant*
daily market 740.1 *market*
daily paper 532.4 *newspaper*
daily round 110.6 *regularity*, 112.4 *monotony*, 214.2 *cycle*, 315.6 *round*, 584.3 *way*
daily routine 110.6 *regularity*
Daimler 52 Scientists
Dai Nichi 8.3 *God*
dainties 350.7 *food*
daintily 260.8 *in a small way*, 370.11 *lightly*, 383.15 *texturally*
daintiness 260.1 *littleness*, 370.5 *lightness*, 383.2 *grain*, 621.1 *cleanness*
dainty 134.14 *purified*, 260.7 *little*, 350.27 *edible*, 370.2 *insubstantial*, 383.10 *delicate*, 411.3 *appetizer*, 411.7 *tasty*, 621.16 *clean*
dainty eater 350.18 *eater*
dainty palate 350.3 *delicate eating*
daiquiri 351.8 *mixed drink*
dairy 68.7 *farm building*, 647.1 *workshop*
dairy farm 68.6 *farm*
dairy farmer 68.15 *agriculturist*
dairy farming 68.3 *livestock farming*
dairyhand 68.16 *farm worker*
dairy ice cream 45.35 *dessert*
dairying 68.3 *livestock farming*
dairymaid 68.16 *farm worker*
dairy products 243.7 *produce*
dais 51.15 *stage*
daisy 84 Flowers and Flowering Plants
daisy chain 84.1 *flower*
daisycutter 27.8 *delivery*, 84.9 *figurative usage*
daisy family 83.3 *seed plant*
daisywheel 84.9 *figurative usage*
daisywheel printer 65.7 *peripheral*
Dakar 93 Cities
dakhma 399.6 *grave*
Dakini 8 Deities
Daksha 8 Deities
Dakshincharin 7 Non-Christian Religions
Dalai Lama 7.8 *priest*, 675.4 *Nobel Peace Prize*, 696.2 *sovereign*
dale 98.8 *valley*
d'Alembert 52 Scientists
Dalesbred 68 Breeds of Sheep
Dales pony 32 Breeds of Horse and Pony
Dall 94 Lakes
Dallas 93 Cities, 93.2 *American cities*
dalliance 328.11 *lingering*, 821.6, 826.2 *courtship*
dally 209.7 *wait*, 328.2 *hesitate*,

576.7 *be irresolute*, 821.26, 826.8 *court*
dallying 328.7 *delayed*, 328.11 *lingering*, 821.6 *courtship*
Dalmatian 77 Breeds of Dogs, 456.5 *variegated thing*
dal segno 49 Musical Terms
dalton 75 Scientific and Technical Units
Dalton 52 Scientists
daltonism 436.2 *poor sight*
Dalton's law 56 Named Laws
dam 63, 32.1 *horse*, 32.13 *breeding*, 63.19 *structure*, 96.9 *stop the flow*, 147.3 *exclusion zone*, 245.5 *propagator*, 323.8 *stop*, 389.16 *water carrier*, 661.3 *barrier*, 661.9 *block*
damage 129.1 *decrease*, 238.1 *weakness*, 238.7 *weaken*, 244.5 *havoc*, 244.10 *lay waste*, 309.11 *deform*, 601.1 *misuse*, 607.1, 607.3 *waste*, 609.7 *make insufficient*, 618.11 *harmfulness*, 618.13 *be worthless*, 620.5 *imperfection*, 628.4 *impair*, 628.10 *impairment*, 722.5 *destruction*, 722.13 *destroy*, 751.5 *cost*, 854.12 *defame*, 862.2 *affliction*, 862.11 *be evil*, 879.10 *affliction*
damaged 620.1 *imperfect*, 628.12 *deteriorated*, 793.4 *blemished*, 862.8 *afflicted*
damages 125.1, 735.2 *compensation*, 746.4 *grant*, 751.6 *business costs*, 878.6 *compensation*, 879.8 *penalty*
damaging 601.5 *abusive*, 618.5 *harmful*, 717.8 *irresolute*, 852.27 *critical*, 854.16 *defamatory*, 862.9 *detrimental*
damagingly 607.11 *destructively*
Damara 5 Languages and Groups of Languages
damascene 456.2 *check*, 456.11 *variegate*
Damascus 93 Cities
damask 57 Alloys, **67** Natural Fabrics, 450.1 *red*
damask rose 84 Flowers and Flowering Plants
dam-breaking 96.10 *fluvial*
dame 402.9 *woman considered as a sex object*, 696.1 *master*
Dame 402.3 *female title of address*
Dame Fortune 229.2 *chance*
Damkina 8 Deities
dammed 323.13 *stopped*, 396.15 *born*
damn 8.18 *devilize*, 16.79 *convict*, 612.8 *trifle*, 827.7 *wish ill*, 827.15 *miscellaneous swearwords*
damnable 618
damn all 172.2 *nothing*
damn and blast 827.6 *vilify*
damnation 199.3 *future condition*, 827.4 *malediction*
damned 8.16 *devilish*, 16.64 *convicted*, 618.6 *damnable*, 827.10 *maledictive*, 864.14 *impious*
damned little difference 114.7 *similar*
damned soul 722.6 *loser*
damnify 628.5 *hurt*
damning 827.10 *maledictive*, 852.29 *blaming*
damningly 827
damn the consequences 574.18 *here goes*
damn with faint praise 542.21 *detract from*
Damodar 96 Rivers
Damona 8 Deities
Damon and Pythias 819.7 *famous friendships*
damp 55.6 *weather data*, 55.52 *humid*, 242.4 *moderate*, 388.3 *miasma*, 389.3 *wateriness*, 391.9 *moist*
dampcourse 280.2 *foot*
damp down 424.6, 428.7 *mute*
damped 424.4 *faint*, 428.2 *nonresonant*
dampen 242.4 *moderate*, 391.13

moisten, 424.6, 428.7 *mute,*
587.5 *discourage,* 770.10 *depress*
dampened 424.4 *faint,* 428.2
nonresonant, 587.10 *dissuaded*
dampener 424.2 *sound reducer*
dampen the spirits of 770.10 *depress*
damper 242.2 *moderator,* 323.2
stopper, 421.3 *inaudibility,*
424.2 *sound reducer,* 428.6 *silencer,* 563.8 *mute,* 587.7 *deterrence,* 661.7 *hinderer,* 661.8 *hinder,* 699.5 *means of restraint,*
699.8 *restrain*
damping 389.26 *wetting,* 587.9
dissuasive
damping-off 69.12 *pests and diseases,* 89.5 *fungal association*
dampish 391.9 *moist*
damply 389.35 *wetly,* 391.17
moistly, 393.27 *slimily*
dampness 777 Phobias by
Topic, 55.6 *weather data,* 389.3
wateriness, 391.1 *moisture*
dampproof 392.10 *waterproof*
damp squib 515.2 *bad outcome,*
683.4 *unsuccessful thing*
damp the ardour 587.5 *discourage*
damsel 402.2 *female*
damselfish 80 Fishes
damselfly 82 Insects
damson 86 Fruits, 455.3 *purple
thing*
damson-coloured 455.6 *purple*
dan 655.4 *skilled person*
dance 46, 46, 161, 773, 46.1
dancing, 46.8 *ballet,* 324.15
walk, 359.17 *spring up,* 364.3
reel, 365.4, 365.11 *rock,* 366.21
be agitated, 366.26 *flicker,*
815.5 *party*
dance about 26.11 *do a combat
sport*
dance attendance on 180.16 *attend,* 467.10 *be attentive,*
808.11 *pander to*
dance attendance upon 697.8
serve
dance costume 295.5 *fancy dress*
dance floor 46.6 *famous dancers,*
376.8 *smooth thing*
dance hall 46
dance lift 41.7 *ice-dancing*
dance music 49
dance of death 397.1 *death*
dance of Siva 10.7 *non-Christian
ritual*
dance of the seven veils 46.2
dance, 296.1 *undress*
dance on ice 41.15 *ice-skate*
dancer 46, 51, 646.1 *worker*
dance step 41.7 *ice-dancing,*
324.12 *gait*
dance upon nothing 879.6 *be
punished*
dancing 46, 26.2 *boxing,* 26.14
combat, 46.8 *ballet,* 365.16
rocking, 366.6 *shaking,* 642.18
active
Dancing and Ballet 46
dancing girl 51.28 *dancer*
dancing light 456.5 *variegated
thing*
dancing on ice 41.7 *ice-dancing*
dandelion 84 Flowers and Flowering Plants, 452.8 *yellow thing*
dander 828.4 *anger*
Dandie Dinmont terrier 77
Breeds of Dogs
dandify 809.17 *be affected*
dandle 821.2 *kiss*
dandruff 132.2 *residue,* 266.4
slice, 384.6 *crumb,* 622.4 *dirt*
dandy 295.27 *model,* 617.1 *worthy,* 861.1 *good,* 861.17 *good
thing*
Danegeld 751.9 *historical taxes*
dang 827.11 *miscellaneous euphemisms*
danged 827.11 *miscellaneous euphemisms*
danger! 41
danger 633, 618.11 *harmfulness,* 635.1 *trap,* 636.1 *warning,*
659.6 *critical situation,* 785.2
disliked thing
Danger 633

danger-loving 778.13 *adventurous,* 780.4 *rash*
dangerous 633, 491.7 *unreliable,* 539.38 *treacherous,* 618.5
harmful, 626.5 *unhygienic,*
772.3 *important,* 828.16 *angry*
dangerous age 207.4 *middle age*
dangerous course 633.5 *danger*
dangerous encounter 785.2 *disliked thing*
dangerous game 780.2 *rash move*
dangerously 633, 491.26 *unreliably*
dangerousness 635.2 *troublemaker*
dangerous person 635.2 *troublemaker*
dangerous situation 633.5 *danger*
dangerous speed 329.8 *speed*
dangerous subject 828.3 *cause of
offence*
dangerous temper 829.1 *irascibility*
dangerous woman 821.9 *lover*
danger past 632.1 *safety*
danger sign 543.1 *sign*
danger signal 633, 636, 450.7
red thing, 517.3 *plan,* 543.4 *signal*
dang it 827.16 *euphemisms*
dangle 139.6 *come unstuck,*
283.1 *suspension,* 283.10 *suspend,* 365.11 *rock,* 526.1 *display*
dangle before one's eyes 586.16
tempt
dangle before the eyes 811.28
flourish
dangler 808.5 *adherent*
dangle the bait 539.33 *snare*
dangling 139.8 *nonadhesive,*
283.1 *suspension,* 283.7 *suspended*
dangling participle 504.11 *grammatical error*
Dan grade 26.7 *judo,* 26.8 *karate*
Dani 5 Languages and Groups
of Languages
Daniel come to judgment 16.23
judge
Daniell 52 Scientists
Daniell cell 56 Named Laws,
57.19 *electrochemistry*
danio 80 Fishes
Danish 5 Languages and
Groups of Languages, 45.36
cake
Danish bacon 45.30 *bacon*
Danish Blue 45 Cheeses
Danish pastry 45.36 *cake,* 414.3
dessert
Danish Red 68 Breeds of Cattle
dank 391.9 *moist,* 415.6 *unpalatable*
dankishness 391.3 *humidity*
dankly 391.17 *moistly*
dankness 391.3 *humidity,* 415.2
unpalatability
D'Annunzio 48 Poets, 48 Dramatists
dansak 45.49 *Indian dish*
Dante Alighieri 48 Poets
Dante and Beatrice 821.10 *lovers*
Dantesque 48.19 *narrative*
Danu 8 Deities
Danube 96 Rivers, 96.5 *other
major rivers*
Danube school 50 Western Art
Styles and Movements
Danubian 32 Breeds of Horse
and Pony
dap 295.30 *dressed up*
daphne 85 Trees and Shrubs
Daphne 85.13 *tree mythology*
daphnia 81.4 *arthropod*
Daphnis and Chloe 821.10 *lovers*
dapper 150.13 *orderly,* 295.30
dressed up, 621.16 *clean*
dapping 20.1 *angling*
dapple 113.6 *assorted,* 133.8
mix, 456.11 *variegate*
dappled 133.12 *mixed,* 456.10
mottled
dapple-grey 32.1 *horse,* 448.1
grey
dappleness 113.2 *assortment*
dappling 133.3 *miscellany,*
456.4 *maculation*
daps 295.19 *footwear*

dapsone 62 Medication
darabukke 49 Musical Instruments
daraf 75 Scientific and Technical Units
Daramulum 8 Deities
darbuk 49 Musical Instruments
Darby and Joan 176.1 *two,* 207.7
older person, 225.5 *stable person,* 823.9 *married couple*
darcy 75 Scientific and Technical Units
Dardanelles 98.9 *inlet*
Dardic 5 Languages and Groups
of Languages
Dards 1 Peoples
dare 807, 479.13 *invent,*
491.22 *risk,* 574.8 *brace oneself,*
597.1 *undertake,* 633.9 *face danger,* 668.3 *act of defiance,* 668.5
defy, 668.6 *be insubordinate,*
778.15 *be courageous,* 778.16
take courage
D area 24.5 *snooker*
daredevil 508.4 *rash person,*
778.7 *courageous person,* 780.3
rash person, 780.4 *rash*
daredevilry 780.1 *rashness*
daresay 488.10 *think likely*
dare say 518.5 *suppose*
Dar es Salaam 93 Cities
daring 237.12 *strong to the
senses,* 479.4 *originality,* 479.9
original, 526.15 *open,* 574.16
fortitude, 596.8 *attempting,*
597.6 *enterprising,* 633.5 *danger,* 668.1 *defiance,* 668.7 *defiant,* 778.1 *courage,* 778.9 *courageous,* 780.1 *rashness,* 780.4
rash, 811.18 *dramatic*
daringly 479.15 *inventively,*
597.9 *enterprisingly,* 668.9 *defiantly,* 811.34 *dramatically*
daringness 668.1 *defiance*
Darjeeling 93 Cities, 351.3 *tea*
dark 440, 447, 55.49 *cloudy,*
205.6 *evening,* 329.4 *be swift,*
399.11 *funeral,* 436.13 *hidden,*
438.2 *difficult to see,* 438.3 *private,* 440.1 *darkness,* 440.10
dark-coloured, 441.5 *dim,* 443.1
opaque, 443.2 *shady,* 444.13
soft-hued, 447.7 *blackness,*
448.3 *dull,* 449.2 *browned,*
527.2 *concealed,* 830.6 *sullen*
Dark Ages 3.10 *past age,* 200.5
historical period, 440.5 *figurative dark thing*
dark blue 454.1 *blue*
dark brown 440.3 *dark colour,*
449.1 *brown*
dark clothes 440.4 *dark thing*
dark cloud 55.18 *cloud*
dark clouds 543.1 *sign,* 687.1 *adversity*
dark colour 440, 447.7 *blackness*
dark-coloured 440
dark colouring 447.7 *blackness*
dark comedy 51.10 *comedy*
dark complexion 449.3 *brownness*
dark-complexioned 447.2 *dark*
Dark Continent 440.5 *figurative
dark thing,* 529.8 *anonymity*
dark corner 438.5 *invisible thing*
darken 55.60 *cloud,* 436.15
blind, 438.7 *become invisible,*
438.8 *make invisible,* 440.13 *become dark,* 440.14 *make dark,*
441.9 *be dim,* 441.10 *make
dim,* 443.11 *make opaque,*
444.15 *colour,* 447.11 *blacken,*
531.9 *disguise*
darkened 438.2 *difficult to see*
darkening 440, 440, 436.11
blinding, 447.7 *blackness*
Darkest Africa 263.3 *distant
place,* 440.5 *figurative dark thing*
darkest hour 440.1 *darkness*
darkfall 205.1 *evening*
dark glasses 56.29 *optical element,* 435.10 *visual aid,* 440.4
dark thing, 440.6 *shade*
dark green 453.1 *green*
dark-grey 448.1 *grey*
dark hair 440.3 *dark colour*
dark-haired 440.10 *dark-coloured,* 447.4 *black-haired*

dark-headed 447.4 *black-haired*
dark horse 32.7 *horseracing,*
440.5 *figurative dark thing,*
502.4 *unknown person,* 527.7 *latent things*
darkish 440.8 *dark,* 441.5 *dim*
dark lantern 439.7 *lantern,*
440.4 *dark thing*
darkling 440.10 *dark-coloured*
darkling beetle 82 Insects
darkly 440, 441.12 *dimly,*
447.12 *blackly,* 830.13 *sullenly*
dark matter 53.4 *cosmological
model,* 440.4 *dark thing*
dark meat 45.28 *poultry*
dark nebula 53.8 *interstellar medium*
darkness 777 Phobias by Topic,
440, 205.2 *night,* 436.1 *blindness,* 438.4 *invisibility,* 438.6
that which makes invisible,
443.6 *opaqueness,* 444.3 *hue,*
447.7 *blackness,* 448.7 *dullness,*
527.11 *mysteriousness,* 658.2
naivety, 687.1 *adversity*
Darkness 440
dark powers 440.7 *spiritual darkness*
dark purple 455.6 *purple*
dark reaction 58.23 *photosynthesis*
darkroom 66.12 *development,*
440.4 *dark thing*
dark rum 351.7 *alcoholic drink*
dark side 305.4 *aspect*
dark skin 440.3 *dark colour,*
449.3 *brownness*
dark-skinned 440.10 *dark-coloured*
dark star 440.4 *dark thing*
dark thing 440
darktime 205.2 *night*
darling 9.4 *idolized person,* 51.22
actor, 206.9 *child,* 784.4 *likable
person,* 821.12 *nicknames for
lovers,* 821.21 *beloved,* 826.4
terms of endearment
Darling 96 Rivers
Darlington 93 Cities
Darmstadt 93 Cities
darn 135.10 *link,* 629.1, 629.8
repair, 827.11 *miscellaneous euphemisms,* 827.16 *euphemisms*
darned 135.12 *united,* 618.6
damnable, 827.11 *miscellaneous euphemisms*
darnel 84 Flowers and Flowering Plants, 87 Grasses
darner 629.12 *repairer*
darning 629.8 *repair*
darshan 7.8 *priest*
dart 224.12 *be irresolute,* 324.15
walk, 338.8 *missile,* 338.10
ball, 338.23 *throw,* 680.6 *historical missile weapon*
Dart 96 Rivers
darted 295.31 *styled*
darter 78 Birds, 80 Fishes
darting 224.2 *irresolution,* 329.1,
329.1 *swift*
Dartmoor 68 Breeds of Sheep,
702.1 *prison*
Dartmoor pony 32 Breeds of
Horse and Pony
Dartmouth 93 Cities
dart off 329.6 *accelerate*
darts 18 Sporting Activities, **42**
darts cricket 18 Sporting Activities
darts football 18 Sporting Activities
darts game 42.1 *game*
dart to and fro 648.2 *make haste*
Darwin 52 Scientists, **93** Cities
Darwinian 59.27 *evolutionary*
Darwinism 59.16 *evolution*
Darwinist 59.19 *life scientist*
Darwin's finches 78.6 *songbird*
Dasehra 10.16 *religious festival*
dash 97.10 *billow,* 133.4 *admixture,* 133.8 *mix,* 136.5 *separator,* 137.4 *means of connection,*
182.1 *few,* 239.1 *vigour,* 241.7
be violent, 324.15 *walk,* 329.4
be swift, 329.6 *accelerate,* 329.9
acceleration, 330.3 *hit,* 330.13
blow, 345.4 *hurry off,* 534.8

data transmission, 542.6 *suggestion,* 543.7 *punctuation,* 543.13 *punctuate,* 554.1 *emphasis,* 554.6 *emphasize,* 574.16 *fortitude,* 642.3 *nimbleness,* 642.12 *be active,* 648.2 *make haste,* 648.4 *haste,* 674.4 *race,* 811.4 *flashiness*
dash at 670.1 *attack*
dashboard 71 *Motor Vehicle Parts,* **73** *Aircraft Parts*
dash down 362.2 *flatten*
dashed 806.3 *humbled*
dashed hopes 776.2 *hopeless situation*
dash for 332.7 *take a direction*
dash forward 329.6 *accelerate*
dashiki 295.8 *shirt*
dashing 329.1 *swift,* 423.1 *loudness,* 554.3 *emphatic,* 642.18 *active,* 811.23 *brave*
Dashing White Sergeant 46.4 *historic dancing*
dash off 329.6 *accelerate,* 345.4 *hurry off,* 648.2 *make haste*
dash one's hopes 515.6 *disappoint*
dash someone's hopes 683.6 *fail*
dash the cup from one's lips 515.6, 776.10 *disappoint*
dash through 648.2 *make haste*
dastard 779.2 *coward,* 822.8 *hated person*
dastardliness 779.1 *cowardice*
dastardly 779.3 *cowardly*
Dastur 7.8 *priest*
dasyure 77 *Marsupials*
data 65.17 *computing term,* 483.1 *evidence,* 501.2 *information,* 518.2 *basis of supposition,* 528.1 *information*
data bank 511.6 *artificial memory,* 605.4 *storage*
database 6.14 *school book,* 65.11 *application,* 171.2 *table,* 511.6 *artificial memory,* 528.6 *information technology,* 545.6 *record book*
database management system 65.11 *application*
data collection 52.57 *population*
data communications 528.6 *information technology*
data entry 65.1 *computing*
data manipulation language 65.11 *application*
Data Post 534.2 *postal communication*
data processing 170.4 *computing,* 235.9 *electronics,* 528.6 *information technology,* 545.6 *record book*
data processing language 5.8 *artificial language*
data summarization 52.57 *population*
data tablet 65.7 *peripheral*
data transfer 65
data transmission 534, 53.32 *satellite*
date 86 *Fruits,* **185, 185,** 51.13 *engagement,* 161.8 *rendezvous,* 180.12 *partner,* 180.14 *keep company with,* 192.3 *chronology,* 192.15 *chronologize,* 401.4 *boyfriend,* 402.4 *girlfriend,* 815.3 *meeting,* 815.13 *fraternize,* 819.14 *seek the friendship of,* 821.9 *lover,* 821.26, 826.8 *court*
dated 3.15 *historic,* 185.25 *of known date*
dateless 186.5 *timeless*
datelessness 186.2 *agelessness*
date line 192.3 *chronology*
date palm 85 *Trees and Shrubs*
date rape 670.16 *terrorist attack,* 736.5 *plundering,* 877.7 *sexual assault*
dating 54, 185, 192.1 *timekeeping,* 821.6, 826.2 *courtship,* 826.9 *endearing*
dating agency 823.13 *matchmaker*
dating error 193.1 *wrong time*
dating service 823.13 *matchmaker*

dative 5.31 *case*
dative bond 57.11 *chemical bond*
datolite 54 *Minerals*
datum 106.6 *aspect,* 518.2 *basis of supposition*
datura 84 *Flowers and Flowering Plants,* 631.12 *poisonous plant*
daub 50.8 *painting,* 50.19 *paint,* 293.24 *coat,* 386.14, 395.18 *anoint,* 521.1 *lack of meaning,* 521.7 *mean nothing,* 548.1 *misrepresentation,* 548.4 *misrepresent,* 622.11 *dirty*
daubed 50.27 *painted*
Daubenton 52 *Scientists*
dauber 50.16 *artist,* 656.10 *unskilled person*
daubing 50.2 *painting,* 548.1 *misrepresentation*
Daudet 48 *Writers*
Daugavpils 93 *Cities*
daughter 402.12 *woman in the family*
daughter nuclide 56.70 *radioactivity*
daughter product 56.70 *radioactivity*
dauli 49 *Musical Instruments*
daunt 587.2 *deter,* 777.13 *frighten,* 806.26 *outdo*
daunted 779.3 *cowardly*
daunting 777.10 *frightening*
dauntless 778.9 *courageous*
dauntlessly 778.18 *courageously*
dauntlessness 574.16 *fortitude,* 778.1 *courage*
Davenant 48 *Dramatists*
davenport 47.4 *table,* 47.6 *bed,* 258.3 *cabinet,* 284.4 *rest*
David and Bathsheba 821.10 *lovers*
David and Jonathan 819.7 *famous friendships*
Davies 48 *Poets,* **49** *Musicians and Composers*
Davis 49 *Musicians and Composers*
Davis Cup 40.1 *tennis*
davit 74 *Parts of a Ship*
Davy 52 *Scientists*
Davy Jones's locker 97.1 *sea,* 277.4 *deep thing,* 397.14 *the spiritual world*
Davy lamp 439.7 *lantern*
dawdle 155.26 *bring up the rear,* 209.7 *wait,* 328.2 *hesitate,* 328.10 *slow motion,* 328.15 *slow person,* 643.12 *be inactive*
dawdler 328.15 *slow person,* 643.8 *nonworker*
dawdling 328.6 *hesitant,* 328.7 *delayed,* 328.11 *lingering,* 642.7 *restlessness,* 643.3 *not participating,* 643.7 *idleness*
Dawkins 52 *Scientists*
dawn 777 *Phobias by Topic,* 156.2 *creation,* 156.27 *emerge,* 204.1, 204.5 *morning,* 208.2 *early hour,* 322.11 *beginning,* 322.24 *begin,* 359.3 *sun rise,* 439.26 *grow light,* 450.7 *red thing,* 457.1 *appearance,* 457.12 *become visible*
dawn chorus 78.18 *birdsong,* 204.1 *morning*
dawn dew 391.6 *dew*
dawning 156.32 *embryonic,* 204.5 *morning,* 322.17 *beginning,* 457.1 *appearance*
dawn of love 821.2 *romantic love*
dawn on 522.4 *be intelligible*
dawn redwood 85 *Trees and Shrubs*
dawn upon 471.14 *have an idea,* 530.9 *be disclosed*
day 185.4 *term,* 185.11 *date,* 187.2 *time period,* 269.8 *measure of time*
day after day 183.23 *repeatedly,* 212.1 *frequently*
Dayak 1 *Peoples*
day and night 212.1 *frequently,* 214.5 *regular thing*
day-and-night attack 670.12 *military attack*
day bed 47.6 *bed*

day-blind 436.9 *weak-sighted*
day blindness 436.2 *poor sight*
daybook 171.4 *bill,* 171.5 *list of appointments,* 185.13 *timer,* 545.2 *certificate,* 750.5 *account book*
daybreak 156.2 *creation,* 204.1 *morning,* 208.2 *early hour*
day by day 185.26 *all the time,* 214.16 *cyclically*
day-care centre 6.12 *educational institution*
daydream 462, 102.2 *illusion,* 102.13 *imagine,* 335.4 *lose track of,* 404.2 *unconsciousness,* 435.5 *imagination,* 435.17 *imagine,* 462.12 *lack thought,* 468.12 *be inattentive,* 471.15 *imagine,* 519.4 *ideality,* 519.6 *reverie,* 519.15 *fantasize*
daydreamer 468.6 *inattentive person,* 519.9 *visionary,* 641.2 *nonacting person,* 685.3 *quitter*
daydreaming 61.14 *trance,* 421.1 *deafness,* 435.5 *imagination,* 461.3 *thoughtfulness,* 468.3 *absent-mindedness,* 468.8 *absent-minded,* 471.7 *idealism,* 519.10 *imaginative*
day dress 814.6 *informal dress*
Day-Glo 439.16 *bright,* 795.7 *vulgar*
day hospital 60.10 *hospital*
day in 212.1 *frequently*
day in day out 159.19 *continuously,* 183.23 *repeatedly,* 185.26 *all the time*
day labourer 646.1 *worker*
Day Lewis 48 *Poets*
daylight 56.23 *light,* 66.15 *lighting,* 204.1 *morning,* 265.1 *interval,* 439.4 *natural light,* 439.19 *sunny*
Daylight Comet 53 *Comets*
daylight robbery 736.1 *stealing,* 753.2 *unfair price*
daylight saving 185.9 *time zone*
daylight-saving 439.19 *sunny*
daylight saving time 192.3 *chronology*
day lily 84 *Flowers and Flowering Plants*
day nurse 60.16 *nurse*
day nursery 6.12 *educational institution*
day of abstinence 871.3 *fast day*
Day of Atonement 10.15 *holy day,* 840.2 *apology*
day off 218.3 *pause,* 254.5 *leave of absence,* 645.2 *time off,* 649.1 *ease*
day of grace 639.2 *deliverance*
day of judgment 492.4 *judgment day,* 879.9 *retribution*
Day of Judgment 157.5 *fate,* 199.3 *future condition*
day of reckoning 879.9 *retribution*
day of rest 649.1 *ease*
day one 156.1 *beginning*
days 110.20 *regularly,* 185.5 *indefinite period,* 188.5 *long duration*
daysack 258.9 *baggage*
days and years to come 199.1 *future time*
day school 6.12 *educational institution*
day's end 205.1 *evening,* 209.2 *late hour*
days gone by 3.8 *past time*
day's march 263.2 *great distance*
days of grace 209.3 *delayed action*
days of innocence 865.3 *naivety*
days of old 3.8, 200.1 *past time*
days of the week 214.5 *regular thing*
days of yore 3.8, 200.1 *past time*
daystar 53.15 *sun*
Daytime 204
Dayton 93 *Cities*
Daytona 200 33.5 *motorcycle racing*
day to remember 511, 812.5 *anniversary*

daze 61.14 *trance,* 491.20 *make uncertain,* 786.10 *be wonderful*
dazed 786.6 *wondering*
dazzle 436.15 *blind,* 439.2 *quality of light,* 439.24 *light,* 786.10 *be wonderful,* 789.7 *be beautiful,* 811.4 *flashiness,* 811.31 *put on a show,* 821.28 *win the love of*
dazzled 436.10 *blinded,* 786.6 *wondering*
dazzler 789.3 *attractive female*
dazzling 237.12 *strong to the senses,* 436.11 *blinding,* 439.16 *bright,* 446.6 *light,* 617.1 *worthy,* 619.1 *perfect,* 811.19 *flashy*
dazzlingly 436.18 *blindingly,* 439.30 *lightly,* 811.35 *flashily,* 821.30 *lovingly*
dBase 65.11 *application*
d-block 57.6 *chemical element*
d.c. transmission 64.33 *power distribution*
D-day 185.11 *date,* 214.6 *annually celebrated day,* 812.5 *anniversary*
DDT 68.14 *pest control*
deacon 7.8 *priest*
deaconess 7.8 *priest*
deaconry 7.9 *priesthood*
deaconship 7.9 *priesthood*
deactivate 125.5 *counterbalance,* 162.13 *dismiss,* 231.3 *counteract,* 242.4 *moderate,* 614.8 *make useless,* 628.4 *impair*
deactivated 57.38 *reactive,* 57.39 *catalytic,* 125.10 *counterbalancing,* 162.21 *disbanded,* 236.10 *powerless,* 240.6 *suspended*
deactivation 57.15 *catalysis,* 125.2 *counterbalance,* 162.2 *disbandment,* 231.1 *counteraction,* 238.1 *weakness*
dead 209, 397, 25.9 *bowls,* 31.8 *hockey,* 100.11 *no more,* 200.18 *over,* 240.5 *inert,* 247.3 *birth control,* 325.5 *sedentary,* 332.9 *directly,* 376.3 *soothing,* 424.4 *faint,* 428.2 *nonresonant,* 444.13 *soft-hued,* 445.6 *drained of colour,* 458.7 *disappeared,* 503.8 *accurately,* 641.3 *inactive,* 704.10 *cancelled,* 761.2 *desensitized*
Dead 97 *Oceans and Seas*
dead ahead 332.9 *directly*
dead and buried 3.18 *in the past,* 157.21 *ended,* 200.18 *over,* 397.19 *dead,* 399.10 *buried,* 512.11 *forgotten,* 722.16 *losing*
dead and gone 3.18 *in the past,* 100.11 *no more,* 200.18 *over,* 397.19 *dead*
dead as a dodo 3.18 *in the past,* 100.11 *no more,* 200.18 *over*
dead ball 23.4 *playing terms,* 24.2 *billiards play,* 29.2 *golfing terms*
dead-ball 35.6 *rugger*
dead-ball foul 19.13 *penalty*
dead-ball line 35.1 *rugger*
dead beat 236.12 *impotent,* 650.1 *fatigued*
deadbeat 808.3 *sycophant*
dead body 397.11 *dead person*
dead bolt 632.4 *safety device*
dead bowl 25.2 *grip*
dead broke 593.5 *necessitous,* 743.2 *insolvent*
dead calm 325.2 *repose,* 376.7 *smoothness*
dead centre 291.1 *centre,* 503.3 *accurate thing*
dead cert 490.12 *something certain,* 589.5 *good chance,* 660.6 *easy thing*
dead certainty 490.12 *something certain*
dead drunk 874
dead duck 397.10 *dying person,* 776.3 *hopeless person*
dead easy 660.9 *easy*
deaden 236.8 *overpower,* 242.4 *moderate,* 404.12 *anaesthetize,* 421.10 *muffle,* 424.6, 428.7 *mute,* 441.11 *tarnish,* 445.6 *decolour,* 563.15 *strike dumb,*

643.14 *make inactive*, 761.7
render insensitive, 783.13 *make
indifferent*
dead end 25.2 *grip*, 323.4 *closed
place*, 327.3 *road*, 659.8 *snag*
deadened 404.7 *anaesthetized*,
424.4 *faint*, 428.2 *nonresonant*
deadening 404.9 *anaesthetic*
deadeye 338.15 *shooter*
dead faint 236.4 *disability*
deadfall 539.13 *snare*
dead from the neck up 502.6 *ignorant*
dead hand 725.2 *legal terms*
deadhead 51.31 *theatregoer*,
69.15 *cultivate*
dead heat 32.7 *horseracing*,
110.5 *equality*, 122.2 *equilibrium*, 198.4 *equal race*
dead-heat 198.11 *equal*
dead-house 397.8 *after death*,
399.1 *burial*
dead jack 25.2 *grip*
dead language 5.9 *ancient language*
dead leaf 379.3 *brittle thing*,
449.5 *brown thing*
dead letter 236.2 *futile effort*,
521.1 *lack of meaning*, 534.3
correspondence
dead-letter office 534.2 *postal
communication*
deadline 157.11 *finality*, 648.4
haste
deadliness 325.1 *motionlessness*,
618.11 *harmfulness*, 626.1 *lack
of hygiene*, 862.1 *evil*
dead load 63.14 *load*, 369.7
weighing
deadlock 110.5 *equality*, 110.10
be equal, 122.2 *equilibrium*,
218.2 *stop*, 323.1 *closure*, 325.1
motionlessness, 487.7 *obstacle*,
632.4 *safety device*, 641.1 *inaction*, 659.8 *snag*, 661.2 *obstacle*,
661.9 *block*, 685.1 *noncompletion*
deadlocked 110.16 *equal*, 641.3
inactive, 659.16 *troubled*,
661.14 *blocked*
dead loss 614.5 *waste of effort*,
722.1 *loss*
deadly 397, 398, 211.14 *accidental*, 244.14 *destructive*,
617.1 *worthy*, 618.5 *harmful*,
626.5 *unhygienic*, 626.7 *toxic*,
633.1 *dangerous*, 788.4 *boring*,
861.1 *good*, 862.7 *evil*, 862.9
detrimental, 866.7 *sinful*
deadly crime 864.7 *criminality*
deadly nightshade 84 Flowers
and Flowering Plants, 631.12
poisonous plant
deadly pale 777.7 *frightened*
deadly sin 864.4, 866.3 *sin*
deadly sin of envy 842.1 *envy*
deadly weapon 680.1 *weapon*
deadman 34.8 *mountaineering*
deadman belay 34.3 *climbing
technique*
dead-man's float 39.1 *swimming*
dead man's hand 42.3 *card game
terms*
dead man's handle 72.5 *locomotive part*, 632.4 *safety device*
dead march 399.2 *funeral*
deadness 440.7 *spiritual darkness*, 444.3 *hue*
deadnettle 84 Flowers and Flowering Plants
dead of winter 409.7 *cold weather*
dead-on 537.21 *accurate*
dead on arrival 397.19 *dead*
deadpan 466.4 *uninterested*,
523.1 *unintelligible*, 772.1 *solemn*, 783.7 *indifferent*, 783.17
indifferently
dead person 397
dead pigeon 397.10 *dying person*
dead puck 31.3 *ice hockey*
dead reckoning 74.5 *navigation*
dead-reckoning position 74.5 *navigation*
dead right 332.9 *directly*, 503.5,
537.21 *accurate*, 537.39 *accurately*
dead-right 843.8 *correct*

dead ringer 110.3 *lookalike*,
176.5 *twin*, 547.1 *representation*
dead room 56.21 *architectural
acoustics*
Dead Sea Scrolls 3.11 *relic*,
202.5 *old thing*
dead set 325.1 *motionlessness*,
596.5 *attempt*, 670.12 *military
attack*
dead shot 338.15 *shooter*, 655.4
skilled person
dead silence 422.4 *silence*
dead simple 660.9 *easy*
dead spit 110.3 *lookalike*, 176.5
twin
deadstock 68.10 *farm tool*
dead stop 218.2 *stop*, 325.1 *motionlessness*, 683.1 *failure*
dead straight 312.1 *straight*
dead tired 650.1 *fatigued*
dead tissue 353
dead to 783.7 *indifferent*, 787.3
unmoved
dead to the world 404.8 *unconscious*, 421.5 *unhearing*, 643.4
not awake, 650.1 *fatigued*,
874.3 *dead drunk*
dead water 94.2 *small lake*,
376.8 *smooth thing*
dead weight 369.7 *weighing*,
661.6 *burden*
dead wood 614.6 *refuse*
deaf 421, 404.6 *unfeeling*,
512.8 *oblivious*, 577.4 *set*,
620.3 *deformed*, 641.3 *inactive*,
761.1 *insensitive*
deaf aid 420.9 *audio device*,
421.1 *deafness*
deaf and dumb 421.4 *deaf*,
563.11 *speechless*, 620.3 *deformed*
deaf-and-dumb language 543.3
gesture, 563.6 *voiceless speech*
deaf and dumb person 563.7
voiceless person
deaf as a post 421.4 *deaf*
deaf ears 421.1 *deafness*
deafen 421, 423.8 *be loud*
deafened 421.4 *deaf*
deafening 421, 423.6 *loud*,
425.8 *banging*, 431.16 *vociferous*
deafeningly 421.12 *deafly*,
431.20 *vociferously*
deafening row 423.2 *outcry*
deafly 421
deaf-mute 421.2 *deaf people*,
421.4 *deaf*, 563.7 *voiceless person*, 620.3 *deformed*
deaf-mutism 421.1 *deafness*,
563.5 *mutism*
deafness 421, 238.3 *poor
health*, 620.5 *imperfection*
Deafness 421
deaf people 421
deaf to 421.5 *unhearing*, 711.8
refused, 783.7 *indifferent*, 787.3
unmoved
deaf to all pleas 421.7 *unheard*
deaginously 395.20 *oilily*
de-air 44.11 *make ceramics*
de-airing 44.5 *ceramic process*
deal 13, 42.3 *card game terms*,
42.10 *play*, 47.12 *wood*, 116.3
arrangement, 116.23 *arrange*,
152.10 *agreement*, 162.16 *distribute*, 223.5 *exchange*, 640.2
deed, 640.4 *act*, 667.2, 667.7
contract, 715.1 *contract*, 716.4
negotiator, 717.1 *compromise*,
731.4 *allot*, 737.1 *trade*, 737.3
bargain, 737.4 *trade*, 737.9 *bargaining*, 739.1 *sell*, 739.3 *selling*
Deal 93 Cities
deal a blow 330.3 *hit*
deal a deathblow 398.19 *execute*
deal destruction 244.10 *lay waste*
dealer 13.9 *economist*, 224.4 *editor*, 230.5 *operator*, 646.3 *agent*,
715.4 *contractor*, 737.10 *trader*,
739.12 *wholesaler*, 739.13 *retailer*
dealer in real property 725.7
property man
deal fairly 857.6 *be honourable*
dealfish 80 Fishes
deal gently 691.3 *be lenient*

deal harshly with 690.5 *be severe*
deal in 640.4 *act*, 737.1 *trade*,
739.1 *sell*
deal in futures 14.5 *invest*, 737.2
speculate
dealing 223.1 *exchange*, 716.1
negotiation, 737.4 *trade*, 739.3
selling
dealing death 398.1 *killing*
deal in generalities 164.27 *make
a generalization*
dealing in the marvellous 541.5
tall story
dealing out 731.1 *allocation*
dealings 640.2 *deed*, 652.8 *treatment*
dealing with 472.7 *focused*
deal in the black market 737.1
trade
deal in the marvellous 541.11
tell a tall story
deal in depth 561.4 *dissertate*
deal off the bottom of the deck
539.30 *be fraudulent*
deal on inside information
539.30, 540.21 *be fraudulent*
deal out 162.16 *distribute*, 729.5
give, 731.4 *allot*
deal underhandedly 540.21 *be
fraudulent*
deal with 107.7 *relate to*, 230.9
take action, 472.11 *raise the
point*, 640.4 *act*, 652.14 *behave
towards*, 737.1 *trade*
deal with in depth 561.4 *dissertate*
dean 6.4 *educator*, 7.8 *priest*,
653.13 *director*, 688.10 *person
of authority*, 696.6 *religious
leader*, 696.9 *educational leader*
deanery 7.9 *priesthood*, 7.10
priestly dwelling, 256.4 *official
residence*
deanship 7.9 *priesthood*
dear 753, 494.6 *overestimated*,
742.3 *opulent*, 753.12 *dearly*,
757.3 *costly*, 784.4 *likable person*, 821.12 *nicknames for lovers*, 821.21 *beloved*, 826.4 *terms
of endearment*
dear at any price 753.7 *dear*
dear at the price 753.7 *dear*
Dearborn 93 Cities
dear departed 397.13 *the dead*
dear friend 819.6 *close friend*
dear heart 821.12 *nicknames for
lovers*, 826.4 *terms of endearment*
dear love 821.11 *loved one*
dearly 738, 753, 821.30 *lovingly*
dearly beloved 821.11 *loved one*
dearly love 821.23 *love*
dearly loved 821.21 *beloved*
dearly love to 784.9 *like to*
dearness 751.1 *price*, 753.1 *high
price*
Dearness 753
dear one 784.4 *likable person*
dearth 182.3 *fewness*, 247.1 *infertility*, 254.2 *disappearance*,
358.5 *shortfall*, 609.9 *scarcity*,
743.9 *inadequacy*, 753.6 *value*
dear to one's heart 821.21 *beloved*
deary 821.12 *nicknames for lovers*, 826.4 *terms of endearment*
death 777 Phobias by Topic,
157, **397**, **512**, 100.8 *extinction*, 141.1 *disintegration*, 211.4
mishap, 218.1 *cessation*, 244.6
destroyer, 325.2 *repose*, 396.5
life cycle, 458.4 *disappearance*,
624.2 *illness*, 649.1 *ease*, 684.2
conclusion, 687.1 *adversity*,
722.1 *loss*, 822.7 *hated thing*,
862.2 *affliction*
Death 397
death and taxes 214.5 *regular
thing*
deathbed 209.11 *late in the day*,
210.8 *in time*, 397.7 *dying day*,
624.2 *illness*
deathbed confession 397.7 *dying
day*, 867.1 *penitence*
deathbed repentance 397.7
dying day, 867.1 *penitence*
deathblow 157.13 *ender*, 398.5

execution, 683.2 *defeat*, 862.2
affliction
death-bringing 398.23 *deadly*
death by a thousand cuts 879.12
corporal punishment
death by misadventure 397.5
ways of dying, 398.8 *accidental
killing*
death cap 89 Fungi, 631.12 *poisonous plant*
death cell 702.3 *prison cell*
death certificate 397.12 *death
count*, 544.3 *means of identification*, 545.2 *certificate*
death chamber 397.4 *death sentence*, 879.16 *instrument of execution*
death count 397
death-dealing 398.24 *murderous*
death-defying 780.4 *rash*
death duty 751.7 *tax*
death grapple 674.6 *fight*
death grip 726.1 *retention*
death house 16.43 *conviction*,
397.4 *death sentence*, 879.16 *instrument of execution*
death instinct 61.22 *libido*
death knell 244.4 *ruin*, 397.4
death sentence, 636.1 *warning*
death knocking at the door
397.18 *dying*
deathless 190.8 *eternal*, 225.9
stable
deathlessness 186.2 *agelessness*,
190.3 *life without end*, 225.1
stability
deathlike 397.18 *dying*, 397.21
deathly, 422.3 *silent*, 445.8
drained of colour
deathlike calm 325.2 *repose*
deathlike silence 422.4 *silence*
deathliness 240.1 *inertness*,
325.1 *motionlessness*, 397.1
death
deathly 397, 211.14 *accidental*,
397.18 *dying*, 398.23 *deadly*,
445.8 *drained of colour*
deathly hush 422.4 *silence*
deathly pale 397.18 *dying*,
445.8 *drained of colour*
death metal 49.9 *popular music*
death notice 397.12 *death count*
death on the roads 398.8 *accidental killing*
death penalty 398.5 *execution*,
879.13 *capital punishment*
death personified 397
death rate 397.12 *death count*
death rattle 397.7 *dying day*
death ray 680.1 *weapon*
death record 397.12 *death count*
death register 397.12 *death count*
death roll 397.12 *death count*
death row 16.43 *conviction*,
397.4 *death sentence*, 702.3
prison cell, 879.16 *instrument of
execution*
death scene 397.7 *dying day*
deaths column 397.12 *death
count*
death seat 71 Motor Vehicle
Parts
death sentence 397, 16.43 *conviction*, 879.13 *capital punishment*
death's-head 397.3 *symbol of
death*
death's-head moth 82 Insects
death spiral 41.6 *ice-skating*
death stroke 157.13 *ender*
death struggle 674.6 *fight*
death throes 397.7 *dying day*
death toll 397.12 *death count*
deathtrap 71.21 *miscellaneous
motoring terms*, 539.13 *snare*,
633.5 *danger*, 635.1 *trap*
Death Valley 98 Deserts, 392.14
desert, 408.8 *hot place*
death warrant 16.43 *conviction*,
879.13 *capital punishment*
deathwatch 397.7 *dying day*
deathwatch beetle 82 Insects,
82.3 *pest*
death wish 61.22 *libido*, 770.2
depression
deb 156.14 *beginner*

debacle 683.1 *failure,* 244.4 *ruin,* 360.4 *fall*

debag 294.11 *uncover,* 296.15 *make nude*

debagged 294.8 *uncovered,* 296.11 *exposed*

debagging 294.3 *nakedness*

de-ball 131.4 *take off,* 236.9 *make impotent,* 628.5 *hurt*

de-balled 236.13 *unsexed*

debar 709.3 *veto*

debark 296.15 *make nude,* 344.4 *land*

debarkation 344.11 *landing*

debarment 709.1 *veto*

de Bary 52 Scientists

debase 362, 133.8 *mix,* 628.3 *make worse,* 628.6 *pervert,* 741.25 *demonetize,* 806.23 *abase,* 854.13 *vilify,* 877.19 *corrupt*

debased 362.21 *degraded,* 858.5 *dishonourable*

debasement 362, 628.8 *perversion,* 628.10 *impairment,* 806.10 *abasement,* 854.5 *scorn,* 858.1 *improbity*

debasing 362.18 *lowering*

debatable 472.8 *problematic,* 473.10 *arguable,* 477.14 *questionable*

debatably 472.13 *problematically,* 477.24 *questionably*

debate 463, 463, 4.5 *philosophical argument,* 4.23 *discuss philosophically,* 472.11 *raise the point,* 473.2 *logical argument,* 473.14 *discuss,* 477.20 *doubt,* 568.4 *conference,* 568.11 *confer,* 576.8 *balance,* 666.2 *argument,* 666.6 *argue,* 674.1 *contention,* 674.13 *conflict,* 679.40 *argue,* 716.3 *discussion*

debater 463.6, 473.6 *arguer,* 674.10 *contender,* 679.5 *arguer*

debating 568.4 *conference*

debauch 628.6 *pervert,* 812.1 *celebration,* 870.11 *overindulge,* 877.19 *corrupt*

debauched 864.12 *immoral,* 870.7 *dissipated,* 877.14 *lecherous*

debauchee 870.5 *self-indulgent person,* 877.8 *immoral man*

debauchery 864.2 *vice,* 870.2 *dissipation,* 877.3 *sexual immorality*

debauching 870.7 *dissipated*

debenture 715.2 *purchase contract,* 718.2 *promise,* 741.14 *paper money*

debenture bond 715.2 *purchase contract*

debilitate 129.5 *make smaller,* 236.7 *remove power from,* 238.7 *weaken,* 650.6 *fatigue*

debilitated 236.12 *impotent,* 238.11 *weakened*

debilitating disease 624.4 *disease*

debilitating illness 236.4 *disability*

debilitation 650.7 *fatigue*

debilitative 129.7 *decrescent*

debility 238.3 *poor health,* 624.1 *ill health*

debit 132.3 *difference,* 722.2 *financial loss,* 745.1 *debt,* 750.1 *accounts,* 750.7 *account*

debit and credit 750.1 *accounts*

debited 750.11 *accounted*

deblossom 69.15 *cultivate*

debouch 345.3 *quit,* 347.10 *emerge,* 349.14 *let out*

deboulé 46.9 *ballet steps*

Debray 4 Philosophers

Debrecen 93 Cities

debris 132.1 *remainder,* 143.8 *bits and pieces,* 326.10 *transferred thing,* 384.9 *grit,* 614.6 *refuse*

debris flow 54.26 *mass movement*

debrisoquine 62 Medication

de Broglie 52 Scientists

de Broglie principle 56 Named Laws

de Broglie wave 365.5 *wave*

debt 745, 593.2 *need,* 733.5 *loan,* 743.6 *insolvency,* 744.1 *credit,* 747.5 *insolvency*

Debt 745

debt capital 745.3 *loan*

debt collector 161.35, 730.7 *collector,* 744.5 *lender*

debt-free 746.16 *paid*

debt of honour 714.1 *promise,* 745.1 *debt*

debtor 745, 683.5 *failing person,* 733.6 *borrower,* 747.6 *non-payer*

debtors budget 750.2 *budgeting*

debtor's prison 702.1 *prison*

debts 661.6 *burden,* 745.1 *debt*

debt to society 879.7 *punishment*

debud 69.15 *cultivate*

debug 65.19 *abort,* 152.19 *tidy*

debugging 65.17 *computing term*

debunk 362.4 *debase,* 799.6 *deride*

debunked 806.3 *humbled*

debus 344.4 *land*

Debussy 49 Musicians and Composers

debut 51.11 *theatrical performance,* 156.9 *premiere,* 156.18 *make a beginning,* 322.11, 322.17 *beginning,* 322.24 *begin,* 344.10 *arrival,* 346.1 *entry,* 457.1 *appearance,* 596.5 *attempt,* 730.4 *reception,* 815.5 *party*

debutant 825.5 *single person*

debutante 156.14 *beginner,* 201.8 *new arrival,* 346.7 *entrant,* 815.6 *social person*

Debye 52 Scientists

deca 75 SI Units

decade 179.6 *ten,* 185.4 *term,* 187.2 *time period,* 269.8 *measure of time*

decadence 48 Literary Groups and Movements, 628.8 *perversion,* 877.3 *sexual immorality*

decadent 48.16 *literary,* 129.7 *decrescent*

decagon 52.44 *polygon,* 179.6 *ten,* 310.3 *angled figure*

decagonal 179.17 *tenth,* 310.9 *angled*

decagram 179.6 *ten*

decahedral 179.17 *tenth,* 310.9 *angled*

decahedron 179.6 *ten,* 310.3 *angled figure*

decahydrate 57.10 *salt*

decal 138.4 *adherent*

decalcomania 44.3 *glaze*

Decalogue 16.1 *the law,* 179.6 *ten,* 847.6 *ethics*

decamp 254.18 *abscond,* 345.3 *quit,* 345.4 *hurry off,* 458.2 *depart,* 591.8 *run away,* 638.5 *escape,* 648.2 *make haste,* 747.7 *not pay*

decampment 345.7 *departure,* 638.1 *escape*

decant 326.11 *transfer,* 354.2 *inject,* 362.6 *throw down,* 621.15 *purify*

decantation 326.3 *transmission*

decanter 258.14 *bottle,* 351.10 *drink container*

decapitate 131.4 *take off,* 136.10 *set apart,* 270.10 *shorten,* 879.5 *execute*

decapitated 131.7 *reduced,* 270.8 *shortened*

decapitation 131.1 *subtraction,* 136.3 *separateness,* 270.2 *shortening,* 879.13 *capital punishment*

decapod 179.6 *ten*

decarbonize 134.10, 621.15 *purify*

decathlete 21.3 *athlete*

decathlon 18 Sporting Activities, 21.2 *field events,* 179.6 *ten,* 674.2 *contest*

decay 628, 56.70 *radioactivity,* 129.1 *decrease,* 136.9 *separate,* 141.1 *disintegration,* 141.3 *disintegrate,* 189.4 *be transient,* 202.3 *antiquity,* 202.17 *grow old,* 238.1 *weakness,* 244.7

agent of destruction, 397.1 *death,* 419.2 *something that makes an unpleasant smell,* 607.1, 607.3 *waste,* 618.10 *poverty,* 618.13 *be worthless,* 622.4 *dirt,* 622.10 *be dirty,* 624.15 *ulcer,* 626.1 *lack of hygiene,* 628.5 *hurt,* 628.9 *dilapidation,* 631.14 *afflict*

decayable 129.7 *decrescent*

decay constant 56.70 *radioactivity*

decayed 141.5 *disintegrated,* 238.9 *dilapidated,* 618.4 *poor,* 626.5 *unhygienic,* 628.12 *deteriorated,* 631.16 *blighting*

decaying 129.6 *decreasing,* 141.6 *disintegrating,* 189.6 *transient,* 419.4 *putrid,* 618.4 *poor,* 624.23 *diseased,* 628.12 *deteriorated,* 631.16 *blighting*

decca phasemeter 74.5 *navigation*

decca system 74.5 *navigation*

decease 157.3, 397.1 *death,* 397.15 *die*

deceased 200.20 *former,* 209.14, 397.19 *dead*

deceit 474.5 *hypocrisy,* 539.1 *deception,* 539.5 *falseness,* 657.1 *cunning,* 858.2 *faithlessness*

deceitful 540, 309.8 *exaggerated,* 474.10 *hypocritical,* 477.14 *questionable,* 538.19 *dishonest,* 538.20 *unfaithful,* 539.35 *deceptive,* 657.4 *cunning,* 858.6 *faithless*

deceitfully 309.14 *distortedly,* 474.15 *hypocritically,* 477.24 *questionably,* 538.28 *dishonestly,* 540.36 *falsely,* 657.6 *cunningly,* 858.11 *dishonourably*

deceitfulness 540, 309.4 *distortion of the truth,* 477.7 *questionableness,* 531.5 *evasion,* 538.10 *dishonesty*

deceive 434, 531, 539, 102.16 *delude,* 115.6 *differentiate,* 286.7 *deviate,* 309.12 *distort the truth,* 436.15 *blind,* 477.21 *confuse,* 497.9 *make someone believe,* 515.8 *be dishonest,* 529.13 *mystify,* 538.24 *pretend,* 538.25 *be dishonest,* 539.27 *be false,* 539.31 *hoax,* 540.16 *be false,* 540.18 *be hypocritical,* 578.1 *be equivocal,* 635.3 *trap,* 657.5 *be cunning,* 734.10 *take away,* 736.16 *act dishonest,* 858.9 *prove false*

deceived 515, 539, 493.7 *misjudging,* 538.16 *misinformed*

deceive oneself 539

deceive one's hopes 515.6 *disappoint*

deceiver 539, 548, 531.7 *concealer,* 657.3 *cunning person,* 797.2 *pretender*

deceiving 539, 309.8 *exaggerated,* 515.12 *deceptive,* 538.17 *duplicitous,* 539.1 *deception,* 657.4 *cunning*

decelerate 129.4 *decrease,* 129.5 *make smaller,* 325.8 *be motionless,* 328.3 *slow down,* 628.1 *deteriorate,* 699.8 *restrain*

deceleration 328, 129.1 *decrease,* 628.7 *deterioration,* 699.1 *restraint*

decelerometer 268.8 *meter*

December 409.7 *cold weather*

decencies 813.5 *etiquette*

decency 134.1 *purity,* 794.1 *elegance,* 817.1 *courtesy,* 843.3 *propernesss,* 857.1 *probity,* 863.1 *virtue,* 876.2 *good morals*

decennial 179.17 *tenth*

decennially 179.24 *fivefold*

decennium 179.6 *ten,* 187.2 *time period*

decent 134.12 *morally pure,* 617.5 *not bad,* 817.7 *courteous,* 831.6 *benevolent,* 843.11 *right-minded,* 847.8 *dutiful,* 857.4 *honourable,* 863.5 *virtuous,* 876.8 *moral*

decent chance 589.4 *fair chance*

decent feeling 831.1 *benevolence*

decently 134.18 *virtuously,* 817.14 *courteously,* 817.15 *genteelly,* 831.10 *benevolently,* 857.7 *honourably,* 863.9 *virtuously*

decentralization 162, 141.2 *deconstruction,* 343.2 *parting,* 703.1 *commission,* 706.3 *delegation*

decentralize 162, 141.4 *deconstruct,* 703.6 *commission,* 706.4 *delegate*

decentralized 162, 706, 703.9 *commissioned*

deception 539, 286.3 *deviousness,* 309.4 *distortion of the truth,* 474.5 *hypocrisy,* 493.1 *misjudgment,* 531.5 *evasion,* 538.8 *pretence,* 539.11 *hoax,* 540.1 *falsehood,* 540.3 *hypocrisy,* 635.1 *trap,* 657.1 *cunning,* 657.2 *stratagem,* 734.3 *taking away,* 736.7 *dishonesty*

Deception 539

deceptive 515, 539, 286.5 *devious,* 309.8 *exaggerated,* 436.11 *blinding,* 457.9 *ostensible,* 474.10 *hypocritical,* 477.14 *questionable,* 538.17 *duplicitous,* 538.18 *pretentious,* 540.25 *false,* 540.27 *hypocritical,* 734.12 *taking,* 736.18 *fraudulent*

deceptive appearance 527.6 *latency*

deceptively 309.14 *distortedly,* 474.15 *hypocritically,* 477.24 *questionably,* 515.13 *disappointingly,* 538.28 *dishonestly,* 540.36 *falsely,* 734.13 *avariciously,* 736.19 *thievishly*

deceptiveness 477.7 *questionableness,* 539.1 *deception,* 797.1 *affectedness*

deci 75 SI Units

decibel 75 Scientific and Technical Units, 56.19 *sound propagation*

decidable 52.73 *numerable*

decide 16.71 *try a case,* 16.76 *judge,* 157.15 *end,* 166.13 *rule,* 226.12 *determine,* 490.21 *make certain,* 492.11 *judge,* 570.12 *choose,* 574.7 *resolve,* 580.1 *select*

decide against 709.3 *veto*

decide beforehand 582.2 *premeditate*

decided 490, 157.21 *ended,* 535.14 *assertive,* 574.1 *resolute*

decidedly 535.24 *truthfully*

decidedness 574.12 *resolution*

decide on 580.1 *select*

decide the issue 226.12 *determine*

decide the outcome 226.12 *determine*

decide the result 226.12 *determine*

deciding 580.14 *selecting*

deciding vote 580.10 *vote*

deciduous 83.14 *of plants,* 360.16 *descending*

deciduous tooth 380.11 *tooth*

deciduous tree 85.1 *tree*

decillion 169.3 *large number,* 179.11 *million*

decimal 52.18 *division,* 52.71 *numerical,* 169.1 *number,* 169.5 *ratio,* 169.9 *fractional,* 173.1 *fraction,* 179.17 *tenth,* 741.22 *monetary*

decimal code 65.10 *character*

decimal coinage 741.9 *British money*

decimal currency 741.1 *money*

decimal fraction 52.18 *division,* 169.5 *ratio,* 173.1 *fraction*

decimalize 52.91 *add,* 179.23 *quintuple*

decimal notation 52.8 *number system*

decimal number 52.8 *number system*

decimal point 52.8 *number system,* 543.1 *sign*

decimal system 52.8 *number sys-tem*, 169.1 *number*
decimate 131.3 *subtract*, 179.23 *quintuple*, 182.8 *reduce*, 238.7 *weaken*, 244.8 *destroy*, 398.18 *slaughter*, 879.5 *execute*
decimated 131.7 *reduced*
decimation 131.1 *subtraction*, 244.2 *destroying*, 398.4 *slaugh-ter*
decipher **524**, 5.46, 524.12 *translate*, 526.3 *reveal*, 550.2 *clarify*
decipherability 522.10 *simplicity*
decipherable 522.2 *simple*
deciphered 5.40 *translated*, 524.15 *interpreted*
decipherment 5.12 *translation*, 524.1 *interpretation*, 524.4 *translation*
decision 16.7 *legal trial*, 26.2 *boxing*, 492.2 *verdict*, 574.12 *resolution*, 580.6 *selection*, 588.4 *formulated intention*
decision-making 653.3 *manage-ment*
decisive 106.8 *difficult*, 210.7 *critical*, 226.13 *causal*, 233.11 *influential*, 535.14 *assertive*, 574.1 *resolute*, 580.14 *selecting*
decisively 210.10 *critically*, 226.14 *causally*, 233.14 *influen-tially*, 574.17 *resolutely*
decisive moment 210.3 *critical time*
decisiveness 535.6 *assertiveness*, 574.12 *resolution*
deck 36.3 *parts of a sailing boat*, 36.6 *canoeing*, 36.8 *punting*, 63.21 *bridge*, 258.4 *rack*, 266.2 *level*, 266.10 *layer*, 280.1 *base*, 330.3 *hit*, 362.3 *bring down*, 557.5 *ornament*
deck bridge 63.21 *bridge*
deck chair 47.2 *chair*
decked 36.12 *canoeing*
decked-canoe race 36.6 *canoeing*
decked kayak 36.6 *canoeing*
decked out 295.29 *dressed*, 791.14 *beautified*
decked out like a Christmas tree 792.8 *decorated*
deckhand 74.7 *nautical person*
deckhead 36.3 *parts of a sailing boat*
deckle edge 375.6 *roughness*
deckle-edged 375.2 *coarse*
deck out 295.33 *dress up*
deck-stepped 36.10 *sailing*
deck-stepped mast 36.3 *parts of a sailing boat*
deck with flowers 812.18 *salute*
declaim 532.14 *proclaim*, 567.7 *address*
declaimer 567.6 *public speaker*
declamation 564.9 *art of public speaking*, 567.1 *address*
declamatory 557.4 *ornate*, 564.20 *eloquent*, 567.13 *oratori-cal*
declaration 483.5 *legal evidence*, 530.2 *divulgence*, 532.1 *publica-tion*, 535.1 *affirmation*, 564.7 *utterance*, 564.8 *speech*, 688.9 *permission*, 692.1 *command*
declaration of faith 497.2 *reli-gious belief*
Declaration of Independence 698.3 *independence*
declaration of intent 714.1 *prom-ise*
declaration of truth 535.3 *vow*
declaration of war 668.3 *act of de-fiance*, 676.4 *belligerency*
declarative 535.10 *affirmative*
declaratory 520.6 *meaningful*, 532.21 *publishing*, 535.10 *affirmative*
declare 4.22 *propound a philoso-phy*, 166.13 *rule*, 483.11 *give ev-idence*, 497.7 *believe*, 520.10 *mean*, 530.6 *divulge*, 532.14 *proclaim*, 535.17 *affirm*, 543.12 *signal*, 564.11 *speak*, 688.21 *grant authority*, 692.9 *command*
declare as true 535.18 *vow*

declare Chapter 11 743.13 *lose one's money*
declared 526.14 *manifest*, 532.19 *published*, 535.11 *stated*
declared innocent 865
declare free 639.1 *deliver*
declare independence 91.17 *be-come a nation*
declare innocent 865
declare one's love 821.26 *court*
declare open 156.24 *open*
declare positively 535.17 *affirm*
declarer 535.9 *affirmer*
declare war 117.14 *disagree*, 666.6 *argue*, 668.6 *be insubordi-nate*, 674.12 *fight*, 676.12 *go to war*, 679.36 *combat*
declaring war 676.8 *warfare*
declension 5.30 *syntax*, 216.1 *change*, 335.13 *deviation*, 335.14 *deviating course*, 360.1 *descent*
declinable 129.7 *decrescent*
declinate 129.7 *decrescent*
declination 53.5 *celestial sphere*, 54.45 *magnetic pole*, 250.2 *exact location*, 268.4 *size*, 335.13 *deviation*, 343.1 *diver-gence*, 360.1 *descent*
decline **129, 337**, 127.2 *defi-ciency*, 127.11 *become inferior*, 129.4 *decrease*, 157.9 *close*, 202.17 *grow old*, 207.5 *old age*, 207.17 *age*, 216.8 *cause change*, 238.6 *be weak*, 337.1 *go back-ward*, 337.4 *slip back*, 358.6 *shortcoming*, 360.1 *descent*, 360.2 *sinkage*, 360.9 *descend*, 536.7 *be negative*, 581.1 *reject*, 598.2 *withdraw*, 600.5 *not use*, 607.1, 607.3 *waste*, 628.1 *dete-riorate*, 628.7 *deterioration*, 683.1 *failure*, 683.6 *fail*, 687.1 *adversity*, 687.9 *be in trouble*, 711.5 *refuse*, 754.12 *be cheap*, 768.7 *become aggravated*
declined 536.12, 581.10 *rejected*
decline in fortune 743.13 *lose one's money*
decline in health 683.1 *failure*, 687.1 *adversity*
declining 129.6 *decreasing*, 207.12 *ageing*, 337.23 *receding*, 360.16 *descending*, 536.2, 581.5 *rejection*, 628.12 *deterio-rated*, 687.6 *adverse*, 754.9 *cheap*
declining prices **754**
declining years 207.5 *old age*
declivitous 360.16 *descending*
declivity 310.2 *obliquity*, 360.6 *slide*
decoagulate 387.23 *dissolve*
decoagulated 387.19 *liquefied*
decoagulation 387.8 *fluidification*
decoct 355.17 *obtain an extract*, 387.23 *dissolve*
decoction 243.3 *product*, 351.2 *drink*, 355.7 *obtaining an ex-tract*, 355.8 *extract*, 387.10 *solu-tion*, 630.2 *medicine*
decode 5.46 *translate*, 65.19 *abort*, 478.20 *solve*, 524.9 *deci-pher*, 524.12 *translate*, 526.3 *re-veal*
decoded 5.40 *translated*, 478.14 *solved*, 522.2 *simple*, 524.15 *in-terpreted*
decoder 478.10 *answerer*, 524.6 *interpreter*, 529.4 *brain-teaser*
decoding 5.12 *translation*, 5.40 *translated*, 478.6 *solution*, 522.10 *simplicity*, 524.1 *inter-pretation*, 524.4 *translation*
decoke 134.10 *purify*
decollate 879.5 *execute*
decollation 879.13 *capital punish-ment*
décolletage 276.4 *low thing*, 296.4 *dishabille*
décolleté 276.5 *low*, 296.10 *in dishabille*
decolorant 445.4 *colour remover*
decoloration 445.1 *colourlessness*
decolorization 445.1 *colourless-ness*
decolorize 446.13 *whiten*

decolorized 446.2 *whitened*
decolour 445
decoloured 445.7 *colourless*
decommission 600.6 *stop using*, 614.8 *make useless*
decommissioned 600.4 *disused*
decompensation 61.12 *stress*, 61.19 *defence mechanism*
decompile 65.19 *abort*
decomposable 141.5 *disintegrated*
decompose 89.11 *moulder*, 136.9 *separate*, 141.3 *disinte-grate*, 162.11 *explode*, 202.17 *grow old*, 384.28 *come to dust*, 397.15 *die*, 628.2 *decay*, 628.5 *hurt*
decomposed 139.8 *nonadhesive*, 141.5 *disintegrated*, 162.20 *sep-arated*, 419.4 *putrid*, 618.4 *poor*, 624.23 *diseased*, 628.12 *deteriorated*
decomposing 141.6 *disintegrating*
decomposition 136.1 *separation*, 141.1 *disintegration*, 162.5 *di-vergence*, 244.2 *destroying*, 384.4 *pulverization*, 419.2 *some-thing that makes an unpleasant smell*, 618.10 *poverty*, 622.2 *un-cleanness*, 628.9 *dilapidation*
decompound 141.4 *deconstruct*
decompressive 129.7 *decrescent*
deconcentrate 162.15 *decentralize*
deconcentrated 162.26 *decentral-ized*
deconcentration 162.6 *decentral-ization*
decongestant 62.4 *drug type*, 62.14 *counteracting*
deconstruct 141
deconstructed 141.5 *disintegrated*
deconstruction 141, 524.1 *inter-pretation*
deconstructionism 4.7 *school of thought*, 382.9 *artistic structure*
Deconstructionism 43 Architec-tural Styles
deconstructionist 4.11 *follower of a doctrine*
deconstructor 48.15 *literary per-son*
decontaminate 134.10, 621.15 *purify*, 625.6 *make hygienic*
decontaminated 621.17 *cleaned*
decontamination 56.75 *nuclear accident*, 134.2 *purification*, 621.2 *cleaning*, 625.1 *hygiene*
decontrol 231.3 *counteract*, 700.1 *liberation*, 700.4 *liberate*, 727.1 *disposal*, 727.9 *dispose of*
decor 51.17 *stage set*
decorate 43, 792, 130.6 *add*, 220.9 *transform*, 300.6 *edge*, 557.5 *ornament*, 627.1 *improve*, 789.8 *beautify*, 792.12 *honour*, 878.9 *reward*
decorate china 44.11 *make ce-ramics*
decorated 792, 792, 43.17 *struc-tured*, 457.10 *aspectual*, 557.4 *ornate*, 791.14 *beautified*
Decorated 43 Architectural Styles
decorate pottery 44.11 *make ce-ramics*
decorating 792
decoration 50.1 *art*, 130.3 *addi-tional item*, 152.2 *array*, 544.4 *insignia*, 545.11 *monument*, 557.1 *ornament*, 627.5 *improve-ment*, 681.1 *trophy*, 789.2 *beau-tiful thing*, 792.3 *honour*, 878.1 *reward*
Decoration 792
decorations 812.8 *salute*
decorative 50.26 *artistic*, 130.9 *extra*, 457.10 *aspectual*, 557.4 *ornate*, 792.8 *decorated*
decorative articles 792
decorative arts 50.1 *art*
decorative glass 44.1 *ceramics*
decoratively 43.20 *architectur-ally*, 50.31 *artistically*
decorative tile 44.8 *ceramic object*
decorative woodwork 47
decorator 792, 216.6 *editor*, 629.12 *repairer*, 646.2 *artisan*

decorous 150.17 *disciplined*, 306.11, 813.6 *formal*
decorousness 813.1 *formality*
decorticate 296.16 *peel*
decortication 296.6 *peeling*
decorum 48.12 *poetic language*, 306.5 *formality*, 794.1 *elegance*, 813.1 *formality*, 813.5 *etiquette*
découpage 42 Hobbies and Pas-times
decoy **539**, 37.3 *hunting equip-ment*, 340.5, 340.12 *lure*, 539.13, 539.33 *snare*, 586.9 *en-ticement*
Decoy 68 Breeds of Fowl
decoy duck 586.9 *enticement*
decrease **129, 129**, 120.2 *cer-tain amount*, 120.8 *quantify*, 121.6 *change gradually*, 129.5 *make smaller*, 131.1 *subtrac-tion*, 131.3 *subtract*, 238.6 *be weak*, 242.1 *moderation*, 242.4 *moderate*, 262.1 *contraction*, 262.5 *make smaller*, 262.6 *be-come smaller*, 360.2 *sinkage*, 360.9 *descend*, 362.1 *lower*, 362.11 *lowering*, 607.1, 607.3 *waste*, 609.9 *scarcity*, 628.1 *de-teriorate*, 628.7 *deterioration*, 722.1 *loss*, 722.9 *lose*, 752.1 *dis-count*
Decrease **129**
decreased 129.6 *decreasing*, 131.7 *reduced*, 262.7 *smaller*, 362.17 *lowered*
decrease in size 262.1 *contrac-tion*, 262.5 *make smaller*
decreasing **129**, 262.8 *contract-ing*, 360.16 *descending*, 628.12 *deteriorated*
decreasingly **129, 131**, 121.10 *by degrees*, 362.24 *down*
decreasing thing **129**
decree 16.3 *law*, 16.68 *legislate*, 16.76 *judge*, 166.1, 166.13 *rule*, 492.2 *verdict*, 492.11 *judge*, 532.1 *publication*, 570.15 *im-pose one's will*, 582.1 *predeter-mine*, 582.5 *predetermination*, 654.3 *precept*, 692.1, 692.9 *com-mand*, 847.17 *impose a duty*
decree absolute 492.2 *verdict*, 692.1 *command*, 824.1 *divorce*
decreed 16.46 *legislated*, 582.3 *predetermined*
decree nisi 492.2 *verdict*, 692.1 *command*, 824.1 *divorce*
decree of nullity 824.1 *divorce*
decrement 52.31 *differentiation*, 129.1 *decrease*, 131.3 *subtracted item*, 722.1 *loss*, 752.1 *discount*
decrepit 202.11 *old*, 207.14 *aged*, 236.12 *impotent*, 238.10 *ill*, 624.21 *unhealthy*, 628.13 *di-lapidated*
decrepitly 202.18 *venerably*
decrepitude 202.1 *oldness*, 236.1 *powerlessness*, 238.3 *poor health*, 628.9 *dilapidation*
decrescendo 129.1 *decrease*, 129.6 *decreasing*
decrescent **129**
decretal 16.45 *legislative*, 653.18 *parliamentary*, 654.3 *precept*
decrial 670.16 *terrorist attack*, 854.1 *disparagement*
decrier 854.7 *disparager*
decriminalization 16.29 *legaliza-tion*, 231.1 *counteraction*
decriminalize 16.65 *make legal*, 116.29 *permit*, 231.3 *counter-act*, 708.3 *permit*
decriminalized 16.44 *legal*, 116.18 *permitting*, 708.7 *permit-ted*
decry 670.10, 852.17 *criticize*, 854.10 *disparage*
decrying 670.25 *critical*, 854.15 *disparaging*
decumbency 282.1 *horizontality*
decumbent 282.10 *lying*
decuple 179.17 *tenth*
decurrence 360.2 *sinkage*
decurrent 89.10 *of fungi*, 360.16 *descending*
decury 679.16 *army unit*
decussation 135.6 *point of union*

dedans 40.5 *real tennis*
dedans penthouse 40.5 *real tennis*
Dedekind 52 Scientists
dedicate 8.17 *deify,* 710.16 *make an offering,* 729.5 *give*
dedicated 7.15 *religious,* 8.15 *deified,* 237.11 *strong in spirit,* 574.2 *tenacious,* 584.14 *habituated,* 772.2 *earnest,* 819.11 *devoted,* 847.9 *loyal*
dedicated to 694.8 *loyal*
dedicate oneself 574.9 *undertake*
dedicate oneself to 9.7 *worship*
dedicate to 599.1 *use*
dedication 7.2 *religiousness,* 8.9 *deification,* 9.1 *worship,* 237.2 *healthiness,* 574.13 *concentration,* 710.6, 729.3 *offering,* 772.5 *earnestness,* 804.1 *right,* 819.3 *familiarity,* 833.1 *philanthropy,* 847.3 *allegiance*
deduce 4.21 *rationalize,* 52.89 *theorize,* 355.15 *draw out,* 459.12 *think,* 461.16 *have an idea,* 463.11 *reason,* 471.14 *have an idea,* 473.14 *discuss,* 492.12 *estimate,* 518.5 *suppose,* 520.11 *infer,* 524.8 *interpret*
deduced 518.8 *supposed*
deduct 131.3 *subtract,* 136.10 *set apart,* 170.9 *add,* 734.10 *take away,* 752.3 *discount*
deducted 131.5 *subtracted*
deductible 129.7 *decrescent,* 751.15 *chargeable*
deduction 4.4 *philosophical investigation,* 4.8 *philosophical term,* 52.64 *reasoning,* 129.1 *decrease,* 131.1 *subtraction,* 459.2 *ways of thinking,* 461.1 *thought,* 463.2 *reasoning,* 473.2 *logical argument,* 492.1 *judgment,* 518.2 *basis of supposition,* 734.3 *taking away,* 747.2 *stoppage,* 751.7 *tax,* 752.1 *discount*
deductive 52.86 *logical,* 131.6 *subtractive,* 459.9 *mental,* 463.8 *rational,* 734.12 *taking*
deductively 4.24 *philosophically,* 131.8 *by subtraction,* 131.9 *decreasingly,* 473.19 *logically,* 734.13 *avariciously*
deductive reasoning 463.2 *reasoning*
Dee 96 Rivers, 96.4 *British rivers*
deed 640, 3.14 *historicalness,* 545.2 *certificate,* 611.2 *important matter,* 644.2 *task,* 652.9 *tactics,* 655.3 *masterpiece,* 715.1, 715.5 *contract,* 718.2 *promise,* 728.3 *transfer property,* 778.8 *courageous act,* 786.3 *wonder-working*
deeded over 728.5 *transferring*
deeding 728.1 *transfer of property*
deed of arms 674.6 *fight*
deed of trust 715.2 *purchase contract*
deed over 728.3 *transfer property*
deeds 652.8 *treatment*
deeds of blood 676.8 *warfare*
deejay 534.29 *broadcaster*
deem 4.22 *propound a philosophy,* 166.13 *rule,* 492.12 *estimate,* 497.8 *be of the opinion*
de-emphasis 542.9 *down-playing*
de-emphasize 555, 542.22 *play down*
de-emphasized 542.19 *downplayed*
deep 277, 277, 427, 4.19 *learned,* 5.43 *phrasal,* 97.7 *oceanic,* 120.6 *quantitative,* 248.13 *spacious,* 271.1 *broad,* 273.1 *thick,* 277.11 *wise,* 290.7 *interior,* 423.6 *loud,* 440.10 *dark-coloured,* 444.11 *colourful,* 447.2 *dark,* 459.11 *thoughtful,* 507.5 *wise,* 523.1 *unintelligible,* 527.1 *latent,* 551.2 *obscure*
deep blue 454.1 *blue*
deep blue sea 97.1 *sea*
deep colour 440.3 *dark colour*
deep-coloured 440.10 *dark-coloured,* 444.11 *colourful*
deep-cut 277.8 *deep*

deep depression 55.11 *weather system*
deep-dish 277.8 *deep*
deep diver 20.2 *artificial fly*
deep down 277.16 *deep*
deep-down 277.8 *deep*
deepen 277, 128.5 *make bigger,* 248.20 *extend,* 440.13 *become dark,* 447.11 *blacken,* 768.6 *aggravate*
deepened 768.4 *aggravated*
deepening 128.1 *increase,* 277.1 *depth,* 768.1 *aggravation*
deepening depression 55.11 *weather system*
deeper 277
deepest 277.10 *deeper*
deepest feelings 759.8 *seat of feelings*
deepfreeze 45.4 *kitchen container,* 605.4 *storage*
deep-freeze 409.4 *cooler*
deep-freezer 409.4 *cooler*
deep-freezing 637.1 *preservation*
deep-fried 45.56 *culinary*
deep frier 45.6 *kitchen equipment*
deep-frozen 371.7 *condensed*
deep-fry 45.55 *cook*
deep-frying 45.8 *cooking technique*
deep in debt 745.9 *in debt*
deep-laid 277.8 *deep,* 594.20 *developed,* 655.9 *well-made*
deep-litter house 68.7 *farm building*
deeply 4.29 *wisely,* 120.7 *quantitatively,* 248.15 *spaciously,* 277.16 *deep,* 277.17 *profoundly,* 290.16 *inwardly,* 427.11 *resonantly,* 447.12 *blackly*
deeply felt 759.14 *emotive*
deep-lying 277.8 *deep*
deeply involved 642.18 *active*
deepmost 277.10 *deeper*
deepness 427, 120.1 *quantity,* 277.1 *depth,* 523.11 *unintelligibility*
deep note 427.3 *deepness*
deep ocean 54.12 *ocean*
deep-pan 277.8 *deep*
deep-pitched 427.8 *deep*
deep purple 455.6 *purple*
deep-reaching 277.8 *deep*
deep red 450.1 *red*
deep-rooted 103.6 *intrinsic,* 225.10 *stabilized,* 237.10 *potent,* 277.9 *deep-seated,* 584.13 *fixed*
deep-rootedness 277.2 *intensity*
deep sea 97.1 *sea,* 277.4 *deep thing*
deep-sea 20.8 *angling,* 54.51 *oceanic,* 74.11 *nautical,* 97.7 *oceanic,* 277.12 *under*
deep-sea diver 97.6 *oceanographer,* 277.5 *submariner*
deep-sea diving 277.1 *depth*
deep-sea drilling 54.17 *ocean research vessel*
deep-sea fish 20.7 *angle*
deep-sea fisherman 20.6 *angler,* 74.7 *nautical person*
deep-sea fishing 20.1 *angling,* 80.7 *fishing,* 590.2 *chase*
deep-seated 277, 103.6 *intrinsic,* 584.13 *fixed*
deep-seatedness 277.2 *intensity*
deep-sea trolling 20.1 *angling*
deep-set 277.8 *deep*
deep six 397.8 *after death,* 397.17 *bury,* 399.6 *grave,* 399.8 *bury*
deep-sounding 427.8 *deep*
Deep South Torrid Zone 408.8 *hot place*
deep space 53.3 *universe,* 263.1 *distance*
deep square 27.4 *team*
deep structure 5.24 *phrasing,* 5.29 *grammar,* 520.1 *meaning,* 527.6 *latency*
deep thing 277
deep thinking 277, 461.2 *intellectual exercise*
deep thought 462.6 *daydream*
deep-throated 432.7 *ululant*
deep tone 447.7 *blackness*

deep-toned 427.8 *deep*
deep-voiced 427.8 *deep*
deep water 277.4 *deep thing*
deep-water 277.12 *under*
deer 77 Placental Mammals, 37.5 *game,* 329.12 *swift animal*
deer farm 68.6 *farm*
deer fly 82 Insects
deerhound 77 Breeds of Dogs
deer hunt 37.2 *hunting*
deer hunter 37.4 *hunter,* 398.13 *animal killer*
deer hunting 37.2 *hunting,* 398.9 *animal killing*
deerlike 77.33 *ungulate*
deer mouse 77 Placental Mammals
deer season 203.1 *season*
deer-stalk 37.7 *shoot,* 590.11 *hunt*
deerstalker 37.4 *hunter,* 77.24 *hunter,* 295.15 *headgear,* 590.6 *hunter*
deerstalking 18 Sporting Activities, 37.2 *hunting,* 77.23 *mammal hunting,* 590.2 *chase*
de-escalate 129.4 *decrease*
de-escalation 129.1 *decrease,* 362.11 *lowering*
de-escalation of the arms race 677.1 *pacification*
def 617.1 *worthy*
deface 244.11 *ruin,* 309.11 *deform,* 546.1 *obliterate,* 614.8 *make useless,* 628.5 *hurt,* 704.6 *cancel,* 790.5 *make ugly,* 793.7 *blemish*
defaced 309.7 *deformed,* 704.10 *cancelled,* 790.4 *ugly,* 793.4 *blemished*
defacement 309.3 *deformity,* 546.3 *obliteration,* 704.1 *cancellation,* 790.1 *hideousness*
defacer 309, 244.6 *destroyer,* 704.5 *abrogator*
de facto 99.13 *real,* 99.22, 101.13 *really*
de facto possession 723.2 *legal terms*
defalcate 747.7 *not pay*
defalcation 145.2 *omission,* 358.6 *shortcoming,* 747.1 *non-payment*
defalcator 747.6 *nonpayer*
defamation 854, 525.2 *misinterpretation,* 540.6 *lying,* 670.16 *terrorist attack,* 827.3 *vilification,* 850.1 *disrespect,* 856.2 *false accusation*
defamation of character 854.3 *defamation*
defamatorily 827.13 *vituperatively,* 856.10 *accusingly*
defamatory 854, 670.25 *critical,* 827.9 *vituperative,* 850.11 *insulting,* 852.27 *critical,* 856.9 *perjurious*
defamatory remark 854.4 *aspersion*
defame 854, 525.1 *misinterpret,* 670.10 *criticize,* 766.7 *be dissatisfied,* 827.6 *vilify,* 844.20 *wrong,* 850.20 *scorn,* 852.22 *vituperate,* 856.6 *accuse falsely*
defamed 856.9 *perjurious*
defamer 854
default 145.1 *incompleteness,* 145.2 *omission,* 145.5 *be incomplete,* 358.6 *shortcoming,* 609.5 *be insufficient,* 683.1 *failure,* 711.1 *refusal,* 711.5 *refuse,* 720.2 *nonperformance,* 720.8 *not perform,* 745.8 *not pay,* 747.1 *nonpayment,* 747.7 *not pay*
defaulted 720.12 *nonperforming*
defaulted match 29.2 *golfing terms*
defaulter 720.6 *evader,* 722.6 *loser,* 745.6 *debtor,* 747.6 *nonpayer*
defaulting 720.12 *nonperforming,* 745.5 *amount owing,* 745.10 *unable to pay,* 747.13 *nonpaying*

defaulting in arrears 145.4 *incomplete*
defeasibility 476.4 *refutability*
defeasible 476.6 *refutable*
defeasibly 476.12 *refutably*
defeat 683, 701, 126.8 *be superior,* 218.2 *stop,* 218.8 *cause to cease,* 476.8 *refute,* 515.2 *bad outcome,* 581.6 *discarding,* 618.14 *ill-treat,* 682.9 *be victorious,* 687.1 *adversity,* 687.11 *cause adversity,* 696.14 *master,* 701.1 *subjection,* 722.1 *loss,* 785.2 *disliked thing*
defeat comprehensively 244.11 *ruin*
defeat easily 682.10 *defeat heavily*
defeated 683, 127.18 *outclassed,* 515.9 *disappointed,* 776.4 *hopeless,* 806.3 *humbled*
defeated candidate 581.9 *rejected person*
defeated player 683.5 *failing person*
defeater 682.5 *victorious person*
defeat heavily 682
defeatism 495.1 *underestimation,* 536.1 *negation,* 641.1 *inaction,* 776.1 *hopelessness,* 779.1 *cowardice*
defeatist 495.2 *pessimist,* 495.4 *underestimating,* 536.11 *negative,* 641.2 *nonacting person,* 641.3 *inactive,* 673.2 *appeaser,* 685.3 *quitter,* 776.3 *hopeless person,* 776.4 *hopeless,* 779.3 *cowardly*
defeat of the enemy 682.2 *victory*
defeat of the prosecution 16.42 *acquittal*
defeat one's hopes 515.6 *disappoint*
defeat the enemy 682.9 *be victorious*
defecate 353, 349.14 *let out*
defecation 353, 621.2 *cleaning,* 624.8 *indigestion*
defect 620, 123.1 *inequality,* 127.2 *deficiency,* 238.1 *weakness,* 254.18 *abscond,* 358.6 *shortcoming,* 578.3 *apostatize,* 609.8 *insufficiency,* 618.8 *inferiority,* 633.7 *vulnerability,* 693.15 *be disobedient,* 720.2 *nonperformance,* 720.9 *disregard orders,* 793.1, 793.1 *spot,* 864.3 *venial sin*
defected 254.11 *truant*
defecting 720.13 *noncompliant*
defection 254.4 *absenteeism,* 578.7 *apostasy,* 598.3 *relinquishment,* 693.1 *disobedience,* 720.3 *disregard of orders,* 858.2 *faithlessness*
defective 127, 358, 123.3 *unequal,* 145.4 *incomplete,* 618.2 *inferior,* 620.1 *imperfect,* 720.12 *nonperforming,* 793.4 *blemished,* 844.18 *gone wrong,* 864.13 *venial*
defective hearing 421.1 *deafness*
defectively 123.7 *unequally,* 127.21 *badly,* 358.10 *not enough,* 620.11 *imperfectly,* 720.15 *inattentively*
defectiveness 145.1 *incompleteness,* 620.5 *imperfection*
defective sight 436.2 *poor sight*
defect of character 633.7 *vulnerability*
defector 254.6 *absentee,* 578.9 *equivocator,* 598.4 *deserter*
defence 19, 671, 855, 16.7 *legal trial,* 31.8 *hockey,* 35.3 *rugby play,* 231.1 *counteraction,* 341.7 *deflection,* 463.4 *explanation,* 473.5 *plea,* 476.3 *countercharge,* 478.5 *counterstatement,* 484.1 *counterevidence,* 632.2 *protection,* 663.3 *conflict,* 676.8 *warfare,* 676.9 *battle,* 680.1 *weapon,* 680.3 *arms race,* 718.1 *protection*
Defence 671
Defence Council 17.5 *military staff*

defence cuts 677.1 *pacification*
defenceless 236.11 *unprotected,* 238.8 *weak,* 633.3 *vulnerable*
defencelessly 236.14 *powerlessly,* 633.11 *dangerously*
defencelessness 236.3 *helplessness,* 238.1 *weakness,* 633.7 *vulnerability*
defence mechanism 61, 591.14 *evasion*
defence mechanism camouflage 671.4 *defensiveness*
defence player 31.6 *lacrosse player*
defence reaction 61.19 *defence mechanism*
defences 632.2 *protection*
defence zone 31.3 *ice hockey*
defend 671, 679, 284.14 *give moral support,* 293.30 *protect,* 463.14 *premise,* 473.16 *plead,* 478.18 *answer back,* 632.9 *protect,* 637.5 *preserve,* 663.15 *object,* 676.13 *be at war,* 718.10 *secure,* 855.8 *justify*
defend against 231.3 *counteract*
defend an action 16.72 *stand trial*
defendant 16.8 *litigant,* 463.6 *arguer,* 476.5 *refuter,* 477.10 *person questioned,* 478.10 *answerer,* 483.7 *person who gives evidence,* 663.9 *opposer,* 856.4 *accused person*
defended 671, 463.10 *causal,* 632.5 *safe*
defender 671, 679, 18.3 *sportsman ,* 31.4 *ice hockey player,* 35.4 *rugby player,* 38.3 *football player,* 231.2 *counteracting thing,* 284.8 *supporter,* 632.3 *protector,* 669.5 *resister,* 855.5 *vindicator*
defending 671, 676.15 *warring,* 855.11 *vindicatory*
defensible 632.6 *invulnerable,* 855.13 *vindicable*
defensive 341, 17.8 *military,* 19.19 *varsity,* 463.10 *causal,* 473.12 *apologetic,* 478.13 *retaliatory,* 484.5 *countering,* 591.18 *avoiding,* 661.13 *hindering,* 671.29 *defending,* 855.11 *vindicatory*
defensive backfield 19.10 *defence*
defensive backs 19.10 *defence*
defensive battle 676.9 *battle*
defensive circle 671.9 *barrier*
defensive coordinator 19.2 *football player*
defensive end 19.10 *defence*
defensive formation 19.10 *defence*
defensive foul 19.13 *penalty*
defensive huddle 19
defensive line 19.10 *defence,* 671.8 *military defences*
defensive lineman 19.10 *defence*
defensively 341, 671, 17.11 *militarily,* 476.11 *in reply,* 478.24 *in answer,* 484.9 *to the contrary,* 661.16 *with delay,* 855.15 *in vindication*
defensive measure 231.1 *counteraction*
defensive missile 680.5 *missile weapon*
defensive move 671.1 *defence*
defensiveness 671
defensive reaction 591.14 *evasion*
defensive stroke 27.9 *stroke*
defensive tackle 19.10 *defence*
defensive tactic 671.1 *defence*
defensive team 19.10 *defence*
defensive wall 147.3 *exclusion zone*
defensive warfare 676.8 *warfare*
defensive weapon 680.1 *weapon*
defensive weapons 676.1 *war*

defer 209.8 *delay,* 283.12 *interrupt,* 499.5 *assent to,* 641.4 *not act,* 694.5 *obey*
deference 817, 362.16 *courtesy,* 673.1, 673.1 *submission,* 694.1 *obedience,* 806.11 *self-abasement,* 808.1 *servility,* 847.3 *allegiance,* 849.3 *respectfulness*
deferent 806.4 *self-abasing*
deferential 817, 362.21 *degraded,* 694.9 *obedient,* 808.6 *servile,* 847.9 *loyal,* 849.9 *showing respect*
deferentially 817, 694.10 *obediently,* 806.28 *subserviently,* 849.22 *respectfully*
deferment 209.3 *delayed action,* 283.6 *interruption,* 752.1 *discount*
defer payment 744.9 *acquire credit,* 752.5 *buy at a discount*
deferral 209.3 *delayed action*
deferred 209.10 *held up,* 283.9 *interrupted,* 600.1 *unused,* 744.12 *charged*
deferred payment 738.7 *purchasing,* 744.1 *credit,* 746.1 *payment,* 747.2 *stoppage*
defer to 817, 673.3 *submit,* 694.5 *obey,* 808.10 *knuckle under,* 849.18 *show respect*
defiance 668, 111.3 *opposition,* 117.4 *disagreement,* 536.3 *rebuttal,* 663.2 *objection,* 669.1 *resistance,* 693.1 *disobedience,* 713.1 *protest,* 807.5 *bravado,* 807.9 *discourtesy*
Defiance 668
defiance of authority 689.1 *anarchy*
defiance of gravity 361.6 *raising,* 370.5 *lightness*
defiance of orders 693.1 *disobedience*
defiant 668, 111.5 *opposing,* 117.10 *disagreeing,* 168.12 *nonconformist,* 526.15 *open,* 536.11 *negative,* 663.20 *discordant,* 669.10 *resistant,* 670.24 *counterattacking,* 693.13 *disobedient,* 713.9 *protesting,* 807.20 *discourteous*
defiantly 668, 111.7 *disapprovingly,* 117.16 *disagreeably,* 526.17 *frankly,* 535.25 *explicitly,* 536.15 *negatively,* 663.23 *opposingly,* 669.14 *resistingly,* 693.17 *disobediently,* 713.11 *disapprovingly,* 778.18 *courageously*
defiant person 668
deficiency 127, 123.1 *inequality,* 145.1 *incompleteness,* 145.2 *omission,* 182.3 *fewness,* 254.2 *disappearance,* 358.6 *shortcoming,* 609.8 *insufficiency,* 620.5 *imperfection,* 620.7 *defect,* 722.2 *financial loss,* 743.9 *inadequacy,* 864.3 *venial sin*
deficiency disease 624.4 *disease*
deficient 123.3 *unequal,* 127.17 *defective,* 145.4 *incomplete,* 238.13 *insufficient,* 254.12 *missing,* 358.7 *short,* 595.7 *unequipped,* 609.1 *insufficient,* 620.2 *incomplete,* 722.17 *unprofitable,* 743.4 *inadequate,* 864.13 *venial*
deficiently 123.7 *unequally,* 145.6 *incompletely,* 358.10 *not enough,* 722.20 *at a loss*
deficit 132.3 *difference,* 145.2 *omission,* 358.5 *shortfall,* 609.8 *insufficiency,* 722.2 *financial loss,* 745.5 *amount owing*
deficit finance 14.1, 741.7 *finance*
deficit financing 13.2 *economy*
deficit spending 13.2 *economy*
defile 265.3 *gulf,* 272.6 *narrow place,* 322.7 *passageway,* 601.1 *misuse,* 622.11 *dirty,* 628.3 *make worse,* 801.4 *disreputable,* 850.27 *desecrate,* 854 13 *vilify,* 862.11 *be evil,* 877.19 *corrupt*
defiled 601.4 *misused,* 622.7 *dirty,* 862.7 *evil*
defilement 601.2 *misuse,* 622.1

dirtiness, 628.10 *impairment,* 854.5 *scorn,* 862.1 *evil,* 877.2 *indecency*
defiling 877.12 *indecent*
define 560, 4.21 *rationalize,* 5.47 *word,* 165.24 *specify,* 302.7 *limit,* 485.16, 490.22 *specify,* 524.8 *interpret,* 537.31 *be accurate,* 550.2 *clarify,* 561.4 *dissertate*
defined 437.2 *clear,* 485.12 *conditional,* 522.3 *recognizable,* 524.15 *interpreted,* 526.14 *manifest,* 537.21 *accurate*
definer 524.6 *interpreter*
defining 103.9 *characteristic,* 163.11 *typical,* 524.14 *interpretive*
definite 535, 5.44 *grammatical,* 302.5 *limited,* 490.1 *certain,* 490.7 *particular,* 522.1 *intelligible,* 522.3 *recognizable,* 526.14 *manifest,* 528.16 *informative,* 550.3 *clear,* 554.3 *emphatic*
definite article 5.35 *part of speech*
definite integral 52.31 *differentiation*
definitely 490.23, 490.26 *certainly,* 535.23 *affirmatively,* 772.12 *indeed*
definiteness 535, 490.9 *certainty,* 490.18 *particularity,* 522.9 *intelligibility,* 522.11 *recognizability,* 550.1 *clarity*
definition 302.1 *limitation,* 437.4 *clarity,* 485.6 *specification,* 520.4 *type of meaning,* 522.11 *recognizability,* 524.1 *interpretation,* 534.23 *television reception,* 537.8 *accuracy,* 550.1 *clarity*
definitional 485.12 *conditional,* 524.14 *interpretive*
definitive 157.20 *ending,* 163.11 *typical,* 524.14 *interpretive,* 537.21 *accurate,* 688.12 *authoritative*
definitively 157.28 *conclusively,* 163.16 *taxonomically*
deflagrating spoon 57 Laboratory Apparatus
deflatability 262.2 *contractibility*
deflatable 262.9 *contractible*
deflate 806, 236.8 *overpower,* 238.7 *weaken,* 262.5 *make smaller,* 262.6 *become smaller,* 362.1 *lower,* 362.4 *debase,* 476.8 *refute,* 542.21 *detract from,* 799.6 *deride*
deflated 542, 238.9 *dilapidated,* 262.7 *smaller,* 362.17 *lowered,* 806.3, 806.3 *humbled*
deflate one's ego 612.13 *make unimportant*
deflation 542, 13.2 *economy,* 13.6 *economics,* 14.1 *finance,* 129.2 *decline,* 129.3 *decreasing thing,* 238.3 *poor health,* 262.1 *contraction,* 362.11 *lowering,* 741.7 *finance,* 754.2 *declining prices,* 806.9 *humiliation*
deflationary 13.13 *economic,* 14.6 *financial,* 129.7 *decrescent,* 262.8 *contracting,* 741.22 *monetary*
deflationist 129.7 *decrescent*
deflect 335, 587, 26.13 *do martial arts,* 252.14 *displace,* 286.6 *be oblique,* 341.3 *fend off,* 591.6 *evade,* 671.24 *parry*
deflected 252.8 *displaced,* 286.4 *oblique,* 335.21 *indirect*
deflection 341, 26.9 *tae kwon do,* 56.15 *wave property,* 162.5 *divergence,* 252.1 *displacement,* 286.1 *obliqueness,* 335.13 *deviation,* 587.7 *deterrence,* 591.14 *evasion*
deflective 286.4 *oblique,* 335.21 *indirect*
defloration 877.3 *sexual immorality*
deflower 734.7 *take,* 877.20 *seduce*
deflowerment 734.1 *taking*

defluxion 347.2 *outflow,* 360.3 *downflow*
Defoe 48 Writers
defoliant 244.7 *agent of destruction,* 631.10 *warfare*
defoliate 244.10 *lay waste*
defoliation 85.10 *tree disease,* 244.2 *destroying,* 247.1 *infertility*
deforest 244.10 *lay waste,* 247.10 *waste,* 355.12 *displace*
De Forest 52 Scientists
deforestation 85.5 *forestry,* 247.1 *infertility,* 355.2 *displacement*
deform 309, 63.31 *load,* 220.9 *transform,* 307.3 *make shapeless,* 309.12 *distort the truth,* 548.4 *misrepresent,* 628.6 *pervert,* 790.5 *make ugly,* 793.7 *blemish*
deformation 63, 54.20 *earth movement,* 548.1 *misrepresentation,* 628.8 *perversion*
deformational 54.54 *tectonic*
deformed 309, 620, 548.6 *misrepresented,* 790.4 *ugly,* 793.4 *blemished*
deformity 309, 620.5 *imperfection,* 790.1 *hideousness*
defraud 538.25 *be dishonest,* 539.30 *be fraudulent,* 601.1 *misuse,* 657.5 *be cunning,* 736.16 *act dishonest,* 747.7 *not pay,* 750.7 *account,* 858.10 *be criminal*
defrauder 538.12, 539.17 *cheat,* 736.11 *dishonest person,* 747.6 *nonpayer*
defrauding 538.19 *dishonest,* 747.1 *nonpayment*
defray 738, 746, 748.3 *donate*
defrayal 746.1 *payment*
defraying 746.1 *payment*
defrayment 746.1 *payment*
defray the cost 746.8 *defray*
defrock 147.8 *eject,* 349.3 *disbar*
defrocking 349.18 *dismissal*
defrost 387.24 *melt,* 408.14 *be hot*
defrosted 408.13 *heated*
deft 655.6 *skilful,* 861.5 *proficient*
deft fingers 655.1 *skill*
deftly 655.12 *skilfully*
deftness 567.3, 655.1 *skill,* 861.12 *proficiency*
defunct 3.18 *in the past,* 100.11 *no more,* 397.19 *dead,* 585.2 *not customary*
defuse 643.14 *make inactive*
defy 668, 111.9 *oppose,* 117.14 *disagree,* 536.8 *rebut,* 574.8 *brace oneself,* 633.9 *face danger,* 642.14 *push,* 663.15 *object,* 663.17 *withstand,* 669.6 *resist,* 670.8 *counterattack,* 693.15 *be disobedient,* 713.6 *protest,* 720.9 *disregard orders,* 778.15 *be courageous*
defy authority 689.4 *be anarchic*
defy comprehension 523.7 *be unintelligible*
defy gravity 370.9 *be light*
defying 668, 668.1 *defiance*
defying comprehension 523.4 *difficult*
defying gravity 359.1 *ascent*
defy orders 693.15 *be disobedient*
defy the law 16.73 *be illegal*
degage 698.13 *informal*
degass 57.29 *absorb*
degassed 57.43 *absorbed*
degassing 57.20 *surface chemistry*
degauss 231.3 *counteract*
degausser 231.2 *counteracting thing*
degeneracy 628.8 *perversion,* 864.2 *vice,* 877.3 *sexual immorality*
degenerate 129.4 *decrease,* 151.25 *be disordered,* 216.7 *be changed,* 220.8 *be transformed,* 628.1 *deteriorate,* 628.12 *deteriorated,* 687.9 *be in trouble,* 768.7 *become aggravated,* 864.9 *wicked person,* 864.12 *immoral,*

877.8 *immoral man*, 877.16 *do wrong*
degenerated 216.12 *changed*, 220.13 *converted*
degenerately 864.20 *immorally*
degenerateness 628.8 *perversion*
degenerating 220.14 *converting*
degeneration 129.1 *decrease*, 216.1 *change*, 220.2 *evolution*, 628.8 *perversion*, 864.2 *vice*
degenerative 618.5 *harmful*, 624.23 *diseased*, 628.12 *deteriorated*
degenerative disease 624.4 *disease*
degenerative joint disease 624.16 *rheumatism*
deglaciation 54.40 *glaciation*
deglutition 350.1 *eating*
degradation 349.18 *dismissal*, 362.15 *debasement*, 628.8 *perversion*, 801.1 *disrespect*, 806.10 *abasement*, 850.8 *indignity*, 854.5 *scorn*, 864.2 *vice*
degrade 57.27 *synthesize*, 129.5 *make smaller*, 136.9 *separate*, 349.3 *disbar*, 362.4 *debase*, 612.13 *make unimportant*, 628.6 *pervert*, 806.23 *abase*, 850.27 *desecrate*, 854.13 *vilify*, 879.1 *punish*
degraded 362, 806.3 *humbled*, 864.12 *immoral*
degrade oneself 801.4 *disreputable*
degrading 801.4 *disreputable*, 850.16 *humiliating*, 879.7 *punishment*
degradingly 362.25 *courteously*
degree 75 *General Units*, 121, 52.27 *equation*, 107.3 *relative position*, 150.4 *position*, 268.4 *size*, 319.3 *rung*, 485.3 *qualifications*, 611.1 *importance*
Degree 121
degree-day 75 *Scientific and Technical Units*
degree of difference 121.3 *gradation*
degrees 332.3 *orientation*
degust 411.9 *taste*
degustation 411.3 *appetizer*
dehisce 83.21 *vegetate*, 86.10 *fruit*
dehiscent 86.9 *of a fruit*, 265.7 *cracked*
dehiscent fruit 86.2 *botanical fruit*
dehorn 68.18 *practise livestock farming*
dehors 49 *Musical Terms*
dehumanization 628.8 *perversion*
dehumanize 628.6 *pervert*, 864.17 *make wicked*
dehumanized 832.11 *cruel*
dehumidification 392.13 *drying*
dehumidifier 392.15 *dryer*
dehumidify 392.17 *dry*
dehydrant 392.15 *dryer*
dehydrate 220.7 *convert into*, 392.17 *dry*, 637.5 *preserve*
dehydrated 392.3 *dried-up*, 637.7 *preserved*, 782.10 *hungry*
dehydrated food 350.7 *food*, 637.3 *preserved thing*
dehydrating 392.9 *drying*
dehydration 220.1 *conversion*, 392.12 *thirst*, 392.13 *drying*, 637.1 *preservation*
dehydrator 392.15 *dryer*
dehydrogenase 58.11 *enzyme*
de-ice 408.14 *be hot*
de-icer 73 *Aircraft Parts*, 408.3 *heater*
deictic 4.16 *dialectical*
deification 8, 361.7 *lift*, 851.3 *praise*
deified 8, 361.12 *exalted*
deified person 8
deify 8, 9.8 *idolatrize*, 361.3 *promote*, 849.10 *revere*, 851.14 *praise*
deifying 849.10 *reverent*
deign 806.18 *condescend*
deigning 806.15 *condescension*
deil 8.7 *devil*

deism 4.7 *school of thought*, 7.2 *religiousness*
deist 4.11 *follower of a doctrine*, 497.5 *believer*
deistic 4.14 *of a philosophy*, 8.13 *divine*
deity 8, 8.1 *divinity*, 9.3 *idol*, 99.7 *self-existence*, 226.7 *Prime Mover*
déjà vu 3.13*looking back*, 11.10 *psychic phenomenon*
deject 440.14 *make dark*, 830.10 *make sullen*
dejecta 353.4 *excrement*
dejected 440.11 *benighted*, 454.3 *depressed*, 515.9 *disappointed*, 770.6 *depressed*, 776.4 *hopeless*, 806.3 *humbled*, 830.6 *sullen*
dejectedly 776.11 *hopelessly*, 830.13 *sullenly*
dejectedness 770.2 *depression*
dejection 61.13 *depression*, 353.2 *defecation*, 353.4 *excrement*, 440.7 *spiritual darkness*, 687.1 *adversity*, 770.2 *depression*, 776.1 *hopelessness*, 830.1 *sullenness*
dejecture 353.4 *excrement*
de jure 16.44 *legal*, 16.81 *legally*
de jure possession 723.2 *legal terms*
deke 31.3 *ice hockey*, 31.9 *play hockey*
deked 31.8 *hockey*
deking 31.8 *hockey*
Dekker 48 *Dramatists*
dekko 435.6 *look*
del 52.50 *scalar quantity*
de la Mare 48 *Poets*
delaminate 266.11 *scale*
delamination 266.6 *layering*
de la Rôche 48 *Writers*
delate 528.13 *inform on*
delator 528.10 *informer*
Delaware 5 *Languages and Groups of Languages*, **86** *Fruits*, **92** *American States*
delay 209, 573, 209.1 *lateness*, 209.3 *delayed action*, 209.7 *wait*, 218.3 *pause*, 283.6 *interruption*, 283.12 *interrupt*, 328.2 *hesitate*, 328.3 *slow down*, 328.12 *hesitation*, 470.2 *indifference*, 470.6 *be neglectful*, 573.8 *hold back*, 576.7 *be irresolute*, 591.7 *be evasive*, 639.2 *deliverance*, 641.1 *inaction*, 641.4 *not act*, 643.7 *idleness*, 643.12 *be inactive*, 652.9 *tactics*, 661.2 *obstacle*, 661.9 *block*, 671.25 *stall*, 685.1 *noncompletion*, 685.5 *not complete*
delayed 328, 209.9 *late*, 283.9 *interrupted*
delayed action 209
delayed dribble 31.3 *ice hockey*
delayed dribbling 31.3 *ice hockey*
delayed reaction 209.3 *delayed action*
delayer 209, 209.4 *latecomer*
delaying 209, 470.5 *indifferent*, 573.4 *procrastinating*, 641.3 *inactive*, 685.4 *uncompleted*
delaying action 591.15 *evasiveness*
delaying tactics 209.3 *delayed action*
delay of game 19.13 *penalty*
dele 546.1 *obliterate*, 546.3 *obliteration*
delectability 763.9 *tastiness*
delectable 405.6 *pleasant*, 411.7, 763.4 *tasty*
delectation 762.1 *happiness*
d-electron 56.65 *atom*
delegable 706.6 *delegated*
delegate 706, 706, 141.4 *deconstruct*, 547.8 *representative*, 564.10 *speaker*, 580.4 *pick*, 646.3 *agent*, 653.16 *official*, 678.4 *representative*, 688.21 *grant authority*, 703.5 *commissioner*, 703.6 *commission*, 703.7 *agent*, 707.6 *deputize*, 728.3 *transfer property*, 729.5 *give*
Delegate 706

delegate authority 688.21 *grant authority*, 703.8 *authorize*
delegated 706, 688.13 *elected*, 703.9 *commissioned*
delegated authority 688.1, 703.3 *authority*
delegating 703.9 *commissioned*
delegation 706, 141.2 *deconstruction*, 688.3 *acquisition of power*, 703.1 *commission*, 703.4 *council*, 706.2 *representative body*, 728.1 *transfer of property*
delegation of power 706.3 *delegation*
delegation of work 706.3 *delegation*
delete 65.19 *abort*, 131.3 *subtract*, 147.8 *eject*, 244.8 *destroy*, 438.8 *make invisible*, 546.1 *obliterate*, 704.6 *cancel*, 709.4 *censor*, 734.10 *take away*
deleted 131.5 *subtracted*, 147.11 *excluded*, 254.12 *missing*, 546.6 *obliterated*, 704.10 *cancelled*, 709.6 *censored*
deleterious 618.5 *harmful*, 862.9 *detrimental*
deleteriously 862.13 *destructively*
deletion 131.1 *subtraction*, 147.2 *ejection*, 244.1 *destruction*, 546.3 *obliteration*, 704.1 *cancellation*, 709.2 *censorship*, 734.3 *taking away*
Delft 44 *Types of Ceramics*
Delhi belly 353.2 *defecation*
deli 350.17 *food shop*
Delia 10.16 *religious festival*
deliberate 268, 582, 4.20 *philosophize*, 38.5 *soccer*, 328.5 *unhurried*, 461.15 *think about*, 471.15 *imagine*, 473.14 *discuss*, 520.9 *meant*, 570.6 *willed*, 574.1 *resolute*, 588.12 *intended*, 645.7 *leisurely*, 654.6 *consult*, 716.4 *negotiator*
deliberate kicking 38.2 *football play*
deliberately 328.16 *slowly*, 471.21 *purposively*, 473.19 *logically*, 574.17 *resolutely*, 588.13 *intentionally*
deliberateness 328.8 *slowness*, 588.2 *intentionality*
deliberate over 568.11 *confer*
deliberate tripping 38.2 *football play*
deliberation 461, 4.4 *philosophical investigation*, 328.8 *slowness*, 473.2 *logical argument*, 654.2 *consultation*, 781.1 *caution*
deliberative 4.17 *thoughtful*, 461.10 *speculative*, 653.18 *parliamentary*, 654.7 *advising*
deliberative assembly 653.10 *legislative body*
deliberative body 653.10 *legislative body*
deliberatively 4.28 *thoughtfully*
Delibes 49 *Musicians and Composers*
delicacies 350.7 *food*, 414.2 *sweetener*
delicacy 134.1 *purity*, 238.1 *weakness*, 274.11 *fineness*, 370.5 *lightness*, 372.3 *sparseness*, 374.12 *gentleness*, 379.2 *brittleness*, 383.2 *grain*, 403.2 *ability to sense*, 411.3 *appetizer*, 481.2 *judiciousness*, 537.8 *accuracy*, 542.3 *subtlety*, 558.1 *elegance*, 624.1 *ill health*, 655.1 *skill*, 760.5 *sensitivity*, 763.10 *pleasant thing*, 789.1 *gorgeousness*, 794.1 *elegance*, 794.2 *subtlety*
delicate 383, 238.8 *weak*, 272.2, 274.4 *fine*, 370.2 *insubstantial*, 372.1 *sparse*, 374.6 *softhearted*, 379.1 *brittle*, 403.7 *susceptible*, 407.10 *handed*, 444.13 *soft-hued*, 481.9 *discriminating*, 537.21 *accurate*, 542.13 *subtle*, 558.3 *elegant*, 624.21 *unhealthy*, 633.2 *un-*

safe, 659.12 *problematic*, 760.1 *sensitive*, 794.5 *refined*
delicate eating 350
delicate flavour 411.4 *flavour*
delicate health 624.1 *ill health*
delicately 370.11 *lightly*, 372.7 *sparsely*, 374.18 *softheartedly*, 379.5 *fragilely*, 383.15 *texturally*, 481.16 *judiciously*, 558.5 *elegantly*, 659.27 *problematically*, 760.12 *sensitively*
delicate move 34.3 *climbing technique*
delicateness 238.1 *weakness*, 537.8 *accuracy*
delicate situation 659.7 *awkward situation*
delicatessen 350.17 *food shop*
delicious 350.27 *edible*, 405.6 *pleasant*, 411.7 *tasty*, 617.1 *worthy*, 763.4 *tasty*
deliciously 350.29 *edibly*, 411.11 *tastily*
deliciousness 411.1 *taste*, 763.9 *tastiness*
delict 866.3 *sin*
delight 405.1 *physical pleasure*, 405.9 *give pleasure*, 762.1 *happiness*, 762.8 *cause joy*, 763.11 *pleasant person*, 763.13 *give pleasure*, 773.1 *rejoicing*
delighted 405.7 *pleased*, 762.4 *happy*
delightful 762, 405.6, 763.1 *pleasant*
delightfulness 763.6 *pleasantness*
delight in 405.8 *feel pleasure*, 762.6 *enjoy*, 763.14 *like*, 765.7 *be satisfied*, 784.7 *like*, 821.23 *love*
delimit 485.16 *specify*, 544.10 *identify*, 731.4 *allot*
delimitation 485.6 *specification*, 731.1 *allocation*
delimited 485.12 *conditional*
delineate 48.21 *write*, 103.11 *characterize*, 165.24 *specify*, 299.5 *outline*, 475.16 *explain*, 543.9 *use signs*, 547.9 *represent*, 560.14 *describe*
delineated 50.27 *painted*, 475.11 *explanatory*
delineating 50.3 *drawing*
delineation 50.3, 50.9 *drawing*, 299.1 *outline*, 475.3 *explanation*, 547.1 *representation*, 560.1 *description*, 767.6 *profile*
delineative 299.6 *outlined*
delineator 50.16 *artist*
delineatory 547.13 *representational*
delinquency 16.38 *lawbreaking*, 693.1 *disobedience*, 720.4 *infraction*, 844.6 *unlawfulness*, 864.1 *wickedness*, 864.7 *criminality*, 866.1 *guilt*
delinquent 16.40 *lawbreaker*, 635.2 *troublemaker*, 693.13 *disobedient*, 720.14 *violating*, 844.10 *wrongdoer*, 844.16 *in the wrong*, 864.11 *wicked*, 864.15 *criminal*, 866.4 *guilty person*
delinquently 598.8 *apathetically*, 693.17 *disobediently*, 864.21 *criminally*
deliquation 387.8 *fluidification*
deliquesce 89.11 *moulder*, 141.4 *deconstruct*, 387.24 *melt*
deliquescence 129.1 *decrease*, 141.2 *deconstruction*, 162.3 *dilution*, 387.8 *fluidification*
deliquescent 89.10 *of fungi*, 129.7 *decrescent*, 141.6 *disintegrating*, 387.19 *liquefied*
delirious 510.12 *manic*, 521.10 *meaningless*, 624.23 *diseased*, 762.4 *happy*
delirium 510.4 *delusion*, 519.6 *reverie*, 521.1 *lack of meaning*, 624.3 *symptom*, 762.1 *happiness*
delirium tremens 366.7 *shake*, 510.4 *delusion*, 874.16 *alcoholism*
delish 617.1 *worthy*
delitescence 527.6 *latency*
delitescent 527.1 *latent*

Delius 49 Musicians and Composers
deliver 639, 70.4, 326.12 *transport*, 534.31 *correspond*, 606.5 *provision*, 629.3 *restore*, 632.9 *protect*, 637.5 *preserve*, 662.17 *help*, 671.23 *rescue*, 698.15 *set free*, 700.4, 700.4 *liberate*, 728.3 *transfer property*, 729.5 *give*, 735.4 *give back*, 767.10 *save*, 839.10 *absolve*
deliverable 639
deliver an address 567.7 *address*
deliverance 639, 16.42 *acquittal*, 629.9 *restoration*, 632.1 *safety*, 637.1 *preservation*, 638.1 *escape*, 662.2 *support*, 698.1 *freedom*, 700.1 *liberation*, 735.1 *giving back*, 767.2 *aid*, 839.3 *absolution*
Deliverance 639
deliver a sermon 852.20 *censure*
deliver a speech 564.14 *speak to*
delivered 639.4 *deliverable*, 839.6 *forgiven*
deliverer 639, 637.4 *preservationist*, 671.15 *protector*, 700.3 *liberator*
deliver oneself 638.5 *escape*
deliver the goods 606.5 *provision*, 615.6 *be convenient*, 684.4 *complete*
delivery 27, 25.2 *grip*, 40.4 *tennis terms*, 156.4 *conception*, 245.7 *obstetrics*, 326.2 *transportation*, 396.4 *biological function*, 564.4 *articulation*, 601.1 *provision*, 639.2 *deliverance*, 652.1 *conduct*, 700.1 *liberation*, 728.1 *transfer of property*, 729.1 *giving*
delivery date 714.1 *promise*
delivery truck 71 Motor Vehicles
delivery van 326.5 *means of transport*
dell 98.8 *valley*, 265.3 *gulf*, 317.2 *concave land*
dell pony 32.5 *pony*
delocalization 326.1 *transfer*
delocalized 57.35 *combined*
delousing 134.2 *purification*, 621.2 *cleaning*
Delphic oracle 517.8 *oracle*
delphinium 84 Flowers and Flowering Plants
Delphinus 53 The Constellations
delta 54.27 *sediment*, 96.2 *channel*, 98.9 *inlet*, 327.11 *channel*, 343.5 *fork*
Delta 534 Phonetic Alphabet, 53.35 *rocketry*
deltaic 98.11 *continental*
delta-like 343.8 *fanlike*
delta-shaped 343.8 *fanlike*
deltoid 177.8 *three-sided*, 261.8 *growing*, 343.8 *fanlike*
delude 102, 515.8 *be dishonest*, 538.24 *pretend*, 539.27, 540.16 *be false*, 540.18 *be hypocritical*
deluded 493.7 *misjudging*, 504.17 *mistaken*, 510.12 *manic*, 515.10 *deceived*, 811.17 *lofty*
delude oneself 539.25 *deceive oneself*
deluder 539.15 *deceiver*
deluge 55.15 *rain*, 96.6 *river flow*, 161.22 *flood*, 389.29 *water*, 610.1 *excess*, 610.4 *be excessive*
deluged 96.11, 389.24 *flooded*
delusion 102, 510, 504.6 *fallibility*, 519.5 *fantasy*, 538.9 *hypocrisy*, 539.2 *self-deception*, 540.1 *falsehood*, 540.3 *hypocrisy*
delusions of grandeur 510.4 *delusion*, 811.2 *airs*
delusive 539.40 *illusory*, 540.25 *false*, 540.27 *hypocritical*
delusively 538.27 *pretentiously*
delusiveness 539.2 *self-deception*
delusory 102.9, 539.40 *illusory*
de luxe 405.6 *pleasant*, 742.3 *opulent*, 811.24 *grand*
delve 68.17 *farm*, 69.15 *cultivate*
delve into 317.7 *make concave*

delve into the supernatural 104.16 *be external*
demagnetize 231.3 *counteract*
demagnetization 231.1 *counteraction*
demagogic 474.8 *cunning*, 567.13 *oratorical*
demagogical 567.13 *oratorical*
demagogically 474.15 *hypocritically*
demagogue 228.7 *motivator*, 474.6 *sophist*, 564.10 *speaker*, 567.6 *public speaker*, 586.14 *motivator*, 653.14 *leader*, 693.8 *agitator*
demagoguery 12.1 *government*, 474.3 *cunning*, 688.7 *type of rule*
demagogy 12.1 *government*, 688.7 *type of rule*
demand 513, 692, 692, 712, 712, 355.6 *extorsion*, 355.16 *extort*, 570.15 *impose one's will*, 571.14 *necessitate*, 593.2 *need*, 593.10 *necessitate*, 599.6 *use*, 695.6 *compel*, 738.11 *custom*, 751.3 *fee*, 751.12 *charge*, 782.1, 782.12 *desire*, 832.18 *torment*, 845.3 *prerogative*, 845.14 *be entitled*
demand an answer 712.6 *request*
demand assurances 632.8 *be safe*
demand backed by threats 712.2 *demand*
demanded 593.4 *required*, 712.10 *demanding*
demand for payment 712.2 *demand*
demanding 593, 712, 191.6 *allowing no delay*, 619.2 *perfectionist*, 650.4 *fatiguing*, 659.10 *difficult*, 659.12 *problematic*, 659.14 *troublesome*, 782.9 *desirous*, 879.21 *punishing*
demanding pity 835.7 *pitiful*
demand one's rights 845.14 *be entitled*
demand payment 712.7 *demand*
demands 513.2 *expectations*
demand tax payment 692.10 *demand*
demand too much 609.7 *make insufficient*, 650.6 *fatigue*
demand with threats 712.7 *demand*
demarcate 103.11 *characterize*, 302.7 *limit*, 481.12 *discriminate*, 485.16 *specify*, 543.9 *use signs*, 699.8 *restrain*, 731.4 *allot*
demarcated 481.11 *judged*, 485.12 *conditional*
demarcation 302.1 *limitation*, 481.1 *discrimination*, 485.6 *specification*, 699.1 *restraint*, 731.1 *allocation*
dematerialization 254.2 *disappearance*, 368.2 *unworldliness*, 458.4 *disappearance*
dematerialize 11.20 *occult*, 254.18 *abscond*, 368.12 *enter a nonmaterial world*, 458.1 *disappear*
dematerialized 254.9 *away*, 368.8 *nonmaterial*
dematerializing 368.8 *nonmaterial*
demean 806.23 *abase*
demeaning 362.18 *lowering*
demean oneself 652.13 *behave badly*, 801.4 *disreputable*, 806.18 *condescend*, 806.21 *humble oneself*, 808.10 *knuckle under*
demeanour 306.6 *nature*, 457.3 *external appearance*, 543.3 *gesture*, 652.1 *conduct*
dement 510.15 *make insane*
demented 153.16 *deranged*, 460.5 *lacking intellect*, 510.11 *insane*, 510.12 *manic*
dementedly 510.17 *insanely*
dementia 236.4 *disability*, 460.1 *lack of intellect*, 510.3 *mental deterioration*
dementia praecox 61.11, 510.5 *psychosis*
demerara 449.5 *brown thing*
Demerara 96 Rivers

demerara rum 351.7 *alcoholic drink*
demerara sugar 45.7 *basic ingredient*, 414.2 *sweetener*
demerge 141.4 *deconstruct*
demerger 141.2 *deconstruction*
demerging 141.2 *deconstruction*
demerit 846.5 *undueness*, 864.3 *venial sin*
demesne 68.6 *farm*, 725.2 *legal terms*
Demeter 8 Deities, 246.4 *fertility cult*
demibastion 671.11 *fortification*
demi-column 43.8 *column*
demi-glace 45.15 *sauce*
demigod 8.5 *deity*
demijohn 258.14 *bottle*
demilitarization 236.1 *powerlessness*
demilitarize 236.7 *remove power from*, 677.5 *make peace*
demilune 671.11 *fortification*
demimonde 864.9 *wicked person*
Demiourgos 8.3 *God*
Demi-Sang 32 Breeds of Horse and Pony
demise 157.3, 397.1 *death*
demised 397.19 *dead*
demisemiquaver 49.17 *notation*
demist 442.12 *make transparent*
demiurge 8.3 *God*
demo 161.4 *rally*, 475.6 *mass demonstration*
demob 17.10 *enlist*, 162.2 *disbandment*, 162.13 *dismiss*, 675.1 *peace*, 677.1 *pacification*, 700.4 *liberate*
demobbed 162.21 *disbanded*
demobilization 162.2 *disbandment*, 675.1 *peace*, 677.1 *pacification*, 700.1 *liberation*
demobilize 17.10 *enlist*, 136.9 *separate*, 162.13 *dismiss*, 643.14 *make inactive*, 677.5 *make peace*, 700.4 *liberate*
demobilized 162.21 *disbanded*
democracy 12.1 *government*, 91.1 *country*, 122.1 *equality*, 400.11 *nation*, 580.11 *franchise*, 665.3 *political grouping*, 688.7 *type of rule*, 724.1 *joint possession*
democracy unlimited 12.1 *government*
democrat 12.6 *political party*
Democrat 665.6 *political party member*
democratic 12.9 *governmental*, 91.16 *national*, 122.6 *equal*, 249.17, 400.13 *national*, 688.14 *governmental*
Democratic 665.10 *political*
democratically 12.14 *politically*, 91.19 *nationally*, 122.13 *equitably*, 249.20 *nationally*, 688.24 *ministerially*
democratic behaviour 652.1 *conduct*
Democratic Left 665.3 *political grouping*
Democratic Party 12.6 *political party*, 665.3 *political grouping*
democratic republic 249.4 *territorial division*
Democratic Social Centre 12.6 *political party*
democratic state 400.11 *nation*
democratic system 580.11 *franchise*
Democratic whip 688.10 *person of authority*, 696.3 *leader*
democratize 91.17 *become a nation*, 665.15 *politicize*
Democritean 4.11 *follower of a doctrine*, 4.14 *of a philosophy*
Democritus 4 Philosophers
demodulate 534.30 *communicate*
demodulated 534.34 *communicated*
demodulation 534.14 *radio transmission*
demodulator 534.14 *radio transmission*
demographer 1.3 *anthropologist*, 2.11 *sociologist*, 400.6 *studier of mankind*

demographic 1.11 *anthropological*, 2.14 *socioeconomic*
demographically 1.16 *anthropologically*, 2.16 *sociologically*
demographic research 2.2 *sociological research*
demographic survey 2.2 *sociological research*
demographic transition 13.4 *economic development*
demography 1.1 *anthropology*, 2.1 *sociology*, 2.2 *sociological research*, 400.5 *study of mankind*
demoiselle crane 78 Birds
de Moivre's formula 52 Named Concepts
demolish 244, 141.4 *deconstruct*, 362.2 *flatten*, 476.8 *refute*, 546.1 *obliterate*, 607.2 *lay waste*, 676.13 *be at war*
demolished 141.5 *disintegrated*, 362.17 *lowered*, 546.6 *obliterated*
demolisher 244.6 *destroyer*
demolishment 244.2 *destroying*
demolition 141.2 *deconstruction*, 244.2 *destroying*, 362.11 *lowering*, 476.1 *refutation*, 546.3 *obliteration*, 628.10 *impairment*
demon 8.7 *devil*, 11.11 *ghost*, 241.4 *violent person or animal*, 618.12 *bad person*, 864.9 *wicked person*
demonetize 741, 747.12 *devalue the currency*
demonetized 741.22 *monetary*
demonetized coinage 741.15 *false money*
demon for work 642.10 *busy person*
demoniac 8.16 *devilish*, 832.11 *cruel*
demoniacal 832.11 *cruel*
demonic 8.16 *devilish*, 9.10 *idolatrous*, 11.15, 11.15 *witchlike*, 642.18 *active*, 862.7 *evil*
demonically 8.20 *devilishly*, 11.26 *magically*
demonism 9.2 *idolatry*
demonize 8.18 *devilize*, 11.21 *bewitch*
demonkind 8.7 *devil*
demon-like 8.16 *devilish*
demonophobia 777 Phobias by Name
demons 777 Phobias by Topic
demonstrability 475
demonstrable 475, 490.1 *certain*
demonstrable existence 99
demonstrableness 475.5 *demonstrability*
demonstrably 475, 99.22 *really*
demonstrate 475, 4.21 *rationalize*, 4.22 *propound a philosophy*, 52.89 *theorize*, 101.12 *establish reality*, 435.18, 437.10 *make visible*, 473.15 *state*, 475.19 *protest*, 480.2 *prove*, 490.21 *make certain*, 524.8 *interpret*, 526.1 *display*, 537.30 *prove true*, 550.2 *clarify*, 642.14 *push*, 655.11 *be expert*, 668.6 *be insubordinate*, 811.27 *show*, 855.8 *justify*
demonstrate against 711.6 *dissent*, 713.8 *cause mischief*
demonstrated 475, 475.11 *explanatory*, 475.13 *proven*, 490.1 *certain*, 537.20 *proved*
demonstrate ill 785.5 *dislike*
demonstrate self-control 699.10 *restrain oneself*, 859.6 *be disinterested*
demonstrate style 549.9 *style*
demonstrating 475
demonstration 475, 16.7 *legal trial*, 52.66 *proof*, 161.4 *rally*, 437.5 *manifestation*, 475.3 *explanation*, 475.4, 480.5 *proof*, 483.2 *proof*, 490.13 *confirmation*, 524.1 *interpretation*, 526.6 *display*, 537.7 *confirmation*, 668.3 *act of defiance*, 711.2 *dissent*, 713.3 *gesture of protest*, 811.14 *show*
Demonstration 475
demonstrative 475, 480.9 *verifi-*

catory, 483.8 *evidential,* 524.14
interpretive, 543.14 *signifying,*
811.16 *showy,* 819.8 *friendly,*
821.17 *loving,* 826.9 *endearing*
demonstratively 475, 480.11
verifiably, 483.14 *as evidence,*
543.18 *indicatively,* 811.32
showily, 826.10 *endearingly*
demonstrativeness 475, 811.1
showiness, 821.3 *lovingness*
demonstrator 475, 475.8 *protester,* 526.12 *displayer,* 668.4
defiant person, 693.7, 713.4 *protester*
demophobia 777 Phobias by
Name
demoralization 628.11 *hurt,*
777.4 *intimidation*
demoralize 628.5 *hurt,* 864.17
make wicked, 877.19 *corrupt*
demoralized 236.12 *impotent,*
777.7 *frightened*
De Morgan 52 Scientists
demos 400.11 *nation*
demote 15.11 *conduct industrial
relations,* 252.17 *relegate,* 349.3
disbar, 362.4 *debase,* 612.13
make unimportant, 704.7 *terminate,* 879.1 *punish*
demoted 252.11 *relegated,*
360.17 *drooping,* 362.21 *degraded*
demotion 252.4 *relegation,*
349.18 *dismissal,* 360.1 *descent,* 360.4 *fall,* 362.15 *debasement,* 879.7 *punishment*
Dempsey 18 Sporting Personalities
demulce 374.14 *ease,* 630.19
remedy
demulcent 62.4 *drug type,* 62.7
ointment, 62.16 *soothing,* 242.2
moderator, 242.8 *moderating,*
386.5, 395.6 *ointment,* 630.5
analgesic, 630.17 *remedial*
demur 117.14 *disagree,* 476.10
countercharge, 484.7 *counter,*
498.1 *disbelief,* 500.2 *disapproval,* 500.9 *refuse,* 536.3 *rebuttal,* 536.8 *rebut,* 573.8 *hold
back,* 573.11 *unwillingness,*
591.4 *shy,* 663.2 *objection,*
663.15 *object,* 711.7 *refuse oneself*
demure 810.10 *bashful*
demurely 810.17 *modestly*
demureness 810.3 *bashfulness*
demuring 810.10 *bashful*
demurity 810.3 *bashfulness*
demurral 476.3 *countercharge,*
536.3 *rebuttal,* 663.2 *objection*
demurrer 16.5 *litigation,* 476.3
countercharge, 484.1 *counterevidence*
demurring 573.1 *unwilling,*
711.9 *dissenting*
demystify 524.9 *decipher*
demythologization 524.1 *interpretation*
demythologizer 524.6 *interpreter*
demythologizing 524.14 *interpretive*
den 77.20 *abode of mammals,*
256.7 *room,* 256.13 *lair,* 293.15
shelter, 317.2 *concave land,*
531.6 *privacy,* 634.3 *animal
shelter,* 647.1 *workshop,* 727.8
sink, 816.5 *solitary place*
denarius 741.12 *ancient coins*
denary 52.71 *numerical,* 179.17
tenth
denationalization 13.1 *economics*
denationalize 628.6 *pervert*
denaturalization 220.2 *evolution,*
846.2 *disentitlement*
denaturalize 220.8 *be transformed,* 220.12 *naturalize,*
628.6 *pervert,* 846.16 *disentitle*
denaturalized 220.17 *naturalized,* 846.12 *disentitled*
denature 628.3 *make worse,*
628.6 *pervert*
denaturization 58.9 *protein*
dendriform 85.14 *treelike,*
162.24 *divergent,* 343.9
branched

dendritic 85.14 *treelike,* 162.24
divergent, 343.9 *branched*
dendrochronology 54.42 *dating,*
85.3 *timber,* 185.8 *dating,*
192.3 *chronology*
dendroid 69.16 *horticultural,*
85.14 *treelike,* 90.7 *algal*
dendrolater 9.6 *idolater*
dendrolatrous 9.10 *idolatrous*
dendrolatry 9.2 *idolatry*
dendrologic 85.17 *arboricultural*
dendrologically 83.25 *botanically,* 85.20 *arboriculturally*
dendrologist 83.12 *plant scientist,* 85.8 *forester*
dendrologous 85.17 *arboricultural*
dendrology 59.1 *life science,*
83.10 *plant science,* 85.5 *forestry*
Deneb 53 Named Stars
Denebola 53 Named Stars
dengue 624.7 *tropical disease*
deniably 536.15 *negatively*
denial 476, 52.63 *mathematical
logic,* 61.19 *defence mechanism,*
100.3 *negativeness,* 147.1 *exclusion,* 484.1 *counterevidence,*
484.2 *reversal,* 491.10 *suspicion,* 498.3 *incredulity,* 500.2
disapproval, 536.2 *rejection,*
536.3 *rebuttal,* 578.8 *recantation,* 581.7 *abrogation,* 591.15
evasiveness, 663.2 *objection,*
669.4 *desisting,* 709.1 *veto,*
711.1 *refusal,* 713.1 *protest,*
722.1 *loss*
denied 484.6 *countered,* 487.4
forbidden, 515.9 *disappointed,*
536.12 *rejected,* 709.5 *vetoed,*
711.9 *dissenting,* 713.9 *protesting*
denier 75 General Units, 67.1
fibre, 383.2 *grain,* 476.5 *refuter,*
484.3 *counterclaimant*
denigrate 612.13 *make unimportant,* 670.10 *criticize,* 711.5 *refuse,* 850.20 *scorn,* 852.17 *criticize,* 854.10 *disparage*
denigrated 850.18 *undervalued*
denigrating 670.25 *critical*
denigration 670.16 *terrorist attack,* 711.1 *refusal,* 854.1 *disparagement*
denigratory 854.15 *disparaging*
denim 67 Natural Fabrics,
288.4 *textile*
denims 295.4 *informal dress,*
295.9 *trousers*
denizen 255.1 *inhabitant*
Denmark 91 Countries
den of iniquity 864.8 *wicked place*
den of vice 864.8 *wicked place*
denominate 165.24 *specify*
denomination 7.1 *religion,* 163.8
genealogy, 544.1 *identification,*
560.7 *nomenclature,* 665.1 *party*
denominational 7, 665.8 *leagued*
denominationally 665.18 *cliquishly*
denominational school 6.12 *educational institution*
denominator 52.18 *division,*
169.5 *ratio*
denotation 520.1 *meaning,* 520.4
type of meaning, 537.10 *literalness*
denotative 520.6 *meaningful,*
537.23 *literal,* 543.14 *signifying*
denote 473.15 *state,* 520.10
mean, 543.10 *signify,* 547.12
stand for
denoted 544.12 *identified*
denouement 48.3 *aspect of fiction, ,*51.6 *scene,* 157.10 *ending,*
195.9 *sequel,* 227.1 *effect,*
478.6 *solution,* 530.1 *disclosure,*
684.2 *conclusion*
denounce 10.18 *perform rites,*
528.13 *inform on ,* 670.10 *criticize,* 799.6 *deride,* 822.14 *hate,*
852.19 *blame,* 856.5 *accuse*
denounced 856.8 *accusatory*
denouncement 852.7 *blame,*
856.1 *accusation*
denouncer 856.3 *accuser*
denouncing 827.9 *vituperative*
dense 273, 371, 83.13 *plant-*

like, 138.9 *adhesive,* 161.50
crowded, 273.3 *thick-witted,*
369.1 *heavy,* 381.3 *dull,* 441.8
stupid, 443.1 *opaque,* 443.5,
460.6 *unintelligent*
dense cloud 55.19 *cloud cover*
dense fog 55.33 *fog,* 441.2 *murk*
densely 371, 138.11 *cohesively,*
273.9 *thick,* 369.16 *heavily,*
443.13 *opaquely*
densely arrayed 371.6 *dense*
denseness 273, 371.1 *density,*
441.4 *stupidity,* 460.2 *unintelligence*
densify 371.8 *be dense*
densimeter 268.8 *meter,* 371.3
relative density
densimetric 268.16 *micrometric*
densimetry 268.2 *micrometry*
densitometer 268.8 *meter*
densitometric 268.16 *micrometric*
density 371, 56.9 *mass,* 273.5
thickness, 273.6 *denseness,*
367.1 *material world,* 373.5
hardness, 443.6 *opaqueness*
Density 371
density current 54.13 *ocean current*
dent 317.3 *cavity,* 317.7 *make
concave,* 319.1, 319.5 *notch,*
330.3 *hit,* 330.13 *blow,* 362.2
flatten, 362.14 *depression,*
380.7 *sharp point*
dental 60
dental auxiliary 60.17 *paramedic*
dental corps 17.4 *military organization*
dental floss 621.10 *cleaning object*
dental hygienist 60.17 *paramedic*
dental powder 621.9 *cleaning
agent*
dental record 544.3 *means of
identification*
dental surgeon 60.14 *dentist,*
630.15 *healer*
dental surgery 60.4 *dentistry,*
60.9, 630.12 *surgery*
dental surgery assistant 60.17
paramedic
dental technician 60.17 *paramedic*
dental therapist 60.17 *paramedic*
dentate 83.18 *of leaves,* 319.4
notched
dentately 319.7 *jaggedly*
dented 317.5 *concave*
denticle 380.11 *tooth*
denticulate 380.4 *toothed*
denticulately 319.7 *jaggedly*
denticulation 380.6 *sharpness*
dentiform 380.4 *toothed*
dentifrice 134.3 *purifier,* 621.9
cleaning agent, 630.3 *prophylactic*
dentil 43 Architectural Decoration
dentist 60, 630.15 *healer*
dentistry 60
dentist's chair 284.4 *rest*
dentition 380.6 *sharpness*
denudate 296.15 *make nude*
denudation 54.35 *weathering,*
294.1 *uncovering,* 296.1 *undress,* 722.5 *destruction*
denude 131.4 *take off,* 136.10
set apart, 238.7 *weaken,* 244.10
lay waste, 296.15 *make nude,*
530.5 *disclose,* 722.13 *destroy*
denuded 296.11 *exposed*
denuder 294.4 *exposer,* 296.7
depilation
denuding 296.1 *undress*
denumerable 52.73 *numerable*
denunciate 827.6 *vilify,* 852.19
blame, 856.5 *accuse*
denunciated 856.8 *accusatory*
denunciation 10.5 *Christian rite,*
670.16 *terrorist attack,* 799.2
act of derision, 827.3 *vilification,* 852.7 *blame,* 856.1 *accusation*
denunciatory 670.25 *critical,*
827.9 *vituperative,* 852.29 *blaming,* 856.8 *accusatory*
de-nut 236.9 *make impotent*
de-nutted 236.13 *unsexed*

Denver 93 Cities, 93.2 *American
cities*
Denver boot 661.4 *restraint*
Denver Stock Show 32.12 *rodeo*
deny 476, 4.23 *discuss philosophically,* 147.7 *exclude,* 484.7
counter, 487.8 *make impossible,*
498.8 *disbelieve,* 500.9 *refuse,*
515.7 *thwart,* 536.7 *be negative,*
536.8 *rebut,* 578.4 *recant,*
581.4 *revoke,* 591.7 *be evasive,*
663.15 *object,* 709.3 *veto,* 711.5
refuse, 713.6 *protest*
deny entry 147.7 *exclude*
denying 484.5 *countering,*
536.13 *rebutting,* 669.13 *desisting,* 711.9 *dissenting,* 713.9 *protesting*
denying oneself 669.4 *desisting,*
711.3 *abnegation*
deny oneself 591.3 *abstain,*
598.1 *relinquish,* 669.9 *desist,*
699.10 *restrain oneself,* 711.7 *refuse oneself,* 869.5 *be self-
restrained*
deny oneself nothing 870.10 *indulge oneself*
deny the possibility 536.8 *rebut*
deobstruent 62.4 *drug type*
deoch-an-doruis 345.9 *parting*
deodand 879.7 *punishment*
deodar 85 Trees and Shrubs
deodorant 417, 62.4 *drug type,*
134.3 *purifier,* 417.4 *deodorizing,* 621.9 *cleaning agent*
deodorization 134.2 *purification,*
417.1 *odourlessness,* 540.12 *facade,* 621.2 *cleaning*
deodorize 417, 134.10 *purify,*
390.20 *aerate,* 540.24 *mask,*
621.15 *purify*
deodorized 134.14 *purified,*
417.3 *odourless*
deodorizer 417.2 *deodorant*
deodorizing 417
deontic logic 4.6 *branch of
philosophy*
deontology 4.6 *branch of philosophy*
deoxycorticosterone 58 Hormones
deoxynucleotide 58.10 *nucleoside*
depaganize 7.20 *preach*
depart 345, 458, 136.13 *diverge,* 254.16 *absent oneself,*
347.9 *exit,* 397.15 *die,* 591.8
run away, 598.2 *withdraw,*
638.5 *escape,* 705.5 *resign*
departed 345, 254.9 *away,*
397.19 *dead*
departed this life 397.19 *dead*
departer 347.8 *outgoer*
depart from 115.5 *be dissimilar,*
335.1 *deviate*
departing 345, 347.15 *outgoing,*
458.6 *disappearing*
department 6.3 *subject,* 92.3
other, 143.1 *part,* 148.2 *piece,*
152.6 *category,* 163.2 *class,*
653.3 *management*
departmental 92.6 *administrative,* 143.11 *partial,* 148.6 *component*
departmentalized 143.11 *partial*
departmentally 92.8 *administratively,* 148.14 *constituently*
Department of Defense 17.4 *military organization*
department store 63.20 *building,*
740.8 *store*
department store account 744.1
credit
depart this life 345.2 *withdraw,*
397.15 *die*
departure 345, 157.3 *death,*
165.6 *exception,* 254.2 *disappearance,* 324.4 *backward motion,* 335.13 *deviation,* 347.1
exit, 359.4 *taking off,* 397.1
death, 458.4 *disappearance,*
553.2 *circumlocution,* 591.16 *desertion,* 598.3 *relinquishment,*
638.1 *escape,* 705.1 *resignation*
Departure 345
departure platform 345.10 *place
of departure*
dependability 217.1 *permanence,*

490.17 *infallibility*, 719.1 *observance*, 857.1 *probity*
dependable 217.7 *permanent*, 225.9 *stable*, 490.6 *infallible*, 574.5 *steady*, 632.5 *safe*, 719.7 *observant*, 857.4 *honourable*
dependably 225.12 *stably*, 719.8 *observantly*, 857.7 *honourably*
dependant 127.6 *inferior*, 180.9, 195.8 *follower*
dependence 127.1 *inferiority*, 497.3 *believing*, 701.1 *subjection*, 743.6 *insolvency*
dependency 12.5 *political organization*, 249.4 *territorial division*, 688.8 *governmental organization*, 701.1 *subjection*, 723.4 *possession*, 724.1 *joint possession*, 725.1 *property*
dependent **701**, 52.77 *given*, 127.15 *subordinate*, 138.5 *follower*, 138.10 *tenacious*, 227.10 *caused*, 236.11 *unprotected*, 249.17 *national*, 701.9 *subject*, 730.5 *recipient*, 808.5 *adherent*, 808.6 *servile*
dependently 127.22 *basely*, 227.12 *with the effect of*, 236.14 *powerlessly*, 701.11 *under subjection*, 875.11 *in a trance*
dependent on 227.10 *caused*
dependent on circumstances 106.7 *circumstantial*
dependent relative 195.8 *follower*
dependents 661.6 *burden*
dependent variable 52.29 *mathematical function*
depending on 227.10 *caused*
depend on 227.7 *follow from*, 490.20 *be certain*, 497.7 *believe*, 701.8 *be subject to*
depeople 349.9 *depopulate*
depersonalization 61.16 *dissociation*, 512.1 *oblivion*
depersonalized 512.8 *oblivious*
depict 50.20 *draw*, 103.11 *characterize*, 165.24 *specify*, 299.5 *outline*, 475.11 *explain*, 547.9 *represent*, 760.14 *describe*
depicted 475.11 *explanatory*
depict falsely 525.1 *misinterpret*
depict in glowing terms 541.10 *boast*
depiction 299.1 *outline*, 475.3 *explanation*, 547.1 *representation*, 560.1 *description*
depiction in glowing terms 541.4 *bombast*
depictive 48.18 *descriptive*, 299.6 *outlined*, 547.13 *representational*
depictively 299.7 *essentially*
depilate 294.13 *remove*
depilation **296**, 294.5 *shedding*, 791.9 *shave*
depilatory 62.4 *drug type*, 294.5 *shedding*, 296.7 *depilation*, 296.13 *hairless*
deplane 344.4 *land*
deplete 238.7 *weaken*, 349.11 *void*, 607.1 *waste*, 609.7 *make insufficient*, 648.5 *hurt*, 722.12 *lessen*, 748.2 *consume*
depleted 238.9 *dilapidated*, 722.16 *losing*, 748.13 *used*
depleted supply 605.3 *supply*
depletion 238.3 *poor health*, 349.21 *removal*, 607.3 *waste*, 628.11 *hurt*, 722.4 *lessening*
deplorable 618.4 *poor*, 774.5 *lamentable*, 862.7 *evil*
deplorably 862.12 *evilly*
deplore 766.7 *be dissatisfied*, 774.6 *lament*, 852.17 *criticize*
deploy 162.16 *distribute*, 251.10 *situate*, 343.11 *move apart*, 599.5 *dispose of*
deployed 162.22 *distributed*
deployment 162.1 *dispersion*, 343.2 *parting*, 599.6 *use*
deplume 296.15 *make nude*, 349.3 *disbar*
depluming 349.18 *dismissal*
depopulate **349**, 162.15 *decentralize*, 244.10 *lay waste*, 254.19 *leave empty*

depopulated 254.14 *unoccupied*
deport 147.8 *eject*, 252.16 *replace*, 326.14 *bring back*, 347.13 *emigrate*, 349.4 *ostracize*, 816.13 *ignore*, 846.16 *disentitle*, 879.1 *punish*
deportation 147.2 *ejection*, 252.3 *replacement*, 326.1 *transfer*, 347.4 *emigration*, 349.19 *ostracism*, 816.3 *separation*, 864.2 *disentitlement*, 879.7 *punishment*
deported 252.10 *replaced*, 816.10 *lonely*, 846.12 *disentitled*
deported person 816.7 *outsider*
deportee 252.7 *displaced person*, 349.27 *expellee*, 816.7 *outsider*
deportment 457.3 *external appearance*, 652.1 *conduct*
deport oneself 652.11 *conduct oneself*
deposal 846.2 *disentitlement*
depose 252.16 *replace*, 349.3 *disbar*, 535.20 *admit*, 581.2 *discard*, 689.4 *be anarchic*, 704.7 *terminate*, 846.16 *disentitle*
deposed 236.10 *powerless*, 252.10 *replaced*, 846.12 *disentitled*
deposed champion 683.5 *failing person*
deposit **744**, **744**, 14.4 *personal finance*, 54.27 *sediment*, 57.24 *ore*, 132.2 *residue*, 132.8 *leave*, 143.2 *particular*, 161.26 *mass*, 371.4 *solid body*, 371.8 *be dense*, 605.1, 605.6 *store*, 622.4 *dirt*, 741.26 *bank*, 746.1 *payment*
deposit account 741.6 *funds*, 744.3 *deposit*, 750.1 *accounts*
depositary 741.18 *treasurer*
deposited 132.9 *remaining*, 750.11 *accounted*
deposition 54.35 *weathering*, 252.3 *replacement*, 483.5 *legal evidence*, 535.3 *vow*, 535.5 *admission*, 545.2 *certificate*, 714.1 *promise*
depositional 535.12 *vowed*
depositor 744
depository 258.1 *container*, 605.4 *storage*, 741.20 *money store*
deposits 605.2 *resource*
depot 72.8 *railway station*, 291.4 *centre of activity*, 344.15 *destination*, 605.4 *storage*, 740.7 *emporium*
depot ship 679.24 *warship*
depravation 628.8 *perversion*
deprave 618.13 *be worthless*, 628.6 *pervert*, 877.19 *corrupt*
depraved 618.3 *bad*, 628.12 *deteriorated*, 858.5 *dishonourable*, 862.7 *evil*, 864.12 *immoral*, 877.14 *lecherous*
depraving 877.12 *indecent*
depravity 618.9 *badness*, 628.8 *perversion*, 858.1 *improbity*, 862.1 *evil*, 864.2 *vice*, 877.2 *indecency*, 877.3 *sexual immorality*
deprecate 536.8 *rebut*, 542.22 *play down*, 663.15 *object*, 669.6 *resist*, 713.6 *protest*, 766.7 *be dissatisfied*, 852.17 *criticize*, 854.10 *disparage*
deprecated 536.12 *rejected*
deprecate oneself 806.21 *humble oneself*, 810.14 *be modest*
deprecating 495.4 *underestimating*, 536.13 *rebutting*, 669.10 *resistant*, 810.12 *self-deprecating*
deprecatingly 669.14 *resistingly*
deprecation 495.1 *underestimation*, 536.3 *rebuttal*, 542.9 *down-playing*, 654.1 *advice*, 669.1 *resistance*, 713.1 *protest*, 766.1 *dissatisfaction*, 854.1 *disparagement*
deprecative 536.11 *negative*, 669.10 *resistant*
deprecatively 536.15 *negatively*
deprecatorily 713.11 *disapprovingly*
deprecatory 713.9 *protesting*,

852.27 *critical*, 854.15 *disparaging*
depreciable 129.7 *decrescent*
depreciate 129.4 *decrease*, 542.21 *detract from*, 628.1 *deteriorate*, 722.12 *lessen*, 741.25 *demonetize*, 752.3 *discount*, 754.12 *be cheap*, 850.20 *scorn*, 852.17 *criticize*, 854.10 *disparage*
depreciated 14.6 *financial*, 542.18 *deflated*, 741.22 *monetary*, 754.9 *cheap*
depreciated currency 741.15 *false money*
depreciate the currency 747.12 *devalue the currency*
depreciation **747**, 14.1 *finance*, 129.1 *decrease*, 495.1 *underestimation*, 542.10 *deflation*, 599.6 *use*, 628.7 *deterioration*, 722.4 *lessening*, 741.7 *finance*, 754.2 *declining prices*, 854.1 *disparagement*
depreciative 129.7 *decrescent*
depreciator 854.7 *disparager*
depreciatory 129.7 *decrescent*, 495.4 *underestimating*, 854.15 *disparaging*
depredate 736.14 *plunder*
depredation 244.5 *havoc*, 736.5 *plundering*
depredator 736.9 *plunderer*
depress **770**, 129.5 *make smaller*, 276.9 *lower*, 317.7 *make concave*, 362.1 *lower*, 440.14 *make dark*, 517.11 *predict*, 587.5 *discourage*, 830.10 *make sullen*
depressant 62.4 *drug type*, 62.15 *sedative*
depressed **454**, **770**, 247.3 *birth control*, 276.7 *lowered*, 317.5 *concave*, 360.17 *drooping*, 362.17 *lowered*, 362.21 *degraded*, 440.11 *benighted*, 447.6 *sad*, 510.13 *mentally ill*, 515.9 *disappointed*, 774.4 *lamenting*, 776.4 *hopeless*, 830.6 *sullen*, 862.8 *afflicted*
depressed arch 43.5 *arch*
depressing 362.18 *lowering*, 447.6 *sad*, 770.7 *distressing*, 774.5 *lamentable*
depressingly 788.8 *boringly*, 830.13 *sullenly*, 862.13 *destructively*
depressing person 770
depression 61, 362, 770, 13.2 *economy*, 55.11 *weather system*, 61.10 *neurosis*, 127.5 *inferior state*, 129.2 *decline*, 247.1 *infertility*, 276.2 *lowland*, 317.1 *concavity*, 360.2 *sinkage*, 362.11 *lowering*, 440.7 *spiritual darkness*, 510.6 *mental breakdown*, 624.3 *symptom*, 628.7 *deterioration*, 643.6 *unemployment*, 687.2 *economic adversity*, 739.5 *sales*, 743.6 *insolvency*, 754.2 *declining prices*, 776.1 *hopelessness*, 862.2 *affliction*
depressive 129.7 *decrescent*, 362.21 *degraded*, 510.7 *insane person*, 510.13 *mentally ill*, 770.4 *depressing person*
depressively 61.39 *psychologically*
depressive reaction 61.13 *depression*
depress the market 754.13 *make cheap*
deprivation 136.2 *setting apart*, 349.20 *eviction*, 609.9 *scarcity*, 722.1 *loss*, 734.2 *taking back*, 743.5 *poverty*, 846.2 *disentitlement*, 879.7 *punishment*
deprive 238.7 *weaken*, 349.8 *evict*, 609.7 *make insufficient*, 722.9 *lose*, 734.8 *take back*, 743.14 *impoverish*, 846.16 *disentitle*, 879.1 *punish*
deprived 593.5 *necessitous*, 722.16 *losing*, 743.1 *poor*, 846.12 *disentitled*
deprived of 593.5 *necessitous*
deprived of strength 238.8 *weak*

deprived of vision 436.8 *blind*
deprive of authority 236.7 *remove power from*
deprive of life 398.16 *kill*
deprive of power 236.7 *remove power from*
deprive of sight 436.15 *blind*
deprive of sleep 650.6 *fatigue*
deprive oneself of 711.7 *refuse oneself*
depriver 349.26 *ejector*
depriving 722.16 *losing*
depth **777** Phobias by Topic, **277**, 52.37 *line*, 120.1 *quantity*, 121.1 *degree*, 237.3 *intensity*, 248.1 *space*, 259.1, 268.4 *size*, 273.5 *thickness*, 290.1 *interior*, 447.7 *blackness*, 490.6 *thoughtfulness*, 527.6 *latency*, 551.1 *obscurity*
Depth **277**
depth charge 679.26 *naval mine*, 680.16 *bomb*
depth indicator 543.5 *indicator*
depth of field 56.32 *optical instrument*, 66.8 *composition*
depth of focus 56.32 *optical instrument*, 66.18 *exposure time*
depth of space 248.1 *space*
depth psychology 61.1 *psychology*
depths 290.2 *inside*
depths of space 263.1 *distance*
depths of winter 409.7 *cold weather*
depth sounder 277.4 *deep thing*
depth sounding 56.22 *sounding*, 277.6 *bathymetry*, 277.13 *bathymetric*
depurate 134.10, 621.15 *purify*
deputation 688.3 *acquisition of power*, 703.1 *commission*, 703.4 *council*, 706.3 *delegation*
deputative 707.7 *deputizing*
depute 222.2 *substitute person*, 703.6 *commission*, 706.1, 706.4 *delegate*, 707.6 *deputize*
deputed 706.7 *decentralized*
deputing 222.1 *substitution*, 706.3 *delegation*
deputize **707**, 222.4 *be a substitute*, 478.23 *answer for*, 688.21 *grant authority*, 703.6 *commission*, 706.4 *delegate*
deputized 222.8 *substituted*, 688.13 *elected*, 703.9 *commissioned*, 706.7 *decentralized*
deputize for 767.11 *assist*
deputizing **707**, 222.1 *substitution*, 706.3 *delegation*
deputy **707**, 127.6 *inferior*, 222.2 *substitute person*, 222.7 *substitute*, 547.8 *representative*, 646.3 *agent*, 653.16 *official*, 662.11 *helper*, 703.5 *commissioner*, 706.1 *delegate*, 706.6 *delegated*, 707.7 *deputizing*, 767.5 *helper*
Deputy 707
deputy chairman 707.1 *deputy*
deputy chief of staff 17.5 *military staff*
deputy prime minister 707.1 *deputy*
deputy sheriff 707.1 *deputy*
dequalinium 62 *Medication*
De Quincey 48 *Writers*
deracinate 244.8 *destroy*, 349.10 *exterminate*, 355.11 *extract*
deracinated 355.19 *dislodged*
deracination 244.2 *destroying*, 355.1 *extraction*
derail 153.9 *disperse*, 252.14 *displace*
derailed 153.14 *dispersed*, 252.8 *displaced*
derailleur 71.11 *bicycle part*
derailment 153.3 *dispersion*, 252.1 *displacement*
derange **153**, 141.4 *deconstruct*, 151.21 *disorder*, 153.8 *disarrange*, 510.15 *make insane*, 628.4 *impair*
deranged **153**, 151.12 *disordered*, 151.17 *discomposed*, 153.13 *disarranged*, 252.8 *displaced*, 510.11 *insane*

derangement 153, 141.1 *disintegration,* 151.1 *disorder,* 153.2 *disarrangement,* 252.1 *displacement,* 628.10 *impairment*
deration 727.9 *dispose of*
derby 295.15 *headgear*
Derby 45 Cheeses, **93** Cities
Derby day 674.2 *contest*
Derbyshire 92 Counties
Derbyshire Gritstone 68 Breeds of Sheep
deregulate 231.1 *counteract,* 700.4 *liberate,* 727.9 *dispose of*
deregulated 700.7 *liberated*
deregulation 231.1 *counteraction,* 700.1 *liberation*
dereism 61.19 *defence mechanism*
derelict 598.5 *relinquished,* 600.4 *disused,* 628.13 *dilapidated,* 727.15 *unclaimed*
derelict house 256.8 *shelter*
dereliction 470.1 *negligence,* 573.14 *disobedience,* 598.3 *relinquishment,* 600.10 *disuse,* 683.1 *failure*
dereliction of duty 720.2 *nonperformance,* 848.3 *self-exemption,* 866.3 *sin*
derestrict 231.3 *counteract,* 727.9 *dispose of*
derestriction 231.1 *counteraction,* 629.9 *restoration*
deri 256.8 *shelter*
deride 799, 429.5 *catcall,* 581.3 *exclude,* 766.7 *be dissatisfied,* 807.29, 850.24 *ridicule,* 852.23 *show disapproval,* 854.14 *ridicule*
derided 852.35 *hissed*
derider 799
de rigueur 166.9 *legal,* 584.12 *established,* 817.8 *good-mannered*
derision 429.2 *catcall,* 668.2 *disobedience,* 766.1 *dissatisfaction,* 807.8 *rudeness,* 818.1 *discourtesy,* 850.4 *ridicule,* 852.9 *show of disapproval,* 854.5 *scorn*
Derision 799
derisive 799, 429.7 *catcalling,* 668.7 *defiant,* 766.4 *dissatisfied,* 807.19 *rude,* 850.14 *ridiculing,* 854.17 *scornful*
derisively 668.9 *defiantly,* 807.35, 818.10 *rudely,* 850.29 *mockingly,* 854.18 *disparagingly*
derisiveness 799.1 *mockery*
derisory 766.4 *dissatisfied,* 798.5 *ridiculous,* 850.14 *ridiculing*
derisory amount 182.1 *few*
derivation 52.64 *reasoning,* 226.1 *cause,* 227.1 *effect,* 355.5 *drawing out,* 520.4 *type of meaning*
derivation of words 5.1 *linguistics*
derivative 5.38 *linguistic,* 52.31 *differentiation,* 118.12 *imitative,* 227.1 *effect,* 227.10 *caused*
derivatively 118.14 *imitatively,* 227.12 *with the effect of*
derive 52.89 *theorize,* 226.9 *be the cause of,* 355.15 *draw out*
derived 227.10 *caused*
derived authority 688.1 *authority*
derived unit 75.2 *unit system*
derive from 227.7 *follow from*
deriving from 227.10 *caused*
Dermaptera 82 Orders of Insects
dermapteran 82.10 *insectan*
dermatitis 624.13 *skin disease*
dermatological 60.22 *medical*
dermatological disease 624.4 *disease*
dermatologist 60.13 *medical specialist*
dermatology 60.3 *medical specialty*
dermatopathophobia 777 Phobias by Name
dermatophyte 89.5 *fungal association*
dermatophytosis 89.5 *fungal association*
dermatoplasty 60 Surgical Operations
dermatosiophobia 777 Phobias by Name

Dermoptera 77.7 *flying mammal*
dermopteran 77.7 *flying mammal,* 77.27 *chiropteran*
derogate 852.18 *find fault,* 854.10 *disparage*
derogation 854.1 *disparagement*
derogator 854.7 *disparager*
derogatorily 854.18 *disparagingly*
derogatory 854.15 *disparaging*
derrick 63.29 *construction equipment,* 275.6 *tall thing,* 361.9 *lifter*
Derrida 4 Philosophers
derriere 304.2 *rear end*
derring-do 778.1 *courage,* 778.8 *courageous act*
derris 69.8 *weedkiller*
derv 410.6 *oil*
dervish 7.7 *monk*
Derwent 96 Rivers
Derwent Water 94 Lakes, 94.4 *British lakes*
desalinate 134.10, 621.15 *purify*
desalination 621.2 *cleaning*
desalinize 621.15 *purify*
desalt 621.15 *purify*
descale 60.21 *practise dentistry*
descant 49.13 *melody,* 49.39 *sing,* 433.1 *melody,* 561.1 *dissertation,* 561.4 *dissertate*
Descartes 4 Philosophers
descend 360, 34.9 *mountaineer,* 127.11 *become inferior,* 277.14 *deepen,* 324.13 *be in motion,* 337.4 *slip back,* 369.12 *be heavy,* 728.4 *be transferred*
descendant 132.6 *person remaining,* 155.12, 195.5 *successor,* 360.16 *descending*   .
descendants 199.2 *future generation*
descended 227.10 *caused*
descend en rappel 34.9 *mountaineer*
descendent 362.18 *lowering*
descender 360, 34.4 *climbing equipment*
descend from 227.7 *follow from*
descend in a diving bell 97.9 *sail the high seas*
descending 360, 34.3 *climbing technique,* 324.17 *directional,* 360.1 *descent,* 362.18 *lowering,* 628.12 *deteriorated*
descending en rappel 34.3 *climbing technique*
descending from 227.10 *caused*
descending motion 324
descending order 159.2 *consecution,* 312.7 *straight line*
descend into the arena 674.11 *contend*
descend on 360.12 *drop*
descend to particulars 165.23 *particularize*
descension 360.1 *descent*
descent 161 Collective Names for Birds and Animals, **195, 360,** 1.5 *anthropological concept,* 34.3 *climbing technique,* 73.5 *flight,* 159.3 *line,* 163.8 *genealogy,* 324.6 *descending motion,* 362.11 *lowering,* 628.7 *deterioration,* 806.9 *humiliation*
Descent 360
describe 560, 3.20 *chronicle,* 48.21 *write,* 165.24 *specify,* 475.16 *explain,* 524.8 *interpret,* 528.12 *communicate,* 547.11 *paint*
describe a circle 560, 334.3 *circuit*
describe briefly 299.5 *outline*
described 3.19 *chronicled,* 475.11 *explanatory*
describe in a circle 363.6 *orbit*
description 560, 3.7 *narrative,* 48.3 *aspect of fiction,* 475.3 *explanation,* 524.1 *interpretation,* 547.1 *representation,* 560.7 *nomenclature*
Description 560
descriptive 48, 560, 3.19 *chronicled,* 4.13 *of philosophy,* 5.38 *linguistic,* 5.44 *grammatical,* 299.6 *outlined,* 475.11 *explanatory,* 522.1 *intelligible,* 524.14

interpretive, 547.13 *representational*
descriptive grammar 5.29 *grammar*
descriptive linguistics 5.1 *linguistics*
descriptively 48, 560, 3.25 *reportedly,* 5.48 *linguistically,* 5.52 *grammatically,* 475.22 *demonstrably,* 547.14 *representationally*
descriptiveness 522.9 *intelligibility*
descriptive statistics 52.53 *statistics*
descriptive writer 560
descriptive writing 48.4 *nonfiction,* 560.5 *fiction*
descriptivism 4.7 *school of thought*
descriptivist 4.11 *follower of a doctrine,* 4.14 *of a philosophy*
descry 435.12 *see,* 496.1 *discover,* 522.7 *recognize*
desecrate 850, 601.1 *misuse,* 622.11 *dirty,* 628.3 *make worse,* 801.4 *disreputable*
desecrated 601.4 *misused*
desecration 601.2 *misuse,* 864.6 *religious sin*
desecrator 601.3 *abuser*
deselect 580.5 *vote,* 581.1 *reject*
deselected 580.15 *chosen*
deselection 581.6 *discarding*
desensitization 761, 61.3 *psychiatric treatment*
desensitize 404.12 *anaesthetize,* 761.7 *render insensitive,* 783.13 *make indifferent*
desensitized 761
desensitizing substance 761
deserpidine 62 Medication
desert 161 Collective Names for Birds and Animals, **392, 392, 824,** 98.10 *miscellaneous,* 220.10 *be converted,* 244.5 *havoc,* 247.1 *infertility,* 247.3 *birth control,* 248.3 *geographical space,* 254.18 *abscond,* 254.19 *leave empty,* 271.5 *broad thing,* 322.8 *open space,* 376.8 *smooth thing,* 408.8 *hot place,* 484.8 *reverse,* 578.3 *apostatize,* 591.8 *run away,* 598.2 *withdraw,* 617.6 *worth,* 672.1 *retaliation,* 693.15 *be disobedient,* 705.5 *resign,* 720.8 *not perform,* 720.9 *disregard orders,* 779.4 *be a coward,* 843.6 *right,* 863.3 *worth*
desert boots 295.19 *footwear*
desert climate 55.38 *climate*
desert dune 54.37 *dune*
deserted 174.16 *alone,* 254.11 *truant,* 254.14 *unoccupied,* 598.5 *relinquished,* 633.3 *vulnerable,* 816.10 *lonely,* 816.11 *secluded,* 824.11 *divorced*
deserter 598, 254.6 *absentee,* 484.4 *tergiversator,* 578.9 *equivocator,* 590.7 *the hunted,* 591.17 *avoider,* 711.4 *refuser,* 720.6 *evader,* 779.2 *coward*
desertification 55.40 *climatic change,* 247.1 *infertility*
deserting 693.13 *disobedient,* 720.12 *nonperforming,* 720.13 *noncompliant,* 858.6 *faithless*
deserting husband 591.17 *avoider*
desertion 591, 254.4 *absenteeism,* 458.4 *disappearance,* 578.7 *apostasy,* 598.3 *relinquishment,* 693.1 *disobedience,* 720.3 *disregard of orders,* 779.1 *cowardice,* 824.2 *separation,* 858.2 *faithlessness*
desertion of principles 717.3 *irresolution*
desert island 247.1 *infertility,* 531.6 *privacy,* 816.5 *solitary place*
desert oak 85 Trees and Shrubs
desert one's principles 717.5 *be irresolute*
desert rat 77 Placental Mammals
deserts 652.1 *conduct,* 672.1 *re-

taliation, 845.2 *due,* 878.1 *reward,* 879.9 *retribution*
desert sands 98.10 *miscellaneous,* 247.1 *infertility*
desert war 676.1 *war*
desert warfare 676.8 *warfare*
desert waste 244.5 *havoc*
deserve 485.14 *be qualified,* 617.9 *be worthy,* 804.7 *be entitled to,* 843.13 *be right,* 845.15 *merit*
deserved 485.9 *qualified,* 843.9 *in the right,* 845.10 *due*
deservedly 845, 485.17 *capably,* 843.16 *right*
deservedness 485.1 *qualification,* 845.1 *entitlement*
deserved reward 878.1 *reward*
deserved tribute 878.1 *reward*
deserve ill of 652.13 *behave badly*
deserve notice 611.7 *be important*
deserve well of 652.12 *behave well*
deserving 617.1 *worthy,* 782.8 *desirable,* 804.5 *entitled,* 845.9 *meritorious,* 851.21 *praiseworthy*
deservingness 845.1 *entitlement*
deserving punishment 879.22 *punishable*
deservings 845.2 *due*
desiccant 392.9 *drying*
desiccate 392.17 *dry*
desiccated 392.3 *dried-up,* 637.7 *preserved*
desiccation 392.13 *drying,* 637.1 *preservation*
desiccative 392.9 *drying,* 392.15 *dryer*
desiccator 392.15 *dryer*
desiderate 593.8 *miss,* 609.6 *be unsatisfied*
desideratum 571.1 *necessity,* 593.1 *requirement,* 782.5 *object of desire*
design 50, 796, 43.18 *be an architect,* 50.1 *art,* 50.4 *treatment,* 50.6 *work of art,* 50.9 *drawing,* 63.30 *engineer,* 119.7 *originate,* 152.2 *array,* 228.1 *motive,* 243.1 *production,* 243.10 *produce,* 295.35 *make clothing,* 306.1, 306.7 *form,* 382.9 *artistic structure,* 382.14 *structure,* 471.4 *purpose,* 471.18 *aim,* 496.4 *invent,* 496.9 *invention,* 520.5 *point,* 520.12 *intend,* 539.8, 539.28 *trick,* 547.11 *paint,* 560.14 *describe,* 588.3 *future intention,* 588.8 *resolve,* 592.1, 592.9 *plan,* 592.10 *plan out,* 597.2 *undertaking,* 792.2 *pattern*
design a prototype 592.10 *plan*
designate 103.11 *characterize,* 163.13 *class,* 165.24 *specify,* 520.10 *mean,* 544.10 *identify,* 580.4 *pick,* 580.15 *chosen,* 707.6 *deputize*
designated 513.7 *expected,* 544.12 *identified*
designated hitter 22.2 *baseball player*
designated runner 22.2 *baseball player*
designation 544.1 *identification,* 560.7 *nomenclature,* 580.6 *selection*
design body 11.7 *spirit*
design buildings 43.18 *be an architect*
designed 43.11 *architectural,* 43.12 *structural,* 50.27 *painted,* 471.12 *purposive,* 518.9, 520.9 *meant,* 582.4 *deliberate,* 588.12 *intended,* 592.14 *planned*
designedly 588.13 *intentionally*
designer 43.2 *architect,* 50.16 *artist,* 51.25 *producer,* 119.3 *originator,* 243.9 *producer,* 295.31 *styled,* 306.10 *prototypical,* 496.12 *discoverer,* 592.8 *planner*
designer drug 630.8, 875.6 *drug*

designer gene 59.12 *molecular biology*
designer label 796.1 *fashion*
designer stubble 375.7 *rough thing*
design houses 43.18 *be an architect*
designing 306.1 *form,* 496.9 *invention,* 539.34 *deceiving*
designing of furniture 47.1 *furniture*
design school 6.12 *educational institution*
desipramine 62 Medication
desirability 782, 580.7 *preference,* 593.3 *needfulness,* 615.3 *convenience,* 821.4 *lovability*
desirable 782, 580.15 *chosen,* 615.1 *convenient,* 782.7 *desired,* 821.22 *lovable*
desirably 782, 821.30 *lovingly*
desire 782, 782, 821, 228.1 *motive,* 340.1 *attraction,* 519.6 *reverie,* 570.1 *will,* 570.11 *wish,* 588.3 *future intention,* 593.8 *miss,* 609.6 *be unsatisfied,* 712.1, 712.6 *request,* 714.11 *promise oneself,* 775.3 *aspiration,* 775.7 *aspire,* 782.13 *like,* 784.1 *liking,* 784.7 *like,* 821.23 *love,* 842.1 *envy,* 842.3 *be envious of*
Desire 782
desire concentration 61.28 *cathexis*
desired 782, 513.7 *expected,* 593.4 *required,* /12.9 *requesting*
desired object 782.5 *object of desire*
desire for knowledge 465.1, 477.8 *curiosity*
desire knowledge 465.7 *be curious*
desirer 782
desires 513.2 *expectations*
desires of the flesh 821.5 *desire*
desiring 513.5 *expecting,* 782.9 *desirous,* 842.2 *envious*
desirous 782, 775.13 *aspirant,* 784.6 *liking,* 821.20 *amorous,* 842.2 *envious*
desirously 782, 784.11 *admiringly,* 842.4 *enviously*
desist 669, 218.6 *cease,* 641.4 *not act*
desistance 218.1 *cessation,* 669.4 *desisting*
desisting 669, 669
desk 47.4 *table,* 258.3 *cabinet*
desk dictionary 5.28 *dictionary*
desk editor 532.12 *publisher*
desk lamp 439.6 *electric light*
desk sergeant 16.17 *police officer*
desktop publishing 235.9 *electronics*
desk worker 646.1 *worker*
desman 77 Placental Mammals
desmid 90 Algae
Des Moines 93 Cities
desolate 244.10 *lay waste,* 247.3 *birth control,* 247.10 *waste,* 349.9 *depopulate,* 770.5 *sad,* 776.4 *hopeless,* 816.10 *lonely,* 816.11 *secluded*
desolation 244.5 *havoc,* 247.1 *infertility,* 687.1 *adversity,* 770.1 *sorrow*
desorb 57.29 *absorb*
desorbed 57.43 *absorbed*
desorption 57.20 *surface chemistry*
despair 770, 440.7 *spiritual darkness,* 515.1 *disappointment,* 515.5 *be crestfallen,* 641.4 *not act,* 770.2 *depression,* 776.1 *hopelessness,* 776.9 *be hopeless*
despairing 776.4 *hopeless*
despairingly 776.11 *hopelessly*
desperado 241.4 *violent person or animal,* 398.11 *murderer,* 780.3 *rash person,* 832.8 *malefactor,* 864.9 *wicked person*
desperate 241.6 *violent,* 574.2 *tenacious,* 642.18 *active,* 776.4 *hopeless,* 780.4 *rash*
desperately 776.11 *hopelessly*

desperate move 34.3 *climbing technique*
desperateness 780.1 *rashness*
desperate remedy 602.1 *means*
desperate situation 633.5 *danger*
desperate straits 659.6 *critical situation*
desperation 574.13 *concentration,* 776.1 *hopelessness,* 780.1 *rashness*
despicability 822.4 *hatefulness*
despicable 618.4 *poor,* 758.2 *unpleasant,* 822.12 *hated,* 850.12 *disregardful,* 862.7 *evil,* 864.11 *wicked*
despicableness 618.10 *poverty*
despicably 618.2 *hatefully*
despise 785.5 *dislike,* 805.28 *disdain,* 807.29 *ridicule,* 822.14 *hate,* 850.20 *scorn*
despised 785.9 *disliked*
despising 785.8 *disliking,* 805.23 *prejudiced*
despite 117.16 *disagreeably,* 130.10 *additionally,* 231.5 *counter,* 663.27 *opposed to,* 666.11 *in disagreement,* 850.3 *contempt,* 852.2 *disrespect*
despiteful 832.14 *hostile*
despitefulness 820.1 *enmity,* 822.1 *hate*
despoil 244.10, 607.2 *lay waste,* 722.13 *destroy,* 734.10 *take away,* 736.14 *plunder,* 850.27 *desecrate,* 862.11 *be evil*
despoiler 244.6 *destroyer,* 734.6 *taker,* 736.9 *plunderer*
despoiling 244.5 *havoc,* 734.3 *taking away,* 736.5 *plundering*
despoilment 722.5 *destruction,* 736.5 *plundering*
despoliation 736.5 *plundering*
despond 770.9 *despair*
despondence 536.1 *negation*
despondency 536.1 *negation,* 687.1 *adversity,* 770.2 *depression,* 776.1 *hopelessness*
despondent 454.3 *depressed,* 536.11 *negative,* 770.6 *depressed,* 776.4 *hopeless*
despondently 536.15 *negatively,* 776.11 *hopelessly*
despot 688.10 *person of authority,* 690.4 *strict person,* 696.4 *absolute ruler*
despotic 16.62 *above the law,* 653.17 *managerial,* 690.8 *severe,* 696.12 *masterful*
despotically 16.85 *summarily*
despotism 688.7 *type of rule,* 690.2 *suppression*
despumate 134.10, 621.15 *purify*
desquamate 266.11 *scale,* 294.13 *remove,* 296.16 *peel,* 353.23 *cast*
desquamated 353.32 *cast-off*
desquamation 266.6 *layering,* 294.5 *shedding,* 296.6 *peeling,* 353.12 *dead tissue*
desquamative 296.12 *peeling*
dessert 45, 414, 45.9 *dish,* 350.14 *mouthful*
dessertspoon 258.17 *ladle,* 350.16 *eating utensil*
dessert wine 351.9 *wine,* 414.5 *sweet drink*
dessicator 57 Laboratory Apparatus
destabilize 57.25 *solidify,* 123.5 *be unequal*
destabilized 57.32 *solid*
destabilizer 57.3 *phase*
De Stijl 43 Architectural Styles, **50** Schools and Groups of Artists
destination 344, 157.6 *end point,* 588.6 *objective*
destine 520.12 *intend,* 571.17 *preordain,* 582.1 *predetermine*
destined 157.23 *annihilated,* 199.11 *future,* 490.5 *inevitable,* 520.9 *meant,* 571.12 *inevitable,* 582.3 *predetermined,* 714.15 *future*
destine for 588.9 *intend for*
destiny 157.5 *fate,* 199.3 *future condition,* 226.4 *contributing*

factor, 233 *influence,* 490.16, 571.5 *inevitability,* 582.5 *predetermination,* 589.2 *luck*
destitute 571.11 *needy,* 593.5 *necessitous,* 687.5 *person in adversity,* 743.1 *poor*
destitution 571.4 *need,* 687.1 *adversity,* 743.5 *poverty*
destrier 32.3 *warhorse,* 679.19 *cavalry*
destroy 244, 722, 100.14 *cause not to exist,* 136.9 *separate,* 141.4 *deconstruct,* 157.17 *kill,* 216.8 *cause change,* 241.8 *use violence,* 349.10 *exterminate,* 398.16 *kill,* 398.18 *slaughter,* 458.3 *cause to disappear,* 476.8 *refute,* 546.1 *obliterate,* 607.2 *lay waste,* 614.8 *make useless,* 618.14 *ill-treat,* 628.4 *impair,* 676.13 *be at war,* 682.10 *defeat heavily,* 704.6 *cancel,* 722.13 *destroy,* 727.9 *dispose of,* 862.11 *be evil*
destroyed 244, 100.11 *no more,* 141.5 *disintegrated,* 157.23 *annihilated,* 546.6 *obliterated,* 628.12 *deteriorated,* 722.16 *losing*
destroyer 244, 607, 216.6 *editor,* 476.5 *refuter,* 679.24 *warship,* 832.8 *malefactor*
destroyer division 17.4 *military organization*
destroyer escort 679.24 *warship*
destroyer flotilla 17.4 *military organization*
destroy good will 822.16 *cause hate*
destroying 244, 62.14 *counteracting,* 244.14 *destructive,* 476.7 *refuting*
destroying angel 89 Fungi
destruct 244.8 *destroy*
destruction 244, 607, 722, 141.2 *deconstruction,* 157.4 *annihilation,* 398.1 *killing,* 398.4 *slaughter,* 458.5 *disguise,* 476.1 *refutation,* 546.3 *obliteration,* 618.11 *harmfulness,* 628.9 *dilapidation,* 628.10 *impairment,* 862.2 *affliction*
Destruction 244
destructionist 244.6 *destroyer*
destruction of life 398.1 *killing*
destruction of weapons 677.1 *pacification*
destructive 244, 241.6 *violent,* 398.24 *murderous,* 618.5 *harmful,* 670.23 *attacking,* 687.6 *adverse,* 854.16 *defamatory,* 862.9 *detrimental*
destructively 141, 244, 607, 862, 476.11 *in reply*
destructiveness 244, 241.1 *violence,* 607.4 *destruction*
Destutt 4 Philosophers
desuetude 598.3 *relinquishment,* 600.10 *disuse,* 727.1 *disposal*
desultorily 160.18 *disconnectedly,* 215.8 *irregularly,* 216.15, 224.15 *changeably,* 685.7 *incompletely*
desultoriness 215.1 *irregularity,* 216.2 *change of mind,* 224.2 *irresolution,* 468.1 *inattention,* 642.7 *restlessness,* 685.1 *noncompletion*
desultory 151.14 *irregular,* 160.8 *discontinuous,* 215.4 *irregular,* 216.11 *changeable,* 224.14 *irresolute,* 335.25 *wandering,* 468.11 *perfunctory,* 482.5 *vague,* 685.4 *uncompleted*
detach 104.15, 136.9 *separate,* 139.5 *unstick,* 162.12 *disperse,* 174.20 *single out,* 252.18 *disconnect*
detached 4, 43.12 *structural,* 104.11 *separate,* 108.6 *unrelated,* 136.17 *unjoined,* 174.16 *alone,* 252.12 *disconnected,* 256.16 *manorial,* 333.4 *middle,* 466.4 *uninterested,* 468.7 *inattentive,* 512.8 *oblivious,* 698.10 *independent,* 783.7 *indifferent,*

816.8 *unsociable,* 859.4 *disinterested*
detached house 43.3 *building,* 256.5 *house*
detachedly 252.21 *disconnectedly*
detached retina 436.2 *poor sight*
detachment 4, 17.4 *military organization,* 61.13 *depression,* 104.3 *separateness,* 136.1 *separation,* 150.8 *harmony,* 174.5 *aloneness,* 252.5 *disconnection,* 468.1 *inattention,* 512.1 *oblivion,* 679.14 *armed forces,* 679.16 *army unit,* 783.1 *indifference,* 816.1 *unsociability,* 859.1 *disinterestedness*
detach oneself 466.6 *be incurious,* 783.12 *be indifferent*
detail 17.4 *military organization,* 106.6 *aspect,* 106.11 *circumstantiate,* 143.2 *particular,* 148.1 *component,* 174.2 *item,* 537.8 *accuracy,* 537.31 *be accurate,* 553.1 *diffuseness,* 553.5 *be diffuse,* 560.15 *recount,* 560.16 *define,* 580.4 *pick,* 612.8 *trifle,* 679.14 *armed forces,* 679.16 *army unit,* 731.6 *assign,* 792.2 *pattern*
detailed 106, 144.7 *complete,* 503.5, 537.21 *accurate,* 553.3 *diffuse,* 560.11 *descriptive,* 644.11 *laborious*
detailed account 553.1 *diffuseness,* 560.1 *description*
detailed description 560.1 *description*
details 165.4 *specifications,* 560.1 *description,* 612.8 *trifle*
detain 699, 726, 209.8 *delay,* 328.3 *slow down,* 661.8 *hinder,* 702.9 *imprison*
detain at His Majesty's pleasure 702.9 *imprison*
detained 699, 209.10 *held up,* 328.7 *delayed,* 702.8 *imprisoned,* 726.10 *retained*
detained at His Majesty's pleasure 702.8 *imprisoned*
detainee 323.6 *closed-in person,* 702.5 *prisoner*
detaining 209.12 *delaying*
detainment 661.1 *hindrance*
detainment at His Majesty's pleasure 702.7 *imprisonment*
detect 496, 250.11 *find,* 348.12 *draw in,* 403.11 *sense,* 522.7 *recognize,* 544.10 *identify*
detectability 437.3 *visibility*
detectable 435.23, 437.1 *visible,* 496.15 *discoverable*
detected 250.7 *found*
detecting 250.3 *locating*
detection 496, 544.1 *identification*
detective 16.17 *police officer,* 465.3 *curious person,* 477.9 *questioner,* 496.12 *discoverer,* 632.3 *protector*
detective novel 560.5 *fiction*
detective story 48.2 *fiction*
detector 496, 53.27 *imaging*
detente 667.1 *agreement*
détente 677.1 *pacification*
detention 699, 726, 16.6 *legal process,* 209.3 *delayed action,* 328.12 *hesitation,* 661.1 *hindrance,* 702.7 *imprisonment,* 879.7 *punishment*
detention centre 702.1 *prison*
detention home 702.1 *prison*
detention in a young offender institution 702.7 *imprisonment*
deter 587, 661.8 *hinder,* 661.9 *block,* 785.7 *cause dislike*
detergent 57 Types of Compounds, 134.2 *purifier,* 134.15 *purifying,* 621.9 *cleaning agent,* 621.18 *cleansing*
deteriorate 628, 127.11 *become inferior,* 202.17 *grow old,* 207.17 *age,* 216.7 *be changed,* 220.8 *be transformed,* 362.1 *lower,* 379.4 *be brittle,* 585.4 *be unaccustomed,* 606.6 *stop using,* 607.1 *waste,* 624.24 *be unhealthy,* 628.3 *make worse,*

687.9 *be in trouble*, 722.12
lessen, 768.7 *become aggravated*
deteriorated 628, 216.12
changed, 362.17 *lowered*
deteriorating 55.46 *seasonal*,
220.14 *converting*, 628.12 *deteriorated*, 864.11 *wicked*
deterioration 628, 14.1 *finance*,
127.2 *deficiency*, 216.1 *change*,
220.2 *evolution*, 337.14 *decline*,
362.11 *lowering*, 362.15 *debasement*, 379.2 *brittleness*, 585.3
unaccustomedness, 607.3 *waste*,
683.1 *failure*, 687.1 *adversity*,
722.4 *lessening*, 768.1 *aggravation*, 864.1 *wickedness*
Deterioration 628
determent 661.1 *hindrance*
determinability 268.3 *measurability*
determinable 268.14 *measurable*,
479.8 *experimental*
determinant 52.22 *matrix*, 226.1
cause, 226.13 *causal*
determination 225, 577, 138.2
tenacity, 237.1 *strength*, 268.1
measurement, 475.4 *proof*,
479.3 *experimentation*, 480.5
proof, 485.6 *specification*,
490.1 *inevitability*, 490.18 *particularity*, 537.7 *confirmation*,
570.2 *willpower*, 574.12 *resolution*, 575.1 *perseverance*, 580.6
selection, 588.2 *intentionality*,
642.8 *assiduity*, 772.5 *earnestness*, 778.3 *steadfastness*
determine 226, 52.90 *enumerate*, 165.24 *specify*, 166.13 *rule*,
170.8 *calculate*, 268.10 *measure*, 332.6 *direct*, 475.17 *prove*,
479.11 *experiment*, 480.2 *prove*,
485.16 *specify*, 490.21 *make certain*, 490.22 *specify*, 492.11
judge, 496.3 *find out*, 537.30
prove true, 570.13 *intend*, 574.7
resolve, 580.1 *select*, 588.8 *resolve*
determined 225, 138.10 *tenacious*, 237.11 *strong in spirit*,
268.13 *measured*, 475.13
proven, 479.10 *tested*, 485.12
conditional, 490.5 *inevitable*,
490.7 *particular*, 537.20 *proved*,
570.7 *iron-willed*, 574.1 *resolute*, 575.10 *persevering*, 577.3
unyielding, 588.12 *intended*,
642.18 *active*, 772.2 *earnest*,
778.12 *self-reliant*
determined effort 596.5 *attempt*
determinedly 225, 138.12 *tenaciously*
determined to 588.11 *intending*
determine to 588.8 *resolve*
determining 170.1 *calculation*,
479.8 *experimental*, 480.9 *verificatory*
determinism 4.7 *school of
thought*, 56.81 *causality*, 571.6
necessitarianism
determinist 4.11 *follower of a doctrine*, 4.14 *of a philosophy*
deterministic 571.12 *inevitable*
deterministic law 56.81 *causality*
deterrence 587
deterrent 231.1 *counteraction*,
587.7 *deterrence*, 587.9 *dissuasive*, 632.2 *protection*, 632.4
safety device, 636.1, 636.8 *warning*, 661.2 *obstacle*, 661.13 *hindering*, 661.14 *blocked*, 680.1
weapon, 718.1 *protection*, 718.6
secure
detest 785.5 *dislike*, 820.11 *be
hostile*, 822.14 *hate*
detestable 618.4 *poor*, 822.12
hated, 862.7 *evil*
detestably 862.12 *evilly*
detestation 785.1 *dislike*, 820.3
ill feeling, 822.1 *hate*
detested 820.10 *hated*
detesting 785.8 *disliking*, 822.10
hating
dethrone 252.16 *replace*, 349.3
disbar, 689.4 *be anarchic*, 704.7
terminate, 846.16 *disentitle*
dethroned 846.12 *disentitled*

---

dethronement 689.1 *anarchy*,
846.2 *disentitlement*
detonate 338.28 *shoot*, 410.11
fuel, 423.8 *be loud*, 425.5 *bang*
detonation 241.3 *instance of violence*, 338.7 *shot*, 425.1 *bang*
detonator 338.12 *propellant*,
410.2 *lighter*, 680.15 *explosive*
detour 334, 334, 363, 216.1
change, 216.7 *be changed*,
311.2 *bend*, 311.6 *curve*, 313.2,
313.6 *circle*, 327.2 *route*,
327.14 *find one's way*, 335.1 *deviate*, 335.14 *deviating course*,
363.5 *ringroad*
detoxify 629.6 *cure*, 873.5 *sober
up*
detract 136.10 *set apart*, 713.6
protest, 854.10 *disparage*
detract from 542, 131.3 *subtract*
detracting 495.4 *underestimating*
detraction 542, 131.1 *subtraction*, 495.1 *underestimation*,
854.1 *disparagement*
detract nothing 122.11 *equalize*
detractor 477.9 *questioner*, 495.2
pessimist, 498.5 *disbeliever*,
500.5 *dissenter*, 713.4 *protester*,
854.7 *disparager*
detractory 854.15 *disparaging*
detrain 344.4 *land*
detribalize 628.6 *pervert*
detriment 616.3 *inconvenience*,
618.11 *harmfulness*, 628.10 *impairment*, 722.1 *loss*
detrimental 862, 616.1 *inconvenient*, 618.5 *harmful*, 687.6 *adverse*
detrimentally 687.12 *in adversity*
detrimental to health 626.5 *unhygienic*
detrital 54.56 *petrographic*,
384.18 *grainy*
detrited 384.18 *grainy*
detrition 384.4 *pulverization*,
385.2 *wearing away*
detritus 132.2 *residue*, 143.8 *bits
and pieces*, 326.10 *transferred
thing*, 384.9 *grit*
Detroit 93 Cities, 93.2 *American
cities*
detrude 349.14 *let out*, 362.5
bear down on
detrusion 349.22 *disgorgement*,
362.13 *submergence*
Dettol 62 Medication
detumesce 129.4 *decrease*
detumescence 129.1 *decrease*
detumescent 129.6 *decreasing*
deuce 42.3 *card game terms*,
110.5 *equality*, 122.2 *equilibrium*, 176.1 *two*
deuced 827.11 *miscellaneous euphemisms*
deuteragonist 51.21 *role*
deuteranopia 436.2 *poor sight*
deuteranopic 436.9 *weak-sighted*
deuterate 57.26 *react*
deuteration 57 Types of Chemical Reaction
deuterogamy 823.3 *types of marriage*
deuteromycetes 89.3 *fungi*
Deuteromycotina 89.3 *fungi*
Deutsche Industrie Normen 75.4
standard
deutsche schalmei 49 Musical
Instruments
Deutschmark 741.11 *national
coins*
deva 8.5 *deity*
devaluated 14.6 *financial*
devaluation 14.1 *finance*, 131.1
subtraction, 628.8 *perversion*,
741.7 *finance*, 747.4 *depreciation*, 754.2 *declining prices*
devalue 131.3 *subtract*, 614.8
make useless, 628.6 *pervert*,
741.25 *demonetize*, 754.13
make cheap
devalued 131.7 *reduced*, 741.22
monetary, 754.9 *cheap*
devalued currency 741.15 *false
money*, 747.4 *depreciation*
devalue the currency 747
Devanagari 5.13 *letter*
devastate 244.10 *lay waste*,

349.9 *depopulate*, 607.2 *lay
waste*
devastated 244.15 *destroyed*,
515.9 *disappointed*
devastating 241.6 *violent*,
244.14 *destructive*
devastatingly 244.16, 607.11 *destructively*
devastation 244.5 *havoc*, 607.4
destruction, 628.10 *impairment*,
670.14 *siege*
develop 82, 336, 594, 6.22 *educate*, 66.21 *photograph*, 99.18
come to be, 128.4 *increase*,
128.5 *make bigger*, 206.18
grow, 207.18 *mature*, 220.8 *be
transformed*, 227.7 *follow from*,
227.8 *grow*, 243.10 *produce*,
261.5 *make bigger*, 261.6 *become bigger*, 324.13 *be in motion*, 336.8 *further*, 526.3 *reveal*,
627.1 *improve*, 627.2 *get better*,
714.10 *show potential*, 721.10
augment
developable 261.9 *enlargeable*
develop a habit 584.18 *habituate*
develop a literary style 549.9
style
develop a method 602.6 *find
means*
develop an attitude 234.4 *tend*
develop a power play 31.9 *play
hockey*
develop a thesis 561.4 *dissertate*
developed 594, 207.11 *adult*,
227.10 *caused*, 243.11 *productive*, 261.7 *bigger*
developed countries 13.4 *economic development*
developed world 249.7 *regions of
the world*
develop engine trouble 661.9
block
developer 66.12 *development*,
243.9 *producer*, 261.4 *enlarger*,
725.7 *property man*
develop from 227.8 *grow*
develop fully 144.5 *be complete*
develop industrially 243.10 *produce*
developing 594, 59.26 *developmental*, 145.4 *incomplete*,
156.32 *embryonic*, 206.13 *maturing*, 220.14 *converting*,
227.11 *growing*, 243.11 *productive*, 261.8 *growing*, 457.7 *appearing*
developing from 227.10 *caused*
developing nations 249.7 *regions
of the world*
developing world 12.5 *political
organization*
develop into 220.7 *convert into*
develop late 209.6 *be late*
development 66, 245, 336,
594, 48.3 *aspect of fiction*,
128.1 *increase*, 154.3 *preparation*, 195.9 *sequel*, 220.2 *evolution*, 227.3 *growth*, 243.2 *manufacture*, 261.1 *growth*, 721.2
augmentation
developmental 59, 154.14 *preparatory*
developmental biologist 59.19
life scientist
developmental biology 59, 59.1
life science
developmental psychology 61.1
psychology
développés 46.10 *positions at
the barre*
develop technical problems
661.9 *block*
devi 8.5 *deity*
Devi 8 Deities
deviance 168.6 *deviation*, 334.2
detour, 335.13 *deviation*, 363.2
circuitousness
deviancy 334.2 *detour*, 335.13
deviation, 504.7 *errancy*
deviant 335, 113.5 *diverse*,
168.10 *eccentric*, 168.17 *abnormal*, 286.5 *devious*, 335.19 *deviant person*, 504.16 *errant*,
844.14 *abnormal*
deviant person 335
deviate 286, 335, 113.8 *be di-

---

verse, 115.5 *be dissimilar*,
117.12 *be disparate*, 136.13 *diverge*, 168.19 *be independent*,
216.7 *be changed*, 286.6 *be
oblique*, 305.8 *move sideways*,
324.13 *be in motion*, 334.4 *detour*, 335.19 *deviant person*,
343.10 *diverge*, 363.8 *detour*,
504.20 *transgress*, 553.6 *be circuitous*, 666.8 *be different*
deviate from the path of virtue
864.16 *be wicked*
deviating 104.10 *foreign*, 286.4
oblique, 334.7 *circuitous*,
335.20 *deviant*, 343.6 *divergent*,
363.9 *orbital*, 553.4 *circumlocutory*, 666.10 *different*
deviating course 335
deviating motion 335
deviation 168, 335, 61.10 *neurosis*, 113.1 *diversity*, 136.1 *separation*, 216.1 *change*, 263.1 *distance*, 286.1 *obliqueness*, 334.2
detour, 343.1 *divergence*, 363.2
circuitousness, 553.2 *circumlocution*, 578.6 *equivocation*, 666.3
difference
Deviation 335
deviationism 168.3 *nonconformism*
deviationist 335.19 *deviant person*, 578.9 *equivocator*, 693.6
nonconformist
deviative 335.20 *deviant*
deviatory 216.11 *changeable*,
335.20 *deviant*
device 48.3 *aspect of fiction*,
232.2 *instrument*, 499.9 *invention*, 539.8 *trick*, 544.8 *heraldic
device*, 592.3 *expedient plan*,
602.1 *means*, 603.1 *tool*, 638.2
means of escape, 657.2 *stratagem*
devil 8, 45.55 *cook*, 241.4 *violent person or animal*, 618.12
bad person, 822.8 *hated person*,
862.6 *evil person*, 864.6 *religious sin*, 864.9 *wicked person*
devil dance 46.4 *historic dancing*
devil incarnate 864.9 *wicked person*
devilish 8, 11.15 *witchlike*,
618.5 *harmful*, 618.6 *damnable*, 832.11 *cruel*, 864.14 *impious*
devilishly 8, 864.20 *immorally*
devilishment 832.1 *malevolence*
devilize 8
devilled 45.56 *culinary*
devilled kidneys 45.44 *British
dish*
devil-like 8.6 *devilish*
devil-may-care 462.8 *thoughtless*, 508.5 *foolish*, 780.4 *rash*,
783.8 *careless*
devil of a lot 181.3 *profuseness*
devil ray 80 Fishes
devilry 832.1 *malevolence*, 862.1
evil, 864.6 *religious sin*
devil's advocate 484.3 *counterclaimant*, 668.4 *defiant person*
devil's coach horse 82 Insects
devil's food cake 45.36 *cake*
Devil's Island 702.1 *prison*,
816.4 *place of confinement*
devil's tattoo 426.1 *drumming*,
788.1 *boredom*
devil worship 9.2 *idolatry*, 864.6
religious sin
devil worshipper 9.6 *idolater*,
864.9 *wicked person*
devil-worshipping 9.10 *idolatrous*
devious 286, 334.7 *circuitous*,
335.25 *wandering*, 539.34 *deceiving*, 657.4 *cunning*, 801.4
disreputable, 858.5 *dishonourable*
deviously 286, 334.8, 363.12
circuitously, 858.11 *dishonourably*
deviousness 286, 335.13 *deviation*, 539.1 *deception*, 858.1 *improbity*
devisable 728.5 *transferring*
devise 99.20 *bring into being*,
119.7 *originate*, 152.18 *make arrangements*, 243.10 *produce*,

382.16 *construct*, 496.4 *invent*, 519.14 *imagine*, 539.28 *trick*, 583.3 *improvise*, 592.11 *invent*, 657.5 *be cunning*, 725.9 *own property*
devise countermeasures 661.8 *hinder*
devised 243.12 *produced*, 519.12 *imaginary*, 582.4 *deliberate*
devisee 730.6 *beneficiary*
deviser 119.3 *originator*, 592.8 *planner*
devisor 729.4 *giver*
devitalize 236.9 *make impotent*
devitrified 44.10 *ceramic*
devitrified glass 44.9 *industrial ceramics*
devitrify 44.11 *make ceramics*, 443.11 *make opaque*
Devizes 93 Cities
devoid 100.9 *nonexistent*, 254.11 *vacant*
devoirs 849.7 *respects*
devolution 141.2 *deconstruction*, 703.1 *commission*, 706.3 *delegation*, 728.1 *transfer of property*
devolutionary 703.9 *commissioned*
devolve 141.4 *deconstruct*, 703.6 *commission*, 706.4 *delegate*, 728.3 *transfer property*, 728.4 *be transferred*
devolved 706.7 *decentralized*
devolvement 703.1 *commission*, 706.3 *delegation*
devolve upon 847.14 *be the duty of*
Devon 68 Breeds of Cattle, **92** Counties, **98** Islands
Devon and Cornwall Longwool 68 Breeds of Sheep
Devon Closewool 68 Breeds of Sheep
Devonian 54 Geological Time Intervals
Devonian period 200.3 *geological period*
Devon minnow 20.2 *artificial fly*
Devon rex 77 Breeds of Cats
Devonshire cream 395.8 *fat*
devote 729.5 *give*
devoted 819, 7.15 *religious*, 9.9 *worshipful*, 574.2 *tenacious*, 584.14 *habituated*, 694.8 *loyal*, 784.6 *liking*, 821.17 *loving*, 821.19 *enamoured*, 847.9 *loyal*, 857.4 *honourable*
devotedly 819, 9.12 *worshipfully*, 694.10 *obediently*, 821.30 *lovingly*, 857.7 *honourably*
devotedness 9.1 *worship*, 574.13 *concentration*, 642.8 *assiduity*, 819.3 *familiarity*
devoted to 694.8 *loyal*
devotee 7.3 *religious person*, 9.5 *worshipper*, 155.14 *follower*, 497.5 *believer*, 584.8 *creature of habit*, 642.10 *busy person*, 782.6 *desirer*
devotee of Bacchus 874.17 *drunkard*
devote oneself 7.19 *be religious*, 574.9 *undertake*
devote oneself to 567.12 *address oneself to*, 597.1 *undertake*
devote to 599.1 *use*
devotion 7.2 *religiousness*, 9.1 *worship*, 10.9 *prayer*, 574.13 *concentration*, 694.2 *loyalty*, 759.5 *good feeling*, 784.1 *liking*, 819.3 *familiarity*, 821.1 *love*, 847.3 *allegiance*, 849.3 *respectfulness*, 857.1 *probity*
devotional 7.15 *religiousness*, 9.9 *worshipful*, 10.22 *worshipping*
devotionally 9.12 *worshipfully*
devotion to duty 847.4 *sense of duty*
devour 244.12 *consume*, 350.21 *eat*, 350.22 *eat well*, 607.1 *waste*, 872.5 *be greedy*
devoured with jealousy 841.4 *jealous*
devouring 350.2 *appetite*, 350.26 *eating*, 872.6 *gluttonous*

devourment 350.2 *appetite*
devour with one's eyes 435.13 *look*
devout 7.15 *religious*, 10.22 *worshipping*, 719.7 *observant*
devoutly 7.23 *religiously*, 10.23 *ritually*, 719.8 *observantly*
de Vries 52 Scientists
dew 55, 391
Dewar 637.2 *preserver*
Dewar flask 56 Named Laws
Dewar structure 57 Named Reactions
dewberry 86 Fruits
dewdrop 55.37 *dew*, 315.3 *round thing*
dewdrops 391.6 *dew*
Dewey 4 Philosophers
dewily 201.24 *immaturely*
dewiness 201.3 *immaturity*, 389.3 *wateriness*, 391.7 *bogginess*, 621.1 *cleanness*
dewpoint 55.6 *weather data*, 55.37 *dew*, 391.3 *humidity*
dew pond 94.2 *small lake*
dewy 201.12 *immature*, 204.5 *morning*, 391.10 *misty*, 621.16 *clean*
dex 875.6 *drug*
dexamethasone 62 Medication
dexamphetamine 62 Medication
dexie 875.6 *drug*
dexo 875.6 *drug*
dexter 544.81 *heraldic device*, 544.13 *heraldic*
Dexter 68 Breeds of Cattle
dexterity 567.3, 655.1 *skill*, 660.1 *easiness*
dexterous 655.6 *skilful*, 861.5 *proficient*
dexterously 655.12 *skilfully*, 861.25 *skillfully*
dexterousness 655.1 *skill*, 861.12 *proficiency*
dexter side 305.1 *side*
dextral 407.10 *handed*
dextrality 407.7 *sense organ*
dextran 58.4 *polysaccharide*, 387.4 *blood*
dextro form 57.13 *structure*
dextromethorphan 62 Medication
dextromoramide 62 Medication
dextropropoxyphene 62 Medication
dextrose 414.2 *sweetener*
dextrothyroxine 62 Medication
D-form 57.13 *structure*
dhak 85 Trees and Shrubs
Dhaka 93 Cities
dhal 45.49 *Indian dish*
Dhamma 7.12 *religious text*
dhammaduta 7.8 *priest*
Dhammapada 7.12 *religious text*
dharana 11.10 *psychic phenomenon*
dharani 11.10 *prayer*
Dhatri 8 Deities
dhobi 625.1 *cleaner*
dhobi itch 89.5 *fungal association*, 624.7 *tropical disease*, 624.13 *skin disease*
dhola 49 Musical Instruments
dhole 77 Placental Mammals
dhoti 295.25 *accessories*
dhow 74 Sailing Ships and Boats
dhyana 11.10 *psychic phenomenon*
DI 245.3 *propagation*
diabetes 777 Phobias by Topic, 624.4 *disease*
diabetic 624.19 *sick person*, 624.23 *diseased*
diabetic diet 350.6 *nutrition*
diabetic retinopathy 436.2 *poor sight*
diabetophobia 777 Phobias by Name
diablerie 11.3 *witchcraft*
diabolic 8.16 *devilish*, 9.10 *idolatrous*, 11.15 *witchlike*, 618.6 *damnable*, 862.7 *evil*
diabolical 8.16 *devilish*, 9.10 *idolatrous*, 11.15 *witchlike*, 618.6 *damnable*, 832.11 *cruel*, 864.14 *impious*

diabolically 8.20 *devilishly*, 11.26 *magically*, 862.12 *evilly*, 864.20 *immorally*
diabolism 9.2 *idolatry*, 864.6 *religious sin*
diabolist 9.6 *idolater*
diabolize 8.18 *devilize*, 11.21 *bewitch*, 864.17 *make wicked*
Diabolus 8.7 *devil*
diachronic 3.15 *historic*, 5.38 *linguistic*, 200.21 *retrospective*
diachronically 3.24 *historically*
diachronic linguistics 5.1 *linguistics*
diacidic 57.36 *acid*
diacidic base 57.9 *base*
diacritic 543.7 *punctuation*
diacritical 5.44 *grammatical*
diacritical mark 543.7 *punctuation*
diacritical work 5.36 *accent*
diaeresis 5.36 *accent*, 48.9 *metre*, 136.5 *separator*, 160.5 *caesura*
diagnose 60.19 *practise medicine*, 481.12 *discriminate*, 530.5 *disclose*, 544.10 *identify*
diagnosed 481.11 *judged*
diagnosis 60, 479.1 *experiment*, 481.1 *discrimination*, 530.1 *disclosure*, 544.1 *identification*, 624.20 *pathology*
diagnostic 60, 481.9 *discriminating*, 543.14 *signifying*
diagnostically 136.22 *in isolation*, 481.15 *discriminatingly*, 543.18 *indicatively*
diagnostician 60.13 *medical specialist*, 654.4 *adviser*
diagnostic instrument 60.7 *diagnosis*
diagnostic procedure 60.7 *diagnosis*
diagnostic radiology 60.7 *diagnosis*
diagnostics 60.7 *diagnosis*, 65.17 *computing term*, 524.5 *science of interpretation*
diagnostic test 60.7 *diagnosis*
diagonal 41.12 *ski*, 52.37 *line*, 286.1 *obliqueness*, 286.2 *oblique line*, 286.4, 310.8 *oblique*
diagonal gate 41.3 *ski racing*
diagonally 41.17 *on a ski run*, 286.8 *obliquely*, 310.12 *askew*, 335.28 *indirectly*
diagonal matrix 52.22 *matrix*
diagonal relationship 57.6 *chemical element*
diagonal side-step 41.2 *cross-country skiing*
diagonal stride 41.2 *cross-country skiing*
diagonal stride with pole planting 41.2 *cross-country skiing*
diagram 50.9 *drawing*, 152.8 *chart*, 299.1, 299.5 *outline*, 547.2 *reproduction*, 547.11 *paint*, 592.5 *map*
diagrammatic 152, 52.78 *pictorial*, 543.14 *signifying*, 547.13 *representational*, 560.13 *representing*
diagrammatically 152.28 *in place*, 543.18 *indicatively*
dial 192.8, 303.2 *face*
dial 999 636.7 *raise the alarm*
dialect 5, 5.4 *parent language*, 165.10 *specialized language*, 564.1 *faculty of speech*
dialectal 5.39 *of language*
dialectic 4.5 *philosophical argument*, 473.2 *logical argument*, 568.4 *conference*
dialectical 4, 463.9 *argumentative*
dialectically 4.24 *philosophically*, 473.19 *logically*, 478.24 *in answer*
dialectical materialism 4.7 *school of thought*, 367.2 *materialization*
dialectical materialist 367.3 *materialist*
dialectician 4.10 *philosopher*, 5.2 *linguist*, 463.5 *reasoner*, 478.10 *answerer*
dialecticism 463.3 *debate*

dialectics 463.3 *debate*
dialectological 5.38 *linguistic*
dialectologist 5.2 *linguist*
dialectology 5.1 *linguistics*, 5.26 *dialect*
dial gauge 268.8 *meter*
diallage 54 Minerals
dialling 534
dialling code 534.11 *dialling*
dialling tone 534.11 *dialling*
dialogical theology 7.13 *theology*
dialogue 4.5 *philosophical argument*, 51.2 *play*, 51.7 *dramaturgy*, 473.2 *logical argument*, 478.3 *question and answer*, 564.1 *faculty of speech*, 568.1 *conversation*
dial telephone 534.9 *telephone*
dial tone 534.11 *dialling*
dialyse 60.20 *practise surgery*, 134.10, 621.15 *purify*
dialysis 60.8 *treatment*, 134.2 *purification*, 621.2 *cleaning*, 630.12 *surgery*
diamagnetic 341.9 *abducent*
diamagnetism 56.59 *ferromagnetism*, 341.5 *repulsion*
diamanté 439.2 *quality of light*, 439.16 *bright*
diameter 52.37 *line*, 52.42 *circle*, 56.7 *space*, 122.7 *dividing line*, 158.4 *midline*, 176.8 *half*, 248.1 *space*, 259.1 *size*, 271.4 *breadth*, 313.4 *parts of a circle*, 333.1 *middle way*
diametral 52.81 *curvilinear*
diametral pitch 63.7 *gear*
diametric 52.81 *curvilinear*, 111.4 *opposite*, 158.11 *midway*, 663.21 *contrary*
diametrically 111.6 *oppositely*
diametrically opposed 663.21 *contrary*
diametrically opposite 111.4 *opposite*
diamond 54 Minerals, 54 Gemstones, 57 Chemical Elements, 22.1 *baseball*, 24.4 *carom*, 42.3 *card game terms*, 52.44 *polygon*, 310.3 *angled figure*, 310.9 *angled*, 373.7 *hard substance*, 617.8 *exceller*
diamondback 79 Reptiles
diamondbird 78 Birds
diamond in the rough 307.2 *shapeless thing*
diamond jubilee 214.6 *annually celebrated day*, 812.5 *anniversary*
diamond knot 74 Knots
diamond-like 373.1 *hard*
diamond mine 317.2 *concave land*
Diamond of Virgo 53 Other Groups of Stars
Diamond Sculls 36.5 *Henley trophies*
diamond-shaped 52.82 *polygonal*
diamond-studded 742.3 *opulent*, 811.24 *grand*
diamond wedding 812.5 *anniversary*
diamorphine 62 Medication
Diana 8 Deities, 37.4 *hunter*, 53.17 *moon*, 590.6 *hunter*, 825.4 *celibate person*
Diana complex 61.18 *complex*
dianetics 61.1 *psychology*
dianthus 84 Flowers and Flowering Plants
diapason 49.13 *melody*, 49.16 *musical note*, 423.1 *loudness*
diapedesis 326.3 *transmission*
diaper 295.23 *children's clothes*
diaphanous 274.4 *fine*, 442.2 *translucent*
diaphanously 442.13 *transparently*
diaphanousness 274.11 *fineness*, 442.6 *translucency*
diaphoresis 347.2 *outflow*, 353.8 *sweat*
diaphoretic 62.4 *drug type*, 62.17 *stimulating*, 353.48 *sweaty*
diaphragm 51.18 *stage lighting*, 66.18 *exposure time*, 247.3 *birth control*, 661.3 *barrier*
diapositive 66.12 *development*

diarist 48.14 *author*, 185.14 *time keeper*, 192.13 *chronicler*, 545.9 *recorder*, 560.10 *descriptive writer*
diaristic 192.17 *timekeeping*
diarize 171.8 *list*, 192.15 *chronologize*
diarrhoea 353.2 *defecation*, 624.3 *symptom*, 624.4 *disease*, 624.8 *indigestion*
diary 3.5 *chronicle*, 48.4 *nonfiction*, 171.5 *list of appointments*, 185.13 *timer*, 192.2 *timetable*, 511.4 *reminder*, 545.6 *record book*, 560.3 *narration*, 560.4 *factual account*, 605.5 *collection*
diaspora 162.7 *sprawl*, 252.3 *replacement*, 335.18 *diffraction*
Diaspora 104.7 *new arrival*
diaspore 54 Minerals
diastase 58.11 *enzyme*
diastasic 370.4 *leavening*
diaster 59.10 *cell division*
diastole 261.1 *growth*
diastrophic 54.54 *tectonic*
diastrophism 54.20 *earth movement*
diastyle 43.8 *column*
diatessaron 49.16 *musical note*
diathesis 624.1 *ill health*
diathiazinine 62 Medication
diatom 90 Algae
diatomaceous 90.7 *algal*
diatomaceous earth 90.5 *algal product*
diatomic 57.35 *combined*
diatonic scale 49.20 *key*
diatribe 564.8 *speech*, 567.1 *address*, 852.8 *berating*
diazepam 62 Medication, 630.8 *drug*
diazonium salt 57 Types of Compounds
diazotization 57 Types of Chemical Reaction
diazotize 57.26 *react*
dib 69.15 *cultivate*, 741.2 *cash*
dibasic 57.36 *acid*
dibasic acid 57.8 *acid*
dibber 69.6, 603.2 *garden tool*
dibble 69.6 *garden tool*, 69.15 *cultivate*
dibucaine 62 Medication
dice 42, 45.55 *cook*, 517.10 *cards*
diced 143.11 *partial*
dice game 42.1 *game*
dice with death 633.9 *face danger*
dicey 229.6 *motiveless*, 589.8 *chance*, 633.1 *dangerous*, 633.2 *unsafe*
dichasial cyme 84.4 *flower head*
dichasium 84.4 *flower head*
dichloralphenazone 62 Medication
dichlorophen 62 Medication
dichlorophenamide 62 Medication
dichotomic 176.13 *half*
dichotomize 176.16 *halve*
dichotomous 136.15 *separate*, 176.13 *half*
dichotomously 136.20 *separately*
dichotomy 4.8 *philosophical term*, 136.3 *separateness*, 176.7 *halving*
dichroic 456.6 *variegated*
dichroism 456.1 *variegation*
dick 16.17 *police officer*, 245.8 *organs of reproduction*
Dickens 48 Writers
dicker 737.3 *bargain*
dickhead 502.5 *ignorant person*
Dickinson 48 Poets
Dick Turpin 736.8 *thief*
dicky 295.8 *shirt*, 633.2 *unsafe*
dicky bow 295.3 *formal dress*, 295.14 *neckwear*
dicotyledon 83.3 *seed plant*
Dicotyledonae 83.3 *seed plant*
dicotyledonous 83.16 *taxonomic*
dicoumarol 62 Medication
dictaphone 545.10 *recording instrument*
dictate 12.11 *govern*, 571.15 *compel*, 593.10 *necessitate*,

653.2 *direct*, 654.5 *advise*, 692.1, 692.9 *command*, 695.6 *compel*, 696.14 *master*
dictate of conscience 586.11 *motive*
dictate to 688.19 *be authoritarian*, 692.11 *have authority over*
dictating 12.10 *governing*
dictator 653.14 *leader*, 688.10 *person of authority*, 690.4 *strict person*, 696.4 *absolute ruler*, 699.6 *law-maker*
dictatorial 12.9 *governmental*, 16.62 *above the law*, 126.13 *dominant*, 570.9 *autocratic*, 653.17 *managerial*, 688.14 *governmental*, 690.8 *severe*, 692.14 *commanding*, 695.9 *compelling*, 696.12 *masterful*
dictatorially 12.14 *politically*, 16.85 *summarily*, 126.16 *superiorly*, 690.11 *severely*, 692.16 *commandingly*, 696.16 *masterfully*
dictatorship 91.1 *country*, 400.11 *nation*, 653.4 *directorship*, 688.7 *type of rule*, 690.2 *suppression*
dictatorship of the proletariat 12.1 *government*, 688.7 *type of rule*
diction 520.1 *meaning*, 549.4 *literary style*, 564.4 *articulation*
dictionary 5, 171, 6.14 *school book*, 65.11 *application*, 528.5 *reference book*, 532.6 *book publishing*, 605.5 *collection*
dictionary compiler 5.2 *linguist*
dictionary of dialects 5.28 *dictionary*
dictionary of names 5.28 *dictionary*
dictionary of quotations 5.28 *dictionary*
dictionary of slang 5.28 *dictionary*
dictum 505.1 *maxim*, 535.2 *statement*, 537.4 *truism*, 564.7 *utterance*, 692.1 *command*
Dictyoptera 82 Orders of Insects
dictyopteran 82.10 *insectan*
dicynodon 79 Fossil Reptiles
didactic 586.19 *persuasive*, 654.7 *advising*
didactically 654.9 *advisably*
didacticism 654.1 *advice*
didactic poetry 48.6 *poetry*
didder 366.24 *shake*
diddle 539.8 *trick*, 539.10 *fraud*, 539.28 *trick*, 821.29 *make love*
diddled 539.36 *deceived*
diddler 539.17 *cheat*, 736.11 *dishonest person*
diddling 539.7 *tricking*, 821.5 *desire*
Diderot 4 Philosophers
didgeridoo 49 Musical Instruments
did you ever 786.14 *wonderful*
die 397, 42.3 *dice*, 43.9 *miscellaneous architectural features*, 100.13 *cease to exist*, 157.19 *expire*, 211.9 *have a mishap*, 218.6 *cease*, 306.2 *prototype*, 325.8 *be motionless*, 345.2 *withdraw*, 347.9 *exit*, 458.1 *disappear*, 641.4 *not act*, 684.5 *conclude*, 687.9 *be in trouble*, 722.9 *lose*
die a natural death 397.16 *meet one's fate*
die at one's post 575.8 *hold out*
die a violent death 397.16 *meet one's fate*
die away 100.13 *cease to exist*, 121.6 *change gradually*, 129.4 *decrease*, 157.18 *come to an end*, 218.6 *cease*, 424.5 *sound faint*
dieback 69.12 *pests and diseases*, 85.10 *tree disease*, 89.5 *fungal association*
die before one's spouse 824.9 *widow*
die before one's time 397.16 *meet one's fate*
die by one's own hand 397.16

meet one's fate, 398.21 *commit suicide*
died out 100.11 *no more*
die down 129.4 *decrease*, 325.8 *be motionless*
die fighting 397.16 *meet one's fate*, 574.11 *persist*
die for a cause 710.12 *offer one's life*
die for food 871.5 *fast*
die hard 397.16 *meet one's fate*, 574.11 *persist*
die-hard 217.3 *conservative person*, 217.8 *conservative*, 577.8 *obstinate person*, 575.5 *tenacious person*, 663.9 *opposer*, 669.5 *resister*, 669.11 *obstinate*
die in action 397.16 *meet one's fate*
die in bed 397.16 *meet one's fate*
die in combat 397.16 *meet one's fate*
die in harness 397.16 *meet one's fate*, 575.6 *persevere*
die in one's sleep 397.16 *meet one's fate*
die in poverty 397.16 *meet one's fate*
die in the attempt 596.3 *tackle*
dieldrin 68.14 *pest control*
dielectric 56.48 *insulation*, 64.7 *nonconductor*
dielectric coefficient 56.48 *insulation*
dielectric constant 56.48 *insulation*, 64.7 *nonconductor*
dielectric polarization 56.48 *insulation*
Diels 52 Scientists
Dien Bien Phu 93 Cities
dienoestrol 62 Medication
die of embarrassment 810.16 *be self-conscious*
die off 218.6 *cease*
die of love 821.24 *be in love*
die of neglect 397.16 *meet one's fate*
die of old age 397.16 *meet one's fate*
die of shame 810.16 *be self-conscious*
die on the ear 424.5 *sound faint*
die out 100.13 *cease to exist*, 129.4 *decrease*, 157.19 *expire*, 200.14 *pass*, 458.1 *disappear*
die peacefully 397.16 *meet one's fate*
die prematurely 397.16 *meet one's fate*
dieresis 543.7 *punctuation*
die Roman fashion 398.21 *commit suicide*
diesel 338.13 *fuel*
Diesel cycle 56.38 *thermodynamics*, 63.13 *engine cycle*
diesel-electric 72.4 *locomotive*
diesel-electric propulsion 338.2 *method of propulsion*
diesel engine 63.11 *engine*, 603.4 *machine*
diesel locomotive 72.4 *locomotive*
diesel oil 395.9 *petroleum*, 410.6 *oil*
diesel-propelled 338.19 *propelled*
diesel propulsion 338.2 *method of propulsion*
diet 274, 161.5 *conference*, 262.6 *become smaller*, 274.14 *become thin*, 350.6 *nutrition*, 350.23 *taste*, 630.13 *therapy*, 653.7 *council*, 699.5 *means of restraint*, 699.10 *restrain oneself*, 722.9 *lose*, 869.1 *self-restraint*, 869.5 *be self-restrained*, 871.1 *fasting*, 871.5 *fast*
dietary 350.6 *nutrition*, 350.27 *edible*, 630.13 *therapy*
dietary expert 350.19 *dietitian*
dietary plan 350.6 *nutrition*
dieter 722, 274.9 *thin person*, 350.18 *eater*, 869.4 *self-restrained person*, 871.4 *fasting person*
dietetic 350.27 *edible*, 630.17 *remedial*

dietetics 60.6 *health care*, 350.6 *nutrition*
die the death 397.16 *meet one's fate*, 879.6 *be punished*
diethylene glycol 57 Common Chemical Compounds
diethylpropion 62 Medication
diethylstilbesterol 62 Medication
dietician 350, 60.17 *paramedic*, 625.3 *hygienist*, 630.15 *healer*
dieting 274.3 *slimming*, 274.10 *diet*, 350.3 *delicate eating*, 350.6 *nutrition*, 699.14 *self-restrained*, 722.1 *loss*, 869.1 *self-restraint*, 869.8 *self-restrained*, 871.1 *fasting*
dietitian 350
diet of bread and water 871.2 *short rations*
diet plan 274.10 *diet*
diet programme 274.10 *diet*
diet regimen 350.6 *nutrition*
diet sheet 350.6 *nutrition*
die well 397.16 *meet one's fate*
die with honour 397.16 *meet one's fate*
die with one's boots on 397.16 *meet one's fate*, 574.11 *persist*, 575.6 *persevere*
die without issue 247.7 *be infertile*
die young 397.16 *meet one's fate*
differ 113.8 *be diverse*, 115.5 *be dissimilar*, 117.12 *be disparate*, 117.14, 434.11 *disagree*, 473.13 *argue*, 500.8 *dissent*, 666.5 *disagree*, 674.13 *conflict*, 820.12 *oppose*
difference 132, 666, 52.16 *subtraction*, 104.2 *foreignness*, 108.1 *unrelatedness*, 108.6 *unrelated*, 113.1 *diversity*, 115.1 *dissimilarity*, 117.1 *disparity*, 123.1 *inequality*, 136.3 *separateness*, 168.1 *nonconformity*, 169.4 *mathematical result*, 216.1 *change*, 309.1 *distortion*, 343.1 *divergence*, 434.6 *disagreement*, 456.1 *variegation*, 473.1 *argument*, 478.7 *numerical result*, 500.1 *dissent*, 544.8 *heraldic device*, 544.10 *identify*, 663.6 *contrariety*, 666.1 *disagreement*
difference machine 170.5 *computer*
difference of degree 123.1 *inequality*
difference of opinion 500.1 *dissent*, 666.1 *disagreement*, 764.8 *quarrel*
differences 500.1 *dissent*
differencing 544.8 *heraldic device*
different 666, 104.10 *foreign*, 113.5 *diverse*, 115.4 *dissimilar*, 117.7 *disparate*, 119.5 *novel*, 123.3 *unequal*, 165.15 *special*, 168.11 *nonconforming*, 216.11 *changeable*, 343.6 *divergent*, 473.7 *arguing*, 663.20 *discordant*
differential 52.31 *differentiation*, 52.76 *functional*, 63.8 *machine element*, 121.3 *gradation*, 121.7 *gradational*, 169.9 *fractional*, 170.15 *mathematical*, 481.9 *discriminating*
differential calculus 52.30 *calculus*
differential diagnosis 60.7 *diagnosis*
differential equation 52.27 *equation*, 52.31 *differentiation*
differential focusing 66.13 *framing*
differential gear 71 Motor Vehicle Parts
differential geometry 52.34 *geometry*
differentially 121, 481.15 *discriminatingly*
differential operator 52.50 *scalar quantity*
differential psychology 61.1 *psychology*
differentiate 115, 52.95 *evalu-*

ate, 103.11 *characterize,* 113.8
be diverse, 121.5 *measure,*
136.10 *set apart,* 165.22 *characterize,* 170.9 *add,* 481.12 *discriminate,* 544.10 *identify*
differentiated 121.7 *gradational,*
136.17 *unjoined,* 481.11 *judged*
differentiation 52, 115.1 *dissimilarity,* 121.3 *gradation,* 165.1
speciality, 170.1 *calculation,*
481.1 *discrimination,* 492.1
judgment, 544.1 *identification*
differently 666, 104.18 *extraneously,* 113.10, 113.10 *diversely,*
115.7, 117.15 *dissimilarly,*
119.8 *originally,* 123.7 *unequally,* 216.15 *changeably,*
309.13 *asymmetrically,* 343.16
divergently, 473.17 *argumentatively*
differentness 165.1 *speciality*
different opinions 113.4 *dissension*
different time 197
Different Time 197
different wavelength 525.2 *misinterpretation*
differing 117.10 *disagreeing,*
500.7 *dissenting,* 666.9 *disagreeing,* 666.10 *different*
differ with 666.5 *disagree*
difficult 106, 523, 659, 41.13
ice-skating, 251.8 *circumstantial,* 373.4 *mentally hard,*
477.13 *problematic,* 491.3 *confused,* 529.11 *mysterious,* 551.2
obscure, 633.1 *dangerous,*
644.11 *laborious,* 687.6 *adverse,*
818.6 *bad-mannered*
difficult character 713.4 *protester*
difficult choice 580.8 *choice*
difficult circumstances 106, 251
difficulties 105.2 *predicament,*
743.5 *poverty*
difficultly 106, 659
difficult person 659
difficult position 659.5 *predicament*
difficult problem 529
difficult question 477
difficult task 659
difficult terrain 659.3 *difficult task*
difficult to comprehend 314.5 *ambiguous*
difficult to handle 659.14 *troublesome*
difficult to hear 421.7 *unheard*
difficult to live with 659.14 *troublesome*
difficult to see 438
difficult word 5.17 *word*
difficulty 659, 30.1 *gymnastics,*
41.7 *ice-dancing,* 477.1 *question,* 523.11 *unintelligibility,*
529.3 *mystification,* 551.1 *obscurity,* 616.3 *inconvenience,*
620.7 *defect,* 661.2 *obstacle,*
666.1 *disagreement,* 687.1 *adversity*
Difficulty 659
difficulty in speaking 563.2 *inarticulation*
difficulty of the dive 39.6 *diving*
diffidence 542.5 *reserve,* 566.4
taciturnity, 810.4, 816.2 *shyness*
diffident 542.15 *reserved,* 566.1
taciturn, 810.11 *shy*
diffidently 542.25 *reservedly,*
810.18 *shyly*
diffract 162.12 *disperse,* 335.12
deflect
diffracted 335.26 *diffractive*
diffracted wave 365.5 *wave*
diffraction 335, 56.15 *wave property,* 56.29 *optical element,*
162.5 *divergence,* 365.5 *wave*
diffraction grating 56.29 *optical element*
diffractive 335, 162.28 *dispersive*
diffractively 162.29 *dispersively*
diffuse 553, 5.43 *phrasal,*
162.12 *disperse,* 162.19 *dispersed,* 164.25 *broadcast,*
253.11 *be present,* 326.11 *transfer,* 334.7 *circuitous,* 335.12 *deflect,* 335.26 *diffractive,* 343.13

radiate, 532.13 *make public,*
551.2 *obscure,* 557.4 *ornate,*
610.7 *superfluous*
diffused 162.22 *distributed,*
335.26 *diffractive,* 441.6 *murky*
diffusely 162, 553, 343.16 *divergently*
diffuse nebula 53.8 *interstellar medium*
diffuseness 553, 5.24 *phrasing,*
521.5 *empty talk,* 551.1 *obscurity,* 557.2 *affectation,* 610.3 *superfluity*
Diffuseness 553
diffuser 66.15 *lighting,* 326.9 *disease carrier*
diffusing filter 66.20 *filter*
diffusion 56.15 *wave property,*
162.1 *dispersion,* 253.2 *omnipresence,* 326.3 *transmission,*
335.18 *diffraction,* 343.3 *radiation,* 528.2 *communication,*
553.1 *diffuseness*
diffusionism 1.5 *anthropological concept*
diffusionist 1.11 *anthropological*
diffusion pump 57.20 *surface chemistry*
diffusive 162.28 *dispersive,*
253.7 *present,* 553.3 *diffuse*
diffusively 162.29 *dispersively,*
553.7 *diffusely*
diffusiveness 253.2 *omnipresence,* 553.1 *diffuseness*
dig 63.30 *engineer,* 68.17 *farm,*
69.15 *cultivate,* 200.8 *excavation,* 277.14 *deepen,* 317.7
make concave, 326.15 *take away,* 330.1 *impel,* 330.13
blow, 366.9 *jolt,* 522.6 *understand,* 644.6 *work,* 850.6 *taunt*
dig a foundation 284.11 *support*
dig a hole 322.20 *hole*
digamous 823.23 *monogamous*
digamy 823.3 *types of marriage*
dig a pit for 592.13 *plot,* 657.5
be cunning
dig at 850.25 *taunt*
dig coal 410.11 *fuel*
dig down 360.15 *tunnel*
digest 140.5 *combine,* 152.7 *catalogue,* 152.15 *categorize,* 262.3
contracted thing, 270.3 *shortened version,* 270.10 *shorten,*
299.1, 299.5 *outline,* 348.13 *absorb,* 350.21 *eat,* 562.1 *summary,* 562.8 *summarize,* 673.4
succumb
Digest 16.1 *the law*
digested 140.7 *combined,* 270.8
shortened
digestible 350.27 *edible*
digestibly 350.29 *edibly*
digestion 140.1 *combination,*
348.5 *absorption,* 350.1 *eating,*
393.5 *pulping*
digestive 348.17 *absorbent,*
630.6 *purgative,* 630.17 *remedial*
digestive biscuit 45.39 *loaf*
digestive juice 352.2 *secreted substance*
dig for 590.8 *pursue*
digger 71 Motor Vehicles, **317,**
63.29 *construction equipment,*
322.3 *person who opens,* 355.10
excavator
Diggers 7 Christian Movements
digger wasp 82 Insects
digging 277.1 *depth,* 360.7 *tunnelling*
digging in one's toes 573.2 *refusing*
digging out 355
digging up 355.3 *digging out*
digging up the body 399.7 *inquest*
digging up the past 3.12 *historicism*
dight 295.33 *dress up*
dig in 574.10 *insist,* 671.21 *entrench,* 676.14 *battle*
dig in one's heels 217.5 *be permanent,* 490.20 *be certain,*
669.7 *be obstinate*
dig in one's toes 575.8 *hold out,*
577.9 *be obstinate*
digit 52.9 *numeral,* 169.1 *number*

digital 52.71, 169.7 *numerical,*
169.8 *odd*
digital circuit 64.13 *circuit*
digital clock 191 Timepieces
and Timers, 56.87, 192.6 *clock*
digital computer 65.3 *computer*
digital display 192.8 *face*
digitalin 58.3 *carbohydrate*
digitalis 62 Medication
digitally 52.87 *mathematically,*
169.12 *numerically*
digital meter 56.82 *measuring instrument*
digital reading 56.82 *measuring instrument*
digital readout 56.82 *measuring instrument*
digital watch 192.7 *watch*
digitizer 65.7 *peripheral*
digitoxin 62 Medication
diglyceride 58.7 *fat*
dignification 8.9 *deification,* 9.1
worship
dignified 8.15 *deified,* 10.21 *ritualistic,* 558.3 *elegant,* 611.6 *notable,* 652.17 *well-behaved,*
794.5 *refined,* 805.18 *prestigious,* 811.22 *majestic,* 813.6
formal
dignify 8.17 *deify,* 9.7 *worship,*
813.10 *celebrate*
dignitary 696.3 *leader*
dignities 817.3 *courtesies*
dignity 558.1 *elegance,* 652.2
good conduct, 794.1 *elegance,*
805.4 *prestige,* 813.1 *formality*
dig one's heels in 663.17 *withstand*
dig one's toes in 574.10 *insist*
dig one's toes into 726.6 *retain*
dig out 355, 317.7 *make concave*
digoxin 62 Medication
digraph 5.13 *letter,* 5.16 *spoken letter*
digraphic 5.41 *lettered*
digress 104.13 *be extraneous,*
108.10 *be unrelated,* 160.15
lose one's train of thought, 286.6
be oblique, 334.4 *detour,* 335.1
deviate, 363.8 *detour,* 335.6 *be circuitous*
digressing 335.25 *wandering*
digression 48.3 *aspect of fiction,*
160.7 *broken thread,* 286.1
obliqueness, 334.2 *detour,*
335.13 *deviation,* 335.16 *wandering,* 363.2 *circuitousness,*
553.2 *circumlocution*
digressive 160, 286.4 *oblique,*
334.7 *circuitous,* 335.25 *wandering,* 553.4 *circumlocutory*
digressively 553.8 *circuitously*
digs 256.1 *habitat*
dig up 355.13 *dig out,* 399.9 *exhume,* 496.2 *detect,* 530.5 *disclose,* 721.11 *acquire*
dig up the past 3.21 *antiquarianize,* 200.16 *excavate*
dihedral 73.7 *miscellaneous aviation terms*
dihedral angle 52.39 *angle*
dihydralazine 62 Medication
dihydrate 57.10 *salt*
dihydrocodeine 62 Medication,
62 Medication
dihydroergotamine 62 Medication
dihydrogen 57 Chemical Elements
dihydrostreptomycin 62 Medication
diiodohydroxyquinoline 62 Medication
Dijon 93 Cities
dik-dik 77 Placental Mammals
dike 327.11 *channel,* 661.3 *barrier*
dikephobia 777 Phobias by Name
dilacerate 136.9 *separate*
dilaceration 136.3 *separateness*
dilapidate 628.5 *hurt*
dilapidated 238, 628, 141.5 *disintegrated,* 111.6 *disintegrating,*
244.15 *destroyed,* 379.1 *brittle,*
599.9 *used,* 633.2 *unsafe,* 743.3
beggarly

dilapidation 628, 129.1 *decrease,*
238.1 *weakness,* 244.4 *ruin,*
599.6 *use,* 743.7 *beggary*
dilatability 261.2 *enlargeability*
dilatable 261.9 *enlargeable,*
372.2 *rarefied*
dilatableness 261.2 *enlargeability*
dilatant 261.9 *enlargeable,* 372.2
rarefied
dilatation 52.48 *transformation,*
261.1 *growth,* 372.4 *rarefaction,*
541.2 *enlargement*
dilatational 372.2 *rarefied*
dilate 128.4 *increase,* 248.20 *extend,* 261.5 *make bigger,* 261.6
become bigger, 271.11 *broaden,*
372.6 *make sparse,* 541.8 *enlarge,* 553.5 *be diffuse,* 721.10
augment
dilated 261.7 *bigger,* 541.13 *enlarged*
dilater 261.4 *enlarger*
dilating 261.8 *growing,* 372.2 *rarefied*
dilation 52.48 *transformation,*
128.1 *increase,* 261.1 *growth,*
271.4 *breadth,* 372.4 *rarefaction,* 541.2 *enlargement,* 721.2
augmentation
dilational 261.9 *enlargeable*
dilative 261.9 *enlargeable,* 372.2
rarefied
dilatometer 268.8 *meter*
dilatometric 268.16 *micrometric*
dilatometry 268.2 *micrometry*
dilator 62.4 *drug type,* 261.4 *enlarger*
dilatorily 209.15 *late,* 328.16
slowly
dilatoriness 209.3 *delayed action,*
328.8 *slowness*
dilatory 209.9 *late,* 328.7 *delayed,* 643.3 *not participating*
dilemma 105.2 *predicament,*
106.4 *difficult circumstances,*
477.4 *difficult question,* 580.8
choice, 659.4 *problem*
dilettante 481.6 *discriminating person,* 502.5 *ignorant person,*
502.7 *semi-skilled,* 576.15 *indecisive person,* 794.4 *refined person*
dilettantism 481.2 *judiciousness,*
502.2 *half-knowledge*
diligence 467, 469.1 *carefulness,*
575.3 *constancy,* 642.8 *assiduity,* 719.1 *observance*
diligent 467, 469.9 *careful,*
575.10 *persevering,* 642.20 *industrious,* 644.10 *working,*
719.7 *observant*
diligently 467.15 *attentively,*
469.12 *carefully,* 719.8 *observantly*
dill 45 Herbs and Spices, 413.5
herbs
dill pickle 413.2 *seasoning*
dillseed 45 Herbs and Spices
dill water 630.6 *purgative*
dilly 861.17 *good thing*
dilly-dally 209.7 *wait,* 328.2 *hesitate,* 576.7 *be irresolute*
dilly-dallying 328.7 *delayed,*
328.11 *lingering*
diloxanide 62 Medication
Dilthey 4 Philosophers
diluent 387.9 *solvent*
dilute 162, 162, 389, 412,
57.25 *solidify,* 57.32 *solid,*
129.5 *make smaller,* 133.8 *mix,*
133.12 *mixed,* 140.5 *combine,*
216.8 *cause change,* 233.9
change, 238.7 *weaken,* 274.16
make thin, 362.4 *debase,* 372.2
rarefied, 372.6 *make sparse,*
412.5 *tasteless,* 542.22 *play down*
diluted 389, 133.12 *mixed,*
162.27 *dilute,* 238.13 *insufficient,* 274.5 *thinned,* 351.17
drinkable, 372.2 *rarefied,* 412.5
tasteless, 542.17 *insipid,* 542.19
downplayed
diluter 274.13 *thinner*
dilute solution 57.3 *phase*
dilution 162, 389, 412, 133.1
mixture, 216.1 *change,* 238.1

weakness, 274.12 *thinning*, 372.4 *rarefaction*, 412.1 *tastelessness*, 542.9 *down-playing*
dim 49 Musical Terms, **441**, 273.3 *thick-witted*, 438.2 *difficult to see*, 438.7 *become invisible*, 438.8 *make invisible*, 440.8 *dark*, 440.13 *become dark*, 440.14 *make dark*, 441.8 *stupid*, 443.2 *shady*, 443.5 *unintelligent*, 443.11 *make opaque*, 445.6 *decolour*, 445.7 *colourless*, 447.2 *dark*, 460.6 *unintelligent*, 502.6 *ignorant*, 523.4 *difficult*, 531.9 *disguise*, 555.4 *deemphasize*, 722.12 *lessen*
dim and distant past 3.9 *distant past*
dimbo 502.5 *ignorant person*, 508.3 *foolish person*
dime 612.8 *trifle*, 741.8 *American money*
dime defence 19.10 *defence*
dimenhydrinate 62 Medication
dimension 75, 52.35 *space*, 120.1 *quantity*, 248.1 *space*, 259.1 *size*
dimensional 248.11 *spatial*
dimensional analysis 75.5 *dimension*
dimensions 52.35 *space*, 457.3 *external appearance*
dime-store 754.9 *cheap*
dime's worth 875.6 *drug*
dimeter 48.9 *metre*
dimethisterone 62 Medication
dimethoate 69.8 *weedkiller*
dimethothiazine 62 Medication
dimethylchlortetracycline 62 Medication
dimethylsulphoxide 62 Medication
dimethyltriptomine 62 Medication
Dimetrodon 79 Fossil Reptiles
dimidiate 544.10 *identify*
dimidiation 54.8 *heraldic device*
diminish 121.6 *change gradually*, 127.11 *become inferior*, 129.4 *decrease*, 131.3 *subtract*, 182.8 *reduce*, 238.6 *be weak*, 238.7 *weaken*, 242.4 *moderate*, 542.22 *play down*, 607.1 *waste*, 722.12 *lessen*, 767.9 *relieve*, 806.23 *abase*
diminished 127.13 *insignificant*, 129.6 *decreasing*, 131.7 *reduced*, 182.7 *fewer*, 238.9 *dilapidated*, 542.19 *downplayed*, 806.3 *humbled*, 806.4 *self-abasing*
diminished responsibility 510.1 *insanity*
diminished seventh 179.3 *seven*
diminishing 121.7 *gradational*, 182.7 *fewer*
diminishingly 129.8, 131.9 *decreasingly*
diminishing returns 129.1 *decrease*, 722.2 *financial loss*
diminishment 542.9 *downplaying*, 806.11 *self- abasement*
diminuendo 49 Musical Terms, 129.1 *decrease*, 129.6 *decreasing*, 262.1 *contraction*
diminution 129.1 *decrease*, 131.1 *subtraction*, 242.1 *moderation*, 362.11 *lowering*, 562.2 *outline*, 609.9 *scarcity*, 722.4 *lessening*
diminutive 5.35 *part of speech*, 5.44 *grammatical*, 260.7 *little*, 270.7 *short*, 560.8 *name*
diminutively 260.8 *in a small way*, 270.12 *short*
diminutiveness 260.1 *littleness*, 270.1 *shortness*
dimity 67 Natural Fabrics
dim lighting 441.1 *dimness*
dimly 441, 438.9 *invisibly*, 440.15 *darkly*, 445.9 *colourlessly*
dimly lit 441.5 *dim*
dimmed 441
dimmed headlights 439.6 *electric light*
dimmed lights 441.1 *dimness*
dim memory 512.3 *poor memory*

dimmer 71 Motor Vehicle Parts, 64.28 *plug*
dimmer switch 440.2 *darkening*, 441.1 *dimness*
dimming 441, 129.1 *decrease*, 440.2, 440.9 *darkening*, 722.4 *lessening*
dimming switch 64.28 *plug*
dimness 441, 440.1 *darkness*, 441.4 *stupidity*, 443.6 *opaqueness*, 460.2 *unintelligence*, 519.5 *fantasy*, 527.11 *mysteriousness*, 628.7 *deterioration*
Dimness 441
dimple 317.3 *cavity*
dimpled 317.5 *concave*
dims 439.6 *electric light*
dim sight 436.2 *poor sight*
dim-sighted 436.9 *weak-sighted*
dim sum 45.48 *Chinese dish*
dim view 852.2 *disrespect*
dimwit 460.3 *unintelligent person*, 508.3 *foolish person*
dim-witted 238.10 *ill*, 441.8 *stupid*, 443.5, 460.6 *unintelligent*, 502.6 *ignorant*, 508.5 *foolish*, 656.1 *unskilful*
dim-wittedness 441.4 *stupidity*, 460.2 *unintelligence*
din 153.5 *commotion*, 366.2 *tumult*, 423.2 *outcry*, 423.8 *be loud*, 434.2 *dissonant noise*
DIN 75 General Units
dinar 741.11 *national coins*
dine 350.24 *have a meal*, 350.25 *provide food*
dine alfresco 289.12 *be outside*
dined 815.11 *popular*
dine out 350.24 *have a meal*, 815.11 *be sociable*
diner 350.15, 350.15 *eating place*, 350.18 *eater*, 411.5 *taster*
diner-in 350.18 *eater*
diner-out 350.18 *eater*
Diners' Club 744.2 *credit card*
Dinesen 48 Writers
dinette 256.7 *room*, 350.15 *eating place*
ding 91 Names for Inhabitants, 36.7 *windsurfing*
dingbat 508.3 *foolish person*
ding-dong 112.4 *monotony*, 112.8 *monotonous*, 122.8 *on equal terms*, 426.5 *ringing*, 674.16 *competitive*
ding-dong battle 674.1 *contention*
ding-dong fight 674.6 *fight*
ding-dong race 122.2 *equilibrium*
ding-dong theory 5.37 *linguistic theory*
dinge 91 Names for Inhabitants
dinghy 74 Ships and Boats, 36.2 *sailing boat*, 36.4 *rowing*
dinghy racing 36.1 *sailing*
dingily 441.12 *dimly*, 445.9 *colourlessly*
dinginess 441.2 *murk*, 622.1 *dirtiness*
dingle 98.8 *valley*, 317.2 *concave land*
dingleberry 353.5 *faeces*
dingo 77 Placental Mammals
dingy 440.8 *dark*, 441.7 *dimmed*, 444.13 *soft-hued*, 445.7 *colourless*, 447.2 *dark*, 559.10 *ugly*, 622.7 *dirty*, 628.13 *dilapidated*
din in 554.6 *emphasize*
dining 350.4 *eating meals*, 350.26 *eating*
dining car 72.6 *rolling stock*, 350.15 *eating place*
dining chair 47.2 *chair*
dining-club member 350.18 *eater*
dining hall 256.7 *room*, 350.15 *eating place*
dining kitchen 256.7 *room*
dining out 350.4 *eating meals*
dining room 6.15 *schoolroom*, 256.7 *room*, 350.15 *eating place*
dining table 47.4 *table*
dining together 819.4 *act of friendship*
din into 183.18 *harp*
dinitro ortho cresol 69.8 *weedkiller*

Dinka 1 Peoples, **5** Languages and Groups of Languages
dinkiness 260.1 *littleness*
dinkum 537.19 *authentic*
dinkum oil 537.1 *truth*
dinky 150.13 *orderly*, 260.7 *little*, 612.4 *trivial*
dinner 205.5 *night thing*, 350.12 *meal*, 815.5 *party*
dinner bell 543.4 *signal*
dinner dance 350.13 *feast*
dinner dress 295.3 *formal dress*, 295.7 *frock*
dinner gong 543.4 *signal*
dinner gown 295.7 *frock*
dinner jacket 813.4 *formal dress*
dinner party 665.7 *social gathering*, 815.5 *party*
dinner plate 258.16 *crockery*
dinner service 258.16 *crockery*
dinning 423.6 *loud*
DIN number 66.10 *graininess*
dinoflagellate 90 Algae
dinosaur 79.6 *extinct reptile*, 200.10 *fossilization*, 202.5 *old thing*, 202.8 *prehistoric animal*, 259.9 *big thing*
dint 330.3 *hit*, 330.13 *blow*
diocesan 7.8 *priest*, 7.17 *priestly*, 249.18 *local*
diocese 7.9 *priesthood*, 249.5 *state*
Dio Chrysostom 4 Philosophers
diode 64, 56.44 *semiconductor*, 56.55 *circuit*
diode rectifier 64.18 *diode*
dioecious 84.12 *of flowers*
Diogenes 834.2 *misanthrope*
Diogenes Laertius 4 Philosophers
Diogenes of Sinope 4 Philosophers
diol 57 Types of Compounds
Dionaea 539.13 *snare*
Dionysia 10.16 *religious festival*
dionysiac dance 46.4 *historic dancing*
Dionysus 8 Deities
Diophantine equation 52 Named Concepts
Diophantus of Alexandria 52 Scientists
diopside 54 Minerals, **54** Gemstones
dioptase 54 Minerals
dioptre 75 Scientific and Technical Units
dioptric 442.1 *transparent*
diorite 54 Common Rocks, **54** Minerals
Dioscorides Pedanius 52 Scientists
dioxin 631.9 *pollution*
dioxygen 57 Chemical Elements
dip 45.15 *sauce*, 54.45 *magnetic pole*, 73.7 *miscellaneous aviation terms*, 98.8 *valley*, 317.2 *concave land*, 326.15 *take away*, 354.4 *immerse*, 354.10 *immersion*, 360.5 *dive*, 360.6 *slide*, 360.12 *drop*, 360.14 *slide*, 362.3 *bring down*, 362.14 *depression*, 389.11 *wash*, 439.5 *incandescent light*, 440.14 *make dark*, 441.10 *make dim*, 621.5 *ablutions*, 621.14 *bathe*, 736.8 *thief*
dip a toe in the water 596.4 *test*
Dipavamsa 7.12 *religious text*
dip down 360.9 *descend*
dipenzepin 62 Medication
dipeptide 58.8 *amino acid*
diphenhydramine 62 Medication
diphenoxylate 62 Medication
diphtheria 624.6 *infection*, 624.9 *respiratory disease*
diphthong 5.16 *spoken letter*, 564.7 *utterance*
dip into 748.1 *expend*
dipipanone 62 Medication
diplegia 624.17 *nervous disorder*
diplice 49 Musical Instruments
Diplodocus 79 Fossil Reptiles
diploid 59.25 *genetic*, 69.5 *gardening*
diploid number 59.14 *chromosome*

diploidy 59.14 *chromosome*
diplo-kithara 49 Musical Instruments
diploma 485.3 *qualifications*, 545.2 *certificate*, 703.3 *authority*, 708.2 *permit*
diplomacy 12.2 *politics*, 592.2 *policy*, 652.8 *treatment*, 652.9 *tactics*, 657.1 *cunning*, 678.2 *mediation*, 716.1 *negotiation*, 817.2 *good manners*
Diploma in Education 485 Educational Qualifications
Diploma in Higher Education 485 Educational Qualifications
diplomat 592.8 *planner*, 657.3 *cunning person*, 678.3 *mediator*, 703.5 *commissioner*, 706.1 *delegate*, 707.3 *agent*, 715.4 *contractor*, 716.4 *negotiator*
diplomatic 507.5 *wise*, 655.6 *skilful*, 678.6 *mediatory*, 706.6 *delegated*, 707.7 *deputizing*, 716.8 *negotiated*, 817.8 *good-mannered*
diplomatic agent 707.3 *agent*
diplomatically 507.9 *wisely*, 678.7 *mediatorially*, 706.8 *representatively*, 707.8 *by proxy*, 716.9 *feasibly*, 817.15 *genteelly*
diplomatic bag 534.3 *correspondence*
diplomatic code 813.5 *etiquette*
diplomatic corps 706.2 *representative body*
diplomatic excuse 538.5 *half-truth*
diplomatic immunity 698.1 *freedom*, 848.1 *exemption*
diplomatic incident 659.7 *awkward situation*
diplomatic language 5.7 *international language*
diplomatic officer 706.1 *delegate*
diplomatic pouch 258.8 *bag*
diplomatic service 706.2 *representative body*
diplomatic staff 706.2 *representative body*
diplomatist 655.5 *expert*, 657.3 *cunning person*, 678.3 *mediator*
diplopia 436.2 *poor sight*
diplopod 81.4 *arthropod*
Diplopoda 81.4 *arthropod*
Diplura 82 Orders of Insects
dipluran 82.10 *insectan*
dipnoan 80.2 *fish*
dipody 48.9 *metre*
dipole 56.50 *electric charge*, 534.17 *antenna*
dipole antenna 534.17 *antenna*
dipole–dipole interaction 57.11 *chemical bond*
dipole moment 56.50 *electric charge*
dip out of 685.6 *drop out*
dipped 389.24 *flooded*
dipped headlights 439.6 *electric light*
dipped lights 441.1 *dimness*
dipper 78 Birds, 258.17 *ladle*, 440.2 *darkening*
dipping 360.4 *fall*, 360.18 *falling*, 440.9 *darkening*, 621.5 *ablutions*
dipping the colours 849.5 *presenting arms*
dippy 510.11 *insane*
diprophylline 62 Medication
Diprotodon 77 Marsupials
dipsomania 61.15 *compulsion*, 351.1 *drinking*, 510.4 *delusion*, 874.16 *alcoholism*
dipsomaniac 874.5 *drunken*, 874.17 *drunkard*
dipsomaniacal 351.16 *drinking*
dipstick 268.6 *measuring instrument*, 656.10 *unskilled person*
dip switch 440.2 *darkening*
Diptera 82 Orders of Insects
dipteran 82.10 *insectan*
diptych 50.8 *painting*, 176.2 *double*
Dirac 52 Scientists
Dirac notation 56.80 *quantum theory*
Dirac's equation 56 Named Laws
dire 618.5 *harmful*, 687.6 *ad-*

verse, 777.10 *frightening*, 862.9
detrimental
**direct 134, 166, 332, 332,
653**, 5.44 *grammatical*, 12.11
govern, 38.5 *soccer*, 41.12 *ski*,
49.40 *conduct*, 51.36 *dramatize*,
126.10 *lead*, 191.5 *immediate*,
228.9 *motivate*, 233.8 *influence*,
243.10 *produce*, 251.10 *situate*,
271.3 *broad-minded*, 312.1
straight, 312.2 *straightforward*,
312.5 *honourable*, 332.9 *directly*, 333.5 *undeviating*, 381.2
outspoken, 442.4 *easily seen
through*, 483.8 *evidential*, 522.2
simple, 537.18 *truthful*, 543.9
use signs, 550.3 *clear*, 556.3 *natural*, 567.10 *send*, 597.1 *undertake*, 640.4 *act*, 640.6 *effective*,
652.14 *behave towards*, 652.15
conduct, 653.1 *manage*, 688.18
have authority, 692.9 *command*,
696.14 *master*
directable 332.14 *directed*
direct access 65.17 *computing
term*
direct approach 327.2 *route*
direct belay 34.3 *climbing technique*
direct cannon 24.3 *English billiards*
direct carving 50.12 *sculpture*
direct communication 8.8 *divine
manifestation*
direct current 56.51, 64.9 *electric
current*, 235.7 *electrical power*
direct debit 746.1 *payment*
direct descent 41.2 *cross-country
skiing*
direct dialling 534.11 *dialling*
direct distance dialing 534.11 *dialling*
direct drill 68.17 *farm*
direct dye 67.6 *dye*
directed 332, 51.37 *dramatic*,
228.12 *motivated*, 490.5 *inevitable*
directed energy 644.4 *exertion*
directed number 52.5 *number*
directed towards 251.6 *situated*,
332.14 *directed*
direct evidence 483.5 *legal evidence*
direct free kick 38.2 *football play*
direct hit 25.2 *grip*
directing 332, 16.48 *jurisdictional*, 233.11 *influential*, 653.4
directorship, 653.17 *managerial*
direct intuition 8.8 *divine manifestation*
direction 332, 12.1 *government*,
12.3 *governance*, 51.12 *production*, 52.37 *line*, 52.50 *scalar
quantity*, 166.4 *guide*, 166.8 *authority*, 230.4 *management*,
251.1 *situation*, 327.2 *route*,
332.5 *directions*, 586.11 *motive*,
640.1 *action*, 652.8 *treatment*,
653.4 *directorship*, 653.5 *guide*,
654.3 *precept*, 688.1 *authority*,
688.4 *governance*, 692.1 *command*
Direction 332
directional 324, 332, 228.11
motivational, 251.7 *situational*,
543.14 *signifying*, 653.17 *managerial*
directional antenna 534.17 *antenna*
directional reference 74.5 *navigation*
directional sign 543.1 *sign*
direction finder 332.3 *orientation*
direction-finding 653.5 *guide*
direction indicator 543.5 *indicator*
directions 332
directive 16.48 *jurisdictional*,
166.1 *rule*, 228.11 *motivational*, 332.16 *directing*, 586.19
persuasive, 692.1 *command*,
692.14 *commanding*
directive therapy 61.3 *psychiatric
treatment*
directly 332, 5.52 *grammatically*, 134.20 *homogenously*,
208.17 *early*, 208.18 *soon*,
312.12 *straight*, 312.13 *straight-*

forwardly, 381.12 *bluntly*,
442.13 *transparently*, 520.13
meaningfully, 537.36 *truthfully*,
537.39 *accurately*, 550.4
clearly, 556.8 *simply*, 640.8 *effectively*
directly proportional to 52.88
equal to
direct mail 586.6 *advertising*
directness 312, 191.1 *immediacy*, 271.6 *broad-mindedness*,
312.6 *straightness*, 381.6 *outspokenness*, 522.10 *simplicity*,
537.5 *truthfulness*, 550.1 *clarity*, 556.6 *naturalness*
direct object 5.35 *part of speech*
direct one's course for 332.7 *take
a direction*
direct oneself 332.7 *take a direction*
director 653, 15.6 *employer*,
51.25 *producer*, 230.5 *operator*,
233.5 *influential person*, 243.9
producer, 298.3 *interfacer*,
534.17 *antenna*, 640.3 *doer*,
652.10 *conductor*, 653.14
leader, 688.10 *person of authority*, 696.9 *company leader*
directorate 653.6 *governing body*
direct order 692.1 *command*
directorial 653.17 *managerial*
director of studies 653.13 *director*
directors 653.6 *governing body*
directorship 653, 12.3 *governance*, 126.2 *leadership*, 688.5
position of authority
directory 65.17 *computing term*,
152.7 *catalogue*, 171.3 *dictionary*, 528.5 *reference book*,
545.6 *record book*
direct primary 580.12 *election*
direct proof 52.66 *proof*
direct proportion 107.2 *interrelatedness*
direct radiation 55.22 *sun*
direct ratio 107.2 *interrelatedness*
directrix 52.42 *circle*
direct tax 749.2 *money received*,
751.7 *tax*
direct tide 97.2 *tide*
direct to 332.6 *direct*
direct vote 580.10 *vote*
direct wave 534.15 *transmitted
wave*
dire necessity 743.5 *poverty*
dire straits 633.5 *danger*, 743.5
poverty
dirge 48.7 *poem*, 399.2 *funeral*,
774.2 *lament*
dirgeful 399.11 *funeral*
dirgelike 399.11 *funeral*, 774.4
lamenting
dirham 741.11 *national coins*
Dirichlet series 52 Named Concepts
dirigible 73.8 *aircraft*, 332.14 *directed*
dirigisme 12.3 *governance*
dirk 380.8 *sharp-pointed thing*,
680.8 *sharp weapon*
dirndl 295.6 *skirt*
dirofilariasis 81.11 *helminthic
disease*
Dirona 8 Deities
dirt 777 Phobias by Topic,
622, 132.2 *residue*, 353.5 *faeces*, 384.5 *powder*, 393.13 *mud*,
440.3 *dark colour*, 528.1 *information*, 614.6 *refuse*, 618.10
poverty, 877.2 *indecency*
dirt-cheap 754.9 *cheap*
dirt-encrusted 622.7 *dirty*
dirt farmer 68.15 *agriculturist*
dirt farming 68.4 *arable farming*
dirt-free 621.16 *clean*
dirtily 622, 384.30 *flakily*,
626.8 *unhygienically*, 827.12
swearingly
dirtiness 622, 151.3 *untidiness*,
393.3 *muddiness*, 443.6 *opaqueness*, 618.10 *poverty*, 626.1 *lack
of hygiene*, 628.10 *impairment*
Dirtiness 622
dirt road 71.2, 327.3 *road*, 375.8
rough ground
dirt track 32.7 *horseracing*, 375.8
rough ground

dirt-track 33.11 *racing*
dirt-track race 33.5 *motorcycle
racing*
dirt-track racing 33.5 *motorcycle
racing*, 674.4 *race*
dirty 622, 622, 55.48 *stormy*,
97.7 *oceanic*, 151.15 *untidy*,
384.16 *powdery*, 393.17 *muddy*,
440.10 *dark-coloured*, 441.7
dimmed, 441.11 *tarnish*, 443.2
shady, 447.11 *blacken*, 470.5 *indifferent*, 618.4 *poor*, 622.9 *obscene*, 626.5 *unhygienic*, 626.6
contagious, 628.3 *make worse*,
743.3 *beggarly*, 827.8 *cursing*,
877.12 *indecent*
dirty book 622.3 *obscenity*
dirty books 877.2 *indecency*
dirty clothes 621.8 *laundry*
dirty dealings 858.3 *criminality*
dirty dishes 621.8 *laundry*
dirty film 622.3 *obscenity*
dirty habits 622.2 *uncleanness*,
626.1 *lack of hygiene*
dirty hands 866.2 *signs of guilt*
dirty joke 622.3 *obscenity*, 818.3
act of discourtesy, 827.1 *curse*,
877.2 *indecency*
dirty language 827.2 *offensive
language*
dirty liar 538.11, 539.16 *liar*
dirty lie 538.4 *lie*
dirty linen 621.8 *laundry*
dirty look 435.6 *look*, 852.10 *disapproving look*
dirty magazine 622.3 *obscenity*
dirty mouth 827.1 *curse*
dirty old man 622.6 *dirty person*,
877.8 *immoral man*
dirty person 622, 626.3 *unhygienic person*
dirty snowball 53.19 *comet*
dirty story 775.5 *joke*, 877.2 *indecency*
dirty talk 827.1 *curse*
dirty trick 539.8 *trick*, 801.3 *disreputable action*, 858.1 *improbity*
dirty water 622.5 *swill*
dirty weather 241.5 *violent
weather*
dirty weekend 815.3 *meeting*
dirty word 827.1 *curse*
Dis 8 Deities, 8.11 *heaven*
disability 236, 616.3 *inconvenience*, 620.7 *defect*, 624.2 *illness*
disable 236.7 *remove power
from*, 238.7 *weaken*, 487.8
make impossible, 614.8 *make
useless*, 628.5 *hurt*, 643.14
make inactive, 661.8 *hinder*
disabled 236.12 *impotent*, 325.5
sedentary, 620.3 *deformed*
disabled person 624.19 *sick person*
disablement 628.11 *hurt*
disablement benefit 662.4 *social
assistance*
disabling 628.11 *hurt*
disabuse 528.11 *inform*
disaccharide 33.4 *carbohydrate*
disaccord 117.4 *disagreement*,
168.1 *nonconformity*, 434.6 *disagreement*, 663.3 *conflict*, 666.1
disagreement
disaccordance 117.4 *disagreement*, 168.1 *nonconformity*
disaccordant 117.10 *disagreeing*
disaccustom 585, 587.3 *deflect*,
598.1 *relinquish*, 656.5 *be unskilful*
disaccustomed 585.1 *unaccustomed*
disadvantage 123.1 *inequality*,
123.5 *be unequal*, 127.2 *deficiency*, 616.3 *inconvenience*,
616.5 *be inconvenient*, 620.7 *defect*, 722.1 *loss*
disadvantaged 593.5 *necessitous*
disadvantageous 616.1 *inconvenient*, 618.5 *harmful*, 687.6 *adverse*
disaffect 587.4 *put off*
disaffected 766.4 *dissatisfied*,
785.8 *disliking*, 820.8 *estranged*
disaffectedly 820.14 *hostilely*
disaffection 500.3 *dissentience*,

587.7 *deterrence*, 785.1 *dislike*,
822.1 *hate*
disaffiliated 104.11 *separate*
disaffiliation 104.3 *separateness*
disaffinity 341.5 *repulsion*, 820.1
enmity
disaffirm 476.9 *deny*, 536.8 *rebut*
disaffirmation 476.1 *refutation*,
476.2 *denial*, 536.3 *rebuttal*
disaffirming 536.13 *rebutting*
**disagree 117, 136, 434, 666,
852**, 111.9 *oppose*, 113.9 *dissent*, 123.5 *be unequal*, 473.13
argue, 477.20 *doubt*, 498.8 *disbelieve*, 500.8 *dissent*, 520.10
mean, 536.8 *rebut*, 573.6 *be unwilling*, 663.15 *object*, 668.6 *be
insubordinate*, 674.13 *conflict*,
679.40 *argue*, 711.6 *dissent*,
764.11 *quarrel*, 785.5 *dislike*,
785.7 *cause dislike*
disagreeable 136, 117.10 *disagreeing*, 415.6 *unpalatable*,
473.8 *argumentative*, 618.3
bad, 764.1 *unpleasant*, 785.9
disliked, 818.5 *discourteous*,
830.7 *irritable*
disagreeableness 764.5 *unpleasantness*, 818.1 *discourtesy*
disagreeably 117, 136, 473.17
argumentatively, 764.13 *unpleasantly*, 818.9 *discourteously*,
830.14 *irritably*
**disagreeing 117, 434, 666,
852**, 113.7 *dissenting*, 123.3
unequal, 136.18 *disagreeable*,
444.12 *gaudy*, 536.13 *rebutting*,
573.2 *refusing*, 663.20 *discordant*, 668.8 *defying*, 711.9 *dissenting*, 785.8 *disliking*, 785.9
disliked
**disagreement 117, 434, 666,
852**, 111.3 *opposition*, 113.4
dissension, 136.4 *disunity*,
168.1 *nonconformity*, 168.2 *dissent*, 473.1 *argument*, 498.1 *disbelief*, 500.1 *dissent*, 536.3 *rebuttal*, 573.11 *unwillingness*,
659.7 *awkward situation*, 663.2
objection, 663.6 *contrariety*,
668.2 *disobedience*, 711.2 *dissent*, 713.1 *protest*, 764.7 *dissension*, 785.1 *dislike*
Disagreement 666
disagree with 663.14 *be against*,
713.6 *protest*, 785.7 *cause dislike*
disallow 147.7 *exclude*, 476.8 *refute*, 536.7 *be negative*, 581.1 *reject*, 704.6 *cancel*, 709.3 *veto*,
711.6 *dissent*, 852.15 *withhold
approval*
disallowal 476.1 *refutation*
disallowance 536.2 *rejection*,
704.1 *cancellation*, 709.1 *veto*
disallowed 487.4 *forbidden*,
536.12 *rejected*, 711.9 *dissenting*
disallow payment 747.8 *stop payment*
disambiguate 524.8 *interpret*,
550.2 *clarify*
disappear 458, 100.13 *cease to
exist*, 129.4 *decrease*, 162.11 *explode*, 172.8 *not exist*, 189.4 *be
transient*, 218.6 *cease*, 244.13
be destroyed, 254.18 *abscond*,
345.3 *quit*, 438.7 *become invisible*, 531.11 *conceal oneself*,
638.5 *escape*
disappearance 254, 458, 129.1
decrease, 162.3 *dilution*, 438.4
invisibility, 531.1 *concealment*,
638.1 *escape*
Disappearance 458
disappeared 458, 254.9 *away*
disappear in a puff of smoke
189.4 *be transient*
disappearing 458, 189.6 *transient*, 458.4 *disappearance*
disappearing act 458.4 *disappearance*
disappearing trick 638.1 *escape*
disappear into thin air 458.1 *disappear*
disappoint 515, 776, 358.2 *fail*,
514.11 *amaze*, 609.5 *be insufficient*, 683.6 *fail*, 766.6 *dissatisfy*
disappointed 515, 514.7

amazed, 766.4 *dissatisfied*, 852.25 *disapproving*
disappointing 515, 358.8 *defective*, 609.1 *insufficient*, 766.5 *unsatisfactory*
disappointingly 515, 609.10 *insufficiently*
disappointment 515, 411.2 *taste of life*, 514.2 *amazement*, 609.8 *insufficiency*, 683.1 *failure*, 766.1 *dissatisfaction*, 776.2 *hopeless situation*, 835.5 *misfortune*
Disappointment 515
disapprobation 500.2 *disapproval*, 663.1 *opposition*, 713.1 *protest*, 766.1 *dissatisfaction*, 822.1 *hate*, 828.1 *resentment*, 850.2 *disesteem*, 852.1 *disapproval*
disapprobatory 852.25 *disapproving*
disapproval 500, 852, 111.3 *opposition*, 581.5 *rejection*, 663.1 *opposition*, 713.1 *protest*, 766.1 *dissatisfaction*, 785.1 *dislike*, 822.1 *hate*, 828.1 *resentment*, 850.2 *disesteem*
Disapproval 852
disapprove 852, 16.79 *convict*, 111.9 *oppose*, 500.9 *refuse*, 766.7 *be dissatisfied*, 785.5 *dislike*, 822.14 *hate*
disapproved 852, 16.64 *convicted*, 111.5 *opposing*, 785.9 *disliked*, 806.3 *humbled*
disapproved of 766.5 *unsatisfactory*
disapprove of 492.11 *judge*, 663.14 *be against*, 713.6 *protest*, 852.14 *disapprove*
disapprover 852
disapproving 852, 111.5 *opposing*, 429.7 *catcalling*, 492.8 *judging*, 659.14 *troublesome*, 663.19 *oppositional*, 713.9 *protesting*, 766.4 *dissatisfied*, 785.8 *disliking*, 828.15 *resentful*
disapproving look 852
disapprovingly 111, 713, 852, 492.13 *judicially*, 659.29 *perversely*, 766.8 *discontentedly*, 828.17 *resentfully*
disarm 236.7 *remove power from*, 236.8 *overpower*, 238.7 *weaken*, 242.3 *be moderate*, 242.4 *moderate*, 614.8 *make useless*, 675.6 *make peace*, 677.4 *pacify*, 677.5 *make peace*, 835.11 *excite pity*
disarmament 236.1 *powerlessness*, 675.1 *peace*, 677.1 *pacification*
disarmament treaty 675.1 *peace*
disarmed 236.1 *unprotected*
disarming 242.8 *moderating*, 677.6 *pacificatory*
disarrange 153, 151.21 *disorder*, 252.14 *displace*
disarranged 153, 151.12 *disordered*, 252.8 *displaced*
disarrangement 153, 151.1 *disorder*, 252.1 *displacement*
disarray 151.1 *disorder*
disarticulate 252.18 *disconnect*
disarticulated 252.12 *disconnected*
disarticulation 252.5 *disconnection*
disassemble 136.9 *separate*, 614.8 *make useless*
disassociate 136.9 *separate*
disassociated 108.6 *unrelated*
disassociate oneself 536.7 *be negative*
disassociation 108.1 *unrelatedness*, 536.2 *rejection*
disassociative 536.11 *negative*
disaster 211.4 *mishap*, 244.4 *ruin*, 515.2 *bad outcome*, 618.11 *harmfulness*, 687.1 *adversity*, 862.2 *affliction*
disaster area 244.5 *havoc*, 607.4 *destruction*
disaster relief 767.4, 833.5 *charity*
disastrous 211.14 *accidental*,

244.14 *destructive*, 618.5 *harmful*, 687.6 *adverse*
disastrously 211.17 *mistakenly*, 244.16 *destructively*, 687.12 *in adversity*, 862.13 *destructively*
disavow 476.9 *deny*, 484.8 *reverse*, 536.7 *be negative*, 578.4 *recant*, 581.4 *revoke*, 713.6 *protest*
disavowal 476.2 *denial*, 484.2 *reversal*, 536.2 *rejection*, 578.8 *recantation*, 581.7 *abrogation*, 713.1 *protest*
disavowed 484.6 *countered*, 536.12 *rejected*
disbalance 123.5 *be unequal*
disband 136.9 *separate*, 141.4 *deconstruct*, 162.13 *dismiss*, 700.4 *liberate*
disbanded 162
disbanding 677.1 *pacification*, 700.1 *liberation*
disbandment 162
disbar 349, 147.8 *eject*, 816.13 *ignore*
disbarment 147.2 *ejection*
disbarred 147.11 *excluded*, 816.10 *lonely*
disbelief 498, 491.10 *suspicion*, 536.2 *rejection*
Disbelief 498
disbelieve 498, 477.20 *doubt*, 491.18 *be uncertain*, 536.7 *be negative*, 720.7 *not observe*
disbelieved 498, 536.12 *rejected*
disbeliever 498, 720.5 *nonobserver*
disbelieving 498, 720.11 *nonobservant*
disbelievingly 498
disburden 349.12 *unload*, 370.10 *lighten*, 639.1 *deliver*, 660.18 *disentangle*
disburdening 370.3 *lightening*
disburdenment 660.8 *disentanglement*
disburse 746.6 *pay*, 748.1 *expend*
disbursed 748.12 *expended*
disbursement 746.1 *payment*, 748.4 *expenditure*
disbursing 746.15 *paying*
disc 52.42 *circle*, 53.7 *galaxy*, 68.10 *farm tool*, 266.4 *slice*, 282.3 *flat thing*, 313.3 *circular thing*, 364.6 *rotator*, 420.9 *audio device*
discalced 296.11 *exposed*
discard 581, 132.8 *leave*, 349.13 *throw away*, 581.8 *rejected thing*, 598.1 *relinquish*, 600.6 *stop using*, 600.11 *unused thing*, 727.9 *dispose of*
discarded 132.9 *remaining*, 581.10 *rejected*, 585.2 *not customary*, 600.4 *disused*, 727.12 *disposed*
discarded matter 614.6 *refuse*
discarding 581, 600.10 *disuse*, 727.1 *disposal*
disc brake 71 Motor Vehicle Parts
disc camera 66.16 *camera*
discern 6.24 *know*, 136.10 *set apart*, 380.17 *be mentally sharp*, 435.12 *see*, 435.16 *visualize*, 481.12 *discriminate*, 501.11 *know*, 507.7 *be wise*, 522.7 *recognize*
discernibility 437.3 *visibility*
discernible 136.19 *separable*, 435.23, 437.1 *visible*
discernibly 437.11 *visibly*
discerning 6.20 *refined*, 277.11 *wise*, 380.5 *mentally sharp*, 435.21 *seeing*, 481.9 *discriminating*, 492.8 *judging*, 492.9 *judicious*, 580.14 *selecting*
discerningly 6, 380.18 *sharply*, 481.16 *judiciously*
discernment 6.11 *refinement*, 277.3 *profundity*, 380.13 *mental sharpness*, 435.4 *visualization*, 459.5 *common sense*, 481.2 *judiciousness*, 492.1 *judgment*, 507.1 *wisdom*
disc floret 84.4 *flower head*
discharge 16.42 *acquittal*, 16.78

acquit, 64.35 *conduct*, 144.4 *complete*, 162.13 *dismiss*, 252.4 *relegation*, 252.17 *relegate*, 338.7 *shot*, 338.28 *shoot*, 344.4 *land*, 347.2 *outflow*, 347.12 *leak*, 349.2 *dismiss*, 349.12 *unload*, 349.14 *let out*, 349.18 *dismissal*, 352.1 *secretion*, 352.7 *secrete*, 353.1 *excretion*, 353.7 *pus*, 353.15 *excrete*, 387.3 *body fluid*, 425.1, 425.5 *bang*, 600.7 *stop work*, 600.10 *disuse*, 624.3 *symptom*, 624.15 *ulcer*, 638.4 *leak*, 639.2 *deliverance*, 640.4 *act*, 645.3 *unemployment*, 645.5 *dismiss*, 684.1 *completion*, 684.4 *complete*, 694.5 *obey*, 698.1 *freedom*, 700.1 *liberation*, 700.4, 700.4 *liberate*, 704.2 *termination*, 704.7 *terminate*, 719.3 *performance*, 719.6 *perform*, 727.10 *dismiss*, 746.1 *payment*, 746.7 *pay off*, 839.3 *absolution*, 839.10 *absolve*, 845.19 *pay*, 848.2 *acquittal*, 848.10 *acquit*, 855.1 *vindication*, 855.7 *vindicate*
discharge a bankrupt 747.10 *forgive a debt*
discharged 16.63 *acquitted*, 252.11 *relegated*, 600.3 *not wanted*, 645.7 *leisurely*, 684.7 *completed*, 698.9 *free*, 704.10 *cancelled*, 727.13 *dismissed*, 746.16 *paid*, 839.6 *forgiven*, 848.6 *acquitted*, 855.12 *innocent*
discharged bankrupt 747.6 *nonpayer*
discharge of duty 847, 684.1 *completion*
discharge one's duty 684.4 *complete*, 847.16 *do one's duty*
discharge one's obligations 863.8 *be virtuous*
discharge one's responsibility 719.6 *perform*
disc harrows 68.10 *farm tool*
disciple 7.3 *religious person*, 118.7 *imitator*, 138.5, 155.14 *follower*, 284.8 *supporter*
disciplinarian 653.15 *manager*, 690.4 *strict person*, 699.6 *lawmaker*
disciplinary 879.19 *punitive*
disciplinary action 879.7 *punishment*
disciplinary procedure 15.2 *industrial negotiations*
discipline 150, 6.3 *subject*, 6.22 *educate*, 15.2 *industrial negotiations*, 15.11 *conduct industrial relations*, 150.7 *method*, 150.22 *pacify*, 167.10 *assimilate*, 203.7 *season*, 249.14, 472.4 *sphere*, 652.8 *treatment*, 688.19 *be authoritarian*, 690.1 *severity*, 690.5 *be severe*, 695.6 *compel*, 699.1 *restraint*, 699.3 *self-restraint*, 699.8 *restrain*, 701.2 *domination*, 701.7 *defeat*, 879.1 *punish*, 879.7 *punishment*
disciplined 150, 15.9 *negotiated*, 690.8 *severe*, 694.7 *obedient*, 699.13 *restraining*, 879.20 *punished*
discipline oneself 869.5 *be self-restrained*
discipliner 879.17 *punisher*
disciplining 15.9 *negotiated*
discipular 284.9 *supportive*
disc jockey 534.29 *broadcaster*
disclaim 476.9 *deny*, 484.8 *reverse*, 536.7 *be negative*, 578.4 *recant*, 581.4 *revoke*, 713.6 *protest*, 727.9 *dispose of*
disclaimed 484.6 *countered*, 536.12 *rejected*
disclaimer 476.2 *denial*, 536.2 *rejection*, 578.8 *recantation*, 713.1 *protest*
disclaiming 476.7 *refuting*
disclamation 484.2 *reversal*, 536.2 *rejection*
dislike 52.83 *spherical*
disclose 530, 6.22 *educate*, 296.14 *undress*, 322.18 *open*, 437.10 *make visible*, 457.14

present, 475.15 *demonstrate*, 496.2 *detect*, 526.1 *display*, 526.3 *reveal*, 532.13 *make public*, 533.13 *report*, 535.20 *admit*, 543.10 *signify*, 564.11 *speak*
disclosed 530, 475.9 *demonstrated*, 526.14 *manifest*, 532.19 *published*, 535.11 *stated*
discloser 530, 535.9 *affirmer*
disclosing 530, 543.14 *signifying*
disclosure 530, 457.1 *appearance*, 475.1 *demonstration*, 496.7 *detection*, 526.10 *manifestation*, 532.1 *publication*, 535.5 *admission*
Disclosure 530
disco 46.1 *dancing*, 46.6 *famous dancers*, 49.7 *dance music*, 161.10 *dance*, 815.5 *party*
discobolus 338.14 *thrower*
disco-dance 46.15 *dance*
disco dancer 46.5, 51.28 *dancer*
disco dancing 46.1 *dancing*
discography 171.2 *table*
discoid 313.5 *circular*
discoloration 444.3 *hue*, 628.9 *dilapidation*
discolour 216.8 *cause change*, 444.15 *colour*, 445.6 *decolour*, 456.11 *variegate*
discoloured 444.13 *soft-hued*, 445.7 *colourless*, 628.12 *deteriorated*
discomfit 153.7 *disturb*, 764.10 *displease*
discomfited 151.17 *discomposed*, 153.12 *disturbed*, 806.3 *humbled*
discomfiting 764.1 *unpleasant*
discomfiture 151.1 *disorder*, 153.1 *disturbance*, 764.5 *unpleasantness*
discomfort 406.1 *pain*, 616.3 *inconvenience*, 764.5 *unpleasantness*, 764.10 *displease*, 862.2 *affliction*
discomforting 764.2 *objectionable*
discommode 616.5 *be inconvenient*, 659.23 *cause difficulties*
discommodious 616.1 *inconvenient*
discommodiously 616.6 *inconveniently*
discompose 151, 153.7 *disturb*, 366.22 *agitate*
discomposed 151, 153.12 *disturbed*, 366.15 *agitated*, 491.3 *confused*
discomposure 151.1 *disorder*, 153.1 *disturbance*, 366.1 *agitation*, 491.12 *confusion*
disconcert 151.22 *discompose*, 153.7 *disturb*, 491.20 *make uncertain*, 514.11 *amaze*, 515.7 *thwart*, 806.11 *humiliate*
disconcerted 151.17 *discomposed*, 153.12 *disturbed*, 491.3 *confused*, 514.7 *amazed*, 515.9 *disappointed*, 806.3 *humbled*
disconcertedness 151.1 *disorder*, 153.1 *disturbance*, 491.12 *confusion*
disconcerting 153.17 *disturbing*, 491.3 *confused*
disconcertingly 153.18 *disturbingly*
disconcertion 491.12 *confusion*
disconcertment 514.2 *amazement*
disconfirm 476.8 *refute*
disconfirmation 476.1 *refutation*
disconformity 720.1 *nonobservance*
disconnect 160, 252, 64.35 *conduct*, 136.9 *separate*, 215.6 *be irregular*, 218.8 *cause to cease*
disconnected 252, 61.36 *psychologically disturbed*, 104.8 *intruder*, 108.6 *unrelated*, 136.15 *separate*, 160.8 *discontinuous*, 215.4 *irregular*, 555.1 *unemphatic*
disconnectedly 160, 252
disconnectedness 104.2 *foreignness*, 160.1 *discontinuity*
disconnection 252, 61.16 *dissociation*, 108.1 *unrelatedness*,

136.1 *separation*, 160.1 *discontinuity*, 215.1 *irregularity*, 555.2 *lack of emphasis*
disconsolate 770.5 *sad*, 774.4 *lamenting*, 776.4 *hopeless*
discontent 515.2 *bad outcome*, 515.7 *thwart*, 609.8 *insufficiency*, 713.1 *protest*, 713.9 *protesting*, 766.1 *dissatisfaction*, 766.4 *dissatisfied*, 785.1 *dislike*, 828.1 *resentment*, 830.3 *irritableness*, 830.12 *make irritable*, 852.1 *disapproval*
discontented 515.9 *disappointed*, 609.2 *unprovided*, 659.14 *troublesome*, 713.9 *protesting*, 766.4 *dissatisfied*, 785.8 *disliking*, 818.5 *discourteous*, 828.15 *resentful*, 830.7 *irritable*, 852.25 *disapproving*
discontentedly 766, 785, 818.9 *discourteously*, 828.17 *resentfully*, 830.14 *irritably*
discontentedness 852.1 *disapproval*
discontenting 515.11 *disappointing*
discontentment 766.1 *dissatisfaction*, 852.1 *disapproval*
discontinuance 160.1 *discontinuity*, 218.1 *cessation*, 283.6 *interruption*, 323.1 *closure*, 585.3 *unaccustomedness*, 598.3 *relinquishment*, 683.1 *failure*, 704.1 *cancellation*, 704.2 *termination*
discontinuation 160.1 *discontinuity*, 215.1 *irregularity*, 218.1 *cessation*, 683.1 *failure*, 704.1 *cancellation*
discontinue 160, 157.16, 218.6 *cease*, 283.12 *interrupt*, 323.9 *close down*, 683.6 *fail*, 704.7 *terminate*
discontinued 160, 283.9 *interrupted*, 598.5 *relinquished*, 600.4 *disused*
discontinuity 160, 54.18 *earth's crust*, 113.1 *diversity*, 136.1 *separation*, 213.3 *infrequency*, 215.1 *irregularity*, 218.1 *cessation*, 265.1 *interval*
Discontinuity 160
discontinuous 160, 136.15 *separate*, 187.9 *periodic*, 213.2 *infrequent*, 215.4 *irregular*, 265.6 *spaced*
discontinuously 160, 136.20 *separately*, 213.1 *infrequently*, 215.8 *irregularly*, 265.8 *apart*
discontinuousness 160.1 *discontinuity*
discord 117.4 *disagreement*, 151.1 *disorder*, 430.1 *stridency* , 430.4 *be strident*, 434.1 *dissonance*, 434.6 *disagreement*, 473.1 *argument*, 500.3 *dissentience*, 663.3 *conflict*, 666.2 *argument*, 666.3 *difference*, 764.7 *dissension*
discordance 113.4 *dissension*, 117.4 *disagreement*, 430.1 *stridency* , 434.1 *dissonance*, 500.3 *dissentience*, 666.1 *disagreement*, 711.2 *dissent*, 764.7 *dissension*
discordancy 117.4 *disagreement*
discordant 663, 108.8 *distorted*, 113.7 *dissenting*, 117.10 *disagreeing*, 423.6 *loud*, 430.7 *strident*, 434.7 *dissonant*, 444.12 *gaudy*, 473.7 *arguing*, 666.9 *disagreeing*, 666.10 *different*, 711.9 *dissenting*, 764.1 *unpleasant*, 820.6 *hostile*
discordantly 108.13 *disproportionately*, 115.7 *dissimilarly*, 117.16 *disagreeably*, 430.10 *stridently*, 434.12 *dissonantly*, 473.17 *argumentatively*, 666.11 *in disagreement*, 666.12 *differently*, 711.11 *uncooperatively*, 820.14 *hostilely*
discotheque 46.6 *famous dancers*, 815.5 *party*
discount 752, 752, 131.1 *subtraction*, 131.2 *subtracted item*, 131.3 *subtract*, 495.3 *underestimate*, 754.1 *cheapness*, 754.9 *cheap*, 754.13 *make cheap*
Discount 752
discounted 752, 131.7 *reduced*
discountenance 663.14 *be against*, 852.14 *disapprove*
discounter 754
discounting 131.1 *subtraction*
discount price 751.1 *price*
discount store 754.7 *discounter*
discount ticket 754.4 *bargain*
discourage 587, 233.9 *change*, 587.1 *dissuade*, 661.8 *hinder*
discouraged 515.9 *disappointed*, 587.10 *dissuaded*, 776.4 *hopeless*
discouragement 515.1 *disappointment*, 587.6 *dissuasion*, 661.1 *hindrance*, 776.1 *hopelessness*
discouraging 587.9 *dissuasive*, 661.13 *hindering*
discouragingly 587.11 *dissuasively*, 661.16 *with delay*
discourse 48.4 *non-fiction*, 473.2 *logical argument*, 475.3 *explanation*, 561.1 *dissertation*, 561.4 *dissertate*, 564.1 *faculty of speech*, 564.14 *speak to*, 567.1, 567.7 *address*, 568.1 *conversation*, 568.9 *converse*
discourse at length 553.5 *be diffuse*
discourser 567.6 *public speaker*, 568.7 *conversationalist*
discourteous 795, 807, 818, 462.10 *inconsiderate*, 559.8 *indecorous*, 652.18 *badly behaved*, 656.3 *clumsy*, 720.11 *nonobservant*, 764.2 *objectionable*, 816.8 *unsociable*, 838.3 *ungrateful*, 850.10 *disrespectful*
discourteous driver 462.7 *inconsiderate person*
discourteously 807, 818, 462.14 *thoughtlessly*, 652.20 *badly*, 720.16 *disobediently*, 764.13 *unpleasantly*, 816.14 *unsocially*, 838.7 *ungratefully*, 850.28 *disrespectfully*
discourteousness 818.1 *discourtesy*, 838.1 *ingratitude*
discourteous person 818
discourtesy 807, 818, 559.2 *impropriety*, 652.4 *bad conduct*, 720.1 *nonobservance*, 764.6 *objectionability*, 795.3 *grossness*, 816.1 *unsociability*, 850.1 *disrespect*
Discourtesy 818
discover 496, 6.23 *learn*, 154.18 *forerun*, 156.22 *invent*, 208.8 *precede*, 243.10 *produce*, 250.11 *find*, 344.2 *reach*, 435.12 *see*, 478.20 *solve*, 501.13 *get to know*, 514.9 *surprise*, 526.3 *reveal*, 528.15 *be informed*, 530.5 *disclose*, 590.9 *follow*, 592.11 *invent*
discoverable 496, 437.1 *visible*
discover a treasure trove 721.14 *profit*
discover by chance 229.5 *happen by chance*
discovered 496, 243.12 *produced*, 250.7 *found*, 478.14 *solved*, 501.10 *known*, 526.14 *manifest*
discoverer 496, 154.8 *precursor*, 208.4 *early comer*, 243.9 *producer*, 530.4 *discloser*
discovering 496, 154.14 *preparatory*, 250.3 *locating*
discover the secret of eternal life 184.9 *be infinite*
discovery 496, 154.3 *preparation*, 156.5 *invention*, 243.1 *production*, 478.6 *solution*, 496.10 *find*, 517.2 *divination*, 526.10 *manifestation*, 530.1 *disclosure*, 605.2 *resource*, 721.5 *profit*
Discovery 496
discredit 476.8 *refute*, 498.3 *incredulity*, 498.8 *disbelieve*, 498.9 *cause disbelief*, 801.1 *disrespect*, 801.4 *disreputable*, 822.4 *hatefulness*, 854.12 *defame*
discreditable 618.4 *poor*
discredited 498.7 *disbelieved*, 600.4 *disused*, 717.8 *irresolute*, 822.12 *hated*
discrediting 476.1 *refutation*, 476.7 *refuting*
discreet 444.13 *soft-hued*, 507.5 *wise*, 531.17 *noncommittal*, 781.4 *cautious*, 817.7 *courteous*
discreetly 507.9 *wisely*, 817.14 *courteously*
discrepancy 115.1 *dissimilarity*, 117.1 *disparity*, 123.1 *inequality*, 132.3 *difference*, 663.6 *contrariety*, 666.3 *difference*
discrepant 115.4 *dissimilar*, 117.7 *disparate*, 666.10 *different*
discrepantly 132.11 *residually*, 666.12 *differently*
discrete 52.70 *universal*, 104.11 *separate*, 108.6 *unrelated*, 136.17 *unjoined*, 139.9 *aloof*, 160.8 *discontinuous*, 162.20 *separated*, 481.11 *judged*
discrete component 64.16 *circuit element*
discrete distribution 52.59 *probability distribution*
discretely 52.87 *mathematically*, 104.18 *extraneously*, 136.22 *in isolation*, 139.11 *aloofly*, 817.15 *genteelly*
discreteness 104.3 *separateness*, 139.2 *aloofness*
discretion 481.2 *judiciousness*, 492.1 *judgment*, 507.1 *wisdom*, 531.4 *silence*, 570.4 *free will*, 580.6 *selection*, 655.1 *skill*, 698.1 *freedom*, 781.1 *caution*, 817.1 *courtesy*
discretional 580.14 *selecting*
discretionary 570.10 *free*, 698.12 *unconditional*
discriminate 481, 844, 6.24 *know*, 115.6 *differentiate*, 123.6 *be unjust*, 136.10 *set apart*, 493.11 *be unjust*, 507.7 *be wise*, 580.4 *pick*, 655.10 *be skilful*
discriminate against 481, 147.7 *exclude*, 844.22 *discriminate*
discriminated against 481.11 *judged*
discriminating 481, 4.15 *rational*, 6.20 *refined*, 103.9 *characteristic*, 411.8 *tasteful*, 492.8 *judging*, 492.9 *judicious*, 542.13 *subtle*, 580.14 *selecting*, 794.5 *refined*
discriminatingly 481, 4.29 *wisely*, 6.27 *discerningly*
discriminating person 481
discrimination 481, 6.11 *refinement*, 115.1 *dissimilarity*, 123.2 *injustice*, 136.2 *setting apart*, 147.1 *exclusion*, 411.2 *taste of life*, 481.2 *judiciousness*, 481.3 *prejudice*, 492.1 *judgment*, 493.3 *injustice*, 507.1 *wisdom*, 542.3 *subtlety*, 580.6 *selection*, 655.1 *skill*, 844.1 *unfairness*
Discrimination 481
discriminatorily 123.8 *unjustly*
discriminatory 481, 123.4, 493.8 *unjust*, 844.11 *wrong*
disc-shaped 52.83 *spherical*
discursion 335.16 *wandering*, 553.2 *circumlocution*
discursive 334.7 *circuitous*, 335.25 *wandering*, 553.4 *circumlocutory*, 561.5 *expository*
discursively 334.8 *circuitously*, 335.27 *astray*, 553.8 *circuitously*
discursiveness 335.16 *wandering*
discursive reasoning 463.2 *reasoning*
discus 21.2 *field events*, 313.3 *circular thing*, 338.10 *ball*
discuss 473, 472.11 *raise the point*, 477.20 *doubt*, 561.4 *dissertate*, 568.11 *confer*, 576.8 *balance*, 654.6 *consult*
discussing 568
discussion 716, 4.5 *philosophical argument*, 163.7 *lecture*, 473.2 *logical argument*, 561.1 *dissertation*, 568.4 *conference*, 654.2 *consultation*
discussion group 161.6 *sitting*, 163.6 *students*
discussions 716.1 *negotiation*
discuss philosophically 4
discus throw 21.2 *field events*
discus thrower 21.3 *athlete*, 338.14 *thrower*
discus throwing 18 Sporting Activities, 21.2 *field events*
disc wheel 71.11 *bicycle part*
disdain 805, 581.3 *exclude*, 668.2 *disobedience*, 720.1 *nonobservance*, 805.2 *unapproachability*, 807.6, 850.3 *contempt*, 850.20, 854.5 *scorn*
disdainful 668.7 *defiant*, 720.11 *nonobservant*, 805.15 *unapproachable*, 807.17, 850.13 *contemptuous*
disdainfully 668.9 *defiantly*, 807.34, 850.30 *contemptuously*
disdainfulness 850.3 *contempt*
disease 777 Phobias by Topic, **624,** 244.7 *agent of destruction*, 618.10 *poverty*, 624.2 *illness*, 628.9 *dilapidation*, 631.1 *affliction*
disease carrier 326
diseased 624, 618.4 *poor*
disease prevention 625.1 *hygiene*
disect 52.97 *align*
disedge 381.10 *blunt*
disembark 74.10 *sail*, 344.4 *land*
disembarkation 344.11 *landing*
disembarkment 344.11 *landing*
disembarrass 660.18 *disentangle*
disembarrassment 660.8 *disentanglement*
disembodied 11.18 *spiritual*, 368.8 *nonmaterial*
disembodiment 368.2 *unworldliness*, 458.4 *disappearance*
disembody 368.12 *enter a nonmaterial world*, 458.3 *cause to disappear*
disembogue 347.11 *run out*, 349.14 *let out*
disemboguement 349.22 *disgorgement*
disembowel 136.11 *divide*, 349.11 *void*, 355.14 *suck*
disembowelled 136.15 *separate*
disembowelment 355.4 *sucking*
disemplane 344.4 *land*
disemploy 349.2 *dismiss*
disemployment 581.6 *discarding*
disenable 487.8 *make impossible*
disenchant 515.6 *disappoint*, 587.5 *discourage*
disenchanted 515.9 *disappointed*, 587.10 *dissuaded*, 785.8 *disliking*
disenchantment 515.2 *bad outcome*, 587.7 *deterrence*
disencumber 370.10 *lighten*, 639.1 *deliver*, 660.18 *disentangle*, 700.4 *liberate*, 767.14 *take away*
disencumbering 370.3 *lightening*
disencumberment 639.2 *deliverance*, 660.8 *disentanglement*, 700.1 *liberation*
disendow 743.14 *impoverish*
disenfranchise 701.6 *subject*, 846.16 *disentitle*
disenfranchised 846.12 *disentitled*
disenfranchisement 701.1 *subjection*, 722.1 *loss*, 846.2 *disentitlement*
disengage 28.3 *fencing movements*, 28.5 *fence*, 136.9 *separate*, 337.2 *retreat*, 355.11 *extract*, 466.6 *be incurious*, 660.18 *disentangle*, 700.4 *liberate*
disengaged 28.6 *fencing*, 252.12 *disconnected*, 355.19 *dislodged*, 466.4 *uninterested*, 643.2 *not working* , 645.7 *leisurely*
disengagement 252.5 *disconnection*, 337.11 *retreat*, 355.1 *extraction*, 660.8 *disentanglement*, 700.1 *liberation*
disentangle 660, 136.9 *separate*, 152.19 *tidy*, 312.10 *straighten*, 524.9 *decipher*, 727.9 *dispose of*

disentangled 134.16 simple, 152.27 tidied
disentanglement 660
disentitle 846
disentitled 846
disentitlement 846, 722.1 loss
disentomb 355.13 dig out, 399.9 exhume
disentombment 355.3 digging out, 399.7 inquest
disequilibrium 123.1 inequality, 224.1 changeableness
disestablish 846.16 disentitle
disestablished 846.12 disentitled
disestablishment 846.2 disentitlement
disesteem 850, 852.2 disrespect
diseur 51.27 entertainer
diseuse 51.27 entertainer
disfavour 766.7 be dissatisfied, 785.1, 785.5 dislike, 801.1 disrespect, 822.1 hate, 850.2 disesteem, 852.1 disapproval, 852.14 disapprove
disfavoured 785.9 disliked
disfellowship 349.18 dismissal
disfigure 309.11 deform, 544.10 identify, 628.5 hurt, 790.5 make ugly, 793.7 blemish
disfigured 309.7 deformed, 790.4 ugly, 793.4 blemished
disfigurement 309.3 deformity, 790.1 hideousness, 793.1 spot
disfranchise 701.6 subject, 846.16 disentitle
disfranchised 236.10 powerless, 846.12 disentitled
disfranchisement 701.1 subjection, 846.2 disentitlement
disgorge 349.14 let out
disgorgement 349
disgorger 20.3 fishing tackle
disgrace 618.10 poverty, 801.1 disrespect, 806.13 disrepute, 806.22 shame, 827.6 vilify, 844.9 dishonour, 850.21 disregard, 858.1 improbity, 877.19 corrupt
disgraceful 618.4 poor, 844.15 immoral, 858.5 dishonourable, 864.11 wicked
disgracefully 618.15 worthlessly, 858.11 dishonourably, 864.18 wickedly
disgrace oneself 801.4 disreputable, 864.16 be wicked
disgruntled 515.9 disappointed, 766.4 dissatisfied, 852.25 disapproving
disgruntlement 766.1 dissatisfaction, 852.1 disapproval
disguise 115, 293, 458, 531, 539, 539, 115.6 differentiate, 118.2 copy, 118.4 camouflage, 293.31 hide, 295.5 fancy dress, 438.6 that which makes invisible, 438.8 make invisible, 457.4 something that appears, 457.14 present, 458.3 cause to disappear, 474.11 practise sophistry, 531.3 covering up, 540.3 hypocrisy, 540.12 facade, 540.18 be hypocritical, 540.24 mask, 638.2 means of escape, 657.1 cunning
disguised 531, 539, 540, 293.37 protected, 438.3 private, 458.7 disappeared, 527.2 concealed, 529.11 mysterious
disguised war 676.1 war
disguise oneself 458.1 disappear
disguise oneself as 457.11 appear
disguiser 293.17 coverer
disgust 415, 233.9 change, 341.4 be repulsive, 587.4 put off, 764.10 displease, 766.1 dissatisfaction, 766.6 dissatisfy, 785.1 dislike, 785.7, 785.7 cause dislike, 822.1 hate, 822.16 cause hate
disgusted 766.4 dissatisfied, 785.8 disliking
disgustedly 766.8 discontentedly
disgusting 341.8 repulsive, 415.6 unpalatable, 618.4 poor, 622.8 unclean, 764.1 unpleasant,

785.9 disliked, 822.12, 822.12 hated
disgustingly 785
disgustingly rich 742.1 wealthy
dish 45, 244.11 ruin, 258.16 crockery, 326.15 take away, 350.14 mouthful, 350.16 eating utensil, 401.4 boyfriend, 534.17 antenna, 789.4 attractive male
dishabille 296, 294.2 undressing, 295.4, 814.6 informal dress
dish antenna 534.17 antenna
disharmonious 117.10, 666.9 disagreeing
disharmoniously 117.16 disagreeably, 434.12 dissonantly, 666.11 in disagreement
disharmony 117.4 disagreement, 151.1 disorder, 434.1 dissonance, 500.3 dissentience, 666.1 disagreement, 764.7 dissension
dishcloth 621.11 cleaning cloth
dishcloth gourd 45 Vegetables, 621.10 cleaning object
dishclout 621.11 cleaning cloth
dishearten 515.6 disappoint, 587.5 discourage, 770.10 depress
disheartened 515.9 disappointed, 587.10 dissuaded, 770.5 sad
disheartening 587.9 dissuasive
dishearteningly 587.11 dissuasively
disheartenment 587.7 deterrence
dished 244.15 destroyed
dishevel 151.24 make disordered
dishevelled 151.15 untidy
dishevelment 151.3 untidiness
dish fit for a king 45.9 dish
dish of the day 45.9 dish, 165.9 special
dishonest 538, 16.60 offending, 474.10 hypocritical, 491.7 unreliable, 515.12 deceptive, 539.34 deceiving, 539.35 deceptive, 540.25 false, 540.31 fraudulent, 618.3 bad, 657.4 cunning, 736.18 fraudulent, 844.15 immoral, 858.5 dishonourable, 864.11 wicked, 877.11 immoral
dishonestly 16, 538, 474.15 hypocritically, 491.26 unreliably, 540.36 falsely, 657.6 cunningly, 736.19 thievishly, 844.28 immorally, 858.11 dishonourably, 864.18 wickedly
dishonest person 736, 858.4 dishonourable person
dishonest politician 601.3 abuser
dishonesty 538, 736, 16.38 lawbreaking, 531.5 evasion, 539.1 deception, 539.10 fraud, 540.1 falsehood, 540.8 fraud, 618.9 badness, 858.1 improbity, 864.1 wickedness, 877.1 immorality
dishonour 844, 717.3 irresolution, 801.1 disrespect, 801.4 disreputable, 850.2 disesteem, 850.21 disregard, 854.12 defame, 858.1 improbity, 877.19 corrupt
dishonourable 858, 717.8 irresolute, 801.4 disreputable, 844.15 immoral, 850.12 disregardful
dishonourable discharge 704.2 termination
dishonourable person 858
dishonourably 858, 717.10 irresolutely
dishonour a cheque 747.8 stop payment
dishonoured 717.8 irresolute
dishonoured cheque 747.3 bad payment
dishonour one's pledge 720.7 not observe
dish out 606.5 provision, 729.5 give, 731.4 allot, 746.11 remunerate
dish out claptrap 538.23 talk nonsense
dishrag 621.11 cleaning cloth
dish up 606.5 provision
dishware 258.16 crockery
dishwasher 258.3 cabinet, 621.7 washer, 621.12 cleaner, 697.6 domestic servant
dishwashing liquid 134.3 purifier

dishwater 238.5 weak thing, 412.3 tasteless items, 622.5 swill
dishy 340.9 attractive
disillusion 515.2 bad outcome, 515.6 disappoint, 528.11 inform, 587.5 discourage, 683.6 fail, 766.6 dissatisfy
disillusioned 515.9 disappointed, 587.10 dissuaded, 766.4 dissatisfied, 785.8 disliking
disillusionment 515.2 bad outcome, 766.1 dissatisfaction
disincarnate 368.12 enter a non-material world
disincarnated 368.8 nonmaterial
disincarnation 368.2 unworldliness
disincentive 587.7 deterrence
disinclination 573.11 unwillingness, 587.7 deterrence, 785.1 dislike
disincline 587.4 put off, 785.7 cause dislike
disinclined 573.1 unwilling, 785.8 disliking
disinfect 134.10 purify, 417.5 deodorize, 621.13 clean, 621.15 purify, 625.6 make hygienic, 630.20 doctor, 632.9 protect
disinfectant 62.4 drug type, 62.14 counteracting, 134.3 purifier, 134.15 purifying, 417.2 deodorant, 417.4 deodorizing, 621.9 cleaning agent, 621.18 cleansing, 630.3 prophylactic, 630.17 remedial, 632.7 tutelary
disinfected 134.14 purified, 417.3 odourless, 621.17 cleaned, 625.4 hygienic, 632.5 safe
disinfection 134.2 purification, 621.2 cleaning, 625.1 hygiene, 630.3 prophylactic
disinfestation 134.2 purification, 621.2 cleaning
disinflation 13.2 economy, 14.1, 741.7 finance
disinflationary 14.6 financial
disinform 548.5 misinform
disinformation 309.4 distortion of the truth, 474.2 sophism, 531.5 evasion, 538.1 untruth, 548.2 misinformation
disinformed 538.16 misinformed
disingenuous 474.10 hypocritical, 538.19 dishonest, 540.27 hypocritical, 657.4 cunning, 858.5 dishonourable
disingenuously 474.15 hypocritically, 538.27 pretentiously
disingenuousness 474.5, 538.9 hypocrisy, 540.3 hypocrisy, 858.1 improbity
disinherit 609.7 make insufficient, 727.9 dispose of, 734.8 take back, 743.14 impoverish
disinheritance 734.2 taking back, 743.6 insolvency
disinherited 727.12 disposed, 743.2 insolvent
disintegrate 141, 136.9 separate, 151.25 be disordered, 162.11 explode, 244.13 be destroyed, 379.4 be brittle, 384.23 pulverize, 384.28 come to dust, 628.1 deteriorate
disintegrated 141, 162.20 separated, 244.15 destroyed, 384.19 pulverized
disintegrating 141
disintegration 141, 56.71 nuclear reaction, 136.1 separation, 151.1 disorder, 162.5 divergence, 244.2 destroying, 384.4 pulverization, 628.9 dilapidation
Disintegration 141
disintegration of personality 61.16 dissociation
disinter 355.13 dig out, 399.9 exhume, 496.2 detect, 530.5 disclose
disinterest 466.2 lack of interest, 783.3 impartiality, 787.1 lack of wonder, 859.1 disinterestedness
disinterested 859, 271.3 broadminded, 482.2 impartial, 783.7

indifferent, 783.9 impartial, 787.3 unmoved, 788.5 bored, 806.5 submissive, 843.7 right, 863.5 virtuous
disinterestedly 466, 859, 482.15 impartially, 783.17 indifferently
disinterestedness 859, 482.7 impartiality, 783.1 indifference, 806.12 submissiveness, 863.1 virtue
Disinterestedness 859
disinterment 355.3 digging out, 399.7 inquest
disinvest 748.1 expend
disinvestment 748.6 extravagance
disinvolve 660.18 disentangle
disinvolvement 660.8 disentanglement
disiplinary 15.9 negotiated
disjoin 136.9 separate, 160.14 disconnect
disjoint 252.18 disconnect
disjointed 136.15 separate, 151.12 disordered, 160.8 discontinuous, 252.12 disconnected, 555.1 unemphatic
disjointedly 160.18, 252.21 disconnectedly
disjointedness 160.1 discontinuity, 252.5 disconnection
disjoint sets 52.21 set
disjunct 108.6 unrelated
disjunction 4.8 philosophical term, 52.63 mathematical logic, 136.1 separation, 151.1 disorder, 160.1 discontinuity
disjunctive 136.15 separate
disjunctively 136.20 separately
disjuncture 108.1 unrelatedness, 136.1 separation
disk 65.7 peripheral, 545.6 record book
diskette 65.7 peripheral
Diskman 65.6 memory
disk operating system 65.8 software
disk pack 65.7 peripheral
disk reader 65.7 peripheral
disk sander 47.11 woodworking tool
dislike 785, 785, 573.11 unwillingness, 603.1 opposition, 663.14 be against, 759.6 bad feeling, 766.1 dissatisfaction, 766.7 be dissatisfied, 788.1 boredom, 788.7 suffer boredom, 820.1 enmity, 822.1, 822.14 hate, 852.1 disapproval, 852.14 disapprove
Dislike 785
dislikeable 785.9 disliked
disliked 785, 764.1 unpleasant, 788.4 boring, 820.10, 822.12 hated
disliked person 785
disliked thing 785
disliking 785
dislocate 136.9 separate, 153.9 disperse, 241.8 use violence, 252.14 displace, 252.18 disconnect
dislocate circle 30.7 stationary rings
dislocated 30.11 gymnastic, 136.15 separate, 151.12 disordered, 153.14 dispersed, 252.8 displaced, 252.12 disconnected
dislocated grip 30.5 horizontal bar
dislocation 136.1 separation, 153.3 dispersion, 241.3 instance of violence, 252.1 displacement, 252.5 disconnection, 628.11 hurt
dislocation metamorphism 54.32 metamorphism
dislodge 153.9 disperse, 252.14 displace, 326.15 take away, 349.8 evict, 355.12 displace
dislodged 355, 153.14 dispersed, 252.8 displaced
dislodgment 153.3 dispersion, 252.1 displacement, 349.20 eviction, 355.2 displacement
disloyal 224.14 irresolute, 578.11 equivocating, 693.13 dis-

obedient, 720.13 *noncompliant*, 820.8 *estranged*, 858.6 *faithless*
disloyal friend 578.9 *equivocator*
disloyally 224.15 *changeably*, 578.13 *perfidiously*, 693.17, 720.16 *disobediently*, 820.14 *hostilely*, 858.11 *dishonourably*
disloyalty 224.2 *irresolution*, 683.3 *personal fault*, 693.1 *disobedience*, 720.3 *disregard of orders*, 820.2 *personal conflict*, 858.2 *faithlessness*
dismal 440.11 *benighted*, 770.6 *depressed*, 830.6 *sullen*, 830.8 *overcast*
dismally 770.12 *joylessly*, 830.13 *sullenly*
dismantle 136.9 *separate*, 141.4 *deconstruct*, 143.10 *part*, 244.9 *demolish*, 600.6 *stop using*, 614.8 *make useless*, 628.4 *impair*, 643.14 *make inactive*
dismantled 595.7 *unequipped*
dismantling 141.2 *deconstruction*
dismast 614.8 *make useless*, 628.4 *impair*
dismasted 595.7 *unequipped*
dismay 777.2 *fearfulness*, 777.13 *frighten*
dismaying 777.10 *frightening*
dismember 136.11 *divide*, 141.4 *deconstruct*, 252.18 *disconnect*, 879.5 *execute*
dismembered 136.15 *separate*, 252.12 *disconnected*
dismemberment 141.2 *deconstruction*, 252.5 *disconnection*
dismiss 27, 162, 349, 645, 727, 15.11 *conduct industrial relations*, 147.8 *eject*, 218.8 *cause to cease*, 252.17 *relegate*, 341.2 *eject*, 347.13 *emigrate*, 458.3 *cause to disappear*, 476.8 *refute*, 581.2 *discard*, 600.7 *stop work*, 643.14 *make inactive*, 700.4 *liberate*, 704.7 *terminate*, 767.12 *relieve from duty*, 783.12 *be indifferent*, 839.10 *absolve*, 848.10 *acquit*, 855.7 *vindicate*
dismissal 27, 349, 10.6 *Eucharist*, 15.2 *industrial negotiations*, 147.2 *ejection*, 162.2 *disbandment*, 218.2 *stop*, 252.4 *relegation*, 341.6 *repulse*, 345.9 *parting*, 347.4 *emigration*, 476.1 *refutation*, 581.6 *discarding*, 600.10 *disuse*, 645.3 *unemployment*, 700.1 *liberation*, 704.2 *termination*, 727.1 *disposal*, 855.1 *vindication*
dismissal for lack of evidence 16.42 *acquittal*
dismiss charges 16.78 *acquit*
dismissed 727, 15.9 *negotiated*, 147.11 *excluded*, 162.21 *disbanded*, 252.11 *relegated*, 581.10 *rejected*, 600.3 *not wanted*, 645.7 *leisurely*, 855.12 *innocent*
dismiss from one's thoughts 839.9 *forgive*
dismissive 341.10 *defensive*
dismissively 341.12 *defensively*, 476.11 *in reply*
dismiss out of hand 581.1 *reject*
dismount 136.9 *separate*, 344.4 *land*, 360.9 *descend*
Disneyland 786.4 *wonder*
disobedience 573, 668, 693, 151.8 *lawlessness*, 168.2 *dissent*, 500.3 *dissentience*, 536.2 *rejection*, 577.5 *obstinacy*, 663.5 *contrariness*, 689.1 *anarchy*, 713.1 *protest*, 720.3 *disregard of orders*, 858.2 *faithlessness*, 864.1 *wickedness*
Disobedience 693
disobedient 693, 151.20 *disorderly*, 577.2 *refractory*, 659.14 *troublesome*, 663.22 *uncooperative*, 668.8 *defying*, 689.6 *anarchic*, 713.9 *protesting*, 720.13 *noncompliant*, 858.6 *faithless*, 864.11 *wicked*
disobediently 693, 720, 659.29

perversely, 668.10 *in defiance*, 689.8 *anarchically*, 713.11 *disapprovingly*, 858.11 *dishonourably*, 864.18 *wickedly*
disobey 151.26 *be disorderly*, 168.20 *infringe a law*, 536.7 *be negative*, 663.17 *withstand*, 668.6 *be insubordinate*, 689.4 *be anarchic*, 693.15 *be disobedient*, 713.6 *protest*, 720.9 *disregard orders*
disobeyed 536.12 *rejected*
disobeying 693.13 *disobedient*
disoblige 832.16 *be malevolent*
disobliging 832.15 *inconsiderate*
disopyramide 62 *Medication*
disorder 151, 151, 151, 307, 713, 113.1 *diversity*, 133.1 *mixture*, 139.1 *nonadhesion*, 141.1 *disintegration*, 141.4 *deconstruct*, 151.8 *lawlessness*, 153.2 *disarrangement*, 153.5 *commotion*, 153.8 *disarrange*, 160.1 *discontinuity*, 215.1 *irregularity*, 252.14 *displace*, 366.2 *tumult*, 618.10 *poverty*, 624.2 *illness*, 689.1 *anarchy*, 693.2 *violation of the law*, 720.4 *infraction*
Disorder 151
disordered 151, 133.12 *mixed*, 141.5 *disintegrated*, 153.13 *disarranged*, 153.16 *deranged*, 215.4 *irregular*, 482.3 *indiscriminate*, 618.4 *poor*, 624.23 *diseased*
disordered personality 61
disorderliness 151.1 *disorder*
disorderly 151, 215.4 *irregular*, 423.6 *loud*, 689.6 *anarchic*, 693.13 *disobedient*, 720.14 *violating*, 795.8 *discourteous*
disorderly behaviour 151.8 *lawlessness*
disorderly house 877.6 *brothel*
disorganization 151.1 *disorder*, 153.2 *disarrangement*, 595.8 *lack of preparation*, 628.10 *impairment*, 689.1 *anarchy*
disorganize 151.21 *disorder*, 153.8 *disarrange*, 252.14 *displace*, 628.4 *impair*
disorganized 151.12 *disordered*, 151.16 *confused*, 153.13 *disarranged*, 482.3 *indiscriminate*, 595.1 *unprepared*, 689.6 *anarchic*
disorient 151.22 *discompose*, 153.9 *disperse*
disorientate 153.14 *dispersed*
disorientation 153.3 *dispersion*, 335.13 *deviation*
disoriented 722.18 *at a loss*
disown 108.11 *be unconcerned*, 476.9 *deny*, 484.8 *reverse*, 536.7 *be negative*, 591.7 *be evasive*, 727.9 *dispose of*
disowned 484.6 *countered*, 536.12 *rejected*, 727.12 *disposed*
disowning 476.7 *refuting*
disownment 476.2 *denial*, 484.2 *reversal*, 536.2 *rejection*
disparage 854, 429.5 *catcall*, 495.5 *underestimate*, 612.13 *make unimportant*, 670.10 *criticize*, 850.20 *scorn*, 852.17 *criticize*
disparaged 850.18 *undervalued*
disparagement 854, 670.16 *terrorist attack*, 807.6 *contempt*
Disparagement 854
disparager 854
disparaging 854, 117.10 *disagreeing*, 495.4 *underestimating*, 670.25 *critical*, 807.17 *contemptuous*, 852.27 *critical*
disparagingly 854, 117.16 *disagreeably*, 495.6 *pessimistically*, 807.34 *contemptuously*
disparaging remark 854.4 *aspersion*
disparate 117, 115.4 *dissimilar*, 123.3 *unequal*
disparately 115.7 *dissimilarly*, 123.7 *unequally*
disparity 117, 108.4 *distortion*, 115.1 *dissimilarity*, 123.1 *in-*

equality, 168.1 *nonconformity*, 663.6 *contrariety*, 666.3 *difference*
Disparity 117
dispassion 4.3 *detachment*, 783.1 *indifference*, 859.1 *disinterestedness*
dispassionate 4.18 *detached*, 492.9 *judicious*, 783.7 *indifferent*, 859.4 *disinterested*
dispassionately 4.27 *stoically*, 783.17 *indifferently*, 859.8 *disinterestedly*
dispatch 70.4 *transport*, 208.1 *earliness*, 208.7 *be early*, 244.8 *destroy*, 324.14 *set in motion*, 326.2 *transportation*, 326.12 *transport*, 329.8 *speed*, 350.22 *eat well*, 398.5 *execution*, 398.16 *kill*, 528.2 *communication*, 533.13 *report*, 534.31 *correspond*, 567.10 *send*, 640.1 *action*, 640.4 *act*, 642.3 *nimbleness*, 642.15 *try*, 648.1 *hasten*, 648.4 *haste*, 652.14 *behave towards*, 684.4 *complete*, 729.5 *give*
dispatch box 258.6 *box*, 534.3 *correspondence*
dispatch rider 71.9 *animal transport*
dispel 136.9 *separate*, 162.12 *disperse*, 244.8 *destroy*, 349.10 *exterminate*, 458.3 *cause to disappear*, 651.1 *refresh*
dispensability 612.5 *unimportance*, 614.3 *uselessness*
dispensable 612.1 *unimportant*, 614.1 *useless*, 855.13 *vindicable*
dispensary 60.10, 630.14 *hospital*
dispensation 116.8 *permit*, 147.1 *exclusion*, 162.1 *dispersion*, 639.2 *deliverance*, 708.1 *permission*, 727.1 *disposal*, 731.1 *allocation*, 839.1 *forgiveness*, 848.1 *exemption*
dispense 162.16 *distribute*, 639.1 *deliver*, 729.5 *give*, 731.4 *allot*
dispensed 162.22 *distributed*
dispensed with 600.3 *not wanted*, 727.12 *disposed*
dispenser 62.2 *pharmacologist*, 630.16 *druggist*
dispense with 147.8 *eject*, 600.5 *not use*, 727.9 *dispose of*
dispensing 731.1 *allocation*
dispeople 349.9 *depopulate*
dispersal 136.1 *separation*, 141.2 *deconstruction*, 162.1 *dispersion*, 326.3 *transmission*, 458.4 *disappearance*
disperse 153, 162, 57.25 *solidify*, 57.32 *solid*, 136.9 *separate*, 136.13 *diverge*, 141.4 *deconstruct*, 151.21 *disorder*, 162.9 *be dispersed*, 164.25 *broadcast*, 182.9 *scatter*, 244.8 *destroy*, 261.5 *make bigger*, 261.6 *become bigger*, 324.14 *set in motion*, 326.11 *transfer*, 326.14 *bring back*, 335.12 *deflect*, 343.13 *radiate*, 362.6 *throw down*, 458.3 *cause to disappear*, 607.1 *waste*
dispersed 153, 162, 136.16 *apart*, 182.6 *sparse*, 261.7 *bigger*, 335.26 *diffractive*, 458.7 *disappeared*
dispersed population 162.7 *sprawl*
disperse phase 57.3 *phase*
disperser 261.4 *enlarger*
dispersion 153, 162, 52.60 *parameter*, 56.15 *wave property*, 136.1 *separation*, 261.1 *growth*, 263.1 *distance*, 326.3 *transmission*, 335.18 *diffraction*, 343.3 *radiation*, 458.4 *disappearance*, 607.3 *waste*
Dispersion 162
dispersion force 57.11 *chemical bond*
dispersive 162, 261.9 *enlargeable*
dispersively 162

dispirit 587.5 *discourage*, 770.10 *depress*
dispirited 770.6 *depressed*, 783.7 *indifferent*, 806.4 *self-abasing*
dispiritedly 783.17 *indifferently*
dispiritedness 770.2 *depression*, 783.1 *indifference*
dispiriting 770.7 *distressing*
displace 252, 355, 136.9 *separate*, 153.9 *disperse*, 216.10 *exchange*, 222.4 *be a substitute*, 324.14 *set in motion*, 326.15 *take away*, 349.5 *take the place of*, 816.13 *ignore*
displaceable 326.17 *transferable*
displaced 252, 151.12 *disordered*, 153.14 *dispersed*, 168.15 *irregular*, 355.19 *dislodged*, 816.10 *lonely*
displaced person 252, 104.7 *new arrival*, 108.3 *unconnected person*, 591.17 *avoider*, 816.7 *outsider*
displacement 252, 355, 369, 36.13 *windsurfing*, 56.54 *electric field*, 57.14 *chemical reaction*, 61.19 *defence mechanism*, 64.11 *electric field*, 153.3 *dispersion*, 216.4 *exchange*, 259.1 *size*, 277.6 *bathymetry*, 326.1 *transfer*
Displacement 252
displacement activity 642.9 *over-activity*
displacement board 36.7 *windsurfing*
displacement current 56.51 *electric current*
displacement sailing 36.7 *windsurfing*
displacer 349.26 *ejector*
display 526, 526, 65.17 *computing term*, 152.2 *array*, 152.12 *arrange*, 161.31 *exhibition*, 303.3 *show*, 435.7 *view*, 435.18 *make visible*, 437.5 *manifestation*, 437.10 *make visible*, 457.2 *being in view*, 457.14 *present*, 475.1 *demonstration*, 475.15 *demonstrate*, 532.8 *public relations*, 534.28 *radar*, 805.9 *ostentation*, 811.14, 811.14 *show*, 811.27 *show*
Display 526
display bad manners 818.7 *be discourteous*
display board 532.9 *advertisement*
display cabinet 526.8 *showplace*
display case 442.8 *transparent thing*, 526.8 *showplace*
displayed 526, 303.7 *outward*, 457.7 *appearing*, 475.9 *demonstrated*
displayer 526
display hauteur 805.28 *disdain*
display of disapproval 852.9 *show of disapproval*
display one's skill 655.11 *be expert*
display something 526
display the flag 676.12 *go to war*
displease 764, 766.6 *dissatisfy*, 785.7 *cause dislike*
displeased 766.4 *dissatisfied*, 785.8 *disliking*, 828.15 *resentful*, 852.25 *disapproving*
displeasing 764.1 *unpleasant*
displeasure 766.1 *dissatisfaction*, 785.1 *dislike*, 822.1 *hate*, 828.1 *resentment*, 852.1 *disapproval*
displume 349.3 *disbar*
displuming 349.18 *dismissal*
disposability 614.3 *uselessness*, 727.1 *disposal*, 727.2 *disposal of property*
disposable 141.5 *disintegrated*, 599.10 *usable*, 613.1 *useful*, 614.1 *useless*, 614.6 *refuse*
disposable camera 66.16 *camera*
disposable lenses 435.10 *visual aid*
disposable things 727
disposably 727
disposal 727, 152.1 *arrangement*, 599.6 *use*, 600.10 *disuse*,

728.1 transfer of property, 739.3 selling
Disposal 727
disposal of property 727
disposal of the dead 399.1 burial
dispose 150.18 order, 152.12 arrange, 163.13 class, 228.9 motivate, 233.8 influence, 332.7 take a direction, 586.15 persuade, 728.3 transfer property
disposed 727, 150.10 ordered, 152.20 arranged, 570.6 willed, 572.1 willing, 588.11 intending, 784.6 liking
disposed of 684.7 completed
dispose of 599, 727, 157.16 cease, 244.8 destroy, 476.8 refute, 684.5 conclude, 739.1 sell
dispose of property 727
disposition 103.4 nature, 105.4 state of mind, 150.1 order, 152.1 arrangement, 234.2 attitude, 570.1 will, 728.1 transfer of property, 771.8 temperament, 784.2 inclination, 810.4 shyness
dispossess 349.8 evict, 722.9 lose, 734.8 take back, 743.14 impoverish, 767.14 take away, 846.16 disentitle
dispossessed 743.2 insolvent, 846.12 disentitled
dispossession 349.20 eviction, 722.1 loss, 734.2 taking back, 743.6 insolvency, 846.2 disentitlement
dispossessor 349.26 ejector
dispraise 852.5 criticism, 852.17, 854.11 criticize
dispraised 852.33 criticized
dispraising 852.27 critical
disproof 16.7 legal trial, 476.1 refutation, 536.3 rebuttal
disproportion 108.4 distortion, 117.1 disparity, 123.1 inequality, 123.5 be unequal, 151.2 irregular order, 309.1 distortion, 309.9 distort
disproportional 117.7 disparate
disproportionate 108.8 distorted, 117.7 disparate, 123.3 unequal, 151.14 irregular, 309.6 distorted, 610.6 excessive
disproportionately 108, 117.15 dissimilarly, 123.7 unequally, 309.13 asymmetrically
disproportionateness 117.1 disparity
disproportionation 57.14 chemical reaction
disproportioned 123.3 unequal
disprovability 476.4 refutability
disprovable 476.6 refutable
disprovably 476.12 refutably
disproval 476.1 refutation
disprove 52.89 theorize, 476.8 refute, 536.8 rebut
disproved 536.12 rejected
disproving 476.7 refuting, 536.3 rebuttal
disputability 491.9 uncertainty
disputable 16.54 litigated, 473.10 arguable, 477.14 questionable, 491.1 uncertain, 498.7 disbelieved
disputably 477.24 questionably, 491.23 uncertainly, 498.11 unbelievably
disputant 463.6, 473.6 arguer, 663.9 opposer
disputation 4.5 philosophical argument, 463.3 debate, 473.2 logical argument, 663.2 objection
disputatious 16.52 legalistic, 473.8 argumentative, 500.7 dissenting, 670.21 aggressive, 829.4 irascible
disputatiousness 829.1 irascibility
dispute 4.23 discuss philosophically, 16.5 litigation, 117.14 disagree, 463.3, 463.13 debate, 473.1 argument, 473.13 argue, 476.9 deny, 477.20 doubt, 491.18 be uncertain, 498.8 disbelieve, 500.1, 500.8 dissent, 659.7 awkward situation, 663.15 object, 666.2 argument, 666.6 argue, 674.1 contention, 674.13 conflict, 676.14 battle, 679.40 argue, 829.6 be irascible
disputed 16.54 litigated
disputed area 666.1 disagreement
disputedly 473.18 arguably, 476.12 refutably
disputer 473.6 arguer, 500.5, 666.4 dissenter, 679.5 arguer
disputes procedure 15.4 industrial dispute
disputing 16.53 litigating, 463.9 argumentative, 666.9 disagreeing
disqualification 21.1 track events, 147.2 ejection, 236.1 powerlessness, 349.18 dismissal, 595.8 lack of preparation, 656.8 unskilfulness, 722.1 loss, 846.2 disentitlement
disqualified 236.10 powerless, 595.7 unequipped, 656.1 unskilful, 846.12 disentitled
disqualified athlete 722.6 loser
disqualify 147.8 eject, 236.7 remove power from, 349.3 disbar, 487.8 make impossible, 614.8 make useless, 846.16 disentitle
disquiet 153.1 disturbance, 153.7 disturb, 224.2 irresolution, 366.1 agitation, 366.22 agitate, 777.2 fearfulness
disquieted 153.12 disturbed, 777.8 fearful
disquietingly 153.18 disturbingly
disquietude 366.1 agitation
disquisition 553.1 diffuseness, 561.1 dissertation, 567.1 address
disquisitional 561.5 expository
disregard 850, 147.7 exclude, 436.7 figurative blindness, 436.16 be blind to, 466.6 be incurious, 468.1 inattention, 468.4 thoughtlessness, 468.12 be inattentive, 468.13 be thoughtless, 470.1 negligence, 470.6 be neglectful, 482.11 not discriminate, 512.4 unthinkingness, 542.9 down-playing, 542.22 play down, 581.1 reject, 600.5 not use, 612.12 think unimportant, 641.4 not act, 668.2 disobedience, 668.6 be insubordinate, 673.3 submit, 720.1 nonobservance, 720.7 not observe, 783.2 carelessness, 783.12 be indifferent, 783.14 be careless, 839.2 forgivingness, 839.11 condone, 850.2 disesteem
disregarded 147.11 excluded, 542.19 downplayed, 612.2 obscure, 839.8 overlooked, 850.18 undervalued
disregardful 850, 470.4 negligent, 720.11 nonobservant
disregarding 468.7 inattentive, 512.10 unthinking, 720.11 nonobservant, 783.8 careless
disregard of orders 720
disregard orders 720
disrelated 104.8 intruder, 108.6 unrelated
disrelish 785.1, 785.5 dislike, 822.14 hate
disrepair 628.9 dilapidation
disreputability 618.10 poverty, 801.1 disrespect
disreputable 801, 618.4 poor, 850.12 disregardful, 858.5 dishonourable, 864.11 wicked
disreputable action 801
disreputable character 801
disreputably 822.18 hatefully, 864.18 wickedly
disrepute 806, 822.4 hatefulness, 850.2 disesteem, 852.2 disrespect, 858.1 improbity, 864.1 wickedness
Disrepute 801
disrespect 801, 850, 850, 852, 720.3 disregard of orders, 807.11 sauciness, 858.1 improbity
Disrespect 850
disrespected 850.17 unrespected
disrespectful 850, 720.13 noncompliant, 807.19 rude, 807.20 discourteous, 816.8 unsociable, 818.5 discourteous, 852.25 disapproving, 858.5 dishonourable
disrespectfully 850, 720.16 disobediently, 807.35 rudely, 807.36 discourteously, 816.14 unsocially, 818.10 rudely, 858.11 dishonourably
disrespectfulness 807.8 rudeness, 807.9 discourtesy, 850.1 disrespect
disrobe 294.11 uncover, 296.14 undress, 296.15 make nude
disrobed 296.9 undressed
disrobement 294.2 undressing, 296.1 undress
disrober 296.8 nude person
disrobing 296.1 undress
disrupt 153, 151.21 disorder, 160.16 interrupt, 211.5 take untimely action, 252.14 displace, 616.5 be inconvenient, 659.23 cause difficulties, 689.4 be anarchic
disrupted 153, 151.12 disordered, 160.10 interrupted
disrupting 211.10 untimely, 616.1 inconvenient
disruption 153, 136.1 separation, 151.1, 151.9 disorder, 160.6 intervention, 211.1 untimeliness, 244.2 destroying, 616.3 inconvenience, 689.1 anarchy
disruptive 151.20 disorderly, 153.17 disturbing, 616.1 inconvenient, 659.14 troublesome
disruptive discharge 64.6 electric discharge
disruptively 151.29 riotously, 153.18 disturbingly, 211.15 at the wrong time, 616.6 inconveniently, 659.29 perversely
disruptiveness 151.8 lawlessness
disruptive pupil 659.9 difficult person
dissatisfaction 766, 145.1 incompleteness, 412.1 tastelessness, 500.2 disapproval, 515.2 bad outcome, 713.1 protest, 785.1 dislike, 788.1 boredom, 828.1 resentment, 830.3 irritableness, 852.1 disapproval
Dissatisfaction 766
dissatisfactory 766.5 unsatisfactory
dissatisfied 766, 500.7 dissenting, 515.9 disappointed, 713.9 protesting, 785.8 disliking, 788.5 bored, 830.7 irritable, 852.25 disapproving
dissatisfied customer 713.4 protester, 766.3 dissatisfied person
dissatisfied person 766
dissatisfy 766, 515.6 disappoint, 620.9 be imperfect, 788.6 be boring, 830.12 make irritable
dissave 748.1 expend
dissaving 748.6 extravagance
dissect 136.11 divide, 141.4 deconstruct, 143.10 part
dissection 59.4 anatomy, 136.1 separation, 141.2 deconstruction
dissemblance 286.3 deviousness, 540.1 falsehood, 540.12 facade
dissemble 115.6 differentiate, 286.7 deviate, 309.12 distort the truth, 474.12 deceive, 527.13 hide, 531.9 disguise, 538.24 pretend, 540.16 be false, 540.20 pretend, 540.24 mask, 578.1 be equivocal, 640.4 act, 858.9 prove false
dissembled 540.35 disguised
dissembler 531.7 concealer, 548.3 deceiver, 657.3 cunning person
dissembling 286.5 devious, 474.10 hypocritical, 538.9 hypocrisy, 538.17 duplicitous, 538.18 pretentious, 540.25 false, 540.30 pretending
disseminate 162.16 distribute, 164.25 broadcast, 326.11 transfer, 528.12 communicate, 532.13 make public
disseminated 162.22 distributed, 532.19 published
disseminated sclerosis 624.17 nervous disorder
dissemination 162.1 dispersion, 326.3 transmission, 528.2 communication, 532.1 publication
disseminative 162.28 dispersive
disseminatively 162.29 dispersively
dissension 113, 764, 117.4 disagreement, 136.4 disunity, 434.6 disagreement, 500.3 dissentience, 663.3 conflict, 666.1 disagreement, 674.1 contention, 693.1 disobedience, 820.1 enmity, 852.4 disagreement
dissent 113, 168, 500, 500, 711, 711, 4.23 discuss philosophically, 117.4 disagreement, 117.14, 136.12 disagree, 168.18 not conform, 434.6 disagreement, 463.3, 463.13 debate, 473.13 argue, 475.19 protest, 477.20 doubt, 498.1 disbelief, 498.8 disbelieve, 536.3 rebuttal, 536.8 rebut, 573.6 be unwilling, 573.9 not cooperate, 663.2 objection, 663.15 object, 666.1 disagreement, 666.5 disagree, 668.2 disobedience, 668.6 be insubordinate, 669.1 resistance, 669.6 resist, 674.1 contention, 674.13 conflict, 693.15 be disobedient, 713.1, 713.6 protest, 720.7 not observe, 764.11 quarrel, 785.1, 785.5 dislike, 820.12 oppose
Dissent 500
dissenter 168, 500, 666, 117.6 misfit, 139.4 individualist, 335.19 deviant person, 475.8 protester, 477.9 questioner, 498.5 disbeliever, 536.6 negativist, 573.16 reluctant person, 663.9 opposer, 713.4 protester, 720.5 nonobserver
dissenters 500
dissentience 500
dissentient 168.8 dissenter, 168.12 nonconformist, 473.7 arguing, 500.5 dissenter, 500.7 dissenting, 663.9 opposer, 663.20 discordant, 666.4 dissenter, 666.9 disagreeing, 713.4 protester
dissentiently 500
dissenting 113, 500, 711, 117.10 disagreeing, 136.18 disagreeable, 168.12 nonconformist, 463.9 argumentative, 473.7 arguing, 475.14 demonstrating, 498.6 disbelieving, 536.13 rebutting, 573.2 refusing, 573.5 reluctant, 663.20 discordant, 666.9 disagreeing, 669.10 resistant, 693.13 disobedient, 698.10 independent, 713.9 protesting, 785.8 disliking, 820.9 aggressive, 852.26 disagreeing
dissentingly 113.10 diversely, 536.15 negatively, 666.11 in disagreement, 669.14 resistingly, 693.17 disobediently, 711.11 uncooperatively
dissentious 473.8 argumentative
dissertate 561
dissertation 561, 48.4 nonfiction, 492.1 judgment, 553.1 diffuseness, 564.8 speech
Dissertation 561
dissertator 561
disservice 614.3 uselessness, 832.7 act of malevolence
dissidence 117.4 disagreement, 168.2 dissent, 500.3 dissentience, 663.2 objection, 666.1 disagreement, 711.2 dissent, 720.3 disregard of orders
dissident 117.6 misfit, 117.10 disagreeing, 168.8 dissenter, 168.12 nonconformist, 335.19 deviant person, 475.8 protester, 498.5 disbeliever, 500.5 dissenter, 500.7 dissenting, 573.2 refusing, 573.16 reluctant person, 663.9 opposer, 663.20 dis-

cordant, 666.4 *dissenter,* 666.9 *disagreeing,* 693.7 *protester,* 711.4 *refuser,* 711.9 *dissenting,* 713.4 *protester,* 720.5 *nonobserver,* 720.11 *nonobservant,* 720.13 *noncompliant*

dissidently 711.11 *uncooperatively*

dissidents 500.6 *dissenters*

dissilience 241.3 *instance of violence*

dissimilar 115, 108.8 *distorted,* 113.5 *diverse,* 117.7 *disparate,* 123.3 *unequal,* 548.6 *misrepresented,* 666.10 *different*

dissimilarity 115, 108.4 *distortion,* 113.1 *diversity,* 117.1 *disparity,* 119.1 *originality,* 123.1 *inequality,* 548.1 *misrepresentation,* 666.3 *difference*

Dissimilarity 115

dissimilarly 115, 117, 108.13 *disproportionately,* 113.10 *diversely,* 123.7 *unequally,* 666.12 *differently*

dissimilation 5.30 *syntax*

dissimilitude 115.1 *dissimilarity,* 117.1 *disparity*

dissimulate 474.12 *deceive,* 540.20 *pretend,* 540.24 *mask*

dissimulated 540.35 *disguised*

dissimulating 474.10 *hypocritical,* 540.30 *pretending*

dissimulation 118.4 *camouflage,* 531.5 *evasion,* 540.7 *pretence,* 540.12 *facade,* 640.2 *deed*

dissimulator 548.3 *deceiver*

dissipate 162.11 *explode,* 162.14 *dilute,* 244.8 *destroy,* 458.3 *cause to disappear,* 607.1 *waste,* 722.11 *be wasteful,* 722.14 *go to waste,* 748.1 *expend,* 757.7 *waste,* 870.11 *overindulge*

dissipated 870, 162.27 *dilute,* 238.11 *weakened,* 458.7 *disappeared,* 877.14 *lecherous*

dissipated person 722.6 *loser*

dissipating 870.7 *dissipated*

dissipation 870, 56.15 *wave property,* 162.3 *dilution,* 238.3 *poor health,* 405.1 *physical pleasure,* 458.4 *disappearance,* 607.3, 722.3 *waste,* 757.5 *unrestrainedness,* 877.3 *sexual immorality*

dissipative 162.28 *dispersive*

dissipatively 162.29 *dispersively*

dissociability 816.1 *unsociability*

dissociable 816.8 *unsociable*

dissociableness 816.1 *unsociability*

dissocial 816.8 *unsociable*

dissociate 57.26 *react,* 136.9 *separate*

dissociated 61.36 *psychologically disturbed,* 104.11 *separate*

dissociate oneself 536.7 *be negative,* 573.9 *not cooperate*

dissociate oneself from 663.14 *be against*

dissociation 61, 573, 104.3 *separateness,* 536.2 *rejection,* 663.4 *uncooperativeness*

dissociation energy 57.11 *chemical bond*

dissociation of personality 61.16 *dissociation*

dissociation reaction 61.10 *neurosis*

dissociative 536.11 *negative*

dissociative hysteria 61.12 *stress*

dissoluble 136.19 *separable,* 387.21 *liquefiable*

dissolute 870.7 *dissipated,* 877.14 *lecherous*

dissoluteness 870.2 *dissipation,* 877.3 *sexual immorality*

dissolution 136.1 *separation,* 141.2 *deconstruction,* 157.4 *annihilation,* 162.2 *disbandment,* 244.2 *destroying,* 387.8 *fluidification,* 458.4 *disappearance,* 727.1 *disposal*

dissolutional 387.20 *liquefying*

dissolution of marriage 824.1 *divorce*

dissolvable 136.19 *separable,* 387.21 *liquefiable*

dissolve 387, 57.25 *solidify,* 100.13 *cease to exist,* 121.6 *change gradually,* 136.9 *separate,* 141.4 *deconstruct,* 157.17 *kill,* 162.13 *dismiss,* 162.14 *dilute,* 244.8 *destroy,* 389.30 *dilute,* 458.1 *disappear,* 727.9 *dispose of*

dissolved 133.12 *mixed,* 141.5 *disintegrated,* 157.23 *annihilated,* 162.21 *disbanded,* 387.19 *liquefied,* 824.11 *divorced*

dissolve into 220.7 *convert into*

dissolve into chaos 151.25 *be disordered*

dissolvent 387.9 *solvent*

dissolve one's marriage 824.7 *divorce*

dissolver 387.9 *solvent*

dissolving 387.8 *fluidification,* 387.20 *liquefying,* 458.6 *disappearing*

dissolving agent 387.9 *solvent*

dissonance 434, 117.4 *disagreement,* 423.1 *loudness,* 430.1 *stridency*

Dissonance 434

dissonant 434, 117.10 *disagreeing,* 430.7 *strident*

dissonant chord 434.3 *musical dissonance*

dissonantly 434, 117.16 *disagreeably*

dissonant noise 434

dissuade 587, 636.5 *warn,* 654.5 *advise,* 661.8 *hinder*

dissuaded 587

dissuasion 587, 636.1 *warning,* 661.1 *hindrance*

Dissuasion 587

dissuasive 587, 636.8 *warning,* 654.7 *advising,* 661.13 *hindering*

dissuasively 587, 661.16 *with delay*

distaff 288.3 *weaving,* 364.4 *vortex*

distaff side 402.13 *womenfolk*

distal 263.8 *distant*

distance 263, 616, 248.8 *intervening space,* 265.1 *interval,* 268.4 *size,* 269.4 *length,* 336.9 *maintain progress,* 438.6 *that which makes invisible,* 441.2 *murk,* 591.10 *avoidance,* 816.1 *unsociability*

Distance 263

distance between 265.1 *interval*

distance event 20.1 *angling*

distance learning 6.2 *educational system*

distance onself 263.6 *keep away*

distant 263, 616, 104.12 *external,* 108.7 *illogical,* 209.13 *later,* 238.13 *insufficient,* 424.4 *faint,* 428.1 *faint-sounding,* 438.2 *difficult to see,* 441.6 *murky,* 466.4 *uninterested,* 598.6 *apathetic,* 805.15 *unapproachable,* 816.8 *unsociable,* 820.8 *estranged*

distantly 263, 104.18 *extraneously,* 424.7 *faintly,* 591.21 *away,* 598.8 *apathetically,* 816.14 *unsocially*

distant past 3, 202.3 *antiquity*

distant place 263

distant sound 424.1 *faintness*

distant time 197.1 *different time*

distaste 785.1 *dislike,* 852.1 *disapproval*

distasteful 764.1 *unpleasant,* 785.9 *disliked,* 790.4 *ugly*

distastefully 764.13 *unpleasantly*

distastefulness 764.5 *unpleasantness*

distemper 50.11 *artist's materials,* 444.4 *pigment,* 444.15 *colour,* 624.2 *illness,* 624.18 *veterinary disease*

distempered 624.23 *diseased*

distend 128.4 *increase,* 248.20 *extend,* 261.5 *make bigger,* 261.6 *become bigger,* 316.5 *be convex,* 377.8 *be elastic,* 541.8 *enlarge*

distended 259.16 *fat,* 261.7 *bigger,* 316.4 *convex,* 377.6 *elastic*

distender 261.4 *enlarger*

distending 377.6 *elastic*

distensibility 261.2 *enlargeability*

distensible 261.9 *enlargeable,* 377.6 *elastic*

distension 261.1 *growth,* 377.1 *elasticity*

distensive 261.9 *enlargeable*

distention 261.1 *growth,* 316.1 *convexity*

distich 48.8 *part of poem,* 48.9 *metre,* 176.2 *double*

distil 57.25 *solidify,* 134.10 *purify,* 355.17 *obtain an extract,* 388.25 *gasify,* 621.15 *purify,* 794.6 *refine*

distillate 103.3 *quintessence,* 355.8 *extract*

distillation 57.5 *process,* 103.3 *quintessence,* 355.7 *obtaining an extract,* 388.10 *vaporization,* 621.2 *cleaning*

distilled 57.32 *solid,* 351.17 *drinkable,* 621.17 *cleaned*

distilled essence 617.6 *worth*

distilled water 389.1 *water*

distillery 647.1 *workshop*

distinct 52.70 *universal,* 117.9 *nonconforming,* 136.17 *unjoined,* 165.15 *special,* 174.14 *singular,* 237.10 *potent,* 318.7 *conspicuous,* 423.7 *heard,* 435.23, 437.1 *visible,* 437.2 *clear,* 475.12 *demonstrable,* 481.11 *judged,* 490.7 *particular,* 522.2 *simple,* 522.3 *recognizable,* 550.3 *clear,* 611.5 *important*

distinction 163, 115.1 *dissimilarity,* 318.1 *prominence,* 481.1 *discrimination,* 492.1 *judgment,* 522.11 *recognizability,* 558.1 *elegance,* 611.1 *importance,* 794.1 *elegance,* 794.2 *subtlety,* 800.1 *estimation,* 802.3 *nobleness*

distinctive 103.9 *characteristic,* 115.4 *dissimilar,* 136.17 *unjoined,* 163.11 *typical,* 165.15 *special,* 318.6 *eminent,* 558.3 *elegant*

distinctive feature 165.3 *characteristic*

distinctively 115.7 *dissimilarly,* 136.22 *in isolation,* 163.16 *taxonomically,* 165.30 *characteristically,* 318.11 *eminently*

distinctiveness 165.1 *speciality,* 174.4 *singularity,* 522.11 *recognizability,* 544.2 *identity*

distinctly 136.22 *in isolation,* 165.28 *specially,* 237.15 *acutely,* 318.10 *protuberantly,* 423.10 *aloud,* 435.25, 437.11 *visibly,* 481.15 *discriminatingly,* 522.13 *intelligibly,* 550.4 *clearly*

distinctness 117.3 *nonconformity,* 318.4 *conspicuousness,* 423.3 *audibility,* 437.3 *visibility,* 490.18 *particularity,* 522.10 *simplicity,* 550.1 *clarity*

distingué 794.5 *refined*

distinguish 103.11 *characterize,* 115.6 *differentiate,* 136.10 *set apart,* 165.22 *characterize,* 435.12 *see,* 481.12 *discriminate,* 501.11 *know,* 507.7 *be wise,* 522.7 *recognize,* 544.10 *identify,* 580.4 *pick*

distinguishability 522.11 *recognizability*

distinguishable 136.19 *separable,* 437.1 *visible,* 522.3 *recognizable*

distinguished 126.15 *excellent,* 165.17 *exceptional,* 558.3 *elegant,* 611.6 *notable,* 617.1 *worthy,* 800.3 *reputable*

Distinguished Conduct Medal 17 British Military Medals and Decorations

Distinguished Flying Cross 17 British Military Medals and Decorations

Distinguished Flying Medal 17

British Military Medals and Decorations

Distinguished Service Cross 17 British Military Medals and Decorations, **17** US Military Medals and Decorations

Distinguished Service Medal 17 British Military Medals and Decorations, **17** US Military Medals and Decorations

distinguishing 103.9, 165.16 *characteristic,* 544.1 *identification*

distinguishing feature 103.4 *nature*

distort 309, 335, 102.16 *delude,* 115.6 *differentiate,* 117.12 *be disparate,* 216.8 *cause change,* 220.9 *transform,* 286.7 *deviate,* 307.3 *make shapeless,* 314.6 *convolute,* 474.11 *practise sophistry,* 493.10 *misjudge,* 504.19 *make a mistake,* 525.1 *misinterpret,* 538.21 *lie,* 540.22 *falsify,* 548.4 *misrepresent,* 601.1 *misuse,* 628.6 *pervert,* 790.5 *make ugly,* 793.7 *blemish,* 864.17 *make wicked*

distorted 108, 309, 52.79 *spatial,* 117.8 *contradictory,* 123.3 *unequal,* 286.5 *devious,* 335.23 *oblique,* 474.7 *sophistic,* 504.15 *erroneous,* 525.3 *misinterpreted,* 531.15 *disguised,* 538.13 *untrue,* 540.32 *falsified,* 548.6 *misrepresented,* 601.4 *misused,* 620.3 *deformed*

distorted image 548.1 *misrepresentation*

distortedly 309, 525.5 *misrepresentedly,* 538.26 *untruthfully,* 601.6 *abusively*

distorted truth 538.5 *half-truth*

distorter 309.5 *defacer*

distorting mirror 435.8 *reflection,* 436.5 *visual distortion,* 548.1 *misrepresentation*

distortion 108, 309, 63.16 *deformation,* 64.14 *terminal,* 117.2 *contradiction,* 123.1 *inequality,* 216.1 *change,* 286.3 *deviousness,* 335.17 *torsion,* 474.1 *sophistry,* 493.1 *misjudgment,* 504.5 *misrepresentation,* 525.2 *misinterpretation,* 534.19 *radio reception,* 534.23 *television reception,* 538.1 *untruth,* 540.9 *falsification,* 548.1 *misrepresentation,* 601.2 *misuse,* 620.5 *imperfection,* 628.8 *perversion,* 793.1 *spot*

Distortion 309

distortion of the truth 309

distortive 286.5 *devious*

distort the truth 309, 538.21 *lie*

distract 153.10 *disrupt*

distracted 153.15 *disrupted,* 468.7 *inattentive,* 512.8 *oblivious*

distractedly 153, 512.16 *obliviously*

distracting 153.4 *disturbing*

distraction 153.4 *disruption,* 468.1 *inattention*

distrain 125.4 *compensate,* 734.8 *take back*

distraint 125.1 *compensation,* 734.2 *taking back*

distress 153.7 *disturb,* 406.1 *pain,* 618.9 *badness,* 618.14 *illtreat,* 631.1 *affliction,* 648.4 *haste,* 650.6 *fatigue,* 687.1 *adversity,* 743.5 *poverty,* 770.1 *sorrow,* 777.13 *frighten,* 862.2 *affliction,* 862.11 *be evil*

distress call 543.6 *word*

distressed 153.12 *disturbed,* 406.7 *feeling pain,* 659.16 *troubled,* 770.5 *sad,* 777.8 *fearful,* 862.8 *afflicted*

distress flare 636.2 *danger signal*

distressing 770, 153.17 *disturbing,* 406.5 *painful,* 618.3 *bad,* 774.5 *lamentable,* 835.7 *pitiful,* 862.9 *detrimental*

distressingly 862.13 *destructively*

distress signal 543.4 *signal*, 636.2 *danger signal*
distributary 96.1 *river*
distribute 162, 70.4 *transport*, 124.10 *make average*, 152.12 *arrange*, 163.13 *class*, 532.15 *publish*, 606.5 *provision*, 731.4 *allot*, 746.11 *remunerate*
distributed 162, 532.19 *published*, 731.7 *allocated*
distributer 70.3 *transporter*
distribution 13.6 *economic factors*, 70.1 *transport*, 150.1 *order*, 162.1 *dispersion*, 606.1 *provision*, 731.1 *allocation*, 739.3 *selling*
distribution network 64.33 *power distribution*
distributive 162.28 *dispersive*
distributive law 52 Theorems and Laws
distributively 162.29 *dispersively*, 727.16 *disposably*
distributive operation 52.14 *operation*
distributor 71 Motor Vehicle Parts, 69.6 *garden tool*, 158.9 *middleman*, 235.7 *electrical power*, 737.10 *trader*
distributor of largess 729.4 *giver*
district 12.5 *political organization*, 92.1 *administrative area*, 93.7 *city district*, 143.1 *part*, 249.5 *state*, 249.17 *national*, 567.5 *place of residence*, 688.8 *governmental organization*
district attorney 16.10 *law officer*, 16.12 *US law officer*, 492.6 *justice*, 856.3 *accuser*
District Attorney 699.6 *law-maker*
district council 16.2 *jurisdiction*, 653.8 *British administrative council*
District Court 16.21 *US court*
district court martial 17.6 *military law*
district judge 16.24 *US judge*
district magistrate 16.23 *US judge*
district nurse 60.16 *nurse*
district officer 653.16 *official*
district official 15.7 *employee*
distrust 841, 841, 477.6 *uncertainty*, 477.20 *doubt*, 491.10 *suspicion*, 491.18 *be uncertain*, 498.1 *disbelief*, 498.8 *disbelieve*, 810.5 *self-depreciation*
distrustful 841, 477.15 *sceptical*, 491.1 *uncertain*, 498.6 *disbelieving*
distrustfully 498.10 *disbelievingly*, 841.9 *jealously*
distrustfulness 841.2 *distrust*
distrust of mankind 834.1 *misanthropy*
distrust people 834.4 *become a misanthrope*
disturb 153, 141.4 *deconstruct*, 151.21 *disorder*, 151.22 *discompose*, 160.16 *interrupt*, 211.5 *take untimely action*, 252.14 *displace*, 366.22 *agitate*, 403.13 *arouse sensation*, 491.20 *make uncertain*, 616.5 *be inconvenient*, 659.23 *cause difficulties*
disturbance 153, 141.1 *disintegration*, 151.1, 151.9 *disorder*, 153.4 *disruption*, 153.5 *commotion*, 160.6 *intervention*, 211.1 *untimeliness*, 241.3 *instance of violence*, 252.1 *displacement*, 366.2 *tumult*, 366.13 *tempest*, 616.3 *inconvenience*, 642.1 *activity*
Disturbance 153
disturbed 153, 61.36 *psychologically disturbed*, 151.17 *discomposed*, 153.16 *deranged*, 160.10 *interrupted*, 241.6 *violent*, 252.8 *displaced*, 366.15 *agitated*, 510.11 *insane*, 510.13 *mentally ill*
disturbed person 61.8 *disordered personality*
disturbing 153, 211.10 *untimely*, 252.8 *displaced*, 616.1 *inconvenient*

disturbingly 153, 141.8 *destructively*, 211.15 *at the wrong time*
disturb one's equanimity 828.14 *make angry*
disulfiram 62 Medication
disulphide bond 58.8 *amino acid*
disunion 117.4 *disagreement*, 136.1 *separation*, 141.2 *deconstruction*, 500.3 *dissentience*
disunite 117.14 *disagree*, 136.9 *separate*, 160.14 *disconnect*, 727.9 *dispose of*, 820.13 *antagonize*
disunited 117.10 *disagreeing*, 136.15 *separate*, 160.8 *discontinuous*, 820.8 *estranged*
disunity 136, 117.4 *disagreement*, 136.1 *separation*, 666.1 *disagreement*, 764.7 *dissension*
disusage 585.3 *unaccustomedness*
disuse 600, 581.6 *discarding*, 585.3 *unaccustomedness*, 598.3 *relinquishment*, 600.6 *stop using*, 727.1 *disposal*
disused 600, 581.10 *rejected*, 585.2 *not customary*
dit 534.8 *data transmission*
ditali 45 Types of Pasta
ditalini 45 Types of Pasta
ditalini rigati 45 Types of Pasta
ditaloni 45 Types of Pasta
ditch 25.1 *green bowling*, 98.8 *valley*, 147.3 *exclusion zone*, 265.2, 265.5 *crack*, 272.6 *narrow place*, 301.3 *enclosing thing*, 321.1, 321.6 *furrow*, 327.11 *channel*, 581.2 *discard*, 598.2 *withdraw*, 600.6 *stop using*, 632.2 *protection*, 657.2 *stratagem*, 661.3 *barrier*, 671.8 *military defences*, 727.9 *dispose of*
ditchwater 622.5 *swill*
diterpene 58.20 *terpene*
dither 365.10 *vacillate*, 366.1 *agitation*, 366.21 *be agitated*, 366.25 *pitch*, 491.19 *hesitate*, 576.5 *vacillate*
ditherer 576.15 *indecisive person*, 641.2 *nonacting person*
dithering 238.12 *weak-willed*, 365.15, 576.1 *vacillating*
dithranol 62 Medication
dithyramb 48.7 *poem*, 812.1 *celebration*
dithyrambic 564.20 *eloquent*, 812.10 *celebrative*
dithyrambist 48.14 *author*
Diti 8 Deities
ditties 48.6 *poetry*
ditto 110.4, 110.9 *duplicate*, 110.18 *identically*, 118.14 *imitatively*, 183.1 *repetition*, 183.24 *again*, 499.9 *yes*, 667.6 *agree with*
diuretic 62.4 *drug type*, 62.17 *stimulating*, 134.4 *purgative*, 353.26 *urinary*, 630.6 *purgative*
diuretically 353.33 *scatologically*
diurnal 76.15 *of animals*, 214.12 *cyclic*
diurnally 214.16 *cyclically*
diva 51.22 *actor*, 126.6 *paragon*, 655.4 *skilled person*
divagate 334.4 *detour*, 335.3 *go astray*
divagation 334.2 *detour*, 335.13 *deviation*
divagatory 335.25 *wandering*
divalent 57.35 *combined*
Divali 10.16 *religious festival*
divan 47.2 *chair*, 47.6 *bed*
divaricate 335.1 *deviate*, 343.6 *divergent*, 343.10 *diverge*
divaricating 335.24 *diverging*
divarication 335.13 *deviation*, 343.1 *divergence*
dive 39, 360, 36.16 *row*, 38.4 *play soccer*, 39.6 *diving*, 73.5 *flight*, 74.10 *sail*, 256.8 *shelter*, 277.14 *deepen*, 281.1 *verticality*, 281.7 *fall vertically*, 329.4 *be swift*, 329.9 *acceleration*, 360.9 *descend*, 360.12 *drop*
dive bomber 73 Types of Aircraft

dive-bomber 670.19 *attacker*
dive-bombing 670.13 *air attack*
dive brake 73 Aircraft Parts
Divehi 5 Languages and Groups of Languages
dive in 156.18 *make a beginning*
dive into 346.13 *fall into*
diver 78 Birds, 78.3 *water bird*, 360.8 *descender*
diverge 136, 162, 343, 52.97 *align*, 113.8 *be diverse*, 115.5 *be dissimilar*, 117.12 *be disparate*, 271.11 *broaden*, 286.6 *be oblique*, 334.4 *detour*, 335.1 *deviate*, 335.12 *deflect*, 553.6 *be circuitous*, 666.8 *be different*
divergence 162, 343, 52.50 *scalar quantity*, 113.1 *diversity*, 115.1 *dissimilarity*, 117.1 *disparity*, 136.1 *separation*, 263.1 *distance*, 286.1 *obliqueness*, 335.13 *deviation*, 666.3 *difference*
Divergence 343
divergence zone 54.19 *plate tectonics*
divergency 343.1 *divergence*
divergent 162, 343, 52.80 *linear*, 115.4 *dissimilar*, 117.7 *disparate*, 136.16 *apart*, 286.4 *oblique*, 335.24 *diverging*, 666.10 *different*
divergently 343, 115.7 *dissimilarly*, 136.21 *apart*, 666.12 *differently*
divergent opinions 117.4 *disagreement*
divergent series 52.20 *sequence*
divergent strabismus 436.2 *poor sight*
diverging 335, 113.5 *diverse*, 343.6 *divergent*
diverging lens 56.29 *optical element*
diverging lines 52.37 *line*
divers 113.6 *assorted*, 175.7 *various*
diverse 113, 115.4 *dissimilar*, 117.7 *disparate*, 123.3 *unequal*, 175.7 *various*, 215.4 *irregular*, 216.11 *changeable*, 473.7 *arguing*
diversely 113, 115.7, 117.15 *dissimilarly*, 123.7 *unequally*, 175.10 *plurally*, 216.15 *changeably*, 456.12 *variedly*, 473.17 *argumentatively*
diverse thing 113
diversification 113.1 *diversity*, 216.1 *change*, 456.1 *variegation*
diversified 164.15 *general*, 216.12 *changed*
diversiform 113.5 *diverse*, 113.6 *assorted*
diversify 113.8 *be diverse*, 117.12 *be disparate*, 216.7 *be changed*, 216.8 *cause change*, 456.11 *variegate*
diversion 216.1 *change*, 334.2 *detour*, 335.13 *deviation*, 335.14 *deviating course*, 356.2 *passing along*, 539.8 *trick*, 539.12 *disguise*, 539.13 *snare*, 601.2 *misuse*, 612.8 *trifle*, 763.7 *pleasure*, 771.2 *amusement*
diversity 113, 115.1 *dissimilarity*, 117.1 *disparity*, 123.1 *inequality*, 168.1 *nonconformity*, 175.2 *multiplicity*, 215.1 *irregularity*, 216.1 *change*, 456.1 *variegation*, 473.1 *argument*
Diversity 113
diversity of colours 456.1 *variegation*
divert 335, 216.7 *be changed*, 216.8 *cause change*, 335.1 *deviate*, 335.7 *misdirect*, 539.28 *trick*, 539.32 *disguise*, 539.33 *snare*, 601.1 *misuse*, 747.7 *not pay*, 771.13 *be humorous*
divert a river 96.8 *cause to flow*
diverted 601.4 *misused*
diverted call 534.10 *telephone call*
diverting 769.2 *cheering*, 771.9 *funny*
divertissement 51.2 *play*

Dives 742.10 *wealthy person*
Dives and Lazarus 111.2 *opposites*
divest 131.4 *take off*, 294.11 *uncover*, 296.14 *undress*, 598.1 *relinquish*, 704.7 *terminate*, 722.9 *lose*, 734.8 *take back*
divested 294.8 *uncovered*, 296.11 *exposed*
divestiture 294.1 *uncovering*
divestment 294.1 *uncovering*, 296.1 *undress*, 722.1 *loss*, 734.2 *taking back*
dividable 731.7 *allocated*
divide 136, 173, 52.91 *add*, 54.8 *drainage*, 60.20 *practise surgery*, 104.15 *separate*, 117.14 *disagree*, 120.8 *quantify*, 124.10 *make average*, 136.14 *come between*, 141.4 *deconstruct*, 143.10 *part*, 162.12 *disperse*, 163.14 *sort*, 170.9 *add*, 257.9 *itemize*, 275.4 *mountain range*, 298.4 *interface*, 343.12 *separate*, 481.12 *discriminate*, 500.8 *dissent*, 580.5 *vote*, 598.2 *withdraw*, 666.5 *disagree*, 666.7 *pick a fight*, 731.4 *allot*, 820.13 *antagonize*
divide and rule 12.11 *govern*
divide by four 178.12 *quadrisect*
divide by three 177.11 *trisect*
divide by two 176.16 *halve*
divided 136.15 *separate*, 143.11 *partial*, 257.12 *itemized*, 481.11 *judged*, 731.7 *allocated*, 820.8 *estranged*
divided by 52.88 *equal to*
divided by two 176.13 *half*
divided into 52.88 *equal to*
divided skirt 295.6 *skirt*
divide fifty-fifty 158.17 *average*
divide in half 176.16 *halve*
divide into four 178.12 *quadrisect*
dividend 32.7 *horseracing*, 52.18 *division*, 132.4 *surplus*, 143.1 *part*, 243.7 *produce*, 724.1 *joint possession*, 730.2 *something received*, 731.2 *portion*
dividends 14.2 *stock exchange*, 721.5 *profit*
divide proportionately 731.4 *allot*
dividers 52.49 *geometric construction*, 170.5 *computer*, 268.6 *measuring instrument*
divide up 136.11 *divide*, 731.4 *allot*
dividing 136.15 *separate*
dividing by four 178.5 *quadrisection*
dividing by three 177.5 *trisection*
dividing by two 176.7 *halving*
dividing line 122, 136.5 *separator*
divi-divi 85 Trees and Shrubs
divination 11, 517, 8.8 *divine manifestation*, 11.1 *occultism*, 464.2 *precognition*, 516.3 *foresight*, 524.5 *science of interpretation*, 759.2 *impression*
divinatory 11, 464.7 *precognitive*
divine 8, 11, 517, 7.14 *theologian*, 7.18 *theological*, 99.14 *self-existent*, 199.9 *look ahead*, 464.9 *be intuitive*, 516.1 *foresee*, 518.5 *suppose*, 696.12 *masterful*, 763.1 *pleasant*, 821.22 *lovable*
divine afflatus 519.2 *inspiration*
divine attribute 8
Divine Creator 226.7 *Prime Mover*
divine essence 8.1 *divinity*
divine justice 879.9 *retribution*
divine king 696.2 *sovereign*
divinely 8
divine manifestation 8
divine nature 8.1 *divinity*
divineness 8.1 *divinity*
divine office 10.4 *public worship*
divine principle 8.1 *divinity*
diviner 11, 199.5 *predictor*, 464.5 *intuitive person*, 517.9 *forecaster*, 519.9 *visionary*, 524.6 *interpreter*, 464.5 *warner*
divine revelation 8.8 *divine manifestation*
divine right 688.1 *authority*
divine service 10.4 *public worship*

diving **18** Sporting Activities, **39**, 36.4, 36.11 rowing, 277.1 depth, 360.18 falling

diving beetle **82** Insects

diving bell 97.5 oceanography, 277.4 deep thing, 360.8 descender

diving bird 78.3 water bird, 360.8 descender

diving board 39.6 diving, 283.5 projecting object, 377.3 elastic thing

diving duck 78.3 water bird

diving mask 39.8 swimwear

diving position 39.6 diving

diving vessel 97.5 oceanography

divining 11.9 divination

divining rod 496.11 detector

divining rods 11.9 divination

divinity **8**, 7.13 theology, 8.5 deity, 99.7 self-existence

Divinity **8**

divinization 8.9 deification

divinize 8.17 deify

divinized 8.15 deified

divisi **49** Musical Terms

divisibility 52.18 division

divisible **52**, 136.19 separable, 731.7 allocated

division **52**, 17.4 military organization, 18.1 sport, 59.17 taxonomy, 60.9 surgery, 92.1 administrative area, 136.2 setting apart, 136.3 separateness, 140.3 assembly, 141.2 deconstruction, 143.1 part, 148.2 piece, 152.6 category, 161.14 force, 163.2 class, 170.1 calculation, 173.2 fractional part, 249.5 state, 343.2 parting, 481.1 discrimination, 500.4 faction, 665.10 legislative body, 666.1 disagreement, 679.16 army unit, 731.1 allocation

divisional 92.6 administrative, 173.5 fractional, 249.17 national, 481.9 discriminating

divisional commander 17.5 military staff

divisionally 92.8 administratively, 249.20 nationally, 257.15 thematically

division championship 682.3 successful thing

Division I 36.7 windsurfing

Division II 36.7 windsurfing

Division III 36.7 windsurfing

divisionism **50** Western Art Styles and Movements

divisionist 50.29 realist

division line 298.1 interface

divisions **257**

division sign 52.13 mathematical symbol, 543.1 sign

divisive 298.5 interfacial, 500.7 dissenting, 666.9 disagreeing

divisively 141.8 destructively, 481.15 discriminatingly, 500.10 dissentiently, 666.11 in disagreement

divisiveness 666.1 disagreement

divisor 52.18 division, 143.1 part

divorce **824**, **824**, 108.1 unrelatedness, 136.1 separation, 136.9 separate, 136.11 divide, 174.6 singleness, 727.1 disposal, 727.9 dispose of, 820.2 personal conflict

divorcé 824.4 divorced person

divorce case 824.3 divorce court

divorce court **824**, 16.19 lawcourt

divorced **824**, 108.6 unrelated, 136.15 separate, 174.17 single, 727.12 disposed , 816.10 lonely

divorce decree 824.1 divorce

divorced man 824.4 divorced person

divorced person **824**

divorced woman 824.4 divorced person

divorcée 174.7 single person, 401.5 single man, 402.5 single girl, 824.4 divorced person

divorcement 136.1 separation, 824.1 divorce

divorcer 824.4 divorced person

divorce settlement 824.3 divorce court

Divorce; Widowhood **824**

divot 29.2 golfing terms, 87.2 grassland, 143.7 piece

divulgation 532.1 publication

divulge **530**, 6.22 educate, 496.2 detect, 526.3 reveal, 532.13 make public

divulged 526.14 manifest

divulgence **530**, 496.7 detection, 532.1 publication

divulging 530.11 disclosing

divvying up 731.1 allocation

divvy up 731.4 allot

Dixie 249.8 regions of the US

Dixieland 49.8, 49.33 jazz, 249.8 regions of the US

DIY 656.4 bungled, 658.1 naive

DIY type 655.4 skilled person

dizzily 224.15 changeably

dizziness 123.1 inequality, 238.3 poor health, 364.1 rotation, 468.3 absent-mindedness, 543.1 sign, 624.3 symptom, 874.10 drunkenness, 874.15 crapulence

dizzy 123.3 unequal, 224.14 irresolute, 275.9 high, 364.12 rotary, 468.10 careless, 874.2 slightly drunk, 874.4 crapulous

dizzy round 364.3 reel

Djibouti **91** Countries

djunadjan **49** Musical Instruments

D-layer 534.15 transmitted wave

DML 65.9 programming language

DNA 58.10 nucleoside, 59.9 cell nucleus, 59.13 genetic material

DNA double helix 59.12 molecular biology

DNA fingerprinting 544.3 means of identification

Dnieper **96** Rivers

Dniester **96** Rivers

D-notice 531.4 silence, 699.1 restraint, 709.2 censorship

do 144.4 complete, 161.9 social gathering, 230.7 be operational, 232.4 be an instrument, 243.10 produce, 350.13 feast, 597.1 undertake, 608.4 suffice, 615.6 be convenient, 640.4 act, 642.12 be active, 652.11 conduct oneself, 652.14 behave towards, 682.8 be effective, 684.4 complete, 719.6 perform, 753.10 overcharge, 765.10 suffice, 812.1 celebration

do a backward somersault 30.10 compete in gymnastics

do a bad job 656.7 be clumsy

doable 230.11 workable, 486.5 possible

do a bunk 254.18 abscond, 591.9 play truant, 638.5 escape, 685.6 drop out, 779.4 be a coward

do a cartwheel vault 30.10 compete in gymnastics

do a christie 41.14 ski

do a combat sport **26**

do addition 130.6 add

do a deal 667.7 contract

do a favour 662.22 improve, 831.8 be benevolent

do again 183.16 repeat, 221.7 restore

do a good deed 833.7 be charitable

do a good turn 617.10 do good, 662.22 improve, 833.7 be charitable

do a handspring 30.10 compete in gymnastics

do a handstand 30.10 compete in gymnastics

do aid climbing 34.9 mountaineer

do a job 736.12 steal

do a job on 674.11 contend

do a kindness 831.8 be benevolent

do all one can 648.8 exert oneself

do all right by oneself 686.5 be prosperous

do all that is possible 608.4 suffice

do all the talking 569.4 monopolize the conversation

do alpine racing 41.14 ski

do a moonlight flit 345.3 quit, 638.5 escape, 745.8, 747.7 not pay

do an about-turn 221.6 reverse

do and no more 608.4 suffice

do a nine-to-five 644.6 work

do an optional exercise 30.10 compete in gymnastics

do a paper on 561.4 dissertate

do a parallel turn 41.14 ski

do a poo 353.16 defecate

do a portrait 560.14 describe

do a prescribed exercise 30.10 compete in gymnastics

do a project on 472.11 raise the point

do a repeat 183.16 repeat

do artistically 558.4 be elegant

do a runner 458.2 depart, 632.8 be safe

do a slow burn 828.12 become angry

do as one chooses 698.16 be independent

do as one is told 694.5 obey

do as one likes 570.14 follow one's own will

do as one pleases 689.4 be anarchic, 698.16 be independent

do as one would be done by 831.8 be benevolent

do as others do 167.8 comply

do as the Romans do 167.8 comply

do a swap 737.1 trade

do at the last moment 648.2 make haste

do a turn-around 536.9 renounce

do a U-turn 216.7 be changed, 221.6, 484.8 reverse, 536.9 renounce, 578.2 equivocate, 734.9 withdraw a statement

do away with 244.8 destroy, 349.10 exterminate, 398.16 kill, 704.6 cancel

do away with oneself 398.21 commit suicide

do a wheelie 33.10 be on the track

do a world of good 617.10, 861.20 do good

dob 480.3 testify, 483.13 turn Queen's evidence

do badly 618.13 be worthless, 656.7 be clumsy, 663.6 fail

do battle 676.14 battle

dobber 480.7 verifier, 483.7 person who gives evidence

dobbin 32.1 horse

do before **194**

Döbereiner's triads 57.6 chemical element

Doberman pinscher **77** Breeds of Dogs

do bird 699.11 detain, 702.10 be in prison

do boring work 788.7 suffer boredom

dobro **49** Musical Instruments

dobsonfly **82** Insects

Dobsonian telescope 53.24 telescope

do business 640.4 act, 716.4 negotiator, 737.1 trade

do business with 664.14 join with, 737.1 trade

do by fits and starts 579.5 be capricious

do by halves 685.5 not complete

doc 60.11 doctor, 630.15 healer

docent 6.4 educator

Docetism **7** Christian Movements

do charity work 710.11 volunteer

do chores 697.8 serve

docile 6.17 educatable, 150.17 disciplined, 228.13 suggestible, 572.3 amenable, 586.20 persuadable, 660.13 easygoing, 673.5 submitting, 694.7 obedient, 847.9 loyal, 861.4 well-behaved

docilely 6.26 studiously, 228.14

influentially, 694.10, 861.24 obediently

docility 6.10 educatability, 228.6 suggestibility, 572.8 acquiescence, 586.7 persuadability, 694.1 obedience, 847.3 allegiance, 861.11 good behaviour

dock **84** Flowers and Flowering Plants, 16.27 courtroom, 63.24 water system, 74.10 sail, 129.5 make smaller, 131.4 take off, 136.10 set apart, 270.10 shorten, 344.4 land, 344.10 stopover, 345.10 place of departure, 492.3 place of judgment, 605.4 storage, 628.5 hurt, 634.2 shelter, 647.1 workshop

dock at a port 98.12 be marooned

docked 131.7 reduced, 145.4 incomplete, 270.8, 562.7 shortened

docker 70.3 transporter, 646.1 worker

docket 171.4 bill, 171.5 list of appointments, 544.3 means of identification, 544.10 identify, 545.1 record, 545.15 register, 708.2 permit, 718.2 promise, 730.3 acknowledgment of payment

docking 53.35 rocketry, 131.1 subtraction, 136.3 separateness, 270.2 shortening, 327.13 flight path, 344.11 landing

Docklands 93.5 London

dockyard 647.1 workshop

Doc Martens 295.19 footwear

do compulsory figures 41.15 iceskate

do cross-country skiing 41.14 ski

doctor **60**, **630**, 6.4 educator, 60.19 practise medicine, 133.8 mix, 216.8 cause change, 233.5 influential person, 397.9 person dealing with the dead, 467.6 attentive person, 469.7 caring person, 485.8 qualified person, 540.22 falsify, 629.6 cure, 629.12 repairer, 630.15 healer, 654.4 adviser, 662.19 support, 750.7 account, 767.5 helper

doctoral 6.21 curricular

doctoring 540.9 falsification

Doctor Jekyll and Mister Hyde 224.5 changeable person

Doctor of Divinity **485** Educational Qualifications

Doctor of Education **485** Educational Qualifications

Doctor of Jurisprudence **485** Educational Qualifications

Doctor of Laws **485** Educational Qualifications

Doctor of Letters **485** Educational Qualifications

Doctor of Medicine **485** Educational Qualifications

Doctor of Music **485** Educational Qualifications

Doctor of Philosophy **485** Educational Qualifications

doctors and nurses **42** Children's Games and Party Games

doctrinaire 490.2 convinced, 490.11 opinionist, 518.4 theorist

doctrinal 6.21 curricular, 7.18 theological, 497.14 believed

doctrinalism 7.13 theology

doctrinally 7.23 religiously

doctrinarian 4.10 philosopher, 518.4 theorist

doctrine 4.1 philosophy, 7.1 religion, 497.2 religious belief

doctrine of chance 589.7 calculation of chance

doctrinism 7.13 theology

docudrama 51.2 play, 534.25 broadcast material, 560.3 narration

document **528**, 3.20 chronicle, 106.11 circumstantiate, 258.5 packet, 480.1 verify, 483.6 documentation, 528.12 communicate, 533.13 report, 537.31 be accurate, 545.1, 545.13 record, 594.2 do the groundwork

documental 537.21 accurate

documentary 3.5 *chronicle*, 101.3 *realism*, 483.8 *evidential*, 533.6 *radio news*, 537.21 *accurate*, 545.16 *recorded*, 560.3 *narration*, 560.4 *factual account*, 560.12 *narrative*

documentary account 560.4 *factual account*

documentary drama 51.2 *play*, 560.3 *narration*

documentary evidence 483.5 *legal evidence*

documentary photography 66.1 *photography*

documentary theatre 51.8 *theatre movements*

documentation 483, 3.5 *chronicle*, 356.6 *passport*, 480.4 *verification*, 480.6 *evidence*, 485.3 *qualifications*, 537.8 *accuracy*, 545.1 *record*

documented 3.19 *chronicled*, 480.8 *verifiable*, 480.10 *verified*, 483.8 *evidential*, 485.10 *authorized*, 490.1 *certain*, 537.21 *accurate*, 545.16 *recorded*

documented fact 503.3 *accurate thing*

documents 480.6 *evidence*, 545.1 *record*

do curling 41.16 *bobsled*

dodder 202.17 *grow old*, 207.17 *age*, 238.6 *be weak*

dodderer 207.7 *older person*

doddering 202.11 *old*, 207.14 *aged*, 366.18 *shaky*

doddle 477.5 *easy question*, 660.6 *easy thing*

dodecagon 179.7 *double figures*

dodecahedron 52.46 *polyhedron*, 179.7 *double figures*

dodecahydrate 57.10 *salt*

dodecaphony 434.4 *atonality*

dodge 324.15 *walk*, 331.2 *respond*, 331.6 *response*, 474.2 *sophism*, 474.12 *deceive*, 531.11 *conceal oneself*, 538.10 *dishonesty*, 539.8 *trick*, 539.10 *fraud*, 539.28 *trick*, 539.30 *be fraudulent*, 578.1 *be equivocal*, 591.6 *evade*, 591.14 *evasion*, 592.3 *expedient plan*, 638.2 *means of escape*, 638.6 *elude*, 655.1 *skill*, 657.2 *stratagem*, 657.5 *be cunning*, 720.8 *not perform*, 722.15 *lose someone*

dodge about 224.12 *be irresolute*

dodger 591.17 *avoider*, 720.6 *evader*

dodgery 539.7 *tricking*

dodge the draft 720.8 *not perform*

dodgily 474.15 *hypocritically*

dodging 539.34 *deceiving*, 540.11 *evasion*, 540.34 *evasive*, 720.12 *nonperforming*

dodgy 474.8 *cunning*, 539.34 *deceiving*, 620.1 *imperfect*, 633.1 *dangerous*, 801.4 *disreputable*

do dirt-track racing 33.9 *race*

do displacement sailing 36.18 *windsurf*

dodo 78 Birds, 78.8 *extinct bird*, 584.8 *creature of habit*

Dodoma 93 Cities

do down 854.10 *disparage*

do dull work 788.7 *suffer boredom*

do duty for 222.4 *be a substitute*, 707.4 *substitute for*, 767.11 *assist*

doe 77.18 *female mammal*, 329.12 *swift animal*, 402.14 *female animal*

do easily 660

do easy work 644.6 *work*

doer 640, 336.16 *progressive person*, 642.10 *busy person*, 646.3 *agent*, 653.15 *manager*, 715.4 *contractor*

doeskin 67 *Natural Fabrics*, 293.14 *animal covering*, 604.1 *materials*

do evil 618.13 *be worthless*, 862.11 *be evil*

doff 131.4 *take off*, 296.14 *un-*

dress, 598.1 *relinquish*, 600.6 *stop using*

doffing one's cap 817.4 *deference*

doff one's cap 294.11 *uncover*

doff one's cap to 849.19 *take off one's hat to*

doff one's hat 817.13 *defer to*

doff one's hat to 851.15 *compliment*

do for 244.8 *destroy*, 398.17 *murder*, 606.5 *provision*, 618.13 *be worthless*, 662.25 *serve*, 682.9 *be victorious*, 697.8 *serve*

do for effect 811.29 *show off*, 811.31 *put on a show*

do Formula 1 racing 33.9 *race*

do for oneself 606.5 *provision*

do free climbing 34.9 *mountaineer*

do freestyle sailing 36.18 *windsurf*

dog 77 Placental Mammals, **77**, 19.11 *defensive huddle*, 19.16 *play defence*, 37.7 *shoot*, 77.17 *male mammal*, 264.10 *stay near*, 401.16 *male animal*, 590.9 *follow*

dog and bone 534.9 *telephone*

dogbane 84 Flowers and Flowering Plants

dog box 72.6 *rolling stock*

dogbreath 419.2 *something that makes an unpleasant smell*

dog brush 621.10 *cleaning object*

dogcart 71 Carriages and Carts

dog collar 7.11 *vestment*, 295.14 *neckwear*, 313.3 *circular thing*

dog days 55.3 *weather*, 203.3 *summer*, 408.5 *hot weather*

dog-ear 320.1, 320.7 *fold*

dog-eared 320.5 *folded*, 599.9 *used*, 628.13 *dilapidated*, 793.6 *seedy*

dog-eat-dog 674.16 *competitive*, 689.1 *anarchy*, 689.6 *anarchic*

dog-eat-dog competition 674.1 *contention*

dog-end 413.7 *tobacco*

dogfight 674.1 *contention*, 674.6 *fight*, 674.9 *duel*, 676.9 *battle*

dog-fighting 77.23 *mammal hunting*

dogfish 80 Fishes, 45.18 *sea fish*

dog flea 82 Insects, 82.3 *pest*

dog food 350.8 *animal food*

dogfood 875.6 *drug*

dog fox 401.16 *male animal*

dogged 570.8 *wilful*, 574.2 *tenacious*, 575.10 *persevering*, 577.3 *unyielding*, 778.12 *self-reliant*

doggedly 574.17 *resolutely*, 575.13 *persistently*, 577.9 *be obstinate*

doggedness 570.3 *wilfulness*, 574.12 *resolution*, 575.1 *perseverance*, 577.6 *determination*

dogger 37.4 *hunter*, 590.5 *pursuer*

doggerel 48.6 *poetry*, 48.19 *narrative*, 506.1 *nonsense*, 559.9 *inelegant*

dogging 37.2 *hunting*, 590.1 *pursuit*

doggish 77.28 *carnivorous*

doggone 827.11 *miscellaneous euphemisms*

doggy 77.28 *carnivorous*

dog howling at night 618.11 *harmfulness*

dogie 77.19 *young mammal*

dog in the manger 661.7 *hinderer*, 860.3 *selfish person*

dog-in-the-manger 577.1 *obstinate*

dog-in-the-manger policy 147.4 *exclusiveness*

dog Latin 5.18 *slang*

dogleg 286.2 *oblique line*, 310.1 *angle*, 335.5 *twist*, 335.14 *deviating course*

doglegged 310.7 *angular*

dogleg hole 29.1 *golf*

doglike 77.28 *carnivorous*

dog lover 76.10 *animal welfarist*

dogma 4.1 *philosophy*, 7.1 *religion*, 497.2 *religious belief*

dogmatic 481.10 *discriminatory*,

490.2 *convinced*, 497.11 *believing*, 535.14 *assertive*, 554.3 *emphatic*, 577.4 *set*, 809.13 *boastful*, 809.14 *opinionated*

dogmatically 481.17 *prejudicially*, 490.24 *with certainty*, 497.15 *believingly*, 535.25 *explicitly*, 554.7 *emphatically*, 809.24 *pompously*

dogmatic theology 7.13 *theology*

dogmatism 490.10 *conviction*, 577.7 *opinionatedness*

dogmatist 481.7 *bigot*, 490.11 *opinionist*, 577.8 *obstinate person*

dogmatize 490.20 *be certain*, 577.9 *be obstinate*

dognap 736.13 *kidnap*

dognapper 736.8 *thief*

dognapping 736.2 *kidnapping*

dog one's every step 590.9 *follow*

dog one's footsteps 590.9 *follow*

do good 617, 861, 613.10 *benefit*, 615.6 *be convenient*, 833.7 *be charitable*, 863.8 *be virtuous*

do-gooder 572.12 *philanthropist*, 640.3 *doer*, 710.8 *volunteer*, 831.5 *benevolent person*, 833.3 *philanthropist*

do-gooding 833.1 *philanthropy*

dog-paddle 39.1 *swimming*, 39.9 *swim*

dog-paddling 39.1, 39.11 *swimming*

dog racing 674.4 *race*

do grasstrack racing 33.9 *race*

do great deeds 640.4 *act*

dog rose 84 Flowers and Flowering Plants

dogs 161 Collective Names by Animal, **777** Phobias by Topic

dogsbody 642.10 *busy person*, 646.1 *worker*, 697.5 *office assistant*

dog's breakfast 493.2 *mistake*, 559.6 *blunder*, 790.2 *ugly person*

dog's dinner 133.3 *miscellany*, 656.9 *bungling*

dog's home 634.3 *animal shelter*

dog show 526.6 *display*

dogsled 71.10 *sled*

dog someone's footsteps 155.23 *follow close*

dog's-tail 87 Grasses

Dog Star 53 Named Stars

dog's-tooth violet 84 Flowers and Flowering Plants

dog tag 544.3 *means of identification*

dog the footsteps of 180.16 *attend*

dog tick 82 Arachnids, 82.3 *pest*

dog-tired 650.1 *fatigued*

dogtooth 43 Architectural Decoration, 319.2 *notched thing*

dogtrot 324.12 *gait*, 328.1 *move slowly*, 328.10 *slow motion*

dog violet 84 Flowers and Flowering Plants

dogwatch 205.4 *evening thing*

dog-weary 650.1 *fatigued*

dogwood 85 Trees and Shrubs

do habitually 212.7 *be frequent*

do hard work 644.6 *work*

Dohnányi 49 Musicians and Composers

do homage 673.4 *succumb*, 849.18 *show respect*

do housework 697.8 *serve*

doism 11.3 *witchcraft*

do ill 862.11 *be evil*

doily 293.12 *protective covering*, 621.11 *cleaning cloth*

do in 244.8 *destroy*, 398.17 *murder*, 650.6 *fatigue*

doing 230.1 *operation*, 243.1 *production*, 640.1 *action*, 640.5 *acting*

doing again 183.1 *repetition*

doing away with oneself 398.7 *suicide*

doing business 737.4 *trade*

doing chores 642.19 *busy*

doing fine 721.17 *well-off*

doing great 721.17 *well-off*

doing nicely thank you 742.1 *wealthy*

doing nothing 641.3 *inactive*

doing one's best 596.8 *attempting*

doing one's duty for king and country 676.7 *war measures*

doing penance 840.4 *atoning*, 867.7 *penitential*

doing porridge 699.15 *detained*, 702.8 *imprisoned*

doings 640.2 *deed*

doing the right thing 813.1 *formality*

doing time 699.15 *detained*, 702.8 *imprisoned*

doing up 201.5 *fresh start*

doing very nicely 721.17 *well-off*

doing well 686.8 *prosperous*

doing without 669.4 *desisting*

do insider trading 737.2 *speculate*

do it 245.14 *have sex*

doit 612.8 *trifle*

doited 510.11 *insane*

do it the hard way 659.19 *have difficulty*

do-it-yourself 603.1 *tool*, 629.8 *repair*, 656.4 *bungled*, 658.1 *naive*

do-it-yourselfer 629.12 *repairer*, 655.4 *skilled person*

dojo 26.7 *judo*, 26.8 *karate*

do justice to 350.22 *eat well*, 855.7 *vindicate*

dolally 168.14 *eccentric*, 510.11 *insane*

dolce 49 Musical Terms

Dolcelatte 45 Cheeses

doldrums 55.11 *wind system*, 325.2 *repose*, 641.1 *inaction*

dole 609.8 *insufficiency*, 662.4 *social assistance*, 729.3 *offering*, 731.2 *portion*

doleful 770.5 *sad*, 774.4 *lamenting*

dolefully 770.11 *sadly*, 774.8 *mournfully*

dolefulness 774.1 *lamentation*

Dølehest 32 Breeds of Horse and Pony

dolente 49 Musical Terms

dole out 162.16 *distribute*, 268.11 *measure out*, 729.5 *give*, 731.4 *allot*, 746.11 *remunerate*

dolerite 54 Common Rocks

doling out 731.1 *allocation*

doll 260.2 *little thing*, 402.9 *woman considered as a sex object*, 547.6 *image*, 821.12 *nicknames for lovers*, 826.4 *terms of endearment*

dollar 741.8 *American money*

dollar diplomacy 741.7 *finance*

dollar reserves 741.6 *funds*

dolled up 295.30, 813.7 *dressed up*

dollop 143.7 *piece*, 259.7 *mass*, 731.2 *portion*

doll's house 260.5 *little space*

doll up 295.33 *dress up*, 791.16 *make up*, 809.17 *be affected*

dolly 41.10 *curling*, 44.6 *ceramic workshop*, 71.7 *handcart*, 621.7 *washer*

dolly bird 402.9 *woman considered as a sex object*

dolly mixture 414.4 *confectionery*

Dolly Varden 80 Fishes

dolmades 45.52 *Greek dish*

dolman jacket 295.11 *jacket*

dolmen 3.11 *relic*, 200.7 *thing of the past*, 399.6 *grave*, 545.11 *monument*

dolmen sleeve 295.24 *part of garment*

Dolmetsch 49 Musicians and Composers

dolomite 54 Minerals

Dolomites 95 Mountains

dolorimetry 268.2 *micrometry*

dolorous 770.5 *sad*

dolour 406.1 *pain*, 770.1 *sorrow*

dolphin 77 Placental Mammals, 39.11 *swimming*, 76.5 *aquatic animal*, 815.10 *social animal*

Dolphin 53 The Constellations

dolphinarium 76.8 *animal welfare*

dolphin-butterfly stroke 39.2 *swimming technique*
dolphin kick 39.2 *swimming technique*
dolphins 161 Collective Names by Animal
dolt 240.2 *inert person,* 460.3 *unintelligent person,* 508.3 *foolish person,* 656.10 *unskilled person,* 658.3 *naive person*
doltish 240.5 *inert,* 441.8 *stupid,* 443.5, 460.6 *unintelligent,* 508.5 *foolish*
dom 401.3 *male title of address*
do magic 786.11 *do wonders*
domain 6.3 *subject,* 52.29 *mathematical function,* 56.59 *ferromagnetism,* 91.3 *dominion,* 163.4 *type,* 249.4 *territorial division,* 249.14 *sphere,* 256.2 *environment,* 472.4 *sphere,* 725.1 *property,* 725.2 *legal terms*
do martial arts 26
dome 316, 43.6 *roof,* 43.10 *church architecture,* 43.19 *decorate,* 53.23 *observatory,* 63.27 *superstructure,* 243.8 *construction,* 275.8 *high thing,* 293.7 *overhead covering,* 293.27 *roof,* 311.3 *curved things*
domed 43.14 *roofed*
domestic 68.21 *domesticated,* 290.8 *internal,* 472.9 *local,* 621.12 *cleaner,* 646.1, 646.1 *worker,* 662.16 *home help,* 697.1 *servant,* 697.6 *domestic servant,* 816.8 *unsociable*
domestically 43.20 *architecturally,* 472.12 *topically,* 816.14 *unsocially*
domestic architect 43.2 *architect*
domestic architecture 43.1 *architecture*
domesticate 584.18 *habituate*
domesticated 68, 76.15 *of animals,* 325.5 *sedentary*
domesticated animal 76
domestic cat 77.10 *cat*
domestic drudge 697.6 *domestic servant*
domestic fowl 78.4 *table bird*
domestic help 621.12 *cleaner,* 662.16 *home help*
domesticity 816.1 *unsociability*
domestic long-hair 77 Breeds of Cats
domestic mail 534.2 *postal communication*
domestic science 45.1 *cookery*
domestic servant 697, 621.12 *cleaner*
domestic tabby 77 Breeds of Cats
domestic trade 737.5 *commercial trade*
domestic tragedy 51.9 *tragedy*
domestic wiring 64.34 *power supply*
domical 311.4 *curved*
domical vault 43.7 *vault*
domicile 255.15 *settle,* 256.1 *habitat,* 567.5 *place of residence*
domiciled 255.13 *resident,* 256.14 *inhabiting*
domiciliary midwife 60.16 *nurse*
dominance 59.11 *genetics,* 233.3 *personal influence,* 688.1 *authority*
dominant 126, 233, 49.16 *musical note,* 59.25 *genetic,* 126.14 *best,* 164.19 *prevailing,* 166.12 *ruling,* 688.12 *authoritative*
dominantly 126.16 *superiorly,* 688.23 *authoritatively*
dominate 95.9 *tower,* 164.28 *prevail,* 166.11 *direct,* 233.10 *be a prevailing influence,* 235.10 *be powerful,* 275.15 *be high,* 570.15 *impose one's will,* 688.19 *be authoritarian,* 692.11 *have authority over,* 696.14 *master,* 701.7 *defeat*
dominating 701, 126.13 *dominant,* 275.9 *high,* 690.8 *severe,* 696.12 *masterful*
dominatingly 126.16 *superiorly,* 696.16 *masterfully*

domination 701, 12.3 *governance,* 126.1 *superiority,* 166.8 *authority,* 233.3 *personal influence,* 688.1, 692.3 *authority*
dominations 8.6 angel
domineer 688.19 *be authoritarian*
domineering 688.12 *authoritative,* 690.8 *severe,* 692.15 *self-assured,* 696.12 *masterful*
domineeringly 692.16 *commandingly,* 696.16 *masterfully*
Domingo 49 Musicians and Composers
Dominica 91 Countries, **98** Islands
Dominican 7 Members of Religious Orders
Dominican Republic 91 Countries
dominie 6.4 *educator*
dominion 91, 12.3 *governance,* 12.5 *political organization,* 126.2 *leadership,* 154.2 *priority,* 166.8 *authority,* 233.3 *personal influence,* 249.4 *territorial division,* 688.4 *governance,* 688.8 *governmental organization,* 692.3 *authority,* 723.1, 723.4 *possession,* 724.1 *joint possession,* 725.1 *property*
dominium 723.2 *legal terms*
domino 293.16 *disguise,* 438.6 *that which makes invisible,* 539.12 *disguise*
dominoes 42.7 *other games*
domino theory 159.4 *repercussion*
do mischief to 862.11 *be evil*
do missionary work 710.11 *volunteer*
do more than enough 610.4 *be excessive*
don 6.4 *educator,* 295.34 *wear,* 501.6 *knowledgeable person,* 688.11 *expert,* 696.9 *educational leader*
Don 32 Breeds of Horse and Pony, **96** Rivers, 96.5 *other major rivers,* 401.3 *male title of address*
don a hair shirt 840.6 *apologize*
donate 748, 116.30 *grant,* 662.29 *finance,* 710.16 *make an offering,* 729.6 *give to charity,* 746.8 *defray,* 755.11 *give*
donated 116.19 *granted,* 710.19 *sacrificial*
donation 748, 116.9 *grant,* 228.5 *positive stimulus,* 662.6 *financial assistance,* 710.6 *offering,* 729.1 *giving,* 729.3 *offering,* 746.1 *payment,* 746.4 *grant,* 755.7 *gift,* 767.4, 833.5 *charity*
donation party 665.7 *social gathering*
donative 729.3 *offering,* 729.7 *given*
donator 729.4 *giver,* 755.9 *generous person*
Doncaster 93 Cities
done 45.56 *culinary,* 144.7 *complete,* 157.21 *ended,* 200.18 *over,* 539.36 *deceived,* 584.12 *established,* 597.5 *undertaken,* 684.8 *concluded,* 718.8 *accomplished*
done by hand 243.12 *produced*
donee 730.5 *recipient*
done for 244.15 *destroyed,* 397.18 *dying,* 397.19 *dead,* 628.12 *deteriorated,* 650.1 *fatigued*
Donegal 92 Counties
Donegal tweed 67 Natural Fabrics
done in 236.12 *impotent,* 628.12 *deteriorated,* 650.1 *fatigued*
done in haste 648.3 *hasty*
done thing 166.6 *custom,* 167.5 *convention*
done to a turn 411.7 *tasty*
Donetsk 93 Cities
done up 201.14 *renewed,* 650.1 *fatigued*

done up like a dog's dinner 295.30 *dressed up*
done with 157.21 *ended,* 600.4 *disused*
donga 265.3 *gulf*
Dongola 32 Breeds of Horse and Pony, **93** Cities
Dongting 94 Lakes
donjon 671.12 *fort*
Don Juan 340.6 *charmer,* 401.7 *libertine,* 482.9 *undiscriminating person,* 539.15 *deceiver,* 540.15 *false person,* 821.9 *lover,* 877.8 *immoral man*
donkey 77 Placental Mammals, 326.6 *beast of burden*
donkey dropper 27.8 *delivery*
donkey-grey 448.1 *grey*
donkey jacket 295.11 *jacket*
donkey's years 188.5 *long duration*
donkey-work 644.1 *work*
Donleavy 48 Writers
Donna 402.3 *female title of address*
Donne 48 Poets
donner kebab 45.54 *other dishes*
donnish 501.9 *literate*
donnybrook 151.9 *disorder,* 473.1, 666.2 *argument*
do no evil 863.8 *be virtuous*
do no good 618.13 *be worthless,* 628.5 *hurt*
do no harm 617.10 *do good*
donor 57.11 *chemical bond,* 606.3 *provider,* 729.4 *giver,* 755.9 *generous person*
donor impurity 56.44, 64.4 *semiconductor*
do nothing 236.6 *be powerless,* 641.4 *not act,* 643.12 *be inactive*
do-nothing 641.3 *inactive*
do nothing but 212.7 *be frequent*
do nothing in excess 869.6 *moderate*
do-nothingism 641.1 *inaction*
do no wrong 876.11 *be moral*
Don Quixote 519.9 *visionary*
Don Quixote and Sancho Panza 819.7 *famous friendships*
don't-care 783.12 *be indifferent*
don't-care 783.9 *impartial*
don't-care attitude 783.3 *impartiality*
don't-know 576.15 *indecisive person,* 698.7 *free person*
don't move 325.11 *stop*
do number ones 353.17 *urinate*
do number twos 353.16 *defecate*
doodah 603.1 *tool,* 612.9 *bauble*
doodle 50.9 *drawing,* 50.20 *draw,* 521.1 *lack of meaning,* 523.7 *be unintelligible,* 560.14 *describe*
doodlebug 82.5 *larva,* 680.16 *bomb*
doodler 50.16 *artist*
doodling 50.3 *drawing*
doohickey 603.1 *tool*
Doolittle 48 Poets
dooly 71.6 *litter*
doom 157.5 *fate,* 244.4 *ruin,* 397.4 *death sentence,* 571.5 *inevitability,* 571.17 *preordain,* 582.5 *predetermination,* 862.11 *be evil,* 879.9 *retribution*
doomed 157.23 *annihilated,* 244.15 *destroyed,* 397.18 *dying,* 571.12 *inevitable,* 582.3 *predetermined,* 687.6 *adverse,* 776.6 *inauspicious*
doom merchant 517.8 *oracle,* 777.5 *frightener*
doomsday 157.5 *fate,* 199.3 *future condition,* 244.4 *ruin,* 879.9 *retribution*
Doomsday 492.4 *judgment day*
doomster 517.8 *oracle*
doomwatcher 517.8 *oracle*
Doon 96 Rivers
do one a bad turn 832.16 *be malevolent*
do one a mischief 618.13 *be worthless*

do one a world of good 662.21 *be helpful*
do one good 625.5 *by hygienic,* 662.21 *be helpful*
do one proud 812.18 *salute*
do one's best 596.2 *try hard,* 642.15 *try*
do one's bidding 694.5 *obey*
do one's bit 847.16 *do one's duty*
do one's damnedest 596.2 *try hard,* 642.15 *try*
do one's duty 847, 694.5 *obey,* 719.6 *perform,* 729.6 *give to charity,* 863.8 *be virtuous*
do oneself in 398.21 *commit suicide*
do oneself proud 682.6 *be successful*
do one's homework 594.8 *prepare oneself*
do one's job 230.7 *be operational*
do one's own thing 104.17, 117.13 *not conform,* 168.19 *be independent,* 174.18 *be one,* 698.16 *be independent,* 720.7 *not observe*
do one's stuff 230.7 *be operational*
do one's thing 230.7 *be operational*
do one's utmost 644.8 *exert oneself*
do one's worst 832.16 *be malevolent*
door 40.5 *real tennis,* 327.2 *route,* 346.6 *means of entry ,* 347.6 *way out*
doorbell 420.8 *something heard,* 427.4 *sources of resonance,* 543.4 *signal*
door buzzer 543.4 *signal*
do-or-die 780.4 *rash*
doorframe 382.4 *framework*
doorkeeper 323.5 *person who closes*
door knocker 423.4 *sound maker,* 543.4 *signal*
door-knocker 330.15 *ram*
doorman 51.26 *stagehand,* 322.3 *person who opens,* 323.5 *person who closes,* 632.3 *protector,* 671.14 *guard*
doormat 238.4 *weakling,* 293.9 *floor covering,* 531.2 *hiding place,* 621.10 *cleaning object,* 673.2 *appeaser,* 808.3 *sycophant,* 810.7 *modest person*
doorpost 346.6 *means of entry*
doorstep 273.5 *thickness,* 359.10 *step*
doorstepping 580.12 *election*
doorstop 661.4 *restraint*
doorstopping 533.3 *reporting*
door-to-door 70.5 *transportable,* 70.6 *commercially*
door-to-door salesman 739.10 *salesman*
doorway 322.7 *passageway,* 327.2 *route,* 346.6 *means of entry*
do out of 539.30 *be fraudulent,* 767.14 *take away*
do over 832.18 *torment*
doowop 49.8 *jazz*
doozy 861.17 *good thing*
dopa 62 Medication
dopamine 58.16 *hormone*
dopant 64.4 *semiconductor*
dope 404.4 *anaesthetic,* 460.3 *unintelligent person,* 508.3 *foolish person,* 528.1 *information,* 630.8 *drug,* 630.20 *doctor,* 631.11 *intoxicant,* 643.14 *make inactive,* 761.6 *desensitizing substance,* 761.7 *render insensitive,* 875.6 *drug*
doped 643.4 *not awake,* 875.7 *drugged*
dope fiend 875.4 *drug taker*
do penance 867, 125.4 *compensate,* 840.6 *apologize,* 867.4 *be penitent*
dope out 169.10 *number,* 170.8 *calculate*
dopey 325.5 *sedentary,* 404.10 *sleepy,* 460.6 *unintelligent,* 643.3 *not awake,* 650.1 *fatigued,* 761.2 *desensitized*
dopiaza 45.49 *Indian dish*

dopily 643.17 *sleepily,* 650.8 *tiredly,* 875.11 *in a trance*
doping 56.44, 64.4 *semiconductor*
do poorly 105.6 *be in a state of*
do porridge 699.11 *detain,* 702.10 *be in prison*
doppelgänger 102.2 *illusion,* 110.3 *lookalike,* 114.5 *counterpart,* 116.5 *conformity,* 128.1 *copy,* 176.5 *twin,* 547.1 *representation*
Doppelgänger 222.2 *substitute person*
doppio 49 Musical Terms
Doppler 52 Scientists
Doppler effect 56 Named Laws
do proud 748.1 *expend,* 805.30 *make proud*
do public relations 524.13 *interpret news*
dorado 80 Fishes
Dorado 53 The Constellations
doraphobia 777 Phobias by Name
dor beetle 82 Insects
Dorcas gazelle 77 Placental Mammals
Dorchester 93 Cities
Dordogne 96 Rivers
Dordrecht 93 Cities
do regularly 584.16 *have a habit*
do repairs 629.1 *repair*
do reverence 362.9 *bow*
Dorian mode 49.20 *key*
Dorians 1 Peoples
Doric 43 Architectural Styles, 43.16 *columned*
Doric mode 49.20 *key*
Doric order 43.8 *column*
do right by 831.8 *be benevolent*
do-right man 167.6 *conformist*
Dorking 68 Breeds of Fowl
dormancy 83.8 *bud,* 240.1 *inertness,* 283.6 *interruption,* 325.1 *motionlessness,* 527.6 *latency,* 641.1 *inaction,* 643.9 *sleep*
dormant 240.5 *inert,* 283.9 *interrupted,* 325.5 *sedentary,* 486.6 *potential,* 527.1 *latent,* 641.3 *inactive,* 643.4 *not awake*
dormant condition 527.6 *latency*
dormant disease 527.7 *latent things*
dormantly 325.10 *motionlessly*
dormant volcano 240.3 *inert thing,* 527.7 *latent things*
dormer 322.7 *passageway*
dormer bungalow 256.5 *house*
dormie side 29.2 *golfing terms*
dormitory 6.15 *schoolroom,* 256.7 *room*
dormitory suburb 93.8 *suburb*
dormitory town 124.8 *middle classes,* 249.11 *settlement*
Dormobile 71 Motor Vehicles
dormouse 77 Placental Mammals, 643.11 *sleeper*
dorsal 304.4 *rear*
dorsal fin 80.5 *fish anatomy*
dorsal region 304.2 *rear end*
Dorset 92 Counties
Dorset Down 68 Breeds of Sheep
Dorset Horn 68 Breeds of Sheep
Dorset Vinney 45 Cheeses
Dortmund 93 Cities
dory 74 Ships and Boats, 80 Fishes
DOS 65.8 *software*
dosage 120.2 *certain amount,* 268.4 *size,* 731.2 *portion .*
Dosanko 32 Breeds of Horse and Pony
dose 62.3 *drug,* 62.5 *prescription,* 120.2 *certain amount,* 143.7 *piece,* 302.2 *limiting factor,* 624.14 *venereal disease,* 630.2 *medicine,* 630.20 *doctor,* 731.2 *portion,* 731.4 *allot,* 879.10 *affliction*
dose equivalent 56.70 *radioactivity*
do serious climbing 34.9 *mountaineer*
do service 613.9 *be useful,* 694.5 *obey,* 697.8 *serve,* 808.11 *pander to*

do set pattern dancing 41.15 *iceskate*
dosh 741.2 *cash*
dosimeter 268.8 *meter*
dosimetric 268.16 *micrometric*
dosimetry 268.2 *micrometry*
dosology 62.1 *pharmacology*
do someone a favour 861.20 *do good*
do someone out of 858.10 *be criminal*
do something 640.4 *act,* 662.17 *help*
do something about 596.1 *attempt*
do something for 662.22 *improve*
Dos Passos 48 Writers
do speed-skiing 41.14 *ski*
doss down 256.18 *take up residence,* 325.8 *be motionless*
dosshouse 256.8 *shelter*
dossier 3.5 *chronicle,* 16.7 *legal trial,* 528.3 *document,* 545.1 *record*
do standing on one's head 660.17 *do easily*
Dostoievskii 48 Writers
do stunt-skiing 41.14 *ski*
do subtraction 131.3 *subtract*
do sums 130.6 *add*
do sustained climbing 34.9 *mountaineer*
dot 162.18 *sprinkle,* 182.9 *scatter,* 250.2 *exact location,* 260.2 *little thing,* 456.4 *maculation,* 456.11 *variegate,* 534.8 *data transmission,* 543.13 *punctuate,* 725.6 *marriage settlement*
dot about 182.9 *scatter*
dotage 202.1 *oldness,* 207.5 *old age,* 508.1 *folly*
dotard 207.7 *older person,* 508.3 *foolish person*
dote on 821.24 *be in love*
do the bidding of 808.11 *pander to*
do the cleaning 621.13 *clean*
do the deed 640.4 *act*
do the dirty on 858.8 *be dishonourable*
do the dirty work of 808.11 *pander to*
do the fair thing 859.6 *be disinterested*
do the Fosbury flop 21.6 *jump*
do the groundwork 594
do the honours 815.11 *be sociable,* 819.15 *be hospitable,* 849.18 *show respect*
do the job 682.8 *be effective*
do the laundry 621.13 *clean*
do the necessary thing 652.14 *behave towards*
do the needful 640.4 *act,* 652.14 *behave towards,* 746.6 *pay,* 847.16 *do one's duty*
do the offices 831.8 *be benevolent*
do the right thing 843.14 *be fair*
do the right thing by 859.7 *be unselfish*
do the rounds 356.9 *proceed*
do the same old thing 788.7 *suffer boredom*
do the splits 30.10 *compete in gymnastics*
do the trick 478.22 *be the answer,* 682.8 *be effective*
do the washing 621.13 *clean*
do the will of 694.5 *obey*
do the work 644.6 *work*
do things backwards 656.5 *be unskilful*
do things by halves 656.5 *be unskilful*
do things by the book 813.11 *be formal*
do things halfway 656.5 *be unskilful*
do things the usual way 327.14 *find one's way*
do thoroughly 144.4, 684.4 *complete*
do time 702.10 *be in prison*
doting 821.19 *enamoured*
dotingly 821.30 *lovingly*
dot-matrix printer 65.7 *peripheral*
dot one's i's and cross one's t's

537.31 *be accurate,* 543.13 *punctuate*
dot product 52.50 *scalar quantity*
do transactions 716.4 *negotiator*
dotted 160.8 *discontinuous,* 162.23 *sprinkled,* 456.10 *mottled*
dotted about 162.19 *dispersed,* 182.6 *sparse*
dotterel 78 Birds
dot the i's and cross the t's 503.7 *be accurate*
dotting 162.4 *sprinkling*
dottle 132.1 *remainder*
dotty 510.11 *insane*
do twice over 610.5 *be superfluous*
do two jobs 644.6 *work*
Douala 93 Cities
double 176, 176, 176, 22.5 *batting terms,* 22.7 *play baseball,* 32.7 *horseracing,* 32.9 *jumping,* 36.11 *rowing,* 39.11 *swimming,* 41.10 *curling,* 42.5 *dice,* 42.6 *darts,* 42.10 *play,* 110.3 *lookalike,* 114.5 *counterpart,* 128.5 *make bigger,* 158.17 *average,* 176.5 *twin,* 176.9 *two,* 183.7 *replica,* 183.16 *repeat,* 222.2 *substitute person,* 239.3 *invigorate,* 293.21 *substitution,* 320.7 *fold,* 335.14 *deviating course,* 337.5 *turn back,* 337.9 *turn round,* 457.5 *impression,* 547.1, 560.9 *representation,* 578.10 *equivocal,* 707.2 *alternative*
double agent 176.3 *duality,* 529.2 *secretiveness,* 539.21 *traitor,* 540.15 *false person*
Double-A league 22.1 *baseball*
double-arm 39.11 *swimming*
double-arm movement 39.2 *swimming technique*
double back 337.3 *reverse,* 337.5 *turn back*
double-barrelled 176.11 *doubleedged*
double-barrelled gun 680.9 *firearm*
double-barrelled shotgun 338.9 *firearm*
double bass 49 Musical Instruments
double bassoon 49 Musical Instruments
double bed 47.6 *bed*
double bill 51.2 *play*
double-bladed 36.12 *canoeing*
double-bladed paddle 36.6 *canoeing*
double-blade race 36.6 *canoeing*
double-blind trial 479.2 *rehearsal*
double boiler 258.15 *pot*
double-breasted 295.31 *styled*
double check 480.4 *verification*
double-check 480.1 *verify*
double-checked 480.10 *verified*
double-checking 480.9 *verificatory*
double chin 259.8 *fat*
double-chinned 259.16 *fat*
double coconut 86 Nuts
double coverage 19.10 *defence*
double cream 395.8 *fat*
double-cross 539.23 *deceive,* 657.5 *be cunning,* 858.9 *prove false*
double-crosser 539.21 *traitor,* 540.15 *false person,* 657.3 *cunning person,* 832.8 *malefactor,* 858.4 *dishonourable person*
double-crossing 176.3 *duality,* 176.11 *double-edged,* 657.1 *cunning,* 858.2 *faithlessness,* 858.6 *faithless*
doubled 176.9 *two,* 183.9 *repeated*
double date 815.3 *meeting*
double-deal 540, 474.12, 539.23 *deceive*
double-dealer 224.6 *fickle person,* 539.21 *traitor,* 578.9 *equivocator,* 858.4 *dishonourable person*
double-dealing 176.3 *duality,* 176.11 *double-edged,* 474.5 *hy-

pocrisy,* 474.10 *hypocritical,* 538.7 *duplicity,* 538.17 *duplicitous,* 539.1 *deception,* 539.34 *deceiving,* 539.38 *treacherous,* 540.2 *duplicity,* 540.26 *duplicitous,* 578.11 *equivocating,* 657.1 *cunning,* 858.2 *faithlessness,* 858.6 *faithless*
double-decker 71.19 *bus,* 45.11 *sandwich,* 176.2 *double,* 266.5 *layered thing,* 266.7 *layered*
double declutch 71.21 *miscellaneous motoring terms*
double-dig 69.15 *cultivate*
doubled over 320.5 *folded*
double dresser 47.5 *cabinet*
double-dribble 23.6 *play basketball*
double-dribbling 23.5 *penalties*
double Dutch 521.4 *senseless talk,* 523.12 *unintelligible thing*
double-edged 176, 380.3 *sharpedged*
double-ended 36.12 *canoeing*
double-ended paddle 36.6 *canoeing*
double-ender 36.2 *sailing boat*
double entendre 176.3 *duality,* 877.2 *pleasantry*
double entry 545.8 *registration,* 750.1 *accounts*
double exposure 176.4 *doubling*
double facade 540.2 *duplicity*
double-faced 176.11 *double-edged*
double fault 504.13 *sporting error*
double figures 179
double flat 49.16 *musical note*
double for 222.4 *be a substitute,* 293.34 *cover for,* 707.4 *substitute for*
double foul 23.4 *playing terms*
double-fry 45.55 *cook*
double glaze 292.3 *line,* 408.14 *be hot*
double-glazed 408.13 *heated*
double glazing 292.1 *lining,* 408.3 *heater,* 424.2 *sound reducer*
Double Gloucester 45 Cheeses
double-handed 20.8 *angling*
double-handed rod 20.3 *fishing tackle*
double harness 176.1 *two*
double-harness 176.14 *pair*
double header 72.7 *train*
double helix 58.10 *nucleoside*
double hook 20.3 *fishing tackle*
double integral 52.31 *differentiation*
double-jointed 374.2 *pliant*
double kayak race 36.6 *canoeing*
double-leg 30.11 *gymnastic*
double-leg circle 30.6 *pommel horse*
double life 176.3 *duality,* 540.2 *duplicity*
double march 329.11 *swift thing*
double meaning 176.3 *duality,* 520.3 *comprehension,* 578.5 *equivocalness ⌐*
double-minded 540.26 *duplicitous*
double-mindedness 540.2 *duplicity*
double negative 504.11 *grammatical error*
doubleness 176.3 *duality,* 538.7, 540.2 *duplicity*
double-oar 36.11 *rowing*
double-oar rowing 36.4 *rowing*
double one's efforts 575.6 *persevere,* 596.2 *try hard*
double over 320.7 *fold*
double overarm 39.2 *swimming technique*
double paddle 36.17 *canoe*
double-paddle 36.12 *canoeing*
double-paddle canoeing 36.6 *canoeing*
double parking 71.21 *miscellaneous motoring terms*
double personality 61.8 *disordered personality,* 61.16 *dissociation*
double play 22.6 *fielding terms*
double-pole 41.2 *cross-country skiing,* 41.12, 41.14 *ski*

double-pole with leg kick 41.2 *cross-country skiing*
double punt 36.19 *punt*
double punting 36.8 *punting*
double-quick 329.1 *swift,* 329.14 *swiftly*
double quotes 543.7 *punctuation*
double rainbow 55.27 *rainbow*
double recessiveness 59.11 *genetics*
double rhyme 48.11 *rhyme*
doubles 40.4 *tennis terms,* 40.14 *forehand*
double salt 57.10 *salt*
doubles court 40.3 *tennis equipment,* 40.8 *squash*
double sculling 36.4 *rowing*
double sculls 36.4 *rowing*
Double Sculls 36.5 *Henley trophies*
double sharp 49.16 *musical note*
double-sided 41.12 *ski,* 176.10 *two-sided*
double-sidedness 176.3 *duality*
double-sided skating 41.3 *ski racing*
double somersault 39.6 *diving*
double space 265.1 *interval*
doubles player 40.6 *tennis player*
double star 53.9 *constellation*
double-strength 874.6 *intoxicating*
double stroke 24.4 *carom*
Double Summer Time 185.9 *time zone*
doublet 5.17 *word,* 176.2 *double,* 222.3 *substitute thing,* 295.8 *shirt*
double take 155.7 *afterthought*
double take-out 41.10 *curling*
double talk 5.22 *many words,* 521.4 *senseless talk,* 521.9 *talk nonsense,* 578.5 *equivocalness*
double-talk 540.11 *evasion,* 540.23 *evade,* 781.1 *be equivocal*
double-talking 540.34 *evasive*
double tenoner 47.11 *woodworking tool*
doublethink 538.7 *duplicity*
double throw axel 41.6 *ice-skating*
double tongue 540.2 *duplicity*
double-tongue 49.38 *sound*
double-tongued 540.26 *duplicitous,* 578.10 *equivocal*
double top 42.6 *darts*
double up 650.6 *fatigue*
double vision 436.2 *poor sight*
double whammy 822.2 *curse,* 827.4 *malediction,* 862.4 *evil power*
double-wing formation 19.7 *offence*
doubl indemnity 735.2 *compensation*
doubling 176, 128.1 *increase,* 183.1 *repetition,* 183.12 *repetitious,* 320.1 *fold*
doubling over 320.1 *fold*
doubly 320, 176.19 *twice*
Doubs 96 Rivers
doubt 477, 473.2 *logical argument,* 473.14 *discuss,* 477.1 *question,* 477.6 *uncertainty,* 489.4 *improbability,* 491.10 *suspicion,* 491.18 *be uncertain,* 498.1 *disbelief,* 498.8 *disbelieve,* 536.8 *rebut,* 573.13 *dissociation,* 576.11 *vacillation,* 776.1 *hopelessness,* 776.9 *be hopeless,* 781.1 *caution,* 781.5 *be cautious,* 841.2, 841.8 *distrust*
doubter 477.9 *questioner,* 491.17 *uncertain person,* 498.5 *disbeliever,* 781.3 *cautious person*
doubtful 238.12 *weak-willed,* 473.10 *arguable,* 477.14 *questionable,* 489.1 *improbable,* 491.1 *uncertain,* 498.6 *disbelieving,* 536.11 *negative,* 633.2 *unsafe,* 781.4 *cautious,* 841.5 *distrustful*
doubtfully 473.18 *arguably,* 477.24 *questionably,* 489.8 *improbably,* 491.23 *uncertainly,* 498.10 *disbelievingly,* 536.15 *negatively,* 841.9 *jealously*

doubtfulness 238.2 *indecisiveness,* 477.6 *uncertainty,* 477.7 *questionableness,* 489.4 *improbability,* 491.9 *uncertainty,* 498.1 *disbelief,* 536.3 *rebuttal*
doubtful war 676.1 *war*
doubting 477.12 *questioning,* 477.15 *sceptical,* 498.6 *disbelieving,* 536.13 *rebutting*
doubting Thomas 477.9 *questioner,* 491.17 *uncertain person,* 498.5 *disbeliever*
doubtless 488.11 *probably*
douceur 729.2 *gift*
douche 62.11 *linctus,* 389.11 *wash,* 389.34 *hose,* 621.6 *bath,* 621.14 *bathe,* 630.6 *purgative*
dough 45.38 *bread,* 374.11 *soft thing,* 393.8 *pulp,* 741.2 *cash*
doughboy 679.8 *soldier*
doughiness 374.10 *compressibility,* 393.4 *pulpiness,* 394.1 *viscosity*
doughnut 45.36 *cake*
doughnut hole 45.36 *cake*
doughtiness 778.1 *courage*
doughty 778.9 *courageous*
doughy 374.2 *pliant,* 393.18 *pulpy,* 445.8 *drained of colour*
Douglas 93 Cities, **93** Cities
Douglas fir 85 Trees and Shrubs
dou louf 45.53 *African dish*
Doulton ware 44 Types of Ceramics
doum palm 85 Trees and Shrubs
do unto others as you would be done by 672.3 *retaliate*
do up 135.10 *link,* 201.20 *make new,* 295.34 *wear,* 323.7 *close,* 627.1 *improve,* 629.2 *refurbish,* 650.6 *fatigue*
dour 577.3 *unyielding,* 772.1 *solemn,* 830.6 *sullen,* 832.12 *callous*
dour ice 41.10 *curling*
dourly 830.13 *sullenly*
dourness 577.5 *obstinacy,* 772.4 *solemnity*
Douro 96 Rivers
douroucouli 77 Placental Mammals
douse 362.3 *bring down,* 389.29 *water,* 440.14 *make dark*
douse the flames 677.4 *pacify*
dout 161 Collective Names for Birds and Animals
dove 78 Birds, 78.1 *birds,* 675.2 *symbol of peace,* 675.3 *pacifist,* 678.3 *mediator,* 865.4 *innocent person*
Dove 53 The Constellations, **96** Rivers
dovecote 78.19 *ornithology,* 256.12 *stall*
dove-grey 448.1 *grey*
dovelike 78.23 *avian,* 675.7 *peaceful,* 865.5 *innocent,* 677.6 *pacificatory*
dove of peace 677.2 *peace offering*
Dover 93 Cities, **93** Cities
Dover sole 45.18 *sea fish,* 45.44 *British dish*
dovetail 47.17 *carpenter,* 135.10 *link,* 298.2 *interaction,* 298.5 *co-operate,* 354.5 *inset*
dovetail and mortise joint 135.5 *joint*
dovetailed 47.16 *joined,* 298.6 *interfacial*
dovetailing 47.10 *carpenter's term,* 47.16 *joined*
dovetail joint 135.5 *joint*
Dovey 96 Rivers
do violence to 241.8 *use violence,* 601.1 *misuse*
do violence to the meaning 525.1 *misinterpret*
do volunteer work 710.11 *volunteer*
dowager 402.2 *female,* 696.1 *master,* 824.6 *surviving spouse*
dowager queen 824.6 *surviving spouse*
dowdy 549.8 *inelegant,* 559.10 *ugly*
dowel 137.8 *fastening*

do well 861, 105.6 *be in a state of,* 336.5 *develop,* 627.2 *get better,* 655.10 *be skilful,* 682.6 *be successful,* 686.5 *be prosperous*
do well at 861.19 *be good at*
dower 725.6 *marriage settlement,* 725.9 *own property,* 729.5 *give,* 749.4 *legacy*
dowered 725.8 *propertied,* 729.7 *given*
dowerless 743.2 *insolvent*
do what is expected 847.16 *do one's duty*
do what is necessary 847.16 *do one's duty*
do what is required 608.4 *suffice,* 640.4 *act*
do what one can with 599.5 *dispose of*
do what one has to do 847.16 *do one's duty*
do what one likes 570.14 *follow one's own will,* 698.16 *be independent*
do what one likes with 599.5 *dispose of,* 701.6 *subject*
do wildwater canoeing 36.17 *canoe*
Dow Industrials 14.2 *stock exchange*
do with a heavy heart 573.10 *grudge*
do with both eyes shut 660.17 *do easily*
do with one hand tied behind one's back 660.17 *do easily*
do without 591.3 *abstain,* 600.5 *not use,* 669.9 *desist,* 711.7 *refuse oneself,* 727.9 *dispose of,* 869.5 *be self-restrained*
Dow Jones Industrial Index 14.2 *stock exchange*
Dowland 49 Musicians and Composers
down 161 Collective Names for Birds and Animals, **360, 362,** 56.78 *quantum,* 78.17 *plumage,* 275.2 *heights,* 276.10 *low,* 281.12 *perpendicularly,* 292.2 *filling,* 351.13 *drink,* 360.1 *descent,* 360.9 *descend,* 360.16 *descending,* 362.2 *flatten,* 370.7 *light thing,* 374.11 *soft thing,* 376.8 *smooth thing,* 383.2 *grain,* 614.1 *useless,* 628.14 *worse,* 770.6 *depressed,* 774.4 *lamenting,* 776.4 *hopeless*
Down 92 Counties
down and down 129.8 *decreasingly*
down-and-out 244.15 *destroyed,* 628.13 *dilapidated,* 687.5 *person in adversity,* 687.7 *unprosperous,* 722.6 *loser,* 743.3 *beggarly,* 743.10 *poor person*
down at heart 360.17 *drooping*
down at heel 151.15 *untidy,* 743.3 *beggarly*
down-at-heel 599.9 *used,* 628.13 *dilapidated,* 793.6 *seedy*
down at the mouth 776.4 *hopeless*
downbear 362.5 *bear down on*
downbeat 49.19 *tempo*
down below 276.10 *low,* 360.19 *down*
downbend 360.1 *descent*
downcast 360.17 *drooping,* 362.12 *downthrow,* 362.19 *fallen,* 362.21 *degraded,* 454.3, 770.6 *depressed,* 776.4 *hopeless*
downcome 360.1 *descent*
downcurve 338.5 *throw,* 360.1 *descent*
downdraught 55.10 *air movement,* 360.1 *descent,* 390.4 *air flow*
down-drawn 44.10 *ceramic*
down-drawn kiln 44.6 *ceramic workshop*
downer 242.2 *moderator,* 360.1 *descent,* 687.1 *adversity,* 770.3 *sad person,* 776.2 *hopeless situation,* 788.2 *boring thing,* 875.6 *drug*
downers 761.6 *desensitizing substance*

downfall 55.25 *rain,* 244.4 *ruin,* 360.4 *fall,* 362.11 *lowering,* 683.1 *failure,* 687.1 *adversity*
downfallen 628.12 *deteriorated*
down feathers 78.17 *plumage*
downflow 360
downflowing 360.16 *descending*
down-force 33.6 *motor racing terms*
down for hearing 16.54 *litigated*
downgrade 65.19 *abort,* 129.5 *make smaller,* 252.17 *relegate,* 349.3 *disbar,* 360.2 *sinkage,* 360.19 *down,* 362.4 *debase,* 879.1 *punish*
downgraded 252.11 *relegated,* 362.21 *degraded*
downgrading 252.4 *relegation,* 362.15 *debasement,* 879.7 *punishment*
downhaul 36.3 *parts of a sailing boat,* 36.13 *windsurfing*
downhaul line 36.7 *windsurfing*
downhearted 770.5 *sad*
downheartedness 770.1 *sorrow*
downhill 41.12 *ski,* 41.17 *on a ski run,* 360.16 *descending,* 360.19 *down,* 628.14 *worse,* 660.9 *easy*
downhill all the way 660.9 *easy*
downhill race 41.3 *ski racing*
downhill racing 18 Sporting Activities, 41.3 *ski racing,* 674.4 *race*
downhill ski 41.5 *ski equipment*
downhill ski run 41.1 *skiing*
downiness 370.5 *lightness,* 374.9 *smoothness,* 383.2 *grain*
downing 350.1 *eating*
Downing Street 179.6 *ten,* 688.6 *place of authority,* 696.8 *the power structure*
down in the dumps 770.6 *depressed,* 776.4 *hopeless*
down in the mouth 360.17 *drooping*
down in the world 628.14 *worse*
downkick 39.2 *swimming technique*
downland 87.2 *grassland,* 98.7 *upland,* 98.11 *continental*
downlight 439.12 *highlight*
down line 72.2 *track*
download 65.17 *computing term,* 65.19 *abort*
downmarket 124.3 *mediocre,* 164.21 *common,* 754.9 *cheap*
down-motion turn 41.4 *skiing technique*
down on one's luck 687.8 *unlucky*
down on one's uppers 593.5 *necessitous*
down on the farm 68.22 *agriculturally*
Downpatrick 93 Cities
down payment 143.2 *particular,* 746.1 *payment*
downplay 542.22 *play down*
downplayed 542
down-playing 542
downpour 55.25 *rain,* 241.5 *violent weather,* 360.3 *downflow*
downright 134.17 *direct,* 144.7 *complete,* 144.9 *completely,* 360.19 *down,* 522.2 *simple,* 526.15 *open,* 530.11 *disclosing,* 537.18 *truthful*
downright lie 538.4 *lie*
downrightness 522.10 *simplicity,* 530.3 *openness,* 537.5 *truthfulness*
downrush 360.3 *downflow*
downrushing 360.16 *descending*
downs 87.2 *grassland,* 95.1 *mountain,* 98.7 *upland*
down side 29.2 *golfing terms*
downsize 65.17 *computing term,* 182.8 *reduce*
down south 360.19 *down*
Downs process 57 Named Reactions
Down's syndrome 510.2 *subnormality*
downstage 51.15 *stage,* 51.41 *onstage*

downstairs 276.10 *low*, 360.19 *down*
downstream 332.11 *in all directions*, 360.19 *down*, 660.9 *easy*
downstreet 360.19 *down*
downsweep method 21.1 *track events*
downswing 29.3 *golf shots*
down the hatch 351.18 *cheers*
down-the-line shooting 18 Sporting Activities
down the middle 176.22 *in half*
downthrow 362, 360.1 *descent*
downthrown 362.19 *fallen*
downtime 65.17 *computing term*
down-to-earth 4.15 *rational*, 101.8 *practical*, 658.1 *naive*
down tools 598.2 *withdraw*
down to one's last penny 743.2 *insolvent*
downtown 93.7 *city district*, 93.14 *urban*, 249.10 *urban area*, 249.18 *local*, 332.11 *in all directions*, 332.14 *directed*, 360.19 *down*
downtowner 93.11 *urbanite*
downtrend 628.7 *deterioration*
downturn 129.2, 337.14 *decline*, 360.1 *descent*, 628.7 *deterioration*
downturning 360.16 *descending*
down under 249.7 *regions of the world*
down-unweighting 41.4 *skiing technique*
downward 2.14 *socioeconomic*, 324.17 *directional*, 360.16 *descending*
downward course 628.7 *deterioration*
downward curve 129.2 *decline*
downward mobility 2.7 *social stratification*
downward motion 324.6 *descending motion*
downwards 129.4 *decrease*, 129.8 *decreasingly*, 276.10 *low*, 360.19, 362.24 *down*
downward spiral 129.2 *decline*
downward trend 129.2, 337.14 *decline*, 360.2 *sinkage*
downwash 73.7 *miscellaneous aviation terms*
down-welling 54.13 *ocean current*
downwind 332.11 *in all directions*, 332.14 *directed*
downwind of 416.5 *odorous*
downy 370.2 *insubstantial*, 374.3, 376.1 *smooth*, 383.11 *fluffy*
downy mildew 89 Fungi, 69.12 *pests and diseases*
do wonders 786, 682.6 *be successful*, 682.8 *be effective*
do wonders with 629.2 *refurbish*
do worse 628.1 *deteriorate*
Dow process 57 Named Reactions
do wrong 844, 877, 16.73 *be illegal*, 133.9 *mix up*, 618.13 *be worthless*, 862.11 *be evil*, 864.16 *be wicked*
do wrong by 862.11 *be evil*
dowry 62.6 *financial assistance*, 721.5 *profit*, 725.6 *marriage settlement*, 728.1 *transfer of property*, 729.1 *giving*
dowse 11.23 *divine*
dowser 11.13 *diviner*, 496.12 *discoverer*, 517.9 *forecaster*
dowsing 11.9, 517.2 *divination*
dowsing rods 11.9 *divination*
Dowson 48 Poets
doxepin 62 Medication, **62** Medication
doxological 10.21 *ritualistic*
doxologically 10.23 *ritually*
doxology 10.8 *hymn*, 49.5 *sacred music*
doxorubicin 62 Medication
doxycycline 62 Medication
doyen 207.7 *older person*, 655.5 *expert*, 696.5 *company leader*
doyenne 696.5 *company leader*
Doyle 48 Writers

doylt 161 Collective Names for Birds and Animals
doze 240.4 *be inert*, 404.2 *unconsciousness*, 404.11 *be unfeeling*, 643.9, 643.13 *sleep*, 649.2 *take it easy*
dozen 179.7 *double figures*
dozens 181.2 *multitude*
dozer 63.29 *construction equipment*, 643.11 *sleeper*
dozily 643.17 *sleepily*, 650.8 *tiredly*
doziness 643.9 *sleep*
dozing 643.4 *not awake*
dozy 643.4 *not awake*, 650.1 *fatigued*
DP 65.1 *computing*
DP manager 65.2 *operator*
drab 112.8 *monotonous*, 440.10 *dark-coloured*, 444.17 *dimmed*, 444.13 *soft-hued*, 448.3 *dull*, 559.10 *ugly*, 622.6 *dirty person*, 788.4 *boring*
drabble 622.11 *dirty*
Drabble 48 Writers
drably 112.15 *monotonously*, 441.12 *dimly*, 448.9 *greyly*, 788.8 *boringly*
drabness 112.4 *monotony*, 440.1 *darkness*, 440.3 *dark colour*, 441.2 *murk*, 448.7 *dullness*, 559.3 *ugliness*
drachm 369.9 *avoirdupois weight*
drachma 75 Some Foreign Units, 741.11 *national coins*
Draco 53 The Constellations
Draconian 237.10 *potent*, 690.8 *severe*
Draconian measures 690.1 *severity*
draff 622.4 *dirt*
draft 17.10 *enlist*, 23.2 *basketball player*, 50.9 *drawing*, 50.20 *draw*, 145.3 *incomplete thing*, 145.5 *be incomplete*, 306.7 *form*, 375.10 *rough idea*, 375.13 *be unfinished*, 518.5 *suppose*, 547.2 *reproduction*, 547.11 *paint*, 560.14 *describe*, 592.6 *outline*, 592.10 *plan out*, 594.2 *do the groundwork*, 594.10 *preparations*, 676.12 *go to war*, 679.14 *armed forces*, 695.3 *coercive methods*, 695.7 *force*, 741.14 *paper money*
draft-card burner 675.3 *pacifist*
draft dodger 108.3 *unconnected person*, 675.3 *pacifist*, 711.4 *refuser*
draft-dodger 591.17 *avoider*, 720.6 *evader*
drafted 17.9 *enlisted*, 50.27 *painted*, 676.15 *warring*, 679.35 *martial*
draftee 676.11 *recruit*, 679.8 *soldier*
draft evader 675.3 *pacifist*
draft exile 675.3 *pacifist*
drafting 50.3 *drawing*
draft pick 19.2 *football player*, 23.2 *basketball player*
draft player 23.2 *basketball player*
draft protester 675.3 *pacifist*
drag 71 Carriages and Carts, **339,** 32.8 *hunting*, 41.16 *bobsled*, 71.10 *sled*, 73.7 *miscellaneous aviation terms*, 185.15 *pass*, 231.1 *counteraction*, 231.3 *counteract*, 233 *influence*, 233.10 *be a prevailing influence*, 302.2 *limiting factor*, 307.2 *limit*, 328.2 *hesitate*, 339.2 *pull*, 339.4 *friction*, 340.1 *attraction*, 340.11 *attract*, 369.8 *weighing down*, 385.1 *friction*, 413.8 *smoking*, 413.14 *smoke*, 661.2 *obstacle*, 661.11 *be inhibited*, 699.5 *means of restraint*, 699.8 *restrain*, 776.3 *hopeless person*, 788.2 *boring thing*, 788.3 *boring person*, 788.6 *be boring*
drag artist 118.7 *imitator*, 547.5 *performer*
drag artiste 51.27 *entertainer*
drag-ass 788.3 *boring person*
drag by 185.15 *pass*
drag down 339.12 *drag*

drag down to one's level 628.6 *pervert*
dragée 62.6 *pill*, 414.4 *confectionery*
drag from 695.7 *force*
dragged out 269.1 *long*
dragging 41.9 *bobsledding*, 41.13 *ice-skating*, 328.4 *slow*, 328.10 *slow motion*, 340.8 *attracting*, 788.4 *boring*
dragging out 269.4 *length*
draggle 339.12 *drag*, 622.11 *dirty*
draggletail 622.6 *dirty person*
draggy 788.4 *boring*
draghound 32.8 *hunting*
draghunt 32.8 *hunting*
drag in 354.1 *insert*
drag in the mud 850.21 *disregard*
drag lift 41.1 *skiing*
dragline 63.29 *construction equipment*
dragnet 164.3 *nonspecificness*, 339.6 *towline*, 539.13 *snare*, 590.1 *pursuit*, 590.3 *hunting and fishing equipment*
dragon 74 Sailing Ships and Boats, 76.7 *legendary beast*
drag on 110.11 *be regular*, 112.12 *be monotonous*, 185.15 *pass*, 209.6 *be late*
dragon 241.4 *violent person or animal*, 829.3 *irascible person*
Dragon 53 The Constellations
drag one's feet 127.8 *be inferior*, 209.6 *be late*, 328.2 *hesitate*, 573.8 *hold back*, 591.4 *shy*, 661.8 *hinder*, 661.11 *be inhibited*
dragonet 80 Fishes
dragonfish 80 Fishes
dragonfly 82 Insects, 82.1 *insect*, 456.5 *variegated thing*
dragonnade 670.14 *siege*
dragon's blood 85 Tree Products, 450.6 *red pigment*
dragon's lair 633.5 *danger*
dragon's teeth 635.1 *trap*
dragon tree 85 Trees and Shrubs
dragoon 32.15 *horse person*, 679.20 *cavalryman*, 695.7 *force*
drag out 269.10 *lengthen*, 526.3 *reveal*
drag race 33.1 *motor racing*
drag-race 33.9 *race*
drag racer 33.8 *driver*
drag racing 18 Sporting Activities, 33.1 *motor racing*, 674.4 *race*
dragster 71 Motor Vehicles
drag through the gutter 854.12 *defame*
drag through the mud 854.12 *defame*
drag up 339.12 *drag*, 361.4 *gather up*
drain 54.63 *ebb*, 63.22 *tunnel*, 64.19 *transistor*, 96.8 *cause to flow*, 129.1, 129.4 *decrease*, 131.3 *subtract*, 134.10 *purify*, 238.7 *weaken*, 322.7 *passageway*, 322.21 *provide passage for*, 347.7 *outlet*, 347.11 *run out*, 349.11 *void*, 351.13 *drink*, 355.14 *suck*, 392.17 *dry*, 599.3 *exploit*, 605.4 *storage*, 607.1 *waste*, 609.7 *make insufficient*, 614.6 *refuse*, 621.15 *purify*, 625.6 *make hygienic*, 628.5 *hurt*, 650.6 *fatigue*, 722.4 *lessening*, 722.12 *lessen*, 727.4 *wastebin*, 727.8 *sink*
drain a bumper 812.17 *congratulate*
drainage 54, 349.21 *removal*, 607.3 *waste*, 621.2 *cleaning*, 622.5 *swill*
drainage basin 54.8 *drainage*
drainage channel 54.8 *drainage*
drainage pattern 54.8 *drainage*
drainage system 54.8 *drainage*, 63.24 *water system*
drain away 129.4 *decrease*
drain cleaner 417.2 *deodorant*
drained 238.9 *dilapidated*, 392.4 *dried-out*, 628.12 *deteriorated*, 650.1 *fatigued*

drained of colour 445
drain electrode 64.19 *transistor*
draining 322.15 *providing passage*, 349.21 *removal*, 355.4 *sucking*, 628.11 *hurt*, 722.4 *lessening*
draining board 727.8 *sink*
drain of colour 445.6 *decolour*
drain one's glass 351.13 *drink*
drain out 347.11 *run out*
drainpipe 347.7 *outlet*, 621.10 *cleaning object*
drainpipes 295.9 *trousers*
drain the lifeblood of 398.18 *slaughter*
drain tile 44.9 *industrial ceramics*
drain to the dregs 349.11 *void*
drake 68.8 *livestock*, 76.7 *legendary beast*, 78.10 *male bird*, 401.16 *male animal*
Drakensberg 95 Mountains
Drakensberger 68 Breeds of Cattle
dram 369.9 *avoirdupois weight*, 874.13 *drink*
DRAM 65.6 *memory*
drama 51, 51.2 *play*, 560.3 *narration*, 640.1 *action*, 640.2 *deed*, 642.1 *activity*, 786.4 *wonder*
drama college 6.12 *educational institution*
drama-documentary 51.2 *play*
drama of fate 51.9 *tragedy*
drama of suspense 51.2 *play*
dramatherapist 61.30 *psychiatrist*
drama therapy 61.3 *psychiatric treatment*
dramatic 51, 811, 48.19 *narrative*, 49.32 *instrumental*, 475.10 *demonstrative*, 640.5 *acting*, 786.8 *wonderful*
dramatically 51, 811, 48.23 *descriptively*, 475.21 *demonstratively*
dramatic art 51.1 *drama*, 51.7 *dramaturgy*
dramatic conflict 51.7 *dramaturgy*
dramatic convention 51.7 *dramaturgy*
dramatic coup 51.7 *dramaturgy*
dramatic cycle 51.2 *play*
dramatic dance 46.4 *historic dancing*
dramatic entertainment 51.1 *drama*, 51.2 *play*
dramatic form 51.7 *dramaturgy*
dramatic irony 48.3 *aspect of fiction*, 51.7 *dramaturgy*
dramaticism 51.1 *drama*
dramatic monologue 48.7 *poem*, 51.2 *play*
dramatic poet 48.14 *author*
dramatic poetry 48.6 *poetry*
dramatic recital 51.2 *play*
dramatic representation 51.2 *play*
dramatics 811, 51.1 *drama*, 51.7 *dramaturgy*, 475.2 *demonstrativeness*
dramatic stroke 51.7 *dramaturgy*
dramatic structure 51.7 *dramaturgy*
dramatic tension 51.7 *dramaturgy*
dramatic unities 51.7 *dramaturgy*
dramatis personae 171.6 *list of names*, 400.7 *person*, 646.4 *personnel*
dramatist 51, 48.14 *author*, 243.9 *producer*, 560.10 *descriptive writer*
dramatize 51, 48.21 *write*, 475.18 *appear*, 526.1 *display*, 547.10 *act*, 560.15 *recount*
dramatize oneself 811.29 *show off*
dramatizer 51.24 *dramatist*
dramaturge 48.14 *author*, 51.24 *dramatist*
dramaturgic 51.37 *dramatic*
dramaturgy 51, 786.3 *wonderworking*
Drambuie 351.7 *alcoholic drink*
drape 51.17 *stage set*, 283.1 *suspension*, 283.10 *suspend*, 293.8 *wall covering*, 293.28 *face*, 295.32 *dress*
draped 295.29 *dressed*

drape oneself 362.8 *sit*
draper 293.17 *coverer*, 295.26 *fashion designer*
drapery 67.3 *fabric*, 243.7 *produce*, 293.8 *wall covering*
drapes 443.7 *opaque thing*
drastic 237.10 *potent*
drastically 237.15 *acutely*
dratted 618.6 *damnable*
draught 62.3 *drug*, 277.6 *bathymetry*, 339.1 *traction*, 339.2 *pull*, 351.2 *drink*, 355.4 *sucking*, 369.6 *displacement*, 630.2 *medicine*
draught animal 71.9 *animal transport*, 76.3 *domesticated animal*
draught beer 351.7 *alcoholic drink*
draughtboard 456.5 *variegated thing*
draught horse 32.2 *thoroughbred*, 71.9 *animal transport*
draughts 777 Phobias by Topic
draughtsman 50.16 *artist*, 545.9 *recorder*
draughtsmanship 50.3 *drawing*, 50.4 *treatment*
Drava 96 Rivers
Dravidian 5 Languages and Groups of Languages, 5.11 *family of languages*
draw 50, 19.9 *play*, 25.9 *bowls*, 29.3 *golf shots*, 31.3 *ice hockey*, 31.9 *play hockey*, 45.55 *cook*, 52.96 *represent*, 74.10 *sail*, 110.5 *equality*, 122.2 *equilibrium*, 122.10 *be equal*, 198.4 *equal race*, 198.8 *run equally*, 218.2 *stop*, 228.9 *motivate*, 262.5 *make smaller*, 265.3 *gulf*, 269.10 *lengthen*, 272.10 *narrow*, 306.7 *form*, 324.14 *set in motion*, 339.2, 339.11 *pull*, 340.1 *attraction*, 340.11 *attract*, 349.11 *void*, 355.14 *suck*, 413.8 *smoking*, 413.14 *smoke*, 547.11 *paint*, 560.14 *describe*, 589.3 *equal chance*, 606.5 *provision*, 630.20 *doctor*, 685.1 *noncompletion*, 741.26 *bank*, 749.5 *winnings*, 782.5 *object of desire*, 782.15 *cause desire*
draw a bead on 37.7, 338.28 *shoot*, 670.2 *fire*
draw a blank 683.6 *fail*, 722.11 *be wasteful*
draw a blueprint 547.11 *paint*
draw a circle 313.7 *make circular*, 560.17 *describe a circle*
draw a kiln 44.11 *make ceramics*
draw a large income 742.12 *be rich*
draw a match 110.10 *be equal*
draw a meaning 520.11 *infer*
draw a mental picture 518.5 *suppose*
draw an allowance 721.14 *profit*
draw an outline 299.5 *outline*
draw a parallel between 114.11 *make similar*
draw a parallel with 107.8 *be proportionate to*
draw a pay cheque 721.12 *earn*
draw a penalty 23.6 *play basketball*, 31.9 *play hockey*
draw a pension 730.9 *receive*
draw a personal foul 19.18 *be penalized*, 23.6 *play basketball*, 31.9 *play hockey*
draw a red herring 108.10 *be unrelated*
draw a salary 721.12 *earn*, 878.13 *get paid*
draw a shot 25.7 *bowl*
draw a suspension 31.9 *play hockey*
draw a technical foul 23.6 *play basketball*, 31.9 *play hockey*
draw attention 467.13 *attract attention*
draw attention to 526.1 *display*, 526.3 *reveal*
draw attention to oneself 117.12 *be disparate*, 475.18 *appear*
draw a veil over 531.8 *conceal*
drawback 131.2 *subtracted item*

draw back 331.2 *respond*, 337.2 *retreat*, 339.14 *draw in*, 591.4 *shy*
drawback 616.3 *inconvenience*, 620.7 *defect*, 659.8 *snag*, 661.2 *obstacle*, 752.1 *discount*
draw back 777.11 *be afraid*
draw back the curtains 439.29 *clarify*
drawbar 72.7 *train*, 137.9 *yoke*
draw blood 406.11 *inflict pain*
draw blood from a stone 487.10 *attempt the impossible*
draw blueprints 43.18 *be an architect*
draw breath 396.16 *live*, 396.18 *be born*, 651.2 *be refreshed*
drawbridge 63.21, 327.9 *bridge*, 638.2 *means of escape*, 671.12 *fort*
draw close to jack 25.7 *bowl*
drawee 745.6 *debtor*
drawer 50.16 *artist*, 258.3 *cabinet*, 339.6 *towline*, 605.4 *storage*
drawers 295.18 *underwear*
draw first breath 396.18 *be born*
draw forth 526.3 *reveal*
draw gear 72.7 *train*
draw harrows 68.10 *farm tool*
draw hoe 69.6 *garden tool*
draw in 339, 348, 262.5 *make smaller*, 262.6 *become smaller*, 340.12 *lure*
drawing 50, 50, 31.3 *ice hockey*, 31.8 *hockey*, 43.1 *architecture*, 50.7 *picture*, 52.49 *geometric construction*, 235.15 *full of energy*, 339.1 *traction*, 339.8 *tractional*, 340.8 *attracting*, 355.1 *extraction*, 355.4 *sucking*, 435.7 *view*, 547.2 *reproduction*, 560.9 *representation*, 630.12 *surgery*
drawing aside 331.6 *response*
drawing back 785.4 *sign of dislike*
drawing board 592.7 *planning*
drawing frame 50.11 *artist's materials*
drawing in 262.1 *contraction*
drawing off 355.4 *sucking*
drawing on the imagination 541.9 *tall story*
drawing out 355, 261.1 *growth*, 269.4 *length*, 355.1 *extraction*, 788.1 *boredom*
drawing paper 50.11 *artist's materials*
drawing pencil 50.11 *artist's materials*
drawing pin 137.8 *fastening*, 380.8 *sharp-pointed thing*
drawing power 339.5 *magnetism*
drawing room 256.7 *room*, 730.4 *reception*, 815.4 *meeting place*
drawing-room comedy 51.10 *comedy*
drawing together 262.1 *contraction*
draw in one's horns 806.20 *submit*
draw interest 721.14 *profit*, 821.25 *be loved*
drawknife 47.11 *woodworking tool*, 376.9 *smoother*, 380.9 *sharp-edged thing*
drawl 328.2 *hesitate*, 564.3 *mode of speech*, 564.13 *speak in a particular way*
drawling 328.6 *hesitant*, 328.12 *hesitation*
drawn 31.8 *hockey*, 50.27 *painted*, 110.16 *equal*, 122.8 *on equal terms*, 252.9 *removed*, 274.2 *emaciated*, 339.8 *tractional*
drawn battle 122.2 *equilibrium*
draw near 199.7 *be in the future*, 264.9 *near*, 342.9 *converge*
drawn game 122.2 *equilibrium*, 685.1 *noncompletion*
draw nigh 199.7 *be in the future*, 264.9 *near*
drawn-in 262.7 *smaller*
drawn match 110.5 *equality*, 122.2 *equilibrium*
drawn out 269.1 *long*, 553.3 *diffuse*, 788.4 *boring*

drawn-out 219.6 *protracted*, 261.7 *bigger*
drawn-together 262.7 *smaller*
drawn up 592.14 *planned*
draw off 131.3 *subtract*, 355.14 *suck*
draw on 599.4 *resort to*, 606.5 *provision*, 821.26 *court*
draw oneself to one's full height 361.5 *arise*
draw one's last breath 157.19 *expire*
draw one's pension 705.5 *resign*
draw one's social security benefits 705.5 *resign*
draw on one's savings 748.1 *expend*
draw on the imagination 541.11 *tell a tall story*
draw out 355, 219.4 *protract*, 226.10 *awaken*, 252.15 *remove*, 261.5 *make bigger*, 261.6 *become bigger*, 269.10 *lengthen*, 355.11 *extract*, 526.3 *reveal*, 553.5 *be diffuse*, 788.6 *be boring*
draw poker 42 Card Games
draw rein 328.3 *slow down*
draw retirement pay 721.12 *earn*
draw shot 25.2 *grip*
drawstring 137.6 *line*
draw stroke 36.6 *canoeing*
draw stumps 27.15 *play*, 157.16 *cease*
draw the cork 351.13 *drink*
draw the curtains 440.14 *make dark*
draw the line 699.8 *restrain*, 726.7 *detain*
draw the line at 147.7 *exclude*, 302.7 *limit*, 581.1 *reject*
draw the teeth of 381.10 *blunt*
draw tight 135.8 *unite*
draw to a close 157.18 *come to an end*
draw to a peak 97.10 *billow*
draw together 135.8 *unite*, 161.37 *assemble*, 262.5 *make smaller*
draw towards 340.11 *attract*
draw tube 53.25 *mounting*
draw up 150.24 *line up*, 218.6 *cease*, 344.3 *approach*, 361.4 *gather up*, 382.14 *structure*, 592.10 *plan out*
draw up an itinerary 327.14 *find one's way*
draw up a programme 592.10 *plan out*
draw up a schedule 592.10 *plan out*
draw up a will 729.5 *give*
draw up birth charts 11.23 *divine*
draw-weight 25.9 *bowls*
dray 71 Carriages and Carts, 71 Motor Vehicles, 71.9 *animal transport*, 71.10 *sled*
drayage 326.2 *transportation*, 339.1 *traction*
drayhorse 32.2 *thoroughbred*
drayman 326.7 *transferor*
Drayton 48 Poets
dread 513.1 *expectation*, 513.8 *expect*, 777.1 *fear*, 777.11 *be afraid*
dreaded 513.7 *expected*
dreadful 618.3 *bad*, 618.5 *harmful*, 687.6 *adverse*, 777.10 *frightening*, 862.7 *evil*
dreadfully 687.12 *in adversity*, 777.16 *frighteningly*, 862.12 *evilly*
dreadfulness 618.9 *badness*, 862.1 *evil*
dreading 513.5 *expecting*
dreadlocks 375.7 *rough thing*, 791.8 *hair cut*
dreadnought 295.12 *coat*, 679.24 *warship*
dreads 791.8 *hair cut*
dream 4.20 *philosophize*, 102.2 *illusion*, 102.13 *imagine*, 435.5 *imagination*, 435.17 *imagine*, 457.4 *something that appears*, 471.6 *ideal*, 471.15 *imagine*, 489.7 *be improbable*, 513.2 *expectations*, 518.5 *suppose*, 519.5 *fantasy*, 519.14 *imagine*, 588.6

objective, 775.3 *aspiration*, 775.7 *aspire*, 789.3 *attractive female*, 861.17 *good thing*
dreamboat 789.4 *attractive male*, 821.9 *lover*
dream dreams 519.15 *fantasize*
dreamed up 243.12 *produced*
dreamed-up 519.12 *imaginary*, 538.13 *untrue*, 539.40 *illusory*
dreamer 4.10 *philosopher*, 102.6 *unrealistic person*, 461.7 *thinker*, 468.6 *inattentive person*, 471.9 *person of ideas*, 519.9 *visionary*, 591.17 *avoider*, 641.2 *nonacting person*, 643.8 *nonworker*, 775.5 *hoper*
dream girl 821.9 *lover*
dreamily 4.28 *thoughtfully*, 471.22 *imaginatively*
dreaming 4.17 *thoughtful*, 435.5 *imagination*, 519.10 *imaginative*, 643.4 *not awake*, 775.13 *aspirant*
dream interpretation 11.9 *divination*
dream interpreter 11.13 *diviner*
dreamland 519, 643.9 *sleep*
dreamlike 102.9 *illusory*, 457.9 *ostensible*, 519.12 *imaginary*
dreamlike thinking 61.19 *defence mechanism*
dream man 789.4 *attractive male*, 821.9 *lover*
dream of 588.10 *aim*, 782.12 *desire*
dream of other worlds 519.15 *fantasize*
dreams 205.5 *night thing*
dream state 61.14 *trance*
dream-symbol interpretation 61.24 *symbolism*
dream up 119.7 *originate*, 156.22 *invent*, 243.10 *produce*, 435.17, 471.15 *imagine*, 519.14 *imagine*, 538.21 *lie*, 583.3 *improvise*
dream world 519.8 *dreamland*, 775.3 *aspiration*
dreamy 461.10 *speculative*, 471.13 *ideal*, 519.10 *imaginative*, 519.12 *imaginary*
drearily 448.9 *grevly*, 770.12 *joylessly*, 788.8 *boringly*
dreariness 448.7 *dullness*, 770.2 *depression*, 788.1 *boredom*
dreary 448.3 *dull*, 559.10 *ugly*, 770.6 *depressed*, 788.4 *boring*, 788.5 *bored*
dreary routine 644.1 *work*
dredge 63.29 *construction equipment*, 63.30 *engineer*, 162.18 *sprinkle*, 317.4 *digger*, 339.12 *drag*, 355.10 *excavator*, 355.11 *extract*, 384.22 *powder*
dredger 74 Ships and Boats, 63.29 *construction equipment*, 317.4 *digger*, 355.10 *excavator*, 361.9 *lifter*, 727.4 *wastebin*
dredge up 361.4 *gather up*
dredging 355.1 *extraction*
D region 390.3 *atmospheric layers*
dregs 132.2 *residue*, 157.8 *tail*, 393.13 *mud*, 622.4 *dirt*
dregs of society 864.9 *wicked person*
dreich 55.49 *cloudy*, 788.4 *boring*
Dreiser 48 Writers
drench 68.18 *practise livestock farming*, 144.6 *fill*, 354.4 *immerse*, 374.13 *soften*, 389.9 *soaking*, 389.29 *water*, 610.4 *be excessive*, 621.14 *bathe*, 630.2 *medicine*, 630.20 *doctor*
drenched 389.23 *wet*, 610.6 *excessive*
drenched with sweat 353.28 *sweaty*
drenching 389.9 *soaking*
drenching rain 55.25 *rain*
Dresden 93 Cities, 398.15 *slaughterhouse*
Dresden china 44 Types of Ceramics
dress 295, 295, 45.55 *cook*, 246.7 *make fertile*, 293.25 *wrap*, 295.7 *frock*, 385.12 *rub*, 386.14, 395.18 *anoint*, 411.10

make taste, 457.3 external appearance, 594.5 equip, 603.6 equipment, 627.1 improve, 630.20 doctor
Dress 295
dress a fly 20.7 angle
dressage 18 Sporting Activities, **32**, 32.6 horsemanship, 32.11 eventing
dressage movement 32.10 dressage
dress blues 295.3 formal dress
dress circle 51.16 auditorium, 435.9 viewpoint
dress down 852.20 censure, 879.1 punish
dressed 295, 20.8 angling, 45.56 culinary, 594.18 prepared
dressed fit to kill 813.7 dressed up
dressed fly 20.2 artificial fly
dressed to kill 295.30 dressed up, 811.19 flashy, 813.7 dressed up
dressed up 295, 813, 130.9 extra
dressed-up 540.35 disguised
dressed up like a dog's dinner 559.10 ugly
dressed up to the nines 295.30 dressed up, 796.7 fashionable, 813.7 dressed up
dresser 47.5 cabinet, 51.26 stagehand, 60.17 paramedic, 258.3 cabinet, 295.28 valet
dressily 295
dress in 295.34 wear
dressing 295, 130.3 additional item, 180.5 side dish, 246.3 fertilizer, 293.6 medical covering, 385.5 polishing, 413.2 seasoning, 630.10 surgical dressing
dressing-down 852.7 blame, 879.7 punishment
dressing gown 295.4 informal dress, 295.16 robe, 295.22 nightwear, 296.4 dishabille, 814.6 informal dress
dressing room 51.15 stage, 256.7 room
dressing ship 812.8 salute
dressing station 630.14 hospital
dressing table 47.4 table
dressing-table mirror 435.8 reflection
dressing up 295.2 dressing, 457.3 external appearance, 540.12 facade
dress in one's best bib and tucker 295.33 dress up
dressmaker 135.7 joiner, 216.6 editor, 295.26 fashion designer
dressmaking 42 Hobbies and Pastimes, 295.2 dressing
dress rehearsal 51.12 production, 594.10 preparations
dress shirt 295.8 shirt
dress suit 295.3 formal dress, 295.10 suit, 813.4 formal dress
dress to kill 295.33 dress up
dress uniform 295.3, 813.4 formal dress
dress up 295, 309.12 distort the truth, 474.11 practise sophistry, 540.24 mask, 627.1 improve, 809.17 be affected
dress up as 457.11 appear
dress up to the nines 295.33 dress up
dress warmly 408.16 feel hot
dress whites 295.3 formal dress
dressy 295.31 styled, 796.7 fashionable
drey 77.20 abode of mammals, 256.13 lair
Dreyer 52 Scientists
Dr Fell 822.8 hated person
dribble 23.4 playing terms, 23.6 play basketball, 31.1 hockey, 31.3 ice hockey, 31.8 hockey, 31.9 play hockey, 96.7 flow, 120.2 certain amount, 338.5 throw, 338.27 kick, 347.3 leakage, 347.12 leak, 349.14 let out, 353.9 saliva, 353.20 salivate, 389.32, 389.32 seep, 391.16 seep, 656.7 be clumsy

dribble away 722.12 lessen
dribbled 31.8 hockey, 38.5 soccer
dribbler 22.5 batting terms
dribbling 23.4 playing terms, 31.1 hockey, 31.3 ice hockey, 31.8 hockey, 38.2 football play, 38.5 soccer, 347.3 leakage, 353.29 salivating, 389.25, 391.12 seeping, 656.3 clumsy
dribbling away 722.4 lessening
dried 392.3 dried-up, 637.7 preserved
dried-blood meal 68.13 fertilizer
dried flower 84.1 flower
dried food 350.7 food, 637.3 preserved thing
dried fruit 45.42 preserve, 86.1 fruits
dried grass 68.9 animal feedstuff
dried milk 351.5 milk, 637.3 preserved thing
dried-out 392
dried-up 392
dried vegetable 69.11 vegetable
drier 55.45 fine
Driesch 52 Scientists
drift 54.38 glacier, 73.7 miscellaneous aviation terms, 96.6 river flow, 96.7 flow, 157.14 aim, 161.26 mass, 224.12 be irresolute, 227.4 significance, 234.1 tendency, 324.2 momentum, 324.13 be in motion, 324.15 walk, 326.10 transferred thing, 332.2 bearing, 335.3 go astray, 335.15 deviating motion, 370.9 be light, 472.1 topic, 488.2 tendency, 520.1 meaning, 534.19 radio reception, 562.1 summary, 641.4 not act, 643.12 be inactive, 698.16 be independent, 754.12 be cheap
driftage 73.7 miscellaneous aviation terms, 96.6 river flow, 324.2 momentum
drift along 336.6 march on
drift apart 162.9 be dispersed
drifter 74 Ships and Boats, 74.3 vessel, 643.8 nonworker
drifting 162.25 sprawled, 236.12 impotent, 324.16 moving, 335.16, 335.25 wandering, 488.6 probable, 633.4 endangered
drifting apart 343.2 parting
drifting snow 55.30 snow
drift net 80.7 fishing
drift off 162.9 be dispersed
drift with the current 660.20 take it easy
driftwood 162, 326.10 transferred thing
drill 67 Natural Fabrics, 77 Placental Mammals, 6.22 educate, 47.11 woodworking tool, 47.17 carpenter, 50.14 sculptor's materials, 63.9 machine tool, 63.30 engineer, 68.10 farm tool, 68.11 farmland, 68.17 farm, 69.6 garden tool, 69.15 cultivate, 112.4 monotony, 112.10 conform, 166.6 custom, 167.10 assimilate, 287.14 deepen, 288.4 textile, 322.2 opener, 322.20 hole, 355.13 dig out, 364.6 rotator, 380.8 sharp-pointed thing, 380.16 use a sharp tool, 423.8 be loud, 584.6 procedure, 594.6 brief, 594.12 briefing, 603.1 tool, 603.9 use tools, 644.5, 644.9 exercise, 688.19 be authoritarian, 811.11 ritual, 813.3 formal occasion
drill attention 813.3 formal occasion
drilled 322.14 holed
driller 317.4 digger
drilling 6.1 education, 63.29 construction equipment, 277.1 depth, 355.3 digging out, 584.7 habituation
drilling machine 63.9 machine tool
drilling vessel 54.17 ocean research vessel
drillmaster 594.15 preparer

drill sergeant 423.5 loud person, 594.15 preparer, 653.13 director
drily 392, 412.10 without taste, 415.10 sourly, 771.16 humorously, 788.8 boringly
drink 777 Phobias by Topic, **351, 351, 874**, 348.11 ingest, 387.1 fluid, 411.9 taste, 651.7 refreshments, 874.8 get drunk, 874.12 alcohol
drinkable 351, 411.7 tasty, 632.5 safe
drinkables 606.2 provisions
drink container 351
drink deep 874.8 get drunk
drinker 351, 68.10 farm tool, 411.5 taster, 874.17 drunkard
drink hard 874.8 get drunk
drinking 351, 351, 874, 348.4 intake
Drinking 351
drinking bout 874, 812.1 celebration
drinking cup 258.13 drinking vessel
drinking horn 258.13 drinking vessel
drinking place 351.11 drink provider
drinking to excess 351.1 drinking
drinking vessel 258
drinking water 389, 351.6 soft drink
drinking yoghurt 351.5 milk
drink in moderation 869.5 be self-restrained
drink like a fish 351.13 drink, 874.8 get drunk
drink moderately 873.3 be sober
drink of the gods 351.2 drink
drink one's fill 351.13 drink, 608.6 have enough
drink problem 874.16 alcoholism
drink provider 351
drinks 180.5 side dish
drinks cabinet 47.5, 258.3 cabinet
drink sociably 873.3 be sober
drinks party 665.7 social gathering, 815.5 party
drink the cup of humiliation 806.24 be humiliated
drink the health of 351.14 drink to, 812.17 congratulate
drink to 351, 812.17 congratulate, 815.11 be sociable, 817.10 be courteous
drink up 348.11 ingest, 349.11 void, 351.13 drink, 392.20 absorb
drink water 873.3 be sober
drip 360, 43.9 miscellaneous architectural features, 62.12 injection, 238.4 weakling, 328.1 move slowly, 346.11 infiltrate, 347.3 leakage, 347.12 leak, 389.32, 391.16 seep, 426.11 knock, 630.2 medicine, 630.13 therapy, 788.3 boring person
drip-drop 426.4 knocking
drip-dropping 391.12 seeping
drip-dry 392, 67.11 treated, 621.13 clean
drip-feed 350.25 provide food, 630.13 therapy
dripping 45.7 basic ingredient, 347.3 leakage, 389.23 wet, 389.25, 391.12 seeping, 742.1 wealthy
dripping wet 389.23 wet
dripping with 144.8 full
dripping with oil 395.5 basted
dripping with wealth 742.1 wealthy
dripstone 43.9 miscellaneous architectural features
drip with wealth 742.12 be rich
drive 23.6 play basketball, 25.2 grip, 27.9 stroke, 27.17 bat, 29.7 golf, 35.5 play rugby, 37.7 shoot, 40.2 tennis strokes, 40.12 badminton terms, 40.13 serve, 68.18 practise livestock farming, 161.23 flock, 161.43 herd, 228.10 manipulate, 230.9 take action, 233 influence, 235.3 vitality, 235.11 give power, 239.1

vigour, 239.2 be full of vigour, 324.14 set in motion, 327.2 route, 327.3 road, 329.7 hurry someone up, 329.9 acceleration, 330.1 impel, 330.10 bat, 330.14 sporting hit, 337.29 in reverse, 338.5 throw, 338.20 propel, 338.21 move forward, 338.26 bat, 535.6 assertiveness, 535.21 be assertive, 554.1 emphasis, 574.13 concentration, 590.2 chase, 599.1 use, 642.4 energy, 642.14 push, 644.4 exertion, 648.1 hasten, 648.4 haste, 650.6 fatigue, 670.1 attack, 670.12 military attack, 695.1 compulsion, 695.6 compel
drive a bargain 737.3 bargain
drive a coach and horses through the law 16.73 be illegal
drive against 670.1 attack
drive a hard bargain 13.11 deal
drive apart 136.14 come between
drive a trade 737.1 trade
drive away 341.1 repel
drive a wedge between 136.14 come between
drive back 341.1 repel
drive crazy 510.15 make insane
drive dangerously 633.10 endanger
drive-foot landing 21.2 field events
drive forward 324.13 be in motion
drive headlong 633.10 endanger
drive home 554.6 emphasize, 684.4 complete
drive in 354.3 impact
drive-in 350.15 eating place
drive insane 153.11 derange
drive into 586.15 persuade
drive into a frenzy 828.14 make angry
drive into the open 349.7 drive out
drive-in window 350.15 eating place
drivel 347.12 leak, 353.9 saliva, 353.20 salivate, 506.1 nonsense, 521.4 senseless talk, 521.5 empty talk, 521.9 talk nonsense
drive like leaves 338.21 move forward
driveller 565.4 talker
drivelling 391.12 seeping
drive mad 153.11 derange, 510.15 make insane
driven 235.15 full of energy, 535.14 assertive, 648.3 hasty
driven snow 55.30 snow, 409.5 ice, 446.9 white thing
drive on 219.8 go on, 228.9 motivate, 330.1 impel, 336.3 press on
drive out 349
drive out of baulk 24.8 play billiards
drive quickly 329.4 be swift
driver 33, 29.4 golf club, 65.8 software, 230.5 operator, 326.7 transferor, 338.11 propeller, 599.8 user, 603.7 machinist, 652.10 conductor, 697.4 personal attendant, 697.6 domestic servant
driver ant 82 Insects
drive recklessly 633.10 endanger
driverless car 71.4 personal transport
drive round the bend 153.11 derange, 510.15 make insane
drive through 644.8 exert oneself
drive to death 398.16 kill
drive to despair 776.10 disappoint
drive together 161.43 herd
drive to one's wits end 460.10 bemuse
drive to the wall 682.10 defeat heavily
drive up the wall 153.11 derange, 510.15 make insane, 828.14 make angry
driveway 327.3 road
drive wheel 364.6 rotator

drive without due care and attention 633.10 *endanger*

drive with the bowl 25.7 *bowl*

driving 37.2 *hunting,* 55.53 *rainy,* 71.1 *road transport,* 71.15 *motor transport,* 161.2 *herding,* 324.16 *moving,* 329.8 *speed,* 330.17 *impelling,* 338.17 *propulsive,* 356.2 *passing along,* 574.2 *tenacious,* 695.9 *compelling*

driving ambition 228.1 *motive*

driving force 228.1 *motive,* 235.1 *power,* 330.11 *impulsion,* 337.29 *in reverse,* 338.12 *propellant,* 586.11 *motive*

driving gloves 295.25 *accessories*

driving iron 29.4 *golf club*

driving licence 71.21 *miscellaneous motoring terms,* 708.2 *permit*

driving licence number 544.3 *means of identification*

driving off 29.3 *golf shots*

driving rain 55.25 *rain*

driving wheel 71 Motor Vehicle Parts

drizzle 55.25, 55.62 *rain,* 360.13 *drip,* 391.2 *mistiness,* 391.15 *be moist*

drizzling 55.53 *rainy,* 391.10 *misty*

drizzly 55.53 *rainy,* 391.10 *misty*

Dr Johnson's Dictionary 5.28 *dictionary*

drogue 73 Aircraft Parts, 36.3 *parts of a sailing boat,* 55.7 *weather instruments,* 632.4 *safety device*

droit de seigneur 225.4 *stable thing*

droll 506.5 *nonsensical,* 771.10 *humorous,* 798.5 *ridiculous*

drollery 506.3 *tomfoolery,* 771.1 *humorousness,* 798.1 *ludicrousness,* 798.4 *joke*

drolly 771.16 *humorously*

dromedary 77 Placental Mammals, 326.6 *beast of burden*

dromond 74 Sailing Ships and Boats

dromophobia 777 Phobias by Name

drone 73 Types of Aircraft, 49.21 *tone,* 82.4 *social insect,* 82.16 *infest,* 110.11 *be regular,* 112.4 *monotony,* 328.15 *slow person,* 424.1 *faintness,* 424.5 *sound faint,* 426.2 *humming,* 426.9 *hum,* 428.4 *faint sound,* 428.8 *sound faint,* 430.2 *hoarseness,* 430.5 *sound hoarse,* 432.6 *buzz,* 434.10 *lack harmony,* 643.8 *nonworker*

drone on 112.12 *be monotonous,* 565.8 *talk too much,* 788.6 *be boring*

drongo 78 Birds, 776.3 *hopeless person*

droning 112.4 *monotony,* 112.8 *monotonous,* 426.16 *humming,* 428.4 *faint sound,* 430.8 *hoarse,* 432.3 *insect noise,* 432.9 *humming,* 434.9 *unmelodious*

drool 347.12 *leak,* 349.14 *let out,* 350.22 *eat well,* 353.20 *salivate,* 391.16 *seep,* 521.5 *empty talk,* 521.9 *talk nonsense*

drooling 353.29 *salivating,* 391.12 *seeping*

drool over 821.27 *kiss*

droop 360, 238.6 *be weak,* 283.1 *suspension,* 283.10 *suspend,* 360.2 *sinkage,* 624.24 *be unhealthy,* 628.1 *deteriorate,* 650.5 *be fatigued,* 683.6 *fail,* 770.9 *despair*

droopiness 770.2 *depression*

drooping 360, 238.8 *weak,* 360.2 *sinkage,* 624.22 *sick,* 650.1 *fatigued*

droopy 360.17 *drooping,* 770.6 *depressed*

drop 360, 35.6 *rugger,* 36.8 *punting,* 36.19 *punt,* 51.17 *stage set,* 77.35 *give birth,* 126.3

advantage, 129.2 *decline,* 129.4 *decrease,* 143.7 *piece,* 160.12 *discontinue,* 238.6 *be weak,* 245.11 *have young,* 260.3 *little piece,* 269.10 *lengthen,* 277.1 *depth,* 277.14 *deepen,* 281.1 *verticality,* 281.7 *fall vertically,* 296.14 *undress,* 315.3 *round thing,* 337.4 *slip back,* 337.14 *decline,* 338.28 *shoot,* 349.2 *dismiss,* 360.5 *dive,* 360.12 *drop,* 362.6 *throw down,* 362.11 *lowering,* 411.3 *appetizer,* 598.1 *relinquish,* 600.6 *stop using,* 612.8 *trifle,* 624.24 *be unhealthy,* 650.5 *be fatigued,* 656.7 *be clumsy,* 673.4 *succumb,* 705.5 *resign,* 727.10 *dismiss,* 874.13 *drink,* 875.10 *drug oneself,* 879.16 *instrument of execution*

drop a brick 656.7 *be clumsy*

drop a catch 656.7 *be clumsy*

drop acid 875.10 *drug oneself*

drop a clanger 211.8 *make a mistake,* 683.6 *fail*

drop a hint 636.5 *warn*

drop a line to 326.13 *post,* 534.31 *correspond*

drop anchor 74.10 *sail,* 256.18 *take up residence,* 344.4 *land*

drop an oar 36.16 *row*

drop a pop-up 656.7 *be clumsy*

drop a sitter 656.7 *be clumsy*

drop ball 38.2 *football play*

drop behind 304.6 *be in the rear*

drop bombs 670.3 *bomb*

drop by 815.12 *visit*

drop by drop 121.10 *by degrees,* 143.12 *partly*

dropcloth 293.9 *floor covering*

drop-crotching 85.6 *tree management*

drop curtain 51.17 *stage set*

drop dead 397.16 *meet one's fate*

drop from the sky 360.12 *drop*

drop from view 512.12 *be forgotten*

drop handlebars 71.11 *bicycle part*

drophead coupé 71.16 *car*

drop in 344.11 *arrive,* 354.1 *insert*

drop in on 815.12 *visit*

drop in the bucket 609.8 *insufficiency,* 612.8 *trifle*

drop in the ocean 609.8 *insufficiency,* 612.8 *trifle*

drop into 346.13 *fall into*

drop it 218.12 *stop,* 598.1 *relinquish*

drop kick 35.3 *rugby play,* 330.13 *blow*

drop-kick 330.7 *kick*

drop-kick the ball 35.5 *play rugby*

drop-leaf 47.14 *wooden*

drop-leaf table 47.14 *table*

droplet 260.3 *little piece,* 315.3 *round thing*

drop like a stone 281.7 *fall vertically*

drop off 139.6 *come unstuck,* 360.9 *descend,* 397.15 *die,* 404.11 *be unfeeling*

drop of the curtain 51.6 *scene*

drop on 360.12 *drop*

drop one 349.16 *belch,* 419.5 *stink*

drop one in it 659.23 *cause difficulties*

drop one's eyes 436.16 *be blind to*

drop one's guard 595.12 *be unprepared,* 780.5 *be rash*

drop one's guts 349.16 *belch*

drop one's voice 424.5, 428.8 *sound faint,* 563.16 *speak in a low voice*

drop out 685

drop out 117.13 *not conform,* 168.19 *be independent,* 573.9 *not cooperate,* 598.2 *withdraw,* 698.16 *be independent,* 720.8 *not perform*

dropout 108.3 *unconnected person,* 168.7 *nonconformist,* 335.19 *deviant person,* 500.5 *dissenter,* 573.16 *reluctant per-*

son, 598.4 *deserter,* 683.5 *failing person,* 685.3 *quitter,* 713.4 *protester,* 720.6 *evader,* 720.12 *nonperforming*

drop-out 35.3 *rugby play*

drop over the side 362.6 *throw down*

drop pass 31.3 *ice hockey*

drop-pass 31.9 *play hockey*

drop-passed 31.8 *hockey*

drop-passing 31.3 *ice hockey,* 31.8 *hockey*

dropped 35.6 *rugger,* 41.13 *ice-skating,* 396.15 *born,* 598.5 *relinquished*

dropped catch 504.13 *sporting error,* 656.9 *bungling*

dropped goal 35.3 *rugby play*

dropped mohawk 41.7 *ice-dancing*

dropped three 41.7 *ice-dancing*

dropper 57 Laboratory Apparatus, 62.8 *drops*

dropping 360.4 *fall,* 360.18, 362.20 *falling,* 650.1 *fatigued*

dropping anchor 344.11 *landing*

dropping in 815.3 *meeting*

dropping one's aitches 504.11 *grammatical error*

droppings 353.5 *faeces,* 622.4 *dirt*

drops 62

drop scene 51.17 *stage set*

drop scone 45.39 *loaf*

drop-shot 40.12 *badminton terms*

dropsical 261.7 *bigger,* 624.23 *diseased*

drop sprogs 245.10 *reproduce oneself*

dropsy 261.1 *growth,* 387.3 *body fluid,* 624.4 *disease*

drop tank 73 Aircraft Parts

drop the bomb 676.13 *be at war*

drop the idea 598.1 *relinquish*

drop the payload 670.3 *bomb*

drop the pilot 345.5 *set out*

droshky 71 Carriages and Carts

drosophila 82 Insects

dross 132.2 *residue,* 266.3 *coat,* 614.6 *refuse,* 622.4 *dirt*

drossy 266.9 *platelike*

drostanolone 62 Medication

drought 55.28, 392.11 *dryness,* 392.12 *thirst,* 609.9 *scarcity*

Droughtmaster 68 Breeds of Cattle

drought-stricken 247.3 *birth control*

drought-stricken land 247.1 *infertility*

droughty 392.1 *dry*

drouk 389.29 *water*

drouthy 392.2 *thirsty*

drove 161 Collective Names for Birds and Animals, 68.18 *practise livestock farming,* 77.21 *assemblage of mammals,* 161.23 *flock,* 181.4 *throng*

drover 32.15 *horse person,* 68.16 *farm worker,* 653.14 *leader*

drown 144.6 *fill,* 244.8 *destroy,* 244.12 *consume,* 360.9 *descend,* 362.3 *bring down,* 389.29 *water,* 397.16 *meet one's fate,* 398.17 *murder,* 422.2 *silence,* 546.1 *obliterate*

drowned 96.11 *flooded,* 144.8 *full,* 389.24 *flooded*

drowning 360.2 *sinkage,* 360.16 *descending,* 389.9 *soaking,* 397.5 *ways of dying,* 398.2 *murder,* 879.13 *capital punishment*

drown oneself 398.21 *commit suicide*

drown one's sorrows 874.8 *get drunk*

drown out 421.10 *muffle*

drown-proofed 39.11 *swimming*

drown-proofing 39.3 *survival swimming,* 39.11 *swimming*

drown the noise 422.2 *silence*

drowse 404.11 *be unfeeling,* 643.13 *sleep,* 649.2 *take it easy,* 650.5 *be fatigued*

drowser 643.11 *sleeper*

drowsily 643.17 *sleepily,* 650.8 *tiredly*

drowsiness 643.9 *sleep,* 650.7 *fatigue*

drowsy 404.10 *sleepy,* 643.4 *not awake,* 650.1 *fatigued,* 788.5 *bored*

Dr. Strangelove 679.6 *militarist*

drub 330.7 *kick,* 330.13 *blow,* 682.10 *defeat heavily,* 879.3 *hit*

drubbing 683.2 *defeat,* 879.12 *corporal punishment*

drudge 642.10 *busy person,* 644.6 *work,* 646.1 *worker,* 697.1 *servant*

drudgery 642.8 *assiduity,* 644.1 *work*

drudging 644.10 *working*

drug 62, 630, 875, 404.4 *anaesthetic,* 460.10 *bemuse,* 630.2 *medicine,* 630.20 *doctor,* 631.11 *intoxicant,* 631.15 *poison,* 643.14 *make inactive,* 761.6 *desensitizing substance,* 761.7 *render insensitive*

drug abuse 875.1 *drug-taking*

drug addict 584.8 *creature of habit,* 624.19 *sick person,* 875.4 *drug taker*

drug addiction 624.4 *disease,* 875.1 *drug-taking*

drug dealer 875.5 *drug pusher*

drug dependence 62.3 *drug,* 875.1 *drug-taking*

drug-dependent 875.8 *addicted*

drug enforcement officer 632.3 *protector*

drugged 875, 236.12 *impotent,* 643.4 *not awake,* 761.2 *desensitized*

drugget 67 Natural Fabrics, 293.9 *floor covering,* 621.11 *cleaning cloth*

druggie 875.4 *drug taker*

druggist 630, 62.2 *pharmacologist*

drug ice 41.10 *curling*

drug oneself 875

drug on the market 754.2 *declining prices*

drug overdose 398.7 *suicide*

drug party 815.5 *party*

drug peddler 864.9 *wicked person,* 875.5 *drug pusher*

drug peddling 864.7 *criminality,* 875.2 *drug pushing*

drug pusher 875

drug pushing 875

drugs 777 Phobias by Topic, 875.6 *drug*

drug scorer 875.4 *drug taker*

drugs squad 16.15 British police

drug store 62.2 *pharmacologist*

drug-store counter 350.15 *eating place*

drug taker 875

drug-taking 875, 630.8 *drug*

Drug-taking 875

drug test 21.5 *competition*

drug traffic 737.4 *trade*

drug trafficking 875.2 *drug pushing*

drug treatment 60.8 *treatment,* 61.3 *psychiatric treatment*

drug type 62

drug user 875.4 *drug taker*

druid 11.12 *occultist*

druidess 11.12 *occultist*

druidic 7.17 *priestly,* 11.15 *witchlike*

Druidism 7 Non-Christian Religions

drum 49 Musical Instruments, **426,** 43.8 *column,* 55.62 *rain,* 183.22 *resound,* 258.11 *vessel,* 365.9 *vibrate,* 366.24 *shake,* 426.1 *drumming,* 521.7 *mean nothing*

drumbeat 214.5 *regular thing,* 426.1 *drumming,* 543.6 *word*

drum-bed sander 47.11 *woodworking tool*

drum brake 71 Motor Vehicle Parts

drum corps 17.4 *military organization*

drumfish 80 Fishes

drumhead court-martial 16.19 *lawcourt*

drumlin 275.3 *mountain*

drum major 653.14 *leader*

drum majorette 653.14 *leader*

drumming 426, **426,** 55.53 *rainy,* 183.6 *reverberation,* 183.15 *reverberatory,* 330.12 *collision,* 365.2 *vibration*

drumming fingers 543.3 *gesture*

drumming out 349.18 *dismissal*

drum one's fingers 543.11 *gesture,* 642.12 *be active*

drum out 349.3 *disbar,* 349.7 *drive out,* 879.1 *punish*

drum printer 65.7 *peripheral*

drum roll 426.1 *drumming,* 812.8 *salute*

drums 676.2 *glory of war*

drum scale 369.10 *scales*

drumstick 45.28 *poultry*

drunk 874, 870.8 *overindulgent,* 874.17 *drunkard*

drunk and disorderly 874.1 *drunk*

drunkard 874, 351.12 *drinker*

drunk as a fiddler 874.1 *drunk*

drunk as a fiddler's bitch 874.1 *drunk*

drunk as a lord 874.1 *drunk*

drunk as an owl 874.1 *drunk*

drunk as a skunk 874.1 *drunk*

drunk as David's sow 874.1 *drunk*

drunken 874, 351.16 *drinking,* 874.1 *drunk*

drunkenly 874

drunkenness 874, 351.1 *drinking,* 610.2 *overdoing it,* 628.8 *perversion,* 870.3 *overindulgence*

Drunkenness 874

drunken stupor 874.10 *drunkenness*

drupe 86.2 *botanical fruit*

Druse 7.6 *non-Christian*

Druses 7 Non-Christian Religions

dry 392, **392,** 12.6 *political party,* 44.11 *make ceramics,* 55.45 *fine,* 68.21 *domesticated,* 139.8 *nonadhesive,* 217.3 *conservative person,* 247.3 *birth control,* 351.17 *drinkable,* 392.2 *thirsty,* 412.5 *tasteless,* 413.12 *season,* 415.5 *acid,* 430.8 *hoarse,* 512.14 *be forgetful,* 555.1 *unemphatic,* 556.1 *simple,* 577.4 *set,* 577.8 *obstinate person,* 591.19 *abstaining,* 594.7 *decrying,* 621.13 *clean,* 625.6 *make hygienic,* 637.5 *preserve,* 665.6 *political party member,* 690.4 *strict person,* 771.10 *humorous,* 782.10 *hungry,* 788.4 *boring,* 869.4 *self-restrained person,* 869.8 *self-restrained,* 873.1 *sober*

dryad 8.5 *deity,* 85.13 *tree mythology*

dry air 55.10 *air movement*

dry as a biscuit 392.3 *dried-up*

dry as a bone 392.2 *thirsty,* 392.3 *dried-up*

dry as a mummy 392.3 *dried-up*

dry as a stick 392.3 *dried-up*

dry as dust 392.3 *dried-up,* 412.5 *tasteless,* 788.4 *boring*

dry as parchment 392.3 *dried-up*

dry battery 64.29 *power source,* 605.4 *storage*

dry-cargo 70.5 *transportable*

dry cell 57.19 *electrochemistry,* 64.29 *power source,* 235.7 *electrical power*

dry-clean 621.13 *clean*

dry cleaner 621.12 *cleaner*

dry-cleaning 67.8 *fabric treatment,* 621.2 *cleaning*

dry climate 55.38 *climate,* 392.14 *desert*

dry county 873.7 *prohibition*

dry cow 68.8 *livestock*

Dryden 48 Poets

dry dock 344.16 *stopover*

dryer 392

dry farmer 68.15 *agriculturist*

dry farming 68.4 *arable farming*

dry feed 350.8 *animal food*

dry-fly 20.8 *angling*

dry-fly fishing 20.1 *angling*

dry fruit 86.2 *botanical fruit*

dry goods 13.6 *economic factors,* 295.1 *dress,* 739.8 *merchandise*

dry-goods dealer 295.26 *fashion designer*

dry ice 409.5 *ice*

drying 392, **392,** 637.1 *preservation*

drying chamber 44.5 *ceramic process*

drying oil 395.7 *oil*

drying out 873.1 *sober*

drying up 392.13 *drying*

dry land 54.6 *continent*

dry measure 75.1 *unit*

dryness 55, **392,** 247.1 *infertility,* 392.12 *thirst,* 412.1 *tastelessness,* 415.1 *sourness,* 556.4 *simplicity,* 771.1 *humorousness,* 782.3 *appetite,* 788.1 *boredom*

Dryness 392

dry off 68.18 *practise livestock farming,* 392.17 *dry*

Dryopithecus 77 Placental Mammals

dryopteris 88 Ferns

dry out 392.17 *dry,* 873.5 *sober up,* 875.10 *drug oneself*

drypoint 50.15 *engraving*

dry rot 89.1 *fungus,* 244.7 *agent of destruction,* 622.4 *dirt*

dry run 479.2 *rehearsal*

drysalter 606.3 *provider*

dry season 203.1 *season*

dry sherry 351.9 *wine*

dry-shod 392.10 *waterproof*

dry skin 392

dry snow 409.5 *ice*

dry spell 55.28 *dryness*

dry state 873.7 *prohibition*

drysuit 36.7 *windsurfing*

dry throat 782.3 *appetite*

dry up 392, 51.34 *underact,* 129.4 *decrease,* 392.17 *dry,* 422.6 *hush* sh silence quiet shut up that's enough peace soft mum's the word whist, 566.9 *lapse into silence,* 607.1 *waste,* 609.5 *be insufficient*

dry wine 351.9 *wine,* 415.3 *sour thing*

dry wit 771.3 *wit*

DTP 65.1 *computing,* 65.11 *application*

DT's 510.4 *delusion,* 874.16 *alcoholism*

Dua 8 Deities

Duala 5 Languages and Groups of Languages

dual carriageway 71.3 *carriageway,* 285.2 *parallel thing,* 327.3 *road*

dualism 4.7 *school of thought,* 176.3 *duality*

dualist 4.11 *follower of a doctrine*

dualistic 4.14 *of a philosophy,* 176.9 *two*

duality 176

dually 176.19 *twice*

dual personality 61.8 *disordered personality,* 176.3 *duality*

dual-purpose 176.10 *two-sided*

Duat 8.11 *heaven*

dub 29.6 *golfer*

dubbed shot 29.3 *golf shots*

Dubhe 53 Named Stars

dubiety 365.3 *vacillation,* 498.1 *disbelief*

dubious 473.10 *arguable,* 474.7 *sophistic,* 477.14 *questionable,* 489.1 *improbable,* 491.1 *uncertain,* 498.6 *disbelieving*

dubiously 474.14 *sophistically,* 477.24 *questionably,* 489.8 *improbably,* 491.23 *uncertainly,* 498.10 *disbelievingly*

dubiousness 477.7 *questionableness,* 491.9 *uncertainty,* 498.1 *disbelief*

dubitable 489.1 *improbable*

Dublin 92 Counties, **93** Cities

Dublin bay prawn 45.19 *shellfish*

dub poetry 48.6 *poetry*

ducal 802.4 *aristocratic*

ducat 741.12 *ancient coins*

duchess 802.1 *nobleman*

duchy 12.5 *political organization,* 91.3 *dominion,* 249.5 *state,* 688.8 *governmental organization*

duck 67 Natural Fabrics, **71** Motor Vehicles, **78** Birds, 27.10 *score,* 37.5 *game,* 39.11 *swimming,* 45.20 *meat,* 68.8 *livestock,* 78.3 *water bird,* 78.11 *female bird,* 172.1 *zero,* 324.15 *walk,* 331.2 *respond,* 331.6 *response,* 354.4 *immerse,* 360.5 *dive,* 360.12 *drop,* 362.3 *bring down,* 362.8 *sit,* 362.9 *bow,* 362.16 *courtesy,* 389.29 *water,* 573.7 *refuse,* 591.6 *evade,* 591.14 *evasion,* 679.24 *warship,* 808.10 *knuckle under,* 817.13 *defer to,* 821.12 *nicknames for lovers,* 826.4 *terms of endearment,* 879.1 *punish*

duck and dive 224.12 *be irresolute*

duck and run 638.5 *escape*

duckboard 63.21 *bridge*

duckboards 293.9 *floor covering*

duck dive 39.6 *diving*

ducked 389.24 *flooded*

duck-egg blue 454.1 *blue*

duck farming 68.3 *livestock farming*

duck-fit 828.4 *anger*

duck gybe 36.1 *sailing,* 36.15 *sail*

duck hunter 37.4 *hunter,* 398.13 *animal killer*

duck hunting 37.2 *hunting,* 398.9 *animal killing*

ducking 354.10 *immersion,* 360.18 *falling,* 362.13 *submergence,* 389.9 *soaking,* 808.2 *sycophancy,* 879.7 *punishment*

ducking and diving 224.2 *irresolution*

ducking stool 879.14 *instrument of punishment*

duckling 68.8 *livestock,* 78.12 *young bird,* 206.4 *young animal*

duckpins 25.4 *bowling*

duck responsibility 717.5 *be irresolute*

ducks 161 Collective Names by Animal, 27.6 *pad*

ducks and drakes 331.4 *recoil*

duck season 203.1 *season*

duck shoot 78.20 *bird sport,* 590.2 *chase*

duck soup 660.6 *easy thing*

Ducks Unlimited 37.2 *hunting*

duck tack 36.1 *sailing,* 36.15 *sail*

duck the issue 591.7 *be evasive*

ducky 821.12 *nicknames for lovers,* 826.4 *terms of endearment*

duct 322.1 *opening*

ductile 339.9 *retractive,* 374.2 *pliant,* 377.6 *elastic,* 660.12 *wieldy*

ductility 374.8 *softness,* 377.1 *elasticity*

ductless gland 352.3 *gland*

dud 102.5 *insubstantial person,* 236.10 *powerless,* 240.3 *inert thing,* 614.1 *useless,* 680.13 *ammunition,* 683.4 *unsuccessful thing,* 683.5 *failing person,* 683.10 *failed*

dud cheque 741.15 *false money,* 747.3 *bad payment*

dude 401.2 *male,* 539.22 *dupe,* 656.10 *unskilled person*

dudelsack 49 Musical Instruments

dude ranch 68.6 *farm*

dudgeon 680.8 *sharp weapon,* 828.2 *offence*

duds 295.1 *dress*

due 845, 845, 199.11 *future,* 332.9 *directly,* 513.7 *expected,* 615.1 *convenient,* 745.9 *in debt,* 746.17 *payable,* 804.2 *entitlement,* 843.6 *right,* 843.9 *in the right,* 845.11 *entitled to*

due credit 878.1 *reward*

due for demolition 244.15 *destroyed*

duel 674, 28.5 *fence,* 398.4 *slaughter,* 674.12 *fight*

dueller 28.4 *fencer,* 679.1 *combatant*

duelling 28.1 *fencing,* 674.9 *duel*

duelling pistol 680.10 *historical gun*

duelling sword 28.2 *fencing equipment*

duellist 674.10 *contender,* 679.1 *combatant*

duel to the death 674.9 *duel*

due measure 242.1 *moderation*

dueness 485.1 *qualification,* 615.3 *convenience,* 652.1 *conduct,* 672.1 *retaliation,* 845.1 *entitlement,* 879.8 *penalty*

duenna 6.4 *educator,* 180.7 *attendant,* 632.3 *protector*

due north 332.9 *directly*

due payment 746.1 *payment*

due process 16.6 *legal process,* 188.3 *continuity*

due process of law 16.33 *litigation*

due punishment 845.2 *due*

due recognition 878.1 *reward*

due respect 849.3 *respectfulness*

due reward 845.2 *due*

dues 845, 749.2 *money received,* 751.3 *fee,* 751.7 *tax*

dues-paying member 665.5 *member*

duet 140.3 *assembly,* 176.1 *two,* 176.2 *double,* 664.9 *team*

due time 615.3 *convenience*

due to 227.10 *caused*

duff 127.14 *poor,* 236.10 *powerless*

duffel 67 Natural Fabrics, 725.4 *possessions*

duffel bag 258.8 *bag*

duffel coat 295.12 *coat*

duffer 29.6 *golfer,* 502.5 *ignorant person,* 656.10 *unskilled person*

dug 77.2 *mammalian characteristic,* 322.14 *holed*

dugdugi 49 Musical Instruments

dug in 671.31 *entrenched*

dugong 77 Placental Mammals

dugout 22.1 *baseball,* 36.12 *canoeing,* 531.2 *hiding place,* 634.1 *refuge,* 671.8 *military defences*

dugout canoe 36.6 *canoeing*

duiker 77 Placental Mammals

Dukas 49 Musicians and Composers

duke 802.1 *nobleman*

Duke 18 Sporting Personalities

dukedom 12.5 *political organization,* 91.3 *dominion,* 688.8 *governmental organization,* 802.2 *aristocracy*

Duke of Perth 46.4 *historic dancing*

dukes 407.7 *sense organ,* 726.3 *tools for gripping*

DUKW 74 Ships and Boats

dulcet 49.30 *harmonic,* 405.6 *pleasant,* 433.6 *melodious,* 763.3 *comfortable*

dulcify 242.4 *moderate*

dulcimer 49 Musical Instruments

Dulcinea 821.9 *lover*

dull 381, 448, 55.49 *cloudy,* 112.8 *monotonous,* 124.3 *mediocre,* 240.5 *inert,* 242.4 *moderate,* 273.3 *thick-witted,* 325.5 *sedentary,* 381.1, 381.10 *blunt,* 412.5 *tasteless,* 424.4 *faint,* 424.6 *mute,* 428.2 *nonresonant,* 428.7 *mute,* 441.5 *dim,* 441.7 *dimmed,* 441.8 *stupid,* 441.11 *tarnish,* 443.2 *shady,* 443.5 *unintelligent,* 444.13 *soft-hued,* 445.6 *decolour,* 445.7 *colourless,* 460.5 *lacking intellect,* 460.10 *bemuse,* 466.4 *uninterested,* 502.6 *ignorant,* 508.5 *foolish,* 555.1 *unemphatic,* 559.10 *ugly,* 641.3 *inactive,* 643.3 *not participating,* 650.1 *fatigued,* 761.1 *insensitive,* 783.7 *indifferent,* 783.13 *make indifferent,* 787.3 *unmoved,* 788.4 *boring,* 788.6 *be boring*

dullard 240.2 *inert person*, 460.3 *unintelligent person*
dulled 428.2 *nonresonant*, 441.7 *dimmed*
dull-edged 381.1 *blunt*
dull green 453.1 *green*
dull monotony 788.1 *boredom*
dullness 381, 448, 112.4 *monotony*, 240.1 *inertness*, 381.5 *bluntness*, 404.1 *lack of feeling*, 412.1 *tastelessness*, 441.2 *murk*, 443.6 *opaqueness*, 444.3 *hue*, 555.2 *lack of emphasis*, 643.7 *idleness*, 650.7 *fatigue*, 761.3 *insensitiveness*, 783.1 *indifference*, 787.1 *lack of wonder*
dull-pointed 381.1 *blunt*
dull sound 428, 424.1 *faintness*
dull speech 788.2 *boring thing*
dull-witted 273.3 *thick-witted*, 443.5 *unintelligent*
dull-wittedness 443.9 *stupidity*
dull work 788.2 *boring thing*
dully 112.15 *monotonously*, 381.11 *smoothly*, 412.10 *without taste*, 445.9 *colourlessly*, 448.9 *greyly*, 643.16 *impassively*, 787.9 *without wonder*, 788.8 *boringly*
Dülmen 32 Breeds of Horse and Pony
Dulong and Petit's law 56 Named Laws, **57** Named Reactions
dulse 90 Algae
Duluth 93 Cities
duly 845, 714.16 *as promised*
Dumas' method 57 Named Reactions
Du Maurier 48 Writers, **48** Writers
dumb 76.14 *animalian*, 273.3 *thick-witted*, 422.3 *silent*, 460.6 *unintelligent*, 460.8 *nonhuman*, 502.6 *ignorant*, 563.11 *speechless*, 566.2 *silent*, 620.3 *deformed*, 656.1 *unskilful*, 786.7 *wide-eyed*
dumb animal 76.2 *animal*
Dumbarton 93 Cities
dumbbell 460.3 *unintelligent person*, 502.5 *ignorant person*
Dumbbell Nebula 53 Nebulae
dumb cluck 502.5 *ignorant person*
dumb crambo 42 Children's Games and Party Games
dumbfound 514.11 *amaze*, 515.6 *disappoint*, 563.15 *strike dumb*, 786.10 *be wonderful*
dumbfounded 422.3 *silent*, 514.7 *amazed*, 563.11 *speechless*, 786.6 *wondering*
dumbfoundment 786.1 *wonder*
dumb friend 76.2 *animal*
dumbness 422.4 *silence*, 563.5 *mutism*, 566.5 *silence*
dumbo 460.3 *unintelligent person*, 502.5 *ignorant person*, 508.3 *foolish person*
dumbshow 51.2 *play*
dumb show 547.3 *acting*
dumbstruck 722.18 *at a loss*, 786.7 *wide-eyed*
dumb waiter 361.10 *elevator*
dumdum 680.13 *ammunition*
dum-dum 502.5 *ignorant person*
Dumfries 93 Cities
Dumfries and Galloway 92 Counties
dummy 102.5 *insubstantial person*, 102.12 *not the real thing*, 118.2 *copy*, 242.2 *moderator*, 306.2 *prototype*, 306.10 *prototypical*, 460.3 *unintelligent person*, 479.8 *experimental*, 502.5 *ignorant person*, 510.7 *insane person*, 526.7 *showpiece*, 540.10 *fake*, 547.6 *image*
dummying 35.3 *rugby play*, 35.6 *rugger*
dummy run 479.2 *rehearsal*
dumortierite 54 Minerals
dump 65.17 *computing term*, 65.19 *abort*, 111.4 *litter*, 256.8 *shelter*, 349.12 *unload*, 598.2 *withdraw*, 600.6 *stop using*, 605.4 *storage*, 614.6 *refuse*,

727.5 *wasteyard*, 727.8 *sink*, 727.9 *dispose of*, 739.1 *sell*, 752.3 *discount*, 754.13 *make cheap*, 806.10 *abasement*, 806.23 *abase*
dumpbin 526.8 *showplace*
dumpcart 71.7 *handcart*
dumpiness 259.6 *squatness*, 260.1 *littleness*, 270.1 *shortness*
dumping 600.10 *disuse*, 727.1 *disposal*, 752.2 *bargain*
dumpling 259.12 *fat person*
dump on 618.14 *ill-treat*, 850.23 *insult*
dump on the market 610.4 *be excessive*
dump truck 63.29 *construction equipment*
dump upon 360.12 *drop*
dumpy 259.16 *fat*, 260.7 *little*, 270.7 *short*, 549.8 *inelegant*, 559.7 *graceless*
dun 32.1 *horse*, 448.1 *grey*, 449.1 *brown*, 642.17 *meddle*, 712.2, 712.7 *demand*, 744.5 *lender*, 744.8 *credit*
dunce 460.3 *unintelligent person*, 502.5 *ignorant person*, 508.3 *foolish person*
dunce cap 295.15 *headgear*
dunce's cap 544.5 *uniform*, 879.14 *instrument of punishment*
Dundalk 93 Cities
Dundee 93 Cities
Dundee cake 45.36 *cake*
dunderhead 460.3 *unintelligent person*
dune 54, 161.26 *mass*, 275.3 *mountain*
dune buggy 71 Motor Vehicles
Dunedin 93 Cities
Dunfermline 93 Cities
dung 68.13 *fertilizer*, 68.17 *farm*, 69.15 *cultivate*, 246.3 *fertilizer*, 353.5 *faeces*, 410.2 *lighter*, 419.2 *something that makes an unpleasant smell*, 622.4 *dirt*
dungaree 67 Natural Fabrics
dungarees 295.9 *trousers*
dung beetle 82 Insects
dungeon 277.4 *deep thing*, 323.4 *closed place*, 440.4 *dark thing*, 702.1 *prison*
dunghill 727.8 *sink*
dunging 68.5 *cultivation*
dungy 353.25 *faecal*, 622.8 *unclean*
dunk 23.4 *playing terms*, 23.6 *play basketball*, 354.4 *immerse*, 389.29 *water*, 621.14 *bathe*
dunked 389.24 *flooded*
Dunkers 7 Christian Movements
dunking 23.4 *playing terms*, 389.9 *soaking*
Dunkirk 93 Cities
dunlin 78 Birds
Dunlop 45 Cheeses, **52** Scientists
Dunmore 93 Cities
dunning 712.2 *demand*
dunnock 78 Birds
Dunoon 93 Cities
Duns 93 Cities
Duns Scotus 4 Philosophers
duo 49.26 *musical group*, 140.3 *assembly*, 176.1 *two*
duodecahedron 310.3 *angled figure*
duodecillion 169.3 *large number*, 179.11 *million*
duodecimal 179.7 *double figures*, 179.18 *eleventh*
duodecimal notation 52.8 *number system*
duodecimo 179.7 *double figures*, 260.2 *little thing*, 260.7 *little*
duodenal 290.10 *visceral*
duodenal ulcer 624.8 *indigestion*
duodenary 179.18 *eleventh*
duodenitis 624.8 *indigestion*
duodenostomy 60 Surgical Operations
duodenum 290.4 *insides*

duodrama 51.2 *play*
duologue 51.2 *play*, 568.1 *conversation*
dupe 539, 110.4 *duplicate*, 127.6 *inferior*, 238.4 *weakling*, 497.9 *make someone believe*, 515.8 *be dishonest*, 539.28 *trick*, 635.3 *trap*, 658.3 *naive person*, 683.5 *failing person*, 687.5 *person in adversity*, 722.6 *loser*, 734.10 *take away*, 736.16 *act dishonest*, 808.3 *sycophant*, 850.9 *butt*
duped 515.10 *deceived*, 538.16 *misinformed*, 539.36 *deceived*
duper 539.15 *deceiver*
dupery 539.7 *tricking*
duple 176.9 *two*
duple metre 48.9 *metre*
duplex 176.2 *double*, 176.9 *two*, 256.5 *house*, 256.16 *manorial*
duplex apartment 256.5 *house*
duplexity 176.3 *duality*
duplicate 110, 110, 110, 118, 114.2 *copy*, 114.8 *simulated*, 114.12 *imitate*, 118.2, 118.10 *copy*, 128.5 *make bigger*, 176.5 *twin*, 176.12, 176.15 *double*, 183.7 *replica*, 183.16 *repeat*, 245.2 *print*, 245.9 *reproduce*, 544.3 *means of identification*, 545.5 *copy*, 547.1 *representation*, 547.6 *image*, 547.9 *represent*, 560.9 *representation*, 610.5 *be superfluous*
duplicate bridge 42 Card Games
duplicate copy 545.5 *copy*
duplicated 114.7 *similar*, 114.8 *simulated*, 176.12 *double*, 183.9 *repeated*, 245.15 *reproduced*
duplicating the cube 529.5 *difficult problem*
duplication 110.4 *duplicate*, 114.1 *similarity*, 118.2 *copy*, 128.1 *increase*, 176.4 *doubling*, 183.1 *repetition*, 245.1 *reproduction*, 610.3 *superfluity*
duplicative 183.12 *repetitious*
duplicator 114.3 *copier*, 118.6 *photocopier*
duplicitous 538, 540, 176.11 *double-edged*, 538.19 *dishonest*, 539.35 *deceptive*, 539.38 *treacherous*, 540.29 *deceitful*, 858.6 *faithless*
duplicitously 538.28 *dishonestly*
duplicity 538, 540, 176.3 *duality*, 474.5 *hypocrisy*, 531.5 *evasion*, 538.10 *dishonesty*, 539.1 *deception*, 539.4 *false-heartedness*, 540.5 *deceitfulness*, 657.1 *cunning*, 858.2 *faithlessness*
Dupré 49 Musicians and Composers
durability 188.4 *long-lastingness*, 217.1 *permanence*, 225.1 *stability*, 237.1 *strength*, 378.6 *toughness*
durable 188.8 *lasting*, 190.8 *eternal*, 217.7 *permanent*, 225.9 *stable*, 237.13 *strengthened*, 378.1 *tough*
durable goods 13.6 *economic factors*
durableness 188.4 *long-lastingness*
durables 13.6 *economic factors*, 739.8 *merchandise*
durably 378.12 *toughly*
Duralumin 57 Alloys, 373.7 *hard substance*
duramen 85.3 *timber*, 373.7 *hard substance*
durance 699.4 *detention*, 702.7 *imprisonment*
Duras 48 Writers
duration 185, 188, 99.6 *continuing existence*, 121.1 *degree*, 248.8 *intervening space*, 269.4 *length*
Duration 188
Durban 93 Cities
durbar 653.7 *council*
duress 695.2 *coercion*, 699.1 *restraint*
Durga-puja 10.16 *religious festival*

Durham 68 Breeds of Cattle, **92** Counties, **93** Cities
durian 86 Fruits
during 185.26 *all the time*
during the evening 205.7 *evening*
during the past 200.22 *in the past*
durmast 85 Trees and Shrubs
durn 827.11 *miscellaneous euphemisms*
durned 827.11 *miscellaneous euphemisms*
Duroc 68 Breeds of Pig
durra 87 Grasses
Durrell 48 Writers
Dürrenmatt 48 Dramatists
Durrës 93 Cities
dush 614.6 *refuse*
dusk 157.9 *close*, 205.1 *evening*, 441.1 *dimness*
duskily 447.12 *blackly*
duskiness 441.1 *dimness*, 447.7 *blackness*
duskness 622.1 *dirtiness*
dusky 205.6 *evening*, 440.8 *dark*, 440.10 *dark-coloured*, 441.5 *dim*, 447.2 *dark*
Düsseldorf 93 Cities
dust 777 Phobias by Topic, 68.13 *fertilizer*, 69.15 *cultivate*, 162.18 *sprinkle*, 362.6 *throw down*, 370.7 *light thing*, 384.5, 384.22 *powder*, 456.11 *variegate*, 591.9 *play truant*, 612.8 *trifle*, 621.13 *clean*, 622.4 *dirt*
dustball 384.5 *powder*
dustbin 258.11 *vessel*, 614.6 *refuse*, 621.10 *cleaning object*, 727.4 *wastebin*, 727.8 *sink*
dustbin man 727.6 *rubbish collector*
dust bowl 247.1 *infertility*, 392.14 *desert*
dustcart 71 Motor Vehicles, 727.4 *wastebin*
dust cloud 384.5 *powder*
dust cover 301.4 *wrapper*, 621.11 *cleaning cloth*
dust-covered 384.16 *powdery*
dust devil 55.16 *wind vortex*, 384.5 *powder*
dust down 879.1 *punish*
dusted 162.23 *sprinkled*, 456.10 *mottled*
duster 295.12 *coat*, 546.4 *eraser*, 621.10 *cleaning object*, 621.11 *cleaning cloth*
dustheap 614.6 *refuse*, 727.5 *wasteyard*
dustily 384.30 *flakily*, 392.24 *drily*
dustiness 384.1 *powderiness*
dusting 162.4 *sprinkling*, 278.3 *shallowness*, 384.4 *pulverization*, 621.2 *cleaning*, 879.12 *corporal punishment*
dusting down 879.7 *punishment*
dusting off 330.12 *collision*
dusting off the batter 22.4 *pitching terms*
dust jacket 293.4 *wrapping*, 301.4 *wrapper*
dustman 621.12, 621.12 *cleaner*, 646.1 *worker*, 727.6 *rubbish collector*
dust of antiquity 202.3 *antiquity*
dust off 330.5 *beat*
dust-off 22.4 *pitching terms*
dustpan and brush 621.10 *cleaning object*
dust ruffle 291.10 *bed covering*
dust sheet 301.4 *wrapper*, 621.11 *cleaning cloth*
dust storm 55.12 *wind*, 241.5 *violent weather*, 384.5 *powder*, 443.7 *opaque thing*
dust thrown in the eyes 657.2 *stratagem*
dust-up 151.9 *disorder*, 666.2 *argument*, 674.1 *contention*, 674.6 *fight*
dusty 384.16 *powdery*, 392.6 *desert*, 441.7 *dimmed*, 443.2 *shady*, 446.2 *whitened*, 456.10 *mottled*, 622.7 *dirty*
dusty air 441.2 *murk*
Dutch 5 Languages and Groups of Languages, 122.6 *equal*

Dutch auction 727.2 *disposal of property*, 739.4 *sale*, 754.2 *declining prices*
Dutch barn 68.7 *farm building*
Dutch Belted 68 Breeds of Cattle
Dutch cap 247.3 *birth control*, 295.15 *headgear*, 661.3 *barrier*
Dutch courage 778.5 *bold front*, 874.10 *drunkenness*, 874.12 *alcohol*
Dutch Draught 32 Breeds of Horse and Pony
Dutch elm 85 Trees and Shrubs
Dutch elm disease 85.10 *tree disease*, 89.5 *fungal association*
Dutch genre painting 50 Western Art Styles and Movements
Dutch hoe 69.6 *garden tool*
Dutchman's breeches 84 Flowers and Flowering Plants
Dutchman's pipe 84 Flowers and Flowering Plants
Dutch oven 45.5 *cooker*, 408.4 *burner*
Dutch punter 36.8 *punting*
Dutch rush 87 Grasses, 88.1 *fern*
Dutch TT 33.5 *motorcycle racing*
Dutch uncle 654.4 *adviser*, 690.4 *strict person*
Dutch Warmblood 32 Breeds of Horse and Pony
duteous 694.7 *obedient*, 719.7 *observant*, 847.8 *dutiful*
duteously 719.8 *observantly*, 847.18 *on duty*
duteousness 847.4 *sense of duty*
dutiable 751.15 *chargeable*
dutiful 847, 9.9 *worshipful*, 10.22 *worshipping*, 478.16 *answerable*, 694.7 *obedient*, 719.7 *observant*, 849.9 *showing respect*, 857.4 *honourable*, 861.4 *well-behaved*, 863.6 *ethical*
dutifully 10.23 *ritually*, 478.27 *answerably*, 694.10 *obediently*, 719.8 *observantly*, 847.18 *on duty*, 857.7 *honourably*, 861.24 *obediently*, 863.10 *ethically*
dutifulness 694.1 *obedience*, 847.4 *sense of duty*, 861.11 *good behaviour*
duty 845, 847, 9.1 *worship*, 10.1 *ritual*, 143.9 *participation*, 478.9 *answerability*, 571.3 *lack of choice*, 586.11 *motive*, 593.3 *needfulness*, 631.3 *burden*, 644.1 *work*, 694.1 *obedience*, 703.2 *engagement*, 719.1 *observance*, 749.2 *money received*, 751.8 *levy*, 804.2 *entitlement*, 863.2 *virtues*
Duty 847
duty-bound 847, 478.16 *answerable*
duty-free 848.8 *tax-free*, 848.13 *with impunity*
duumvirate 12.1 *government*, 664.9 *team*
duvet 293.10 *bed covering*, 374.11 *soft thing*, 408.3 *heater*
duvetine 67 Natural Fabrics
DV 8.19 *divinely*
dvojachka 49 Musical Instruments
Dvořák 49 Musicians and Composers
dvoynice 49 Musical Instruments
dwarf 11.11 *ghost*, 260.4 *little person*, 260.7 *little*, 270.5 *short person*
dwarf bush tree 69.10 *fruit tree*
dwarf chestnut 86 Nuts
dwarfed 260.7 *little*
dwarf elliptical 53.7 *galaxy*
dwarfish 260.7 *little*
dwarfishness 260.1 *littleness*
dwarf pyramid 69.10 *fruit tree*
dwarf tree 85.1 *tree*
dwell 396, 99.17 *exist*, 250.10 *settle*, 253.13 *reside*, 255.14, 256.17 *inhabit*
dweller 255.1 *inhabitant*
dwellers 255.2 *inhabitants*
dwell in 256.17 *inhabit*, 723.7 *possess*

dwelling 255.13 *resident*, 256.1 *habitat*, 256.14 *inhabiting*
dwelling place 256.1 *habitat*
dwell on 554.6 *emphasize*
dwell on a mountain 95.10 *climb a mountain*
dwell upon 788.6 *be boring*
dwindle 129.4 *decrease*, 238.6 *be weak*, 458.1 *disappear*, 722.12 *lessen*
dwindle away 458.1 *disappear*
dwindling 129.1 *decrease*, 129.6 *decreasing*, 458.4 *disappearance*, 722.4 *lessening*
DX code 66.10 *graininess*
dyad 176.1 *two*
dyadic 4.16 *dialectical*, 176.9 *two*
Dyak 5 Languages and Groups of Languages
Dyaus 8 Deities
Dyaus-Pitar 8 Deities
dybbuk 8.7 *devil*
dydrogesterone 62 Medication
dye 67, 56.28 *colour*, 67.15 *treat*, 133.4 *admixture*, 133.8 *mix*, 439.28 *bleach*, 444.4 *pigment*, 444.15 *colour*
dye blue 454.9 *blue*
dyed 67.11 *treated*, 133.12 *mixed*, 444.10 *coloured*, 584.13 *fixed*
dyed-in-the-wool 67.11 *treated*, 144.7 *complete*, 217.8 *conservative*, 584.13 *fixed*, 868.3 *impenitent*
dyed-in-the-wool conservative 217.3 *conservative person*
dyed-in-the-wool sinner 868.2 *impenitent person*
dyed-in-the-yarn 67.11 *treated*
dyeing 67, 440.9 *darkening*
dye laser 56.26 *laser*
dyer's broom 84 Flowers and Flowering Plants
dyestuff 67.6 *dye*, 444.4 *pigment*
dyestuffs 57.22 *industrial chemistry*
Dyfed 92 Counties
dying 397, 397.1 *death*, 458.4 *disappearance*, 458.6 *disappearing*, 624.22 *sick*
dying away 424.4 *faint*
dying breath 397.7 *dying day*
dying by one's own hand 398.7 *suicide*
dying day 397
dying for 782.9 *desirous*
dying for food 871.6 *fasting*
dying out 458.4 *disappearance*
dying patient 397.10 *dying person*
dying person 397
dying race 247.1 *infertility*
dying star 53.11 *stellar birth*
dying words 155.9 *conclusion*
dyke 54.30 *igneous rock*, 265.2 *crack*, 301.3 *enclosing thing*, 301.5 *enclose*, 402.10 *homosexual*
dykey 402.15 *female*
Dylan 8 Deities, 97.4 *sea god*
dynamic 56.98 *physical*, 235.15 *full of energy*, 239.4 *vigorous*, 324.17 *directional*, 330.17 *impelling*, 396.13 *lively*, 642.18 *active*
dynamically 330, 56.100 *physically*, 235.19 *energetically*, 324.18 *in motion*
dynamic belay 34.3 *climbing technique*
dynamic duo 140.3 *assembly*
dynamic energy 642.4 *energy*
dynamic friction 56.10 *force*
dynamic load 63.14 *load*
dynamic memory 65.6 *memory*
dynamic metamorphism 54.32 *metamorphism*
dynamic psychology 61.1 *psychology*
dynamic range 66.10 *graininess*
dynamics 56.2 *classical physics*, 324.1 *motion*, 330.11 *impulsion*
dynamic structure 63
dynamic system 63.5 *dynamic structure*
dynamism 4.7 *school of thought*,

235.3 *vitality*, 239.1 *vigour*, 642.4 *energy*
dynamist 4.11 *follower of a doctrine*
dynamistic 4.14 *of a philosophy*
dynamite 244.7 *agent of destruction*, 244.9 *demolish*, 338.13 *fuel*, 617.1 *worthy*, 635.1 *trap*, 680.15 *explosive*, 875.6 *drug*
dynamo 64.30 *generator*, 235.6 *source of energy*, 410.4 *electricity*, 603.4 *machine*, 642.10 *busy person*
dynamometer 268.8 *meter*
dynamometric 268.16 *micrometric*
dynamometry 268.2 *micrometry*
dynamotor 603.4 *machine*
dynastic 12.10 *governing*
dynasty 12.3 *governance*, 159.3 *line*, 688.7 *type of rule*, 802.3 *nobleness*
dyne 75 Scientific and Technical Units
dyno 875.6 *drug*
Dyophysites 7 Christian Movements
Dyothelites 7 Christian Movements
dysentery 353.2 *defecation*, 624.8 *indigestion*
dysmenorrhoea 353.11 *menstruation*, 406.2 *painful condition*
dyspepsia 406.2 *painful condition*, 624.8 *indigestion*
dyspeptic 624.19 *sick person*, 829.4 *irascible*, 830.7 *irritable*
dysphasia 563.3 *speech defect*
dysphasic 563.12 *inarticulate*
dysphemia 563.3 *speech defect*
dysphemic 563.12 *inarticulate*
dysphemism 559.4 *inelegance of speech*, 827.1 *curse*
dysphemistic 559.9 *inelegant*, 827.8 *cursing*
dysphemize 827.5 *curse*
dysphonia 563.1 *voicelessness*
dysphonic 563.9 *voiceless*
dyspnoea 624.10 *cardiovascular disease*
dysprosium 57 Chemical Elements
dystopia 48.2 *fiction*
Dyula 5 Languages and Groups of Languages
Dzongka 5 Languages and Groups of Languages

E

E 2.7 *social stratification*
Ea 8 Deities
each 142.6 *whole*, 165.32 *severally*
each according to his share 731.8 *proportionately*
each and every one 164.10 *everyone*
each in his turn 223.8 *in exchange*
each one 164.10 *everyone*
each other 109.2 *interconnection*
each-way bet 32.7 *horseracing*
eager 572, 237.11 *strong in spirit*, 513.5 *expecting*, 642.18 *active*, 772.2 *earnest*, 782.9 *desirous*, 784.6 *liking*
eager beaver 572.11 *willing worker*, 642.10 *busy person*
eagerly 237.15 *acutely*, 642.22 *actively*, 782.18 *desirously*, 784.11 *admiringly*
eagerness 572, 574.13 *concentration*, 642.4 *energy*, 772.5 *earnestness*, 782.1 *desire*, 784.2 *inclination*
eagle 78 Birds, 29.2 *golfing terms*, 78.5 *bird of prey*, 329.12 *swift animal*, 359.11 *ascender*, 435.2 *eye*, 543.1 *sign*, 544.8 *heraldic device*, 741.8 *American money*
Eagle 53 The Constellations
eagle eye 435.2 *eye*

eagle-eyed 435.21 *seeing*
eagle owl 78 Birds
eaglet 78.12 *young bird*
eagle-winged 329.1 *swift*
eaglewood 85 Trees and Shrubs
eagre 97.3 *wave*
ear 420, 56.17 *sound*
ear 60.3 *medical specialty*
ear 87.4 *cereal grass*, 227.3 *growth*, 322.4 *body orifice*, 457.3 *external appearance*
earache 406.2 *painful condition*, 420.6 *otology*
ear attachments 420
ear clip 420.7 *ear attachments*
ear-cuff 792.6 *jewellery*
ear drops 62.8 *drops*, 420.6 *otology*
eardrum 420.5 *internal ear*
eared 420
ear flaps 420.7 *ear attachments*
ear for 655.2 *aptitude*
earful 420.8 *something heard*, 564.8 *speech*, 567.1 *address*, 852.7 *blame*
earhole 420.4 *ear*
earl 802.1 *nobleman*
earldom 91.3 *dominion*, 802.2 *aristocracy*
earldorman 723.6 *lord*
earless 421.4 *deaf*
Earl Grey 351.3 *tea*
earlier 154.11 *prior*, 154.20 *before*, 194.10 *prior*, 194.11 *before*, 197.3 *another time*, 200.17 *past*, 202.20 *formerly*
earlies 68.12 *crop*
earliest 154.10 *preceding*, 156.31 *prime*, 194.10 *prior*, 194.11 *before*, 208.12 *early*
earliest inhabitant 208.4 *early comer*, 255.1 *inhabitant*
earliest settler 208.4 *early comer*
earliest stage 208.3 *early stage*
earlike 420.12 *eared*
earliness 208, 193.1 *wrong time*, 211.1 *untimeliness*
Earliness 208
Earl Marshal 544.9 *herald*
earlobe 420.4 *ear*
Earl of Coventry 42 Card Games
Earl's Court 93.5 *London*
early 208, 208, 156.29 *beginning*, 200.17 *past*, 202.15 *primal*, 202.21 *archaically*, 204.5 *morning*, 211.10 *untimely*, 329.1 *swift*
Early American 47.7 *furniture style*
early arrival 208.4 *early comer*
early bird 204.2 *morning thing*, 208.4 *early comer*
Early Christian 43 Architectural Styles
Early Christian art 50 Western Art Styles and Movements
early civilizations 400.4 *civilized human*
early comer 208
early days 156.12 *first move*
early edition 532.4 *newspaper*
Early English 43 Architectural Styles
early evening 205.1 *evening*
Early Federal 47.7 *furniture style*
early history 208.3 *early stage*
early hour 208
early humanity 400.3 *uncivilized human*
early life 206.1 *youth*
early lift 21.2 *field events*
early man 202.7 *ancient people*, 208.3 *early stage*, 400.3 *uncivilized human*
early maturity 208.5 *prematurity*
early morning 208.2 *early hour*, 441.1 *dimness*
early potatoes 68.12 *crop*
Early Renaissance 43 Architectural Styles
Early Renaissance art 50 Western Art Styles and Movements
early retirement 15.2 *industrial negotiations*
early riser 208.4 *early comer*
early stage 208
early stages 156.12 *first move*

early start 208.1 *earliness*
early time 208.2 *early hour*
early warning 208.3 *early stage*
early warning system 208.3 *early stage*
early wood 85.3 *timber*
earmark 165.3 *characteristic*, 165.22 *characterize*, 544.3 *means of identification*, 544.10 *identify*, 580.4 *pick*, 588.9 *intend for*, 593.10 *necessitate*, 731.4 *allot*, 734.7 *take*
earmarked 544.12 *identified*, 593.4 *required*
earmarking 731.1 *allocation*
earmuffs 295.25 *accessories*, 420.7 *ear attachments*, 632.4 *safety device*
earn 721, 721.9 *gain*, 730.9, 749.7 *receive*, 804.7 *be entitled to*, 845.15 *incur*
earn a black belt 26.13 *do martial arts*
earn a crust 721.12 *earn*
earn a diploma 703.8 *authorize*
earn a dividend 721.14 *profit*
earn a living 721.12 *earn*
earn an income 878.13 *get paid*
earn a standing ovation 682.6 *be successful*
earn a wage 644.6 *work*
earned 845.10 *due*
earned income 721.4 *earnings*
earned-run average 22.4 *pitching terms*
earned-run-average leader 22.2 *baseball player*
earner 646.1 *worker*, 721.7 *gainer*, 730.5 *recipient*
earnest 772, 143.2 *particular*, 277.9 *deep-seated*, 554.3 *emphatic*, 574.2 *tenacious*, 746.1 *payment*
earnestly 772, 554.7 *emphatically*, 574.17 *resolutely*
earnest money 746.1 *payment*
earnestness 772, 574.13 *concentration*, 642.8 *assiduity*
earnest of good faith 143.2 *particular*
earn income 721.12 *earn*
earning 746.19 *receiving pay*
earning capacity 613.8 *benefit*
earnings 721, 721.1 *gain*, 730.2 *something received*, 734.5 *takings*, 746.3 *pay*, 749.3 *income*, 878.4 *reward for service*
earnings per share 14.2 *stock exchange*
earning status 2.7 *social stratification*
earn interest 128.4 *increase*
earn little or nothing 743.12 *be poor*
ear of corn 87.4 *cereal grass*
EAROM 65.6 *memory*
earphone 420.7 *ear attachments*
earphones 420.9 *audio device*, 730.8 *receiver*
earpiece 420.9 *audio device*, 534.9 *telephone*
ear-piercing 430.9 *shrill*
earplug 420.7 *ear attachments*, 421.3 *inaudibility*
earplugs 424.2 *sound reducer*, 632.4 *safety device*
ear-rending 423.6 *loud*
earring 283.3 *suspended object*, 420.7 *ear attachments*, 792.6 *jewellery*
ear-shaped 420.12 *eared*
ear-shattering 421.6 *deafening*
earshot 264.2 *short distance*, 420.1 *hearing*
ear-splitting 420.14 *hearable*, 421.6 *deafening*, 423.6 *loud*, 425.8 *banging*, 430.7 *strident*
ear-splitting noise 423.1 *loudness*
ear stud 420.7 *ear attachments*
earth 54, 32.8 *hunting*, 54.36 *soil*, 56.52, 64.10 *electric potential*, 64.35 *conduct*, 77.20 *abode of mammals*, 235.7 *electrical power*, 256.13 *lair*, 280.1 *base*, 371.4 *solid body*, 622.4 *dirt*, 632.4 *safety device*, 632.9 *protect*, 634.3 *animal shelter*

Earth 53 Planets and their Satellites, 53.16 *planet*
earth, air, fire, and water 367.4 *matter*
earth art 50 Western Art Styles and Movements, 50.12 *sculpture*
earth ball 89 Fungi
earthborn 400.12 *human*
earth closet 353.13 *lavatory*, 727.7 *toilet*
earth dam 63.23 *dam*
earth earth 135.10 *link*
earthed conductor 64.10 *electric potential*
earthenware 44.1 *ceramics*, 243.7 *produce*
earthenware mark 44.4 *porcelain mark*
earthflow 54.26 *mass movement*
earth goddess 8.5 *deity*
Earth Goddess 246.4 *fertility cult*
earthgrazer 53.16 *planet*
earth ground potential 64.10 *electric potential*
earthling 400.7 *person*
earthlings 400.1 *humankind*
earthly 367.7 *material*
earthly paradise 405.5 *idealized pleasure*
earth matter 101.2 *real world*
Earth Mother 246.4 *fertility cult*
earth movement 54
earthmover 63.29 *construction equipment*
earthnut 86 Nuts, 45.33 *vegetable*
earth orbit 53.35 *rocketry*, 327.13 *flight path*
earthquake 54.22 *seismic activity*, 241.3 *instance of violence*, 244.7 *agent of destruction*, 365.5 *wave*, 615.1 *trap*
earthquake magnitude 54.22 *seismic activity*
earthquake zone 54.22 *seismic activity*
earth satellite 53.32 *satellite*
earth's atmosphere 55.8 *atmosphere*
earth science 54
Earth Science 54
earth's crust 54
earth-shaking 233.11 *influential*, 365.17 *waving*, 611.5 *important*, 611.6 *notable*
earthshine 53.14 *solar system*, 439.4 *natural light*
earth's magnetism 56.58 *geomagnetism*
earth's orbit 311.3 *curved things*
earth's surface 54.5 *earth*
earthstar 89 Fungi
earth tongue 89 Fungi
earth tremor 54.22 *seismic activity*
earthward 332.10 *clockwise*
earthwork 3.11 *relic*, 200.7 *thing of the past*, 399.6 *grave*, 543.5 *indicator*, 545.11 *monument*, 661.3 *barrier*, 671.8 *military defences*, 671.12 *fort*
earthworm 81 Worms, 81.6 *worm*
earthy 54
ear trumpet 420.7 *ear attachments*, 420.9 *audio device*, 421.1 *deafness*, 423.4 *sound maker*
ear wax 420.6 *otology*
earwig 82 Insects, 69.12 *pests and diseases*, 82.1 *insect*
ear witness 420.2 *hearer*
ease 374, 386, 649, 649, 767, 60.19 *practise medicine*, 106.5 *comfortable circumstances*, 129.4 *decrease*, 242.4 *moderate*, 370.10 *lighten*, 405.1 *physical pleasure*, 405.10 *comfort*, 558.1 *elegance*, 630.19 *remedy*, 645.1 *leisure*, 651.1 *refresh*, 651.5 *refreshment*, 655.1 *skill*, 660.1 *easiness*, 660.16 *make easy*, 662.2, 662.19 *support*, 677.4 *pacify*, 686.1 *prosperity*, 698.4 *informality*, 742.7 *opulence*, 763.7 *pleasure*, 765.1 *sat-

isfaction*, 767.9 *relieve*, 814.4 *freedom*, 855.8 *justify*
Ease 649
ease along 328.1 *move slowly*, 338.24 *push*
eased 767.7 *relieved*
easeful 405.6 *pleasant*, 649.4 *at ease*
ease in 354.5 *inset*
easel 50.11 *artist's materials*
easel-painter 50.16 *artist*
easel painting 50.8 *painting*
easement 370.6 *lightening*
ease off 242.3 *be moderate*, 328.3 *slow down*
ease of manner 660
ease of viewing 437.4 *clarity*
ease out 727.10 *dismiss*
ease out a line 36.15 *sail*
ease the way 662.28 *further*
ease up 374.15 *be kind*
easier said than done 659.10 *difficult*
easily 660, 106.18 *comfortably*, 328.16 *slowly*, 374.18 *softheartedly*, 558.5 *elegantly*, 649.6 *with ease*, 691.6 *leniently*, 698.22 *informally*, 815.18 *sociably*
easily detected 442.4 *easily seen through*
easily distinguished 437.1 *visible*
easily excused 839.7 *forgivable*
easily led 228.13 *suggestible*
easily mistaken 523.3 *unrecognizable*
easily roused 829.4 *irascible*
easily seen 318.7 *conspicuous*
easily seen through 442
easily tempted 864.13 *venial*
easily understood 522.2 *simple*
easiness 660, 374.12 *gentleness*, 522.10 *simplicity*, 691.1 *leniency*, 708.1 *permission*
Easiness 660
easing 660, 242.1 *moderation*, 242.8 *moderating*, 370.3, 370.6 *lightening*, 374.7 *impressionable*, 629.11 *recuperation*, 767.8 *relieving*
easing off 328.9 *deceleration*
easing up 374.12 *gentleness*
east 332.4 *compass point*, 332.12 *north*, 332.13 *directional*
East African Safari 33.4 *motor rally*
East African Safari rally 33.1 *motor racing*
east and west 111.2 *opposites*
East and West 249.7 *regions of the world*
eastbound 332.13 *directional*
East Bulgarian 32 Breeds of Horse and Pony
East Cape 92 New Zealand Regions and Territories
East China 97 Oceans and Seas
East End 93.5 *London*
Easter 10.16 *religious festival*, 203.2 *spring*, 214.6 *annually celebrated day*
Easter bonnet 295.15 *headgear*
Easter Island 529.6 *natural mystery*
easterly 55.15 *wind direction*, 55.47 *windy*, 332.12 *north*, 332.13 *directional*
eastern 249.16 *regional*, 305.6 *side*, 332.13 *directional*
Eastern bloc 91.2 *union of nations*
Eastern cut-off style 21.2 *field events*
Eastern Daylight Time 185.9 *time zone*
Easterner 255.10 *US inhabitant*
Eastern Hemisphere 249.7 *regions of the world*
easternmost 332.13 *directional*
Eastern Orthodox Church 7 Christian Movements
Eastern Standard Time 185.9 *time zone*
Easter offering 729.3 *offering*
Easter season 203.1 *season*
Eastertide 10.16 *religious festival*, 203.2 *spring*

East Friesian 32 Breeds of Horse and Pony
East Germanic 5 Languages and Groups of Languages
easting 332.4 *compass point*
eastings and northings 250.2 *exact location*
East Kilbride 93 Cities
Eastlander 255.10 *US inhabitant*
east side 305.3 *side direction*
East Side 93.3 *New York*
East Sussex 92 Counties
eastward 332.4 *compass point*, 332.13 *directional*
eastwardly 332.12 *north*
eastwards 332.12 *north*
east wind 55.15 *wind direction*
easy 660, 36.21 *avast*, 106.9 *comfortable*, 328.5 *unhurried*, 374.6 *softhearted*, 522.2 *simple*, 558.3 *elegant*, 645.7 *leisurely*, 649.4 *at ease*, 691.4 *lenient*, 698.13 *informal*, 763.3 *comfortable*, 815.15 *sociable*
easy as falling off a log 660.9 *easy*
easy as pie 660.9 *easy*
easy as winking 660.9 *easy*
easy chair 47.2 *chair*, 284.4 *rest*, 374.11 *soft thing*
easy circumstances 742.7 *opulence*
easy come easy go 708.8 *permitting*, 757.1 *extravagant*
easy death 397.5 *ways of dying*
easy does it 660.20 *take it easy*
easy-flowing 660.12 *wieldy*
easygoing 660, 325.6 *quiescent*, 374.6 *softhearted*, 462.8 *thoughtless*, 576.4 *unsteady*, 595.3 *without preparation*, 656.1 *unskilful*, 675.7 *peaceful*, 691.4 *lenient*, 698.13 *informal*, 708.8 *permitting*, 763.2 *likable*, 783.7 *indifferent*, 814.10 *free*, 815.15 *sociable*
easygoing nature 576.14 *apathy*
easygoingness 814.4 *freedom*
easy in one's mind 660.14 *relaxed*
easy-listening 49.9 *popular music*, 420.14 *hearable*
easy manner 815.2 *social ambition*
easy mark 236.5 *powerless person*, 238.4 *weakling*, 539.22 *dupe*, 850.9 *butt*
easy meat 236.5 *powerless person*, 238.4 *weakling*, 660.6 *easy thing*
easy money 721.5 *profit*
easy on 649.5 *labour-saving*
easy on the ear 420.14 *hearable*
easy on the eye 435.23 *visible*, 457.10 *aspectual*
easy on the pocket 754.9 *cheap*
easy-paced 328.4 *slow*
easy-peasy 660.9 *easy*
easy pickings 539.22 *dupe*
easy question 477
easy ride 660.6 *easy thing*
easy rider 71.14 *cyclist*
easy-running 660.12 *wieldy*
easy stages 328.8 *slowness*
easy street 405.5 *idealized pleasure*, 742.7 *opulence*
Easy Street 686.1 *prosperity*
easy target 633.7 *vulnerability*, 660.6 *easy thing*
easy temper 817.1 *courtesy*
easy terms 677.2 *peace offering*, 754.1 *cheapness*
easy thing 660
easy times 686.3 *time of plenty*
easy to comprehend 522.2 *simple*
easy to follow 522.2 *simple*
easy to grasp 522.2 *simple*
easy to read 522.2 *simple*
easy to see 437.2 *clear*
easy to understand 312.2 *straightforward*
easy virtue 877.3 *sexual immorality*
easy word 5.17 *word*
easy work 641.1 *inaction*, 644.1 *work*

eat 350, 348.11 *ingest,* 411.9 *taste,* 607.1 *waste*

eatable 350.27 *edible,* 632.5 *safe*

eatables 350.7 *food,* 606.2 *provisions*

eatably 350.29 *edibly*

eat away 129.4 *decrease,* 628.5 *hurt*

eat between meals 350.24 *have a meal*

eat crow 578.4 *recant,* 673.4 *succumb*

eat dirt 673.4 *succumb,* 806.20 *submit,* 806.21 *humble oneself*

eat, drink, and be merry 762.6 *enjoy*

eaten up with jealousy 841.4 *jealous*

eater 350, 411.5 *taster*

eatery 350.15 *eating place*

eat everything in sight 350.22 *eat well*

eat grass 87

eat humble pie 578.4 *recant,* 673.4 *succumb,* 734.9 *withdraw a statement,* 806.20 *submit*

eating 350, 350, 348.4 *intake*

Eating 350

eating alone 350.4 *eating meals*

eating crow 578.8 *recantation*

eating for two 245.16 *reproductive*

eating habit 350

eating habits 584.5 *tradition*

eating house 350.15 *eating place*

eating in bed 350.4 *eating meals*

eating meals 350

eating one's words 578.8 *recantation*

eating on the run 350.4 *eating meals*

eating out 350.4 *eating meals*

eating out of one's hands 701.9 *subject*

eating place 350

eating together 350.4 *eating meals*

eating utensil 350

eat in moderation 869.5 *be self-restrained*

eat into 346.11 *infiltrate*

eat less 350.23 *taste,* 871.5 *fast*

eat like a horse 872.5 *be greedy*

eat like a pig 350.22 *eat well*

eat no meat 871.5 *fast*

eat nothing 871.5 *fast*

eat off the same platter 815.11 *be sociable*

eat one's fill 144.5 *be complete,* 608.6 *have enough*

eat one's hat 536.9 *renounce,* 578.4 *recant*

eat one's head off 872.5 *be greedy*

eat one's heart out 770.8 *grieve,* 841.6 *be jealous*

eat one's words 536.9 *renounce,* 578.4 *recant,* 734.9 *withdraw a statement*

eat out 350.24 *have a meal*

eat out of house and home 872.5 *be greedy*

eat out of one's hands 701.8 *be subject to*

eats 350.7 *food*

eat sparingly 869.5 *be self-restrained,* 871.5 *fast*

eat to live, not live to eat 869.5 *be self-restrained*

eat up 244.12 *consume,* 350.22 *eat well,* 872.5 *be greedy*

eat well 350

eau de cologne 791.6 *toiletries*

eau de Cologne 389.14 *lavender water,* 418.2 *fragrant thing*

eau-de-nil 453.1 *green*

eau de toilette 791.6 *toiletries*

eavesdrop 420.15 *hear,* 465.7 *be curious*

eavesdropper 420.2 *hearer,* 465.4 *meddler*

eavesdropping 420.1 *hearing*

ebb 54, 96.6 *river flow,* 96.7 *flow,* 97.7 *oceanic,* 97.10 *billow,* 129.1, 129.4 *decrease,* 276.3 *lowest point,* 324.13 *be in motion,* 337.3 *reverse,* 337.4 *slip*

back, 337.12 *reversal,* 337.14 *decline,* 360.9 *descend,* 458.1 *disappear,* 458.4 *disappearance,* 607.3 *waste,* 609.9 *scarcity,* 628.1 *deteriorate,* 628.7 *deterioration*

ebb and flow 97.2 *tide,* 97.10 *billow,* 214.1 *regularity,* 214.7 *be regular,* 224.11 *be changeable,* 365.1 *oscillation,* 365.8 *oscillate*

ebb away 129.4 *decrease,* 607.1 *waste*

ebbing 96.10 *fluvial,* 97.7 *oceanic,* 129.6 *decreasing,* 337.23 *receding,* 628.12 *deteriorated*

ebb tide 97.2 *tide,* 129.3 *decreasing thing,* 214.5 *regular thing,* 276.3 *lowest point*

Ebbw Vale 93 Cities

Ebionite 7 Non-Christian Religions

Ebisu 8 Deities

Eblis 8.7 *devil*

E-boat 74 Ships and Boats, 679.24 *warship*

ebon 447.1 *black*

ebonite 377.4 *rubber*

ebony 85 Trees and Shrubs, 440.4 *dark thing,* 440.10 *dark-coloured,* 447.1 *black,* 447.9 *black thing*

ebriate 874.1 *drunk*

ebriated 874.1 *drunk*

ebriety 874.10 *drunkenness*

ebriose 874.1 *drunk*

ebriosity 874.10 *drunkenness*

Ebro 96 Rivers

EBSIDIC 65.10 *character*

ebullience 762.1 *happiness*

ebullient 241.6 *violent,* 460.12 *warm-hearted,* 762.3 *happy*

ebullition 56.37 *temperature,* 366.3 *turbulence*

EC 91.2 *union of nations*

eccentric 168, 168, 52.81 *curvilinear,* 104.5 *nonconformist,* 117.6 *misfit,* 117.9 *nonconforming,* 139.4 *individualist,* 149.9 *misfit,* 165.16 *characteristic,* 215.5 *unusual,* 335.19 *deviant person,* 335.20 *deviant,* 491.7 *unreliable,* 508.4 *rash person,* 508.5 *foolish,* 510.7 *insane person,* 519.9 *visionary,* 523.5 *strange,* 579.1 *capricious,* 579.4 *capricious person,* 666.4 *dissenter,* 698.8 *free-thinker,* 698.10 *independent,* 798.3 *object of ridicule,* 798.5 *ridiculous,* 816.6 *unsocial person*

eccentrically 117.15 *dissimilarly,* 149.18 *extraneously,* 215.9 *unusually,* 335.29 *erratically,* 491.26 *unreliably,* 585.8 *unusually,* 698.20 *freely*

eccentric circles 52.42 *circle*

eccentricity 52.42 *circle,* 53.21 *orbit,* 117.3 *nonconformity,* 119.1 *originality,* 165.3 *characteristic,* 168.3 *nonconformism,* 215.2 *unusualness,* 335.13 *deviation,* 491.15 *unreliability,* 508.1 *folly,* 510.1 *insanity,* 579.2 *caprice,* 620.7 *defect,* 798.1 *ludicrousness*

ecchymose 353.21 *bleed*

ecchymosed 353.30 *bleeding*

ecchymosis 353.1 *excretion,* 353.10 *bleeding*

Eccles cake 45.36 *cake*

ecclesia 16.18 *tribunal,* 653.7 *council*

ecclesiarch 7.8 *priest*

ecclesiastic 7.8 *priest,* 7.17 *priestly*

ecclesiastical 121.8 *ranked,* 653.18 *parliamentary*

ecclesiastical council 653.7 *council*

ecclesiastical court 16

ecclesiastical governor 696.6 *religious leader*

ecclesiastical law 16.1 *the law*

ecclesiastically 7.23 *religiously*

ecclesiastical rank 121.2 *rank*

ecclesiastical season 203.1 *season*

ecclesiastical tax 751.7 *tax*

ecclesiasticism 7.9 *priesthood,* 12.1 *government,* 688.7 *type of rule*

ecclesiolater 9.6 *idolater*

ecclesiolatrous 9.10 *idolatrous*

ecclesiolatry 9.2 *idolatry*

ecclesiological 7.18 *theological*

ecclesiologist 7.14 *theologian*

ecclesiology 7.13 *theology*

ecclesiophobia 777 Phobias by Name

eccrine 352.4 *secretory,* 352.5 *of a secretion*

eccrine gland 352.3 *gland*

eccrine secretion 352.1 *secretion*

ecdyse 353.23 *cast*

ecdysial 296.12 *peeling,* 353.32 *cast-off*

ecdysiast 51.28 *dancer,* 294.4 *exposer,* 296.8 *nude person*

ecdysis 296.6 *peeling,* 353.12 *dead tissue*

ecdysone 58 Hormones

ECG 60.7 *diagnosis*

echelon 105.1 *state,* 107.3 *relative position,* 121.2 *rank*

echidna 77.6 *insect-eating mammal*

echinoderm 81, 76.5 *aquatic animal*

echinodermal 81

Echinodermata 81.3 *echinoderm*

echinodermatous 81.17 *echinodermal*

echinoid 81.3 *echinoderm,* 81.17 *echinodermal*

echinus 43 Architectural Decoration

echo 56.21 *architectural acoustics,* 114.10 *be similar,* 116.4 *harmony,* 116.24 *harmonize,* 118.1 *imitation,* 118.9 *imitate,* 176.15 *double,* 183.1 *repetition,* 183.6 *reverberation,* 183.16 *repeat,* 183.22 *resound,* 245.9 *reproduce,* 331.1, 331.4 *recoil,* 420.8 *something heard,* 420.10 *sound quality,* 420.16 *be heard,* 425.5 *bang,* 426.1 *drumming,* 426.8 *drum,* 427.1 *resonance,* 427.9 *resonate,* 478.4 *reaction,* 478.19 *react,* 499.4 *assent,* 534.28 *radar,* 667.6 *agree with*

Echo 534 Phonetic Alphabet

echo chamber 331.5 *reflector*

echoed 183.9 *repeated*

echoic 5.42 *worded,* 118.12 *imitative,* 420.14 *hearable,* 427.6 *resonant*

echoic word 5.17 *word*

echoing 116.13 *harmonious,* 118.12 *imitative,* 183.12 *repetitious,* 420.14 *hearable,* 423.6 *loud,* 427.6 *resonant,* 478.12 *reactive*

echoingly 478.24 *in answer*

echolalia 183.1 *repetition*

echolocating 277.13 *bathymetric*

echolocation 277.6 *bathymetry,* 420.9 *audio device*

echo sounder 268.6 *measuring instrument,* 277.4 *deep thing*

echo sounding 54.17 *ocean research vessel,* 56.22 *sounding,* 277.6 *bathymetry*

eckies 729.2 *gift*

eclair 45.36 *cake*

eclampsia 366.8 *spasm*

eclamptic 366.19 *convulsive*

eclectic 133.12 *mixed,* 164.15 *general,* 580.14 *selecting*

eclectically 50.30 *pictorially,* 580.17 *selectively*

eclecticism 50 Western Art Styles and Movements, 133.1 *mixture,* 164.2 *catholicity,* 580.6 *selection*

eclectic 50.29 *realist*

eclipse 53.21 *orbit,* 53.37 *observe,* 126.8 *be superior,* 293.31 *hide,* 436.6 *blinder,* 436.15 *blind,* 438.6 *that which makes invisible,* 438.8 *make invisible,* 440.1 *darkness,* 440.2 *darkening,* 440.14 *make dark,* 458.5 *disguise,* 531.1 *concealment,* 531.9 *disguise*

eclipsed 438.1 *invisible,* 458.7 *disappeared,* 531.14 *concealed*

eclipse of the moon 440.1 *darkness*

eclipse of the sun 440.1 *darkness*

eclipsing 126.12 *superior,* 293.1 *covering*

eclipsing binary 53.9 *constellation*

ecliptic 53.5 *celestial sphere*

eclogue 48.7 *poem*

Eco 48 Writers

ecodevelopment 243.2 *manufacture*

ecofarming 68.1 *agriculture*

ecological 1.11 *anthropological,* 59.20 *biological,* 627.16 *improving,* 637.6 *preserving*

ecologically 59.29 *biologically,* 68.22 *agriculturally,* 83.25 *botanically,* 637.8 *preservatively*

ecological psychology 61.1 *psychology*

ecologist 59.19 *life scientist,* 217.4 *conservationist,* 627.12 *reformer,* 637.4 *preservationist*

Ecologists 12.6 *political party*

ecology 59, 59.1 *life science,* 453.16 *green politics,* 627.11 *reformism,* 637.1 *preservation*

econometrics 13.3 *economic statistics*

economic 13, 2.14 *socioeconomic,* 14.6 *financial,* 653.17 *managerial,* 737.14 *commercial,* 750.10 *accounting,* 754.9 *cheap*

economic adversity 687

economic aid 662.6 *financial assistance*

economical 756.4 *thrifty,* 781.4 *cautious,* 869.8 *self-restrained*

economically 13, 756, 2.16 *sociologically,* 653.19 *managerially,* 750.13 *financially,* 754.15 *cheaply,* 869.11 *with self-restraint*

economically worded 552.3 *concise*

economical with the truth 309.8 *exaggerated,* 474.7 *sophistic*

economic analysis 13.3 *economic statistics*

economic anthropology 1.1 *anthropology*

economic boom 246.2 *productiveness*

economic botany 83.10 *plant science*

economic class 665.2 *society*

economic decline 247.1 *infertility*

economic determinist 2.11 *sociologist*

economic development 13

economic downturn 13.2 *economy*

economic expert 13.9 *economist*

economic factors 13

economic geology 54.1 *earth science*

economic growth 13.1 *economics,* 13.4 *economic development*

economic history 3.1 *history*

economic integration 737.5 *commercial trade,* 740.4 *free market*

economic materialism 2.7 *social stratification*

economic migrant 104.7 *new arrival*

economic miracle 629.10 *revival*

economic policy 13.1 *economics*

economic power 2.7 *social stratification*

economic pressure 699.2 *economic restraint*

economic productivity 13.3 *economic statistics*

economic progress 336.12 *advance*

economic prosperity 686.1 *prosperity*

economic recovery 629.10 *revival*

economic restraint 699

economics 13, 653.3 *management*

Economics 13

economic sanction 13.6 *economic factors*

economic sanctions 676.8 *warfare*

economic stagnation 247.1 *infertility*
economic statistics 13
economic status 2.7 *social stratification*
economic system 13.1 *economics*
economic theory 13.1 *economics*
economic union 13.5 *international trade*
economic upturn 13.2 *economy*, 246.2 *productiveness*
economic war 676.1 *war*
economic warfare 676.8 *warfare*
economic zone 13.5 *international trade*, 147.3 *exclusion zone*, 249.3 *regional boundary*, 737.5 *commercial trade*, 740.4 *free market*
economist 13
economization 129.1 *decrease*
economize 699, 129.5 *make smaller*, 605.6 *store*, 747.11 *be parsimonious*, 754.1 *buy cheaply*, 756.6 *save*, 781.5 *be cautious*, 869.5 *be self-restrained*
economizer 756.3 *saver*
economizing 129.1 *decrease*, 756.4 *thrifty*
economy 13, 606.1 *provision*, 607.3 *waste*, 637.1 *preservation*, 754.9 *cheap*, 756.1 *thrift*, 869.1 *self-restraint*
economy-class 754.9 *cheap*
economy drive 756.2 *act of thrift*
economy fare 754.4 *bargain*
economy of words 552.1 *conciseness*
economy price 754.1 *cheapness*
economy size 259.3 *large scale*
economy-size 259.15 *big*, 754.9 *cheap*
economy with the truth 309.4 *distortion of the truth*, 538.5 *half-truth*
ecophobia 777 *Phobias by Name*
ecophysiology 59.18 *ecology*
ecosphere 54.5 *earth*, 59.2 *living world*, 390.2 *aerosphere*
ecosystem 59.18 *ecology*, 256.2 *environment*
ecru 446.1 *white*, 448.1 *grey*, 449.1 *brown*
EC snake 741.7 *finance*
ecstasis 512.1 *oblivion*
ecstasy 510.4 *delusion*, 512.1 *oblivion*, 519.2 *inspiration*, 759.4 *emotion*, 762.1 *happiness*, 821.2 *romantic love*, 821.5 *desire*, 875.6 *drug*
ecstatic 11.12 *occultist*, 512.8 *oblivious*, 759.13 *passionate*, 762.4 *happy*, 773.9 *rejoicing*, 821.20 *amorous*
ecstatically 512.16 *obliviously*, 759.20 *with feeling*, 773.11 *rejoicingly*
ectoderm 59.15 *developmental biology*
ectodermal 59.26 *developmental biology*
ectohormone 58.16 *hormone*, 352.2 *secreted substance*
ectomorph 1.9 *physical type*, 61.7 *personality type*, 274.9 *thin person*, 306.6 *nature*
ectomorphic 1.15 *physical*, 274.1 *thin*
ectomorphism 61.7 *personality type*
ectomorphy 1.9 *physical type*, 61.7 *personality type*
ectoparasite 76.4 *type of animal*
ectoparasitic 76.15 *of animals*
ectoplasm 11.10 *psychic phenomenon*, 59.7 *cell*, 457.4 *something that appears*
ectoplasmic 59.23 *cellular*
ectoplasy 11.10 *psychic phenomenon*
ectoproct 81.7 *coelenterate*
Ectoprocta 81.7 *coelenterate*
ectotrophic mycorrhiza 89.5 *fungal association*
ectype 43 *Architectural Decoration*
ECU 741.7 *finance*
Ecuador 91 *Countries*

ecumenic 664.18 *joint*
ecumenical 164.15 *general*
ecumenicalism 164.2 *catholicity*, 664.6 *movement*
ecumenicism 164.2 *catholicity*
ecumenicity 164.2 *catholicity*
ecumenicize 164.23 *generalize*
eczema 624.13 *skin disease*
edacious 872.6 *gluttonous*
edaciously 872.7 *gluttonously*
edaciousness 872.1 *gluttony*
edacity 872.1 *gluttony*
Edam 45 *Cheeses*
Edberg 18 *Sporting Personalities*
Eddington 52 *Scientists*
eddy 55.16 *wind vortex*, 96.6 *river flow*, 96.7 *flow*, 364.4 *vortex*, 364.10 *swirl*, 635.1 *trap*
eddy current 56.51, 64.9 *electric current*
edelweiss 84 *Flowers and Flowering Plants*
edental 381.4 *toothless*
Edentata 77.13 *toothless mammal*
edentate 77.13 *toothless mammal*, 77.26 *insectivorous*, 381.4 *toothless*
edentulous 381.4 *toothless*
Edgar 48 *Dramatists*
edge 299, 300, 300, 27.9 *stroke*, 27.17 *bat*, 34.9 *mountaineer*, 52.37 *line*, 126.3 *advantage*, 157.7 *limit*, 297.7 *surround*, 302.3 *furthest point*, 305.1 *side*, 305.7 *be alongside*, 310.2 *obliquity*, 380.15 *make sharp*, 777.8 *fearful*
Edge 300
edge away 573.7 *refuse*
edged 300.8 *edging*, 300.9 *skirting*
edged tool 603.1 *tool*
edgeless 376.2 *uniform*, 381.1 *blunt*
edge of sight 438.6 *that which makes invisible*
edge out 727.10 *dismiss*
edger 69.6 *garden tool*
edge round 334.3 *circuit*
edge tool 380.9 *sharp-edged thing*
Edgeworth 48 *Writers*
edginess 366.1 *agitation*
edging 300, 300, 34.3 *climbing technique*, 41.4 *skiing technique*, 130.3 *additional item*, 295.24 *part of garment*
edging iron 69.6 *garden tool*
edging tool 69.6 *garden tool*
edgy 366.15 *agitated*
EDI 65.14 *data transfer*
edible 350, 411.7 *tasty*, 632.5 *safe*
edibles 350.7 *food*
edibly 350
edict 16.3 *law*, 166.1 *rule*, 492.2 *verdict*, 532.1 *publication*, 692.1 *command*
edification 6.1 *education*, 861.13 *benefit*
edifice 243.8, 382.6 *construction*
edificial 43.11 *architectural*, 63.32 *structural*
edify 617.10 *do good*
edifying 6.16 *educational*, 613.4 *profitable*, 617.4 *worthwhile*, 861.6 *beneficial*, 876.10 *moralistic*
edifyingly 6.25 *educationally*
Edinburgh 93 *Cities*, 93.4 *British cities*
Edinburgh Castle 43 *Noted Buildings*
Edison 52 *Scientists*
edit 5.46 *translate*, 216.8 *cause change*, 454.10 *blue-pencil*, 524.8 *interpret*, 532.15 *publish*, 533.13 *report*, 558.4 *be elegant*, 627.3 *rectify*, 629.1 *repair*
edit down 129.5 *make smaller*
edited 5.40 *translated*, 524.15 *interpreted*, 546.6 *obliterated*, 627.14 *improved*
edited text 524.1 *interpretation*
editing 131.1 *subtraction*, 524.1 *interpretation*, 546.3 *oblitera-*

tion, 621.4 *censorship*, 627.6 *rectification*, 629.8 *repair*
edition 5.12 *translation*, 143.2 *particular*, 245.2 *print*, 524.1 *interpretation*, 532.4 *newspaper*, 627.6 *rectification*
editor 216, 224, 65.11 *application*, 492.5 *judge*, 524.6 *interpreter*, 532.11 *newspaper man*, 532.12 *publisher*, 533.4 *journalist*, 561.3 *dissertator*, 562.5 *summarizer*, 627.13 *reviser*, 629.12 *repairer*
editorial 524.16 *annotative*, 532.3 *journalism*, 533.9 *news story*, 533.14 *journalistic*, 561.2 *article*, 561.5 *expository*
editorial change 546.3 *obliteration*
editorial comment 524.2 *annotation*, 532.3 *journalism*, 561.2 *article*
editorially 533.15 *journalistically*
editorial writer 524.7 *news interpreter*, 532.11 *newspaper man*
editor-in-chief 532.12 *publisher*
edit out 147.8 *eject*, 546.1 *obliterate*, 621.15 *purify*
Edmonton 93 *Cities*
Edo 1 *Peoples*, 5 *Languages and Groups of Languages*
Edomite 5 *Languages and Groups of Languages*
EDP 65.1 *computing*
educability 6.10 *educatability*
educable 6.17 *educatable*
educatability 6
educatable 6
educate 6, 15.11 *conduct industrial relations*, 243.10 *produce*, 501.14 *cause to know*, 528.11 *inform*, 530.6 *divulge*, 594.6 *brief*
educated 6, 4.19 *learned*, 5.39 *of language*, 6.19 *knowledgeable*, 6.20 *refined*, 243.12 *produced*, 501.9 *literate*
educated palate 350.3 *delicate eating*
educated person 400.4 *civilized human*
educate oneself 594.8 *prepare oneself*
educating 332.16 *directing*
education 6, 6.11 *refinement*, 332.5 *directions*, 501.3 *learning*, 594.12 *briefing*, 627.5 *improvement*
Education 6
educational 6, 2.12 *sociological*, 528.16 *informative*
educational broadcasting 534.25 *broadcast material*
educational institution 6, 2.8 *human institution*
educationalist 6
educational leader 696
educationally 6, 2.16 *sociologically*
educationally subnormal 460.5 *lacking intellect*, 460.7 *intellectually subnormal*
educational psychologist 6.5 *educationalist*
educational psychology 61.1 *psychology*
educational status 2.7 *social stratification*
educational system 6
educational topic 472
Educational Welfare Officer 6.5 *educationalist*
educationist 6.5 *educationalist*
education officer 15.6 *employer*
educative 6.16 *educational*, 233.11 *influential*
educator 6, 48.15 *literary person*, 688.10 *person of authority*
educatory 6.16 *educational*
educe 355.15 *draw out*
educible 355.18 *extractive*
eduction 355.5 *drawing out*
aductive 355.18 *extractive*
edulcorate 134.10, 621.15 *purify*
Edward 94 *Lakes*
Edwardian 43 *Architectural Styles*, 202.14 *historic*

Edward Villella 46.14 *famous ballet dancers*
EEC law 16.1 *the law*
EEG 60.7 *diagnosis*
eel 80 *Fishes*, 20.5 *British game fish*, 45.17 *freshwater fish*
eel basket 80.7 *fishing*
eelgrass 87 *Grasses*
eel-like 80.13 *fishlike*
eel pie and mash 45.44 *British dish*
eelpout 80 *Fishes*
eelworm 81 *Worms*, 69.12 *pests and diseases*
eerie 11.18 *spiritual*
eerie feeling 516.3 *foresight*
eerily 11.26 *magically*
eeriness 11.2 *the occult*
Eeyore 770.4 *depressing person*, 776.3 *hopeless person*
Eeyorish 770.6 *depressed*
efface 244.8 *destroy*, 546.1 *obliterate*, 704.6 *cancel*
effaced 546.6 *obliterated*
effacement 546.3 *obliteration*
eff and blind 827.5 *curse*
effect 227, 56.6 *law*, 132.1 *remainder*, 155.5 *consequence*, 157.12 *end result*, 159.4 *repercussion*, 226.9 *be the cause of*, 227.5 *show an effect*, 232.1 *instrumentality*, 232.4 *be an instrument*, 243.3 *product*, 243.10 *produce*, 457.5 *impression*, 520.1 *meaning*, 570.13 *intend*, 640.1 *action*, 682.6 *be successful*, 684.4 *complete*, 811.10 *exhibitionism*
Effect 227
effect a change 216.8 *cause change*
effected 227.10 *caused*, 684.7 *completed*
effected by 227.10 *caused*
effective 640, 144.7 *complete*, 226.13 *causal*, 230.12 *operative*, 232.6 *instrumental*, 233.11 *influential*, 235.13 *powerful*, 237.10 *potent*, 239.4 *vigorous*, 300.10 *advantaged*, 457.7 *appearing*, 554.3 *emphatic*, 586.19 *persuasive*, 613.3 *instrumental*, 615.1 *convenient*, 679.8 *soldier*, 682.13 *successful*
effective control 12.3 *governance*
effective dose 62.5 *prescription*
effectively 640, 142.13 *on the whole*, 226.14 *causally*, 230.13 *operationally*, 232.9 *instrumentally*, 235.18 *powerfully*, 237.15 *acutely*, 300.12 *at an advantage*, 682.16 *successfully*
effectiveness 126.1 *superiority*, 230.4 *management*, 232.1 *instrumentality*, 235.2 *ability*, 237.1 *strength*
effective procedure 52.28 *algorithm*
effective rate 14.1 *finance*
effectives 679.14 *armed forces*
effect of use 599.6 *use*
effect one's escape 638.5 *escape*
effects 132.5 *estate*, 227.2 *visible effect*, 725.4 *possessions*
effectual 144.7 *complete*, 226.13 *causal*, 230.12 *operative*, 232.6 *instrumental*, 233.11 *influential*, 235.13 *powerful*, 613.3 *instrumental*, 615.1 *convenient*
effectuality 230.4 *management*, 235.2 *ability*, 237.1 *strength*
effectually 103.13 *in essence*, 226.14 *causally*, 230.13 *operationally*, 232.9 *instrumentally*, 233.14 *influentially*, 235.18 *powerfully*
effectuate 226.9 *be the cause of*, 230.8 *activate*, 684.4 *complete*
effectuated 684.7 *completed*
effectuation 590.1 *pursuit*, 640.1 *action*
effeminacy 402.1 *female sex*
effeminate 401.17 *male*, 402.15 *female*
effeminize 236.9 *make impotent*
effervesce 366.21 *be agitated*,

390.24 *bubble*, 425.6 *crack*, 429.4 *hiss*
effervescence 241.1 *violence*, 366.3 *turbulence*, 370.5 *lightness*, 388.7 *gaseousness*, 429.1 *hiss*
effervescent 241.6 *violent*, 366.17 *turbulent*, 370.2 *insubstantial*, 388.21 *gassy*, 390.18 *bubbly*, 429.6 *hissing*
effervescently 370.11 *lightly*, 388.30 *smokily*, 390.25 *airily*, 429.8 *sibilantly*
effervescingly 388.30 *smokily*, 390.25 *airily*
effete 236.13 *unsexed*, 238.12 *weak-willed*, 614.1 *useless*, 628.12 *deteriorated*
effeteness 614.3 *uselessness*
efficacious 230.12 *operative*, 232.6 *instrumental*, 235.13 *powerful*, 613.3 *instrumental*, 682.13 *successful*
efficaciously 230.13 *operationally*, 232.9 *instrumentally*, 235.18 *powerfully*, 682.16 *successfully*
efficacy 232.1 *instrumentality*, 235.2 *ability*, 485.1 *qualification*, 613.7 *instrumentality*
efficiency 63.10 *work*, 230.4 *management*, 235.2 *ability*, 485.1 *qualification*, 613.7 *instrumentality*, 655.1 *skill*, 660.1 *easiness*, 861.12 *proficiency*
efficient 230.12 *operative*, 232.6 *instrumental*, 235.13 *powerful*, 239.4 *vigorous*, 485.9 *qualified*, 501.8 *knowledgeable*, 613.3 *instrumental*, 642.20 *industrious*, 655.6 *skilful*, 655.8 *expert*, 861.5 *proficient*
efficiently 230.13 *operationally*, 232.9 *instrumentally*, 235.18 *powerfully*, 485.17 *capably*, 613.12 *usefully*, 655.12 *skilfully*
effigy 9.3 *idol*, 547.6 *image*
effing and blinding 559.4 *inelegance of speech*, 827.1 *curse*
effloresce 84.13 *flower*, 384.28 *come to dust*
efflorescence 84.5 *flowering*, 245.3 *propagation*, 384.1 *powderiness*, 384.5 *powder*, 594.13 *development*
efflorescent 69.16 *horticultural*, 84.11 *flowering*
effluence 96.6 *river flow*, 347.2 *outflow*
effluent 68.13 *fertilizer*, 96.1 *river*, 96.10 *fluvial*, 347.16 *outflowing*, 353.4 *excrement*
effluvial 388.18 *miasmic*
effluvium 11.10 *psychic phenomenon*, 388.2 *exhalation*, 419.1 *stench*, 631.9 *pollution*
efflux 347.2 *outflow*
effluxion 347.2 *outflow*
effort 63.10 *work*, 235.1 *power*, 239.1 *vigour*, 243.1 *production*, 479.1 *experiment*, 575.2 *commitment*, 596.5 *attempt*, 597.2 *undertaking*, 640.1 *action*, 644.4 *exertion*, 659.1 *difficulty*, 674.2 *contest*
effortful 659.10 *difficult*
effortless 660.9 *easy*
effortlessly 660.21 *easily*
effortlessness 660.1 *easiness*
effort-wasting 614.2 *futile*
effrontery 303.3 *boldness*, 668.1 *defiance*, 807.1 *insolence*
effulgence 439.2 *quality of light*
effulgent 439.16 *bright*
effuse 347.10 *emerge*, 347.12 *leak*, 553.3 *diffuse*
effused 347.16 *outflowing*
effusion 347.2 *outflow*, 347.3 *leakage*, 349.22 *disgorgement*, 353.1 *excretion*, 553.1 *diffuseness*, 565.2 *effusiveness*
effusive 565, 347.16 *outflowing*, 475.10 *demonstrative*, 553.3 *diffuse*, 610.6 *excessive*, 759.13 *passionate*, 819.3 *friendly*
effusively 565, 347.18 *forth*,

475.21 *demonstratively*, 553.7 *diffusely*, 819.17 *in friendship*
effusiveness 565, 475.2 *demonstrativeness*, 553.1 *diffuseness*, 610.2 *overdoing it*
effusive welcome 348.2 *receptivity*
Efik 1 *Peoples*, 5 *Languages and Groups of Languages*
eft 79 *Amphibians*
EFTS 65.12 *electronic office*
e.g. 165.31 *namely*
egalitarian 122.6 *equal*, 627.12 *reformer*
egalitarianism 12.1 *government*, 122.1 *equality*, 688.7 *type of rule*
Egeria 654.4 *adviser*
egest 349.14 *let out*, 353.15 *excrete*
egesta 353.4 *excrement*
egestion 349.23 *vomiting*, 353.1 *excretion*
egestive 353.24 *excretory*
egg 78.15 *eggs*, 156.3 *source*, 226.3 *rudiment*, 243.7 *produce*, 245.8 *organs of reproduction*, 315.3 *round thing*
egg and dart 43 *Architectural Decoration*
egg and spoon race 674.4 *race*
eggbeater 73.8 *aircraft*
eggbeater 364.6 *rotator*, 366.14 *agitator*
eggcup 258.13 *drinking vessel*
egg drop soup 45.48 *Chinese dish*
egged on 228.12 *motivated*, 586.20 *persuadable*
egg flip 351.7 *alcoholic drink*
egg fu yung 45.48 *Chinese dish*
egghead 4.12 *sage*, 6.7 *learner*, 459.8 *intellectual person*, 461.7 *thinker*, 471.9 *person of ideas*, 501.6 *knowledgeable person*, 655.5, 688.11 *expert*, 696.9 *educational leader*, 772.7 *serious person*
egg-laying mammal 77
eggnog 351.7 *alcoholic drink*
egg on 228.10 *manipulate*, 239.3 *invigorate*
egg on one's face 850.8 *indignity*
eggplant 45 *Vegetables*
egg roll 45.48 *Chinese dish*
eggs 78, 45.7 *basic ingredient*, 243.7 *produce*
eggs Benedict 45.43 *US dish*
egg-shaped 313.5 *circular*, 315.9 *round*, 334.6 *circular*
eggshell 78.15 *eggs*, 238.5 *weak thing*, 293.13 *casing*, 379.3 *brittle thing*
eggshell blue 454.1 *blue*
eggshell glaze 44.3 *glaze*
eggshell porcelain 44.1 *ceramics*
eggspoon 258.17 *ladle*
egg timer 191 *Timepieces and Timers*, 192.9 *hourglass*
egg whisk 364.6 *rotator*
egg white 393.11 *mucus*
eglantine 84 *Flowers and Flowering Plants*
Egmont 95 *Mountains*
ego 11.7 *spirit*, 61.21 *psyche*, 165.11 *identity*, 368.6 *internal world*, 860.2 *egoism*
ego analysis 61.3 *psychiatric treatment*
ego-centred 860.5 *egoistic*
ego-centredness 860.2 *egoism*
egocentric 290.12 *internalized*, 809.12 *self-interested*, 860.5 *egoistic*
egocentrically 809.20 *smugly*, 860.9 *egoistically*
egocentricity 860.2 *egoism*
egocentrism 290.6 *internalization*, 860.2 *egoism*
ego-id conflict 61.21 *psyche*
ego ideal 61.21 *psyche*, 519.4 *ideality*
egoism 860, 4.7 *school of thought*, 805.3 *conceit*, 809.5 *self-interest*, 834.1 *misanthropy*, 870.4 *self-absorption*
egoist 4.11 *follower of a doctrine*, 788.3 *boring person*, 805.13

proud person, 834.2 *misanthrope*, 860.3 *selfish person*, 870.5 *self-indulgent person*
egoistic 860, 4.14 *of a philosophy*, 809.12 *self-interested*, 834.3 *misanthropic*
egoistical 860.5 *egoistic*
egoistically 860, 805.32 *proudly*, 834.5 *misanthropically*
egoisticalness 809.5 *self-interest*
egomania 61.15 *compulsion*, 494.1 *overestimation*
egomaniac 652.5 *badly behaved person*, 860.3 *selfish person*
ego therapy 61.3 *psychiatric treatment*
egotism 805.3 *conceit*, 809.5 *self-interest*, 821.1 *love*, 834.1 *misanthropy*, 860.2 *egoism*
egotist 788.3 *boring person*, 809.7 *vain person*, 834.2 *misanthrope*, 860.3 *selfish person*
egotistic 809.12 *self-interested*, 860.5 *egoistic*, 870.9 *self-absorbed*
egotistical 165.18 *subjective*, 834.3 *misanthropic*, 860.5 *egoistic*
egotistically 805.32 *proudly*, 809.22 *selfishly*, 834.5 *misanthropically*, 860.9 *egoistically*
egotisticalness 809.5 *self-interest*
ego trip 860.2 *egoism*
egregious 611.6 *notable*
egress 96.6 *river flow*, 324.4 *backward motion*, 345.7 *departure*, 347.1 *exit*, 347.6 *way out*, 347.9 *exit*, 349.21 *removal*, 638.2 *means of escape*
egression 347.1 *exit*
egressive 347.15 *outgoing*
egret 78 *Birds*
Egypt 91 *Countries*
Egyptian 5 *Languages and Groups of Languages*, 43 *Architectural Styles*, 400.4 *civilized human*
Egyptians 200.6 *people of the past*
Egyptological 3.17 *archaeological*
Egyptologist 1.4 *palaeoanthropologist*, 3.4 *archaeologist*, 200.11 *antiquarian*
Egyptology 1.2 *palaeoanthropology*, 3.2 *archaeology*
EHF 534 *Radio-frequency Bands*
Ehrenberg 48 *Writers*
Eichendorff 48 *Writers*
Eichler 52 *Scientists*
eider 78 *Birds*
eiderdown 78.17 *plumage*, 293.10 *bed covering*, 374.11 *soft thing*
eidetic 114.9 *lifelike*, 519.10 *imaginative*, 560.11 *descriptive*
eidetically 114.14 *comparably*
eidetic image 547.6 *image*
Eid-ul-Adha 10.16 *religious festival*
Eid-ul-Fitr 10.16 *religious festival*
Eiffel Tower 43 *Noted Buildings*, 275.6 *tall thing*
Eiger 95 *Mountains*, 95.6 *other major mountains and ranges*
eight 179, 52.9 *numeral*, 179.15 *eighth*
eight all 40.9 *squash terms*
eight ball 24.6 *pool*
eight-beat crawl 39.2 *swimming technique*
eight bells 204.3 *noon*
eight centuries 179.9 *treble figures*
eighteen-hole course 29.1 *golf*
eighteenth 173.4 *less than one*
Eighteenth Amendment 709.1 *veto*, 869.1 *self-restraint*
eighteen-yard 38.5 *soccer*
eighteen-yard box 38.1 *soccer*
eighter 179.4 *eight*
eighter from Decatur 179.4 *eight*
eight-five-three 42 *Card Games*
eightfold 179.15 *eighth*
eighth 179, 52.75 *equal*, 143.1 *part*, 173.4 *less than one*, 179.4 *eight*
eighth guard 28.3 *fencing movements*

eighth note 49.17 *notation*
eighth part 179.4 *eight*
eightieth 173.4 *less than one*, 179.19 *twentieth*
eight-man 35.6 *rugger*
eight-man shove 35.3 *rugby play*
eights 36.4 *rowing*, 674.4 *race*
eight-sided 52.82 *polygonal*
eightsome reel 46.4 *historic dancing*
eight-step approach 21.2 *field events*
eighty 179.8 *twenty and over*
Eindhoven 93 *Cities*
Einsiedler 32 *Breeds of Horse and Pony*
Einstein 52 *Scientists*
einsteinium 57 *Chemical Elements*
Einstein theory 248.9 *fourth dimension*
Einstein universe 53.4 *cosmological model*
Eir 8 *Deities*
Eire 91.10 *Ireland*
eisegesis 524.1 *interpretation*
Eisenhower jacket 295.11 *jacket*
eisoprophobia 777 *Phobias by Name*
either...or 580.17 *selectively*
ejaculate 349.14 *let out*, 353.15 *excrete*, 431.14 *hiss*, 564.11 *speak*
ejaculation 349.22 *disgorgement*, 353.1 *excretion*, 366.8 *spasm*, 431.7 *cry of disapproval*, 564.7 *utterance*
ejaculative 349.29 *expulsive*
ejaculatory 431.19 *hissing*
eject 147, 338, 341, 131.3 *subtract*, 134.11 *simplify*, 136.9 *separate*, 252.16 *replace*, 326.14 *bring back*, 330.1 *impel*, 349.1 *expel*, 352.7 *secrete*, 353.15 *excrete*, 581.2 *discard*, 600.6 *stop using*, 704.7 *terminate*, 727.9 *dispose of*
ejecta 54.25 *eruption*, 353.4 *excrement*
ejectamenta 338.8 *missile*, 353.4 *excrement*
ejected 131.5 *subtracted*, 136.15 *separate*, 711.8 *refused*
ejecting mechanism 349.28 *propellant*
ejection 147, 338, 131.1 *subtraction*, 136.2 *setting apart*, 252.3 *replacement*, 338.7 *shot*, 341.6 *repulse*, 349.17 *expulsion*, 352.1 *secretion*, 353.1 *excretion*, 581.6 *discarding*, 704.2 *termination*, 727.1 *disposal*
ejective 338.18 *projectile*, 349.29 *expulsive*, 353.24 *excretory*
ejectment 349.17 *expulsion*
ejector 349, 338.8 *missile*
ejector seat 73 *Aircraft Parts*, 338.4 *ejection*, 349.28 *propellant*, 632.4 *safety device*
ejoy 599.5 *dispose of*
eke out 144.4 *complete*
eke out a livelihood 743.12 *be poor*
el 72.1 *railway*, 327.10 *railway*
El 8 *Deities*
elaborate 684, 106.10 *detailed*, 382.15 *shape*, 553.5 *be diffuse*, 557.4 *ornate*, 558.3 *ornament*, 558.3 *elegant*, 558.4 *be elegant*, 594.7 *develop*, 594.20 *developed*, 619.5 *perfect*, 627.1 *improve*, 644.11 *laborious*, 684.7 *completed*, 811.24 *grand*
elaborated 684.7 *completed*
elaborately 106.19 *meticulously*, 549.10 *stylistically*, 557.6 *ornately*, 558.5 *elegantly*, 684.9 *completely*, 811.40 *grandly*
elaborateness 811.9 *grandeur*
elaboration 684, 553.1 *diffuseness*, 558.1 *elegance*, 627.5 *improvement*, 644.4 *exertion*, 684.3 *elaboration*
Elamite 5 *Languages and Groups of Languages*
eland 77 *Placental Mammals*

elapse 185.15 *pass*, 188.7 *go on*, 200.14 *pass*
elasmobranch 80.2 *fish*
elasmosaur 79 Fossil Reptiles
elastic 377, 261.9 *enlargeable*, 331.8 *recoiling*, 337.26 *resilient*, 374.2 *pliant*
elastically 377, 331.10 *on the rebound*, 374.17 *softly*
elasticate 377.9 *make elastic*
elastic band 377.3 *elastic thing*
elastic bandage 293.6 *medical covering*
elastic board 30.6 *pommel horse*
elastic fluid 387.1 *fluid*, 388.1 *gas*
elasticity 377, 56.10 *force*, 63.15 *strength of materials*, 235.4 *energy*, 261.2 *enlargeability*, 331.4 *recoil*, 337.17 *resilience*, 374.8 *softness*
Elasticity 377
elasticize 377.9 *make elastic*
elastic scattering 56.71 *nuclear reaction*
elastic strain 63.14 *load*
elastic thing 377
elastic tissue 377.3 *elastic thing*
elastomer 377.4 *rubber*
Elastoplast 138.3 *adhesive*, 222.3 *substitute thing*, 293.6 *medical covering*, 630.10 *surgical dressing*
Elat 8 Deities
elate 805.30 *make proud*
elated 762.4 *happy*, 805.22 *boastful*
elater 88.4 *moss plant*
elation 510.4 *delusion*
E-layer 534.15 *transmitted wave*
Elbe 96 Rivers, 96.5 *other major rivers*
Elbert 95 Mountains
elbow 31.9 *play hockey*, 135.5 *joint*, 267.4 *meet*, 330.1 *impel*, 407.11 *touch*
elbow aside 850.22 *show disrespect*
elbow-cop 671.7 *armour*
elbowed 31.8 *hockey*
elbow grease 385.5 *polishing*, 644.4 *exertion*
elbow guard 28.2 *fencing equipment*
elbowing 31.3 *ice hockey*, 31.8 *hockey*, 648.3 *hasty*
elbow-joint 310.1 *angle*
elbow one's way 590.13 *follow up*, 642.14 *push*, 644.8 *exert oneself*
elbow out 727.10 *dismiss*
elbow pad 31.3 *ice hockey*
elbow protector 27.6 *pad*
elbowroom 210.2 *opportunity*, 248.6 *available space*, 698.5 *scope*
elbow through 356.10 *enter*
elbow-to-elbow 267.7 *beside*, 264.5 *near*, 267.5 *juxtaposed*
Elbrus 95 Mountains
eld 3.8 *past time*
elder 85 Trees and Shrubs, 7.8 *priest*, 45.31 *offal*, 126.5 *superior*, 126.15 *excellent*, 154.12 *primary*, 194.6 *person having priority*, 194.10 *prior*, 200.17 *past*, 202.11 *old*, 207.7 *older person*, 696.1 *master*, 696.12 *masterful*
elderberry 86 Fruits
elderflower wine 84.8 *flower product*
elderliness 202.1 *oldness*, 207.5 *old age*
elderly 202.11 *old*, 207.14 *aged*, 448.2 *grey-haired*
elders 202.2 *old people*
elders and betters 202.2 *old people*
elder statesman 459.8 *intellectual person*
elder statesmen 653.7 *council*
eldest 154.9 *predecessor*, 194.10 *prior*
El Djazair 93 Cities
El Dorado 519.8 *dreamland*, 588.6 *objective*, 714.4 *promised land*, 742.5 *wealth*

eldritch 11.18 *spiritual*
Eleatic 4.11 *follower of a doctrine*, 4.14 *of a philosophy*
Eleaticism 4.7 *school of thought*
elect 7.21 *ordain*, 580.5 *vote*, 580.15 *chosen*, 688.21 *grant authority*, 703.6 *commission*, 706.4 *delegate*
elected 688, 580.15 *chosen*, 706.6 *delegated*
elected person 706.1 *delegate*
elected representative 15.7 *employee*, 703.5 *commissioner*, 706.1 *delegate*
election 580, 7.9 *priesthood*, 688.3 *acquisition of power*, 703.1 *commission*, 706.3 *delegation*
electioneer 580.5 *vote*
electioneering 580.12 *election*, 580.16 *elective*
elective 580
elector 580.13 *electorate*
electoral 580.16 *elective*
electoral college 580.11 *franchise*
electoral defeat 581.6 *discarding*
electoral district 249.5 *state*, 580.12 *election*
electoral mandate 692.4 *authorization*
electoral roll 171.6 *list of names*, 580.12 *election*
electoral system 580.11 *franchise*
electorate 580, 16.18 *tribunal*, 171.6 *list of names*, 249.5 *state*
Electra complex 61.18 *complex*, 821.2 *romantic love*
electric 56.98 *physical*, 64.36 *electronic*, 235.16 *charged*, 329.1 *swift*, 403.9 *exciting*, 410.10 *powered*
electrical 28.6 *fencing*, 56.98 *physical*, 64.36 *electronic*, 235.16 *charged*, 235.17, 410.10 *powered*
electrical conduction 56
electrical energy 56, 64, 56.11, 235.4 *energy*
electrical engineer 63.2 *engineer*, 64.2 *electronics engineer*, 646.2 *artisan*
electrical engineering 63.1 *engineering*, 64.1 *electronics*, 603.5 *mechanics*
electrical épée 28.2 *fencing equipment*
electrical fault 683.4 *unsuccessful thing*
electrical foil 28.2 *fencing equipment*
electrical instrument 64
electrically 56.100 *physically*, 64.37 *electronically*, 235.19 *energetically*, 410.12 *powerfully*
electrical oscillation 56.14 *sound wave*
electrical porcelain 44.9 *industrial ceramics*
electrical potential 235.4 *energy*
electrical power 235
electrical wheel 44.6 *ceramic workshop*
electric arc 56.46 *electric discharge*
electric battery 410.4 *electricity*
electric blanket 408.3 *heater*
electric blue 454.1 *blue*
electric cable 64.27 *wire*
electric car 71 Motor Vehicles
electric chair 16.43 *conviction*, 397.4 *death sentence*, 398.5 *execution*, 410.4 *electricity*, 879.16 *instrument of execution*
electric charge 56, 64, 235.7 *electrical power*
electric circuit 56.55, 64.13 *circuit*
electric clock 191 Timepieces and Timers, 192.6 *clock*
electric constant 56.50 *electric charge*
electric current 56, 64, 235.7 *electrical power*, 410.4 *electricity*
electric discharge 56, 64
electric drill 603.1 *tool*
electric eel 80 Fishes
electric fence 68.11 *farmland*, 671.9 *barrier*

electric fencer 68.10 *farm tool*
electric field 56, 64
electric field strength 56.54 *electric field*
electric filament 64.27 *wire*
electric fire 408.6 *fire*
electric flux 56.54 *electric field*
electric guitar 49 Musical Instruments
electrician 51.26 *stagehand*, 64.2 *electronics engineer*, 410.9 *power-worker*, 629.12 *repairer*, 646.2 *artisan*
electric iron 376.9 *smoother*, 408.3 *heater*
electricity 777 Phobias by Topic, 56, 64, 410, 56.2 *classical physics*, 235.4 *energy*, 235.7 *electrical power*, 329.11 *swift thing*, 338.13, 410.1 *fuel*
electricity meter 268.8 *meter*, 410.4 *electricity*
electricity substation 235.6 *source of energy*
electricity supply 235.7 *electrical power*, 410.4 *electricity*
electric lead 410.4 *electricity*
electric light 439, 56.23 *light*, 235.7 *electrical power*
electric locomotive 72.4 *locomotive*
electric meter 64.34 *power supply*
electric mixer 45.6 *kitchen equipment*, 133.6 *mixer*
electric motor 4, 56.56 *electrical energy*, 410.4 *electricity*
electric potential 56, 64
electric power 56.56, 64.26 *electrical energy*, 235.4 *energy*
electric railway 327.10 *railway*
electric ray 80 Fishes
electric shock 235.7 *electrical power*
electric storm 56, 55.21 *thunderstorm*
electric switch 410.4 *electricity*
electrification 235.7 *electrical power*, 410.4 *electricity*
electrified 228.12 *motivated*
electrify 228.9 *motivate*, 235.11 *give power*, 239.3 *invigorate*, 410.11 *fuel*, 514.11 *amaze*, 786.10 *be wonderful*
electrifying 228.11 *motivational*, 403.9 *exciting*, 410.10 *powered*
electro 49.9 *popular music*
electroacoustics 56.2 *classical physics*
electroacoustic transducer 64.22 *transformer*
electrobiology 59.1 *life science*
electrocardiography 60.7 *diagnosis*
electrochemical 57
electrochemical series 57.19 *electrochemistry*
electrochemist 57.2 *chemist*
electrochemistry 57
electroconvulsive shock therapy 61.3 *psychiatric treatment*
electroconvulsive therapy 61.3 *psychiatric treatment*, 510.9 *treatment*, 630.13 *therapy*
electrocute 64.35 *conduct*, 398.17 *murder*, 398.19, 879.5 *execute*
electrocution 235.7 *electrical power*, 397.4 *death sentence*, 398.5 *execution*, 410.4 *electricity*, 879.13 *capital punishment*
electrode 56.43 *electrical conduction*, 64.5 *electrolytic conduction*, 235.7 *electrical power*
electrodeposit 57.28 *electrolyse*
electrodeposited 57.42 *electrochemical*
electrodeposition 57.19 *electrochemistry*
electrode potential 57.19 *electrochemistry*
electrodynamic 56.98 *physical*, 64.36 *electronic*
electrodynamically 56.100 *physically*, 64.37 *electronically*
electrodynamics 56.2 *classical physics*, 235.7 *electrical power*
electroencephalogy 60.7 *diagnosis*

electroform 57.28 *electrolyse*
electroformed 57.42 *electrochemical*
electrolyse 57, 141.4 *deconstruct*
electrolysis 56.43 *electrical conduction*, 57.19 *electrochemistry*, 141.2 *deconstruction*, 235.7 *electrical power*, 296.7 *depilation*, 630.12 *surgery*
electrolyte 56.43 *electrical conduction*, 57.19 *electrochemistry*, 64.3 *electricity*, 64.5 *electrolytic conduction*
electrolytic 57.42 *electrochemical*, 64.36 *electronic*
electrolytically 64.37 *electronically*, 141.7 *to pieces*
electrolytic capacitor 64.17 *resistor*
electrolytic cell 56.43 *electrical conduction*, 57.19 *electrochemistry*, 64.5 *electrolytic conduction*
electrolytic conduction 64
electrolytic conductor 56.43 *electrical conduction*
electrolytic corrosion 57.19 *electrochemistry*
electrolytic extraction 57.23 *metallurgy*
electrolytic forming 57.19 *electrochemistry*
electrolytic refining 57.19 *electrochemistry*
electromagnet 56.60, 340.3 *magnet*
electromagnetic 64.36 *electronic*
electromagnetically 64.37 *electronically*
electromagnetic conduction 326.3 *transmission*
electromagnetic field 235.4 *energy*
electromagnetic induction 56, 56.63 *magnetic phenomenon*
electromagnetic interaction 56.79 *fundamental interaction*
electromagnetic radiation 56, 235.9 *electronics*, 439.1 *light*
electromagnetic spectrum 56.13, 56.62 *electromagnetic radiation*
electromagnetic theory 56.5 *theory*
electromagnetic wave 56.62 *electromagnetic radiation*, 365.5 *wave*
electromagnetism 56.2 *classical physics*, 56.57 *magnetism*, 235.4 *energy*, 367.6 *natural science*
electromechanical 64.36 *electronic*
electromechanically 64.37 *electronically*
electrometer 56.90 *ammeter*, 64.23 *electrical instrument*, 268.8 *meter*
electrometric 268.16 *micrometric*
electrometry 268.2 *micrometry*
electromotive 57.42 *electrochemical*, 64.36 *electronic*
electromotive force 56.52, 64.10 *electric potential*, 235.4 *energy*
electromotive series 57.19 *electrochemistry*
electron 56.44 *semiconductor*, 56.50 *electric charge*, 56.65 *atom*, 56.77 *elementary particle*, 64.4 *semiconductor*, 260.2 *little thing*, 367.4 *matter*
electron conduction 56.44, 64.4 *semiconductor*
electron configuration 56.65 *atom*
electron-deficient 57.35 *combined*
electron-deficient bond 57.11 *chemical bond*
electron-deficient compound 57.7 *chemical compound*
electron emission 64
electron gun 64.24 *electron emission*
electronic 64, 232.8 *practical*, 235.16 *charged*, 603.8 *mechanical*
electronically 64, 232.9 *instrumentally*, 235.19 *energetically*, 603.10 *instrumentally*
electronic brain 65.3 *computer*

electronic circuit 56.55, 64.13 *circuit*
electronic clock 191 Timepieces and Timers
electronic communication 534.1 *communications*
electronic component 56.55 *circuit*
electronic computer 65.3 *computer*
electronic data processing 170.4 *computing*
electronic device 56.55 *circuit*, 64.16 *circuit element*
electronic flash 66.19 *flash*
electronic flight information system 73 Aircraft Parts
electronic instrument 49.25 *musical instrument*
electronic journalism 533.1 *news*
electronic listening device 545.10 *recording instrument*
electronic mail 65.12 *electronic office*, 534.8 *data transmission*
electronic means 232.1 *instrumentality*
electronic media 533.5 *mass communication*
electronic office 65, 534.8 *data transmission*
electronics 64, 235, 64.13 *circuit*, 603.5 *mechanics*
Electronics and Electrical Engineering 64
electronics engineer 64
electronics engineering 63.1 *engineering*, 64.1 *electronics*
electronic surveillance 632.2 *protection*
electronic tube 44.9 *industrial ceramics*
electron lens 64.24 *electron emission*
electron mass 56.97 *fundamental constant*
electron microscope 56.85 *microscope*
electron microscopy 59.6 *cell biology*
electron multiplier 56.93 *radiation detector*, 64.24 *electron emission*
electron physics 235.9 *electronics*
electron shell 56.65 *atom*
electron spectroscopy 57.17 *analysis*
electron-transport chain 58.24 *respiration*
electron tube 64, 64.24 *electron emission*
electro-optical effect 56.33 *photosensitivity*
electro-optics 56.2 *classical physics*
electro-osmosis 57.17 *analysis*
electrophile 57.14 *chemical reaction*
electrophilic 57.38 *reactive*
electrophilic reaction 57.14 *chemical reaction*
electrophobia 777 Phobias by Name
electrophoresis 57.17 *analysis*
electrophoretic 57.41 *analytic*
electrophotographic printer 65.7 *peripheral*
electrophotometer 56.32 *optical instrument*
electroplate 57.28 *electrolyse*, 293.3 *coating*, 293.24 *coat*
electroplated 57.42 *electrochemical*
electroplater 293.17 *coverer*
electroplating 57.19 *electrochemistry*, 57.23 *metallurgy*
electrorefining 57.23 *metallurgy*
electroshock 61.3 *psychiatric treatment*
electroshock therapy 61.3 *psychiatric treatment*
electrostatic 64.36 *electronic*
electrostatically 64.37 *electronically*
electrostatic generator 64.30 *generator*
electrostatic induction 56.49 *electromagnetic induction*

electrostatic printer 65.7 *peripheral*
electrostatics 235.7 *electrical power*
electrostriction 56.49 *electromagnetic induction*
electrotechnician 64.2 *electronics engineer*
electrotechnics 64.1 *electronics*
electrotechnology 630.13 *therapy*
electrovalent 57.35 *combined*
electrovalent bond 57.11 *chemical bond*
electrovalently 57.46 *chemically*
electrovoltaic 57.42 *electrochemical*
electroweak interaction 56.79 *fundamental interaction*
electrum 57 Alloys, 133.2 *mixed thing*, 741.16 *bullion*
electrum coinage 741.13 *coinage*
electuary 630.2 *medicine*
eleemosynary 754.11 *free of charge*, 833.6 *philanthropic*
Elegabalus 8 Deities
elegance 558, 794, 5.24 *phrasing*, 6.11 *refinement*, 411.2 *taste of life*, 542.3 *subtlety*, 549.2 *stylishness*, 655.1 *skill*, 789.1 *gorgeousness*, 796.1 *fashion*, 811.9 *grandeur*, 817.2 *good manners*
Elegance 558
elegances 817.3 *courtesies*
elegancies 813.5 *etiquette*
elegancy 558.1 *elegance*
elegant 558, 5.43 *phrasal*, 6.20 *refined*, 411.8 *tasteful*, 542.13 *subtle*, 549.7 *stylish*, 655.9 *well-made*, 789.6 *personable*, 794.5 *refined*, 811.24 *grand*, 813.6 *formal*, 817.8 *good-mannered*
elegantly 558, 5.51 *phraseologically*, 6.27 *discerningly*, 295.36 *dressily*, 411.11 *tastily*, 549.10 *stylistically*, 811.40 *grandly*, 817.15 *genteelly*
elegantly upholstered 742.3 *opulent*
elegant phrase 5.24 *phrasing*
elegiac 48.19 *narrative*, 399.11 *funeral*, 774.4 *lamenting*
elegiacal 399.11 *funeral*
elegiacally 399.12 *funereally*
elegiac couplet 48.9 *metre*
elegiac distich 48.9 *metre*
elegiac pentameter 48.9 *metre*
elegiac poem 48.7 *poem*
elegiac poetry 48.6 *poetry*
eligibility 146.1 *inclusion*
elegist 48.14 *author*, 399.3 *funeral director*, 774.3 *lamenter*
elegize 48.21 *write*, 774.6 *lament*
elegy 48.7 *poem*, 399.2 *funeral*, 774.2 *lament*
element 52.21 *set*, 57.6 *chemical element*, 106.6 *aspect*, 133.4 *admixture*, 143.1 *part*, 143.4 *component*, 146.2 *thing included*, 148.1 *component*, 226.3 *rudiment*, 256.2 *environment*, 305.4 *aspect*, 367.4 *matter*, 400.7 *person*
element 104 57 Chemical Elements
element 105 57 Chemical Elements
element 106 57 Chemical Elements
elemental 57, 11.18 *spiritual*, 55.41 *meteorologic*, 134.16 *simple*, 143.11 *partial*, 148.6 *component*, 226.13 *causal*, 257.10 *containing*
elementally 148.14 *constituently*, 257.13 *structurally*
elemental spirit 11.11 *ghost*
elementary 134.16 *simple*, 148.6 *component*, 154.13 *precursory*, 156.35 *rudimentary*, 226.13 *causal*, 594.16 *preparatory*, 595.5 *immature*, 660.9 *easy*
elementary charge 56.97 *fundamental constant*
elementary particle 56, 367.4 *matter*
elementary unit 367.4 *matter*

elements 55.6 *weather data*, 156.7 *rudiments*, 257.1 *contents*, 604.1 *materials*
elenchus 4.4 *philosophical investigation*, 473.2 *logical argument*
elenctic 4.16 *dialectical*, 473.11 *logical*, 477.12 *questioning*
elephant 77 Placental Mammals, 259.9 *big thing*, 275.6 *tall thing*, 326.6 *beast of burden*
elephant bird 78 Birds, 78.8 *extinct bird*
elephant garlic 45 Vegetables
elephant grass 87 Grasses
elephant gun 338.9, 680.9 *firearm*
elephant hunt 590.2 *chase*
elephantiasis 259.4 *gigantism*
elephantine 77.32 *pachydermatous*, 259.17 *stocky*
elephantoid 77.32 *pachydermatous*
elephants 161 Collective Names by Animal
elephant seal 77 Placental Mammals
elephant's ear 45 Vegetables
elephant's-tusk shell 81 Molluscs
Eleusinianism 7 Non-Christian Religions
eleutherophobia 777 Phobias by Name
elevate 8.17 *deify*, 128.5, 261.5 *make bigger*, 275.17 *raise*, 281.6 *make vertical*, 336.8 *further*, 339.12 *drag*, 361.3 *promote*, 370.9 *be light*, 621.15 *purify*, 627.1 *improve*, 874.9 *be intoxicating*
elevated 8.15 *exalted*, 70.5 *transportable*, 72.1 *railway*, 95.7 *mountainous*, 261.7 *bigger*, 275.9 *high*, 275.11 *exalted*, 361.11 *raised*, 361.12 *exalted*, 554.5 *serious*, 805.19 *stately*, 874.1 *drunk*
elevated railway 72.1 *railway*, 327.10 *railway*
elevate oneself 304.7 *rear up*
elevating 281.2 *making vertical*
elevating oneself 304.3 *rearing up*
elevation 8.9 *deification*, 54.6 *continent*, 128.1 *increase*, 195.4 *accession*, 261.1 *growth*, 275.1 *height*, 281.2 *making vertical*, 336.12 *advance*, 359.2 *upturn*, 361.6 *raising*, 382.6 *construction*, 457.3 *external appearance*, 547.7 *map*, 554.2 *seriousness*, 627.5 *improvement*, 767.6 *profile*, 874.10 *drunkenness*
elevation of the Host 10.6 *Eucharist*
elevator 73 Aircraft Parts, **361,** 63.29 *construction equipment*, 71.4 *personal transport*, 359.8 *lift*
elevatory 261.9 *enlargeable*
eleven 27.4 *team*, 179.7 *double figures*
elevenses 204.2 *morning thing*, 350.12 *meal*, 815.3 *meeting*
eleventh 179, 173.4 *less than one*
eleventh hour 209.2 *late hour*, 210.3 *critical time*
eleventh-hour 209.11 *late in the day*, 210.8 *in time*
eleventh-hour rescue 592.3 *expedient plan*
elevon 73 Aircraft Parts
elf 11.11 *ghost*, 76.7 *legendary beast*, 260.4 *little person*, 270.5 *short person*
elf-cup 89 Fungi
elfin 260.7 *little*
Elgar 49 Musicians and Composers
El Giza 93 Cities
Elgon 95 Mountains
eliche 45 Types of Pasta
elicit 226.10 *awaken*, 355.15 *draw out*
elicitation 355.5 *drawing out*
elicitory 355.18 *extractive*
elide 270.10 *shorten*

elided 270.8 *shortened*
eligibility 485.1 *qualification*
eligible 146.8 *included*, 485.9 *qualified*, 823.22 *marriageable*
eligible bachelor 823.4 *marriageability*
eligible party 823.4 *marriageability*
eliminant 349.29 *expulsive*, 353.24 *excretory*
eliminate 52.92 *manipulate*, 57.26 *react*, 131.3 *subtract*, 134.11 *simplify*, 147.8 *eject*, 157.17 *kill*, 182.8 *reduce*, 349.10 *exterminate*, 349.11 *void*, 353.15 *excrete*, 355.11 *extract*, 398.17 *murder*, 458.3 *cause to disappear*, 546.1 *obliterate*, 581.2 *discard*, 621.15 *purify*, 704.6 *cancel*
eliminated 131.5 *subtracted*, 157.23 *annihilated*, 355.19 *dislodged*, 546.6 *obliterated*
eliminate each other 704.9 *cancel out*
eliminate the alternatives 580.1 *select*
elimination 52.24 *evaluation*, 57.14 *chemical reaction*, 131.1 *subtraction*, 134.2 *purification*, 147.2 *ejection*, 157.4 *annihilation*, 244.1 *destruction*, 349.21 *removal*, 353.1 *excretion*, 355.1 *extraction*, 458.5 *disguise*, 546.3 *obliteration*, 581.6 *discarding*, 704.1 *cancellation*
eliminative 353.24 *excretory*
elinvar 57 Alloys
Eliot 48 Writers, **48** Poets, **48** Dramatists
Elioun 8 Deities
elision 48.12 *poetic language*, 262.1 *contraction*, 270.2 *shortening*, 552.1 *conciseness*, 562.2 *outline*
elite 617, 147.10 *excluding*, 580.9 *chosen thing*, 580.15 *chosen*, 611.3 *chief thing*, 815.7 *human society*, 861.2 *best*, 861.9 *the best*
elitism 12.1 *government*, 481.4 *social discrimination*
elitist 481.7 *bigot*, 481.10 *discriminatory*
elixir 62.3 *drug*, 103.3 *quintessence*, 355.8 *extract*, 630.1 *remedy*, 630.2 *medicine*
Elizabethan 43 Architectural Styles, 3.15 *historic*, 47.7 *furniture style*, 202.14 *historic*
Elizabethan Age 3.10 *past age*
Elizabethan theatre 51.14 *theatre*
Elizabethan tragedy 51.9 *tragedy*
elk 77 Placental Mammals, **161** Collective Names by Animal
elkhound 77 Breeds of Dogs
elk hunt 590.2 *chase*
ell 130.3 *additional item*
Ellesmere 98 Islands
ellipse 52.42 *circle*, 269.6 *oblong*, 334.1 *circuit*, 363.1 *orbital motion*
ellipsis 5.3 *syntax*, 160.5 *caesura*, 270.3 *shortened version*, 543.7 *punctuation*, 551.1 *obscurity*, 552.1 *conciseness*
ellipsoid 52.45 *curved surface*
ellipsoidal 52.83 *spherical*
elliptic 52.81 *curvilinear*, 313.5 *circular*, 552.3 *concise*
elliptical 269.2 *elongated*, 270.8 *shortened*, 334.6, 363.10 *circular*, 551.2 *obscure*
elliptical arch 43.5 *arch*
elliptical galaxy 53.7 *galaxy*
elliptically 270.12 *short*, 313.8 *circularly*, 551.4 *obscurely*, 552.5 *concisely*
elliptically polarized light 56.27 *polarized light*
elliptical orbit 53.21 *orbit*
elm 85 Trees and Shrubs
elm bark beetle 82 Insects
El Nath 53 Named Stars
el Niño 55 Winds
elocution 564.4 *articulation*

Elohim 8.3 *God*
Elohistic 8.13 *divine*
elongate 269.10 *lengthen*
elongated 269
elongation 63.16 *deformation*, 269.4 *length*
elope 345.3 *quit*, 591.8 *run away*, 638.5 *escape*, 823.15 *marry*
elopement 345.7 *departure*, 591.16 *desertion*, 638.1 *escape*, 823.5 *wedding*
eloper 638.3 *escaper*
elope with 734.10 *take away*
eloquence 554.2 *seriousness*, 557.2 *affectation*, 564.2 *power of speech*, 565.1 *talkativeness*
eloquent 564, 520.6 *meaningful*, 554.3 *emphatic*, 557.4 *ornate*, 565.5 *talkative*
eloquently 564.21 *orally*, 565.10 *talkatively*
El Paso 93 *Cities*
El Salvador 91 *Countries*
elsewhere 254.21 *away*
Elton 52 *Scientists*
elucidate 4.21 *rationalize*, 437.10 *make visible*, 439.29 *clarify*, 475.16 *explain*, 522.5 *simplify*, 524.8 *interpret*, 550.2 *clarify*, 561.3 *dissertate*
elucidated 439.22 *enlightened*, 475.11 *explanatory*, 524.15 *interpreted*
elucidation 439.13 *enlightenment*, 475.3 *explanation*, 524.1 *interpretation*
elucidative 524.14 *interpretive*
elucidatory 524.14 *interpretive*, 560.11 *descriptive*
eluctate 700.5 *be liberated*
elude 638, 474.12 *deceive*, 573.7 *refuse*, 591.6 *evade*, 720.8 *not perform*, 722.15 *lose someone*
elude one 523.7 *be unintelligible*
eluent 57.17 *analysis*
elusion 638.1 *escape*
elusive 102.8 *unreal*, 474.8 *cunning*, 523.4 *difficult*, 591.18 *avoiding*, 638.8 *escaping*
elusively 474.15 *hypocritically*, 591.22 *evasively*
elusiveness 591.14 *evasion*, 671.4 *defensiveness*
elution 57.17 *analysis*
elutriate 134.10, 621.15 *purify*
elver 80.3 *young fish*
Elyot 48 *Writers*
Elysia 714.4 *promised land*
Elysian 8.14 *heavenly*, 405.6 *pleasant*, 762.5 *delightful*, 763.1 *pleasant*
Elysian fields 397.14 *the spiritual world*, 405.5 *idealized pleasure*
Elysian Fields 714.4 *promised land*
Elysium 368.1 *nonmaterial world*, 405.5 *idealized pleasure*
Elytis 48 *Poets*
Elzevir edition 260.2 *little thing*
em 75 *General Units*
Ema 8 *Deities*
emaciate 236.7 *remove power from*, 262.5 *make smaller*, 262.6 *become smaller*, 607.1 *waste*
emaciated 274, 238.10 *ill*, 262.7 *smaller*, 445.8 *drained of colour*, 609.3 *underfed*, 624.21 *unhealthy*
emaciating 262.8 *contracting*
emaciation 274, 262.1 *contraction*, 607.3 *waste*
email 534.8 *data transmission*
emanate 155.25 *result*, 343.13 *radiate*, 347.10 *emerge*, 347.12 *leak*, 352.7 *secrete*, 416.8 *have odour*, 526.5 *be visible*
emanate from 227.7 *follow from*
emanating 347.15 *outgoing*
emanation 11.10 *psychic phenomenon*, 343.3 *radiation*, 347.2 *outflow*, 352.1 *secretion*, 353.1 *excretion*, 416.1 *odour*, 416.4

reputation, 457.4 *something that appears*
emanational 352.4 *secretory*
emanative 347.15 *outgoing*, 352.4 *secretory*, 416.5 *odorous*
emanatory 352.4 *secretory*
emancipate 639.1 *deliver*, 698.15 *set free*, 700.4 *liberate*, 767.10 *save*
emancipated 638.8 *escaping*, 698.9 *free*, 700.7 *liberated*
emancipation 639.2 *deliverance*, 698.1 *freedom*, 700.1 *liberation*, 767.2 *aid*
emancipation of the dissonance 434.4 *atonality*
Emancipation Proclamation 698.1 *freedom*, 700.1 *liberation*
emancipator 639.3 *deliverer*, 700.3 *liberator*
emanent 347.15 *outgoing*
emarginate 380.4 *toothed*
emasculate 131.4 *take off*, 236.9 *make impotent*, 247.8 *make infertile*, 614.8 *make useless*
emasculated 236.13 *unsexed*
emasculation 131.1 *subtraction*
embalm 397.17, 399.8 *bury*, 418.6 *perfume*, 637.5 *preserve*
embalmed 397.22 *post-mortem*, 399.10 *buried*, 637.7 *preserved*
embalmed body 397.11 *dead person*
embalmer 397.9 *person dealing with the dead*, 399.3 *funeral director*, 637.4 *preservationist*
embalming 397.8 *after death*, 399.1 *burial*, 637.1 *preservation*
embalmment 399.1 *burial*
embank 284.11 *support*
embankment 63.19 *structure*, 63.23 *dam*, 72.2 *track*, 96.2 *channel*, 161.26 *mass*, 284.2 *supporting part*, 327.10 *railway*, 632.4 *safety device*, 661.3 *barrier*, 671.8 *military defences*, 726.4 *wall*
embargo 13.6 *economic factors*, 147.1 *exclusion*, 147.7 *exclude*, 302.2 *limiting factor*, 302.7 *limit*, 325.1 *motionlessness*, 325.9 *make motionless*, 661.2 *obstacle*, 661.9 *block*, 692.1, 692.9 *command*, 699.2 *economic restraint*, 709.1, 709.3 *veto*, 711.2, 711.6 *dissent*, 747.2 *stoppage*
embargoed 147.11 *excluded*, 692.14 *commanding*, 699.13 *restraining*, 709.5 *vetoed*, 711.9 *dissenting*
embark 345.5 *set out*, 346.9 *enter*
embarkation 156.6 *inauguration*, 345.8 *start*
embarkment 345.8 *start*
embark on 156.18 *make a beginning*, 597.1 *undertake*
embark upon office 195.11 *follow in office*
embarrass 491.20 *make uncertain*, 616.5 *be inconvenient*, 659.23 *cause difficulties*, 661.11 *be inhibited*, 764.10 *displease*, 806.17 *humiliate*
embarrassed 366.15 *agitated*, 491.3 *confused*, 659.16 *troubled*, 661.15 *inhibitive*, 699.14 *self-restrained*, 806.3 *humbled*, 810.11 *shy*
embarrassing 661.15 *inhibitive*, 699.14 *self-restrained*, 806.6, 850.16 *humiliating*
embarrassingly 491.24 *confusingly*, 661.18 *inhibitively*, 699.17 *with self-restraint*
embarrassing position 659.7 *awkward situation*
embarrassing situation 659.7 *awkward situation*, 785.2 *disliked thing*, 822.7 *hated thing*
embarrassment 366.1 *agitation*, 491.12 *confusion*, 661.5 *inhibition*, 699.3 *self-restraint*, 806.9 *humiliation*, 810.4 *shyness*, 850.8 *indignity*, 866.2 *signs of guilt*

embarrassment of riches 246.1 *fertility*
embassy 256.4 *official residence*, 703.4 *council*, 706.2 *representative body*
embattled 676.15 *warring*
Embden 68 *Breeds of Fowl*
Embden–Meyerhof pathway 58.24 *respiration*
embed 354.5 *inset*
embedded 354.12 *inserted*
embedment 354.8 *insertion*
embellish 102.16 *delude*, 130.6 *add*, 540.24 *mask*, 541.7 *exaggerate*, 557.5 *ornament*, 627.1 *improve*, 792.10 *decorate*
embellished 540.35 *disguised*, 541.12 *exaggerated*, 557.4 *ornate*, 791.14 *beautified*, 792.8 *decorated*
embellishment 540.12 *facade*, 541.1 *exaggeration*, 557.1 *ornament*, 627.5 *improvement*, 792.1 *adornment*
embers 408.6, 439.8 *fire*
embezzle 601.1 *misuse*, 734.10 *take away*, 736.16 *act dishonest*, 747.7 *not pay*, 858.10 *be criminal*
embezzlement 601.2 *misuse*, 734.3 *taking away*, 736.7 *dishonesty*, 747.1 *nonpayment*, 858.3 *criminality*
embezzler 734.6 *taker*, 736.11 *dishonest person*, 747.6 *nonpayer*, 858.4 *dishonourable person*
embezzling 858.7 *criminal*
Embioptera 82 *Orders of Insects*
embiopteran 82.10 *insectan*
embitter 415.9 *disgust*, 628.3 *make worse*, 820.13 *antagonize*, 822.16 *cause hate*, 830.12 *make irritable*
embittered 820.6 *hostile*, 828.15 *resentful*
embitter with disappointment 515.7 *thwart*
emblazon 444.15 *colour*, 544.10 *identify*, 792.10 *decorate*, 811.28 *flourish*
emblazoned 544.13 *heraldic*
emblem 11.6 *talisman*, 299.1 *outline*, 543.1 *sign*, 544.3 *means of identification*
emblematic 299.6 *outlined*, 544.13 *heraldic*, 547.13 *representational*, 560.13 *representing*
emblematically 544.14 *identifiably*, 547.14 *representationally*
embodied 140.7 *combined*, 293.39 *inclusive*, 367.7 *material*, 457.7 *appearing*
embodiment 8.8 *divine manifestation*, 103.3 *quintessence*, 140.1 *combination*, 146.1 *inclusion*, 257.1 *contents*, 293.19 *inclusion*, 367.2 *materialization*, 457.1 *appearance*, 547.1 *representation*
embody 103, 257, 140.5 *combine*, 146.4 *include*, 148.11 *consist of*, 293.32 *include*, 367.8 *be material*, 547.9 *represent*
embodying 148.9 *composing*, 257.10 *containing*
embolden 778.17 *give courage*
embolectomy 60 *Surgical Operations*
embolism 354.8 *insertion*, 624.10 *cardiovascular disease*
embolus 323.2 *stopper*, 371.4 *solid body*
embosom 821.27 *kiss*
emboss 50.22 *engrave*, 375.12 *make rough*, 544.10 *identify*, 792.10 *decorate*
embossed 43.17 *structured*, 50.28 *sculpted*
embossing 50.13 *relief-carving*
embossment 50.13 *relief-carving*, 767.6 *profile*
embrace 103.12 *embody*, 135.8 *unite*, 135.10 *link*, 138.6 *adhere*, 142.9 *be whole*, 146.4 *include*, 148.11 *consist of*, 264.10 *stay near*, 320.3 *enfoldment*,

320.9 *enfold*, 334.5 *encircle*, 348.9 *welcome*, 580.3 *side with*, 632.2 *protection*, 632.9 *protect*, 726.1 *retention*, 726.6 *retain*, 815.9 *welcome*, 815.11 *be sociable*, 815.14 *welcome*, 817.5 *sign of courtesy*, 817.12 *greet*, 819.4 *act of friendship*, 819.15 *be hospitable*, 821.14 *communication of love*, 821.24 *be in love*, 821.27 *kiss*, 826.1 *endearment*, 826.7 *show endearment for*
embracing 821.14 *communication of love*
embrasure 671.11 *fortification*
embrocate 386.14, 395.18 *anoint*
embrocation 62.7, 386.5 *ointment*, 395.6 *ointment*, 630.9 *balm*
embroider 102.16 *delude*, 309.12 *distort the truth*, 474.11 *practise sophistry*, 540.24 *mask*, 541.7 *exaggerate*, 557.5 *ornament*, 792.10 *decorate*
embroidered 456.6 *variegated*, 540.35 *disguised*, 541.12 *exaggerated*, 791.14 *beautified*, 792.8 *decorated*
embroiderer 792.7 *decorator*
embroidery 42 *Hobbies and Pastimes*, 50.1 *art*, 540.12 *facade*, 541.1 *exaggeration*, 557.1 *ornament*, 792.2 *pattern*
embroilment 366.3 *turbulence*
embrown 449.7 *brown*
embryo 59.15 *developmental biology*, 83.9 *seed*, 145.3 *incomplete thing*, 156.3 *source*, 226.3 *rudiment*, 245.7 *obstetrics*
embryogenesis 59.15 *developmental biology*
embryogeny 59.15 *developmental biology*
embryological 59.20 *biological*, 76.16 *zoological*
embryologically 59.29 *biologically*
embryologist 59.19 *life scientist*, 60.13 *medical specialist*, 76.11 *zoologist*
embryology 59.1 *life science*, 59.15 *developmental biology*, 60.3 *medical specialty*, 76.9 *animal science*
embryonic 156, 59.26 *developmental*, 201.12 *immature*, 226.13 *causal*, 260.7 *little*, 595.5 *immature*
embryonically 145.6 *incompletely*, 595.16 *immaturely*
embryotomy 60 *Surgical Operations*
embus 345.5 *set out*
emcee 51.25 *producer*, 534.29 *broadcaster*, 653.2 *direct*
emend 524.8 *interpret*, 627.3 *rectify*, 629.1 *repair*
emendation 216.1 *change*, 524.1 *interpretation*, 627.6 *rectification*, 629.8 *repair*
emendator 524.6 *interpreter*, 629.12 *repairer*
emended 216.12 *changed*, 524.15 *interpreted*
emender 524.6 *interpreter*, 627.13 *reviser*
emerald 54 *Gemstones*, 453.1 *green*, 453.11 *green thing*
emerge 156, 347, 227.7 *follow from*, 344.4 *land*, 345.5 *set out*, 435.19 *be visible*, 457.12 *become visible*, 530.9 *be disclosed*, 638.7 *leak*
emergence 156.2 *creation*, 344.10 *arrival*, 347.1 *exit*, 457.1 *appearance*
emergency 106.4 *difficult circumstances*, 191.1 *immediacy*, 210.3 *critical time*, 593.3 *needfulness*, 633.5 *danger*, 659.6 *critical situation*, 687.1 *adversity*
emergency aid 767.4 *charity*
emergency buzzer 636.2 *danger signal*
emergency council 654.4 *adviser*
emergency exit 347.6 *way out*, 638.2 *means of escape*

emergency food supply 350.7 *food*
emergency funds 602.5 *reserves*
emergency light 71 Motor Vehicle Parts
emergency part 632.4 *safety device*
emergency plan 516.4 *prudence*, 517.3 *plan*, 592.2 *policy*
emergency procedure 592.2 *policy*
emergency rations 350.7 *food*, 606.1 *provision*
emergency reserves 605.1 *store*
emergent 156.32 *embryonic*, 227.10 *caused*, 347.15 *outgoing*, 457.7 *appearing*
emerging 344.18 *arriving*, 347.1 *exit*, 347.15 *outgoing*
emeritus 200.20, 202.13 *former*, 705.7 *resigning*, 800.2 *person of repute*, 800.3 *reputable*
emersion 347.1 *exit*
Emerson 48 Poets
emery 54 Minerals, 376.11 *smooth*, 380.12 *sharpener*
emery board 375.7 *rough thing*, 376.9 *smoother*, 380.12 *sharpener*, 384.12 *abrasive*, 385.7 *eraser*
emery paper 375.7 *rough thing*, 376.9 *smoother*, 380.12 *sharpener*, 384.12 *abrasive*, 385.7 *eraser*
emery wheel 375.7 *rough thing*
emesis 349.23 *vomiting*
emetic 62.4 *drug type*, 62.17 *stimulating*, 134.4 *purgative*, 349.28 *propellant*, 349.29 *expulsive*, 630.6 *purgative*, 630.17 *remedial*
emetically 349.32 *expulsively*
emetine 62 Medication
emetocathartic 349.29 *expulsive*
emetophobia 777 Phobias by Name
emigrant 104.7 *new arrival*, 149.8 *exile*, 347.8 *outgoer*
emigrate 347, 104.14 *be foreign*, 149.16 *migrate*, 345.3 *quit*
emigration 347, 162.7 *sprawl*, 345.7 *departure*
emigratory 345.13 *outgoing*
émigré 104.7 *new arrival*
eminence 126.1 *superiority*, 275.1 *height*, 318.1 *prominence*, 361.8 *height*, 611.1 *importance*, 617.6 *worth*, 800.1 *estimation*
eminent 318, 126.15 *excellent*, 275.11, 361.12 *exalted*, 611.5 *important*, 611.6 *notable*, 617.1 *worthy*, 800.3 *reputable*
eminent domain 688.1 *authority*
eminently 318, 126.16 *superiorly*, 611.9 *importantly*
emissary 703.5 *commissioner*, 706.1 *delegate*, 707.3 *agent*
emission 56, 349, 347.2 *outflow*, 352.1 *secretion*, 353.1 *excretion*, 638.4 *leak*
emission nebula 53.8 *interstellar medium*
emission spectrum 56.68 *emission*
emissive 349.29 *expulsive*, 352.4 *secretory*
emissivity 349.25 *emission*
emit 53.37 *observe*, 347.12 *leak*, 349.14 *let out*, 352.7 *secrete*, 353.15 *excrete*, 388.27 *give off*, 727.9 *dispose of*
emit rays 349.14 *let out*
emitter 64.19 *transistor*, 349.28 *propellant*
emitter electrode 64.19 *transistor*
emitting 349.29 *expulsive*
Emmanuel 8.4 *God the Son*
emmenagogic 349.29 *expulsive*
Emmental 45 Cheeses
emmer 87 Grasses
emmet 82.4 *social insect*
Emmy 878.2 *prize*
emollient 62.7 *ointment*, 62.16 *soothing*, 242.8 *moderating*, 386.5 *ointment*, 386.9 *lubricant*, 395.6 *ointment*, 395.13 *lubricant*, 630.9 *balm*, 630.17 *re-*

medial, 677.6 *pacificatory*, 763.3 *comfortable*
emolument 721.5 *profit*, 746.3 *pay*, 749.3 *income*, 878.4 *reward for service*
emotion 759, 233 *influence*, 403.1 *sensation*, 821.3 *lovingness*
emotional 61.36 *psychologically disturbed*, 233.12 *appealing*, 475.10 *demonstrative*, 583.2 *spontaneous*, 759.12, 760.1 *sensitive*, 821.20 *amorous*
emotional instability 759.7 *emotionalism*
emotionalism 759, 475.2 *demonstrativeness*
emotionalist 475.7 *demonstrator*
emotionalistic 475.10 *demonstrative*
emotionality 475.2 *demonstrativeness*, 759.7 *emotionalism*
emotionalize 475.18 *appear*
emotionally 759, 233.14 *influentially*, 403.14 *sensationally*, 475.21 *demonstratively*, 760.13 *oversensitively*, 821.30 *lovingly*
emotionally disturbed person 61.8 *disordered personality*
emotional person 759.9 *feeling person*
emotional strain 61.12 *stress*
emotive 759, 403.9 *exciting*
emotiveness 759.7 *emotionalism*
emotivism 4.7 *school of thought*
emotivist 4.11 *follower of a doctrine*, 4.14 *of a philosophy*
empanada 45.50 *Central American dish*
empanel 545.13 *record*, 545.15 *register*
empanel a jury 16.71 *try a case*
empanelling a jury 16.7 *legal trial*
empanelment 545.8 *registration*
empathetic 284.9 *supportive*, 667.10 *agreeing*, 724.5 *jointly possessing*, 759.12, 760.1 *sensitive*, 784.6 *liking*, 831.6 *benevolent*
empathetically 667.14 *agreeably*, 724.6 *in common*, 784.11 *admiringly*
empathize 116.21 *be in accord*, 519.16 *have insight*, 667.6 *agree with*, 759.18 *feel for*, 760.11 *be sensitive*, 831.8 *be benevolent*, 835.8 *pity*
empathize with 835.8 *pity*
empathizing 116.10 *in accord*
empathizer 724.5 *participant*
empathy 116.1 *accord*, 284.6 *moral support*, 519.3 *insight*, 667.1 *agreement*, 724.2 *participation*, 759.5 *good feeling*, 760.5 *sensitivity*, 784.1 *liking*, 835.1 *pity*
Empedoclean 4.11 *follower of a doctrine*, 4.14 *of a philosophy*
Empedocles 4 Philosophers
empennage 73 Aircraft Parts
emperor 126.5 *superior*, 688.10 *person of authority*, 696.2 *sovereign*
emperor moth 82 Insects
emperor penguin 78 Birds
empery 12.3 *governance*
emphasis 535, 554, 48.9 *metre*, 235.1 *power*, 237.3 *intensity*, 526.10 *manifestation*, 564.3 *mode of speech*, 611.1 *importance*
Emphasis 554
emphasize 535, 554, 237.8 *strengthen*, 522.5 *simplify*, 526.1 *display*, 526.3 *reveal*, 532.16 *publicize*, 543.10 *signify*, 543.13 *punctuate*, 611.8 *make important*, 674.11 *contend*, 695.6 *compel*
emphasized 535, 554, 526.14 *manifest*
emphatic 554, 444.11 *colourful*, 526.15 *open*, 535.14 *assertive*, 668.7 *defiant*
emphatically 554, 535.23 *affirmatively*, 668.9 *defiantly*
emphatically deny 536.8 *rebut*

emphatic denial 536.3 *rebuttal*
emphysema 624.9 *respiratory disease*
empiracle formula 57.13 *structure*
empire 12.3 *governance*, 12.5 *political organization*, 91.3 *dominion*, 249.4 *territorial division*, 688.8 *governmental organization*
Empire 43 Architectural Styles, 47.7 *furniture style*
Empire bed 47.6 *bed*
empire building 357.10 *expansionism*
Empire-line 295.31 *styled*
Empire State Building 43 Noted Buildings, 259.9 *big thing*, 275.6 *tall thing*
empirical 52.69 *theoretic*, 99.13 *real*, 367.7 *material*, 479.8 *experimental*, 483.8 *evidential*
empirically 479.14 *experimentally*
empirical probability 52.62 *probability*, 488.5 *probability theory*
empirical psychology 61.1 *psychology*
empirical sociologist 2.11 *sociologist*
empirical world 367.1 *material world*
empiricism 4.7 *school of thought*, 367.2 *materialization*, 479.3 *experimentation*
empiricist 4.11 *follower of a doctrine*, 4.14 *of a philosophy*, 479.5 *experimenter*
emplace 250.9 *locate*
emplaced 250.6 *located*
emplacement 250.4 *placing*, 671.11 *fortification*
emplane 345.5 *set out*
emplanement 345.8 *start*
employ 2.15 *socialize*, 230.9 *take action*, 599.1 *use*, 613.11 *find useful*, 644.7 *work for*, 701.1 *subjection*, 701.6 *subject*, 703.7 *engage*, 734.7 *take*
employability 613.6 *usability*
employable 15.8 *industrial*, 232.6 *instrumental*, 599.10, 613.2 *usable*, 701.9 *subject*, 703.10 *engaged*
employed 15.8 *industrial*, 251.6 *situated*, 599.9 *used*, 642.19 *busy*, 644.10 *working*, 701.9 *subject*, 703.10 *engaged*
employee 15, 15.8 *industrial*, 230.5 *operator*, 646.1 *worker*, 697.1 *servant*, 697.5 *office assistant*, 701.3 *subordinate*
employee claim 15.4 *industrial dispute*
employee demands 15.1 *industrial relations*
employee dinner 350.13 *feast*
employee jurisdiction 15.1 *industrial relations*
employee practices 15.1 *industrial relations*
employee relations 15.1 *industrial relations*
employee rights 15.1 *industrial relations*
employees 646.4 *personnel*, 662.11 *helper*
employer 15, 13.9 *economist*, 15.8 *industrial*, 646.3 *agent*, 653.13 *director*, 696.5 *company leader*
employer-employee relations 15.1 *industrial relations*
employer jurisdiction 15.1 *industrial relations*
employer rights 15.1 *industrial relations*
employers 653.6 *governing body*
employer's association 15.1 *industrial relations*
employer's liability 15.2 *industrial relations*
employers' organization 15.1 *industrial relations*
employing 15.8 *industrial*
employment 251, 13.6 *economic factors*, 15.8 *industrial*, 232.1 *instrumentality*, 599.6 *use*, 613.5 *usefulness*, 640.1 *action*, 644.3

job, 701.1 *subjection*, 703.2 *engagement*, 734.1 *taking*
employment contract 15.1 *industrial relations*, 715.2 *purchase contract*
employment laws 15.1 *industrial relations*
employment manager 15.6 *employer*
employment relationships 15.1 *industrial relations*
employment rules 15.1 *industrial relations*
employment standards 15.2 *industrial negotiations*
employment status 2.7 *social stratification*
employment training 6.2 *educational system*
employ oneself 640.4 *act*
employ tactics 652.11 *conduct oneself*
emporium 740
empower 235.11 *give power*, 485.13 *qualify*, 486.7 *make possible*, 688.21 *grant authority*, 703.6 *commission*, 706.4 *delegate*, 707.6 *deputize*, 708.3 *permit*, 845.16 *entitle*
empowered 235.13 *powerful*, 485.10 *authorized*, 688.12 *authoritative*, 703.9 *commissioned*
empowerment 485.4 *permission*, 688.3 *acquisition of power*, 703.1 *commission*
empress 688.10 *person of authority*, 696.2 *sovereign*
emprise 597.2 *undertaking*
Empson 48 Poets
emptily 254.20 *absently*, 372.7 *sparsely*, 540.38 *hypocritically*, 683.12 *unsuccessfully*
emptiness 100, 254, 236.1 *powerlessness*, 248.2 *empty space*, 372.3 *sparseness*, 521.1 *lack of meaning*, 536.5 *nonexistence*, 540.3 *hypocrisy*, 555.2 *lack of emphasis*, 612.5 *unimportance*
emptiness of mind 512.2 *blankness*
emptional 738.13 *bought*
emptor 738.12 *purchaser*
empty 100.9 *nonexistent*, 131.3 *subtract*, 247.3 *birth control*, 248.21 *space*, 254.13 *vacant*, 254.14 *unoccupied*, 278.2 *superficial*, 349.11 *void*, 355.14 *suck*, 370.10 *lighten*, 372.1 *sparse*, 372.6 *make sparse*, 474.7 *sophistic*, 521.10 *meaningless*, 536.14 *nonexistent*, 540.27 *hypocritical*, 553.3 *diffuse*, 555.1 *unemphatic*, 607.1 *waste*, 609.2 *unprovided*, 643.2 *not working*, 683.10 *failed*, 782.10 *hungry*, 871.6 *fasting*
empty bottle 614.6 *refuse*
empty chatter 521.5 *empty talk*
empty gesture 521.3 *meaningless thing*, 539.3, 540.3 *hypocrisy*
empty gossip 538.5 *half-truth*
empty-handed 609.2 *unprovided*
empty head 462.1 *lack of thought*, 809.7 *vain person*
empty-headed 460.6 *unintelligent*, 462.8 *thoughtless*, 502.6 *ignorant*, 508.5 *foolish*, 512.9 *blank*
empty-headedly 460.11 *unintelligently*
empty-headedness 460.2 *unintelligence*, 462.1 *lack of thought*, 502.1 *ignorance*, 508.1 *folly*, 512.2 *blankness*
emptying 349.11 *removal*, 355.4 *sucking*
empty larder 743.6 *insolvency*
empty one's pocket 746.6 *pay*, 748.1 *expend*
empty out 349.11 *void*
empty phrase 5.5 *nonstandard language*
empty pride 809.1 *vanity*
empty promises 102.4 *theorization*
empty purse 743.6 *insolvency*

empty set 52.21 *set*
empty shell 132.1 *remainder,* 254.3 *emptiness*
empty sound 521.1 *lack of meaning*
empty space 248, 254.3 *emptiness*
empty stomach 782.3 *appetite*
empty talk 521, 5.5 *nonstandard language,* 102.4 *theorization,* 506.1 *nonsense,* 521.4 *senseless talk,* 553.1 *diffuseness,* 557.2 *affectation,* 565.3 *talk*
empty the glass 351.13 *drink*
empty threats 236.2 *futile effort*
empty words 5.5 *nonstandard language,* 474.1 *sophistry,* 521.1 *lack of meaning,* 538.8 *pretence*
empurple 455
empyreal 8.14 *heavenly*
empyrean 8.11 *heaven,* 8.14 *heavenly,* 53.3 *universe*
em rule 543.7 *punctuation*
Ems 96 *Rivers*
em space 265.1 *interval*
emu 78 Birds, 78.2 *flightless bird*
e.m.u. 75.2 *unit system*
emulate 118, 65.19 *abort,* 114.12, 118.9 *imitate,* 167.8 *comply,* 663.16 *confront,* 674.11 *contend*
emulating 118.12 *imitative*
emulation 118.1 *imitation,* 167.1 *conformity,* 663.3 *conflict,* 674.1 *contention*
emulative 841.4 *jealous*
emulator 65.17 *computing term,* 663.10 *competitor,* 674.10 *contender*
emulous 841.4 *jealous*
emulously 841.9 *jealousy*
emulsification 393.6 *thickening*
emulsifier 350.11 *food content,* 393.11 *thickener*
emulsify 57.25 *solidify,* 387.22 *make fluid,* 393.25, 394.11 *thicken*
emulsion 66, 394, 57.3 *phase,* 387.10 *solution,* 393.1 *semiliquid*
emulsion paint 444.5 *paint*
emulsive 393.16 *semiliquid,* 394.8 *viscous*
emulsoid 57.32 *solid,* 393.1 *semiliquid*
emu wren 78 Birds
en 75 General Units
enable 116.30 *grant,* 235.11 *give power,* 485.13 *qualify,* 486.7 *make possible,* 602.6 *find means,* 660.16 *make easy,* 708.3 *permit,* 845.16 *entitle*
enabled 116.19 *granted,* 485.10 *authorized*
enablement 485.4 *permission*
enabler 662.11 *helper*
enact 16.68 *legislate,* 51.32 *act,* 526.1 *display,* 547.10, 640.4 *act,* 652.14 *behave towards,* 684.4 *complete,* 692.9 *command*
enacted 16.46 *legislated,* 51.37 *dramatic,* 692.14 *commanding*
enacting 16.31 *legislation,* 640.5 *acting*
enactment 16.31 *legislation,* 51.20 *acting,* 166.1 *rule,* 526.9 *production,* 547.3 *acting,* 640.1 *action,* 654.3 *precept,* 692.1 *command*
enamel 44.11 *make ceramics,* 293.3 *coating,* 293.24 *coat,* 376.10 *polish,* 444.4 *pigment,* 444.15 *colour,* 456.11 *variegate*
enamel kiln 44.6 *ceramic workshop*
enamelled 44.10 *ceramic,* 376.4 *polished,* 792.8 *decorated*
enameller 50.16 *artist*
enamelling 42 Hobbies and Pastimes, 44.10 *ceramic,* 50.1 *art*
enamellist 44.7 *potter*
enamelware 44.1 *ceramics*
enamelwork 456.5 *variegated thing*
enamour 821.28 *win the love of*
enamoured 821

enamoured of 821.18 *in love*
enantiomorphic 308.4 *symmetrical*
enantiomorphic figure 52.48 *transformation*
encaenia 10.16 *religious festival*
encamp 256.18 *take up residence*
encapsulate 146.4 *include,* 270.10 *shorten,* 354.5 *inset,* 562.8 *summarize*
encapsulated 270.8 *shortened*
encapsulation 146.1 *inclusion,* 270.2 *shortening*
encase 293.25 *wrap,* 354.5 *inset*
encased 293.37 *protected*
encash 13.10 *trade with,* 739.1 *sell,* 741.26 *bank*
encaustic 44.10 *ceramic,* 50.8 *painting*
encaustically 44.12 *ornamentally*
encaustic tile 44.8 *ceramic object*
enceinte 245.16 *reproductive*
encephalia 624.6 *infection*
encephalitis 624.6 *infection*
encephalitis lethargica 624.6 *infection,* 624.7 *tropical disease*
encephalopathy 510.3 *mental deterioration*
enchant 11.21 *bewitch,* 762.8 *cause joy,* 786.10 *be wonderful,* 821.28 *win the love of*
enchanted 11.19 *bewitched,* 220.13 *converted,* 762.4 *happy,* 821.19 *enamoured*
enchanter 11.4 *witch,* 340.6 *charmer*
enchanter's nightshade 84 Flowers and Flowering Plants
enchanting 11.15 *witchlike,* 762.5 *delightful,* 789.6 *personable,* 821.22 *lovable*
enchantingly 340.14 *attractively,* 821.30 *lovingly*
enchantment 11.3 *witchcraft,* 220.1 *conversion,* 762.1 *happiness,* 821.2 *romantic love,* 821.4 *lovability*
enchantress 11.4 *witch,* 340.6 *charmer*
enchilada 45.50 Central American dish
encipher 523.8 *make unintelligible,* 529.14 *make mysterious*
encircle 334, 52.97 *align,* 146.4 *include,* 297.7 *surround,* 313.6 *circle,* 363.7 *ring,* 670.4 *besiege*
encircled 297.5 *surrounded*
encirclement 297, 146.1 *inclusion,* 301.1 *enclosure ,* 670.14 *siege*
Encke 53 Comets
enclave 92.1 *administrative area,* 301.2 *enclosed place,* 816.4 *place of confinement*
enclitic 5.17 *word,* 5.42 *worded*
enclose 301, 323, 146.4 *include,* 147.7 *exclude,* 248.20 *extend,* 257.6 *contain,* 258.21 *put in a container,* 293.25 *wrap,* 297.7 *surround,* 320.9 *enfold,* 632.9 *protect,* 670.4 *besiege,* 671.18 *fence,* 726.7 *detain*
enclosed 301, 323, 258.20 *containing,* 290.7 *interior,* 293.37 *protected,* 297.5 *surrounded*
enclosed land 681.8 *farmland*
enclosed place 301, 323.4 *closed place*
enclosed places 777 Phobias by Topic
enclosed space 52.35 *space*
enclosement 293.1 *covering*
enclosing 258.20 *containing,* 301.1 *enclosure ,* 726.2 *detention*
enclosing thing 301
enclosure 301, 68.11 *farmland,* 146.1 *inclusion,* 146.2 *thing included,* 147.3 *exclusion zone,* 249.12 *plot,* 301.2 *enclosed place,* 320.3 *enfoldment,* 323.4 *closed place,* 634.2 *shelter,* 676.8 *warfare*
Enclosure 301
encode 11.20 *occult,* 523.8 *make unintelligible,* 524.12 *translate,* 529.14 *make mysterious,* 531.9 *disguise*

encoded 11.14 *occult,* 523.1 *unintelligible,* 524.15 *interpreted*
encoffin 399.8 *bury*
encomiastic 851.18 *approving*
encomium 48.7 *poem,* 564.8 *speech,* 851.4 *compliment*
encompass 103.12 *embody,* 130.6 *add,* 142.9 *be whole,* 146.4 *include,* 148.11 *consist of,* 248.20 *extend,* 293.32 *include,* 297.7 *surround,* 301.6 *wrap,* 313.7 *make circular,* 334.5 *encircle,* 363.7 *ring*
encompassed 297.5 *surrounded*
encompassing 121.7 *gradational,* 293.39 *inclusive*
encompassment 297.2 *encirclement*
encore 51.6 *scene,* 176.19 *twice,* 183.5 *repeat,* 183.24 *again,* 851.5, 851.16 *acclaim,* 851.27 *bravo*
encounter 198.6 *be simultaneous,* 267.2 *meeting,* 267.4 *meet,* 330.2 *collide,* 330.12 *collision,* 344.8 *meet,* 344.14 *meeting,* 496.1 *discover,* 496.6 *discovery,* 674.1 *contention,* 674.6, 674.12 *fight*
encounter aliens 11.24 *experience psychic phenomena*
encounter by chance 589.11 *chance upon*
encounter group 61.3 *psychiatric treatment*
encounter unexpectedly 589.11 *chance upon*
encourage 6.22 *educate,* 226.10 *awaken,* 228.9 *motivate,* 233.8 *influence,* 284.14 *give moral support,* 627.1 *improve,* 654.5, 662.23 *advise,* 769.8 *cheer,* 775.10 *inspire hope,* 778.17 *give courage,* 831.8 *be benevolent*
encouraged 228.12 *motivated,* 586.20 *persuadable*
encouragement 778, 226.1 *cause,* 228.2 *inducement,* 233 *influence,* 284.6 *moral support,* 586.2 *flattery,* 654.1 *advice,* 662.9 *patronage,* 775.4 *comfort*
encouraging 778, 228.11 *motivational,* 233.12 *appealing,* 284.9 *supportive,* 586.19 *persuasive,* 654.7 *advising,* 662.32 *supportive,* 714.14 *auspicious,* 769.2, 775.14 *cheering*
encouragingly 6.25 *educationally,* 228.14, 233.14 *influentially,* 586.21 *persuasively,* 714.17 *auspiciously,* 775.15 *hopefully*
Encratism 825.3 *monasticism,* 876.3 *moral purity*
Encratite 825.4 *celibate person,* 825.8 *monastic,* 876.5 *pure person*
Encratites 7 Christian Movements
encroach 346.10 *invade,* 357.5 *transgress,* 670.4 *besiege,* 846.14 *arrogate*
encroaching 16.60 *offending,* 357.11 *overrun*
encroachment 16.38 *lawbreaking,* 19.13 *penalty,* 336.15 *improvement,* 346.3 *inroad,* 357.8 *transgression,* 670.14 *siege,* 846.3 *arrogation*
encrust 289.11 *be exterior,* 293.28 *face*
encrustation 293.8 *wall covering,* 622.1 *dirtiness*
encrusted 375.2 *coarse,* 622.7 *dirty*
encumber 369.14 *make heavy,* 661.8 *hinder,* 661.12 *burden*
encumbered 661.13 *hindering,* 745.9 *in debt*
encumbering 661.13 *hindering*
encumbrance 130.1 *addition,* 369.8 *weighing down,* 661.1 *hindrance,* 661.6 *burden,* 745.1 *debt*
encyclical 532.1 *publication,* 692.1 *command,* 692.14 *commanding*
encyclopedia 6.14 *school book,*

171.3 *dictionary,* 528.5 *reference book,* 605.5 *collection*
encyclopedic 146.7 *including,* 164.15 *general,* 501.8 *knowledgeable*
encyclopedically 171.13 *inventorially*
Encyclopédistes 48 Literary Groups and Movements
end 157, 157, 25.1 *green bowling,* 100.13 *cease to exist,* 100.14 *cause not to exist,* 142.10 *complete,* 144.3 *completion,* 144.4 *complete,* 144.5 *be complete,* 155.9 *conclusion,* 155.20 *rear,* 157.25 *hindmost,* 160.2 *cessation,* 160.12 *discontinue,* 195.9 *sequel,* 200.14 *pass,* 218.2 *stop,* 218.6 *cease,* 218.8 *cause to cease,* 227.1 *effect,* 244.4 *ruin,* 244.8 *destroy,* 244.13 *be destroyed,* 304.2 *rear end,* 304.4 *rear,* 323.1 *closure,* 323.9 *close down,* 344.15 *destination,* 360.4 *fall,* 397.1 *death,* 458.1 *disappear,* 458.4 *disappearance,* 471.4 *purpose,* 520.5 *point,* 588.6 *objective,* 684.2 *conclusion,* 684.5 *conclude*
End 157
end age discrimination 700.6 *treat equally*
end an affair 598.2 *withdraw*
endanger 633
endangered 633
endangered species 76.1 *animals,* 637.3 *preserved thing*
endangerment 633.5 *danger*
end around 19.9 *play*
endarterectomy 60 Surgical Operations
endboards 31.3 *ice hockey*
endearing 826, 784.5 *likable,* 821.22 *lovable*
endearingly 826, 784.10 *with great liking,* 821.30 *lovingly*
endearing qualities 821.4 *lovability*
endearment 826, 821.4 *lovability*
Endearment 826
endearments 521.5 *empty talk*
endear oneself 821.28 *win the love of*
endeavour 235.1 *power,* 235.10 *be powerful,* 243.1 *production,* 479.1 *experiment,* 479.13 *invent,* 596.2 *try hard,* 596.5 *attempt,* 597.1 *undertake,* 597.2 *undertaking,* 640.1 *action,* 644.4 *exertion,* 644.8 *exert oneself*
ended 157, 3.18 *in the past,* 100.11 *no more,* 144.7 *complete,* 160.9 *discontinued,* 200.18 *over,* 218.10 *finished,* 323.14 *closed down,* 684.8 *concluded*
endemic 164.17 *widespread,* 290.7 *interior,* 626.6 *contagious*
endemic disease 624.4 *disease*
ender 157
Enders 52 Scientists
end game 42.4 *chess terms*
end-grain wood 47.12 *wood*
end hostilities 675.5 *be at peace*
end in 227.5 *show an effect*
end in a point 380.14 *be sharp*
end in futility 683.8 *miscarry*
ending 157, 157, 130.3 *additional item,* 144.3 *completion,* 157.1 *end,* 218.2 *stop,* 684.2 *conclusion,* 684.8 *concluded*
end in smoke 358.3 *fall through*
end in view 588.6 *objective*
end it all 157.9 *expire*
endive 45 Vegetables
endless 159.11 *continuous,* 181.8 *numberless,* 184.1 *infinite,* 184.3 *eternal,* 219.6 *protracted,* 269.1 *long,* 608.2 *plentiful*
endless band 159.6 *continuum*
endlessly 112.13 *uniformly,* 159.19 *continuously,* 184.10 *infinitely,* 186.8 *ever,* 219.7 *continually,* 269.11 *lengthily,* 608.9 *enough*

endlessness 159.5 *continuity*, 184.4 *infinity*, 190.1 *eternity*, 269.4 *length*
endless round 159.6 *continuum*
endless supply 608.8 *plenty*
end line 19.4 *stadium*
end matter 155.8 *addition*, 157.10 *ending*, 304.1 *rear*
endmost 157.25 *hindmost*
endocarditis 624.10 *cardiovascular disease*
endocarp 86.3 *fruit structure*
endocrine 59.20 *biological*, 352.5 *of a secretion*
endocrine disease 624.4 *disease*
endocrine gland 352.3 *gland*
endocrinological 59.20 *biological*
endocrinologist 58.2 *biochemist*, 59.19 *life scientist*, 60.13 *medical specialist*
endocrinology 58.1 *biochemistry*, 59.1 *life science*, 60.3 *medical specialty*
endoderm 59.15 *developmental biology*, 290.1 *interior*
endodermal 59.26 *developmental*, 290.7 *interior*
endodermic 290.7 *interior*
endodermis 290.1 *interior*
endodontic 60.23 *dental*
endodontics 60.4 *dentistry*
endodontist 60.14 *dentist*
end of hostilities 675.1 *peace*
end of life 397.1 *death*
end of play 27.1 *cricket match*
end of steel 72.3 *rail*
end of the affair 684.2 *conclusion*
end of the day 157.9 *close*
end of the line 72.8 *railway station*, 157.3 *death*, 157.6 *end point*, 327.10 *railway*, 344.15 *destination*
end of the matter 684.2 *conclusion*
end of the pier 51.14 *theatre*
end of the rainbow 263.3 *distant place*, 519.7 *idealism*, 714.4 *promised land*, 742.5 *wealth*
end of the road 157.9 *close*
end of the world 157.5 *fate*, 244.4 *ruin*
end of time 4.9 *philosophical problem*, 157.5 *fate*
end of war 675.1 *peace*
endogamy 823.3 *types of marriage*
endogenous depression 61.13 *depression*
endomitosis 59.10 *cell division*
endomorph 1.9 *physical type*, 61.7 *personality type*, 306.6 *nature*
endomorphic 1.15 *physical*, 259.16 *fat*, 273.1 *thick*
endomorphism 61.7 *personality type*
endomorphy 1.9 *physical type*, 61.7 *personality type*, 259.5 *fatness*
end one's life 397.16 *meet one's fate*
endoparasite 76.4 *type of animal*
endoparasitic 76.15 *of animals*
endoplasm 59.7 *cell*
endoplasmic 59.23 *cellular*
endoplasmic reticulum 59.8 *cell organ*
ENDOR 58.7 *analysis*
endorse 16.68 *legislate*, 101.12 *establish reality*, 116.28 *consent*, 284.14 *give moral support*, 480.1 *verify*, 483.12 *prove*, 490.21 *make certain*, 499.4 *assent*, 535.19 *confirm*, 544.11 *identify oneself*, 580.3 *side with*, 662.23 *advise*, 667.7 *contract*, 708.3 *permit*, 715.5 *contract*, 718.11 *promise*, 851.12 *accept*
endorse a cheque 741.26 *bank*
endorsed 116.17 *consenting*, 535.13 *supported*, 667.11 *contractual*, 851.23 *approved*
endorsee 730.5 *recipient*
endorsement 71.21 *miscellaneous motoring terms*, 116.7 *consent*, 284.6 *moral support*, 499.2 *yes*, 535.4 *confirmation*,

544.3 *means of identification*, 667.2 *contract*, 708.1 *permission*, 708.2 *permit*, 718.2 *promise*, 851.1 *approval*
endorser 499.3 *assenter*, 535.9 *affirmer*, 667.5 *assenter*, 715.4 *contractor*
endoscope 60.7 *diagnosis*
endoscopy 60.7 *diagnosis*
endoskeleton 382.7 *skeleton*
endosmosis 348.5 *absorption*, 356.3 *passage into*
endosmotic 348.17 *absorbent*
endosperm 83.9 *seed*
endotrophic mycorrhiza 89.5 *fungal association*
endow 116.30 *grant*, 235.11 *give power*, 485.13 *qualify*, 606.5 *provision*, 662.29 *finance*, 725.9 *own property*, 729.5 *give*, 742.15 *make rich*, 755.11 *give*
endowed 235.13 *powerful*, 485.9 *qualified*, 655.7 *gifted*, 725.8 *propertied*, 729.7 *given*
endowing 729.1 *giving*
endowment 116.9 *grant*, 235.2, 485.2 *ability*, 485.4 *permission*, 655.2 *aptitude*, 662.6 *financial assistance*, 721.5 *profit*, 729.1 *giving*
endow with power 235.11 *give power*
endpiece 304.1 *rear*
end play 27.15 *play*
end point 157, 57.18 *gravimetric analysis*
end product 155.5 *consequence*, 684.2 *conclusion*
end-product 243.3 *product*
end racial discrimination 700.6 *treat equally*
end result 157, 155.5 *consequence*, 227.1 *effect*, 684.2 *conclusion*
end rhyme 48.11 *rhyme*
end sexual discrimination 700.6 *treat equally*
ends of the earth 157.7 *limit*, 263.3 *distant place*
end someone's life 398.16 *kill*
end table 47.4 *table*
end to end 159.20 *in a line*, 267.7 *beside*, 269.11 *lengthily*
end-to-end 267.5 *juxtaposed*
end up 227.9 *take effect*, 358.3 *fall through*
end up in 344.2 *reach*
end up in someone's black books 822.16 *cause hate*
endurable 284.10 *supportable*
endurance 33.11 *racing*, 99.6 *continuing existence*, 138.2 *tenacity*, 188.4 *long-lastingness*, 217.1 *permanence*, 219.2 *protraction*, 235.1 *power*, 237.1 *strength*, 378.8 *physical strength*, 575.4 *stamina*, 778.3 *steadfastness*
endurance event 33.1 *motor racing*
endurance racing 33.1 *motor racing*
endure 575, 99.19 *continue to be*, 188.6 *last*, 217.5 *be permanent*, 219.4 *protract*, 284.12 *bear*, 378.10 *be tough*, 396.16 *live*, 574.11 *persist*, 669.6 *resist*, 673.4 *succumb*, 778.16 *take courage*, 839.12 *show mercy*
endure forever 190.5 *be eternal*
endure hardship 687.9 *be in trouble*
endure longer 721.10 *augment*
enduring 4.18 *detached*, 99.12 *lasting*, 138.10 *tenacious*, 188.8 *lasting*, 190.8 *eternal*, 217.7 *permanent*, 219.6 *protracted*, 225.9 *stable*, 378.4 *powerful*, 575.10 *persevering*
enduringly 4.27 *stoically*, 138.12 *tenaciously*, 217.9 *permanently*, 219.7 *continually*, 225.12 *stably*, 378.13 *powerfully*
endways 269.3 *longitudinal*, 269.12 *longitudinally*, 281.11 *vertically*
endwise 281.11 *vertically*

end zone 19.4 *stadium*
enema 134.4 *purgative*, 354.11 *thing inserted*, 389.11 *wash*, 621.2 *cleaning*, 630.6 *purgative*
enemy 635.2 *troublemaker*, 663.11 *opponent*, 785.3 *disliked person*, 820.5 *hostile person*, 822.8 *hated person*
enemy of marriage 825.5 *single person*
energetic 235.15 *full of energy*, 237.11 *strong in spirit*, 239.4 *vigorous*, 241.6 *violent*, 396.13 *lively*, 554.3 *emphatic*, 574.2 *tenacious*, 623.1 *healthy*, 642.18 *active*, 642.20 *industrious*, 644.10 *working*
energetically 235, 237.14 *strongly*, 237.15 *acutely*, 239.6 *with vigour*, 554.7 *emphatically*, 644.12 *laboriously*
energetic person 642.10 *busy person*
energid 59.7 *cell*
energize 128.5 *make bigger*, 228.9 *motivate*, 235.11 *give power*, 237.8 *strengthen*, 239.3 *invigorate*
energized 228.12 *motivated*
energizing 228.11 *motivational*, 586.19 *persuasive*
energy 56, 235, 642, 235.3 *vitality*, 237.2 *healthiness*, 239.1 *vigour*, 241.1 *violence*, 338.12 *propellant*, 396.1 *life*, 554.1 *emphasis*, 574.13 *concentration*, 623.3 *health*, 644.4 *exertion*
energy balance 55.9 *atmospheric process*
energy band 56.44 *semiconductor*
energy charge 61.28 *cathexis*
energy-consuming 607.8 *wasteful*
energy crisis 609.9 *scarcity*
energy depletion 236.1 *powerlessness*
energy gap 56.44 *semiconductor*
energy imparted 56.70 *radioactivity*
Energy Information Administration 235.8 *nuclear power*
energy level 56.65 *atom*
energy-rich bond 58.22 *bioenergetics*
energy-saving 637.6 *preserving*
enervate 236.9 *make impotent*, 238.7 *weaken*, 650.6 *fatigue*, 777.13 *frighten*
enervated 238.11 *weakened*, 650.1 *fatigued*
enervated style 555.2 *lack of emphasis*
enervating 777.10 *frightening*
enervation 238.3 *poor health*, 555.2 *lack of emphasis*, 650.7 *fatigue*
enetophobia 777 Phobias by Name
enfeeble 129.5 *make smaller*, 238.7 *weaken*
enfeebled 238.8 *weak*
enfeeblement 129.1 *decrease*, 238.1 *weakness*
enfeoffment 729.1 *giving*
Enfield rifle 680.10 *historical gun*
enfilade 670.2 *fire*, 670.12 *military attack*
enfold 320, 135.10 *link*, 293.25 *wrap*, 295.32 *dress*, 297.7 *surround*, 301.6 *wrap*, 632.9 *protect*, 821.27 *kiss*
enfolded 297.5 *surrounded*
enfoldment 320, 293.1 *covering*, 297.2 *encirclement*, 821.14 *communication of love*
enforce 695.6 *compel*
enforce a speed limit 699.8 *restrain*
enforce celibacy on oneself 825.9 *be celibate*
enforce civil rights 700.6 *treat equally*
enforced repatriation 252.3 *replacement*
enforcement 695.2 *coercion*
enforcer 699.6 *law-maker*
enforcing 695.9 *compelling*
enfranchise 698.15 *set free*,

700.6 *treat equally*, 845.16 *entitle*
enfranchised 580.16 *elective*, 698.9 *free*
enfranchisement 698.3 *independence*
engage 703, 135.8 *unite*, 135.10 *link*, 208.9 *prepare*, 586.15 *persuade*, 588.8 *resolve*, 597.1 *undertake*, 670.1 *attack*, 674.12 *fight*, 676.14 *battle*, 734.7 *take*, 847.17 *impose a duty*
engaged 703, 107.5 *interrelated*, 135.12 *united*, 211.12, 642.19 *busy*, 676.15 *warring*, 714.12 *promised*, 823.22 *marriageable*, 826.9 *endearing*, 847.11 *duty-bound*
engaged column 43.8 *column*
engaged couple 821.10 *lovers*
engaged in war 676.15 *warring*
engaged man 401.4 *boyfriend*
engaged person 714.6 *someone promised*
engaged to 821.18 *in love*
engaged tone 534.11 *dialling*
engaged woman 402.4 *girlfriend*
engage in 567.12 *address oneself to*, 597.1 *undertake*
engage in a forlorn hope 633.9 *face danger*
engage in conversation 568.9 *converse*
engage in dialectic 4.23 *discuss philosophically*
engage in fisticuffs 26.11 *do a combat sport*, 666.6 *argue*, 674.12 *fight*
engage in war 676.13 *be at war*
engagement 51, 703, 107.2 *interrelatedness*, 588.4 *formulated intention*, 597.2 *undertaking*, 597.3 *contract*, 674.1 *contention*, 674.6 *fight*, 676.9 *battle*, 714.1 *promise*, 715.1 *contract*, 724.2 *participation*, 734.1 *taking*, 815.3 *meeting*, 821.8 *love affair*, 826.2 *courtship*, 847.2 *task*, 847.7 *commitment*
engagement book 171.5 *list of appointments*
engagement diary 171.5 *list of appointments*, 511.4 *reminder*
engagement party 665.7 *social gathering*
engagement ring 826.3 *love token*
engage oneself 847.15 *be liable*
engage with 674.11 *contend*
engaging 763.2 *likable*, 821.22 *lovable*
Engels 4 Philosophers
engender 156.26, 243.10 *produce*, 243.13 *propagate*
engine 63, 53.35 *rocketry*, 56.11 *energy*, 63.5 *dynamic structure*, 72.4 *locomotive*, 148.4 *components*, 603.4 *machine*
engine cycle 63
engine driver 72.9 *railway worker*
engineer 63, 63, 72.9 *railway worker*, 226.10 *awaken*, 243.9 *producer*, 243.10 *produce*, 592.11 *invent*, 603.7 *machinist*, 629.12 *repairer*, 646.2 *artisan*
engineer battalion 17.4 *military organization*
engineering 63, 243.2 *manufacture*, 603.5 *mechanics*
Engineering 63
engineering brick 43.4 *building material*
engineering design 63.1 *engineering*
engineering drawing 63.1 *engineering*
engineering geology 63.1 *engineering*
engine failure 683.4 *unsuccessful thing*
engine lathe 63.9 *machine tool*
engine pod 73 Aircraft Parts
engine power 235.4 *energy*
engine room 74 Parts of a Ship
engine trouble 661.2 *obstacle*
England 91
Engler 52 Scientists

English 5 Languages and Groups of Languages, **43** Architectural Styles, **777** Phobias by Topic, 24.2 billiards play
English as she is spoken 5.3 spoken language, 564.1 faculty of speech
English billiards Sporting Activities, **24**, 24.1 billiards
English bond 63.26 masonry
English bone china 44.1 ceramics
English breakfast 45.44 British dish, 350.12 meal
English Classics 32.7 horseracing
English lakes 94.4 British lakes
English Longwool 68 Breeds of Sheep
Englishman 91.9 England, 255.9 British inhabitant
Englishman's tie 74 Knots
English mountains 95.5 British mountains
English muffin 45.39 loaf
English mustard 413.5 herbs
Englishness 91.9 England
English one-step 46.2 dance
English rose 544.6 national emblem
English ryegrass 87 Grasses
English saddle 32.14 horse-riding terms
English setter 77 Breeds of Dogs, 37.6 sporting dog
English sonnet 48.7 poem
English-speaking 564.19 speaking
English springer 37.6 sporting dog
English stroke 36.4 rowing
English thoroughbred 32.2 thoroughbred
English waltz 46.2 dance
engobe 44.4 raw material
engorge 348.11 ingest, 350.22 eat well, 872.5 be greedy
engorged 872.6 gluttonous
engorgement 348.4 intake, 350.2 appetite, 610.2 overdoing it
engraft 130.6 add, 354.6 plant
engrail 375.12 make rough
engram 61.23 memory
engrave 50, 225.7 make stable, 299.5 outline, 321.6 furrow, 544.10 identify, 545.14 inscribe, 547.11 paint, 792.10 decorate
engraved 50.28 sculpted, 225.10 stabilized, 277.8 deep, 321.4 furrowed
engraver 50, 545.9 recorder, 547.4 person who makes a representation
engraving 50, 50.1 art, 50.7 picture, 50.13 relief-carving, 225.4 stable thing, 299.1 outline, 321.3 furrowed thing, 545.8 registration, 547.2 reproduction
engross 59.13 absorb, 723.7 possess, 738.1 purchase
engrossed 290.12 internalized, 467.8 diligent
engrossment 290.6 internalization, 348.5 absorption, 723.1 possession
engulf 96.7 flow, 244.12 consume, 348.11 ingest, 350.21 eat, 610.4 be excessive
engulfed 96.11, 389.24 flooded
engulfing 348.4 intake
engulfment 96.6 river flow, 348.4 intake, 350.1 eating
enhance 128.5 make bigger, 361.3 promote, 411.10 make taste, 541.7 exaggerate, 554.6 emphasize, 557.5 ornament, 611.8 make important, 627.1 reveal, 541.7 exaggerate, 554.6 emphasize, 557.5 ornament, 611.8 make important, 627.1, 662.22 improve, 742.15 make rich, 768.6 aggravate, 792.10 decorate
enhanced 128.7 increased, 541.12 exaggerated, 554.4 emphasized, 627.14 improved, 768.4 aggravated, 792.8 decorated
enhanced radiation bomb 680.16 bomb
enhancement 128.1 increase, 541.1 exaggeration, 627.5 im-

provement, 768.1 aggravation, 792.1 adornment
enhancing 62.17 stimulating
enharmonic 116.13 harmonious
enharmonic scale 49.20 key
ENIAC 65.3 computer
enigma 11.2 the occult, 477.4 difficult question, 491.9 uncertainty, 502.3 unknown thing, 523.12 unintelligible thing, 529.3 mystification, 551.1 obscurity, 578.5 equivocalness, 786.5 person of wonder
enigmatic 11.14 occult, 440.11 benighted, 443.4 inscrutable, 477.13 problematic, 491.3 confused, 505.2 proverbial, 523.1 unintelligible, 523.4 difficult, 529.11 mysterious, 551.2 obscure, 786.8 wonderful
enigmatically 11.25 occultly, 477.24 questionably, 491.24 confusingly, 523.13 unintelligibly, 551.4 obscurely
enigmatic question 523.12 unintelligible thing
enjoin 654.5 advise, 847.17 impose a duty
enjoy 762, 135.11 make love, 405.8 feel pleasure, 411.9 taste, 723.7 possess, 763.14 like, 769.7 be cheerful, 784.7 like
enjoyable 405.6, 763.1 pleasant
enjoyably 405.11 pleasingly
enjoy company 815.11 be sociable
enjoy diplomatic immunity 848.11 be exempt
enjoy friendship with 819.13 befriend
enjoy good fortune 106.14 be comfortable
enjoy good health 623.5 be healthy
enjoy His Majesty's hospitality 702.10 be in prison
enjoy immunity 848.11 be exempt
enjoying 723.8 possessing
enjoying liberty 698.10 independent
enjoy liberty 698.14 be free
enjoy life 239.2 be full of vigour
enjoyment 405.1 physical pleasure, 411.2 taste of life, 599.6 use, 723.1 possession, 762.1 happiness, 763.7 pleasure, 765.1 satisfaction, 771.2 amusement, 805.7 fulfilment, 815.1 sociability
enjoy oneself 405.8 feel pleasure
enjoy peace 675.5 be at peace, 677.4 pacify
enjoy prosperity 686.5 be prosperous
enjoy sex 405.8 feel pleasure
enjoy success 682.6 be successful
enjoy the open air 289.12 be outside
enjoy the power of 235.10 be powerful
enlace 288.8 interweave, 314.6 convolute
enlarge 541, 66.21 photograph, 110.9 duplicate, 128.5 make bigger, 259.18 measure, 261.5 make bigger, 261.6 become bigger, 271.11 broaden, 547.9 represent, 611.8 make important
enlargeability 261
enlargeable 261
enlarged 541, 128.7 increased, 768.4 aggravated
enlarged heart 624.10 cardiovascular disease
enlarged thing 261
enlargement 541, 66.12, 66.12 development, 110.4, 118.5 duplicate, 128.1 increase, 130.1 addition, 261.1 growth, 261.3 enlarged thing, 553.1 diffuseness
enlarger 261, 66.12 development
enlarge upon 553.5 be diffuse
enlighten 6.22 educate, 8.17 deify, 528.11 inform, 550.2 clarify
enlightened 439, 4.19 learned, 6.19 knowledgeable, 8.13 di-

vine, 501.8 knowledgeable, 528.18 informed, 833.6 philanthropic
enlightening 6.16 educational, 528.16 informative
enlightenment 439, 6.1 education, 8.1 divinity, 496.8 finding out, 501.1 knowledge, 507.1 wisdom, 524.1 interpretation
Enlightenment 3.10 past age
Enlil 8 Deities
enlist 17, 171, 128.5 make bigger, 228.9 motivate, 346.14 enrol, 348.10 introduce, 354.7 install, 545.15 register, 586.15 persuade, 665.13 be a member, 676.12 go to war, 703.7 engage
enlisted 17, 679.35 martial
enlisted man 679.8 soldier
enlisted person 679.17 army person
enlisting 676.7 war measures
enlist in one's service 599.4 resort to
enlistment 346.1 entry, 348.3 introduction, 545.8 registration, 703.2 engagement
enliven 237.8 strengthen, 239.3 invigorate, 403.13 arouse sensation, 471.16 inspire, 629.5 revive, 651.1 refresh, 769.6 bring cheer
enlivened 396.12 alive, 651.4 refreshed
en masse 161.51 together, 181.14 in crowds
enmesh 539.28 trick
Enmesharra 8 Deities
enmeshed 539.36 deceived
enmeshment 539.7 tricking
enmist 55.64 fog
enmity 820, 111.3 opposition, 117.4 disagreement, 663.3 conflict, 666.1 disagreement, 785.1 dislike, 822.1 hate, 832.1 malevolence
Enmity 820
ennead 179.5 nine
enneadic 179.16 ninth
enneagon 179.5 nine
enneagonal 179.16 ninth
enneahedral 179.16 ninth
enneahedron 179.5 nine
Ennerdale 94 Lakes
Ennis 93 Cities
Enniskillen 93 Cities
Ennius 48 Poets
ennoble 8.17 deify, 802.5 make noble
ennobled 8.15 deified
ennobled titled 802.4 aristocratic
ennoblement 8.9 deification, 804.1 right
ennui 788.1 boredom
enormity 259.2 bigness, 864.1 wickedness, 866.3 sin
enormous 184.2 immeasurable, 248.13 spacious, 259.15 big
enormously 120.7 quantitatively, 259.20 largely
enough 608, 120.6 quantitative, 218.12 stop, 608.1 sufficient, 608.7 sufficiency, 673.7 I/we surrender, 765.6 satisfactory, 765.12 satisfactorily
enough and to spare 608.2 plentiful, 610.8 excessively
enough noise to wake the dead 423.2 outcry
enough rope to hang oneself 698.6 liberality
enough to get by 608.7 sufficiency
enough to go round 608.1 sufficient
enough to keep body and soul together 608.7 sufficiency
enough to live on 608.7 sufficiency
enough to wake the dead 423.6 loud
en passant 356.14 by the way
enplane 345.5 set out
enplanement 345.8 start
enprint 66.12 development
enrage 153.11 derange, 241.9 make violent, 764.10 displease,

785.7 cause dislike, 822.16 cause hate, 828.14 make angry
enraged 241.6 violent, 828.16 angry
enrapture 762.8 cause joy, 821.28 win the love of
enraptured 762.4 happy, 821.19 enamoured
enrich 128.5 make bigger, 246.7 make fertile, 557.5 ornament, 627.1 improve, 729.5 give, 742.15 make rich
enriched 792.8 decorated
enriched bread 45.38 bread
enriched uranium 56.73 nuclear reactor, 410.7 nuclear power
enrichment 128.1 increase, 627.5 improvement, 792.1 adornment
enrich oneself 742.13 get rich
enrobe 295.32 dress
enrol 156, 346, 171.9 enlist, 348.10 introduce, 354.7 install, 545.13 record, 545.15 register, 665.13 be a member, 676.12 go to war, 703.7 engage
enrolled 156, 545.16 recorded
Enrolled Nurse 60.16 nurse
enrolment 156, 346.1 entry, 348.3 introduction, 545.8 registration, 703.2 engagement
en route 70.6 commercially, 220.18 convertibly, 324.18 in motion, 326.18 in transit, 356.14 by the way
en route to 327.17 via, 336.19 forward
en rule 137.4 means of connection, 543.7 punctuation
ens 99.1 existence
ensanguined 398.24 murderous, 450.4 bloody
ensconce 250.9 locate, 531.8 conceal, 632.9 protect
ensconced 250.6 located
ensconce oneself 250.10 settle
ensemble 49.26 musical group, 51.23 cast, 142.2 whole thing, 142.5 unit, 295.10 suit
ensepulchre 399.8 bury
ensheathe 354.5 inset
enshrine 8.17 deify, 361.3 promote
enshrined 8.15 deified, 361.12 exalted
enshrinement 8.9 deification, 361.7 lift
enshroud 55.64 fog, 293.25 wrap
enshrouded 55.56 foggy, 293.37 protected
ensiform 380.3 sharp-edged
ensign 36.3 parts of a sailing boat, 544.7 flag, 679.8 soldier
Ensign 17 US Military Ranks
ensilage 605.4 storage
enslave 690.6 suppress, 734.10 take away
enslaved 699.15 detained, 701.9 subject, 821.19 enamoured
enslavement 701.1 subjection
enslaving 701.9 subject
ensnare 228.10 manipulate, 340.12 lure, 496.2 detect, 514.10 ambush, 539.28 trick, 539.33 snare, 586.16 tempt, 590.11 hunt, 592.13 plot, 635.3 trap, 734.10 take away, 821.28 win the love of
ensnared 539.36 deceived, 821.19 enamoured
ensnarement 539.7 tricking
ensnaring 821.20 amorous
ensnarl 539.33 snare
en space 265.1 interval
enstatite 54 Minerals
ensue 155.25 result, 195.10 succeed
ensuing 155.18 consequent, 195.12 succeeding, 227.10 caused
ensure 225.7 make stable, 227.7 follow from, 480.1 verify, 490.21 make certain
ensure a result 582.2 premeditate
ENT 60.3 medical specialty, 420.6 otology, 420.13 otological
entablature 43.8 column, 279.3 architectural summit

entail 520.12 *intend*, 571.14 *necessitate*, 725.2 *legal terms*
entamoeba 81.10 *parasite*
entangle 133.9 *mix up*, 137.11 *connect*, 137.13 *intercommunicate*, 288.8 *interweave*, 523.7 *be unintelligible*, 539.28 *trick*, 539.33 *snare*
entangled 133.12 *mixed*, 137.15 *connected*, 539.36 *deceived*
entanglement 133.1 *mixture*, 133.3 *miscellany*, 137.1 *connection*, 288.1 *interweaving*, 539.7 *tricking*, 821.8 *love affair*
entanglements 671.9 *barrier*
entangle one's line 20.7 *angle*
entasis 43.8 *column*
Entebbe 93 Cities
entelechial 101.6 *real*
entelechy 101.1 *reality*, 103.3 *quintessence*
entellus 77 Placental Mammals
entente 116.2 *alliance*, 135.2 *agreement*, 667.2 *contract*, 677.1 *pacification*, 819.2 *friendly relations*
entente cordiale 667.2 *contract*, 819.2 *friendly relations*
enter 346, 356, 18.6 *participate*, 51.32 *act*, 146.6 *subsume*, 171.8 *list*, 290.14 *go inside*, 327.14 *find one's way*, 344.5 *get in*, 354.2 *inject*, 457.12 *become visible*, 545.15 *register*, 674.11 *contend*, 750.7 *account*
enter a different phase 220.8 *be transformed*
enteral administration 62.13 *administration*
enter a new phase 220.8 *be transformed*
enter a nonmaterial world 368
enter as 146.5 *subsume*
enterectomy 60 Surgical Operations
entered 146.8 *included*, 171.11 *listed*, 545.11 *recorded*
enter for 346.14 *enrol*, 674.11 *contend*
enteric 290.10 *visceral*
enter in a book 545.14 *inscribe*
entering 346, 344.18 *arriving*, 457.7 *appearing*
entering the crease area 31.5 *lacrosse*
enter into 146.5 *be included*, 724.4 *have joint possession*
enter into a contract 715.5 *contract*
enter into an agreement 714.7 *promise*
enter into an alliance 715.5 *contract*
enter into argument 463.13 *debate*
enter into the spirit of 759.18 *feel for*
enteritis 624.8 *indigestion*
enter names 545.15 *register*
enterogastrone 58 Hormones
enter one's head 471.14 *have an idea*
enter orbit 53.38 *launch*
enterostomy 60 Surgical Operations
enterotomy 60 Surgical Operations
enterprise 226.6 *undertaking*, 243.1 *production*, 336.12 *advance*, 519.1 *imagination*, 588.3 *future intention*, 597.2 *undertaking*, 642.2 *social activity*, 642.4 *energy*, 665.1 *party*, 737.6 *business*
enterprising 597, 239.4 *vigorous*, 336.17 *forward*, 479.9 *original*, 519.10 *imaginative*, 596.8 *attempting*, 642.18 *active*
enterprising businessman 597.4 *volunteer*
enterprisingly 597
entertain 405.9 *give pleasure*, 665.16 *host*, 729.5 *give*, 730.10 *receive someone*, 771.13 *be humorous*, 815.11 *be sociable*, 819.15 *be hospitable*

entertained 730.13 *received*, 815.16 *popular*
entertainer 51, 46.5 *dancer*
entertain friends 819.15 *be hospitable*
entertaining 42.9 *recreational*, 730.4 *reception*, 769.2 *cheering*, 771.9 *funny*, 815.17 *festive*
entertainingly 42.11 *recreationally*, 815.18 *sociably*
entertainment 771, 42.8 *pastime*, 350.4 *eating meals*, 405.4 *pleasurable things*, 606.1 *provision*, 762.2 *fun*, 763.7 *pleasure*, 771.2 *amusement*, 815.3 *meeting*, 815.5 *party*
entertainment industry 51.4 *show business*
entertain respect for 849.15 *respect*
enter the church 7.19 *be religious*
enter the crease area 31.9 *play hockey*
enter the Golden Gate 397.15 *die*
enter the lion's den 633.8 *be in danger*
enter the lists 674.11 *contend*, 679.37 *fight*
enter the race 710.13 *be a candidate*
enter the ring 26.11 *do a combat sport*
enter upon 195.11 *follow in office*
enthalpy 56.38 *thermodynamics*
enthral 340.12 *lure*, 762.8 *cause joy*, 821.28 *win the love of*
enthralling 762.5 *delightful*
enthrone 703.6 *commission*, 812.19 *install*
enthronement 703.1 *commission*, 804.1 *right*, 812.3 *ceremony*
enthuse 239.2 *be full of vigour*
enthusiasm 7.2 *religiousness*, 237.2 *healthiness*, 239.1 *vigour*, 554.1 *emphasis*, 572.7 *eagerness*, 642.4 *energy*, 772.5 *earnestness*
enthusiast 51.31 *theatregoer*, 155.14 *follower*, 519.9 *visionary*, 584.8 *creature of habit*, 642.10 *busy person*
enthusiastic 237.11 *strong in spirit*, 239.4 *vigorous*, 519.10 *imaginative*, 554.3 *emphatic*, 572.8 *eager*, 642.18 *active*, 772.8 *earnest*
enthusiastically 237.15 *acutely*, 554.7 *emphatically*, 642.22 *actively*
entice 228.10 *manipulate*, 340.12 *lure*, 586.16 *tempt*
enticed 228.12 *motivated*
enticement 586, 228.2 *inducement*, 340.4 *allurement*, 586.2 *flattery*, 878.4 *reward for service*
enticing 340.9 *attractive*
entire 83.18 *of leaves*, 120.6 *quantitative*, 134.16 *simple*, 142.7 *uncut*, 144.7 *complete*, 174.13 *whole*, 619.1 *perfect*, 684.7 *completed*
entire horse 401.16 *male animal*
entirely 120.7 *quantitatively*, 142.11 *wholly*, 144.9 *completely*, 621.20 *clean*, 684.9 *completely*
entirety 120.4 *total*, 142.2 *whole thing*, 144.1 *completeness*, 684.1 *completion*
entitle 845, 116.29 *permit*, 567.11 *title*
entitled 804, 845, 116.18 *permitting*, 485.10 *authorized*, 843.9 *in the right*
entitledness 845.1 *entitlement*
entitled to 845
entitlement 804, 845, 116.8 *permit*, 485.1 *qualification*, 843.6 *right*
Entitlement 845
entity 59.3 *organism*, 99.1 *existence*, 99.2 *thing*, 142.2 *whole thing*, 174.1 *one*, 396.1 *life*
entoloma 89 Fungi
entomb 258.21 *put in a container*, 311.10 *enclose*, 397.17, 399.8 *bury*

entombed 258.20 *containing*, 399.10 *buried*
entombment 399.1 *burial*
entomological 82, 81.18 *arthropodous*
entomologist 82, 76.11 *zoologist*, 81.15 *invertebrate zoologist*
entomology 76.9 *animal science*, 81.14 *invertebrate zoology*, 82.7 *study*
entomophobia 777 Phobias by Name
entoproct 81.7 *coelenterate*
Entoprocta 81.7 *coelenterate*
entourage 180.10 *attendance*, 195.1 *succession*
entr'acte 51.2 *play*, 51.6 *scene*
entrails 257.3, 290.4 *insides*, 517.10 *cards*
entrain 345.5 *set out*
entrainment 345.8 *start*
entrance 346, 51.20 *acting*, 303.1, 303.6 *front*, 322.7 *passageway*, 327.2 *route*, 344.10 *arrival*, 346.1 *entry*, 348.2 *receptivity*, 356.3 *passage into*, 457.1 *appearance*
entranced 11.19 *bewitched*
entrance fee 751.3 *fee*
entrance hall 256.7 *room*, 303.1 *front*
entrancing 11.15 *witchlike*, 762.5 *delightful*
entrant 346, 674.10 *contender*
entrap 228.10 *manipulate*, 539.28 *trick*, 539.33 *snare*, 635.3 *trap*
entrapment 539.7 *tricking*
entrapped 539.36 *deceived*
entreat 473.16 *plead*, 477.17 *question*, 567.8 *appeal to*, 712.6 *request*
entreating 712.9 *requesting*
entreatingly 712.12 *by request*
entreaty 473.5 *plea*, 477.1 *question*, 712.1 *request*
entrechat 46.9 *ballet steps*
entrée 45.9 *dish*, 348.2 *receptivity*, 350.14 *mouthful*
entremets 45.9 *dish*, 350.14 *mouthful*
entrench 671, 225.7 *make stable*, 237.8 *strengthen*, 357.5 *transgress*, 632.9 *protect*
entrenched 671, 217.7 *permanent*, 225.10 *stabilized*
entrenchment 217.1 *permanence*, 671.8 *military defences*
entrepot 605.4 *storage*, 740.7 *emporium*
entrepreneur 135.7 *joiner*, 243.9 *producer*, 596.7 *attempter*, 597.4 *volunteer*, 640.3 *doer*, 715.4 *contractor*, 739.12 *wholesaler*
entropy 56.38 *thermodynamics*, 133.1 *mixture*, 139.1 *nonadhesion*
entrust 326.14 *bring back*, 703.6 *commission*, 706.4 *delegate*, 707.6 *deputize*, 729.5 *give*
entrusting 703.1 *commission*
entrustment 703.1 *commission*
entry 346, 32.7 *horseracing*, 39.6 *diving*, 39.11 *swimming*, 346.5 *entrance*, 348.2 *receptivity*, 354.9 *injection*, 356.3 *passage into*, 545.1 *record*, 545.8 *registration*, 750.1 *accounts*
Entry 346
entry dive 39.6 *diving*
entry into office 195.4 *accession*
Entryphone 420.8 *something heard*
entry upon 195.4 *accession*
ENT specialist 420.6 *otology*
entwine 135.10 *link*, 137.11 *connect*, 288.8 *interweave*, 311.6 *curve*, 314.6 *convolute*, 320.9 *enfold*
entwined 314.4 *convolutional*
entwining 320.3 *enfoldment*
enucleate 524.9 *decipher*
Enugu 93 Cities
E number 350.11 *food content*
enumerable 52.73 *numerable*
enumerate 52, 165.24 *specify*,

169.10, 170.11 *number*, 171.8 *list*, 257.9 *itemize*
enumerated 171.11 *listed*
enumerate with 146.6 *subsume*
enumeration 52.12 *numeration*, 170.1 *calculation*, 171.1 *list*, 171.7 *listing*, 750.3 *accounting*
enumeration district 249.5 *state*
enumerative 170.13 *calculative*
enumerator 170.6 *calculator*
enunciate 535.17 *affirm*, 564.11 *speak*
enunciated 535.11 *stated*, 564.16 *speech*
enunciation 535.2 *statement*, 564.4 *articulation*
enunciative 535.10 *affirmative*
enunciator 535.9 *affirmer*
enunciatory 535.10 *affirmative*
enuresis 353.3 *urination*
enuretic 353.26 *urinary*
Enurta 8 Deities
envelop 146.4 *include*, 244.12 *consume*, 289.11 *be exterior*, 293.25 *wrap*, 295.32 *dress*, 297.7 *surround*, 301.6 *wrap*, 320.9 *enfold*, 632.9 *protect*, 726.7 *detain*
envelope 258.5 *packet*, 258.21 *put in a container*, 289.1 *exterior*, 293.4 *wrapping*, 301.4 *wrapper*, 534.3 *correspondence*
enveloped 258.20 *containing*, 289.6 *exterior*, 297.5 *surrounded*
enveloping 258.20 *containing*
envelopment 28.3 *fencing movements*, 293.1 *covering*, 297.2 *encirclement*, 301.1 *enclosure*, 320.3 *enfoldment*, 726.2 *detention*
envenom 628.3 *make worse*, 822.16 *cause hate*, 828.14 *make angry*, 830.12 *make irritable*
envenomed 618.4 *poor*, 626.7 *toxic*, 832.14 *hostile*
enviable 782.7 *desired*
envied 782.7 *desired*
envier 782.6 *desirer*
envious 842, 453.5 *green-eyed*, 759.13 *passionate*, 782.9 *desirous*, 820.6 *hostile*, 822.10 *hating*, 828.15 *resentful*, 841.4 *jealous*, 860.4 *selfish*
envious-eyed 842.2 *envious*
enviously 842, 782.18 *desirously*, 820.14 *hostilely*, 822.18 *hatefully*, 828.17 *resentfully*, 841.9 *jealously*, 860.8 *selfishly*
enviousness 841.1 *jealousy*, 842.1 *envy*
environ 248.20 *extend*, 297.7 *surround*
environment 256, 50.12 *sculpture*, 106.1 *circumstances*, 250.1 *location*, 297.1 *surroundings*
environmental 256, 453, 2.12 *sociological*, 106.7 *circumstantial*, 297.4 *surrounding*, 627.16 *improving*, 637.6 *preserving*
environmental abuse 601.2 *misuse*
environmental art 50 Western Art Styles and Movements
environmental engineering 63.1 *engineering*
environmental health officer 625.3 *hygienist*
environmentalism 217.1 *permanence*, 453.16 *green politics*
environmentalist 217.4 *conservationist*, 627.12 *reformer*, 637.7 *preservationist*
environmentally 256, 2.16 *sociologically*, 106.16 *relatively*, 637.8 *preservatively*
environmental movement 637.1 *preservation*
environment-friendly 453.7 *environmental*, 637.6 *preserving*
environs 249.13 *locality*, 250.1 *location*, 264.3 *near place*, 297.1 *surroundings*
envisage 471.15 *imagine*, 513.8 *expect*, 516.1 *foresee*, 519.14 *imagine*, 592.12 *plan ahead*
envision 471.15 *imagine*, 516.1 *foresee*, 519.14 *imagine*

envoi 48.8 *part of poem*
envoy 130.3 *additional item,* 157.10 *ending,* 547.8 *representative,* 653.16 *official,* 703.4 *council,* 703.5 *commissioner,* 706.1 *delegate,* 707.3 *agent*
envoy extraordinary 653.16 *official*
envy 842, 453.14 *green-eyed monster,* 759.6 *bad feeling,* 782.12 *desire,* 820.2 *personal conflict,* 822.1, 822.14 *hate,* 828.1 *resentment,* 841.1 *jealousy,* 841.6 *be jealous,* 842.3 *be envious of,* 860.1 *selfishness,* 860.6 *be selfish,* 864.5 *seven deadly sins*
Envy 842
envying 842.2 *envious*
enwrap 293.25 *wrap*
enwrapment 293.1 *covering*
Enzensberger 48 Poets
enzenze 49 Musical Instruments
enzootic 626.6 *contagious*
Enzu 8 Deities
enzyme 57 Types of Compounds, **58,** 57.15 *catalysis,* 216.5 *changer,* 370.8 *leavening*
enzyme class 58.11 *enzyme*
enzymic 58.26 *biochemical,* 370.4 *leavening*
enzymically 58.27 *biochemically*
enzymologist 58.2 *biochemist*
enzymology 58.1 *biochemistry,* 59.1 *life science*
Eocene 54 Geological Time Intervals
Eocene period 200.3 *geological period*
eohippus 77 Placental Mammals
eolith 3.11 *relic,* 200.7 *thing of the past*
eon 54.41 *geological time,* 187.3 *geological period*
eonothem 54.41 *geological time*
Eos 8 Deities, 204.1 *morning*
eosin 67.6 *dye*
eosophobia 777 Phobias by Name
Eostre 8 Deities
Eötvös 52 Scientists
EP 545.7 *recording*
eparchy 92.3 *other*
epaulette 544.4 *insignia*
epeirogenic 54.54 *tectonic*
epexegesis 524.1 *interpretation*
ephemera 562.3 *compendium*
ephemeral 83.2 *plant,* 83.14 *of plants,* 84.2 *flowering plant,* 189.6 *transient,* 224.13 *changeable,* 397.20 *deadly*
ephemerality 189.1 *transience,* 397.1 *death*
ephemerally 83.24 *herbaceously,* 189.8 *transiently,* 224.15 *changeably*
ephemeris 53.6 *star catalogue,* 74.5 *navigation,* 528.5 *reference book*
ephemeris time 185.9 *time zone*
Ephemeroptera 82 Orders of Insects
ephemeropteran 82.10 *insectan*
ephod 7.11 *vestment*
epic 48.7 *poem,* 48.19 *narrative,* 259.15 *big,* 553.3 *diffuse,* 560.3 *narration,* 560.12 *narrative,* 696.11 *masterpiece*
epicalyx 84.3 *flower part*
epicene 578.10 *equivocal*
epicentral 291.6 *central*
epicentre 54.22 *seismic activity,* 158.1 *middle,* 291.1 *centre*
epic length 553.1 *diffuseness*
epic novel 48.2 *fiction*
epic poet 48.14 *author*
epic poetry 48.6 *poetry*
epic simile 48.12 *poetic language*
Epictetus 4 Philosophers
epic theatre 51.8 *theatre movements*
epicure 350.18 *eater,* 403.4 *someone or something that feels,* 405.3 *pleasure-seeker,* 411.5 *taster,* 481.6 *discriminating per-*

son, 870.5 *self-indulgent person,* 872.4 *glutton*
epicurean 4.11 *follower of a doctrine,* 4.14 *of a philosophy,* 45.56 *culinary,* 403.4 *someone or something that feels,* 403.7 *susceptible,* 405.3 *pleasure-seeker,* 411.7 *tasty,* 481.9 *discriminating,* 763.5 *pleasure-loving,* 763.12 *pleasure-loving person,* 870.6 *self-indulgent,* 872.4 *glutton,* 872.6 *gluttonous*
epicureanism 4.7 *school of thought,* 405.1 *physical pleasure,* 763.7 *pleasure,* 870.1 *self-indulgence,* 872.2 *epicurism*
epicurism 872, 350.3 *delicate eating*
Epicurus 4 Philosophers
epicycle 313.2 *circle*
epicycloid 52.40 *curve*
epidemic 164.17 *widespread,* 624.5 *plague,* 626.6 *contagious*
epidemic disease 624.4 *disease*
epidemiological 60.22 *medical*
epidemiologist 60.13 *medical specialist*
epidemiology 59.1 *life science,* 60.3 *medical specialty,* 624.20 *pathology*
epidermal 278.2 *superficial,* 289.6 *exterior,* 293.38 *covering*
epidermic 289.6 *exterior*
epidermis 83.5 *stem,* 278.4 *shallow thing,* 289.1 *exterior,* 293.14 *animal covering*
epidermoid 289.6 *exterior*
epididymectomy 60 Surgical Operations
epididymovasostomy 60 Surgical Operations
epidiorite 54 Common Rocks
epidote 54 Minerals
epidural 62.12 *injection,* 245.7 *obstetrics*
epigeal 89.10 *of fungi*
epiglottis 564.5 *organ of speech*
epigram 48.7 *poem,* 505.1 *maxim,* 506.2 *solecism,* 552.2 *outline,* 876.7 *moral*
epigrammatic 505.2 *proverbial,* 552.3 *concise,* 562.6 *summary*
epigrammatical 562.6 *summary*
epigrammatically 505.4 *proverbially,* 562.12 *in brief*
epigrammatist 5.2 *linguist*
epigrammatize 505.3 *aphorize,* 552.4 *be concise,* 562.8 *summarize*
epigraph 3.11 *relic,* 505.1 *maxim*
epigrapher 1.4 *palaeoanthropologist,* 3.4 *archaeologist*
epigraphic 1.12 *palaeoanthropological,* 5.40 *translated*
epigraphical 1.12 *palaeoanthropological,* 3.17 *archaeological*
epigraphically 1.17 *palaeoanthropologically,* 3.25 *reportedly,* 5.48 *linguistically*
epigraphist 1.4 *palaeoanthropologist,* 5.2 *linguist,* 524.6 *interpreter*
epigraphy 1.2 *palaeoanthropology,* 5.12 *translation,* 524.5 *science of interpretation,* 545.8 *registration*
epigynous 84.12 *of flowers*
epilepsy 366.8 *spasm,* 510.3 *mental deterioration,* 624.4 *disease,* 624.17 *nervous disorder*
epileptic 366.19 *convulsive,* 624.23 *diseased*
epileptic fit 510.3 *mental deterioration*
epilithic 90.7 *algal*
epilogue 51.6 *scene,* 130.3 *additional item,* 157.10 *ending,* 195.9 *sequel,* 304.1 *rear,* 684.2 *conclusion*
epimenorrhoea 353.11 *menstruation*
epimer 57.13 *structure*
epimeric 57.37 *structural*
epimerism 57.13 *structure*

epiphanic 8.13 *divine,* 457.7 *appearing,* 530.12 *revelatory*
epiphany 8.8 *divine manifestation,* 367.2 *materialization,* 457.4 *something that appears,* 526.10 *manifestation,* 530.1 *disclosure*
Epiphany 10.15 *holy day*
epiphenomenal 589.8 *chance*
epiphenomenalism 4.7 *school of thought*
epiphenomenalist 4.11 *follower of a doctrine,* 4.14 *of a philosophy*
epiphyllum 84 Flowers and Flowering Plants
epiphyte 83.2 *plant*
epiphytic 83.14 *of plants,* 90.7 *algal*
epiphytically 83.24 *herbaceously,* 90.9 *algologically*
episcopal 7.17 *priestly*
Episcopal Church 7 Christian Movements
Episcopalian 7.5 *Christian,* 7.16 *denominational*
episcopal ring 7.11 *vestment*
episcopal vestment 7.11 *vestment*
episcopate 7.9 *priesthood*
episiotomy 60 Surgical Operations
episode 3.14 *historicalness,* 48.3 *aspect of fiction,* 51.6 *scene,* 106.2 *occurrence,* 143.2 *particular*
episodic 160.8 *discontinuous*
epispastic 62.4 *drug type*
epistemologically 4.24 *philosophically*
epistemology 4.6 *branch of philosophy*
Epistle 10.6 *Eucharist*
Epistles 7.12 *religious text*
epistolary 534.33 *communicational*
epistolary novel 48.2 *fiction*
epistrophe 48.12 *poetic language,* 183.1 *repetition,* 426.7 *repeated word*
epistyle 43 Architectural Decoration, 279.3 *architectural summit*
epitaph 5.25 *inscription,* 345.9 *parting,* 399.4 *funeral objects*
epitaphic 5.43 *phrasal,* 399.11 *funeral*
epitaphist 399.3 *funeral director*
epithalamium 48.7 *poem,* 823.6 *general terms*
epitheca 90.3 *plant body*
epithelioma 624.12 *cancer*
epithet 505.1 *maxim,* 560.8 *name*
epitome 5.12 *translation,* 103.3 *quintessence,* 262.3 *contracted thing,* 270.3 *shortened version,* 299.1 *outline,* 471.6 *ideal,* 547.1 *representation,* 552.2 *outline,* 562.1 *summary*
epitomical 471.13 *ideal,* 552.3 *concise*
epitomization 270.2 *shortening*
epitomize 471, 103.12 *embody,* 270.10 *shorten,* 299.5 *outline,* 547.9 *represent,* 552.4 *be concise,* 562.8 *summarize*
epitomized 270.8 *shortened*
epitomizer 562.5 *summarizer*
epizootic 626.6 *contagious*
epoch 75 Scientific and Technical Units, 54.41 *geological time,* 185.4 *term,* 187.2 *time period,* 187.3 *geological period,* 192.3 *chronology*
epoch-making 611.6 *notable*
epode 48.7 *poem,* 48.8 *part of poem*
Epona 8 Deities
eponym 560.8 *name*
eponymy 560.7 *nomenclature*
epos 48.6 *poetry,* 48.7 *poem*
EPOS 65.12 *electronic office*
epoxide 57 Types of Compounds
epoxide resin 57.21 *polymer*
epoxy 604.1 *materials*
epoxy resin 138.3 *adhesive*

Epsilon Eridani 53 Named Stars
Epsilon Indi 53 Named Stars
Epsom 674.5 *racecourse*
Epsom salt 57 Common Chemical Compounds, **62** Medication
Epsom salts 630.6 *purgative*
Epunamun 8 Deities
equable 4.18 *detached,* 122.6 *equal,* 242.6 *moderate*
equably 4.27 *stoically,* 122.13 *equitably,* 242.9 *moderately*
equal 52, 110, 122, 122, 198, 52.93 *equate,* 107.5 *interrelated,* 110.10 *be equal,* 112.5 *uniform,* 112.6, 116.14 *conforming,* 169.11, 170.10 *total,* 225.9 *stable,* 285.4 *correlated,* 285.6 *correlate,* 308.4 *symmetrical,* 608.1 *sufficient,* 617.9 *be worthy,* 667.8 *be compatible,* 667.12 *compatible,* 843.7 *right*
equal chance 589, 229.2 *chance*
equal contest 674.2 *contest*
equal exchange 109.1 *interchange,* 110.2 *equivalence*
equal footing 122.1 *equality*
equality 52, 110, 122, 14.1 *finance,* 107.2 *interrelatedness,* 112.2 *conformity,* 112.4 *similarity,* 225.1 *stability,* 285.1 *parallelism,* 308.1 *symmetry,* 667.3 *compatibility,* 843.1 *fairness*
Equality 122
equalization 122, 125.2 *counterbalance,* 420.10 *sound quality*
equalization fund 14.1, 741.7 *finance*
equalize 122, 52.93 *equate,* 107.8 *be proportionate to,* 109.9 *correlate,* 110.10 *be equal,* 112.9 *be uniform,* 114.11 *make similar,* 116.24 *harmonize,* 116.26 *make uniform,* 124.10 *make average,* 125.5 *counterbalance,* 225.7 *make stable,* 282.7 *make horizontal,* 308.6 *symmetrize,* 333.7 *be halfway,* 704.9 *cancel out*
equalized 122.6 *equal,* 125.10 *counterbalancing,* 704.10 *cancelled*
equalizing 125.10 *counterbalancing,* 704.4 *cancelling out*
equally 110, 122, 308, 843, 52.87 *mathematically,* 106.15 *under the circumstances,* 107.10 *relevantly,* 109.10 *reciprocally,* 112.13 *uniformly,* 114.14 *comparably,* 116.34 *uniformly,* 225.12 *stably,* 333.8 *medially,* 667.16 *compatibly*
equally divided 122.8 *on equal terms*
equalness 843.1 *fairness*
equal opportunity 700, 110.5, 122.1 *equality*
equal race 198
equal rights 110.5, 122.1 *equality,* 402.1 *female sex,* 698.2 *free speech,* 700.2 *equal opportunity*
equal sign 543.1 *sign*
equals sign 52.13 *mathematical symbol*
equal standing 110.5 *equality*
equal status 700.2 *equal opportunity*
equal swap 717.1 *compromise*
equal the best 617.9 *be worthy*
equal to 52, 235.13 *powerful,* 608.1 *sufficient*
equal value 110.5 *equality*
equal weight 704.4 *cancelling out*
equal with 198
equanimity 4.3 *detachment,* 112.3 *agreement,* 242.1 *moderation,* 303.4 *assurance,* 482.7 *impartiality,* 765.1 *satisfaction*
equanimous 4.18 *detached,* 112.7 *agreeing,* 482.2 *impartial*
equanimously 112, 482.15 *impartially*
equate 52, 107.8 *be proportionate to,* 110.8 *make the same,* 122.11 *equalize,* 124.10 *make average,* 478.20 *solve*
equation 52, 52.65 *theory,* 56.6

law, 122.3 *equalization,* 170.1
calculation, 478.7 *numerical result*
equation of state 56.6 *law,* 56.38
thermodynamics
equation of time 185.9 *time zone*
equator 59.10 *cell division,*
122.7 *dividing line,* 158.4 *midline,* 176.8 *half,* 249.2 *geographical region,* 313.3 *circular thing,*
408.8 *hot place*
equatorial 158.11 *midway,*
408.11 *warm*
Equatorial Guinea 91 Countries
equatorially 249.19 *geographically*
equatorial mounting 53.25
mounting
equatorial rain forest 408.8 *hot
place*
equatorial rainy zone 55.39 *climatic zone*
equestrian 32.15 *horse person,*
32.17 *equine*
equestrian director 51.29 *circus
performer*
equestrianism 32.6 *horsemanship*
equestrian painter 50.16 *artist*
equestrian painting 50.10 *art subject*
equestrienne 32.15 *horse person*
equidistance 158.5 *middle distance,* 285.1 *parallelism*
equidistant 52.80 *linear,* 110.16,
122.6 *equal,* 158.11 *midway,*
285.3 *parallel,* 333.4 *middle*
equidistantly 122.13 *equitably*
equilateral 52.80 *linear,* 122.6
equal, 308.4 *symmetrical*
equilaterally 308.7 *symmetrically*
equilateral triangle 52.43 *triangle,* 310.3 *angled figure*
equilibrant 125.2 *counterbalance*
equilibrate 110.10 *be equal,*
116.24 *harmonize,* 125.5 *counterbalance,* 308.6 *symmetrize*
equilibrated 57.38 *reactive,*
125.10 *counterbalancing*
equilibrating 125.10 *counterbalancing*
equilibration 110.5 *equality,*
122.3 *equalization,* 125.2 *counterbalance*
equilibrist 51.29 *circus performer*
equilibrium 122, 56.10 *force,*
57.14 *chemical reaction,* 110.6
regularity, 116.4 *harmony,*
125.2 *counterbalance,* 159.7 *stability,* 308.1 *symmetry,* 325.1
motionlessness
equilibrium constant 57.14 *chemical reaction*
equilizer 122
equine 32, 77.33 *ungulate*
equine distemper 624.18 *veterinary disease*
equine species 32.1 *horse*
equinoctial 97.7 *oceanic,* 203.9
seasonal
equinoctially 203.18 *seasonally*
equinoctial tide 97.2 *tide,* 275.8
high thing
equinox 3.5 *celestial sphere*
equip 594, 6.22 *educate,* 295.35
make clothing, 485.13 *qualify,*
602.6 *find means,* 606.5 *provision*
equipage 71 Carriages and
Carts
equipment 603, 232.2 *instrument,* 485.1 *qualification,* 485.4
permission, 594.11 *fitting out,*
602.2 *supplies,* 606.1 *provision*
equipoise 122.2 *equilibrium,*
125.5 *counterbalance,* 325.1 *motionlessness*
equipoised 125.10 *counterbalancing*
equipollence 110.2 *equivalence,*
116.5 *conformity,* 122.3 *equalization*
equipollent 110.13 *equivalent,*
116.14 *conforming,* 122.6 *equal*
equiponderance 110.5, 122.1
equality, 125.2 *counterbalance*
equiponderant 110.16 *equal,*
125.10 *counterbalancing*

equiponderate 110.10 *be equal,*
125.5 *counterbalance*
equip oneself 605.6 *store*
equipose 308.1 *symmetry*
equipped 485.9 *qualified,*
594.18 *prepared,* 606.8 *provisional*
equipper 594.15 *preparer*
equipping 606.1 *provision,* 606.7
provisioning
equisetum 88.1 *fern*
equitable 122.6 *equal,* 843.7
right, 857.4 *honourable,* 859.4
disinterested
equitableness 843.1 *fairness,*
859.1 *disinterestedness*
equitably 122, 859.8 *disinterestedly*
equitation 32.6 *horsemanship,*
324.2 *momentum*
equity 843.1 *fairness,* 857.1 *probity*
equity law 16.1 *the law*
equivalence 110, 4.8 *philosophical term,* 52.26 *equality,* 52.63
mathematical logic, 109.3 *correlation,* 114.1 *similarity,* 116.5
conformity, 122.1 *equality,*
222.1 *substitution,* 478.8
correspondence, 520.4 *type of
meaning*
equivalence point 57.18 *gravimetric analysis*
equivalence relation 52.63 *mathematical logic*
equivalency 122.1 *equality*
equivalent 110, 52.86 *logical,*
57.41 *analytic,* 109.6 *correlative,* 110.2 *equivalence,* 114.5
counterpart, 114.7 *similar,*
116.14 *conforming,* 122.6
equal, 222.1 *substitution,* 222.7
substitute, 223.1 *exchange,*
223.6 *in exchange,* 478.15 *correspondent,* 520.6 *meaningful,*
524.17 *translational*
equivalent circuit 64.13 *circuit*
equivalently 109.11 *correlatively,*
110.18 *identically,* 114.14 *comparably,* 122.12 *equally,* 222.9
instead, 223.8 *in exchange,*
478.26 *correspondingly*
equivalent meaning 520.4 *type of
meaning*
equivalent triangles 52.43 *triangle*
equivocal 578, 5.42 *worded,*
117.7 *disparate,* 286.5 *devious,*
314.5 *ambiguous,* 474.7 *sophistic,* 474.9 *quibbling,* 477.14
questionable, 484.5 *countering,*
491.6 *indeterminate,* 520.6
meaningful, 523.4 *difficult,*
538.17 *duplicitous,* 540.34 *evasive,* 551.2 *obscure,* 576.1 *vacillating,* 591.18 *avoiding,* 657.4
cunning
equivocality 117.1 *disparity,*
531.5 *evasion*
equivocally 578, 5.50 *lexically,*
117.15 *dissimilarly,* 286.9 *deviously,* 314.8 *circularly,* 474.14
sophistically, 477.24 *questionably,* 484.9 *to the contrary,*
491.25 *indeterminately,* 538.26
untruthfully, 551.4 *obscurely,*
576.16 *irresolutely,* 591.22 *evasively*
equivocalness 578, 5.22 *many
words,* 117.1 *disparity,* 491.14
indeterminacy, 520.3 *comprehension,* 523.11 *unintelligibility,*
525.2 *misinterpretation,* 531.5
evasion, 538.7 *duplicity,* 551.1
obscurity, 553.2 *circumlocution*
equivocal passage 520.3 *comprehension*
equivocate 531, 578, 117.12 *be
disparate,* 286.7 *deviate,* 314.7
be ambiguous, 333.7 *be halfway,* 474.13 *quibble,* 484.8 *reverse,* 491.19 *hesitate,* 525.1
misinterpret, 540.23 *evade,*
576.5 *vacillate,* 578.1 *be equivocal,* 591.7 *be evasive*
equivocating 578, 474.9 *quib-

bling,* 538.15 *lying,* 578.10
equivocal
equivocatingly 538.26 *untruthfully*
equivocation 578, 224.2 *irresolution,* 286.3 *deviousness,* 365.3
vacillation, 474.1 *sophistry,*
484.1 *counterevidence,* 531.5
evasion, 538.5 *half-truth,*
540.11 *evasion,* 576.11 *vacillation,* 578.5 *equivocalness,*
591.15 *evasiveness*
Equivocation 578
equivocator 578, 474.6 *sophist,*
484.4 *tergiversator,* 538.11,
539.16 *liar*
equivoque 578.5 *equivocalness*
equotidian 164.21 *common*
Equuleus 53 The Constellations
era 54.41 *geological time,* 185.4
term, 187.2 *time period,* 187.3
geological period, 192.3 *chronology*
ERA 700.2 *equal opportunity*
eradicable 131.6 *subtractive,*
355.18 *extractive*
eradicably 131.9 *decreasingly*
eradicate 100.14 *cause not to
exist,* 131.3 *subtract,* 147.8
eject, 172.9 *annihilate,* 244.8 *destroy,* 349.10 *exterminate,*
355.11 *extract,* 546.1 *obliterate,*
734.10 *take away*
eradicated 131.5 *subtracted,*
546.6 *obliterated*
eradication 131.1 *subtraction,*
147.2 *ejection,* 244.2 *destroying,*
355.1 *extraction,* 546.3 *obliteration,* 734.3 *taking away*
eradicative 355.18 *extractive*
erasable 65.20 *on-line*
erase 65.20 *short,* 131.3 *subtract,* 244.8 *destroy,* 349.10 *exterminate,* 385.14 *erode,* 438.8
make invisible, 458.3 *cause to
disappear,* 546.1 *obliterate,*
621.13 *clean,* 704.6 *cancel,*
734.10 *take away*
erased 131.5 *subtracted,* 546.6
obliterated
erased from the record 839.8
overlooked
erase from one's memory 512.13
forget
eraser 385, 546, 244.6 *destroyer,* 438.6 *that which makes
invisible,* 621.10 *cleaning object*
erasing 546.3 *obliteration*
erassitude 393.2 *semiliquidity*
ERA supporter 700.3 *liberator*
erasure 131.1 *subtraction,* 244.1
destruction, 385.2 *wearing
away,* 458.5 *disguise,* 546.3
obliteration, 734.3 *taking away*
erathem 54.41 *geological time*
Eratosthenes 52 Named Concepts, **53** Lunar Features
Eratosthenes of Cyrene 52 Scientists
erbium 57 Chemical Elements
Ercilla 48 Poets
ere 194.11 *before*
Erebus 8.11 *heaven*
erect 275, 43.18 *be an architect,*
63.30 *engineer,* 83.14 *of plants,*
128.5 *make bigger,* 148.13
make, 161.44 *put together,*
225.7 *make stable,* 226.11 *inaugurate,* 243.10 *produce,* 281.6
make vertical, 281.8 *vertical,*
361.1 *raise,* 382.16 *construct,*
805.15 *unapproachable*
erected 43.12 *structural,* 361.11
raised
Erectheum 43 Noted Buildings
erectile 361.11 *raised*
erecting 281.2 *making vertical*
erection 43.3 *building,* 161.33
putting together, 243.2 *manufacture,* 281.1 *verticality,* 281.2
making vertical, 316.2 *bulge,*
361.6 *raising,* 382.6 *construction*
erectly 281.11 *vertically,* 805.32
proudly
erectness 281.1 *verticality*
E region 390.3 *atmospheric layers*

eremite 168.9 *hermit,* 174.8
loner, 816.6 *unsocial person*
Erewhon 519.8 *dreamland,*
714.4 *promised land,* 775.3 *aspiration*
Erfurt 93 Cities
erg 75 Scientific and Technical
Units, 63.10 *work,* 235.5 *unit
of work*
ergo 227.12 *with the effect of*
ergonomics 644.4 *exertion*
ergophobia 777 Phobias by
Name
ergot 89 Fungi
ergotism 89.5 *fungal association*
erh-hu 49 Musical Instruments
eric 125.1 *compensation*
erica 84 Flowers and Flowering
Plants
Ericht 94 Lakes
Eridanus 53 The Constellations
Erie 5 Languages and Groups
of Languages, **94** Lakes, 94.3
US lakes
Erigena 4 Philosophers
Erin 91.10 *Ireland*
Eris 8 Deities, 676.3 *god of war*
eristic 4.5 *philosophical argument,* 473.2 *logical argument,*
473.6 *arguer,* 473.9 *hostile*
Erlenmeyer flask 57 Laboratory
Apparatus
ERM 741.7 *finance*
ermine 77 Placental Mammals,
293.14 *animal covering,* 544.8
heraldic device, 544.13 *heraldic*
ermines 544.8 *heraldic device*
erminites 544.8 *heraldic device*
erminois 544.8 *heraldic device*
ermitophobia 777 Phobias by
Name
erne 78 Birds
Erne 94 Lakes
Ernie 224.3 *changeable thing*
ERNIE 65.3 *computer*
erode 385, 131.3 *subtract,*
141.3 *disintegrate,* 384.29
weather, 607.1 *waste,* 628.5
hurt, 722.12 *lessen*
eroded 54.59 *weathered,* 131.7
reduced, 247.3 *birth control,*
458.7 *disappeared*
erogena 821.20 *amorous*
Eros 8 Deities, **53** Minor Planets, 61.22 *libido,* 821.16 *gods
and goddesses of love*
erosian 56.10 *force*
erosion 54.35 *weathering,* 129.1
decrease, 131.1 *subtraction,*
141.1 *disintegration,* 244.7
agent of destruction, 384.4 *pulverization,* 385.2 *wearing away,*
458.4 *disappearance,* 607.3
waste, 628.9 *dilapidation,* 722.4
lessening
erosive 385.10 *frictional*
erotic 405.6 *pleasant,* 821.20 *amorous,* 877.12 *indecent*
erotica 296.3 *pornography,* 877.2
indecency
erotic dancer 51.28 *dancer*
erotic desire 61.22 *libido*
eroticism 61.22 *libido,* 405.1
physical pleasure, 821.5 *desire,*
877.3 *sexual immorality*
erotic literature 877.2 *indecency*
erotic novel 48.2 *fiction*
erotic poetry 48.6 *poetry*
erotomania 510.4 *delusion,*
821.5 *desire*
erotophobia 777 Phobias by
Name
err 211.8 *make a mistake,* 335.3
go astray, 504.19 *make a mistake,* 504.20 *transgress,* 525.1
misinterpret, 656.5 *be unskilful,*
844.23 *sin,* 864.16 *be wicked,*
877.16 *do wrong*
errancy 504
errand 703.2 *engagement*
errand boy 697.5 *office assistant*
errant 504, 335.25 *wandering*
errantry 335.16 *wandering*
erratic 54.38 *glacier,* 113.5 *diverse,* 151.14 *irregular,* 160.8
discontinuous, 215.4 *irregular,*
215.5 *unusual,* 324.16 *moving,*

335.25 *wandering*, 491.7 *unreliable*, 491.17 *uncertain person*, 579.1 *capricious*
erratically 335, 113.11 *irregularly*, 151.27 *in disorder*, 215.8 *irregularly*, 491.26 *unreliably*, 579.6 *capriciously*
erraticism 224.2 *irresolution*
erratum 504.12 *typing error*
erring 211.13 *mistaken*, 504.16 *errant*, 864.11 *wicked*
erroneous 504, 211.13 *mistaken*, 474.7 *sophistic*, 538.13 *untrue*, 540.25 *false*, 844.12 *incorrect*
erroneously 504, 211.17 *mistakenly*, 474.14 *sophistically*, 525.4 *mistakenly*, 538.26 *untruthfully*, 540.36 *falsely*, 844.26 *wrong*
erroneousness 504, 538.1 *untruth*, 540.1 *falsehood*, 620.5 *imperfection*, 844.2 *incorrectness*
error 25.5 *bowling delivery*, 52.66 *proof*, 56.83 *sensitivity*, 211.3 *lost chance*, 335.16 *wandering*, 468.5 *inattentive act*, 493.2, 504.1 *mistake*, 508.2 *act of folly*, 519.5 *fantasy*, 525.2 *misinterpretation*, 540.1 *falsehood*, 616.3 *inconvenience*, 620.5 *imperfection*, 620.7 *defect*, 656.9 *bungling*, 683.1 *failure*, 844.2 *incorrectness*, 844.8 *wrong-doing*
Error 504
error of law 16.4 *bad law*
ersatz 114.8 *simulated*, 118.13 *imitation*, 707.7 *deputizing*, 733.11 *borrowed*
erstwhile 154.11 *prior*, 202.13 *former*, 209.14 *dead*
eruct 349.14 *let out*, 349.16, 425.7 *belch*
eructate 349.16 *belch*
eructation 349.24, 388.5 *belch*, 425.4 *belch*
eructative 349
erudite 4.19 *learned*, 6.18 *educated*, 48.16 *literary*, 459.10 *intelligent*, 501.9 *literate*, 507.5 *wise*
erudition 6.9 *learnedness*, 48.1 *literature*, 459.4 *cleverness*, 501.3 *learning*, 507.1 *wisdom*
erupt 156.27 *emerge*, 322.18 *open*, 347.10 *emerge*, 349.14 *let out*
erupting 347.15 *outgoing*
eruption 54, 241.3 *instance of violence*, 347.1 *exit*, 349.22 *disgorgement*, 624.13 *skin disease*
eruptive 54.55 *volcanic*, 241.6 *violent*, 347.15 *outgoing*, 349.29 *expulsive*
eruptively 347.18 *forth*, 349.32 *expulsively*
eruptiveness 349.22 *disgorgement*
erysipelas 624.13 *skin disease*
erysipelatous 624.23 *diseased*
erythema 624.13 *skin disease*
erythrite 54 Minerals
erythritol 62 Medication
erythrocyte 387.4 *blood*
erythromycin 62 Medication
erythrophobia 777 Phobias by Name
erythropoietin 58 Hormones
Erzurum 93 Cities
ESA 53.31 *space travel*
Esbjerg 93 Cities
escalade 346.10 *invade*, 359.14 *climb*, 670.9 *attack successfully*, 670.14 *siege*
escalader 670.19 *attacker*, 679.1 *combatant*
escalate 128.4 *increase*, 128.5 *make bigger*, 361.2 *send up*, 721.10 *augment*, 753.9 *be dear*
escalated 361.11 *raised*
escalating 128.6 *increasing*, 359.23 *rising*
escalation 128.1 *increase*, 361.6 *raising*, 721.2 *augmentation*
escalator 265.5 *means of transport*, 359.8 *lift*, 361.10 *elevator*
escapable 591.20 *avoidable*

escapade 579.3 *whim*
escape 638, 638, 83.2 *plant*, 136.13 *diverge*, 254.18 *abscond*, 345.3 *quit*, 345.7 *departure*, 347.10 *emerge*, 458.2 *depart*, 458.4 *disappearance*, 591.6 *evade*, 591.8 *run away*, 591.14 *evasion*, 632.8 *be safe*, 639.2 *deliverance*, 671.28 *survive*, 682.7 *overcome obstacles*, 698.14 *be free*, 700.1 *liberation*, 700.4 *liberate*, 722.15 *lose someone*, 848.12 *exempt oneself*
Escape 638
escape artist 51.27 *entertainer*
escape by the skin of one's teeth 638.5 *escape*
escape character 65.10 *character*
escape clause 485.7 *condition*, 632.1 *safety*, 632.8 *means of escape*, 716.2 *basis for negotiations*
escaped 83.15 *wild*, 591.18 *avoiding*, 638.8 *escaping*, 698.9 *free*
escape detection 638.6 *elude*
escaped prisoner 638.3 *escaper*
escapee 458.4 *disappearance*, 590.7 *the hunted*, 591.17 *avoider*, 638.3 *escaper*, 698.7 *free person*, 700.3 *liberator*
escape from jail 638.5 *escape*
escape hatch 347.6 *way out*, 632.4 *safety device*, 638.2 *means of escape*
escape lane 71.3 *carriageway*
escape notice 810, 138.7 *be come invisible*, 638.6 *elude*
escape observation 527.13 *hide*
escape one 523.7 *be unintelligible*
escaper 638, 591.17 *avoider*
escape route 347.6 *way out*
escape sequence 65.10 *character*
escape velocity 53.35 *rocketry*
escape wheel 364.6 *rotator*
escaping 638, 458.6 *disappearing*
escapism 61.19 *defence mechanism*, 519.6 *reverie*, 591.12 *shyness*, 638.1 *escape*, 848.3 *self-exemption*
escapist 61.8 *disordered personality*, 519.9 *visionary*, 591.17 *avoider*, 638.3 *escaper*
escapologist 51.27 *entertainer*, 638.3 *escaper*
escapology 458.4 *disappearance*, 638.1 *escape*
escargots 45.45 *French dish*
escarp 671.11 *fortification*
escarpment 275.2 *heights*, 281.3 *vertical thing*, 310.2 *obliquity*
eschar 293.14 *animal covering*
eschatological 7.18 *theological*, 157.20 *ending*, 588.12 *intended*
eschatologist 7.14 *theologian*
eschatology 7.13 *theology*, 157.5 *fate*, 199.4 *looking to the future*, 588.5 *final intention*
escheat 879.7 *punishment*
eschew 591.1 *avoid*, 869.5 *be self-restrained*
eschewal 869.1 *self-restraint*
eschew artifice 658.4 *be naive*
escort 180, 180.7 *attendant*, 180.12 *partner*, 180.14 *keep company with*, 401.4 *boyfriend*, 402.4 *girlfriend*, 632.2 *protection*, 632.9 *protect*, 652.10 *conductor*, 652.15 *conduct*, 653.2 *direct*, 671.14 *guard*, 821.9 *lover*, 821.26 *court*
escorted 180.20 *accompanied*
escribed figure 52.41 *geometric figure*
escritoire 47.4 *table*, 258.3 *cabinet*
escudo 741.11 *national coins*
esculent 350.27 *edible*, 411.7 *tasty*
escutcheon 544.8 *heraldic device*
Esk 96 Rivers
esker 275.4 *mountain range*
Eskimo 5 Languages and Groups of Languages, **7** Non-Christian Religions, 409.6 *Arctic*

Eskimo dog 77 Breeds of Dogs
Eskimo roll 36.6 *canoeing*
Esky 258.6 *box*, 409.4 *cooler*
ESN 6.17 *educatable*
esoteric 4.13 *of philosophy*, 11.12 *occultist*, 11.14 *occult*, 165.17 *exceptional*, 440.11 *benighted*, 523.1, 523.1 *unintelligible*, 527.5, 529.11 *mysterious*, 551.2 *obscure*, 659.12 *problematic*
esoterica 11.2 *the occult*, 529.7 *esotericism*
esoterically 4.25 *theoretically*, 11.25 *occultly*, 523.13 *unintelligibly*
esotericism 529, 11.1 *occultism*, 523.11 *unintelligibility*, 527.11 *mysteriousness*
esoterics 11.1 *occultism*
esoteric sense 520.4 *type of meaning*
esotropia 436.2 *poor sight*
ESP 368.3 *spiritual world*, 403.1 *sensation*
espadrilles 295.19 *footwear*
espalier 69.10 *fruit tree*, 288.2 *braid*, 288.8 *interweave*
especial 165.15 *special*
especially 126.16 *superiorly*, 165.28 *specially*
Esperanto 5.7 *international language*
espionage 435.3 *observation*, 529.2 *secretiveness*, 693.3 *subversion*
esplanade 282.3 *flat thing*, 303.1 *front*, 327.7 *arcade*
espousal 821.8 *love affair*, 823.5 *wedding*
espouse 580.3 *side with*, 714.7 *promise*, 823.15 *marry*
espouse a theory 4.22 *propound a philosophy*
espoused 823.8 *spouse*, 823.21 *married*
espouser 823.8 *spouse*
espresso café 350.15 *eating place*
esprit de corps 819.2 *friendly relations*
esprit d'escalier 209.3 *delayed action*
espy 435.12 *see*, 496.1 *discover*
Esq. 401.3 *male title of address*
esquire 401.3 *male title of address*
ESR 57.17 *analysis*
essay 48.4 *non-fiction*, 479.1, 479.11 *experiment*, 560.3 *narration*, 561.1 *dissertation*, 596.1, 596.5 *attempt*, 674.2 *contest*, 674.11 *contend*
essayed 479.10 *tested*
essayer 596.7 *attempter*
essaying 596.8 *attempting*
essayist 560.10 *descriptive writer*, 561.3 *dissertator*
esse 99.1 *existence*
Essen 93 Cities
essence 62.5 *prescription*, 99.3 *nature*, 134.8 *simplicity*, 243.3 *product*, 257.1 *contents*, 306.1 *form*, 355.8 *extract*, 418.2 *fragrant thing*, 471.1 *idea*, 472.1 *topic*, 473.4 *gist*, 520.1 *meaning*, 611.3 *chief thing*, 617.6 *worth*, 619.3 *perfection*, 861.9 *the best*
Essence 103
Essene 7.6 *non-Christian*
Essenes 7 Non-Christian Religions
essential 103, 99.11 *intrinsic*, 148.8 *belonging*, 257.10 *containing*, 280.3 *base*, 571.1 *necessity*, 571.9 *necessary*, 593.1 *requirement*, 593.4 *required*, 611.3 *chief thing*, 611.5 *important*, 695.1 *compulsion*, 861.2 *best*
essential amino acid 58.8 *amino acid*
essential clause 716.2 *basis for negotiations*
essential content 103
essential element 58

essential facts 165.4 *specifications*
essential fatty acid 58.7 *fat*
essentialism 4.7 *school of thought*
essentialist 4.11 *follower of a doctrine*, 4.14 *of a philosophy*
essentiality 593.3 *needfulness*, 611.1 *importance*
essentialize 355.17 *obtain an extract*
essentially 299, 99.22 *really*, 103.13 *in essence*, 142.13 *on the whole*, 148.14 *constituently*, 257.13 *structurally*, 280.5 *basically*, 472.14 *thematically*, 593.12 *in need*
essential nature 99.3 *nature*
essentialness 571.2 *indispensability*
essential oil 57.7 *oil*, 418.2 *fragrant thing*, 791.6 *toiletries*
essential part 143.5 *largest part*, 396.1 *life*, 611.3 *chief thing*
essentials 165.4 *specifications*
Essequibo 96 Rivers
Essex 92 Counties
est 61.3 *psychiatric treatment*
establish 16.68 *legislate*, 101.12 *establish reality*, 156.17 *begin*, 156.23 *inaugurate*, 166.13 *rule*, 190.7, 217.6 *make permanent*, 225.7 *make stable*, 226.11 *inaugurate*, 243.10 *produce*, 250.9 *locate*, 280.4 *base*, 473.15 *state*, 475.17, 480.2 *prove*, 490.21 *make certain*, 535.19 *confirm*, 537.30 *prove true*, 544.10 *identify*, 594.2 *do the groundwork*
establish a connection 107.7 *relate to*
establish a mean 124.10 *make average*
establish an interrelationship 109.8 *interrelate*
establish a right 845.16 *entitle*
established 584, 1.14 *societal*, 124.1 *average*, 202.12 *olden*, 217.7 *permanent*, 225.10 *stabilized*, 235.14 *operative*, 250.6 *located*, 490.1 *certain*, 490.3 *decided*, 535.13 *supported*, 537.20 *proved*, 544.12 *identified*, 725.8 *propertied*
established custom 584.4 *custom*
established practice 10.1 *ritual*
established ways 584.3 *way*
establisher 243.9 *producer*
establishing 156.34 *inaugural*, 480.9 *verificatory*, 544.1 *identification*
establishment 156.6 *inauguration*, 217.1 *permanence*, 243.2 *manufacture*, 250.4 *placing*, 382.6 *construction*, 480.5 *proof*, 490.13, 535.4 *confirmation*, 537.7 *confirmation*, 544.1 *identification*, 665.1 *party*, 703.4 *council*, 740.8 *store*
establish reality 101
establish residence 250.10 *settle*
establish the trend 233.8 *influence*
Estanatlehi 8 Deities
estate 132, 68.6 *farm*, 71.16 *car*, 105.1 *state*, 251.5 *rank*, 256.4 *official residence*, 570.5 *will*, 723.4 *possession*, 725.1 *property*, 742.5 *wealth*
estate agent 725.7 *property man*, 739.12 *wholesaler*
estate and effects 725.4 *possessions*
estate car 71 Motor Vehicles
estate duty 751.7 *tax*
estate management 68.1 *agriculture*
esteem 9.1, 9.7 *worship*, 318.1 *prominence*, 492.12 *estimate*, 497.8 *be of the opinion*, 611.8 *make important*, 617.6 *worth*, 784.7 *like*, 800.1 *estimation*, 821.23 *love*, 849.1, 849.15 *respect*, 851.2 *admiration*, 851.11 *approve*
esteemed 9.11 *worshipped*, 318.6 *eminent*, 617.1 *worthy*, 821.21 *beloved*, 849.12 *respected*

ester 57 Types of Compounds, 395.7 *oil*, 395.8 *fat*
esterification 57 Types of Chemical Reaction
esterify 57.26 *react*
Esthwaite 94 Lakes
estimable 170.14 *calculable*, 268.14 *measurable*, 617.1 *worthy*, 849.13 *respectable*, 851.21 *praiseworthy*
estimably 170.16 *mathematically*
estimate 492, 52.93 *equate*, 121.5 *measure*, 170.8 *calculate*, 268.1 *measurement*, 268.10 *measure*, 471.17 *theorize*, 479.11 *experiment*, 492.1 *judgment*, 513.9 *predict*, 524.1 *interpretation*, 524.8 *interpret*, 528.3 *document*, 654.1 *advice*, 750.7 *account*, 751.1 *price*, 751.7 *tax*
estimated 268.13 *measured*, 471.10 *theoretical*, 479.10 *tested*
estimated position 74.5 *navigation*
estimated value 56.83 *sensitivity*
estimation 800, 52.66 *proof*, 170.1 *calculation*, 268.1 *measurement*, 471.1 *idea*, 479.3 *experimentation*, 492.1 *judgment*
estimative 170.13 *calculative*
estimator 16.23 *judge*, 170.6 *calculator*, 268.9 *measurer*, 654.4 *adviser*
estinto 49 Musical Terms
Estonia 91 Countries
Estonian 5 Languages and Groups of Languages
Estonians 1 Peoples
estrange 136.11 *divide*, 820.13 *antagonize*, 822.16 *cause hate*
estranged 820, 824.11 *divorced*
estrangement 666.1 *disagreement*, 820.2 *personal conflict*, 822.4 *hatefulness*, 824.2 *separation*
estuarial 98.11 *continental*
estuarine 97.7 *oceanic*
estuary 98.9 *inlet*, 327.11 *channel*
Estuary English 5.26 *dialect*
e.s.u. 75.2 *unit system*
esurient 872.6 *gluttonous*
E.T. 104.6 *outsider*
etc. 146.9 *inclusively*, 175.12 *et cetera*
Etc. 31, 36, 40
et cetera 175, 130.10 *additionally*, 146.9 *inclusively*
etch 50.22 *engrave*, 299.5 *outline*, 321.6 *furrow*, 544.10 *identify*, 545.14 *inscribe*, 547.11 *paint*, 792.10 *decorate*
etched 321.4 *furrowed*
etcher 50.18 *engraver*, 547.4 *person who makes a representation*
etching 50.1 *art*, 50.15 *engraving*, 299.1 *outline*, 321.3 *furrowed thing*, 547.2 *reproduction*, 792.2 *pattern*
etching point 50.15 *engraving*
eternal 184, 190, 8.13 *divine*, 185.21 *lasting through time*, 186.5 *timeless*, 188.9, 217.7 *permanent*, 219.6 *protracted*, 368.8 *nonmaterial*
eternal damnation 8.11 *heaven*
eternal fire 199.3 *future condition*
eternalization 190
eternalize 186.4 *perpetuate*
eternal life 368.1 *nonmaterial world*, 396.5 *life cycle*, 714.4 *promised land*
eternally 184, 190, 8.19 *divinely*, 185.30 *chronologically*, 186.8 *ever*, 188.12 *everlastingly*, 217.9 *permanently*, 219.7 *continually*, 368.13 *metaphysically*
eternal peace 649.1 *ease*
eternal rest 190.3 *life without end*, 325.2 *repose*, 397.1 *death*
eternal return 183.4 *return*
eternal triangle 821.8 *love affair*, 841.1 *jealousy*, 877.4 *illicit love*
eternal verities 537.1 *truth*
eternal youth 714.4 *promised land*
eternity 184, 190, 8.2 *divine at-*

tribute, 186.1 *timelessness*, 217.1 *permanence*, 368.1 *nonmaterial world*, 396.5 *life cycle*
Eternity 190
etesian 55 Winds
ethacrynic acid 62 Medication
ethambutol 62 Medication
ethane 57 Common Chemical Compounds
ethanol 57 Common Chemical Compounds
ethebenecid 62 Medication
ether 57 Types of Compounds, 275.8 *high thing*, 370.7 *light thing*, 372.5, 388.1 *gas*, 390.1 *air*, 404.4 *anaesthetic*
ethereal 8.14 *heavenly*, 11.18 *spiritual*, 102.8 *unreal*, 275.9 *high*, 368.8 *nonmaterial*, 370.2 *insubstantial*, 372.1 *sparse*, 388.17, 390.12 *airy*, 519.12 *imaginary*
etherealism 388.9 *aeriness*
ethereality 102.1 *unreality*, 370.5 *lightness*, 372.3 *sparseness*, 390.9 *airiness*
etherealization 372.4 *rarefaction*, 388.10 *vaporization*
etherealize 11.20 *occult*, 372.6 *make sparse*
etherealized 372.2 *rarefied*
ethereally 368.13 *metaphysically*, 370.11 *lightly*, 372.7 *sparsely*, 388.28 *aerily*
ethereal world 368.1 *nonmaterial world*
Etherege 48 Dramatists
etheriability 388.9 *aeriness*
etheric body 11.7 *spirit*
etherification 388.10 *vaporization*
etherify 388.25 *gasify*
ethering 68.5 *cultivation*
etherism 404.2 *unconsciousness*
etherize 388.26 *aerate*, 404.12 *anaesthetize*
etherized 404.7 *anaesthetized*
Ethernet 65.15 *network*
ethical 863, 4.13 *of philosophy*, 652.17 *well-behaved*, 843.10 *moral*, 847.8 *dutiful*, 857.4 *honourable*, 876.8 *moral*
ethical drug 62.3 *drug*, 630.2 *medicine*
ethically 863, 4.25 *theoretically*, 652.19 *well*, 847.18 *on duty*, 857.7 *honourably*, 876.13 *morally*
ethicalness 876.1 *morality*
ethical self 61.21 *psyche*
ethical system 4.2 *philosophical system*
ethics 847, 4.6 *branch of philosophy*, 7.1 *religion*, 857.1 *probity*, 863.2 *virtues*, 876.1 *morality*
ethinamate 62 Medication
ethinyloestradiol 62 Medication
ethionamide 62 Medication
Ethiopia 91 Countries
Ethiopian 5 Languages and Groups of Languages, 400.4 *civilized human*
Ethiopians 200.6 *people of the past*
Ethiopic 5 Languages and Groups of Languages
ethisterone 62 Medication
ethmoid bone 382 Bones
ethnic 1.13 *racial*, 1.14 *societal*, 149.11 *foreign*, 255.12 *native*, 400.12 *human*
ethnically 1.18 *societally*, 2.16 *sociologically*, 400.15 *humanly*
ethnic cleansing 252.3 *replacement*, 398.3 *homicide*, 481.4 *social discrimination*
ethnic group 1.7 *society*, 2.6 *social group*, 400.9 *group*
ethnic minority 400.9 *group*
ethnic music 49.10 *world music*
ethnic origin 1.6 *race*
ethnobiological 59.20 *biological*
ethnobiologist 59.19 *life scientist*
ethnobiology 59.1 *life science*
ethnobotanical 83.20 *botanical*
ethnobotanist 83.12 *plant scientist*

ethnobotany 1.1 *anthropology*, 83.10 *plant science*
ethnocentric 481.10 *discriminatory*
ethnocentrically 481.17 *prejudicially*
ethnocentricity 481.4 *social discrimination*
ethnogenic 1.11 *anthropological*
ethnogenist 1.3 *anthropologist*
ethnogeny 1.1 *anthropology*
ethnographer 1.3 *anthropologist*, 400.6 *studier of mankind*
ethnographic 1.11 *anthropological*
ethnographical 400.12 *human*
ethnographically 1.16 *anthropologically*, 400.15 *humanly*
ethnography 1.1 *anthropology*, 400.5 *study of mankind*
ethnological 1.11 *anthropological*
ethnologically 1.16 *anthropologically*
ethnologist 1.3 *anthropologist*
ethnology 1.1 *anthropology*, 400.5 *study of mankind*
ethnomusicologist 1.3 *anthropologist*
ethnomusicology 1.1 *anthropology*
ethnoscientific 1.11 *anthropological*
ethnoscientific studies 1.1 *anthropology*
ethological 76.16 *zoological*, 652.16 *behaving*
ethologist 76.11 *zoologist*
ethology 61.1 *psychology*, 76.9 *animal science*
ethos 4.2 *philosophical system*, 652.6 *way of life*, 876.1 *morality*
ethosuximide 62 Medication
ethotoin 62 Medication
ethychloride 62 Medication
ethyl alcohol 57 Common Chemical Compounds
ethyl biscoumacetate 62 Medication
ethylene 57 Common Chemical Compounds, **62** Medication, 58.17 *plant hormone*
ethylene glycol 408.3 *heater*
ethyloestrenol 62 Medication
ethynodiol 62 Medication
etiolate 445.6 *decolour*, 446.13 *whiten*
etiolated 236.12 *impotent*, 445.7 *colourless*
etiolation 445.1 *colourlessness*, 446.7 *whiteness*
etiological 226.13 *causal*
etiology 226.1 *cause*, 624.20 *pathology*
etiquette 794, 813, 167.4 *conventionalism*, 306.5 *formality*, 584.5 *tradition*, 652.2 *good conduct*, 813.1 *formality*, 817.2 *good manners*, 843.3 *properness*
Etna 95 Mountains, 408.8 *hot place*
etoglucid 62 Medication
Eton collar 295.14 *neckwear*
Eton crop 791.8 *hair cut*
Eton jacket 295.11 *jacket*
Etruscan 5 Languages and Groups of Languages, **7** Non-Christian Religions, 50.29 *realist*, 202.14 *historic*
Etruscan art 50 Western Art Styles and Movements
Etruscans 1 Peoples, 200.6 *people of the past*
etymological 5.38 *linguistic*, 520.6 *meaningful*
etymologically 5.48 *linguistically*
etymologist 5.2 *linguist*
etymology 5.1 *linguistics*, 226.1 *cause*, 520.4 *type of meaning*
etymon 5.17 *word*, 5.35 *part of speech*, 226.3 *rudiment*
Eubransdal 32 Breeds of Horse and Pony
eucalyptus 85 Trees and Shrubs, 418.3 *incense*
eucharis 84 Flowers and Flowering Plants
Eucharist 10, 10.5 *Christian rite*, 837.2 *thanks*
eucharistial 10.14 *sacred object*

eucharistic 10.21 *ritualistic*
euchre 42 Card Games
euchromosome 59.14 *chromosome*
Eucken 4 Philosophers
Euclid 4 Philosophers, **52** Scientists
Euclidean geometry 52 Named Concepts, 52.34 *geometry*
Euclidean space 52.35 *space*
Euclidian 4.11 *follower of a doctrine*, 4.14 *of a philosophy*
Euclid's axioms 52 Named Concepts
eucryphia 85 Trees and Shrubs
eudaemonism 4.7 *school of thought*
eudaemonist 4.11 *follower of a doctrine*
eudaemonistic 4.14 *of a philosophy*
eudemonia 649.1 *ease*
eudemonic 649.4 *at ease*
eudiometer 388.15 *vaporimeter*
Eudoxus of Cnidus 52 Scientists
Eugene 93 Cities
eugenics 59.11 *genetics*, 60.3 *medical specialty*, 245.3 *propagation*
euglena 90 Algae, 260.2 *little thing*
euhemerism 4.7 *school of thought*, 524.1 *interpretation*
euhemerist 4.11 *follower of a doctrine*, 524.6 *interpreter*
euhemeristic 4.14 *of a philosophy*, 524.14 *interpretive*
Euhemerus 4 Philosophers
eukaryote 59.3 *organism*
eukaryotic 59.23 *cellular*
eukaryotic cell 59.7 *cell*
Euler 52 Scientists
Euler's constant 52 Named Concepts
Euler's formula 52 Named Concepts
eulogia 10.9 *prayer*
eulogist 399.3 *funeral director*, 851.9 *praiser*
eulogistic 399.11 *funeral*, 851.18 *approving*
eulogistical 399.11 *funeral*
eulogistically 399.12 *funereally*
eulogize 397.17 *bury*, 851.15 *compliment*
eulogizer 399.3 *funeral director*, 851.9 *praiser*
eulogy 397.8 *after death*, 399.2 *funeral*, 564.8 *speech*, 851.4 *compliment*
Eumenides 8 Deities
eumitosis 59.10 *cell division*
Eumycota 89.3 *fungi*
Eunomia 53 Minor Planets
eunuch 401, 825.4 *celibate person*
euonymus 85 Trees and Shrubs
eupepsia 623.3 *health*
eupeptic 623.1 *healthy*
euphemism 134.1 *purity*, 286.3 *deviousness*, 557.1 *ornament*, 797.1 *affectedness*, 876.4 *self-righteousness*
euphemisms 827
euphemistic 134.12 *morally pure*, 286.5 *devious*, 557.4 *ornate*, 797.3 *affected*, 876.10 *moralistic*
euphemistically 286.9 *deviously*
euphemize 242.4 *moderate*, 557.5 *ornament*
euphonic 116.13 *harmonious*, 433.6 *melodious*
euphonically 116.33 *harmoniously*
euphonious 116.13 *harmonious*, 405.6 *pleasant*, 433.6 *melodious*, 558.3 *elegant*
euphoniously 116.33 *harmoniously*, 433.11 *melodiously*, 558.5 *elegantly*
euphoniousness 116.4 *harmony*, 433.3 *melodiousness*
euphonium 49 Musical Instruments
euphony 48.12 *poetic language*, 49.13 *melody*, 116.4 *harmony*,

433.3 *melodiousness*, 558.1 *elegance*
euphorbia 84 Flowers and Flowering Plants
euphoria 405.1 *physical pleasure*, 762.1 *happiness*
euphoric 405.7 *pleased*, 762.4 *happy*, 773.9 *rejoicing*
euphorically 773.11 *rejoicing*
Euphrates 96 Rivers, 96.5 *other major rivers*
Euphrosyne 8 Deities, **53** Minor Planets
euphuism 557.1 *ornament*, 797.1 *affectedness*
Euphuism 48 Literary Groups and Movements
euphuist 557.3 *phrasemonger*, 558.2 *stylist*
euphuistic 557.4 *ornate*
euphuize 557.5 *ornament*
Eupolis 48 Dramatists
Eurasia 98.1 *continent*
Eurasian 133.5 *hybrid*
eureka 471.25 *got it*
eurhythmic 308.5 *even*
eurhythmical 308.5 *even*
eurhythmics 46.1 *dancing*, 627.9 *physical improvement*, 644.5 *exercise*
eurhythmy 308.3 *evenness*
Euripidean tragedy 51.9 *tragedy*
Euripides 48 Dramatists
Eurobond market 741.7 *finance*
Eurocheque 741.14 *paper money*
Eurocrat 653.16 *official*
Eurocurrency market 741.7 *finance*
euro-disco 49.7 *dance music*
Eurodollar 741.7 *finance*
Eurodollar market 14.1, 741.7 *finance*
Euromarket 13.5 *international trade*, 737.5 *commercial trade*, 740.4 *free market*, 741.7 *finance*
Euro-MP 653.16 *official*
Euronet 65.15 *network*
Europe 98.1 *continent*
European Bank 732.4 *lending institution*, 741.7 *finance*
European Boxing Union 26.2 *boxing*
European commissioner 653.16 *official*
European Community 13.5 *international trade*, 400.9 *group*, 724.1 *joint possession*, 737.5 *commercial trade*, 740.4 *free market*
European Community law 16.1 *the law*
European Cup 38.1 *soccer*
European Cup Winners' Cup 38.1 *soccer*
European Currency Unit 14.1 *finance*
European Economic Area 740.4 *free market*
European Economic Community 13.5 *international trade*, 400.9 *group*, 737.5 *commercial trade*, 740.4 *free market*
European Free Trade Association 13.5 *international trade*, 737.5 *commercial trade*, 740.4 *free market*
European Games 21.5 *competition*
Europeanize 220.12 *naturalize*
Europeanized 220.17 *naturalized*
European Luge Championships 41.9 *bobsledding*
European Monetary System 14.1, 741.7 *finance*
European Organization for Nuclear Research 235.8 *nuclear power*
European Parliament 653.10 *legislative body*
European Parliament member 653.16 *official*
European sea bass 20.5 *British game fish*
European Southern Observatory 53.23 *observatory*
Europe class 36.2 *sailing boat*
europium 57 Chemical Elements

Eurus 55.15 *wind direction*
Euryale 11.4 *witch*
eurypterid 81.4 *arthropod*
Eustachian tube 420.5 *internal ear*
Euston Road school 50 Schools and Groups of Artists
eutectic 57.3 *phase*, 57.7 *chemical compound*, 57.32 *solid*
Eutelsat 534.7 *satellite communication*
euthanasia 397.5 *ways of dying*, 398.1 *killing*
Eutheria 77.5 *placental mammal*
eutherian 77.5 *placental mammal*, 77.25 *mammalian*
eutherian characteristic 77.5 *placental mammal*
eutrophication 90.1 *alga*
euxenite 54 Minerals
evacuant 134.4 *purgative*
evacuate 254.19 *leave empty*, 345.2 *withdraw*, 347.10 *emerge*, 349.11 *void*, 353.16 *defecate*, 598.2 *withdraw*
evacuated 252.10 *replaced*
evacuation 252.3 *replacement*, 345.7 *departure*, 347.1 *exit*, 349.21 *removal*, 353.2 *defecation*, 598.3 *relinquishment*
evacuation service 17.4 *military organization*
evacuee 149.8 *exile*, 252.7 *displaced person*, 816.7 *outsider*
evade 540, 591, 286.7 *deviate*, 331.2 *respond*, 474.12 *deceive*, 531.11 *conceal oneself*, 531.13 *equivocate*, 538.24 *pretend*, 576.6 *hesitate*, 578.1 *be equivocal*, 638.6 *elude*, 720.8 *not perform*, 722.15 *lose someone*, 858.8 *be dishonourable*
evade detection 527.13 *hide*
evade liability 848.12 *exempt oneself*
evade one's creditors 747.7 *not pay*
evade one's responsibilities 717.5 *be irresolute*, 848.12 *exempt oneself*
evader 720, 531.7 *concealer*, 591.17 *avoider*, 638.3 *escaper*
evade tax 113.12 *cheat*
evade taxes 638.6 *elude*, 711.5 *refuse*, 736.16 *act dishonest*, 747.7 *not pay*
evading 720.12 *nonperforming*
evaginate 287.3 *invert*
evagination 287.1 *inversion*
evaluate 52, 4.21 *rationalize*, 52.90 *enumerate*, 121.5, 268.10 *measure*, 492.12 *estimate*, 524.11 *criticize*, 751.11 *price*
evaluation 52, 52.66 *proof*, 268.1 *measurement*, 492.1 *judgment*
evaluation of returns 580.12 *election*
evanesce 129.4 *decrease*, 189.4 *be transient*, 458.1 *disappear*
evanescence 129.1 *decrease*, 189.1 *transience*, 458.4 *disappearance*
evanescent 129.6 *decreasing*, 189.6 *transient*, 458.6 *disappearing*
evangelical 7.15 *religious*
Evangelical 7.5 *Christian*
Evangelicalism 7 Christian Movements
evangelism 220.3 *persuasion*, 629.10 *revival*
evangelist 7.5 *Christian*, 220.5 *converter*
evangelization 220.3 *persuasion*
evangelize 7.20 *preach*, 220.11 *persuade*, 497.9 *make someone believe*
evangelized 220.16 *influenced*
Evans 49 Musicians and Composers
Evansville 93 Cities
evaporability 388.8 *volatility*
evaporable 388.23 *volatile*
evaporate 54.5 *ebb*, 57.25 *solidify*, 100.13 *cease to exist*, 129.4 *decrease*, 162.11 *explode*,

162.14 *dilute*, 189.4 *be transient*, 244.8 *destroy*, 371.8 *be dense*, 388.25 *gasify*, 392.17 *dry*, 392.23 *drip-dry*, 458.1 *disappear*, 607.1 *waste*, 722.12 *lessen*
evaporated 55.43 *atmospheric*, 57.32 *solid*, 162.27 *dilute*, 392.4 *dried-out*
evaporated milk 351.5 *milk*
evaporating 458.6 *disappearing*
evaporating dish 57 Laboratory Apparatus
evaporation 54.10 *water cycle*, 55.9 *atmospheric process*, 56.37 *temperature*, 57.3 *phase*, 129.1 *decrease*, 162.3 *dilution*, 347.2 *outflow*, 388.10 *vaporization*, 458.4 *disappearance*, 607.3 *waste*, 722.4 *lessening*
evaporative 388.23 *volatile*, 392.9 *drying*
evaporator 392.15 *dryer*
evaporimeter 268.8 *meter*
evasion 531, 540, 591, 26.9 *tae kwon do*, 286.3 *deviousness*, 331.6 *response*, 474.5 *hypocrisy*, 538.8 *pretence*, 578.5 *equivocalness*, 592.3 *expedient plan*, 638.1 *escape*, 657.1 *cunning*, 657.2 *stratagem*
evasion of responsibility 717.3 *irresolution*, 848.3 *self-exemption*
evasive 540, 286.5 *devious*, 309.8 *exaggerated*, 474.8 *cunning*, 531.17 *noncommittal*, 538.15 *lying*, 566.3 *sparing with words*, 576.1 *vacillating*, 578.10 *equivocal*, 591.18 *avoiding*, 638.8 *escaping*, 717.8 *irresolute*
evasive action 591.14 *evasion*
evasively 591, 26.16 *professionally*, 309.14 *distortedly*, 474.15 *hypocritically*, 538.27 *pretentiously*, 578.12 *equivocally*, 717.10 *irresolutely*
evasiveness 591, 531.5 *evasion*, 566.4 *taciturnity*
eve 205.1 *evening*
Eve 402.2 *female*, 586.13 *tempter*
Evelyn 48 Writers
even 308, 52.71 *numerical*, 110.17 *regular*, 112.5 *uniform*, 116.14 *conforming*, 122.8 *on equal terms*, 122.11 *equalize*, 169.8 *odd*, 214.11 *regular*, 214.14 *orderly*, 282.7 *make horizontal*, 282.8 *horizontal*, 308.6 *symmetrize*, 333.4 *middle*, 376.1 *smooth*, 376.2 *uniform*, 376.11 *smooth*, 537.39 *accurately*
even as 198.15 *as*
even break 110.5 *equality*, 122.2 *equilibrium*, 843.1 *fairness*
even chance 229.2 *chance*, 486.3 *strong possibility*, 488.4 *chance*, 589.3 *equal chance*
even deal 843.1 *fairness*
evened up 125.10 *counterbalancing*
even-handed 843.7 *right*
even-handedness 843.1 *fairness*
even if 518.11 *supposing*
evening 205, 205, 205, 157.9 *close*
evening bag 258.8 *bag*
evening class 205.4 *evening thing*
evening damp 391.6 *dew*
evening dress 295.3, 813.4 *formal dress*
evening gloves 295.25 *accessories*
evening gown 295.3 *formal dress*, 295.7 *frock*, 813.4 *formal dress*
evening light 441.1 *dimness*
evening meal 350.12 *meal*
evening news 205.4 *evening thing*, 533.6 *radio news*
evening of one's life 207.5 *old age*
evening paper 532.4 *newspaper*
evening prayers 10.4 *public worship*
evening primrose 205.4 *evening thing*

evenings 110.20 *regularly*, 205.7 *evening*
evening service 10.4 *public worship*
evening shirt 295.8 *shirt*
evening star 53.10 *star*, 205.4 *evening thing*
evening thing 205
evening time 205.1 *evening*
evening twilight 205.1 *evening*
evening up 122.3 *equalization*, 125.10 *counterbalancing*
even keel 122.2 *equilibrium*
Evenki 5 Languages and Groups of Languages
even less 129.8 *decreasingly*
evenly 110.20 *regularly*, 112.13 *uniformly*, 116.35 *consistently*, 122.12 *equally*, 214.15 *regularly*, 214.17 *orderly*, 282.11 *horizontally*, 308.8 *equally*, 376.14 *smoothly*
evenly matched 122.8 *on equal terms*
even match 674.2 *contest*
even money 110.5, 122.1 *equality*
even more 126.17 *supremely*
even more so 128.8 *increasingly*
evenness 308, 110.6 *regularity*, 112.1 *uniformity*, 122.1 *equality*, 122.2 *equilibrium*, 214.4 *orderliness*, 282.1 *horizontality*, 376.7 *smoothness*
even number 52.5 *number*, 169.2 *kind of number*
even out 116.26 *make uniform*, 124.10 *make average*
even pace 110.6 *regularity*, 112.1 *uniformity*
even rhythm 112.1 *uniformity*
evens 32.7 *horseracing*, 486.3 *strong possibility*
even-sided 122.6 *equal*, 308.4 *symmetrical*, 308.5 *even*
even-siddedly 308.8 *equally*
even sides 308.1 *symmetry*
evensong 10.4 *public worship*, 205.1 *evening*
even Stevens 308.8 *equally*
event 3.14 *historicalness*, 18.1 *sport*, 52.58 *frequency distribution*, 106.2 *occurrence*, 227.1 *effect*, 665.7 *social gathering*, 674.2 *contest*
even temper 4.3 *detachment*, 817.1 *courtesy*
even-tempered 4.18 *detached*, 817.7 *courteous*
eventer 32.15 *horse person*
eventful 106.7 *circumstantial*, 611.6 *notable*, 642.19 *busy*
event horizon 53.11 *stellar birth*
eventide 205.1 *evening*
eventing 32, 32.6 *horsemanship*
even-toed 77.33 *ungulate*
even-toed ungulate 77.15 *hoofed mammal*
events 472.3 *matter of interest*
eventual 106.7 *circumstantial*, 157.24 *limiting*, 199.11 *future*, 227.10 *caused*, 486.6 *potential*, 714.15 *future*
eventuality 106.1 *circumstances*, 486.1 *possibility*
eventually 106.16 *relatively*, 157.26 *finally*, 199.14 *in the future*, 227.12 *with the effect of*, 486.11, 714.18 *potentially*
eventuate in 227.5 *show an effect*
even up 110.8 *make the same*, 112.9 *be uniform*, 122.11 *equalize*, 125.5 *counterbalance*, 308.6 *symmetrize*
even with 130.10 *additionally*
ever 186, 185.26 *all the time*
ever and anon 212.1 *frequently*
ever-changing 216.11, 224.13 *changeable*
Everest 95 Mountains, 95.6 *other major mountains and ranges*, 126.4 *summit*, 275.3 *mountain*
evergreen 83.2 *plant*, 83.14 *of plants*, 85.1 *tree*, 85.14 *treelike*, 188.8 *lasting*, 190.8 *eternal*,

217.7 *permanent*, 225.9 *stable*, 453.4 *fresh*, 453.8 *greenness*
evergreen copy 533.10 *copy*
ever higher 359.26 *up*
ever-increasing 128.6 *increasing*
everlasting 184.3 *eternal*, 185.21 *lasting through time*, 186.5 *timeless*, 188.9 *permanent*, 190.8 *eternal*, 217.7 *permanent*, 219.6 *protracted*
Everlasting Father 8.3 *God*
everlasting flower 84.1 *flower*
everlastingly 188, 186.8 *ever*, 217.9 *permanently*, 219.7 *continually*
everlastingness 184.7 *eternity*, 186.2 *agelessness*, 190.1 *eternity*, 217.1 *permanence*
ever less 129.3 *decreasingly*
evermore 186.8 *ever*, 190.11 *eternally*
eversion 216.1 *change*
ever so many 181.6 *many*
evert 216.8 *cause change*
Evert 18 Sporting Personalities
ever-victorious 682.15 *victorious*
ever-welcome 815.16 *popular*
every 142.6 *whole*, 195.12 *succeeding*
every afternoon 205.7 *evening*
every bit 142.11 *wholly*
everybody 142.4 *all*, 164.10 *everyone*, 400.1 *humankind*
everybody's fool 850.9 *butt*
everybody under the sun 164.10 *everyone*
everyday 167, 5.39 *of language*, 124.1 *average*, 164.21 *common*, 214.14 *orderly*
every day 214.16 *cyclically*
everyday 556.1 *simple*, 584.9 *habitual*, 584.10 *familiar*, 599.9 *used*, 620.4 *ordinary*
everyday knowledge 655.1 *skill*
everyday occurrence 212.4 *frequency*
everyday practice 652.7 *way*
everyday speech 544.1 *simplicity*
everyday work 644.1 *work*
every evening 205.7 *evening*
every hour 212.1 *frequently*
every inch 142.11 *wholly*, 144.10 *fully*
every inch a king 126.15 *excellent*
every living soul 400.1 *humankind*
everyman 164, 124.7 *average person*, 400.7 *person*, 803.1 *plebeian*
every man for himself 689.1 *anarchy*, 860.1 *selfishness*
every-man-for-himself 16.61 *lawless*
every man Jack 164.10 *everyone*
every minute 212.1 *frequently*
every month 214.16 *cyclically*
every morning 204.8 *in the morning*
every mother's son 161.20 *crowd*, 164.10 *everyone*
every night 205.7 *evening*, 214.16 *cyclically*
every now and again 212.2 *sometimes*, 215.8 *irregularly*
everyone 164, 142.4 *all*, 400.1 *humankind*
everyone and everything 142.4 *all*
every other 155.16 *alternating*, 195.12 *succeeding*
every other day 214.16 *cyclically*
every other month 214.16 *cyclically*
every other night 214.16 *cyclically*
every other week 214.16 *cyclically*
every other year 214.16 *cyclically*
every second 155.16 *alternating*, 195.12 *succeeding*, 212.1 *frequently*
every so often 212.2 *sometimes*, 265.8 *apart*
everything 777 Phobias by Topic, 142.4 *all*, 164.10 *everyone*

everything being equal 492.14 *considering*
everything but the kitchen sink 113.2 *assortment*, 142.4 *all*, 326.10 *transferred thing*
every Tom, Dick, and Harry 161.20 *crowd*, 164.10 *everyone*
every way 332.11 *in all directions*
every week 214.16 *cyclically*
everywhere 162, 164.32 *universally*, 248.16 *extensively*, 253.7 *present*, 253.15 *here*, 332.11 *in all directions*
every which way 113.11 *irregularly*, 151.28 *anyhow*
every which way 248.16 *extensively*, 332.11 *in all directions*
every whit 144.10 *fully*
everywoman 124.7 *average person*, 164.9 *everyman*, 400.7 *person*
every year 214.16 *cyclically*
evict 349, 147.8 *eject*, 252.16 *replace*, 722.9 *lose*, 734.8 *take back*
evicted 147.11 *excluded*, 252.10 *replaced*
eviction 349, 147.2 *ejection*, 252.3 *replacement*, 722.1 *loss*, 734.2 *taking back*
evictor 349.26 *ejector*
evidence 480, 483, 16.7 *legal trial*, 437.3 *visibility*, 473.3 *line of argument*, 475.4 *proof*, 475.17 *prove*, 490.9 *certainty*, 490.13 *confirmation*, 518.2 *basis of supposition*, 520.10 *mean*, 526.3 *reveal*, 526.10 *manifestation*, 537.7 *confirmation*, 543.1 *sign*, 688.9 *permission*, 856.1 *accusation*
Evidence 483
evidence in chief 483.5 *legal evidence*
evident 483, 322.13 *opened up*, 435.23, 437.1 *visible*, 442.4 *easily seen through*, 457.7 *appearing*, 475.12 *demonstrable*, 488.6 *probable*, 526.14 *manifest*
evidential 483, 475.13 *proven*, 480.9 *verificatory*, 543.14 *signifying*
evidentially 543.18 *indicatively*
evidently 483, 322.25 *obviously*, 435.25, 437.11 *visibly*, 457.15 *apparently*, 526.16 *manifestly*
evidentness 483
evil 862, 862, 8.16 *devilish*, 440.7 *spiritual darkness*, 440.11 *benighted*, 447.5 *black-hearted*, 601.2 *misuse*, 601.5 *abusive*, 618.3 *bad*, 618.5 *harmful*, 618.9 *badness*, 631.1 *affliction*, 631.16 *blighting*, 687.1 *adversity*, 832.10 *malevolent*, 844.16 *in the wrong*, 858.5 *dishonourable*, 864.1 *wickedness*, 864.11 *wicked*, 877.1 *immorality*, 877.11 *immoral*
Evil 862
evil act 832.7 *act of malevolence*
evil deed 844.8 *wrong-doing*
evil-disposed 832.10 *malevolent*
evil disposition 832.1 *malevolence*
evildoer 618.12 *bad person*, 640.3 *doer*, 832.8 *malefactor*, 862.6 *evil person*, 864.9 *wicked person*
evildoing 864.1 *wickedness*, 864.11 *wicked*
evil eye 11.5 *spell*, 435.6 *look*, 822.2 *curse*
evil genius 618.12 *bad person*, 862.6 *evil person*
evil intent 832.1 *malevolence*
evilly 862, 601.6 *abusively*, 864.18 *wickedly*
evil-minded 832.10 *malevolent*
evil nature 877.1 *immorality*
evilness 618.9 *badness*, 832.1 *malevolence*, 844.5 *unrighteousness*, 858.1 *improbity*, 862.1 *evil*
evil omen 636.1 *warning*
evil person 862
evil plight 862.5 *evil thing*
evil portent 636.1 *warning*

evil power 862
evil ruler 862.6 *evil person*
evil-smelling 419.3 *stinking*
evil-speaking 822.13 *angry*, 827.3 *vilification*
evil spell 822.2 *curse*, 862.4 *evil power*
evil spirit 8.7 *devil*, 618.12 *bad person*
evil star 618.11 *harmfulness*, 687.3 *bad fortune*, 862.3 *bad luck*
evil thing 862
evil wish 862.5 *evil thing*
evince 473.15 *state*, 475.17, 480.2 *prove*, 490.21 *make certain*, 526.3 *reveal*
evirate 236.9 *make impotent*
evirate 236.9 *make impotent*
eviscerate 349.11 *void*, 355.14 *suck*, 628.5 *hurt*
evisceration 355.4 *sucking*
evocation 11.5 *spell*, 59.15 *developmental biology*, 226.1 *cause*, 355.5 *drawing out*, 511.1 *memory*, 547.1 *representation*
evocative 355.18 *extractive*, 511.7 *memorable*, 520.6 *meaningful*, 547.13 *representational*, 560.11 *descriptive*
evocatively 355.22 *expressively*
evocative psychotherapy 61.3 *psychiatric treatment*
evoke 11.22 *conjure*, 114.10 *be similar*, 226.10 *awaken*, 228.9 *motivate*, 355.15 *draw out*, 547.9 *represent*, 560.15 *recount*
evolute 52.40 *curve*
evolution 59, 220, 59.1 *life science*, 99.8 *creation*, 170.1 *calculation*, 324.3 *motion towards*, 336.14 *development*, 396.8 *theories of life*, 640.1 *action*, 640.2 *deed*
evolutionary 59, 59.20 *biological*
evolutionist 59.19 *life scientist*
evolve 99.18 *come to be*, 121.6 *change gradually*, 220.8 *be transformed*, 227.7 *follow from*, 243.10 *produce*, 324.13 *be in motion*, 336.5 *develop*, 382.15 *shape*, 627.2 *get better*, 714.10 *show potential*
evolved 99.15 *created*, 227.10 *caused*
evolve into 220.7 *convert into*
evolving 220.2 *evolution*, 220.14 *converting*
evolving from 227.10 *caused*
evulse 355.11 *extract*
evulsion 355.1 *extraction*
ewe 68.8 *livestock*, 77.18 *female mammal*, 402.14 *female animal*
Ewe 1 Peoples, **5** Languages and Groups of Languages
ewe-lamb 402.14 *female animal*
ewer 44.8 *ceramic object*, 258.11 *vessel*, 389.16 *water carrier*
ex 154.11 *prior*, 200.20 *former*
exa 75 SI Units
exacerbate 128.5 *make bigger*, 241.9 *make violent*, 541.7 *exaggerate*, 628.3 *make worse*, 768.6 *aggravate*, 822.16 *cause hate*, 830.12 *make irritable*
exacerbated 541.12 *exaggerated*, 628.12 *deteriorated*, 768.4 *aggravated*
exacerbation 128.1 *increase*, 541.1 *exaggeration*, 628.10 *impairment*, 768.1 *aggravation*
exact 106.10 *detailed*, 114.9 *lifelike*, 355.16 *extort*, 469.9 *careful*, 503.5, 537.21 *accurate*, 550.3 *clear*, 552.3 *concise*, 619.1 *perfect*, 690.8 *severe*, 692.10 *demand*, 695.7 *force*, 712.7 *demand*, 719.7 *observant*, 751.12 *charge*, 813.6 *formal*, 843.8 *correct*
exacta 32.7 *horseracing*
exact amount 608.7 *sufficiency*
exact a penalty 879.2 *penalize*
exact compensation 672.3 *retaliate*
exact image 547.6 *image*
exacting 355, 593.6 *demanding*, 619.2 *perfectionist*, 650.4 *fatigu-*

ing, 659.10 *difficult*, 659.12 *problematic*, 690.8 *severe*
exactingly 355.21 *away*, 690.11 *severely*
exaction 355.6 *extortion*, 712.2 *demand*, 751.8 *levy*
exaction of penalty 879.8 *penalty*
exactitude 469.4 *fastidiousness*, 503.1, 537.8 *accuracy*
exactive 355.20 *exacting*
exact likeness 547.1 *representation*
exact location 250
exactly 106.19 *meticulously*, 114.14 *comparably*, 165.28 *specially*, 332.9 *directly*, 503.8, 537.39 *accurately*, 550.4 *clearly*, 552.5 *concisely*, 619.7 *perfectly*, 719.8 *observantly*
exactly enough 608.9 *enough*
exactness 469.1 *carefulness*, 503.1, 537.8 *accuracy*, 550.1 *clarity*, 552.1 *conciseness*, 619.3 *perfection*
exact picture 547.6 *image*
exact retribution 879.2 *penalize*
exact revenge 832.19 *be pitiless*
exact science 56.1 *physics*
exact time 185.7 *time measurement*
exaggerate 357, 541, 128.5 *make bigger*, 309.12 *distort the truth*, 494.4 *overestimate*, 519.14 *imagine*, 519.15 *fantasize*, 525.1 *misinterpret*, 548.4 *misrepresent*, 610.4 *be excessive*, 611.8 *make important*, 768.6 *aggravate*, 811.30 *put on airs*
exaggerated 309, 357, 541, 494.6 *overestimated*, 519.10 *imaginative*, 521.10 *meaningless*, 525.3 *misinterpreted*, 535.15 *emphasized*, 538.13 *untrue*, 540.32 *falsified*, 548.6 *misrepresented*, 557.4 *ornate*, 610.6 *excessive*, 620.2 *incomplete*, 757.2 *unrestrained*
exaggerated lengths 541.1 *exaggeration*
exaggeratedly 541, 525.5 *misrepresentedly*, 538.26 *untruthfully*
exaggerating 541.1 *exaggeration*
exaggeration 541, 128.1 *increase*, 309.4 *distortion of the truth*, 357.9 *excessiveness*, 494.1 *overestimation*, 519.4 *ideality*, 521.5 *empty talk*, 525.2 *misinterpretation*, 532.8 *public relations*, 538.1 *untruth*, 548.1 *misrepresentation*, 557.2 *affectation*, 610.1 *excess*, 757.5 *unrestrainedness*, 768.1 *aggravation*
Exaggeration 541
exaggerator 541, 494.3 *optimist*
exalt 8.17 *deify*, 9.7 *worship*, 10.19 *offer worship*, 128.5 *make bigger*, 275.17 *raise*, 361.3 *promote*, 611.8 *make important*, 849.17, 851.14 *praise*
exaltation 8.9 *deification*, 9.1 *worship*, 10.3 *rite of worship*, 78.13 *assemblage of birds*, 128.1 *increase*, 275.1 *height*, 361.7 *lift*, 762.1 *happiness*, 851.3 *praise*
exalted 275, 361, 8.15 *deified*, 318.6 *eminent*, 611.6 *notable*
exaltedly 318.11 *eminently*
exaltedness 318.1 *prominence*
exalting 804.1 *right*
examination 4.4 *philosophical investigation*, 16.7 *legal trial*, 435.3 *observation*, 467.2 *close attention*, 477.3 *questionnaire*, 479.3 *experimentation*, 561.1 *dissertation*, 568.6 *interview*
examinational 477.13 *problematic*
examination paper 6.14 *school book*
examinations 485.3 *qualifications*
examine 4.20 *philosophical investigate*, 16.71 *try a case*, 60.19 *practise medicine*, 435.14 *inspect*, 467.11 *take note of*, 477.17 *question*, 477.18 *interrogate*,

479.11 *experiment*, 492.12 *estimate*
examined 477.16 *questioned*
examinee 477.10 *person questioned*, 674.10 *contender*
examiner 465.3 *curious person*, 467.6 *attentive person*, 477.9 *questioner*, 492.5 *judge*, 568.7 *conversationalist*
examiner of accounts 750.6 *accountant*
examine the accounts 750.8 *audit*
examining 477.12 *questioning*
example 143.2 *particular*, 154.4, 166.5 *precedent*, 305.2 *prototype*, 471.6 *ideal*, 475.3 *explanation*, 524.1 *interpretation*, 526.7 *showpiece*, 547.8 *representative*, 636.1 *warning*, 652.1 *conduct*, 654.3 *precept*, 879.7 *punishment*
exam success 682.3 *successful thing*
exanimate 397.19 *dead*
exasperate 241.9 *make violent*, 650.6 *fatigue*, 659.22 *cause trouble*, 768.8 *annoy*, 828.9 *offend*
exasperated 828.15 *resentful*
exasperating 659.13 *inconvenient*, 768.5 *aggravating*
exasperatingly 828.17 *resentfully*
exasperation 768.2 *annoyance*, 828.1 *resentment*
ex cathedra 535.14 *assertive*, 535.25 *explicitly*, 688.23 *authoritatively*
excavate 200, 3.21 *antiquarianize*, 63.30 *engineer*, 277.14 *deepen*, 317.7 *make concave*, 322.20 *hole*, 355.13 *dig out*, 360.15 *tunnel*
excavated 322.14 *holed*
excavate the past 200.16 *excavate*
excavation 200, 3.12 *historicism*, 63.29 *construction equipment*, 277.1 *depth*, 317.2 *concave land*, 322.5 *hole*, 355.3 *digging out*, 360.7 *tunnelling*, 496.7 *detection*
excavation site 647.1 *workshop*
excavator 355, 63.29 *construction equipment*, 317.4 *digger*, 322.3 *person who opens*, 646.1 *worker*
exceed 357, 126.8 *be superior*, 128.4 *increase*
exceeding 126.12 *superior*
exceedingly 126.16 *superiorly*
exceeding the law 16.55 *illegal*
exceed one's authority 16.74 *be lawless*
exceed requirements 610.5 *be superfluous*
excel 165, 126.8 *be superior*, 357.3 *exceed*, 617.9 *be worthy*, 655.10 *be skilful*, 861.19 *be good at*
excellence 126.1 *superiority*, 163.9 *distinction*, 611.1 *importance*, 617.6 *worth*, 619.3 *perfection*, 655.1 *skill*, 861.8 *good*, 863.3 *worth*
excellent 126, 696, 611.6 *notable*, 617.1 *worthy*, 619.1 *perfect*, 655.6 *skilful*, 786.8 *wonderful*, 861.1 *good*, 863.7 *worthy*
excellently 126.16 *superiorly*, 617.11 *worthily*, 619.7 *perfectly*, 696.16 *masterfully*, 861.22 *well*, 863.11 *worthily*
exceller 617, 655.3 *masterpiece*, 655.4 *skilled person*
excelsior 359.26 *up*
excelsior figure 359.11 *ascender*
except 106.15 *under the circumstances*, 131.3 *subtract*, 131.8 *by subtraction*, 132.8 *leave*, 136.10 *set apart*, 147.7 *exclude*, 147.12 *exclusively*, 581.3 *exclude*, 698.15 *set free*, 848.9 *exempt*
excepted 131.5 *subtracted*, 136.17 *unjoined*, 147.11 *excluded*, 698.9 *free*, 848.5 *exempt*
except for 147.12 *exclusively*
excepting 131.8 *by subtraction*, 147.12 *exclusively*

exception 165, 113.1 *diversity*, 131.1 *subtraction*, 136.2 *setting apart*, 147.1 *exclusion*, 168.6 *deviation*, 581.5 *rejection*, 698.1 *freedom*, 848.1 *exemption*, 852.4 *disagreement*
exceptional 165, 113.5 *diverse*, 168.14 *eccentric*, 215.5 *unusual*, 489.2 *questionable*, 786.8 *wonderful*
exceptionality 168.4 *unusualness*
exceptionally 113.10 *diversely*, 165.30 *characteristically*, 215.9 *unusually*, 489.10 *rarely*
exceptionalness 215.2 *unusualness*
exceptional person 786.5 *person of wonder*
exception to the rule 113.1 *diversity*, 165.6 *exception*
excerpt 562.9 *compile*, 580.4 *pick*
excerpts 562.3 *compendium*, 580.9 *chosen thing*
excess 610, 128.1 *increase*, 132.3 *difference*, 132.4, 132.10 *surplus*, 241.1 *violence*, 357.9 *excessiveness*, 553.1 *diffuseness*, 608.8 *plenty*, 610.7 *superfluous*, 642.9 *overactivity*, 698.6 *liberality*, 698.12 *unconditional*, 870.3 *overindulgence*
Excess 610
excessive 357, 610, 132.10 *surplus*, 241.6 *violent*, 541.12 *exaggerated*, 541.14 *extravagant*, 553.3 *diffuse*, 614.1 *useless*, 698.12 *unconditional*, 753.7 *dear*, 757.2 *unrestrained*, 846.10 *undue*, 870.8 *overindulgent*
excessive bureaucracy 610.2 *overdoing it*
excessive charge 751.3 *fee*, 753.2 *unfair price*
excessive consumption 350.2 *appetite*
excessive drinking 874.11 *drinking*
excessive frankness 818.1 *discourtesy*
excessive interest 745.4 *interest*
excessive loyalty 541.4 *bombast*
excessively 357, 541, 610, 698, 132.11 *residually*, 753.12 *dearly*, 757.9 *extravagantly*, 846.18 *unduly*, 870.12 *self-indulgently*
excessiveness 357, 846, 541.1 *exaggeration*, 541.3 *extravagance*, 610.1 *excess*, 870.3 *overindulgence*
excessive praise 853.1 *flattery*
excessive speed 329.8 *speed*
excessive zeal 572.7 *eagerness*
excess of freedom 698.6 *liberality*
excess profit 13.7 *corporation*
excess profits tax 751.7 *tax*
exchange 216, 216, 223, 223, 14.2 *stock exchange*, 109.1 *interchange*, 109.7 *reciprocate*, 122.3 *equalization*, 135.1 *union*, 222.1 *substitution*, 222.5 *take a substitute*, 222.6 *give a substitute*, 326.1, 326.11 *transfer*, 478.3 *question and answer*, 478.19 *react*, 534.12 *public telephone system*, 716.1 *negotiation*, 728.1 *transfer of property*, 728.3 *transfer property*, 737.1, 737.4 *trade*, 739.1 *sell*, 739.3 *selling*, 740.1 *market*, 741.7 *finance*, 741.26 *bank*
Exchange 223
exchangeable 216, 109.4 *reciprocal*, 223.6 *in exchange*, 326.17 *transferable*, 716.8 *negotiated*, 728.5 *transferring*, 737.13 *mercantile*
exchangeably 326.18 *in transit*, 478.24 *in answer*
exchange blows 674.12 *fight*
exchange control 741.7 *finance*
exchanged 223, 109.4 *reciprocal*, 222.8 *substituted*
exchanged vow 715.1 *contract*
exchange for 222.5 *take a substitute*, 223.5 *exchange*

exchange force 56.79 *fundamental interaction*
exchange gifts 216.10 *exchange*
exchange goods 216.10 *exchange*
exchange ideas 4.23 *discuss philosophically*
exchange letters 534.31 *correspond*
exchange meaningful looks 563.14 *have difficulty speaking*
exchange of blows 330.12 *collision*
exchange of gases 390.8 *respiration*
exchange of gifts 216.4 *exchange*
exchange of goods 216.4 *exchange*, 737.4 *trade*
exchange of views 568.4 *conference*, 654.2 *consultation*, 716.3 *discussion*
exchange of vows 714.1 *promise*
exchange opinions 463.13 *debate*, 473.14 *discuss*
exchange pleasantries 568.9 *converse*
exchange premium 14.1 *finance*
exchanger 224.4 *editor*
exchange rate 13.6 *economic factors*, 14.1, 741.7 *finance*
Exchange Rate Mechanism 13.5 *international trade*, 14.1 *finance*
exchange rate parity 741.7 *finance*
exchange shots 674.12 *fight*
exchange signals 543.12 *signal*
exchange student 223.4 *person who exchanges*
exchange value 122.3 *equalization*, 751.2 *value*
exchange views 568.11 *confer*
exchange vows 714.7 *promise*
exchange words 568.9 *converse*
exchanging 737.13 *mercantile*
exchanging favours 664.3 *mutual relationship*
exchequer 605.4 *storage*, 741.6 *funds*, 741.19 *treasury*
excipient 62.5 *prescription*
excise 60.20 *practise surgery*, 131.4 *take off*, 355.13 *dig out*, 751.8 *levy*
excise duty 13.6 *economic factors*
exciseman 730.7 *collector*
excise officer 730.7 *collector*
excision 60.9 *surgery*, 131.1 *subtraction*, 355.3 *digging out*
excitability 642.7 *restlessness*, 759.7 *emotionalism*, 780.1 *rashness*
excitable 642.18 *active*, 759.13 *passionate*
excitant 875.6 *drug*
excitation 56.67 *excited atom*, 642.1 *activity*, 874.10 *drunkenness*
excitation energy 56.67 *excited atom*
excite 226.10 *awaken*, 228.9 *motivate*, 239.3 *invigorate*, 366.22 *agitate*, 403.13 *arouse sensation*, 405.9 *give pleasure*, 413.13 *be piquant*, 782.15 *cause desire*, 821.25 *be loved*, 874.9 *be intoxicating*
excited 366.16 *restless*, 403.7 *susceptible*, 405.7 *pleased*, 513.5 *expecting*, 821.20 *amorous*
excited atom 56
excitedly 541.18 *exaggeratedly*, 821.30 *lovingly*
excited state 56.67 *excited atom*
excite expectations 517.11 *predict*
excite hate 785.7 *cause dislike*, 822.16 *cause hate*
excite love 786.10 *be wonderful*
excitement 239.1 *vigour*, 366.2 *tumult*, 403.1 *sensation*, 541.1 *exaggeration*
excite pity 835
excite the attention of 467.13 *attract attention*
exciting 403, 239.5 *invigorating*, 413.10 *stimulating*, 560.11 *descriptive*, 586.19 *persuasive*, 874.6 *intoxicating*
excitingly 403.14 *sensationally*

exclaim 431.14 *hiss*, 564.11 *speak*, 564.12 *speak loudly*
exclamation 431.7 *cry of disapproval*, 564.7 *utterance*, 786.2 *sign of wonderment*
exclamation mark 543.7 *punctuation*, 786.2 *sign of wonderment*
exclamatory 431.19 *hissing*
exclude 147, 581, 131.3 *subtract*, 132.8 *leave*, 134.11 *simplify*, 136.10 *set apart*, 145.5 *be incomplete*, 302.7 *limit*, 349.4 *ostracize*, 487.8 *make impossible*, 699.8 *restrain*, 709.3 *veto*, 816.13 *ignore*, 848.9 *exempt*, 852.15 *withhold approval*
excluded 147, 131.5 *subtracted*, 136.17 *unjoined*, 254.12 *missing*, 581.10 *rejected*, 711.8 *refused*, 848.5 *exempt*, 852.31 *disapproved*
excluded person 147
excluding 147, 131.8 *by subtraction*, 147.12 *exclusively*
exclusion 147, 131.1 *subtraction*, 136.2 *setting apart*, 302.1 *limitation*, 349.18 *dismissal*, 349.19 *ostracism*, 581.5 *rejection*, 709.1 *veto*, 816.3 *separation*, 848.1 *exemption*
Exclusion 147
exclusionary 147.10 *excluding*
exclusion order 147.1 *exclusion*
exclusion zone 147, 249.3 *regional boundary*
exclusive 147.10 *excluding*, 302.5 *limited*, 533.3 *reporting*, 533.9 *news story*, 617.1 *worthy*, 665.8 *leagued*, 699.13 *restraining*, 709.5 *vetoed*, 723.8 *possessing*, 723.9 *possessed*, 753.8 *valuable*, 816.8 *unsociable*
exclusively 147, 174.24 *once*, 665.18 *cliquishly*, 699.16 *under restraints*, 709.7 *by veto*, 723.10 *possessively*, 753.13 *valuably*, 816.14 *unsocially*
exclusiveness 147, 665.4 *partisanship*
exclusive of 131.8 *by subtraction*, 147.12 *exclusively*
exclusive possession 723.1 *possession*
exclusive rights 699.1 *restraint*
exclusive sale 739.3 *selling*
exclusivity 147.4 *exclusiveness*, 699.1 *restraint*, 816.1 *unsociability*
exclusory 147.10 *excluding*
excogitate 4.20 *philosophize*, 519.14 *imagine*
excogitation 4.4 *philosophical investigation*
excommunicate 10.18 *perform rites*, 16.79 *convict*, 147.8 *eject*, 349.3 *disbar*, 709.3 *veto*, 827.7 *wish ill*
excommunicated 10.21 *ritualistic*, 709.5 *vetoed*, 827.10 *maledictive*
excommunication 10.5 *Christian rite*, 147.2 *ejection*, 349.18 *dismissal*, 709.1 *veto*, 827.4 *malediction*
ex-con 698.7 *free person*
ex-convict 698.7 *free person*
excoriate 294.13 *remove*, 296.16 *peel*
excoriation 294.5 *shedding*, 296.6 *peeling*
excrement 353, 132.2 *residue*, 387.3 *body fluid*, 419.2 *something that makes an unpleasant smell*, 622.4 *dirt*
excremental 353.25 *faecal*, 622.8 *unclean*
excrementary 353.25 *faecal*
excrementitious 622.8 *unclean*
excrescence 316.1 *convexity*, 610.3 *superfluity*
excrescent 316.6 *convex*
excrescently 316.6 *convexly*
excreta 353.4 *excrement*
excrete 353, 347.12 *leak*, 349.14 *let out*, 352.7 *secrete*
excretion 353, 59.5 *physiology*, 347.2 *outflow*, 349.22 *disgorge-*

ment, 352.1 secretion, 621.2 cleaning, 622.2 uncleanness, 727.1 disposal
Excretion 353
excretionary 353.24 excretory
excretive 353.24 excretory
excretory 353, 59.22 physiological, 347.17 leaky, 352.4 secretory
excruciate 406.11 inflict pain
excruciating 406.5 painful
excruciatingly 406.13 painfully
exculpate 16.78 acquit, 839.10 absolve, 848.10 acquit, 855.7 vindicate, 865.9 declare innocent
exculpated 16.63 acquitted, 839.6 forgiven, 865.6 declared innocent
exculpating 855.11 vindicatory
exculpation 16.42 acquittal, 839.3 absolution, 855.1 vindication, 865.2 legal innocence
exculpatory 855.11 vindicatory
excurse 335.3 go astray
excursion 334.2 detour, 335.13 deviation, 357.7 crossing, 363.2 circuitousness, 553.2 circumlocution, 754.9 cheap
excursion fare 754.4 bargain
excursive 334.7 circuitous, 553.4 circumlocutory
excursus 335.16 wandering, 553.2 circumlocution
excusable 839.7 forgivable, 843.9 in the right, 855.13 vindicable
excusatory 855.11 vindicatory
excuse 147.7 exclude, 226.5 reason, 228.1 motive, 463.4 explanation, 463.14 premise, 473.5 plea, 538.8 pretence, 639.1 deliver, 639.2 deliverance, 657.2 stratagem, 698.15 set free, 839.1 forgiveness, 839.9 forgive, 840.2 apology, 848.2 acquittal, 848.10 acquit, 855.2 defence, 855.7 vindicate
excused 147.11 excluded, 463.10 causal, 839.6 forgiven, 848.6 acquitted
excuse-me dance 46.2 dance
excuse oneself 848.12 exempt oneself
excuser 855.5 vindicator
excusing 671.29 defending, 839.4 forgiving, 855.11 vindicatory
excusing the liberty 849.23 saving your grace
Exe 96 Rivers
exec 688.10 person of authority, 696.7 military leader
execrable 618.3 bad, 618.6 damnable, 822.12 hated
execrableness 618.9 badness
execrate 820.11 be hostile, 822.14 hate, 827.6 vilify, 852.22 vituperate
execration 822.1 hate, 827.3 vilification, 852.8 berating
execrative 822.10 hating, 827.10 maledictive
execratively 822.18 hatefully, 827.14 damningly
execratory 852.27 critical
executant 640.3 doer, 646.1 worker
execute 398, 879, 144.4 complete, 230.9 take action, 243.10 produce, 590.14 carry on, 597.1 undertake, 619.5 perfect, 640.4 act, 652.14 behave towards, 684.4 complete, 690.6 suppress, 719.6 perform
execute a contract 715.5 contract
execute a gymnastic movement 30.10 compete in gymnastics
execute a sentence 879.2 penalize
execute a will 729.5 give
executed 597.5 undertaken, 684.7 completed, 690.9 suppressed, 879.20 punished
execute justice 879.2 penalize
execution 398, 16.7 legal trial, 30.1 gymnastics, 39.6 diving, 230.1 operation, 243.1 produc-

tion, 397.4 death sentence, 398.1 killing, 590.1 pursuit, 640.1 action, 655.1 skill, 684.1 completion, 690.2 suppression, 719.3 performance, 879.13 capital punishment
execution chamber 16.43 conviction
executioner 398, 241.4 violent person or animal, 244.6 destroyer, 398.10 killer, 879.17 punisher
execution of judgment 16.7 legal trial, 492.2 verdict
execution of justice 879.8 penalty
execution of sentence 879.8 penalty
executive 12.1 government, 12.9 governmental, 15.6 employer, 16.48 jurisdictional, 126.5 superior, 230.5 operator, 640.3 doer, 640.6 effective, 646.1 worker, 646.3 agent, 653.6 governing body, 653.15 manager, 653.17 managerial, 688.10 person of authority, 696.5 company leader, 696.12 masterful
executive assistant 646.1 worker, 697.5 office assistant, 707.1 deputy
executively 16.86 jurisdictionally, 696.16 masterfully
executive office 647.1 workshop
executive officer 688.10 person of authority, 696.7 military leader
executor 640.3 doer, 646.3 agent, 653.15 manager, 703.5 commissioner
executorship 703.4 council
executrix 646.3 agent
exegesis 5.12 translation, 475.3 explanation, 524.1 interpretation, 524.2 annotation, 561.1 dissertation
exegete 5.2 linguist, 524.6 interpreter, 561.3 dissertator
exegetic 5.40 translated, 475.11 explanatory, 524.14 interpretive
exegetical 524.14 interpretive, 561.5 expository
exegetically 5.48 linguistically, 475.22 demonstrably, 524.18 in other words
exegetics 5.12 translation, 524.5 science of interpretation
exegetist 475.7 demonstrator, 524.6 interpreter
exemplar 471.6 ideal, 547.1 representation
exemplary 306.10 prototypical, 471.13 ideal, 524.14 interpretive, 547.13 representational, 617.1 worthy, 619.1 perfect, 636.8 warning, 863.7 worthy
exemplification 475.3 explanation, 524.1 interpretation
exemplificatory 475.11 explanatory
exemplified 475.11 explanatory
exemplify 4.21 rationalize, 471.19 epitomize, 475.16 explain, 524.8 interpret, 547.12 stand for
exemplifying 475.11 explanatory
exempt 848, 848, 16.63 acquitted, 16.78 acquit, 116.18 permitting, 116.29 permit, 136.17 unjoined, 147.7 exclude, 147.11 excluded, 581.3 exclude, 638.8 escaping, 639.1 deliver, 698.9 free, 698.15 set free, 700.4 liberate, 708.3 permit, 839.9 forgive
exempted 16.63 acquitted, 116.18 permitting, 147.11 excluded, 700.7 liberated, 848.5 exempt
exemptibility 700.1 liberation
exemptible 700.7 liberated, 855.13 vindicable
exemption 848, 16.42 acquittal, 116.8 permit, 136.2 setting apart, 147.1 exclusion, 581.5 rejection, 638.1 escape, 639.2 deliverance, 698.1 freedom, 700.1 liberation, 708.1 permission, 727.1 disposal, 839.1 forgiveness
Exemption 848

exemptive 147.10 excluding
exempt oneself 848
exequies 399.2 funeral
exercise 644, 644, 30.10 compete in gymnastics, 230.1 operation, 324.11 bodily movement, 594.6 brief, 594.8 prepare oneself, 594.12 briefing, 596.6 venture, 597.2 undertaking, 599.1, 599.6 use, 625.1 hygiene, 627.9 physical improvement, 640.2 deed, 640.4 act, 644.2 task, 703.2 engagement
exercise a pull 340.11 attract
exercise book 6.14 school book
exercised 599.9 used
exercised in arms 676.17 military
exercise discretion 655.10 be skilful
exercise divine right 845.14 be entitled
exercise influence 233.8 influence
exercise judgment 16.76 judge
exercise one's discretion 580.1 select
exercise one's intellect 461.12 think
exercise one's prerogative 845.14 be entitled
exercise power 235.10 be powerful, 688.18 have authority
exercise self-control 869.5 be self-restrained
exercising 644.10 working
exercising choice 580.14 selecting
exert authority 12.11 govern, 690.5 be severe
exert energy 235.10 be powerful
exert influence 233.8 influence, 235.10 be powerful
exertion 644, 235.1 power, 239.1 vigour, 575.2 commitment, 640.1 action, 650.7 fatigue, 674.2 contest
exert no authority 689.5 misgovern
exert oneself 644, 239.2 be full of vigour, 596.2 try hard, 642.15 try
exert pressure 228.10 manipulate
exert sovereignty 91
exert weight 369.12 be heavy
exes 721.5 profit
Exeter 93 Cities
exfiltrate 347.12 leak
exfiltration 347.3 leakage
exfoliate 266.11 scale, 294.13 remove, 296.16 peel
exfoliation 266.6 layering, 294.5 shedding, 296.6 peeling
exfoliatory 296.12 peeling
ex-gratia payment 729.2 gift, 746.3 pay
exhalation 388, 388.10 vaporization, 390.8 respiration, 416.1 odour, 419.1 stench, 441.2 murk
exhale 347.12 leak, 349.14 let out, 388.27 give off, 390.21 respire, 416.8 have odour
exhaling 390.19 respiratory
exhaust 218.8 cause to cease, 236.7 remove power from, 347.2 outflow, 349.11 void, 349.14 let out, 372.6 make sparse, 599.1 use, 607.1 waste, 609.7 make insufficient, 614.8 make useless, 628.5 hurt, 650.6 fatigue, 684.4 complete, 748.2 consume, 757.7 waste
exhausted 200.18 over, 236.12 impotent, 238.11 weakened, 555.1 unemphatic, 599.9 used, 624.21 unhealthy, 628.12 deteriorated, 628.13 dilapidated, 650.1 fatigued, 748.13 used
exhaust fan 417.2 deodorant
exhaust fumes 419.2 something that makes an unpleasant smell, 631.8 poison
exhausting 644.11 laborious, 650.4 fatiguing, 659.10 difficult, 879.21 punishing
exhaustingly 650.9 tiringly
exhausting work 644.1 work
exhaustion 129.1 decrease, 236.4 disability, 238.3 poor health, 349.21 removal, 555.2 lack of

emphasis, 599.6 use, 607.3 waste, 628.11 hurt, 650.7 fatigue, 722.4 lessening
exhaustion of supplies 628.7 deterioration
exhaustive 144.7 complete, 684.7 completed
exhaustively 277.17 profoundly, 684.9 completely
exhaustiveness 684.1 completion
exhaust the possibilities of 599.3 exploit
exhibit 4.22 propound a philosophy, 294.11 uncover, 435.18 make visible, 437.6 visible thing, 437.10 make visible, 457.14 present, 475.15 demonstrate, 483.5 legal evidence, 526.1 display, 526.2 display something, 526.7 showpiece, 544.10 identify, 605.5 collection, 811.27 show
exhibited 475.9 demonstrated, 526.13 displayed
exhibition 161, 51.11 theatrical performance, 435.7 view, 437.5 manifestation, 457.2 being in view, 475.1 demonstration, 526.6 display, 532.8 public relations, 605.5 collection, 740.2 fair, 797.1 affectedness, 811.14 show, 878.3 grant
exhibitional 475.9 demonstrated
exhibition centre 526.8 showplace
exhibitioner 730.5 recipient
exhibition game 19.1 football
exhibition hall 526.8 showplace
exhibitionism 811, 294.1 uncovering, 296.1 undress, 475.2 demonstrativeness, 809.6 boastfulness
exhibitionist 296.8 nude person, 475.7 demonstrator, 475.10 demonstrative, 490.11 opinionist, 526.12 displayer, 797.2 pretender, 809.7 vain person, 811.15 showman, 811.19 flashy exhibitionistic** 475.10 demonstrative, 809.13 boastful
exhibitor 51.25 producer, 526.12 displayer
exhilarate 239.3 invigorate, 471.16 inspire, 651.1 refresh, 769.6 bring cheer, 874.9 be intoxicating
exhilarated 651.4 refreshed, 769.1 cheerful, 874.1 drunk
exhilarating 239.5 invigorating, 651.3 refreshing, 874.6 intoxicating
exhilaratingly 651.8 refreshingly
exhilaration 239.1 vigour, 651.5 refreshment, 762.1 happiness, 769.3 cheerfulness, 874.10 drunkenness
exhort 228.9 motivate, 654.5 advise, 778.17 give courage
exhortation 586, 564.8 speech, 567.2 salutation, 778.6 encouragement
exhorted 228.12 motivated
exhumation 3.12 historicism, 355.3 digging out, 399.7 inquest
exhume 399, 3.21 antiquarianize, 200.16 excavate, 355.13 dig out
ex-husband 401.5 single man
ex hypothesi 4.25 theoretically, 518.10 supposedly
exigency 106.4 difficult circumstances, 191.1 immediacy, 593.3 needfulness, 659.6 critical situation
exigent 106.8 difficult, 191.6 allowing no delay, 593.6 demanding
exigently 106.17 difficultly, 355.21 away
exiguity 182.3 fewness, 260.1 littleness, 272.7 fineness
exiguous 182.6 sparse, 260.7 little, 272.2 fine
exiguously 182.11 sparsely
exile 149, 104.7 new arrival, 147.2 ejection, 147.5 excluded person, 147.8 eject, 252.7 displaced person, 252.16 replace,

347.4 *emigration,* 347.8 *out-goer,* 347.13 *emigrate,* 349.4 *ostracize,* 349.19 *ostracism,* 816.3 *separation,* 816.7 *outsider,* 816.13 *ignore,* 879.1 *punish,* 879.7 *punishment*
exiled 147.11 *excluded,* 252.10 *replaced,* 816.10 *lonely*
exilement 349.19 *ostracism*
exist 99, 83.22 *be dormant,* 101.10 *be real,* 196.5, 253.11 *be present,* 367.8 *be material,* 396.16 *live*
existence 99, 196.3 *actuality,* 253.1 *presence,* 367.1 *material world,* 396.1 *life,* 396.10 *life-style,* 457.2 *being in view,* 537.2 *reality*
Existence 99
existence of god 4.9 *philosophical problem*
existent 99.10 *existing,* 196.6, 253.7 *present,* 396.12 *alive*
existentialism 48 Literary Groups and Movements, 4.7 *school of thought,* 99.1 *existence*
existentialist 4.11 *follower of a doctrine,* 4.14 *of a philosophy*
existentially 99.22 *really*
existential psychology 61.1 *psychology*
existential quantifier 52.63 *mathematical logic*
existential theology 7.13 *theology*
existential therapy 61.3 *psychiatric treatment*
existing 99, 537, 101.6 *real,* 196.6, 253.7 *present,* 396.1 *life*
existing conditions 106.1 *circumstances*
existing together 198.1 *same time*
exist outside 104.16 *be external*
exist simultaneously 198.6 *be simultaneous*
exist together 198.6 *be simultaneous*
exit 347, 347, 51.20 *acting,* 51.32 *act,* 137.5 *road,* 157.3 *death,* 254.16 *absent oneself,* 322.7 *passageway,* 324.4 *backward motion,* 327.11 *channel,* 345.2 *withdraw,* 345.7 *departure,* 347.6 *way out,* 397.1 *death,* 458.4 *disappearance,* 531.11 *conceal oneself,* 638.2 *means of escape*
Exit 347
ex-libris 544.3 *means of identification*
Exmoor Horn 68 Breeds of Sheep
Exmoor pony 32 Breeds of Horse and Pony
exobiology 53.1 *astronomy,* 59.1 *life science*
exocarp 86.3 *fruit structure*
Exocet 338.8 *missile,* 680.5 *missile weapon*
exocrine 352.5 *of a secretion*
exocrine gland 352.3 *gland*
exode 51.6 *scene*
exodontic 60.23 *dental*
exodontics 60.5 *dentistry*
exodontist 60.14 *dentist*
exodus 51.6 *scene,* 345.7 *departure,* 347.1 *exit*
ex officio 653.19 *managerially,* 688.12 *authoritative*
exogamy 823.3 *types of marriage*
exon 59.13 *genetic material*
exonerate 16.78 *acquit,* 839.10 *absolve,* 848.10 *acquit,* 885.7 *vindicate,* 865.9 *declare innocent*
exonerated 16.63 *acquitted,* 839.6 *forgiven,* 848.6 *acquitted,* 865.6 *declared innocent*
exonerating 839.4 *forgiving,* 855.11 *vindicatory*
exoneration 16.42 *acquittal,* 839.3 *absolution,* 848.2 *acquittal,* 855.1 *vindication,* 865.2 *legal innocence*
exonerative 855.11 *vindicatory*
exorbitance 541.1 *exaggeration,* 541.3 *extravagance,* 610.1 *excess,* 753.2 *unfair price*
exorbitant 335.20 *deviant,* 357.12 *excessive,* 541.12 *exag-*

gerated, 541.14 *extravagant,* 610.6 *excessive,* 753.7 *dear,* 757.3 *costly*
exorbitantly 541.17 *excessively,* 753.12 *dearly*
exorbitant price 753.2 *unfair price*
exorbitation 335.13 *deviation*
exorcise 10.18 *perform rites,* 349.10 *exterminate*
exorcised 10.21 *ritualistic*
exorcism 10.5 *Christian rite*
exorcist 11.12 *occultist*
exorcizer 11.12 *occultist*
exordium 156.10 *introduction*
exoskeletal 289.6 *exterior*
exoskeleton 289.1 *exterior,* 382.7 *skeleton*
exosmosis 348.5 *absorption*
exosmotic 348.17 *absorbent*
exosphere 55.8 *atmosphere,* 275.8 *high thing,* 279.1 *summit,* 390.3 *atmospheric layers*
exoteric 522.2 *simple*
exotic 69.19 *ornamental,* 83.2 *plant,* 83.15 *wild,* 104.10 *foreign,* 108.6 *unrelated,* 117.7 *disparate,* 149.11 *foreign,* 165.17 *exceptional,* 168.14 *eccentric,* 263.8 *distant,* 289.10 *extraneous,* 786.8 *wonderful*
exotically 69.20 *horticulturally,* 83.24 *herbaceously,* 104.18 *extraneously,* 108.12 *irrelevantly,* 149.18 *extraneously*
exotic dancer 51.28 *dancer,* 294.4 *exposer,* 296.8 *nude person*
exoticism 149.3 *foreignness*
exoticness 104.2, 149.3 *foreignness*
exotropia 436.2 *poor sight*
expand 52.92 *manipulate,* 121.6 *change gradually,* 128.4 *increase,* 128.5 *make bigger,* 130.6 *add,* 164.24 *broaden,* 227.8 *grow,* 248.20 *extend,* 261.5 *make bigger,* 261.6 *become bigger,* 271.11 *broaden,* 372.6 *make sparse,* 377.8 *be elastic,* 541.8 *enlarge,* 553.5 *be diffuse,* 721.10 *augment*
expandable 261.9 *enlargeable*
expanded 128.7 *increased,* 261.7 *bigger,* 372.2 *rarefied,* 541.13 *enlarged,* 553.3 *diffuse*
expanded palette 444.5 *paint*
expanded polystyrene 57.21 *polymer*
expander 261.4 *enlarger*
expanding 128.6 *increasing,* 227.11, 261.8 *growing,* 372.2 *rarefied*
expanding bullet 680.13 *ammunition*
expanding economy 686.1 *prosperity*
expanding universe 53.4 *cosmological model*
expanse 248.1 *space,* 248.3 *geographical space,* 259.1 *size,* 271.4 *breadth*
expansibility 261.2 *enlargeability*
expansible 261.9 *enlargeable*
expansile 261.9 *enlargeable*
expansion 56, 12.3 *governance,* 52.24 *evaluation,* 128.1 *increase,* 227.3 *growth,* 248.1 *space,* 261.1 *growth,* 372.4 *rarefaction,* 541.2 *enlargement,* 553.1 *diffuseness,* 721.2 *augmentation*
Expansion 261
expansionary 261.9 *enlargeable*
expansion coefficient 56.39 *expansion*
expansionism 357, 346.4 *right of entry,* 400.11 *nation,* 676.5 *bellicosity*
expansionist 679.6 *militarist*
expansionistic 679.33 *combative*
expansive 146.7 *including,* 248.13 *spacious,* 259.15 *big,* 261.9 *enlargeable,* 271.1 *broad,* 372.2 *rarefied,* 475.10 *demonstrative,* 565.6 *effusive,* 721.18 *acquisitional*
expansively 248.15 *spaciously,* 261.10 *largely,* 372.7 *sparsely,*

475.21 *demonstratively,* 565.11 *effusively,* 721.20 *gainfully*
expansiveness 248.4 *spaciousness,* 259.2 *bigness,* 271.4 *breadth,* 475.2 *demonstrativeness*
expat 816.7 *outsider*
expatiate 553.5 *be diffuse,* 565.8 *talk too much*
expatiation 553.1 *diffuseness*
expatriate 104.7 *new arrival,* 108.3 *unconnected person,* 147.8 *eject,* 149.6, 149.13 *immigrant,* 345.3 *quit,* 347.8 *outgoer,* 347.13 *emigrate,* 349.4 *ostracize,* 816.7 *outsider*
expatriation 147.2 *ejection,* 347.4 *emigration,* 349.19 *ostracism*
expect 199, 513, 208.9 *prepare,* 488.10 *think likely,* 516.1 *foresee,* 588.7 *intend,* 592.12 *plan ahead,* 594.3 *be prepared,* 775.7 *aspire,* 787.5 *not wonder about,* 804.7 *be entitled to,* 845.14 *be entitled,* 847.17 *impose a duty*
expectance 513.1 *expectation*
expectancy 199.4 *looking to the future,* 513.1 *expectation*
expectant 513, 775, 245.16 *reproductive,* 513.4 *expectant person,* 513.5 *expecting,* 516.6 *foreseeing*
expectantly 513, 516.8 *foresightedly,* 775.15 *hopefully*
expectant mother 513.4 *expectant person*
expectant person 513
expectation 513, 775, 199.4 *looking to the future,* 208.5 *prematurity,* 488.1 *probability,* 497.3 *believing,* 516.3 *foresight,* 517.1 *prediction,* 804.2, 845.1 *entitlement*
Expectation 513
expectation neurosis 61.10 *neurosis*
expectations 513, 775.2 *expectation*
expectative 208.16 *premature*
expect better 515.4 *be disappointed*
expected 513, 199.13 *foreseen,* 488.6 *probable,* 518.9 *meant,* 787.4 *predictable*
expectedly 513, 488.11 *probably*
expected soon 208.13 *imminent*
expected value 52.60 *parameter*
expecting 513, 245.16 *reproductive,* 513.6, 775.12 *expectant*
expecting a baby 245.16 *reproductive*
expecting a happy event 245.16 *reproductive*
expecting better 515.9 *disappointed*
expecting more 515.9 *disappointed*
expecting otherwise 515.9 *disappointed*
expect it of 847.17 *impose a duty*
expect more 515.4 *be disappointed*
expectorant 62.4 *drug type,* 62.17 *stimulating,* 353.29 *salivating,* 630.6 *purgative*
expectorate 353.15 *excrete,* 353.20 *salivate*
expectoration 353.1 *excretion,* 353.9 *saliva*
expect otherwise 515.4 *be disappointed*
expect the worst 513.8 *expect*
expect too much 609.7 *make insufficient*
expedience 615.3 *convenience,* 782.2 *desirability*
expediency 613.5 *usefulness,* 615.3 *convenience*
expedient 101.8 *practical,* 116.16 *fitting,* 222.1 *substitution,* 232.2 *instrument,* 592.3 *expedient plan,* 602.1 *means,* 613.1 *useful,* 615.1 *convenient,* 615.5 *convenience,* 654.8 *advisable,* 657.2 *stratagem,* 662.34 *beneficial,* 782.8 *desirable*

expediential 615.1 *convenient*
expediently 116.38 *fittingly,* 615.7 *conveniently,* 782.17 *desirably*
expedient plan 592
expedite 208.7 *be early,* 232.4 *be an instrument,* 326.12 *transport,* 329.4, 329.4 *be swift,* 648.1 *hasten,* 660.16 *make easy,* 662.28 *further*
expedite one's end 615.6 *be convenient*
expediting 660.7 *easing,* 662.8 *furtherance*
expedition 208.1 *earliness,* 329.8 *speed,* 642.3 *nimbleness,* 648.4 *haste,* 676.8 *warfare*
expeditionary force 679.14 *armed forces*
expeditious 208.12 *early,* 329.1, 329.1 *swift,* 642.18 *active,* 648.3 *hasty*
expeditiously 208.17 *early,* 329.14 *swiftly*
expeditiousness 329.8 *speed,* 648.4 *haste*
expel 349, 131.3 *subtract,* 134.11 *simplify,* 136.9 *separate,* 147.8 *eject,* 252.16 *replace,* 326.14 *bring back,* 330.1 *impel,* 338.25, 341.2 *eject,* 347.13 *emigrate,* 349.3 *disbar,* 353.15 *excrete,* 355.12 *displace,* 458.3 *cause to disappear,* 581.2 *discard,* 816.13 *ignore,* 846.16 *disentitle,* 879.1 *punish*
expelled 131.5 *subtracted,* 136.15 *separate,* 147.11 *excluded,* 252.10 *replaced,* 816.10 *lonely,* 846.12 *disentitled*
expellee 349, 347.8 *outgoer*
expellent 349.29 *expulsive*
expeller 349.26 *ejector*
expend 748, 599.1 *use,* 599.5 *dispose of,* 607.1 *waste,* 738.2 *shop,* 746.6 *pay*
expendability 612.5 *unimportance,* 614.3 *uselessness*
expendable 612.1 *unimportant,* 614.1 *useless*
expended 748, 347.16 *outflowing*
expending 748, 746.15 *paying*
expenditure 748, 347.5 *export,* 607.3 *waste,* 722.2 *financial loss,* 738.8 *shopping,* 746.1 *payment,* 751.5 *cost*
Expenditure 748
expense 748, 607.3 *waste,* 722.2 *financial loss*
expense account 721.5 *profit,* 729.2 *gift,* 748.5 *expense,* 750.1 *accounts,* 878.4 *reward for service*
expenses 748.5 *expense,* 751.5 *cost*
expensive 494.6 *overestimated,* 617.3 *valuable,* 742.3 *opulent,* 753.7 *dear,* 757.3 *costly,* 811.24 *grand*
expensively 738.16, 753.12 *dearly,* 811.40 *grandly*
expensiveness 753.1 *high price*
experience 3.14 *historicalness,* 207.3 *maturity,* 403.1 *sensation,* 403.11 *sense,* 411.2 *taste of life,* 411.9 *taste,* 485.3 *qualifications,* 501.3 *learning,* 501.13 *get to know,* 507.1 *wisdom,* 655.1 *skill,* 759.1 *feeling,* 759.15 *feel*
experienced 6.19 *knowledgeable,* 207.11 *adult,* 485.9 *qualified,* 501.8 *knowledgeable,* 594.18 *prepared,* 655.8 *expert,* 657.4 *cunning,* 696.13 *excellent*
experienced hand 655.5 *expert*
experience growth 721.10 *augment*
experience psychic phenomena 11
experiences 3.6 *biography*
experiencing the sour taste of failure 411.8 *tasteful*
experiencing the sweet taste of success 411.8 *tasteful*
experiential 52.69 *theoretic*

experiment 479, 479, 496.9 *invention,* 594.10 *preparations,* 596.4 *test,* 596.6 *venture*
Experiment 479
experimental 479, 56.99 *theoretical,* 477.15 *sceptical,* 479.9 *original,* 491.5 *uncertified,* 496.13 *discovering,* 585.2 *not customary,* 596.9 *tentative,* 656.3 *clumsy,* 781.4 *cautious*
experimental animal 76.3 *domesticated animal*
experimentalism 479.3 *experimentation*
experimentalist 479.5 *experimenter*
experimentalize 479.11 *experiment*
experimentally 479, 477.23 *questioningly,* 479.15 *inventively,* 496.16 *originally,* 585.8 *unusually,* 596.10 *ambitiously*
experimental method 652.7 *way*
experimental physics 56
experimental psychology 61.1 *psychology*
experimental scientist 518.4 *theorist*
experimental taxonomy 59.17 *taxonomy*
experimental theatre 51.1 *drama*
experimentation 479, 479.4 *originality*
experimented upon 479.10 *tested*
experimentee 479
experimenter 479, 475.7 *demonstrator,* 477.9 *questioner,* 518.4 *theorist,* 596.7 *attempter*
experimenting 479.8 *experimental*
experiment on 398.22 *kill animals*
expert 655, 655, 688, 688, 696, 4.12 *sage,* 4.19 *learned,* 6.4 *educator,* 6.16 *educational,* 126.6 *paragon,* 165.14 *specialist,* 165.21 *specialized,* 485.8 *qualified person,* 485.9 *qualified,* 492.5 *judge,* 501.6 *knowledgeable person,* 501.8 *knowledgeable person,* 611.4 *bigwig,* 619.1 *perfect,* 619.4 *perfectionist,* 640.3 *doer,* 654.4 *adviser,* 655.4 *skilled person,* 655.6 *skilful,* 696.13 *excellent,* 861.5 *proficient*
expertise 165.7 *special skill,* 485.3 *qualifications,* 501.2 *information,* 567.3 *skill,* 567.3 *perfection,* 655.1 *skill,* 861.12 *proficiency*
expertly 688, 4.29 *wisely,* 6.25 *educationally,* 655.12 *skilfully,* 696.16 *masterfully,* 861.25 *skilfully*
expertly made 655.9 *well-made*
expert mechanic 619.4 *perfectionist*
expertness 567.3, 655.1 *skill*
expert system 65.16 *artificial intelligence*
expiate 125.4 *compensate,* 710.14 *offer reparation,* 765.11 *recompense,* 840.5 *atone*
expiated 125.7 *compensated*
expiating 125.9 *compensatory*
expiation 125.1 *compensation,* 222.1 *substitution,* 630.1 *remedy,* 710.6 *offering,* 765.2 *reparation,* 840.1 *atonement*
expiator 840.3 *atoner*
expiatory 125.9 *compensatory,* 710.19 *sacrificial,* 840.4 *atoning*
expiatory offering 840.2 *apology*
expiration 144.3 *completion,* 157.2 *cessation,* 157.3 *death,* 390.8 *respiration,* 397.1 *death*
expire 157, 100.13 *cease to exist,* 200.14 *pass,* 349.14 *let out,* 390.21 *respire,* 397.15 *die,* 458.1 *disappear*
expired 3.18 *in the past*
expiring 397.18 *dying*
expiry 157.2 *cessation,* 397.1 *death*
explain 475.4, 4.21 *rationalize,* 463.14 *premise,* 473.16 *plead,* 478.20 *solve,* 522.5 *simplify,*

524.8 *interpret,* 526.1 *display,* 526.3 *reveal,* 560.16 *define,* 561.4 *dissertate,* 660.16 *make easy,* 855.8 *justify*
explainable 855.13 *vindicable*
explained 473.12 *apologetic,* 475.11 *explanatory,* 478.14 *solved,* 522.2 *simple,* 524.15 *interpreted*
explainer 475.7 *demonstrator,* 524.6 *interpreter*
explaining 524.14 *interpretive*
explain wrongly 525.1 *misinterpret*
explanation 463, 475, 4.1 *philosophy,* 226.5 *reason,* 473.5 *plea,* 478.6 *solution,* 518.1 *supposition,* 520.4 *type of meaning,* 522.10 *simplicity,* 524.1 *interpretation,* 530.1 *disclosure,* 560.1 *description,* 561.1 *dissertation,* 855.2 *defence*
explanatory 475, 226.13, 463.10 *causal,* 478.14 *solved,* 522.1 *intelligible,* 524.14 *interpretive,* 524.16 *annotative,* 530.12 *revelatory,* 543.14 *signifying,* 560.11 *descriptive,* 855.11 *vindicatory*
explanatory remark 524.2 *annotation*
expletive 5.19 *swearword,* 431.7 *cry of disapproval,* 553.1 *diffuseness,* 610.3 *superfluity,* 827.1 *curse*
explicability 522.9 *intelligibility*
explicable 473.12 *apologetic,* 522.1 *intelligible*
explicably 473.20 *apologetically*
explicate 4.21 *rationalize,* 522.5 *simplify,* 524.8 *interpret,* 550.2 *clarify*
explication 524.1 *interpretation*
explicative 524.14 *interpretive*
explicator 475.7 *demonstrator*
explicatory 475.11 *explanatory,* 522.1 *intelligible,* 524.14 *interpretive,* 530.12 *revelatory,* 560.11 *descriptive*
explicit 52.77 *given,* 271.3 *broadminded,* 322.16 *open,* 475.9 *demonstrated,* 520.6 *meaningful,* 522.2 *simple,* 526.15 *open,* 528.16 *informative,* 535.14 *assertive,* 550.3 *clear*
explicitly 535, 296.17 *nakedly,* 322.26 *openly,* 520.13 *meaningfully,* 522.13 *intelligibly,* 550.4 *clearly*
explicitness 271.6 *broad-mindedness,* 322.9 *openness,* 520.3 *comprehension,* 522.10 *simplicity,* 535.6 *assertiveness,* 550.1 *clarity*
explode 162, 141.3 *disintegrate,* 244.9 *demolish,* 322.18 *open,* 338.28 *shoot,* 359.17 *spring up,* 379.4 *be brittle,* 410.11 *fuel,* 423.8 *be loud,* 425.5 *bang,* 431.10 *cry out,* 476.8 *refute,* 642.12 *be active,* 759.17 *feel deeply,* 828.12 *become angry*
exploded 498.7 *disbelieved*
exploding 425.8 *banging,* 476.7 *refuting*
exploit 599, 210.5 *take the opportunity,* 243.10 *produce,* 481.14 *discriminate against,* 601.1 *misuse,* 611.2 *important matter,* 627.1 *improve,* 640.2 *deed,* 640.4 *act,* 655.3 *masterpiece,* 655.10 *be skilful,* 690.6 *suppress,* 701.6 *subject,* 778.8 *courageous act,* 786.3 *wonderworking,* 861.19 *be good at*
exploitable 599.10 *usable*
exploitation 599.6 *use,* 601.2 *misuse,* 655.1 *skill,* 690.2 *suppression*
exploitative 601.5 *abusive,* 690.8 *severe*
exploitatively 601.6 *abusively*
exploited 481.11 *judged,* 599.9 *used,* 601.4 *misused,* 690.9 *suppressed*
exploiter 599.8 *user*
exploration 154.3 *preparation,*

479.3 *experimentation,* 496.9 *invention*
exploratory 154.14 *preparatory,* 208.15 *precursory,* 477.12 *questioning,* 479.8 *experimental,* 496.13 *discovering*
explore 4.20 *philosophize,* 54.65 *map,* 154.18 *forerun,* 156.21 *pioneer,* 208.8 *precede,* 479.11 *experiment,* 496.4 *invent*
explored 501.10 *known*
explorer 154.8 *precursor,* 208.4 *early comer,* 224.7 *person who moves around,* 465.3 *curious person,* 496.12 *discoverer*
explore underwater 97.9 *sail the high seas*
explosion 141.1 *disintegration,* 241.3 *instance of violence,* 244.5 *havoc,* 423.1 *loudness,* 425.1 *bang,* 828.4 *anger*
explosive 680, 241.6 *violent,* 244.7 *agent of destruction,* 338.18 *projectile,* 347.15 *outgoing,* 349.28 *propellant,* 349.29 *expulsive,* 379.1 *brittle,* 410.2 *lighter,* 410.10 *powered,* 425.3 *banger,* 425.8 *banging,* 633.1 *dangerous*
explosive device 338.12 *propellant,* 680.16 *bomb*
explosively 425, 141.8 *destructively,* 338.34 *forward,* 347.18 *forth,* 349.32 *expulsively,* 379.5 *fragilely,* 410.12 *powerfully*
explosives 57.22 *industrial chemistry*
expo 475.1 *demonstration,* 526.6 *display*
exponent 52.17 *multiplication,* 169.6 *power,* 475.7 *demonstrator,* 524.6 *interpreter,* 561.3 *dissertator*
exponential 52.76 *functional,* 169.9 *fractional*
exponential distribution 52.59 *probability distribution*
exponential function 52.29 *mathematical function*
exponentially 52.87, 170.16 *mathematically*
exponential series 52.20 *sequence*
exponentiation 52.17 *multiplication*
export 347, 13.10 *trade with,* 13.13 *economic,* 70.4 *transport,* 326.2 *transportation,* 326.12 *transport,* 347.13 *emigrate,* 606.5 *provision*
export and import 737.1 *trade,* 737.5 *commercial trade*
exportation 326.2 *transportation,* 347.5 *export*
exporter 13.9 *economist,* 326.7 *transferor ,* 737.10 *trader,* 739.12 *wholesaler*
exporting 13.2 *economy,* 347.5 *export*
exporting and importing 737.5 *commercial trade*
exposable 296.11 *exposed*
expose 66.21 *photograph,* 238.7 *weaken,* 294.11 *uncover,* 296.14 *undress,* 322.18 *open,* 390.20 *aerate,* 435.18, 437.10 *make visible,* 457.14 *present,* 475.15 *demonstrate,* 476.8 *refute,* 496.2 *detect,* 526.1 *display,* 526.3 *reveal,* 530.5 *disclose,* 532.13 *make public*
exposé 530.2 *divulgence ,* 560.2 *brief description*
exposed 296, 236.11 *unprotected,* 294.8 *uncovered,* 322.12 *open,* 390.12 *airy,* 437.1 *visible,* 437.2 *clear,* 457.7 *appearing,* 475.9 *demonstrated,* 496.14 *discovered,* 526.14 *manifest,* 530.10 *disclosed,* 532.19 *published,* 595.1 *unprepared,* 633.3 *vulnerable*
exposed flank 633.7 *vulnerability*
exposed part 633.7 *vulnerability*
exposed to view 437.2 *clear*
expose oneself 296.14 *undress,* 457.14 *present,* 633.9 *face danger*

exposer 294, 296.8 *nude person,* 530.4 *discloser*
expose the trick 657.5 *be cunning*
expose to danger 633.10 *endanger*
expose to sunlight 392.19 *bake*
expose to view 526.1 *display*
exposing 296.1 *undress*
exposing oneself 877.7 *sexual assault*
exposition 437.5 *manifestation,* 475.1 *demonstration,* 475.3 *explanation,* 524.1 *interpretation,* 526.6 *display,* 561.1 *dissertation,* 740.2 *fair*
expositional 475.9 *demonstrated*
expositive 524.14 *interpretive,* 560.11 *descriptive*
expositor 5.2 *linguist,* 475.7 *demonstrator,* 561.3 *dissertator,* 567.6 *public speaker*
expository 561, 475.9 *demonstrated,* 524.14 *interpretive,* 528.16 *informative,* 530.12 *revelatory,* 560.11 *descriptive*
expository prose 48.5 *prose*
expository scene 51.6 *scene*
expostulate 587.1 *dissuade,* 663.15 *object,* 713.6 *protest*
expostulation 587.6 *dissuasion,* 636.1 *warning,* 663.2 *objection,* 713.1 *protest*
expostulatory 587.9 *dissuasive*
exposure 66.12 *development,* 294.1 *uncovering,* 296.1 *undress,* 390.5 *open air,* 409.3 *chill,* 437.4 *clarity,* 437.5 *manifestation,* 457.1 *appearance,* 496.7 *detection,* 526.10 *manifestation,* 530.1 *disclosure,* 633.7 *vulnerability*
exposure meter 439.11 *photoelectricity*
exposure of infants 398.3 *homicide*
exposure scene 51.6 *scene*
exposure time 66
expound 4.21 *rationalize,* 4.22 *propound a philosophy,* 475.16 *explain,* 524.8 *interpret,* 561.4 *dissertate*
expounded 475.11 *explanatory*
expounder 475.7 *demonstrator,* 524.6 *interpreter,* 561.3 *dissertator,* 567.6 *public speaker*
expounding 475.3 *explanation*
express 5.45 *use language,* 48.21 *write,* 70.5 *transportable,* 72.7 *train,* 165.15 *special,* 306.7 *form,* 326.13 *post,* 329.1 *swift,* 329.11 *swift thing,* 355.12 *displace,* 475.9 *demonstrated,* 475.16 *explain,* 520.6 *meaningful,* 520.10 *mean,* 526.3 *reveal,* 535.14 *assertive,* 549.9 *style,* 564.11 *speak*
express acknowledgments 837.6 *be grateful*
expressage 326.2 *transportation*
express contempt 807.29 *ridicule*
express delivery 534.2 *postal communication*
express disapprobation 852.14 *disapprove*
express disapproval 663.15 *object,* 852.14 *disapprove*
express doubts 536.8 *rebut,* 711.6 *dissent*
expressed 549.6 *styled*
expressed desire 712.1 *request*
express gratitude 837.6 *be grateful*
expressible 526.13 *displayed*
expressing 355.7 *obtaining an extract*
express in words 549.9 *style*
expression 52.25 *algebraic expression,* 306.4 *forming,* 306.6 *nature,* 355.2 *displacement,* 457.3 *external appearance,* 520.1 *meaning,* 526.10 *manifestation,* 564.7 *utterance*
expressionism 48 *Literary Groups and Movements,* **50** *Western Art Styles and Movements,* 51.8 *theatre movements*

expressionist 50.29 *realist*, 51.40 *activist*

expressionistically 50.30 *pictorially*

expressionless 523.1 *unintelligible*

expressionlessly 523.13 *unintelligibly*

expression of dissatisfaction **766**

expression of ideas 549.4 *literary style*

expression of regret 840.2 *apology*

expressive 48.18 *descriptive*, 306.9 *formed*, 520.6 *meaningful*, 528.16 *informative*, 543.14 *signifying*, 558.3 *elegant*, 560.11 *descriptive*

expressive abstraction **50** Western Art Styles and Movements

expressively **355**, 48.23 *descriptively*, 306.13 *formatively*, 475.21 *demonstratively*, 522.13 *intelligibly*, 543.18 *indicatively*, 558.5 *elegantly*

expressly 165.28 *specially*, 537.39 *accurately*

express mail 534.2 *postal communication*

expressman 326.8 *messenger*

express messenger 329.13 *swift person*

expressness 535.6 *assertiveness*

express one's condolences 835.9 *sorrow*

express one's feelings 828.13 *vent one's anger*

express one's regrets 840.6 *apologize*

express one's remorse 840.6 *apologize*

express pain **406**

express pithily 552.4 *be concise*, 562.8 *summarize*

express regret 840.6 *apologize*

express regrets 817.10 *be courteous*, 867.4 *be penitent*

express speed 329.8 *speed*

express sympathy for 835.9 *sorrow*

express thanks 837.6 *be grateful*

express train 329.11 *swift thing*

expressway 71.2, 137.5 *road*, 327.3 *road*

expropriate 349.8 *evict*, 601.1 *misuse*, 722.9 *lose*, 734.8 *take back*, 846.16 *disentitle*

expropriation 136.2 *setting apart*, 349.20 *eviction*, 722.1 *loss*, 734.2 *taking back*, 846.2 *disentitlement*, 879.7 *punishment*

expropriator 734.6 *taker*

expropriatory 734.12 *taking*

expugnable 633.3 *vulnerable*

expulsion 349, 131.1 *subtraction*, 134.2 *purification*, 136.2 *setting apart*, 147.2 *ejection*, 235.4 *energy*, 252.3 *replacement*, 326.1 *transfer*, 338.4 *ejection*, 341.6 *repulse*, 347.4 *emigration*, 353.1 *excretion*, 355.2 *displacement*, 581.6 *discarding*, 704.2 *termination*, 816.3 *separation*, 846.2 *disentitlement*, 879.7 *punishment*

Expulsion **349**

expulsive **349**

expulsive 338.18 *projectile*

expulsive 347.15 *outgoing*

expulsively **349**

expunction 546.3 *obliteration*

expunge 244.8 *destroy*, 546.1 *obliterate*, 704.6 *cancel*

expunged 546.6 *obliterated*

expurgate 131.3 *subtract*, 134.10 *purify*, 147.8 *eject*, 621.15 *purify*, 628.5 *hurt*, 690.6 *suppress*

expurgated 621.17 *cleaned*, 690.9 *suppressed*, 876.10 *moralistic*

expurgation 131.1 *subtraction*, 134.1 *purity*, 147.2 *ejection*, 621.4 *censorship*, 690.2 *suppression*, 876.4 *self-righteousness*

exquisite 405.6 *pleasant*, 406.5 *painful*, 558.3 *elegant*, 617.1

worthy, 786.8 *wonderful*, 789.5 *beautiful*, 861.1 *good*

exquisitely 861.22 *well*

exquisite manners 817.2 *good manners*

exquisiteness 789.1 *gorgeousness*

exsection 355.3 *digging out*

ex-serviceman 679.11 *former soldier*

ex-servicewoman 679.11 *former soldier*

exsiccant 392.9 *drying*

exsiccate 392.17 *dry*

exsiccated 392.3 *dried-up*

exsiccation 392.13 *drying*

exsiccative 392.9 *drying*, 392.15 *dryer*

exsiccator 392.15 *dryer*

ex-slave 698.7 *free person*

exspiration 388.2 *exhalation*

exsuction 355.4 *sucking*

extant 99.10 *existing*, 196.6, 253.7 *present*, 396.12 *alive*

extemporaneous 583.1 *improvised*

extemporaneously 583.7 *extempore*

extemporary 583.1 *improvised*

extempore **583**, 583.1 *improvised*, 595.15 *spontaneously*

extemporization 583.4 *improvisation*, 595.8 *lack of preparation*

extemporize 583.3 *improvise*, 595.12 *be unprepared*, 595.13 *improvise*

extemporized 595.2 *spontaneous*

extemporizer 583.6 *improviser*

extend **248**, 52.97 *align*, 120.8 *quantify*, 128.5 *make bigger*, 130.6 *add*, 159.14 *continue*, 164.24 *broaden*, 209.8 *delay*, 219.4 *protract*, 261.5 *make bigger*, 261.6 *become bigger*, 263.7 *reach*, 269.9 *be long*, 269.10 *lengthen*, 271.9 *be broad*, 322.19 *open up*, 372.6 *make sparse*, 377.8 *be elastic*, 553.5 *be diffuse*, 610.4 *be excessive*

extendability 261.2 *enlargeability*

extendable 261.9 *enlargeable*

extend an invitation 665.16 *host*

extend credit 744.8 *credit*

extended 120.6 *quantitative*, 128.7 *increased*, 209.10 *held up*, 219.6 *protracted*, 248.13 *spacious*, 261.7 *bigger*, 269.1 *long*, 322.13 *opened up*, 372.2 *rarefied*, 377.6 *elastic*, 520.6 *meaningful*, 553.3 *diffuse*

extended family 161.17 *family*, 665.2 *society*

extendedly 209.15 *late*

extended meaning 520.3 *comprehension*

extender 34.4 *climbing equipment*

extendibility 261.2 *enlargeability*, 374.8 *softness*

extendible 261.9 *enlargeable*, 374.2 *pliant*

extending 261.8 *growing*, 372.2 *rarefied*, 377.6 *elastic*

extend the hand of friendship 819.14 *seek the friendship of*

extend to 144.6 *fill*, 263.7 *reach*

extensibility 261.2 *enlargeable*, 374.8 *softness*, 377.1 *elasticity*

extensible 261.9 *enlargeable*, 374.2 *pliant*, 377.6 *elastic*

extensibleness 261.2 *enlargeability*

extensile 261.9 *enlargeable*, 374.2 *pliant*

extensin 58.4 *polysaccharide*

extension 34.8 *mountaineering*, 120.2 *certain amount*, 128.1 *increase*, 130.1 *addition*, 155.3 *continuity*, 209.3 *delayed action*, 219.2 *protraction*, 248.1 *space*, 259.1 *size*, 261.1 *growth*, 261.3 *enlarged thing*, 269.4 *length*, 372.4 *rarefaction*, 377.1 *elasticity*, 534.9 *telephone*, 553.1 *diffuseness*

extensional 261.9 *enlargeable*

extension ladder 359.9 *ladder*

extension sling 34.4 *climbing equipment*

extensive **248**, 121.7 *grada-*

tional, 146.7 *including*, 164.15 *general*, 164.17 *widespread*, 259.15 *big*, 261.9 *enlargeable*, 269.1 *long*, 271.1 *broad*, 322.13 *opened up*, 372.2 *rarefied*

extensive farming 68.1 *agriculture*

extensively **248**, 121.9 *differentially*, 164.32 *universally*, 261.10 *largely*, 269.11 *lengthily*, 271.7 *broadly*, 277.17 *profoundly*, 322.25 *obviously*, 372.7 *sparsely*

extensiveness 164.4 *widespreadness*, 248.4 *spaciousness*, 259.2 *bigness*, 271.4 *breadth*

extensor 261.4 *enlarger*

extent 52.35 *space*, 52.38 *surface*, 120.1 *quantity*, 121.1 *degree*, 157.7 *limit*, 185.3 *duration*, 248.1 *space*, 259.1 *space*, 268.4 *size*, 269.4 *length*, 271.4 *breadth*, 277.2 *intensity*, 302.2 *limiting factor*

extenuate 129.5 *make smaller*, 238.7 *weaken*, 242.4 *moderate*, 485.15 *modify*, 855.8 *justify*

extenuating 671.29 *defending*, 855.11 *vindicatory*

extenuating circumstances 485.5 *modification*, 855.2 *defence*

extenuatingly 855.15 *in vindication*

extenuation 129.1 *decrease*, 855.2 *defence*

extenuatory 855.11 *vindicatory*

exterior **289**, **289**, 50.10 *art subject*, 52.35 *space*, 104.12 *external*, 437.6 *visible thing*, 457.3 *external appearance*, 457.8 *outer*

Exterior **289**

exterior angle 52.39 *angle*

exteriority 104.4 *externality*, 149.3 *foreignness*, 289.1 *exterior*

exteriorization 289.4 *externalization*

exteriorize 289.14 *externalize*

exteriorized 289.9 *externalized*

exteriorized protoplasm 11.10 *psychic phenomenon*

exterminate **349**, 100.14 *cause not to exist*, 157.17 *kill*, 244.8 *destroy*, 398.18 *slaughter*, 398.22 *kill animals*, 546.1 *obliterate*

exterminated 157.23 *annihilated*, 546.6 *obliterated*

extermination 157.4 *annihilation*, 244.1 *destruction*, 398.4 *slaughter*, 398.9 *animal killing*, 546.3 *obliteration*

exterminator 244.6 *destroyer*

external **104**, 136.17 *unjoined*, 289.1, 289.6 *exterior*, 437.1 *visible*, 457.8 *outer*

external appearance **457**

external application 630.10 *surgical dressing*

external-combustion engine 63.11 *engine*

external evidence 483.5 *legal evidence*

external gear 63.7 *gear*

externality **104**, 289.1 *exterior*

externalization **289**, 104.4 *externality*

externalize **289**, 104.16 *be external*, 367.8 *be material*

externalized **289**, 104.12 *external*

externalizing 104.12 *external*

externally **289**, 104.18 *extraneously*, 136.22 *in isolation*, 437.11 *visibly*, 457.15 *apparently*, 526.16 *manifestly*

externally acting hormone 58.16 *hormone*

externalness 289.1 *exterior*

external respiration 58.24 *respiration*

externals 457.3 *external appearance*

external secretion 352.2 *secreted substance*

external work 56.38 *thermodynamics*

externment 349.18 *dismissal*

extinct 3.18 *in the past*, 100.11 *no more*, 200.18 *over*, 397.19

dead, 458.7 *disappeared*, 641.3, 643.1 *inactive*

extinct arthropod 81.4 *arthropod*

extinct bird **78**

extinction **100**, 129.1 *decrease*, 157.4 *annihilation*, 244.1 *destruction*, 397.1 *death*, 458.4 *disappearance*, 643.5 *inactivity*

extinct reptile **79**

extinct volcano 200.3 *inert thing*

extinguish 100.14 *cause not to exist*, 126.8 *be superior*, 157.17 *kill*, 244.8 *destroy*, 440.14 *make dark*, 587.5 *discourage*, 643.14 *make inactive*

extinguisher 244.6 *destroyer*

extinguishing 440.9 *darkening*

extinguishment 440.2 *darkening*

extirpate 131.3 *subtract*, 244.8 *destroy*, 349.8 *evict*, 546.1 *obliterate*

extirpated 546.6 *obliterated*

extirpation 131.1 *subtraction*, 244.2 *destroying*, 546.3 *obliteration*

extirpative 131.6 *subtractive*

extol 9.7 *worship*, 10.19 *offer worship*, 532.16 *publicize*, 849.17, 851.14 *praise*

extolled 9.11 *worshipped*, 10.21 *ritualistic*

extoller 851.9 *praiser*

extolment 9.1 *worship*, 851.3 *praise*

extorsion **355**

extort **355**, 690.6 *suppress*, 692.10 *demand*, 695.7 *force*, 712.7 *demand*, 732.5 *lend*, 753.10 *overcharge*

extorted 712.10 *demanding*

extorting 712.10 *demanding*, 734.3 *taking away*

extortion **753**, 690.2 *suppression*, 692.2 *demand*, 693.2 *violation of the law*, 695.3 *coercive methods*, 712.2 *demand*, 732.1 *lending*, 734.3 *taking away*, 736.7 *dishonesty*, 751.3 *fee*

extortionary **355**

extortionate **355**, 690.20 *exacting*, 732.6 *loaned*, 734.12 *taking*, 753.7 *dear*, 757.3 *costly*

extortionately 734.13 *avariciously*, 753.12 *dearly*

extortionate price 753.2 *unfair price*

extortioner 734.6 *taker*

extortionist 693.9 *criminal*, 695.4 *coercive person*, 712.4 *requester*, 734.6 *taker*, 744.5 *lender*, 753.5 *overcharger*

extortive **355**, 20 *exacting*, 712.10 *demanding*

extort protection money 734.10 *take away*, 736.16 *act dishonest*

extra **130**, **130**, 27.10 *score*, 51.22 *actor*, 104.8 *intruder*, 123.1 *inequality*, 130.10 *additionally*, 132.10 *surplus*, 147.11 *excluded*, 201.5 *fresh start*, 201.14 *renewed*, 532.4 *newspaper*, 533.5 *mass communication*, 533.9 *news story*, 553.1 *diffuseness*, 600.1 *unused*, 610.3 *superfluity*, 610.7 *superfluous*, 614.1 *useless*, 632.4 *safety device*, 721.5 *profit*, 751.3 *fee*

extrachromosomal genetic element 59.13 *genetic material*

extract **57**, **355**, **355**, 60.21 *practise dentistry*, 103.3 *quintessence*, 131.3 *subtract*, 143.2 *particular*, 243.3 *product*, 243.10 *produce*, 252.15 *remove*, 387.2 *juice*, 526.3 *reveal*, 599.3 *exploit*, 606.5 *provision*, 630.20 *doctor*, 639.1 *deliver*

extract a root 52.91 *add*

extracted 131.5 *subtracted*, 252.9 *removed*, 355.19 *dislodged*

extracting 630.12 *surgery*

extraction **355**, 57.23 *metallurgy*, 60.4 *dentistry*, 131.1 *subtraction*, 163.8 *genealogy*, 252.2 *removal*, 355.7 *obtaining an extract*, 639.2 *deliverance*, 734.3 *taking away*

Extraction **355**

extraction of roots 52.17 *multiplication,* 170.1 *calculation*
extractive 355, 57.45 *metallurgical*
extractor 355
extractor fan 364.6 *rotator,* 417.2 *deodorant*
extract roots 170.9 *add*
extracts 562.3 *compendium*
extracurricular 6.21 *curricular*
extradite 147.8 *eject,* 326.14 *bring back,* 349.4 *ostracize,* 735.4 *give back*
extradition 147.2 *ejection,* 326.1 *transfer,* 349.19 *ostracism,* 735.1 *giving back*
extrados 43.9 *miscellaneous architectural features*
extra edition 532.4 *newspaper*
extra-embryonic membrane 59.15 *developmental biology*
extragalactic 53.36 *astronomical*
extragalactically 53.39 *astronomically*
extra help 130.4 *extra*
extra-high-voltage a.c. transmission 64.33 *power distribution*
extra inning 130.4 *extra*
extra innings 22.1 *baseball*
extrajudicial 16.56 *unauthorized*
extrajudicial execution 398.5 *execution*
extra large 259.15 *big*
extra load 130.1 *addition*
extramarital relations 877.4 *illicit love*
extra money 721.5 *profit*
extra mouth to feed 130.5 *extra person*
extramundane 8.13 *divine,* 11.18 *spiritual,* 53.36 *astronomical,* 368.8 *nonmaterial*
extramural 6.21 *curricular,* 289.7 *outside*
extraneous 104, 289, 108.6 *unrelated,* 147.11 *unfit,* 147.11 *excluded,* 149.11 *foreign*
extraneous element 149.1 *foreign body*
extraneously 104, 149, 108.12 *irrelevantly*
extraneousness 104, 289, 108.1 *unrelatedness,* 115.1 *dissimilarity,* 149.3 *foreignness*
Extraneousness 104
extraordinariness 168.4 *unusualness*
extraordinary 165.16 *characteristic,* 168.14 *eccentric,* 489.2 *questionable,* 786.8 *wonderful*
extra pair of hands 130.5 *extra person*
extra person 130
extra point 19.6 *scoring*
extrapolate 52.93 *equate,* 170.9 *add*
extrapolation 52.66 *proof,* 170.1 *calculation*
extra power 235.1 *power*
extras 130.4 *extra,* 132.4 *surplus,* 748.5 *expense*
extrasensory 1.1.16 *psychic,* 368.9 *parapsychological,* 464.7 *precognitive*
extrasensory perception 11.1 *occultism,* 403.1 *sensation* 459.2 *ways of thinking,* 464.2 *precognition,* 516.3 *foresight,* 759.2 *impression*
extraterrestrial 149, 149, 11.11 *ghost,* 11.18 *spiritual,* 53.36 *astronomical,* 104.6 *outsider,* 104.12 *external*
extraterrestrially 53.39 *astronomically,* 149.18 *extraneously*
extra time 130.4 *extra*
extra-time victory 682.2 *victory*
extravagance 541, 748, 757, 508.1 *folly,* 557.2 *affectation,* 601.2 *misuse,* 607.3 *waste,* 608.8 *plenty,* 811.4 *flashiness,* 811.6 *blatancy,* 870.3 *overindulgence*
Extravagance 757
extravagant 541, 757, 519.11 *fantastical,* 557.4 *ornate,* 601.5 *abusive,* 607.8 *wasteful,* 608.2

plentiful, 748.11 *spendthrift,* 753.7 *dear,* 811.19 *flashy,* 811.21 *blatant,* 870.8 *overindulgent*
extravagantly 757, 541.17 *excessively,* 557.6 *ornately,* 601.6 *abusively,* 607.10 *wastefully,* 748.14 *generously,* 753.12 *dearly,* 811.35 *flashily,* 811.37 *blatantly*
extravaganza 51.5 *show,* 519.4 *ideality*
extravagation 357.7 *crossing*
extravasate 347.12 *leak,* 349.14 *let out,* 353.4 *excrement,* 353.15 *excrete,* 353.21 *bleed*
extravasated 347.16 *outflowing*
extravasation 347.3 *leakage,* 349.22 *disgorgement,* 353.1 *excretion,* 353.4 *excrement*
extravasation of blood 353.10 *bleeding*
extravehicular activity 53.31 *space travel*
extra weight 369.4 *heaviness*
extra work 644.2 *task*
extreme 157.7 *limit,* 157.24 *limiting,* 237.10 *potent,* 241.6 *violent,* 263.8 *distant,* 277.9 *deepseated,* 300.8 *edging,* 302.6 *furthest,* 406.5 *painful,* 541.1 *exaggeration,* 541.12 *exaggerated,* 610.1 *excess,* 610.6 *excessive,* 619.3 *perfection,* 627.16 *improving,* 757.2 *unrestrained*
extremely 121.11 *to a degree,* 126.16 *superiorly,* 237.15 *acutely,* 300.11 *marginally,* 541.17 *excessively*
extremely high frequency 534 Radio-frequency bands
extreme penalty 879.13 *capital punishment*
extremes 111.1 *oppositeness,* 610.1 *excess,* 757.5 *unrestrainedness*
extreme unction 10.5 *Christian rite,* 397.7 *dying day*
extremism 541.1 *exaggeration,* 627.11 *reformism*
extremist 335.19 *deviant person,* 541.6 *exaggerator,* 627.12 *reformer,* 627.16 *improving,* 693.10 *seditionist*
extremity 157.7 *limit,* 279.1 *summit,* 300.1 *edge,* 302.3 *furthest point*
extricable 639.4 *deliverable*
extricably 639
extricate 252.15 *remove,* 355.11 *extract,* 639.1 *deliver,* 660.18 *disentangle,* 698.15 *set free,* 700.4 *liberate*
extricated 252.9 *removed,* 355.19 *dislodged*
extricate oneself 700.5 *be liberated*
extrication 252.2 *removal,* 355.1 *extraction,* 639.2 *deliverance,* 660.8 *disentanglement,* 700.1 *liberation*
extrinsic 104.12 *external,* 108.7 *illogical,* 136.17 *unjoined,* 149.11 *foreign*
extrinsicality 104.4 *externality,* 149.3 *foreignness*
extrinsically 104.18 *extraneously,* 136.22 *in isolation,* 149.18 *extraneously*
extroversion 61.7 *personality type,* 289.4 *externalization*
extroversive 61.35 *extroverted*
extrovert 61.7 *personality type,* 61.35 *extroverted,* 239.4 *vigorous,* 289.4 *externalization,* 815.15 *sociable*
extroverted 61, 239.4 *vigorous,* 289.9 *externalized*
extrovertedness 61.7 *personality type*
extrudable 67.9 *spun*
extrude 67.13 *spin,* 349.14 *let out,* 353.15 *excrete*
extruded 67.9 *spun*
extruder 67.2 *spinning*

extrusion 54.29 *petrogenesis,* 67.2 *spinning,* 347.1 *exit,* 349.22 *disgorgement,* 353.1 *excretion*
extrusive 54.56 *petrographic*
extrusive rock 54.30 *igneous rock*
exuberance 246.1 *fertility,* 553.1 *diffuseness,* 610.1 *excess,* 762.1 *happiness*
exuberant 246.5 *fertile,* 553.3 *diffuse,* 610.6 *excessive,* 762.4 *happy*
exuberate 608.5 *about*
exudate 389, 347.12 *leak,* 353.4 *excrement,* 353.8 *sweat*
exudation 347.2 *outflow,* 352.1 *secretion,* 353.1 *excretion,* 353.4 *excrement,* 353.8 *sweat,* 389.4 *exudate*
exudative 347.17 *leaky,* 352.4 *secretory,* 353.24 *excretory*
exude 347.12 *leak,* 352.7 *secrete,* 353.15 *excrete,* 353.19 *sweat,* 389.32, 391.16 *seep*
exult 773.5 *rejoice*
exultant 773.9 *rejoicing*
exultation 773.1 *rejoicing*
exultet 10.8 *hymn*
exult in 805.25 *be proud of*
exurb 93.8 *suburb*
exurban 93.14 *urban*
exurbia 93.8 *suburb,* 249.11 *settlement*
exuviae 353.12 *dead tissue,* 622.4 *dirt*
exuvial 296.12 *peeling,* 353.32 *cast-off*
exuviate 294.13 *remove,* 296.16 *peel*
exuviation 294.5 *shedding,* 296.6 *peeling*
ex-wife 402.12 *woman in the family*
eyas 78.12 *young bird*
eye 74 Rigging, **435,** 20.3 *fishing tackle,* 56.23 *light,* 60.3 *medical specialty,* 322.5 *hole,* 435.13 *look,* 457.3 *external appearance,* 826.8 *court*
eyeball 435.2 *eye,* 435.14 *inspect*
eyeball to eyeball 111.6 *oppositely,* 267.7 *beside,* 435.24 *visually,* 663.20 *discordant,* 663.25 *at odds*
eyeball-to-eyeball 111.4 *opposite,* 267.5 *juxtaposed*
eyebath 62.11 *linctus,* 258.12 *bath,* 386.6 *pomade*
eyebright 84 Flowers and Flowering Plants
eyebrow 435.2 *eye*
eye-catching 318.7 *conspicuous,* 435.23 *visible,* 437.2 *clear,* 526.14 *manifest*
eye clinic 436.3 *aid for poor sight*
eyed 435.21 *seeing*
eye disease 436.2 *poor sight*
eye drops 62.8 *drops,* 436.3 *aid for poor sight*
eye for 655.2 *aptitude*
eye for an eye 223.1 *exchange,* 840.1 *atonement*
eye-for-eye 109.4 *reciprocal*
eyeful 435.7 *view*
eyeglass 435.10 *visual aid,* 442.8 *transparent thing*
eyehole 322.5 *hole*
eye hospital 436.3 *aid for poor sight*
eyelash 435.2 *eye*
eyeless 145.4 *incomplete,* 436.8 *blind*
eyelessness 436.1 *blindness*
eyelet 137.8 *fastening,* 322.5 *hole*
eyelid 293.14 *animal covering,* 435.2 *eye*
eyelike 435.20 *visual*
eye-liner 791.4 *cosmetics*
eye lotion 386.6 *pomade*
eye make-up 791.4 *cosmetics*
eye muscle 435.2 *eye*
eye of the hurricane 291.2 *central thing,* 325.2 *repose,* 642.1 *activity*
eye of the storm 55.16 *wind vortex*

eye-opener 435.7 *view,* 496.7 *detection,* 514.4 *surprising thing,* 786.4 *wonder*
eye-opening 6.16 *educational,* 435.23 *visible*
eyepatch 436.6 *blinder*
eyepiece 53.25 *mounting,* 56.30 *lens system*
eye rhyme 48.11 *rhyme*
eyes 777 Phobias by Topic
eyeshade 293.12 *protective covering,* 435.10 *visual aid,* 440.6 *shade,* 634.2 *shelter*
eye-shadow 444.9 *complexion,* 791.4 *cosmetics*
eyeshot 435.9 *viewpoint,* 437.3 *visibility*
eyesight 435.1 *vision,* 437.3 *visibility*
eyesocket 435.2 *eye*
eyes on stalks 786.2 *sign of wonderment*
eyesore 43.3 *building,* 435.7 *view,* 790.3 *ugly place,* 793.3 *blot on the landscape*
eyespot 90.3 *plant body*
eyestrain 436.2 *poor sight*
eye test 60.7 *diagnosis*
Eyetie 91 Names for Inhabitants
eye to eye 435.24 *visually,* 667.14 *agreeably*
eyetooth 380.11 *tooth*
eye up 435.13 *look*
eyewash 62.8 *drops,* 386.6 *pomade,* 395.6 *ointment,* 436.3 *aid for poor sight,* 521.5 *empty talk,* 538.6, 540.13 *nonsense,* 630.9 *balm,* 853.1 *flattery*
eyewitness 253.5 *someone present,* 435.11 *observer,* 480.7 *verifier,* 483.7 *person who gives evidence,* 528.9 *informant,* 535.9 *affirmer*
eyewitness account 528.2 *communication,* 533.2 *news event*
eyeworm 81 Worms
eyra 77 Placental Mammals
Eyre 94 Lakes, 94.5 *other major lakes*
Eyre of Justice 16.20 *British court*
eyrie 78.14 *nest,* 256.13 *lair,* 275.8 *high thing,* 634.3 *animal shelter*
Ezekiel 636.4 *warner*

F

f 49 Musical Terms
F1 car 33.1 *motor racing*
Fa 8 Deities
fab 617.1 *worthy,* 786.14 *wonderful,* 861.1 *good,* 861.27 *great super*
Fabian 12.6 *political party,* 328.5 *unhurried,* 627.12 *reformer,* 641.3 *inactive*
Fabianism 12.1 *government,* 328.8 *slowness,* 627.11 *reformism,* 641.1 *inaction*
Fabian policy 641.1 *inaction*
fable 48.2 *fiction,* 519.7 *idealism,* 521.5 *empty talk,* 538.4 *lie,* 540.9 *falsification,* 540.22 *falsify,* 560.3 *narration*
fabled 518.8 *supposed,* 519.12 *imaginary,* 540.32 *falsified,* 800.3 *reputable,* 804.5 *entitled*
fabler 48.14 *author*
Fabre 52 Scientists
fabric 67, 382, 54.28 *rock,* 67.10 *woven,* 103.1 *essence,* 243.7 *produce,* 288.4 *textile,* 367.4 *matter,* 383.5 *textile,* 604.1 *materials*
fabricate 102, 148.13 *make,* 161.44 *put together,* 243.10 *produce,* 309.12 *distort the truth,* 382.15 *shape,* 519.14 *imagine,* 538.21 *lie,* 538.22 *make unreal,* 540.22 *falsify*

fabricated 63.32 *structural*, 309.8 *exaggerated*, 519.12 *imaginary*, 538.13 *untrue*, 540.32 *falsified*
fabricating 538.15 *lying*, 540.29 *deceitful*
fabrication 161.33 *putting together*, 243.2 *manufacture*, 309.4 *distortion of the truth*, 382.3 *form*, 519.5 *fantasy*, 538.1 *untruth*, 538.3, 540.6 *lying*, 540.9 *falsification*
fabricator 243.9 *producer*, 538.11, 539.16 *liar*
fabric dealer 295.26 *fashion designer*
Fabrics and Dyeing 67
fabric treatment 67
fabulist 48.14 *author*, 538.11, 539.16 *liar*, 560.10 *descriptive writer*
fabulous 48.17 *fictional*, 487.2 *unbelievable*, 519.12 *imaginary*, 617.1 *worthy*, 861.1 *good*
fabulous bird 78
fabulously 786.13 *wonderfully*, 861.22 *well*
faburden 433.3 *melodiousness*
façade 40, 289.1 *exterior*, 303.1 *front*, 303.2 *face*, 303.3 *show*, 436.6 *blinder*, 437.6 *visible thing*, 457.3 *external appearance*
face 192, 293, 303, 5.15 *type style*, 29.1 *golf*, 29.4 *golf club*, 52.38 *surface*, 111.8 *be opposite*, 156.18 *make a beginning*, 266.10 *layer*, 281.3 *vertical thing*, 289.1 *exterior*, 289.11 *be exterior*, 292.3 *line*, 295.27 *model*, 303.10 *be in front*, 305.7 *be alongside*, 306.6 *nature*, 318.3 *protuberance*, 457.3 *external appearance*, 513.8 *expect*, 540.12 *facade*, 540.24 *mask*, 574.8 *brace oneself*, 663.16 *confront*, 778.15 *be courageous*, 807.2 *cheek*
face about 335.11, 337.9 *turn round*
face a total loss 722.9 *lose*
face bankruptcy 722.10 *have a financial loss*
face both ways 578.2 *equivocate*
face card 42.3 *card game terms*
face-centred 57.33 *crystalline*
face-centred-cubic crystal 57.4 *crystal*
facecloth 621.11 *cleaning cloth*
face cream 386.6 *pomade*, 395.6 *ointment*, 621.9 *cleaning agent*, 630.9 *balm*
faced 266.8 *coated*, 293.36 *covered*
face danger 633, 668.5 *defy*, 778.15 *be courageous*
face death 633.9 *face danger*
face defeat 722.9 *lose*
face difficulties 659.20 *be in difficulty*
face disaster 656.5 *be unskilful*
face disqualification 722.9 *lose*
face down 282.10 *lying*
face flannel 621.11 *cleaning cloth*
faceguard 19.18 *be penalized*
faceguard 27.6 *pad*, 31.5 *lacrosse*
faceguarding 19.13 *penalty*
face heavy odds 633.9 *face danger*
face in the crowd 531.7 *concealer*
faceless 112.6 *conforming*
face-lift 627.5 *improvement*, 629.8 *repair*, 791.2 *plastic surgery*
face like a tombstone 770.6 *depressed*
face like a wet weekend 770.6 *depressed*
facemask 19.3 *uniform*, 19.18 *be penalized*, 31.3 *ice hockey*, 385.7 *eraser*
face off 31.9 *play hockey*
face-off 31.3 *ice hockey*, 31.8 *hockey*
face-off circle 31.3 *ice hockey*
face pack 791.3 *beauty treatment*
face powder 384.5 *powder*

facer 514.3 *shock*
face reality 673.3 *submit*
face-saving measures 593.3 *needfulness*
facet 43 Architectural Decoration, 106.6 *aspect*, 148.1 *component*, 289.1 *exterior*, 305.4 *aspect*, 457.3 *external appearance*
faceted 289.6 *exterior*, 310.9 *angled*
face the ball 31.9 *play hockey*
face the cameras 51.32 *act*
face the facts 673.3 *submit*
face the issue 574.8 *brace oneself*
face the music 778.15 *be courageous*, 879.6 *be punished*
face the odds 574.8 *brace oneself*, 778.15 *be courageous*
face the other way 335.11 *turn round*
facetiae 877.2 *indecency*
facetious 771.10 *humorous*
facetiously 771.16 *humorously*
facetiousness 771.1 *humorousness*
face to face 111.6 *oppositely*, 267.7 *beside*, 663.20 *discordant*, 663.25 *at odds*
face-to-face 111.4 *opposite*, 267.5 *juxtaposed*, 526.17 *frankly*
face up to 303.10 *be in front*
face value 457.5 *impression*, 751.2 *value*
facial 303.7 *outward*, 385.6 *massage*, 791.3 *beauty treatment*
facial distortion 309
facial expression 457.3 *external appearance*
facially 457.15 *apparently*
facial massage 385.6 *massage*
facial scrub 385.7 *eraser*
facies 54.28 *rock*, 457.3 *external appearance*
facile 49 Musical Terms, 660.9 *easy*
facilely 660.21 *easily*
facileness 660.2 *simplicity*
facilitate 522.5 *simplify*, 524.8 *interpret*, 586.16 *tempt*, 602.6 *find means*, 660.16 *make easy*, 662.28 *further*, 698.15 *set free*, 708.3 *permit*
facilitated 660.11 *made easy*
facilitating 660.10 *feasible*, 662.30 *helping*
facilitation 660.7 *easing*, 662.8 *furtherance*
facilitative 662.30 *helping*
facilitator 662.11 *helper*
facilities 602.1 *means*, 615.5 *convenience*
facility 485.2 *ability*, 486.2 *possibleness*, 522.10 *simplicity*, 655.1 *skill*, 660.1 *easiness*, 662.7 *convenience*
facing 111.4 *opposite*, 111.6 *oppositely*, 266.3 *coat*, 289.6 *exterior*, 292.1 *lining*, 293.8 *wall covering*, 305.2 *surface*, 305.6 *side*, 376.10 *polish*, 457.3 *external appearance*
facing both ways 578.10 *equivocal*
facing death 633.4 *endangered*
facing the ball 31.5 *lacrosse*
facing the firing squad 633.4 *endangered*
facsimile 65.12 *electronic office*, 110.4 *duplicate*, 114.2, 118.2 *copy*, 118.5 *duplicate*, 245.2 *print*, 547.1, 560.9 *representation*
facsimile machine 114.3 *copier*, 118.6 *photocopier*
facsimile transmission 534.8 *data transmission*
fact 99, 3.14 *historicalness*, 101.1 *reality*, 106.6 *aspect*, 490.12 *something certain*, 537.1 *truth*
fact-find 477.17 *question*
fact-finding 477.12 *questioning*
facticity 99.4 *demonstrable existence*
faction 500, 7.1 *religion*, 117.4 *disagreement*, 143.1 *part*, 148.2 *piece*, 161.16 *party*, 500.6 *dis-*

senters, 534.25 *broadcast material*, 538.1 *untruth*, 560.3 *narration*, 663.8 *the opposition*, 665.3 *political grouping*, 693.3 *subversion*
factional 117.10 *disagreeing*, 161.49 *grouped*, 560.12 *narrative*, 665.10 *political*, 693.14 *subversive*
factionalism 500.3 *dissentience*, 665.4 *partisanship*
factionalist 500.5 *dissenter*
factionalized 538.13 *untrue*
factious 473.8 *argumentative*
factitious 540.28 *spurious*
factitiously 540.37 *spuriously*
factitiousness 540.27 *spuriousness*
fact of the matter 99.5 *fact*
factor 52.17 *multiplication*, 59.11 *genetics*, 59.13 *genetic material*, 106.6 *aspect*, 143.1 *part*, 146.2 *thing included*, 148.1 *component*, 169.4 *mathematical result*, 226.4 *contributing factor*, 232.2 *instrument*, 251.2 *circumstances*, 367.4 *matter*, 653.15 *manager*
factorage 737.4 *trade*
factor analysis 52.55 *statistical methods*
factorial 52.17 *multiplication*, 59.25 *genetic*
factorization 52.17 *multiplication*
factorize 52.91 *add*, 136.11 *divide*
factors 257.1 *contents*
factorship 737.4 *trade*
factory 2.8 *human institution*, 63.20 *building*, 243.2 *manufacture*, 647.1 *workshop*
factory discount price 751.1 *price*
factory farm 68.6 *farm*
factory farming 68.1 *agriculture*, 243.2 *manufacture*
factory floor 161.13 *workforce*
factory-gate price 751.1 *price*
factory hand 646.1 *worker*
factory-made 243.12 *produced*
factory mark 44.4 *porcelain mark*
factory of lies 538.5 *half-truth*
factory price 751.1 *price*
factory ship 74 Ships and Boats
factory worker 646.1 *worker*
factotum 642.10 *busy person*, 646.1 *worker*, 697.1 *servant*
facts 483.1 *evidence*, 490.13 *confirmation*, 501.2, 528.1 *information*, 533.1 *news*, 537.3 *the truth*, 537.7 *confirmation*
facts and figures 528.1 *information*
facts of life 101.5 *realities*, 245.3 *propagation*, 537.3 *the truth*
facts of the matter 537.3 *the truth*
factual 3.19 *chronicled*, 99.13, 101.6 *real*, 483.8 *evidential*, 490.1 *certain*, 503.6 *correct*, 537.15 *true*, 560.12 *narrative*
factual account 560
factuality 99.4 *demonstrable existence*, 101.1 *reality*, 490.9 *certainty*
factualize 99.20 *bring into being*, 101.11 *make real*
factually 483.14 *as evidence*, 537.35 *truly*
factualness 3.14 *historicalness*
facula 53.15 *sun*
faculty 6.3 *subject*, 6.6 *instructorship*, 235.2, 485.2 *ability*, 501.4 *intellect*, 655.1 *skill*, 655.2 *aptitude*
faculty of judgment 492.1 *judgment*
faculty of sight 435.1 *vision*
faculty of speech 564
faculty psychology 61.1 *psychology*
fad 114.2 *copy*, 201.2 *trendiness*, 579.3 *whim*, 784.3 *likes*
FAD 58.12 *coenzyme*
faddiness 469.4 *fastidiousness*
faddish 201.10 *new*, 579.1 *capricious*
faddishness 579.2 *caprice*
faddism 579.2 *caprice*

faddist 201.9 *modern person*
faddy 469.9 *careful*, 579.1 *capricious*
fade 29.3 *golf shots*, 29.7 *golf*, 71.21 *miscellaneous motoring terms*, 121.6 *change gradually*, 129.4 *decrease*, 189.4 *be transient*, 202.17 *grow old*, 238.6 *be weak*, 438.7 *become invisible*, 439.28 *bleach*, 441.9 *be dim*, 441.10 *make dim*, 444.15 *colour*, 445.5 *lose colour*, 445.6 *decolour*, 446.13 *whiten*, 458.1 *disappear*, 607.1 *waste*, 628.1 *deteriorate*
fadeaway 22.4 *pitching terms*
fade away 100.13 *cease to exist*, 129.4 *decrease*, 157.18 *come to an end*, 218.6 *cease*, 424.5 *sound faint*, 438.7 *become invisible*, 458.1 *disappear*, 624.24 *be unhealthy*
faded 392.3 *dried-up*, 439.21 *light*, 441.7 *dimmed*, 444.13 *soft-hued*, 445.7 *colourless*, 446.2 *whitened*, 628.12 *deteriorated*
faded hue 444.3 *hue*
fade from one's memory 512.12 *be forgotten*
fade from sight 129.4 *decrease*
fade in 457.12 *become visible*
fade into the background 673.3 *submit*
fade out 121.6 *change gradually*, 157.18 *come to an end*, 218.6 *cease*, 441.9 *be dim*, 458.1 *disappear*, 722.12 *lessen*
fade-out 129.1 *decrease*, 440.2 *darkening*, 458.4 *disappearance*
fading 121.7 *gradational*, 129.1 *decrease*, 129.6 *decreasing*, 189.6 *transient*, 392.13 *drying*, 397.18 *dying*, 445.1 *colourlessness*, 445.7 *colourless*, 458.4 *disappearance*, 458.6 *disappearing*, 534.19 *radio reception*, 628.7 *deterioration*
fading away 458.4 *disappearance*
fading fast 397.18 *dying*
fading out 121.7 *gradational*, 458.4 *disappearance*, 722.4 *lessening*
faecal 353, 622.8 *unclean*
faeces 777 Phobias by Topic, 353, 622.4 *dirt*
Faeroese 5 Languages and Groups of Languages
fag 401.9 *offensive terms for homosexual*, 413.7 *tobacco*, 642.10 *busy person*, 644.1, 644.6 *work*, 646.1 *worker*, 650.6 *fatigue*, 701.3 *subordinate*
fag end 132.1 *remainder*, 157.8 *tail* 413.7 *tobacco*
fagged 650.1 *fatigued*
fagged out 650.1 *fatigued*
faggot 85.3 *timber*, 401.9 *offensive terms for homosexual*, 410.2 *lighter*, 604.1 *materials*
faggots 45.20 *meat*
fag out 650.6 *fatigue*
Fahrenheit scale 75.3 *scale*, 408.2 *heat measurement*
faience 44.1 *ceramics*
fail 358, 683, 63.31 *load*, 127.8 *be inferior*, 129.4 *decrease*, 218.7 *stop working*, 236.6 *be powerless*, 238.6 *be weak*, 244.13 *be destroyed*, 247.7 *be infertile*, 320.10 *close*, 360.10 *droop*, 491.21 *change*, 515.4 *be disappointed*, 515.6 *disappoint*, 609.5 *be insufficient*, 614.7 *be useless*, 620.9 *be imperfect*, 624.24 *be unhealthy*, 628.1 *deteriorate*, 650.5 *be fatigued*, 656.5 *be unskilful*, 656.7 *be clumsy*, 683.9 *malfunction*, 687.9 *be in trouble*, 720.8 *not perform*, 722.9 *lose*, 747.9 *be unable to pay*, 844.24 *go wrong*
failed 683, 127.17 *defective*, 238.11 *weakened*, 247.6 *having no effect*, 320.6 *closed*, 656.1 *unskilful*, 720.12 *nonperforming*, 722.16 *losing*

fail in duty 720.9 *disregard orders*
failing 127.2 *deficiency,* 127.17 *defective,* 207.14 *aged,* 244.15 *destroyed,* 358.8 *defective,* 609.10 *insufficiently,* 620.7 *defect,* 628.12 *deteriorated,* 633.7 *vulnerability,* 683.1 *failure,* 683.3 *personal fault,* 683.10 *failed,* 720.12 *nonperforming,* 722.16 *losing,* 864.3 *venial sin,* 864.13 *venial*
failing grade 302.2 *limiting factor*
failing health 624.1 *ill health,* 683.1 *failure*
failing person 683
failing sight 436.2 *poor sight*
fail in health 683.6 *fail*
fail in one's duties 683.6 *fail*
fail in one's duty 848.12 *exempt oneself*
fail in responsibility 720.8 *not perform*
faille 67 Natural Fabrics
fail-safe 632.6 *invulnerable*
fail-safe device 632.4 *safety device*
fail-safe system 632.4 *safety device*
fail the test 620.9 *be imperfect*
fail to act 641.4 *not act,* 783.12 *be indifferent*
fail to amaze 787.7 *not cause wonder*
fail to appear 254.15 *be absent,* 458.2 *depart*
fail to appreciate 838.6 *be ungrateful*
fail to deliver 515.6 *disappoint,* 685.5 *not complete*
fail to fulfil 145.5 *be incomplete*
fail to fulfil one's duty 720.8 *not perform*
fail to hear 421.8 *be deaf*
fail to heed 783.14 *be careless*
fail to inspire 783.13 *make indifferent,* 787.7 *not cause wonder*
fail to interest 788.6 *be boring*
fail to move 783.12 *be indifferent,* 783.13 *make indifferent*
fail to retract 535.19 *confirm*
fail to score 683.7 *be defeated*
fail to see 460.15 *lack intellect*
fail to take advantage of 600.5 *not use*
failure 777 Phobias by Topic, **683,** 51.11 *theatrical performance,* 63.16 *deformation,* 127.2 *deficiency,* 127.6 *inferior,* 129.1 *decrease,* 218.2 *stop,* 238.3 *poor health,* 244.4 *ruin,* 337.21 *backslider,* 358.6 *shortcoming,* 360.4 *fall,* 411.2 *taste of life,* 515.2 *bad outcome,* 581.8 *rejected thing,* 609.8 *insufficiency,* 614.4 *futility,* 620.5 *imperfection,* 656.9 *bungling,* 656.10 *unskilled person,* 683.5 *failing person,* 685.1 *noncompletion,* 685.3 *quitter,* 720.2 *nonperformance,* 722.1 *loss,* 722.6 *loser,* 747.5 *insolvency,* 776.3 *hopeless person,* 785.2 *disliked thing,* 866.3 *sin*
Failure 683
failure of credit 747.5 *insolvency*
failure to act 641.1 *inaction*
failure to arouse 787.1 *lack of wonder*
failure to finish 685.1 *noncompletion*
failure to hear 421.1 *deafness*
failure to meet one's obligations 747.5 *insolvency*
failure to pay 683.1 *failure*
faint 424, 236.4 *disability,* 236.6 *be powerless,* 238.6 *be weak,* 238.10 *ill,* 238.13 *insufficient,* 404.2 *unconsciousness,* 404.11 *be unfeeling,* 421.7 *unheard,* 422.3 *silent,* 428.1 *faint-sounding,* 438.2 *difficult to see,* 441.6 *murky,* 445.7 *colourless,* 491.6 *indeterminate,* 542.16 *imperceptible,* 563.10 *low-voiced,* 624.24 *be unhealthy,* 650.1 *fatigued,* 650.5 *be fatigued,* 650.7

fatigue, 673.4 *succumb,* 722.9 *lose,* 821.24 *be in love*
faint-coloured 445.8 *drained of colour*
faint heart 779.1 *cowardice*
faint-hearted 576.3 *timid,* 779.3 *cowardly*
faint-heartedly 779.5 *cravenly*
faint-heartedness 573.13 *dissociation,* 576.13 *timidity,* 779.1 *cowardice*
faint hope 477.7 *questionableness,* 486.4 *remote possibility,* 775.1 *hope*
fainting 624.3 *symptom,* 650.1 *fatigued,* 650.7 *fatigue*
faintly 424, 428, 238.14 *weakly,* 422.5 *silently,* 441.12 *dimly,* 445.9 *colourlessly,* 491.25 *indeterminately,* 542.27 *imperceptibly*
faintness 424, 238.3 *poor health,* 421.3 *inaudibility,* 422.4 *silence,* 428.3 *muteness,* 438.4 *invisibility,* 441.1 *dimness,* 445.2 *paleness,* 491.14 *indeterminacy,* 523.11 *unintelligibility,* 527.10 *quietness,* 542.7 *imperceptibility,* 650.7 *fatigue*
Faintness 424
faint praise 542.2 *detraction,* 854.1 *disparagement*
faint resemblance 114.1 *similarity*
faint smell 416.1 *odour*
faint sound 428, 421.3 *inaudibility*
faint-sounding 428
faint-sounding thing 424
fair 740, 4.15 *rational,* 55.45 *fine,* 122.6 *equal,* 124.3 *mediocre,* 158.15 *middling,* 242.6 *moderate,* 392.5 *rainless,* 408.11 *warm,* 439.21 *light,* 446.3 *white-haired,* 482.2 *impartial,* 492.9 *judicious,* 526.6 *display,* 617.5 *not bad,* 714.14 *auspicious,* 727.2 *disposal of property,* 765.6 *satisfactory,* 783.9 *impartial,* 783.10 *mediocre,* 789.5 *beautiful,* 812.1 *celebration,* 817.7 *courteous,* 843.7 *right,* 857.4 *honourable,* 859.4 *disinterested,* 861.3 *kind,* 876.8 *moral*
fair and foul 111.2 *opposites*
fair and square 312.5, 857.4 *honourable*
fair ball 12.5 *batting terms*
Fairbanks 93 Cities
fair catch 19.12 *special team,* 35.3 *rugby play*
fair chance 589, 229.2 *chance*
fair copy 118.2 *copy*
fair crack of the whip 843.1 *fairness*
fair dealing 312.8 *directness*
fair-dealing 857.4 *honourable*
fair dinkum 537.40 *right*
faired 381.1 *blunt*
fair exchange 109.1 *interchange,* 122.3 *equalization,* 737.4 *trade*
fair expectation 488.4 *chance*
fair fighter 857.3 *honourable person*
fair game 539.22 *dupe,* 850.9 *butt*
fair hair 452.6 *yellowness*
fair-haired 446.3 *white-haired,* 452.3 *yellow-haired*
fairing 73 Aircraft Parts, 729.2 *gift*
fairish 124.3 *mediocre,* 158.15 *middling*
fairishness 124.6 *mediocrity*
Fair Isle 295.13 *sweater*
fairlead 36.3 *parts of a sailing boat*
fairly 4.26 *rationally,* 4.27 *stoically,* 121.11 *to a degree,* 122.13 *equitably,* 242.9 *moderately,* 482.15 *impartially,* 700.8 *free,* 783.19 *impartially,* 783.20 *unexceptionally,* 843.19 *equally,* 857.7 *honourably,* 859.8 *disinterestedly*

fair-minded 482.2 *impartial,* 507.5 *wise,* 843.7 *right,* 859.4 *disinterested*
fair-mindedness 482.7 *impartiality,* 843.1 *fairness,* 859.1 *disinterestedness*
fairness 843, 122.1 *equality,* 242.1 *moderation,* 312.8 *directness,* 439.14 *light colour,* 446.7 *whiteness,* 482.7, 783.3 *impartiality,* 789.1 *gorgeousness,* 857.1 *probity,* 859.1 *disinterestedness,* 861.10 *kindness,* 876.2 *good morals*
fair offer 677.2 *peace offering,* 710.3 *business offer*
fair play 843.1 *fairness,* 876.2 *good morals*
fair price 122.3 *equalization*
fair sex 402.1 *female sex*
fair shake 122.2 *equilibrium*
fair share 731.2 *portion*
fair size 259.3 *large scale*
fair-size 259.15 *big*
fair-skinned 446.1 *white*
fair territory 12.1 *baseball*
fair to middling 124.3 *mediocre,* 242.6 *moderate,* 617.5 *not bad,* 623.1 *healthy*
fair trade laws 13.1 *economics*
fair trial 16.7 *legal trial*
fair value 122.3 *equalization,* 751.2 *value*
fairway 29.1 *golf*
fair way 263.2 *great distance*
fair-weather friend 499.3 *assenter,* 538.12 *cheat,* 539.19 *hypocrite,* 579.4 *capricious person*
fair-weather sailor 74.7 *nautical person,* 656.10 *unskilled person*
fair wind 662.1 *help*
fair words 817.1 *courtesy*
fairy 11.11 *ghost,* 11.18 *spiritual,* 260.4 *little person*
fairy bluebird 78 Birds
fairy cycle 71.12 *bicycle*
fairy godmother 8.6 *angel,* 284.8 *supporter,* 632.3 *protector,* 662.15 *benefactor,* 729.4 *giver,* 755.9 *generous person,* 786.5 *person of wonder*
fairyland 519.8 *dreamland,* 786.4 *wonder*
fairy lights 439.6 *electric light*
fairy penguin 78 Birds
fairy ring 11.6 *talisman,* 89.2 *mushroom*
fairy-ring mushroom 89 Fungi
fairy shrimp 81.4 *arthropod*
fairy tale 48.2 *fiction,* 519.4 *ideality,* 538.4 *lie,* 560.3 *narration*
fairy-tale ending 682.1 *success*
Faisalabad 93 Cities
faith 7.1 *religion,* 490.10 *conviction,* 497.2 *religious belief,* 497.3 *believing,* 537.13 *faithfulness,* 632.1 *safety,* 718.1 *protection,* 775.2 *expectation,* 857.2 *purity,* 863.2 *virtues*
faith cure 630.13 *therapy*
faithful 537, 5.40 *translated,* 7.15 *religious,* 101.7 *realistic,* 114.9 *lifelike,* 134.12 *morally pure,* 138.10 *tenacious,* 490.6 *infallible,* 497.11 *believing,* 503.6 *correct,* 524.17 *translational,* 537.21 *accurate,* 575.10 *persevering,* 694.3 *loyal,* 719.7 *observant,* 819.11 *devoted,* 821.17 *loving,* 857.4 *honourable,* 863.6 *ethical*
faithful copy 118.2 *copy*
faithful likeness 114.1 *similarity*
faithful love 821.2 *romantic love*
faithfully 7.23 *religiously,* 114.14 *comparably,* 134.18 *virtuously,* 138.12 *tenaciously,* 497.15 *believingly,* 503.8 *accurately,* 694.10 *obediently,* 719.8 *observantly,* 819.19 *devotedly,* 821.30 *lovingly,* 857.7 *honourably,* 863.10 *ethically*
faithfully rendered 537.25 *lifelike*

faithfulness 537, 7.2 *religiousness,* 503.2 *correctness,* 537.8 *accuracy,* 694.2 *loyalty,* 719.1 *observance,* 857.1 *probity*
faithful rendering 537.12 *true to life*
faithful servant 808.3 *sycophant*
faithful spouse 823.8 *spouse*
faithful translation 5.12, 524.4 *translation*
faith-heal 11.24 *experience psychic phenomena*
faith healer 11.12 *occultist,* 60.12 *healer,* 629.12 *repairer,* 630.15 *healer*
faith healing 11.1 *occultism,* 60.2 *natural medicine,* 630.11 *medical art*
faithless 858, 498.6 *disbelieving,* 538.20 *unfaithful,* 539.38 *treacherous*
faithlessly 538.28 *dishonestly,* 858.11 *dishonourably*
faithlessness 858, 538.10 *dishonesty,* 693.1 *disobedience*
Fajan's rules 57 Named Reactions
fake 540, 540, 19.15 *play offence,* 31.3 *ice hockey,* 31.9 *play hockey,* 102.7 *artificiality,* 102.12 *not the real thing,* 117.11 *unfit,* 117.12 *be disparate,* 118.2, 118.10 *copy,* 118.13 *imitation,* 309.8 *exaggerated,* 309.12 *distort the truth,* 474.10 *hypocritical,* 474.12 *deceive,* 538.12 *cheat,* 538.14 *unreal,* 538.19 *dishonest,* 538.22 *make unreal,* 538.25 *be dishonest,* 539.15 *deceiver,* 539.39 *imitative,* 540.12 *facade,* 540.21 *be fraudulent,* 540.22 *falsify,* 540.24 *mask,* 540.29 *deceitful,* 540.31 *fraudulent,* 540.32 *falsified,* 540.35 *disguised,* 733.3 *illegal borrowing,* 733.9 *borrow illegally,* 733.11 *borrowed,* 736.6 *illegal borrowing*
fake a confession 856.6 *accuse falsely*
fake book 531.2 *hiding place*
fake bottom 539.12 *disguise*
fake conduct 540.5 *deceitfulness*
fake confession 856.2 *false accusation*
faked 31.8 *hockey,* 538.14 *unreal,* 540.32 *falsified*
fake kick 19.12 *special team*
fakely 538.28 *dishonestly*
faker 118.8 *copier,* 474.6 *sophist,* 538.12 *cheat,* 539.15 *deceiver*
fakery 474.5 *hypocrisy,* 540.8 *fraud*
fake someone out 539.28 *trick*
fake suicide 398.7 *suicide*
fake the evidence 856.6 *accuse falsely*
faking 31.3 *ice hockey,* 31.8 *hockey,* 474.10 *hypocritical,* 540.8 *fraud,* 540.9 *falsification*
fakir 7.3 *religious person,* 7.7 *monk,* 11.12 *occultist*
Fal 96 Rivers
Falabella 32 Breeds of Horse and Pony
Falangists 12.6 *political party*
Falasha 7 Non-Christian Religions
falchion 680.8 *sharp weapon*
falcon 78 Birds, 78.5 *bird of prey,* 544.8 *heraldic device,* 590.6 *hunter*
falconer 78.22, 590.6 *hunter*
falconet 680.12 *historical guns*
falconry 18 Sporting Activities, 78.20 *bird sport,* 590.2 *chase*
Faldo 18 Sporting Personalities
Faliscan 5 Languages and Groups of Languages
Falkirk 93 Cities
Falklands War 17 Major Wars
fall 74 Rigging, **360,** 26.5 *wrestling,* 53.20 *meteor,* 55.62 *rain,* 96.7 *flow,* 129.2 *decline,* 129.4 *decrease,* 203.4 *autumn,* 214.5 *regular thing,* 238.6 *be weak,* 244.13 *be destroyed,* 245.10 *re-*

produce oneself, 277.1 *depth*, 277.14 *deepen*, 281.1 *verticality*, 337.4 *slip buck*, 337.14 *decline*, 360.5 *dive*, 360.11 *trip*, 360.12 *drop*, 362.11 *lowering*, 397.16 *meet one's fate*, 504.20 *transgress*, 628.1 *deteriorate*, 633.8 *be in danger*, 683.1 *failure*, 683.6 *fail*, 687.1 *adversity*, 754.2 *declining prices*, 754.12 *be cheap*, 864.16 *be wicked*, 877.16 *do wrong*

fall about 773.8 *laugh*

fallacious 474.7 *sophistic*, 504.15 *erroneous*, 538.13 *untrue*, 539.35 *deceptive*, 540.25 *false*, 844.12 *incorrect*

fallaciously 474.14 *sophistically*, 538.26 *untruthfully*, 540.36 *falsely*

fallaciousness 474.1 *sophistry*, 504.3 *erroneousness*, 538.1 *untruth*, 539.5 *falseness*, 540.1 *falsehood*, 844.2 *incorrectness*

fallacy 102.3 *delusion*, 474.1 *sophistry*, 474.2 *sophism*, 493.1 *misjudgment*, 504.3 *erroneousness*, 504.4 *faulty reasoning*, 538.1 *untruth*, 539.5 *falseness*, 540.1 *falsehood*

fall apart 136.9 *separate*, 141.3 *disintegrate*, 189.4 *be transient*, 628.1 *deteriorate*

fall apart at the seams 238.6 *be weak*

fall asleep 218.9 *pause*, 397.15 *die*, 404.11 *be unfeeling*

fall at a person's feet 808.11 *pander to*

fall at the feet of 849.19 *take off one's hat to*

fall away 136.13 *diverge*

fall back 337.2 *retreat*

fallback 337.11 *retreat*

fall-back 331.6 *response*

fall back on 599.4 *resort to*, 671.28 *survive*

fall behind 127.8 *be inferior*, 337.2 *retreat*

fall below 127.8 *be inferior*, 609.5 *be insufficient*

fall below the poverty line 687.10 *need money*, 743.12 *be poor*

fall between two stools 158.18 *stand in the middle*

fall by the wayside 358.1 *fall short*, 614.7 *be useless*, 683.6 *fail*

fall colours 449.5 *brown thing*

fall dead on the ear 428.9 *be nonresonant*

fall down 358.1 *fall short*, 358.3 *fall through*, 360.10 *droop*, 360.11 *trip*, 360.12 *drop*

fall down before 849.19 *take off one's hat to*

fall due 845.18 *be due*

fallen 362, 8.16 *devilish*, 244.15 *destroyed*, 864.11 *wicked*, 877.13 *unchaste*

fallen angel 8.6 *angel*, 8.7 *devil*, 722.6 *loser*, 864.9 *wicked person*

fallen by the wayside 628.12 *deteriorated*, 722.16 *losing*

fallen nature 864.1 *wickedness*

fallen woman 664.9 *wicked person*, 877.9 *immoral woman*

faller 360.8 *descender*

fall flat 358.3 *fall through*, 683.8 *miscarry*

fall flat on one's face 360.11 *trip*

fall for 228.8 *be motivated*, 497.7 *believe*, 539.24 *be deceived*, 586.18 *be persuaded*, 821.24 *be in love*

fall foul of 674.12 *fight*, 687.9 *be in trouble*

fall from favour 801.4 *disreputable*

fall from grace 687.9 *be in trouble*, 801.4 *disreputable*, 844.23 *sin*, 864.16 *be wicked*

fall guy 222.2 *substitute person*, 539.22 *dupe*, 722.6 *loser*, 850.9 *butt*

fall headlong 360.11 *trip*, 362.7 *lean*

fall head over heels in love 821.24 *be in love*

fall heir to 721.14 *profit*

fallibility 504, 491.15 *unreliability*, 493.1 *misjudgment*, 620.5 *imperfection*, 683.1 *failure*

fallible 491.7 *unreliable*, 493.7 *misjudging*, 504.16 *errant*, 620.1 *imperfect*

fallibly 491.26 *unreliably*, 493.13 *misguidedly*

fall ill 624.24 *be unhealthy*, 628.1 *deteriorate*

fall in 112.10, 116.25 *conform*, 150.24, 159.17 *line up*, 161.41 *band together*, 262.6 *become smaller*, 360.10 *droop*, 379.4 *be brittle*

falling 360, 362, 14.6 *financial*, 96.10 *fluvial*, 123.3 *unequal*, 129.6 *decreasing*, 360.4 *fall*, 360.18 *falling*, 628.12 *deteriorated*, 754.9 *cheap*

falling apart 141.6 *disintegrating*, 244.15 *destroyed*, 628.13 *dilapidated*

falling away 337.14 *decline*

falling back 331.6 *response*

falling birth rate 247.1 *infertility*

falling down 244.15 *destroyed*

falling exchange rate 14.1, 741.7 *finance*

falling hair 294.6 *baldness*, 296.7 *depilation*

falling in love 821.8 *love affair*, 821.18 *in love*

falling leaves 543.1 *sign*

falling off 129.2 *decline*, 628.7 *deterioration*, 628.12 *deteriorated*, 722.4 *lessening*

falling-out 473.1, 666.2 *argument*

falling pressure 55.6 *weather data*

falling price 129.3 *decreasing thing*

falling rocks 34.2 *climbing dangers*

falling short 123.3 *unequal*, 145.1 *incompleteness*, 358.6 *shortcoming*, 515.11 *disappointing*

falling sickness 366.8 *spasm*, 624.4 *disease*, 624.17 *nervous disorder*

falling star 53.20 *meteor*, 439.4 *natural light*

falling to pieces 628.13 *dilapidated*, 633.2 *unsafe*

fall in one's own trap 656.6 *act foolishly*

fall in price 754.12 *be cheap*

fall into 346

fall into a gorge 98.12 *be marooned*

fall into a habit 584.18 *habituate*

fall into a routine 110.11 *be regular*

fall into arrears 747.9 *be unable to pay*

fall into a trap 514.12 *be surprised*

fall into confusion 151.25 *be disordered*

fall into disarray 151.25 *be disordered*

fall into disuse 585.4 *be unaccustomed*

fall into evil ways 864.16 *be wicked*

fall into line 808.13 *conform*

fall into one's hands 730.9 *receive*

fall into place 150.24 *line up*

fall into quicksand 98.12 *be marooned*

fall into ruin 244.13 *be destroyed*

fall into the clutches of 701.8 *be subject to*

fall in with 167.8 *comply*, 342.10 *come together*, 667.6 *agree with*

fall-line 41.1 *skiing*

fall off 139.6 *come unstuck*, 337.1 *go backward*, 337.14 *decline*, 360.9 *descend*, 628.1 *deteriorate*

fall of the leaf 203.4 *autumn*

fall on 592.11 *invent*

fall on bad days 687.9 *be in trouble*

fall on deaf ears 421.11 *be unheard*

fall on hard times 687.9 *be in trouble*, 743.13 *lose one's money*

fall on one's feet 686.6 *be fortunate*

fall on one's knees 808.10 *knuckle under*, 835.12 *ask for mercy*, 849.19 *take off one's hat to*

fall on one's sword 398.21 *commit suicide*

fall on the ear 420.16 *be heard*

Fallopian tubes 245.8 *organs of reproduction*

fallout 56.75 *nuclear accident*, 155.6 *aftermath*, 227.9 *take effect*, 235.8 *nuclear power*, 243.3 *product*, 349.25 *emission*, 384.5 *powder*, 626.1 *lack of hygiene*, 631.10 *warfare*

fall out 117.14 *disagree*, 473.13 *argue*, 685.6 *drop out*, 820.12 *oppose*

fall out of love 783.12 *be indifferent*

fallout shelter 634.1 *refuge*, 671.10 *shelter*

fall out with 500.8 *dissent*, 666.5 *disagree*

fall over 360.11 *trip*, 808.8 *be servile*

fallow 68.20 *farmable*, 240.5 *inert*, 247.3 *birth control*, 452.1 *yellow*, 462.8 *thoughtless*, 595.4 *untrained*, 600.1 *unused*, 641.3 *inactive*, 643.2 *not working*

fallow deer 77 *Placental Mammals*

fallow mind 462.1 *lack of thought*

fallowness 240.1 *inertness*, 247.1 *infertility*

fall prostrate 360.11 *trip*

falls 96.2 *channel*

fall short 358, 123.5 *be unequal*, 127.8 *be inferior*, 145.5 *be incomplete*, 515.4 *be disappointed*, 515.6 *disappoint*, 609.5 *be insufficient*, 620.9 *be imperfect*, 683.6 *fail*, 722.10 *have a financial loss*

fall short of one's goal 685.5 *not complete*

fall short of perfection 620.9 *be imperfect*

fall sick 624.24 *be unhealthy*

fall silent 422.1 *be silent*

fall through 358

fall through the air 360.12 *drop*

fall to 156.18 *make a beginning*, 350.22 *eat well*, 597.1 *undertake*, 847.14 *be the duty of*

fall to bits 384.28 *come to dust*

fall to leeward 74.9 *navigate*

fall to one 749.7 *receive*

fall to one's lot 229.5 *happen by chance*, 589.10 *chance*, 730.9 *receive*

fall to one's share 730.9 *receive*

fall to pieces 141.3 *disintegrate*, 189.4 *be transient*, 379.4 *be brittle*, 683.9 *malfunction*

fall to the ground 358.3 *fall through*

fall to the lot of 847.14 *be the duty of*

fall upon 344.2 *reach*, 670.5 *strike*

fall vertically 281

fall victim to 539.24 *be deceived*

false 540, 28.6 *fencing*, 52.86 *logical*, 102.12 *not the real thing*, 114.8 *simulated*, 309.8 *exaggerated*, 474.10 *hypocritical*, 504.15 *erroneous*, 538.13 *untrue*, 538.14 *unreal*, 538.17 *duplicitous*, 538.18 *pretentious*, 538.19 *dishonest*, 538.20 *unfaithful*, 539.35 *deceptive*, 539.37 *hypocritical*, 540.10 *untrustworthy*, 540.31 *fraudulent*, 540.35 *disguised*, 548.6 *misrepresented*, 578.11 *equivocating*, 844.12 *incorrect*, 846.8 *unentitled*, 858.6 *faithless*

false acacia 85 Trees and Shrubs

false accusation 856

false air 540.12 *facade*

false alarm 636

false alert 636.3 *false alarm*

false arch 43.5 *arch*

false arrest 16.4 *bad law*

false attack 28.3 *fencing movements*

false beard 293.16 *disguise*

false charge 856.2 *false accusation*

false colour 540.12 *facade*

false colours 539.12 *disguise*

false conclusion 504.1 *mistake*

false conduct 540.1 *falsehood*

false construction 525.2 *misinterpretation*

False Cross 53 Other Groups of Stars

false dawn 102.4 *theorization*, 204.1 *morning*, 515.3 *mirage*

false depiction 525.2 *misinterpretation*

false dew 55.37, 391.6 *dew*

false display 797.1 *affectedness*

false evidence 531.5 *evasion*, 856.2 *false accusation*

false excuse 538.1 *untruth*

false expectation 515.1 *disappointment*

false face 538.9, 539.3 *hypocrisy*

false-faced 538.18 *pretentious*, 539.37 *hypocritical*

false friend 538.12 *cheat*, 539.19 *hypocrite*

false front 538.9, 539.3 *hypocrisy*, 539.12 *disguise*, 540.12 *facade*, 557.2 *affectation*

false-fronted 539.37 *hypocritical*

false fruit 86.2 *botanical fruit*

false gold 741.16 *bullion*

false hair 295.15 *headgear*, 791.10 *wig*

false-hearted 538.17 *duplicitous*, 539.38 *treacherous*, 540.29 *deceitful*

false-heartedly 538.28 *dishonestly*

false-heartedness 539, 538.7 *duplicity*, 540.5 *deceitfulness*

falsehood 540, 309.4 *distortion of the truth*, 519.4 *ideality*, 521.5 *empty talk*, 538.1 *untruth*, 539.1 *deception*, 548.1 *misrepresentation*, 858.1 *improbity*

Falsehood 540

false hope 775.1 *hope*

false hopes 515.1 *disappointment*

false idea 525.2 *misinterpretation*

false image 548.1 *misrepresentation*

false impression 102.3 *delusion*, 504.6 *fallibility*, 525.2 *misinterpretation*

false imprisonment 736.2 *kidnapping*

false information 548.2 *misinformation*

false keel 74 Parts of a Ship

false light 525.2 *misinterpretation*, 540.12 *facade*, 548.1 *misrepresentation*

falsely 540, 114.14 *comparably*, 309.14 *distortedly*, 474.14 *sophistically*, 525.4 *mistakenly*, 538.26 *untruthfully*, 548.8 *unrepresentatively*, 844.26 *wrong*, 858.11 *dishonourably*

falsely coloured 540.35 *disguised*

falsely colouring 540.12 *facade*

falsely pious 540.27 *hypocritical*

falsely swearing 540.29 *deceitful*

false modesty 134.1 *purity*, 495.1 *underestimation*, 876.4 *self-righteousness*

false money 741

false morel 89 Fungi

false move 504.1 *mistake*

false name 560.8 *name*

falseness 539, 504.3 *erroneousness*, 538.1 *untruth*, 538.7 *duplicity*, 538.10 *dishonesty*, 539.1 *deception*, 539.3 *hypocrisy*, 540.1 *falsehood*, 540.4 *spu-*

riousness, 844.2 *incorrectness*, 858.2 *faithlessness*
false note 117.2 *contradiction*
false oath 538.3 *lying*
false person 540
false piety 540.3 *hypocrisy*
false plea 538.3 *lying*
false political promises 657.1 *cunning*
false pregnancy 636.3 *false alarm*
false pride 805.3 *conceit*
false promise 484.2 *reversal*
false reading 309.4 *distortion of the truth*, 493.1 *misjudgment*, 525.2 *misinterpretation*
false reasoning 474.1 *sophistry*
false report 636.3 *false alarm*
false reputation 539.5 *falseness*
false root 5.17 *word*
false rumour 538.5 *half-truth*, 636.3 *false alarm*
false scent 614.5 *waste of effort*
false scorpion 82 Arachnids, 82.2 *arachnid*
false sense 525.2 *misinterpretation*
false shame 876.4 *self-righteousness*
false show 538.8 *pretence*, 539.3 *hypocrisy*, 540.12 *facade*, 557.2 *affectation*
false start 19.13 *penalty*, 21.1 *track events*, 156.11 *starting point*
false step 504.1 *mistake*
false swearing 540.6 *lying*
false thing 540
false tooth 380.11 *tooth*
falsetto 49.32 *instrumental*, 430.3 *shrillness*
false warning 636.3 *false alarm*
false witness 538.11, 539.16 *liar*, 540.6 *lying*, 856.3 *accuser*
falsies 295.25 *accessories*
falsification 540, 504.5 *misrepresentation*, 525.2 *misinterpretation*, 538.1 *untruth*, 538.3 *lying*, 548.1 *misrepresentation*
falsified 540, 504.15 *erroneous*, 525.3 *misinterpreted*
falsifier 538.11, 539.16 *liar*
falsify 540, 309.12 *distort the truth*, 474.11 *practise sophistry*, 504.9 *make a mistake*, 525.1 *misinterpret*, 538.21 *lie*, 538.22 *make unreal*, 538.25 *be dishonest*, 540.16 *be false*, 540.21 *be fraudulent*, 548.4 *misrepresent*, 858.8 *be dishonourable*
falsifying 538.15 *lying*, 540.9 *falsification*
falsify the accounts 750.7 *account*
falsity 52.63 *mathematical logic*, 52.64 *reasoning*, 309.4 *distortion of the truth*, 504.3 *erroneousness*, 538.1 *untruth*, 540.1 *falsehood*, 540.8 *fraud*, 797.1 *affectedness*, 858.2 *faithlessness*
Falstaff 259.12 *fat person*
faltboat 74 Ships and Boats, 36.6 *canoeing*
falter 224.11 *be changeable*, 328.2 *hesitate*, 366.7 *shake*, 366.11 *stagger*, 366.24 *shake*, 366.25 *pitch*, 491.19 *hesitate*
faltering 328.4 *slow*, 366.6 *shaking*, 366.18 *shaky*, 491.2 *irresolute*, 491.11 *irresoluteness*
falteringly 328.16 *slowly*
fame 511.5 *day to remember*, 532.7 *publicity*, 682.1 *success*, 686.1 *prosperity*, 804.1 *right*, 861.8 *good*
fame and fortune 682.1 *success*, 686.1 *prosperity*
famed 532.20 *well-known*
familial 665.9 *societal*
familiar 584, 814, 819, 6.19 *knowledgeable*, 11.6 *talisman*, 124.1 *average*, 164.21 *common*, 167.15 *everyday*, 183.13 *monotonous*, 472.9 *local*, 584.14 *habituated*, 698.13 *informal*, 807.15 *audacious*, 818.5 *discourteous*, 819.6 *close friend*, 826.9 *endearing*, 846.9 *presumptive*, 850.10 *disrespectful*

familiarity 814, 819, 124.4 *average*, 183.3 *repetitiveness*, 501.1 *knowledge*, 584.1 *habit*, 698.4 *informality*, 815.1 *sociability*, 826.2 *courtship*, 846.4 *presumptuousness*
familiarize oneself with 501.13 *get to know*
familiarly 698.22 *informally*, 814.13 *casually*, 819.18 *intimately*, 826.10 *endearingly*
familiar name 560.8 *name*
familiar spirit 11.6 *talisman*, 11.11 *ghost*
familiar with 501.8 *knowledgeable*
family 161, 2.4 *social organization*, 2.8 *human institution*, 36.14 *courting*, 52.40 *curve*, 59.17 *taxonomy*, 142.5 *unit*, 143.1 *part*, 152.6 *category*, 163.3 *kingdom*, 163.8 *genealogy*, 195.2 *descent*, 255.2 *inhabitants*, 400.9 *group*, 665.2 *society*, 815.7 *human society*
family allowance 662.4 *social assistance*
family benefit 662.4 *social assistance*
family car 71.16 *car*, 124.8 *middle classes*
family circle 815.7 *human society*
family concern 740.8 *store*
family court 16.21 *US court*
family court judge 16.24 *US judge*
family credit 662.4 *social assistance*
family doctor 60.11 *doctor*
family farm 68.6 *farm*
family feeling 667.1 *agreement*
family group 2.6 *social group*
family history 200.12 *genealogy*
family likeness 114.1 *similarity*
family man 401.13 *man in the family*
family meal 350.12 *meal*
family member 137.3 *associate*
family name 560.8 *name*
family of languages 5
family-oriented 815.18 *sociably*
family pet 821.11 *loved one*, 826.6 *object of endearment*
family planning 247.3 *birth control*
family plot 399.5 *cemetery*
family practitioner 60.11 *doctor*
family punt 36.8 *punting*
family relationship 107.1 *relatedness*
family resemblance 110.3 *lookalike*, 114.1 *similarity*
family responsibilities 661.6 *burden*
family reunion 815.3 *meeting*
family room 256.7 *room*
family secret 529.1 *secrecy*
family size 259.3 *large scale*
family-size 259.15 *big*
family therapy 61.3 *psychiatric treatment*
family training 61.3 *psychiatric treatment*
family tree 85.12 *figurative usage*, 159.3 *line*, 195.2 *descent*, 200.12 *genealogy*
famine 247.1 *infertility*, 350.10 *scarcity*, 358.5 *shortfall*, 609.9 *scarcity*, 743.7 *beggary*, 782.3 *appetite*
famine relief 767.4 *charity*
famine-stricken 609.3 *underfed*
famish 871.5 *fast*
famished 609.3 *underfed*, 782.10 *hungry*, 871.6 *fasting*
famishing 871.6 *fasting*
famishment 871.2 *short rations*
famous 3.19 *chronicled*, 501.10 *known*, 526.14 *manifest*, 532.20 *well-known*, 617.1, 617.1 *worthy*, 682.13 *successful*, 686.8 *prosperous*, 800.3 *reputable*, 804.5 *entitled*, 861.1 *good*
famous ballet dancers 46
famous dancers 46
famous friendships 819
famously 617.11 *worthily*, 686.9 *prosperously*, 861.22 *well*

famousness 532.7 *publicity*, 682.1 *success*
famous tennis players 40
fan 9.5 *worshipper*, 51.31 *theatregoer*, 138.5, 155.14 *follower*, 261.5 *make bigger*, 261.6 *become bigger*, 284.8 *supporter*, 338.11 *propeller*, 343.5 *fork*, 343.11 *move apart*, 390.7 *ventilator*, 390.22 *blow*, 409.4 *cooler*, 409.12 *make cold*, 584.8 *creature of habit*, 621.15 *purify*, 651.1 *refresh*, 821.9 *lover*, 851.8 *admirer*
fanatic 7.4 *religionist*, 168.8 *dissenter*, 335.19 *deviant person*, 481.7 *bigot*, 490.11 *opinionist*, 493.5 *misjudging person*, 541.6 *exaggerator*, 577.8 *obstinate person*, 642.10 *busy person*
fanatical 7.15 *religious*, 481.10 *discriminatory*, 490.2 *convinced*, 493.8 *unjust*, 572.2 *eager*, 577.4 *set*, 642.18 *active*, 759.13 *passionate*
fanatically 7.23 *religiously*, 481.17 *prejudicially*, 493.14 *unjustly*
fanatical worker 642.10 *busy person*
fanaticism 7.2 *religiousness*, 481.4 *social discrimination*, 490.10 *conviction*, 493.3 *injustice*, 572.7 *eagerness*, 577.7 *opinionatedness*, 759.4 *emotion*
fanciable 519.3 *imaginable*, 782.11 *lustful*
fancied 102.9 *illusory*, 518.8 *supposed*, 519.12 *imaginary*, 821.21 *beloved*
fancied up 295.30 *dressed up*
fancier 78.21 *ornithologist*, 655.5 *expert*, 782.6 *desirer*
fanciful 100.10 *unreal*, 102.9 *illusory*, 102.10 *theoretical*, 461.10 *speculative*, 471.11 *ideational*, 489.2 *questionable*, 506.5 *nonsensical*, 518.8 *supposed*, 519.11 *fantastical*, 519.12 *imaginary*, 579.1 *capricious*
fancifully 519.17 *imaginatively*, 579.6 *capriciously*
fancifulness 519.1 *imagination*
fan club 851.8 *admirer*
fancy 39.11 *swimming*, 102.2 *illusion*, 435.17 *imagine*, 461.6 *idea*, 471.2 *theory*, 471.6 *ideal*, 471.15 *imagine*, 497.8 *be of the opinion*, 518.1 *supposition*, 518.5 *suppose*, 519.1 *imagination*, 519.4 *ideality*, 519.5 *fantasy*, 519.14 *imagine*, 557.4 *ornate*, 570.1 *will*, 579.3 *whim*, 580.2 *prefer*, 580.7 *preference*, 580.15 *chosen*, 753.7 *dear*, 759.2 *impression*, 782.1, 782.12 *desire*, 782.13 *like*, 784.3 *likes*, 784.7 *like*, 792.8 *decorated*, 821.2 *romantic love*, 821.23 *love*
fancy diving 39.6 *diving*
fancy dress 295
fancy-dress dance 46.1 *dancing*
fancy-dress party 665.7 *social gathering*, 815.5 *party*
fancy-free 108.6 *unrelated*, 698.10 *independent*, 783.7 *indifferent*, 825.6 *celibate*
fancy-led 519.10 *imaginative*
fancy price 753.1 *high price*
fancy up 295.33 *dress up*
fancywork 792.2 *pattern*
fan dance 46.2 *dance*
fan dancer 294.4 *exposer*
fandango 46.4 *historic dancing*
fandur 49 Musical Instruments
fane 10.11 *place of worship*
fanfare 773, 423.1 *loudness*, 427.2 *ringing*, 543.6 *word*, 812.8, 812.8 *salute*
fanfaron 541.6 *exaggerator*
fanfaronade 540.12 *facade*, 811.12 *magniloquence*, 812.8 *salute*
fang 380.11 *tooth*

Fang 1 Peoples, **5** Languages and Groups of Languages
fanged 380.4 *toothed*
Fangio 18 Sporting Personalities
fanglike 380.4 *toothed*
fangs 380.11 *tooth*, 726.3 *tools for gripping*
fan heater 408.3 *heater*
fanlight 322.7 *passageway*, 439.10 *window*
fanlike 343, 261.8 *growing*
fanned 43.15 *vaulted*, 261.7 *bigger*, 390.17 *ventilated*
fanned out 261.7 *bigger*
fanning 261.1 *growth*, 261.8 *growing*, 343.2 *parting*, 390.6 *ventilation*
fanning out 162.5 *divergence*, 261.1 *growth*, 335.18 *diffraction*, 343.2 *parting*
fanny 245.8 *organs of reproduction*, 304.2 *rear end*
fanon 7.11 *vestment*
fan out 162.10 *diverge*, 261.5 *make bigger*, 261.6 *become bigger*, 343.11 *move apart*
fan oven 45.5 *cooker*
fan palm 85.1 *tree*
fan scale 369.10 *scales*
fan-shape 261.8 *growing*
fan-shaped 177.8 *three-sided*, 343.8 *fanlike*
fan-shaped backboard 23.3 *basketball equipment*
fantail 78 Birds, 43.9 *miscellaneous architectural features*
fan-tan 42 Card Games
fantasia 519.6 *reverie*
fantasist 519.9 *visionary*
fantasize 519, 102.13, 471.15 *imagine*
fantasizing 462.6 *daydream*
fantast 519.9 *visionary*
fantastic! 617
fantastic 102.9 *illusory*, 471.13 *ideal*, 487.2 *unbelievable*, 519.11 *fantastical*, 579.1 *capricious*, 617.1 *worthy*, 786.8 *wonderful*
fantastical 519, 100.10 *unreal*, 757.2 *unrestrained*
fantasticality 519.1 *imagination*
fantastically 471.22 *imaginatively*, 786.13 *wonderfully*
fantasy 519, 61.19 *defence mechanism*, 100.5 *nonreality*, 102.2 *illusion*, 435.5 *imagination*, 471.6 *ideal*, 519.1 *imagination*, 519.4 *ideality*, 538.4 *lie*, 560.3 *narration*, 775.3 *aspiration*, 786.4, 786.4 *wonder*
fantasy novel 48.2 *fiction*
Fanti 5 Languages and Groups of Languages
fantoccini 547.6 *image*
fan-trained tree 69.10 *fruit tree*
fan vault 43.7 *vault*
fan vaulting 43.7 *vault*
fanworm 81 Worms
far 21.7 *fast*, 263.8 *distant*, 263.10 *distantly*, 269.1 *long*, 302.6 *furthest*, 305.6 *side*
far above 115.4 *dissimilar*
farad 75 SI Units, **75** Scientific and Technical Units
faraday 75 Scientific and Technical Units
Faraday 52 Scientists
Faraday constant 56.97 *fundamental constant*
Faraday effect 56 Named Laws
Faraday's laws 56 Named Laws, **57** Named Reactions
far afield 263.10 *distantly*
far and away 126.17 *supremely*
far and near 263.10 *distantly*
farandole 46.4 *historic dancing*
far and wide 248.16 *extensively*, 263.10 *distantly*
far away 263.8 *distant*, 263.10 *distantly*, 357.15 *out of reach*
far back in the past 200.22 *in the past*
far below 115.4 *dissimilar*

farce 51.2 *play*, 51.10 *comedy*, 506.3 *tomfoolery*, 612.8 *trifle*, 771.4 *entertainment*, 798.2 *slapstick comedy*
farcer 51.22 *actor*
farcical 51.38 *tragic*, 506.5 *nonsensical*, 771.10 *humorous*, 798.5 *ridiculous*
farcically 771.16 *humorously*
far cry 263.2 *great distance*
farcy 624.18 *veterinary disease*
fare 105.6 *be in a state of*, 326.10 *transferred thing*, 350.7 *food*, 350.21 *eat*, 751.3 *fee*
Far East 249.7 *regions of the world*, 263.3 *distant place*
fare well 106.14 *be comfortable*, 686.5 *be prosperous*
farewell 345.9 *parting*, 345.11 *departing*, 345.14 *goodbye*
farewell address 345.9 *parting*, 564.8 *speech*
farewell oration 564.8 *speech*
farewell performance 51.11 *theatrical performance*
farfalle 45 Types of Pasta
farfalline 45 Types of Pasta
far-fetched 108.7 *illogical*, 357.13 *exaggerated*, 489.1 *improbable*, 498.7 *disbelieved*, 541.12 *exaggerated*
far-flung 164.18 *far-reaching*, 248.12 *extensive*, 263.8 *distant*
far from it 115.4 *dissimilar*, 358.10 *not enough*, 536.16, 711.12 *no*
far from the madding crowd 325.10 *motionlessly*
far gone 397.18 *dying*, 628.12 *deteriorated*
farina 384.8 *meal*
farinaceous 69.16 *horticultural*, 87.8 *grasslike*, 384.17 *mealy*
far infrared 56.13 *electromagnetic radiation*
farm 68, 68, 68.19 *agricultural*, 70.5 *transportable*, 243.10 *produce*, 304.8 *nurture*, 594.7 *develop*, 647.1 *workshop*, 725.1 *property*
farmable 68
farm agent 68.16 *farm worker*
farm animal 76.3 *domesticated animal*
farm belt 68.11 *farmland*
farm bike 68.10 *farm tool*
farm bottom land 98.12 *be marooned*
farmboy 68.16 *farm worker*
farm building 68
farm business 68.1 *agriculture*
farm club 22.1 *baseball*
farmed 68.20 *farmable*
farmer 68.15 *agriculturist*, 243.9 *producer*, 255.5 *countryman*, 350.20 *food provider*, 594.15 *preparer*, 646.1 *worker*
farmer's almanac 605.5 *collection*
farmer's lung 89.5 *fungal association*
farmers' market 740.1 *market*
farm-gate sale 68.1 *agriculture*
farmhand 68.16 *farm worker*, 646.1 *worker*, 697.1 *servant*
farmhouse 45.39 *loaf*, 68.7 *farm building*, 68.19 *agricultural*, 256.5 *house*
farm implement 68.10 *farm tool*
farming 68.1 *agriculture*, 68.19 *agricultural*, 243.2 *manufacture*
farmland 68, 453.8 *greenness*
farm machinery 68.10 *farm tool*
farm manager 68.16 *farm worker*, 653.15 *manager*
farm office 68.7 *farm building*
farm pond 94.2 *small lake*
farm road 71.2 *road*
farmstead 68.6 *farm*
farm tool 68
farmtoun 68.6 *farm*
farm track 71.2 *road*
farm tractor 71 Motor Vehicles
farmwork 644.1 *work*
farm worker 68, 646.1 *worker*
farmyard 68.7 *farm building*
farmyard manure 68.13, 246.3 *fertilizer*

farmyard smells 419.2 *something that makes an unpleasant smell*
farnesol 58.20 *terpene*
farness 263.1 *distance*, 302.3 *furthest point*
faro 42 Card Games
far off 263.8 *distant*, 263.10 *distantly*
far out 585.2 *not customary*
far-out 168.14 *eccentric*
far-out group 665.3 *political grouping*
Farquhar 48 Dramatists
farrago 133.3 *miscellany*
far-ranging 164.18 *far-reaching*
far-reaching 164, 248.12 *extensive*, 269.1 *long*
farrier 32.15 *horse person*
farriery 32.14 *horse-riding terms*
farrow 77.35 *give birth*, 206.4 *young animal*, 245.11 *have young*
farrowing crate 68.7 *farm building*
farrowing house 68.7 *farm building*
farse 10.10 *religious manual*
far-seeing 435.21 *seeing*
Farsi 5 Languages and Groups of Languages
far side 305.3 *side direction*
far side of the moon 305.2 *surface*
far sight 435.1 *vision*, 436.2 *poor sight*
far-sighted 435.21 *seeing*, 435.22 *bespectacled*, 436.9 *weak-sighted*, 507.6 *intelligent*, 516.6 *foreseeing*
far-sightedly 516.8 *foresightedly*
far-sightedness 435.4 *visualization*, 436.2 *poor sight*, 507.1 *wisdom*, 516.4 *prudence*
fart 349.16, 349.24 *belch*, 388.5 *belch*, 419.2 *something that makes an unpleasant smell*, 419.5 *stink*, 425.4, 425.7 *belch*
farther 263.8 *distant*, 263.10 *distantly*
farthermost 263.8 *distant*
farthest 263.8 *distant*
farthing 741.10 *former British money*
farthingale 295.18 *underwear*
farting 349.24 *belch*
far ultraviolet 56.13 *electromagnetic radiation*
Far West 263.3 *distant place*
fascia 43 Architectural Decoration, 43.9 *miscellaneous architectural features*, 266.3 *coat*, 457.3 *external appearance*, 544.3 *means of identification*
fascial 43.17 *structured*
fasciate 456.8 *checked*
fasciately 456.12 *variedly*
fascicled 161.49 *grouped*
fascicular 161.49 *grouped*
fascicule 143.2 *particular*
fascinate 228.9 *motivate*, 233.10 *be a prevailing influence*, 340.12 *lure*, 821.28 *win the love of*
fascinated 11.19 *bewitched*, 784.6 *liking*, 786.6 *wondering*, 821.19 *enamoured*
fascinating 11.15 *witchlike*, 228.11 *motivational*, 233.12 *appealing*, 340.9 *attractive*, 586.19 *persuasive*, 784.5 *likable*
fascinatingly 228.14 *influentially*, 784.10 *with great liking*
fascination 228.2 *inducement*, 233 *influence*, 340.4 *allurement*, 586.3 *incentive*, 782.1 *desire*, 784.1 *liking*, 786.1 *wonder*, 821.1 *love*, 821.2 *romantic love*
Fasciola 81 Worms
fascioliasis 81.11 *helminthic disease*
fascism 481.4 *social discrimination*
Fascism 12.1 *government*, 688.7 *type of rule*, 690.2 *suppression*
fascist 481.7 *bigot*, 481.10 *discriminatory*, 635.2 *troublemaker*
Fascist 12.9, 688.14 *governmental*, 690.8 *severe*

Fascists 12.6 *political party*
fashion 796, 796, 105.1 *state*, 114.2 *copy*, 148.13 *make*, 167.5 *convention*, 234.1 *tendency*, 243.10 *produce*, 295.2 *dressing*, 306.5 *formality*, 306.7 *form*, 327.1 *way*, 382.3 *form*, 382.15 *shape*, 457.3 *external appearance*, 549.1 *style*, 560.14 *describe*, 584.4 *custom*, 652.1 *conduct*
Fashion 796
fashionable 796, 105.8 *in a state of*, 105.9 *conditionally*, 196.6 *present*, 201.16 *avant-garde*, 295.30 *dressed up*, 306.11 *formal*, 457.10 *aspectual*, 549.7 *stylish*, 584.12 *established*, 805.21 *ostentatious*, 813.7 *dressed up*
fashionable élite 796
fashionableness 796
fashionable set 201.6 *avant-garde*
fashionably 201.23 *trendily*, 295.36 *dressily*, 306.14 *conventionally*
fashion artist 50.16 *artist*
fashion boots 295.15 *footwear*
fashion business 796
fashion designer 295
fashion designing 295.2 *dressing*
fashioned 306.9 *formed*
fashioning 306.4 *forming*
fashion model 796, 295.27 *model*
fashion photography 66.1 *photography*
fashion plate 796.5 *fashion model*
fashion reporter 533.4 *journalist*
fashion show 526.6 *display*
fashion victim 114.4 *person who copies*
fast 21, 718, 871, 9.7 *worship*, 25.9 *bowls*, 27.13 *bowling*, 57.38 *reactive*, 135.15 *tied*, 135.18 *inextricably*, 191.5 *immediate*, 191.7 *prepared for immediate use*, 208.12 *early*, 329.1 *swift*, 444.10 *coloured*, 609.8 *insufficiency*, 642.18 *active*, 642.22 *actively*, 648.3 *hasty*, 648.6 *hastily*, 699.5 *means of restraint*, 699.10 *restrain oneself*, 722.9 *lose*, 726.10 *retained*, 819.11 *devoted*, 840.6 *apologize*, 869.1 *self-restraint*, 869.5 *be self-restrained*, 871.1 *fasting*, 871.3 *fast day*, 877.13 *unchaste*
fast asleep 643.4 *not awake*
fastback 71 Motor Vehicles
fast ball 22.4 *pitching terms*
fastball 338.5 *throw*
fast bowler 27.4 *team*
fast break offence 23.4 *playing terms*
fast-breeder reactor 56.73 *nuclear reactor*, 235.8, 410.7 *nuclear power*
fast by 264.6 *near*
fast colour 225.4 *stable thing*
fast day 871, 10.15 *holy day*, 812.5 *anniversary*
fast delivery 27.8 *delivery*
fast dye 67.6 *dye*, 444.4 *pigment*
fasten 135.10 *link*, 137.11 *connect*, 283.10 *suspend*, 323.7 *close*
fasten down 225.7 *make stable*
fastened 135.15 *tied*, 137.15 *connected*, 323.12 *closed*
fastener 135.5 *joint*, 137.8 *fastening*
fastening 137, 135.5 *joint*, 137.1 *connection*, 726.3 *tools for gripping*
fasten on 611.8 *make important*, 726.10 *retain*
fasten one's seatbelt 594.4 *prepare for action*
fasten up 135.10 *link*
faster 324.19 *go*, 648.8 *hurry up*, 722.7 *dieter*, 840.3 *atoner*, 869.4 *self-restrained person*, 871.4 *fasting person*
faster race 721.2 *augmentation*

faster than a speeding bullet 329.1 *swift*
faster than sound 329.1 *swift*
fast film 66.10 *graininess*
fast food 350.7 *food*
fast-food chef 45.2 *cook*
fast-food counter 350.15 *eating place*
fast-food restaurant 350.15 *eating place*
fast foxtrot 46.2 *dance*
fast friendship 819.3 *familiarity*
fast green 25.1 *green bowling*
fastidious 467.8 *diligent*, 469.9 *careful*, 481.9 *discriminating*, 542.13 *subtle*, 619.2 *perfectionist*, 621.16 *clean*, 659.14 *troublesome*, 690.8 *severe*, 719.7 *observant*, 794.5 *refined*, 813.6 *formal*, 852.28 *fault-finding*, 857.4 *honourable*
fastidiously 467.15 *attentively*, 481.16 *judiciously*, 690.11 *severely*, 719.8 *observantly*
fastidiousness 469, 467.3 *carefulness*, 481.2 *judiciousness*, 503.1, 537.8 *accuracy*, 542.3 *subtlety*, 580.6 *selection*, 621.1 *cleanness*, 690.1 *severity*, 813.1 *formality*, 852.6 *fault-finding*, 857.1 *probity*
fastigiate 380.1 *sharp*
fastigium 279.3 *architectural summit*
fasting 871, 871, 9.1 *worship*, 609.3 *underfed*, 609.8 *insufficiency*, 699.14 *self-restrained*, 722.1 *loss*, 743.7 *beggary*, 840.2 *apology*, 869.1 *self-restraint*, 869.4 *self-restrained person*
Fasting 871
fasting person 871
fast lane 71.3 *carriageway*
fast-liver 870.5 *self-indulgent person*
fast living 870.2 *dissipation*
fast-living 870.7 *dissipated*
fastly 718, 819.19 *devotedly*
fast motion 329.8 *speed*
fastness 329.8 *speed*, 634.1 *refuge*, 671.12 *fort*
Fastnet Race 36.1 *sailing*
Fast of Av 10.16 *religious festival*
fast operator 715.4 *contractor*
fast patrol boat 679.24 *warship*
fast rate 329.8 *speed*
fast reaction 57.14 *chemical reaction*
fast reactor 56.73 *nuclear reactor*
fast talker 657.3 *cunning person*
fast transport ship 679.24 *warship*
fast wicket 27.5 *wicket*
fat 58, 259, 259, 395, 45.7 *basic ingredient*, 58.6 *lipid*, 68.21 *domesticated*, 246.5 *fertile*, 261.5 *make bigger*, 261.6 *become bigger*, 273.1 *thick*, 273.5 *thickness*, 315.10 *well-rounded*, 350.11 *food content*, 369.1 *heavy*, 386.10, 395.11 *oily*, 608.2 *plentiful*, 608.8 *plenty*, 610.2 *overdoing it*, 686.8 *prosperous*, 742.4 *lush*
fatal 211.14 *accidental*, 244.14 *destructive*, 397.20, 398.23 *deadly*, 618.5 *harmful*
fatal accident 397.5 *ways of dying*, 398.8 *accidental killing*
fatal blow 244.4 *ruin*
fatal car crash 398.8 *accidental killing*
fatal disease 397.5 *ways of dying*
fatal flaw 633.7 *vulnerability*, 864.3 *venial sin*
fatal gift 539
fatal illness 624.2 *illness*
fatalism 4.7 *school of thought*, 571.6 *necessitarianism*, 673.1 *submission*
fatalist 4.11 *follower of a doctrine*, 571.7 *necessitarian*, 641.2 *nonacting person*
fatalistic 4.14 *of a philosophy*, 673.5 *submitting*
fatalities 397.12 *death count*

fatality 397.5 *ways of dying,*
397.11 *dead person,* 571.6 *necessitarianism,* 862.2 *affliction*
fatality list 397.12 *death count*
fatally 397, 244.16 *destructively,*
398.25 *lethally,* 862.13 *destructively*
fatal move 683.2 *defeat*
fatal plane crash 398.8 *accidental killing*
fatal train crash 398.8 *accidental killing*
Fata Morgana 102.2 *illusion,*
435.5 *imagination*
fat-arsed 259.16 *fat*
fat as a pig 259.16 *fat,* 273.1 *thick*
fat cat 686.4 *prosperous person,*
721.7 *gainer,* 742.10 *wealthy person,* 800.2 *person of repute*
fat cattle 68.8 *livestock*
fat chance 489.4 *improbability,*
536.17 *never,* 589.6 *poor chance,* 589.15 *good luck*
fat clay 44.2 *raw material*
fate 157, 199.3 *future condition,*
226.4 *contributing factor,* 233 *influence,* 490.16, 571.5 *inevitability,* 571.17 *preordain,* 582.5 *predetermination,* 589.2 *luck*
fated 157.23 *annihilated,*
199.11 *future,* 397.18 *dying,*
490.5, 571.12 *inevitable,* 582.3 *predetermined,* 714.15 *future*
fatedly 571.19 *necessarily*
fateful 490.5 *inevitable,* 517.15 *presageful,* 611.5 *important*
fatefully 490.25 *inevitably,*
517.16 *predictively*
fatefulness 490.16 *inevitability*
fate of Icarus 360.4 *fall*
fat-free diet 350.6 *nutrition*
fathead 36.7 *windsurfing*
father 7.8 *priest,* 156.26 *produce,*
207.8 *man,* 226.7 *Prime Mover,*
226.9 *be the cause of,* 243.9 *producer,* 245.5 *propagator,* 245.13 *propagate,* 401.13 *man in the family*
Father 8.3 *God,* 226.7 *Prime Mover,* 401.3 *male title of address*
Father Christmas 729.4 *giver,*
755.9 *generous person*
father complex 61.18 *complex*
fathered 396.15 *born*
father figure 61.25 *surrogate,*
222.2 *substitute person*
father fixation 61.17 *fixation*
fatherhood 245.4 *development,*
396.4 *biological function,*
401.13 *man in the family*
father image 61.24 *symbolism,*
61.25 *surrogate*
fatherland 91.6 *native land,*
249.4 *territorial division,* 256.3 *home*
fatherly 207.13 *middle-aged,*
831.6 *benevolent*
fatherly eye 632.2 *protection*
Father of Lies 538.11, 539.16 *liar*
father of the chapel 15.7 *employee*
Father of the House 12.8 *politician*
Father's Day 214.6 *annually celebrated day*
father substitute 222.2 *substitute person*
father symbol 61.24 *symbolism*
Father Time 202.2 *old people,*
628.9 *dilapidation*
fathom 75 *Scientific and Technical Units,* 75 *General Units,*
4.21 *rationalize,* 268.10 *measure,* 277.14 *deepen,* 507.7 *be wise,* 522.6 *understand*
fathomable 268.14 *measurable,*
522.1 *intelligible*
fathomableness 522.9 *intelligibility*
fathomer 277.4 *deep thing*
Fathometer 277.4 *deep thing*
fathomless 277.8 *deep*
fathomlessness 277.1 *depth*
fatidic 517.13 *predicting*

fatigue 777 *Phobias by Topic,*
650, 650, 236.4 *disability,*
238.3 *poor health,* 599.1 *use,*
601.1 *misuse,* 624.3 *symptom,*
644.1 *work,* 644.7 *work for,*
788.1 *boredom,* 788.6 *be boring,*
847.2 *task*
Fatigue 650
fatigued 650, 236.12 *impotent,*
238.11 *weakened,* 624.21 *unhealthy,* 788.5 *bored*
fatigue duty 644.1 *work*
fatigues 295.3, 813.4 *formal dress*
fatiguing 650, 618.3 *bad,*
659.10 *difficult*
fat lamb 68.8 *livestock*
fatling 68.8 *livestock*
fatly 259.20 *largely*
fatness 259, 273.5 *thickness,*
315.2 *round body,* 369.4 *heaviness,* 386.2, 395.1 *oiliness*
fat of the land 350.7 *food,* 608.8 *plenty,* 686.1 *prosperity,* 742.7 *opulence*
fat part 51.21 *role*
fat person 259
fatso 259.12 *fat person*
fatstock 68.8 *livestock*
fatted 261.7 *bigger*
fatten 273, 68.18 *practise livestock farming,* 128.4 *increase,*
261.5 *make bigger,* 261.6 *become bigger,* 350.25 *provide food*
fattened 261.7 *bigger*
fattened-up 304.5 *bred*
fattening 128.1 *increase,* 261.1 *growth,* 350.27 *edible*
fattening house 68.7 *farm building*
fatten on 350.22 *eat well,*
808.15 *sponge*
fatten up 304.8 *nurture,* 350.25 *provide food*
fatter 261.7 *bigger*
fattiness 386.2, 395.1 *oiliness,*
610.2 *overdoing it*
fattishness 259.5 *fatness*
fatty 259.12 *fat person,* 386.10,
395.11 *oily*
fatty acid 58.7 *fat*
fatty-acid ester 58.7 *fat*
fatty degeneration of the heart
624.10 *cardiovascular disease*
fatty oil 395.7 *oil*
fatuity 460.2 *unintelligence,*
462.1 *lack of thought,* 798.1 *ludicrousness*
fatuous 460.6 *unintelligent,*
462.8 *thoughtless,* 506.5 *nonsensical,* 508.5 *foolish,* 521.10 *meaningless,* 798.5 *ridiculous*
fatuously 460.11 *unintelligently*
fatuousness 508.1 *folly,* 798.1 *ludicrousness*
faucet 323.2 *stopper*
Faulkner 48 *Writers*
fault 32.9 *jumping,* 40.4 *tennis terms,* 40.12 *badminton terms,*
54.20 *earth movement,* 98.10 *miscellaneous,* 127.2 *deficiency,*
160.4 *interruption,* 265.2 *crack,*
322.1 *opening,* 358.6 *shortcoming,* 504.1 *mistake,* 618.8 *inferiority,* 620.7 *defect,* 852.17 *criticize,* 864.3 *venial sin,* 866.3 *sin*
fault-block mountain 54.21 *mountain building*
fault-finder 785.3 *disliked person,*
818.4 *discourteous person,*
852.12 *critic*
fault-finding 852, 852, 659.14 *troublesome,* 854.1 *disparagement*
faultily 504.22 *wrongly*
faultiness 127.2 *deficiency,*
618.8 *inferiority,* 620.5 *imperfection*
faulting 54.20 *earth movement*
faultless 142.7 *uncut,* 144.7 *complete,* 537.21 *accurate,* 619.1 *perfect,* 865.5 *innocent,* 876.9 *pure*
faultlessly 619.7 *perfectly,*
865.11 *innocently*

faultlessness 134.1 *purity,* 537.8 *accuracy,* 619.3 *perfection,*
865.1 *innocence,* 876.3 *moral purity*
fault line 54.20 *earth movement*
faulty 127.17 *defective,* 238.13 *insufficient,* 358.8 *defective,*
474.7 *sophistic,* 476.6 *refutable,*
504.15 *erroneous,* 618.2 *inferior,* 620.1 *imperfect,* 656.4 *bungled*
faulty logic 474.1 *sophistry*
faulty reasoning 504
faulty syntax 5.29 *grammar,*
504.11 *grammatical error*
faulty vision 436.2 *poor sight*
faun 8.5 *deity*
fauna 76.1 *animals*
Faunus 8 *Deities*
Fauré 49 *Musicians and Composers*
fauteuil 51.16 *auditorium*
Fauvism 50 *Western Art Styles and Movements*
Fauvist 50.29 *realist*
fauxbourdon 433.3 *melodiousness*
faux pas 504.10, 559.6 *blunder,*
656.9 *bungling,* 683.4 *unsuccessful thing* 866.3 *sin*
Faverolle 68 *Breeds of Fowl*
favonian 55.47 *windy*
favour 114.10 *be similar,* 126.3 *advantage,* 233.4 *indirect influence,* 284.6 *moral support,*
284.14 *give moral support,*
336.8 *further,* 481.12 *discriminate,* 570.12 *choose,* 580.2 *prefer,* 580.7 *preference,* 617.10 *do good,* 662.2 *support,* 662.22 *improve,* 662.28 *further,* 686.2 *good fortune,* 686.7 *be auspicious,* 691.1 *leniency,* 691.3 *be lenient,* 708.4 *be permissive,*
712.1 *request,* 729.2 *gift,*
782.12 *desire,* 784.2 *inclination,*
784.8 *prefer,* 800.1 *estimation,*
804.3 *honours,* 831.4 *benevolent act,* 835.3 *mercy,* 844.22 *discriminate,* 849.1, 849.15 *respect,* 851.2 *admiration,* 851.13 *support,* 861.17 *good thing,*
878.1 *reward*
favourable 819, 106.9 *comfortable,* 210.6 *timely,* 284.9 *supportive,* 517.15 *presageful,*
617.4 *worthwhile,* 662.34 *beneficial,* 682.13 *successful,* 686.8 *prosperous,* 714.14 *auspicious,*
775.14 *cheering,* 819.8 *friendly,*
851.18 *approving,* 861.1 *good*
favourable attitude 784.1 *liking*
favourable auspices 714.3 *potential*
favourable chance 229.2 *chance,*
589.5 *good chance*
favourable crisis 851.7 *advocate*
favourableness 210.1 *timeliness,*
861.8 *good*
favourable opportunity 210.2 *opportunity*
favourable outcome 52.62 *probability,* 682.1 *success*
favourable prospect 488.4 *chance*
favourable review 524.3 *criticism,* 851.4 *compliment*
favourable towards 784.6 *liking*
favourable verdict 16.7 *legal trial,* 16.42 *acquittal*
favourable wind 55.15 *wind direction*
favourably 819, 106.18 *comfortably,* 126.16 *superiorly,* 210.9 *opportunely,* 662.36 *helpfully,*
682.16 *successfully,* 686.9 *prosperously,* 714.17 *auspiciously,*
784.11 *admiringly,* 819.17 *in friendship*
favourably disposed 662.35 *benevolent*
favoured 784.5 *likable,* 851.23 *approved*
favoured by 800.3 *reputable*
favoured suitor 821.11 *loved one*
favouring 114.7 *similar,* 580.14 *selecting,* 662.30 *helping,* 784.6 *liking,* 844.11 *wrong*

favourite 9.4 *idolized person,*
32.7 *horseracing,* 126.12 *superior,* 291.8 *focal,* 340.6 *charmer,*
400.7 *person,* 580.15 *chosen,*
611.4 *bigwig,* 617.8 *exceller,*
674.10 *contender,* 800.2 *person of repute,* 805.12 *object of pride,*
819.10 *familiar,* 821.11 *loved one,* 821.21 *beloved*
favourite of the gods 686.4 *prosperous person*
favouritism 481, 493.3 *injustice,*
580.7 *preference,* 819.1 *friendship,* 844.1 *unfairness*
favours 821.6, 826.2 *courtship*
favour with 729.5 *give*
favus 89.5 *fungal association*
fawn 808, 77.19 *young mammal,* 206.4 *young animal,* 449.1 *brown,* 853.11 *be sycophantic*
fawner 499.3 *assenter,* 853.7 *sycophant*
fawning 808.2 *sycophancy,*
808.7 *sycophantic,* 849.9 *showing respect,* 853.5 *sycophancy,*
853.16 *sycophantic*
fawningly grovellingly 808.17 *sycophantically*
fawn on 817.13 *defer to,* 853.11 *be sycophantic*
fawn over 467.14 *be solicitous*
fax 65.12 *electronic office,* 65.15 *network,* 110.4, 110.9 *duplicate,*
114.12 *imitate,* 118.5 *duplicate,*
326.13 *post,* 528.2 *communication,* 528.12 *communicate,*
534.8 *data transmission,*
534.31 *correspond,* 547.1 *representation*
Faxaflói 32 *Breeds of Horse and Pony*
faxed 110.15 *duplicate*
fax machine 534.8 *data transmission*
fax number 534.8 *data transmission*
fay 11.11 *ghost*
fayalite 54 *Minerals*
Faye 53 *Comets*
Fayetteville 93 *Cities*
faze 491.20 *make uncertain,*
786.10 *be wonderful*
fazed 786.6 *wondering*
f-block 57.6 *chemical element*
Fea 8 *Deities,* 676.3 *god of war*
fealty 694.2 *loyalty,* 847.3 *allegiance,* 849.2 *admiration*
fear 777 *Phobias by Topic,*
777, 513.1 *expectation,* 513.8 *expect,* 631.4 *strain,* 633.5 *danger,* 777.11 *be afraid,* 785.1,
785.5 *dislike,* 786.1, 786.9 *wonder,* 822.7 *hated thing*
Fear 777
fear and trembling 777.1 *fear*
feared 513.7 *expected,* 785.9 *disliked*
fear for 777.14 *worry*
fearful 777, 777.10 *frightening,*
779.3 *cowardly,* 785.8, 785.8 *disliking,* 786.8 *wonderful*
fearfully 777, 779.5 *cravenly,*
786.13 *wonderfully*
fearfulness 777, 779.1 *cowardice*
fear God 7.19 *be religious,* 9.7 *worship,* 857.6 *be honourable*
fearing 777.7 *frightened,* 785.8 *disliking*
fearless 778.9 *courageous*
fearlessly 778.18 *courageously*
fearlessness 778.1 *courage*
fearnought 295.12 *coat*
fear of animals 76
fear of God 7.2 *religiousness*
fearsome 777.10 *frightening,*
785.9 *disliked*
fear-stricken 777.7 *frightened*
feasibility 486.2 *possibleness,*
660.3 *wieldiness*
feasible 660, 101.9 *realizable,*
486.5 *possible,* 716.6 *negotiated*
feasibly 716, 486.11 *potentially*
feast 350, 10.15 *holy day,*
10.16 *religious festival,* 350.24 *have a meal,* 350.25 *provide food,* 405.4 *pleasurable things,*
608.8 *plenty,* 773.1 *rejoicing,*

773.5 *rejoice*, 812.1 *celebration*, 815.5 *party*, 872.3 *act of gluttony*
feast and famine 111.2 *opposites*
feast day 10.15 *holy day*, 773.1 *rejoicing*, 812.5 *anniversary*
feaster 350.18 *eater*
feasting 350.2 *appetite*, 350.4 *eating meals*
Feast of Circumcision 10.16 *religious festival*
Feast of Tabernacles 10.16 *religious festival*
Feast of the Annunciation 10.16 *religious festival*
Feast of the Dedication 10.16 *religious festival*
Feast of Weeks 10.16 *religious festival*
feast one's eyes on 435.13 *look*
feat 592.3 *expedient plan*, 597.2 *undertaking*, 640.2 *deed*, 644.2 *task*, 655.3 *masterpiece*, 682.1 *success*, 778.8 *courageous act*, 786.3 *wonder-working*
feather 36.16 *row*, 78.17 *plumage*, 163.4 *type*, 370.7 *light thing*, 374.11 *soft thing*, 576.15 *indecisive person*, 612.8 *trifle*
feather ball 29.5 *golf ball*
featherbed 15.11 *conduct industrial relations*, 374.13 *soften*, 405.10 *comfort*
feather bed 47.6 *bed*, 374.11 *soft thing*, 405.4 *pleasurable things*
featherbedded 15.9 *negotiated*
featherbedding 15.1 *industrial relations*, 15.9 *negotiated*
featherbrain 579.4 *capricious person*
featherbrained 151.16 *confused*, 576.2 *changeable*, 579.1 *capricious*, 612.4 *trivial*
feather duster 81 *Worms*, 621.10 *cleaning object*
feathered friend 78.1 *birds*
feather grass 87 *Grasses*
featherheaded 612.4 *trivial*
featheriness 374.9 *smoothness*
feathering 36.4, 36.11 *rowing*, 73.7 *miscellaneous aviation terms*
feather in one's cap 681.1 *trophy*, 682.1 *success*
feather one's nest 405.8 *feel pleasure*, 686.5 *be prosperous*, 742.13 *get rich*, 860.6 *be selfish*
feather palm 85.1 *tree*
feathers 777 *Phobias by Topic*, 40.11 *badminton equipment*, 78.16 *avian anatomy*, 78.17 *plumage*, 292.2 *filling*, 293.14 *animal covering*, 792.5 *decorative articles*
feather star 81.3 *echinoderm*
featherweight 26.3 *boxing weight divisions*, 26.4 *boxer*, 26.14 *combat*, 260.4 *little person*, 369.1 *heavy*, 369.7 *weighing*, 370.1 *light*, 679.3 *athlete*
feathery 370.2 *insubstantial*, 374.3 *smooth*
feathery cloud 55.20 *cloud appearance*
feat of arms 674.6 *fight*
feat of creation 696.11 *masterpiece*
feat of endurance 778.8 *courageous act*
feat of skill 655.3 *masterpiece*
feature 51.36 *dramatize*, 146.2 *thing included*, 148.1 *component*, 165.3 *characteristic*, 165.9 *special*, 180.4 *concomitant*, 305.4 *aspect*, 437.6 *visible thing*, 457.3 *external appearance*, 526.1 *display*, 532.16 *publicize*, 554.6 *emphasize*
feature article 533.9 *news story*
feature copy 533.10 *copy*
featured 533.13 *displayed*
feature film 243.5 *work of art*
featureless 112.6 *conforming*, 159.11 *continuous*, 214.11 *regular*, 254.13 *vacant*, 307.5 *shapeless*, 576.4 *unsteady*

featurelessness 307.1 *shapelessness*
feature news 533.9 *news story*
features 257.1 *contents*, 306.6 *nature*, 457.3 *external appearance*
features editor 532.11 *newspaper man*
feature story 528.4 *mass communication*, 533.9 *news story*
feature writer 528.9 *informant*
featuring 51.39 *stagestruck*, 257.10 *containing*
febrifugal 62.14 *counteracting*, 630.17 *remedial*
febrifuge 62.4 *drug type*, 630.4 *antidote*
febrile 624.23 *diseased*
febrile disease 624.4 *disease*
febrile seizure 624.4 *disease*
febriphobia 777 *Phobias by Name*
February 270.4 *short thing*, 409.7 *cold weather*
feckless 579.1 *capricious*, 614.1 *useless*, 656.1 *unskilful*
fecklessness 579.2 *caprice*, 614.3 *uselessness*
feculence 353.5 *faeces*, 622.4 *dirt*
feculent 353.25 *faecal*
fecund 243.11 *productive*, 246.5 *fertile*, 519.10 *imaginative*, 742.4 *lush*
fecundate 245.13 *propagate*, 246.7 *make fertile*
fecundated 245.16 *reproductive*
fecundation 245.3 *propagation*, 246.2 *productiveness*
fecundity 246.1 *fertility*, 608.8 *plenty*
fedayeen 679.9 *guerrilla*
federal 12.9 *governmental*, 91.16 *national*, 665.9 *societal*, 688.14 *governmental*
Federal Bureau of Investigation 16.16 *US police*
Federal Communications Commission 534.24 *television broadcasting*
federal council 653.7 *council*
Federal Court 16.21 *US court*
federal debt 745.2 *national debt*
federal depository 741.20 *money store*
federal election 580.12 *election*
federalism 12.1 *government*, 664.5 *joint control*, 665.3 *political grouping*, 688.7 *type of rule*
federalization 162.6 *decentralization*
federalize 665.15 *politicize*
federalized 162.26 *decentralized*
federal judge 16.24 *US judge*
federally 91.19 *nationally*, 116.32 *in alliance*, 665.18 *cliquishly*
federal marshal 16.12 *US law officer*
federal post 688.5 *position of authority*
federal prison 702.1 *prison*
Federal Reserve System 741.19 *treasury*
federate 140.6 *come together*, 664.16 *join*, 665.12 *be in league with*, 665.15 *politicize*
federated 140.8 *cooperative*
federation 12.5 *political organization*, 91.2 *union of nations*, 116.2 *alliance*, 140.2 *cooperation*, 664.5 *joint control*, 664.9 *team*, 665.1 *party*, 665.3 *political grouping*, 688.8 *governmental organization*, 703.1 *commission*, 724.1 *joint possession*
Federation 43 *Architectural Styles*
Fédération Internationale de Bobsleigh et Tobogganing 41.9 *bobsledding*
Fédération Internationale de Football Association 38.1 *soccer*
Fédération Internationale de Gymnastique 30.4 *gymnastic organization*
Fédération Internationale de Hockey 31.1 *hockey*

Fédération Internationale de l'Automobile 33.7 *racing governing body*
Fédération Internationale d'Escrime 28.1 *fencing*
Fédération Internationale de Ski 41.1 *skiing*
Fédération Internationale Motocycliste 33.7 *racing governing body*
Fédération Internationale Sociétés d'Aviron 36.4 *rowing*
fedora 295.15 *headgear*
fed-up 788.5 *bored*
fed up with 650.2 *bored*
fee **751**, 721.4 *earnings*, 723.3 *medieval ownership*, 725.3 *historic property terms*, 729.2 *gift*, 746.3 *pay*, 748.5 *expense*, 878.4 *reward for service*
feeble 127.17 *defective*, 236.12 *impotent*, 238.8 *weak*, 238.10 *ill*, 412.5 *tasteless*, 424.4 *faint*, 441.6 *murky*, 555.1 *unemphatic*, 864.13 *venial*
feeble-minded 238.10 *ill*, 460.5 *lacking intellect*, 460.7 *intellectually subnormal*, 508.5 *foolish*
feeble-mindedly 460.11 *unintelligently*
feeble-mindedness 460.1 *lack of intellect*, 508.1 *folly*, 510.2 *subnormality*
feebleness 238.1 *weakness*, 412.1 *tastelessness*, 555.2 *lack of emphasis*
feebly 127.21 *badly*, 236.14 *powerlessly*, 238.14 *weakly*, 555.3 *unemphatically*
feed 51.21 *role*, 51.27 *entertainer*, 63.9 *machine tool*, 68.9 *animal feedstuff*, 68.18 *practise livestock farming*, 87.12 *manage grassland*, 246.7 *make fertile*, 350.8 *animal food*, 350.21 *eat*, 350.25 *provide food*, 396.20 *support life*, 606.1, 606.5 *provision*, 637.5 *preserve*, 651.1 *refresh*
feedback 64.15 *circuit function*, 221.5 *reply*
feedback inhibition 58.11 *enzyme*
feedbin 68.10 *farm tool*
feeder 51.21 *role*, 64.33 *power distribution*, 68.10 *farm tool*, 96.1 *river*, 350.18 *eater*, 606.3 *provider*
feeder line 327.10 *railway*
feeder road 71.3 *carriageway*
feeding 9.5 *gardening*, 350.1, 350.26 *eating*, 350.27 *edible*, 606.1 *provision*
feeding frenzy 872.3 *act of gluttony*
feeding organ 350.16 *eating utensil*
feedlot 68.7 *farm building*
feed on 808.15 *sponge*
feed oneself full 350.22 *eat well*
feed one's face 350.22 *eat well*
feed one's tapeworm 350.22 *eat well*
feedstore 68.10 *farm tool*
feedstuff 350.8 *animal food*
fee faw fum 11.5 *spell*
feel **759**, 4.22 *propound a philosophy*, 165.3 *characteristic*, 383.1 *texture*, 403.11 *sense*, 407.1, 407.11 *touch*, 407.13 *be touched by*, 464.9 *be intuitive*, 471.15 *imagine*, 481.2 *judiciousness*, 828.8 *resent*
feel an aversion for 785.5 *dislike*
feel an obligation 837.6 *be grateful*
feel at home 698.17 *be informal*, 814.11 *not stand on ceremony*
feel at liberty 698.17 *be informal*
feel bad 624.24 *be unhealthy*
feel cheap 806.24 *be humiliated*
feel cheated 609.6 *be unsatisfied*
feel concern for 465.7 *be curious*
feel confident 775.6 *hope*
feel contrite 867.4 *be penitent*
feel deeply **759**, 760.11 *be sensitive*
feel discontented 828.8 *resent*
feel disgust 785.5 *dislike*

feel dissatisfied 609.6 *be unsatisfied*
feel dizzy 650.5 *be fatigued*
feeler 143.4 *component*, 407.7 *sense organ*, 479.1 *experiment*, 710.2 *tentative offer*, 726.3 *tools for gripping*
feeler gauge 268.6 *measuring instrument*
feel fear 785.5 *dislike*
feel fine 623.5 *be healthy*
feel fondness for 784.7 *like*
feel for **759**, 760.11 *be sensitive*, 821.23 *love*, 835.8 *pity*
feel free 698.17 *be informal*
feel giddy 650.5 *be fatigued*
feel good 405.8 *feel pleasure*, 623.5 *be healthy*
feel great 623.5 *be healthy*
feel guilty 866.9 *appear guilty*, 867.4 *be penitent*
feel helpless 236.6 *be powerless*
feel hot **408**
feel hungry 609.6 *be unsatisfied*
feel hurt 828.10 *be offended*
feel ill 624.24 *be unhealthy*
feeling **759**, **759**, 4.1 *philosophy*, 297.3 *atmosphere*, 403.1 *sensation*, 403.5 *sensible*, 407.1 *touch*, 464.1 *intuition*, 464.3 *insight*, 471.1 *idea*, 471.2 *theory*, 497.1 *belief*, 517.1 *prediction*, 554.1 *emphasis*, 652.1 *conduct*, 759.12, 760.1 *sensitive*, 821.3 *lovingness*, 835.1 *pity*
Feeling **759**
feeling fine 623.1 *healthy*
feeling for 655.2 *aptitude*
feeling for language 549.4 *literary style*
feeling good 405.1 *physical pleasure*, 623.1 *healthy*
feeling great 623.1 *healthy*
feeling guilty 866.6 *appearing guilty*
feeling hot 408.9 *hot*
feeling like a million dollars 623.1 *healthy*
feelingly 403.14 *sensationally*, 759.20 *with feeling*, 760.12 *sensitively*
feeling of frustration 515.1 *disappointment*
feeling of identity 667.1 *agreement*
feeling pain **406**
feeling person **759**, 464.5 *intuitive person*
feelings **759**, 403.2 *ability to sense*
feeling the pinch 593.5 *necessitous*
feeling well 623.1 *healthy*
feel in one's bones **759**
feel instinctively 759.16 *feel in one's bones*
feel insulted 828.8 *resent*
feel it coming 516.1 *foresee*
feel it in one's bones 464.9 *be intuitive*, 516.1 *foresee*
feel kinship for 667.6 *agree with*
feel like a giant refreshed 651.2 *be refreshed*
feel like a kid again 651.2 *be refreshed*
feel like a million dollars 623.5 *be healthy*
feel like a new man 627.2 *get better*, 651.2 *be refreshed*
feel like hell 624.24 *be unhealthy*
feel like oneself again 623.6 *get healthy*
feel no concern for 466.6 *be incurious*
feel no friction 376.12 *go smoothly*
feel no obligation 838.6 *be ungrateful*
feel no remorse 868.5 *be impenitent*
feel nothing 868.5 *be impenitent*
feel offended 828.8 *resent*
feel one's blood turn to water 777.11 *be afraid*
feel oneself again 651.2 *be refreshed*

feel one's hair stand on end
777.11 *be afraid*
feel one's way 436.14 *be blind*,
516.2 *show prudence*, 781.5 *be
cautious*
feel pain **406**, 687.9 *be in trouble*
feel pique 828.10 *be offended*
feel piqued 828.8 *resent*
feel pity 835.8 *pity*
feel pleasure **405**
feel pride **805**, 809.16 *show off*
feel refreshed 651.2 *be refreshed*
feel remorse 867.4 *be penitent*
feel resentment 828.8 *resent*
feel rotten 624.24 *be unhealthy*
feel shame 810.16 *be self-
conscious*, 867.4 *be penitent*
feel sick 624.24 *be unhealthy*
feel sick at 785.5 *dislike*
feel small 806.24 *be humiliated*
feel something is missing 609.6
be unsatisfied
feel sore 828.8 *resent*
feel sorrow for 835.8 *pity*
feel sorry 867.4 *be penitent*
feel sorry for 835.8 *pity*
feel sure 490.20 *be certain*
feel the draught 687.10 *need
money*
feel the ground give way 633.8
be in danger
feel the ground slip away 633.8
be in danger
feel the lack 609.6 *be unsatisfied*
feel the need for 593.7 *require*
feel the pinch 659.20 *be in difficulty*, 687.10 *need money*,
743.12 *be poor*
feel the pulse 479.11 *experiment*
feel the spirit 7.19 *be religious*
feel the urge 228.8 *be motivated*,
586.18 *be persuaded*
feel twice the man one was
651.2 *be refreshed*
feel unfulfilled 609.6 *be unsatisfied*
feel up 407.11 *touch*
feel well 623.5 *be healthy*
fees 749.3 *income*, 845.5 *dues*
fee simple 723.2, 725.2 *legal
terms*
fee tail 725.2 *legal terms*
feet of clay 238.1 *weakness*,
539.5 *falseness*, 620.7 *defect*,
633.7 *vulnerability*
Fehling's solution **57** Named Reactions
Fehling's test 58.5 *sugar test*
feign 474.12 *deceive*, 538.24,
540.20 *pretend*, 640.4 *act*
feigning 474.10 *hypocritical*,
538.8 *pretence*, 538.18 *pretentious*, 540.7 *pretence*, 540.30
pretending
feigningly 538.27 *pretentiously*
feijoa **86** *Fruits*
feint 26.2 *boxing*, 26.11 *do a
combat sport*, 28.3 *fencing movements*, 28.5 *fence*, 539.8,
539.28 *trick*, 540.7 *pretence*,
540.20 *pretend*, 657.2 *stratagem*
feinting 26.2 *boxing*, 26.14 *combat*, 28.6 *fencing*, 539.34 *deceiving*
feisty 237.9 *physically strong*,
239.4 *vigorous*
feldspar 44.2 *raw material*,
54.34 *mineral*
f-electron 56.65 *atom*
felicitate 812.15 *celebrate*
felicitation 851.4 *compliment*
felicitous 210.6 *timely*, 558.3 *elegant*, 655.9 *well-made*, 686.8
prosperous, 762.4 *happy*
felicitously 558.5 *elegantly*,
686.9 *prosperously*
felicity 405.1 *physical pleasure*,
558.1 *elegance*, 686.1 *prosperity*, 762.1 *happiness*
felid 77.8 *flesh-eating mammal*
Felidae 77.8 *flesh-eating mammal*
feline 77.8 *flesh-eating mammal*,
77.10 *cat*, 77.28 *carnivorous*,
657.4 *cunning*
fell 85.18 *manage trees*, 95.1
mountain, 244.9 *demolish*,
275.2 *heights*, 282.7 *make hori-

zontal*, 293.14 *animal covering*,
338.28 *shoot*, 362.2 *flatten*,
398.23 *deadly*
Fell **32** Breeds of Horse and
Pony
fella 821.9 *lover*
fell boots 295.19 *footwear*
felling 85.6 *tree management*
felling licence 85.6 *tree management*
felling saw 85.7 *timber production*
fellow 6.4 *educator*, 114.5 *counterpart*, 122.5 *equal*, 148.5 *member*, 180.11 *companion*, 401.2
male, 401.3 *male title of address*, 664.10 *cooperator*, 665.5
member, 696.9 *educational
leader*, 730.5 *recipient*, 819.5
friend
fellow citizen 255.8 *national*
fellow countryman 255.8 *national*
fellow creature 400.7 *person*,
819.5 *friend*
fellow feeling 664.2 *fellowship*,
667.1 *agreement*, 724.2 *participation*, 759.5 *good feeling*,
819.2 *friendly relations*, 821.1
love, 831.1 *benevolence*, 835.1
pity
fellows 664.9 *team*
fellowship 664, 6.6 *instructorship*, 116.2 *alliance*, 161.15 *association*, 180.3 *companionship*,
662.6 *financial assistance*,
665.1 *party*, 667.1 *agreement*,
721.5 *profit*, 724.2 *participation*, 729.2 *gift*, 730.2 *something received*, 749.3 *income*,
815.8 *good company*, 819.1
friendship, 878.3 *grant*
fellowship winner 730.5 *recipient*
fellow student 6.7 *learner*
fellow tenant 724.3 *participant*
fellow traveller 180.11 *companion*, 284.8 *supporter*, 499.3 *assenter*, 539.20 *plotter*
fellow worker 646.5 *partner*
fell pony 32.5 *pony*
fell running **18** Sporting Activities
fell walker 34.7 *mountaineer*
fell walking 34.1 *mountaineering*
felo-de-se 398.7 *suicide*, 879.11
penance
felon 16.40 *lawbreaker*, 832.8
malefactor, 844.10 *wrongdoer*,
858.4 *dishonourable person*,
864.9 *wicked person*, 866.4
guilty person
felonious 16.60 *offending*,
844.16 *in the wrong*, 858.7,
864.15 *criminal*
feloniously 864.21 *criminally*
felony 16.39 *crime*, 693.2 *violation of the law*, 844.8 *wrong-
doing*, 858.3, 864.7 *criminality*,
866.3 *sin*
felsic rock 54.30 *igneous rock*
felt **67** *Natural Fabrics*, 67.14
weave, 604.1 *materials*
felted 67.10 *woven*
felt hat 295.15 *headgear*
felucca **74** Sailing Ships and
Boats
female **402**, **402**, 84.12 *of flowers*
Female **402**
female animal **402**
female bird **77**
female circumcision 10.7 *non-
Christian ritual*
female condom 247.3 *birth control*
female genital mutilation 10.7
non-Christian ritual
female impersonator 51.27 *entertainer*, 118.7 *imitator*, 224.8 *person who changes costume*, 547.5
performer
female mammal **77**
female person 402.2 *female*
female sex **402**
female sex organs 245.8 *organs
of reproduction*
female title of address **402**

female transvestite 402.10 *homosexual*
female warrior 679.10 *woman
soldier*
feme covert 823.11 *married
woman*
femidom 247.3 *birth control*
feminality 402.1 *female sex*
feminine 5.44 *grammatical*,
402.15 *female*
feminine gender 402.1 *female sex*
feminine intuition 464.1 *intuition*
feminineness 402.1 *female sex*
feminine rhyme 48.11 *rhyme*
femininity 402.1 *female sex*
feminism 402.1 *female sex*,
627.11 *reformism*, 700.2 *equal
opportunity*, 805.11 *prejudice*
feminist 402.11 *liberated
woman*, 402.15 *female*, 627.12
reformer, 805.23 *prejudiced*
feministic 402.15 *female*
feminist theatre 51.8 *theatre
movements*
feminist theology 7.13 *theology*
feminist therapy 61.3 *psychiatric
treatment*
femme fatale 586.13 *tempter*,
789.3 *attractive female*
femto **75** SI Units
femur **382** Bones
fen 98.3, 391.8 *marsh*
fence **28**, **671**, 32.9 *jumping*,
32.11 *eventing*, 68.11 *farmland*,
69.3 *ornamental garden*, 136.6
boundary, 147.3 *exclusion zone*,
301.3 *enclosing thing*, 301.5 *enclose*, 302.4 *boundary marker*,
330.2 *collide*, 531.13 *equivocate*, 540.23 *evade*, 578.1 *be
equivocal*, 591.7 *be evasive*,
634.2 *shelter*, 661.3 *barrier*,
661.9 *block*, 671.9 *barrier*,
671.24 *parry*, 674.12, 679.37
fight, 726.4 *wall*, 730.5 *recipient*, 730.9 *receive*, 736.11 *dishonest person*, 737.1 *trade*,
737.10 *trader*, 739.12 *wholesaler*, 858.10 *be criminal*
fenced-in 301.7 *enclosed*, 661.14
blocked, 726.10 *retained*
fence in 301.5 *enclose*, 632.9 *protect*, 726.7 *detain*
fence off 147.7 *exclude*
fencer **28**, 32.2 *thoroughbred*,
674.10 *contender*, 679.3 *athlete*
fence round 632.9 *protect*
fences 32.7 *horseracing*, 674.4
race
fence-sitter 783.6 *indifferent person*
fencible 679.8 *soldier*
Fencing **28**
fencing area 28.1 *fencing*
fencing assault 28.1 *fencing*
fencing association 28.1 *fencing*
fencing bout 28.1 *fencing*
fencing clothes 28.2 *fencing
equipment*
fencing equipment **28**
fencing movements **28**
fencing sword 680.8 *sharp
weapon*
fencing weapon 28.2 *fencing
equipment*
fender **71** Motor Vehicle Parts,
671.2 *safeguard*
fend for oneself 698.16 *be independent*
fend off **341**, 671.24 *parry*
fenestella 43.9 *miscellaneous architectural features*
fenestra 43.9 *miscellaneous architectural features*
fenestrated 43.17 *structured*
fenestrated cupola 43.9 *miscellaneous architectural features*
fenfluridine **62** Medication
fenland 98.3 *marsh*
fennec **77** Placental Mammals
fennel **45** Herbs and Spices, **45**
Vegetables, 413.5 *herbs*
fenny 98.11 *continental*, 391.11
marshy

fenoprofen **62** Medication
Fens 249.9 *regions of Britain*
fenugreek **45** Herbs and Spices,
413.5 *herbs*
feodal 725.8 *propertied*
feral 76.15 *of animals*
fer-de-lance **79** Reptiles
Fermanagh **92** Counties
Fermat **52** Scientists
fermata 160.5 *caesura*, 218.3
pause
Fermat's last theorem **52** Named
Concepts
Fermat's principle **56** Named
Laws
ferment 57.26 *react*, 89.11
moulder, 151.5 *confusion*, 153.5
commotion, 216.5 *changer*,
216.8 *cause change*, 220.1 *conversion*, 220.7 *convert into*,
220.9 *transform*, 241.1 *violence*,
366.3 *turbulence*, 366.21 *be agitated*, 370.8 *leavening*, 370.10
lighten, 390.11 *aeration*, 390.24
bubble, 415.8 *sour*, 828.4 *anger*
fermentation **57** Types of
Chemical Reaction, 216.1
change, 220.1 *conversion*,
361.10 *elevator*, 366.3 *turbulence*, 370.8 *leavening*, 388.7
gaseousness, 390.11 *aeration*
fermentation vat 220.4 *medium
of conversion*
fermentative 370.4 *leavening*
fermented 89.9 *fungal*, 351.17
drinkable, 415.6 *unpalatable*
fermented drink 351.7 *alcoholic
drink*
fermenting 220.14 *converting*,
243.1 *production*, 370.4 *leavening*
ferment into 220.7 *convert into*
fermi **75** Scientific and Technical Units
Fermi **52** Scientists
Fermi level **56** Named Laws
fermion 56.77 *elementary particle*
fermium **57** Chemical Elements
fern **88**
fern ally 88.1 *fern*
fernlike **88**
fernlike plant 88.1 *fern*
fern plant **88**
Ferns and Mosses **88**
fern seed 88.2 *fern plant*
ferny 88.5 *fernlike*
féroce 45.51 *West Indian dish*
ferocious 241.6 *violent*, 832.11
cruel
ferociously 241.10 *violently*
ferociousness 832.2 *cruelness*
ferocity 241.1 *violence*, 832.2 *cruelness*
Feronia **8** Deities
Ferrarese school **50** Western Art
Styles and Movements
ferret **77** Placental Mammals
ferreting **18** Sporting Activities,
77.23 *mammal hunting*, 590.2
chase
ferreting out 496.7 *detection*
ferret out 496.2 *detect*
ferrets **161** Collective Names
by Animal
ferriage 326.2 *transportation*
ferric 57.34 *elemental*
Ferrier **49** Musicians and Composers
ferriferous plumbous 57.34 *elemental*
ferrimagnetism 56.59 *ferromagnetism*
Ferris wheel 364.6 *rotator*
ferrite 56.60 *magnet*
ferrochromium **57** Alloys
ferroconcrete 43.4 *building material*, 373.7 *hard substance*,
604.2 *building material*
ferromagnetic core 56.60 *magnet*
ferromagnetic material 56.59 *ferromagnetism*
ferromagnetism **56**
ferromanganese **57** Alloys
ferromolybdenum **57** Alloys
ferronickel **57** Alloys
ferrosilicon **57** Alloys
ferrosoferric 57.34 *elemental*

ferrous 57.34 *elemental*
ferrovitreous 43.17 *structured*
ferrovitreous construction 43.4 *building material*
ferruginous 449.1 *brown*
ferrule 20.3 *fishing tackle*
ferry 74.3 *vessel*, 96.2 *channel*, 326.12 *transport*
ferry bridge 63.21 *bridge*
ferry crossing 74.2 *waterway*
ferrying 74.11 *nautical*
ferryman 74.8 *boatman*, 326.7 *transferor*
ferry terminal 218.4 *stopping place*
fertile 246, 68.20 *farmable*, 86.6 *fruiting*, 243.11 *productive*, 519.10 *imaginative*, 553.3 *diffuse*, 608.2 *plentiful*, 721.19 *yielding*, 742.4 *lush*
fertile imagination 246.2 *productiveness*, 519.1 *imagination*
fertilely 721.20 *gainfully*
fertile nuclide 56.72 *nuclear fission*
fertile soil 226.2 *source*
fertility 246, 396.4 *biological function*, 553.1 *diffuseness*, 608.8 *plenty*
Fertility 246
fertility cult 246
fertility dance 46.4 *historic dancing*
fertility drug 246.3 *fertilizer*
fertility god 8.5 *deity*
fertility rite 10.7 *non-Christian ritual*, 246.4 *fertility cult*
fertility symbol 61.24 *symbolism*, 246.4 *fertility cult*
fertilization 245.3 *propagation*, 246.2 *productiveness*
fertilize 68.17 *farm*, 69.15 *cultivate*, 87.12 *manage grassland*, 239.3 *invigorate*, 245.13 *propagate*, 246.7 *make fertile*
fertilized 245.16 *reproductive*
fertilizer 68, 69, 246, 245.5 *propagator*
fertilizers 57.22 *industrial chemistry*
fertilizer spreader 68.10 *farm tool*
fertilizing 68.5 *cultivation*
ferule 879.14 *instrument of punishment*
fervent 7.15 *religious*, 237.10 *potent*, 241.6 *violent*, 554.3 *emphatic*, 642.18 *active*, 648.3 *hasty*, 759.13 *passionate*, 821.19 *enamoured*
fervently 237.15 *acutely*, 554.7 *emphatically*, 759.20 *with feeling*, 821.30 *lovingly*
fervent patriotism 676.5 *bellicosity*
fervid 237.10 *potent*
fervour 7.2 *religiousness*, 554.1 *emphasis*, 572.7 *eagerness*, 642.4 *energy*, 759.4 *emotion*, 821.2 *romantic love*
fescue 87 Grasses, 68.12 *crop*
fesse point 544.8 *heraldic device*
festa 812.1 *celebration*
festal 10.21 *ritualistic*
festal cheer 350.9 *plenty*
festally 10.23 *ritually*
fester 353, 622.10 *be dirty*, 628.2 *decay*
festering 353.7 *pus*, 353.27 *purulent*, 622.8 *unclean*, 624.6 *infection*, 624.15 *ulcer*, 624.23 *diseased*, 626.7 *toxic*
festival 10.16 *religious festival*, 161.9 *social gathering*, 773.1 *rejoicing*
Festival of Lights 10.16 *religious festival*
festive 815, 10.21 *ritualistic*, 665.1 *social*, 812.10 *celebrative*
festive board 350.9 *plenty*
festive gathering 580.13 *feast*
festively 815.18 *sociably*
festive occasion 665.7 *social gathering*, 812.1 *celebration*
festivities 773.1 *rejoicing*, 812.1 *celebration*

festivity 10.16 *religious festival*, 161.9 *social gathering*, 773.1 *rejoicing*, 812.1 *celebration*, 815.1 *sociability*, 815.5 *party*
festoon 43 Architectural Decoration, 557.5 *ornament*, 792.10 *decorate*
festoon blind 440.6 *shade*
FET 64.19 *transistor*
fetal 59.26 *developmental*, 156.32 *embryonic*
fetch 11.11 *ghost*, 36.15 *sail*, 102.2 *illusion*, 326.14 *bring back*, 344.2 *reach*, 539.8, 539.28 *trick*, 751.13 *cost*
fetch a blow 670.5 *strike*
fetch a good price 739.2 *be sold*
fetch and carry 326.14 *bring back*, 808.10 *knuckle under*, 808.11 *pander to*
fetch breath 396.18 *be born*
fetch down 362.2 *flatten*
fetching 340.9 *attractive*
fetch up in 344.2 *reach*
fetch water in a sieve 487.10 *attempt the impossible*
fête 773, 350.25 *provide food*, 665.16 *host*, 811.14 *show*, 812.1 *celebration*, 812.15 *celebrate*, 812.18 *salute*, 813.3 *formal occasion*, 817.12 *greet*
fêted 815.16 *popular*
fetid 419.3 *stinking*, 618.4 *poor*, 622.8 *unclean*
fetidness 419.1 *stench*
fetish 8.5 *deity*, 9.3 *idol*, 10.14 *sacred object*, 11.6 *talisman*
fetishism 9.2 *idolatry*, 10.7 *non-Christian ritual*, 11.3 *witchcraft*, 510.4 *delusion*
fetishist 9.6 *idolater*
fetishistic 9.10 *idolatrous*, 10.21 *ritualistic*, 11.15 *witchlike*
fetishization 8.9 *deification*
fetishize 9.8 *idolatrize*
fetish-like 9.10 *idolatrous*
fetor 419.1 *stench*, 618.10 *poverty*, 622.2 *uncleanness*
fetoscope 60.7 *diagnosis*
fetoscopy 60.7 *diagnosis*
fetter 135.10 *link*, 137.4 *means of connection*, 137.12 *bind*, 632.4 *safety device*, 661.4 *restraint*, 661.10 *restrain*, 699.12 *gag*
fettered 137.16 *bound*
fetters 699.5 *means of restraint*, 879.14 *instrument of punishment*
fettle 44.11 *make ceramics*, 105.1 *state*, 105.4 *state of mind*, 105.5 *physical state*, 306.6 *nature*, 623.3 *health*
fettling 44.5 *ceramic process*
fettuccine 45 Types of Pasta
fetus 59.15 *developmental biology*, 226.3 *rudiment*, 245.7 *obstetrics*
feu 725.3 *historic property terms*
Feuchtwanger 48 Writers, **48** Dramatists
feud 473.1 *argument*, 473.13 *argue*, 500.1 *dissent*, 666.2 *argument*, 666.6 *argue*, 723.3 *medieval ownership*, 725.3 *historic property terms*, 764.8, 764.11 *quarrel*, 820.4 *act of hostility*, 820.12 *oppose*
feudal 12.9 *governmental*, 202.14 *historic*, 701.9 *subject*, 725.8 *propertied*
feudal court 16.19 *lawcourt*
feudalism 12.1 *government*, 701.1 *subjection*
feudality 12.1 *government*, 723.3 *medieval ownership*, 725.3 *historic property terms*
feudal lord 632.3 *protector*
feudal tax 751.9 *historical taxes*
feudatory 725.8 *propertied*
feuding 473.9 *hostile*
Feuerbach 4 Philosophers
feuilleton 532.4 *newspaper*
fever 777 Phobias by Topic, 366.2 *tumult*, 366.5 *restlessness*, 408.1 *heat*, 543.1 *sign*, 624.3 *symptom*, 624.6 *infec-*

tion, 624.7 *tropical disease*, 642.7 *restlessness*
fevered 366.16 *restless*, 408.12 *warm-hearted*, 450.2 *red-faced*, 624.23 *diseased*
feverish 366.16 *restless*, 408.12 *warm-hearted*, 450.2 *red-faced*, 624.22 *sick*, 624.23 *diseased*, 642.18 *active*, 648.3 *hasty*
feverish haste 648.4 *haste*
feverishly 366.27 *agitatedly*, 408.17 *warmly*, 648.6 *hastily*
feverishness 366.5 *restlessness*, 408.1 *heat*, 624.3 *symptom*
fever tree 85 Trees and Shrubs
few 182, **182**, 120.2 *certain amount*, 120.6 *quantitative*, 175.6 *plural*, 213.2 *infrequent*, 274.6 *scant*, 490.8 *unspecified*, 609.4 *scarce*
Few 182
few and far between 162.19 *dispersed*, 182.6 *sparse*, 213.1 *infrequently*, 213.2 *infrequent*, 609.4 *scarce*
fewer 182
few in number 274.6 *scant*
fewness 182, 120.2 *certain amount*, 127.3 *inferior numbers*, 213.3 *infrequency*, 274.12 *thinning*
few words 552.1 *conciseness*
fey 11.18 *spiritual*, 397.18 *dying*, 759.11 *intuitive*
Feydeau 48 Dramatists
Feydeau farce 51.10 *comedy*
feyness 11.8 *psychic power*
Feynman 52 Scientists
ff 49 Musical Terms
fiacre 71 Carriages and Carts
fiancé 401.4 *boyfriend*, 714.6 *someone promised*, 821.9 *lover*
fiancée 402.4 *girlfriend*, 714.6 *someone promised*, 821.9 *lover*
Fianna Fáil 12.6 *political party*
fiasco 515.2 *bad outcome*, 683.1 *failure*, 862.2 *affliction*
fiat 166.1 *rule*, 692.1 *command*
fiat money 741.14 *paper money*
fib 489.6 *implausibility*, 489.7 *be improbable*, 538.4, 538.21 *lie*, 548.1 *misrepresentation*
fibber 538.11, 539.16 *liar*
fibbery 538.3, 540.6 *lying*
fibbing 538.3, 538.15 *lying*, 540.6 *lying*, 540.29 *deceitful*
Fibonacci 52 Scientists
Fibonacci numbers 52 Named Concepts
fibre 67, **383**, 137.6 *line*, 350.11 *food content*, 604.1 *materials*
fibreboard 604.4 *board*
fibre cable 534.6 *telecommunication*
fibreglass 293.12 *protective covering*, 442.9 *glass*, 604.1 *materials*
fibre-optic cable 534.6 *telecommunication*
fibre optics 56.34 *photometry*, 65.14 *data transfer*
fibre-optics transmission 56.34 *photometry*
fibre paper 604.3 *paper*
fibre pole 21.2 *field events*
fibres 57.22 *industrial chemistry*
fibrescope 60.7 *diagnosis*
fibrin 58.9 *protein*
fibrosis 624.4 *disease*
fibrositis 624.16 *rheumatism*
fibrous 81.22 *spongelike*, 378.3 *hard*, 383.8 *rough*
fibrously 383.15 *texturally*
fibrous protein 58.9 *protein*
fibrous root 83.7 *root*
fibrous-rooted 83.19 *of roots*
fibster 538.11, 539.16 *liar*
fibula 382 Bones
Fichte 4 Philosophers
fichu 295.14 *neckwear*
Ficino 4 Philosophers
fickle 216.11 *changeable*, 224.14 *irresolute*, 491.8 *capricious*, 538.20 *unfaithful*, 576.2 *changeable*, 578.11 *equivocating*, 579.1 *capricious*

fickleness 216.2 *change of mind*, 224.2 *irresolution*, 491.16 *capriciousness*, 576.12 *inconstancy*, 579.2 *caprice*
fickle person 224
fictile 306.9 *formed*
fiction 48, **560**, 102.4 *theorization*, 243.4 *mental product*, 309.4 *distortion of the truth*, 519.4 *ideality*, 538.1 *untruth*, 540.9 *falsification*, 560.3 *narration*
fictional 48, 102.10 *theoretical*, 519.10 *imaginative*, 519.12 *imaginary*, 540.32 *falsified*, 560.12 *narrative*
fictional biography 48.2, 560.5 *fiction*
fictional horse 32.1 *horse*
fictionalization 538.1 *untruth*
fictionalize 519.15 *fantasize*, 538.21 *lie*, 560.15 *recount*
fictionalized 48.17 *fictional*, 538.13 *untrue*, 540.32 *falsified*
fiction editor 532.12 *publisher*
fictionist 560.10 *descriptive writer*
fiction writer 48.14 *author*, 560.10 *descriptive writer*
fictitious 102.10 *theoretical*, 309.8 *exaggerated*, 474.7 *sophistic*, 519.12 *imaginary*, 846.8 *unentitled*
fictive 519.12 *imaginary*
fiddle 49 Musical Instruments, 13.12 *cheat*, 49.38 *sound*, 407.11 *touch*, 521.7 *mean nothing*, 539.10 *fraud*, 539.30 *be fraudulent*, 540.9 *falsification*, 540.22 *falsify*, 592.3 *expedient plan*, 642.17 *meddle*, 736.7 *dishonesty*, 736.12 *steal*, 747.1 *nonpayment*, 750.7 *account*, 858.3 *criminality*, 858.10 *be criminal*
fiddle-faddle 521.14 *nonsense*
fiddle one's income tax 747.7 *not pay*
fiddler 736.11 *dishonest person*
fiddler crab 81.4 *arthropod*
fiddlesticks 521.14 *nonsense*
fiddle with 216.8 *cause change*, 407.11 *touch*
fiddling 612.4 *trivial*, 642.7 *restlessness*, 642.21 *meddling*, 644.11 *laborious*, 736.1 *stealing*, 736.18 *fraudulent*
fideism 490.10 *conviction*
fidel 49 Musical Instruments
fidelini 45 Types of Pasta
fidelity 138.2 *tenacity*, 490.17 *infallibility*, 503.2 *correctness*, 537.8 *accuracy*, 537.13 *faithfulness*, 575.3 *constancy*, 694.2 *loyalty*, 719.1 *observance*, 857.1 *probity*
fidget 224.12 *be irresolute*, 366.24 *shake*, 642.10 *busy person*, 648.2 *make haste*, 648.4 *haste*
fidgetiness 366.5, 642.7 *restlessness*
fidgeting 224.2 *irresolution*
fidgety 224.14 *irresolute*, 366.16 *restless*, 576.2 *changeable*, 642.18 *active*
fidla 49 Musical Instruments
Fido 77.9 *dog*
fiducial point 52.36 *point*, 53.21 *orbit*
fiduciary 741.22 *monetary*
fiduciary currency 741.14 *paper money*
fiduciary heir 730.6 *beneficiary*
fief 723.3 *medieval ownership*, 725.3 *historic property terms*
fiefdom 725.3 *historic property terms*
field 27, 6.3 *subject*, 18.2 *sportsground*, 19.4 *stadium*, 21.6 *track*, 31.8 *hockey*, 37.8 *shooting*, 52.1 *mathematics*, 52.21 *set*, 52.23 *algebra*, 56.10 *force*, 65.17 *computing term*, 68.11 *farmland*, 87.2 *grassland*, 98.6 *lowland*, 165.8 *specialization*, 248.7 *range*, 249.14 *sphere*, 301.2 *enclosed place*,

file for divorce 824.7 *divorce*
file past 159.17 *line up*
file server 65.15 *network*
filet steak 45.22 *beef*
filial love 821.1 *love*
filiated 116.11 *allied*
filibeg 295.6 *skirt*
filibuster 209.3 *delayed action*, 209.8 *delay*, 474.13 *quibble*, 565.9 *out-talk*, 573.12 *opposition*, 661.2 *obstacle*, 661.7 *hinderer*, 661.9 *block*
filibusterer 209.5 *delayer*, 663.9 *opposer*
Filicinae 88.1 *fern*
filicopsid 88.1 *fern*
Filicopsida 88.1 *fern*
filiform 272.2 *fine*
filigree 288.2 *braid*, 288.8 *interweave*, 792.2 *pattern*
filing 152.5 *categorization*, 171.7 *listing*, 260.3 *little piece*, 262.1 *contraction*, 385.3 *grinding*, 545.8 *registration*
filing cabinet 258.3 *cabinet*
filing clerk 545.9 *recorder*
filings 132.2 *residue*, 143.8 *bits and pieces*, 384.6 *crumb*
filing system 171.2 *table*
filini 45 Types of Pasta
fill 144, 292, 60.21 *practise dentistry*, 63.28 *substructure*, 128.4 *increase*, 253.11 *be present*, 257.7 *stuff*, 605.6 *store*, 606.6 *replenish*, 608.4 *suffice*, 610.4 *be excessive*, 629.1 *repair*, 630.20 *doctor*, 765.8 *satisfy*
fill a gap 144.4 *complete*
fill a need 144.4 *complete*, 662.26 *be useful*
fill a post 12.11 *govern*
fill a space 130.6 *add*, 144.6 *fill*
filled 608, 144.8 *full*
filled to overflowing 610.6 *excessive*
filled up 144.8 *full*
filled with holes 322.14 *holed*
filler 43.9 *miscellaneous architectural features*, 257.4 *stuffing*, 292.2 *filling*, 553.1 *diffuseness*
filler cap 71 Motor Vehicle Parts
fillet 43 Architectural Decoration, 45.55 *cook*, 137.10 *band*, 295.15 *headgear*, 349.11 *void*
fill in 128.5 *make bigger*, 144.4 *complete*, 222.4 *be a substitute*, 293.34 *cover for*, 528.11 *inform*, 550.2 *clarify*, 629.1 *repair*
fill-in 155.13 *replacement*, 222.2 *substitute person*, 293.21 *substitution*
filling 292, 128.6 *increasing*, 144.2 *fullness*, 232.3 *iteration*, 257.4 *stuffing*, 354.11 *thing inserted*, 630.12 *surgery*, 765.5 *satisfying*
filling depression 55.11 *weather system*
fillings 60.4 *dentistry*
filling station 410.6 *oil*, 605.4 *storage*
filling the bill 608.1 *sufficient*
filling up 144.2 *fullness*
filling-up 606.1 *provision*
fill-in light 66.15 *lighting*
fill in the cracks 629.1 *repair*
fill in the gaps 609.5 *be insufficient*
fillip 228.3 *stimulus*, 330.13 *blow*, 586.8 *incentive*
fillness 427.3 *deepness*
fill oneself 872.5 *be greedy*
fill one's lungs 651.2 *be refreshed*
fill one's stomach 350.22 *eat well*
fill out 128.4 *increase*, 128.5 *make bigger*, 144.4 *complete*, 144.5 *be complete*, 261.6 *become bigger*, 273.8 *fatten*, 315.11 *make round*
fill space 259.19 *be big*
fill the air 423.8 *be loud*
fill the bill 116.27 *fit*, 608.4 *suffice*, 613.9 *be useful*, 615.6 *be convenient*, 682.8 *be effective*, 684.4 *complete*
fill the gap 130.6 *add*
fill the port 41.16 *bobsled*

fill to capacity 144.6 *fill*
fill up 128.5 *make bigger*, 144.6 *fill*, 257.7 *stuff*, 410.11 *fuel*, 605.6 *store*, 606.6 *replenish*
fill-up 144.2 *fullness*
fill up again 629.3 *restore*
fill with conceit 809.18 *make conceited*
fill with desire 782.15 *cause desire*
fill with distaste 587.4 *put off*
fill with holes 322.20 *hole*
fill with longing 782.15 *cause desire*
filly 32.1 *horse*, 77.18 *female mammal*, 77.19 *young mammal*, 206.4 *young animal*, 402.14 *female animal*
film 66, 243.5 *work of art*, 266.3 *coat*, 274.11 *fineness*, 278.4 *shallow thing*, 293.3 *coating*, 435.7 *view*, 438.6 *that which makes invisible*, 441.2 *murk*, 441.10 *make dim*, 442.8 *transparent thing*, 443.7 *opaque thing*, 526.9 *production*, 545.7 *recording*, 545.13 *record*, 547.2 *reproduction*, 547.9 *represent*
film actor 51.22 *actor*
film actress 51.22 *actor*
film advance 66.18 *exposure time*
film camera 66.16 *camera*
film classification 709.2 *censorship*
film director 243.9 *producer*
filmed 545.16 *recorded*
filmgoer 51.31 *theatregoer*
film horse 32.1 *horse*
filminess 383.2 *grain*, 441.2 *murk*, 442.6 *translucency*, 443.6 *opaqueness*
filmography 171.2 *table*
film over 441.9 *be dim*
film plane 66.18 *exposure time*
film producer 243.9 *producer*
film review 524.3 *criticism*
film rewind 66.18 *exposure time*
film school 6.12 *educational institution*
film speed 66.10 *graininess*
film star 51.22 *actor*, 617.8 *exceller*
filmy 266.9 *platelike*, 383.10 *delicate*, 438.2 *difficult to see*, 441.6 *murky*, 442.2 *translucent*, 443.2 *shady*
Filofax 171.5 *list of appointments*
filo pastry 45.37 *pastry*
filoplume 78.12 *plumage*
filter 66, 44.11 *make ceramics*, 56.55 *circuit*, 57.25 *solidify*, 64.22 *transformer*, 64.34 *power supply*, 65.8 *software*, 71.3 *carriageway*, 134.3 *purifier*, 134.10 *purify*, 322.6 *porous thing*, 335.1 *deviate*, 347.12 *leak*, 424.2 *sound reducer*, 621.10 *cleaning depot*, 621.15 *purify*
filter cloth 44.6 *ceramic workshop*
filtered 57.32 *solid*, 621.17 *cleaned*
filtered water 351.6 *soft drink*
filter-feeder 76.4 *type of animal*
filter funnel 57 Laboratory Apparatus
filter in 346.11 *infiltrate*
filtering 64.15 *circuit function*, 347.3 *leakage*
filter paper 57 Laboratory Apparatus
filter press 44.6 *ceramic workshop*
filter pressing 44.5 *ceramic process*
filter pump 57 Laboratory Apparatus, 57.20 *surface chemistry*
filter through 253.11 *be present*
filter-tip 413.7, 413.11 *tobacco*
filth 618.10 *poverty*, 622.4 *dirt*, 626.1 *lack of hygiene*, 822.7 *hated thing*, 827.1 *curse*, 877.2 *indecency*
filthily 626.8 *unhygienically*
filthiness 618.10 *poverty*, 622.1 *dirtiness*, 877.2 *indecency*

filthy 151.15 *untidy*, 618.4 *poor*, 622.7 *dirty*, 622.9 *obscene*, 626.5 *unhygienic*, 795.9 *ribald*, 827.8 *cursing*, 877.12 *indecent*
filthy language 827.2 *offensive language*
filthy lucre 721.5 *profit*, 741.2 *cash*, 742.6 *money*
filthy rich 721.17 *well-off*, 742.1 *wealthy*
filthy talk 877.2 *indecency*
filtrable virus 59.3 *organism*
filtrate 347.12 *leak*
filtration 57.5 *process*, 347.3 *leakage*, 621.2 *cleaning*
fin 36.7 *windsurfing*, 39.1 *swimming*, 80.5 *fish anatomy*, 122.4 *equilizer*, 143.4 *component*, 179.1 *five*, 225.3 *stabilizer*
finagle 858.8 *be dishonourable*
final 21.1 *track events*, 157.20 *ending*, 345.11 *departing*, 674.2 *contest*, 684.8 *concluded*
final arguments 16.7 *legal trial*
final attempt 596.5 *attempt*
final battle 674.6 *fight*
final cause 588.5 *final intention*
final chapter 684.2 *conclusion*
final curtain 51.6 *scene*, 157.10 *ending*, 684.2 *conclusion*
final decision 588.4 *formulated intention*
final defeat 683.2 *defeat*
final demand 61.3 *warning*, 692.2, 712.2 *demand*
finale 51.6 *scene*, 157.1 *end*, 157.10 *ending*, 684.2 *conclusion*
final exam 684.2 *conclusion*
final intention 588
final invoice 636.1 *warning*
finalist 674.10 *contender*
finality 157, 217.1 *permanence*, 397.7 *dying day*, 684.2 *conclusion*
finalization 144.3 *completion*
finalize 142.10, 144.4 *complete*, 157.15 *end*, 217.6 *make permanent*
finalize accounts 750.9 *settle accounts*
finalized 144.7 *complete*, 157.21 *ended*, 684.8 *concluded*
finally 157, 218, 323, 155.30 *behind*
final notice 636.1 *warning*, 712.2 *demand*
final objective 588.6 *objective*
final offer 710.3 *business offer*
final rest 649.1 *ease*
final resting place 218.5, 325.3 *resting place*, 399.5 *cemetery*
final result 227.1 *effect*
final say 233 *influence*
final shot 684.2 *conclusion*
Final Solution 398.4 *slaughter*, 879.13 *capital punishment*
final stage 157.9 *close*
final story 684.2 *conclusion*
final stroke 398.5 *execution*
final touch 144.1 *completeness*, 627.5 *improvement*, 684.3 *elaboration*
final warning 636.1 *warning*, 692.2 *demand*
final word 588.4 *formulated intention*
final words 397.7 *dying day*
finance 14, 662, 741, 13.11 *deal*, 14.5 *invest*, 284.13 *support financially*, 602.6 *find means*, 729.5 *give*, 738.5, 746.8 *defray*, 748.3 *donate*, 748.7 *donation*, 755.11 *give*
Finance 14
finance a purchase 733.7 *borrow*
finance company 732.4 *lending institution*, 744.4 *bank*
finance house 744.4 *bank*
financer 729.4 *giver*
finances 602.4 *financial resources*, 741.6 *funds*
financial 14, 13.13 *economic*, 93.14 *urban*, 737.14 *commercial*, 741.22 *monetary*, 750.10 *accounting*
financial accounting 14.1 *finance*, 750.1 *accounts*

financial adviser 14.3 *stockbroker*
financial affairs 14.1 *finance*
financial aid 284.7 *financial support*
financial assistance 662, 729.2 *gift*
financial backing 662.6 *financial assistance*
financial circles 741.7 *finance*
financial collapse 743.6 *insolvency*
financial company 741.19 *treasury*
financial consultant 654.4 *adviser*
financial control 14.1 *finance*, 688.1 *authority*, 741.7 *finance*
financial crisis 747.5 *insolvency*
financial dealing 223.1 *exchange*
financial disaster 687.2 *economic adversity*
financial district 93.7 *city district*
financial embarrassment 659.7 *awkward situation*, 743.6 *insolvency*
financial escape 638.1 *escape*
financial failure 320.4 *closure*
financial forecaster 517.9 *forecaster*
financial house 741.19 *treasury*
financial institution 732.4 *lending institution*
financial loss 722
financially 741, 750, 13.14 *economically*, 749.8 *profitably*
financially embarrassed 743.2 *insolvent*
financially rewarding 682.14, 878.15 *rewarding*
financially ruined 743.2 *insolvent*
financially sound 742.2 *solvent*
financially stable 742.2 *solvent*
financially worthwhile 721.15 *gainful*
financial plan 592.1 *plan*
financial power 742.5 *wealth*
financial provision 741.6 *funds*
financial records 750.1 *accounts*
financial resources 602
financial reverse 687.2 *economic adversity*
financial reward 878.1 *reward*
financial ruin 687.2 *economic adversity*, 743.6, 747.5 *insolvency*
financial sector 13.2 *economy*
financial security 13.6 *economic factors*
financial setback 687.2 *economic adversity*
financial soundness 742.8 *solvency*
financial stability 742.8 *solvency*
financial statement 528.3 *document*
financial support 284, 749.3 *income*
Financial Times Ordinary Share Index 14.2 *stock exchange*
Financial Times-Stock Exchange 100 Index 14.2 *stock exchange*
financial unsoundness 743.6 *insolvency*
financial upturn 629.10 *revival*
financial world 741.7 *finance*
financial year 14.1 *finance*
financier 741, 14.3 *stockbroker*, 732.3 *lender*, 739.12 *wholesaler*, 741.18 *treasurer*
financing 733.1 *borrowing*
finch 79 Birds, 78.6 *songbird*
finches 161 Collective Names by Animal
finchlike 78.23 *avian*
find 250, 496, 16.71 *try a case*, 53.20 *meteor*, 130.4 *extra*, 166.13 *rule*, 243.10 *produce*, 344.2 *reach*, 492.11 *judge*, 496.1 *discover*, 602.6 *find means*, 606.5 *provision*, 721.5 *profit*, 738.6 *purchase*, 861.17 *good thing*
find a bargain 752.5 *buy at a discount*
findable 496.15 *discoverable*
find a clue 496.2 *detect*
find against 16.79 *convict*, 492.11 *judge*
find agreement 678.1 *mediate*

find a husband for 823.17 *matchmake*
find a joker in the pack 661.9 *block*
find a loophole 682.7 *overcome obstacles*
find a mate for 823.17 *matchmake*
find-and-destroy mission 670.12 *military attack*
find a nigger in the woodpile 661.9 *block*
find an opening 322
find an out 855.8 *justify*
find a remedy 231.3 *counteract*
find a resolution 524.9 *decipher, 684.5 conclude*
find a solution 524.9 *decipher, 684.5 conclude*
find a use for 613.11 *find useful*
find a way 232.5 *find means, 327.14 find one's way, 592.11 invent, 602.6 find means*
find a way out 682.7 *overcome obstacles*
find a way round 231.3 *counteract, 682.7 overcome obstacles*
find a wife for 823.17 *matchmake*
find bargains 754.14 *buy cheaply*
find common ground 298.5 *cooperate*
find credence 497.10 *be believed*
find difficult 659
find engaged 211.5 *take untimely action*
finder 53.25 *mounting, 496.12 discoverer*
find fault 852, 659.23 *cause difficulties,* 659.24 *create difficulties,* 854.11 *criticize*
find fault with 766.7 *be dissatisfied*
find favour 851.17 *meet with approval*
find for 16.78 *acquit,* 492.11 *judge*
find freedom 638.5 *escape*
find guilty 16.79 *convict*
find hard to understand 523.9 *find unintelligible*
find indispensable 593.9 *find necessary*
finding 16.7 *legal trial,* 250.3 *locating,* 492.2 *verdict,* 496.6 *discovery,* 496.13 *discovering,* 721.5 *profit*
finding again 629.9 *restoration*
finding a penny 517.6 *good-luck sign*
finding of innocence 865.2 *legal innocence*
finding out 496
finding the spot 250.3 *locating*
find innocent 865.9 *declare innocent*
find in the cross hairs 670.2 *fire*
find intolerable 828.8 *resent*
find liable 16.79 *convict*
find loathsome 822.14 *hate*
find means 232, 602, 226.10 *awaken*
find necessary 593
find no common ground 136.12 *disagree*
find no fault 851.11 *approve*
find not guilty 16.78 *acquit,* 865.9 *declare innocent*
find not to one's taste 785.5 *dislike*
find one's bearings 74.9 *navigate*
find one's El Dorado 742.13 *get rich*
find oneself in a catch-22 situation 661.9 *block*
find oneself up shit creek 106.13 *get into difficulties*
find one's feet again 629.4 *be restored*
find one's level 150.24 *line up*
find one's match 672.4 *serve one right*
find one's way 327
find one's way into 346.9 *enter*
find out 496, 6.23 *learn,* 490.21 *make certain,* 501.13 *get to know*
find out about 496.3 *find out*

find peace and quiet 649.2 *take it easy*
find problems 659.23 *cause difficulties,* 659.24 *create difficulties*
find relief 638.5 *escape*
find room for 146.4 *include*
find safety 632.8 *be safe*
find shelter 634.4 *shelter*
find space for 146.4 *include*
find the case not proven 16.78 *acquit*
find the key to 524.9 *decipher*
find-the-lady 42 Card Games
find the meaning 524.9 *decipher*
find the means 226.10 *awaken*
find the philosopher's stone 742.13 *get rich*
find the pot of gold 721.14 *profit*
find the pot of gold at the end of the rainbow 742.13 *get rich*
find there is a lack of evidence 16.78 *acquit*
find there is no case to answer 16.78 *acquit*
find the sense of 524.9 *decipher*
find the spot 250.11 *find*
find the very thing 667.9 *be suitable*
find time for 645.4 *have leisure*
find time hangs heavy on one's hands 645.4 *have leisure*
find too difficult 523.9 *find unintelligible*
find to one's cost 515.4 *be disappointed*
find unintelligible 523
find useful 613, 662, 599.3 *exploit*
find words for 5.47 *word,* 564.11 *speak*
find words to express 549.9 *style,* 564.11 *speak*
fine 55, 272, 274, 16.43 *conviction,* 44.10 *ceramic,* 67.10 *woven,* 260.7 *little,* 372.1 *sparse,* 383.9 *smooth,* 392.5 *rainless,* 442.2 *translucent,* 537.21 *accurate,* 558.3 *elegant,* 617.1 *worthy,* 623.1 *healthy,* 695.3 *coercive methods,* 699.1 *restraint,* 751.8 *levy,* 789.5 *beautiful,* 805.21 *ostentatious,* 811.22 *majestic,* 843.12 *all right,* 861.1 *good,* 879.1 *punish,* 879.7 *punishment*
fine adjustment 503.3 *accurate thing,* 537.8 *accuracy*
fine and dandy 861.1 *good*
fine art 547.2 *reproduction*
fine arts 50.1 *art*
fine blade 680.8 *sharp weapon*
fine chemicals 57.22 *industrial chemistry*
fine china 44.1 *ceramics*
fined 879.20 *punished*
fine detail 503.3 *accurate thing*
fine distinction 503.3 *accurate thing*
fine-drawn 272.2 *fine,* 383.10 *delicate*
fine feathers 811.14 *show*
fine fettle 105.4 *state of mind,* 105.5 *physical state,* 150.5 *orderliness*
fine fryer 402.9 *woman considered as a sex object*
Fine Gael 12.6 *political party*
fine grain 66.10 *graininess*
fine-grained 383.9 *smooth*
fine-grained texture 54.28 *rock*
fine kettle of fish 659.5 *predicament*
fine line 503.3 *accurate thing*
finely 260.8 *in a small way,* 372.7 *sparsely,* 383.15 *texturally*
finely adjusted 537.21 *accurate*
fine mess 659.5 *predicament*
fineness 272, 274, 260.1 *littleness,* 372.3 *sparseness,* 383.2 *grain,* 442.6 *translucency,* 537.8 *accuracy*
fineness of grain 383.2 *grain*
fine opportunity 210.2 *opportunity*
fine print 165.4 *specifications*
fine qualities 863.2 *virtues*
finer 126.12 *superior*

fine rain 55.25 *rain*
fine reaching 36.1 *sailing*
finer feelings 759.3 *feelings,* 760.5 *sensitivity*
finer points 503.3 *accurate thing*
finery 295.1 *dress,* 813.4 *formal dress*
finespun 272.2 *fine,* 383.10 *delicate*
finesse 42.3 *card game terms,* 42.10 *play,* 481.2 *judiciousness,* 542.3 *subtlety,* 655.1 *skill,* 657.1 *cunning,* 657.5 *be cunning*
fine-structure constant 56.97 *fundamental constant*
fine-toned 433.6 *melodious*
fine-tune 627.3 *rectify*
fine tuning 503.1, 760.10 *accuracy*
fine-weave 67.10 *woven*
fine workmanship 655.1 *skill*
fine-woven 383.9 *smooth*
fine writer 549.5 *stylist*
finfoot 78 Birds
finger 135.5 *joint,* 143.7 *piece,* 403.4 *someone or something that feels,* 407.7 *sense organ,* 407.11 *touch,* 543.5 *indicator,* 543.9 *use signs,* 599.1 *use,* 726.3 *tools for gripping,* 874.13 *drink*
finger alphabet 421.1 *deafness*
finger bowl 258.16 *crockery*
fingerbreadth 264.2 *short distance*
finger grass 87 Grasses
fingering 407.2 *touching*
finger-licking 350.27 *edible*
finger-lickin' good 411.7 *tasty*
fingerling 80.3 *young fish,* 260.4 *little person*
fingermark 545.12 *vestige*
fingernail 373.7 *hard substance,* 380.9 *sharp-edged thing,* 407.7 *sense organ*
fingernails 726.3 *tools for gripping*
finger painter 50.16 *artist*
finger painting 50.2, 50.8 *painting*
finger post 543.5 *indicator*
fingerprint 132.1 *remainder,* 227.2 *visible effect,* 543.1 *sign,* 543.9 *use signs,* 544.3 *means of identification,* 544.10 *identify*
fingerprinted 544.12 *identified*
finger puppet 547.6 *image*
fingers 272.8 *narrow thing,* 726.3 *tools for gripping*
finger sandwich 45.11 *sandwich*
finger's-breadth 264.2 *short distance*
fingerstall 630.10 *surgical dressing*
finger's width 264.2 *short distance*
fingertip 403.4 *someone or something that feels,* 407.7 *sense organ*
finial 43 Architectural Decoration, 279.3 *architectural summit*
finickiness 467.2 *close attention,* 580.6 *selection*
finicky 106.10 *detailed,* 659.14 *troublesome*
fining 879.7 *punishment*
finis 157.1 *end,* 684.2 *conclusion*
finish 30.5 *horizontal bar,* 30.10 *compete in gymnastics,* 32.7 *horseracing,* 36.4 *rowing,* 36.16 *row,* 130.3 *additional item,* 142.10 *complete,* 144.1 *completeness,* 144.3 *completion,* 144.4 *complete,* 144.5 *be complete,* 155.9 *conclusion,* 157.1 *end,* 157.10 *ending,* 157.15 *end,* 160.2 *cessation,* 160.12 *discontinue,* 200.14 *pass,* 218.2 *stop,* 218.6 *cease,* 295.35 *make clothing,* 323.1 *closure,* 323.9 *close down,* 344.15 *destination,* 376.7 *smoothness,* 376.11 *smooth,* 383.1 *texture,* 558.1 *elegance,* 619.3 *perfection,* 619.5 *perfect,* 655.1 *skill,* 684.2 *conclusion,* 684.5 *conclude,* 794.1 *elegance*

finished 218, 3.18 *in the past,* 36.11 *rowing,* 100.11 *no more,* 144.7 *complete,* 157.21 *ended,* 160.9 *discontinued,* 200.18 *over,* 323.14 *closed down,* 397.19 *dead,* 487.3 *hopeless,* 558.3 *elegant,* 619.1 *perfect,* 655.6 *skilful,* 655.8 *expert,* 655.9 *well-made,* 684.8 *concluded,* 696.13 *excellent*
finished article 243.3 *product*
finished product 684.2 *conclusion*
finished state 144.1 *completeness*
finished up 684.8 *concluded*
finisher 157.13 *ender,* 295.26 *fashion designer,* 640.3 *doer,* 684.3 *elaboration*
finish first 21.6 *race*
finish halfway 620.10 *leave imperfect*
finishing 21.1 *track events,* 144.3 *completion,* 157.20 *ending,* 684.2 *conclusion,* 684.8 *concluded*
finishing line 588.6 *objective*
finishing off 144.3 *completion,* 684.3 *elaboration*
finishing school 6.12 *educational institution*
finishing stroke 157.13 *ender,* 684.3 *elaboration*
finishing tape 588.6 *objective*
finishing touch 130.3 *additional item,* 144.1 *completeness,* 627.5 *improvement,* 684.3 *elaboration*
finish off 157.15 *end,* 157.16 *cease,* 684.5 *conclude*
finish one's preparations 594.4 *prepare for action*
finish tape 21.1 *track events*
finish the job 644.6 *work*
finish the race 344.2 *reach*
finite 52.72 *complex,* 120.6 *quantitative,* 169.9 *fractional,* 302.5 *limited*
finitely 52.87 *mathematically,* 120.7 *quantitatively*
finite number 52.7 *natural number*
finite quantity 302.2 *limiting factor*
finite sequence 52.20 *sequence*
finite set 52.21 *set*
fink 528.10 *informer,* 856.3 *accuser,* 856.5 *accuse*
fin keel 74 Parts of a Ship, 36.3 *parts of a sailing boat*
Finland 91 Countries
finnan haddock 45.16 *fish dish,* 80.8 *food fish*
Finncattle 68 Breeds of Cattle
Finn class 36.2 *sailing boat*
Finnic 5 Languages and Groups of Languages
Finnish 5 Languages and Groups of Languages
Finnish Ayrshire 68 Breeds of Cattle
Finnish Horse 32 Breeds of Horse and Pony
Finnish spitz 77 Breeds of Dogs
Finno-Tartar 5 Languages and Groups of Languages
Finno-Ugric 5 Languages and Groups of Languages, 5.11 *family of languages*
finocchio 45 Vegetables
Finsteraarhorn 95 Mountains
fiord 98.9 *inlet*
fiorin 87 Grasses
fioritura 49 Musical Terms
fipple flute 49 Musical Instruments
fipples 534.23 *television reception*
fir 85 Trees and Shrubs
Firbank 48 Writers
fir cone 85.2 *tree part*
Firdausi 48 Poets
fire 777 Phobias by Topic, **408, 439, 670,** 15.11 *conduct industrial relations,* 37.7 *shoot,* 44.11 *make ceramics,* 147.8 *eject,* 218.8 *cause to cease,* 241.9 *make violent,* 244.7 *agent of destruction,* 252.17 *relegate,* 330.4 *throw,* 338.28 *shoot,* 349.2 *dismiss,* 392.19 *bake,*

408.15 *burn*, 410.11 *fuel*,
423.1 *loudness*, 439.24 *light*,
450.7 *red thing*, 543.4 *signal*,
554.1 *emphasis*, 590.19 *after
him*, 600.7 *stop work*, 643.14
make inactive, 645.5 *dismiss*,
670.15 *firing*, 676.14 *battle*,
679.37 *fight*, 704.7 *terminate*,
727.10 *dismiss*, 759.4 *emotion*,
767.12 *relieve from duty*
fire alarm 543.4 *signal*, 632.4
safety device, 636.2 *danger signal*
fire ant 82 Insects
firearm 338, 680, 425.3 *banger*
firearm silencer 424.2 *sound reducer*
fire a salute 817.12 *greet*, 849.20
salute
fire a salvo 812.18 *salute*
fire a shot 25.7 *bowl*
fire at 338.28 *shoot*, 670.2 *fire*
fire a volley 338.28 *shoot*
fire a warning flare 636.7 *raise
the alarm*
fire a warning shot 543.12 *signal*
fire away 156.18 *make a beginning*
fireball 53.20 *meteor*, 408.6,
439.8 *fire*
firebell 427.4 *sources of resonance*, 636.2 *danger signal*
fire blanket 632.4 *safety device*
fireblight 69.12 *pests and diseases*
firebomb 408.6 *fire*, 410.2 *lighter*, 680.16 *bomb*
firebomber 408.7 *fireman*, 410.9
power-worker
firebox 72.5 *locomotive part*,
408.6 *fire*
firebrand 228.7 *motivator*, 241.4
violent person or animal, 408.6
fire 410.2 *lighter*, 586.14 *motivator*, 635.2 *troublemaker*,
679.5 *arguer*, 693.8 *agitator*
firebrat 82 Insects
firebreak 265.1 *interval*
fire-breathing 408.12 *warm-
hearted*
firebrick 44.9 *industrial ceramics*
firebug 408.7 *fireman*
firecracker 425.3 *banger*
firecrest 78 Birds
fire curtain 51.17 *stage set*,
293.12 *protective covering*
fired 15.9 *negotiated*, 44.10 *ceramic*, 218.10 *finished*, 408.13
heated, 600.3 *not wanted*, 645.7
leisurely, 704.10, 704.10 *cancelled*, 727.13 *dismissed*
firedamp 57 Common Chemical Compounds, 388.3 *miasma*
fired employee 581.9 *rejected person*
fire door 632.4 *safety device*
fired porcelain 44.1 *ceramics*
firedrake 76.7 *legendary beast*
fire-eater 51.29 *circus performer*,
241.4 *violent person or animal*,
679.1 *combatant*
fire engine 71 Motor Vehicles,
389.13 *irrigator*, 450.7 *red thing*
fire-engine siren 423.4 *signal*
fire escape 347.6 *way out*, 359.7
means of ascent, 632.4 *safety device*, 638.2 *means of escape*
fire extinguisher 632.4 *safety device*
firefight 674.1 *contention*, 674.6
fight
fire fighter 408.7 *fireman*, 632.3
protector
firefly 82 Insects, **439**
fireglow 450.7 *red thing*
fireguard 634.2 *shelter*
firehouse 93.13 *municipal building*
fire insurance 632.2 *protection*
firelight 439.8 *fire*
firelighter 410.2 *lighter*, 439.8
fire
firelit 439.18 *lit*
fireman 408, 72.9 *railway
worker*, 543.8 *signer*, 632.3 *protector*
fireman's ladder 327.2 *route*
fire off 338.28 *shoot*
fire of love 821.5 *desire*

fire on 670.2 *fire*
fire one's imagination 471.16 *inspire*
fire opal 54 Gemstones
fireplace 408.6 *fire*
fireproof 378.1 *tough*, 378.11
make tough, 632.6 *invulnerable*
fireproof clothing 671.6 *protective
clothing*
firer 44.7 *potter*
fire raiser 241.4 *violent person or
animal*, 408.7 *fireman*
fire-raising 244.3 *destructiveness*
fire salamander 79 Amphibians
fire sale 739.4 *sale*, 752.2 *bargain*
fire screen 634.2 *shelter*
fire ship 410.2 *lighter*, 679.24
warship
fireside 256.3 *home*
fireside chat 568.2 *chat*
fire station 93.13 *municipal
building*
firestorm 408.6 *fire*
fire the first shot 670.1 *attack*
fire the parting shot 478.18 *answer back*
fire the starting gun 21.6 *race*
firethorn 84 Flowers and Flowering Plants
fire tongs 726.3 *tools for gripping*
firetrap 635.1 *trap*
fire up 239.3 *invigorate*, 241.9
make violent, 410.11 *fuel*
fire wall 632.4 *safety device*
firewatcher 632.3 *protector*
fireweed 84 Flowers and Flowering Plants
firewood 85.3 *timber*, 410.2 *lighter*
fireworks 439.8 *fire*, 655.3 *masterpiece*, 680.15 *explosive*,
811.14 *show*, 812.8 *salute*
fireworks party 665.7 *social gathering*
fire worship 9.2 *idolatry*
fire worshipper 9.6 *idolater*
fire-worshipping 9.10 *idolatrous*
firing 670, 15.2 *industrial negotiations*, 25.9 *bowls*, 44.5 *ceramic
process*, 147.2 *ejection*, 218.2
stop, 338.6 *shooting*, 349.18 *dismissal*, 704.2 *termination*,
727.1 *disposal*
firing line 676.10 *battleground*
firing on all cylinders 239.6 *with
vigour*
firing shot 25.2 *grip*
firing squad 16.43 *conviction*,
397.4 *death sentence*, 398.5 *execution*, 879.16 *instrument of execution*
firing squad member 398.12 *executioner*
firkin 75 General Units, 258.11
vessel
firm 13.7 *corporation*, 135.15
tied, 217.7 *permanent*, 225.9
stable, 237.10 *potent*, 237.11
strong in spirit, 371.6 *dense*,
373.2 *tough*, 373.4 *mentally
hard*, 373.10 *solidify*, 378.3
hard, 490.6 *infallible*, 554.3 *emphatic*, 574.5 *steady*, 577.3 *unyielding*, 647.1 *workshop*,
669.11 *obstinate*, 690.8 *severe*,
726.9 *retentive*, 737.7 *company*,
740.8 *store*, 819.11 *devoted*
firm advice 654.3 *precept*
firmament 8.11 *heaven*, 53.3 *universe*
firm attachment 821.1 *love*
firm control 690.1 *severity*
firm date 714.1 *promise*
firm fixture 225.4 *stable thing*
firm foundation 225.4 *stable thing*
firm hand 690.1 *severity*
firm hold 726.1 *retention*
firming up 225.1 *stability*
firmly 135.18 *inextricably*, 217.9
permanently, 225.12 *stably*,
237.15 *acutely*, 371.10 *densely*,
373.13 *inflexibly*, 378.12
toughly, 490.23 *certainly*,
669.14 *resistingly*, 690.11 *severely*, 726.11 *tenaciously*,
819.19 *devotedly*

firmness 217.1 *permanence*,
225.1 *stability*, 237.1 *strength*,
373.5 *hardness*, 378.6 *toughness*, 490.17 *infallibility*,
574.15 *will*, 669.2 *obstinacy*,
690.1 *severity*, 819.3 *familiarity*
firmness of purpose 570.2 *willpower*
firm-packed 371.6 *dense*
firm price 710.3 *business offer*
firm principle 166.4 *guide*
firm up 225.7 *make stable*, 273.7
thicken, 371.9 *make dense*
firn 34.5 *rock face*
first 154, 156, 52.75 *equal*,
119.4 *original*, 119.8 *originally*,
126.14 *best*, 154.10 *preceding*,
154.12 *primary*, 154.23 *primarily*, 156.29 *beginning*, 174.11
one, 194.10 *prior*, 194.11 *before*, 201.10 *new*, 201.21 *newly*,
208.12, 208.17 *early*, 303.1
front, 322.17 *beginning*, 617.2
best, 682.5 *victorious person*
first aid 630.13 *therapy*, 662.5
medical assistance
first-aid 630.17 *remedial*
first-aid station 630.14 *hospital*
First Amendment 698.2 *free
speech*
first among equals 126.5 *superior*, 194.10 *prior*
first and foremost 154.21,
156.40 *first*
first and last 174.14 *singular*
first appearance 156.9 *premiere*,
457.1 *appearance*
first arrival 208.4 *early comer*
first attack 31.6 *lacrosse player*
first attempt 596.5 *attempt*
first base 22.1 *baseball*, 156.12
first move
first-baseman 22.2 *baseball player*
first-baseman's glove 22.3 *baseball equipment*
first-base umpire 22.2 *baseball
player*
first beginnings 156.2 *creation*
firstborn 154.9 *predecessor*
first cause 4.9 *philosophical problem*
First Cause 8.3 *God*
first choice 580.9 *chosen thing*,
611.3 *chief thing*
first class 194.2 *greater importance*, 861.8 *good*
first-class 126.15 *excellent*,
194.10 *prior*, 611.7 *worthy*,
617.2 *best*, 742.3 *opulent*,
802.4 *aristocratic*, 861.1 *good*
first-class cricket 27.1 *cricket
match*
first-class mail 534.2 *postal communication*
first-class stamp 534.3
correspondence
first comer 255.1 *inhabitant*
first communion 10.5 *Christian
rite*
first concern 154.2 *priority*,
194.3 *matter of priority*
first course 45.9 *dish*, 156.12
first move, 350.14 *mouthful*
first crack 208.2 *early hour*
first crack of dawn 208.2 *early
hour*
first cuckoo 203.2 *spring*
first defence 31.6 *lacrosse player*
first-degree burn 408.1 *heat*
first-degree murder 398.2 *murder*
first derivative 52.31 *differentiation*
first division 194.2 *greater importance*
first-division 194.10 *prior*
first draft 592.6 *outline*, 594.10
preparations
first early 68.12 *crop*
first echelon 679.14 *armed forces*
first edition 119.2 *original*
first eleven 194.2 *greater importance*
first fiddle 611.4 *bigwig*, 655.4
skilled person
first finger 407.7 *sense organ*
first floor 280.2 *foot*
first gallery 40.5 *real tennis*

first go 596.5 *attempt*
first guard 28.3 *fencing movements*
first-hand 119.4 *original*
first house 51.11 *theatrical performance*
first importance 611.1 *importance*
first impression 457.5 *impression*
first innings 156.12 *first move*
first in the field 119.4 *original*,
194.10 *prior*
first lady 126.6 *paragon*
first lap 156.12 *first move*
first law 56.38 *thermodynamics*
first leg 156.12 *first move*
First Lieutenant 17 US Military
Ranks
first light 204.1 *morning*, 359.3
sun rise, 441.1 *dimness*
first love 821.2 *romantic love*
firstly 156.40 *first*, 194.11 *before*, 201.21 *newly*, 208.17 *early*
first move 156
first name 560.8 *name*
first night 51.11 *theatrical performance*, 156.9 *premiere*, 201.4
beginning, 457.1 *appearance*
first-nighter 51.31 *theatregoer*
first-night nerves 51.20 *acting*
first object ball 24.4 *carom*
first of all 126.17 *supremely*,
156.40 *first*
first officer 73.3 *aircraft personnel*
first of its kind 194.10 *prior*
first one and then the other
109.10 *reciprocally*
first-order 57.38 *reactive*
first-past-the-post system 580.11
franchise
first payment 746.1 *payment*
first performance 51.11 *theatrical
performance*
first-person narrative 48.3 *aspect
of fiction*
first place 126.1 *superiority*,
154.2 *priority*, 194.2 *greater importance*
first-place finisher 682.5 *victorious person*
first principle 226.3 *rudiment*,
367.4 *matter*
first principles 52.65 *theory*,
156.7 *rudiments*
first priority 611.3 *chief thing*
first prize 681.1 *trophy*
first quarter 53.17 *moon*
first-rate 126.15 *excellent*, 611.6
notable, 617.1 *worthy*, 617.2
best, 655.6 *skilful*, 696.13 *excellent*, 861.1 *good*
first-rater 617.8 *exceller*, 682.4
successful person, 861.16 *superior person*
first refusal 738.7 *purchasing*
first round 156.12 *first move*
first school 6.12 *educational institution*
first screening 457.1 *appearance*
first secretary 653.16 *official*
first see the light 396.18 *be born*
first slip 27.4 *team*
first stage 156.12 *first move*
first step 156.12 *first move*,
208.3 *early stage*, 226.3 *rudiment*
first steps 156.4 *conception*
first string 655.4 *skilled person*
first-string 617.1 *worthy*
first-string player 655.4 *skilled
person*
first-team player 23.2 *basketball
player*
first thing 156.40 *first*, 208.17
early, 226.3 *rudiment*
first time 156.9 *premiere*
first tooth 380.11 *tooth*
first violin 653.14 *leader*
first wicket down 27.4 *team*
First World War 676.1 *war*
firth 98.9 *inlet*
Firth of Forth 98.9 *inlet*
fiscal 13.13 *economic*, 14.6 *financial*, 737.14 *commercial*, 741.22
monetary, 750.10 *accounting*
fiscal competence 742.8 *solvency*
fiscal incompetence 743.6 *insolvency*

fiscally 13.14 *economically,* 741.28, 750.13 *financially*
fiscal policy 13.1 *economics,* 13.6 *economic factors*
fiscal year 187.4 *period of activity*
Fischer 52 Scientists, 52 Scientists
Fischer-Dieskau 49 Musicians and Composers
Fischer–Tropsch process 57 Named Reactions
fish 42 Card Games, 161 Collective Names by Animal, 777 Phobias by Topic, **80, 80,** 20.7 *angle,* 76.4 *type of animal,* 76.5 *aquatic animal,* 80.1 *fishes,* 355.11 *extract,* 398.22 *kill animals,* 590.11 *hunt*
fishability 80.7 *fishing*
fish anatomy 80
fish and chips 45.16 *fish dish,* 45.44 *British dish*
fish-and-chip shop 350.15 *eating place*
fish ball 45.16 *fish dish*
fishbowl 80.6 *study of fish*
fish breeding 80.6 *study of fish*
fishcake 45.16 *fish dish*
fish course 45.9 *dish,* 350.14 *mouthful*
fish day 869.1 *self-restraint,* 871.3 *fast day*
fish dish 45
fish eagle 80.11 *fishing animal*
fished 20.8 *angling*
fisher 77 Placental Mammals, **80,** 20.6 *angler*
fisherfolk 80.10 *fisher*
fisherman 20.6 *angler,* 74.7 *nautical person,* 80.10 *fisher,* 350.20 *food provider,* 590.6 *hunter*
fisherman's bend 74 Knots
fisherman's jersey 295.13 *sweater*
fisherman's knot 74 Knots
fisherman's tale 541.5, 541.5 *tall story*
fisherman's yarn 538.4 *lie*
fishery 80.7 *fishing*
fishes 80
Fishes 53 The Constellations, 80
fisheye lens 66.17 *lens,* 435.8 *reflection*
fish farm 68.6 *farm,* 80.6 *study of fish*
fish farmer 80.10 *fisher*
fish farming 68.3 *livestock farming,* 80.7 *fishing*
fish-finder 80.7 *fishing*
fish finger 45.16 *fish dish*
fish food 350.8 *animal food*
fish for 590.8 *pursue*
fish for compliments 809.15 *be vain,* 811.29 *show off*
fish for invitations 815.11 *be sociable*
fish fork 350.16 *eating utensil*
fishgig 80.7 *fishing*
fish glue 80.9 *fish product,* 138.3 *adhesive*
Fishguard 93 Cities
fish hawk 78 Birds
fish-hold 80.7 *fishing*
fish-hook 20.3 *fishing tackle,* 80.7 *fishing,* 380.8 *sharppointed thing,* 539.13 *snare*
fishiness 286.3 *deviousness*
fishing **80,** 20.1, 20.8 *angling,* 74.11 *nautical,* 355.1 *extraction,* 590.2 *chase,* 590.16 *hunting*
fishing animal 80
fishing bank 80.7 *fishing*
fishing bird 78.3 *water bird*
fishing boat 74 Ships and Boats, 74.3 *vessel*
fishing cat 80.11 *fishing animal*
fishing fleet 80.7 *fishing*
fishing ground 80.7 *fishing*
fishing licence 708.2 *permit*
fishing line 80.7 *fishing,* 590.3 *hunting and fishing equipment*
fishing net 590.3 *hunting and fishing equipment*

fishing pole 20.3 *fishing tackle,* 590.3 *hunting and fishing equipment*
fishing rod 20.3 *fishing tackle,* 590.3 *hunting and fishing equipment*
fishing season 203.1 *season*
fishing tackle 20
fishing the water 20.1 *angling*
fishing to the rise 20.1 *angling*
fishing with bait 20.1 *angling*
fish in the sea 400.1 *humankind*
fish in troubled waters 659.21 *get into trouble*
fish joint 47.10 *carpenter's term,* 72.3 *rail*
fish kettle 258.15 *pot*
fish knife 350.16 *eating utensil,* 380.10 *knife*
fish ladder 80.7 *fishing*
fishlike 80
fish line 80.7 *fishing*
fish-liver oil 80.9 *fish product*
fish louse 81.4 *arthropod,* 81.10 *parasite*
fish lover 80.12 *ichthyologist*
fishman 80.10 *fisher*
fish market 740.1 *market*
fishmeal 68.9 *animal feedstuff,* 68.13, 69.7 *fertilizer,* 80.9 *fish product,* 246.3 *fertilizer*
fishmonger 80.10 *fisher,* 350.17 *food shop,* 350.20 *food provider,* 606.3 *provider,* 739.13 *retailer*
fishnet 80.7 *fishing,* 288.2 *braid,* 590.3 *hunting and fishing equipment*
fishnet tights 295.20 *legwear*
fish out 355.11 *extract*
fish out of water 108.2 *unrelated thing,* 117.6, 149.9 *misfit,* 168.7 *nonconformist,* 252.7 *displaced person,* 335.19 *deviant person,* 666.4 *dissenter,* 816.6 *unsocial person*
fish owl 78 Birds
fish pie 45.16 *fish dish*
fishplate 72.3 *rail*
fishpond 80.6 *study of fish,* 94.2 *small lake*
fish product 80
fish roe 80.9 *fish product*
fish seller 80.10 *fisher*
fishskin disease 392.16 *dry skin*
fish soup 45.13 *soup*
fish stick 45.16 *fish dish*
fish store 350.17 *food shop*
fish story 538.4 *lie,* 541.5 *tall story*
fishtail 39.11 *swimming*
fishtail kick 39.2 *swimming technique*
fishtank 80.6 *study of fish,* 256.12 *stall*
fish the water 20.7 *angle*
fish to the rise 20.7 *angle*
fishtrap 80.7 *fishing*
fish up 361.4 *gather up*
fish way 80.7 *fishing*
fish weir 80.7 *fishing*
fishwife 80.10 *fisher,* 829.3 *irascible person*
fish with a pole 20.7 *angle*
fish with a rod 20.7 *angle*
fish with bait 20.7 *angle*
fishy 80.13 *fishlike,* 286.5 *devious,* 858.7 *criminal*
fishy transaction 539.7 *tricking,* 858.3 *criminality*
fissile 136.19 *separable,* 265.7 *cracked,* 379.1 *brittle*
fissile nuclide 56.72 *nuclear fission*
fissility 379.2 *brittleness*
fission 56.72 *nuclear fission,* 136.1 *separation,* 141.2 *deconstruction,* 141.4 *deconstruct,* 235.8 *nuclear power*
fissionable 136.19 *separable*
fissionable material 680.15 *explosive*
fissionable nuclide 56.72 *nuclear fission*
fission energy 56.11 *energy*
fission product 56.72 *nuclear fission*

fission reaction 56.72 *nuclear fission,* 57.14 *chemical reaction*
fissure 54.24 *volcanic activity,* 136.3 *separateness,* 160.4 *interruption,* 265.2 *crack,* 321.1, 321.6 *furrow,* 322.1 *opening,* 322.20 *hole*
fissured 265.7 *cracked,* 322.12 *open*
fissure sealing 60.4 *dentistry*
fist 407.7 *sense organ,* 543.3 *gesture,* 543.7 *punctuation,* 680.1 *weapon,* 726.3 *tools for gripping*
fistfight 151.9 *disorder*
fistful 702.4 *prison sentence*
fisticuffs 26.2 *boxing,* 151.9 *disorder,* 241.3 *instance of violence,* 330.12 *collision,* 473.1 *argument,* 500.1 *dissent,* 666.2 *argument,* 674.6 *fight,* 674.7 *boxing,* 764.8, 828.5 *quarrel*
fistula 624.15 *ulcer*
fit 116, 845, 48.8 *part of poem,* 105.1 *state,* 107.8 *be proportionate to,* 122.9 *adequate,* 122.11 *equalize,* 135.10 *link,* 138.6 *adhere,* 142.8 *sound,* 167.7 *conform,* 167.9 *make conform,* 187.1 *period,* 210.6 *timely,* 235.13 *powerful,* 237.9 *physically strong,* 241.3 *instance of violence,* 295.35 *make clothing,* 306.12 *on form,* 366.8 *spasm,* 478.22 *be the answer,* 485.9 *qualified,* 485.14 *be qualified,* 510.3 *mental deterioration,* 579.3 *whim,* 594.5 *equip,* 613.2 *usable,* 615.1 *convenient,* 615.6 *be convenient,* 623.1 *healthy,* 624.2 *illness,* 642.3 *nimbleness,* 667.13 *suitable,* 670.20 *bout,* 843.12 *all right*
fit a beam 47.17 *carpenter*
fit a mould 105.6 *be in a state of*
fit and ready 623.1 *healthy*
fit as a fiddle 237.9 *physically strong,* 623.1 *healthy*
fit as a flea 237.9 *physically strong*
fit badly 666.8 *be different*
fit for habitation 256.14 *inhabiting*
fit for legislation 16.47 *liable to law*
fit for marriage 823.22 *marriageable*
fit for nothing 614.1 *useless*
fit for release 639.4 *deliverable*
fit for use 594.19 *in hand,* 613.2 *usable*
fitful 113.5 *diverse,* 160.8 *discontinuous,* 187.9 *periodic,* 213.2 *infrequent,* 215.4 *irregular,* 224.13 *changeable,* 366.19 *convulsive,* 491.8, 579.1 *capricious*
fitfully 113.11 *irregularly,* 160.17 *discontinuously,* 187.14 *for short periods,* 213.1 *infrequently,* 215.8 *irregularly,* 224.15 *changeably,* 491.27, 579.6 *capriciously*
fitfulness 113.1 *diversity,* 160.1 *discontinuity,* 213.3 *infrequency,* 215.1 *irregularity,* 224.2 *irresolution,* 491.16 *capriciousness,* 579.2 *caprice*
fithele 49 Musical Instruments
fit in 167.8 *comply,* 167.9 *make conform,* 665.13 *be a member*
fit into a category 107.9 *have a relative position*
fit like a glove 138.6 *adhere*
fitly 210.9 *opportunely*
fitness 210.1 *timeliness,* 235.2 *ability,* 237.2 *healthiness,* 306.6 *nature,* 478.8 *correspondence,* 485.1 *qualification,* 594.14 *preparedness,* 615.3 *convenience,* 623.3 *health,* 625.2 *salubrity,* 655.2 *aptitude,* 667.4 *suitability*
fitness for marriage 823.4 *marriageability*
fit of anger 828.4 *anger*
fit of temper 822.5, 828.4 *anger*
fit of terror 777.1 *fear*
fit of the sulks 830.2 *sign of sullenness*

fit on the head of a pin 260.6 *be little*
fit out 295.35 *make clothing,* 594.5 *equip,* 602.6 *find means,* 606.5 *provision*
fit perfectly 667.9 *be suitable*
fits and starts 215.1 *irregularity,* 366.1 *agitation*
fitted 148.7 *modular,* 485.9 *qualified*
fitted carpet 293.9 *floor covering*
fittedness 485.1 *qualification*
fitted sheet 293.10 *bed covering*
fitted unit 258.3 *cabinet*
fitter 63.4 *mechanical engineer,* 295.26 *fashion designer,* 594.15 *preparer,* 603.7 *machinist,* 646.2 *artisan*
fit the bill 782.16 *be desirable*
fit the occasion 210.4 *be timely*
fit tight 138.6 *adhere*
Fittig reaction 57 Named Reactions
fitting 116, 210.6 *timely,* 478.15 *correspondent,* 485.9 *qualified,* 558.3 *elegant,* 608.1 *sufficient,* 615.1 *convenient,* 667.13 *suitable,* 782.8 *desirable,* 845.13 *fit*
fittingly 116, 210.9 *opportunely,* 478.26 *correspondingly,* 485.17 *capably,* 615.7 *conveniently,* 843.18 *properly*
fittingness 558.1 *elegance*
fitting out 594, 606.1 *provision*
fitting retribution 855.4 *revenge,* 879.9 *retribution*
fittings 603.6 *equipment*
fitting the circumstances 106.7 *circumstantial*
fitting together 161.33 *putting together,* 298.2 *interaction*
fit to bust 144.8 *full*
fit to drop 650.1 *fatigued*
fit together 135.8 *unite,* 140.5 *combine,* 148.13 *make,* 161.44 *put together,* 298.5 *cooperate*
fit up 592.13 *plot*
fit-up 592.4 *plot*
fit well 135.8 *unite,* 667.9 *be suitable*
Fitzgerald 48 Writers, 48 Poets, 52 Scientists
Fitzsimmons 18 Sporting Personalities
five 179, 52.9 *numeral,* 179.12 *fifth*
five-act play 51.2 *play*
five-and-dime 612.4 *trivial*
Five and Over 179
five-and-ten 754.9 *cheap*
five and twenty 179.8 *twenty and over*
five-a-side 179.1 *five*
five-barred gate 68.11 *farmland*
five-by-five 179.1 *five*
five cents 741.8 *American money*
five centuries 179.9 *treble figures*
five C's 179.9 *treble figures*
five-dollar bill 179.1 *five,* 741.8 *American money*
five-figure 179.21 *thousandth*
five-finger 179.1 *five*
five fingers 702.4 *prison sentence*
fivefold 179, 179.12 *fifth*
five hundred 42 Card Games, 179.9 *treble figures*
five hundred and one 42.6 *darts*
five-man defence 23.4 *playing terms*
five-metre platform 39.6 *diving*
five-minute penalty 31.3 *ice hockey*
five-nations championship 35.2 *championship*
five o'clock 204.4 *afternoon,* 350.12 *meal*
five-o'clock shadow 375.7 *rough thing*
five pence 741.9 *British money*
five-pound note 179.1 *five,* 741.9 *British money*
fiver 179.1 *five,* 741.8 *American money,* 741.9 *British money*
five shillings 741.10 *former British money*
five-sided 52.82 *polygonal*

fivesome 179.1 *five*
five spices 45 Herbs and Spices
five-spot 179.1 *five*
fivestones 42 Children's Games and Party Games
five stones 179.1 *five*
five-year plan 592.1 *plan*
fix 293, 105.2 *predicament*, 106.4 *difficult circumstances*, 120.8 *quantify*, 131.4 *take off*, 135.10 *link*, 163.13 *class*, 165.24 *specify*, 217.6 *make permanent*, 225.7 *make stable*, 236.9 *make impotent*, 250.9 *locate*, 251.3 *difficult circumstances*, 251.10 *situate*, 280.4 *base*, 332.6 *direct*, 475.17 *prove*, 490.21 *make certain*, 539.10 *fraud*, 539.30 *be fraudulent*, 540.9 *falsification*, 540.22 *falsify*, 574.7 *resolve*, 582.2 *premeditate*, 594.4 *prepare for action*, 627.3 *rectify*, 629.1 *repair*, 630.19 *remedy*, 659.5 *predicament*, 843.15 *put right*, 875.6 *drug*, 879.2 *penalize*
fix a fight 26.11 *do a combat sport*
fix a position 36.15 *sail*
fixated 467.8 *diligent*, 510.13 *mentally ill*
fixation 57 Types of Chemical Reaction, **61**, 59.6 *cell biology*, 250.4 *placing*, 325.1 *motionlessness*, 467.4 *diligence*, 493.4 *prejudgment*, 510.4 *delusion*, 584.1 *habit*
fixation neurosis 61.10 *neurosis*
fixation of affect 61.17 *fixation*
fixative 50.11 *artist's materials*, 138.3 *adhesive*, 418.2 *fragrant thing*, 444.4 *pigment*
fixed 584, 5.43 *phrasal*, 122.6 *equal*, 217.7 *permanent*, 225.10 *stabilized*, 236.12 *impotent*, 250.6 *located*, 325.4 *motionless*, 490.3 *decided*, 490.5 *inevitable*, 490.7 *particular*, 493.8 *unjust*, 539.35 *deceptive*, 582.4 *deliberate*, 629.13 *repaired*, 718.9 *fast*, 725.8 *propertied*
fixed array 534.28 *radar*
fixed assets 13.7 *corporation*, 725.5 *personal estate*
fixed bridge 21.3 *bridge*
fixed costs 13.7 *corporation*
fixed day 185.11 *date*
fixed expression 5.24 *phrasing*
fixed fight 26.2 *boxing*
fixed-focus lens 66.17 *lens*
fixed form 48.10 *verse form*
fixed-head coupé 71.16 *car*
fixed idea 493.4 *prejudgment*
fixedly 217.9 *permanently*, 325.10 *motionlessly*, 718.17 *fastly*
fixedness 217.1 *permanence*, 225.1 *stability*
fixed oil 395.7 *oil*
fixed point 52.36 *point*
fixed-point notation 52.8 *number system*
fixed position 671.8 *military defences*
fixed price 751.1 *price*
fixed resolve 574.12 *resolution*
fixed seat 36.4 *rowing*
fixed-seat 36.11 *rowing*
fixed-seat rowing 36.4 *rowing*
fixed-spool 20.8 *angling*
fixed-spool reel 20.3 *fishing tackle*
fixed star 53.10 *star*
fixed term 185.3 *duration*
fixed ways 584.3 *way*
fixer 293, 66.12 *development*, 629.12 *repairer*
fixing 293, 34.8 *mountaineering*, 131.1 *subtraction*, 250.4 *placing*, 490.18 *particularity*, 629.8 *repair*
fixing point 34.5 *rock face*
fixing solution 66.12 *development*
fix in one's mind 511.11 *memorize*

fixity 188.4 *long-lastingness*, 217.1 *permanence*, 225.1 *stability*, 325.1 *motionlessness*, 577.6 *determination*
fixity of purpose 574.13 *concentration*
fix on 332.7 *take a direction*
fix one's teeth into 726.6 *retain*
fix the date 192.14 *keep time*
fix the day 192.14 *keep time*
fix the game 657.5 *be cunning*
fix the price of 751.11 *price*
fix the time 192.14 *keep time*
fix to 718.14 *make fast*
fixture 180.4 *concomitant*, 225.4 *stable thing*, 603.6 *equipment*, 674.2 *contest*
fixtures 603.6 *equipment*
fixtures and fittings 725.4 *possessions*
fix up 152.17 *come to an arrangement*, 606.5 *provision*, 627.1 *improve*, 629.2 *refurbish*
fix upon 467.12 *scrutinize*
fizz 351.6 *soft drink*, 390.24 *bubble*, 424.1 *faintness*, 424.5 *sound faint*, 429.1, 429.4 *hiss*
fizziness 388.7 *gaseousness*
fizzle 425.6 *crack*, 429.4 *hiss*
fizzle out 157.18 *come to an end*, 358.2, 683.6 *fail*
fizzling 429.6 *hissing*
fizzy 351.17 *drinkable*, 388.21 *gassy*, 390.18 *bubbly*, 429.6 *hissing*
fizzy drink 351.6 *soft drink*
fizzy water 351.6 *soft drink*, 389.2 *drinking water*
fjord 54.7 *landform*
Fjord 32 Breeds of Horse and Pony
flab 259.8 *fat*
flabbergast 514.11 *amaze*, 786.10 *be wonderful*
flabbergasted 514.7 *amazed*, 786.6 *wondering*
flabbiness 259.5 *fatness*, 273.5 *thickness*, 374.8 *softness*, 393.4 *pulpiness*
flabby 259.16 *fat*, 273.1 *thick*, 374.1 *soft*, 393.18 *pulpy*
flabellate 261.8 *growing*
flabelliform 261.8 *growing*
flaccid 238.8 *weak*, 240.5 *inert*, 374.1 *soft*, 555.1 *unemphatic*
flaccidity 238.1 *weakness*, 374.8 *softness*, 555.2 *lack of emphasis*
flaccidly 374.17 *softly*
flaccidness 374.8 *softness*
flack 228.7 *motivator*, 524.7 *news interpreter*, 526.12 *displayer*, 528.9 *informant*, 532.10 *publicizer*
flackery 532.8 *public relations*, 586.6 *advertising*
flacon 418.2 *fragrant thing*
flag 84 Flowers and Flowering Plants, **544**, 29.2 *golfing terms*, 36.3 *parts of a sailing boat*, 238.6 *be weak*, 328.2 *hesitate*, 533.12 *headline*, 604.2 *building material*, 624.24 *be unhealthy*, 650.5 *be fatigued*, 683.6 *fail*, 770.9 *despair*
flag day 729.3 *offering*, 812.5 *anniversary*, 833.5 *charity*
flag down 543.11 *gesture*
flagellant 840.3 *atoner*, 867.3 *penitent person*
flagellate 81.9 *protozoan*, 81.23 *protozoan*, 90.7 *algal*, 879.3 *hit*
flagellate oneself 840.6 *apologize*, 867.5 *do penance*
flagellate protozoan 81.9 *protozoan*
flagellation 840.2 *apology*, 867.2 *type of penance*, 879.12 *corporal punishment*
flagellator 879.17 *punisher*
flagellum 59.8 *cell organ*
flageolet 45 Vegetables, **49** Musical Instruments
flagging 238.3 *poor health*, 328.4 *slow*, 328.9 *deceleration*, 624.22 *sick*, 650.1 *fatigued*
flagitious 864.11 *wicked*
flagitiousness 864.1 *wickedness*

flagman 636.4 *warner*
flag of convenience 544.7 *flag*, 592.3 *expedient plan*, 657.2 *stratagem*
flag officer 17.5 *military staff*
flag of surrender 544.7 *flag*
flag of truce 544.7 *flag*, 675.2 *symbol of peace*, 677.2 *peace offering*
flagon 258.14 *bottle*
flag on a windless day 240.3 *inert thing*
flagpole 544.7 *flag*
flagrancy 526.10 *manifestation*, 807.3 *audacity*, 811.6 *blatancy*, 864.1 *wickedness*
flagrant 526.14 *manifest*, 532.20 *well-known*, 807.15 *audacious*, 811.21 *blatant*, 864.11 *wicked*, 864.13 *venial*
flagrantly 526.16 *manifestly*, 807.32 *audaciously*, 811.37 *blatantly*, 864.18 *wickedly*
flags 812.8 *salute*
flagship 74 Ships and Boats
flag ship 679.24 *warship*
flag signals 534.27 *signalling*
flagstaff 275.6 *tall thing*, 544.7 *flag*
flagstick 29.2 *golfing terms*
flagstone 280.1 *base*, 293.11 *paving*, 327.4 *road surface*, 376.8 *smooth thing*, 604.2 *building material*
flag waving 543.3 *gesture*
flag-waving 812.9 *rejoicing*
flail 330.5 *beat*, 330.16 *weapons*, 670.5 *strike*, 879.3 *hit*
flailing 670.23 *attacking*
flail mower 68.10 *farm tool*
flair 235.2 *ability*, 459.4 *cleverness*, 481.2 *judiciousness*, 485.2 *ability*, 549.2 *stylishness*, 655.2 *aptitude*
flak 680.13 *ammunition*, 852.5, 854.2 *criticism*
flak-catcher 586.12 *persuader*
flake 34.5 *rock face*, 136.10 *set apart*, 143.7 *piece*, 266.4 *slice*, 266.11 *scale*, 296.16 *peel*, 379.4 *be brittle*, 384.6 *crumb*, 384.24 *crumble*, 413.7 *tobacco*
flaked maize 68.9 *animal feedstuff*
flaked out 643.4 *not awake*, 650.1 *fatigued*
flake off 266.11 *scale*, 296.16 *peel*
flake out 650.5 *be fatigued*
flake white 446.8 *whitener*
flakily 384
flakiness 266.6 *layering*, 379.2 *brittleness*, 384.2 *crumbliness*
flaking 379.1 *brittle*, 384.4 *pulverization*
flak jacket 19.3 *uniform*, 671.6 *protective clothing*
flaky 266.9 *platelike*, 379.1 *brittle*, 384.20 *crumbly*
flaky pastry 45.37 *pastry*
flam 538.4 *lie*
flambeau 439.7 *lantern*
flamboyance 475.2 *demonstrativeness*, 541.3 *extravagance*, 811.4 *flashiness*
flamboyant 43 Architectural Styles, 439.16 *bright*, 475.10 *demonstrative*, 541.14 *extravagant*, 557.4 *ornate*, 811.19 *flashy*
flamboyantly 439.30 *lightly*, 475.21 *demonstratively*, 541.17 *excessively*, 557.6 *ornately*, 811.35 *flashily*
flame 408.6 *fire*, 408.15 *burn*, 439.8 *fire*, 439.25 *light up*, 450.7 *red thing*, 821.5 *desire*
flame-coloured 450.1 *red*, 451.1 *orange*
flame gun 69.6 *garden tool*
flamen 7.8 *priest*
flamenco 46.1 *historic dancing*
flame-of-the-forest 85 Trees and Shrubs
flameout 73.7 *miscellaneous aviation terms*

flameproof 67.11 *treated*, 67.15 *treat*
flameproofing 67.8 *fabric treatment*
flames 408.6 *fire*
flames of love 821.5 *desire*
flamethrower 408.6 *fire*, 680.11 *guns*
flame tree 85 Trees and Shrubs
flame with passion 821.24 *be in love*
flaming 241.6 *violent*, 408.10 *on fire*, 439.16 *bright*
flaming June 408.5 *hot weather*
flamingo 78 Birds, 78.3 *water bird*
flammability 408.6 *fire*
flammable 408.10 *on fire*, 410.10 *powered*, 633.1 *dangerous*
Flamsteed 52 Scientists
flan 45.36 *cake*
flanch 544.8 *heraldic device*
flan dish 45.6 *kitchen equipment*
flange 63.27 *superstructure*, 299.3 *edge*
flank 45.22 *beef*, 305.1 *side*, 305.7 *be alongside*, 334.5 *encircle*, 363.7 *ring*, 632.9 *protect*
flanker 19.7 *offence*, 35.4 *rugby player*
flanking 305.6 *side*
flanking attack 670.12 *military attack*
flannel 67 Natural Fabrics, 288.4 *textile*, 521.5 *empty talk*, 621.11 *cleaning cloth*, 853.2, 853.9 *blarney*
flannelette 67 Natural Fabrics, 288.4 *textile*
flannels 295.9 *trousers*
flan ring 45.6 *kitchen equipment*
flap 73 Aircraft Parts, 130.3 *additional item*, 139.6 *come unstuck*, 224.11 *be changeable*, 266.1 *layer*, 293.2 *cover*, 295.24 *part of garment*, 365.12 *wave*, 366.1 *agitation*, 366.4 *fuss*, 366.21 *be agitated*, 648.4 *haste*, 666.2 *argument*
flapdoodle 521.5 *empty talk*
flapjack 45.39, 45.39 *loaf*
flapping 139.8 *nonadhesive*
flapping in the breeze 139.8 *nonadhesive*
flare 36.10 *sailing*, 66.8 *composition*, 73.5 *flight*, 261.1 *growth*, 261.5 *make bigger*, 261.6 *become bigger*, 271.4 *breadth*, 271.9 *be broad*, 408.15 *burn*, 439.2 *quality of light*, 439.8 *fire*, 439.25 *light up*, 543.4 *signal*, 636.2 *danger signal*, 680.5 *missile weapon*
flared 261.7 *bigger*, 271.1 *broad*
flared skirt 295.6 *skirt*
flare gybe 36.1 *sailing*, 36.15 *sail*
flare pass 19.9 *play*
flare path 439.6 *electric light*
flares 295.9 *trousers*
flare star 53.12 *variable star*
flare up 128.4 *increase*, 439.25 *light up*, 828.12 *become angry*
flare-up 241.3 *instance of violence*, 828.4 *anger*
flaring 261.1 *growth*, 261.8 *growing*, 408.10 *on fire*, 439.16 *bright*, 444.12 *gaudy*
flash 66, 94.1 *lake*, 191.3 *instant*, 224.11 *be changeable*, 294.11 *uncover*, 296.14 *undress*, 366.12, 366.26 *flicker*, 439.2 *quality of light*, 439.4 *natural light*, 439.25 *light up*, 457.14 *present*, 464.3 *insight*, 526.1 *display*, 583.5 *spontaneity*, 811.28 *flourish*
flashback 3.13 *looking back*, 511.2 *retrospect*
flashbulb 66.19 *flash*, 439.7 *lantern*
flash by 329.6 *accelerate*, 356.8 *pass*
flash cube 66.19 *flash*
flash desorption 57.20 *surface chemistry*

flasher 71 Motor Vehicle Parts, 294.4 *exposer*, 296.8 *nude person*, 877.10 *sex offender*

flash flood 241.5 *violent weather*, 635.1 *trap*

flash food 96.6 *river flow*

flashgun 66.19 *flash*, 439.7 *lantern*

flashily 811

flashiness 811, 475.2 *demonstrativeness*

flashing 294.1 *uncovering*, 296.1 *undress*, 296.11 *exposed*, 329.1 *swift*, 439.2 *quality of light*, 439.15 *lucent*, 439.16 *bright*, 543.16 *signalling*, 877.7 *sexual assault*

flashing light 439.6 *electric light*, 543.4 *signal*, 636.2 *danger signal*

flash in the pan 189.2 *transient thing*, 270.4 *short thing*, 636.3 *false alarm*, 682.1 *success*

flashlamp 439.7 *lantern*

flashlight 439.7 *lantern*

flashlit 439.18 *lit*

flash note 741.15 *false money*

flash of inspiration 461.6 *idea*

flash on the mind 530.9 *be disclosed*

flash out with 583.3 *improvise*

flash photography 66.1 *photography*

flash point 408.1 *heat*

flashy 811, 439.16 *bright*, 444.12 *gaudy*, 475.10 *demonstrative*, 557.4 *ornate*

flask 57 Laboratory Apparatus, 258.14 *bottle*, 351.10 *drink container*

flask fungi 89.3 *fungi*

flat 49.16 *musical note*, 51.17 *stage set*, 52.79 *spatial*, 52.80 *linear*, 98.3 *marsh*, 98.11 *continental*, 110.17 *regular*, 112.5 *uniform*, 214.11 *regular*, 214.14 *orderly*, 248.11 *spatial*, 256.5 *house*, 262.7 *smaller*, 276.7 *lowland*, 278.2 *superficial*, 278.4 *shallow thing*, 282.2 *horizontal surface*, 282.8 *horizontal*, 282.11 *horizontally*, 325.5 *sedentary*, 376.2 *uniform*, 381.1 *blunt*, 412.5 *tasteless*, 428.2 *nonresonant*, 430.7 *strident*, 434.9 *unmelodious*, 444.13 *softhued*, 555.1 *unemphatic*, 628.12 *deteriorated*, 650.1 *fatigued*, 725.1 *property*, 743.2 *insolvent*, 788.4 *boring*

flat as a pancake 282.8 *horizontal*

flat-bed plotter 65.7 *peripheral*

flatboard 36.7 *windsurfing*

flatboat 74 Ships and Boats

flat broke 593.5 *necessitous*, 687.7 *unprosperous*, 743.2 *insolvent*

flat chest 274.7 *thinness*

flat-chested 274.1 *thin*

flatcoat retriever 37.6 *sporting dog*

flat contradiction 536.3 *rebuttal*

flat country 98.6 *lowland*

flat denial 536.3 *rebuttal*

flat fare 751.3 *fee*

flatfish 80 Fishes, 45.18 *sea fish*, 80.2 *fish*, 80.8 *food fish*, 282.3 *flat thing*

flatfoot 16.17 *police officer*, 718.3 *security officer*

flat-green bowls 18 Sporting Activities

flathead 80 Fishes

Flathead 94 Lakes

flatiron 282.4 *flattener*, 376.9 *smoother*

Flat Iron Building 43 Noted Buildings

flat knot 74 Knots

flat land 282.3 *flat thing*

flatly 110.20, 214.15 *regularly*, 214.17 *orderly*, 282.11 *horizontally*, 376.14, 381.11 *smoothly*, 412.10 *without taste*, 788.8 *boringly*

flatmate 180.11 *companion*, 255.3 *householder*, 724.3 *participant*

flatness 52.38 *surface*, 110.6 *regularity*, 127.5 *inferior state*, 214.4 *orderliness*, 262.1 *contraction*, 276.2 *lowland*, 282.1 *horizontality*, 376.7 *smoothness*, 381.5 *bluntness*, 412.1 *tastelessness*, 434.3 *musical dissonance*, 555.2 *lack of emphasis*, 788.1 *boredom*

flat on one's back 282.11 *horizontally*

flat out 239.6 *with vigour*, 282.10 *lying*, 329.14 *swiftly*, 608.9 *enough*, 650.1 *fatigued*

flat-out 329.1 *swift*

flat-out speed 329.8 *speed*

flat race 674.4 *race*

flat racing 32.7 *horseracing*

flat rate 751.3 *fee*

flat refusal 711.1 *refusal*

flat roll 68.10 *farm tool*

flat roof 43.6 *roof*, 293.7 *overhead covering*

flats 98.6, 276.2 *lowland*, 276.4 *low thing*, 278.4 *shallow thing*, 282.3 *flat thing*

flat screen 65.7 *peripheral*

flat-sharing 724.5 *jointly possessing*

flat shoes 295.19 *footwear*

flat spin 73.5 *flight*

flat surface 52.38 *surface*, 282.3 *flat thing*

flatten 362, 110.8 *make the same*, 214.10 *make regular*, 244.9 *demolish*, 244.11 *ruin*, 262.5 *make smaller*, 274.16 *make thin*, 276.9 *lower*, 282.7 *make horizontal*, 376.11 *smooth*, 381.10 *blunt*, 383.13 *smooth*, 682.10 *defeat heavily*

flatten down 376.11 *smooth*

flattened 282, 274.5 *thinned*, 276.5 *low*, 362.17 *lowered*, 376.2 *uniform*, 381.1 *blunt*

flattener 282, 376.9 *smoother*

flattening 244.2 *destroying*, 262.1 *contraction*, 276.1 *lowness*, 362.12 *downthrow*

flatten oneself 362.8 *sit*

flatten out 214.10 *make regular*, 312.10 *straighten*

flatter 853, 118.9 *imitate*, 228.9 *motivate*, 521.9 *talk nonsense*, 540.18 *be hypocritical*, 541.10 *boast*, 548.4 *misrepresent*, 657.5 *be cunning*, 771.15 *humour*, 808.9 *fawn*, 817.10 *be courteous*, 821.28 *win the love of*, 826.7 *show endearment for*, 851.14 *praise*

flattered 228.12 *motivated*, 541.12 *exaggerated*

flatterer 853, 167.6 *conformist*, 228.7 *motivator*, 499.3 *assenter*, 657.3 *cunning person*, 771.7 *person who humours*

flattering 853, 228.2 *inducement*, 521.12 *unmeant*, 540.27 *hypocritical*, 548.1 *misrepresentation*, 548.6 *misrepresented*, 578.11 *equivocating*, 657.4 *cunning*, 771.11 *humouring*, 808.7 *sycophantic*, 817.8 *good-mannered*, 821.6 *courtship*, 851.18 *approving*

flatteringly 853, 538.27 *pretentiously*

flatter oneself 805.29 *feel pride*, 809.15 *be vain*

flatter to deceive 853.9 *blarney*

flattery 586, 853, 228.5 *positive stimulus*, 521.3 *meaningless thing*, 521.5 *empty talk*, 538.9, 540.3 *hypocrisy*, 541.4 *bombast*, 548.1 *misrepresentation*, 657.1 *cunning*, 763.10 *pleasant thing*, 817.1 *courtesy*, 821.14 *communication of love*, 826.1 *endearment*, 851.3 *praise*

Flattery 853

flat thing 282

flatties 276.4 *low thing*, 295.19 *footwear*

flat-toned 434.9 *unmelodious*

flattop 679.24 *warship*

flat tyre 282.3 *flat thing*, 661.2 *obstacle*

flatulence 349.24, 388.5 *belch*, 425.4 *belch*, 555.2 *lack of emphasis*, 557.2 *affectation*, 624.8 *indigestion*

flatulency 349.24, 388.5 *belch*

flatulent 388, 349.31 *eructative*, 390.14 *aerial*, 553.3 *diffuse*, 555.1 *unemphatic*

flatulous 349.31 *eructative*

flat universe 53.4 *cosmological model*

flatuosity 349.24, 388.5 *belch*

flatus 349.24, 388.5 *belch*, 419.2 *something that makes an unpleasant smell*, 624.8 *indigestion*

flatware 282.3 *flat thing*

flatways 282.11 *horizontally*

flatwise 282.11 *horizontally*

flatworm 81 Worms, 81.6 *worm*

Flaubert 48 Writers

flaunt 475.15 *demonstrate*, 526.1 *display*

flaunted 526.13 *displayed*

flaunter 526.12 *displayer*

flaunting 365.4 *rock*, 444.12 *gaudy*, 526.15 *open*, 805.21 *ostentatious*, 811.10 *exhibitionism*, 877.13 *unchaste*

flaunt oneself 811.29 *show off*

flavescent 452.2 *yellowish*

flavone 58.18 *pigment*

flavonoid 58.18 *pigment*

flavonol 58.18 *pigment*

flavoprotein 58.9 *protein*, 58.12 *coenzyme*

flavour 411, 45.55 *cook*, 130.6 *add*, 133.4 *admixture*, 165.3 *characteristic*, 411.10 *make taste*, 413.12 *season*

flavour enhancer 350.11 *food content*, 411.4 *flavour*

flavourful 411.7 *tasty*, 413.9 *piquant*, 763.4 *tasty*

flavouring 130.3 *additional item*, 411.4 *flavour*, 413.2 *seasoning*

flavourless 412.5 *tasteless*, 542.17 *insipid*

flavourlessness 542.8 *insipidness*

flaw 265.2 *crack*, 322.1 *opening*, 618.8 *inferiority*, 620.7 *defect*, 633.7 *vulnerability*, 661.2 *obstacle*, 793.1 *spot*, 793.7 *blemish*, 864.3 *venial sin*

flawed 145.4 *incomplete*, 474.7 *sophistic*, 476.6 *refutable*, 504.15 *erroneous*, 618.2 *inferior*, 620.1 *imperfect*, 793.4 *blemished*

flawed argument 474.2 *sophism*

flawed logic 504.4 *faulty reasoning*

flawless 142.7 *uncut*, 537.21 *accurate*, 558.3 *elegant*, 617.1 *worthy*, 619.1 *perfect*, 861.2 *best*

flawlessly 619.7 *perfectly*

flawlessness 134.1 *purity*, 537.8 *accuracy*, 617.6 *worth*, 619.3 *perfection*, 861.9 *the best*

flawless performance 619.3 *perfection*

flax 84 Flowers and Flowering Plants, 68.12 *crop*

flaxen 439.21 *light*

flaxen-haired 446.3 *white-haired*, 452.3 *yellow-haired*

flaxseed 83.9 *seed*

flay 136.10 *set apart*, 294.13 *remove*, 296.15 *make nude*, 879.3 *hit*, 879.5 *execute*

flay alive 879.5 *execute*

flayed 294.9 *shed*

flayer 294.7 *shedder*

F-layer 534.15 *transmitted wave*

flaying 294.5 *shedding*

flaying alive 879.13 *capital punishment*

flay one's back 879.3 *hit*

flea 82 Insects, 82.3 *pest*, 622.4 *dirt*

fleabag 256.8 *shelter*

fleabane 84 Flowers and Flowering Plants

flea beetle 82 Insects, 69.12 *pests and diseases*

fleabite 612.8 *trifle*

flea-bitten 82.12 *verminous*, 622.8 *unclean*, 626.5 *unhygienic*, 628.13 *dilapidated*

flea circus 51.5 *show*

flea-flicker 19.9 *play*

flea in one's ear 564.8 *speech*, 852.7 *blame*

fleam 380.8 *sharp-pointed thing*

flea market 740.1 *market*, 754.7 *discounter*

fleapit 51.14 *theatre*, 628.9 *dilapidation*

fleawort 84 Flowers and Flowering Plants

flèche 43.10 *church architecture*, 275.6 *tall thing*, 380.8 *sharp-pointed thing*

fléchette 680.6 *historical missile weapon*

fleck 260.3 *little piece*, 456.4 *maculation*

Flecker 48 Poets

flection 320.1 *fold*

flectional 320.5 *folded*

fled 254.9 *away*

fledge 594.7 *develop*

fledged 594.20 *developed*

fledgling 78.12 *young bird*, 156.15 *baby*, 201.8 *new arrival*, 206.4 *young animal*, 206.11 *young*

flee 254.18 *abscond*, 345.4 *hurry off*, 458.2 *depart*, 591.8 *run away*, 638.5 *escape*, 779.4 *be a coward*

fleece 67 Natural Fabrics, 131.4 *take off*, 136.10 *set apart*, 293.14 *animal covering*, 296.15 *make nude*, 374.11 *soft thing*, 539.30 *be fraudulent*, 734.10 *take away*, 736.16 *act dishonest*, 743.14 *impoverish*, 753.10 *overcharge*

fleeced 743.2 *insolvent*

fleeciness 376.7 *smoothness*

fleecy 374.3, 376.1 *smooth*

fleecy cloud 55.20 *cloud appearance*

flee one's homeland 104.14 *be foreign*

fleer 638.3 *escaper*

fleet 17.4 *military organization*, 74.11 *nautical*, 98.9 *inlet*, 140.3 *assembly*, 161.14 *force*, 181.4 *throng*, 329.1 *swift*, 648.3 *hasty*, 679.22 *navy*, 679.23 *naval unit*

fleet admiral 692.6 *person in command*, 696.7 *military leader*

Fleet Admiral 17 US Military Ranks, 74.7 *nautical person*

Fleet Air Arm 679.23 *naval unit*, 679.29 *air force*

fleet arm 679.22 *navy*

fleet auxiliary vessels 679.24 *warship*

fleet blockade 676.8 *warfare*

fleet chief petty officer 679.27 *naval man*

fleeting 102.8 *unreal*, 189.6 *transient*, 324.16 *moving*, 458.6 *disappearing*, 648.3 *hasty*

fleetingly 458, 189.8 *transiently*

fleetly 329.14 *swiftly*

fleetness 329.8 *speed*

fleet of foot 329.1 *swift*

Fleet Street 532.3 *journalism*

Fleming 48 Writers, **52** Scientists

Flemings 1 Peoples

Flemish 5 Languages and Groups of Languages

Flemish bond 63.26 *masonry*

flesh 45.20 *meat*, 86.3 *fruit structure*, 367.4 *matter*, 400.2 *human nature*

flesh and blood 367.4 *matter*, 367.5 *object*, 400.7 *person*

flesh-coloured 450.1 *red*

flesh-eater 76.4 *type of animal*, 350.18 *eater*

flesh-eating 77.28 *carnivorous*, 350.5 *eating habit*, 350.26 *eating*

flesh-eating mammal 77
fleshiness 259.5 *fatness*, 315.2 *round body*, 393.4 *pulpiness*
fleshings 295.20 *legwear*
fleshliness 877.3 *sexual immorality*
fleshly 367.7 *material*, 400.12 *human*, 877.14 *lecherous*
flesh one's sword 676.13 *be at war*
flesh-pink 450.1 *red*
fleshpots 350.9 *plenty*, 405.4 *pleasurable things* 686.1 *prosperity*, 742.7 *opulence*
flesh show 51.5 *show*
fleshy 86.9 *of a fruit*, 259.16 *fat*, 315.10 *well-rounded*, 393.19 *juicy*, 395.11 *oily*
Fletcher 48 Dramatists
fleur-de-lis 647.8 *heraldic device*
fleur pastry 45.37 *pastry*
fleury 544.13 *heraldic*
flex 64.27 *wire*, 235.7 *electrical power*, 377.1 *elasticity*, 377.8 *be elastic*, 410.4 *electricity*
flexatone 49 Musical Instruments
flex defence 19.10 *defence*
flexed 320.5 *folded*, 377.6 *elastic*
flexibility 167.3 *pliancy*, 224.1 *changeableness*, 374.8 *softness*, 377.1 *elasticity*, 377.2 *adaptability*, 486.2 *possibleness*, 491.16 *capriciousness*, 655.1 *skill*, 660.3 *wieldiness*
flexible 167.11 *conformable*, 374.2 *pliant*, 377.6 *elastic*, 377.7 *adaptive*, 486.5 *possible*, 491.8 *capricious*, 576.4 *unsteady*, 655.6 *skilful*, 660.12 *wieldy*
flexibly 167.16 *adaptably*, 374.17 *softly*, 377.11 *elastically*, 377.12 *adaptably*, 491.27 *capriciously*
flexile 374.2 *pliant*
flexing 377.6 *elastic*
flexitime 13.8 *industrial relations*, 15.2 *industrial negotiations*
flex one's muscles 378.10 *be tough*, 594.8 *prepare oneself*
flexuous 320.5 *folded*
flexuously 320.11 *doubly*
flexure 320.1 *fold*, 335.14 *deviating course*
flick 31.8 *hockey*, 31.9 *play hockey*, 38.4 *play soccer*, 330.6 *tap*, 330.11 *blow*, 339.3 *jerk*, 339.13 *pull at*, 366.26 *flicker*, 407.3 *press*, 407.11 *touch*
flicked 31.8 *hockey*
flicker 78 Birds, **366, 366**, 215.1 *irregularity*, 215.6 *be irregular*, 224.11 *be changeable*, 365.9 *vibrate*, 439.2 *quality of light*, 439.25 *light up*
flickering 366, 215.1 *irregularity*, 215.4 *irregular*, 224.13 *changeable*, 365.2 *vibration*, 365.14 *vibrating*, 439.2 *quality of light*, 439.15 *lucent*
flickeringly 215.8 *irregularly*
flickery 366.20 *flickering*, 439.15 *lucent*
flicking 31.1, 31.8 *hockey*
flick knife 380.10 *knife*, 680.8 *sharp weapon*
flick stroke 31.1 *hockey*
flier 76.6 *flying animal*, 532.9 *advertisement*
flies 161 Collective Names by Animal, 51.15 *stage*
flight 73, 17.4 *military organization*, 27.8 *delivery*, 27.18 *bowl*, 42.6 *darts*, 61.19 *defence mechanism*, 73.1 *aviation*, 78.13 *assemblage of birds*, 181.4 *throng*, 324.2 *momentum*, 345.7 *departure*, 361.2 *send up*, 458.4 *disappearance*, 591.16 *desertion*, 638.1 *escape*, 679.30 *air force unit*
flight attendant 697.3 *attendant*
flight bag 258.9 *baggage*
flight control 73

flight deck 73 Aircraft Parts, **74** Parts of a Ship
flight engineer 73.3 *aircraft personnel*
flight feather 78.17 *plumage*
flight formation 73.5 *flight*
flightiness 224.2 *irresolution*, 468.2 *impetuosity*, 579.2 *caprice*
flight lane 327.2 *route*, 327.13 *flight path*
flightless 78.23 *avian*
flightless bird 78
flight level 73.5 *flight*
Flight Lieutenant 17 British Military Ranks
flight-lieutenant 679.32 *airman*
flight line 73.4 *airport*
flight of fancy 102.2 *illusion*, 519.4 *ideality*, 541.5 *tall story*
flight of stairs 327.2 *route*, 359.7 *means of ascent*
flight path 327
flight reaction 61.10 *neurosis*
flight recorder 73 Aircraft Parts, 545.10 *recording instrument*
flight sergeant 679.32 *airman*
flight sergeant aircrew 679.32 *airman*
flight strip 327.13 *flight path*
flight test 479.2 *rehearsal*
flight-test 479.12 *rehearse*
flighty 224.14 *irresolute*, 468.10 *careless*, 576.2 *changeable*, 579.1 *capricious*
flimflam 515.8 *be dishonest*, 521.5 *empty talk*, 538.4 *lie*, 538.8 *pretence*, 538.25 *be dishonest*, 539.7 *tricking*, 539.10 *fraud*, 539.28 *trick*, 539.30 *be fraudulent*, 540.13 *nonsense*, 540.29 *deceitful*, 657.2 *stratagem*, 657.5 *be cunning*, 736.7 *dishonesty*
flimflam man 539.17 *cheat*, 657.3 *cunning person*, 736.11 *dishonest person*
flimflammed 539.36 *deceived*
flimflammer 539.17 *cheat*
flimflammery 539.7 *tricking*
flimflamming 538.15 *lying*, 538.19 *dishonest*
flimsily 370.11 *lightly*, 374.17 *softly*, 379.5 *fragilely*, 442.13 *transparently*
flimsiness 274.11 *fineness*, 370.5 *lightness*, 372.3 *sparseness*, 379.2 *brittleness*, 442.6 *translucency*
flimsy 102.8 *unreal*, 238.13 *insufficient*, 274.4 *fine*, 278.2 *superficial*, 370.2 *insubstantial*, 372.1 *sparse*, 374.1 *soft*, 379.1 *brittle*, 442.2 *translucent*, 612.4 *trivial*
flimsy item 238.5 *weak thing*
flinch 42 Card Games, 331.2 *respond*, 331.6 *response*, 406.9 *feel pain*, 573.7 *refuse*, 591.4 *shy*, 777.11 *be afraid*
flinch at 711.5 *refuse*
flinching 591.12 *shyness*, 591.18 *avoiding*
Flinders 95 Mountains
fling 46.4 *historic dancing*, 162.17 *sow*, 330.4, 338.5 *throw*, 338.23 *throw*, 362.6 *throw down*, 479.1 *experiment*
fling down 362.6 *throw down*
flinger 338.14 *thrower*
flinging 338.3 *throwing*
fling money around 748.1 *expend*
fling off 345.1 *depart*, 349.10 *exterminate*
fling to the four winds 244.12 *consume*
fling wide the gates 348.9 *welcome*, 812.18 *salute*
flint 54 Common Rocks, 44.2 *raw material*, 373.7 *hard substance*, 410.2 *lighter*
Flint 93 Cities, **93** Cities
flint axe 3.11 *relic*
flint chisel 603.3 *prehistoric tool*
flint glass 442.9 *glass*
flint-hearted 832.12 *callous*
flintiness 836.1 *pitilessness*
flintlock 680.10 *historical gun*

flint pebbles 44.2 *raw material*
flint tool 3.11 *relic*
flinty 54.57 *chalky*, 373.1 *hard*, 832.12 *callous*, 836.4 *pitiless*
flip 45.55 *cook*, 330.6 *tap*, 330.13 *blow*, 338.5, 338.23 *throw*, 339.3 *jerk*, 339.13 *pull at*, 565.6 *effusive*, 807.13 *insolent*
flip-flop 64.13 *circuit*, 65.17 *computing term*, 216.2 *change of mind*, 216.7 *be changed*, 216.11 *changeable*, 579.3 *whim*, 579.5 *be capricious*
flip-flops 295.19 *footwear*
flip of the coin 589.3 *equal chance*
flip one's lid 828.12 *become angry*
flippancy 508.1 *folly*, 612.7 *triviality*, 771.1 *humorousness*, 780.1 *rashness*, 807.10 *impudence*
flippant 508.5 *foolish*, 771.10 *humorous*, 780.4 *rash*, 807.21 *impudent*
flippantly 807.30 *insolently*
flipper 27.8 *delivery*, 39.1 *swimming*, 51.17 *stage set*, 143.4 *component*, 407.7 *sense organ*
flippers 39.8 *swimwear*
flip the switch 230.8 *activate*
flirt 339.3 *jerk*, 339.13 *pull at*, 467.14 *be solicitous*, 578.9 *equivocator*, 579.4 *capricious person*, 579.5 *be capricious*, 821.9 *lover*, 821.26 *court*, 826.5 *courting person*, 826.8 *court*
flirtation 579.3 *whim*, 821.6 *courtship*, 821.8, 821.8 *love affair*, 826.2 *courtship*
flirtatious 579.1 *capricious*, 821.20 *amorous*, 826.9 *endearing*
flirtatiously 821.30 *lovingly*, 826.10 *endearingly*
flirtatiousness 579.2 *caprice*, 821.4 *lovability*, 821.6, 826.2 *courtship*
flirting 821.6 *courtship*
flirty 821.20 *amorous*, 826.9 *endearing*
flit 189.4 *be transient*, 224.12 *be irresolute*, 329.4 *be swift*, 345.3 *quit*, 345.7 *departure*, 366.12 *flicker*, 591.9 *play truant*, 591.16 *desertion*, 638.1 *escape*
flitch 45.30 *bacon*, 85.3 *timber*
flitched 47.16 *joined*
flitched joint 47.10 *carpenter's term*
flitter 224.12 *be irresolute*
float 71 Motor Vehicles, 14.5 *invest*, 20.3 *fishing tackle*, 39.1 *swimming*, 39.3 *survival swimming*, 39.9 *swim*, 90.3 *plant body*, 156.23 *inaugurate*, 224.12 *be irresolute*, 338.33 *start*, 359.20 *hover*, 366.12 *wave*, 370.7 *light thing*, 370.9 *be light*, 376.12 *go smoothly*, 602.6 *find means*, 737.1 *trade*
floatability 370.5 *lightness*
floatable 370.2 *insubstantial*
float a loan 732.5 *lend*, 733.7 *borrow*
floated 39.11 *swimming*
floater 36.7, 36.13 *windsurfing*, 338.10 *ball*
float fishing 20.1 *angling*
floating 14.6 *financial*, 20.8 *angling*, 39.1, 39.11 *swimming*, 74.11 *nautical*, 108.6 *unrelated*, 224.13 *changeable*, 359.23 *rising*, 370.2 *insubstantial*, 370.5 *lightness*, 698.9 *free*, 741.22 *monetary*, 875.7 *drugged*
floating bridge 327.9 *bridge*
floating currency 14.1 *finance*
floating debt 745.1 *debt*
floating device 39.3 *survival swimming*
floating diver 20.2 *artificial fly*
floating exchange rate 741.7 *finance*
floating island 45.35 *dessert*, 98.2 *island*

floating plug 20.2 *artificial fly*
floating-point notation 52.8 *number system*
floating point operation 65.17 *computing term*
floating rib 382 Bones
floating thing 370.7 *light thing*
floating up 359.1 *ascent*
floating vote 576.11 *vacillation*
floating voter 576.15 *indecisive person*, 698.7 *free person*
floating world 50 Non-Western Art
float in the air 359.20 *hover*
float on the air 424.5 *sound faint*
float rod 20.3 *fishing tackle*
float tackle 20.3 *fishing tackle*
float to the surface 370.9 *be light*
float up 359.17 *spring up*
floaty 370.2 *insubstantial*
floccinaucinihilipilification 172.3 *nothingness*
floccose 266.9 *platelike*
flocculate 57.25 *solidify*
flocculence 375.4 *smoothness*
flocculent 266.9 *platelike*, 374.3 *smooth*, 375.3 *barbed*, 384.16 *powdery*
flocculent colloidal 57.32 *solid*
flocculently 266.12 *in layers*
flocculent precipitate 57.3 *phase*
floccus 266.4 *slice*
flock 161 Collective Names for Birds and Animals, **161**, 10.17 *worshipper*, 77.21 *assemblage of mammals*, 78.13 *assemblage of birds*, 181.4 *throng*, 181.11 *crowd*, 266.4 *slice*
flock together 161.39 *come together*
floe 54.39 *iceberg*
flog 330.5 *beat*, 406.11 *inflict pain*, 648.1 *hasten*, 727.11 *dispose of property*, 739.1 *sell*, 879.3 *hit*
flog a dead horse 610.5 *be superfluous*, 614.9 *waste effort*
flogger 879.17 *punisher*
flogging 330.12 *collision*, 330.17 *impelling*, 406.1 *pain*, 879.12 *corporal punishment*
flood 161, 51.18 *stage lighting*, 55.26 *raininess*, 96.6 *river flow*, 96.7 *flow*, 97.2 *tide*, 161.40, 181.11 *crowd*, 241.3 *instance of violence*, 241.5 *violent weather*, 244.7 *agent of destruction*, 275.8 *high thing*, 293.31 *hide*, 336.11 *course*, 346.2 *influx*, 347.2 *outflow*, 347.11 *run out*, 354.4 *immerse*, 357.1 *overstep*, 357.6 *overstepping*, 387.25 *flow*, 389.2 *water*, 608.8 *plenty*, 610.1 *excess*, 610.4 *be excessive*
flood-control system 63.24 *water system*
flooded 96, 389, 357.11 *overrun*, 391.11 *marshy*
floodgate 63.24 *water system*, 347.7 *outlet*
flood in 346
flooding 357.6 *overstepping*, 357.11 *overrun*, 389.9 *soaking*, 610.6 *excessive*
flooding over 293.1 *covering*
floodlight 51.18 *stage lighting*, 66.15 *lighting*, 439.6 *electric light*, 439.24 *light*
floodlit 327.15 *accessible*, 439.18 *lit*
flood of words 551.1 *obscurity*
flood out 347.11 *run out*
flood plain 54.7 *landform*, 98.6 *lowland*, 391.8 *marsh*
flood proof 392.10 *waterproof*
floods 777 Phobias by Topic
flood the market 610.4 *be excessive*, 754.13 *make cheap*
flood the tanks 74.10 *sail*
flood tide 97.2 *tide*, 128.3 *increasing thing*, 275.8 *high thing*
floor 120.2 *certain amount*, 127.5 *inferior state*, 244.11 *ruin*, 258.4 *rack*, 266.2 *level*, 276.4 *low thing*, 280.1 *base*, 282.3 *flat thing*, 362.3 *bring*

down, 476.8 *refute*, 514.11
amaze, 751.3 *fee*
floorboards 293.9 *floor covering*
floor covering 293, 280.1 *base*
floorer 476.1 *refutation*
floor exercises 18 Sporting Activities, **30**
flooring 63.21 *bridge*, 280.1 *base*
floor leader 653.14 *leader*
floor plan 592.5 *map*
floor polish 376.10 *polish*, 621.9 *cleaning agent*
floor polisher 376.9 *smoother*
floors 36.8 *punting*
floor show 51.5 *show*
floor tile 44.9 *industrial ceramics*
flop 21.2 *field events*, 51.11 *theatrical performance*, 139.6 *come unstuck*, 238.6 *be weak*, 360.4 *fall*, 360.10 *droop*, 374.13 *soften*, 581.8 *rejected thing*, 628.1 *deteriorate*, 656.9 *bungling*, 683.4 *unsuccessful thing*, 683.5 *failing person*, 683.6 *fail*, 722.6 *loser*, 739.2 *be sold*
flop down 360.10 *droop*
flophouse 256.8 *shelter*
floppiness 139.1 *nonadhesion*, 238.1 *weakness*, 374.8 *softness*
flopping 139.8 *nonadhesive*, 360.18 *falling*
floppy 65.7 *peripheral*, 139.8 *nonadhesive*, 238.8 *weak*, 374.1 *soft*
floppy disk 56.64 *magnetic recording*, 65.7 *peripheral*, 364.6 *rotator*
flops 65.17 *computing term*
flora 83.1 *plants*, 83.11 *herbarium*
flora and fauna 59.2 *living world*
floral 84, 69.16 *horticultural*, 418.4 *fragrant*
floral arrangement 557.1 *ornament*
floral charge 544.8 *heraldic device*
floral dance 84.9 *figurative usage*
floral diagram 84.3 *flower part*
floral envelope 84.3 *flower part*
floral formula 84.3 *flower part*
Floralia 10.16 *religious festival*
floral leaf 83.6 *leaf*
florally 84, 69.20 *horticulturally*, 418.7 *fragrantly*
floral marquetry 47.9 *decorative woodwork*
floreate 84.10 *floral*
Florence 93 Cities
Florence Cathedral 43 Noted Buildings
Florence Nightingale 60.16 *nurse*
Florentine school 50 Western Art Styles and Movements
Flores 98 Islands
florescence 84.5 *flowering*, 227.3 *growth*, 245.3 *propagation*, 594.13 *development*
florescent 69.16 *horticultural*, 84.11 *flowering*, 594.20 *developed*
floret 84.1 *flower*
floriate 84.10 *floral*
floricultural 69.16 *horticultural*
floriculture 69.1 *horticulture*, 84.7 *flower culture*
floriculturist 69.13 *horticulturist*, 84.7 *flower culture*
florid 84.10 *floral*, 444.11 *colourful*, 450.2 *red-faced*, 456.6 *variegated*, 557.4 *ornate*, 623.1 *healthy*
Florida 92 American States
floridly 84.14 *florally*, 450.10 *ruddily*, 456.12 *variedly*, 557.6 *ornately*
floridness 450.5 *redness*, 557.1 *ornament*
florid style 558.1 *elegance*
florilegium 83.11 *herbarium*
florin 741.10 *former British money*
florist 84.7 *flower culture*, 739.13 *retailer*
floristic 84.10 *floral*
floristically 84.14 *florally*
floristics 84.7 *flower culture*
flossiness 374.9 *smoothness*

flossy 374.3 *smooth*
flotation 156.9 *premiere*, 594.9 *preparation*
flotel 74 Ships and Boats
flotilla 17.4 *military organization*, 140.3 *assembly*, 679.23 *naval unit*
flotilla leader 679.24 *warship*
flotsam 326.10 *transferred thing*, 727.3 *disposable things*, 816.7 *outsider*
flotsam and jetsam 143.8 *bits and pieces*, 162.8 *driftwood*, 727.3 *disposable things*, 816.7 *outsider*
flounce 300.2 *edging*, 320.2, 320.8 *pleat*, 339.3 *jerk*, 339.13 *pull at*, 366.11 *stagger*, 366.25 *pitch*, 792.5 *decorative articles*
flounce off 345.1 *depart*
flounder 80 Fishes, 20.4 *American game fish*, 45.18 *sea fish*, 282.3 *flat thing*, 364.10 *swirl*, 365.12 *wave*, 366.11 *stagger*, 366.25 *pitch*, 656.7 *be clumsy*, 659.19 *have difficulty*, 659.20 *be in difficulty*
flounderer 722.6 *loser*
floundering 722.18 *at a loss*
flour 45.7 *basic ingredient*, 162.18 *sprinkle*, 384.8 *meal*, 384.22 *powder*, 384.25 *grind*, 393.11 *thickener*, 446.9 *white thing*
flour dredger 45.6 *kitchen equipment*
flouriness 384.1 *powderiness*
flourish 811, 49.22 *phrase*, 83.21 *vegetate*, 84.13 *flower*, 89.12 *mushroom*, 106.14 *be comfortable*, 128.4 *increase*, 246.6 *be fertile*, 261.6 *become bigger*, 365.12 *wave*, 366.22 *agitate*, 423.1 *loudness*, 427.2 *ringing*, 475.15 *demonstrate*, 526.1 *display*, 543.6 *word*, 557.1 *ornament*, 558.1 *elegance*, 623.5 *be healthy*, 682.6 *be successful*, 686.5 *be prosperous*, 792.2 *pattern*, 811.12 *magniloquence*, 861.21 *do well*
flourished 526.13 *displayed*
flourishing 83.13 *plantlike*, 84.11 *flowering*, 239.4 *vigorous*, 246.5 *fertile*, 261.1 *growth*, 261.8 *growing*, 365.4 *rock*, 453.4 *fresh*, 623.1 *healthy*, 682.13 *successful*, 686.8 *prosperous*
floury 384.17 *mealy*
flout 668.5 *defy*, 720.9 *disregard orders*
flout authority 693.15 *be disobedient*, 720.9 *disregard orders*
flout etiquette 818.7 *be discourteous*
flouting 850.15 *taunting*
flow 96, 387, 387, 54.63 *ebb*, 56.8 *time*, 97.2 *tide*, 155.25 *result*, 159.7 *stability*, 161.40 *crowd*, 185.15 *pass*, 195.1 *succession*, 219.1 *continuity*, 219.3 *continue*, 324.2 *momentum*, 324.13 *be in motion*, 336.6 *march on*, 353.1 *excretion*, 424.5 *sound faint*, 553.1 *diffuseness*, 553.5 *be diffuse*, 558.1 *elegance*, 608.5 *about*, 610.4 *be excessive*, 642.12 *be active*, 660.19 *go easily*
flowage 96.6 *river flow*
flow back 96.7 *flow*, 337.3 *reverse*
flow between 136.14 *come between*
flow by 185.15 *pass*
flow chart 152.8 *chart*, 592.5 *map*
flow down 360.13 *drip*
flower 84, 84, 69.9 *garden plant*, 83.2 *plant*, 83.21 *vegetate*, 85.19 *grow*, 103.3 *quintessence*, 128.4 *increase*, 206.18 *grow*, 207.18 *mature*, 227.3 *growth*, 227.8 *grow*, 243.7 *produce*, 245.11 *have young*, 261.6 *become bigger*, 418.2 *fragrant thing*, 617.7 *elite*, 682.6 *be suc-*

cessful, 686.5 *be prosperous*, 721.10 *augment*, 861.9 *the best*
flowerage 84.5 *flowering*
flower arrangement 84.1 *flower*, 152.2 *array*, 557.1 *ornament*
flower arranging 42 Hobbies and Pastimes
flower basket 258.7 *basket*
flowerbed 69.3 *ornamental garden*
flower bud 83.8 *bud*
flower child 84.9 *figurative usage*, 168.7 *nonconformist*
flower cluster 84.4 *flower head*
flower culture 84
flowered 84.10 *floral*
flowerer 84.2 *flowering plant*
floweret 84.1 *flower*
flower garden 69.2 *garden*, 69.3 *ornamental garden*, 418.2 *fragrant thing*
flower girl 84.7 *flower culture*, 823.7 *bridal party*
flower grower 69.13 *horticulturist*, 84.7 *flower culture*
flower growing 69.1 *horticulture*, 84.7 *flower culture*
flower head 84, 143.6 *branch*
floweriness 557.1 *ornament*
flowering 84, 84, 83.16 *taxonomic*, 206.13 *maturing*, 227.11 *growing*, 245.3 *propagation*, 261.1 *growth*, 261.8 *growing*, 594.13 *development*, 594.20 *developed*
flowering ash 85 Trees and Shrubs
flowering currant 84 Flowers and Flowering Plants
flowering plant 84, 83.3 *seed plant*
flowering quince 84 Flowers and Flowering Plants
flower-like 84.10 *floral*
flower market 740.1 *market*
flower painter 50.16 *artist*
flower painting 50.10 *art subject*
flower part 84
flowerpecker 78 Birds
flowerpot 69.4 *nursery*
flower power 84.9 *figurative usage*
flower pressing 42 Hobbies and Pastimes
flower product 84
flowers 777 Phobias by Topic, 84.1 *flower*, 384.5 *powder*, 399.4 *funeral objects*, 826.3 *love token*
Flowers 84
flower seller 84.7 *flower culture*
flower selling 84.7 *flower culture*
flowers of speech 557.1 *ornament*
flowers of sulphur 384.5 *powder*
flower stalk 83.5 *stem*
flowery 69.16 *horticultural*, 84.10 *floral*, 203.10 *spring*, 418.4 *fragrant*, 557.4 *ornate*, 702.3 *prison cell*
flowery speaker 557.3 *phrasemonger*
flowery speech 564.2 *power of speech*
flowery writer 557.3 *phrasemonger*
flow from 227.7 *follow from*
flow in 96.7 *flow*, 97.10 *billow*, 346.12 *flood in*
flowing 387, 96.6 *river flow*, 96.10 *fluvial*, 219.5 *continual*, 224.13 *changeable*, 324.16 *moving*, 553.3 *diffuse*, 610.6 *excessive*
flowing bowl 874.13 *drink*
flowing on 336.18 *ongoing*
flowing river 96.1 *river*
flowing together 96.6 *river flow*
flowing with milk and honey 742.4 *lush*
flowmeter 387, 56.88 *barometer*
flown 254.9 *away*
flow of electricity 56.51 *electric current*
flow of ideas 461.5 *creative thought*
flow of time 188.2 *time*

flow of traffic 324.2 *momentum*
flow of words 565.1 *talkativeness*
flow on 336.6 *march on*, 389.29 *water*
flow onwards 185.15 *pass*
flow out 96.7 *flow*, 97.10 *billow*, 347.11 *run out*, 359.17 *spring up*, 607.1 *waste*, 610.4 *be excessive*, 638.7 *leak*
flow over 96.7 *flow*
flow sheet 152.8 *chart*
flow together 96.7 *flow*, 291.9 *centre*
flow with milk and honey 608.5 *about*
flu 624.6 *infection*, 624.9 *respiratory disease*
flub 656.9 *bungling*
flubbed 620.1 *imperfect*
fluctuant 365.13 *oscillating*
fluctuate 123.5 *be unequal*, 215.6 *be irregular*, 216.7 *be changed*, 224.11 *be changeable*, 365.8 *oscillate*, 365.10 *vacillate*, 491.21 *change*, 576.5 *vacillate*, 579.5 *be capricious*
fluctuating 215.4 *irregular*, 216.11, 224.13 *changeable*, 324.17 *directional*, 365.13 *oscillating*, 491.8 *capricious*
fluctuating currency 741.1 *money*
fluctuation 215.1 *irregularity*, 216.1 *change*, 224.1 *changeableness*, 324.5 *circuition*, 365.1 *oscillation*, 491.16 *capriciousness*, 576.12 *inconstancy*, 737.5 *commercial trade*
fludrocortisone 62 Medication
flue 322.7 *passageway*, 408.6 *fire*
fluency 30.1 *gymnastics*, 96.6 *river flow*, 387.6 *flow*, 558.1 *elegance*, 564.2 *power of speech*, 565.1 *talkativeness*, 660.1 *easiness*
fluent 96.10 *fluvial*, 324.16 *moving*, 387.15 *flowing*, 553.3 *diffuse*, 558.3 *elegant*, 564.19 *speaking*, 565.5 *talkative*
fluently 96, 387.26 *fluidly*, 549.10 *stylistically*, 558.5 *elegantly*, 565.10 *talkatively*
fluent tongue 565.1 *talkativeness*
flufenamic acid 62 Medication
fluff 51.34 *underact*, 370.7 *light thing*, 370.10 *lighten*, 374.11 *soft thing*, 374.13 *soften*, 383.2 *grain*, 384.5 *powder*, 390.10 *air bubble*, 434.10 *lack harmony*, 504.10 *blunder*, 656.7 *be clumsy*, 656.9 *bungling*
fluff one's lines 512.14 *be forgetful*, 656.5 *be unskilful*
fluff up 374.13 *soften*
fluffily 370.11 *lightly*, 374.17 *softly*
fluffiness 370.5 *lightness*, 374.9 *smoothness*, 383.2 *grain*
fluffy 383, 370.2 *insubstantial*, 374.3 *smooth*
flugelhorn 49 Musical Instruments
fluid 387, 387, 139.8 *nonadhesive*, 224.13 *changeable*, 374.1 *soft*, 389.1 *water*, 389.21 *watery*, 491.8 *capricious*, 558.3 *elegant*
Fluid 387
fluidal 387.14 *fluid*
fluid dram 75 General Units
fluid drive 71 Motor Vehicle Parts
fluid extract 387.1 *fluid*
fluidic 387.14 *fluid*
fluidification 387
fluidify 387.22 *make fluid*
fluid intake 348.4 *intake*, 351.1 *drinking*
fluidity 387, 139.1 *nonadhesion*, 224.1 *changeableness*, 491.16 *capriciousness*, 558.1 *elegance*
fluidize 387.22 *make fluid*, 388.26 *aerate*
fluidly 387, 139.10 *noncohesively*, 224.15 *changeably*, 374.17 *softly*, 389.35 *wetly*, 491.27 *capriciously*

fluid mechanics 387, 56.2 *classical physics*
fluidmeter 387.12 *flowmeter*
fluidness 387.5 *fluidity*
fluid ounce 75 General Units
fluke 80 Fishes, **81** Worms, 81.6 *worm,* 81.10 *parasite,* 229.3 *coincidence,* 380.8 *sharppointed thing,* 489.5 *unexpectedness,* 589.2 *luck*
fluky 81.20 *wormlike,* 229.6 *motiveless,* 489.3 *unexpected,* 589.8 *chance*
flume 265.3 *gulf,* 347.7 *outlet*
flummery 521.5 *empty talk,* 538.8 *pretence*
flummox 460.10 *bemuse,* 491.20 *make uncertain,* 523.7 *be unintelligible*
flummoxed 523.6 *confused*
flunk 683.5 *fail*
flunked 683.10 *failed*
flunkey 701.3 *subordinate*
flunky 127.6 *inferior,* 646.1 *worker,* 697.1 *servant*
fluorapatite 54 Minerals
fluoresce 439.25 *light up*
fluorescence 56.24 *light emission,* 439.1 *light*
fluorescent 439.15 *lucent,* 439.16 *bright*
fluorescent clothing 437.7 *that which makes visible*
fluorescent lamp 64.20 *electron tube*
fluorescent light 56.25 *light source,* 439.6 *electric light*
fluorescent paint 437.7 *that which makes visible*
fluorescent tube 44.9 *industrial ceramics,* 56.25 *light source*
fluoric 57.34 *elemental*
fluoridate 57.26 *react,* 632.9 *protect*
fluoridated 57.34 *elemental*
fluoridation 60.6 *health care*
fluoride 57 Types of Compounds, 630.3 *prophylactic*
fluorinate 632.9 *protect*
fluorinated 57.34 *elemental*
fluorination 57 Types of Chemical Reaction
fluorine 57 Chemical Elements
fluormate 57.26 *react*
fluorocarbon 57 Types of Compounds, 604.1 *materials*
fluorometer 268.8 *meter*
fluorometric 268.16 *micrometric*
fluorometry 268.2 *micrometry*
fluorspar 54 Minerals
fluoxuridine 62 Medication
fluphenazine 62 Medication
flurazepam 62 Medication
flurried 366.15 *agitated*
flurry 55.25 *rain,* 55.30 *snow,* 329.8 *speed,* 366.4 *fuss,* 409.5 *ice,* 642.3 *nimbleness,* 648.4 *haste*
flush 37.7 *shoot,* 41.12 *ski,* 42.3 *card game terms,* 96.6 *river flow,* 96.7 *flow,* 112.5 *uniform,* 122.6 *equal,* 134.10 *purify,* 144.8 *full,* 282.7 *make horizontal,* 282.8 *horizontal,* 282.11 *horizontally,* 332.9 *directly,* 376.1 *smooth,* 408.1 *heat,* 408.16 *feel hot,* 444.9 *complexion,* 444.16 *make up,* 450.5 *redness,* 450.9 *redden,* 590.11 *hunt,* 608.3 *filled,* 621.13 *clean,* 721.17 *well-off,* 742.1 *wealthy,* 805.30 *make proud,* 810.2 *blushing,* 810.16 *be self-conscious*
flushed 408.12 *warm-hearted,* 450.2 *red-faced,* 810.9 *blushing,* 874.1 *drunk*
flushed with pride 805.22 *boastful*
flushed with rage 828.16 *angry*
flushed with victory 682.15 *victorious*
flush gate 41.3 *ski racing*
flushing 134.2 *purification,* 450.2 *red-faced,* 810.2 *blushing*
flushing out 621.2 *cleaning*
flushly 376.14 *smoothly*

flushness 282.1 *horizontality,* 376.7 *smoothness*
flush out 134.10 *purify,* 621.13 *clean,* 621.15 *purify*
flush with anger 828.12 *become angry*
fluspirilene 62 Medication
fluster 153.7 *disturb,* 366.4 *fuss,* 366.22 *agitate*
flustered 153.12 *disturbed,* 366.15 *agitated,* 366.16 *restless,* 874.2 *slightly drunk*
flute 43 Architectural Decoration, **49** Musical Instruments, 43.8 *column,* 43.19 *decorate,* 49.39 *sing,* 321.1, 321.6 *furrow,* 564.13 *speak in a particular way*
fluted 43.16 *columned,* 321.4 *furrowed*
fluted armour 671.7 *armour*
fluted funnel 57 Laboratory Apparatus
flutes 777 Phobias by Topic
fluther 161 Collective Names for Birds and Animals
fluting 43.8 *column,* 792.2 *pattern*
flutter 39.11 *swimming,* 73.5 *flight,* 224.11 *be changeable,* 365.2 *vibration,* 365.9 *vibrate,* 365.11 *rock,* 365.12 *wave,* 366.10 *beat,* 366.12 *flicker,* 366.21 *be agitated,* 366.22 *agitate,* 366.26 *flicker,* 434.5 *atmospheric dissonance,* 648.4 *haste,* 777.12 *be fearful*
flutteration 366.4 *fuss*
flutter down 360.12 *drop*
fluttering 366.16 *restless,* 403.3 *stimulus*
fluttering eyelashes 543.3 *gesture*
flutter kick 39.2 *swimming technique*
flutter one's eyelashes 435.13 *look,* 543.11 *gesture*
flutter someone's heart 821.28 *win the love of*
fluttery 366.16 *restless*
fluvial 96
fluviomarine 96.10 *fluvial*
fluvioterrestrial 96.12 *hydrologic*
flux 56.10 *force,* 64.11 *electric field,* 96.6 *river flow,* 97.2 *tide,* 195.1 *succession,* 224.1 *changeableness,* 324.2 *momentum,* 353.1 *excretion,* 353.2 *defecation,* 387.6 *flow,* 387.9 *solvent,* 387.10 *solution,* 387.24 *melt*
flux and reflux 97.2 *tide,* 365.1 *oscillation*
flux collector 53.24 *telescope*
flux density 56.10 *force*
flexibility 387.8 *fluidification*
fluxible 387.15 *flowing*
fluxile 387.15 *flowing*
fluxility 387.5 *fluidity,* 387.6 *flow*
fluxion 52.31 *differentiation,* 387.6 *flow*
fluxional 387.15 *flowing*
fluxionary 387.15 *flowing*
fluxive 387.15 *flowing*
fluxure 387.5 *fluidity*
fly 71 Carriages and Carts, **82** Insects, **78,** 22.5 *batting terms,* 70.4 *transport,* 76.6 *flying animal,* 82.1 *insect,* 185.15 *pass,* 189.4 *be transient,* 254.18 *abscond,* 275.15 *be high,* 295.24 *part of garment,* 324.15 *walk,* 326.12 *transport,* 327.14 *find one's way,* 329.4 *be swift,* 359.19 *take off,* 365.12 *wave,* 458.2 *depart,* 539.13 *snare,* 544.7 *flag,* 590.3 *hunting and fishing equipment,* 591.8 *run away,* 638.5 *escape,* 642.12 *be active,* 648.2 *make haste,* 657.4 *cunning*
Fly 53 The Constellations
fly about 532.17 *be published*
fly a flag 366.22 *agitate*
fly against 670.1 *attack*
fly agaric 89 Fungi
fly a kite 532.13 *make public,* 596.4 *test*
fly aloft 359.19 *take off*

fly apart 162.11 *explode*
fly at 829.6 *be irascible*
fly away 189.4 *be transient*
fly ball 22.5 *batting terms*
flyblow 82.16 *infest*
flyblown 82.12 *verminous,* 622.8 *unclean,* 626.5 *unhygienic*
fly-boy 676.11 *recruit*
flyby 53.35 *rocketry*
fly by 185.15 *pass*
fly-by-light 73.6 *flight control*
fly-by-night 591.18 *avoiding,* 657.3 *cunning person,* 683.5 *failing person,* 685.3 *quitter*
fly by the seat of one's pants 657.5 *be cunning*
fly-by-wire 73.6 *flight control,* 436.7 *figurative blindness*
flycatcher 78 Birds, 78.6 *songbird*
fly dick 16.17 *police officer*
fly down 360.12 *drop*
flyer 73.3 *aircraft personnel,* 532.9 *advertisement*
fly-fish 20.7 *angle,* 80.15 *fish,* 590.11 *hunt*
fly-fisher 20.6 *angler*
fly-fishing 18 Sporting Activities, 20.1 *angling,* 80.7 *fishing,* 590.2 *chase*
fly floor 51.15 *stage*
fly gallery 51.15 *stage*
fly in 606.5 *provision*
fly in all directions 162.11 *explode*
flying 26.15 *wrestling,* 41.13 *iceskating,* 73.1 *aviation,* 77.27 *chiropteran,* 139.8 *nonadhesive,* 189.6 *transient,* 275.9 *high,* 324.16 *moving,* 329.1 *swift,* 356.2 *passing along*
flying animal 76
flying axel 41.6 *ice-skating*
flying back kick 26.9 *tae kwon do*
flying boat 679.31 *military aircraft*
flying bomb 680.16 *bomb*
flying buttress 43.8 *column,* 43.10 *church architecture,* 284.2 *supporting part,* 726.4 *wall*
flying circus 73.1 *aviation*
flying column 679.14 *armed forces*
flying corps 679.29 *air force*
flying doctor 73.1 *aviation,* 630.15 *healer*
Flying Dutchman 74.7 *nautical person*
Flying Dutchman class 36.2 *sailing boat*
flying fish 80 Fishes, 76.6 *flying animal,* 80.2 *fish*
Flying Fish 53 The Constellations
flying fox 77 Placental Mammals, 76.6 *flying animal*
flying gurnard 80 Fishes
flying insect 76.6 *flying animal*
flying kick 26.9 *tae kwon do*
flying lap 33.6 *motor racing terms*
flying lemur 77 Placental Mammals
flying lizard 79 Reptiles
flying mammal 77, 76.6 *flying animal*
flying mare 26.5 *wrestling*
flying officer 679.32 *airman*
Flying Officer 17 British Military Ranks
flying phalanger 77 Marsupials
flying picket 15.4 *industrial dispute*
flying reptile 79.6 *extinct reptile*
flying reverse crescent kick 26.9 *tae kwon do*
flying saucer 53.34 *SETI*
flying saucers 529.6 *natural mystery*
flying snake 79 Reptiles
flying squad 16.15 *British police*
flying squirrel 77 Placental Mammals
flying start 126.3 *advantage,* 156.11 *starting point,* 194.5 *gift of priority,* 300.4 *advantage,* 329.9 *acceleration*
flying up 359.4 *taking off*
flying wing 73 Types of Aircraft

fly in the face of 668.5 *defy*
fly in the face of reason 487.9 *be impossible*
fly in the ointment 620.7 *defect,* 631.6 *source of trouble,* 635.2 *troublemaker,* 661.2 *obstacle*
fly into a passion 828.12 *become angry*
fly into a rage 828.12 *become angry*
fly into the arms of 826.7 *show endearment for*
fly like a bat out of hell 648.2 *make haste*
flyman 51.26 *stagehand*
fly off 335.8 *sidestep,* 343.15 *change direction*
fly off at a tangent 343.15 *change direction*
fly off the handle 828.12 *become angry*
fly one's flag 676.12 *go to war*
fly out 22.7 *play baseball*
fly-out 22.6 *fielding terms*
flyover 63.21 *bridge,* 137.5, 327.3 *road,* 327.15 *accessible,* 356.5 *crossing point*
flypaper 138.3 *adhesive,* 539.13 *snare*
fly past 811.27 *show,* 813.3 *formal occasion*
flypast 849.5 *presenting arms*
fly-past 73.7 *miscellaneous aviation terms,* 811.13 *ceremonial,* 812.8 *salute*
fly pattern 19.9 *play*
fly rod 20.3 *fishing tackle*
fly spoon 20.2 *artificial fly*
fly-spotted 456.10 *mottled*
fly the nest 254.18 *abscond*
fly to arms 676.12 *go to war*
flytrap 539.13 *snare*
fly up 359.17 *spring up*
flyweight 26.3 *boxing weight divisions,* 26.4 *boxer,* 26.14 *combat,* 369.7 *weighing,* 674.10 *contender,* 679.3 *athlete*
flywheel 71 Motor Vehicle Parts, 364.6 *rotator*
FM transmitter 534.16 *transmitter*
f-number 56.31 *lens element,* 66.18 *exposure time*
Fo 48 Dramatists
foal 32.1 *horse,* 77.19 *young mammal,* 77.35 *give birth,* 206.4 *young animal,* 245.11 *have young*
foaled 396.15 *born*
foam 97.3 *wave,* 97.10 *billow,* 292.2 *filling,* 353.9 *saliva,* 370.7 *light thing,* 374.11 *soft thing,* 390.10 *air bubble,* 390.24 *bubble,* 612.9 *bauble*
foam at the mouth 366.21 *be agitated,* 828.11 *be angry*
foam-filled 374.4 *compressible*
foam-filling 374.11 *soft thing*
foam-flecked 446.2 *whitened*
foam glass 44.9 *industrial ceramics*
foamily 446.14 *whitely*
foaminess 370.5 *lightness*
foaming 353.29 *salivating,* 370.2 *insubstantial,* 446.2 *whitened,* 828.16 *angry*
foaming at the mouth 510.12 *manic,* 828.16 *angry*
foam rubber 377.4 *rubber*
foamy 370.2 *insubstantial,* 390.18 *bubbly*
fob 192.7 *watch*
f.o.b. 754.11 *free of charge*
fob off 222.6 *give a substitute*
fob off on 695.7 *force*
focal 291, 52.81 *curvilinear,* 126.14 *best,* 158.12 *core,* 342.7 *convergent*
focalization 291.3 *centrality,* 342.5 *focus*
focalize 291.9 *centre*
focalized 291.7 *centralized*
focalizing 291.3 *centrality*
focal length 56.31 *lens element,* 66.17 *lens*
focal plane 56.31 *lens element*

focal point 56.31 *lens element,* 158.2 *core,* 291.1 *centre,* 291.5 *focus,* 340.7 *centre of attraction*
focus 291, 342, 342, 52.42 *circle,* 54.22 *seismic activity,* 56.31 *lens element,* 66.8 *composition,* 66.17 *lens,* 66.21 *photograph,* 103.2 *essential content,* 135.6 *point of union,* 158.2 *core,* 158.16 *place in the middle,* 291.1, 291.9 *centre,* 340.7 *centre of attraction,* 435.13 *look,* 437.4 *clarity,* 437.10 *make visible,* 472.2 *issue,* 594.4 *prepare for action*
focused 472, 342.7 *convergent,* 522.1 *intelligible*
focusing 56.32 *optical instrument,* 291.3 *centrality,* 342.7 *convergent*
focusing screen 66.18 *exposure time*
focus on 472, 291.9 *centre,* 437.10 *make visible,* 588.10 *aim*
fodder 68.9 *animal feedstuff,* 68.18 *practise livestock farming,* 87.11 *eat grass,* 350.8 *animal food,* 604.1 *materials*
fodder beet 68.12 *crop*
fodder crop 68.12 *crop*
fodder grass 87.1 *grass*
fodder peas 68.12 *crop*
fodder rape 68.12 *crop*
Fodor 528.5 *reference book*
foe 663.11 *opponent,* 820.5 *hostile person,* 822.8 *hated person*
foetid 388.18 *miasmic*
foetid air 388.3 *miasma*
fog 777 Phobias by Topic, **55, 55,** 57.3 *phase,* 66.8 *composition,* 307.1 *shapelessness,* 307.3 *make shapeless,* 388.4 *water vapour,* 389.3 *wateriness,* 391.2 *mistiness,* 438.4 *invisibility,* 438.6 *that which makes invisible,* 441.2 *murk,* 441.10 *make dim,* 443.7 *opaque thing,* 443.10 *be opaque,* 491.20 *make uncertain,* 531.9 *disguise,* 626.1 *lack of hygiene*
fog band 391.2 *mistiness*
fog bank 55.33 *fog*
fogbound 55.56 *foggy,* 699.15 *detained*
fogbow 55.27 *rainbow*
fog drip 55.37, 391.6 *dew*
foggily 55.65 *meteorologically,* 307.6 *shapelessly,* 441.12 *dimly,* 443.13 *opaquely,* 448.9 *greyly,* 491.25 *indeterminately*
fogginess 55.35 *visibility,* 307.1 *shapelessness,* 391.2 *mistiness,* 438.4 *invisibility,* 441.2 *murk,* 443.6 *opaqueness,* 491.14 *indeterminacy,* 551.1 *obscurity*
foggy 55, 371.7 *condensed,* 388.19 *smoky,* 391.10 *misty,* 438.2 *difficult to see,* 441.6 *murky,* 443.2 *shady,* 448.3 *dull,* 491.6 *indeterminate,* 523.4 *difficult,* 551.2 *obscure*
foghorn 543.4 *signal,* 636.2 *danger signal,* 653.5 *guide*
fog lamp 439.6 *electric light*
fog level 66.10 *graininess*
fog light 71 Motor Vehicle Parts
fogou 3.11 *relic,* 200.7 *thing of the past,* 399.6 *grave*
fog signal 72.2 *track,* 636.2 *danger signal*
Föhn 55 Winds
foible 620.7 *defect,* 683.3 *personal fault,* 864.3 *venial sin*
foil 43 Architectural Decoration, 28.2 *fencing equipment,* 28.6 *fencing,* 51.27 *entertainer,* 266.3 *coat,* 293.4 *wrapping,* 301.4 *wrapper,* 341.7 *deflection,* 381.9 *blunt instrument,* 515.7 *thwart,* 591.2 *avert,* 661.8 *hinder,* 663.18 *counteract,* 680.8 *sharp weapon*
foil button 28.2 *fencing equipment*
foiled 515.9 *disappointed*
foil-fence 28.5 *fence*
foil fencing 28.1 *fencing*
foil grip 28.2 *fencing equipment*

foil guard 28.2 *fencing equipment*
foiling 661.1 *hindrance*
foilsman 28.4 *fencer,* 674.10 *contender,* 679.3 *athlete*
foin 670.18 *hit*
foison 608.8 *plenty*
foist on 695.7 *force*
Fokker 52 Scientists
fold 54, 320, 320, 10.17 *worshipper,* 42.3 *card game terms,* 42.10 *play,* 54.20 *earth movement,* 68.7 *farm building,* 135.5 *joint,* 218.6 *cease,* 256.12 *stall,* 266.1 *layer,* 295.24 *part of garment,* 295.35 *make clothing,* 301.2 *enclosed place,* 323.4 *closed place,* 323.10 *enclose,* 364.9 *roll,* 375.12 *make rough,* 634.3 *animal shelter,* 683.6 *fail,* 821.27 *kiss*
Fold 320
foldable 262.9 *contractible*
fold around 320.7 *fold*
foldaway 47.14 *wooden*
foldaway bed 47.6 *bed*
fold-belt mountain 54.21 *mountain building*
foldboat 36.6 *canoeing*
folded 320, 295.31 *styled*
folded arms 543.3 *gesture*
folded dipole 534.17 *antenna*
folded over 320.5 *folded*
folder 258.5 *packet,* 301.4 *wrapper,* 605.5 *collection*
fold-hinge 54.20 *earth movement*
fold in 45.55 *cook*
folding 36.12 *canoeing,* 47.14 *wooden,* 54.20 *earth movement,* 68.3 *livestock farming*
folding cabbage 741.2 *cash*
folding canoe 36.6 *canoeing*
folding chair 47.2 *chair*
folding cycle 71.12 *bicycle*
folding green 741.2 *cash*
folding ladder 359.9 *ladder*
folding money 741.2 *cash*
folding up 320.4 *closure*
fold in two 158.17 *average*
fold mountain 54.21 *mountain building*
fold one's arms 543.11 *gesture*
fold over 320.7 *fold*
fold to one's heart 821.27 *kiss*
fold up 157.16, 218.6 *cease,* 262.6 *become smaller,* 320.7 *fold,* 320.10 *close,* 605.6 *store*
foliage 83.6 *leaf,* 143.6 *branch,* 453.8 *greenness*
foliage bud 83.8 *bud*
foliar feed 69.7 *fertilizer*
foliate 83.14 *of plants,* 266.9 *platelike*
foliated 54.56 *petrographic,* 266.7 *layered*
foliated rock 54.33 *metamorphic rock*
foliation 43 Architectural Decoration, 54.29 *petrogenesis,* 266.6 *layering*
folic acid 57 Common Chemical Compounds, 58.13 *vitamin*
folie à deux 510.4 *delusion*
folio 143.2 *particular*
foliose 90.8 *lichenoid*
foliose lichen 90.6 *lichen*
folium 52.40 *curve*
folk 1.7 *society,* 1.14 *societal,* 49.33 *jazz,* 400.9 *group*
folk art 50 Western Art Styles and Movements, 1.8 *tradition*
folk ballad 49.11 *folk music*
folk costume 295.3 *formal dress*
folk dance 46.4 *historic dancing*
folk dancing 46.1 *dancing*
Folkestone 93 Cities
Folketing 653.10 *legislative body*
folk etymology 5.1 *linguistics,* 504.11 *grammatical error*
folk history 1.8 *tradition,* 3.7 *narrative*
folk literature 48.1 *literature*
folklore 1.8, 202.6 *tradition,* 400.5 *study of mankind,* 497.2 *religious belief,* 584.4 *custom*
folklorist 400.6 *studier of mankind*

folk medicine 60.2 *natural medicine,* 630.11 *medical art*
folkmoot 653.7 *council*
folk motif 1.8 *tradition*
folk music 49
folk play 51.2 *play*
folk poetry 48.6 *poetry*
folk psychology 61.1 *psychology*
folk rock 49.9 *popular music,* 49.11 *folk music*
folks 161.17 *family*
folksiness 814.3 *familiarity*
folk society 2.5 *society*
folksong 1.8 *tradition,* 49.11 *folk music,* 433.2 *song*
folk story 48.2 *fiction*
folksy 49.33 *jazz,* 814.9 *familiar*
folk tale 1.8 *tradition,* 3.7 *narrative,* 48.2 *fiction,* 560.3 *narration*
foller 262.4 *contractor*
follicle 86.2 *botanical fruit*
follicle mite 82 Arachnids
follicle-stimulating hormone 58 Hormones
follicularly challenged 294.10 *bald*
Follies 51.5 *show*
follow 127, 590, 808, 4.21 *rationalize,* 4.22 *propound a philosophy,* 116.25 *conform,* 118.9 *imitate,* 118.11 *emulate,* 155.21 *follow in sequence,* 155.26 *bring up the rear,* 165.27 *specialize,* 167.8 *comply,* 180.16 *attend,* 195.10 *succeed,* 227.7 *follow from,* 264.10 *stay near,* 304.6 *be in the rear,* 522.6 *understand,* 599.1 *use,* 697.8 *serve,* 719.4 *observe*
follow a course 652.11 *conduct oneself*
follow advice 654.6 *consult*
follow a pattern 21.7 *be regular*
follow a plan 592.12 *plan ahead*
follow a procedure 719.6 *perform*
follow at heel 808.14 *follow*
follow a trend 105.6 *be in a state of*
follow bad advice 515.4 *be disappointed*
follow close 155
follow custom 817.11 *have good manners*
followed 590.17 *pursued*
follower 138, 155, 180, 195, 9.5, 10.17 *worshipper,* 118.7 *imitator,* 127.6 *inferior,* 167.6 *conformist,* 284.8 *supporter,* 590.5 *pursuer,* 667.5 *assenter,* 697.1 *servant,* 701.4 *dependent,* 808.5 *adherent,* 821.9 *lover,* 851.8 *admirer*
follower of a doctrine 4
follower of fashion 114.4 *person who copies*
followers 155.14 *follower*
follow from 227
follow in a series 159.13 *be consecutive*
following 114.7 *similar,* 118.1 *imitation,* 118.12 *imitative,* 155.1 *sequence,* 155.14 *follower,* 155.15 *sequential,* 155.28 *after,* 159.9 *consecutive,* 180.10 *attendance,* 195.1 *succession,* 195.12 *succeeding,* 202.12 *delaying,* 227.10 *caused,* 324.10 *regular movement,* 590.1 *pursuit,* 590.15 *pursuing,* 719.1 *observance*
following from 227.10 *caused*
following spot 51.18 *stage lighting*
following the letter 537.10 *literalness,* 537.23 *literal*
following upon 227.12 *with the effect of*
following wind 55.15 *wind direction,* 338.12 *propellant,* 390.4 *air flow,* 662.1 *help*
follow in office 195
follow in sequence 155, 195.10 *succeed*
follow in the footsteps of 155.21 *follow in sequence*

follow in the position of 195.11 *follow in office*
follow in the steps of 118.11 *emulate*
follow in the wake 304.6 *be in the rear*
follow in the wake of 118.11 *emulate*
follow in turn 155.24 *alternate*
follow like sheep 118.11 *emulate,* 694.5 *obey*
follow on 118.11 *emulate,* 155.21 *follow in sequence,* 159.13 *be consecutive*
follow one's bent 698.16 *be independent*
follow one's career 652.11 *conduct oneself*
follow one's conscience 228.8 *be motivated,* 863.8 *be virtuous*
follow one's hunch 464.9 *be intuitive*
follow one's instincts 228.8 *be motivated*
follow one's nose 332.7 *take a direction,* 416.7 *smell*
follow one's own will 570
follow one's routine 112.12 *be monotonous*
follow on from 227.7 *follow from*
follow orders 694.5 *obey*
follow protocol 306.8, 813.11 *be formal*
follow separate paths 136.13 *diverge*
follow suit 118.11 *emulate,* 167.8 *comply*
follow that car 590.19 *after him*
follow the beaten path 167.8 *comply*
follow the book 694.5 *obey*
follow the chase 590.11 *hunt*
follow the crowd 112.10, 116.25 *conform,* 499.5 *assent to,* 808.14 *follow*
follow the example of 118.11 *emulate*
follow the fashion 167.8 *comply*
follow the golden mean 242.3 *be moderate*
follow the herd 118.11 *emulate*
follow the law 16
follow the letter 537.32 *be literal*
follow the letter of the law 16.67 *follow the law*
follow the party line 166.17 *obey orders,* 694.5 *obey*
follow the rising star 578.3 *apostatize*
follow the scent 37.7 *shoot,* 416.7 *smell,* 590.9 *follow*
follow the straight and narrow 863.8 *be virtuous,* 876.11 *be moral*
follow the trail 590.9 *follow*
follow the trend 167.8 *comply,* 201.18 *be trendy*
follow through 219.3 *continue,* 575.7 *maintain,* 684.4 *complete*
follow-through 25.2 *grip,* 25.5 *bowling delivery,* 25.9 *bowls,* 25.10 *bowling,* 29.3 *golf shots,* 40.2 *tennis strokes,* 155.3 *continuity*
follow to the ends of the earth 694.5 *obey*
follow up 590, 60.19 *practise medicine,* 219.4 *protract,* 684.4 *complete*
follow-up 60.6 *health care,* 155.3 *continuity,* 195.9 *sequel,* 219.1 *continuity*
folly 508, 243.8 *construction,* 460.2 *unintelligence,* 462.1 *lack of thought,* 502.1 *ignorance,* 780.1 *rashness,* 798.1 *ludicrousness*
Folly 508
Fomalhaut 53 Named Stars
foment 226.10 *awaken,* 241.9 *make violent,* 630.20 *doctor*
fomentation 62.7 *ointment,* 226.1 *cause,* 408.3 *heater,* 630.10 *surgical dressing,* 630.13 *therapy*
fomenter 226.8 *contributor*

fond 759.12 *sensitive,* 782.9 *desirous,* 821.17 *loving,* 826.9 *endearing*

fondant 45.41 *sweet,* 414.4 *confectionery*

fond farewell 817.3 *courtesies*

fond feeling 784.1 *liking*

fond illusion 539.2 *self-deception*

fondle 405.9 *give pleasure,* 407.4 *kiss,* 407.11 *touch,* 821.14 *communication of love,* 821.27 *kiss,* 826.7 *show endearment*

fondling 407.2, 407.2 *touching,* 821.14 *communication of love,* 826.1 *endearment,* 826.9 *endearing*

fond look 821.14 *communication of love,* 826.2 *courtship*

fondly 821.30 *lovingly,* 826.10 *endearingly*

fondness 759.5 *good feeling,* 782.1 *desire,* 784.1 *liking,* 821.1 *love,* 826.1 *endearment*

fondness for company 815.1 *sociability*

fondness for society 815.1 *sociability*

fondness for the bottle 874.11 *drinking*

fond of 821.18 *in love*

fond of a drink 874.5 *drunken*

fond of company 815.15 *sociable*

fondue 45.15 *sauce,* 45.34 *vegetarian dish,* 45.45 *French dish*

fondue fork 350.16 *eating utensil*

fondus 46.10 *positions at the barre*

font 5.15 *type style,* 10.12 *church*

Fontainebleau school 50 Western Art Styles and Movements

Fontainebleu 45 Cheeses

Fontane 48 Writers

Fontrevault 7 Members of Religious Orders

food 777 Phobias by Topic, **350,** 396.3 *life requirements,* 604.1 *materials,* 606.2 *provisions,* 651.7 *refreshments*

food aid 729.3 *offering*

food chain 59.18 *ecology*

food-combining diet 350.6 *nutrition*

food content 350

food department 350.17 *food shop*

food fish 80, 80.2 *fish*

food for powder 679.17 *army person*

food for the body 350.7 *food*

food for the mind 350.7 *food*

food for the spirit 350.7 *food*

food for worms 397.11 *dead person*

food hall 350.17 *food shop*

foodie 350.18 *eater,* 411.5 *taster,* 872.4 *glutton*

food mixer 45.6 *kitchen equipment*

food mountain 161.25 *assemblage,* 350.9 *plenty,* 605.1 *store*

food of the gods 350.7 *food*

food orgy 872.3 *act of gluttony*

food parcel 729.3 *offering*

food plant 83.2 *plant*

food poisoning 624.2 *illness,* 624.6 *infection,* 624.8 *indigestion,* 631.7 *poisoning*

food preparation 45.1 *cookery*

food processing 45.1 *cookery*

food processor 45.6 *kitchen equipment,* 133.6 *mixer,* 346.4 *rotator,* 366.14 *agitator,* 384.11 *pulverizer,* 387.11 *liquidizer,* 393.15 *pulper*

food provider 350

food pyramid 59.18 *ecology*

food rations 606.1 *provision*

food shop 350

food stamp 729.3 *offering*

food stamps 606.1 *provision,* 833.4 *welfare state*

food store 90.3 *plant body*

foodstuffs 350.7 *food,* 606.2 *provisions*

food supply 606.1 *provision*

food web 59.18 *ecology*

---

fool 506, 45.35 *dessert,* 51.21 *role,* 51.30 *clown,* 393.8 *pulp,* 460.3 *unintelligent person,* 493.5 *misjudging person,* 502.5 *ignorant person,* 506.4 *buffoon,* 508.3 *foolish person,* 539.22 *dupe,* 539.28 *trick,* 656.10 *unskilled person,* 658.3 *naive person,* 734.10 *take away,* 798.3 *object of ridicule,* 850.9 *butt*

fool around 506.8 *fool,* 640.4 *act,* 821.27 *kiss*

fooled 538.16 *misinformed,* 539.36 *deceived*

foolery 508.2 *act of folly*

foolhardiness 468.2 *impetuosity,* 778.4 *adventurousness,* 780.1 *rashness*

foolhardy 508.5 *foolish,* 778.13 *adventurous,* 780.4 *rash*

fooling 539.7 *tricking*

fooling around 821.6 *courtship,* 826.1 *endearment,* 877.3 *sexual immorality*

foolish 508, 278.2 *superficial,* 460.6 *unintelligent,* 462.8 *thoughtless,* 493.9 *misjudged,* 506.5 *nonsensical,* 521.10 *meaningless,* 612.4 *trivial,* 656.1 *unskilful,* 780.4 *rash,* 798.5 *ridiculous*

foolish hope 489.4 *improbability*

foolishly 508, 460.11 *unintelligently,* 493.13 *misguidedly,* 506.9 *nonsensically,* 656.11 *unskilfully,* 780.6 *rashly*

foolishness 460.2 *unintelligence,* 508.1 *folly,* 798.1 *ludicrousness*

foolish person 508

foolish talk 521.4 *senseless talk*

foolproof 632.6 *invulnerable,* 660.12 *wieldy*

fool's errand 614.5 *waste of effort,* 722.3 *waste*

fool's gold 54 Minerals, 515.3 *mirage,* 539.6 *imitation,* 540.14 *false thing,* 614.5 *waste of effort,* 636.3 *false alarm,* 741.16 *bullion*

fool's paradise 102.4 *theorization,* 493.1 *misjudgment,* 494.2 *overestimate,* 515.3 *mirage,* 775.3 *aspiration*

fool with 628.4 *impair,* 656.7 *be clumsy*

foot 75 General Units, **280,** 48.8 *part of poem,* 48.9 *metre,* 88.4 *moss plant,* 143.4 *component,* 269.7 *measure of length,* 276.4 *low thing,* 679.17 *army person*

footage 269.4 *length*

foot-and-mouth disease 624.18 *veterinary disease*

football 19, 38.1, 38.5 *soccer,* 258.19 *inflatable,* 338.10 *ball*

Football Association 38.1 *soccer*

Football Association Challenge Cup 38.1 *soccer*

football boots 295.19 *footwear*

football championship 38.1 *soccer*

football club 38.1 *soccer*

football coach 38.3 *football player*

footballer 237.5 *athlete*

Footballer of the Year 38.3 *football player*

football fan 38.3 *football player*

football field 38.1 *soccer*

football game 19.1 *football,* 38.1 *soccer*

football ground 38.1 *soccer*

football helmet 632.4 *safety device*

football kit 38.1 *soccer*

Football League 38.1 *soccer*

football manager 38.3 *football player*

football match 38.1 *soccer*

football organization 38.1 *soccer*

football pitch 38.1 *soccer*

football play 38

football player 19, 38, 237.5 *athlete*

football referee 38.3 *football player*

football season 203.1 *season*

---

football side 38.1 *soccer*

football stadium 38.1 *soccer*

football team 38.1 *soccer*

football trainer 38.3 *football player*

football uniform 38.1 *soccer*

footbath 258.12 *bath*

foot bath 621.6 *bath*

footboard 47.6 *bed*

footbridge 63.21, 327.9 *bridge*

foot-candle 75 Scientific and Technical Units

foot-dragger 328.15 *slow person*

foot-dragging 328.6 *hesitant,* 328.12 *hesitation,* 661.5 *inhibition,* 661.15 *inhibitive,* 663.4 *uncooperativeness*

foot fault 25.2 *grip,* 40.4 *tennis terms*

footgear 295.19 *footwear*

Foot Guard 679.12 *ceremonial troops*

foothill 95.1 *mountain,* 318.2 *projection*

foothills 275.2 *heights,* 276.2 *lowland*

foothold 34.5 *rock face,* 322.10 *opportunity,* 726.1 *retention*

footing 63.28 *substructure,* 105.1 *state,* 106.1 *circumstances,* 121.2 *rank,* 233 *influence,* 251.2 *circumstances,* 280.1 *base,* 726.1 *retention*

foot-lambert 75 Scientific and Technical Units

footlicking 808.2 *sycophancy,* 808.7 *sycophantic*

footlights 51.18 *stage lighting,* 439.6 *electric light*

foot line 41.10 *curling*

footling 612.4 *trivial*

footloose 335.25 *wandering,* 698.10 *independent*

footloose and fancy free 335.25 *wandering,* 698.10 *independent*

footman 697.6 *domestic servant*

footnote 130.3 *additional item,* 280.2 *foot,* 524.2 *annotation,* 524.10 *annotate*

footpath 327.6 *path,* 356.4 *access*

footplate 72.5 *locomotive part*

foot-pound 75 Scientific and Technical Units, 235.5 *unit of work*

foot-poundal 75 Scientific and Technical Units

footprint 73.7 *miscellaneous aviation terms,* 132.1 *remainder,* 227.2 *visible effect,* 317.3 *cavity,* 483.4 *indication,* 544.3 *means of identification,* 545.12 *vestige*

foot race 674.4 *race*

foot regiment 679.16 *army unit*

footrest 284.4 *rest,* 359.10 *step*

foot rule 268.6 *measuring instrument*

foots 51.18 *stage lighting*

footsie 543.3 *gesture,* 821.14 *communication of love,* 826.1 *endearment*

Footsie 14.2 *stock exchange*

footslogger 679.17 *army person*

foot soldier 679.17 *army person*

footsore 650.1 *fatigued*

foot-spinner 82 Insects

foot spot 24.4 *carom,* 24.6 *pool*

foot steering 36.7 *windsurfing*

footstep 359.10 *step,* 545.12 *vestige*

footstone 399.4 *funeral objects*

footstool 284.4 *rest,* 808.3 *sycophant*

footstrap 36.7 *windsurfing*

foot string 24.4 *carom*

foot the bill 746.8 *defray*

foot-ton 75 Scientific and Technical Units

foot transport 71.1 *road transport*

foot-warmer 408.3 *heater*

footway 327.6 *path*

footwear 295

footweary 650.1 *fatigued*

footwork 26.2 *boxing*

foozle 656.7 *be clumsy,* 656.9 *bungling*

foozled 656.4 *bungled*

---

fop 295.27 *model,* 809.7 *vain person*

foppish 809.11 *cocky,* 811.19 *flashy*

foppishly 809.21 *cockily,* 811.35 *flashily*

foppishness 295.2 *dressing*

for 588, 707.8 *by proxy,* 851.19 *supporting*

for a beginning 156.40 *first*

forage 87.11, 87.11 *eat grass,* 350.8 *animal food,* 606.5 *provision,* 736.14 *plunder*

forage cap 295.15 *headgear*

forage harvester 68.10 *farm tool*

foraging 736.5 *plundering,* 736.17 *stolen*

for a kick-off 156.40 *first*

for all ages 613.1 *useful*

for all one is worth 329.14 *swiftly,* 642.22 *actively,* 644.12 *laboriously*

for all one knows 486.9 *possibly,* 502.12 *ignorantly,* 589.14 *perchance*

for all practical purposes 103.13 *in essence,* 264.7 *nearly*

for all that 130.10 *additionally*

for all to see 437.2 *clear,* 475.20 *manifestly,* 483.15 *evidently,* 526.16 *manifestly,* 532.22 *publicly*

for a long time 188.11 *long*

for always 157.27 *to the end,* 185.30 *chronologically,* 190.11 *eternally,* 726.11 *tenaciously*

for a moment 189.8 *transiently*

for a purpose 588.12 *intended,* 588.14 *for*

for a rainy day 516.8 *foresightedly*

for a reason 588.12 *intended*

for a season 185.26 *all the time*

for a song 738.14 *buying,* 754.15 *cheaply*

for a start 156.40 *first*

for a time 185.26 *all the time*

for a while 196.10 *for the present*

foray 670.1 *attack,* 736.5 *plundering,* 736.14 *plunder*

for aye 190.11 *eternally*

forbear 591.3 *abstain,* 591.24 *hands off,* 600.5 *not use,* 669.9 *desist,* 691.3 *be lenient,* 835.10, 839.12 *show mercy,* 869.5 *be self-restrained*

forbearance 591.11 *abstinence,* 600.8 *nonuse,* 669.4 *desisting,* 691.1 *leniency,* 814.4 *freedom,* 835.3 *mercy,* 839.2 *forgivingness,* 869.1 *self-restraint*

forbearant 835.6 *pitying*

forbearer 669.5 *resister*

forbearing 669.4, 669.13 *desisting,* 691.4 *lenient,* 839.5 *merciful,* 869.8 *self-restrained*

forbearingly 669.15 *abstemiously,* 869.11 *with self-restraint*

for better or for worse 575.13 *persistently*

for better or worse 190.11 *eternally*

forbid 16.75 *make illegal,* 147.7 *exclude,* 476.8 *refute,* 487.8 *make impossible,* 661.8 *hinder,* 709.3 *veto,* 711.6 *dissent,* 846.17 *criminalize*

forbiddance 147.1 *exclusion*

forbidden 487, 16.55 *illegal,* 147.11 *excluded,* 357.15 *out of reach,* 709.5 *vetoed,* 846.12 *disentitled*

forbidden fruit 86.5 *figurative usage,* 782.5 *object of desire,* 877.4 *illicit love*

forbidden love 821.8 *love affair,* 877.4 *illicit love*

forbidding 440.11 *forbidment,* 709.1 *veto,* 816.8 *unsociable*

forbiddingly 816.14 *unsociably*

force 56, 161, 695, 27.17 *bat,* 96.2 *channel,* 140.3 *assembly,* 226.1 *cause,* 226.10 *awaken,* 228.10 *manipulate,* 230.1 *operation,* 232.2 *instrument,* 233 *influence,* 233.10 *be a prevailing influence,* 235.1 *power,* 235.4

energy, 235.10 *be powerful*, 237.1 *strength*, 239.1 *vigour*, 241.1 *violence*, 241.8 *use violence*, 330.11 *impulsion*, 336.8 *further*, 385.1 *friction*, 520.1 *meaning*, 537.11 *pedantry*, 554.1 *emphasis*, 570.15 *impose one's will*, 571.15 *compel*, 586.15 *persuade*, 594.7 *develop*, 601.1, 601.2 *misuse*, 618.14 *illtreat*, 640.1 *action*, 644.4 *exertion*, 665.1 *party*, 695.2 *coercion*, 877.20 *seduce*
force a card 539.30 *be fraudulent*
force a confrontation 526.4 *show oneself*
force a passage 356.10 *enter*
force a surrender 682.9 *be victorious*
forced 69.19 *ornamental*, 108.7 *illogical*, 595.5 *immature*, 648.3 *hasty*
forced entry 346.3 *inroad*
forced labour 644.1 *work*, 695.3 *coercive methods*, 702.7 *imprisonment*
forced landing 360.5 *dive*
forced march 329.11 *swift thing*, 648.4 *haste*
forced out 22.6 *fielding terms*, 705.7 *resigning*
forced reconciliation 677.1 *pacification*
forced resignation 689.1 *anarchy*, 705.1 *resignation*
forced saving 751.8 *levy*
forced vibration 56.14 *sound wave*
force eight 55.14 *windiness*
force-feed 350.25 *provide food*, 695.7 *force*
force-feeding 695.3 *coercive methods*
forceful 233.11 *influential*, 235.13 *powerful*, 237.10 *potent*, 239.4 *vigorous*, 241.6 *violent*, 300.10 *advantaged*, 535.14 *assertive*, 537.24 *pedantic*, 554.3 *emphatic*, 560.11 *descriptive*, 574.2 *tenacious*, 586.19 *persuasive*, 601.5 *abusive*, 640.6 *effective*, 642.18 *active*, 695.9 *compelling*
forcefully 233.14 *influentially*, 235.18 *powerfully*, 237.14 *strongly*, 239.6 *with vigour*, 241.10 *violently*, 300.12 *at an advantage*, 330.18 *dynamically*, 338.34 *forward*, 554.7 *emphatically*, 586.21 *persuasively*, 601.6 *abusively*, 640.8 *effectively*, 642.22 *actively*, 670.26 *aggresively*, 695.11 *compellingly*
forcefulness 235.1 *power*, 239.1 *vigour*, 241.1 *violence*, 535.6 *assertiveness*, 554.1 *emphasis*
forceful person 695.4 *coercive person*
force in 354.3 *impact*
force into a mould 167.9 *make conform*
force into oblivion 546.1 *obliterate*
force majeure 490.16 *inevitability*, 571.6 *necessitarianism*, 695.2 *coercion*
force nine 55.14 *windiness*
force of circumstances 571.6 *necessitarianism*
force of gravity 235.4 *energy*, 340.2 *pulling power*, 369.5 *gravity*
force of habit 584.1 *habit*
force of inertia 235.4 *energy*
force oneself 573.10 *grudge*
force one's way 590.13 *follow up*, 644.8 *exert oneself*
force open 241.8 *use violence*
force out 22.7 *play baseball*, 349.7 *drive out*, 355.16 *extort*
forcep 23.7 *fishing tackle*
force play 22.6 *fielding terms*
forceps 355.10 *excavator*, 726.3 *tools for gripping*
forceps delivery 245.7 *obstetrics*
for certain 480.12 *assuredly*
forces 63.14 *load*

forces of law and order 16.14 *police*
force someone's hand 695.6 *compel*
force someone to strip 296.15 *make nude*
force ten 55.14 *windiness*
force to accept 695.7 *force*
force to be reckoned with 233 *influence*
force to resign 689.4 *be anarchic*
force to step down 476.8 *refute*
force to the wall 659.23 *cause difficulties*
force upon 695.7 *force*
forcible 235.13 *powerful*, 239.4 *vigorous*, 241.6 *violent*, 695.9 *compelling*, 712.10 *demanding*
forcible demand 712.2 *demand*
forcible removal 252.3 *replacement*
forcible wedlock 823.5 *wedding*
forcibly 235.18 *powerfully*, 237.14 *strongly*, 239.6 *with vigour*, 241.10 *violently*, 695.11 *compellingly*, 712.12 *by request*
forcing 695.2 *coercion*
forcing a card 539.10 *fraud*
forcing a run 22.4 *pitching terms*
forcing bag 45.6 *kitchen equipment*
forcing bed 69.4 *nursery*
forcing house 69.4 *nursery*
ford 63.21 *bridge*, 96.2 *channel*, 272.6 *narrow place*, 278.4 *shallow thing*, 356.5 *crossing point*, 356.11 *cross*
Ford 48 *Writers*, **48** *Dramatists*
for dear life 642.22 *actively*
fore 303.1, 303.6 *front*, 636.10 *look out*
fore and aft 144.9 *completely*
fore-and-aft 36.10 *sailing*
fore-and-aft sail 36.3 *parts of a sailing boat*
forearm 143.4 *component*, 594.3 *be prepared*, 636.5 *warn*
forearmed 513.5 *expecting*, 594.18 *prepared*, 636.9 *warned*
forebear 154.9 *predecessor*, 711.7 *refuse oneself*
forebears 202.2 *old people*
forebode 511.6 *foresee*, 517.11 *predict*, 633.10 *endanger*
foreboding 464.3 *insight*, 513.1 *expectation*, 516.3 *foresight*, 517.1 *prediction*, 517.13 *predicting*, 633.1 *dangerous*, 636.1, 636.8 *warning*, 777.2 *fearfulness*
forecaddie 29.6 *golfer*
forecast 55, **154**, 11.23 *divine*, 55.4 *weather forecast*, 199.4 *looking to the future*, 488.1 *probability*, 513.2 *expectations*, 513.9 *predict*, 516.1 *foresee*, 516.3 *foresight*, 517.6 *foreseeable*, 517.1 *prediction*, 517.11 *predict*, 517.14 *predicted*, 592.2 *policy*, 592.12 *plan ahead*
forecaster 517.1 *diviner*, 199.5, 516.5 *predictor*
forecasting 11.9 *divination*, 517.1 *prediction*
forecastle 74 *Parts of a Ship*, 303.1 *front*
forecheck 31.3 *ice hockey*, 31.9 *play hockey*
forechecker 31.4 *ice hockey player*
forechecking 31.3 *ice hockey*
foreclose 323.9 *close down*, 734.8 *take back*
foreclosed 745.10 *unable to pay*
foreclosing 734.2 *taking back*
foreclosure 323.1 *closure*, 734.2 *taking back*, 745.5 *amount owing*
foreconscious 61.21 *psyche*
forecourt 303.1 *front*
foredeck 303.1 *front*
forefather 154.9 *predecessor*, 208.4 *early comer*
forefathers 397.13 *the dead*
forefinger 407.7 *sense organ*, 543.5 *indicator*
forefront 154.2 *priority*, 303.1 *front*
foregoer 154.8 *precursor*

foregoing 154.11 *prior*, 200.19 *antiquarian*
foregone conclusion 490.12 *something certain*, 493.4 *prejudgment*, 516.3 *foresight*, 582.6 *premeditation*
foreground 264.3 *near place*, 303.1, 303.6 *front*
forehand 40, 25.9 *bowls*, 208.16 *premature*, 208.17 *early*, 208.20 *prematurely*
forehand drive 40.2 *tennis strokes*
forehand grip 25.2 *grip*
forehand volley 40.2 *tennis strokes*
forehead 318.3 *protuberance*, 457.3 *external appearance*
foreign 104, **149**, 108.6 *unrelated*, 117.7 *disparate*, 136.17 *unjoined*, 147.11 *excluded*, 289.10 *extraneous*, 822.12 *hated*
foreign accent 564.3 *mode of speech*
foreign body 149, 147.6 *thing excluded*
Foreign Body 149
foreign-born 149.13 *immigrant*
foreign coins 741.11 *national coins*
foreign correspondent 528.9 *informant*, 532.11 *newspaper man*, 533.4 *journalist*
foreign currency reserves 14.1 *finance*
foreign editor 533.4 *journalist*
foreign element 149.1 *foreign body*
foreigner 149, 104.6 *outsider*, 108.3 *unconnected person*, 117.6 *misfit*, 201.8 *new arrival*, 816.7 *outsider*
foreigners 777 Phobias by Topic, 289.5 *extraneousness*
foreign exchange dealer 739.12 *wholesaler*
foreign exchange market 14.1, 741.7 *finance*
foreign influx 346.4 *right of entry*
foreign language dictionary 5.28 *dictionary*
foreign-language student 5.2 *linguist*
foreign-language study 5.1 *linguistics*
foreign loan 732.2 *loan*
foreign-made 104.12 *external*, 149.14 *imported*
foreign matter 149.1 *foreign body*
foreignness 104, **149**, 108.1 *unrelatedness*, 289.5 *extraneousness*
foreign product 104.4 *externality*
foreign resident 149.6 *immigrant*
foreign rule 12.3 *governance*
foreign sector 13.2 *economy*
foreign service 706.2 *representative body*
foreign substance 149.1 *foreign body*
foreign trade 737.5 *commercial trade*
forejudge 481.13 *prejudge*, 516.1 *foresee*
foreknow 516.1 *foresee*
foreknowledge 199.4 *looking to the future*, 501.1 *knowledge*, 516.3 *foresight*
foreland 98.5 *peninsula*
forelimb 143.4 *component*
forelock-tugging 849.11 *in a respectful stance*
foreman 126.5 *superior*, 653.15 *manager*
foreman of the jury 16.26, 492.7 *jury*
foremast 74 *Rigging*, 303.1 *front*
foremost 126.14 *best*, 154.12 *primary*, 156.30 *front*, 194.10 *prior*, 611.5 *important*
forename 560.8 *name*
forenamed 154.11 *prior*
forenoon 204.1, 204.5 *morning*
forensic 16.49 *judicatory*, 60.22 *medical*
forensic medicine 60.3 *medical specialty*
forensic pathologist 60.13 *medical specialist*

forensic pathology 624.20 *pathology*
foreordain 582.1 *predetermine*
foreordained 582.3 *predetermined*
foreordination 582.5 *predetermination*
fore rib 45.22 *beef*
foreroyal 74 Sails
forerun 154, 194.8 *be before*, 517.11 *predict*
forerunner 154.8 *precursor*, 166.5 *precedent*, 194.6 *person having priority*, 194.7 *foretaste*, 496.12 *discoverer*, 517.5 *omen*, 653.13 *director*
foresail 74 Sails, 36.3 *parts of a sailing boat*
foresee 516, 11.23 *divine*, 199.9 *look ahead*, 208.9 *prepare*, 435.16 *visualize*, 435.17 *imagine*, 488.10 *think likely*, 513.9, 517.11 *predict*, 588.7 *intend*, 592.12 *plan ahead*
foreseeable 516, 199.12 *predictable*, 513.7 *expected*, 517.14 *predicted*, 714.15 *future*
foreseeably 513.13 *expectedly*, 517.16 *predictively*
foreseeing 516, 517.13 *predicting*
foreseen 199, 513.7 *expected*
foreshadow 194.8 *be before*, 516.1 *foresee*, 517.11 *predict*
fore shank 45.23 *beef*, 45.27 *lamb*
foreshock 54.22 *seismic activity*
foreshorten 50.23 *design*, 270.10 *shorten*
foreshortened 50.27 *painted*, 270.8 *shortened*
foreshortening 50.4 *treatment*, 270.2 *shortening*
foreshow 517.11 *predict*
foresight 516, 11.8 *psychic power*, 199.4 *looking to the future*, 208.5 *prematurity*, 435.4 *visualization*, 435.10 *visual aid*, 501.1 *knowledge*, 507.1 *wisdom*, 517.1 *prediction*, 592.2 *policy*, 594.9 *preparation*, 781.1 *caution*
Foresight 516
foresighted 208.16 *premature*, 516.6 *foreseeing*
foresightedly 516, 208.20 *prematurely*
foreskin 245.8 *organs of reproduction*
forest 83.1 *plants*, 85.4 *trees*, 371.4 *solid body*
forestage 51.15 *stage*
forestal 85.16 *wooded*
forestall 147.7 *exclude*, 194.9 *do before*, 199.10 *expect*, 208.9 *prepare*, 516.1 *foresee*, 661.8 *hinder*, 723.7 *possess*
forestalled 147.11 *excluded*
forestalling 661.1 *hindrance*, 738.7 *purchasing*
forestalment 723.1 *possession*
forestay 36.3 *parts of a sailing boat*
forestaysail 74 Sails
forested 83.13 *plantlike*, 85.16 *wooded*
forester 85, 632.3 *protector*, 637.4 *preservationist*
Forester 48 *Writers*
forest fire 408.6 *fire*
forest green 453.1 *green*
forest manager 85.8 *forester*
forest of 181.4 *throng*
forest ranger 85.8 *forester*
forestry 85, 68.4 *arable farming*, 83.10 *plant science*
forest spirit 8.5 *deity*
foretaste 194, 143.2 *particular*, 154.6 *preview*, 516.3 *foresight*
foretell 11.23 *divine*, 154.19 *forecast*, 199.9 *look ahead*, 516.1 *foresee*, 517.11 *predict*
foreteller 11.13 *diviner*
foretelling 517.1 *prediction*, 517.13 *predicting*
for eternity 368.13 *metaphysically*

forethought 507.1 *wisdom*, 516.4 *prudence*, 592.2 *policy*, 594.9 *preparation*, 781.1 *caution*
foretime 3.8 *past time*
foretoken 517.5 *omen*, 517.11 *predict*
foretold 199.13 *foreseen*, 517.14 *predicted*
foretop 74 Sails
fore-topgallant 74 Sails
foretopman 74.7 *nautical person*, 359.11 *ascender*
fore-topmast 74 Rigging
fore-topsail 74 Sails
for ever 144.10 *fully*, 188.10 *for the duration*, 185.30 *chronologically*
forever 184.3 *eternal*, 184.7 *eternity*, 184.12 *eternally*, 185.26 *all the time*, 186.8 *ever*, 190.11 *eternally*, 217.9 *permanently*, 219.7 *continually*, 368.13 *metaphysically*, 726.11 *tenaciously*
for ever and a day 190.11 *eternally*
for ever and ever 190.11 *eternally*, 217.9 *permanently*
forever in one's memory 511.7 *memorable*
forever more 186.8 *ever*
for evermore 188.10 *for the duration*, 190.11 *eternally*
forever tired 650.1 *fatigued*
for everyday use 613.1 *useful*
for everyone 522.2 *simple*
forewarn 199.10 *expect*, 516.1 *foresee*, 517.11 *predict*, 636.5 *warn*, 781.6 *caution*
forewarned 513.5 *expecting*, 594.18 *prepared*, 636.9 *warned*
forewarning 516.3 *foresight*, 517.1 *prediction*, 517.5 *omen*, 517.13 *predicting*, 636.1 *warning*
foreword 154.5 *preface*, 156.10 *introduction*, 194.7 *foretaste*, 303.11 *front*, 564.8 *speech*
Forfar 93 Cities
forfeit 131.2 *subtracted item*, 598.1 *relinquish*, 598.3 *relinquishment*, 722.1 *loss*, 722.9 *lose*, 846.16 *disentitle*, 879.1 *punish*, 879.7 *punishment*
forfeit one's reputation 801.4 *disreputable*
forfeiture 722.1 *loss*, 846.2 *disentitlement*, 879.7 *punishment*
forfeiture of deposit 581.6 *discarding*
for free 710.20 *persuasively*, 729.9 *as a gift*, 754.11 *free of charge*
for fun 771.17 *jokingly*
forgather 161.39 *come together*
forgathering 135.1 *union*, 161.1 *assembly*
forge 118.10 *copy*, 243.10 *produce*, 306.7 *form*, 309.12 *distort the truth*, 408.6 *fire*, 538.22 *make unreal*, 538.25 *be dishonest*, 539.30, 540.21 *be fraudulent*, 540.22 *falsify*, 647.1 *workshop*, 741.24 *monetize*, 796.8 *fashion*
forge ahead 336.3 *press on*
forged 118.13 *imitation*, 538.14 *unreal*, 539.39 *imitative*, 540.28 *spurious*, 540.31 *fraudulent*, 540.32 *falsified*
forged note 741.15 *false money*
forged passport 540.14 *false thing*
forger 114.4 *person who copies*, 118.8 *copier*, 538.12 *cheat*, 547.4 *person who makes a representation*, 646.2 *artisan*, 736.11 *dishonest person*, 741.17 *financier*
forgery 118.2 *copy*, 538.2 *unrealness*, 538.10 *dishonesty*, 539.10 *fraud*, 540.4 *spuriousness*, 540.8 *fraud*, 540.9 *falsification*, 736.7 *dishonesty*, 741.15 *false money*
forget 512, 546, 133.11 *be mixed up*, 462.12 *lack thought*, 470.6 *be neglectful*, 691.3 *be le-*

nient, 722.9 *lose*, 838.6 *be ungrateful*, 839.9 *forgive*
forgetful 133.13 *mixed-up*, 404.6 *unfeeling*, 468.7 *inattentive*, 470.4 *negligent*, 512.9 *blank*, 720.11 *nonobservant*, 838.3 *ungrateful*
forgetfully 468.14 *inattentively*, 512.16 *obliviously*, 720.15 *inattentively*, 838.7 *ungratefully*
forgetfulness 546, 468.1 *inattention*, 470.1 *negligence*, 512.2 *blankness*, 720.1 *nonobservance*, 838.1 *ingratitude*
forgetful person 512
forget grievances 677.5 *make peace*
forget it! 598
forget it 218.12 *stop*, 536.17 *never*, 598.1 *relinquish*
forget-me-not 84 Flowers and Flowering Plants, 454.6 *blue thing*
forget one's differences 675.5 *be at peace*
forget oneself 828.12 *become angry*
forget one's lines 512.14 *be forgetful*
forget one's manners 478.18 *answer back*
forget one's place 807.22 *be rude*, 807.28 *get above oneself*
forget one's principles 858.8 *be dishonourable*
forget one's problems 649.2 *take it easy*
forget one's words 656.5 *be unskilful*
forgettable 512.11 *forgotten*, 612.1 *unimportant*
forgetting 61.23 *memory*, 512.9 *blank*, 546.5 *forgetfulness*
forget work 649.2 *take it easy*
forging 382.5 *structuring*
forgivable 839, 612.1 *unimportant*, 843.9 *in the right*, 855.13 *vindicable*
forgivably 855.15 *in vindication*
forgive 512, 839, 16.78 *acquit*, 691.3 *be lenient*, 831.8 *be benevolent*, 835.10 *show mercy*, 848.10 *acquit*
forgive a debt 747
forgive and forget 512.15 *forgive*, 677.5 *make peace*, 839.9 *forgive*
forgiven 839, 16.63 *acquitted*, 691.5 *given consideration*
forgiveness 839, 16.42 *acquittal*, 512.6 *amnesty*, 675.1 *peace*, 677.2 *peace offering*, 691.1 *leniency*, 700.1 *liberation*, 831.1 *benevolence*, 835.3 *mercy*
Forgiveness 839
forgiveness of debts 747.1 *nonpayment*
forgiveness of sin 839.1 *forgiveness*
forgiveness of sins 700.1 *liberation*
forgive one's sins 839.9 *forgive*
forgiving 839, 691.4 *lenient*, 831.6 *benevolent*, 835.6 *pitying*
forgivingly 16, 839, 677.7 *pacifically*, 831.10 *benevolently*
forgiving nature 839.2 *forgivingness*
forgivingness 839
forgo 598.1 *relinquish*, 705.5 *resign*, 727.9 *dispose of*, 869.5 *be self-restrained*
forgoing 598.3 *relinquishment*, 727.1 *disposal*
forgone 598.5 *relinquished*, 727.12 *disposed*
for good 144.10 *fully*, 157.28 *conclusively*, 188.10 *for the duration*, 190.11 *eternally*, 217.9 *permanently*, 726.11 *tenaciously*
for good and all 144.10 *fully*, 157.28 *conclusively*, 188.10 *for the duration*, 190.11 *eternally*, 217.9 *permanently*, 726.11 *tenaciously*
forgo repayment 744.9 *acquire credit*

forgo sex 825.10 *be continent*, 876.11 *be moral*
forgotten 512, 546.6 *obliterated*, 722.16 *losing*, 838.4 *unthanked*
forgotten anniversary 468.5 *inattentive act*
forgotten birthday 468.5 *inattentive act*
forgotten man 147.5 *excluded person*
forgotten name 468.5 *inattentive act*
for humane reasons 835.13 *pitifully*
foritified line 671.8 *military defences*
fork 343, 42.4 *chess terms*, 69.6 *garden tool*, 69.15 *cultivate*, 71.11 *bicycle part*, 85.2 *tree part*, 96.1 *river*, 162.10 *diverge*, 176.8 *half*, 176.16 *halve*, 310.1, 310.11 *angle*, 326.15 *take away*, 338.24 *push*, 343.14 *branch*, 350.16 *eating utensil*, 380.8 *sharp-pointed thing*, 380.16 *use a sharp tool*, 603.2 *garden tool*
fork bender 11.12 *occultist*
fork bending 11.1 *occultism*
forked 176.13 *half*, 310.7 *angular*, 343.9 *branched*
forked tongue 540.2 *duplicity*, 657.3 *cunning person*
for keeps 184.12, 190.11 *eternally*, 726.11 *tenaciously*
for kicks 405.11 *pleasingly*
fork in 350.22 *eat well*
forking 162.24 *divergent*, 176.7 *halving*, 343.4 *branching*, 343.9 *branched*
forklift 361.9 *lifter*
fork-lift truck 71 Motor Vehicles
fork lightning 55.21 *thunderstorm*
forklike 343.9 *branched*
fork out 729.5 *give*, 746.6 *pay*, 748.1 *expend*
fork supper 350.12 *meal*
for long 188.11 *long*
forlorn 770.5 *sad*, 776.4 *hopeless*, 816.10 *lonely*
forlorn hope 515.1 *disappointment*
form 306, 306, 382, 6.22 *educate*, 10.1 *ritual*, 16.34 *legal formality*, 32.7 *horseracing*, 39.6 *diving*, 50.4 *treatment*, 50.21 *sculpt*, 57.4 *crystal*, 59.4 *anatomy*, 59.17 *taxonomy*, 61.26 *gestalt*, 77.20 *abode of mammals*, 99.20 *bring into being*, 105.1 *state*, 148.13 *make*, 150.18 *order*, 156.22 *invent*, 163.4 *type*, 163.6 *students*, 166.6 *custom*, 167.5 *convention*, 167.9 *make conform*, 243.10 *produce*, 299.2 *shadow*, 306.2 *prototype*, 306.3 *kind*, 327.1 *way*, 382.15 *shape*, 457.3 *external appearance*, 544.1 *identification*, 545.1 *record*, 547.11 *paint*, 560.14 *describe*, 584.5 *tradition*, 592.10 *plan out*, 599.1 *use*, 623.3 *health*, 654.3 *precept*, 767.6 *profile*, 796.4 *design*, 811.11 *ritual*, 813.1 *formality*
Form 306
formable 374.7 *impressionable*
form a cartel 699.9 *economize*, 715.5 *contract*
form a clique 665.12 *be in league with*
form a club 665.12 *be in league with*
form a coalition 665.15 *politicize*
form a community 2.15 *socialize*
form a core 371.8 *be dense*
form a crocodile 159.17 *line up*
form a government 12.12 *take authority*
form a hypothesis 518.5 *suppose*
form a kernel 371.8 *be dense*
formal 306, 813, 5.39 *of language*, 48.16 *literary*, 52.69 *theoretic*, 150.10 *ordered*, 150.14 *well-ordered*, 167.14 *conformist*, 295.3 *formal dress*, 306.9 *formed*, 382.12 *organic*, 559.9

inelegant, 690.8 *severe*, 699.14 *self-restrained*, 811.22 *majestic*, 811.26 *ritualistic*, 817.8 *good-mannered*
formal agreement 715.1 *contract*, 851.1 *approval*
formal argument 463.3 *debate*
formal attire 813.4 *formal dress*
formal cause 226.1 *cause*
formal clothes 295.1 *dress*
formal contract 715.1 *contract*
formaldehyde 57 Common Chemical Compounds, **62** Medication, 637.2 *preserver*
formal dining 350.4 *eating meals*
formal dinner 350.13 *feast*
formal dress 295, 813
formal expression 52.65 *theory*
formal garden 69.2 *garden*
form a line 159.17 *line up*
formalism 813, 10.2 *ritualism*, 51.8 *theatre movements*, 150.1 *order*, 167.4 *conventionalism*
formalist 7.4 *religionist*, 51.40 *activist*, 167.6 *conformist*
formalistic 7.15 *religious*, 150.10 *ordered*, 813.6 *formal*
formalistically 150.25 *in order*
formalities 813.5 *etiquette*, 817.3 *courtesies*
formality 306, 813, 10.1 *ritual*, 16.34 *legal formality*, 167.4 *conventionalism*, 477.5 *easy question*, 584.5 *tradition*, 690.1 *severity*, 699.3 *self-restraint*, 811.7 *pomp*, 817.2 *good manners*
Formality 813
formalization 150.1 *order*
formalize 813, 16.68 *legislate*, 306.7 *form*
formalized 150.10 *ordered*
formal language 5.6 *official language*, 5.29 *grammar*
formal logic 4.6 *branch of philosophy*, 52.63 *mathematical logic*
formally 813, 5.52 *grammatically*, 306.13 *formatively*, 690.11 *severely*, 699.17 *with self-restraint*, 811.38 *majestically*, 811.42 *ritualistically*, 817.15 *genteelly*
formally dressed 813.7 *dressed up*
formal meal 350.12 *meal*
formalness 813.1 *formality*
formal occasion 813, 350.13 *feast*
form a loose scrum 35.5 *play rugby*
formal reasoning 459.2 *ways of thinking*
formal speech 567.1 *address*
formal usage 5.29 *grammar*
formal visit 815.3 *meeting*
form an alliance 116, 137.13 *intercommunicate*
form an image of 519.14 *imagine*
form a partnership 665.12 *be in league with*, 715.5 *contract*, 823.19 *merge*
form a party 665.14 *be a party member*
form a picket line 661.9 *block*
form a queue 159.17 *line up*
form a scab 135.10 *link*, 629.6 *cure*
form a scrum 35.5 *play rugby*
format 65.17 *computing term*, 65.19 *abort*, 306.1 *form*, 306.2 *prototype*, 306.7, 382.3 *form*, 457.3 *external appearance*
form a tight scrum 35.5 *play rugby*
formation 35.3 *rugby play*, 150.1 *order*, 156.5 *invention*, 306.1, 382.3 *form*, 382.5 *structuring*, 457.1 *appearance*
formational 152.22 *organizational*
formative 5.35 *part of speech*, 5.44 *grammatical*, 148.6 *component*, 156.29 *beginning*, 226.13 *causal*, 243.11 *productive*, 306.9 *formed*, 374.7 *impressionable*
formatively 306
form a whole 142.9 *be whole*
form criticism 524.3 *criticism*

formed 306, 43.17 *structured*
form engraver 47.13 *carpenter*
former 200, 202, 3.15 *historic,* 154.11, 194.10 *prior,* 200.22 *dead,* 705.7 *resigning*
former British coinage 741.10 *former British money*
former British divisions 92
former British money 741
for mercy's sake 835.14 *have pity*
formerly 202, 209, 3.24 *historically,* 154.20 *before,* 200.22 *in the past,* 705.10 *by resigning*
former soldier 679
former time 197.1 *different time*
former times 3.8, 200.1 *past time*
formic 58 Common Fatty Acids
Formica 266.5 *layered thing,* 293.12 *protective covering,* 604.1 *materials*
formic acid 57 Common Chemical Compounds
formication 366.5 *restlessness,* 403.3 *stimulus,* 624.13 *skin disease*
formidable 237.10 *potent,* 611.6 *notable,* 659.10 *difficult,* 777.10 *frightening*
formidably 659.26 *arduously*
forming 306, 243.1 *production,* 306.1 *form*
formless 151.14 *irregular,* 307.5 *shapeless*
formlessly 307.6 *shapelessly*
formlessness 307.1 *shapelessness*
form letters 5.47 *word*
form of government 12.1 *government*
form of law 16.34 *legal formality,* 306.5 *formality*
form of speech 5.49 *literary style*
form of worship 10.1 *ritual,* 10.4 *public worship*
for money 721.20 *gainfully*
Formosan 5 Languages and Groups of Languages
form part of 148.10 *compose*
formroom 6.15 *schoolroom*
form teacher 6.4 *educator*
formula 5.23 *phrase,* 10.1 *ritual,* 16.34 *legal formality,* 52.14 *operation,* 52.65 *theory,* 57.13 *structure,* 62.5 *prescription,* 166.5 *precedent,* 306.2 *prototype,* 505.1 *maxim,* 592.2 *policy,* 630.1 *remedy,* 654.3 *precept*
Formula 1 33.11 *racing*
Formula 1 car 33.1 *motor racing*
Formula 1 driver 33.8 *driver*
Formula 1 race 33, 33.1 *motor racing*
Formula 1 racer 33.8 *driver*
Formula 1 racing 33.1 *motor racing,* 674.4 *race*
Formula 2 33.11 *racing*
Formula 2 racing 33.1 *motor racing*
Formula 3 33.1 *motor racing*
Formula 3000 33.1 *motor racing*
Formula 40 class 36.2 *sailing boat*
formulaic 10.21 *ritualistic*
formulary 10.1 *ritual,* 654.3 *precept,* 813.1 *formal*
Formula Super Vee racing 33.1 *motor racing*
formulate 5.45 *use language,* 243.10 *produce,* 306.7 *form,* 382.15 *shape,* 471.15 *imagine,* 505.3 *aphorize,* 526.3 *reveal,* 549.9 *style,* 564.11 *speak,* 592.11 *invent,* 796.8 *fashion*
formulated intention 588
formulation 243.1 *production,* 306.4 *forming,* 526.10 *manifestation*
Formula Vauxhall Lotus 33.1 *motor racing*
Fornax 53 The Constellations
fornicate 821.29 *make love,* 877.17 *be sexually immoral*
fornication 135.4 *sexual union,* 821.5 *desire,* 877.3 *sexual immorality*
for nickels and dimes 754.15 *cheaply*
for noble reasons 863.9 *virtuously*

for no good reason 229.8 *by chance*
for nothing 729.7 *given,* 754.11 *free of charge,* 754.15 *cheaply*
for now 185.26 *all the time*
for one's benefit 613.4 *profitable*
for oneself 577.9 *be obstinate*
for one's own part 165.29 *personally*
for one's own sake 860.8 *selfishly*
for one's service 878.19 *rewardingly*
for peanuts 754.9 *cheap*
for pennies 754.15 *cheaply*
for pity's sake 835.14 *have pity*
for private ends 860.8 *selfishly*
for profit 737.15 *profitable,* 860.8 *selfishly*
for public notice 526.16 *manifestly*
forrard 336.19 *forward*
forray 670.12 *military attack*
for real 99.13 *real*
for recreation 39.12 *by swimming*
for rent 710.17 *offered*
for revenge 862.12 *evilly*
forsake 254.19 *leave empty,* 578.2 *equivocate,* 598.2 *withdraw,* 858.9 *prove false*
forsaken 174.16 *alone,* 254.14 *unoccupied,* 598.5 *relinquished*
forsakenly 598.7 *on hold*
forsake one's duties 598.2 *withdraw*
for sale 727, 710.17 *offered,* 710.20 *persuasively,* 729.7 *given,* 739.18 *on sale*
Forseti 8 Deities, **8** Deities
for short periods 187
forsooth 537.35 *truly*
for specified periods 187
for sport 771.17 *jokingly*
for starters 156.40 *first*
Forster 48 Writers
for sure 480.12 *assuredly*
forswear 484.8 *reverse,* 536.9 *renounce,* 578.4 *recant,* 591.3 *abstain,* 598.1 *relinquish,* 727.9 *dispose of*
forswearer 578.9 *equivocator*
forswearing 484.2 *reversal,* 536.4 *renunciation,* 536.13 *rebutting,* 540.6 *lying,* 540.29 *deceitful,* 578.8 *recantation,* 591.11 *abstinence,* 727.1 *disposal*
forsworn 727.12 *disposed*
forsythia 84 Flowers and Flowering Plants
fort 671, 243.8 *construction,* 634.1 *refuge*
Fortaleza 93 Cities
fortalice 671.12 *fort*
forte 49 Musical Terms, 165.7 *special skill,* 249.14 *sphere,* 423.1 *loudness,* 423.6 *loud,* 423.9 *loudly,* 501.2 *information,* 617.6 *worth,* 655.1 *skill*
Fortean animals 529.6 *natural mystery*
forth 347, 336.19 *forward*
Forth 65 Programming Languages, **96** Rivers, 96.4 *British rivers*
for that reason 116.36 *accordingly*
forthcoming 199.11 *future,* 208.13 *imminent,* 264.5 *near,* 347.15 *outgoing,* 530.11 *disclosing,* 594.17 *developing*
forthcoming event 199.6 *future event*
for the asking 729.7 *given*
for the benefit of others 863.9 *virtuously*
for the better 627.17 *better*
for the chop 244.15 *destroyed*
for the count 26.16 *professionally*
for the duration 188, 185.26 *all the time*
for the first time 479.15 *inventively*
for the general public 522.2 *simple,* 522.13 *intelligibly*
for the interim 185.26 *all the time*
for the layman 522.2 *simple,* 522.13 *intelligibly*

for the love of God 835.14 *have pity*
for the moment 196.10 *for the present*
for the most part 103.13 *in essence,* 124.11 *on average,* 142.13 *on the whole,* 164.31 *overall,* 166.18 *as a rule*
for the nonce 189.9 *for the time being,* 196.10 *for the present*
for the occasion 196.10 *for the present,* 210.6 *timely,* 210.9 *opportunely*
for the present 196
for the price of 751.16 *at a price*
for the public good 613.12 *usefully,* 833.8 *philanthropically*
for the sake of 662.37 *in aid of*
for the sake of appearances 457.15 *apparently*
for the sake of argument 518.10 *supposedly*
for the sake of others 859.9 *unselfishly*
for the time being 189, 185.26 *all the time,* 196.10 *for the present*
for the worse 628.14 *worse*
for this occasion 196.10 *for the present*
forthright 332.9 *directly,* 442.4 *easily seen through,* 522.2 *simple,* 526.15 *open,* 537.18 *truthful,* 556.3 *natural*
forthrightly 526.17 *frankly,* 530.13 *openly*
forthrightness 442.10 *openness,* 522.10 *simplicity,* 537.5 *truthfulness*
forthwith 191.8 *immediately,* 208.17 *early*
fortieth 173.4 *less than one,* 179.19 *twentieth*
fortification 671, 237.1 *strength,* 318.2 *projection,* 535.4 *confirmation,* 634.1 *refuge,* 676.6 *art of war*
fortified 237.13 *strengthened,* 373.3 *hardened,* 535.13 *supported,* 651.4 *refreshed,* 671.30 *defended*
fortified wine 351.9 *wine*
fortifier 535.9 *affirmer*
fortify 133.8 *mix,* 237.8 *strengthen,* 535.19 *confirm,* 632.9 *protect,* 651.1 *refresh,* 671.20 *reinforce,* 718.14 *make fast*
fortifying 237.4 *strengthening,* 651.3 *refreshing*
fortissimo 49 Musical Terms, 423.1 *loudness,* 423.6 *loud,* 423.9 *loudly*
fortitude 574, 575.4 *stamina,* 778.3 *steadfastness,* 863.2 *virtues*
Fort Knox 741.20 *money store*
Fort Lauderdale 93 Cities
fortnight 179.7 *double figures,* 185.4 *term,* 187.2 *time period*
fortnightly 214.12 *cyclic,* 214.16 *cyclically,* 532.5 *journal*
Fortran 65 Programming Languages
fortress 243.8 *construction,* 634.1 *refuge,* 671.12 *fort*
Fortress America 676.1 *war*
fortuitous 229.6 *motiveless,* 489.3 *unexpected,* 589.8 *chance*
fortuitously 229.8 *by chance,* 489.11 *luckily,* 589.13 *by chance*
fortuitousness 229.1 *lack of motive,* 589.1 *chance*
fortuity 229.1 *lack of motive,* 589.1 *chance*
Fortuna 8 Deities
fortunate 210.6 *timely,* 229.7 *adventurous,* 517.15 *presageful,* 589.8 *chance,* 682.13 *successful,* 686.8 *prosperous,* 714.14 *auspicious*
Fortunate Isles 519.8 *dreamland*
fortunately 210.9 *opportunely,* 229.9 *luckily,* 589.13 *by chance,* 682.16 *successfully,* 686.9 *prosperously,* 714.17 *auspiciously*

fortune 741, 224.3 *changeable thing,* 229.2 *chance,* 516.3 *foresight,* 517.1 *prediction,* 589.2 *luck,* 682.1 *success,* 686.1 *prosperity,* 686.2 *good fortune,* 742.5 *wealth*
fortune's favourite 686.4 *prosperous person*
fortunes of war 676.1 *war*
fortune teller 11.13 *diviner,* 199.5 *predictor,* 368.7 *believer in a nonmaterial world,* 516.5 *predictor,* 517.9 *forecaster*
fortune telling 11.1 *occultism,* 11.9 *divination,* 199.4 *looking to the future,* 516.3 *foresight,* 517.2 *divination,* 517.13 *predicting*
Fort Wayne 93 Cities
Fort William 93 Cities
Fort Worth 93 Cities
forty 179.8 *twenty and over*
forty acres and a mule 657.1 *cunning*
forty-ninth parallel 298.1 *interface*
forty-one 24.6 *pool*
fortysomething 207.13 *middle-aged*
forty winks 643.9 *sleep,* 649.1 *ease*
forum 16.18 *tribunal,* 93.7 *city district,* 291.4 *centre of activity,* 568.4 *conference,* 706.2 *representative body,* 740.6 *marketplace*
for want of 609.10 *insufficiently*
for want of anything better 222.9 *instead*
forward 336, 336, 338, 23.2 *basketball player,* 30.11 *gymnastic,* 31.2 *hockey player,* 31.4 *ice hockey player,* 35.4 *rugby player,* 36.10 *sailing,* 70.4 *transport,* 194.10 *prior,* 208.16 *premature,* 284.14 *give moral support,* 303.6 *front,* 303.11 *in front,* 324.19 *go,* 326.12 *transport,* 326.13 *post,* 326.8 *further,* 534.31 *correspond,* 567.10 *send,* 595.5 *immature,* 615.6 *be convenient,* 627.1 *improve,* 660.16 *make easy,* 662.28 *further,* 818.6 *bad-mannered,* 850.10 *disrespectful*
forwardal 336.10 *forward motion*
forward bow 36.12 *canoeing*
forward bow stroke 36.6 *canoeing*
forward dislocate circle 30.7 *stationary rings*
forward dive 39.6 *diving*
forwarded 70.5 *transportable*
forwarded mail 534.2 *postal communication*
forwarder 85.7 *timber production*
forwarding 70.1 *transport,* 70.5 *transportable,* 336.10 *forward motion,* 662.8 *furtherance*
forward line 303.1 *front*
forward-looking 336.17 *forward*
forwardly 208.20 *prematurely*
forward march 336.10 *forward motion*
forward mast 36.3 *parts of a sailing boat*
forward motion 336, 195.1 *succession*
Forward Motion 336
forward movement 195.1 *succession*
forwardness 595.10 *immaturity*
forward pass 338.5 *throw*
forward planning 516.4 *prudence,* 517.3 *plan*
forward progress 19.7 *offence*
forwards 30.12 *competitively,* 336.19 *forward*
forward somersault 30.5 *horizontal bar,* 30.8 *floor exercises*
forward uprise 30.7 *stationary rings*
forward upstart 30.7 *stationary rings*
for what purpose? 613.12 *usefully*
for what reason? 477.25 *what?*
for your ears only 529.15 *in secret*
Fosbury flop 21.2 *field events*

Foscolo 48 Poets
fossa 77 Placental Mammals
fosse 301.3 *enclosing thing,* 317.2 *concave land,* 671.8 *military defences*
fossil 54, 3.11 *relic,* 59.3 *organism,* 132.1 *remainder,* 200.10 *fossilization,* 202.5 *old thing,* 397.11 *dead person,* 637.3 *preserved thing*
fossil algae 90.5 *algal product*
fossil animal 54.43 *fossil*
fossil bird 78.8 *extinct bird*
fossil fish 80
fossil footprint 54.43 *fossil*
fossil fuel 200.10 *fossilization,* 235.6 *source of energy,* 410.1 *fuel*
fossil hunting 42 Hobbies and Pastimes
fossiliferous 54.61 *fossilized*
fossilization 200, 54.43 *fossil,* 371.2 *concentration,* 373.6 *solidification*
fossilize 54.62 *lithify,* 371.8 *be dense,* 373.10 *solidify*
fossilized 54, 200.19 *antiquarian,* 373.3 *hardened,* 397.22 *post-mortem*
fossilized remains 200.7 *thing of the past*
fossil man 54.43 *fossil*
fossil oil 395.9 *petroleum*
fossilology 3.2 *archaeology*
fossil plant 54.43 *fossil*
fossil record 54.43 *fossil,* 59.16 *evolution,* 200.10 *fossilization*
fossil reptile 79.6 *extinct reptile*
fossil resin 395.9 *resin*
fossil track 54.43 *fossil*
foster 6.22 *educate,* 222.4 *be a substitute,* 226.12 *determine,* 284.14 *give moral support,* 293.34 *cover for,* 293.40 *substitutive,* 336.8 *further,* 627.1 *improve,* 632.9 *protect,* 637.5 *preserve,* 662.23 *advise*
fosterage 662.9 *patronage*
foster child 701.4 *dependent*
fostering 662.32 *supportive*
foster parent 222.2 *substitute person,* 293.21 *substitution*
fou as a coot 874.1 *drunk*
fou as a wulk 874.1 *drunk*
Foucault 4 Philosophers, **52** Scientists
fouetté 46.9 *ballet steps*
fouetté en tournant 46.9 *ballet steps*
fought to the death 674.16 *competitive*
fought to the finish 674.16 *competitive*
foul 22.7 *play baseball,* 23.4 *playing terms,* 23.6 *play basketball,* 24.4 *carom,* 24.9 *billiard,* 25.10 *bowling,* 26.2 *boxing,* 26.11 *do a combat sport,* 31.5 *lacrosse,* 31.9 *play hockey,* 38.2 *football play,* 38.4 *play soccer,* 55.48 *stormy,* 74.9 *navigate,* 330.2 *collide,* 341.8 *repulsive,* 353.16 *defecate,* 618.4 *poor,* 622.7 *dirty,* 622.8 *unclean,* 622.11 *dirty,* 626.5 *unhygienic,* 628.3 *make worse,* 785.9 *disliked,* 827.8 *cursing,* 844.7 *sense of wrong,* 862.7 *evil,* 864.11 *wicked,* 864.15 *criminal*
foulard 67 Natural Fabrics
foul ball 22.5 *batting terms*
fouled 38.5 *soccer,* 622.7 *dirty*
fouled-up 151.19 *mixed-up,* 656.4 *bungled*
fouling 38.2 *football play,* 38.5 *soccer*
foul language 827.2 *offensive language*
foul line 22.1 *baseball,* 25.4 *bowling*
foul mouth 822.6 *swearing,* 827.1 *curse*
foul-mouthed 818.6 *bad-mannered,* 822.13 *angry,* 827.8 *cursing*
foul-mouthing 827.1 *curse*

foulness 618.10 *poverty,* 622.1 *dirtiness,* 622.2 *uncleanness,* 862.1 *evil*
foul off 22.7 *play baseball*
foul out 23.6 *play basketball*
foul play 16.39 *crime,* 481.3 *prejudice,* 493.3 *injustice,* 539.10 *fraud,* 640.2 *deed,* 657.1 *cunning,* 670.16 *terrorist attack,* 801.3 *disreputable action,* 832.7 *act of malevolence,* 844.6 *unlawfulness,* 844.7 *sense of wrong,* 858.1 *improbity,* 862.5 *evil thing,* 864.7 *criminality*
foul shooter 23.3 *basketball player*
foul shot 23.4 *playing terms*
foul-smelling 419.3 *stinking*
foul stroke 24.3 *English billiards*
foul taste 415.2 *unpalatability*
foul-tasting 415.6 *unpalatable*
foul territory 22.1 *baseball*
foul the line 335.3 *go astray*
foul tip 22.5 *batting terms*
foul-tongued 827.8 *cursing*
foul up 151.21 *confuse,* 504.19 *make a mistake,* 622.10 *be dirty,* 656.7 *be clumsy,* 661.8 *hinder*
foul-up 151.6 *mix-up,* 504.10 *blunder,* 656.9 *bungling,* 661.2 *obstacle*
foul weather 241.5 *violent weather*
foumart 77 Placental Mammals
found 250, 154.18 *forerun,* 156.23 *inaugurate,* 225.7 *make stable,* 226.11 *inaugurate,* 243.10 *produce,* 284.6 *base,* 306.7 *form,* 496.14 *discovered,* 594.2 *do the groundwork,* 629.13 *repaired*
foundation 63.28 *substructure,* 154.3 *preparation,* 156.6 *inauguration,* 226.3 *rudiment,* 280.1 *base,* 284.2 *supporting part,* 472.1 *topic,* 594.10 *preparations,* 665.1 *party*
foundational 63.32 *structural,* 154.14 *preparatory,* 156.34 *inaugural,* 226.13 *causal,* 284.9 *supportive*
foundation garment 295.18 *underwear*
foundations 63.28 *substructure,* 382.6 *construction*
foundation stone 284.2 *supporting part*
founded 472.7 *focused*
founded on a rock 632.6 *invulnerable*
founder 226.7 *Prime Mover,* 243.9 *producer,* 244.13 *be destroyed,* 277.14 *deepen,* 360.9 *descend,* 366.25 *pitch,* 369.12 *be heavy,* 397.16 *meet one's fate,* 496.12 *discoverer,* 592.8 *planner,* 687.9 *be in trouble*
foundering 360.16 *descending*
founder member 243.9 *producer*
found guilty 866.5 *guilty*
founding 154.1 *preparatory*
founding father 154.8 *precursor,* 243.9 *producer*
found innocent 865.6 *declared innocent*
foundling 816.7 *outsider*
found not guilty 865.6 *declared innocent*
found object 50.12 *sculpture*
foundry 220.4 *medium of conversion,* 647.1 *workshop*
foundryman 646.2 *artisan*
found wanting 609.1 *insufficient,* 852.32 *unsatisfactory*
fount 5.15 *type style,* 226.2 *source,* 605.2 *resource*
fountain 69.3 *ornamental garden,* 226.2 *source,* 347.2 *outflow,* 359.2 *upturn,* 359.12 *geyser,* 359.17 *spring up,* 389.1 *water,* 605.2 *resource*
fountainhead 96.2 *channel,* 156.3, 226.2 *source*
Fountain of Youth 588.6 *objective,* 714.4 *promised land*
fountain syringe 389.11 *wash*

Fouqué 48 Writers, **48** Dramatists
four 178, 178, 27.10 *score,* 52.9 *numeral*
Four 178
four and twenty 179.8 *twenty and over*
four-ball match 29.1 *golf*
four-beat trudgen crawl 39.2 *swimming technique*
four bits 741.8 *American money*
four by four 178.14 *in fours*
four-colour theorem 52 Theorems and Laws
four corners of the earth 142.2 *whole thing,* 178.3 *foursome,* 263.3 *distant place*
four corners of the law 16.34 *legal formality*
four-dimensional continuum 56.7 *space*
four-dimensional space 52.35, 56.7 *space*
four-eyed 435.22 *bespectacled*
four-eyed fish 80 Fishes
four-figure 179.21 *thousandth*
four-flush 538.25 *be dishonest*
four-flusher 538.12 *cheat,* 539.15 *deceiver*
four-flushing 538.19 *dishonest*
fourfold 178.7 *four,* 178.13 *four times*
fourfoldness 178.4 *quadruplication*
four-footed 178.9 *tetramerous*
four-handed 178.10 *quartered*
four humours 771
four hundred 179.9 *treble figures*
Fourier 52 Scientists
Fourier analysis 52 Named Concepts
Fourier series 52 Named Concepts, 52.20 *sequence*
four-in-hand 71 Carriages and Carts, 178.3 *foursome,* 295.14 *neckwear*
four-leaf clover 11.6 *talisman,* 178.3 *foursome,* 213.4 *rare things,* 517.6 *good-luck sign*
four-legged 178.9 *tetramerous*
four-legged friend 76.2 *animal*
four-letter 5.39 *of language,* 827.8 *cursing*
four-letter word 5.19 *swearword,* 178.3 *foursome,* 827.1 *curse*
four-man bobsled 41.9 *bobsledding*
four-man kayak race 36.6 *canoeing*
four-master 74 Sailing Ships and Boats
four-minute warning 192.10 *signal*
four of a kind 42.3 *card game terms*
four-part 178.10 *quartered*
four-parted 178.10 *quartered*
four-poster 178.3 *foursome*
four-poster bed 47.6 *bed*
fours 25.9 *bowls,* 36.4 *rowing*
fourscore 179.8 *twenty and over*
fourscore and ten 179.8 *twenty and over*
four seasons 178.3 *foursome*
four-sided 52.82 *polygonal,* 178.8 *quadrilateral*
fours match 25.1 *green bowling*
foursome 178, 29.1 *golf,* 178.1 *four*
foursome reel 46.4 *historic dancing*
foursquare 178.8 *quadrilateral,* 178.13 *four times*
four-star 395.9 *petroleum*
four-step 25.10 *bowling*
four-step delivery 25.5 *bowling delivery*
four-stroke 178.10 *quartered*
four-stroke cycle 63.13 *engine cycle*
fourteen 179.7 *double figures*
fourteenth 173.4 *less than one,* 179.18 *eleventh*
fourth 178, 49.16 *musical note,* 52.75 *equal,* 173.4 *less than one,* 178.6 *quarter,* 178.7 *four*

fourth-class mail 534.2 *postal communication*
fourth dimension 248
fourth-dimensional 248.11 *spatial*
fourth estate 533.2 *journalism*
Fourth Estate 533.1 *news*
fourth finger 407.7 *sense organ*
fourth guard 28.3 *fencing movements*
fourthly 178.15 *fourth*
Fourth of July 214.6 *annually celebrated day,* 812.5 *anniversary*
fourth part 178.6 *quarter*
fourth power 52.17 *multiplication*
four times 178
four-wheel drive 71 Motor Vehicle Parts
four winds 178.3 *foursome*
foutou 45.53 *African dish*
fowl 68.8 *livestock,* 78.1 *birds,* 590.11 *hunt*
fowler 590.6 *hunter*
Fowles 48 Writers
fowling 78.20 *bird sport,* 590.2 *chase*
fowling-piece 590.3 *hunting and fishing equipment,* 680.9 *firearm*
fowl-like 78.23 *avian*
fowl of the air 78.1 *birds*
fowl tick 82 Arachnids
fox 74 Rigging, **77** Placental Mammals, 32.8 *hunting,* 329.12 *swift animal,* 456.11 *variegate,* 657.3 *cunning person*
Fox 5 Languages and Groups of Languages, **53** The Constellations
FOX 534.24 *television broadcasting*
fox and geese 42 Children's Games and Party Games
foxdog 32.8 *hunting*
foxes 161 Collective Names by Animal
foxglove 84 Flowers and Flowering Plants, 455.3 *purple thing*
fox grape 86 Fruits
foxhole 317.2 *concave land,* 322.7 *passageway,* 531.2 *hiding place,* 634.1 *refuge,* 671.8 *military defences*
foxhound 77 Breeds of Dogs, 32.8 *hunting*
fox hound 590.6 *hunter*
fox hunt 32.8 *hunting,* 590.2 *chase*
fox hunter 32.2 *thoroughbred,* 77.24 *hunter,* 398.13 *animal killer,* 590.6 *hunter*
fox hunting 18 Sporting Activities, 32.8 *hunting,* 32.17 *equine* 77.23 *mammal hunting*
fox hunting 398.9 *animal killing*
foxiness 474.3, 657.1 *cunning*
foxing 456.4 *maculation*
fox in the henhouse 661.2 *obstacle*
foxlike 77.28 *carnivorous*
foxtail 87 Grasses
fox terrier 77 Breeds of Dogs
foxtrot 46.2, 46.15 *dance*
Foxtrot 534 Phonetic Alphabet
foxtrotter 46.5 *dancer*
foxy 77.28 *carnivorous,* 449.1 *brown,* 474.8, 657.4 *cunning,* 858.5 *dishonourable*
foxy lady 340.6 *charmer*
foyer 51.16 *auditorium,* 256.7 *room,* 303.1 *front,* 346.6 *means of entry*
Foyle 94 Lakes
f.p.s. system 75.2 *unit system*
f.p.s. unit 75.2 *unit system*
fracas 153.5 *commotion,* 241.3 *instance of violence,* 473.1 *argument,* 500.1 *dissent,* 666.2 *argument,* 674.6 *fight*
fracastorius 563.7 *voiceless person*
fractal 52.28 *algorithm,* 52.41 *geometric figure*
fraction 173, 52.6 *complex number,* 52.18 *division,* 57.22 *industrial chemistry,* 120.2 *certain amount,* 143.1 *part,* 145.3 *incomplete thing,* 148.2 *piece,* 169.5 *ratio,* 612.8 *trifle*
Fraction 173

fractional 169, 173, 52.71 *numerical*, 120.6 *quantitative*, 143.11 *partial*, 148.6 *component*
fractional crystallization 57.5 *process*
fractional currency 741.13 *coinage*
fractional distillation 57.5 *process*, 57.22 *industrial chemistry*
fractionalize 136.11 *divide*
fractionally 173, 120.7 *quantitatively*, 143.12 *partly*, 148.14 *constituently*
fractional part 173
fractionate 57.25 *solidify*, 136.11 *divide*, 388.25 *gasify*
fractionation 57.22 *industrial chemistry*, 388.10 *vaporization*, 410.6 *oil*
fractionize 136.11 *divide*
fractious 473.8 *argumentative*, 663.22 *uncooperative*, 829.4 *irascible*
fractiousness 573.14 *disobedience*, 663.5 *contrariness*, 829.1 *irascibility*
fracture 54.20 *earth movement*, 54.64 *fold*, 63.16 *deformation*, 63.31 *load*, 136.9 *separate*, 160.4 *interruption*, 241.3 *instance of violence*, 241.8 *use violence*, 265.2, 265.5 *crack*, 322.1 *opening*, 322.18 *open*, 379.4 *be brittle*, 406.3 *injury*, 406.11 *inflict pain*
fractured 265.7 *cracked*, 322.12 *open*, 406.6 *injured*
fractureproof 378.1 *tough*
fradicin 62 *Medication*
fraenectomy 60 *Surgical Operations*
fragile 139.8 *nonadhesive*, 189.7 *impermanent*, 238.8 *weak*, 272.2 *fine*, 379.1 *brittle*
fragile as an eggshell 379.1 *brittle*
fragile item 238.5 *weak thing*
fragilely 379, 139.10 *noncohesively*
fragileness 139.1 *nonadhesion*, 379.2 *brittleness*
fragility 236.1 *powerlessness*, 238.1 *weakness*, 272.7 *fineness*, 379.2 *brittleness*
fragment 173, 136.11 *divide*, 143.1, 143.10 *part*, 148.2 *piece*, 149.2 *impurity*, 162.11 *explode*, 173.8 *divide*, 260.3 *little piece*, 379.4 *be brittle*, 384.6 *crumb*, 384.23 *pulverize*
fragmentary 143.11 *partial*, 145.4 *incomplete*, 173.5 *fractional*, 620.2 *incomplete*, 685.4 *uncompleted*
fragmentation 136.1 *separation*, 162.5 *divergence*, 384.4 *pulverization*
fragmentation bomb 680.16 *bomb*
fragmented 143.11 *partial*, 160.8 *discontinuous*, 162.20 *separated*
fragments 132.1 *remainder*
fragrance 418, 405.1 *physical pleasure*, 414.1 *sweetness*, 416.1 *odour*
Fragrance 418
fragrance-free 417.3 *odourless*
fragrancy 418.1 *fragrance*
fragrant 418, 84.10 *floral*, 405.6, 414.7 *pleasant*, 416.5 *odorous*
fragrantly 418, 84.14 *florally*, 414.9 *sweetly*
fragrant thing 418
frail 236.12 *impotent*, 238.10 *ill*, 274.2 *emaciated*, 379.1 *brittle*, 633.2 *unsafe*, 864.13 *venial*, 877.13 *unchaste*
frailly 379.5 *fragilely*
frailty 207.5 *old age*, 236.1 *powerlessness*, 238.3 *poor health*, 274.4 *emaciation*, 379.2 *brittleness*, 620.5 *imperfection*, 864.3 *venial sin*
framboesia 624.7 *tropical disease*, 624.13 *skin disease*

frame 73 *Aircraft Parts*, 24.5 *snooker*, 25.4 *bowling*, 47.17 *carpenter*, 63.27 *superstructure*, 66.12 *development*, 69.4 *nursery*, 71.11 *bicycle part*, 163.4 *type*, 243.10 *produce*, 258.1 *container*, 280.2 *foot*, 284.2 *supporting part*, 284.11 *support*, 297.7 *surround*, 299.1 *outline*, 299.2 *shadow*, 299.5 *outline*, 301.4 *wrapper*, 301.6 *wrap*, 306.1 *form*, 306.2 *prototype*, 306.7 *form*, 354.5 *inset*, 367.4 *matter*, 382.4 *framework*, 382.15 *shape*, 485.16 *specify*, 534.21 *television*, 540.9 *falsification*, 540.22 *falsify*, 549.9 *style*, 582.2 *premeditate*, 592.10 *plan out*, 592.13 *plot*, 594.10 *preparations*, 856.2 *false accusation*, 856.6 *accuse falsely*
framed 47.16 *joined*, 582.4 *deliberate*, 856.9 *perjurious*
frame frequency 534.21 *television*
frame of mind 105.2 *state of mind*, 759.4 *emotion*
frame of reference 52.33 *coordinates*, 485.6 *specification*, 716.2 *basis for negotiations*
framer 592.8 *planner*
frames 435.10 *visual aid*
frame someone 538.21 *lie*
frame-up 538.3 *lying*, 540.8 *fraud*, 540.9 *falsification*, 582.6 *premeditation*, 592.4 *plot*, 856.2 *false accusation*
framework 382, 284.2 *supporting part*, 299.2 *shadow*, 301.4 *wrapper*, 594.10 *preparations*
framing 66, 47.10 *carpenter's term*, 47.16 *joined*, 66.8 *composition*, 382.4 *framework*
framycetin 62 *Medication*
franc 741.11 *national coins*
France 48 *Writers*, **91** *Countries*
franchise 580, 698.15 *set free*, 845.6 *bond*, 848.4 *licence*
franchised 698.9 *free*
franchisement 698.3 *independence*
Franciscan 7 *Members of Religious Orders*, 743.10 *poor person*
francium 57 *Chemical Elements*
Franck 49 *Musicians and Composers*
francolin 78 *Birds*
Franconian 5 *Languages and Groups of Languages*
Francophobe 820.5 *hostile person*, 822.9 *hater*
Francophobia 777 *Phobias by Name*, 822.3 *race hatred*
Francophobic 820.7 *intolerant*, 822.11 *racist*
Franco-Prussian War 17 *Major Wars*
frangibility 139.1 *nonadhesion*, 379.2 *brittleness*
frangible 139.8 *nonadhesive*, 379.1 *brittle*
frangibleness 379.2 *brittleness*
frangipani 84 *Flowers and Flowering Plants*, 418.3 *incense*
Franglais 5.26 *dialect*
frank 271.3 *broad-minded*, 312.5 *honourable*, 322.16 *open*, 381.2 *outspoken*, 442.4 *easily seen through*, 475.10 *demonstrative*, 526.15 *open*, 530.11 *disclosing*, 534.31 *correspond*, 537.18 *truthful*, 556.3 *natural*, 565.6 *effusive*, 567.10 *send*, 658.1 *naive*, 698.13 *informal*, 857.4 *honourable*
frankalmoign 723.3 *medieval ownership*, 725.3 *historic property terms*
Frankenstein's monster 396.6 *things brought to life*
Frankfurt 93 *Cities*
Frankfurt am Main 93 *Cities*
Frankfurt an der Oder 93 *Cities*
Frankfurt Book Fair 532.6 *book publishing*
frankfurter 45.29 *sausage*

Frankfurt School 4.7 *school of thought*
frankincense 85 *Tree Products*, 418.3 *incense*
franking machine 534.3 *correspondence*
Frankish 5 *Languages and Groups of Languages*
Frankism 7 *Christian Movements*
franklinite 54 *Minerals*
frankly 526, 312.13 *straightforwardly*, 322.26 *openly*, 381.12 *bluntly*, 475.21 *demonstratively*, 530.13 *openly*, 537.36 *truthfully*, 556.8 *simply*, 565.11 *effusively*, 658.5 *naively*, 698.22 *informally*, 857.7 *honourably*
frankness 322.9 *openness*, 381.6 *outspokenness*, 442.10 *openness*, 475.2 *demonstrativeness*, 530.3 *openness*, 537.5 *truthfulness*, 556.6 *naturalness*, 565.2 *effusiveness*, 658.2 *naivety*, 698.4 *informality*, 857.1 *probity*
frantic 241.6 *violent*, 510.12 *manic*, 642.18 *active*
frantic haste 642.3 *nimbleness*
Franzlisp 65 *Programming Languages*
frap 135.8 *unite*
frappé 351.7 *alcoholic drink*, 409.8 *cold*
Fraser 96 *Rivers*
frat 819.14 *seek the friendship of*
Fratello 7 *Members of Religious Orders*
fraternal 116.11 *allied*, 664.19 *associating*, 665.8 *leagued*, 819.8 *friendly*, 821.17 *loving*, 831.6 *benevolent*
fraternalism 664.2 *fellowship*, 819.1 *friendship*
fraternally 665.18 *cliquishly*, 819.17 *in friendship*, 831.10 *benevolently*
fraternal order 665.1 *party*
fraternal society 665.1 *party*
fraternal twins 176.6 *twins*
fraternity 161.15 *association*, 400.9 *group*, 664.2 *fellowship*, 664.9 *team*, 665.1 *party*, 815.8 *good company*, 819.1 *friendship*
fraternity house 6.15 *schoolroom*
fraternization 815.1 *sociability*, 819.1 *friendship*
fraternize 815, 116.22 *form an alliance*, 140.6 *come together*, 665.12 *be in league with*
fraternizer 539.20 *plotter*
fraternize with 819.13 *befriend*
fraternizing 116.11 *allied*
fraticide 832.7 *act of malevolence*
fratricide 398.3 *homicide*, 398.11 *murderer*
fratting 815.1 *sociability*
Frau 402.3 *female title of address*
fraud 539, 540, 16.38 *lawbreaking*, 16.39 *crime*, 538.10 *dishonesty*, 538.12 *cheat*, 538.25 *be dishonest*, 539.15 *deceiver*, 540.15 *false person*, 548.3 *deceiver*, 601.2 *misuse*, 655.5 *expert*, 657.2 *stratagem*, 657.3 *cunning person*, 736.7 *dishonesty*, 801.3 *disreputable action*, 858.3 *criminality*, 858.4 *dishonourable person*
fraud squad 16.15 *British police*
fraudulence 286.3 *deviousness*, 538.10 *dishonesty*, 539.1 *deception*, 539.10 *fraud*, 540.5 *deceitfulness*, 540.8 *fraud*, 858.3 *criminality*
fraudulency 539.1 *deception*, 858.3 *criminality*
fraudulent 540, 736, 16.60 *offending*, 286.5 *devious*, 474.10 *hypocritical*, 538.19 *dishonest*, 539.35 *deceptive*, 540.29 *deceitful*, 601.5 *abusive*, 801.4 *disreputable*, 858.7 *criminal*
fraudulently 16.83, 538.28 *dishonestly*, 601.6 *abusively*, 736.19 *thievishly*, 858.11 *dishonourably*
fraught 144.8 *full*

fraught with danger 633.1 *dangerous*
fraught with difficulties 661.14 *blocked*
Fraulein 402.3 *female title of address*
Fraunhofer 52 *Scientists*
Fraunhofer diffraction 56 Named Laws
Fraunhofer lines 56 Named Laws, 53.15 *sun*
fray 151.9 *disorder*, 153.5 *commotion*, 385.14 *erode*, 473.1 *argument*, 628.1 *deteriorate*, 628.5 *hurt*, 642.1 *activity*, 644.4 *exertion*, 674.6 *fight*
frayed 628.13 *dilapidated*
Frayn 48 *Dramatists*
Frazier 18 *Sporting Personalities*
frazzle 385.14 *erode*, 628.5 *hurt*
frazzled 408.10 *on fire*
freak 113.1 *diversity*, 117.6 *misfit*, 168.10 *eccentric*, 335.19 *deviant person*, 579.3 *whim*, 579.4 *capricious person*, 666.4 *dissenter*, 786.5 *person of wonder*, 875.4 *drug taker*
freak accident 489.5 *unexpectedness*
freaked out 875.7 *drugged*
freakish 113.5 *diverse*, 117.9 *nonconforming*, 168.14 *eccentric*, 489.3 *unexpected*, 514.8 *surprising*, 579.1 *capricious*
freakishly 113.10 *diversely*
freakishness 117.3 *nonconformity*, 168.4 *unusualness*, 510.1 *insanity*, 579.2 *caprice*
freak out 759.17 *feel deeply*, 875.10 *drug oneself*
freaky 117.9 *nonconforming*, 168.14 *eccentric*, 514.8 *surprising*
freckle 162.18 *sprinkle*, 449.3 *brownness*, 456.4 *maculation*, 456.11 *variegate*, 624.13 *skin disease*
freckled 162.23 *sprinkled*, 456.10 *mottled*
freckling 162.4 *sprinkling*, 456.4 *maculation*
Fred Astaire and Ginger Rogers 46.6 *famous dancers*
Frederick Ashton 46.14 *famous ballet dancers*
Fredericton 93 *Cities*
Frederiksborg 32 *Breeds of Horse and Pony*
Fred Perry 40.7 *famous tennis players*
free 570, 698, 700, 814, 5.40 *translated*, 16.63 *acquitted*, 16.78 *acquit*, 24.9 *billiard*, 30.11 *gymnastic*, 34.8 *mountaineering*, 38.5 *soccer*, 41.13 *ice-skating*, 108.6 *unrelated*, 136.15 *separate*, 139.5 *unstick*, 139.8 *nonadhesive*, 139.9 *aloof*, 271.3 *broad-minded*, 322.13 *opened up*, 322.19 *open up*, 355.11 *extract*, 524.17 *translational*, 526.15 *open*, 600.3 *not wanted*, 629.3 *restore*, 638.8 *escaping*, 639.1 *deliver*, 639.4 *deliverable*, 639.6 *extricably*, 643.2 *not working*, 645.6 *leisure*, 645.7 *leisurely*, 660.16 *make easy*, 660.18 *disentangle*, 698.20 *freely*, 700.4 *liberate*, 700.7 *liberated*, 727.9 *dispose of*, 729.7 *given*, 729.9 *as a gift*, 754.11 *free of charge*, 767.10 *save*, 825.6 *celibate*, 839.10 *absolve*, 848.6 *acquitted*, 848.7 *independent*, 848.10 *acquit*, 855.7 *vindicate*
free admission 754.6 *absence of charge*
free agent 19.2 *football player*, 698.7 *free person*
free-and-easiness 814.4 *freedom*
free-and-easy 698.13 *informal*, 780.4 *rash*, 814.10 *free*, 815.15 *sociable*, 819.10 *familiar*
free as a bird 698.10 *independent*
free as air 698.10 *independent*

free association 61.27 *association of ideas*
free-association test 61.5 *psychological test*
free as the wind 698.10 *independent*
free ball 24.5 *snooker*
freebase 875.10 *drug oneself*
freebasing 875.1 *drug-taking*
freebie 130.4 *extra*, 228.5 *positive stimulus*, 710.1 *offer*, 721.5 *profit*, 729.2 *gift*, 754.6 *absence of charge*
freeboard 74 Parts of a Ship, 265.1 *interval*
free board 754.6 *absence of charge*
freeboot 736.14 *plunder*
freebooter 679.6 *militarist*, 712.5 *beggar*, 736.9 *plunderer*
freebooting 736.5 *plundering*
freeborn 698.9 *free*
Free Church of Scotland 7 Christian Movements
free citizen 698.7 *free person*
free city 12.5 *political organization*
free climbing 34.1 *mountaineering*
free country 91.1 *country*
freed 698.9 *free*, 700.7 *liberated*, 727.12 *disposed* , 839.6 *forgiven*
free-dancing 41.7 *ice-dancing*
free delivery 754.6 *absence of charge*
freed from blame 848.6 *acquitted*
freedman 698.7 *free person*
freedom 777 Phobias by Topic, **698, 814**, 16.42 *acquittal*, 108.1 *unrelatedness*, 139.2 *aloofness*, 271.6 *broad-mindedness*, 638.1 *escape*, 639.2 *deliverance*, 645.1 *leisure*, 660.5 *smoothness*, 700.1 *liberation*, 708.1 *permission*, 848.2 *acquittal*
Freedom 698
freedom fighter 669.5 *resister*, 679.9 *guerrilla*, 713.5 *seditionist*
freedom from artifice 658.2 *naivety*
freedom from blame 865.1 *innocence*
freedom from dirt 621.1 *cleanness*
freedom from fear 698.2 *free speech*
freedom from sin 865.1 *innocence*
freedom from want 698.2 *free speech*
freedom from war 675.1 *peace*, 677.1 *pacification*
freedom of action 698.1, 814.4 *freedom*
freedom of choice 570.4 *free will*, 580.6 *selection*, 602.1 *means*, 698.1 *freedom*
freedom of movement 698.1 *freedom*
freedom of religion 698.2 *free speech*
freedom of speech and expression 698.2 *free speech*
freedom of the press 698.2 *free speech*
freedom of thought 698.1 *freedom*
freedom of worship 698.2 *free speech*
free drink 754.6 *absence of charge*
free duty 13.6 *economic factors*
freedwoman 698.7 *free person*
free economy 737.5 *commercial trade*
free enterprise 698.1 *freedom*, 737.5 *commercial trade*
free entry 754.6 *absence of charge*
free exchange rate 741.7 *finance*
free exercises 30.1 *gymnastics*
free fall 53.31 *space travel*
free-faller 360.8 *descender*
freefalling 18 Sporting Activities
free fight 674.6 *fight*, 698.6 *liberality*
free-floating anxiety 61.12 *stress*
Freefone 754.6 *absence of charge*
Freefone call 534.10 *telephone call*

free-for-all 151.9 *disorder*, 674.2 *contest*, 674.6 *fight*, 698.6 *liberality*, 698.12 *unconditional*
free for the asking 754.11 *free of charge*
free from 134.13 *pure*
free from blame 855.7 *vindicate*
free from guile 658.1 *naive*
free from impurities 134.10, 621.15 *purify*
free from sin 865.5 *innocent*
free gift 130.4 *extra*, 721.5 *profit*, 729.2 *gift*, 754.6 *absence of charge*
free goods 13.6 *economic factors*
free hand 570.4 *free will*, 698.6 *liberality*, 708.1 *permission*
freehand drawing 50.3 *drawing*, 560.9 *representation*
free hit 31.1 *hockey*
freehold 255.11 *inhabited*, 723.1, 723.4 *possession*, 725.1 *property*, 725.8 *propertied*
freeholder 255.3 *householder*, 725.7 *property man*
freeing 136.1 *separation*, 660.8 *disentanglement*, 700.1 *liberation*, 727.1 *disposal*, 839.3 *absolution*
free kick 19.12 *special team*, 35.3 *rugby play*, 38.2 *football play*
freelance 533.13 *report*, 644.6 *work*, 646.1 *worker*, 679.6 *militarist*, 698.10 *independent*, 698.16 *be independent*
freelance pay 749.3 *income*
freelancer 528.9 *informant*, 532.11 *newspaper man*, 646.1 *worker*, 679.6 *militarist*, 698.7 *free person*
freelance reporter 528.9 *informant*
free-lance reporter 533.4 *journalist*
free-lance writer 533.4 *journalist*
free-liver 870.5 *self-indulgent person*
free living 870.2 *dissipation*
free-living 870.7 *dissipated*
free-living flatworm 81.6 *worm*
freeload 712.8 *solicit money*, 754.14 *buy cheaply*, 815.11 *be sociable*
freeloader 643.8 *nonworker*, 712.5 *beggar*, 743.10 *poor person*, 754.8 *bargain hunter*, 808.3 *sycophant*
freeloading 712.3 *solicitation*, 712.11 *begging*
free-loading 808.7 *sycophantic*
free lodging 754.6 *absence of charge*
free love 698.6 *liberality*, 708.1 *permission*, 821.2 *romantic love*, 823.3 *types of marriage*, 877.3 *sexual immorality*
free lunch 405.4 *pleasurable things*, 754.6 *absence of charge*
freely 698, 16.88 *forgivingly*, 108.12 *irrelevantly*, 136.20 *separately*, 139.11 *aloofly*, 271.7 *broadly*, 530.13 *openly*, 638.9 *fugitively*, 660.21 *easily*, 698.22 *informally*, 700.8 *free*, 755.12 *generously*, 825.12 *celibately*, 848.13 *with impunity*
freeman 93.11 *urbanite*, 698.7 *free person*
free market 740, 346.4 *right of entry*, 698.1 *freedom*
free-market economy 13.2 *economy*, 737.5 *commercial trade*
Freemason 527.9 *backstage manipulator*, 529.7 *esotericism*, 531.7 *concealer*
freemasonry 664.2 *fellowship*, 819.1 *friendship*
Freemasonry 529.7 *esotericism*
free meal 729.3 *offering*
free mentally 700.4 *liberate*
free-minded 698.10 *independent*
free-mindedly 698.20 *freely*
free moments 645.1 *leisure*
free of charge 754
free oneself 136.13 *diverge*, 700.5 *be liberated*

free pardon 839.1 *forgiveness*
free pass 754.6 *absence of charge*
free person 698
free pistol shooting 18 Sporting Activities
free play 31.5 *lacrosse*, 698.5 *scope*
free port 13.6 *economic factors*, 346.4 *right of entry*, 698.1 *freedom*, 740.7 *emporium*, 754.6 *absence of charge*
free position 31.5 *lacrosse*
Freepost 534.2 *postal communication*, 754.6 *absence of charge*
free postage 754.6 *absence of charge*
free quarters 754.6 *absence of charge*
free radical 224.3 *changeable thing*
free range 698.5 *scope*
free-range 698.11 *ranging*
free-range hen 68.8 *livestock*
free ride 754.6 *absence of charge*
free-rider 643.8 *nonworker*
free sail 36.18 *windsurf*
free sailing 36.7 *windsurfing*
free scope 698.5 *scope*
free seat 754.6 *absence of charge*
free service 754.6 *absence of charge*
freesheet 532.4 *newspaper*, 754.6 *absence of charge*
free shot 23.4 *playing terms*
freesia 84 Flowers and Flowering Plants
free-skate 41.15 *ice-skate*
free-skating 41.6, 41.13 *ice-skating*
free-skating movement 41.6 *ice-skating*
free socage 723.3 *medieval ownership*, 725.3 *historic property terms*
free space 56.7 *space*
free-speaking 564.19 *speaking*, 698.13 *informal*
free speech 698, 814.4 *freedom*
free spirit 139.4 *individualist*, 168.7 *nonconformist*, 570.4 *free will*, 698.7 *free person*
free-spirited 698.10 *independent*
free-spoken 658.1 *naive*
freestyle 26.15 *wrestling*, 26.16 *professionally*, 36.13 *windsurfing*, 39.11 *swimming*, 41.12 *ski*
free-style 32.10 *dressage*
freestyle event 39.1 *swimming*
freestyle sailing 36.7 *windsurfing*
freestyle skiing 18 Sporting Activities, 41.1 *skiing*
freestyle wrestler 26.6 *wrestler*, 674.10 *contender*, 679.3 *athlete*
freestyle wrestling 26.5, 674.8 *wrestling*
free-thinker 698, 168.7 *nonconformist*, 168.13 *unconventional*, 271.6 *broad-mindedness*, 498.5 *disbeliever*
free-thinking 271.3 *broad-minded*, 698.1 *freedom*, 698.10 *independent*
free thought 814.4 *freedom*
free-throw 23.4 *playing terms*
free-throw lane 23.1 *basketball*
free ticket 754.6 *absence of charge*
free time 645.1 *leisure*, 649.1 *ease*
free to choose 698.10 *independent*
Freetown 93 Cities
free trade 13.5 *international trade*, 346.4 *right of entry*, 698.1 *freedom*, 698.9 *free*, 737.5 *commercial trade*, 754.6 *absence of charge*
free-trade area 698.1 *freedom*, 737.5 *commercial trade*, 740.4 *free market*
free-trader 698.7 *free person*
free-trade zone 13.5 *international trade*
free translation 5.12, 524.4 *translation*
free union 823.3 *types of marriage*
free verse 48.10 *verse form*

freeway 71.2, 137.5 *road*, 327.3 *road*
freewheel 71 Motor Vehicle Parts, 324.15 *walk*, 376.12 *go smoothly*, 641.4 *not act*, 660.17 *do easily*, 660.19 *go easily*
freewheeling 698.10 *independent*
free will 570, 4.9 *philosophical problem*, 580.6 *selection*, 698.1, 814.4 *freedom*
freewoman 698.7 *free person*
free world 12.5 *political organization*
freezable 409.9 *heat-resistant*
freeze 55, 41.10 *curling*, 55.63 *snow*, 57.25 *solidify*, 138.6 *adhere*, 218.8 *cause to cease*, 225.7 *make stable*, 240.4 *be inert*, 325.1 *motionlessness*, 325.8 *be motionless*, 325.9 *make motionless*, 371.8 *be dense*, 373.9 *harden*, 404.12 *anaesthetize*, 409.10 *be cold*, 409.11 *become cold*, 409.12 *make cold*, 600.6 *stop using*, 637.5 *preserve*, 699.2 *economic restraint*, 747.2 *stoppage*, 747.8 *stop payment*, 761.7 *render insensitive*
freeze-dried 409.9 *heat-resistant*, 632.6 *invulnerable*, 637.7 *preserved*
freeze-dried food 350.7 *food*, 637.3 *preserved thing*
freeze-dry 392.17 *dry*, 409.12 *make cold*, 637.5 *preserve*
freeze-drying 637.1 *preservation*
freeze in one's tracks 218.6 *cease*
freeze onto 138.6 *adhere*
freeze out 349.7 *drive out*, 581.3 *exclude*, 816.13 *ignore*
freeze over 409.11 *become cold*
freeze pay 699.9 *economize*
freeze prices 302.7 *limit*, 699.9 *economize*
freezer 45.4 *kitchen container*, 56.35 *heat*, 258.3 *cabinet*, 409.4 *cooler*, 605.4 *storage*, 637.2 *preserver*
freezer bag 258.8 *bag*
freezer stock 350.7 *food*
freeze the ball 23.6 *play basketball*
freeze to death 409.11 *become cold*
freeze-up 55.32 *freeze*, 409.5 *ice*
freeze with horror 777.11 *be afraid*
freezing 409, 23.4 *playing terms*, 55.47 *windy*, 55.55 *cool*, 56.37 *temperature*, 57.3 *phase*, 371.7 *condensed*, 409.8 *cold*, 409.9 *heat-resistant*, 454.2 *bluish*, 626.5 *unhygienic*, 637.1 *preservation*
freezing cold 409.2 *freezing*
freezing fog 55.33 *fog*
freezing point 56.37 *temperature*
freezing rain 55.29 *hail*
Frege 4 Philosophers, **52** Scientists
Fregean 4.14 *of a philosophy*
F region 390.3 *atmospheric layers*
Freiberger 32 Breeds of Horse and Pony
freight 70.2 *thing transported*, 70.4 *transport*, 70.5 *transportable*, 144.6 *fill*, 257.2 *load*, 257.6 *contain*, 326.2 *transportation*, 326.10 *transferred thing*, 326.12 *transport*, 369.6 *displacement*, 739.8 *merchandise*
freightage 326.2 *transportation*, 326.10 *transferred thing*, 751.6 *business costs*
freight car 72.6 *rolling stock*
freight carriage 70.1 *transport*
freight charges 751.6 *business costs*
freighted 144.8 *full*
freighter 73 Types of Aircraft, **74** Ships and Boats, 74.3 *vessel*, 326.5 *means of transport*, 326.7 *transferor*
freightliner 72.6 *rolling stock*
freight ton 75 General Units

freight train 72.7 *train*, 258.10 *cart*, 326.5 *means of transport*
French 1 Peoples, **5** Languages and Groups of Languages, **43** Architectural Styles, **777** Phobias by Topic
French and Indian War 17 Major Wars
French art nouveau glass 44.1 *ceramics*
French bean 45 Vegetables
French billiards 24.1 *billiards*, 24.4 *carom*
French blue 454.5 *blueness*
French bread 45.39 *loaf*
French bulldog 77 Breeds of Dogs
French-Canadian dialect 5.26 *dialect*
French cricket 18 Sporting Activities
French curve 52 Named Concepts
French dip sandwich 45.11 *sandwich*
French dish 45
French door 346.6 *means of entry*
French dressing 45.15 *sauce*, 413.2 *seasoning*
French farce 51.10 *comedy*
French fleur-de-lis 544.6 *national emblem*
French GP at Bandol 33.2 *Formula 1 race*
french horn 49 Musical Instruments
Frenchified 220.17 *naturalized*
Frenchify 220.12 *naturalize*
French kiss 821.14 *communication of love*, 826.1 *endearment*
French knickers 295.18 *underwear*
French knot 74 Knots
French leave 254.4 *absenteeism*, 591.16 *desertion*, 638.1 *escape*
French letter 247.3 *birth control*
French mustard 413.5 *herbs*
French navy 454.1 *blue*
French Open 40.1 *tennis*
French perfume 418.2 *fragrant thing*
French polish 376.10 *polish*
French provincial 47.7 *furniture style*
French Saddle Horse 32 Breeds of Horse and Pony
French stick 45.39 *loaf*
French toast 45.38 *bread*
French Trotter 32 Breeds of Horse and Pony
Freneau 48 Poets
frenetic 241.6 *violent*, 510.12 *manic*, 642.18 *active*
frenzied 241.6 *violent*, 510.12 *manic*, 521.10 *meaningless*, 642.18 *active*, 670.23 *attacking*, 828.16 *angry*
frenzy 241.1 *violence*, 366.2 *tumult*, 366.8 *spasm*, 510.4 *delusion*, 519.2 *inspiration*, 519.6 *reverie*, 521.1 *lack of meaning*, 642.1 *activity*, 642.4 *energy*
Freon 388.11 *vaporizer*
frequence 212.4 *frequency*
frequency 212, 52.58 *frequency distribution*, 56.8 *time*, 56.16 *waveform*, 56.51, 64.9 *electric current*, 121.1 *degree*, 214.1 *regularity*, 235.7 *electrical power*, 365.1 *oscillation*, 365.5 *wave*
Frequency 212
frequency allocation 534.14 *radio transmission*
frequency band 56.16 *waveform*, 212.6 *radio frequency*, 365.5 *wave*, 534.14 *radio transmission*
frequency distribution 52
frequency-division multiplex 534.14 *radio transmission*
frequency function 52.59 *probability distribution*
frequency modulation 212.6 *radio frequency*, 534.14 *radio transmission*
frequency response 56.83 *sensitivity*

frequency spectrum 56.16 *waveform*, 212.6 *radio frequency*, 365.5 *wave*
frequent 212, 212, 256, 599, 121.7 *gradational*, 180.14 *keep company with*, 214.11 *regular*, 219.4 *protract*, 253.12 *attend*, 584.14 *habituated*, 584.16 *have a habit*
frequentation 815.3 *meeting*
frequenter 253.5 *someone present*, 584.8 *creature of habit*
frequenter of restaurants 350.18 *eater*
frequenting 212, 253.2 *omnipresence*, 815.3 *meeting*
frequently 212, 121.9 *differentially*, 183.23 *repeatedly*, 214.15 *regularly*
frequentness 212.4 *frequency*
frequent occurrence 212.4 *frequency*
frequent patron 584.8 *creature of habit*
fresco 50.8 *painting*
fresh 453, 55.45 *fine*, 55.47 *windy*, 119.5 *novel*, 130.9 *extra*, 134.14 *purified*, 156.32 *embryonic*, 201.12 *immature*, 201.24 *immaturely*, 204.5 *morning*, 239.5 *invigorating*, 390.15 *breezy*, 390.17 *ventilated*, 409.8 *cold*, 414.7 *pleasant*, 417.3 *odourless*, 453.2 *verdant*, 585.1 *unaccustomed*, 600.2 *new*, 617.5 *not bad*, 621.16 *clean*, 623.1 *healthy*, 637.7 *preserved*, 651.3 *refreshing*, 807.21 *impudent*, 850.10 *disrespectful*
fresh air 390.5 *open air*, 417.1 *odourlessness*, 625.2 *salubrity*
fresh-air fiend 625.3 *hygienist*
fresh as a daisy 134.14 *purified*, 201.12 *immature*, 621.16 *clean*, 623.1 *healthy*
fresh as paint 201.12 *immature*
fresh blood 155.13 *replacement*, 195.5 *successor*
fresh breeze 55.13 *wind strength*
fresh coffee 418.2 *fragrant thing*
freshen 55.58 *blow*, 134.10 *purify*, 239.3 *invigorate*, 390.20 *aerate*, 409.12 *make cold*, 417.5 *deodorize*, 621.13 *clean*, 621.15 *purify*, 625.6 *make hygienic*, 629.5 *revive*, 651.1 *refresh*
freshened 621.17 *cleaned*
freshened up 201.14 *renewed*, 651.4 *refreshed*
freshener 621.9 *cleaning agent*
freshening 417.4 *deodorizing*, 621.2 *cleaning*
freshening up 651.5 *refreshment*
freshen up 201.20 *make new*, 621.13 *clean*, 627.1 *improve*, 629.2 *refurbish*, 651.1 *refresh*
fresher 149.7 *newcomer*, 156.14 *beginner*, 201.8 *new arrival*
freshet 96.1, 96.1 *river*, 96.6 *river flow*
fresh fields 156.13 *new beginnings*
fresh fish 45.16 *fish dish*
fresh fruit 45.35 *dessert*
freshly 119.8 *originally*, 201.24 *immaturely*, 414.9 *sweetly*, 417.7 *odourlessly*, 453.18 *greenly*, 600.13 *newly*, 651.8 *refreshingly*
freshman 6.7 *learner*, 156.14 *beginner*, 201.8 *new arrival*
fresh milk 351.5 *milk*
freshness 119.1 *originality*, 134.1 *purity*, 201.3 *immaturity*, 206.2 *youthfulness*, 239.1 *vigour*, 409.1 *coldness*, 414.1 *sweetness*, 417.1 *odourlessness*, 600.9 *newness*, 621.1 *cleanness*, 651.5 *refreshment*, 807.10 *impudence*, 807.11 *sauciness*
fresh news 533.9 *news story*
fresh smell 416.1 *odour*
fresh spurt 629.10 *revival*
fresh start 201, 156.13 *new beginnings*, 704.3 *new beginning*
freshwater 20.8 *angling*
fresh water 389.1 *water*

freshwater bait fishing 20.1 *angling*
freshwater fish 45, 80.1 *fishes*
freshwater fishing 590.2 *chase*
freshwater lake 94.1 *lake*
freshwater sailor 656.10 *unskilled person*
fresh wind 55.14 *windiness*
fresnel 75 Scientific and Technical Units
Fresnel 52 Scientists
Fresnel diffraction 56 Named Laws
Fresnel lens 56 Named Laws
Fresnel's biprism 56 Named Laws
Fresno 93 Cities
fret 43 Architectural Decoration, 43.19 *decorate*, 55.34 *mist*, 385.15 *grind*, 431.13 *cry*, 544.8 *heraldic device*, 628.5 *hurt*, 642.7 *restlessness*, 642.12 *be active*, 648.2 *make haste*, 777.14 *worry*, 828.4 *anger*, 828.9 *offend*, 828.11 *be angry*, 829.6 *be irascible*, 830.9 *be sullen*
fretful 579.1 *capricious*, 642.18 *active*, 829.4 *irascible*
fretfully 829.9 *irascibly*
fretfulness 579.2 *caprice*, 829.1 *irascibility*
fretsaw 603.1 *tool*
fretting 385.3 *grinding*, 385.11 *rough*, 777.3 *worry*, 777.9 *worried*
fret vapour 441.2 *murk*
fretwork 42 Hobbies and Pastimes, 288.2 *braid*
Freud 61.29 *psychologist*
Freudian 61
Freudian analysis 61.3 *psychiatric treatment*
Freudian fixation 61.17 *fixation*
Freudianism 61.1 *psychology*
Freudian psychology 61.1 *psychology*
Freudian slip 504.9 *trivial error*, 506.2 *solecism*
Frey 8 Deities
Freya 821.16 *gods and goddesses of love*
friability 139.1 *nonadhesion*, 379.2 *brittleness*, 384.2 *crumbliness*
friable 139.8 *nonadhesive*, 379.1 *brittle*, 384.20 *crumbly*
friableness 379.2 *brittleness*, 384.2 *crumbliness*
friable rock 34.2 *climbing dangers*
friar 7.7 *monk*
friarbird 78 Birds
Friar Preacher 7 Members of Religious Orders
friary 7.10 *priestly dwelling*
fribble 612.10 *nonentity*
fricassée 45.32 *meat dish*
frication 385.1 *friction*
fricative 5.16 *spoken letter*, 5.41 *lettered*
friction 339, 385, 56.10 *force*, 231.1 *counteraction*, 235.4 *energy*, 328.9 *deceleration*, 330.12 *collision*, 385.10 *frictional*, 430.2 *hoarseness*, 500.1 *dissent*, 661.1 *hindrance*, 663.3 *conflict*, 666.1 *disagreement*, 764.7 *dissension*, 820.1 *enmity*
Friction 385
frictional 385, 231.4 *counteracting*
frictional electricity 56.42 *electricity*
frictionize 385.13 *abrade*
frictionless 5.41 *lettered*, 116.10 *in accord*, 376.1 *smooth*, 660.12 *wieldy*
frictionless continuant 5.16 *spoken letter*
friction match 439.8 *fire*
Friday 871.3 *fast day*
fridge 45.4 *kitchen container*, 258.3 *cabinet*, 409.4 *cooler*, 605.4 *storage*, 637.2 *preserver*
fridge-freezer 258.3 *cabinet*, 409.4 *cooler*, 605.4 *storage*
fried 45.56 *culinary*, 874.1 *drunk*

fried bread 45.38 *bread*
fried catfish 45.43 *US dish*
Friedel–Crafts reaction 57 Named Reactions
fried fish 45.16 *fish dish*
fried noodles 45.48 *Chinese dish*
fried rice 45.48 *Chinese dish*
Friel 48 Dramatists
friend 819, 137.3 *associate*, 180.11 *companion*, 198.5 *contemporary*, 284.8 *supporter*, 654.4 *adviser*, 759.9 *feeling person*, 784.4 *likable person*, 815.6 *social person*, 861.15 *good person*
Friend 7.5 *Christian*
friend at court 233.4 *indirect influence*, 527.9 *backstage manipulator*
friend in need 662.13 *supporter*, 819.5 *friend*
friendless 174.16 *alone*, 236.11 *unprotected*, 816.10 *lonely*
friendlessness 174.5 *aloneness*
friendlike 819.8 *friendly*
friendlily 861.23 *nicely*
friendliness 677.2 *peace offering*, 698.4 *informality*, 759.5 *good feeling*, 763.8 *amiability*, 784.1 *liking*, 815.1 *sociability*, 817.1 *courtesy*, 819.1 *friendship*, 861.10 *kindness*
friendly 819, 662.35 *benevolent*, 664.19 *associating*, 667.10 *agreeing*, 674.2 *contest*, 675.7 *peaceful*, 677.6 *pacificatory*, 759.12 *sensitive*, 763.2, 784.5 *likable*, 815.15 *sociable*, 817.7 *courteous*, 821.17 *loving*, 831.6 *benevolent*, 861.3 *kind*
friendly approach 677.2 *peace offering*
friendly critic 662.13 *supporter*
friendly match 38.1 *soccer*
friendly relations 819
friendly society 732.4 *lending institution*, 744.4 *bank*
friendly takeover 13.7 *corporation*
friendly talk 568.2 *chat*
friendly with 819.9 *friends with*
friend of the family 819.6 *close friend*
friend of the human race 833.3 *philanthropist*
friends and acquaintances 815.7 *human society*
friends and relations 815.7 *human society*
friendship 819, 2.3 *social environment*, 107.1 *relatedness*, 180.3 *companionship*, 273.6 *denseness*, 284.6 *moral support*, 664.2 *fellowship*, 667.1 *agreement*, 675.1 *peace*, 784.1 *liking*, 815.8 *good company*, 821.1 *love*, 831.1 *benevolence*
Friendship 819
friends in high places 527.9 *backstage manipulator*
Friends of the Earth 453.16 *green politics*, 627.11 *reformism*, 637.1 *preservation*
Friends of the Earth member 637.4 *preservationist*
friends with 819
frier 45.6 *kitchen equipment*
Friese-Greene 52 Scientists
Friesian 32 Breeds of Horse and Pony, **68** Breeds of Cattle
frieze 43 Architectural Decoration, **67** Natural Fabrics, 43.9 *miscellaneous architectural features*, 279.3 *architectural summit*
frig 34.9 *mountaineer*
frigate 74 Sailing Ships and Boats, 679.24 *warship*
frigate bird 78 Birds, 78.3 *water bird*
Frigg 8 Deities, 823.14 *gods and goddesses of marriage*
frigging 34.3 *climbing technique*
fright 42 Card Games, 435.7 *view*, 514.3 *shock*, 777.1 *fear*, 777.13 *frighten*, 790.2 *ugly person*
frighten 777, 514.9 *surprise*, 636.7 *raise the alarm*, 690.5 *be severe*, 785.7 *cause dislike*,

786.10 *be wonderful*, 832.18
torment
frighten away 587.2 *deter*
frightened 777, 779.3 *cowardly,*
810.11 *shy*
frightened out of one's wits
777.7 *frightened*
frightened person 777
frightened to death 777.7 *frightened*
frightener 777
frightening 777, 633.1 *dangerous,* 636.8 *warning,* 777.4 *intimidation,* 786.8 *wonderful*
frighteningly 777
frighten off 587.2 *deter*
**frighten someone out of their
wits** 777.13 *frighten*
frightful 777.10 *frightening*
frightfully 777.16 *frighteningly*
fright neurosis 61.10 *neurosis*
frigid 55.55 *cool,* 409.8 *cold,*
761.1 *insensitive,* 783.7 *indifferent,* 816.8 *unsociable,* 876.9
pure
frigidarium 409.6 *Arctic*
frigidity 409.2 *freezing,* 816.1 *unsociability,* 876.3 *moral purity*
frigidly 409.13 *coldly,* 816.14 *unsociably*
frigid zone 409.6 *Arctic*
frigorific 409.9 *heat-resistant*
frill 78.17 *plumage,* 130.3 *additional item,* 610.3 *superfluity,*
792.5 *decorative articles*
frilled lizard 79 Reptiles
frills 557.1 *ornament*
frilly 811.19 *flashy*
Frimla 8 Deities
fringe 15.9 *negotiated,* 130.3 *additional item,* 157.7 *limit,*
168.13 *unconventional,* 283.3
suspended object, 289.1 *exterior,*
289.11 *be exterior,* 299.3, 300.1
edge, 300.2 *edging,* 300.6 *edge,*
791.8 *hair cut,* 792.5 *decorative
articles*
fringe adjustments 15.2 *industrial negotiations*
fringe benefit 721.5 *profit,* 730.2
something received
fringe benefits 878.4 *reward for
service*
fringed 300.9 *skirting*
fringe group 665.3 *political
grouping*
fringe medicine 60.2 *natural medicine*
fringe theatre 51.1 *drama*
fringe tree 85 Trees and Shrubs
fringilline 78.23 *avian*
fringing 157.24 *limiting*
frippery 295.1 *dress,* 612.9 *bauble,* 754.5 *cheap item,* 792.5 *decorative articles*
Frisch 48 Writers, **52** Scientists,
52 Scientists
Frisian 5 Languages and
Groups of Languages
Frisians 1 Peoples
frisky 642.18 *active*
frisson 403.3 *stimulus*
frit 777.7 *frightened*
fritillary 82 Insects, **84** Flowers
and Flowering Plants
fritted glaze 44.3 *glaze*
fritter 45.36 *cake,* 601.1 *misuse,*
607.1, 757.7 *waste*
fritter away 722.11 *be wasteful,*
748.1 *expend,* 757.7 *waste*
frittering 607.3 *waste*
Friulian 5 Languages and
Groups of Languages
frivolity 468.3 *absent-mindedness,* 508.1 *folly,* 579.2 *caprice,*
612.7 *triviality,* 780.1 *rashness*
frivolous 278.2 *superficial,* 508.5
foolish, 579.1 *capricious,* 612.4
trivial, 780.4 *rash*
frivolously 579.6 *capriciously*
frivolousness 579.2 *caprice,*
612.7 *triviality*
frizz 791.8 *hair cut*
Fizzle 68 Breeds of Fowl
Frizzles 68 Breeds of Fowl
frizzy 375.3 *barbed*

frock 295, 7.11 *vestment,* 7.21
ordain, 295.1 *dress*
frock coat 295.12 *coat*
frocked 295.29 *dressed*
Froebel system 6.2 *educational
system*
frog 42 Card Games, **79** Amphibians, 39.11 *swimming,*
72.3 *rail,* 137.8 *fastening*
Frog 91 Names for Inhabitants
frog-bit 84 Flowers and Flowering Plants
frogfish 80 Fishes
froggy 79.13 *amphibian*
froghopper 82 Insects
frog in the throat 430.2 *hoarseness*
frog kick 39.2 *swimming technique*
froglet 79.8 *young amphibian*
froglike 79.13 *amphibian*
frogman 360.8 *descender*
frogmarch 330.1 *impel*
frogmouth 78 Birds
frogs legs 45.45 *French dish*
frogspawn 79.8 *young amphibian*
frog spit 90.1 *alga*
Froissart 48 Poets
frolic 46.15, 773.7 *dance*
frolic about 640.4 *act*
from 347.19 *out of*
from a biased standpoint 234.6
probably
from a distance 104.18 *extraneously*
fromage frais 45 Cheeses, 393.8
pulp
from age to age 190.11 *eternally*
from a historical perspective 3.24
historically
from all directions 293.42 *inclusively*
from all points of the compass
248.18 *from everywhere*
from a selfish standpoint 834.5
misanthropically
from a sense of obligation 837.8
gratefully
from A to Z 144.9 *completely,*
146.9 *inclusively*
from bad to worse 768, 687.12
in adversity
from before the Flood 202.12
olden
from beginning to end 144.9
completely
from behind 123.7 *unequally*
from coast to coast 112.14
equanimously, 144.9 *completely,*
248.17 *from end to end*
from day to day 185.26 *all the
time*
from door to door 326.18 *in transit*
from end to end 248, 144.9 *completely*
from every place 248.18 *from everywhere*
from every quarter 332.11 *in all
directions*
from everywhere 248
from experience 200.24 *retrospectively*
from far and near 144.9 *completely*
from first to last 144.9 *completely*
from generation to generation
190.11 *eternally*
from hand to hand 326.18 *in
transit*
from head to foot 144.9 *completely*
from hell to breakfast 248.17
from end to end
from here to eternity 248.17
from end to end
from here to the back of beyond
248.17 *from end to end*
from here until kingdom come
248.17 *from end to end*
from instinct 460.12 *nonhumanly*
from its birth 156.39 *from the beginning*
from its inception 156.39 *from
the beginning*

from Land's End to John o' Groats
112.14 *equanimously,* 144.9
completely, 248.17 *from end to
end*
from loyalty 819.19 *devotedly*
from necessity 571.19 *necessarily*
from north to south 248.17 *from
end to end*
from now on 199.15 *after*
from one end to the other 144.9
completely
from one extreme to the other
579.6 *capriciously*
from one side to the other 271.8
breadthwise
from outer space 104.18 *extraneously,* 149.19 *abroad*
from past experience 200.24 *retrospectively*
from personal motives 860.8 *selfishly*
from pillar to post 324.18 *in motion,* 326.18 *in transit,* 334.8 *circuitously,* 365.18 *to and fro,*
576.16 *irresolutely*
from pole to pole 248.17 *from
end to end*
from scratch 156.39 *from the beginning,* 201.22 *again*
from sea to sea 144.9 *completely*
from sea to shining sea 144.9
completely
from side to side 214.15 *regularly*
from stem to stern 144.9 *completely*
from that angle 106.15 *under the
circumstances*
from the beginning 156, 183.24,
201.22 *again*
from the bottom of one's heart
759.20 *with feeling*
from the context 520.13 *meaningfully*
from the first 156.39 *from the beginning*
from the foundations 156.39
from the beginning
from the four corners of the earth
248.18 *from everywhere,* 332.11
in all directions
**from the four corners of the
world** 144.9 *completely*
**from the four points of the com-
pass** 144.9 *completely*
from the four winds 332.11 *in all
directions*
from the frying pan into the fire
687.12 *in adversity*
**from the furthest corners of the
earth** 248.18 *from everywhere*
from the grapevine 529.18 *reportedly*
from the ground up 201.22 *again*
from the heart 833.8 *philanthropically*
from the rear 123.7 *unequally*
from the start 201.22 *again*
from the top 201.22 *again,*
221.13 *reversibly*
from the word go 156.39 *from
the beginning*
from this moment on 199.15 *after*
from this time forth 199.15 *after*
from time immemorial 3.24 *historically,* 200.22 *in the past*
from time to time 185.28, 212.2
sometimes
from top to bottom 144.9 *completely,* 248.17 *from end to end*
from top to toe 144.9 *completely*
from wall to wall 144.9 *completely*
from what one can gather 528.19
reportedly
from what place? 477.25 *what?*
frond 83.6 *leaf,* 88.2 *fern plant,*
90.3 *plant body*
Frondeur 693.6 *nonconformist*
front 156, 303, 303, 25.9
bowls, 55.10 *air movement,*
126.10 *lead,* 154.2 *priority,*
154.15 *precede,* 264.3 *near
place,* 289.1, 289.6 *exterior,*
289.11 *be exterior,* 293.28 *face,*
295.1 *dress,* 303.5 *boldness,*
303.10 *be in front,* 438.6 *that
which makes invisible,* 457.3 *ex-

ternal appearance,* 540.12 *facade,* 663.16 *confront,* 676.10
battleground
Front 303
frontage 251.1 *situation,* 303.1
front
frontal 55, 156.30, 303.6 *front*
frontal bone 382 Bones
frontal system 55.11 *weather system*
frontbencher 298.3 *interfacer*
front bowls 25.2 *grip*
front court 23.1 *basketball*
front crawl 39.1 *swimming*
front door 303.1 *front,* 346.6
means of entry
front elevation 303.1 *front*
front-end loader 63.29 *construction equipment,* 68.10 *farm tool*
Fronte Nuovo delle Arti 50
Schools and Groups of Artists
front for 707.4 *substitute for*
frontier 136.6 *boundary,* 157.7
limit, 157.24 *limiting,* 267.1
juxtaposition, 300.1 *edge,* 302.3
furthest point
frontier post 356.5 *crossing point*
frontiersman 154.8 *precursor,*
255.5 *countryman,* 298.3 *interfacer*
fronting 303.6 *front*
frontispiece 43 Architectural
Decoration, 154.5 *preface,*
156.10 *introduction,* 279.3 *architectural summit,* 303.1 *front*
front kick 26.9 *tae kwon do*
front line 303.1 *front,* 676.10 *battleground,* 679.14 *armed forces*
front-line soldier 298.3 *interfacer*
front-line troops 679.14 *armed
forces*
front matter 154.5 *preface,*
156.10 *introduction,* 303.1 *front*
front of house 51.16 *auditorium*
front-of-house staff 51.26 *stagehand*
front of the queue 154.2 *priority*
front page 303.1 *front*
front-page 528.17 *newsworthy,*
611.6 *notable*
front-point 34.9 *mountaineer*
front-pointing 34.3 *climbing technique,* 34.8 *mountaineering*
front position 154.2 *priority*
front room 256.7 *room*
front row 35.4 *rugby player*
front rows 51.16 *auditorium*
frontrunner 154.8 *precursor,*
674.10 *contender*
front scale 30.6 *pommel horse*
front side 305.2 *surface*
frontstage 51.15 *stage,* 51.41
onstage
front stalls 51.16 *auditorium*
front-surfaced 56.29 *optical element*
front tooth 380.11 *tooth*
front up to 303.10 *be in front*
frost 55, 55.63 *snow,* 279.7 *top,*
293.24 *coat,* 409.2 *freezing,*
409.5 *ice,* 414.8 *sweeten,*
443.11 *make opaque,* 446.9
white thing, 446.13 *whiten,*
448.8 *grey*
Frost 48 Poets
frostbite 34.2 *climbing dangers,*
409.3 *chill*
frost-bitten 409.8 *cold*
frost-covered 55.55 *cool*
frost damage 55.36 *frost*
frosted 55.55 *cool,* 279.6 *topped,*
409.8 *cold,* 414.6 *sweet,* 441.6
murky, 442.3 *semitransparent,*
443.2 *shady,* 446.2 *whitened*
frosted glass 439.10 *window,*
441.2 *murk,* 442.9 *glass,* 443.7
opaque thing
frost hollow 55.36 *frost,* 409.5 *ice*
frostily 55.65 *meteorologically,*
409.13 *coldly,* 820.14 *hostilely*
frostiness 409.5 *ice,* 816.1 *unsociability,* 820.1 *enmity*
frosting 279.4 *top layer,* 293.3
coating, 384.4 *pulverization,*
409.5 *ice,* 414.3 *dessert*

frosty 55.55 *cool,* 409.8 *cold,* 446.2 *whitened,* 783.7 *indifferent,* 816.8 *unsociable,* 820.6 *hostile*
froth 97.3 *wave,* 97.10 *billow,* 353.9 *saliva,* 370.7 *light thing,* 390.10 *air bubble,* 390.24 *bubble,* 612.9 *bauble,* 622.4 *dirt*
froth at the mouth 353.20 *salivate*
froth-blower 874.17 *drunkard*
froth flotation 57.23 *metallurgy*
frothily 390.25 *airily*
frothiness 370.5 *lightness*
frothing 353.29 *salivating*
frothy 370.2 *insubstantial,* 390.18 *bubbly,* 557.4 *ornate,* 612.4 *trivial,* 811.19 *flashy*
frottage 50.7 *picture,* 385.1 *friction*
froufrou 424.1 *faintness,* 429.1 *hiss*
froward 577.1 *obstinate*
frown 829, 309.2 *facial distortion,* 309.10 *make faces,* 543.3, 543.11 *gesture,* 772.8 *be serious,* 785.4 *sign of dislike,* 818.3 *act of discourtesy,* 818.8 *get angry,* 828.6 *sign of anger,* 828.11 *be angry,* 829.2 *sign of irascibility,* 830.4 *sign of irritableness,* 830.11 *be irritable,* 852.10 *disapproving look,* 852.23 *show disapproval*
frown down 806.26 *outdo*
frowning 772.1 *solemn,* 829.5 *showing irascibility,* 830.7 *irritable*
frown on 816.13 *ignore,* 852.14 *disapprove*
frowns of fortune 687.3 *bad fortune*
frowstiness 419.1 *stench*
frowsty 419.3 *stinking*
frowziness 419.1 *stench*
frowzy 419.3 *stinking,* 622.7 *dirty*
frozen 57.32 *solid,* 225.9 *stable,* 302.5 *limited,* 325.4 *motionless,* 371.7 *condensed,* 373.3 *hardened,* 404.7 *anaesthetized,* 409.8 *cold,* 600.4 *disused,* 632.6 *invulnerable,* 637.7 *preserved,* 641.3 *inactive,* 699.13 *restraining,* 725.8 *propertied,* 761.2 *desensitized*
frozen assets 725.5 *personal estate,* 745.5 *amount owing*
frozen balance 745.5 *amount owing*
frozen ball 24.2 *billiards play*
frozen collocation 5.23 *phrase*
frozen corn snow 41.1 *skiing*
frozen food 350.7 *food,* 637.3 *preserved thing*
frozen like a statue 225.9 *stable*
frozen-out 816.10 *lonely*
frozen over 373.3 *hardened*
frozen rain 409.5 *ice*
frozen shoulder 624.16 *rheumatism*
frozen solid 373.3 *hardened,* 409.8 *cold*
fructan 58.4 *polysaccharide*
fructiferous 86.6 *fruiting,* 246.5 *fertile*
fructiferously 86
fructification 245.3 *propagation,* 246.2 *productiveness,* 594.13 *development*
fructify 86.10 *fruit,* 245.11 *have young,* 246.6 *be fertile,* 246.7 *make fertile,* 627.2 *get better*
fructose 58 Common Sugars, 350.11 *food content,* 414.2 *sweetener*
fructuous 86.6 *fruiting*
fructuously 86.11 *fructiferously*
frugal 756.4 *thrifty,* 781.4 *cautious,* 869.8 *self-restrained*
frugality 637.1 *preservation,* 756.1 *thrift,* 869.1 *self-restraint*
frugally 756.7 *economically,* 869.11 *with self-restraint*
frugivore 86.4 *fruit eating*
frugivorous 86.8 *fruit-eating,* 350.26 *eating*

frugivorousness 86.4 *fruit eating,* 350.5 *eating habit*
fruit 86, 45.9 *dish,* 69.10 *fruit tree,* 85.9 *tree product,* 155.11 *progeny,* 227.3 *growth,* 243.7 *produce,* 245.11 *have young,* 414.2 *sweetener,* 721.6 *yield*
fruitage 69.1 *horticulture*
fruitarian 86.4 *fruit eating*
fruitarianism 86.4 *fruit eating*
fruit basket 787.3 *basket*
fruit bat 77 Placental Mammals, 86.4 *fruit eating*
fruit-bearing 86.6 *fruiting,* 227.11 *growing,* 246.5 *fertile*
fruit belt 243.11 *farmland*
fruitcake 45.36 *cake,* 168.10 *eccentric*
fruit cake 414.3 *dessert*
fruitcake 510.7 *insane person*
fruit crush 414.5 *sweet drink*
fruit cup 45.35 *dessert,* 414.5 *sweet drink*
fruit diet 350.6 *nutrition*
fruit drop 69.12 *pests and diseases*
fruit-eater 86.4 *fruit eating*
fruit eating 86
fruit-eating 86
fruit-eating animal 86.4 *fruit eating*
fruit-eating person 86.4 *fruit eating*
fruiter 69.13 *horticulturist,* 85.1 *tree*
fruiterer 86.4 *fruit eating*
fruit farm 68.6 *farm,* 69.2 *garden*
fruit farmer 68.15 *agriculturist,* 69.13 *horticulturist*
fruit farming 68.4 *arable farming*
fruit flan 45.35 *dessert*
fruit fly 82 Insects
fruitful 68.20 *farmable,* 86.6 *fruiting,* 243.11 *productive,* 246.5 *fertile,* 613.4 *profitable,* 682.13 *successful,* 721.19 *yielding*
fruitfully 246, 68.22 *agriculturally,* 86.11 *fructiferously,* 243.13 *productively,* 682.16 *successfully,* 721.20 *gainfully*
fruitfulness 246.1 *fertility,* 613.8 *benefit*
fruit grower 69.13 *horticulturist*
fruit growing 69.1 *horticulture,* 86.4 *fruit eating*
fruit gum 414.4 *confectionery*
fruitily 86.11 *fructiferously*
fruitiness 416.1 *odour*
fruiting 86, 594.20 *developed*
fruiting body 86.2 *botanical fruit,* 89.4 *fungal body*
fruition 144.3 *completion,* 245.3 *propagation,* 594.13 *development,* 684.1 *completion*
fruit juice 351.6 *soft drink,* 414.5 *sweet drink*
fruitless 247.3 *birth control,* 614.2 *futile,* 683.10 *failed,* 838.5 *thankless*
fruitlessly 247.11 *unproductively,* 358.11 *in vain,* 683.12 *unsuccessfully,* 838.7 *ungratefully*
fruitlessness 247.1 *infertility,* 614.4 *futility,* 722.3 *waste*
fruitlike 86
fruit of someone's loins 245.6 *progeny*
fruit picker 68.16 *farm worker,* 69.13 *horticulturist*
fruits 86
Fruits 86
fruit salad 45.35 *dessert*
fruit seller 86.4 *fruit eating*
fruit selling 86.4 *fruit eating*
fruits of the earth 86.1 *fruits*
fruit squash 414.5 *sweet drink*
fruit stall 350.17 *food shop*
fruit structure 86
fruit tree 69, 85.1 *tree*
fruit wall 86.3 *fruit structure*
fruity 69.17 *botanical,* 86.7 *fruitlike,* 418.4 *fragrant,* 877.12 *indecent*
frumpish 151.15 *untidy*
frumpy 549.8 *inelegant*
frusemide 62 Medication

frustrate 231.3 *counteract,* 515.7 *thwart,* 661.8 *hinder,* 663.18 *counteract*
frustrated 515.9 *disappointed*
frustrated expectations 515.1 *disappointment*
frustrating 231.4 *counteracting,* 515.11 *disappointing*
frustratingly 515.13 *disappointingly*
frustration 61.12 *stress,* 231.1 *counteraction,* 236.2 *futile effort,* 515.1 *disappointment,* 661.1 *hindrance,* 683.1 *failure*
frustration test 61.5 *psychological test*
frustrator 661.7 *hinderer*
frustule 90.3 *plant body*
frustum 43.9 *miscellaneous architectural features,* 52.45 *curved surface,* 52.46 *polyhedron,* 132.1 *remainder*
fruticose 90.8 *lichenoid*
fruticose lichen 90.6 *lichen*
fry 45.55 *cook,* 76.5 *aquatic animal,* 80.3 *young fish,* 206.4 *young animal,* 408.14 *be hot*
Fry 48 Dramatists
frying 45.8 *cooking technique*
frying in hell 16.64 *convicted*
frying pan 45.6 *kitchen equipment,* 258.15 *pot*
fry over lightly 45.55 *cook*
fry sunny side up 45.55 *cook*
fry-up 133.2 *mixed thing*
F star 53.13 *luminosity*
f-stop 66.18 *exposure time*
Fuchi 8 Deities
fuchsia 84 Flowers and Flowering Plants, 450.1 *red,* 455.6 *purple*
fuchsine 67.6 *dye*
fuck 135.11 *make love,* 245.14 *have sex,* 821.29 *make love,* 827.15 *miscellaneous swearwords*
fuck all 172.2 *nothing*
fucked 135.14 *conjunctive,* 236.10 *powerless,* 244.15 *destroyed*
fucked up 236.10 *powerless,* 656.4 *bungled*
fucked-up 151.19 *mixed-up,* 614.1 *useless*
fucking 135.4 *sexual union,* 821.5 *desire*
fucking hell 827.15 *miscellaneous swearwords*
fuck it 827.15 *miscellaneous swearwords*
fuck me 827.15 *miscellaneous swearwords*
fuck off 345.1 *depart,* 345.15 *go,* 349.33 *go away,* 827.15 *miscellaneous swearwords*
fuck up 151.23 *confuse,* 504.19 *make a mistake,* 601.1 *misuse,* 628.4 *impair,* 656.7 *be clumsy*
fuck-up 151.6 *mix-up,* 504.10 *blunder,* 661.2 *obstacle*
fuckwit 502.5 *ignorant person,* 508.3 *foolish person*
fuck with 628.4 *impair*
fuckwitted 502.6 *ignorant*
fuck you 827.15 *miscellaneous swearwords*
fucoid 90 Algae, 90.7 *algal*
fucose 58 Common Sugars
fucoxanthin 58.18 *pigment,* 90.3 *plant body*
fucus 90 Algae
fuddle 460.10 *bemuse,* 874.8 *get drunk,* 874.9 *be intoxicating*
fuddled 874.2 *slightly drunk*
fudge 45.41 *sweet,* 102.16 *delude,* 414.4 *confectionery,* 474.11 *practise sophistry,* 539.28 *trick,* 578.1 *be equivocal,* 591.7 *be evasive,* 750.7 *account*
fudge cake 45.36 *cake*
fudge the issue 540.23 *evade*
fudging the issue 540.11 *evasion*
Fudo 8 Deities

fuel 338, 410, 410, 56.35 *heat,* 128.5 *make bigger,* 235.12 *generate power,* 604.1 *materials,* 605.6 *store,* 606.5 *provision*
Fuel 410
fuel assembly 56.73 *nuclear reactor*
fuel cell 56.43 *electrical conduction,* 57.19 *electrochemistry,* 64.29 *power source,* 235.7 *electrical power,* 410.4 *electricity*
fuel-efficient 410.10 *powered*
fuel element 56.73 *nuclear reactor*
fuel filter 621.10 *cleaning object*
fuel injection 410.6 *oil*
fuel oil 395.7 *oil,* 395.9 *petroleum*
fuel rod 56.73 *nuclear reactor,* 235.8, 410.7 *nuclear power*
fuel ship 679.24 *warship*
fuel stop 33.6 *motor racing terms*
fuel to the flame 606.1 *provision*
fuel up 605.6 *store*
Fufluns 8 Deities
fug 408.1 *heat,* 419.1 *stench*
fugacious 189.6 *transient*
fugacity 189.1 *transience*
fugal 118.12 *imitative*
Fugard 48 Dramatists
fuggy 408.9 *hot,* 419.3 *stinking,* 626.5 *unhygienic*
fugitate 349.4 *ostracize*
fugitation 349.19 *ostracism*
fugitive 102.8 *unreal,* 136.16 *apart,* 189.6 *transient,* 458.6 *disappearing,* 590.7 *the hunted,* 591.17 *avoider,* 591.18 *avoiding,* 638.3 *escaper,* 638.8 *escaping*
fugitively 638, 458.8 *fleetingly*
fugleman 126.5 *superior,* 653.14 *leader*
fugue 61.14 *trance,* 118.1 *imitation,* 328.13 *slow thing*
fugue state 61.14 *trance*
fujara 49 Musical Instruments
Fujiwara style 50 Non-Western Art
Fujiyama 95 Mountains, 10.13 *shrine*
Fukuoka 93 Cities
Fukurokuju 8 Deities
Fula 5 Languages and Groups of Languages
Fulani 1 Peoples, **5** Languages and Groups of Languages, **68** Breeds of Cattle
fulcrum 158.2 *core,* 284.2 *supporting part,* 291.1 *centre,* 364.4 *vortex,* 611.3 *chief thing*
fulfil 142.10 *complete,* 144.4 *complete,* 323.9 *close down,* 608.4 *suffice,* 619.5 *perfect,* 640.4 *act,* 684.4 *complete,* 719.6 *perform,* 765.8 *satisfy*
fulfil expectations 478.22 *be the answer*
fulfilled 805, 619.1 *perfect,* 684.7 *completed,* 765.4 *satisfied*
fulfilling 684.7 *completed,* 765.5 *satisfying*
fulfilment 805, 144.1 *completeness,* 144.3 *completion,* 323.1 *closure,* 344.17 *achievement,* 608.7 *sufficiency,* 684.1 *completion,* 719.3 *performance,* 765.1 *satisfaction*
fulfil one's duty 847.16 *do one's duty*
fulfil one's role 719.6 *perform*
fulguration 241.5 *violent weather*
fulgurite 54 Minerals
fuliginous 447.1 *black,* 448.1 *grey*
full 144, 106.10 *detailed,* 142.6 *whole,* 257.11 *loaded,* 259.16 *fat,* 271.1 *broad,* 323.13 *stopped,* 332.9 *directly,* 350.26 *eating,* 371.6 *dense,* 423.6 *loud,* 427.8 *deep,* 433.6 *melodious,* 560.11 *descriptive,* 608.3 *filled,* 610.6 *excessive,* 619.1 *perfect,* 765.4 *satisfied*
full armour 671.7 *armour*
fullback 19.7 *offence,* 31.2 *hockey player,* 35.4 *rugby player,* 38.3 *football player*
full-ball 24.9 *billiard*

full-ball aim 24.2 *billiards play*
full-bellied 259.16 *fat*
full blast 423.1 *loudness*, 423.9 *loudly*
full bloom 84.5 *flowering*
full blow 84.5 *flowering*
full-blown 144.7 *complete*, 259.15 *big*, 261.7 *bigger*, 684.7 *completed*
full-bodied 273.2 *dense*, 351.17 *drinkable*
full-bodied wine 351.9 *wine*
full-bosomed 259.16 *fat*
full capacity 144.2 *fullness*
full career 329.8 *speed*
full chorus 423.1 *loudness*, 423.9 *loudly*
full circle 313.2 *circle*, 334.1 *circuit*, 363.3 *orbit*, 364.1 *rotation*
full-coloured 444.11 *colourful*
full complement 144.2 *fullness*, 146.1 *inclusion*
full course 142.3 *whole situation*
full coverage 146.1 *inclusion*
full crew 144.2 *fullness*
full cycle 313.2 *circle*
full details 530.3 *openness*
full dress 295.3, 813.4 *formal dress*
full-dress uniform 295.3 *formal dress*
Fuller 48 Writers, **48** Poets
full extent 144.2 *fullness*
full-face 457.3 *external appearance*
full-faced 259.16 *fat*, 303.6 *front*
full-face picture 303.2 *face*
full-face portrait 50.10 *art subject*
full-fledged 144.7 *complete*, 261.7 *bigger*
full-frontal 303.6 *front*
full gale 55.14 *windiness*
full-grown 144.7 *complete*, 207.11 *adult*, 259.15 *big*, 261.7 *bigger*, 594.20 *developed*, 684.7 *completed*
full growth 259.2 *bigness*
full head of steam 235.4 *energy*
full house 42.3 *card game terms*, 51.11 *theatrical performance*, 51.31 *theatregoer*, 144.2 *fullness*
full length 144.2 *fullness*, 269.4 *length*
full-length 269.1 *long*
full-length mirror 56.29 *optical element*, 435.8 *reflection*
full-length novel 243.5 *work of art*
full-length portrait 50.10 *art subject*
full lick 329.8 *speed*
full list 142.5 *unit*
full load 144.2 *fullness*
full meal 350.12 *meal*
full measure 144.2 *fullness*, 608.7 *sufficiency*
full military rites 399.1 *burial*
full moon 53.17 *moon*, 439.4 *natural light*
full name 560.8 *name*
full nelson 26.5 *wrestling*, 726.1 *retention*
fullness 144, 142.1 *whole*, 259.5 *fatness*, 271.4 *breadth*, 273.5 *thickness*, 608.8 *plenty*, 684.1 *completion*
full observance 719.1 *observance*
full of 144.8 *full*
full of beans 239.4 *vigorous*, 623.1 *healthy*, 642.18 *active*
full of difficult words 551.2 *obscure*
full of energy 235
full of flavour 411.11 *tastily*
full of forgiveness 835.6 *pitying*
full of grace 8.13 *divine*
full of guilt 867.6 *penitent*
full of hate 820.6 *hostile*, 822.10 *hating*, 828.15 *resentful*, 832.10 *malevolent*
full of holes 317.5 *concave*
full of hope 513.5 *expecting*, 714.14 *auspicious*, 714.17 *auspiciously*, 775.11 *hopeful*
full of joy 762.4 *happy*
full of labour 644.11 *laborious*
full of loathing 832.10 *malevolent*

full of malice 822.10 *hating*
full of meaning 520.6 *meaningful*
full of mercy 835.6 *pitying*
full of news 533.14 *journalistic*
full of noise 423.6 *loud*
full of Old Nick 618.5 *harmful*
full of oneself 809.11 *cocky*
full of pep 239.4 *vigorous*
full of potential 714.14 *auspicious*
full of praises 9.9 *worshipful*
full of promise 714.14 *auspicious*, 714.17 *auspiciously*
full of regrets 867.6 *penitent*
full of remorse 867.6 *penitent*
full of revenge 832.13 *merciless*
full of ruses 657.4 *cunning*
full of sin 864.11 *wicked*
full of snares 657.4 *cunning*
full of stamina 642.20 *industrious*
full of steam 623.1 *healthy*
full of surprises 514.8 *surprising*
full of the devil 618.5 *harmful*
full of the milk of human kindness 831.6 *benevolent*
full of vitality 378.4 *powerful*, 623.1 *healthy*, 642.18 *active*
full of years 202.11 *old*
full opportunity 698.5 *scope*
full out 144.10 *fully*
full pardon 677.2 *peace offering*, 839.1 *forgiveness*
full particulars 106.1 *circumstances*
full pelt 239.6 *with vigour*, 329.8 *speed*
full play 698.5 *scope*
full pressure 644.4 *exertion*
full quota 144.2 *fullness*, 146.1 *inclusion*
full radiator 56.40 *heating effect*
full report 530.2 *divulgence*
full sail 329.8 *speed*
full satisfaction 746.1 *payment*
full-scale 144.7 *complete*, 259.15 *big*
full scope 698.5 *scope*
full set 146.1 *inclusion*
full settlement 746.1 *payment*
full size 144.2 *fullness*, 259.2 *bigness*
full-size 259.15 *big*
full skirt 295.6 *skirt*
full speed 329.8 *speed*
full speed ahead 329.14 *swiftly*, 574.18 *here goes*
full steam ahead 239.6 *with vigour*
full stop 136.5 *separator*, 325.1 *motionlessness*, 543.7 *punctuation*
full stride 21.1 *track events*
full-throated 423.6 *loud*, 427.8 *deep*, 431.16 *vociferous*, 432.7 *ululant*
full tide 97.2 *tide*
full tilt 332.9 *directly*, 642.22 *actively*
full to bursting 144.8 *full*
full-toned 433.6 *melodious*
full to overflowing 144.8 *full*
full toss 27.8 *delivery*, 338.5 *throw*
full to the brim 144.8 *full*
full turn 30.5 *horizontal bar*
full up 144.8 *full*, 608.3 *filled*
full-up 350.26 *eating*, 765.4 *satisfied*
full value 144.2 *fullness*
full view 142.3 *whole situation*
full volume 144.2 *fullness*
full-wave rectifier 64.21 *rectifier*
fully 144, 106.19 *meticulously*, 142.11 *wholly*, 257.14 *internally*, 371.10 *densely*, 684.9 *completely*
fully armed 594.18 *prepared*
fully charged 144.8 *full*
fully comprehensive 142.6 *whole*, 164.15 *general*
fully developed 261.7 *bigger*, 684.7 *completed*
fully dressed 594.18 *prepared*
fully engaged 642.19 *busy*
fully fashioned 795.31 *styled*
fully fledged 144.7 *complete*, 261.7 *bigger*, 594.20 *developed*
fully furnished 594.18 *prepared*

fully grown 144.7 *complete*, 261.7 *bigger*
fully laden 144.8 *full*
fully mature 619.1 *perfect*
fully occupied 642.19 *busy*
fully occupied person 642.10 *busy person*
fully realized 684.7 *completed*
fully restored 142.8 *sound*
fully ripe 619.1 *perfect*
fully trained 594.18 *prepared*
fulmar 78 Birds, 78.3 *water bird*
fulminate 338.30 *blow up*, 423.8 *be loud*, 827.6 *vilify*
fulmination 827.3 *vilification*
fulsome 817.9 *deferential*, 851.18 *approving*
fulsomely 817.16 *deferentially*
fulsomeness 817.4 *deference*
Fulton 52 Scientists
Fulton Street 740.1 *market*
fulvous 449.1 *brown*, 452.2 *yellowish*
fumaric 58 Common Fatty Acids
fumaric acid 57 Common Chemical Compounds
fumble 19.9 *play*, 407.11 *touch*, 656.7 *be clumsy*, 656.9 *bungling*
fumbler 656.10 *unskilled person*
fumbling 656.3 *clumsy*
fume 349.14 *let out*, 366.3 *turbulence*, 388.27 *give off*, 408.15 *burn*, 642.12 *be active*, 648.2 *make haste*, 828.11 *be angry*
fume cupboard 57 Laboratory Apparatus
fumigant 630.3 *prophylactic*
fumigate 134.10 *purify*, 388.26 *aerate*, 417.5 *deodorize*, 621.15 *purify*, 625.6 *make hygienic*
fumigated 417.3 *odourless*
fumigation 134.2 *purification*, 388.10 *vaporization*, 417.1 *odourlessness*, 621.2 *cleaning*, 625.1 *hygiene*
fumigator 417.2 *deodorant*
fuming 241.6 *violent*, 366.17 *turbulent*, 388.18 *miasmic*, 828.16 *angry*
fumitory 84 Flowers and Flowering Plants
fumy 388.18 *miasmic*
fumarole 54.25 *eruption*
fun 762, 405.1 *physical pleasure*, 405.6 *pleasant*, 769.3 *cheerfulness*, 771.2 *amusement*, 815.17 *festive*
funambulist 237.5 *athlete*
funboard 36.7 *windsurfing*
funboard storm sail 36.7 *windsurfing*
function 4.8 *philosophical term*, 16.2 *jurisdiction*, 52.29 *mathematical function*, 65.17 *computing term*, 150.23 *be in order*, 161.9 *social gathering*, 232.4 *be an instrument*, 471.4 *purpose*, 599.6 *use*, 613.6 *usability*, 613.9 *be useful*, 640.4 *act*, 703.2 *engagement*, 811.13 *ceremonial*, 812.1 *celebration*, 812.3 *ceremony*, 847.2 *task*
functional 43 Architectural Styles, **52**, 52.29 *mathematical function*, 101.8 *practical*, 230.10 *operational*, 471.12 *purposive*, 613.1 *useful*, 640.6 *effective*, 703.10 *engaged*
functional analysis 52.30 *calculus*
functional calculus 52.63 *mathematical logic*
functional disease 624.4 *disease*
functional equation 52.27 *equation*
functionalism 1.5 *anthropological concept*, 4.7 *school of thought*, 613.5 *usefulness*
functionalist 1.11 *anthropological*, 4.11 *follower of a doctrine*, 4.14 *of a philosophy*
functionality 232.1 *instrumentality*
functionally 52.87 *mathematically*, 230.13 *operationally*, 471.21 *purposively*, 640.8 *effectively*

functional nervous disorder 61.9 *psychological disorder*
functional psychology 61.1 *psychology*
functional psychosis 61.11 *psychosis*
functionary 646.3 *agent*, 653.16 *official*, 703.5 *commissioner*
functioning 230.10 *operational*, 232.8 *practical*, 471.12 *purposive*, 599.6 *use*, 599.10 *usable*, 640.1 *action*
functionless 614.1 *useless*
fund 14.5 *invest*, 161.25 *assemblage*, 284.13 *support financially*, 602.6 *find means*, 605.1, 605.6 *store*, 662.29 *finance*, 741.19 *treasury*, 746.8 *defray*, 755.11 *give*, 833.5 *charity*
fundament 280.1 *base*, 304.2 *rear end*
fundamental 52.70 *universal*, 56.20 *musical note*, 99.11, 103.6 *intrinsic*, 134.16 *simple*, 148.8 *belonging*, 156.35 *rudimentary*, 226.13 *causal*, 280.3 *base*, 290.11 *intrinsic*, 571.1 *necessity*, 571.9 *necessary*, 611.5 *important*, 690.8 *severe*
fundamental constant 56
fundamental interaction 56
fundamentalism 7 Christian Movements, 7.2 *religiousness*, 481.4 *social discrimination*, 690.1 *severity*
fundamentalist 7.5 *Christian*, 7.6 *non-Christian*, 7.15 *religious*, 7.16 *denominational*, 481.7 *bigot*, 481.10 *discriminatory*, 635.2 *troublemaker*
fundamentally 52.87 *mathematically*, 99.22 *really*, 103.14 *at heart*, 134.20 *homogeneously*, 148.14 *constituently*, 156.42 *principally*, 226.14 *causally*, 280.5 *basically*, 690.11 *severely*
fundamental nature 99.3 *nature*
fundamental note 49.16 *musical note*
fundamental particle 56.77 *elementary particle*, 367.4 *matter*
fundamentals 101.5 *realities*, 165.4 *specifications*, 226.3 *rudiment*, 611.3 *chief thing*
fundamental standard 75.4 *standard*
fundamental unit 75.2 *unit system*
funded 605.7 *stored*
funded debt 745.2 *national debt*
funder 729.4 *giver*
funding 662.6 *financial assistance*
fund-raiser 284.8 *supporter*, 712.4 *requester*, 721.7 *gainer*, 733.6 *borrower*, 833.5 *charity*
fund-raising 712.3 *solicitation*, 712.11 *begging*, 721.1 *gain*, 721.15 *gainful*, 733.1 *borrowing*
funds 741, 602.4 *financial resources*, 725.5 *personal estate*
funds for investment 741.6 *funds*
funds in hand 741.6 *funds*
fundus 280.1 *base*
funebrial 399.11 *funeral*
funeral 399, 399, 397.8 *after death*, 813.3 *formal occasion*
funeral ceremony 399.2 *funeral*
funeral colour 455.1 *purpleness*
funeral director 399, 397.9 *person dealing with the dead*
funeral hymn 399.2 *funeral*
funeral march 328.13 *slow thing*
funeral objects 399
funeral oration 345.9 *parting*, 399.2 *funeral*, 774.2 *lament*
funeral parlour 397.8 *after death*, 399.2 *funeral*
funeral pile 399.1 *burial*
funeral procession 159.8 *procession*, 328.13 *slow thing*, 399.2 *funeral*
funeral pyre 408.6 *fire*
funeral rites 397.7 *dying day*, 399.2 *funeral*
funeral sermon 399.2 *funeral*
funeral service 399.2 *funeral*
funeral urn 399.4 *funeral objects*

funerary 399.11 *funeral*
funerary sculpture 50.12 *sculpture*
funereal 10.21 *ritualistic*, 397.22 *post-mortem*, 399.11 *funeral*, 440.10 *dark-coloured*, 447.6 *sad*
funereally 399
fungal 89
fungal antibiotic 89
fungal association 89
fungal body 89
fungal constituent 90.6 *lichen*
fungal disease 89.5 *fungal association*
fungi 89, 396.9 *classifications of life*
Fungi 89, 89.3 *fungi*
fungicidal 62.14 *counteracting*, 69.18 *herbicidal*
fungicide 62.4 *drug type*, 68.14 *pest control*, 69.8 *weedkiller*, 89.7 *antifungal agent*, 398.14 *plant killer*
fungiform 89.9 *fungal*
fungistat 89.7 *antifungal agent*
fungoid 89.9 *fungal*
fungology 59.1 *life science*
fungosity 89.1 *fungus*
fungous 89.9 *fungal*
fungus 89, 83.4 *lower plant*, 141.1 *disintegration*, 622.4 *dirt*
funicle 83.5 *stem*, 83.9 *seed*
funicular 41.1 *skiing*, 72.1 *railway*, 327.12 *cableway*, 359.8 *lift*, 361.10 *elevator*
funk 591.4 *shy*, 777.1 *fear*, 777.12 *be fearful*, 779.1 *cowardice*, 779.2 *coward*, 779.4 *be a coward*
funker 576.15 *indecisive person*
funk hole 634.1 *refuge*
funkster 49.24 *musician*
fun-loving 405.7 *pleased*
funnel 33.10 *be on the track*, 72.5 *locomotive part*, 322.7 *passageway*, 322.21 *provide passage for*, 326.11 *transfer*, 342.6 *narrowing*, 342.9 *converge*, 653.2 *direct*
funnel cap 89 *Fungi*
funnelling 33.6 *motor racing terms*
funnel weaver 82 *Arachnids*
funnily 771.16 *humorously*
funniness 771.1 *humorousness*
funny 771, 168.14 *eccentric*, 506.5 *nonsensical*, 510.11 *insane*, 769.1 *cheerful*, 771.10 *humorous*, 798.5 *ridiculous*
funny bone 382 *Bones*
funny farm 510.8 *mental hospital*
funny ha-ha 798.5 *ridiculous*
funny house 510.8 *mental hospital*
funny money 741.15 *false money*
funny peculiar 798.5 *ridiculous*
funny place 510.8 *mental hospital*
funny side 305.4 *aspect*
funny story 771.5 *joke*
fun run 674.4 *race*
fun time 405.2 *good time*
fur 777 *Phobias by Topic*, 77.2 *mammalian characteristic*, 243.7 *produce*, 293.14 *animal covering*, 295.12 *coat*, 295.14 *neckwear*, 374.11 *soft thing*, 544.8 *heraldic device*, 622.4 *dirt*
furanose 57 *Types of Compounds*, 58.3 *carbohydrate*
furbelow 300.2 *edging*, 300.6 *edge*, 792.5 *decorative articles*
furbish 385.12 *rub*
furcate 343.9 *branched*, 343.14 *branch*
furcation 343.4 *branching*
fur coat 408.3 *heater*
furcula 343.5 *fork*
furculum 343.5 *fork*
furfuraceous 266.9 *platelike*, 384.17 *mealy*
furfuraceously 266.12 *in layers*
fur hat 408.3 *heater*
Furioso 32 *Breeds of Horse and Pony*
furious 455, 241.6 *violent*, 618.5 *harmful*, 648.3 *hasty*, 822.13, 828.16 *angry*

furiously 828.18 *angrily*
furious rage 828.4 *anger*
furl 320.1, 320.7 *fold*, 364.9 *roll*
furl a sail 36.15 *sail*
fur-lined 408.13 *heated*
furlong 75 *General Units*
furlough 254.5 *leave of absence*, 349.2 *dismiss*, 349.18 *dismissal*, 645.2 *time off*, 649.1 *ease*, 704.2 *termination*, 708.2 *permit*
furnace 44.6 *ceramic workshop*, 56.35 *heat*, 408.6 *fire*, 635.1 *trap*, 647.1 *workshop*
Furnace 53 The Constellations
furnish 243.10 *produce*, 594.5 *equip*, 602.6 *find means*, 606.5 *provision*, 710.11 *volunteer*
furnish a good excuse 855.8 *justify*
furnished 594.18 *prepared*, 606.8 *provisional*
furnishing 594.11 *fitting out*, 603.6 *equipment*, 606.1 *provision*, 606.7 *provisioning*
furnishings 47.1 *furniture*, 130.3 *additional item*
furniture 47, 603.6 *equipment*, 725.4 *possessions*
Furniture and Woodwork 47
furniture cover 293.12 *protective covering*
furniture-designing 47.1 *furniture*
furniture factory 47.1 *furniture*
furniture-maker 47.13 *carpenter*
furniture-making 47.1 *furniture*
furniture polish 293.3 *coating*, 376.10 *polish*, 621.9 *cleaning agent*
furniture store 47.1 *furniture*
furniture style 47
furore 153.5 *commotion*, 366.2 *tumult*
furred up 622.7 *dirty*
furrier 293.17 *coverer*, 295.26 *fashion designer*
furriness 374.9 *smoothness*
furrow 321, 321, 68.11 *farmland*, 265.2, 265.5 *crack*, 320.2, 320.8 *pleat*, 375.8 *rough ground*, 375.12 *make rough*
Furrow 321
furrowed 321, 265.7 *cracked*, 375.2 *coarse*
furrowed thing 321
furry 374.3 *smooth*, 375.3 *barbed*
furry friend 76.2 *animal*
further 336, 662, 130.8 *additional*, 130.10 *additionally*, 219.4 *protract*, 263.8 *distant*, 263.10 *distantly*, 284.14 *give moral support*, 627.1 *improve*, 660.16 *make easy*
furtherance 662, 219.2 *protraction*, 284.6 *moral support*, 336.12 *advance*, 336.14 *development*, 627.5 *improvement*
further education college 6.12 *educational institution*
furthering 336.12 *advance*, 662.33 *helpful*
furthermore 130.10 *additionally*
furthermost 263.8 *distant*
further oneself 336.7 *make one's way*
further one's purpose 613.9 *be useful*
further promote 6.22 *educate*
further reflection 627.7 *reconsideration*
further throw 721.2 *augmentation*
furthest 302, 157.24 *limiting*, 263.8 *distant*
furthest point 302
furtive 286.5 *devious*, 529.10 *secretive*, 539.34 *deceiving*
furtively 286.9 *deviously*, 529.16 *stealthily*
furtiveness 286.3 *deviousness*, 529.2 *secretiveness*, 539.1 *deception*
fury 241.1 *violence*, 241.4 *violent person or animal*, 759.6 *bad feeling*, 822.5, 828.4 *anger*, 829.3 *irascible person*, 832.9 *vixen*
Fury 244.7 *agent of destruction*

furze 84 Flowers and Flowering Plants
fuscous 449.1 *brown*
fuse 64.28 *plug*, 64.35 *conduct*, 133.8 *mix*, 135.10 *link*, 140.5 *combine*, 174.19 *become one*, 387.24 *melt*, 408.14 *be hot*, 410.2 *lighter*, 632.4 *safety device*, 664.16 *join*, 680.15 *explosive*
fused 133.12 *mixed*, 140.7 *combined*
fuselage 73 Aircraft Parts
Fushun 93 Cities
fusible 387.21 *liquefiable*
fusible alloy 57 Alloys
fusiform 89.10 *of fungi*, 272.3 *tapered*, 380.1 *sharp*
fusil 544.8 *heraldic device*, 680.10 *historical gun*
fusilier 679.13 *historical soldiery*
fusillade 338.7 *shot*, 670.2 *fire*, 670.15 *firing*
fusilli 45 Types of Pasta
fusing 387.8 *fluidification*, 387.20 *liquefying*
fusion 49.8 *jazz*, 49.9 *popular music*, 56.37 *temperature*, 56.72 *nuclear fission*, 133.1 *mixture*, 133.2 *mixed thing*, 135.1 *union*, 140.1 *combination*, 235.8 *nuclear power*, 387.8 *fluidification*, 664.7 *association*
fusion bomb 235.8 *nuclear power*
fusion energy 56.11 *energy*
fusion reaction 56.72 *nuclear fission*
fusion reactor 56
Fuso Kyo 7 Non-Christian Religions
fuss 366, 151.9 *disorder*, 153.5 *commotion*, 366.21 *be agitated*, 494.2 *overestimate*, 541.1 *exaggeration*, 541.7 *exaggerate*, 642.3 *nimbleness*, 642.12 *be active*, 648.4 *haste*, 663.2 *objection*, 666.2 *argument*, 666.6 *argue*, 811.6 *blatancy*
fuss and bother 642.3 *nimbleness*
fuss-budget 642.11 *meddler*
fussily 106.19 *meticulously*, 811.37 *blatantly*
fussiness 627.5 *improvement*
fussing 366.16 *restless*, 852.6 *fault-finding*
fussing like a hen with chickens 642.19 *busy*
fussing over 467.5 *solicitude*
fuss over 467.14 *be solicitous*
fusspot 481.6 *discriminating person*, 642.11 *meddler*
fussy 106.10 *detailed*, 557.4 *ornate*, 619.2 *perfectionist*, 642.18 *active*, 644.11 *laborious*, 659.14 *troublesome*, 811.21 *blatant*
fussy eater 350.18 *eater*, 659.9 *difficult person*
fust 419.1 *stench*
fustian 67 Natural Fabrics, 541.15 *bombastic*, 553.3 *diffuse*, 557.2 *affectation*, 557.4 *ornate*
fustic 85 Tree Products
fustigate 879.3 *hit*
fustily 419.6 *stinkingly*
fustiness 419.1 *stench*
fusty 419.3 *stinking*, 622.7 *dirty*, 626.5 *unhygienic*
futhark 5.14 *alphabet*
futile 614, 776, 521.11 *aimless*, 614.1 *useless*, 618.1 *worthless*, 656.1 *unskilful*, 683.10 *failed*
futile activity 642.9 *overactivity*
futile effort 236, 683.1 *failure*
futile exploit 236.2 *futile effort*
futilely 683.12 *unsuccessfully*
futilitarianism 614.5 *waste of effort*
futility 614, 236.1 *powerlessness*, 521.2, 521.6 *aimlessness*, 614.3 *uselessness*, 618.7 *worthlessness*, 683.1 *failure*
futon 47.6 *bed*
Futsunushi 8 Deities
futtock 74 Parts of a Ship
future 199, 714, 5.34 *tense*, 199.1 *future time*, 209.13 *later*,

486.6 *potential*, 513.7 *expected*, 821.11 *loved one*
future condition 199
future event 199
future generation 199
future generations 155.12 *successor*, 195.6 *posterity*
future intention 588
future interrogative 477.11 *question mark*
future perfect 5.34 *tense*
future state 199.3 *future condition*, 396.5 *life cycle*, 397.14 *the spiritual world*
future time 199, 197.1 *different time*
Future Time 199
future years 199.1 *future time*
futurism 50 Western Art Styles and Movements, 201.2 *trendiness*
Futurism 48 Literary Groups and Movements
futurist 201.9 *modern person*
futuristic 48.16 *literary*, 201.10 *new*
futuristically 201.21 *newly*
futurity 199.1 *future time*
futurologist 516.5 *predictor*, 517.9 *forecaster*
futurology 516.4 *prudence*
fuye 49 Musical Instruments
fuzz 370.7 *light thing*
fuzzily 307.6 *shapelessly*, 383.15 *texturally*, 491.25 *indeterminately*, 551.4 *obscurely*
fuzziness 307.1 *shapelessness*, 383.2 *grain*, 438.4 *invisibility*, 441.2 *murk*, 443.6 *opaqueness*, 491.14 *indeterminacy*, 551.1 *obscurity*
fuzzy 307.5 *shapeless*, 375.3 *barbed*, 383.11 *fluffy*, 404.10 *sleepy*, 438.2 *difficult to see*, 441.6 *murky*, 443.2 *shady*, 491.6 *indeterminate*, 523.4 *difficult*, 551.2 *obscure*
fuzzy tongue 874.15 *crapulence*
fylfot 11.6 *talisman*, 544.6 *national emblem*
fylker 92.3 *other*

G

G 179.10 *thousand*, 369.5 *gravity*
Ga 5 Languages and Groups of Languages
gab 565.3 *talk*, 565.7 *be talkative*
gabber 565.4 *talker*
gabbiness 565.1 *talkativeness*
gabble 506.6 *talk nonsense*, 521.5 *empty talk*, 521.9 *talk nonsense*, 565.3 *talk*, 565.7 *be talkative*
gabbling 565.5 *talkative*
gabbro 54 Common Rocks
gabby 565.5 *talkative*
gabelle 751.9 *historical taxes*
gaberdine 67 Natural Fabrics
gaberdine coat 295.12 *coat*
gabert 74 Sailing Ships and Boats
gabion 671.11 *fortification*
gabionade 671.11 *fortification*
gable 43.9 *miscellaneous architectural features*, 279.3 *architectural summit*, 283.5 *projecting object*
gable end 43.9 *miscellaneous architectural features*
gable roof 293.7 *overhead covering*
Gabon 91 Countries
gaboon 85 Trees and Shrubs
gaboon viper 79 Reptiles
Gabor 52 Scientists
Gabriel 8.6 *angel*
Gadaba 5 Languages and Groups of Languages
Gadarene swine 398.9 *animal killing*
gad fly 82 Insects
gadget 232.2 *instrument*, 367.5

object, 592.3 *expedient plan,* 603.1 *tool*
gadget play 19.9 *play*
gadoid 80.13 *fishlike*
gadolinite 54 Minerals
gadolinium 57 Chemical Elements
gadroon 43 Architectural Decoration
gadulka 49 Musical Instruments
gadwall 78 Birds
Gael 255.9 *British inhabitant*
Gaelic 5 Languages and Groups of Languages
Gaelic Athletic Association 31.7 *hurling*
Gaelic football 18 Sporting Activities
gaff 74 Rigging, 20.3 *fishing tackle,* 36.3 *parts of a sailing boat,* 36.10 *sailing,* 380.8 *sharp-pointed thing,* 380.16 *use a sharp tool* , 680.8 *sharp weapon*
gaffe 504.10 *blunder,* 508.2 *act of folly,* 559.6 *blunder,* 656.9 *bungling,* 814.5 *nonobservance*
gaffer 126.5 *superior,* 653.15 *manager*
gaff rig 36.3 *parts of a sailing boat*
gaff-rigged 36.10 *sailing*
gaffsail 36.3 *parts of a sailing boat*
gag 699, 349.15 *vomit,* 422.2 *silence,* 424.2 *sound reducer,* 506.2 *solecism,* 506.6 *talk nonsense,* 563.15 *strike dumb,* 699.5 *means of restraint,* 771.5 *joke*
gaga 153.16 *deranged,* 207.14 *aged,* 460.7 *intellectually subnormal,* 508.5 *foolish*
Gagauzi 5 Languages and Groups of Languages
gage 875.6 *drug*
gagged 563.11 *speechless,* 699.15 *detained*
gagging 349.23 *vomiting*
gaggle 161 Collective Names for Birds and Animals, 78.13 *assemblage of birds,* 432.5 *sing*
gag man 51.24 *dramatist*
gagster 771.6 *humorist*
gag writer 51.24 *dramatist,* 771.6 *humorist*
gahnite 54 Minerals
Gaia 8 Deities, 54.5 *earth*
gaiety 762.1 *happiness,* 769.3 *cheerfulness,* 812.1 *celebration,* 815.1 *sociability*
gaillardia 84 Flowers and Flowering Plants
gaily 762.9 *joyfully,* 769.9 *cheerfully*
gain 721, 721, 878, 64.15 *circuit function,* 128.1, 128.4 *increase,* 130.4 *extra,* 227.3 *growth,* 227.8 *grow,* 243.7 *produce,* 319.6 *notch up,* 336.12 *advance,* 344.9 *achieve,* 606.1 *provision,* 613.8, 613.10 *benefit,* 662.21 *be helpful,* 725.5 *profit,* 730.9 *receive,* 737.1 *trade,* 739.1 *sell,* 742.5 *wealth,* 742.13 *get rich,* 749.2 *money received,* 749.7 *receive,* 861.13 *benefit,* 861.21 *do well,* 878.5 *turnover*
Gain 721
gain acceptance 497.10 *be believed*
gain access 322.19 *open up*
gain admittance 346.9 *enter*
gain a flying start 208.7 *be early*
gain a foothold 322.23 *find an opening*
gain a footing 233.8 *influence*
gain a hearing 233.8 *influence*
gain altitude 359.19 *take off*
gain a reward 878.12 *be rewarded*
gain ascendancy over 806.26 *outdo*
gain credit 851.17 *meet with approval*
gained 730.13, 749.6 *received*
gainer 721
gain from 613.11 *find useful*

gainful 721, 613.4 *profitable,* 662.34 *beneficial,* 682.14 *rewarding,* 749.6 *received,* 878.15 *rewarding*
gain full play 233.10 *be a prevailing influence*
gainfully 721, 682.16 *successfully,* 749.8, 878.20 *profitably*
gainfulness 721.1 *gain*
gain ground 128.4 *increase,* 336.3 *press on,* 721.10 *augment*
gain height 336.3 *press on,* 359.19 *take off,* 721.10 *augment*
gain immortality 184.9 *be infinite*
gaining 721.1 *gain,* 721.18 *acquisitional*
gaining altitude 359.4 *taking off*
gaining ground 721.2 *augmentation*
gaining height 359.1 *ascent,* 359.23 *rising,* 721.2 *augmentation*
gaining on 721.2 *augmentation*
gaining time 721.2 *augmentation*
gaining weight 721.2 *augmentation*
gain in value 128.4 *increase,* 721.2 *augmentation,* 721.10 *augment*
gain mastery 233.10 *be a prevailing influence*
gain on 329.6 *accelerate,* 336.9 *maintain progress,* 721.10 *augment*
gain one's end 682.6 *be successful*
gain one's freedom 700.5 *be liberated*
gain one's goal 682.6 *be successful*
gain one's spurs 851.17 *meet with approval*
gain power 12.12 *take authority,* 235.10 *be powerful*
gains 721.5 *profit,* 742.5 *wealth*
gainsay 473.13 *argue,* 476.9 *deny,* 536.8 *rebut,* 663.15 *object,* 711.6 *dissent,* 713.6 *protest*
gainsayer 536.6 *negativist,* 663.9 *opposer,* 711.4 *refuser*
gainsaying 536.3 *rebuttal,* 536.13 *rebutting,* 711.2 *dissent,* 713.1 *protest*
gain self-determination 91.17 *become a nation*
gain strength 128.4 *increase*
gain the friendship of 819.13 *befriend*
gain the upper hand 233.10 *be a prevailing influence,* 688.20 *take authority,* 806.26 *outdo*
gain the weather gauge 74.9 *navigate*
gain time 208.7 *be early,* 209.8 *delay,* 336.4 *make good time,* 721.10 *augment*
gain weight 261.6 *become bigger,* 369.12 *be heavy,* 721.10 *augment*
gait 324, 32.10 *dressage*
gaita 49 Musical Instruments
gaiter 41.5 *ski equipment*
gaiters 295.20 *legwear*
gajdy 49 Musical Instruments
gal 75 Scientific and Technical Units, 402.2 *female*
gala 665.7 *social gathering,* 665.11 *social,* 811.14 *show,* 812.1 *celebration,* 813.3 *formal occasion,* 815.5 *party*
galactic 53.36 *astronomical,* 164.16 *universal*
galactically 53.39 *astronomically*
galactic centre 53.7 *galaxy*
galactic latitude 53.5 *celestial sphere*
galactic longitude 53.5 *celestial sphere*
galactic nebula 53.7 *galaxy*
galactose 58 Common Sugars
gala day 812.5 *anniversary*
galago 77 Placental Mammals
Galahad 825.4 *celibate person,* 857.3 *honourable person*
gala night 51.11 *theatrical performance*

Galápagos giant tortoise 79 Reptiles
gala performance 813.3 *formal occasion*
Galashiels 93 Cities
galaxy 53, 161.28 *cluster,* 181.4 *throng*
Galcha 5 Languages and Groups of Languages
gale 55.13 *wind strength,* 241.5 *violent weather,* 329.11 *swift thing,* 635.1 *trap*
gale-force 55.47 *windy*
Galen 630.15 *healer*
galena 54 Minerals, **57** Common Chemical Compounds, **57** Common Metal Ores
Galenic 630.18 *medical*
galenical 62.5 *prescription,* 630.2 *medicine*
gale warning 636.2 *danger signal*
Galibi 5 Languages and Groups of Languages
Galiceño 32 Breeds of Horse and Pony
Galician 5 Languages and Groups of Languages
Galician Blond 68 Breeds of Cattle
Galilean satellite 53.18 *satellite*
Galilean telescope 53.24 *telescope*
Galilee 97 Oceans and Seas
galilee porch 43.10 *church architecture*
Galileo Galilei 52 Scientists
galimatias 521.5 *empty talk*
Galina Ulanova 46.14 *famous ballet dancers*
galiot 74 Sailing Ships and Boats
gall 352.2 *secreted substance,* 385.15 *grind,* 415.2 *unpalatability,* 618.11 *harmfulness,* 631.4 *strain,* 807.2 *cheek,* 822.1 *hate,* 828.1 *resentment,* 829.1 *irascibility,* 832.4 *bitterness*
Galla 1 Peoples, **5** Languages and Groups of Languages
gallamine 62 Medication
gall and wormwood 415.3 *sour thing,* 785.1 *dislike*
gallant 467.9 *solicitous,* 778.9 *courageous,* 778.10 *chivalrous,* 811.23 *brave,* 817.6 *courteous person,* 817.7 *courteous,* 821.9 *lover,* 821.19 *enamoured*
gallant company 679.17 *army person*
gallantly 811.39 *bravely,* 817.14 *courteously*
gallantry 467.5 *solicitude,* 778.2 *heroism,* 778.8 *courageous act,* 817.1 *courtesy,* 821.6, 826.2 *courtship*
galleass 679.25 *historical naval ships*
galleon 74 Sailing Ships and Boats, 679.25 *historical naval ships*
Galleria Vittorio Emanuele II 43 Noted Buildings
gallery 51.16 *auditorium,* 51.31 *theatregoer,* 161.31 *exhibition,* 256.7 *room,* 327.7 *arcade,* 435.9 *viewpoint,* 526.8 *showplace,* 605.5 *collection*
gallery forest 85.4 *trees*
galley 73 Aircraft Parts, **74** Ships and Boats, **74** Parts of a Ship, 45.3 *kitchen,* 256.7 *room*
galleys 879.7 *punishment*
galley salve 701.5 *subjected person*
galley slave 74.8 *boatman,* 642.10 *busy person,* 646.1 *worker,* 697.7 *slave*
galliard 46.4 *historic dancing*
Gallicism 5.26 *dialect*
galliform 78.23 *avian*
galligaskins 295.9 *trousers,* 295.20 *legwear*
gallimaufry 133.3 *miscellany*
gallinaceous 78.23 *avian*
galling 385.3 *grinding,* 385.11 *rough*
gallinule 78 Birds
gallium 57 Chemical Elements

gallium arsenide 57 Common Chemical Compounds, 64.4 *semiconductor*
gall midge 82 Insects
gallon 75 Scientific and Technical Units, **75** General Units
gallonage 75 General Units
gallop 32.16 *ride,* 324.12 *gait,* 324.15 *walk,* 329.4 *be swift,* 329.9 *acceleration*
gallop at 670.1 *attack*
galloper 329.12 *swift animal*
Gallophobia 777 Phobias by Name
galloping 329.1 *swift*
galloping guns 680.11 *guns*
galloping rhythm 624.10 *cardiovascular disease*
Gallo-Romance 5 Languages and Groups of Languages
galloway 32.5 *pony*
Galloway 68 Breeds of Cattle
gallows 283.4 *hanger,* 398.5 *execution,* 879.16 *instrument of execution*
gallows humour 771.3 *wit*
Gallup poll 580.10 *vote*
gall wasp 82 Insects
gally 807.14 *cheeky*
Galois 52 Scientists
Galois group 52 Named Concepts
galop 46.4 *historic dancing*
galore 181.9 *ample,* 608.8 *plenty*
galoshes 295.19 *footwear*
Galton 52 Scientists
galumph 656.7 *be clumsy*
Galvani 52 Scientists
galvanic electricity 235.7 *electrical power*
galvanize 228.9 *motivate,* 239.3 *invigorate,* 330.1 *impel,* 403.13 *arouse sensation*
galvanized 228.12 *motivated*
galvanizing 228.11 *motivational*
galvanometer 56.90 *ammeter,* 64.23 *electrical instrument,* 268.8 *meter*
galvanometric 268.16 *micrometric*
galvanometry 268.2 *micrometry*
Galveston 93 Cities
Galway 68 Breeds of Sheep, **92** Counties, **93** Cities
gam 161 Collective Names for Birds and Animals
gama grass 87 Grasses
gambang kaya 49 Musical Instruments
Gambia 91 Countries, **96** Rivers
gambit 156.10 *introduction,* 479.1 *experiment,* 539.8 *trick,* 596.5 *attempt,* 652.9 *tactics*
gamble 42.10 *play,* 229.2, 229.4 *chance,* 479.13 *invent,* 486.7 *make possible,* 488.10 *think likely,* 491.15 *unreliability,* 491.22 *risk,* 517.12 *divine,* 518.3 *conjecture,* 518.5 *suppose,* 589.1 *chance,* 589.12 *take a chance,* 596.3 *tackle,* 633.9 *face danger,* 633.10 *endanger,* 737.2 *speculate,* 780.2 *rash move,* 780.5 *be rash*
gambler 517.9 *forecaster,* 518.4 *theorist,* 780.3 *rash person*
gambling 215.3 *irregular thing,* 229.7 *adventurous,* 518.3 *conjecture,* 589.3 *equal chance,* 589.7 *calculation of chance,* 597.2 *undertaking,* 633.5 *danger,* 737.8 *speculation*
gambling chance 589.4 *fair chance*
gambling den 864.8 *wicked place*
gambling game 42.1 *game*
gamboge 85 Tree Products, 452.7 *yellow pigment*
gambol 46.15 *dance*
gambrel roof 43.6 *roof*
game 37, 42, 18.1 *sport,* 40.4 *tennis terms,* 45.20 *meat,* 76.1 *animals,* 238.10 *ill,* 539.11 *hoax,* 572.1 *willing,* 574.4 *undaunted,* 575.12 *indomitable,* 588.6 *objective,* 590.7 *the hunted,* 592.4 *plot,* 596.8 *attempting,* 644.3 *job,* 652.9 *tac-*

tics, 657.2 *stratagem*, 674.2 *contest*, 778.13 *adventurous*, 850.9 *butt*
game bag 258.8 *bag*
game bird 78.4 *table bird*
game birds 37.5 *game*
Gameboy 65.18 *computer game*
gamecock 674.10 *contender*, 679.4 *fighting animal*
game fish 45.17 *freshwater fish*, 80.2 *fish*, 80.8 *food fish*
game fishing 18 Sporting Activities, 20.1 *angling*, 80.7 *fishing*, 590.2 *chase*
game fowl 78.4 *table bird*
gamekeeper 632.3, 671.15 *protector*
game licence 37.2 *hunting*
gameness 572.6 *willingness*, 575.4 *stamina*, 778.4 *adventurousness*
game of chance 229.2 *chance*, 589.3 *equal chance*
game of golf 29.1 *golf*
game of tenpins 25.4 *bowling*
game plan 19.14 *miscellaneous terms*, 652.9 *tactics*
game-playing 65.16 *artificial intelligence*
game reserve 76.8 *animal welfare*, 637.1 *preservation*
game rules 652.9 *tactics*
games 21.5 *competition*, 644.5 *exercise*, 674.1 *contention*, 674.2 *contest*
Games and Pastimes 42
games computer 65.3 *computer*
game, set, and match 682.2 *victory*
game shooting 37.2 *hunting*
game show 51.5 *show*, 534.25 *broadcast material*
game-show host 51.27 *entertainer*
game show presenter 477.9 *questioner*
gamesmanship 652.9 *tactics*, 657.1 *cunning*, 674.1 *contention*
games room 256.7 *room*
gamete 59.7 *cell*, 90.4 *reproductive body*
game terms 40.5 *real tennis*
game theory 52 Mathematical Theories, 4.7 *school of thought*, 65.16 *artificial intelligence*
game time 19
gametophobia 777 Phobias by Name
gametophyte 88.4 *moss plant*
game to the last 575.12 *indomitable*
game warden 76.10 *animal welfarist*
game-winning 682.15 *victorious*
gaminess 413.1 *piquancy*, 419.2 *something that makes an unpleasant smell*
gaming 589.3 *equal chance*
gaming table 47.4 *table*
gamma 75 Scientific and Technical Units, 66.10 *graininess*
gamma camera 66.16 *camera*
gammadion 11.6 *talisman*
gamma distribution 52.59 *probability distribution*
gamma function 52.29 *mathematical function*
gamma-ray astronomy 53.1 *astronomy*
gamma rays 56.13 *electromagnetic radiation*, 56.70 *radioactivity*
gammon 45.30 *bacon*, 538.8 *pretence*, 538.24 *pretend*, 540.13 *nonsense*
gammy 238.10 *ill*
Gamow 52 Scientists
gamut 49.16 *musical note*, 49.20 *key*, 159.2 *consecution*, 248.7 *range*
gamy 413.9 *piquant*, 419.4 *putrid*
Ganda 1 Peoples, **5** Languages and Groups of Languages
gander 68.8 *livestock*, 78.10 *male bird*, 401.16 *male animal*, 435.6 *look*
gandery 792.5 *decorative articles*

Gandharan art 50 Non-Western Art
gandy 795.7 *vulgar*
gandy dancer 72.9 *railway worker*
ganef 736.11 *dishonest person*
Ganesha 8 Deities
gang 161 Collective Names for Birds and Animals, 116.2 *alliance*, 161.11 *group*, 646.4 *personnel*, 665.1 *party*
gang along 345.1 *depart*
gangbang 877.7 *sexual assault*
ganger 646.1 *worker*, 653.15 *manager*
Ganges 96 Rivers, 96.5 *other major rivers*
ganging up 116.11 *allied*
gangland 864.7 *criminality*
gangliness 274.7 *thinness*
gangling 274.1 *thin*, 275.12 *tall*, 656.3 *clumsy*
gangly 275.12 *tall*
gang member 398.11 *murderer*, 693.9 *criminal*, 736.11 *dishonest person*, 862.6 *evil person*
gang murder 398.2 *murder*
Gangotri 10.13 *shrine*
gangplank 74 Parts of a Ship, 63.21 *bridge*, 327.2 *route*
gang rape 241.2 *physical violence*, 736.5 *plundering*, 877.7 *sexual assault*
gangrene 141.1 *disintegration*, 141.3 *disintegrate*, 622.10 *be dirty*, 624.6 *infection*, 624.15 *ulcer*, 628.2 *decay*, 628.9 *dilapidation*
gangrenous 141.5 *disintegrated*, 141.6 *disintegrating*, 624.23 *diseased*
gangrenously 141.8 *destructively*
gang rule 16.41 *lawlessness*
gangster 398.11 *murderer*, 640.3 *doer*, 693.9 *criminal*, 736.11 *dishonest person*, 832.8 *malefactor*, 858.4 *dishonourable person*, 864.9 *wicked person*, 875.6 *drug*
gang together 664.14 *join with*, 665.12 *be in league with*
gangue 57.24 *ore*
gang up 116.22 *form an alliance*, 161.41 *band together*, 180.14 *keep company with*
gang up with 664.14 *join with*, 815.13 *fraternize*
gang warfare 674.6 *fight*, 693.2 *violation of the law*
gangway 74 Parts of a Ship, 63.21 *bridge*, 322.7 *passageway*, 327.2 *route*
gangway ladder 359.9 *ladder*
ganja 875.6 *drug*
gannet 78 Birds, 78.3 *water bird*, 350.18 *eater*, 852.4 *glutton*
gannet-like 350.26 *eating*
ganoid scale 80.5 *fish anatomy*
gansa gambang 49 Musical Instruments
gansa jongkok 49 Musical Instruments
gantry crane 361.9 *lifter*
Ganymede 326.7 *transferor*
Gaoh 8 Deities
gap 100.4 *emptiness*, 117.1 *disparity*, 136.3 *separateness*, 145.2 *omission*, 160.4 *interruption*, 218.3 *pause*, 248.8 *intervening space*, 254.3 *emptiness*, 265.1 *interval*, 317.2 *concave land*, 322.1 *opening*, 593.2 *need*, 607.2 *defect*
gape 265.3 *gulf*, 265.5 *crack*, 277.14 *deepen*, 322.1 *opening*, 322.18 *open*, 435.6, 435.13 *look*, 786.9 *wonder*
gaper 435.11 *observer*
gaping 265.7 *cracked*, 277.8 *deep*, 322.12 *open*, 786.7 *wide-eyed*
gapingly 322.27 *cavernously*
gap in the market 593.2 *need*
gappy 160.8 *discontinuous*, 265.7 *cracked*
gar 80 Fishes
garage 49.9 *popular music*, 63.20 *building*, 71.21 *miscellaneous motoring terms*, 256.7

room, 258.21 *put in a container*, 605.4 *storage*, 632.9 *protect*, 637.5 *preserve*
garaged 258.20 *containing*
garage sale 727.2 *disposal of property*, 739.4 *sale*, 752.2 *bargain*, 754.7 *discounter*
garaging 71.21 *miscellaneous motoring terms*
garam masala 45 Herbs and Spices
Garamond type 5.15 *type style*
garance 67.6 *dye*
Garand rifle 680.11 *guns*
garb 295.1, 295.32 *dress*, 457.3 *external appearance*
garbage 31.8 *hockey*, 151.4 *litter*, 607.5 *waste product*, 622.4 *dirt*, 727.3 *disposable things*
garbage can 727.4 *wastebin*
garbage goal 31.3 *ice hockey*
garbage man 727.6 *rubbish collector*
garbage truck 71 Motor Vehicles
garbed 295.29 *dressed*
garble 131.3 *subtract*, 506.6 *talk nonsense*, 523.8 *make unintelligible*, 525.1 *misinterpret*, 525.2 *misinterpretation*, 540.9 *falsification*, 540.22 *falsify*, 548.5 *misinform*, 555.2 *lack of emphasis*, 750.7 *account*
garbled 145.4 *incomplete*, 523.1 *unintelligible*, 525.3 *misinterpreted*, 548.7 *misinformed*, 555.1 *unemphatic*, 659.12 *problematic*
garbling 525.2 *misinterpretation*, 540.9 *falsification*, 548.2 *misinformation*
García Lorca 48 Poets, **48** Dramatists
Gariciá Márquez 48 Writers
Garda 94 Lakes
gardant 544.13 *heraldic*
garden 69, 34.9 *mountaineer*, 69.14 *practise horticulture*
garden centre 69.2 *garden*
garden chair 69.3 *ornamental garden*
garden city 69.2 *garden*, 93.4 *British cities*, 249.10 *urban area*
gardener 69.13 *horticulturist*, 243.9 *producer*, 646.1 *worker*, 697.6 *domestic servant*
garden flower 84.1 *flower*
garden gate 179.4 *gate*
garden gnome 69.3 *ornamental garden*
garden hose 389.13 *irrigator*
gardenia 84 Flowers and Flowering Plants, 418.2 *fragrant thing*
gardening 42 Hobbies and Pastimes, **69**, 34.3 *climbing technique*, 34.8 *mountaineering*, 69.1 *horticulture*
garden line 69.6 *garden tool*
Garden of Eden 69.2 *garden*, 519.8 *dreamland*
garden of remembrance 69.2 *garden*, 399.5 *cemetery*
garden of rest 69.2 *garden*, 399.5 *cemetery*
Garden of the Hesperides 69.2 *garden*
garden party 665.7 *social gathering*, 815.5 *party*
garden path 69.3 *ornamental garden*, 327.2 *route*
garden plant 69, 83.2 *plant*
garden roller 282.4 *flattener*, 376.9 *smoother*
garden room 256.7 *room*
garden sculpture 50.12 *sculpture*
garden seat 69.3 *ornamental garden*
garden shed 69.4 *nursery*
garden shop 69.2 *garden*
garden suburb 69.2 *garden*, 93.8 *suburb*
garden tool 69, 603, 603.1 *tool*
garden-variety 556.1 *simple*
garden work 644.1 *work*
garganey 78 Birds
Gargantua 259.10 *big person*
Gargantuan 259.15 *big*

gargle 62.11 *linctus*, 134.3 *purifier*, 621.9 *cleaning agent*, 630.3 *prophylactic*
gargoyle 347.7 *outlet*, 547.6 *image*, 790.2 *ugly person*
gari 45.53 *African dish*
garish 437.2 *clear*, 439.16 *bright*, 444.12 *gaudy*, 559.10 *ugly*, 795.7 *vulgar*, 811.19 *flashy*
garishly 444.18 *colourfully*, 811.35 *flashily*
garishness 559.3 *ugliness*, 811.4 *flashiness*
garland 74 Rigging, 84.1 *flower*, 544.4 *insignia*, 544.8 *heraldic device*, 681.1 *trophy*, 792.10 *decorate*, 812.18 *salute*, 817.12 *greet*
Garland 93 Cities
garlic 45 Herbs and Spices, **45** Vegetables, 11.6 *talisman*, 413.2 *seasoning*, 419.2 *something that makes an unpleasant smell*
garlic dip 45.15 *sauce*
garlic mustard 84 Flowers and Flowering Plants
garlic press 393.15 *pulper*
garlic salt 45 Herbs and Spices, 413.2 *seasoning*
garlic sausage 45.29 *sausage*
garment 295.1, 295.32 *dress*
Garment District 295.2 *dressing*
garmentmaker 295.26 *fashion designer*
garment-making 295.2 *dressing*
garmentworker 295.26 *fashion designer*
garner 605.4 *storage*, 605.6 *store*
garnering 605.4 *storage*
garnet 54 Minerals, **54** Gemstones, 137.7 *tackle*, 450.7 *red thing*
Garnet star 53 Named Stars
garnierite 54 Minerals
garnish 45.55 *cook*, 130.3 *additional item*, 130.6 *add*, 411.10 *make taste*, 413.2 *seasoning*, 557.1, 557.5 *ornament*, 792.1 *adornment*
garnished 557.4 *ornate*, 792.8 *decorated*
garnishing 130.3 *additional item*
garniture 295.24 *part of garment*
Garo 5 Languages and Groups of Languages
Garonne 96 Rivers
Garranos 32 Breeds of Horse and Pony
garret 256.7 *room*, 275.8 *high thing*
garrison 632.3 *protector*, 632.9 *protect*, 671.14 *guard*, 671.21 *entrench*, 679.14 *armed forces*
garrisoned 632.5 *safe*
garron 32.5 *pony*
garrotte 236.8 *overpower*, 398.17 *murder*, 398.19, 879.5 *execute*, 879.13 *capital punishment*, 879.16 *instrument of execution*
garrotter 398.11 *murderer*, 879.17 *punisher*
garrotting 398.2 *murder*
garrulity 565.1 *talkativeness*
garrulous 530.11 *disclosing*, 565.5 *talkative*
garrulously 565.10 *talkatively*
garrulousness 565.1 *talkativeness*
garter 137.8 *fastening*, 295.20 *legwear*, 681.1 *trophy*, 792.3 *honour*
garter belt 295.18 *underwear*
garter snake 79 Reptiles
garuda 78.9 *fabulous bird*
Garuda 8 Deities
Gary 93 Cities
gas 372, 388, 410, 71.21 *miscellaneous motoring terms*, 102.4 *theorization*, 235.6 *source of energy*, 338.13 *fuel*, 349.24 *belch*, 361.10 *elevator*, 388.5 *belch*, 390.1 *air*, 398.7 *suicide*, 398.17 *murder*, 398.19 *execute*, 410.1 *fuel*, 410.3 *gas*, 419.1 *stench*, 521.5 *empty talk*, 565.3 *talk*, 565.7 *be talkative*, 604.1 *materials*, 624.8 *indigestion*,

879.5 *execute*, 879.13 *capital punishment*, 879.16 *instrument of execution*
Gas 388
gas analysis 57.18 *gravimetric analysis*
gasbag 258.19 *inflatable*, 565.4 *talker*, 568.8 *chatterer*
gas balloon 388
gas burner 410.3 *gas*
gas chamber 16.43 *conviction*, 397.4 *death sentence*, 398.5 *execution*, 398.15 *slaughterhouse*, 879.16 *instrument of execution*
Gascony 68 Breeds of Cattle
gas-cooled reactor 56.73 *nuclear reactor*, 410.7 *nuclear power*
gas discharge 56.46, 64.6 *electric discharge*
gas-discharge tube 56.25 *light source*, 56.46 *electric discharge*, 64.6 *electric discharge*, 64.20 *electron tube*
gaseity 388.7 *gaseousness*
gaseous 388, 57.32 *solid*, 370.2 *insubstantial*, 372.1 *sparse*, 410.10 *powered*
gaseous medium 390.1 *air*
gaseous nebula 53.8 *interstellar medium*
gaseousness 388, 370.5 *lightness*, 372.3 *sparseness*
gaseous state 388.7 *gaseousness*
gasfield 410.3 *gas*, 605.2 *resource*
gas fire 408.6 *fire*
gas-fired 408.13 *heated*, 410.10 *powered*
gas-fitter 410.9 *power-worker*
gas gangrene 388.6 *aerogastria*
gas gun 68.14 *pest control*
gash 136.3 *separateness*, 136.9 *separate*, 265.2, 265.5 *crack*, 319.1, 319.5 *notch*, 322.20 *hole*, 406.3 *injury*, 406.11 *inflict pain*
gas heater 408.3 *heater*
gashed 322.14 *holed*
gasholder 388.14 *gasworks*, 410.3 *gas*, 605.4 *storage*
gasification 388.10 *vaporization*
gasified 388.16 *gaseous*
gasiform 388.16 *gaseous*
gasify 388, 370.10 *lighten*, 372.6 *make sparse*
gas jar 57 Laboratory Apparatus
gas jet 408.6 *fire*, 439.5 *incandescent light*
Gaskell 48 Writers
gasket 74 Rigging, 36.3 *parts of a sailing boat*
gaslamp 388.14 *gasworks*, 439.5 *incandescent light*
gas laser 56.26 *laser*
gas leakage 638.4 *leak*
gaslight 56.23 *light*, 388.14 *gasworks*, 439.5 *incandescent light*
gaslike 388.16 *gaseous*
gas main 410.3 *gas*
gasman 410.9 *power-worker*, 646.2 *artisan*
gas mantle 439.5 *incandescent light*
gas mask 632.4 *safety device*, 637.2 *preserver*, 671.6 *protective clothing*
gas meter 268.8 *meter*, 388.15 *vaporimeter*, 410.3 *gas*
gas oil 410.6 *oil*
gasolier 388.14 *gasworks*, 439.5 *incandescent light*
gasoline 410.6 *oil*
gasometer 388.14 *gasworks*, 388.15 *vaporimeter*, 410.3 *gas*, 605.4 *storage*
gas oneself 398.21 *commit suicide*
gas oven 398.15 *slaughterhouse*, 408.6 *fire*
gasp 406.12 *express pain*, 430.5 *sound hoarse*, 431.6 *cry of pain*, 431.13 *cry*, 564.7 *utterance*, 564.13 *speak in a particular way*, 650.5 *be fatigued*, 786.9 *wonder*
gasping 650.7 *fatigue*
gasping for breath 650.3 *panting*
gas pipe 410.3 *gas*

gas plant 388.14 *gasworks*
gasp of admiration 786.2 *sign of wonderment*
gas poker 410.3 *gas*
gasproof 632.6 *invulnerable*
gas-propelled 338.19 *propelled*
gas propulsion 338.2 *method of propulsion*
gasp with admiration 786.9 *wonder*
gas ring 45.5 *cooker*, 408.4 *burner*
Gassendi 52 Scientists, **53** Lunar Features
gasser 565.4 *talker*, 568.8 *chatterer*
gas shell 680.5 *missile weapon*
gassiness 388.7 *gaseousness*, 565.1 *talkativeness*
gassing oneself 398.7 *suicide*
gassy 388, 388.16 *gaseous*, 388.20 *flatulent*, 419.3 *stinking*, 565.5 *talkative*
gas tank 410.3 *gas*
gas thermometer 56.89 *thermometer*
gastralgia 624.8 *indigestion*
gastrectomy 60 Surgical Operations
gastric 290.10 *visceral*, 352.5 *of a secretion*
gastric gland 352 Exocrine Glands
gastric juice 352.2 *secreted substance*
gastric ulcer 624.8 *indigestion*
gastrin 58.11 *enzyme*
gastritis 624.8 *indigestion*
gastroduodenostomy 60 Surgical Operations
gastroenteritis 624.4 *disease*, 624.6 *infection*
gastroenterologist 60.13 *medical specialist*
gastroenterology 60.3 *medical specialty*
gastroenterostomy 60 Surgical Operations
gastrointestinal disease 624.4 *disease*
gastrojejunostomy 60 Surgical Operations
gastronome 872.4 *glutton*
gastronomic 45.56 *culinary*, 872.6 *gluttonous*
gastronomically 45.57 *culinarily*, 872.7 *gluttonously*
gastronomy 45.1 *cookery*, 872.2 *epicurism*
gastro-oesophagostomy 60 Surgical Operations
gastroplasty 60 Surgical Operations
gastropod 76.4 *type of animal*, 81.5 *mollusc*
Gastropoda 81.5 *mollusc*
gastropodan 81.19 *molluscan*
gastropodous 81.19 *molluscan*
gastroscope 60.7 *diagnosis*
gastroscopy 60.7 *diagnosis*
gastrostomy 60 Surgical Operations
gastrotomy 60 Surgical Operations
gastrotrich 81.6 *worm*
Gastrotricha 81.6 *worm*
gastrula 59.15 *developmental biology*
gastrulation 59.15 *developmental biology*
gas turbine 63.12 *turbine*, 410.3 *gas*
gas vapour 57.3 *phase*
gas vent 54.25 *eruption*
gas warfare 676.8 *warfare*
gasworks 388, 410.3 *gas*, 647.1 *workshop*
gat 680.9 *firearm*, 680.11 *guns*
gate 71 Motor Vehicle Parts, 32.9 *jumping*, 36.6 *canoeing*, 41.3 *ski racing*, 64.13 *circuit*, 64.19 *transistor*, 68.11 *farmland*, 322.7 *passageway*, 345.10 *place of departure*, 346.6 *means of entry* , 347.6 *way out*, 671.12 *fort*, 721.4 *earnings*, 749.2 *money received*, 879.1 *punish*

gateau 45.36 *cake*, 414.3 *dessert*
gate-crash 104.16 *be external*, 149.17 *intrude*, 255.15 *settle*, 346.10 *invade*, 666.7 *pick a fight*, 815.11 *be sociable*
gate-crasher 104.8 *intruder*, 108.3 *unconnected person*, 149.10 *intruder*, 255.6 *illegal occupant*, 346.8 *intruder*, 661.7 *hinderer*, 666.4 *dissenter*, 754.8 *bargain hunter*, 815.6 *social person*
gate-crashing 104.4 *externality*, 104.12 *external*
gated 322.15 *providing passage*, 879.20 *punished*
gated crossing 72.2 *track*
gate electrode 64.19 *transistor*
gatehouse 671.12 *fort*
gatekeeper 323.5 *person who closes*, 533.4 *journalist*
gate-leg 47.14 *wooden*
gate-leg table 47.4 *table*
gate money 721.4 *earnings*, 730.2 *something received*, 749.2 *money received*
gate of ivory 538.5 *half-truth*
gate post 34.6 *means of entry*
gateway 65.15 *network*, 65.17 *computing term*, 346.6 *means of entry*
gather 55.59 *storm*, 68.17 *farm*, 135.8 *unite*, 161.37 *assemble*, 261.6 *become bigger*, 262.5 *make smaller*, 295.35 *make clothing*, 320.2, 320.8 *pleat*, 324.14 *set in motion*, 342.10 *come together*, 344.8 *meet*, 420.15 *hear*, 518.5 *suppose*, 605.6 *store*, 665.17 *socialize*
gather dust 641.4 *not act*, 739.2 *be sold*
gathered 135.15 *tied*, 161.46 *assembled*, 262.7 *smaller*, 295.31 *styled*
gathered to one's fathers 397.19 *dead*
gatherer 161.35 *collector*, 721.7 *gainer*
gather food 606.5 *provision*
gather in 721.9 *gain*, 721.11 *acquire*
gathering 10.17 *worshipper*, 135.1 *union*, 161.1 *assembly*, 161.3 *meeting*, 261.8 *growing*, 262.1 *contraction*, 262.8 *contracting*, 568.4 *conference*, 605.4 *storage*, 624.15 *ulcer*, 626.7 *toxic*, 721.3 *acquisition*, 815.3 *meeting*
gathering clouds 517.7 *bad-luck sign*, 633.6 *danger signal*, 636.1 *warning*, 667.1 *adversity*
gathering in 721.1 *gain*
gathering of the clans 161.9 *social gathering*
gathering storm 633.6 *danger signal*, 636.1 *warning*
gather momentum 329.6 *accelerate*
gather notes 594.2 *do the groundwork*
gather round 161.39 *come together*
gather speed 329.6 *accelerate*
gather together 135.8 *unite*, 161.39 *come together*, 721.11 *acquire*
gather up 361
gather way 74.9 *navigate*, 324.13 *be in motion*, 336.3 *press on*
gating 879.7 *punishment*
Gatling gun 680.12 *historical guns*
gator 79.5 *crocodilian*
GATT 715.3 *alliance*, 737.9 *bargaining*
Ga-tum-dag 8 Deities
gauche 412.6 *coarse*, 453.3 *raw*, 502.6 *ignorant*, 559.7 *graceless*, 585.2 *not customary*, 656.3 *clumsy*, 795.8 *discourteous*
gauchely 412.11 *tastelessly*
gaucheness 412.4 *bad taste*, 559.1 *inelegance*
gaucherie 502.1 *ignorance*,

559.1 *inelegance*, 559.6 *blunder*, 656.8 *unskilfulness*, 814.5 *nonobservance*
gaucho 32.15 *horse person*, 68.16 *farm worker*
gaud 754.5 *cheap item*
gaudily 444.18 *colourfully*, 811.35 *flashily*
gaudiness 437.4 *clarity*, 559.3 *ugliness*, 754.3 *shoddiness*, 795.1 *tastelessness*, 811.4 *flashiness*
gaudy 444, 412.6 *coarse*, 437.2 *clear*, 526.14 *manifest*, 559.10 *ugly*, 754.10 *shoddy*, 811.19 *flashy*
gauge 71 Motor Vehicle Parts, **75** Scientific and Technical Units, 56.82 *measuring instrument*, 67.5 *knitting*, 72.3 *rail*, 170.5 *computer*, 170.11 *number*, 259.1 *size*, 259.18 *measure*, 268.8 *meter*, 268.10 *measure*, 271.4 *breadth*, 327.10 *railway*, 329.8 *speed*, 332.3 *orientation*, 492.12 *estimate*, 543.5 *indicator*, 545.10 *recording instrument*
gaugeable 268.14 *measurable*
gauged 268.13 *measured*
gauger 268.9 *measurer*
gauging 268.1 *measurement*
gauleiter 696.4 *absolute ruler*
Gaulish 5 Languages and Groups of Languages
Gauls 1 Peoples
gaum 393.2 *semiliquidity*
gauminess 394.1 *viscosity*
gaumy 394.8 *viscous*
gaunt 247.3 *birth control*, 274.2 *emaciated*
gauntlet 671.7 *armour*
gauntlets 295.25 *accessories*, 671.6 *protective clothing*
gauntness 274.8 *emaciation*
gaur 77 Placental Mammals
gauss 75 Scientific and Technical Units
Gauss 52 Scientists
Gaussian distribution 52 Named Concepts, 52.59 *probability distribution*
Gauss's theorem 52 Named Concepts
Gautier 48 Poets
gauze 67 Natural Fabrics, 51.17 *stage set*, 274.11 *fineness*, 442.8 *transparent thing*, 630.10 *surgical dressing*
gauziness 274.11 *fineness*, 442.6 *translucency*
gauzy 274.4 *fine*, 442.2 *translucent*
gavel 544.4 *insignia*
gavial 79 Reptiles
gavotte 46.4 *historic dancing*
gawk 435.13 *look*, 786.9 *wonder*
gawkiness 274.7 *thinness*, 559.1 *inelegance*
gawkish 559.7 *graceless*, 656.3 *clumsy*
gawkishness 559.1 *inelegance*
gawky 274.1 *thin*, 559.7 *graceless*, 656.3 *clumsy*
gawp 435.13 *look*, 786.9 *wonder*
gawper 435.11 *observer*
gay 401.8 *homosexual*, 401.17 *male*, 402.10 *homosexual*, 444.11 *colourful*, 762.4 *happy*, 769.1 *cheerful*, 811.19 *flashy*, 812.10 *celebrative*
Gay 48 Poets, **48** Dramatists
gayal 77 Placental Mammals
gayatri 10.9 *prayer*
gay dog 401.2 *male*
Gay Gordons 46.4 *historic dancing*
gay liberation 698.1 *freedom*, 700.2 *equal opportunity*
Gay-Lussac 52 Scientists
Gay-Lussac's law 56 Named Laws, 57 Named Reactions
Gayoe 32 Breeds of Horse and Pony
gay rights 845.3 *prerogative*
Gaza 93 Cities
gaze 435.6, 435.13 *look*, 543.11 *gesture*, 818.7 *be discourteous*

genetic element 59.13 *genetic material*

genetic engineering 59.1 *life science*, 59.11 *genetics*, 59.12 *molecular biology*, 245.3 *propagation*

genetic fingerprinting 59.12 *molecular biology*, 544.3 *means of identification*

geneticist 59.19 *life scientist*

genetic likeness 114.1 *similarity*

genetic mapping 59.12 *molecular biology*

genetic material 59

genetic psychology 61.1 *psychology*

genetics 59, 59.1 *life science*, 396.7 *studies of life*

genetic screening 60.7 *diagnosis*

Geneva 93 Cities, 94 Lakes

Geneva Bible 7.12 *religious text*

genial 763.9 *likable*, 769.1, 769.1 *cheerful*, 815.15 *sociable*, 817.7 *courteous*, 819.8 *friendly*, 831.6 *benevolent*

geniality 763.8 *amiability*, 769.3, 769.3 *cheerfulness*, 815.1 *sociability*, 819.1 *friendship*, 831.1 *benevolence*

genially 763.15 *pleasantly*, 815.18 *sociably*, 819.17 *in friendship*

genic 59.25 *genetic*

genie 662.15 *benefactor*

genie of the lamp 232.3 *assistant*

genioplasty 60 Surgical Operations

genipap 86 Fruits

genital 245.16 *reproductive*

genitalia 226.2 *source*, 245.8 *organs of reproduction*

genitally 245.18 *reproductively*

genitals 245.8 *organs of reproduction*

genitive 5.31 *case*

genitourinary 60.22 *medical*

genitourinary medicine 60.3 *medical specialty*

genius 4.12 *sage*, 8.5 *deity*, 11.11 *ghost*, 50.5 *artistry*, 126.6 *paragon*, 165.7 *special skill*, 234.2 *attitude*, 459.4 *cleverness*, 459.8 *intellectual person*, 461.7 *thinker*, 485.2 *ability*, 501.6 *knowledgeable person*, 507.2 *intelligence*, 507.4 *intellectual*, 519.2 *inspiration*, 617.8 *exceller*, 655.2 *aptitude*, 655.4 *skilled person*, 688.11, 696.10 *expert*, 786.5 *person of wonder*, 861.16 *superior person*

genius for 655.2 *aptitude*

genned up 528.18 *informed*, 6.19 *knowledgeable*

Genoa 74 Sails, 93 Cities, 36.3 *parts of a sailing boat*

genocidal 398.24 *murderous*

genocide 244.2 *destroying*, 398.3 *homicide*, 398.4 *slaughter*, 832.7 *act of malevolence*, 879.13 *capital punishment*

Genoese pastry 45.37 *pastry*

genome 59.13 *genetic material*

genomic 59.25 *genetic*

genophobia 777 Phobias by Name

genotype 59.11 *genetics*, 59.12 *molecular biology*

genotypic 59.25 *genetic*

genre 163.4 *type*, 306.3 *kind*, 560.6 *sort*

genre painter 50.16 *artist*

genre painting 50.10 *art subject*

genro 653.7 *council*

gent 401.2 *male*, 802.1 *nobleman*

gentamycin 62 Medication

genteel 794.5 *refined*, 817.8 *good-mannered*, 876.10 *moralistic*

genteelism 876.4 *self-righteousness*

genteelly 817

genteelness 817.2 *good manners*

gentian 84 Flowers and Flowering Plants, 413.5 *herbs*

gentian blue 454.5 *blueness*

---

gentian violet 455.2 *purple pigment*

Gentile 4 Philosophers

gentilities 817.3 *courtesies*

gentility 400.9 *group*, 558.1 *elegance*, 802.3 *nobleness*, 817.2 *good manners*

gentle 242.6 *moderate*, 328.5 *unhurried*, 370.2 *insubstantial*, 374.6 *softhearted*, 424.4 *faint*, 428.1 *faint-sounding*, 660.14 *relaxed*, 691.4 *lenient*, 817.7 *courteous*, 835.6 *pitying*, 865.5 *innocent*

gentle as a lamb 242.6 *moderate*

gentle breeze 55.13 *wind strength*

gentlefolk 802.2 *aristocracy*

gentle handling 652.8 *treatment*

gentleman 400.4 *civilized human*, 400.10 *member of society*, 401.2 *male*, 401.3 *male title of address*, 652.3 *well-behaved person*, 697.6 *domestic servant*, 794.4 *refined person*, 802.1 *nobleman*, 817.6 *courteous person*

gentleman farmer 68.15 *agriculturist*

gentlemanliness 817.2 *good manners*

gentlemanly 401.17 *male*, 652.17 *well-behaved*, 794.5 *refined*, 802.4 *aristocratic*, 817.8 *good-mannered*, 857.4 *honourable*

gentlemanly behaviour 652.2 *good conduct*

gentleman of the road 168.7 *nonconformist*

gentleman's agreement 667.2 *contract*, 714.1 *promise*, 715.1 *contract*, 847.7 *commitment*

gentleman's club 657.1 *cunning*

gentleman's gentleman 697.6 *domestic servant*

Gentlemen 727.7 *toilet*

gentlemen's agreement 597.3 *contract*

gentleness 374, 242.1 *moderation*, 370.5 *lightness*, 691.1 *leniency*, 817.1 *courtesy*, 835.1 *pity*

gentle sex 402.1 *female sex*

gentlewoman 794.4 *refined person*, 802.1 *nobleman*

gently 242.9 *moderately*, 328.16 *slowly*, 370.11 *lightly*, 374.18 *softheartedly*, 691.6 *leniently*, 817.14 *courteously*, 835.13 *pitifully*

gentrification 93.1 *city*

gentrified 93.14 *urban*

gentrify 93.15 *urbanize*, 629.2 *refurbish*

gentry 617.7 *elite*, 815.7 *human society*

gents 353.13 *lavatory*

genuflect 9.7 *worship*, 10.19 *offer worship*, 362.9 *bow*, 362.16 *courtesy*, 696.6 *show obeisance to*, 806.21 *humble oneself*, 849.19 *take off one's hat to*

genuflection 9.1 *worship*, 673.1 *submission*, 694.3 *obeisance*, 806.11 *self-abasement*, 849.4 *mark of respect*

genuine 3.19 *chronicled*, 16.51 *legitimate*, 101.7 *realistic*, 119.6, 537.19 *authentic*, 688.15 *true*, 772.2 *earnest*, 843.8 *correct*

genuinely 3.25 *reportedly*, 480.11 *veritably*, 537.37, 688.25 *authentically*, 772.11 *earnestly*, 843.20 *correctly*

genuineness 3.14 *historicalness*, 16.30 *legitimacy*, 119.1 *originality*, 537.6 *authenticity*, 843.2 *correctness*

genus 59.17 *taxonomy*, 143.1 *part*, 163.3 *kingdom*, 163.4 *type*

geocentric 53.36 *astronomical*, 291.6 *central*

geochemical 54.48 *geological*

---

geochemist 54.3 *geologist*, 57.2 *chemist*

geochemistry 54.1 *earth science*, 57.1 *chemistry*

geochronological 54.48 *geological*

geochronological unit 54.41 *geological time*

geochronologist 54.3 *geologist*

geochronology 54.1 *earth science*

geodesic 43.17 *structured*, 52.37 *line*

geodesic dome 43.6 *roof*, 63.27 *superstructure*

geodesist 54.3 *geologist*, 170.7 *mathematician*, 268.9 *measurer*

geodesy 54.1 *earth science*, 250.5 *topography*, 268.1 *measurement*

geodetic 54.48 *geological*, 250.8 *locational*, 268.12 *metrical*

geodetically 54.66 *geographically*, 250.13 *topographically*, 268.17 *measurably*

geodetics 268.1 *measurement*

geoduck 81 Molluscs

geographic 1.11 *anthropological*

geographical 1.11 *anthropological*, 249.16 *regional*, 250.8 *locational*, 251.7 *situational*

geographical feature 54.7 *landform*

geographically 54, 249.1, 1.16 *anthropologically*, 250.13 *topographically*

geographical mile 75 General Units

geographical region 249

geographical space 248

geographical unit 249.1 *region*

geography 54.1 *earth science*, 250.5 *topography*, 251.1 *situation*

geoid 54.5 *earth*

geolinguist 5.2 *linguist*

geolinguistic 5.38 *linguistic*

geolinguistics 5.1 *linguistics*

geological 54

geological epoch 200.3 *geological period*

geological fold 320.1 *fold*

geologically 54.66 *geographically*

geological period 187, 200, 185.4 *term*

geological time 54

geological time scale 54.41 *geological time*

geological time unit 54.41 *geological time*

geologist 54

geology 54.1 *earth science*

geomagnetic 54.49 *geophysical*

geomagnetic field 54.44 *geomagnetism*

geomagnetic pole 54.45 *magnetic pole*

geomagnetics 54.2 *geophysics*

geomagnetism 54, 56, 54.2 *geophysics*

geomagnetist 54.4 *geophysicist*

geomancer 11.13 *diviner*, 199.5 *predictor*

geomancy 11.9, 517.2 *divination*

geometer 170.7 *mathematician*

geometric 50.24 *pictorial*, 52.68, 170.15 *mathematical*

geometrical 169.8 *odd*

geometrical abstraction 50 Western Art Styles and Movements

geometrically 50.30 *pictorially*, 169.12 *numerically*, 170.16 *mathematically*

geometric construction 52

geometric figure 52

geometrician 52.2, 170.7 *mathematician*

geometric instrument 52.49 *geometric construction*

geometric mean 52.60 *parameter*

geometric optics 56.2 *classical physics*

geometric perspective 50.4 *treatment*

geometric progression 52.20 *sequence*, 336.10 *forward motion*

geometric series 52.20 *sequence*

geometric shape 52.41 *geometric figure*

---

geometrid moth 82 Insects

geometry 52, 52.1 *mathematics*, 170.1 *calculation*, 310.4 *angular measurement*

geomorphic feature 54.7 *landform*

geomorphological 54.48 *geological*

geomorphologically 54.66 *geographically*

geomorphologist 54.3 *geologist*, 382.10 *anatomist*

geomorphology 54.1 *earth science*, 382.8 *science of structure*

geophysical 54

geophysical satellite 53.32 *satellite*

geophysicist 54, 367.3 *materialist*

geophysics 54, 56.4 *experimental physics*, 367.6 *natural science*

geopolitical 54.48 *geological*

geopolitics 54.1 *earth science*

geoponic 68.19 *agricultural*

geoponics 68.1 *agriculture*

Geordie 255.9 *British inhabitant*

Geordie dialect 5.26 *dialect*

George 617.1 *worthy*

George Balanchine 46.14 *famous ballet dancers*

George Cross 544.4 *insignia*, 681.1 *trophy*

Georgette crepe 67 Natural Fabrics

George Washington 537.14 *truthful person*

Georgia 91 Countries, 92 American States

Georgian 5 Languages and Groups of Languages, 43 Architectural Styles, 47.7 *furniture style*, 202.14 *historic*

Georgian poetry 48 Literary Groups and Movements

Georgians 1 Peoples

georgic 48.7 *poem*, 68.19 *agricultural*

geoscience 54.1 *earth science*

geosphere 54.5 *earth*

geospheric 54.50 *terrestrial*

geostationary orbit 53.32 *satellite*

geostationary satellite 534.7 *satellite communication*

geostrophic 55.43 *atmospheric*

geostrophic force 55.9 *atmospheric process*

geostrophic wind 55.12 *wind*

geosynchronous orbit 53.32 *satellite*

geotechnical engineering 63.17 *civil engineering*

geothermal 235.17, 410.10 *powered*

geothermal energy 56.11 *energy*, 410.8 *renewable energy*

geothermal power 235.6 *source of energy*

geothermal power station 64.32 *power station*

gephyrophobia 777 Phobias by Name

geraniol 58.20 *terpene*

geranium 84 Flowers and Flowering Plants, 450.7 *red thing*

gerbil 77 Placental Mammals

gerbil food 350.8 *animal food*

Gerda 8 Deities

gerenuk 77 Placental Mammals

geriatric 60.22 *medical*, 207.7 *older person*, 207.14 *aged*, 207.15 *age-related*, 630.18 *medical*

geriatrician 60.13 *medical specialist*, 207.6 *gerontology*

geriatric medicine 207.6 *gerontology*

geriatric patient 624.19 *sick person*

geriatrics 60.3 *medical specialty*

germ 626, 59.3 *organism*, 59.15 *developmental biology*, 59.26 *developmental*, 156.3 *source*, 226.3 *rudiment*, 260.2 *little thing*, 624.6 *infection*, 631.7 *poisoning*

German 5 Languages and Groups of Languages, 43 Ar-

chitectural Styles, 30.11 *gymnastic*
German chocolate cake 45.36 *cake*
germander 84 Flowers and Flowering Plants
German dish 45
germane 107.4 *related*, 116.16 *fitting*
germanely 107.10 *relevantly*
germaneness 107.1 *relatedness*
German GP at Hockenheim 33.2 *Formula 1 race*
German gymnastics 30.1 *gymnastics*
germanic 57.34 *elemental*
Germanic 5 Languages and Groups of Languages, **7** Non-Christian Religions, 5.11 *family of languages*
germanite 54 Minerals
germanium 57 Chemical Elements, 64.4 *semiconductor*
Germanize 220.12 *naturalize*
Germanized 220.17 *naturalized*
German measles 624.6 *infection*
Germanophobia 777 Phobias by Name
germanous 57.34 *elemental*
German Red Pied 68 Breeds of Cattle
Germans 1 Peoples, **777** Phobias by Topic
German shepherd 77 Breeds of Dogs
German short-haired pointer 37.6 *sporting dog*
German silver 57 Alloys, 539.6 *imitation*
German Trotter 32 Breeds of Horse and Pony
Germany 91 Countries
German Yellow 68 Breeds of Cattle
germ-carrier 626.4 *infectious person*, 624.6 *infection*
germ-carrying 626.6 *contagious*
germ cell 59.7 *cell*
germen 59.7 *cell*
germ-free 625.4 *hygienic*
germicidal 62.14 *counteracting*, 134.15 *purifying*
germicide 62.4 *drug type*, 398.13 *animal killer*, 630.3 *prophylactic*
germinal 59.26 *developmental*, 156.32 *embryonic*, 226.13 *causal*, 245.16 *reproductive*, 260.7 *little*
germinant 59.26 *developmental*
germinate 83.21 *vegetate*, 89.12 *mushroom*, 156.26 *produce*, 156.27 *emerge*, 227.8 *grow*, 245.11 *have young*, 246.6 *be fertile*, 261.6 *become bigger*
germinating 59.26 *developmental*, 261.8 *growing*
germinating seed 83.9 *seed*
germination 59.15 *developmental biology*, 83.9 *seed*, 245.3 *propagation*, 261.1 *growth*
germinative 59.26 *developmental*
germ-laden 657.4 *toxic*
germ layer 59.15 *developmental biology*
germ plasm 59.7 *cell*
germs 777 Phobias by Topic
germ warfare 831.10, 676.8 *warfare*
Geronimo 590.19 *after him*
gerontocracy 12.1 *government*
gerontologic 207.15 *age-related*
gerontologist 60.13 *medical specialist*, 207.6 *gerontology*
gerontology 207, 60.3 *medical specialty*
gerrymander 657.5 *be cunning*
gerrymandered 539.35 *deceptive*
gerrymandering 539.10 *fraud*, 657.1 *cunning*
Gershwin 49 Musicians and Composers
Gesell's development schedule 61.5 *psychological test*
gesso 50.11 *artist's materials*
gestalt 61, 306.1 *form*
Gestalt 4.8 *philosophical term*, 142.2 *whole thing*

Gestaltism 61.1 *psychology*
Gestalt psychology 61.1 *psychology*
Gestalt theory 61.1 *psychology*
Gestalt therapy 61.3 *psychiatric treatment*, 630.13 *therapy*
Gestalt whole 306.1 *form*
gestate 594.7 *develop*
gestation 245.3 *propagation*, 594.13 *development*
gestatory 156.32 *embryonic*
geste 48.2 *fiction*
gesticulate 324.15 *walk*, 543.11 *gesture*, 563.14 *have difficulty speaking*, 652.11 *conduct oneself*
gesticulation 324.11 *bodily movement*, 543.3 *gesture*, 563.6 *voiceless speech*, 564.4 *articulation*, 640.2 *deed*, 652.1 *conduct*
gesticulative 543.15 *gestural*
gesticulator 543.8 *signer*
gestural 543
gesture 543, 543, 5.5 *nonstandard language*, 51.7 *dramaturgy*, 324.11 *bodily movement*, 324.15 *walk*, 528.7 *advice*, 543.9 *use signs*, 543.11 *gesture*, 563.6 *voiceless speech*, 563.14 *have difficulty speaking*, 564.4 *articulation*, 640.2 *deed*, 652.1 *conduct oneself*, 807.7 *insult*
gesture of equality 652.1 *conduct*
gesture of protest 713
gesturer 543.8 *signer*
get 220.7 *convert into*, 326.14 *bring back*, 345.15 *go*, 355.15 *draw out*, 471.14 *have an idea*, 522.6 *understand*, 715.6 *catch*, 721.9 *gain*, 730.9 *receive*, 734.7 *take*, 738.1 *purchase*, 749.7 *receive*
get a bad name 852.24 *be open to criticism*
get a bad press 852.24 *be open to criticism*
get a bearing 250.11 *find*
get about 815.11 *be sociable*
get above oneself 807, 809.15 *be vain*
get a break 322.23 *find an opening*, 686.6 *be fortunate*
get a corner on 723.7 *possess*
get acquainted 819.13 *befriend*
get across 520.10 *mean*, 522.4 *be intelligible*
get a dose of one's own medicine 672.4 *serve one right*
get a firm hold 726.6 *retain*
get a firm hold on 726.7 *detain*
get a fix 250.11 *find*
get a foothold 34.9 *mountaineer*, 726.6 *retain*
get a free hit 31.9 *play hockey*
get a free position 31.9 *play hockey*
get after 574.9 *undertake*
get agitated about 759.17 *feel deeply*
get a half-nelson on 726.6 *retain*
get ahead 126, 208, 336.9 *maintain progress*, 344.9 *achieve*, 682.6 *be successful*
get ahead of 126.8 *be superior*, 208.8 *precede*
get a head start 126.11 *get ahead*, 208.7 *be early*
get a hold on 12.12 *take authority*
get a kick out of 405.8 *feel pleasure*
get all snarled up 659.18 *find difficult*
get all tangled up 659.18 *find difficult*
get along 336.1 *go forward*, 345.1 *depart*
get along with 815.13 *fraternize*
get along without 727.9 *dispose of*
get a medal 721.14 *profit*, 878.12 *be rewarded*
get a mental picture of 519.14 *imagine*
get a middle-aged spread 207.17 *age*

get a move on 329.4 *be swift*, 329.6 *accelerate*, 336.9 *maintain progress*, 574.9 *undertake*, 648.8 *hurry up*
get an earful 420.15 *hear*
get angry 818, 828.12 *become angry*, 829.6 *be irascible*
get a penalty stroke 31.9 *play hockey*
get a piece of the action 642.16 *be sociable*, 731.5 *get one's allotment*
get a reaction 331.3 *get a response*
get a receipt 746.6 *pay*
get a reprieve 638.5 *escape*
get a response 331
get a reward 878.12 *be rewarded*
get a rise out of 331.3 *get a response*
get around 532.17 *be published*, 655.10 *be skilful*
get a running start 126.11 *get ahead*
get a second wind 126.11 *get ahead*
get a share 731.5 *get one's allotment*
get a slap in the face 806.24 *be humiliated*
get a stranglehold on 726.6 *retain*
get-at-able 264.5 *near*, 344.20 *attainable*, 407.8 *touchable*
get a tan 408.16 *feel hot*
get a tight grip 726.6 *retain*
get a toehold 726.6 *retain*
get at the truth 537.31 *be accurate*
get away 136.13 *diverge*
getaway 329.3 *accelerating*, 329.9 *acceleration*
get away 345.1 *depart*
getaway 345.7 *departure*, 638.1 *escape*
get away 638.5 *escape*, 700.5 *be liberated*
get away with it 638.5 *escape*, 708.5 *be permitted*, 848.12 *exempt oneself*
get away with murder 708.5 *be permitted*, 848.12 *exempt oneself*
get a wiggle on 208.10 *hasten*
get back 125.6 *be compensated*, 231.3 *counteract*, 478.17 *answer*
get back at 221.7 *restore*
get back on one's feet 623.6 *get healthy*
get back to normal 629.4 *be restored*
get behind 662.24 *back*
get behindhand 747.9 *be unable to pay*
get better 627, 216.7 *be changed*, 359.21 *upturn*, 629.4 *be restored*, 714.10 *show potential*, 861.21 *do well*
get bogged down 358.1 *fall short*
get by 105.6 *be in a state of*, 124.9 *be average*, 783.16 *be mediocre*
get by any means 602.6 *find means*
get by fair means or foul 602.6 *find means*
get by hook or crook 232.5, 602.6 *find means*
get by on 599.5 *dispose of*
get caught in the act 866.8 *be guilty*
get caught red-handed 866.8 *be guilty*
get caught with one's hand in the till 866.8 *be guilty*
get caught with one's pants down 866.8 *be guilty*
get caught with one's trousers down 866.8 *be guilty*
get changed 295.34 *wear*
get chummy with 819.13 *befriend*
get close 264.9 *near*
get cold feet 578.2 *equivocate*, 777.12 *be fearful*, 779.4 *be a coward*

get compensation 125.6 *be compensated*
get cracking 156.18 *make a beginning*, 329.4 *be swift*, 640.4 *act*
get credit 745.7 *be in debt*
get cross 828.12 *become angry*
get crow's-feet 207.17 *age*
get cut down 397.16 *meet one's fate*
get dirty 622.10 *be dirty*
get divorced 824.7 *divorce*
get done 230.9 *take action*
get down 344.4 *land*, 350.21 *eat*, 360.9 *descend*, 360.12 *drop*, 362.8 *sit*, 597.1 *undertake*
get down from one's high horse 806.21 *humble oneself*
get down on one's haunches 362.8 *sit*
get down on one's knees 840.6 *apologize*, 849.19 *take off one's hat to*
get down to 574.9 *undertake*, 596.3 *tackle*
get down to brass tacks 107.7 *relate to*, 165.23 *particularize*, 552.4 *be concise*, 556.7 *be simple*
get down to it 644.6 *work*
get down to the nitty-gritty 107.7 *relate to*, 165.23 *particularize*
get down to the nuts and bolts 552.4 *be concise*
get dressed 295.34 *wear*
get drunk 874, 351.13 *drink*
get egg on one's face 656.7 *be clumsy*
get engaged 477.22 *pop the question*
get engaged to 714.7 *promise*
get even 746.13 *retaliate*
get even with 672.3 *retaliate*, 879.2 *penalize*
get fat 261.6 *become bigger*, 686.5 *be prosperous*
get fatter 721.10 *augment*
get fired 347.14 *be dismissed*, 645.4 *have leisure*
get for a song 752.5 *buy at a discount*
get free 136.13 *diverge*, 638.5 *escape*, 698.14 *be free*, 700.5 *be liberated*
get fresh 807.22 *be rude*, 826.8 *court*
get frostbite 409.11 *become cold*
get going 156.18 *make a beginning*, 345.15 *go*, 574.9 *undertake*, 640.4 *act*, 686.5 *be prosperous*
get healthy 623
get hitched 135.11 *make love*, 823.15 *marry*
get hold of 522.6 *understand*, 721.9 *gain*, 734.7 *take*
get hold of the wrong end of the stick 493.10 *misjudge*, 525.1 *misinterpret*
get hot 264.9 *near*
get hot under the collar 828.12 *become angry*
get huffy 828.10 *be offended*
get hung up 358.3 *fall through*
get ideas 471.18 *aim*
get in 344, 346.9 *enter*
get in advance 721.12 *earn*
get in a mess 659.20 *be in difficulty*
get in a pickle 106.13 *get into difficulties*
get in a rut 110.11 *be regular*
get in back of 662.24 *back*
get in early 208.11 *get ahead*
get in first 194.9 *do before*
get in line 159.17 *line up*
get in one's corner 586.15 *persuade*
get in on the act 640.4 *act*, 724.4 *have joint possession*
get in on the ground floor 208.11 *get ahead*
get in print 532.17 *be published*
get in the way 656.7 *be clumsy*, 661.9 *block*
get in the way of 661.8 *hinder*
get into a fix 105.7 *be in a predic-*

getting rid of 727.1 *disposal*
getting round 853.3 *cajolery*
gettings 721.5 *profit*
getting well 623.1 *healthy*
getting worse 628.12 *deteriorated*
get to 263.7, 344.2 *reach*, 721.10 *augment*
get together 161.41 *band together*, 342.10 *come together*, 664.14 *join with*, 677.5 *make peace*, 721.11 *acquire*, 815.11 *be sociable*
get-together 161.9, 665.7 *social gathering*, 815.3 *meeting*
get together with 664.14 *join with*
get to grips with 596.3 *tackle*
get to hear of 528.15 *be informed*
get to know 501, 522.6 *understand*, 819.13 *befriend*
get too dear 753.9 *be dear*
get to one 828.9 *offend*
get to the bottom of 522.6 *understand*
get to the heart of the matter 472.11 *raise the point*
get to the top 344.9 *achieve*
get tough 690.5 *be severe*
get tough with 690.6 *suppress*
Gettysburg 93 *Cities*
get under one's feet 661.9 *block*
get under way 74.9 *navigate*, 156.19 *start off*, 345.5 *set out*
get up 55.58 *blow*, 243.10 *produce*, 281.5 *be vertical*, 359.16 *stand up*, 361.5 *arise*, 382.16 *construct*, 629.4 *be restored*, 642.12 *be active*
get-up 295.1 *dress*, 306.6 *nature*, 382.3 *form*
get up a good head of steam 239.2 *be full of vigour*
get-up-and-go 235.3 *vitality*, 239.1 *vigour*, 535.6 *assertiveness*, 642.4 *energy*
get up one's nose 415.9 *disgust*, 764.10 *displease*, 785.7 *cause dislike*
get up steam 74.9 *navigate*
get up to date 201.17 *become new*
get used to 584.18 *habituate*
get warm 264.9 *near*, 496.2 *detect*
get weaving 156.18 *make a beginning*, 574.9 *undertake*
get well 623.6 *get healthy*, 629.4 *be restored*
get what is coming to one 878.12 *be rewarded*
get what one deserves 672.4 *serve one right*
get what one was asking for 879.6 *be punished*
get what was coming 672.4 *serve one right*
get what was due 672.4 *serve one right*
get wind of 416.7 *smell*, 496.2 *detect*, 528.15 *be informed*
get wise to 501.13 *get to know*, 522.6, 787.6 *understand*
get with it 201.18 *be trendy*
get working 629.1 *repair*
get worse 127.11 *become inferior*, 624.24 *be unhealthy*, 628.1 *deteriorate*, 768.7 *become aggravated*
get wrong 133.11 *be mixed up*, 493.10 *misjudge*, 523.9 *find unintelligible*, 525.1 *misinterpret*
get you gone 349.33 *go away*
Geulincx 4 *Philosophers*
geullah 10.9 *prayer*
geumatophobia 777 *Phobias by Name*
gewgaw 612.9 *bauble*, 754.5 *cheap item*
gewgaws 792.5 *decorative articles*
Geyaguga 8 *Deities*
geyser 359, 54.25 *eruption*, 98.10 *miscellaneous*, 408.3 *heater*, 408.8 *hot place*
geyserite 54 *Minerals*
G force 369.5 *gravity*
G-force loading 33.6 *motor racing terms*

Ghana 91 *Countries*
gharry 71 *Carriages and Carts*
ghastliness 618.9 *badness*
ghastly 397.21 *deathly*, 445.8 *drained of colour*, 446.4 *pale*, 618.3 *bad*, 777.10 *frightening*
ghat 265.3 *gulf*, 634.2 *shelter*
Ghats 95 *Mountains*
ghazi 7.4 *religionist*
Ghazi 679.6 *militarist*
ghee 45.7 *basic ingredient*, 387.2 *juice*
Ghegs 1 *Peoples*
Ghent 93 *Cities*
gherkin 45 *Vegetables*, 413.2 *seasoning*
ghetto 93.7 *city district*, 136.2 *setting apart*, 147.3 *exclusion zone*, 249.10 *urban area*, 323.4 *closed place*, 400.9 *group*, 816.4 *place of confinement*
ghetto blaster 420.9 *audio device*, 423.4 *sound maker*, 534.18 *radio*
ghettoization 147.1 *exclusion*, 481.4 *social discrimination*
ghettoize 147.7 *exclude*
ghettoized 249.18 *local*
ghetto resident 743.10 *poor person*
ghibli 55 *Winds*
ghost 11, 102.2 *illusion*, 253.6 *ghostly presence*, 368.3 *spiritual world*, 435.5 *imagination*, 457.4 *something that appears*, 519.5 *fantasy*, 777.5 *frightener*
ghostbuster 11.12 *occultist*
ghost dance 10.7 *non-Christian ritual*, 11.1 *occultism*
Ghost Dance 7 *Non-Christian Religions*
ghost-fire 44.11 *make ceramics*
ghost firing 44.5 *ceramic process*
ghost gum 85 *Trees and Shrubs*
ghostlike 445.8 *drained of colour*
ghostliness 11.2 *the occult*, 368.2 *unworldliness*
ghostly 11.18 *spiritual*, 102.8 *unreal*, 253.7 *present*, 368.8 *nonmaterial*, 397.21 *deathly*, 445.8 *drained of colour*
ghostly presence 253
ghost of a chance 229.2 *chance*, 489.4 *improbability*
ghost-ridden 11.19 *bewitched*
ghosts 777 *Phobias by Topic*, 397.14 *the spiritual world*, 529.6 *natural mystery*
ghost shark 80 *Fishes*
ghost story 48.2, 560.5 *fiction*
ghost town 93.9 *town*, 240.3 *inert thing*, 249.11 *settlement*
ghost word 5.17 *word*
ghostwrite 222.2 *be a substitute*, 293.34 *cover for*, 707.4 *substitute for*
ghostwriter 222.2 *substitute person*, 293.21 *substitution*, 532.12 *publisher*, 560.10 *descriptive writer*, 707.2 *alternative*
ghoul 11.11 *ghost*, 864.9 *wicked person*
ghoulish 832.11 *cruel*
ghoulishly 11.26 *magically*
GI 674.10 *contender*, 676.11 *recruit*, 679.8 *soldier*
Giacobini–Zinner 53 *Comets*
giant 53.13 *luminosity*, 237.6 *muscleman*, 259.9 *big thing*, 259.10 *big person*, 259.11 *tall person*, 259.15 *big*, 275.7 *tall person*, 275.12 *tall*
giant cartwheel vault 30.6 *pommel horse*
giant circles 30.5 *horizontal bar*
giant clam 81 *Molluscs*
giant elliptical 53.7 *galaxy*
giantess 259.10 *big person*
giantism 259.4 *largeness*
giant planet 53.16 *planet*
giant reptile 79.6 *extinct reptile*
giant size 259.3 *large scale*
giant-size 259.15 *big*
giant slalom 18 *Sporting Activities*

giant slalom in one run 41.3 *ski racing*
giant slalom race 41.3 *ski racing*
giant slalom racing 41.3 *ski racing*
giant slalom ski 41.5 *ski equipment*
giant sloth 202.8 *prehistoric animal*
giant spiral 53.7 *galaxy*
Giant's Ridge International Classic Marathon 41.2 *cross-country skiing*
giant star 53.13 *luminosity*
giant water bug 82 *Insects*
giardia 81.10 *parasite*
giardiasis 81.12 *protozoal disease*
gib 77.10 *cat*
gibber 432.4 *cry*, 521.9 *talk nonsense*, 523.7 *be unintelligible*, 565.7 *be talkative*
gibbering 521.10 *meaningless*, 523.1 *unintelligible*
gibberish 5.5 *nonstandard language*, 506.1 *nonsense*, 521.4 *senseless talk*, 523.12 *unintelligible thing*
gibbet 283.4 *hanger*, 398.5 *execution*, 879.5 *execute*, 879.16 *instrument of execution*
gibbon 45 *Vegetables*, 77 *Placental Mammals*
Gibbons 49 *Musicians and Composers*
gibbous 315.9 *round*, 316.4 *convex*
gibbous moon 53.17 *moon*
gibbousness 315.1 *roundness*, 316.1 *convexity*
Gibbs 52 *Scientists*
Gibbs function 56 *Named Laws*, 57 *Named Reactions*, 56.38 *thermodynamics*
gibbsite 54 *Minerals*
giberellin 58.17 *plant hormone*
Gibil 8 *Deities*
Gibran 48 *Poets*
Gibson 98 *Deserts*
giddiness 238.3 *poor health*, 364.1 *rotation*, 508.1 *folly*, 579.2 *caprice*, 874.15 *crapulence*
giddy 123.3 *unequal*, 224.14 *irresolute*, 275.9 *high*, 364.12 *rotary*, 366.16 *restless*, 576.2 *changeable*, 579.1 *capricious*, 656.1 *unskilful*, 874.2 *slightly drunk*, 874.4 *crapulous*
Gide 48 *Writers*
Gideon Bible 7.12 *religious text*
Gideons 7 *Christian Movements*
gidgee 85 *Trees and Shrubs*
Gidran 32 *Breeds of Horse and Pony*
gift 729, 755, 116.9 *grant*, 165.7 *special skill*, 228.5 *positive stimulus*, 234.3 *aptitude*, 235.2 *ability*, 326.10 *transferred thing*, 485.2 *ability*, 655.2 *aptitude*, 710.6 *offering*, 721.5 *profit*, 721.1 *transfer of property*, 729.5 *give*, 730.2 *something received*, 754.6 *absence of charge*, 767.4, 833.5 *charity*, 861.12 *proficiency*, 861.13 *benefit*, 878.7 *bounty*
GIFT 245.3 *propagation*
gift child 617.8 *exceller*
gifted 655, 235.13 *powerful*, 459.10 *intelligent*, 485.9 *qualified*, 501.8 *knowledgeable*, 507.6 *intelligent*, 655.6 *skilful*, 861.5 *proficient*
gifted child 655.4 *skilled person*
giftedly 861.25 *skillfully*
gifting 729.1 *giving*
gift of healing 630.11 *medical art*
gift of life 396.4 *biological function*
gift of pleasing 821.4 *lovability*
gift of priority 194
gift of the gab 564.2 *power of speech*, 565.1 *talkativeness*
gift tax 751.7 *tax*
gift token 729.2 *gift*
gift voucher 729.2 *gift*

giftwrap 293.25 *wrap*, 457.14 *present*
giftwrapper 293.17 *coverer*
giftwrapping 293.4 *wrapping*
gig 71 *Carriages and Carts*, 74 *Ships and Boats*, 49.27 *performance*, 51.13 *engagement*
giga 75 *SI Units*
gigabyte 65.17 *computing term*, 179.10 *thousand*
gigahertz 75 *Scientific and Technical Units*
gigantesque 259.15 *big*
gigantic 259.15 *big*, 275.12 *tall*
gigantism 259
gigantomachy 674.6 *fight*
giggle 431.2 *cry of joy*, 431.11 *laugh*, 762.7 *show joy*, 771.14 *laugh*, 773.3 *laughter*, 773.8 *laugh*
giggler 773.4 *rejoicer*
giggling 431.17 *cheering*, 773.3 *laughter*, 773.10 *laughing*
gigolo 401.7 *libertine*, 808.3 *sycophant*, 821.9 *lover*, 877.8 *immoral man*
gigue 46.4 *historic dancing*
GI Joe 124.7 *average person*, 255.10 *US inhabitant*
Gila monster 79 *Reptiles*
gilbert 75 *Scientific and Technical Units*
Gilbert 48 *Dramatists*, 52 *Scientists*
Gilbert and Sullivan 51.3 *musical drama*
Gilbertese 5 *Languages and Groups of Languages*
Gilbertine 7 *Members of Religious Orders*
gild 44.11 *make ceramics*, 102.16 *delude*, 293.24 *coat*, 444.15 *colour*, 452.10 *make yellow*, 474.11 *practise sophistry*, 540.12 *facade*, 557.5 *ornament*
gilded 44.10 *ceramic*, 452.1 *yellow*, 540.35 *disguised*, 557.4 *ornate*, 742.3 *opulent*, 792.8 *decorated*
gilded decoration 44.3 *glaze*
gilder 792.7 *decorator*
gilding 792.2 *pattern*
gilding the lily 541.1 *exaggeration*
gild the lily 541.7 *exaggerate*, 548.4 *misrepresent*, 557.5 *ornament*, 610.5 *be superfluous*, 627.1 *improve*
gild the pill 405.2 *give pleasure*, 586.16 *tempt*
gilt 6.8 *livestock*, 77.18 *female mammal*, 402.14 *female animal*, 452.1 *yellow*, 540.24 *mask*, 792.2 *pattern*, 792.8 *decorated*
gilt-edged 617.3 *valuable*, 718.7 *guaranteed*
gilt-edged security 718.2 *promise*
gimbal 36.3 *parts of a sailing boat*, 364.4 *vortex*
gimcrack 238.8 *weak*, 379.1 *brittle*, 612.4 *trivial*, 612.9 *bauble*, 633.2 *unsafe*, 754.5 *cheap item*
gimlet 380.8 *sharp-pointed thing*
gimlet eye 435.2 *eye*
gimlet-eyed 435.21 *seeing*
gimmick 201.7 *new thing*, 539.8 *trick*, 592.3 *expedient plan*, 655.1 *skill*
gimmickry 201.1 *newness*
gimmicky 201.10 *new*, 539.35 *deceptive*
gimp 300.2 *edging*
gimpy 238.10 *ill*
gin 539.13, 539.33 *snare*, 635.1 *trap*
gin and It 351.8 *mixed drink*

gin and Jaguar belt 249.11 *settlement*

gin and tonic 351.8 *mixed drink*

ginger 45 Herbs and Spices, 396.1 *life*, 413.5 *herbs*, 451.1 *orange*

ginger ale 351.6 *soft drink*

ginger beer 351.6 *soft drink*

gingerbread 45.36 *cake*

gingerbread man 547.6 *image*

gingerbread plum 86 Fruits

ginger group 228.7, 586.14 *motivator*

ginger-haired 450.3 *red-haired*

gingerly 469.12 *carefully*, 781.4 *cautious*, 781.7 *cautiously*

gingernob 450.7 *red thing*

ginger up 239.3 *invigorate*

gingery 396.13 *lively*

gingham 67 Natural Fabrics

gingivectomy 60 Surgical Operations

ginglymus 135.5 *joint*

ginkgo 85 Trees and Shrubs

ginned 539.42 *trapped*

ginned up 874.1 *drunk*

ginormous 259.15 *big*

gin rummy 42 Card Games

Ginsberg 48 Poets

ginseng 45 Herbs and Spices, 630.7 *tonic*

gin sling 351.8 *mixed drink*

gin-sodden 874.5 *drunken*

gintrap 68.14 *pest control*

giocoso 49 Musical Terms

Giordano Bruno 53 Lunar Features

Giorgi system 75.2 *unit system*

gippo 387.2 *juice*

Gir 68 Breeds of Cattle

giraffe 77 Placental Mammals, 77.15 *hoofed mammal*, 275.6 *tall thing*

Giraffe 53 The Constellations

Giraudoux 48 Writers, 48 Dramatists

gird 135.10 *link*, 363.7 *ring*

girded 297.5 *surrounded*

girder 43.4 *building material*, 63.27 *superstructure*, 137.4 *means of connection*, 284.2 *supporting part*

girder bridge 63.21 *bridge*

girdle 135.10 *link*, 137.10 *band*, 284.5 *supporting garment*, 295.18 *underwear*, 313.3 *circular thing*, 313.7 *make circular*, 334.5 *encircle*, 363.7 *ring*, 699.5 *means of restraint*, 699.12 *gag*

girdle the earth 363.7 *ring*

gird one's loins 237.7 *be strong*

gird up one's loins 594.8 *prepare oneself*

girl 206.8 *young woman*, 206.9 *child*, 400.7 *person*, 402.2 *female*, 402.4 *girlfriend*, 402.12 *woman in the family*, 697.6 *domestic servant*, 821.9 *lover*, 875.6 *drug*

girl Friday 646.1 *worker*, 662.11 *helper*, 707.1 *deputy*, 767.5 *helper*

girlfriend 402, 180.12 *partner*, 819.6 *close friend*, 821.9 *lover*, 826.5 *courting person*

girlhood 206.1 *youth*

girlie magazine 877.2 *indecency*

girlish 206.11 *young*, 274.1 *thin*, 402.15 *female*, 595.5 *immature*

girlish figure 274.7 *thinness*

girlishly 206.14 *youthfully*

girlishness 206.2 *youthfulness*, 402.1 *female sex*

girllike 206.11 *young*

girl next door 164.9 *everyman*

girly show 51.5 *show*

girn 309.2 *facial distortion*, 309.10 *make faces*

giro cheque 741.14 *paper money*

Gironde 96 Rivers

Girondists 12.6 *political party*

girth 137.10 *band*, 259.1 *size*

GI's 353.2 *defecation*

gisarme 680.8 *sharp weapon*

Giselle 46.11 *classical ballets*

Gissing 48 Writers

gist 473, 103.2 *essential content*, 143.5 *largest part*, 257.1 *contents*, 472.1 *topic*, 520.1 *meaning*, 562.1 *summary*, 611.3 *chief thing*

git 345.15 *go*, 652.5 *badly behaved person*, 758.6 *nasty person*, 822.8 *hated person*

gittern 49 Musical Instruments

give 729, 755, 116.30 *grant*, 243.10 *produce*, 374.8 *softness*, 374.16 *yield*, 377.1 *elasticity*, 377.8 *be elastic*, 570.16 *bequeath*, 606.5 *provision*, 710.11 *volunteer*, 725.9 *own property*, 746.8 *defray*, 748.3 *donate*, 878.11 *pay*

give a bear hug 726.6 *retain*

give a big hand 851.16 *acclaim*

give a birthday present 729.5 *give*

give a black mark 852.20 *censure*

give a blank cheque to 708.4 *be permissive*

giveable 728.5 *transferring*, 729.7 *given*

give a bonus 837.6 *be grateful*

give a boost to 128.5 *make bigger*

give a bouquet 851.15 *compliment*

give a break 651.1 *refresh*, 835.10 *show mercy*

give a breather 651.1 *refresh*

give a catcall 543.11 *gesture*, 713.7 *complain*

give access to 734.11 *be hospitable*

give a chance to 486.7 *make possible*

give a Christmas present 729.5 *give*

give a cold reception to 581.3 *exclude*

give a come-hither look 821.26 *court*

give a commission 676.12 *go to war*

give a concession 752.3 *discount*

give a cool welcome to 581.3 *exclude*

give a deserved reward 878.9 *reward*

give a direction 692.9 *command*

give a dishonourable discharge to 704.7 *terminate*

give admittance to 348.7 *admit*

give a dressing-down 852.20 *censure*, 879.1 *punish*

give a drubbing 682.10 *defeat heavily*

give advice 654.5 *advise*

give a face-lift to 629.2 *refurbish*

give a face-lift to 627.1 *improve*, 792.11 *paint and decorate*

give a false alarm 636.7 *raise the alarm*

give a false idea 525.1 *misinterpret*

give a false impression 525.1 *misinterpret*, 539.23 *deceive*

give a false plea 538.21 *lie*

give a false reading 309.12 *distort the truth*

give a false show 540.24 *mask*

give a firm date 714.7 *promise*

give a flawless performance 619.6 *be perfect*

give a free hand 698.15 *set free*

give a French kiss 821.27 *kiss*, 826.7 *show endearment for*

give a good hiding 330.5 *beat*

give a good reason 855.8 *justify*

give a gratuity 729.5 *give*

give a guided tour 526.1 *display*

give a hand 662.17 *help*, 837.6 *be grateful*

give a hand-signal 543.11 *gesture*

give a hearing 16.76 *judge*, 420.15 *hear*

give a hero's welcome 817.12 *greet*

give a hero's welcome to 773.6 *fête*

give a hiding 879.3 *hit*

give a Judas kiss 540.19 *be deceitful*

give a knee-jerk reaction 464.10 *be instinctive*

give a last chance 835.10 *show mercy*

give a lead 228.9 *motivate*

give a leg-up 361.3 *promote*, 662.22 *improve*

give a lesson 879.1 *punish*

give a lethal injection 398.19, 879.5 *execute*

give a lick and a promise 145.5 *be incomplete*, 470.6 *be neglectful*

give a lift 361.3 *promote*

give a literal translation of 524.12 *translate*

give allegiance to 694.5 *obey*

give alms 10.18 *perform rites*, 729.6 *give to charity*

give a long-term loan 732.5 *lend*

give a look 543.11 *gesture*

give a loose translation 5.46 *translate*

give a mandate 692.9 *command*, 703.8 *authorize*

give a miss 591.4 *shy*

give an advantage 615.6 *be convenient*

give a name to 544.10 *identify*

give an anniversary gift 729.5 *give*

give an assist 662.17 *help*

give an audition 477.17 *question*

give and go 31.3 *ice hockey*, 31.9 *play hockey*

give-and-go 31.8 *hockey*

give and take 109.1 *interchange*, 109.7 *reciprocate*, 221.4, 221.8 *return*, 223.5 *exchange*, 242.1 *moderation*, 664.3 *mutual relationship*, 664.12 *reciprocate*, 672.3 *retaliate*, 674.6, 674.12 *fight*, 715.1, 715.5 *contract*, 717.4 *compromise*

give-and-take 109.4 *reciprocal*, 223.1 *exchange*, 678.2 *mediation*, 717.1 *compromise*, 717.6 *compromising*

give an earful 852.20 *censure*

give an edge to 239.3 *invigorate*

give an encore 183.17 *iterate*

give an equal exchange 109.7 *reciprocate*

give an equivalent 223.5 *exchange*

give a new lease of life 201.20 *make new*, 396.21 *invigorate*, 629.5 *revive*

give an example 524.8 *interpret*

give an impetus to 330.1 *impel*

give an impression 289.13 *appear outwardly*

give an inch and take a mile 846.15 *presume*

give an intentional walk 22.7 *play baseball*

give a nod and a wink 540.22 *falsify*

give an order 692.9 *command*

give an outline of 562.8 *summarize*

give a party 665.16 *host*

give a password 543.9 *use signs*

give a piece of one's mind 852.20 *censure*

give a prison sentence 16.79 *convict*

give a prize 729.5 *give*

give a quid pro quo 672.3 *retaliate*

give a raspberry 713.7 *complain*

give a rebel yell 668.6 *be insubordinate*

give a receipt 730.9 *receive*

give a reference for 851.13 *support*

give a roasting 852.21 *berate*

give a rough idea 375.13 *be unfinished*

give a ruling 692.11 *have authority over*

give a scholarship 878.10 *grant*

give a second chance 835.10 *show mercy*

give a second wind to 651.1 *refresh*

give a sense of security 718.10 *secure*

give a sense to 524.8 *interpret*

give as good as one gets 223.5 *exchange*, 331.2 *respond*, 674.12 *fight*

give as good as one got 672.3 *retaliate*

give a short-term loan 732.5 *lend*

give a shot 630.20 *doctor*

give a shot in the arm 396.21 *invigorate*

give a sop to Cerberus 586.17 *bribe*

give a spin 524.13 *interpret news*

give assistance 662.17 *help*

give assurances 632.9 *protect*

give a standing ovation 851.16 *acclaim*

give a start 338.33 *start*

give a subordinate role to 701.6 *subject*

give a substitute 222

give a sworn statement 535.18 *vow*

give asylum to 734.11 *be hospitable*

give a talk 567.7 *address*

give a ticket to 348.7 *admit*

give a true report 537.31 *be accurate*

give attention to 719.4 *observe*

give attention to details 537.31 *be accurate*

give a twist to 525.1 *misinterpret*

give authority 688.21 *grant authority*

give a verbatim account 537.32 *be literal*

give a viva voce examination 477.17 *question*

give a warm reception to 671.26 *act on the defensive*

giveaway 130.4 *extra*

give away 526.3 *reveal*

giveaway 530.2 *divulgence*

give away 530.7 *betray*

giveaway 532.4 *newspaper*, 721.5 *profit*, 721.15 *gainful*, 729.2 *gift*, 729.3 *offering*

give away 729.5 *give*

giveaway 729.7 *given*, 754.6 *absence of charge*, 754.9 *cheap*, 754.11 *free of charge*

give away 754.13 *make cheap*, 755.10 *be generous*, 823.16 *join in marriage*

giveaway price 754.1 *cheapness*

give a wide berth 632.8 *be safe*

give a wide berth to 263.6 *keep away*, 334.4 *detour*, 591.1 *avoid*

give a wigging 852.20 *censure*

give a wolf whistle 543.11 *gesture*

give a word in the ear 636.5 *warn*

give a word of warning 636.5 *warn*

give a word to the wise 636.5 *warn*

give a written guarantee 714.8 *guarantee*

give a wrong idea 102.16 *delude*

give back 735, 221.7, 629.3 *restore*

give back one's position 735.4 *give back*

give battle 674.12 *fight*, 676.14 *battle*

give birth 77, 156.26 *produce*, 245.10 *reproduce oneself*, 246.6 *be fertile*

give birth to 396, 201.19 *begin*, 243.10 *produce*

give blow for blow 109.7 *reciprocate*, 223.5 *exchange*

give by will 729.5 *give*

give carte blanche to 708.4 *be permissive*

give chase 590.10 *chase*

give consideration 817.10 *be courteous*

give constructive criticism 524.11 *criticize*

give counsel 654.5 *advise*

give courage 778

give credit 732.5 *lend*, 744.8 *credit*, 837.6 *be grateful*

give credit where credit is due 845.17 *credit*
give credit where it's due 744.11 *recognize*
give criticism 524.11 *criticize*
give delivery 728.3 *transfer property*
give details of 165.23 *particularize*
give diplomatic immunity 698.15 *set free*
give directions 332.6 *direct*
give dispensation 708.3 *permit*
give ear 420.15 *hear*
give enlightenment 524.8 *interpret*
give every man his due 845.17 *credit*
give evidence **483,** 16.72 *stand trial,* 480.3 *testify*
give evidence of 543.10 *signify*
give fair warning 636.5 *warn*
give false evidence 856.6 *accuse falsely*
give false information 548.5 *misinform*
give feedback 221.9 *reply*
give final notice 692.10 *demand*
give financial reward 878.9 *reward*
give financial support 831.9 *be charitable*
give first aid 630.20 *doctor*
give fitting retribution 855.10 *avenge*
give food and drink 651.1 *refresh*
give forgiveness 839.9 *forgive*
give free 729.5 *give*
give freely 729.6 *give to charity,* 755.10 *be generous,* 831.9 *be charitable*
give free rein 700.4 *liberate*
give free rein to 698.15 *set free*
give generously 729.6 *give to charity,* 755.10 *be generous,* 859.7 *be unselfish*
give ground 337.2 *retreat*
give hard knocks 674.12 *fight*
give heart to 239.3 *invigorate*
give her ten 36.21 *avast*
give his comeuppance 879.2 *penalize*
give hope 396.21 *invigorate,* 517.11 *predict*
give in 218.6 *cease,* 228.8 *be motivated,* 374.16 *yield,* 499.4 *assent,* 598.2 *withdraw,* 673.3 *submit*
give in exchange 109.7 *reciprocate,* 222.6 *give a substitute,* 223.5 *exchange*
give in marriage 823.16 *join in marriage*
give in return 223.5 *exchange*
give insight 524.8 *interpret*
give instances 475.16 *explain*
give in to 127.9 *yield to*
give it a go 479.13 *invent,* 596.1 *attempt*
give it a try 596.1 *attempt,* 674.11 *contend*
give it a whirl 596.1 *attempt*
give it one's all 596.2 *try hard*
give it one's best shot 596.2 *try hard*
give it some welly 235.11 *give power,* 239.2 *be full of vigour*
give it straight 552.4 *be concise,* 857.6 *be honourable*
give it the gun 235.11 *give power,* 239.2 *be full of vigour*
give it to someone straight 312.11 *be straight*
give job satisfaction 878.9 *reward*
give laws 16.68 *legislate*
give laws to 12.11 *govern*
give leave 116.29 *permit*
give life to 245.13 *propagate,* 396.19 *give birth to*
give light 439.24 *light*
give lines 879.1 *punish*
give lip 807.25 *answer back*
give lip service 538.24 *pretend*
give money 748.3 *donate*
give moral support **284**
given **52, 729,** 106.7 *circumstantial,* 490.1 *certain,* 518.8

supposed, 584.14 *habituated,* 606.8 *provisional,* 730.11 *receiving,* 754.11 *free of charge*
given a bad press 852.33 *criticized*
given away 729.7 *given,* 754.11 *free of charge*
given consideration **691**
give new life to 662.19 *support*
give news coverage to 293.33 *fix*
given free 754.11 *free of charge*
given name 560.8 *name*
given notice to quit 727.13 *dismissed*
give no clue 523.10 *be unexplained*
give no credit 838.6 *be ungrateful*
given one's marching orders 727.13 *dismissed*
give no quarter 398.18 *slaughter,* 690.5 *be severe,* 836.6 *be pitiless*
give nothing away 529.12 *keep secret*
give notice 517.11 *predict,* 636.5 *warn,* 705.5 *resign,* 727.10 *dismiss*
give no trouble 660.15 *be easy*
given out 162.22 *distributed*
given permission 691.5 *given consideration*
given status 107.6 *ranked*
given that 106.15 *under the circumstances*
given the boot 727.13 *dismissed*
given the chop 727.13 *dismissed*
given the heave-ho 727.13 *dismissed*
given the red light 711.8 *refused*
given the rough edge of one's tongue 852.34 *censured*
given the sack 727.13 *dismissed*
given the third degree 477.16 *questioned*
given the thumbs down 711.8 *refused*
given to drink 874.5 *drunken*
given up 160.9 *discontinued*
give occasion for 226.9 *be the cause of*
give off **388,** 352.7 *secrete,* 353.15 *excrete*
give one a bellyful 788.6 *be boring*
give one a fright 514.9 *surprise*
give one a hard time 659.23 *cause difficulties*
give one a knuckle sandwich 674.12 *fight*
give one a loan 732.5 *lend*
give one a necklace 879.5 *execute*
give one a run for one's money 638.6 *elude*
give one a turn 514.9 *surprise*
give one his head 698.15 *set free*
give one leeway 698.15 *set free*
give one pause 587.2 *deter*
give one's all 644.8 *exert oneself*
give one's assent 851.12 *accept*
give one's best regards 817.10 *be courteous*
give one's best wishes 817.10 *be courteous*
give one's blessing 116.28 *consent,* 708.3 *permit,* 831.8 *be benevolent,* 851.12 *accept*
give one's blessing to 284.14 *give moral support,* 667.6 *agree with*
give one's cards 252.17 *relegate*
give one's consent 851.12 *accept*
give oneself airs 805.26 *be too proud,* 809.15 *be vain,* 811.30 *put on airs*
give oneself a pat on the back 809.15 *be vain*
give oneself to 574.9 *undertake*
give oneself up 673.3 *submit*
give one's IOU 667.7 *contract,* 714.8 *guarantee,* 718.11 *promise,* 733.7 *borrow*
give one's life for another 397.16 *meet one's fate*
give one's marching orders 252.17 *relegate,* 349.2 *dismiss*
give one's money back 735.5 *compensate*
give one's oath 535.18 *vow*

give one's quietus 398.19 *execute*
give one's walking papers 252.17 *relegate*
give one's word 535.18 *vow,* 714.7, 718.11 *promise*
give one's word as a gentleman 535.18 *vow*
give one's word of honour 535.18 *vow*
give one the benefit of the doubt 839.11 *condone*
give one the bird 850.25 *taunt*
give one the giggles 798.7 *make one laugh*
give one the right 845.16 *entitle*
give one the slip 591.6 *evade,* 638.6 *elude*
give one trouble 659.17 *be difficult*
give one what for 852.21 *berate*
give or take a little 264.7 *nearly*
give out 349.14 *let out,* 530.6 *divulge,* 532.13 *make public,* 607.1 *waste,* 729.5 *give*
give out the bull 538.23 *talk nonsense*
give over 218.6 *cease,* 218.12 *stop,* 729.5 *give*
give peace to 677.4 *pacify*
give permission 667.6 *agree with,* 688.21 *grant authority,* 703.8 *authorize,* 708.3 *permit*
give personal recognizance 718.11 *promise*
give personal reward 878.9 *reward*
give place 337.2 *retreat*
give pleasure **405, 763**
give points to 123.5 *be unequal*
give power **235**
give praise to 729.5 *give*
give precedence to 194.9 *do before*
give priority **154**
give quarter 691.3 *be lenient,* 835.10 *show mercy*
giver **729,** 606.3 *provider*
give recognition 744.11 *recognize*
give refuge to 1008.9 *welcome*
give rein to one's imagination 519.14 *imagine*
give relief to 662.19 *support*
give renewed strength to 651.1 *refresh*
give respect 817.10 *be courteous*
give respite 835.10 *show mercy*
give responsibility 703.6 *commission*
give rise to 226.9 *be the cause of*
give sanctuary to 348.9 *welcome,* 734.11 *be hospitable*
give satisfaction 674.12 *fight,* 710.14 *offer reparation,* 840.5 *atone*
give scope 660.16 *make easy,* 698.15 *set free*
give security 718.12 *certify*
give shelter to 734.11 *be hospitable*
give some lip 478.18 *answer back*
give someone a bad time 406.11 *inflict pain*
give someone a bell 534.32 *telephone*
give someone a black eye 330.9 *fight*
give someone a black look 435.13 *look*
give someone a blank cheque 698.15 *set free*
give someone a bloody nose 330.9 *fight*
give someone a bum steer 539.27 *be false*
give someone a buzz 534.32 *telephone*
give someone a call 534.32 *telephone*
give someone a chance 116.30 *grant,* 708.4 *be permissive*
give someone a free hand 708.4 *be permissive*
give someone a fright 777.13 *frighten*
give someone a good sendoff 345.6 *part*

give someone an inferiority complex 841.7 *arouse jealousy*
give someone a refill 351.15 *provide drink*
give someone a secret sign 543.9 *use signs*
give someone a tinkle 534.32 *telephone*
give someone carte blanche 698.15 *set free*
give someone his head 708.4 *be permissive*
give someone his marching orders 341.2 *eject*
give someone his money's worth 754.13 *make cheap*
give someone lip 818.7 *be discourteous*
give someone some lip 668.5 *defy*
give someone the axe 704.7 *terminate*
give someone the bird 341.1 *repel,* 713.7 *complain*
give someone the blues 830.10 *make sullen*
give someone the boot 727.10 *dismiss*
give someone the Bronx cheer 713.7 *complain*
give someone the chop 704.7 *terminate,* 727.10 *dismiss*
give someone the cold shoulder 468.13 *be thoughtless*
give someone the evil eye 822.15 *curse*
give someone the finger 713.7 *complain*
give someone the glad eye 435.13 *look*
give someone the golden handshake 704.7 *terminate*
give someone the heave-ho 704.7 *terminate,* 727.10 *dismiss*
give someone their marching orders 704.7 *terminate,* 727.10 *dismiss*
give someone the once-over 435.14 *inspect*
give someone the pip 830.10 *make sullen*
give someone the slip 345.3 *quit,* 722.15 *lose someone*
give someone the third degree 477.18 *interrogate*
give straight from the shoulder 526.4 *show oneself*
give strength to 237.8 *strengthen*
give stripes 879.3 *hit*
give strokes 879.3 *hit*
give suck 350.25 *provide food,* 351.15 *provide drink*
give support 662.23 *advise*
give supportive evidence 855.8 *justify*
give sworn testimony 535.18 *vow*
give teeth 235.11 *give power*
give temporarily 732.5 *lend*
give terms 677.4 *pacify*
give thanks **837,** 9.7 *worship,* 10.19 *offer worship,* 10.20 *pray,* 773.7 *dance,* 837.6 *be grateful*
give the alarm 636.7 *raise the alarm*
give the all clear 116.28 *consent,* 708.3 *permit*
give the appearance of truth 537.33 *seem lifelike*
give the axe 349.2 *dismiss*
give the battle cry 668.6 *be insubordinate*
give the benefit of the doubt 16.78 *acquit*
give the big E 147.8 *eject,* 252.17 *relegate*
give the boot 349.2 *dismiss*
give the brown envelope 252.17 *relegate*
give the bum's rush 349.1 *expel*
give the cat 879.3 *hit*
give the cold shoulder 349.4 *ostracize,* 850.23 *insult,* 852.15 *withhold approval*
give the coup de grâce 684.6 *elaborate*
give the Devil his due 843.14 *be fair*

give the elbow 147.8 *eject*, 252.17 *relegate*
give the evil eye to 827.7 *wish ill*
give the freedom of 698.15 *set free*
give the game away 530.7 *betray*
give the glad eye 826.8 *court*
give the go ahead 116.28 *consent*
give the go-ahead 708.3 *permit*, 851.12 *accept*
give the go-by 591.1 *avoid*, 850.23 *insult*
give the green light 499.4 *assent*, 667.6 *agree with*, 708.3 *permit*, 851.12 *accept*
give the green light to 855.7 *vindicate*
give the heave-ho 252.17 *relegate*
give the hook 349.2 *dismiss*
give the kiss of life 630.20 *doctor*
give the lie to 536.8 *rebut*
give the nod 116.28 *consent*, 708.3 *permit*
give the nod to 667.6 *agree with*
give the OK 116.28 *consent*, 499.4 *assent*, 667.6 *agree with*, 708.3 *permit*, 851.12 *accept*
give the OK to 855.7 *vindicate*
give the old heave-ho 349.1 *expel*
give the red light 500.9 *refuse*, 852.15 *withhold approval*
give the red light to 573.6 *be unwilling*, 709.3 *veto*
give the rough edge of one's tongue 852.21 *berate*
give the rough edge of one's tongue to 827.6 *vilify*
give the run of 698.15 *set free*
give the sack 349.2 *dismiss*
give the sack to 712.10 *dismiss*
give the seal of approval to 284.14 *give moral support*
give the shirt off one's back 729.6 *give to charity*
give the silent treatment 349.4 *ostracize*
give the stamp of approval 851.12 *accept*
give the third degree 879.4 *torture*
give the thumbs down 500.9 *refuse*, 709.3 *veto*, 852.15 *withhold approval*
give the thumbs down to 573.6 *be unwilling*, 711.5 *refuse*
give the thumbs up 116.28 *consent*, 499.4 *assent*, 851.12 *accept*
give the thumbs up to 667.6 *agree with*
give the true story 537.29 *be truthful*
give the V-sign 543.11 *gesture*, 713.7 *complain*
give the word 535.17 *affirm*
give the works 879.4 *torture*
give the wrong answer 844.19 *be wrong*
give three cheers 431.12, 769.8 *cheer*, 837.6 *be grateful*, 851.16 *acclaim*
give thumbs up for 109.7 *reciprocate*, 223.5 *exchange*, 746.13 *retaliate*
give tit for tat 109.7 *reciprocate*, 223.5 *exchange*, 746.13 *retaliate*
give to 599.1 *use*, 703.6 *commission*
give to charity 729, 748.3 *donate*
give to eat 350.25 *provide food*
give tongue 423.8 *be loud*, 432.4 *cry*
give to understand 528.11 *inform*
give trouble 659.22 *cause trouble*
give two cheers 542.21 *detract from*
give umbrage 828.9 *offend*
give undivided attention to 467.11 *take note of*
give up 147.7 *exclude*, 160.12 *discontinue*, 218.6 *cease*, 352.7 *secrete*, 502.9 *be ignorant*, 576.10 *commemorate*, 581.2 *discard*, 585.5 *disaccustom*, 586.18 *be persuaded*, 598.1 *relinquish*, 598.2 *withdraw*, 600.6 *stop using*, 641.4 *not act*, 673.3 *submit*, 685.5 *not complete*, 705.5 *resign*, 727.9 *dispose of*, 729.5

give, 776.9 *be hopeless*, 869.5 *be self-restrained*
give up alcohol 873
give up arms 242.3 *be moderate*
give up drinking 873.4 *give up alcohol*
give up eating 871.5 *fast*
give up everything for 574.9 *undertake*
give up hope 776.9 *be hopeless*
give up one's friends 816.12 *be unsocial*
give up one's social life 816.12 *be unsocial*
give up the crown 705.5 *resign*
give up the ghost 157.19 *expire*, 397.15 *die*
give up the idea 598.1 *relinquish*
give up work 645.4 *have leisure*
give utterance to 564.11 *speak*
give vent to 349.14 *let out*, 530.6 *divulge*
give voice 431.15 *sing out*
give voice to 535.17 *affirm*
give vows 632.9 *protect*
give warning 517.11 *predict*
give way 238.6 *be weak*, 337.2 *retreat*, 360.10 *droop*, 374.16 *yield*, 379.4 *be brittle*, 576.10 *compromise*, 673.3 *submit*, 770.9 *despair*
give weight to 611.8 *make important*
give what for 879.2 *penalize*
give what is due 878.11 *pay*
give what was coming to him 879.2 *penalize*
give with both hands 755.10 *be generous*
give written authority 703.8 *authorize*
giving 729, 729, 878, 374.2 *pliant*, 377.6 *elastic*, 732.1 *lending*, 748.7 *donation*, 755.1 *generous*, 831.7 *charitable*
Giving 729
giving away 543.14 *signifying*
giving back 735, 221.2, 629.9 *restoration*
Giving Back 735
giving credit 732.1 *lending*, 837.5 *thanking*
giving in 673.1 *submission*
giving light 439.3 *lightening*
giving notice 705.1 *resignation*
giving out 162.1 *dispersion*
giving temporarily 732.1 *lending*
giving up 598.3 *relinquishment*, 727.1 *disposal*
giving up the fort 673.1 *submission*
giving way 673.1 *submission*
gizmo 232.2 *instrument*, 592.3 *expedient plan*, 603.1 *tool*
gizzard 78.16 *avian anatomy*
glabrous 296.13 *hairless*, 376.1 *smooth*
glacé 376.4 *polished*, 376.11 *smooth*
glacé fruit 414.2 *sweetener*
glacial 54.60 *glaciated*, 202.15 *primal*, 409.8 *cold*
glacial advance 54.40 *glaciation*
glacial deposit 54.27 *sediment*
glacial erosion 54.35 *weathering*
glacial lake 94.1 *lake*
glacial maximum 54.40 *glaciation*
glacial period 54.40 *glaciation*, 200.3 *geological period*
glacial recession 54.40 *glaciation*
glacial surge 54.40 *glaciation*
glacial valley 54.7 *landform*
glaciate 371.8 *be dense*, 373.10 *solidify*, 409.12 *make cold*
glaciated 54
glaciation 54, 55.40 *climatic change*, 371.2 *concentration*, 373.6 *solidification*
glacier 54, 54.5 *rock face*, 55.32 *freeze*, 409.5 *ice*
glacier milk 54.38 *glacier*
glaciological 54.48 *geological*
glaciologist 54.3 *geologist*
glaciology 54.1 *earth science*
glacis 34.5 *rock face*, 671.11 *fortification*
glad 762.4 *happy*, 769.1 *cheerful*

gladden 405.9 *give pleasure*, 762.8 *cause joy*, 769.6 *bring cheer*
gladdon 84 Flowers and Flowering Plants
glade 85.4 *trees*, 248.3 *geographical space*, 322.8 *open space*
glad eye 435.6 *look*
glad-hand 815.13 *fraternize*
gladiator 674.10 *contender*, 679.3 *athlete*
gladiatorial 17.8 *military*, 674.15 *contentious*, 679.35 *martial*
gladiatorial combat 398.4 *slaughter*, 674.9 *duel*
gladiolus 84 Flowers and Flowering Plants
gladly 572.16 *willingly*, 762.9 *joyfully*, 769.9 *cheerfully*
gladness 762.1 *happiness*
glad rags 295.1 *dress*
gladsome 762.4 *happy*
Gladstone 71 Carriages and Carts
Gladstone bag 258.9 *baggage*
glair 393.10 *mucus*, 394.3 *paste*
glaive 680.8 *sharp weapon*
glamorize 789.8, 791.15 *beautify*
glamorous 789.5 *beautiful*, 796.7 *fashionable*
glamorously 295.36 *dressily*
glamour 11.5 *spell*, 789.1 *gorgeousness*
glance 54 Minerals, 27.9 *stroke*, 27.17 *bat*, 267.2 *meeting*, 267.4 *meet*, 335.2 *divert*, 338.26 *bat*, 343.15 *change direction*, 407.12 *abut*, 435.6, 435.13 *look*, 439.25 *light up*, 543.3, 543.11 *gesture*
glancing 267.6 *meeting*, 407.9 *touching*, 543.15 *gestural*
glancing light 456.5 *variegated thing*
glancingly 435.26 *watchfully*
gland 352, 290.4 *insides*
glanders 624.18 *veterinary disease*
glandular 290.10 *visceral*, 352.4 *secretory*, 352.5 *of a secretion*
glandular fever 624.6 *infection*
glandularly 352
glandulous 352.5 *of a secretion*
glandulously 352.8 *glandularly*
glans penis 245.8 *organs of reproduction*
glare 55.61 *shine*, 435.6, 435.13 *look*, 439.2 *quality of light*, 439.25 *light up*, 772.8 *be serious*, 828.6 *sign of anger*, 828.11 *be angry*, 829.2 *sign of irascibility*, 830.4 *sign of irritableness*, 830.11 *be irritable*, 852.10 *disapproving look*
glaring 237.12 *strong to the senses*, 435.21 *seeing*, 437.2 *clear*, 439.16 *bright*, 444.12 *gaudy*, 526.14 *manifest*, 532.20 *well-known*
glaring error 504.10 *blunder*
Glaser 52 Scientists
Glasgow 93 Cities, 93.4 *British cities*
Glasgow Boys 50 Schools and Groups of Artists
glasnost 526.11 *openness*
glass 442, 43.4 *building material*, 43.18 *be an architect*, 44.9 *industrial ceramics*, 44.11 *make ceramics*, 55.7 *weather instruments*, 57.4 *crystal*, 120.3 *container*, 238.5 *weak thing*, 258.13 *drinking vessel*, 351.2 *drink*, 351.10 *drink container*, 376.8 *smooth thing*, 379.3 *brittle thing*, 435.8 *reflection*, 442.8 *transparent thing*, 442.1 *materials*
glass-blower 646.2 *artisan*
glass case 442.8 *transparent thing*
glass electrode 57.19 *electrochemistry*
glass engraving 12 Hobbies and Pastimes
glasses 56.29 *optical element*, 435.10 *visual aid*, 436.3 *aid for*

poor sight, 442.8 *transparent thing*
glass eye 436.3 *aid for poor sight*
glass fibre 44.9 *industrial ceramics*, 63.25 *construction material*
glassfish 80 Fishes
glassful 351.2 *drink*
glasshouse 69.4 *nursery*, 256.7 *room*, 379.3 *brittle thing*, 442.8 *transparent thing*, 702.2 *the inside*
glassiness 376.7 *smoothness*, 439.2 *quality of light*, 442.5 *transparency*
glass-like 442.1 *transparent*
glasspaper 375.7 *rough thing*, 376.9 *smoother*, 380.12 *sharpener*, 384.12 *abrasive*, 385.7 *eraser*
glass sculpture 50.12 *sculpture*
glass snake 79 Reptiles, 79.2 *lizard*
glassware 44.1 *ceramics*, 258.16 *crockery*, 442.9 *glass*
glasswort 84 Flowers and Flowering Plants
glassy 373.1 *hard*, 376.4 *polished*, 439.17 *lustrous*, 442.1 *transparent*, 443.3 *mirror-like*, 445.8 *drained of colour*
glassy-eyed 874.2 *slightly drunk*
glassy rock 54.30 *igneous rock*
Glaswegian 255.9 *British inhabitant*
Glauber's salt 57 Common Chemical Compounds, 62 Medication
glaucoma 436.1 *blindness*, 624.7 *tropical disease*
glaucomatous 436.8 *blind*
glauconite 54 Minerals
glaucous 453.1 *green*
glaze 44, 439, 44.11 *make ceramics*, 293.3 *coating*, 293.24 *coat*, 376.10 *polish*, 376.11 *smooth*, 393.12 *poultice*, 394.3 *paste*, 409.5 *ice*, 414.8 *sweeten*, 441.10 *make dim*, 444.4 *pigment*
glazed 44.10 *ceramic*, 293.36 *covered*, 376.4 *polished*, 409.8 *cold*, 414.6 *sweet*, 874.2 *slightly drunk*
glazed frost 55.29 *hail*
glazed ware 44.1 *ceramics*
glaze-fire 44.11 *make ceramics*
glaze firing 44.5 *ceramic process*
glaze ice 55.29 *hail*
glaze kiln 44.6 *ceramic workshop*
glaze over 441.9 *be dim*
glazer 44.7 *potter*
glazing 44.5 *ceramic process*, 44.10 *ceramic*
GLC 57.17 *analysis*
gleam 439.2 *quality of light*, 439.25 *light up*
gleaming 376.4 *polished*, 439.17 *lustrous*
gleamingly 439.30 *lightly*
glean 68.17 *farm*, 355.15 *draw out*, 580.4 *pick*, 605.6 *store*, 721.11 *acquire*
gleaner 161.35 *collector*, 621.12 *cleaner*, 721.7 *gainer*
gleaning 721.3 *acquisition*
gleanings 580.9 *chosen thing*, 721.4 *earnings*, 721.6 *yield*, 734.5 *takings*, 736.4 *stolen goods*
glebe 68.11 *farmland*
glee 433.2 *song*, 762.1 *happiness*
gleefully 762.9 *joyfully*
gleefulness 762.1 *happiness*
gleet 353.7 *pus*, 387.3 *body fluid*
gleg 642.18 *active*
glen 98.8 *valley*, 317.2 *concave land*
Glencoe 93 Cities
glengarry 295.15 *headgear*
Glenrothes 93 Cities
glib 376.6 *smooth-mannered*, 565.5 *talkative*, 660.9 *easy*, 817.9 *deferential*
glibenclamide 62 Medication
glibly 376.16 *suavely*, 565.10 *talkatively*, 817.16 *deferentially*

glibness 565.1 *talkativeness*, 660.2 *simplicity*, 817.4 *deference*
glib talk 521.5 *empty talk*
glib tongue 657.3 *cunning person*
glide 27.9 *stroke*, 27.17 *bat*, 28.3 *fencing movements*, 28.5 *fence*, 54.26 *mass movement*, 79.15 *live as a reptile*, 96.7 *flow*, 360.6, 360.14 *slide*, 370.9 *be light*, 376.12 *go smoothly*, 531.11 *conceal oneself*, 641.4 *not act*, 660.19 *go easily*
glide path 73.5 *flight*
glide plane 308.2 *symmetry operation*
glider 73.8 *aircraft*
glide reflection 52.48 *transformation*
glider pilot 73.3 *aircraft personnel*
gliding 18 Sporting Activities, 73.1 *aviation*, 360.18 *falling*
glimmer 55.61 *shine*, 439.25 *light up*
glimmering 439.15 *lucent*
glimpse 435.6 *look*, 435.12 *see*, 496.1 *discover*, 496.6 *discovery*
gling-bu 49 Musical Instruments
Glinka 49 Musicians and Composers
glint 439.2 *quality of light*, 439.25 *light up*
glinting 439.16 *bright*
glissade 34.9 *mountaineer*, 46.9 *ballet steps*, 360.6, 360.14 *slide*
glissading 34.3 *climbing technique*, 34.8 *mountaineering*
glissando 49 Musical Terms, 360.6 *slide*
glissées 46.10 *positions at the barre*
glisten 439.25 *light up*
glistening 439.2 *quality of light*, 439.17 *lustrous*
glister 439.2 *quality of light*
glitch 218.2 *stop*, 504.14 *computer error*, 618.8 *inferiority*, 661.2 *obstacle*
glitter 439.2 *quality of light*, 439.25 *light up*, 811.4 *flashiness*, 811.31 *put on a show*
glitterati 721.8 *wealthy people*
glittering 439.16 *bright*, 742.3 *opulent*, 811.19 *flashy*
glitteringly 811.35 *flashily*
glittery 439.16 *bright*
glitz 437.4 *clarity*, 795.1 *tastelessness*
glitzily 811.40 *grandly*
glitzy 437.2 *clear*, 742.3 *opulent*, 795.7 *vulgar*, 811.24 *grand*, 813.7 *dressed up*
GLM 41.1 *skiing*
gloaming 205.1 *evening*, 441.1 *dimness*
gloating 832.3 *callousness*
gloating pleasure 832.3 *callousness*
glob 259.7 *mass*
global 54.50 *terrestrial*, 142.6 *whole*, 146.7 *including*, 164.16 *universal*, 248.12 *extensive*, 482.4 *wholesale*, 724.5 *jointly possessing*
global approach 146.1 *inclusion*
globality 164.1 *generality*
globalize 164.23 *generalize*
globally 146.9 *inclusively*, 248.16 *extensively*, 724.6 *in common*
global outlook 91.5 *internationalism*
global view **164**
global village 724.1 *joint possession*
global war 676.1 *war*
global warming 55.40 *climatic change*, 408.5 *hot weather*
globe 142.2 *whole thing*, 299.4 *map*, 315.3 *round thing*, 547.7 *map*
globe artichoke 45 Vegetables
globefish 80 Fishes
globe flower 84 Flowers and Flowering Plants
globe thistle 84 Flowers and Flowering Plants

globose 315.9 *round*
globosely 315.13 *roundly*
globosity 315.1 *roundness*
globous 315.9 *round*
globular 315.9 *round*
globular cloud 55.20 *cloud appearance*
globular cluster 53.9 *constellation*
globularity 315.1 *roundness*
globularly 315.13 *roundly*
globular protein 58.9 *protein*
globule 315.3 *round thing*
globulin 58.9 *protein*, 387.4 *blood*
glockenspiel 49 Musical Instruments
glomerate 161.48 *cumulate*
Glomma 96 Rivers
glom on to 721.9 *gain*
gloom 440.1 *darkness*, 440.7 *spiritual darkness*, 770.2 *depression*, 772.4 *solemnity*, 776.1 *hopelessness*
gloom and doom 687.1 *adversity*, 776.1 *hopelessness*
gloomily 440.15 *darkly*, 447.12 *blackly*, 448.9 *greyly*, 770.12 *joylessly*, 776.11 *hopelessly*, 830.13 *sullenly*
gloominess 440.1 *darkness*, 448.7 *dullness*, 770.2 *depression*, 776.1 *hopelessness*
gloomy 55.49 *cloudy*, 440.8 *dark*, 440.11 *benighted*, 441.7 *dimmed*, 447.6 *sad*, 448.3 *dull*, 454.3 *depressed*, 687.6 *adverse*, 770.6 *depressed*, 776.4 *hopeless*, 830.6 *sullen*
gloomy day 687.4 *time of adversity*
glop 393.1 *semiliquid*, 394.7 *slime*
Gloria 10.6 *Eucharist*, 10.8 *hymn*
Gloria in Excelsis 10.8 *hymn*
Gloria Patri 10.8 *hymn*
glorification 8.9 *deification*, 9.1 *worship*, 10.3 *rite of worship*, 128.1 *increase*, 804.1 *right*, 851.3 *praise*
glorified 8.15 *deified*, 9.11 *worshipped*, 10.21 *ritualistic*
glorify 8.17 *deify*, 9.7 *worship*, 10.19 *offer worship*, 128.5 *make bigger*, 532.16 *publicize*, 611.8 *make important*, 849.17, 851.14 *praise*
gloriole 439.12 *highlight*
glorious 10.21 *ritualistic*, 318.6 *eminent*, 617.1 *worthy*, 773.9 *rejoicing*, 811.24 *grand*
gloriously 318.11 *eminently*, 617.11 *worthily*, 811.40 *grandly*
gloriously drunk 874.1 *drunk*
glory 318.1 *prominence*, 686.1 *prosperity*, 773.2 *fanfare*, 773.5 *rejoice*, 804.1 *right*, 811.9 *grandeur*, 851.3 *praise*
glory hole 74 Parts of a Ship, 256.7 *room*
glory in 805.25 *be proud of*
glory of war 676
gloss 5.28 *dictionary*, 5.46 *translate*, 376.10 *polish*, 376.11 *smooth*, 439.2 *quality of light*, 474.11 *practise sophistry*, 524.2 *annotation*, 524.10 *annotate*, 539.12, 539.32 *disguise*, 540.12 *facade*, 540.24 *mask*, 561.1 *dissertation*, 561.4 *dissertate*, 660.16 *make easy*
glossarial 5.42 *worded*, 171.12 *inventorial*, 524.16 *annotative*, 561.5 *expository*
glossarially 5.50 *lexically*, 171.13 *inventorially*
glossarist 524.6 *interpreter*, 561.3 *dissertator*
glossary 5.28, 171.3 *dictionary*, 257.5 *divisions*
glossator 524.6 *interpreter*
glossectomy 60 Surgical Operations
glossed 524.15 *interpreted*, 539.41, 540.35 *disguised*
glosseme 5.17 *word*
gloss finish 66.12 *development*
glossiness 376.7 *smoothness*
glossolalia 5.5 *nonstandard lan-*

guage, 7.2 *religiousness*, 11.5 *spell*, 431.3 *cry of praise*, 564.2 *power of speech*
glossological 5.38 *linguistic*
glossologist 5.2 *linguist*
glossology 5.1 *linguistics*
gloss over 531.8 *conceal*, 540.24 *mask*
gloss paint 444.5 *paint*
glossy 376.4 *polished*, 439.17 *lustrous*
glossy magazine 532.5 *journal*
glossy paper 604.3 *paper*
glottal stop 5.16 *spoken letter*
glottis 564.5 *organ of speech*
glottochronological 5.38 *linguistic*
glottochronology 5.1 *linguistics*
glottological 5.38 *linguistic*
Gloucester 45 Cheeses, 93 Cities
Gloucester Old Spot 68 Breeds of Pig
Gloucestershire 92 Counties
glove 27.6 *pad*, 31.1 *hockey*, 31.5 *lacrosse*, 295.32 *dress*
gloved 295.29 *dressed*
glove puppet 547.6 *image*
glover 295.26 *fashion designer*
gloves 38.1 *soccer*, 41.5 *ski equipment*, 295.25 *accessories*, 671.6 *protective clothing*
glow 353.19 *sweat*, 408.6 *fire*, 408.14 *be hot*, 439.2 *quality of light*, 439.8 *fire*, 439.25 *light up*, 444.9 *complexion*, 444.16 *make up*, 450.5 *redness*, 450.9 *redden*, 554.1 *emphasis*, 554.6 *emphasize*, 789.7 *be beautiful*
glow discharge 56.46, 64.6 *electric discharge*
glower 435.6, 435.13 *look*, 772.8 *be serious*, 818.8 *get angry*, 828.6 *sign of anger*, 828.11 *be angry*, 829.2 *sign of irascibility*, 830.4 *sign of irritableness*, 830.11 *be irritable*
glowering 829.5 *showing irascibility*, 830.7 *irritable*, 830.8 *overcast*
glower lour 829.7 *frown*
glowing 353.28 *sweaty*, 408.9 *hot*, 439.15 *lucent*, 444.11 *colourful*, 450.2 *red-faced*, 554.3 *emphatic*, 623.1 *healthy*
glowing health 623.3 *health*
glowingly 439.30 *lightly*
glowing terms 851.4 *compliment*
glow lamp 64.20 *electron tube*
glow-worm 82 Insects, 81.6 *worm*, 82.5 *larva*, 439.9 *firefly*
gloxinia 84 Flowers and Flowering Plants
glucagon 58 Hormones, 62 Medication
Gluck 49 Musicians and Composers
glucocorticoid 58.16 *hormone*
glucose 58 Common Sugars, 350.11 *food content*, 414.2 *sweetener*
glucoside 58.3 *carbohydrate*
glue 135.10 *link*, 137.11 *connect*, 138.3 *adhesive*, 138.7 *cause to adhere*, 393.10 *mucus*, 394.2 *adhesive*, 394.10 *stick*, 726.3 *tools for gripping*, 726.6 *retain*
glued 135.15 *tied*, 137.15 *connected*, 726.10 *retained*
gluelike 394.8 *viscous*, 726.9 *retentive*
gluelikeness 394.1 *viscosity*
glue onto 130.6 *add*
glue-sniffing 875.1 *drug-taking*
glue together 130.6 *add*, 629.1 *repair*
gluey 138.9 *adhesive*, 393.22 *mucilaginous*, 394.8 *viscous*, 726.9 *retentive*
glueyness 394.1 *viscosity*
gluhwein 414.5 *sweet drink*
glulam timber 63.25 *construction material*
glum 454.3, 770.6 *depressed*, 772.1 *solemn*, 830.6 *sullen*
glume 87.3 *grass plant*
glumly 770.12 *joylessly*, 772.10 *solemnly*, 830.13 *sullenly*

glumness 770.2 *depression*, 830.1 *sullenness*
glut 132.4 *surplus*, 246.2 *productiveness*, 608.8 *plenty*, 610.1 *excess*, 610.3 *superfluity*, 610.4 *be excessive*, 754.2 *declining prices*, 788.6 *be boring*, 872.5 *be greedy*
glutamic acid 58 Amino Acids
glutamine 58 Amino Acids
gluten 58.9 *protein*, 393.10 *mucus*, 394.2 *adhesive*
glutenous 394.8 *viscous*
glutethimidine 62 Medication
glutinose 394.8 *viscous*
glutinosity 394.1 *viscosity*
glutinous 393.22 *mucilaginous*, 394.8 *viscous*
glutinousness 394.1 *viscosity*
glut oneself 608.4 *suffice*, 872.5 *be greedy*
glutted 608.3 *filled*
glut the market 754.13 *make cheap*
glutting 872.6 *gluttonous*
glutton 77 Placental Mammals, **872**, 350.18 *eater*, 482.9 *undiscriminating person*, 782.6 *desirer*, 870.5 *self-indulgent person*
glutton for punishment 642.10 *busy person*
glutton for work 642.10 *busy person*
gluttonize 350.22 *eat well*, 872.5 *be greedy*
gluttonizing 872.6 *gluttonous*
gluttonous **872**, 350.26 *eating*, 782.9 *desirous*, 870.8 *overindulgent*
gluttonously **872**, 350.28 *carnivorously*
gluttony **872**, 350.2 *appetite*, 610.2 *overdoing it*, 864.5 *seven deadly sins*, 870.3 *overindulgence*
Gluttony **872**
glycan 58.4 *polysaccharide*
glyceride 58.7 *fat*
glycerinate 386.13 *lubricate*
glycerine 57 Common Chemical Compounds, 62 Medication, 58.3 *carbohydrate*, 386.4, 395.5 *lubricant*, 414.2 *sweetener*
glycerine trinitrate 62 Medication
glycerinize 386.13 *lubricate*, 395.18 *anoint*
glycerol 58.3 *carbohydrate*
glycerolate 386.13 *lubricate*, 395.18 *anoint*
glycerophosphatide 58.6 *lipid*
glyceryl ester 395.7 *oil*
glycine 58 Amino Acids
glycogen 58.4 *polysaccharide*
glycolipid 58.6 *lipid*
glycolysis 58.24 *respiration*, 59.6 *cell biology*
glycolytic 58.26 *biochemical*
glycoprotein 58.9 *protein*
glycosaminoglycan 58.4 *polysaccharide*
glycoside 58.3 *carbohydrate*
glymidine 62 Medication
glyph 50.13 *relief-carving*
glyptic 50.25 *sculptural*
Glyptodon 77 Placental Mammals
glyptography 50.15 *engraving*
gnarl 85.2 *tree part*, 85.13 *make rough*, 383.12 *coarsen*
gnarled 85.14 *treelike*, 371.7 *condensed*, 375.2 *coarse*
gnarly 375.2 *coarse*
gnash 350.21 *eat*
gnashing 241.6 *violent*, 350.1 *eating*, 828.16 *angry*
gnashing the teeth 828.4 *anger*
gnash one's teeth 236.6 *be powerless*, 543.11 *gesture*
gnat 82.1 *insect*
gnatcatcher 78 Birds
gnat's piss 874.12 *alcohol*
gnaw 136.9 *separate*, 350.21 *eat*, 385.13 *abrade*, 406.10 *be painful*, 607.1 *waste*, 628.5 *hurt*
gnaw at the roots 628.5 *hurt*
gnaw away 385.13 *abrade*

gnawing 77.30 *rodent-like*, 385.10 *frictional*, 406.5 *painful*
gnawing mammal 77
gneiss 54 Common Rocks
gneissic 54.57 *chalky*
gneissoid 54.57 *chalky*
gneissose 54.57 *chalky*
gnocchi 45 Types of Pasta
gnome 11.11 *ghost*, 76.7 *legendary beast*, 260.4 *little person*, 270.5 *short person*, 505.1 *maxim*
gnomic 505.2 *proverbial*
gnomic formula 505.1 *maxim*
gnomon 191 Timepieces and Timers, 192.8 *face*
gnomonic projection 547.7 *map*
gnosiology 4.6 *branch of philosophy*
gnosis 501.1 *knowledge*, 529.7 *esotericism*
gnostic 6.18 *educated*, 523.1 *unintelligible*, 527.5 *mysterious*, 551.2 *obscure*
Gnosticism 4.7 *school of thought*
gnotobiotic 59.20 *biological*
gnotobiotically 68.22 *agriculturally*
gnotobiotics 59.1 *life science*, 68.3 *livestock farming*
GNP 721.4 *earnings*
gnu 77 Placental Mammals
go 42 Board Games
go! 324, 345
go 150.23 *be in order*, 187.4 *period of activity*, 214.2 *cycle*, 230.7 *be operational*, 239.1 *vigour*, 248.8 *intervening space*, 263.7 *reach*, 324.13 *be in motion*, 332.7 *take a direction*, 345.1 *depart*, 347.9 *exit*, 353.15 *excrete*, 356.9 *proceed*, 458.2 *depart*, 479.1 *experiment*, 535.6 *assertiveness*, 591.8 *run away*, 596.5 *attempt*, 598.2 *withdraw*, 629.7 *resort*, 642.4 *energy*, 682.8 *be effective*
go aboard 345.5 *set out*, 346.9 *enter*, 359.15 *mount*
go about 36.15 *sail*, 363.6 *orbit*, 597.1 *undertake*
go absent without leave 591.8 *run away*, 598.2 *withdraw*, 638.5 *escape*
go across 356.11 *cross*
goad 228.3 *stimulus*, 228.10 *manipulate*, 241.9 *make violent*, 330.1 *impel*, 380.8 *sharp-pointed thing*, 380.16 *use a sharp tool* , 403.3 *stimulus*, 413.13 *be piquant*, 586.8 *incentive*, 648.1 *hasten*, 648.4 *haste*, 710.9 *offer*, 768.8 *annoy*, 828.9, 828.9 *offend*
goaded 228.12 *motivated*
go adrift 335.3 *go astray*
go after 155.21 *follow in sequence*, 326.14 *bring back*, 574.9 *undertake*, 590.8 *pursue*
go against 231.3 *counteract*, 663.13 *be contrary*
go against the grain 383, 168.19 *be independent*, 375.12 *make rough*, 666.8 *be different*, 785.7 *cause dislike*
go ahead 156.18 *make a beginning*, 336.3 *press on*, 336.9 *maintain progress*, 336.11 *course*, 490.26 *certainly*
go-ahead 116.7 *consent*, 239.4 *vigorous*, 336.17 *forward*, 453.15 *green light*, 597.6 *enterprising*, 851.1 *approval*
go ahead of 154.15 *precede*
goal 23.4 *playing terms*, 31.1 *hockey*, 31.3, 31.3 *ice hockey*, 31.5 *lacrosse*, 31.7 *hurling*, 35.1 *rugger*, 38.1 *soccer*, 157.14 *aim*, 228.1 *motive*, 332.1 *direction*, 344.15 *destination*, 471.4 *purpose*, 586.1 *motive*, 588.6 *objective*, 596.6 *venture*, 682.3 *successful thing*, 782.5 *object of desire*
goal area 31.5 *lacrosse*, 38.1 *soccer*

goal crease 31.3 *ice hockey*, 31.5 *lacrosse*
goal-directed 471.12 *purposive*
goalie 31.2 *hockey player*, 31.4 *ice hockey player*
goalkeeper 31.2 *hockey player*, 31.4 *ice hockey player*, 38.3 *football player*, 671.15 *protector*
goalkeeper's protective clothing 31.1 *hockey*, 31.3 *ice hockey*
goalkeeper's stick 31.3 *ice hockey*
goal kick 38.2 *football play*
goal line 19.4 *stadium*, 35.1 *rugger*, 38.1 *soccer*
go all out 329.4 *be swift*, 596.2 *try hard*, 644.8 *exert oneself*, 698.19 *liberalize*
go all out for 471.18 *aim*
go all round the houses 334.4, 363.8 *detour*
go all the way with 499.4 *assent*
go all ways at once 642.13 *be busy*
goalminder 31.4 *ice hockey player*
go along with 116.21 *be in accord*, 167.8 *comply*, 499.4 *assent*, 572.13 *be willing*, 664.15 *concur*, 673.3 *submit*, 694.5 *obey*
goal-oriented 228.12 *motivated*, 586.20 *persuadable*
goalpost 38.1 *soccer*
goalposts 19.4 *stadium*, 35.1 *rugger*
goal-tend 23.6 *play basketball*
goaltender 31.2 *hockey player*, 31.4 *ice hockey player*
goal-tending 23.5 *penalties*
go amiss 358.4 *miss*, 616.5 *be inconvenient*, 683.8 *miscarry*
go and get 326.14 *bring back*
go and return 214.8 *be cyclic*
go ape 510.14 *become insane*
go around 363.6 *orbit*
go around with 819.13 *befriend*
go as 547.10 *act*
go astern 36.15 *sail*, 74.9 *navigate*
go as the crow flies 270.11 *short-cut*
go astray 335, 358.4 *miss*, 633.8 *be in danger*, 844.23 *sin*, 877.16 *do wrong*
go as white as a sheet 445.5 *lose colour*
goat 77 Placental Mammals, 45.20 *meat*, 68.8 *livestock*
Goat 53 The Constellations
goat antelope 77 Placental Mammals
go at a snail's pace 328.1 *move slowly*
goatee 375.7 *rough thing*
goatherd 68.16 *farm worker*
goathide 604.1 *materials*
goatish 877.14 *lecherous*
goatlike 77.33 *ungulate*
goat moth 82 Insects
goats 161 Collective Names by Animal
goatsbeard 84 Flowers and Flowering Plants
goatskin 604.1 *materials*
goat's milk 351.5 *milk*
goatsucker 78 Birds
go away! 349
go away 136.13 *diverge*, 345.1 *depart*, 345.5 *go*, 458.2 *depart*
go AWOL 254.18 *abscond*, 458.2 *depart*, 598.2 *withdraw*, 693.15 *be disobedient*, 700.5 *be liberated*, 720.9 *disregard orders*
go awry 683.8 *miscarry*
gob 120.2 *certain amount*, 259.7 *mass*, 322.4 *body orifice*
go back 183.19 *return to*, 221.6 *reverse*, 335.11 *turn round*, 337.5 *turn back*
go back a long way 202.16 *be old*
go back and forth 214.7 *be regular*, 576.5 *vacillate*

go back in time 202.16 *be old*
go back on 578.4 *recant*, 720.7 *not observe*
go back on one's promises 858.9 *prove false*
go back on one's word 536.9 *renounce*, 598.2 *withdraw*
go back to square one 156.28 *begin again*, 627.4 *reconsider*, 629.4 *be restored*
go back to the beginning 183.20 *renew*, 221.7 *restore*
go back to the drawing board 156.28 *begin again*, 337.1 *go backward*
go back to the past 200.15 *look back*
go backward(s 337
go backwards 304.7 *rear up*
go bad 415.8 *sour*, 622.10 *be dirty*, 628.1 *deteriorate*, 628.2 *decay*
go bail for 632.9 *protect*, 700.4 *liberate*, 745.7 *be in debt*
go bald 294.12 *shed*
go bananas 759.17 *feel deeply*
go bankrupt 218.7 *stop working*, 683.6 *fail*, 687.10 *need money*, 743.13 *lose one's money*, 747.9 *be unable to pay*
gobbet 143.2 *particular*, 143.7 *piece*, 350.14 *mouthful*
gobble 29.3 *golf shots*, 348.11 *ingest*, 350.22 *eat well*, 432.5 *sing*, 872.5 *be greedy*
gobbledegook 5.5 *nonstandard language*, 506.1 *nonsense*, 521.4 *senseless talk*, 551.1 *obscurity*, 564.1 *faculty of speech*, 578.5 *equivocalness*
gobbler 78.10 *male bird*, 350.18 *eater*, 872.4 *glutton*
gobble up 244.12 *consume*, 607.1 *waste*
gobbling 350.2 *appetite*, 872.6 *gluttonous*
go before 154.15 *precede*, 194.8 *be before*, 208.8 *precede*, 348.8 *show in*, 517.11 *predict*, 594.1 *prepare*
go begging 610.5 *be superfluous*, 614.7 *be useless*
go belly up 218.7 *stop working*, 397.15 *die*, 683.6 *fail*, 687.10 *need money*, 743.13 *lose one's money*
go belly-up 722.10 *have a financial loss*, 747.9 *be unable to pay*
go below 276.8 *be low*
go below the surface 527.13 *hide*
go berserk 241.7 *be violent*, 670.5 *strike*, 828.11 *be angry*
go-between 135.7 *joiner*, 158.9 *middleman*, 232.3 *assistant*, 646.3 *agent*, 678.3 *mediator*, 707.3 *agent*, 716.4 *negotiator*, 823.11 *matchmaker*
go beyond 357.1 *overstep*
go beyond belief 489.7 *be improbable*
go beyond the bounds of reason 489.7 *be improbable*
Gobi 98 Deserts, 392.14 *desert*, 408.8 *hot place*
go big-game hunting 37.7 *shoot*, 590.11 *hunt*
go blank 51.34 *underact*
goblet 258.13 *drinking vessel*
goblin 11.11 *ghost*, 76.7 *legendary beast*
go blind 436.14 *be blind*
goblin shark 80 Fishes
gobo 51.18 *stage lighting*
go bond for 714.8 *guarantee*
go broke 722.10 *have a financial loss*, 743.13 *lose one's money*
gobs 259.7 *mass*
gobsmack 514.11 *amaze*, 563.15 *strike dumb*
gobsmacked 514.7 *amazed*, 563.11 *speechless*, 722.18 *at a loss*, 786.6 *wondering*
gobstopper 45.41 *sweet*
go bust 320.10 *close*, 683.6 *fail*, 722.10 *have a financial loss*, 737.2 *speculate*, 743.13 *lose*

one's money, 747.9 *be unable to pay*
go busted 743.13 *lose one's money*
goby 80 Fishes
go by 167.8 *comply*
go by fits and starts 215.6 *be irregular*
go by the board 683.8 *miscarry*
go by the book 166.17 *obey orders*, 503.7 *be accurate*, 857.6 *be honourable*
go by the card 74.9 *navigate*
go by the letter of the law 537.32 *be literal*
go by the rule book 836.6 *be pitiless*
go cap in hand 712.6 *request*
go cap in hand to 567.8 *appeal to*
go cart 71.8 *baby carriage*
go catting 576.9 *change sides*
go chase yourself 349.33 *go away*
go clubbing 815.11 *be sociable*
go cold turkey 598.1 *relinquish*, 875.10 *drug oneself*
go contemporary 201.18 *be trendy*
go courting 821.26, 826.8 *court*
god 8.5 *deity*, 9.3 *idol*
God 777 Phobias by Topic, **8**, 156.16 *originator*, 226.7 *Prime Mover*, 243.9 *producer*
go dancing 46.15 *dance*
Godavari 96 Rivers
Goddard 52 Scientists
goddaughter 402.12 *woman in the family*
goddess 8.5 *deity*, 821.9 *lover*
goddess of health 623.3 *health*
go dead slow 328.1 *move slowly*
go deaf 421.8 *be deaf*
Gödel 52 Scientists
Gödel numbers 52 Named Concepts
godfather 401.13 *man in the family*, 611.4 *bigwig*
God-fearing 7.15 *religious*
God forbid 536.17 *never*
godforsaken 254.14 *unoccupied*, 263.8 *distant*, 816.10 *lonely*, 864.14 *impious*
godforsaken hole 816.5 *solitary place*
godforsaken place 263.3 *distant place*
God-given 729.7 *given*
godhead 8.1 *divinity*
godhood 8.1 *divinity*
go directly 332.7 *take a direction*
go dirt-cheap 754.12 *be cheap*
God knows 502.13 *who knows?*
God knows where 263.3 *distant place*
godless 864.14 *impious*
godlike 8.13 *divine*, 99.14 *self-existent*
godliness 8.1 *divinity*, 843.4 *righteousness*, 857.2 *purity*, 863.1 *virtue*
godly 7.15 *religious*, 8.13 *divine*, 619.1 *perfect*, 843.10 *moral*, 857.5 *pure*, 863.5 *virtuous*
god-making 361.7 *lift*
godmother 402.12 *woman in the family*
god of war 676
go down 129.4 *decrease*, 244.13 *be destroyed*, 262.6 *become smaller*
go downhill 244.13 *be destroyed*, 360.9 *descend*, 628.1 *deteriorate*, 687.9 *be in trouble*
go downhill fast 244.13 *be destroyed*
go down in the world 687.9 *be in trouble*
go down on bended knee 712.6 *request*
go down on one's knees to 712.6 *request*
go down the drain 607.1 *waste*, 722.14 *go to waste*
go down the tubes 337.1 *go backward*
go down well 497.10 *be believed*

go down with 624.24 *be unhealthy*
go down with (colours) flying 574.11 *persist*
go down with one's ship 574.11 *persist*, 575.8 *hold out*, 847.16 *do one's duty*
go dry 869.5 *be self-restrained*, 873.4 *give up alcohol*
gods 435.9 *viewpoint*
God's acre 399.5 *cemetery*
gods and goddesses of anger 828
gods and goddesses of love 821
gods and goddesses of marriage 823
God's answer to 617.1 *worthy*
God's country 91.6 *native land*
God's creation 400.7 *person*
godsend 861.17 *good thing*
God's gift to women 809.7 *vain person*
godship 8.1 *divinity*
God's image 400.7 *person*
God's in heaven 179.3 *seven*
godson 401.13 *man in the family*
God's own 580.15 *chosen*, 617.1 *worthy*
God's plenty 608.8 *plenty*
God's purpose 588.5 *final intention*
God's truth 537.3 *the truth*
God's will 571.5 *inevitability*
God the Father 8.3 *God*
God the Son 8
go Dutch 122.10 *be equal*, 124.10 *make average*, 176.17 *go halves*, 717.4 *compromise*, 724.4 *have joint possession*, 746.9 *pay one's way*, 815.11 *be sociable*
Godwin 4 Philosophers
Godwin Austen 95 Mountains
godwit 78 Birds
go easily 660
go easy 242.3 *be moderate*, 660.20 *take it easy*
go easy on 691.3 *be lenient*, 835.10 *show mercy*
goer 32.2 *thoroughbred*, 347.8 *outgoer*, 402.6 *loose woman*
Goethe 48 Poets
goethite 54 Minerals
go even-Stephen 724.4 *have joint possession*
go far 686.5 *be prosperous*
go farther and fare worse 628.1 *deteriorate*
go fast 336.9 *maintain progress*, 648.2 *make haste*
go faster 648.2 *make haste*
go fell walking 34.9 *mountaineer*
gofer 127.6 *inferior*, 642.10 *busy person*, 646.1 *worker*, 662.11 *helper*, 673.2 *appeaser*, 694.4 *obedient person*, 697.5 *office assistant*, 701.3 *subordinate*
go fifty-fifty 110.10 *be equal*, 124.10 *make average*, 176.17 *go halves*, 717.4 *compromise*, 724.4 *have joint possession*
go first 154.15 *precede*
go fish 42 Card Games
go fishing 590.11 *hunt*
go flat 628.2 *decay*
go flat out 596.2 *try hard*, 698.19 *liberalize*
go for 326.14 *bring back*, 332.7 *take a direction*, 588.10 *aim*, 670.1 *attack*, 670.5 *strike*, 674.12 *fight*, 821.23 *love*
go for a burton 360.11 *trip*, 397.15 *die*
go for a good price 739.2 *be sold*
go for a song 754.12 *be cheap*
go for broke 574.8 *brace oneself*, 596.2 *try hard*
go for help 662.17 *help*
go for it 574.8 *brace oneself*, 574.18, 596.11 *here goes*
go for the jack 25.7 *bowl*
go forward 336, 336.1 *go forward*
go free 698.14 *be free*, 700.5 *be liberated*
go from bad to worse 127.11 *become inferior*, 628.1 *deteriorate*, 768.7 *become aggravated*
go from door to door 712.8 *solicit money*
go from the sublime to the ridiculous 798.6 *be ridiculous*
go full bat 329.4 *be swift*
go full belt at 670.1 *attack*
go full pelt 329.4 *be swift*
go full steam 329.4 *be swift*
go full tilt 329.4 *be swift*
go get it 574.9 *undertake*
go-getter 336.16 *progressive person*, 592.8 *planner*, 597.4 *volunteer*, 640.3 *doer*, 642.10 *busy person*
go-getting 239.4 *vigorous*, 336.12 *advance*, 336.17 *forward*, 642.18 *active*, 775.13 *aspirant*
goggle 435.13 *look*
goggle at 786.9 *wonder*
goggled 34.8 *mountaineering*
goggle-eyed 435.21 *seeing*
goggles 34.4 *climbing equipment*, 39.8 *swimwear*, 41.5 *ski equipment*, 435.10 *visual aid*, 634.2 *shelter*, 671.6 *protective clothing*
go-go 329.1 *motion*
go-go dancer 46.5, 51.28 *dancer*
Gogol 48 Writers, 48 Dramatists
go great guns 682.6 *be successful*
go grey 207.17 *age*, 448.8 *grey*
gogsee 41.10 *curling*
go half and half 717.4 *compromise*
go halfway 124.10 *make average*, 333.7 *be halfway*
go halves 176, 122.10 *be equal*, 124.10 *make average*, 724.4 *have joint possession*, 731.5 *get one's allotment*
go hand in glove with 180.13 *accompany*
go hand in hand 198.7 *synchronize*
go hand in hand with 180.13 *accompany*
go hatless 294.11 *uncover*
go home 337.5 *turn back*
go hungry 871.5 *fast*
go hunting 37.7 *shoot*, 590.11 *hunt*
Goidelic 5 Languages and Groups of Languages
go in 27.15 *play*, 346.9 *enter*
go in a huddle 568.10 *chat*
go in for 165.27 *specialize*, 567.12 *address oneself to*, 574.9 *undertake*, 584.16 *have a habit*, 597.1 *undertake*
going 230.10 *operational*, 324.1 *motion*, 324.16 *moving*, 345.7 *departure*, 347.15 *outgoing*, 397.18 *dying*, 458.4 *disappearance*, 458.6 *disappearing*, 598.3 *relinquishment*, 642.18 *active*
going after 155.1 *sequence*, 590.1 *pursuit*
going around the corner 22.6 *fielding terms*
going away 345.7 *departure*, 458.4 *disappearance*
going back 221.1 *reversion*, 337.10 *backward motion*, 345.7 *departure*, 578.11 *equivocating*
going backwards 304.3 *rearing up*
going before 154.1 *precedence*
going belly-up 722.2 *financial loss*
going blind 436.1 *blindness*
going by the letter of the law 537.11 *pedantry*
going cheap 754.9 *cheap*
going down 16.43 *conviction*, 129.6 *decreasing*, 360.1 *descent*
going down fighting 575.12 *indomitable*
going downhill 628.12 *deteriorated*
going down of the sun 205.1 *evening*
going down the tubes 337.19 *backsliding*
going down with guns blazing 575.12 *indomitable*

going Dutch 122.1 *equality*
going for a song 754.9 *cheap*
going forward 336.10 *forward motion*
going grey 207.12 *ageing*
going halves 122.1 *equality*
going home 162.2 *disbandment*
going on 145.4 *incomplete*, 336.20 *in progress*
going on and on 190.10 *continuing forever*, 553.3 *diffuse*
going on board 345.8 *start*
going on the rampage 828.4 *anger*
going out 347.1 *exit*, 821.6, 826.2 *courtship*
going out of business 320.4 *closure*
going-out-of-business sale 739.4 *sale*, 752.2 *bargain*
going over 578.7 *apostasy*
going over again 183.2 *iteration*
going rate 751.3 *fee*
going round in circles 685.1 *noncompletion*
goings-on 472.3 *matter of interest*
going steady 821.6, 826.2 *courtship*
going the rounds 533.14 *journalistic*
going through the roof 753.7 *dear*, 757.3 *costly*
going to extremes 541.3 *extravagance*
going together 821.6, 826.2 *courtship*
going to hell in a basket 628.7 *deterioration*
going to law 16.5 *litigation*, 16.53 *litigating*
going too far 541.3 *extravagance*
going to pot 628.12 *deteriorated*
going to the head 874.6 *intoxicating*
going to the root 611.5 *important*
going to the wall 722.2 *financial loss*
going under 320.4 *closure*
going up 359.6 *mounting*
going up on hind legs 304.3 *rearing up*
going with 821.6, 826.2 *courtship*
going without 591.19 *abstaining*, 871.6 *fasting*
go in one ear and out of the other 512.12 *be forgotten*
go in one ear and out the other 421.11 *be unheard*
go in opposition 663.12 *oppose*
go inside 290
go into 561.4 *dissertate*
go into a brown study 519.15 *fantasize*
go into a decline 624.24 *be unhealthy*
go into a huddle 161.39 *come together*
go into a partnership 715.5 *contract*
go into a tailspin 129.4 *decrease*
go into a trance 11.24 *experience psychic phenomena*
go into debt 743.13 *lose one's money*
go into detail 106.11 *circumstantiate*, 165.23 *particularize*, 553.5 *be diffuse*
go into details 503.7 *be accurate*
go into ecstasies over 759.17 *feel deeply*
go into exile 147.9 *be excluded*
go into hiding 438.7 *become invisible*
go into league with 715.5 *contract*
go into liquidation 218.7 *stop working*, 747.9 *be unable to pay*
go into mourning for 774.6 *lament*
go into orbit 313.6 *circle*, 363.6 *orbit*, 364.8 *rotate*
go into overdrive 235.11 *give power*, 648.2 *make haste*
go into particulars 503.7 *be accurate*
go into partnership 664.14 *join with*

go into partnership with 140.6 *come together*
go into purdah 438.7 *become invisible*
go into receivership 218.7 *stop working*
go into recession 129.4 *decrease*
go into retirement 458.2 *depart*, 645.4 *have leisure*, 705.5 *resign*, 816.12 *be unsocial*
go into retreat 458.2 *depart*
go into reverse 337.3 *reverse*
go into seclusion 139.7 *be aloof*, 816.12 *be unsocial*
go into the red 722.10 *have a financial loss*, 744.9 *acquire credit*, 745.7 *be in debt*, 753.11 *overpay*
go into training 6.23 *learn*
go into voluntary exile 147.9 *be excluded*
go in with 664.14 *join with*
go it alone 174.18 *be one*, 698.16 *be independent*
goitre 624.4 *disease*
go kaput 683.9 *malfunction*, 844.24 *go wrong*
go-kart 71 Motor Vehicles
Go-Kart 33.11 *racing*
Go-Karting 33.1 *motor racing*
go lame 238.6 *be weak*, 328.2 *hesitate*
Golan Heights 95 Mountains
Golconda 742.5 *wealth*
gold 57 Chemical Elements, 777 Phobias by Topic, 21.6 *track*, 291.2 *central thing*, 452.1 *yellow*, 452.8 *yellow thing*, 617.8 *exceller*, 741.1 *money*, 741.16 *bullion*
Gold 52 Scientists
gold and silver standard 741.7 *finance*
goldarn 827.11 *miscellaneous euphemisms*
gold bar 741.16 *bullion*
gold-based 741.22 *monetary*
gold brick 328.15 *slow person*, 539.8 *trick*, 591.5 *shirk*, 591.17 *avoider*
gold bricker 591.17 *avoider*
gold coinage 741.13 *coinage*
goldcrest 78 Birds
gold cup 681.1 *trophy*
gold decoration 44.3 *glaze*
gold-digger 721.7 *gainer*, 821.9 *lover*, 826.5 *courting person*
gold-digging 721.16 *greedy*
golden 203.12 *autumn*, 451.1 *orange*, 452.1 *yellow*, 617.3 *valuable*, 675.7 *peaceful*, 686.8 *prosperous*, 775.14 *cheering*
golden age 106.5 *comfortable circumstances*, 200.1 *past time*, 686.3 *time of plenty*, 865.3 *naivety*
golden apple 228.5 *positive stimulus*
golden bell 84 Flowers and Flowering Plants
golden-brown algae 90.2 *algae*
golden calf 9.3 *idol*
golden cat 77 Placental Mammals
golden days 686.3 *time of plenty*
Golden Delicious 86 Fruits
golden dream 519.6 *reverie*
golden eagle 78 Birds
goldeneye 78 Birds
golden goose 742.5 *wealth*
golden-haired 446.3 *white-haired*, 452.3 *yellow-haired*
golden handcuffs 746.3 *pay*, 878.4 *reward for service*
golden handshake 125.1 *compensation*, 130.4 *extra*, 345.9 *parting*, 704.2 *termination*, 721.5 *profit*, 729.2 *gift*, 746.3 *pay*, 837.3 *recognition*, 878.4 *reward for service*
golden hello 746.3 *pay*, 878.4 *reward for service*
golden jubilee 812.5 *anniversary*
goldenly 452.11 *yellowly*
golden mean 50.4 *treatment*, 52.44 *polygon*, 124.5 *medium*, 158.3 *median*, 242.1 *modera-*

tion, 333.1 *middle way*, 869.2 *moderation*
golden mole 77 Placental Mammals
golden oldie 207.7 *older person*
golden opportunity 210.2, 322.10 *opportunity*, 710.2 *tentative offer*
golden parachute 125.1 *compensation*, 721.5 *profit*, 746.3 *pay*, 878.4 *reward for service*
golden pheasant 78 Birds
golden rectangle 52.44 *polygon*
golden retriever 77 Breeds of Dogs, 37.6 *sporting dog*
goldenrod 84 Flowers and Flowering Plants
golden rule 654.3 *precept*
golden section 50.4 *treatment*, 52.44 *polygon*
Golden Temple of Amritsar 10.13 *shrine*
golden time 686.3 *time of plenty*
golden times 675.1 *peace*
golden-toned 433.6 *melodious*
golden touch 742.5 *wealth*
golden wedding 812.5 *anniversary*
golden wedding anniversary 214.6 *annually celebrated day*
golden years 207.5 *old age*
golden-yellow 452.1 *yellow*
goldfinch 78 Birds
goldfinches 161 Collective Names by Animal
goldfish 80 Fishes, 451.3 *orange thing*
goldfish bowl 442.8 *transparent thing*
Golding 48 Writers
gold leaf 792.2 *pattern*
gold medal 21.5 *competition*, 30.1 *gymnastics*, 126.14 *best*, 544.4 *insignia*, 611.6 *notable*, 617.2 *best*, 681.1 *trophy*
gold-medallist 21.3, 237.5 *athlete*, 655.4 *skilled person*
gold mine 317.2 *concave land*, 742.5 *wealth*, 605.2 *resource*
Goldoni 48 Dramatists
gold plate 293.3 *coating*
gold-plate 293.24 *coat*
gold reserves 741.6 *funds*
gold-rimmed glasses 435.10 *visual aid*
Goldschmidt 52 Scientists
gold-sheet inlay 47.9 *decorative woodwork*
goldsmith 646.2 *artisan*
Goldsmith 48 Writers
gold sovereign 741.10 *former British money*
gold standard 14.1, 741.7 *finance*
gold star 792.3 *honour*
Gold Star 17 US Military Medals and Decorations
Goldstein-Sheerer test 61.6 *intelligence test*
gold tooth 380.11 *tooth*
gold vault 605.4 *storage*
gold watch 837.3 *recognition*
Goldwynism 504.11 *grammatical error*
golf 18 Sporting Activities, **29, 29**
Golf 534 Phonetic Alphabet, **29**
golf bag 258.8 *bag*
golf ball 29, 29.2 *golfing terms*, 338.10 *ball*
golfball printer 65.7 *peripheral*
golf bodies 29.1 *golf*
golf cart 71 Motor Vehicles
golf club 29
golf club part 29.4 *golf club*
golf course 29.1 *golf*
golfer 29
golf game 29.1 *golf*
golfing 29.1 *golf*
golfing terms 29
golf match 29.1 *golf*
golf rules 29.2 *golfing terms*
golf shots 29
golf widow 824.6 *surviving spouse*
Golgi apparatus 59.8 *cell organ*
Golgi body 59.8 *cell organ*

Golgi complex 59.8 *cell organ*
Golgi vesicle 59.8 *cell organ*
golgotha 399.5 *cemetery*
goliard 51.27 *entertainer*
Goliath 237.6 *muscleman*, 259.10 *big person*, 275.7 *tall person*
goliath beetle 82 Insects
goliath frog 79 Amphibians
go light 543.4 *signal*
go like a bat out of hell 239.2 *be full of vigour*
go like a rocket 648.2 *make haste*
go like clockwork 150.23 *be in order*, 660.19 *go easily*
go like gangbusters 239.2 *be full of vigour*
golliwog 547.6 *image*
go looking for trouble 666.7 *pick a fight*
go lower 277.14 *deepen*
go mad 508.6 *be foolish*, 510.14 *become insane*, 759.17 *feel deeply*
gombroon 44 Types of Ceramics
go missing 254.18 *abscond*
go modern 201.18 *be trendy*
go mouldy 415.8 *sour*
go mountaineering 34.9 *mountaineer*
gomuti 85 Trees and Shrubs
gonadotrophic hormone 58.16 *hormone*
gonadotrophin 58.16 *hormone*, 246.3 *fertilizer*
go native 814.11 *not stand on ceremony*
Goncharov 48 Writers
Goncourt 48 Writers
Gondi 5 Languages and Groups of Languages
gondola 74 Ships and Boats, 72.6 *rolling stock*, 327.12 *cableway*
gondola lift 41.1 *skiing*
gondolier 74.8 *boatman*, 326.7 *transferor*
Gondwana 54.19 *plate tectonics*
gone 3.18 *in the past*, 172.7 *null*, 200.18 *over*, 254.9 *away*, 345.12 *departed*, 397.19 *dead*, 458.7 *disappeared*, 487.3 *hopeless*, 512.11 *forgotten*, 641.3 *inactive*, 776.5 *past hope*, 874.3 *dead drunk*
gone away 345.12 *departed*, 458.7 *disappeared*
gone bad 618.4 *poor*, 626.5 *unhygienic*, 628.12 *deteriorated*
gone before 397.19 *dead*
gone but not forgotten 397.19 *dead*
gone by the board 722.16 *losing*
gone down the drain 722.16 *losing*
gone for a burton 397.19 *dead*
gone forever 200.18 *over*, 722.16 *losing*
gone for good 200.18 *over*, 722.16 *losing*
gone from bad to worse 628.12 *deteriorated*
gone missing 252.13 *misplaced*, 722.16 *losing*
gone off 345.12 *departed*, 626.5 *unhygienic*, 628.12 *deteriorated*
goner 397.10 *dying person*, 776.3 *hopeless person*
gone to Elysium 397.19 *dead*
gone to ground 458.7 *disappeared*
gone to join one's ancestors 397.19 *dead*
gone to pot 207.13 *middle-aged*, 743.3 *beggarly*
gone to ruin 743.3 *beggarly*
gone to seed 69.17 *botanical*, 83.13 *plantlike*
gone to the Elysian fields 397.19 *dead*
gone to the happy hunting grounds 397.19 *dead*
gone wrong 844
gonfalon 544.7 *flag*
gong 49 Musical Instruments, 192.10 *signal*, 423.4 *sound maker*, 427.4 *sources of resonance*, 544.4 *insignia*, 681.1 *tro-*

phy, 792.3 *honour*, 804.3 *honours*
gong ageng 49 Musical Instruments
gong chimes 49 Musical Instruments
gong drum 49 Musical Instruments
Góngora y Argote 48 Poets
Gongorism 48 Literary Groups and Movements
gongue 49 Musical Instruments
gonidium 90.4 *reproductive body*
go nightclubbing 815.11 *be sociable*
goniometer 268.8 *meter*, 310.4 *angular measurement*
goniometric 268.16 *micrometric*
goniometry 268.2 *micrometry*, 310.4 *angular measurement*
gonion 310.1 *angle*
goniotomy 60 Surgical Operations
gonorrhoea 624.4 *disease*, 624.14 *venereal disease*
gonorrhoeic 626.4 *infectious person*
goo 393.1 *semiliquid*, 394.7 *slime*, 622.4 *dirt*
Gooch 18 Sporting Personalities
good 861, 861, 350.27 *edible*, 558.3 *elegant*, 599.6 *use*, 613.2, 613.3 *usable*, 613.4 *profitable*, 613.5 *usefulness*, 613.6 *usability*, 617.1 *worthy*, 617.4 *worthwhile*, 632.5 *safe*, 652.17 *well-behaved*, 655.6 *skilful*, 662.34 *beneficial*, 694.7 *obedient*, 714.14 *auspicious*, 782.8 *desirable*, 784.5 *likable*, 831.6 *benevolent*, 857.4 *honourable*, 863.5 *virtuous*, 865.5 *innocent*, 876.8 *moral*
Good 861
good acquaintance 784.4 *likable person*
good and bad 620.1 *imperfect*
good and early 208.12, 208.17 *early*
good and evil 111.2 *opposites*
good and mad 828.16 *angry*
good and tired 788.5 *bored*
good as gold 617.1 *worthy*, 863.5 *virtuous*
good as new 201.14 *renewed*
good as one's word 617.1 *worthy*
good at 501.8 *knowledgeable*, 655.6 *skilful*, 696.13 *excellent*
good bargain 738.6 *purchase*
good behaviour 861, 652.2 *good conduct*, 694.2 *loyalty*, 817.2 *good manners*, 863.1 *virtue*
good books 851.2 *admiration*
good break 686.2 *good fortune*
good breeding 794.1 *elegance*, 802.3 *nobleness*, 817.2 *good manners*
good buy 738.6 *purchase*, 748.4 *expenditure*, 754.4 *bargain*
goodbye! 345
goodbye 345.9 *parting*
good chance 589, 210.2 *opportunity*, 229.2 *chance*, 486.3 *strong possibility*, 488.4 *chance*
good character 857.1 *probity*
good cheer 350.7 *food*, 769.3 *cheerfulness*, 815.1 *sociability*
good child 652.3 *well-behaved person*
good citizenship 833.2 *public spiritedness*
good climate 625.2 *salubrity*
good clip 329.8 *speed*
good colour 800.1 *estimation*
good companion 815.6 *social person*
good company 815, 763.8 *amiability*, 815.6 *social person*
good condition 105.5 *physical state*, 150.5 *orderliness*, 623.3 *health*
good conduct 652
good conscience 863.1 *virtue*
good constitution 623.3 *health*
good credit risk 744.1 *credit*
good deal 754.4 *bargain*
good debt 745.1 *debt*

good deed 640.2 *deed*, 662.2 *support*, 831.4 *benevolent act*
good deportment 817.2 *good manners*
good ear 420.1 *hearing*
good eater 872.4 *glutton*
good English 5.29 *grammar*
good enough 617.5 *not bad*, 765.6 *satisfactory*
good example 863.4 *virtuous person*
good excuse 855.2 *defence*
good eyesight 435.1 *vision*
good faith 694.2 *loyalty*, 857.1 *probity*
good feeling 759
good fellow 815.6 *social person*
good fellowship 815.8 *good company*
good fit 667.3 *compatibility*
good food 350.7 *food*
good for it 742.2 *solvent*
good form 306.5 *formality*, 811.11 *ritual*, 813.5 *etiquette*
good-for-nothing 236.10 *powerless*, 612.2 *obscure*, 614.1 *useless*, 722.6 *loser*, 858.4 *dishonourable person*, 858.5 *dishonourable*, 864.9 *wicked person*
good-for-nothingness 858.1 *improbity*
good for one 623.2 *healthful*
good fortune 686, 106.5 *comfortable circumstances*, 229.2 *chance*, 589.2 *luck*
Good Friday 10.15 *holy day*, 871.3 *fast day*
good giver 729.4 *giver*
good graces 851.2 *admiration*
good grammar 5.29 *grammar*
good grounds 855.2 *defence*
good head for 655.2 *aptitude*
good health 623.3 *health*
good-hearted 831.6 *benevolent*
good-heartedly 831.10 *benevolently*
good heavens! 514
good host 815.6 *social person*
good housekeeping 756.1 *thrift*
good humour 105.4 *state of mind*, 769.3 *cheerfulness*, 817.1 *courtesy*
good-humoured 105.8 *in a state of*, 769.1 *cheerful*, 817.7 *courteous*, 831.6 *benevolent*
good-humouredly 105.9 *conditionally*, 817.14 *courteously*
good husbandry 756.1 *thrift*
good idea 461.6 *idea*
goodies 350.7 *food*
goodies and baddies 111.2 *opposites*
good influence 216.6 *editor*, 627.5 *improvement*
good in law 16.46 *legislated*
good in parts 620.1 *imperfect*
good intention 588.1 *intention*
good intentions 652.1 *conduct*
good lady 823.1 *married woman*
good light 439.10 *window*
good likeness 114.1 *similarity*
goodliness 861.10 *kindness*, 861.14 *largeness*
good listener 760.8 *sensitive person*
good-looking 340.9 *attractive*, 789.5 *beautiful*
good looks 457.3 *external appearance*, 789.1 *gorgeousness*
good loser 857.3 *honourable person*
good luck! 589, 686
good luck 210.2 *opportunity*, 229.2 *chance*, 589.2 *luck*, 686.2 *good fortune*, 861.17 *good thing*
good-luck charm 11.6 *talisman*, 517.6 *good-luck sign*, 637.2 *preserver*
good-luck sign 517
good lungs 423.4 *sound maker*
goodly 259.15 *big*, 861.3 *kind*, 861.7 *large*, 863.9 *virtuously*
goodman 401.3 *male title of address*, 823.10 *married man*
good management 756.1 *thrift*
good-mannered 817

good manners 817, 652.2 *good conduct,* 794.1 *elegance,* 813.5 *etiquette,* 815.2 *social ambition,* 861.11 *good behaviour*
good match 823.4 *marriageability*
good memory 511.1 *memory,* 726.5 *retentiveness*
good mixer 815.6 *social person*
good morals 876
good move 682.3 *successful thing*
good-natured 576.4 *unsteady,* 675.7 *peaceful,* 763.2 *likable,* 769.1 *cheerful,* 831.6 *benevolent,* 861.3 *kind*
good-naturedly 831.10 *benevolently,* 861.23 *nicely*
good-naturedness 831.1 *benevolence,* 861.10 *kindness*
good neighbour 662.13 *supporter,* 784.4 *likable person,* 815.6 *social person,* 831.5 *benevolent person,* 833.3 *philanthropist,* 861.15 *good person*
goodness 617.6 *worth,* 623.4 *healthfulness,* 652.2 *good conduct,* 655.1 *skill,* 694.1 *obedience,* 831.1 *benevolence,* 857.1 *probity,* 861.8 *good,* 863.1 *virtue,* 865.1 *innocence,* 876.2 *good morals*
goodness and mercy 831.1 *benevolence*
goodness gracious 786.14 *wonderful*
goodness-of-fit test 52.54 *hypothesis testing*
Good News Bible 7.12 *religious text*
good nick 150.5 *orderliness*
goodnight 345.9 *parting,* 345.14 *goodbye*
good nose 416.2 *sense of smell*
good notice 851.4 *compliment*
good nutrition 625.2 *salubrity*
good occasion 210.1 *timeliness*
good odds 589.5 *good chance*
good odour 416.4 *reputation*
good offices 632.2 *protection,* 662.2 *support,* 677.1 *pacification,* 678.2 *mediation,* 831.4 *benevolent act*
good old days 3.8, 200.1 *past time*
good old summertime 203.3 *summer*
good omen 517.5 *omen,* 714.3 *potential*
good opinion 849.1 *respect,* 851.2 *admiration*
good opportunity 210.2 *opportunity,* 486.3 *strong possibility*
good pair of lungs 423.4 *sound maker*
good part 51.21 *role*
good person 861, 784.4 *likable person,* 857.3 *honourable person,* 863.4 *virtuous person,* 865.4 *innocent person*
good piste 41.3 *skiing*
good point 617.6 *worth*
good policy 615.3 *convenience*
good press 851.4 *compliment*
good prospects 714.3 *potential*
good quality 617.1 *worthy,* 617.6 *worth,* 861.8 *good*
good reason 855.2 *defence*
good reference 800.1 *estimation*
good report 800.1 *estimation*
good review 524.3 *criticism*
good riddance 639.2 *deliverance,* 722.1 *loss*
good right arm 767.5 *helper*
good role model 640.3 *doer*
goods 13.2 *economy,* 13.6 *economic factors,* 70.2 *thing transported,* 70.5 *transportable,* 243.7 *produce,* 326.10 *transferred thing,* 725.5 *personal estate,* 739.8 *merchandise*
good sales 739.5 *sales*
Good Samaritan 662.13 *supporter,* 710.8 *volunteer,* 729.4 *giver,* 755.9 *generous person,* 760.8 *sensitive person,* 831.5 *benevolent person,* 833.3 *philanthropist,* 861.15 *good person,* 863.4 *virtuous person*

goods and chattels 725.4 *possessions*
goods and services 243.7 *produce*
good sense 507.2 *intelligence,* 509.2 *rationality*
good shot 338.15 *shooter,* 590.6 *hunter,* 682.3 *successful thing*
good size 259.3 *large scale*
good-size 259.15 *big*
goods on approval 739.8 *merchandise*
goods on assignment 739.8 *merchandise*
good sort 857.3 *honourable person*
good spirits 105.4 *state of mind,* 769.3 *cheerfulness*
good sport 857.3 *honourable person*
good stead 613.5 *usefulness*
goods train 72.7 *train,* 326.5 *means of transport*
good sword 679.1 *combatant*
good table 350.9 *plenty*
good taste 134.1 *purity,* 411.2 *taste of life,* 481.2 *judiciousness,* 542.3 *subtlety,* 558.1, 794.1 *elegance,* 876.2 *good morals*
good temper 4.3 *detachment*
good-tempered 4.18 *detached*
good terms 819.2 *friendly relations*
good thing 861
good things to come 714.3 *potential*
good time 405
good time coming 199.3 *future condition*
good-time girl 405.3 *pleasure-seeker*
good times 686.3 *time of plenty,* 742.7 *opulence*
good times coming 519.7 *idealism*
good trim 150.5 *orderliness*
good try 596.5 *attempt*
good turn 662.2 *support,* 831.4 *benevolent act,* 861.10 *kindness*
good understanding 819.2 *friendly relations*
good usage 599.6 *use*
good value 754.1 *cheapness*
good-value 754.9 *cheap*
good vibes 667.1 *agreement*
good vibrations 667.1 *agreement*
good visibility 55.35 *visibility*
good way 263.2 *great distance*
good wheeze 461.6 *idea*
goodwife 402.3 *female title of address,* 823.11 *married woman*
goodwill 572, 662.10 *helpfulness,* 667.1 *agreement,* 819.1 *friendship,* 831.1 *benevolence,* 833.1 *philanthropy*
goodwill towards man 831.1 *benevolence*
good wishes 849.7 *respects*
good with money 756.4 *thrifty*
good word 851.4 *compliment*
good work 831.4 *benevolent act*
good works 2.10 *social services,* 831.2, 833.5 *charity*
goody 402.3 *female title of address,* 823.11 *married woman*
goody-goody 134.5 *pure person,* 540.15 *false person,* 540.27 *hypocritical,* 831.5 *benevolent person,* 863.4 *virtuous person,* 865.4 *innocent person,* 865.5 *innocent*
goody-goodyism 813.2 *formalism*
gooey 393.16 *semiliquid,* 726.9 *retentive*
gooeyness 394.1 *viscosity*
goof 504.10 *blunder*
go off 335.8 *sidestep,* 343.11 *move apart,* 415.8 *sour,* 423.8 *be loud,* 622.10 *be dirty,* 628.2 *decay*
go off at a tangent 104.13 *be extraneous,* 160.15 *lose one's train of thought,* 334.4 *detour,* 335.1 *deviate*
go off at half cock 193.3 *mistime*
go off at half-cock 595.12 *be unprepared*

go off at the drop of a hat 572.13 *be willing*
go off half-cocked 208.10 *hasten*
go off like a shot 572.13 *be willing*
go off on a tangent 310.11 *angle,* 553.6 *be circuitous*
go off one's head 510.14 *become insane*
go off sick 624.24 *be unhealthy*
go offside 38.4 *play soccer*
go offsides 31.9 *play hockey*
go off-sides 35.5 *play rugby*
go off the air 421.11 *be unheard,* 458.1 *disappear*
go off the beaten track 117.13 *not conform,* 168.19 *be independent*
go off the deep end 828.12 *become angry*
go off the gold standard 747.12 *devalue the currency*
go off the point 108.10 *be unrelated,* 160.15 *lose one's train of thought*
goofing off 328.11 *lingering*
goof off 328.2 *hesitate*
goof-off 328.15 *slow person*
googly 27.8 *delivery,* 539.9 *sleight of hand*
googol 169.3 *large number,* 179.11 *million*
googolplex 169.3 *large number,* 179.11 *million*
goo-goo eyes 821.6, 826.2 *courtship*
gook 91 Names for Inhabitants, 393.1 *semiliquid,* 394.7 *slime*
goolies 245.8 *organs of reproduction*
go on 188
go on! 219
go on 159.14 *continue,* 212.7 *be frequent,* 219.3 *continue,* 324.13 *be in motion,* 345.1 *depart,* 575.7 *maintain,* 786.14 *wonderful*
go on a bender 870.11 *overindulge,* 874.8 *get drunk*
go on a binge 773.5 *rejoice,* 872.5 *be greedy*
go on a blind 874.8 *get drunk*
go on about 183.18 *harp,* 876.12 *moralize*
go on a climbing expedition 34.9 *mountaineer*
go on a crash diet 871.5 *fast*
go on active service 676.13 *be at war*
go on a diet 869.5 *be self-restrained,* 871.5 *fast*
go on a fool's errand 656.6 *act foolishly,* 722.11 *be wasteful*
go on a furlough 645.4 *have leisure,* 649.2 *take it easy*
go on a hunger strike 722.9 *lose,* 871.5 *fast*
go on a liquid diet 871.5 *fast*
go on a mission 703.7 *engage*
go on and on 183.18 *harp,* 184.9 *be infinite,* 553.5 *be diffuse,* 565.7 *be talkative,* 788.6 *be boring*
go on a pilgrimage 7.19 *be religious,* 9.7 *worship*
go on a protest march 713.8 *cause mischief*
go on a pub-crawl 874.8 *get drunk*
go on a rampage 423.8 *be loud*
go on as before 629.4 *be restored*
go on a spending spree 748.1 *expend,* 757.8 *overspend*
go on a spree 815.11 *be sociable,* 874.8 *get drunk*
go on a starvation diet 871.5 *fast*
go on at 183.18 *harp*
go on a wild goose chase 656.6 *act foolishly*
go on a wild-goose chase 722.11 *be wasteful*
go on board 359.15 *mount*
go one better 126.8 *be superior,* 657.5 *be cunning*
go one-on-one 31.9 *play hockey*

go one's own sweet way 174.18 *be one*
go one's own way 168.19 *be independent,* 570.14 *follow one's own will,* 577.9 *be obstinate,* 698.16 *be independent*
go one's separate ways 162.9 *be dispersed*
go on for a long time 219.4 *protract*
go on forever 190.5 *be eternal,* 788.6 *be boring*
go on furlough 254.17 *take leave of absence*
go on holiday 254.17 *take leave of absence*
go on honeymoon 823.15 *marry*
go on hunger strike 713.8 *cause mischief*
go on leave 254.17 *take leave of absence,* 649.2 *take it easy,* 651.2 *be refreshed,* 848.12 *exempt oneself*
go on location 254.17 *take leave of absence*
go on oiled wheels 660.19 *go easily*
go on one's feelings 464.9 *be intuitive*
go on relief 743.12 *be poor*
go on sabbatical 254.17 *take leave of absence*
go onside 38.4 *play soccer*
go on strike 218.7 *stop working,* 711.5 *refuse,* 713.8 *cause mischief*
go on the air 420.16 *be heard*
go on the attack 670.1 *attack*
go on the blink 844.24 *go wrong*
go on the dole 743.12 *be poor*
go on the fuddle 874.8 *get drunk*
go on the lam 527.13 *hide,* 531.11 *conceal oneself,* 591.6 *evade,* 632.8 *be safe,* 634.4 *shelter,* 700.5 *be liberated*
go on the parish 743.12 *be poor*
go on the pill 247.9 *practise birth control*
go on the rampage 151.26 *be disorderly,* 241.7 *be violent,* 670.9 *attack successfully*
go on the rocks 244.13 *be destroyed,* 683.6 *fail,* 687.9 *be in trouble*
go on the stock exchange 14.5 *invest,* 737.2 *speculate*
go on the wagon 591.3 *abstain,* 699.10 *restrain oneself,* 869.5 *be self-restrained,* 873.4 *give up alcohol*
go on the warpath 241.7 *be violent,* 666.7 *pick a fight,* 676.13 *be at war*
go onto the offensive 670.1 *attack*
go on trial 856.7 *be accused*
go on vacation 254.17 *take leave of absence,* 649.2 *take it easy*
go on welfare 743.12 *be poor*
goop 393.1 *semiliquid*
goosander 78 Birds
goose 78 Birds, 37.5 *game,* 45.20 *meat,* 68.8 *livestock,* 78.3 *water bird,* 78.11 *female bird,* 407.4 *kiss,* 407.11 *touch,* 429.3 *hisser,* 543.3 *gesture,* 821.14 *communication of love,* 826.7 *show endearment for*
goose barnacle 81.4 *arthropod*
gooseberry 86 Fruits, 108.3 *unconnected person*
gooseberry bush 245.7 *obstetrics*
gooseberry sawfly 69.12 *pests and diseases*
gooseboy 68.16 *farm worker*
goose bumps 375.7 *rough thing,* 777.2 *fearfulness*
goose egg 172.1 *zero*
goose fair 740.1 *market*
goosefish 80 Fishes
goose flesh 375.7 *rough thing,* 403.3 *stimulus,* 777.2 *fearfulness*
goosefoot 84 Flowers and Flowering Plants
goosefoot family 83.3 *seed plant*
goosegirl 68.16 *farm worker*

goosegrass 84 Flowers and Flowering Plants, **87** Grasses
gooselike 78.23 *avian*
gooseneck 74 Rigging, 36.3 *parts of a sailing boat*
goosenecked 36.10 *sailing*
goose pimples 375.7 *rough thing*
goose-pimples 403.3 *stimulus*
goose someone 543.11 *gesture*
goosestep 324.12 *gait*
goosewing 36.15 *sail*
goosing 407.12 *touching*
Goossens 49 Musicians and Composers
goosy 78.23 *avian*
go OTT 357.4 *exaggerate,* 359.14 *climb*
go out 157.18 *come to an end,* 347.9 *exit,* 440.13 *become dark,* 815.11 *be sociable*
go out for trade 737.1 *trade*
go out like a lamb 242.3 *be moderate*
go out of business 218.7 *stop working,* 320.10 *close*
go out of commission 844.24 *go wrong*
go out of one's way 334.4, 363.8 *detour*
go out of one's way to 572.13 *be willing*
go out of print 458.1 *disappear*
go out of style 202.17 *grow old*
go out of town 254.17 *take leave of absence*
go out of use 458.1 *disappear*
go out on a limb 168.19 *be independent,* 229.4 *chance,* 589.12 *take a chance*
go out on the ale 351.13 *drink*
go out on the town 815.11 *be sociable*
go out to the middle 27.17 *bat*
go out with 135.8 *unite,* 180.14 *keep company with,* 819.14 *seek the friendship of,* 821.26, 826.8 *court*
go over 576.9 *change sides,* 578.3 *apostatize,* 598.2 *withdraw,* 682.6 *be successful*
go over again 183.17 *iterate*
go over again and again 183.18 *harp*
go over big 682.6 *be successful*
go overboard 610.4 *be excessive*
go over one's head 523.7 *be unintelligible*
go over the bounding main 97.9 *sail the high seas*
go over the hill 700.4 *liberate*
go over the limit 357.4 *exaggerate*
go over the same ground 183.17 *iterate,* 183.19 *return to*
go over the top 357.4 *exaggerate,* 359.14 *climb,* 610.4 *be excessive,* 670.14 *attack,* 676.14 *battle,* 811.29 *show off*
go over the wall 638.5 *escape,* 700.4 *liberate*
go over to the enemy 858.9 *prove false*
GOP 665.3 *political grouping*
go partners 664.14 *join with*
go partying 815.11 *be sociable*
gopher 77 Placental Mammals
go phut 844.24 *go wrong*
go pitapat 365.9 *vibrate,* 366.24 *shake*
go pubbing 815.11 *be sociable*
go pub-crawling 815.11 *be sociable*
go public 530.5 *disclose,* 532.13 *make public*
go quietly 242.3 *be moderate*
go racing 33.9 *race*
goral 77 Placental Mammals
Gordian knot 529.5 *difficult problem,* 659.4 *problem*
Gordimer 48 Writers
Gordon setter 77 Breeds of Dogs
gore 295.24 *part of garment,* 380.14 *be sharp,* 387.4 *blood,* 393.10 *mucus,* 450.7 *red thing*
gored skirt 295.6 *skirt*
go regularly 584.16 *have a habit*
gorge 54.7 *landform,* 98.8 *valley,* 265.3 *gulf,* 317.2 *concave*

land, 322.7 *passageway,* 608.4 *suffice,* 610.4 *be excessive,* 870.11 *overindulge,* 872.5 *be greedy*
gorged 144.8 *full,* 610.6 *excessive,* 872.6 *gluttonous*
gorge oneself 350.22 *eat well*
gorgeous 617.1 *worthy,* 762.5 *delightful,* 789.5 *beautiful,* 811.24 *grand*
gorgeousness 789, 811.9 *grandeur*
gorger 872.4 *glutton*
gorgerin 43 Architectural Decoration, 279.3 *architectural summit*
gorget 671.7 *armour*
gorging 350.2 *appetite,* 872.6 *gluttonous*
Gorgon 435.2 *eye*
Gorgonzola 45 Cheeses
go right through one 430.4 *be strident*
gorilla 77 Placental Mammals
goriness 387.5 *fluidity*
goring 670.18 *hit*
Gorki 48 Writers
Gorky 93 Cities
gormandize 350.22 *eat well,* 405.8 *feel pleasure,* 872.5 *be greedy*
gormandizer 872.4 *glutton*
gormandizing 350.2 *appetite*
gormless 508.5 *foolish*
go round 297.7 *surround,* 313.6 *circle,* 324.13 *be in motion,* 327.14 *find one's way,* 334.3 *circuit,* 364.8 *rotate*
go round and round 334.3 *circuit*
go round in circles 334.3 *circuit,* 363.6 *orbit,* 576.7 *be irresolute,* 614.9 *waste effort*
go round the bend 510.14 *become insane*
gorse 84 Flowers and Flowering Plants
go rusty 656.5 *be unskilful*
gory 387.18 *bloody,* 393.22 *mucilaginous,* 398.24 *murderous,* 450.4 *bloody*
Gosain 7.8 *priest*
go scot-free 638.5 *escape,* 700.5 *be liberated*
go separate ways 136.13 *diverge,* 343.12 *separate*
go septic 628.2 *decay*
gosh 786.14 *wonderful,* 827.16 *euphemisms*
go shares 122.10 *be equal,* 124.10 *make average,* 724.4 *have joint possession,* 731.5 *get one's allotment,* 815.11 *be sociable*
goshawk 78 Birds, 78.5 *bird of prey*
goshdarn 827.11 *miscellaneous euphemisms,* 827.16 *euphemisms*
goshdarned 827.11 *miscellaneous euphemisms*
Goshen 714.4 *promised land*
go shooting 37.7 *shoot,* 590.11 *hunt*
go shopping 738.2 *shop*
go short and wide 25.7 *bowl*
Goshute 1 Peoples
go sidewards 324.13 *be in motion*
go sideways 305.8 *move sideways*
gosling 68.8 *livestock,* 78.12 *young bird*
go slow 15.12 *have an industrial dispute,* 328.1 *move slowly,* 328.12 *hesitation,* 644.6 *work,* 713.8 *cause mischief*
go-slow 13.8 *industrial relations,* 15.4 *industrial dispute,* 713.3 *gesture of protest*
go smoothly 376, 660.19 *go easily*
go so far but no further 717.4 *compromise*
go solo 174.18 *be one*
go sour 415.8 *sour,* 628.2 *decay*
go spare 828.12 *become angry*

gospel 49.5 *sacred music,* 537.3 *the truth,* 537.15 *true*
Gospel 10.6 *Eucharist*
gospel music 49.5 *sacred music*
Gospels 7.12 *religious text*
gospel song 10.8 *hymn*
gossamer 67 Natural Fabrics, 238.5 *weak thing,* 274.4 *fine,* 274.11 *fineness,* 370.7 *light thing,* 383.10 *delicate,* 442.8 *transparent thing,* 612.8 *trifle*
gossameriness 383.2 *grain*
gossamer thread 238.5 *weak thing*
gossamery 370.2 *insubstantial,* 383.10 *delicate*
gossip 420.8 *something heard,* 465.2 *prying,* 465.4 *meddler,* 465.7 *be curious,* 472.3 *matter of interest,* 528.7 *advice,* 528.10 *informer,* 532.13 *publication,* 532.13 *make public,* 538.21 *lie,* 564.10 *speaker,* 565.3 *talk,* 565.4 *talker,* 568.2 *chat,* 568.8 *chatterer,* 568.10 *chat,* 854.3 *defamation,* 854.8 *defamer,* 854.13 *vilify*
gossip column 532.3 *journalism,* 533.9 *news story*
gossip columnist 528.9 *informant,* 532.11 *newspaper man,* 533.4 *journalist,* 560.10 *descriptive writer,* 854.8 *defamer*
gossiper 564.10 *speaker,* 854.8 *defamer*
gossiping 854.16 *defamatory*
gossipmonger 465.4 *meddler*
gossip writer 528.9 *informant*
gossipy 465.6 *prying,* 472.9 *local,* 528.16 *informative,* 565.6 *effusive,* 568.14 *conversational*
go stale 628.2 *decay*
go steady with 135.8 *unite,* 821.26, 826.8 *court*
go straight 332.7 *take a direction,* 627.2 *get better,* 863.8 *be virtuous*
Göteborg 93 Cities
Gotham 93.3 *New York,* 249.10 *urban area*
go the long way round 334.4, 363.8 *detour*
go the pretty way 363.8 *detour*
go the round 334.3 *circuit,* 363.7 *ring*
go the rounds 532.12 *be published*
go the way of all flesh 397.15 *die*
go the whole hog 574.6 *be resolute,* 642.15 *try,* 684.4 *complete*
go the wrong way about it 656.5 *be unskilful*
gothic 47.7 *furniture style*
Gothic 5 Languages and Groups of Languages, **43** Architectural Styles, 5.41 *lettered,* 50.29 *realist,* 202.14 *historic*
Gothic art 50 Western Art Styles and Movements
gothic horror 48.2 *fiction*
gothic novel 560.5 *fiction*
Gothic novel 48.2 *fiction*
Gothic Revival 43 Architectural Styles
Gothic type 5.15 *type style*
go through 599.1 *use,* 599.5 *dispose of,* 652.14 *behave towards,* 748.2 *consume,* 757.7 *waste,* 759.15 *feel*
go through fire and water 574.6 *be resolute*
go through hell 406.9 *feel pain*
go through one's paces 811.31 *put on a show*
go through phases 224.11 *be changeable*
go through the bankruptcy court 747.9 *be unable to pay*
go through the books 750.8 *audit*
go through the ceiling 753.9 *be dear*
go through the roof 128.4 *increase*
Goths 1 Peoples, 200.6 *people of the past*
got it! 471
Gotland 98 Islands

goto 65.17 *computing term*
go to 263.7 *reach*
go to a funeral 399.8 *bury*
go to all lengths 574.6 *be resolute*
go to and fro 214.7 *be regular,* 576.5 *vacillate*
go to any length 574.6 *be resolute*
go to any lengths 644.8 *exert oneself*
go to arbitration 717.4 *compromise*
go to bat for 662.24 *back*
go to bed 325.8 *be motionless,* 649.2 *take it easy*
go to bed late 642.13 *be busy*
go to bed with 135.11 *make love*
go to blazes 244.13 *be destroyed*
go to church 7.19 *be religious*
go to confession 840.6 *apologize,* 867.4 *be penitent*
go to court 666.6 *argue*
go to Davy Jones's locker 397.16 *meet one's fate*
go to earth 531.11 *conceal oneself*
go to exaggerated lengths 541.7 *exaggerate*
go to extremes 541.9 *be extravagant*
go together 180.13 *accompany,* 605.6 *store*
go together with 180.13 *accompany*
go to glory 397.15 *die*
go to ground 458.1 *disappear*
go to heaven 8.17 *deify,* 368.12 *enter a nonmaterial world*
go to hell 244.13 *be destroyed,* 368.12 *enter a nonmaterial world*
go to hospital 624.24 *be unhealthy*
go to it 156.18 *make a beginning,* 574.9 *undertake*
go to law 16.70 *litigate*
go to meet 344.8 *meet*
go too far 357.1 *overstep,* 541.9 *be extravagant,* 698.19 *liberalize,* 846.15 *presume*
go to one's corner 26.11 *do a combat sport*
go to one's eternal rest 325.8 *be motionless*
go to one's head 809.16 *show off,* 874.9 *be intoxicating*
go to one's last home 397.15 *die*
go to one's long account 397.15 *die*
go to one's reward 397.15 *die*
go to parties 815.11 *be sociable*
go to pieces 141.3 *disintegrate,* 244.13 *be destroyed,* 628.1 *deteriorate*
go topless 296.14 *undress*
go to pot 207.17 *age,* 244.13 *be destroyed,* 607.1 *waste,* 628.1 *deteriorate,* 687.9 *be in trouble,* 722.14 *go to waste,* 743.13 *lose one's money,* 877.16 *do wrong*
go to press 532.15 *publish*
go to rack and ruin 244.13 *be destroyed,* 628.1 *deteriorate,* 687.9 *be in trouble,* 877.16 *do wrong*
go to ruin 607.1 *waste,* 628.1 *deteriorate,* 743.13 *lose one's money*
go to school 6.23 *learn*
go to seed 207.17 *age,* 628.1 *deteriorate,* 722.14 *go to waste*
go to sleep 404.11 *be unfeeling,* 649.2 *take it easy*
go to the bad 844.23 *sin,* 864.16 *be wicked,* 877.16 *do wrong*
go to the big house 699.11 *detain*
go to the block 739.2 *be sold*
go to the bog 767.13 *relieve oneself*
go to the country 580.5 *vote*
go to the devil 628.1 *deteriorate*
go to the dogs 244.13 *be destroyed,* 628.1 *deteriorate,* 683.6 *fail,* 687.9 *be in trouble,* 722.14 *go to waste,* 844.23 *sin,* 864.16 *be wicked,* 877.16 *do wrong*

go to the happy hunting ground 325.8 *be motionless*
go to the john 767.13 *relieve oneself*
go to the last roundup 397.15 *die*
go to the little boys' room 767.13 *relieve oneself*
go to the men's room 767.13 *relieve oneself*
go to the penalty box 31.9 *play hockey*
go to the polls 580.5 *vote*
go to the relief of 662.17 *help*
go to the rest room 767.13 *relieve oneself*
go to the starting grid 33.10 *be on the track*
go to the toilet 353.15 *excrete*
go to the wall 244.13 *be destroyed*, 320.10 *close*, 659.20 *be in difficulty*, 683.6 *fail*, 722.10 *have a financial loss*, 743.13 *lose one's money*, 747.9 *be unable to pay*
go to the witness box 16.70 *litigate*
go to war 676, 473.13, 666.6 *argue*, 674.12 *fight*
go to waste 722, 244.13 *be destroyed*, 607.1 *waste*, 614.7 *be useless*
got rid of 727.12 *disposed*
gotten 749.6 *received*
Götterdämmerung 157.5 *fate*
gouache 50.11 *artist's materials*, 444.5 *paint*
Gouda 45 Cheeses
gouge 26.5 *wrestling*, 26.12 *wrestle*, 319.1, 319.5 *notch*, 753.10 *overcharge*
gouged 54.59 *weathered*
gouge out 317.7 *make concave*, 355.13 *dig out*
gouging 26.5 *wrestling*, 753.4 *extortion*, 753.7 *bear*
goulash 45.32 *meat dish*, 133.2 *mixed thing*
Gould Belt 53 Clusters
go under 244.13 *be destroyed*, 320.10 *close*, 360.9 *descend*, 659.20 *be in difficulty*
go underground 360.15 *tunnel*, 527.13 *hide*, 531.11 *conceal oneself*, 632.8 *be safe*, 689.4 *be anarchic*
go under water 360.9 *descend*
go unnoticed 124.9 *be average*
go unpunished 638.5 *escape*
go up 359.13 *ascend*
go up a blind alley 327.14 *find one's way*
go up in a puff of smoke 100.13 *cease to exist*
go up in flames 408.15 *burn*
go up in smoke 683.8 *miscarry*, 722.14 *go to waste*
go up on hind legs 304.7 *rear up*
go up Salt River 397.15 *die*
go upstairs 359.15 *mount*
go up the spout 722.14 *go to waste*
go up the wall 828.12 *become angry*
gourami 80 Fishes
gourd 45 Vegetables, 86 Fruits, 258.14 *bottle*
Gourlay 29.5 *golf ball*
gourmand 350.18 *eater*, 405.3 *pleasure-seeker*, 411.5 *taster*, 482.9 *undiscriminating person*, 763.5 *pleasure-loving*, 870.5 *self-indulgent person*, 872.4 *glutton*
gourmandise 872.2 *epicurism*
gourmandising 405.1 *physical pleasure*
gourmandism 350.2 *appetite*, 350.3 *delicate eating*, 872.2 *epicurism*
gourmandizing 870.3 *overindulgence*, 870.8 *overindulgent*
gourmet 350.18 *eater*, 405.3 *pleasure-seeker*, 411.5 *taster*, 481.6 *discriminating person*, 763.5 *pleasure-loving*, 870.5 *self-indulgent person*, 872.4 *glutton*
gout 624.16 *rheumatism*

goutweed 84 Flowers and Flowering Plants
gouty 624.23 *diseased*, 874.5 *drunken*
govern 12, 92.7 *administer*, 150.22 *pacify*, 166.16 *direct*, 235.10 *be powerful*, 242.4 *moderate*, 653.1 *manage*, 688.18 *have authority*, 692.11 *have authority over*, 696.14 *master*
governance 12, 688, 235.1 *power*, 652.9 *tactics*, 653.3 *management*, 688.1 *authority*
governess 6.4 *educator*, 632.3 *protector*, 697.4 *personal attendant*
governing 12, 126.13 *dominant*, 653.17 *managerial*, 688.12 *authoritative*
governing body 12, 653, 6.5 *educationalist*
government 12, 235.1 *power*, 653.3 *management*, 653.10 *legislative body*, 688.4 *governance*, 692.3 *authority*
governmental 12, 688, 92.6 *administrative*, 400.13 *national*, 652.16 *behaving*, 653.17 *managerial*, 692.14 *commanding*
governmental architecture 43.1 *architecture*
governmental area 92.1 *administrative area*
governmental committee 654.4 *adviser*
governmental funds 741.19 *treasury*
governmentally 2.16 *sociologically*, 12.14 *politically*, 92.8 *administratively*, 692.16 *commandingly*
governmental organization 688
governmental power 12.3 *governance*
Government and Politics 12
government by estates 12.1 *government*
government by the ballot box 12.1 *government*
Government Communications Headquarters 17.4 *military organization*
government debt 745.2 *national debt*
government documents 528.3 *document*
government institution 2.8 *human institution*
government man 702.5 *prisoner*
government office 653.3 *management*
government offices 647.1 *workshop*
government of the people, by the people, for the people 688.7 *type of rule*
government papers 545.1 *record*
government post 688.5 *position of authority*
government servant 653.16 *official*
governor 12, 6.5 *educationalist*, 63.11 *engine*, 126.5 *superior*, 401.3 *male title of address*, 653.13 *director*, 653.14 *leader*, 661.4 *restraint*, 688.10 *person of authority*, 696.1 *master*, 696.3 *leader*, 696.9 *educational leader*, 699.5 *means of restraint*, 703.5 *commissioner*
governor general 653.13 *director*, 696.3 *leader*
Governor of the Bank of England 741.18 *treasurer*
governorship 688.5 *position of authority*, 703.4 *council*
governor's mansion 256.4 *official residence*
Gower 48 Poets
go west 244.13 *be destroyed*, 397.15 *die*
go where the wind blows 576.7 *be irresolute*
go white around the gills 445.5 *lose colour*
go with 135.8 *unite*, 180.13 *accompany*, 264.10 *stay near*

go without 711.7 *refuse oneself*, 871.5 *fast*
go without food 871.5 *fast*
go without saying 526.5 *be visible*
go with the crowd 124.9 *be average*
go with the flow 116.25 *conform*, 167.8 *comply*
go with the stream 167.8 *comply*, 336.6 *march on*, 808.14 *follow*
go with the tide 660.20 *take it easy*
gown 7.11 *vestment*, 295.5 *fancy dress*, 295.7 *frock*, 295.16 *robe*, 295.32 *dress*
gowned 295.29 *dressed*
go wrong 844, 515.6 *disappoint*, 683.8 *miscarry*, 683.9 *malfunction*, 877.16 *do wrong*
goy 91 Names for Inhabitants
Goytisolo 48 Poets
GPO 534.2 *postal communication*
grab 71.21 *miscellaneous motoring terms*, 407.11 *touch*, 726.6 *retain*, 734.7 *take*, 734.10 *take away*, 736.3 *theft*
grab away 590.10 *chase*
grab bag 113.3 *diverse thing*, 133.3 *miscellany*
grabber 734.6 *taker*
grabbing 726.1 *retention*, 734.1 *taking*, 734.3 *taking away*
grab bucket 63.29 *construction equipment*
grabby 721.16 *greedy*
grab one 471.14 *have an idea*
grab one's opportunity 210.5 *take the opportunity*
grab the limelight 811.29 *show off*
grace 10.9 *prayer*, 49.16 *musical note*, 549.2 *stylishness*, 557.5 *ornament*, 558.1 *elegance*, 655.1 *skill*, 729.2 *gift*, 789.1 *gorgeousness*, 794.1 *elegance*, 831.1 *benevolence*, 833.1 *philanthropy*, 835.3 *mercy*, 837.2 *thanks*, 839.1 *forgiveness*, 861.10 *kindness*, 863.2 *virtues*
Grace 18 Sporting Personalities
grace-and-favour 754.11 *free of charge*
grace-and-favour flat 754.6 *absence of charge*
grace before meals 837.2 *thanks*
graceful 549.7 *stylish*, 558.3 *elegant*, 794.5 *refined*, 817.7 *courteous*, 821.22 *lovable*
graceful gesture 817.5 *sign of courtesy*
gracefully 8.19 *divinely*, 549.10 *stylistically*, 558.5 *elegantly*, 817.14 *courteously*
gracefulness 558.1 *elegance*, 789.1 *gorgeousness*, 817.1 *courtesy*
graceless 559, 656.3 *clumsy*, 790.4, 790.4 *ugly*
gracelessly 559.11 *inelegantly*
gracelessness 559.1 *inelegance*, 790.1 *hideousness*
grace note 49.16 *musical note*
grace of God 831.1 *benevolence*
graces 817.3 *courtesies*
grace the occasion 253.12 *attend*
gracile 274.1 *thin*, 558.3 *elegant*, 789.5 *beautiful*
gracility 274.7 *thinness*
gracious 572.4 *helpful*, 652.17 *well-behaved*, 691.4 *lenient*, 814.8 *sociable*, 817.7 *courteous*, 819.8 *friendly*, 833.6 *philanthropic*, 835.6 *pitying*, 849.9 *showing respect*, 861.3 *kind*
gracious host 652.3 *well-behaved person*
gracious living 794.1 *elegance*
graciously 652.19 *well*, 691.6 *leniently*, 817.14 *courteously*, 819.17 *in friendship*, 835.13 *pitifully*, 849.22 *respectfully*
gracious manners 652.2 *good conduct*
graciousness 572.9 *goodwill*, 652.2 *good conduct*, 691.1 *le-

niency*, 814.2 *sociability*, 817.1, 817.1 *courtesy*, 861.10 *kindness*
grackle 78 Birds
gradation 121, 5.30 *syntax*, 150.3 *hierarchy*, 152.5 *categorization*, 319.3 *rung*
gradational 121, 150.12 *hierarchical*
grade 75 Scientific and Technical Units, 112.10 *conform*, 121.2 *rank*, 121.5 *measure*, 150.4 *position*, 150.19 *systematize*, 152.6 *category*, 152.15 *categorize*, 163.5 *social class*, 163.6 *students*, 163.14 *sort*, 259.18, 268.10 *measure*, 282.7 *make horizontal*, 284.1 *obliqueness*, 319.3 *rung*, 481.12 *discriminate*
grade crossing 327.10 *railway*
graded 121.7 *gradational*, 150.12 *hierarchical*, 152.24 *categorized*, 163.12 *classed*, 481.11 *judged*
grade school 6.12 *educational institution*
gradient 52.37 *line*, 52.50 *scalar quantity*, 72.2 *track*, 359.2 *upturn*
gradient post 72.2 *track*
gradient wind 55.12 *wind*
grading 63.29 *construction equipment*, 121.2 *rank*, 121.3 *gradation*, 152.5 *categorization*, 163.1 *classification*
gradual 121.7 *gradational*, 328.5 *unhurried*
Gradual 10.6 *Eucharist*, 10.8 *hymn*
gradualism 121.1 *degree*, 328.8 *slowness*, 627.11 *reformism*
gradualist 627.12 *reformer*
gradually 121.10 *by degrees*, 143.12 *partly*, 328.16 *slowly*
gradualness 121.1 *degree*
graduate 6.21 *curricular*, 121.5, 259.18 *measure*, 268.10 *measure*, 481.12 *discriminate*, 485.8 *qualified person*, 627.2 *get better*, 655.4 *skilled person*, 682.4 *successful person*, 682.6 *be successful*, 696.10 *expert*, 812.20 *come out*
graduated 121.7 *gradational*, 268.13 *measured*, 481.11 *judged*
graduated flask 57 Laboratory Apparatus
graduated reciprocation in tension reduction 61.5 *psychological test*
graduated scale 56.82, 268.6 *measuring instrument*
graduate school 6.12 *educational institution*
graduation 121.3 *gradation*, 152.5 *categorization*, 481.1 *discrimination*, 627.5 *improvement*, 812.3 *ceremony*, 813.3 *formal occasion*
gradus 5.28 *dictionary*
Graeco-Roman 43 Architectural Styles, 26.15 *wrestling*
Graeco-Roman art 50 Western Art Styles and Movements
Graeco-Roman wrestler 26.6 *wrestler*, 679.3 *athlete*
Graeco-Roman wrestling 26.5, 674.8 *wrestling*
Graf 18 Sporting Personalities
graffiti 545.4 *inscription*
graffito 50.9 *drawing*
graft 69.5 *gardening*, 69.15 *cultivate*, 130.4 *extra*, 137.1 *connection*, 137.11 *connect*, 245.13 *propagate*, 354.6 *plant*, 354.8 *insertion*, 630.12 *surgery*, 736.4 *stolen goods*, 736.7 *dishonesty*, 858.3 *criminality*
grafted 69.19 *ornamental*, 354.12 *inserted*
grafting 60.9 *surgery*, 69.5 *gardening*, 354.8 *insertion*, 630.12 *surgery*
graft union 69.5 *gardening*
Graham 52 Scientists
Grahame 48 Writers

Graham's law 57 Named Reactions
grain 75 General Units, **383, 384,** 83.9 *seed*, 86.1 *fruits*, 86.3 *fruit structure*, 87.4 *cereal grass*, 163.4 *type*, 234.2 *attitude*, 260.2 *little thing*, 350.8 *animal food*, 383.12 *coarsen*, 384.25 *grind*, 444.4 *pigment*, 604.1 *materials*
grain bin 68.10 *farm tool*
grain drier 68.10 *farm tool*
grained 383.8 *rough*
grain elevator 68.7 *farm building*
grain farming 68.6 *farm*
grain farming 68.11 *arable farming*
graininess 66, 384, 383.2 *grain*
grain of sand 54.27 *sediment*, 260.2 *little thing*
Grain scan 60.7 *diagnosis*
grains of sand 400.1 *humankind*
grain weevil 82 Insects, 82.3 *pest*
grainy 384, 375.2 *coarse*, 383.8 *rough*
grainy picture 534.23 *television reception*
gram 75 Scientific and Technical Units, 369.9 *avoirdupois weight*
grama grass 87 Grasses
gram atom 75 Scientific and Technical Units
gram calorie 75 Scientific and Technical Units
gramercy 837.9 *thank you*
gramigna 45 Types of Pasta
graminaceous 87.8 *grasslike*
graminaceous plant 87.1 *grass*
Gramineae 87.1 *grass*
gramineous 87.8 *grasslike*
graminiferous 87.8 *grasslike*
graminivore 87.6 *grass-eater*
graminivorous 87.10 *grass-eating*, 350.26 *eating*
graminivorousness 350.5 *eating habit*
grammar 5, 6.14 *school book*
grammar book 6.14 *school book*
grammarian 5.2 *linguist*
grammatical 5, 5.38 *linguistic*
grammatical analysis 5.30 *syntax*
grammatical error 504
grammatically 5, 5.48 *linguistically*
grammatical meaning 520.4 *type of meaning*
grammaticalness 5.29 *grammar*
grammatical rules 5.29 *grammar*
grammatical studies 5.30 *syntax*
grammatic character 5.13 *letter*
grammatologist 5.2 *linguist*
grammatology 5.1 *linguistics*
gram molecule 75 Scientific and Technical Units
gramophone record 364.6 *rotator*, 545.7 *recording*
Grampian 92 Counties, **95** Mountains
Grampian Mountains 95.5 *British mountains*
grampus 77 Placental Mammals
gramyre 11.3 *witchcraft*
Grana 45 Cheeses
Granada 93 Cities
granadilla 84 Flowers and Flowering Plants, **86** Fruits
granary 68.7 *farm building*, 605.4 *storage*
granary bread 45.38 *bread*
grand 811, 179.10 *thousand*, 256.16 *manorial*, 259.15 *big*, 554.5 *serious*, 611.5 *important*, 617.1 *worthy*, 741.3 *fortune*, 805.19 *stately*, 805.21 *ostentatious*, 811.22 *majestic*
Grand Canyon 98.8 *valley*
grand-champion 617.2 *best*
granddaughter 402.12 *woman in the family*
grand design 142.3 *whole situation*
grand duchy 91.3 *dominion*
grand duke 802.1 *nobleman*
grande dame 805.13 *proud person*
grandee 611.4 *bigwig*
grandeur 811, 259.2 *bigness*,

554.2 *seriousness*, 558.1 *elegance*, 805.6 *majesty*
grandfather 207.8 *man*, 401.13 *man in the family*
grandfather clock 191 Timepieces and Timers, 192.6 *clock*
grand fellow 617.8 *exceller*
grand finale 811.14 *show*
Grand Guignol 51.2 *play*, 51.7 *dramaturgy*
Grand hama 7.8 *priest*
grandiloquence 541.4 *bombast*, 554.2 *seriousness*, 557.2 *affectation*, 559.4 *inelegance of speech*, 564.2 *power of speech*, 811.5 *pomposity*
grandiloquent 357.13 *exaggerated*, 541.15 *bombastic*, 554.5 *serious*, 557.4 *ornate*, 559.9 *inelegant*, 564.20 *eloquent*, 811.20 *pompous*
grandiloquently 541.16 *exaggeratedly*, 554.7 *emphatically*, 557.6 *ornately*, 564.21 *orally*, 811.36 *pompously*
grandiose 357.13 *exaggerated*, 541.14 *extravagant*, 557.4 *ornate*, 811.24 *grand*
grandiosely 811.40 *grandly*
grandiosity 805.6 *majesty*, 811.9 *grandeur*
grand jury 16.26, 492.7 *jury*
grand larceny 736.1 *stealing*
grandly 811, 805.34 *imposingly*, 811.38 *majestically*
grand mal 510.3 *mental deterioration*, 624.17 *nervous disorder*
Grand Manner 50 Western Art Styles and Movements
grand master 696.10 *expert*
grandmother 207.9 *woman*, 402.12 *woman in the family*
grandmother clock 191 Timepieces and Timers, 192.6 *clock*
grandmother's footsteps 42 Children's Games and Party Games
Grand National 32.7 *horseracing*
grandness 259.2 *bigness*, 811.9 *grandeur*
Grand Old Party 12.6 *political party*
grand opening 201.4 *beginning*
grand opening sale 739.4 *sale*, 752.2 *bargain*
grand opera 49.4 *opera*
grand panjandrum 611.4 *bigwig*
grand parade 811.13 *ceremonial*
grandparents 202.2 *old people*
grand piano 49 Musical Instruments
Grand Prix 33.2 *Formula 1 race*, 33.11 *racing*
Grand Prix car 33.1 *motor racing*
Grand Prix driver 33.8 *driver*
Grand Prix Formula One Class 33.1 *motor racing*
Grand Prix race 33.1 *motor racing*, 33.5 *motorcycle racing*
Grand Prix racer 33.8 *driver*
Grand Prix racing 33.1 *motor racing*, 674.4 *race*
Grand Prix World Championship 33.1 *motor racing*
Grand Prix yacht racing 36.1 *sailing*
Grand Rapids 93 Cities
grands battements 46.10 *positions at the barre*
Grandsire Triple 49.6 *campanology*
grand slam 42.3 *card game terms*, 682.3 *successful thing*
grand-slam home run 22.5 *batting terms*
grand-slammer 22.5 *batting terms*
grandson 401.13 *man in the family*
grandstand 435.9 *viewpoint*
grandstander 811.15 *showman*
grand strategy 17.1 *military affairs*, 676.6 *art of war*
grand theft 736.1 *stealing*
grand toilette 813.4 *formal dress*
grand view 142.3 *whole situation*
grand vizier 653.16 *official*

grange 68.7 *farm building*, 256.4 *official residence*
granger 68.15 *agriculturist*
granita 45.35 *dessert*
granite 54 Common Rocks, 43.4 *building material*, 50.14 *sculptor's materials*, 63.26 *masonry*, 373.1 *hard*, 373.7 *hard substance*, 604.2 *building material*
granite moss 88.3 *moss*
Granite Peak 95 Mountains
granite rock 225.4 *stable thing*
granitic 54.57 *chalky*, 373.1 *hard*
Grannos 8 Deities
granny 207.9 *woman*
granny-bash 481.14 *discriminate against*
granny-basher 481.7 *bigot*
granny-bashing 481.4 *social discrimination*
granny flat 256.5 *house*
granny glasses 435.10 *visual aid*
granny knot 74 *Knots*, 137.6 *line*
Gran Paradiso 95 Mountains
Gran Premio de Barcelona 33.5 *motorcycle racing*
grant 116, 116, 746, 878, 878, 68.2 *Common Agricultural Policy* , 284.7 *financial support*, 284.13 *support financially*, 499.4 *assent*, 530.8 *admit*, 662.6 *financial assistance*, 673.3 *submit*, 688.3 *acquisition of power*, 688.21 *grant authority*, 708.2 *permit*, 721.5 *profit*, 725.9 *own property*, 729.1 *giving*, 729.2 *gift*, 729.5 *give*, 732.1 *lending*, 732.5 *lend*, 744.8 *credit*, 749.3 *income*, 845.6 *bond*
grant absolution 839.9 *forgive*, 848.10 *acquit*
grant a decree of nullity 824.7 *divorce*
grant a final decree 824.7 *divorce*
grant a loan 744.8 *credit*
grant amnesty 691.3 *be lenient*
grant amnesty to 839.9 *forgive*, 848.10 *acquit*
grant an annulment 824.7 *divorce*
grant an armistice 677.4 *pacify*
grant a pardon 835.10 *show mercy*
grant a respite 16.78 *acquit*
grant asylum 348.9 *welcome*, 632.9 *protect*
grant a truce 677.4 *pacify*
grant a visa to 734.11 *be hospitable*
grant bail to 700.4 *liberate*
grant clemency 677.4 *pacify*
granted 116, 518.8 *supposed*, 688.13 *elected*, 729.7 *given*, 749.6 *received*
granted amnesty 691.5 *given consideration*, 839.6 *forgiven*
granted for the sake of argument 518.8 *supposed*
grantee 730.5 *recipient*
grant equality to 700.6 *treat equally*
grant equal rights to 700.6 *treat equally*
Granth 7.12 *religious text*
grant immunity 698.15 *set free*, 708.3 *permit*, 839.9 *forgive*, 848.9 *exempt*
grant impunity 848.9 *exempt*
grant-in-aid 729.2 *gift*, 746.4 *grant*
granting 106.15 *under the circumstances*, 729.1, 729.8 *giving*
granting a visa 734.4 *taking in*
grant-maintained school 6.12 *educational institution*
grantor 729.4 *giver*
grant peace 677.4 *pacify*
grant permission 851.12 *accept*
grant power of attorney 703.6 *commission*
grant remission 855.7 *vindicate*
granular 260.7 *little*, 383.8 *rough*, 384.18 *grainy*
granularity 384.3 *graininess*
granularly 384.30 *flakily*

granular snow 55.30 *snow*, 409.5 *ice*
granular texture 383.2 *grain*
granulate 373.10 *solidify*, 375.12 *make rough*, 383.12 *coarsen*, 384.25 *grind*, 384.28 *come to dust*
granulated 373.3 *hardened*, 375.2 *coarse*, 383.8 *rough*, 384.19 *pulverized*
granulated sugar 45.7 *basic ingredient*, 414.2 *sweetener*
granulation 373.6 *solidification*, 375.6 *roughness*, 383.2 *grain*, 384.3 *graininess*, 384.4 *pulverization*
granule 53.15 *sun*, 68.13 *fertilizer*, 260.2 *little thing*, 384.7 *grain*
granules 54.27 *sediment*
granulet 384.7 *grain*
granulite 54 Common Rocks
granulization 384.4 *pulverization*
granulize 384.25 *grind*
grape 54 Fruits, 338.8 *missile*
grape fern 88 Ferns
grapefruit 86 Fruits
grapefruit juice 351.6 *soft drink*
grape hyacinth 84 Flowers and Flowering Plants
grapeshot 338.8 *missile*, 680.14 *historical ammunition*
grapevine 86.5 *figurative usage*, 420.8 *something heard*, 528.8 *source of information*
graph 52, 50.9 *drawing*, 52.96 *represent*, 118.5 *duplicate*, 152.8 *chart*, 299.1, 299.5 *outline*, 547.2 *reproduction*
grapheme 5.13 *letter*, 5.16 *spoken letter*
graphemics 5.1 *linguistics*
graphic 5.41 *lettered*, 48.18 *descriptive*, 50.24, 52.78 *pictorial*, 101.7 *realistic*, 114.9 *lifelike*, 152.26 *diagrammatic*, 522.1 *intelligible*, 547.13 *representational*, 554.3 *emphatic*, 560.11 *descriptive*
graphically 5.48 *linguistically*, 50.30 *pictorially*, 114.14 *comparably*, 547.14 *representationally*, 560.18 *descriptively*
graphic artist 50.16 *artist*, 547.4 *person who makes a representation*
graphic arts 50.1 *art*
graphic character 65.10 *character*
graphic equalizer 420.10 *sound quality*
graphicness 522.9 *intelligibility*
graphic representation 52.32 *graph*
graphics 547.2 *reproduction*
graphite 57 Chemical Elements, 384.6, 395.5 *lubricant*, 621.9 *cleaning agent*
graphitic 57.34 *elemental*
graphology 524.5 *science of interpretation*
graphophobia 777 Phobias by Name
graph paper 52.32 *graph*
grapnel 632.4 *safety device*, 726.3 *tools for gripping*
grapple 26.5 *wrestling*, 26.12 *wrestle*, 85.7 *timber production*, 135.8 *unite*, 135.10 *link*, 137.9 *yoke*, 670.9 *attack successfully*, 674.8 *wrestling*, 674.11 *contend*, 674.12, 679.37 *fight*, 726.6 *retain*
grappler 26.6 *wrestler*, 674.10 *contender*, 699.3 *athlete*
grapple with 138.6 *adhere*, 574.9 *undertake*, 663.16 *confront*, 670.5 *strike*, 674.11 *contend*
grappling 674.14 *contending*
grappling iron 137.9 *yoke*, 632.4 *safety device*, 726.3 *tools for gripping*
graptolite 54.43 *fossil*
Grasmere 94 Lakes, 94 4 *British lakes*
grasp 4.21 *rationalize*, 138.6 *adhere*, 235.2 *ability*, 248.7 *range*,

407.11 *touch*, 471.14 *have an idea*, 501.1 *knowledge*, 501.13 *get to know*, 507.7 *be wise*, 522.6 *understand*, 522.12 *understanding*, 632.2 *protection*, 637.5 *preserve*, 696.15 *learn*, 723.1 *possession*, 726.1 *retention*, 726.6 *retain*, 734.7 *take*
grasped 726.10 *retained*
grasping 407.2 *touching*, 721.16 *greedy*, 726.9 *retentive*, 734.1, 734.12 *taking*
graspingly 734.13 *avariciously*
grasping nature 734.1 *taking*
grasp the meaning 522.6 *understand*
grasp the nettle 574.9, 597.1 *undertake*
grass 87, 25.2 *grip*, 77.37 *graze*, 87.2 *grassland*, 87.12 *manage grassland*, 350.8 *animal food*, 453.8 *greenness*, 480.3 *testify*, 480.7 *verifier*, 483.7 *person who gives evidence*, 528.10 *informer*, 528.13 *inform on*, 530.4 *discloser*, 530.7 *betray*, 565.4 *talker*, 578.9 *equivocator*, 856.3 *accuser*, 856.5 *accuse*, 875.6 *drug*
Grass 48 Writers
grass-covered 87.9 *grassy*
grass cutter 380.9 *sharp-edged thing*
grass-cutter 87
grass-eater 87
grass-eating 87
grasses 83.3 *seed plant*
Grasses 87
grass family 87.1 *grass*
grassfinch 78 Birds
grass flower 87.3 *grass plant*
grass-green 87.9 *grassy*, 453.1 *green*
grasshopper 82 Insects, 82.1 *insect*
grassland 87, 68.11 *farmland*, 83.1 *plants*, 98.6 *lowland*, 248.3 *geographical space*, 453.8 *greenness*
grassless 392.6 *desert*
grasslike 87
grasslike plant 87.1 *grass*
grass monkey 77 Placental Mammals
grass of Parnassus 84 Flowers and Flowering Plants, **87** Grasses
grass on 483.13 *turn Queen's evidence*
grass over 87.12 *manage grassland*
grass plant 87
grass roots 87.7 *figurative usage*, 164.11 *general public*, 611.3 *chief thing*, 611.5 *important*
grass-roots 803.2 *the common people*
grass-roots movement 665.3 *political grouping*
grass silage 68.9 *animal feedstuff*
grass-skiing 41.1 *skiing*
grass skirt 295.6 *skirt*
grass snake 79 Reptiles
grasstrack 33.11 *racing*
grasstrack racing 33.1 *motor racing*
grass tree 87 Grasses
grass up 483.13 *turn Queen's evidence*
grass widow 87.7 *figurative usage*, 824.4 *divorced person*, 824.6 *surviving spouse*
grass widower 824.6 *surviving spouse*
grass widowerhood 824.1 *divorce*, 824.5 *widowhood*
grass widowhood 824.1 *divorce*, 824.5 *widowhood*
grassy 87, 69.17 *botanical*, 83.13 *plantlike*, 374.4 *compressible*, 453.2 *verdant*
grate 384, 45.55 *cook*, 117.12 *be disparate*, 322.6 *porous thing*, 375.12 *make rough*, 385.15 *grind*, 408.6 *fire*, 430.4 *be strident*, 430.5 *sound hoarse*, 432.6 *buzz*, 434.10 *lack harmony*,

785.7 *cause dislike*, 822.16 *cause hate*
grated 375.2 *coarse*, 384.19 *pulverized*
grated cheese 45 Cheeses
grateful 837, 851.18 *approving*
gratefully 837
gratefulness 837.1 *gratitude*
grateful thanks 837.2 *thanks*
grate on one's ears 430.4 *be strident*
grater 384, 45.6 *kitchen equipment*, 375.7 *rough thing*
gratification 405.1 *physical pleasure*, 691.1 *leniency*, 765.1 *satisfaction*
gratified 405.7 *pleased*, 691.5 *given consideration*, 765.4 *satisfied*, 837.4 *grateful*
gratify 405.9 *give pleasure*, 691.3 *be lenient*, 765.3 *give pleasure*, 765.8 *satisfy*, 771.15 *humour*, 805.30 *make proud*
gratifying 405.6, 763.1 *pleasant*, 765.5 *satisfying*
gratifyingly 691.6 *leniently*
gratin dish 45.6 *kitchen equipment*
grating 36.8 *punting*, 56.29 *optical element*, 117.2 *contradiction*, 117.8 *contradictory*, 384.4 *pulverization*, 385.9 *irritation*, 385.11 *rough*, 430.7 *strident*, 434.7 *dissonant*, 559.9 *inelegant*
gratis 729.7 *given*, 729.9 *as a gift*, 754.11 *free of charge*
gratitude 837, 851.2 *admiration*, 878.1 *reward*
Gratitude 837
gratuitous 518.7 *suppositional*, 721.15 *gainful*, 729.7 *given*, 754.11 *free of charge*, 807.18 *insulting*, 846.10 *undue*
gratuitously 721.20 *gainfully*, 729.9 *as a gift*, 846.18 *unduly*
gratuitousness 754.6 *absence of charge*, 846.5 *undueness*
gratuity 130.4 *extra*, 228.5 *positive stimulus*, 721.5 *profit*, 729.2 *gift*, 746.3 *pay*, 754.6 *absence of charge*, 837.3 *recognition*, 878.7 *bounty*
grav 75 Scientific and Technical Units
gravadlax 45.16 *fish dish*
gravamen 103.2 *essential content*, 856.1 *accusation*
grave 399, 5.36 *accent*, 50.22 *engrave*, 218.5 *resting place*, 277.4 *deep thing*, 317.2 *concave land*, 323.4 *closed place*, 325.3 *resting place*, 397.8 *after death*, 554.5 *serious*, 611.5 *important*, 772.1 *solemn*, 805.19 *stately*, 813.6 *formal*, 876.10 *moralistic*
grave accent 543.7 *punctuation*
grave affair 611.2 *important matter*
grave clothes 295, 399.4 *funeral objects*
grave digger 317.4 *digger*, 399.3 *funeral director*
gravel 54.27 *sediment*, 54.36 *soil*, 63.26 *masonry*, 293.11 *paving*, 293.29 *surface*, 384.9 *grit*, 604.2 *building material*
gravelliness 384.3 *graininess*
gravelly 54.58 *earthy*, 373.1 *hard*, 375.2 *coarse*, 384.18 *grainy*, 424.4 *faint*, 430.8 *hoarse*
gravel road 327.3 *road*
gravely 554.7 *emphatically*, 772.10 *solemnly*, 805.33 *with dignity*
graven 50.25 *sculptural*
graveness 876.4 *self-righteousness*
graven image 9.3 *idol*, 547.6 *image*
grave note 427.3 *deepness*
graveolent 419.3 *stinking*
grave pit 399.6 *grave*
graver 47.11 *woodworking tool*, 50.15 *engraving*
grave-robber 736.9 *plunderer*
grave-robbing 355.3 *digging out*, 736.5 *plundering*, 736.17 *stolen*

Graves 48 Writers, **48** Poets
graveside service 399.2 *funeral*
graveside services 397.8 *after death*
gravestone 293.2 *cover*, 399.4 *funeral objects*, 545.11 *monument*
grave-wax 141.1 *disintegration*
graveyard 218.5, 325.3 *resting place*, 397.8 *after death*, 399.5 *cemetery*
graveyard poetry 48 Literary Groups and Movements
gravid 245.16 *reproductive*, 513.6 *expectant*
gravimetric 54.49 *geophysical*, 57.41 *analytic*
gravimetric analysis 57
gravimetry 54.2 *geophysics*, 57.18 *gravimetric analysis*
gravitas 772.4 *solemnity*
gravitate 360.9 *descend*, 369.12 *be heavy*
gravitate towards 234.4 *tend*
gravitation 234.2 *attitude*, 235.1 *power*, 360.2 *sinkage*, 369.5 *gravity*
gravitational 340.10 *magnetic*
gravitational collapse 53.11 *stellar birth*
gravitational constant 53.4 *cosmological model*
gravitational force 53.4 *cosmological model*, 56.10 *force*
gravitational interaction 56.79 *fundamental interaction*
gravitational pull 369.5 *gravity*
gravitational redshift 53.7 *galaxy*
gravity 777 Phobias by Topic, **369**, 120.1 *quantity*, 233 *influence*, 235.1 *power*, 340.2 *pulling power*, 367.1 *material world*, 554.2 *seriousness*, 611.1 *importance*, 772.4 *solemnity*, 772.6 *importance*, 805.6 *majesty*, 813.1 *formality*, 876.4 *self-righteousness*
gravity dam 63.23 *dam*
gravity geophysics 54.2 *geophysics*
gravity-operated railway 327.10 *railway*
gravy 45.15 *sauce*, 387.2 *juice*, 393.7 *soup*, 721.5 *profit*, 729.2 *gift*, 741.2 *cash*
gravy boat 258.16 *crockery*
gray 75 SI Units, **75** Scientific and Technical Units
Gray 48 Poets, **52** Scientists
grayhound 329.4 *be swift*
grayling 80 Fishes, 20.5 *British game fish*, 45.17 *freshwater fish*
gray panther 207.7 *older person*
Gray Panther 448.6 *figurative usage*
Graz 93 Cities
graze 77, 68.18 *practise livestock farming*, 87.11 *eat grass*, 267.2 *meeting*, 267.4 *meet*, 278.4 *shallow thing*, 278.6 *be shallow*, 350.21 *eat*, 350.24 *have a meal*, 350.25 *provide food*, 385.13 *abrade*, 406.3 *injury*, 406.11 *inflict pain*, 407.3 *press*, 407.11 *touch*, 407.12 *abut*, 872.5 *be greedy*
grazed 68.20 *farmable*, 406.6 *injured*
grazer 76.4 *type of animal*, 87.6 *grass-eater*
grazier 68.15 *agriculturist*, 243.9 *producer*
grazing 68.3 *livestock farming*, 68.11 *farmland*, 87.2 *grassland*, 87.10 *grass-eating*, 267.6 *meeting*, 350.4 *eating meals*, 350.5 *eating habit*, 350.26 *eating*, 385.4 *scraping*
grazing-incidence telescope 53.26 *radio telescope*
grease 45.7 *basic ingredient*, 374.13 *soften*, 376.10 *polish*, 376.11 *smooth*, 386.4 *lubricant*, 386.13 *lubricate*, 395.5 *lubricant*, 395.7, 395.17 *oil*, 424.2 *sound reducer*, 622.11 *dirty*, 660.16 *make easy*, 729.2 *gift*

greaseball 91 Names for Inhabitants
greased 376.4 *polished*, 395.15 *basted*, 395.16 *lubricated*
greased lightning 329.11 *swift thing*
greased palm 586.9 *enticement*
grease gun 376.10 *polish*, 386.7 *lubricator*, 395.5 *lubricant*
grease job 386.1, 395.3 *lubrication*
grease leather 386.13 *lubricate*, 395.17 *oil*
grease monkey 646.2 *artisan*
greasepaint 51.1 *drama*, 51.19 *stage requisite*, 295.5 *fancy dress*, 791.4 *cosmetics*
grease pit 395.5 *lubricant*
greaseproof paper 45.6 *kitchen equipment*, 604.3 *paper*
greaser 91 Names for Inhabitants, 71.14 *cyclist*
grease rack 395.5 *lubricant*
grease the palm 586.17 *bribe*, 729.5 *give*, 878.11 *pay*
grease the ways 660.16 *make easy*
grease the wheels 395.17 *oil*, 586.16 *tempt*, 660.16 *make easy*, 662.28 *further*
greasewood 85 Trees and Shrubs
greasily 386.16, 395.20 *oilily*
greasiness 376.7 *smoothness*, 386.2, 395.1 *oiliness*
greasing 395.3 *lubrication*
greasy 376.4 *polished*, 386.10, 395.11 *oily*, 395.16 *lubricated*, 622.7 *dirty*, 853.15 *unctuous*
greasy junkie 875.4 *drug taker*
greasy rock 34.2 *climbing dangers*
greasy spoon 350.15 *eating place*
great 861, 233.11 *influential*, 235.13 *powerful*, 237.10 *potent*, 248.13 *spacious*, 259.15 *big*, 369.1 *heavy*, 608.2 *plentiful*, 611.5 *important*, 617.1 *worthy*, 696.12 *masterful*, 861.1 *good*
great and small 111.2 *opposites*
great auk 78.8 *extinct bird*
Great Australian Bight 98.9 *inlet*
Great Barrier Reef 98.2 *island*
Great Bear 53 The Constellations, **94** Lakes, 94.5 *other major lakes*
great big 259.15 *big*
great bloodshed 398.4 *slaughter*
Great Britain 98 Islands, **91**
great catch 611.4 *bigwig*
great circle 52.42 *circle*, 176.8 *half*
great-circle sailing 74.5 *navigation*
Great Cluster in Hercules 53 Clusters
greatcoat 295.12 *coat*
great crested grebe 78 Birds
Great Dane 77 Breeds of Dogs
great day 611.2 *important matter*, 773.1 *rejoicing*, 812.5 *anniversary*
great distance 263
Great Divide 275.4 *mountain range*
Great Dog 53 The Constellations
great doings 611.2 *important matter*, 642.1 *activity*
greaten 261.6 *become bigger*
greater 52.75 *equal*, 120.6 *quantitative*, 126.12 *superior*
greater and greater 128.8 *increasingly*
greater city 93.1 *city*
greater doxology 10.8 *hymn*
greater good 580.8 *choice*
greater importance 194
Greater London 93.5 London
Greater New York 93.3 *New York*
greater number 175.3 *majority*
greater part 143.5 *largest part*, 175.3 *majority*
greater proportion 175.3 *majority*
greater than 52.88 *equal to*
greater than or equal to 52.88 *equal to*

greatest 52.75 *equal*, 126.14 *best*
greatest elongation 53.16 *planet*
greatest good of the greatest
number 833.2 *public spiritedness*
greatest number 175.3 *majority*
great expectations 199.4 *looking to the future*, 775.3 *aspiration*
great gun 680.11 *guns*
great house 243.8 *construction*
great hundred 179.9 *treble figures*
Great Lake 94 *Lakes*
Great Looped Nebula 53 *Nebulae*
greatly 259.20 *largely*, 369.16 *heavily*, 611.1 *worthily*
great man 611.4 *bigwig*
Great Mogul 696.2 *sovereign*
Great Mother 8.3 *God*
Great Nebula in Orion 53 *Nebulae*
greatness 126.1 *superiority*, 233 *influence*, 235.1 *power*, 237.1 *strength*, 259.2 *bigness*, 611.1 *importance*, 617.6 *worth*, 688.2 *authoritativeness*, 861.8 *good*
great news 611.2 *important matter*
great number 181.2 *multitude*
Great Ouse 96 *Rivers*
great quantity 120.2 *certain amount*, 608.8 *plenty*, 610.1 *excess*
great respect 849.2 *admiration*
Great Salt Lake 94 *Lakes*, 98 *Deserts*, 94.3 *US lakes*
Great Sandy 98 *Deserts*
great seal 544.3 *means of identification*
Great Slave 94 *Lakes*, 94.5 *other major lakes*
great speed 329.8 *speed*
Great Square of Pegasus 53 *Other Groups of Stars*
great success 682.1 *success*
great thing 611.3 *chief thing*
great tit 78 *Birds*
great unwashed 803.2 *the common people*
Great Victoria 98 *Deserts*
Great Vowel Shift 5.37 *linguistic theory*
Great Wall of China 661.3, 671.9 *barrier*
great waters 97.1 *sea*
great way 263.2 *great distance*
Great White Hope 674.10 *contender*
great work 243
great work of literature 655.3 *masterpiece*
great worth 753.6 *value*
Great Yarmouth 93 *Cities*
greave 671.7 *armour*
grebe 78 *Birds*, 78.3 *water bird*
grebo 49.9 *popular music*
Grecian 43 *Architectural Styles*
Grecian couch 47.2 *chair*
Greece 91 *Countries*
greed 350.2 *appetite*, 357.9 *excessiveness*, 721.1 *gain*, 734.1 *taking*, 782.1 *desire*, 860.1 *selfishness*, 870.3 *overindulgence*, 872.1 *gluttony*
greedily 350.28 *carnivorously*, 357.16 *excessively*, 721.20 *gainfully*, 734.13 *avariciously*, 860.8 *selfishly*, 872.7 *gluttonously*
greediness 872.1 *gluttony*
greedy 721, 350.26 *eating*, 609.2 *unprovided*, 734.12 *taking*, 782.9 *desirous*, 860.4 *selfish*, 870.8 *overindulgent*, 872.6 *gluttonous*
greedy guts 872.4 *glutton*
greedy person 734.6 *taker*, 872.4 *glutton*
greedy pig 782.6 *desirer*, 872.4 *glutton*
Greek 5 *Languages and Groups of Languages*, 5.41 *lettered*, 400.4 *civilized human*, 521.4 *senseless talk*
Greek alphabet 5.14 *alphabet*
Greek chorus 51.21 *role*
Greek cross plan 43.10 *church architecture*
Greek dish 45
Greek drama 51.2 *play*

Greek fire 408.6 *fire*, 680.16 *bomb*
Greek gift 539.14 *fatal gift*, 657.2 *stratagem*
Greek meeting Greek 122.8 *on equal terms*
Greek meets Greek 122.2 *equilibrium*
Greek Orthodox 7 *Christian Movements*
Greek Revival 43 *Architectural Styles*
Greek salad 45.52 *Greek dish*
Greek theatre 51.14 *theatre*
Greek tragedy 51.9 *tragedy*
green 453, 453, 18.2 *sportsground*, 25.1 *green bowling*, 25.2 *grip*, 29.1 *golf*, 41.12 *ski*, 56.28, 56.28 *colour*, 74.11 *nautical*, 83.13 *plantlike*, 83.14 *of plants*, 87.2 *grassland*, 87.9 *grassy*, 201.12, 206.12 *immature*, 217.4 *conservationist*, 282.3 *flat thing*, 415.5 *acid*, 453.2 *verdant*, 453.3 *raw*, 453.6 *sick*, 453.7 *environmental*, 453.8 *greenness*, 497.12 *gullible*, 502.6 *ignorant*, 585.1 *unaccustomed*, 595.5 *immature*, 624.21 *unhealthy*, 637.4 *preservationist*, 637.6 *preserving*, 656.2 *unskilled*, 658.1 *naive*, 665.10 *political*, 741.2 *cash*, 820.6 *hostile*, 841.4 *jealous*, 865.7 *naive*
Green 48 *Writers*, 48 *Writers*, 12.9 *governmental*, 665.6 *political party member*
green about the gills 238.10 *ill*
green algae 90.2 *algae*
green and blacks 761.6 *desensitizing substance*
green apple 415.3 *sour thing*
green around the gills 453.6, 624.22 *sick*
greenback 453.12 *figurative usage*, 741.8 *American money*
green bacon 45.30 *bacon*
green ball 24.5 *snooker*
Green Bay 93 *Cities*, 453.12 *figurative usage*
green bean 453.9 *greenstuff*
green belt 93.8 *suburb*, 248.3 *geographical space*, 249.6 *regions*, 297.1 *surroundings*, 453.8 *greenness*
Green Berets 453.12 *figurative usage*
green-blue 454.1 *blue*
greenbottle 82 *Insects*
green bowling 25
green cabbage 45 *Vegetables*
green card 71.21 *miscellaneous motoring terms*, 453.11 *green thing*, 708.2 *permit*
green dragon 453.11 *green thing*, 875.6 *drug*
Greene 48 *Writers*
green envy 453.14 *green-eyed monster*
greenery 83.1 *plants*, 83.6 *leaf*, 453.8 *greenness*
green-eyed 453, 820.6 *hostile*, 822.10 *hating*, 841.4 *jealous*, 842.2 *envious*
green-eyed jealousy 841.1 *jealousy*
green-eyed monster 453, 841.1 *jealousy*, 842.1 *envy*
greenfinch 78 *Birds*, 453.11 *green thing*
green-fingered 655.6 *skilful*
green fingers 69.5 *gardening*, 453.8 *greenness*, 485.2 *ability*, 655.2 *aptitude*
greenfly 82 *Insects*, 69.12 *pests and diseases*, 82.3 *pest*, 453.11 *green thing*
greengage 86 *Fruits*, 453.9 *greenstuff*
greengrocer 86.4 *fruit eating*, 350.17 *food shop*, 350.20 *food provider*, 453.9 *greenstuff*, 606.3 *provider*, 739.13 *retailer*
greenheart 85 *Trees and Shrubs*, 453.11 *green thing*
greenhorn 104.7 *new arrival*,

149.7 *newcomer*, 156.14 *beginner*, 201.8 *new arrival*, 453.13 *young thing*, 502.5 *ignorant person*, 539.22 *dupe*, 656.10 *unskilled person*, 658.3 *naive person*, 865.4 *innocent person*
green hornet 453.11 *green thing*, 875.6 *drug*
greenhouse 69.4 *nursery*, 226.2 *source*, 256.7 *room*, 379.3 *brittle thing*, 408.8 *hot place*, 442.8 *transparent thing*, 453.12 *figurative usage*
greenhouse effect 55.40 *climatic change*, 408.5 *hot weather*, 453.12 *figurative usage*, 626.1 *lack of hygiene*, 631.9 *pollution*
greenhouse gas 631.9 *pollution*
greenhouse gases 408.5 *hot weather*
green ice 453.11 *green thing*
greening 453.16 *green politics*
greenish 453.1 *green*
greenish-yellow 452.1 *yellow*
greenkeeper 453.8 *greenness*
green labelling 453.16 *green politics*
Greenland 97 *Oceans and Seas*, 98 *Islands*, 453.12 *figurative usage*
Greenland Sea 453.12 *figurative usage*
Greenland shark 80 *Fishes*
green leek 453.9 *greenstuff*
greenlet 453.11 *green thing*
green light 453, 116.7 *consent*, 439.6 *electric light*, 499.2 *yes*, 543.4 *signal*, 851.1 *approval*
greenly 453, 206.15 *immaturely*
greenmail 453.12 *figurative usage*, 737.9 *bargaining*, 738.7 *purchasing*
green man 439.6 *electric light*
green manure 68.12 *crop*, 68.13 *fertilizer*
green monkey disease 624.7 *tropical disease*
Green Mountains 453.12 *figurative usage*
green movement 637.1 *preservation*
greenness 453, 201.3, 206.3 *immaturity*, 415.1 *sourness*, 595.10 *immaturity*, 656.8 *unskilfulness*, 658.2, 865.3 *naivety*
Greenness 453
Greenock 93 *Cities*
greenockite 54 *Minerals*
green old age 207.5 *old age*
green paper 453.11 *green thing*, 528.3 *document*
Green Party 12.6 *political party*, 453.16 *green politics*, 665.3 *political grouping*
Green Party member 217.4 *conservationist*
Greenpeace 453.16 *green politics*, 627.11 *reformism*, 637.1 *preservation*
Greenpeace member 637.4 *preservationist*
green pepper 45 *Vegetables*, 453.9 *greenstuff*
green pigment 453
green plant 83.2 *plant*
green plants 83.1 *plants*
green politics 453
green porphyry 453.11 *green thing*
green pound 14.1 *finance*, 68.2 *Common Agricultural Policy*, 453.12 *figurative usage*, 741.7 *finance*
Green Revolution 68.4 *arable farming*, 246.1 *fertility*
Green River 453.12 *figurative usage*
greenroom 51.15 *stage*, 453.12 *figurative usage*
green run 41.1 *skiing*
greens 45.33 *vegetable*, 453.9 *greenstuff*
Greens 453.16 *green politics*
green salad 45.14 *salad*
greensand 453.11 *green thing*
Greensboro 93 *Cities*

greenshank 78 *Birds*, 453.11 *green thing*
greensick 453.6 *sick*
green snake 453.11 *green thing*
Green's theorem 52 *Named Concepts*
greenstick fracture 453.13 *young thing*
greenstone 453.11 *green thing*
greenstuff 453
green stuff 741.2 *cash*
greensward 87.2 *grassland*
green tea 351.3 *tea*, 453.13 *young thing*
green the desert 246.7 *make fertile*
green thing 453
greentop 27.5 *wicket*
green turtle 79 *Reptiles*, 453.11 *green thing*
green vegetable 45.33, 69.11 *vegetable*
green vegetables 86.1 *fruits*
Greenville 93 *Cities*
Greenwich Mean Time 185.9 *time zone*
Greenwich Village 93.3 *New York*
green with envy 453.5 *green-eyed*, 828.15 *resentful*, 842.2 *envious*
greenwood 85.4 *trees*, 453.8 *greenness*
greet 817, 543.11 *gesture*, 567.9 *approach*, 730.10 *receive someone*, 815.14 *welcome*, 819.15 *be hospitable*, 849.20 *salute*
greeting 849, 344.12 *reception*, 564.7 *utterance*, 567.2 *salutation*, 730.4 *reception*, 815.9 *welcome*, 817.5 *sign of courtesy*
greetings 344.24 *welcome*, 431.4 *cry of greeting*, 567.15 *hail*, 849.7 *respects*
gregale 55 *Winds*
gregarious 815.15 *sociable*
gregariously 815.18 *sociably*
gregariousness 815.1 *sociability*
Gregorian calendar 185.13 *timer*, 192.3 *chronology*
Gregorian chant 10.8 *hymn*
Gregorian mode 49.20 *key*
Gregory 52 *Scientists*
Gregory's series 52 *Named Concepts*
greige 446.1 *white*, 448.1 *grey*, 448.4 *greyness*
gremlin 11.11 *ghost*, 73.7 *miscellaneous aviation terms*, 618.11 *harmfulness*, 661.7 *hinderer*
Grenada 91 *Countries*, 98 *Islands*
grenade 425.3 *banger*, 680.16 *bomb*
grenadier 80 *Fishes*, 679.13 *historical soldiery*
Grenadier Guard 679.12 *ceremonial troops*
grenadine 67 *Natural Fabrics*, 351.7 *alcoholic drink*
Grenoble 93 *Cities*
Gresham's law 628.7 *deterioration*
Gretna Green wedding 823.5 *wedding*
grey 448, 448, 32.1 *horse*, 55.49 *cloudy*, 112.8 *monotonous*, 124.3 *mediocre*, 167.6, 167.14 *conformist*, 202.11 *old*, 207.17 *age*, 333.4 *middle*, 441.5 *dim*, 445.7 *colourless*, 446.3 *white-haired*, 770.6 *depressed*
grey area 158.6 *middle ground*, 448.6 *figurative usage*
grey arsenic 57 *Chemical Elements*
greybeard 207.7 *older person*, 207.8 *man*, 448.6 *figurative usage*
grey-black 447.1 *black*
grey-blue 454.1 *blue*
grey colour 448.4 *greyness*
grey eminence 233.4 *indirect influence*
Grey Friar 7 *Members of Reli-*

gious Orders, 448.5 *grey thing*, 743.10 *poor person*

grey-green 453.1 *green*

grey hair 448.5 *grey thing*

grey-haired 448, 202.11 *old*, 207.14 *aged*, 446.3 *white-haired*

grey-headed 448.2 *grey-haired*

greyhen 78.11 *female bird*

grey hen 448.5 *grey thing*

greyhound 77 Breeds of Dogs, 329.12 *swift animal*, 448.5 *grey thing*

greyhound racing 18 Sporting Activities, 674.4 *race*

greying 207.12 *ageing*, 448.2 *grey-haired*

greyish 448.1 *grey*

greyishness 448.4 *greyness*

grey knight 448.6 *figurative usage*

greylag 448.5 *grey thing*

greylag goose 78 Birds

greyly 448, 202.11 *venerably*

grey man 448.6 *figurative usage*

grey market 448.6 *figurative usage*, 740.3 *sellers' market*

grey matter 448.6 *figurative usage*, 459.7 *brain*, 507.2 *intelligence*

grey mould 69.12 *pests and diseases*

grey mullet 80 Fishes, 20.5 *British game fish*

greyness 448, 112.4 *monotony*, 207.5 *old age*, 441.2 *murk*, 446.7 *whiteness*

Greyness 448

Grey Nun 7 Members of Religious Orders

grey pigment 448.4 *greyness*

grey population 448.6 *figurative usage*

grey squirrel 77 Placental Mammals, 448.5 *grey thing*

grey thing 448

greywacke 448.5 *grey thing*

grey whale 448.5 *grey thing*

grey wolf 77 Placental Mammals, 448.5 *grey thing*

gribble 81.4 *arthropod*

gricer 72.10 *miscellaneous*

grid 33.6 *motor racing terms*, 51.15 *stage*, 64.20 *electron tube*, 235.7 *electrical power*, 288.2 *braid*

griddle 45.5 *cooker*, 45.55 *cook*, 408.4 *burner*

gridiron 19.4 *stadium*, 51.15 *stage*, 282.3 *flat thing*

gridlock 71.21 *miscellaneous motoring terms*, 159.8 *procession*, 218.2 *stop*, 325.1 *motionlessness*

grid reference 250.2 *exact location*

grief 631.2 *adversity*, 770.1 *sorrow*, 862.2 *affliction*

grief-stricken 770.5 *sad*, 862.8 *afflicted*

Grieg 49 Musicians and Composers

grievance 15.4 *industrial dispute*, 844.7 *sense of wrong*

grievance procedure 15.4 *industrial dispute*

grieve 770, 397.17 *bury*, 687.9 *be in trouble*, 774.6 *lament*, 828.9 *offend*, 835.9 *sorrow*, 835.11 *excite pity*

grieve for 759.18 *feel for*, 835.9 *sorrow*

griever 774.3 *lamenter*

grieving 774.1 *lamentation*, 774.4 *lamenting*

grievous 618.4 *poor*, 770.7 *distressing*, 835.7 *pitiful*, 862.8 *afflicted*

grievous bodily harm 330.12 *collision*, 670.16 *terrorist attack*, 832.7 *act of malevolence*

grievously 687.12 *in adversity*, 862.13 *destructively*

griffin 76.7 *legendary beast*, 78.9 *fabulous bird*, 544.8 *heraldic device*

Griffiths 48 Dramatists

griffon 77 Breeds of Dogs

griffon vulture 78 Birds

Grigg–Skjellerup 53 Comets

grill 45.5 *cooker*, 45.32 *meat dish*, 45.55 *cook*, 408.4 *burner*, 408.14 *be hot*, 449.7 *brown*, 477.18 *interrogate*

grille 71 Motor Vehicle Parts

grille 40.5 *real tennis*, 322.6 *porous thing*

grilled 45.56 *culinary*, 449.2 *browned*, 477.16 *questioned*

grille penthouse 40.5 *real tennis*

grilling 45.8 *cooking technique*, 477.2 *questioning*

grill room 350.15 *eating place*

grilse 80.3 *young fish*

grim 440.11 *benighted*, 574.3 *strong-willed*, 577.3 *unyielding*, 618.3 *bad*, 772.1 *solemn*, 777.10 *frightening*, 818.5 *discourteous*, 830.6 *sullen*, 832.12 *callous*

grimace 309.2 *facial distortion*, 309.10 *make faces*, 435.6, 435.13 *look*, 543.3, 543.11 *gesture*, 785.6 *react against*, 829.2 *sign of irascibility*, 829.7 *frown*, 830.4 *sign of irritableness*, 830.11 *be irritable*

grimacing 543.15 *gestural*, 829.5 *showing irascibility*

Grimaldi 53 Lunar Features

grimalkin 77.10 *cat*

grim determination 574.12 *resolution*

grime 440.3 *dark colour*, 622.4 *dirt*, 622.11 *dirty*

griminess 622.1 *dirtiness*

grimly 440.15 *darkly*, 818.9 *discourteously*, 830.13 *sullenly*

Grimm's law 5.37 *linguistic theory*

grimness 440.7 *spiritual darkness*, 577.6 *determination*, 618.9 *badness*, 772.4 *solemnity*, 830.1 *sullenness*, 832.3 *callousness*

Grimsby 93 Cities

grim-visaged war 676.1 *war*

grimy 440.10 *dark-coloured*, 443.2 *shady*, 622.7 *dirty*

grin 762.7 *show joy*, 769.7 *be cheerful*

grin and bear it 574.11 *persist*, 673.4 *succumb*, 769.7 *be cheerful*, 778.5 *take courage*

grind 384, 385, 44.11 *make ceramics*, 45.55 *cook*, 136.9 *separate*, 244.9 *demolish*, 262.5 *make smaller*, 350.21 *eat*, 380.15 *make sharp*, 406.10 *be painful*, 430.4 *be strident*, 430.5 *sound hoarse*, 584.3 *way*, 644.1, 644.6 *work*

grind down 807.26 *oppress*

grinder 45.6 *kitchen equipment*, 45.11 *sandwich*, 63.9 *machine tool*, 262.4 *contractor*, 380.11 *tooth*, 384.11 *pulverizer*

grinding 385, 44.5 *ceramic process*, 244.2 *destroying*, 262.1 *contraction*, 384.4 *pulverization*, 385.11 *rough*, 406.5 *painful*, 644.10 *working*

grind into the dust 244.9 *demolish*

grindstone 380.12 *sharpener*, 384.11 *pulverizer*, 644.1 *work*, 788.2 *boring thing*

grind to a halt 218.6 *cease*

grind to dust 244.9 *demolish*

grind to powder 244.9 *demolish*

grind underfoot 244.9 *demolish*

grind under one's heel 244.9 *demolish*

gringo 91 Names for Inhabitants

grinning 769.1 *cheerful*

grip 25, 12.3 *governance*, 29.4 *golf clip*, 135.8 *unite*, 135.10 *link*, 137.8 *fastening*, 137.12 *bind*, 138.6 *adhere*, 233 *influence*, 258.8 *bag*, 258.9 *baggage*, 339.4 *friction*, 366.8 *spasm*, 406.10 *be painful*, 407.11 *touch*, 543.3 *gesture*, 603.1 *tool*, 632.2 *protection*, 655.1 *skill*, 688.4 *governance*, 723.1 *possession*, 726.1 *retention*, 726.3 *tools for gripping*, 726.6 *retain*

gripe 74 Rigging, 663.15 *object*, 713.7 *complain*, 726.6 *retain*, 766.2 *expression of dissatisfaction*, 766.7 *be dissatisfied*, 844.7 *sense of wrong*

griper 766.3 *dissatisfied person*

gripes 624.8 *indigestion*

grip of iron 726.1 *retention*

grip of steel 726.1 *retention*

gripped 137.16 *bound*, 726.10 *retained*

gripping 233.12 *appealing*, 406.5 *painful*, 407.2 *touching*, 726.9 *retentive*

grips 406.2 *painful condition*

Griqua 5 Languages and Groups of Languages

grisaille 50.8 *painting*, 448.4 *greyness*

griseofulvin 62 Medication

griseous 448.1 *grey*

grisette 402.2 *female*

grisly 790.4 *ugly*

grison 77 Placental Mammals

grist 384.8 *meal*, 604.1 *materials*

gristle 371.4 *solid body*, 373.7 *hard substance*, 378.7 *tough thing*

gristly 373.1, 378.3 *hard*

grist to the mill 606.1 *provision*, 721.1 *gain*

grit 384, 237.1 *strength*, 373.7 *hard substance*, 383.2 *grain*, 574.16 *fortitude*, 575.4 *stamina*, 778.1 *courage*

grit one's teeth 543.11 *gesture*, 574.8 *brace oneself*, 575.8 *hold out*

grits 45.40 *breakfast cereal*, 45.43 *US dish*

gritstone 34.5 *rock face*

Gritstone 68 Breeds of Sheep

gritted teeth 574.16 *fortitude*

gritter 71 Motor Vehicles, 71.21 *miscellaneous motoring terms*

grittily 373.12 *toughly*, 384.30 *flakily*

grittiness 373.5 *hardness*, 383.2 *grain*, 384.3 *graininess*

gritting 71.21 *miscellaneous motoring terms*

gritty 373.1 *hard*, 383.8 *rough*, 384.18 *grainy*

grizzle 446.13 *whiten*, 456.11 *variegate*

grizzled 202.11 *old*, 446.3 *white-haired*, 448.2 *grey-haired*, 456.10 *mottled*

grizzly 448.2 *grey-haired*

grizzly bear 77 Placental Mammals

groan 406.12 *express pain*, 431.6 *cry of pain*, 431.13 *cry*, 713.3 *gesture of protest*, 713.7 *complain*, 774.2 *lament*

groaning 431.18 *crying*

groaning board 350.9, 608.8 *plenty*

groat 741.10 *former British money*

groats 384.8 *meal*

grocer 350.20 *food provider*, 606.3 *provider*, 739.13 *retailer*

groceries 350.7 *food*, 606.2 *provisions*

grocer's 350.17 *food shop*

grocery 350.17 *food shop*

groceryman 739.13 *retailer*

Groenendael 77 Breeds of Dogs

grog 351.7 *alcoholic drink*, 874.12 *alcohol*

grog-blossom 874.16 *alcoholism*

grogginess 761.4 *desensitization*

groggy 238.10 *ill*, 325.5 *sedentary*, 624.22 *sick*, 761.2 *desensitized*

grogram 67 Natural Fabrics

groin 43.9 *miscellaneous architectural features*, 343.5 *fork*

groin vault 43.7 *vault*

grommet 420.7 *ear attachments*, 544.7 *flag*

Groningen 32 Breeds of Horse and Pony

Groningen Whiteheaded 68 Breeds of Cattle

groom 32.15 *horse person*, 32.16 *ride*, 68.16 *farm worker*, 68.18 *practise livestock farming*, 150.21 *tidy*, 401.4 *boyfriend*, 594.6 *brief*, 621.13 *clean*, 697.6 *domestic servant*, 823.7 *bridal party*, 823.8 *spouse*

groomed 150.13 *orderly*, 295.30 *dressed up*, 376.1 *smooth*, 594.18 *prepared*

grooming 32.14 *horse-riding terms*

grooming kit 32.14 *horse-riding terms*

groove 34.5 *rock face*, 112.4 *monotony*, 166.6 *custom*, 265.2, 265.5 *crack*, 315.6 *round*, 319.1 *notch*, 321.1, 321.6 *furrow*, 327.6 *path*, 584.3 *way*

grooved 265.7 *cracked*, 321.4 *furrowed*

groover 762.3 *joyful person*

groovy 617.1 *worthy*, 796.7 *fashionable*

grope 407.4 *kiss*, 407.11, 407.11 *touch*, 436.14 *be blind*, 656.7 *be clumsy*, 821.14 *communication of love*

grope one's way 328.2 *hesitate*

groping 328.6 *hesitant*, 407.2 *touching*, 656.3 *clumsy*, 821.14 *communication of love*

grosbeak 78 Birds

grosgrain 67 Natural Fabrics

gross 120.4 *total*, 142.6 *whole*, 179.9 *treble figures*, 259.16 *fat*, 412.6 *coarse*, 559.8 *indecorous*, 618.3 *bad*, 721.5 *profit*, 721.13 *be profitable*, 721.15 *gainful*, 730.9, 749.7 *receive*, 790.4 *ugly*, 795.7 *vulgar*, 818.6 *bad-mannered*, 864.12 *immoral*

gross behaviour 818.2 *bad manners*

gross domestic product 13.3 *economic statistics*, 243.7 *produce*

gross indecency 877.7 *sexual assault*

grossly 559.11 *inelegantly*, 753.12 *dearly*, 818.10 *rudely*

gross national product 13.3 *economic statistics*, 243.7 *produce*

grossness 795, 259.5 *fatness*, 559.2 *impropriety*, 618.9 *badness*, 818.2 *bad manners*, 877.2 *indecency*

gross out 785.7 *cause dislike*

gross-out 864.10 *bad person*

gross profit 13.7 *corporation*, 878.5 *turnover*

gross profits 721.5 *profit*, 749.2 *money received*

gross receipts 721.4 *earnings*, 730.2 *something received*, 749.2 *money received*

gross return 721.4 *earnings*

gross revenue 721.4 *earnings*

gross score 29.2 *golfing terms*

gross someone out 864.16 *be wicked*

gross structure 59.4 *anatomy*

gross ton 75 General Units

grossularite 54 Gemstones

gross weight 369.7 *weighing*

grotesque 168.14 *eccentric*, 309.7 *deformed*, 519.11 *fantastical*, 548.6 *misrepresented*, 559.9 *inelegant*, 786.8 *wonderful*

grotesquely 309.13 *asymmetrically*

grotesqueness 168.4 *unusualness*

grotesquerie 168.4 *unusualness*, 309.3 *deformity*, 548.1 *misrepresentation*

grottiness 618.10 *poverty*

grotto 69.3 *ornamental garden*

grottty 618.4 *poor*

grotty 470.5 *indifferent*, 612.4 *trivial*, 622.8 *unclean*, 624.22 *sick*, 790.4 *ugly*

grouch 818.4 *discourteous person*, 829.3 *irascible person*, 830.5 *sullen person*, 830.11, 830.11 *be irritable*, 852.13 *pessimist*

grouchily 829.9 *irascibly*, 830.14 *irritably*

grouchiness 829.1 *irascibility*, 830.3 *irritableness*
grouchy 473.8 *argumentative*, 829.4 *irascible*, 830.7 *irritable*
ground 27, 6.22 *educate*, 18.2 *sportsground*, 20.8 *angling*, 45.56 *culinary*, 50.11 *artist's materials*, 54.6 *continent*, 64.35 *conduct*, 74.10 *sail*, 135.10 *link*, 143.11 *partial*, 226.5 *reason*, 235.7 *electrical power*, 244.15 *destroyed*, 249.1 *region*, 251.2 *circumstances*, 280.1, 280.3 *base*, 280.4 *base*, 284.9 *supportive*, 344.4 *land*, 362.2 *flatten*, 384.19 *pulverized*, 490.21 *make certain*, 879.1 *punish*
ground-attack aircraft 679.31 *military aircraft*
ground bait 20.1 *angling*, 539.13 *snare*
ground ball 22.5 *batting terms*
ground-based observatory 53.23 *observatory*
ground bass 433.3 *melodiousness*
ground beetle 82 Insects
groundbreaker 154.8 *precursor*
ground-breaking 154.14 *preparatory*
ground bug 82 Insects
ground clearance 33.6 *motor racing terms*
ground control 73.6 *flight control*
ground cover 69.9 *garden plant*
groundcrew 73.3 *aircraft personnel*
ground drive 40.2 *tennis strokes*
grounded 6.19 *knowledgeable*, 225.10 *stabilized*, 236.12 *impotent*, 251.8 *circumstantial*, 362.17 *lowered*, 879.20 *punished*
ground elder 84 Flowers and Flowering Plants
ground engineer 73.3 *aircraft personnel*
grounder 22.5 *batting terms*
ground floor 280.2 *foot*
ground fog 55.33 *fog*
ground-force attack 670.12 *military attack*
ground forces 17.2 *the military*
ground frost 55.36 *frost*
ground gained 336.12 *advance*, 721.2 *augmentation*
ground game 19.9 *play*
ground glass 442.9 *glass*, 443.7 *opaque thing*
groundhog 77 Placental Mammals
Groundhog Day 55.3 *weather*
groundhog hunting 590.2 *chase*
grounding 35.6 *rugger*, 362.12 *downthrow*, 879.7 *punishment*
grounding the ball 35.3 *rugby play*
grounding the club 29.3 *golf shots*
ground intentionally 19.18 *be penalized*
groundless 229.6 *motiveless*, 474.7 *sophistic*, 476.6 *refutable*, 589.9 *causeless*
groundlessly 474.14 *sophistically*, 476.12 *refutably*
ground-level 280.3 *base*
groundling 51.31 *theatregoer*, 73.3 *aircraft personnel*
ground meat 45.20 *meat*
ground money 32.12 *rodeo*
groundnut 86 Nuts
groundnut meal 68.9 *animal feedstuff*
groundnuts 68.12 *crop*
ground out 22.7 *play baseball*
ground pine 88.1 *fern*
ground plan 299.1 *outline*, 592.5 *map*
ground-reflected wave 534.15 *transmitted wave*
ground rent 751.3 *fee*
ground run 73.5 *flight*
grounds 132.2 *residue*, 226.5 *reason*, 228.1 *motive*, 393.13 *mud*, 463.4 *explanation*, 473.3 *line of argument*, 483.1 *evidence*, 485.7 *condition*, 490.13 *confirmation*,

586.11 *motive*, 622.4 *dirt*, 725.1 *property*, 855.2 *defence*
groundsel 84 Flowers and Flowering Plants
grounds for dismissal 15.2 *industrial negotiations*
grounds for divorce 824.3 *divorce court*
groundsheet 293.9 *floor covering*
groundspeed 73.5 *flight*
ground speed 329.8 *speed*
ground squirrel 77 Placental Mammals
ground staff 679.32 *airman*
ground state 56.67 *excited atom*
ground station 55.5 *weather station*
ground stroke 40.2 *tennis strokes*
ground swell 366.13 *tempest*
ground to dust 384.19 *pulverized*
ground under repair 29.1 *golf*
groundwater 54
ground wave 534.15 *transmitted wave*
groundwork 152.11 *arrangements*, 154.3 *preparation*, 156.7 *rudiments*, 226.3 *rudiment*, 284.2 *supporting part*
ground work 365.5 *wave*
groundwork 594.10 *preparations*
group 161, 161, 400, 2.4 *social organization*, 17.4 *military organization*, 50.12 *sculpture*, 50.23 *design*, 52.21 *set*, 52.23 *algebra*, 57.6 *chemical element*, 116.2 *alliance*, 140.3 *assembly*, 140.5 *combine*, 143.1 *part*, 150.19 *systematize*, 152.6 *category*, 152.12 *arrange*, 152.15 *categorize*, 161.25 *assemblage*, 161.37 *assemble*, 161.39 *come together*, 163.2 *class*, 163.5 *social class*, 163.13 *class*, 259.18 *measure*, 305.5 *team*, 665.1 *party*, 679.16 *army unit*, 703.4 *council*
Group 48 Literary Groups and Movements
group activity 642.2 *social activity*, 815.1 *sociability*
group behaviour 2.6 *social group*
group captain 679.32 *airman*
Group Captain 17 British Military Ranks
group dynamics 61.3 *psychiatric treatment*
grouped 150, 161, 152.20 *arranged*, 152.24 *categorized*, 163.12 *classed*
Groupe de Recherche d'Art Visuel 50 Schools and Groups of Artists
grouper 80 Fishes
groupie 9.5 *worshipper*, 127.6 *inferior*, 138.5, 155.14 *follower*, 180.9, 195.8 *follower*, 206.6 *young person*, 584.8 *creature of habit*, 821.9 *lover*, 851.8 *admirer*
group influence 233
grouping 150, 50.4 *treatment*, 140.3 *assembly*, 152.1 *arrangement*, 152.5 *categorization*, 161.1 *assembly*, 161.11 *group*, 163.1 *classification*, 163.2 *class*
group interaction 2.6 *social group*
Group of Seven 50 Schools and Groups of Artists, 13.5 *international trade*
group participation 724.2 *participation*
group photograph 66.4 *portrait*
group practice 60.1 *medicine*
group psychology 61.1 *psychology*
group psychotherapy 61.3 *psychiatric treatment*
group relations training 61.3 *psychiatric treatment*
group solidarity 2.6 *social group*
group test 61.5 *psychological test*
group theory 52 Mathematical Theories
group therapy 630.13 *therapy*
group together 161.37 *assemble*, 665.12 *be in league with*
Group Zero 50 Schools and Groups of Artists
grouse 161 Collective Names

by Animal, 37.5 *game*, 45.20 *meat*, 78.4 *table bird*, 663.15 *object*, 713.7 *complain*, 766.7 *be dissatisfied*, 830.11 *be irritable*, 844.7 *sense of wrong*
grouse moor 98.6 *lowland*
grouser 713.4 *protester*, 766.3 *dissatisfied person*, 818.4 *discourteous person*, 830.5 *sullen person*, 852.13 *pessimist*
grouse season 203.1 *season*
grouse shoot 590.2 *chase*
grouse shooter 398.13 *animal killer*
grouse shooting 18 Sporting Activities, 37.2 *hunting*, 398.9 *animal killing*
grousing 830.7 *irritable*
grout 63.26 *masonry*, 138.3 *adhesive*, 293.8 *wall covering*, 293.28 *face*
grouts 622.4 *dirt*
Grove 49 Musicians and Composers
grovel 276.8 *be low*, 282.6 *be horizontal*, 362.9 *bow*, 364.10 *swirl*, 467.14 *be solicitous*, 673.4 *succumb*, 694.6 *show obeisance to*, 701.8 *be subject to*, 806.20 *submit*, 808.9 *fawn*, 849.19 *take off one's hat to*
groveller 673.2 *appeaser*, 808.3 *sycophant*
grovelling 362.15 *debasement*, 362.21 *degraded*, 673.1 *submission*, 694.3 *obeisance*, 808.2 *sycophancy*, 808.7 *sycophantic*
groves of academe 501.7 *academia*
grow 85, 206, 227, 68.17 *farm*, 68.18 *practise livestock farming*, 83.21 *vegetate*, 99.18 *come to be*, 121.6 *change gradually*, 128.4 *increase*, 128.5 *make bigger*, 207.18 *mature*, 220.8 *be transformed*, 243.10 *produce*, 261.6 *become bigger*, 275.16 *rise*, 336.8 *further*, 594.7 *develop*, 721.10 *augment*
grow bag 69.4 *nursery*, 226.2 *source*
grow better 627.2 *get better*
grow by leaps and bounds 128.4 *increase*
grow dark 55.60 *cloud*, 440.13 *become dark*
grow dim 129.4 *decrease*, 441.9 *be dim*
grower 68.15 *agriculturist*, 243.9 *producer*, 594.15 *preparer*
grow fat 686.5 *be prosperous*
grow from 227.8 *grow*
grow fruit 69.14 *practise horticulture*
growing 227, 261, 83.13 *plantlike*, 121.7 *gradational*, 128.6 *increasing*, 206.13 *maturing*, 220.14 *converting*, 239.4 *vigorous*, 243.2 *manufacture*
growing apart 136.1 *separation*
growing medium 226.2 *source*
growing old 207.12 *ageing*
growing pains 206.2 *youthfulness*
growing plants 69.5 *gardening*
growing season 203.3 *summer*
growing soft 129.1 *decrease*
growing together 140.1 *combination*
grow in profusion 608.5 *about*
growl 432.1 *animal cry*, 432.4 *cry*, 564.13 *speak in a particular way*, 818.8 *get angry*, 828.6 *sign of anger*, 828.11 *be angry*, 829.2 *sign of irascibility*, 829.7 *frown*, 830.4 *sign of irritableness*, 830.11 *be irritable*
growler 54.39 *iceberg*
growless 129.4 *decrease*
grow light 439
grow like a weed 261.6 *become bigger*
growling 818.5 *discourteous*, 818.6 *bad-mannered*, 828.16 *angry*, 829.5 *showing irascibility*
grow moss 628.2 *decay*
grown 243.12 *produced*, 261.7

bigger, 304.5 *bred*, 594.20 *developed*
grown old 207.14 *aged*
grown up 594.20 *developed*
grown-up 207.7 *older person*, 207.11 *adult*
grow old 202, 207.17 *age*, 628.1 *deteriorate*
grow on one 584.17 *become a habit*
grow pale 439.28 *bleach*, 441.9 *be dim*
grow plants 304.8 *nurture*
grow rank 622.10 *be dirty*
grow rich 128.4 *increase*, 686.5 *be prosperous*
grow rusty 585.4 *be unaccustomed*
grow smaller 129.4 *decrease*
grow soft 129.4 *decrease*
grow stale 628.2 *decay*
growth 227, 261, 57.4 *crystal*, 59.5 *physiology*, 83.1 *plants*, 128.1 *increase*, 220.2 *evolution*, 243.2 *manufacture*, 245.4, 336.14 *development*, 624.3 *symptom*, 624.12 *cancer*, 721.2 *augmentation*
growth hormone 58 Hormones
growth ring 85.3 *timber*
growth study 1.10 *measurement*
growth substance 58.17 *plant hormone*
grow together 138.6 *adhere*, 140.5 *combine*
grow up 128.4 *increase*, 207.17 *age*, 207.18 *mature*, 261.6 *become bigger*, 359.13 *ascend*, 359.18 *jump*
grow vegetables 69.14 *practise horticulture*
grow weak 238.6 *be weak*, 624.24 *be unhealthy*
grow weary of the world 788.7 *suffer boredom*
groyne 63.24 *water system*, 632.4 *safety device*
GRP 36.10 *sailing*
GRP board 36.7 *windsurfing*
GRP hull 36.3 *parts of a sailing boat*
grub 82.5 *larva*, 85.18 *manage trees*, 206.4 *young animal*, 350.7 *food*, 606.2 *provisions*
grubbily 622.12 *dirtily*
grubbiness 151.3 *untidiness*, 618.10 *poverty*, 622.1 *dirtiness*
grubby 82.12 *verminous*, 151.15 *untidy*, 618.4 *poor*, 622.7 *dirty*
grub out 355.11 *extract*
grub's on! 45
grudge 573, 758, 609.7 *make insufficient*, 759.6 *bad feeling*, 820.3 *ill feeling*, 820.11 *be hostile*, 822.1 *hate*, 828.1 *resentment*, 832.4 *bitterness*, 842.1 *envy*, 842.3 *be envious of*
grudge match 674.2 *contest*
grudging 659.14 *troublesome*, 758.1 *mean*, 820.6 *hostile*, 822.10 *hating*, 828.15 *resentful*, 842.2 *envious*
grudging apology 867.1 *penitence*
grudgingly 758.9 *meanly*, 820.14 *hostilely*, 822.18 *hatefully*, 828.17 *resentfully*, 842.4 *enviously*
grudgingness 842.1 *envy*
grudging service 573.14 *disobedience*
grudging thanks 838.1 *ingratitude*
gruel 45.40 *breakfast cereal*, 393.7 *soup*, 412.3 *tasteless items*
gruelling 644.11 *laborious*, 650.4 *fatiguing*, 659.10 *difficult*, 879.21 *punishing*
gruesome 618.3 *bad*, 790.4 *ugly*
gruff 270.9 *abrupt*, 430.8 *hoarse*, 818.5 *discourteous*, 829.4 *irascible*, 830.7 *irritable*, 832.12 *callous*
gruffly 818.9 *discourteously*, 829.9 *irascibly*, 830.14 *irritably*
gruffness 270.6 *abruptness*, 430.2 *hoarseness*, 566.4 *taci-*

turnity, 818.1 *discourtesy,* 829.1 *irascibility,* 830.3 *irritableness*
grugru nut 86 Nuts
Grumbacher red 450.6 *red pigment*
grumble 426.8 *drum,* 713.7 *complain,* 766.7 *be dissatisfied,* 830.11 *be irritable*
grumbler 713.4 *protester,* 766.3 *dissatisfied person,* 830.5 *sullen person*
grumbling 426.1 *drumming,* 818.6 *bad-mannered,* 830.7 *irritable*
grume 393.10 *mucus*
grump 829.3 *irascible person,* 830.5 *sullen person*
grumpily 415.11 *splenetically,* 829.9 *irascibly,* 830.14 *irritably*
grumpiness 829.1 *irascibility,* 830.3 *irritableness*
grumpishness 830.1 *sullenness*
grumpy 415.7 *splenetic,* 829.4 *irascible,* 830.7 *irritable*
Grundyism 134.1 *purity,* 876.4 *self-righteousness*
grunge 49.9 *popular music,* 622.4 *dirt*
grungy 618.4 *poor*
grunion 80 Fishes
grunt 80 Fishes, 79.16 *live as an amphibian,* 430.2 *hoarseness,* 430.5 *sound hoarse,* 432.4 *cry,* 650.5 *be fatigued,* 673.2 *appeaser,* 701.3 *subordinate*
grunt-and-groan 26.15 *wrestling*
grunt-and-groaner 26.6 *wrestler,* 674.10 *contender,* 679.3 *athlete*
grunting 430.8 *hoarse*
gruntled 405.7 *pleased*
Grus 53 The Constellations
Gruyère 45 Cheeses
Grylloblatodea 82 Orders of Insects
grylloblatodean 82.10 *insectan*
GSC 57.17 *analysis*
G star 53.13 *luminosity*
G-strings 295.25 *accessories,* 296.4 *dishabille*
G-suit 295.10 *suit*
guacamole 45.50 *Central American dish*
Guadalajara 93 Cities
Guadalcanal 98 Islands
guaiacum 85 Trees and Shrubs
guaiphenesin 62 Medication
Guam 98 Islands
guanaco 77 Placental Mammals
guanethidine 62 Medication
guanine 58.10 *nucleoside,* 59.12 *molecular biology*
guano 246.3 *fertilizer,* 353.5 *faeces,* 622.4 *dirt*
Guantánamo 93 Cities
Guarani 1 Peoples, **5** Languages and Groups of Languages, **7** Non-Christian Religions
guarantee 490, 714, 714, 480.1 *verify,* 490.21 *make certain,* 535.3, 535.18 *vow,* 597.3 *contract,* 632.1 *safety,* 632.9 *protect,* 662.29 *finance,* 718.2, 718.11 *promise,* 845.6 *bond*
guaranteed 490, 718, 535.12 *vowed,* 632.5 *safe,* 714.13 *guaranteeing,* 718.7 *guaranteed*
guaranteed annual income 662.4 *social assistance*
guaranteed loan 745.3 *loan*
guaranteeing 714
guarantee payments 15.2 *industrial negotiations*
guarantor 490, 535.9 *affirmer,* 714.5 *promise-maker,* 745.6 *debtor*
guaranty 745.3 *loan*
Guarapuavano 32 Breeds of Horse and Pony
guard 671, 19.7 *offence,* 23.2 *basketball player,* 23.6 *play basketball,* 28.3 *fencing movements,* 28.5 *fence,* 41.10 *curling,* 72.9 *railway worker,* 180.7 *attendant,* 180.15 *escort,* 293.30 *protect,* 435.11 *observer,* 469.8 *watchful person,* 469.11 *care for,* 632.2 *protection,* 632.3

protector, 632.9 *protect,* 636.4 *warner,* 637.5 *preserve,* 671.17, 679.39 *defend,* 699.11 *detain,* 718.10 *secure*
guard against 467.11 *take note of,* 516.2 *show prudence,* 594.3 *be prepared*
guard cell 83.6 *leaf*
guard dog 77.9 *dog,* 632.3 *protector,* 671.5 *self-defence*
guard-duty 469.5 *watchfulness*
guarded 180.20 *accompanied,* 566.3 *sparing with words,* 632.5 *safe,* 781.4 *cautious*
guardedness 469.5 *watchfulness,* 781.1 *caution*
guarded speech 566
guardhouse 702.1 *prison*
guardian 284.8 *supporter,* 284.9 *supportive,* 469.8 *watchful person,* 632.3 *protector,* 632.7 *tutelary,* 671.15 *protector*
guardian angel 8.6 *angel,* 284.8 *supporter,* 632.3 *protector,* 662.15 *benefactor*
Guardian Angel 469.8 *watchful person,* 679.2 *defender*
Guardian Angels 632.3 *protector*
guardian of morality 876.6 *moralist*
guardianship 632.2 *protection*
guarding 23.4 *playing terms,* 469.5 *watchfulness,* 469.9 *careful,* 632.7 *tutelary,* 699.4 *detention*
guard of honour 849.5 *presenting arms*
guard one's pride 805.31 *save face*
guard one's reputation 857.6 *be honourable*
guardrail 632.4 *safety device*
Guards 679.14 *armed forces*
guard ship 679.24 *warship*
Guardsman 679.8 *soldier,* 679.12 *ceremonial troops*
guard's van 72.6 *rolling stock*
guar gum 394.2 *adhesive*
Guatemala 91 Countries
Guatemala City 93 Cities
guava 86 Fruits
Guayaquil 93 Cities
guayule 85 Trees and Shrubs
gubernatorial 12.9 *governmental,* 653.17 *managerial,* 688.14 *governmental,* 703.9 *commissioned*
guberniya 92.3 *other*
guck 393.1 *semiliquid,* 394.7 *slime*
guddle 590.11 *hunt*
guddler 590.6 *hunter*
gudgeon 74 Parts of a Ship, **80** Fishes, 364.4 *vortex*
guelder rose 84 Flowers and Flowering Plants
guellemin 816.6 *unsocial person*
guenon 77 Placental Mammals
guerdon 125.1 *compensation,* 125.4 *compensate,* 878.1, 878.9 *reward*
guerdoner 125.3 *compensator*
Guericke 52 Scientists
Guernsey 68 Breeds of Cattle, **98** Islands, 295.13 *sweater*
guerrilla 679, 398.10 *killer,* 670.19 *attacker,* 672.2 *revenger,* 689.3 *anarchist,* 693.10 *seditionist,* 713.10 *law-breaking*
guerrilla attack 670.16 *terrorist attack*
guerrilla force 679.14 *armed forces*
guerrilla tactics 689.1 *anarchy*
guerrilla war 713.2 *disorder*
guerrilla warfare 669.3 *resistance movement,* 676.8 *warfare,* 693.4 *revolution*
guess 102.14 *theorize,* 471.2 *theory,* 471.17 *theorize,* 477.20 *doubt,* 479.11 *experiment,* 491.9 *uncertainty,* 492.1 *judgment,* 492.12 *estimate,* 497.8 *be of the opinion,* 517.11 *predict,* 518.3 *conjecture,* 518.5 *suppose*
guess at 759.16 *feel in one's bones*
guessed 518.8 *supposed*

guesser 518.4 *theorist*
guessing 477.15 *sceptical,* 518.3 *conjecture,* 518.7 *suppositional*
guesstimate 170.8 *calculate,* 471.17 *theorize,* 517.11 *predict,* 518.3 *conjecture,* 518.5 *suppose*
guesstimated 471.10 *theoretical*
guesstimating 518.7 *suppositional*
guesswork 102.4 *theorization,* 477.6 *uncertainty,* 479.3 *experimentation,* 491.9 *uncertainty,* 492.1 *judgment,* 502.3 *unknown thing,* 504.2 *inaccuracy,* 517.2 *divination,* 518.3 *conjecture*
guest 149.6 *immigrant,* 255.3 *householder,* 346.7 *entrant,* 723.5 *possessor,* 804.4 *titleholder,* 815.6 *social person*
guest house 256.10 *hotel*
guest of His Majesty 702.5 *prisoner*
guest pass 754.6 *absence of charge*
guest rope 137.6 *line*
guest soap 621.9 *cleaning agent*
guest ticket 754.6 *absence of charge*
guest worker 104.7 *new arrival,* 149.6 *immigrant*
guff 521.5 *empty talk,* 538.6 *nonsense,* 565.3 *talk*
guffaw 431.2 *cry of joy,* 431.11 *laugh,* 762.7 *show joy,* 771.14 *laugh*
Guggenheim Museum 43 Noted Buildings
guidable 332.14 *directed*
guidance 6.1, 6.1 *education,* 332.5 *directions,* 652.8 *treatment,* 653.4 *directorship,* 654.1 *advice,* 662.2 *support*
guidance counsellor 654.4 *adviser*
guide 166, 653, 6.22 *educate,* 27.17 *bat,* 34.7 *mountaineer,* 154.8 *precursor,* 154.15 *precede,* 156.21 *pioneer,* 166.16 *direct,* 180.8 *usher,* 180.15 *escort,* 233.8 *influence,* 332.6 *direct,* 543.5 *indicator,* 543.9 *use signs,* 652.10 *conductor,* 652.15 *conduct,* 653.2 *direct,* 653.13 *director,* 654.3 *precept,* 654.4 *adviser,* 654.5 *advise,* 662.14 *adviser,* 662.23 *advise,* 688.11, 696.10 *expert*
guidebook 171.3 *dictionary,* 528.5 *reference book,* 532.6 *book publishing*
guided 6.19 *knowledgeable,* 180.20 *accompanied*
guided missile 680.5 *missile weapon*
guided-missile destroyer 679.24 *warship*
guide dog 77.9 *dog,* 436.3 *aid for poor sight*
guided wave 365.5 *wave*
guideless 633.3 *vulnerable*
guideline 166.4 *guide,* 654.3 *precept*
guide number 66.15 *lighting*
guidepost 543.5 *indicator*
guide telescope 53.25 *mounting*
guiding 6.16 *educational,* 154.14 *preparatory,* 233.11 *influential,* 332.5 *directions,* 332.16 *directing,* 653.17 *managerial*
guiding light 228.1, 586.11 *motive*
guiding principle 228.1, 586.11 *motive*
guiding spirit 8.5 *deity*
guiding star 228.1 *motive,* 439.13 *enlightenment,* 543.5 *indicator*
Guido d'arezzo 49 Musicians and Composers
guidon 544.7 *flag*
guild 15.3 *organized labour,* 116.2 *alliance,* 161.15 *association,* 665.1 *party*
guilder 741.11 *national coins*
guildsman 737.11 *chamber of commerce member*
guild socialism 12.1 *government*

guile 474.5 *hypocrisy,* 539.1 *deception,* 540.5 *deceitfulness,* 657.1 *cunning*
guileful 539.34 *deceiving,* 540.29 *deceitful,* 657.4 *cunning*
guilefully 657.6 *cunningly*
guileless 442.4 *easily seen through,* 537.18 *truthful,* 556.3 *natural,* 658.1, 865.7 *naive*
guilelessly 865.12 *naively*
guilelessness 442.10 *openness,* 537.5 *truthfulness,* 658.2, 865.3 *naivety*
guillemot 78 Birds
guilloche 43 Architectural Decoration
guillotine 218.2 *stop,* 218.8 *cause to cease,* 397.4 *death sentence,* 398.5 *execution,* 398.19, 879.5 *execute,* 879.16 *instrument of execution*
guillotining 879.13 *capital punishment*
guilt 866, 16.38 *lawbreaking,* 864.7 *criminality,* 867.1 *penitence*
Guilt 866
guilt complex 866.2 *signs of guilt*
guilt feelings 867.1 *penitence*
guiltily 16, 866, 864.21 *criminally,* 867.8 *penitently*
guiltiness 504.7 *errancy,* 866.1 *guilt*
guiltless 16.63 *acquitted,* 619.1 *perfect,* 863.5 *virtuous,* 865.5 *innocent*
guiltlessly 16.88 *forgivingly,* 863.9 *virtuously,* 865.11 *innocently*
guiltlessness 619.3 *perfection,* 863.1 *virtue,* 865.1 *innocence*
guilt-offering 222.3 *substitute thing*
guilty 866, 16.7 *legal trial,* 16.60 *offending,* 16.64 *convicted,* 504.16 *errant,* 844.16 *in the wrong,* 852.36 *blameworthy,* 864.15 *criminal,* 867.6 *penitent*
guilty act 844.8 *wrong-doing,* 864.7 *criminality,* 866.3 *sin*
guilty behaviour 866.2 *signs of guilt*
guilty conscience 866.2 *signs of guilt,* 867.1 *penitence*
guilty feelings 866.2 *signs of guilt*
guilty love 877.4 *illicit love*
guilty party 856.4 *accused person,* 866.4 *guilty person*
guilty person 866
guimpe 295.14 *neckwear*
guinea 91 Names for Inhabitants, 741.10 *former British money*
Guinea 91 Countries
Guinea-Bissau 91 Countries
guinea cock 78.10 *male bird*
guinea fowl 78 Birds, 78.4 *table bird*
guinea pig 77 Placental Mammals, 479.7 *experimentee*
guinea worm 81 Worms, 81.10 *parasite*
guisard 539.15 *deceiver*
guise 105.1 *state,* 289.3 *appearance,* 295.5 *fancy dress,* 327.1 *way,* 457.4 *something that appears,* 652.1 *conduct*
guiser 539.15 *deceiver*
guitar 49 Musical Instruments
guitar-banjo 49 Musical Instruments
guitar fish 80 Fishes
guitar-violin 49 Musical Instruments
Gujarati 5 Languages and Groups of Languages
Gula 8 Deities
Gulag 702.1 *prison,* 879.7 *punishment*
gulch 265.3 *gulf*
gules 450.1 *red,* 544.8 *heraldic device,* 544.13 *heraldic*
gulf 265, 96.6 *river flow,* 98.9 *inlet,* 277.4 *deep thing,* 317.2 *concave land,* 327.11 *channel*
Gulf of Alaska 98.9 *inlet*
Gulf of California 98.9 *inlet*

Gulf of Campeche 98.9 *inlet*
Gulf of Guinea 98.9 *inlet*
Gulf of Mexico 98.9 *inlet*
Gulf of Saint Lawrence 98.9 *inlet*
Gulf Stream 54.13 *ocean current*,
408.8 *hot place*
Gulf War **17** Major Wars
gulfweed **90** Algae
gull **78** Birds, 78.3 *water bird*,
539.22 *dupe*, 539.30 *be fraudulent*
gullet 350.16 *eating utensil*
gullibility 466.1 *incuriousness*,
493.1 *misjudgment*, 497.3 *believing*, 658.2 *naivety*
gullible **497**, 453.3 *raw*, 466.3
incurious, 493.7 *misjudging*,
497.11 *believing*, 658.1 *naive*
gullibly 466.7 *incuriously*,
493.13 *misguidedly*, 497.15
believingly, 658.5 *naively*
gullied 34.8 *mountaineering*
gull wing **73** Aircraft Parts
gully 27.4 *team*, 34.5 *rock face*,
98.8 *valley*, 265.3 *gulf*, 272.6
narrow place, 317.2 *concave land*
gully washer 241.5 *violent
weather*
gulp **161** Collective Names for
Birds and Animals, 348.4 *intake*, 348.11 *ingest*, 350.21 *eat*,
351.2, 351.13 *drink*, 872.5 *be
greedy*
gulp down 348.11 *ingest*, 350.21
eat, 351.13 *drink*
gulping 348.4 *intake*, 350.1 *eating*, 351.1 *drinking*, 872.6 *gluttonous*
gum **85** Trees and Shrubs,
45.41 *sweet*, 85.9 *tree product*,
138.3 *adhesive*, 138.4 *adherent*,
138.7 *cause to adhere*, 352.2 *secreted substance*, 377.3 *elastic
thing*, 394.2 *adhesive*, 394.10
stick, 395.10 *resin*, 726.3 *tools
for gripping*, 726.6 *retain*
gum acaroides 395.10 *resin*
gum arabic 58.4 *polysaccharide*
gumball 746.5 *drug*
gumbo **45** Vegetables, 45.13
soup, 13.2 *mixed thing*, 393.7
soup, 394.8 *viscous*
gumbolike 394.8 *viscous*
gumdrop 45.41 *sweet*, 414.4 *confectionery*
gum elastic 377.4 *rubber*
gumlike 394.8 *viscous*, 395.14
resinous
gumlikeness 394.1 *viscosity*
gummed 726.10 *retained*
gummic 395.14 *resinous*
gummiferous 395.14 *resinous*
gumminess 394.1 *viscosity*
gummite **54** Minerals
gummosity 394.1 *viscosity*
gummous 394.8 *viscous*, 395.14
resinous
gummy 138.9 *adhesive*, 394.8
viscous, 395.14 *resinous*, 726.9
retentive
gum nut **86** Nuts
gum print 66.12 *development*
gumption 507.2 *intelligence*
gum resin 395.10 *resin*
gum rosin 395.10 *resin*
gumshoe 496.12 *discoverer*
gumshoes 295.19 *footwear*
gum turpentine 85.9 *tree product*
gum up 394.10 *stick*, 661.9 *block*
gum up the works 661.9 *block*
gun 36.7 *windsurfing*, 244.7
agent of destruction, 338.9 *firearm*, 338.15 *shooter*, 338.28
shoot, 398.2 *murder*, 425.3
banger, 590.3 *hunting and fishing equipment*, 590.6 *hunter*,
680.9 *firearm*
gunbarrel 41.1 *skiing*
gunbearer 326.7 *transferor*
gunboat 679.24 *warship*
gunboat diplomacy 676.1 *war*,
678.2 *mediation*, 679.22 *navy*
guncarriage 680.11 *guns*
guncotton 338.13 *fuel*
gun cotton 680.15 *explosive*
gun deck **74** Parts of a Ship

gundog 37.6 *sporting dog*, 77.9
dog, 590.6 *hunter*
gun down 338.28 *shoot*, 398.17
murder, 398.18 *slaughter*,
679.37 *fight*
gun emplacement 671.11 *fortification*, 680.11 *guns*
gunfire 338.7 *shot*, 423.1 *loudness*, 670.15 *firing*
gun for 338.28 *shoot*
gunge 393.1 *semiliquid*, 394.7
slime
gungeon 875.6 *drug*
gunge yuck 622.4 *dirt*
gung ho
gung-ho 17.8 *military*, 91.16 *national*, 572.2 *eager*, 574.2 *tenacious*, 676.16 *warlike*, 679.33
combative
gung-ho attitude 17.7 *miscellaneous terms*, 642.8 *assiduity*
gung-ho nationalism 91.4 *nationalism*
gungy 393.16 *semiliquid*, 618.4
poor
gunk 393.1 *semiliquid*, 394.7
slime, 622.4 *dirt*
gunky 393.16 *semiliquid*, 618.4
poor
gunman 338.15 *shooter*, 398.11
murderer, 671.1 *combatant*,
695.4 *coercive person*, 736.11
dishonest person, 832.8 *malefactor*
gun metal **57** Alloys
gunmetal 448.5 *grey thing*
gunnel **80** Fishes
gunner 338.15 *shooter*, 679.17
army person, 679.32 *airman*
gunnery 338.6 *shooting*, 670.15
firing, 676.6 *art of war*, 680.2
arms
gunning 37.2 *hunting*, 590.2
chase
gunny 67 Natural Fabrics
gun park 680.11 *guns*
gunpowder 244.7 *agent of destruction*, 338.13 *fuel*, 351.3
tea, 680.15 *explosive*
gun rack 680.4 *arsenal*
gunroom 605.4 *storage*, 680.4 *arsenal*
gun-running 680.3 *arms race*
guns **680**
gunshot 264.2 *short distance*,
338.7 *shot*, 633.6 *danger signal*
gunsight 435.10 *visual aid*
gunsmith 646.2 *artisan*
gunstock 680.9 *firearm*
gunter 36.10 *sailing*
gunter rig 36.3 *parts of a sailing
boat*
gunter-rigged 36.10 *sailing*
Gunter's chain **75** General
Units, 268.6 *measuring instrument*
gunwale **74** Parts of a Ship,
36.4 *rowing*, 36.6 *canoeing*
guppy **80** Fishes
Gur **5** Languages and Groups of
Languages
gurge 364.4 *vortex*, 364.10 *swirl*
gurgle 96.7 *flow*, 390.24 *bubble*,
424.1 *faintness*, 424.5 *sound
faint*
gurgling 424.4 *faint*
gurgling brook 424.3 *faint-
sounding thing*
Gurindji **5** Languages and
Groups of Languages
gurk 349.16 *belch*
Gurkha 679.6 *militarist*
Gurkhali **5** Languages and
Groups of Languages
gurnard **80** Fishes
guru 4.12 *sage*, 6.4 *educator*, 7.8
priest, 459.8 *intellectual person*,
507.3 *wise man*, 653.14 *leader*,
655.5 *expert*, 688.10 *person of
authority*, 696.6 *religious leader*,
696.9 *educational leader*
gush 96.6 *river flow*, 96.7 *flow*,
128.2 *spread*, 347.2 *outflow*,
347.11 *run out*, 359.2 *upturn*,
359.17 *spring up*, 387.25 *flow*,
521.9 *talk nonsense*, 553.1 *diffuseness*, 553.5 *be diffuse*, 565.2

effusiveness, 565.8 *talk too
much*, 638.7 *leak*
gusher 347.2 *outflow*, 359.12
geyser, 605.2 *resource*
gushiness 565.2 *effusiveness*
gushing 96.10 *fluvial*, 347.2 *outflow*, 553.3 *diffuse*, 565.6 *effusive*, 610.6 *excessive*
gushingly 565.11 *effusively*
gush out 347.11 *run out*
gusle **49** Musical Instruments
gusset 295.24 *part of garment*
gusseted 295.31 *styled*
gussied up 295.30 *dressed up*
gussy up 295.33 *dress up*
gust 55.12 *wind*, 55.58 *blow*,
390.4 *air flow*, 390.22 *blow*
gustation 411.3 *appetizer*
gustiness 55.14 *windiness*
gusto 239.1 *vigour*, 411.4 *flavour*, 554.1 *emphasis*, 762.1
happiness
gusty 55.47 *windy*, 390.15
breezy
gut 45.55 *cook*, 98.9 *inlet*,
244.10 *lay waste*, 258.18 *stomach*, 349.11 *void*, 355.14 *suck*,
607.1 *waste*
gut-ache 406.2 *painful condition*
Gutai group **50** Schools and
Groups of Artists
gutless 238.12 *weak-willed*,
240.5 *inert*, 779.3 *cowardly*
gutlessness 238.2 *indecisiveness*,
240.1 *inertness*
gut reaction 462.3, 464.4 *instinct*, 759.2 *impression*
guts 148.4 *components*, 237.1
strength, 239.1 *vigour*, 257.3,
290.4 *insides*, 350.16 *eating
utensil*, 574.16 *fortitude*, 575.4
stamina, 759.8 *seat of feelings*,
778.1 *courage*
gutsiness 575.4 *stamina*
gutsy 575.12 *indomitable*, 778.9
courageous
gutta **43** Architectural Decoration, 29.5 *golf ball*
guttae 62.8 *drops*
gutta-percha **85** Tree Products,
377.4 *rubber*
gutta-percha ball 29.5 *golf ball*
guttation 59.5 *physiology*, 352.1
secretion, 391.6 *dew*
gutter 25.4, 25.10 *bowling*,
224.11 *be changeable*, 321.1,
321.6 *furrow*, 347.7 *outlet*,
366.26 *flicker*, 441.9 *be dim*,
727.8 *sink*
gutteral 430.8 *hoarse*
gutteral consonant 5.16 *spoken
letter*
gutteralize 430.5 *sound hoarse*
gutterally 430.10 *stridently*
gutteralness 430.2 *hoarseness*
gutteral sound 430.2 *hoarseness*
gutter ball 25.5 *bowling delivery*
guttering 366.20 *flickering*
gutter press 532.3 *journalism*,
533.5 *mass communication*
gutter shot 25.5 *bowling delivery*
gutting 355.4 *sucking*
guttural 5.16 *spoken letter*, 5.39
of language, 5.41 *lettered*,
564.18 *phonetic*
guttural accent 5.26 *dialect*
guv 401.3 *male title of address*
guvnor 401.3 *male title of address*, 696.1 *master*
guy 36.3 *parts of a sailing boat*,
137.6 *line*, 137.7 *tackle*, 401.2
person, 401.2 *male*, 493.6 *misjudged person*, 525.1 *misinterpret*, 547.6 *image*, 548.1 *misrepresentation*, 548.4 *misrepresent*,
799.6 *deride*, 807.29 *ridicule*,
850.25 *taunt*, 854.14 *ridicule*
Guyana **91** Countries
guy derrick 63.29 *construction
equipment*
Guy Fawkes 539.20 *plotter*,
547.6 *image*, 693.10 *seditionist*
Guy Fawkes Day 214.6 *annually
celebrated day*
guyot 54.16 *ocean floor*
guy rope 137.6 *line*
guy wires 30.5 *horizontal bar*

guzzle 350.22 *eat well*, 872.5 *be
greedy*, 874.8 *get drunk*
guzzler 351.12 *drinker*, 872.4
glutton
guzzling 350.2 *appetite*, 350.26
eating, 872.6 *gluttonous*, 874.5
drunken
Gwalior **93** Cities
Gwalu **8** Deities
Gwent **92** Counties
Gwynedd **92** Counties
gyaku-zuki 26.8 *karate*
gybe 36.1 *sailing*, 36.15 *sail*,
74.9 *navigate*
gymkhana **18** Sporting Activities, 32.6 *horsemanship*, 674.2
contest
gymnasium 6.15 *schoolroom*,
30.1 *gymnastics*
gymnast 237.5 *athlete*, 655.4
skilled person, 674.10 *contender*,
811.15 *showman*
gymnastic **30**, 18.5 *sporting*,
644.10 *working*
gymnastic apparatus **30**
gymnastic clothing **30**
gymnastic mat 30.3 *gymnastic
apparatus*
gymnastic organization **30**
gymnastic routine 30.1 *gymnastics*
gymnastics **30**, 324.11 *bodily
movement*, 644.5 *exercise*,
674.1 *contention*, 674.2 *contest*
Gymnastics **30**
gymnastics association 30.4 *gymnastic organization*
gymnastics club 30.4 *gymnastic
organization*
gymnastics coach 30.9 *gymnasts*
gymnastic scoring 30.1 *gymnastics*
gymnastics display 811.14 *show*
gymnastic shoes 30.2 *gymnastic
clothing*
gymnastics judge 30.9 *gymnasts*
gymnasts **30**
gymnosophical 296.9 *undressed*
gymnosophist 296.8 *nude person*
gymnosophy 296.1 *undress*
gymnosperm 83.3 *seed plant*
Gymnospermae 83.3 *seed plant*
gymnure **77** Placental Mammals
gym pants 295.9 *trousers*
gympie **85** Trees and Shrubs
gym shoes 23.3 *basketball equipment*, 295.19 *footwear*
gymslip 295.7 *frock*
gynaeceum 821.13 *abode of love*
gynaecocracy 12.1 *government*
gynaecological 60.22, 630.18
medical
gynaecologist 60.13 *medical specialist*, 245.7 *obstetrics*
gynaecology 60.3 *medical specialty*, 402.1 *female sex*
gynarchy 12.1 *government*,
402.1 *female sex*
gynephobia **777** Phobias by
Name
gyniatrics 402.1 *female sex*
gyniatry 402.1 *female sex*
gynocracy 12.1 *government*,
402.1 *female sex*
gynoecium 84.3 *flower part*,
245.8 *organs of reproduction*
gynography 402.1 *female sex*
gyp 539.10 *fraud*, 539.17 *cheat*,
539.30 *be fraudulent*
gypper 539.17 *cheat*
gyppo **91** Names for Inhabitants
gyppy 624.8 *indigestion*
Gypsies **1** Peoples
gypsophila **84** Flowers and
Flowering Plants
gypsum **54** Minerals, **57** Common Chemical Compounds,
44.2 *raw material*, 604.1 *materials*
gypsy 11.13 *diviner*, 104.5 *nonconformist*, 104.10 *foreign*
Gypsy **5** Languages and Groups
of Languages, 739.11 *pedlar*
Gypsy dance 46.4 *historic dancing*

gypsy moth 82 Insects
gypsy signs 543.1 sign
gyrate 324.13 be in motion, 364.8 rotate
gyrating 324.17 directional, 363.11 orbiting, 364.11 rotating
gyration 324.5 circuition, 364.1 rotation
gyrational 324.17 directional, 364.12 rotary
gyratory 324.17 directional, 363.10 circular, 364.12 rotary
gyre 8.7 devil, 54.13 ocean current, 334.1, 334.3 circuit, 363.1 orbital motion, 363.6 orbit, 364.8 rotate
gyre upward 359.19 take off
gyrfalcon 78 Birds
gyring 363.1 orbital motion, 363.11 orbiting
gyring up 359.4 taking off
gyro 364.6 rotator
gyrocompass 56.84 altimeter, 74.5 navigation, 364.6 rotator, 653.5 guide
gyrocopter 73 Types of Aircraft
gyrodyne 73 Types of Aircraft
gyron 544.8 heraldic device
gyroplane 364.6 rotator
gyroscope 56.84 altimeter, 364.6 rotator
gyroscopic 364.12 rotary
gyrostabilizer 364.6 rotator
gyrostat 56.84 altimeter
gyrostatic 364.12 rotary
gyrostatics 364.7 science of rotation

H

H 875.6 drug
H₂O 389.1 water
haar 441.2 murk
Haavikko 48 Poets
habanera 46.2 dance
habeas corpus 16.6 legal process, 692.2 demand
Haber 52 Scientists
haberdasher 295.26 fashion designer, 739.13 retailer
habergeon 671.7 armour
Haber process 57 Named Reactions
habiliment 295.2 dressing
habilimented 295.29 dressed
habiliments 295.1 dress
habit 584, 1.8 tradition, 7.11 vestment, 10.1 ritual, 32.10 dressage, 57.4 crystal, 112.1 uniformity, 116.6 convention, 150.7 method, 164.5 averageness, 166.6 custom, 183.3 repetitiveness, 306.5 formality, 513.3 the expected thing, 599.6 use, 875.1 drug-taking
Habit 584
habit and repute 654.3 precept
habitat 256, 250.1 location, 256.2 environment, 567.5 place of residence
Habitat 256
habitation 243.8 construction, 253.3 residence, 256.1 habitat, 567.5 place of residence
habited 295.29 dressed
habit-forming 584, 233.12 appealing, 586.19 persuasive, 874.6 intoxicating
habits 652.6 way of life, 876.1 morality
habitual 150, 584, 112.5 uniform, 116.15 conventional, 124.1 average, 164.21 common, 166.10 customary, 183.13 monotonous, 212.3 frequent, 306.11 formal, 584.14 habituated
habitual action 584.1 habit
habitual drunkard 874.17 drunkard
habitual liar 538.11, 539.16 liar
habitually 584, 112.13 uniformly, 116.37 conventionally,

124.11 on average, 164.30 usually, 166.18 as a rule, 212.1 frequently, 306.14 conventionally, 875.11 in a trance
habitually drunk 874.5 drunken
habitual lying 538.3, 540.6 lying
habitualness 164.5 averageness, 212.4 frequency
habituate 584, 116.26 make uniform, 584.16 have a habit
habituated 584, 253.8 attendant, 577.4 set
habituation 584
habitude 584.2 tendency
habitué 253.5 someone present, 584.8 creature of habit, 815.6 social person
hacek 5.1 linguistics, 543.7 punctuation
Hachiman 8 Deities
hacienda 68.6 farm, 725.1 property
hack 23.6 play basketball, 32.1 horse, 32.4 saddle horse, 33.10 be on the track, 41.10 curling, 41.13 ice-skating, 71.18 cab, 136.9 separate, 319.1, 319.5 notch, 322.18 open, 375.12 make rough, 528.9 informant, 532.11 newspaper man, 533.4 journalist, 560.10 descriptive writer, 646.1 worker, 656.10 unskilled person
hackberry 86 Fruits
hackbrett 49 Musical Instruments
hackbut 680.10 historical gun
hacked 322.12 open, 375.3 barbed
hacker 65.2 operator
hacking 23.5 penalties, 33.6 motor racing terms
hacking jacket 295.11 jacket
hackle 544.4 insignia
hackney 71 Carriages and Carts, 32.1 horse, 32.2 thoroughbred
Hackney 32 Breeds of Horse and Pony
hackney cab 71.18 cab
hackneyed 5.42 worded, 164.22 commonplace, 183.13 monotonous, 505.2 proverbial, 521.10 meaningless, 555.1 unemphatic, 584.10 familiar, 599.9 used
hackneyed expression 5.21 catchword
hackneyed phrase 505.1 maxim
Hackney pony 32 Breeds of Horse and Pony
hack weight 41.10 curling
hack work 644.1 work
had 539.36 deceived
hadal 54.51 oceanic
Hadar 53 Named Stars
had best 847.14 be the duty of
had better 847.14 be the duty of
haddock 80 Fishes, 45.18 sea fish, 80.8 food fish
hadephobia 777 Phobias by Name
Hades 8 Deities, 8.11 heaven, 368.1 nonmaterial world, 397.14 the spiritual world, 864.8 wicked place
Hadith 7.12 religious text
Hadlee 18 Sporting Personalities
Hadley 53 Rills and Valleys
Hadrianic art 50 Western Art Styles and Movements
Hadrian's wall 298.1 interface
Hadrian's Wall 661.3, 671.9 barrier
hadron 56.77 elementary particle
hadrosaur 79 Fossil Reptiles
Haeckel 52 Scientists
Haeckel's law 59.16 evolution
haem 58.24 respiration
haemal 387.18 bloody
haematemesis 353.10 bleeding
haematite 57 Common Metal Ores
haematologist 60.13 medical specialist
haematology 60.3 medical specialty

haematopoietic disease 624.4 disease
haematoxylin 85 Tree Products
haematoxylon 85 Trees and Shrubs
haematuria 353.10 bleeding
haemic 387.18 bloody
haemogenic 387.18 bloody
haemoglobin 58.18 pigment, 58.24 respiration, 387.4 blood
haemolytic anaemia 624.11 blood disease
haemophilia 353.10 bleeding, 387.5 fluidity, 624.11 blood disease
haemophiliac 624.19 sick person
haemophilic 387.18 bloody, 624.23 diseased
haemoprotein 58.9 protein
haemoptysis 353.10 bleeding
haemorrhage 347.2 outflow, 353.10 bleeding, 353.21 bleed, 387.6 flow, 624.11 blood disease, 722.4 lessening, 722.12 lessen
haemorrhaging 353.30 bleeding
haemorrhoea 353.10 bleeding
haemorrhoidectomy 60 Surgical Operations
haemostasis 371.2 concentration
haemostatic 371.6 dense
Haemus 53 Mountains
Haflinger 32 Breeds of Horse and Pony
hafnium 57 Chemical Elements
haft 603.1 tool
hag 832.9 vixen
hagbut 680.10 historical gun
Hagen 18 Sporting Personalities
hagfish 80 Fishes
haggard 274.2 emaciated, 397.21 deathly, 650.1 fatigued
Haggard 48 Writers
haggardness 274.8 emaciation
haggis 45.29 sausage, 45.32 meat dish, 45.44 British dish
haggle 710.10 offer to buy, 737.3 bargain, 754.14 buy cheaply
haggler 737.10 trader, 738.12 purchaser
haggling 716.1 negotiation, 716.8 negotiated, 737.9 bargaining, 738.14 buying
Hagia Sophia 43 Noted Buildings
hagiographer 560.10 descriptive writer
hagiographical 7.18 theological
hagiography 7.13 theology, 48.4 non-fiction, 560.4 factual account, 853.1 flattery
hagiological 7.18 theological
hagiologist 7.14 theologian
hagiology 7.13 theology
hagiophobia 777 Phobias by Name
hag-ridden 11.19 bewitched
Hague 93 Cities
Hague school 50 Western Art Styles and Movements
ha-ha 69.3 ornamental garden, 136.6 boundary, 265.2 crack, 301.3 enclosing thing
Hahn 52 Scientists
hahnium 57 Chemical Elements
Haida 1 Peoples, 5 Languages and Groups of Languages
Haifa 93 Cities
haiku 48.7 poem, 552.2 outline
hail 55
hail! 567
hail 55.24 precipitation, 55.63 snow, 161.22 flood, 181.4 throng, 344.23 hello, 409.5 ice, 431.4 cry of greeting, 543.6 word, 543.12 signal, 567.2 salutation, 567.9 approach, 817.12 greet, 851.16 acclaim
hailer 543.8 signaller
hail-fellow-well-met 815.15 sociable, 819.10 familiar
hailing 543.16 signalling
Hail Mary 10.9 prayer
hail-Mary 19.9 play
hailstone 55.24 precipitation, 409.5 ice

hailstorm 55.29 hail, 241.5 violent weather, 409.5 ice
Hailwood 18 Sporting Personalities
Hainan 98 Islands
Haiphong 93 Cities
hair 777 Phobias by Topic, 77.2 mammalian characteristic, 272.8 narrow thing, 293.14 animal covering, 374.11 soft thing, 376.8 smooth thing, 380.8 sharp-pointed thing
hairband 313.3 circular thing
hairbreadth escape 633.5 danger, 638.1 escape
hairbrush 376.9 smoother, 621.10 cleaning object, 879.14 instrument of punishment
haircloth 67 Natural Fabrics
hair colour 791.7 hairdressing
hair conditioner 386.6 pomade
hair cut 791
haircut 296.7 depilation
hair cutting 791.7 hairdressing
hair disease 777 Phobias by Topic
hair-do 791.8 hair cut
hairdresser 621.12 cleaner, 697.4 personal attendant, 791.13 beautician
hairdressers 791.11 hairdressing salon
hairdressing 791
hairdressing salon 791
hair-dryer 392.15 dryer
hair dyeing 791.7 hairdressing
hair grass 87 Grasses
hairgrip 137.8 fastening
hair hygrometer 389.19 measuring instrument
hairiness 375.6 roughness
hairless 296, 294.10 bald, 376.1 smooth
hairlessness 294.6, 296.5 baldness
hairlike 272.2 fine
hairline crack 265.2 crack, 322.1 opening
hair moss 88.3 moss
hair of the dog 874.13 drink
hair oil 395.6 ointment
hair on end 636.2 danger signal
hairpiece 295.15 headgear
hairpin 33.6 motor racing terms, 41.3 ski racing, 41.12 ski, 137.8 fastening, 335.5 twist
hairpin bend 71.3 carriageway, 310.1 angle, 335.14 deviating course
hairpin curve 286.2 oblique line
hair-pulling 26.5 wrestling
hair-raising 403.9 exciting, 777.10 frightening
hair remover 294.5 shedding, 296.7 depilation
hair-removing 296.13 hairless
hair's-breadth 264.2 short distance
hair shirt 295.8 shirt, 840.2 apology, 867.1 penitence
hair space 265.1 interval
hairsplitter 503.4 accurate person
hair-splitter 474.6 sophist, 481.6 discriminating person
hairsplitting 503.1 accuracy, 503.5 accurate, 852.6, 852.28 fault-finding
hair-splitting 474.4, 474.9 quibbling, 481.2 judiciousness, 481.9 discriminating
hairspring 377.5 spring, 603.4 machine
hair standing on end 777.1 fear
hairstreak 82 Insects
hairstyle 791.8 hair cut
hair styling 791.7 hairdressing
hair-stylist 791.13 beautician
hair transplant 295.15 headgear
hair-trigger 329.1 swift
hairworm 81 Worms
hairy 375.3 barbed, 383.8 rough, 633.1 dangerous, 659.12 problematic, 661.14 blocked
hairy frog 79 Amphibians
Haiti 11 Countries, 98 Islands
Haitian 5 Languages and Groups of Languages

hajj 9.1 *worship*
hajji 7.3 *religious person,* 9.5 *worshipper,* 497.5 *believer*
haka 46.4 *historic dancing*
hakam 7.8 *priest*
hake 80 *Fishes,* 45.18 *sea fish*
hakea 85 *Trees and Shrubs*
hakim 60.12, 630.15 *healer*
halal 134.14 *purified*
halberd 680.8 *sharp weapon*
halberdier 679.13 *historical soldiery*
halcyon 325.6 *quiescent,* 675.7 *peaceful,* 686.8 *prosperous*
halcyon days 55.3 *weather,* 106.5 *comfortable circumstances,* 686.3 *time of plenty,* 762.2 *fun,* 861.17 *good thing*
hale 142.8 *sound,* 237.9 *physically strong,* 239.4 *vigorous,* 306.12 *on form,* 339.11 *pull,* 623.1 *healthy*
hale and hearty 142.8 *sound,* 237.9 *physically strong,* 239.4 *vigorous,* 623.1 *healthy*
haleness 623.3 *health*
Hale Observatories 53.23 *observatory*
Hale Telescope 53.24 *telescope*
half 176, 176, 19.5 *game time,* 23.1 *basketball,* 143.1 *part,* 143.12 *partly,* 145.4 *incomplete,* 145.6 *incompletely,* 173.4 *less than one,* 173.5 *fractional,* 173.7 *fractionally,* 176.22 *in half*
half a chance 486.3 *strong possibility,* 589.6 *poor chance*
half-a-crown 741.10 *former British money*
half-a-dozen 179.2 *six*
half a gale 55.14 *windiness*
half a hundred 179.8 *twenty and over*
half a mo 189.3 *short duration,* 191.3 *instant*
half and half 158, 124.2 *medium,* 124.12 *mediumly,* 143.12 *partly*
half-and-half 110.16 *equal,* 122.8 *on equal terms,* 133.12 *mixed,* 176.22 *in half,* 333.4 *middle*
half-and-halfer 333.3 *moderate person*
half-and-half measures 333.2 *middle of the road*
half-and-half split 110.5 *equality*
half a sec 191.3 *instant*
half-asleep 643.3 *not awake,* 650.1 *fatigued*
half-assed 656.4 *bungled*
half a tick 191.3 *instant*
half-awake 650.1 *fatigued*
halfback 19.7 *offence,* 31.2 *hockey player,* 35.4 *rugby player*
half-bagged 874.2 *slightly drunk*
half-baked 208.16 *premature,* 502.7 *semi-skilled,* 595.3 *without preparation,* 595.6 *uncooked,* 656.4 *bungled,* 685.4 *uncompleted*
half-ball 24.9 *billiard*
half-ball stroke 24.2 *billiards play*
halfbeak 80 *Fishes*
half begin 685.5 *not complete*
half-begun 685.4 *uncompleted*
half-believe 498.8 *disbelieve*
half-blood 133.5 *hybrid*
half-blooded 133.12 *mixed*
half-blown 595.5 *immature*
half-bred 68.21 *domesticated*
half-breed 1.6 *race,* 1.13 *racial,* 133.5 *hybrid,* 133.12 *mixed*
half-butt cue 24.3 *English billiards*
half-butt rest 24.3 *English billiards*
half-caste 1.6 *race,* 1.13 *racial,* 133.5 *hybrid,* 133.12 *mixed*
half cell 57.19 *electrochemistry*
half century 179.8 *twenty and over*
half circle 313.2 *circle*
half-clothed 296.10 *in dishabille*
half-cocked 208.16 *premature*
half-cooked 595.6 *uncooked*

half-crown 741.10 *former British money*
half-cut 874.2 *slightly drunk*
half-dark 441.5 *dim*
half-dead 397.18 *dying,* 641.3 *inactive,* 650.1 *fatigued*
half deck 74 *Parts of a Ship*
half-developed 595.5 *immature*
half do 685.5 *not complete*
half-dollar 741.8 *American money*
half-done 145.4 *incomplete,* 358.7 *short,* 470.5 *indifferent,* 685.4 *uncompleted*
half-dressed 296.10 *in dishabille*
half-face 457.3 *external appearance*
half fare 754.4 *bargain*
half-fed 609.3 *underfed*
half-filled 620.2 *incomplete*
half finish 685.5 *not complete*
half-finished 143.11 *partial,* 145.4 *incomplete,* 595.5 *immature,* 620.2 *incomplete,* 685.4 *uncompleted*
half-formed 595.5 *immature*
half-frozen 393.23 *thawing*
half-furnished 595.7 *unequipped*
half-gone 641.3 *inactive*
half-grown 595.5 *immature*
half-hardy 69.17 *botanical,* 83.15 *wild*
half-heard 424.4 *faint,* 428.1 *faint-sounding*
half-hearted 145.4 *incomplete,* 238.12 *weak-willed,* 542.17 *insipid,* 573.3 *cautious,* 783.7 *indifferent,* 838.1 *ingratitude*
half-hearted attempt 596.5 *attempt*
halfheartedly 242.9 *moderately*
half-heartedly 238.14 *weakly,* 542.26 *insipidly,* 573.17 *unwillingly,* 783.17 *indifferently*
half-heartedness 145.1 *incompleteness,* 542.8 *insipidness,* 573.13 *dissociation,* 576.14 *apathy,* 783.1 *indifference*
halfhearted thanks 838.1 *ingratitude*
half hitch 74 *Knots*
half-holiday 645.2 *time off*
half-hose 295.20 *legwear*
half-hunter 191 *Timepieces and Timers,* 192.7 *watch*
half-knowledge 502, 501.2 *information*
half-length portrait 50.10 *art subject*
half-lie 538.5 *half-truth,* 538.21 *lie*
half-life 56.70 *radioactivity*
half-light 441.1 *dimness,* 444.3 *hue*
half line 48.8 *part of poem*
halfling 260.4 *little person*
half-lit 441.5 *dim*
half-mast 362.10 *lower the flag*
half measure 538.5 *shortfall*
half-measure 717, 717, 124.6 *mediocrity*
half measures 333.2 *middle of the road,* 609.8 *insufficiency,* 614.5 *waste of effort,* 685.1 *non-completion*
half-measures 656.9 *bungling*
half-melted 393.23 *thawing*
half-moon 53.17 *moon,* 311.3 *curved things*
half-moon glasses 435.10 *visual aid*
half-nelson 26.5 *wrestling,* 726.1 *retention*
half pay 749.3 *income*
halfpenny 741.10 *former British money*
half-pint 260.4 *little person,* 270.5 *short person*
half pint glass 258.13 *drinking vessel*
half-point 332.4 *compass point*
half-price 754.9 *cheap*
half rations 609.8 *insufficiency*
half relief 50.13 *relief-carving*
half-remembered 512.11 *forgotten*
half rhyme 48.11 *rhyme*
half-ripe 595.5 *immature*
half-seas over 874.1 *drunk*

half-seen 438.2 *difficult to see*
half-shot 874.2 *slightly drunk*
half shove 36.19 *punt*
half-shove 36.8 *punting*
half-skilled 656.2 *unskilled*
half-slip 295.18 *underwear*
half sovereign 741.10 *former British money*
half space 265.1 *interval*
half-spoken 527.4 *unsaid*
half-spoken word 527.10 *quietness*
half standard 69.10 *fruit tree*
half starve 869.5 *be self-restrained,* 871.5 *fast*
half-starved 609.3 *underfed,* 782.10 *hungry,* 871.6 *fasting*
half the battle 611.3 *chief thing*
half-timbered building 43.3 *building*
half-timbering 243.8 *construction*
half time 19.5 *game time*
half-time 23.1 *basketball,* 187.4 *period of activity*
half tone 66.3 *photograph*
half-tone 439.12 *highlight,* 444.3 *hue*
half-tonner 36.10 *sailing*
half-tonner class 36.2 *sailing boat*
half-track 71 *Motor Vehicles*
half-true 540.32 *falsified*
half-truth 538
half-truthfully 538.26 *untruthfully*
half-turn 30.8 *floor exercises*
half-volley 40.5 *real tennis*
half volte 32.10 *dressage*
half-war 676.1 *war*
half-wave rectifier 64.21 *rectifier*
halfway 124.2 *medium,* 124.12 *mediumly,* 158.5 *middle distance,* 158.11, 158.21 *midway,* 176.13 *half,* 333.4 *middle,* 717.1 *compromise,* 717.6 *compromising,* 717.9 *compromisingly*
half-way 35.6 *rugger,* 38.5 *soccer*
halfway house 124.5 *medium,* 158.1 *middle,* 242.1 *moderation,* 256.11 *retreat,* 634.2 *shelter,* 702.1 *prison*
half-way line 35.1 *rugger,* 38.1 *soccer*
halfway measures 333.2 *middle of the road*
halfway point 124.5 *medium,* 158.1 *middle*
half-white 446.1 *white*
halfwit 460.3 *unintelligent person,* 508.3 *foolish person*
halibut 80 *Fishes,* 45.18 *sea fish,* 80.8 *food fish*
halide 57 *Types of Compounds*
Halifax 93 *Cities,* **93** *Cities*
halite 54 *Minerals*
halitosis 419.2 *something that makes an unpleasant smell*
hall 6.15 *schoolroom,* 51.14 *theatre,* 243.8 *construction,* 256.4 *official residence,* 256.7 *room,* 327.2 *route,* 420.3 *auditorium,* 526.8 *showplace*
Halle 93 *Cities*
Hallé 49 *Musicians and Composers*
Hall effect 56 *Named Laws*
hallelujah 431.3 *cry of praise,* 773.2 *fanfare,* 773.12 *hurrah,* 812.7 *thanksgiving*
Hallelujah 10.8 *hymn*
hallelujah chorus 773.2 *fanfare*
Halley 52 *Scientists,* **53** *Comets*
Halley's Comet 213.4 *rare things,* 214.5 *regular thing,* 439.4 *natural light*
hallmark 165.3 *characteristic,* 543.1 *sign,* 543.3 *means of identification,* 544.10 *identify,* 560.8 *name*
hallmarked 544.12 *identified*
hall-marked 537.19 *authentic*
hallmarked silver 537.6 *authenticity*
halloa 32.8 *hunting*
hall of mirrors 436.5 *visual distortion*
hall of residence 6.15 *schoolroom*
halloo 431.5 *hunting cry,* 590.10 *chase,* 590.19 *after him*

hallow 8.17 *deify,* 9.7 *worship,* 812.16 *commemorate*
hallowed 8.13 *divine*
hallowed by custom 584.12 *established*
hallowedness 8.1 *divinity*
Hallowe'en 10.16 *religious festival,* 11.3 *witchcraft,* 214.6 *annually celebrated day*
Hallowe'en party 665.7 *social gathering*
halls of death 397.14 *the spiritual world*
hallucinate 11.24 *experience psychic phenomena,* 102.13, 435.17 *imagine,* 519.14 *imagine,* 539.25 *deceive oneself*
hallucinating 510.12 *manic*
hallucination 11.10 *psychic phenomenon,* 102.2 *illusion,* 435.5 *imagination,* 457.4 *something that appears,* 504.6 *fallibility,* 510.4 *delusion,* 519.5 *fantasy,* 539.5 *falseness*
hallucinatory 102.9 *illusory,* 457.9 *ostensible,* 539.40 *illusory*
hallucinogen 62.4 *drug type,* 875.6 *drug*
hallucinogenic 62.17 *stimulating,* 875.9 *addictive*
hallux 382 *Bones,* 407.7 *sense organ*
hallway 322.7 *passageway,* 327.2 *route*
halma 42 *Board Games*
Halmahera 98 *Islands*
halo 53.7 *galaxy,* 55.22 *sun,* 313.3 *circular thing,* 439.12 *highlight*
haloalkane 57 *Types of Compounds*
halocaine 62 *Medication*
haloed 8.15 *deified,* 439.17 *lustrous*
haloform 57 *Types of Compounds*
halogen 57.6 *chemical element*
halogenate 57.26 *react*
halogenation 57 *Types of Chemical Reaction*
halogen light 439.6 *electric light*
halon 631.9 *pollution*
haloperidol 62 *Medication*
halothane 62 *Medication,* 404.4 *anaesthetic*
Hälsingborg 93 *Cities*
halt 72.8 *railway station,* 157.2 *cessation,* 157.16 *cease,* 160.2 *cessation,* 160.12 *discontinue,* 209.3 *delayed action,* 209.8 *delay,* 218.2 *stop,* 218.4 *stopping place,* 218.6 *cease,* 238.6 *be weak,* 325.1 *motionlessness,* 325.8 *be motionless,* 325.11 *stop,* 328.2 *hesitate,* 344.16 *stopover,* 620.3 *deformed,* 659.8 *snag,* 683.1 *failure*
halted 160.9 *discontinued,* 209.10 *held up*
halter 137.9 *yoke,* 295.8 *shirt,* 699.5 *means of restraint,* 879.16 *instrument of execution*
halt hostilities 677.5 *make peace*
halting 145.4 *incomplete,* 215.4 *irregular,* 328.4 *slow*
haltingly 215.8 *irregularly,* 328.16 *slowly*
halt one's progress 587.3 *deflect*
halt the arms race 675.6 *make peace,* 677.4 *pacify*
halvah 45.54 *other dishes*
halve 176, 124.10 *make average,* 136.11 *divide,* 158.17 *average*
halved 136.15 *separate,* 176.13 *half*
halved hole 29.2 *golfing terms*
halving 176
halyard 36.3 *parts of a sailing boat,* 137.9 *tackle,* 544.7 *flag*
ham 45.30 *bacon,* 51.7 *dramaturgy,* 51.22 *actor,* 51.33 *overact,* 541.7 *exaggerate,* 656.2 *unskilled,* 656.10 *unskilled person*
ham acting 51.20 *acting*
hamadryad 79 *Reptiles,* 8.5 *deity,* 85.13 *tree mythology*

hamadryas 77 Placental Mammals

ham and cheese sandwich 45.11 *sandwich*

hamartophobia 777 Phobias by Name

ham-bone soup 45.43 *US dish*

Hamburg 93 Cities

hamburger 45.11 *sandwich*, 45.20 *meat*

hamburger place 350.15 *eating place*

Hamburgh 68 Breeds of Fowl

Hamersley 95 Mountains

ham-fisted 559.7 *graceless*, 776.8 *bad*

ham-fistedness 659.2 *awkwardness*

ham-handed 656.3 *clumsy*

ham-handedness 656.8 *unskilfulness*

Hamilton 52 Scientists, **93** Cities, **93** Cities

Hamitic 5 Languages and Groups of Languages, 5.11 *family of languages*

Hamito-Semitic 5 Languages and Groups of Languages, 5.11 *family of languages*

ham it up 51.33 *overact*, 541.7 *exaggerate*, 656.5 *be unskilful*

hamlet 92.4 *community*, 93.1 *city*, 93.10 *village*, 249.11 *settlement*

Hamlet 48 Shakespeare's plays

hammed up 51.38 *tragic*

hammer 382 Bones, **384**, 21.2 *field events*, 34.4 *climbing equipment*, 126.8 *be superior*, 183.22 *resound*, 330.2 *collide*, 330.5 *beat*, 330.15 *ram*, 338.10 *ball*, 373.7 *hard substance*, 384.27 *beat*, 420.5 *internal ear*, 423.8 *be loud*, 603.1 *tool*, 603.9 *use tools*, 670.5 *strike*, 680.7 *blunt weapon*

hammer and sickle 543.1 *sign*

hammer and tongs 239.6 *with vigour*, 241.10 *violently*, 330.12 *collision*, 644.12 *laboriously*

hammer at 644.8 *exert oneself*

hammer away at 183.18 *harp*, 575.6 *persevere*

hammer blows 241.2 *physical violence*

hammer glove 21.2 *field events*

hammerhead 78 Birds

hammer head 330.15 *ram*

hammerhead shark 80 Fishes

hammer home 554.6 *emphasize*

hammer in 135.10 *link*, 354.3 *impact*

hammering 183.6 *reverberation*, 183.15 *reverberatory*, 330.12 *collision*

hammer into 183.18 *harp*

hammerlock 726.1 *retention*

hammer out 306.7 *form*, 796.8 *fashion*

hammerstone 330.15 *ram*

hammer throw 21.2 *field events*

hammer-thrower 21.3 *athlete*

hammer throwing 18 Sporting Activities

hammer-throwing 21.2 *field events*

Hammett 48 Writers

hamming 51.20 *acting*, 541.1 *exaggeration*

hamming it up 51.20 *acting*

hammock 47.6 *bed*, 283.3 *suspended object*, 325.3 *resting place*

Hammond 18 Sporting Personalities

hammy 51.38 *tragic*

hamper 258.7 *basket*, 302.7 *limit*, 369.14 *make heavy*, 515.7 *thwart*, 628.5 *hurt*, 659.23 *cause difficulties*, 661.8 *hinder*

hampered 515.9 *disappointed*

hampering 661.1 *hindrance*

Hampshire 4 Philosophers, **68** Breeds of Pig, **92** Counties

Hampshire Down 68 Breeds of Sheep

Hampstead 93.5 *London*

Hampton 93 Cities

ham sandwich 45.11 *sandwich*

hamse 543.7 *punctuation*

hamster 77 Placental Mammals

hamster food 350.8 *animal food*

hamstring 236.8 *overpower*, 244.11 *ruin*, 628.5 *hurt*

Hamsun 48 Writers

hamzah 5.36 *accent*

Han 96 Rivers

hand 42.2 *contest*, 42.3 *card game terms*, 45.24 *pork* , 143.4 *component*, 230.6 *operative*, 232.3 *assistant*, 400.7 *person*, 407.7 *sense organ*, 543.7 *punctuation*, 640.3 *doer*, 646.1 *worker*, 662.1 *help*, 726.3 *tools for gripping*, 851.5 *acclaim*

hand back 629.3 *restore*, 735.4 *give back*

handbag 258.8 *bag*, 326.10 *transferred thing*, 741.20 *money store*

handball 38.2 *football play*, 377.3 *elastic thing*

handbarrow 71.7 *handcart*

hand beater 45.6 *kitchen equipment*

handbell 49 Musical Instruments, 49.6 *campanology*, 427.4 *sources of resonance*

handbill 532.9 *advertisement*

handbook 6.14 *school book*, 528.5 *reference book*

handbrake turn 71.21 *miscellaneous motoring terms*

handbreadth 271.4 *breadth*

handcart 71, 258.10 *cart*

handclap 851.5 *acclaim*

handclapping 851.5 *acclaim*

handclasp 815.9 *welcome*, 817.5 *sign of courtesy*, 819.4 *act of friendship*

hand cream 134.3 *purifier*, 395.6 *ointment*

handcuff 135.10 *link*, 137.12 *bind*, 323.11 *restrain*, 699.12 *gag*

handcuffed 137.16 *bound*

handcuffs 137.8 *fastening*, 323.3 *restrainer*, 699.5 *means of restraint*

hand down 570.16 *bequeath*, 728.3 *transfer property*

hand down a judgment 166.13 *rule*

handed 407

handed down 1.14 *societal*

Handel 49 Musicians and Composers

handfork 69.6 *garden tool*

handful 120.3 *container*, 182.1 *few*, 659.3 *difficult task*, 659.9 *difficult person*, 693.5 *troublemaker*, 693.9 *criminal*, 702.4 *prison sentence*

hand grenade 680.16 *bomb*

handgrip 20.3 *fishing tackle*

handgun 680.9 *firearm*

hand-held computer game 65.18 *computer game*

handhold 726.1 *retention*

hand horn 49 Musical Instruments

handicap 29.2 *golfing terms*, 32.7 *horseracing*, 36.10 *sailing*, 123.1 *inequality*, 123.5 *be unequal*, 126.3 *advantage*, 127.2 *deficiency*, 369.8 *weighing down*, 369.14 *make heavy*, 616.3 *inconvenience*, 616.5 *be inconvenient*, 620.7 *defect*, 624.2 *illness*, 661.6, 661.12 *burden*, 674.2 *contest*

handicapped 369.3 *ponderous*, 620.8 *deformed*, 661.14 *blocked*

handicap race 36.1 *sailing*

handicap score 29.2 *golfing terms*

handicap stroke 29.3 *golf shots*

handicraft 50.1 *art*, 640.2 *deed*

handicraftsman 640.3 *doer*, 646.2 *artisan*

handicraft worker 640.3 *doer*

handily 232.9 *instrumentally*, 613.12 *usefully*, 615.7 *conveniently*, 655.12 *skilfully*

hand in 40.9 *squash terms*

handiness 232.1 *instrumentality*, 253.4 *availability*, 260.1 *littleness*, 264.1 *nearness*, 613.5 *usefulness*, 615.3 *convenience*, 655.1 *skill*, 660.3 *wieldiness*, 861.12 *proficiency*

handing back 735.1 *giving back*

handing in one's notice 705.1 *resignation*

hand in glove 180.22 *hand in hand*, 664.19 *associating*, 664.20 *cooperatively*, 819.10 *familiar*, 819.18 *intimately*

hand-in-glove 180.19 *associated*, 407.9 *touching*

handing over 598.3 *relinquishment*

hand in hand 180, 116.32 *in alliance*, 135.12 *united*, 664.20 *cooperatively*, 815.18 *sociably*, 819.10 *familiar*, 819.18 *intimately*

hand-in-hand 264.5 *near*, 305.10 *laterally*, 407.9 *touching*

hand in one's notice 705.5 *resign*

hand in one's resignation 705.5 *resign*

hand it to 851.15 *compliment*

hand it to one 845.17 *credit*

handiwork 227.2 *visible effect*, 243.1 *production*, 640.2 *deed*

Handke 48 Dramatists

handkerchief 295.25 *accessories*, 621.11 *cleaning cloth*

hand-knit sweater 295.13 *sweater*

handle 36.4 *rowing*, 230.9 *take action*, 293.33 *fix*, 407.11 *touch*, 560.8 *name*, 599.1 *use*, 603.1 *tool*, 652.14 *behave towards*, 653.1 *manage*, 737.1 *trade*, 739.1 *sell*, 804.1 *right*

handle a consignment 70.4 *transport*

handlebars 71.11 *bicycle part*, 375.7 *rough thing*

handle cargo 70.4 *transport*

handled 38.5 *soccer*

handle drum 49 Musical Instruments

handler 230.5 *operator*, 293.18 *fixer*

handle tenderly 691.3 *be lenient*

handle the ball 35.5 *play rugby*

handle with kid gloves 691.3 *be lenient*

handling 38.2 *football play*, 230.4 *management*, 293.20 *fixing*, 407.2 *touching*, 599.6 *use*, 640.1 *action*, 652.8 *treatment*, 653.3 *management*

handling the ball in a scrum 35.3 *rugby play*

hand loom 67.4, 288.3 *weaving*

hand lotion 134.3 *purifier*, 386.6 *pomade*, 621.9 *cleaning agent*

handmade 243.12 *produced*

handmaid 232.3 *assistant*, 697.6 *domestic servant*

handmaiden 697.6 *domestic servant*

hand-me-down 295.1 *dress*, 599.9 *used*

hand me downs 296.4 *dishabille*

hand-milk 68.18 *practise livestock farming*

hand mirror 56.29 *optical element*, 435.8 *reflection*

hand of death 397.1 *death*

handoff 19.9 *play*, 19.15 *play offence*

hand of friendship 677.2 *peace offering*

hand of God 631.1 *affliction*

hand on 326.14 *bring back*, 728.3 *transfer property*

hand-operated 232.8 *practical*, 407.10 *handed*

hand out 40.9 *squash terms*, 228.5 *positive stimulus*, 528.4 *mass communication*, 532.9 *advertisement*, 533.9 *news story*, 606.5 *provision*, 662.4 *social assistance*, 729.3 *offering*, 755.7 *gift*, 833.5 *charity*

hand out a sample 710.9 *offer*

hand out bouquets 878.9 *reward*

hand out brickbats 852.17 *criticize*

handover 326.2 *transportation*

hand over 326.11 *transfer*, 326.12 *transport*, 356.11 *cross*, 598.1 *relinquish*

handover 728.1 *transfer of property*

hand over 728.3 *transfer property*, 729.5 *give*

hand over fist 359.26 *up*

hand over one's sword 673.3 *submit*

hand over the baton 21.6 *race*

hand-paint 44.11 *make ceramics*

hand-painted 44.10 *ceramic*

hand-painted decorations 44.3 *glaze*

hand-pick 131.3 *subtract*, 580.4 *pick*

hand-picked 580.15 *chosen*, 617.1 *worthy*

handprop 51.19 *stage requisite*

hand round 606.5 *provision*

hands 192.8 *face*, 646.4 *personnel*, 662.11 *helper*

hands across the sea 819.2 *friendly relations*

hands down 660.21 *easily*

handsel 729.2 *gift*, 746.1 *payment*

handset 420.9 *audio device*, 534.9 *telephone*

handshake 65.14 *data transfer*, 65.17 *computing term*, 344.12 *reception*, 543.3 *gesture*, 714.1 *promise*, 808.9 *fawn*, 815.9 *welcome*, 817.5 *sign of courtesy*, 819.4 *act of friendship*

handshaking 808.2 *sycophancy*, 808.7 *sycophantic*

hand signal 543.3 *gesture*

hands in pockets 543.3 *gesture*

hands off! 591

hands off 641.1 *inaction*

hands-off 641.3 *inactive*

handsome 755.1 *generous*, 789.5 *beautiful*

handsome fortune 742.5 *wealth*

handsomeness 789.1 *gorgeousness*

hands-on 407.10 *handed*

hands on hips 543.3 *gesture*

handspike 603.1 *tool*

handspring 30.6 *pommel horse*, 30.8 *floor exercises*, 287.1 *inversion*, 287.3 *invert*, 359.5 *jump*

handstand 30.5 *horizontal bar*, 30.7 *stationary rings*, 39.11 *swimming*

handstand dive 39.6 *diving*

handstand position 30.5 *horizontal bar*

handstrap 30.2 *gymnastic clothing*

hand's turn 644.2 *task*

hand that rocks the cradle 233.4 *indirect influence*

hand to hand 407.17 *manually*

hand-to-hand 70.6 *commercially*, 674.15 *contentious*

hand-to-hand fight 674.9 *duel*

hand-to-hand fighting 674.6 *fight*

hand-to-mouth 608.1 *sufficient*, 743.1 *poor*

hand-to-mouth existence 743.5 *poverty*

hand tool 603.1 *tool*

hand to on a plate 127.9 *yield to*

hand towel 621.11 *cleaning cloth*

hand trumpet 49 Musical Instruments

hand-turn 44.11 *make ceramics*

hand-turned 44.10 *ceramic*

hand-turned wheel 44.6 *ceramic workshop*

handwoven 288.6 *interwoven*

handy 232.6 *instrumental*, 253.10 *available*, 260.7 *little*, 264.5 *near*, 370.1 *light*, 407.8 *touchable*, 613.1 *useful*, 615.1 *convenient*, 655.6 *skilful*, 660.12 *wieldy*, 662.33 *helpful*, 861.5 *proficient*

handyman 629.12 *repairer*, 642.10 *busy person*, 646.1

worker, 655.4 *skilled person*, 697.1 *servant*

Han dynasty art 50 Non-Western Art

hanepoot 86 Fruits

Han fei zi 4 Philosophers

hang 30.7 *stationary rings*, 30.10 *compete in gymnastics*, 68.14 *pest control*, 283.1 *suspension*, 283.10 *suspend*, 359.20 *hover*, 397.16 *meet one's fate*, 398.19, 879.5 *execute*

hang about 209.7 *wait*, 264.10 *stay near*, 643.12 *be inactive*

hang a picture 526.2 *display something*

hangar 73.4 *airport*, 256.7 *room*

hang around 209.7 *wait*, 253.12 *attend*, 264.10 *stay near*

hang around with 180.14 *keep company with*, 815.13 *fraternize*

hang back 209.7 *wait*, 491.19 *hesitate*, 573.8 *hold back*, 591.4 *shy*, 661.11 *be inhibited*, 781.5 *be cautious*, 810.15 *escape notice*

hang by a thread 633.8 *be in danger*

hang by the neck 879.5 *execute*

hangdog 806.3 *humbled*, 808.7 *sycophantic*, 866.6 *appearing guilty*

hangdog look 806.9 *humiliation*, 830.2 *sign of sullenness*

hang down 283.10 *suspend*, 360.10 *droop*

hang, draw, and quarter 879.5 *execute*

hang 'em high 398.26 *no quarter*, 879.24 *string him up*

hanger 283, 23.4 *playing terms*, 603.1 *tool*, 680.8 *sharp weapon*

hanger-on 138.5, 155.14 *follower*, 180.9, 195.8 *follower*, 701.4 *dependent*, 712.5 *beggar*, 808.5 *adherent*, 853.7 *sycophant*

hang fire 209.7 *wait*, 218.9 *pause*, 240.4 *be inert*, 247.7 *be infertile*, 325.8 *be motionless*, 573.8 *hold back*, 641.4 *not act*, 643.12 *be inactive*

hang glide 283.10 *suspend*

hang glider 73.8 *aircraft*

hang-glider 360.8 *descender*

hang-gliding 18 Sporting Activities

hang in 574.11 *persist*

hanging 51.17 *stage*, 139.8 *nonadhesive*, 238.8 *weak*, 283.1 *suspension*, 283.7 *suspended*, 293.8 *wall covering*, 397.4 *death sentence*, 398.2 *murder*, 398.5 *execution*, 879.13 *capital punishment*

hanging back 491.2 *irresolute*, 661.5 *inhibition*

hanging ball 29.2 *golfing terms*

hanging basket 69.3 *ornamental garden*

hanging by a thread 397.18 *dying*, 633.2 *unsafe*

hanging by the wrists 879.12 *corporal punishment*

hanging, drawing, and quartering 879.13 *capital punishment*

hanging garden 69.2 *garden*

Hanging Gardens of Babylon 69.2 *garden*

hanging in there 575.10 *persevering*

hanging judge 16.23 *judge*, 690.4 *strict person*, 879.17 *punisher*

hanging object 283.3 *suspended object*

hanging offence 864.7 *criminality*

hanging on 726.1 *retention*

hanging oneself 398.7 *suicide*

hanging out 212.5 *frequenting*

hanging rope 879.15 *instrument of execution*

hanging together 116.14 *conforming*

hanging up 218.2 *stop*

hanging valley 54.7 *landform*

hang it up 600.7 *stop work*, 673.3 *submit*

hang like a millstone 369.13 *weigh on*

hang loose 218.9 *pause*, 374.14 *ease*

hangman 42 Children's Games and Party Games, 241.4 *violent person or animal*, 244.6 *destroyer*, 398.10 *killer*, 398.12 *executioner*, 879.17 *punisher*

hangman's knot 74 Knots

hang on 135.10 *link*, 138.8 *be tenacious*, 188.6 *last*, 209.8 *delay*, 219.4 *protract*, 575.8 *hold out*, 726.6 *retain*, 808.14 *follow*

hang on by one's teeth 225.8 *show determination*, 575.8 *hold out*

hang oneself 398.21 *commit suicide*

hang one's head 806.24 *be humiliated*

hang one's head in shame 867.4 *be penitent*

hang one's lip 830.9 *be sullen*

hang on for dear life 575.8 *hold out*, 726.6 *retain*

hang on in there 188.6 *last*, 219.4 *protract*

hang on like grim death 575.8 *hold out*

hang on someone's words 420.15 *hear*

hang on the skirts of 808.14 *follow*

hang on to 605.6 *store*

hang onto 860.6 *be selfish*

hang on with all one's might 726.6 *retain*

hang out 253.12 *attend*

hangout 256.2 *environment*

hang out 392.23 *drip-dry*

hang out a signal 543.12 *signal*

hang out at 212.8, 256.19 *frequent*

hang out the flags 812.18 *salute*

hang out to dry 392.23 *drip-dry*

hang out with 180.14 *keep company with*, 815.13 *fraternize*

hangover 155.6 *aftermath*

hang over 283.11 *project*, 328.2 *hesitate*

hangover 874.15 *crapulence*

Hang Seng Index 14.2 *stock exchange*

hang technique 21.2 *field events*

hang time 19.12 *special team*

hang together 116.5 *conform*, 135.8 *unite*, 138.6 *adhere*, 664.13 *work together*

hang tough 378.10 *be tough*

hang up 218.6 *cease*, 283.10 *suspend*, 534.32 *telephone*, 600.6 *stop using*

hang-up 467.4 *diligence*, 620.7 *defect*, 661.2 *obstacle*

hang upon 227.7 *follow from*

hang up on 563.15 *strike dumb*

hang up one's hat 256.18 *take up residence*

hang up one's spikes 600.7 *stop work*

hang weights on 369.14 *make heavy*

hank 74 Rigging, **75** General Units, 36.3 *parts of a sailing boat*, 161.27 *bundle*

hanker after 782.12 *desire*, 784.7 *like*, 842.3 *be envious of*

hankering 782.1 *desire*, 784.1, 784.6 *liking*

hanky-panky 539.7 *tricking*, 801.3 *disreputable action*, 821.8 *love affair*

Hannibal 93 Cities

Hannukah 10.16 *religious festival*

Hanoi 52 Named Concepts, **93** Cities

Hanover 93 Cities

Hanoverian 32 Breeds of Horse and Pony, 202.14 *historic*

Hansard 545.1 *record*

Hansen's disease 624.7 *tropical disease*

hansom 71 Carriages and Carts

Hanuman 8 Deities

Haokah 8 Deities

hap 229.5 *happen by chance*

ha'penny 741.10 *former British money*

haphazard 113.5 *diverse*, 151.14, 215.4 *irregular*, 229.6 *motiveless*, 482.3 *indiscriminate*, 491.8 *capricious*, 589.8 *chance*, 648.3 *hasty*, 656.3 *clumsy*

haphazardly 113.11 *irregularly*, 151.27 *in disorder*, 215.8 *irregularly*, 229.8 *by chance*, 482.14 *indiscriminately*, 589.13 *by chance*

haphazardness 113.1 *diversity*, 151.2 *irregular order*, 215.1 *irregularity*, 229.1 *lack of motive*

haphido 18 Sporting Activities

Hapi 8 Deities

hapless 687.8 *unlucky*

haploid 59.25 *genetic*

haploid number 59.14 *chromosome*

haploidy 59.14 *chromosome*

haplomitosis 59.10 *cell division*

haply 486.9 *possibly*

happen 101.10 *be real*, 227.5 *show an effect*, 227.9 *take effect*, 229.5 *happen by chance*, 457.13 *occur*, 589.10 *chance*, 640.4 *act*

happen again 183.21 *be repeated*

happen at the same time 198.6 *be simultaneous*

happen by chance 229

happen by coincidence 229.5 *happen by chance*

happen every day 212.7 *be frequent*

happening 3.14 *historicalness*, 51.2 *play*, 99.2 *thing*, 106.2 *occurrence*, 196.3 *actuality*, 227.1 *effect*, 457.2 *being in view*, 472.6 *topical*, 640.1 *action*, 640.5 *acting*

happening late 209.9 *late*

happenings 472.3 *matter of interest*

happen often 212.7 *be frequent*

happen upon 229.5 *happen by chance*, 496.1 *discover*

happen yearly 214.8 *be cyclic*

happiest days of one's life 206.1 *youth*

happily 210.9 *opportunely*, 405.11 *pleasingly*, 489.11 *luckily*, 686.9 *prosperously*, 762.9 *joyfully*, 765.13 *with satisfaction*, 769.9 *cheerfully*

happily in love 821.18 *in love*

happiness 762, 405.1 *physical pleasure*, 682.1 *success*, 686.1 *prosperity*, 765.1 *satisfaction*, 769.3 *cheerfulness*, 773.1 *rejoicing*, 861.13 *benefit*

happy 762, 210.6 *timely*, 405.7 *pleased*, 655.9 *well-made*, 677.6 *pacificatory*, 686.8 *prosperous*, 765.4 *satisfied*, 769.1 *cheerful*, 773.9 *rejoicing*, 874.1 *drunk*

happy as a sandboy 762.4 *happy*

happy chance 210.2 *opportunity*

happy coincidence 210.1 *timeliness*

happy dreams 649.1 *ease*

happy either way 783.9 *impartial*

happy ending 682.1 *success*, 861.17 *good thing*

happy event 245.3 *propagation*

happy family 116.1 *accord*

happy few 126.7 *the best people*

happy fortune 686.2 *good fortune*

happy-go-lucky 462.8 *thoughtless*, 595.3 *without preparation*, 656.1 *unskilful*, 780.4 *rash*

happy hour 405.2 *good time*

happy hunting ground 8.11 *heaven*, 325.3 *resting place*, 368.1 *nonmaterial world*

happy hunting grounds 397.14 *the spiritual world*

happy medium 124.5 *medium*, 158.3 *median*, 242.1 *moderation*, 333.1 *middle way*, 717.1 *compromise*, 869.2 *moderation*

happy release 397.5 *ways of dying*

happy thought 592.3 *expedient plan*

Happy Valley 519.8 *dreamland*

hapteron 90.3 *plant body*

haptophobia 777 Phobias by Name

har 55.35 *visibility*

hara-kiri 10.7 *non-Christian ritual*, 398.7 *suicide*, 879.11 *penance*

harangue 553.5 *be diffuse*, 561.1 *dissertation*, 561.4 *dissertate*, 564.8 *speech*, 564.14 *speak to*, 567.1, 567.7 *address*, 876.12 *moralize*

haranguer 564.10 *speaker*

Harare 93 Cities

harass 153.7 *disturb*, 481.14 *discriminate against*, 590.8 *pursue*, 618.13 *be worthless*, 618.14 *ill-treat*, 642.17 *meddle*, 650.6 *fatigue*, 690.6 *suppress*, 777.14 *worry*, 828.9 *offend*, 832.18 *torment*, 862.11 *be evil*

harassed 659.16 *troubled*, 690.9 *suppressed*, 777.9 *worried*

harassing 832.10 *malevolent*

harassment 618.11 *harmfulness*, 670.11 *attack*, 690.2 *suppression*, 768.3 *nuisance*, 832.5 *intolerance*

Harbin 93 Cities

harbinger 154.8 *precursor*, 517.5 *omen*, 517.11 *predict*

Harbinger 53 Mountains

harbour 63.24 *water system*, 218.4 *stopping place*, 301.2 *enclosed place*, 344.15 *destination*, 632.9 *protect*, 634.2 *shelter*

harbour a design 588.8 *resolve*

harbourage 634.2 *shelter*

harbour seal 77 Placental Mammals

hard 373, 378, 44.10 *ceramic*, 225.9 *stable*, 225.11 *determined*, 239.6 *with vigour*, 273.4 *thick-skinned*, 351.17 *drinkable*, 415.5 *acid*, 551.2 *obscure*, 574.3 *strong-willed*, 644.11 *laborious*, 659.16 *difficult*, 669.11 *obstinate*, 687.6 *adverse*, 690.8 *severe*, 761.1 *insensitive*, 832.12 *callous*, 836.4 *pitiless*, 868.3 *impenitent*, 874.6 *intoxicating*, 879.21 *punishing*

hard and fast rule 166.4 *guide*

hardangerfele 49 Musical Instruments

hard as a rock 373.1 *hard*

hard as iron 373.1 *hard*, 574.3 *strong-willed*

hard as nails 373.1 *hard*, 577.3 *unyielding*, 690.8 *severe*

hard-ass 577.8 *obstinate person*

hard as steel 373.1 *hard*

hard as stone 373.1 *hard*

hard at it 642.19 *busy*, 644.10 *working*

hard at work 642.19 *busy*

hardback 532.6 *book publishing*

hard bargaining 716.1 *negotiation*, 737.9 *bargaining*

hard blow 687.1 *adversity*

hardboard 47.12 *wood*, 604.4 *board*

hard-boil 373.9 *harden*

hardboiled 378.3 *hard*

hard-boiled 373.3 *hardened*, 373.4 *mentally hard*, 378.5 *mentally tough*, 577.3 *unyielding*

hard breathing 650.7 *fatigue*

hard by 264.6 *near*

hard case 836.3 *pitiless person*, 868.2 *impenitent person*

hard cash 741.2 *cash*

hard centre 373.5 *hardness*

hard coal 604.1 *materials*

hardcore 49.9 *popular music*

hard core 63.25 *construction material*, 371.4 *solid body*, 373.5 *hardness*, 604.2 *building material*

hard-core 577.3 *unyielding*, 669.10 *resistant*

hard-core pornography 877.2 *indecency*

hard-core supporter 575.5 *tenacious person*

hard corn 624.15 *ulcer*

hard currency 741.1 *money*
hard disk 56.64 *magnetic record-*
ing, 65.7 *peripheral*
hard dose 879.10 *affliction*
hard drink 874.12 *alcohol*
hard drinker 351.12 *drinker*,
874.17 *drunkard*
hard drinking 874.11 *drinking*
hard-drinking 874.5 *drunken*
hard driving 329.8 *speed*
hard drug 875.6 *drug*
hard ECU 741.7 *finance*
harden 373, 203.7 *season*,
225.6 *be stable*, 237.8
strengthen, 273.7 *thicken*, 371.8
be dense, 378.10 *be tough*,
378.11 *make tough*, 584.18 *ha-*
bituate, 594.7 *develop*, 753.9 *be*
dear, 783.12 *be indifferent*
hardened 373, 203.15 *seasoned*,
378.2 *toughened*, 404.6 *unfeel-*
ing, 577.3 *unyielding*, 584.14
habituated, 594.20 *developed*,
761.1 *insensitive*, 805.15 *un-*
approachable, 832.12 *callous*,
836.4 *pitiless*, 864.11 *wicked*,
868.3 *impenitent*
hardened face 807.3 *audacity*
hardened sinner 868.2 *impenit-*
ent person
hardening 225.1 *stability*, 237.4
strengthening, 371.1 *density*,
373.6 *solidification*, 584.7 *habit-*
uation, 594.13 *development*
hardening of the arteries 236.4
disability, 373.6 *solidification*,
624.10 *cardiovascular disease*,
628.9 *dilapidation*
harden one's heart 783.12 *be in-*
different, 820.11 *be hostile*,
836.6 *be pitiless*, 868.5 *be im-*
penitent
harden one's heart to 711.5 *re-*
fuse
harden up 36.15 *sail*
hard facts 611.3 *chief thing*
hard fate 687.3 *bad fortune*
hard feelings 759.6 *bad feeling*,
820.3 *ill feeling*, 822.1 *hate*,
828.1 *resentment*
hard fern 88 *Ferns*
hard-fire 44.11 *make ceramics*
hard firing 44.5 *ceramic process*
hard-fought 644.11 *laborious*
hard freeze 55.32 *freeze*
hard frost 55.36 *frost*, 409.5 *ice*
hard furrow to plough 659.3 *diffi-*
cult task
hard going 659.3 *difficult task*
hard graft 659.3 *difficult task*
hard-grained 85.15 *woody*
hard hand 690.1 *severity*
hard hat 293.5 *body covering*,
295.15 *headgear*
hard-head 577.8 *obstinate per-*
son, 669.5 *resister*
hard-headed 101.8 *practical*,
577.3 *unyielding*, 669.10 *resis-*
tant, 690.8 *severe*
hard-headedly 669.14 *resistingly*
hardhearted 373.4 *mentally*
hard, 378.5 *mentally tough*,
690.8 *severe*, 836.4 *pitiless*
hard-hearted 832.12 *callous*,
864.11 *wicked*, 868.3 *impenitent*
hardheartedly 373.13 *inflexibly*,
378.14 *single-mindedly*, 690.11
severely
hard-heartedly 864.18 *wickedly*,
868.6 *impenitently*
hardheartedness 373.8 *mental*
hardness, 378.9 *mental tough-*
ness, 832.3 *callousness*, 836.1
pitilessness
hard-heartedness 404.3 *heedless-*
ness, 868.1 *impenitence*
hard-hearted person 868.2 *im-*
penitent person
hard-hitting 574.2 *tenacious*
hardihood 778.1 *courage*
hardily 237.14 *strongly*, 378.13
powerfully
hardiness 378.8 *physical*
strength, 778.1 *courage*
hard knocks 674.6 *fight*
hard labour 644.1 *work*, 879.7
punishment

hard landing 53.35 *rocketry*
hard lenses 435.10 *visual aid*
hard life 659.6 *critical situation*,
687.1 *adversity*
hard light 66.15 *lighting*
hard line 577.6 *determination*,
679.33 *combative*
hard-line 577.4 *set*
hardliner 577.8 *obstinate person*,
665.6 *political party member*,
669.5 *resister*, 679.6 *militarist*,
690.4 *strict person*
hard-liner 12.6 *political party*,
217.3 *conservative person*,
584.8 *creature of habit*
hard lines 879.10 *affliction*
hard luck 213.1 *lost chance*,
589.15 *good luck*, 687.3 *bad for-*
tune
hardly 182.11 *sparsely*, 213.1 *in-*
frequently, 272.11 *narrowly*,
659.25 *difficultly*
hardly a chance 489.4 *im-*
probability
hardly any 182.5 *few*
hardly breathing 641.3 *inactive*
hardly ever 186.10 *seldom*,
213.1 *infrequently*, 489.10 *rarely*
hardly like 115.4 *dissimilar*
hardly possible 786.8 *wonderful*
hard master 690.4 *strict person*
hard-mouthed 577.2 *refractory*
hardness 373, 225.2 *determina-*
tion, 371.1 *density*, 378.6 *tough-*
ness, 383.2 *grain*, 404.3 *heed-*
lessness, 574.14 *tenacity*, 577.6
determination, 659.1 *difficulty*,
669.2 *obstinacy*, 690.1 *severity*,
761.3 *insensitiveness*, 832.3 *cal-*
lousness, 836.1 *pitilessness*,
868.1 *impenitence*
Hardness 373
hardness of heart 373.8 *mental*
hardness, 836.1 *pitilessness*,
864.1 *wickedness*, 868.1 *im-*
penitence
hard news 533.1 *news*, 533.9
news story
hard-nose 577.8 *obstinate person*
hard-nosed 378.5 *mentally*
tough, 577.3 *unyielding*, 669.10
resistant
hardnut 761.5 *insensitive person*
hard nut to crack 523.12 *unintel-*
ligible thing, 529.5 *difficult prob-*
lem, 659.4 *problem*
hard of hearing 421.4 *deaf*
hard of heart 832.12 *callous*
hard pad 624.18 *veterinary dis-*
ease
hard palate 564.5 *organ of speech*
hardpan 280.1 *base*, 371.4 *solid*
body
hard-paste 44.10 *ceramic*
hard-paste porcelain 44.1 *ceram-*
ics
hard pitch 22.4 *pitching terms*
hard porn 877.2 *indecency*
hard-pressed 648.3 *hasty*, 743.2
insolvent
hard pruning 69.5 *gardening*
hard pull 659.3 *difficult task*
hard put to it 743.2 *insolvent*
hard resin 395.10 *resin*
hard return 65.17 *computing term*
hard-right 217.8 *conservative*
hard road to travel 659.3 *diffi-*
cult task
hard rock 49.9 *popular music*
hard roe 45.16 *fish dish*, 80.5
fish anatomy
hard row 879.10 *affliction*
hard row of stumps 659.3 *diffi-*
cult task
hard row to hoe 659.3 *difficult*
task
hard rubber 377.4 *rubber*
hard sector 65.17 *computing term*
hard sell 228.2 *inducement*,
586.6 *advertising*, 739.6 *sales-*
manship
hard selling 586.5 *propaganda*
hard-shell 81 *Molluscs*, 669.10
resistant
hard-shelled 577.4 *set*
hardship 571.4 *need*, 659.6 *criti-*

cal situation, 687.1 *adversity*,
743.5 *poverty*
hard shoulder 71.3 *carriageway*,
300.1 *edge*
hard standing 71.21 *miscella-*
neous motoring terms, 73.4 *air-*
port
hard steel 373.7 *hard substance*
hard substance 373
hard-surface 41.12 *ski*
hard-surface snow 41.1 *skiing*
hard tack 350.7 *food*
hard task 597.2 *undertaking*,
659.3 *difficult task*
hard thinking 461.2 *intellectual*
exercise
hard tick 82.2 *arachnid*
hard times 659.6 *critical situa-*
tion, 659.7 *awkward situation*,
687.4 *time of adversity*, 743.6
insolvency
hard to believe 489.2 *question-*
able, 498.7 *disbelieved*
hard to catch 591.18 *avoiding*
hard to come by 609.4 *scarce*
hard to decode 523.1 *unintelligi-*
ble
hard to get 609.4 *scarce*
hardtop 71 *Motor Vehicles*
hard to pin down 518.7 *supposi-*
tional
hard to please 659.14 *trouble-*
some
hard to satisfy 659.14 *trouble-*
some
hard to swallow 489.2 *question-*
able
hard to understand 523.4 *difficult*
hard up 571.11 *needy*, 609.2 *un-*
provided, 743.1 *poor*, 743.2 *in-*
solvent
hard-up 687.7 *unprosperous*
hard usage 599.6 *use*
hard vacuum 57.20 *surface chem-*
istry
hardware 65.4 *computer part*,
243.7 *produce*, 373.7 *hard sub-*
stance
hard water 389.1 *water*
hard-wearing 237.13 *strength-*
ened, 378.1 *tough*
hard winter 55.31 *coldness*
hardwire 65.19 *abort*
hard-won 644.11 *laborious*
hardwood 36.12 *canoeing*, 47.12
wood, 85.1 *tree*, 85.15 *woody*,
373.7 *hard substance*
hardwood paddle 36.6 *canoeing*
hard word 5.17 *word*
hard words 551.1 *obscurity*
hard work 575.2 *commitment*,
642.8 *assiduity*, 644.1 *work*,
659.3 *difficult task*
hard worker 597.4 *volunteer*,
642.10 *busy person*
hard-working 642.20 *industrious*,
644.10 *working*
hardy 69.17 *botanical*, 83.15
wild, 237.9 *physically strong*,
239.4 *vigorous*, 378.4 *powerful*,
623.1 *healthy*, 778.9 *courageous*
Hardy 48 *Writers*, **48** *Poets*, **52**
Scientists
hare 77 *Placental Mammals*,
45.20 *meat*, 324.15 *walk*,
329.12 *swift animal*
Hare 4 *Philosophers*, **48** *Drama-*
tists, **53** *The Constellations*
hare and hounds race 674.4 *race*
harebell 84 *Flowers and Flower-*
ing Plants
harebrained 508.5 *foolish*, 780.4
rash
hare coursing 77.23 *mammal*
hunting
hare hunting 32.8, 37.2 *hunting*
Hare Krishna 7 *Non-Christian*
Religions
harelike 77.31 *rabbit-like*
harem 402.13 *womenfolk*,
821.13 *abode of love*
hare off 329.4 *be swift*
hares 161 *Collective Names by*
Animal, 77.12 *gnawing mam-*
mal
hare's ear 89 *Fungi*
hare's fur glaze 44.3 *glaze*

hare's-tail 87 *Grasses*
hare wallaby 77 *Marsupials*
Hargreaves 52 *Scientists*
haricot bean 45 *Vegetables*
hark 420.15 *hear*, 590.10 *chase*
hark back 3.22 *remember*,
200.15 *look back*, 221.6 *reverse*,
337.8 *look back*, 511.12 *remem-*
ber
harking back 3.13 *looking back*
harking-back 337.15 *looking back*
Harlem 93.3 *New York*
Harlem Renaissance 48 *Literary*
Groups and Movements
Harlequin 51.21 *role*, 51.30
clown, 456.5 *variegated thing*
harlequinade 51.2 *play*
Harlequin and Columbine 821.10
lovers
harlequin bug 82 *Insects*
harlequin duck 78 *Birds*
harlequin snake 79 *Reptiles*
harlot 402.7 *prostitute*, 877.9 *im-*
moral woman
harlotry 877.3 *sexual immorality*,
877.5 *prostitution*
harlot's trade 877.5 *prostitution*
harm 238.7 *weaken*, 601.1,
601.2 *misuse*, 616.3 *inconve-*
nience, 616.5 *be inconvenient*,
618.11 *harmfulness*, 628.5,
628.11 *hurt*, 631.1 *affliction*,
631.14 *afflict*, 722.5 *destruc-*
tion, 722.13 *destroy*, 832.7,
832.7 *act of malevolence*,
832.18 *torment*, 844.8 *wrong-*
doing, 844.20 *wrong*, 862.2 *af-*
fliction, 862.11 *be evil*
harmattan 55 *Winds*
harmed 628.12 *deteriorated*
harmful 618, 244.14 *destructive*,
601.5 *abusive*, 616.1 *inconve-*
nient, 626.5 *unhygienic*, 628.12
deteriorated, 631.16 *blighting*,
633.1 *dangerous*, 687.6 *adverse*,
844.16 *in the wrong*, 862.9 *detri-*
mental
harmfully 601.6 *abusively*,
631.17 *banefully*, 687.12 *in ad-*
versity, 862.13 *destructively*
harmfulness 618, 862.2 *affliction*
harmless 236.11 *unprotected*,
242.6 *moderate*, 617.4 *worth-*
while, 625.4 *hygienic*, 632.5
safe, 675.7 *peaceful*, 806.1 *hum-*
ble, 865.5 *innocent*
harmless joke 612.8 *trifle*
harmlessly 236.14 *powerlessly*,
865.11 *innocently*
harmlessness 236.3 *helplessness*,
238.1 *weakness*, 632.1 *safety*,
865.1 *innocence*
harmonic 49, 49.16 *musical*
note, 49.21 *tone*, 52.85 *cyclic*,
56.20 *musical note*, 116.13 *har-*
monious, 365.13 *oscillating*,
433.7 *harmonious*
harmonica 49 *Musical Instru-*
ments
harmonic minor scale 49.20 *key*
harmonic progression 52.20 *se-*
quence, 433.3 *melodiousness*
harmonics 49, 433
harmonic scale 49.20 *key*
harmonious 116, 150, 433,
49.30 *harmonic*, 110.13 *equiva-*
lent, 116.10 *in accord*, 135.13
agreeable, 140.8 *cooperative*,
166.11 *uniform*, 167.12 *con-*
forming, 285.4 *correlated*, 308.4
symmetrical, 308.5 *even*, 433.6
melodious, 444.11 *colourful*,
558.3 *elegant*, 664.19 *associat-*
ing, 667.10 *agreeing*, 675.7
peaceful, 819.8 *friendly*
harmoniously 116, 433, 110.18
identically, 116.31 *in accord*,
135.17 *agreeably*, 140.10 *in*
combination, 167.17 *con-*
formingly, 558.5 *elegantly*,
664.20 *cooperatively*, 667.14
agreeably, 819.17 *in friendship*
harmoniousness 433.3 *melodious-*
ness
harmonist 433.5 *melodist*
harmonium 49 *Musical Instru-*
ments

harmonization 116.4 *harmony,*
133.1 *mixture,* 433.3 *melodiousness,* 667.1 *agreement*
harmonize 49, 116, 150, 433,
49.39 *sing,* 110.7 *be the same,*
110.8 *make the same,* 112.10
conform, 133.8 *mix,* 140.6 *come
together,* 167.7 *conform,* 285.6
correlate, 308.6 *symmetrize,*
433.9 *set to music,* 664.15 *concur,* 667.6 *agree with,* 677.4 *pacify*
harmonized 133.12 *mixed,* 140.7
combined
harmonizing 49.30 *harmonic,*
433.7 *harmonious*
harmonograph 365.6 *measuring
instrument*
harmony 116, 150, 30.8 *floor
exercises,* 49.1 *music,* 49.13 *melody,* 110.2 *equivalence,* 116.1
accord, 133.2 *mixed thing,*
135.2 *agreement,* 140.2 *cooperation,* 144.1 *completeness,* 166.7
uniformity, 167.1 *conformity,*
285.1 *parallelism,* 308.1 *symmetry,* 308.3 *evenness,* 433.3
melodiousness, 499.1 *assent,*
558.1 *elegance,* 664.2 *fellowship,* 667.1 *agreement,* 675.1
peace, 789.1 *gorgeousness,*
819.1 *friendship,* 819.2 *friendly
relations*
harmotome 54 Minerals
harness 20.1 *angling,* 34.4 *climbing equipment,* 36.7 *windsurfing,* 68.18 *practise livestock
farming,* 135.10 *link,* 137.7
tackle, 137.9 *yoke,* 137.12 *bind,*
603.6 *equipment,* 671.7 *armour,*
699.5 *means of restraint,*
699.12 *gag*
harnessed 137.16 *bound,*
671.30 *defended*
harness hitch 74 Knots
harness horse racing 18 Sporting Activities
harness line 36.7 *windsurfing*
harness racing 674.4 *race*
harness together 135.8 *unite*
harp 49 Musical Instruments,
183
harpaxophobia 777 Phobias by
Name
harping 183.12 *repetitious*
harp on 110.11 *be regular,*
183.18 *harp,* 219.3 *continue,*
788.6 *be boring*
harpoon 380.8 *sharp-pointed
thing,* 380.16 *use a sharp tool ,*
680.6 *historical missile weapon,*
680.8 *sharp weapon*
harpsichord 49 Musical Instruments
harpy 76.7 *legendary beast,* 78.9
fabulous bird
harpy eagle 78 Birds
harridan 829.3 *irascible person*
harrier 77 Breeds of Dogs, 78
Birds, 21.3 *athlete,* 78.5 *bird of
prey,* 329.13 *swift person*
Harrington 4 Philosophers
Harrisburg 93 Cities
Harrison 48 Poets
Harris tweed 67 Natural Fabrics
Harrogate 93 Cities
harrow 68.17 *farm,* 376.9
smoother, 376.11 *smooth,* 380.8
sharp-pointed thing, 380.16 *use
a sharp tool ,* 406.11 *inflict pain*
harrowed 376.2 *uniform*
harrowing 68.5 *cultivation,*
406.5 *painful,* 770.7 *distressing*
harrows 68.10 *farm tool*
harry 590.8 *pursue,* 670.1 *attack,*
832.18 *torment*
harrying 670.23 *attacking*
Harry Tate 179.4 *eight*
harsh 241.6 *violent,* 415.6 *unpalatable,* 415.7 *splenetic,*
420.14 *hearable,* 430.7 *strident,*
434.7 *dissonant,* 444.12 *gaudy,*
618.5 *harmful,* 690.8 *severe,*
818.5 *discourteous,* 832.12 *callous,* 836.4 *pitiless*
harshly 241.10 *violently,* 385.17
abrasively, 415.13 *sourly,*

415.11 *splenetically,* 430.10 *stridently,* 434.12 *dissonantly,*
690.11 *severely,* 818.9 *discourteously,* 832.20 *malevolently,*
836.7 *pitilessly*
harshness 241.1 *violence,* 413.4
stimulation, 430.1 *stridency ,*
434.1 *dissonance,* 618.11 *harmfulness,* 690.1 *severity,* 818.1
discourtesy, 832.3 *callousness*
harsh sound 430.1 *stridency*
Harsh Sound 430
harsh treatment 690.1 *severity*
harsh voice 563.2 *inarticulation*
harsh words 852.8 *berating*
hart 77.17 *male mammal,*
401.16 *male animal*
Hart 48 Dramatists
Harte 48 Writers
hartebeest 77 Placental Mammals
Hartford 93 Cities
Hartley 48 Writers
Hartmann 4 Philosophers, 4 Philosophers
hartshorn 630.7 *tonic*
hart's-tongue 88 Ferns
harum-scarum 113.11 *irregularly,*
151.20 *disorderly,* 151.28 *anyhow*
haruspex 7.8 *priest,* 11.13 *diviner,* 517.9 *forecaster*
haruspical 11.17 *divinatory,*
517.15 *presageful*
haruspicate 199.9 *look ahead*
haruspication 11.9 *divination*
haruspicy 11.9, 517.2 *divination*
Harvard-Yale race 36.4 *rowing*
harvest 68.17 *farm,* 203.4 *autumn,* 227.3 *growth,* 227.8
grow, 243.7 *produce,* 605.1,
605.6 *store,* 721.6 *yield,* 721.11
acquire
harvest dance 46.4 *historic dancing*
harvested 721.19 *yielding*
harvester 68.10 *farm tool,*
161.35 *collector*
Harvest Festival 10.16 *religious
festival*
harvest home 350.13 *feast,*
812.7 *thanksgiving*
harvesting 68.5 *cultivation*
harvestman 82 Arachnids, 82.2
arachnid
harvest mite 82 Arachnids, 82.3
pest
harvest moon 53.17 *moon,* 203.4
autumn, 439.4 *natural light*
harvest mouse 77 Placental
Mammals
harvest supper 350.13 *feast*
harvest time 203.4 *autumn*
Harvey Smith salute 543.3 *gesture,* 850.7 *sign of disrespect*
Harwich 93 Cities
Harz 95 Mountains
has been 3.18 *in the past*
has-been 683.5 *failing person*
hash 45.32 *meat dish,* 133.2
mixed thing, 133.3 *miscellany,*
151.4 *litter,* 151.6 *mix-up,*
151.23 *confuse,* 875.6 *drug*
hashish 631.11 *intoxicant,*
875.6 *drug*
hash mark 19.4 *stadium,* 544.4
insignia
Hasidic 7.16 *denominational*
Hasidism 7 Non-Christian Religions
hasp 135.5 *joint,* 137.8 *fastening,* 323.3 *restrainer*
hassle 151.22 *discompose,* 153.7
disturb, 616.5 *be inconvenient,*
642.3 *nimbleness,* 642.17 *meddle ,* 644.4 *exertion,* 648.4 *haste,*
659.17 *be difficult,* 661.8 *hinder,* 666.2 *argument,* 666.6
argue, 674.1 *contention,* 690.5
be severe, 768.3 *nuisance,* 768.8
annoy, 852.18 *find fault*
hassock 87.2 *grassland,* 161.27
bundle
hastate 83.18 *of leaves,* 380.1
sharp
haste 648, 208.1 *earliness,*
208.5 *prematurity,* 329.8 *speed,*

595.8 *lack of preparation,* 642.3
nimbleness, 780.1 *rashness*
Haste 648
hasten 208, 648, 208.7 *be
early,* 226.10 *awaken,* 329.4 *be
swift,* 329.7 *hurry someone up,*
336.8 *further,* 642.12 *be active,*
648.2 *make haste,* 660.16 *make
easy,* 662.28 *further*
hasten away 648.2 *make haste*
hastening 648.3 *hasty,* 648.4
haste, 660.7 *easing*
hasten off 345.4 *hurry off*
hasten someone's end 398.16 *kill*
hastily 648, 208.17 *early,*
208.20 *prematurely,* 329.14
swiftly, 595.14 *unreadily,* 780.6
rashly
hastiness 648, 208.1 *earliness,*
208.5 *prematurity,* 329.8 *speed,*
595.8 *lack of preparation,* 780.1
rashness
Hastings 93 Cities
hasty 648, 208.12 *early,* 208.16
premature, 278.2 *superficial,*
329.1 *swift,* 595.3 *without preparation,* 656.3 *clumsy,* 780.4
rash
hasty retreat 638.1 *escape*
hat 293.5 *body covering,* 295.15
headgear
hat brim 283.5 *projecting object*
hatch 74 Parts of a Ship, 50.20
draw, 78.12 *young bird,* 78.15
eggs, 78.26 *nest,* 82.17 *develop,*
102.17 *fabricate,* 243.10 *produce,* 245.11 *have young,*
245.13 *propagate,* 346.6 *means
of entry ,* 440.14 *make dark,*
519.14 *imagine,* 592.11 *invent,*
592.13 *plot,* 594.7 *develop*
hatch a plot 592.13 *plot*
hatchback 71 Motor Vehicles,
71.16 *car*
hatcheck girl 697.3 *attendant*
hatched 243.12 *produced,*
396.15 *born*
hatcher 592.8 *planner*
hatchery 78.14 *nest,* 78.19 *ornithology,* 226.2 *source*
hatches, matches, and dispatches
528.4 *mass communication*
hatchet 85.7 *timber production,*
380.9 *sharp-edged thing,* 680.8
sharp weapon
hatchet face 274.7 *thinness*
hatchet-faced 274.1 *thin*
hatchetfish 80 Fishes
hatchet job 244.2 *destroying,*
854.2 *criticism*
hatchet man 244.6 *destroyer,*
398.11 *murderer,* 832.8 *malefactor,* 854.7 *disparager,* 879.17
punisher
hatching 245.3 *propagation,*
440.2 *darkening,* 594.13 *development,* 594.17 *developing*
hatchment 399.4 *funeral objects,*
544.8 *heraldic device*
hatchway 74 Parts of a Ship,
346.6 *means of entry*
hate 822, 822, 663.1 *opposition,* 663.14 *be against,* 666.5
disagree, 785.1, 785.5 *dislike,*
820.1 *enmity,* 820.11 *be hostile,*
832.1 *malevolence,* 832.16 *be
malevolent*
Hate 822
hated 820, 822
hated person 822
hated thing 822
hate evil 863.8 *be virtuous*
hateful 618.4 *poor,* 666.9 *disagreeing,* 764.1 *unpleasant,*
785.8 *disliking,* 820.10 *hated,*
822.10 *hating,* 822.12 *hated,*
832.10 *malevolent,* 862.7 *evil*
hatefully 822, 666.11 *in disagreement,* 820.15 *aggressively,*
832.20 *malevolently,* 862.12
evilly
hatefulness 822, 801.1 *disrespect,* 832.1 *malevolence,* 862.1
evil
hate mankind 834.4 *become a
misanthrope*

hate men 834.4 *become a misanthrope*
hate one's guts 822.14 *hate*
hater 822
hater of man 834.2 *misanthrope*
hater of mankind 834.2 *misanthrope*
hater of women 834.2 *misanthrope*
hate the world 834.4 *become a
misanthrope*
Hathor 8 Deities
hating 822, 666.9 *disagreeing,*
785.8 *disliking,* 832.10 *malevolent*
hatless 294.8 *uncovered,* 296.10
in dishabille
hatmaking 295.2 *dressing*
hatpin 137.8 *fastening,* 380.8
sharp-pointed thing, 792.6
jewellery
hat rack 283.4 *hanger*
hatred 663.1 *opposition,* 666.1
disagreement, 759.6 *bad feeling,*
785.1 *dislike,* 820.1 *enmity,*
822.1 *hate,* 832.1 *malevolence*
hatred of mankind 834.1 *misanthropy*
hatted 295.29 *dressed*
hatter 295.26 *fashion designer*
hatting 295.2 *dressing*
hat trick 27.8 *delivery,* 177.2 *trident,* 655.3 *masterpiece,* 682.3
successful thing
hat waving 543.3 *gesture*
hauberk 671.7 *armour*
Haugeanism 7 Christian Movements
haughtily 807.33 *arrogantly,*
816.14 *unsocially*
haughtiness 805.3 *conceit,* 807.4
arrogance, 816.1 *unsociability*
haughty 805.17 *conceited,*
807.16 *arrogant,* 816.8 *unsociable,* 850.13 *contemptuous*
haul 16.36 *stolen property,* 63.30
engineer, 70.4 *transport,* 74.9
navigate, 324.14 *set in motion,*
326.12 *transport,* 339.2, 339.11
pull, 644.6 *work,* 721.3 *acquisition,* 734.5 *takings,* 736.4 *stolen
goods*
haulage 70.1 *transport,* 326.2
transportation, 339.1 *traction*
haul ass 329.4 *be swift*
haul before the court 16.70 *litigate*
haul down 362.10 *lower the flag*
haul down the flag 673.3 *submit*
hauled before the court 16.54 *litigated*
hauled up 856.8 *accusatory*
hauler 63.29 *construction equipment,* 326.7 *transferor ,* 339.6
towline
haulier 339.6 *towline*
haul in 20.7 *angle,* 699.11 *detain*
hauling 63.29 *construction equipment,* 326.2 *transportation,*
339.1 *traction,* 339.8 *tractional*
hauling freightage 70.1 *transport*
hauling over the coals 852.7
blame
haulm 87.3 *grass plant*
haul over the coals 852.20 *censure*
haul up 361.4 *gather up,* 856.5
accuse
haunch 43.9 *miscellaneous architectural features*
haunch bone 382 Bones
haunches 304.2 *rear end*
haunt 212.8 *frequent,* 219.4 *protract,* 249.13 *locality,* 250.1 *location,* 253.12 *attend,* 256.2 *environment,* 256.19 *frequent,*
511.13 *remind,* 584.16 *have a
habit,* 777.14 *worry*
haunted 11.19 *bewitched,* 253.7
present, 777.9 *worried*
haunter 253.5 *someone present*
haunting 183.14 *recurrent,* 212.3
frequent, 212.5 *frequenting,*
511.7 *memorable,* 584.15 *habit-
forming*
hauntingly 212.1 *frequently*
Hauptmann 48 Dramatists

Haurvatat 8.6 *angel*
Hausa 1 Peoples, 5 Languages and Groups of Languages
hausfrau 646.1 *worker*
haustorium 89.4 *fungal body*
hautboy 86 Fruits
haute couture 796.1 *fashion*
haute cuisine 45.1 *cookery*
hauteur 805.5 *stateliness*
Havana 77 Breeds of Cats, 93 Cities, 413.7 *tobacco*
have 135.11 *make love*, 146.4 *include*, 522.6 *understand*, 723.7 *possess*
have a baby 245.10 *reproduce oneself*
have a bachelor's apartment 825.9 *be celibate*
have a bachelor's flat 825.9 *be celibate*
have a bad conscience 866.9 *appear guilty*
have a bad liver 829.6 *be irascible*
have a bad outcome 515.4 *be disappointed*
have a bad result 515.4 *be disappointed*
have a bad temper 829.6 *be irascible*
have a bad time 687.9 *be in trouble*
have a bag of tricks 539.28 *trick*
have a ball 405.8 *feel pleasure*, 773.5 *rejoice*
have a bash 674.11 *contend*
have a bath 621.14 *bathe*
have a bearing on 107.7 *relate to*
have a bee in one's bonnet 579.5 *be capricious*
have a bellyful 608.4 *suffice*
have a bent 234.4 *tend*
have a bias 580.2 *prefer*
have a big appetite 872.5 *be greedy*
have a big heart 831.8 *be benevolent*, 859.7 *be unselfish*
have a big mouth 565.8 *talk too much*
have a birdie 29.7 *golf*
have a birthday 214.9 *commemorate*
have a birthmark 544.11 *identify oneself*
have a bite 20.7 *angle*
have a bit of slap and tickle 821.27 *kiss*
have a bit on the side 877.17 *be sexually immoral*
have a blank cheque 698.19 *liberalize*, 708.5 *be permitted*
have a blind spot 436.14 *be blind*, 523.9 *find unintelligible*
have a bogey 29.7 *golf*
have a bone to pick 666.5 *disagree*, 666.7 *pick a fight*, 822.14 *hate*, 828.8 *resent*
have a bowel movement 353.16 *defecate*
have a brainstorm 462.12 *lack thought*
have a brainwave 461.16 *have an idea*
have a break 160.13 *pause*
have a breakdown 661.9 *block*
have a breakout play 31.9 *play hockey*
have a bright future 714.10 *show potential*
have a brush with 674.12 *fight*
have a bumper crop 721.11 *acquire*
have a bumpy face 375.11 *be rough*
have a burst of anger 822.17 *anger*
have a burst of energy 329.6 *accelerate*
have a burst of speed 329.6 *accelerate*
have a butcher's 435.14 *inspect*
have a buyer 739.2 *be sold*
have a cameo role 51.34 *underact*
have a card up one's sleeve 126.11 *get ahead*, 657.5 *be cunning*

have a cash-flow crisis 747.9 *be unable to pay*
have a cast of mind 784.8 *prefer*
have a catnap 649.2 *take it easy*
have a chance 589.12 *take a chance*
have a change 651.2 *be refreshed*
have a change of pace 651.2 *be refreshed*
have a cheek 668.5 *defy*
have a cheque bounce 687.10 *need money*
have a chink in one's armour 620.9 *be imperfect*
have a chinwag 568.10 *chat*
have a chip on one's shoulder 666.7 *pick a fight*
have a choice 580.1 *select*
have a circulation 532.18 *become famous*
have a claim to 843.13 *be right*, 845.14 *be entitled*
have a classification 107.9 *have a relative position*
have a clean bill of health 623.5 *be healthy*
have a clear conscience 865.8 *be innocent*
have a close call 638.5 *escape*
have a closed mind 577.9 *be obstinate*
have a close shave 638.5 *escape*
have acne 375.11 *be rough*
have a cockup 661.9 *block*
have a cold heart 787.5 *not wonder about*
have a cold in the nose 417.6 *have no smell*
have a comedown 687.9 *be in trouble*
have a complaint 624.24 *be unhealthy*
have a conference on the mound 22.7 *play baseball*
have a connection with 107.7 *relate to*
have a conservative outlook 661.11 *be inhibited*
have a constitution 12.13 *be governed*
have a corner 31.9 *play hockey*
have a cosy chat 568.10 *chat*
have a crack 620.9 *be imperfect*
have a crack at 596.1 *attempt*
have a credibility gap 666.8 *be different*
have a credit facility 733.10 *buy on credit*
have a crisis of faith 7.19 *be religious*
have a cross to bear 661.12 *burden*
have a crush on 784.7 *like*, 821.24 *be in love*
have a cut at 670.6 *stab*
have a date 821.26, 826.8 *court*
have a dead puck 31.9 *play hockey*
have a dekko 435.14 *inspect*
have a denouement 684.5 *conclude*
have a difference of opinion with 500.8 *dissent*
have a dilemma 105.7 *be in a predicament*
have a discussion 716.4 *negotiator*
have a distinctive appearance 522.8 *be recognizable*
have a donnybrook 666.6 *argue*
have a double meaning 578.1 *be equivocal*
have a down on 822.14 *hate*
have a drink 351.13 *drink*
have a dust-up 666.6 *argue*
have advance knowledge 516.1 *foresee*
have a fair chance 229.4 *chance*
have a falling-out 666.5 *disagree*
have a false front 539.32 *disguise*
have a false start 19.18 *be penalized*
have a fancy for 821.23 *love*
have a fault 620.9 *be imperfect*
have a feed 350.24 *have a meal*
have a feeling about 464.9 *be intuitive*

have a fencing bout 28.5 *fence*
have affection for 826.7 *show endearment*
have a fight 674.12 *fight*
have a financial loss **722**
have a financial reverse 687.10 *need money*
have a financial setback 687.10 *need money*
have a finger in 640.4 *act*, 724.4 *have joint possession*
have a finger in every pie 642.17 *meddle*
have a fit of temper 822.17 *anger*
have a flair 235.10 *be powerful*
have a flair for 655.10 *be skilful*
have a flat 661.9 *block*
have a flight of fancy 541.11 *tell a tall story*
have a fling 479.13 *invent*, 870.11 *overindulge*
have a fling at 670.5 *strike*
have a flying start 300.7 *have an advantage*
have a fly in the ointment 661.9 *block*
have a fondness for 821.23 *love*
have a foot in both camps 540.17 *double-deal*, 717.4 *compromise*
have a foul mouth 822.17 *anger*
have a foul stroke 24.8 *play billiards*
have a foursome 29.7 *golf*
have a free hand 698.18 *have scope*, 698.19 *liberalize*, 708.5 *be permitted*
have a free kick 38.4 *play soccer*
have a free mind 698.14 *be free*
have a free play 31.9 *play hockey*
have a fresh start 201.17 *become new*, 704.8 *be reborn*
have a frog in one's throat 430.5 *sound hoarse*
have a full nelson on 26.12 *wrestle*
have a funny feeling about 464.9 *be intuitive*
have a gainful occupation 878.13 *get paid*
have a generous heart 831.8 *be benevolent*
have a generous nature 729.5 *give*
have a genius for 234.4 *tend*
have a gift 234.4 *tend*, 235.10 *be powerful*
have a gift for 655.10 *be skilful*, 861.19 *be good at*
have a go 214.7 *be regular*, 479.13 *invent*, 596.1 *attempt*, 596.11 *here goes*
have a goal kick 38.4 *play soccer*
have a go at 502.10 *know little*, 670.5 *strike*, 674.11 *contend*
have a good appetite 350.22 *eat well*
have a good ear 420.15 *hear*
have a good effect 617.10 *do good*
have a good head for 655.10 *be skilful*
have a good idea 461.16 *have an idea*
have a good influence on 627.1 *improve*
have a good memory 726.8 *remember*
have a good mind to 572.13 *be willing*
have a good reputation 800.5 *have repute*
have a good style 558.4 *be elegant*
have a good time 686.10 *good luck*, 762.6 *enjoy*
have a good time of it 686.5 *be prosperous*
have a grand opening 201.19 *begin*
have a grasping nature 734.7 *take*
have a grip of iron 726.6 *retain*
have a grip of steel 726.6 *retain*
have a grudge against 785.5 *dislike*
have a habit **584**

have a haemorrhage 828.12 *become angry*
have a hairbreadth escape 638.5 *escape*
have a hand in 226.12 *determine*, 232.4 *be an instrument*, 640.4 *act*, 662.28 *further*, 724.4 *have joint possession*
have a hard time of it 659.20 *be in difficulty*, 687.9 *be in trouble*
have a head on one's shoulders 459.13 *be intelligent*
have a head start 300.7 *have an advantage*
have a heart 835.14 *have pity*
have a heart attack 624.24 *be unhealthy*
have a heart of gold 831.8 *be benevolent*
have a heart of stone 783.12 *be indifferent*
have a heart-to-heart 568.10 *chat*
have a hiccup 661.9 *block*
have a high opinion of 849.15 *respect*
have a high opinion of oneself 809.15 *be vain*
have a high profile 437.8 *be visible*
have a high regard for 821.23 *love*
have a hold over 233.10 *be a prevailing influence*
have a hole in one 29.7 *golf*
have a honeymoon period 667.6 *agree with*
have a hopeless case 236.6 *be powerless*
have a house-warming 201.19 *begin*
have a hunch 471.17 *theorize*, 518.5 *suppose*
have a hunch about 759.16 *feel in one's bones*
have a jagged edge 380.14 *be sharp*
have a Jimmy Riddle 353.17 *urinate*
have a kind heart 821.23 *love*
have a kindness for 821.23 *love*
have a knack for 655.10 *be skilful*
have a knees-up 773.5 *rejoice*
have a knock-down-drag-out fight 666.6 *argue*
have a large part in 226.12 *determine*
have a leaning 234.4 *tend*
have a Le Mans start 36.18 *windsurf*
have a liberated mind 698.14 *be free*
have a light touch 558.4 *be elegant*
have a line of attack 28.5 *fence*
have a little chat 568.10 *chat*
have all one could ask for 765.7 *be satisfied*
have all the appearances of 114.10 *be similar*
have all the earmarks of 114.10 *be similar*
have all the fight knocked out of one 673.3 *submit*
have all the hallmarks of 114.10 *be similar*
have all the luck 686.6 *be fortunate*
have all the signs of 114.10 *be similar*
have all the time in the world 645.4 *have leisure*
have all the virtues 863.8 *be virtuous*
have all to oneself 723.7 *possess*
have a long face 830.9 *be sullen*
have a long winter's sleep 203.6 *spend the season*
have a look at 435.14 *inspect*
have a look 457.11 *appear*
have a look-see 435.14 *inspect*
have a lot of bottle 778.15 *be courageous*
have a lot of get-up-and-go 239.2 *be full of vigour*
have a lot of pizzazz 239.2 *be full of vigour*

have a lot to learn 502.9 *be ignorant*
have a low IQ 460.9 *lack intellect*
have a low opinion of 850.19 *disrespect*, 852.14 *disapprove*
have a lucky break 686.5 *be prosperous*, 686.6 *be fortunate*
have a malignant growth 227.8 *grow*
have a market 739.2 *be sold*
have a mash on 821.24 *be in love*
have ambition 860.6 *be selfish*
have a meal 350
have a meaning 520.10 *mean*
have a meltdown 410.11 *fuel*
have a mental block 546.2 *forget*
have a method 327.14 *find one's way*
have a mild manner 817.10 *be courteous*
have a millstone round one's neck 661.12 *burden*
have a mind like a sieve 512.14 *be forgetful*
have a mind of one's own 570.14 *follow one's own will*
have a mind to 572.13 *be willing*, 588.8 *resolve*
have a misadventure 211.9 *have a mishap*
have a mishap 211, 661.9 *block*, 687.9 *be in trouble*
have a monkey on one's back 661.12 *burden*
have a monotonous job 788.7 *suffer boredom*
have a motive 588.8 *resolve*
have a mutual dependence 701.8 *be subject to*
have a mutual relationship 107.8 *be proportionate to*
have an accident 211.9 *have a mishap*, 661.9 *block*, 687.9 *be in trouble*
have an account with 744.9 *acquire credit*, 745.7 *be in debt*
have an ace in the hole 126.11 *get ahead*, 300.7 *have an advantage*
have an active interest 642.16 *be sociable*
have an advantage 300, 721.9 *gain*
have an affair 864.16 *be wicked*
have an affinity 140.5 *combine*
have an affinity for 667.6 *agree with*, 784.7 *like*
have an affliction 624.24 *be unhealthy*
have an ague 366.24 *shake*
have an albatross round one's neck 661.12 *burden*
have an anniversary 214.9 *commemorate*
have an aptitude 234.4 *tend*
have an area of disagreement 666.5 *disagree*
have a narrow escape 638.5 *escape*
have a narrow outlook 302.7 *limit*
have a narrow squeak 638.5 *escape*
have an athletic build 378.10 *be tough*
have an attachment for 784.7 *like*
have an attack 624.24 *be unhealthy*
have an attraction 340.11 *attract*
have an auction 727.11 *dispose of property*
have an audience of one 569.3 *soliloquize*
have an axe to grind 657.5 *be cunning*, 860.6 *be selfish*
have and hold 723.7 *possess*
have an ear for 420.15 *hear*, 655.10 *be skilful*
have an edge 380.14 *be sharp*
have a need for 712.6 *request*
have an effect 226.12 *determine*, 227.5 *show an effect*
have an emergency 106.13 *get into difficulties*
have an empty stomach 871.5 *fast*
have a nervous breakdown 759.17 *feel deeply*

have an estate 725.9 *own property*
have a new beginning 704.8 *be reborn*
have a new look 201.17 *become new*
have a new start 201.17 *become new*
have an expense account 721.14 *profit*
have an extra mouth to feed 396.19 *give birth to*
have an eye for 655.10 *be skilful*
have an eye for business 737.1 *trade*
have an eye on the main chance 516.2 *show prudence*
have an eye to 199.8, 588.7 *intend*
have an eye to the future 516.2 *show prudence*
have a nice day 345.14 *goodbye*
have an idea 461, 471, 518.5 *suppose*
have an illness 687.9 *be in trouble*
have an impact with 228.9 *motivate*
have an in 346.9 *enter*
have an income 730.9 *receive*
have an independent mind 700.4 *liberate*
have an industrial dispute 15
have an infatuation 821.24 *be in love*
have an inkling 518.5 *suppose*
have an inspiration 519.14 *imagine*
have an instinct 234.4 *tend*
have an iron grip 726.6 *retain*
have an open day 815.11 *be sociable*
have an orgasm 405.8 *feel pleasure*, 684.5 *conclude*
have another 351.13 *drink*
have another think coming 504.18 *be in error*
have a notion 518.5 *suppose*
have an overdraft 733.7 *borrow*
have an oversight 720.7 *not observe*
have ants in one's pants 366.24 *shake*
have an ulterior motive 657.5 *be cunning*
have an uncontrollable temper 829.6 *be irascible*
have an unfair advantage 721.9 *gain*
have a part to play 233.8 *influence*
have a party 773.5 *rejoice*
have a payoff 684.5 *conclude*
have a penalty shot 31.9 *play hockey*
have a penalty stroke 29.7 *golf*
have a penalty try 35.5 *play rugby*
have a photographic memory 726.8 *remember*
have a piece of 724.4 *have joint possession*
have a piece of luck 721.14 *profit*
have a place 12.11 *govern*
have a point 107.7 *relate to*, 380.14 *be sharp*
have a policy 592.12 *plan ahead*
have a poor appetite 350.23 *taste*
have a poor ear 420.15 *hear*
have a poor return 722.10 *have a financial loss*
have a portfolio 725.9 *own property*
have a powwow with 654.6 *consult*
have a practice 630.20 *doctor*
have a predicament 105.7 *be in a predicament*
have a predisposition 234.4 *tend*
have a preference 580.2 *prefer*
have a preference for 784.8 *prefer*
have a premonition 199.9 *look ahead*
have a price war 739.1 *sell*
have a prior engagement 211.7 *be busy*

have a private income 721.12 *earn*
have a prizefight 26.11 *do a combat sport*
have a problem 105.7 *be in a predicament*, 659.20 *be in difficulty*
have a prominent feature 318.8 *protrude*
have a propensity 234.4 *tend*
have a propensity for 784.8 *prefer*
have aptitude 235.10 *be powerful*
have a punch-up 674.12 *fight*
have a purpose 588.8 *resolve*
have a quick word with 568.9 *converse*
have a rapid heartbeat 214.7 *be regular*
have a red face 806.24 *be humiliated*
have a refill 351.13 *drink*
have a relationship 107.7 *relate to*
have a relative position 107
have a request to make 712.6 *request*
have a rest 649.2 *take it easy*, 651.2 *be refreshed*
have a reversal 722.9 *lose*
have a rightful claim to 845.14 *be entitled*
have a right to 845.14 *be entitled*
have a roof over one's head 632.8 *be safe*
have a rough surface 375.11 *be rough*
have a route 327.14 *find one's way*
have a rowing race 36.16 *row*
have artistic licence 698.14 *be free*
have a run-in 666.6 *argue*
have a run of good luck 686.6 *be fortunate*
have a sale 727.11 *dispose of property*
have a say 580.5 *vote*
have a say in 233.8 *influence*
have a say-so 698.14 *be free*
have a screw loose 510.14 *become insane*
have a seat 344.24 *welcome*
have a second childhood 207.17 *age*
have a second meaning 578.1 *be equivocal*
have a sense 520.10 *mean*
have a sense of community 2.15 *socialize*
have a sense of idiom 5.45 *use language*
have a sense of loyalty 719.4 *observe*
have a sense of responsibility 719.4 *observe*
have a setback 722.9 *lose*
have a set to 473.13 *argue*
have a set-to 666.6 *argue*
have a sharp tongue 829.6 *be irascible*
have a shit 353.16 *defecate*
have a shopping list 738.2 *shop*
have a shortcoming 720.8 *not perform*
have a short fuse 829.6 *be irascible*
have a short memory 512.14 *be forgetful*
have a short temper 829.6 *be irascible*
have a shot at 596.1 *attempt*
have a shot in one's locker 657.5 *be cunning*
have a shower 621.14 *bathe*
have a show of force 690.6 *suppress*
have a side effect 227.5 *show an effect*, 227.6 *have a visible effect*
have a simple answer 660.15 *be easy*
have a sister city 135.8 *unite*
have a sit-down strike 711.5 *refuse*
have a slanging match 666.6 *argue*, 827.6 *vilify*
have a slash 353.17 *urinate*
have as many phases as the moon 224.11 *be changeable*

have a smattering of knowledge 502.10 *know little*
have a social conscience 833.7 *be charitable*
have a soft spot for 821.23 *love*
have a stab at 479.13 *invent*, 596.1 *attempt*
have a stake in 724.4 *have joint possession*
have a standing 105.6 *be in a state of*
have a start on 194.9 *do before*
have a station in life 105.6 *be in a state of*
have a stroke 624.24 *be unhealthy*
have a stroke of luck 686.6 *be fortunate*
have a sudden brainwave 583.3 *improvise*
have a sudden flight of fancy 579.5 *be capricious*
have a summit meeting 716.4 *negotiator*
have a suspicion 786.12 *wonder whether*
have a suspicion about 491.18 *be uncertain*
have a sweet tongue 817.10 *be courteous*
have at 674.12 *fight*
have a talk 568.9 *converse*
have a tantrum 828.11 *be angry*
have a temper 829.6 *be irascible*
have a tendency 234.4 *tend*, 584.16 *have a habit*
have a tête-à-tête with 654.6 *consult*
have a theory 518.5 *suppose*
have a thick skin 783.12 *be indifferent*
have a thing about 821.18 *in love*
have a tiff 828.11 *be angry*
have a tiger by the tail 659.22 *cause trouble*
have a title to 845.14 *be entitled*
have at one's beck and call 692.12 *be available to one*
have at one's command 599.5 *dispose of*, 692.12 *be available to one*, 723.7 *possess*
have at one's disposal 599.5 *dispose of*, 692.12 *be available to one*, 723.7 *possess*
have at one's elbow 654.6 *consult*
have at one's mercy 701.6 *subject*
have a touchback 19.17 *kick*
have a turn 214.7 *be regular*
have a twin town 135.8 *unite*
have a use for 613.11 *find useful*
have authority 688, 12.11 *govern*, 235.10 *be powerful*, 698.16 *be independent*
have authority over 692
have authorization 708.5 *be permitted*
have a vacancy for 593.7 *require*
have a vantage point 126.11 *get ahead*
have a vicelike grip 726.6 *retain*
have a visible effect 227
have a voice 233.8 *influence*, 580.1 *select*, 580.5 *vote*
have a voice in 724.4 *have joint possession*
have a vote 580.5 *vote*
have a walkover 660.17 *do easily*
have a water start 38.16 *windsurf*
have a way with 653.1 *manage*
have a weakness for 821.23 *love*
have a weight on one's shoulders 661.12 *burden*
have a whip-round 729.6 *give to charity*
have a wide acquaintance with 819.13 *befriend*
have a will of one's own 698.16 *be independent*
have a wolf by the ears 659.22 *cause trouble*
have a word with 568.9 *converse*
have bad breath 419.5 *stink*
have bad luck 211.6 *lose one's chance*, 229.4 *chance*, 683.6 *fail*
have bad taste 412
have balls 239.2 *be full of vigour*

have barefaced cheek 668.5 *defy*
have bats in the belfry 510.14 *become insane*
have being 396.16 *live*
have belongings 725.9 *own property*
have bills to pay 745.7 *be in debt*
have blood on one's hands 866.8 *be guilty*
have BO 419.5 *stink*
have bought it 244.13 *be destroyed*
have bought the farm 244.13 *be destroyed*
have brains 507.8 *be intelligent*
have buoyancy 377.10 *be adaptable*
have by the throat 726.6 *retain*
have cancer 227.8 *grow*
have capital gains 721.14 *profit*
have carnal knowledge 135.11 *make love*
have carte blanche 698.19 *liberalize*
have certain status 107.9 *have a relative position*
have charge of 632.9 *protect*, 653.1 *manage*
have charges brought against one 856.7 *be accused*
have charisma 233.8 *influence*, 235.10 *be powerful*
have children 245.10 *reproduce oneself*
have chutzpah 668.5 *defy*
have clairvoyance 516.1 *foresee*
have clean hands 865.8 *be innocent*
have clearance 708.5 *be permitted*
have clout 233.8 *influence*, 318.9 *be prominent*, 688.18 *have authority*
have cold feet 627.4 *reconsider*
have coming 845.14 *be entitled*
have company 665.16 *host*
have compassion 374.15 *be kind*, 691.3 *be lenient*
have composure 869.7 *be calm*
have concord 135.9 *agree*
have conformity 667.8 *be compatible*
have consequence 227.5 *show an effect*
have continuity 212.7 *be frequent*
have coverage 19.16 *play defence*
have crimes to answer for 866.8 *be guilty*
have currency 164.28 *prevail*
have dealings with 737.1 *trade*, 819.13 *befriend*
have debts 661.12 *burden*
have decency 857.6 *be honourable*
have deep understanding 277.15 *be profound*
have defective sight 436.14 *be blind*
have dependents to support 661.12 *burden*
have designs 592.13 *plot*, 784.7 *like*
have designs on 588.10 *aim*, 714.11 *promise oneself*
have differences with 500.8 *dissent*, 666.5 *disagree*, 764.11 *quarrel*
have different opinions 113.9 *dissent*
have difficulties 105.7 *be in a predicament*, 687.9 *be in trouble*
have difficulty 659
have difficulty speaking 563
have diminishing returns 722.10 *have a financial loss*
have discord 113.9 *dissent*
have dissention 136.12 *disagree*
have distinction 318.9 *be prominent*
have done with 600.6 *stop using*
have doubts about 498.8 *disbelieve*
have drive 235.10 *be powerful*
have egg on one's face 656.6 *act foolishly*
have elbowroom 698.18 *have scope*

have encroachment 19.18 *be penalized*
have enough 608, 144.5 *be complete*
have enough of 684.5 *conclude*
have enough rope to hang oneself 698.18 *have scope*
have every intention 588.8 *resolve*
have every intention to 199.8 *intend*
have everything 144.5 *be complete*
have everything going one's way 686.5 *be prosperous*
have excess 610.4 *be excessive*
have exclusive possession of 723.7 *possess*
have exclusive rights to 723.7 *possess*
have experience 655.11 *be expert*
have expertise 688.22 *be an authority on*
have expired 200.13 *be past*
have extra money 721.14 *profit*
have extrasensory perception 516.1 *foresee*
have eyes bigger than one's stomach 872.5 *be greedy*
have eyes for 821.23 *love*
have eyes in the back of one's head 435.12 *see*
have faith 7.19 *be religious*, 775.8 *be optimistic*
have faith in 490.20 *be certain*, 497.7 *believe*
have false piety 540.18 *be hypocritical*
have family responsibilities 661.12 *burden*
have fatigue 683.6 *fail*
have feet of clay 539.27 *be false*, 620.9 *be imperfect*
have fighting skills 26.11 *do a combat sport*
have fish to fry 597.1 *undertake*
have flexibility 377.8 *be elastic*
have fond illusions 539.25 *deceive oneself*
have for sale 739.1 *sell*
have forty winks 240.4 *be inert*, 643.13 *sleep*, 649.2 *take it easy*
have freedom of choice 698.14 *be free*
have free time 641.4 *not act*, 645.4 *have leisure*
have free will 580.1 *select*, 698.14 *be free*
have friends 815.13 *fraternize*, 819.13 *befriend*
have friends in high places 233.8 *influence*
have from 730.9 *receive*
have fun 405.8 *feel pleasure*, 686.10 *good luck*, 762.6 *enjoy*, 769.7 *be cheerful*, 815.13 *fraternize*
have gainful employment 721.12 *earn*
have gangrene 622.10 *be dirty*
have G-force loading 33.10 *be on the track*
have gone out with the Ark 200.13 *be past*
have good breeding 817.11 *have good manners*
have good hang time 19.17 *kick*
have good luck 229.4 *chance*
have good manners 817
have good prospects 714.10 *show potential*
have good vibes 667.6 *agree with*
have good vibrations 667.6 *agree with*
have gooseflesh 403.11 *sense*
have goose flesh 407.13 *be touched by*
have goosebumps 409.10 *be cold*
have goose-pimples 403.11 *sense*
have got to 695.8 *be compelled*
have ground clearance 33.10 *be on the track*
have grounds for 843.13 *be right*
have growing pains 206.18 *grow*
have guilt feelings 867.4 *be penitent*
have guts 778.15 *be courageous*

have had a bellyful 608.6 *have enough*
have had enough 608.6 *have enough*, 673.3 *submit*
have had it 244.13 *be destroyed*
have had it up to here 608.6 *have enough*
have had more than enough 608.6 *have enough*
have had one's chips 397.15 *die*
have had one's day 200.13 *be past*, 207.17 *age*
have had one's lesson 672.4 *serve one right*
have had one too many 874.7 *be drunk*
have had too much 874.7 *be drunk*
have halitosis 419.5 *stink*
have hard feelings towards 822.14 *hate*
have harmony 135.9 *agree*
have heartburn 841.6 *be jealous*
have high hopes 775.7 *aspire*
have high regard for 784.7 *like*
have histrionics 541.7 *exaggerate*
have hoped better of 515.4 *be disappointed*
have hoped for better 515.4 *be disappointed*
have hoped for something better 515.4 *be disappointed*
have horns 380.14 *be sharp*
have hysterics 759.17 *feel deeply*
have illegal motion 19.18 *be penalized*
have illegal use of hands 19.18 *be penalized*
have impact 227.5 *show an effect*
have importance 233.8 *influence*
have independent means 698.16 *be independent*
have inferior rank 701.8 *be subject to*
have influence 233.8 *influence*
have in hand 723.7 *possess*, 726.7 *detain*
have in mind 497.8 *be of the opinion*, 520.10 *mean*, 588.7 *intend*, 714.11 *promise oneself*
have in mind to 199.8 *intend*
have in one's book 652.14 *behave towards*
have in one's charge 653.1 *manage*
have in one's grasp 723.7 *possess*
have in one's grip 723.7 *possess*
have in one's name 723.7 *possess*
have in one's possession 723.7 *possess*
have in one's power 233.10 *be a prevailing influence*
have in prospect 513.8 *expect*
have in reserve 600.5 *not use*
have insight 519, 522.6 *understand*
have integrity 134.9 *be pure*
have intercourse 821.29 *make love*
have in the bag 718.13 *secure one's objective*
have in view 588.7 *intend*
have irons in the fire 597.1 *undertake*
have it all 144.5 *be complete*
have it all one's own way 570.15 *impose one's will*, 660.17 *do easily*
have it all one's way 682.10 *defeat heavily*
have it away 245.14 *have sex*
have it bad 821.24 *be in love*
have it both ways 176, 474.12 *deceive*, 540.17 *double-deal*
have it coming 845.15 *merit*
have it coming to one 879.6 *be punished*
have it easy 660.17 *do easily*, 686.5 *be prosperous*
have it from 528.15 *be informed*
have it from the horse's mouth 528.15 *be informed*
have it in for 785.5 *dislike*, 822.14 *hate*, 832.18 *torment*
have it in one's power 235.10 *be powerful*

have it in the bag 660.17 *do easily*
have it made 686.5 *be prosperous*
have it off 135.11 *make love*, 245.14 *have sex*, 821.29 *make love*
have it one's own way 698.16 *be independent*
have it on good authority 528.15 *be informed*
have it over one 126.8 *be superior*
have it soft 660.17 *do easily*
have its roots in 227.7 *follow from*
have joint possession 724
have jurisdiction 92.7 *administer*
have jurisdiction over 16
have kittens 777.12 *be fearful*
have know 528.11 *inform*
have know-how 235.10 *be powerful*
Havel 48 *Dramatists*
have laws 12.13 *be governed*
have leisure 645
have life 396.16 *live*
have little in common 115.5 *be dissimilar*
have little to say 566.8 *be taciturn*
have little weight 370.9 *be light*
have long ears 420.15 *hear*
have losses 722.10 *have a financial loss*
have love for 821.23 *love*
have luck 589.12 *take a chance*, 686.6 *be fortunate*
have many dates 821.25 *be loved*
have many irons in the fire 113.8 *be diverse*
have many strings to one's bow 113.8 *be diverse*
have mercy 835.14 *have pity*
have mercy on 835.10 *show mercy*
have merit 617.9 *be worthy*
have method in one's madness 657.5 *be cunning*
have misfortune 211.6 *lose one's chance*
have misgivings 477.20 *doubt*
have mobility 324.13 *be in motion*
have money 742.12 *be rich*
have money coming in 721.12 *earn*
have money coming out of one's ears 742.12 *be rich*
have money to burn 742.12 *be rich*
have morals 134.9 *be pure*
have more than enough 659.20 *be in difficulty*
haven 256.11 *retreat*, 325.3 *resting place*, 344.15 *destination*, 632.2 *protection*, 634.2 *shelter*, 816.4 *place of confinement*
have natural talent 234.4 *tend*
have need of 593.7 *require*
have nerve 668.5 *defy*
have never felt better 623.5 *be healthy*
have nine lives 396.16 *live*, 632.8 *be safe*
have no affectations 658.4 *be naive*
have no alibi 866.8 *be guilty*
have no alternative 571.16 *be compelled*
have no ambition 641.4 *not act*
have no answer 523.10 *be unexplained*
have no aspirations 783.16 *be mediocre*
have no bearing 521.7 *mean nothing*
have no bearing on 108.10 *be unrelated*
have no bounds 184.8 *have no limit*
have no business with 117.12 *be disparate*
have no censorship 698.14 *be free*
have no chance 236.6 *be powerless*, 614.7 *be useless*
have no choice 695.8 *be compelled*

have no claim to 846.13 *not be entitled*
have no clout 612.11 *be unimportant*
have no concern with 108.11 *be unconcerned*
have no conscience 868.5 *be impenitent*
have no control 236.6 *be powerless*
have no desire for 785.5 *dislike*
have no desires 783.12 *be indifferent*
have no doubt 490.20 *be certain*
have no doubts about 497.7 *believe*
have no ear 420.15 *hear*
have no ear for 421.8 *be deaf*
have no end 190.5 *be eternal*
have no enjoyment from 788.7 *suffer boredom*
have no excuse 866.8 *be guilty*
have no existence 100.12 *not exist*, 536.10 *be nothing*
have no faults 134.9 *be pure*
have no fault to find 851.11 *approve*
have no feelings 378.10 *be tough*, 836.6 *be pitiless*
have no fight left 673.3 *submit*
have no function 641.4 *not act*
have no grasp of 523.9 *find unintelligible*
have no guile 658.4, 865.10 *be naive*
have no guilt 865.8 *be innocent*
have no guts 779.4 *be a coward*
have no hand in 591.1 *avoid*
have no hang-ups 658.4 *be naive*
have no heart 836.6 *be pitiless*
have no heart for 785.5 *dislike*
have no hope 641.4 *not act*
have no inclination for 785.5 *dislike*
have no influence 236.6 *be powerless*
have no interest in 108.11 *be unconcerned*
have no issue 247.7 *be infertile*
have no law 16.74 *be lawless*
have no liability 848.11 *be exempt*
have no life 641.4 *not act*
have no liking for 785.5 *dislike*
have no limit **184**
have no love for 822.14 *hate*
have no luck 687.9 *be in trouble*
have no manners 818.7 *be discourteous*
have no meaning 506.7 *be nonsense*, 521.7 *mean nothing*
have no meaning for 521.8 *not understand*
have no mercy 832.19, 836.6 *be pitiless*
have no money 687.10 *need money*
have no morals 783.14 *be careless*, 858.8 *be dishonourable*, 877.17 *be sexually immoral*
have no more 722.9 *lose*
have no more shots in one's locker 743.12 *be poor*
have no objection 116.21 *be in accord*
have no objection to 667.6 *agree with*
have no offers 825.9 *be celibate*
have no offspring 247.7 *be infertile*
have no option 695.8 *be compelled*
have no passion 783.12 *be indifferent*
have no pity 836.6 *be pitiless*
have no plans 595.12 *be unprepared*
have no point 104.13 *be extraneous*
have no power 236.6 *be powerless*
have no prejudice 783.15 *be impartial*
have no prospects 743.12 *be poor*
have no pull 612.11 *be unimportant*
have no purpose 614.7 *be useless*

have no questions about 787.6 *understand*
have no ready cash 747.9 *be unable to pay*
have no recollection of 512.13 *forget*
have no regard for 850.19 *disrespect*, 852.14 *disapprove*
have no regrets 868.5 *be impenitent*
have no relation to 104.13 *be extraneous*
have no relevance 104.13 *be extraneous*
have no remorse 868.5 *be impenitent*
have no resistance 236.6 *be powerless*
have no respect for 850.19 *disrespect*, 852.14 *disapprove*
have no responsibility 848.11 *be exempt*
have no right 846.13 *not be entitled*
have no say 236.6 *be powerless*
have no secrets 522.4 *be intelligible*, 526.4 *show oneself*
have no self-doubt 809.15 *be vain*
have no sense of pride 806.19 *be humble*
have no sex 825.10 *be continent*
have no shame 526.4 *show oneself*
have no sin 134.9 *be pure*
have no smell **417**
have no solution 523.10 *be unexplained*
have no stomach for 573.6 *be unwilling*, 779.4 *be a coward*, 785.5 *dislike*
have no strength left 650.5 *be fatigued*
have no taste 412.7 *be tasteless*
have no taste for 783.12 *be indifferent*
have nothing in common 115.5 *be dissimilar*
have nothing left to give 650.5 *be fatigued*
have nothing on 129.7 *yield to*
have nothing to add 144.4 *complete*
have nothing to be ashamed of 865.8 *be innocent*
have nothing to complain about 765.7 *be satisfied*
have nothing to confess 865.8 *be innocent*
have nothing to declare 865.8 *be innocent*
have nothing to do 641.4 *not act*
have nothing to do with 108.11 *be unconcerned*, 591.1 *avoid*, 666.5 *disagree*, 816.13 *ignore*
have nothing to go on 502.9 *be ignorant*
have nothing to grumble about 765.7 *be satisfied*
have nothing to hide 865.8 *be innocent*
have nothing to it 787.8 *be predictable*
have nothing to say for oneself 866.8 *be guilty*
have nothing to show for 722.10 *have a financial loss*
have no thought for others 860.7 *be egoistic*
have no thought for the consequences 508.6 *be foolish*
have no time for 785.5 *dislike*, 818.7 *be discourteous*, 850.19 *disrespect*
have no time to lose 642.12 *be active*, 648.2 *make haste*
have no time to spare 648.2 *make haste*
have no title to 846.13 *not be entitled*
have no tricks 658.4 *be naive*
have no truck with 573.9 *not cooperate*
have no nous 803.2 *the common people*
have no use 610.5 *be superfluous*, 614.7 *be useless*

have no use for 600.5 *not use*, 785.5 *dislike*
have no value 618.13 *be worthless*
have no way out 571.16 *be compelled*
have no weight 612.11 *be unimportant*
have no words to express 786.9 *wonder*
have no work 645.4 *have leisure*
have occasion for 593.7 *require*
have odour **416**
have offspring 245.11 *have young*
have on 295.34 *wear*
have one foot in the grave 207.17 *age*
have one for the road 345.6 *part*, 351.13 *drink*
have one hand tied behind one's back 659.19 *have difficulty*
have one over the eight 874.8 *get drunk*
have one's back to the wall 633.9 *face danger*, 659.20 *be in difficulty*
have one's birth 245.11 *have young*
have one's cake and eat it 176.18 *have it both ways*
have one's cake and eat it too 540.17 *double-deal*
have one's conviction overturned 638.5 *escape*
have one's doubts 477.20 *doubt*, 491.18 *be uncertain*
have one's eye on 714.11 *promise oneself*, 782.12 *desire*
have one's eyes opened 522.6 *understand*
have one's fill 144.5 *be complete*
have one's fling 642.12 *be active*, 698.19 *liberalize*
have one's foibles 864.16 *be wicked*
have one's friends and relations 353.22 *menstruate*
have one's hand in 655.10 *be skilful*
have one's hands full 642.13 *be busy*, 659.20 *be in difficulty*
have one's head 698.18 *have scope*
have one's head for 879.1 *punish*
have one's head in the clouds 462.12 *lack thought*
have one's head screwed on 459.13 *be intelligent*
have one's head screwed on the right way 507.8 *be intelligent*
have one's heart in one's work 644.8 *exert oneself*
have one's heart in the right place 831.8 *be benevolent*, 833.7 *be charitable*
have one's heart's desire 765.7 *be satisfied*
have one's knife in 785.6 *react against*
have one's mind in the mud 652.13 *behave badly*
have one's nativity 396.18 *be born*
have one's nerves stretched 403.12 *awake*
have one's nose out of joint 828.10 *be offended*
have one's nose to the grindstone 788.7 *suffer boredom*
have one's own way 570.15 *impose one's will*
have one's palm greased 878.13 *get paid*
have one's period 214.8 *be cyclic*, 353.22 *menstruate*
have one's plans ruined 515.4 *be disappointed*
have one's plate full 642.13 *be busy*
have one's pound of flesh 690.5 *be severe*
have one's pride 805.24 *be proud*
have one's reward 878.12 *be rewarded*
have one's say 535.17 *affirm*, 535.21 *be assertive*, 564.11 *speak*

have one's self-respect 805.24 *be proud*
have one's senses 403.11 *sense*
have one's ship come in 742.13 *get rich*
have one's way 698.16 *be independent*
have one's way with 821.29 *make love*, 877.20 *seduce*
have one's weak side 864.16 *be wicked*
have one's wicked way with 135.11 *make love*
have one's wits about one 403.12 *awake*, 459.13 *be intelligent*, 507.7 *be wise*, 509.6 *be sane*, 655.10 *be skilful*
have one's work cut out 659.19 *have difficulty*
have one too many 874.8 *get drunk*
have only oneself to blame 845.15 *merit*
have on offer 13.10 *trade with*, 739.1 *sell*
have on one's hands 610.5 *be superfluous*
have on one's plate 652.14 *behave towards*
have on the carpet 879.1 *punish*
have on the side 600.5 *not use*
have openness 322.22 *be open*
have other fish to fry 211.7 *be busy*, 598.1 *relinquish*, 642.12 *be active*
have other things to do 211.7 *be busy*, 642.12 *be active*
have over a barrel 688.18 *have authority*
have overall responsibility 653.2 *direct*
have passion for 784.7 *like*
have perfect pitch 420.15 *hear*
have permission 708.5 *be permitted*
have persistence 726.6 *retain*
have personal motives 860.6 *be selfish*
have pertinence 667.9 *be suitable*
have physical strength 378.10 *be tough*
have pity! **835**
have pity 691.3 *be lenient*, 835.10 *show mercy*
have pity for 835.8 *pity*
have play 698.18 *have scope*
have plenty of rope 698.18 *have scope*
have plenty of time 645.4 *have leisure*
have poor health 624.24 *be unhealthy*
have possession 19.15 *play offence*
have possibilities 714.10 *show potential*
have power 12.11 *govern*, 235.10 *be powerful*, 688.18 *have authority*
have power over 233.10 *be a prevailing influence*, 692.11 *have authority over*
have precedence 154.16 *take precedence*
have prior information 516.1 *foresee*
have priority 154.16 *take precedence*, 611.7 *be important*
have progeny 245.11 *have young*
have prongs 380.14 *be sharp*
have prospects 199.10 *expect*
have pull 233.8 *influence*
have pulling power 233.8 *influence*
have quality 617.9 *be worthy*
have qualms 777.12 *be fearful*
have quick wits 380.17 *be mentally sharp*
have ready 594.4 *prepare for action*
have recourse 629.7 *resort*
have recourse to 599.4 *resort to*
have regard for 719.4 *observe*, 831.8 *be benevolent*
have regrets 867.4 *be penitent*
have regular wages 721.12 *earn*
have relevance 107.7 *relate to*

have relevancy 667.9 *be suitable*
have repute 800
have reservations 498.8 *disbelieve*
have resilience 377.10 *be adaptable*
have resources 725.9 *own property*
have responsibility 653.2 *direct*
Haverfordwest 93 *Cities*
have right on one's side 843.13 *be right*
have room to breathe 698.18 *have scope*
have round 734.11 *be hospitable*
haversack 258.9 *baggage*
have saving grace 863.8 *be virtuous*
have scope 698
have scruples 573.6 *be unwilling*
have second sight 435.17 *imagine*, 516.1 *foresee*
have second thoughts 461, 484.8 *reverse*, 576.6 *hesitate*, 627.4 *reconsider*, 781.5 *be cautious*, 867.4 *be penitent*
have seen better days 207.17 *age*, 628.1 *deteriorate*, 687.9 *be in trouble*
have seen it all before 787.6 *understand*
have self-control 302.7 *limit*
have self-motivation 228.8 *be motivated*
have self-reliance 698.16 *be independent*
have self-restraint 302.7 *limit*
have several irons in the fire 642.13 *be busy*
have sex 245, 821.29 *make love*
have sexual intercourse 135.11 *make love*, 245.14 *have sex*
have sexual relations 135.11 *make love*
have sex with 135.11 *make love*
have sharp wits 380.17 *be mentally sharp*
have simplicity 690.7 *be unadorned*
have small chance 589.12 *take a chance*
have solidarity 135.9 *agree*
have someone on 539.28 *trick*
have someone on the ropes 26.11 *do a combat sport*
have someone's blessing 708.5 *be permitted*
have someone's ear 420.15 *hear*
have something extra 126.11 *get ahead*
have something in hand 126.11 *get ahead*
have something in one's eye 436.14 *be blind*
have something in reserve 126.11 *get ahead*
have some use 613.9 *be useful*
have sovereignty 91.17 *become a nation*
have spare time 645.4 *have leisure*
have spots in front of one's eyes 436.14 *be blind*
have stamina 235.10 *be powerful*
have staying power 235.10 *be powerful*
have sticky fingers 736.12 *steal*
have substance 725.9 *own property*
have success 682.6 *be successful,* 721.9 *gain*
have superiority 123.5 *be unequal*
have survivability 378.10 *be tough*
have sway 233.10 *be a prevailing influence,* 235.10 *be powerful*
have sway over 692.11 *have authority over*
have taped 653.1 *manage*
have taste 558.4 *be elegant*
have tea 350.24 *have a meal*
have teething troubles 661.9 *block*
have temerity 668.5 *defy*
have tenacity 378.10 *be tough,* 726.6 *retain*
have tenure of 723.7 *possess*

have that little extra something 300.7 *have an advantage*
have the advantage 123.5 *be unequal*
have the appearance of 457.11 *appear*
have the audacity 807.22 *be rude*
have the ball at one's feet 698.16 *be independent*
have the best intentions 831.8 *be benevolent,* 865.8 *be innocent*
have the best of both worlds 176.18 *have it both ways*
have the best of it 682.9 *be victorious*
have the blarney 657.5 *be cunning*
have the bloom of youth 206.16 *be young*
have the blues 830.9 *be sullen*
have the brass neck 807.22 *be rude*
have the casting vote 226.12 *determine,* 233.10 *be a prevailing influence*
have the cheek 807.22 *be rude*
have the common touch 817.10 *be courteous*
have the courage of one's convictions 778.15 *be courageous*
have the curse 353.22 *menstruate*
have the deck stacked against one 633.9 *face danger*
have the deed for 723.7 *possess*
have the desired effect 615.6 *be convenient*
have the disadvantage 123.5 *be unequal*
have the ear of 233.8 *influence*
have the edge on 126.8 *be superior*
have the effect of 226.9 *be the cause of*
have the feel of a language 5.45 *use language*
have the final say 233.10 *be a prevailing influence,* 478.18 *answer back*
have the freedom of 698.18 *have scope*
have the gall 807.22 *be rude*
have the game in one's hands 660.17 *do easily*
have the golden touch 742.12 *be rich*
have the habit of 584.16 *have a habit*
have the hots for 782.13 *like,* 877.17 *be sexually immoral*
have the innocence of a child 865.10 *be naive*
have the innocence of a newborn babe 865.10 *be naive*
have the inside track 126.11 *get ahead,* 300.7 *have an advantage*
have the jump on 300.7 *have an advantage*
have the knack 485.14 *be qualified,* 655.10 *be skilful,* 861.19 *be good at*
have the know-how 655.11 *be expert,* 688.22 *be an authority on*
have the knowledge 655.11 *be expert*
have the last laugh 126.8 *be superior*
have the last word 209.8 *delay,* 476.8 *refute,* 478.18 *answer back,* 535.21 *be assertive*
have the law on 16.70 *litigate*
have the lion's share 126.11 *get ahead*
have the look of power 692.11 *have authority over*
have the makings of 488.8 *be probable*
have the means 602.6 *find means,* 608.6 *have enough*
have the measure of 653.1 *manage*
have the Midas touch 721.14 *profit*
have the morals of an alley cat 877.17 *be sexually immoral*
have them rolling in the aisles 798.7 *make one laugh*

have the nerve 807.22 *be rude*
have the odds against one 633.9 *face danger*
have the pip 830.9 *be sullen*
have the pole position 33.10 *be on the track,* 126.11 *get ahead*
have the right 845.14 *be entitled*
have the right connections 233.8 *influence*
have the right moral attitude 876.12 *moralize*
have the right touch 655.10 *be skilful*
have the run of 698.18 *have scope*
have the runs 353.16 *defecate*
have the same meaning 520.10 *mean*
have the say-so 688.18 *have authority*
have the shivers 409.10 *be cold*
have the skids put under one 127.11 *become inferior*
have the spotlight on one 526.5 *be visible*
have the talent for 235.10 *be powerful*
have the trick of 655.10 *be skilful*
have the upper hand 688.18 *have authority*
have the use of 599.5 *dispose of*
have the usufruct 599.5 *dispose of*
have the verdict read 16.71 *try a case*
have the vote 580.5 *vote*
have the whip hand 126.8 *be superior,* 688.18 *have authority*
have the wolf at one's door 687.10 *need money*
have the words taken out of one's mouth 566.9 *lapse into silence*
have the world at one's feet 682.6 *be successful*
have thoughts above one's station 471.18 *aim*
have time for 729.5 *give*
have time on one's hand 645.4 *have leisure*
have time on one's hands 788.7 *suffer boredom*
have time to kill 788.7 *suffer boredom*
have time to spare 208.7 *be early*
have title to 723.7 *possess*
have to 695.8 *be compelled*
have to dinner 350.25 *provide food*
have to do with 107.7 *relate to,* 640.4 *act,* 652.14 *behave towards,* 724.4 *have joint possession*
have to hand it to 127.9 *yield to*
have tone 377.8 *be elastic*
have too many irons in the fire 597.1 *undertake,* 610.4 *be excessive,* 656.6 *act foolishly*
have too much 874.8 *get drunk*
have too much on one's plate 596.3 *tackle,* 597.1 *undertake,* 610.4 *be excessive*
have to one's name 725.9 *own property*
have to repay 745.7 *be in debt*
have to run for it 633.8 *be in danger*
have to spare 599.5 *dispose of*
have trouble 659.19 *have difficulty,* 687.9 *be in trouble*
have two meanings 578.1 *be equivocal*
have under one's belt 718.13 *secure one's objective*
have under one's thumb 233.10 *be a prevailing influence,* 688.18 *have authority*
have understanding 519.16 *have insight,* 522.6 *understand*
have up 16.70 *litigate*
have virtue 134.9 *be pure,* 857.6 *be honourable*
have visions 4.20 *philosophize*
have visitors 353.22 *menstruate*
have vitality 721.12 *earn,* 742.12 *be rich*
have weight 369.12 *be heavy*

have what it takes 235.10 *be powerful,* 237.7 *be strong,* 575.9 *endure*
have withdrawal symptoms 875.10 *drug oneself*
have words 117.14 *disagree,* 473.13 *argue*
have x-ray eyes 435.12 *see,* 442.12 *make transparent*
have young 245
have zest 239.2 *be full of vigour*
having 146.7 *including,* 723.8 *possessing*
having a closed mind 443.5 *unintelligent*
having a light touch 370.1 *light*
having and holding 723.8 *possessing*
having an excuse 855.13 *vindicable*
having a part 724.1 *joint possession*
having a prior engagement 211.12 *busy*
having a share 724.1 *joint possession*
having a touch of human frailty 864.13 *venial*
having a weaker side 864.13 *venial*
having bad taste 411.8 *tasteful,* 412.6 *coarse*
having ears 420.12 *eared*
having flavour 411.7 *tasty*
having full play 698.11 *ranging*
having good taste 411.8 *tasteful*
having had it 397.18 *dying*
having had one too many 874.1 *drunk*
having had too much 874.1 *drunk*
having in view 588.11 *intending*
having it good 686.1 *prosperity*
having it off 821.5 *desire*
having meaning 520.6 *meaningful*
having motion 324.16 *moving*
having no case 16.64 *convicted*
having no effect 247
having no legal protection 16.56 *unauthorized*
having no regrets 868.3 *impenitent*
having no remorse 868.3 *impenitent*
having no sorrow 868.3 *impenitent*
having nothing to eat 871.5 *fast*
having one's foibles 864.13 *venial*
having other fish to fry 211.12 *busy*
having other things to do 211.12 *busy*
having poor sight 436.9 *weak-sighted*
having possessions 723.8 *possessing*
having sense 520.6 *meaningful*
having tea 350.4 *eating meals*
having teeth 235.14 *operative*
having the right 845.11 *entitled to*
having weight 369.1 *heavy*
havoc 244, 607.4 *destruction,* 628.10 *impairment,* 670.14 *siege*
haw 335.8 *sidestep*
Hawaii 92 *American States,* **98** *Islands*
Hawaiian 5 *Languages and Groups of Languages*
Hawaiian goose 78 *Birds*
Hawes Water 94 *Lakes,* 94.4 *British lakes*
hawfinch 78 *Birds*
Hawick 93 *Cities*
hawk 78 *Birds,* 78.5 *bird of prey,* 353.20 *salivate,* 430.5 *sound hoarse,* 435.2 *eye,* 590.6 *hunter,* 590.11 *hunt,* 670.19 *attacker,* 679.6 *militarist,* 690.4 *strict person,* 712.6 *request,* 727.11 *dispose of property,* 739.1 *sell*
hawk about 532.13 *make public*
hawkbell 49 *Musical Instruments*
hawkbit 84 *Flowers and Flowering Plants*

hawker 78.22 *hunter,* 431.9 *crier,* 590.6 *hunter,* 739.11 *pedlar*

Hawke's Bay 92 New Zealand Regions and Territories

hawk-eyed 435.21 *seeing*

hawking 78.20 *bird sport,* 590.2 *chase*

hawkish 78.23 *avian,* 670.22 *militant,* 674.15 *contentious,* 676.16 *warlike*

hawkishness 676.5 *bellicosity*

hawk moth 82 Insects

hawk owl 78 Birds

hawksbill turtle 79 Reptiles

hawk's-eye 54 Minerals, **54** Gemstones

hawkweed 84 Flowers and Flowering Plants

hawsehole 74 Parts of a Ship

hawser 36.3 *parts of a sailing boat,* 137.6 *line*

hawser bend 74 Knots

hawthorn 85 Trees and Shrubs

Hawthorn 18 Sporting Personalities

Hawthorne 48 Writers

hay 46.4 *historic dancing,* 68.9 *animal feedstuff,* 350.8 *animal food*

Haya 8 Deities

haybarn 68.7 *farm building*

haybox 408.4 *burner*

haycock 68.10 *farm tool,* 605.1 *store*

Hay Diet 350.6 *nutrition*

Haydn 49 Musicians and Composers

hay fever 624.1 *ill health*

hayfield 68.11 *farmland*

haylage 68.9 *animal feedstuff*

hayloft 68.7 *farm building*

haymaker 330.14 *sporting hit*

haymaking 203.3 *summer*

hay-making 68.5 *cultivation*

hayrack 68.10 *farm tool*

hayrick 68.10 *farm tool,* 161.27 *bundle,* 605.1 *store*

hayseed 83.9 *seed,* 93.12 *rural dweller,* 255.5 *countryman,* 658.3 *naive person*

haystack 68.10 *farm tool,* 161.27 *bundle,* 605.1 *store*

hay turner 68.10 *farm tool*

haywain 72.1 *Carriages and Carts,* 68.10 *farm tool*

haywire 151.18 *muddled*

hazard 24.2 *billiards play,* 491.15 *unreliability,* 491.22 *risk,* 589.1 *chance,* 589.12 *take a chance,* 633.5 *danger,* 633.9 *face danger,* 633.10 *endanger,* 635.1 *trap,* 661.2 *obstacle*

hazard a guess 518.5 *suppose,* 786.12 *wonder whether*

hazarding 633.5 *danger*

hazardous 491.7 *unreliable,* 633.1 *dangerous,* 661.14 *blocked*

hazardously 491.26 *unreliably,* 633.11 *dangerously,* 661.17 *in the way*

hazardousness 633.5 *danger*

hazard side 40.5 *real tennis*

hazard warning light 71 Motor Vehicle Parts

haze 55.34 *mist,* 55.64 *fog,* 389.3 *wateriness,* 438.4 *invisibility,* 438.6 *that which makes invisible,* 441.2 *murk,* 442.8 *transparent thing,* 443.7 *opaque thing,* 491.20 *make uncertain*

hazel 85 Trees and Shrubs, 449.1 *brown*

hazelnut 86 Nuts

hazily 55.65 *meteorologically,* 307.6 *shapelessly,* 438.9 *invisibly,* 441.12 *dimly,* 491.25 *indeterminately*

haziness 55.35 *visibility,* 307.1 *shapelessness,* 438.4 *invisibility,* 441.2 *murk,* 443.6 *opaqueness,* 491.14 *indeterminacy*

hazy 55.56 *foggy,* 102.8 *unreal,* 307.5 *shapeless,* 438.2 *difficult to see,* 441.6 *murky,* 443.2

shady, 456.10 *mottled,* 491.6 *indeterminate,* 523.4 *difficult*

hazy recollection 512.3 *poor memory*

hazzan 7.8 *priest*

H-beam 63.27 *superstructure*

H-bomb 680.16 *bomb*

HCFC 631.9 *pollution*

H-D curve 66.10 *graininess*

he 401.2 *male*

head 43 Architectural Decoration, **74** Parts of a Ship, **279,** 25.2 *grip,* 25.10 *bowling,* 29.4 *golf club,* 38.2 *football play,* 38.4 *play soccer,* 50.10 *art subject,* 50.12 *sculpture,* 96.2 *channel,* 98.5 *peninsula,* 126.5 *superior,* 126.10 *lead,* 152.6 *category,* 154.15 *precede,* 156.21 *pioneer,* 156.30 *front,* 163.2 *class,* 194.8 *be before,* 235.4 *energy,* 243.7 *produce,* 279.5, 279.7 *top,* 291.5 *focus,* 291.8 *focal,* 303.10 *be in front,* 332.7 *take a direction,* 353.13 *lavatory,* 389.17 *water cycle,* 400.7 *person,* 459.7 *brain,* 517.10 *cards,* 533.12 *headline,* 547.6 *image,* 611.3 *chief thing,* 611.4 *bigwig,* 653.2 *direct,* 653.13 *director,* 681.2 *spoils,* 688.10 *person of authority,* 696.5 *company leader,* 696.9 *educational leader,* 696.12 *masterful,* 696.14 *master,* 727.7 *toilet,* 875.4 *drug taker*

headache 406.2 *painful condition,* 624.3 *symptom,* 659.4 *problem*

headachy 624.22 *sick*

head-and-shoulders 303.6 *front*

head and shoulders above 126.12 *superior*

head-and-shoulders shot 303.2 *face*

head an institution 696.14 *master*

head a school 696.14 *master*

headband 137.10 *band,* 295.15 *headgear,* 313.3 *circular thing*

headboard 47.6 *bed*

head bobbing 39.1 *swimming*

head boy 126.5 *superior*

headcase 168.10 *eccentric,* 510.7 *insane person*

head coach 19.2 *football player,* 22.2 *baseball player,* 23.2 *basketball player*

head cold 417.1 *odourlessness,* 624.9 *respiratory disease*

head count 170.3 *count,* 171.6 *list of names*

head cushion 24.4 *carom*

head doctor 510.10 *psychiatrist*

headdress 7.11 *vestment,* 295.15 *headgear*

headed 38.5 *soccer,* 279.6 *topped*

headed for 332.14 *directed,* 490.5 *inevitable*

header 63.26 *masonry,* 65.17 *computing term,* 360.4 *fall,* 360.5 *dive*

header forward straight 39.6 *diving*

header forward with tuck 39.6 *diving*

head first 241.10 *violently*

headfirst 780.6 *rashly*

head for 74.9 *navigate,* 332.7 *take a direction,* 471.18 *aim,* 629.7 *resort*

head foremost 241.10 *violently*

headgear 295

head guard 671.6 *protective clothing*

head honcho 126.5 *superior,* 688.10 *person of authority,* 696.5 *company leader*

headhunter 590.6 *hunter*

head-hunter 398.10 *killer*

head-hunting 398.24 *murderous*

headily 416.10 *odorously*

heading 38.2 *football play,* 38.5 *soccer,* 73.5 *flight,* 152.6 *category,* 163.2 *class,* 279.2 *head,* 332.2 *bearing,* 544.7 *flag,* 560.2 *brief description*

heading for 199.14 *in the future*

heading for the scrap heap 244.15 *destroyed*

heading up 36.1 *sailing,* 653.17 *managerial*

head in the clouds 462.1 *lack of thought,* 468.3 *absent-mindedness,* 512.8 *oblivious,* 519.6 *reverie*

head in the sand 641.1 *inaction*

head into 156.18 *make a beginning*

head into the wind 74.9 *navigate*

headlamp 439.6 *electric light*

headland 68.11 *farmland,* 98.5 *peninsula,* 318.2 *projection*

headless 131.7 *reduced,* 143.11 *partial*

headlight 71 Motor Vehicle Parts, 439.6 *electric light*

headline 533, 526.1 *display,* 528.17 *newsworthy,* 532.3 *journalism,* 532.16 *publicize,* 611.8 *make important*

head linesman 19.2 *football player*

headlock 26.5 *wrestling,* 726.1 *retention*

headlong 241.10 *violently,* 329.1 *swift,* 329.14 *swiftly,* 595.14 *unreadily,* 648.3 *hasty,* 780.4 *rash,* 780.6 *rashly*

headlong plunge 329.9 *acceleration*

headlong rush 329.9 *acceleration*

head louse 82 Insects, 82.3 *pest*

headman 31.9 *play hockey,* 653.13 *director,* 696.3 *leader*

headmanned 31.8 *hockey*

headmanning 31.8 *hockey*

headmanning the puck 31.3 *ice hockey*

headmaster 6.4 *educator,* 126.5 *superior,* 653.13 *director,* 688.10 *person of authority,* 696.9 *educational leader*

headmistress 6.4 *educator,* 126.5 *superior,* 688.10 *person of authority,* 696.9 *educational leader*

headmost 126.14 *best,* 154.12 *primary*

head mould 43 Architectural Decoration

head moulding 43 Architectural Decoration

head nurse 60.16 *nurse*

head of department 15.6 *employer,* 696.9 *educational leader*

head off 341.1 *repel,* 341.3 *fend off,* 587.3 *deflect*

head office 647.1 *workshop*

head of pressure 389.17 *water cycle*

head of sixth-form 696.9 *educational leader*

head of state 653.13 *director,* 692.6 *person in command,* 696.3 *leader*

head of the household 255.3 *householder,* 653.13 *director*

head-on 663.20 *discordant*

head-on collision 330.12 *collision*

head over heels 151.18 *muddled*

head over heels 144.9 *completely,* 364.13 *round*

head-over-heels 287.2 *inverted,* 287.4 *inversely*

head over heels in love 821.18 *in love*

head patting 543.3 *gesture*

headphones 420.9 *audio device,* 534.9 *telephone,* 730.8 *receiver*

headpiece 43 Architectural Decoration, 279.2 *head*

head pin 25.4 *bowling*

headquarter 291.9 *centre*

headquarters 17.1 *military affairs,* 92.5 *administrative headquarters,* 291.4 *centre of activity,* 592.7 *planning*

headrest 71 Motor Vehicle Parts, 284.4 *rest*

headroom 248.6 *available space,* 265.1 *interval*

headsail 74 Sails, 36.3 *parts of a sailing boat*

heads and tails 111.2 *opposites*

head scanner 630.14 *hospital*

headscarf 295.15 *headgear*

headset 420.9 *audio device,* 534.9 *telephone,* 730.8 *receiver*

headship 126.2 *leadership,* 688.5 *position of authority*

headshrinker 61.30, 510.10 *psychiatrist,* 630.15 *healer*

headsman 879.17 *punisher*

headsman's axe 879.16 *instrument of execution*

heads or tails 229.2 *chance*

head spot 24.4 *carom,* 24.6 *pool*

headstand 287.1 *inversion*

head start 126.3 *advantage,* 194.5 *gift of priority,* 208.1 *earliness,* 300.4 *advantage*

headstock 364.4 *vortex*

heads together 654.2 *consultation*

headstone 43.9 *miscellaneous architectural features,* 279.3 *architectural summit,* 399.4 *funeral objects*

head straight on 332.7 *take a direction*

headstream 96.2 *channel*

head string 24.4 *carom,* 24.6 *pool*

headstrong 241.6 *violent,* 508.5 *foolish,* 570.8 *wilful,* 577.1 *obstinate,* 659.14 *troublesome,* 689.6 *anarchic*

headstrongness 138.2 *tenacity*

heads will roll 879.24 *string him up*

head teacher 6.4 *educator,* 696.9 *educational leader*

head to head 111.6 *oppositely*

head-to-head 674.15 *contentious*

head-to-head contest 674.9 *duel*

head-to-wind 36.10 *sailing*

head up 36.15 *sail,* 154.15 *precede,* 194.8 *be before,* 653.2 *direct*

head-up display 73 Aircraft Parts

head waiter 606.4 *caterer,* 697.3 *attendant*

headwaters 96.2 *channel,* 226.2 *source*

headway 248.6 *available space,* 324.3 *motion towards,* 336.10 *forward motion,* 627.5 *improvement,* 721.2 *augmentation*

head wind 55.15 *wind direction*

headwind 73.5 *flight,* 111.3 *opposition,* 231.2 *counteracting thing*

head wind 390.4 *air flow*

headwork 461.2 *intellectual exercise*

heady 237.12 *strong to the senses,* 416.5 *odorous,* 418.4 *fragrant,* 689.6 *anarchic,* 874.6 *intoxicating*

heady scent 416.1 *odour*

heal 60.19 *practise medicine,* 623.7 *make healthy,* 629.6 *cure,* 630.19 *remedy,* 677.4 *pacify*

heal-all 630.1 *remedy*

healed 623.1 *healthy,* 629.15 *cured*

healer 60, 630, 629.12 *repairer*

healing 60.2 *natural medicine,* 60.25 *therapeutic,* 629.11 *recuperation,* 629.16 *restorative,* 630.11 *medical art,* 630.17 *remedial*

healing agent 62.3 *drug*

healing art 630.13 *therapy*

healing gift 630.1 *remedy*

healing over 629.11 *recuperation*

healing quality 630.1 *remedy*

healing touch 630.11 *medical art*

heal itself 629.6 *cure*

heal over 135.10 *link,* 629.6 *cure*

health 623, 239.1 *vigour,* 306.6 *nature,* 351.2 *drink,* 617.6 *worth,* 625.2 *salubrity,* 812.6 *tribute*

Health 623

health and safety representative 15.7 *employee*

health and strength 623.3 *health*

health and wealth 686.1 *prosperity*

health care 60, 60.1 *medicine,* 831.3 *welfare*

health centre 60.10 *hospital*

health club 625.1 *hygiene*

health diet 871.1 *fasting*
health education 60.6 *health care*
health farm 625.1 *hygiene*
health food 350.7 *food*, 625.2 *salubrity*
health-food restaurant 350.15 *eating place*
health-food shop 350.17 *food shop*
healthful 623, 625.4 *hygienic*
healthfully 623.8 *healthily*, 625.7 *hygienically*
healthfulness 623, 625.2 *salubrity*
health-giving 623.2 *healthful*, 625.4 *hygienic*, 630.17 *remedial*
healthily 623, 306.13 *formatively*, 625.7 *hygienically*
healthiness 237, 623.3 *health*, 625.2 *salubrity*, 861.8 *good*
health inspector 625.3 *hygienist*
health insurance 662.4 *social assistance*, 718.1 *protection*
health officer 60.11 *doctor*
health promotion 60.6 *health care*
health resort 625.1 *hygiene*
health salts 630.6 *purgative*
health spa 625.1 *hygiene*
health visitor 60.16 *nurse*
healthy 623, 142.8 *sound*, 237.9 *physically strong*, 239.4 *vigorous*, 239.5 *invigorating*, 259.15 *big*, 306.12 *on form*, 617.4 *worthwhile*, 625.4 *hygienic*, 629.15 *cured*, 843.12 *all right*, 861.1 *good*
healthy diet 625.2 *salubrity*
healthy eating 350.6 *nutrition*
healthy food 350.7 *food*
healthy hue 444.9 *complexion*
healthy state 623.3 *health*
Heaney 48 Poets
heap 71.16 *car*, 120.2 *certain amount*, 143.7 *piece*, 161.26 *mass*, 161.37 *assemble*, 259.7 *mass*, 482.8 *indiscriminateness*, 482.11 *not discriminate*, 605.1, 605.6 *store*, 721.3 *acquisition*, 721.11 *acquire*
heap abuse upon 827.6 *vilify*
heap coals of fire on one's head 672.3 *retaliate*
heaped 161.47 *collected*, 605.7 *stored*
heaped cloud 55.20 *cloud appearance*
heaped up 140.9 *assembled*
heaping coals of fire 672.1 *retaliation*
heap on 130.6 *add*
heaps 181.3 *profuseness*
heaps of money 741.3 *fortune*, 742.6 *money*
heap up 140.5 *combine*
hear 420, 403.11 *sense*, 477.17 *question*, 492.11 *judge*, 528.15 *be informed*
hearable 420, 423.7 *heard*
hearably 420.17 *aurally*
hear a case 16.69 *have jurisdiction over*, 16.71 *try a case*, 16.76 *judge*
hear a cause 16.69 *have jurisdiction over*, 16.71 *try a case*
hear a complaint 16.69 *have jurisdiction over*
hear both sides 843.14 *be fair*
heard 423, 534.34 *communicated*, 730.13 *received*
heard of 501.10 *known*
hearer 420, 730.5 *recipient*
hear from 420.15 *hear*
hear, hear 499.9 *yes*
hear hear 851.27 *bravo*
hear hear! 420
hearing 420, 16.7 *legal trial*, 396.4 *biological function*, 403.1 *sensation*, 420.11 *aural*, 477.3 *questionnaire*, 479.2 *rehearsal*, 653.7 *council*
Hearing 420
hearing aid 56.18 *source of sound*, 420.7 *ear attachments*, 420.9 *audio device*, 421.1 *deafness*, 423.8 *sound maker*
hearing distance 420.1 *hearing*
hearing-impaired 421.4 *deaf*

hearing impairment 421.1 *deafness*
hearing loss 421.1 *deafness*
hearing of evidence 16.7 *legal trial*
hearing specialist 420.6 *otology*
hearing test 60.7 *diagnosis*
hearken 420.15 *hear*
hearkener 420.2 *hearer*
hear no evil, see no evil, speak no evil 863.8 *be virtuous*
hear of 420.15 *hear*
hear on the grapevine 420.15 *hear*
hear out 420.15 *hear*
hearsay 106.7 *circumstantial*, 420.8 *something heard*, 532.1 *publication*
hearsay evidence 420.8 *something heard*, 483.5 *legal evidence*
hearse 71 Motor Vehicles, 399.4 *funeral objects*
hear sentence 16.72 *stand trial*
heart 42.3 *card game terms*, 45.31 *offal*, 103.2 *essential content*, 158.2 *core*, 243.7 *produce*, 257.3 *insides*, 290.2 *inside*, 290.4 *insides*, 290.5 *inner nature*, 291.1 *centre*, 396.3 *life requirements*, 611.3 *chief thing*, 759.8 *seat of feelings*
heartache 770.1 *sorrow*
heart and soul 142.11 *wholly*, 144.9 *completely*
heart attack 236.4 *disability*, 624.10 *cardiovascular disease*
heartbeat 214.5 *regular thing*, 365.2 *vibration*, 424.3 *faint-sounding thing*
heartbreak 770.1 *sorrow*
heartbreaker 401.7 *libertine*, 821.9 *lover*, 826.5 *courting person*
heartbreaking 770.7 *distressing*, 835.7 *pitiful*
heartbroken 515.9 *disappointed*, 770.5 *sad*
heartburn 406.2 *painful condition*, 624.8 *indigestion*, 841.1 *jealousy*
heartburning 828.1 *resentment*, 841.1 *jealousy*
heart condition 624.10 *cardiovascular disease*
heart disease 777 Phobias by Topic, 624.4 *disease*, 624.10 *cardiovascular disease*
hear tell 420.15 *hear*
hear tell of 420.15 *hear*
hearten 239.3 *invigorate*, 662.19 *support*, 769.6 *bring cheer*, 778.17 *give courage*
heartening 662.32 *supportive*, 775.14 *cheering*, 778.6 *encouragement*, 778.14 *encouraging*
heart failure 624.10 *cardiovascular disease*
heartfelt 777.9 *deep-seated*, 759.14 *emotive*
heartfelt apology 867.1 *penitence*
hearth 256.3 *home*, 408.6 *fire*, 634.1 *refuge*
hearth and home 256.3 *home*
hear the call 586.18 *be persuaded*
hear the case 492.11 *judge*
hear the patter of little feet 396.19 *give birth to*
hear things 102.13 *imagine*, 420.15 *hear*
hearth rug 293.9 *floor covering*
hearthstone 408.6 *fire*, 621.9 *cleaning agent*
heartily 237.15 *acutely*, 306.13 *formatively*, 623.8 *healthily*, 644.12 *laboriously*, 815.18 *sociably*, 819.17 *in friendship*
heartiness 623.3 *health*, 819.1 *friendship*
heartland 158.2 *core*, 249.6 *regions*, 290.3 *inland*
heartless 373.4 *mentally hard*, 761.1 *insensitive*, 832.12 *callous*, 836.4 *pitiless*, 868.3 *impenitent*
heartlessly 761.8 *unfeelingly*, 832.20 *malevolently*, 836.7 *pitilessly*

heartlessness 404.3 *heedlessness*, 761.3 *insensitiveness*, 832.3 *callousness*, 836.1 *pitilessness*
heart-lung machine 630.14 *hospital*
heart of flint 832.3 *callousness*, 836.1 *pitilessness*
heart of gold 831.1 *benevolence*
heart of marble 832.3 *callousness*
heart of oak 373.7 *hard substance*, 778.7 *courageous person*
heart of stone 832.3 *callousness*, 836.1 *pitilessness*, 868.1 *impenitence*
heart of the matter 158.2 *core*, 472.1 *topic*, 611.3 *chief thing*
heart pain 406.2 *painful condition*, 650.7 *fatigue*
heart-rending 835.7 *pitiful*
heart rot 69.12 *pests and diseases*, 85.10 *tree disease*
hearts 42 Card Games
heart's blood 396.3 *life requirements*
heart's desire 588.6 *objective*
heartsmitten 821.19 *enamoured*
hearts of oak 574.16 *fortitude*
heart-stopping 633.2 *unsafe*
heart surgeon 60.13 *medical specialist*
heart surgery 60.9, 630.12 *surgery*
heart-throb 365.2 *vibration*, 821.9 *lover*, 826.5 *courting person*
heart-to-heart 526.15 *open*, 568.2 *chat*
heart trouble 624.10 *cardiovascular disease*
heart urchin 81.3 *echinoderm*
heart-warming 405.6 *pleasant*, 408.12 *warm-hearted*, 769.2 *cheering*
heartwood 47.12 *wood*, 85.3 *timber*, 373.7 *hard substance*
heartworm 81 Worms
hearty 74.7 *nautical person*, 306.12 *on form*, 404.5 *unfeeling person*, 623.1 *healthy*, 815.15 *sociable*, 819.8 *friendly*
hearty assent 116.7 *consent*
hearty eater 350.18 *eater*, 872.4 *glutton*
hearty thanks 837.2 *thanks*
hearty welcome 815.9 *welcome*
hear voices 420.15 *hear*
heat 777 Phobias by Topic, **55, 56, 408**, 21.1 *track events*, 45.55 *cook*, 56.2 *classical physics*, 143.3 *stage*, 235.4 *energy*, 235.12 *generate power*, 373.9 *harden*, 392.14 *desert*, 408.14 *be hot*, 674.2 *contest*, 759.4 *emotion*, 828.4 *anger*
Heat 408
heat capacity 56.36 *heat flow*
heated 408, 241.6 *violent*, 759.13 *passionate*
heatedly 828.18 *angrily*
heated pool 39.7 *swimming pool*
heated up 408.13 *heated*
heat-engine cycle 63.13 *engine cycle*
heater 408, 56.35 *heat*, 235.6 *source of energy*
heat exchange 56.36 *heat flow*
heat exchanger 235.6 *source of energy*
heat exhaustion 408.5 *hot weather*
heat flow 56
heat flow rate 56.36 *heat flow*
heath 84 Flowers and Flowering Plants, 87.2 *grassland*, 98.6 *lowland*
heat haze 55.34 *mist*
heat-haze 408.5 *hot weather*
Heathcliff and Cathy 821.10 *lovers*
heathcock 78.10 *male bird*
heathen 9.6 *idolater*, 9.10 *idolatrous*, 498.5 *disbeliever*, 498.6 *disbelieving*, 720.5 *nonobserver*
heathenism 9.2 *idolatry*, 498.4 *unbelief*
heathenize 9.8 *idolatrize*
heathenry 9.2 *idolatry*

heather 84 Flowers and Flowering Plants, 455.3 *purple thing*
heathering 68.5 *cultivation*
heath hen 78.11 *female bird*
Heath Robinson 519.11 *fantastical*
heating 408.9 *hot*
heating device 56.35 *heat*
heating effect 56
heating element 408.3 *heater*
heating system 56.35 *heat*
heat lamp 408.6 *fire*
heat measurement 408
heat-proof 409.9 *heat-resistant*
heat rash 408.5 *hot weather*, 624.13 *skin disease*
heat-resistant 409
heat retention 617.1 *preservation*
heat-seeking missile 338.8 *missile*
heatstroke 408.5 *hot weather*
heat the boiler 594.4 *prepare for action*
heat through 408.14 *be hot*
heat transfer 55.9 *atmospheric process*, 56.36 *heat flow*
heat transport 55.9 *atmospheric process*
heat-treat 373.9 *harden*
heat-treated 373.3 *hardened*
heat treatment 630.13 *therapy*
heat unit 408.2 *heat measurement*
heat up 45.55 *cook*, 128.5 *make bigger*, 408.14 *be hot*, 820.13 *antagonize*, 821.25 *be loved*
heatwave 55.23 *heat*
heat wave 365.5 *wave*, 408.5 *hot weather*
heat with solar power 410.11 *fuel*
heave 97.3 *wave*, 97.10 *billow*, 326.12 *transport*, 330.1 *impel*, 330.4 *throw*, 330.13 *blow*, 338.5, 338.23 *throw*, 339.2, 339.11 *pull*, 349.15 *vomit*, 361.1 *raise*, 361.6 *raising*, 365.9 *vibrate*, 644.4 *exertion*, 644.6 *work*
heave a brick 670.7 *stone*
heaved 361.11 *raised*
heave in sight 437.9 *appear*, 457.12 *become visible*
heaven 777 Phobias by Topic, **8**, 51.16 *auditorium*, 190.3 *life without end*, 199.3 *future condition*, 233.2 *occult influence*, 275.8 *high thing*, 279.1 *summit*, 325.3 *resting place*, 368.1 *nonmaterial world*, 396.5 *life cycle*, 397.14 *the spiritual world*, 405.5 *idealized pleasure*, 762.2 *fun*, 763.6 *pleasantness*
Heaven 714.4 *promised land*
heaven be praised 837.9 *thank you*
heavenly 8, 53.36 *astronomical*, 368.8 *nonmaterial*, 617.1 *worthy*, 762.5 *delightful*, 763.1 *pleasant*
heavenly being 8.6 *angel*
heavenly body 53.10 *star*
heavenly host 8.6 *angel*
heavenly kingdom 368.1 *nonmaterial world*
heaven on earth 405.5 *idealized pleasure*
heavens 53.3 *universe*, 248.2 *empty space*, 275.8 *high thing*, 279.1 *summit*
heaven-sent 210.6 *timely*, 861.1 *good*
heavenward 275.20 *higher*, 332.10 *clockwise*, 359.26 *up*
heave out 349.1 *expel*
heaver 338.14 *thrower*
heave the lead 74.9 *navigate*, 277.14 *deepen*
heave to 36.15, 74.10 *sail*
heavier-than-air craft 73.8 *aircraft*
heavily 369, 120.7 *quantitatively*, 325.10 *motionlessly*, 371.10 *densely*, 788.8 *boringly*
heavily built 259.17 *stocky*
heaviness 369, 120.1 *quantity*, 259.6 *squatness*, 273.5 *thickness*, 393.4 *pulpiness*, 549.3 *in-*

elegance, 643.9 sleep, 788.1 boredom

Heaviness 369

heaving 36.10 sailing, 338.3 throwing, 339.1 traction, 349.23 vomiting

heaving line 36.3 parts of a sailing boat

heaving stomach 785.4 sign of dislike

Heaviside 52 Scientists

Heaviside layer 390.3 atmospheric layers

heavy 369, 41.10 curling, 51.21 role, 55.49 cloudy, 55.52 humid, 55.53 rainy, 97.7 oceanic, 120.6 quantitative, 180.7 attendant, 237.6 muscleman, 240.5 inert, 259.10 big person, 259.17 stocky, 273.1 thick, 325.5 sedentary, 369.16 heavily, 371.6 dense, 393.20 thick, 394.8 viscous, 428.2 nonresonant, 533.5 mass communication, 549.8 inelegant, 554.5 serious, 611.5 important, 644.11 laborious, 659.10 difficult, 788.4, 788.4 boring

heavy-armed 671.30 defended

heavy-armed soldier 679.8 soldier

heavy artillery 680.11 guns

heavy as a horse 369.1 heavy

heavy as lead 369.1 heavy

heavy bombardment 670.12 military attack

heavy bomber 679.31 military aircraft

heavy brigade 679.16 army unit

heavy build 259.6 squatness

heavy cavalry 679.19 cavalry

heavy clothing 34.4 climbing equipment

heavy dragoon 32.15 horse person, 679.20 cavalryman

heavy drinker 351.12 drinker

heavy-duty 237.13 strengthened

heavy eater 350.18 eater, 872.4 glutton

heavy-eyed 643.4 not awake, 650.1 fatigued

heavy father 51.21 role

heavy food 350.7 food

heavy-footed 559.7 graceless, 656.3 clumsy

heavy-going 659.11 rough

heavy gun 680.11 guns

heavy-handed 241.6 violent, 369.3 ponderous, 404.6 unfeeling, 407.10 handed, 549.8 inelegant, 559.7 graceless, 656.3 clumsy, 690.8 severe

heavy-handedly 407.15 insensitively, 690.11 severely

heavy-handedness 404.1 lack of feeling, 549.3 inelegance, 656.8 unskilfulness

heavyhearted 770.5 sad

heavyheartedness 770.1 sorrow

heavy hog 68.8 livestock

heavy industry 243.2 manufacture

heavy-laden 144.8 full, 661.14 blocked

heavy-lidded 650.1 fatigued

heavy metal 49.9 popular music, 57.6 chemical element, 680.11 guns

heavy-metal poisoning 631.9 pollution

heavy scene 611.2 important matter

heavy sea 97.3 wave, 366.13 tempest

heavyset 259.17 stocky

heavy sledding 659.3 difficult task

heavy sleep 643.9 sleep

heavy sleeper 240.2 inert person

heavy socks 34.4 climbing equipment

heavy sound 428.5 dull sound

heavy swell 97.3 wave

heavy traffic 642.6 business

heavy water 389.1 water

heavyweight 26.3 boxing weight divisions, 26.4 boxer, 26.14 com-

bat, 259.12 fat person, 369.1 heavy, 369.7 weighing

heavy weight 369.11 weight

heavyweight 611.4 bigwig, 674.10 contender, 679.3 athlete, 772.7 serious person

heavyweight champion 26.4 boxer

heavy wet snow 41.1 skiing

heavy wine 351.9 wine

heavy with 245.16 reproductive, 246.5 fertile

heavy woman 51.21 role

heavy work 644.1 work

hebdomadal 214.12 cyclic

hebdomadary 214.12 cyclic

Hebe 8 Deities, 53 Minor Planets

hebephrenia 61.11, 510.5 psychosis

hebetude 381.7 dullness, 443.9 stupidity, 460.2 unintelligence

hebetudinous 381.3 dull

Hebraist 200.11 antiquarian

Hebrew 5 Languages and Groups of Languages, 7.16 denominational, 400.4 civilized human

Hebrew alphabet 5.14 alphabet

Hebridean 68 Breeds of Sheep

Hecate 8 Deities, 11.4 witch

hecatomb 244.5 havoc, 710.6 offering

heckelclarina 49 Musical Instruments

heckelphone 49 Musical Instruments

heckle 661.8 hinder, 850.25 taunt, 852.23 show disapproval

heckler 500.5 dissenter, 661.7 hinderer, 663.9 opposer

heck of a lot 181.3 profuseness

hectic 450.2 red-faced, 642.19 busy

hectic flush 450.5 redness

hecto 75 SI Units

hectograph copy 110.4 duplicate

hector 541.6 exaggerator, 807.26 oppress

hectoring 777.4 intimidation

hedge 68.11 farmland, 69.3 ornamental garden, 136.6 boundary, 286.7 deviate, 301.3 enclosing thing, 302.4 boundary marker, 474.13 quibble, 531.13 equivocate, 578.1 be equivocal, 591.7 be evasive, 634.2 shelter, 671.18 fence, 781.5 be cautious

hedge clipper 603.2 garden tool

hedgecutter 68.10 farm tool

hedgehog 77 Placental Mammals, 380.8 sharp-pointed thing

hedgehog cactus 84 Flowers and Flowering Plants

hedgehopping 73.5 flight

hedge-laying 68.5 cultivation

hedge one's bets 333.7 be halfway, 632.8 be safe, 716.6 make conditions, 781.5 be cautious

hedgerow 68.11 farmland, 301.3 enclosing thing

hedgerow tree 85.1 tree

hedge sparrow 78 Birds

hedge trimmer 69.6 garden tool

hedging 68.5 cultivation, 286.3 deviousness, 286.5 devious, 474.4, 474.9 quibbling

hedonism 4.7 school of thought, 405.1 physical pleasure, 763.7 pleasure, 870.1 self-indulgence, 872.1 gluttony

hedonist 4.11 follower of a doctrine, 405.3 pleasure-seeker, 763.12 pleasure-loving person, 870.5 self-indulgent person

hedonistic 4.14 of a philosophy, 405.7 pleased, 763.5 pleasure-loving, 870.6 self-indulgent, 872.6 gluttonous

hedonize 872.5 be greedy

hedonophobia 777 Phobias by Name

hedonics 61.1 psychology

heebie-jeebies 366.1 agitation, 403.3 stimulus, 874.16 alcoholism

heed 420.1 hearing, 420.15 hear, 467.3 carefulness, 467.12

scrutinize, 469.1 carefulness, 469.10 be careful, 694.5 obey, 719.1 observance, 719.4 observe, 781.1 caution, 849.18 show respect

heeded 719.7 observant

heedful 467.7 watchful, 469.9 careful, 719.7 observant, 781.4 cautious

heedfully 719.8 observantly, 781.7 cautiously

heedfulness 781.1 caution

heeding 420.1 hearing, 719.1 observance, 719.7 observant

heedless 404.6 unfeeling, 421.5 unhearing, 462.10 inconsiderate, 464.4 uninterested, 468.7 inattentive, 470.4 negligent, 508.5 foolish, 512.10 unthinking, 648.3 hasty, 720.11 nonobservant, 780.4 rash, 783.8 careless, 832.15 inconsiderate, 838.3 ungrateful

heedlessly 466.8 disinterestedly, 468.14 inattentively, 512.16 obliviously, 648.7 rashly, 720.15 inattentively, 780.6 rashly, 783.18 carelessly, 838.7 ungratefully

heedlessness 404, 421.1 deafness, 468.1 inattention, 470.1 negligence, 508.1 folly, 512.4 unthinkingness, 720.1 nonobservance, 780.1 rashness, 783.2 carelessness, 832.6 inconsiderateness

heed the call 228.8 be motivated

hee-haw 432.1 animal cry

heel 29.4 golf club, 36.15 sail, 123.5 be unequal, 280.2 foot, 304.1 rear, 335.1 deviate, 629.1 repair

heel bone 382 Bones

heel hook 34.3 climbing technique

heel-hook 34.9 mountaineer

heel in 69.15 cultivate

heeling 35.3 rugby play, 35.6 rugger, 123.3 unequal, 629.8 repair

heel over 74.10 sail

heel piece 304.1 rear

heels over head 364.13 round

heeltaps 132.2 residue

heel the ball 35.5 play rugby

heft 361.1 raise, 369.4 heaviness, 369.15 weigh

heftiness 259.6 squatness, 369.4 heaviness

hefting 369.7 weighing

hefty 259.17 stocky, 369.1 heavy, 659.10 difficult

Hegel 4 Philosophers

Hegelian 4.11 follower of a doctrine, 4.14 of a philosophy, 368.7 believer in a nonmaterial world, 368.10 idealist

Hegelian dialectic 4.5 philosophical argument

Hegelianism 4.7 school of thought, 368.5 idealism

hegemonic 126.14 best, 235.13 powerful, 653.17 managerial

hegemony 126.2 leadership, 233.3 personal influence, 235.1 power, 688.1 authority

Hegira 345.7 departure

he-goat 401.16 male animal

Hehe 7 Non-Christian Religions

Heian style 50 Non-Western Art

Heidegger 4 Philosophers

Heidelberg 93 Cities

Heidelberg man 202.7 ancient people

Heidelberg school 50 Schools and Groups of Artists

heifer 68.8 livestock, 77.18 female mammal, 402.14 female animal

height 275, 361, 52.37 line, 56.7 space, 120.1 quantity, 121.1 degree, 126.4 summit, 248.1 space, 259.1, 268.4 size, 269.4 length

Height 275

heighten 128.5, 261.5 make bigger, 275.17 raise, 361.3 pro-

mote, 541.8 enlarge, 768.6 aggravate

heighten awareness 403.13 arouse sensation

heightened 128.7 increased, 261.7 bigger, 541.13 enlarged, 768.4 aggravated

heightener 403.3 stimulus

heightening 128.1 increase, 261.1 growth, 261.8 growing, 541.2 enlargement, 768.1 aggravation

height measure 275

height of perfection 619.3 perfection

heights 275, 95.1 mountain, 98.7 upland

height-weight ratio 1.10 measurement

Heimdal 8 Deities

Heine 48 Poets

Heinkel 52 Scientists

heinous 16.60 offending, 447.5 black-hearted, 618.3 bad, 832.11 cruel, 864.11 wicked, 866.7 sinful

heinousness 618.9 badness, 832.2 cruelness, 864.1 wickedness

heir 132.6 person remaining, 155.12, 195.5 successor, 513.4 expectant person, 721.7 gainer, 730.6 beneficiary, 742.10 wealthy person, 845.7 beneficiary

heir apparent 195.5 successor, 730.6, 845.7 beneficiary

heir-at-law 730.6, 845.7 beneficiary

heirdom 723.1 possession

heiress 195.5 successor, 513.4 expectant person, 721.7 gainer, 730.6 beneficiary, 742.10 wealthy person, 845.7 beneficiary

heirloom 3.11 relic, 202.5 old thing, 725.5 personal estate, 730.1 receiving

heir presumptive 195.5 successor, 730.6 beneficiary

heirs 199.2 future generation

heirship 723.1 possession, 730.1 receiving

heir to a fortune 742.10 wealthy person

Heisenberg 52 Scientists

Heisenberg uncertainty principle 56 Named Laws, 56.81 causality

heist 361.1 raise, 734.3 taking away, 734.10 take away, 736.3 theft, 736.12 steal

Hel 8 Deities, 8.11 heaven

helcoplasty 60 Surgical Operations

held 31.8 hockey, 38.5 soccer, 225.9 stable, 258.20 containing, 605.7 stored, 632.5 safe, 723.9 possessed, 726.10 retained

held back 302.5 limited, 661.13 hindering

held ball 23.4 playing terms

held in 726.10 retained

held in low esteem 850.17 unrespected

held in respect 849.12 respected

held position 30.6 pommel horse

held together 116.14 conforming

held up 209, 661.13 hindering

held-up 209.10 held up, 328.7 delayed

Helena 93 Cities

Heley 29.5 golf ball

heliacal 53.36 astronomical, 363.10 circular

helical 52.81 curvilinear, 314.4 convolutional, 334.6 circular

helical gear 63.7 gear

helically 314.8 circularly

helicon 49 Musical Instruments

Helicon 48.13 poetic genius

helicopter 73.8 aircraft, 679.31 military aircraft

helicopter flying 18 Sporting Activities

helicopter gunship 679.31 military aircraft

helicopter skiing 41.1 skiing

heliocentric 53.36 *astronomical*, 291.6 *central*
heliocentrically 53.39 *astronomically*
heliodor 54 Gemstones
heliograph 534.8 *data transmission*, 543.4 *signal*
heliographer 543.8 *signer*
heliographic 543.16 *signalling*
heliolater 9.6 *idolater*
heliolatrous 9.10 *idolatrous*
heliolatry 9.2 *idolatry*
heliometer 268.8 *meter*
heliometric 268.16 *micrometric*
heliometry 268.2 *micrometry*
heliophobia 777 Phobias by Name
Helios 8 Deities, 53.15 *sun*
heliostat 53.24 *telescope*
heliotrope 84 Flowers and Flowering Plants, 455.3 *purple thing*, 455.6 *purple*
heliport 184.5 *destination*
helium 57 Chemical Elements, 338.13 *fuel*, 361.10 *elevator*, 370.7 *light thing*
helium balloon 73.8 *aircraft*, 361.10 *elevator*, 388.13 *gas balloon*
helium-neon laser 56.26 *laser*
helix 43 Architectural Decoration, 52.40 *curve*, 363.1 *orbital motion*
Helix Nebula 53 Nebulae
hell 777 Phobias by Topic, **8**, 151.5 *confusion*, 199.3 *future condition*, 277.4 *deep thing*, 368.1 *nonmaterial world*, 397.14 *the spiritual world*, 406.1 *pain*, 687.1 *adversity*, 864.8 *wicked place*
Hell 408.8 *hot place*
Helladic 202.14 *historic*
hellbender 79 Amphibians
hellbent 508.5 *foolish*, 588.11 *intending*
hell-bent 574.1 *resolute*
hell-born 8.16 *devilish*
hellcat 241.4 *violent person or animal*, 832.9 *vixen*
hell-driver 329.13 *swift person*
hellebore 84 Flowers and Flowering Plants, 631.12 *poisonous plant*
helleborine 84 Flowers and Flowering Plants
Hellenes 1 Peoples
Hellenic 5 Languages and Groups of Languages, 5.11 *family of languages*, 202.14 *historic*
Hellenistic 3.15 *historic*, 50.29 *realist*, 202.14 *historic*
Hellenistic Age 3.10 *past age*
Hellenistic art 50 Western Art Styles and Movements
Heller 48 Writers
Hellespont 98.9 *inlet*
hellfire 199.3 *future condition*, 408.8 *hot place*
hell for leather 329.14 *swiftly*
hell-hag 832.9 *vixen*
hellhound 241.4 *violent person or animal*
hellish 8.16 *devilish*, 11.15 *witchlike*, 618.6 *damnable*, 832.11 *cruel*, 864.11 *wicked*
hellishly 8.20 *devilishly*
hellishness 864.1 *wickedness*
Hellman 48 Dramatists
hello! 344
hello 344.12 *reception*, 431.4 *cry of greeting*, 567.15 *hail*
hell of a lot 181.3 *profuseness*
hell on earth 406.1 *pain*
hell-raiser 241.4 *violent person or animal*
hell-raising 151.20 *disorderly*
Hell's Angel 679.1 *combatant*
Hell's Kitchen 93.3 *New York*
hell to pay 879.9 *retribution*
Hell–Volard–Zelinsky reaction 57 Named Reactions
hell west and crooked 248.16 *extensively*
helm 36.3 *parts of a sailing boat*,

74.5 *navigation*, 603.1 *tool*, 653.5 *guide*, 671.7 *armour*
helmet 19.3 *uniform*, 27.6 *pad*, 31.1 *hockey*, 31.3 *ice hockey*, 31.5 *lacrosse*, 34.4 *climbing equipment*, 295.15 *headgear*, 544.8 *heraldic device*, 671.6 *protective clothing*, 671.7 *armour*
helmet shell 81 Molluscs
Helmholtz 52 Scientists
Helmholtz coils 56 Named Laws
Helmholtz function 56 Named Laws, **57** Named Reactions, 56.38 *thermodynamics*
helminth 81.6 *worm*, 81.10 *parasite*
helminthic 81.20 *wormlike*
helminthic disease 81
helminthoid 81.20 *wormlike*
helminthological 81.20 *wormlike*
helminthologist 76.11 *zoologist*, 81.15 *invertebrate zoologist*
helminthology 76.9 *animal science*, 81.14 *invertebrate zoology*
helminthophobia 777 Phobias by Name
Helmont 52 Scientists
helmsman 36.9 *sailor*, 74.7 *nautical person*, 653.13 *director*
helmsmanship 74.5 *navigation*, 332.1 *direction*, 653.4 *directorship*
Heloha 8 Deities
Heloise and Abelard 821.10 *lovers*
helot 808.3 *sycophant*
helotism 808.1 *servility*
help 662, 662, 65.17 *computing term*, 226.12 *determine*, 232.1 *instrumentality*, 232.3 *assistant*, 232.4 *be an instrument*, 284.6 *moral support*, 284.14 *give moral support*, 572.14 *cooperate*, 613.5 *usefulness*, 613.9 *be useful*, 615.6 *be convenient*, 617.10 *do good*, 621.12 *cleaner*, 630.1, 630.19 *remedy*, 639.5 *to the rescue*, 640.4 *act*, 646.1 *worker*, 660.5 *smoothness*, 660.16 *make easy*, 662.16 *home help*, 664.1 *cooperation*, 664.11 *cooperate*, 697.1 *servant*, 697.8 *serve*, 707.5 *represent*, 729.2 *gift*, 729.6 *give to charity*, 734.10 *take away*, 767.2 *aid*, 767.11 *assist*, 817.1 *courtesy*, 819.16 *be favourable*, 833.7 *be charitable*, 861.20 *do good*
Help 662
help a lame dog over a stile 662.22 *improve*
help a lame duck 662.22 *improve*
help along 660.16 *make easy*, 662.28 *further*
help decide 226.12 *determine*
helper 662, 767, 226.8 *contributor*, 232.3 *assistant*, 284.8 *supporter*, 654.4 *adviser*, 664.10 *co-operator*, 701.3 *subordinate*, 707.1 *deputy*, 729.4 *giver*, 833.3 *philanthropist*, 861.15 *good person*
helpful 572, 662, 6.16 *educational*, 232.6 *instrumental*, 284.9 *supportive*, 611.5 *important*, 613.1 *useful*, 615.1 *convenient*, 630.17 *remedial*, 660.10 *feasible*, 664.17 *cooperative*, 767.8 *relieving*, 819.12 *favourable*, 831.6 *benevolent*, 861.3 *kind*
helpful act 831.4 *benevolent act*
helpfully 662, 625 *educationally*, 232.9 *instrumentally*, 613.12 *usefully*, 767.15 *comfortingly*, 819.20 *favourably*, 831.10 *benevolently*, 861.23 *nicely*
helpful neighbour 817.6 *courteous person*
helpfulness 662, 572.9 *goodwill*, 613.5 *usefulness*, 615.3 *convenience*, 664.1 *cooperation*, 831.1 *benevolence*, 833.1 *philanthropy*, 861.10 *kindness*
helpful person 784.4 *likable person*
help fund 729.6 *give to charity*

helping 662, 143.7 *piece*, 232.6 *instrumental*, 350.14 *mouthful*, 606.1 *provision*, 697.9 *serving*, 731.2 *portion*, 767.8 *relieving*
helping hand 284.8 *supporter*, 572.11 *willing worker*, 662.1 *help*, 662.11 *helper*, 767.2 *aid*, 833.3 *philanthropist*
helpless 236.12 *impotent*, 238.8 *weak*, 633.3 *vulnerable*
helplessly 236.14 *powerlessly*, 238.14 *weakly*, 633.11 *dangerously*
helplessness 236, 238.1 *weakness*, 633.7 *vulnerability*
helpmate 284.8 *supporter*, 535.9 *affirmer*, 662.13 *supporter*, 767.5 *helper*, 823.8 *spouse*
helpmeet 662.13 *supporter*, 767.5 *helper*, 823.8 *spouse*
help on 660.16 *make easy*
help out 662.17 *help*, 662.29 *finance*
help the police with their inquiries 477.19 *be questioned*, 856.7 *be accused*
help up 361.1 *raise*
help with money 729.6 *give to charity*
help yourself 344.24 *welcome*, 490.26 *certainly*
Helsinki 93 Cities
helter-skelter 113.11 *irregularly*, 151.28 *anyhow*, 329.14 *swiftly*, 648.6 *hastily*
helve 603.1 *tool*
helvella 89 Fungi
Helvellyn 95 Mountains, 95.5 *British mountains*
Helvétius 4 Philosophers
hem 300.2 *edging*, 300.6 *edge*, 430.5 *sound hoarse*
he-man 237.6 *muscleman*, 241.4 *violent person or animal*, 401.6 *macho man*, 778.7 *courageous person*
hemaphobia 777 Phobias by Name
hematite 54 Minerals
hemeralopia 436.2 *poor sight*
hemeralopic 436.9 *weak-sighted*
hemiacetal 58.3 *carbohydrate*
hemicellulose 58.4 *polysaccharide*
Hemichordata 81.2 *protochordate*
hemichordate 81.2 *protochordate*, 81.6 *worm*, 81.16 *invertebrate*
hemicolectomy 60 Surgical Operations
hemidemisemiquaver 49.17 *notation*
hemihydrate 57.10 *salt*
hemiketal 58.3 *carbohydrate*
hemimorphite 54 Minerals
hem in 301.5 *enclose*, 670.4 *besiege*, 699.8 *restrain*
Hemingway 48 Writers
hemiplegia 236.4 *disability*, 624.17 *nervous disorder*
hemiplegic 236.12 *impotent*, 624.19 *sick person*
Hemiptera 82 Orders of Insects
hemipteran 82.10 *insectan*
hemisphere 143.1 *part*, 176.8 *half*, 315.3 *round thing*
hemispherical 315.9 *round*
hemistich 48.8 *part of poem*
hemline 295.24 *part of garment*, 300.2 *edging*
hemlock 84 Flowers and Flowering Plants, **85** Trees and Shrubs, 631.8 *poison*, 631.12 *poisonous plant*, 879.16 *instrument of execution*
hemmed 295.31 *styled*
hemmed-in 297.5 *surrounded*, 301.7 *enclosed*
hemp 875.6 *drug*
hempen collar 879.16 *instrument of execution*
hen 68.8 *livestock*, 78.11 *female bird*, 402.14 *female animal*
henbane 84 Flowers and Flowering Plants, 631.12 *poisonous plant*
hence 116.36 *accordingly*, 227.12 *with the effect of*
henceforth 199.15 *after*

henceforward 199.15 *after*
henchman 127.6 *inferior*, 662.11 *helper*, 671.13 *defender*, 697.1 *servant*, 697.4 *personal attendant*
hen coop 68.7 *farm building*
hendecagon 179.7 *double figures*
hendecagonal 179.18 *eleventh*
hendecahedron 179.7 *double figures*
hendecasyllabic 48.20 *metrical*
Hendry 18 Sporting Personalities
henequen 84 Flowers and Flowering Plants
henhouse 68.7 *farm building*, 256.12 *stall*
Henley 674.4 *race*
Henley stewart 36.9 *sailor*
Henley trophies 36
henna 85 Tree Products, 450.6 *red pigment*, 451.2 *orangeness*
hen party 161.9 *social gathering*, 402.13 *womenfolk*, 665.7 *social gathering*, 815.5 *party*
henpeck 701.6 *subject*, 852.18 *find fault*
henpecked 701.9 *subject*
henpecked husband 694.4 *obedient person*, 823.10 *married man*
henpecking 852.6 *fault-finding*
hen run 68.7 *farm building*
henry 75 SI Units, **75** Scientific and Technical Units
Henry 48 Writers, **52** Scientists
Henry IV Part 1 48 Shakespeare's plays
Henry IV Part 2 48 Shakespeare's plays
Henry V 48 Shakespeare's plays
Henry VI Part 1 48 Shakespeare's plays
Henry VI Part 2 48 Shakespeare's plays
Henry VI Part 3 48 Shakespeare's plays
Henry VIII 48 Shakespeare's plays
Henry Kissinger 675.4 *Nobel Peace Prize*
Henry's law 57 Named Reactions
Henryson 48 Poets
Henze 49 Musicians and Composers
heparin 62 Medication
hepatectomy 60 Surgical Operations
hepatic 88.6 *mosslike*
Hepaticae 88.3 *moss*
Hepaticopsida 88.3 *moss*
hepaticostomy 60 Surgical Operations
Hephaestus 8 Deities
heptabarbitone 62 Medication
heptad 179.3 *seven*
heptadic 179.14 *seventh*
heptagon 52.44 *polygon*, 179.3 *seven*, 310.3 *angled figure*
heptagonal 52.82 *polygonal*, 179.14 *seventh*, 310.9 *angled*
heptahedral 179.14 *seventh*
heptahedron 179.3 *seven*
heptahydrate 57.10 *salt*
heptameter 48.9 *metre*, 179.3 *seven*
heptangular 179.14 *seventh*
heptastich 48.8 *part of poem*
Heptateuch 179.3 *seven*
heptathlete 21.3 *athlete*
heptathlon 18 Sporting Activities, 21.2 *field events*
heptatonic 179.14 *seventh*
heptavalent 57.35 *combined*
heptose 58.3 *carbohydrate*
Hequet 8 Deities
her 402.2 *female*
Hera 8 Deities, 823.14 *gods and goddesses of marriage*
Heraclitean 4.11 *follower of a doctrine*, 4.14 *of a philosophy*
Heraclitus 4 Philosophers
herald 544, 154.8 *precursor*, 154.19 *forecast*, 194.7 *foretaste*, 496.4 *invent*, 496.12 *discoverer*, 517.5 *omen*, 517.11 *predict*, 528.9 *informant*, 532.10

publicizer, 532.14 proclaim, 543.12 signal
herald extraordinary 544.9 *herald*
heraldic 544
heraldically 544.14 *identifiably*
heraldic bird 78.9 *fabulous bird*
heraldic colour 44.1 *colour*
heraldic device 544
heraldic official 544.9 *herald*
heraldic register 544.9 *herald*
heraldic tincture 544.8 *heraldic device*
heralding 517.13 *predicting*
heraldist 544.9 *herald*
Herat 93 Cities
herb 45.7 *basic ingredient,* 69.9 *garden plant,* 69.11 *vegetable,* 83.2 *plant,* 133.4 *admixture,* 630.2 *medicine*
herbaceous 69.16 *horticultural,* 83.13 *plantlike,* 83.14 *of plants*
herbaceous border 69.3 *ornamental garden*
herbaceously 83
herbaceous perennial 83.2 *plant*
herbaceous plant 83.2 *plant*
herbage 83.1 *plants,* 87.2 *grassland*
herbal 69.16 *horticultural,* 83.11 *herbarium,* 83.13 *plantlike,* 630.18 *medical*
herbalism 60.2 *natural medicine,* 60.8 *treatment*
herbalist 60.12 *healer,* 83.12 *plant scientist,* 630.15 *healer*
herbal remedy 630.2 *medicine*
herbal tea 531.3 *tea*
herbarium 83
Herbart 4 Philosophers
herb doctor 630.15 *healer*
Herbert 48 Poets, **48** Poets
herb garden 69.2 *garden,* 418.2 *fragrant thing*
herbicidal 69
herbicide 68.14 *pest control,* 69.8 *weedkiller,* 398.14 *plant killer*
herbivore 76.4 *type of animal,* 87.6 *grass-eater,* 350.18 *eater*
herbivorous 76.15 *of animals,* 87.10 *grass-eating,* 350.26 *eating*
herbivorously 87, 350.28 *carnivorously*
herbivorousness 350.5 *eating habit*
herb Paris 84 Flowers and Flowering Plants
herb Robert 84 Flowers and Flowering Plants
herbs 413, 416.2 *sense of smell,* 418.2 *fragrant thing*
herb sausage 45.29 *sausage*
herb tea 630.7 *tonic*
herby 413.9 *piquant,* 416.5 *odorous*
herculean 237.9 *physically strong,* 644.11 *laborious,* 659.10 *difficult*
herculean task 659.3 *difficult task*
Hercules 53 The Constellations, **53** The Constellations, 237.6 *muscleman,* 259.10 *big person*
hercules beetle 82 Insects
Hercules'club 85 Trees and Shrubs
hercules moth 82 Insects
herd 161 Collective Names for Birds and Animals, **161,** 68.18 *practise livestock farming,* 77.21 *assemblage of mammals,* 161.23 *flock,* 167.6 *conformist*
herded 161.46 *assembled*
herder 68.16 *farm worker*
Herder 4 Philosophers
herdic 71 Carriages and Carts
herding 161, 68.3 *livestock farming*
herd manager 68.16 *farm worker*
herd's grass 87 Grasses
herdsman 68.16 *farm worker,* 161.34 *assembler,* 653.14 *leader*
Herdsman 53 The Constellations
Herdwick 68 Breeds of Sheep

here 253, 196.8 *available,* 250.12 *where,* 344.22 *on arrival*
hereabouts 250.12 *where,* 264.6 *near*
hereafter 199.15 *after,* 368.1 *nonmaterial world,* 397.14 *the spiritual world,* 492.4 *judgment day*
here and there 160.17 *discontinuously,* 162.30 *diffusely,* 182.10 *in ones and twos,* 250.12 *where,* 327.17 *via*
hereat 250.12 *where*
hereby 384.5 *thus*
hereditament 132.5 *estate,* 227.2 *visible effect,* 725.2 *legal terms,* 730.1 *receiving*
hereditarily 725.10 *proprietarily,* 730.15 *receptively*
hereditary 59.25 *genetic,* 132.9 *remaining,* 227.10 *caused,* 725.8 *propertied,* 730.14 *receivable,* 749.6 *received*
hereditary character 59.11 *genetics*
heredity 777 Phobias by Topic, 59.11 *genetics*
Hereford 68 Breeds of Cattle, **68** Breeds of Pig, **93** Cities
Hereford and Worcester 92 Counties
here goes! 574, 596
hereinafter 199.15 *after*
here lies 399.4 *funeral objects*
Herero 1 Peoples, **5** Languages and Groups of Languages
Heres 8 Deities
here's health 351.18 *cheers*
here's looking at you 351.18 *cheers*
here's mud in your eye 351.18 *cheers*
here's to you 351.18 *cheers*
heresy 117.3 *nonconformity,* 168.3 *nonconformism,* 498.4 *unbelief,* 504.7 *errancy*
heresy-hunt 7.20 *preach*
heresy-hunting 7.2 *religiousness,* 481.4 *social discrimination*
here, there, and everywhere 113.11 *irregularly,* 248.16 *extensively*
heretic 117.6 *misfit,* 117.9 *nonconforming,* 168.8 *dissenter,* 335.19 *deviant person,* 498.5 *disbeliever,* 720.5 *nonobserver,* 720.11 *nonobservant,* 822.8 *hated person*
heretical 168.12 *nonconformist,* 498.6 *disbelieving,* 500.7 *dissenting,* 504.16 *errant*
heretically 117.16 *disagreeably,* 720.16 *disobediently*
here today and gone tomorrow 189.6 *transient*
here today gone tomorrow 458.6 *disappearing*
heretofore 194.11 *before,* 200.23 *before now*
herewith 232.9 *instrumentally*
heritability 728.1 *transfer of property*
heritable 725.8 *propertied*
heritably 725.10 *proprietarily*
heritage 723.1 *possession,* 730.1 *receiving,* 749.4 *legacy*
heritor 730.6 *beneficiary*
herky-jerky 215.4 *irregular*
her ladyship 402.3 *female title of address*
herm 50.12 *sculpture*
Her Majesty's Loyal Opposition 663.8 *the opposition*
hermaphrodite 236.5 *powerless person*
hermaphrodite brig 74 Sailing Ships and Boats
hermeneutic 5.40 *translated,* 473.2 *logical argument,* 524.14 *interpretive*
hermeneutically 5.48 *linguistically*
hermeneutics 5.12 *translation,* 524.5 *science of interpretation*
Hermes 8 Deities, **53** Minor Planets, 326.8 *messenger,* 329.13 *swift person,* 423.5 *loud person*

hermetic 11.14 *occult*
hermetically 323.16 *impermeably*
hermetically seal 372.6 *make sparse*
hermetically sealed 323.12 *closed,* 632.6 *invulnerable*
hermeticism 48 Literary Groups and Movements, 11.1 *occultism*
hermetics 11.1 *occultism*
hermetism 11.1 *occultism*
hermit 168, 7.7 *monk,* 108.3 *unconnected person,* 139.4 *individualist,* 174.8 *loner,* 335.19 *deviant person,* 531.7 *concealer,* 598.4 *deserter,* 816.6 *unsocial person,* 825.4 *celibate person*
hermitage 7.10 *priestly dwelling,* 634.1 *refuge*
Hermitage 43 Noted Buildings
hermit crab 81.4 *arthropod*
Hermite 52 Scientists
hermit-like 7.15 *religious*
Hermod 8 Deities
Hermon 95 Mountains
herms 43 Architectural Decoration
hernia 406.2 *painful condition*
hernioplasty 60 Surgical Operations
hero 9.4 *idolized person,* 45.11 *sandwich,* 51.21 *role,* 617.8 *exceller,* 640.3 *doer,* 679.8 *soldier,* 682.4 *successful person,* 778.7 *courageous person,* 786.5 *person of wonder,* 821.11 *loved one*
Hero and Leander 821.10 *lovers*
Herod 241.4 *violent person or animal*
heroic 1.14 *societal,* 48.19 *narrative,* 49.32 *instrumental,* 202.14 *historic,* 560.12 *narrative,* 574.4 *undaunted,* 640.5 *acting,* 644.11 *laborious,* 679.35 *martial,* 778.9 *courageous,* 778.10 *chivalrous,* 811.23 *brave*
heroic age 200.5 *historical period*
Heroic Age 3.10 *past age*
heroically 679.42 *martially,* 778.18 *courageously,* 811.39 *bravely*
heroic couplet 48.9 *metre*
heroic drama 51.2 *play*
heroic exploit 778.8 *courageous act*
heroic poetry 48.6 *poetry*
heroic qualities 863.2 *virtues*
heroics 778.8 *courageous act,* 811.8 *bravado*
heroin 62 Medication, 630.8 *drug,* 631.11 *intoxicant,* 875.6 *drug*
heroine 9.4 *idolized person,* 51.21 *role,* 640.3 *doer,* 679.10 *woman soldier,* 682.4 *successful person,* 778.7 *courageous person,* 786.5 *person of wonder,* 821.11 *loved one*
heroism 778
heron 78 Birds, 78.3 *water bird*
herons 161 Collective Names by Animal
Heron's 52 Named Concepts
Hero of Alexandria 52 Scientists
hero's welcome 812.4 *reception*
hero worship 9.2 *idolatry,* 786.1 *wonder,* 821.1 *love,* 851.3 *praise*
hero-worship 9.8 *idolatrize,* 786.9 *wonder,* 849.2 *admiration,* 849.16 *revere,* 851.14 *praise*
hero worshipper 9.5 *worshipper*
hero-worshipper 821.9 *lover,* 851.8 *admirer*
hero-worshipping 9.9 *worshipful,* 849.10 *reverent,* 851.18 *approving*
herpes 624.13 *skin disease,* 624.14 *venereal disease*
herpes simplex 624.4 *disease,* 624.14 *venereal disease*
herpes zoster 624.13 *skin disease*
herpetological 79
herpetologist 79, 76.11 *zoologist*
herpetology 79, 76.9 *animal science,* 79.14 *herpetological*
herpetophobia 777 Phobias by Name

Herr 401.3 *male title of address*
Herrick 48 Poets
herring 80 Fishes, 45.18 *sea fish,* 80.8 *food fish*
herringbone 67 Natural Fabrics, 41.2 *cross-country skiing,* 41.4 *skiing technique,* 47.16 *joined*
herringbone strutting 47.10 *carpenter's term*
herring gull 78 Birds
herring-like 80.13 *fishlike*
herring pond 97.1 *sea*
herring roe 80.9 *fish product*
Herschel 52 Scientists
herself 165.12 *I,* 402.2 *female*
Hershef 8 Deities
Hershey bar 544.4 *insignia*
Hertford 93 Cities
Hertfordshire 92 Counties
hertz 75 SI Units, **75** Scientific and Technical Units, 56.16 *waveform,* 212.6 *radio frequency*
Hertz 52 Scientists
Hertzsprung–Russell diagram 53.13 *luminosity*
Hesiod 48 Poets
hesitance 238.2 *indecisiveness,* 781.1 *caution*
hesitancy 498.1 *disbelief,* 576.11 *vacillation,* 781.1 *caution*
hesitant 328, 238.12 *weakwilled,* 365.15 *vacillating,* 491.2 *irresolute,* 498.6 *disbelieving,* 573.3 *cautious,* 576.1 *vacillating,* 781.4 *cautious*
hesitantly 491.23 *uncertainly,* 498.10 *disbelievingly,* 573.17 *unwillingly,* 576.16 *irresolutely,* 591.23 *shyly,* 781.7 *cautiously*
hesitate 328, 491, 576, 224.12 *be irresolute,* 365.10 *vacillate,* 477.20 *doubt,* 498.8 *disbelieve,* 573.8 *hold back,* 781.5 *be cautious,* 810.15 *escape notice*
hesitating 224.14 *irresolute,* 477.15 *sceptical,* 491.2 *irresolute,* 576.1 *vacillating*
hesitatingly 477.24 *questionably*
hesitation 328, 224.2 *irresolution,* 365.3 *vacillation,* 477.6 *uncertainty,* 491.11 *irresoluteness,* 498.1 *disbelief,* 573.13 *dissociation,* 576.11 *vacillation,* 717.3 *irresolution,* 781.1 *caution*
hesitation waltz 46.2 *dance*
hesitator 641.2 *nonacting person,* 781.3 *cautious person*
hesperidium 86.2 *botanical fruit*
Hesperornis 78 Birds
Hesperus 53.10 *star,* 205.4 *evening thing*
Hess 49 Musicians and Composers, **52** Scientists
Hesse 48 Writers
Hesse's law 57 Named Reactions
hessian 67 Natural Fabrics
Hessian 679.6 *militarist*
hessite 54 Minerals
Hestia 8 Deities
Hesus 8 Deities
heterochromatin 59.9 *cell nucleus*
heterochromosome 59.14 *chromosome*
heteroclite 5.44 *grammatical*
heterocyclic 57.7 *chemical compound,* 57.35 *combined*
heterodox 117.9 *nonconforming,* 168.12 *nonconformist,* 500.7 *dissenting*
heterodoxy 117.3 *nonconformity,* 168.3 *nonconformism,* 504.7 *errancy*
heterogeneity 108.1 *unrelatedness,* 113.1 *diversity,* 115.1 *dissimilarity,* 117.1 *disparity,* 123.1 *inequality,* 133.1 *mixture*
heterogeneous 2.13 *communal,* 113.5 *diverse,* 117.7 *disparate,* 133.12 *mixed*
heterogeneous catalysis 57.15 *catalysis*
heterogeneously 2.16 *sociologically,* 113.10 *diversely,* 133.12 *in the midst*
heterogenous 108.6 *unrelated,* 164.15 *general*

heterolyse 57.26 *react*
heterolysis 57.14 *chemical reaction*
heterolytic 57.38 *reactive*
heterolytic fission 57.14 *chemical reaction*
heteromorphism 113.2 *assortment*
heteromorphous 113.6 *assorted*
heteronomy 12.3 *governance*, 688.7 *type of rule*
heterophony 433.3 *melodiousness*
heteropolar bond 57.11 *chemical bond*
heteropolysaccharide 58.4 *polysaccharide*
heteropteran 82.10 *insectan*
heterosexual 312.4 *traditional*, 312.9 *straight person*
heterosome 59.14 *chromosome*
heterothallic 89.10 *of fungi*
heterotropia 436.2 *poor sight*
hetoheptose 58.3 *carbohydrate*
het up 828.16 *angry*
heulandite 54 Minerals
heuristic 4.16 *dialectical*, 52.69 *theoretic*, 473.2 *logical argument*, 473.11 *logical*, 496.15 *discoverable*
heuristic solution 52.64 *reasoning*
Heu T'U 8 Deities
hevea 85 Trees and Shrubs
Hevesy 52 Scientists
hew 136.9 *separate*, 306.7 *form*, 322.18 *open*, 362.2 *flatten*, 796.8 *fashion*
hew down 362.2 *flatten*
hewer of wood and drawer of water 646.1 *worker*
hewn 322.12 *open*
hex 11.5 *spell*, 11.21 *bewitch*, 687.11 *cause adversity*, 822.2 *curse*, 827.4 *malediction*, 827.7 *wish ill*, 862.4 *evil power*, 862.11 *be evil*
hexacanth 81.13 *invertebrate larva*
hexachlorophane 62 Medication
hexachord 179.2 *six*
hexad 179.2 *six*
hexadecimal 179.7 *double figures*, 179.18 *eleventh*
hexadecimal code 65.10 *character*
hexadecimal notation 52.8 *number system*
hexadic 179.13 *sixth*
hexagon 52.44 *polygon*, 179.2 *six*, 310.3 *angled figure*
hexagonal 52.82 *polygonal*, 57.33 *crystalline*, 179.13 *sixth*, 310.9 *angled*
hexagonal close packed 57.33 *crystalline*
hexagonal close packing 57.4 *crystal*
hexagonal crystal 57.4 *crystal*
hexagram 52.44 *polygon*, 179.2 *six*, 310.3 *angled figure*
hexagrammoid 310.9 *angled*
hexahedral 52.84 *cubic*, 179.13 *sixth*
hexahedron 52.46 *polyhedron*, 179.2 *six*
hexahydrate 57.10 *salt*
hexameter 48.9 *metre*, 179.2 *six*
hexamine 62 Medication
hexane 57 Common Chemical Compounds
hexangular 179.13 *sixth*
hexapod 179.2 *six*
Hexapoda 82.1 *insect*
hexastich 48.8 *part of poem*
hexastyle 43.8 *column*
Hexateuch 179.2 *six*
hexatonic 179.13 *sixth*
hexavalent 57.35 *combined*
hexed 11.19 *bewitched*, 827.10, 827.10 *maledictive*, 862.10 *inauspicious*
hexentric 34.8 *mountaineering*
hexentric nut 34.4 *climbing equipment*
hexobarbitone 62 Medication
hexose 57 Types of Compounds, 58.3 *carbohydrate*
heyday 185.5 *indefinite period*, 686.3 *time of plenty*
heyday of the blood 206.1 *youth*

Hey rube 543.6 *word*
Hey-tau 8 Deities
HF high frequency 534 Radio-frequency Bands
HGV 71 Motor Vehicles
H-hour 185.11 *date*
hi 344.23 *hello*, 567.15 *hail*
hiatus 160.5 *caesura*, 248.8 *intervening space*, 265.1 *interval*
hibernacle 409.6 Arctic
hibernaculum 409.6 Arctic
hibernal 203.13 *winter*
hibernate 203.6 *spend the season*, 527.12 *be latent*, 643.13 *sleep*
hibernating 240.5 *inert*, 527.1 *latent*, 643.4 *not awake*
hibernation 203.5 *winter*, 240.1 *inertness*, 527.6 *latency*, 643.9 *sleep*
hibernator 643.11 *sleeper*
Hibernia 91.10 *Ireland*
Hibernicism 5.26 *dialect*
hibiscus 84 Flowers and Flowering Plants
hiccup 349.16, 349.24 *belch*, 388.5, 425.4 *belch*, 425.7 *belch*, 618.8 *inferiority*, 661.2 *obstacle*, 874.7 *be drunk*, 874.10 *drunkenness*
hiccupping 874.2 *slightly drunk*, 874.10 *drunkenness*
hick 93.14 *urban*, 127.13 *insignificant*, 255.5 *countryman*, 656.10 *unskilled person*, 658.3 *naive person*, 803.1 *plebeian*
hickdom 249.6 *regions*
Hickling Broad 94 Lakes, 94.4 *British lakes*
hickory 85 Trees and Shrubs, 86 Nuts
Hicksites 7 Christian Movements
Hickstead 32.11 *eventing*
hick town 93.10 *village*, 127.7 *inferior thing*, 816.5 *solitary place*
Hidalgo 53 Minor Planets
Hidatsa 1 Peoples
hidden 436, 290.12 *internalized*, 293.37 *protected*, 438.3 *private*, 440.11 *benighted*, 458.7 *disappeared*, 523.1 *unintelligible*, 523.3 *unrecognizable*, 527.2 *concealed*, 529.11 *mysterious*, 531.14 *concealed*, 539.41 *disguised*, 591.18 *avoiding*, 816.11 *secluded*
hidden away 527.2 *concealed*
hidden camera 438.5 *invisible thing*
hidden cause 226.4 *contributing factor*
hidden cave 531.2 *hiding place*
hidden danger 527.7 *latent things*
hidden depths 527.6 *latency*
hidden fires 527.6 *latency*
hidden hand 233.4 *indirect influence*, 527.9 *backstage manipulator*, 635.2 *troublemaker*, 653.13 *director*
hidden income 878.4 *reward for service*
hidden influence 233.4 *indirect influence*
hiddenite 54 Minerals, 54 Gemstones
hidden meaning 520.4 *type of meaning*, 527.11 *mysteriousness*
hidden panel 293.15 *shelter*, 638.2 *means of escape*
hidden persuader 532.10 *publicizer*
hidden power 688.1 *authority*
hidden self 165.11 *identity*
hide 293, 527, 11.20 *occult*, 139.7 *be aloof*, 243.7 *produce*, 290.15 *keep inside*, 293.14 *animal covering*, 293.15 *shelter*, 438.6 *that which makes invisible*, 438.7 *become invisible*, 438.8 *make invisible*, 458.1 *disappear*, 458.3 *cause to disappear*, 529.12 *keep secret*, 531.8 *conceal*, 591.6 *evade*, 604.1 *materials*, 605.6 *store*, 632.8 *be safe*, 632.9 *protect*, 637.5 *pre-*

serve, 638.6 *elude*, 657.5 *be cunning*, 879.3 *hit*
hide-and-seek 42 Children's Games and Party Games, 438.5 *invisible thing*, 591.14 *evasion*
hideaway 256.11 *retreat*, 293.15 *shelter*
hide away 438.8 *make invisible*
hideaway 531.2 *hiding place*
hide away 531.8 *conceal*, 632.9 *protect*
hide behind the skirts of 634.4 *shelter*
hidebound 302.5 *limited*, 493.8 *unjust*, 577.4 *set*
hideboundness 813.1 *formality*
hide from 531.11 *conceal oneself*
hide one's abilities 247.7 *be infertile*
hide one's face 806.24 *be humiliated*
hide one's light under a bushel 247.7 *be infertile*, 810.15 *escape notice*
hideosity 790.1 *hideousness*
hideous 309.7 *deformed*, 341.8 *repulsive*, 777.10 *frightening*, 790.4 *ugly*
hideously 309.13 *asymmetrically*, 341.11 *repulsively*, 777.16 *frighteningly*
hideousness 790, 309.3 *deformity*
hideout 293.15 *shelter*
hide out 293.30 *protect*, 531.11 *conceal oneself*
hide-out 531.2 *hiding place*, 634.1 *refuge*, 816.5 *solitary place*
hider 531.7 *concealer*, 657.3 *cunning person*
hide under a bushel 438.8 *make invisible*
hiding 293.1 *covering*, 330.12 *collision*, 436.11 *blinding*, 438.4 *invisibility*, 458.5 *disguise*, 458.6 *disappearing*, 527.2 *concealed*, 527.8, 531.1 *concealment*, 591.18 *avoiding*, 682.2 *victory*, 683.2 *defeat*, 879.12 *corporal punishment*
hiding place 531, 293.15 *shelter*, 438.6 *that which makes invisible*, 605.1 *store*, 634.1 *refuge*, 816.5 *solitary place*
hidrotic 62.4 *drug type*, 62.17 *stimulating*
hidy-hole 438.6 *that which makes invisible*, 531.2 *hiding place*, 634.1 *refuge*
hie 329.4 *be swift*
hiemal 203.13 *winter*
hierarch 7.8 *priest*
hierarchic 121.8 *ranked*
hierarchical 121.8 *ranked*, 152.25 *categorical*, 163.10 *classificatory*
hierarchical database 65.11 *application*
hierarchically 121.9 *differentially*, 150.25 *in order*, 163.16 *taxonomically*
hierarchy 150, 12.1 *government*, 121.2 *rank*, 152.5 *categorization*, 163.1 *classification*, 195.1 *succession*
hierarchy of authority 2.7 *social stratification*
hieratic 7.17 *priestly*
hierocracy 7.9 *priesthood*, 12.1 *government*
hierocratic 7.17 *priestly*
hieroglyph 5.13 *letter*, 543.1 *sign*
hieroglyphic 5.41 *lettered*, 547.13 *representational*
hieroglyphically 5.48 *linguistically*
hieroglyphics 529.4 *brain-teaser*, 543.1 *sign*, 547.1 *representation*
hierographical 7.18 *theological*
hierography 7.13 *theology*
hierological 7.18 *theological*
hierologist 7.14 *theologian*
hierology 7.13 *theology*
hieromancer 11.13 *diviner*
hieromancy 11.9 *divination*
hieromarch 7.7 *monk*

Hieronymite 816.6 *unsocial person*
hierophant 7.8 *priest*
hierophantic 7.17 *priestly*
hierophobia 777 Phobias by Name
hieroscopy 11.9 *divination*
hi-fi 760.10 *accuracy*
hi-fi enthusiast 420.2 *hearer*
hi-fi unit 258.3 *cabinet*
higgle 737.3 *bargain*
higgledy-piggledy 113.11 *irregularly*, 133.12 *mixed*, 133.14 *in the midst*, 151.4 *litter*, 151.18 *muddled*, 151.28 *anyhow*, 482.3 *indiscriminate*
higgling 737.9 *bargaining*
high 275, 275, 21.7 *fast*, 55.11 *weather system*, 55.47 *windy*, 95.7 *mountainous*, 95.11 *on the mountain*, 120.6 *quantitative*, 141.5 *disintegrated*, 248.13 *spacious*, 269.1 *long*, 405.7 *pleased*, 415.6 *unpalatable*, 419.4 *putrid*, 430.9 *shrill*, 611.5 *important*, 762.2 *fun*, 769.1 *cheerful*, 773.9 *rejoicing*, 874.1 *drunk*, 875.7 *drugged*
high achiever 640.3 *doer*, 861.16 *superior person*
high-altitude wind 55.12 *wind*
high and dry 225.9 *stable*, 392.1 *dry*
high and low 111.2 *opposites*, 144.9 *completely*, 248.16 *extensively*
high-and-mightiness 811.2 *airs*
high-and-mighty 805.19 *stately*, 811.17 *lofty*
high antiquity 200.1 *past time*
high approval 611.1 *importance*
high as a kite 405.7 *pleased*, 762.4 *happy*
highball 72.2 *track*, 351.8 *mixed drink*
highball glass 258.13 *drinking vessel*
highball it 329.5 *run like a shot*
high baroque 50 Western Art Styles and Movements
high birth rate 246.2 *productiveness*
high blood pressure 624.3 *symptom*, 624.10 *cardiovascular disease*
high boots 295.19 *footwear*
high-born 802.4 *aristocratic*
highboy 47.5, 258.3 *cabinet*
highbrow 4.12 *sage*, 4.19 *learned*, 6.18 *educated*, 459.8 *intellectual person*, 461.7 *thinker*, 461.11 *reasoning*, 501.6 *knowledgeable person*, 501.9 *literate*, 507.5 *wise*, 655.5, 688.11 *expert*, 696.9 *educational leader*, 696.13 *excellent*, 772.7 *serious person*
high buildings 777 Phobias by Topic
high calibre 126.1 *superiority*
high-calorie 350.27 *edible*
high camp 51.10 *comedy*
high-caste 802.4 *aristocratic*
high casualties 398.4 *slaughter*
high chair 47.2 *chair*, 275.8 *high thing*
High Church 7 Christian Movements
High-Church 7.16 *denominational*
high-class 802.4 *aristocratic*, 861.1 *good*
high cloud 55.18 *cloud*
high collar 295.14 *neckwear*
high colour 450.7 *red thing*
high-coloured 444.11 *colourful*
high comedy 51.10 *comedy*
high commissioner 688.10 *person of authority*, 696.3 *leader*, 706.1 *delegate*
high-cost 753.7 *dear*
high country 98.7 *upland*
high court 16.19 *lawcourt*
High Court 16.20 British court, 492.3 *place of judgment*
High Court of Justiciary 16.20 British court
high day 812.5 *anniversary*

high days and holidays 773.1 *rejoicing*
high definition 534.23 *television reception*
high-definition 437.2 *clear*
high-definition television 534.21 *television*
high-density 181.10 *crowded*
high diving 39.6 *diving*
high dudgeon 828.2 *offence*
high endeavour 596.6 *venture*
high-energy radiation 56.70 *radioactivity*
higher 275, 275, 52.75 *equal*, 126.12 *superior*, 368.8 *nonmaterial*
higher arithmetic 52.4 *simple arithmetic*
higher criticism 524.3 *criticism*
higher education 6.2 *educational system*
Higher Grade 485 Educational Qualifications
higher interest rate account 741.6 *funds*
higher jump 721.2 *augmentation*
higher mathematics 52.1 *mathematics*
Higher National Certificate 485 Educational Qualifications
Higher National Diploma 485 Educational Qualifications
higher position 154.2 *priority*
higher rank 154.2 *priority*
higher-up 126.5 *superior*
higher-ups 688.4 *governance*, 696.8 *the power structure*
highest 52.75 *equal*, 95.7 *mountainous*, 126.14 *best*, 275.10 *higher*, 279.5 *top*
highest bidder 738.12 *purchaser*
highest common factor 52.17 *multiplication*
highest level 279.1 *summit*
highest point 279.1 *summit*
high executioner 879.17 *punisher*
high explosive 410.2 *lighter*, 680.15 *explosive*
highfalutin 557.4 *ornate*
high-falutin 805.18 *prestigious*, 811.17 *lofty*
high-falutin ways 811.2 *airs*
high fashion 201.2 *trendiness*, 295.2 *dressing*, 796.1 *fashion*
high-fibre 625.4 *hygienic*
high-fibre food 350.7 *food*
high fidelity 503.2 *correctness*, 537.8, 760.10 *accuracy*
high-fidelity 503.6 *correct*
high finance 14.1, 741.7 *finance*
high-flier 126.6 *paragon*, 640.3 *doer*, 805.4 *prestige*
high-flown 361.12 *exalted*, 519.10 *imaginative*, 557.4 *ornate*
high flyer 861.16 *superior person*
high-flyer 682.4 *successful person*
high-flying 557.4 *ornate*, 805.18 *prestigious*
Highgate 93.5 *London*
high-geared 329.1 *swift*
High German 5 Languages and Groups of Languages
high-grade rock 54.33 *metamorphic rock*
high ground 126.4 *summit*, 235.1 *power*
high-handed 688.12 *authoritative*, 690.9 *severe*, 692.15 *self-assured*, 805.19 *stately*
high-handedly 241.10 *violently*, 688.23 *authoritatively*, 690.11 *severely*, 692.16 *commandingly*
high hat 295.15 *headgear*
high-hatted 805.14 *proud*
high heels 275.8 *high thing*, 295.19 *footwear*
high hopes 775.3 *aspiration*
high ideals 857.1 *probity*
high income 742.5 *wealth*
high-inside 28.3 *fencing movements*, 28.6 *fencing*, 28.7 *on guard*
high interest 745.4 *interest*
high IQ 507.2 *intelligence*
high jinks 506.3 *tomfoolery*, 812.1 *celebration*

high jump 21.2 *field events*, 359.5 *jump*, 879.7 *punishment*
high jumper 21.3, 237.5 *athlete*
high jumping 18 Sporting Activities, 21.2 *field events*
high key 66.8 *composition*
high-kicker 46.5 *dancer*
high kicks 46.2 *dance*
highland 95.7 *mountainous*, 98.7 *upland*, 98.11 *continental*, 249.16 *regional*, 275.2 *heights*
high land 359.2 *upturn*
Highland 68 Breeds of Cattle, 92 Counties
Highland dancing 46.1 *dancing*
highlander 255.5 *countryman*
Highlander 91.11 *Scotland*
Highland fling 46.4 *historic dancing*
Highland Games 674.2 *contest*
Highland pony 32 Breeds of Horse and Pony
highlands 53.17 *moon*, 95.1 *mountain*, 249.6 *regions*
high-level 611.5 *important*, 653.17 *managerial*
high-level bombing 670.13 *air attack*
high-level language 65.9 *programming language*
high-level talks 568.5 *talks*, 716.3 *discussion*
high-level waste 56.74 *nuclear waste*
highlight 439, 103.2 *essential content*, 165.22 *characterize*, 437.10 *make visible*, 439.24 *light*, 457.14 *present*, 526.3 *reveal*, 526.10 *manifestation*, 532.16 *publicize*, 543.10 *signify*, 554.6 *emphasize*, 580.4 *pick*, 611.3 *chief thing*, 611.8 *make important*
highlighted 437.2 *clear*, 439.18 *lit*, 526.14 *manifest*, 554.4 *emphasized*
highlighter 437.7 *that which makes visible*
highlights 66.8 *composition*
high-liver 870.5 *self-indulgent person*
high living 870.2 *dissipation*
high-living 870.7 *dissipated*
high low 42 Card Games
highly 361, 120.7 *quantitatively*
highly capable 507.6 *intelligent*
highly coloured 522.1 *intelligible*, 541.12 *exaggerated*, 560.11 *descriptive*
highly-coloured imagination 519.1 *imagination*
highly considered 849.12 *respected*
highly flavoured 237.12 *strong to the senses*, 413.9 *piquant*
highly productive 246.5 *fertile*
highly qualified 501.9 *literate*, 655.6 *skilful*, 655.8 *expert*
highly regarded 849.12 *respected*
highly seasoned 237.12 *strong to the senses*, 413.9 *piquant*
highly strung 759.12 *sensitive*, 760.2 *oversensitive*, 777.8 *fearful*
highly-strung 829.4 *irascible*
highly thought of 800.3 *reputable*, 849.12 *respected*
highly wrought 594.20 *developed*, 684.7 *completed*
High Mass 10.6 *Eucharist*
high-minded 134.12 *morally pure*, 805.19 *stately*, 857.4 *honourable*, 859.5 *unselfish*, 876.8 *moral*
high-mindedly 134.18 *virtuously*, 857.7 *honourably*, 859.9 *unselfishly*
high-mindedness 134.1 *purity*, 857.1 *probity*, 859.2 *unselfishness*
high moral tone 134.1 *purity*
high muck-a-muck 661.4 *bigwig*
highness 275.1 *height*
high noon 204.3 *noon*
high-noon 204.6 *noon*
high-nosed 805.19 *stately*
high note 49.21 *tone*, 430.3 *shrillness*

high-octane 410.10 *powered*
high-octane petrol 395.9 *petroleum*
high office 688.5 *position of authority*
high official 653.16 *official*
high on the hog 686.8 *prosperous*, 686.9 *prosperously*, 742.16 *wealthily*
high opinion 849.1 *respect*
high-outside 28.3 *fencing movements*, 28.6 *fencing*, 28.7 *on guard*
high-pass filter 64.22 *transformer*
high pitch 49.21 *tone*, 430.3 *shrillness*
high-pitched 430.9 *shrill*, 557.4 *ornate*
high places 777 Phobias by Topic
highpockets 259.11 *tall person*
high point 103.2 *essential content*
high post 23.4 *playing terms*
high-powered 37.8 *shooting*, 237.10 *potent*
high-powered rifle 37.3 *hunting equipment*
high-pressure 695.9 *compelling*
high-pressure worker 642.10 *busy person*
high price 753
high-price 753.7 *dear*
high-priced 753.7 *dear*, 757.3 *costly*
high priest 7.8 *priest*, 653.14 *leader*, 696.6 *religious leader*
high-principled 843.10 *moral*, 857.4 *honourable*, 863.6 *ethical*
high principles 857.1 *probity*, 863.2 *virtues*
high-priority 611.5 *important*
high productivity 246.2 *productiveness*
high profile 437.4 *clarity*
high-profile 437.2 *clear*
high-ranking 611.6 *notable*
high rate 751.3 *fee*
high regard 849.2 *admiration*
high relief 50.13 *relief-carving*, 437.6 *visible thing*, 437.7 *that which makes visible*, 767.6 *profile*
High Renaissance 43 Architectural Styles
High Renaissance art 50 Western Art Styles and Movements
high resolution 136.1 *separation*
high-resolution 136.19 *separable*
high-rise 43.12 *structural*, 256.16 *manorial*, 275.9 *high*
high-rise building 43.3, 63.20 *building*, 243.8 *construction*
high-rise flats 256.6 *apartment block*, 275.6 *tall thing*
high road 327.3 *road*
high saturation 56.28 *colour*
high school 6.12 *educational institution*, 32.6 *horsemanship*
high-school football 19.1 *football*
high seas 97.1 *sea*, 698.1 *freedom*
high sign 543.1 *sign*
Highsmith 48 Writers
high society 796.6 *fashionable élite*, 802.2 *aristocracy*, 815.7 *human society*
high-sounding 423.6 *loud*, 557.4 *ornate*
high-sounding words 557.2 *affectation*
high-speed 329.1, 329.1 *swift*
high-speed steel 57 Alloys, 63.9 *machine tool*
high-spirited 105.8 *in a state of*, 769.1 *cheerful*, 805.14 *proud*
high spirits 105.4 *state of mind*, 642.4 *energy*, 762.1 *happiness*, 769.3 *cheerfulness*
high spot 611.3 *chief thing*
high standard of living 686.1 *prosperity*
high standing 611.1 *importance*, 849.1 *respect*
high-stepper 32.2 *thoroughbred*
highstick 31.9 *play hockey*
highsticked 31.8 *hockey*

highsticking 31.1 *hockey*, 31.3 *ice hockey*, 31.8 *hockey*
high street 93.7 *city district*, 327.3 *road*, 642.6 *business*
high-street 93.14 *urban*
high summer 203.3 *summer*, 408.5 *hot weather*
high table 301.2 *enclosed place*
high tackle 35.3 *rugby play*
hightail 345.4 *hurry off*
high tar 413.7 *tobacco*
high-tar 413.11 *tobacco*
high tax bracket 742.5 *wealth*
high tea 350.12 *meal*, 815.3 *meeting*
high tech 602.1 *means*, 603.5 *mechanics*
high-tech 243.11 *productive*
high technology 243.2 *manufacture*, 602.1 *means*, 603.5 *mechanics*
high-technology 243.11 *productive*
high-tech war 676.1 *war*
high temperature 408.1 *heat*, 624.3 *symptom*
high-temperature gas-cooled reactor 56.73 *nuclear reactor*
high-temperature superconductor 56.45 *superconductivity*
high-tensile steel 74.4 *shipbuilding*
high tension 235.4 *energy*
high-tension 235.16 *charged*
high-test gas 395.9 *petroleum*
high thing 275
high tide 54.15, 97.2 *tide*, 275.8 *high thing*
high time 209.2 *late hour*, 615.3 *convenience*
high tone 557.2 *affectation*
high tragedy 51.9 *tragedy*
high treason 693.3 *subversion*, 713.2 *disorder*, 858.2 *faithlessness*
high turnout 181.4 *throng*
high up 95.11 *on the mountain*, 275.19 *high*
high-up 275.9 *high*
high vacuum 57.20 *surface chemistry*
high value 753.6 *value*
high-value 753.8 *valuable*
high-velocity 329.1, 329.1 *swift*
high-voltage a.c. transmission 64.33 *power distribution*
high-voltage d.c. transmission 64.33 *power distribution*
high volume 423.1 *loudness*
high water 97.2 *tide*, 275.8 *high thing*
high-water mark 268.6 *measuring instrument*, 302.2 *limiting factor*
highway 71.2, 137.5 *road*, 327.3 *road*, 356.2 *passing along*
highway engineering 63.17 *civil engineering*
highwayman 736.8 *thief*
highway patrolman 718.3 *security officer*
highway ramp 137.5 *road*
highway restaurant 218.4 *stopping place*
highway robber 736.8 *thief*
highway robbery 736.1 *stealing*, 753.2 *unfair price*
highways and by-ways 327.3 *road*
highway sign 543.1 *sign*, 543.5 *indicator*
high wind 55.14 *windiness*
high-wire artist 51.29 *circus performer*
high yellow 133.5 *hybrid*
high-yielding 243.11 *productive*, 246.5 *fertile*
hi-hat cymbals 49 Musical Instruments
HII region 53.8 *interstellar medium*
hijack 539.33 *snare*, 734.10 *take away*, 736.12 *steal*
hijacked 539.42 *trapped*, 736.17 *stolen*
hijacker 695.4 *coercive person*, 734.6 *taker*, 736.8 *thief*

hijacking 539.13 *snare*, 734.3 *taking away*, 736.1 *stealing*, 736.17 *stolen*

hike 261.5 *make bigger*, 361.1 *raise*

hiked 128.7 *increased*

hike up 128.5 *make bigger*, 239.13 *invigorate*, 261.5 *make bigger*

hiking **18** *Sporting Activities*, 261.1 *growth*

hiking trail 327.6 *path*

hilarious 771.9 *funny*, 773.10 *laughing*, 798.5 *ridiculous*

hilariously 771.16 *humorously*

hilarity 771.2 *amusement*, 773.3 *laughter*

Hilbert 52 *Scientists*

Hilbert space 52 *Named Concepts*

Hilbert's problems 52 *Named Concepts*

hill 34.8 *mountaineering*, 54.7 *landform*, 95.1, 275.3 *mountain*, 310.2 *obliquity*, 359.2 *upturn*, 360.6 *slide*

Hill 18 *Sporting Personalities*, **48** *Writers*, **48** *Poets*

hill and dale 111.2 *opposites*

hillbilly 95.3 *mountaineer*, 255.5 *countryman*, 658.3 *naive person*, 803.1 *plebeian*

hillbilly music 49.11 *folk music*

hill climb 33.1 *motor racing*

hillclimbing 33.1 *motor racing*

hill climbing 34.1 *mountaineering*

hill-climbing 359.6 *mounting*

hill-dweller 95.3 *mountaineer*

hill-dwelling 95.7, 275.13 *mountainous*

hill farm 68.6 *farm*

hill farmer 68.15 *agriculturist*

hill fog 55.33 *fog*

hill mist 55.34 *mist*

hill mynah 78 *Birds*

hillock 95.1, 275.3 *mountain*, 276.2 *lowland*, 316.3 *dome*

hillocky 275.13 *mountainous*

Hill Radnor 68 *Breeds of Sheep*

hillside 305.1 *side*

hilltop 95.1 *mountain*, 275.2 *heights*, 279.1 *summit*

hilly 95.7, 275.13 *mountainous*, 310.8 *oblique*

hilum 83.9 *seed*

him 401.2 *male*, 534.19 *radio reception*

Himalayan 95.7, 275.13 *mountainous*

Himalayas 95 *Mountains*, 95.6 *other major mountains and ranges*, 275.4 *mountain range*

himation 295.16 *robe*

himbo 502.5 *ignorant person*

himself 165.12 *I*, 401.2 *male*

Himyaritic 5 *Languages and Groups of Languages*

hind 77.18 *female mammal*, 304.4 *rear*, 402.14 *female animal*

hinder 661, 111.9 *oppose*, 153.10 *disrupt*, 209.8 *delay*, 218.2 *cause to cease*, 231.3 *counteract*, 302.7 *limit*, 323.8 *stop*, 328.3 *slow down*, 369.14 *make heavy*, 515.7 *thwart*, 591.2 *avert*, 609.5 *be insufficient*, 614.7 *be useless*, 616.5 *be inconvenient*, 628.5 *hurt*, 659.23 *cause difficulties*, 663.7 *withstand*, 669.6 *resist*, 693.15 *be disobedient*, 699.8 *restrain*

hindered 111.5 *opposing*, 153.15 *disrupted*, 209.10 *held up*, 515.9 *disappointed*, 609.2 *unprovided*, 661.13 *hindering*

hinderer 661

hindering 661, 111.5 *opposing*, 209.12 *delaying*, 616.1 *inconvenient*, 661.1 *hindrance*, 663.22 *uncooperative*

Hindi 5 *Languages and Groups of Languages*

hindlimb 143.4 *component*

hindmost 157, 155.20, 340.40 *rear*

hindquarters 304.2 *rear end*

hindrance 661, 111.3 *opposition*, 153.4 *disruption*, 209.3 *delayed action*, 218.2 *stop*, 231.1 *counteraction*, 302.2 *limiting factor*, 323.1 *closure*, 573.12 *opposition*, 587.6 *dissuasion*, 591.10 *avoidance*, 616.3 *inconvenience*, 620.7 *defect*, 659.8 *snag*, 661.7 *hinderer*, 693.1 *disobedience*, 699.1 *restraint*

Hindrance 661

hind shank 45.23 *beef* , 45.27 *lamb*

hindsight 511.1 *memory*

Hind's Nebula 53 *Nebulae*

Hindu 7.6 *non-Christian*, 7.16 *denominational*

Hindu Kush 95 *Mountains*

Hindustani 5 *Languages and Groups of Languages*

Hindu text 7.12 *religious text*

hindward 337.28 *backward*

hinge 135.5 *joint*, 137.4 *means of connection*, 137.8 *fastening*, 137.11 *connect*, 364.4 *vortex*, 364.8 *rotate*

hinged 137.15 *connected*

hingle 364.4 *vortex*

Hinman Cup 36.1 *sailing*

hinny 77 *Placental Mammals*, 133.5 *hybrid*, 402.3 *female title of address*

hint 182.1 *few*, 228.10 *manipulate*, 471.2 *theory*, 517.3 *plan*, 517.11 *predict*, 518.2 *basis of supposition*, 518.6 *propound*, 527.10 *quietness*, 527.14 *imply*, 528.7 *advice*, 528.14 *tip*, 530.2 *divulgence* , 530.6 *divulge*, 636.1 *warning*, 636.5 *warn*, 654.1 *advice*, 654.5 *advise*, 759.2 *impression*

hint at 520.10 *mean*, 543.10 *signify*

hinted 527.4 *unsaid*

hinter 586.14 *motivator*

hinterland 92.4 *community*, 248.3 *geographical space*, 249.6 *regions*, 289.2 *outside*, 290.3 *inland*, 304.1 *rear*

hinting 518.7 *suppositional*, 636.8 *warning*

Hinun 8 *Deities*

hip 6.19 *knowledgeable*, 43.9 *miscellaneous architectural features*, 135.5 *joint*, 305.1 *side*, 796.7 *fashionable*

hip bath 258.12, 621.6 *bath*

hipbone 382 *Bones*

hip boots 295.19 *footwear*

hip flask 258.14 *bottle*, 351.10 *drink container*

hip, hip, hooray 773.12 *hurrah*

hip, hip, hurrah 773.12 *hurrah*

hip-hip hurrah 431.3 *cry of praise*

hip-hop 49.9 *popular music*

hip-huggers 295.9 *trousers*

Hipparchus 52 *Scientists*

Hipparion 77 *Placental Mammals*

hipped 43.14 *roofed*

hipped on 821.18 *in love*

hippie 104.5, 168.7 *nonconformist*, 168.13 *unconventional*, 500.5 *dissenter*, 698.8 *free-thinker*, 713.4 *protester*, 720.5 *nonobserver*

hippiedom 168.3 *nonconformism*

hippo 259.12 *fat person*

hippocampus 80 *Fishes*

hippocras 351.7 *alcoholic drink*

Hippocrates 630.15 *healer*

Hippocratic 60.22, 630.18 *medical*

Hippocratic oath 60.1 *medicine*, 847.6 *ethics*

Hippocrene 48.13 *poetic genius*

hippodrome 51.14 *theatre*

hippogriff 76.7 *legendary beast*

hippophobia 77 *Phobias by Name*

hippopotami 161 *Collective Names by Animal*

hippopotamus 77 *Placental Mammals*, 77.14 *pachyderm*,

77.15 *hoofed mammal*, 259.9 *big thing*

hippy 259.16 *fat*

hip roof 43.6 *roof*

hipsters 295.9 *trousers*

Hirado ware 44 *Types of Ceramics*

hircine 77.33 *ungulate*

hire 15.11 *conduct industrial relations*, 703.7 *engage*, 728.1 *transfer of property*, 728.3 *transfer property*, 751.3 *fee*

hire car 71.18 *cab*

hired 15.9 *negotiated*, 746.19 *receiving pay*

hired assassin 398.11 *murderer*, 832.8 *malefactor*

hired gun 398.11 *murderer*

hired hand 697.1 *servant*

hired help 662.16 *home help*, 697.1 *servant*

hired killer 398.11 *murderer*, 864.9 *wicked person*

hired mourner 399.3 *funeral director*

hireling 127.6 *inferior*, 697.1 *servant*

hire personnel 602.6 *find means*

hire purchase 733.4 *credit*, 738.7 *purchasing*, 744.1 *credit*, 747.2 *stoppage*

hire-purchase 728.1 *transfer of property*

hire-purchase dealer 732.3 *lender*

hire-purchase payment 746.1 *payment*

hirer 728.2 *person transferring property*

Hiri Motu 5 *Languages and Groups of Languages*

hiring 15.9 *negotiated*

hiring practices 15.2 *industrial negotiations*

Hiroshima 93 *Cities*, 398.15 *slaughterhouse*

hirple 328.1 *move slowly*

hirsute 375.3 *barbed*

hirudin 62 *Medication*

Hirudinea 81.6 *worm*

hirudinean 81.6 *worm*, 81.20 *wormlike*

hirundine 78.23 *avian*

Hisakitaimisi 8 *Deities*

His Excellency 696.3 *leader*

His Highness 611.4 *bigwig*, 696.2 *sovereign*

his Honour 16.23 *judge*

his lordship 401.3 *male title of address*

his Lordship 492.6 *justice*

his nibs 16.23 *judge*, 611.4 *bigwig*, 805.13 *proud person*

Hispaniola 98 *Islands*

Hispano Arab 32 *Breeds of Horse and Pony*

Hispano-Moresque ware 44 *Types of Ceramics*

hispid 375.2 *coarse*, 375.3 *barbed*, 380.2 *spiked*

hispidity 375.6 *roughness*

His Royal Highness 696.2 *sovereign*

hiss 429, 429, 431, 79.15 *live as a reptile*, 424.1 *faintness*, 424.5 *sound faint*, 431.7 *cry of disapproval*, 432.1 *animal cry*, 432.2 *bird song*, 432.4 *cry*, 434.5 *atmospheric dissonance*, 534.19 *radio reception*, 543.3, 543.11 *gesture*, 563.4 *whispering*, 563.14 *have difficulty speaking*, 713.3 *gesture of protest*, 713.7 *complain*, 766.2 *expression of dissatisfaction*, 766.7 *be dissatisfied*, 850.6, 850.25 *taunt*, 852.9 *show of disapproval*, 852.23 *show disapproval*

His Satanic Majesty 8.7 *devil*

hissed 852

hisser 429

hissing 429, 431, 79.12 *snakelike*, 423.1 *loudness*, 424.4 *faint*, 429.1 *hiss*, 563.12 *inarticulate*, 713.9 *protesting*,

850.15 *taunting*, 852.9 *show of disapproval*

hissingly 434.12 *dissonantly*

Hissing Sound 429

hist 429.9 *sh*

histidine 58 *Amino Acids*

histochemistry 59.6 *cell biology*

histogram 52.32 *graph*, 52.58 *frequency distribution*

histological 59.20 *biological*

histologically 59.29 *biologically*

histologist 59.19 *life scientist*, 382.10 *anatomist*

histology 59.1 *life science*, 59.4 *anatomy*, 59.6 *cell biology*, 382.8 *science of structure*

histone 58.9 *protein*

histoplasmosis 89.5 *fungal association*

historian 3, 48.14 *author*, 192.13 *chronicler*, 545.9 *recorder*, 560.10 *descriptive writer*, 688.11 *expert*

historic 3, 202, 200.17 *past*

historical 3, 3.18 *in the past*, 3.19 *chronicled*, 99.13, 101.6 *real*, 200.17 *past*, 202.14 *historic*, 490.1 *certain*

historical ammunition 680

historical documents 545.1 *record*

historical geology 3.2 *archaeology*, 54.1 *earth science*

historical gun 680

historical guns 680

historical linguistics 5.1 *linguistics*

historically 3, 200.24 *retrospectively*, 202.21 *archaically*

historical map 299.4 *map*

historical materialism 3.1 *history*

historical method 3.12 *historicism*

historical methodology 3.1 *history*

historical missile weapon 680

historical naval ships 679

historicalness 3

historical novel 48.2, 560.5 *fiction*

historical painter 50.16 *artist*

historical painting 50.10 *art subject*

historical period 200

historical record 3.5 *chronicle*, 545.1 *record*

historical soldiery 679

historical taxes 751

historic building 202.5 *old thing*

historic dancing 46

Historic District 202.5 *old thing*

historic fencing 28.1 *fencing*

historicism 3

historicity 3.14 *historicalness*, 99.4 *demonstrable existence*, 101.1 *reality*, 490.9 *certainty*

historic present 5.34 *tense*

historic property terms 725

historiographer 3.3 *historian*, 48.14 *author*, 192.13 *chronicler*, 560.10 *descriptive writer*

historiographical 3.16 *historical*, 48.19 *narrative*

historiography 3.1 *history*, 48.4 *non-fiction*

history 3, 3.5 *chronicle*, 3.8 *past time*, 48.4 *non-fiction*, 200.1 *past time*, 396.11 *life story*, 485.3 *qualifications*, 511.2 *retrospect*, 545.1 *record*, 560.3 *narration*, 652.1 *conduct*

History 3

history of ideas 3.1 *history*

history of illness 624.2 *illness*

history of science 3.1 *history*

histricomorphs 77.12 *gnawing mammal*

histrionic 51.37 *dramatic*, 475.10 *demonstrative*, 541.12 *exaggerated*, 797.3 *affected*, 811.18 *dramatic*

histrionical 541.12 *exaggerated*

histrionically 51.42 *dramatically*, 475.21 *demonstratively*, 541.16 *exaggeratedly*, 811.34 *dramatically*

histrionic art 51.1 *drama*

histrionics 51.1 *drama*, 51.7 *dramaturgy*, 51.20 *acting*, 475.2 *demonstrativeness*, 541.1 *exaggera-*

tion, 797.1 *affectedness*, 811.3 *dramatics*

historionism 51.1 *drama*

his Worship 16.23 *judge*, 492.6 *justice*

hit 330, 670, 879, 22.5 *batting terms*, 22.7 *play baseball*, 25.2 *grip*, 26.14 *combat*, 28.3 *fencing movements*, 28.5 *fence*, 31.9 *play hockey*, 49.9 *popular music*, 51.11 *theatrical performance*, 241.8 *use violence*, 267.4 *meet*, 330.10 *bat*, 330.13 *blow*, 330.14 *sporting hit*, 338.28 *shoot*, 344.1 *arrive*, 406.3 *injury*, 406.11 *inflict pain*, 407.3 *press*, 407.11 *touch*, 617.8 *exceller*, 618.14 *ill-treat*, 655.3 *masterpiece*, 670.5 *strike*, 674.12, 679.37 *fight*, 682.1 *success*, 682.3 *successful thing*, 682.4 *successful person*, 785.6 *react against*, 786.5 *person of wonder*, 861.17 *good thing*, 875.6 *drug*, 879.12 *corporal punishment*

hit a bad patch 687.9 *be in trouble*

hit a clinker 434.10 *lack harmony*

hit a double 22.7 *play baseball*

hit a fly 22.7 *play baseball*

hit a grand-slam home run 22.7 *play baseball*

hit a grand-slammer 22.7 *play baseball*

hit a grounder 22.7 *play baseball*

hit a home run 22.7 *play baseball*

hit a mental block 462.12 *lack thought*

hit and miss 479.1 *experiment*

hit-and-miss 780.4 *rash*

hit-and-run accident 71.21 *miscellaneous motoring terms*

hit-and-run play 22.5 *batting terms*

hit a nerve 331.3 *get a response*

hit an iceberg 98.12 *be marooned*

hit a receiver 19.15 *play offence*

hit a reef 98.12 *be marooned*

hit a sandbar 98.12 *be marooned*

hit a shot 23.6 *play basketball*

hit a single 22.7 *play baseball*

hit a slalom pole 41.14 *ski*

hit a snag 661.9 *block*

hit a straight 33.10 *be on the track*

hit a streak of luck 686.6 *be fortunate*

hit a triple 22.7 *play baseball*

hit back 672.3 *retaliate*

hit below the belt 26.11 *do a combat sport*, 844.21 *do wrong*

hit bottom 770.9 *despair*

hitch 74 Knots, 36.15 *sail*, 68.18 *practise livestock farming*, 135.5 *joint*, 135.10 *link*, 218.2 *stop*, 339.3 *jerk*, 339.13 *pull at*, 515.2 *bad outcome*, 659.8 *snag*, 661.2 *obstacle*

hitch and hike 365.8 *oscillate*, 365.18 *to and fro*

hitched 135.14 *conjunctive*, 135.15 *tied*, 823.21 *married*

hitch-hike 46.2 *dance*

hitchhiker 71.21 *miscellaneous motoring terms*

hitchhiking 71.21 *miscellaneous motoring terms*

Hitchi 8 Deities

hitchkick technique 21.2 *field events*

hitch to 130.6 *add*

hitch up to 130.6 *add*

hit for 332.7 *take a direction*

hit from the penalty corner 31.9 *play hockey*

hit hard 239.2 *be full of vigour*

hit hard times 659.20 *be in difficulty*

hitherto 3.24 *historically*, 194.11 *before*, 200.23 *before now*

hit home 331.3 *get a response*

hit in 31.9 *play hockey*

hit-in 31.1, 31.8 *hockey*

hit into a double play 22.7 *play baseball*

hit it 682.6 *be successful*

hit it off 667.6 *agree with*, 682.6 *be successful*

hit it off with 116.21 *be in accord*, 819.13 *befriend*

hit it on the nose 537.31 *be accurate*

Hitler 618.12 *bad person*, 696.4 *absolute ruler*, 822.8 *hated person*, 862.6 *evil person*

Hitler diaries 540.14 *false thing*

hit man 244.6 *destroyer*, 398.11 *murderer*, 679.1 *combatant*, 832.8 *malefactor*, 864.10 *bad person*, 879.17 *punisher*

hit one 471.14 *have an idea*

hit one in the eye 437.8 *be visible*

hit or miss 504.2 *inaccuracy*

hit-or-miss 151.14 *irregular*, 229.6 *motiveless*, 468.10 *careless*, 589.8 *chance*

hit over the head 330.3 *hit*, 330.8 *club*

hit rock bottom 172, 687.9 *be in trouble*, 770.9 *despair*

hit someone up 733.7 *borrow*

hitter 22.2 *baseball player*

hit the batter 22.7 *play baseball*

hit the big time 686.5 *be prosperous*

hit the bottle 874.8 *get drunk*

hit the bottom cushion 24.8 *play billiards*

hit the crossbar 19.17 *kick*, 21.6 *jump*

hit the finish tape 21.6 *race*

hit the headlines 532.18 *become famous*

hit the jackpot 682.6 *be successful*, 721.14 *profit*, 742.13 *get rich*

hit the mark 682.6 *be successful*

hit the nail on the head 503.7, 537.31 *be accurate*

hit the puck 31.9 *play hockey*

hit the road 156.19 *start off*, 345.5 *set out*, 531.11 *conceal oneself*

hit the roof 128.4 *increase*, 759.17 *feel deeply*, 818.8 *get angry*, 828.12 *become angry*

hit the shops 738.2 *shop*

hit the skids 127.11 *become inferior*, 628.1 *deteriorate*

hit the spot 615.6 *be convenient*

hit the target 670.3 *bomb*

hitting 26.14 *combat*, 31.1 *hockey*, 879.12 *corporal punishment*

hitting below the belt 26.2 *boxing*, 858.1 *improbity*

hitting it on the fly 40.2 *tennis strokes*

hitting on 250.3 *locating*

hitting the nail on the head 537.8 *accuracy*

hitting up 733.1 *borrowing*, 734.1 *taking*, 875.1 *drug-taking*

Hittite 5 Languages and Groups of Languages, 400.4 *civilized human*

Hittites 1 Peoples

hit town 344.1 *arrive*

hit tune 49.9 *popular music*

hit up 734.7 *take*

hit upon 250.11 *find*, 344.2 *reach*, 360.12 *drop*, 496.1 *discover*, 589.11 *chance upon*, 592.11 *invent*

hit upon an idea 496.4 *invent*

hit wicket 27.11 *dismissal*, 504.13 *sporting error*

HIV 624.6 *infection*

HIV-carrier 626.4 *infectious person*

hive 161 Collective Names for Birds and Animals, 82.4 *social insect*, 181.4 *throng*, 605.4 *storage*, 605.6 *store*, 642.6 *business*

hived off 136.17 *unjoined*

hive of activity 642.6 *business*

hive off 136.10 *set apart*, 162.12 *disperse*

hive of industry 642.6 *business*, 647.1 *workshop*

hives 624.13 *skin disease*

hiya 344.23 *hello*

Hizen porcelain 44 Types of Ceramics

Ho 5 Languages and Groups of Languages

Hoad 18 Sporting Personalities

hoagie 45.11 *sandwich*

hoar 55.36 *frost*, 409.8 *cold*, 446.9 *white thing*, 448.2 *grey-haired*

hoard 758, 161.25 *assemblage*, 161.37 *assemble*, 605.1 *store*, 606.5 *provision*, 632.9 *protect*, 721.3 *acquisition*, 721.11 *acquire*, 738.1 *purchase*

hoarded 161.47 *collected*, 605.7 *stored*

hoarder 161, 469.6 *careful person*, 721.7 *gainer*, 738.12 *purchaser*, 758.5 *miser*

hoarding 526.8 *showplace*, 532.9 *advertisement*

hoard supplies 594.3 *be prepared*

hoar frost 55.29 *hail*, 55.36 *frost*, 409.5 *ice*

hoarily 207.16 *maturely*

hoariness 207.5 *old age*, 446.7 *whiteness*

hoarse 430, 424.4 *faint*, 563.10 *low-voiced*

hoarsely 434.12 *dissonantly*, 563.17 *voicelessly*

hoarseness 430, 424.1 *faintness*, 434.1 *dissonance*, 563.2 *inarticulation*, 624.3 *symptom*

hoary 202.11 *old*, 207.14 *aged*, 446.2 *whitened*, 446.3 *white-haired*, 448.2 *grey-haired*

hoary age 202.1 *oldness*

hoatzin 78 Birds

hoax 539, 539, 538.8 *pretence*, 538.25 *be dishonest*, 540.8 *fraud*, 540.21 *be fraudulent*, 636.3 *false alarm*

hoaxed 539.36 *deceived*

hoaxer 539.15 *deceiver*, 540.15 *false person*, 548.3 *deceiver*

hob 45.5 *cooker*, 408.4 *burner*

Hobart 93 Cities

Hobbes 4 Philosophers

Hobbism 4.7 *school of thought*

Hobbist 4.11 *follower of a doctrine*, 4.14 *of a philosophy*

hobbit 260.4 *little person*

hobble 135.10 *link*, 236.8 *overpower*, 244.11 *ruin*, 328.1 *move slowly*, 328.10 *slow motion*, 659.5 *predicament*, 661.8 *hinder*, 699.5 *means of restraint*, 699.12 *gag*

hobble skirt 295.6 *skirt*

hobbling 238.10 *ill*, 328.4 *slow*, 628.11 *hurt*

Hobbs 18 Sporting Personalities

hobby 78 Birds, 42.8 *pastime*, 590.4 *activity*, 642.2 *social activity*, 784.3 *likes*

hobbyhorse 71.12 *bicycle*

hobgoblin 11.11 *ghost*

hobnail boots 295.19 *footwear*

hobnob 180.14 *keep company with*, 815.13 *fraternize*

hobnobbing 815.1 *sociability*

hobnob with 819.13 *befriend*

hobo 168.7 *nonconformist*, 224.7 *person who moves around*, 622.6 *dirty person*, 643.8 *nonworker*, 712.5 *beggar*, 743.10 *poor person*

Hoboken 93 Cities

Hobson's choice 477.4 *difficult question*, 571.3 *lack of choice*, 580.8 *choice*, 695.1 *compulsion*

Hochhuth 48 Dramatists

Ho Chi Minh City 93 Cities

hock 45.24, 45.25 *pork* , 351.9 *wine*, 733.7 *borrow*

hocked 718.7 *guaranteed*

hockey 31, 31

hockey association 31.1 *hockey*

hockey ball 31.1 *hockey*, 338.10 *ball*

hockey clothing 31.1 *hockey*

Hockey, Ice Hockey, Lacrosse, Etc. 31

hockey player 31, 31.4 *ice hockey player*

hockey stick 31.1 *hockey*, 31.3 *ice hockey*, 330.15 *ram*

hockey stop 41.4 *skiing technique*

hockey technique 31.1 *hockey*

hocking 732.1 *lending*, 733.1 *borrowing*

hock shop 732.4 *lending institution*

hocus-pocus 11.5 *spell*, 521.1 *lack of meaning*, 539.9 *sleight of hand*, 539.40 *illusory*

Hod 8 Deities

hodden 383.8 *rough*

Hodeida 93 Cities

hodgepodge 113.2 *assortment*, 151.4 *litter*

Hodgkin 52 Scientists, 52 Scientists

Hodgkin's disease 624.11 *blood disease*

hodophobia 777 Phobias by Name

Hödur 8 Deities

hoe 68.17 *farm*, 69.6 *garden tool*, 69.15 *cultivate*, 603.2 *garden tool*, 603.9 *use tools*, 621.10 *cleaning object*

hoed 69.19 *ornamental*

hoedown 46.4 *historic dancing*, 815.5 *party*

hoe one's own row 174.18 *be one*

Hofmann 49 Musicians and Composers

Hofmann degradation 57 Named Reactions

Hofmann's method 57 Named Reactions

Hofmeister 52 Scientists

hog 77 Placental Mammals, 68.8 *livestock*, 350.18 *eater*, 401.16 *male animal*, 723.7 *possess*, 860.3 *selfish person*, 860.6 *be selfish*, 872.4 *glutton*

hogahn 10.7 *non-Christian ritual*

Hogan 18 Sporting Personalities

hogback 275.4 *mountain range*

hog caller 423.5 *loud person*

hogfish 80 Fishes

hogg 68.8 *livestock*

Hoggar 95 Mountains

hogget 68.8 *livestock*

hoggish 77.33 *ungulate*, 622.8 *unclean*, 872.6 *gluttonous*

hoggishly 872.7 *gluttonously*

hoggishness 872.1 *gluttony*

hog line 41.10 *curling*

hognose snake 79 Reptiles

hognut 86 Nuts

hog's back 32.9 *jumping*, 275.4 *mountain range*

hogshead 72 General Units, 258.11 *vessel*

hog wallow 393.14 *puddle*

hog-wallow 622.5 *swill*

hogwash 474.2 *sophism*, 538.6, 540.13 *nonsense*, 622.5 *swill*

hoick 361.1 *raise*

hoick back 33.10 *be on the track*

hoicking back 33.6 *motor racing terms*

hoick out 131.3 *subtract*

hoi polloi 124.7 *average person*, 127.6 *inferior*, 164.11 *general public*, 400.9 *group*, 642.6 *business*, 795.6 *vulgar herd*

hoi-polloi 803.2 *the common people*

hoist 63.29 *construction equipment*, 63.30 *engineer*, 275.17, 361.1 *raise*, 361.6 *raising*, 361.9 *lifter*, 544.7 *flag*

hoisted 361.11 *raised*

hoisting 63.29 *construction equipment*

hoisting one's flag over 723.1 *possession*

hoist sail 74.9 *navigate*

hoist the Blue Peter 345.5 *set out*

hoity-toity 805.14 *proud*

hoke 540.13 *nonsense*

hokey 118.13 *imitation*, 538.14 *unreal*

hokey cokey 46.2 *dance*

hoki 45.18 *sea fish*

hoking 51.20 *acting*

hoking it up 51.20 *acting*

Hokkaido 98 Islands

hokum 474.2 *sophism*, 521.5 *empty talk*, 538.6, 540.13 *nonsense*

Holborn 93.5 *London*
hold 73 Aircraft Parts, **74** Parts of a Ship, 12.3 *governance*, 19.18 *be penalized*, 30.10 *compete in gymnastics*, 31.1 *hockey*, 31.9 *play hockey*, 34.5 *rock face*, 38.4 *play soccer*, 41.7 *ice-dancing*, 42.3 *card game terms*, 42.10 *play*, 99.19 *continue to be*, 138.6 *adhere*, 146.4 *include*, 209.8 *delay*, 218.8 *cause to cease*, 225.6 *be stable*, 233 *influence*, 233.4 *indirect influence*, 248.20 *extend*, 257.6 *contain*, 280.2 *foot*, 325.11 *stop*, 407.11 *touch*, 473.15 *state*, 497.7 *believe*, 522.6 *understand*, 605.4 *storage*, 605.6 *store*, 637.5 *preserve*, 674.8 *wrestling*, 688.4 *governance*, 699.11 *detain*, 723.1 *possession*, 723.7 *possess*, 726.1 *retention*, 726.6 *retain*, 734.10 *take away*, 759.19 *believe*, 875.10 *drug oneself*
hold a boxing match 26.11 *do a combat sport*
hold a brief for 662.23 *advise*, 671.22 *plead for*
hold a card 665.13 *be a member*
hold a certain position 107.9 *have a relative position*
hold a charity event 712.8 *solicit money*
hold a clearance sale 739.1 *sell*
hold a conference 568.11 *confer*, 716.4 *negotiator*
hold a confidential discussion 654.6 *consult*
hold a consultation 654.6 *consult*
hold a conversation 568.9 *converse*
hold a council of war 568.11 *confer*, 654.6 *consult*
hold a court case 856.5 *accuse*
hold a demonstration 668.6 *be insubordinate*
hold a directorship 696.14 *master*
hold a finger to the wind 596.4 *test*
hold a fire sale 739.1 *sell*
hold a going-out-of-business sale 739.1 *sell*
hold a heading 332.7 *take a direction*
hold a healthy lead 126.10 *lead*
holdall 258.8 *bag*, 258.9 *baggage*, 605.4 *storage*
hold all the aces 126.8 *be superior*, 233.10 *be a prevailing influence*, 688.19 *be authoritarian*
hold all the cards 126.8 *be superior*, 233.10 *be a prevailing influence*
hold all the trumps 660.17 *do easily*
hold a meeting 161.42 *call together*
hold an advantage 126.11 *get ahead*
hold an election 580.5 *vote*
hold an exhibition 526.2 *display something*
hold an opinion 4.22 *propound a philosophy*
hold a point of view 461.16 *have an idea*
hold a position 30.10 *compete in gymnastics*
hold a protest meeting 713.8 *cause mischief*
hold a public inquiry 654.6 *consult*
hold a referendum 580.5 *vote*
hold a responsible position 653.2 *direct*
hold a sale 739.1 *sell*
hold a séance 11.22 *conjure*
hold a special sale 710.9 *offer*
hold a subordinate position 701.8 *be subject to*
hold a summit 568.11 *confer*, 716.4 *negotiator*
hold a symposium 561.4 *dissertate*
hold at bay 671.24 *parry*, 699.8 *restrain*

hold a trial 856.5 *accuse*
hold a wake 399.8 *bury*
hold a wrestling match 26.12 *wrestle*
hold back 573, 209.8 *delay*, 218.9 *pause*, 328.3 *slow down*, 587.3 *deflect*, 591.3 *abstain*, 609.7 *make insufficient*, 661.8 *hinder*, 695.6 *compel*, 699.8 *restrain*, 699.10 *restrain oneself*, 781.5 *be cautious*, 869.5 *be self-restrained*
hold centre stage 526.5 *be visible*
hold cheap 950.3 *underestimate*, 612.12 *think unimportant*, 850.19 *disrespect*
hold court 16.69 *have jurisdiction over*, 16.76 *judge*
hold dear 784.7 *like*, 821.23 *love*, 849.15 *respect*
hold down 362.5 *bear down on*, 699.8 *restrain*, 701.6 *subject*, 726.7 *detain*
hold down inflation 699.9 *economize*
holder 19.12 *special team*, 258.1 *container*, 605.4 *storage*, 723.5 *possessor*, 725.7 *property man*, 730.5 *recipient*, 804.4 *titleholder*
holder of dual nationality 255.8 *national*
hold exclusive rights 699.8 *restrain*
holdfast 90.3 *plant body*, 137.8 *fastening*
hold fast 138.6 *adhere*, 407.11 *touch*, 574.10 *insist*, 575.8 *hold out*
hold for 588.9 *intend for*
hold for questioning 477.18 *interrogate*
hold forth 564.14 *speak to*, 565.8 *talk too much*, 567.7 *address*, 876.12 *moralize*
hold forth without interruption 569.4 *monopolize the conversation*
hold good 537.27 *be true*
hold hands 135.8 *unite*, 826.8 *court*
hold hard 325.11 *stop*
hold honorary membership in 665.13 *be a member*
hold in 302.7 *limit*, 726.7 *detain*
hold in abeyance 600.5 *not use*
hold in affection 821.23 *love*
hold in captivity 699.11 *detain*
hold in check 328.3 *slow down*, 699.8 *restrain*
hold in common 298.4 *interface*, 724.4 *have joint possession*
hold incommunicado 699.11 *detain*
hold in contempt 807.22 *be rude*, 822.14 *hate*, 850.19 *disrespect*, 850.20 *scorn*, 852.14 *disapprove*
hold in disgust 822.14 *hate*
holding 19.13 *penalty*, 23.4 *playing terms*, 30.8 *floor exercises*, 31.1 *hockey*, 31.3 *ice hockey*, 31.8 *hockey*, 38.2 *football play*, 38.5 *soccer*, 68.6 *farm*, 146.7 *including*, 249.12 *plot*, 257.11 *loaded*, 258.20 *containing*, 407.2 *touching*, 605.1 *store*, 723.1 *possession*, 723.8 *possessing*, 725.1 *property*, 726.1 *retention*, 875.2 *drug pushing*
holding back 726.2 *detention*
holding good 537.15 *true*
holding hands 819.4 *act of friendship*
holding in 726.2 *detention*
holding on 138.2 *tenacity*
holding one's own 623.1 *healthy*
holdings 161.25 *assemblage*
holding the faith 7.15 *religious*
holding the reins 653.17 *managerial*
holding the reins of government 12.10 *governing*, 688.12 *authoritative*
holding the sceptre 12.10 *governing*
holding together 138.1 *adhesion*
holding true 537.15 *true*

holding up 284.1 *support*, 537.15 *true*
holding up in the wash 537.15 *true*
holding water 537.15 *true*
hold in high esteem 849.15 *respect*
hold in high regard 849.15 *respect*, 851.11 *approve*
hold in low esteem 850.19 *disrespect*, 852.14 *disapprove*
hold in one's arms 826.7 *show endearment for*
hold in one's mind 511.11 *memorize*, 726.8 *remember*
hold in perpetuity 186.4 *perpetuate*
hold in reverence 849.16 *revere*
hold in solution 387.23 *dissolve*
hold in the palm of one's hand 688.18 *have authority*
hold in thrall 821.28 *win the love of*
hold in trust 707.5 *represent*
hold it 325.11 *stop*
hold it against 820.11 *be hostile*
hold mass executions 879.5 *execute*
hold membership 665.13 *be a member*
hold no brief for 641.4 *not act*
hold off 591.1 *avoid*, 600.5 *not use*, 669.6 *resist*, 671.24 *parry*
hold office 12.11 *govern*, 653.2 *direct*, 688.18 *have authority*
hold off the wet 392.22 *keep dry*
hold on 138.8 *be tenacious*, 209.8 *delay*, 407.11 *touch*
hold one back 302.7 *limit*, 661.8 *hinder*
hold one's breath 240.4 *be inert*, 325.8 *be motionless*, 422.1 *be silent*, 786.9 *wonder*
hold oneself back 699.10 *restrain oneself*
hold oneself erect 805.24 *be proud*
hold oneself in readiness 594.8 *prepare oneself*
hold oneself straight 281.5 *be vertical*
hold oneself up 361.5 *arise*
hold one's fire 240.4 *be inert*
hold one's ground 574.10 *insist*, 676.13 *be at war*
hold one's hand out 879.6 *be punished*
hold one's head 805.24 *be proud*
hold one's head up 361.5 *arise*
hold one's horses 209.8 *delay*, 218.9 *pause*, 240.4 *be inert*
hold one's lead 336.9 *maintain progress*
hold one's liquor 873.3 *be sober*
hold one's nose 417.6 *have no smell*
hold one's nose in the air 805.26 *be too proud*
hold one's own 122.10 *be equal*, 663.17 *withstand*, 671.28 *survive*
hold one's tongue 422.1 *be silent*, 529.12 *keep secret*, 531.12 *be silent*, 563.13 *be voiceless*, 566.8 *be taciturn*
hold on life 396.5 *life cycle*
hold on like a bulldog 138.8 *be tenacious*, 726.6 *retain*
hold on like a snapping turtle 726.6 *retain*
hold on to 726.7 *detain*
hold open house 815.11 *be sociable*
hold opposite opinions 113.9 *dissent*
hold opposite views 666.5 *disagree*
hold out 575, 188.6 *last*, 225.8 *show determination*, 237.7 *be strong*, 574.11 *persist*, 663.17 *withstand*, 710.9 *offer*
hold out a carrot 228.9 *motivate*, 586.17 *bribe*
hold out a carrot to 586.16 *tempt*
hold out a hand to 662.23 *advise*
hold out an incentive 710.9 *offer*

hold out for 575.8 *hold out*, 737.3 *bargain*
hold out hopes 517.11 *predict*
hold out hopes for 714.9 *be auspicious*
hold out one's hand 543.11 *gesture*, 677.4 *pacify*, 712.8 *solicit money*
hold out one's hand to 730.10 *receive someone*
hold out one's own 574.11 *persist*
hold out the olive branch 677.4 *pacify*
hold out the peace pipe 677.4 *pacify*
hold out to the bitter end 225.8 *show determination*
hold out to the last 575.8 *hold out*
hold over 209.8 *delay*
hold over one's head 633.10 *endanger*
hold power 653.2 *direct*, 688.18 *have authority*
hold prisoner 618.14 *ill-treat*
hold responsible 852.19 *blame*
hold someone's hand 662.20 *sustain*
hold someone up 736.12 *steal*
hold steady 332.7 *take a direction*
hold straight 333.6 *be in the middle*
hold surgery 60.19 *practise medicine*
hold sway 12.11 *govern*, 166.15 *be the rule*, 688.18 *have authority*
hold sway over 166.16 *direct*
hold talks 568.11 *confer*, 716.4 *negotiator*
hold the ball 23.6 *play basketball*
hold the edge 126.11 *get ahead*
hold the faith 7.19 *be religious*
hold the floor 535.21 *be assertive*
hold the fort 222.4 *be a substitute*
hold the helm 74.9 *navigate*
hold the lead 126.10 *lead*
hold the line 209.8 *delay*, 332.7 *take a direction*
hold the L position 30.10 *compete in gymnastics*
hold the portfolio 653.1 *manage*
hold the purse strings 14.5 *invest*, 653.1 *manage*
hold the reins 12.11 *govern*, 653.1 *manage*, 653.2 *direct*
hold the reins of government 688.18 *have authority*
hold the ring of truth 537.33 *seem lifelike*
hold the road 122.11 *equalize*, 225.8 *show determination*
hold the scales 16.76 *judge*, 333.7 *be halfway*
hold the tiller 653.2 *direct*
hold the trump hand 126.11 *get ahead*
hold the upper hand 126.11 *get ahead*
hold the whip hand 126.11 *get ahead*, 233.10 *be a prevailing influence*
hold tight 726.6 *retain*
hold tightly 826.7 *show endearment for*
hold to 719.4 *observe*
hold together 116.25 *conform*, 135.8 *unite*, 138.6 *adhere*, 138.7 *cause to adhere*, 664.13 *work together*
hold to ransom 695.7 *force*, 832.18 *torment*
hold true 537.27 *be true*
hold up 209.8 *delay*
holdup 218.2 *stop*
hold up 218.6 *cease*, 218.8 *cause to cease*, 218.9 *pause*, 225.6 *be stable*, 237.7 *be strong*, 275.17 *raise*, 283.12 *interrupt*, 284.11 *support*, 361.1 *raise*, 370.10 *lighten*, 537.27 *be true*, 726.7 *detain*, 753.10 *overcharge*
hold-up 209.3 *delayed action*, 328.12 *hesitation*, 736.3 *theft*
hold up in the wash 537.27 *be true*

hold-up man 736.11 *dishonest person*
hold up one's hands 673.3 *submit*
hold up to view 530.5 *disclose*
hold water 463.12 *be reasonable, 537.27 be true*
hold with 851.11 *approve*
hold within 290.15 *keep inside*
hold your tongue 422.6 *hush, 566.11 hush*
hole 322, **322**, 29.1 *golf, 29.2 golfing terms, 29.7 golf, 56.44, 64.4 semiconductor, 100.4 emptiness, 106.4 difficult circumstances, 136.3 separateness, 250.1 location, 256.8 shelter, 256.13 lair, 260.5 little space, 265.2 crack, 277.4 deep thing, 317.2 concave land, 322.1 opening, 354.1 insert, 634.1 refuge, 634.3 animal shelter, 659.5 predicament*
hole conduction 56.44, 64.4 *semiconductor*
holed **322**
hole-high ball 29.2 *golfing terms*
hole in one 29.3 *golf shots, 503.3 accurate thing, 682.3 successful thing*
hole in the wall 258.2 *compartment*
hole out 29.3 *golf shots*
holey 628.13 *dilapidated*
Holi 10.16 *religious festival*
holiday 10.15 *holy day, 214.5 regular thing, 214.7 be regular, 218.3, 218.9 pause, 254.5 leave of absence, 645.2 time off, 649.1 ease, 649.4 at ease, 651.6 refresher, 686.3 time of plenty, 708.2 permit, 762.2 fun, 763.10 pleasant thing, 773.1 rejoicing, 812.1 celebration, 812.2 commemoration*
holidays 15.2 *industrial negotiations*
holiday town 93.1 *city*
holier than thou 805.14 *proud, 865.5 innocent*
holier-than-thou 7.15 *religious, 876.10 moralistic*
holiness 8.1 *divinity, 857.2 purity, 863.1 virtue*
holism 4.7 *school of thought, 142.1 whole*
holistic 142.6 *whole*
holistically 142.11 *wholly*
holistic approach 142.1 *whole*
holistic medicine 60.2 *natural medicine, 630.11 medical art*
hollandaise sauce 45.15 *sauce*
Holle **8** *Deities*
holler 431.1 *cry, 431.10 cry out*
hollow 102.8 *unreal, 144.9 completely, 145.4 incomplete, 238.13 insufficient, 254.13 vacant, 276.2 lowland, 317.2 concave land, 317.5 concave, 317.7 make concave, 322.1 opening, 322.20 hole, 362.2 flatten, 362.14 depression, 427.6 resonant, 521.10 meaningless, 538.18 pretentious, 539.37 hypocritical, 540.28 spurious*
hollow-cheeked 274.2 *emaciated*
hollow cheeks 274.8 *emaciation*
hollow-chisel mortiser 47.11 *woodworking tool*
hollowed 322.14 *holed*
hollow-eyed 274.2 *emaciated, 650.1 fatigued*
hollow eyes 274.8 *emaciation*
hollowly 254.20 *absently, 317.8 concavely*
hollow man 102.5 *insubstantial person*
hollowness 145.1 *incompleteness, 254.3 emptiness, 317.1 concavity, 427.1 resonance, 538.8 pretence, 539.3 hypocrisy, 540.4 spuriousness*
hollow out 317.7 *make concave*
hollow tile 44.9 *industrial ceramics*
hollow tree 531.2 *hiding place*
holly **85** *Trees and Shrubs*

holly fern **88** *Ferns*
hollyhock **84** *Flowers and Flowering Plants*
Hollywood **93** *Cities, 51.4 show business*
Hollywood costume 295.5 *fancy dress*
holm 98.2 *island*
Holmes **48** *Writers,* **48** *Poets*
holmium **57** *Chemical Elements*
holm oak **85** *Trees and Shrubs*
holocaust 244.5 *havoc, 398.4 slaughter, 408.6 fire*
Holocene **54** *Geological Time Intervals*
Holocene period 200.3 *geological period*
holocephalan 80.2 *fish*
holocrine 352.4 *secretory*
holocrine secretion 352.1 *secretion*
holoenzyme 58.11 *enzyme*
hologram 66.5 *stereoscopic image, 110.4 duplicate, 439.12 highlight, 457.4 something that appears, 547.6 image*
holograph 119.2 *original*
holographic 110.15 *duplicate*
holographically 110.18 *identically*
holographic image 66.5 *stereoscopic image*
holography 66.1 *photography, 439.12 highlight*
holophrastic 5.39 *of language*
holothurian 81.3 *echinoderm, 81.17 echinodermal*
Holst **49** *Musicians and Composers*
Holstein **32** *Breeds of Horse and Pony*
Holstein-Friesian **68** *Breeds of Cattle*
holster 680.4 *arsenal*
holt 85.4 *trees, 256.13 lair*
Holtzman inkblot technique 61.5 *psychological test*
holy 7.15 *religious, 8.13 divine, 863.5 virtuous*
Holy Bible 7.12 *religious text*
Holy Communion 10.6 *Eucharist*
holy cow 786.14 *wonderful*
holy cross 10.14 *sacred object*
holy day 10, 214.6 *annually celebrated day, 812.5 anniversary*
holy fear 9.1 *worship*
Holy Grail 10.14 *sacred object, 588.6 objective, 714.4 promised land*
Holyhead **93** *Cities*
Holy Joe 7.8 *priest*
holy mackerel 786.14 *wonderful*
holyman 7.3 *religious person*
Holy Mary 8.10 *deified person*
holy matrimony 715.1 *contract, 823.1 marriage*
Holy Matrimony 10.5 *Christian rite*
holy Moses 786.14 *wonderful*
Holy Office 16.22 *ecclesiastical court*
holy of holies 10.13 *shrine, 301.2 enclosed place, 634.1 refuge*
holy orders 7.9 *priesthood, 10.5 Christian rite, 825.3 monasticism*
holy place 10.13 *shrine, 291.4 centre of activity*
holy rite 10.5 *Christian rite*
holy roller 7.5 *Christian*
Holy Roman Empire 3.10 *past age, 91.3 dominion*
holy shit 786.14 *wonderful*
holy smoke 786.14 *wonderful*
holystone 621.9 *cleaning agent, 621.13 clean*
holy terror 241.4 *violent person or animal, 631.13 oppressor, 862.6 evil person*
Holy Trinity 8.3 *God*
holy war 674.6 *fight, 676.1 war*
holy warrior 670.19 *attacker*
holy water **389**, 10.14 *sacred object*
holy wedlock 823.1 *marriage*
Holywell **93** *Cities*
Holy Writ 537.3 *the truth*

homage 9.1 *worship, 673.1 submission, 694.3 obeisance, 847.3 allegiance, 849.2 admiration*
homaloid 282.2 *horizontal surface*
homaloidal 282.8 *horizontal*
homburg 295.15 *headgear*
Homburg **93** *Cities*
home **777** *Phobias by Topic,* **256**, 91.6 *native land, 226.2 source, 256.1 habitat, 264.5 near, 290.2 inside, 290.8 internal, 290.14 go inside, 325.3 resting place, 344.4 land, 344.15 destination, 344.22 on arrival, 567.5 place of residence, 634.1 refuge*
home again 344.22 *on arrival*
home and dry 632.5 *safe, 682.13 successful*
home and hosed 632.5 *safe*
home base 22.1 *baseball*
homebody 816.6 *unsocial person*
home brew 874.12 *alcohol*
home circle 815.7 *human society*
homecoming 344.13 *return*
home-coming 337.20 *return*
homecoming queen 617.8 *exceller*
home computer 65.3 *computer*
Home Counties 124.8 *middle classes, 249.9 regions of Britain*
home economics 45.1 *cookery, 653.3 management*
home farm 68.6 *farm*
home for the dying 630.14 *hospital, 634.2 shelter*
home free 632.5 *safe, 682.13 successful*
home furnishings 47.1 *furniture*
home ground 91.6 *native land, 256.2 environment*
home-grown food 350.7 *food*
Home Guard 17.2 *the military, 632.3 protector, 679.2 defender, 679.15 army*
Home Guardsman 679.8 *soldier*
home help **662**, 621.12 *cleaner, 646.1 worker*
home in 342.11 *focus*
home in on 250.11 *find, 291.9 centre*
homeland 91.6 *native land, 249.4 territorial division, 256.3 home, 816.4 place of confinement*
home learning 6.2 *educational system*
homeless 104.10 *foreign, 108.6 unrelated, 224.13 changeable, 252.10 replaced, 687.4 unprosperous, 743.3 beggarly*
homelessness 108.1 *unrelatedness, 687.1 adversity, 743.7 beggary*
homeless person 104.7 *new arrival, 252.7 displaced person, 622.6 dirty person, 687.5 person in adversity, 743.10 poor person, 816.7 outsider*
homeless shelter 632.2 *protection*
homelife 816.1 *unsociability*
homelike 290.8 *internal*
homeliness 457.3 *external appearance, 556.4 simplicity, 790.1 hideousness, 814.3 familiarity*
home-loving 325.5 *sedentary*
homely 457.10 *aspectual, 556.1 simple, 790.4 ugly, 814.9 familiar*
home-made 243.12 *produced, 656.4 bungled, 658.1 naive*
home movie 66.14 *cine film*
home nurse 60.16 *nurse*
Home Office 16.2 *jurisdiction*
homeopath 60.12, 630.15 *healer*
homeopathic 60.22 *medical*
homeopathy 60.2 *natural medicine, 60.8 treatment*
homeostasis 110.6 *regularity, 122.2 equilibrium, 225.1 stability*
homeostatic 110.17 *regular, 122.6 equal, 225.9 stable*
home-plate umpire 22.2 *baseball player*
homer 682.3 *successful thing*
Homer **48** *Poets*

Homeric 48.19 *narrative, 259.15 big*
Homeric epithet 48.12 *poetic language*
Homeric hymn 10.8 *hymn*
Homeric simile 48.12 *poetic language*
home rule 12.1 *government, 688.7 type of rule, 698.3 independence*
home run 22.5 *batting terms, 330.14 sporting hit, 682.3 successful thing*
home-run hitter 22.2 *baseball player*
home-run leader 22.2 *baseball player*
homesick 782.9 *desirous*
homesickness 782.1 *desire*
home side 305.5 *team*
homespun **67** *Natural Fabrics, 134.17 direct, 243.12 produced, 288.4 textile, 375.7 rough thing, 383.8 rough, 556.1 simple, 658.1 naive*
homestead 68.6 *farm, 256.3 home, 725.1 property*
home stretch 157.9 *close*
home-sweet-home 256.3 *home*
home-thrust 670.18 *hit*
home town 256.3 *home*
home towner 255.8 *national*
home trade 737.5 *commercial trade*
home truth 526.11 *openness, 556.6 naturalness*
home truths 101.5 *realities, 537.3 the truth, 852.7 blame*
home tutor 6.4 *educator*
home visit 60.6 *health care*
homeward 332.10 *clockwise, 344.19 approaching*
homeward-bound 337.27 *returning, 344.19 approaching*
homeward journey 337.20 *return*
homework 594.10 *preparations, 644.1 work*
homeyness 556.4 *simplicity, 814.3 familiarity*
homichlophobia **777** *Phobias by Name*
homicidal 398.24 *murderous, 832.11 cruel*
homicidally 398.25 *lethally*
homicidal mania 510.4 *delusion*
homicidal maniac 241.4 *violent person or animal, 398.11 murderer, 510.7 insane person, 832.8 malefactor, 862.6 evil person*
homicide **398**, 16.39 *crime, 241.2 physical violence, 398.11 murderer, 693.2 violation of the law, 832.7 act of malevolence*
homilist 6.4 *educator*
homily 48.4 *non-fiction, 561.1 dissertation, 564.8 speech, 567.1 address, 876.7 moral*
homing 337.27 *returning, 346.15 entering*
homing in on 250.3 *locating*
homing pigeon 326.8 *messenger*
hominid 54.43 *fossil, 77.34 primate, 202.7 ancient people, 400.1 humankind*
Hominidae 77.16 *primate*
hominids 77.16 *primate*
hominoid 400.12 *human*
homo 401.9 *offensive terms for homosexual, 401.17 male*
homocentric 291.7 *centralized*
homocyclic 57.7 *chemical compound, 57.35 combined*
homoeopathic 630.18 *medical*
homoeopathy 630.11 *medical art*
Homo erectus 202.7 *ancient people, 400.3 uncivilized human*
homogeneity 2.5 *society, 110.2 equivalence, 110.6 regularity, 112.1 uniformity, 116.5 conformity, 134.8 simplicity*
homogeneous 110.12 *same, 110.13 equivalent, 112.5 uniform, 114.7 similar, 134.16 simple*
homogeneous catalysis 57.15 *catalysis*

homogeneously 112.13 *uniformly*, 114.14 *comparably*
homogenetic 116.14 *conforming*
homogenize 110.8 *make the same*, 112.9 *be uniform*, 112.10 *conform*, 114.11 *make similar*, 116.26 *make uniform*
homogenized milk 351.5 *milk*
homogenous 110.17 *regular*, 116.14 *conforming*
homogeneously 134, 110.18 *identically*
homograph 5.17 *word*, 110.2 *equivalence*
homographic 5.42 *worded*, 110.13 *equivalent*
homoiotherm 77.1 *mammal*
homoiothermic 77.25 *mammalian*, 408.12 *warm-hearted*
homoiousia 110.2 *equivalence*
homoiousian 110.13 *equivalent*
homologous 107.5 *interrelated*, 116.14 *conforming*, 122.6 *equal*
homologous chromosome 59.14 *chromosome*
homology 107.1 *relatedness*, 107.2 *interrelatedness*, 116.5 *conformity*
homolysis 57.14 *chemical reaction*
homolytic 57.38 *reactive*
homolytic fission 57.14 *chemical reaction*
Homo neanderthalensis 400.3 *uncivilized human*
homonym 5.17 *word*, 110.2 *equivalence*
homonymic 5.42 *worded*, 110.13 *equivalent*
homonymous 520.6 *meaningful*, 578.10 *equivocal*
homonymy 114.1 *similarity*
homoousia 110.1 *sameness*
homoousian 110.12 *same*
homophobe 481.7 *bigot*, 493.5 *misjudging person*, 822.9 *hater*
homophobia 481.4 *social discrimination*, 493.3 *injustice*
homophobic 481.10 *discriminatory*, 493.8 *unjust*
homophobically 481.17 *prejudicially*
homophone 5.17 *word*, 110.2 *equivalence*
homophonic 5.42 *worded*, 49.30 *harmonic*, 110.13 *equivalent*, 116.13, 433.7 *harmonious*
homophonically 116.33 *harmoniously*
homophony 49.13 *melody*, 116.4 *harmony*, 433.3 *melodiousness*
homophyllic 110.14 *lookalike*
homophyly 110.3 *lookalike*
homopolar bond 57.11 *chemical bond*
homopolymer 57.21 *polymer*
homopolysaccharide 58.4 *polysaccharide*
homopteran 82.10 *insectan*
Homo sapiens 202.7 *ancient people*, 400.1 *humankind*
homosexual 401, 402, 401.17 *male*
homosexual marriage 823.3 *types of marriage*
homosexual neurosis 61.10 *neurosis*
homothallic 89.10 *of fungi*
homothety 52.48 *transformation*
Homs 93 Cities
homunculus 260.4 *little person*
homy 290.8 *internal*, 556.1 *simple*
hon 821.12 *nicknames for lovers*, 826.4 *terms of endearment*
honcho 632.9 *protect*, 653.2 *direct*
Honduras 91 Countries
hone 380.12 *sharpener*, 380.15 *make sharp*, 503.7 *be accurate*
honed 380.3 *sharp-edged*
Honegger 49 Musicians and Composers
honest 16.50 *law-abiding*, 134.17 *direct*, 312.5 *honourable*, 322.16 *open*, 480.13 *really*, 526.15 *open*, 537.18 *truth-*

ful, 556.3 *natural*, 658.1 *naive*, 843.10 *moral*, 857.4 *honourable*, 859.5 *unselfish*, 861.3 *kind*, 863.6 *ethical*, 876.8 *moral*
honest John 537.14 *truthful person*
honestly 101.14 *certainly*, 119.8 *originally*, 134.20 *homogeneously*, 312.13 *straightforwardly*, 322.26 *openly*, 480.13 *really*, 526.17 *frankly*, 537.36 *truthfully*, 772.11 *earnestly*, 857.7 *honourably*, 859.9 *unselfishly*, 861.23 *nicely*, 863.10 *ethically*
honest money 741.1 *money*
honest person 857.3 *honourable person*, 863.4 *virtuous person*
honest sweat 353.8 *sweat*
honest to God 101.14 *certainly*, 526.15 *open*
honest-to-God 99.13 *real*, 537.15 *true*, 537.19 *authentic*
honest to goodness 526.15 *open*
honest-to-goodness 537.15 *true*, 537.19 *authentic*
honesty 84 Flowers and Flowering Plants, 134.1 *purity*, 312.8 *directness*, 322.9, 530.3 *openness*, 537.5 *truthfulness*, 556.6 *naturalness*, 658.2 *naivety*, 843.3 *properness*, 857.1 *probity*, 859.2 *unselfishness*, 861.10 *kindness*, 863.2 *virtues*, 876.2 *good morals*
honey 82.4 *social insect*, 393.9 *jelly*, 394.6 *gelatin*, 402.9 *woman considered as a sex object*, 414.2 *sweetener*, 414.8 *sweeten*, 452.8 *yellow thing*, 821.12 *nicknames for lovers*, 826.4 *terms of endearment*
honey ant 82 Insects
honey badger 77 Placental Mammals
honey bear 77 Placental Mammals
honeybee 82 Insects, 82.4 *social insect*
honey-blond 452.3 *yellow-haired*
honeybun 826.4 *terms of endearment*
honeybunch 821.12 *nicknames for lovers*, 826.4 *terms of endearment*
honey child 821.12 *nicknames for lovers*, 826.4 *terms of endearment*
honey-coloured 452.1, 452.1 *yellow*
honeycomb 317.3 *cavity*, 317.7 *make concave*, 322.6 *porous thing*, 322.20 *hole*, 414.2 *sweetener*, 605.4 *storage*, 628.5 *hurt*
honeycombed 322.14 *holed*, 628.12 *deteriorated*
honeycreeper 78 Birds
honeydew 86 Fruits, 352.2 *secreted substance*, 414.2 *sweetener*
honeyeater 78 Birds
honeyed 853, 414.6 *sweet*, 433.6 *melodious*
honeyed phrases 853.2 *blarney*
honeyed tongue 817.1 *courtesy*
honeyed words 586.2 *flattery*, 821.14 *communication of love*, 826.1 *endearment*, 853.2 *blarney*
honey fungus 89 Fungi, 69.12 *pests and diseases*
honey guide 78 Birds
honeying 821.6 *courtship*
honey locust 85 Trees and Shrubs
honeymoon 156.8 *enrolment*, 763.10 *pleasant thing*, 821.28 *win the love of*, 823.6 *general terms*, 823.15 *marry*
honeymoon cottage 821.13 *abode of love*
honeymooners 823.9 *married couple*
honeymoon period 667.1 *agreement*, 686.3 *time of plenty*, 762.2 *fun*
honeymoon suite 821.13 *abode of love*, 823.6 *general terms*
honey mouse 77 Marsupials

honeypot 258.15 *pot*
honeysuckle 84 Flowers and Flowering Plants, 418.2 *fragrant thing*
honey-tongued 817.8 *good-mannered*, 853.13 *honeyed*
Hong Kong 98 Islands, 93.6 *other cities*
honk 423.1 *loudness*, 432.5 *sing*, 543.12 *signal*, 636.2 *danger signal*, 636.7 *raise the alarm*
honky 91 Names for Inhabitants
Honolulu 93 Cities
honorarium 721.5 *profit*, 729.2 *gift*, 746.3 *pay*, 878.4 *reward for service*
honorary 754.11 *free of charge*
honorary degree 878.1 *reward*
honorary member 665.5 *member*
honorary title 878.1 *reward*
honorary treasurer 741.18 *treasurer*
honorific 849.8 *respectful*
honorifically 9.12 *worshipfully*
honour 792, 792, 7.2 *religiousness*, 7.19 *be religious*, 9.1, 9.7 *worship*, 10.3 *rite of worship*, 10.19 *offer worship*, 29.3 *golf shots*, 134.1 *purity*, 284.14 *give moral support*, 511.14 *commemorate*, 586.11 *motive*, 611.8 *make important*, 681.1 *trophy*, 718.2 *promise*, 746.7 *pay off*, 763.10 *pleasant thing*, 773.6 *fête*, 804.1 *right*, 805.1 *pride*, 812.16 *commemorate*, 817.12 *greet*, 843.3 *properness*, 845.19 *pay*, 849.1 *respect*, 849.16 *revere*, 851.2 *admiration*, 851.3 *praise*, 857.1 *probity*, 863.1 *virtue*, 876.2 *good morals*, 878.1, 878.9 *reward*
honour a bill 746.7 *pay off*
honourable 312, 857, 134.12 *morally pure*, 134.17 *direct*, 658.1 *naive*, 719.7 *observant*, 800.3 *reputable*, 805.14 *proud*, 812.11 *commemorative*, 843.10 *moral*, 847.8 *dutiful*, 859.5 *unselfish*, 861.3 *kind*, 863.5 *virtuous*, 876.8 *moral*
honourable discharge 704.2 *termination*
honourable mention 851.4 *compliment*
honourableness 857.1 *probity*, 859.2 *unselfishness*, 861.10 *kindness*
honourable person 857
honourably 857, 9.12 *worshipfully*, 134.18 *virtuously*, 134.20 *homogeneously*, 312.13 *straightforwardly*, 719.8 *observantly*, 859.9 *unselfishly*, 863.9 *virtuously*
honour and glory 686.1 *prosperity*
honoured 9.11 *worshipped*, 792.9 *decorated*, 800.3 *reputable*, 804.4 *titleholder*, 804.6 *worshipful*, 849.12 *respected*
honour graduate 682.4 *successful person*
honouring 812.2 *commemoration*
honour one's obligations 719.6 *perform*
honour point 544.8 *heraldic device*
honours 804, 792.3 *honour*, 878.1 *reward*
honours list 681.1 *trophy*
honour system 29.2 *golfing terms*
honour the dead 214.9 *commemorate*
honour with 729.5 *give*
honour with a title 878.7 *reward*
honour with one's presence 253.12 *attend*
Honshu 98 Islands
hooch 351.7 *alcoholic drink*, 874.12 *alcohol*
hood 71 Motor Vehicle Parts, 7.11 *vestment*, 41.9 *bobsledding*, 293.5 *body covering*, 293.31 *hide*, 295.15 *headgear*, 295.32 *dress*, 440.6 *shade*, 440.14 *make dark*, 693.9 *crimi-*

nal, 832.8 *malefactor*, 864.10 *bad person*
Hood 48 Poets, **95** Mountains
hooded 293.37 *protected*, 295.29 *dressed*, 531.14 *concealed*
hooded crow 78 Birds
hooded seal 77 Placental Mammals
hoodlum 679.1 *combatant*, 693.9 *criminal*, 736.11 *dishonest person*, 832.8 *malefactor*, 864.9 *wicked person*
hood mould 43 Architectural Decoration
hoodoo 11.3 *witchcraft*, 618.11 *harmfulness*, 862.4 *evil power*
hoodooed 862.10 *inauspicious*
hoodwink 436.15 *blind*, 539.28 *trick*
hoodwinking 539.7 *tricking*
hooey 474.2 *sophism*, 506.1 *nonsense*, 521.5 *empty talk*, 521.14, 538.6 *nonsense*, 540.13 *nonsense*
hoof and horn 246.3 *fertilizer*
hoof-and-horn meal 68.13 *fertilizer*
hoof-and-mouth disease 624.18 *veterinary disease*
hoofed 77.33 *ungulate*
hoofed mammal 77
hoofer 46.5, 51.28 *dancer*
hoof it 46.15 *dance*
Hooghly 96 Rivers
hook 20.7 *angle*, 25.5 *bowling delivery*, 27.9 *stroke*, 27.17 *bat*, 29.3 *golf shots*, 29.7 *golf*, 31.1, 31.8 *hockey*, 31.9 *play hockey*, 98.5 *peninsula*, 135.5 *joint*, 137.8 *fastening*, 137.9 *yoke*, 137.11 *connect*, 283.4 *hanger*, 330.14 *sporting hit*, 335.2 *divert*, 380.8 *sharp-pointed thing*, 380.16 *use a sharp tool*, 539.13, 539.33 *snare*, 590.11 *hunt*, 603.1 *tool*, 603.9 *use*, *tools*, 726.3 *tools for gripping*, 877.18 *prostitute*
hookah 413.7 *tobacco*
hook and eye 137.8 *fastening*, 295.24 *part of garment*
Hooke 52 Scientists
hooked 25.10 *bowling*, 31.8 *hockey*, 135.14 *conjunctive*, 137.15 *connected*, 310.7 *angular*, 539.42 *trapped*, 821.18 *in love*, 823.21 *married*, 875.8 *addicted*
hooked-in 36.13 *windsurfing*
hooked rug 293.9 *floor covering*
hooker 74 Ships and Boats, **74** Sailing Ships and Boats, 35.4 *rugby player*, 864.10 *bad person*, 877.9 *immoral woman*
Hooker 52 Scientists
Hooker's green 453.10 *green pigment*
Hooke's law 56 Named Laws
hookey 591.16 *desertion*
hook in 36.18 *windsurf*, 539.33 *snare*
hooking 31.1 *hockey*, 31.3 *ice hockey*, 31.8 *hockey*
hooking off 33.6 *motor racing terms*
hook, line, and sinker 142.11 *wholly*, 144.9 *completely*
hook off 33.10 *be on the track*
Hook of Holland 98.5 *peninsula*
hook on 135.10 *link*
hook over 310.11 *angle*
hook pass 19.9 *play*, 23.4 *playing terms*
hooks 726.3 *tools for gripping*
hook shot 23.4 *playing terms*
hook up 283.10 *suspend*, 664.16 *join*
hookup 823.2 *alliance*
hook-up 73.7 *miscellaneous aviation terms*, 135.1 *union*, 664.7 *association*
hook up to 130.6 *add*
hook up with 135.10 *link*, 815.13 *fraternize*, 823.15 *marry*, 823.19 *merge*
hookwinked 539.36 *deceived*

horse-riding 32.17 *equine*
horse-riding terms 32
horses 161 Collective Names by Animal, **777** Phobias by Topic
Horses 32
horse sense 4.3 *detachment*, 459.5 *common sense*, 507.2 *intelligence*
horseshoe 11.6 *talisman*, 32.14 *horse-riding terms*, 311.3 *curved things*, 517.6 *good-luck sign*
horseshoe arch 43.5 *arch*
horseshoe bat 77 Placental Mammals
horseshoe crab 81.4 *arthropod*
horseshoe magnet 56.60, 340.3 *magnet*
horseshoe pitching 18 Sporting Activities
horse show 32.6 *horsemanship*, 674.2 *contest*
horse soldier 32.15 *horse person*, 679.20 *cavalryman*
horsetail 87 Grasses, 88.1 *fern*
horsetrader 539.17 *cheat*
horse-trader 737.10 *trader*
horse trading 716.1 *negotiation*
horse-trading 32.14 *horse-riding terms*, 737.9 *bargaining*
horse transport 71.1 *road transport*
horsewhip 32.14 *horse-riding terms*, 879.3 *hit*, 879.14 *instrument of punishment*
horsewhipping 879.12 *corporal punishment*
horsewomanship 32.6 *horsemanship*
horsy 77.33 *ungulate*
Horta 8 Deities
hortative 228.11 *motivational*, 654.7 *advising*
hortatively 228.14 *influentially*, 654.9 *advisably*
hortatorily 228.14 *influentially*, 654.9 *advisably*
hortatory 228.11 *motivational*, 586.19 *persuasive*, 654.7 *advising*
horticultural 69
horticulturally 69, 83.25 *botanically*
horticulture 69, 83.10 *plant science*
Horticulture 69
horticulturist 69
hortus siccus 83.11 *herbarium*
Horus 8 Deities, 78.9 *fabulous bird*
hosanna 431.3 *cry of praise*, 773.2 *fanfare*, 773.12 *hurrah*
Hosanna 10.8 *hymn*
hosannah 812.7 *thanksgiving*
hose 389, 69.6 *garden tool*, 295.20 *legwear*, 322.7 *passageway*, 391.14 *sprinkle*
hose down 389.34 *hose*
hosel 29.4 *golf club*
hosepipe 389.31 *irrigator*
hosier 295.26 *fashion designer*
hosiery 243.7 *produce*, 295.2 *dressing*, 295.20 *legwear*
hosing 389.8 *watering*, 391.5 *sprinkle*
hosing down 389.8 *watering*
hospice 60.10 *hospital*, 256.11 *retreat*, 630.14 *hospital*, 634.2 *shelter*
hospitable 344.21 *welcoming*, 348.15 *receptive*, 665.11 *social*, 755.1 *generous*, 815.15 *sociable*, 819.8 *friendly*, 831.7 *charitable*
hospitably 348.18 *receptively*, 815.18 *sociably*, 819.17 *in friendship*, 831.11 *charitably*
hospital 60, 630.14, 63.20 *building*, 218.5 *resting place*, 243.8 *construction*
hospital administrator 60.17 *paramedic*
hospital bed 630.14 *hospital*
hospital case 624.19 *sick person*
hospital doctor 60.11 *doctor*
hospitality 344.21 *reception*, 348.2 *receptivity*, 350.4 *eating meals*, 734.4 *taking in*, 755.5

generosity, 815.1 *sociability*, 815.8 *good company*, 819.1 *friendship*, 831.2 *charity*
hospitalize 630.20 *doctor*
hospitalized 624.22 *sick*
Hospitaller 7 Members of Religious Orders
hospital patient 624.19 *sick person*
hospital ship 630.14 *hospital*, 679.24 *warship*
hospital social worker 60.17 *paramedic*
hospital train 630.14 *hospital*
hospital ward 60.10, 630.14 *hospital*
host 665, 51.27 *entertainer*, 59.18 *ecology*, 76.4 *type of animal*, 161.20 *crowd*, 161.23 *flock*, 181.4 *throng*, 534.29 *broadcaster*, 606.4 *caterer*, 624.6 *infection*, 653.2 *direct*, 679.18 *army of people*, 730.10 *receive someone*, 815.11 *be sociable*
hostage 224.10 *person who is exchanged*, 699.7 *charge*, 701.5 *subjected person*, 702.5 *prisoner*
hostage taking 670.16 *terrorist attack*
hostel 256.10 *hotel*
hostelry 256.10 *hotel*
hostess 697.3 *attendant*
hostile 473, 820, 832, 111.5 *opposing*, 117.10 *disagreeing*, 136.18 *disagreeable*, 231.4 *counteracting*, 341.10 *defensive*, 663.19 *oppositional*, 666.9 *disagreeing*, 670.21 *aggressive*, 679.33 *combative*, 687.6 *adverse*, 713.9 *protesting*, 785.8 *disliking*, 822.10 *hating*, 841.4 *jealous*, 852.26 *disagreeing*
hostile attack 670.12 *military attack*
hostile critic 854.7 *disparager*
hostile criticism 852.5, 854.2 *criticism*
hostile jury 16.43 *conviction*
hostilely 820, 111.7 *disapprovingly*, 117.16, 136.23 *disagreeably*, 231.5 *counter*, 666.11 *in disagreement*, 713.11 *disapprovingly*, 822.18 *hatefully*, 841.9 *jealously*
hostile person 820
hostile personality 61.8 *disordered personality*
hostile takeover 13.7 *corporation*
hostile verdict 16.43 *conviction*
hostile witness 484.4 *tergiversator*, 856.3 *accuser*
hostilities 674.6 *fight*, 676.4 *belligerency*, 820.4 *act of hostility*
hostility 111.3 *opposition*, 117.4 *disagreement*, 136.4 *disunity*, 231.1 *counteraction*, 618.11 *harmfulness*, 663.1 *opposition*, 666.1 *disagreement*, 670.11 *attack*, 713.1 *protest*, 785.1 *dislike*, 820.1 *enmity*, 822.1 *hate*, 832.1 *malevolence*, 841.1 *jealousy*, 852.4 *disagreement*
hostler 68.16 *farm worker*
hot 55, 408, 16.59 *stolen*, 237.12 *strong to the senses*, 241.6 *violent*, 264.5 *near*, 392.5 *rainless*, 413.9 *piquant*, 736.17 *stolen*, 877.14 *lecherous*
hot air 102.4 *theorization*, 361.10 *elevator*, 370.7 *light thing*, 494.2 *overestimate*, 521.5 *empty talk*, 541.4 *bombast*, 565.3 *talk*
hot-air balloon 73.8 *aircraft*, 361.10 *elevator*
hot-air current 408.8 *hot place*
hot-air vent 408.3 *heater*
hot and bothered 366.16 *restless*, 408.12 *warm-hearted*
hot and cold 111.2 *opposites*
hot as hell 408.10 *on fire*
hot bath 621.6 *bath*
hotbed 69.4 *nursery*, 226.2 *source*, 246.1 *fertility*, 291.4 *centre of activity*, 408.8 *hot place*, 624.6 *infection*, 635.1 *trap*

hot-blooded 241.6 *violent*, 403.7 *susceptible*, 408.12 *warm-hearted*, 829.4 *irascible*
hot-bloodedly 829.9 *irascibly*
hot body 56.35 *heat*
hotbox 364.4 *vortex*
hot chocolate 351.5 *milk*, 414.5 *sweet drink*
hotchpotch 113.2 *assortment*, 161.32 *miscellany*
hot climate 55.38 *climate*
hot corner 22.6 *fielding terms*
hot dog 45.11 *sandwich*
hot-dog 41.14 *ski*
hot-dogging 41.1 *skiing*, 41.12 *ski*
hot-dog stand 350.15 *eating place*
Hotei 8 Deities
hotel 256, 63.20 *building*, 218.5 *resting place*
Hotel 534 Phonetic Alphabet
hotelier 606.4 *caterer*
hotelkeeper 606.4 *caterer*
hotel manager 606.4 *caterer*
hot enough to fry an egg on 408.10 *on fire*
hot flush 408.1 *heat*
hotfoot 648.3 *hasty*, 648.6 *hastily*
hotfoot it 329.4 *be swift*
hot for 782.11 *lustful*
hot goods 734.5 *takings*, 736.4 *stolen goods*
hot gospeller 7.5 *Christian*
hot grog 351.7 *alcoholic drink*
hothead 462.7 *inconsiderate person*, 508.4, 780.3 *rash person*, 829.3 *irascible person*, 830.5 *sullen person*
hot-head 759.9 *feeling person*
hotheaded 241.6 *violent*, 508.5 *foolish*, 780.4 *rash*
hot-headed 648.3 *hasty*, 759.13 *passionate*
hotheadedness 780.1 *rashness*
hothouse 69.4 *nursery*, 226.2 *source*, 408.8 *hot place*
hot-house plant 83.2 *plant*
hot item 16.36 *stolen property*
hot line 534.12 *public telephone system*
hotly 55.65 *meteorologically*, 408.17 *warmly*
hot-metal printing 245.1 *reproduction*
hot money 741.6 *funds*
hotness 56.35, 408.1 *heat*
hot news 533.9 *news story*
hot off the press 201.10 *new*, 472.6 *topical*, 533.14 *journalistic*
hot on the trail 37.9 *on the trail*, 590.18 *pursuant to*
hot pants 295.9 *trousers*, 296.4 *dishabille*, 782.4 *sexual desire*
hot place 408
hotplate 57 Laboratory Apparatus, 45.5 *cooker*, 408.4 *burner*
hot press 376.9 *smoother*
hot-press 376.11 *smooth*
hot property 734.5 *takings*, 736.4 *stolen goods*
hot pursuit 590.2 *chase*
hot rod 71 Motor Vehicles
hot-rod race 33.1 *motor racing*
hot-rod racing 33.1 *motor racing*
hot-shoe 66.19 *flash*
hot shot 811.15 *showman*, 875.6 *drug*
hot-shot 875.10 *drug oneself*
hot shower 621.6 *bath*
hot spell 55.23 *heat*, 408.5 *hot weather*
hot spot 408.8 *hot place*
hot spring 54.25 *eruption*, 98.10 *miscellaneous*, 408.8 *hot place*
hot springs 625.1 *hygiene*, 630.14 *hospital*
hotspur 241.4 *violent person or animal*
hot substance 56.35 *heat*
hotted-up 329.1 *swift*
hot-tempered 408.12 *warm-hearted*, 829.4 *irascible*
Hottentot 1 Peoples, **5** Languages and Groups of Languages

hotter 55.50 *warm*
hottie 408.3 *heater*
hot toddy 351.7 *alcoholic drink*, 414.5 *sweet drink*
hot tub 621.6 *bath*
hot under the collar 828.16 *angry*
hot up 128.5 *make bigger*
hot war 676.1 *war*
hot water 134.3 *purifier*, 251.3 *difficult circumstances*, 621.9 *cleaning agent*, 659.5 *predicament*
hot-water bottle 258.14 *bottle*, 408.3 *heater*
hot-water crust pastry 45.37 *pastry*
hot-water pipes 408.3 *heater*
hot-water tank 408.3 *heater*
hot weather 408, 55.23 *heat*
hot-wiring 71.21 *miscellaneous motoring terms*
Houdan 68 Breeds of Fowl
Houdini 638.3 *escaper*
hound 74 Rigging, 32.8 *hunting*, 77.9 *dog*, 590.6 *hunter*, 820.12 *oppose*, 832.18 *torment*
hounded 590.17 *pursued*
hounding 590.1 *pursuit*, 590.2 *chase*
hound of Hell 241.4 *violent person or animal*
Hound of the Baskervilles 241.4 *violent person or animal*
hounds 161 Collective Names by Animal, 590.6 *hunter*
hound's tooth check 456.2 *check*
houngan 7.8 *priest*, 11.12 *occultist*
hour 106.2 *occurrence*, 185.4 *term*, 187.2 *time period*, 192.3 *chronology*, 269.8 *measure of time*
hour angle 53.5 *celestial sphere*
hour by hour 214.16 *cyclically*
hourglass 191 Timepieces and Timers, **192**, 262.3 *contracted thing*
hourglass figure 262.3 *contracted thing*, 274.7 *thinness*
hour hand 543.5 *indicator*
hourly 110.17 *regular*, 110.20 *regularly*, 185.22 *periodic*, 187.13 *for specified periods*, 212.1 *frequently*, 214.12 *cyclic*, 214.16 *cyclically*
hour of decision 106.3 *critical moment*
hours worked 15.2 *industrial negotiations*
house 256, 41.10 *curling*, 49.9 *popular music*, 51.14 *theatre*, 51.31 *theatregoer*, 63.20 *building*, 243.8 *construction*, 256.1 *habitat*, 293.30 *protect*, 346.7 *entrant*, 382.6 *construction*, 420.2 *hearer*, 567.5 *place of residence*, 632.9 *protect*, 665.1 *party*, 725.1 *property*, 740.8 *store*
House 12.4 *governing body*, 653.12 *US government*
house agent 739.12 *wholesaler*
house arrest 699.4 *detention*, 879.7 *punishment*
houseboat 74 Ships and Boats, 256.9 *mobile home*
housebound 325.5 *sedentary*, 699.15 *detained*
house boy 697.6 *domestic servant*
housebreak 736.12 *steal*
housebreaker 16.40 *lawbreaker*, 346.8 *intruder*, 736.8 *thief*
house-breaker 693.9 *criminal*
housebreaking 346.3 *inroad*, 736.1 *stealing*
housebuilder 646.2 *artisan*
house built on sand 238.5 *weak thing*
housecarl 679.12 *ceremonial troops*
house cat 77.10 *cat*
housecleaner 621.12 *cleaner*
housecleaning 621.2 *cleaning*
housecoat 295.4 *informal dress*, 295.15 *robe*, 296.4 *dishabille*, 814.6 *informal dress*
house curtain 51.17 *stage set*

housed 47.16 *joined*, 256.14 *inhabiting*

house divided against itself 666.1 *disagreement*

housed joint 47.10 *carpenter's term*

house fire 408.6 *fire*

housefly 82 Insects

household 124.1 *average*, 161.17 *family*, 167.15 *everyday*, 255.2 *inhabitants*, 584.10 *familiar*

Household Cavalry 679.14 *armed forces*

householder 255, 723.5 *possessor*, 725.7 *property man*

household gods 8.5 *deity*

household insurance 632.2 *protection*

household management 653.3 *management*

household servant 697.1 *servant*

household troops 679.14 *armed forces*

household words 556.4 *simplicity*

house husband 401.13 *man in the family*

househusband 653.15 *manager*, 823.10 *married man*

housekeeper 606.4 *caterer*, 653.15 *manager*, 662.16 *home help*, 697.6 *domestic servant*

housekeeping 653.3 *management*

houseleek 84 Flowers and Flowering Plants

houseless 252.10 *replaced*

houselights 51.18 *stage lighting*

house lights 439.6 *electric light*

house magazine 532.5 *journal*

housemaid 621.12 *cleaner*, 697.6 *domestic servant*

housemaid's knee 624.16 *rheumatism*

House majority leader 12.8 *politician*, 653.14 *leader*

houseman 60.11 *doctor*

house martin 78 Birds

housemaster 696.9 *educational leader*

House minority leader 12.8 *politician*, 653.14 *leader*

housemistress 696.9 *educational leader*

housemother 696.1 *master*

house number 567.5 *place of residence*

house of cards 238.5 *weak thing*, 379.3 *brittle thing*

House of Commons 12.4 *governing body*, 653.11 *British government*

house of correction 627.10 *reformatory*, 702.1 *prison*

house of detention 702.1 *prison*

house of God 10.11 *place of worship*

house of ill repute 877.6 *brothel*

House of Lords 12.4 *governing body*, 16.20 *British court*, 653.11 *British government*

House of Peers 12.4 *governing body*, 653.11 *British government*

house of prayer 10.11 *place of worship*

house of prostitution 864.8 *wicked place*

House of Representatives 12.4 *governing body*, 653.12 *US government*

house organ 532.5 *journal*

housepainting 792.4 *decorating*

house party 815.5 *party*

house pet 76.3 *domesticated animal*

house physician 60.11 *doctor*

house plant 83.2 *plant*

house-proud 805.14 *proud*

house-raising 665.7 *social gathering*, 815.5 *party*

house rent 751.3 *fee*

house rules 584.5 *tradition*

house-sharing 724.5 *jointly possessing*

Houses of Parliament 43 Noted Buildings

house sparrow 78 Birds

house steward 697.6 *domestic servant*

house surgeon 60.11 *doctor*

housetop 279.3 *architectural summit*, 293.7 *overhead covering*

house-trained 353.26 *urinary*

house-tree-person projective test 61.5 *psychological test*

house-warming 156.8 *enrolment*, 161.9 *social gathering*, 201.4 *beginning*, 665.7 *social gathering*, 815.5 *party*

housewife 402.12 *woman in the family*, 606.4 *caterer*, 646.1 *worker*, 653.15 *manager*, 823.11 *married woman*

housewifery 653.3 *management*

housework 644.1 *work*

housing 293.12 *protective covering*

housing benefit 662.4 *social assistance*

housing estate 93.7 *city district*, 256.6 *apartment block*

Housman 43 Poets

Houston 93 Cities, 93.2 *American cities*

Houyhnhnm 32.1 *horse*

hovel 256.8 *shelter*

hover 161 Collective Names for Birds and Animals, **359,** 78.27 *fly*, 224.12 *be irresolute*, 283.11 *project*, 328.2 *hesitate*, 370.9 *be light*

hovercraft 74 Ships and Boats

hoverfly 82 Insects

hovering 275.9 *high*

hover mower 69.6 *garden tool*

hover on the brink 633.8 *be in danger*

hover over 264.10 *stay near*, 275.15 *be high*, 467.10 *be attentive*

how 327

how? 477.25 *what?*

how about that 786.14 *wonderful*

how are you? 344.23 *hello*

how dare you! 668.11

how do you do? 344.23 *hello*

how-do-you-do 659.5 *predicament*

however 327.16 *how*

however little 121.10 *by degrees*

however much 121.10 *by degrees*

how it goes 106.1 *circumstances*

how it is 105.3 *state of affairs*, 251.2 *circumstances*, 537.3 *the truth*

howitzer 680.11 *guns*

howl 55.58 *blow*, 406.12 *express pain*, 423.2 *outcry*, 423.8 *be loud*, 430.1 *stridency*, 430.4 *be strident*, 431.6 *cry of pain*, 431.13, 432.4 *cry*, 713.3 *gesture of protest*, 713.7 *complain*, 770.8 *grieve*, 771.14 *laugh*, 774.2 *lament*, 774.7 *weep*

howler 493.2 *mistake*, 504.10 *blunder*, 506.2 *solecism*, 559.6 *blunder*, 798.4 *joke*

howler monkey 77 Placental Mammals

howling 241.6 *violent*, 430.7 *strident*, 431.18 *crying*, 432.1 *animal cry*, 432.7 *ululant*

howling gale 55.14 *windiness*

howlingly 432

howling success 682.1 *success*

how much? 477.25 *what?*

Howrah 93 Cities

how's that! 27

how things stack up 105.3 *state of affairs*

how things stand 105.3 *state of affairs*, 251.2 *circumstances*

howzat 27.21 *how's that*

hoya 84 Flowers and Flowering Plants

hoyden 206.8 *young woman*

hoydenish 658.1 *naive*

Hoyle 18 Sporting Personalities, **52** Scientists

HPLC 57.17 *analysis*

Hsi Chiang 96 Rivers

Hsuan-wu 8 Deities

Hu 32 Breeds of Horse and Pony

huaca 8.5 *deity*

Huaca 8 Deities

Huahuantli 8 Deities

Hua-yen 7 Non-Christian Religions

hub 63.8 *machine element*, 158.2 *core*, 291.1 *centre*, 342.5 *focus*, 364.4 *vortex*, 611.3 *chief thing*

hubbie 180.12 *partner*

Hubble 52 Scientists

hubble-bubble 413.7 *tobacco*

Hubble classification 53.7 *galaxy*

Hubble constant 53.7 *galaxy*

Hubble Nebula 53 Nebulae

Hubble Space Telescope 53.24 *telescope*

hub brake 71.11 *bicycle part*

hubbub 151.5 *confusion*, 153.5 *commotion*, 366.2 *tumult*, 423.2 *outcry*, 431.1 *cry*, 434.2 *dissonant noise*, 674.6 *fight*

hubby 823.10 *married man*

hub gear 71.11 *bicycle part*

hubris 51.9 *tragedy*, 494.1 *overestimation*, 805.3 *conceit*, 807.3 *audacity*

hubristic 494.5 *overestimating*, 805.16 *oppressive*

hu ch'in 49 Musical Instruments

huck 67 Natural Fabrics

huckleberry 86 Fruits

huckster 541.10 *boast*, 737.3 *bargain*, 739.11 *pedlar*

huckstering 541.4 *bombast*

Huddersfield 93 Cities

huddle 19, 161.21 *scrum*, 161.39 *come together*, 262.6 *become smaller*, 568.4 *conference*, 654.2 *consultation*, 654.6 *consult*

huddled 262.7 *smaller*

Hudibrastic verse 48.6 *poetry*

Hudson 96 Rivers, 96.3 *US rivers*

Hudson Bay 98.9 *inlet*

Hudson River school 50 Schools and Groups of Artists

hue 444, 56.28 *colour*, 103.4 *nature*, 133.4 *admixture*, 163.4 *type*

hue and cry 431.5 *hunting cry*, 494.2 *overestimate*, 543.6 *word*, 590.2 *chase*, 636.2 *danger signal*

hueless 445.7 *colourless*

huff 36.8 *punting*, 390.22 *blow*, 828.2 *offence*, 828.9 *offend*, 828.14 *make angry*

huffed 828.16 *angry*

huffiness 829.1 *irascibility*

huffy 829.4 *irascible*

hug 138.6 *adhere*, 264.10 *stay near*, 320.3 *enfoldment*, 320.9 *enfold*, 405.9 *give pleasure*, 405.10 *comfort*, 543.3, 543.11 *gesture*, 637.5 *preserve*, 726.1 *retention*, 726.6 *retain*, 815.9 *welcome*, 815.11 *be sociable*, 817.5 *sign of courtesy*, 817.12 *greet*, 819.4 *act of friendship*, 821.14 *communication of love*, 826.1 *endearment*, 826.7 *show endearment for*

huge 259.15 *big*

hugely 120.7 *quantitatively*, 259.20 *largely*

hugeness 259.2 *bigness*

huggable 821.22 *lovable*

huggermugger 113.11 *irregularly*, 529.16 *stealthily*

hugging 821.14 *communication of love*

Hughes 48 Writers, **48** Poets

Hugo 48 Writers, **48** Poets

hug oneself 805.29 *feel pride*, 809.16 *show off*

Huguenot 7.5 *Christian*

Huguenotism 7 Christian Movements

Hui 1 Peoples

huia 78 Birds

Huitzilopochtli 8 Deities

Huixtochuatl 8 Deities

hula 46.2 *dance*

hula ipu 49 Musical Instruments

Hulda 8 Deities

hulk 237.6 *muscleman*, 241.4 *violent person or animal*, 259.10

big person, 656.7 *be clumsy*, 656.10 *unskilled person*

hulkiness 259.6 *squatness*

hulking 259.17 *stocky*, 616.1 *inconvenient*, 656.3, 659.15 *clumsy*

hulky 259.17 *stocky*

hull 36.3 *parts of a sailing boat*, 36.7 *windsurfing*, 289.1 *exterior*, 293.13 *casing*

Hull 93 Cities

hullabaloo 151.5 *confusion*, 153.5 *commotion*, 423.2 *outcry*, 431.1 *cry*, 434.2 *dissonant noise*

hum 426, 55.58 *blow*, 110.11 *be regular*, 181.11 *crowd*, 419.1 *stench*, 419.5 *stink*, 424.1 *faintness*, 424.5 *sound faint*, 426.2 *humming*, 427.9 *resonate*, 428.8 *sound faint*, 432.6 *buzz*, 642.6 *business*, 642.13 *be busy*

human 400, 400.7 *person*, 835.6 *pitying*, 864.13 *venial*

human being 396.1 *life*, 400.7 *person*

human cannonball 51.29 *circus performer*

human communications 2.3 *social environment*

Human Cry 431

human development 2.9 *social change*

hum and haw 576.8 *balance*

human dynamo 642.10 *busy person*

humane 691.4 *lenient*, 831.6 *benevolent*, 833.6 *philanthropic*, 835.6 *pitying*

human ecologist 1.3 *anthropologist*

human ecology 1.1 *anthropology*, 2.1 *sociology*, 59.18 *ecology*

humanely 691.6 *leniently*, 831.10 *benevolently*, 833.8 *philanthropically*, 835.13 *pitifully*

humaneness 691.1 *leniency*, 831.1 *benevolence*, 833.1 *philanthropy*

human error 504.6 *fallibility*

human failing 400.2 *human nature*, 633.7 *vulnerability*

human fallibility 400.2 *human nature*

human flea 82.3 *pest*

human frailty 400.2 *human nature*, 864.3 *venial sin*

human garbage can 872.4 *glutton*

human geography 1.1 *anthropology*, 54.1 *earth science*

human institution 2

human interaction 2.3 *social environment*

humanism 7 Non-Christian Religions, 4.7 *school of thought*, 400.5 *study of mankind*, 627.11 *reformism*

humanist 4.11 *follower of a doctrine*, 367.3 *materialist*, 400.6 *studier of mankind*, 627.12 *reformer*, 698.8 *free-thinker*, 698.10 *independent*, 720.5 *non-observer*

humanistic 4.14 *of a philosophy*, 48.16 *literary*, 400.12 *human*, 698.10 *independent*

humanistically 400.15 *humanly*

humanistic psychology 61.1 *psychology*

humanistic therapy 61.3 *psychiatric treatment*

humanitarian 710.8 *volunteer*, 710.18 *voluntary*, 755.2 *magnanimous*, 755.9 *generous person*, 831.5 *benevolent person*, 833.3 *philanthropist*, 833.6 *philanthropic*

humanitarianism 400.5 *study of mankind*, 831.1 *benevolence*, 833.1 *philanthropy*, 833.2 *public spiritedness*

humanities 6.3 *subject*, 396.7 *studies of life*

humanity 400.1 *humankind*, 691.1 *leniency*, 815.7 *human society*, 831.1 *benevolence*, 833.1 *philanthropy*, 835.1 *pity*

humanize 400.14 *make human*

humankind 400, 396.1 *life,* 815.7 *human society*
Humankind 400
human life 396.1 *life*
humanlike 400.12 *human*
humanlike machine 400
humanly 400, 2.16 *sociologically*
human nature 400
human object 367.5 *object*
humanoid 202.7 *ancient people,* 400.8 *humanlike machine,* 400.12 *human*
human palaeontology 3.2 *archaeology*
human race 400.1 *humankind*
human relations 653.3 *management*
human resources 602
human rights 698.2 *free speech,* 845.3 *prerogative*
human sacrifice 710.7 *martyr*
human scientist 1.3 *anthropologist*
human social behaviour 2.3 *social environment*
human society 815
human species 400.1 *humankind*
human studies 1.1 *anthropology*
human weakness 400.2 *human nature,* 864.3 *venial sin*
Humber 96 *Rivers,* 96.4 *British rivers*
Humberside 92 *Counties*
humble 806, 7.15 *religious,* 9.9 *worshipful,* 127.15 *subordinate,* 362.4 *debase,* 495.4 *underestimating,* 515.7 *thwart,* 556.1 *simple,* 612.2 *obscure,* 673.5, 673.5 *submitting,* 694.9 *obeisant,* 701.6 *subject,* 806.17 *humiliate,* 810.8 *modest,* 817.7 *courteous,* 859.9 *showing respect,* 859.5 *unselfish*
humble apology 867.1 *penitence*
humble confession 867.1 *penitence*
humbled 806, 9.9 *worshipful,* 127.18 *outclassed,* 515.9 *disappointed*
humbleness 127.1 *inferiority,* 556.4 *simplicity,* 806.7 *humility,* 849.3 *respectfulness*
humble oneself 806, 7.19 *be religious,* 9.7 *worship*
humble person 806
humble pie 578.8 *recantation*
humble servant 697.1 *servant*
humble submission 673.1 *submission*
humbling 515.2 *bad outcome*
humbling oneself 9.1 *worship*
humbly 806, 7.23 *religiously,* 9.12 *worshipfully,* 127.22 *basely,* 362.25 *courteously,* 495.6 *pessimistically,* 673.6 *with humility,* 810.17 *modestly,* 817.14 *courteously,* 849.22 *respectfully,* 859.9 *unselfishly*
humbug 474.5 *hypocrisy,* 502.5 *ignorant person,* 521.5 *empty talk,* 521.14 *nonsense,* 538.12 *cheat,* 538.19 *dishonest,* 538.24 *pretend,* 539.11 *hoax,* 539.15 *deceiver,* 540.4 *spuriousness,* 540.13 *nonsense,* 540.15 *false person,* 540.28 *spurious,* 797.2 *pretender*
humbuggery 538.8 *pretence,* 540.4 *spuriousness,* 540.13 *nonsense*
humdinger 259.9 *big thing,* 617.8 *exceller,* 861.17 *good thing*
humdrum 112.8 *monotonous,* 183.3 *repetitiveness,* 183.13 *monotonous,* 412.5 *tasteless,* 556.1 *simple,* 788.1 *boredom,* 788.4 *boring*
humdrumness 112.4 *monotony,* 788.1 *boredom*
Hume 4 *Philosophers*
humect 391.13 *moisten*
humectant 62.4 *drug type,* 389.26 *wetting,* 391.9 *moist*
humectate 391.13 *moisten*
humectus 391.1 *moisture*
humerus 382 *Bones*

Hume's Law 4.8 *philosophical term*
humid 55, 391.9 *moist,* 408.11 *warm,* 626.5 *unhygienic*
humid climate 55.38 *climate*
humidification 391.3 *humidity*
humidify 391.13 *moisten*
humidity 391, 55.6 *weather data,* 55.23 *heat*
humidly 55.65 *meteorologically,* 391.17 *moistly*
humidness 55.23 *heat,* 391.3 *humidity*
humidor 389.19 *measuring instrument,* 413.7 *tobacco*
humiliate 806, 362.4 *debase,* 515.7 *thwart,* 612.13 *make unimportant,* 687.11 *cause adversity,* 701.6 *subject,* 850.27 *desecrate*
humiliated 127.18 *outclassed,* 362.21 *degraded,* 515.9 *disappointed,* 806.3 *humbled,* 867.7 *penitential*
humiliate oneself 801.4 *disreputable,* 867.5 *do penance*
humiliating 806, 850, 362.18 *lowering,* 867.7 *penitential*
humiliatingly 867.8 *penitently*
humiliation 806, 360.4 *fall,* 362.15 *debasement,* 515.2 *bad outcome,* 687.1 *adversity,* 850.8 *indignity*
humility 806, 7.2 *religiousness,* 9.1 *worship,* 127.1 *inferiority,* 495.1 *underestimation,* 673.1 *submission,* 694.3 *obeisance,* 810.1 *modesty,* 817.1 *courtesy,* 849.3 *respectfulness,* 859.2 *unselfishness*
Humility 806
Humism 4.7 *school of thought*
Humist 4.11 *follower of a doctrine*
hummel 49 *Musical Instruments*
humming 426, 426, 432, 427.1 *resonance,* 427.6 *resonant,* 428.4 *faint sound,* 432.3 *insect noise,* 642.19 *busy*
hummingbird 78 *Birds*
humming top 364.6 *rotator*
hummock 95.1, 275.3 *mountain,* 276.2 *lowland,* 316.3 *dome*
hummocky 275.13 *mountainous*
hummus 45.12 *hors d'oeuvre,* 45.34 *vegetarian dish,* 45.52 *Greek dish*
hum of activity 642.6 *business*
humoral 387.16 *rheumy*
humorist 771, 51.27 *entertainer,* 506.4 *buffoon*
humorous 771, 506.5 *nonsensical,* 773.10 *laughing*
humorously 771, 506.9 *nonsensically*
humorousness 771
humour 771, 103.4 *nature,* 105.4 *state of mind,* 234.2 *attitude,* 387.3 *body fluid,* 391.1 *moisture,* 579.3 *whim,* 691.3 *be lenient,* 771.1 *humorousness,* 771.8 *temperament*
Humour 771
humour column 533.9 *news story*
humouring 771, 691.1 *leniency*
humourless 772.1 *solemn,* 788.4 *boring*
humourless comedian 788.3 *boring person*
humourlessness 772.4 *solemnity*
humourous 798.5 *ridiculous*
humoursome 579.1 *capricious*
hump 275.3 *mountain,* 316.2 *bulge,* 316.3 *dome,* 316.5 *be convex,* 326.12 *transport,* 644.6 *work*
humpback bridge 63.21, 327.9 *bridge*
hump-back bridge 327.9 *bridge*
humpback whale 77 *Placental Mammals*
humped 316.4 *convex*
Humperdinck 49 *Musicians and Composers*
Humphreys Peak 95 *Mountains*
humping 326.2 *transportation,* 821.5 *desire*

Hun 5 *Languages and Groups of Languages,* **91** *Names for Inhabitants,* 244.6 *destroyer,* 832.8 *malefactor*
hunch 362.8 *sit,* 362.16 *courtesy,* 464.3 *insight,* 471.2 *theory,* 517.1 *prediction,* 518.2 *basis of supposition,* 583.5 *spontaneity,* 759.2 *impression*
hunchback 309.3 *deformity*
hunchbacked 309.7 *deformed*
hunch down 362.8 *sit*
hunched 362.23 *sedentary*
hundred 92.2 *former British divisions,* 179.9 *treble figures,* 181.7 *myriad,* 249.5 *state*
hundred and forty-four 179.9 *treble figures*
hundred and twenty 179.9 *treble figures*
hundredfold 179.20 *hundredth,* 179.24 *fivefold*
hundred percent 179.9 *treble figures*
hundreds 181.2 *multitude*
hundreds and hundreds 179.9 *treble figures*
hundreds and thousands 179.9 *treble figures,* 181.2 *multitude*
hundreds of thousands 181.2 *multitude*
hundreds place 52.8 *number system*
hundredth 179, 173.4 *less than one*
hundred thousand 179.10 *thousand*
hundred-to-one chance 489.4 *improbability*
hundredweight 75 *General Units,* 179.9 *treble figures,* 369.9 *avoirdupois weight*
Hundred Years' War 17 *Major Wars*
hung 283.7 *suspended*
Hungarian 5 *Languages and Groups of Languages*
Hungarian goulash 45.54 *other dishes,* 133.2 *mixed thing*
Hungarian GP at Hungaroring 33.2 *Formula 1 race*
Hungarian puli 77 *Breeds of Dogs*
Hungarian vizsla 77 *Breeds of Dogs*
Hungary 91 *Countries*
hunger 350.2 *appetite,* 350.22 *eat well,* 743.7 *beggary,* 782.1 *desire,* 782.3 *appetite,* 782.14 *be hungry,* 871.2 *short rations,* 871.5 *fast*
hunger for 782.12 *desire*
hunger pains 406.2 *painful condition*
hunger strike 713.3 *gesture of protest*
hunger striker 871.4 *fasting person*
hunger striking 871.2 *short rations*
hunging 534.10 *telephone call*
hung jury 16.7 *legal trial,* 122.2 *equilibrium*
hung over 874.4 *crapulous*
hung parliament 122.2 *equilibrium*
hungrily 782, 350.28 *carnivorously,* 871.7 *abstemiously,* 872.7 *gluttonously*
hungriness 782.3 *appetite*
hungry 782, 350.26 *eating,* 593.5 *necessitous,* 609.3 *underfed,* 743.3 *beggarly,* 871.6 *fasting*
hungry as a bear 609.3 *underfed*
hungry enough to eat a horse 871.6 *fasting*
hungry for knowledge 6.17 *educatable*
hung-up 153.16 *deranged,* 467.8 *diligent*
hunk 120.2 *certain amount,* 143.7 *piece,* 237.6 *muscleman,* 259.7 *mass,* 340.6 *charmer,* 401.4 *boyfriend,* 789.4 *attractive male*
Hunk 91 *Names for Inhabitants*

hunkers 304.2 *rear end*
hunk of a man 237.6 *muscleman*
hunky 340.9 *attractive*
hunky-dory 617.1 *worthy,* 861.1 *good*
Huns 200.6 *people of the past*
hunt 590, 32.8 *hunting,* 32.15 *horse person,* 32.16 *ride,* 37.2 *hunting,* 37.7 *shoot,* 398.22 *kill animals,* 477.17 *question,* 496.2 *detect,* 496.7 *detection,* 590.2 *chase,* 670.1 *attack*
Hunt 18 *Sporting Personalities,* **48** *Poets*
hunt ball 161.10 *dance,* 815.5 *party*
hunt button 32.8 *hunting*
hunt down 690.6 *suppress,* 820.12 *oppose*
hunted 590.17 *pursued,* 591.18 *avoiding*
hunter 191 *Timepieces and Timers,* **37, 77, 78, 590,** 32.1 *horse,* 32.2 *thoroughbred,* 32.8 *hunting,* 32.15 *horse person,* 192.7 *watch,* 338.16 *archer,* 398.13 *animal killer*
Hunter 32 *Breeds of Horse and Pony,* **96** *Rivers*
hunter-killer 679.24 *warship*
Hunter's bend 74 *Knots*
hunter's moon 53.17 *moon,* 203.4 *autumn*
hunter trials 32.8 *hunting*
hunt for 37.7 *shoot,* 590.8 *pursue*
Hunthaca 8 *Deities*
Huntin 8 *Deities*
hunting 32, 37, 590, 32.17 *equine,* 37.8 *shooting,* 73.5 *flight,* 398.9 *animal killing,* 496.7 *detection,* 590.1 *pursuit,* 590.2 *chase*
hunting accessories 37.3 *hunting equipment*
hunting and fishing equipment 590
hunting association 37.2 *hunting*
hunting at force 37.2 *hunting*
hunting boots 37.3 *hunting equipment*
hunting cap 32.8 *hunting*
hunting clothes 37.3 *hunting equipment*
hunting cry 431
hunting dance 46.4 *historic dancing*
hunting dog 37.6 *sporting dog,* 77.9 *dog*
Hunting Dogs 53 *The Constellations*
Huntingdon Beach 93 *Cities*
Huntingdon's chorea 624.17 *nervous disorder*
hunting equipment 37
hunting horn 32.8 *hunting*
hunting jacket 37.3 *hunting equipment,* 295.11 *jacket*
hunting knife 380.10 *knife*
hunting licence 37.2 *hunting*
hunting limit 37.2 *hunting*
hunting lodge 37.2 *hunting*
hunting party 37.2 *hunting*
hunting rifle 37.3 *hunting equipment*
hunting rifle 590.3 *hunting and fishing equipment*
hunting season 37.2 *hunting,* 203.1 *season*
hunting, shooting, and fishing 590.2 *chase*
hunting spider 82 *Arachnids*
hunt livery 32.8 *hunting*
hunt master 32.8 *hunting,* 32.15 *horse person*
hunt out 349.7 *drive out*
huntress 37.4, 590.6 *hunter*
hunt sab 76.10 *animal welfarist*
hunt saboteur 76.10 *animal welfarist*
hunt secretary 32.15 *horse person*
hunt servant 32.15 *horse person*
huntsman 32.15 *horse person,* 398.13 *animal killer,* 431.9 *crier,* 590.6 *hunter,* 653.15 *manager*
Huntsville 93 *Cities*
hunt terrier 32.8 *hunting*

hunt the facts 477.17 *question*
Huon pine 85 Trees and Shrubs
Hupa 1 Peoples
Hurakan 8 Deities
hurdle 21.1 *track events*, 21.6 *race*, 68.11 *farmland*, 359.5 *jump*, 359.14 *climb*, 359.18 *jump*, 659.8 *snag*, 661.2 *obstacle*
hurdler 21.3 *athlete*, 32.2 *thoroughbred*
hurdle racing 32.7 *horseracing*
hurdles 21.1 *track events*, 21.6 *track*, 32.7 *horseracing*, 674.4 *race*
hurdling 18 Sporting Activities, 359.5 *jump*
hurdy-gurdy 49 Musical Instruments
hurl 330.4, 338.5, 338.23 *throw*
hurl at 670.7 *stone*
hurl a volley of abuse at 827.6 *vilify*
hurl defiance at 668.5 *defy*
hurler 338.14 *thrower*
hurley 31.7 *hurling*
hurling 18 Sporting Activities, **31**, 338.3 *throwing*
hurling association 31.7 *hurling*
hurling ball 31.7 *hurling*
hurling stick 31.7 *hurling*
hurl oneself 241.7 *be violent*
hurly-burly 151.9 *disorder*, 153.5 *commotion*, 366.2 *tumult*
Huron 1 Peoples, **5** Languages and Groups of Languages, **94** Lakes, 94.3 *US lakes*
hurrah 773, 431.3 *cry of praise*, 431.12, 769.8 *cheer*, 773.2 *fanfare*, 851.27 *bravo*
Hurrians 1 Peoples
hurricane 55.13 *wind strength*, 55.16 *wind vortex*, 241.5 *violent weather*, 329.11 *swift thing*, 375.9 *broken water*, 635.1 *trap*
hurricane-force 55.47 *windy*
hurricane lamp 439.5 *incandescent light*
hurricane warning 55.4 *weather forecast*, 636.1 *warning*, 636.2 *danger signal*
hurried 208.12 *early*, 329.1 *swift*, 648.3 *hasty*
hurriedly 208.17 *early*, 648.6 *hastily*
hurriedness 208.1 *earliness*
hurry 208.1 *earliness*, 208.7 *be early*, 228.9 *motivate*, 329.4 *be swift*, 329.8 *speed*, 642.3 *nimbleness*, 642.12 *be active*, 648.1 *hasten*, 648.2 *make haste*, 648.4 *haste*
hurrying 329.1 *swift*
hurryingly 329.14 *swiftly*
hurry off 345
hurry-scurry 642.3 *nimbleness*, 648.4 *haste*
hurry someone up 329
hurry up! 648
hurry-up offence 19.8 *huddle*
hurst 85.4 *trees*
hurt 628, 628, 238.7 *weaken*, 406.1 *pain*, 406.7 *feeling pain*, 406.9 *feel pain*, 406.10 *be painful*, 406.11 *inflict pain*, 616.3 *inconvenience*, 618.11 *harmfulness*, 618.13 *be worthless*, 628.12 *deteriorated*, 631.5 *pain*, 764.12 *be painful*, 828.2 *offence*, 828.9 *offend*, 828.15, 828.15 *resentful*, 832.7 *act of malevolence*, 832.18 *torment*, 844.8 *wrongdoing*, 844.20 *wrong*, 862.2 *affliction*, 862.8 *afflicted*, 862.11 *be evil*, 879.1 *punish*
hurtful 406.8 *inflicting pain*, 616.1 *inconvenient*, 618.5 *harmful*, 758.2 *unpleasant*, 844.16 *in the wrong*, 862.9 *detrimental*
hurtfully 406.13 *painfully*, 828.17 *resentfully*, 862.13 *destructively*
hurtfulness 406.1 *pain*, 618.11 *harmfulness*, 758.4 *unpleasantness*, 862.2 *affliction*
hurting 406.5 *painful*, 406.7 *feel-*

ing pain, 406.8 *inflicting pain*, 743.2 *insolvent*
hurtle 241.7 *be violent*, 329.4 *be swift*, 330.2 *collide*, 330.4 *throw*
hurtless 617.4 *worthwhile*
hurtling 329.1 *swift*
hurt one's pocket 753.9 *be dear*
hurt pride 806.9 *humiliation*
hurt the ears 434.10 *lack harmony*
huruk 49 Musical Instruments
husband 180.12 *partner*, 207.8 *man*, 401.13 *man in the family*, 605.6 *store*, 696.1 *master*, 756.5 *be thrifty*, 823.10 *married man*
husbandhood 823.1 *marriage*
husbandless 824.12 *widowed*, 825.6 *celibate*
husbandly 823.20 *matrimonial*
husbandman 68.15 *agriculturist*, 803.1 *plebeian*
husband one's resources 756.5 *be thrifty*
husbandry 68.1 *agriculture*, 653.3 *management*
hush 422, 566, 129.5 *make smaller*, 422.4 *moderate*, 325.2 *repose*, 422.2, 422.4 *silence*, 424.6, 428.7 *mute*, 429.1, 429.4 *hiss*, 563.15 *strike dumb*
hushed 325.6 *quiescent*, 422.3 *silent*, 424.4 *faint*, 428.1 *faint-sounding*
hushed tones 424.1 *faintness*
hush-hush 527.3 *unsolved*, 529.9 *secret*, 611.5 *important*
hush money 228.5 *positive stimulus*, 729.2 *gift*, 751.8 *levy*, 878.8 *secret money*
Hush Puppies 45.38 *bread*, 295.19 *footwear*
hush up 529.12 *keep secret*
husk 86.3 *fruit structure*, 87.4 *cereal grass*, 132.1 *remainder*, 254.3 *emptiness*, 289.1 *exterior*, 293.13 *casing*
huskily 563.17 *voicelessly*
huskiness 430.2 *hoarseness*, 563.2 *inarticulation*
husks 132.2 *residue*, 614.6 *refuse*
husky 77 Breeds of Dogs, 326.6 *beast of burden*, 424.4 *faint*, 430.8 *hoarse*, 563.10 *low-voiced*
hussar 32.15 *horse person*, 679.20 *cavalryman*
Husserl 4 Philosophers
Hussism 7 Christian Movements
Hussite 7.5 *Christian*
hussy 206.8 *young woman*, 402.6 *loose woman*, 807.12 *impudent person*, 864.9 *wicked person*
hustings 532.7 *publicity*, 580.12 *election*
hustle 228.9 *motivate*, 324.14 *set in motion*, 329.4 *be swift*, 330.1 *impel*, 330.13 *blow*, 338.21 *move forward*, 366.23 *jolt*, 642.3 *nimbleness*, 642.12 *be active*, 648.1 *hasten*, 648.2 *make haste*, 648.4 *haste*, 712.6 *request*, 736.12 *steal*, 877.18 *prostitute*
hustle and bustle 642.3 *nimbleness*
hustle away 648.1 *hasten*
hustle out 339.1 *expel*
hustler 329.13 *swift person*, 336.16 *progressive person*, 642.10 *busy person*, 712.4 *requester*, 877.8 *immoral man*
hustling 329.1 *swift*, 642.19 *busy*, 736.1 *stealing*
hut 256.8 *shelter*
hutch 68.7 *farm building*, 77.20 *abode of mammals*, 256.8 *shelter*, 323.4 *closed place*, 323.10 *enclose*, 634.3 *animal shelter*
Hutcheson 4 Philosophers
hutia 77 Placental Mammals
Hutton 18 Sporting Personalities, **52** Scientists
Hutu 5 Languages and Groups of Languages
Huxley 52 Scientists

Huygens 52 Scientists
Huygens' principle 365.5 *wave*
Huysmans 48 Writers
huzzah 431.3 *cry of praise*, 773.2 *fanfare*, 851.5, 851.16 *acclaim*
Hwange 93 Cities
hyacinth 54 Minerals, **54** Gemstones, **84** Flowers and Flowering Plants, 454.6 *blue thing*
hyacinthine 454.1 *blue*, 455.6 *purple*
Hyadese 53 Clusters
hyaenid 77.8 *flesh-eating mammal*
Hyaenidae 77.8 *flesh-eating mammal*
hyalin 442.8 *transparent thing*
hyaline 442.1 *transparent thing*
hyalite 442.8 *transparent thing*
hyaloplasm 79.7 *cell*
hyacinth 455.3 *purple thing*
hybrid 133, 5.17 *word*, 133.12 *mixed*, 140.4 *compound*
hybrid computer 65.3 *computer*
hybrid expression 5.17 *word*
hybrid flower 133.5 *hybrid*
hybridization 57.12 *valence*, 133.1 *mixture*
hybridize 133.8 *mix*
hybrid language 5.26 *dialect*
hybrid orbital 57.12 *valence*
hybrid rose 133.5 *hybrid*
hydathode 352.3 *gland*
hydatid 81.13 *invertebrate larva*
Hyde Park 93.5 *London*
Hyderabad 93 Cities
hydnum 89 Fungi
Hydra 53 The Constellations
hydragogue 62.4 *drug type*, 387.9 *solvent*
hydra-headed 245.15 *reproduced*
hydrallazine 62 Medication
hydrangea 84 Flowers and Flowering Plants
hydrant 389.13 *irrigator*
hydrargaphen 62 Medication
hydrate 389, 57.10 *salt*, 57.26 *react*, 140.5 *combine*, 389.29 *water*
hydrated 57.36 *acid*, 389.21 *watery*
hydration 57 Types of Chemical Reaction, 389.6 *hydrate*
hydraulic 389.21 *watery*, 603.8 *mechanical*
hydraulically 389, 603.10 *instrumentally*
hydraulic brake 71 Motor Vehicle Parts
hydraulic lift 361.9 *lifter*
hydraulic power 235.4 *energy*
hydraulic press 63.6 *simple machine*
hydraulics 387.13 *fluid mechanics*, 389.18 *hydrography*, 603.5 *mechanics*
hydraulic suspension 71 Motor Vehicle Parts
hydraulic tailgate 361.9 *lifter*
hydraulis 49 Musical Instruments
hydrazine 57 Common Chemical Compounds
hydro 630.14 *hospital*
hydrocele 387.3 *body fluid*, 624.4 *disease*
hydrocephalic 624.23 *diseased*
hydrocephalous 624.23 *diseased*
hydrochloric acid 57 Common Chemical Compounds
hydrochlorothiazide 62 Medication
hydrocortisone 58 Hormones, **62** Medication
hydrocybe 89 Fungi
hydrodynamic 56.98 *physical*, 389.21 *watery*
hydrodynamically 56.100 *physically*, 389.36 *hydraulically*
hydrodynamics 56.2 *classical physics*, 387.13 *fluid mechanics*, 389.18 *hydrography*, 603.5 *mechanics*
hydroelectric 64.36 *electronic*, 235.17, 410.10 *powered*
hydroelectrically 410.12 *powerfully*

hydroelectricity 235.6 *source of energy*, 410.4 *electricity*
hydroelectric power 235.4 *energy*
hydroelectric power station 64.32 *power station*
hydroelectric station 235.6 *source of energy*
hydroflumethiazide 62 Medication
hydrofoil 74 Ships and Boats
hydrogen 57 Chemical Elements, 58.15 *essential element*, 338.13 *fuel*, 361.10 *elevator*, 372.5 *gas*
hydrogenate 57.26 *react*, 388.26 *aerate*
hydrogenated fat 395.8 *fat*
hydrogenation 57 Types of Chemical Reaction
hydrogen balloon 361.10 *elevator*, 388.13 *gas balloon*
hydrogen bomb 235.8 *nuclear power*, 680.16 *bomb*
hydrogen bond 57.11 *chemical bond*
hydrogencarbonate 57 Types of Compounds
hydrogen cyanide 631.8 *poison*
hydrogen electrode 57.19 *electrochemistry*
hydrogenous 57.34 *elemental*
hydrogen peroxide 57 Common Chemical Compounds, **62** Medication, 445.4 *colour remover*, 630.3 *prophylactic*
hydrogen sulphide 57 Common Chemical Compounds, 419.2 *something that makes an unpleasant smell*
hydrogeology 387.13 *fluid mechanics*
hydrograph 389.19 *measuring instrument*
hydrographer 97.6 *oceanographer*, 389.20 *hydrologist*
hydrographic 54.49 *geophysical*, 97.8 *oceanographic*
hydrographically 97.12 *oceanographically*
hydrography 389, 54.17 *ocean research vessel*, 97.5 *oceanography*
hydroid 81.21 *coelenterate*
hydrokinetics 387.13 *fluid mechanics*, 389.18 *hydrography*
hydrol 389.1 *water*
hydrolase 58.11 *enzyme*
hydrolic cement 44.9 *industrial ceramics*
hydrological 96, 54.48 *geological*
hydrological cycle 54.10, 389.17 *water cycle*
hydrologically 54.66 *geographically*, 96.13 *fluently*
hydrologist 389, 54.3 *geologist*
hydrology 54.1 *earth science*, 387.13 *fluid mechanics*, 389.18 *hydrography*
hydrolyse 57.26 *react*, 141.4 *deconstruct*
hydrolysis 57 Types of Chemical Reaction, 141.2 *deconstruction*, 389.6 *hydrate*
hydrolytically 141.7 *to pieces*
hydromancy 11.9 *divination*, 389.15 *holy water*, 517.2 *divination*
hydromechanics 389.18 *hydrography*, 603.5 *mechanics*
hydrometeor 55.24 *precipitation*, 389.17 *water cycle*
hydrometeorologic 55.54 *pluvial*
hydrometeorology 55.1 *meteorology*
hydrometer 56.88 *barometer*, 268.8 *meter*, 371.3 *relative density*, 387.12 *flowmeter*
hydrometric 268.16 *micrometric*, 389.21 *watery*
hydrometrically 389.36 *hydraulically*
hydrometry 268.2 *micrometry*, 387.13 *fluid mechanics*, 389.18 *hydrography*
hydropathy 389.7 *hydrotherapeutics*
hydrophilic 57.32 *solid*

hydrophilic colloid 57.3 *phase*
hydrophobia 777 Phobias by Name, 510.3 *mental deterioration*, 624.6 *infection*
hydrophobic 57.32 *solid*
hydrophobic colloid 57.3 *phase*
hydrophobophobia 777 Phobias by Name
hydrophyte 83.2 *plant*
hydrophytic 83.14 *of plants*
hydroponic 69.16 *horticultural*
hydroponically 68.22 *agriculturally*, 69.20 *horticulturally*
hydroponic food 350.7 *food*
hydroponics 68.4 *arable farming*, 69.5 *gardening*, 389.18 *hydrography*
hydroscopically 389.36 *hydraulically*
hydrosol 57.3 *phase*
hydrosphere 54.5 *earth*, 389.17 *water cycle*
hydrospheric 54.50 *terrestrial*, 96.12 *hydrologic*
hydrostat 389.19 *measuring instrument*
hydrostatic 96.12 *hydrologic*, 389.21 *watery*
hydrostatically 389.36 *hydraulically*
hydrostatic head 389.17 *water cycle*
hydrostatics 387.13 *fluid mechanics*, 389.18 *hydrography*
hydrotherapeutic 389.27 *cleansing*
hydrotherapeutics 389
hydrotherapy 389.7 *hydrotherapeutics*, 630.13 *therapy*
hydrothermal water 389.1 *water*
hydrous 389.21 *watery*
hydroxyamphetamine 62 Medication
hydroxyprogesterone 62 Medication
hydroxystilbamidine 62 Medication
hydroxyurea 62 Medication
hydroxyzine 62 , 62 Medication
Hydrozoa 81.7 *coelenterate*
hydrozoan 81.7, 81.21 *coelenterate*
Hydrus 53 The Constellations
hyena 77 Placental Mammals, 350.18 *eater*, 832.8 *malefactor*, 872.4 *glutton*
hyetographic 55.54 *pluvial*
hyetography 55.1 *meteorology*
Hygeia 623.3 *health*
Hygiea 53 Minor Planets
hygiene 625, 60.6 *health care*, 621.2 *cleaning*, 621.5 *ablutions*, 623.4 *healthfulness*, 630.3 *prophylactic*, 632.2 *protection*, 637.1 *preservation*
Hygiene 625
hygienic 625, 134.15 *purifying*, 621.16 *clean*, 621.18 *cleansing*, 623.2 *healthful*, 630.17 *remedial*, 632.5 *safe*, 632.7 *tutelary*, 637.6 *preserving*
hygienically 625, 134.19 *purely*, 621.19 *cleanly*, 623.8 *healthily*, 632.10 *safely*
hygienics 625.1 *hygiene*
hygienist 625, 60.17 *paramedic*
Hyginus 53 Rills and Valleys
hygric 389
hygrodeik 389.19 *measuring instrument*
hygrograph 55.7 *weather instruments*, 389.19 *measuring instrument*
hygrographic 55.42 *barometric*
hygrometer 55.7 *weather instruments*, 56.88 *barometer*, 268.8 *meter*, 389.19 *measuring instrument*
hygrometric 55.42 *barometric*, 268.16 *micrometric*, 389.28 *hygric*
hygrometry 268.2 *micrometry*, 389.18 *hydrography*
hygrophilous 389.28 *hygric*
hygrophobia 777 Phobias by Name

hygroscope 389.19 *measuring instrument*
hygroscopic 389.28 *hygric*
hygrothermagraph 389.19 *measuring instrument*
hygrothermal 389.28 *hygric*
hylomorphism 4.7 *school of thought*
hylozoism 4.7 *school of thought*
Hymen 823.14 *gods and goddesses of marriage*
hymenal rites 823.5 *wedding*
hymeneal 823.6 *general terms*, 823.20 *matrimonial*
hymenium 89.4 *fungal body*
Hymenoptera 82 Orders of Insects
hymenopteran 82.10 *insectan*
hymenotomy 60 Surgical Operations
Hymettus 95 Mountains
Hymettus honey 414.2 *sweetener*
hymn 10, 48.7 *poem*, 49.5 *sacred music*, 433.2 *song*, 773.2 *fanfare*, 837.2 *thanks*
hymnal 10.8 *hymn*, 49.32 *instrumental*
hymnary 10.8 *hymn*
hymning 10.8 *hymn*
hymnody 49.5 *sacred music*
hymnographical 10.21 *ritualistic*
hymnography 10.8 *hymn*
hymnological 10.21 *ritualistic*
hymnology 10.8 *hymn*, 49.5 *sacred music*
hymn-singing 9.1 *worship*, 10.3 *rite of worship*, 10.8 *hymn*
hymn tune 49.5 *sacred music*
hymn writer 49.24 *musician*
hynotic trance 11.10 *psychic phenomenon*
hyoid bone 382 Bones
hyoscine 62 Medication
hyoscyamine 62 Medication
hypabyssal intrusion 54.30 *igneous rock*
Hypatia 4 Philosophers
hype 494.1 *overestimation*, 494.4 *overestimate*, 532.8 *public relations* , 532.16 *publicize*, 541.1 *exaggeration*, 541.4 *bombast*, 541.7 *exaggerate*, 541.10 *boast*, 586.6 *advertising*, 627.1 *improve*, 851.15 *compliment*, 853.1 *flattery*, 853.8 *flatter*, 875.4 *drug taker*
hyped 541.12 *exaggerated*
hyped up 403.7 *susceptible*
hypegiaphobia 777 Phobias by Name
hyper 642.18 *active*
hyperacidity 624.8 *indigestion*
hyperactive 403.7 *susceptible*, 642.18 *active*
hyperactive child 642.10 *busy person*
hyperactivity 642.9 *overactivity*
hyperaesthesia 403.2 *ability to sense*
hyperbaton 557.1 *ornament*
hyperbola 52.42 *circle*, 311.2 *bend*
hyperbole 357.9 *excessiveness*, 494.1 *overestimation*, 541.1 *exaggeration*, 557.2 *affectation*, 757.5 *unrestrainedness*
hyperbolic 52.81 *curvilinear*, 311.4 *curved*, 357.13, 541.12 *exaggerated*, 557.4 *ornate*, 757.2 *unrestrained*
hyperbolically 311.7 *curvedly*, 357.16 *excessively*, 494.7 *overoptimistically*, 541.16 *exaggeratedly*, 557.6 *ornately*
hyperbolic cosine 52.52 *trigonometric function*
hyperbolic function 52.52 *trigonometric function*
hyperbolic orbit 53.21 *orbit*
hyperbolic sine 52.52 *trigonometric function*
hyperbolic spiral 52.40 *curve*
hyperbolic tangent 52.52 *trigonometric function*
hyperbolism 541.1 *exaggeration*
hyperbolize 541.7 *exaggerate*

hyperboloid 52.45 *curved surface*, 52.83 *spherical*
hyperborean 263.8 *distant*, 332.13 *directional*
hypercathexis 61.28 *cathexis*
hypercritical 659.14 *troublesome*, 852.28 *fault-finding*
hypercriticalness 852.6 *fault-finding*
hypercriticism 852.6 *fault-finding*
hypercube 52.35 *space*
hyperfocal distance 66.18 *exposure time*
hypericum 84 Flowers and Flowering Plants
Hyperion 8 Deities, 53.15 *sun*
hypermarket 350.17 *food shop*, 740.8 *store*
hypermetropia 436.2 *poor sight*
hypermetropic 436.9 *weak-sighted*
hyperphysical 11.16 *psychic*
hyperphysics 11.1 *occultism*
hyperplasia 259.4 *gigantism*
hyperpyrexia 624.3 *symptom*
hypersensitive 759.21 *sensitive*
hypersensitization 66.10 *graininess*
hypersonic 329.1 *swift*
hypersonically 329.14 *swiftly*
hypersonic speed 329.8 *speed*
hyperspace 52.35 *space*
hypersphere 52.35 *space*
hypersthene 54 Minerals
hypertension 624.3 *symptom*, 624.10 *cardiovascular disease*
hyperthermia 624.3 *symptom*
hyperthermy 624.3 *symptom*
hyperthyroidism 624.4 *disease*, 642.9 *overactivity*
hypertrophied 261.7 *bigger*
hypertrophy 259.4 *gigantism*, 261.1 *growth*, 261.5 *make bigger*, 261.6 *become bigger*
hype up 851.15 *compliment*
hypha 89.4 *fungal body*
hyphal 89.10 *of fungi*
hyphen 135.5 *joint*, 136.5 *separator*, 137.4 *means of connection*, 543.7 *punctuation*
hyphenate 135.8 *unite*, 543.13 *punctuate*
hyphenated 137.15 *connected*, 543.17 *punctuated*
hyphenation 135.1 *union*
hyping 541.15 *bombastic*
hypnophobia 777 Phobias by Name
Hypnos 8 Deities
hypnosis 11.10 *psychic phenomenon*, 404.4 *anaesthetic*, 512.1 *oblivion*, 630.5 *analgesic*, 643.9 *sleep*, 761.4 *desensitization*
hypnotherapeutic 61.32 *psychological*
hypnotherapist 61.30 *psychiatrist*
hypnotherapy 61.3 *psychiatric treatment*, 630.13 *therapy*
hypnotic 11.15 *witchlike*, 62.4 *drug type*, 62.15 *sedative*, 228.11 *motivational*, 233.12 *appealing*, 242.8 *moderating*, 404.9 *anaesthetic*, 512.8 *oblivious*, 586.19 *persuasive*, 630.17 *remedial*, 695.9 *compelling*, 767.3 *reliever*, 767.8 *relieving*
hypnotically 11.25 *occultly*, 228.14, 233.14 *influentially*, 340.13 *attractionally*, 512.16 *obliviously*, 695.11 *compellingly*
hypnotic suggestion 61.3 *psychiatric treatment*
hypnotic trance 61.14 *trance*
hypnotism 11.1 *occultism*, 233.2 *occult influence*, 340.2 *pulling power*
hypnotist 11.12 *occultist*, 51.27 *entertainer*, 228.7 *motivator*, 629.12 *repairer*, 630.15 *healer*
hypnotize 11.21 *bewitch*, 228.10 *manipulate*, 233.10 *be a prevailing influence*, 340.12 *lure*, 404.12 *anaesthetize*, 761.7 *render insensitive*
hypnotized 11.19 *bewitched*, 228.12 *motivated*, 404.7 *anaesthetized*, 643.4 *not awake*

hypnotizer 228.7 *motivator*
hypo 66.12 *development*
hypocaust 408.3 *heater*
hypochondria 61.10 *neurosis*, 510.4 *delusion*, 624.1 *ill health*
hypochondriac 238.4 *weakling*, 510.7 *insane person*, 539.15 *deceiver*, 624.19 *sick person*, 624.21 *unhealthy*
hypocrisy 474, 538, 539, 540, 484.2 *reversal*, 539.4 *false-heartedness*, 657.1 *cunning*, 853.1 *flattery*, 858.1 *improbity*
hypocrite 539, 117.6 *misfit*, 118.7 *imitator*, 224.6 *fickle person*, 309.5 *defacer*, 474.6 *sophist*, 484.4 *tergiversator*, 499.3 *assenter*, 538.12 *cheat*, 539.15 *deceiver*, 540.15 *false person*, 657.3 *cunning person*, 797.2 *pretender*
hypocritical 474, 539, 540, 117.11 *unfit*, 176.11 *double-edged*, 484.5 *countering*, 538.18 *pretentious*, 578.11 *equivocating*, 657.4 *cunning*, 853.12 *flattering*, 858.5 *dishonourable*
hypocritically 474, 540, 117.17 *unsuitably*, 309.14 *distortedly*, 484.9 *to the contrary*, 538.27 *pretentiously*, 540.36 *falsely*, 858.11 *dishonourably*
hypocriticalness 538.9, 539.3, 540.3 *hypocrisy*
hypocycloid 52.40 *curve*
hypodermic 276.6 *lower*
hypodermic needle 322.2 *opener*, 380.8 *sharp-pointed thing*
hypogastric 276.6 *lower*
hypogeal 277.12 *under*
hypogene 277.12 *under*
hypogeous 277.12 *under*
hypogeum 277.4 *deep thing*
hypoglycaemic shock therapy 61.3 *psychiatric treatment*
hypogynous 84.12 *of flowers*
hypoid gear 71 Motor Vehicle Parts
hypolimnion 276.4 *low thing*
hypomania 510.4 *delusion*
hypomaniac 510.7 *insane person*
hypomenorrhoea 353.11 *menstruation*
hypophyge 43 Architectural Decoration
hypophysectomy 60 Surgical Operations
hypotaxis 5.30 *syntax*
hypotension 624.3 *symptom*, 624.10 *cardiovascular disease*
hypotenuse 52.43 *triangle*
hypotheca 90.3 *plant body*
hypothecator 4.10 *philosopher*
hypothermia 409.3 *chill*, 624.3 *symptom*
hypothesis 4.1 *philosophy*, 4.8 *philosophical term*, 52.65 *theory*, 56.6 *law*, 102.4 *theorization*, 226.3 *rudiment*, 461.6 *idea*, 463.4 *explanation*, 471.2 *theory*, 473.3 *line of argument*, 497.1 *belief*, 518.1 *supposition*
hypothesist 4.10 *philosopher*, 518.4 *theorist*
hypothesis testing 52
hypothesize 4.20 *philosophize*, 52.89, 102.14 *theorize*, 461.16 *have an idea*, 471.17 *theorize*, 473.15 *state*, 518.5 *suppose*
hypothesized 518.8 *supposed*
hypothesizer 4.10 *philosopher*
hypothetic 52.69 *theoretic*
hypothetical 4.13 *of philosophy*, 56.99, 102.10 *theoretical*, 471.10 *theoretical*, 473.11 *logical*, 491.1 *uncertain*, 497.14 *believed*, 518.7 *suppositional*, 519.12 *imaginary*
hypothetical argument 518.1 *supposition*
hypothetically 4.25 *theoretically*, 102.18 *ideally*, 471.20 *theoretically*, 473.18 *arguably*, 497.16 *believably*, 518.10 *supposedly*
hypsographic 275.14 *altimetric*
hypsography 275.5 *height measure*

identifying sign 543.1 *sign*
identifying with 116.10 *in accord*
identify oneself 544
identify with 109.9 *correlate*, 116.21 *be in accord*
identikit 167.15 *everyday*
Identikit 544.3 *means of identification*, 547.2 *reproduction*
identity 165, 544, 4.8 *philosophical term*, 52.21 *set*, 52.26 *equality*, 109.3 *correlation*, 116.1 *accord*, 165.2 *personality*, 174.4 *singularity*, 520.4 *type of meaning*
identity card 483.6 *documentation*, 544.3 *means of identification*
identity element 52.21 *set*
identity matrix 52.22 *matrix*
identity number 544.3 *means of identification*
ideogram 5.13 *letter*
ideograph 5.13 *letter*
ideographic 5.41 *lettered*
ideological 4.13 *of philosophy*, 461.11 *reasoning*, 471.13 *ideal*
ideologically 471, 4.25 *theoretically*
ideological war 676.1 *war*
ideologist 461.7 *thinker*, 471.9 *person of ideas*, 833.3 *philanthropist*
ideologue 4.10 *philosopher*, 471.9 *person of ideas*
ideology 471, 4.2 *philosophical system*, 497.2 *religious belief*
ideophobia 777 Phobias by Name
Ides 185.11 *date*
idiochromosome 59.14 *chromosome*
idiocy 460.1 *lack of intellect*, 508.1 *folly*, 510.1 *insanity*, 510.2 *subnormality*
idioglossia 5.5 *nonstandard language*
idiolect 5.5 *nonstandard language*, 165.10 *specialized language*, 523.12 *unintelligible thing*, 549.4 *literary style*, 564.1 *faculty of speech*
idiom 5.3 *spoken language*, 5.26 *dialect*, 165.10 *specialized language*, 520.4 *type of meaning*, 549.1 *style*, 556.4 *simplicity*, 564.1 *faculty of speech*
idiomatic 5.39 *of language*, 165.16 *characteristic*, 520.6 *meaningful*, 558.3 *elegant*
idiomatically 5.49 *colloquially*, 549.10 *stylistically*
idiomatic speech 5.3 *spoken language*, 564.1 *faculty of speech*
idiophone 49.25 *musical instrument*
idioplasm 59.7 *cell*
idiosyncrasy 168, 117.3 *nonconformity*, 119.1 *originality*, 165.3 *characteristic*, 234.2 *attitude*, 549.1 *style*, 579.3 *whim*, 584.2 *tendency*, 620.7 *defect*
idiosyncratic 103.9 *characteristic*, 117.9 *nonconforming*, 165.16 *characteristic*, 168.14 *eccentric*, 215.5 *unusual*, 579.1 *capricious*
idiosyncratically 117.15 *dissimilarly*, 549.10 *stylistically*
idiot 460.3 *unintelligent person*, 508.3 *foolish person*, 510.7 *insane person*, 798.3 *object of ridicule*
idiot box 534.22 *television set*
idiotic 460.5 *lacking intellect*, 460.7 *intellectually subnormal*, 506.5 *nonsensical*, 508.5 *foolish*
idiotically 460.11 *unintelligently*, 508.8 *foolishly*
idiot savant 510.7 *insane person*, 786.5 *person of wonder*
I disagree 476.13 *no*
idle 230.7 *be operational*, 240.5 *inert*, 278.2 *superficial*, 325.5 *sedentary*, 325.8 *be motionless*, 328.1 *move slowly*, 328.5 *unhurried*, 466.4 *uninterested*, 600.1 *unused*, 600.3 *not wanted*, 614.2 *futile*, 641.3 *inactive*,

641.4 *not act*, 643.2 *not working*, 643.3 *not participating*, 643.12 *be inactive*, 645.7 *leisurely*, 649.4 *at ease*
idle fancy 519.7 *idealism*
idle gossip 565.3 *talk*, 568.2 *chat*
idle hours 641.1 *inaction*
idle moments 645.1 *leisure*
idleness 777 Phobias by Topic, **643**, 240.1 *inertness*, 466.2 *lack of interest*, 600.10 *disuse*, 614.4 *futility*, 641.1 *inaction*, 645.1 *leisure*, 649.1 *ease*
idler 209.4 *latecomer*, 328.15 *slow person*, 470.3 *negligent person*, 591.17 *avoider*, 641.2 *nonacting person*, 643.8 *nonworker*, 685.3 *quitter*, 720.6 *evader*
idle rich 641.2 *nonacting person*, 643.8 *nonworker*
idler wheel 364.6 *rotator*
idle speech 521.5 *empty talk*
idle talk 568.2 *chat*
idly 240.7 *inertly*, 328.16 *slowly*, 466.8 *disinterestedly*, 600.12 *out of use*, 641.5 *without action*
Ido 5 Languages and Groups of Languages
idol 9, 8.5 *deity*, 51.22 *actor*, 547.6 *image*, 617.8 *exceller*, 786.5 *person of wonder*, 821.11 *loved one*
idolater 9, 864.9 *wicked person*
idolatrize 9, 849.16 *revere*
idolatrous 9, 851.18 *approving*
idolatrously 9.12 *worshipfully*
idolatry 9, 821.1 *love*, 851.3 *praise*, 864.6 *religious sin*
idolism 9.2 *idolatry*
idolization 8.9 *deification*, 9.2 *idolatry*, 821.1 *love*, 849.2 *admiration*
idolize 8.17 *deify*, 9.8 *idolatrize*, 786.9 *wonder*, 821.23 *love*, 849.16 *revere*, 851.14 *praise*
idolized 8.15 *deified*, 9.11 *worshipped*
idolized person 9
idolizer 9.5 *worshipper*, 9.6 *idolater*
idolizing 849.10 *reverent*
I don't believe it 514.14 *good heavens*, 786.14 *wonderful*
idoxuridine 62 Medication
Idun 8 Deities
idyll 48.7 *poem*
idyllic 48.19 *narrative*, 405.6, 763.1 *pleasant*
i.e. 165.31 *namely*, 524.18 *in other words*
if 106.15 *under the circumstances*, 518.11 *supposing*
iffy 589.8 *chance*, 633.1 *dangerous*, 801.4 *disreputable*
if not 106.15 *under the circumstances*
if one can trust one's ears 528.19 *reportedly*
I-formation 19.7 *offence*
if possible 486.9 *possibly*
if so 106.15 *under the circumstances*
if worst comes to worst 687.12 *in adversity*
I give up 502.13 *who knows?*
igloo 409.6 *Arctic*
igneous 54.56 *petrographic*, 408.10 *on fire*
igneous rock 54, 54.28 *rock*
ignis fatuus 102.2 *illusion*, 439.9 *firefly*
ignite 408.15 *burn*, 439.24 *light*, 828.12 *become angry*
ignition 71 Motor Vehicle Parts, 408.6, 439.8 *fire*
ignition key 71 Motor Vehicle Parts
ignition system 410.2 *lighter*
ignoble 858.5 *dishonourable*
ignobly 858.11 *dishonourably*
ignominious 801.4 *disreputable*, 827.9 *vituperative*
ignominiously 827.13 *vituperatively*
ignominy 801.1 *disrespect*
ignoramus 460.3 *unintelligent person*, 502.5 *ignorant person*

ignorance 462, 502, 404.1 *lack of feeling*, 436.7 *figurative blindness*, 440.7 *spiritual darkness*, 460.2 *unintelligence*, 508.1 *folly*, 577.7 *opinionatedness*, 656.8 *unskilfulness*, 658.2 *naivety*
ignorance 502
ignorant 502, 436.12 *blind to*, 440.11 *benighted*, 460.6 *unintelligent*, 462.8 *thoughtless*, 508.5 *foolish*, 595.4 *untrained*, 656.2 *unskilled*, 658.2 *naive*
ignorantly 502, 460.11 *unintelligently*, 585.6 *unaccustomedly*
ignorant of 585.1 *unaccustomed*
ignorant person 502
ignore 816, 147.7 *exclude*, 404.11 *be unfeeling*, 421.8 *be deaf*, 436.16 *be blind to*, 468.12 *be inattentive*, 468.13 *be thoughtless*, 470.6 *be neglectful*, 577.9 *be obstinate*, 581.1 *reject*, 591.1 *avoid*, 600.5 *not use*, 641.4 *not act*, 668.6 *be insubordinate*, 673.3 *submit*, 720.7 *not observe*, 818.7 *be discourteous*, 838.6 *be ungrateful*, 839.11 *condone*, 850.21 *disregard*
ignored 838.4 *unthanked*, 850.18 *undervalued*
ignore formalities 648.2 *make haste*
ignore instructions 693.15 *be disobedient*
ignore the consequences 462.12 *lack thought*, 780.5 *be rash*
ignoring 147.12 *exclusively*, 468.4 *thoughtlessness*
Igorot 5 Languages and Groups of Languages
iguana 79 Reptiles, 79.2 *lizard*
iguanodon 79 Fossil Reptiles
IJsselmeer 94 Lakes
Ik 1 Peoples
ikat weave 67.10 *woven*
ikkyo 26.10 *aikido*
Ilah 8 Deities
Ilamatecuhtli 8 Deities
Ilat 8 Deities
Ile de France 68 Breeds of Sheep
ileectomy 60 Surgical Operations
ileocolostomy 60 Surgical Operations
ileoproctostomy 60 Surgical Operations
ileostomy 60 Surgical Operations
Iliamna 94 Lakes
ilium 382 Bones
ilk 163.4 *type*, 163.8 *genealogy*, 560.6 *sort*
ill 238, 618.11 *harmfulness*, 618.15 *worthlessly*, 624.21 *unhealthy*, 624.22 *sick*, 659.25 *difficultly*, 687.6 *adverse*, 862.8 *afflicted*, 862.12 *evilly*
ill-adapted 117.11 *unfit*
ill-advised 493.9 *misjudged*, 508.5 *foolish*, 616.1 *inconvenient*, 656.4 *bungled*, 780.4 *rash*
ill-assorted 117.8 *contradictory*
ill-balanced 123.3 *unequal*
ill-behaved 659.14 *troublesome*
ill-bred 652.18 *badly behaved*, 658.1 *naive*, 795.7 *vulgar*, 818.6 *bad-mannered*
ill-breeding 652.4 *bad conduct*, 795.3 *grossness*, 818.2 *bad manners*
ill-chosen 117.8 *contradictory*
ill-considered 508.5 *foolish*, 616.1 *inconvenient*, 648.3 *hasty*, 656.1 *unskilful*, 656.4 *bungled*, 780.4 *rash*
ill-contrived 616.1 *inconvenient*, 656.4 *bungled*
ill-defined 164.20 *generalized*, 307.5 *shapeless*, 438.2 *difficult to see*, 441.6 *murky*, 482.5 *vague*, 656.4 *bungled*
ill-devised 656.4 *bungled*
ill-disciplined 870.8 *overindulgent*
ill-disposed 618.5 *harmful*, 820.6 *hostile*, 832.10 *malevolent*
ill disposition 832.1 *malevolence*

ill-dressed 457.10 *aspectual*
illegal 16, 236.10 *powerless*, 618.3 *bad*, 709.5 *vetoed*, 710.17 *offered*, 720.14 *violating*, 844.16 *in the wrong*, 846.8 *unentitled*, 864.15 *criminal*, 866.7 *sinful*, 877.11 *immoral*
illegal alien 201.8 *new arrival*
illegal bodycheck 31.5 *lacrosse*
illegal borrowing 733, 736
illegal entry 346.3 *inroad*
illegal execution 879.13 *capital punishment*
illegal gain 721.5 *profit*
illegal hold 26.5 *wrestling*
illegal hooking 35.3 *rugby play*
illegal immigrant 255.6 *illegal occupant*
illegality 16, 618.9 *badness*, 709.1 *veto*, 720.4 *infraction*, 844.6 *unlawfulness*, 864.7 *criminality*, 866.1 *guilt*, 866.3 *sin*
illegalize 16.75 *make illegal*, 846.17 *criminalize*
illegally 16, 16.89 *guiltily*, 236.14 *powerlessly*, 709.7 *by veto*, 710.20 *persuasively*, 720.16 *disobediently*, 846.19 *unrightfully*, 864.21 *criminally*
illegally ground the ball 19.18 *be penalized*
illegal motion 19.13 *penalty*
illegal occupant 255, 846.7 *usurper*
illegal occupation 846.3 *arrogation*
illegal occupier 846.7 *usurper*
illegal offer 710
illegal speed 329.8 *speed*
illegal use of hands 19.13 *penalty*
illegibility 521.1 *lack of meaning*, 523.11 *unintelligibility*, 546.3 *obliteration*
illegible 521.10 *meaningless*, 523.1 *unintelligible*, 546.6 *obliterated*, 659.12 *problematic*
illegibly 523.13 *unintelligibly*
illegitimacy 16.35 *illegality*, 540.4 *spuriousness*, 709.1 *veto*, 844.6 *unlawfulness*
illegitimate 16.55 *illegal*, 540.28 *spurious*, 709.5 *vetoed*, 844.16 *in the wrong*, 846.8 *unentitled*
illegitimately 16.82 *illegally*, 709.7 *by veto*, 846.19 *unrightfully*
illegitimize 16.75 *make illegal*
ill-equipped 236.11 *unprotected*, 609.2 *unprovided*
ill-fated 687.8 *unlucky*
ill-favoured 790.4 *ugly*
ill feeling 820, 785.1 *dislike*, 822.1 *hate*, 832.4 *bitterness*
ill feelings 828.1 *resentment*
ill-fitted 117.11 *unfit*
ill fortune 211.3 *lost chance*, 589.2 *luck*, 687.3 *bad fortune*, 862.3 *bad luck*
ill-fortune 229.2 *chance*
ill-furnished 609.2 *unprovided*
ill-gotten 736.17 *stolen*
ill-gotten gains 721.5 *profit*, 730.2 *something received*, 734.5 *takings*, 736.4 *stolen goods*
ill health 624, 620.5 *imperfection*
Ill Health 624
ill humour 828.1 *resentment*, 830.1 *sullenness*
ill-humoured 828.15 *resentful*, 829.4 *irascible*, 830.6 *sullen*
ill-humouredly 829.9 *irascibly*, 830.13 *sullenly*
illiberality 577.7 *opinionatedness*
Illich 4 Philosophers
illicit 16.55 *illegal*, 539.35 *deceptive*, 540.31 *fraudulent*, 709.5 *vetoed*, 844.16 *in the wrong*, 846.8 *unentitled*
illicit love 877, 698.6 *liberality*, 821.8 *love affair*
illicitly 16.82 *illegally*, 538.28 *dishonestly*, 709.7 *by veto*, 844.28 *immorally*, 846.19 *unrightfully*
illicitness 16.35 *illegality*, 709.1 *veto*, 844.6 *unlawfulness*
illicit practice 538.10 *dishonesty*,

539.10, 540.8 *fraud*
illimitability 184.4 *infinity*
illimitable 184.1 *infinite*
illimitably 184.1 *infinitely*
Illinois 1 Peoples, **92** American States, **96** Rivers
ill-intentioned 832.10 *malevolent*
illite 54 Minerals
illiteracy 502.1 *ignorance*
illiterate 5.39 *of language*, 502.5 *ignorant person*, 502.6 *ignorant*
illiterately 5.49 *colloquially*
illiterate speech 5.5 *nonstandard language*
ill-judged 5.6 *bungled*
ill-lit 440.8 *dark*, 441.5 *dim*
ill luck 211.3 *lost chance*
ill-made 309.7 *deformed*
ill-mannered 652.18 *badly behaved*, 656.3 *clumsy*, 818.6 *bad-mannered*, 838.3 *ungrateful*
ill-mannered person 652.5 *badly behaved person*
ill-matched 117.8 *contradictory*, 123.3 *unequal*, 823.21 *married*
ill-matching 117.8 *contradictory*
ill-mated 117.8 *contradictory*
ill nature 822.1 *hate*, 830.1 *sullenness*, 832.1 *malevolence*
ill-natured 822.10 *hating*, 830.6 *sullen*, 832.10 *malevolent*
ill-naturedly 822.18 *hatefully*, 830.14 *irritably*
illness 624, 624.1 *ill health*, 628.9 *dilapidation*, 687.1 *adversity*, 822.7 *hated thing*, 862.2 *affliction*
illogical 108, 229.6 *motiveless*, 460.6 *unintelligent*, 474.7 *sophistic*, 487.1 *impossible*, 504.15 *erroneous*, 521.10 *meaningless*
illogicality 108.1 *unrelatedness*, 229.1 *lack of motive*, 460.2 *unintelligence*, 474.1 *sophistry*, 487.5 *impossibility*, 521.1 *lack of meaning*
illogically 229.8 *by chance*, 460.11 *unintelligently*, 474.14 *sophistically*, 487.11 *impossibly*, 521.13 *meaninglessly*
illogicalness 474.1 *sophistry*
ill-omened 211.10 *untimely*, 636.8 *warning*, 776.6 *inauspicious*
ill person 626.4 *infectious person*
ill-planned 616.1 *inconvenient*
ill-prepared 656.4 *bungled*
ill-proportioned 559.7 *graceless*
ill-provided 595.7 *unequipped*
ill-repute 801.1 *disrepute*
ill service 832.7 *act of malevolence*
ill-sorted 117.8 *contradictory*, 123.3 *unequal*
ill-sounding 559.9 *inelegant*
ill-spent 614.2 *futile*
ill-starred 211.10 *untimely*, 687.8 *unlucky*, 776.6 *inauspicious*
ill-suited 117.11 *unfit*
ill-supplied 609.2 *unprovided*
ill temper 830.3 *irritableness*
ill-tempered 830.7 *irritable*
ill-timed 117.11 *unfit*, 211.10 *untimely*, 493.9 *misjudged*, 616.1 *inconvenient*, 656.4 *bungled*
ill-treat 618, 241.8 *use violence*, 601.1 *misuse*, 832.18 *torment*, 844.20 *wrong*
ill-treated 601.4 *misused*
ill-treatment 599.6 *use*, 601.2 *misuse*, 618.11 *harmfulness*, 832.7 *act of malevolence*
ill turn 832.7 *act of malevolence*
illuminance 56.24 *light emission*
illuminate 4.21 *rationalize*, 6.22 *educate*, 50.19 *paint*, 437.10 *make visible*, 439.24 *light*, 444.15 *colour*, 475.16 *explain*, 524.8 *interpret*, 526.1 *display*, 526.3 *reveal*, 550.2 *clarify*, 792.10 *decorate*
illuminated 50.27 *painted*, 437.2 *clear*, 439.18 *lit*, 439.22 *enlightened*, 475.11 *explanatory*
illuminated sign 439.6 *electric*

light
illuminati 459.8 *intellectual person*, 501.7 *academia*
Illuminati 7 Christian Movements, 439.13 *enlightenment*
illuminating 6.16 *educational*, 439.15 *lucent*, 475.11 *explanatory*, 524.14 *interpretive*, 528.16 *informative*, 560.11 *descriptive*, 561.5 *expository*
illuminatingly 6.25 *educationally*, 439.30 *lightly*, 475.22 *demonstrably*
illumination 6.1 *education*, 50.2 *painting*, 50.7 *picture*, 56.24 *light emission*, 437.7 *that which makes visible*, 439.1 *light*, 439.3 *lightening*, 439.13 *enlightenment*, 475.3 *explanation*, 496.8 *finding out*, 501.1 *knowledge*, 524.1 *interpretation*, 547.2 *reproduction*, 792.2 *pattern*
illuminations 812.8 *salute*
illuminator 50.16 *artist*, 792.7 *decorator*
illumine 439.24 *light*
ill-use 601.1, 601.2 *misuse*, 618.14 *ill-treat*, 844.20 *wrong*
illusion 102, 11.10 *psychic phenomenon*, 435.5 *imagination*, 457.4 *something that appears*, 504.6 *fallibility*, 510.4 *delusion*, 519.5 *fantasy*, 539.5 *falseness*, 539.9 *sleight of hand*
illusionary 435.20 *visual*
illusionism 50.4 *treatment*, 102.3 *delusion*
illusionist 50.24 *pictorial*, 118.7 *imitator*
illusive 519.12 *imaginary*, 539.40 *illusory*
illusorily 368.13 *metaphysically*
illusory 102, 539, 100.10 *unreal*, 368.8 *nonmaterial*, 435.20 *visual*, 457.9 *ostensible*, 474.7 *sophistic*, 519.12 *imaginary*
illustrate 4.21 *rationalize*, 299.5 *outline*, 437.10 *make visible*, 475.16 *explain*, 480.2 *prove*, 524.8 *interpret*, 547.11 *paint*, 560.14 *describe*, 792.10 *decorate*
illustrated 475.11 *explanatory*, 524.15 *interpreted*
illustrated dictionary 5.28 *dictionary*
illustrated lecture 51.5 *show*
illustration 50.7 *picture*, 299.1 *outline*, 437.6 *visible thing*, 475.3 *explanation*, 480.5 *proof*, 524.1 *interpretation*, 547.2 *reproduction*, 792.2 *pattern*
illustrative 50.26 *artistic*, 475.11 *explanatory*, 480.7 *verificatory*, 522.1 *intelligible*, 524.14 *interpretive*, 547.13 *representational*, 560.11 *descriptive*
illustratively 50.31 *artistically*, 475.22 *demonstrably*, 480.11 *verifiably*, 524.18 *in other words*, 547.14 *representationally*, 560.18 *descriptively*
illustrator 50.16 *artist*, 475.7 *demonstrator*, 547.4 *person who makes a representation*, 792.7 *decorator*
illustrious 804.5 *entitled*
ill will 759.6 *bad feeling*, 785.1 *dislike*, 820.3 *ill feeling*, 822.1 *hate*, 832.1 *malevolence*, 842.1 *envy*, 862.1 *evil*
ill-willed 832.10 *malevolent*
ill wind 618.11 *harmfulness*, 687.1 *adversity*, 862.3 *bad luck*
ill-wisher 635.2 *troublemaker*, 785.3 *disliked person*, 820.5 *hostile person*
ill wishes 822.1 *hate*, 827.4 *malediction*
ill-wishing 832.10 *malevolent*
Illyrian 5 Languages and Groups of Languages
Ilmagah 8 Deities
ilmenite 54 Minerals
Ilokano 5 Languages and Groups of Languages
Ilythyia-Leucothea 8 Deities
Ilyushin 52 Scientists

image 547, 9.3 *idol*, 50.7 *picture*, 52.29 *mathematical function*, 61.24 *symbolism*, 66.3 *photograph*, 102.7 *artificiality*, 114.5 *counterpart*, 118.2 *copy*, 289.3 *appearance*, 435.8 *reflection*, 457.4 *something that appears*, 519.4 *ideality*, 543.1 *sign*, 547.9 *represent*
image blur 66.8 *composition*
image-building 519.1 *imagination*
image distance 56.31 *lens element*
image-maker 532.10 *publicizer*
image recorder 435.8 *reflection*
imagery 48.12 *poetic language*, 519.1 *imagination*
imaginable 519, 486.5 *possible*, 518.8 *supposed*
imaginably 486.11 *potentially*
imaginal 289.8 *apparent*
imaginary 519, 52.72 *complex*, 100.10 *unreal*, 102.9 *illusory*, 102.10 *theoretical*, 169.8 *odd*, 289.8 *apparent*, 368.8 *nonmaterial*, 435.20 *visual*, 457.9 *ostensible*, 518.8 *supposed*, 786.8 *wonderful*
imaginary number 52.6 *complex number*, 169.2 *kind of number*
imaginary part 52.6 *complex number*
imaginary world 368.1 *nonmaterial world*, 519.4 *ideality*
imagination 435, 471, 519, 100.5 *nonreality*, 119.1 *originality*, 435.4 *visualization*, 540.9 *falsification*, 657.1 *cunning*
Imagination 519
imaginative 519, 50.26 *artistic*, 119.4 *original*, 435.21 *seeing*, 471.11 *ideational*, 506.5 *nonsensical*, 540.32 *falsified*, 560.12 *narrative*, 657.4 *cunning*
imaginative exercise 519.4 *ideality*
imaginative journalism 309.4 *distortion of the truth*
imaginatively 471, 519, 50.31 *artistically*, 119.8 *originally*, 560.18 *descriptively*
imaginativeness 246.2 *productiveness*, 471.8, 519.1 *imagination*
imagine 102, 435, 471, 519, 119.7 *originate*, 243.10 *produce*, 435.16 *visualize*, 461.12 *think*, 497.8 *be of the opinion*, 518.5 *suppose*, 538.21 *lie*, 540.22 *falsify*, 560.15 *recount*
imagined 243.12 *produced*, 471.11 *ideational*, 518.8 *supposed*, 519.12 *imaginary*, 538.13 *untrue*, 539.40 *illusory*
imaging 53
imaging system 53.27 *imaging*
Imagism 48 Literary Groups and Movements
imago 61.24 *symbolism*, 82.5 *larva*, 471.1 *idea*
I'm all right Jack 870.4 *self-absorption*
imam 7.8 *priest*, 126.5 *superior*, 696.6 *religious leader*
Imari ware 44 Types of Ceramics
imbalance 108.4 *distortion*, 123.1 *inequality*, 224.1 *changeableness*, 309.1 *distortion*, 309.9 *distort*
imbalanced 108.8 *distorted*, 224.13 *changeable*
imbecile 238.10 *ill*, 460.3 *unintelligent person*, 508.3 *foolish person*, 510.7 *insane person*
imbecilic 460.5 *lacking intellect*, 460.7 *intellectually subnormal*, 508.5 *foolish*
imbecility 460.1 *lack of intellect*, 508.1 *folly*, 510.2 *subnormality*
imbibe 348.11 *ingest*, 351.13 *drink*
imbibing 351.1, 351.16 *drinking*
imbibition 348.4 *intake*, 351.1 *drinking*
imbibitory 348.17 *absorbent*
imbricate 43.14 *roofed*, 293.26 *overlie*

imbricated roof 43.6 *roof*
imbrication 293.1 *covering*
imbroglio 133.3 *miscellany*, 659.4 *problem*
imbrue 389.29 *water*, 444.15 *colour*
imbruement 389.9 *soaking*
imbu 86 Fruits
imbue 133.8 *mix*, 140.5 *combine*, 167.10 *assimilate*, 253.11 *be present*, 354.2 *inject*, 389.31 *steep*, 444.15 *colour*, 584.18 *habituate*
imbued 584.13 *fixed*
I'm done for 397.24 *I'm dying*
I'm dying! 397
IMF 732.4 *lending institution*
I'm guilty 867.9 *sorry*
Imhotep 8 Deities
imine 57 Types of Compounds
imino acid 58.8 *amino acid*
imipramine 62 Medication
imitate 114, 118, 51.32 *act*, 102.17 *fabricate*, 110.7 *be the same*, 110.9 *duplicate*, 167.8 *comply*, 183.16 *repeat*, 222.4 *be a substitute*, 457.11 *appear*, 538.24, 540.20 *pretend*, 543.11 *gesture*, 547.9 *represent*, 733.9 *borrow illegally*, 734.10 *take away*, 736.15 *infringe*, 850.24 *ridicule*
imitated 114.8 *simulated*, 118.12 *imitative*, 519.12 *imaginary*, 733.11 *borrowed*
imitating 733.3, 736.6 *illegal borrowing*, 850.14 *ridiculing*
imitation 118, 118, 539, 102.7 *artificiality*, 102.12 *not the real thing*, 110.4 *duplicate*, 114.1 *similarity*, 114.2 *copy*, 114.8 *simulated*, 118.2 *copy*, 167.1 *conformity*, 183.1 *repetition*, 457.5 *impression*, 460.2 *unintelligence*, 539.39 *imitative*, 540.7 *pretence*, 540.10 *fake*, 540.35 *disguised*, 547.1, 560.9 *representation*, 707.7 *deputizing*, 733.3 *illegal borrowing*, 734.3 *taking away*, 736.6 *illegal borrowing*, 850.4 *ridicule*
Imitation 118
imitative 118, 539, 114.8 *simulated*, 183.9 *repeated*, 460.6 *unintelligent*, 540.33 *fake*, 540.35 *disguised*, 547.13 *representational*, 707.7 *deputizing*
imitatively 118, 110.18 *identically*, 114.14 *comparably*, 460.11 *unintelligently*, 707.8 *by proxy*
imitativeness 460.2 *unintelligence*
imitator 118, 114.4 *person who copies*, 167.6 *conformist*, 733.6 *borrower*, 736.10 *infringer*
immaculacy 134.1 *purity*, 619.3 *perfection*, 865.1 *innocence*, 876.3 *moral purity*
immaculate 134.13, 446.5 *pure*, 619.1 *perfect*, 621.16 *clean*, 863.5 *virtuous*, 865.5 *innocent*, 876.9 *pure*
Immaculate Conception 876.3 *moral purity*
immaculately 134.19 *purely*, 619.7 *perfectly*, 863.9 *virtuously*, 865.11 *innocently*
immaculateness 619.3 *perfection*, 621.1 *cleanness*, 876.3 *moral purity*
immanent 103.6 *intrinsic*
immaterial 11.18 *spiritual*, 104.8 *intruder*, 108.7 *illogical*, 368.8 *nonmaterial*, 372.1 *sparse*, 438.1 *invisible*, 612.1 *unimportant*, 783.11 *insignificant*
immaterialism 102.1 *unreality*, 368.2 *unworldliness*
immaterialist 368.8 *nonmaterial*
immaterialistic 368.8 *nonmaterial*
immateriality 102.1 *unreality*, 104.1 *extraneousness*, 368.2 *unworldliness*, 372.3 *sparseness*, 612.5 *unimportance*, 783.5 *insignificance*
immaterialize 11.20 *occult*,

368.12 *enter a nonmaterial world*
immaterially 104.18 *extraneously,* 368.13 *metaphysically*
immaterialness 368.2 *unworldliness*
immature 82, 201, 206, 595, 145.4 *incomplete,* 211.10 *untimely,* 415.5 *acid,* 453.3 *raw,* 460.6 *unintelligent,* 585.1 *unaccustomed,* 620.2 *incomplete,* 656.2 *unskilled,* 658.1 *naive,* 685.4 *uncompleted,* 865.7 *naive*
immature amphibian 79.8 *young amphibian*
immaturely 201, 206, 595, 211.15 *at the wrong time,* 460.11 *unintelligently,* 585.6 *unaccustomedly,* 685.7 *incompletely,* 865.12 *naively*
immature personality 61.8 *disordered personality*
immature thing 453.13 *young thing*
immaturity 201, 206, 595, 145.1 *incompleteness,* 206.1 *youth,* 211.1 *untimeliness,* 460.2 *unintelligence,* 620.5 *imperfection,* 656.8 *unskilfulness,* 658.2 *naivety,* 685.1 *noncompletion,* 865.3 *naivety*
immeasurability 184
immeasurable 184, 8.13 *divine,* 181.8 *numberless*
immeasurably 184, 181.13 *numerously*
immediacy 191, 208.1 *earliness,* 253.4 *availability,* 264.1 *nearness,* 648.4 *haste*
Immediacy 191
immediate 191, 208.12 *early,* 253.10 *available,* 264.5 *near,* 329.1 *swift,* 332.15 *direct,* 472.6 *topical,* 648.3 *hasty*
immediate circle 253.4 *availability*
immediate constituent analysis 5.30 *syntax*
immediately 191, 99.23 *now,* 208.17 *early,* 329.14 *swiftly,* 648.6 *hastily*
immediateness 191.1 *immediacy*
Immelann turn 73.5 *flight*
immemorial 1.14 *societal,* 185.21 *lasting through time,* 190.9 *agelong,* 202.12 *olden*
immemorially 202.21 *archaically*
immemorial wisdom 1.8 *tradition*
immense 184.2 *immeasurable,* 248.13 *spacious,* 259.15 *big*
immensely 184.11 *immeasurably,* 248.15 *spaciously,* 259.20 *largely*
immenseness 184.6 *vastness,* 259.2 *bigness*
immensity 184.6 *vastness,* 248.4 *spaciousness,* 259.2 *bigness*
immerge 354.4 *immerse*
immerse 354, 277.14 *deepen,* 389.29 *water*
immersed 354, 277.12 *under,* 389.24 *flooded*
immerse oneself in 354.4 *immerse*
immersion 354, 10.5 *Christian rite,* 277.1 *depth,* 360.2 *sinkage,* 389.9 *soaking,* 389.15 *holy water*
immersion heater 408.3 *heater*
immigrant 149, 149, 104.7, 201.8 *new arrival,* 255.7 *settler,* 255.13 *resident,* 344.18 *arriving,* 346.7 *entrant,* 346.15 *entering*
immigrate 104.14 *be foreign,* 149.16 *migrate,* 255.15 *settle,* 346.14 *enrol*
immigration 346.4 *right of entry*
imminent 208, 199.11 *future,* 344.19 *approaching,* 513.7 *expected*
imminently 199.14 *in the future,* 208.18 *soon*
immiscibility 136.3 *separateness,* 139.1 *nonadhesion*
immiscible 117.7 *disparate,* 136.17 *unjoined,* 139.8 *nonad-*

hesive
immiscibly 139.10 *noncohesively*
immission 348.1 *admittance*
immix 133.8 *mix*
immobile 217.7 *permanent,* 225.9 *stable,* 240.5 *inert,* 325.4 *motionless,* 641.3, 643.1 *inactive*
immobility 217.1 *permanence,* 225.1 *stability,* 240.1 *inertness,* 325.1 *motionlessness,* 641.1 *inaction,* 643.5 *inactivity*
immobilization 225.1 *stability*
immobilization techniques 26.10 *aikido*
immobilize 26.13 *do martial arts,* 217.6 *make permanent,* 325.9 *make motionless,* 643.14 *make inactive*
immobilized 26.15 *wrestling*
immoderate 241.6 *violent,* 610.6 *excessive,* 698.12 *unconditional,* 757.2 *unrestrained,* 846.10 *undue,* 870.8 *overindulgent*
immoderately 610.8, 698.21 *excessively,* 757.9 *extravagantly,* 870.12 *self-indulgently*
immoderateness 846.6 *excessiveness*
immoderation 610.2 *overdoing it,* 698.6 *liberality,* 757.5 *unrestrainedness,* 870.3 *overindulgence*
immodest 526.15 *open,* 809.8 *vain,* 877.13 *unchaste*
immodestly 809.19 *vainly,* 877.21 *immorally*
immodesty 809.1 *vanity,* 877.3 *sexual immorality*
immolate 398.20 *kill ritually*
immolation 398.6 *ritual killing*
immoral 844, 864, 877, 618.3 *bad,* 693.1 *disobedient,* 795.9 *ribald,* 801.4 *disreputable,* 858.5 *dishonourable,* 862.7 *evil*
immoralist 652.5 *badly behaved person*
immorality 877, 618.9 *badness,* 628.8 *perversion,* 693.1 *disobedience,* 858.1 *improbity,* 862.1 *evil,* 864.2 *vice*
Immorality 877
immorally 844, 864, 877, 693.17 *disobediently,* 858.11 *dishonourably,* 862.12 *evilly*
immoral man 877
immoral woman 877
immortal 8.13 *divine,* 126.14 *best,* 184.3 *eternal,* 186.5 *timeless,* 188.9 *permanent,* 190.8 *eternal,* 217.7 *permanent*
immortality 8.2 *divine attribute,* 184.7 *eternity,* 186.2 *agelessness,* 190.3 *life without end,* 217.1 *permanence,* 396.5 *life cycle*
immortalization 8.9 *deification*
immortalize 8.17 *deify,* 186.4 *perpetuate,* 190.6 *make eternal,* 217.6 *make permanent*
immortalized 8.15 *deified*
immortal life 396.5 *life cycle*
immortally 184.12 *eternally,* 217.9 *permanently*
immotive 325.4 *motionless*
immovability 225.1 *stability,* 373.8 *mental hardness,* 577.6 *determination*
immovable 135.15 *tied,* 217.7 *permanent,* 225.9 *stable,* 325.4 *motionless,* 574.5 *steady,* 577.3 *unyielding,* 718.9 *fast,* 725.8 *propertied*
immovables 725.2 *legal terms*
immovably 135.18 *inextricably,* 718.17 *fastly*
immune 16.63 *acquitted,* 625.4 *hygienic,* 632.6 *invulnerable,* 638.8 *escaping,* 698.9 *free,* 718.6 *secure,* 761.1 *insensitive,* 848.5 *exempt*
immunity 625.1 *hygiene,* 632.1 *safety,* 638.1 *escape,* 698.1 *freedom,* 718.1 *protection,* 839.1 *forgiveness,* 848.1 *exemption*
immunization 60.6 *health care,* 625.1 *hygiene,* 630.3 *prophylactic,* 632.2 *protection*

immunize 60.19 *practise medicine,* 625.6 *make hygienic,* 630.20 *doctor,* 632.9 *protect*
immunized 625.4 *hygienic,* 632.5 *safe*
immunizing 625.4 *hygienic*
immunoglobulin 58.9 *protein*
immunological 59.20 *biological*
immunologically 59.29 *biologically*
immunologist 59.19 *life scientist,* 60.13 *medical specialist*
immunology 59.1 *life science,* 60.3 *medical specialty*
immunosuppressant 630.4 *antidote*
immunosuppressive 62.4 *drug type,* 62.14 *counteracting*
immunotherapy 60.8 *treatment,* 630.13 *therapy*
immure 323.10 *enclose,* 702.9 *imprison*
immurement 699.4 *detention,* 702.7 *imprisonment*
immutability 186, 217.1 *permanence,* 225.1 *stability*
immutable 112.5 *uniform,* 186.6 *changeless,* 190.8 *eternal,* 217.7 *permanent,* 225.9 *stable,* 373.4 *mentally hard*
immutable law 225.4 *stable thing*
immutably 217.9 *permanently,* 225.12 *stably,* 373.13 *inflexibly*
imp 8.7 *devil,* 11.11 *ghost,* 354.6 *plant,* 579.4 *capricious person,* 693.5 *troublemaker*
impact 354, 135.8 *unite,* 227.1 *effect,* 233 *influence,* 330.2 *collide,* 330.12 *collision,* 407.12 *abut,* 457.5 *impression*
impacted 354.12 *inserted*
impaction 354.8 *insertion*
impactment 354.8 *insertion*
impact printer 65.7 *peripheral*
impact upon 227.5 *show an effect*
impair 628, 169.8 *odd,* 216.8 *cause change,* 233.9 *change,* 238.7 *weaken,* 309.11 *deform,* 357.5 *transgress,* 601.1 *misuse,* 607.1 *waste,* 609.7 *make insufficient,* 614.8 *make useless,* 618.13 *be worthless,* 642.17 *meddle,* 656.7 *be clumsy,* 661.8 *hinder,* 722.13 *destroy,* 790.5 *make ugly,* 793.7, 793.7 *blemish,* 862.11 *be evil*
impaired 145.4 *incomplete,* 628.12 *deteriorated*
impaired visibility 441.2 *murk*
impaired vision 436.2 *poor sight*
impairment 628, 127.2 *deficiency,* 145.1 *incompleteness,* 238.1 *weakness,* 722.5 *destruction*
impala 77 Placental Mammals
impale 406.11 *inflict pain,* 544.10 *identify,* 670.6 *stab,* 879.5 *execute*
impalement 544.8 *heraldic device,* 670.18 *hit,* 879.13 *capital punishment*
impaling 544.8 *heraldic device*
impalpability 102.1 *unreality,* 260.1 *littleness,* 368.2 *unworldliness*
impalpable 102.8 *unreal,* 260.7 *little,* 368.8 *nonmaterial,* 542.16 *imperceptible*
impalpably 260.9 *microscopically,* 368.13 *metaphysically*
impanation 10.6 *Eucharist*
imparity 123.1 *inequality*
impart 6.22 *educate,* 528.12 *communicate,* 564.11 *speak,* 729.5 *give*
impartable 729.7 *given*
impartation 729.1 *giving*
imparter 729.4 *giver*
impartial 482, 783, 4.15 *rational,* 110.16, 122.6 *equal,* 271.3 *broad-minded,* 333.4 *middle,* 507.5 *wise,* 843.7 *right,* 857.4 *honourable,* 859.4 *disinterested*
impartiality 482, 783, 110.5 *equality,* 242.1 *moderation,* 271.6 *broad-mindedness,* 333.2 *middle of the road,* 843.1 *fair-*

ness, 857.1 *probity,* 859.1 *disinterestedness*
impartially 482, 783, 4.26 *rationally,* 110.19 *equally,* 122.13 *equitably,* 333.8 *medially,* 843.19 *equally,* 857.7 *honourably,* 859.8 *disinterestedly*
impartial person 482, 859
imparting 729.1, 729.8 *giving*
imparting of life 396.1 *life*
impart life 396.19 *give birth to*
impart momentum 329.6 *accelerate*
impart odour to 416
impassability 323.1 *closure*
impassable 323.13 *stopped,* 659.11 *rough*
impassably 323.16 *impermeably*
impasse 323.1 *closure,* 487.7 *obstacle,* 659.8 *snag,* 661.2 *obstacle*
impassioned 241.6 *violent,* 554.3 *emphatic,* 759.13 *passionate*
impassive 240.5 *inert,* 325.6 *quiescent,* 404.6 *unfeeling,* 466.4 *uninterested,* 523.1 *unintelligible,* 641.3 *inactive,* 643.3 *not participating,* 761.1 *insensitive,* 783.7 *indifferent,* 787.3 *unmoved,* 836.4 *pitiless*
impassively 643, 240.7 *inertly,* 325.10 *motionlessly,* 466.8 *disinterestedly,* 523.13 *unintelligibly,* 641.5 *without action,* 783.17 *indifferently,* 787.9 *without wonder,* 836.7 *pitilessly*
impassivity 240.1 *inertness,* 404.3 *heedlessness,* 466.2 *lack of interest,* 523.11 *unintelligibility,* 641.1 *inaction,* 643.7 *idleness,* 761.3 *insensitiveness,* 787.1 *lack of wonder*
impasto 50.8 *painting*
impatience 648.5 *hastiness,* 780.1 *rashness,* 818.2 *bad manners,* 829.1 *irascibility*
impatiens 84 Flowers and Flowering Plants
impatient 648.3 *hasty,* 780.4 *rash,* 818.5 *discourteous,* 828.15 *resentful,* 829.4 *irascible*
impatiently 648.7, 780.6 *rashly,* 818.9 *discourteously,* 829.9 *irascibly*
impeach 16.70 *litigate,* 852.19 *blame,* 856.5 *accuse*
impeachability 866.1 *guilt*
impeachable 852.36 *blameworthy,* 856.8 *accusatory,* 866.5 *guilty*
impeached 856.8 *accusatory*
impeacher 856.3 *accuser*
impeachment 16.5 *litigation,* 852.7 *blame,* 856.1 *accusation*
impeccability 619.3 *perfection,* 865.1 *innocence*
impeccable 619.1 *perfect,* 863.5 *virtuous,* 865.5 *innocent*
impeccably 619.7 *perfectly,* 863.9 *virtuously,* 865.11 *innocently*
impeccancy 619.3 *perfection*
impeccant 619.1 *perfect*
impecuniosity 743.5 *poverty*
impecunious 687.7 *unprosperous,* 743.1 *poor*
impecuniously 743.15 *poorly*
impecuniousness 743.5 *poverty*
impedance 56.53, 64.12 *resistance*
impede 328.3 *slow down,* 661.8 *hinder,* 661.9 *block,* 699.8 *restrain,* 709.3 *veto*
impeded 328.7 *delayed,* 661.13 *hindering*
impeder 661.7 *hinderer*
impediment 515.2 *bad outcome,* 616.3 *inconvenience,* 661.1 *hindrance,* 661.2 *obstacle,* 699.1 *restraint,* 709.1 *veto,* 824.2 *separation*
impedimenta 326.10 *transferred thing,* 603.6 *equipment,* 725.4 *possessions*
impeding 661.13 *hindering*
impel 330, 226.10 *awaken,*

228.9 *motivate*, 324.14 *set in motion*, 338.20 *propel*, 571.15 *compel*, 586.15 *persuade*, 642.14 *push*, 648.1 *hasten*, 695.6 *compel*
impelled 228.12 *motivated*
impellent 330.11 *impulsion*, 330.17 *impelling*
impeller 338.11 *propeller*, 364.6 *rotator*
impelling 330, 226.13 *causal*, 235.15 *full of energy*, 324.16 *moving*
impelling force 330.11 *impulsion*
impend 488.8 *be probable*
impending 199.11 *future*, 208.13 *imminent*, 344.19 *approaching*, 513.7 *expected*, 594.17 *developing*
impending disaster 633.5 *danger*
impenetrability 237.1 *strength*, 273.6 *denseness*, 323.1 *closure*, 371.1 *density*, 373.5 *hardness*, 443.6 *opaqueness*, 487.6 *hopelessness*, 523.11 *unintelligibility*
impenetrable 273.2 *dense*, 323.13 *stopped*, 371.6 *dense*, 443.1 *opaque*, 487.3 *hopeless*, 523.1 *unintelligible*, 527.2 *concealed*, 659.11 *rough*, 659.12 *problematic*
impenetrably 323.16 *impermeably*, 443.13 *opaquely*, 523.13 *unintelligibly*
impenitence 868
Impenitence 868
Impenitent 868
impenitently 868
impenitentness 868.1 *impenitence*
impenitent person 868
imperative 4.8 *philosophical term*, 5.33 *mood*, 103.5 *essential*, 191.6 *allowing no delay*, 571.1 *necessity*, 571.9 *necessary*, 571.10 *obligatory*, 593.6 *demanding*, 611.5 *important*, 688.12 *authoritative*, 692.14 *commanding*, 695.9 *compelling*, 847.12 *obligatory*
imperatively 571.19 *necessarily*, 593.12 *in need*, 692.16 *commandingly*, 695.11 *compellingly*
imperativeness 688.2 *authoritativeness*
imperceptibility 542, 260.1 *littleness*, 438.4 *invisibility*, 527.8 *concealment*
imperceptible 542, 238.13 *insufficient*, 260.7 *little*, 328.5 *unhurried*, 428.1 *faint-sounding*, 438.1 *invisible*
imperceptibleness 542.7 *imperceptibility*
imperceptibly 542, 238.14 *weakly*, 260.9 *microscopically*, 404.13 *insensibly*, 438.9 *invisibly*
imperceptive 436.12 *blind to*, 761.1 *insensitive*
imperceptively 381.13 *obtusely*, 460.11 *unintelligently*, 482.13 *unselectively*
impercipience 381.7 *dullness*
impercipient 761.1 *insensitive*
imperfect 620, 5.34 *tense*, 84.12 *of flowers*, 127.17 *defective*, 143.11 *partial*, 145.4 *incomplete*, 309.7 *deformed*, 358.8 *defective*, 595.5 *immature*, 618.2 *inferior*, 656.4 *bungled*, 685.4 *uncompleted*, 793.4 *blemished*, 864.13 *venial*
imperfect cadence 434.4 *atonality*
imperfect fungi 89.3 *fungi*
imperfection 777 Phobias by Topic, **620**, 127.2 *deficiency*, 145.1 *incompleteness*, 309.3 *deformity*, 358.6 *shortcoming*, 595.10 *immaturity*, 609.8 *insufficiency*, 618.8 *inferiority*, 633.7 *vulnerability*, 658.2 *naivety*, 685.1 *noncompletion*, 793.1 *spot*, 864.3 *venial sin*
Imperfection 620
imperfect item 620
imperfectly 620, 127.21 *badly*, 309.13 *asymmetrically*, 595.16

immaturely, 656.11 *unskilfully*, 685.7 *incompletely*, 864.19 *vulnerably*
imperfectness 620.5 *imperfection*
imperia 43.9 *miscellaneous architectural features*
imperial 12.10 *governing*, 126.13 *dominant*, 268.12 *metrical*, 688.14 *governmental*
Imperial Defence College 17.3 *military training*
imperialism 12.3 *governance*, 91.3 *dominion*, 357.10 *expansionism*, 400.11 *nation*, 688.7 *type of rule*
imperialist 679.6 *militarist*
imperialistic 91.16 *national*, 679.33 *combative*
imperialistically 91.19 *nationally*, 679.41 *aggressively*
imperialist war 676.1 *war*
imperial paper 604.3 *paper*
imperial purple 455.1 *purpleness*
imperial system 268.5 *measuring system*
Imperial units 75.2 *unit system*
imperial wood pulp 604.3 *paper*
imperil 633.10 *endanger*
imperilment 633.5 *danger*
imperious 688.12 *authoritative*, 692.15 *self-assured*, 696.12 *masterful*, 805.19 *stately*
imperiously 692.16 *commandingly*, 696.16 *masterfully*
imperiousness 688.2 *authoritativeness*
imperishability 190.1 *eternity*, 217.1 *permanence*
imperishable 186.6 *changeless*, 190.8 *eternal*, 217.7 *permanent*, 225.9 *stable*
imperishably 217.9 *permanently*, 225.12 *stably*
imperium 126.2 *leadership*
imperium in imperio 12.1 *government*
impermanence 189.1 *transience*, 224.1 *changeableness*
impermanent 189, 224.13 *changeable*
impermanently 189.8 *transiently*, 224.15 *changeably*
impermeability 323.1 *closure*, 371.1 *density*, 443.6 *opaqueness*
impermeable 323.12 *closed*, 371.6 *dense*, 443.1 *opaque*
impermeably 323, 443.13 *opaquely*
impermissibility 16.35 *illegality*
impermissible 16.55 *illegal*, 709.5 *vetoed*
impermissibly 709.7 *by veto*
impersonal 367.7 *material*, 783.7 *indifferent*, 859.4 *disinterested*
impersonally 367.9 *materially*, 783.17 *indifferently*, 859.8 *disinterestedly*
impersonate 51.32 *act*, 118.9 *imitate*, 538.24, 540.20 *pretend*, 540.24 *mask*, 547.9 *represent*, 547.10 *act*
impersonating 538.8 *pretence*, 538.19 *dishonest*, 547.3 *acting*
impersonation 51.20 *acting*, 118.1 *imitation*, 118.3 *mockery*, 540.7 *pretence*, 547.1 *representation*, 547.3 *acting*, 890.4 *ridicule*
impersonator 51.27 *entertainer*, 114.4 *person who copies*, 118.7 *imitator*, 224.8 *person who changes costume*, 538.12 *cheat*, 539.15 *deceiver*, 547.5 *performer*
impertinence 668.1 *defiance*, 764.6 *objectionability*, 807.1 *insolence*, 807.10 *impudence*, 807.11 *sauciness*, 846.4 *presumptuousness*, 850.1 *disrespect*
impertinent 668.7 *defiant*, 764.2 *objectionable*, 807.13 *insolent*, 807.21 *impudent*, 818.6 *bad-mannered*, 846.9 *presumptive*, 850.10 *disrespectful*
impertinently 668.9 *defiantly*, 807.30 *insolently*, 818.10 *rudely*, 846.18 *unduly*, 850.28 *disrespectfully*

imperturbability 4.3 *detachment*, 225.2 *determination*, 325.2 *repose*, 466.2 *lack of interest*, 787.1 *lack of wonder*
imperturbable 4.18 *detached*, 225.11 *determined*, 325.6 *quiescent*, 466.4 *uninterested*, 787.3 *unmoved*
imperturbably 4.27 *stoically*, 225.13 *determinedly*, 466.8 *disinterestedly*, 787.9 *without wonder*
imperturbed 787.3 *unmoved*
impervious 323.12 *closed*, 371.6 *dense*, 404.6 *unfeeling*, 443.1 *opaque*, 487.3 *hopeless*, 577.4 *set*, 761.1 *insensitive*
imperviously 323.16 *impermeably*, 371.10 *densely*, 443.13 *opaquely*
imperviousness 323.1 *closure*, 371.1 *density*, 443.6 *opaqueness*, 487.6 *hopelessness*
impetigo 624.13 *skin disease*
impetrate 10.20 *pray*
impetration 10.9 *prayer*
impetrational 10.21 *ritualistic*
impetuosity 468, 208.5 *prematurity*, 241.1 *violence*, 648.5 *hastiness*, 780.1 *rashness*
impetuous 208.16 *premature*, 241.6 *violent*, 583.2 *spontaneous*, 648.3 *hasty*, 759.13 *passionate*, 780.4 *rash*
impetuously 208.20 *prematurely*, 468.14 *inattentively*, 595.14 *unreadily*, 648.7, 780.6 *rashly*
impetuousness 595.8 *lack of preparation*, 648.5 *hastiness*, 780.1 *rashness*
impetus 228.1 *motive*, 235.4 *energy*, 239.1 *vigour*, 324.2 *momentum*, 329.9 *acceleration*, 330.11 *impulsion*, 337.29 *in reverse*, 586.11 *motive*
Imphal 93 Cities
impiety 601.2 *misuse*, 864.6 *religious sin*
impinge 267.4 *meet*, 357.5 *transgress*, 407.12 *abut*
impingement 267.2 *meeting*
impinge upon 330.2 *collide*
impinging 267.6 *meeting*
impious 864, 601.5 *abusive*
impiously 601.6 *abusively*, 864.20 *immorally*
impish 618.5 *harmful*
implacability 574.14 *tenacity*, 836.2 *inflexibility*
implacable 574.3 *strong-willed*, 577.3 *unyielding*, 822.13 *angry*, 836.5 *inflexible*
implant 62.12 *injection*, 62.19 *administer*, 167.10 *assimilate*, 354.2 *inject*, 354.6 *plant*, 584.18 *habituate*
implantation 354.8 *insertion*, 354.9 *injection*
implanted 354.13 *injected*, 584.13 *fixed*
implausibility 489, 477.7 *questionableness*, 498.2 *unbelievability*
implausible 477.14, 489.2 *questionable*, 498.7 *disbelieved*
implausibly 477.24 *questionably*, 498.11 *unbelievably*
implead 16.70 *litigate*
implement 230.9 *take action*, 232.2 *instrument*, 232.4 *be an instrument*, 243.10 *produce*, 603.1 *tool*, 640.4 *act*, 684.4 *complete*
implementation 230.1 *operation*, 640.1 *action*, 684.1 *completion*
implemented 684.7 *completed*
implicate 146.4 *include*, 527.14 *imply*, 856.5 *accuse*
implicated 107.4 *related*, 856.8 *accusatory*, 866.5 *guilty*
implication 52.63 *mathematical logic*, 107.1 *relatedness*, 146.1 *inclusion*, 520.1 *meaning*, 527.10 *quietness*, 856.1 *accusation*, 866.1 *guilt*
implication sign 52.13 *mathematical symbol*

implicative 527.4 *unsaid*, 543.14 *signifying*
implicit 52.77 *given*, 520.6 *meaningful*, 527.4 *unsaid*
implicitly 527.15 *latently*
implied 106.7 *circumstantial*, 520.6 *meaningful*, 520.9 *meant*, 527.4 *unsaid*
implied consent 708.1 *permission*
implied sense 520.4 *type of meaning*
implode 262.5 *make smaller*, 262.6 *become smaller*
implore 10.20 *pray*, 712.6 *request*
imploring 712.1 *request*
implosion 262.1 *contraction*
implosive 262.8 *contracting*
imply 527, 473.15 *state*, 483.10 *make evident*, 520.10 *mean*, 527.14 *imply*, 528.14 *tip*, 543.10 *signify*
impolite 559.8 *indecorous*, 652.18 *badly behaved*, 764.2 *objectionable*, 816.8 *unsociable*, 818.5 *discourteous*, 850.10 *disrespectful*
impolitely 652.20 *badly*, 816.14 *unsocially*, 818.9 *discourteously*
impoliteness 764.6 *objectionability*, 818.1 *discourtesy*, 850.1 *disrespect*
impolitic 616.1 *inconvenient*, 656.1 *unskilful*
imponderability 260.1 *littleness*, 368.2 *unworldliness*, 370.5 *lightness*
imponderable 260.7 *little*, 368.8 *nonmaterial*, 370.1 *light*
imponderableness 370.5 *lightness*
imponderably 260.9 *microscopically*, 368.13 *metaphysically*, 370.11 *lightly*
imponderous 370.1 *light*
import 13.10 *trade with*, 13.13 *economic*, 104.16 *be external*, 227.4 *significance*, 326.2 *transportation*, 326.12 *transport*, 346.1 *entry*, 348.1 *admittance*, 348.7 *admit*, 354.1 *insert*, 354.8 *insertion*, 520.1 *meaning*, 520.2 *significance*, 520.10 *mean*, 606.5 *provision*, 611.1 *importance*, 611.7 *be important*, 772.6 *importance*
importable 326.17 *transferable*
importance 611, 772, 154.2 *priority*, 233 *influence*, 318.1 *prominence*, 520.2 *significance*, 554.2 *seriousness*, 648.4 *haste*
Importance 611
important 611, 772, 126.15 *excellent*, 230.12 *operative*, 233.11 *influential*, 318.6 *eminent*, 520.7 *significant*, 554.5 *serious*, 617.2 *best*, 653.17 *managerial*, 849.14 *awe-inspiring*
important figure 400.7 *person*
importantly 611, 126.16 *superiorly*, 230.13 *operationally*, 233.14 *influentially*, 318.11 *eminently*
important matter 611
important occasion 611.2 *important matter*
important person 400.7 *person*, 611.4 *bigwig*
importation 104.4 *externality*, 326.2 *transportation*, 346.4 *right of entry*, 348.1 *admittance*, 354.8 *insertion*
import duty 13.6 *economic factors*
imported 149, 104.12 *external*, 346.15 *entering*, 354.12 *inserted*
imported word 5.17 *word*
importer 13.9 *economist*, 326.7 *transferor*, 737.10 *trader*, 739.12 *wholesaler*
importing 13.2 *economy*, 104.12 *external*, 346.4 *right of entry*, 348.1 *admittance*, 520.6 *meaningful*
import levy 749.2 *money received*
import momentum 330.1 *impel*
importunate 191.6 *allowing no delay*
importune 642.17 *meddle*,

877.18 *prostitute*
importuning 877.5 *prostitution*
importunity 712.1 *request*
impose 130.6 *add*, 571.15 *compel*, 692.10 *demand*, 692.11 *have authority over*, 695.6 *compel*, 849.21 *command respect*, 879.1 *punish*
impose a ban 692.9 *command*, 709.3 *veto*
impose a curfew 699.11 *detain*
impose a duty 847, 695.6 *compel*
impose a fine 699.8 *restrain*
impose an embargo 692.9 *command*, 699.9 *economize*
impose a penalty 879.2 *penalize*
impose a tariff 699.9 *economize*
impose conditions 716.6 *make conditions*
imposed peace 675.1 *peace*, 677.1 *pacification*
impose martial law 690.5 *be severe*
impose on 599.4 *resort to*
impose one's will 570
impose order upon 214.10 *make regular*
impose peace 677.4 *pacify*
imposing 259.15 *big*, 611.6 *notable*, 805.19 *stately*, 811.24 *grand*, 849.14 *awe-inspiring*
imposingly 805
imposition 130.1 *addition*, 631.3 *burden*, 751.8 *levy*, 847.1 *duty*, 879.10 *affliction*
imposition on one's time 642.6 *business*
impossibility 487, 52.62 *probability*, 487.6 *hopelessness*, 498.2 *unbelievability*, 589.6 *poor chance*
Impossibility 487
impossibility of discovery 523.11 *unintelligibility*
impossible 487
impossible! 487
impossible 498.7 *disbelieved*, 659.10 *difficult*, 711.12 *no*, 776.7 *futile*, 786.8 *wonderful*
impossibleness 487.5 *impossibility*
impossible to explain 523.1 *unintelligible*
impossibly 487
impost 43.8 *column*, 43.9 *miscellaneous architectural features*, 751.8 *levy*
imposter 118.7 *imitator*, 538.12 *cheat*, 539.15 *deceiver*, 540.15 *false person*, 656.10 *unskilled person*, 846.7 *usurper*
impostor 222.2 *substitute person*
impostrous 538.18 *pretentious*, 540.28 *spurious*, 540.31 *fraudulent*
imposture 118.1 *imitation*, 538.8 *pretence*, 539.5 *falseness*, 539.10 *fraud*, 540.4 *spuriousness*, 540.8 *fraud*, 657.1 *cunning*
impotence 236.1 *powerlessness*, 238.1 *weakness*, 247.1 *infertility*, 612.6 *obscurity*, 614.3 *uselessness*, 641.1 *inaction*, 656.8 *unskilfulness*, 689.1 *anarchy*
impotent 236, 238.8 *weak*, 247.3 *birth control*, 612.2 *obscure*, 614.1 *useless*, 641.3 *inactive*, 656.1 *unskilful*
impotent fury 236.2 *futile effort*
impotently 236.14 *powerlessly*, 238.14 *weakly*, 247.11 *unproductively*
impound 323.10 *enclose*, 699.11 *detain*, 702.9 *imprison*, 734.8 *take back*
impounding 734.2 *taking back*
impoundment 63.23 *dam*, 699.4 *detention*
impoverish 743, 129.5 *make smaller*, 259.8 *weaken*, 607.1 *waste*, 609.7 *make insufficient*, 722.12 *lessen*, 727.9 *dispose of*
impoverished 238.11 *weakened*, 612.2 *obscure*, 628.12 *deteriorated*, 722.17 *unprofitable*, 743.2 *insolvent*
impoverishment 129.1 *decrease*,

238.3 *poor health*, 628.7 *deterioration*, 722.4 *lessening*, 743.5 *poverty*
impracticability 487.6 *hopelessness*, 614.3 *uselessness*
impracticable 117.11 *unfit*, 614.1 *useless*, 659.10 *difficult*
impractically 117.17 *unsuitably*
impractical 4.13 *of philosophy*, 108.7 *illogical*, 471.13 *ideal*, 487.3 *hopeless*, 519.11 *fantastical*, 600.1 *unused*, 614.1 *useless*
impracticality 471.7 *idealism*, 487.6 *hopelessness*, 614.3 *uselessness*
impractically 471.22 *imaginatively*, 487.12 *hopelessly*, 600.12 *out of use*, 614.10 *uselessly*
imprecate 827.7 *wish ill*
imprecation 827.1 *curse*, 827.4 *malediction*
imprecatory 827.10 *maledictive*
imprecise 164.20 *generalized*, 491.6 *indeterminate*, 551.2 *obscure*, 844.12 *incorrect*
imprecisely 491.25 *indeterminately*, 504.22 *wrongly*, 551.4 *obscurely*, 844.26 *wrong*
impreciseness 551.1 *obscurity*
imprecision 164.3 *nonspecificness*, 490.19, 491.14 *indeterminacy*, 504.2 *inaccuracy*, 551.1 *obscurity*
impregnability 237.1 *strength*, 632.1 *safety*, 718.1 *protection*
impregnable 632.6 *invulnerable*, 718.6 *secure*
impregnably 632.10 *safely*, 718.15 *surely*
impregnate 133.8 *mix*, 140.5 *combine*, 245.13 *propagate*, 246.7 *make fertile*, 253.11 *be present*, 354.2 *inject*, 389.31 *steep*
impregnated 140.7 *combined*, 245.16 *reproductive*, 354.13 *injected*
impregnation 133.1 *mixture*, 245.3 *propagation*, 354.9 *injection*, 389.10 *steeping*
impresario 51.25 *producer*, 526.12 *displayer*
impress 17.10 *enlist*, 50.22 *engrave*, 227.2 *visible effect*, 228.9 *motivate*, 233.8 *influence*, 317.7 *make concave*, 374.13 *soften*, 403.13 *arouse sensation*, 514.11 *amaze*, 544.3 *means of identification*, 544.10 *identify*, 695.7 *force*, 736.13 *kidnap*, 786.10, 786.10 *be wonderful*, 849.21 *command respect*
impressed 514.7 *amazed*, 786.6 *wondering*
impressed with oneself 809.10 *self-admiring*
impressibility 228.6 *suggestibility*, 374.8 *softness*, 576.14 *apathy*, 586.7 *persuadability*, 760.5 *sensitivity*
impressible 228.13 *suggestible*, 374.2 *pliant*, 760.1 *sensitive*
impression 457, 759, 110.4 *duplicate*, 233 *influence*, 289.3 *appearance*, 310.5 *viewpoint*, 317.1 *concavity*, 403.1 *sensation*, 407.1 *touch*, 464.3 *insight*, 497.1 *belief*, 519.4 *ideality*, 547.1, 560.9 *representation*
impressionability 576.14 *apathy*, 760.5 *sensitivity*
impressionable 374, 6.17 *educatable*, 220.15 *convertible*, 224.14 *irresolute*, 403.7 *susceptible*, 576.4 *unsteady*, 759.10 *feeling*, 760.1 *sensitive*
impressionably 224.15 *changeably*, 374.18 *softheartedly*
impressional 289.8 *apparent*
impressionism 50 Western Art Styles and Movements
impressionist 49.32 *instrumental*, 50.29 *realist*, 51.27 *entertainer*
impressionistic 299.6 *outlined*, 547.13 *representational*, 560.11

descriptive, 560.13 *representing*
impressionistically 50.30 *pictorially*
impressionist music 49.3 *classical music*
impressive 233.11 *influential*, 318.6 *eminent*, 403.9 *exciting*, 457.7 *appearing*, 497.13 *believable*, 554.5 *serious*, 586.19 *persuasive*, 611.6 *notable*, 786.8 *wonderful*, 805.18 *prestigious*, 811.24 *grand*, 849.14 *awe-inspiring*, 861.1 *good*
impressive effort 644.4 *exertion*
impressively 233.14 *influentially*, 318.11 *eminently*, 586.21 *persuasively*, 861.22 *well*
impressiveness 318.1 *prominence*, 554.2 *seriousness*
impressment 17.1 *military affairs*, 695.3 *coercive methods*, 736.2 *kidnapping*
impress no-one 787.7 *not cause wonder*
impress on 554.6 *emphasize*
impress upon 227.6 *have a visible effect*
imprimatur 708.2 *permit*, 851.1 *approval*
imprint 227.2 *visible effect*, 227.6 *have a visible effect*, 317.7 *make concave*, 543.1 *sign*, 544.3 *means of identification*, 544.10 *identify*
imprinted 544.12 *identified*
imprinter 543.8 *signer*
imprison 702, 290.15 *keep inside*, 301.5, 323.10 *enclose*, 632.9 *protect*, 699.11, 726.7 *detain*, 816.13 *ignore*, 879.1 *punish*
imprisoned 702, 301.7, 323.15 *enclosed*, 632.5 *safe*, 699.15 *detained*, 726.10 *retained*, 879.20 *punished*
imprisoning 726.2 *detention*
imprisonment 702, 699.4 *detention*, 879.7 *punishment*
improbability 489, 477.7 *questionableness*, 491.13 *indemonstrability*, 498.2 *unbelievability*, 514.1 *surprise*, 589.6 *poor chance*
Improbability 489
improbable 489, 108.7 *illogical*, 477.14 *questionable*, 491.4 *indemonstrable*, 498.7 *disbelieved*, 786.8 *wonderful*
improbably 489, 477.24 *questionably*, 491.26 *unreliably*
improbity 858, 16.38 *lawbreaking*, 538.10 *dishonesty*, 540.1 *falsehood*, 540.5 *deceitfulness*, 578.7 *apostasy*, 657.1 *cunning*, 747.1 *nonpayment*, 862.1 *evil*, 864.1 *wickedness*
Improbity 858
impromptu 583.1 *improvised*, 583.7 *extempore*, 595.2 *spontaneous*, 595.8 *lack of preparation*, 595.15 *spontaneously*
impromptu talk 583.4 *improvisation*
improper 844, 117.11 *unfit*, 559.8 *indecorous*, 616.1 *inconvenient*, 618.4 *poor*, 864.11 *wicked*, 877.12 *indecent*
improper fraction 169.5 *ratio*, 173.1 *fraction*
improperly 844, 117.17 *unsuitably*, 145.6 *incompletely*, 616.6 *inconveniently*
impropriety 559, 844, 117.5 *unfitness*, 616.3 *inconvenience*, 618.10 *poverty*, 795.3 *grossness*, 864.3 *venial sin*, 866.3 *sin*
improvable 627, 220.15 *convertible*, 721.18 *acquisitional*
improvably 627.17 *better*
improve 627, 662, 6.22 *educate*, 128.4 *increase*, 216.7 *be changed*, 216.8 *cause change*, 220.8 *be transformed*, 233.9 *change*, 336.8 *further*, 359.21 *upturn*, 485.15 *modify*, 592.10 *plan out*, 617.10 *do good*, 619.5 *perfect*, 627.2 *get better*, 629.2

refurbish, 714.10 *show potential*, 721.10 *augment*, 742.15 *make rich*, 861.20 *do good*, 861.21 *do well*
improved 627, 216.12 *changed*, 220.13 *converted*, 485.11 *modified*, 629.13 *repaired*, 721.18 *acquisitional*, 791.14 *beautified*
improved mileage 721.2 *augmentation*
improved productivity 13.4 *economic development*
improved relations 677.1 *pacification*
improved technology 13.4 *economic development*
improved version 627.8 *better thing*
improve living conditions 2.15 *socialize*
improvement 336, 627, 14.1 *finance*, 128.1 *increase*, 216.1 *change*, 220.2 *evolution*, 485.5 *modification*, 662.1 *help*, 721.2 *augmentation*, 791.1 *transfiguration*, 861.13 *benefit*
Improvement 627
improve on 126.8 *be superior*
improve oneself 627.2 *get better*
improve on nature 627.1 *improve*
improve out of all recognition 627.1 *improve*
improver 216.6 *editor*, 336.16 *progressive person*, 627.13 *reviser*
improve the occasion 210.5 *take the opportunity*
improve upon 627.1 *improve*
improvidence 595.8 *lack of preparation*, 607.3 *waste*, 757.4 *extravagance*, 780.1 *rashness*
improvident 595.3 *without preparation*, 607.8 *wasteful*, 757.1 *extravagant*, 780.4 *rash*
improvidently 595.14 *unreadily*, 607.10 *wastefully*
improving 627, 6.16 *educational*, 220.14 *converting*, 861.6 *beneficial*
improvingly 6.25 *educationally*
improvisation 583, 49.2 *music making*, 51.2 *play*, 51.20 *acting*, 519.5 *fantasy*, 592.3 *expedient plan*, 595.8 *lack of preparation*
Improvisation 583
improvisatore 583.6 *improviser*
improvisatrice 583.6 *improviser*
improvise 583, 595, 49.36 *play*, 519.14 *imagine*, 547.10 *act*, 594.2 *do the groundwork*, 595.12 *be unprepared*
improvised 583, 51.37 *dramatic*, 595.2 *spontaneous*
improvised drama 51.2 *play*
improviser 583, 51.22 *actor*
improvising 51.20 *acting*
improvize 51.33 *overact*
improvized 49.31 *composed*
imprudence 508.1 *folly*, 616.3 *inconvenience*, 780.1 *rashness*
imprudent 508.5 *foolish*, 530.11 *disclosing*, 616.1 *inconvenient*, 780.4 *rash*
imprudently 508.8 *foolishly*
impudence 807, 668.1 *defiance*, 807.1 *insolence*, 807.11 *sauciness*, 818.2 *bad manners*, 850.1 *disrespect*
impudent 807, 526.15 *open*, 668.7 *defiant*, 807.13 *insolent*, 818.6 *bad-mannered*, 850.10 *disrespectful*
impudently 668.9 *defiantly*, 807.30 *insolently*, 818.10 *rudely*, 850.28 *disrespectfully*
impudent person 807
impudent talk 668.3 *act of defiance*
impugn 111.9 *oppose*, 477.20 *doubt*, 536.8 *rebut*, 663.15 *object*
impugnation 111.3 *opposition*, 536.3 *rebuttal*, 663.2 *objection*
impugning 536.13 *rebutting*
impugnment 111.3 *opposition*, 663.2 *objection*
impulse 228.1 *motive*, 233 *influence*, 329.9 *acceleration*, 330.11

impulsion, 464.3 *insight*, 571.8 *involuntariness*, 579.3 *whim*, 583.5 *spontaneity*, 586.11 *motive*, 759.2 *impression*, 782.1 *desire*

impulse-reaction turbine 63.12 *turbine*

impulse turbine 63.12 *turbine*

impulsion 330, 61.15 *compulsion*, 226.1 *cause*, 324.2 *momentum*, 337.29 *in reverse*, 648.4 *haste*

Impulsion 330

impulsive 330.17 *impelling*, 462.9 *instinctive*, 571.13 *involuntary*, 583.2 *spontaneous*, 648.3 *hasty*, 656.1 *unskilful*, 759.11 *intuitive*, 780.4 *rash*

impulsively 330.18 *dynamically*, 338.34 *forward*, 468.14 *inattentively*, 648.7, 780.6 *rashly*

impulsiveness 468.2 *impetuosity*, 583.5 *spontaneity*, 648.5 *hastiness*, 780.1 *rashness*

impunity 16.42 *acquittal*, 638.1 *escape*, 884.11 *exemption*

impure 622.8 *unclean*, 698.12 *unconditional*, 864.12 *immoral*, 877.12 *indecent*

impurely 698.21 *excessively*

impureness 628.8 *perversion*

impure thoughts 877.2 *indecency*

impurity 149, 147.6 *thing excluded*, 622.2 *uncleanness*, 628.8 *perversion*, 864.2 *vice*

impurity atom 56.44, 64.4 *semiconductor*

imputation 856.1 *accusation*

imputative 856.8 *accusatory*

impute 856.5 *accuse*

Imran Khan 18 *Sporting Personalities*

I myself 165.12 *I*

in 27, 346, 354, 27.12 *cricketing*, 40.4 *tennis terms*, 201.10 *new*, 253.17 *at home*, 346.18 *into*, 584.12 *established*, 702.8 *imprisoned*

in A1 condition 623.1 *healthy*

in a bad humour 830.7 *irritable*

in a bad mood 105.8 *in a state of*

in a bad temper 822.13 *angry*

in a bad way 624.22 *sick*, 628.12 *deteriorated*, 633.4 *endangered*, 687.6 *adverse*

in a beeline 332.9 *directly*

in a belligerent way 668.10 *in defiance*

in abeyance 236.10 *powerless*, 240.6 *suspended*, 240.7 *inertly*, 527.1 *latent*, 598.7 *on hold*, 600.1 *unused*, 641.3 *inactive*

in a big way 259.20 *largely*

inability 236.1 *powerlessness*, 614.3 *uselessness*, 656.8 *unskilfulness*, 683.1 *failure*

inability to act 641.1 *inaction*

inability to pay 683.1 *failure*, 745.5 *amount owing*, 747.5 *insolvency*

inability to see 436.7 *figurative blindness*

inability to wait 648.5 *hastiness*

in a bind 633.4 *endangered*

in a black hole 770.6 *depressed*

in a blissful manner 686.9 *prosperously*

in a blue funk 777.7 *frightened*

in a body 161.51, 180.21 *together*

in Abraham's bosom 397.19 *dead*

in a brown study 4.17 *thoughtful*, 461.10 *speculative*, 468.8 *absent-minded*, 519.10 *imaginative*

in absentia 254.20 *absently*

in abundance 181.9 *ample*

in a carefree manner 649.6 *with ease*

in a catch-22 situation 576.16 *irresolutely*, 633.4 *endangered*

inaccessibility 263.1 *distance*, 487.6 *hopelessness*, 616.4 *distance*, 816.1 *unsociability*

inaccessible 263.8 *distant*, 487.3

hopeless, 816.8 *unsociable*

inaccessibly 816.14 *unsociably*

in accord 116, 116, 167.12 *conforming*, 167.17 *conformingly*, 433.12 *harmoniously*

in accordance 167.17 *conformingly*

inaccordant 117.10 *disagreeing*

in accord with 667.10 *agreeing*

inaccuracy 504, 482.6 *lack of discrimination*, 491.14 *indeterminacy*, 538.1 *untruth*, 551.1 *obscurity*, 844.2 *incorrectness*

inaccurate 482.1 *undiscriminating*, 491.6 *indeterminate*, 504.15 *erroneous*, 538.13 *untrue*, 548.6 *misrepresented*, 551.2 *obscure*, 844.12 *incorrect*

inaccurately 482.14 *indiscriminately*, 491.25 *indeterminately*, 504.22 *wrongly*, 538.26 *untruthfully*, 548.8 *unrepresentatively*, 551.4 *obscurely*, 844.26 *wrong*

in accusation 856.10 *accusingly*

in a certain state 105.8 *in a state of*, 105.9 *conditionally*

in a circle 364.13 *round*

in a class by itself 617.1 *worthy*

in a clear style 522.13 *intelligibly*

in a cold sweat 777.7 *frightened*

in a coma 404.8 *unconscious*, 624.22 *sick*

in a constrained manner 542.28 *moderately*

in a context 107.10 *relevantly*

in a controversial way 666.11 *in disagreement*, 711.11 *uncooperatively*

in a corner 659.16 *troubled*, 661.14 *blocked*, 661.17 *in the way*

in a courageous way 668.9 *defiantly*

in a cowardly way 238.14 *weakly*

in a critical condition 397.18 *dying*

in a critical way 713.11 *disapprovingly*

in a crocodile 159.20 *in a line*, 180.21 *together*

inaction 641, 240.1 *inertness*, 325.1 *motionlessness*, 591.13 *shirking*

in action 640.5 *acting*, 642.18 *active*

inaction 643.5 *inactivity*

Inaction 641

inactivate 643.14 *make inactive*

inactive 641, 643, 57.38 *reactive*, 240.5 *inert*, 325.4 *motionless*, 464.4 *uninterested*, 527.1 *latent*, 591.18 *avoiding*, 600.3 *not wanted*, 645.7 *leisurely*, 694.7 *obedient*, 783.7 *indifferent*, 788.4 *boring*

inactively 643, 240.7 *inertly*, 325.10 *motionlessly*, 694.10 *obediently*, 783.17 *indifferently*, 788.8 *boringly*

inactive volcano 54.24 *volcanic activity*

inactivity 643, 240.1 *inertness*, 325.1 *motionlessness*, 466.2 *lack of interest*, 527.6 *latency*, 591.13 *shirking*, 600.10 *disuse*, 610.3 *superfluity*, 641.1 *inaction*, 645.1 *leisure*, 649.1 *ease*, 673.1 *submission*, 694.1 *obedience*, 783.1 *indifference*, 788.1 *boredom*

Inactivity 643

in actuality 101.13 *really*

in addition 128.8 *increasingly*, 130.10 *additionally*

in a dead heat 198.14 *equal with*

in a decline 624.22 *sick*

in a delicate condition 245.16 *reproductive*

in a demonstrative way 826.10 *endearingly*

inadequacy 743, 127.3 *inferior numbers*, 145.1 *incompleteness*, 358.6 *shortcoming*, 609.8 *insufficiency*, 614.3 *uselessness*, 620.5 *imperfection*

inadequate 743, 123.3 *unequal*, 143.11 *partial*, 145.4 *incom-

plete, 238.13 *insufficient*, 260.7 *little*, 358.7 *short*, 358.8 *defective*, 515.11 *disappointing*, 595.3 *without preparation*, 609.1 *insufficient*, 614.1 *useless*, 620.2 *incomplete*, 656.1 *unskilful*, 852.32 *unsatisfactory*

inadequately 743, 123.7 *unequally*, 143.12 *partly*, 145.6 *incompletely*, 238.14 *weakly*, 358.10 *not enough*, 585.7 *unskilfully*, 609.10 *insufficiently*

in a destructive manner 862.13 *destructively*

in a different class 126.12 *superior*

in a different way 666.12 *differently*

in a dilemma 477.13 *problematic*, 659.16 *troubled*

in a direct fashion 134.20 *homogenously*

in a direct line 332.9 *directly*

in a dishonest way 736.19 *thievishly*

in a disorderly manner 215.8 *irregularly*

in a dither 366.27 *agitatedly*

inadmissibility 117.5 *unfitness*

inadmissible 117.11 *unfit*, 147.11 *excluded*, 616.1 *inconvenient*

inadmissible evidence 483.5 *legal evidence*

inadmissibly 117.17 *unsuitably*

in a downward curve 131.9 *decreasingly*

in a dream 512.16 *obliviously*

in a drunken stupor 874.3 *dead drunk*, 874.18 *drunkenly*

in advance 154.21 *first*, 208.17 *early*, 303.11 *in front*, 746.21 *cash down*

in adverse circumstances 687.7 *unprosperous*, 687.12 *in adversity*

in adversity 687

inadvertent 589.9 *causeless*

inadvertently 589.13 *by chance*

inadvisability 616.3 *inconvenience*

inadvisable 616.1 *inconvenient*

inadvisably 616.6 *inconveniently*

in a fair way 122.13 *equitably*

in a false light 548.8 *unrepresentatively*

in a few words 562.12 *in brief*

in a firm grip 726.11 *tenaciously*

in a fit of depression 830.13 *sullenly*

in a fix 106.8 *difficult*, 659.16 *troubled*, 661.14 *blocked*

in a fixed position 718.17 *fastly*

in a flap 366.16 *restless*

in a flash 191.9 *in the shortest possible time*, 648.6 *hastily*

in a foreign country 104.18 *extraneously*

in a Formula 1 car 33.12 *in a race*

in a frame-up 856.10 *accusingly*

in a friendly fashion 815.18 *sociably*

in a friendly spirit 819.17 *in friendship*

in a friendly way 819.17 *in friendship*

in a funk 777.7 *frightened*

in a generous-hearted manner 730.15 *receptively*

in a gentlemanly manner 652.19 *well*

in agony 406.7 *feeling pain*

in a good mood 105.8 *in a state of*

in a gracious manner 691.6 *leniently*

in a greedy fashion 734.13 *avariciously*

in agreement 140.8 *cooperative*, 167.12 *conforming*, 499.6 *assenting*, 677.7 *pacifically*

in a groove 110.20 *regularly*

in a gruff manner 829.9 *irascibly*

in a harmless way 865.11 *innocently*

in a hateful manner 666.11 *in disagreement*, 822.18 *hatefully*

in a heap 482.14 *indiscriminately*

in a heart-to-heart way 526.17 *frankly*

in a helpful manner 831.10 *benevolently*

in a high-handed manner 690.11 *severely*

in a hole-and-corner way 529.16 *stealthily*

in a huff 828.16 *angry*

in a humble manner 859.9 *unselfishly*

in a hurry 648.3 *hasty*

in a hurtful manner 828.17 *resentfully*

in aid of 662

in a jam 106.8 *difficult*, 633.4 *endangered*, 659.16 *troubled*

in a jumble 151.27 *in disorder*

in a kindhearted way 835.13 *pitifully*

in a lather 366.15 *agitated*

in a liberating atmosphere 700.8 *free*

inalienable 103.5 *essential*, 698.9 *free*, 845.8 *entitled*

inalienable rights 698.2 *free speech*

in a line 159, 269.12 *longitudinally*

in all 144.9 *completely*

in all areas 248.16 *extensively*

in all conscience 535.24 *truthfully*, 772.12 *indeed*, 857.7 *honourably*

in all directions 332, 162.31 *everywhere*, 595.1 *unprepared*

in all directions at once 332.11 *in all directions*

in all haste 648.3 *hasty*

in alliance 116

in all innocence 134.18 *virtuously*, 857.8 *purely*, 863.9 *virtuously*, 865.11 *innocently*

in all lands 248.16 *extensively*

in all likelihood 101.13 *really*, 475.22 *demonstrably*, 486.11 *potentially*, 488.11 *probably*

in all manner of ways 113.11 *regularly*, 332.11 *in all directions*

in all places 248.16 *extensively*

in all probability 488.11 *probably*

in all quarters 162.31 *everywhere*

in all respects 144.9 *completely*, 537.39 *accurately*

in all seriousness 535.24 *truthfully*, 772.11 *earnestly*

in all truth 142.13 *on the whole*

in a loose manner 139.10 *noncohesively*

in a loving manner 826.10 *endearingly*

inalterable 225.9 *stable*

in a luge 41.17 *on a ski run*

in a manipulative way 734.13 *avariciously*

in a mass 161.51 *together*

in amazement 786.13 *wonderfully*

in ambush 438.1 *invisible*

in a measure 121.11 *to a degree*

in amends 735.7 *redemptively*

in a mess 151.15 *untidy*, 151.27 *in disorder*, 482.14 *indiscriminately*, 659.16 *troubled*

in a minority 182.7 *fewer*

in a moment 189.8 *transiently*

in a muddle 151.27 *in disorder*, 482.14 *indiscriminately*

in an abusive manner 827.13 *vituperatively*

in an accommodating manner 717.9 *compromisingly*

in an active manner 230.13 *operationally*

in an affectionate way 821.30 *lovingly*

in an aggressive way 666.11 *in disagreement*

in an alien way 136.22 *in isolation*

in an amusing way 815.18 *sociably*

in an antagonistic way 822.18 *hatefully*

in an apt way 667.17 *suitably*

in an aside 428.10 *faintly*

in a natural state 595.4 *untrained*

in a natural way 367.9 *materially*

in ancient times 202.19 *anciently*
in and out 216.15, 224.15 *changeably*, 365.18 *to and fro*
inane 460.6 *unintelligent*, 462.8 *thoughtless*, 508.5 *foolish*, 521.10 *meaningless*, 555.1 *unemphatic*
in a negative manner 661.18 *inhibitively*
in an egotistical manner 834.5 *misanthropically*
in an elaborate manner 106.19 *meticulously*
inanely 460.11 *unintelligently*
in a nervous state 829.9 *irascibly*
in an evasive manner 717.10 *irresolutely*
in an everyday manner 214.17 *orderly*
in an excellent manner 863.11 *worthily*
in an expert manner 688.26 *expertly*
in an explicit way 271.7 *broadly*
in anger 828.18 *angrily*
in an ill humour 830.13 *sullenly*
inanimate 397.19 *dead*, 460.8 *nonhuman*, 643.1 *inactive*
inanimately 397.23 *fatally*, 460.12 *nonhumanly*, 643.15 *inactively*
inanimate nature 460.4 *nonhuman existence*
inanimate object 240.3 *inert thing*, 367.5 *object*
inanimate objects 460.4 *nonhuman existence*
in an impersonal manner 783.17 *indifferently*
in an indecent manner 827.12 *swearingly*
in an indifferent way 787.9 *without wonder*
in an inferior place 127.19 *inferiorly*
in an inferior state 127.19 *inferiorly*
in an informal way 698.22 *informally*
in an inhibited way 661.18 *inhibitively*
in an instant 189.8 *transiently*, 191.9 *in the shortest possible time*
in an interesting condition 245.16 *reproductive*
in an intimate fashion 819.18 *intimately*
in an intrusive manner 661.16 *with delay*
in an irritable mood 829.9 *irascibly*
inanity 460.2 *unintelligence*, 462.1 *lack of thought*, 508.1 *folly*, 521.1 *lack of meaning*
in a noble manner 696.16 *masterfully*
in an obscene manner 864.20 *immorally*
in an offensive way 818.10 *rudely*
in an offhand manner 583.7 *extempore*, 595.2 *spontaneous*
in a nonpartisan way 665.18 *cliquishly*
in an open-minded way 730.15 *receptively*
in an optimistic way 714.17 *auspiciously*
in answer 478, 473.20 *apologetically*, 476.11 *in reply*
in anticipation 154, 488.11 *probably*, 594.22 *in preparation*
in an uncompromising way 577.9 *be obstinate*
in an undertone 424.7, 428.10 *faintly*, 529.15 *in secret*, 563.17 *voicelessly*
in an ungentlemanly manner 652.20 *badly*
in an unpleasant manner 818.9 *discourteously*
in a nutshell 260.8 *in a small way*, 270.12 *short*, 505.4 *proverbially*, 552.3 *concise*, 552.5 *concisely*, 562.12 *in brief*
in any case 327.16 *how*
in any event 327.16 *how,*

589.14 *perchance*
in a paddy 828.16 *angry*, 828.18 *angrily*
in a passionate moment 784.11 *admiringly*
in a patriotic way 91.19 *nationally*
in a peaceful manner 667.14 *agreeably*
in a peaceful way 675.8 *peacefully*
in a perfect way 126.17 *supremely*, 134.18 *virtuously*, 865.11 *innocently*
in a perfect world 471.23 *ideally*
in a permissive fashion 708.9 *with permission*
in a persuasive manner 710.20 *persuasively*
in a pertinent way 667.17 *suitably*
in a pet 828.15 *resentful*
in a pickle 106.8 *difficult*, 659.16 *troubled*, 661.14 *blocked*
in a pinch 593.12 *in need*
in a pleasing way 784.10 *with great liking*
in a polite manner 817.14 *courteously*
in a political context 688.24 *ministerially*
in a political way 665.18 *cliquishly*
in a possessive manner 841.9 *jealously*
in a possessive way 135.16 *as one*
inappetence 783.1 *indifference*
inappetency 783.1 *indifference*
inappetent 783.7 *indifferent*
in apple-pie order 150.13 *orderly*
inapplicability 104.1 *extraneousness*, 108.1 *unrelatedness*, 117.5 *unfitness*, 614.3 *uselessness*
inapplicable 104.8 *intruder*, 108.6 *unrelated*, 117.11 *unfit*, 614.1 *useless*
inapplicably 104.18 *extraneously*, 108.12 *irrelevantly*
inapposite 108.6 *unrelated*, 117.11 *unfit*
inappositely 108.12 *irrelevantly*
inappositeness 108.1 *unrelatedness*, 117.5 *unfitness*
inappreciability 260.1 *littleness*
inappreciable 260.7 *little*, 438.1 *invisible*, 612.1 *unimportant*
inappreciably 260.8 *in a small way*
inapprehensibility 523.11 *unintelligibility*
inapprehensible 523.1 *unintelligible*
inappropriate 108.6 *unrelated*, 117.11 *unfit*, 211.10 *untimely*, 616.1 *inconvenient*, 844.13 *improper*
inappropriately 108.12 *irrelevantly*, 117.17 *unsuitably*, 211.15 *at the wrong time*, 844.27 *improperly*
inappropriateness 108.1 *unrelatedness*, 117.5 *unfitness*, 211.1 *untimeliness*, 616.3 *inconvenience*
in a predicament 659.16 *troubled*
in a profitable way 819.20 *favourably*
inapt 108.6 *unrelated*, 117.11 *unfit*, 211.10 *untimely*, 614.1 *useless*, 844.13 *improper*
inaptitude 108.1 *unrelatedness*, 117.5 *unfitness*, 614.3 *uselessness*, 616.3 *inconvenience*
inaptly 108.12 *irrelevantly*, 117.17 *unsuitably*
inaptness 108.1 *unrelatedness*, 117.5 *unfitness*
in a quandary 491.3 *confused*, 491.24 *confusingly*, 659.16 *troubled*
in a race 33
in a rage 828.16 *angry*
in a receptive way 730.15 *receptively*
in a relative way 106.16 *relatively*
in a repressive way 709.7 *by veto*

in a resolute manner 225.13 *determinedly*
in a respectful stance 849
Inari 8 Deities
in armour 594.18 *prepared*
in arms 206.11 *young*
in a roundabout way 334.8, 363.12 *circuitously*, 553.8 *circuitously*
in a row 155.15 *sequential*, 159.20 *in a line*, 195.14 *in succession*
in arrears 132.12 *with a remainder*, 145.6 *incompletely*, 358.9 *behind*, 745.11 *insolvently*, 747.13 *nonpaying*, 747.15 *without paying*, 845.12 *owed*
inarticulacy 566.5 *silence*
inarticulate 563, 523.1 *unintelligible*, 563.11 *speechless*, 566.2 *silent*, 658.1 *naive*, 786.7 *wide-eyed*, 810.11 *shy*
inarticulately 523.13 *unintelligibly*
inarticulateness 563.2 *inarticulation*
inarticulation 563
inartistic 656.4 *bungled*, 658.1 *naive*
in a rush 648.3 *hasty*
in a rut 110.20 *regularly*, 112.15 *monotonously*
in a safe manner 718.16 *surely*
in ascendency 126.12 *superior*
in a scrape 659.16 *troubled*
in a secret manner 709.8 *under censorship*
in a seductive manner 228.14 *influentially*
in a sense 520.13 *meaningfully*
in a series 159.18 *consecutively*
in a serious mood 830.13 *sullenly*
in a sexual way 135.16 *as one*
in a sharp tone 818.9 *discourteously*, 829.9 *irascibly*
in a short time 208.18 *soon*
in a short while 208.18 *soon*
in a shy manner 699.17 *with self-restraint*, 816.14 *unsocially*
in a similar situation 114.13 *similarly*
in a similar way 667.16 *compatibly*
in a slalom race 41.17 *on a ski run*
in a small way 260
in a sour disposition 829.9 *irascibly*
in a Spartan manner 871.7 *abstemiously*
in a speculative way 518.10 *supposedly*
in a spin 364.13 *round*, 366.16 *restless*
in a spiteful manner 855.16 *vindictively*
in a spiteful way 820.15 *aggressively*
in association 140.8 *cooperative*, 665.18 *cliquishly*
in association with 180.24, 664.22 *with*
in a standoffish mood 263.11 *reservedly*
in a state of 105, 105.9 *conditionally*
in a state of flux 224.13 *changeable*
in a state of nature 296.9 *undressed*, 658.1 *naive*
in a state of war 676.15 *warring*
in a stew 828.16 *angry*
in astonishment 786.13 *wonderfully*
in a strange way 104.18 *extraneously*, 115.7 *dissimilarly*
in a stubborn manner 373.13 *inflexibly*
in a suggestive manner 543.18 *indicatively*
in a swinging motion 214.15 *regularly*
in a sympathetic manner 784.11 *admiringly*
in a tangle 659.16 *troubled*
in a temper 828.16 *angry*
in a temporary manner 717.9

compromisingly
in a tense manner 373.12 *toughly*
in a three-man combination 31.10 *on the field*
in a tight corner 633.4 *endangered*
in a tight spot 659.16 *troubled*
in a tizzy 153.12 *disturbed*, 366.27 *agitatedly*
in a toboggan 41.17 *on a ski run*
in atonement 735.7 *redemptively*
in a trance 875, 512.16 *obliviously*, 519.10 *imaginative*
in a trice 189.8 *transiently*, 191.9 *in the shortest possible time*
in a trickle 182.10 *in ones and twos*
in attendance 196.8 *available*, 253.8 *attendant*
inattention 468, 421.1 *deafness*, 462.4 *inconsideration*, 470.1 *negligence*, 512.4 *unthinkingness*, 642.7 *restlessness*, 656.9 *bungling*, 685.1 *noncompletion*, 720.1 *nonobservance*, 780.1 *rashness*, 783.2 *carelessness*, 818.1 *discourtesy*
Inattention 468
inattention to detail 685.1 *noncompletion*
inattentive 468, 335.25 *wandering*, 421.5 *unhearing*, 462.10 *inconsiderate*, 470.4 *negligent*, 508.5 *foolish*, 512.10 *unthinking*, 656.1 *unskilful*, 685.4 *uncompleted*, 720.11 *nonobservant*, 780.4 *rash*, 783.8 *careless*, 818.5 *discourteous*
inattentive act 468
inattentively 468, 720, 512.16 *obliviously*, 685.7 *incompletely*, 783.18 *carelessly*, 818.9 *discourteously*
inattentiveness 468.1 *inattention*
inattentive person 468
in at the death 398.25 *lethally*
in at the kill 398.25 *lethally*
in a twinkling 189.8 *transiently*, 191.9 *in the shortest possible time*
inaudibility 421, 56.17 *sound*, 422.4 *silence*, 424.1 *faintness*, 523.11 *unintelligibility*
inaudible 238.13 *insufficient*, 421.7 *unheard*, 422.3 *silent*, 424.4 *faint*, 428.1 *faint-sounding*, 523.1 *unintelligible*, 563.10 *low-voiced*
inaudibly 238.14 *weakly*, 421.12 *deafly*, 422.5 *silently*, 523.13 *unintelligibly*
inaugural 156, 154.13 *precursory*, 322.17 *beginning*, 703.9 *commissioned*
inaugural address 156.9 *premiere*, 567.2 *salutation*
inaugurate 156, 226, 154.18 *forerun*, 201.19, 322.24 *begin*, 348.10 *introduce*, 354.7 *install*, 703.6 *commission*, 812.19 *install*
inaugurated 201, 156.37 *enrolled*
inauguration 156, 195.4 *accession*, 201.4, 322.11 *beginning*, 348.3 *introduction*, 594.9 *preparation*, 703.1 *commission*, 812.3 *ceremony*, 813.3 *formal occasion*
inauguratory 156.34 *inaugural*
inauspicious 776, 862, 211.10 *untimely*, 489.1 *improbable*, 517.15 *presageful*, 687.6 *adverse*
inauspiciously 862, 211.15 *at the wrong time*, 517.16 *predictively*, 687.12 *in adversity*
inauspiciousness 211.1 *untimeliness*, 862.3 *bad luck*
inauthentic 538.14 *unreal*
in authority 126.13 *dominant*, 233.11 *influential*, 688.23 *authoritatively*
in autumn 203.18 *seasonally*
in a vacuum 372.7 *sparsely*
in a vindictive way 862.12 *evilly*
in a warmhearted manner 835.13 *pitifully*
in a way 114.13 *similarly,*

121.11 *to a degree*
in awe 786.13 *wonderfully,*
849.10 *reverent*
in a while 208.18 *soon,* 209.17
later
in a whirl 364.13 *round*
in a whisper 424.7 *faintly,*
529.15 *in secret,* 563.17 *voicelessly*
in a wicked way 693.17 *disobediently*
in a word 270.12 *short,* 552.5
concisely, 562.12 *in brief*
in a world of one's own 461.10
speculative, 468.8 *absent-minded,* 512.8 *oblivious*
in back of 304.9 *in the rear*
in bad condition 105.8 *in a state of*
in bad form 105.8 *in a state of,*
105.9 *conditionally*
in bad health 624.22 *sick*
in bad nick 624.22 *sick*
in bad odour with 820.8 *estranged*
in bad spirits 105.8 *in a state of,*
105.9 *conditionally*
in bad taste 559.8 *indecorous,*
559.10 *ugly,* 795.9 *ribald*
in battle 473.9 *hostile,* 676.15
warring
in baulk 24.9 *billiard*
in bed 624.22 *sick*
in behalf of 293.43 *alternatively,*
707.8 *by proxy*
in being 253.7 *present*
in between 124.12 *mediumly,*
158.20 *in the middle*
in bits 136.20 *separately,* 136.21
apart, 141.5 *disintegrated,*
143.11 *partial*
in bits and pieces 628.13 *dilapidated*
in black 774.8 *mournfully*
in black and white 545.16 *recorded,* 545.17 *on the record*
in bliss 686.8 *prosperous*
in bloom 69.16 *horticultural,*
84.11 *flowering,* 206.13 *maturing*
in blossom 84.11 *flowering*
in blue water 97.11 *nautically*
in bold relief 437.2 *clear,* 526.14
manifest
in bondage 701.9 *subject*
in bonds 697.9 *serving,* 699.15
detained, 701.9 *subject*
inborn 103.6 *intrinsic*
inborn aptitude 655.2 *aptitude*
inbound 344.19 *approaching,*
346.15 *entering*
in brackets 354.15 *in*
inbred 103.6 *intrinsic,* 140.7
combined
in-bred 68.21 *domesticated*
in brief 562, 270.12 *short,*
299.7 *essentially,* 552.5 *concisely*
in broad daylight 475.20 *manifestly,* 483.15 *evidently,* 526.16
manifestly
in bulk 142.12 *one and all*
in business 737.20 *in trade*
Inca 1 Peoples, **5** Languages
and Groups of Languages,
400.4 *civilized human*
in cahoots 116.32 *in alliance,*
135.16 *as one,* 664.19 *associating,* 664.21 *in cooperation*
incalculability 184.5 *immeasurability*
incalculable 181.8 *numberless,*
184.2 *immeasurable,* 589.8
chance
incalculably 181.13 *numerously,*
184.11 *immeasurably*
in camera 438.3 *private,* 438.9
invisibly, 529.15 *in secret*
Incan 7 Non-Christian Religions
incandesce 439.25 *light up*
incandescence 56.24 *light emission,* 56.40 *heating effect,* 408.1
heat, 439.1 *light*
incandescent 408.9 *hot,* 439.15
lucent
incandescent lamp 56.25 *light
source*

incandescent light 439
incandescently 439.30 *lightly*
incant 10.20 *pray,* 11.21 *bewitch,* 712.6 *request*
incantation 11.5 *spell,* 712.1 *request*
incantational 11.15 *witchlike,*
712.9 *requesting*
incantatory 11.15 *witchlike*
incapability 236.1 *powerlessness*
incapable 117.11 *unfit,* 236.10
powerless, 595.7 *unequipped,*
609.1 *insufficient,* 656.1 *unskilful*
incapable of thought 462.8
thoughtless
incapably 585.7 *unskilfully*
incapacitate 236.7 *remove power
from,* 643.14 *make inactive,*
661.8 *hinder*
incapacitated 236.12 *impotent,*
875.7 *drugged*
incapacity 117.5 *unfitness,* 236.1
powerlessness, 656.8 *unskilfulness,* 683.1 *failure*
in captivity 697.9 *serving,*
697.10 *obediently,* 699.15 *detained,* 701.9 *subject,* 701.11
under subjection, 702.8 *imprisoned*
incarcerate 323.10 *enclose,*
699.11 *detain,* 702.9 *imprison,*
879.1 *punish*
incarcerated 699.15 *detained,*
702.8 *imprisoned*
incarceration 699.4 *detention,*
879.7 *punishment*
incarnadine 450.4 *bloody,* 450.9
redden
incarnate 8.13 *divine,* 103.12 *embody,* 367.7 *material,* 367.8 *be
material,* 396.12 *alive,* 457.7 *appearing,* 547.9 *represent*
incarnation 8.8 *divine manifestation,* 103.3 *quintessence,* 367.2
materialization, 457.1 *appearance,* 526.10 *manifestation,*
547.1 *representation*
Incas 200.6 *people of the past*
in cash 742.2 *solvent*
incautious 508.5 *foolish,* 583.2
spontaneous, 780.4 *rash*
incautiousness 780.1 *rashness*
incendiary 244.14 *destructive,*
408.7 *fireman,* 408.10 *on fire,*
410.10 *powered*
incendiary bomb 408.6 *fire,*
680.16 *bomb*
incense 418, 10.14 *sacred object,* 710.6 *offering,* 822.16
cause hate, 828.9 *offend*
incense cedar 85 Trees and
Shrubs
incensed 828.16 *angry*
incensory 10.14 *sacred object*
incentive 586, 586, 228.2 *inducement,* 228.11 *motivational,*
330.11 *impulse,* 586.19 *persuasive,* 752.2 *bargain,* 878.4 *reward for service*
incentive pay 729.2 *gift*
inception 156.6 *inauguration,*
201.4, 322.11 *beginning*
inceptive 156.34 *inaugural,*
226.13 *causal,* 322.17 *beginning*
inceptively 226.14 *causally*
incertitude 491.9 *uncertainty*
incessancy 159.5 *continuity,*
212.4 *frequency*
incessant 159.11 *continuous,*
183.14 *recurrent,* 188.9 *permanent,* 190.10 *continuing forever,*
212.3 *frequent,* 219.5 *continual,*
426.15 *drumming,* 642.18 *active*
incessantly 159.19 *continuously,*
183.23 *repeatedly,* 186.8 *ever,*
188.12 *everlastingly,* 212.1 *frequently,* 219.7 *continually,*
426.19 *repeatedly*
incest 877.7 *sexual assault*
incestuous 877.15 *unlawful*
inch 75 General Units, 98.2 *island,* 98.6 *lowland,* 264.2 *short
distance,* 269.7 *measure of
length*
in chains 701.9 *subject*
inch along 328.1 *move slowly*

in character 165.16 *characteristic,* 584.11 *normal*
in charge 12.10 *governing,*
653.17 *managerial,* 653.19
managerially, 688.23 *authoritatively*
inch by inch 121.10 *by degrees,*
328.16 *slowly*
in check 302.5 *limited,* 699.13 *restraining*
inches taller 805.17 *conceited*
inch forward 336.7 *make one's
way*
inchmeal 121.10 *by degrees*
inchoate 156.32 *embryonic,*
156.34 *inaugural,* 201.12,
595.5 *immature*
inchoation 156.6 *inauguration*
inchoative 156.34 *inaugural*
in chorus 116.33 *harmoniously,*
198.13 *synchronously,* 433.7
harmonious, 433.12 *harmoniously,* 667.10 *agreeing*
incident 3.14 *historicalness,* 48.3
aspect of fiction, 106.2 *occurrence*
incidental 104.8 *intruder,* 106.6
aspect, 106.7 *circumstantial,*
106.10 *detailed,* 108.7 *illogical,*
180.17 *accompanying,* 229.6
motiveless, 589.8 *chance,* 612.3
secondary
incidentally 104.18 *extraneously,*
106.16 *relatively,* 106.19 *meticulously,* 108.12 *irrelevantly,*
229.8 *by chance,* 612.14 *unimportantly*
incidentalness 104.1 *extraneousness*
incinerate 244.12 *consume,*
399.8 *bury,* 408.15 *burn*
incineration 244.2 *destroying,*
399.1 *burial*
incinerator 408.6 *fire,* 727.4
wastebin
incipience 156.6 *inauguration*
incipient 156.34 *inaugural,*
260.7 *little*
incircle 52.42 *circle*
in circles 364.13 *round*
in circulation 532.19 *published*
incise 50.22 *engrave,* 60.20 *practise surgery,* 265.5 *crack,* 319.5
notch, 545.14 *inscribe*
incised 277.8 *deep*
incision 60.9 *surgery,* 136.3 *separateness,* 265.2 *crack,* 319.1
notch
incisive 300.10 *advantaged,*
535.14 *assertive,* 552.3 *concise,*
554.3 *emphatic*
incisively 300.12 *at an advantage,* 552.5 *concisely,* 554.7 *emphatically*
incisiveness 459.4 *cleverness,*
535.6 *assertiveness,* 552.1 *conciseness,* 554.1 *emphasis*
incisor 380.11 *tooth*
incisural 319.4 *notched*
incisure 319.1 *notch*
incite 226.10 *awaken,* 228.10
manipulate, 241.9 *make violent,*
330.1 *impel,* 648.1 *hasten,*
654.5 *advise,* 778.17 *give courage*
incited 228.12 *motivated,*
586.20 *persuadable*
incitement 330.11 *impulsion,*
586.2 *flattery,* 778.6 *encouragement*
inciting 228.11 *motivational*
incitive 228.11 *motivational*
incivility 764.6 *objectionability,*
795.3 *grossness,* 807.1 *insolence,* 818.1 *discourtesy,* 850.1
disrespect
in civvies 675.7 *peaceful*
inclemency 409.7 *cold weather,*
690.1 *severity,* 836.1 *pitilessness*
inclement 55.48 *stormy,* 409.8
cold, 690.8 *severe*
inclement weather 241.5 *violent
weather*
inclination 784, 53.21 *orbit,*
54.45 *magnetic pole,* 234.2
attitude, 286.1 *obliqueness,*
332.2 *bearing,* 360.6 *slide,*

411.2 *taste of life,* 570.1 *will,*
580.7 *preference,* 655.2 *aptitude,* 782.1 *desire,* 821.7 *choice,*
849.4 *mark of respect*
inclinational 286.4 *oblique*
inclination of balance 123.1 *inequality*
incline 228.9 *motivate,* 234.4
tend, 275.2 *heights,* 286.6 *be
oblique,* 310.11 *angle,* 332.7
take a direction, 359.2 *upturn,*
360.14 *slide,* 362.7 *lean,* 580.2
prefer, 586.15 *persuade,* 594.2
do the groundwork
inclined 286.4, 310.8 *oblique,*
572.1 *willing,* 588.11 *intending*
inclined fold 54.20 *earth movement*
inclined plane 52.38 *surface,*
63.6 *simple machine*
inclined railway 72.1 *railway*
inclined towards 234.5 *tending
to,* 784.6 *liking*
incline one's head 362.9 *bow*
incline the head 849.19 *take off
one's hat to*
incline towards 234.4 *tend*
inclining 234.5 *tending to,* 286.4
oblique
inclining towards 234.5 *tending to*
inclinometer 73 Aircraft Parts
in clover 405.7 *pleased,* 686.8
prosperous, 686.9 *prosperously,*
742.1 *wealthy,* 742.16 *wealthily*
include 146, 293, 103.12 *embody,* 130.6 *add,* 135.8 *unite,*
148.11 *consist of,* 257.8 *embody,* 348.7 *admit,* 354.1 *insert,*
472.10 *focus on*
included 146, 130.8 *additional,*
354.12 *inserted*
include out 147.7 *exclude*
including 146, 130.10 *additionally,* 148.9 *composing,* 257.10
containing
inclusion 146, 293, 130.1 *addition,* 146.2 *thing included,*
348.1 *admittance,* 354.11 *thing
inserted,* 724.2 *participation*
Inclusion 146
inclusive 293, 130.8 *additional,*
146.7 *including,* 164.15 *general,*
257.10 *containing*
inclusively 146, 293, 148.14
constituently, 257.14 *internally*
inclusiveness 142.1 *whole,* 146.1
inclusion, 164.1 *generality*
inclusive of 130.10 *additionally,*
148.9 *composing*
incognito 529.11 *mysterious,*
529.15 *in secret,* 531.15 *disguised,* 539.12 *disguise,* 539.15
deceiver, 539.41 *disguised*
incognizable 523.3 *unrecognizable*
incognizance 502.1 *ignorance*
incognizant 502.6 *ignorant*
incoherence 139.1 *nonadhesion,*
151.1 *disorder,* 160.1 *discontinuity,* 491.14 *indeterminacy,*
510.1 *insanity,* 521.1 *lack of
meaning*
incoherent 139.8 *nonadhesive,*
151.16 *confused,* 160.8 *discontinuous,* 215.5 *unusual,* 460.7
intellectually subnormal, 491.6
indeterminate, 521.10 *meaningless,* 523.1 *unintelligible,* 553.3
diffuse
incoherently 139.10 *noncohesively,* 491.25 *indeterminately,* 523.13 *unintelligibly*
in cold blood 588.13 *intentionally,* 761.8 *unfeelingly,* 783.17
indifferently, 836.7 *pitilessly*
in cold storage 209.10 *held up,*
240.7 *inertly*
in collaboration 130.10 *additionally,* 664.21 *in cooperation*
in collaboration with 664.22 *with*
in collusion 664.21 *in cooperation*
in colour 444.10 *coloured*
in combat 670.26 *aggressively*
in combination 140
income 749, 13.6 *economic factors,* 243.7 *produce,* 602.4 *financial resources,* 721.4 *earnings,*

725.5 *personal estate*, 730.2 *something received*, 742.5 *wealth*, 746.3 *pay*, 878.4 *reward for service*

incomer 147.5 *excluded person*, 149.6 *immigrant*, 195.8 *follower*, 201.8 *new arrival*, 255.7 *settler*, 346.7 *entrant*

income support 662.4 *social assistance*, 833.4 *welfare state*

income tax 13.6 *economic factors*, 729.2 *gift*, 751.7 *tax*

income-tax haven 592.3 *expedient plan*

income tax return 545.1 *record*

in comfort 686.9 *prosperously*

incoming 104.4 *externality*, 104.12 *external*, 149.13 *immigrant*, 344.18 *arriving*, 344.19 *approaching*, 346.1 *entry*, 346.15 *entering*

incomings 749.2 *money received*

incoming tide 214.5 *regular thing*, 635.1 *trap*

in command 653.19 *managerially*, 688.23 *authoritatively*

in commemoration of 812.21 *in honour of*

incommensurability 115.2 *unlikeness*, 117.1 *disparity*

incommensurate 52.74 *divisible*, 108.7 *illogical*, 115.4 *dissimilar*, 117.7 *disparate*

incommensurate 115.4 *dissimilar*, 117.7 *disparate*

incommensurately 115.7 *dissimilarly*

in commerce 737.20 *in trade*

in committee 568.13 *discussing*

incommode 616.5 *be inconvenient*

incommodious 272.1 *narrow*, 616.1 *inconvenient*

incommodiously 616.6 *inconveniently*

incommodiousness 272.5 *narrowness*, 616.3 *inconvenience*

in common 724, 724.5 *jointly possessing*

in common parlance 556.8 *simply*

incommunicability 523.11 *unintelligibility*

incommunicable 523.1 *unintelligible*

incommunicado 531.14 *concealed*

incommunicative 566.1 *taciturn*

incommunicatively 566.10 *taciturnly*

incommunicativeness 566.4 *taciturnity*

in communion 116.11 *allied*

incommutable 225.9 *stable*

in-company 15.10 *unionized*

in-company union 15.3 *organized labour*

in company with 180.24 *with*

incomparability 126.1 *superiority*

incomparable 115.4 *dissimilar*, 119.5 *novel*, 126.14, 617.2 *best*

incomparably 115.7 *dissimilarly*, 119.8 *originally*, 126.17 *supremely*

in comparison 107.10 *relevantly*

incompatibility 52.64 *reasoning*, 115.2 *unlikeness*, 117.4 *disagreement*, 168.1 *nonconformity*, 473.1 *argument*, 661.1 *disagreement*, 666.3 *difference*, 816.1 *unsociality*, 820.1 *enmity*, 824.3 *divorce court*

incompatible 52.86 *logical*, 115.4 *dissimilar*, 117.10 *disagreeing*, 117.11 *unfit*, 168.11 *nonconforming*, 473.7 *arguing*, 663.21 *contrary*, 666.9 *disagreeing*, 666.10 *different*, 816.10 *lonely*

incompatibly 115.7 *dissimilarly*, 117.16 *disagreeably*, 473.17 *argumentatively*, 666.11 *in disagreement*, 666.12 *differently*, 816.14 *unsocially*

in compensation 125, 735.7 *redemptively*, 878.19 *rewardingly*

incompetence 117.5 *unfitness*, 236.1 *powerlessness*, 595.8 *lack of preparation*, 609.8 *insufficiency*, 614.3 *uselessness*, 618.8 *inferiority*, 656.8 *unskilfulness*

incompetent 117.11 *unfit*, 236.10 *powerless*, 595.7 *unequipped*, 609.1 *insufficient*, 614.1 *useless*, 618.2 *inferior*, 656.1 *unskilful*, 656.10 *unskilled person*, 722.6 *loser*, 776.8 *bad*

incompetently 117.17 *unsuitably*, 236.14 *powerlessly*, 585.7 *unskilfully*, 609.10 *insufficiently*, 614.10 *uselessly*, 656.11 *unskilfully*

in competition 39.12 *by swimming*

incomplete 145, 620, 52.86 *logical*, 143.11 *partial*, 173.5 *fractional*, 307.5 *shapeless*, 358.7 *short*, 375.5 *unfinished*, 470.5 *indifferent*, 609.1 *insufficient*, 685.4 *uncompleted*

incompletely 145, 375, 685, 143.12 *partly*, 595.16 *immaturely*, 620.11 *imperfectly*

incompleteness 145, 307.1 *shapelessness*, 358.5 *shortfall*, 375.10 *rough idea*, 595.10 *immaturity*, 609.8 *insufficiency*, 620.5 *imperfection*, 685.1 *noncompletion*

Incompleteness 145

incomplete pass 19.9 *play*

incomplete set 620.6 *imperfect item*

incomplete thing 145

incomplete work 685.1 *noncompletion*

incompletion 307.1 *shapelessness*, 685.1 *noncompletion*

in compliance with 694.10 *obediently*

incomprehensibility 184.5 *immeasurability*, 523.11 *unintelligibility*, 551.1 *obscurity*

incomprehensible 184.2 *immeasurable*, 523.1 *unintelligible*, 551.2 *obscure*

incomprehensibly 523.13 *unintelligibly*, 551.4 *obscurely*

incomprehension 460.2 *unintelligence*, 502.1 *ignorance*

incompressibility 371.1 *density*

incompressible 371.6 *dense*

inconceivability 487.5 *impossibility*, 523.11 *unintelligibility*

inconceivable 487.1 *impossible*, 523.1 *unintelligible*, 786.8 *wonderful*

inconceivably 487.11 *impossibly*, 523.13 *unintelligibly*

in concert 116.10 *in accord*, 116.13 *harmonious*, 116.31 *in accord*, 116.33 *harmoniously*, 135.13 *agreeable*, 135.17 *agreeably*, 140.10 *in combination*, 198.13 *synchronously*, 664.21 *in cooperation*

in concert with 664.22 *with*

in conclusion 157.26 *finally*, 478.25 *conclusively*

inconclusive 238.13 *insufficient*, 476.6 *refutable*

inconclusively 238.14 *weakly*, 476.12 *refutably*

in concord 433.7 *harmonious*, 433.12 *harmoniously*

in condition 105.8 *in a state of*, 623.1 *healthy*

in conference 568.13 *discussing*

in confidence 529.15 *in secret*

in confinement 879.20 *punished*

in conflict 473.17 *argumentatively*

in conflict with 663.27 *opposed to*, 713.11 *disapprovingly*

in conformity with 694.10 *obediently*

in confrontation 663.25 *at odds*

in confusion 13.11 *irregularly*, 151.27 *in disorder*

in Congress 706.8 *representatively*

incongruence 117.1 *disparity*

incongruent 108.8 *distorted*, 117.7 *disparate*, 123.23 *unequal*

incongruently 108.13 *disproportionately*, 117.15 *dissimilarly*

incongruity 113.1 *diversity*, 115.2 *unlikeness*, 117.1 *dispar-*

ity, 168.1 *nonconformity*, 666.3 *difference*

incongruous 113.5 *diverse*, 115.4 *dissimilar*, 168.11 *nonconforming*, 215.5 *unusual*, 666.10 *different*, 844.13 *improper*

incongruously 115.7 *dissimilarly*, 168.21 *unconformably*, 666.12 *differently*, 722.21 *out of place*

incongruousness 215.2 *unusualness*

in conjunction 135.16 *as one*, 664.21 *in cooperation*

in conjunction with 130.10 *additionally*, 180.24, 664.22 *with*

in connection with 137

in consent 433.7 *harmonious*, 433.12 *harmoniously*

in consequence 155.29 *consequently*, 227.12 *with the effect of*

inconsequence 612.5 *unimportance*, 783.5 *insignificance*

inconsequential 117.11 *unfit*, 474.7 *sophistic*, 521.11 *aimless*, 612.1 *unimportant*, 783.11 *insignificant*

inconsequentially 612.14 *unimportantly*

inconsiderable 127.13 *insignificant*, 260.7 *little*, 612.1 *unimportant*

inconsiderably 127.20 *insignificantly*, 260.8 *in a small way*

inconsiderate 462, 832, 436.12 *blind to*, 468.9 *thoughtless*, 652.18 *badly behaved*, 780.4 *rash*, 818.5 *discourteous*, 838.3 *ungrateful*

inconsiderate driver 652.5 *badly behaved person*

inconsiderately 468.14 *inattentively*, 652.20 *badly*, 818.9 *discourteously*, 832.20 *malevolently*, 838.7 *ungratefully*

inconsiderateness 832, 818.1 *discourtesy*, 838.1 *ingratitude*

inconsiderate person 462

inconsideration 462, 468.4 *thoughtlessness*, 780.1 *rashness*, 832.6 *inconsiderateness*

inconsistency 52.64 *reasoning*, 113.1 *diversity*, 117.1 *disparity*, 168.1 *nonconformity*, 215.1 *irregularity*, 216.1 *change*, 224.1 *changeableness*, 229.1 *lack of motive*, 474.1 *sophistry*, 491.15 *unreliability*, 504.4 *faulty reasoning*, 578.6 *equivocation*, 579.2 *caprice*, 663.6 *contrariety*, 666.3 *difference*

inconsistent 52.86 *logical*, 113.5 *diverse*, 117.7 *disparate*, 168.11 *nonconforming*, 215.4 *irregular*, 216.11, 224.13 *changeable*, 229.6 *motiveless*, 474.7 *sophistic*, 491.7 *unreliable*, 504.15 *erroneous*, 579.1 *capricious*, 663.21 *contrary*, 666.10 *different*

inconsistently 113.10 *diversely*, 117.15 *dissimilarly*, 168.21 *unconformably*, 215.8 *irregularly*, 216.15, 224.15 *changeably*, 229.8 *by chance*, 474.14 *sophistically*, 491.26 *unreliably*, 666.12 *differently*

inconsolable 770.5 *sad*

inconsonance 117.1 *disparity*

inconsonant 117.7 *disparate*

inconsonantly 117.16 *disagreeably*

inconspicuous 438.2 *difficult to see*, 542.16 *imperceptible*

inconspicuously 542.27 *imperceptibly*

inconspicuousness 542.7 *imperceptibility*

inconstancy 576, 215.1 *irregularity*, 216.1 *change*, 224.1 *changeableness*, 491.16 *capriciousness*, 579.2 *caprice*

inconstant 113.5 *diverse*, 215.4 *irregular*, 216.11, 224.13 *changeable*, 491.8 *capricious*, 539.38 *treacherous*, 576.2 *changeable*, 579.1 *capricious*

inconstantly 113.10 *diversely*,

215.8 *irregularly*, 216.15, 224.15 *changeably*, 491.27 *capriciously*

in constant use 599.9 *used*

in contact 137.14 *connective*, 267.5 *juxtaposed*, 267.7 *beside*

in contempt of 666.11 *in disagreement*

incontestable 526.14 *manifest*

incontinence 236.4 *disability*, 353.3 *urination*, 698.6 *liberality*, 727.1 *disposal*, 870.3 *overindulgence*, 877.3 *sexual immorality*

incontinent 236.12 *impotent*, 353.26 *urinary*, 698.12 *unconditional*, 870.8 *overindulgent*, 877.14 *lecherous*

incontinently 698.21 *excessively*, 870.12 *self-indulgently*

in contradiction 536.15 *negatively*, 711.11 *uncooperatively*

in contrast 107.10 *relevantly*, 231.5 *counter*

in contrast to 663.27 *opposed to*

in control 653.19 *managerially*, 688.23 *authoritatively*

incontrovertible 116.20 *agreeable*, 225.9 *stable*, 490.3 *decided*

inconvenience 616, 153.4 *disruption*, 153.10 *disrupt*, 211.1 *untimeliness*, 614.3 *uselessness*, 616.5 *be inconvenient*, 659.8 *snag*, 659.23 *cause difficulties*, 661.2 *obstacle*, 661.6 *burden*, 661.9 *block*, 661.12 *burden*

Inconvenience 616

inconvenienced 153.15 *disrupted*, 659.16 *troubled*

inconvenient 616, 659, 211.10 *untimely*, 493.9 *misjudged*, 614.1 *useless*, 661.14 *blocked*

inconveniently 616, 153.18 *disturbingly*, 211.15 *at the wrong time*, 614.10 *uselessly*, 659.28 *awkwardly*, 661.17 *in the way*

in conversation 478.24 *in answer*

in convoy 180.21 *together*

in cooperation 664

in cooperation with 664.22 *with*, 724.6 *in common*

incorporate 103.12 *embody*, 135.8 *unite*, 140.5 *combine*, 146.4 *include*, 148.11 *consist of*, 293.32 *include*, 348.13 *absorb*, 368.8 *nonmaterial*, 665.12 *be in league with*, 737.1 *trade*

incorporated 135.12 *united*, 140.7 *combined*, 293.39 *inclusive*, 665.8 *leagued*, 737.19 *corporate*

incorporated company 13.7 *corporation*, 737.7 *company*

incorporating 146.7 *including*, 148.9 *composing*

incorporation 140.1 *combination*, 146.1, 293.19 *inclusion*, 348.5 *absorption*, 664.7 *association*

incorporative 146.7 *including*

incorporator 293.17 *coverer*

incorporeal 11.18 *spiritual*, 102.8 *unreal*, 368.8 *nonmaterial*, 372.1 *sparse*

incorporeality 102.1 *unreality*, 372.3 *sparseness*

incorporeally 368.13 *metaphysically*

incorporealness 368.2 *unworldliness*

incorporeity 368.2 *unworldliness*

incorrect 844, 52.86 *logical*, 504.15 *erroneous*, 548.6 *misrepresented*, 559.9 *inelegant*, 844.13 *improper*

incorrectly 504.22 *wrongly*, 548.8 *unrepresentatively*, 844.26 *wrong*

incorrectness 844, 504.3 *erroneousness*, 559.4 *inelegance of speech*, 795.3 *grossness*, 814.5 *nonobservance*

incorrect spelling 5.27 *spelling*

incorrect usage 5.29 *grammar*, 504.11 *grammatical error*

incorrigibility 577.5 *obstinacy*, 868.1 *impenitence*

incorrigible 577.2 *refractory*,

722.16 *losing*, 776.5 *past hope*, 864.11 *wicked*, 868.3 *impenitent*
incorrigibly 864.18 *wickedly*
incorrupt 865.5 *innocent*
incorruptedness 865.1 *innocence*
incorruptibility 190.1 *eternity*, 623.3 *health*, 857.1 *probity*, 865.1 *innocence*
incorruptible 186.6 *changeless*, 190.8 *eternal*, 857.4 *honourable*, 865.5 *innocent*
incorruption 623.3 *health*, 865.1 *innocence*
in court 16.81 *legally*, 16.87 *in litigation*
incrassate 261.7 *bigger*, 273.1 *thick*, 393.16 *semiliquid*, 393.25 *thicken*, 394.8 *viscous*, 394.11 *thicken*
incrassation 393.6 *thickening*, 394.1 *viscosity*
increase **128, 128,** 120.2 *certain amount*, 120.8 *quantify*, 121.6 *change gradually*, 128.5 *make bigger*, 130.1 *addition*, 175.4 *multiplication*, 175.9 - *pluralize*, 227.3 *growth*, 227.8 *grow*, 243.7 *produce*, 261.1 *growth*, 261.5 *make bigger*, 261.6 *become bigger*, 269.10 *lengthen*, 359.2 *upturn*, 361.2 *send up*, 605.6 *store*, 606.1 - *provision*, 610.1 *excess*, 627.2 *get better*, 627.5 *improvement*, 721.2 *augmentation*, 721.10 *augment*, 768.6 *aggravate*
Increase 128
increased 128, 120.6 *quantitative*, 175.8 *multiplicative*, 261.7 *bigger*, 768.4 *aggravated*
increased output 243.2 *manufacture*
increase fourfold 178.11 *quadruple*
increase in size 261.1 *growth*, 261.5 *make bigger*, 261.6 *become bigger*
increase numbers 128.5 *make bigger*
increase one's demands 609.6 *be unsatisfied*
increaser 261.4 *enlarger*
increase the chances 488.9 *make probable*
increase the odds 488.9 *make probable*
increase threefold 177.10 *triple*
increasing 128, 121.7 *gradational*, 175.8 *multiplicative*, 227.11, 261.8 *growing*, 627.14 *improved*
increasingly 128, 121.10 *by degrees*, 261.10 *largely*
increasing thing 128
incredibility 489.6 *implausibility*, 498.2 *unbelievability*
incredible 487.2 *unbelievable*, 489.2 *questionable*, 498.7 *disbelieved*, 786.8, 786.14 *wonderful*
incredibly 487.11 *impossibly*, 489.8 *improbably*, 498.11 *unbelievably*
in credit 744, 750.13 *financially*
incredulity 498, 491.10 *suspicion*, 514.2 *amazement*
incredulous 498.6 *disbelieving*
incredulously 498.10 *disbelievingly*
increment 52.31 *differentiation*, 128.1 *increase*, 130.1 *addition*, 721.2 *augmentation*, 878.4 *reward for service*
incremental 130.8 *additional*
incriminate 852.19 *blame*, 856.5 *accuse*
incriminated 856.8 *accusatory*
incriminating evidence 483.5 *legal evidence*
incrimination 856.1 *accusation*
incriminator 856.3 *accuser*
incriminatory 856.8 *accusatory*
in-crowd 161.19 *clique*, 201.6 *avant-garde*
in crowds 181
incrusted 373.1 *hard*
incubate 245.13 *propagate*, 304.8 *nurture*, 594.7 *develop*

incubating 594.17 *developing*
incubation 245.3 *propagation*, 594.13 *development*
incubator 226.2 *source*, 637.2 *preserver*
incubus 8.7 *devil*, 369.8 *weighing down*
incudectomy 60 Surgical Operations
inculcate 6.22 *educate*, 140.5 *combine*
inculpability 865.1 *innocence*
inculpable 865.5 *innocent*
inculpate 856.5 *accuse*
inculpated 866.5 *guilty*
inculpation 866.1 *guilt*
incumbent 255.1 *inhabitant*
incumbent on 369.3 *ponderous*, 847.12 *obligatory*
incurable 398.23 *deadly*, 577.3 *unyielding*, 618.4 *poor*, 624.22 *sick*, 776.5 *past hope*
incurably 776.11 *hopelessly*
incur a duty 653.2 *direct*, 847.15 *be liable*
incur a penalty 722.9 *lose*
incur a responsibility 847.15 *be liable*
incur blame 785.7 *cause dislike*
incur costs 748.1 *expend*
incur expenses 748.1 *expend*
incuriosity 466.1 *incuriousness*, 468.1 *inattention*, 783.1 *indifference*
incurious 466, 468.7 *inattentive*, 783.7 *indifferent*
incuriously 466, 468.14 *inattentively*, 783.17 *indifferently*
incuriousness 466, 783.1 *indifference*
incur liabilities 733.10 *buy on credit*
incur loss 722.9 *lose*
incur losses 722.10 *have a financial loss*
incurred 597.5 *undertaken*
incursion 346.3 *inroad*, 357.8 *transgression*, 670.14 *siege*, 676.8 *warfare*
incursive 346.16 *invasive*
incursively 346.17 *in*
incur upon 670.9 *attack successfully*
incurvate 317.5 *concave*
incurvation 317.1 *concavity*
incurvature 311.1 *curvature*
incus 382 Bones, 420.5 *internal ear*
in custody 632.5 *safe*, 699.15 *detained*
in danger 633.3 *vulnerable*, 633.4 *endangered*
in date order 185.25 *of known date*
in Davy Jones' locker 362.24 *down*
in days gone by 3.24 *historically*
in days of yore 200.22 *in the past*
in debt 745, 661.14 *blocked*, 743.2 *insolvent*, 745.11 *insolvently*, 747.15 *without paying*, 750.13 *financially*
indebted 661.14 *blocked*, 743.2 *insolvent*, 745.9 *in debt*, 747.13 *nonpaying*, 837.4 *grateful*
indebtedness 743.6 *insolvency*, 745.1 *debt*
indecency 877, 412.4 *bad taste*, 618.10 *poverty*, 622.3 *obscenity*, 858.1 *improbity*, 864.2 *vice*
indecent 454, 877, 412.6 *coarse*, 618.4 *poor*, 622.9 *obscene*, 795.9 *ribald*, 827.8 *cursing*, 858.5 *dishonourable*, 864.12 *immoral*
indecent assault 241.2 *physical violence*, 670.16 *terrorist attack*, 877.7 *sexual assault*
indecent exposure 294.1 *uncovering*, 296.1 *undress*, 877.7 *sexual assault*
indecently 296.17 *nakedly*, 412.11 *tastelessly*, 622.12 *dirtily*, 827.12 *swearingly*, 858.11 *dishonourably*, 864.20, 877.21 *immorally*
indecently assault 877.20 *seduce*

indecently dressed 296.11 *exposed*
indecipherable 659.12 *problematic*
indecision 238.2 *indecisiveness*, 240.1 *inertness*, 365.3 *vacillation*, 491.11 *irresoluteness*, 576.11 *vacillation*
indecisive 216.11 *changeable*, 238.12 *weak-willed*, 240.5 *inert*, 491.2 *irresolute*, 576.1 *vacillating*
indecisively 216.15 *changeably*, 238.14 *weakly*, 491.23 *uncertainly*, 576.16 *irresolutely*
indecisiveness 238, 240.1 *inertness*, 491.11 *irresoluteness*
indecisive person 576
in decline 129.8 *decreasingly*, 628.12 *deteriorated*
indecorous 559, 844.13 *improper*, 864.13 *venial*
indecorously 559.11 *inelegantly*, 844.27 *improperly*, 864.19 *vulnerably*
indecorousness 844.3 *impropriety*
indecorum 864.3 *venial sin*
in deduction 131.8 *by subtraction*
indeed 772, 101.14 *certainly*, 480.12 *assuredly*, 537.35 *truly*, 537.37 *authentically*
in deep 592.15 *planning*
in deep water 659.16 *troubled*
indefatigability 575.2 *commitment*, 642.8 *assiduity*
indefatigable 378.4 *powerful*, 574.2 *tenacious*, 575.11 *steady*, 642.20 *industrious*
in default 132.12 *with a remainder*, 145.4 *incomplete*, 145.6 *incompletely*, 609.10 *insufficiently*
in default of 222.9 *instead*
indefeasible 225.9 *stable*
indefectability 619.3 *perfection*
indefectible 619.1 *perfect*
in defence 473.12 *apologetic*, 473.20 *apologetically*, 476.11 *in reply*, 478.24 *in answer*, 471.32 *defensively*
indefensible 236.11 *unprotected*
indefensibly 236.14 *powerlessly*
in defiance 668
in defiance of 666.11 *in disagreement*, 713.11 *disapprovingly*
indefinable 523.1 *unintelligible*
indefinableness 523.11 *unintelligibility*
indefinite 5.44 *grammatical*, 102.8 *unreal*, 164.20 *generalized*, 307.5 *shapeless*, 438.2 *difficult to see*, 443.4 *inscrutable*, 490.8 *unspecified*, 491.6 *indeterminate*, 523.3 *unrecognizable*, 551.2 *obscure*
indefinite article 5.35 *part of speech*
indefinite integral 52.31 *differentiation*
indefinitely 184.10 *infinitely*, 307.6 *shapelessly*, 438.9 *invisibly*, 491.25 *indeterminately*, 551.4 *obscurely*
indefiniteness 491.14 *indeterminacy*, 551.1 *obscurity*, 578.5 *equivocalness*
indefinite period 185
indefinite time 185.5 *indefinite period*
indehiscent 86.9 *of a fruit*
indehiscent fruit 86.2 *botanical fruit*
indelible 225.9 *stable*, 511.7 *memorable*
indelible ink 225.4 *stable thing*, 447.8 *black pigment*
indelibly 225.12 *stably*
indelicacy 482.6 *lack of discrimination*, 559.2 *impropriety*, 877.2 *indecency*
indelicate 482.1 *undiscriminating*, 559.8 *indecorous*, 790.4 *ugly*, 827.8 *cursing*, 877.12 *indecent*
indelicate language 827.2 *offensive language*
indelicately 482.13 *unselectively*, 559.11 *inelegantly*, 827.12

swearingly
in demand 593.4 *required*, 739.16 *sold*, 782.7 *desired*, 851.24 *admired*
indemnification 125.1, 735.2 *compensation*, 840.1 *atonement*, 878.6 *compensation*
indemnificatory 125.9 *compensatory*, 735.6 *restoring*, 840.4 *atoning*, 878.17 *compensatory*
indemnified 125.7 *compensated*
indemnifier 125.3 *compensator*
indemnify 125.4 *compensate*, 718.11 *promise*, 735.5 *compensate*, 746.10 *pay back*, 765.11 *recompense*, 839.9 *forgive*, 840.5 *atone*, 878.11 *pay*
indemnifying 125.9 *compensatory*, 735.6 *restoring*
indemnity 125.1 *compensation*, 718.2 *promise*, 735.2 *compensation*, 746.2 *repayment*, 746.4 *grant*, 765.2 *reparation*, 839.1 *forgiveness*, 840.1 *atonement*, 878.6 *compensation*
indemonstrability 491
indemonstrable 491
in denial 536.15 *negatively*
indent 317.7 *make concave*, 319.5 *notch*, 375.12 *make rough*, 543.13 *punctuate*, 593.1 *requirement*, 593.10 *necessitate*, 692.10, 712.2 *demand*, 712.7 *demand*, 715.5 *contract*, 734.1 *taking*, 734.7 *take*
indentation 317.1 *concavity*, 319.1 *notch*, 362.14 *depression*, 383.3 *nap*
indented 317.5 *concave*, 319.4 *notched*, 543.17 *punctuated*
indention 317.1 *concavity*, 543.7 *punctuation*, 734.1 *taking*
indenture 667.2, 667.7 *contract*, 701.6 *subject*
indentured 701.9 *subject*
indentured servant 701.5 *subjected person*
indentureship 701.1 *subjection*
independence 698, 12.1 *government*, 104.3 *separateness*, 108.1 *unrelatedness*, 119.1 *originality*, 139.2 *aloofness*, 570.4 *free will*, 662.4 *social assistance*, 742.8 *solvency*, 805.2 *unapproachability*, 814.4 *freedom*, 825.1 *celibacy*, 848.2 *acquittal*
Independence 93 Cities
Independence Day 214.6 *annually celebrated day*, 812.5 *anniversary*
independent 698, 848, 12.9 *governmental*, 15.10 *unionized*, 52.77 *given*, 91.16 *national*, 104.11 *separate*, 108.6 *unrelated*, 139.4 *individualist*, 139.9 *aloof*, 168.7 *nonconformist*, 168.13 *unconventional*, 174.15 *solo*, 333.4 *middle*, 570.10 *free*, 576.15 *indecisive person*, 665.6 *political party member*, 665.10 *political*, 688.14 *governmental*, 698.7 *free person*, 720.5 *nonobserver*, 720.11 *nonobservant*, 805.15 *unapproachable*, 814.10 *free*, 825.6 *celibate*
Independent Broadcasting Authority 534.24 *television broadcasting*
independently 15.13 *industrially*, 91.19 *nationally*, 104.18 *extraneously*, 108.12 *irrelevantly*, 139.11 *aloofly*, 168.22 *out of step*, 174.21 *alone*, 665.18 *cliquishly*, 688.24 *ministerially*, 698.20 *freely*, 720.16 *disobediently*, 825.12 *celibately*
independent means 698.3 *independence*
independent mind 700.1 *liberation*
independent-minded 700.7 *liberated*
independent referee 654.4 *adviser*
independent rule 698.3 *independence*
independent school 6.12 *educational institution*

independent state 91.1 *country*
independent television 534.24 *television broadcasting*
Independent Television Authority 534.24 *television broadcasting*
Independent Television Commission 534.24 *television broadcasting*
independent union 15.3 *organized labour*
independent variable 52.29 *mathematical function*
independent voter 698.7 *free person*
independent worker 646.1 *worker*
in deposit 605.7 *stored*
in depth 277.17 *profoundly*
in-depth reporting 533.3 *reporting*
in descending order 129.8 *decreasingly*
indescribable 786.8 *wonderful*
indescribably 786.13 *wonderfully*
indestructibility 217.1 *permanence,* 225.1 *stability*
indestructible 186.6 *changeless,* 217.7 *permanent,* 225.9 *stable,* 373.2, 378.1 *tough*
indestructibly 217.9 *permanently,* 225.12 *stably,* 378.12 *toughly*
in detail 143.12 *partly,* 165.32 *severally,* 277.17 *profoundly,* 469.12 *carefully,* 553.7 *diffusely*
in detention 702.8 *imprisoned*
indeterminable 184.2 *immeasurable,* 589.8 *chance*
indeterminableness 184.5 *immeasurability*
indeterminably 184.11 *immeasurably*
indeterminacy 490, 491, 56.81 *causality,* 229.1 *lack of motive,* 589.1 *chance*
indeterminant 229.6 *motiveless*
indeterminantly 229.8 *by chance*
indeterminate 491, 102.8 *unreal,* 164.20 *generalized,* 490.8 *unspecified*
indeterminately 491
indetermination 589.1 *chance*
index 52.17 *multiplication,* 150.19 *systematize,* 152.7 *catalogue,* 152.15 *categorize,* 163.14 *sort,* 169.6 *power,* 171.2 *table,* 171.8 *list,* 257.5 *divisions,* 257.9 *itemize,* 303.2 *face,* 528.5 *reference book,* 543.5 *indicator,* 543.7 *punctuation,* 545.6 *record book,* 545.13 *record*
index card 545.6 *record book*
indexed 150.11 *grouped,* 152.24 *categorized,* 171.11 *listed,* 257.12 *itemized,* 544.12 *identified,* 545.16 *recorded*
indexes 170.2 *statistics*
index finger 407.7 *sense organ,* 543.5 *indicator*
index fossil 54.43 *fossil*
indexical 150.11 *grouped,* 163.10 *classificatory*
indexically 152.28 *in place,* 257.15 *thematically*
indexing 150.2 *grouping,* 152.5 *categorization,* 171.7 *listing,* 545.8 *registration*
India 91 Countries, **534** Phonetic Alphabet, 98.1 *continent*
Indiaman 74 Ships and Boats
indian 255.1 *inhabitant*
Indian 5 Languages and Groups of Languages, **53** The Constellations, **97** Oceans and Seas, 1.6 *race,* 1.13 *racial*
Indiana 92 American States
Indianapolis 93 Cities
Indianapolis 500 674.4 *race*
Indian corn 87 Grasses
Indian dish 45
Indian elephant 77 Placental Mammals
Indian Game 68 Breeds of Fowl
Indian horse 32.1 *horse*
Indian ink 447.8 *black pigment*
Indianize 220.12 *naturalize*
Indian mode 49.20 *key*
Indian mulberry 85 Trees and Shrubs

Indian paintbrush 84 Flowers and Flowering Plants
Indian red 450.6 *red pigment*
Indian rice 87 Grasses
Indian Runner 68 Breeds of Fowl
Indian summer 55.3 *weather,* 55.23 *heat,* 203.3 *summer,* 408.5 *hot weather,* 629.10 *revival*
Indian tea 351.3 *tea*
Indian temple dance 46.4 *historic dancing*
Indian yellow 452.7 *yellow pigment*
India paper 604.3 *paper*
india rubber 377.4 *rubber*
Indic 5 Languages and Groups of Languages
indicate 154.15 *precede,* 332.6 *direct,* 437.10 *make visible,* 471.19 *epitomize,* 473.15 *state,* 475.16 *explain,* 483.10 *make evident,* 490.22 *specify,* 517.11 *predict,* 520.10 *mean,* 526.1 *display,* 526.3 *reveal,* 527.14 *imply,* 528.14 *tip,* 543.9 *use signs,* 543.10 *signify,* 544.10 *identify,* 653.2 *direct*
indicated 490.7 *particular,* 527.4 *unsaid*
indicated value 56.82 *measuring instrument*
indicating 520.6 *meaningful,* 528.16 *informative,* 544.1 *identification*
indicating instrument 56.82 *measuring instrument*
indication 483, 52.64 *reasoning,* 180.4 *concomitant,* 471.2 *theory,* 475.3 *explanation,* 490.18 *particularity,* 517.5 *omen,* 526.10 *manifestation,* 528.7 *advice,* 543.1 *sign,* 544.1 *identification,* 547.1 *representation,* 560.2 *brief description,* 560.7 *nomenclature,* 624.3 *symptom,* 636.1 *warning*
indicative 5.33 *mood,* 60.24 *diagnostic,* 471.10 *theoretical,* 475.11 *explanatory,* 483.8 *evidential,* 517.13 *predicting,* 520.6 *meaningful,* 526.14 *manifest,* 543.14 *signifying*
indicatively 543, 471.21 *purposively,* 475.22 *demonstrably,* 483.14 *as evidence,* 544.14 *identifiably*
indicator 71 Motor Vehicle Parts, **543,** 57.18 *gravimetric analysis,* 268.8 *meter,* 439.6 *electric light,* 483.4 *indication,* 543.1 *sign,* 636.1 *warning*
indicator light 439.6 *electric light*
indicatory 543.14 *signifying*
indict 16.70 *litigate,* 856.5 *accuse*
indictability 866.1 *guilt*
indictable 856.8 *accusatory*
indictable offence 16.39 *crime*
indicted 856.8 *accusatory*
indicter 856.3 *accuser*
indictment 856.1 *accusation*
indie 49.9 *popular music*
indifference 470, 783, 61.13 *depression,* 124.6 *mediocrity,* 240.1 *inertness,* 325.1 *motionlessness,* 412.1 *tastelessness,* 421.1 *deafness,* 466.2 *lack of interest,* 468.1 *inattention,* 468.4 *thoughtlessness,* 482.6 *lack of discrimination,* 512.4 *unthinkingness,* 573.13 *dissociation,* 576.14 *apathy,* 641.1 *inaction,* 643.7 *idleness,* 675.1 *peace,* 705.2 *stoicism,* 720.1 *nonobservance,* 761.3 *insensitiveness,* 787.1 *lack of wonder,* 788.1 *boredom,* 814.1 *informality,* 816.1 *unsociability,* 859.1 *disinterestedness*
Indifference 783
indifference to art 658.2 *naivety*
indifferent 470, 783, 124.3 *mediocre,* 158.15 *middling,* 240.5 *inert,* 242.6 *moderate,* 325.5 *sedentary,* 333.4 *middle,* 412.5 *tasteless,* 421.5 *unhearing,* 466.4 *uninterested,* 482.1 *undis-*

criminating, 512.10 *unthinking,* 576.4 *unsteady,* 598.6 *apathetic,* 617.5 *not bad,* 641.3 *inactive,* 643.3 *not participating,* 698.10 *independent,* 705.8 *resigned,* 720.11 *nonobservant,* 761.1 *insensitive,* 787.3 *unmoved,* 788.4 *boring,* 814.7 *informal,* 816.8 *unsociable,* 859.4 *disinterested*
in different directions 115.7 *dissimilarly*
indifferentism 783.1 *indifference*
indifferentist 783.6 *indifferent person*
indifferently 783, 240.7 *inertly,* 466.8 *disinterestedly,* 468.14 *inattentively,* 482.13 *unselectively,* 512.16 *obliviously,* 598.8 *apathetically,* 641.5 *without action,* 643.16 *impassively,* 698.20 *freely,* 705.9 *stoically,* 761.8 *unfeelingly,* 787.9 *without wonder,* 788.8 *boringly,* 816.14 *unsocially,* 859.8 *disinterestedly*
indifferent person 783
in different ways 113.10 *diversely*
in difficulties 659.16 *troubled,* 687.6 *adverse,* 743.2 *insolvent,* 745.9 *in debt*
indigence 571.4 *need,* 743.5 *poverty*
indigene 255.1 *inhabitant*
indigenous 1.13 *racial,* 83.15 *wild,* 208.15 *precursory,* 255.12 *native*
indigenously 208.19 *primevally*
indigenous race 1.6 *race*
indigent 571.11 *needy,* 743.1 *poor,* 743.10 *poor person*
indigestibility 378.6 *toughness*
indigestible 378.3 *hard,* 595.6 *uncooked,* 626.5 *unhygienic*
indigestibly 378.12 *toughly*
indigestion 624, 406.2 *painful condition*
indignant 828.15 *resentful,* 828.16 *angry,* 852.25 *disapproving*
indignantly 828.17 *resentfully,* 828.18 *angrily*
indignation 852.1 *disapproval*
indignity 850, 828.2 *offence*
indigo 56.28 *colour,* 444.4 *pigment,* 454.1 *blue,* 454.5 *blueness,* 455.6 *purple*
in diplomatic language 716.9 *feasibly*
indirect 335, 5.44 *grammatical,* 38.5 *soccer,* 106.7 *circumstantial,* 286.4 *oblique,* 286.5 *devious,* 334.7 *circuitous,* 363.9 *orbital,* 527.5 *mysterious,* 539.34 *deceiving,* 551.2 *obscure,* 553.4 *circumlocutory*
indirect authority 688.1 *authority*
indirect cannon 24.3 *English billiards*
indirect costs 13.7 *corporation*
indirect course 335.14 *deviating course*
in-directed 61.34 *introverted*
indirect election 580.12 *election*
indirect evidence 483.5 *legal evidence*
indirect free kick 38.2 *football play*
indirect influence 233
indirection 286.1 *obliqueness,* 286.3 *deviousness,* 335.13 *deviation,* 363.2 *circuitousness,* 539.1 *deception*
indirectly 335, 5.52 *grammatically,* 106.16 *relatively,* 286.9 *deviously,* 334.8, 363.12 *circuitously,* 527.15 *latently,* 551.4 *obscurely,* 553.8 *circuitously,* 707.8 *by proxy*
indirect motion 335.15 *deviating motion*
indirectness 286.1 *obliqueness,* 551.1 *obscurity,* 553.2 *circumlocution*
indirect object 5.35 *part of speech*
indirect proof 52.66 *proof*
indirect question 5.23 *phrase,* 477.11 *question mark*

indirect radiation 55.22 *sun*
indirect speech 5.23 *phrase*
indirect tax 749.2 *money received,* 751.7 *tax*
indirect wave 534.15 *transmitted wave*
in dire straits 687.7 *unprosperous,* 745.9 *in debt*
in disagreement 666
in disarray 151.12 *disordered,* 151.27 *in disorder*
indiscernibility 438.4 *invisibility*
indiscernible 260.7 *little,* 438.1 *invisible*
indiscernibly 260.9 *microscopically,* 438.9 *invisibly*
indiscipline 689.1 *anarchy,* 693.1 *disobedience,* 870.3 *overindulgence*
indiscreet 482.1 *undiscriminating,* 528.16 *informative,* 530.11 *disclosing,* 656.3 *clumsy,* 780.4 *rash,* 864.13 *venial*
indiscreetly 530.13 *openly,* 864.19 *vulnerably*
indiscretion 482.6 *lack of discrimination,* 508.1 *folly,* 530.3 *openness,* 656.9 *bungling,* 780.1 *rashness,* 864.3 *venial sin,* 866.3 *sin*
indiscriminate 482, 783.9 *impartial*
indiscriminate bombing 670.13 *air attack*
indiscriminately 482, 151.27 *in disorder,* 783.19 *impartially*
indiscriminateness 482
indiscriminating 656.3 *clumsy*
indiscrimination 482.6 *lack of discrimination,* 783.3 *impartiality*
in disequilibrium 123.3 *unequal*
in dishabille 296
in disorder 151, 151.12 *disordered*
indispensability 571, 593.3 *needfulness*
indispensable 103.5 *essential,* 571.9 *necessary,* 593.4 *required,* 611.5 *important*
indispensableness 571.2 *indispensability*
indispensably 593.12 *in need*
indispose 587.4 *put off*
indisposed 573.1 *unwilling,* 624.22 *sick*
indisposition 573.11 *unwillingness,* 624.1 *ill health,* 624.2 *illness*
indisputability 490.9 *certainty*
indisputable 99.13 *real,* 225.9 *stable,* 475.12 *demonstrable,* 535.16 *definite*
indisputably 225.12 *stably,* 480.12 *assuredly,* 535.23 *affirmatively*
in disrepair 628.13 *dilapidated*
indissolubility 174.3 *oneness,* 371.1 *density*
indissoluble 135.12 *united,* 174.13 *whole,* 225.9 *stable,* 371.7 *condensed,* 726.9 *retentive*
indissolubly 135.16 *as one,* 225.12 *stably,* 726.11 *tenaciously*
indistinct 424.4 *faint,* 428.1 *faint-sounding,* 436.13 *hidden,* 438.2 *difficult to see,* 441.6 *murky,* 482.5 *vague,* 491.6 *indeterminate,* 523.3 *unrecognizable,* 542.16 *imperceptible,* 551.2 *obscure*
indistinctive 482.5 *vague*
indistinctly 424.7 *faintly,* 438.9 *invisibly,* 441.12 *dimly,* 491.25 *indeterminately,* 542.27 *imperceptibly,* 551.4 *obscurely*
indistinctness 424.1 *faintness,* 428.3 *muteness,* 438.4 *invisibility,* 441.2 *murk,* 491.14 *indeterminacy,* 551.1 *obscurity*
indistinguishability 110.1 *sameness,* 116.5 *conformity,* 438.4 *invisibility*
indistinguishable 110.12 *same,* 116.14 *conforming,* 438.1 *invisible,* 441.6 *murky,* 523.3 *unrecognizable*

indistinguishably 110.18 *identically*, 116.34 *uniformly*, 438.9 *invisibly*, 482.14 *indiscriminately*

in distress 743.1 *poor*

indium 57 Chemical Elements

individual 59.3 *organism*, 108.6 *unrelated*, 113.5 *diverse*, 117.9 *nonconforming*, 119.5 *novel*, 142.6 *whole*, 144.7 *complete*, 165.13 *person*, 165.15 *special*, 168.14 *eccentric*, 174.1, 174.11 *one*, 174.14 *singular*, 215.5 *unusual*, 396.1 *life*, 400.7 *person*, 400.12 *human*, 490.7 *particular*, 543.14 *signifying*, 698.10 *independent*

individualism 4.7 *school of thought*, 698.3 *independence*, 860.1 *selfishness*

individualist 139, 4.11 *follower of a doctrine*, 41.11 *skier*, 117.6 *misfit*, 698.7 *free person*

individualistic 4.14 *of a philosophy*, 165.15 *special*, 165.18 *subjective*, 168.14 *eccentric*, 698.10 *independent*, 860.4 *selfish*

individualistically 698.20 *freely*, 860.8 *selfishly*

individuality 108.1 *unrelatedness*, 113.1 *diversity*, 117.3 *nonconformity*, 119.1 *originality*, 165.1 *speciality*, 168.4 *unusualness*, 174.4 *singularity*, 367.1 *material world*, 544.2 *identity*, 698.3 *independence*

individualize 117.13 *not conform*, 165.26 *personalize*

individualized 165.20 *personalized*

individually 108.12 *irrelevantly*, 113.10 *diversely*, 117.15 *dissimilarly*, 119.8 *originally*, 165.29 *personally*, 174.22 *one by one*, 400.15 *humanly*, 543.18 *indicatively*, 698.20 *freely*

individual project 472.5 *educational topic*

individual psychology 61.1 *psychology*

individual retirement account 13.6 *economic factors*

individual test 61.5 *psychological test*

indivisibility 134.8 *simplicity*, 138.1 *adhesion*, 142.1 *whole*, 174.3 *oneness*, 371.1 *density*

indivisible 52.74 *divisible*, 103.7 *integral*, 134.16 *simple*, 135.12 *united*, 138.9 *adhesive*, 174.13 *whole*, 371.6 *dense*

indivisibly 135.16 *as one*, 138.11 *cohesively*, 174.23 *wholly*

Indo-Chinese 5 Languages and Groups of Languages

indocile 577.2 *refractory*

indocility 573.14 *disobedience*, 577.5 *obstinacy*

indoctrinate 6.22 *educate*, 167.10 *assimilate*, 220.11 *persuade*, 497.9 *make someone believe*, 584.18 *habituate*, 586.15 *persuade*

indoctrination 6.1 *education*, 220.3 *persuasion*, 584.7 *habituation*, 586.5 *propaganda*

indoctrinator 220.5 *converter*

Indo-European 5 Languages and Groups of Languages, 5.11 *family of languages*

Indo-Germanic 5 Languages and Groups of Languages, 5.11 *family of languages*

Indo-Hittite 5 Languages and Groups of Languages

Indo-Iranian 5 Languages and Groups of Languages, 5.11 *family of languages*

indolence 99.9 *mere existence*, 240.1 *inertness*, 325.1 *motionlessness*, 328.8 *slowness*, 641.1 *inaction*, 643.7 *idleness*

indolent 99.16 *vegetating*, 240.5 *inert*, 325.5 *sedentary*, 328.5 *unhurried*, 641.3 *inactive*, 643.3 *not participating*

indolently 240.7 *inertly*, 328.16

slowly, 643.16 *impassively*

indomethacin 62 Medication

Indomitable 575, 574.4 *undaunted*, 778.9 *courageous*

Indonesia 91 Countries

Indonesian 5 Languages and Groups of Languages

indoor 31.8 *hockey*, 39.11 *swimming*, 290.8 *internal*, 301.7 *enclosed*

indoor game 42.1 *game*

indoor garden 69.2 *garden*

indoor gardening 69.1 *horticulture*

indoor hockey 31.1 *hockey*

indoors 290.2 *inside*

indoor sport 18.4 *sporting activity*

indoor swimming pool 39.7 *swimming pool*

indoor track events 21.1 *track events*

Indo-Pacific 5 Languages and Groups of Languages

Indore 93 Cities

in double harness 823.21 *married*, 823.24 *matrimonially*

in double jeopardy 633.4 *endangered*

in double-quick time 329.14 *swiftly*

in double-time 329.14 *swiftly*

in doubt 477.14 *questionable*, 477.24 *questionably*

Indra 8 Deities, 676.3 *god of war*

in draft 592.14 *planned*

indraught 346.2 *influx*, 348.4 *intake*

indrawal 346.2 *influx*, 348.4 *intake*

indrawing 346.2 *influx*

indri 77 Placental Mammals

in dribs and drabs 143.12 *partly*, 160.17 *discontinuously*, 182.10 *in ones and twos*

indubitability 490.9 *certainty*, 535.8 *definiteness*

indubitable 488.6 *probable*, 490.3 *decided*, 535.16 *definite*

indubitableness 535.8 *definiteness*

indubitably 101.14 *certainly*, 488.11 *probably*, 490.23 *certainly*, 535.23 *affirmatively*, 537.37 *authentically*

induce 60.20 *practise surgery*, 226.10 *awaken*, 228.9 *motivate*, 340.11 *attract*, 355.15 *draw out*, 459.12 *think*, 463.11 *reason*, 473.14 *discuss*, 586.15 *persuade*, 710.9 *offer*

induced 228.12 *motivated*, 586.20 *persuadable*

induced current 56.51, 64.9 *electric current*

induced electricity 235.7 *electrical power*

induced sweat 353.8 *sweat*

inducement 228, 340.2 *pulling power*, 586.1 *persuasion*, 586.8 *incentive*, 729.2 *gift*, 878.4 *reward for service*

inducing 586.19 *persuasive*

inducing secretion 352

induct 156.23 *inaugurate*, 156.25, 346.14 *enrol*, 354.7 *install*, 703.6 *commission*, 812.19 *install*

inductance 56.53, 64.12 *resistance*, 235.7 *electrical power*

induction 4.4 *philosophical investigation*, 7.9 *priesthood*, 52.64 *reasoning*, 59.15 *developmental biology*, 60.9 *surgery*, 156.8 *enrolment*, 235.7 *electrical power*, 346.1 *entry*, 348.3 *introduction*, 459.2 *ways of thinking*, 463.2 *reasoning*, 473.2 *logical argument*, 518.2 *basis of supposition*, 703.1 *commission*

induction coil 64.17 *resistor*

induction motor 64.31 *electric motor*

induction training 15.2 *industrial negotiations*

inductive 52.86 *logical*, 64.36 *electronic*, 340.10 *magnetic*, 463.8 *rational*

inductively 473.19 *logically*

inductive reasoning 463.2 *reasoning*

inductor 56.55 *circuit*, 64.17 *resistor*

in due course 199.14 *in the future*, 209.17 *later*

in due form 813.12 *formally*

indulge 351.13 *drink*, 405.9 *give pleasure*, 467.14 *be solicitous*, 662.22 *improve*, 691.3 *be lenient*, 708.4 *be permissive*, 765.8 *satisfy*, 771.15 *humour*, 831.8 *be benevolent*

indulged 691.5 *given consideration*, 839.6 *forgiven*

indulge in 640.4 *act*, 652.11 *conduct oneself*, 870.10 *indulge oneself*

indulge in wishful thinking 539.25 *deceive oneself*

indulgence 405.1 *physical pleasure*, 467.5 *solicitude*, 628.8 *perversion*, 691.1 *leniency*, 708.1 *permission*, 814.4 *freedom*, 839.1 *forgiveness*, 839.2 *forgivingness*

indulgent 467.9 *solicitous*, 660.13 *easygoing*, 662.35 *benevolent*, 691.4 *lenient*, 708.8 *permitting*, 814.10 *free*, 831.6 *benevolent*, 839.5 *merciful*

indulgently 405.11 *pleasingly*, 691.6 *leniently*, 708.9 *with permission*, 831.10 *benevolently*, 839.14 *forgivingly*

indulge one's appetite 872.5 *be greedy*

indulge oneself 870, 405.8 *feel pleasure*, 689.4 *be anarchic*, 860.6 *be selfish*, 872.5 *be greedy*

indulge one's fancy 580.4 *pick*

indulging 771.11 *humouring*

in duplicate 110.18 *identically*, 245.17 *repeatedly*

indurate 373.3 *hardened*, 868.5 *be impenitent*

indurated 373.3 *hardened*

induration 868.1 *impenitence*

indurative 868.3 *impenitent*

Indus 53 The Constellations, **96** Rivers

indusium 88.2 *fern plant*

industrial 15, 15, 2.13 *communal*, 44.10 *ceramic*, 243.11 *productive*, 737.17 *professional*

industrial action 15.4 *industrial dispute*, 218.2 *stop*, 475.6 *mass demonstration*, 711.1 *refusal*

industrial archaeology 3.2 *archaeology*, 200.9 *antiquarianism*

industrial architect 43.2 *architect*

industrial architecture 43.1 *architecture*

industrial area 647.1 *workshop*

industrial art 50.1 *art*

industrial artist 50.16 *artist*

industrial ceramics 44

industrial chemistry 57, 57.1 *chemistry*

industrial city 93.1 *city*

industrial conflict 15.4 *industrial dispute*

industrial design 50.1 *art*

industrial designer 50.16 *artist*

industrial dispute 15

industrial engineering 63.3 *mechanical engineering*

industrial espionage 529.2 *secretiveness*

industrial estate 647.1 *workshop*

industrial institution 2.8 *human institution*

industrialist 243.9 *producer*, 646.3 *agent*

industrialization 13.4 *economic development*, 243.2 *manufacture*

industrialize 2.15 *socialize*, 243.10 *produce*

industrialized 2.13 *communal*, 243.11 *productive*

industrialized society 2.5 *society*

industrializing governmental 2.13 *communal*

industrial law 15.5 *labour law*

industrially 15, 2.16 *sociologically*, 43.20 *architecturally*,

44.12 *ornamentally*

industrial medicine 60.1 *medicine*

industrial negotiations 15

industrial organization 2.4 *social organization*

industrial psychologist 61.29 *psychologist*

industrial psychology 61.1 *psychology*

Industrial Relations 15

industrial relations 13

Industrial Relations Act 15.5 *labour law*

industrial revolution 13.6 *economic factors*

Industrial Revolution 200.5 *historical period*

industrial rock 49.9 *popular music*

industrial safety 13.8 *industrial relations*

industrial spy 713.5 *seditionist*

industrial strife 15.4 *industrial dispute*

industrial town 647.1 *workshop*

industrial tribunal 15.1 *industrial relations*

industrial union 15.3 *organized labour*

industrial unionism 15.1 *industrial relations*

industries fair 740.2 *fair*

industrious 642, 575.10 *persevering*, 640.5 *acting*, 644.10 *working*

industriously 642.22 *actively*

industriousness 575.2 *commitment*, 642.8 *assiduity*

industry 243.2 *manufacture*, 642.6 *business*, 642.8 *assiduity*, 644.1 *work*, 737.6 *business*

industry-wide 15.10 *unionized*

industry-wide strike 15.4 *industrial dispute*

in Dutch 659.16 *troubled*

indweller 255.1 *inhabitant*

indwelt 255.11 *inhabited*

IndyCar racing 33.11 *motor racing*, 674.4 *race*

in earnest 535.24 *truthfully*, 574.17 *resolutely*

in easy circumstances 742.1 *wealthy*

inebriant 874.6 *intoxicating*

inebriate 874.5 *drunken*, 874.9 *be intoxicating*, 874.17 *drunkard*

inebriated 874.1 *drunk*

inebriating 874.6 *intoxicating*

inebriation 874.10 *drunkenness*

inebriative 874.6 *intoxicating*

inebriety 874.10 *drunkenness*

inedibility 378.6 *toughness*

inedible 378.3 *hard*, 415.6 *unpalatable*, 595.6 *uncooked*, 626.5 *unhygienic*, 764.3 *unpalatable*

inedibly 415.10 *sourly*

ineffability 523.11 *unintelligibility*

ineffable 8.13 *divine*, 487.2 *unbelievable*, 502.8 *unknown*, 523.1 *unintelligible*, 786.8 *wonderful*

ineffably 8.19 *divinely*, 786.13 *wonderfully*

in effect 99.10 *existing*, 101.13 *really*, 142.13 *on the whole*

ineffective 145.4 *incomplete*, 236.10 *powerless*, 247.6 *having no effect*, 521.10 *meaningless*, 555.1 *unemphatic*, 614.1 *useless*, 683.10 *failed*

ineffectively 145.6 *incompletely*, 236.14 *powerlessly*, 614.10 *uselessly*, 683.12 *unsuccessfully*

ineffectiveness 145.1 *incompleteness*, 236.1 *powerlessness*, 555.2 *lack of emphasis*, 614.3 *uselessness*, 683.1 *failure*

ineffectual 145.4 *incomplete*, 236.10 *powerless*, 238.8 *weak*, 521.10 *meaningless*, 521.11 *aimless*, 576.3 *timid*, 612.1 *unimportant*, 614.1 *useless*, 656.1 *unskilful*, 683.10 *failed*

ineffectuality 145.1 *incompleteness*, 236.1 *powerlessness*, 238.2 *indecisiveness*, 521.1 *lack of meaning*, 521.2 *aimlessness*, 656.8 *unskilfulness*

ineffectually 145.6 *incompletely*, 236.14 *powerlessly*, 238.14 *weakly*, 612.14 *unimportantly*, 614.10 *uselessly*, 683.12 *unsuccessfully*

ineffectualness 614.3 *uselessness*

inefficacious 236.10 *powerless*, 683.10 *failed*

inefficaciously 683.12 *unsuccessfully*

inefficacy 614.3 *uselessness*

inefficiency 236.1 *powerlessness*, 614.3 *uselessness*, 618.8 *inferiority*, 656.8 *unskillfulness*, 683.1 *failure*

inefficient 236.10 *powerless*, 614.1 *useless*, 618.2 *inferior*, 656.1 *unskilful*

inefficiently 236.14 *powerlessly*, 656.11 *unskilfully*

inelastic 371.6 *dense*, 373.2 *tough*, 378.3 *hard*, 379.1 *brittle*, 577.3 *unyielding*

inelasticity 373.5 *hardness*, 379.2 *brittleness*, 577.6 *determination*, 669.2 *obstinacy*

inelastic scattering 56.71 *nuclear reaction*

inelastic strain 63.14 *load*

inelegance 549, 559, 795, 117.5 *unfitness*, 412.4 *bad taste*, 551.1 *obscurity*

Inelegance 559

inelegance of speech 559

inelegancy 559.1 *inelegance*

inelegant 549, 559, 117.11 *unfit*, 412.6 *coarse*, 551.2 *obscure*, 559.7 *graceless*, 656.3 *clumsy*, 790.4 *ugly*, 795.7 *vulgar*

inelegantly 559, 117.17 *unsuitably*, 412.11 *tastelessly*, 551.4 *obscurely*

ineligible 117.11 *unfit*, 581.10 *rejected*, 616.1 *inconvenient*

ineligible athlete 581.9 *rejected person*

ineligible receiver 19.13 *penalty*

ineluctability 490.16, 571.5 *inevitability*

ineluctable 490.5, 571.12 *inevitable*, 695.10 *compulsory*

ineluctably 490.25 *inevitably*

in embryo 145.6 *incomplete*, 156.41 *in the bud*, 594.17 *developing*

in employment 697.9 *serving*

inept 117.11 *unfit*, 236.10 *powerless*, 508.5 *foolish*, 614.1 *useless*, 616.1 *inconvenient*, 656.1 *unskilful*, 776.8 *bad*

ineptitude 236.1 *powerlessness*, 508.1 *folly*, 614.3 *uselessness*, 656.8 *unskilfulness*

ineptly 117.17 *unsuitably*, 236.14 *powerlessly*, 656.11 *unskilfully*

ineptness 656.8 *unskilfulness*

inequal 375.1 *rough*

inequality 123, 52.26 *equality*, 108.4 *distortion*, 113.1 *diversity*, 117.1 *disparity*, 215.1 *irregularity*, 375.6 *roughness*, 493.3 *injustice*, 666.3 *difference*

Inequality 123

inequally 375.14 *roughly*

in equal measures 717.9 *compromisingly*

in equal parts 717.9 *compromisingly*

in equal portions 667.16 *compatibly*

in equilibrium 116.13 *harmonious*, 122.12 *equally*, 125.10 *counterbalancing*

inequitable 123.4 *unjust*, 481.10 *discriminatory*, 844.11 *wrong*

inequitably 123.8 *unjustly*, 481.17 *prejudicially*

inequity 123.2 *injustice*, 481.3 *prejudice*, 844.1 *unfairness*

ineradicable 103.7 *integral*, 225.9 *stable*

inerrantist 7.4 *religionist*

in error 493.7 *misjudging*, 493.13 *misguidedly*, 504.17 *mistaken*, 504.21 *erroneously*, 525.4 *mistakenly*

inert 240, 57.34 *elemental*, 99.16 *vegetating*, 325.5 *sedentary*, 328.5 *unhurried*, 527.1 *latent*, 591.18 *avoiding*, 641.3, 643.1 *inactive*, 761.2 *desensitized*, 783.7 *indifferent*

inert gas 57.6 *chemical element*

inertia 56.9 *mass*, 99.9 *mere existence*, 240.1 *inertness*, 325.1 *motionlessness*, 328.8 *slowness*, 641.1 *inaction*, 643.5 *inactivity*, 783.1 *indifference*

inertial navigation 74.5 *navigation*

inertly 240, 325.10 *motionlessly*, 466.8 *disinterestedly*, 641.5 *without action*, 643.15 *inactively*, 783.17 *indifferently*

inertness 240, 325.1 *motionlessness*, 328.8 *slowness*, 527.6 *latency*, 576.14 *apathy*, 641.1 *inaction*, 643.5 *inactivity*

Inertness 240

inert person 240

inert thing 240

inescapable 490.5, 571.12 *inevitable*, 847.12 *obligatory*

inescapableness 490.16 *inevitability*

inescapably 490.25 *inevitably*

in essence 103, 142.13 *on the whole*, 257.13 *structurally*, 472.14 *thematically*

inessential 104.8 *intruder*, 612.1 *unimportant*, 612.8 *trifle*

inessentiality 104.1 *extraneousness*, 612.5 *unimportance*

inestimable 184.2 *immeasurable*, 617.3, 753.8 *valuable*

inestimably 184.11 *immeasurably*, 753.13 *valuably*

in estrangement 824.13 *without one's spouse*

inevasible 490.5 *inevitable*

inevasibleness 490.16 *inevitability*

in everyday use 599.9 *used*

in every detail 537.39 *accurately*

in every direction 332.11 *in all directions*

in every nook and cranny 248.16 *extensively*

in every place 248.16 *extensively*

in every quarter 248.16 *extensively*, 332.11 *in all directions*

in every respect 142.11 *wholly*

in every way 144.9 *completely*

in evidence 475.22 *demonstrably*, 483.14 *as evidence*

inevitability 490, 571, 112.1 *uniformity*

inevitable 490, 571, 112.5 *uniform*, 695.9 *compelling*

inevitableness 490.16 *inevitability*

inevitably 490, 112.13 *uniformly*, 571.19 *necessarily*, 695.11 *compellingly*

inexact 164.20 *generalized*, 470.5 *indifferent*, 482.5 *vague*, 491.6 *indeterminate*, 504.15 *erroneous*, 538.13 *untrue*, 551.2 *obscure*, 555.1 *unemphatic*, 656.3 *clumsy*

inexactitude 164.3 *nonspecificness*, 470.2 *indifference*, 482.8 *indiscriminateness*, 504.2 *inaccuracy*, 555.2 *lack of emphasis*

inexactly 482.14 *indiscriminately*, 504.22 *wrongly*, 538.26 *untruthfully*, 551.4 *obscurely*, 555.3 *unemphatically*

inexactness 490.19, 491.14 *indeterminacy*, 493.1 *misjudgment*, 504.2 *inaccuracy*, 538.1 *untruth*, 551.1 *obscurity*

in excess 870.12 *self-indulgently*

in excess of requirements 610.8 *excessively*

in exchange 223, 223, 109.10 *reciprocally*, 728.6 *by transfer*

in exchange for 223.8 *in exchange*

inexcitability 4.3 *detachment*, 240.1 *inertness*, 783.1 *indifference*, 787.1 *lack of wonder*

inexcitable 325.6 *quiescent*,

783.7 *indifferent*, 787.3 *unmoved*

inexcusable 844.17 *unforgivable*, 864.11 *wicked*, 866.5 *guilty*

inexcusably 864.18 *wickedly*, 866.11 *guiltily*

inexhaustible 181.8 *numberless*, 219.6 *protracted*, 608.2 *plentiful*

inexhaustibly 219.7 *continually*, 608.9 *enough*, 757.9 *extravagantly*

in existence 253.14 *in person*

inexistence 254.1 *absence*

inexistent 254.8 *absent*

inexorability 490.16, 571.5 *inevitability*, 574.14 *tenacity*

inexorable 336.18 *ongoing*, 490.5, 571.12 *inevitable*, 574.3 *strong-willed*, 577.3 *unyielding*, 836.5 *inflexible*

inexorableness 836.2 *inflexibility*

inexorably 490.25 *inevitably*, 577.9 *be obstinate*

inexpectant 595.1 *unprepared*, 786.6 *wondering*

in expectation 133.5 *expecting*

inexpedience 117.5 *unfitness*, 211.1 *untimeliness*, 614.3 *uselessness*, 616.3 *inconvenience*

inexpediency 614.3 *uselessness*, 616.3 *inconvenience*

inexpedient 117.11 *unfit*, 211.10 *untimely*, 614.1 *useless*, 616.1 *inconvenient*

inexpediently 117.17 *unsuitably*, 211.15 *at the wrong time*, 616.6 *inconveniently*

inexpensive 754.9 *cheap*

inexpensively 738.15, 754.15 *cheaply*

inexpensiveness 754.1 *cheapness*

inexperience 201.3, 206.3 *immaturity*, 502.2 *half-knowledge*, 585.3 *unaccustomedness*, 656.8 *unskilfulness*, 658.2, 865.3 *naivety*

inexperienced 201.12, 206.12 *immature*, 453.3 *raw*, 502.7 *semi-skilled*, 585.1 *unaccustomed*, 595.4 *untrained*, 656.2 *unskilled*, 658.1, 865.7 *naive*

inexpert 453.3 *raw*, 502.7 *semi-skilled*, 656.2 *unskilled*

inexpertly 585.7, 656.11 *unskilfully*

inexpertness 502.2 *half-knowledge*, 656.8 *unskilfulness*

inexpiable 864.11 *wicked*

in explanation 524.18 *in other words*, 855.15 *in vindication*

inexplicability 229.1 *lack of motive*, 523.11 *unintelligibility*, 589.1 *chance*

inexplicable 229.6 *motiveless*, 523.1 *unintelligible*, 589.9 *causeless*

inexplicably 229.8 *by chance*, 523.13 *unintelligibly*, 589.13 *by chance*

inexpressibility 523.11 *unintelligibility*

inexpressible 523.1 *unintelligible*, 786.8 *wonderful*

inexpugnable 632.6 *invulnerable*

inextensibility 373.5 *hardness*

inextinguishable 225.9 *stable*, 241.6 *violent*

inextricable 135.12 *united*, 138.9 *adhesive*

inextricably 135, 135.16 *as one*, 138.11 *cohesively*

in fact 99.22, 101.13 *really*, 537.35 *truly*

in fair condition 617.5 *not bad*

in fair health 623.1 *healthy*

in fairness 843.17 *by rights*

infallibility 490, 619.3 *perfection*

infallible 490, 619.1 *perfect*

infamous 501.10 *known*, 526.14 *manifest*, 532.20 *well-known*, 801.4 *disreputable*, 844.15 *immoral*, 864.11 *wicked*

infamy 532.7 *publicity*, 801.1 *disrespect*, 864.1 *wickedness*

infancy 156.4 *conception*, 206.1 *youth*, 236.3 *helplessness*

infant 156.15 *baby*, 156.32 *embryonic*, 206.9 *child*, 206.11 *young*, 238.4 *weakling*, 563.7 *voiceless person*, 563.9 *voiceless*, 865.4 *innocent person*

infanticide 10.7 *non-Christian ritual*, 398.3 *homicide*, 398.11 *murderer*, 832.7 *act of malevolence*

infantile 206.11 *young*, 460.6 *unintelligent*

infantile fixation 61.17 *fixation*

infantile paralysis 624.17 *nervous disorder*

infant prodigy 786.5 *person of wonder*

infantry 679.16 *army unit*

infantry assault 670.12 *military attack*

infantry battalion 17.4 *military organization*

infantry division 17.4 *military organization*

infantry engagement 676.9 *battle*

infantryman 676.11 *recruit*, 679.17 *army person*

infantry regiment 17.4 *military organization*

infantry service 676.8 *warfare*

infant school 6.12 *educational institution*

infants' wear 295.23 *children's clothes*

infarct 323.2 *stopper*

infarction 624.10 *cardiovascular disease*

in fashion 105.9 *conditionally*, 196.6 *present*, 201.23 *trendily*, 584.12 *established*

infatuated 784.6 *liking*, 821.19 *enamoured*

infatuated with 821.18 *in love*

infatuating 784.5 *likable*

infatuatingly 784.10 *with great liking*

infatuation 784.1 *liking*, 784.3 *likes*, 821.2 *romantic love*

in favour 572.1 *willing*, 819.9 *friends with*, 851.19 *supporting*

in favour of 222.9 *instead*

in favour with 800.3 *reputable*

in fear and trembling 777.7 *frightened*

in fear of 777.15 *fearfully*

infect 133.10 *become mixed*, 228.10 *manipulate*, 233.9 *change*, 326.11 *transfer*, 618.13 *be worthless*, 622.11 *dirty*, 628.3 *make worse*, 631.15 *poison*

infected 618.4 *poor*, 624.23 *diseased*, 626.6 *contagious*

infection 624, 133.1 *mixture*, 233 *influence*, 326.3 *transmission*, 618.10 *poverty*, 622.2 *uncleanness*, 624.5 *plague*, 626.2 *germ*, 628.10 *impairment*, 631.7 *poisoning*, 687.1 *adversity*

infectious 233.12 *appealing*, 326.17 *transferable*, 618.5 *harmful*, 622.8 *unclean*, 624.23 *diseased*, 626.6 *contagious*, 633.1 *dangerous*

infectious disease 326.10 *transferred thing*, 624.4 *disease*

infectiously 133.14 *in the midst*, 233.14 *influentially*, 326.18 *in transit*, 626.8 *unhygienically*

infectious mononucleosis 624.6 *infection*

infectiousness 624.6 *infection*, 626.1 *lack of hygiene*

infectious person 626, 326.9 *disease carrier*

infective 626.6 *contagious*

infective hepatitis 624.6 *infection*

infecund 247.3 *birth control*

infecundity 247.1 *infertility*

infelicitous 117.11 *unfit*, 211.14 *accidental*, 616.1 *inconvenient*, 656.4 *bungled*

infelicitously 117.17 *unsuitably*

infelicity 117.5 *unfitness*, 656.7 *bungling*

infer 520, 4.21 *rationalize*, 52.89 *theorize*, 461.16 *have an idea*, 463.11 *reason*, 492.12 *estimate*, 518.5 *suppose*, 524.8 *in-*

terpret, 528.15 *be informed*
inference 4.4 *philosophical investigation*, 4.8 *philosophical term*, 52.64 *reasoning*, 227.1 *effect*, 463.2 *reasoning*, 492.1 *judgment*, 518.2 *basis of supposition*, 527.10 *quietness*, 528.7 *advice*
inferential 52.86 *logical*, 106.7 *circumstantial*, 463.8 *rational*, 527.4 *unsaid*
inferentially 106.16 *relatively*
inferior 127, 127, 618, 115.4 *dissimilar*, 123.3 *unequal*, 124.3 *mediocre*, 195.7, 195.13 *subordinate*, 276.6 *lower*, 358.8 *defective*, 515.11 *disappointing*, 609.1 *insufficient*, 612.4 *trivial*, 612.10 *nonentity*, 620.1 *imperfect*, 577.1 *servant*, 701.3 *subordinate*, 701.9 *subject*, 754.10 *shoddy*, 776.8 *bad*
inferiority 127, 618, 123.1 *inequality*, 124.6 *mediocrity*, 195.3 *subordination*, 276.1 *lowness*, 358.6 *shortcoming*, 609.8 *insufficiency*, 612.7 *triviality*, 620.5 *imperfection*, 701.1 *subjection*, 754.3 *shoddiness*
inferiority 127
inferiority complex 61.18 *complex*
inferiorly 127
inferior numbers 127
inferior personality 61.8 *disordered personality*
inferior planet 53.16 *planet*
inferior rank 701.1 *subjection*
inferior standing 127.1 *inferiority*
inferior state 127
inferior status 127.1 *inferiority*, 701.1 *subjection*
inferior thing 127
inferior version 620.6 *imperfect item*
infernal 8.16 *devilish*, 618.6 *damnable*, 832.11 *cruel*, 864.14 *impious*
infernally 8.20 *devilishly*
infernal machine 680.16 *bomb*
inferno 8.11 *heaven*, 151.5 *confusion*, 408.8 *hot place*
inferred 518.8 *supposed*, 520.6 *meaningful*, 527.4 *unsaid*
infertile 247, 236.13 *unsexed*
infertility 247, 236.4 *disability*, 609.9 *scarcity*
Infertility 247
infest 82, 181.12 *overcrowd*, 357.5 *transgress*, 631.14 *afflict*
infestation 357.8 *transgression*, 626.1 *lack of hygiene*, 631.1 *affliction*
infested 82.12 *verminous*, 144.8 *full*, 357.11 *overrun*
infeudation 729.1 *giving*
infidel 7.6 *non-Christian*, 498.5 *disbeliever*, 720.5 *nonobserver*
infidelity 224.2 *irresolution*, 498.4 *unbelief*, 821.8 *love affair*, 858.2 *faithlessness*, 877.4 *illicit love*
infield 22.1 *baseball*
infielder 22.2 *baseball player*
infielder's glove 22.3 *baseball equipment*
infield fly 22.6 *fielding terms*
infield fly rule 22.6 *fielding terms*
infighting 666.1 *disagreement*, 674.6 *fight*, 674.7 *boxing*
in file 159.20 *in a line*
infiltrate 346, 133.10 *become mixed*, 253.11 *be present*, 348.13 *absorb*, 356.10 *enter*, 389.31 *steep*, 693.16 *be subversive*
infiltrating 356.13 *penetrating*
infiltration 133.1 *mixture*, 346.3 *inroad*, 356.3 *passage into*, 389.10 *steeping*, 693.3 *subversion*
infiltrator 693.10 *seditionist*
in fine feather 295.30 *dressed up*, 623.1 *healthy*
in fine fettle 813.7 *dressed up*
in fine fettle 105.8 *in a state of*, 105.9 *conditionally*, 142.8 *sound*, 150.13 *orderly*, 237.9

physically strong, 306.12 *on form*, 623.1 *healthy*
in fine form 623.1 *healthy*
in fine trim 623.1 *healthy*
infinite 184, 8.13 *divine*, 52.72 *complex*, 53.36 *astronomical*, 120.6 *quantitative*, 169.9 *fractional*, 181.8 *numberless*, 190.8 *eternal*, 248.12 *extensive*, 253.7 *present*, 259.15 *big*
infinitely 184, 8.19 *divinely*, 52.87 *mathematically*, 53.39 *astronomically*, 120.7 *quantitatively*, 181.13 *numerously*, 259.20 *largely*
infiniteness 184.4 *infinity*
infinite number 52.7 *natural number*, 52.11 *infinity*
infinite regress 337.10 *backward motion*
infinite sequence 52.20 *sequence*
infinite set 52.21 *set*
infinitesimal 52.72 *complex*, 172.6 *zero*, 173.6 *small*, 260.7 *little*, 438.2 *difficult to see*
infinitesimal calculus 52.30 *calculus*
infinitesimally 52.87 *mathematically*, 260.9 *microscopically*
infinitesimal number 52.10 *zero*
infinite space 184.6 *vastness*, 248.2 *empty space*
infinite supply 184.4 *infinity*
infinitive 5.33 *mood*
infinitude 52.11, 184.4 *infinity*, 190.1 *eternity*
infinity 777 Phobias by Topic, **52**, **184**, 8.2 *divine attribute*, 66.18 *exposure time*, 120.5 *numbers*, 169.3 *large number*, 181.1 *multiplicity*, 190.1 *eternity*, 248.2 *empty space*, 263.1 *distance*, 269.4 *length*
Infinity 184
infirm 238.10 *ill*, 491.7 *unreliable*, 624.21 *unhealthy*, 864.13 *venial*
infirmary 60.10, 630.14 *hospital*
infirmity 207.5 *old age*, 238.3 *poor health*, 491.15 *unreliability*, 620.5 *imperfection*, 624.1 *ill health*, 624.2 *illness*, 864.3 *venial sin*
infirmity of purpose 576.11 *vacillation*
in first place 194.11 *before*
in fits 366.29 *jerkily*
in fits and starts 160.17 *discontinuously*
infix 5.35 *part of speech*, 130.3 *additional item*, 130.6 *add*, 135.10 *link*, 354.5 *inset*
infixed 354.12 *inserted*
infixion 354.8 *insertion*
in flagrante delicto 640.7 *actively*, 866.11 *guiltily*
inflame 239.3 *invigorate*, 241.9 *make violent*, 768.6 *aggravate*, 821.25 *be loved*, 828.9 *offend*
inflamed 228.12 *motivated*, 241.6 *violent*, 624.23 *diseased*, 759.13 *passionate*
in flames 408.10 *on fire*
inflaming 228.11 *motivational*, 408.12 *warm-hearted*, 586.19 *persuasive*
inflammability 408.6 *fire*
inflammable 408.10 *on fire*, 410.10 *powered*, 633.1 *dangerous*
inflammation 406.1 *pain*, 408.1 *heat*, 624.3 *symptom*, 624.15 *ulcer*
inflammatory 228.11 *motivational*
inflatable 74 Ships and Boats, **258**, 261.3 *enlarged thing*, 261.9 *enlargeable*
inflate 121.6 *change gradually*, 128.5, 261.5 *make bigger*, 261.6 *become bigger*, 525.1 *misinterpret*, 541.8 *enlarge*, 541.10 *boast*, 721.10 *augment*, 741.25 *demonetize*, 753.10 *overcharge*, 809.18 *make conceited*
inflated 261.7 *bigger*, 390.14 *aerial*, 525.3 *misinterpreted*, 541.12 *exaggerated*, 541.13 *en-

larged*, 557.4 *ornate*, 805.22 *boastful*
inflatedness 541.4 *bombast*
inflater 261.4 *enlarger*
inflating 541.15 *bombastic*
inflation 13.2 *economy*, 13.3 *economic statistics*, 13.6 *economic factors*, 14.1 *finance*, 128.3 *increasing thing*, 261.1 *growth*, 525.2 *misinterpretation*, 541.2 *enlargement*, 610.3 *superfluity*, 721.2 *augmentation*, 741.7 *finance*, 751.5 *cost*, 753.3 *inflationary price*
inflationary 13.13 *economic*, 14.6 *financial*, 261.9 *enlargeable*, 721.18 *acquisitional*, 741.22 *monetary*, 753.7 *dear*, 757.3 *costly*
inflationary pressure 753.3 *inflationary price*
inflationary price 753
inflationary spiral 13.6 *economic factors*, 14.1, 741.7 *finance*, 753.3 *inflationary price*
inflationary universe 53.4 *cosmological model*
inflator 261.4 *enlarger*
inflect 216.8 *cause change*
inflected 5.39 *of language*, 5.44 *grammatical*
inflected language 5.10 *language type*
inflection 5.16 *spoken letter*, 5.30 *syntax*, 5.35 *part of speech*, 130.3 *additional item*, 216.1 *change*, 564.3 *mode of speech*
inflectional 5.42 *worded*, 5.44 *grammatical*
inflectionally 5.50 *lexically*
inflexibility 836, 225.1 *stability*, 225.2 *determination*, 373.5 *hardness*, 373.8 *mental hardness*, 378.9 *mental toughness*, 574.14 *tenacity*, 577.6 *determination*, 669.2 *obstinacy*, 690.1 *severity*
inflexible 836, 225.9 *stable*, 225.11 *determined*, 373.2 *tough*, 373.4 *mentally hard*, 378.5 *mentally tough*, 490.5 *inevitable*, 574.3 *strong-willed*, 577.3 *unyielding*, 669.11 *obstinate*, 690.8 *severe*
inflexibly 373, 225.12 *stably*, 225.13 *determinedly*, 378.14 *single-mindedly*, 669.14 *resistingly*, 690.11 *severely*
inflict 695.7 *force*, 879.1 *punish*
inflicting pain 406
infliction 879.10 *affliction*
inflict pain 406, 879.1 *punish*, 879.4 *torture*
inflict punishment 672.3 *retaliate*, 879.1 *punish*
in flight 638.9 *fugitively*
in-flight magazine 532.5 *journal*
in flood 96.11 *flooded*, 96.13 *fluently*
Inflood 346.12 *flood in*
inflooding 346.2 *influx*, 346.16 *invasive*
inflorescence 84.4 *flower head*
inflorescent 84.11 *flowering*
inflow 96.6 *river flow*, 346.2 *influx*, 346.12 *flood in*
in flower 84.11 *flowering*, 594.20 *developed*
inflowing 346.16 *invasive*
influence 233, 233, 126.1 *superiority*, 154.18 *forerun*, 166.8 *authority*, 216.8 *cause change*, 220.11 *persuade*, 226.4 *contributing factor*, 226.10 *awaken*, 228.2 *inducement*, 228.9 *motivate*, 230.8 *activate*, 232.1 *instrumentality*, 232.2 *instrument*, 232.4 *be an instrument*, 234.1 *tendency*, 234.4 *tend*, 235.1 *power*, 235.10 *be powerful*, 340.11 *attract*, 497.9 *make someone believe*, 518.6 *propound*, 527.13 *hide*, 586.1 *persuasion*, 586.14 *motivator*, 586.15 *persuade*, 611.1 *importance*, 611.7 *be important*, 613.7 *instrumentality*, 640.1 *action*,

640.4 *act*, 653.1 *manage*, 653.13 *director*, 688.1 *authority*, 688.18 *have authority*
Influence 233
influenceable 220.15 *convertible*
influenced 220, 228.12 *motivated*
influence in a bad way 216.8 *cause change*
influence in a good way 216.8 *cause change*
influence negatively 233.9 *change*
influence of alcohol 874.10 *drunkenness*
influence pedlar 233.5 *influential person*
influence positively 233.9 *change*
influencing 228.11 *motivational*
influential 233, 166.12 *ruling*, 226.13 *causal*, 228.11 *motivational*, 230.12 *operative*, 232.7 *causal*, 235.13 *powerful*, 340.10 *magnetic*, 586.19 *persuasive*, 611.6 *notable*, 640.6 *effective*, 688.12 *authoritative*, 695.9 *compelling*
influentially 228, 233, 226.14 *causally*, 230.13 *operationally*, 232.9 *instrumentally*, 235.18 *powerfully*, 340.14 *attractively*, 640.8 *effectively*, 695.11 *compellingly*
influential person 233, 611.4 *bigwig*
influenza 624.4 *disease*, 624.6 *infection*, 624.9 *respiratory disease*
influx 346
info 528.1 *information*
in focus 437.1 *visible*, 437.2 *clear*
Infoniwoo 8 Deities
in force 99.10 *existing*, 230.12, 235.14 *operative*, 237.14 *strongly*
in foreign lands 104.18 *extraneously*
in foreign parts 104.18 *extraneously*, 149.19 *abroad*
inform 528, 3.20 *chronicle*, 6.22 *educate*, 103.11 *characterize*
in form 105.8 *in a state of*
inform 480.3 *testify*, 483.13 *turn Queen's evidence*, 501.14 *cause to know*, 520.10 *mean*, 524.8 *interpret*, 530.6 *divulge*, 532.13 *make public*, 534.30 *communicate*, 543.12 *signal*, 594.6 *brief*, 636.5 *warn*, 665.4 *advise*
inform against 856.5 *accuse*
informal 698, 814, 5.39 *of language*, 16.56 *unauthorized*, 295.31 *styled*, 470.5 *indifferent*, 568.14 *conversational*, 720.11 *nonobservant*
informal agreement 715.1 *contract*
informal clothes 295.1 *dress*
informal dress 295, 814, 296.4 *dishabille*
informality 698, 814, 296.4 *dishabille*, 470.2 *indifference*, 720.1 *nonobservance*
Informality 814
informal language 5.3 *spoken language*
informally 698, 814, 5.49 *colloquially*, 295.36 *dressily*, 296.17 *nakedly*, 568.15 *conversationally*, 720.15 *inattentively*
informally dressed 296.10 *in dishabille*
informal meal 350.12 *meal*
informalness 814.1 *informality*
informal speech 5.3 *spoken language*
informant 528, 480.7 *verifier*, 483.7 *person who gives evidence*, 530.4 *discloser*, 534.29 *broadcaster*, 636.4 *warner*
information 501, 528, 3.5 *chronicle*, 483.1 *evidence*, 533.1 *news*, 636.1 *warning*, 654.1 *advice*
Information 528
informational 6.16 *educational*, 528.16 *informative*
information centre 528.8 *source of information*

information office 528.8 *source of information*
information processing 170.4 *computing*, 528.6 *information technology*
information retrieval 170.4 *computing*, 528.6 *information technology*
information technology 528, 65.1, 170.4 *computing*
information theory 528.6 *information technology*
informative 528, 6.16 *educational*, 522.1 *intelligible*, 530.11 *disclosing*, 533.14 *journalistic*, 560.11 *descriptive*, 568.14 *conversational*, 636.8 *warning*, 654.7 *advising*, 662.33 *helpful*
informatively 3.25 *reportedly*, 6.25 *educationally*, 533.15 *journalistically*, 654.9 *advisably*
informativeness 522.9 *intelligibility*
informatory 528.16 *informative*
informed 528, 4.19 *learned*, 483.8 *evidential*, 501.8 *knowledgeable*
informedly 6.25 *educationally*
informer 528, 16.8 *litigant*, 480.7 *verifier*, 528.9 *informant*, 530.4 *discloser*, 539.21 *traitor*, 540.15 *false person*, 565.4 *talker*, 578.9 *equivocator*, 856.3 *accuser*
inform on 528, 530.7 *betray*
in fours 178
infracostal 276.6 *lower*
infraction 720, 168.2 *dissent*, 357.8 *transgression*, 693.2 *violation of the law*, 844.6 *unlawfulness*, 844.8 *wrong-doing*
infractor 844.10 *wrongdoer*
infra dig 559.8 *indecorous*, 795.7 *vulgar*, 803.4 *common*
Infralapsarianism 7 Christian Movements
infrangibility 378.6 *toughness*
infrangible 138.9 *adhesive*, 371.6 *dense*, 378.1 *tough*
infrangibly 378.12 *toughly*
infrared astronomy 53.1 *astronomy*
infrared film 66.9 *film*
infrared observatory 53.23 *observatory*
infrared photography 66.1 *photography*
infrared radiation 56.13 *electromagnetic radiation*, 439.1 *light*
infrared spectrometry 57.17 *analysis*
infrared spectrum 56.68 *emission*
infrared telescope 53.24 *telescope*
infrasound 56.17 *sound*
infrastructural 382.11 *structural*
infrastructure 280.2 *foot*, 382.6 *construction*
infrequence 213.3 *infrequency*
infrequency 213, 182.4 *rarity*, 215.1 *irregularity*
Infrequency 213
infrequent 213, 162.19 *dispersed*, 182.6 *sparse*, 185.23 *occasional*, 215.4 *irregular*, 609.4 *scarce*, 753.8 *valuable*
infrequently 213, 160.17 *discontinuously*, 162.30 *diffusely*, 182.11 *sparsely*, 185.28 *sometimes*, 215.8 *irregularly*, 609.10 *insufficiently*, 753.13 *valuably*
infrequent occurrence 213.3 *infrequency*
in friendship 819, 815.18 *sociably*
infringe 736, 104.16 *be external*, 357.5 *transgress*, 670.4 *besiege*, 693.15 *be disobedient*, 844.21 *do wrong*, 846.14 *arrogate*
infringe a copyright 733.9 *borrow illegally*, 734.7 *take*
infringe a law 168
infringed 720.14 *violating*, 733.11 *borrowed*, 736.18 *fraudulent*
infringement 16.38 *lawbreaking*, 104.4 *externality*, 168.2 *dissent*, 357.8 *transgression*, 670.14

siege, 693.2 *violation of the law*, 720.4 *infraction*, 844.8 *wrongdoing*, 846.3 *arrogation*
infringement of copyright 733.3 *illegal borrowing*, 734.1 *taking*, 736.6 *illegal borrowing*
infringe on 720.10 *violate the law*
infringer 736, 734.6 *taker*
infringing 16.60 *offending*, 104.12 *external*, 720.14 *violating*, 844.16 *in the wrong*
in front 303, 154.21 *first*, 194.11 *before*, 263.10 *distantly*, 357.17 *ahead*
in front of 194.11 *before*
in front of one's face 437.2 *clear*
in full 106.19 *meticulously*, 144.10 *fully*, 553.7 *diffusely*
in full bloom 84.11 *flowering*, 207.11 *adult*, 207.16 *maturely*
in full blow 84.11 *flowering*
in full career 329.14 *swiftly*
in full control 235.13 *powerful*
in full cry 423.9 *loudly*, 590.15 *pursuing*, 590.18 *pursuant to*
in full dress 295.30, 813.7 *dressed up*
in full gallop 329.14 *swiftly*
in full possession of one's faculties 509.4 *sane*
in full sail 329.14 *swiftly*
in full swing 642.19 *busy*
in full view 437.1 *visible*, 526.16 *manifestly*, 532.22 *publicly*
in full war-paint 594.18 *prepared*
in fun 771.17 *jokingly*
in funds 742.2 *solvent*
infuriate 241.9 *make violent*, 820.13 *antagonize*, 828.14 *make angry*
infuriated 241.6 *violent*, 828.16 *angry*
infuriatingly 828.18 *angrily*
infuse 62.19 *administer*, 133.8 *mix*, 140.5 *combine*, 354.2 *inject*, 355.17 *obtain an extract*, 387.23 *dissolve*, 389.31 *steep*
infused 354.13 *injected*
infuse new blood into 627.1 *improve*
infusible 371.7 *condensed*
infusion 62.13 *administration*, 133.1 *mixture*, 133.2 *mixed thing*, 133.4 *admixture*, 351.2 *drink*, 354.9 *injection*, 355.7 *obtaining an extract*, 355.8 *extract*, 387.10 *solution*, 389.10 *steeping*, 630.2 *medicine*, 630.7 *tonic*
in future 199.14 *in the future*
ingathering 161.1 *assembly*
in general 124.11 *on average*, 142.13 *on the whole*, 164.29 *generally*
Ingenhousz 52 Scientists
ingenious 471.11 *ideational*, 519.10 *imaginative*, 592.15 *planning*, 655.6 *skilful*, 657.4 *cunning*
ingeniously 471.22, 519.17 *imaginatively*, 592.17 *conspiratorially*, 655.12 *skilfully*
ingenious plan 592.3 *expedient plan*
ingenue 51.21 *role*, 497.6 *trusting person*, 658.3 *naive person*, 865.4 *innocent person*
@RHEAD = ingenuity
ingenuity 471.8, 519.1 *imagination*, 567.3, 655.1 *skill*, 657.1 *cunning*
ingenuous 201.12, 206.12 *immature*, 322.16 *open*, 442.4 *easily seen through*, 453.3 *raw*, 537.18 *truthful*, 556.3 *natural*, 658.1, 865.7 *naive*
ingenuously 322.26 *openly*, 658.5, 865.12 *naively*
ingenuousness 201.3, 206.3 *immaturity*, 322.9, 442.10 *openness*, 537.5 *truthfulness*, 658.2, 865.3 *naivety*
ingenuous person 658.3 *naive person*
ingest 348, 62.19 *administer*, 350.21 *eat*
ingesting 350.1 *eating*

ingestion 348.4 *intake*, 350.1 *eating*
ingestive 348.17 *absorbent*
Ingleborough 95 Mountains
inglenook 256.3 *home*, 258.2 *compartment*, 408.6 *fire*
in glowing terms 554.7 *emphatically*
in-goal 35.6 *rugger*
in-goal area 35.1 *rugger*
ingoing 61.34 *introverted*, 346.1 *entry*, 346.15 *entering*
ingoingness 61.7 *personality type*
Ingolstadt 93 Cities
in good condition 105.8 *in a state of*, 150.13 *orderly*, 306.12 *on form*, 617.5 *not bad*, 623.1 *healthy*
in good faith 857.7 *honourably*
in good form 105.8 *in a state of*, 105.9 *conditionally*
in good health 142.8 *sound*, 237.9 *physically strong*, 623.1 *healthy*, 843.12 *all right*
in good heart 623.1 *healthy*
in good nick 150.13 *orderly*, 237.9 *physically strong*, 306.12 *on form*, 623.1 *healthy*
in good odour 851.24 *admired*
in good odour with 800.3 *reputable*
in good order 150.13 *orderly*
in good shape 237.9 *physically strong*, 623.1 *healthy*
in good spirits 105.8 *in a state of*, 105.9 *conditionally*, 769.1 *cheerful*
in good time 208.17 *early*
in good trim 150.13 *orderly*
in good trust 819.19 *devotedly*
ingot 604.1 *materials*, 741.16 *bullion*
ingraft 354.6 *plant*, 584.18 *habituate*
ingrained 103.6 *intrinsic*, 140.7 *combined*, 225.10 *stabilized*, 584.13 *fixed*
in Grand Prix competition 33.12 *in a race*
ingrate 838.2 *thankless person*
ingratiate 376.13 *smooth over*
ingratiate oneself 808.9 *fawn*, 817.13 *defer to*, 821.28 *win the love of*, 853.10 *cajole*
ingratiating 376.6 *smooth-mannered*, 771.11 *humouring*, 808.7 *sycophantic*, 817.9 *deferential*, 849.9 *showing respect*, 853.14 *cajoling*
ingratiatingly 808.17 *sycophantically*, 817.16 *deferentially*
ingratiation 808.2 *sycophancy*, 817.4 *deference*, 853.3 *cajolery*
ingratitude 838, 512.4 *unthinkingness*
Ingratitude 838
ingredient 130.3 *additional item*, 133.4 *admixture*, 143.4 *component*, 146.2 *thing included*, 148.1, 148.6 *component*, 367.4 *matter*
ingredients 257.1 *contents*
ingress 96.6 *river flow*, 324.3 *motion towards*, 346.1 *entry*, 346.5 *entrance*, 354.9 *injection*, 356.3 *passage into*, 670.14 *siege*
ingression 346.1 *entry*
ingressive 346.15 *entering*
in-group 161.19 *clique*, 201.6 *avant-garde*
ingrowing 346.16 *invasive*
inguen 343.5 *fork*
ingungu 49 Musical Instruments
ingurgitate 348.11 *ingest*, 350.21 *eat*
ingurgitation 348.4 *intake*, 350.1 *eating*
Ingush 5 Languages and Groups of Languages
inhabit 255, 256, 99.17 *exist*, 250.10 *settle*, 253.13 *reside*, 396.17 *dwell*
inhabitance 253.3 *residence*
inhabitant 255
Inhabitant 255
inhabitants 255, 400.9 *group*

inhabited 255
inhabiter 255.1 *inhabitant*
inhabiting 256
inhalant 62
inhalation 62.13 *administration*, 346.2 *influx*, 348.4 *intake*, 390.8 *respiration*, 416.2 *sense of smell*
inhale 62.19 *administer*, 348.12 *draw in*, 390.21 *respire*, 413.14 *smoke*, 416.7 *smell*
inhalement 348.4 *intake*
in half 176
inhaling 390.19 *respiratory*
in halves 136.20 *separately*, 176.22 *in half*
in hand 594, 382.19 *in production*, 594.22 *in preparation*, 600.1 *unused*, 605.7 *stored*
in-handle 41.13 *ice-skating*
in-handle turn 41.10 *curling*
in harbour 632.5 *safe*
inharmonious 117.10 *disagreeing*, 430.7 *strident*, 434.7 *dissonant*
inharmoniousness 117.4 *disagreement*
in harmony 140.8 *cooperative*, 167.17 *conformingly*, 433.7 *harmonious*, 433.12 *harmoniously*, 667.14 *agreeably*
in harness 594.18 *prepared*, 640.5 *acting*, 642.19 *busy*, 701.9 *subject*
in haste 648.3 *hasty*
in health 623.1 *healthy*
in heaps 181.14 *in crowds*
in heat 203.17 *in season*, 821.30 *lovingly*
in hell 8.20 *devilishly*, 16.64 *convicted*
in hellfire 8.20 *devilishly*
inhere 148.12 *be one of*
inherent 99.11, 103.6 *intrinsic*, 146.8 *included*, 148.8 *belonging*, 280.3 *base*, 290.11 *intrinsic*
inherent ability 655.2 *aptitude*
inherently 99.22 *really*, 146.9 *inclusively*, 148.14 *constitutively*
inherit 155.22 *succeed*, 227.6 *have a visible effect*, 227.7 *follow from*, 682.12 *succeed to*, 721.14 *profit*, 725.9 *own property*, 728.3 *transfer property*, 730.9 *receive*, 734.7 *take*, 742.13 *get rich*, 749.7 *receive*
inheritable 727.14 *for sale*, 728.5 *transferring*
inheritance 59.11 *genetics*, 132.5 *estate*, 195.4 *accession*, 227.2 *visible effect*, 570.5 *will*, 721.5 *profit*, 723.1 *possession*, 725.5 *personal estate*, 728.1 *transfer of property*, 729.2 *gift*, 730.1 *receiving*, 734.1 *taking*, 749.4 *legacy*
inheritance of acquired characteristics 59.16 *evolution*
inheritance tax 751.7 *tax*
inherited 227.10 *caused*, 721.15 *gainful*, 730.13, 749.6 *received*
inheriting 721.15 *gainful*, 734.12 *taking*
inheriting from 227.10 *caused*
inheritor 132.6 *person remaining*, 155.12, 195.5 *successor*, 513.4 *expectant person*, 730.6, 845.7 *beneficiary*
inheritors 199.2 *future generation*
inheritress 730.6 *beneficiary*
inhibit 231.3 *counteract*, 302.7 *limit*, 709.3 *veto*
inhibited 61.37 *subconscious*, 699.14 *self-restrained*
inhibitedly 61.39 *psychologically*
inhibiting 62.14 *counteracting*, 302.5 *limited*, 699.14 *self-restrained*, 709.5 *vetoed*
inhibition 661, 58.11 *enzyme*, 61.19 *defence mechanism*, 302.1 *limitation*, 699.3 *self-restraint*
inhibitive 661
inhibitively 661
inhibitor 62.4 *drug type*, 231.1 *counteraction*
in hiding 438.9 *invisibly*, 458.8 *fleetingly*, 638.9 *fugitively*

in high 329.14 *swiftly*
in high cotton 742.1 *wealthy*
in high dudgeon 828.16 *angry*
in high esteem 851.24 *admired*
in high gear 329.14, 329.14 *swiftly*
in high hopes 513.5 *expecting*
in high relief 437.2 *clear*
in high spirits 769.1 *cheerful*
in his prime 218.11 *finally*
in hock 593.5 *necessitous*, 718.7 *guaranteed*, 743.2 *insolvent*, 745.9 *in debt*, 745.11 *insolvently*
in holes 628.13 *dilapidated*
in holy wedlock 823.24 *matrimonially*
in honour of 812
inhospitable 820.6 *hostile*, 832.15 *inconsiderate*
inhospitably 816.14 *unsociably*, 820.14 *hostilely*
in hospital 624.22 *sick*, 624.25 *unhealthily*
inhospitality 816.1 *unsociability*
in hot blood 828.18 *angrily*
in hot pursuit 37.9 *on the trail*, 590.15 *pursuing*, 590.18 *pursuant to*
in hot water 659.16 *troubled*
in-house 253.9 *resident*, 290.8 *internal*
in-house magazine 532.5 *journal*
inhuman 618.5 *harmful*, 832.11 *cruel*, 834.3 *misanthropic*, 864.11 *wicked*
inhumane 690.8 *severe*, 832.11 *cruel*
inhumanely 690.11 *severely*
inhumaneness 832.2 *cruelness*
inhumanity 618.11 *harmfulness*, 690.1 *severity*, 832.2 *cruelness*, 834.1 *misanthropy*, 836.1 *pitilessness*, 864.1 *wickedness*
inhumanly 834.5 *misanthropically*, 864.18 *wickedly*
inhumation 399.1 *burial*
inhume 399.8 *bury*
inhumed 399.10 *buried*
in hysterics 241.6 *violent*
in ICU 624.22 *sick*
in ignorance 502.12 *ignorantly*
inimical 111.5 *opposing*, 117.10 *disagreeing*, 136.18 *disagreeable*, 231.4 *counteracting*, 473.9 *hostile*, 663.19 *oppositional*, 666.9 *disagreeing*, 670.21 *aggressive*, 679.33 *combative*, 785.8 *disliking*, 820.6 *hostile*
inimicality 111.3 *opposition*, 820.1 *enmity*
inimically 111.7 *disapprovingly*, 136.23 *disagreeably*, 231.5 *counter*, 473.17 *argumentatively*, 663.23 *opposingly*, 666.11 *in disagreement*, 679.41 *aggressively*, 820.14 *hostilely*
inimitability 126.1 *superiority*, 537.6 *authenticity*
inimitable 119.5 *novel*, 126.14 *best*, 165.17 *exceptional*, 537.19 *authentic*
inimitably 119.8 *originally*, 126.17 *supremely*
in imitation of 707.8 *by proxy*
in Indian file 159.20 *in a line*
in instalments 143.12 *partly*, 145.6 *incompletely*, 733.13 *on loan*, 746.21 *cash down*
in intensive care 397.18 *dying*, 624.22 *sick*
in inverted order 287.2 *inverted*
iniquitous 862.7 *evil*, 864.11 *wicked*
iniquitously 864.18 *wickedly*
iniquity 862.1 *evil*, 864.1 *wickedness*, 866.3 *sin*
in irons 36.10 *sailing*, 699.15 *detained*
in isolation 136, 139.11 *aloofly*
in italics 554.4 *emphasized*
initial 5.13 *letter*, 5.41 *lettered*, 5.47 *word*, 154.13 *precursory*, 156.29, 322.17 *beginning*, 513.9 *use signs*, 544.11 *identify oneself*
initially 156.38 *in the beginning*
initial rhyme 48.11 *rhyme*

initials 544.3 *means of identification*, 545.4 *inscription*
initial teaching alphabet 5.14 *alphabet*
initiate 6.7 *learner*, 119.7 *originate*, 154.18 *forerun*, 156.14 *beginner*, 156.17 *begin*, 156.23 *inaugurate*, 156.25 *enrol*, 201.19 *begin*, 226.11 *inaugurate*, 228.9 *motivate*, 322.24 *begin*, 346.14 *enrol*, 348.10 *introduce*, 354.7 *install*, 529.7 *esotericism*, 597.1 *undertake*, 652.14 *behave towards*, 665.5 *member*, 665.13 *be a member*, 812.19 *install*
initiate a buyout 737.3 *bargain*
initiated 156.37 *enrolled*, 201.13 *inaugurated*
initiation 119.1 *originality*, 156.8 *enrolment*, 201.4 *beginning*, 226.1 *cause*, 322.11 *beginning*, 346.1 *entry*, 348.3 *introduction*, 730.4 *reception*, 812.3 *ceremony*, 813.3 *formal occasion*
initiation ceremony 156.8 *enrolment*
initiation rite 10.7 *non-Christian ritual*
initiative 156.11 *starting point*, 156.29 *beginning*, 348.16 *introductory*, 642.4 *energy*, 698.1 *freedom*
initiator 156.16 *originator*
initiatory 154.13 *precursory*, 156.29 *beginning*, 156.36 *introductory*, 226.13 *causal*, 348.16 *introductory*
in its infancy 156.41 *in the bud*
in its own way 165.30 *characteristically*
inject 354, 60.19 *practise medicine*, 62.19 *administer*, 322.20 *hole*, 389.31 *steep*, 389.34 *hose*, 630.20 *doctor*
injected 354, 322.14 *holed*
injecting 875.1 *drug-taking*
injection 62, 354, 53.35 *rocketry*, 389.10 *steeping*, 630.2 *medicine*, 879.13 *capital punishment*
inject oneself 875.10 *drug oneself*
in jeopardy 633.4 *endangered*
injudicial 16.56 *unauthorized*
injudicious 508.5 *foolish*, 616.1 *inconvenient*, 780.4 *rash*
injudiciously 616.6 *inconveniently*
injunction 15.4 *industrial dispute*, 16.6 *legal process*, 166.1 *rule*, 593.1 *requirement*, 654.3 *precept*, 661.1 *hindrance*, 692.2 *demand*, 699.1 *restraint*, 709.1 *veto*, 712.2 *demand*
injunctive 15.10 *unionized*, 166.9 *legal*, 692.14 *commanding*, 699.13 *restraining*, 709.5 *vetoed*, 712.10 *demanding*
injunctively 709.7 *by veto*
injure 238.7 *weaken*, 406.11 *inflict pain*, 601.1 *misuse*, 618.13 *be worthless*, 628.5 *hurt*, 687.11 *cause adversity*, 722.13 *destroy*, 832.18 *torment*, 844.20 *wrong*, 862.11 *be evil*
injured 406, 628.12 *deteriorated*, 862.8 *afflicted*
injured husband 51.21 *role*, 823.10 *married man*
injured pride 806.9 *humiliation*
injurious 244.14 *destructive*, 601.5 *abusive*, 618.5 *harmful*, 626.5 *unhygienic*, 628.12 *deteriorated*, 818.6 *bad-mannered*, 844.16 *in the wrong*, 854.16 *defamatory*, 862.9 *detrimental*
injuriously 601.6 *abusively*, 818.10 *rudely*
injuriousness 628.11 *hurt*
injury 777 *Phobias by Topic*, 406, 601.2 *misuse*, 618.11 *harmfulness*, 628.11 *hurt*, 687.1 *adversity*, 722.5 *destruction*, 822.7 *hated thing*, 844.7 *sense of wrong*, 844.8 *wrongdoing*, 862.2 *affliction*, 866.3 *sin*, 879.10 *affliction*
injury time 130.4 *extra*
injustice 123, 493, 16.4 *bad*

law, 618.9 *badness*, 670.16 *terrorist attack*, 844.1 *unfairness*, 844.7 *sense of wrong*, 858.1 *improbity*, 862.1 *evil*, 866.3 *sin*
in juxtaposition 267.7 *beside*
ink 50.11 *artist's materials*, 440.4 *dark thing*, 447.8 *black pigment*, 447.9 *black thing*, 447.11 *blacken*
inkberry 85 *Trees and Shrubs*
inkblot test 61.5 *psychological test*
ink cap 89 *Fungi*
inked 50.27 *painted*
in keeping 116.38 *fittingly*, 167.12 *conforming*, 167.17 *conformingly*
in keeping with 112.13 *uniformly*, 667.10 *agreeing*
in key 49.41 *in tune*
inkily 447.12 *blackly*
ink in 50.19 *paint*, 447.11 *blacken*
in kind 223.8 *in exchange*
in kindness 831.10 *benevolently*
inkiness 447.7 *blackness*
ink-jet printer 65.7 *peripheral*
inkling 461.6 *idea*, 501.2 *information*, 518.2 *basis of supposition*, 542.6 *suggestion*, 759.2 *impression*
ink-slinging 674.1 *contention*
inky 440.10 *dark-coloured*, 447.1 *black*
in labour 245.16 *reproductive*
inlaid 47.14 *wooden*, 354.12 *inserted*, 456.8 *checked*, 792.8 *decorated*
inlaid decoration 47.1 *furniture*
inlaid tile 44.8 *ceramic object*
inland 290, 290, 70.5 *transportable*, 74.11 *inward*
Inland 97 *Oceans and Seas*
inland navigation 74.1 *water travel*
inland post 534.2 *postal communication*
Inland Revenue 13.6 *economic factors*, 751.7 *tax*
inlands 290.3 *inland*
inland sea 94.1 *lake*
inland waterway 74.2 *waterway*
inlay 47.18 *work wood*, 354.5 *inset*, 354.11 *thing inserted*, 456.2 *check*, 456.11 *variegate*
in layers 266, 266.7 *layered*
in league 116.32 *in alliance*, 135.16 *as one*, 140.8 *cooperative*, 140.10 *in combination*, 664.21 *in cooperation*
in league with 665.8 *leagued*
in left field 510.11 *insane*
in length 269.11 *lengthily*
inlet 98, 317.2 *concave land*, 327.11 *channel*, 346.5 *entrance*
in lieu 252.20 *out of place*, 478.27 *answerably*
in lieu of 222.9 *instead*
in life 396.12 *alive*
in like manner 114.13 *similarly*, 116.34 *uniformly*
in limbo 600.4 *disused*
in line 112.6 *conforming*, 112.13 *uniformly*, 167.12 *conforming*, 167.17 *conformingly*, 195.14 *in succession*
in line with 332.9 *directly*
in liquidation 244.15 *destroyed*, 320.12 *in the red*
in liquor 874.1 *drunk*
in litigation 16
in loads 181.14 *in crowds*
in lock step 198.10 *synchronized*
in loco 615.1 *convenient*
in lots 143.12 *partly*
in love 821
in love with 821.18 *in love*
in love with one's own voice 553.3 *diffuse*
in low gear 328.17 *in slow motion*
in luck 686.8 *prosperous*
in luxury 686.8 *prosperous*
in majority 175
in malice 618.15 *worthlessly*
in masses 181.14 *in crowds*
inmate 255.1 *inhabitant*, 323.6

closed-in person, 699.7 *charge*, 701.5 *subjected person*, 702.5 *prisoner*
in memoriam 399.12 *funereally*
in memory of 511.16 *memorably*, 812.21 *in honour of*
in mid air 283.13 *pendulously*
in mid-progress 336.20 *in progress*
in mid-stream 326.18 *in transit*
immigrant 346.7 *entrant*
immigration 346.4 *right of entry*
in miniature 260.8 *in a small way*
in mint condition 629.13 *repaired*
in moderation 242.9 *moderately*, 333.8 *medially*, 699.17 *with self-restraint*
in modo di 49 *Musical Terms*
in more than one way 666.12 *differently*
in mortal fear 777.15 *fearfully*
inmost 290.12 *internalized*
in mothballs 605.7 *stored*
in motion 324, 324.16 *moving*
in mourning 774.8 *mournfully*
inn 256.10 *hotel*
innaccessible 616.2 *distant*
in name only 102.19 *apparently*, 540.37 *spuriously*
Innana 8 *Deities*
in nappies 206.11 *young*
innards 148.4 *components*, 257.3, 290.4 *insides*
innate 99.11, 103.6 *intrinsic*, 290.11 *intrinsic*, 464.8 *instinctive*
innate ability 485.2 *ability*, 655.2 *aptitude*
innately 290.16 *inwardly*
innateness 99.3 *nature*
innate reaction 464.4 *instinct*
in nature's garb 296.9 *undressed*
in need 593, 593.5 *necessitous*, 743.1 *poor*, 743.15 *poorly*
in need of 145.4 *incomplete*
in need of repair 844.18 *gone wrong*
inner 146.8 *included*, 158.12 *core*, 165.19 *personal*, 290.7 *interior*
inner being 11.7 *spirit*
inner block 26.9 *tae kwon do*
inner cabinet 653.3 *management*, 653.6 *governing body*
inner circle 147.4 *exclusiveness*, 665.1 *party*
inner-circle 665.8 *leagued*
inner city 93.7 *city district*, 249.10 *urban area*
inner-city 256.15 *environmental*
inner-city ghetto 628.9 *dilapidation*
inner-directed 117.9 *nonconforming*, 698.10 *independent*
inner-directedness 117.3 *nonconformity*
inner-directed person 117.6 *misfit*
inner ear 420.5 *internal ear*
inner form 306.1 *form*
inner layer 290.1 *interior*
inner life 290.5 *inner nature*
inner man 165.11 *identity*, 290.5 *inner nature*
inner mind 11.7 *spirit*
innermost 290.11 *intrinsic*
innermost being 290.5 *inner nature*
innermost recesses 527.10 *quietness*
innermost thought 461.3 *thoughtfulness*
inner nature 290
inner part 290.2 *inside*
inner person 290.5 *inner nature*, 527.10 *quietness*
inner product 52.50 *scalar quantity*
inner self 165.11 *identity*
inner sense 11.8 *psychic power*
inner side 290.1 *interior*
inner ski turn 41.4 *skiing technique*
inner surface 290.1 *interior*
inner tube 39.3 *survival swimming*, 258.19 *inflatable*, 388.13 *gas balloon*
inner voice 847.4 *sense of duty*

inner wall 290.1 *interior*
inner workings 257.3 *insides*
inning 22.1 *baseball*, 24.1 *billiards*, 187.4 *period of activity*
innings 27.1 *cricket match*, 187.4 *period of activity*
innkeeper 606.4 *caterer*
in no case 536.16 *no*
innocence 865, 16.42 *acquittal*, 134.1 *purity*, 201.3 *immaturity*, 236.3 *helplessness*, 238.1 *weakness*, 502.1 *ignorance*, 619.3 *perfection*, 633.7 *vulnerability*, 658.2 *naivety*, 857.2 *purity*, 863.1 *virtue*, 876.3 *moral purity*
Innocence 865
innocent 855, 865, 16.63 *acquitted*, 134.12 *morally pure*, 201.12 *immature*, 206.11 *young*, 236.11 *unprotected*, 453.3 *raw*, 497.6 *trusting person*, 497.12 *gullible*, 502.6 *ignorant*, 539.22 *dupe*, 585.1 *unaccustomed*, 617.4 *worthwhile*, 619.1 *perfect*, 632.5 *safe*, 658.1 *naive*, 658.3 *naive person*, 675.7 *peaceful*, 825.7 *virginal*, 857.5 *pure*, 863.5 *virtuous*, 865.4 *innocent person*, 876.9 *pure*
innocent as a child 865.7 *naive*
innocent as a dove 865.5 *innocent*
innocent as a lamb 632.5 *safe*, 865.5 *innocent*
innocent as a newborn babe 865.7 *naive*
innocent intentions 865.1 *innocence*
innocently 865, 16.88 *forgivingly*, 134.18 *virtuously*, 206.14 *youthfully*, 236.14 *powerlessly*, 585.6 *unaccustomedly*, 658.5 *naively*, 857.8 *purely*, 863.9 *virtuously*
innocentness 865.1 *innocence*
innocent party 865.4 *innocent person*
innocent person 865
innocent tumour 624.12 *cancer*
innocuous 617.4 *worthwhile*, 625.4 *hygienic*, 632.5 *safe*, 865.5 *innocent*
innocuously 865.11 *innocently*
innominate bone 382 *Bones*
in no place 100.17 *nowhere*
in nothing flat 329.14 *swiftly*
in no time 191.9 *in the shortest possible time*, 329.14 *swiftly*
in no uncertain terms 522.13 *intelligibly*, 554.7 *emphatically*
innovate 115.6 *differentiate*, 119.7 *originate*, 154.18 *forerun*, 156.22 *invent*, 201.18 *be trendy*, 216.8 *cause change*, 243.10 *produce*, 479.13 *invent*
innovation 119.1 *originality*, 154.3 *preparation*, 156.5 *invention*, 201.1 *newness*, 216.1 *change*, 243.1 *production*, 479.4 *originality*
innovational 216.11 *changeable*
innovative 119.4 *original*, 154.14 *preparatory*, 156.33 *inventive*, 201.10 *new*, 216.11 *changeable*, 243.11 *productive*, 479.9 *original*, 519.10 *imaginative*, 597.6 *enterprising*
innovatively 119.8 *originally*, 201.21 *newly*, 216.15 *changeably*, 243.13 *productively*, 479.15 *inventively*, 597.9 *enterprisingly*
innovator 119.3 *originator*, 154.8 *precursor*, 216.6 *editor*, 243.9 *producer*, 479.5 *experimenter*, 583.6 *improviser*, 597.4 *volunteer*
innovatory 154.14 *preparatory*
in no way 100.15 *not at all*, 172.11 *none*
innoxious 625.4 *hygienic*
Innsbruck 93 *Cities*
inn sign 544.3 *means of identification*
innuendo 527.10 *quietness*, 854.4 *aspersion*
innumerability 181.1 *multiplicity*,

184.5 *immeasurability*
innumerable 181.8 *numberless*, 184.2 *immeasurable*
innumerably 181.13 *numerously*, 184.11 *immeasurably*
in numerical order 169.12 *numerically*
in obedience to 694.10 *obediently*
in oblivion 783.17 *indifferently*
inobservance 720.1 *nonobservance*
inobservant 720.11 *nonobservant*
in occupation 253.9 *resident*
inoculate 60.19 *practise medicine*, 62.19 *administer*, 140.5 *combine*, 354.2 *inject*, 625.6 *make hygienic*, 630.20 *doctor*, 632.9 *protect*
inoculated 354.13 *injected*, 625.4 *hygienic*, 632.5 *safe*
inoculation 777 Phobias by Topic, 60.6 *health care*, 354.9 *injection*, 625.1 *hygiene*, 630.3 *prophylactic*, 632.2 *protection*
inocybe 89 Fungi
inodorous 417.3 *odourless*
inodorousness 417.1 *odourlessness*
in-off 24.3 *English billiards*
inoffensive 617.4 *worthwhile*, 675.7 *peaceful*, 806.1 *humble*, 865.5 *innocent*
inoffensively 865.11 *innocently*
inoffensiveness 865.1 *innocence*
in oils 50.30 *pictorially*
in olden days 202.19 *anciently*
in olden times 3.24 *historically*
in on 528.18 *informed*, 724.5 *jointly possessing*
in one piece 142.6 *whole*
in one's absence 254.20 *absently*
in ones and twos 182
in one's bad book 785.9 *disliked*
in one's behalf 222.9 *instead*
in one's best bib and tucker 295.30 *dressed up*, 594.18 *prepared*, 813.7 *dressed up*
in one's birthday suit 294.8 *uncovered*, 296.9 *undressed*, 296.17 *nakedly*
in one's control 701.9 *subject*
in one's crystal ball 516.8 *foresightedly*
in one's cups 874.1 *drunk*
in one's debt 837.4 *grateful*
in one's employ 697.9 *serving*
in one's grasp 723.9 *possessed*
in one's hands 723.9 *possessed*
in one's head 471.11 *ideational*, 471.20 *theoretically*
in one's infancy 206.11 *young*, 206.14 *youthfully*
in one's name 723.9 *possessed*, 723.10 *possessively*
in one's old age 207.16 *maturely*
in one's opinion 471.24 *ideologically*
in one's own back yard 264.6 *near*
in one's own time 645.7 *leisurely*
in one's pay 697.9 *serving*
in one's place 222.9 *instead*
in one's pocket 701.9 *subject*
in one's power 701.9 *subject*
in one's prime 207.11 *adult*, 207.16 *maturely*
in one's right mind 509.4 *sane*, 629.15 *cured*
in one's second childhood 460.5 *lacking intellect*
in one's shell 783.7 *indifferent*, 816.8 *unsociable*
in one's shirtsleeves 296.10 *in dishabille*, 296.17 *nakedly*, 649.4 *at ease*
in one's shoes 222.9 *instead*
in one's sleep 404.13 *insensibly*
in one's spare time 645.7 *leisurely*
in one's stride 584.19 *habitually*, 655.12 *skilfully*
in one's teens 179.18 *eleventh*, 206.11 *young*, 206.14 *youthfully*
in one's thoughts 472.12 *topically*
in one way or another 327.16 *how*

in open court 526.16 *manifestly*, 532.22 *publicly*
in open rebellion 668.10 *in defiance*
inoperability 487.6 *hopelessness*
inoperable 398.23 *deadly*, 487.3 *hopeless*, 624.22 *sick*, 776.5 *past hope*
inoperably 487.12 *hopelessly*
in operation 230.10 *operational*, 599.10 *usable*, 640.5 *acting*
inoperational 600.1 *unused*
inoperative 236.10 *powerless*, 614.1 *useless*, 641.3 *inactive*
inopportune 117.11 *unfit*, 211.10 *untimely*, 616.1 *inconvenient*
inopportunely 117.17 *unsuitably*, 211.15 *at the wrong time*, 616.6 *inconveniently*
inopportune moment 211.1 *untimeliness*
inopportuneness 211.1 *untimeliness*, 616.3 *inconvenience*
in opposition 663, 117.10 *disagreeing*, 475.23 *in protest*, 536.15 *negatively*, 663.20 *discordant*, 687.6 *adverse*, 713.11 *disapprovingly*
in opposition to 231.5 *counter*, 663.27 *opposed to*
in orbit 275.19 *high*
in order 150, 105.8 *in a state of*, 150.12 *hierarchical*, 150.26 *orderly*, 152.20 *arranged*, 152.28 *in place*, 155.15 *sequential*, 155.27 *in sequence*, 159.9 *consecutive*, 159.18 *consecutively*, 171.13 *inventorially*, 195.14 *in succession*
in orderly fashion 150.26 *orderly*
in order to 588.14 *for*
in order to influence 228.14 *influentially*
in order to oppress 696.16 *masterfully*
in order to prevent 709.7 *by veto*
in order to provoke 666.11 *in disagreement*
inordinacy 541.1 *exaggeration*, 541.3 *extravagance*
inordinancy 870.3 *overindulgence*
inordinate 541.12 *exaggerated*, 541.14 *extravagant*, 610.6 *excessive*, 757.2 *unrestrained*, 870.8 *overindulgent*
inordinately 541.17 *excessively*, 757.9 *extravagantly*
inordinateness 870.3 *overindulgence*
inorganic 57.31 *chemical*, 57.35 *combined*, 460.8 *nonhuman*
inorganic base 57.9 *base*
inorganic chemist 57.2 *chemist*
inorganic chemistry 57.1 *chemistry*, 367.6 *natural science*
inorganic compound 57.7 *chemical compound*
inorganic pigment 444.4 *pigment*
inorganic sediment 54.27 *sediment*
inosculation 135.1 *union*
inosilicate 54.34 *mineral*
inositol 58.3 *carbohydrate*
in other words 524, 475.22 *demonstrably*, 520.13 *meaningfully*
in outline 299.6 *outlined*, 299.7 *essentially*, 457.15 *apparently*, 552.5 *concisely*, 685.4 *uncompleted*
in outline form 685.7 *incompletely*
in over one's head 236.14 *powerlessly*, 745.11 *insolvently*
in pain 862.8 *afflicted*
in pairs 176.9 *two*, 176.20 *two by two*
in pantomime 543.18 *indicatively*
in par 110.19 *equally*
in Paradise 397.19 *dead*
in parallel 285, 64.37 *electronically*, 478.26 *correspondingly*
in parenthesis 354.15 *in*
in Parliament 706.8 *representatively*
in part 143.12 *partly*, 145.6 *incompletely*

in particular 165.28 *specially*
in partnership 116.32 *in alliance*, 135.16 *as one*, 140.8 *cooperative*, 140.10 *in combination*, 665.18 *cliquishly*
in parts 141.7 *to pieces*, 143.12 *partly*
in passage to 327.17 *via*
in passing 326.18 *in transit*
in pastels 50.30 *pictorially*
in past times 200.22 *in the past*
in-patient 60.18 *patient*, 624.19 *sick person*
in peace 675.8 *peacefully*
in peak condition 623.1 *healthy*
in pencil 50.30 *pictorially*
in perfect condition 619.1 *perfect*
in perfect health 619.1 *perfect*
in perfect order 150.13 *orderly*
in peril 633.4 *endangered*
in perpetuity 184.12 *eternally*
in person 253, 165.29 *personally*
in phase 110.20 *regularly*, 365.5 *wave*
in pieces 136.16 *apart*, 136.20 *separately*, 136.21 *apart*, 141.5 *disintegrated*, 143.11 *partial*
in place 152, 167.17 *conformingly*, 250.12 *where*, 251.11 *geographically*, 253.16 *on the spot*, 478.27 *answerably*
in place of 222.9 *instead*, 252.20 *out of place*
in places 162.30 *diffusely*, 182.10 *in ones and twos*, 250.12 *where*
in plain English 522.13 *intelligibly*, 524.18 *in other words*, 660.11 *made easy*, 857.7 *honourably*
in plain terms 522.13 *intelligibly*
in plain view 437.11 *visibly*
in plain words 322.26 *openly*, 520.13 *meaningfully*, 524.18 *in other words*, 556.8 *simply*, 857.7 *honourably*
in play 230.10 *operational*
in-play wall 40.9 *squash terms*
in plenty 181.9 *ample*
in point of fact 99.22 *really*, 537.35 *truly*
in poor condition 624.22 *sick*
in poor health 624.22 *sick*, 687.6 *adverse*
in poor shape 624.22 *sick*, 687.6 *adverse*
in port 632.5 *safe*
in position 251.11 *geographically*
in possession 723.8 *possessing*
inpouring 346.16 *invasive*
in power 12.10 *governing*, 688.23 *authoritatively*
in practice 101.13 *really*, 594.18 *prepared*, 599.9 *used*
in preparation 594, 145.4 *incomplete*, 154.22 *in anticipation*, 594.17 *developing*, 685.7 *incompletely*
in pretence 474.10 *hypocritical*
in print 532.19 *published*
in prison 702.8 *imprisoned*
in private 139.11 *aloofly*, 438.9 *invisibly*, 531.18 *privately*, 816.14 *unsocially*
in process of 685.7 *incompletely*
in production 382
in profit 749.8 *profitably*
in profusion 181.9 *ample*
in progress 336, 145.4 *incomplete*, 219.5 *continual*, 594.17 *developing*
in proof 475.22 *demonstrably*, 483.14 *as evidence*, 592.14 *planned*
in proportion 52.74 *divisible*
in proportion to 107.10 *relevantly*
in prose 556.8 *simply*
in protest 475, 500.10 *dissentiently*
in public 437.11 *visibly*, 475.20, 526.16 *manifestly*
in purdah 816.10 *lonely*
in pursuance of 588.14 *for*, 590.18 *pursuant to*
in pursuit 590.15 *pursuing*, 590.18 *pursuant to*
input 64.35 *conduct*, 65.17 *com-*

puting term, 65.19 *abort,* 346.1 *entry,* 545.13 *record,* 545.16 *recorded,* 593.2 *need*
input impedance 64.12 *resistance*
input-output device 65.7 *peripheral*
input signal 64.14 *terminal*
input terminal 64.14 *terminal*
input voltage 64.14 *terminal*
in queer street 743.2 *insolvent*
inquest 399, 16.7 *legal trial,* 397.8 *after death,* 477.2 *questioning*
in question 472.13 *problematically,* 473.10 *arguable,* 473.18 *arguably,* 477.14 *questionable,* 477.24 *questionably,* 491.23 *uncertainly,* 633.1 *dangerous*
in quest of 590.15 *pursuing,* 590.18 *pursuant to*
in quick succession 212.1 *frequently*
inquietude 224.2 *irresolution,* 366.1 *agitation*
inquire 4.20 *philosophize,* 465.7 *be curious,* 472.11 *raise the point,* 473.14 *discuss,* 477.17 *question,* 479.11 *experiment*
inquire after 465.7 *be curious*
inquire into 561.4 *dissertate*
inquirer 4.10 *philosopher,* 465.3 *curious person,* 478.10 *answerer,* 479.5 *experimenter,* 568.7 *conversationalist,* 596.7 *attempter,* 712.4 *requester*
inquiring 465.5 *curious,* 477.12 *questioning,* 479.8 *experimental,* 596.9 *tentative*
inquiring mind 465.1, 477.8 *curiosity*
inquiry 16.7 *legal trial,* 465.1 *curiosity,* 473.2 *logical argument,* 477.2 *questioning,* 479.1 *experiment,* 561.1 *dissertation,* 597.2 *undertaking*
inquisition 16.7 *legal trial,* 465.1 *curiosity,* 477.2 *questioning,* 690.2 *suppression*
Inquisition 16.22 *ecclesiastical court*
inquisitional 16.49 *judicatory,* 492.8 *judging*
inquisitive 6.17 *educatable,* 465.5 *curious,* 477.12 *questioning*
inquisitively 465.8 *curiously,* 477.23 *questioningly*
inquisitiveness 6.10 *educatability,* 465.1, 477.8 *curiosity*
inquisitive person 642.11 *meddler*
inquisitor 465.3 *curious person,* 477.9 *questioner,* 690.4 *strict person,* 879.17 *punisher*
inquisitorial 465.5 *curious,* 690.8 *severe*
inquisitorially 465.8 *curiously*
inquorate 182.7 *fewer*
in rags 151.15 *untidy,* 628.13 *dilapidated,* 743.3 *beggarly*
in rapid succession 212.1 *frequently*
in rapport 116.10 *in accord*
in rapport with 667.10 *agreeing*
in readiness 594.18 *prepared,* 594.22 *in preparation*
in reality 101.13 *really,* 537.35 *truly*
in rebellion 693.14 *subversive*
in rebellion against 713.11 *disapprovingly*
in receipt 749.8 *profitably*
in receivership 244.15 *destroyed,* 320.12 *in the red*
in recess 218.10 *finished*
in recession 628.12 *deteriorated*
in recognition of one's service 837.8 *gratefully*
in recompense 735.7 *redemptively*
in redemption 735.7 *redemptively*
in reduced circumstances 743.1 *poor,* 743.15 *poorly*
in regard to 107.10 *relevantly*
in relation to 107.10 *relevantly,* 137.17 *in connection with*
in relays 155.27 *in sequence*
in relief 50.30 *pictorially,* 526.14 *manifest*

in remembrance of 812.21 *in honour of*
in repentance 840.8 *penitently*
in reply 476, 478.24 *in answer,* 484.9 *to the contrary*
in repose 325.10 *motionlessly*
in reprisal 672.5 *retaliatory*
in requital 672.6 *with vengeance,* 735.7 *redemptively*
in reserve 240.6 *suspended,* 240.7 *inertly,* 600.1 *unused,* 605.7 *stored*
in residence 253.9 *resident,* 253.17 *at home,* 256.14 *inhabiting*
in response 473.20 *apologetically,* 476.11 *in reply,* 478.24 *in answer,* 484.9 *to the contrary*
in restitution 735.7 *redemptively*
in retaliation 672.5 *retaliatory*
in retirement 645.7 *leisurely,* 705.7 *resigning,* 705.10 *by resigning*
in retreat 683.11 *defeated*
in return 223.8 *in exchange*
in return for 223.8 *in exchange*
in reverse 337, 287.4 *inversely,* 337.28 *backward*
inroad 346, 670.14 *siege*
inroads 607.3 *waste*
in round numbers 264.7 *nearly*
in round terms 5.51 *phraseologically*
in ruins 141.5 *disintegrated,* 244.15 *destroyed,* 628.13 *dilapidated*
inrun 346.2 *influx*
in running order 230.10 *operational*
inrush 346.2 *influx,* 346.12 *flood in*
inrushing 346.16 *invasive*
in sackcloth and ashes 774.8 *mournfully,* 867.8 *penitently*
in safe hands 632.5 *safe*
in safe keeping 632.5 *safe*
in safety 632.5 *safe,* 632.10 *safely*
insalubrious 398.23 *deadly,* 618.5 *harmful,* 622.8 *unclean,* 624.23 *diseased,* 626.5 *unhygienic,* 877.12 *indecent*
insalubriously 626.8 *unhygienically*
insalubrity 618.11 *harmfulness,* 626.1 *lack of hygiene*
ins and outs 106.11 *circumstances,* 165.4 *specifications*
ins-and-outs 36.7 *windsurfing*
insane 510, 153.15 *deranged,* 241.6 *violent,* 460.5 *lacking intellect,* 508.5 *foolish,* 821.19 *inamoured*
insane asylum 510.8 *mental hospital*
insanely 510, 153.19 *distractedly,* 460.11 *unintelligently,* 508.8 *foolishly*
insane person 510
insanitariness 626.1 *lack of hygiene*
insanitary 622.8 *unclean,* 626.5 *unhygienic*
insanitation 626.1 *lack of hygiene*
insanity 777 Phobias by Topic, **510,** 153.6 *derangement,* 460.1 *lack of intellect,* 508.1 *folly*
Insanity 510
insatiability 872.1 *gluttony*
insatiable 609.2 *unprovided,* 782.9 *desirous,* 872.6 *gluttonous*
insatiable curiosity 477.8 *curiosity*
in scale 121.7 *gradational*
inscape 306.3 *kind*
inscribe 545, 5.47 *word,* 52.97 *align,* 346.14 *enrol,* 348.10 *introduce,* 524.10 *annotate,* 544.11 *identify oneself,* 545.13 *record*
inscribed 5.43 *phrasal,* 545.16 *recorded*
inscribed figure 52.41 *geometric figure*
Inscribing 545.8 *registration*
inscription 5, 545, 3.11 *relic,* 399.4 *funeral objects,* 524.2 *annotation*

inscrutability 443.8 *obscurity,* 523.11 *unintelligibility*
inscrutable 443, 440.11 *benighted,* 523.1 *unintelligible,* 523.4 *difficult,* 529.11 *mysterious*
inscrutably 440.15 *darkly,* 443.13 *opaquely,* 523.13 *unintelligibly,* 787.9 *without wonder*
in search of 590.18 *pursuant to*
in season 203, 203.9 *seasonal,* 245.16 *reproductive*
in seclusion 139.11 *aloofly*
in second place 195.15 *as follows*
in secrecy 529.16 *stealthily*
in secret 529, 531.18 *privately*
insect 82, 20.1 *angling,* 76.4 *type of animal,* 81.4 *arthropod,* 81.6 *worm*
Insecta 81.4 *arthropod,* 82.1 *insect*
insectan 82
insect-eating mammal 77
insecticidal 69.18 *herbicidal*
insecticide 62.4 *drug type,* 68.14 *pest control,* 69.8 *weedkiller,* 398.13 *animal killer,* 630.3 *prophylactic,* 631.8 *poison*
insectiform 82.10 *insectan*
insectile 81.18 *arthropodous,* 82.10 *insectan*
Insectivora 77.6 *insect-eating mammal*
insectivore 76.4 *type of animal,* 77.6 *insect-eating mammal,* 350.18 *eater*
insectivorous 77, 76.15 *of animals,* 83.14 *of plants,* 350.26 *eating*
insectivorously 350.28 *carnivorously*
insectivorousness 350.5 *eating habit*
insect larva 81.6 *worm*
insect-like 81.18 *arthropodous,* 82.10 *insectan*
insect noise 432
insects 777 Phobias by Topic
Insects and Arachnids 82
insect stings 777 Phobias by Topic
insecure 491.7 *unreliable,* 633.2 *unsafe*
insecurely 491.26 *unreliably*
insecurity 491.15 *unreliability*
in security 632.5 *safe*
insecurity 633.5 *danger,* 633.7 *vulnerability*
inselberg 275.3 *mountain*
in self-defence 26.16 *professionally,* 671.32 *defensively,* 672.5 *retaliatory*
in self-reproach 867.8 *penitently*
inseminate 245.13 *propagate,* 246.7 *make fertile*
insemination 245.3 *propagation*
insensate 761.1 *insensitive*
insensibility 61.13 *depression,* 240.1 *inertness,* 325.2 *repose,* 466.2 *lack of interest,* 502.1 *ignorance,* 512.1 *oblivion,* 519.6 *reverie,* 624.3 *symptom,* 624.17 *nervous disorder,* 641.1 *inaction,* 643.9 *sleep,* 650.7 *fatigue,* 761.3 *insensitiveness,* 783.1 *indifference*
Insensibility 404
insensible 236.12 *impotent,* 240.5 *inert,* 325.6 *quiescent,* 404.7 *anaesthetized,* 466.4 *uninterested,* 512.8 *oblivious,* 630.17 *remedial,* 641.3 *inactive,* 643.4 *not awake,* 761.1 *insensitive,* 783.7 *indifferent,* 875.7 *drugged*
insensible to 783.7 *indifferent*
insensibly 404, 240.7 *inertly,* 643.17 *sleepily,* 783.17 *indifferently,* 875.11 *in a trance*
insensitive 761, 273.4 *thickskinned,* 373.4 *mentally hard,* 381.3 *dull,* 404.6 *unfeeling,* 412.6 *coarse,* 421.5 *unhearing,* 462.10 *inconsiderate,* 468.9 *thoughtless,* 482.1 *undiscriminating,* 783.7 *indifferent,* 818.5 *discourteous,* 832.15 *inconsiderate*

insensitively 407, 381.13 *obtusely,* 404.13 *insensibly,* 412.11 *tastelessly,* 462.14 *thoughtlessly,* 466.8 *disinterestedly,* 482.13 *unselectively,* 761.8 *unfeelingly,* 783.17 *indifferently,* 818.9 *discourteously*
insensitiveness 761, 381.7 *dullness,* 404.1 *lack of feeling,* 462.4 *inconsideration*
insensitive person 761
insensitivity 381.7 *dullness,* 412.4 *bad taste,* 421.1 *deafness,* 462.4 *inconsideration,* 468.4 *thoughtlessness,* 482.6 *lack of discrimination,* 783.1 *indifference,* 818.1 *discourtesy,* 832.6 *inconsiderateness*
Insensitivity 761
in sentences 5.51 *phraseologically*
insentient 404.6 *unfeeling*
inseparability 138.1 *adhesion,* 264.1 *nearness,* 371.1 *density,* 819.3 *familiarity*
inseparable 103.7 *integral,* 135.12 *united,* 138.9 *adhesive,* 174.13 *whole,* 180.19 *associated,* 264.5 *near,* 371.6 *dense,* 819.10 *familiar*
inseparables 819.6 *close friend*
inseparably 135.16 *as one,* 135.18 *inextricably,* 138.11 *cohesively,* 180.21 *together,* 819.18 *intimately*
in sequence 155, 171.13 *inventorially,* 195.14 *in succession*
in series 64.37 *electronically,* 150.25 *in order,* 171.13 *inventorially*
insert 354, 62.19 *administer,* 130.6 *add,* 155.8 *addition,* 257.7 *stuff,* 346.11 *infiltrate,* 348.7 *admit,* 354.11 *thing inserted,* 532.9 *advertisement*
inserted 354, 130.8 *additional*
insertion 354, 53.35 *rocketry,* 130.1 *addition,* 143.7 *piece,* 346.3 *inroad,* 348.1 *admittance,* 354.11 *thing inserted,* 532.9 *advertisement,* 629.8 *repair*
Insertion 354
in service 599.9 *used,* 697.9 *serving*
in-service training 6.2 *educational system*
in servitude 697.9 *serving,* 697.10 *obediently*
inset 354, 354.11 *thing inserted*
in-set 201.6 *avant-garde*
in set form 813.12 *formally*
in set phrases 5.51 *phraseologically*
in set terms 5.51 *phraseologically*
in seventh heaven 279.8 *on top,* 762.4 *happy*
in shallow water 633.4 *endangered*
in shape 306.12 *on form*
inshore 264.5 *near*
inshore fishing 590.2 *chase*
in short 270.12 *short,* 472.14 *thematically,* 552.5 *concisely,* 562.12 *in brief*
in short supply 609.4 *scarce*
in shreds 628.13 *dilapidated*
in sickness 624.25 *unhealthily*
inside 290, 38.5 *soccer*
in side 40.12 *badminton terms*
inside 52.35 *space,* 146.9 *inclusively,* 158.2, 158.12 *core,* 257.3 *insides,* 257.14 *internally,* 290.7 *interior,* 290.16 *inwardly,* 354.15 *in,* 702.8 *imprisoned*
inside agent 528.10 *informer*
inside and out 248.16 *extensively*
inside home 31.6 *lacrosse player*
inside information 528.7 *advice*
inside job 592.4 *plot*
inside left 38.3 *football player*
inside out 221.13 *reversibly*
inside-out 287.2 *inverted*
inside-out and back-to-front 287.2 *inverted*
insider 146.3 *person included,* 665.5 *member*
insider dealing 539.10, 540.8 *fraud,* 592.4 *plot,* 737.8 *specula-*

tion
inside right 38.3 *football player*
insider trading 592.4 *plot,* 737.8 *speculation*
inside run 19.9 *play*
insides 257, 290, 148.4 *components*
inside ski 41.5 *ski equipment*
inside the boom 36.20 *offshore*
inside-the-park home run 22.5 *batting terms*
inside track 126.3, 300.4 *advantage*
insidious 244.14 *destructive,* 474.8 *cunning,* 527.5 *mysterious,* 539.35 *deceptive,* 657.4 *cunning*
insidiously 474.15 *hypocritically*
insidiousness 244.1 *destruction,* 474.3 *cunning,* 539.1 *deception*
insight 464, 519, 6.11 *refinement,* 11.8 *psychic power,* 277.3 *profundity,* 435.4 *visualization,* 439.13 *enlightenment,* 459.2 *ways of thinking,* 464.1 *intuition,* 481.2 *judiciousness,* 507.1 *wisdom,* 516.4 *prudence,* 524.1 *interpretation,* 759.2 *impression*
in sight 435.24 *visually,* 437.1 *visible,* 437.11 *visibly,* 457.7 *appearing*
insightful 6.20 *refined,* 464.6 *intuitive,* 481.9 *discriminating,* 524.14 *interpretive*
insightfully 6.27 *discerningly,* 481.16 *judiciously*
in sight of 336.20 *in progress*
insignia 544, 437.6 *visible thing*
insignificance 783, 104.1 *extraneousness,* 127.1 *inferiority,* 521.1 *lack of meaning,* 612.5 *unimportance,* 618.7 *worthlessness*
insignificant 127, 783, 104.8 *intruder,* 173.6 *small,* 260.7 *little,* 521.10 *meaningless,* 612.11 *unimportant,* 618.1 *worthless*
insignificantly 127, 104.18 *extraneously,* 260.8 *in a small way,* 521.13 *meaninglessly,* 612.14 *unimportantly,* 783.20 *unexceptionally*
insignificant matter 612.8 *trifle*
in sign language 543.18 *indicatively*
in silence 422.5 *silently*
insincere 474.10 *hypocritical,* 521.12 *unmeant,* 538.18 *pretentious,* 538.19 *dishonest,* 539.37, 540.27 *hypocritical,* 657.4 *cunning,* 853.12 *flattering,* 858.5 *dishonourable*
insincerely 474.15 *hypocritically,* 538.27 *pretentiously,* 540.38 *hypocritically,* 858.11 *dishonourably*
insincere praise 853.1 *flattery*
insincerity 474.5 *hypocrisy,* 521.3 *meaningless thing,* 538.8 *pretence,* 538.9, 539.3 *hypocrisy,* 540.3 *hypocrisy,* 657.1 *cunning,* 853.1 *flattery,* 858.1 *improbity*
in single file 159.20 *in a line,* 269.12 *longitudinally*
insinuate 228.10 *manipulate,* 346.11 *infiltrate,* 354.1 *insert,* 527.14 *imply,* 528.14 *tip,* 854.13 *vilify,* 856.5 *accuse*
insinuated 354.12 *inserted,* 527.4 *unsaid*
insinuate oneself 808.9 *fawn,* 853.11 *be sycophantic*
insinuating 228.11 *motivational,* 527.4 *unsaid,* 528.16 *informative,* 854.16 *defamatory*
insinuatingly 228.14 *influentially*
insinuation 346.3 *inroad,* 354.8 *insertion,* 527.10 *quietness,* 528.7 *advice,* 854.4 *aspersion,* 856.1 *accusation*
insipid 542, 238.13 *insufficient,* 412.5 *tasteless,* 445.8 *drained of colour,* 555.1 *unemphatic,* 576.3 *timid,* 788.4 *boring*
insipidity 412.1 *tastelessness,* 542.8 *insipidness,* 555.2 *lack of*

emphasis, 788.1 *boredom*
insipidly 542, 238.14 *weakly,* 412.10 *without taste,* 788.8 *boringly*
insipidness 542, 412.1 *tastelessness*
insist 574, 535.21 *be assertive,* 554.6 *emphasize,* 577.9 *be obstinate,* 586.15 *persuade,* 674.11 *contend,* 695.6 *compel,* 712.6 *request*
insistence 535.6 *assertiveness,* 554.1 *emphasis,* 574.14 *tenacity,* 575.1 *perseverance,* 586.1 *persuasion,* 611.1 *importance,* 712.1 *request*
insistent 426.15 *drumming,* 535.14 *assertive,* 554.3 *emphatic,* 574.2 *tenacious,* 712.9 *requesting*
insistently 426.19 *repeatedly,* 535.25 *explicitly,* 554.7 *emphatically,* 712.12 *by request*
insister 535.9 *affirmer*
insist on 513.11, 692.10 *demand,* 695.6 *compel*
insist on one's pound of flesh 836.6 *be pitiless*
insist on one's rights 845.14 *be entitled*
in slavery 697.9 *serving,* 697.10 *obediently,* 701.9 *subject,* 701.11 *under subjection*
in slight measure 121.10 *by degrees*
in slow motion 328
in smithereens 143.11 *partial*
insobriety 874.10 *drunkenness*
insolate 392.8 *bake*
insolated 392.8 *baked*
insolation 392.13 *drying*
insolence 807, 478.1 *answer,* 668.1 *defiance,* 805.3 *conceit,* 818.2 *bad manners,* 850.1 *disrespect*
Insolence 807
insolent 807, 478.11 *answering,* 668.7 *defiant,* 805.17 *conceited,* 818.6 *bad-mannered,* 850.10 *disrespectful*
insolently 807, 478.24 *in answer,* 668.9 *defiantly,* 818.8 *rudely,* 850.28 *disrespectfully*
insolent person 818.4 *discourteous person*
in solitary 702.8 *imprisoned*
in solitary confinement 702.8 *imprisoned*
insoluble 52.73 *numerable,* 371.7 *condensed,* 523.2 *unexplained*
insolubly 371.10 *densely*
insolvable 52.73 *numerable*
insolvency 743, 747, 244.4 *ruin,* 609.8 *insufficiency,* 663.1 *failure,* 722.2 *financial loss*
insolvent 743, 683.5 *failing person,* 683.10 *failed,* 722.17 *unprofitable,* 743.10 *poor person,* 745.6 *debtor,* 745.10 *unable to pay,* 747.13 *nonpaying*
insolvent debtor 747.6 *nonpayer*
insolvently 745, 683.12 *unsuccessfully,* 747.15 *without paying*
in some degree 107.10 *relevantly*
in some measure 121.11 *to a degree,* 143.12 *partly*
in someone's bad books 820.8 *estranged,* 822.12 *hated*
in someone's black books 820.8 *estranged,* 822.12 *hated*
in someone's wake 180.21 *together*
in some sense 520.13 *meaningfully*
in some way 327.16 *how*
insomnia 642.7 *restlessness*
insomniac 403.6 *conscious,* 624.19 *sick person*
insouciance 466.2 *lack of interest,* 470.1 *negligence,* 660.4 *ease of manner,* 783.1 *indifference,* 787.1 *lack of wonder*
insouciant 466.4 *uninterested,* 470.4 *negligent,* 783.7 *indifferent,* 787.3 *unmoved*

insouciantly 783.17 *indifferently,* 787.9 *without wonder*
in spasms 366.29 *jerkily*
in spate 96.11 *flooded*
inspect 435, 469.11 *care for,* 477.17 *question,* 492.12 *estimate*
inspect accounts 750.8 *audit*
inspected 477.16 *questioned*
inspection 435.3 *observation,* 469.5 *watchfulness,* 477.2 *questioning,* 492.1 *judgment*
inspection of accounts 750.3 *accounting*
inspection of books 750.3 *accounting*
inspector 72.9 *railway worker,* 435.11 *observer,* 477.9 *questioner,* 492.5 *judge,* 653.15 *manager*
inspector of accounts 750.6 *accountant*
inspectorship 688.5 *position of authority*
inspiration 519, 8.5 *deity,* 48.13 *poetic genius,* 226.1 *cause,* 228.1 *motive,* 233 *influence,* 239.1 *vigour,* 243.1 *production,* 348.4 *intake,* 390.8 *respiration,* 459.2 *ways of thinking,* 461.5 *creative thought,* 464.1 *intuition,* 471.8 *imagination,* 496.9 *invention,* 507.2 *intelligence,* 554.1 *emphasis,* 583.5 *spontaneity,* 592.3 *expedient plan*
inspirational 226.13 *causal,* 233.12 *appealing,* 759.11 *intuitive*
inspirationally 4.29 *wisely,* 226.14 *causally,* 228.14, 233.14 *influentially,* 471.22 *imaginatively*
inspiration from the muse 519.2 *inspiration*
inspire 471, 226.10 *awaken,* 228.9 *motivate,* 239.3 *invigorate,* 348.12 *draw in,* 390.21 *respire,* 778.17 *give courage*
inspire awe 786.10 *be wonderful*
inspired 228.12 *motivated,* 464.6 *intuitive,* 471.11 *ideational,* 519.10 *imaginative,* 553.3 *diffuse,* 554.3 *emphatic,* 586.20 *persuadable*
inspire hope 775
inspirer 226.7 *Prime Mover,* 586.14 *motivator*
inspire respect 849.21 *command respect*
inspiring 226.13 *causal,* 233.12 *appealing,* 239.5 *invigorating,* 695.9 *compelling*
inspiringly 4.29 *wisely,* 226.14 *causally*
inspirit 228.9 *motivate,* 471.16 *inspire,* 778.17 *give courage*
inspissate 371.8 *be dense,* 393.16 *semiliquid,* 393.25 *thicken,* 394.8 *viscous,* 394.11 *thicken*
inspissation 393.6 *thickening,* 394.1 *viscosity*
in spite 832.20 *malevolently*
in spite of 117.16 *disagreeably,* 130.10 *additionally,* 231.5 *counter,* 659.25 *difficulty,* 663.27 *opposed to,* 666.11 *in disagreement*
in spite of oneself 573.17 *unwillingly*
in spitting distance 264.6 *near*
in splendid isolation 136.22 *in isolation*
in sport 771.17 *jokingly*
in spots 160.17 *discontinuously,* 182.10 *in ones and twos,* 215.8 *irregularly,* 250.12 *where*
in spring 203.18 *seasonally*
instability 63.16 *deformation,* 113.1 *diversity,* 153.6 *derangement,* 189.1 *transience,* 215.1 *irregularity,* 224.1 *changeableness,* 238.1 *weakness,* 491.15 *unreliability,* 579.2 *caprice,* 633.7 *vulnerability*
install 354, 812, 156.23 *inaugurate,* 156.25 *enrol,* 250.9 *locate,*

251.10 *situate,* 348.10 *introduce,* 703.6 *commission*
installation 50.12 *sculpture,* 156.6 *inauguration,* 156.8 *enrolment,* 250.4 *placing,* 348.3 *introduction,* 647.1 *workshop,* 703.1 *commission*
installed 156.37 *enrolled,* 250.6 *located*
instalment 143.2 *particular,* 703.1 *commission,* 733.4 *credit,* 733.11 *borrowed,* 746.1 *payment*
instalment buying 744.1 *credit*
instalment loan 732.2 *loan*
instalment plan 733.4, 744.1 *credit,* 747.2 *stoppage*
instalment-plan payment 746.1 *payment*
Instamatic 66.16 *camera*
instance 106.2 *occurrence,* 106.11 *circumstantiate*
instance of violence 241
instant 191, 185.11 *date,* 187.2 *time period,* 189.3 *short duration,* 191.4 *point in time,* 191.5 *immediate,* 196.6 *present,* 594.21 *ready-made,* 642.18 *active*
instantaneity 191.1 *immediacy,* 329.8 *speed*
instantaneous 191.5 *immediate,* 329.1 *swift*
instantaneous current 64.9 *electric current*
instantaneously 191.8 *immediately,* 329.14 *swiftly*
instantaneousness 191.1 *immediacy,* 329.8 *speed*
instantaneous voltage 64.10 *electric potential*
instant dislike 785.1 *dislike*
instantly 191.8 *immediately*
instate 354.7 *install,* 703.6 *commission,* 812.19 *install*
instatement 348.3 *introduction,* 703.1 *commission*
in statu quo 217.9 *permanently*
instead 222, 252.20 *out of place,* 478.27 *answerably*
instead of 222.9 *instead*
in step 167.12 *conforming,* 198.10 *synchronized,* 198.13 *synchronously,* 667.10 *agreeing*
instigate 156.23, 226.11 *inaugurate,* 228.9 *motivate,* 586.15 *persuade*
instigating 228.11 *motivational*
instigation 156.6 *inauguration,* 226.1 *cause*
instigative 156.34 *inaugural,* 228.11 *motivational*
instigator 226.7 *Prime Mover,* 228.7 *motivator,* 243.9 *producer,* 586.14 *motivator*
instigatory 156.34 *inaugural*
instil 6.22 *educate,* 62.19 *administer,* 133.8 *mix,* 140.5 *combine,* 167.10 *assimilate,* 354.2 *inject*
instillation 133.1 *mixture*
instinct 462, 464, 234.3 *aptitude,* 459.2 *ways of thinking,* 460.4 *nonhuman existence,* 518.2 *basis of supposition,* 583.5 *spontaneity,* 584.2 *tendency,* 759.2 *impression*
instinctive 462, 464, 459.9 *mental,* 460.8 *nonhuman,* 571.13 *involuntary,* 583.2 *spontaneous,* 759.11 *intuitive*
instinctive dislike 785.1 *dislike*
instinctive feeling 759.2 *impression*
instinctively 459.14 *mentally,* 460.12 *nonhumanly,* 462.14 *thoughtlessly,* 464.11 *intuitively,* 583.7 *extempore*
instinctiveness 462.3 *instinct,* 571.8 *involuntariness*
instinctual 460.8 *nonhuman,* 464.8 *instinctive*
instinctually 460.12 *nonhumanly*
in stir 702.8 *imprisoned*
institute 6.12 *educational institution,* 156.23 *inaugurate,* 156.25 *enrol,* 226.11 *inaugurate,* 243.10 *produce,* 665.1 *party*
instituted 584.12 *established*

institute legal proceedings 16.70 *litigate*
institution 7.9 *priesthood*, 10.1 *ritual*, 16.1 *the law*, 116.6 *convention*, 156.6 *inauguration*, 584.4 *custom*, 665.1 *party*
institutional 116.15 *conventional*, 665.8 *leagued*
institutional building 63.20 *building*
institutionalization 584.7 *habituation*
institutionalize 116.26 *make uniform*
institutionalized 116.15 *conventional*, 584.12 *established*
institutionally 665.18 *cliquishly*
institutionary 156.34 *inaugural*
in stock 605.7 *stored*, 606.7 *provisioning*, 739.18 *on sale*
in storage 605.7 *stored*
in store 594.19 *in hand*, 605.7 *stored*, 723.9 *possessed*
in strips 266.12 *in layers*
instruct 6.22 *educate*, 167.10 *assimilate*, 475.16 *explain*, 501.14 *cause to know*, 526.1 *display*, 528.11 *inform*, 594.6 *brief*, 654.5 *advise*, 692.9 *command*, 696.14 *master*
instructable 6.17 *educatable*
instructed 501.8 *knowledgeable*, 594.18 *prepared*, 655.8 *expert*
instructing 332.16 *directing*
instruction 6.1 *education*, 166.4 *guide*, 332.5 *directions*, 501.3 *learning*, 528.2 *communication*, 594.12 *briefing*, 654.1 *advice*, 654.3 *precept*, 692.1 *command*
instructional 6.16 *educational*, 41.12 *ski*, 528.16 *informative*
instructional ski 41.5 *ski equipment*
instructions 475.3 *explanation*
instructive 6.16 *educational*, 233.11 *influential*, 528.16 *informative*, 636.8 *warning*, 654.7 *advising*, 879.19 *punitive*
instructively 6.25 *educationally*, 654.9 *advisably*
instructor 6.4 *educator*, 475.7 *demonstrator*, 653.13 *director*, 696.9 *educational leader*
instructorship 6
instrument 232, 12.1 *government*, 56.82 *measuring instrument*, 127.6 *inferior*, 152.16 *adapt*, 539.22 *dupe*, 602.1 *means*, 603.1 *tool*, 612.10 *nonentity*, 646.3 *agent*, 662.1 *help*, 808.3 *sycophant*
instrumental 49, 232, 613, 232.7 *causal*, 479.8 *experimental*, 599.9 *used*, 603.8 *mechanical*, 662.30 *helping*
instrumentalism 4.7 *school of thought*, 479.3 *experimentation*
instrumentalist 4.11 *follower of a doctrine*, 4.14 *of a philosophy*, 49.24 *musician*
instrumentality 232, 613
Instrumentality 232
instrumentally 232, 603, 599.11 *usefully*
instrumentate 49.35 *compose*
instrumentation 49.2 *music making*, 56.82 *measuring instrument*, 152.9 *musical arrangement*, 232.1 *instrumentality*, 433.3 *melodiousness*
instrument of execution 879
instrument of punishment 879
instrument of torture 879
instrument transformer 64.22 *transformer*
in style 105.9 *conditionally*
in subjection 701.9 *subject*
insubordinate 151.20 *disorderly*, 689.6 *anarchic*, 693.13 *disobedient*, 713.10 *law-breaking*, 720.13 *noncompliant*, 850.10 *disrespectful*
insubordinately 689.8 *anarchically*, 693.17 *disobediently*, 713.11 *disapprovingly*
insubordination 668.2 *disobedience*, 689.1 *anarchy*, 693.1 *dis-*

obedience, 720.3 *disregard of orders*
in substance 103.14 *at heart*, 142.13 *on the whole*
insubstantial 370, 11.18 *spiritual*, 102.8 *unreal*, 145.4 *incomplete*, 238.13 *insufficient*, 274.4 *fine*, 368.8 *nonmaterial*, 372.1 *sparse*, 379.1 *brittle*, 390.12 *airy*, 438.1 *invisible*, 442.2 *translucent*, 491.7 *unreliable*, 519.12 *imaginary*, 539.40 *illusory*, 609.1 *insufficient*, 612.1 *unimportant*, 612.4 *trivial*, 809.8 *vain*
insubstantiality 145.1 *incompleteness*, 274.1 *fineness*, 368.2 *unworldliness*, 372.3 *sparseness*, 438.4 *invisibility*, 442.6 *translucency*, 491.15 *unreliability*, 539.5 *falseness*, 612.5 *unimportance*, 809.1 *vanity*
insubstantialize 368.12 *enter a nonmaterial world*
insubstantially 145.6 *incompletely*, 368.13 *metaphysically*, 370.11 *lightly*, 372.7 *sparsely*, 379.5 *fragilely*, 442.13 *transparently*, 491.26 *unreliably*, 609.10 *insufficiently*
insubstantial person 102
insubstantial thing 238.5 *weak thing*
in succession 195, 155.27 *in sequence*, 159.18 *consecutively*
insufferable 785.9 *disliked*
insufficience 123.1 *inequality*
insufficiency 609, 52.64 *reasoning*, 123.1 *inequality*, 127.2 *deficiency*, 145.1 *incompleteness*, 145.2 *omission*, 254.2 *disappearance*, 358.5 *shortfall*, 593.2 *need*, 620.5 *imperfection*, 683.1 *failure*, 720.2 *nonperformance*, 722.2 *financial loss*, 743.9 *inadequacy*
Insufficiency 609
insufficient 238, 609, 123.3 *unequal*, 143.11 *partial*, 145.4 *incomplete*, 358.7 *short*, 515.11 *disappointing*, 620.2 *incomplete*, 656.1 *unskilful*, 683.10 *failed*, 720.12 *nonperforming*, 722.17 *unprofitable*, 743.4 *inadequate*, 852.32 *unsatisfactory*
insufficient diet 350.10 *scarcity*, 871.2 *short rations*
insufficient evidence 16.7 *legal trial*
insufficient funds 743.6 *insolvency*, 745.5 *amount owing*
insufficient income 743.5 *poverty*
insufficiently 609, 123.7 *unequally*, 145.6 *incompletely*, 238.14 *weakly*, 620.11 *imperfectly*, 683.12 *unsuccessfully*, 720.15 *inattentively*, 722.20 *at a loss*, 743.17 *inadequately*
insular 98.11 *continental*, 136.17 *unjoined*, 174.16 *alone*, 249.16 *regional*, 249.18 *local*, 481.10 *discriminatory*, 493.8 *unjust*
insularism 481.3 *prejudice*
insularity 104.3 *separateness*, 108.1 *unrelatedness*, 136.2 *setting apart*, 174.5 *aloneness*, 493.3 *injustice*
insularly 98.13 *continentally*
insulate 44.11 *make ceramics*, 64.35 *conduct*, 136.10 *set apart*, 292.3 *line*, 293.30 *protect*, 408.14 *be hot*, 421.10 *muffle*, 632.9 *protect*
insulated 408.13 *heated*, 409.9 *heat-resistant*
insulating 292.1 *lining*
insulating material 64.7 *nonconductor*
insulation 56, 64.7 *nonconductor*, 292.1 *lining*, 293.12 *protective covering*, 408.3 *heater*, 637.1 *preservation*
insulator 56.43 *electrical conduction*, 56.48 *insulation*, 64.7 *nonconductor*, 235.7 *electrical power*
insulin 58 *Hormones*, 62 *Medi-*

cation, 58.9 *protein*, 630.8 *drug*
insulin shock therapy 61.3 *psychiatric treatment*
insult 807, 850, 850, 478.18 *answer back*, 628.10 *impairment*, 668.3 *act of defiance*, 668.6 *be insubordinate*, 764.11 *quarrel*, 818.3 *act of discourtesy*, 818.7 *be discourteous*, 828.2 *offence*, 828.9 *offend*, 854.5 *scorn*
insulted 828.15 *resentful*
insulting 807, 850, 668.7 *defiant*, 854.16 *defamatory*
insultingly 668.9 *defiantly*
in sum 142.12 *one and all*
in summer 203.18 *seasonally*
in Sunday best 295.30, 813.7 *dressed up*
in Sunday go-to-meeting clothes 295.30 *dressed up*
insuperability 487.6 *hopelessness*
insuperable 487.3 *hopeless*
insuperably 487.12 *hopelessly*
in support 819.19 *devotedly*, 855.15 *in vindication*
insurable 729.7 *given*
insurance 781, 490.14 *guarantee*, 589.7 *calculation of chance*, 632.2 *protection*, 718.2 *promise*
insurance certificate 545.2 *certificate*
insurance papers 545.2 *certificate*
insurance policy 715.2 *purchase contract*, 718.2 *promise*, 781.2 *insurance*
insurance premium 714.2 *guarantee*
insurance spraying 68.5 *cultivation*
insure 594.3 *be prepared*, 714.8 *guarantee*, 718.11 *promise*, 718.12 *certify*
insured 490.4 *guaranteed*, 632.5 *safe*, 718.7 *guaranteed*
insured mail 534.2 *postal communication*
insurer 490.15 *guarantor*
insurgence 16.41 *lawlessness*, 669.3 *resistance movement*, 693.4 *revolution*
insurgency 693.4 *revolution*, 713.2 *disorder*
insurgent 16.61 *lawless*, 669.12 *resisting*, 693.10 *seditionist*, 693.14 *subversive*, 713.10 *law-breaking*
insurmountability 487.6 *hopelessness*
insurmountable 487.3 *hopeless*
insurmountable debt 747.5 *insolvency*
insurmountably 487.12 *hopelessly*
insurrection 668.3 *act of defiance*, 669.3 *resistance movement*, 693.4 *revolution*, 713.2 *disorder*
insurrectional 693.14 *subversive*
insurrectionary 693.14 *subversive*, 713.10 *law-breaking*
insurrectionist 693.10 *seditionist*
in suspense 240.7 *inertly*, 283.13 *pendulously*, 513.5 *expecting*, 513.12 *expectantly*
in suspension 387.19 *liquefied*
in swarms 181.14 *in crowds*
inswinger 27.8 *delivery*
in sworn testimony 535.24 *truthfully*
in sympathy 835.13 *pitifully*
in sync 116.13 *harmonious*, 198.10 *synchronized*, 198.13 *synchronously*, 433.12 *harmoniously*
intact 142.7 *uncut*, 144.7 *complete*, 619.1 *perfect*, 632.5 *safe*, 637.7 *preserved*, 684.7 *completed*, 825.7 *virginal*
intaglio 50.13 *relief-carving*
in tails 295.30, 813.7 *dressed up*
intake 348, 346.2 *influx*, 346.7 *entrant*, 593.2 *need*
in tandem 269.12 *longitudinally*, 664.21 *in cooperation*
in tandem with 180.24 *with*
intangibility 102.1 *unreality*, 260.1 *littleness*, 368.2 *unworldliness*

intangible 11.18 *spiritual*, 102.8 *unreal*, 260.7 *little*, 368.8 *nonmaterial*, 725.8 *propertied*
intangible assets 725.5 *personal estate*
intangibles 725.5 *personal estate*
intangibly 260.9 *microscopically*, 368.13 *metaphysically*
intarsia 47.9 *decorative woodwork*
in tatters 244.15 *destroyed*, 628.13 *dilapidated*
in Technicolor 444.10 *coloured*, 444.18 *colourfully*
integer 52.6 *complex number*, 142.2 *whole thing*, 169.2 *kind of number*, 174.1 *one*
integers 120.5 *numbers*
integral 103, 52.31 *differentiation*, 52.71 *numerical*, 52.76 *functional*, 142.6 *whole*, 144.7 *complete*, 148.6 *component*, 148.7 *modular*, 148.8 *belonging*, 169.9 *fractional*, 170.15 *mathematical*, 174.13 *whole*
integral calculus 52.30 *calculus*
integral equation 52.27 *equation*, 52.31 *differentiation*
integrality 142.1 *whole*, 144.1 *completeness*, 174.3 *oneness*
integrally 142.11 *wholly*, 148.14 *constituently*, 174.23 *wholly*
integral part 148.1 *component*
integral sign 52.13 *mathematical symbol*
integrant 148.1, 148.6 *component*
integrate 52.95 *evaluate*, 122.11 *equalize*, 133.8 *mix*, 133.10 *become mixed*, 140.5 *combine*, 142.9 *be whole*, 144.4 *complete*, 146.4 *include*, 170.9 *add*, 174.19 *become one*
integrated 103.7 *integral*, 133.12 *mixed*, 140.7 *combined*, 142.6 *whole*, 146.8 *included*
integrated circuit 64.13 *circuit*, 235.9 *electronics*, 260.2 *little thing*
integration 52.31 *differentiation*, 133.1 *mixture*, 140.1 *combination*, 142.1 *whole*, 146.1 *inclusion*, 170.1 *calculation*, 627.11 *reformism*, 664.7 *association*
integrationist 627.12 *reformer*
integrity 134.1 *purity*, 142.1 *whole*, 174.3 *oneness*, 843.3 *properness*, 843.4 *righteousness*, 857.1 *probity*, 863.1 *virtue*, 876.2 *good morals*
integument 289.1 *exterior*, 293.13 *casing*
integumental 289.6 *exterior*, 293.38 *covering*
intellect 501, 368.6 *internal world*, 459.3 *intelligence*, 459.8 *intellectual person*, 463.1 *reason*, 507.2 *intelligence*
Intellect 459
intellectual 507, 4.12 *sage*, 4.19 *learned*, 6.18 *educated*, 277.7 *deep thinking*, 459.8 *intellectual person*, 459.9 *mental*, 461.7 *thinker*, 461.8 *thoughtful*, 461.11 *reasoning*, 463.5 *reasoner*, 463.7 *reasoning*, 471.11 *ideational*, 501.6 *knowledgeable person*, 501.9 *literate*, 507.5 *wise*, 646.1 *worker*, 655.4 *skilled person*, 655.5, 688.11 *expert*, 688.17 *expert*, 696.9 *educational leader*, 696.13 *excellent*, 772.7 *serious person*
intellectual exercise 461
intellectualism 459.1 *mind*, 507.2 *intelligence*
intellectuality 6.9 *learnedness*, 459.1 *mind*
intellectualize 4.21 *rationalize*, 461.17 *philosophize*
intellectually 4.24 *philosophically*, 6.26 *studiously*, 459.14 *mentally*, 501.15 *knowledgeably*, 688.26 *expertly*, 696.16 *masterfully*
intellectually subnormal 460
intellectually weak 460.5 *lacking intellect*
intellectual person 459

intellectual subnormality 61.9 *psychological disorder*, 510.2 *subnormality*
intellectual weakness 460.1 *lack of intellect*
intelligence **459, 507,** 6.10 *educatability*, 380.13 *mental sharpness*, 463.1 *reason*, 483.1 *evidence*, 501.3 *learning*, 501.4 *intellect*, 509.2 *rationality*, 528.1 *information*, 533.1 *news*, 636.1 *warning*, 654.1 *advice*, 657.1 *cunning*
intelligence quotient 61.6 *intelligence test*
intelligence service 529.2 *secretiveness*
intelligence staff 17.5 *military staff*
intelligence test **61,** 61.5 *psychological test*
intelligence testing 61.4 *psychometrics*
intelligent **459, 507,** 4.19 *learned*, 6.17 *educatable*, 380.5 *mentally sharp*, 439.22 *enlightened*, 461.11, 463.7 *reasoning*, 501.8 *knowledgeable*, 509.5 *rational*, 655.6 *skilful*, 657.4 *cunning*
intelligent anticipation 516.4 *prudence*
intelligently **459, 507,** 6.26 *studiously*, 380.18 *sharply*, 501.15 *knowledgeably*, 655.12 *skilfully*
intelligentsia 501.7 *academia*
intelligibility **522,** 509.2 *rationality*, 520.4 *type of meaning*, 550.1 *clarity*, 556.4, 660.2 *simplicity*
Intelligibility **522**
intelligible **522,** 134.16 *simple*, 150.14 *well-ordered*, 509.5 *rational*, 520.6 *meaningful*, 526.14 *manifest*, 550.3 *clear*, 660.9 *easy*
intelligibly **522,** 520.13 *meaningfully*, 550.4 *clearly*, 556.8 *simply*
Intelsat 534.7 *satellite communication*
intemperance 357.9 *excessiveness*, 541.3 *extravagance*, 610.2 *overdoing it*, 698.6 *liberality*, 870.3 *overindulgence*, 872.1 *gluttony*, 874.11 *drinking*
intemperate 241.6 *violent*, 541.14 *extravagant*, 698.12 *unconditional*, 870.8 *overindulgent*, 872.6 *gluttonous*, 874.5 *drunken*
intemperately 541.17, 698.21 *excessively*, 870.12 *self-indulgently*
in tempo 49.41 *in tune*
intend **199, 520, 570, 588,** 471.18 *aim*, 513.8 *expect*, 520.10 *mean*, 574.7 *resolve*, 582.1 *predetermine*, 592.9 *plan*, 784.8 *prefer*
intendant 653.16 *official*
intended **588,** 518.9, 520.9 *meant*, 592.14 *planned*, 821.11 *loved one*
intend for **588**
intending **588,** 234.5 *tending to*, 784.6 *liking*
intense 237.10 *potent*, 239.4 *vigorous*, 241.6 *violent*, 277.9 *deepseated*, 444.11 *colourful*, 554.5 *serious*, 759.13 *passionate*
intensely 237.15 *acutely*, 241.10 *violently*, 759.20 *with feeling*
intensification 128.1 *increase*, 541.1 *exaggeration*, 768.1 *aggravation*
intensified 128.7 *increased*, 273.2 *dense*, 541.12 *exaggerated*, 768.4 *aggravated*
intensify 128.5 *make bigger*, 239.3 *invigorate*, 273.7 *thicken*, 541.7 *exaggerate*, 768.6 *aggravate*
intensity **237, 277,** 121.1 *degree*, 239.1 *vigour*, 241.1 *violence*, 273.6 *denseness*, 444.3 *hue*, 554.1 *emphasis*, 759.4 *emotion*
intensive 5.17 *word*, 5.35 *part of speech*, 5.42 *worded*, 5.44 *gram-*

matical
intensive farming 68.1 *agriculture*
intensively 5.50 *lexically*
intensive therapy 60.8 *treatment*
intensive therapy unit 60.10 *hospital*
intent 157.14 *aim*, 520.5 *point*, 570.1 *will*, 574.1 *resolute*, 574.15 *will*, 588.1 *intention*, 772.2 *earnest*
intention **588,** 10.9 *prayer*, 157.14 *aim*, 228.1 *motive*, 471.3 *plan*, 520.4 *type of meaning*, 520.5 *point*, 570.1 *will*, 574.12 *resolution*, 582.6 *premeditation*, 586.11 *motive*, 592.1 *plan*, 596.6 *venture*, 714.1 *promise*, 775.3 *aspiration*, 784.2 *inclination*
Intention **588**
intentional 471.12 *purposive*, 570.6 *willed*, 582.4 *deliberate*, 588.12 *intended*, 592.14 *planned*
intentional bias 588.5 *final intention*
intentional grounding 19.13 *penalty*
intentionality **588**
intentional knock-on 35.3 *rugby play*
intentionally **588,** 471.21 *purposively*, 592.16 *as planned*
intentional pass 22.4 *pitching terms*
intentions 652.1 *conduct*
intently 574.17 *resolutely*
intentness 642.8 *assiduity*
intent on 588.11 *intending*
intent upon 574.1 *resolute*
inter 277.14 *deepen*, 354.4 *immerse*, 399.8 *bury*, 531.8 *conceal*
interact 2.15 *socialize*, 107.8 *be proportionate to*, 109.7 *reciprocate*, 298.4 *interface*, 478.19 *react*, 642.16 *be sociable*, 664.12 *reciprocate*
interacting 107.5 *interrelated*, 109.1 *interchange*, 109.4 *reciprocal*, 308.4 *symmetrical*
interaction **298,** 2.3 *social environment*, 107.2 *interrelatedness*, 109.1 *interchange*, 230.2 *joint operation*, 308.1 *symmetry*, 478.3 *question and answer*, 640.1 *action*, 642.2 *social activity*, 664.3 *mutual relationship*
interactive 2.12 *sociological*, 298.6 *interfacial*, 478.12 *reactive*, 640.5 *acting*, 642.18 *active*, 664.18 *joint*
interactively 2.16 *sociologically*, 298.7 *interfacially*, 478.24 *in answer*
interalliance 107.2 *interrelatedness*
interallied 107.5 *interrelated*
interassociate 107.8 *be proportionate to*, 109.8 *interrelate*
interassociated 107.5 *interrelated*
interassociation 107.2 *interrelatedness*
interbraiding 67.2 *spinning*
interbred 133.12 *mixed*
interbreed 133.8 *mix*, 133.10 *become mixed*
interbreeding 133.1 *mixture*
intercalary 185.24 *between times*
intercalate 354.1 *insert*
intercalated 185.24 *between times*, 354.12 *inserted*
intercalation 354.8 *insertion*
intercalative 354.12 *inserted*
intercallation compound 57.7 *chemical compound*
intercaste marriage 823.3 *types of marriage*
intercede 158.19 *mediate*, 284.14 *give moral support*, 662.23 *advise*, 678.1 *mediate*, 713.6 *protest*
intercede for 232.4 *be an instrument*
interceder 678.3 *mediator*
intercept 52.32 *graph*, 420.15 *hear*, 661.8 *hinder*
intercepted pass 19.9 *play*

interception 35.3 *rugby play*, 661.1 *hindrance*
interceptor **73** *Types of Aircraft*, 679.31 *military aircraft*
intercession 10.9 *prayer*, 232.1 *instrumentality*, 284.6 *moral support*, 662.2 *support*, 678.2 *mediation*, 713.1 *protest*
intercessional 232.7 *causal*, 284.9 *supportive*, 678.6 *mediatory*
intercessor 158.9 *middleman*, 678.3 *mediator*, 716.4 *negotiator*
intercessory 678.6 *mediatory*
interchange **109,** 107.2 *interrelatedness*, 109.7 *reciprocate*, 110.7 *be the same*, 122.3 *equalization*, 135.1 *union*, 137.5 *road*, 216.4, 216.10 *exchange*, 222.6 *give a substitute*, 223.1, 223.5 *exchange*, 288.5 *crossroads*, 288.9 *cross*, 324.15 *walk*, 326.1, 326.11 *transfer*, 478.3 *question and answer*, 478.19 *react*, 728.1 *transfer of property*, 728.3 *transfer property*
interchangeability 109.1 *interchange*, 110.2 *equivalence*, 116.5 *conformity*, 122.3 *equalization*
interchangeable 109.4 *reciprocal*, 110.13 *equivalent*, 116.14 *conforming*, 216.14 *exchangeable*, 223.6 *in exchange*, 326.17 *transferable*, 482.5 *vague*
interchangeably 109.10 *reciprocally*, 223.8 *in exchange*, 288.10 *interlacedly*, 326.18 *in transit*, 478.24 *in answer*
interchanged 107.5 *interrelated*, 109.4 *reciprocal*, 223.7 *exchanged*
interchanging 107.2 *interrelatedness*, 288.7 *crossing*
intercollegiate 36.11 *rowing*
intercollegiate rowing 36.4 *rowing*
Intercollegiate Yacht Racing Association 36.1 *sailing*
intercolumniation 43.8 *column*
intercom 420.9 *audio device*, 534.9 *telephone*
intercommunicate **137,** 135.10 *link*, 267.4 *meet*
intercommunicating 267.5 *juxtaposed*
intercommunication 107.2 *interrelatedness*, 135.1 *union*, 137.2 *association*, 267.2 *meeting*, 288.1 *interweaving*, 568.1 *conversation*, 716.1 *negotiation*, 815.1 *sociability*
intercommunicative 716.8 *negotiated*
intercommunion 815.1 *sociability*
interconnect 107.8 *be proportionate to*, 109.8 *interrelate*, 135.10 *link*, 137.11 *connect*, 219.3 *continue*
interconnected **109,** 107.5 *interrelated*, 137.15 *connected*, 219.5 *continual*
interconnected circuits 56.55 *circuit*
interconnectedness 308.1 *symmetry*
interconnecting 288.7 *crossing*
interconnection **109,** 107.1 *relatedness*, 107.2 *interrelatedness*, 135.1 *union*, 137.1 *connection*, 137.4 *means of connection*, 219.1 *continuity*
interconnective 137.14 *connective*
intercontinental ballistic missile 680.5 *missile weapon*
intercourse 2.3 *social environment*, 107.2 *interrelatedness*, 135.1 *union*, 135.4 *sexual union*, 137.2 *association*, 568.1 *conversation*, 815.1 *sociability*
intercrop 288.8 *interweave*
intercrossing 356.5 *crossing point*
interdepend 109.8 *interrelate*
interdependence 107.2 *interrelatedness*, 109.2 *interconnection*, 308.1 *symmetry*
interdependent 107.5 *interrelated*, 109.5 *interconnected*,

308.4 *symmetrical*
interdependently 107.10 *relevantly*, 109.10 *reciprocally*
interdict 147.7 *exclude*, 692.1 *command*, 692.2 *demand*, 692.9 *command*, 692.10 *demand*, 699.1 *restraint*, 699.8 *restrain*, 699.12 *gag*, 709.1, 709.3 *veto*, 711.2, 711.6 *dissent*
interdicted 692.14 *commanding*
interdiction 147.1 *exclusion*, 661.1 *hindrance*, 709.1 *veto*, 711.2 *dissent*
interdictive 699.13 *restraining*, 709.5 *vetoed*, 711.9 *dissenting*
interdictively 699.16 *under restraints*, 709.7 *by veto*, 711.11 *uncooperatively*
interdictor 679.31 *military aircraft*
interdictory 147.10 *excluding*
interdigitate 288.8 *interweave*
interdigitated 288.6 *interwoven*
interdigitation 288.1 *interweaving*
interdisciplinary education 6.3 *subject*
interest **745,** 107.7 *relate to*, 128.3 *increasing thing*, 130.4 *extra*, 228.9 *motive*, 233 *influence*, 243.7 *produce*, 249.14 *sphere*, 413.13 *be piquant*, 465.1 *curiosity*, 472.1 *topic*, 590.4 *activity*, 611.1 *importance*, 611.7 *be important*, 642.2 *social activity*, 721.5 *profit*, 749.2 *money received*, 861.13 *benefit*
interest-bearing 243.11 *productive*
interested 465.5 *curious*
interesting 413.10 *stimulating*, 472.8 *problematic*, 821.22 *lovable*
interestingly 413.16 *stimulatingly*, 472.13 *problematically*
interest oneself in 642.16 *be sociable*
interest rate 14.1 *finance*
interface **298, 298,** 64.28 *plug*, 65.17 *computing term*, 65.19 *abort*, 137.13 *intercommunicate*, 267.2 *meeting*, 267.4 *meet*, 292.3 *line*, 407.6 *contiguity*, 407.12 *abut*
Interface **298**
interfaced 137.15 *connected*
interfacer **298**
interfacial **298**
interfacially **298**
interfacing 292.1 *lining*, 407.9 *touching*
interfaith 133.12 *mixed*
interfaith marriage 133.2 *mixed thing*, 823.3 *types of marriage*
interfere 19.18 *be penalized*, 31.9 *play hockey*, 153.10 *disrupt*, 640.4 *act*, 642.17 *meddle*, 661.8 *hinder*, 678.1 *mediate*, 709.3 *veto*
interfered 31.8 *hockey*
interfered with 153.15 *disrupted*
interference 22.5 *batting terms*, 31.1 *hockey*, 31.3 *ice hockey*, 31.5 *lacrosse*, 56.15 *wave property*, 153.4 *disruption*, 231.1 *counteraction*, 232.1 *instrumentality*, 365.5 *wave*, 421.3 *inaudibility*, 434.5 *atmospheric dissonance*, 438.6 *that which makes invisible*, 534.19 *radio reception*, 534.23 *television reception*, 642.9 *overactivity*, 661.1 *hindrance*, 709.1 *veto*
interference pattern 56.28 *colour*
interferer 642.17 *meddler*, 661.7 *hinderer*
interfere with 133.8 *mix*, 216.8 *cause change*, 231.3 *counteract*, 877.20 *seduce*
interfering 31.8 *hockey*, 231.4 *counteracting*, 232.7 *causal*, 233.11 *influential*, 642.9 *overactivity*, 642.21 *meddling*, 661.13 *hindering*
interfering so-and-so 661.7 *hinderer*

interferometer 56.32 *optical instrument,* 56.92 *light meter,* 268.8 *meter*
interferometric 268.16 *micrometric*
interferometry 53.27 *imaging,* 56.96 *microscopy,* 268.2 *micrometry*
interferon 58.9 *protein,* 630.4 *antidote*
interfile 288.8 *interweave*
interfuse 288.8 *interweave*
interfusion 133.1 *mixture,* 288.1 *interweaving*
intergalactic 53.36 *astronomical,* 248.12 *extensive*
intergalactically 53.39 *astronomically,* 248.16 *extensively*
intergalactic space 248.2 *empty space*
interglacial 54.40 *glaciation,* 54.60 *glaciated,* 55.40 *climatic change,* 185.24 *between times*
interglaciation 55.40 *climatic change*
intergression 346.1 *entry*
interim 158.14 *mediatory,* 160.3, 185.6 *interval,* 185.24 *between times,* 196.7 *occasional,* 218.3 *pause,* 649.1 *ease*
interim period 185.6 *interval,* 218.3 *pause*
interior 290, 290, 50.10 *art subject,* 52.35 *space,* 146.8 *included,* 158.2, 158.12 *core,* 290.9 *inland*
Interior 290
interior angle 52.39 *angle*
interior decorating 792.4 *decorating*
interior decoration 557.1 *ornament*
interior decorator 629.12 *repairer*
interior design 792.4 *decorating*
interiority 290.1 *interior,* 527.10 *quietness*
interior light 439.6 *electric light*
interior monologue 48.3 *aspect of fiction,* 569.1 *soliloquy*
interjacence 348.1 *admittance*
interject 130.6 *add,* 160.16 *interrupt,* 354.1 *insert,* 478.18 *answer back,* 564.11 *speak*
interjected 478.13 *retaliatory*
interjecting 478.13 *retaliatory*
interjection 5.35 *part of speech,* 130.1 *addition,* 160.6 *intervention,* 348.1 *admittance,* 354.8 *insertion,* 431.7 *cry of disapproval,* 478.5 *counterstatement,* 564.7 *utterance,* 567.2 *salutation*
interjectional 5.44 *grammatical*
interlace 133.8 *mix,* 135.10 *link,* 288.8 *interweave*
interlaced 133.12 *mixed,* 288.6 *interwoven*
interlacedly 288
interlaced scanning 534.21 *television*
interlacement 288.1 *interweaving*
interlacing 107.2 *interrelatedness,* 288.1 *interweaving*
interlard 133.8 *mix*
interlay 133.8 *mix,* 288.8 *interweave*
interleave 113.8 *be diverse,* 133.8 *mix*
interline 288.8 *interweave,* 292.3 *line*
interlineally 288.10 *interlacedly*
interlinearly 288.10 *interlacedly*
interlineation 130.3 *additional item,* 288.1 *interweaving*
interlingua 5 Languages and Groups of Languages
interling 257.4 *stuffing,* 266.1 *layer,* 292.1, 292.1 *lining*
interlink 107.8 *be proportionate to,* 109.8 *interrelate*
interlinkage 107.2 *interrelatedness*
interlinked 107.5 *interrelated,* 109.5 *interconnected*
interlock 107.8 *be proportionate to,* 109.8 *interrelate,* 135.8 *unite,* 135.10 *link,* 288.8 *inter-*

weave
interlocked 107.5 *interrelated*
interlocking 107.2 *interrelatedness,* 109.5 *interconnected,* 135.1 *union,* 288.1 *interweaving*
interlock stitch 67.5 *knitting*
interlocute 478.19 *react*
interlocution 4.5 *philosophical argument,* 478.3 *question and answer,* 568.1 *conversation,* 568.6 *interview*
interlocutor 477.9 *questioner,* 478.10 *answerer,* 564.10 *speaker,* 568.7 *conversationalist*
interlocutory 478.12 *reactive,* 568.12 *conversing*
interlope 104.16 *be external,* 149.17 *intrude*
interloper 104.8 *intruder,* 147.5 *excluded person,* 149.10 *intruder*
interloping 104.4 *externality,* 104.12 *external*
interlude 51.2 *play,* 51.6 *scene,* 51.10 *comedy,* 130.3 *additional item,* 185.6 *interval,* 218.3 *pause*
interlunar 185.24 *between times*
intermarriage 133.1 *mixture,* 823.3 *types of marriage*
intermarried 133.12 *mixed*
intermarry 133.10 *become mixed,* 823.15 *marry*
intermeddle 642.17 *meddle,* 678.1 *mediate*
intermeddler 642.11 *meddler*
intermeddling 678.2 *mediation*
intermediacy 232.1 *instrumentality*
intermediary 124.2 *medium,* 135.7 *joiner,* 158.9 *middleman,* 158.14 *mediatory,* 232.3 *assistant,* 298.3 *interfacer,* 298.6 *interfacial,* 564.10 *speaker,* 675.3 *pacifist,* 678.3 *mediator,* 706.1 *delegate,* 706.6 *delegated,* 707.3 *agent,* 707.7 *deputizing,* 716.4 *negotiator*
intermediate 124.2 *medium,* 158.3 *median,* 158.14 *mediatory,* 185.24 *between times,* 232.4 *be an instrument,* 232.7 *causal,* 333.4 *middle,* 678.1 *mediate*
intermediate bond 57.11 *chemical bond*
intermediate-frequency amplifier 534.18 *radio*
intermediate host 76.4 *type of animal*
intermediate-level waste 56.74 *nuclear waste*
intermediately 124.12 *mediumly,* 333.8 *medially,* 678.7 *mediatorially*
intermediateness 232.1 *instrumentality*
intermediate rock 54.30 *igneous rock*
intermediate technology 243.2 *manufacture*
intermediation 678.2 *mediation*
intermediator 678.3 *mediator*
intermedin 58 Hormones
intermedium 124.5 *medium,* 137.4 *means of connection*
interment 277.1 *depth,* 354.10 *immersion,* 399.1 *burial,* 546.3 *obliteration*
intermeshed 107.5 *interrelated*
intermeshing 107.2 *interrelatedness*
intermetallic compound 57.7 *chemical compound*
intermezzo 49.4 *opera,* 51.2 *play,* 51.6 *scene,* 130.3 *additional item*
interminability 184.4 *infinity,* 269.4 *length*
interminable 159.11 *continuous,* 184.1 *infinite,* 190.10 *continuing forever,* 219.6 *protracted,* 269.1 *long*
interminably 184.10 *infinitely,* 219.7 *continually,* 269.11 *lengthily,* 608.9 *enough*
intermingle 2.15 *socialize,* 133.8 *mix,* 288.8 *interweave*
intermingled 133.12 *mixed,*

482.3 *indiscriminate*
intermingling 133.1 *mixture*
intermission 51.6 *scene,* 160.3 *interval,* 248.8 *intervening space*
intermit 214.7 *be regular,* 215.6 *be irregular*
intermittence 160.1 *discontinuity,* 182.4 *rarity,* 213.3 *infrequency,* 215.1 *irregularity*
intermittent 160.8 *discontinuous,* 182.6 *sparse,* 185.23 *occasional,* 187.9 *periodic,* 213.2 *infrequent,* 215.4 *irregular*
intermittently 160.17 *discontinuously,* 185.28 *sometimes,* 213.1 *infrequently,* 215.8 *irregularly,* 491.27 *capriciously*
intermittent showers 55.25 *rain*
intermix 113.8 *be diverse,* 133.8 *mix*
intermixed 133.12 *mixed*
intermixture 133.1 *mixture*
intermodal transportation 70.1 *transport*
intern 6.4 *educator,* 60.11 *doctor,* 323.10 *enclose,* 699.11 *detain,* 702.9 *imprison,* 879.1 *punish*
internal 290, 368, 158.12 *core,* 290.1, 290.7 *interior,* 290.10 *visceral,* 438.3 *private*
internal bleeding 624.11 *blood disease*
internal-combustion engine 63.11 *engine,* 603.4 *machine*
internal ear 420
internal energy 56.38 *thermodynamics,* 235.4 *energy*
internal evidence 483.5 *legal evidence*
internal examination 60.6 *health care*
internal friction 385.1 *friction*
internal gear 63.7 *gear*
internality 290.1 *interior*
internalization 290
internalize 290.15 *keep inside,* 348.13 *absorb,* 461.17 *philosophize*
internalized 290
internally 257, 290.16 *inwardly,* 368.14 *subjectively,* 438.9 *invisibly*
internal medicine 60.1 *medicine,* 60.3 *medical specialty*
internalness 290.1 *interior*
internal organs 290.4 *insides*
internal resistance 64.12 *resistance*
internal respiration 58.24 *respiration,* 59.6 *cell biology*
Internal Revenue 13.6 *economic factors*
internal rhyme 48.11 *rhyme*
internal secretion 352.2 *secreted substance*
internal world 368
international 43 Architectural Styles, 33.11 *racing,* 91.16 *national,* 142.6 *whole,* 164.16 *universal,* 233.13 *dominant,* 400.13 *national,* 724.5 *jointly possessing*
international 10 square metre canoe 36.6 *canoeing*
international agreement 667.2 *contract,* 715.3 *alliance*
International Atomic Energy Agency 235.8 *nuclear power*
International Badminton Federation 40.10 *badminton*
International Bank for Reconstruction and Development 13.4 *economic development*
International Boxing Federation 26.2 *boxing*
international candle 75 Scientific and Technical Units
International Canoe Federation 36.6 *canoeing*
International Casting Federation 20.1 *angling*
International Challenge Cup 36.6 *canoeing*
international code 534.11 *dialling*
International Confederation of Free Trade Unions 15.3 *organized labour*

international cooperation 400.9 *group*
International Date Line 185.9 *time zone,* 192.3 *chronology*
international date line 302.4 *boundary marker*
International Development Association 13.4 *economic development*
international direct dialling 534.11 *dialling*
international fair 740.2 *fair*
International Federation of Christian Trade Unions 15.3 *organized labour*
international finance 14.1 *finance*
International Finance Corporation 13.4 *economic development,* 741.7 *finance*
International Gothic 50 Western Art Styles and Movements
international government 12.1 *government*
International Hockey Board 31.1 *hockey*
International Ice Hockey Federation 31.3 *ice hockey*
internationalism 91, 164.1 *generality*
internationalist 91, 833.3 *philanthropist*
internationality 91.5 *internationalism*
internationalize 220.12 *naturalize,* 724.4 *have joint possession*
internationalized 220.17 *naturalized*
International Labour Organisation 13.8 *industrial relations*
international language 5
international law 16.1 *the law*
international loan 732.2 *loan*
International Luge Federation 41.9 *bobsledding*
internationally 33.12 *in a race,* 91.19 *nationally,* 164.32 *universally,* 233.14 *influentially,* 249.20 *nationally,* 400.15 *humanly,* 724.6 *in common*
international mail 534.2 *postal communication*
International Monetary Fund 13.4 *economic development,* 14.1, 741.7 *finance*
international nautical mile 75 General Units
international organization 724.1 *joint possession*
international pact 715.3 *alliance*
international paper 532.4 *newspaper*
International Phonetic Alphabet 5.14 *alphabet*
international police 16.14 *police*
international racing 33.1 *motor racing*
International Red Cross 675.2 *symbol of peace*
international sailing 36.1 *sailing*
International Scientific Vocabulary 5.7 *international language*
international show jumping 32.9 *jumping*
International Skating 135 Union 41.6 *ice-skating*
International Socialists 12.6 *political party*
International society 400.9 *group*
International Swimming Federation 39.5 *swimming association*
international trade 13, 737.5 *commercial trade*
international union organization 15.3 *organized labour*
International Yacht Racing Union 36.1 *sailing*
internecine 244.14 *destructive,* 398.24 *murderous*
internecine war 676.1 *war*
interned 702.8 *imprisoned*
internee 323.6 *closed-in person*
internetworking 65.15 *network*
internment 676.7 *war measures,* 699.4 *detention,* 702.7 *imprisonment,* 879.7 *punishment*
internode 83.5 *stem*
interpellant 477.12 *questioning*

interpellate 477.17 *question*
interpellation 477.2 *questioning*, 567.2 *salutation*
interpellator 477.9 *questioner*, 568.7 *conversationalist*
interpenetrate 107.8 *be proportionate to*, 288.8 *interweave*, 298.5 *cooperate*, 346.11 *infiltrate*
interpenetration 107.2 *interrelatedness*, 288.1 *interweaving*, 298.2 *interaction*, 346.3 *inroad*, 356.3 *passage into*
interpenetrative 298.6 *interfacial*
interpenetratively 288.10 *interlacedly*
interpersonal relations 2.3 *social environment*
interphase 59.10 *cell division*
interplanetary 53.36 *astronomical*
interplanetary space 53.14 *solar system*, 248.2 *empty space*
interplay 107.8 *be proportionate to*, 109.1 *interchange*, 109.7 *reciprocate*, 223.1 *exchange*, 664.3 *mutual relationship*, 664.12 *reciprocate*
interplaying 107.2 *interrelatedness*, 109.4 *reciprocal*
Interpol 16.14 *police*
interpolate 52.93 *equate*, 130.6 *add*, 158.16 *place in the middle*, 160.16 *interrupt*, 170.9 *add*, 354.1 *insert*
interpolated 130.8 *additional*, 354.12 *inserted*
interpolation 52.66 *proof*, 130.3 *additional item*, 143.7 *piece*, 160.6 *intervention*, 170.1 *calculation*, 354.8 *insertion*
interpolative 354.12 *inserted*
interpose 130.6 *add*, 136.14 *come between*, 158.16 *place in the middle*, 160.16 *interrupt*, 232.4 *be an instrument*, 642.17 *meddle*, 661.8 *hinder*, 678.1 *mediate*
interposition 130.1 *addition*, 232.1 *instrumentality*, 661.1 *hindrance*, 678.2 *mediation*
interpret 524, 4.21 *rationalize*, 5.46 *translate*, 49.36 *play*, 152.16 *adapt*, 216.8 *cause change*, 220.9 *transform*, 478.20 *solve*, 481.12 *discriminate*, 522.5 *simplify*, 524.12 *translate*, 526.3 *reveal*, 550.2 *clarify*, 560.16 *define*, 561.4 *dissertate*, 616.16 *make easy*
interpretability 522.9 *intelligibility*
interpretable 522.1 *intelligible*
interpretation 524, 51.20 *acting*, 152.9 *musical arrangement*, 216.1 *change*, 220.1 *conversion*, 478.6 *solution*, 481.1 *discrimination*, 520.4 *type of meaning*, 522.10 *simplicity*, 561.1 *dissertation*
Interpretation 524
interpretational 478.14 *solved*, 481.9 *discriminating*, 524.14 *interpretive*
interpretative 520.6 *meaningful*, 522.1 *intelligible*, 524.14 *interpretive*, 561.5 *expository*
interpretatively 524.18 *in other words*
interpret dreams 11.23, 517.12 *divine*
interpreted 524, 51.37 *dramatic*, 478.14 *solved*, 481.11 *judged*, 522.2 *simple*
interpreted language 65.9 *programming language*
interpreter 524, 5.2 *linguist*, 65.8 *software*, 561.3 *dissertator*
interpreter of dreams 517.9 *forecaster*
interpreting dreams 517.2 *divination*
interpretive 524, 48.16 *literary*, 520.6 *meaningful*, 522.1 *intelligible*, 530.12 *revelatory*, 543.14 *signifying*, 560.11 *descriptive*, 561.5 *expository*
interpretively 524.18 *in other*

words, 543.18 *indicatively*
interpretive reporting 533.3 *reporting*
interpret news 524
interpret the part 51.35 *rehearse*
interpret the scriptures 7.22 *theologize*
interquartile range 52.60 *parameter*
interracial 133.12 *mixed*, 400.13 *national*
interracially 133.14 *in the midst*
interracial marriage 133.2 *mixed thing*, 823.3 *types of marriage*
Interrail Card 754.4 *bargain*
interred 354.14 *immersed*, 399.10 *buried*
interregnum 12.1 *government*, 185.6 *interval*, 689.1 *anarchy*
interrelate 109, 116.25 *conform*, 219.3 *continue*, 664.12 *reciprocate*
interrelated 107, 109.5 *interconnected*, 116.14 *conforming*, 219.5 *continual*
interrelatedness 107, 219.1 *continuity*
interrelating 664.18 *joint*
interrelation 219.1 *continuity*, 308.1 *symmetry*
interrelationship 109.2 *interconnection*
interrobang 543.7 *punctuation*
interrogate 477, 465.7 *be curious*
interrogated 477.16 *questioned*
interrogation 477.2 *questioning*, 568.6 *interview*
interrogation mark 477.11 *question mark*
interrogation point 477.11 *question mark*
interrogative 477.12 *questioning*
interrogative clause 477.11 *question mark*
interrogative pronoun 477.11 *question mark*
interrogator 477.9 *questioner*, 568.7 *conversationalist*
interrupt 160, 283, 117.12 *be disparate*, 145.5 *be incomplete*, 153.10 *disrupt*, 211.5 *take untimely action*, 218.8 *cause to cease*, 218.9 *pause*, 346.10 *invade*, 564.11 *speak*, 642.17 *meddle*, 661.8 *hinder*, 818.7 *be discourteous*
interrupted 160, 283, 136.15 *separate*, 145.4 *incomplete*, 153.15 *disrupted*, 218.10 *finished*
interrupted state 145.1 *incompleteness*
interrupter 661.7 *hinderer*
interrupting 211.10 *untimely*
interruption 160, 283, 117.5 *unfitness*, 153.4 *disruption*, 160.6 *intervention*, 211.1 *untimeliness*, 218.2 *stop*, 218.3 *pause*, 248.8 *intervening space*, 265.1 *interval*, 642.9 *overactivity*, 661.1 *hindrance*, 818.2 *bad manners*
intersect 52.97 *align*, 288.9 *cross*, 310.11 *angle*, 342.9 *converge*, 407.12 *abut*
intersecting 314.17 *structured*, 52.80 *linear*, 288.7 *crossing*, 407.9 *touching*
intersecting lines 52.37 *line*
intersecting road 137.5 *road*
intersecting vault 43.7 *vault*
intersection 52.21 *set*, 71.3 *carriageway*, 135.6 *point of union*, 288.5 *crossroads*, 310.1 *angle*, 327.3 *road*, 343.4 *branching*, 356.5 *crossing point*, 407.6 *contiguity*
intersectional 288.7 *crossing*
interspace 265.1 *interval*, 265.4 *space*
interspaced 265.6 *spaced*
interspatial 265.6 *spaced*
interspatially 265.8 *apart*, 288.10 *interlacedly*
intersperse 113.8 *be diverse*, 133.8 *mix*
interspersed 133.12 *mixed*

interstate 70.5 *transportable*, 137.5 *road*
interstate commerce 13.1 *economics*
interstate highway 71.2, 327.3 *road*
interstellar 53.36 *astronomical*, 248.12 *extensive*
interstellar dust 53.8 *interstellar medium*
interstellar gas 53.8 *interstellar medium*
interstellar medium 53
interstellar molecule 53.8 *interstellar medium*
interstellar space 248.2 *empty space*
interstice 265.2 *crack*
interstitial 265.6 *spaced*
interstitial-cell-stimulating hormone 58 Hormones
interstitial compound 57.7 *chemical compound*
interstitially 265.8 *apart*
intertexture 288.1 *interweaving*, 383.1 *texture*
intertidal 54.52 *coastal*, 97.7 *oceanic*
intertidal zone 54.15 *tide*
intertropical convergence zone 55.17 *wind system*
intertwine 133.8 *mix*, 135.10 *link*, 140.5 *combine*, 288.8 *interweave*, 320.9 *enfold*
intertwined 107.5 *interrelated*, 133.12 *mixed*, 140.7 *combined*, 288.6 *interwoven*
intertwinement 288.1 *interweaving*
intertwining 67.2 *spinning*, 107.2 *interrelatedness*, 288.1 *interweaving*
intertwiningly 288.10 *interlacedly*
intertwist 133.8 *mix*
intertwisted 133.12 *mixed*
interurban 93.14 *urban*
interval 121, 160, 185, 265, 49.16 *musical note*, 49.17 *notation*, 51.6 *scene*, 55.3 *weather*, 56.8 *time*, 100.4 *emptiness*, 145.2 *omission*, 187.1 *period*, 203.1 *season*, 218.3 *pause*, 248.8 *intervening space*, 322.1 *opening*, 649.1 *ease*
Interval 265
intervallic 185.24 *between times*, 265.6 *spaced*
interval scale 52.56 *nonparametric methods*
intervene 153.10 *disrupt*, 158.19 *mediate*, 160.16 *interrupt*, 185.15 *pass*, 232.4 *be an instrument*, 640.4 *act*, 642.17 *meddle*, 661.8 *hinder*, 661.9 *block*, 678.1 *mediate*, 699.9 *economize*, 737.1 *trade*
intervener 16.8 *litigant*
intervening 232.7 *causal*, 356.13 *penetrating*, 661.13 *hindering*
intervening space 248, 265.1 *interval*
intervention 160, 13.6 *economic factors*, 153.4 *disruption*, 232.1 *instrumentality*, 356.3 *passage into*, 661.1 *hindrance*, 661.2 *obstacle*, 676.1 *war*, 678.2 *mediation*, 699.2 *economic restraint*, 737.5 *commercial trade*
interventional 232.7 *causal*, 661.13 *hindering*, 661.14 *blocked*, 699.13 *restraining*
interventionalist 699.6 *law-maker*
interventionally 661.17 *in the way*
interventionism 699.2 *economic restraint*, 737.5 *commercial trade*
interventionist 158.9 *middleman*
interview 568, 477.3 *questionnaire*, 477.17 *question*, 478.3 *question and answer*, 478.19 *react*, 533.13 *report*, 815.3 *meeting*
interviewee 477.10 *person questioned*, 478.10 *answerer*
interviewer 477.9 *questioner*, 568.7 *conversationalist*
interwar 185.24 *between times*

interweave 288, 133.8 *mix*, 135.10 *link*, 137.11 *connect*, 140.5 *combine*
interweaving 288, 67.4 *weaving*, 107.2 *interrelatedness*
Interweaving 288
interwork 107.8 *be proportionate to*, 288.1 *interweaving*
interworking 107.2 *interrelatedness*, 107.5 *interrelated*
interwoven 288, 107.5 *interrelated*, 133.12 *mixed*, 135.15 *tied*, 137.15 *connected*, 140.7 *combined*
intestate 546.6 *obliterated*
intestinal 290.10 *visceral*, 322.15 *providing passage*
intestinal gland 352.3 *gland*
intestinally 322.27 *cavernously*
intestines 290.4 *insides*, 314.3 *convoluted thing*, 322.7 *passageway*, 350.16 *eating utensil*
in that case 106.15 *under the circumstances*, 116.36 *accordingly*
in that place 250.12 *where*
in that way 116.36 *accordingly*
in the abstract 4.25 *theoretically*
in the act 640.7 *actively*, 866.11 *guiltily*
in the affirmative 116.39 *with consent*, 499.8 *unanimously*
in the aftermath 155.28 *after*
in the afternoon 205.7 *evening*
in the aggregate 142.12 *one and all*
in the air 275.19 *high*, 297.6 *atmospheric*, 532.19 *published*, 685.7 *incompletely*
in the altogether 294.8 *uncovered*, 296.9 *undressed*, 296.17 *nakedly*
in the army 676.15 *warring*
in the ascendant 233.11 *influential*, 126.12 *superior*, 359.22 *ascending*
in the background 226.14 *causally*, 263.10 *distantly*, 304.9 *in the rear*, 527.2 *concealed*
in the back of beyond 263.10 *distantly*
in the bag 258.20 *containing*, 684.7 *completed*, 718.8 *accomplished*
in the bank 723.9 *possessed*
in the bargain bin 752.7 *at a discount*
in the beginning 156
in the big house 699.15 *detained*, 702.8 *imprisoned*
in the black 721.17 *well-off*, 721.20 *gainfully*, 742.2 *solvent*, 744.13 *in credit*, 746.16 *paid*
in the book 545.16 *recorded*
in the boondocks 263.10 *distantly*
in the boonies 263.10 *distantly*
in the bud 156, 59.26 *developmental*, 156.32 *embryonic*
in the buff 294.8 *uncovered*, 296.9 *undressed*, 296.17 *nakedly*
in the business 642.21 *meddling*
in the can 684.8 *concluded*
in the cannon's mouth 679.42 *martially*
in the case 106.15 *under the circumstances*
in the centre of 291.10 *centrally*
in the chair 653.17 *managerial*, 653.19 *managerially*
in the chips 742.1 *wealthy*
in the circumstances 105.9 *conditionally*
in the clear 16.63 *acquitted*, 632.5 *safe*, 865.5 *innocent*
in the clink 632.5 *safe*
in the clouds 95.11 *on the mountain*, 275.19 *high*
in the club 245.16 *reproductive*
in the clutches of 701.9 *subject*
in the cooler 702.8 *imprisoned*
in the corner 26.14 *combat*
in the course of 185.26 *all the time*
in the cradle 206.11 *young*, 206.14 *youthfully*
in the current mode 201.23 *trend-*

ily
in the dark 436.12 *blind to,*
440.15 *darkly,* 502.6 *ignorant*
in the database 545.16 *recorded*
in the days of 185.29 *one day*
in the dead of night 205.7 *evening*
in the deepfreeze 240.7 *inertly*
in the depths 770.6 *depressed*
in the dim and distant past 3.24
historically
in the direction of 327.17 *via*
in the dirt 362.24 *down*
in the distance 263.10 *distantly*
in the doctor's hands 624.25 *unhealthily*
in the doldrums 770.6 *depressed,*
776.4 *hopeless*
in the dough 742.1 *wealthy*
in the driving seat 233.13 *dominant,* 653.19 *managerial,*
653.19 *managerially,* 688.23 *authoritatively*
in the dust 806.3 *humbled*
in the embryonic stage 594.17
developing
in the end 155.30 *behind,*
157.26, 218.11 *finally,* 323.17
finally, 478.25 *conclusively,*
490.25 *inevitably*
in the evening 205.7 *evening*
in the event 106.15 *under the circumstances*
in the event of death 397.23 *fatally*
in the event that 518.11 *supposing*
in the expected way 788.8 *boringly*
in the eye of the law 16.81 *legally*
in the eyes of the law 16.81 *legally*
in the face of 253.16 *on the spot,*
663.27 *opposed to,* 668.9 *defiantly,* 713.11 *disapprovingly*
in the face of death 633.11 *dangerously,* 676.18 *so war*
in the family way 245.16 *reproductive,* 513.6 *expectant*
in the file 545.16 *recorded*
in the final analysis 157.26 *finally*
in the first place 156.40 *first,*
194.11 *before*
in the flesh 165.29 *personally,*
253.14 *in person,* 367.7 *material,* 396.12 *alive*
in the flower of youth 206.11
young, 206.14 *youthfully*
in the foreground 526.14 *manifest*
in the fourth place 178.15 *fourth*
in the freezer 637.7 *preserved*
in the fresh air 417.3 *odourless,*
417.7 *odourlessly*
in the fullness of time 199.14 *in the future*
in the future 199, 197.3 *another time,* 209.17 *later*
in the gaseous state 388.16 *gaseous*
in the gloaming 441.12 *dimly*
in the good books of 819.9
friends with
in the good graces of 819.9
friends with
in the good old days 3.24 *historically,* 202.19 *anciently*
in the grave 397.19 *dead,*
399.10 *buried*
in the gravy 742.1 *wealthy*
in the grip of 726.10 *retained*
in the groove 112.13 *uniformly*
in the habit 584.14 *habituated*
in the hands of 701.9 *subject,*
723.9 *possessed*
in the hands of the receiver
244.15 *destroyed,* 745.10 *unable to pay*
in the headlines 532.20 *well-known*
in the heat of passion 828.18 *angrily*
in the heat of the moment
828.18 *angrily*

in the height of passion 828.18
angrily
in the hoosegow 632.5 *safe*
in the hot seat 633.4 *endangered,* 653.19 *managerially*
in the index 545.16 *recorded*
in the interim 185.26 *all the time,* 196.10 *for the present*
in the know 6.19, 501.8 *knowledgeable,* 528.18 *informed*
in the land of the living 396.12
alive
in the large 259.20 *largely*
in the lead 194.11 *before,*
303.11 *in front,* 357.14 *surpassing,* 357.17 *ahead*
in the lee of 632.10 *safely*
in the limelight 526.14 *manifest,*
532.22 *publicly*
in the line of duty 847.18 *on duty*
in the lion's den 633.4 *endangered*
in the long run 124.11 *on average,* 157.26 *finally,* 164.31 *overall*
in the lowest position 127.19 *inferiorly*
in the L position 30.12 *competitively*
in the main 103.13 *in essence,*
126.16 *superiorly,* 142.13 *on the whole,* 164.31 *overall,*
166.18 *as a rule,* 611.9 *importantly*
in the majority 175.11 *in majority*
in the making 685.7 *incompletely*
in the marketplace 737.20 *in trade*
in the mass 142.12 *one and all*
in the meantime 185.26 *all the time,* 189.9 *for the time being,*
196.10 *for the present*
in the melting pot 133.12 *mixed*
in the middle 158, 124.12
mediumly, 333.8 *medially*
in the middle of 133.14 *in the midst,* 291.10 *centrally,* 724.5
jointly possessing
In the midst 133
in the midst of 133.14 *in the midst,* 158.20 *in the middle,*
291.10 *centrally,* 640.7 *actively*
in the mind 471.11 *ideational,*
471.20 *theoretically,* 472.12 *topically*
in the mind's eye 471.11 *ideational,* 471.20 *theoretically,*
519.17 *imaginatively*
in the minutes 545.16 *recorded*
in the mists of time 3.24 *historically,* 200.22 *in the past*
in the mode 584.12 *established*
in the money 686.8 *prosperous,*
741.28 *financially,* 742.1
wealthy
in the morning 204
in the name of 12.14 *politically,*
662.37 *in aid of,* 688.23 *authoritatively*
in the negative 536.15 *negatively*
in the neighbourhood 256.20 *environmentally,* 264.5, 264.6
near, 297.8 *round*
in the news 472.6 *topical,*
472.12 *topically,* 532.19 *published*
in the nick 702.8 *imprisoned*
in the nick of time 210.11 *in time*
in the night 440.15 *darkly*
in the nude 296.9 *undressed,*
296.17 *nakedly*
in the offing 199.14 *in the future,* 263.10 *distantly,* 594.17
developing
in the open 289.15 *externally,*
322.25 *obviously,* 390.26 *out-of-doors,* 526.14 *manifest,* 530.13
openly, 532.19 *published*
in the open air 289.15 *externally,* 390.26 *out-of-doors*
in the open water 39.12 *by swimming*
in theory 102.18 *ideally,* 471.20
theoretically, 518.10 *supposedly*
in the ownership of 723.9 *possessed*
in the past 3, 200, 197.3 *an-*

other time
in the pay of 701.9 *subject,*
701.11 *under subjection*
in the picture 403.5 *sensible,*
501.8 *knowledgeable,* 528.18 *informed*
in the pink 150.13 *orderly,* 237.9
physically strong, 306.12 *on form,* 405.7 *pleased,* 450.10 *ruddily,* 619.1 *perfect,* 623.1
healthy, 843.12 *all right*
in the pipeline 70.6 *commercially,* 145.4 *incomplete*
in the plural 175.6 *plural*
in the possession of 723.9 *possessed,* 723.10 *possessively*
in the poverty trap 593.5 *necessitous,* 743.1 *poor,* 743.15 *poorly*
in the presence of 253.16 *on the spot*
in the present case 105.9 *conditionally*
in the public eye 437.2 *clear,*
532.20 *well-known,* 532.22 *publicly*
in the pudding club 245.16 *reproductive*
in the raw 294.8 *uncovered,*
296.9 *undressed,* 296.17 *nakedly*
in the rear 304
in the red 320, 722.17 *unprofitable,* 722.20 *at a loss,* 743.2 *insolvent,* 744.12 *charged,* 745.9
in debt, 745.11 *insolvently,*
747.15 *without paying*
in the refrigerator 637.7 *preserved*
in the right 843, 843
**in the right place at the right
time** 615.7 *conveniently*
in the ring 26.16 *professionally*
in the rough 335.21 *indirect,*
375.14 *roughly*
in the running 674.14 *contending*
in the saddle 594.18 *prepared,*
653.19 *managerially,* 688.23 *authoritatively*
in the sale 752.7 *at a discount*
in the same boat 114.13 *similarly,* 724.5 *jointly possessing*
in the same breath 191.9 *in the shortest possible time*
in the same breath as 198.15 *as*
in the same category 114.13 *similarly*
in the same class 146.8 *included*
in the same league 146.8 *included*
in the same place 110.18 *identically*
in the same way 110.18 *identically,* 114.14 *comparably,*
116.34 *uniformly,* 667.16 *compatibly*
in the same words 537.38 *literally*
in the second place 176.21 *second,* 195.15 *as follows*
in the Senate 706.8 *representatively*
in the sense that 520.13 *meaningfully*
in the service of 662.37 *in aid of*
in the shade 440.15 *darkly*
in the shops 739.18 *on sale*
in the shortest possible time 191
in the singular 174.22 *one by one*
in the small hours 205.7 *evening,*
208.17 *early*
in the soup 633.4 *endangered,*
659.16 *troubled*
in the spotlight 51.41 *onstage*
in the stars 199.16 *predictably*
in the sticks 263.10 *distantly*
in the sun 390.26 *out-of-doors*
in the swim 686.9 *prosperously*
in the teeth of 659.25 *difficultly,*
668.9 *defiantly*
in the thick of 158.20 *in the middle,* 640.7 *actively*
in the thick of the fray 679.42
martially
in the third place 177.14 *third*
in the twilight 441.12 *dimly*
in the twinkling of an eye 189.8
transiently, 191.9 *in the shortest possible time*
in the usual course 164.30 *usu-*

ally
in the vanguard 194.11 *before,*
303.11 *in front*
in the vernacular 556.8 *simply*
in the very moment that 198.15
as
in the vicinity 256.20 *environmentally,* 264.5, 264.6 *near,*
297.8 *round,* 615.8 *nearby*
in the way 661, 661.14 *blocked*
in the way of marriage 823.24
matrimonially
in the wee small hours 205.7 *evening,* 208.17 *early*
in the wind 199.14 *in the future*
in the wind's eye 332.11 *in all directions*
in the wings 51.41 *onstage*
in the worst possible taste 795.9
ribald
in the wrong 844, 866.5 *guilty*
in the wrong place 252.10 *replaced,* 252.20 *out of place*
in the year of 185.29 *one day*
in this vicinity 250.12 *where*
in this way 106.15 *under the circumstances,* 327.16 *how*
in threes 177
inti 741.11 *national coins*
intimacy 135.4 *sexual union,*
264.1 *nearness,* 784.1 *liking,*
815.1 *sociability,* 819.3 *familiarity,* 821.5 *desire*
intimate 135.12 *united,* 165.19
personal, 264.5 *near,* 290.12 *internalized,* 520.10 *mean,*
527.14 *imply,* 528.14 *tip,* 529.9
secret, 543.10 *signify,* 784.5 *likable,* 819.6 *close friend,* 819.10
familiar
intimated 527.4 *unsaid*
intimate friend 784.4 *likable person,* 819.6 *close friend*
intimately 819, 135.16 *as one,*
135.18 *inextricably,* 290.16 *inwardly,* 784.10 *with great liking*
intimate review 51.5 *show*
intimation 501.2 *information,*
517.3 *plan,* 518.2 *basis of supposition,* 528.7 *advice,* 542.6
suggestion, 759.2 *impression*
in time 210, 210, 49.41 *in tune,*
198.10 *synchronized,* 198.13
synchronously, 208.17 *early,*
209.17 *later*
in times gone by 200.22 *in the past*
intimidate 586.15 *persuade,*
587.2 *deter,* 633.10 *endanger,*
690.5 *be severe,* 695.7 *force,*
701.7 *defeat,* 777.13 *frighten,*
832.18 *torment*
intimidated 777.7 *frightened*
intimidating 701.10 *dominating,*
777.10 *frightening*
intimidation 777, 587.7 *deterrence,* 670.11 *attack,* 676.1 *war,*
695.2 *coercion,* 701.2 *domination,* 832.5 *intolerance,* 832.7
act of malevolence
intimidatory 832.10 *malevolent*
intimisme 50 Western Art Styles
and Movements
intinction 10.6 *Eucharist*
in tip-top condition 623.1 *healthy*
into 346, 642.18 *active*
in token of 543.18 *indicatively*
intolerable 406.5 *painful,* 618.3
bad, 785.9 *disliked*
intolerance 832, 231.1 *counteraction,* 481.3 *prejudice,* 493.3 *injustice,* 500.3 *dissentience,*
577.7 *opinionatedness,* 618.11
harmfulness, 690.1 *severity,*
759.6 *bad feeling,* 820.1 *enmity,*
836.1 *pitilessness*
intolerant 820, 231.4 *counteracting,* 481.10 *discriminatory,*
493.8 *unjust,* 500.7 *dissenting,*
618.5 *harmful,* 690.8 *severe,*
832.10 *malevolent*
intolerantly 231.5 *counter,*
481.17 *prejudicially,* 493.14 *unjustly,* 690.11 *severely,* 820.14
hostilely, 832.20 *malevolently*
intonation 564.3 *mode of speech*
intone 49.39 *sing*

in torment 8.20 *devilishly*
into sight 437.11 *visibly*, 457.15 *apparently*
into the bargain 130.10 *additionally*
into the black 744
into the red 744.15 *into the black*
in touch 6.19 *knowledgeable*, 35.6 *rugger*, 528.18 *informed*
into view 437.11 *visibly*
in tow 180.21 *together*
intoxicant 631, 630.8 *drug*, 874.6 *intoxicating*
intoxicate 239.3 *invigorate*, 631.15 *poison*, 762.8 *cause joy*
intoxicated 762.4 *happy*, 874.1 *drunk*
intoxicated person 874.17 *drunkard*
intoxicating 874, 237.12 *strong to the senses*
intoxicating liquor 874.12 *alcohol*
intoxication 628.8 *perversion*, 628.10 *impairment*, 762.1 *happiness*, 874.10 *drunkenness*
intractability 373.8 *mental hardness*, 577.5, 669.2 *obstinacy*, 693.1 *disobedience*, 836.2 *inflexibility*
intractable 231.4 *counteracting*, 373.4 *mentally hard*, 577.2 *refractory*, 659.14 *troublesome*, 669.11 *obstinate*, 693.13 *disobedient*, 836.5 *inflexible*
intractably 231.5 *counter*, 373.13 *inflexibly*, 669.14 *resistingly*, 693.17 *disobediently*
intractile 373.4 *mentally hard*
intracutaneous injection 62.12 *injection*
in trade 737
intradermal injection 62.12 *injection*
intrados 43.9 *miscellaneous architectural features*
in training 656.2 *unskilled*
intramural 6.21 *curricular*, 301.7 *enclosed*
intramurally 301.8 *confinedly*
intramuscular injection 62.12 *injection*
intransigence 373.8 *mental hardness*, 570.3 *wilfulness*, 577.6 *determination*
intransigent 373.4 *mentally hard*, 570.8 *wilful*, 577.3 *strongwilled*, 663.9 *opposer*
intransigently 373.13 *inflexibly*, 577.9 *be obstinate*
in transit 326, 70.6 *commercially*, 220.18 *convertibly*, 252.20 *out of place*, 324.18 *in motion*, 336.20 *in progress*, 356.14 *by the way*
in transition 220.18 *convertibly*
intransitive 5.44 *grammatical*
intransitively 5.52 *grammatically*
intransitive verb 5.35 *part of speech*
in transit to 327.17 *via*
intransmutable 225.9 *stable*
intrauterine 290.10 *visceral*
intravenous 290.7 *interior*
intravenous injection 62.12 *injection*, 630.13 *therapy*
intravenous pyelogram 60.7 *diagnosis*
intrepid 778.12 *self-reliant*
intrepidity 778.3 *steadfastness*
intrepidly 778.18 *courageously*
intricacy 314.1 *convolution*, 314.2 *coil*, 529.3 *mystification*, 659.1 *difficulty*
intricate 135.12 *united*, 314.4 *convolutional*, 529.11 *mysterious*, 659.12 *problematic*
intricately 135.16 *as one*, 314.8 *circularly*, 659.27 *problematically*
intricateness 314.1 *convolution*
intrigant 592.8 *planner*
intrigue 228.9 *motivate*, 413.13 *be piquant*, 527.8 *concealment*, 529.2 *secretiveness*, 592.4, 592.13 *plot*, 642.9 *overactivity*, 657.1 *cunning*, 657.5 *be cun-*

-ning, 693.3 *subversion*, 821.8 *love affair*, 877.4 *illicit love*
intriguer 539.20 *plotter*, 592.8 *planner*, 642.11 *meddler*, 657.3 *cunning person*
intriguing 413.10 *stimulating*, 592.15 *planning*, 642.21 *meddling*, 657.4 *cunning*, 821.22 *lovable*
intriguingly 413.16 *stimulatingly*, 592.17 *conspiratorially*
in trim 623.1 *healthy*
intrinsic 99, 103, 290, 134.16 *simple*, 146.8 *included*, 148.8 *belonging*, 165.15 *special*, 226.13 *causal*, 537.17 *truistic*
intrinsicality 290.5 *inner nature*
intrinsically 103.13 *in essence*, 134.20 *homogenously*, 146.9 *inclusively*, 226.14 *causally*, 290.16 *inwardly*
intrinsic truth 537.4 *truism*
in triplicate 110.18 *identically*, 177.12 *thrice*, 245.17 *repeatedly*
in triumph 682.16 *successfully*
introception 348.1 *admittance*
introceptive 348.14 *admissive*
introduce 348, 130.6 *add*, 154.19 *forecast*, 194.9 *do before*, 303.10 *be in front*, 346.14 *enrol*, 348.8 *show in*, 354.1 *insert*, 354.2 *inject*, 594.1 *prepare*, 653.2 *direct*, 817.10 *be courteous*, 819.15 *be hospitable*
introduce a red herring 539.32 *disguise*
introduced 83.15 *wild*, 354.12 *inserted*
introduce oneself 815.13 *fraternize*
introduction 156, 348, 51.6 *scene*, 154.5 *preface*, 194.7 *foretaste*, 303.1 *front*, 346.1 *entry*, 354.8 *insertion*, 457.1 *appearance*, 817.3 *courtesies*
introductive 348.16 *introductory*
introductorily 594.23 *preparatorily*
introductory 156, 348, 154.13 *precursory*, 322.17 *beginning*, 594.16 *preparatory*
introit 10.6 *Eucharist*, 49.5 *sacred music*
introject 354.1 *insert*
introjected 354.12 *inserted*
introjection 354.8 *insertion*
intromission 348.1 *admittance*, 354.8 *insertion*
intromissive 348.14 *admissive*
intromit 348.7 *admit*, 354.1 *insert*
intromittent 348.14 *admissive*
intromittent organ 245.8 *organs of reproduction*
intron 59.13 *genetic material*
introspect 4.20, 461.17 *philosophize*, 477.17 *question*
introspection 4.4 *philosophical investigation*, 461.3 *thoughtfulness*, 512.1 *oblivion*
introspection psychology 61.1 *psychology*
introspective 4.17 *thoughtful*, 461.10 *speculative*, 477.12 *questioning*, 512.8 *oblivious*
introspectively 4.28, 461.18 *thoughtfully*, 477.23 *questioningly*
in trouble 659.16 *troubled*, 687.6 *adverse*
introversion 61.7 *personality type*, 287.1 *inversion*, 290.6 *internalization*, 661.5 *inhibition*, 699.3 *self-restraint*, 816.2 *shyness*
introversive 61.34 *introverted*, 661.15 *inhibitive*, 699.14 *self-restrained*
introvert 61.7 *personality type*, 61.34 *introverted*, 287.3 *invert*, 290.6 *internalization*, 542.11 *modest person*, 661.7 *hinderer*
introverted 61, 290.12 *internalized*, 816.9 *shy*
introvertedness 61.7 *personality type*
intrude 149, 104.16 *be external*, 153.10 *disrupt*, 211.5 *take un-*

-timely action, 357.5 *transgress*, 642.17 *meddle*, 666.7 *pick a fight*
intruder 104, 149, 346, 147.5 *excluded person*, 661.7 *hinderer*, 666.4 *dissenter*
intruding 117.11 *unfit*
intrusion 54.29 *petrogenesis*, 104.4 *externality*, 117.5 *unfitness*, 153.4 *disruption*, 211.1 *untimeliness*, 346.3 *inroad*, 357.8 *transgression*
intrusive 54.56 *petrographic*, 104.12 *external*, 117.11 *unfit*, 211.10 *untimely*, 346.16 *invasive*, 357.11 *overrun*, 642.21 *meddling*, 661.13 *hindering*
intrusively 104.18 *extraneously*, 117.17 *unsuitably*, 153.18 *disturbingly*, 211.15 *at the wrong time*, 346.17 *in*, 357.16 *excessively*, 661.16 *with delay*
intrusiveness 117.5 *unfitness*, 642.9 *overactivity*
intrusive person 654.4 *adviser*
in truth 101.14 *certainly*, 480.12 *assuredly*, 537.35 *truly*, 857.7 *honourably*
intubation 62.12 *injection*
intuit 11.23 *divine*, 459.12 *think*, 464.9 *be intuitive*, 471.14 *have an idea*, 507.7 *be wise*, 518.5 *suppose*, 759.16 *feel in one's bones*
intuition 464, 4.4 *philosophical investigation*, 11.8 *psychic power*, 459.2 *ways of thinking*, 461.6 *idea*, 462.3 *instinct*, 471.2 *theory*, 497.1 *belief*, 501.1 *knowledge*, 507.1 *wisdom*, 518.2 *basis of supposition*, 518.3 *conjecture*, 583.5 *spontaneity*, 759.2 *impression*
Intuition 464
intuitionism 4.7 *school of thought*
intuitive 464, 759, 459.9 *mental*, 462.9 *instinctive*, 516.6 *foreseeing*, 518.7 *suppositional*, 571.13 *involuntary*, 583.2 *spontaneous*
intuitively 464, 459.14 *mentally*, 461.18 *thoughtfully*
intuitiveness 464.1 *intuition*
intuitive person 464
intuitive reasoning 464.1 *intuition*
intumesce 128.4 *increase*
intumescence 128.2 *spread*, 261.1 *growth*
in tune 49, 49.30 *harmonic*, 116.13, 433.7 *harmonious*, 433.12 *harmoniously*, 667.10 *agreeing*
in turmoil 113.11 *irregularly*
in turn 150.25 *in order*, 155.27 *in sequence*, 159.18 *consecutively*, 165.32 *severally*
in-turn 41.16 *bobsled*
in twain 136.20 *separately*, 176.22 *in half*
in two 136.20 *separately*, 176.22 *in half*, 320.11 *doubly*
in twos 176.9 *two*, 176.20 *two by two*
in twos and threes 182.10 *in ones and twos*
in two shakes of a lamb's tail 191.8 *immediately*
Inuktitut 5 Languages and Groups of Languages
inulin 58.4 *polysaccharide*
inunction 386.3 *anointment*, 386.5 *ointment*, 395.4 *anointment*
inunctum 386.5 *ointment*, 395.4 *anointment*
inundant 96.10 *fluvial*
inundate 96.7 *flow*, 293.31 *hide*, 347.11 *run out*, 389.29 *water*, 610.4 *be excessive*
inundated 96.11 *flooded*, 357.11 *overrun*, 389.24 *flooded*
inundation 96.6 *river flow*, 244.7 *agent of destruction*, 347.2 *outflow*, 357.6 *overstepping*, 389.9 *soaking*, 610.1 *excess*
inundatorily 96.13 *fluently*

in unfinished form 375.15 *incompletely*
in union 135.16 *as one*
in unison 116.33 *harmoniously*, 138.11 *cohesively*, 180.21 *together*, 198.13 *synchronously*, 433.7 *harmonious*, 433.12 *harmoniously*, 667.10 *agreeing*
inurbane 818.5 *discourteous*
inurbanity 818.1 *discourtesy*
inure 203.7 *season*, 584.18 *habituate*, 594.7 *develop*
inured 203.15 *seasoned*, 404.7 *anaesthetized*, 584.14 *habituated*
inurement 584.7 *habituation*, 594.13 *development*
in use 230.10 *operational*, 599.9 *used*
inutile 614.1 *useless*
inutility 236.1 *powerlessness*, 610.3 *superfluity*, 612.7 *triviality*, 614.3 *uselessness*
invade 346, 82.16 *infest*, 104.16 *be external*, 149.17 *intrude*, 357.5 *transgress*, 628.5 *hurt*, 670.9 *attack successfully*, 676.13 *be at war*, 679.38 *conquer*, 846.18 *arrogate*
invader 147.5 *excluded person*, 149.10 *intruder*, 255.6 *illegal occupant*, 346.8 *intruder*, 670.19 *attacker*, 820.5 *hostile person*, 846.7 *usurper*
invading 104.12 *external*, 670.23 *attacking*
invaginate 287.3 *invert*
invagination 287.1 *inversion*
in vain 358, 614.2 *futile*, 614.10 *uselessly*, 683.12 *unsuccessfully*
invalid 52.86 *logical*, 60.18 *patient*, 236.5 *powerless person*, 236.10 *powerless*, 238.4 *weakling*, 238.13 *insufficient*, 474.7 *sophistic*, 521.10 *meaningless*, 598.5 *relinquished*, 614.1 *useless*, 624.19 *sick person*, 624.21 *unhealthy*, 626.4 *infectious person*, 704.10 *cancelled*, 844.12 *incorrect*, 846.8 *unentitled*
invalid argument 52.64 *reasoning*
invalidate 52.89 *theorize*, 100.14 *cause not to exist*, 231.3 *counteract*, 236.7 *remove power from*, 238.7 *weaken*, 244.8 *destroy*, 476.8 *refute*, 484.7 *counter*, 536.7 *be negative*, 536.9 *renounce*, 598.2 *withdraw*, 704.6 *cancel*
invalidated 236.10 *powerless*, 484.6 *countered*, 536.12 *rejected*, 704.10 *cancelled*
invalidating 231.4 *counteracting*, 476.7 *refuting*
invalidation 231.1 *counteraction*, 236.1 *powerlessness*, 476.1 *refutation*, 484.1 *counterevidence*, 536.2 *rejection*, 536.4 *renunciation*, 704.1 *cancellation*
invalided 624.22 *sick*
invalidism 624.1 *ill health*
invalidity 52.64 *reasoning*, 236.4 *disability*, 474.1 *sophistry*, 521.1 *lack of meaning*, 844.2 *incorrectness*
invalidly 704, 536.15 *negatively*, 598.7 *on hold*
invaluable 613.4 *profitable*, 617.3, 753.8 *valuable*
invaluableness 753.6 *value*
invaluably 753.13 *valuably*
invar 57 Alloys
invariability 110.6 *regularity*, 112.4 *monotony*, 183.3 *repetitiveness*, 225.1 *stability*
invariable 52.77 *given*, 110.17 *regular*, 112.8 *monotonous*, 116.14 *conforming*, 183.13 *monotonous*, 217.7 *permanent*, 225.4 *stable thing*, 225.9 *stable*, 584.9 *habitual*, 788.4 *boring*
invariable quantity 225.4 *stable thing*
invariably 110.20 *regularly*, 112.13 *uniformly*, 116.35 *consistently*, 164.30 *usually*, 164.32 *universally*, 217.9 *permanently*, 584.19 *habitually*,

788.8 *boringly*

invariant 52.25 *algebraic expression*, 110.6 *regularity*, 110.17 *regular*

invasion 104.4 *externality*, 346.3 *inroad*, 357.8 *transgression*, 670.14 *siege*, 676.8 *warfare*, 846.3 *arrogation*

invasive 346, 104.12 *external*, 357.11 *overrun*

invasively 346.17 *in*, 357.16 *excessively*

invective 564.8 *speech*, 567.1 *address*, 827.1 *curse*, 827.8 *cursing*

inveigh against 670.10 *criticize*, 827.6 *vilify*

inveigle 228.10 *manipulate*, 586.16 *tempt*, 635.3 *trap*, 853.10 *cajole*

inveiglement 853.3 *cajolery*

inveigler 853.6 *flatterer*

inveigling 853.14 *cajoling*

invent 156, 479, 496, 592, 99.20 *bring into being*, 102.17 *fabricate*, 119.7 *originate*, 154.18 *forerun*, 201.18 *be trendy*, 216.8 *cause change*, 226.9 *be the cause of*, 243.10 *produce*, 382.14 *structure*, 461.16 *have an idea*, 471.15, 519.14 *imagine*, 526.3 *reveal*, 538.22 *make unreal*, 540.22 *falsify*, 583.3 *improvise*

invented 243.12 *produced*, 519.12 *imaginary*, 538.14 *unreal*, 540.32 *falsified*

invention 156, 496, 50.5 *artistry*, 119.2 *original*, 201.1 *newness*, 216.1 *change*, 226.1 *cause*, 243.1 *production*, 471.3 *plan*, 519.1 *imagination*, 538.2 *unrealness*, 540.9 *falsification*, 583.4 *improvisation*, 592.3 *expedient plan*

inventive 156, 119.4 *original*, 201.10 *new*, 216.11 *changeable*, 226.13 *causal*, 243.11 *productive*, 246.5 *fertile*, 461.10 *speculative*, 471.11 *ideational*, 479.9 *original*, 496.13 *discovering*, 519.10 *imaginative*, 583.1 *improvised*, 657.4 *cunning*

inventively 479, 119.8 *originally*, 201.21 *newly*, 216.15 *changeably*, 226.14 *causally*, 243.13 *productively*, 246.8 *fruitfully*, 461.18 *thoughtfully*, 471.22 *imaginatively*, 496.16 *originally*, 519.17 *imaginatively*

inventiveness 119.1 *originality*, 246.2 *productiveness*, 461.5 *creative thought*, 471.8 *imagination*, 479.4 *originality*, 519.1 *imagination*, 657.1 *cunning*

inventive power 461.5 *creative thought*

inventor 119.3 *originator*, 154.8 *precursor*, 156.16 *originator*, 226.7 *Prime Mover*, 243.9 *producer*, 471.9 *person of ideas*, 479.5 *experimenter*, 496.12 *discoverer*, 583.6 *improviser*, 592.8 *planner*

inventorial 171, 750.10 *accounting*

inventorially 171

inventoried 171.11 *listed*

inventorize 560.16 *define*

inventory 142.5 *unit*, 152.7 *catalogue*, 152.15 *categorize*, 170.3 *count*, 170.11 *number*, 171.1, 171.8 *list*, 257.5 *divisions*, 545.1 *record*, 605.5 *collection*, 750.8 *audit*

inveracious 540.25 *false*

inveracity 540.1 *falsehood*

Inverness 93 *Cities*, 93.4 *British cities*

inverse 52.18 *division*, 52.21 *set*, 52.22 *matrix*, 52.74 *divisible*, 111.1 *oppositeness*, 111.4 *opposite*

inverse cosine 52.52 *trigonometric function*

inverse function 52.29 *mathematical function*

inversely 287, 111.6 *oppositely*

inversely proportional to 52.88 *equal to*

inverse proportion 107.2 *interrelatedness*

inverse ratio 107.2 *interrelatedness*

inverse sine 52.52 *trigonometric function*

inverse tangent 52.52 *trigonometric function*

inverse trigonometric function 52.52 *trigonometric function*

inversion 287, 48.12 *poetic language*, 57.13 *structure*, 111.1 *oppositeness*, 170.1 *calculation*, 216.1 *change*, 308.2 *symmetry operation*, 337.12 *reversal*

Inversion 287

invert 287, 43.9 *miscellaneous architectural features*, 57.26 *react*, 111.8 *be opposite*, 216.8 *cause change*, 244.9 *demolish*

invertebrate 81, 81, 76.4 *type of animal*, 76.15 *of animals*

invertebrate chordate 81.1 *invertebrate*

invertebrate larva 81

Invertebrates 81

invertebrate zoologist 81, 76.11 *zoologist*

invertebrate zoology 81, 76.9 *animal science*

inverted 287, 30.11 *gymnastic*, 111.4 *opposite*

inverted comma 543.7 *punctuation*

inverted grip 30.5 *horizontal bar*

inverted hang 30.7 *stationary rings*

invertedly 221.13 *reversibly*

inverted order 287.1 *inversion*

inverted snobbery 805.3 *conceit*

inverter 64.34 *power supply*

invert sugar 57.13 *structure*

invest 14, 741, 7.21 *ordain*, 156.25 *enrol*, 295.32 *dress*, 348.10 *introduce*, 354.7 *install*, 485.13 *qualify*, 605.6 *store*, 670.4 *besiege*, 676.13 *be at war*, 703.6 *commission*, 737.2 *speculate*, 748.1 *expend*

invested 295.29 *dressed*, 605.7 *stored*, 748.12 *expended*

investigate 4.20 *philosophize*, 477.17 *question*, 479.11 *experiment*, 492.12 *estimate*

investigated 477.16 *questioned*

investigation 4.4 *philosophical investigation*, 477.2 *questioning*, 479.1 *experiment*, 479.3 *experimentation*, 568.6 *interview*

investigation into first causes 4.4 *philosophical investigation*

investigative 477.12 *questioning*, 479.8 *experimental*

investigative journalism 530.2 *divulgence*

investigative journalist 530.4 *discloser*, 532.11 *newspaper man*

investigatively 477.23 *questioningly*, 479.14 *experimentally*

investigative reporting 533.3 *reporting*

investigator 4.10 *philosopher*, 465.3 *curious person*, 477.9 *questioner*, 479.5 *experimenter*, 530.4 *discloser*

invest in 14.5 *invest*, 738.1 *purchase*

investing 738.14 *buying*

investiture 7.9 *priesthood*, 116.9 *grant*, 156.8 *enrolment*, 295.2 *dressing*, 348.3 *introduction*, 703.1 *commission*, 729.1 *giving*

investment 14.1 *finance*, 295.2 *dressing*, 485.4 *permission*, 605.1 *store*, 670.14 *siege*, 676.8 *warfare*, 729.1 *giving*, 737.8 *speculation*, 748.5 *expense*

investment account 742.5 *wealth*

investment capital 602.4 *financial resources*

investment portfolio 602.4 *financial resources*

investments 602.4 *financial resources*, 742.5 *wealth*

investor 14.3 *stockbroker*, 725.7

property man , 738.12 *purchaser*, 744.6 *depositor*, 748.8 *spender*

invest with 116.30 *grant*, 729.5 *give*

invest with power 235.11 *give power*

inveteracy 584.1 *habit*

inveterate 202.12 *olden*, 584.14 *habituated*, 868.3 *impenitent*

inveterately 202.21 *archaically*

inveterate sinner 868.2 *impenitent person*

invidious 764.1 *unpleasant*, 822.12 *hated*, 841.4 *jealous*

invidiously 841.9 *jealously*

in view 253.10 *available*, 435.23, 437.1 *visible*, 437.11 *visibly*

invigilate 435.15 *watch*, 469.11 *care for*, 653.1 *manage*

invigilation 469.5 *watchfulness*

invigilator 435.11 *observer*

invigorate 239, 396, 128.5 *make bigger*, 237.8 *strengthen*, 403.13 *arouse sensation*, 629.5 *revive*, 651.1 *refresh*

invigorated 651.4 *refreshed*

invigorating 239, 55.45 *fine*, 62.17 *stimulating*, 237.4 *strengthening*, 409.8 *cold*, 623.2 *healthful*, 651.3 *refreshing*

invigoratingly 651.5 *refreshingly*

invigoration 128.1 *increase*, 237.4 *strengthening*, 239.1 *vigour*, 651.5 *refreshment*

invincibility 237.1 *strength*

invincible 126.14 *best*, 669.12 *resisting*, 682.15 *victorious*

invincible ignorance 436.7 *figurative blindness*

invincibly 126.17 *supremely*, 669.14 *resistingly*, 682.16 *successfully*

in vindication 855

inviolability 237.1 *strength*

inviolable 217.7 *permanent*, 845.8 *entitled*

inviolable place 634.1 *refuge*

inviolably 217.9 *permanently*

inviolate 142.7 *uncut*

in virtue of one's authority 12.14 *politically*, 688.23 *authoritatively*

invisibility 438, 260.1 *littleness*, 458.4 *disappearance*, 523.11 *unintelligibility*, 527.8, 531.1 *concealment*

Invisibility 438

invisible 438, 238.13 *insufficient*, 260.7 *little*, 436.13 *hidden*, 458.7 *disappeared*, 523.1 *unintelligible*, 527.2 *concealed*

invisible earnings 737.5 *commercial trade*

invisible goods 737.5 *commercial trade*

invisible imports 438.5 *invisible thing*

invisible ink 438.5 *invisible thing*

invisible man 528.9 *anonymity*

invisible mending 629.8 *repair*

invisibles 737.5 *commercial trade*

invisible thing 438

invisible trade 13.5 *international trade*, 737.5 *commercial trade*

invisible writing 527.8 *concealment*

invisibly 438, 260.9 *microscopically*, 458.8 *fleetingly*, 529.16 *stealthily*

invitation 228.2 *inducement*, 348.1 *admittance*, 543.6 *word*, 586.2 *flattery*, 692.1 *command*, 710.1 *offer*, 712.1 *request*, 817.3 *courtesies*

invitational 712.9 *requesting*

invitatory 348.15 *receptive*

invite 348.9 *welcome*, 665.16 *host*, 692.9 *command*, 712.6 *request*, 815.11 *be sociable*, 817.10 *be courteous*

invite difficulties 659.19 *have difficulty*

invite offers 710.9 *offer*

invite over 350.25 *provide food*

inviter 543.8 *signer*

inviting 228.11 *motivational*, 344.21 *welcoming*, 348.15 *receptive*, 405.6 *pleasant*, 411.7 *tasty*, 543.16 *signalling*, 586.19 *persuasive*, 710.17 *offered*, 712.9 *requesting*, 763.1 *pleasant*, 782.8 *desirable*, 815.15 *sociable*

invitingly 228.14 *influentially*, 348.18 *receptively*, 586.21 *persuasively*

invocation 10.9 *prayer*, 11.5 *spell*, 567.2 *salutation*, 712.1 *request*

invocational 10.21 *ritualistic*, 11.15 *witchlike*, 712.9 *requesting*

invocatory 567.14 *vocative*

in vogue 295.36 *dressily*, 584.12 *established*

invoice 171.4 *bill*, 171.8 *list*, 544.3 *means of identification*, 545.1 *record*, 712.7 *demand*, 750.4 *statement*, 750.9 *settle accounts*, 751.4 *bill*

invoiced 750.11 *accounted*

invoke 10.20 *pray*, 11.22 *conjure*, 564.14 *speak to*, 567.8 *appeal to*, 712.6 *request*

invoke a blessing 10.20 *pray*

invoke the Official Secrets Act 709.4 *censor*

involucre 83.6 *leaf*, 84.3 *flower part*, 293.4 *wrapping*

involuntarily 583.7 *extempore*, 695.11 *compellingly*, 701.11 *under subjection*

involuntariness 571, 583.5 *spontaneity*

involuntary 571, 462.9 *instinctive*, 521.12 *unmeant*, 583.2 *spontaneous*, 695.9 *compelling*, 701.9 *subject*

involuntary saving 751.8 *levy*

involuntary servitude 701.1 *subjection*

involute 52.40 *curve*

involution 170.1 *calculation*, 314.1 *convolution*

involutional 314.4 *convolutional*

involutional melancholia 61.13 *depression*, 510.6 *mental breakdown*

involve 137.13 *intercommunicate*, 146.4 *include*, 148.11 *consist of*, 520.12 *intend*, 527.14 *imply*, 571.14, 593.10 *necessitate*

involved 107.4 *related*, 133.12 *mixed*, 135.12 *united*, 314.5 *ambiguous*, 551.2 *obscure*, 592.15 *planning*, 642.18 *active*, 659.12 *problematic*, 724.5 *jointly possessing*

involved in 133.12 *mixed*

involved style 551.1 *obscurity*

involved with 759.12 *sensitive*

involvement 107.1 *relatedness*, 133.1 *mixture*, 135.1 *union*, 137.1 *connection*, 146.1 *inclusion*, 724.2 *participation*, 759.5 *good feeling*

involve oneself 724.4 *have joint possession*

involving effort 644.11 *laborious*

invulnerability 237.1 *strength*, 632.1 *safety*, 718.1 *protection*

invulnerable 632, 225.9 *stable*, 625.4 *hygienic*, 671.31 *entrenched*, 718.6 *secure*

invulnerably 225.12 *stably*, 237.14 *strongly*, 632.10 *safely*, 718.16 *surely*

in want 593.5 *necessitous*, 593.12 *in need*, 743.1 *poor*

inward 39.11 *swimming*, 290.7 *interior*, 290.8 *internal*, 290.12 *private*

inwardly 290, 346.17 *in*, 438.9 *invisibly*, 158.8 *fleetingly*

inwardness 290.1 *interior*, 290.6 *internalization*

inwards 438.9 *invisibly*

in water colours 50.30 *pictorially*

in waves 155.27 *in sequence*
inweave 288.8 *interweave*
in what position? 477.25 *what?*
in what way? 477.25 *what?*
in white tie and tails 295.30, 813.7 *dressed up*
in-wick 41.10 *curling,* 41.13 *ice-skating*
in winter 203.18 *seasonally*
in with 819.9 *friends with*
in with a chance 674.14 *contending*
in wonder 786.13 *wonderfully*
in wonderment 786.6 *wondering*
in words of one syllable 522.13 *intelligibly,* 552.5 *concisely,* 556.8 *simply*
in words to that effect 524.18 *in other words*
in working order 101.8 *practical,* 230.10 *operational,* 594.19 *in hand*
Io 8 Deities
I object 476.13 *no*
I/O device 65.7 *peripheral*
iodic 57.34 *elemental*
iodide 57 Types of Compounds
iodine 57 Chemical Elements, 58.15 *essential element,* 630.3 *prophylactic*
iodochlorhydroxyquin 62 Medication
iodoform 62 Medication
iodometric 268.16 *micrometric*
iodometry 268.2 *micrometry*
iodous 57.34 *elemental*
io moth 82 Insects
Iomud 32 Breeds of Horse and Pony
ion 56, 56.50 *electric charge,* 64.5 *electrolytic conduction,* 260.2 *little thing,* 367.4 *matter*
Ionesco 48 Dramatists
ion-exchange chromatography 57.17 *analysis*
ion gauge 57.20 *surface chemistry*
Ionian 97 Oceans and Seas
Ionian mode 49.20 *key*
ionic 48.9 *metre,* 57.35 *combined*
Ionic 43 Architectural Styles
ionically 57.46 *chemically*
ionic bond 57.11 *chemical bond*
ionic compound 57.7 *chemical compound*
Ionic order 43.8 *column*
ionization 56.66 *ion,* 57.14 *chemical reaction*
ionization chamber 56.93 *radiation detector*
ionization energy 56.66 *ion*
ionization potential 56.66 *ion*
ionize 57.26 *react*
ionizing radiation 56.70 *radioactivity*
ionographic printer 65.7 *peripheral*
ionosphere 55.8 *atmosphere,* 390.3 *atmospheric layers,* 534.15 *transmitted wave*
ionospheric 55.43 *atmospheric*
ionospheric disturbance 534.15 *transmitted wave*
ionospheric reflection 534.15 *transmitted wave*
ionospheric storm 534.15 *transmitted wave*
ionospheric wave 534.15 *transmitted wave*
ion pump 57.20 *surface chemistry*
iota 173.3 *fragment,* 260.3 *little piece,* 542.6 *suggestion,* 612.8 *trifle*
IOU 667.2 *contract,* 714.2 *guarantee,* 715.2 *purchase contract,* 718.2 *promise,* 733.5 *loan,* 741.14 *paper money*
Iowa 1 Peoples, 92 American States
ipecacuanha 62 Medication, 630.6 *purgative*
iprindole 62 Medication
iproniazid 62 Medication
ipso facto 99.22 *really*
Ipswich 93 Cities
IPTS 75.3 *scale*
IQ 459.3 *intelligence*

Iqbal 4 Philosophers, 48 Poets
IQ meter 61.4 *psychometrics*
IQ test 61.6 *intelligence test*
Ira 828.7 *gods and goddesses of anger*
IRA 679.14 *armed forces*
IRA member 679.9 *guerrilla,* 693.10, 713.5 *seditionist*
Iran 91 Countries
Irangate 531.5 *evasion*
Iranian 5 Languages and Groups of Languages
Iran-Iraq War 17 Major Wars
Iraq 91 Countries
Iraqi Republican Guards 679.14 *armed forces*
irascibility 829, 270.6 *abruptness,* 385.9 *irritation,* 579.2 *caprice,* 666.1 *disagreement,* 760.6 *oversensitivity,* 830.3 *irritableness*
Irascibility 829
irascible 829, 270.9 *abrupt,* 473.8 *argumentative,* 500.7 *dissenting,* 577.2 *refractory,* 579.1 *capricious,* 666.9 *disagreeing,* 674.15 *contentious,* 760.2 *oversensitive,* 818.6 *bad-mannered,* 830.7 *irritable*
irascible person 829
irascibly 829, 666.11 *in disagreement,* 674.17 *contentiously,* 818.10 *rudely,* 830.14 *irritably*
irate 822.13, 828.16 *angry*
irately 828.18 *angrily*
ire 822.5, 828.4 *anger*
ireful 828.16 *angry*
Ireland 49 Musicians and Composers, 91 Countries, 98 Islands, 91
Irene and Vernon Castle 46.6 *famous dancers*
irenic 675.7 *peaceful,* 677.6 *pacificatory*
irenical 677.6 *pacificatory*
irenically 677.7 *pacifically*
irenicon 677.2 *peace offering*
irenics 675.1 *peace,* 677.1 *pacification*
irenic theology 675.1 *peace*
I repent 867.9 *sorry*
iridectomy 60 Surgical Operations
iridesce 439.25 *light up*
iridescence 56.28 *colour,* 224.1 *changeableness,* 439.2 *quality of light,* 456.1 *variegation*
iridescent 456, 224.13 *changeable,* 439.17 *lustrous*
iridescent cloud 55.20 *cloud appearance*
iridescently 224.15 *changeably,* 456.12 *variedly*
iridic 57.34 *elemental*
iridium 57 Chemical Elements
iridotomy 60 Surgical Operations
iridous 57.34 *elemental*
irimi nage 26.10 *aikido*
iris 84 Flowers and Flowering Plants, 51.18 *stage lighting,* 435.2 *eye,* 454.6 *blue thing*
Iris 8 Deities, 8 Deities, 53 Minor Planets, 326.8 *messenger,* 329.13 *swift person*
iris diaphragm 51.18 *stage lighting,* 66.18 *exposure time*
Irish 5 Languages and Groups of Languages, 97 Oceans and Seas
Irish accent 5.26 *dialect*
Irish bull 504.11 *grammatical error*
Irish dancing 46.1 *dancing*
Irish Draught 32 Breeds of Horse and Pony
Irish elk 77 Placental Mammals
Irish Gaelic 5 Languages and Groups of Languages
Irish government 12.4 *governing body*
Irish Guard 679.12 *ceremonial troops*
Irish hockey 31.7 *hurling*
Irish Hunter 32 Breeds of Horse and Pony
Irishism 5.26 *dialect,* 91.10 *Ire-*

land
Irish jig 46.4 *historic dancing*
Irishman 91.10 *Ireland*
Irish Moiled 68 Breeds of Cattle
Irish moss 88.3 *moss*
Irishness 91.10 *Ireland*
Irish setter 77 Breeds of Dogs, 37.6 *sporting dog*
Irish shamrock 544.6 *national emblem*
Irish stew 45.44 *British dish,* 133.2 *mixed thing*
Irish terrier 77 Breeds of Dogs
Irish wake 397.8 *after death,* 399.2 *funeral*
Irish water spaniel 37.6 *sporting dog*
Irish whiskey 351.7 *alcoholic drink*
Irish wolfhound 77 Breeds of Dogs
irk 153.7 *disturb,* 616.5 *be inconvenient,* 650.6 *fatigue,* 659.22 *cause trouble,* 788.6 *be boring*
irksome 616.1 *inconvenient,* 650.4 *fatiguing,* 659.13 *inconvenient,* 764.1 *unpleasant,* 788.4 *boring*
irksomeness 788.1 *boredom*
Irkutsk 93 Cities
iroko 85 Trees and Shrubs
iron 57 Chemical Elements, 29.4 *golf club,* 56.59 *ferromagnetism,* 58.15 *essential element,* 282.4 *flattener,* 282.7 *make horizontal,* 350.11 *food content,* 373.1 *hard,* 373.7 *hard substance,* 376.9 *smoother,* 376.11 *smooth,* 385.16 *massage,* 408.3 *heater,* 448.5 *grey thing,* 574.3 *strong-willed,* 574.16 *fortitude,* 621.13 *clean,* 630.7 *tonic*
Iron Age 3.10 *past age,* 200.4 *prehistoric age*
Iron-Age 202.15 *primal*
Iron-Age man 202.7 *ancient people*
iron boot 879.15 *instrument of torture*
ironbound 375.2 *coarse*
ironbound coast 98.4 *coast,* 635.1 *trap*
ironclad 679.25 *historical naval ships*
iron-clad 671.30 *defended*
iron club 29.4 *golf club*
iron constitution 623.3 *health*
Iron Cross 544.4 *insignia*
Iron Curtain 136.6 *boundary,* 147.3 *exclusion zone,* 298.1 *interface,* 661.3 *barrier*
Iron Curtain country 91.1 *country*
ironed 282.9 *flattened,* 376.2 *uniform,* 621.17 *cleaned*
iron-grey 448.1 *grey*
iron grip 726.1 *retention*
iron hand 652.8 *treatment,* 690.2 *suppression*
iron hand in a velvet glove 527.7 *latent things,* 652.8 *treatment*
iron horse 72.4 *locomotive*
iron-horse 71.12 *bicycle*
ironic 176.11 *double-edged,* 771.10 *humorous,* 797.3 *affected,* 850.14 *ridiculing*
ironical 797.3 *affected*
ironically 538.28 *dishonestly,* 771.16 *humorously*
ironist 771.6 *humorist,* 797.2 *pretender*
iron lung 630.14 *hospital,* 637.2 *preserver*
Iron Maiden 879.15 *instrument of torture*
iron meteorite 53.20 *meteor*
ironmonger 739.13 *retailer*
ironmongery 243.7 *produce*
iron nerve 225.2 *determination*
iron-nerved 225.11 *determined*
iron out 152.19 *tidy,* 312.10 *straighten,* 376.11, 383.13 *smooth,* 385.16 *massage,* 660.16 *make easy*
iron out problems 654.6 *consult*
iron rations 350.7 *food,* 606.1 *provision,* 609.8 *insufficiency,* 871.2 *short rations*

iron rule 690.2 *suppression*
irons 699.5 *means of restraint,* 879.14 *instrument of punishment*
iron shot 29.3 *golf shots*
iron sickle 603.3 *prehistoric tool*
Ironsides 32.15 *horse person,* 679.20 *cavalryman*
ironstone 57 Common Metal Ores, 44.1 *ceramics*
iron sway 12.3 *governance*
iron throat 423.4 *sound maker*
ironware 243.7 *produce*
iron will 225.2 *determination,* 570.2 *willpower,* 574.15 *will*
iron-willed 570, 225.11 *determined,* 574.3 *strong-willed*
ironwood 85 Trees and Shrubs
irony 48.12 *poetic language,* 176.3 *duality,* 538.7 *duplicity,* 771.3 *wit,* 797.1 *affectedness,* 850.4 *ridicule*
Iroquoian 5 Languages and Groups of Languages
Iroquois 1 Peoples, 5 Languages and Groups of Languages
irradiate 57.26 *react,* 439.24 *light,* 637.5 *preserve*
irradiation 637.1 *preservation*
irrational 52.6 *complex number,* 52.72 *complex,* 52.74 *divisible,* 169.8 *odd,* 229.6 *motiveless,* 460.5 *lacking intellect,* 460.8 *nonhuman,* 474.7 *sophistic,* 487.1 *impossible*
irrationality 229.1 *lack of motive,* 460.1 *lack of intellect,* 460.4 *nonhuman existence,* 474.1 *sophistry,* 510.1 *insanity*
irrationally 229.8 *by chance,* 460.11 *unintelligently,* 460.12 *nonhumanly,* 474.14 *sophistically,* 487.11 *impossibly*
irrational number 52.6 *complex number,* 169.2 *kind of number*
Irrawaddy 96 Rivers
irreclaimable 722.16 *losing,* 864.11 *wicked,* 868.3 *impenitent*
irreclaimably 722.19 *irrecoverably*
irreconcilability 117.4, 666.1 *disagreement*
irreconcilable 117.10 *disagreeing,* 663.21 *contrary,* 666.9 *disagreeing,* 820.8 *estranged*
irreconcilably 117.16 *disagreeably,* 666.11 *in disagreement*
irrecoverable 200.18 *over,* 487.3 *hopeless,* 722.16 *losing*
irrecoverably 722, 487.12 *hopelessly*
irredeemability 618.9 *badness*
irredeemable 618.3 *bad,* 722.16 *losing,* 747.14 *unpaid,* 776.5 *past hope,* 864.11 *wicked,* 868.3 *impenitent*
irredeemably 722.19 *irrecoverably,* 776.11 *hopelessly,* 864.18 *wickedly*
irreducible 134.16 *simple,* 562.6 *summary*
irreducibly 134.20 *homogenously*
irreflexive relation 52.63 *mathematical logic*
irrefutable 490.3 *decided*
irregardless 327.16 *how*
irregular 151, 168, 215, 5.44 *grammatical,* 16.56 *unauthorized,* 17.9 *enlisted,* 52.79 *spatial,* 57.33 *crystalline,* 84.12 *of flowers,* 117.7 *disparate,* 123.3 *unequal,* 160.8 *discontinuous,* 187.9 *periodic,* 213.2 *infrequent,* 224.13 *changeable,* 309.6 *distorted,* 324.17 *directional,* 375.1 *rough,* 491.7 *unreliable,* 620.1 *imperfect,* 679.8 *soldier,* 814.10 *free,* 844.14 *abnormal*
irregular forces 17.2 *the military*
irregular galaxy 53.7 *galaxy*
irregularity 215, 16.35 *illegality,* 113.1 *diversity,* 117.1 *disparity,* 123.1 *inequality,* 151.2 *irregular order,* 160.1 *discontinuity,* 165.6 *exception,* 213.3 *infrequency,* 224.1 *changeableness,*

309.1 *distortion*, 375.6 *rough-ness*, 491.15 *unreliability*, 620.5 *imperfection*, 814.4 *freedom*, 844.4 *abnormality*
Irregularity 215
irregularly 113, 215, 5.52 *grammatically*, 117.15 *dissimilarly*, 123.7 *unequally*, 151.27 *in disorder*, 160.17 *discontinuously*, 187.14 *for short periods*, 213.1 *infrequently*, 224.15 *changeably*, 309.13 *asymmetrically*, 375.14 *roughly*, 491.26 *unreliably*, 620.11 *imperfectly*
irregular motion 324.5 *circuition*
irregular order 151
irregular polyhedron 52.46 *polyhedron*
irregulars 17.2 *the military*
irregular thing 215
irregular union 877.4 *illicit love*
irrelation 108.1 *unrelatedness*
irrelative 104.8 *intruder*
irrelatively 108.12 *irrelevantly*
irrelevance 104.1 *extraneousness*, 108.1 *unrelatedness*, 117.5 *unfitness*, 521.1 *lack of meaning*, 553.2 *circumlocution*, 612.5 *unimportance*, 783.5 *insignificance*
irrelevancy 104.1 *extraneousness*, 108.1 *unrelatedness*, 117.5 *unfitness*, 612.5 *unimportance*
irrelevant 104.8 *intruder*, 108.6 *unrelated*, 117.11 *unfit*, 521.10 *meaningless*, 553.4 *circumlocutory*, 612.1 *unimportant*, 783.11 *insignificant*
irrelevantly 108, 104.18 *extraneously*, 117.17 *unsuitably*, 521.13 *meaninglessly*, 612.14 *unimportantly*, 783.20 *unexceptionally*
irreligion 498.4 *unbelief*
irreligionist 498.5 *disbeliever*
irreligious 864.14 *impious*
irreligiously 864.20 *immorally*
irremediable 618.4 *poor*, 776.5 *past hope*
irremissible 864.11 *wicked*
irremovable 577.3 *unyielding*, 718.9 *fast*
irreparable 487.3 *hopeless*, 776.5 *past hope*
irreparable loss 722.1 *loss*
irreparably 487.12 *hopelessly*
irreplaceability 611.1 *importance*
irreplaceable 611.5 *important*, 617.3 *valuable*
irreprehensible 865.5 *innocent*
irrepressible 241.6 *violent*, 577.2 *refractory*
irreproachability 619.3 *perfection*, 863.1 *virtue*, 865.1 *innocence*
irreproachable 619.1 *perfect*, 863.5 *virtuous*, 865.5 *innocent*
irreproachably 619.7 *perfectly*, 863.9 *virtuously*, 865.11 *innocently*
irresistibility 695.1 *compulsion*
irresistible 228.11 *motivational*, 233.12 *appealing*, 235.13 *powerful*, 340.9 *attractive*, 586.19 *persuasive*, 695.9 *compelling*
irresistible force 330.11 *impulsion*, 695.1 *compulsion*
irresistible progress 336.15 *improvement*
irresistibly 228.14, 233.14 *influentially*, 235.18 *powerfully*, 340.13 *attractionally*, 586.21 *persuasively*, 695.11 *compellingly*
irresolute 224, 491, 717, 236.12 *impotent*, 238.12 *weak-willed*, 240.5 *inert*, 333.4 *middle*, 706.5 *vacillating*, 578.11 *equivocating*, 708.8 *permitting*
irresolutely 576, 717, 224.15 *changeably*, 236.14 *impotently*, 238.14 *weakly*, 491.23 *uncertainly*, 708.9 *with permission*
irresoluteness 491
irresolution 224, 717, 238.2 *indecisiveness*, 240.1 *inertness*, 365.3 *vacillation*, 491.11 *irresoluteness*, 576.11 *vacillation*,

578.6 *equivocation*
irresponsibility 508.1 *folly*, 576.12 *inconstancy*, 579.2 *caprice*, 689.1 *anarchy*, 780.1 *rashness*
irresponsible 491.8 *capricious*, 576.2 *changeable*, 579.1 *capricious*, 689.6 *anarchic*, 780.4 *rash*
irresponsibly 491.27 *capriciously*, 689.8 *anarchically*, 780.6 *rashly*
irretrievable 722.16 *losing*, 776.5 *past hope*
irretrievable breakdown 244.4 *ruin*
irretrievable loss 722.1 *loss*
irretrievably 722.19 *irrecoverably*
irreverence 787.1 *lack of wonder*, 850.1 *disrespect*
irreverent 787.3 *unmoved*, 850.10 *disrespectful*
irreverential 850.10 *disrespectful*
irreverently 787.9 *without wonder*, 850.28 *disrespectfully*
irreversibility 225.1 *stability*, 336.15 *improvement*, 577.6 *determination*
irreversible 57.38 *reactive*, 225.9 *stable*, 332.15 *direct*, 336.18 *ongoing*, 577.3 *unyielding*, 776.5 *past hope*
irreversible reaction 57.14 *chemical reaction*
irreversibly 225.12 *stably*
irrevocability 490.16 *inevitability*
irrevocable 225.9 *stable*, 487.3 *hopeless*, 776.5 *past hope*
irrevocably 225.12 *stably*, 487.12 *hopelessly*, 490.25 *inevitably*
irrigate 68.17 *farm*, 96.8 *cause to flow*, 246.7 *make fertile*, 389.29 *water*
irrigation 68.5 *cultivation*, 389.7 *hydrotherapeutics*, 389.8 *watering*
irrigational 389.26 *wetting*
irrigation system 63.24 *water system*
irrigator 389, 68.10 *farm tool*
irriguous 389.26 *wetting*
irritability 403.2 *ability to sense*, 760.6 *oversensitivity*, 829.1 *irascibility*, 830.3 *irritableness*
irritable 830, 403.7 *susceptible*, 473.8 *argumentative*, 674.15 *contentious*, 760.2 *oversensitive*, 829.4 *irascible*
irritableness 830
irritably 830, 473.17 *argumentatively*, 674.17 *contentiously*, 760.13 *oversensitively*, 829.9 *irascibly*
irritant 151.11 *troublemaker*, 385.10 *frictional*
irritate 153.7 *disturb*, 241.9 *make violent*, 385.15 *grind*, 616.5 *be inconvenient*, 628.3 *make worse*, 642.17 *meddle*, 650.6 *fatigue*, 768.8 *annoy*, 820.13 *antagonize*, 828.9 *offend*, 829.8 *make irascible*, 830.12 *make irritable*
irritated 153.12 *disturbed*, 403.7 *susceptible*, 828.15 *resentful*
irritating 616.1 *inconvenient*, 642.21 *meddling*, 768.5 *aggravating*
irritatingly 153.18 *disturbingly*, 385.17 *abrasively*, 616.6 *inconveniently*, 768.10 *annoyingly*, 828.17 *resentfully*
irritation 385, 406.1 *pain*, 616.3 *inconvenience*, 768.2 *annoyance*, 828.1 *resentment*
irrupt 346.10 *invade*, 357.1 *overstep*
irruption 346.3 *inroad*, 357.6 *overstepping*, 459.10 *siege*
irruptive 346.16 *invasive*
Irtysh 96 Rivers
Irving 48 Writers
Isabella 32 Breeds of Horse and Pony
isangoma 11.4 *witch*
ISBN 544.3 *means of identifica-*

tion
ischium 382 Bones
I see 471.25 *got it*
Isherwood 48 Writers
isidium 90.6 *lichen*
isigubu 49 Musical Instruments
isinglass 80.9 *fish product*, 393.9 *jelly*
Isis 8 Deities, **96** Rivers, 96.4 *British rivers*
I-ski 41.5 *ski equipment*
Islamabad 93 Cities
Islamic 43 Architectural Styles, 7.16 *denominational*
Islamic art 50 Non-Western Art
Islamic text 7.12 *religious text*
Islamize 7.20 *preach*
island 98, 98.2 *island*, 249.1 *region*, 318.2 *projection*, 356.5 *crossing point*
island arc 54.20 *earth movement*
island chain 98.2 *island*
island continent 98.2 *island*
islander 98.11 *continental*
island group 98.2 *island*
island universe 53.7 *galaxy*
Islay 93 Cities
isle 98.2 *island*
Isle of Man 98 Islands
Isle of Man TT 33.5 *motorcycle racing*
Isle of Man TT Races 674.4 *race*
Isle of Wight 98 Islands
Isle of Youth 98 Islands
Isles of the Blest 519.8 *dreamland*
islet 98.2 *island*, 249.1 *region*
isleted 98.11 *continental*
islets of Langerhans 352 Endocrine Glands
ism 497.2 *religious belief*
Ismailia 93 Cities
ISO 75.4 *standard*
ISO-7 65.10 *character*
isoantibody 387.4 *blood*
isobar 55.4 *weather forecast*
isobaric 55.42 *barometric*
isochronal 198.10 *synchronized*, 214.11 *regular*
isochronally 198.13 *synchronously*
isochronism 198.3 *synchronism*
isochronon 191 Timepieces and Timers
isochronous 198.10 *synchronized*, 214.11 *regular*
isochronously 198.13 *synchronously*
isocracy 12.1 *government*
isogamy 90.4 *reproductive body*
isogesis 524.1 *interpretation*
isogete 524.6 *interpreter*
isogloss 5.26 *dialect*
isokont 90.2 *algae*
isolate 104.15 *separate*, 136.10 *set apart*, 139.5 *unstick*, 147.7 *exclude*, 174.20 *single out*, 580.4 *pick*, 625.6 *make hygienic*, 816.13 *ignore*
isolated 61.34 *introverted*, 104.11 *separate*, 136.17 *unjoined*, 139.9 *aloof*, 168.16 *solitary*, 174.16 *alone*, 529.9 *secret*, 633.3 *vulnerable*, 816.10 *lonely*, 816.11 *secluded*
isolated case 174.2 *item*
isolated instance 165.6 *exception*, 174.2 *item*
isolate oneself 174.18 *be one*
isolation 61.19 *defence mechanism*, 104.3 *separateness*, 108.1 *unrelatedness*, 136.2 *setting apart*, 139.2 *aloofness*, 147.3 *exclusion zone*, 174.5 *aloneness*, 625.1 *hygiene*, 630.3 *prophylactic*, 632.2 *protection*, 816.3 *separation*
isolation block 19.9 *play*
isolationism 4.7 *school of thought*, 91.4 *nationalism*, 108.1 *unrelatedness*, 136.3 *separateness*, 174.5 *aloneness*, 400.11 *nation*, 591.12 *shyness*, 698.1 *freedom*
isolationist 4.11 *follower of a doctrine*, 4.14 *of a philosophy*, 91.14 *nationalist*, 136.8 *person*

who separates, 139.4 *individualist*, 168.9 *hermit*, 174.8 *loner*, 174.16 *alone*, 698.7 *free person*, 698.9 *free*
isolationist nation 91.1 *country*
isolation ward 60.10, 630.14 *hospital*
isoleucine 58 Amino Acids
isolex 5.26 *dialect*
isomer 57.13 *structure*
isomerase 58.11 *enzyme*
isomeric 57.37 *structural*
isomerism 57.13 *structure*
isometric drawing 547.2 *reproduction*
isometric projection 52.48 *transformation*, 547.2 *reproduction*
isometrics 644.5 *exercise*
isomorphic 306.9 *formed*
isomorphism 306.1 *form*
isomorphous 306.9 *formed*
isoniazid 62 Medication
isophone 5.26 *dialect*
isopod 81.4 *arthropod*
isoprenaline 62 Medication
isoprene rubber 57.21 *polymer*
isoprene unit 58.20 *terpene*
Isoptera 82 Orders of Insects
isopteran 82.10 *insectan*
ISO rating 66.10 *graininess*
isosceles 308.4 *symmetrical*
isosceles triangle 52.43 *triangle*, 310.3 *angled figure*
isospin 56.78 *quantum*
isostacy 54.18 *earth's crust*
isostatic 54.53 *solid-earth*
isostatic equilibrium 54.18 *earth's crust*
isotactic 57.44 *polymeric*
isotactic polymer 57.21 *polymer*
isotherm 55.4 *weather forecast*
isothermal 55.42 *barometric*, 55.43 *atmospheric*
isothermal change 56.39 *expansion*
isothermal layer 390.3 *atmospheric layers*
isotope 56, 367.4 *matter*
isotope effect 57.14 *chemical reaction*
isotrophic 110.12 *same*
isotrophically 110.18 *identically*
isotrophy 110.1 *sameness*
isotropic 116.14 *conforming*
isotropy 116.5 *conformity*, 122.3 *equalization*
isoxuprine 62 Medication
I-spy 42 Children's Games and Party Games, 435.3 *observation*
Israel 91 Countries, 714.4 *promised land*
Israelis 1 Peoples
Israfel 8.6 *angel*
Issas 1 Peoples
issuance 162.1 *dispersion*, 347.1 *exit*
issue 472, 14.2 *stock exchange*, 16.5 *litigation*, 103.2 *essential content*, 143.2 *particular*, 155.11 *progeny*, 155.25 *result*, 156.27 *emerge*, 157.12 *end result*, 162.16 *distribute*, 227.1 *effect*, 227.5 *show an effect*, 243.3 *product*, 345.5 *set out*, 347.1 *exit*, 347.10 *emerge*, 457.1 *appearance*, 457.12 *become visible*, 457.14 *present*, 473.3 *line of argument*, 473.4 *gist*, 477.1 *question*, 478.6 *solution*, 532.15 *publish*, 533.13 *report*, 611.3 *chief thing*, 638.4, 638.7 *leak*, 741.13 *coinage*, 741.24 *monetize*
issue a caveat 636.5 *warn*
issue a command 692.9 *command*
issue a counterorder 704.9 *cancel out*
issue a diploma 703.8 *authorize*
issue a D-notice 709.4 *censor*
issue a flat contradiction 536.8 *rebut*
issue a flat denial 536.8 *rebut*
issue a manifesto 535.17 *affirm*, 692.9 *command*

issue an edict 692.9 *command*
issue an injunction 692.10 *demand*, 699.8 *restrain*
issue an ultimatum 712.7 *demand*
issue a passport 703.8 *authorize*
issue a press release 535.17 *affirm*
issue a publication 532.15 *publish*
issue a public relations release 535.17 *affirm*
issue a public warning 636.5 *warn*
issue a statement 692.9 *command*
issue a suit 712.6 *request*
issue a supportive statement 535.19 *confirm*
issue a warning notice 692.10 *demand*
issue a warrant 692.10 *demand*
issue a writ 703.8 *authorize*
issued 162.22 *distributed*, 741.22 *monetary*
issue forth 156.27 *emerge*, 345.5 *set out*, 347.10 *emerge*
issue from 227.7 *follow from*
issue price 14.2 *stock exchange*
issuing 347.15 *outgoing*, 478.14 *solved*
issuing forth 457.1 *appearance*
Issyk-kul 94 Lakes
Istanbul 93 Cities

isthmian 98.11 *continental*, 272.4 *narrow-leaved*
isthmus 98.5 *peninsula*, 137.4 *means of connection*, 262.3 *contracted thing*, 272.6 *narrow place*
istoriato ware 44 Types of Ceramics
I swear 480.13 *really*
it 119.2 *original*, 537.6 *authenticity*, 586.3 *incentive*
IT 528.6 *information technology*
Italian 5 Languages and Groups of Languages, **43** Architectural Styles
Italian dish 45
Italian friction hitch 34.3 *climbing technique*
Italian GP at Monza 33.2 Formula 1 *race*
Italian Heavy Draught 32 Breeds of Horse and Pony
Italian ryegrass 87 Grasses, 68.12 *crop*
Italian sonnet 48.7 *poem*
italic 5.41 *lettered*
Italic 5 Languages and Groups of Languages, 5.11 *family of languages*
italicize 543.13 *punctuate*, 554.6 *emphasize*
italicized 543.17 *punctuated*
italics 554.1 *emphasis*
italic type 5.15 *type style*
Italy 91 Countries, 33.2 Formula 1 *race*
itch 340.1 *attraction*, 366.24 *shake*, 403.3 *stimulus*, 403.11 *sense*, 407.13 *be touched by*, 624.13 *skin disease*, 782.1 *desire*
Itchen 96 Rivers
itch for 782.12 *desire*
itchiness 366.5 *restlessness*, 760.7 *soreness*
itching 777 Phobias by Topic, 366.5 *restlessness*, 821.5 *desire*
itching for 782.9 *desirous*
itch mite 82 Arachnids, 82.3 *pest*
itchy 366.16 *restless*, 403.9 *exciting*, 760.3 *sore*
itchy feet 642.7 *restlessness*
item *174*, 51.6 *scene*, 99.2 *thing*, 106.6 *aspect*, 143.2 *particular*, 146.2 *thing included*, 148.1 *component*, 174.1 *one*, 243.3 *product*, 367.5 *object*, 472.2 *issue*, 545.1 *record*, 750.1 *accounts*
itemization 171.1 *list*, 171.7 *listing*
itemize *257*, 106.11 *circumstantiate*, 165.24 *specify*, 171.8 *list*, 475.16 *explain*, 545.15 *register*, 560.16 *define*

itemized *257*, 171.11 *listed*, 750.10 *accounting*
itemized account 171.4 *bill*
items 130.4 *extra*, 171.1 *list*, 257.5 *divisions*
iterate *183*, 110.11 *be regular*, 187.10 *be periodical*, 575.6 *persevere*
iterated *183*, 575.11 *steady*
iteration *183*, 52.28 *algorithm*, 187.5 *recurrent period*, 554.1 *emphasis*, 575.3 *constancy*
iterative 183.12 *repetitious*, 187.8 *periodical*, 554.3 *emphatic*
it follows that 116.36 *accordingly*, 227.12 *with the effect of*
I think not 536.16 *no*
itinerary 171.5 *list of appointments*, 327.2 *route*, 517.3 *plan*
it is all up with me 397.24 *I'm dying*
it's all over 397.24 *I'm dying*
it's curtains 397.24 *I'm dying*
itself 165.12 *I*
it serves you right 672.7 *revenge*
itsy-bitsy 260.7 *little*
itty-bitty 260.7 *little*
ITV 534.24 *television broadcasting*
Itzamna 8 Deities
Itzanagi 8 Deities
Itzanami 8 Deities
Itzlacoliuhqui 8 Deities
Itzli 8 Deities
Itzpapalotl 8 Deities
IUCD 247.3 *birth control*
IUD 247.3 *birth control*
Ivan Lendl 40.7 *famous tennis players*
I've had it 397.24 *I'm dying*
Ives 49 Musicians and Composers
IVF 245.3 *propagation*
ivories 49.16 *musical note*, 380.11 *tooth*
ivory 373.7 *hard substance*, 376.8 *smooth thing*, 439.14 *light colour*, 439.21 *light*, 446.1 *white*, 446.9 *white thing*
ivory-billed woodpecker 78 Birds
ivory black 447.8 *black pigment*
ivory-carving 50.12 *sculpture*
ivory nut 86 Nuts
ivory palm 85 Trees and Shrubs
ivory tower 531.6 *privacy*, 634.1 *refuge*, 816.5 *solitary place*
ivorywood 85 Trees and Shrubs
Ivy League 6.13 *university*
I/we surrender! 673
Ix 8 Deities
Ixazalvoh 8 Deities
Ixcuina 8 Deities
Ixion's wheel 364.6 *rotator*
Ixtlilton 8 Deities
Ixworth 68 Breeds of Fowl
Izmir 93 Cities

J

J 36.12 *canoeing*
Ja'alin 7 Non-Christian Religions
jab 26.9 *tae kwon do*, 26.11 *do a combat sport*, 330.3 *hit*, 330.13 *blow*, 330.14 *sporting hit*, 406.3 *injury*, 406.11 *inflict pain*, 407.3 *press*, 407.11 *touch*, 596.5 *attempt*, 630.2 *medicine*, 670.18 *hit*
jabbed 26.14 *combat*
jabber 5.5 *nonstandard language*, 26.4 *boxer*, 521.5 *empty talk*, 521.9 *talk nonsense*, 565.3 *talk*, 565.7 *be talkative*
jabberer 565.4 *talker*
jabbering 565.3 *talk*, 565.5 *talkative*
jabbing 26.2 *boxing*, 26.14 *combat*, 674.7 *boxing*
jabiru 78 Birds
jabot 295.14 *neckwear*
jaboticaba 86 Fruits
jab throw a left hook 26.11 *do a*

combat sport
jacamar 78 Birds
jacana 78 Birds
jacaranda 85 Trees and Shrubs
jacaré 79 Reptiles
jack 74 Rigging, 25.1 *green bowling*, 71.21 *miscellaneous motoring terms*, 77.17 *male mammal*, 361.9 *lifter*, 401.16 *male animal*, 544.7 *flag*, 603.1 *tool*, 741.2 *cash*
jackal 77 Placental Mammals, 808.3 *sycophant*
jackass 77.17 *male mammal*, 508.3 *foolish person*
jackboot 652.8 *treatment*, 690.2 *suppression*
jackboots 295.19 *footwear*
Jack Buchanan 46.6 *famous dancers*
jack-by-the-hedge 84 Flowers and Flowering Plants
jackdaw 78 Birds, 78.6 *songbird*
jackdaw in peacock's feathers 539.15 *deceiver*, 656.10 *unskilled person*
jacket *295*, 258.5 *packet*, 293.5 *body covering*, 293.13 *casing*
Jackfield ware 44 Types of Ceramics
Jack Frost 55.36 *frost*, 409.5 *ice*
jackfruit 86 Fruits
jack-high 25.9 *bowls*
Jackie 91 Names for Inhabitants
jack-in-office 696.4 *absolute ruler*
Jack-in-office 653.16 *official*, 807.12 *impudent person*
jack-in-the-pulpit 84 Flowers and Flowering Plants
jack it in 598.2 *withdraw*, 705.5 *resign*
Jack Ketch 879.17 *punisher*
jackknife 380.10 *knife*
jack of all trades 642.10 *busy person*, 646.1 *worker*, 655.4 *skilled person*
jack of all trades and master of none 612.10 *nonentity*, 656.10 *unskilled person*
jack-o'-lantern 102.2 *illusion*, 319.2 *notched thing*
Jack-o'-lantern 439.9 *firefly*
jack pine 85 Trees and Shrubs
jack plane 47.11 *woodworking tool*
jackpot 721.5 *profit*, 878.2 *prize*
jack-pudding 51.30 *clown*
jackrabbit 77 Placental Mammals
Jack Russell terrier 77 Breeds of Dogs
jacks 42 Children's Games and Party Games
jackscrew 361.9 *lifter*
Jack shit 172.2 *nothing*
Jackson 93 Cities
Jacksonville 93 Cities
jackstraw 102.5 *insubstantial person*
jackstraws 42 Children's Games and Party Games
Jack Tar 74.7 *nautical person*
jack up 128.5 *make bigger*, 361.1 *raise*
Jacob 68 Breeds of Sheep
Jacobean 43 Architectural Styles, 47.7 *furniture style*, 202.14 *historic*
Jacobean tragedy 51.9 *tragedy*
Jacobin 7 Members of Religious Orders, 693.6 *nonconformist*
Jacobins 12.6 *political party*
Jacobites 7 Christian Movements
Jacob's ladder 359.9 *ladder*
Jacquard 52 Scientists, 67 Natural Fabrics
Jacquard loom 67.4 *weaving*
Jacques Cousteau 97.6 *oceanographer*
jactitate 366.21 *be agitated*
jactitation 366.5 *restlessness*
jaculate 338.20 *propel*
jaculation 337.29 *in reverse*, 338.3 *throwing*
jaculatory 338.18 *projectile*
jacuzzi 258.12 *bath*

Jacuzzi 385.6 *massage*, 389.11 *wash*, 408.8 *hot place*, 621.6 *bath*
Jacy 8 Deities
jade 32.1 *horse*, 32.4 *saddle horse*, 402.8 *nasty woman*, 453.1 *green*, 453.11 *green thing*, 650.6 *fatigue*, 785.7 *cause dislike*, 788.6 *be boring*
jaded 164.22 *commonplace*, 650.2, 788.5 *bored*
jadedness 650.7 *fatigue*
Jade Emperor 8 Deities
jadeite 54 Minerals
Jaffa 86 Fruits, 93 Cities
jag 874.14 *drinking bout*
Jagannath 8 Deities
jagged 319.4 *notched*, 375.2 *coarse*, 380.4 *toothed*
jagged edge 380.7 *sharp point*
jaggedly 319, 375.14 *roughly*
jaggedness 375.6 *roughness*
jaggy 319.4 *notched*, 375.2 *coarse*
jaguar 77 Placental Mammals, 456.5 *variegated thing*
jaguarundi 77 Placental Mammals
Jah 8 Deities, 8.3 *God*
jahannan 8.11 *heaven*
jai alai 18 Sporting Activities
jail 218.5 *resting place*, 290.2 *inside*, 290.15 *keep inside*, 323.4 *closed place*, 323.10 *enclose*, 695.3 *coercive methods*, 702.1 *prison*, 702.9 *imprison*, 816.4 *place of confinement*, 816.13 *ignore*, 879.1 *punish*, 879.14 *instrument of punishment*
jailbird 16.40 *lawbreaker*, 699.7 *charge*, 702.5 *prisoner*, 866.4 *guilty person*
jailbreak 638.1 *escape*
jail-breaker 638.3 *escaper*
jail cell 702.3 *prison cell*
jailed 323.15 *enclosed*
jailer 323.5 *person who closes*, 692.6 *person in command*, 699.6 *law-maker*, 702.6 *prison officer*
jail fever 624.6 *infection*
jailhouse 702.1 *prison*
jailhouse lawyer 463.6 *arguer*
Jain 7.6 *non-Christian*
Jainist text 7.12 *religious text*
jainpan 71.6 *litter*
Jaipur 93 Cities
Jakarta 93 Cities
jakes 353.5 *faeces*, 727.7 *toilet*
jalap 62 Medication
jalopy 71.16 *car*
jam 34.9 *mountaineer*, 45.42 *preserve*, 49.37 *syncopate*, 105.2 *predicament*, 106.4 *difficult circumstances*, 135.10 *link*, 144.6 *fill*, 161.21 *scrum*, 181.4 *throng*, 181.11 *crowd*, 209.3 *delayed action*, 209.8 *delay*, 218.6 *cease*, 251.3 *difficult circumstances*, 257.7 *stuff*, 262.5 *make smaller*, 325.9 *make motionless*, 393.9 *jelly*, 394.6 *gelatin*, 414.2 *sweetener*, 421.10 *muffle*, 583.3 *improvise*, 637.3 *preserved thing*, 659.5 *predicament*, 661.2 *obstacle*, 683.9 *malfunction*
Jamaica 91 Countries, **98** Islands
Jamaica Hope 68 Breeds of Cattle
Jamaican ganga 875.6 *drug*
Jamaica rum 351.7 *alcoholic drink*
jambalaya 45.43 *US dish*
jamboree 405.4 *pleasurable things*, 812.1 *celebration*
jam doughnut 45.36 *cake*
James 48 Writers, **48** Writers, **96** Rivers, 61.29 *psychologist*
James-Lange theory 61.3 *psychiatric treatment*
jam in 346.12 *flood in*, 354.3 *impact*
jamjar 258.15 *pot*
jammed 135.15 *tied*, 144.8 *full*, 181.10 *crowded*, 209.10 *held up*, 273.2 *dense*, 323.13

stopped, 327.15 *accessible*
jammed tight 144.8 *full*
jamming 34.3 *climbing technique*, 36.10 *sailing*, 36.12 *canoeing*, 49.2 *music making*, 421.3 *inaudibility*, 438.6 *that which makes invisible*
jamming cleat 36.3 *parts of a sailing boat*
jamming stroke 36.6 *canoeing*
jammy 394.9 *gelatinous*, 617.1 *worthy*
jam-packed 144.8 *full*, 161.50, 181.10 *crowded*
jam sandwich 45.11 *sandwich*, 71.17 *police car*
jam session 46.1 *dancing*, 583.4 *improvisation*
Jamshedpur 93 Cities
jam tart 45.36 *cake*
jam tomorrow 199.3 *future condition*, 519.7 *idealism*, 586.8 *incentive*
Janáček 49 Musicians and Composers
JANET 65.15 *network*
jangle 427.10 *ring*, 430.4 *be strident*, 434.10 *lack harmony*
jangling 434.1 *dissonance*, 434.7 *dissonant*
janissary 679.12 *ceremonial troops*
janitor 435.11 *observer*, 697.3 *attendant*
Janrt 61.29 *psychologist*
Jansenism 7 Christian Movements
jansky 75 Scientific and Technical Units
Jansky 52 Scientists
January 409.7 *cold weather*
Janus 176.3 *duality*, 578.9 *equivocator*
Janus-faced 540.26 *duplicitous*
Janus-like 176.11 *double-edged*
Jap 91 Names for Inhabitants
japan 293.3 *coating*, 293.24 *coat*, 395.10 *resin*, 447.8 *black pigment*, 447.11 *blacken*
Japan 91 Countries, **97** Oceans and Seas
Japanese 5 Languages and Groups of Languages, **68** Breeds of Fowl, **87** Grasses, **777** Phobias by Topic
Japanese cedar 85 Trees and Shrubs
Japanese chin 77 Breeds of Dogs
Japanese garden 69.2 *garden*
Japanese GP at Suzuka 33.2 *Formula 1 race*
Japanese maple 85 Trees and Shrubs
Japanese persimmon 86 Fruits
Japanese quince 86 Fruits
Japanese rising sun 544.6 *national emblem*
Japanese scroll painting 50 Non-Western Art
Japanese woodblocks 50 Non-Western Art
japanned 395.14 *resinous*
japanning 47.1 *furniture*
Japanophobia 777 Phobias by Name
jape 771.5 *joke*
japer 506.4 *buffoon*
japonica 84 Flowers and Flowering Plants
jar 44.8 *ceramic object*, 117.2 *contradiction*, 117.12 *be disparate*, 120.3 *container*, 258.11 *vessel*, 366.9, 366.23 *jolt*, 430.4 *be strident*, 434.10 *lack harmony*, 637.2 *preserver*, 785.7 *cause dislike*, 822.16 *cause hate*
jardinière 69.4 *nursery*
jargon 5.3 *spoken language*, 5.20 *jargon word*, 165.10 *specialized language*, 520.4 *type of meaning*, 521.1 *lack of meaning*, 564.1 *faculty of speech*
jargonal 5.39 *of language*
jargonish 5.39 *of language*
jargonistic 5.39 *of language*
jargonize 5.45 *use language*
jargon word 5

jarhead 676.11 *recruit*, 679.28 *marines*
jarosite 54 Minerals
jarrah 85 Trees and Shrubs
jarring 117.2 *contradiction*, 117.8 *contradictory*, 366.19 *convulsive*, 430.7 *strident*, 434.1 *dissonance*, 434.7 *dissonant*, 559.9 *inelegant*
Jarry 48 Dramatists
jasmine 418.2 *fragrant thing*
jasmine tea 351.3 *tea*
Jason 74.7 *nautical person*
jaspé 456.9 *striped*
jasper 44 Types of Ceramics, **54** Gemstones, 456.5 *variegated thing*
Jaspers 4 Philosophers
Jataka 7.12 *religious text*
jaundice 452.6 *yellowness*, 481.3 *prejudice*, 493.12 *bias*, 841.1 *jealousy*
jaundiced 452.4 *yellow-faced*, 481.10 *discriminatory*, 493.8 *unjust*, 624.21 *unhealthy*, 841.4 *jealous*, 842.2 *envious*
jaundiced eye 493.3 *injustice*, 841.1 *jealousy*
jaundiced look 841.1 *jealousy*
jaundiced view 841.1 *jealousy*
jaundice-eyed 841.4 *jealous*
jauntily 769.9 *cheerfully*, 811.35 *flashily*
jauntiness 769.3 *cheerfulness*
jaunting car 71 Carriages and Carts
jaunty 769.1 *cheerful*, 811.19 *flashy*
java 351.4 *coffee*
Java 97 Oceans and Seas, **98** Islands
Java man 202.7 *ancient people*, 400.3 *uncivilized human*
Javanese 5 Languages and Groups of Languages
javelin 21.2 *field events*, 338.10 *ball*, 680.6 *historical missile weapon*, 680.8 *sharp weapon*
javelin-carrying 21.2 *field events*
javelin throw 21.2 *field events*
javelin thrower 338.14 *thrower*
javelin-thrower 21.3 *athlete*
javelin throwing 18 Sporting Activities
javelin-throwing 21.2 *field events*
jaw 305.1 *side*, 457.3 *external appearance*, 521.5 *empty talk*, 521.9 *talk nonsense*, 565.3 *talk*, 565.7 *be talkative*
jawbone 382 Bones
jawbreaker 5.17 *word*, 373.7 *hard substance*, 414.4 *confectionery*
jawbreaking 659.12 *problematic*
jaw-jaw 565.3 *talk*
jaw, jaw – not war, war 675.5 *be at peace*
jawless fish 80.2 *fish*
jaws 350.16 *eating utensil*
jaws of death 397.1 *death*, 633.5 *danger*
jaws of life 71.21 *miscellaneous motoring terms*
jay 78 Birds, 565.4 *talker*
Jaycee 13.9 *economist*, 737.11 *chamber of commerce member*
jazz 49, 49, 521.5 *empty talk*
jazz band 49.26 *musical group*
jazzed up 128.7 *increased*
jazz-funk 49.9 *popular music*
jazzman 49.24 *musician*
jazz up 128.5 *make bigger*
JCB 71 Motor Vehicles, 63.29 *construction equipment*, 355.10 *excavator*
JCL 65.9 *programming language*
J-cloth 621.11 *cleaning cloth*
jealous 841, 453.5 *green-eyed*, 759.13 *passionate*, 820.6 *hostile*, 821.20 *amorous*, 822.10 *hating*, 828.15 *resentful*, 842.2 *envious*, 860.4 *selfish*
jealously 841, 820.11 *hostilely*, 821.30 *lovingly*, 822.18 *hatefully*, 828.17 *resentfully*, 842.4 *enviously*, 860.8 *selfishly*
jealousness 841.1 *jealousy*

jealousy 777 Phobias by Topic, **841**, 453.14 *green-eyed monster*, 674.1 *contention*, 759.6 *bad feeling*, 820.2 *personal conflict*, 821.2 *romantic love*, 822.1 *hate*, 828.1 *resentment*, 842.1 *envy*, 860.1 *selfishness*
Jealousy 841
jean 67 Natural Fabrics
Jean Lafitte 736.9 *plunderer*
jeans 295.9 *trousers*, 814.6 *informal dress*
Jeans 52 Scientists
Jeep 71 Motor Vehicles
jeepers 827.11 *miscellaneous euphemisms*
jeepers-creepers 827.16 *euphemisms*
Jeeps 18 Sporting Personalities
jeer 429.2, 429.5 *catcall*, 431.7 *cry of disapproval*, 431.14 *hiss*, 713.3 *gesture of protest*, 713.7 *complain*, 807.29 *ridicule*, 818.3 *act of discourtesy*, 850.6, 850.25 *taunt*, 852.9 *show of disapproval*, 852.23 *show disapproval*
jeer at 799.6 *deride*
jeer capstan 361.9 *lifter*
jeered 852.35 *hissed*
jeering 429.7 *catcalling*, 431.19 *hissing*, 713.9 *protesting*, 818.1 *discourtesy*, 850.15 *taunting*
jeeringly 818.10 *rudely*
jeers 361.9 *lifter*
Jeffers 48 Poets
Jefferson City 93 Cities
Jefferson Memorial 43 Noted Buildings
Jehovah 8.3 *God*
Jehovah's Witness 7.5 *Christian*
Jehovah's Witnesses 7 Christian Movements
Jehu 329.13 *swift person*
jejunal 290.10 *visceral*
jejune 412.5 *tasteless*, 609.1 *insufficient*
jejunectomy 60 Surgical Operations
jejuneness 412.1 *tastelessness*
jejunoileostomy 60 Surgical Operations
jejunostomy 60 Surgical Operations
jejunotomy 60 Surgical Operations
jejunum 290.4 *insides*
Jekyll and Hyde 111.2 *opposites*, 176.3 *duality*
jell 371.8 *be dense*, 373.10 *solidify*, 393.9 *jelly*, 393.26 *gelatinize*
jelled 371.7 *condensed*, 394.9 *gelatinous*
jellied 394.9 *gelatinous*
jellied eel 45.16 *fish dish*, 80.8 *food fish*
jellification 394.1 *viscosity*
jellify 371.8 *be dense*, 393.26 *gelatinize*, 394.11 *thicken*
jelling 371.7 *condensed*
jelly 393, 45.35 *dessert*, 45.42 *preserve*, 393.26 *gelatinize*, 394.6 *gelatin*, 394.11 *thicken*, 414.2 *sweetener*, 637.2 *preserver*, 637.3 *preserved thing*
jelly bean 45.41 *sweet*
jellyfish 161 Collective Names by Animal, 76.5 *aquatic animal*, 238.4 *weakling*, 307.2 *shapeless thing*, 779.2 *coward*
jelly fungi 89.3 *fungi*
jelly-like 393.21, 394.9 *gelatinous*
jelly-likeness 394.1 *viscosity*
jelly mould 258.16 *crockery*
jelutong 85 Trees and Shrubs
jemmy 603.1 *tool*
jennet 32.4 *saddle horse*
jenny 74 Sails, 77.18 *female mammal*
jeopardize 633.10 *endanger*
jeopardy 589.1 *chance*, 633.5 *danger*
jerboa 77 Placental Mammals
jeremiad 567.1 *address*
jerid 680.8 *sharp weapon*
jerk 339, 46.2 *dance*, 215.1 *irreg-*

ularity, 215.6 *be irregular*, 330.1 *impel*, 338.23 *throw*, 339.13 *pull at*, 366.9 *jolt*, 366.21 *be agitated*, 366.23 *jolt*, 366.24 *shake*, 375.11 *be rough*, 508.3 *foolish person*, 656.10 *unskilled person*
jerkily 366, 215.8 *irregularly*
jerkin 295.11 *jacket*
jerkiness 160.1 *discontinuity*, 215.1 *irregularity*, 366.1 *agitation*
jerking 215.4 *irregular*
jerkwater 93.14 *urban*, 127.13 *insignificant*, 612.4 *trivial*
jerkwater engine 72.4 *locomotive*
jerkwater town 93.10 *village*, 127.7 *inferior thing*, 816.5 *solitary place*
jerky 160.8 *discontinuous*, 215.4 *irregular*, 366.19 *convulsive*
jeroboam 258.14 *bottle*
Jeronymite 7 Members of Religious Orders
jerry 353.14, 727.7 *toilet*
Jerry 91 Names for Inhabitants
jerry-built 127.14 *poor*, 238.8 *weak*, 379.1 *brittle*, 595.3 *without preparation*, 612.4 *trivial*, 620.2 *incomplete*, 633.2 *unsafe*, 656.4 *bungled*
jerry-built house 379.3 *brittle thing*
jerrycan 71.21 *miscellaneous motoring terms*
jersey 67 Natural Fabrics, 19.3 *uniform*, 23.3 *basketball equipment*, 295.13 *sweater*
Jersey 68 Breeds of Cattle, **98** Islands
Jersey City 93 Cities
Jersey Giant 68 Breeds of Fowl
Jerusalem 93 Cities, 10.13 *shrine*, 291.4 *centre of activity*
Jerusalem artichoke 45 Vegetables
Jerusalem Bible 7.12 *religious text*
Jerusalem cherry 86 Fruits
Jesse James 736.8 *thief*
jest 612.8 *trifle*, 771.5 *joke*, 771.13 *be humorous*, 850.9 *butt*
jester 51.30 *clown*, 506.4 *buffoon*, 771.6 *humorist*
jester's cap 295.15 *headgear*
jesting 771.3 *wit*
Jesuit 7 Members of Religious Orders, 474.6 *sophist*
jesuitic 474.7 *sophistic*
jesuitically 474.14 *sophistically*
Jesuitism 540.4 *spuriousness*
jesuitry 474.1 *sophistry*
Jesus 8.4 *God the Son*
Jesus boots 295.19 *footwear*
Jesus Christ 8.4 *God the Son*, 827.15 *miscellaneous swearwords*
Jesus freak 7.5 *Christian*
Jesus-freak 497.5 *believer*
Jesus wept 827.15 *miscellaneous swearwords*
jet 33.10 *be on the track*, 41.4 *skiing technique*, 41.12 *ski*, 235.4 *energy*, 329.11 *swift thing*, 338.12 *propellant*, 347.2 *outflow*, 347.11 *run out*, 349.14 *let out*, 349.22 *disgorgement*, 359.2 *upturn*, 359.17 *spring up*, 440.4 *dark thing*, 447.1 *black*, 447.9 *black thing*
JET 235.8 *nuclear power*
jet-black 440.10 *dark-coloured*, 447.1 *black*
jet-boat 74 Ships and Boats
jeté 46.9 *ballet steps*
jet engine 73 Aircraft Parts, 63.11 *engine*
jet flight 329.11 *swift thing*
jet lag 73.1 *aviation*
jet-lagged 650.1 *fatigued*
jet pipe 73 Aircraft Parts
jet plane 73 Types of Aircraft
jet-propelled 329.1 *swift*, 338.19 *propelled*
jet propulsion 235.4 *energy*, 338.2 *method of propulsion*
jetsam 326.10 *transferred thing*, 727.3 *disposable things*

jet set 201.6 *avant-garde*, 617.7
elite, 796.6 *fashionable élite*,
802.2 *aristocracy*
jet setter 796.6 *fashionable élite*
jet-setter 405.3 *pleasure-seeker*,
642.10 *busy person*
jet skiing 18 Sporting Activities
jetstream 55.10 *air movement*,
390.4 *air flow*
jetting 33.6 *motor racing terms*
jettison 349.13 *throw away*,
349.20 *eviction*, 370.10 *lighten*,
581.2 *discard*, 598.1 *relinquish*,
600.6 *stop using*, 727.9 *dispose
of*
jettisoned 598.5 *relinquished*,
600.4 *disused*
jet turn 41.4 *skiing technique*
jetty 63.24 *water system*, 318.2
projection, 447.1 *black*, 634.2
shelter, 661.3 *barrier*
Jeune Peinture Belge 50 Schools
and Groups of Artists
Jew 7.6 *non-Christian*
jewel 364.4 *vortex*, 617.8 *exceller*, 655.3 *masterpiece*, 789.3
attractive female, 861.17 *good
thing*
Jewel Box 53 Clusters
jewel in the crown 526.7 *showpiece*, 805.12 *object of pride*,
821.11 *loved one*, 861.9 *the best*
jeweller 646.2 *artisan*, 792.7 *decorator*
jeweller's rouge 57 Common
Chemical Compounds
jewellery 792
jewellery box 258.6 *box*
jewfish 80 Fishes
Jewish 7.16 *denominational*
Jewish ghetto 93.7 *city district*
Jewish text 7.12 *religious text*
Jews 1 Peoples, **777** Phobias by
Topic
jew's ear 89 Fungi
jew's harp 49 Musical Instruments
Jewtown 93.7 *city district*
Jhansi 93 Cities
jib 74 Sails, 36.3 *parts of a sailing boat*, 331.2 *respond*, 335.8
sidestep, 337.6 *shrink back*,
573.7 *refuse*, 576.6 *hesitate*,
591.4 *shy*
jib at 711.5 *refuse*
jibbering 551.2 *obscure*, 565.5
talkative
jibberish 551.1 *obscurity*
jibbing 591.12 *shyness*
jibe 116.27 *fit*, 850.6 *taunt*
jibe at 850.25 *taunt*
jibing 850.15 *taunting*
Jidda 93 Cities
jiffy 191.3 *instant*
jig 20.2 *artificial fly*, 46.4 *historic dancing*, 46.15 *dance*, 51.6
scene, 306.2 *prototype*, 339.3
jerk, 339.11 *pull at*, 366.9 *jolt*,
366.24 *shake*, 513.9 *snare*
jig about 46.15 *dance*
jigger 71 Motor Vehicles, **74**
Sails, **74** Rigging, **82** Insects,
44.6 *ceramic workshop*, 44.11
make ceramics, 72.4 *locomotive*,
82.3 *pest*, 258.13 *drinking vessel*, 366.24 *shake*
jiggery-pokery 474.4 *quibbling*,
538.8 *pretence*, 539.7 *tricking*
jigget 366.9 *jolt*, 366.24 *shake*
jiggle 339.3 *jerk*, 339.11 *pull at*,
366.24 *shake*
jiggler 366.14 *agitator*
jigsaw 47.11 *woodworking tool*,
140.2 *cooperation*, 603.1 *tool*
jigsaw piece 148.3 *unit*
jihad 676.1 *war*
jill 77.18 *female mammal*
jillion 169.3 *large number*,
179.11 *million*, 181.7 *myriad*
jillions 181.2 *multitude*
jilt 515.7 *thwart*, 578.9 *equivocator*, 598.2 *withdraw*
jilted 515.9 *disappointed*, 598.5
relinquished, 785.9 *disliked*,
822.12 *hated*
jilter 598.4 *deserter*
jim crow 91 Names for Inhabi-

tants
jim-dandy 861.1 *good*, 861.17
good thing
jimjams 874.16 *alcoholism*
Jimmy 255.9 *British inhabitant*,
401.3 *male title of address*
Jimmy Connors 40.7 *famous tennis players*
Jimmy Hix 179.2 *six*
Jimmy Riddle 353.3 *urination*
jimson weed 62 Medication, **84**
Flowers and Flowering Plants
Jinan 93 Cities
jingle 427.2 *ringing*, 427.10 *ring*
jingles 48.6 *poetry*
jingling 427.7 *ringing*
jingling Johnny 49 Musical Instruments
jingo 5.21 *catchword*, 481.7 *bigot*
Jingo 8 Deities
jingoism 91.4 *nationalism*,
400.11 *nation*, 481.4 *social discrimination*, 676.5 *bellicosity*
jingoist 91.14 *nationalist*, 481.7
bigot, 679.6 *militarist*
jingoistic 5.39 *of language*, 91.16
national, 481.10 *discriminatory*,
679.33 *combative*
jingoistically 91.19 *nationally*,
481.17 *prejudicially*, 679.41 *aggressively*
jinn 76.7 *legendary beast*
jinni 11.11 *ghost*
jinx 11.5 *spell*, 11.21 *bewitch*,
618.11 *harmfulness*, 687.11
cause adversity, 827.4 *malediction*, 862.4 *evil power*, 862.11
be evil
jinxed 11.19 *bewitched*, 827.10
maledictive, 862.10 *inauspicious*
jinxed again 862.15 *bad luck*
jitterbug 46.2 *dance*, 46.5
dancer, 46.15 *dance*, 760.9 *oversensitive person*
jitteriness 576.13 *timidity*
jitters 366.1 *agitation*
jittery 366.15 *agitated*, 576.3
timid, 777.8 *fearful*
jive 46.2, 46.15 *dance*, 49.8
jazz, 521.5 *empty talk*, 521.9
talk nonsense
jiver 46.5 *dancer*
jizo 8 Deities
jo 821.9 *lover*
Joachim 49 Musicians and Composers
Joan of Arc 679.10 *woman soldier*
job 644, 65.17 *computing term*,
230.3 *business*, 251.4 *employment*, 322.10 *opportunity*,
597.2 *undertaking*, 640.2 *deed*,
644.2 *task*, 703.2 *engagement*,
736.3 *theft*, 737.6 *business*
Job 743.10 *poor person*
job allocation 731.1 *allocation*
jobber 715.4 *contractor*, 737.10
trader, 739.12 *wholesaler*
jobbery 657.1 *cunning*
jobbing 737.4 *trade*
job description 15.2 *industrial negotiations*
job due yesterday 648.4 *haste*
job flexibility 15.2 *industrial negotiations*
jobless 600.3 *not wanted*, 641.3
inactive, 643.2 *not working*,
645.7 *leisurely*
joblessness 641.1 *inaction*,
645.3 *unemployment*
job lot hotchpotch 133.3 *miscellany*
job of work 644.2 *task*
job satisfaction 878.1 *reward*
Job's comforter 770.4 *depressing
person*, 776.3 *hopeless person*
job-share 706.4 *delegate*
job sharing 706.3 *delegation*
job-sharing 731.1 *allocation*
jobsworth 653.7 *official*
job training 6.2 *educational system*
Jock 91 Names for Inhabitants,
255.9 *British inhabitant*, 401.3
male title of address
jockette 32.15 *horse person*
jockey 32.15 *horse person*,
652.11 *conduct oneself*, 657.5

be cunning, 674.10 *contender*
jockey cap 295.15 *headgear*
jockeying 652.9 *tactics*
jockeying for position 652.9 *tactics*
jockey's colours 544.5 *uniform*
jockey shorts 295.18 *underwear*
jockstrap 21.4 *sports equipment*,
284.5 *supporting garment*,
295.18 *underwear*, 295.25 *accessories*
jockstrap 296.4 *dishabille*
jocose 771.10 *humorous*
jocular 506.5 *nonsensical*,
771.10 *humorous*
jodan-uke 26.8 *karate*
Jodhpur 93 Cities
jodhpurs 295.9 *trousers*
Jodo 7 Non-Christian Religions
Jodrell Bank 53.23 *observatory*
joe 400.7 *person*
Joe Bloggs 124.7 *average person*,
164.9 *everyman*, 400.7 *person*
Joe Public 124.7 *average person*,
164.9 *everyman*, 400.9 *group*
Joe Six-Pack 164.9 *everyman*
Joe Soap 124.7 *average person*,
400.7 *person*
joey 77.19 *young mammal*
jog 228.9 *motivate*, 324.12 *gait*,
324.15 *walk*, 328.10 *slow motion*, 330.1 *impel*, 330.13 *blow*,
339.3 *jerk*, 339.13 *pull at*,
366.9, 366.23 *jolt*, 543.11 *gesture*, 644.9 *exercise*
joggers 295.9 *trousers*
jogging 625.1 *hygiene*, 627.9
physical improvement, 644.5 *exercise*
jogging suit 21.4 *sports equipment*, 295.10 *suit*
joggle 330.1 *impel*, 330.13 *blow*,
339.3 *jerk*, 339.13 *pull at*,
366.9, 366.23 *jolt*
joggling 366.18 *shaky*
jog on 336.6 *march on*
jog one's memory 511.13 *remind*
jog suit 295.10 *suit*
jog trot 112.1 *uniformity*,
324.12 *gait*, 328.10 *slow motion*
jog-trot 328.1 *move slowly*
Johannesburg 93 Cities
john 353.13 *lavatory*, 727.7 *toilet*
John 18 Sporting Personalities
John Barleycorn 351.7 *alcoholic
drink*, 874.12 *alcohol*
John Brown 693.10 *seditionist*
John Bull 91.9 *England*, 255.9
British inhabitant
John Doe 164.9 *everyman*, 400.7
person, 502.4 *unknown person*
John Dory 80 Fishes
John Hancock Center 43 Noted
Buildings
John McEnroe 40.7 *famous tennis
players*
John Newcombe 40.7 *famous ten-
nis players*
johnny 247.3 *birth control*
Johnny 401.3 *male title of address*
Johnny come lately 149.7 *new-
comer*
Johnny-come-lately 201.8 *new ar-
rival*, 209.4 *latecomer*
Johnny on the spot 208.4 *early
comer*
John o'Groats 93 Cities
John Q. Public 124.7 *average person*, 164.9 *everyman*
John Smith and Pocahontas
819.7 *famous friendships*
Johnsonese 551.1 *obscurity*,
557.2 *affectation*
Johnsonian 551.2 *obscure*, 557.4
ornate
Johnstown 93 Cities
John Thomas 245.8 *organs of reproduction*
join 664, 110.8 *make the same*,
130.6 *add*, 130.7 *support*, 135.5
joint, 135.8, 135.8 *unite*,
135.10 *link*, 137.11 *connect*,
138.7 *cause to adhere*, 140.5
combine, 144.4 *complete*,
148.10 *compose*, 159.15 *concatenate*, 161.44 *put together*,
174.19 *become one*, 267.3 *juxta-

pose*, 344.8 *meet*, 346.14 *enrol*,
407.12 *abut*, 629.1 *repair*,
665.13 *be a member*, 724.4
have joint possession, 823.16
join in marriage
join a charmed circle 699.8 *restrain*
join a consortium 715.5 *contract*
join a party 665.14 *be a party
member*
join a shooting party 37.7 *shoot*
join battle 663.16 *confront*,
676.14 *battle*
joined 47, 107.4 *related*, 130.8
additional, 135.12 *united*,
137.15 *connected*, 140.7 *combined*, 146.8 *included*, 148.7
modular, 161.48 *cumulate*,
174.13 *whole*, 180.19 *associated*, 267.5 *juxtaposed*, 823.21
married
joiner 135, 47.13 *carpenter*,
646.2 *artisan*, 815.6 *social person*
joinery 47.8 *woodwork*
join forces 161.41 *band together*,
664.14 *join with*
join forces with 140.6 *come together*
join hands 140.6 *come together*
join hands with 664.14 *join with*
join in 2.15 *socialize*, 18.6 *participate*, 42.10 *play*, 253.12 *attend*,
642.16 *be sociable*, 664.13 *work
together*, 724.4 *have joint possession*, 815.11 *be sociable*
joining 47.16 *joined*, 130.1 *addition*, 135.1 *union*, 137.1 *connection*, 267.1 *juxtaposition*, 407.6
contiguity
joining of forces 664.4 *joint operation*
joining together 135.3 *unification*, 140.1 *combination*, 161.1
assembly
joining up 676.7 *war measures*
join in holy wedlock 823.16 *join
in marriage*
join in marriage 823
join in the melee 674.12 *fight*
join issue with 674.13 *conflict*
join one's fortunes to 664.14 *join
with*
joint 135, 664, 47.10
carpenter's term, 54.20 *earth
movement*, 116.11 *allied*, 137.4
means of connection, 137.14
connective, 140.7 *combined*,
256.8 *shelter*, 407.6 *contiguity*,
724.5 *jointly possessing*, 875.6
drug
joint action 664.4 *joint operation*,
724.2 *participation*
joint bank account 724.1 *joint
possession*
Joint Chiefs of Staff 17.5 *military
staff*
joint consultation committee 15.4
industrial dispute
joint control 664
joint dominion 12.3 *governance*
jointed 20.8 *angling*, 47.16
joined, 81.18 *arthropodous*,
135.12 *united*, 310.7 *angular*
jointed plugs 20.2 *artificial fly*
joint effort 664.4 *joint operation*
jointer 47.11 *woodworking tool*
Joint European Torus 56.94 *particle accelerator*
joint government 724.1 *joint possession*
join the angels 397.15 *die*
join the army 676.12 *go to war*
join the Band of Hope 873.4 *give
up alcohol*
join the chain gang 702.10 *be in
prison*
join the choir invisible 397.15 *die*
join the colours 17.10 *enlist*
join the dance 46.15 *dance*
join the inner circle 665.12 *be in
league with*
joint heir 730.6 *beneficiary*
join the majority 397.15 *die*
join the opposition 578.3 *apostatize*
join the rat race 642.13 *be busy*

join the traffic 356.9 *proceed*
jointing 54.20 *earth movement*, 135.3 *unification*
jointly 130.10 *additionally*, 135.16 *as one*, 137.17 *in connection with*, 140.10 *in combination*, 664.20 *cooperatively*, 665.18 *cliquishly*, 724.6 *in common*
jointly possessed 724.5 *jointly possessing*
jointly possessing 724
jointly with 664.22 *with*
joint-master 32.15 *horse person*
join together 140.5 *combine*
joint operation 230, 664, 676.8 *warfare*
joint owner 724.3 *participant*
joint ownership 724.1 *joint possession*
joint possession 724
Joint Possession 724
joint regulations 15.1 *industrial relations*
joint rule 12.3 *governance*
joint stock 724.1 *joint possession*
joint tenancy 724.1 *joint possession*
jointure 725.2 *legal terms*
joint venture 230.2 *joint operation*
join up 17.10 *enlist*, 161.41 *band together*, 676.12 *go to war*
join up with 664.14 *join with*
join Weightwatchers 871.5 *fast*
join with 664, 116.22 *form an alliance*, 135.8 *unite*
joist 47.10 *carpenter's term*, 47.12 *wood*, 47.17 *carpenter*, 63.27 *superstructure*, 225.3 *stabilizer*
joisted 47.16 *joined*
jojoba 85 *Trees and Shrubs*
jo kata 26.10 *aikido*
joke 771, 798, 506.2 *solecism*, 506.6 *talk nonsense*, 539.11 *hoax*, 612.8 *trifle*, 656.10 *unskilled person*, 771.13 *be humorous*, 799.2 *act of derision*, 850.9 *butt*
joker 42.3 *card game terms*, 401.2 *male*, 506.4 *buffoon*, 539.8 *trick*, 661.2 *obstacle*, 771.6 *humorist*, 799.3 *derider*
joker in the pack 335.19 *deviant person*
jokesmith 51.24 *dramatist*, 771.6 *humorist*
joke writer 51.24 *dramatist*
jokey 771.10 *humorous*
jokiness 771.1 *humorousness*
joking 771.3 *wit*, 771.10 *humorous*
jokingly 771
jollification 773.1 *rejoicing*, 812.1 *celebration*
jolliness 773.1 *rejoicing*
jollity 769.3 *cheerfulness*, 812.1 *celebration*, 815.1 *sociability*
jolly 44.6 *ceramic workshop*, 44.10 *ceramic*, 679.28 *marines*, 769.1 *cheerful*, 773.9 *rejoicing*, 815.15 *sociable*
jolly a cup 44.11 *make ceramics*
jolly along 769.6 *bring cheer*
jolly boat 74 Ships and Boats, **74** Sailing Ships and Boats
Jolly Roger 544.7 *flag*
jolt 366, 366, 228.9 *motivate*, 241.9 *make violent*, 330.1 *impel*, 330.2 *collide*, 330.12 *collision*, 330.13 *blow*, 339.3 *jerk*, 339.13 *pull at*, 375.11 *be rough*, 514.3 *shock*, 514.9 *surprise*
joltiness 160.1 *discontinuity*, 366.3 *turbulence*, 375.6 *roughness*
jolting 366.19 *convulsive*, 375.4 *bumpy*
jolty 160.8 *discontinuous*, 366.19 *convulsive*
Joly steam calorimeter 56 Named Laws
Jonah 770.4 *depressing person*
jones 875.4 *drug taker*
Jones 18 Sporting Personalities
jongleur 48.14 *author*, 51.27 *entertainer*

jonquil 84 Flowers and Flowering Plants
Jonson 48 Poets, **48** Dramatists
Jonsonian comedy 51.10 *comedy*
Jophiel 8.6 *angel*
Jordan 91 Countries, **96** Rivers, 96.5 *other major rivers*
Jorojin 8 Deities
Joselito 18 Sporting Personalities
Joseph's coat 456.5 *variegated thing*
Josephson 52 Scientists
Joseph Surface 538.12 *cheat*, 539.19 *hypocrite*
josh 771.13 *be humorous*
joshing 771.3 *wit*
Joshua tree 85 Trees and Shrubs
joss 9.3 *idol*
joss stick 418.3 *incense*
jostle 267.4 *meet*, 330.1 *impel*, 330.13 *blow*, 366.9, 366.23 *jolt*, 674.12 *fight*, 850.22 *show disrespect*
jostling crowd 642.6 *business*
jo suburi 26.10 *aikido*
jot 173.3 *fragment*, 260.3 *little piece*, 542.6 *suggestion*, 545.14 *inscribe*, 612.8 *trifle*
jot down 545.14 *inscribe*
jotter 545.6 *record book*
jottings 545.3 *notes*
Jo-Uk 8 Deities
joule 75 SI Units, **75** Scientific and Technical Units, 235.5 *unit of work*, 408.2 *heat measurement*
Joule 52 Scientists
Joule–Kelvin 56 Named Laws
Joule's laws 56 Named Laws
jounce 366.9, 366.23 *jolt*
journal 532, 3.5 *chronicle*, 48.4 *non-fiction*, 63.8 *machine element*, 171.4 *bill*, 187.7 *periodical*, 192.2 *timetable*, 364.4 *vortex*, 545.6 *record book*, 560.3 *narration*, 560.4 *factual account*, 750.5 *account book*
journal box 364.4 *vortex*
journalese 5.20 *jargon word*, 533.9 *news story*
journalism 532, 528.4 *mass communication*, 533.1 *news*, 560.4 *factual account*
journalist 533, 293.18 *fixer*, 465.3 *curious person*, 477.9 *questioner*, 524.7 *news interpreter*, 528.9 *informant*, 532.11 *newspaper man*, 545.9 *recorder*, 560.10 *descriptive writer*, 561.3 *dissertator*, 646.1 *worker*
journalistic 533, 5.39 *of language*, 477.15 *sceptical*
journalistically 533, 5.49 *colloquially*
journalize 750.7 *account*
journals 528.4 *mass communication*
journey 356.1 *passage*, 356.9 *proceed*
journeyman 191 Timepieces and Timers, 646.2 *artisan*
journey's end 157.6 *end point*, 325.3 *resting place*, 344.15 *destination*
journeywork 644.1 *work*
journo 533.4 *journalist*
joust 674.9 *duel*, 679.37 *fight*
jouster 679.3 *athlete*
jousting 674.9 *duel*
jousting armour 671.7 *armour*
joust with 674.12 *contend*
jovial 769.1 *cheerful*, 815.15 *sociable*
JOVIAL 65 Programming Languages
joviality 769.3 *cheerfulness*, 815.1 *sociability*
Jovian 53.36 *astronomical*
Jovian planet 53.16 *planet*
jowl 305.1 *side*
joy 762
Joyce 48 Writers
joyful 762.4 *happy*, 769.1 *cheer-*

-ful, 773.9 *rejoicing*
joyfully 762, 769.9 *cheerfully*, 773.11 *rejoicingly*
joyfulness 762.1 *happiness*, 773.1 *rejoicing*
joyful person 762
joyless 770.6 *depressed*
joylessly 770
joylessness 770.2 *depression*
joyous 762.4 *happy*, 815.17 *festive*
joyously 815.18 *sociably*
joyousness 762.1 *happiness*
joyride 736.6 *illegal borrowing*, 736.15 *infringe*
joy-ride 733.9 *borrow illegally*
joyrider 736.10 *infringer*
joyriding 733.3, 736.6 *illegal borrowing*, 736.18 *fraudulent*
joystick 73 Aircraft Parts, 65.7 *peripheral*, 653.5 *guide*
J. Paul Getty Museum 43 Noted Buildings
J stroke 36.6 *canoeing*
Juárez 93 Cities
Juba 96 Rivers
jubbah 295.16 *robe*
jubilant 762.4 *happy*, 773.9 *rejoicing*
jubilantly 773.11 *rejoicingly*
jubilate 773.5 *rejoice*, 812.16 *commemorate*
Jubilate Deo 10.8 *hymn*
jubilation 773.1 *rejoicing*, 812.1 *celebration*
jubilee 179.8 *twenty and over*, 214.6 *annually celebrated day*, 773.1 *rejoicing*, 812.1 *celebration*, 812.2 *commemoration*, 812.5 *anniversary*
Jubilee Indian Game 68 Breeds of Fowl
jubilize 812.16 *commemorate*
Judaeo-Christian 7.16 *denominational*
Judaic 7.16 *denominational*
Judaize 7.20 *preach*
Judas 539.21 *traitor*, 578.9 *equivocator*, 832.8 *malefactor*, 858.4 *dishonourable person*, 864.9 *wicked person*
Judas Iscariot 539.21 *traitor*, 540.15 *false person*
Judas kiss 538.7 *duplicity*, 540.5 *deceitfulness*, 858.2 *faithlessness*
Judas tree 85 Trees and Shrubs
judas-window 435.9 *viewpoint*
judder 71.21 *miscellaneous motoring terms*, 366.7 *shake*, 366.9, 366.23 *jolt*, 366.24 *shake*
juddering 366.6 *shaking*, 366.18 *shaky*
Judeophobia 777 Phobias by Name
judge 16, 16, 492, 492, 4.22 *propound a philosophy*, 6.24 *know*, 16.10 *law officer*, 16.13 *lawyer*, 16.69 *have jurisdiction over*, 16.71 *try a case*, 21.3 *athlete*, 26.8 *karate*, 26.9 *tae kwon do*, 31.6 *lacrosse player*, 136.8 *person who separates*, 166.13 *rule*, 185.16 *time*, 242.2 *moderator*, 242.4 *moderate*, 463.11 *reason*, 481.6 *discriminating person*, 481.12 *discriminate*, 482.10 *impartial person*, 492.6 *justice*, 492.12 *estimate*, 507.1 *be wise*, 524.8 *interpret*, 580.1 *select*, 654.4 *adviser*, 678.1 *mediate*, 678.3 *mediator*, 688.10 *person of authority*, 692.6 *person in command*, 692.11 *have authority over*, 696.3 *leader*, 699.6 *law-maker*, 859.3 *impartial person*, 879.17 *punisher*
judge advocate 16.10 *law officer*, 492.6 *justice*
judge advocate general 16.23 *judge*, 492.6 *justice*
judge and jury 16.18 *tribunal*
judge by eye 492.12 *estimate*
judged 481, 492
Judge Jeffreys 16.23 *judge*
Judge Roy Bean 16.23 *judge*
judgeship 688.5 *position of au-*

-thority
judging 492, 492.1 *judgment*
judgingly 16.81 *legally*
judgment 492, 4.1 *philosophy*, 6.11 *refinement*, 16.7 *legal trial*, 16.33 *litigation*, 16.43 *conviction*, 459.3 *intelligence*, 463.1 *reason*, 481.2 *judiciousness*, 492.2 *verdict*, 497.1 *belief*, 507.1 *wisdom*, 524.1 *interpretation*, 580.6 *selection*, 588.4 *formulated intention*, 653.3 *management*, 654.3 *precept*, 678.2 *mediation*, 879.9 *retribution*
Judgment 492
judgment according to the law 16.33 *litigation*
judgmental 463.7 *reasoning*, 492.8 *judging*, 852.29 *blaming*
judgmentally 4.29 *wisely*, 6.27 *discerningly*, 481.16 *judiciously*, 678.7 *mediatorially*
judgment day 492
Judgment Day 16.18 *tribunal*, 199.3 *future condition*
judgment seat 16.18 *tribunal*, 16.27 *courtroom*, 492.3 *place of judgment*
judicative 16.49 *judicatory*
judicatorial 16.48 *jurisdictional*, 16.49 *judicatory*
judicatory 16, 16.18 *tribunal*, 16.48 *jurisdictional*, 492.9 *judicious*
judicature 16.2 *jurisdiction*
judicial 16.49 *judicatory*, 492.9 *judicious*, 653.17 *managerial*
judicial assembly 16.18 *tribunal*
judicially 492, 16.81 *legally*
judicial murder 398.5 *execution*, 879.13 *capital punishment*
judicial oath 535.3 *vow*
judicial officer 653.16 *official*
judicial separation 824.2 *separation*
judiciary 16.23 *judge*, 16.48 *jurisdictional*
judicious 492, 4.15 *rational*, 6.20 *refined*, 16.49 *judicatory*, 242.6 *moderate*, 459.11 *thoughtful*, 481.9 *discriminating*, 507.5 *wise*, 615.1 *convenient*, 654.8 *advisable*, 781.4 *cautious*
judiciously 481, 4.29 *wisely*, 6.27 *discerningly*, 242.9 *moderately*, 459.15 *intelligently*, 492.13 *judicially*, 507.9 *wisely*, 654.9 *advisably*, 781.7 *cautiously*
judiciousness 481, 242.1 *moderation*, 459.6 *thoughtfulness*, 507.1 *wisdom*, 781.1 *caution*
judo 18 Sporting Activities, **26,** 26.1 *combat sports*, 26.15 *wrestling*, 671.5 *self-defence*, 674.8 *wrestling*
judo club 26.7 *judo*
judo grade 26.7 *judo*
judoist 26.7 *judo*, 679.3 *athlete*
judoka 26.7 *judo*
judo kata 26.7 *judo*
judo mat 26.7 *judo*
judo match 26.7 *judo*
judo practitioner 26.7 *judo*
judo referee 26.7 *judo*
judo technique 26.7 *judo*
jug 44.8 *ceramic object*, 258.11 *vessel*, 389.16 *water carrier*, 702.2 *the inside ,* 702.9 *imprison*
jug-eared 420.12 *eared*
jug ears 420.4 *ear*
Jugendstil 50 Western Art Styles and Movements
juggernaut 71 Motor Vehicles, 244.7 *agent of destruction*, 326.5 *means of transport*
Juggernaut 9.3 *idol*
juggle 539, 474.11 *practise sophistry*, 540.21 *be fraudulent*, 657.5 *be cunning*
juggled 539.40 *illusory*
juggled figures 540.8 *fraud*
juggler 51.29 *circus performer*, 657.3 *cunning person*
jugglery 539.9 *sleight of hand*, 657.1 *cunning*
juggling 539.9 *sleight of hand*,

540.9 *falsification*
jug kettle 258.15 *pot*
juice 387, 56.51, 64.9 *electric current*, 355.8 *extract*, 874.12 *alcohol*
juiced 874.3 *dead drunk*
juice extractor 355.9 *extractor*, 387.11 *liquidizer*
juice head 874.17 *drunkard*
juiceless 392.3 *dried-up*
juice of the grape 351.9 *wine*
juicer 45.6 *kitchen equipment*
juicily 387.26 *fluidly*
juiciness 387, 206.2 *youthfulness*, 387.5 *fluidity*, 393.4 *pulpiness*
juicy 393, 203.10 *spring*, 374.4 *compressible*, 387.15 *flowing*, 405.6 *pleasant*, 617.1 *worthy*, 763.4 *tasty*
juicy part 51.21 *role*
jujitsu 674.8 *wrestling*
jujitsuist 679.3 *athlete*
juju 10.14 *sacred object*, 11.6 *talisman*
jujube 86 Fruits, 45.41 *sweet*
jujuism 11.3 *witchcraft*
juke house 877.6 *brothel*
julep 351.6 *soft drink*, 351.8 *mixed drink*
Jules Verne 53 Lunar Features
Julian calendar 185.13 *timer*, 192.3 *chronology*
Julia set 52 Named Concepts
julienne 45.13 *soup*
Juliet 534 Phonetic Alphabet
Juliet cap 295.15 *headgear*
Julius Caesar 48 Shakespeare's plays
jumble 113.8 *be diverse*, 132.2 *residue*, 133.1 *mixture*, 133.3 *miscellany*, 133.9 *mix up*, 151.4 *litter*, 151.5 *confusion*, 151.21 *disorder*, 161.32 *miscellany*, 307.4 *disorder*, 482.8 *indiscriminateness*, 482.11 *not discriminate*, 628.1 *impair*, 727.3 *disposable things*, 754.5 *cheap item*
jumbled 133.12 *mixed*, 133.13 *mixed-up*, 151.12 *disordered*, 151.18 *muddled*, 482.3 *indiscriminate*, 659.12 *problematic*
jumble sale 727.2 *disposal of property*, 739.4 *sale*, 740.10 *bazaar*, 752.2 *bargain*, 754.7 *discounter*
jumbo 70.5 *transportable*, 259.9 *big thing*, 259.15 *big*
jumbo jet 73 Types of Aircraft
Jumna 96 Rivers
jump 21, 359, 359, 21.2 *field events*, 28.3 *fencing movements*, 30.6 *pommel horse*, 30.8 *floor exercises*, 30.10 *compete in gymnastics*, 32.16 *ride*, 35.5 *play rugby*, 41.1 *skiing*, 41.6 *ice-skating*, 41.12 *ski*, 41.15 *ice-skate*, 126.3 *advantage*, 128.2 *spread*, 265.1 *interval*, 324.12 *gait*, 329.4 *be swift*, 329.9 *acceleration*, 336.13 *step*, 357.7 *crossing*, 366.9 *jolt*, 366.21 *be agitated*, 366.23 *jolt*, 514.3 *shock*, 514.12 *be surprised*, 670.5 *strike*, 674.4 *race*
jump about 366.21 *be agitated*
jump ahead 329.6 *accelerate*
jump at 572.13 *be willing*, 590.10 *chase*
jump at the bidding of 808.11 *pander to*
jump at the chance 208.11 *get ahead*, 499.4 *assent*
jump a wave 36.18 *windsurf*
jump bail 591.8 *run away*, 638.5 *escape*
jump ball 23.4 *playing terms*
jump down one's throat 828.13 *vent one's anger*
jump down someone's throat 829.6 *be irascible*
jumped ball 24.6 *pool*
jumped ship 254.11 *truant*
jumper 21.3 *athlete*, 32.2 *thoroughbred*, 35.4 *rugby player*, 46.5 *dancer*, 71.10 *sled*, 295.7 *frock*, 295.13 *sweater*

jumpers 295.23 *children's clothes*
Jumpers 7 Christian Movements
jump forward 28.5 *fence*
jump from a high place 398.21 *commit suicide*
jump from the frying pan into the fire 628.1 *deteriorate*
jump higher 721.10 *augment*
jump in 39.10 *dive*, 359.15 *mount*
jumpiness 366.1 *agitation*, 576.13 *timidity*, 642.7 *restlessness*
jumping 32, 21.2 *field events*, 21.6 *track*, 30.6 *pommel horse*, 30.8 *floor exercises*, 32.17 *equine*, 359.24 *leaping*, 366.19 *convulsive*
jumping at the chance 208.6 *getting ahead*
jumping from a high place 398.7 *suicide*
jumping jack 377.3 *elastic thing*, 439.8 *fire*
jumping lane 32.9 *jumping*
jumping mouse 77 Placental Mammals
jumping-off place 93.10 *village*
jumping-off point 345.10 *place of departure*
jumping with 144.8 *full*
jump in the middle of 678.1 *mediate*
jump in time 160.3 *interval*
jump jet 73 Types of Aircraft, 679.31 *military aircraft*
jump jockey 32.15 *horse person*
jump leads 71 Motor Vehicle Parts
jump-off 32.9 *jumping*, 156.11 *starting point*
jump on 345.5 *set out*
jump on the band wagon 116.25 *conform*
jump on the bandwagon 167.8 *comply*, 499.5 *assent to*, 578.3 *apostatize*, 808.14 *follow*
jump out 347.10 *emerge*
jump out of one's skin 514.12 *be surprised*, 777.11 *be afraid*
jump overboard 398.21 *commit suicide*
jumps 32.7 *horseracing*
jump seat 71 Motor Vehicle Parts
jump ship 254.18 *abscond*, 576.9 *change sides*, 578.3 *apostatize*
jump shot 23.4 *playing terms*
jump suit 295.10 *suit*
jump the gun 193.3 *mistime*, 208.7 *be early*, 208.10 *hasten*
jump the queue 194.9 *do before*
jump the wall 700.5 *be liberated*
jump to it 208.10 *hasten*, 642.14 *push*
jump to one's feet 361.5 *arise*
jump turn 41.4 *skiing technique*
jump up 359.17 *spring up*, 361.5 *arise*
jumpy 366.19 *convulsive*, 403.7 *susceptible*, 576.3 *timid*, 642.18 *active*, 760.2 *oversensitive*, 777.8 *fearful*, 829.4 *irascible*
juncaceous 83.16 *taxonomic*
junco 78 Birds
junction 135.1 *union*, 135.5 *joint*, 135.6 *point of union*, 137.4 *means of connection*, 161.1 *assembly*, 267.1 *juxtaposition*, 310.1 *angle*, 327.10 *railway*, 342.4 *meeting place*, 344.15 *destination*, 356.5 *crossing point*, 407.6 *contiguity*
junction box 135.6 *point of union*, 235.7 *electrical power*
juncture 106.2 *occurrence*, 121.4 *interval*, 135.5 *joint*, 135.6 *point of union*, 185.11 *date*, 191.4 *point in time*, 251.2 *circumstances*, 264.1 *nearness*
Juneau 93 Cities
June beetle 82 Insects
Jung 61.29 *psychologist*
Jungfrau 95 Mountains
Jungian 61.33 *Freudian*
Jungian psychology 61.1 *psychol-*

ogy
jungle 83.1 *plants*, 85.4 *trees*, 151.7 *tangle*, 408.8 *hot place*
jungle fowl 78 Birds
jungle green 453.1 *green*
jungle telegraph 420.8 *something heard*
jungle warfare 676.8 *warfare*
junior 127.6 *inferior*, 127.15 *subordinate*, 206.6 *young person*, 206.11 *young*, 701.4 *dependent*, 701.9 *subject*
junior chamber of commerce 13.7 *corporation*, 737.5 *commercial trade*
junior chamber of commerce member 13.9 *economist*, 737.11 *chamber of commerce member*
junior high 6.12 *educational institution*
juniority 701.1 *subjection*
junior judo 26.7 *judo*
junior-lightweight 26.3 *boxing weight divisions*, 26.14 *combat*
junior minister 12.8 *politician*, 653.16 *official*
junior officer 17.5 *military staff*
junior rank 701.1 *subjection*
junior school 6.12 *educational institution*
junior technician 679.32 *airman*
juniper 85 Trees and Shrubs, 413.5 *herbs*
juniper berries 45 Herbs and Spices
junk 74 Sailing Ships and Boats, 132.2 *residue*, 349.13 *throw away*, 521.5 *empty talk*, 540.10 *fake*, 581.2 *discard*, 598.1 *relinquish*, 600.6 *stop using*, 614.6 *refuse*, 618.8 *inferiority*, 727.3 *disposable things*, 754.5 *cheap item*, 875.6 *drug*
junk art 50 Western Art Styles and Movements
junked 600.4 *disused*
Junkers 52 Scientists
junket 350.13 *feast*, 393.8 *pulp*, 812.15 *celebrate*
junk food 350.7 *food*
junkie 875.4 *drug taker*
junk mail 528.4 *mass communication*
junkman 727.6 *rubbish collector*, 739.11 *pedlar*
junk pile 727.5 *wasteyard*
junk room 256.7 *room*
junk sale 739.4 *sale*
junk shop 754.7 *discounter*
junky 540.33 *fake*, 618.2 *inferior*
junkyard 727.5 *wasteyard*
Juno 8 Deities, **53** Minor Planets, 823.14 *gods and goddesses of marriage*
Junoesque 789.5 *beautiful*
junta 161.16 *party*, 665.3 *political grouping*
jun-zuki 26.8 *karate*
Jupiter 8 Deities, **53** Planets and their Satellites, 53.16 *planet*
Jura 95 Mountains
jural 16.49 *judicatory*
jurally 16.81 *legally*
Jurassic 54 Geological Time Intervals
Jurassic period 200.3 *geological period*
jurat 16.26 *jury*
juridical 16.48 *jurisdictional*, 492.9 *judicious*
jurisdiction 16, 16.6 *legal process*, 16.33 *litigation*, 126.2 *leadership*, 249.14 *sphere*, 688.4 *governance*
jurisdictional 16, 16.49 *judicatory*, 688.14 *governmental*
jurisdictionally 16, 16.81 *legally*
jurisdictive 16.48 *jurisdictional*, 16.49 *judicatory*
jurisprudence 16, 166.2 *canon*
jurisprudential 16.45 *legislative*, 16.49 *judicatory*
jurisprudently 16.81 *legally*
jurist 16.13 *lawyer*, 16.26 *jury*, 463.6 *arguer*, 492.5 *judge*
juristically 16.81 *legally*

juror 16.26, 492.7 *jury*
juror's panel 16.26 *jury*
Juruá 96 Rivers
Jurupari 8 Deities
jury 16, 492, 16.13 *lawyer*, 26.9 *tae kwon do*, 36.10 *sailing*, 492.5 *judge*, 492.7 *jury*
jury box 16.27 *courtroom*, 492.3 *place of judgment*
jury list 16.26, 492.7 *jury*, 545.1 *record*
jury man 16.26 *jury*
juryman 492.7 *jury*
jury mast 632.4 *safety device*
jury member 859.3 *impartial person*
jury panel 16.26 *jury*
jury poll 580.10 *vote*
jury rig 36.3 *parts of a sailing boat*, 632.4 *safety device*
jury-rig 36.15 *sail*
jury-rigged 583.1 *improvised*
jurywoman 492.7 *jury*
jus canonicum 16.1 *the law*
jus gentium 16.1 *the law*
jus naturale 16.1 *the law*
jussive 5.33 *mood*
just 16.44 *legal*, 122.6 *equal*, 201.21 *newly*, 242.6 *moderate*, 492.9 *judicious*, 503.8 *accurately*, 507.5 *wise*, 698.9 *free*, 783.9 *impartial*, 843.7 *right*, 845.8 *entitled*, 857.4 *honourable*, 859.4 *disinterested*, 863.6 *ethical*, 876.8 *moral*
just a bit 121.10 *by degrees*
just about 124.11 *on average*, 264.7 *nearly*
just a few 182.1 *few*
just a minute 189.3 *short duration*
just around the corner 264.6 *near*
just as 114.13 *similarly*, 198.15 *as*
just a second 189.3 *short duration*
just as one thought 787.4 *predictable*
just as one would wish 619.7 *perfectly*
just a tick 189.3 *short duration*
just before 194.11 *before*
just caught 424.4 *faint*
just cause 855.2 *defence*
just deserts 672.1 *retaliation*, 845.2 *due*, 878.1 *reward*, 879.9 *retribution*
just do 608.4 *suffice*
just enough 608.9 *enough*
just happen 580.10 *chance*
just heard 424.4 *faint*
just here 250.12 *where*
justice 777 Phobias by Topic, **492**, 16.23 *judge*, 16.28 *legality*, 16.33 *litigation*, 109.1 *interchange*, 110.5, 122.1 *equality*, 242.1 *moderation*, 482.7 *impartiality*, 672.1 *retaliation*, 696.3 *leader*, 783.3 *impartiality*, 843.1 *fairness*, 857.1 *probity*, 859.1 *disinterestedness*, 863.2 *virtues*, 876.2 *good morals*, 878.1 *reward*, 879.9 *retribution*
Justice Department 16.2 *jurisdiction*
justice of the peace 16.10 *law officer*, 16.23 *judge*, 492.6 *justice*, 653.16 *official*, 688.10 *person of authority*, 696.3 *leader*
justice seen to be done 16.7 *legal trial*
justiceship 16.23 *judge*
justice under the law 16.33 *litigation*
justiciable 16.47 *liable to law*, 16.48 *jurisdictional*, 16.54 *litigated*, 16.58 *unjust*
justiciary 16.23 *judge*, 16.48 *jurisdictional*, 16.49 *judicatory*, 879.17 *punisher*
justifiable 473.12 *apologetic*, 843.9 *in the right*, 855.13 *vindicable*
justifiable homicide 16.39 *crime*
justifiably 4.26 *rationally*, 473.20 *apologetically*, 475.22 *demonstrably*, 845.21 *deservedly*

560.15 *recount*
keep private 816.13 *ignore*
keep quiet 325.8 *be motionless*, 422.1 *be silent*, 527.12 *be latent*, 527.13 *hide*, 563.13 *be voiceless*, 566.8 *be taciturn*, 641.4 *not act*, 673.3 *submit*, 699.10 *restrain oneself*
keep running 637.5 *preserve*
keep safe 632.9 *protect*, 637.5 *preserve*
keep safe and sound 718.10 *secure*
keepsake 511.3, 681.3 *memento*, 729.2 *gift*
keep score 171.10 *score*
keep secret 529, 726.7 *detain*
keep shtoom 563.13 *be voiceless*, 566.8 *be taciturn*
keep sight of 437.10 *make visible*
keep silent 422.1 *be silent*
keep smiling 775.9 *be hopeful*
keep someone guessing 491.20 *make uncertain*
keep stable 225.7 *make stable*
keep steadfast 857.6 *be honourable*
keep-stepped mast 36.3 *parts of a sailing boat*
keep still 325.8 *be motionless*
keep stored away 600.5 *not use*
keep straight 863.8 *be virtuous*
keep supplied 606.5 *provision*
keep sweet 242.4 *moderate*
keep tabs on 469.11 *care for*, 544.10 *identify*, 781.5 *be cautious*
keep the ball in play 219.3 *continue*
keep the ball rolling 219.3 *continue*, 575.7 *maintain*
keep the books 750.7 *account*
keep the faith 694.6 *show obeisance to*
keep the field 676.13 *be at war*
keep the golden mean 333.7 *be halfway*, 869.6 *moderate*
keep the law 694.5 *obey*
keep the nose down 332.7 *take a direction*
keep the peace 242.3 *be moderate*, 667.7 *contract*, 675.5 *be at peace*, 677.4 *pacify*
keep the pot boiling 219.3 *continue*, 575.7 *maintain*, 642.13 *be busy*
keep the proper observance 719.4 *observe*
keep the same beat 198.7 *synchronize*
keep the score 170.8 *calculate*
keep the wolf from the door 396.20 *support life*, 721.12 *earn*
keep things moving 219.3 *continue*
keep time 192, 185.16 *time*, 192.16 *measure time*
keep time with 180.13 *accompany*, 198.7 *synchronize*
keep together 664.13 *work together*
keep to mid-stream 333.6 *be in the middle*
keep to oneself 529.12 *keep secret*, 726.7 *detain*, 816.12 *be unsocial*
keep to one side 726.7 *detain*
keep to the circumference 334.3 *circuit*
keep to the middle 333.6 *be in the middle*
keep to the middle way 869.6 *moderate*
keep to the point 312.11 *be straight*
keep to the spirit of 719.4 *observe*
keep to the straight and narrow 134.9 *be pure*, 857.6 *be honourable*
keep to the straight and narrow path 863.8 *be virtuous*
keep under 362.5 *bear down on*
keep under cover 293.31 *hide*, 632.9 *protect*, 637.5 *preserve*
keep under lock and key 699.11 *detain*, 718.10 *secure*
keep under observation 435.15

watch
keep under one's hat 529.12 *keep secret*
keep under one's thumb 701.6 *subject*
keep under wraps 529.12 *keep secret*, 531.8 *conceal*
keep up 217.6 *make permanent*, 219.3 *continue*, 575.7 *maintain*, 637.5 *preserve*
keep up the good work 219.8 *go on*
keep up with 122.10 *be equal*, 815.12 *visit*
keep up with the Joneses 167.8 *comply*, 815.11 *be sociable*
keep warm 408.16 *feel hot*
keep watertight 392.22 *keep dry*
keep well 623.5 *be healthy*
keep wicket 27.16 *field*
keep within bounds 242.4 *moderate*, 699.8 *restrain*, 869.6 *moderate*
keep within limits 242.4 *moderate*
keep within the law 16.67 *follow the law*
keep your distance 591.24 *hands off*
keeshond 77 *Breeds of Dogs*
kef 875.6 *drug*
kefta 45.52 *Greek dish*
keg 258.11 *vessel*
keg beer 351.7 *alcoholic drink*
Kegon 7 *Non-Christian Religions*
keister Gary Glitter 304.2 *rear end*
Kekulé structure 57 *Named Reactions*
Kekulé von Stradonitz 52 *Scientists*
Kells 93 *Cities*
kelontong 49 *Musical Instruments*
kelp 90 *Algae*, 90.1 *alga*
kelpie 77 *Breeds of Dogs*
Kelpie 8 *Deities*
Kelso 93 *Cities*
kelvin 75 *SI Units*, 75 *Scientific and Technical Units*
Kelvin 52 *Scientists*
Kelvin scale 75.3 *scale*
kemanak 49 *Musical Instruments*
kempt 150.13 *orderly*
ken 501.1 *knowledge*, 501.11 *know*, 522.7 *recognize*
kena 49 *Musical Instruments*
Kendall 52 *Scientists*
kendo 18 *Sporting Activities*, 674.9 *duel*
Kendrew 52 *Scientists*
kenipo 18 *Sporting Activities*
kennel 161 *Collective Names for Birds and Animals*, 161.23 *flock*, 256.12 *stall*, 323.4 *closed place*, 323.10 *enclose*
kennel huntsman 32.15 *horse person*
Kennelly 52 *Scientists*
kennel man 32.15 *horse person*
kennels 634.3 *animal shelter*
kenning 48.12 *poetic language*
ken no kamae 26.10 *aikido*
Kenny 4 *Philosophers*
keno 42 *Card Games*
kenong 49 *Musical Instruments*
kenophobia 777 *Phobias by Name*
kenosis 806.9 *humiliation*
Kensington 93.5 *London*
ken suburi 26.10 *aikido*
Kent 92 *Counties*
Kent mental test 61.6 *intelligence test*
Kentucky 92 *American States*
Kentucky bluegrass 87 *Grasses*
Kentucky coffee tree 85 *Trees and Shrubs*
Kentucky Derby 32.7 *horseracing*
Kentucky Fried Chicken 45.43 *US dish*
Kenya 91 *Countries*, 95 *Mountains*
kepi 295.15 *headgear*
Kepler 52 *Scientists*, 53 *Lunar Features*
Keplerian telescope 53.24 *tele-*

scope
Kepler's laws 56 *Named Laws*, 53.14 *solar system*
Kepler's star 53 *Named Stars*
kept 637.7 *preserved*, 726.10 *retained*
kept back 711.8 *refused*
kept by 605.7 *stored*
kept in 726.10 *retained*
kept on a lead 699.13 *restraining*
kept quiet 527.2 *concealed*
kept under constraint 699.13 *restraining*
kept woman 402.4 *girlfriend*, 821.11 *loved one*, 877.9 *immoral woman*
kerar 49 *Musical Instruments*
keratectomy 60 *Surgical Operations*
keratin 58.9 *protein*, 382.7 *skeleton*
keratoplasty 60 *Surgical Operations*
keratotomy 60 *Surgical Operations*
keraunophobia 777 *Phobias by Name*
kerb 300.1 *edge*, 327.4 *road surface*
kerb crawling 877.5 *prostitution*
kerb market 740.3 *sellers' market*
kerbside parking 356.2 *passing along*
kerbstone 327.4 *road surface*
kerchief 295.14 *neckwear*
kerf 319.1, 319.5 *notch*
kermes 85 *Tree Products*, 450.6 *red pigment*
kern 679.8 *soldier*
kernel 83.9 *seed*, 86.3 *fruit structure*, 103.2 *essential content*, 158.2 *core*, 257.3 *insides*, 291.1 *centre*, 611.3 *chief thing*
kernels 86.1 *fruits*
kernite 54 *Minerals*
kernmantel rope 34.4 *climbing equipment*
kerosene 395.9 *petroleum*
Kerouac 48 *Writers*
kerplunk 332.9 *directly*
Kerr effect 56 *Named Laws*
Kerry 68 *Breeds of Cattle*, 92 *Counties*
Kerry blue terrier 77 *Breeds of Dogs*
Kerry Hill 68 *Breeds of Sheep*
Kesey 48 *Writers*
kestrel 78 *Birds*, 78.5 *bird of prey*
ketal 57 *Types of Compounds*
ketch 74 *Sailing Ships and Boats*
ketchup 413.2 *seasoning*
ketohexose 57 *Types of Compounds*, 58.3 *carbohydrate*
ketone 57 *Types of Compounds*
ketooctose 58.3 *carbohydrate*
ketopentose 57 *Types of Compounds*, 58.3 *carbohydrate*
ketoprofen 62 *Medication*
ketose 57 *Types of Compounds*, 58.3 *carbohydrate*
ketotetrose 58.3 *carbohydrate*
ketotriose 58.3 *carbohydrate*
kettle 45.5 *cooker*, 258.15 *pot*, 408.4 *burner*
kettledrum 49 *Musical Instruments*
kettle of fish 251.2 *circumstances*
kevel 384.27 *beat*
Kew Gardens 69.2 *garden*
kewpie doll 878.2 *prize*
key 49, 98.2 *island*, 121.1 *degree*, 210.7 *critical*, 226.5 *reason*, 230.12 *operative*, 291.6 *central*, 291.8 *focal*, 322.2 *opener*, 524.1 *interpretation*, 524.4 *translation*, 543.1 *sign*, 611.5 *important*, 632.4 *safety device*
keyboard 49.16 *musical note*, 65.7 *peripheral*
keyboarder 545.9 *recorder*
keyboard instrument 49.25 *musical instrument*
key card 322.2 *opener*
key centre 49.21 *tone*
keyed up 594.18 *prepared*
key figure 291.5 *focus*

keyhole 322.5 *hole*
keyhole limpet 81 *Molluscs*
Keyhole Nebula 53 *Nebulae*
keyhole surgery 60.9 *surgery*
key man 655.5 *expert*
Keynes 4 *Philosophers*
Keyneseanism 4.7 *school of thought*
Keynesian 4.11 *follower of a doctrine*, 4.14 *of a philosophy*
Keynesian economics 13.1 *economics*
keynote 49.16 *musical note*, 166.4 *guide*, 472.1 *topic*, 611.3 *chief thing*
key person 611.4 *bigwig*, 653.15 *manager*
key point 210.3 *critical time*, 611.2 *important matter*
keys 49.16 *musical note*, 544.4 *insignia*
key signature 49.17 *notation*
keystone 103.2 *essential content*, 158.2 *core*, 279.3 *architectural summit*, 284.2 *supporting part*
keystone combination 22.2 *baseball player*
Key West 93 *Cities*, 98 *Islands*, 98.2 *island*
KGB 529.2 *secretiveness*
Khachaturian 49 *Musicians and Composers*
khaddar 288.4 *textile*
khaki 449.1 *brown*, 813.4 *formal dress*
Khaki Campbell 68 *Breeds of Fowl*
khakis 295.3 *formal dress*
khaki uniform 295.3 *formal dress*
Khalkha 5 *Languages and Groups of Languages*
khamsin 55 *Winds*
khan 696.2 *sovereign*
Khan 18 *Sporting Personalities*
Kharkov 93 *Cities*
Khartoum 93 *Cities*
Khasi 5 *Languages and Groups of Languages*
khazi 353.13 *lavatory*, 727.7 *toilet*
khen 49 *Musical Instruments*
Khensu 8 *Deities*
Khepera 8 *Deities*
Khillari 68 *Breeds of Cattle*
Khmer 1 *Peoples*, 5 *Languages and Groups of Languages*
Khnemu 8 *Deities*
Khoisan 1 *Peoples*, 5 *Languages and Groups of Languages*
Kholmogor 68 *Breeds of Cattle*
Khond 5 *Languages and Groups of Languages*, 7 *Non-Christian Religions*
Khors 8 *Deities*
Khoser-et-hasis 8 *Deities*
Khshathra Vairya 8.6 *angel*
Khulna 93 *Cities*
khumbgwe 49 *Musical Instruments*
kiaat 85 *Trees and Shrubs*
kiang 77 *Placental Mammals*
kibble 384.27 *beat*
kibbutz 68.6 *farm*, 724.1 *joint possession*
kibbutznik 68.15 *agriculturist*, 724.3 *participant*
kibe 624.15 *ulcer*
kibitzer 465.4, 642.11 *meddler*
kick 19, 330, 338, 26.5 *wrestling*, 26.12 *wrestle*, 35.3 *rugby play*, 35.5 *play rugby*, 38.2 *football play*, 38.4 *play soccer*, 39.2 *swimming technique*, 41.12 *ski*, 231.1 *counteraction*, 239.1 *vigour*, 330.13 *blow*, 331.1 *recoil*, 337.29 *in reverse*, 338.5 *throw*, 338.20 *propel*, 403.3 *stimulus*, 407.3 *press*, 407.11 *touch*, 413.1 *piquancy*, 528.7 *advice*, 543.3, 543.11 *gesture*, 581.5 *rejection*, 585.5 *disaccustom*, 598.1 *relinquish*, 642.1 *activity*, 663.15 *object*, 670.5 *strike*, 670.18 *hit*, 674.12 *fight*, 713.1, 713.6 *protest*, 762.2 *fun*
kick against the pricks 713.6 *protest*

kick-ahead 35.3 *rugby play*
Kickapoo 1 Peoples
kick around 701.6 *subject*
kick ass 670.5 *strike*, 676.13 *be at war*
kick at goal 35.3 *rugby play*
kick back 221.8 *return*
kickback 228.5 *positive stimulus*, 231.1 *counteraction*
kick back 231.3 *counteract*, 331.1 *recoil*
kickback 331.4 *recoil*, 478.4 *reaction*
kick back 478.19 *react*
kickback 586.10 *bribe*
kick back 672.3 *retaliate*
kickback 710.4 *illegal offer*, 729.2 *gift*, 878.8 *secret money*
kick boxing 18 Sporting Activities
kick downstairs 252.17 *relegate*, 349.3 *disbar*, 581.2 *discard*
kickean 42 Children's Games and Party Games
kicked 38.5 *soccer*
kicked around 701.9 *subject*
kicker 19.12 *special team*, 42.3 *card game terms*
kick in 729.5 *give*
kicking 19.19 *varsity*, 26.5, 26.15 *wrestling*, 38.2 *football play*, 38.5 *soccer*, 241.6 *violent*, 670.23 *attacking*
kicking against the pricks 713.1 *protest*
kicking ass 879.7 *punishment*
kicking downstairs 252.4 *relegation*
kicking out 349.17 *expulsion*
kicking strap 36.3 *parts of a sailing boat*
kicking team 19.12 *special team*
kicking tee 19.12 *special team*
kicking the ball 23.5 *penalties*
kicking upstairs 252.4 *relegation*
kick in the ass 652.8 *treatment*
kick in the pants 652.8 *treatment*
kick in the teeth 711.2 *dissent*
kick it 397.15 *die*
kickoff 19.12 *special team*
kick off 19.19 *kick*, 38.4 *play soccer*, 156.18 *make a beginning*, 338.33 *start*
kick-off 35.3 *rugby play*, 38.2 *football play*, 156.11 *starting point*
kick one's heels 209.7 *wait*, 641.4 *not act*, 643.12 *be inactive*
kick out 147.8 *eject*, 252.17 *relegate*, 349.1 *expel*, 349.2 *dismiss*, 581.2 *discard*, 727.10 *dismiss*
kick over 244.9 *demolish*
kick over the traces 168.18 *not conform*, 693.16 *be subversive*, 864.16 *be wicked*
kick pleat 295.24 *part of garment*
kickshaw 754.5 *cheap item*
kick someone in the teeth 711.6 *dissent*
kickstand 71.11 *bicycle part*
kick-start 156.20 *activate*
kickstool 359.10 *step*
kick the air 879.6 *be punished*
kick the ball 23.6 *play basketball*
kick the bucket 100.13 *cease to exist*, 397.15 *die*
kick the habit 591.3 *abstain*, 873.4 *give up alcohol*
kick turn 41.2 *cross-country skiing*, 41.4 *skiing technique*
kick under the table 528.7 *advice*, 543.3 *gesture*, 636.1 *warning*, 636.5 *warn*
kick up a fuss about 713.7 *complain*
kick up a row 151.26 *be disorderly*, 241.7 *be violent*, 666.6 *argue*, 828.11 *be angry*
kick up a shindy 423.8 *be loud*, 642.12 *be active*, 666.6 *argue*
kick up bobsy-die 666.6 *argue*
kick up dirt 828.11 *be angry*
kick up one's heels 762.6 *enjoy*
kick up shit 828.12 *become angry*
kick upstairs 252.17 *relegate*, 349.2 *dismiss*, 627.5 *improve-*

ment, 802.5 *make noble*
kick wheel 44.6 *ceramic workshop*
kid 68.8 *livestock*, 77.19 *young mammal*, 206.4 *young animal*, 206.6 *young person*, 206.7 *young man*, 206.9 *child*, 245.6 *progeny*, 293.14 *animal covering*, 539.28 *trick*, 771.13 *be humorous*
kidder 539.15 *deceiver*
kiddie 206.9 *child*
kidding 539.7 *tricking*, 771.3 *wit*
kid-glove 691.4 *lenient*
kid gloves 295.25 *accessories*, 652.8 *treatment*, 691.1 *leniency*
kidglove treatment 691.1 *leniency*
kidnap 736, 539.33 *snare*, 695.7 *force*, 699.11 *detain*, 734.10 *take away*, 866.10 *sin*
kidnapped 539.42 *trapped*, 699.15 *detained*, 736.17 *stolen*
kidnapper 695.4 *coercive person*, 699.6 *law-maker*, 734.6 *taker*, 736.8 *thief*, 862.6 *evil person*
kidnapping 736, 539.13 *snare*, 670.16 *terrorist attack*, 695.3 *coercive methods*, 699.4 *detention*, 734.3 *taking away*, 736.17 *stolen*
kidney 45.31 *offal*, 163.4 *type*, 290.4 *insides*, 560.6 *sort*
kidney bean 45 Vegetables
kidney donor 729.4 *giver*
kidney machine 630.14 *hospital*
kidney worm 81 Worms
kids 155.11 *progeny*, 206.10 *the young*
kid's stuff 660.6 *easy thing*
Kiel 93 Cities
Kierkegaard 4 Philosophers
Kierkegaardian 4.11 *follower of a doctrine*, 4.14 *of a philosophy*
kieserite 54 Minerals
Kiev 93 Cities
Kiho Tumi 8 Cities
kike 91 Names for Inhabitants
Kikuyu 1 Peoples, **5** Languages and Groups of Languages
Kilconnell 93 Cities
Kildare 92 Counties, **93** Cities
kilderkin 75 General Units
Kilimanjaro 95 Mountains, 95.6 *other major mountains and ranges*
Kilkenny 92 Counties, **93** Cities
kill 157, 398, 832, 37.7 *shoot*, 96.1 *river*, 100.14 *cause not to exist*, 131.4 *take off*, 218.8 *cause to cease*, 236.8 *overpower*, 244.8 *destroy*, 338.5 *throw*, 607.2 *lay waste*, 670.9 *attack successfully*, 676.13 *be at war*, 679.38 *conquer*, 704.6 *cancel*, 709.4 *censor*, 862.11 *be evil*, 879.5 *execute*
kill animals 398
Killarney 93 Cities
killdeer 78 Birds
killed 37.8 *shooting*, 397.19 *dead*, 704.10 *cancelled*
killed spirits 57 Common Chemical Compounds
killer 398, 42.6 *darts*, 244.6 *destroyer*, 398.11 *murderer*, 607.7 *destroyer*, 670.19 *attacker*, 679.1 *combatant*, 693.9 *criminal*, 832.8 *malefactor*, 861.17 *good thing*, 862.6 *evil person*, 864.9 *wicked person*
killer-diller 861.17 *good thing*
killer disease 624.4 *disease*
killer dog 398.10 *killer*
killer whale 77 Placental Mammals
killian 41.7 *ice-dancing*, 41.13 *ice-skating*
killian hold 41.7 *ice-dancing*
killick 632.4 *safety device*
killifish 80 Fishes
kill in cold blood 832.17 *kill*
killing 397, 398, 37.2 *hunting*, 244.2 *destroying*, 398.2 *deadly*, 618.5 *harmful*, 644.11 *laborious*, 682.1 *success*, 721.5 *profit*, 832.7 *act of malevolence*
Killing 398
killing field 676.10 *battleground*

killing fields 398.15 *slaughterhouse*, 674.6 *fight*
killing oneself 398.7 *suicide*
killjoy 242.2 *moderator*, 587.8 *cautionary person*, 641.2 *nonacting person*, 661.7 *hinderer*, 770.4 *depressing person*, 788.3 *boring person*, 852.13 *pessimist*
kill off 157.16 *cease*
kill oneself 397.16 *meet one's fate*, 398.21 *commit suicide*
kill ritually 398
kill the fatted calf 405.8 *feel pleasure*, 812.18 *salute*, 815.11 *be sociable*
kill the fatted calf for 773.6 *fête*
kill the goose that lays the golden eggs 656.6 *act foolishly*
kill time 641.4 *not act*, 643.12 *be inactive*
kill with kindness 628.5 *hurt*, 826.7 *show endearment for*
Kilmarnock 93 Cities
kiln 44.6 *ceramic workshop*, 392.19 *bake*, 408.6 *fire*
kilner jar 45.6 *kitchen equipment*, 258.11 *vessel*
kiln furniture 44.6 *ceramic workshop*
kilo 75 SI Units, **75** General Units, 179.10 *thousand*, 369.9 *avoirdupois weight*
Kilo 534 Phonetic Alphabet
kilobyte 65.17 *computing term*, 179.10 *thousand*
kilocalorie 408.2 *heat measurement*
kilocycle 75 Scientific and Technical Units
kilogram 75 SI Units, **75** Scientific and Technical Units, 179.10 *thousand*, 369.9 *avoirdupois weight*
kilogram calorie 75 Scientific and Technical Units
kilohertz 212.6 *radio frequency*
kilometre 179.10 *thousand*, 269.7 *measure of length*
kilometres per hour 329.8 *speed*
kiloton 75 Scientific and Technical Units
kilowatt 235.5 *unit of work*
kilowatt-hour 75 Scientific and Technical Units
kilt 295.3 *formal dress*, 295.6 *skirt*, 544.5 *uniform*
kilter 105.5 *physical state*
Kimberley 93 Cities
kimono 295.16 *robe*, 296.4 *dishabille*
kin 137.3 *associate*, 163.8 *genealogy*
kind 306, 861, 163.4 *type*, 374.6 *softhearted*, 560.5 *sort*, 617.4 *worthwhile*, 662.35 *benevolent*, 691.4 *lenient*, 763.2 *likable*, 817.7 *courteous*, 819.8 *friendly*, 821.17 *loving*, 831.6 *benevolent*, 833.6 *philanthropic*, 835.6 *pitying*, 839.5 *merciful*, 859.5 *unselfish*
kind act 831.4 *benevolent act*, 861.10 *kindness*
kind deed 831.4 *benevolent act*
kindergarten 6.12 *educational institution*
kindest regards 849.7 *respects*
kind-hearted 374.6 *softhearted*, 831.6 *benevolent*, 833.6 *philanthropic*, 835.6 *pitying*
kind-heartedly 831.10 *benevolently*, 833.8 *philanthropically*, 835.13 *pitifully*
kind-heartedness 831.1 *benevolence*, 833.1 *philanthropy*, 861.10 *kindness*
kindle 77.35 *give birth*, 226.10 *awaken*, 239.3 *invigorate*, 408.15 *burn*, 410.11 *toil*, 439.24 *light*, 828.12 *become angry*
kindliness 691.1 *leniency*, 763.8 *amiability*, 817.1 *courtesy*, 819.1 *friendship*, 831.1 *benevolence*, 861.10 *kindness*
kindling 85.3 *timber*, 410.2 *lighter*
kindly 284.9 *supportive*, 662.35

benevolent, 662.38 *benevolently*, 691.4 *lenient*, 691.6 *leniently*, 763.2 *likable*, 817.7 *courteous*, 817.14 *courteously*, 819.8 *friendly*, 819.17 *in friendship*, 821.30 *lovingly*, 831.10 *benevolently*, 833.6 *philanthropic*, 835.13 *pitifully*, 839.14 *forgivingly*, 859.9 *unselfishly*
kindly disposition 831.1 *benevolence*
kindness 861, 374.12 *gentleness*, 662.2 *support*, 662.10 *helpfulness*, 691.1 *leniency*, 815.1 *sociability*, 817.1 *courtesy*, 819.1 *friendship*, 821.3 *lovingness*, 831.1 *benevolence*, 831.4 *benevolent act*, 833.1 *philanthropy*, 835.1 *pity*, 839.2 *forgivingness*, 859.2 *unselfishness*
kind of 121.11 *to a degree*
kind offices 662.2 *support*
kind of number 169
kind person 729.4 *giver*, 784.4 *likable person*, 831.5 *benevolent person*, 833.3 *philanthropist*
kindred 107.4 *related*
kindred spirit 114.5 *counterpart*
kind regards 849.7 *respects*
kind remembrances 817.3 *courtesies*
kinematic 56.98 *physical*, 324.17 *directional*
kinematically 56.100 *physically*
kinematics 56.2 *classical physics*, 324.1 *motion*
kinesiatrics 324.1 *motion*
kinesics 543.3 *gesture*
kinesipathic 324.17 *directional*
kinesipathy 324.1 *motion*
kinesis 324.1 *motion*
kinesitherapy 324.1 *motion*
kinesodic 324.17 *directional*
kinetic 56.98 *physical*, 57.31 *chemical*, 228.11 *motivational*, 235.15 *full of energy*, 324.17 *directional*
kinetically 56.100 *physically*, 324.18 *in motion*
kinetic art 50 Western Art Styles and Movements, 50.1 *art*
kinetic energy 56.11, 235.4 *energy*, 324.1 *motion*
kineticist 57.2 *chemist*
kinetics 57.1 *chemistry*, 57.14 *chemical reaction*, 324.1 *motion*
kinetic sculpture 50.12 *sculpture*
kinetic theory 56.5 *theory*
kinetochore 59.14 *chromosome*
kinetophobia 777 Phobias by Name
kinetosome 59.8 *cell organ*
king 42.4 *chess terms*, 82.4 *social insect*, 126.5 *superior*, 688.10 *person of authority*, 696.2 *sovereign*
King 18 Sporting Personalities
kingbird 78 Birds
king bolt 72.7 *train*
King Charles spaniel 77 Breeds of Dogs
king cobra 79 Reptiles
kingcup 84 Flowers and Flowering Plants
kingdom 163, 12.5 *political organization*, 59.17 *taxonomy*, 91.3 *dominion*, 249.4 *territorial division*, 400.11 *nation*, 688.8 *governmental organization*
kingdom come 199.3 *future condition*
King Edward and Wallis Simpson 821.10 *lovers*
kin-geri 26.8 *karate*
kingfish 80 Fishes, 45.18 *sea fish*, 696.5 *company leader*
kingfisher 78 Birds, 78.3 *water bird*, 80.11 *fishing animal*, 360.8 *descender*
kingfisher-blue 454.1 *blue*
King James' Bible 7.12 *religious text*
King John 48 Shakespeare's plays
King Kong 259.9 *big thing*
King Lear 48 Shakespeare's plays

kinglet 78 Birds
kinglike 12.10 *governing*, 688.14 *governmental*
kingliness 802.3 *nobleness*
kingly 12.10 *governing*, 688.14 *governmental*, 805.19 *stately*
kingmaker 233.4 *indirect influence*, 653.13 *director*
King of Arms 544.9 *herald*
King of Death 397.2 *death personified*
King of Kings 8.3 *God*
King of Terrors 397.2 *death personified*
King of the Jews 8.4 *God the Son*
king pair 27.10 *score*
kingpin 75 *Motor Vehicle Parts*, 137.8 *fastening*, 611.3 *chief thing*, 611.4 *bigwig*, 653.15 *manager*, 696.5 *company leader*
king post 284.2 *supporting part*
king-post truss 47.10 *carpenter's term*
kingprawn 45.19 *shellfish*
King's Bench 16.20 *British court*
King's College Chapel 43 *Noted Buildings*
King's Colour 544.7 *flag*
King's highway 327.3 *road*
kingship 12.1 *government*, 126.2 *leadership*
king size 259.3 *large scale*
king-size 259.15 *big*, 413.7, 413.11 *tobacco*
klng-slze bed 47.6 *bed*
Kingsley 48 *Writers*
King's Lynn 93 *Cities*
king snake 79 *Reptiles*
Kings Peak 95 *Mountains*
King's Proctor 16.11 *British law officer*
king's ransom 742.6 *money*
Kingston 93 *Cities*, 98 *Cities*
King Tutankhamen's tomb 200.7 *thing of the past*
King Tut's tomb 399.6 *grave*
Kingu 8 *Deities*
Kingwana 5 *Languages and Groups of Languages*
kingwood 85 *Trees and Shrubs*
Kinich-ahau 8 *Deities*
kinin 58.8 *amino acid*
kink 168.5 *idiosyncrasy*, 314.2 *coil*, 375.7 *rough thing*, 375.12 *make rough*, 579.3 *whim*, 620.7 *defect*
kinkajou 77 *Placental Mammals*
kinkiness 510.1 *insanity*
Kinkozan ware 44 *Types of Ceramics*
kinky 510.11 *insane*
kino 85 *Tree Products*
kinorhynch 81.6 *worm*
Kinorhyncha 81.6 *worm*
Kinross 93 *Cities*
Kinsey 52 *Scientists*
Kinshasa 93 *Cities*
kinship 1.5 *anthropological concept*, 2.8 *human institution*, 107.1 *relatedness*, 114.1 *similarity*, 116.1 *accord*, 667.1 *agreement*
kinship group 400.9 *group*
kinsman 137.3 *associate*
kiosk 740.9 *stall*
Kiowa 1 *Peoples*
kip 75 *General Units*, 643.9, 643.13 *sleep*, 741.11 *national coins*
kip down 649.2 *take it easy*
kiphouse 256.8 *shelter*
Kipling 48 *Writers*, 48 *Poets*
kipper 91 *Names for Inhabitants*, 45.16 *fish dish*, 80.8 *food fish*, 392.17 *dry*, 413.12 *season*, 637.5 *preserve*
kippered 413.9 *piquant*
kippered fish 45.16 *fish dish*
kippered herring 45.16 *fish dish*
kippers 45.44 *British dish*
Kipp's apparatus 57 *Laboratory Apparatus*, 57 *Named Reactions*
kir 351.8 *mixed drink*
Kirchhoff 52 *Scientists*
Kirchoff's laws 56 *Named Laws*
Kirghiz 5 *Languages and*

Groups of Languages
Kirghizia 91 *Countries*
kirk 10.11 *place of worship*
Kirkcaldy 93 *Cities*
Kirkcudbright 93 *Cities*
Kirkuk 93 *Cities*
Kirkwall 93 *Cities*
Kirlian photography 11.1 *occultism*
Kirovabad 93 *Cities*
Kirovakan 93 *Cities*
Kirov Ballet 46.12 *ballet companies*
kir rose 351.8 *mixed drink*
kirtle 295.6 *skirt*
Kirundi 5 *Languages and Groups of Languages*
Kishar 8 *Deities*
Kishi Bojin 8 *Deities*
kismet 582.5 *predetermination*
Kiso 32 *Breeds of Horse and Pony*
kiss 407, 821, 267.4 *meet*, 407.11 *touch*, 407.12 *abut*, 815.9, 815.14 *welcome*, 817.5 *sign of courtesy*, 817.12 *greet*, 819.4 *act of friendship*, 821.14 *communication of love*, 826.1 *endearment*, 826.7 *show endearment for*
kissable 821.22 *lovable*
kiss and make up 677.5 *make peace*, 839.9 *forgive*
kiss-and-tell confession 48.4 *nonfiction*
kissar 49 *Musical Instruments*
kisser 303.2 *face*, 322.4 *body orifice*
kiss goodbye 722.9 *lose*
kiss hands 362.9 *bow*
kissing 821.14 *communication of love*, 826.1 *endearment*
kissing bug 82 *Insects*
kissing disease 624.6 *infection*
kissing hands 362.16 *courtesy*
kissing someone's hand 817.4 *deference*
kissing the hem 849.4 *mark of respect*
kiss off 704.7 *terminate*
kiss of life 39.3 *survival swimming*
kiss of peace 10.5 *Christian rite*
kiss shot 24.4 *carom*
kiss someone's hand 817.13 *defer to*
kiss the book 535.18 *vow*
kiss the hand of 634.4 *shelter*
kiss the hem of one's garment 849.19 *take off one's hat to*
kiss the ring of 849.19 *take off one's hat to*
kiss the rod 673.4 *succumb*
kit 49 *Musical Instruments*, 77.10 *cat*, 77.19 *young mammal*, 142.5 *unit*, 295.1 *dress*, 594.11 *fitting out*, 603.6 *equipment*
Kitakyushu 93 *Cities*
kitbag 258.8 *bag*
Kitche Manitou 8 *Deities*
kitchen 45, 256.7 *room*, 647.1 *workshop*
kitchen boy 697.6 *domestic servant*
kitchen cabinet 653.7 *council*
kitchen container 45
kitchen equipment 45
kitchenette 256.7 *room*
kitchen garden 69.2 *garden*
kitchen knife 380.10 *knife*
kitchen maid 697.6 *domestic servant*
kitchen police 17.4 *military organization*
kitchen range 45.5 *cooker*, 408.4 *burner*
kitchen scales 369.10 *scales*
kitchen sink 258.12 *bath*, 727.8 *sink*
kitchen-sink 560.12 *narrative*
kitchen-sink drama 48 *Literary Groups and Movements*, 51.2 *play*, 51.8 *theatre movements*, 101.3 *realism*, 560.3 *narration*
kitchen table 47.4 *table*
kitchen unit 258.3 *cabinet*

kitchenware 243.7 *produce*
kitchen work 644.1 *work*
kite 74 *Sails*, 78 *Birds*, 73.8 *aircraft*, 78.5 *bird of prey*, 359.19 *take off*, 741.15 *false money*
kite a check 741.24 *monetize*
kite flying 42 *Hobbies and Pastimes*
Kitemark 75.4 *standard*
kit fox 77 *Placental Mammals*
kith 137.3 *associate*
kith and kin 161.17 *family*
kithara 49 *Musical Instruments*
kiting 18 *Sporting Activities*
kit out 594.5 *equip*, 606.5 *provision*
kitsch 50 *Western Art Styles and Movements*, 127.4 *poor quality*, 754.3 *shoddiness*
kitted out 295.29 *dressed*
kitten 77.10 *cat*, 77.19 *young mammal*, 77.35 *give birth*, 206.4 *young animal*, 238.4 *weakling*, 245.11 *have young*
kittenish 77.28 *carnivorous*
kittens 161 *Collective Names by Animal*, 384.5 *powder*
kittiwake 78 *Birds*
Kitt Peak National Observatory 53.23 *observatory*
kitty 25.1 *green bowling*, 605.1 *store*, 724.1 *joint possession*, 878.2 *prize*
kitty-cornered 286.4 *oblique*, 286.8 *obliquely*
Kitwe 93 *Cities*
Kivu 94 *Lakes*
kiwi 78 *Birds*, 78.2 *flightless bird*
kiwi fruit 86 *Fruits*
Kjeldahl's method 57 *Named Reactions*
Kladrub 32 *Breeds of Horse and Pony*
Klansman 529.7 *esotericism*, 531.7 *concealer*
Klaproth 52 *Scientists*
klaxon 423.4 *sound maker*, 636.2 *danger signal*
Kleenex 621.11 *cleaning cloth*
Klein 61.29 *psychologist*
Klein bottle 52 *Named Concepts*, 52.47 *topology*, 159.6 *continuum*
Kleinian 61.33 *Freudian*
kleptomania 510.4 *delusion*, 736.1 *stealing*
kleptomaniac 510.7 *insane person*, 695.5 *compulsive person*, 736.8 *thief*, 736.17 *stolen*
kleptophobia 777 *Phobias by Name*
kletterschuh 34.4 *climbing equipment*
klieg light 51.18 *stage lighting*, 439.6 *electric light*
klipspringer 77 *Placental Mammals*
klister 41.12 *ski*
klister wax 41.5 *ski equipment*
kloof 265.3 *gulf*
klutz 460.3 *unintelligent person*
klutziness 559.1 *inelegance*, 618.8 *inferiority*
klutzy 460.6 *unintelligent*, 559.7 *graceless*, 618.2 *inferior*
klystron 64.20 *electron tube*
K meson 56.77 *elementary particle*
kmukamtch 8.7 *devil*
Knabstrup 32 *Breeds of Horse and Pony*
knack 485.2 *ability*, 584.2 *tendency*, 592.3 *expedient plan*, 602.1 *means*, 655.2 *aptitude*, 657.1 *cunning*
knacker 398.13, 398.13 *animal killer*
knackered 650.1 *fatigued*
knacker's yard 398.15 *slaughterhouse*
knackery 398.9 *animal killing*
knap 275.2 *heights*
knapsack 258.9 *baggage*, 326.10 *transferred thing*
knapsack sprayer 69.6 *garden tool*
knapweed 84 *Flowers and Flow-*

ering Plants
knave 657.3 *cunning person*, 858.4 *dishonourable person*, 864.9 *wicked person*
knavery 657.1 *cunning*, 858.1 *improbity*, 864.1 *wickedness*
knavish 657.4 *cunning*, 864.11 *wicked*
knead 45.55 *cook*, 133.8 *mix*, 306.7 *form*, 374.13 *soften*, 384.27 *beat*, 385.16 *massage*, 407.11 *touch*
kneading 385.6 *massage*
knee 31.9 *play hockey*, 36.8 *punting*, 135.5 *joint*, 330.7 *kick*
knee breeches 295.9 *trousers*
kneecap 382 *Bones*, 879.4 *torture*
kneed 31.8 *hockey*
knee-deep 277.8 *deep*, 278.1 *shallow*
knee guard 23.3 *basketball equipment*
knee-high 206.11 *young*, 260.7 *little*, 275.12 *tall*, 276.5 *low*
knee-high 206.11 *young*, 276.5 *low*
knee-high to a grasshopper 206.11 *young*, 276.5 *low*
knee-hole 47.14 *wooden*
knee-hole desk 47.4 *table*
kneeing 31.3 *ice hockey*, 31.8 *hockey*
kneejerk 583.2 *spontaneous*
knee-jerk 331.9 *reactive*, 464.4 *instinct*, 464.8 *instinctive*
knee-jerk journalism 533.3 *reporting*
knee-jerk reaction 571.8 *involuntariness*, 583.5 *spontaneity*
kneejerk response 462.3 *instinct*
knee-joint 310.1 *angle*
kneel 9.7 *worship*, 10.19 *offer worship*, 362.9 *bow*, 673.4 *succumb*, 694.6 *show obeisance to*, 808.10 *knuckle under*, 817.13 *defer to*, 849.19 *take off one's hat to*
knee-length 269.1 *long*
knee-length socks 295.20 *legwear*
kneeling 9.1 *worship*, 362.16 *courtesy*, 362.21 *degraded*, 673.1 *submission*, 673.5 *submitting*, 694.3 *obeisance*, 694.9 *obeisant*, 849.4 *mark of respect*, 849.11 *in a respectful stance*
kneel on 330.7 *kick*
kneel to 712.6 *request*
knee pad 31.3 *ice hockey*
kneepan 382 *Bones*
knees-up 46.1 *dancing*, 161.10 *dance*, 815.5 *party*
knell 244.4 *ruin*, 397.4 *death sentence*, 399.2 *funeral*, 427.2 *ringing*, 427.10 *ring*, 543.4 *signal*, 636.1 *warning*, 636.7 *raise the alarm*, 774.2 *lament*
knickerbocker glory 45.35 *dessert*
knickerbockers 295.9 *trousers*
knickers 295.9 *trousers*, 295.18 *underwear*
knick-knack 754.5 *cheap item*, 612.9 *bauble*
knick-knacks 792.5 *decorative articles*
knife 380, 34.4 *climbing equipment*, 37.3 *hunting equipment*, 322.2 *opener*, 322.20 *hole*, 350.16 *eating utensil*, 380.16 *use a sharp tool*, 398.2, 398.17 *murder*, 406.11 *inflict pain*, 603.1 *tool*, 670.6 *stab*, 680.8 *sharp weapon*
knifeblade 34.8 *mountaineering*
knifeblade piton 34.4 *climbing equipment*
knife block 26.9 *tae kwon do*
knifed 322.14 *holed*
knife edge 34.5 *rock face*, 300.3 *cutting edge*, 380.7 *sharp point*
knife-edge 34.8 *mountaineering*, 272.8 *narrow thing*
knife-edged 380.3 *sharp-edged*
knife-grinder 629.12 *repairer*, 646.2 *artisan*
knifelike 380.3 *sharp-edged*
knife pleat 320.2 *pleat*
knife point 380.7 *sharp point*
knife sharpener 380.12 *sharpener*

knife-thrower 338.14 *thrower*
knifing 398.2 *murder,* 670.18 *hit*
knight 32.15 *horse person,* 42.4
chess terms, 671.13 *defender,*
679.1 *combatant,* 679.20 *caval-*
ryman, 778.7 *courageous person,*
792.12 *honour,* 802.1 *noble-*
man, 802.5 *make noble,* 804.4
titleholder, 817.6 *courteous per-*
son
knighted 792.9 *decorated*
knight errant 32.15 *horse person,*
519.9 *visionary,* 671.13 *de-*
fender, 679.1 *combatant*
knight errantry 519.4 *ideality*
knighthood 804.1 *right*
knighting 804.1 *right*
Knight in Shining Armour 134.5
pure person
knight in shining armour 632.3
protector, 778.7 *courageous per-*
son, 857.3 *honourable person,*
863.4 *virtuous person*
knightliness 778.2 *heroism*
knightly 676.17 *military,* 778.10
chivalrous, 817.14 *courteously*
knightly deed 778.8 *courageous*
act
knight of the road 739.10 *sales-*
man
Knightsbridge 93.5 *London*
knight's-move 335.15 *deviating*
motion
knight's-move thought 61.16 *dis-*
sociation
knit 67.5 *knitting,* 67.14 *weave,*
135.10 *link,* 243.10 *produce,*
262.5 *make smaller,* 262.6 *be-*
come smaller, 288.8 *interweave,*
295.13 *sweater,* 321.7 *wrinkle*
knit one's brows 830.11 *be irrita-*
ble
knitted 67.10 *woven,* 262.7
smaller, 321.5 *wrinkly*
knitted brow 321.2 *wrinkle*
knitted fabric 67.3 *fabric*
knitted sweater 295.13 *sweater*
knitter 288.3 *weaving*
knitting 42 Hobbies and Pastimes, **67,** 135.3 *unification,*
262.1 *contraction,* 288.2 *braid,*
306.4 *forming*
knitting machine 67.5 *knitting*
knitting needle 380.8 *sharp-*
pointed thing
knit together 135.10 *link,* 629.6
cure
knob 34.5 *rock face,* 245.8 *or-*
gans of reproduction, 275.3
mountain, 283.4 *hanger,* 316.2
bulge, 383.12 *coarsen*
knobbliness 375.6 *roughness*
knobbly 375.2 *coarse*
knobby 375.2 *coarse*
knobkerrie 680.7 *blunt weapon*
knobstick 680.7 *blunt weapon*
knock 426, 245.14 *have sex,*
330.3 *hit,* 330.13 *blow,* 338.5
throw, 396.9 *jolt,* 407.3 *press,*
407.11 *touch,* 423.8 *be loud,*
425.2 *crack,* 670.18 *hit,* 852.5
criticism, 852.17, 854.11 *criti-*
cize
knockabout 51.10 *comedy,* 51.38
tragic
knock about 601.1 *misuse*
knock-about 798.2 *slapstick com-*
edy, 798.5 *ridiculous*
knockabout farce 51.10 *comedy*
knock about with 819.13 *befriend*
knock at the door 344.3 *approach*
knock back 351.13 *drink*
knock back a few 874.8 *get drunk*
knock cold 330.3 *hit*
knock down 26.11 *do a combat*
sport, 236.8 *overpower,* 244.9 *de-*
molish, 276.9 *lower,* 282.7
make horizontal, 330.9 *fight,*
476.8 *refute,* 670.5 *strike,* 752.3
discount
knockdown 754.9 *cheap*
knock down 754.13 *make cheap*
knock-down 26.2 *boxing,* 26.14
combat
knock down a few rungs 612.13
make unimportant
knock down a hurdle 21.6 *race*

knockdown argument 476.1 *refu-*
tation
knock-down-drag-out 666.9 *dis-*
agreeing
knock-down-drag-out fight 666.2
argument, 674.1 *contention*
knock down pins 25.8 *bowl*
knockdown price 752.2 *bargain,*
754.1 *cheapness*
knock-down punch 26.2 *boxing*
knock down to 739.1 *sell*
knocked down 276.5 *low,*
282.10 *lying*
knocked flat 276.5 *low,* 282.10
lying
knocked off course 252.8 *dis-*
placed
knocked out 26.14 *combat,*
404.7 *anaesthetized,* 404.8 *un-*
conscious, 683.11 *defeated*
knocked over 276.5 *low*
knocked up 650.1 *fatigued*
knocker 330.15 *ram,* 852.12
critic, 854.7 *disparager*
knockers 316.2 *bulge*
knock flat 244.11 *ruin,* 276.9
lower, 282.7 *make horizontal*
knock for a loop 514.11 *amaze*
knock-for-knock 71.21 *miscella-*
neous motoring terms
knock for six 514.11 *amaze*
knock galley-west 151.22 *discom-*
pose
knock hard 423.8 *be loud*
knock heads together 330.2 *col-*
lide
knock in 135.10 *link,* 354.3 *im-*
pact
knocking 426, 426.17 *rattling,*
854.2 *criticism,* 854.15 *disparag-*
ing
knocking down 244.2 *destroying*
knocking knees 777.1 *fear*
knocking off course 252.1 *dis-*
placement
knocking on wood 517.6 *good-*
luck sign
knocking shop 877.6 *brothel*
knock into 344.8 *meet*
knock into shape 167.10 *assimi-*
late, 220.9 *transform,* 306.7
form, 796.8 *fashion*
knock it off 218.12 *stop,* 422.1
be silent, 422.6 *hush* sh silence
quiet shut up that's enough
peace soft mum's the word
whist
knock-kneed 342.7 *convergent*
knock-knock 426.4 *knocking*
knock off 131.4 *take off,* 135.11
make love, 139.5 *unstick,*
245.14 *have sex,* 736.12 *steal,*
752.3 *discount*
knock off course 252.14 *displace*
knock off one's perch 806.23
abase
knock-on 35.3 *rugby play,*
159.10 *repercussive*
knock-on effect 159.4 *repercus-*
sion
**knock one's head against a brick
wall** 656.6 *act foolishly*
knockout 18.1 *sport*
knock out 26.11 *do a combat*
sport
knockout 157.13 *ender*
knock out 157.17 *kill,* 236.8 *over-*
power, 243.10 *produce,* 244.11
ruin, 330.9 *fight,* 404.12 *an-*
aesthetize, 460.10 *bemuse*
knockout 617.8 *exceller*
knock out 643.14 *make inactive*
knockout 682.2 *victory*
knock out 682.10 *defeat heavily,*
761.7 *render insensitive*
knockout 786.5 *person of wonder,*
861.17 *good thing*
knock-out 26.2 *boxing,* 26.14
combat
knockout blow 157.13 *ender,*
244.4 *ruin*
knockout competition 674.2 *con-*
test
knockout drops 404.4 *anaesthetic*
knock-out drops 761.6 *desensitiz-*
ing substance
knock out of shape 307.3 *make*

shapeless
knock out of true alignment
309.9 *distort*
knockout punch 244.4 *ruin*
knock-out punch 26.2 *boxing,*
330.14 *sporting hit*
knockout whist 42 Card Games
knock over 244.9 *demolish,*
276.9 *lower*
knock senseless 761.7 *render in-*
sensitive
knock the bottom out 23.6 *play*
basketball
**knock the bottom out of the mar-
ket** 754.13 *make cheap*
knock the cover off 27.17 *bat*
knock the shit out of 682.10 *de-*
feat heavily
knock the stuffing out of 682.10
defeat heavily
knock together 148.13 *make*
knock up 245.13 *propagate,*
361.2 *send up,* 650.6 *fatigue*
knoll 275.3 *mountain*
knot 75 General Units, **78**
Birds, 52.47 *topology,* 74.6 *nau-*
tical speed, 85.2 *tree part,* 135.5
joint, 135.10 *link,* 137.6 *line,*
137.11 *connect,* 161.27 *bundle,*
269.7 *measure of length,* 288.8
interweave, 316.2 *bulge,* 329.8
speed, 371.4 *solid body,* 375.7
rough thing, 375.12 *make*
rough, 661.4 *restraint*
knot garden 69.2 *garden*
knothole 322.5 *hole*
knotted 135.15 *tied,* 137.15 *con-*
nected, 371.7 *condensed,* 375.2
coarse
knotted score 122.2 *equilibrium*
knot theory 52 Mathematical
Theories
knottiness 159.1 *difficulty*
knotting 52.47 *topology,* 135.3
unification, 288.2 *braid*
knotty 371.7 *condensed,* 375.2
coarse, 477.13 *problematic,*
529.11 *mysterious,* 659.12 *prob-*
lematic
knotty problem 477.4 *difficult*
question, 523.12 *unintelligible*
thing, 529.5 *difficult problem,*
659.4 *problem*
knotweed 84 Flowers and Flowering Plants
knout 879.14 *instrument of pun-*
ishment
know 6, **501,** 135.11 *make love,*
490.20 *be certain,* 497.7 *believe,*
507.8 *be intelligent,* 522.6 *un-*
derstand, 528.15 *be informed,*
653.1 *manage,* 655.11 *be ex-*
pert, 688.22 *be an authority on*
knowability 522.9 *intelligibility*
knowable 501.10 *known,* 522.1
intelligible, 522.3 *recognizable*
know again 511.12 *remember*
knowall
know-all 4.12 *sage,* 459.8 *intellec-*
tual person, 501.6 *knowledge-*
able person, 809.7 *vain person*
know all about 688.22 *be an au-*
thority on
know all the answers 501.12
know by heart, 655.10 *be skil-*
ful, 657.5 *be cunning,* 696.15
learn
know all the ins and outs 655.11
be expert
know a trick or two 657.5 *be cun-*
ning
know back to front 688.22 *be an*
authority on
know backwards 6.24 *know,*
501.12 *know by heart,* 655.11
be expert
know by heart 501, 6.24 *know*
know by instinct 759.16 *feel in*
one's bones
know for sure 490.20 *be certain*
know forward and backward
501.12 *know by heart,* 655.11
be expert
know from A to Z 501.12 *know*
by heart
know full well 501.12 *know by*
heart

knowhow 485.2 *ability*
know how 485.14 *be qualified*
know-how 235.2 *ability,* 327.1
way, 501.2 *information,* 602.1
means, 655.2 *aptitude,* 657.1
cunning
know how many beans make five
507.8 *be intelligent*
know how to 696.15 *learn*
know how to mix 815.11 *be so-*
ciable
know in advance 516.1 *foresee*
knowing 135.4 *sexual union,*
501.1 *knowledge,* 501.8 *knowl-*
edgeable, 507.5 *wise,* 657.4 *cun-*
ning, 759.10 *feeling*
knowingly 501.15 *knowledge-*
ably, 588.13 *intentionally*
knowing no better 865.7 *naive*
knowing no wrong 865.7 *naive*
knowing one's place 849.9 *show-*
ing respect
knowing person 655.5 *expert*
know inside out 6.24 *know,*
501.12 *know by heart,* 688.22
be an authority on
know it all 787.5 *not wonder*
about
know-it-all 459.8 *intellectual per-*
son, 809.7 *vain person,* 809.13
boastful
know just when to stop 655.10
be skilful
knowledge 501, 439.13 *enlight-*
enment, 490.9 *certainty,* 507.1
wisdom, 522.12 *understanding,*
528.1 *information,* 602.1
means, 655.1 *skill,* 657.1 *cun-*
ning, 688.2 *authoritativeness,*
759.1 *feeling*
Knowledge 501
knowledgeable 6, **501,** 4.19
learned, 165.21 *specialized,*
277.11 *wise,* 459.10 *intelligent,*
463.7 *reasoning,* 507.5 *wise,*
657.4 *cunning,* 688.12 *authori-*
tative, 688.17 *expert*
knowledgeableness 459.4 *clever-*
ness
knowledgeable person 501
knowledgeably 501, 4.29 *wisely,*
459.15 *intelligently,* 655.12
skilfully, 688.23 *authoritatively,*
688.26 *expertly*
knowledge of law 16.32 *jurispru-*
dence
knowledge of the enemy 676.6
art of war
knowledge-seeking 477.12 *ques-*
tioning
know like a book 6.24 *know*
know like the back of one's hand
6.24 *know,* 501.12 *know by*
heart
know little 502
known 501, 52.77 *given,* 490.1
certain, 544.12 *identified,*
584.10 *familiar,* 599.9 *used*
known as 544.12 *identified*
known attitudes 652.1 *conduct*
known by 544.12 *identified*
know no better 658.4 *be naive,*
818.7 *be discourteous,* 865.10
be naive
know no bounds 610.4 *be excess-*
ive
know no law 16.74 *be lawless*
know no limit 184.8 *have no limit*
know nothing 502.9 *be ignorant*
Know-Nothings 529.7 *esotericism*
know no wrong 865.10 *be naive*
know one's onions 655.11 *be ex-*
pert
know one's own mind 570.14 *fol-*
low one's own will, 574.6 *be res-*
olute
know one's place 116.25 *con-*
form, 673.4 *succumb,* 810.14 *be*
modest
know one's stuff 501.12 *know by*
heart, 655.11 *be expert,* 688.22
be an authority on
know the ins and outs 106.11 *cir-*
cumstantiate
**know the price of everything and
the value of nothing** 737.1 *trade*

know the real world 537.28 *bring into existence*
know the right people 233.8 *influence*
know the ropes 6.24 *know,* 501.12 *know by heart,* 655.11 *be expert,* 688.22 *be an authority on*
know the score 6.24 *know,* 507.7 *be wise,* 787.6 *understand*
know what one is about 655.10 *be skilful*
know what's what 6.24 *know,* 459.13 *be intelligent,* 507.7 *be wise,* 655.10 *be skilful*
know when one has had enough 869.5 *be self-restrained*
know when to stop 699.10 *restrain oneself,* 869.5 *be self-restrained*
Knoxville 93 Cities
knub 383.3 *nap*
knuckle 135.5 *joint*
knuckle ball 22.4 *pitching terms,* 338.5 *throw*
knuckle-duster 330.16 *weapons,* 680.7 *blunt weapon*
knuckle sandwich 407.7 *sense organ*
knuckle under 808, 127.9 *yield to,* 673.4 *succumb,* 806.20 *submit*
knurled 375.2 *coarse*
KO 236.8 *overpower,* 244.11 *ruin,* 682.2 *victory,* 682.3 *successful thing,* 682.10 *defeat heavily*
koa 85 Trees and Shrubs
koala 77 Marsupials
Koan 7 Non-Christian Religions
kob 77 Placental Mammals
Kobe 93 Cities
Koblenz 93 Cities
kobold 11.11 *ghost*
koboro 49 Musical Instruments
Koch 52 Scientists
KO'd 683.11 *defeated*
Kodagu 5 Languages and Groups of Languages
Kodály 49 Musicians and Composers
Kodiak 98 Islands
Kodiak bear 77 Placental Mammals
Koestler 48 Writers
Koffka 4 Philosophers
koheleth 7.8 *priest*
kohen 7.8 *priest*
Kohima 93 Cities
kohl 791.4 *cosmetics*
kohlrabi 45 Vegetables
Kohoutek 53 Comets
Koibal 5 Languages and Groups of Languages
koine 5.7 *international language*
koji 7.7 *monk*
ko-kiu 49 Musical Instruments
Ko-Kutani ware 44 Types of Ceramics
kola nut 86 Nuts
Kolbe 52 Scientists
Kolbe electrolysis 57 Named Reactions
kolkhoz 724.1 *joint possession,* 68.6 *farm*
Kolmogorov 52 Scientists
kol nidre 10.9 *prayer*
Kolyma 96 Rivers
kombu 90.5 *algal product*
Komi 5 Languages and Groups of Languages
kominuter 384.11 *pulverizer*
Komodo dragon 79 Reptiles, 79.2 *lizard*
Komoku 8 Deities
Komondor 77 Breeds of Dogs
komungo 49 Musical Instruments
Kongo 5 Languages and Groups of Languages
kōnighorn 49 Musical Instruments
konimeter 384.15 *koniology*
koniology 384
koniophobia 777 Phobias by Name
kontakion 10.8 *hymn*

kook 510.7 *insane person*
kookaburra 78 Birds
kooky 168.14 *eccentric*
kop 275.3 *mountain*
kopasetic 617.1 *worthy*
kopeck 741.4 *change*
Kopff 53 Comets
kopje 275.3 *mountain*
kopophobia 777 Phobias by Name
Koran 7.12 *religious text*
Korchnoi 18 Sporting Personalities
Kordofanian 5 Languages and Groups of Languages
Korea 91 Countries, 91 Countries
Korean 5 Languages and Groups of Languages
Korean War 17 Major Wars
korfball 18 Sporting Activities
korma 45.49 *Indian dish*
Korsakoff's psychosis 61.11, 510.5 *psychosis*
Korwa 5 Languages and Groups of Languages
Kosciusko 95 Mountains
kosher 134.14 *purified,* 167.14 *conformist,* 621.16 *clean*
koshi-waza 26.7 *judo*
Košice 93 Cities
kote gaeshi 26.10 *aikido*
koto 49 Musical Instruments
kowhai 85 Trees and Shrubs
kowtow 362.9 *bow,* 362.16 *courtesy,* 673.1 *submission,* 673.4 *succumb,* 694.3 *obeisance,* 694.6 *show obeisance to,* 808.10 *knuckle under,* 817.13 *defer to,* 849.4 *mark of respect,* 849.19 *take off one's hat to*
kowtower 808.3 *sycophant*
kowtowing 362.21 *degraded,* 808.7 *sycophantic,* 817.4 *deference,* 817.9 *deferential,* 849.9 *showing respect*
krait 79 Reptiles
kraken 76.7 *legendary beast*
Kranj 93 Cities
K rations 606.1 *provision,* 871.2 *short rations*
Kraut 91 Names for Inhabitants
Krebs 52 Scientists
Krebs cycle 58.24 *respiration,* 59.6 *cell biology*
Kreisler 49 Musicians and Composers
krill 76.5 *aquatic animal*
Krio 5 Languages and Groups of Languages
Kriol 5 Languages and Groups of Languages
Kripke 4 Philosophers
kris 380.10 *knife,* 680.8 *sharp weapon*
Krishna 8 Deities
Kristeva 4 Philosophers
Krivoy Rog 93 Cities
krona 741.11 *national coins*
krone 741.11 *national coins*
Kruger 33 Named Stars
Kruševac 93 Cities
krypton 57 Chemical Elements
Kshatriya 679.6 *militarist*
K star 53.13 *luminosity*
Kuala Lumpur 93 Cities
Kuban 96 Rivers
Kubera 8 Deities
Kubachi ware 44 Types of Ceramics
kudos 318.1 *prominence,* 851.4 *compliment*
kudu 77 Placental Mammals
Kuki 5 Languages and Groups of Languages
Ku Klux Klan 529.7 *esotericism*
kukri 680.8 *sharp weapon*
Kukulcan 8 Deities
kulfi 45.49 *Indian dish*
Kumasi 93 Cities
Kumbum 10.13 *shrine*
kumi jo 26.10 *aikido*
kumiss 351.5 *milk*
kumi tachi 26.10 *aikido*
kumquat 86 Fruits
Kundera 48 Writers

kung fu 18 Sporting Activities, 674.8 *wrestling*
Kunlun 95 Mountains
Kunming 93 Cities
kunzite 54 Minerals, 54 Gemstones
kur 32.10 *dressage*
Kura 96 Rivers
Kurchatov 52 Scientists
Kurdish 5 Languages and Groups of Languages
Kurds 1 Peoples
Kuri 68 Breeds of Cattle
Kuril Trench 54.16 *ocean floor*
Kurma 8 Deities
kurrajong 85 Trees and Shrubs
kurtosis 52.59 *probability distribution*
kuru 510.3 *mental deterioration*
Kurukh 5 Languages and Groups of Languages
Kustanair 32 Breeds of Horse and Pony
Kutenai 1 Peoples
kuting 41.10 *curling*
kuting stone 41.10 *curling*
Kuvasz 77 Breeds of Dogs
Kuwait 91 Countries, 93 Cities
kvetch 766.3 *dissatisfied person,* 766.7 *be dissatisfied*
Kwa 5 Languages and Groups of Languages
Kwakiutl 1 Peoples, 5 Languages and Groups of Languages
kwashiorkor 624.4 *disease,* 624.7 *tropical disease*
kwela 49.10 *world music*
Kyd 48 Dramatists
Kyle of Lochalsh 98.9 *inlet*
Kyloe 68 Breeds of Cattle
kymograph 73 Aircraft Parts, 365.6 *measuring instrument*
Kyoga 94 Lakes
Kyokushinkai 26.8 *karate*
Kyoto 93 Cities
Kyrie Eleison 10.9 *prayer*
Kyries 10.6 *Eucharist*
Kyu grade 26.7 *judo*
Kyushu 98 Islands

L

laager 671.9 *barrier,* 671.12 *fort*
lab 479.6 *place of experimentation,* 647.1 *workshop*
labarum 544.7 *flag*
label 43 Architectural Decoration, 163.4 *type,* 163.13 *class,* 165.22 *characterize,* 526.8 *showplace,* 544.3 *means of identification,* 544.8 *heraldic device,* 544.10 *identify,* 560.8 *name*
labelled 544.12 *identified*
labelling 544.1 *identification*
labial 5.16 *spoken letter,* 5.41 *lettered*
labia majora 245.8 *organs of reproduction*
labia minora 245.8 *organs of reproduction*
labiate 83.16 *taxonomic*
labile 224.13 *changeable*
labiodental 5.16 *spoken letter*
labionasal 5.16 *spoken letter*
labioplasty 60 Surgical Operations
labour 161 Collective Names for Birds and Animals
laboratory 6.15 *schoolroom,* 220.4 *medium of conversion,* 479.6 *place of experimentation,* 647.1 *workshop*
laboratory animal 76.3 *domesticated animal,* 479.7 *experimentee*
laboratory test 60.7 *diagnosis*
Labor Day 214.6 *annually celebrated day*
laborious 644, 642.20 *industrious,* 650.4 *fatiguing,* 659.10 *difficult,* 879.21 *punishing*

laboriously 644, 650.9 *tiringly,* 659.26 *arduously*
laboriousness 642.8 *assiduity,* 659.1 *difficulty*
labor union 13.8 *industrial relations,* 737.5 *commercial trade*
labor union member 13.9 *economist,* 737.11 *chamber of commerce member*
labour 15.1 *industrial relations,* 15.8 *industrial,* 108.10 *be unrelated,* 183.18 *harp,* 245.7 *obstetrics,* 366.25 *pitch,* 541.7 *exaggerate,* 596.2 *try hard,* 611.8 *make important,* 640.1 *action,* 640.4 *act,* 642.8 *assiduity,* 644.1 *work,* 644.6 *work,* 646.4 *personnel,* 659.3 *difficult task*
Labour 12.9 *governmental,* 665.10 *political*
labour camp 695.3 *coercive methods,* 702.1 *prison,* 879.7 *punishment*
labour costs 13.8 *industrial relations*
labour dispute 15.4 *industrial dispute*
laboured 108.7 *illogical,* 541.12 *exaggerated,* 559.9 *inelegant,* 594.20 *developed,* 644.11 *laborious*
laboured breathing 650.7 *fatigue*
labourer 124.7 *average person,* 230.6 *operative,* 243.9 *producer,* 646.1 *worker,* 697.1 *servant*
labour force 13.4 *economic development,* 13.8 *industrial relations,* 15.1 *industrial relations,* 646.4 *personnel*
labouring 541.1 *exaggeration,* 642.20 *industrious,* 644.10 *working*
labour in vain 358.2 *fail,* 607.1 *waste,* 614.9 *waste effort,* 656.6 *act foolishly,* 722.11 *be wasteful*
Labourite 12.6 *political party,* 665.6 *political party member*
labour law 15, 13.8 *industrial relations*
labour-management body 15.1 *industrial relations*
Labour Management Relations Act 15.5 *labour law*
labour of love 572.10 *voluntary work,* 597.2 *undertaking,* 644.1 *work,* 729.1 *giving,* 754.6 *absence of charge,* 831.4 *benevolent act*
labour of Sisyphus 236.2 *futile effort,* 614.5 *waste of effort,* 722.3 *waste*
labour on behalf of 662.25 *serve*
labour pains 245.7 *obstetrics,* 406.2 *painful condition*
Labour Party 12.6 *political party,* 665.3 *political grouping*
labour pool 646.4 *personnel*
labour relations 15.1 *industrial relations*
labour resources 602.3 *human resources*
labour-saving 649, 603.8 *mechanical,* 645.7 *leisurely,* 660.10 *feasible,* 756.4 *thrifty*
labour-saving device 662.7 *convenience*
labour the obvious 522.5 *simplify,* 610.5 *be superfluous,* 614.9 *waste effort*
labour under 105.7 *be in a predicament,* 624.24 *be unhealthy*
labour under a disadvantage 659.19 *have difficulty*
labour under a false impression 504.18 *be in error*
labour under difficulties 659.19 *have difficulty*
labour union 15.3 *organized labour,* 665.1 *party*
Labrador 37.6 *sporting dog*
Labrador retriever 77 Breeds of Dogs
lab rat 479.7 *experimentee*
La Bruyère 48 Writers
laburnum 84 Flowers and Flowering Plants

labyrinth 151.7 *tangle*, 314.3 *convoluted thing*, 420.5 *internal ear*, 529.4 *brain-teaser*
labyrinth fish 80 *Fishes*
labyrinthine 151.18 *muddled*, 314.4 *convolutional*, 335.21 *indirect*, 529.11 *mysterious*, 659.12 *problematic*
labyrinthitis 420.6 *otology*
labyrinthodont 79 *Amphibians*
Lacan 4 *Philosophers*, 61.29 *psychologist*
Lacanian 61.33 *Freudian*
Lacanian psychology 61.1 *psychology*
Lacaune 68 *Breeds of Sheep*
laccolith 54.28 *rock*, 54.30 *igneous rock*
lace 67.4 *weaving*, 133.8 *mix*, 135.10 *link*, 137.6 *line*, 137.11 *connect*, 274.11 *fineness*, 288.2 *braid*, 288.4 *textile*, 288.8 *interweave*, 442.8 *transparent thing*, 792.2 *pattern*
laced 137.15 *connected*, 288.6 *interwoven*, 295.31 *styled*
lace into 670.5 *strike*
lacemaker 792.7 *decorator*
lace making 42 *Hobbies and Pastimes*, 288.2 *braid*
lacerate 136.9 *separate*
lacerated 406.6 *injured*
laceration 136.3 *separateness*, 406.3 *injury*
Lacerta 53 The Constellations
Lacertilia 79.2 *lizard*
lacertilian 79.2 *lizard*, 79.11 *reptilian*
lace up 135.10 *link*, 295.34 *wear*
lace-ups 295.19 *footwear*
lace up tight 135.8 *unite*
lacewing 82 *Insects*
lacework 288.2 *braid*, 792.2 *pattern*
laches 720.1 *nonobservance*
Lachesis 8 *Deities*
Lachlan 96 *Rivers*
lachrymal 387.16 *rheumy*
lachrymator 62.4 *drug type*
lachrymatory 387.16 *rheumy*
lachrymose 774.4 *lamenting*
laciness 274.11 *fineness*, 288.2 *braid*
lacing 67.4 *weaving*, 288.1 *interweaving*
lac insect 82 *Insects*
lack 127.11 *become inferior*, 145.1 *incompleteness*, 145.2 *omission*, 145.5 *be incomplete*, 182.3 *fewness*, 254.2 *disappearance*, 358.1 *fall short*, 358.5 *shortfall*, 593.2 *need*, 593.7 *require*, 609.5 *be insufficient*, 609.9 *scarcity*, 620.5 *imperfection*, 620.7 *defect*, 685.1 *noncompletion*, 685.5 *not complete*, 712.6 *request*, 743.5 *poverty*, 743.9 *inadequacy*, 743.12 *be poor*
lackadaisical 466.4 *uninterested*, 468.11 *perfunctory*, 470.5, 783.7 *indifferent*
lackadaisicalness 783.1 *indifference*
lack amazement 787.5 *not wonder about*
lack awe 787.5 *not wonder about*
lack bias 537.29 *be truthful*, 859.6 *be disinterested*
lack candour 540.18 *be hypocritical*
lack compassion 836.6 *be pitiless*
lack conviction 717.5 *be irresolute*
lack courage 779.4 *be a coward*
lack courtesy 850.22 *show disrespect*
lack definition 307.3 *make shapeless*
lack discipline 698.19 *liberalize*
lack disguise 537.29 *be truthful*
lack emotion 859.6 *be disinterested*, 869.7 *be calm*
lack equality 375.11 *be rough*
lack experience 865.10 *be naive*
lackey 232.3 *assistant*, 697.1 *servant*, 701.3 *subordinate*
lack fairness 123.6 *be unjust*

lack harmony 434, 136.12 *disagree*
lack honesty 858.8 *be dishonourable*
lack hope 776.9 *be hopeless*
lackie 808.3 *sycophant*
lack information 502.9 *be ignorant*
lacking 100.9 *nonexistent*, 145.4 *incomplete*, 172.7 *null*, 238.13 *insufficient*, 254.12 *missing*, 358.7 *short*, 593.4 *required*, 593.5 *necessitous*, 609.1 *insufficient*, 609.2 *unprovided*, 620.2 *incomplete*, 685.4 *uncompleted*, 722.16 *losing*, 743.4 *inadequate*
lacking application 600.1 *unused*
lacking ceremony 720.11 *nonobservant*
lacking definition 307.5 *shapeless*
lacking emotion 869.10 *calm*
lacking intellect 460
lacking maturity 595.5 *immature*
lacking nothing 144.7 *complete*
lacking refinement 412.6 *coarse*
lacking self-control 236.12 *impotent*
lacking sight 436.8 *blind*
lacking strength 238.8 *weak*
lacking style 411.8 *tasteful*
lacking substance 519.12 *imaginary*
lacking taste 412.6 *coarse*
lack integrity 538.25 *be dishonest*, 540.16 *be false*
lack intellect 460
lack interest 788.6 *be boring*
lack light 440.12 *be dark*
lacklustre 441.7 *dimmed*, 445.7 *colourless*, 445.8 *drained of colour*, 770.6 *depressed*
lack maturity 865.10 *be naive*
lack mercy 690.5 *be severe*
lack of ability 656.8 *unskilfulness*
lack of action 641.1 *inaction*
lack of admiration 787.1 *lack of wonder*
lack of advantage 614.4 *futility*
lack of amazement 787.1 *lack of wonder*
lack of ambition 641.1 *inaction*
lack of appetite 350.3 *delicate eating*, 624.3 *symptom*, 783.1 *indifference*
lack of appreciation 838.1 *ingratitude*
lack of assumption 537.5 *truthfulness*
lack of attention 421.1 *deafness*
lack of authority 236.1 *powerlessness*
lack of awareness 404.1 *lack of feeling*
lack of awe 787.1 *lack of wonder*
lack of benefit 614.4 *futility*
lack of betterment 628.7 *deterioration*
lack of bias 537.5 *truthfulness*, 843.1 *fairness*, 859.1 *disinterestedness*
lack of bite 381.8 *toothlessness*
lack of brains 460.1 *lack of intellect*
lack of care 832.6 *inconsiderateness*
lack of cause 229.1 *lack of motive*
lack of censorship 698.2 *free speech*
lack of ceremony 720.1 *nonobservance*, 814.1 *informality*
lack of change 112.4 *monotony*, 112.8 *monotonous*
lack of choice 571
lack of claim 846.1 *lack of entitlement*
lack of clarity 428.3 *muteness*, 520.3 *comprehension*, 523.11 *unintelligibility*, 551.1 *obscurity*
lack of colour 556.5 *unadornment*
lack of commitment 576.11 *vacillation*, 598.3 *relinquishment*
lack of committal 717.3 *irresolution*
lack of communication 830.1 *sullenness*
lack of concealment 437.3 *visibility*

lack of concentration 642.7 *restlessness*
lack of concern 832.6 *inconsiderateness*
lack of confession 868.1 *impenitence*
lack of confinement 698.1 *freedom*
lack of conscience 858.1 *improbity*
lack of consent 711.1 *refusal*, 711.2 *dissent*
lack of consideration 436.7 *figurative blindness*, 818.1 *discourtesy*
lack of continuity 160.1 *discontinuity*
lack of contrition 868.1 *impenitence*
lack of convention 814.1 *informality*
lack of conviction 717.3 *irresolution*
lack of courage 779.1 *cowardice*
lack of credit 838.1 *ingratitude*
Lack of Curiosity 466
lack of danger 632.1 *safety*
lack of decoration 556.5 *unadornment*
lack of definition 307.1 *shapelessness*
lack of delay 191.1 *immediacy*
lack of democracy 123.2 *injustice*
lack of depth 278.3 *shallowness*
lack of deviation 537.9 *uniformity*
lack of discernment 436.7 *figurative blindness*
lack of discipline 151.8 *lawlessness*, 698.6 *liberality*
Lack of Discrimination 482
lack of discrimination 482
lack of disguise 537.5 *truthfulness*
lack of drive 576.12 *inconstancy*
lack of ease 659.2 *awkwardness*
lack of emotion 859.1 *disinterestedness*, 869.3 *calmness*
lack of emphasis 555
Lack of Emphasis 555
lack of enjoyment 788.1 *boredom*
lack of enlightenment 436.7 *figurative blindness*
lack of entitlement 846
Lack of Entitlement 846
lack of exaggeration 537.5 *truthfulness*
lack of expectation 514.1 *surprise*, 595.8 *lack of preparation*, 786.1 *wonder*
lack of expression 523.11 *unintelligibility*
lack of fairness 123.2 *injustice*
lack of feeling 404, 761.3 *insensitiveness*
lack of finesse 559.1 *inelegance*
lack of fitness 624.1 *ill health*
lack of flattery 537.5 *truthfulness*
lack of food 350.10 *scarcity*
lack of force 555.2 *lack of emphasis*
lack of formality 814.1 *informality*
lack of function 614.3 *uselessness*
lack of grace 659.2 *awkwardness*
lack of gratitude 838.1 *ingratitude*
lack of harmony 136.4 *disunity*
lack of haste 328.8 *slowness*
lack of heat 409.1 *coldness*
lack of hindrance 660.5 *smoothness*
lack of hope 776.1 *hopelessness*
lack of humanity 832.1 *malevolence*
lack of hygiene 626
Lack of Hygiene 626
lack of importance 104.1 *extraneousness*
lack of improvement 628.7 *deterioration*
lack of incisiveness 381.8 *toothlessness*
lack of inspiration 555.2 *lack of emphasis*
lack of integrity 538.10 *dishonesty*, 540.1 *falsehood*, 858.1 *improbity*
lack of intellect 460

Lack of Intellect 460
lack of intelligence 441.4 *stupidity*
lack of intention 229.1 *lack of motive*
lack of interest 466, 783.1 *indifference*, 787.1 *lack of wonder*, 788.1 *boredom*
lack of knowledge 460.2 *unintelligence*, 502.1 *ignorance*
lack of light 440.1 *darkness*
lack of maintenance 628.9 *dilapidation*
lack of manners 818.2 *bad manners*
lack of meaning 521, 523.11 *unintelligibility*
Lack of Meaning 521
lack of memory 462.5 *mental block*
lack of mercy 690.1 *severity*
lack of moral fibre 779.1 *cowardice*
lack of morals 858.1 *improbity*, 877.1 *immorality*
lack of motive 229
Lack of Motive 229
lack of naturalness 551.1 *obscurity*
lack of order 139.1 *nonadhesion*
lack of ornamentation 556.5 *unadornment*
lack of oxygen 34.2 *climbing dangers*
lack of passion 555.2 *lack of emphasis*
lack of perception 436.7 *figurative blindness*
lack of pigment 446.7 *whiteness*
lack of pity 836.1 *pitilessness*
lack of planning 616.3 *inconvenience*
lack of polish 559.1 *inelegance*, 559.4 *inelegance of speech*
lack of politeness 818.2 *bad manners*
lack of power 236.1 *powerlessness*
lack of practice 585.3 *unaccustomedness*, 656.8 *unskilfulness*
lack of prejudice 271.6 *broadmindedness*, 859.1 *disinterestedness*
lack of preparation 595
Lack of Preparation 595
lack of pretence 537.5 *truthfulness*
lack of pretension 537.5 *truthfulness*
lack of principle 864.3 *venial sin*
lack of principles 858.1 *improbity*, 877.1 *immorality*
lack of professionalism 656.8 *unskilfulness*
lack of proficiency 656.8 *unskilfulness*
lack of profit 722.2 *financial loss*
lack of progress 641.1 *inaction*
lack of protection 236.3 *helplessness*, 633.7 *vulnerability*
lack of protocol 616.3 *inconvenience*
lack of purpose 521.2, 521.6 *aimlessness*, 614.4 *futility*
lack of reason 460.1 *lack of intellect*, 521.1 *lack of meaning*
lack of refinement 412.4 *bad taste*, 549.3 *inelegance*
lack of repair 628.9 *dilapidation*
lack of resolution 576.11 *vacillation*, 717.3 *irresolution*
lack of respect 850.1 *disrespect*
lack of restraint 482.6 *lack of discrimination*, 698.1 *freedom*
lack of retraction 535.4 *confirmation*
lack of risk 632.1 *safety*
lack of sanitation 626.1 *lack of hygiene*
lack of satisfaction 609.8 *insufficiency*
lack of self-confidence 810.5 *self-deprecation*
lack of self-respect 808.1 *servility*
lack of sensation 404.1 *lack of feeling*

lack of sense 523.11 *uni-intelligibility*
lack of sense of smell 417.1 *odourlessness*
lack of seriousness 612.7 *triviality*
lack of sex 825.2 *virginity*
lack of sight 436.1 *blindness*
lack of skill 614.3 *uselessness*, 618.8 *inferiority*, 656.8 *unskilfulness*, 659.2 *awkwardness*
lack of smell 417.1 *odourlessness*
lack of solidity 372.3 *sparseness*
lack of sparkle 555.2 *lack of emphasis*
lack of spirit 555.2 *lack of emphasis*, 779.1 *cowardice*, 787.1 *lack of wonder*
lack of strength 238.1 *weakness*, 624.1 *ill health*
lack of style 411.2 *taste of life*, 555.2 *lack of emphasis*, 559.1 *inelegance*
lack of substance 372.3 *sparseness*, 612.5 *unimportance*
lack of success 683.1 *failure*
lack of surprise 787.2 *predictability*
lack of talent 656.8 *unskilfulness*
lack of talk 830.1 *sullenness*
lack of taste 412.4 *bad taste*
lack of thoroughness 620.5 *imperfection*
lack of thought 462
Lack of Thought 462
lack of training 595.8 *lack of preparation*
lack of transparency 551.1 *obscurity*
lack of understanding 460.2 *unintelligence*, 523.11 *unintelligibility*
lack of unity 136.4 *disunity*, 139.1 *nonadhesion*
lack of use 600.8 *nonuse*, 614.3 *uselessness*
lack of value 618.7 *worthlessness*
lack of variation 788.1 *boredom*
lack of variety 112.1 *uniformity*
lack of veneration 850.1 *disrespect*
lack of ventilation 419.1 *stench*
lack of viscosity 139.1 *nonadhesion*
lack of warning 514.1 *surprise*
lack of weight 370.5 *lightness*
lack of willpower 576.12 *inconstancy*
lack of wisdom 460.2 *unintelligence*
lack of wit 460.2 *unintelligence*
lack of wonder 787
Lack of Wonder 787
lack of zeal 573.13 *dissociation*
lack order 720.10 *violate the law*
lack planning 595.12 *be unprepared*
lack prejudice 271.12 *be broadminded*, 859.6 *be disinterested*
lack preparation 595.12 *be unprepared*
lack reason 460.9 *lack intellect*
lack refinement 412.9 *have bad taste*
lack regularity 215.6 *be irregular*, 375.11 *be rough*
lack resolution 717.5 *be irresolute*
lack restraint 698.14 *be free*, 698.19 *liberalize*
lack sincerity 538.25 *be dishonest*
lack skill 656.5 *be unskilful*
lack sophistication 865.10 *be naive*
lack talent 656.5 *be unskilful*
lack taste 412.9 *have bad taste*
lack thought 462
lack uniformity 375.11 *be rough*
lack unity 136.12 *disagree*
lack variation 788.6 *be boring*
lack variety 112.10 *conform*, 788.6 *be boring*
lack weight 370.9 *be light*
Laclos 48 Writers
laconic 552.3 *concise*, 562.6 *summary*, 566.3 *sparing with words*
laconically 552.5 *concisely*, 562.11 *summarily*

laconicism 552.1 *conciseness*, 562.4 *summariness*, 566.6 *guarded speech*
laconicness 566.6 *guarded speech*
laconism 552.1 *conciseness*, 562.4 *summariness*, 566.6 *guarded speech*
lacquer 47.18 *work wood*, 293.3 *coating*, 293.24 *coat*, 444.4 *pigment*, 444.15 *colour*
lacquered 47.14 *wooden*, 376.4 *polished*
lacquered furniture 47.1 *furniture*
lacquering 47.1 *furniture*
lacquer tree 85 Trees and Shrubs
lac resin 395.10 *resin*
lacrimal 352.5 *of a secretion*
lacrimal gland 352 Exocrine Glands, 352.3 *gland*
lacrimate 352.7 *secrete*
lacrimation 352.1 *secretion*
lacrimatory 352.4 *secretory*, 352.5 *of a secretion*, 352.6 *inducing secretion*
lacrosse 18 Sporting Activities, **31**, 31.8 *hockey*
Lacrosse 31
lacrosse association 31.5 *lacrosse*
lacrosse ball 31.5 *lacrosse*
lacrosse player 31
lacrosse stick 31.5 *lacrosse*
lacrosse techniques 31.5 *lacrosse*
lactam 57 Types of Compounds
lactarius 89 Fungi
lactase 58.11 *enzyme*
lactate 57 Types of Compounds, **77**, 352.7 *secrete*
lactating 352.4 *secretory*
lactation 352.1 *secretion*, 387.3 *body fluid*, 387.7 *juiciness*
lactational 352.4 *secretory*
lactationally 352.8 *glandularly*
lacteal 352.5 *of a secretion*, 387.17 *milky*, 393.19 *juicy*
lacteally 352.8 *glandularly*, 387.26 *fluidly*
lacteous 387.17 *milky*
lactescence 387.7 *juiciness*, 446.7 *whiteness*
lactescent 352.4 *secretory*, 387.17 *milky*, 393.19 *juicy*, 446.1 *white*
lactic 58 Common Fatty Acids, 351.17 *drinkable*, 387.17 *milky*
lactiferous 352.4 *secretory*, 387.17 *milky*, 393.19 *juicy*
lactifugal 62.14 *counteracting*
lactifuge 62.4 *drug type*
lactogenic 352.6 *inducing secretion*
lactogenic hormone 58 Hormones
lactone 57 Types of Compounds
lactose 58 Common Sugars, 350.11 *food content*, 414.2 *sweetener*
lacuna 100.4 *emptiness*, 145.2 *omission*, 160.5 *caesura*, 218.3 *pause*, 248.8 *intervening space*, 265.1 *interval*, 593.2 *need*, 620.7 *defect*
Lacus Autumni 53 Seas
lacuscular 94.9 *lakelike*
Lacus Mortis 53 Seas
Lacus Somniorum 53 Seas
lacustral 94.9 *lakelike*
lacustrian 94.6 *lake dweller*, 94.9 *lakelike*
lacustrine 94.9 *lakelike*
lacustrine dweller 94.6 *lake dweller*
lacustrine dwelling 94.7 *lake dwelling*
Lacus Veris 53 Seas
lacy 274.4 *fine*, 288.6 *interwoven*
lad 206.7 *young man*, 206.9 *child*, 401.2 *male*, 401.3 *male title of address*
Ladakh 95 Mountains
ladder **359**, 136.3 *separateness*, 136.9 *separate*, 137.4 *means of connection*, 159.2 *consecution*, 275.8 *high thing*, 327.2 *route*, 638.2 *means of escape*
ladder-back 47.14 *wooden*
ladder-back chair 47.2 *chair*
ladder-climbing 359.6 *mounting*

ladder-like **359**
laddie 206.7 *young man*, 206.9 *child*
laddish 151.20 *disorderly*, 401.17 *male*
laddishness 151.8 *lawlessness*, 401.1 *male sex*
lade 144.6 *fill*, 257.6 *contain*, 369.14 *make heavy*
laden 144.8 *full*, 257.11, 369.2 *loaded*
laden weight 369.9 *avoirdupois weight*
ladies 353.13 *lavatory*
Ladies 727.7 *toilet*
ladies' man 224.6 *fickle person*, 340.6 *charmer*, 401.7 *libertine*, 821.9 *lover*, 826.5 *courting person*
ladies of the chorus 51.23 *cast*
Ladies Plate 36.5 Henley trophies
ladies' room 353.13 *lavatory*
lading 257.2 *load*, 369.6 *displacement*
Ladino 5 Languages and Groups of Languages
ladle **258**, 45.6 *kitchen equipment*, 326.15 *take away*
ladled 258.20 *containing*
Ladoga 94 Lakes, 94.5 *other major lakes*
lady 400.4 *civilized human*, 400.10 *member of society*, 402.2 *female*, 402.3 *female title of address*, 652.3 *well-behaved person*, 696.1 *master*, 802.1 *nobleman*, 804.4 *titleholder*, 817.6 *courteous person*, 823.11 *married woman*
Lady 402.3 *female title of address*
ladybird beetle 82 Insects
Lady Bountiful 729.4 *giver*, 755.9 *generous person*
Lady chapel 10.11 *place of worship*
Lady Day 10.15 *holy day*
lady fern 88 Ferns
lady in amorata 821.9 *lover*
lady-in-waiting 697.6 *domestic servant*
lady-killer 821.9 *lover*, 826.5 *courting person*
ladylike 402.15 *female*, 652.17 *well-behaved*, 794.5 *refined*, 802.4 *aristocratic*, 817.8 *good-mannered*
ladylike behaviour 652.2 *good conduct*
ladylikeness 817.2 *good manners*
lady luck 589.2 *luck*
Lady Luck 229.2 *chance*
Lady Mayor 696.3 *leader*
Lady Muck 802.1 *nobleman*
lady of the bedchamber 697.6 *domestic servant*
lady of the house 696.1 *master*
lady of the manor 696.1 *master*
lady of the night 402.7 *prostitute*
Lady Poverty 743.5 *poverty*
lady's fingers 45 Vegetables
lady's maid 295.28 *valet*, 697.6 *domestic servant*
Ladysmith 93 Cities
lady's slipper 84 Flowers and Flowering Plants
lady's smock 84 Flowers and Flowering Plants
lady with a lamp 60.16 *nurse*
Laestadianism 7 Christian Movements
laetrile 62 Medication
laevo form 57.13 *structure*
La Fayette 48 Writers
La Fleche 68 Breeds of Fowl
La Fontaine 48 Poets
Laforgue 48 Poets
lag 16.40 *lawbreaker*, 24.6 *pool*, 127.8 *be inferior*, 155.26 *bring up the rear*, 209.1 *lateness*, 209.6 *be late*, 293.30 *protect*, 328.2 *hesitate*, 358.1 *fall short*, 408.14 *be hot*, 480.3 *testify*, 483.13 *turn Queen's evidence*, 699.4 *detention*, 699.11 *detain*, 702.4 *prison sentence*, 702.10 *be in prison*
lag behind 155.26 *bring up the*

rear, 193.3 *mistime*, 209.6 *be late*, 304.6 *be in the rear*
lager glass 258.13 *drinking vessel*
Lagerkvist 48 Writers
laggard 209.4 *latecomer*, 328.15 *slow person*, 643.3 *not participating*
lagged 408.13 *heated*
lagger 480.7 *verifier*, 483.7 *person who gives evidence*
lagging 24.4 *carom*, 209.1 *lateness*, 209.12 *delaying*, 293.12 *protective covering*, 328.6 *hesitant*, 328.11 *lingering*, 408.3 *heater*
lagging behind 209.12 *delaying*
lagniappe 130.4 *extra*, 610.3 *superfluity*, 721.5 *profit*, 729.2 *gift*
lagomorph 77.12 *gnawing mammal*
Lagomorpha 77.12 *gnawing mammal*
lagomorphic 77.31 *rabbit-like*
lagomorphous 77.31 *rabbit-like*
lagoon 54.11 *coast*, 94.1 *lake*, 98.2 *island*
Lagoon Nebula 53 Nebulae
Lagos 93 Cities
Lagrange 52 Scientists
Lagrange's theorem 52 Named Concepts
lahar 54.26 *mass movement*
La Hire 53 Scientists
Lahnda 5 Languages and Groups of Languages
Lahore 93 Cities
laid 135.14 *conjunctive*, 396.15 *born*
laid-back 374.6 *softhearted*, 649.4 *at ease*, 783.7 *indifferent*
laid bare 238.9 *dilapidated*, 294.8 *uncovered*, 296.11 *exposed*, 530.10 *disclosed*
laid into 852.34 *censured*
laid low 238.11 *weakened*, 276.5 *low*, 806.3 *humbled*
laid off 15.9 *negotiated*, 252.11 *relegated*, 600.3 *not wanted*, 641.3 *inactive*, 643.2 *not working*, 645.7 *leisurely*, 704.10 *cancelled*, 727.13 *dismissed*
laid out 748.12 *expended*
laid to rest 399.10 *buried*
laid up 236.10 *powerless*, 238.9 *dilapidated*, 600.4 *disused*, 605.7 *stored*, 624.22 *sick*, 643.2 *not working*
laid up in lavender 637.7 *preserved*
Laing 61.29 *psychologist*
Laingian 61.33 *Freudian*
lair **256**, 77.20 *abode of mammals*, 293.15 *shelter*, 531.6 *privacy*, 634.3 *animal shelter*
laird 696.1 *master*, 723.6 *lord*
laissez faire 737.5 *commercial trade*
laissez-faire attitude 708.1 *permission*
lake **94**, 56.28 *colour*, 67.6 *dye*, 74.2 *waterway*, 120.2 *certain amount*
lake dweller 94
lake dwelling 94
lake-dwelling 94.9 *lakelike*
lake fog 55.33 *fog*
lake house 94.7 *lake dwelling*
Lakeland terrier 77 Breeds of Dogs
lakelet 94.2 *small lake*
lakelike 94
lake lodge 94.7 *lake dwelling*
lake naphthol 67.6 *dye*
Lakenfelder 68 Breeds of Fowl
lake of fire and brimstone 8.11 *heaven*
Lake of the Woods 94 Lakes
lake poet 48.14 *author*
Lake poets 48 Literary Groups and Movements
laker 94.6 *lake dweller*
lakes 777 Phobias by Topic
Lakes 94
lake sediment 54.27 *sediment*
lakeside dweller 94.6 *lake dweller*
lakeside house 94.7 *lake dwelling*

lakeside village 94.7 *lake dwelling*
lake trout 80 Fishes, 20.4 *American game fish*
lakh 179.10 *thousand*
Lakhame 8 Deities
Lakhmu 8 Deities
lakhs 741.3 *fortune*
Lakshmi 8 Deities
Lalande 52 Scientists, **53** Named Stars
Lallans 5.26 *dialect*
lallation 563.3 *speech defect*
lalophobia 777 Phobias by Name
lam 345.4 *hurry off*
lama 7.8 *priest*
Lamaism 7 Non-Christian Religions
Lamarck 52 Scientists
Lamarckian 59.27 *evolutionary*
Lamarckism 59.16 *evolution*
Lamartine 48 Poets
lamasery 7.10 *priestly dwelling*
lamb 45.20 *meat*, 68.8 *livestock*, 68.18 *practise livestock farming*, 77.19 *young mammal*, 77.35 *give birth*, 206.4 *young animal*, 245.11 *have young*, 658.3 *naive person*, 675.2 *symbol of peace*, 821.12 *nicknames for lovers*, 826.4 *terms of endearment*, 865.4 *innocent person*
Lamb 48 Writers
lambast 852.21 *berate*
lambaste 330.5 *beat*, 879.3 *hit*
lambasted 852.34 *censured*
lambasting 674.7 *boxing*, 852.8 *berating*
lambent 439.15 *lucent*
Lambert 52 Scientists
Lambert's law 56 Named Laws
Lambeth 93.5 *London*
Lambeth Palace 7.10 *priestly dwelling*
Lambeth Walk 46.2 *dance*
lambing house 68.7 *farm building*
lambkin 77.19 *young mammal*, 206.4 *young animal*
lambkins 821.12 *nicknames for lovers*, 826.4 *terms of endearment*
lamblike 865.5 *innocent*
Lamb of God 8.4 *God the Son*
lambrequin 544.8 *heraldic device*
lamb: scrag end 45
lamb: shoulder 45
lamb's liver 45.31 *offal*
lamb to the slaughter 222.3 *substitute thing*, 497.6 *trusting person*
lame 145.4 *incomplete*, 236.8 *overpower*, 238.7 *weaken*, 238.10 *ill*, 555.1 *unemphatic*, 614.8 *make useless*, 620.3 *deformed*, 628.5 *hurt*
lamé 67 Natural Fabrics
lamebrain 460.3 *unintelligent person*
lame dog 238.4 *weakling*, 722.6 *loser*
lame duck 238.4 *weakling*, 687.5 *person in adversity*, 722.6 *loser*, 747.6 *nonpayer*
lamella 89.4 *fungal body*, 266.3 *coat*
lamellar 266.9 *platelike*
lamellar compound 57.7 *chemical compound*
lamellate 266.9 *platelike*
lamellated 266.9 *platelike*
lamellation 266.6 *layering*
lamellibranch 81.5 *mollusc*
lamelliform 266.9 *platelike*
lamely 555.3 *unemphatically*
lameness 238.3 *poor health*, 555.2 *lack of emphasis*, 620.5 *imperfection*, 628.11 *hurt*
lament 774, **774**, 397.17 *bury*, 399.2 *funeral*, 399.8 *bury*, 431.13 *cry*, 770.8 *grieve*, 835.2 *condolence*, 835.9 *sorrow*
lamentable 774, 618.4 *poor*, 770.7 *distressing*, 776.8 *bad*
lamentation 774, 397.8 *after death*, 399.2 *funeral*, 431.6 *cry of pain*, 774.2 *lament*

Lamentation 774
lamented 397.19 *dead*
lamenter 774
lamenting 774, 399.11 *funeral*, 774.1 *lamentation*, 867.6 *penitent*
lame verse 48.6 *poetry*
lamia 11.4 *witch*, 76.7 *legendary beast*
lamina 47.11 *woodworking tool*, 52.38 *surface*, 83.6 *leaf*, 90.3 *plant body*, 266.3 *coat*, 379.3 *brittle thing*
laminaria 90 Algae
laminate 44.11 *make ceramics*, 47.18 *work wood*, 266.5 *layered thing*, 266.7 *layered*, 266.10 *layer*
laminated 266.7 *layered*, 266.8 *coated*
laminated furniture 47.1 *furniture*
laminated glass 44.9 *industrial ceramics*, 266.5 *layered thing*, 442.9 *glass*
laminated paper 604.3 *paper*
laminated wood 266.5 *layered thing*
lamination 266.6 *layering*
Lammas 10.15 *holy day*
lammergeier 78 Birds
Lammermuir 95 Mountains
lamp 56.25 *light source*, 439.5 *incandescent light*
Lampang 93 Cities
lampblack 447.8 *black pigment*
Lampedusa 48 Writers
lampholder 439.6 *electric light*
lamping 590.2 *chase*
lamplight 439.5 *incandescent light*
lamplighter 439.7 *lantern*
lamplit 439.18 *lit*
Lampong 5 Languages and Groups of Languages
lampoon 771.4 *entertainment*, 771.13 *be humorous*, 799.2 *act of derision*, 799.6 *deride*, 850.4, 854.6 *ridicule*, 854.14 *ridicule*
lampooner 771.6 *humorist*, 799.3 *derider*, 854.9 *ridiculer*
lampoonist 799.3 *derider*, 854.9 *ridiculer*
lamppost 275.6 *tall thing*, 439.6 *electric light*
lamprey 80 Fishes
lampshade 293.12 *protective covering*, 441.1 *dimness*, 634.2 *shelter*
lampshade making 42 Hobbies and Pastimes
lampshell 81.5 *mollusc*
lamp-standard 439.6 *electric light*
Lamut 5 Languages and Groups of Languages
Lān 92.3 *other*
LAN 65.15 *network*
Lanark 93 Cities
lanate 375.3 *barbed*
Lancashire 45 Cheeses, **92** Counties
Lancashire hotpot 45.44 *British dish*
Lancaster 93 Cities, **93** Cities
lance 69.6 *garden tool*, 322.2 *opener*, 322.20 *hole*, 338.23 *throw*, 380.8 *sharp-pointed thing*, 380.16 *use a sharp tool*, 398.17 *murder*, 670.6 *stab*, 679.37 *fight*, 680.8 *sharp weapon*
lance-corporal 679.17 *army person*
lanced 322.14 *holed*
lancelet 81.2 *protochordate*
Lancelot 134.5 *pure person*
Lancelot and Guinevere 821.10 *lovers*
lanceolate 83.18 *of leaves*, 380.1 *sharp*
lancer 32.15 *horse person*, 679.13 *historical soldiery*, 679.20 *cavalryman*
lance rest 671.7 *armour*
Lancers 46.2 *dance*
lance-shaped 380.1 *sharp*
lancet 43.13 *arched*, 322.2

opener, 380.8 *sharp-pointed thing*
lancet arch 43.5, 43.5 *arch*
lancet fish 80 Fishes
lancet window 43.9 *miscellaneous architectural features*
lancewood 85 Trees and Shrubs
Lanchow 93 Cities
lancinating 406.5 *painful*
lancination 406.1 *pain*
land 344, 21.6 *jump*, 30.10 *compete in gymnastics*, 54.6 *continent*, 74.10 *sail*, 83.14 *of plants*, 91.1 *country*, 249.1 *region*, 325.8 *be motionless*, 360.12 *drop*, 725.1 *property*
Land 52 Scientists, 92.3 *other*
land a blow 26.11 *do a combat sport*
Landais Pony 32 Breeds of Horse and Pony
land and sea 111.2 *opposites*
land a rabbit punch 26.11 *do a combat sport*
land art 50 Western Art Styles and Movements
land attack 670.12 *military attack*
landau 71 Carriages and Carts, **71** Motor Vehicles
Landau 52 Scientists
land breeze 36.1 *sailing*, 55.12 *wind*
land bridge 54.16 *ocean floor*, 98.5 *peninsula*
land crab 81.4 *arthropod*
landed 723.8 *possessing*, 725.8 *propertied*
landed estate 723.4 *possession*, 725.1 *property*
landed property 725.1 *property*
lander 53.33 *planetary probe*
landfall 344.11 *landing*
landfill 605.4 *storage*, 614.6 *refuse*, 727.8 *sink*
landfill site 727.5 *wasteyard*
land flowing with milk and honey 246.1 *fertility*, 714.4 *promised land*
land forces 17.2 *the military*
landform 54
land-grabber 539.17 *cheat*
landholding 723.1 *possession*
landing 344, 21.2 *field events*, 21.6 *track*, 30.5 *horizontal bar*, 73.5 *flight*, 256.7 *room*, 266.2 *level*, 279.3 *architectural summit*, 359.7 *means of ascent*, 360.5 *dive*
landing area 21.2 *field events*
landing beam 73.6 *flight control*
landing craft 679.24 *warship*
landing field 73.4 *airport*, 327.13 *flight path*
landing on one's feet 682.1 *success*
landing stage 359.7 *means of ascent*
landing strip 73.4 *airport*
land in the cooler 702.10 *be in prison*
landlady 606.4 *caterer*, 696.1 *master*
landlocked 94.9 *lakelike*, 290.9 *inland*
landlocked water 94.2 *small lake*
landlord 606.4 *caterer*, 696.1 *master*, 723.5 *possessor*, 804.4 *titleholder*
landlubber 656.10 *unskilled person*
landmark 103.2 *essential content*, 437.6 *visible thing*, 543.5 *indicator*, 611.2 *important matter*
landmass 54.6 *continent*, 98.1 *continent*, 249.1 *region*
landmine 680.16 *bomb*
land-office business 686.1 *prosperity*
Land of Liberty 91.7 *United States*
land of milk and honey 405.5 *idealized pleasure*, 519.8 *dreamland*, 588.6 *objective*
land of Nod 540.9 *sleep*
land of our fathers 249.4 *territorial division*
land of promise 714.4 *promised land*

Land of the Midnight Sun 409.6 *Arctic*
land on a beach 98.12 *be marooned*
land one in trouble 618.13 *be worthless*
land on one's feet 632.8 *be safe*, 682.7 *overcome obstacles*
land operations 676.8 *warfare*
Landor 48 Writers, **48** Poets
landowner 696.1 *master*, 723.5 *possessor*, 725.7 *property man*, 804.4 *titleholder*
landownership 723.1 *possession*
landowning 723.1 *possession*, 723.8 *possessing*
land pirate 539.17 *cheat*
Landrace 68 Breeds of Pig
Land Rover 71 Motor Vehicles
lands 725.1 *property*
landscape 50.10 *art subject*, 54.6 *continent*, 66.4 *portrait*, 69.19 *practise horticulture*, 435.7 *view*
landscape architect 43.2 *architect*, 69.13 *horticulturist*
landscape architecture 43.1 *architecture*, 69.1 *horticulture*
landscaped 69.19 *ornamental*
landscape gardener 69.13 *horticulturist*
landscape gardening 69.1 *horticulture*
landscape painter 50.16 *artist*
landscape photography 66.1 *photography*
landscapist 69.13 *horticulturist*
land shark 539.17 *cheat*
landside 73.4 *airport*
landslide 54.26 *mass movement*, 244.7 *agent of destruction*, 360.3 *downflow*
landslide victory 682.2 *victory*
landslip 244.7 *agent of destruction*, 360.3 *downflow*
land station 55.5 *weather station*
land tenure 723.1 *possession*
land travel 324.2 *momentum*
land-use planning 63.17 *civil engineering*
landward 332.10 *clockwise*
lane 21.1 *track events*, 71.3 *carriageway*, 137.5 *road*, 327.2 *route*, 327.3 *road*, 327.11 *channel*
Lange 61.29 *psychologist*
Langland 48 Poets
langlauf 18 Sporting Activities
langleik 49 Musical Instruments
Langley 52 Scientists
Langmuir 52 Scientists
Langobardic 5 Languages and Groups of Languages
Langrenus 53 Lunar Features
langspil 49 Musical Instruments
language 6.3 *subject*, 65.8 *software*, 65.9 *programming language*, 549.4 *literary style*, 564.1 *faculty of speech*
language group 5.11 *family of languages*
language laboratory 6.15 *schoolroom*
language of confusion 5.5 *nonstandard language*
language student 5.2 *linguist*
language type 5
langue 564.1 *faculty of speech*
languid 238.10 *ill*, 240.5 *inert*, 325.5 *sedentary*, 328.5 *unhurried*, 555.1 *unemphatic*, 643.3 *not participating*, 650.1 *fatigued*
languidly 238.14 *weakly*, 240.7 *inertly*, 325.10 *motionlessly*, 328.16 *slowly*, 643.16 *impassively*
languish 238.6 *be weak*, 624.24 *be unhealthy*, 650.5 *be fatigued*, 770.8 *grieve*
languisher 770.3 *sad person*
languishing 624.22 *sick*, 770.5 *sad*, 821.19 *enamoured*
languishing look 821.14 *communication of love*, 826.2 *courtship*
languishment 650.7 *fatigue*, 770.1 *sorrow*
languor 240.1 *inertness*, 325.1

motionlessness, 328.8 *slowness*, 643.7 *idleness*, 650.7 *fatigue*, 788.1 *boredom*

languorous 325.5 *sedentary*, 328.5 *unhurried*, 650.1 *fatigued*, 788.4 *boring*

languorously 325.10 *motionlessly*, 328.16 *slowly*, 788.8 *boringly*

langur 77 *Placental Mammals*

Lanier 48 Poets

lank 559.10 *ugly*

Lankester 52 Scientists

lankiness 274.7 *thinness*, 275.1 *height*

lanky 274.1 *thin*, 275.12 *tall*

lanner falcon 78 Birds

lanolin 386.6 *pomade*, 395.6 *ointment*, 395.8 *fat*, 630.9 *balm*

Lansing 93 Cities

lansquenet 42 Card Games

lantana 85 Trees and Shrubs

lantern 439, 43.9 *miscellaneous architectural features*, 275.8 *high thing*

lantern cupola 43.9 *miscellaneous architectural features*

lantern fish 80 Fishes

lantern fly 82 Insects

lantern-jawed 274.1 *thin*

lantern jaws 274.7 *thinness*

lanternslide 66.12 *development*

lanthanoid 57.6 *chemical element*

lanthanum 57 Chemical Elements

lanyard 74 Rigging, 36.3 *parts of a sailing boat*, 137.7 *tackle*

Lao 5 Languages and Groups of Languages

laodicean 783.6 *indifferent person*

Laodicean 333.3 *moderate person*

Laois 92 Counties

Laos 91 Countries

Lao Zi 4 Philosophers

lap 21.6 *race*, 33.6 *motor racing terms*, 33.10 *be on the track*, 39.1 *swimming*, 96.6 *river flow*, 96.7 *flow*, 142.3 *whole situation*, 143.3 *stage*, 214.2 *cycle*, 266.1 *layer*, 293.26 *overlie*, 313.2, 313.6 *circle*, 315.6 *round*, 315.12 *move round*, 320.7 *fold*, 329.6 *accelerate*, 334.1, 334.3 *circuit*, 351.13 *drink*, 357.3 *exceed*, 363.3 *orbit*, 363.7 *ring*, 424.5 *sound faint*, 634.1 *refuge*

laparoscope 60.7 *diagnosis*

laparoscopy 60.7 *diagnosis*

laparotomy 60 Surgical Operations, 630.12 *surgery*

La Paz 93 Cities

lapdog 77.9 *dog*, 167.6 *conformist*, 808.3 *sycophant*

lapel 130.3 *additional item*, 295.24 *part of garment*

lapel pin 544.5 *uniform*

lap fence 69.3 *ornamental garden*

lapidary 42 Hobbies and Pastimes, 5.43 *phrasal*, 50.18 *engraver*, 399.11 *funeral*

lapidary inscription 5.25 *inscription*

lapidary phrases 399.4 *funeral objects*

lapidate 338.23 *throw*, 670.7 *stone*, 879.5 *execute*

lapidation 670.18 *hit*, 879.13 *capital punishment*

lapideous 373.1 *hard*

lapidification 373.6 *solidification*

lapis lazuli 54 Minerals, **54** Gemstones, 454.6 *blue thing*

lap joint 47.10 *carpenter's term*

Laplace 52 Scientists

Laplace operator 52 Named Concepts

La Plata 93 Cities

lap of luxury 106.5 *comfortable circumstances*, 686.1, 686.1 *prosperity*

lap organ 49 Musical Instruments

Lapp 5 Languages and Groups of Languages

lapped 33.11 *racing*, 329.3 *accelerating*

lappet 130.3 *additional item*

lapping 33.11 *racing*, 96.6 *river flow*, 329.3 *accelerating*, 329.9 *acceleration*, 351.1 *drinking*

Lapps 1 Peoples

lap robe 293.5 *body covering*

Lapsang Souchong 351.3 *tea*

lapse 248.8 *intervening space*, 248.21 *space*, 335.16 *wandering*, 337.1 *go backward*, 337.19 *backsliding*, 360.2 *sinkage*, 468.5 *inattentive act*, 498.8 - *disbelieve*, 504.9 *trivial error*, 504.19 *make a mistake*, 504.20 *transgress*, 585.4 *be unaccustomed*, 628.1 *deteriorate*, 628.7 *deterioration*, 864.16 *be wicked*, 866.3 *sin*, 877.16 *do wrong*

lapsed 3.18 *in the past*, 628.12 *deteriorated*

lapsed believer 720.5 *nonobserver*

lapse into disorder 151.25 *be disordered*

lapse into oblivion 127.10 *follow*

lapse into silence 566

lapse into unconsciousness 236.6 *be powerless*

lapse of memory 512.3 *poor memory*

lapse of time 185.2 *passage of time*, 188.2 *time*

lapsing 337.23 *receding*

Laptev 97 Oceans and Seas

lap-top computer 65.3 *computer*

lap up 348.11 *ingest*, 351.13 *drink*

Laputan 519.11 *fantastical*

lapwing 78 Birds, 78.3 *water bird*

lapwings 161 Collective Names by Animal

larboard 74 Parts of a Ship

larcenist 736.8 *thief*

larcenous 736.17 *stolen*

larcenously 736.19 *thievishly*

larceny 736.1 *stealing*

larch 85 Trees and Shrubs

lard 45.7 *basic ingredient*, 45.55 *cook*, 259.8 *fat*, 386.13 *lubricate*, 386.14 *anoint*, 395.8 *fat*, 395.18 *anoint*

lardaceous 386.10, 395.11 *oily*

larder 45.3 *kitchen*, 45.4 *kitchen container*, 256.7 *room*, 605.4 *storage*

larder-fridge 45.4 *kitchen container*

larding needle 45.6 *kitchen equipment*

Lardner 48 Writers

lardy 386.10, 395.11 *oily*

lardy cake 45.36 *cake*

Lares 8 Deities

large 861, 259.15 *big*, 369.1 *heavy*, 755.4 *big*

large amount 120.2 *certain amount*, 181.2 *multitude*

large-animal practice 60.5 *veterinary medicine*

large as life 259.15 *big*

Large Black 68 Breeds of Pig

large-format camera 66.16 *camera*

large-hearted 833.6 *philanthropic*

large inheritance 742.5 *wealth*

large-lettered 5.41 *lettered*

largely 259, 261, 142.13 *on the whole*, 164.31 *overall*, 369.16 *heavily*, 611.9 *importantly*

Large Magellanic Cloud 53 Galaxies

largemouth black bass 20.4 *American game fish*

Large Munsterlander 77 Breeds of Dogs

largeness 861, 259.2 *bigness*

large number 169

large numbers 181.2 *multitude*

large office 647.1 *workshop*

large order 659.3 *difficult task*

large-print book 436.3 *aid for poor sight*

larger 261.7 *bigger*

larger than life 259.15 *big*

large scale 259

large-scale 259.15 *big*

large size 259.3 *large scale*, 861.14 *largeness*

large-size 259.15 *big*, 861.7 *large*

largess 729.1 *giving*, 729.3 *offering*

largest 52.75 *equal*

largest part 143

large turnout 181.4 *throng*

Large White 68 Breeds of Pig

larghetto 328.16 *slowly*

largo 49 Musical Terms, 328.16 *slowly*

lariat 137.9 *yoke*

lark 78 Birds, 78.6 *songbird*, 359.11 *ascender*, 762.2 *fun*, 771.5 *joke*

lark about 506.8 *fool*

lark around 640.4 *act*

Larkin 48 Poets

larks 161 Collective Names by Animal

larkspur 84 Flowers and Flowering Plants

Larne 93 Cities

larrikin 832.8 *malefactor*

larrup 879.3 *hit*

larva 82, 59.15 *developmental biology*, 76.5 *aquatic animal*, 206.4 *young animal*, 226.3 *rudiment*

larval 59.26 *developmental*, 82.13 *immature*

laryngectomy 60 Surgical Operations

laryngitis 406.2 *painful condition*, 422.4 *silence*, 424.2 *sound reducer*, 624.9 *respiratory disease*

laryngotomy 60 Surgical Operations

larynx 423.4 *sound maker*, 564.5 *organ of speech*

lasagne 45 Types of Pasta

lasagnette 45 Types of Pasta

lascivious 622.9 *obscene*, 782.11 *lustful*, 821.20 *amorous*, 877.14 *lecherous*

lasciviously 622.12 *dirtily*, 782.20 *lustfully*, 821.30 *lovingly*

lasciviousness 622.3 *obscenity*, 821.5 *desire*, 877.3 *sexual immorality*

laser 56, 235.9 *electronics*, 439.12 *highlight*, 680.1 *weapon*

laser copy 545.5 *copy*

laserprinter 65.7 *peripheral*

laser printer 114.3 *copier*

laser sailing 18 Sporting Activities

laser show 51.5 *show*, 439.12 *highlight*

laser surgery 60.9 *surgery*

laser targeting 670.13 *air attack*

lash 135.10 *link*, 137.11 *connect*, 228.4 *negative stimulus*, 228.10 *manipulate*, 241.9 *make violent*, 330.5 *beat*, 330.13 *blow*, 648.1 *hasten*, 852.21 *berate*, 879.3 *hit*, 879.14 *instrument of punishment*

lash back 331.1 *recoil*

lashed 135.15 *tied*, 137.15 *connected*

lashing 137.6 *line*

lashings 608.8 *plenty*

lash into a fury 241.9 *make violent*

lash out at 670.5 *strike*

lash up 135.10 *link*

Lasker 18 Sporting Personalities

lass 206.8 *young woman*, 206.9 *child*, 402.3 *female title of address*, 821.9 *lover*

Lassa fever 624.7 *tropical disease*

lassi 45.49 *Indian dish*, 351.5 *milk*

lassie 206.8 *young woman*, 206.9 *child*, 402.2 *female*, 402.3 *female title of address*

lassitude 650.7 *fatigue*

lasso 137.9 *yoke*, 137.12 *bind*, 680.6 *historical missile weapon*

lassoed 137.16 *bound*

lasso lift 41.6 *ice-skating*

last 75 General Units, **188**, 99.19 *continue to be*, 154.11 *prior*, 155.20 *rear*, 157.20 *ending*, 157.24 *limiting*, 195.12 *suc-*

ceeding, 195.15 *as follows*, 217.5 *be permanent*, 219.4 *protract*, 345.11 *departing*, 378.10 *be tough*, 396.16 *live*, 684.8 *concluded*

last act 157.10 *ending*, 684.2 *conclusion*

last agony 397.7 *dying day*

last an eternity 217.5 *be permanent*

last a round 26.12 *wrestle*

last arrival 209.1 *lateness*

last arriver 209.4 *latecomer*

last ball 157.9 *close*

last bid 596.5 *attempt*

last breath 157.3 *death*, 397.7 *dying day*

last cent 157.8 *tail*

last challenge 596.5 *attempt*

last-ditcher 577.8 *obstinate person*, 663.9 *opposer*

last-ditch stand 209.3 *delayed action*

last forever 184.9 *be infinite*, 190.5 *be eternal*, 217.5 *be permanent*

last frontier 157.7 *limit*

last gallery 40.5 *real tennis*

last gasp 157.3 *death*, 397.7 *dying day*, 602.1 *means*

last handshake 345.9 *parting*

last hope 602.1 *means*, 775.1 *hope*

last hour 397.7 *dying day*

lasting 99, 188, 186.5 *timeless*, 217.7 *permanent*, 219.6 *protracted*, 378.1 *tough*, 396.12 *alive*, 584.11 *normal*

lastingly 217.9 *permanently*, 219.7 *continually*, 378.12 *toughly*

lastingness 378.6 *toughness*

lasting peace 675.1 *peace*

lasting power 378.8 *physical strength*

lasting through time 185

last innings 157.9 *close*

last in the field 195.8 *follower*

last judgment 157.5 *fate*

Last Judgment 199.3 *future condition*, 492.4 *judgment day*

last lap 157.9 *close*, 344.15 *destination*

last laugh 157.10 *ending*

lastly 157.26 *finally*, 195.15 *as follows*

last man in 195.8 *follower*

last minute 209.2 *late hour*, 210.3 *critical time*

last-minute 209.11 *late in the day*, 210.8 *in time*, 633.2 *unsafe*, 648.3 *hasty*

last-minute preparations 209.3 *delayed action*

last-minute rescue 592.3 *expedient plan*

last-minute rush 648.4 *haste*

last moment 172.4 *zero level*

last month 200.1 *past time*, 200.22 *in the past*

last name 560.8 *name*

last night 200.1 *past time*

last of the big spenders 607.6 *waster*

last one out 132.6 *person remaining*

last orders 157.11 *finality*

last out 188.6 *last*

last outpost 302.3 *furthest point*

last over 157.9 *close*

last penny 157.8 *tail*

last place 155.10 *rear*, 195.3 *subordination*

last post 345.9 *parting*, 399.2 *funeral*, 543.6 *word*, 774.2 *lament*

last quarter 53.17 *moon*

last resort 592.3 *expedient plan*, 602.1 *means*, 615.5 *convenience*, 634.1 *refuge*

last rest 325.3 *resting place*

last rites 10.5 *Christian rite*, 397.7 *dying day*, 774.1 *lamentation*

last round 157.9 *close*

last season 200.22 *in the past*

last-second 633.2 *unsafe*

last shot 596.5 *attempt*

last stage 157.9 *close*
last stop 157.6 *end point,* 344.15 *destination*
last straw 610.2 *overdoing it,* 661.6 *burden,* 684.3 *elaboration,* 828.3 *cause of offence*
last stroke 684.3 *elaboration*
last throw 602.1 *means*
last time of asking 712.2 *demand*
last touch 144.1 *completeness,* 684.3 *elaboration*
last try 596.5 *attempt*
last waltz 46.2 *dance*
last week 200.1 *past time,* 200.22 *in the past*
last will and testament 570.5 *will,* 718.2 *promise,* 729.1 *giving*
last word 157.10 *ending,* 209.3 *delayed action,* 478.5 *counterstatement,* 617.8 *exceller,* 619.3 *perfection,* 627.5 *improvement,* 654.4 *adviser,* 710.3 *business offer*
last words 155.9 *conclusion,* 157.3 *death,* 345.9 *parting,* 397.7 *dying day,* 684.2 *conclusion*
last year 200.1 *past time,* 200.22 *in the past*
Las Vegas 93 Cities, 93.2 *American cities*
Las Vegas wedding 823.5 *wedding*
latch 135.5 *joint,* 137.8 *fastening,* 137.12 *bind,* 323.3 *restrainer,* 323.7 *close*
latched 137.16 *bound,* 323.12 *closed*
latch on to 522.6 *understand,* 808.14 *follow*
late 209, 209, 154.11 *prior,* 195.12 *succeeding,* 200.20 *former,* 205.7 *evening,* 209.14 *dead,* 211.10 *untimely,* 328.7 *delayed,* 397.19 *dead,* 595.1 *unprepared,* 705.7 *resigning*
late arrival 209.1 *lateness*
late arriver 209.4 *latecomer*
late at night 205.7 *evening*
late bloomer 209.4 *latecomer*
latecomer 209, 195.8 *follower,* 201.8 *new arrival*
late developer 209.4 *latecomer*
late edition 532.4 *newspaper*
lateen 74 Sailing Ships and Boats
lateen sail 74 Sails
late evening 441.1 *dimness*
late extra 532.4 *newspaper*
Late Greek 5 Languages and Groups of Languages
late hour 209
late in the day 209
late lamented 209.14 , 397.19 *dead*
late lift 21.2 *field events*
lately 200.22 *in the past,* 201.21 *newly,* 209.15 *late,* 209.18 *formerly,* 211.15 *at the wrong time,* 705.10 *by resigning*
latency 527, 240.1 *inertness,* 325.1 *motionlessness,* 438.4 *invisibility,* 520.4 *type of meaning,* 542.4 *plot,* 657.1 *cunning*
Latency 527
lateness 209, 193.1 *wrong time,* 211.1 *untimeliness,* 595.8 *lack of preparation,* 648.4 *haste*
Lateness 209
late-night review 51.5 *show*
latent 527, 11.14 *occult,* 240.5 *inert,* 325.5 *sedentary,* 438.1 *invisible,* 531.15 *disguised,* 591.18 *avoiding*
latent heat 56.38 *thermodynamics,* 408.2 *heat measurement*
latent image 66.11 *emulsion*
latently 527, 240.7 *inertly,* 325.10 *motionlessly*
latent meaning 520.4 *type of meaning,* 527.11 *mysteriousness*
latentness 527.6 *latency*
latent things 527
later 209, 209, 155.17 *next,* 155.28 *after,* 195.12 *succeeding,* 197.3 *another time,* 199.11 *future,* 199.14 *in the future*

lateral 19.9 *play,* 19.15 *play-offence,* 305.6 *side*
lateral bud 83.8 *bud*
laterality 305.1 *side*
lateral line 80.5 *fish anatomy*
laterally 305
lateral movement 54.13 *ocean current*
lateral root 83.7 *root*
laterals 237.1 *strength*
lateral thinking 461.5 *creative thought,* 518.2 *basis of supposition*
lateral water hazard 29.1 *golf*
later generations 155.12 *successor,* 195.6 *posterity*
late riser 209.4 *latecomer*
lateritic soil 54.36 *soil*
later on 199.14 *in the future,* 209.17 *later*
later time 197.1 *different time*
late-running 209.12 *delaying*
latest 195.12 *succeeding,* 201.10 *new*
latest news 533.9 *news story*
late wood 85.3 *timber*
latex 85 Tree Products, 352.2 *secreted substance,* 377.4 *rubber,* 387.2 *juice,* 604.1 *materials*
lath 47.12 *wood,* 47.17 *carpenter,* 266.4 *slice,* 274.11 *fineness,* 604.1 *materials*
lath and plaster 604.2 *building material*
lathe 47.11 *woodworking tool,* 47.17 *carpenter,* 63.9 *machine tool,* 220.4 *medium of conversion*
lather 386.4 *lubricant,* 386.13 *lubricate,* 390.10 *air bubble,* 395.5 *lubricant,* 395.17 *oil,* 621.14 *bathe,* 879.3 *hit*
lathering 621.5 *ablutions*
lathery 446.2 *whitened*
lathi 680.7 *blunt weapon*
lathing 47.12 *wood*
laths 47.10 *carpenter's term*
lathwork 47.12 *wood*
laticifer 352.3 *gland*
laticiferous 352.4 *secretory*
Latimeria 80 Fishes
Latin 5 Languages and Groups of Languages
Latin American Integration Association 13.5 *international trade*
Latinate 557.4 *ornate*
Latino 1.6 *race*
latitude 52.39 *angle,* 248.6 *available space,* 249.2 *geographical region,* 251.1 *situation,* 268.4 *size,* 271.4 *breadth,* 302.4 *boundary marker,* 698.5 *scope,* 814.4 *freedom*
latitude and longitude 250.2 *exact location*
latitudinal 249.16 *regional,* 302.6 *furthest*
latitudinal line 122.7 *dividing line*
latitudinally 249.19 *geographically*
latitudinarian 691.2 *lenient person,* 698.8 *free-thinker,* 698.10 *independent*
latitudinarianism 698.1 *freedom*
Latitudinarianism 7 Christian Movements
latrine 353.13 *lavatory,* 419.2 *something that makes an unpleasant smell,* 727.7 *toilet*
latter 155.17 *next,* 195.12 *succeeding,* 304.4 *rear*
latter days 199.3 *future condition*
Latter-Day Saint 7.5 *Christian*
latter end 304.2 *rear end*
latterly 201.21 *newly*
lattice 57.4 *crystal,* 288.2 *braid,* 322.6 *porous thing,* 382.4 *framework*
latticework 382.4 *framework*
Latvia 91 Countries
Latvian 5 Languages and Groups of Languages
Latvian Harness Horse 32 Breeds of Horse and Pony
laud 9.7 *worship,* 10.19 *offer worship,* 849.17, 851.3 *praise,* 851.14 *praise*

Lauda 18 Sporting Personalities
laudable 617.1 *worthy,* 782.8 *desirable,* 849.13 *respectable,* 851.21 *praiseworthy*
laudably 617.11 *worthily*
laudanum 242.2 *moderator,* 404.4 *anaesthetic,* 630.5 *analgesic*
laudation 9.1 *worship,* 10.3 *rite of worship,* 851.3 *praise*
laudational 10.21 *ritualistic*
laudator 851.9 *praiser*
laudatory 851.18 *approving,* 853.12 *flattering*
lauds 10.4 *public worship*
Laue 52 Scientists
laugh 431, 771, 773, 423.8 *be loud,* 431.2 *cry of joy,* 506.2 *solecism,* 543.3, 543.11 *gesture,* 762.7 *show joy,* 769.7 *be cheerful,* 773.3 *laughter*
laughable 506.5 *nonsensical,* 771.9 *funny,* 773.10 *laughing,* 798.5 *ridiculous*
laughableness 798.1 *ludicrousness*
laughably 771.16 *humorously*
laugh all the way to the bank 721.14 *profit*
laugh at 581.3 *exclude,* 799.6 *deride,* 850.25 *taunt*
laugh at an offer 609.6 *be unsatisfied*
laugh at danger 778.15 *be courageous*
laugher 773.4 *rejoicer*
laughing 773, 431.17 *cheering,* 543.15 *gestural,* 769.1 *cheerful*
laughing gas 87 Common Chemical Compounds, 62 Medication, 630.5 *analgesic*
laughing jackass 78 Birds
laughing owl 78 Birds
laughing stock 799, 117.6 *misfit,* 539.22 *dupe,* 666.4 *dissenter,* 850.9 *butt*
laugh in someone's face 668.6 *be insubordinate*
laugh in the face of 807.29 *ridicule*
laugh like a drain 771.14 *laugh*
laugh-line 321.2 *wrinkle*
laugh one's head off 771.14 *laugh*
laugh on the other side of one's face 515.5 *be crestfallen*
laugh out of court 807.29 *ridicule*
laughter 773, 423.1 *loudness,* 431.2 *cry of joy,* 769.3 *cheerfulness,* 771.2 *amusement*
laughter and tears 111.2 *opposites*
laugh till one cries 771.14 *laugh*
launch 74 Ships and Boats, 53, 74.9 *navigate,* 156.1 *beginning,* 156.6 *inauguration,* 156.9 *premiere,* 156.20 *activate,* 156.23 *inaugurate,* 201.19 *begin,* 226.11 *inaugurate,* 322.11 *beginning,* 322.24 *begin,* 330.4 *throw,* 338.20 *propel,* 338.33 *start,* 359.19 *take off,* 457.1 *appearance,* 457.14 *present,* 597.1 *undertake,* 812.19 *install*
launch a balloon d'essai 596.4 *test*
launch an appeal 712.8 *solicit money,* 721.9 *gain,* 729.6 *give to charity*
launch an attack 670.1 *attack*
launch a sailing boat 36.15 *sail*
launch a trial balloon 532.13 *make public,* 596.4 *test*
launched 74.11 *nautical,* 156.37 *enrolled,* 201.13 *inaugurated*
launched into eternity 397.19 *dead*
launcher 53.35 *rocketry*
launching 74.4 *shipbuilding,* 156.9 *premiere,* 201.4 *beginning,* 594.9 *preparation*
launching ceremony 74.4 *shipbuilding*
launching pad 680.5 *missile weapon*

launching site 327.13 *flight path*
launch into 597.1 *undertake*
launch into eternity 398.16 *kill*
launch out at 670.5 *strike*
launch party 665.7 *social gathering*
launch vehicle 53.35 *rocketry*
launder 376.11 *smooth,* 621.13 *clean*
laundered 621.17 *cleaned*
laundered money 878.8 *secret money*
launderer 621.12 *cleaner*
laundering 67.8 *fabric treatment*
laundress 621.12 *cleaner*
laundrette 621.7 *washer*
laundry 621, 621.2 *cleaning,* 647.1 *workshop*
laundry basket 258.7 *basket*
laundry maid 697.6 *domestic servant*
laundryman 621.12 *cleaner*
laundry room 256.7 *room,* 647.1 *workshop*
launeddas 49 Musical Instruments
Laurasia 54.19 *plate tectonics*
laureate 126.6 *paragon*
laurel 85 Trees and Shrubs
laurels 588.6 *objective,* 681.1 *trophy*
laurel wreath 681.1 *trophy*
lauric 58 Common Fatty Acids
Lausanne 93 Cities
Lautréamont 48 Writers
lav 256.7 *room*
lava 54.25 *eruption,* 393.13 *mud,* 408.8 *hot place*
lavabo 10.6 *Eucharist*
lava flow 54.25 *eruption*
lavage 621.5 *ablutions*
laval 54.55 *volcanic*
lavation 621.5 *ablutions*
lavatory 353, 256.7 *room,* 727.7 *toilet*
lavatory attendant 621.12 *cleaner*
lavatory bowl 727.7 *toilet*
lavatory paper 621.11 *cleaning cloth*
lave 134.10 *purify,* 389.34 *hose,* 621.15 *purify*
lavender 45 Herbs and Spices, 84 Flowers and Flowering Plants, 418.2 *fragrant thing,* 455.3 *purple thing,* 455.6 *purple*
Lavender 68 Breeds of Fowl
lavender bag 418.2 *fragrant thing*
lavender sachet 418.2 *fragrant thing*
lavender water 389, 84.8 *flower product,* 418.2 *fragrant thing*
laver 90 Algae, 45.33 *vegetable*
Laver 18 Sporting Personalities
laverbread 45.33 *vegetable*
laver bread 90.5 *algal product*
laverock 359.11 *ascender*
laving 389.11 *wash*
lavish 541.9 *be extravagant,* 541.14 *extravagant,* 607.1 *waste,* 607.8 *wasteful,* 608.2 *plentiful,* 610.4 *be excessive,* 742.3 *opulent,* 755.1 *generous,* 755.3 *abundant,* 757.1 *extravagant,* 757.7 *waste,* 811.24 *grand*
lavishly 541.17 *excessively,* 607.10 *wastefully,* 742.16 *wealthily,* 755.12 *generously,* 757.9 *extravagantly,* 811.40 *grandly*
lavishness 541.3 *extravagance,* 607.3 *waste,* 742.7 *opulence,* 757.4 *extravagance,* 811.9 *grandeur*
lavish upon 610.4 *be excessive,* 729.5 *give*
Lavoisier 52 Scientists
Lavumisa 93 Cities
law 16, 56, 16.1 *the law,* 52.65 *theory,* 150.9 *discipline,* 166.1 *rule,* 214.4 *orderliness,* 492.2 *verdict,* 505.1 *maxim,* 584.5 *tradition,* 654.3 *precept,* 688.1 *authority,* 692.1 *command,* 708.1 *permission*
Law 16
law-abiding 16, 150.17 *disci-*

plined, 167.14 *conformist*, 652.17 *well-behaved*, 673.5 *submitting*, 675.7 *peaceful*, 694.7 *obedient*, 843.11 *right-minded*, 857.4 *honourable*
law-abiding citizen 652.3 *well-behaved person*, 694.4 *obedient person*
law and equity 16.1 *the law*
law and order 150.9 *discipline*, 675.1 *peace*
lawbreaker 16, 693.9 *criminal*, 832.8 *malefactor*, 844.10 *wrongdoer*, 858.4 *dishonourable person*, 864.9 *wicked person*
lawbreaking 16, 713, 693.2 *violation of the law*, 693.13 *disobedient*, 858.3 *criminality*, 858.7 *criminal*, 864.7 *criminality*, 864.15 *criminal*
law consultancy 16.32 *jurisprudence*
law court 16, 16.7 *legal trial*, 492.3 *place of judgment*
law courts 16.27 *courtroom*
Law Courts 43 Noted Buildings
law-enforcer 16.17 *police officer*
lawful 16.44 *legal*, 150.17 *disciplined*, 537.24 *pedantic*, 688.12 *authoritative*, 708.7 *permitted*, 845.8 *entitled*
lawful authority 688.1 *authority*
lawfully 16.81 *legally*, 16.86 *jurisdictionally*, 688.23 *authoritatively*, 708.9 *with permission*
lawfulness 16.28 *legality*, 537.11 *pedantry*
lawful possession 723.1 *possession*
lawgiver 12.7 *governor*, 16.9 *lawmaker*, 653.13 *director*
lawgiving 16.31 *legislation*, 16.45 *legislative*
lawless 16, 151.20 *disorderly*, 689.6 *anarchic*, 693.13 *disobedient*, 713.10 *law-breaking*, 844.16 *in the wrong*
lawlessly 16, 689.8 *anarchically*, 693.17 *disobediently*, 713.11 *disapprovingly*
lawlessness 16, 151, 689.1 *anarchy*, 693.2 *violation of the law*, 713.2 *disorder*, 844.6 *unlawfulness*
Law Lord 16.9 *lawmaker*
lawmaker 16, 699, 12.7 *governor*, 653.13 *director*
lawmaking 16.31 *legislation*, 16.45 *legislative*, 653.3 *management*
lawn 67 Natural Fabrics, 69.3 *ornamental garden*, 87.2 *grassland*, 376.8 *smooth thing*, 453.8 *greenness*
lawn bowls 25.1 *green bowling*
lawn grass 87.1 *grass*
lawn meet 32.8 *hunting*
lawn mower 69.6 *garden tool*, 87.5 *grass-cutter*, 380.9 *sharp-edged thing*, 603.2 *garden tool*
lawn party 815.5 *party*
lawn rake 69.6 *garden tool*
lawn tennis 18 Sporting Activities, 40.1 *tennis*
law of averages 166.3 *rule of nature*, 488.5 *probability theory*
law of commerce 16.1 *the law*
law of contract 16.1 *the law*
law of crime 16.1 *the law*
law of diminishing returns 628.7 *deterioration*
law officer 16
law of nations 16.1 *the law*
law of the air 16.1 *the law*
law of the jungle 166.3 *rule of nature*, 689.1 *anarchy*
law of the land 16.1 *the law*
law of the Medes and the Persians 225.4 *stable thing*
law of the sea 16.1 *the law*
Lawrence 48 Writers, **48** Willers, **48** Poets, **52** Scientists
lawrencium 57 Chemical Elements
law reports 16.7 *legal trial*
laws 12.5 *political organization*

law school 6.12 *educational institution*
laws of Medes and the Persians 654.3 *precept*
laws of motion 56.6 *law*, 324.1 *motion*
laws of nature 367.1 *material world*
laws of reflection 56.6 *law*
laws of refraction 56.6 *law*
laws of thermodynamics 56.6 *law*
lawsuit 16.5, 16.33 *litigation*, 640.1 *action*, 856.1 *accusation*
lawyer 16, 228.7 *motivator*, 233.5 *influential person*, 465.3 *curious person*, 467.6 *attentive person*, 473.6 *arguer*, 477.9 *questioner*, 654.4 *adviser*, 679.5 *arguer*, 707.3 *agent*, 716.4 *negotiator*
lax 139.8 *nonadhesive*, 240.5 *inert*, 374.1 *soft*, 374.6 *soft-hearted*, 470.5 *indifferent*, 482.1 *undiscriminating*, 491.6 *indeterminate*, 643.3 *not participating*, 691.4 *lenient*, 698.12 *unconditional*, 708.8 *permitting*, 720.11 *nonobservant*, 783.8 *careless*, 814.10 *free*, 831.6 *benevolent*, 864.13 *venial*
laxation 374.12 *gentleness*
laxative 62.4 *drug type*, 62.17 *stimulating*, 134.4 *purgative*, 349.28 *propellant*, 349.29 *expulsive*, 353.25 *faecal*, 621.2 *cleaning*, 630.6 *purgative*, 630.17 *remedial*
laxity 240.1 *inertness*, 374.12 *gentleness*, 491.14 *indeterminacy*, 504.2 *inaccuracy*, 691.1 *leniency*, 698.6 *liberality*, 720.1 *nonobservance*, 783.2 *carelessness*, 814.4 *freedom*, 864.3 *venial sin*, 877.3 *sexual immorality*
laxly 139.10 *noncohesively*, 374.17 *softly*, 374.18 *softheartedly*, 708.9 *with permission*
laxness 374.12 *gentleness*, 698.6 *liberality*
lay 48.7 *poem*, 63.30 *engineer*, 135.11 *make love*, 245.11 *have young*, 245.14 *have sex*, 266.10 *layer*, 282.7 *make horizontal*, 332.2 *bearing*, 433.2 *song*, 502.7 *semi-skilled*, 656.2 *unskilled*
lay a block 25.7 *bowl*
lay aboard 670.9 *attack successfully*
layabout 641.2 *nonacting person*, 643.8 *nonworker*
lay about one 670.5 *strike*, 674.12 *fight*
lay a cornerstone 284.11 *support*
lay a false scent 531.11 *conceal oneself*, 539.27 *be false*
lay a foundation stone 284.11 *support*
lay a hand on 862.11 *be evil*
Layamon 48 Writers
lay an embargo on 325.9 *make motionless*
lay aside 326.15 *take away*, 581.2 *discard*, 600.6 *stop using*
lay at one's feet 710.11 *volunteer*
lay a trap for 539.33 *snare*
lay at the feet of 729.5 *give*
layaway 34.8 *mountaineering*
lay away 605.6 *store*
layaway move 34.3 *climbing technique*
laybacking 34.3 *climbing technique*, 34.8 *mountaineering*
lay-back spin 41.6 *ice-skating*
lay bare 294.11 *uncover*, 296.14 *undress*, 437.10 *make visible*, 496.2 *detect*, 526.3 *reveal*, 530.5 *disclose*
lay before 710.9 *offer*
lay bricks 293.28 *face*
lay by 605.6 *store*
lay-by 72.2 *track*, 218.4 *stopping place*, 356.2 *passing along*
lay claim to 845.14 *be entitled*
lay disciple 7.7 *monk*
lay down 4.22 *propound a philos-*

ophy, 166.13 *rule*, 266.10 *layer*, 282.7 *make horizontal*, 362.1 *lower*, 518.5 *suppose*
lay down a cellar 351.15 *provide drink*
lay down conditions of employment 15.11 *conduct industrial relations*
lay down guidelines 302.7 *limit*
lay down one's arms 673.3 *submit*, 677.5 *make peace*
lay down one's life 397.16 *meet one's fate*
lay down the law 12.11 *govern*, 166.13 *rule*, 490.20 *be certain*, 535.21 *be assertive*, 688.19 *be authoritarian*, 692.9 *command*, 807.27 *dare*
lay eggs 670.3 *bomb*
layer 266, 266, 68.8 *livestock*, 69.15 *cultivate*, 245.13 *propagate*, 258.4 *rack*, 282.3 *flat thing*, 293.3 *coating*, 293.24 *coat*, 320.1, 320.7 *fold*, 390.3 *atmospheric layers*
Layer 266
layer cake 266.5 *layered thing*
layer cloud 55.20 *cloud appearance*
layered 266
layered thing 266
layering 266, 69.5 *gardening*
layer-on of hands 630.15 *healer*
layette 295.23 *children's clothes*
lay eyes on 435.12 *see*
lay for 332.7 *take a direction*
lay hands on 407.11 *touch*, 721.9 *gain*
lay in 605.6 *store*
lay in ashes 244.10 *lay waste*
lay in a stock 606.5 *provision*
lay in drink 351.15 *provide drink*
laying bare 294.1 *uncovering*, 296.1 *undress*
laying claim to 723.1 *possession*
laying hen 68.8 *livestock*
laying into 852.8 *berating*
laying it on 817.4 *deference*
laying off 15.2 *industrial negotiations*, 349.18 *dismissal*
laying on 293.1 *covering*
laying one's hands on 250.3 *locating*
laying on of hands 10.5 *Christian rite*, 407.2 *touching*, 630.11 *medical art*
laying open 526.10 *manifestation*
laying siege 821.6, 826.2 *courtship*
laying the first stone 156.9 *premiere*
laying waste 244.5 *havoc*, 670.14 *siege*
lay in ruins 244.10 *lay waste*
lay in the dust 244.9 *demolish*
lay in the grave 399.8 *bury*
lay into 350.22 *eat well*, 670.5 *strike*, 852.21 *berate*
lay it on 350.22 *eat well*, 541.10 *boast*, 817.13 *defer to*, 853.8 *flatter*
lay it on thick 541.10 *boast*, 586.15 *persuade*, 610.4 *be excessive*, 853.8 *flatter*
lay it on with a trowel 541.10 *boast*, 610.4 *be excessive*, 853.8 *flatter*
lay low 276.9 *lower*, 670.5 *strike*
layman 502.5 *ignorant person*
lay off 15.11 *conduct industrial relations*, 218.8 *cause to cease*, 218.12 *stop*, 252.17 *relegate*, 325.11 *stop*, 349.2 *dismiss*, 600.7 *stop work*, 643.14 *make inactive*, 645.5 *dismiss*, 704.7 *terminate*, 727.10 *dismiss*, 767.12 *relieve from duty*
lay-off 218.2 *stop*, 252.4 *relegation*, 643.6, 645.3 *unemployment*, 704.2 *termination*
lay-offs 15.2 *industrial negotiations*
lay of the land 106.1, 251.2 *circumstances*
lay on 130.6 *add*, 293.23 *cover*, 674.12 *fight*
lay one's back open 879.3 *hit*

lay oneself open to 633.9 *face danger*
lay one's hands on 250.11 *find*, 734.7 *take*
lay one's head on the block 879.6 *be punished*
lay on the lash 879.3 *hit*
lay on the scale 369.15 *weigh*
lay on the table 209.8 *delay*
lay open 296.14 *undress*, 526.3 *reveal*, 530.5 *disclose*
lay out 50.23 *design*
layout 150.1 *order*
lay out 150.18 *order*
layout 152.2 *array*
lay out 152.12 *arrange*, 248.21 *space*
layout 251.2 *circumstances*, 299.1 *outline*
lay out 299.5 *outline*, 306.7 *form*, 362.3 *bring down*, 399.8 *bury*, 543.9 *use signs*
layout 592.5 *map*
lay out 592.10 *plan out*, 607.1 *waste*, 746.6 *pay*, 748.1 *expend*
lay over 160.13 *pause*, 293.23 *cover*
lay siege to 670.4 *besiege*, 679.36 *combat*, 821.26 *court*
lay the blame on 856.5 *accuse*
lay the cornerstone 592.10 *plan out*
lay the first stone 156.24 *open*
lay the foundation 592.10 *plan out*
lay the foundations 226.11 *inaugurate*, 594.2 *do the groundwork*
lay the foundation stone 156.24 *open*
lay to 74.10 *sail*
lay together 135.8 *unite*
lay to rest 399.8 *bury*
lay traps 590.11 *hunt*
lay up 136.10 *set apart*, 140.5 *combine*, 600.6 *stop using*, 605.6 *store*, 614.8 *make useless*, 643.14 *make inactive*
lay-up 23.4 *playing terms*
lay up a sailboat 36.15 *sail*
lay up for a rainy day 516.2 *show prudence*
lay up in lavender 418.6 *perfume*
lay upon 692.10 *demand*
lay waste 244, 607, 247.10 *waste*, 614.8 *make useless*, 628.4 *impair*, 670.9 *attack successfully*, 676.13 *be at war*
lay waste with fire and the sword 244.10 *lay waste*
Laza 8.11 *heaven*
lazar 743.10 *poor person*
lazaretto 74 Parts of a Ship, 630.14 *hospital*
lazar-house 630.14 *hospital*
Lazarus 396.5 *life cycle*, 743.10 *poor person*
laze 328.1 *move slowly*, 643.12 *be inactive*, 649.2 *take it easy*
laze around 240.4 *be inert*
lazily 240.7 *inertly*, 328.16 *slowly*, 641.5 *without action*, 643.16 *impassively*
laziness 240.1 *inertness*, 328.8 *slowness*, 470.2 *indifference*, 573.15 *delay*, 641.1 *inaction*, 643.7 *idleness*
lazulite 54 Minerals
lazy 240.5 *inert*, 328.5 *unhurried*, 470.5 *indifferent*, 573.4 *procrastinating*, 641.3 *inactive*, 643.3 *not participating*, 649.4 *at ease*
lazy river 96.1 *river*
lbw 27.11 *dismissal*
LCD 439.11 *photoelectricity*
L-dopa 62 Medication
lea 75 General Units, 68.11 *farmland*, 87.2 *grassland*, 98.6 *lowland*
Lea 96 Rivers
leach 134.10 *purify*, 347.12 *leak*, 387.23 *dissolve*, 389.29 *water*, 621.15 *purify*
leaching 347.3 *leakage*, 387.8

fluidification, 389.9 *soaking*,
631.9 *pollution*
lead 57 Chemical Elements,
74 Rigging, **126**, 12.11 *govern*,
20.3 *fishing tackle*, 21.6 *race*,
41.11 *skier*, 49.40 *conduct*,
51.21 *role*, 51.22 *actor*, 64.27
wire, 74.5 *navigation*, 121.5
measure, 126.3 *advantage*,
137.9 *yoke*, 154.4 *precedent*,
154.15 *precede*, 156.21 *pioneer*,
166.16 *direct*, 180.15 *escort*,
194.2 *greater importance*, 194.8
be before, 228.9 *motivate*, 233.8
influence, 235.7 *electrical power*,
268.6 *measuring instrument*,
277.4 *deep thing*, 279.7 *top*,
303.10 *in front*, 323.3 -
restrainer, 332.6 *direct*, 332.7
take a direction, 369.11 *weight*,
448.5 *grey thing*, 543.1 *sign*,
632.4 *safety device*, 652.14 -
behave towards, 652.15 *conduct*, 653.1 *manage*, 653.2 *direct*, 661.4 *restraint*, 688.18
have authority, 696.14 *master*,
699.5 *means of restraint*,
699.12 *gag*
lead a bad life 652.13 *behave
badly*
leadable 332.14 *directed*
lead a boring life 788.7 *suffer
boredom*
lead a charmed life 686.6 *be fortunate*
lead a cloistered life 816.12 *be
unsocial*
lead a coup 689.4 *be anarchic*,
693.16 *be subversive*, 734.7 *take*
lead a coup d'état 688.20 *take
authority*, 689.4 *be anarchic*
lead a good life 652.12 *behave
well*
lead a life of crime 858.10 *be
criminal*
lead a monotonous life 112.12 *be
monotonous*
lead an uprising 713.8 *cause mischief*
lead a putsch 713.8 *cause mischief*
lead a rebellion 693.16 *be subversive*
lead astray 228.10 *manipulate*,
864.17 *make wicked*, 877.19
corrupt
lead balloon 369.11 *weight*
lead block 19.9 *play*, 19.15 *play
offence*
lead by the nose 233.10 *be a prevailing influence*, 688.19 *be authoritarian*, 701.6 *subject*
lead captive 701.7 *defeat*
lead crystal 44.1 *ceramics*, 442.9
glass
leaded petrol 395.9 *petroleum*
leaden 325.5 *sedentary*, 369.1
heavy, 440.10 *dark-coloured*,
441.5 *dim*, 445.7 *colourless*,
448.1 *grey*, 448.3 *dull*, 788.4
boring
leaden hours 788.2 *boring thing*
leadenly 369.16 *heavily*
leadenness 440.1 *darkness*
leader 74 Rigging, **653**, **696**,
25.3 *bowls player*, 65.17 *computing term*, 85.2 *tree part*,
126.5 *superior*, 154.8 *precursor*,
165.9 *special*, 180.8 *usher*,
194.6 *person having priority*,
532.3 *journalism*, 533.9 *news
story*, 561.2 *article*, 611.4 *bigwig*, 652.10 *conductor*, 688.10
person of authority
leader of the House of Commons
12.8 *politician*, 653.14 *leader*
leader of the House of Lords
653.14 *leader*
leader of the Opposition 12.8 *politician*, 653.14 *leader*
leader of the opposition 668.4 *defiant person*
leader of the orchestra 653.14
leader
leadership 126, 121.2 *rank*,
207.3 *maturity*, 233.3 *personal
influence*, 652.8 *treatment*,

653.4 *directorship*, 688.1 *authority*
leader writer 524.7 *news interpreter*, 532.11 *newspaper man*,
533.4 *journalist*, 561.3 *dissertator*
lead glass 442.9 *glass*
lead-in 156.10 *introduction*
leading 12.10 *governing*, 121.8
ranked, 126.12 *superior*, 154.10
preceding, 154.12 *primary*,
154.14 *preparatory*, 156.30
front, 194.10 *prior*, 233.11 *influential*, 234.5 *tending to*, 279.5
top, 332.5 *directions*, 332.16 *directing*, 611.5 *important*, 611.6
notable, 653.17 *managerial*,
688.12 *authoritative*, 696.12
masterful
leading aircraftman 679.32 *airman*
leading article 532.3 *journalism*,
561.2 *article*
leading case 654.3 *precept*
leading item 165.9 *special*
leading lady 51.22 *actor*
leading light 439.13 *enlightenment*, 611.4 *bigwig*
leading man 51.22 *actor*
leading note 49.16 *musical note*
leading part 233 *influence*
leading question 477.4 *difficult
question*
leading role 51.21 *role*
leading sense 520.4 *type of
meaning*
leading to 234.5 *tending to*
lead into temptation 228.10 *manipulate*, 586.16 *tempt*
lead in triumph 701.7 *defeat*
lead line 74.5 *navigation*, 277.4
deep thing
lead-off man 22.2 *baseball player*
lead on 340.12 *lure*, 653.2 *direct*, 821.26 *court*
lead one a dance 591.6 *evade*
lead one a merry dance 659.22
cause trouble
lead one to expect 488.8 *be probable*
lead over 653.2 *direct*
lead poisoning 624.2 *illness*
lead role 51.21 *role*
lead runner 154.8 *precursor*
lead sinker 20.3 *fishing tackle*
leadsman 74.7 *nautical person*
lead the dance 126.10 *lead*,
154.18 *forerun*
lead the way 156.21 *pioneer*,
594.1 *prepare*, 653.2 *direct*
lead the way to 496.4 *invent*
lead the world 194.8 *be before*
lead the worship 710.15 *offer
worship*, 719.5 *observe religious
ceremony*
lead through 653.2 *direct*
lead to 226.9 *be the cause of*,
234.4 *tend*, 263.7 *reach*
lead to the altar 821.28 *win the
love of*, 823.15 *marry*
lead up the garden path 309.12
distort the truth, 539.27 *be false*
lead up to 594.1 *prepare*
lead vocalist 49.23 *singer*
leaf 83, 83.21 *vegetate*, 85.2 *tree
part*, 87.3 *grass plant*, 88.2 *fern
plant*, 143.2 *particular*, 143.6
branch, 243.7 *produce*, 266.3
coat, 319.2 *notched thing*
leaf beetle 82 Insects
leaf blade 83.6 *leaf*
leaf bud 83.8 *bud*
leaf cast 85.10 *tree disease*
leaf curl 69.12 *pests and diseases*, 85.10 *tree disease*
leafcutter ant 82 Insects
leafcutter bee 82 Insects
leaf cutting 69.5 *gardening*
leaf fall 83.6 *leaf*
leaf-green 453.1 *green*
leaf hopper 82 Insects
leaf-hopper 69.12 *pests and diseases*, 82.1 *insect*
leaf insect 82 Insects
leafless 296.12 *peeling*
leaflet 83.6 *leaf*, 88.2 *fern plant*,

143.6 *branch*, 532.9 *advertisement*
leaflike 266.9 *platelike*
leaflike part 83.6 *leaf*
leaf litter 85.4 *trees*
leaf miner 69.12 *pests and diseases*
leaf mould 69.12 *pests and diseases*, 85.4 *trees*
leaf out 85.19 *grow*
leaf spot 69.12 *pests and diseases*
leaf spring 377.5 *spring*
leafstalk 83.5 *stem*, 83.6 *leaf*
leaf sweeper 69.6 *garden tool*
leaf tissue 83.6 *leaf*
leafy 83.13 *plantlike*, 83.14 *of
plants*, 453.2 *verdant*
leafy liverwort 88.3 *moss*
league 75 General Units, 18.1
sport, 116.2 *alliance*, 140.2 *cooperation*, 163.4 *type*, 163.5 *social class*, 664.9 *team*, 665.1
party, 665.3 *political grouping*,
715.3 *alliance*
league championship 682.3 *successful thing*
league cricket 27.1 *cricket match*
leagued 665, 140.8 *cooperative*
League match 38.1 *soccer*
League of Nations 653.7 *council*
league with 140.6 *come together*,
715.5 *contract*
leak 347, 638, 638, 347.3 *leakage*, 353.3 *urination*, 391.16
seep, 496.7 *detection*, 528.7 *advice*, 530.2 *divulgence* , 530.6 *divulge*, 607.1 *waste*, 620.7 *defect*, 620.9 *be imperfect*, 722.12
lessen, 727.9 *dispose of*
leakage 347, 129.1 *decrease*,
346.3 *inroad*, 607.3 *waste*,
638.4 *leak*, 722.4 *lessening*
leak air 638.7 *leak*
leak away 638.7 *leak*
leak detector 57.20 *surface chemistry*
leaked 530.10 *disclosed*
leak gas 638.7 *leak*
leak in 346.11 *infiltrate*
leaking 144.8 *full*, 347.3 *leakage*, 628.13 *dilapidated*
leaking tyre 429.3 *hisser*
leak out 347.12 *leak*, 530.9 *be
disclosed*
leakproof 392.10 *waterproof*,
632.6 *invulnerable*
leaky 347, 322.14 *holed*,
530.11 *disclosing*, 620.1 *imperfect*, 633.2 *unsafe*
leal 769.8 *loyal*
lean 362, 123.5 *be unequal*,
234.4 *tend*, 274.1 *thin*, 286.6
be oblique, 310.11 *angle*, 378.4
powerful, 580.2 *prefer*, 609.3 *underfed*
lean and hungry look 274.8 *emaciation*
lean backwards 304.7 *rear up*
lean-burn engine 603.4 *machine*
lean clay 44.2 *raw material*
lean cuisine 45.1 *cookery*, 871.1
fasting
lean forward 362.7 *lean*
leaning 123.3 *unequal*, 234.2
attitude, 234.5 *tending to*, 286.1
obliqueness, 286.4 *oblique*,
580.7 *preference*, 584.2 *tendency*, 782.1 *desire*, 784.2 *inclination*, 784.6 *liking*
leaning backwards 304.3 *rearing
up*
leaning over backwards 541.1 *exaggeration*
leaning to one side 844.11 *wrong*
leaning towards 234.5 *tending to*
Leaning Tower of Pisa 43 *Noted
Buildings*
lean-limbed 274.1 *thin*
leanly 378.13 *powerfully*
leanness 274.7 *thinness*, 378.8
physical strength, 609.9 *scarcity*
lean on 695.6 *compel*
lean on a broken reed 633.8 *be
in danger*, 656.6 *act foolishly*
lean over backward 362.7 *lean*
lean over backwards 125.4 *com-

pensate, 541.7 *exaggerate*,
572.13 *be willing*
lean period 687.4 *time of adversity*
lean-to 256.7 *room*, 256.8 *shelter*
lean to one side 844.22 *discriminate*
lean towards 234.4 *tend*, 784.8
prefer, 844.22 *discriminate*
leap 161 Collective Names for
Birds and Animals, 21.6 *jump*,
32.7 *horseracing*, 46.15 *dance*,
77.21 *assemblage of mammals*,
128.2 *spread*, 154.3 *preparation*,
265.1 *interval*, 324.12 *gait*,
324.15 *walk*, 329.4 *be swift*,
329.9 *acceleration*, 336.13 *step*,
359.5, 359.18 *jump*, 596.5 *attempt*, 674.4 *race*
leap at 572.13 *be willing*,
590.10 *chase*
leap for joy 773.5 *rejoice*
leapfrog 42 Children's Games
and Party Games, 357.1 *overstep*, 357.7 *crossing*, 359.5
jump, 365.8 *oscillate*
leaping 359, 366.15 *agitated*
leap in the dark 633.5 *danger*,
780.2 *rash move*
leap into 580.3 *side with*
leap out 522.8 *be recognizable*
leaps and bounds 336.13 *step*
leap to one's feet 361.5 *arise*
leap up 359.17 *spring up*, 361.5
arise
leap year 213.4 *rare things*,
214.5 *regular thing*
learn 6, 696, 420.15 *hear*,
496.3 *find out*, 501.13 *get to
know*, 511.11 *memorize*, 522.6
understand, 528.15 *be informed*,
627.2 *get better*
learn a habit 584.18 *habituate*
learn a trade 696.15 *learn*
learn by experience 627.2 *get better*
learn by heart 511.11 *memorize*,
696.15 *learn*
learn by rote 501.12 *know by
heart*, 511.11 *memorize*
learned 4, 6.18 *educated*, 48.16
literary, 459.10 *intelligent*,
507.5 *wise*
learned in the law 16.45 *legislative*
learned journal 187.7 *periodical*
learnedness 6
learned person 655.5 *expert*
learner 6, 156.14 *beginner*,
646.2 *artisan*, 656.10 *unskilled
person*, 701.3 *subordinate*
learner's dictionary 5.28 *dictionary*
learn from 654.6 *consult*
learn from experience 867.4 *be
penitent*
learning 6, 501, 48.1 *literature*,
496.8 *finding out*, 507.1 *wisdom*, 522.12 *understanding*,
594.17 *developing*
learning by heart 511.1 *memory*
learning difficulties 510.2 *subnormality*
learn obedience 673.4 *succumb*
learn one's lesson 636.6 *be
warned*, 867.4 *be penitent*
learn one's lines 51.35 *rehearse*
learnt by heart 511.9 *memorized*
learn to live together 677.5 *make
peace*
lease 255.14 *inhabit*, 715.2 *purchase contract*, 723.1 *possession*,
728.1 *transfer of property*, 728.3
transfer property
leased 255.11 *inhabited*
leasehold 723.1 *possession*,
725.1 *property*, 725.8 *propertied*
leaseholder 255.3 *householder*,
723.5 *possessor*, 725.7 *property
man*
leash 135.10 *link*, 137.9 *yoke*,
137.12 *bind*, 323.3 *restrainer*,
323.11 *restrain*, 661.4 *restraint*,
661.10 *restrain*, 699.5 *means of
restraint*, 699.12 *gag*
leashed 137.16 *bound*, 661.14
blocked

leash the dogs of war 677.5 *make peace*

leasing contract 715.2 *purchase contract*

least 182, 52.75 *equal,* 120.2 *certain amount,* 120.6 *quantitative,* 127.12 *inferior,* 182.7 *fewer*

least bit 612.8 *trifle*

least one can do 608.7 *sufficiency*

leather 243.7 *produce,* 293.14 *animal covering,* 330.5 *beat,* 378.7 *tough thing,* 604.1 *materials,* 621.11 *cleaning cloth,* 879.3 *hit*

leatherback 79 Reptiles

leather chair 47.2 *chair*

Leatherette 67 Synthetic Fibres and Fabrics

leatheriness 378.6 *toughness*

leathering 330.12 *collision*

leatherjacket 82 Insects, 69.12 *pests and diseases,* 82.5 *larva*

leather jacket 295.11 *jacket*

leather leg-guard 31.3 *ice hockey*

leatherlike 378.3 *hard*

leatherneck 679.28 *marines*

leather punch 322.2 *opener*

leather shoes 295.19 *footwear*

leathery 373.1, 378.3 *hard*

leave 132, 116.7 *consent,* 136.13 *diverge,* 147.7 *exclude,* 254.5 *leave of absence,* 254.16 *absent oneself,* 326.14 *bring back,* 345.1 *depart,* 345.9 *parting,* 347.9 *exit,* 347.14 *be dismissed,* 570.16 *bequeath,* 591.1 *avoid,* 591.8 *run away,* 598.2 *withdraw,* 600.6 *stop using,* 605.6 *store,* 645.2 *time off,* 649.1 *ease,* 651.6 *refresher,* 673.3 *submit,* 691.1 *leniency,* 705.5 *resign,* 708.1 *permission,* 708.2 *permit,* 729.5 *give,* 814.4 *freedom,* 824.8 *desert,* 848.4 *licence*

leave a clean plate 350.22 *eat well*

leave a deposit 718.15 *reserve*

leave a fingerprint 227.6 *have a visible effect*

leave a footprint 227.6 *have a visible effect*

leave a gap 609.5 *be insufficient*

leave ajar 322.18 *open*

leave a lacuna 609.5 *be insufficient*

leave alone 600.5 *not use,* 641.4 *not act*

leave a loophole 716.6 *make conditions*

leave a remainder 123.5 *be unequal*

leave a runner stranded 22.7 *play baseball*

leave a trace 227.6 *have a visible effect*

leave at the starting post 329.6 *accelerate*

leave behind 132.8 *leave,* 329.6 *accelerate,* 336.9 *maintain progress,* 357.3 *exceed,* 512.13 *forget,* 721.10 *augment,* 722.15 *lose someone*

leave dangling 145.5 *be incomplete*

leave destitute 743.14 *impoverish*

leave empty 254

leave fingerprints 544.11 *identify oneself*

leave footprints 544.11 *identify oneself*

leave for 629.7 *resort*

leave half-done 470.6 *be neglectful*

leave hanging 145.5 *be incomplete,* 685.5 *not complete*

leave holding the baby 539.30 *be fraudulent*

leave hold of 598.1 *relinquish*

leave home 345.3 *quit*

leave imperfect 620

leave incomplete 685.5 *not complete*

leave in high dudgeon 345.1 *depart*

leave in suspense 576.7 *be irresolute*

leave in the air 145.5 *be incomplete,* 685.5 *not complete*

leave in the lurch 515.6 *disappoint,* 539.30 *be fraudulent*

leave it to 703.6 *commission*

leave it to chance 589.12 *take a chance*

leave it to fate 589.12 *take a chance*

leave land behind 345.5 *set out*

leaven 45.7 *basic ingredient,* 203.8 *mitigate,* 216.5 *changer,* 216.8 *cause change,* 220.1 *conversion,* 220.7 *convert into,* 220.9 *transform,* 226.4 *contributing factor,* 233.9 *change,* 370.8 *leavening,* 370.10 *lighten,* 390.11 *aeration,* 627.1 *improve*

leavened 203.16 *mitigated*

leavening 370, 370, 216.1 *change,* 220.14 *converting,* 390.11 *aeration*

leavening agent 216.5 *changer*

leave no address 531.11 *conceal oneself*

leave no choice 571.15, 695.6 *compel*

leave no escape 695.6 *compel*

leave no loose ends 142.10, 684.4 *complete*

leave no option 695.6 *compel*

leave no remainder 122.11 *equalize*

leave no space 253.11 *be present*

leave no stone unturned 644.8 *exert oneself,* 684.4 *complete*

leave no survivors 546.1 *obliterate*

leave nothing out 144.4 *complete*

leave nothing to be desired 619.6 *be perfect*

leave nothing to chance 144.4 *complete,* 781.5 *be cautious*

leave no trace 100.13 *cease to exist,* 345.3 *quit,* 546.1 *obliterate*

leave of absence 254, 708.2 *permit,* 848.4 *licence*

leave off 160.12 *discontinue,* 218.6 *cease,* 218.12 *stop,* 600.6 *stop using*

leave one cold 466.6 *be incurious,* 783.12 *be indifferent,* 788.6 *be boring*

leave one's bills unpaid 745.8 *not pay*

leave one's body 11.24 *experience psychic phenomena*

leave one's calling card 815.12 *visit*

leave one's husband a widower 824.9 *widow*

leave one's job 218.7 *stop working*

leave one's post 705.5 *resign*

leave one's wife a widow 824.9 *widow*

leave one to his own devices 698.15 *set free*

leave on one side 356.8 *pass*

leave on the cutting-room floor 546.1 *obliterate*

leave out 131.3 *subtract,* 132.8 *leave,* 147.7 *exclude,* 248.21 *space,* 525.1 *misinterpret,* 566.9 *lapse into silence,* 848.9 *exempt*

leave over 132.8 *leave*

leaver 347.8 *outgoer*

leaves 83.6 *leaf,* 453.8 *greenness,* 614.6 *refuse*

leave senseless 330.9 *fight*

leave something to be desired 358.2 *fail*

leave speechless 514.11 *amaze*

leave standing 329.6 *accelerate,* 357.3 *exceed*

leave stranded 598.2 *withdraw*

leavetaking 345.9 *parting*

leave-taking 345.11 *departing*

leave the beaten path 168.19 *be independent*

leave the country 345.3 *quit*

leave the door open 710.9 *offer*

leave the earth 359.19 *take off*

leave the field 27.15 *play*

leave the ground 359.19 *take off*

leave the neighbourhood 345.3 *quit*

leave the nest 207.18 *mature,* 345.3 *quit*

leave the options open 716.6 *make conditions*

leave the pocket 19.15 *play offence*

leave the scene 254.16 *absent oneself*

leave the stage 345.2 *withdraw*

leave the straight and narrow 335.1 *deviate*

leave to chance 229.4 *chance*

leave to one's own choice 698.15 *set free*

leave unavenged 839.12 *show mercy*

leave undecided 576.7 *be irresolute*

leave undeveloped 307.3 *make shapeless*

leave undone 145.5 *be incomplete,* 470.6 *be neglectful,* 685.5 *not complete*

leave unfinished 145.5 *be incomplete,* 375.13 *be unfinished,* 614.9 *waste effort,* 620.10 *leave imperfect,* 685.5 *not complete*

leave unsatisfied 515.6 *disappoint*

leave work 345.2 *withdraw*

leaving 345.7 *departure,* 345.11 *departing,* 347.15 *outgoing,* 598.3 *relinquishment,* 729.1 *giving*

leaving behind 721.2 *augmentation*

leaving ground 359.4 *taking off*

leaving present 837.3 *recognition*

leavings 127.7 *inferior thing,* 132.2 *residue,* 143.8 *bits and pieces,* 243.3 *product,* 614.6 *refuse,* 622.4 *dirt*

Leavis 48 Writers

Leavisite 48.15 *literary person,* 524.6 *interpreter,* 561.3 *dissertator*

Lebanon 91 Countries

Lebensraum 91.3 *dominion,* 400.11 *nation*

Leblanc process 57 Named Reactions

Le Carré 48 Writers

lech 782.6 *desirer,* 877.17 *be sexually immoral*

Le Châtelier 52 Scientists

Le Châtelier's principle 57 Named Reactions

lecher 482.9 *undiscriminating person,* 782.6 *desirer,* 821.9 *lover,* 826.5 *courting person,* 864.9 *wicked person,* 877.8 *immoral man*

lecherous 877, 782.11 *lustful*

lecherously 782.20 *lustfully*

lecherousness 782.4 *sexual desire,* 877.3 *sexual immorality*

lechery 782.4 *sexual desire,* 877.3 *sexual immorality*

leching 203.17 *in season*

Lech Wałęsa 675.4 *Nobel Peace Prize*

lecithin 58.6 *lipid*

Leclanché cell 56 Named Laws, 57.19 *electrochemistry*

Leconte de Lisle 48 Poets

Lecoq de Boisbaudran 52 Scientists

lectern 10.12 *church,* 47.4 *table*

lection 524.1 *interpretation*

lectionary 10.10 *religious manual*

lecture 163, 51.5 *show,* 475.3 *explanation,* 475.16 *explain,* 561.1 *dissertation,* 564.8 *speech,* 564.14 *speak to,* 567.1, 567.7 *address,* 586.2 *flattery,* 852.7 *blame,* 852.20 *censure,* 876.12 *moralize*

lecture course 472.5 *educational topic*

lecture hall 6.15 *schoolroom*

lecturer 6.4 *educator,* 475.7 *demonstrator,* 561.3 *dissertator,* 564.10 *speaker,* 567.6 *public speaker,* 696.9 *educational leader*

lectureship 6.6 *instructorship*

led 180.20 *accompanied*

LED 64.18 *diode,* 439.11 *photoelectricity*

led by the nose 701.9 *subject*

lederhosen 295.9 **trousers**, 544.5 *uniform*

ledge 34.5 *rock face,* 41.1 *skiing,* 266.2 *level,* 282.3 *flat thing,* 318.2 *projection*

ledged 34.8 *mountaineering,* 41.12 *ski*

ledger 171.4 *bill,* 545.6 *record book,* 750.5 *account book*

ledgering 20.1 *angling*

ledger line 49.17 *notation*

ledger rod 20.3 *fishing tackle*

lee 634.2 *shelter*

leeboards 36.3 *parts of a sailing boat*

leech 81 Worms, 60.11 *doctor,* 81.6 *worm,* 81.10 *parasite,* 138.4 *adherent,* 630.15 *healer,* 643.8 *nonworker,* 734.6 *taker,* 808.3 *sycophant*

Leech 94 Lakes

leechcraft 630.11 *medical art*

leechlike 81.20 *wormlike,* 808.7 *sycophantic*

Leeds 93 Cities, 93.4 *British cities*

Leeds pottery 44 Types of Ceramics

leek-green 453.1 *green*

Lee Lincoln Scarp 53 Rills and Valleys

leer 309.2 *facial distortion,* 309.10 *make faces,* 435.6, 435.13 *look,* 543.3, 543.11 *gesture,* 826.8 *court*

lees 132.2 *residue,* 157.8 *tail,* 393.13 *mud,* 622.4 *dirt*

Lees' disk 56 Named Laws

lee shore 635.1 *trap*

lee side 305.3 *side direction*

Leeuwenhoek 52 Scientists

lee wall 634.2 *shelter*

leeward 74 Parts of a Ship, 332.10 *clockwise*

lee-wave cloud 55.20 *cloud appearance*

leeway 248.6 *available space,* 265.1 *interval,* 335.15 *deviating motion,* 698.5 *scope,* 814.4 *freedom*

Le Fanu 48 Writers

left 12.6 *political party,* 26.14 *combat,* 38.5 *soccer,* 56.78 *quantum,* 132.9 *remaining,* 136.17 *unjoined,* 305.6 *side,* 330.14 *sporting hit,* 345.12 *departed*

left behind 132.9 *remaining,* 727.15 *unclaimed*

left centre three-quarter 35.4 *rugby player*

left defence 31.4 *ice hockey player*

left field centre field 22.1 *baseball*

left fielder 22.2 *baseball player*

left half 38.3 *football player*

left hand 305.1 *side*

left-hand 33.11 *racing*

left-handed 407.5 *toucher,* 407.10 *handed,* 578.10 *equivocal,* 656.3 *clumsy,* 850.11 *insulting*

left-handed compliment 850.5 *insult*

left-handed hitter 22.2 *baseball player*

left-handed marriage 823.3 *types of marriage*

left-handedness 407.7 *sense organ,* 656.8 *unskilfulness*

left-hander 33.6 *motor racing terms*

left-hand kink 33.6 *motor racing terms*

left-hand side 305.3 *side direction*

left hanging 145.4 *incomplete,* 685.4 *uncompleted*

left high and dry 633.3 *vulnerable*

left hook 26.2 *boxing*

leftie 12.6 *political party,* 693.11 *rebel*

left in the air 145.4 *incomplete,* 685.4 *uncompleted*

leftist 12.6 *political party,* 665.6

political party member, 665.10 *political*
left jab 26.2 *boxing*
left-luggage office 72.8 *railway station*
left of centre 242.7 *politically moderate*, 665.3 *political grouping*
left out 147.11 *excluded*, 254.12 *missing*
leftover 130.3 *additional item*, 132.10 *surplus*, 600.3 *not wanted*, 607.9 *waste*, 610.7 *superfluous*
leftovers 127.7 *inferior thing*, 132.2 *residue*, 132.4 *surplus*, 607.5 *waste product*, 610.3 *superfluity*, 614.6 *refuse*, 622.4 *dirt*
left side 305.3 *side direction*
left stick 31.3 *ice hockey*
left to one's own devices 698.10 *independent*
left to right 365.18 *to and fro*
left to rot 600.1 *unused*
left unfinished 145.4 *incomplete*, 685.4 *uncompleted*
left uppercut 26.2 *boxing*
leftward 332.10 *clockwise*
left wing 31.4 *ice hockey player*, 31.6 *lacrosse player*
left-wing 665.10 *political*
left-winger 12.6 *political party*, 665.6 *political party member*
left wing three-quarter 35.4 *rugby player*
left without words 786.7 *wide-eyed*
lefty 665.6 *political party member*
leg 21.1 *track events*, 27.14 *positioned*, 45.22 *beef*, 45.25 *pork*, 45.26, 45.27 *lamb*, 45.28 *poultry*, 143.3 *stage*, 143.4 *component*
legacy 749, 155.6 *aftermath*, 227.2 *visible effect*, 326.10 *transferred thing*, 570.5 *will*, 721.5 *profit*, 725.5 *personal estate*, 729.2 *gift*, 730.1 *receiving*
legal 16, 166, 116.18 *permitting*, 214.14 *orderly*, 477.15 *sceptical*, 537.24 *pedantic*, 688.12 *authoritative*, 708.7 *permitted*, 845.8 *entitled*
legal action 16.5, 16.33 *litigation*, 640.1 *action*
legal administration 16.2 *jurisdiction*
legal administrator 16.10 *law officer*
legal advice 16.32 *jurisprudence*
legal adviser 16.13 *lawyer*, 654.4 *adviser*
legal agreement 711.1 *contract*
legal argument 463.3 *debate*
legal authority 16.2 *jurisdiction*
legal beagle 16.13 *lawyer*
legal case 16.5 *litigation*
legal chicanery 539.10 *fraud*
legal claim 723.1 *possession*
legal code 16.1 *the law*
legal competence 16.2 *jurisdiction*
legal costs 751.6 *business costs*
legal counsel 654.4 *adviser*
legal debt 879.8 *penalty*
legal defence 855.2 *defence*
legal dispute 16.5 *litigation*
legal eagle 16.13 *lawyer*
legalese 5.6 *official language*, 5.20 *jargon word*
legal estate 725.1 *property*
legal ethics 4.6 *branch of philosophy*
legal evidence 483
legal flaw 16.4 *bad law*
legal force 695.2 *coercion*
legal formality 16
legal government 12.1 *government*
legal heir 730.6 *beneficiary*
legal history 3.1 *history*
legal innocence 865
legalism 16.28 *legality*
legal issue 16.5 *litigation*
legalistic 16, 813.6 *formal*
legality 16, 12.1 *government*,

537.11 *pedantry*, 688.1 *authority*, 708.1 *permission*
legalization 16
legalize 16.65 *make legal*, 116.29 *permit*, 688.21 *grant authority*, 708.3 *permit*
legalized 16.44 *legal*, 116.18 *permitting*, 688.16 *authorized*, 708.7 *permitted*
legalized killing 397.4 *death sentence*, 398.5 *execution*, 879.13 *capital punishment*
legal learning 16.32 *jurisprudence*
legal liability 879.8 *penalty*
legally 16, 16.86 *jurisdictionally*, 214.17 *orderly*, 688.23 *authoritatively*, 708.9 *with permission*, 845.20 *duly*
legally separated 824.11 *divorced*
legally sound 16.46 *legislated*
legal obligation 879.8 *penalty*
legal order 692.1 *command*, 692.2 *demand*
legal possession 723.1 *possession*
legal power 688.1 *authority*
legal practitioner 16.13 *lawyer*
legal precedent 584.5 *tradition*
legal procedure 16.6 *legal process*
legal proceeding 640.1 *action*
legal proceedings 16.6 *legal process*
legal process 16, 16.33 *litigation*
legal punishment 879.8 *penalty*
legal quibble 503.3 *accurate thing*
legal remedy 16.5 *litigation*
legal representative 16.13 *lawyer*
legal restraint 699.1 *restraint*
legal right 845.3 *prerogative*
legal rights 698.2 *free speech*
legal separation 824.2 *separation*
legal tender 741.1 *money*
legal terms 723, 725
legal trial 16
legate 703.5 *commissioner*, 706.1 *delegate*, 707.3 *agent*
legatee 730.6 *beneficiary*
legatine 706.6 *delegated*
legation 703.4 *council*, 706.2 *representative body*
legato 49 Musical Terms
legator 729.4 *giver*
Legba 8 Deities
leg break 27.8 *delivery*, 335.15 *deviating motion*
leg-break 27.13 *bowling*
leg bye 27.10 *score*
leg cutter 27.8 *delivery*
legend 1.8 *tradition*, 3.7 *narrative*, 5.25 *inscription*, 48.2 *fiction*, 202.6 *tradition*, 524.2 *annotation*, 540.9 *falsification*, 545.4 *inscription*, 560.2 *brief description*, 560.3 *narration*
legendary 1.14 *societal*, 3.19 *chronicled*, 48.17 *fictional*, 519.12 *imaginary*, 540.32 *falsified*
legendary beast 76
legendary horse 32.1 *horse*
legendary serpent 79.3 *snake*
Legendre 52 Scientists
Legendre polynomials 52 Named Concepts
legerdemain 539.9 *sleight of hand*
leg fillet 45.24 *pork*
leggeramente 49 Musical Terms
leggings 295.20 *legwear*
leg glance 27.9 *stroke*
leg glide 27.9 *stroke*
leggy 275.12 *tall*
Leghorn 68 Breeds of Fowl
legibility 522.10 *simplicity*
legible 522.2 *simple*
legion 161.14 *force*, 181.4 *throng*, 181.5 *multitudinous*, 679.16 *army unit*, 679.18 *army of people*
legionary 679.11 *former soldier*
legionnaire 676.11 *recruit*, 679.11 *former soldier*
legionnaire's disease 624.9 *respiratory disease*

Legion of Merit 17 US Military Medals and Decorations
legislate 16, 640.4 *act*, 653.1 *manage*, 688.18 *have authority*, 692.9 *command*
legislated 16
legislate for 12.11 *govern*
legislation 16, 492.2 *verdict*, 653.3 *management*, 654.3 *precept*, 692.1 *command*
legislational 16.45 *legislative*
legislative 16, 653.17 *managerial*, 653.18 *parliamentary*, 692.14 *commanding*
legislative assembly 653.10 *legislative body*
legislative body 653
legislative branch 653.10 *legislative body*
legislator 12.7 *governor*, 16.9 *lawmaker*, 653.13 *director*, 699.6 *law-maker*
legislatorial 16.45 *legislative*
legislatorship 16.31 *legislation*
legislature 16.31 *legislation*, 161.5 *conference*, 653.10 *legislative body*
legit 16.44 *legal*, 51.1 *drama*, 708.7 *permitted*
legitimacy 16, 16.28 *legality*, 537.6 *authenticity*, 537.11 *pedantry*, 688.1 *authority*, 843.2 *correctness*
legitimate 16, 16.44 *legal*, 537.19 *authentic*, 537.24 *pedantic*, 688.12 *authoritative*, 688.15 *true*, 708.7 *permitted*, 843.8 *correct*, 845.8 *entitled*
legitimately 16.81 *legally*, 537.37 *authentically*, 537.38 *literally*, 688.23 *authoritatively*, 688.25 *authentically*, 708.9 *with permission*
legitimateness 16.28 *legality*
legitimate succession 688.3 *acquisition of power*
legitimate theatre 51.1 *drama*
legitimatize 16.65 *make legal*, 688.21 *grant authority*
legitimatized 16.44 *legal*
legitimation 16.29 *legalization*
legitimize 16.65 *make legal*, 708.3 *permit*
legitimized 16.44 *legal*
legless 143.11 *partial*, 145.4 *incomplete*, 620.3 *deformed*, 874.3 *dead drunk*
legless lizard 79.2 *lizard*
Lego 148.3 *unit*
leg-of-mutton sleeve 295.24 *part of garment*
leg-pull 539.11 *hoax*, 771.5 *joke*
leg-puller 539.15 *deceiver*
legroom 248.6 *available space*
legs eleven 179.7 *double figures*
leg show 51.5 *show*
leg slip 27.4 *team*
leg theory 27.8 *delivery*
leg trap 27.8 *delivery*
legume 45.33, 69.11 *vegetable*, 86.2 *botanical fruit*
legumes 86.1 *fruits*
leguminous 69.16 *horticultural*, 83.16 *taxonomic*, 86.6 *fruiting*
leg-up 336.12 *advance*, 361.7 *lift*, 662.1 *help*
legwarmers 295.20 *legwear*
legwear 295
legwork 644.1 *work*
leg-work 533.3 *reporting*
Le Havre 93 Cities
Leibig condenser 57 Laboratory Apparatus
Leibnitz 4 Philosophers
Leibnitzian 4.11 *follower of a doctrine*, 4.14 *of a philosophy*
Leibnitz's Law 4.8 *philosophical term*
Leibnitz's theorem 52 Named Concepts
Leicester 45 Cheeses, **93** Cities
Leicester Longwool 68 Breeds of Sheep
Leicestershire 92 Counties
Leiden 93 Cities
Leinster 92 Counties
Leipzig 93 Cities

leishmania 81.10 *parasite*
leishmaniasis 81.12 *protozoal disease*
leisure 645, 645, 218.3 *pause*, 641.1 *inaction*, 649.1 *ease*
Leisure 645
leisured 325.6 *quiescent*, 641.3 *inactive*, 645.7 *leisurely*, 649.4 *at ease*
leisured class 742.11 *the rich*
leisured classes 641.2 *nonacting person*, 643.8 *nonworker*
leisureliness 328.8 *slowness*
leisurely 645, 645, 209.15 *late*, 268.15 *deliberate*, 328.15 *unhurried*, 328.16 *slowly*, 641.3 *inactive*, 649.4 *at ease*, 660.14 *relaxed*
leisurely gait 328.10 *slow motion*
leisurely progress 328.8 *slowness*
leisure pool 39.7 *swimming pool*
leisure pursuit 590.4 *activity*
leisure suit 295.10 *suit*
leisure time 218.3 *pause*
leisure wear 295.4, 814.6 *informal dress*
leitmotif 49.4 *opera*, 433.1 *melody*
leitmotiv 48.3 *aspect of fiction*, 472.1 *topic*
Leitrim 92 Counties
lek 78.14 *nest*, 741.11 *national coins*
Lemaître 52 Scientists
Léman 94 Lakes
Le Mans 93 Cities
Le Mans 24-hour race 33.3 *sports car race*
Le Mans start 36.7 *windsurfing*
lemma 52.65 *theory*, 87.3 *grass plant*
lemming 77 Placental Mammals
lemming-like 167.13 *compliant*
lemmings 398.9 *animal killing*
lemniscate 52.40 *curve*
lemon 86 Fruits, 86.5 *figurative usage*, 127.7 *inferior thing*, 415.3 *sour thing*, 452.8 *yellow thing*, 683.4 *unsuccessful thing*, 683.5 *failing person*
lemonade 351.6 *soft drink*, 414.5 *sweet drink*
lemon chicken 45.48 *Chinese dish*
lemon grove 69.2 *garden*
lemon meringue pie 45.36 *cake*
lemon mint 45 Herbs and Spices
lemon sole 80 Fishes, 45.18 *sea fish*
lemon squeezer 45.6 *kitchen equipment*, 86.5 *figurative usage*, 355.9 *extractor*
lemon tea 351.3 *tea*
lemon thyme 413.5 *herbs*
lemon verbena 413.5 *herbs*
lemonwood 85 Trees and Shrubs
lemony 415.5 *acid*
lemon yellow 452.7 *yellow pigment*
lemon-yellow 452.1 *yellow*
lemur 77 Placental Mammals
lemures 11.11 *ghost*
Lena 96 Rivers
lend 732, 606.5 *provision*, 662.29 *finance*, 710.11 *volunteer*, 728.3 *transfer property*, 729.5 *give*, 744.8 *credit*
lend a hand 572.14 *cooperate*, 662.17 *help*
lend a helping hand 284.14 *give moral support*, 710.11 *volunteer*
lend an ear 420.15 *hear*
lend at interest 732.5 *lend*
lender 732, 744, 606.3 *provider*, 728.2 *person transferring property*, 739.12 *wholesaler*
lender of last resort 744.5 *lender*
lend force to 237.8 *strengthen*
lending 732, 606.1 *provision*, 732.6 *loaned*, 745.3 *loan*
Lending 732
lending at interest 732.1 *lending*
lending institution 732
lending money 732.1 *lending*
lending on collateral 732.1 *lending*
lending on security 732.1 *lending*
lend itself 662.26 *be useful*

lend-lease 732.2 *loan*
lend money 732.5 *lend*
lend one's backing to 851.13 *support*
lend oneself 662.23 *advise*, 664.12 *reciprocate*
lend oneself to 232.4 *be an instrument*
lend on security 732.5 *lend*
lend wings to 329.7 *hurry someone up*, 662.28 *further*
length 269, 52.37 *line*, 56.7 *space*, 75.5 *dimension*, 120.1 *quantity*, 143.7 *piece*, 248.1 *space*, 259.1, 268.4 *size*
Length 269
lengthen 269, 128.5 *make bigger*, 248.20 *extend*, 261.5 *make bigger*, 261.6 *become bigger*, 553.5 *be diffuse*
lengthened 269.6 *protracted*, 261.7 *bigger*, 269.1 *long*
lengthener 261.4 *enlarger*
lengthening 261.1 *growth*, 261.8 *growing*, 269.4 *length*
lengthily 269
lengthiness 269.4 *length*
lengthman 72.9 *railway worker*
length of time 188.2 *time*
lengthways 269.3 *longitudinal*, 269.12 *longitudinally*, 282.11 *horizontally*
lengthwise 282.11 *horizontally*
lengthy 269.1 *long*, 553.3 *diffuse*
lenience 691.1 *leniency*
leniency 691, 374.12 *gentleness*, 652.8 *treatment*, 677.2 *peace offering*, 708.1 *permission*, 835.3 *mercy*
Leniency 691
lenient 691, 374.6 *softhearted*, 660.13 *easygoing*, 708.8 *permitting*, 817.7 *courteous*, 831.6 *benevolent*, 835.6 *pitying*, 839.5 *merciful*
leniently 691, 16.88 *forgivingly*, 374.18 *softheartedly*, 677.7 *pacifically*, 708.9 *with permission*, 817.14 *courteously*
lenient person 691
Lenin 95 Mountains
Leninism 12.1 *governmental*, 688.7 *type of rule*
Leninist 12.9 *governmental*
lenitive 242.2 *moderator*, 242.8 *moderating*, 386.5 *ointment*, 386.9 *lubricant*, 395.6 *ointment*, 395.13 *lubricant*, 630.17 *remedial*, 677.6 *pacificatory*
lenity 691.1 *leniency*, 839.2 *forgivingness*
lens 66, 44.9 *industrial ceramics*, 56.29 *optical element*, 316.2 *bulge*, 435.2 *eye*, 442.8 *transparent thing*
lens aperture 56.31 *lens element*
lens attachment 66.17 *lens*
lens cap 66.17 *lens*
lens cover 66.17 *lens*
lens element 56
lenses 435.10 *visual aid*
lens hood 66.17 *lens*
lens mount 66.17 *lens*
lens system 56, 66.17 *lens*
lent 732.6 *loaned*
Lent 10.16 *religious festival*, 871.3 *fast day*
Lenten 698.8 *self-restrained*, 871.6 *fasting*
Lenten fare 609.8 *insufficiency*, 869.1 *self-restraint*, 871.1 *fasting*
lenticular 52.81 *curvilinear*, 316.4 *convex*
lenticular cloud 55.20 *cloud appearance*
lenticular galaxy 53.7 *galaxy*
lentiform 316.4 *convex*
lentil 45 Vegetables
lentitude 328.8 *slowness*
lentivirus 624.6 *infection*
lentivirus disease 624.4 *disease*
lento 49 Musical Terms
lentor 334.1 *viscosity*
Lenz's law 56 Named Laws
Leo 53 The Constellations, **53** Zodiac Constellations

Leo Minor 53 The Constellations
Leonids 53 Meteor Showers
leonine 77.28 *carnivorous*
Leonov 48 Dramatists
leopard 77 Placental Mammals, 456.5 *variegated thing*
Leopard 679.21 *armoured cavalry*
leopardess 77.18 *female mammal*
Leopardi 48 Poets
leopard lily 84 Flowers and Flowering Plants
leopards 161 Collective Names by Animal
leopard seal 77 Placental Mammals
leotard 30.2 *gymnastic clothing*, 295.10 *suit*
Lepcha 5 Languages and Groups of Languages
lepe 161 Collective Names for Birds and Animals
leper 816.7 *outsider*
leper asylum 630.14 *hospital*
leper colony 630.14 *hospital*
Lepidoptera 82 Orders of Insects
lepidopteran 82.10 *insectan*
lepidopterist 82.8 *entomologist*
lepidoptery 42 Hobbies and Pastimes
lepista 89 Fungi
leporid 77.31 *rabbit-like*
leporids 77.12 *gnawing mammal*
leporine 77.31 *rabbit-like*
leprechaun 11.11 *ghost*, 260.4 *little person*
leprosy 624.7 *tropical disease*, 624.13 *skin disease*
leprous 622.8 *unclean*, 624.23 *diseased*
leptocephalic 272.4 *narrow-leaved*
lepton 75 Some Foreign Units, 56.77 *elementary particle*
leptonia 89 Fungi
leptophyllous 272.4 *narrow-leaved*
leptorrhine 272.4 *narrow-leaved*
leptosome 274.9 *thin person*
leptosomic 274.1 *thin*
Lepus 53 The Constellations
lergy 626.2 *germ*
Lermontov 48 Poets
Lerwick 93 Cities
les 402.10 *homosexual*
Lesage 48 Writers
lesbian 402.10 *homosexual*, 402.15 *female*
lesbian marriage 823.3 *types of marriage*
lese-majesty 693.3 *subversion*
Leslie's cube 56 Named Laws
Lesotho 91 Countries
less 120.2 *certain amount*, 127.19 *inferiorly*, 131.8 *by subtraction*, 182.2 *least*, 182.7 *fewer*
less and less 121.10 *by degrees*, 129.8, 131.9 *decreasingly*
lessee 255.3 *householder*, 723.5 *possessor*, 725.7 *property man*, 730.5 *recipient*
lessen 722, 129.4 *decrease*, 238.7 *weaken*, 242.4 *moderate*, 262.5 *make smaller*, 262.6 *become smaller*, 374.14 *ease*, 627.1 *improve*, 767.9 *relieve*
lessened 131.7 *reduced*
lessening 722, 129.1 *decrease*, 242.1 *moderation*, 262.1 *contraction*, 262.8 *contracting*
lesser 52.75 *equal*, 127.12 *inferior*
lesser creation 127.6 *inferior*
lesser doxology 10.8 *hymn*
lesser evil 580.8 *choice*
lesser importance 195.3 *subordination*
lesser of two evils 580.8 *choice*
lesser quaking grass 87 Grasses
less important 195.13 *subordinule*
Lessing 48 Writers
lesson 163.7 *lecture*, 561.1 *dissertation*, 636.1 *warning*, 852.7 *blame*, 876.7 *moral*, 879.7 *punishment*

Lesson 10.6 *Eucharist*
less so 129.8 *decreasingly*
less sound 424.1 *faintness*
less than 52.88 *equal to*, 127.19 *inferiorly*
less than one 173
less than one's hopes 515.11 *disappointing*
less than or equal to 52.88 *equal to*
less than perfect 620.1 *imperfect*
less than somewhat 609.10 *insufficiently*
less than the going rate 752.7 *at a discount*
less than the market rate 752.7 *at a discount*
less than the truth 538.1 *untruth*
Les Sylphides 46.11 *classical ballets*
Les Vingt 50 Schools and Groups of Artists
let 40.4 *tennis terms*, 40.12 *badminton terms*, 255.11 *inhabited*, 323.1 *closure*, 518.5 *suppose*, 708.3 *permit*, 723.7 *possess*, 728.1 *transfer of property*, 728.3 *transfer property*
let alone 130.10 *additionally*, 147.12 *exclusively*, 217.6 *make permanent*, 219.3 *continue*, 591.1 *avoid*, 641.4 *not act*
let an opportunity slip 211.6 *lose one's chance*
let be 217.6 *make permanent*, 219.3 *continue*
let bygones be bygones 512.15 *forgive*, 677.5 *make peace*, 839.9 *forgive*
let down 269.10 *lengthen*, 362.1 *lower*
letdown 515.2 *bad outcome*
let down 515.6 *disappoint*, 515.9 *disappointed*
letdown 683.1 *failure*
let down 806.3 *humbled*
letdown 806.10 *abasement*
let down 858.9 *prove false*
let-down 776.2 *hopeless situation*
let down one's side 858.9 *prove false*
let down the portcullis 634.4 *shelter*
let drop 362.6 *throw down*, 530.6 *divulge*
let fall 362.6 *throw down*, 530.6 *divulge*, 656.7 *be clumsy*
let fly 36.15 *sail*, 330.4 *throw*, 338.28 *shoot*, 419.5 *stink*, 670.2 *fire*, 828.12 *become angry*
let fly at 670.5 *strike*
let go 16.63 *acquitted*, 16.78 *acquit*, 252.17 *relegate*, 349.2 *dismiss*, 362.6 *throw down*, 598.9 *forget it*, 639.1 *deliver*, 698.15 *set free*, 698.19 *liberalize*, 727.9 *dispose of*, 767.12 *relieve from duty*, 783.12 *be indifferent*, 848.10 *acquit*
let go for a song 754.13 *make cheap*
let go free 700.4 *liberate*
let go no further 529.12 *keep secret*
let go of 598.1 *relinquish*, 700.4 *liberate*, 705.5 *resign*
lethal 244.14 *destructive*, 397.20, 398.23 *deadly*, 626.7 *toxic*
lethal chamber 879.16 *instrument of execution*
lethal dose 631.11 *intoxicant*
lethal injection 397.4 *death sentence*, 398.5 *execution*, 879.16 *instrument of execution*
lethally 398, 244.16 *destructively*
lethargic 328.5 *unhurried*, 643.3 *not participating*, 650.1 *fatigued*, 783.7 *indifferent*
lethargically 643.16 *impassively*, 650.8 *tiredly*
lethargy 61.13 *depression*, 328.8 *slowness*, 643.7 *idleness*, 650.7 *fatigue*, 783.1 *submission*, 783.1, 783.1 *indifference*
let have it 330.3 *hit*
Lethean 512.9 *blank*

let in 130.6 *add*, 348.7 *admit*
let in daylight 530.5 *disclose*
let it all hang out 530.6 *divulge*, 698.19 *liberalize*
let it be known 532.13 *make public*
let it go 839.9 *forgive*, 839.11 *condone*
let it pass 839.9 *forgive*
let it rip 329.6 *accelerate*
let judgment go by default 673.3 *submit*
let know 528.11 *inform*
let loose 700.4 *liberate*
let loose of 727.9 *dispose of*
let nature take its course 219.3 *continue*
let nothing stand in one's way 836.6 *be pitiless*
let off 16.63 *acquitted*, 16.78 *acquit*, 338.28 *shoot*, 419.5 *stink*, 639.1 *deliver*, 698.15 *set free*, 839.6 *forgiven*, 839.10 *absolve*, 848.6 *acquitted*, 848.10 *acquit*
let-off 16.42 *acquittal*, 639.2 *deliverance*
let off scot-free 848.10 *acquit*
let off steam 388.27 *give off*
let off the hook 16.63 *acquitted*, 16.78 *acquit*, 691.3 *be lenient*, 700.4 *liberate*, 839.6 *forgiven*
let on 530.6 *divulge*
let one in on 530.6 *divulge*
let one off the hook 839.10 *absolve*
let one off this time 839.10 *absolve*
let one's breath out 349.14 *let out*
let oneself be walked all over 808.8 *be servile*
let oneself go 553.5 *be diffuse*, 628.1 *deteriorate*, 689.4 *be anarchic*, 698.19 *liberalize*
let oneself in 346.9 *enter*
let oneself in for 597.1 *undertake*, 659.19 *have difficulty*
let one's hair down 698.17 *be informal*, 698.19 *liberalize*, 720.7 *not observe*, 814.11 *not stand on ceremony*
let one's imagination run riot 519.14 *imagine*
let or hindrance 661.1 *hindrance*
let out 349, 349.2 *dismiss*, 530.5 *disclose*, 530.6 *divulge*, 639.1 *deliver*, 700.4 *liberate*, 727.9 *dispose of*
let-out 16.4 *bad law*, 602.1 *means*, 638.2 *means of escape*, 639.2 *deliverance*
let-out clause 716.2 *basis for negotiations*
let out on bail 700.4 *liberate*
let pass 641.4 *not act*, 839.11 *condone*
let rip 349.16 *belch*
let sleeping dogs lie 217.6 *make permanent*, 219.3 *continue*, 641.4 *not act*, 698.15 *set free*
let slip 362.6 *throw down*, 493.10 *misjudge*, 530.5 *disclose*
let slip through one's fingers 211.6 *lose one's chance*, 722.11 *be wasteful*
let some light in 530.5 *disclose*
let someone down 683.6 *fail*, 720.8 *not perform*
let someone get away with it 708.4 *be permissive*
let someone get away with murder 708.4 *be permissive*
let someone have it 670.5 *strike*
let stick to one's finger 752.4 *take a discount*
let stick to one's fingers 736.12 *steal*
letter 5, 5.47 *word*, 534.3 *correspondence*, 543.1 *sign*, 544.10 *identify*, 560.4 *factual account*
letter bomb 539.13 *snare*, 680.16 *bomb*
letter bombing 670.16 *terrorist attack*
letterbox 534.3 *correspondence*
letter by letter 503.8 *accurately*

letter carrier 326.8 *messenger*, 534.4 *postal worker*
lettered 5, 4.19 *learned*, 48.16 *literary*, 544.12 *identified*
lettered player 655.4 *skilled person*
letterer 543.8 *signer*
letter for letter 118.14 *imitatively*, 537.38 *literally*
letter-for-letter 5.48 *linguistically*
letterhead 544.3 *means of identification*
lettering 5.13 *letter*, 5.41 *lettered*, 792.2 *pattern*
letterman 237.5 *athlete*
letter of credit 741.14 *paper money*, 744.2 *credit card*
letter of introduction 544.3 *means of identification*, 851.6 *recommendation*
letter of the law 16.34 *legal formality*, 690.1 *severity*
letter post 534.2 *postal communication*
letterpress printing 245.1 *reproduction*
letter-quality printer 65.7 *peripheral*
letters 48.1 *literature*, 326.10 *transferred thing*
letter s 429.3 *hisser*
letters 501.3 *learning*, 501.5 *science*
letters a foot high 532.8 *public relations*
letters after one's name 544.3 *means of identification*, 878.1 *reward*
letters of fire 532.8 *public relations*
letters patent 692.4 *authorization*, 708.2 *permit*
letters to the editor 528.4 *mass communication*, 532.3 *journalism*
letter writer 534.5 *correspondent*
let the air out of 542.21 *detract from*
let the air out of one's tyres 614.8 *make useless*
let the ayes have it 499.5 *assent to*
let the cat get one's tongue 563.14 *have difficulty speaking*
let the cat out of the bag 528.13 *inform on* , 530.7 *betray*, 656.7 *be clumsy*
let the good times roll 641.4 *not act*
let the side down 578.3 *apostatize*
let the world go by 641.4 *not act*
let things take care of themselves 641.4 *not act*
let things take their course 219.3 *continue*, 641.4 *not act*
letting go 727.1 *disposal*
letting off 835.3 *mercy*
Lettish 5 Languages and Groups of Languages
let tomorrow take care of itself 595.12 *be unprepared*
lettuce 45 Vegetables, 453.9 *greenstuff*
lettuce and tomato sandwich 45.11 *sandwich*
let up 160.13 *pause*
letup 218.3 *pause*
let up 218.6 *cease*, 218.9 *pause*, 218.12 *stop*
letup 242.1 *moderation*
let up 328.3 *slow down*, 649.2 *take it easy*
let-up 160.3 *interval*, 649.1 *ease*
let well alone 641.4 *not act*
let well enough alone 217.6 *make permanent*
Leucetios 8 Deities
leucine 58 Amino Acids
Leucippus 4 Philosophers
leucite 54 Minerals
leucocyte 387.4 *blood*
leucoderma 446.7 *whiteness*, 624.13 *skin disease*
leucoplast 59.8 *cell organ*
leucorrhoea 353.7 *pus*, 387.3 *body fluid*

leucotomy 60 Surgical Operations, 61.3 *psychiatric treatment*
leukaemia 624.4 *disease*, 624.11 *blood disease*, 624.12 *cancer*
leukaemic 624.23 *diseased*
levant 745.8, 747.7 *not pay*
levanter 55 Winds
levee 96.2 *channel*, 661.3 *barrier*
level 266, 63.17 *civil engineering*, 98.6 *lowland*, 107.3 *relative position*, 110.8 *make the same*, 110.16 *equal*, 110.17 *regular*, 112.5 *uniform*, 116.14 *conforming*, 116.26 *make uniform*, 121.2 *rank*, 121.4 *interval*, 121.7 *gradational*, 122.8 *on equal terms*, 122.11 *equalize*, 124.10 *make average*, 125.5 *counterbalance*, 127.5 *inferior state*, 152.6 *category*, 163.5 *social class*, 198.11 *equal*, 214.10 *make regular*, 214.11 *regular*, 214.14 *orderly*, 244.9 *demolish*, 258.4 *rack*, 282.2 *horizontal surface*, 282.7 *make horizontal*, 282.8 *horizontal*, 282.11 *horizontally*, 319.3 *rung*, 362.2 *flatten*, 376.2 *uniform*, 376.11 *smooth*, 420.10 *sound quality*, 670.2 *fire*
level-action 37.8 *shooting*
level-action rifle 37.3 *hunting equipment*
level crossing 72.2 *track*, 327.10 *railway*, 356.5 *crossing point*
level-green 25.9 *bowls*
level-green bowls 25.1 *green bowling*
level ground 276.2 *lowland*, 282.3 *flat thing*
level-headed 4.18 *detached*, 101.8 *practical*, 507.5 *wise*, 509.5 *rational*
level-headedness 4.3 *detachment*, 507.1 *wisdom*
levelled 125.10 *counterbalancing*, 282.9 *flattened*, 362.17 *lowered*
leveller 244.6 *destroyer*
Leveller 627.12 *reformer*
Levellers 7 Christian Movements
levelling 125.10 *counterbalancing*, 362.11 *lowering*, 362.12 *downthrow*
levelling off 129.2 *decline*, 262.1 *contraction*
levelling out 129.2 *decline*
levelling up 122.3 *equalization*
levelly 110.19 *equally*, 110.20 *regularly*, 112.13 *uniformly*, 121.9 *differentially*, 376.14 *smoothly*
Lion
Level N53 The Constellations
Lion 53 The Constellations
levelness 110.6 *regularity*, 112.1 *uniformity*, 122.1 *equality*, 214.4 *orderliness*, 282.1 *horizontality*, 376.7 *smoothness*
level off 112.9 *be uniform*, 129.4 *decrease*
level of meaning 520.4 *type of meaning*
level out 129.4 *decrease*, 214.10 *make regular*, 282.7 *make horizontal*
level pegged 122.8 *on equal terms*, 198.14 *equal with*
level pegging 110.5, 122.1 *equality*, 198.4 *equal race*, 264.2 *short distance*, 264.5 *near*
level-pegging 110.16, 198.11 *equal*
level up 122.11 *equalize*, 124.10 *make average*
level with 144.8 *full*, 198.14 *equal with*, 857.6 *be honourable*
leven 361.10 *elevator*
Leven 51 Lakes
lever 30.7 *stationary rings*, 36.19 *punt*, 63.6 *simple machine*, 233.4 *indirect influence*, 338.11 *propeller*, 355.10 *excavator*, 361.1 *raise*, 361.9 *lifter*, 603.1 *tool*, 603.9 *use tools*
leverage 126.1 *superiority*, 233

influence, 603.1 *tool*, 698.5 *scope*, 745.3 *loan*
leveraged 737.18 *contractual*
leveraged buyout 13.7 *corporation*
levered 36.14 *punting*
leveret 77.19 *young mammal*
levering 36.8 *punting*
lever out 355.12 *displace*
Levi 48 Writers, **48** Writers
leviathan 259.9 *big thing*
levigate 376.11 *smooth*, 384.23 *pulverize*, 385.12 *rub*
levigated 384.19 *pulverized*
levigation 376.7 *smoothness*, 384.4 *pulverization*, 385.3 *grinding*
levigator 384.11 *pulverizer*
levirate 823.3 *types of marriage*
leviration 823.3 *types of marriage*
Levi's 295.9 *trousers*
levitate 11.24 *experience psychic phenomena*, 359.13 *ascend*, 359.20 *hover*, 361.1 *raise*, 370.9 *be light*
levitated 361.11 *raised*
levitating 370.2 *insubstantial*, 370.5 *lightness*
levitation 11.1 *occultism*, 359.1 *ascent*, 361.6 *raising*, 370.5 *lightness*
levitational 370.2 *insubstantial*
levitative 370.2 *insubstantial*
Levite 7.8 *priest*
levity 370.5 *lightness*, 576.12 *inconstancy*, 579.2 *caprice*, 769.3 *cheerfulness*, 780.1 *rashness*
levorphanol 62 Medication
levy 751, 68.2 *Common Agricultural Policy* , 679.14 *armed forces*, 692.2, 692.10 *demand*, 712.7 *demand*, 734.5 *takings*, 734.8 *take back*, 751.12 *charge*, 845.5 *dues*
levying 734.2 *taking back*
lewd 622.9 *obscene*, 795.9 *ribald*, 877.12 *indecent*, 877.14 *lecherous*
lewdly 622.12 *dirtily*
lewdness 622.3 *obscenity*, 877.2 *indecency*
Lewes 4 Philosophers
Lewis 48 Writers, **48** Writers, **48 Writers**
Lewis acid 57.8 *acid*
Lewis base 57.9 *base*
Lewis Carroll and Alice 819.7 *famous friendships*
Lewis gun 680.12 *historical guns*
lewisite 631.10 *warfare*
Lexell 53 Comets
lexical 5.42 *worded*, 520.8 *semantic*
lexically 5
lexical meaning 520.4 *type of meaning*
lexicographer 5.2 *linguist*, 524.6 *interpreter*, 688.11 *expert*
lexicographic 5.38 *linguistic*
lexicographical 5.41 *lettered*
lexicographically 5.48 *linguistically*
lexicography 5.1 *linguistics*, 5.28 *dictionary*, 524.5 *science of interpretation*
lexicological 5.38 *linguistic*
lexicologist 5.2 *linguist*
lexicology 5.1 *linguistics*
lexicon 5.28 *dictionary*, 6.14 *school book*, 171.3 *dictionary*
lexicostatistical 5.38 *linguistic*
lexicostatistics 5.1 *linguistics*
lexigraphy 5.13 *letter*
Lexington 93 Cities
lex mercatoria 16.1 *the law*
lex non scripta 16.1 *the law*
lex scripta 16.1 *the law*
ley 87.2 *grassland*
Leyden jar 56 Named Laws
ley grass 87.1 *grass*
Leyte 98 Islands
lez 402.10 *homosexual*
L-form 57.13 *structure*
LGM 53.34 *SETI*
Lha 8.6 *angel*
Lhasa apso 77 Breeds of Dogs

L'Hospital's rule 52 Named Concepts
li 75 Some Foreign Units
liability 234.2 *attitude*, 478.9 *answerability*, 488.1 *probability*, 633.7 *vulnerability*, 745.1 *debt*, 847.1 *duty*, 866.1 *guilt*, 879.8 *penalty*
liable 847, 16.64 *convicted*, 478.16 *answerable*, 488.6 *probable*, 633.3 *vulnerable*, 745.9 *in debt*, 879.22 *punishable*
liableness 488.1 *probability*
liable to 234.5 *tending to*
liable to illness 624.21 *unhealthy*
liable to law 16
liable to prosecution 856.8 *accusatory*
liable to the law 16.48 *jurisdictional*
liaise 135.8 *unite*, 137.13 *intercommunicate*
liaise with 107.7 *relate to*
liaising 137.14 *connective*
liaison 107.1 *relatedness*, 135.1 *union*, 137.2 *association*, 678.3 *mediator*, 821.8 *love affair*, 877.4 *illicit love*
liana 83.2 *plant*
liar 538, 539, 309.5 *defacer*, 474.6 *sophist*, 539.15 *deceiver*, 540.15 *false person*, 541.6 *exaggerator*, 548.3 *deceiver*, 657.3 *cunning person*
liar's promise 521.3 *meaningless thing*
libation 349.22 *disgorgement*, 351.2, 874.13 *drink*
libational 10.21 *ritualistic*
libationary 10.21 *ritualistic*
libations 874.12 *alcohol*
libation to Bacchus 874.13 *drink*
libeccio 55 Winds
libel 525.1 *misinterpret*, 525.2 *misinterpretation*, 538.1 *untruth*, 538.3 *lying*, 538.21 *lie*, 540.6 *lying*, 618.11 *harmfulness*, 618.14 *ill-treat*, 670.10 *criticize*, 670.16 *terrorist attack*, 827.3 *vilification*, 827.6 *vilify*, 854.3 *defamation*, 854.12 *defame*, 856.2 *false accusation*, 856.6 *accuse falsely*
libellant 16.8 *litigant*, 856.3 *accuser*
libelled 856.9 *perjurious*
libellee 16.8 *litigant*
libeller 854.8 *defamer*, 856.3 *accuser*
libelling 538.15 *lying*, 540.29 *deceitful*
libellous 525.3 *misinterpreted*, 538.13 *untrue*, 540.32 *falsified*, 670.25 *critical*, 827.9 *vituperative*, 854.16 *defamatory*, 856.9 *perjurious*
libellously 525.5 *misrepresentedly*, 538.26 *untruthfully*, 827.13 *vituperatively*, 854.18 *disparagingly*, 856.10 *accusingly*
liberal 6.21 *curricular*, 164.15 *general*, 242.7 *politically moderate*, 271.3 *broad-minded*, 333.3 *moderate person*, 482.2 *impartial*, 482.10 *impartial person*, 608.2 *plentiful*, 627.12 *reformer*, 665.6 *political party member*, 665.10 *political*, 675.7 *peaceful*, 691.2 *lenient person*, 698.7 *free person*, 698.9 *free*, 729.8 *giving*, 748.10 *expending*, 755.1 *generous*, 831.7 *charitable*, 833.6 *philanthropic*, 878.18 *giving*
Liberal 12.9 *governmental*
Liberal Democrat 665.6 *political party member*
Liberal Democrat Party 12.6 *political party*
liberal education 6.2 *educational system*
liberalism 627.11 *reformism*, 665.3 *political grouping*, 698.1 *freedom*, 831.3 *welfare*
liberality 698, 271.6 *broad-mindedness*, 729.1 *giving*, 748.7 *do-*

nation, 755.5 generosity, 831.2 charity, 833.1 philanthropy
liberalization 700.1 liberation
liberalize 698, 665.15 politicize, 700.4 liberate
liberalized 700.7 liberated
liberally 665.18 cliquishly, 729.9 as a gift, 748.14, 755.12 generously, 831.11 charitably
Liberals 12.6 political party
liberal thinking 700.1 liberation
liberate 700, 16.78 acquit, 136.9 separate, 352.7 secrete, 355.11 extract, 629.3 restore, 639.1 deliver, 730.18 disentangle, 698.15 set free, 727.9 dispose of, 767.10 save, 848.10 acquit, 855.7 vindicate
liberated 700, 16.63 acquitted, 136.15 separate, 355.19 dislodged, 638.8 escaping, 639.4 deliverable, 698.9 free, 698.12 unconditional, 727.12 disposed, 848.6 acquitted
liberated man 401
liberated mind 698.1 freedom
liberated spirit 700.1 liberation
liberated woman 402
liberating 136.1 separation, 700.7 liberated, 727.1 disposal
liberation 700, 16.42 acquittal, 355.1 extraction, 638.1 escape, 639.2 deliverance, 698.1 freedom, 727.1 disposal, 767.2 aid, 848.2 acquittal
Liberation 700
liberation theology 7.13 theology
liberator 700, 639.3 deliverer
Liberia 91 Countries
libertarian 698.8 free-thinker, 698.9 free
libertarianism 698.1 freedom
libertinage 821.5 desire
libertine 401, 405.3 pleasure-seeker, 698.8 free-thinker, 782.6 desirer, 821.9 lover, 826.5 courting person, 877.8 immoral man, 877.14 lecherous
libertinism 698.6 liberality, 877.3 sexual immorality
liberty 116.7 consent, 645.1 leisure, 698.1 freedom, 848.2 acquittal
Liberty Bell 698.3 independence
liberty cap 89 Fungi
Liberty Hall 698.6 liberality
liberty horse 32.1 horse
liberty ship 74 Ships and Boats
libidinal energy 61.22 libido
libidinal object 61.22 libido
libidinous 782.11 lustful, 877.14 lecherous
libidinously 782.20 lustfully
libidinousness 782.4 sexual desire
libido 61, 782.4 sexual desire, 821.5 desire, 877.3 sexual immorality
libido analogue 61.22 libido
libido arrest 61.17 fixation
libido fixation 61.17 fixation
libra 75 Some Fixed Units
Libra 53 The Constellations, **53** Zodiac Constellations
librarian 532.12 publisher, 653.15 manager
library 6.15 schoolroom, 161.31 exhibition, 256.7 room, 531.6 privacy, 532.6 book publishing, 605.5 collection, 647.1 workshop
library school 6.12 educational institution
library table 47.4 table
libration 53.17 moon, 365.1 oscillation
libratory 365.13 oscillating
librettist 48.14 author, 49.24 musician, 51.24 dramatist, 560.10 descriptive writer
libretto 49.4 opera, 51.2 play
Libya 91 Countries
Libyan 5 Languages and Groups of Languages
lice 777 Phobias by Topic
licence 848, 16.29 legalization, 116.8 permit, 485.3 qualifications, 688.9 permission, 698.1 freedom, 698.6 liberality, 703.3

authority, 708.1 permission, 708.2 permit, 814.4 freedom, 845.6 bond, 851.1 approval
licenced 688.16 authorized
license 16.65 make legal, 116.29 permit, 485.13 qualify, 688.21 grant authority, 703.8 authorize, 708.3 permit, 845.16 entitle, 851.12 accept
licensed 16.44 legal, 16.50 law-abiding, 116.18 permitting, 485.10 authorized, 708.7 permitted
Licensed Practical Nurse 60.16 nurse
licensed premises 351.11 drink provider
licensee 606.4 caterer, 703.5 commissioner, 730.5 recipient
license plate 71 Motor Vehicle Parts
license plate number 544.3 means of identification
licentiate 485.3 qualifications
licentious 16.61 lawless, 405.7 pleased, 622.9 obscene, 698.12 unconditional, 870.7 dissipated, 877.14 lecherous
licentiously 698.21 excessively
licentiousness 622.3 obscenity, 698.6 liberality, 821.5 desire, 846.4 presumptuousness, 870.2 dissipation, 877.3 sexual immorality
lichen 90, 83.4 lower plant, 88.3 moss, 89.5 fungal association, 90.1 alga
lichened 90.8 lichenoid
licheniform 90.8 lichenoid
lichenized 90.8 lichenoid
lichenoid 90
lichenological 90.8 lichenoid
lichenologist 83.12 plant scientist, 90.6 lichen
lichenology 83.10 plant science, 90.6 lichen
lichenometry 90.6 lichen
lichenose 90.8 lichenoid
lichenous 90.8 lichenoid
licit 16.44 legal, 116.18 permitting, 708.7 permitted, 845.8 entitled
licitly 16.81 legally
licitness 16.28 legality
lick 126.8 be superior, 324.12 gait, 330.5 beat, 350.23 taste, 621.5 ablutions, 682.10 defeat heavily
licked 683.11 defeated
lickerish 877.14 lecherous
lickerishness 877.3 sexual immorality
lickety-split 329.14 swiftly, 648.6 hastily
licking 330.12 collision, 350.3 delicate eating, 682.2 victory, 683.2 defeat
lick into shape 150.21 tidy, 220.9 transform, 306.7 form, 594.6 brief
lick one's lips 782.14 be hungry
lickspit 808.3 sycophant
lickspittle 808.9 fawn
lick the arse of 808.9 fawn
lick the boots of 673.4 succumb
lick the dust 673.4 succumb, 806.20 submit, 808.10 knuckle under
lick the feet of 808.9 fawn
lick the hem of one's garment 808.9 fawn
lick the platter clean 350.22 eat well
lick the shoes of 808.9 fawn
lid 293.2 cover, 295.15 headgear, 323.2 stopper, 440.6 shade
lie 538, 538, 30.10 compete in gymnastics, 105.6 be in a state of, 240.4 be inert, 251.9 be situated, 282.6 be horizontal, 309.4 distortion of the truth, 309.12 distort the truth, 332.2 bearing, 474.12 deceive, 489.6 implausibility, 489.7 be improbable, 531.5 evasion, 540.16 be false, 548.1 misrepresentation, 548.4 misrepresent, 657.2 strata-

gem, 858.1 improbity, 858.8 be dishonourable
lie-abed 643.11 sleeper
lie ahead 199.7 be in the future
lie around 297.7 surround, 643.12 be inactive
lie a sailboat 36.15 sail
lie at the bottom of 226.9 be the cause of
lie at the door of 847.14 be the duty of
lie back 649.2 take it easy
lie below the surface 290.13 be interior, 527.13 hide
lie beneath 290.13 be interior, 527.12 be latent
Lieberkühn's gland 352 Exocrine Glands
lie betwixt and between 158.18 stand in the middle
Liebig 52 Scientists
Liechtenstein 91 Countries
lied 433.2 song
lie dead 641.4 not act
lieder singer 433.5 melodist
lie detector 61.4 psychometrics, 496.11 detector
lie doggo 240.4 be inert, 527.13 hide, 531.11 conceal oneself
lie dormant 527.12 be latent, 643.13 sleep
lie down 276.8 be low, 282.6 be horizontal, 362.8 sit, 649.2 take it easy
lie fallow 247.7 be infertile, 595.12 be unprepared, 600.6 stop using, 641.4 not act
lie flat 282.6 be horizontal
liege 696.1 master, 701.5 subjected person
liege lord 632.3 protector, 696.1 master
Liège 93 Cities
liegeman 697.1 servant
Lie group 52 Named Concepts
lie heavy upon 369.14 make heavy
lie hidden 527.13 hide
lie idle 240.4 be inert, 600.6 stop using, 641.4 not act
lie in ambush 527.13 hide
lie in one's power 235.10 be powerful
lie in the future 199.7 be in the future
lie in the grave 397.15 die
lie in the neighbourhood of 264.8 be near
lie in the vicinity of 264.8 be near
lie in wait 240.4 be inert, 635.3 trap
lie just around the corner 199.7 be in the future
lie low 276.8 be low, 438.7 become invisible, 458.1 disappear, 527.13 hide, 531.11 conceal oneself, 632.8 be safe, 638.6 elude, 657.5 be cunning
lientery 353.2 defecation
lie of the ball 29.2 golfing terms
lie of the land 106.1 circumstances, 332.1 direction
lie on a bed of nails 840.6 apologize
lie on one's back 282.6 be horizontal
lie on the ball 35.5 play rugby
lie on velvet 686.5 be prosperous
lie opposite 111.8 be opposite
lie out of the way 263.5 be distant
lie over 293.26 overlie
lie parallel 285.5 parallel
lierne 43 Architectural Decoration
lierne vault 43.7 vault
lie still 240.4 be inert
lie to 74.10 sail
lie under the surface 527.12 be latent
lieutenant 662.11 helper, 679.17 army person, 679.27 naval man, 707.1 deputy
Lieutenant 17 British Military Ranks, **17** British Military Ranks, **17** US Military Ranks, **17** US Military Ranks

Lieutenant Colonel 17 British Military Ranks, **17** US Military Ranks
lieutenant-colonel 679.17 army person
Lieutenant Commander 17 British Military Ranks, **17** US Military Ranks
lieutenant-commander 679.27 naval man
lieutenant general 692.6 person in command
Lieutenant General 17 British Military Ranks, **17** US Military Ranks
lieutenant-general 679.17 army person
lieutenant governor 696.3 leader
lie with 135.11 make love
lie within 290.13 be interior
life 396, 3.6 biography, 48.4 non-fiction, 99.1 existence, 239.1 vigour, 642.1 activity, 642.4 energy, 702.4 prison sentence
Life 396
life activity 396.4 biological function
life a curfew 700.4 liberate
life after death 199.3 future condition, 368.1 nonmaterial world
life-and-death 772.3 important
life and soul of the party 769.4 cheerful person
life assurance 632.2 protection
life belt 39.3 survival swimming, 293.3 protective covering, 370.7 light thing, 632.4 safety device, 637.2 preserver
lifeblood 103.2 essential content, 387.4 blood, 396.3 life requirements
lifeboat 74 Ships and Boats, 632.4 safety device, 639.3 deliverer
lifeboatman 639.3 deliverer
life buoy 39.3 survival swimming, 370.7 light thing, 632.4 safety device
life cycle 396, 214.2 cycle, 220.2 evolution
life everlasting 190.3 life without end
life expectancy 396.5 life cycle
life force 396.1 life
life-giving 245.16 reproductive, 396.12 alive
lifeguard 39.4 swimmer, 632.3 protector, 637.4 preservationist, 671.14 guard, 718.3 security officer
Life Guard 679.12 ceremonial troops
lifeguarding 39.3 survival swimming
life instinct 61.22 libido
life insurance 632.2 protection
life jacket 39.3 survival swimming, 293.12 protective covering, 370.7 light thing, 632.4 safety device, 637.2 preserver
lifeless 240.5 inert, 325.5 sedentary, 397.19 dead, 412.5 tasteless, 643.1 inactive
lifelessly 240.7 inertly, 325.10 motionlessly, 397.23 fatally, 643.15 inactively
lifelessness 240.1 inertness, 412.1 tastelessness, 573.13 dissociation, 643.5 inactivity
lifelike 114, 537, 101.7 realistic, 503.6 correct
lifelikeness 537.12 true to life
lifeline 36.3 parts of a sailing boat, 137.6 line, 632.4 safety device, 637.2 preserver
lifelong 188.8 lasting, 396.12 alive
lifelong dream 588.6 objective
lifelong friend 819.6 close friend
lifemanship 652.9 tactics
life member 665.5 member
life of abstinence 825.2 virginity
life of ease 106.5 comfortable circumstances, 686.1 prosperity
life of Riley 686.1 prosperity, 742.7 opulence

life of the party 815.6 *social person*
life on earth 396.1 *life*
life on the ocean wave 74.1 *water travel*
life peer 12.8 *politician*, 653.16 *official*, 802.1 *nobleman*
life preserver 39.3 *survival swimming*, 370.7 *light thing*, 680.7 *blunt weapon*
lifer 702.5 *prisoner*
life raft 632.4 *safety device*
life requirements 396
lifesaver 39.4 *swimmer*
life-saver 632.3 *protector*, 637.4 *preservationist*, 639.3 *deliverer*
lifesaving 39.3 *survival swimming*
life-saving 639.2 *deliverance*, 639.4 *deliverable*
life science 59
Life Science 59
life sciences 396.7 *studies of life*
life scientist 59
life senses 396.4 *biological function*
life size 259.2 *bigness*
life-size 259.15 *big*
life space 142.2 *whole thing*
life span 185.3 *duration*, 207.1 *age*, 396.5 *life cycle*
life story 396, 3.6 *biography*, 48.4 *non-fiction*, 560.4 *factual account*
lifestyle 396, 105.1 *state*, 584.3 *way*, 652.6 *way of life*
life support system 637.2 *preserver*
life-support system 396.5 *life cycle*, 630.14 *hospital*
life-threatening 244.14 *destructive*, 398.23 *deadly*, 633.1 *dangerous*
lifetime 207.1 *age*, 269.8 *measure of time*, 396.5 *life cycle*
life to come 199.3 *future condition*, .396.5 *life cycle*
life vest 39.3 *survival swimming*, 632.4 *safety device*
life without end 190
Liffey 96 Rivers
Lifford 93 Cities
lift 359, 361, 21.2 *field events*, 27.8 *delivery*, 36.3 *parts of a sailing boat*, 41.1 *skiing*, 41.6 *ice-skating*, 41.16 *bobsled* , 71.4 *personal transport*, 275.1 *height*, 275.17 *raise*, 326.5 *means of transport*, 326.12 *transport*, 330.10 *bat*, 336.8 *further*, 336.12 *advance*, 339.12 *drag*, 359.13 *ascend*, 361.1 *raise*, 361.9 *lifter*, 361.10 *elevator*, 390.1 *air*, 627.5 *improvement*, 644.4 *exertion*, 644.6 *work*, 662.2, 662.19 *support*, 727.9 *dispose of*, 736.3 *theft*, 736.12 *steal*, 736.15 *infringe*
lift a finger 640.4 *act*
lift an oar 36.16 *row*
lift bridge 63.21 *bridge*
lift controls 700.4 *liberate*
lifted 41.13 *ice-skating*, 361.11 *raised*
lifter 361, 736.8 *thief*
lift front legs 304.7 *rear up*
lifting 41.9 *bobsledding* , 41.13 *ice-skating*, 359.23 *rising*, 361.6 *raising*, 736.1 *stealing*, 736.6 *illegal borrowing*
lifting body 73 Types of Aircraft
lifting front legs 304.3 *rearing up*
liftoff 345.8 *start*, 359.4 *taking off*
lift off 359.19 *take off*
lift-off 359.27 *alley-oop*
lift oneself 361.5 *arise*
lift restrictions 727.9 *dispose of*
lift the ban on 708.3 *permit*
lift the roof 430.4 *be strident*
lift the veil 530.5 *disclose*
lift the veil on 496.2 *detect*
lift up 275.17, 361.1 *raise*
ligament 137.6 *line*, 382.7 *skeleton*
ligand 57.11 *chemical bond*
ligase 58.11 *enzyme*

ligate 137.11 *connect*
ligation 135.3 *unification*
ligature 135.1 *union*, 137.6 *line*
liger 77 Placental Mammals
ligger 712.5 *beggar*
light 777 Phobias by Topic, 56, 370, 439, 439, 439, 446, 446, 41.10 *curling*, 56.13 *electromagnetic radiation*, 56.25 *light source*, 105.1 *state*, 120.6 *quantitative*, 182.6 *sparse*, 235.9 *electronics*, 235.12 *generate power*, 238.13 *insufficient*, 274.4 *fine*, 278.2 *superficial*, 351.17 *drinkable*, 359.23 *rising*, 365.5 *wave*, 372.1 *sparse*, 390.12 *airy*, 410.11 *fuel*, 437.2 *clear*, 437.6 *visible thing*, 437.7 *that which makes visible*, 437.10 *make visible*, 439.18 *lit*, 442.9 *glass*, 444.13 *soft-hued*, 524.1 *interpretation*, 612.1 *unimportant*, 636.2 *danger signal*, 660.9 *easy*, 796.4 *design*, 877.13 *unchaste*
Light 439
light air 55.13 *wind strength*
light-armed soldier 679.8 *soldier*
light artillery 680.11 *guns*
light as a fairy 370.1 *light*
light as a feather 370.1 *light*
light as air 370.1 *light*
light as day 439.19 *sunny*
light as thistledown 370.1 *light*
light beam 56.24 *light emission*
light blue 454.1 *blue*
lightboard 51.15 *stage*, 51.18 *stage lighting*
light bomber 679.31 *military aircraft*
light breeze 55.13 *wind strength*, 424.3 *faint-sounding thing*
light brigade 679.16 *army unit*
light bulb 44.9 *industrial ceramics*, 56.25 *light source*, 439.6 *electric light*
light buoy 439.6 *electric light*
light cavalry 679.19 *cavalry*
light coat 295.12 *coat*
light colour 439
light-coloured 439.21 *light*
light comedian 51.22 *actor*
light comedy 51.10 *comedy*
light complexioned 446.1 *white*
light cruiser 679.24 *warship*
light dragoon 32.15 *horse person*, 679.20 *cavalryman*
light drinker 351.12 *drinker*
light eater 350.18 *eater*
light emission 56
light-emitting diode 56.25 *light source*
lighten 370, 55.61 *shine*, 242.4 *moderate*, 439.24 *light*, 439.26 *grow light*, 439.28 *bleach*, 660.18 *disentangle*, 769.6 *bring cheer*
lightened 439.18 *lit*, 439.21 *light*
lightener 361.10 *elevator*
light engine 72.4 *locomotive*
lightening 370, 370, 439, 439.15 *lucent*
lighten ship 370.10 *lighten*
lighter 74 Ships and Boats, 410, 439.8 *fire*
lighterage 326.2 *transportation*, 751.6 *business costs*
lighter fuel 410.3 *gas*
lighter in one's purse 748.10 *expending*
lighter than air 370.1 *light*
lighter-than-air 390.12 *airy*
lighter-than-air craft 73.8 *aircraft*
light filter 441.1 *dimness*
light-fingered 370.1 *light*, 736.17 *stolen*, 858.7 *criminal*
light-fingeredness 736.1 *stealing*
light fingers 736.1 *stealing*, 858.3 *criminality*
light fitting 439.6 *electric light*
light-flyweight 26.3 *boxing weight divisions*, 26.14 *combat*
light-footed 329.1 *swift*, 370.1 *light*, 642.18 *active*
light-gathering power 53.28 *resolution*
light-grey 448.1 *grey*

light guide 56.29 *optical element*
light hand 691.1 *leniency*
light-handed 370.1 *light*, 407.10 *handed*
light-handedly 407.16 *sensitively*
light-headed 224.14 *irresolute*
light-hearted 769.1 *cheerful*
light-heartedly 769.9 *cheerfully*
lightheartedness 762.1 *happiness*
light-heartedness 769.3 *cheerfulness*
light heavyweight 369.7 *weighing*
light-heavyweight 26.3 *boxing weight divisions*, 26.14 *combat*
light horse 32.1 *horse*, 32.15 *horse person*, 679.19 *cavalry*
lighthouse 74.5 *navigation*, 275.6 *tall thing*, 281.3 *vertical thing*, 439.6 *electric light*, 531.6 *privacy*, 543.5 *indicator*, 632.4 *safety device*, 653.5 *guide*
lighthouse beacon 543.4 *signal*
lighthouse-keeper 636.4 *warner*
lighthouse operator 543.8 *signer*
light industry 243.2 *manufacture*
light infantry 679.16 *army unit*
lighting 66, 56.25 *light source*, 439.5 *incandescent light*, 439.15 *lucent*
lighting board 51.18 *stage lighting*
lighting desk 51.18 *stage lighting*
lighting man 51.26 *stagehand*
lighting plot 51.18 *stage lighting*
lighting-up time 71.21 *miscellaneous motoring terms*, 205.1 *evening*, 439.6 *electric light*
lightish 439.21 *light*
lightless 440.8 *dark*
light lunch 350.12 *meal*
lightly 370, 439, 120.7 *quantitatively*, 182.11 *sparsely*, 238.14 *weakly*, 278.8 *shallowly*, 372.7 *sparsely*, 390.25 *airily*, 446.14 *whitely*
lightly built 1.15 *physical*
light machine gun 680.11 *guns*
light meal 350.12 *meal*
light meter 56, 66.18 *exposure time*
light microscopy 59.6 *cell biology*
light-middleweight 26.3 *boxing weight divisions*, 26.14 *combat*
light-minded 224.14 *irresolute*, 576.2 *changeable*, 579.1 *capricious*, 656.1 *unskilful*
light-mindedness 224.2 *irresolution*, 579.2 *caprice*
light music 49.9 *popular music*
lightness 370, 120.1 *quantity*, 123.1 *inequality*, 274.11 *fineness*, 278.3 *shallowness*, 372.3 *sparseness*, 390.9 *airiness*, 439.14 *light colour*, 445.2 *paleness*, 877.3 *sexual immorality*
Lightness 370
lightning 777 Phobias by Topic, 15.10 *unionized*, 55.21 *thunderstorm*, 55.59 *storm*, 56.47 *electric storm*, 235.7 *electrical power*, 329.11 *swift thing*, 439.4 *natural light*
lightning arrester 56.47 *electric storm*
lightning conductor 55.21 *thunderstorm*, 56.47 *electric storm*, 235.7 *electrical power*, 632.4 *safety device*
lightning flash 55.21 *thunderstorm*, 329.11 *swift thing*
lightning sketch 50.9 *drawing*
lightning speed 329.8 *speed*
lightning strike 15.4 *industrial dispute*, 55.21 *thunderstorm*
light of love 821.2 *romantic love*
light of one's life 821.11 *loved one*
light on 609.1 *insufficient*
light on one's feet 370.1 *light*
light pen 65.7 *peripheral*, 439.11 *photoelectricity*
light pipe 56.29 *optical element*
light pocket 743.6 *insolvency*
light pollution 53.23 *observatory*
lightproof 323.12 *closed*, 440.8 *dark*, 443.1 *opaque*

light railway 72.1 *railway*, 327.10 *railway*
light rain 55.25 *rain*
light ray 439.1 *light*
light reaction 58.23 *photosynthesis*
light red oxide 450.6 *red pigment*
light rein 691.1 *leniency*
light relief 51.10 *comedy*
light rum 351.7 *alcoholic drink*
lights 51.18 *stage lighting*, 71.3 *carriageway*, 72.2 *track*
light-sensitive 439.23 *photoelectric*
light-sensitive cell 435.2 *eye*
light-sensitive material 56.33 *photosensitivity*
lightship 74 Ships and Boats, 74.5 *navigation*, 439.6 *electric light*, 543.5 *indicator*, 632.4 *safety device*
light ship 653.5 *guide*
light show 51.5 *show*, 439.12 *highlight*
light shower 55.25 *rain*
light signal 439.6 *electric light*
light-skinned 445.8 *drained of colour*
light sleep 643.9 *sleep*
light socket 439.6 *electric light*
lightsome 642.18 *active*
light source 56, 66.15 *lighting*
light-source 439.5 *incandescent light*
lights out 440.2 *darkening*, 543.6 *word*
light switch 410.4 *electricity*, 439.6 *electric light*
light the fuse 156.20 *activate*
light the touchpaper 410.11 *fuel*
light thing 370
light-tight 440.8 *dark*, 443.1 *opaque*
light up 439, 439.24 *light*
light upon 229.5 *happen by chance*, 344.2 *reach*, 360.12 *drop*, 589.11 *chance upon*, 721.14 *profit*
light verse 48.6 *poetry*
light vessel 653.5 *guide*
light water reactor 235.8 *nuclear power*
light wave 439.1 *light*
lightweight 26.3 *boxing weight divisions*, 26.14 *combat*, 127.13 *insignificant*, 238.4 *weakling*, 238.8 *weak*, 260.4 *little person*, 278.2 *superficial*, 278.5 *shallow person*, 369.1 *heavy*, 369.7 *weighing*, 370.1 *light*, 612.10 *nonentity*, 674.10 *contender*, 679.3 *athlete*
light-weight 612.4 *trivial*
light-welterweight 26.3 *boxing weight divisions*, 26.14 *combat*
light wine 351.9 *wine*
light year 75 Scientific and Technical Units
light-year 53.22 *astronomical unit*, 269.7 *measure of length*
light years 263.1 *distance*
ligneous 85.15 *woody*, 378.3 *hard*, 410.10 *powered*
ligniform 85.15 *woody*
lignin 58.4 *polysaccharide*, 59.7 *cell*, 85.3 *timber*
lignite 410.5 *coal*, 449.5 *brown thing*
lignitic 410.10 *powered*
lignocaine 62 Medication, 404.4 *anaesthetic*
lignography 47.8 *woodwork*, 50.15 *engraving*
lignum vitae 85 Trees and Shrubs
ligule 83.6 *leaf*, 87.3 *grass plant*
Ligurian 97 Oceans and Seas
likability 821.4 *lovability*
likable 763, 784, 405.6 *pleasant*, 782.8 *desirable*, 821.22 *lovable*
likable person 784
likable trait 617.6 *worth*
like 763, 782, 784, 110.14 *lookalike*, 114.7 *similar*, 114.13 *similarly*, 116.14 *conforming*, 116.34 *uniformly*, 234.4 *tend,*

327.16 *how*, 547.13 *representational*, 782.12 *desire*, 821.1, 821.23 *love*, 851.11 *approve*
like a bat out of hell 239.6 *with vigour*, 648.6 *hastily*
like a battering ram 241.10 *violently*
like a bear with a sore head 764.2 *objectionable*, 829.4 *irascible*
like a bird 329.1 *swift*
like a bitch 829.9 *irascibly*
like a bolt from the blue 425.10 *explosively*, 514.13 *surprisingly*
like a bomb 642.22 *actively*
like a boor 818.10 *rudely*
like a breath of fresh air 649.5 *labour-saving*
like a brother 831.10 *benevolently*
like a bucket in a well 365.18 *to and fro*
like a bull at a gate 241.10 *violently*
like a bureaucracy 703.11 *under commission*
like a cat on a hot tin roof 366.29 *jerkily*, 642.18 *active*, 760.2 *oversensitive*
like a cat on hot bricks 366.29 *jerkily*, 642.18 *active*
like a cat that got the cream 805.17 *conceited*
like a chicken with its head cut off 239.6 *with vigour*
like a child with a new toy 762.4 *happy*
like a chip off the old block 114.13 *similarly*
like a clan 665.18 *cliquishly*
like a diplomat 707.8 *by proxy*, 716.9 *feasibly*, 817.15 *genteelly*
like a drowned rat 389.23 *wet*
like a father 831.10 *benevolently*
like a fish 74.11 *nautical*
like a fish out of water 252.10 *replaced*, 656.1 *unskilful*, 666.10 *different*, 666.12 *differently*, 722.18 *at a loss*, 722.21 *out of place*, 816.10 *lonely*
like a fossil 132.12 *with a remainder*
like a giant refreshed 651.4 *refreshed*
like a Good Samaritan 710.20 *persuasively*
like a hen on a hot griddle 642.18 *active*
like a hog 872.7 *gluttonously*
like a horse 369.16 *heavily*, 872.7 *gluttonously*
like a horse in a mill 364.13 *round*
like a kid again 651.4 *refreshed*
like a knight in shining armour 817.14 *courteously*
like a lamb to the slaughter 497.15 *believingly*
like a lead balloon 369.16 *heavily*
like a leech 808.18 *parasitically*
like a limpet 138.11 *cohesively*
like all hell let loose 423.9 *loudly*
like a long-tailed cat in a room full of rocking chairs 642.18 *active*
like a lord 805.36 *majestically*
like a machine 655.12 *skilfully*
like a mad bull 241.6 *violent*
like a mad dog 241.6 *violent*
like a man 574.17 *resolutely*
like a master 655.12 *skilfully*
like a maze 314.4 *convolutional*
like a monk 825.12 *celibately*
like a mother 831.10 *benevolently*
like a mule 577.9 *be obstinate*
like an acrobat 374.17 *softly*
like an ambassador 706.8 *representatively*
like an ape 118.14 *imitatively*
like an athlete 374.17 *softly*
like an eagle 329.1 *swift*
like a nerd 818.10 *rudely*
like a new beginning 704.11 *invalidly*
like a new man 651.4 *refreshed*
like an expert 655.12 *skilfully*

like an illusion 368.13 *metaphysically*
like an innocent child 865.12 *naively*
like a nomad 104.18 *extraneously*
like a nun 825.12 *celibately*
like a parrot 118.14 *imitatively*
like a pendulum 139.10 *non-cohesively*
like a penitent 867.8 *penitently*
like a phoenix from the ashes 629.13 *repaired*
like a photograph 114.14 *comparably*
like a pig 872.7 *gluttonously*
like a pirate 736.19 *thievishly*
like a predator 734.13 *avariciously*, 736.19 *thievishly*
like a puppet on a string 694.7 *obedient*, 701.9 *subject*
like a Puritan 134.18 *virtuously*
like a raging bull 241.6 *violent*
like a relic 132.12 *with a remainder*
like a rocket 648.6 *hastily*
like a sailor 74.11 *nautical*, 74.12 *nautically*
like a servant 701.11 *under subjection*
like a shot 572.17 *spontaneously*
like a shrew 829.9 *irascibly*
like a square peg in a round hole 252.10 *replaced*, 666.10 *different*, 666.12 *differently*, 722.18 *at a loss*, 722.21 *out of place*
like a thief in the night 529.16 *stealthily*, 858.11 *dishonourably*
like a ton of bricks 369.16 *heavily*
like a torrent 96.13 *fluently*
like a tribe 665.18 *cliquishly*
like a vice 726.11 *tenaciously*
like a vixen 829.9 *irascibly*
like a volcano 98.13 *continentally*
like a war 668.10 *in defiance*
like a wolf 872.7 *gluttonously*
like a yob 818.10 *rudely*
like best 580.2 *prefer*
like better 580.2 *prefer*
like cats and dogs 666.9 *disagreeing*, 666.11 *in disagreement*
like clockwork 110.20 *regularly*, 112.13 *uniformly*, 214.15 *regularly*, 660.21 *easily*
like crazy 239.6 *with vigour*
liked 784.5 *likable*, 815.16 *popular*, 821.21 *beloved*
like death warmed up 624.22 *sick*
like double Dutch 523.1 *unintelligible*
like father like son 114.13 *similarly*
like for like 672.1 *retaliation*, 672.5 *retaliatory*
like friends 815.18 *sociably*
like Gadarene swine 241.10 *violently*
like gangbusters 239.6 *with vigour*
like glue 726.11 *tenaciously*
like gold dust 213.2 *infrequent*, 753.8 *valuable*
like grains of sand 139.8 *nonadhesive*
like greased lightning 191.8 *immediately*, 329.1 *swift*, 648.6 *hastily*
like Hamlet without the Prince 145.4 *incomplete*
like hell 239.6 *with vigour*, 711.12 *no*
like ivy 138.11 *cohesively*
like lead 369.16 *heavily*
likelihood 52.62 *probability*, 199.4 *looking to the future*, 475.5 *demonstrably*, 486.1 *possibility*, 488.1 *probability*, 513.1 *expectation*, 589.5 *good chance*
likeliness 488.1 *probability*
likely 101.9 *realizable*, 199.12 *predictable*, 199.16 *predictably*, 234.5 *tending to*, 475.22 *demonstrably*, 486.5 *possible*, 488.6 *probable*, 488.11 *proba-

bly*, 497.13 *believable*, 513.7 *expected*, 714.14 *auspicious*
like mad 239.6 *with vigour*, 241.10 *violently*
like magic 786.8 *wonderful*
like man and wife 823.24 *matrimonially*
like-minded 116.10 *in accord*, 499.6 *assenting*, 667.10 *agreeing*
like-mindedly 667.14 *agreeably*
like-mindedness 116.1 *accord*, 499.1 *assent*, 667.1 *agreement*
liken 107.8 *be proportionate to*, 114.11 *make similar*, 116.26 *make uniform*
likeness 50.7 *picture*, 114.1 *similarity*, 116.5 *conformity*, 118.2 *copy*, 122.1 *equality*, 167.1 *conformity*, 435.8 *reflection*, 457.5 *impression*, 547.1 *representation*, 547.6 *image*, 560.9 *representation*
like new 201.21 *newly*, 629.13 *repaired*, 629.15 *cured*
like no other 165.30 *characteristically*
like nothing 660.21 *easily*
like parchment 379.1 *brittle*
like putty in one's hands 599.9 *used*, 694.7 *obedient*, 701.9 *subject*
like putty in someone's hands 224.14 *irresolute*
likes 784
like sheep 116.31 *in accord*
like shooting fish in a barrel 660.9 *easy*
like snow in August 213.2 *infrequent*
like so 106.15 *under the circumstances*
like something the cat brought in 151.15 *untidy*
like stroke 29.2 *golfing terms*
like taking candy from a baby 660.9 *easy*
like that 106.15 *under the circumstances*, 116.36 *accordingly*
like the back of a bus 273.1 *thick*
like the curate's egg 127.17 *defective*, 620.1 *imperfect*
like the end of the world 618.5 *harmful*
like the idea 667.6 *agree with*
like the idea of 499.4 *assent*
like the Rock of Gibraltar 225.9 *stable*, 574.5 *steady*
like the sound of one's own voice 565.8 *talk too much*
like the spitting image 114.13 *similarly*
like this 106.15 *under the circumstances*
like to 784
like two peas in a pod 110.14 *lookalike*
like water off a duck's back 617.4 *worthwhile*
likewise 110.18 *identically*, 114.13 *similarly*, 116.34 *uniformly*
liking 784, 784, 234.2 *attitude*, 411.2 *taste of life*, 580.7 *preference*, 759.5 *good feeling*, 782.1 *desire*, 821.1 *love*, 851.2 *admiration*
Liking 784
lilac 84 Flowers and Flowering Plants, 455.3 *purple thing*, 455.6 *purple*
lilac-pointed Siamese 77 Breeds of Cats
liliaceous 83.16 *taxonomic*
Lill 49 Musicians and Composers
Lille 93 Cities
Lilliputian 260.7 *little*, 270.5 *short person*
lilly-pilly 85 Trees and Shrubs
Lilongwe 93 Cities
lilt 123.5 *be unequal*, 433.2 *song*, 433.10 *sing*
lilting 433.6 *melodious*
lily 84 Flowers and Flowering Plants, 418.2 *fragrant thing*, 446.9 *white thing*
lily family 83.3 *seed plant*

lily-livered 238.12 *weak-willed*, 452.5, 779.3 *cowardly*
lily-of-the-valley 84 Flowers and Flowering Plants
lily pond 69.3 *ornamental garden*
lily-white 446.1 *white*
Lima 93 Cities, 93 Cities, 534 Phonetic Alphabet
lima bean 45 Vegetables
limation 384.4 *pulverization*, 385.3 *grinding*
limb 85.2 *tree part*, 143.4 *component*, 143.6 *branch*
limber 74 Parts of a Ship, 374.2 *pliant*, 680.11 *guns*
limber hole 74 Parts of a Ship
limberly 374.17 *softly*
limberness 374.8 *softness*
limber up 374.14 *ease*, 594.8 *prepare oneself*, 644.9 *exercise*
limb from limb 136.21 *apart*
limbless 131.7 *reduced*, 143.11 *partial*, 145.4 *incomplete*
limbless amphibian 79.7 *amphibian*
limbo 8.11 *heaven*, 100.4 *emptiness*, 600.10 *disuse*
Limburger 45 Cheeses
lime 85 Trees and Shrubs, 86 Fruits, 68.13 *fertilizer*, 138.3 *adhesive*, 246.3 *fertilizer*, 415.3 *sour thing*, 445.4 *colour remover*, 453.9 *greenstuff*, 539.33 *snare*
lime-green 453.1 *green*
limekiln 44.6 *ceramic workshop*
limelight 51.18 *stage lighting*, 439.6 *electric light*, 532.7 *publicity*
limerick 48.7 *poem*
Limerick 92 Counties, 93 Cities
limestone 54 Common Rocks, 63.26 *masonry*, 68.13 *fertilizer*
lime twig 539.13 *snare*
limewater 389.1 *water*
limey 91 Names for Inhabitants, 86.5 *figurative usage*, 679.27 *naval man*
Limey 255.9 *British inhabitant*
Limeyland 91.8 *Great Britain*
liminal 298.6 *interfacial*
limit 157, 302, 42.3 *card game terms*, 52.29 *mathematical function*, 52.31 *differentiation*, 120.2 *certain amount*, 120.8 *quantify*, 129.5 *make smaller*, 136.6 *boundary*, 147.7 *exclude*, 242.4 *moderate*, 259.1 *size*, 262.5 *make smaller*, 272.10 *narrow*, 279.1 *summit*, 300.1 *edge*, 302.1 *limitation*, 485.16 *specify*, 544.10 *identify*, 609.5 *be insufficient*, 661.8 *hinder*, 684.3 *elaboration*, 699.1 *restraint*, 699.8 *restrain*, 731.4 *allot*
Limit 302
limitability 262.2 *contractibility*
limitable 262.9 *contractible*
limitation 302, 121.1 *degree*, 129.1 *decrease*, 131.2 *subtracted item*, 147.1 *exclusion*, 262.1 *contraction*, 272.5 *narrowness*, 485.6 *specification*, 620.7 *defect*, 661.1 *hindrance*, 699.1 *restraint*, 725.2 *legal terms*, 864.3 *venial sin*
limitations 699.1 *restraint*
limited 302, 120.6 *quantitative*, 121.7 *gradational*, 147.10 *excluding*, 242.6 *moderate*, 249.18 *local*, 260.7 *little*, 262.7 *smaller*, 272.1 *narrow*, 485.12 *conditional*, 609.1 *insufficient*, 612.4 *trivial*, 661.13 *hindering*, 699.13 *restraining*, 725.8 *propertied*, 737.19 *corporate*, 869.9 *moderate*
limited choice 580.8 *choice*
limited company 13.7 *corporation*, 737.7 *company*
limited nuclear warfare 676.8 *warfare*
limited offer 228.5 *positive stimulus*
limited options 580.8 *choice*

limited-over match 27.1 *cricket match*
limited period 185.3 *duration*
limited war 676.1 *war*
limiting 157, 262.8 *contracting,* 485.12 *conditional,* 699.13 *restraining,* 869.9 *moderate*
limiting condition 485.7 *condition*
limiting factor 302, 699.1 *restraint*
limiting magnitude 53.28 *resolution*
limitless 181.8 *numberless,* 184.1 *infinite,* 259.15 *big*
limitlessly 184.10 *infinitely,* 259.20 *largely*
limitlessness 184.4 *infinity*
limitless resources 742.5 *wealth*
limit of endurance 650.7 *fatigue*
limit oneself 869.5 *be self-restrained*
limit one's speed 302.7 *limit*
limits 300.1 *edge*
limn 50.20 *draw,* 299.5 *outline,* 560.14 *describe*
limner 50.16 *artist*
limnetic zone 94.8 *limnology*
limning 50.3 *drawing,* 299.1 *outline*
limnograph 94.8 *limnology*
limnologic 94.9 *lakelike*
limnologically 94
limnologist 94.8 *limnology*
limnology 94
limnometer 94.8 *limnology*
limnophilous 94.9 *lakelike*
limnophobia 777 Phobias by Name
limo 71.16 *car*
Limoges 44 Types of Ceramics, **93** Cities
limonene 58.20 *terpene*
limonite 54 Minerals, **57** Common Metal Ores
Limousin 68 Breeds of Cattle
limousine 71 Motor Vehicles, 71.16 *car*
Limousin Half-bred 32 Breeds of Horse and Pony
limp 238.6 *be weak,* 238.8 *weak,* 240.5 *inert,* 328.1 *move slowly,* 328.10 *slow motion,* 374.1 *soft,* 555.1 *unemphatic*
limpet 81 Molluscs, 138.4 *adherent*
limpet mine 680.16 *bomb*
limpid 442.1 *transparent,* 522.2 *simple,* 550.3 *clear*
limpidity 442.5 *transparency,* 522.10 *simplicity,* 550.1 *clarity*
limpidly 442.13 *transparently,* 550.4 *clearly*
limpidness 442.5 *transparency*
limping 145.4 *incomplete,* 238.10 *ill,* 328.4 *slow*
limply 240.7 *inertly,* 374.17 *softly*
limpness 238.1 *weakness,* 374.8 *softness,* 555.2 *lack of emphasis*
Limpopo 96 Rivers
limp-wristed 238.12 *weak-willed*
limulus 81.4 *arthropod*
linchpin 137.8 *fastening,* 158.2 *core,* 611.3 *chief thing*
Lincoln 68 Breeds of Sheep, **93** Cities, **93** Cities, 93.4 *British cities*
Lincoln green 453.1 *green*
Lincoln Red 68 Breeds of Cattle
Lincolnshire 92 Counties
lincomycin 62 Medication
linctus 62, 133.2 *mixed thing,* 630.2 *medicine*
Lind 49 Musicians and Composers
linden 85 Trees and Shrubs
Linde process 56 Named Laws
Lindsay 48 Poets
Lindwall 18 Sporting Personalities
Lindy-hop 46.2 *dance*
line 75 Scientific and Technical Units, **52, 137, 159, 292,** 20.3 *fishing tackle,* 29.3 *golf shots,* 48.8 *part of poem,* 49.13 *melody,* 49.17 *notation,* 50.4 *treatment,* 74.5 *navigation,*

121.3 *gradation,* 132.6 *person remaining,* 144.6 *fill,* 155.2 *series,* 159.2 *consecution,* 159.8 *procession,* 159.16 *arrange consecutively,* 163.4 *type,* 163.8 - *genealogy,* 165.8 *specialization,* 167.1 *conformity,* 195.1 *succession,* 249.14 *sphere,* 266.10 *layer,* 268.6 *measuring instrument,* 269.5 *piece,* 272.8 *narrow thing,* 302.4 *boundary marker,* 321.2, 321.7 *wrinkle,* 327.1 *way,* 327.2 *route,* 327.10 *railway,* 332.1 *direction,* 332.2 *bearing,* 408.14 *be hot,* 433.1 *melody,* 456.3 *striping,* 521.5 *empty talk,* 534.21 *television,* 567.4 *approach,* 629.1 *repair,* 652.9 *tactics,* 679.14 *armed forces,* 679.16 *army unit,* 739.8 - *merchandise,* 802.3 *nobleness*
lineage 132.6 *person remaining,* 159.3 *line,* 163.8 *genealogy,* 195.2 *descent,* 200.12 *genealogy,* 802.3 *nobleness*
lineal 52.80 *linear,* 159.9 *consecutive*
lineament 306.6 *nature,* 767.6 *profile*
lineaments 457.3 *external appearance*
linear 52, 50.24 *pictorial,* 52.76 *functional,* 83.18 *of leaves,* 159.9 *consecutive,* 268.12 *metrical,* 269.3 *longitudinal,* 312.1 *straight*
linear accelerator 56.94 *particle accelerator,* 235.8 *nuclear power*
linear algebra 52.23 *algebra*
linear build 1.9 *physical type*
linear circuit 64.13 *circuit*
linear equation 52.27 *equation*
linear extent 52.37 *line*
linearity 52.37 *line,* 312.6 *straightness*
linear measure 75.1 *unit*
linear measurement 52.37 *line*
linear motion 56.8 *time*
linear perspective 50.4 *treatment*
linear response 56.83 *sensitivity*
linear scale 52.32 *graph,* 75.3 *scale*
linear strain 63.14 *load*
Line-Backed Welsh 68 Breeds of Cattle
linebacker 19.10 *defence*
line call 19.8 *huddle*
lined 130.8 *additional,* 207.14 *aged,* 257.11 *loaded,* 266.8 *coated,* 321.5 *wrinkly,* 408.13 *heated,* 456.9 *striped*
lined coat 292.1 *lining*
line drawing 50.9 *drawing*
line drive 22.5 *batting terms,* 330.14 *sporting hit*
line engraving 50.15 *engraving*
line graph 299.1 *outline*
line infantry 679.16 *army unit*
line integral 52.31 *differentiation*
line in the sand 302.4 *boundary marker*
line judge 19.2 *football player*
line management 15.1 *industrial relations*
line manager 15.6 *employer*
linen 67 Natural Fabrics, 67.12 *natural,* 288.4 *textile,* 295.1 *dress*
line of action 327.1 *way,* 652.1 *conduct*
line of advance 327.2 *route*
line of argument 473
line of attack 28.3 *fencing movements,* 327.1 *way*
line of battle 676.9 *battle*
line of business 644.3 *job*
line of credit 602.4 *financial resources,* 744.1 *credit*
line of descent 195.2 *descent*
line of direction 332.1 *direction*
line of duty 847.2 *task*
line of least resistance 673.1 *submission*
line of reasoning 473.3 *line of argument*
line of retreat 327.2 *route*

line of sight 332.2 *bearing,* 437.3 *visibility*
line-of-sight transmission 534.15 *transmitted wave*
line of succession 730.1 *receiving*
line of symmetry 52.41 *geometric figure*
line of tenpins 25.4 *bowling*
line of work 644.3 *job*
line one's pocket 742.13 *get rich*
line one's pockets 686.5 *be prosperous,* 721.14 *profit*
line-out 35.3 *rugby play*
line printer 65.7 *peripheral*
liner 74.3 *vessel,* 292.1 *lining*
lines 51.2 *play,* 306.1 *form,* 879.7 *punishment*
line segment 52.37 *line*
linesman 31.4 *ice hockey player,* 38.3 *football player,* 40.6 *tennis player,* 534.13 *telephoner*
linesman's chair 40.3 *tennis equipment*
line spectrum 56.68 *emission*
lines per frame 534.21 *television*
line up 150, 159, 52.97 *align,* 116.25 *conform,* 150.18 *order,* 152.12 *arrange,* 159.16 *arrange consecutively*
lineup 171.6 *list of names*
line-up 24.6 *pool,* 150.1 *order,* 152.1 *arrangement,* 159.1 *consecutiveness*
line up with 664.14 *join with*
ling 80 Fishes
lingam 9.3 *idol,* 246.4 *fertility cult*
linga sharira 11.7 *spirit*
Lingayata 7 Non-Christian Religions
linger 209.7 *wait,* 328.2 *hesitate*
lingerer 328.15 *slow person*
lingerie 295.18 *underwear*
lingerie party 665.7 *social gathering*
lingering 328, 328.7 *delayed,* 427.6 *resonant*
lingeringly 328.16 *slowly*
lingering note 427.1 *resonance*
lingo 5.4 *parent language,* 5.20 *jargon word,* 564.1 *faculty of speech*
lingonberry 86 Fruits
lingua franca 5.7 *international language,* 5.26 *dialect*
lingual 5.38 *linguistic,* 564.16 *speech*
linguini 45 Types of Pasta
linguist 5, 5.24.6 *interpreter*
linguistic 5, 520.8 *semantic,* 564.16 *speech*
linguistically 5, 549.10 *stylistically,* 564.21 *orally*
linguistic analysis 5.1 *linguistics*
linguistic analyst 5.2 *linguist*
linguistic distribution 5.1 *linguistics*
linguistic geographer 5.2 *linguist*
linguistic geography 5.1 *linguistics*
linguistician 5.2 *linguist*
linguistics 5, 520.1 *meaning,* 524.5 *science of interpretation,* 564.6 *phonetics*
Linguistics 5
linguistic scholar 5.2 *linguist*
linguistic science 5.1 *linguistics*
linguistic scientist 5.2 *linguist*
linguistic structure 5.1 *linguistics*
linguistic theory 5
linguistic typology 5.1 *linguistics*
liniment 62.7, 395.6 *ointment,* 630.9 *balm*
lining 292, 130.3 *additional item,* 257.4 *stuffing,* 266.1 *layer*
Lining 292
lining paper 292.1 *lining*
link 75 General Units, **135,** 107.1 *relatedness,* 135.1 *union,* 135.5 *joint,* 135.8 *unite,* 135.10 *link,* 137.4 *means of connection,* 137.11 *connect,* 140.5 *combine,* 148.1 *component,* 159.15 *concatenate,* 271.10 *span,* 439.7 *lantern,* 716.4 *negotiator,* 823.2 *alliance,* 823.19 *merge*
linkage 59.10 *cell division,* 107.1

relatedness, 135.1 *union,* 138.1 *adhesion*
link-boy 439.7 *lantern*
linked 107.4 *related,* 116.11 *allied,* 137.15 *connected,* 138.9 *adhesive,* 140.7 *combined,* 146.8 *included,* 148.7 *modular,* 327.15 *accessible*
linking 61.27 *association of ideas,* 137.1 *connection,* 267.5 *juxtaposed*
linkman 135.7 *joiner,* 298.3 *interfacer*
links 18.2 *sportsground,* 29.1 *golf*
linksman 29.6 *golfer*
link together 135.10 *link*
link up 161.41 *band together,* 407.12 *abut,* 534.30 *communicate*
link up with 135.8 *unite,* 135.10 *link*
link with 107.7 *relate to*
linn 94.2 *small lake,* 96.2 *channel*
Linnaean system 59.17 *taxonomy*
Linnaeus 52 Scientists
linnet 78 Birds
lino 293.9 *floor covering*
linocut 50.15 *engraving*
linoleum 280.1 *base,* 293.9 *floor covering*
linonophobia 777 Phobias by Name
linsang 77 Placental Mammals
linseed 68.12 *crop,* 83.9 *seed*
linseed meal 68.9 *animal feedstuff*
linsey-woolsey 67 Natural Fabrics, 133.3 *miscellany,* 375.7 *rough thing,* 383.8 *rough*
lint 384.5 *powder,* 630.10 *surgical dressing*
lintel 43.9 *miscellaneous architectural features,* 279.3 *architectural summit,* 284.2 *supporting part,* 346.6 *means of entry*
lint remover 621.10 *cleaning object*
lion 77 Placental Mammals, 401.16 *male animal,* 544.8 *heraldic device,* 611.4 *bigwig,* 778.7 *courageous person,* 815.10 *social animal*
lion couchant 544.8 *heraldic device*
lioness 77.18 *female mammal,* 402.14 *female animal*
lion-hearted 778.9 *courageous*
lion-heartedness 778.1 *courage*
lion hunt 590.2 *chase*
lion hunter 590.6 *hunter*
lionization 8.9 *deification,* 361.7 *lift,* 804.1 *right,* 851.3 *praise*
lionize 9.8 *idolatrize,* 361.3 *promote,* 611.8 *make important,* 773.6 *fête,* 812.18 *salute,* 849.16 *revere,* 851.14 *praise*
lionized 9.11 *worshipped,* 361.12 *exalted*
lionizer 9.5 *worshipper*
lionizing 851.18 *approving*
lion-like 77.28 *carnivorous*
lion rampant 544.8 *heraldic device*
lions 161 Collective Names by Animal
lion's mouth 633.5 *danger*
lion's share 126.3 *advantage,* 143.5 *largest part,* 175.3 *majority,* 610.1 *excess*
lion tamer 51.29 *circus performer*
liothyronine 62 Medication
Liouville 52 Scientists
lip 49.38 *sound,* 300.1 *edge,* 668.1 *defiance,* 807.2 *cheek,* 807.25 *answer back,* 818.2 *bad manners*
lipase 58.11 *enzyme*
lipid 58
lipoamide 58.12 *coenzyme*
lip off 478.18 *answer back*
lipoic acid 58.13 *vitamin*
lipolysis 58.7 *fat*
lipoprotein 58.6 *lipid,* 58.9 *protein*
lipotrophin 58 Hormones
Lippe 96 Rivers

Lippershey 52 Scientists
Lippizaner 32 Breeds of Horse and Pony
Lippizaner stallion 32.10 *dressage*
lippy 565.6 *effusive*, 818.6 *bad-mannered*
lip-read 421.8 *be deaf*, 524.12 *translate*
lip-reader 421.1 *deafness*, 524.6 *interpreter*
lip-reading 421.1 *deafness*, 524.4 *translation*
lips 457.3 *external appearance*, 564.5 *organ of speech*
Lipscomb 52 Scientists
lip service 538.8 *pretence*, 538.9, 539.3 *hypocrisy*, 540.3 *hypocrisy*
lipstick 295.5 *fancy dress*, 444.9 *complexion*, 450.6 *red pigment*, 791.4 *cosmetics*
lip-sync 198.3 *synchronism*
liquate 387.22 *make fluid*
liquefacient 387.9 *solvent*, 387.19 *liquefied*
liquefaction 56.37 *temperature*, 141.2 *deconstruction*, 162.3 *dilution*, 387.5 *fluidity*, 387.8 *fluididization*, 607.3 *waste*
liquefactive 387.20 *liquefying*
liquefiable 387
liquefied 387, 141.5 *disintegrated*, 162.27 *dilute*
liquefy 57.25 *solidify*, 139.6 *come unstuck*, 141.4 *deconstruct*, 162.14 *dilute*, 374.13 *soften*, 387.22 *make fluid*, 442.11 *be transparent*, 607.1 *waste*
liquefying 387
liquesce 387.22 *make fluid*
liquescence 387.8 *fluididization*
liquescency 387.8 *fluididization*
liquescent 387.19 *liquefied*
liqueur 351.7 *alcoholic drink*, 414.5 *sweet drink*
liqueur glass 258.13 *drinking vessel*
liquid 5.16 *spoken letter*, 5.41 *lettered*, 57.3 *phase*, 57.32 *solid*, 139.1 *nonadhesion*, 139.8 *nonadhesive*, 387.1, 387.14 *fluid*, 389.1 *water*, 389.21 *watery*, 442.1 *transparent*, 725.8 *propertied*
liquidambar 85 Trees and Shrubs
liquid assets 725.5 *personal estate*, 741.6 *funds*, 742.5 *wealth*
liquidate 157.17 *kill*, 244.8 *destroy*, 349.10 *exterminate*, 398.18 *slaughter*, 458.3 *cause to disappear*, 546.1 *obliterate*, 741.26 *bank*, 746.7 *pay off*
liquidated 157.23 *annihilated*, 546.6 *obliterated*, 746.16 *paid*
liquidation 13.7 *corporation*, 157.4 *annihilation*, 244.1 *destruction*, 398.4 *slaughter*, 546.3 *obliteration*, 746.1 *payment*
liquidator 244.6 *destroyer*, 730.7 *collector*
liquid conductor 56.43 *electrical conduction*, 64.3 *electricity*
liquid diet 350.6 *nutrition*, 871.1 *fasting*
liquidescence 387.5 *fluidity*
liquid extract 387.1 *fluid*
liquid fuel 53.35 *rocketry*
liquidity 139.1 *nonadhesion*, 387.5 *fluidity*, 402.4 *financial resources*, 741.6 *funds*
liquidity ratio 744.1 *credit*
liquidization 387.8 *fluididization*
liquidize 45.55 *cook*, 387.22 *make fluid*, 393.24 *pulp*
liquidizer 387, 45.6 *kitchen equipment*, 133.6 *mixer*
liquidly 139.10 *noncohesively*, 387.26 *fluidly*, 389.35 *wetly*
liquid measure 75.1 *unit*
liquidness 387.5 *fluidity*
liquid oxygen 409.4 *cooler*, 410.3 *gas*
liquid paraffin 62 Medication
liquid state 387.1 *fluid*
liquifier 387.9 *solvent*
liquiform 387.14 *fluid*

liquor 351.7 *alcoholic drink*, 387.1 *fluid*, 874.12 *alcohol*
liquor cabinet 47.5 *cabinet*
liquored up 874.1 *drunk*
liquorice 45.41 *sweet*, 413.5 *herbs*, 414.4 *confectionery*, 630.6 *purgative*
liquorice allsort 45.41 *sweet*
liquor store 351.11 *drink provider*
liquor up 874.8 *get drunk*
Lir 8 Deities
lira 49 Musical Instruments, 741.11 *national coins*
lirica 49 Musical Instruments
liriodendron 85 Trees and Shrubs
lirone 49 Musical Instruments
Lisbon 93 Cities, 93.6 *other cities*
Lisburn 93 Cities
lisle 67 Natural Fabrics
lisle stockings 295.20 *legwear*
lisp 429.1, 429.4 *hiss*, 563.14 *have difficulty speaking*
lisping 563.3 *speech defect*, 563.12 *inarticulate*, 564.3 *mode of speech*
Lissa 8 Deities
Lissajous' figures 56 Named Laws
lissom 374.2 *pliant*
lissomly 374.17 *softly*
list 43 Architectural Decoration, **171, 171,** 67.4 *weaving*, 74.10 *sail*, 123.1 *inequality*, 123.5 *be unequal*, 146.6 - *subsume*, 152.7 *catalogue*, 152.15 *categorize*, 163.2 *class*, 165.24 *specify*, 170.11 *number*, 192.2 *timetable*, 195.1 *succession*, 257.5 *divisions*, 257.9 *itemize*, 286.1 *obliqueness*, 286.6 *be oblique*, 360.14 *slide*, 545.1, 545.13 *record*, 545.15 *register*, 580.6 *selection*, 750.8 *audit*
List 171
listed 171, 43.12 *structural*, 146.8 *included*, 150.11 *grouped*, 152.24 *categorized*, 257.12 *itemized*, 545.16 *recorded*
listed building 43.3 *building*, 202.5 *old thing*, 637.3 *preserved thing*
listel 43 Architectural Decoration
listen 420.15 *hear*
listenability 420.10 *sound quality*
listenable 420.14 *hearable*
listener 420.2 *hearer*, 730.5 *recipient*
listener in 420.2 *hearer*
listening 420.1 *hearing*, 420.11 *aural*
listening in 420.1 *hearing*
listening post 420.3 *auditorium*
listen to 420.15 *hear*, 654.6 *consult*
listen to a false prophet 515.4 *be disappointed*
listen with deaf ears 481.13 *prejudge*
listeria 631.7 *poisoning*
listeriosis 631.7 *poisoning*
listing 171, 123.3 *unequal*, 150.2 *grouping*, 152.5 - *categorization*, 163.2 *class*, 171.1 *list*, 286.4 *oblique*, 545.8 *registration*
listless 328.5 *unhurried*, 468.7 *inattentive*, 643.3 *not participating*, 650.1 *fatigued*, 770.6 *depressed*, 783.7 *indifferent*
listlessly 643.16 *impassively*, 650.8 *tiredly*, 770.12 *joylessly*, 783.17 *indifferently*
listlessness 576.14 *apathy*, 643.7 *idleness*, 650.7 *fatigue*, 783.1 *indifference*
list of appointments 171
list of characters 400.7 *person*
list of names 171
list price 751.1 *price*
list requirements 699.8 *restrain*
lists 674.9 *duel*
Liszt 49 Musicians and Composers

lit 439, 327.15 *accessible*, 437.2 *clear*
litany 10.9 *prayer*
litchi 86 Fruits
litchi nut 86 Nuts
literacy 6.9 *learnedness*, 501.3 *learning*
literal 537, 5.40 *translated*, 5.41 *lettered*, 503.6 *correct*, 504.12 *typing error*, 520.6 *meaningful*, 524.17 *translational*, 658.1 *naive*, 719.7 *observant*
literalism 118.1 *imitation*, 503.2 *correctness*, 537.10 *literalness*
literality 520.4 *type of meaning*, 537.10 *literalness*
literally 537, 5.48 *linguistically*, 118.14 *imitatively*, 503.8 *accurately*, 520.13 *meaningfully*, 619.7 *perfectly*, 719.8 *observantly*
literal meaning 520.4 *type of meaning*, 537.10 *literalness*
literal-minded 537.24 *pedantic*, 658.1 *naive*
literal-mindedness 537.11 *pedantry*
literalness 537, 7.2 *religiousness*, 503.2 *correctness*
literal translation 5.12, 524.4 *translation*
literarily 5.48 *linguistically*
literary 48, 5.39 *of language*, 6.18 *educated*
literary agent 532.12 *publisher*, 707.3 *agent*
literary composition 243.1 *production*, 243.5 *work of art*
literary conversion 326.4 *translation*
literary critic 48.15 *literary person*, 524.6 *interpreter*
literary criticism 524.3 *criticism*
literary language 5.6 *official language*
literary magazine 532.5 *journal*
literary person 48, 560.10 *descriptive writer*
literary scholar 48.15 *literary person*
literary style 549
literary theft 736.6 *illegal borrowing*
literary work 243.1 *production*, 243.5 *work of art*
literate 501, 4.19 *learned*, 6.18 *educated*
literati 501.7 *academia*
literatim 118.14 *imitatively*
literature 48, 6.14 *school book*, 501.5 *science*
Literature 48
lithagogue 62.4 *drug type*
litharge 57 Common Metal Ores
lithe 374.2 *pliant*
lithely 374.17 *softly*
litheness 374.8 *softness*
lithesome 374.2 *pliant*
lithia 57 Common Chemical Compounds
lithic 54.56 *petrographic*, 373.1, 373.1 *hard*
lithification 54.29 *petrogenesis*
lithified sediment 54.31 *sedimentary rock*
lithify 54
lithium 57 Chemical Elements
lithium carbonate 62 Medication
lithograph 50.15 *engraving*, 547.2 *reproduction*, 560.9 *representation*
lithography 50.1 *art*
lithoid 373.1 *hard*
lithophone 49 Musical Instruments
lithosphere 54.18 *earth's crust*
lithospheric 54.53 *solid-earth*
lithospheric plate 54.19 *plate tectonics*
lithotomy 60 Surgical Operations
Lithuania 91 Countries
Lithuanian 5 Languages and Groups of Languages
Lithuanian Heavy Draught 32 Breeds of Horse and Pony
Lithuanians 1 Peoples

litigable 16.54 *litigated*
litigant 16, 16.53 *litigating*, 663.9 *opposer*, 679.5 *arguer*, 856.3 *accuser*
litigate 16, 463.13 *debate*, 663.15 *object*, 856.5 *accuse*
litigated 16
litigating 16
litigation 16, 16, 306.5 *formality*, 463.3 *debate*, 856.1 *accusation*
litigator 16.8 *litigant*, 463.6 *arguer*
litigious 16.52 *legalistic*, 16.53 *litigating*, 306.11 *formal*, 463.9, 473.8 *argumentative*, 670.21 *aggressive*, 679.34 *argumentative*, 856.8 *accusatory*
litigiously 16.87 *in litigation*, 306.14 *conventionally*, 679.41 *aggressively*, 856.10 *accusingly*
litigiousness 16.5 *litigation*
litigious person 16.8 *litigant*
litmus 57.18 *gravimetric analysis*
litmus paper 57.18 *gravimetric analysis*
litotes 495.1 *underestimation*
litter 161 Collective Names for Birds and Animals, **71, 151,** 77.35 *give birth*, 132.2 *residue*, 161.24 *brace*, 162.17 *sow*, 206.4 *young animal*, 245.11 *have young*, 326.5 *means of transport*, 607.5 *waste product*, 614.6 *refuse*, 622.4 *dirt*
littérateur 459.8 *intellectual person*
litter bearer 326.7 *transferor*
litter bin 258.11 *vessel*, 621.10 *cleaning object*, 727.4 *wastebin*
litterbug 151.10 *slattern*, 622.6 *dirty person*
littered 396.15 *born*, 622.7 *dirty*
litter lout 151.10 *slattern*, 622.6 *dirty person*
litter picker 727.6 *rubbish collector*
little 260, 182.1, 182.5 *few*, 182.6 *sparse*, 182.11 *sparsely*, 213.1 *infrequently*, 238.13 *insufficient*, 270.7 *short*, 612.1 *unimportant*
little angel 206.9 *child*
Little Bear 53 The Constellations
Little Bighorn 398.15 *slaughterhouse*
little bit 612.8 *trifle*
little black dress 295.7 *frock*, 440.4 *dark thing*
little black number 295.7 *frock*
little boy 401.2 *male*
little boys' room 353.13 *lavatory*, 727.7 *toilet*
little by little 121.10 *by degrees*, 143.12 *partly*, 328.16 *slowly*
little cherub 206.9 *child*
Little Dog 53 The Constellations
little extra 130.4 *extra*
little few 609.8 *insufficiency*
little finger 407.7 *sense organ*
little game 652.9 *tactics*
little girl 402.2 *female*
little girls' room 353.13 *lavatory*, 727.7 *toilet*
little green man 104.6 *outsider*, 149.5 *extraterrestrial*
little green men 11.11 *ghost*, 453.11 *green thing*
little grey cells 507.2 *intelligence*
little Hitler 696.4 *absolute ruler*
Little Horse 53 The Constellations
little imp 206.9 *child*
Little Italy 93.3 *New York*
little jobs 353.6 *urine*
Little League baseball 22.1 *baseball*
Little League World Series 22.1 *baseball*
Little Lion 53 The Constellations
little mama 402.9 *woman considered as a sex object*
little man 164.9 *everyman*, 803.1 *plebeian*

little monkey 206.9 *child*, 693.5 *troublemaker*
littleness 260, 127.3 *inferior numbers*, 270.1 *shortness*, 860.1 *selfishness*
Littleness 260
little one 206.9 *child*
little owl 78 *Birds*
little person 260
little piece 260
Little Rock 93 *Cities*
little school 702.2 *the inside*
little ships 679.23 *naval unit*
little something extra 300.4 *advantage*
little space 260
little theatre 51.14 *theatre*
little thing 260
little toe 407.7 *sense organ*
little way 264.2 *short distance*
little worth 195.3 *subordination*
littoral 54.52 *coastal*, 76.15 *of animals*, 97.7 *oceanic*, 98.11 *continental*, 300.1 *edge*, 300.8 *edging*
lit up 439.18 *lit*, 874.1 *drunk*
liturgic 813.8 *ceremonious*
liturgical 10.21 *ritualistic*, 49.32 *instrumental*
liturgical drama 51.2 *play*
liturgical east end 43.10 *church architecture*
liturgical garment 7.11 *vestment*
liturgically 10.23 *ritually*
liturgical music 49.5 *sacred music*
liturgics 10.2 *ritualism*
liturgism 10.2 *ritualism*
liturgology 10.2 *ritualism*
liturgy 10.1 *ritual*, 10.4 *public worship*, 719.2 *religious observance*, 812.3 *ceremony*, 813.3 *formal occasion*
lituus 49 *Musical Instruments*
Livarot 45 *Cheeses*
live 396, 25.9 *bowls*, 34.8 *mountaineering*, 56.52 *electric potential*, 59.21 *living*, 64.36 *electronic*, 99.17 *exist*, 196.5 *be present*, 235.11 *full of energy*, 253.11 *be present*, 253.14 *in person*, 396.12 *alive*, 642.18 *active*
live a bohemian life 720.7 *not observe*
live abroad 149.16 *migrate*
live a certain way 105.6 *be in a state of*
live again 629.4 *be restored*
Live Aid 729.3 *offering*
live a life of ease 106.14 *be comfortable*, 686.5 *be prosperous*
live alone 825.9 *be celibate*
live ammunition 315.8 *round*, 680.13 *ammunition*
live and let live 217.6 *make permanent*, 641.4 *not act*, 698.15 *set free*, 859.6 *be disinterested*
live-and-let-live 691.4 *lenient*
live apart 824.7 *divorce*
live as an amphibian 79
live as a reptile 79
live a simple life 658.4 *be naive*
live as man and wife 823.15 *marry*
live a spartan life 690.7 *be unadorned*
live at 396.17 *dwell*
live at the same time 198.6 *be simultaneous*
live ball 23.4 *playing terms*
live-bearing 245.16 *reproductive*
live beyond one's means 757.8 *overspend*
live bowl 25.2 *grip*
live by a creed 535.17 *affirm*
live by one's wits 655.10 *be skilful*, 657.5 *be cunning*, 858.8 *be dishonourable*
live by the golden rule 672.3 *retaliate*
live cartridge 680.13 *ammunition*
live circuit 64.10 *electric potential*
live conductor 64.10 *electric potential*
live coverage 533.3 *reporting*, 534.25 *broadcast material*

lived in 255.11 *inhabited*
live for the day 196.5 *be present*
live for today 196.5 *be present*
live from day to day 595.12 *be unprepared*
live from hand to mouth 593.11 *be needy*, 743.12 *be poor*
live frugally 869.5 *be self-restrained*
live high on the hog 686.5 *be prosperous*
live honourably 134.9 *be pure*
live immoderately 698.19 *liberalize*
live in 99.17 *exist*, 253.13 *reside*, 255.14, 256.17 *inhabit*, 697.8 *serve*
live-in 253.9 *resident*
live in a bohemian way 698.16 *be independent*
live in a dream world 519.15 *fantasize*
live in a glass house 379.4 *be brittle*
live in an ivory tower 466.6 *be incurious*
live in another land 104.14 *be foreign*
live in a spartan way 699.10 *restrain oneself*
live in a state of grace 865.8 *be innocent*
live in a state of nature 658.4 *be naive*
live in a whirl 642.13 *be busy*
live in cloud-cuckoo land 539.25 *deceive oneself*
live in clover 686.5 *be prosperous*
live in hope 775.6 *hope*
live in ignorance 658.4 *be naive*
live-in lover 180.12 *partner*, 401.13 *man in the family*, 402.12 *woman in the family*, 823.12 *partner*
live-in maid 697.6 *domestic servant*
live in one's own little world 539.25 *deceive oneself*
live in peace 677.4 *pacify*
live in poverty 593.11 *be needy*, 743.12 *be poor*
live in sin 135.11 *make love*
live in single blessedness 825.9 *be celibate*
live in the lap of luxury 106.14 *be comfortable*, 686.5 *be prosperous*
live in the modern world 196.5 *be present*
live in the past 200.15 *look back*
live in the present 196.5 *be present*
live it up 686.10 *good luck*, 815.13 *fraternize*
live jack 25.2 *grip*
live life to the fullest 396.16 *live*
livelihood 251.4 *employment*, 662.3 *sustenance*
live like a Christian 857.6 *be honourable*
live like a hermit 825.11 *be monastic*
live like a monk 134.9 *be pure*, 699.10 *restrain oneself*, 825.11 *be monastic*
live like a nun 134.9 *be pure*, 825.11 *be monastic*
live like a Puritan 134.9 *be pure*
liveliness 235.3 *vitality*, 237.2 *healthiness*, 239.1 *vigour*, 329.10 *quickness of mind*, 377.2 *adaptability*, 396.1 *life*, 413.4 *stimulation*, 554.1 *emphasis*, 642.4 *energy*, 769.3 *cheerfulness*
live load 63.14 *load*, 369.7 *weighing*
lively 396, 235.11 *full of energy*, 239.4 *vigorous*, 329.2 *mentally quick*, 377.7 *adaptive*, 396.22 *vitally*, 413.10 *stimulating*, 519.10 *imaginative*, 554.3 *emphatic*, 642.18 *active*, 642.9 *busy*, 769.1 *cheerful*, 815.15 *sociable*
lively imagination 519.1 *imagination*

liven 396.16 *live*, 396.19 *give birth to*
live off 808.15 *sponge*
live on 99.19 *continue to be*, 219.4 *protract*, 511.15 *be remembered*
live on a budget 756.5 *be thrifty*
live on air 871.5 *fast*
live on a pittance 593.11 *be needy*, 743.12 *be poor*
live on bread and water 871.5 *fast*
live on capital 748.1 *expend*
live on credit 745.7 *be in debt*
live on Easy Street 686.5 *be prosperous*
live on easy street 742.12 *be rich*
live one's life 396.16 *live*
live one's own life 104.17 *not conform*
live on immoral earnings 877.18 *prostitute*
live on rations 871.5 *fast*
live on the breadline 593.11 *be needy*
live on the fat of the land 686.5 *be prosperous*
live on the road 104.14 *be foreign*
live or die 574.17 *resolutely*
live out one's time 219.4 *protract*
live plainly 869.5 *be self-restrained*
live poorly 743.12 *be poor*
live purely 134.9 *be pure*
liver 352 *Exocrine Glands*, 45.31 *offal*, 290.4 *insides*, 830.3 *irritableness*
liver-coloured 449.1 *brown*
liver relay 534.25 *broadcast material*
liver fluke 81 *Worms*, 81.6 *worm*, 81.10 *parasite*, 624.18 *veterinary disease*
liveried 295.29 *dressed*
liverish 874.5 *drunken*
liverishness 624.8 *indigestion*
live rope 34.4 *climbing equipment*
Liverpool 93 *Cities*, 93.4 *British cities*
Liverpool poets 48 *Literary Groups and Movements*
Liverpudlian 255.9 *British inhabitant*
liver sausage 45.29 *sausage*
liverwort 88.3 *moss*
livery 295.3 *formal dress*, 544.5 *uniform*, 813.4 *formal dress*
liveryman 13.9 *economist*, 737.11 *chamber of commerce member*
livery stable 32.14 *horse-riding terms*
live separately 824.7 *divorce*
live shot 680.13 *ammunition*
live show 51.5 *show*
live side by side 2.15 *socialize*
live simply 711.7 *refuse oneself*, 869.5 *be self-restrained*
livestock 68, 76.3 *domesticated animal*
livestock farm 68.6 *farm*
livestock farmer 68.15 *agriculturist*
livestock farming 68, 68.1 *agriculture*
livestock market 740.1 *market*
live theatre 51.1 *drama*
live the life of Riley 686.5 *be prosperous*, 742.12 *be rich*
live through 629.4 *be restored*, 759.15 *feel*
live to a ripe old age 207.17 *age*
live to eat 872.5 *be greedy*
live to fight another day 632.8 *be safe*, 671.28 *survive*, 779.4 *be a coward*
live together 823, 180.14 *keep company with*, 823.15 *marry*
liveware 65.2 *operator*, 170.6 *calculator*
live well 686.5 *be prosperous*
live wire 235.7 *electrical power*, 336.16 *progressive person*, 640.3 *doer*, 642.10 *busy person*
live with 135.11 *make love*, 180.14 *keep company with*, 482.12 *be fair*

live within one's means 754.14 *buy cheaply*, 756.5 *be thrifty*
livid 455, 397.21 *deathly*, 440.10 *dark-coloured*, 441.5 *dim*, 445.8 *drained of colour*, 446.4 *pale*, 454.2 *bluish*, 455.8 *furious*, 828.16 *angry*
lividity 454.8 *bluishness*, 455.5 *lividness*
lividly 828.18 *angrily*
lividness 455, 440.1 *darkness*, 454.8 *bluishness*
living 59, 5.39 *of language*, 99.10 *existing*, 114.9 *lifelike*, 256.14 *inhabiting*, 396.1 *life*, 396.12 *alive*, 662.3 *sustenance*, 725.1 *property*
living apart 824.2 *separation*, 824.11 *divorced*
living area 730.4 *reception*
living as man and wife 823.1 *marriage*
living being 59.3 *organism*, 396.1 *life*
living fossil 80.4 *fossil fish*, 81.4 *arthropod*
living hell 687.1 *adversity*
living image 110.3 *lookalike*, 114.5 *counterpart*
living in 255.13 *resident*
living in a fool's paradise 539.2 *self-deception*
living in an ivory tower 539.2 *self-deception*
living in cloud-cuckoo land 539.2 *self-deception*
living in clover 686.1 *prosperity*
living in one's own little world 539.2 *self-deception*
living issue 472.2 *issue*
living language 5.3 *spoken language*, 564.1 *faculty of speech*
living matter 396
living off one's capital 748.6 *extravagance*
living on borrowed time 207.14 *aged*
living on capital 748.11 *spendthrift*
living on immoral earnings 877.5 *prostitution*
living organism 59.3 *organism*
living person 396.1 *life*
living quarters 256.1 *habitat*
living room 256.7 *room*, 698.5 *scope*, 730.4 *reception*
living soul 396.1 *life*, 400.7 *person*
living space 248.6 *available space*, 698.5 *scope*
living thing 59.3 *organism*
living things 396.1 *life*
living tissue 396.2 *living matter*
living wage 608.7 *sufficiency*
living world 59
Livonian 5 *Languages and Groups of Languages*
Livy 48 *Writers*
lixiviate 134.10 *purify*, 347.12 *leak*, 387.23 *dissolve*, 389.29 *water*, 621.15 *purify*
lixiviation 347.3 *leakage*, 387.8 *fluidification*, 389.9 *soaking*
lixivium 387.10 *solution*
lizard 79 *Reptiles*, **79**
Lizard 53 *The Constellations*
lizard fish 80 *Fishes*
lizard-like 79.11 *reptilian*
lizard-like reptile 79.2 *lizard*
Ljubljana 93 *Cities*
Lladro 44 *Types of Ceramics*
llama 77 *Placental Mammals*, 326.6 *beast of burden*
Llandrindod Wells 93 *Cities*
Llandudno 93 *Cities*
Llanelly 93 *Cities*
Llanero 32 *Breeds of Horse and Pony*
Llangollen 93 *Cities*
llano 87.2 *grassland*, 98.6 *lowland*
Llanwenog 68 *Breeds of Sheep*
Llewellyn 18 *Sporting Personalities*
Lleyn 68 *Breeds of Sheep*
Lloyd 18 *Sporting Personalities*
   18 *Sporting Personalities*

Lloyd's mirror 56 Named Laws
llyn 94.1 *lake*
loach 80 Fishes
load 63, 63, 257, 338, 63.10
work, 64.14 *terminal,* 65.19
abort, 70.2 *thing transported,*
70.4 *transport,* 120.2 *certain
amount,* 130.1 *addition,* 130.6
add, 144.6 *fill,* 257.6 *contain,*
326.10 *transferred thing,* 369.6
displacement, 369.14 *make
heavy,* 540.21 *be fraudulent,*
605.1, 605.6 *store,* 610.2 *overdoing it,* 687.1 *adversity,* 739.8
merchandise
load-bearing capacity 237.1
strength
load-bearing wall 43.9 *miscellaneous architectural features*
loaded 257, 369, 70.5 *transportable,* 130.8 *additional,* 144.8
full, 582.4 *deliberate,* 605.7
stored, 721.17 *well-off,* 742.1
wealthy, 874.3 *dead drunk,*
875.7 *drugged*
loaded dice 123.1 *inequality,*
540.8 *fraud*
loaded table 350.9, 608.8 *plenty*
loader 70.3 *transporter,* 594.15
preparer
load factor 73.7 *miscellaneous
aviation terms*
loading 70.1 *transport,* 70.5
transportable, 73.7 *miscellaneous aviation terms,* 356.2
passing along, 369.6 *displacement,* 594.9 *preparation*
loading the bases 22.4 *pitching
terms*
load line 268.6 *measuring instrument,* 543.5 *indicator*
load of bull 521.4 *senseless talk*
load of old rubbish 614.6 *refuse*
load of rubbish 521.4 *senseless
talk*
loads 181.3 *profuseness*
load the bases 22.7 *play baseball*
load the dice 539.30 *be fraudulent,* 582.2 *premeditate*
load the gun 594.4 *prepare for action*
load tightly 371.9 *make dense*
load with ornament 557.5 *ornament*
loaf 45, 641.4 *not act,* 643.12 *be
inactive*
loafer 641.2 *nonacting person,*
643.8 *nonworker*
loafers 295.19 *footwear*
loafing 641.1 *inaction,* 643.3 *not
participating*
loam 54.36 *soil,* 622.4 *dirt*
loamy 54.58 *earthy,* 374.4 *compressible*
loan 732, 733, 745, 662.6 *financial assistance,* 662.29 *finance,* 710.11 *volunteer,* 732.5
lend, 744.1, 744.8 *credit,* 831.4
benevolent act
loan agreement 733.1 *borrowing*
loan applicant 745.6 *debtor*
loan application 733.1 *borrowing*
loan capital 745.3 *loan*
loaned 732, 733.11 *borrowed*
loanee 745.6 *debtor*
loaner 728.2 *person transferring
property,* 732.3 *lender*
loaning 732.1 *lending*
loan-maker 744.5 *lender*
loan office 732.4 *lending institution*
loan officer 732.3 *lender*
loan repayment 745.3 *loan*
loan shark 732.3, 744.5 *lender,*
753.5 *overcharger,* 836.3 *pitiless
person*
loan-sharking 732.1 *lending,*
753.4 *extortion*
loan transaction 733.1 *borrowing*
loan translation 5.17 *word*
loan word 5.17 *word*
loath 573.1 *unwilling,* 785.8 *disliking*
loathe 785.5 *dislike,* 820.11 *be
hostile,* 822.14 *hate,* 832.16 *be
malevolent*
loathed 820.10, 822.12 *hated*

loathing 785.1 *dislike,* 785.8 *disliking,* 820.1 *enmity,* 822.1
hate, 822.10 *hating,* 832.1 *malevolence*
loathingly 822.18 *hatefully*
loathness 573.11 *unwillingness*
loathsome 341.8 *repulsive,* 618.4
poor, 764.1 *unpleasant,* 785.9
disliked, 801.1 *disrespect,* 822.4
hatefulness, 822.12 *hated*
lob 40.2 *tennis strokes,* 40.13
serve, 330.4, 338.5 *throw,*
338.23 *throw,* 361.2 *send up*
Lobachevski 52 Scientists
Lobachevskian geometry 52
Named Concepts
lobbed 361.11 *raised*
lobbied 228.12 *motivated*
lobbing 338.3 *throwing*
lobby 228.7 *motivator,* 228.10
manipulate, 233.6 *group influence,* 233.8 *influence,* 256.7
room, 303.1 *front,* 327.2 *route,*
346.6 *means of entry* , 586.14
motivator, 586.15 *persuade,*
730.4 *reception*
lobby correspondent 533.4 *journalist*
lobbyer 586.14 *motivator*
lobbying 228.2 *inducement,*
586.1 *persuasion*
lobbyist 228.7 *motivator,* 233.5
influential person, 586.14 *motivator,* 596.7 *attempter,* 640.3
doer, 712.4 *requester*
lobectomy 60 Surgical Operations
lobed 83.18 *of leaves*
lobe-finned fish 80.2 *fish*
lobelia 84 Flowers and Flowering Plants
Lobito 93 Cities
loblolly 85 Trees and Shrubs,
393.7 *soup,* 393.14 *puddle*
lobotomy 60 Surgical Operations, 630.12 *surgery*
lobster 45.19 *shellfish,* 81.4 *arthropod*
lobster bisque 45.13 *soup*
lobstertails 624.14 *venereal disease*
lobster thermidor 45.45 *French
dish*
local 249, 472, 93.11 *native,*
93.11 *urbanite,* 93.14 *urban,*
251.7 *situational,* 255.1 *inhabitant,* 255.12 *native,* 256.10
hotel, 256.15 *environmental,*
264.5 *near,* 290.8 *internal*
local anaesthesia 630.5 *analgesic*
local anaesthetic 630.5 *analgesic*
local area network 135.1 *union*
local authority 16.2 *jurisdiction*
local call 534.10 *telephone call*
local climate 55.38 *climate*
local code 534.11 *dialling*
local colour 48.3 *aspect of fiction,*
50.4 *treatment*
locale 249.13 *locality,* 250.1 *location,* 251.1 *situation,* 256.2
environment, 297.1 *surroundings*
local election 580.12 *election*
local exchange 534.12 *public telephone system*
local government 12.1 *government*
local-government election 580.12
election
Local Group 53.7 *galaxy*
local history 3.1 *history*
local-history topic 472.5 *educational topic*
local-interest 472.9 *local*
localism 5.26 *dialect*
locality 249, 250.1 *location,*
251.1 *situation,* 256.2 *environment,* 264.3 *near place*
localization 162.6 *decentralization*
localize 162.15 *decentralize,*
699.8 *restrain*
localized 162.26 *decentralized,*
249.18 *local*
localized war 676.1 *war*
local jurisdiction 16.2 *jurisdiction*
locally 93.16 *municipally,*
249.20 *nationally,* 251.11 *geographically,* 256.20 *environmen-*

tally, 264.6 *near,* 472.12 *topically*
local newspaper 533.5 *mass communication*
local paper 532.4 *newspaper*
local pronunciation 5.26 *dialect*
local radio 534.20 *radio broadcasting*
local road 327.3 *road*
local tax 751.7 *tax*
local television 534.24 *television
broadcasting*
local time 185.9 *time zone,*
192.3 *chronology*
local wind 55.12 *wind*
local worthy 611.4 *bigwig*
locatable 250.7 *found*
locate 250, 152.12 *arrange,*
250.10 *settle,* 251.10 *situate,*
291.9 *centre,* 496.1 *discover*
located 250, 250.7 *found,* 251.6
situated, 496.14 *discovered*
locating 250, 250.4 *placing,*
291.3 *centrality*
location 250, 52.36 *point,* 152.1
arrangement, 251.1 *situation,*
332.1 *direction,* 496.6 *discovery,*
567.5 *place of residence*
Location 250
locational 250, 2.14 *socioeconomic*
locational theory 2.2 *sociological
research*
locative 5.31 *case*
loch 94.1 *lake*
Loch Leven 94.4 *British lakes*
Loch Lomond 94.4 *British lakes*
Loch Ness 94.4 *British lakes*
Loch Ness Monster 76.7 *legendary beast*
Loch Ness Monster 529.6 *natural
mystery*
Loch Ness monster 539.11 *hoax*
Loch Rannoch 94.4 *British lakes*
Loch Tay 94.4 *British lakes*
Lochy 94 Lakes
lock 35.4 *rugby player,* 63.24
water system, 71.21 *miscellaneous motoring terms,* 135.10
link, 137.8 *fastening,* 137.12
bind, 323.3 *restrainer,* 323.7
close, 325.1 *motionlessness,*
325.9 *make motionless,* 327.11
channel, 632.4 *safety device,*
680.9 *firearm,* 726.1 *retention,*
726.6 *retain*
lock and key 137.8 *fastening*
lock away 632.9 *protect,* 718.10
secure
lockbox 718.5 *safe*
Locke 4 Philosophers
locked 137.16 *bound,* 323.12
closed
locked away 718.6 *secure*
locked up 258.20 *containing,*
702.8 *imprisoned,* 718.6 *secure*
locker 36.8 *punting,* 258.6 *box*
Lockerbie 93 Cities
lock horns 666.6 *argue,* 674.12
fight
lock horns with 674.11 *contend*
lock in 726.7 *detain*
locking in 726.2 *detention*
locking karabiner 34.4 *climbing
equipment*
locking the blade 36.6 *canoeing*
lockjaw 624.6 *infection*
lock oneself in 634.4 *shelter*
lock out 15.12 *have an industrial
dispute*
lockout 147.1 *exclusion,* 218.2
stop
lock out 218.8 *cause to cease*
lockout 661.2 *obstacle*
lock out 661.9 *block,* 711.5 *refuse*
lock-out 13.8 *industrial relations,*
711.1 *refusal*
locksmith 322.3 *person who
opens,* 646.2 *artisan*
lock step 198.4 *equal race*
lock, stock, and barrel 120.4
total, 142.11 *wholly,* 144.9 *completely*
lock the blade 36.17 *canoe*
lock together 135.10 *link*
lock up 135.10 *link,* 323.7 *close,*

323.10 *enclose,* 531.8 *conceal,*
671.17 *defend*
lockup 702.1 *prison*
lock up 702.9 *imprison,* 718.10
secure, 879.1 *punish*
lock up and throw away the key
702.9 *imprison*
Lockyer 52 Scientists
loco 72.4 *locomotive,* 510.11 *insane*
locomotion 59.5 *physiology,*
324.1 *motion*
Locomotion 72.10 *miscellaneous*
locomotive 72, 235.15 *full of energy,* 324.16 *moving,* 339.6 *towline*
locomotive part 72
locomotory 59.22 *physiological*
Locrian mode 49.20 *key*
locum 60.11 *doctor,* 130.5 *extra
person,* 155.13 *replacement,*
222.2 *substitute person,* 293.21
substitution, 293.40 *substitutive,* 707.2 *alternative,* 767.5
helper
locum tenens 222.2 *substitute
person,* 767.5 *helper*
locus 52.36 *point*
locust 82 Insects, **85** Trees and
Shrubs, 82.1 *insect,* 82.3 *pest,*
350.18 *eater,* 734.6 *taker,* 872.4
glutton
locusts 161 Collective Names
by Animal, 244.7 *agent of destruction*
locution 5.24 *phrasing,* 564.7 *utterance*
locutionary 5.43 *phrasal*
lode 57.24 *ore,* 266.1 *layer,*
605.2 *resource*
loden 67 Natural Fabrics,
295.11 *jacket*
loden green 453.1 *green*
lodestar 228.1 *motive,* 340.3
magnet, 543.5 *indicator,* 653.5
guide
lodestone 57 Common Metal
Ores, 56.60, 339.7 *magnet,*
340.3 *magnet,* 517.6 *good-luck
sign*
lodestuff 57.24 *ore*
lodge 77.20 *abode of mammals,*
255.14 *inhabit,* 256.4 *official
residence,* 256.18 *take up residence,* 325.9 *make motionless,*
396.17 *dwell,* 529.7 *esotericism,*
665.1 *party*
Lodge 48 Writers, **52** Scientists
lodge a complaint 856.5 *accuse*
lodged 256.14 *inhabiting*
lodger 255.3 *householder,* 723.5
possessor
lodging 218.5 *resting place,*
256.1 *habitat*
lodgings 256.1 *habitat*
lodicule 87.3 *grass plant*
Lodz 93 Cities
loess 54.27 *sediment,* 132.2 *residue,* 326.10 *transferred thing*
Lofri 8 Deities
loft 27.17 *bat,* 256.7 *room,*
275.8 *high thing,* 338.26 *bat,*
361.2 *send up,* 605.4 *storage*
lofted shot 29.3 *golf shots*
loftily 811, 805.34 *imposingly,*
807.33 *arrogantly,* 869.9 *unselfishly*
loftiness 126.1 *superiority,*
275.1, 361.8 *height,* 554.2 -
seriousness, 557.2 *affectation,*
805.5 *stateliness,* 807.4 -
arrogance, 811.2 *airs,* 850.3 -
contempt, 859.2 *unselfishness*
loft ladder 359.9 *ladder*
lofty 811, 95.7 *mountainous,*
248.13 *spacious,* 275.9 *high,*
361.12 *exalted,* 554.5 *serious,*
557.4 *ornate,* 805.19 *stately,*
807.16 *arrogant,* 850.13 *contemptuous,* 859.5 *unselfish*
lofty ground 126.4 *summit*
log 3.5, 3.20 *chronicle,* 47.12
wood, 52.19 *logarithm,* 74.5
navigation, 85.3 *timber,* 85.18
manage trees, 169.6 *power,*
268.6 *measuring instrument,*
329.8 *speed,* 410.2 *lighter,*

545.6 *record book*, 545.13 *re-cord*, 604.1 *materials*
Logan 95 Mountains
loganberry 86 Fruits, 133.5 *hy-brid*
logan stone 365.7 *oscillator*
logarithm 52, 169.6 *power*, 170.1 *calculation*
logarithmic 52.76 *functional*, 169.9 *fractional*, 170.15 *mathe-matical*
logarithmically 52.87, 170.16 *mathematically*
logarithmic function 52.29 *mathe-matical function*
logarithmic paper 52.32 *graph*
logarithmic scale 52.19 *loga-rithm*, 52.32 *graph*, 75.3 *scale*
logarithmic series 52.20 *sequence*
logarithmic spiral 52.40 *curve*
logarithm tables 52.19 *logarithm*
log basket 258.7 *basket*
logbook 3.5 *chronicle*, 71.21 *mis-cellaneous motoring terms*, 545.6 *record book*
log cabin 256.5 *house*
loge 51.16 *auditorium*
logged 3.19 *chronicled*, 545.16 *recorded*
logger 85.8 *forester*
loggerhead 79 Reptiles
loggia 43.9 *miscellaneous architectural features*, 327.7 *ar-cade*
logging 85.6 *tree management*
logic 4.6 *branch of philosophy*, 459.2 *ways of thinking*, 463.2 *reasoning*, 473.2 *logical argument*, 537.7 *confirmation*
logical 52, 473, 4.15 *rational*, 459.9 *mental*, 461.11 *reason-ing*, 463.8 *rational*
logical argument 473
logical connective 52.63 *mathe-matical logic*
logical empiricism 4.7 *school of thought*
logical empiricist 4.11 *follower of a doctrine*
logical expression 52.63 *mathe-matical logic*
logical formula 52.63 *mathemati-cal logic*
logical impossibility 487.5 *im-possibility*
logicalize 4.21 *rationalize*, 463.11 *reason*
logically 473, 4.24 *philosophi-cally*, 4.26 *rationally*, 52.87 *mathematically*, 459.15 *intelli-gently*, 461.18 *thoughtfully*, 463.15 *reasonably*, 537.37 au-thentically
logically demonstrated 537.20 *proved*
logically proven 537.20 *proved*
logical operation 52.14 *operation*, 52.63 *mathematical logic*
logical operator 52.13 *mathemat-ical symbol*, 52.63 *mathemati-cal logic*
logical order 150.3 *hierarchy*
logical outcome 227.1 *effect*
logical positivism 4.7 *school of thought*
logical positivist 4.11 *follower of a doctrine*
logical process 463.2 *reasoning*
logical product 52.63 *mathemati-cal logic*
logical proposition 52.63 *mathe-matical logic*
logical reasoning 52.64 *reasoning*
logical sequence 155.1 *sequence*
logical sum 52.63 *mathematical logic*
logical thinker 461.7 *thinker*
logical thought 463.2 *reasoning*
logical value 52.63 *mathematical logic*
logic chopper 474.6 *sophist*
logic-chopper 657.3 *cunning per-son*
logic chopping 474.1 *sophistry*
logic-chopping 474.7 *sophistic*
logic circuit 64.13 *circuit*

logician 4.10 *philosopher*, 463.5 *reasoner*, 473.6 *arguer*
logicize 4.21 *rationalize*, 473.14 *discuss*
login 65.17 *computing term*, 65.19 *abort*
logistic 52.40 *curve*
logistics 17.1 *military affairs*, 594.11 *fitting out*, 606.1 *provi-sion*, 652.9 *tactics*, 676.6 *art of war*
log jam 122.2 *equilibrium*, 209.3 *delayed action*, 218.2 *stop*, 641.1 *inaction*
logjam 659.8 *snag*
log jam 661.2 *obstacle*
log-jammed 209.10 *held up*
log-line knot 74.6 *nautical speed*
logo 544.3 *means of identifica-tion*
Logo 65 Programming Lan-guages
logoff 65.17 *computing term*, 65.19 *abort*
logomachize 4.23 *discuss philo-sophically*, 473.14 *discuss*
logomachy 4.5 *philosophical argu-ment*
logomancy 11.9 *divination*
logomania 565.1 *talkativeness*
logometric 169.9 *fractional*
logon 65.17 *computing term*, 65.19 *abort*
logophile 5.2 *linguist*
logophobia 777 Phobias by Name
logorrhoea 553.1 *diffuseness*, 564.2 *power of speech*, 565.1 *talkativeness*
Logos 5.17 *word*
logotherapy 61.3 *psychiatric treatment*
logotype 544.3 *means of identifi-cation*
logout 65.17 *computing term*, 65.19 *abort*
log paper 52.32 *graph*
logroll 223.5 *exchange*
logrolling 223.1 *exchange*, 664.3 *mutual relationship*
log scale 75.3 *scale*
log table 170.5 *computer*
log tables 52.19 *logarithm*
logwood 85 Trees and Shrubs
loin 45.24, 45.25 *pork* , 45.26, 45.27 *lamb*
loin chop 45.27 *lamb*
loincloth 295.25 *accessories*
loins 245.4 *development*
loipe 41.1 *skiing*
Loire 96 Rivers
loiter 209.7 *wait*, 328.2 *hesitate*
loiterer 328.15 *slow person*
loitering 328.7 *delayed*, 328.11 *lingering*
loiteringly 328.16 *slowly*
Lokai 32 Breeds of Horse and Pony
Lokayata 7 Non-Christian Reli-gions, 4.7 *school of thought*
Loki 8 Deities, 8.7 *devil*, 539.15 *deceiver*
loll 649.2 *take it easy*
lollapalooza 617.8 *exceller*, 861.17 *good thing*
Lollard 7.5 *Christian*
Lollardy 7 Christian Movements
lolling 643.3 *not participating*
lollipop 45.41 *sweet*, 414.4 *con-fectionery*
lolly 741.2 *cash*
lollygag 328.2 *hesitate*, 821.27 *kiss*, 826.7 *show endearment for*
lollygagging 328.7 *delayed*, 328.11 *lingering*, 821.6 *court-ship*, 826.1 *endearment*
Lombardy poplar 85 Trees and Shrubs
Lomé 93 Cities
lomentum 86.2 *botanical fruit*
Lomond 95 Lakes, **95** Moun-tains
London 48 Writers, **93** Cities, **93**, 93.4 *British cities*, 249.10 *urban area*
Londonderry 92 Counties, **93** Cities

Londoner 255.9 *British inhabi-tant*
London pride 84 Flowers and Flowering Plants
lone 168.16 *solitary*, 174.11 *one*, 174.16 *alone*
loneliness 777 Phobias by Topic, 136.2 *setting apart*, 174.5 *aloneness*, 816.3 *separa-tion*
lonely 816, 136.17 *unjoined*, 174.16 *alone*
lonely hearts club 823.13 *match-maker*
lonely hearts column 823.13 *matchmaker*
lonely pride 816.1 *unsociability*
loneness 174.5 *aloneness*
lone pair 57.11 *chemical bond*
loner 174, 117.6 *misfit*, 139.4 *individualist*, 168.9 *hermit*, 335.19 *deviant person*, 698.8 *free-thinker*, 816.6 *unsocial per-son*
lonesome 174.16 *alone*, 816.10 *lonely*
lonesomeness 174.5 *aloneness*
lone wolf 139.4 *individualist*, 168.9 *hermit*, 174.8 *loner*, 335.19 *deviant person*, 531.7 *concealer*, 698.8 *free-thinker*, 816.6 *unsocial person*
lone woman 825.5 *single person*
long 188, 269, 30.11 *gymnas-tic*, 41.12 *ski*, 120.6 *quantita-tive*, 248.13 *spacious*, 553.3 *dif-fuse*, 775.7 *aspire*, 784.7 *like*
long ago 3.8 *past time*, 3.24 *his-torically*, 200.22 *in the past*
longan 86 Fruits
long arm 12.3 *governance*
long arm of the law 16.1 *the law*
long-awaited 513.7 *expected*
Long Beach 93 Cities
longboat 74 Ships and Boats, **74** Sailing Ships and Boats
longbow 244.7 *agent of destruc-tion*, 338.9 *firearm*, 680.6 *histor-ical missile weapon*
long bread 742.6 *money*
long-butt cue 24.3 *English bil-liards*
longcase clock 192.6 *clock*
long chalk 263.2 *great distance*
Longchamp 674.5 *racecourse*
long circuit 33.6 *motor racing terms*
longcloth 67 Natural Fabrics
long-course 39.11 *swimming*
long-course pool 39.7 *swimming pool*
long-distance 21.6 *track*, 39.11 *swimming*, 41.13 *ice-skating*, 263.8 *distant*
long-distance call 534.10 *tele-phone call*
long-distance communication 534.1 *communications*
long-distance hitter 22.2 *baseball player*
long-distance race 21.1 *track events*, 674.4 *race*
long-distance racing 21.1 *track events*, 41.8 *speed-skating*
long-distance runner 21.3 *athlete*
long-distance running 18 Sport-ing Activities, 21.1 *track events*
long-distance swimmer 39.4 *swimmer*
long-distance swimming 39.1 *swimming*
long division 52.18 *division*
long dozen 179.7 *double figures*
long-drawn-out 269.1 *long*, 553.3 *diffuse*, 811.20 *pompous*
long dress 813.4 *formal dress*
long drink 351.2 *drink*
long drink of water 259.11 *tall person*, 274.9 *thin person*, 275.7 *tall person*
long duration 188, 219.2 *protrac-tion*
long-eared 420.12 *eared*
longed for 782.7 *desired*
longer endurance 721.2 *augmen-tation*
longeron 73 Aircraft Parts

long established 202.12 *olden*
longest way 334.2 *detour*
longevity 207.5 *old age*, 396.5 *life cycle*, 623.3 *health*
long face 772.4 *solemnity*, 830.2 *sign of sullenness*
long-faced 770.6 *depressed*, 772.1 *solemn*
Longfellow 48 Poets
long-focus lens 66.17 *lens*
long for 593.8 *miss*, 609.6 *be un-satisfied*, 782.12 *desire*, 821.24 *be in love*, 842.3 *be envious of*
Longford 92 Counties, **93** Cities
long game 29.3 *golf shots*
long gloves 295.25 *accessories*
long gone 397.19 *dead*
long green 742.6 *money*
long habit 584.1 *habit*
long-haired blue 77 Breeds of Cats
long-haired weirdo 720.5 *non-observer*
long haul 263.2 *great distance*
long home 399.6 *grave*
long hop 27.8 *delivery*
Longhorn 68 Breeds of Cattle
long hot summer 408.5 *hot weather*
longing 775.3 *aspiration*, 775.13 *aspirant*, 782.1 *desire*, 784.1, 784.6 *liking*, 821.5 *desire*, 821.20 *amorous*, 842.2 *envious*
longing for 593.5 *necessitous*, 782.9 *desirous*
longingly 784.11 *admiringly*, 842.4 *enviously*
long in-off 24.2 *billiards play*
long in the tooth 207.13 *middle-aged*
Long Island 98 Islands
longitude 52.39 *angle*, 249.2 *geo-graphical region*, 251.1 *situa-tion*, 268.4 *size*, 269.4 *length*, 302.4 *boundary marker*
longitudinal 269, 249.16 *re-gional*, 302.6 *furthest*
longitudinal dune 54.37 *dune*
longitudinal line 122.7 *dividing line*
longitudinally 269, 249.19 *geo-graphically*
longitudinal strain 63.14 *load*
longitudinal wave 56.12, 365.5 *wave*
long johns 295.18 *underwear*, 408.3 *heater*
long jump 21.2 *field events*
long jumper 21.3 *athlete*
long jumping 18 Sporting Activ-ities, 21.2 *field events*
long-lasting 185.21 *lasting through time*, 188.8 *lasting*, 217.7 *permanent*, 225.9 *stable*, 378.1 *tough*
long-lastingness 188
longleaf pine 85 Trees and Shrubs
long-legged 275.12 *tall*
longlegs 259.11, 275.7 *tall per-son*
long life 623.3 *health*
long-life food 350.7 *food*, 637.3 *preserved thing*
long-life milk 351.5 *milk*, 637.3 *preserved thing*
long-limbed 275.12 *tall*
long-lived 188.8 *lasting*, 396.12 *alive*
long loser 24.2 *billiards play*
long-lost 722.16 *losing*
Long Melford 330.14 *sporting hit*
long moss 88.3 *moss*
long-necked 275.12 *tall*
longness 269.4 *length*
long note 49.19 *tempo*
long odds 229.2 *chance*, 486.4 *remote possibility*, 489.4 *im-probability*, 589.5 *good chance*
long off 27.4 *team*
long on 27.4 *team*
long on-off 24.2 *billiards play*
long pants 295.9 *trousers*
long past 200.19 *antiquarian*
long period 57.6 *chemical ele-ment*
long range 263.1 *distance*

long-range 70.5 *transportable, 263.8 distant*
long-range forecast 55.4 *weather forecast*
long-range plan 516.4 *prudence, 517.3 plan*
long run 51.11 *theatrical performance, 263.2 great distance*
longship 74 Sailing Ships and Boats
long shot 66.4 *portrait, 229.2 chance, 486.4 remote possibility, 489.4 improbability, 589.6 poor chance*
long sight 435.1 *vision, 436.2 poor sight*
longsighted 516.6 *foreseeing*
long-sighted 435.22 *bespectacled, 436.9 weak-sighted*
longsightedly 516.8 *foresightedly*
longsightedness 516.4 *prudence*
long-sightedness 436.2 *poor sight*
long since 3.24 *historically, 200.22 in the past*
long ski 41.5 *ski equipment*
long sleeve 295.24 *part of garment*
long-sleeved 295.31 *styled*
long-sleeved shirt 295.8 *shirt*
longstanding 188.8 *lasting, 202.12 olden*
long standing 217.1 *permanence*
longstanding 217.7 *permanent*
long-standing client 584.8 *creature of habit*
longstop 27.4 *team*
long story made short 299.1 *outline*
long string 24.6 *pool*
long-suffering 691.4 *lenient, 835.3 mercy, 839.2 forgivingness, 839.5 merciful*
long suit 617.6 *worth*
long sword 46.4 *historic dancing*
long-tailed tit 78 Birds
long-term 188.8 *lasting*
long-term forecast 55.4 *weather forecast*
long-term loan 732.2 *loan*
long-term soldier 679.8 *soldier*
long to 784.9 *like to*
long trail 263.2 *great distance*
long trousers 295.9 *trousers*
longueur 788.1 *boredom*
long underwear 295.18 *underwear*
long use 599.6 *use*
long wave 212.6 *radio frequency, 534.14 radio transmission*
long way 263.2 *great distance*
long way round 334.2 *detour, 335.14 deviating course, 363.5 ringroad*
longways 269.3 *longitudinal, 269.12 longitudinally*
long-winded 269.1 *long, 334.7 circuitous, 553.3 diffuse, 565.5 talkative, 788.4 boring*
long-windedly 553.7 *diffusely, 788.8 boringly*
long-windedness 553.1 *diffuseness, 559.4 inelegance of speech, 564.2 power of speech, 565.1 talkativeness, 788.1 boredom*
long-winded speaker 788.3 *boring person*
long-wire antenna 534.17 *antenna*
long word 5.17 *word*
long-worded 557.4 *ornate*
long words 557.2 *affectation*
Longworth trap 539.13 *snare*
Lonk 68 Breeds of Sheep
Lonsdale 52 Scientists
lontar 49 Musical Instruments
loo 42 Card Games, 256.7 *room, 353.13 lavatory, 727.7 toilet*
looby 656.10 *unskilled person*
loofah 621.10 *cleaning object*
loofie 41.10 *curling*
look 435, 435, 289.13 *appear outwardly, 306.6 nature, 457.3 external appearance, 457.11 appear, 528.7 advice, 543.3 gesture, 652.1 conduct, 796.1 fashion*

look after 60.19 *practise medicine, 632.9 protect, 637.5 preserve, 653.1 manage, 662.19 support, 662.25, 697.8 serve*
look after number one 174.18 *be one, 870.10 indulge oneself*
look after oneself 623.5 *be healthy*
look aghast 786.9 *wonder*
look a gift horse in the mouth 581.1 *reject, 838.6 be ungrateful*
look ahead 199, 516.2 *show prudence, 592.12 plan ahead*
lookalike 110, 110, 51.22 *actor*
look alike 110.7 *be the same*
lookalike 114.5 *counterpart, 176.5 twin, 222.2 substitute person, 222.7 substitute, 547.1 representation*
look-alike 116.5 *conformity, 457.5 impression*
look as good as new 629.4 *be restored*
look ashamed 866.9 *appear guilty*
look as if butter would not melt in one's mouth 865.8 *be innocent*
look as if one had seen a ghost 777.11 *be afraid*
look askance 435.13 *look, 785.6 react against*
look askance at 766.7 *be dissatisfied*
look as young as ever 217.5 *be permanent*
look at 435.13 *look, 513.8 expect*
look at in the light of 4.22 *propound a philosophy*
look away 436.16 *be blind to*
look back 200, 337, 3.21 *antiquarianize, 221.6 reverse, 511.12 remember*
look before one leaps 516.2 *show prudence, 573.8 hold back, 781.5 be cautious*
look big 811.30 *put on airs*
look black 517.11 *predict, 828.11 be angry, 830.11 be irritable*
look blank 515.5 *be crestfallen, 523.7 be unintelligible, 531.12 be silent*
look blue 515.5 *be crestfallen*
look closely at 435.14 *inspect*
look daggers 435.13 *look, 543.11 gesture, 828.11 be angry*
look danger in the face 633.9 *face danger*
look deadpan 523.7 *be unintelligible*
look down a gun barrel 633.9 *face danger*
look down on 275.15 *be high, 805.28 disdain, 850.20 scorn, 852.14 disapprove*
look down one's nose 435.13 *look*
look down one's nose at 850.20 *scorn, 852.14 disapprove*
look down upon 95.9 *tower*
looked for 199.13 *foreseen, 714.15 future*
look embarrassed 866.9 *appear guilty*
looker 435.11 *observer, 789.3 attractive female, 789.4 attractive male*
looker-on 253.5 *someone present, 435.11 observer*
look expressionless 523.7 *be unintelligible*
look foolish 806.24 *be humiliated*
look for 488.10 *think likely, 513.8 expect, 516.1 foresee, 588.7 intend, 590.8 pursue, 594.3 be prepared*
look for a disagreement 666.7 *pick a fight*
look for a needle in a haystack 487.10 *attempt the impossible*
look for a short cut 660.20 *take it easy*
look for a welcome 344.3 *approach*
look for trouble 666.7 *pick a fight*
look forward 199.9 *look ahead*
look forward to 513.8 *expect,*

714.11 *promise oneself, 775.7 aspire*
look guilty 866.9 *appear guilty*
look in 346.9 *enter*
look-in 210.2 *opportunity*
look inferior 115.5 *be dissimilar*
looking 435.21 *seeing, 543.15 gestural*
looking after number one 860.1 *selfishness*
looking ahead 199.4 *looking to the future, 516.6 foreseeing*
looking back 3, 337, 200.2 *retrospection, 200.21 retrospective, 221.1 reversion*
looking for 590.1 *pursuit*
looking for a needle in a haystack 685.2 *never-ending task*
looking glass 435.8 *reflection*
looking guilty 866.6 *appearing guilty*
looking neither left nor right 333.5 *undeviating*
looking to the future 199
looking true 537.25 *lifelike*
looking up 627.14 *improved*
look in mint condition 629.4 *be restored*
look in on 253.12 *attend*
look in one's eyes 652.1 *conduct*
look in the face 778.15 *be courageous*
look into 4.20 *philosophize*
look into a crystal 199.9 *look ahead*
look into one's crystal ball 516.1 *foresee*
look in vain for 722.9 *lose*
look kindly on 686.7 *be auspicious*
look like 116.25 *conform, 457.11 appear, 547.9 represent*
look like new 629.4 *be restored*
look like rain 440.13 *become dark*
look like the cat that swallowed the canary 765.7 *be satisfied, 866.9 appear guilty*
look like thunder 828.11 *be angry*
look natural 531.12 *be silent*
look neither right nor left 333.6 *be in the middle*
look of power 692.5 *self-assurance*
look of reality 537.12 *true to life*
look ominous 517.11 *predict*
look on 236.6 *be powerless, 253.12 attend, 641.4 not act*
look one in the face 658.4 *be naive, 805.24 be proud*
look one straight in the eyes 658.4 *be naive*
look one up and down 826.8 *court*
look on the black side 776.9 *be hopeless*
look on the bright side 769.7 *be cheerful, 775.8 be optimistic*
look out! 636
look out 41.18 *danger*
lookout 435.11 *observer, 469.5 watchfulness, 632.3 protector, 636.4 warner*
look out 781.5 *be cautious*
look out for 469.11 *care for, 513.10 wait*
look out for number one 590.12 *aim at*
lookout man 74.7 *nautical person*
look out the window 641.4 *not act*
look over 435.14 *inspect*
look over one's shoulder 200.15, 337.8 *look back, 573.8 hold back*
look right through 818.7 *be discourteous*
looks 457.3 *external appearance*
look-see 435.3 *observation*
look serious 772.8 *be serious*
look sheepish 866.9 *appear guilty*
look sideways 435.13 *look*
look someone in the face 435.13 *look*
look straight at 435.13 *look*
look superior 115.5 *be dissimilar*
look the other way 436.16 *be blind to, 591.1 avoid, 783.12 be indifferent*

look through rose-coloured glasses 775.8 *be optimistic*
look to 847.17 *impose a duty*
look to be 457.11 *appear*
look to one's profits 737.1 *trade*
look to the future 516.2 *show prudence*
look true 537.33 *seem lifelike*
look twice 781.5 *be cautious*
look up 815.12 *visit*
look up to 9.8 *idolatrize, 276.8 be low, 849.15 respect, 849.16 revere*
look volumes 543.11 *gesture*
look where you're going 636.10 *look out*
look with a favourable eye 831.8 *be benevolent*
look young 623.5 *be healthy*
loom 36.4 *rowing, 67.4 weaving, 259.19 be big, 288.3 weaving, 359.20 hover, 437.9 appear, 457.12 become visible, 633.10 endanger, 647.1 workshop*
loomed 288.6 *interwoven*
looming 208.13 *imminent*
loom large 101.10 *be real, 259.19 be big, 435.19, 526.5 be visible*
loom over 359.20 *hover*
loom up 435.19 *be visible*
loon 78.3 *water bird, 510.7 insane person*
loony 61.8 *disordered personality, 168.10 eccentric, 460.6 unintelligent, 510.7 insane person*
loony bin 510.8 *mental hospital*
loony school 510.8 *mental hospital*
loony tune 510.7 *insane person*
loop 41.6 *ice-skating, 41.16 bobsled , 65.17 computing term, 65.19 abort, 72.2 track, 73.5 flight, 137.8 fastening, 137.9 yoke, 247.3 birth control, 311.2 bend, 311.6 curve, 313.2 circle, 314.2 coil, 314.6 convolute, 334.1 circuit, 334.2 detour, 334.3 circuit, 363.3 orbit, 363.7 ring*
loop antenna 534.17 *antenna*
looped 67.10 *woven, 311.4 curved, 363.10 circular*
looper 82.5 *larva*
loophole 16.4 *bad law, 347.6 way out, 592.3 expedient plan, 620.7 defect, 638.2 means of escape, 671.11 fortification*
loopholed 671.30 *defended*
looping 35.3 *rugby play, 35.6 rugger*
looping the loop 73.5 *flight, 334.1 circuit*
loop jump 41.6 *ice-skating*
loop knot 74 Knots
loop line 334.2 *detour*
Loop Nebula 53 Nebulae
loop the loop 334.3 *circuit*
loopy 510.11 *insane*
loose 5.40 *translated, 35.6 - rugger, 136.9, 136.15 separate, 139.5 unstick, 139.8 nonadhesive, 162.25 sprawled, 164.20 generalized, 224.13 changeable, 238.8 weak, 335.25 wandering, 374.1 soft, 482.1 undiscriminating, 491.6 indeterminate, 504.15 erroneous, 524.17 translational, 555.1 unemphatic, 598.1 relinquish, 638.8 escaping, 660.16 make easy, 698.12 unconditional, 698.15 set free, 700.4 liberate, 708.8 permitting, 814.10 free, 877.13 unchaste*
loose a rope 36.15 *sail*
loose ball 23.4 *playing terms*
loose bowels 353.2 *defecation*
loosebox 68.7 *farm building*
loose ends 685.1 *noncompletion*
loose-fitting 139.8 *nonadhesive*
loose-footed 36.10 *sailing*
loose-footed sail 36.3 *parts of a sailing boat*
loose forward 35.4 *rugby player*
loose impediments 29.1 *golf*
loose in the attic 510.11 *insane*

loose in the head 510.11 *insane*
loose-knit 553.3 *diffuse*
loose-limbed 374.2 *pliant*
loosely 136.20 *separately,*
139.10 *noncohesively,* 164.29
generally, 374.17 *softly,* 491.25
indeterminately, 504.22
wrongly, 555.3 *unemphatically,*
698.21 *excessively,* 708.9 *with
permission*
loose morals 864.2 *vice,* 877.3
sexual immorality
loosen 136.9 *separate,* 139.5 *unstick,* 238.7 *weaken,* 374.13
soften, 374.14, 649.3 *ease,*
700.4 *liberate*
loosened 136.15 *separate*
looseness 139.1 *nonadhesion,*
164.3 *nonspecificness,* 238.1
weakness, 374.8 *softness,* 384.2
crumbliness, 491.14 *indeterminacy,* 504.2 *inaccuracy,* 555.2
lack of emphasis, 814.4 *freedom*
loosening 136.1 *separation*
loosen one's grip 598.1 *relinquish*
loosen up 374.14 *ease*
loose off 338.28 *shoot*
loose rocks 34.2 *climbing dangers*
loose screw 620.7 *defect*
loose scrum 35.3 *rugby play*
loose talk 877.2 *indecency*
loose translation 5.12, 524.4
translation
loose woman 402, 877.9 *immoral woman*
loosing 136.1 *separation,* 700.1
liberation
loot 151.11 *troublemaker,*
244.10, 607.2 *lay waste,* 681.2
spoils, 734.10 *take away,* 736.4
stolen goods, 736.14 *plunder,*
741.2 *cash*
loot and pillage 736.14 *plunder*
looter 244.6 *destroyer,* 734.6
taker
looting 244.5 *havoc,* 607.4 *destruction,* 734.3 *taking away,*
736.5 *plundering,* 736.17 *stolen*
looting and pillaging 736.5 *plundering*
lop 69.15 *cultivate,* 85.18 *manage trees,* 131.4 *take off,* 136.10
set apart, 270.10 *shorten*
lope 324.12 *gait,* 324.15 *walk,*
329.4 *be swift*
lop-eared 420.12 *eared*
Lop Nur 94 Lakes
lopolith 54.28 *rock*
lopped 131.7 *reduced,* 145.4 *incomplete*
lopper 69.6 *garden tool,* 393.25,
394.11 *thicken,* 603.2 *garden
tool*
loppered 393.20 *thick*
loppering 394.1 *viscosity*
lopping 85.6 *tree management,*
131.1 *subtraction*
lopsided 123.3 *unequal,* 309.6
distorted, 656.3 *clumsy*
lopsidedly 309.13 *asymmetrically*
lopsidedness 123.1 *inequality,*
309.1 *distortion*
loquacious 5.42 *worded,* 528.16
informative, 530.11 *disclosing,*
553.3 *diffuse,* 564.19 *speaking,*
565.5 *talkative,* 568.12 *conversing*
loquaciously 5.50 *lexically,*
553.7 *diffusely,* 565.10 *talkatively,* 568.15 *conversationally*
loquaciousness 565.1 *talkativeness*
loquacity 5.22 *many words,*
553.1 *diffuseness,* 564.2 *power
of speech,* 565.1 *talkativeness*
loquat 86 Fruits
loran 73.6 *flight control*
loran-A system 74.5 *navigation*
loran-B system 74.5 *navigation*
loran system 74.5 *navigation*
lorazepam 62 Medication
lord 723, 696.1 *master,* 802.1
nobleman, 804.4 *titleholder*
Lord 8.3 *God,* 401.3 *male title of
address*

Lord Advocate 16.11 *British law
officer*
lord and master 696.1 *master,*
723.6 *lord,* 823.10 *married man*
Lord Chancellor 16.11 *British law
officer,* 16.25 *British judge*
Lord Chancellor's Court 16.20
British court
Lord Chief Justice 16.25 *British
judge*
lord-in-waiting 697.6 *domestic
servant*
lord it 807.27 *dare,* 807.28 *get
above oneself*
lord it over 688.19 *be authoritarian,* 696.14 *master,* 805.28 *disdain*
Lord Jesus 8.4 *God the Son*
lordliness 688.2 *authoritativeness,* 805.6 *majesty*
lordly 12.10 *governing,* 688.12
authoritative, 692.15 *self-assured,* 696.12 *masterful,* 802.4
aristocratic, 804.6 *worshipful,*
805.19 *stately*
Lord Lyon 544.9 *herald*
lord mayor 16.11 *British law officer*
Lord Mayor 696.3 *leader*
Lord Mayor's show 811.13 *ceremonial,* 813.3 *formal occasion*
Lord Muck 802.1 *nobleman,*
805.23 *proud person*
Lord Nelson and Lady Hamilton
821.10 *lovers*
Lord of Appeal 16.25 *British
judge*
Lord of Creation 400.7 *person,*
805.13 *proud person*
Lord of Lords 8.3 *God*
lord of misrule 151.11 *troublemaker*
lord of the bedchamber 697.6 *domestic servant*
Lord of the Flies 8.7 *devil*
lord of the manor 611.4 *bigwig,*
696.1 *master,* 723.6 *lord,* 725.7
property man
lord paramount 696.1 *master*
lord provost 16.11 *British law officer*
Lord's 27.2 *ground,* 674.3 *stadium*
lords-and-ladies 84 Flowers and
Flowering Plants
Lord's day 649.1 *ease*
Lord's Day 10.15 *holy day*
lordship 126.2 *leadership,* 723.1
possession, 802.2 *aristocracy*
Lords Spiritual 12.4 *governing
body,* 653.16 *official*
Lord's Supper 10.6 *Eucharist*
Lords Temporal 12.4 *governing
body,* 653.16 *official*
lore 1.8 *tradition,* 48.1 *literature,*
202.6 *tradition,* 501.3 *learning,*
584.4 *custom,* 657.1 *cunning*
lorelei 11.4 *witch*
Lorelei 586.13 *tempter*
Lorentz 52 Scientists
Lorentz–Fitzgerald contraction 56
Named Laws
Lorenz 52 Scientists
lorgnette 435.10 *visual aid*
lorica 293.14 *animal covering,*
671.7 *armour*
loriner 32.15 *horse person*
loris 77 Placental Mammals
lorn 816.10 *lonely*
lorry 71 Motor Vehicles, 70.5
transportable, 71.20 *truck,*
258.10 *cart,* 326.5 *means of
transport*
lorryload 120.3 *container*
lory 78 Birds
Los Angeles 93 Cities, 93.2
American cities
lose 722, 129.4 *decrease,* 244.8
destroy, 252.19 *misplace,* 358.1
fall short, 598.1 *relinquish,*
683.7 *be defeated,* 687.9 *be in
trouble,* 739.1 *sell*
lose a battle 701.8 *be subject to*
lose a chance 722.9 *lose*
lose an opportunity 211.6 *lose
one's chance*
lose badly 683.7 *be defeated*

lose by a whisker 683.7 *be defeated,* 722.9 *lose*
lose colour 445, 439.28 *bleach*
lose consciousness 236.6 *be powerless,* 722.9 *lose*
lose contact with 722.9 *lose*
lose control 241.7 *be violent,*
628.1 *deteriorate,* 828.12 *become angry*
lose currency 202.17 *grow old*
lose earnings 722.10 *have a financial loss*
lose everything 743.13 *lose one's
money*
lose face 127.9 *yield to,* 656.6
act foolishly
lose faith in human nature 834.4
become a misanthrope
lose feathers 296.16 *peel*
lose flavour 628.2 *decay*
lose ground 328.3 *slow down,*
337.1 *go backward,* 358.1 *fall
short,* 628.1 *deteriorate*
lose hair 294.12 *shed*
lose handle 41.10 *curling*
lose hands down 683.7 *be defeated*
lose health 628.1 *deteriorate*
lose heart 770.9 *despair,* 776.9
be hopeless
lose heat 409.11 *become cold*
lose height 360.9 *descend*
lose hope 770.9 *despair,* 776.9
be hopeless
lose interest 412.7 *be tasteless,*
598.1 *relinquish,* 783.12 *be indifferent*
lose interest in 722.12 *lessen*
lose it 656.5 *be unskilful*
lose leaves 85.19 *grow*
lose momentum 328.3 *slow down*
lose money 722.10 *have a financial loss*
lose money on 739.1 *sell*
lose not a moment 648.2 *make
haste*
lose no time 208.10 *hasten,*
648.2 *make haste*
lose one 523.7 *be unintelligible*
lose one's bearings 335.3 *go
astray*
lose one's bottle 779.4 *be a coward*
lose one's chance 211, 209.7
wait
lose one's cunning 656.5 *be unskilful*
lose one's feel 656.5 *be unskilful*
lose one's fortune 687.10 *need
money*
lose one's freedom 701.8 *be subject to,* 722.9 *lose*
lose one's head 508.6 *be foolish,*
656.5 *be unskilful*
lose one's hearing 421.8 *be deaf*
lose one's heart 821.24 *be in
love,* 821.26 *court*
lose one's husband 824.10 *be
widowed*
lose one's inheritance 687.10
need money
lose one's life 397.15 *die*
lose one's marbles 510.14 *become insane*
lose one's memory 462.12 *lack
thought,* 722.9 *lose*
lose one's money 743
lose one's nerve 656.5 *be unskilful,* 779.4 *be a coward*
lose one's powers of speech
563.14 *have difficulty speaking*
lose one's rag 828.12 *become
angry*
lose one's rights 701.8 *be subject
to,* 722.9 *lose*
lose one's self-respect 808.8 *be
servile*
lose one's sense of direction
335.3 *go astray*
lose one's sense of smell 417.6
have no smell
lose one's sight 436.14 *be blind*
lose one's skill 656.5 *be unskilful*
lose one's temper 818.8 *get
angry,* 828.12 *become angry*
lose one's tongue 563.14 *have
difficulty speaking*

lose one's touch 656.5 *be unskilful*
lose one's train of thought 160
lose one's voice 129.4 *decrease,*
422.1 *be silent,* 563.14 *have difficulty speaking,* 566.9 *lapse
into silence*
lose one's way 335.3 *go astray*
lose one's wits 510.14 *become insane*
lose out 656.5 *be unskilful,*
683.6 *fail,* 683.7 *be defeated,*
722.9 *lose*
lose out on love 687.9 *be in trouble*
lose patience 828.12 *become
angry*
lose power 683.9 *malfunction*
lose profits 722.10 *have a financial loss*
loser 722, 127.6 *inferior,* 581.9
rejected person, 656.10 *unskilled
person,* 683.5 *failing person,*
687.5 *person in adversity,* 701.5
subjected person, 776.3 *hopeless
person*
lose repute 801.4 *disreputable*
lose shine 441.11 *tarnish*
lose sight of 438.7 *become invisible,* 722.9 *lose*
lose someone 722, 329.6 *accelerate*
lose someone's attention 783.13
make indifferent
lose speed 328.3 *slow down*
lose strength 624.24 *be unhealthy*
lose taste 412.7 *be tasteless,*
628.2 *decay*
lose the baby 247.7 *be infertile*
lose the ball 31.9 *play hockey*
lose the battle 683.7 *be defeated,*
687.9 *be in trouble,* 722.9 *lose,*
722.12 *lessen*
lose the day 722.9 *lose*
lose the election 683.7 *be defeated,* 722.9 *lose*
lose the game 683.7 *be defeated,*
687.9 *be in trouble*
lose the match 683.7 *be defeated,* 687.9 *be in trouble,*
722.9 *lose*
lose the race 683.7 *be defeated*
lose the scent 417.6 *have no
smell*
lose the thread 108.10 *be unrelated,* 335.4 *lose track of*
lose the upper hand 127.9 *yield
to*
lose the vote 683.7 *be defeated*
lose the war 683.7 *be defeated,*
687.9 *be in trouble*
lose time 209.6 *be late,* 211.5
take untimely action
lose track of 335, 252.19 *misplace,* 722.9 *lose*
lose value 628.1 *deteriorate*
lose water 438.7 *leak*
lose weight 129.5 *make smaller,*
262.6 *become smaller,* 274.14
become thin, 370.10 *lighten,*
722.9 *lose,* 869.5 *be self-restrained,* 871.5 *fast*
losing 722, 252.6 *misplacement,*
722.1 *loss*
losing balance 123.3 *unequal*
losing battle 722.3 *waste*
losing candidate 580.13 *electorate*
losing game 683.2 *defeat*
losing general 683.5 *failing person*
losing ground 628.7 *deterioration*
losing hazard 24.3 *English billiards*
losing it 656.3 *clumsy*
losing move 683.2 *defeat*
losing one's feel 656.3 *clumsy*
losing one's touch 656.3 *clumsy*
losing person 683.5 *failing person*
losings 722.2 *financial loss*
losing weight 262.1 *contraction,*
350.6 *nutrition,* 871.1 *fasting*
Losna 8 Deities
loss 722, 129.1 *decrease,* 131.2
subtracted item, 132.3 *difference,* 145.2 *omission,* 244.4
ruin, 254.2 *disappearance,*

347.5 *export*, 358.5 *shortfall*, 458.5 *disguise*, 607.3 *waste*, 614.4 *futility*, 628.10 *impairment*, 638.4 *leak*, 683.2 *defeat*, 879.10 *affliction*
Loss 722
losses 722.2 *financial loss*
Lossiemouth 93 Cities
loss leader 228.5 *positive stimulus*, 586.9 *enticement*, 722.2 *financial loss*, 752.2, 754.4 *bargain*
loss-leader 739.8 *merchandise*
loss-leading 722.17 *unprofitable*
loss-making 129.7 *decrescent*, 614.2 *futile*, 722.17, 737.16 *unprofitable*
loss of ball 31.5 *lacrosse*
loss of battle 701.1 *subjection*
loss of condition 624.1 *ill health*
loss of consciousness 236.4 *disability*, 624.3 *symptom*, 650.7 *fatigue*, 722.1 *loss*
loss of control 236.4 *disability*
loss of earnings 722.2 *financial loss*
loss of face 850.8 *indignity*
loss of faith 498.4 *unbelief*
loss of fortune 743.6 *insolvency*
loss of freedom 701.1 *subjection*, 722.1 *loss*
loss of hope 776.1 *hopelessness*
loss of innocence 864.1 *wickedness*
loss of interest 722.3 *waste*
loss of life 397.1 *death*
loss of memory 512.2 *blankness*, 546.5 *forgetfulness*
loss of morale 628.11 *hurt*
loss of nerve 576.13 *timidity*
loss of profit 722.2 *financial loss*
loss of right 846.2 *disentitlement*
loss of rights 701.1 *subjection*, 722.1 *loss*
loss of strength 238.3 *poor health*
loss of value 129.1 *decrease*
loss of vision 436.1 *blindness*
loss of voice 563.1 *voicelessness*
loss of weight 722.1 *loss*
lost 16.64 *convicted*, 145.4 *incomplete*, 252.13 *misplaced*, 254.9 *away*, 335.21 *indirect*, 458.7 *disappeared*, 512.11 *forgotten*, 683.11 *defeated*, 722.16 *losing*, 776.5 *past hope*, 868.3 *impenitent*
lost and gone 200.18 *over*
lost art 722.8 *lost thing*
lost at sea 722.16 *losing*
lost battle 683.2 *defeat*, 687.1 *adversity*, 722.8 *lost thing*
lost bet 683.4 *unsuccessful thing*
lost cause 581.8 *rejected thing*, 683.2 *defeat*, 722.8 *lost thing*, 776.2 *hopeless situation*, 868.2 *impenitent person*
lost chance 211, 722.8 *lost thing*
lost child 590.7 *the hunted*
lost connection 160.7 *broken thread*
lost election 581.6 *discarding*, 683.4 *unsuccessful thing*, 722.8 *lost thing*
lost forever 200.18 *over*
lost fortune 717.2 *economic adversity*
lost from view 722.16 *losing*
lost game 687.1 *adversity*, 722.8 *lost thing*
Lost Generation 722.8 *lost thing*
lost ground 722.8 *lost thing*
lost hope 722.8 *lost thing*
lost in amazement 722.18 *at a loss*, 786.6 *wondering*
lost inheritance 687.2 *economic adversity*
lost in the distance 438.2 *difficult to see*
lost in thought 4.17 *thoughtful*, 461.9 *concentrating*, 468.8 *absent-minded*, 722.18 *at a loss*
lost in wonder 786.6 *wondering*
lost labour 614.5 *waste of effort*, 642.9 *overactivity*, 656.9 *bungling*, 683.1 *failure*, 722.8 *lost thing*

lost language 5.9 *ancient language*
lost leader 578.9 *equivocator*
lost life 722.8 *lost thing*
lost love 687.1 *adversity*, 722.8 *lost thing*
lost match 687.1 *adversity*
lost melody 433.1 *melody*
lost memory 722.8 *lost thing*
lost opportunity 211.3 *lost chance*, 722.8 *lost thing*
lost sheep 722.6 *loser*, 864.9 *wicked person*
lost shot 602.1 *means*
lost soul 8.7 *devil*, 722.6 *loser*, 864.9 *wicked person*
lost thing 722
lost time 722.8 *lost thing*
lost to 783.7 *indifferent*
lost to oblivion 512.11 *forgotten*
lost to sight 458.7 *disappeared*
lost tribes 722.8 *lost thing*
lost war 683.2 *defeat*, 687.1 *adversity*, 722.8 *lost thing*
lost-wax casting 50.12 *sculpture*
lost youth 722.8 *lost thing*
lot 105.1 *state*, 120.2 *certain amount*, 229.2 *chance*, 249.12 *plot*, 302.2 *limiting factor*, 517.10 *cards*, 582.5 *predetermination*, 589.2 *luck*, 725.1 *property*, 731.2 *portion*
Lothario 340.6 *charmer*, 821.9 *lover*
Lothian 92 Counties
lotion 62.7 *ointment*, 134.3 *purifier*, 386.5, 395.6 *ointment*, 630.9 *balm*
lots 181.2 *multitude*, 608.8 *plenty*
lots of luck 589.15, 686.10 *good luck*
lottery 229.2 *chance*, 589.3 *equal chance*, 749.5 *winnings*
lotus 84 Flowers and Flowering Plants
Lotus-123 65.11 *application*
lotus-eater 86.5 *figurative usage*, 405.3 *pleasure-seeker*, 519.9 *visionary*, 643.8 *nonworker*
lotus-eating 325.1 *motionlessness*
Lotus of the True Law 7.12 *religious text*
lotus root 45 Vegetables
louche 877.12 *indecent*
loud 423, 237.12 *strong to the senses*, 420.14 *hearable*, 426.15 *drumming*, 427.7 *ringing*, 430.7 *strident*, 431.16 *vociferous*, 444.12 *gaudy*, 526.14 *manifest*, 557.4 *ornate*, 559.10 *ugly*, 795.7 *vulgar*, 811.19 *flashy*
loud breathing 423.1 *loudness*
loud cry 431.1 *cry*
loud drunk 652.5 *badly behaved person*
loud enough to wake the dead 420.14 *hearable*
loud-hailer 420.9 *audio device*, 423.4 *sound maker*, 532.1 *publication*
loud instrument 423.4 *sound maker*
loud laughter 423.1 *loudness*
loudly 423.1 *loudness*, 430.10 *stridently*, 431.20 *vociferously*, 811.35 *flashily*
loudmouth 601.3 *abuser*, 785.3 *disliked person*, 818.4 *discourteous person*
loudmouthed 431.16 *vociferous*
loud-mouthed 423.6 *loud*
loudness 423, 56.17 *sound*, 444.3 *hue*, 521.1 *lack of meaning*, 559.3 *ugliness*, 811.4 *flashiness*
Loudness 423
loudness level 56.19 *sound propagation*
loud noise 423.1 *loudness*
loud pedal 423.4 *sound maker*
loud person 423
loud report 423.1 *loudness*
loudspeaker 56.18 *source of sound*, 64.22 *transformer*, 420.9 *audio device*, 423.4 *sound*

maker, 532.1 *publication*, 534.18 *radio*
loudspeaker van 71 Motor Vehicles, 420.9 *audio device*
loud-speaking 564.19 *speaking*
loud-spoken 564.19 *speaking*
lough 94.1 *lake*
Lough Neagh 94.4 *British lakes*
Louis 18 Sporting Personalities
Louisiana 92 American States
Louis Quatorze 43 Architectural Styles, 47.7 *furniture style*
Louis Quinze 43 Architectural Styles, 47.7 *furniture style*
Louis Seize 43 Architectural Styles, 47.7 *furniture style*
Louis Treize 43 Architectural Styles
Louisville 93 Cities
Louisville slugger 22.3 *baseball equipment*
lounge 256.7 *room*, 643.12 *be inactive*, 649.2 *take it easy*, 727.7 *toilet*
lounge chair 47.2 *chair*
lounger 643.8 *nonworker*
lounge suit 295.4 *informal dress*, 295.10 *suit*, 813.4 *formal dress*
loungewear 814.6 *informal dress*
lounging pyjamas 295.4 *informal dress*
lounging robe 295.16 *robe*
loupe 435.10 *visual aid*
lour 440.13 *become dark*, 441.9 *be dim*, 636.5 *warn*, 818.8 *get angry*, 828.11 *be angry*, 829.2 *sign of irascibility*, 830.4 *sign of irritableness*, 830.11 *be irritable*
Lourdes 93 Cities, 291.4 *centre of activity*, 529.6 *natural mystery*, 588.6 *objective*
louring 440.8 *dark*, 441.5 *dim*, 829.5 *showing irascibility*, 830.7 *irritable*, 830.8 *overcast*
louse 82 Insects, 82.3 *pest*, 622.4 *dirt*, 864.10 *bad person*
louse up 504.19 *make a mistake*, 661.8 *hinder*
louse-up 504.10 *blunder*
lousiness 618.10 *poverty*
lousy 82.12 *verminous*, 618.4 *poor*, 622.8 *unclean*, 754.10 *shoddy*, 862.7 *evil*
lousy with 144.8 *full*
lousy with money 742.1 *wealthy*
lout 652.5 *badly behaved person*, 656.10 *unskilled person*, 764.9 *unpleasant person*, 818.4 *discourteous person*, 832.8 *malefactor*
Louth 92 Counties
loutish 818.6 *bad-mannered*
loutishly 818.10 *rudely*
loutishness 818.2 *bad manners*
louvre 43.9 *miscellaneous architectural features*
Louvre 43 Noted Buildings
lovability 821
lovable 821, 405.6 *pleasant*, 784.5 *likable*
lovableness 821.4 *lovability*
lovably 784.10 *with great liking*, 821.30 *lovingly*
lovage 45 Herbs and Spices, 413.5 *herbs*
love 821, 821, 8.2 *divine attribute*, 100.2 *nothingness*, 172.1 *zero*, 759.5 *good feeling*, 782.1 *desire*, 782.13 *like*, 784.1 *liking*, 784.4 *likable person*, 784.7 *like*, 786.1 *wonder*, 817.3 *courtesies*, 817.10 *be courteous*, 819.1 *friendship*, 821.11 *loved one*, 821.12 *nicknames for lovers*, 826.1 *endearment*, 826.4 *terms of endearment*, 826.7 *show endearment for*, 831.1 *benevolence*, 831.8 *be benevolent*, 851.2 *admiration*, 863.2 *virtues*
Love 821
love affair 821
love all 122.2 *equilibrium*
love-all 110.16 *equal*
love-all score 110.5 *equality*
love and peace 667.1 *agreement*
love a party 815.11 *be sociable*
love apple 86 Fruits

lovebird 78 Birds
lovebirds 821.10 *lovers*
lovebite 821.14 *communication of love*, 826.1 *endearment*
love charm 11.5 *spell*
love company 815.11 *be sociable*
Lovecraft 48 Writers
loved 821.21 *beloved*
love deuce 40.4 *tennis terms*
loved one 821
loved ones 397.13 *the dead*
love feast 10.16 *religious festival*
love food 872.5 *be greedy*
love for one's country 821.1 *love*
love game 682.2 *victory*
love good 863.8 *be virtuous*
lovegrass 87 Grasses
love-hate relationship 821.2 *romantic love*
love-in 405.4 *pleasurable things*
love-in-a-mist 84 Flowers and Flowering Plants
love interest 51.21 *role*
love item 821
love knot 74 Knots
Lovelace 48 Poets
loveless 785.8 *disliking*, 822.12 *hated*
love letter 821.15 *love item*, 826.3 *love token*
love-lies-bleeding 84 Flowers and Flowering Plants
loveliness 405.1 *physical pleasure*, 763.6 *pleasantness*, 789.1 *gorgeousness*, 821.4 *lovability*
Lovell 52 Scientists
lovelorn 821.19 *enamoured*, 822.12 *hated*
lovelornness 821.3 *lovingness*
Loveltine 7 Members of Religious Orders
lovely 405.6 *pleasant*, 617.1 *worthy*, 762.5 *delightful*, 763.1 *pleasant*, 784.5 *likable*, 789.3 *attractive female*, 789.5 *beautiful*, 821.22 *lovable*
lovely child 826.6 *object of endearment*
love lyric 821.15 *love item*
lovemaking 821.5 *desire*, 826.2 *courtship*
love match 823.3 *types of marriage*
love nest 256.5 *house*, 815.4 *meeting place*, 821.13 *abode of love*
love of mankind 831.1 *benevolence*
love of war 676.5 *bellicosity*
love oneself 860.7 *be egoistic*
love one's job 644.8 *exert oneself*
love-play 826.2 *courtship*
love poem 821.15 *love item*, 826.3 *love token*
love potion 11.5 *spell*
love-potion 405.4 *pleasurable things*
lover 821, 180.12 *partner*, 401.4 *boyfriend*, 402.4 *girlfriend*, 467.6 *attentive person*, 712.4 *requester*, 784.4 *likable person*, 821.12 *nicknames for lovers*, 826.4 *terms of endearment*, 826.5 *courting person*, 826.6 *object of endearment*
lover boy 401.4 *boyfriend*
lovers 821
love scene 51.6 *scene*
love seat 47.2 *chair*
lovesick 821.19 *enamoured*
lovesickness 821.3 *lovingness*
Love's Labour's Lost 48 Shakespeare's plays
love slap 821.14 *communication of love*, 826.1 *endearment*
lovesome 821.22 *lovable*
love song 433.2 *song*, 821.15 *love item*
love sonnet 821.15 *love item*, 826.3 *love token*
love story 48.2, 560.5 *fiction*
love suit 826.2 *courtship*
love the sound of one's own voice 809.15 *be vain*
love to 784.9 *like to*
love to distraction 821.23 *love*
love to eat 872.5 *be greedy*

love token **826**, 681.3 *memento*,
821.15 *love item*
loveworthy 821.22 *lovable*
lovey 821.12 *nicknames for lovers*, 826.4 *terms of endearment*
lovey-dovey 826.9 *endearing*
lovie 51.22 *actor*
loving **821**, 784.6 *liking*, 826.9
endearing, 831.6 *benevolent*,
863.6 *ethical*
loving care 469.2 *consideration*
loving couple 821.10 *lovers*
loving cup 258.13 *drinking vessel*, 351.10 *drink container*,
681.1 *trophy*
loving kindness 831.1 *benevolence*
loving looks 821.14 *communication of love*
lovingly **821**, 784.11 *admiringly*, 826.10 *endearingly*,
831.10 *benevolently*, 863.10 *ethically*
lovingness **821**
loving touch 821.14 *communication of love*
loving words 821.14 *communication of love*, 826.1 *endearment*
low **276, 276**, 5.39 *of language*,
55.11 *weather system*, 127.5 *inferior state*, 238.13 *insufficient*,
270.7 *short*, 278.2 *superficial*,
362.18 *lowering*, 424.4 *faint*,
424.7 *faintly*, 427.8 *deep*, 428.1
faint-sounding, 430.8 *hoarse*,
432.4 *cry*, 563.10 *low-voiced*,
563.17 *voicelessly*, 618.4 *poor*,
673.5 *submitting*, 754.9 *cheap*,
754.10 *shoddy*, 770.6 *depressed*,
806.2 *lowly*, 850.12 *disregardful*
low attendance 182.1 *few*
low birth rate 247.1 *infertility*
low blood pressure 624.3 *symptom*, 624.10 *cardiovascular disease*
low-born 803.3 *common*, 806.2
lowly
lowboy 47.5, 258.3 *cabinet*
low-brow 502.6 *ignorant*
low-budget 754.9 *cheap*
low-built 276.5 *low*
low-calorie 350.27 *edible*
low-calorie drink 351.6 *soft drink*
low camp 51.10 *comedy*
low-caste 127.12 *inferior*, 803.3
common
Löwchen **77** Breeds of Dogs
low-cholesterol diet 350.6 *nutrition*
Low Church **7** Christian Movements
Low-Church 7.16 *denominational*
low-class 127.12 *inferior*
low cloud 55.18 *cloud*
low comedian 51.22 *actor*
low comedy 51.10 *comedy*
low cunning 538.10 *dishonesty*,
540.5 *deceitfulness*
low-cut 276.5 *low*, 296.10 *in dishabille*
low-cut neckline 276.4 *low thing*
low definition 438.4 *invisibility*,
441.2 *murk*
low-definition 438.2 *difficult to
see*, 441.6 *murky*
low-density 182.6 *sparse*
low down 276.10 *low*
low-down 528.1 *information*,
803.3 *common*, 858.5 *dishonourable*
low ebb 127.5 *inferior state*
Lowell **48** Poets, **48** Poets, **48**
Poets, **52** Scientists, **93** Cities
lower **276, 276, 362**, 2.14 *socioeconomic*, 52.75 *equal*, 121.6
change gradually, 127.12 *inferior*, 129.5 *make smaller*,
277.14 *deepen*, 304.4 *rear*,
360.9 *descend*, 428.7 *mute*,
441.10 *make dim*, 517.11 *predict*, 628.6 *pervert*, 701.6, 701.9
subject, 752.3 *discount*, 795.10
vulgarize, 806.23 *abase*, 850.27
desecrate
lower animal 81.1 *invertebrate*
lower atmosphere 390.2 *atmospheric layers*

lower back 304.2 *rear end*
lower bound 52.21 *set*
Lower Carboniferous **54** Geological Time Intervals
lower-case 5.41 *lettered*
lower-case letter 5.15 *type style*
Lower Chamber 12.4, 12.4 *governing body*, 653.11 *British government*, 653.12 *US government*
lower charges 754.13 *make cheap*
lower class 2.7 *social stratification*, 127.1 *inferiority*, 400.9
group
lower classes 127.6 *inferior*
Lower Cretaceous **54** Geological
Time Intervals
lower criticism 524.3 *criticism*
lower deck **74** Parts of a Ship,
280.2 *foot*
lower depths 277.4 *deep thing*
lowered **362**, 276.5 *low*, 806.3
humbled
lower ground floor 280.2 *foot*
Lower House 12.4, 12.4 *governing body*, 653.11 *British government*, 653.12 *US government*
lowering **362, 362**, 276.1 *lowness*, 277.1 *depth*, 360.1 *descent*, 360.2 *sinkage*, 360.16 *descending*
Lowering **362**
lowering oneself 806.15 *condescension*
lowering the body 399.2 *funeral*
Lower Jurassic **54** Geological
Time Intervals
lower limit 52.31 *differentiation*,
120.2 *certain amount*, 302.2
limiting factor
Lower Lough Erne 94.4 *British
lakes*
lower merit 195.3 *subordination*
lower middle class 158.8 *middle
class*, 400.9 *group*
lower oneself 801.4 *disreputable*,
806.18 *condescend*
lower one's sights 598.1 *relinquish*
lower one's tone 806.20 *submit*
lower one's voice 424.5 *sound
faint*
lower orders 127.6 *inferior*,
803.2 *the common people*
lower plant **83**
lower standards 362.4 *debase*
lower status 701.1 *subjection*
lower the body 399.8 *bury*
lower the flag **362**
lower the official rate of exchange 747.12 *devalue the currency*
lower the price 754.13 *make
cheap*
lower the standard 362.10 *lower
the flag*
lower the tone 795.10 *vulgarize*
Lower Triassic **54** Geological
Time Intervals
lower world 8.11 *heaven*, 368.1
nonmaterial world
lowest 52.75 *equal*, 127.12 *inferior*, 276.6 *lower*, 277.10 *deeper*,
280.3 *base*
lowest common denominator
164.6 *average*, 522.10 *simplicity*
lowest common multiple 52.17
multiplication
low esteem 850.3 *contempt*,
852.2 *disrespect*
lowest level 276.3 *lowest point*,
280.1 *base*
lowest of the low 127.6 *inferior*
Lowestoft ware **44** Types of Ceramics
lowest point **276**, 127.5 *inferior
state*, 172.4 *zero level*, 280.1
base
low-fat 350.27 *edible*, 625.4 *hygienic*
low-fat diet 350.6 *nutrition*
low-fat food 350.7 *food*
low frequency **534** Radio-
frequency Bands
low gear 328.10 *slow motion*
Low German **5** Languages and
Groups of Languages

low grade 618.8 *inferiority*,
754.10 *shoddy*
low-grade 127.12, 618.2 *inferior*
low-grade rock 54.33 *metamorphic rock*
low-heeled 276.5 *low*
low heels 276.4 *low thing*
low-hung 276.5 *low*
low income 743.5 *poverty*
low-inside 28.3 *fencing movements*, 28.6 *fencing*, 28.7 *on
guard*
low in tone 447.2 *dark*
low IQ 460.1 *lack of intellect*,
508.1 *folly*
low key 66.8 *composition*
low-key 242.6 *moderate*
lowland **98, 276**, 98.11 *continental*, 249.16 *regional*
lowlander 255.5 *countryman*
Lowlander 91.11 *Scotland*
lowlands **276**, 249.6 *regions*
low language 5.19 *swearword*
low-level 276.5 *low*, 612.3 *secondary*
low-level bombing 670.13 *air attack*
low-level flying 73.5 *flight*
low-level language 65.9 *programming language*
low-level waste 56.74 *nuclear
waste*
low life 127.6 *inferior*, 127.15
subordinate, 801.2 *disreputable
character*, 806.8 *lowliness*,
864.10 *bad person*
lowliness **806**, 127.1 *inferiority*,
556.4 *simplicity*, 758.4 *unpleasantness*
low-loader **71** Motor Vehicles,
72.6 *rolling stock*
lowly **806**, 556.1 *simple*, 612.2
obscure, 673.5 *submitting*,
758.2 *unpleasant*
low-lying 276.7 *lowland*
low man on the totem pole 701.3
subordinate
Low Mass 10.6 *Eucharist*
low mental age 460.1 *lack of intellect*
low-necked 276.5 *low*, 296.10 *in
dishabille*
lowness **276**, 127.5 *inferior
state*, 270.1 *shortness*, 427.3
deepness, 428.3 *muteness*,
430.2 *hoarseness*, 618.10 *poverty*, 754.3 *shoddiness*, 770.2 *depression*
Lowness **276**
low note 49.21 *tone*, 427.3 *deepness*
low on 609.1 *insufficient*
low opinion 850.3 *contempt*,
852.2 *disrespect*
low-outside 28.3 *fencing movements*, 28.6 *fencing*, 28.7 *on
guard*
lowpaid 743.1 *poor*
low-pass filter 64.22 *transformer*
low pay 609.8 *insufficiency*,
743.5 *poverty*
low pitch 49.21 *tone*
low point 127.5 *inferior state*
low post 23.4 *playing terms*
low pressure 372.3 *sparseness*
low-pressure 372.1 *sparse*
low-price 754.9 *cheap*
low-priced 612.4 *trivial*
low price tag 754.1 *cheapness*
low profile 438.4 *invisibility*
low-profile 438.2 *difficult to see*,
542.15 *reserved*
low quality 618.8 *inferiority*,
754.10 *shoddy*
low-quality 618.2 *inferior*
low rate 751.3 *fee*
low reading age 460.1 *lack of intellect*
low relief 50.13 *relief-carving*,
767.6 *profile*
low resolution 136.1 *separation*
low-resolution 136.19 *separable*
low-rise 43.12 *structural*, 276.5
low
low-rise building 43.3 *building*
Lowry **48** Writers
Lowry–Brønsted acid 57.8 *acid*

Lowry–Brønsted base 57.9 *base*
Lowry–Brønsted theory **57**
Named Reactions
low-salt 625.4 *hygienic*
low-salt food 350.7 *food*
low saturation 56.28 *colour*
low-set 276.5 *low*
low-slung 276.5 *low*
low-spirited 105.8 *in a state of*
low spirits 105.4 *state of mind*,
770.2 *depression*
low standard 618.8 *inferiority*,
620.5 *imperfection*
low-standard 618.2 *inferior*
low tar 413.7 *tobacco*
low-tar 413.11 *tobacco*
low tech 603.5 *mechanics*
low-tech 243.11 *productive*
low technology 243.2 *manufacture*, 603.5 *mechanics*
low-technology 243.11 *productive*
low temperature 409.1 *coldness*
low-temperature physics 56.3
modern physics
low thing **276**
low tide 54.15, 97.2 *tide*, 276.3
lowest point, 278.4 *shallow thing*
low-toned 447.2 *dark*
low turnout 182.1 *few*
low vacuum 57.20 *surface chemistry*
low visibility 441.2 *murk*
low voice 427.3 *deepness*, 563.4
whispering
low-voiced **563**
low volume 424.1 *faintness*
low water 97.2 *tide*, 276.3 *lowest
point*, 278.4 *shallow thing*,
609.9 *scarcity*, 743.6 *insolvency*
low-water mark 302.2 *limiting
factor*
low-weight 370.1 *light*
low yield 247.1 *infertility*
low-yield 247.3 *birth control*
lox 45.16 *fish dish*, 409.4 *cooler*,
410.3 *gas*
loyal **694, 847**, 138.10 *tenacious*, 490.6 *infallible*, 537.26
faithful, 658.1 *naive*, 719.7 *observant*, 819.11 *devoted*, 821.17
loving, 857.4 *honourable*
loyal customer 738.12 *purchaser*
loyal devotion 784.1 *liking*
loyalist 167.6 *conformist*, 665.6
political party member, 694.4
obedient person
loyally 138.12 *tenaciously*,
694.10 *obediently*, 719.8 *observantly*, 819.19 *devotedly*,
847.18 *on duty*, 857.7 *honourably*
loyal party member 694.4 *obedient person*
loyal support 819.1 *friendship*
loyal supporter 575.5 *tenacious
person*
loyalty **694**, 138.2 *tenacity*,
490.17 *infallibility*, 537.13
faithfulness, 719.1 *observance*,
821.1 *love*, 847.3 *allegiance*,
849.3 *respectfulness*, 857.1 *probity*
loyalty oath 535.3 *vow*
Loyolite **7** Members of Religious Orders
lozenge 52.44 *polygon*, 62.6 *pill*,
310.3 *angled figure*, 544.8 *heraldic device*, 630.2 *medicine*
Lozi **1** Peoples, **5** Languages
and Groups of Languages
LP 545.7 *recording*
L position 30.7 *stationary rings*
LSD **62** Medication, 875.6 *drug*
LSI 64.13 *circuit*
Lualaba **96** Rivers
Luanda **93** Cities
Luba **5** Languages and Groups
of Languages
lubber 656.10 *unskilled person*
lubber line 332.3 *orientation*
lubberliness 656.8 *unskilfulness*
lubberly 656.3 *clumsy*
Lubbock **93** Cities
lube 386.1, 395.3 *lubrication*
Lübeck **93** Cities
Lublin **93** Cities
lubricant 386, **386**, 395, **395**,

376.10 *polish*, 424.2 *sound re-ducer*
lubricate 386, 374.13 *soften*, 376.11 *smooth*, 395.17 *oil*, 660.16 *make easy*
lubricated 386, 395, 376.4 *pol-ished*, 660.12 *wieldy*
lubricating 242.8 *moderating*, 386.1 *lubrication*, 386.9 *lubri-cant*, 395.3 *lubrication*, 395.13 *lubricant*
lubricating agent 386.4, 395.5 *lu-bricant*
lubricating oil 386.4, 395.5 *lubri-cant*
lubrication 386, 395, 376.7 *smoothness*
Lubrication 386
lubricational 386.9, 395.13 *lubri-cant*
lubricative 386.9, 395.13 *lubri-cant*
lubricator 386, 376.10 *polish*, 386.4, 395.5 *lubricant*
lubricatory 386.9, 395.13 *lubri-cant*
lubricious 376.4 *polished*, 877.12 *indecent*
lubricitate 386.13 *lubricate*
lubricity 376.7 *smoothness*, 386.1 *lubrication*, 395.1 *oili-ness*, 877.3 *sexual immorality*
lubrification 386.1, 395.3 *lubrica-tion*
lubrify 386.13 *lubricate*, 395.17 *oil*
lubritary 395.5 *lubricant*
lubritorium 71.21 *miscellaneous motoring terms*, 395.5 *lubricant*
Lubumbashi 93 Cities
Lucan 48 Poets
lucency 439.1 *light*
lucent 439, 442.2 *translucent*
lucerne 68.12 *crop*, 350.8 *animal food*
Lucerne 93 Cities, **94** Lakes
lucid 4.15 *rational*, 437.2 *clear*, 439.22 *enlightened*, 442.4 *easily seen through*, 509.5 *rational*, 520.6 *meaningful*, 522.2 *sim-ple*, 550.3 *clear*
lucidity 4.3 *detachment*, 442.10 *openness*, 509.2 *rationality*, 522.10 *simplicity*, 550.1 *clarity*, 660.2 *simplicity*
lucidly 4.26 *rationally*, 509.7 *sanely*, 522.13 *intelligibly*, 550.4 *clearly*
lucifer 410.2 *lighter*, 439.8 *fire*
Lucifer 8.6 *angel*, 8.7 *devil*, 53.10 *star*
luck 589, 106.5 *comfortable cir-cumstances*, 210.2 *opportunity*, 224.3 *changeable thing*, 229.2 *chance*, 486.3 *strong possibility*, 682.1 *success*, 686.2 *good for-tune*
luckily 229, 489, 106.18 *com-fortably*, 210.9 *opportunely*, 589.13 *by chance*, 682.16 *suc-cessfully*, 686.9 *prosperously*
luckiness 106.5 *comfortable cir-cumstances*
luckless 687.8 *unlucky*
Lucknow 93 Cities
luck of the draw 589.2 *luck*, 686.2 *good fortune*
luck on one's side 589.2 *luck*
luck piece 11.6 *talisman*
lucky 106.9 *comfortable*, 210.6 *timely*, 229.7 *adventurous*, 589.8 *chance*, 682.13 *success-ful*, 686.8 *prosperous*, 861.1 *good*
lucky bean 11.6 *talisman*
lucky break 210.2 *opportunity*, 229.3 *coincidence*, 322.10 *oppor-tunity*, 682.1 *success*, 686.2 *good fortune*
lucky charm 11.6 *talisman*
lucky devil 686.4 *prosperous per-son*
lucky dip 113.3 *diverse thing*, 133.3 *miscellany*, 589.3 *equal chance*, 749.5 *winnings*
lucky dog 589.15 *good luck*, 686.4 *prosperous person*
lucky draw 749.5 *winnings*

lucky fellow 686.4 *prosperous per-son*
lucky find 130.4 *extra*, 496.10 *find*
lucky man 714.6 *someone prom-ised*, 821.11 *loved one*
lucky shot 229.3 *coincidence*, 489.5 *unexpectedness*, 589.2 *luck*, 686.2 *good fortune*
lucky strike 229.3 *coincidence*, 589.2 *luck*, 686.2 *good fortune*
lucky stroke 682.1 *success*
lucrative 243.11 *productive*, 246.5 *fertile*, 613.4 *profitable*, 682.14 *rewarding*, 721.15 *gain-ful*, 746.18 *profitable*, 878.15 *re-warding*
lucrative deal 721.1 *gain*
lucratively 682.16 *successfully*, 721.20 *gainfully*, 878.20 *profit-ably*
lucre 721.5 *profit*, 741.2 *cash*, 742.6 *money*
Lucretia 825.4 *celibate person*
Lucretian 4.11 *follower of a doc-trine*, 4.14 *of a philosophy*
Lucretius 4 Philosophers
Lucretius 48 Poets
lucubration 561.1 *dissertation*
Lucullan banquet 350.13 *feast*, 872.3 *act of gluttony*
Lucullus 350.18 *eater*, 872.4 *glut-ton*
Lüda 93 Cities
Luddite 244.6 *destroyer*, 693.10 *seditionist*
ludicrous 506.5 *nonsensical*, 508.5 *foolish*, 559.9 *inelegant*
ludicrously 508.8 *foolishly*
ludicrousness 798, 508.1 *folly*
Ludjatako 8 Deities
ludo 42 Board Games, **42** Children's Games and Party Games
luff 74.9 *navigate*, 36.15 *sail*
luffing 36.1, 36.10 *sailing*
luff-tackle 361.9 *lifter*
lug 322.4 *body orifice*, 326.12 *transport*, 339.2, 339.11 *pull*, 420.4 *ear*, 603.1 *tool*
Lug 8 Deities
Luganda 5 Languages and Groups of Languages
Lugano 93 Cities
luge 18 Sporting Activities, 41.9 *bobsledding* , 41.16 *bob-sled* , 71.10 *sled*
lugeing 41.9 *bobsledding* , 41.13 *ice-skating*
luge race 41.9 *bobsledding*
luge techniques 41.9 *bobsledding*
luggage 70.2 *thing transported*, 258.9 *baggage*, 326.10 *trans-ferred thing*, 725.4 *possessions*
luggage label 544.3 *means of identification*
luggage rack 258.10 *cart*
luggage trolley 71.7 *handcart*
luggage van 72.6 *rolling stock*
lugger 74, 74 Sailing Ships and Boats, 36.2 *sailing boat*
lughole 420.4 *ear*
lugsail 74 Sails, 36.3 *parts of a sailing boat*
lugubrious 770.6 *depressed*
lugubriously 770.12 *joylessly*
lugworm 81 Worms
Luing 68 Breeds of Cattle
Lukacs 4 Philosophers
lukewarm 124.3 *mediocre*, 333.4 *middle*, 573.3 *cautious*, 717.8 *ir-resolute*, 783.7 *indifferent*
lukewarmly 717.10 *irresolutely*
lukewarmness 333.2 *middle of the road*, 408.1 *heat*, 576.14 *ap-athy*, 717.3 *irresolution*, 783.1 *indifference*
lukewarm support 854.1 *dispar-agement*
lull 160.3, 185.6 *interval*, 209.3 *delayed action*, 218.3 *pause*, 242.4 *moderate*, 325.1 *motion-lessness*, 325.2 *repose*, 325.9 *make motionless*, 422.2, 422.4 *silence*, 643.5 *inactivity*, 649.1 *ease*, 651.6 *refresher*, 677.1 *paci-*

fication, 765.9 *comfort*, 767.1 *ease*
lullaby 242.2 *moderator*, 433.2 *song*
lull in hostilities 675.1 *peace*
Lullism 7 Christian Movements
lulu 789.3 *attractive female*
lumache 45 Types of Pasta
Luma white 446.8 *whitener*
lumbago 406.2 *painful condition*, 624.16 *rheumatism*
lumbar 304.4 *rear*
lumbar puncture 60.7 *diagnosis*
lumbar region 304.2 *rear end*
lumber 47.12 *wood*, 63.25*con-struction material*, 85.3 *timber*, 85.18 *manage trees*, 132.2 *re-sidue*, 151.4 *litter*, 362.2 *flatten*, 614.6 *refuse*, 656.7 *be clumsy*
lumbered with 661.14 *blocked*
lumberer 85.8 *forester*
lumbering 85.6 *tree manage-ment*, 259.17 *stocky*, 328.4 *slow*, 328.10 *slow motion*, 616.1 *inconvenient*, 656.3, 659.15 *clumsy*
lumberjack 85.8 *forester*, 295.11 *jacket*, 410.9 *power-worker*
lumber-jacket 295.11 *jacket*
lumber room 256.7 *room*
lumber yard 85.7 *timber produc-tion*
lumbricoid 81.20 *wormlike*
lumen 75 SI Units, **75** Scien-tific and Technical Units
Lumière 52 Scientists
luminance 56.24 *light emission*
luminary 53.10 *star*
luminescence 56.24 *light emis-sion*, 439.1 *light*
Luminists 50 Schools and Groups of Artists
luminosity 53, 439.1 *light*, 444.3 *hue*, 446.12 *light*
luminosity class 53.13 *luminosity*
luminous 439.15 *lucent*, 446.6 *light*, 522.1 *intelligible*
luminous efficacy 56.24 *light emission*
luminous efficiency 56.24 *light emission*
luminous flux 56.24 *light emis-sion*
luminous glaze 444.4 *pigment*
luminously 439.30 *lightly*, 446.14 *whitely*
luminousness 439.1 *light*
Lummi 1 Peoples
lump 143.7 *piece*, 227.3 *growth*, 259.7 *mass*, 369.4 *heaviness*, 371.4 *solid body*, 373.7 *hard substance*, 624.3 *symptom*, 656.10 *unskilled person*
lumpectomy 60 Surgical Opera-tions
lumpfish caviar 45.16 *fish dish*
lumpily 375.14 *roughly*
lumpiness 259.6 *squatness*, 369.4 *heaviness*, 373.5 *hard-ness*, 375.6 *roughness*
lumpish 240.5 *inert*, 259.17 *stocky*, 369.1 *heavy*
lumpishness 259.6 *squatness*, 549.3 *inelegance*
lump it 673.4 *succumb*
lumpsucker 80 Fishes
lump sum 741.5 *sum*
lump together 135.8 *unite*, 140.5 *combine*, 482.11 *not discrimi-nate*
lumpy 259.17 *stocky*, 369.1 *heavy*, 371.7 *condensed*, 373.1 *hard*, 375.2 *coarse*, 393.20 *thick*
Luna 8 Deities
lunacy 508.1 *folly*, 510.1 *insanity*
luna moth 82 Insects
lunar 53.36 *astronomical*, 97.7 *oceanic*, 311.4 *curved*
lunar base 53.31 *space travel*
lunar eclipse 53.17 *moon*, 440.1 *darkness*
lunar landscape 247.1 *infertility*
lunar module 53.30 *spacecraft*
lunar month 53.17 *moon*, 185.4 *term*
lunar motion 365.1 *oscillation*
lunar tide 97.2 *tide*

lunate 52.81 *curvilinear*
lunatic 61.8 *disordered personal-ity*, 508.5 *foolish*, 510.7 *insane person*
lunatic asylum 510.8 *mental hos-pital*
lunatic fringe 335.19 *deviant per-son*, 665.3 *political grouping*
lunch 350.12 *meal*, 350.24 *have a meal*
lunch counter 350.15 *eating place*
luncheon 350.12 *meal*
luncheonette 350.15 *eating place*
luncher 350.18 *eater*
lunching 350.4 *eating meals*
lunch party 665.7 *social gathering*
lunchroom 350.15 *eating place*
Lunda 1 Peoples
Lundy Island 32 Breeds of Horse and Pony
lune 52.42 *circle*
Lune 96 Rivers
Lüne 96 Rivers
lunette 43.9 *miscellaneous archi-tectural features*, 671.8 *military defences*
lung 290.4 *insides*, 390.8 *respira-tion*
lung cancer 413.8 *smoking*, 624.9 *respiratory disease*, 624.12 *cancer*
lunge 26.15 *wrestling*, 28.3 *fenc-ing movements*, 28.5 *fence*, 329.4 *be swift*, 670.6 *stab*, 670.18 *hit*
lunge punch 26.9 *tae kwon do*
lungfish 80 Fishes
lungi 295.25 *accessories*
lunging 28.6 *fencing*
lungs 423.4 *sound maker*
lungs of brass 423.4 *sound maker*
lungworm 81 Worms
lungwort 84 Flowers and Flow-ering Plants
lunker 259.9 *big thing*
Lun-yu 7.12 *religious text*
Luo 1 Peoples, **5** Languages and Groups of Languages
Lupercalia 10.6 *religious festival*
lupin 84 Flowers and Flowering Plants, 68.12 *crop*
lupine 77.28 *carnivorous*
lupus 624.13 *skin disease*
Lupus 53 The Constellations
lur 49 Musical Instruments
lurch 36.16 *row*, 215.1 *irregular-ity*, 215.6 *be irregular*, 360.11 *trip*, 365.4, 365.11 *rock*, 366.11 *stagger*, 366.25 *pitch*, 874.7 *be drunk*
lurcher 77.9 *dog*
lurching 215.1 *irregularity*, 215.4 *irregular*, 360.18 *falling*, 365.16 *rocking*
lure 340, 340, 20.2 *artificial fly*, 228.2 *inducement*, 228.5 *positive stimulus*, 228.10 *manip-ulate*, 233.8 *influence*, 539.13, 539.33 *snare*, 586.3 *incentive*, 586.9 *enticement*, 586.16 *tempt*, 710.9 *offer*, 782.5 *object of desire*, 782.15 *cause desire*, 821.26 *court*, 878.4 *reward for service*
lured 228.12 *motivated*
Lurex 439.2 *quality of light*, 439.16 *bright*
Lurgan 93 Cities
lurid 437.2 *clear*, 439.16 *bright*, 444.12 *gaudy*, 445.8 *drained of colour*, 811.21 *blatant*
luridly 811.37 *blatantly*
luridness 811.6 *blatancy*
lurk 240.4 *be inert*, 438.7 *be-come invisible*, 458.1 *disappear*, 527.13 *hide*, 657.5 *be cunning*
lurker 657.3 *cunning person*
lurking 438.1 *invisible*, 527.2 *concealed*, 527.8 *concealment*
lurk in the shadows 440.12 *be dark*
Lusaka 93 Cities
Lusatian 5 Languages and Groups of Languages
Lüscher colour test 61.5 *psycho-logical test*

luscious 405.6 *pleasant*, 763.4 *tasty*
lusciousness 763.9 *tastiness*
lush 742, 83.13 *plantlike*, 246.5 *fertile*, 351.12 *drinker*, 405.6 *pleasant*, 608.2 *plentiful*, 789.5 *beautiful*, 874.8 *get drunk*, 874.14 *drinking bout*
lushed 874.3 *dead drunk*
lushness 246.1 *fertility*, 608.8 *plenty*
Lüshun 93 Cities
Lusitano 32 Breeds of Horse and Pony
lust 782.1 *desire*, 782.4 *sexual desire*, 821.2 *romantic love*, 821.5 *desire*, 864.2 *vice*, 864.5 *seven deadly sins*, 877.3 *sexual immorality*
lust after 782.12 *desire*, 782.13 *like*, 842.3 *be envious of*
lustful 782, 821.20 *amorous*, 864.12 *immoral*, 877.14 *lecherous*
lustfully 782, 821.30 *lovingly*, 864.20 *immorally*
lustily 237.15 *acutely*, 239.6 *with vigour*, 423.9 *loudly*, 644.12 *laboriously*
lustiness 239.1 *vigour*
lusting 203.17 *in season*
lustral 134.15 *purifying*, 621.18 *cleansing*, 840.4 *atoning*
lustrate 134.10, 621.15 *purify*
lustration 10.5 *Christian rite*, 134.2 *purification*, 621.3 *religious cleansing*, 840.2 *apology*
lustrational 840.4 *atoning*
lustrative 840.4 *atoning*
lustre 376.7 *smoothness*, 439.1 *light*, 439.2 *quality of light*
lustreless 441.7 *dimmed*, 443.2 *shady*, 445.7 *colourless*
lustreware 44.1 *ceramics*
lustrous 439
lusty 237.9 *physically strong*, 239.4 *vigorous*, 259.17 *stocky*, 423.6 *loud*, 623.1 *healthy*
lute 49 Musical Instruments, 44.11 *make ceramics*, 138.3 *adhesive*, 138.7 *cause to adhere*
luteal 352.5 *of a secretion*
luteinizing hormone 58 Hormones
luteolin 452.7 *yellow pigment*
luteotrophic hormone 58 Hormones
luteous 452.2 *yellowish*
lutetium 57 Chemical Elements
Lutheran 7.5 *Christian*
Lutheranism 7 Christian Movements
Lutine bell 543.4 *signal*
luting 44.5 *ceramic process*
Luton 93 Cities
lux 75 SI Units
luxate 252.18 *disconnect*
luxation 252.5 *disconnection*
Luxembourg 91 Countries, **93** Cities
Luxor 93 Cities
luxuriance 246.1 *fertility*, 608.8 *plenty*, 610.1 *excess*
luxuriant 83.13 *plantlike*, 246.5 *fertile*, 371.6 *dense*, 405.6 *pleasant*, 557.4 *ornate*, 608.2 *plentiful*, 610.6 *excessive*, 811.24 *grand*
luxuriantly 608.9 *enough*, 811.40 *grandly*
luxuriate 405.8 *feel pleasure*, 608.5 *about*, 610.4 *be excessive*
luxuriate in 870.10 *indulge oneself*
luxuriating 608.2 *plentiful*
luxuries 350.7 *food*
luxurious 405.6 *pleasant*, 686.8 *prosperous*, 742.3 *opulent*, 811.24 *grand*
luxuriously 405.11 *pleasingly*, 686.9 *prosperously*, 742.16 *wealthily*, 811.40 *grandly*
luxuriousness 610.3 *superfluity*, 811.9 *grandeur*
luxury 405.1 *physical pleasure*, 608.8 *plenty*, 610.3 *superfluity*, 610.7 *superfluous*, 682.1 *suc-*

cess, 686.1 *prosperity*, 742.7 *opulence*, 753.7 *dear*, 763.7 *pleasure*, 763.10 *pleasant thing*, 811.9 *grandeur*, 870.1 *self-indulgence*
luxury article 610.3 *superfluity*
luxury car 610.3 *superfluity*
luxury coach 71.19 *bus*
luxury flat 610.3 *superfluity*
luxury goods 405.4 *pleasurable things*
luxury hotel 610.3 *superfluity*
luxury price 753.1 *high price*
Luyten 53 Named Stars
Luzon 98 Islands
Lvov 93 Cities
LW transmitter 534.16 *transmitter*
lyase 58.11 *enzyme*
lyceum 6.12 *educational institution*
lychgate 346.6 *means of entry*
Lycian 5 Languages and Groups of Languages
lycine 58 Amino Acids
lycopod 88.1 *fern*
lycopodium 88.1 *fern*
lycopsid 88.1 *fern*
Lycra 67 Synthetic Fibres and Fabrics, 377.3 *elastic thing*
lyddite 680.15 *explosive*
Lydian 5 Languages and Groups of Languages
Lydian mode 49.20 *key*
lye 62 Medication, 387.10 *solution*
Lyell 52 Scientists
lying 282, 538, 538, 540, 30.6 *pommel horse*, 282.1 *horizontality*, 309.8 *exaggerated*, 474.10 *hypocritical*, 525.2 *misinterpretation*, 539.1 *deception*, 540.5 *deceitfulness*, 540.29 *deceitful*, 858.5 *dishonourable*
lying down 276.1 *lowness*, 276.5 *low*, 282.10 *lying*, 673.5 *submitting*
lying flat 282.10 *lying*
lying-in 245.7 *obstetrics*
lying-in-state 399.2 *funeral*
lying in wait 635.1 *trap*
lying low 527.2 *concealed*
lying on the ball 35.3 *rugby play*
Lyle 18 Sporting Personalities
Lyly 48 Dramatists
Lyman series 56 Named Laws
lyme grass 87 Grasses
Lymeswold 45 Cheeses
lymph 387.3 *body fluid*
lymphadenectomy 60 Surgical Operations
lymphocyte 387.4 *blood*
lymphogram 60.7 *diagnosis*
lymphography 60.7 *diagnosis*
lymphoma 624.11 *blood disease*
lynch 398.19 *execute*, 852.23 *show disapproval*, 879.5 *execute*
lyncher 879.17 *punisher*
lynch him 879.24 *string him up*
lynching 398.5 *execution*, 879.13 *capital punishment*
lynch law 16.41 *lawlessness*, 689.1 *anarchy*, 879.13 *capital punishment*
lynoestrenol 62 Medication
lynx 77 Placental Mammals, 435.2 *eye*
Lynx 53 The Constellations, **53** The Constellations
lynx-eyed 435.21 *seeing*, 841.4 *jealous*
Lyon King of Arms 544.9 *herald*
Lyonnesse 519.8 *dreamland*
Lyons 93 Cities
lyophilic 57.32 *solid*
lyophilic colloid 57.3 *phase*
lyophobic 57.32 *solid*
lyophobic colloid 57.3 *phase*
Lyotard 4 Philosophers
lyra 49 Musical Instruments
Lyra 53 The Constellations
lyre 49 Musical Instruments
Lyre 53 The Constellations
lyrebird 78 Birds
lyrenaic philosophy 4.7 *school of thought*
lyric 48.7 *poem*, 49.30 *harmonic*, 433.2 *song*

lyrical 48.19 *narrative*, 433.6 *melodious*
lyrical abstraction 50 Western Art Styles and Movements
lyrically 48.22 *poetically*, 433.11 *melodiously*
lyricist 48.14 *author*, 49.24 *musician*, 433.5 *melodist*
lyric poet 48.14 *author*
lyric poetry 48.6 *poetry*
Lyrids 53 Meteor Showers
Lysenko 52 Scientists
Lysenkoism 59.16 *evolution*
lysosome 59.8 *cell organ*
lysozyme 58.11 *enzyme*
Lyssa 8 Deities
lyssophobia 777 Phobias by Name

M

M 875.6 *drug*
M1A1 679.21 *armoured cavalry*
M-1 rifle 680.11 *guns*
M25 363.5 *ringroad*
M-60 machine gun 680.11 *guns*
Ma 8 Deities
Maahes 8 Deities
ma'am 402.3 *female title of address*
maarib 10.4 *public worship*
Maas 96 Rivers
Maastricht 93 Cities
Maat 8 Deities
Mab 11.11 *ghost*
mac 295.12 *coat*
Mac 401.3 *male title of address*
macadam 45.51 *West Indian dish*, 293.11 *paving*, 604.2 *building material*
McAdam 52 Scientists
macadamia nut 86 Nuts
macadamize 293.29 *surface*
macaque 77 Placental Mammals
macaroni 45 Types of Pasta
macaroni cheese 45.34 *vegetarian dish*
macaronics 48.6 *poetry*
macaroon 45.36 *cake*
macassar 386.5 *ointment*
Macau Grand Prix 33.5 *motorcycle racing*
Macaulay 48 Writers
macaw 78 Birds
Macbeth 48 Shakespeare's plays
McBride 18 Sporting Personalities
McCarthy 48 Writers
McCarthyism 481.4 *social discrimination*, 590.1 *pursuit*
maccheronici 45 Types of Pasta
McCullers 48 Writers
Macdiarmid 48 Poets
McDonald's 350.15 *eating place*
Macdonnell 95 Mountains
mace 45 Herbs and Spices, 330.16 *weapons*, 413.5 *herbs*, 544.4 *insignia*, 680.7 *blunt weapon*
Mace 231.2 *counteracting thing*, 631.10 *warfare*, 671.5 *self-defence*
macebearer 16.10 *law officer*
macedoine 45.14 *salad*
Macedonian 5 Languages and Groups of Languages
Macedonianism 7 Christian Movements
macerate 374.13 *soften*, 389.31 *steep*
macerated 609.3 *underfed*
maceration 389.10 *steeping*, 393.5 *pulping*, 840.2 *apology*
macerator 393.15 *pulper*
McEwan 48 Writers
Mach 52 Scientists
Mach 1 56.19 *sound propagation*
Macha 8 Deities
macher 611.4 *bigwig*
machete 49 Musical Instruments, 380.10 *knife*, 680.8 *sharp weapon*

Machiavelli 592.8 *planner*, 657.3 *cunning person*
Machiavellian 538.19 *dishonest*, 540.25 *false*, 592.15 *planning*, 657.4 *cunning*
Machiavellianism 538.10 *dishonesty*, 540.1 *falsehood*, 657.1 *cunning*
machicolated 671.30 *defended*
machicolation 671.11 *fortification*
machinate 474.11 *practise sophistry*, 539.28 *trick*, 592.13 *plot*
machination 474.3 *cunning*, 539.4 *false-heartedness*, 539.7 *tricking*, 592.4 *plot*, 657.2 *stratagem*
machinator 539.20 *plotter*
machine 603, 56.11 *energy*, 63.5 *dynamic structure*, 65.3 *computer*, 232.2 *instrument*, 243.2 *manufacture*, 243.10 *produce*, 603.1 *tool*
machine code 5.8 *artificial language*, 65.9 *programming language*
machine-design engineering 63.3 *mechanical engineering*
machine element 63
machine gun 244.7 *agent of destruction*, 680.11 *guns*
machine-gun fire 670.15 *firing*
machine-gunner 679.17 *army person*
machine knitting 67.5 *knitting*
machine loom 67.4 *weaving*
machine-made 243.12 *produced*
machine-milk 68.18 *practise livestock farming*
machine-minded 603.8 *mechanical*
machine-minder 603.7 *machinist*
machine part 63.8 *machine element*
machinery 777 Phobias by Topic, 63.5 *dynamic structure*, 148.4 *components*, 243.2 *manufacture*, 602.2 *supplies*, 603.4 *machine*
machine tool 63, 603.1 *tool*
machining 243.2 *manufacture*
machinist 603, 51.26 *stagehand*, 230.6 *operative*, 646.2 *artisan*
machismo 401.1 *male sex*, 811.23 *bravado*
Machmeter 73 Aircraft Parts
Mach number 56 Named Laws, **75** Scientific and Technical Units, 56.19 *sound propagation*, 329.8 *speed*
macho 401.17 *male*, 811.23 *brave*
macho man 401
machzor 10.10 *religious manual*
Macintosh 52 Scientists
Mackenzie 96 Rivers, 96.5 *other major rivers*
mackerel 80 Fishes, 20.4 *American game fish*, 20.5 *British game fish*, 45.18 *sea fish*, 80.8 *food fish*
mackerel shark 80 Fishes
mackerel sky 55.20 *cloud appearance*, 456.5 *variegated thing*
mackerel spinner 20.2 *artificial fly*
mackinaw 67 Natural Fabrics
Mackinaw coat 295.11 *jacket*
McKinley 95 Mountains, 275.3 *mountain*
mackintosh 67 Natural Fabrics, 295.12 *coat*
Maclaurin series 52 Named Concepts
McLeod gauge 57.20 *surface chemistry*
Maclisp 65 Programming Languages
McMillan 52 Scientists
McNaghten Rules 510.1 *insanity*
MacNeice 48 Poets
Mâcon 93 Cities
macramé 42 Hobbies and Pastimes, 288.2 *braid*, 288.8 *interweave*
macrobiotic diet 350.6 *nutrition*
macrocarpa 85 Trees and Shrubs
macroclimate 55.38 *climate*

macrocosm 53.3 *universe*, 142.2 *whole thing*
macroeconomics 13.1 *economics*
macro lens 66.17 *lens*
macrometeorology 55.1 *meteorology*
macromolecular structure 59.12 *molecular biology*
macromolecule 57.21 *polymer*, 59.12 *molecular biology*, 396.2 *living matter*
macron 5.36 *accent*, 543.7 *punctuation*
macronucleus 59.9 *cell nucleus*
macronutrient 58.15 *essential element*
macrophotography 66.1 *photography*
macroscopic 259.15 *big*
macroseism 54.22 *seismic activity*
macrosociology 2.1 *sociology*
Macuilxochitl 5 Deities
macula 456.4 *maculation*, 624.13 *skin disease*
macular 456.10 *mottled*
maculate 456.10 *mottled*, 456.11 *variegate*, 622.11 *dirty*
maculation 456
macumba 49.10 *world music*
mad 153.16 *deranged*, 241.6 *violent*, 506.5 *nonsensical*, 508.5 *foolish*, 510.11 *insane*, 579.1 *capricious*, 821.19 *enamoured*, 828.16 *angry*
mad about 821.18 *in love*
Madagascar 91 Countries, **98** Islands
Madagascar aquamarine 54 Gemstones
madam 696.1 *master*, 877.9 *immoral woman*
Madam 402.3 *female title of address*
madame 402.3 *female title of address*, 807.12 *impudent person*
Madame Tussaud's 605.5 *collection*
mad as a hatter 510.11 *insane*
mad as a hornet 828.16 *angry*
mad as a march hare 510.11 *insane*
mad as a wet hen 828.16 *angry*
madcap 241.4 *violent person or animal*, 508.4, 780.3 *rash person*, 780.4 *rash*
mad-cow disease 510.3 *mental deterioration*, 624.18 *veterinary disease*
mad dash 642.3 *nimbleness*
madden 241.9 *make violent*, 510.15 *make insane*, 820.13 *antagonize*, 828.14 *make angry*
maddened 241.6 *violent*
maddeningly 828.17 *resentfully*
madder 67.6 *dye*, 444.4 *pigment*, 450.6 *red pigment*
madding crowd 642.6 *business*
mad doctor 61.30, 510.10 *psychiatrist*
mad dog 241.4 *violent person or animal*
made 99.15 *created*, 243.12 *produced*, 306.9 *formed*
made a joke of 539.36 *deceived*
made easier 660.11 *made easy*
made easy 660, 522.2 *simple*
made in heaven 632.6 *invulnerable*
madeira 351.9 *wine*
Madeira 96 Rivers, **98** Islands
Madeira cake 45.36 *cake*
made law 16.46 *legislated*
made legal 688.16 *authorized*
madeleine 45.36 *cake*
made light of 542.19 *downplayed*
made man 336.16 *progressive person*
made man and wife 823.21 *married*
mademoiselle 206.8 *young woman*, 402.3 *female title of address*
made of money 742.1 *wealthy*
made one 823.21 *married*
made over 728.5 *transferring*
made public 475.9 *demonstrated*,

526.13 *displayed*, 532.19 *published*
made ready 594.18 *prepared*
made redundant 727.13 *dismissed*
made simple 522.2 *simple*
made sport of 539.36 *deceived*
made to feel at home 815.16 *popular*
made to grovel 701.9 *subject*
made to measure 165.20 *personalized*
made-to-measure 295.31 *styled*
made-to-order 295.31 *styled*
made-up 45.56 *culinary*, 102.10 *theoretical*, 135.12 *united*, 257.10 *containing*, 540.32 *falsified*
made up of 146.7 *including*
madhouse 151.5 *confusion*, 510.8 *mental hospital*
Madhva 7 Non-Christian Religions
Madison 93 Cities
Madison Avenue 586.6 *advertising*
madly 510.17 *insanely*, 821.30 *lovingly*
madman 241.4 *violent person or animal*, 510.7 *insane person*
madness 153.6 *derangement*, 508.1 *folly*, 510.1 *insanity*
Madonna 8.10 *deified person*
Madonna lily 84 Flowers and Flowering Plants
mad race 642.3 *nimbleness*
madras 67 Natural Fabrics, 45.49 *Indian dish*, 288.4 *textile*
Madras 93 Cities, 413.2 *seasoning*
Madrid 93 Cities, 93.6 *other cities*
madrigal 48.7 *poem*, 49.3 *classical music*, 315.7 *round*, 433.2 *song*
madroña 85 Trees and Shrubs
mad round 815.3 *meeting*
mad scramble 642.3 *nimbleness*
Madura 98 Islands
Madura foot 89.5 *fungal association*
Madurese 5 Languages and Groups of Languages
madwoman 510.7 *insane person*
mae-geri 26.8 *karate*
maelstrom 96.6 *river flow*, 364.4 *vortex*, 366.2 *tumult*, 635.1 *trap*, 642.1 *activity*
Maelstrom 96.6 *river flow*
maenad 874.17 *drunkard*
maestà 50.10 *art subject*
Maesteg 93 Cities
maestoso 49 Musical Terms
maestro 6.4 *educator*, 49.24 *musician*, 619.4 *perfectionist*, 655.4 *skilled person*, 688.11, 696.10 *expert*
Maeterlinck 48 Poets, **48** Dramatists
mae west 370.7 *light thing*
Mae West 39.3 *survival swimming*, 632.4 *safety device*
Maffei 1 53 Galaxies
Maffei 2 53 Galaxies
maffick 812.15 *celebrate*
mafficking 812.9 *rejoicing*
Mafia 529.7 *esotericism*
Mafia hit man 398.11 *murderer*
Mafia member 693.9 *criminal*
mafic rock 54.30 *igneous rock*
Mafikeng 93 Cities
mafioso 529.7 *esotericism*, 531.7 *concealer*, 662.6 *evil person*
Mafioso 693.9 *criminal*
maftir 7.8 *priest*
magazine 187.7 *periodical*, 532.5 *journal*, 605.4 *storage*, 680.4 *arsenal*, 680.9 *firearm*
magazine rifle 680.9 *firearm*
magazines 528.4 *mass communication*
magazine section 532.4 *newspaper*
magdalen 867.3 *penitent person*
Magdalena 96 Rivers
Magdeburg 93 Cities
mage 11.4 *witch*

magenta 56.28 *colour*, 450.1 *red*, 455.6 *purple*
maggid 7.8 *priest*
Maggiore 94 Lakes
maggot 20.1 *angling*, 82.5 *larva*, 519.4 *ideality*, 579.3 *whim*
maggoty 82.12 *verminous*, 622.8 *unclean*
magianism 11.3 *witchcraft*
magic 777 Phobias by Topic, 11.1 *occultism*, 11.3 *witchcraft*, 102.3 *delusion*, 220.1 *conversion*, 233.2 *occult influence*, 235.1 *power*, 539.9 *sleight of hand*, 539.40 *illusory*, 617.1 *worthy*, 786.3 *wonder-working*, 786.8, 786.14 *wonderful*
magical 11.15 *witchlike*, 539.40 *illusory*
magically 11
magical power 235.1 *power*
magic belt 11.6 *talisman*
magic carpet 11.6 *talisman*, 329.11 *swift thing*, 396.6 *things brought to life*
magic circle 11.6 *talisman*
magician 11.4 *witch*, 51.27 *entertainer*, 216.6, 224.4 *editor*, 514.5 *surpriser*
magic lantern 66.12 *development*, 435.8 *reflection*
magic mushroom 89.2 *mushroom*, 875.6 *drug*
magic realism 48 Literary Groups and Movements, **50** Western Art Styles and Movements
magic ring 11.6 *talisman*
magic show 51.5 *show*
magic spell 11.5 *spell*, 233.2 *occult influence*
magic sword 11.6 *talisman*
magic symbol 543.1 *sign*
magic words 11.5 *spell*
Maginot line 298.1 *interface*
Maginot Line 671.9 *barrier*
magism 11.3 *witchcraft*
magisterial 12.10 *governing*, 16.49 *judicatory*, 126.13 *dominant*, 655.6 *skilful*, 696.12 *masterful*
magisterially 126.16 *superiorly*, 805.34 *imposingly*
magistracy 16.2 *jurisdiction*, 16.23 *judge*, 688.5 *position of authority*
magistral 696.12 *masterful*
magistrality 688.1 *authority*
magistrate 16.13 *lawyer*, 16.23 *judge*, 492.6 *justice*, 653.16 *official*, 688.10 *person of authority*, 696.3 *leader*, 879.17 *punisher*
magistrates' court 16.20 *British court*
magistrate's court 492.3 *place of judgment*
magma 54.24 *volcanic activity*, 133.2 *mixed thing*, 408.8 *hot place*
magma chamber 54.24 *volcanic activity*
magmatic 54.56 *petrographic*
magmatic rock 54.30 *igneous rock*
magmatism 54.29 *petrogenesis*
magmatite 54.34 *mineral*
Magna Carta 16.1 *the law*, 845.3 *prerogative*
magnanimity 755, 691.1 *leniency*, 831.2 *charity*, 839.2 *forgivingness*, 859.2 *unselfishness*, 863.1 *virtue*
magnanimous 755, 691.4 *lenient*, 831.7 *charitable*, 839.5 *merciful*, 859.5 *unselfish*, 863.5 *virtuous*
magnanimously 691.6 *leniently*, 831.11 *charitably*, 839.14 *forgivingly*, 859.9 *unselfishly*, 863.9 *virtuously*
magnate 611.4 *bigwig*, 721.7 *gainer*, 741.17 *financier*, 742.10 *wealthy person*
magnesia 57 Common Chemical Compounds
magnesite 54 Minerals
magnesium 57 Chemical Elements, 58.15 *essential element*

magnesium alloy 63.25 *construction material*
magnesium carbonate 62 Medication
magnesium hydroxide 62 Medication
magnesium sulphate 62 Medication
magnet 56, 339, 340, 138.3 *adhesive*
magnetic 339, 340, 56.98 *physical*, 228.11 *motivational*, 233.12 *appealing*, 235.16 *charged*, 586.19 *persuasive*
magnetic alloy 56.59 *ferromagnetism*
magnetically 339, 56.100 *physically*, 235.19 *energetically*, 340.13 *attractionally*
magnetic anomaly 54.44 *geomagnetism*
magnetic attaction 56.57 *magnetism*
magnetic card 56.64 *magnetic recording*
magnetic compass 74.5 *navigation*
magnetic constant 56.61 *magnetic quantity*
magnetic damping 56.63 *magnetic phenomenon*
magnetic declination 56.58 *geomagnetism*
magnetic deflection 56.63 *magnetic phenomenon*
magnetic dip 56.58 *geomagnetism*
magnetic dipole moment 56.61 *magnetic quantity*
magnetic disk 56.64 *magnetic recording*
magnetic epoch 56.58 *geomagnetism*
magnetic equator 54.45 *magnetic pole*, 56.58 *geomagnetism*
magnetic field 56.61 *magnetic quantity*, 235.4 *energy*
magnetic field strength 56.61 *magnetic quantity*
magnetic flux 56.61 *magnetic quantity*
magnetic focusing 56.63 *magnetic phenomenon*
magnetic force 235.4 *energy*
magnetic hysteresis 56.63 *magnetic phenomenon*
magnetic induction 56.61 *magnetic quantity*
magnetic ink 56.64 *magnetic recording*
magnetic ink character recognition 56.64 *magnetic recording*
magnetic iron ore 56.60 *magnet*
magnetic lens 56.63 *magnetic phenomenon*
magnetic levitation 56.63 *magnetic phenomenon*
magnetic memory 56.64 *magnetic recording*
magnetic meridian 56.58 *geomagnetism*
magnetic mine 680.16 *bomb*
magnetic mirror 56.63 *magnetic phenomenon*
magnetic moment 56.61 *magnetic quantity*
magnetic monopole 56.60 *magnet*
magnetic needle 74.5 *navigation*, 340.3 *magnet*, 543.5 *indicator*, 653.5 *guide*
magnetic North 56.58 *geomagnetism*, 332.4 *compass point*
magnetic North Pole 56.58 *geomagnetism*
magnetic personality 228.2 *inducement*, 233.3 *personal influence*
magnetic phenomenon 56
magnetic pole 54
magnetic potential difference 56.61 *magnetic quantity*
magnetic quantity 56
magnetic recording 56
magnetic repulsion 56.57 *magnetism*, 341.5 *repulsion*
magnetic resonance imaging 56.64 *magnetic recording*

magnetic reversal 54.44, 56.58 *geomagnetism*
magnetics 56.2 *classical physics*
magnetic separating 44.5 *ceramic process*
magnetic South 56.58 *geomagnetism*
magnetic South Pole 56.58 *geomagnetism*
magnetic storage 56.64 *magnetic recording*
magnetic storm 54.44, 56.58 *geomagnetism*, 241.5 *violent weather*, 366.13 *tempest*
magnetic stripe 56.64 *magnetic recording*
magnetic tape 56.64 *magnetic recording*, 545.6 *record book*, 545.7 *recording*
magnetic track 56.64 *magnetic recording*
magnetic variable 56.61 *magnetic quantity*
magnetism 56, 339, 56.2 *classical physics*, 228.2 *inducement*, 233 *influence*, 235.4 *energy*, 340.2 *pulling power*, 586.3 *incentive*
magnetite 54 Minerals, 57 Common Metal Ores, 56.60, 340.3 *magnet*
magnetization 56.61 *magnetic quantity*, 340.2 *pulling power*
magnetize 235.11 *give power*, 339.15 *pull towards*, 340.11 *attract*
magnetized 340.10 *magnetic*
magnetized iron 340.3 *magnet*
magnetizer 339.7 *magnet*
magnetizing coil 56.60 *magnet*
magneto 64.30 *generator*, 235.6 *source of energy*, 410.4 *electricity*
magnetohydrodynamically 56.100 *physically*
magnetohydrodynamic nonclassical 56.98 *physical*
magnetohydrodynamics 56.3 *modern physics*
magnetometer 56.90 *ammeter*, 268.8 *meter*
magnetometric 268.16 *micrometric*
magnetometry 268.2 *micrometry*
magnetomotive force 56.61 *magnetic quantity*
magneton 75 Scientific and Technical Units, 56.61 *magnetic quantity*
magneto-optical effect 56.63 *magnetic phenomenon*
magnetopause 54.44 *geomagnetism*
magnetosphere 53.16 *planet*, 54.44, 56.58 *geomagnetism*
magnetostriction 56.63 *magnetic phenomenon*
magnetron 64.20 *electron tube*
magnifiable 261.9 *enlargeable*
Magnificat 10.8 *hymn*, 837.2 *thanks*
magnification 8.9 *deification*, 9.1 *worship*, 10.3 *rite of worship*, 56.32 *optical instrument*, 128.1 *increase*, 261.1 *growth*, 435.10 *visual aid*, 541.2 *enlargement*, 768.1 *aggravation*
magnificence 617.6 *worth*, 789.1 *gorgeousness*, 811.9 *grandeur*, 861.8 *good*
magnificent 617.1 *worthy*, 811.24 *grand*, 861.1 *good*
magnificently 811.40 *grandly*, 861.22 *well*
magnified 8.15 *deified*, 128.7 *increased*, 261.7 *bigger*, 541.13 *enlarged*, 757.2 *unrestrained*, 768.4 *aggravated*
magnifier 435.10 *visual aid*
magnify 8.17 *deify*, 9.7 *worship*, 10.19 *offer worship*, 128.5, 261.5 *make bigger*, 261.6 *become bigger*, 541.8 *enlarge*, 611.8 *make important*, 768.6 *aggravate*, 851.14 *praise*
magnifying glass 435.10 *visual aid*
magnifying mirror 435.8 *reflection*

magnifying power 56.32 *optical instrument*
magniloquence 811, 541.4 *bombast*, 554.2 *seriousness*, 557.2 *affectation*, 564.2 *power of speech*
magniloquent 541.15 *bombastic*, 553.3 *diffuse*, 554.5 *serious*, 557.4 *ornate*, 564.20 *eloquent*
magniloquently 541.16 *exaggeratedly*, 554.7 *emphatically*, 557.6 *ornately*, 564.21 *orally*
magnitude 52.50 *scalar quantity*, 53.13 *luminosity*, 120.1 *quantity*, 121.1 *degree*, 233 *influence*, 259.1, 268.4 *size*, 611.1 *importance*
magnolia 84 Flowers and Flowering Plants, 446.1 *white*
magnolia metal 57 Alloys
magnox 57 Alloys
magnox reactor 56.73 *nuclear reactor*, 410.7 *nuclear power*
magnum 258.14 *bottle*
magnum opus 243.6 *great work*, 655.3, 696.11 *masterpiece*
magnus hitch 74 Knots
magpie 78 Birds, 78.6 *songbird*, 161.36 *hoarder*, 565.4 *talker*
Magpie 68 Breeds of Fowl
magpies 161 Collective Names by Animal
magsman 539.17 *cheat*
magus 11.4 *witch*
Magyar 5 Languages and Groups of Languages
Magyars 1 Peoples
Maha Bodhi 7 Non-Christian Religions
Mahadeva 8 Deities
Mahadevi 8 Deities
maharajah 653.14 *leader*, 696.2 *sovereign*
mahatma 11.12 *occultist*
Mahavastu 7.12 *religious text*
Mahayanan 7 Non-Christian Religions
Mahdi 653.14 *leader*
Mahfouz 48 Writers
Mahican 5 Languages and Groups of Languages
Mah Jong 42 Board Games
Mahler 49 Musicians and Composers
mahlstick 50.11 *artist's materials*
mahogany 85 Trees and Shrubs, 376.8 *smooth thing*, 449.1 *brown*
Mahon 5 Languages and Groups of Languages
maid 134.5 *pure person*, 206.8 *young woman*, 621.12 *cleaner*, 646.1 *worker*, 697.3 *attendant*, 697.6 *domestic servant*, 825.5 *single person*
maiden 27.8 *delivery*, 32.7 *horseracing*, 69.5 *gardening*, 85.1 *tree*, 134.5 *pure person*, 156.29 *beginning*, 201.12 *immature*, 206.8 *young woman*, 402.2 *female*, 402.15 *single girl*, 825.5 *single person*, 825.6 *celibate*, 876.5 *pure person*, 879.16 *instrument of execution*
Maiden 53 The Constellations
maiden aunt 174.7, 825.5 *single person*
maidenhair fern 88 Ferns
maidenhair tree 85 Trees and Shrubs
maidenhead 825.2 *virginity*, 876.3 *moral purity*
Maidenhead 93 Cities
maidenhood 206.1 *youth*, 698.3 *independence*, 825.2 *virginity*, 876.3 *moral purity*
maiden lady 825.5 *single person*
maidenliness 206.2 *youthfulness*
maidenly 201.24 *immaturely*, 206.11 *young*, 402.15 *female*, 825.6 *celibate*, 825.7 *virginal*, 876.9 *pure*
maiden name 560.8 *name*
maiden over 27.8 *delivery*
maiden race 32.7 *horseracing*
maiden speech 156.9 *premiere*

maiden voyage 156.9 *premiere*, 201.4 *beginning*
maid-in-waiting 697.6 *domestic servant*
maid of all work 642.10 *busy person*, 646.1 *worker*
maid of honour 819.6 *close friend*, 823.7 *bridal party*
maidservant 697.6 *domestic servant*
maids of honour 45.36 *cake*
Maidstone 93 Cities
maieusis 530.4 *discloser*
maieutic 232.7 *causal*, 473.2 *logical argument*, 530.11 *disclosing*
mail 70.2 *thing transported*, 293.12 *protective covering*, 326.10 *transferred thing*, 326.13 *post*, 534.3 *correspondence*, 534.31 *correspond*, 567.10 *send*, 632.4 *safety device*, 671.7 *armour*, 680.1 *weapon*
mailable 326.17 *transferable*
mailbag 534.3 *correspondence*
mail boat 74 Ships and Boats
mailbomb 680.16 *bomb*
mailbombing 670.16 *terrorist attack*
mailbox 65.12 *electronic office*, 534.3 *correspondence*
mail carrier 326.8 *messenger*, 534.4 *postal worker*
mail-clad 671.30 *defended*
mailcoach 72.6 *rolling stock*
mailed 671.30 *defended*
mailed fist 690.2 *suppression*
Mailer 48 Writers
mailing 326.2 *transportation*
mailing list 528.4 *mass communication*
mail-in vote 580.10 *vote*
maillot 295.21 *beachwear*
mailman 326.8 *messenger*, 534.4 *postal worker*
mail pouch 534.3 *correspondence*
mailsack 534.3 *correspondence*
mailshot 528.4 *mass communication*
mail train 72.7 *train*
mail van 72.6 *rolling stock*
mailwoman 534.4 *postal worker*
maim 236.8 *overpower*, 238.7 *weaken*, 628.5 *hurt*
maimed 145.4 *incomplete*, 620.3 *deformed*
Maimonides 3 Philosophers
main 70.5 *transportable*, 97.1 *sea*, 126.14 *best*, 291.8 *focal*, 327.15 *accessible*, 611.5 *important*, 696.12 *masterful*, 727.8 *sink*
Main 96 Rivers
main attraction 611.3 *chief thing*
main body 143.5 *largest part*, 679.14 *armed forces*
main chance 229.2, 488.4 *chance*, 589.5 *good chance*, 611.3 *chief thing*
main course 74 Sails, 45.9 *dish*, 350.14 *mouthful*
maincrop potatoes 68.12 *crop*
main deck 74 Parts of a Ship
main drag 327.5 *crossing*
Maine 92 American States
Maine Anjou 68 Breeds of Cattle
Maine lobster 45.43 *US dish*
main entrance 303.1 *front*
main feature 165.9 *special*, 611.3 *chief thing*
main force 235.1 *power*, 695.2 *coercion*
mainframe 65.3 *computer*
main interest 291.5 *focus*
mainland 54.6 *continent*
main line 72.2 *track*, 327.10 *railway*
mainline 875.10 *drug oneself*
mainliner 875.4 *drug taker*
main-line railway 72.1 *railway*
main-line station 72.8 *railway station*
mainlining 875.1 *drug-taking*
mainly 103.13 *in essence*, 124.11 *on average*, 126.16 *superiorly*, 142.13 *on the whole*, 156.42 *principally*, 164.31 *overall*,

166.18 *as a rule*, 611.9 *importantly*
mainmast 36.3 *parts of a sailing boat*
main meaning 520.4 *type of meaning*
main memory 65.6 *memory*
main office 291.4 *centre of activity*, 647.1 *workshop*
main part 143.5 *largest part*, 610.1 *excess*, 611.3 *chief thing*
main place 291.4 *centre of activity*
main plane 73 Aircraft Parts
main point 472.1 *topic*, 611.3 *chief thing*
main reaction 57.14 *chemical reaction*
main road 71.2, 137.5, 327.3 *road*
mainsail 74 Sails, 36.3 *parts of a sailing boat*
main sequence 53.11 *stellar birth*
main-sequence star 53.13 *luminosity*
main shock 54.22 *seismic activity*
mainspring 226.2 *source*, 377.5 *spring*, 586.11 *motive*, 603.4 *machine*
mains supply 64.34 *power supply*
mainstay 74 Rigging, 284.2 *supporting part*, 611.3 *chief thing*, 634.1 *refuge*, 662.13 *supporter*, 718.1 *protection*
mainstream 49.33 *jazz*
mainstream jazz 49.8 *jazz*
main street 93.7 *city district*, 93.14 *urban*, 137.5, 327.3 *road*
maintain 575, 4.22 *propound a philosophy*, 60.20 *practise surgery*, 186.4 *perpetuate*, 219.3 *continue*, 219.4 *protract*, 230.9 *take action*, 284.13 *support financially*, 396.20 *support life*, 473.15 *state*, 497.7 *believe*, 606.5 *provision*, 629.1 *repair*, 637.5 *preserve*, 662.20 *sustain*, 674.13 *conflict*, 726.7 *detain*, 759.19 *believe*
maintain a certain footing 105.6 *be in a state of*
maintain consistency 667.8 *be compatible*
maintain control 235.10 *be powerful*
maintain course 36.15 *sail*
maintained 497.14 *believed*
maintainer 284.8 *supporter*
maintain firm control 690.5 *be severe*
maintaining 284.9 *supportive*
maintaining one's distance 816.1 *unsociability*
maintain one's grip 575.8 *hold out*
maintain one's ground 575.8 *hold out*
maintain one's hold 726.6 *retain*
maintain one's status 105.6 *be in a state of*
maintain progress 336
maintain supply 606.5 *provision*
maintain the status quo 217.6 *make permanent*
maintain tradition 306.8 *be formal*
maintenance 16.39 *crime*, 219.1 *continuity*, 230.4 *management*, 284.7 *financial support*, 575.3 *constancy*, 606.1 *provision*, 629.8 *repair*, 637.1 *preservation*, 662.3 *sustenance*, 662.4 *social assistance*, 721.4 *earnings*, 725.6 *marriage settlement*, 726.2 *detention*, 730.2 *something received*, 749.3 *income*, 824.3 *divorce court*
maintenance service 17.4 *military organization*
main thing 611.3 *chief thing*
maintop 74 Parts of a Ship
main topic 611.3 *chief thing*
maintopsail 74 Sails
main wall 40.5 *real tennis*
Mainz 93 Cities
Maiso 8 Deities
maisonette 256.5 *house*
maître d' 697.3 *attendant*

maître d'hôtel 606.4 *caterer*

maître d'hôtel 697.3 *attendant*

maize 87 *Grasses*, 68.12 *crop*

maize silage 68.9 *animal feedstuff*

majesterial 805.19 *stately*

majestic 811, 8.13 *divine*, 12.10 *governing*, 554.5 *serious*, 558.3 *elegant*, 688.14 *governmental*, 696.12 *masterful*, 804.6 *worshipful*, 805.19 *stately*

majestically 805, 811, 8.19 *divinely*, 554.7 *emphatically*

majestic progress 336.15 *improvement*

majesty 805, 8.2 *divine attribute*, 688.2 *authoritativeness*, 811.7 *pomp*

Majlis 653.10 *legislative body*

majolica 44 Types of Ceramics

majolica painter 44.7 *potter*

major 126.15 *excellent*, 165.8 *specialization*, 611.5 *important*, 655.1 *skill*, 679.17 *army person*, 696.12 *masterful*

Major 17 British Military Ranks, 17 US Military Ranks

major axis 52.42 *circle*

major championships 29.1 *golf*

major-domo 697.6 *domestic servant*

major earthquake 54.22 *seismic activity*

major element 58.15 *essential element*

major general 679.17 *army person*, 692.6 *person in command*

Major General 17 British Military Ranks, 17 US Military Ranks

major golf courses 29.1 *golf*

major in 6.23 *learn*, 165.27 *specialize*

major interval 49.16 *musical note*

majority 175, 120.2 *certain amount*, 120.6 *quantitative*, 121.4 *interval*, 121.7 *gradational*, 126.1 *superiority*, 143.1 *part*, 143.5 *largest part*, 175.6 *plural*

majority rule 12.1 *government*, 688.7 *type of rule*

majority verdict 16.7 *legal trial*

majority vote 580.10 *vote*

majority whip 12.8 *politician*, 653.15 *manager*

major key 49.20 *key*

major league baseball 22.1 *baseball*

major part 143.5 *largest part*

major planet 53.16 *planet*

major poet 48.14 *author*

major scale 49.20 *key*

major subject 655.1 *skill*

major suit 655.1 *skill*

major surgery 60.9 *surgery*

major term 4.8 *philosophical term*

major third 177.6 *third*

major war 676.1 *war*

majuscule 5.15 *type style*, 5.41 *lettered*

Makassar 5 Languages and Groups of Languages

make 148, 99.20 *bring into being*, 161.44 *put together*, 163.4 *type*, 169.11, 170.10 *total*, 226.9 *be the cause of*, 226.10 *awaken*, 243.10 *produce*, 306.7 *form*, 382.15 *shape*, 594.7 *develop*, 627.1 *improve*, 695.6 *compel*, 721.9 *gain*

make a 180-degree turn 536.9 *renounce*

make a back pass 38.4 *play soccer*

make a bad buy 738.1 *purchase*

make a bad match 823.15 *marry*

make a bad move 683.6 *fail*

make a balls-up of 628.4 *impair*

make a bank shot 23.6 *play basketball*, 24.8 *play billiards*

make a beeline for 332.7 *take a direction*, 333.6 *be in the middle*

make a beginning 156

make a bequest 728.3 *transfer property*, 729.5 *give*

make a bid 13.11 *deal*, 596.1 *attempt*, 716.6 *make conditions*, 737.3 *bargain*

make a bid for 710.10 *offer to buy*

make a blocking kick 26.13 *do martial arts*

make a bloomer 844.19 *be wrong*

make a bomb 742.13 *get rich*

make a boo-boo 211.8 *make a mistake*

make a bounce pass 23.6 *play basketball*

make a bow 362.9 *bow*

make a break 24.8 *play billiards*, 216.7 *be changed*

make a break for 332.7 *take a direction*

make abstruse 551.3 *make obscure*

make a bundle 742.13 *get rich*

make a burnt offering 710.16 *make an offering*

make a buy 738.1 *purchase*

make a buyout 738.1 *purchase*

make a call 534.32 *telephone*

make a cat's paw of 599.3 *exploit*

make a change 216.8 *cause change*

make a changeover 21.6 *race*

make a charity appeal 712.8 *solicit money*

make a choice 580.1 *select*

make a circle 313.6 *circle*

make a circuit 334.3 *circuit*, 363.6 *orbit*

make a clean breast of 312.11 *be straight*

make a clean breast of it 530.8 *admit*, 537.29 *be truthful*

make a clean sweep 349.11 *void*, 621.13 *clean*

make a comeback 627.2 *get better*, 629.4 *be restored*

make a commotion 541.7 *exaggerate*

make a compact 667.7, 715.5 *contract*

make a conquest 821.28 *win the love of*

make a contract 714.8 *guarantee*

make a copy 326.16 *translate*

make a copy of 245.9 *reproduce*

make a corner in 738.1 *purchase*

make acquaintance 815.13 *fraternize*

make a crossing 356.11 *cross*

make a cynosure of 532.16 *publicize*

make a date 815.13 *fraternize*, 821.26, 826.8 *court*

make a dead reckoning 36.15 *sail*

make a dead set at 670.1 *attack*

make a deal 152.17 *come to an arrangement*, 667.7 *contract*, 677.5 *make peace*, 716.4 *negotiator*, 717.4 *compromise*, 737.3 *bargain*

make a dent in 607.1 *waste*

make a deposit 744.10 *deposit*, 752.5 *buy at a discount*

make a disposition 535.18 *vow*

make adequate provision 608.4 *suffice*

make a detour 313.6 *circle*, 334.4, 363.8 *detour*

make a devil of a row 423.8 *be loud*

make a diagram 547.11 *paint*

make a diagram of 560.14 *describe*

make a disposition 728.3 *transfer property*

make a diversion 334.4 *detour*

make adjustments 717.4 *compromise*

make a double play 22.7 *play baseball*

make a downhill run 41.14 *ski*

make a down payment 746.6 *pay*

make a draught 390.22 *blow*

make advances 819.14 *seek the friendship of*, 821.26, 826.8 *court*

make a face 785.6 *react against*

make a fair catch 19.17 *kick*

make a fair exchange 737.1 *trade*

make a fair offer 710.9 *offer*

make a false attack 28.5 *fence*

make a false image 548.4 *misrepresent*

make a false start 21.6 *race*

make a faux pas 656.7 *be clumsy*

make a feint 28.5 *fence*

make a field goal 23.6 *play basketball*

make a final demand 712.7 *demand*

make a find 738.1 *purchase*

make a flying kick 26.13 *do martial arts*

make a fool of 539.28 *trick*, 599.3 *exploit*, 734.10 *take away*, 806.22 *shame*

make a fool of oneself 508.7 *play the fool*, 656.6 *act foolishly*

make a forced march 648.2 *make haste*

make a fortune 686.5 *be prosperous*, 721.14 *profit*, 742.13 *get rich*

make a fresh start 156.28 *begin again*, 867.4 *be penitent*

make a fuel stop 33.10 *be on the track*

make a fuss 663.15 *object*

make a fuss about 494.4 *overestimate*, 611.8 *make important*

make a generalization 164

make a gentleman's agreement 714.7 *promise*

make a getaway 638.5 *escape*

make a gift 729.5 *give*

make a good buy 738.1 *purchase*

make a good fit 135.8 *unite*

make a good guess 516.1 *foresee*

make a good living 721.14 *profit*

make a good match 823.15 *marry*

make a good start 336.2 *start*

make a go of 682.6 *be successful*

make a guess 518.5 *suppose*

make a habit of 112.9 *be uniform*, 584.16 *have a habit*

make a hash of 151.23 *confuse*, 656.7 *be clumsy*, 683.6 *fail*

make a high tackle 35.5 *play rugby*

make a hit 682.6 *be successful*, 821.28 *win the love of*

make a hole in one's pocket 753.9 *be dear*

make a hook pass 23.6 *play basketball*

make a hook shot 23.6 *play basketball*

make a hostage of 701.7 *defeat*

make a house call 60.19 *practise medicine*

make a jump shot 23.6 *play basketball*

make a killing 682.6 *be successful*, 721.14 *profit*, 737.1 *trade*, 737.2 *speculate*, 739.1 *sell*, 742.13 *get rich*, 752.5 *buy at a discount*

make a kiss shot 24.8 *play billiards*

make a landfall 74.10 *sail*, 344.4 *land*

make a last-ditch stand 209.8 *delay*

make a laughing stock of 850.24 *ridicule*

make a legal defence 855.8 *justify*

make a lip 830.9 *be sullen*

make a list 171.8 *list*

make a little go a long way 871.5 *fast*

make all clear for 660.16 *make easy*

make all hell break loose 828.14 *make angry*

make all-out war 666.6 *argue*

make allowances 485.15 *modify*

make allowances for 839.12 *show mercy*, 855.7 *vindicate*

make a loan application 733.7 *borrow*

make a loss 358.1 *fall short*, 683.6 *fail*

make a man of 617.10 *do good*

make a match 823.17 *matchmake*

make amends 9.7 *worship*, 125.4 *compensate*, 629.3 *restore*, 710.14 *offer reparation*, 746.14 *atone*, 765.11 *recompense*, 867.5 *do penance*, 878.11 *pay*

make amends for 735.5 *compensate*, 840.5 *atone*

make a mess 622.11 *dirty*

make a mess of 656.7 *be clumsy*

make a mint 742.13 *get rich*

make a mistake 211, 504, 656.5 *be unskilful*, 844.19 *be wrong*, 864.16 *be wicked*

make a mockery of 799.6 *deride*

make a mountain out of a molehill 494.4 *overestimate*, 541.7 *exaggerate*

make a move 156.19 *start off*, 324.15 *walk*

make an addition to 130.7 *support*

make an alliance 140.6 *come together*

make a name for oneself 800.5 *have repute*

make an appearance 344.1 *arrive*, 457.12 *become visible*

make an arrest 699.11 *detain*

make an ass of 539.28 *trick*

make an ass of oneself 656.6 *act foolishly*

make an attempt 596.1 *attempt*

make an educated guess 517.11 *predict*

make an effort 640.4 *act*, 642.15 *try*, 644.8 *exert oneself*

make an empty gesture 539.26 *be a hypocrite*, 540.18 *be hypocritical*

make an end of 157.16 *cease*

make an entrance 51.32 *act*, 344.5 *get in*, 346.9 *enter*, 437.9 *appear*

make an error 540.16 *be false*

make a nest egg 605.6 *store*

make a net profit 721.14 *profit*

make a new version 524.12 *translate*

make an example of 879.1 *punish*

make an exception 131.3 *subtract*, 147.7 *exclude*

make an exit 347.9 *exit*

make angry 828, 829.8 *make irascible*

make an honest woman of 823.15 *marry*

make an idol of 9.8 *idolatrize*

make an impression 110.9 *duplicate*, 239.2 *be full of vigour*, 511.15 *be remembered*, 526.5 *be visible*, 611.7 *be important*

make an impression in 374.13 *soften*

make an incision 60.20 *practise surgery*

make an offer 710.9 *offer*, 737.3 *bargain*, 738.1 *purchase*

make an offer for 710.10 *offer to buy*

make an offering 710

make an off-the-lip turn 36.18 *windsurf*

make a note 511.13 *remind*

make an outward show 540.24 *mask*

make an overture 710.9 *offer*

make a nuisance of oneself 616.5 *be inconvenient*

make an unlawful entry 736.12 *steal*

make an unsecured loan 732.5 *lend*

make a packet 742.13 *get rich*

make a pact 140.6 *come together*

make a pass 38.4 *play soccer*, 826.8 *court*

make a pass at 670.6 *stab*

make a patsy of 599.3 *exploit*

make a pawn of 599.3 *exploit*

make a payment 746.6 *pay*

make a peace offering 710.16 *make an offering*

make a pig of oneself 872.5 *be greedy*

make a pig's ear of 151.23 *confuse*

make a pile 742.13 *get rich*

make a pit stop 33.10 *be on the track*
make a plan 592.9 *plan*
make a point 472.11 *raise the point*, 518.6 *propound*, 674.11 *contend*
make a point of 695.6 *compel*
make a poor likeness 548.4 *misrepresent*
make apparent 457.14 *present*
make appointments 12.12 *take authority*
make a prediction 517.11 *predict*
make a preliminary sketch 375.13 *be unfinished*
make a presentation 729.5 *give*
make a present of 729.5 *give*
make a press announcement 535.17 *affirm*
make a pretense of 540.20 *pretend*
make a prisoner 734.10 *take away*
make a profit 13.10 *trade with*, 686.5 *be prosperous*, 721.9 *gain*, 721.14 *profit*, 737.1 *trade*, 739.1 *sell*, 742.13 *get rich*, 861.21 *do well*
make a prognosis 517.11 *predict*
make a promise 714.7 *promise*
make a public exhibition of one-self 811.29 *show off*
make a purchase 738.1 *purchase*
make a reference to 107.7 *relate to*
make a report on 492.12 *estimate*
make a request 712.6 *request*
make a requital 672.3 *retaliate*
make a reservation 718.15 *reserve*
make a resolution 574.7 *resolve*
make a résumé 562.8 *summarize*
make a rough copy 375.13 *be unfinished*
make a rough sketch 594.2 *do the groundwork*
make a round trip 221.8 *return*, 313.6 *circle*, 334.3 *circuit*, 363.6 *orbit*
make arrangements 152
make artificial 538.22 *make unreal*
make a rude remark 668.6 *be insubordinate*
make a ruling 166.13 *rule*
make a run 41.16 *bobsled*
make a running attack 28.5 *fence*
make a sacrifice 859.7 *be unselfish*
make a sacrificial offering 710.16 *make an offering*
make a sale 739.1 *sell*
make a scene 828.11 *be angry*
make a scissors turn 41.14 *ski*
make a secured loan 732.5 *lend*
make as good as new 629.3 *restore*
make a shindy 828.11 *be angry*
make a show 811.31 *put on a show*
make a show of 526.1 *display*, 540.20 *pretend*
make a side move 305.8 *move sideways*
make as if 540.20 *pretend*
make a signal 543.12 *signal*
make a silk purse from a sow's ear 487.10 *attempt the impossible*
make a sortie 670.8 *counterattack*
make a space 265.4 *space*
make a special request 712.6 *request*
make a speech 567.7 *address*
make a splash 610.4 *be excessive*, 811.31 *put on a show*
make a stand 669.6 *resist*, 671.21 *entrench*, 674.11 *contend*, 676.14 *battle*
make a start 156.18 *make a beginning*
make a statement 535.17 *affirm*, 560.15 *recount*
make a stir 611.7 *be important*, 611.8 *make important*
make a straight thrust 28.5 *fence*
make a strike 25.8 *bowl*

make a success of 682.6 *be successful*
make a suggestion 518.6 *propound*
make a sweeping statement 164.27 *make a generalization*
make a synopsis of 562.8 *summarize*
make a takeover bid 728.3 *transfer property*, 737.3 *bargain*
make a thumbnail sketch 299.5 *outline*
make a toast 819.15 *be hospitable*
make a to-do 541.7 *exaggerate*
make a tool of 599.3 *exploit*
make a trade-off 728.3 *transfer property*
make a treaty 716.4 *negotiator*
make a trial of 596.4 *test*
make a true representation 537.31 *be accurate*
make a U-turn 337.9 *turn round*
make available to all 522.5 *simplify*
make average 124
make a virtue of necessity 571, 673.3 *submit*, 717.4 *compromise*
make a V sign 807.29 *ridicule*
make a wally of 539.28 *trick*
make a way 327.14 *find one's way*
make away with 244.8 *destroy*, 398.16 *kill*
make away with oneself 398.21 *commit suicide*
make a weak effort 620.10 *leave imperfect*
make a whole 144.5 *be complete*
make a widow 824.9 *widow*
make a widower 824.9 *widow*
make a wilderness and call it peace 244.10 *lay waste*
make a will 729.5 *give*
make a word-for-word translation 5.46 *translate*
make a wry face 830.11 *be irritable*
make bad blood 785.7 *cause dislike*, 820.13 *antagonize*
make badly 618.13 *be worthless*
make barren 236.9 *make impotent*, 614.8 *make useless*
make basic plans 594.2 *do the groundwork*
make believe 519.14 *imagine*, 538.24 *pretend*
make-believe 100.5 *nonreality*, 102.10 *theoretical*, 519.5 *fantasy*, 519.12 *imaginary*, 538.8 *pretence*, 538.14 *unreal*, 539.2 *self-deception*, 539.25 *deceive oneself*, 539.40 *illusory*
make better 216.8 *cause change*, 233.9 *change*, 617.10 *do good*, 627.1 *improve*, 861.20 *do good*
make bigger 128, 261
make bitter 830.12 *make irritable*
make blind 436.15 *blind*
make bold 807.22 *be rude*, 818.7 *be discourteous*, 846.15 *presume*
make bold to 698.19 *liberalize*
make both ends meet 756.5 *be thrifty*
make bright 376.11 *smooth*
make by hand 344.10 *produce*
make capital out of 599.3 *exploit*, 613.11 *find useful*, 627.2 *get better*, 721.14 *profit*
make captive 699.11 *detain*
make ceramics 44
make certain 490, 480.1 *verify*, 632.9 *protect*, 718.11 *promise*, 781.5 *be cautious*
make cheap 754
make circular 313
make claims upon 692.10 *demand*
make clean 621.13 *clean*
make clear 4.21 *rationalize*, 475.16 *explain*, 522.5 *simplify*, 524.8 *interpret*, 550.2 *clarify*, 627.3 *rectify*, 660.16 *make easy*
make clothing 295
make coarse 628.6 *pervert*
make cold 409
make comfortable 405.10 *comfort*

make common cause 664.13 *work together*
make complete 144.4, 684.4 *complete*, 684.6 *elaborate*
make complex 314.7 *be ambiguous*
make concave 317
make conceited 809
make concessions 708.3 *permit*
make concise 625.3 *rectify*
make concrete 367.8 *be material*
make conditions 716
make conform 167
make consistent 112.9 *be uniform*, 214.10 *make regular*, 308.6 *symmetrize*
make constant 214.10 *make regular*
make contact 135.10 *link*, 267.3 *juxtapose*, 298.4 *interface*, 407.12 *abut*, 534.30 *communicate*, 594.1 *prepare*
make content 677.4 *pacify*
make continual 214.10 *make regular*
make corrections 627.3 *rectify*
make crystal-clear 522.5 *simplify*
make dark 440
make deaf 421.9 *deafen*
make deliveries 606.5 *provision*
make demands 593.10 *necessitate*, 692.10 *demand*, 716.6 *make conditions*
make dense 371
make dependent 701.6 *subject*
make different 216.8 *cause change*
make difficulties 663.17 *withstand*
make dim 441
make dirty 622.11 *dirty*
make disappear 189.5 *make transient*
make disordered 151
make disproportionate 123.5 *be unequal*
make dissimilar 548.4 *misrepresent*
make diverse 113.8 *be diverse*
make do 124.9 *be average*, 583.3 *improvise*, 756.5 *be thrifty*
make do with 222.5 *take a substitute*, 599.5 *dispose of*
make drunk 874.9 *be intoxicating*
make due provision 606.5 *provision*
make easier 660.16 *make easy*
make easily understood 522.5 *simplify*
make easy 660, 522.5 *simplify*
make elastic 377
make ends meet 396.20 *support life*, 747.11 *be parsimonious*
make enemies 136.11 *divide*, 820.13 *antagonize*, 822.16 *cause hate*
make equal 704.9 *cancel out*
make eternal 190
make even 214.10 *make regular*
make every second count 648.2 *make haste*
make evident 483
make exception 485.15 *modify*
make excuses 591.5 *shirk*
make excuses for 855.8 *justify*
make exempt 16.78 *acquit*
make extra demands 650.6 *fatigue*
make eyes 821.26 *court*
make eyes at 435.13 *look*, 826.8 *court*
make faces 309
make faces at 850.26 *cock a snook*
make famous 532.16 *publicize*
make fast 718, 36.15 *sail*, 135.8 *unite*, 225.7 *make stable*
make fertile 246
make few demands 691.3 *be lenient*
make fine 537.31 *be accurate*
make fine adjustments 537.31 *be accurate*
make firm 135.8 *unite*, 718.14 *make fast*
make fluid 387
make for 74.9 *navigate*, 332.7

take a direction, 336.8, 662.28 *further*
make fragrant 414.8 *sweeten*
make free 846.15 *presume*
make free with 698.19 *liberalize*, 807.22 *be rude*, 818.7 *be discourteous*
make fresh 621.13 *clean*
make friendly overtures to 819.14 *seek the friendship of*
make friends 677.5 *make peace*, 815.13 *fraternize*, 819.13 *befriend*
make friends with 140.6 *come together*, 819.13 *befriend*
make full 257.7 *stuff*
make fun of 539.28 *trick*, 771.13 *be humorous*, 850.24, 854.14 *ridicule*
make glow 239.3 *invigorate*
make good 122.11 *equalize*, 125.4 *compensate*, 344.9 *achieve*, 480.1 *verify*, 606.6 *replenish*, 627.2 *get better*, 627.3 *rectify*, 629.1 *repair*, 672.3 *retaliate*, 682.6 *be successful*, 686.5 *be prosperous*, 719.6 *perform*, 735.5 *compensate*, 840.5 *atone*, 855.7 *vindicate*
make good one's escape 638.5 *escape*
make good one's word 719.6 *perform*
make good progress 336.2 *start*
make good time 336
make green 453.17 *green*
make happen 226.9 *be the cause of*, 230.8 *activate*
make happy 677.4 *pacify*
make hard 373.9 *harden*
make haste 648
make hay of 599.3 *exploit*
make hay while the sun shines 210.5 *take the opportunity*, 642.13 *be busy*, 655.10 *be skilful*
make headway 336.1 *go forward*, 627.2 *get better*, 721.10 *augment*
make headway against 682.7 *overcome obstacles*
make healthy 623, 627.1 *improve*
make heavy 369
make heavy weather of 659.18 *find difficult*
make hell freeze over 487.10 *attempt the impossible*
make history 511.15 *be remembered*, 640.4 *act*
make horizontal 282
make human 400
make hygienic 623
make ignorant 502
make ill 687.11 *cause adversity*
make illegal 16, 16.79 *convict*, 709.3 *veto*, 846.17 *criminalize*
make illegible 546.1 *obliterate*
make immaculate 621.13 *clean*
make immovable 718.14 *make fast*
make immune 16.78 *acquit*
make impatient 829.8 *make irascible*
make important 611, 526.3 *reveal*
make impossible 487, 536.7 *be negative*
make impotent 236
make improvements 627.1 *improve*, 627.3 *rectify*
make inactive 643, 614.8 *make useless*, 628.4 *impair*
make incumbent 847.17 *impose a duty*
make indifferent 783
make inferior 701.6 *subject*
make infertile 247
make initial progress 336.2 *start*
make inoperative 628.4 *impair*
make inroads 357.5 *transgress*
make inroads on 607.1 *waste*
make insane 510
make insensitive 783.13 *make indifferent*
make insufficient 609
make into 220.9 *transform*
make into a novel 48.21 *write*

make into a play 48.21 *write*
make into a whole 144.4 *complete*
make invisible 438
make irascible 829
make irritable 830
make it 344.2 *reach,* 344.9 *achieve,* 627.2 *get better,* 682.6 *be successful,* 686.5 *be prosperous,* 742.13 *get rich*
make it all square 122.10 *be equal,* 124.10 *make average*
make it big 611.7 *be important,* 627.2 *get better*
make it easy for 708.4 *be permissive*
make it hard on oneself 659.19 *have difficulty*
make it one's aim 596.1 *attempt*
make it one's business to 590.12 *aim at*
make it one's duty 714.8 *guarantee,* 847.15 *be liable*
make it to the top 532.18 *become famous*
make it tough for 659.23 *cause difficulties*
make it up 125.4 *compensate,* 677.5 *make peace,* 839.9 *forgive*
make it up as one goes along 595.13 *improvise*
make it with 135.11, 821.29 *make love*
make it worth one's while 878.11 *pay*
make jealous 841.7 *arouse jealousy*
make known 528.12 *communicate,* 530.5 *disclose,* 532.13 *make public*
make lame 614.8 *make useless*
make larger 261.5 *make bigger*
make law 692.9 *command*
make laws 16.68 *legislate*
make leeway 336.3 *press on*
make legal 16, 653.1 *manage,* 688.21 *grant authority,* 708.3 *permit*
make less 129.5 *make smaller*
make light 370.10 *lighten*
make lighter 370.10 *lighten*
make light of 495.3 *underestimate,* 542.22 *play down,* 660.17 *do easily*
make light work of 660.17 *do easily*
make like 114.12 *imitate,* 540.20 *pretend*
make likely 488.9 *make probable*
make like new 629.3 *restore*
make little of 495.3 *underestimate*
make love 135, 821, 245.14 *have sex,* 826.8 *court*
make love not war 675.5 *be at peace,* 831.8 *be benevolent*
make love to 405.9 *give pleasure*
make mad 241.9 *make violent,* 828.14 *make angry*
make matters up 840.5 *atone*
make merry 405.8 *feel pleasure,* 665.17 *socialize,* 773.5 *rejoice*
make mincemeat of 244.9 *demolish,* 244.11 *ruin*
make mincemeat of someone 126.8 *be superior*
make mischief 635.3 *trap,* 693.15 *be disobedient*
make money 682.6 *be successful,* 686.5 *be prosperous,* 721.9 *gain,* 742.13 *get rich,* 861.21 *do well*
make money by 721.12 *earn*
make more 128.5 *make bigger*
make motionless 325
make much ado 611.8 *make important*
make much of 532.16 *publicize,* 541.10 *boast,* 611.8 *make important,* 812.18 *salute,* 821.23 *love,* 826.7 *show endearment for*
make music 49.36 *play*
make mute 563.15 *strike dumb*
make mutual concessions 717.4 *compromise*
make mysterious 529
make neat 621.13 *clean,* 627.1 *improve*

make neither head nor tail of 523.9 *find unintelligible*
make neutral 704.9 *cancel out*
make new 201
make no answer 566.8 *be taciturn*
make noble 802
make no bones about 526.4 *show secret,* 535.21 *be assertive*
make no bones about it 537.29 *be truthful,* 556.7 *be simple*
make no comment 529.12 *keep secret*
make no confession 868.5 *be impenitent*
make no demands 660.15 *be easy,* 691.3 *be lenient*
make no difference 122.11 *equalize*
make no distinction between 482.11 *not discriminate*
make no impact upon 783.13 *make indifferent*
make no impression 612.11 *be unimportant*
make no mistake 522.7 *recognize*
make no mystery 526.4 *show oneself*
make no noise 422.1 *be silent*
make nonsense of 521.7 *mean nothing*
make no point 553.6 *be circuitous*
make no preparations 595.12 *be unprepared*
make no profit 722.10 *have a financial loss*
make no secret of 526.4 *show oneself*
make no sense 521.7 *mean nothing*
make no sign 527.13 *hide,* 529.12 *keep secret*
make notes 545.14 *inscribe*
make nothing of 523.9 *find unintelligible*
make no use of 607.1 *waste*
make no waves 673.3 *submit*
make nude 296
make null and void 16.77 *annul,* 704.6 *cancel*
make obeisance 362.9 *bow,* 808.10 *knuckle under,* 817.13 *defer to,* 849.19 *take off one's hat to*
make obligatory 692.10 *demand*
make obscure 551
make obvious 526.3 *reveal*
make off 345.4 *hurry off,* 591.8 *run away*
make off-limits 709.3 *veto*
make off with 736.12 *steal*
make one 134.11 *simplify,* 135.8 *unite,* 174.19 *become one,* 823.16 *join in marriage*
make one eat dirt 806.17 *humiliate*
make one fed-up 788.6 *be boring*
make one feel small 806.17 *humiliate*
make one jump 514.9 *surprise*
make one laugh 798
make one look silly 539.28 *trick*
make one more 130.7 *support*
make one of us 586.15 *persuade*
make one's adieus 345.6 *part*
make one's apologies 840.6 *apologize*
make one's bed and lie in it 672.4 *serve one right*
make one's blood boil 828.14 *make angry*
make one's contribution 130.6 *add*
make one's daily round 112.12 *be monotonous,* 214.8 *be cyclic*
make one's debut 156.27 *emerge*
make one's defence 16.72 *stand trial*
make oneself 573.10 *grudge*
make oneself at home 698.17 *be informal,* 814.11 *not stand on ceremony,* 815.12 *visit*
make oneself attractive 821.28 *win the love of*
make oneself conspicuous 811.29 *show off*
make oneself felt 233.8 *influence*

make oneself liable 847.15 *be liable*
make oneself one of the family 815.12 *visit*
make oneself responsible 745.7 *be in debt*
make oneself scarce 254.16 *absent oneself,* 345.4 *hurry off,* 591.8 *run away,* 638.5 *escape,* 648.2 *make haste*
make oneself useful 613.9 *be useful,* 662.17 *help,* 697.8 *serve*
make oneself welcome 815.12 *visit*
make one's excuses 711.5 *refuse*
make one's exit 345.6 *part*
make one's eyes open 786.10 *be wonderful*
make one's fortune 686.5 *be prosperous,* 742.13 *get rich*
make one's gorge rise 341.4 *be repulsive,* 828.14 *make angry*
make one's head spin 460.10 *bemuse*
make one's head swim 523.7 *be unintelligible,* 786.10 *be wonderful,* 874.9 *be intoxicating*
make one sick 785.7 *cause dislike*
make one sit up and take notice 786.10 *be wonderful*
make one's mark 682.6 *be successful,* 686.5 *be prosperous*
make one's money work for one 737.2 *speculate*
make one's mouth water 586.16 *tempt,* 782.15 *cause desire*
make one's name 532.16 *publicize*
make one's nest 256.18 *take up residence*
make one's own 165.26 *personalize,* 721.9 *gain*
make one's pile 686.5 *be prosperous,* 721.14 *profit*
make one's point 228.9 *motivate*
make one's presence felt 253.12 *attend*
make one's quarry 590.12 *aim at*
make one's rounds 334.3 *circuit,* 363.7 *ring*
make one's submission 518.6 *propound*
make one stop in one's tracks 587.2 *deter*
make one's voice heard 233.8 *influence*
make one's way 336, 324.13 *be in motion,* 627.2 *get better*
make one tired 788.6 *be boring*
make one yawn 788.6 *be boring*
make opaque 443
make operate 230.8 *activate*
make operational 230.8 *activate,* 594.4 *prepare for action*
make ordinary 214.10 *make regular*
make or mar 226.9 *be the cause of,* 233.9 *change*
make out 105.6 *be in a state of,* 435.12 *see,* 522.7 *recognize,* 524.9 *decipher,* 821.27 *kiss,* 826.7 *show endearment for*
make-out artist 821.9 *lover,* 826.5 *courting person*
make out like a bandit 627.2 *get better*
make over 326.11 *transfer,* 629.2 *refurbish,* 728.3 *transfer property,* 729.5 *give*
make overtures 716.4 *negotiator,* 819.13 *befriend,* 826.8 *court*
make overtures to 712.6 *request*
make overweight 369.14 *make heavy*
make passes 821.26 *court*
make peace 675, 677, 218.9 *pause,* 677.4 *pacify,* 839.9 *forgive*
make people stare 811.29 *show off*
make periodical 187
make permanent 190, 217
make plain 522.5 *simplify,* 526.3 *reveal*
make play with 599.3 *exploit*
make pleasant 414.8 *sweeten*
make pointed 380.15 *make sharp*

make poor 743.14 *impoverish*
make porous 322.20 *hole*
make port 74.10 *sail,* 344.4 *land,* 634.4 *shelter*
make possible 486, 660.16 *make easy,* 708.3 *permit*
make pregnant 245.13 *propagate*
make preparations 594.1 *prepare*
make probable 488
make progress 219.3 *continue,* 336.1 *go forward,* 627.2 *get better,* 642.13 *be busy*
make proposals 716.6 *make conditions*
make proud 805
make provision 606.5 *provision*
make provisions 516.2 *show prudence*
make public 532
make quiet 422.2 *silence*
maker 156.16 *originator,* 243.9 *producer,* 646.3 *agent*
Maker 226.7 *Prime Mover*
make rapid strides 721.10 *augment*
make ready 6.22 *educate,* 594.1 *prepare,* 594.4 *prepare for action,* 602.6 *find means,* 606.5 *provision*
make real 101, 367.8 *be material*
make red 450.9 *redden*
make redress 735.5 *compensate*
make redundant 15.11 *conduct industrial relations,* 147.8 *eject,* 218.8 *cause to cease,* 252.17 *relegate,* 349.2 *dismiss,* 600.7 *stop work,* 645.5, 727.10 *dismiss*
make reference to 526.3 *reveal*
make regular 214
make reparation 878.11 *pay*
make reparation for 843.15 *put right*
make reparations 735.5 *compensate*
make restitution 125.4 *compensate,* 221.7 *restore,* 735.4 *give back*
make rich 742
make right 840.5 *atone*
make rivers run uphill 487.10 *attempt the impossible*
make room 265.4 *space*
make room for 248.2 *space*
make rough 375
make round 315, 313.7 *make circular*
make routine 214.10 *make regular*
make safe 632.9 *protect,* 718.10 *secure*
make sane 509.6 *be sane*
make sense 463.12 *be reasonable,* 522.4 *be intelligible*
make sense of 524.8 *interpret*
make shallow 278
make shapeless 307
make sharp 380
make sheep's eyes 826.8 *court*
makeshift 127.14 *poor,* 222.7 *substitute,* 583.1 *improvised,* 592.3 *expedient plan*
make shift 592.11 *invent*
makeshift 594.16 *preparatory,* 595.3 *without preparation,* 599.9 *used,* 602.1 *means,* 608.1 *sufficient,* 609.8 *insufficiency,* 620.2 *incomplete,* 620.6 *imperfect item*
make shift to 596.1 *attempt*
make shift with 599.5 *dispose of*
make shipshape 312.10 *straighten,* 627.1 *improve*
make short shrift of 836.6 *be pitiless*
make short work of 244.11 *ruin,* 350.22 *eat well,* 642.15 *try,* 644.6 *work,* 648.2 *make haste,* 660.17 *do easily*
make silent 422.2 *silence*
make similar 114, 112.9 *be uniform*
make simple 134.11 *simplify,* 556.7 *be simple*
make small 628.5 *hurt*
make smaller 129, 262, 371.9 *make dense*

make smell like roses 540.24 *mask*
make someone 135.11 *make love,* 532.16 *publicize,* 821.29 *make love*
make someone believe 497
make someone eat dust 648.2 *make haste*
make someone jump 777.13 *frighten*
make someone keep his distance 341.1 *repel*
make someone's blood run cold 777.13 *frighten*
make someone's ears burn 420.15 *hear*
make someone's hackles rise 407.12 *abut*
make someone sit up and notice 611.7 *be important*
make someone's mouth water 228.9 *motivate*
make something happen 574.10 *insist*
make sore 828.14 *make angry*
make sound 718.14 *make fast*
make sparse 372
make speeches 564.14 *speak to*
make spherical 315.11 *make round*
make stable 225
make steadfast 718.14 *make fast*
make straight 312.10 *straighten*
make strides 336.3 *press on*
make strong 237.8 *strengthen*
make sullen 830
make sure 225.7 *make stable,* 490.21 *make certain,* 781.5 *be cautious*
make symmetric 112.9 *be uniform*
make taboo 709.4 *censor*
make tangible 537.28 *bring into existence*
make taste 411
make terms 116.23 *arrange,* 667.7, 715.5 *contract*
make the air blue 827.5 *curse*
make the best of a bad job 717.4 *compromise*
make the best of it 571.18 *make a virtue of necessity,* 775.8 *be optimistic*
make the best of one's way 336.4 *make good time*
make the big time 682.6 *be successful*
make the desert bloom 246.7 *make fertile*
make the effort 596.1 *attempt*
make the first move 156.21 *pioneer*
make the front page 532.18 *become famous*
make the grade 344.9 *achieve,* 608.4 *suffice,* 627.2 *get better,* 682.6 *be successful*
make the leopard change its spots 487.10 *attempt the impossible*
make the lion lie down with the lamb 675.6 *make peace*
make the most of 494.4 *overestimate,* 599.3 *exploit,* 995.5 *dispose of,* 627.1 *improve,* 640.4 *act*
make the point 477.20 *doubt*
make the rubble bounce 670.3 *bomb*
make the running 329.6 *accelerate,* 357.3 *exceed*
make the same 110
make the sign of the cross 10.19 *offer worship*
make the sparks fly 642.15 *try*
make the supreme sacrifice 397.16 *meet one's fate*
make the welkin ring 423.8 *be loud*
make the world a safer place 675.6 *make peace*
make thin 274
make things awkward 659.23 *cause difficulties*
make things difficult 487.8 *make impossible,* 659.24 *create difficulties*

make things easy for 228.9 *motivate,* 586.16 *tempt*
make things hum 642.15 *try*
make things worse 628.3 *make worse,* 659.23 *cause difficulties*
make tidy 621.13 *clean*
make time for 729.5 *give*
make time stand still 186.4 *perpetuate*
make to order 295.35 *make clothing*
make tough 378
make to walk the plank 398.17 *murder*
make tracks 329.4 *be swift,* 345.1 *depart,* 591.8 *run away,* 648.2 *make haste*
make transient 189
make transparent 442
make trouble 151.26 *be disorderly,* 666.7 *pick a fight,* 679.36 *combat*
make ugly 790, 628.5 *hurt*
make unbreakable 378.11 *make tough*
make uncertain 491
make unclean 601.1 *misuse,* 622.11 *dirty,* 628.3 *make worse*
make uniform 116, 112.9 *be uniform,* 112.10 *conform,* 134.11 *simplify,* 214.10 *make regular,* 308.6 *symmetrize,* 537.31 *be accurate*
make unimportant 612
make unintelligible 523
make unlike 115.6 *differentiate*
make unreal 538
make unwelcome 341.3 *fend off,* 349.4 *ostracize,* 468.13 *be thoughtless,* 581.3 *exclude,* 818.7 *be discourteous*
make up 444, 791, 99.20 *bring into being,* 102.17 *fabricate,* 115.3 *disguise,* 140.5 *combine,* 144.4 *complete,* 146.5 *be included,* 148.10 *compose,* 148.13 *make,* 243.10 *produce,* 257.8 *embody,* 519.14 *imagine,* 606.6 *replenish,* 627.1 *improve*
makeup 103.4 *nature,* 306.4 *forming*
make-up 51.19 *stage requisite,* 118.4 *camouflage,* 140.4 *compound,* 146.1 *inclusion,* 165.2 *personality,* 257.1 *contents,* 295.5 *fancy dress,* 382.3 *form,* 444.9 *complexion,* 791.4 *cosmetics*
make up an account 750.7 *account*
make-up artist 51.26 *stagehand,* 791.13 *beautician*
make-up box 791
make up for 125.4 *compensate,* 840.5 *atone*
make up for lost time 329.6 *accelerate,* 336.4 *make good time,* 644.6 *work,* 648.2 *make haste*
make up for one's error 710.14 *offer reparation*
make up leeway 336.4 *make good time*
make-up man 51.26 *stagehand*
make up one's mind 574.7 *resolve,* 580.1 *select*
make up the numbers 130.7 *support*
make up the shortfall 130.6 *add*
make uptight 829.8 *make irascible*
make up time 329.6 *accelerate*
make up to 808.9 *fawn,* 819.14 *seek the friendship of,* 853.10 *cajole*
make useless 614
make use of 599.1 *use,* 613.11 *find useful,* 808.15 *sponge*
make vertical 281
make violent 241
make visible 435, 437
make war 816.13 *be at war*
make war on 820.12 *oppose*
make waves 168.18 *not conform,* 611.7 *be important*
make way 74.9 *navigate*
make way for 335.8 *sidestep,*

591.1 *avoid,* 660.16 *make easy,* 673.3 *submit*
make weak 238.7 *weaken*
makeweight 122.4 *equalizer,* 125.2 *counterbalance,* 144.2 *fullness,* 369.10 *scales*
make welcome 730.10 *receive someone,* 815.11 *be sociable*
make well 623.7 *make healthy,* 629.6 *cure,* 677.4 *pacify*
make whole 144.4 *complete,* 629.3 *restore*
make whoopee 773.5 *rejoice,* 821.27 *kiss*
make wicked 864
make work 230.8 *activate,* 642.15 *try,* 644.6 *work*
make-work 15.9 *negotiated*
make-work rules 15.2 *industrial negotiations*
make worse 628, 768.6 *aggravate*
make yellow 452
make young 206
make yourself at home 344.24 *welcome*
making 243.1 *production,* 243.2 *manufacture,* 344.17 *achievement,* 382.5 *structuring,* 594.13 *development*
making a break 24.3 *English billiards*
making amends 735.2 *compensation,* 840.1 *atonement,* 840.4 *atoning*
making a mountain out of a molehill 541.1 *exaggeration*
making a prisoner 734.3 *taking away*
making a profit 613.4 *profitable*
making arrangements 152.11 *arrangements*
making as good as new 629.8 *repair*
making dim 441.3 *dimming*
making equal 704.4 *cancelling out*
making friends 819.1 *friendship*
making good 627.6 *rectification,* 735.2 *compensation,* 840.1 *atonement*
making infertile 247
making it with 821.5 *desire*
making light 439.3 *lightening*
making light of 542.9 *down-playing*
making like new 629.8 *repair*
making love 821.5 *desire*
making much of 541.4 *bombast*
making of furniture 47.1 *furniture*
making one's own 723.1 *possession*
making out 821.6 *courtship,* 826.1 *endearment*
making progress 293.22 *progression*
making ready 594.9 *preparation*
making right 840.1 *atonement*
makings 721.1 *gain,* 721.4 *earnings*
making sense 522.1 *intelligible*
making smooth 376.7 *smoothness*
making someone 821.5 *desire*
making terms 716.1 *negotiation*
making tracks 329.8 *speed*
making up for 840.1 *atonement*
making up one's mind 580.6 *selection*
making vertical 281
making war 676.8 *warfare*
making whoopee 821.6 *courtship,* 826.1 *endearment*
mako 85 *Trees and Shrubs*
mako shark 80 *Fishes*
Makuna 1 *Peoples*
malachite 54 *Minerals,* 453.11 *green thing*
malacologist 76.11 *zoologist,* 81.15 *invertebrate zoologist*
malacology 76.9 *animal science,* 81.14 *invertebrate zoology*
malacostracan 81.4 *arthropod*
maladjusted 117.8 *contradictory,* 153.16 *deranged*
maladjusted personality 61.8 *disordered personality*

maladjustment 117.2 *contradiction*
maladminister 601.1 *misuse,* 656.5 *be unskilful*
maladministered 656.4 *bungled*
maladministration 601.2 *misuse,* 656.9 *bungling*
maladroit 656.3 *clumsy*
malady 624.2 *illness,* 631.1 *affliction*
mala fide 858.11 *dishonourably*
Málaga 93 *Cities*
Malagasy 5 *Languages and Groups of Languages*
malaise 406.1 *pain,* 624.3 *symptom,* 770.2 *depression,* 862.2 *affliction*
Malamud 48 *Writers*
malamute 326.6 *beast of burden*
malapert 807.13 *insolent*
malapropism 5.29 *grammar,* 504.11 *grammatical error,* 506.2 *solecism,* 601.2 *misuse,* 798.4 *joke*
malapropos 117.11 *unfit,* 117.17 *unsuitably,* 211.10 *untimely,* 211.15 *at the wrong time,* 616.1 *inconvenient*
malaria 81.12 *protozoal disease,* 388.3 *miasma,* 624.6 *infection,* 624.7 *tropical disease*
malarial 626.6 *contagious*
malarial fever 624.6 *infection,* 624.7 *tropical disease*
malarious 626.6 *contagious*
malarkey 521.5 *empty talk*
Malathion 69.8 *weedkiller*
Malawi 91 *Countries,* 94 *Lakes,* 94.5 *other major lakes*
Malay 5 *Languages and Groups of Languages,* 68 *Breeds of Fowl,* 5.11 *family of languages*
malaya 45.49 *Indian dish*
Malayalam 5 *Languages and Groups of Languages*
Malayo-Javanese 5 *Languages and Groups of Languages*
Malayo-Polynesian 5 *Languages and Groups of Languages,* 5.11 *family of languages*
Malaysia 91 *Countries*
malcological 81.19 *molluscan*
malcontent 500.5 *dissenter,* 659.9 *difficult person,* 693.6 *nonconformist,* 713.4 *protester,* 713.9 *protesting,* 766.3 *dissatisfied person,* 766.4 *dissatisfied*
malcontented 766.4 *dissatisfied*
Maldives 91 *Countries*
Maldonado 93 *Cities*
male 401, 401, 84.12 *of flowers*
Male 401
male animal 401
male bird 78
Malebranche 4 *Philosophers*
male chauvinism 401.1 *male sex,* 481.4 *social discrimination*
male chauvinist 481.7 *bigot,* 834.2 *misanthrope*
male chauvinist pig 401.6 *macho man,* 481.7 *bigot,* 834.2 *misanthrope*
malediction 827, 618.11 *harmfulness,* 822.1 *hate,* 862.4 *evil power*
maledictive 827, 822.10 *hating*
maledictively 822.18 *hatefully*
maledictory 827.10 *maledictive*
male-dominated society 401.1 *male sex*
male exclusiveness 401.1 *male sex*
malefactor 832, 16.40 *lawbreaker,* 640.3 *doer,* 844.10 *wrongdoer,* 862.6 *evil person,* 864.9 *wicked person,* 866.4 *guilty person*
male feminist 401.14 *liberated man*
male fern 88 *Ferns*
malefic 618.5 *harmful,* 832.10 *malevolent*
maleficence 832.1 *malevolence,* 862.1 *evil*
maleficent 862.7 *evil,* 864.11 *wicked*
maleic 58 *Common Fatty Acids*

male mammal 77
male member 245.8 *organs of reproduction*
male menopause 207.4 *middle age*
male model 295.27 *model*, 526.12 *displayer*
male nurse 60.16 *nurse*
male person 401.2 *male*
male pill 247.3 *birth control*
male prostitute 401.7 *libertine*, 877.8 *immoral man*
male rape 241.2 *physical violence*
male sex 401
male sex organs 245.8 *organs of reproduction*
male stripper 296.8 *nude person*
male title of address 401
malevolence 832, 233.2 *occult influence*, 618.11 *harmfulness*, 820.1 *enmity*, 822.1 *hate*, 834.1 *misanthropy*, 862.1 *evil*, 864.1 *wickedness*
Malevolence 832
malevolent 832, 618.5 *harmful*, 631.16 *blighting*, 820.6 *hostile*, 822.10 *hating*, 855.14 *vindictive*, 862.7 *evil*, 864.11 *wicked*
malevolently 832, 631.17 *banefully*, 820.15 *aggressively*, 822.18 *hatefully*, 855.16 *vindictively*, 862.12 *evilly*, 864.18 *wickedly*
malfeasance 16.39 *crime*
malfeasant 832.8 *malefactor*
malform 309.11 *deform*
malformation 309.3 *deformity*
malformed 309.7 *deformed*
malfunction 683, 661.2 *obstacle*, 661.9 *block*, 844.24 *go wrong*
malfunctioning 661.14 *blocked*, 844.18 *gone wrong*
Malherbe 48 Poets
Mali 91 Countries
malic 58 Common Fatty Acids
malic acid 57 Common Chemical Compounds
malice 618.11 *harmfulness*, 820.1 *enmity*, 822.1 *hate*, 828.1 *resentment*, 832.1 *malevolence*, 862.1 *evil*
malice aforethought 822.1 *hate*, 832.1 *malevolence*
malicious 618.5 *harmful*, 820.6 *hostile*, 822.10 *hating*, 828.15 *resentful*, 832.10 *malevolent*, 842.2 *envious*, 855.14 *vindictive*, 862.7 *evil*
malicious gossip 854.3 *defamation*
maliciously 822.18 *hatefully*, 828.17 *resentfully*, 832.20 *malevolently*, 842.4 *enviously*, 855.16 *vindictively*, 862.12 *evilly*
maliciousness 832.1 *malevolence*
malign 618.5 *harmful*, 670.10 *criticize*, 832.10 *malevolent*, 844.20 *wrong*, 854.12 *defame*
malignance 832.1 *malevolence*
malignancy 618.11 *harmfulness*
malignancy malignity 862.2 *affliction*
malignant 398.23 *deadly*, 618.5 *harmful*, 820.6 *hostile*, 822.10 *hating*, 832.10 *malevolent*, 862.7 *evil*, 862.9 *detrimental*
malignant growth 227.3 *growth*
malignantly 398.25 *lethally*, 822.18 *hatefully*
malignant tumour 624.12 *cancer*
malign influence 233.2 *occult influence*, 687.3 *bad fortune*, 862.4 *evil power*
maligning 670.25 *critical*
malignity 440.7 *spiritual darkness*, 618.11 *harmfulness*, 820.1 *enmity*, 822.1 *hate*, 832.1 *malevolence*, 862.1 *evil*
Malikite 5 Non-Christian Religions
malines 67 Natural Fabrics
Malines 68 Breeds of Fowl
malinger 540.19 *be deceitful*, 591.5 *shirk*
malingerer 539.15 *deceiver*, 624.19 *sick person*

malingering 540.5 *deceitfulness*, 540.29 *deceitful*
Malinke 1 Peoples, **5** Languages and Groups of Languages
Maliseet 1 Peoples
malison 827.4 *malediction*
mall 291.4 *centre of activity*, 740.7 *emporium*
mallard 78 Birds
Mallarmé 48 Poets
malleability 6.10 *educatability*, 167.3 *pliancy*, 228.6 *suggestibility*, 374.8 *softness*, 694.1 *obedience*
malleable 6.17 *educatable*, 167.11 *conformable*, 224.14 *irresolute*, 228.13 *suggestible*, 374.2 *pliant*, 660.12 *wieldy*, 673.5 *submitting*, 694.7 *obedient*
malleably 6.26 *studiously*, 167.16 *adaptably*
mallee fowl 78 Birds
mallee tree 85 Trees and Shrubs
mallet 50.14 *sculptor's materials*, 330.15 *ram*, 384.14 *hammer*
malleus 382 Bones, 420.5 *internal ear*
Mallophaga 82 Orders of Insects
mallophagan 82.10 *insectan*
mallow 84 Flowers and Flowering Plants
Malmö 93 Cities
malnourished 274.2 *emaciated*, 624.21 *unhealthy*
malnutrition 274.8 *emaciation*, 350.10 *scarcity*, 609.8 *insufficiency*, 624.4 *disease*
malodorous 419.3 *stinking*, 622.8 *unclean*
malodorously 419.6 *stinkingly*
malodorousness 419.1 *stench*
malodour 419.1 *stench*
Malory 48 Writers
malpractice 16.39 *crime*, 601.2 *misuse*, 866.3 *sin*
Malraux 48 Writers
Malta 91 Countries, **98** Islands
malt bread 45.38 *bread*
malt culms 68.9 *animal feedstuff*
malted milk 351.5 *milk*
Maltese 5 Languages and Groups of Languages, **77** Breeds of Dogs
Malthusianism 628.7 *deterioration*
malting 647.1 *workshop*
malt house 647.1 *workshop*
malt liquor 351.7 *alcoholic drink*
maltose 58 Common Sugars
maltreat 601.1 *misuse*, 618.14 *illtreat*, 832.18 *torment*, 844.20 *wrong*, 862.11 *be evil*
maltreated 601.4 *misused*
maltreatment 601.2 *misuse*, 618.11 *harmfulness*, 832.7 *act of malevolence*
malt vinegar 45.7 *basic ingredient*
Malvern 95 Mountains
Malvern Hills 95.5 *British mountains*
Mama Allpa 8 Deities
Mama Cocha 8 Deities
mamaloi 7.8 *priest*
mamba 79 Reptiles, 79.3 *snake*
mambo 46.2 *dance*
Mameluke 679.6 *militarist*
Mamet 48 Dramatists
mamilla 77.2 *mammalian characteristic*, 316.2 *bulge*
mamma 77.2 *mammalian characteristic*
mammal 77, 76.4 *type of animal*
mammal hunting 77
Mammalia 77.1 *mammal*
mammalian 77
mammalian characteristic 77
mammal-like 77.25 *mammalian*
mammal-like reptile 79.6 *extinct reptile*
mammals 396.9 *classifications of life*
Mammals 77
mammary 352.5 *of a secretion*
mammary gland 352 Exocrine Glands, 77.2 *mammalian characteristic*, 352.3 *gland*
mammee apple 86 Fruits

mammogram 60.7 *diagnosis*
mammography 60.7 *diagnosis*
mammologist 77, 76.11 *zoologist*
mammology 76.9 *animal science*, 77.1 *mammal*
Mammonism 7 Non-Christian Religions, 9.2 *idolatry*
Mammonist 9.6 *idolater*
Mammonistic 9.10 *idolatrous*
mammonolater 9.6 *idolater*
mammonolatrous 9.10 *idolatrous*
mammonolatry 9.2 *idolatry*
mammoplasty 60 Surgical Operations
mammoth 77 Placental Mammals, 200.10 *fossilization*, 259.9 *big thing*, 259.15 *big*
Mammoth Bronze 68 Breeds of Fowl
mammothermography 60.7 *diagnosis*
mammy 632.3 *protector*
mammy wagon 71 Motor Vehicles
man 207, 230.9 *take action*, 400.1 *humankind*, 400.7 *person*, 401.1 *male sex*, 401.2 *male*, 401.3 *male title of address*, 594.5 *equip*, 606.5 *provision*, 671.21 *entrench*, 697.6 *domestic servant*, 808.3 *sycophant*, 808.5 *adherent*
mana 8.5 *deity*, 235.1 *power*
man about the house 401.13 *man in the family*
man about town 655.5 *expert*, 815.6 *social person*
manacle 135.10 *link*, 137.12 *bind*, 699.12 *gag*
manacled 137.16 *bound*
manacles 137.8 *fastening*, 699.5 *means of restraint*
man after one's own heart 821.11 *loved one*
manage 12.11 *govern*, 105.6 *be in a state of*, 126.10 *lead*, 150.18 *order*, 152.18 *make arrangements*, 166.16 *direct*, 226.10 *awaken*, 230.9 *take action*, 235.10 *be powerful*, 597.1 *undertake*, 640.4 *act*, 652.14 *behave towards*, 682.7 *overcome obstacles*, 688.18 *have authority*, 696.14 *master*, 707.5 *represent*
manageability 660.3 *wieldiness*
manageable 230.11 *workable*, 284.10 *supportable*, 572.3 *amenable*, 660.12 *wieldy*, 694.7 *obedient*, 754.9 *cheap*
managed 14.6 *financial*, 15.8 *industrial*
managed currency 14.1 *finance*, 741.1 *money*, 741.7 *finance*
manage grassland 87
management 230, 653, 12.1 *government*, 15.1 *industrial relations*, 126.2 *leadership*, 166.8 *authority*, 599.6 *use*, 640.1 *action*, 652.8 *treatment*, 653.6 *governing body*, 688.4 *governance*
Management 653
management accounting 750.1 *accounts*
management buyout 13.7 *corporation*, 738.7 *purchasing*
management by objectives 592.1 *plan*
management consultant 654.4 *adviser*
management demands 15.1 *industrial relations*
management-employee relations 15.1 *industrial relations*
management engineering 63.1 *engineering*
management lock-out 15.4 *industrial dispute*
management practices 15.1 *industrial relations*
management review 592.2 *policy*
management study 653.3 *management*
manager 653, 15.6 *employer*, 22.2 *baseball player*, 26.4 *boxer*,

51.25 *producer*, 126.5 *superior*, 228.7 *motivator*, 230.5 *operator*, 233.5 *influential person*, 586.14 *motivator*, 592.8 *planner*, 640.3 *doer*, 646.3 *agent*, 653.13 *director*, 688.10 *person of authority*, 696.5 *company leader*
manageress 653.15 *manager*
managerial 653, 15.8 *industrial*, 597.6 *enterprising*, 640.6 *effective*, 688.14 *governmental*, 696.12 *masterful*
managerial control 653.4 *directorship*
managerially 653, 15.13 *industrially*, 696.16 *masterfully*
managers 653.6 *governing body*
managership 653.3 *management*
manage the business of 707.5 *represent*
manage the interests of 707.5 *represent*
manage trees 85
managing 15.8 *industrial*, 332.5 *directions*, 653.3 *management*, 653.17 *managerial*
managing director 15.6 *employer*, 640.3 *doer*, 653.15 *manager*
managing editor 532.12 *publisher*, 533.4 *journalist*
Managua 93 Cities
manakin 78 Birds
mañana attitude 573.15 *delay*
man and beast 111.2 *opposites*
man and wife 823.9 *married couple*
man a ship 74.9 *navigate*
man-at-arms 679.1 *combatant*, 679.8 *soldier*, 679.17 *army person*, 679.20 *cavalryman*
manatee 77 Placental Mammals
man at the top 400.7 *person*
man at the wheel 74.2 *nautical person*
Manawatu 92 New Zealand Regions and Territories, **96** Rivers
Manchester 93 Cities, 93.4 *British cities*
Manchester terrier 77 Breeds of Dogs
manchineel 85 Trees and Shrubs
Manchu 5 Languages and Groups of Languages, 5.11 *family of languages*
man-crazy 877.13 *unchaste*
Mancunian 255.9 *British inhabitant*
mandala 11.6 *talisman*, 313.2 *circle*, 543.1 *sign*
Mandalay 93 Cities
mandamus 16.6 *legal process*
Mandan 1 Peoples
mandarin 86 Fruits, 451.3 *orange thing*, 611.4 *bigwig*, 653.16 *official*, 696.3 *leader*
Mandarin Chinese 5 Languages and Groups of Languages
Mandarin collar 25 neckwear
mandarin duck 78 Birds
mandate 12.1 *government*, 12.5 *political organization*, 16.2 *jurisdiction*, 91.3 *dominion*, 91.18 *exert sovereignty*, 249.4 *territorial division*, 485.6 *specification*, 571.15 *compel*, 592.2 *policy*, 654.3 *precept*, 688.8 *governmental organization*, 692.4 *authorization*, 692.13 *authorize*, 695.2 *coercion*, 695.6 *compel*, 703.3 *authority*, 703.8 *authorize*, 708.1 *permission*, 851.1 *approval*
mandated 91.16 *national*, 692.15 *self-assured*, 703.9 *commissioned*
mandated territory 12.1 *government*, 12.5 *political organization*, 91.3 *dominion*
mandatory 91.3 *dominion*, 103.5 *essential*, 166.9 *legal*, 485.12 *conditional*, 571.10 *obligatory*, 692.14 *commanding*, 695.10 *compulsory*, 847.12 *obligatory*
Mande 5 Languages and Groups of Languages
Mandeism 7 Christian Movements

Mandelbrot set 52 Named Concepts
mandible 382 Bones
mandibles 350.16 eating utensil
Mandingo 1 Peoples
mandobass 49 Musical Instruments
mandocello 49 Musical Instruments
mandola 49 Musical Instruments
mandolin 49 Musical Instruments
mandolinetto 49 Musical Instruments
mandolone 49 Musical Instruments
mandrel 364.4 vortex
mandrill 77 Placental Mammals
manducate 350.21 eat
manducation 350.1 eating
man-eater 340.6 charmer, 350.18 eater, 398.10 killer, 590.6 hunter
man-eating 350.5 eating habit, 350.26 eating, 398.24 murderous
man-eating shark 79 Fishes
manège 32.6 horsemanship
manes 11.11 ghost
man Friday 232.3 assistant, 662.11 helper, 697.5 office assistant
man from Mars 104.6 outsider
manfully 574.17 resolutely
mangabey 77 Placental Mammals
Mangalarga 32 Breeds of Horse and Pony
Mangalitsa 68 Breeds of Pig
manganese 57 Chemical Elements, 58.15 essential element
manganese bronze 57 Alloys
manganic 57.34 elemental
manganite 54 Minerals
manganous 57.34 elemental
mange 624.13 skin disease, 624.18 veterinary disease
mangels 68.12 crop
mangetout 45 Vegetables
manginess 624.1 ill health
mangle 262.4 contractor, 282.4 flattener, 355.9 extractor, 376.9 smoother, 376.11 smooth, 392.15 dryer, 392.23 drip-dry, 406.11 inflict pain, 621.13 clean
mangled 145.4 incomplete, 392.4 dried-out, 618.2 inferior
mango 86 Fruits
Mango 93 Cities
mangonel 338.9 firearm, 680.6 historical missile weapon
mangosteen 86 Fruits
mangrove 85 Trees and Shrubs
mangrove snake 79 Reptiles
mangrove sudd 98.3 marsh
mangy 618.4 poor, 622.8 unclean, 624.21 unhealthy, 624.23 diseased, 754.10 shoddy
manhandle 326.12 transport, 326.15 take away, 601.1 misuse
man-hater 820.5 hostile person, 822.9 hater, 834.2 misanthrope
man-hating 834.3 misanthropic
Manhattan 98 Islands, 93.3 New York, 351.8 mixed drink
manhole 322.7 passageway
manhood 207.2 adulthood, 401.1 male sex
manhood suffrage 580.11 franchise
man-hour 75 General Units, 187.4 period of activity
man-hours 644.2 task
manhunt 590.1 pursuit
mania 61.15 compulsion, 510.4 delusion, 584.1 habit, 759.4 emotion, 784.3 likes
maniac 510.7 insane person
manic 510, 642.18 active, 759.13 passionate
manic-depressive 224.5 changeable person, 510.7 insane person
manic-depressive psychosis 61.11, 510.5 psychosis
Manichaeism 4.7 school of thought

manicotti 45 Types of Pasta
manicure 791.3 beauty treatment
manicured 558.3 elegant
manicure set 791.5 make-up box
manicurist 791.13 beautician
manifest 526, 99.10 existing, 171.4 bill, 253.7 present, 312.5 honourable, 322.13 opened up, 435.23, 437.1 visible, 437.9 appear, 437.10 make visible, 442.4 easily seen through, 457.7 appearing, 475.9 demonstrated, 475.15 demonstrate, 483.9 evident, 526.1 display, 526.3 reveal, 530.5 disclose, 532.20 well-known, 547.9 represent, 750.4 statement, 811.27 show
manifestation 437, 526, 11.11 ghost, 253.1 presence, 253.6 ghostly presence, 367.2 materialization, 457.1 appearance, 475.1 demonstration, 483.3 evidentness, 496.7 detection, 530.1 disclosure, 532.7 publicity, 543.4 signal, 547.1 representation, 811.14 show
manifested 526.13 displayed
manifesting 530.12 revelatory
manifestly 475, 526, 99.22 really, 322.25 obviously, 435.25, 437.11 visibly, 457.15 apparently, 483.15 evidently, 496.16 originally
manifestness 253.1 presence, 526.10 manifestation
manifesto 4.2 philosophical system, 497.2 religious belief, 532.1 publication, 535.2 statement, 580.12 election, 592.2 policy, 692.1 command
manifold 71 Motor Vehicle Parts, 52.47 topology, 113.5 diverse, 175.8 multiplicative, 181.5 multitudinous
manikin 260.4 little person, 547.6 image
Manila 93 Cities
man in the family 401
man in the moon 53.17 moon
man in the street 124.7 average person, 164.9 everyman, 400.7 person
man-in-the-street 803.1 plebeian
manioc 45 Vegetables
maniphobia 777 Phobias by Name
maniple 7.11 vestment, 679.16 army unit
manipulatable 230.11 workable
manipulate 52, 228, 230.9 take action, 407.11 touch, 474.11 practise sophistry, 539.28 trick, 540.22 falsify, 592.13 plot, 599.1 use, 630.20 doctor, 640.4 act, 652.11 conduct oneself, 652.14 behave towards, 653.1 manage, 688.18 have authority, 734.10 take away
manipulated 539.36 deceived, 540.32 falsified
manipulate market prices 737.2 speculate
manipulate the truth 525.1 misinterpret
manipulating 407.2 touching, 474.8 cunning
manipulation 52.24 evaluation, 230.4 management, 474.3 cunning, 525.2 misinterpretation, 539.7 tricking, 540.9 falsification, 592.4 plot, 601.2 misuse, 630.13 therapy, 652.8 treatment, 653.3 management, 688.1 authority, 734.3 taking away
manipulative 540.29 deceitful, 734.12 taking
manipulatively 734.13 avariciously
manipulative treatment 60.8 treatment
manipulator 228.7 motivator, 233.5 influential person, 586.14 motivator, 640.3 doer
Manipur pony 32 Breeds of Horse and Pony
Manitoba 92 Canadian Prov-

inces and Territories, 94 Lakes, 94.5 other major lakes
manitou 8.5 deity
mankind 396.1 life, 400.1 humankind, 401.1 male sex, 815.7 human society
mankind-hater 834.2 misanthrope
manky 618.4 poor, 622.8 unclean
manlike 401.17 male
manliness 237.1 strength, 401.1 male sex, 778.2 heroism
manly 237.9 physically strong, 401.17 male, 778.10 chivalrous, 789.5 beautiful
man-mad 877.13 unchaste
man-made 102.12 not the real thing, 118.13 imitation, 243.12 produced, 539.39 imitative
man-made lake 94.1 lake, 539.6 imitation
man-management 653.3 management
man mountain 259.10 big person
Mann 48 Writers
manna 85 Trees and Shrubs, 350.7 food, 396.3 life requirements, 662.3 sustenance, 729.3 offering
mannan 58.4 polysaccharide
manned crossing 72.2 track
manned flight 53.31 space travel
mannequin 526.12 displayer, 796.5 fashion model
manner 105.1 state, 163.4 type, 327.1 way, 457.3 external appearance, 549.1 style, 602.1 means, 652.1 conduct
mannered 559.9 inelegant, 797.3 affected
mannerism 48 Literary Groups and Movements, 50 Western Art Styles and Movements, 117.3 nonconformity, 165.3 characteristic, 168.5 idiosyncrasy, 544.1 identification, 549.1 style, 584.2 tendency
mannerist 43 Architectural Styles, 50.29 realist
mannerless brat 785.3 disliked person
mannerless imp 818.4 discourteous person
mannerliness 817.2 good manners
mannerly 150.17 disciplined
manner of speaking 549.4 literary style
manner of working 327.1 way
manners 584.5 tradition, 652.1 conduct, 652.6 way of life, 876.1 morality
manners and customs 584.4 custom
Mannheim 93 Cities
mannikin 78 Birds
Manning 48 Writers
mannish 401.17 male
mannishness 401.1 male sex
mannitol 62 Medication, 58.3 carbohydrate
mannomustine 62 Medication
mannose 58 Common Sugars
Manobo 5 Languages and Groups of Languages
manoeuvrability 660.3 wieldiness, 698.5 scope
manoeuvrable 230.11 workable, 660.12 wieldy, 698.11 ranging
manoeuvre 175.3 flight, 230.9 take action, 324.15 walk, 407.11 touch, 592.13 plot, 599.1 use, 640.2 deed, 640.4 act, 652.9 tactics, 652.11 conduct oneself, 653.1 manage, 657.2 stratagem, 657.5 be cunning, 676.13 be at war
manoeuvres 652.9 tactics, 676.6 art of war
manoeuvring 230.4 management, 652.9 tactics, 657.1 cunning
man of action 336.16 progressive person, 640.3 doer, 642.10 busy person
man of blood 241.4 violent person or animal, 398.10 killer

man of dishonour 858.4 dishonourable person
man of genius 786.5 person of wonder
man of goodwill 831.5 benevolent person
man of high standing 800.2 person of repute
man of his word 857.3 honourable person
man of honour 800.2 person of repute, 857.3 honourable person
man of impulse 579.4 capricious person
man of letters 48.15 literary person, 560.10 descriptive writer
man of means 686.4 prosperous person, 742.10 wealthy person
man of peace 675.3 pacifist
man of prayer 7.3 religious person, 497.5 believer
man of property 686.4 prosperous person, 723.6 lord, 725.7 property man
man of straw 102.5 insubstantial person, 236.5 powerless person, 238.4 weakling, 278.5 shallow person, 576.15 indecisive person, 612.10 nonentity
man of substance 686.4 prosperous person, 723.6 lord
man of taste 794.4 refined person
man of the cloth 7.8 priest
man of the house 696.1 master, 725.7 property man
man of the match 682.4 successful person
man of the world 207.8 man, 401.7 libertine, 655.5 expert
man of the year 682.4 successful person
man-of-war 78 Birds, 679.24 warship
manometer 268.8 meter, 388.15 vaporimeter
manometric 268.16 micrometric
manometry 268.2 micrometry
man on the Clapham omnibus 124.7 average person, 164.9 everyman, 400.7 person
man on the make 821.9 lover, 826.5 courting person
manor 249.13 locality, 250.1 location, 725.1 property
manor house 256.4 official residence
manorial 256, 725.8 propertied
manorial court 16.19 lawcourt
man overboard 639.5 to the rescue
manpower 161.13 workforce, 235.1 power, 235.4 energy, 602.3 human resources, 644.4 exertion, 646.4 personnel
mansard 275.8 high thing
mansard roof 43.6 roof
man's best friend 77.9 dog
manse 7.10 priestly dwelling, 256.4 official residence
manservant 697.6 domestic servant
man's evening dress 440.4 dark thing
Mansfield 48 Writers
mansion 243.8 construction, 256.4 official residence, 725.1 property
Mansion House 256.4 official residence
man-size 259.15 big
manslaughter 16.39 crime, 398.1 killing, 398.2 murder, 398.8 accidental killing
mansuetude 817.1 courtesy
manta ray 80 Fishes
mantelet 671.7 armour
mantelpiece 283.5 projecting object, 284.2 supporting part
mantelshelf 34.5 rock face
manteltree 85.12 figurative usage
man the breach 671.21 entrench
man the defences 671.21 entrench
man the fort 671.21 entrench
man the guns 671.21 entrench
mantic 517.13 predicting
manticore 76.7 legendary beast

mantilla 295.15 *headgear*

mantis 82 *Insects*, 82.1 *insect*

mantissa 52.19 *logarithm*, 169.6 *power*

mantis shrimp 81.4 *arthropod*

mantle 7.11 *vestment*, 54.18 *earth's crust*, 295.25 *accessories*, 295.32 *dress*, 450.9 *redden*

mantled 295.29 *diseased*

mantle of snow 55.30 *snow*

mantling 544.8 *heraldic device*

mantology 11.9 *divination*

man-to-man 31.8 *hockey*

man-to-man assignment 31.3 *ice hockey*

man-to-man defence 19.10 *defence*, 23.4 *playing terms*

mantra 10.8 *hymn*, 10.9 *prayer*, 505.1 *maxim*

mantua 295.7 *frock*

manual 6.14 *school book*, 15.8 *industrial*, 49.16 *musical note*, 232.8 *practical*, 407.10 *handed*, 528.5 *reference book*

manual labour 644.1 *work*

manually 407, 15.13 *industrially*, 232.9 *instrumentally*, 644.12 *laboriously*

manual skill 655.1 *skill*

manual work 644.1 *work*

manual worker 15.7 *employee*, 124.7 *average person*, 603.7 *machinist*, 640.3 *doer*, 646.1 *worker*

manubrium 90.4 *reproductive body*

manufacture 243, 102.17 *fabricate*, 161.33 *putting together*, 161.44 *put together*, 243.3 *product*, 243.10 *produce*, 382.15 *shape*, 594.13 *development*, 640.1 *action*

manufactured 243.12 *produced*

manufactured item 243.3 *product*

manufacturer 243.9 *producer*, 646.3 *agent*

manufacturing 13.2 *economy*, 243.2 *manufacture*, 243.11 *productive*

manufacturing plant 647.1 *workshop*

manufacturing town 647.1 *workshop*

manuka 85 *Trees and Shrubs*

Manukau 93 *Cities*

manumission 700.1 *liberation*

manumit 698.15 *set free*, 700.4 *liberate*

manumitter 700.3 *liberator*

manure 68.13 *fertilizer*, 68.17 *farm*, 69.7 *fertilizer*, 69.15 *cultivate*, 246.3 *fertilizer*, 246.7 *make fertile*, 353.5 *faeces*, 622.4 *dirt*

manure heap 68.10 *farm tool*

manuscript 3.11 *relic*, 119.2 *original*

manuscript editor 532.12 *publisher*

Man/Woman of the Year 878.2 *prize*

Manx 5 *Languages and Groups of Languages*, **77** *Breeds of Cats*

Manx Loghtan 68 *Breeds of Sheep*

many 181, 120.6 *quantitative*, 175.1 *plurality*, 175.6 *plural*, 181.2 *multitude*, 212.3 *frequent*, 490.8 *unspecified*

many a time 212.1, 212.1 *frequently*

many a time and oft 212.1 *frequently*

many-celled invertebrate 81.1 *invertebrate*

many-coloured 444.10 *coloured*, 456.6 *variegated*

many-hued 456.6 *variegated*

many-one 52.76 *functional*

many-sided 175.7 *various*, 305.6 *side*, 655.6 *skilful*

many-sidedness 175.2 *multiplicity*, 655.1 *skill*

many thanks 837.9 *thank you*

many times 212.1 *frequently*

many times over 183.23 *repeatedly*

many-tongued 423.6 *loud*

many voices 113.4 *dissension*

many words 5

manzanilla 86 *Fruits*

Manzoni 48 *Writers*, 48 *Poets*

MAO inhibitor 62.4 *drug type*

Maoism 12.1 *government*

Mao jacket 295.11 *jacket*

Maori 5 *Languages and Groups of Languages*, 200.6 *people of the past*

Maoris 1 *Peoples*

Maou 8 *Deities*

maoz tzur 10.8 *hymn*

map 54, 299, 547, 592, 34.4 *climbing equipment*, 63.30 *engineer*, 250.2 *exact location*, 332.3 *orientation*, 547.11 *paint*

maple 85 *Trees and Shrubs*

maple syrup 414.2 *sweetener*

mapmaker 547.4 *person who makes a representation*

mapmaking 547.7 *map*

map of the heavens 547.7 *map*

map out 154.18 *forerun*, 592.10 *plan out*

map out a course 592.10 *plan out*

mapped 268.13 *measured*

mapping 52.29 *mathematical function*, 63.17 *civil engineering*

map reference 250.2 *exact location*

maprotiline 62 *Medication*

Maputo 93 *Cities*

maquette 50.12 *sculpture*

Maquis 679.9 *guerrilla*, 679.14 *armed forces*

mar 133.8 *mix*, 233.9 *change*, 238.7 *weaken*, 244.11 *ruin*, 628.4 *impair*, 631.14 *afflict*, 656.7 *be clumsy*, 793.7 *blemish*

mara 77 *Placental Mammals*

Mara 8.7 *devil*

marabenta 49.10 *world music*

marabi 49.10 *world music*

marabou 78 *Birds*

marabout 7.3 *religious person*, 168.9 *hermit*, 174.8 *loner*, 816.6 *unsocial person*

Maracaibo 93 *Cities*, 94 *Lakes*, 94.5 *other major lakes*

maracas 49 *Musical Instruments*

marae 10.13 *shrine*

marang 86 *Fruits*

Marans 68 *Breeds of Fowl*

marasca 86 *Fruits*

marasmic 274.2 *emaciated*

marasmus 262.1 *contraction*, 274.8 *emaciation*, 624.4 *disease*, 628.9 *dilapidation*

Maratha 1 *Peoples*

Marathi 5 *Languages and Groups of Languages*

marathon 21.6 *track*, 41.2 *cross-country skiing*, 263.2 *great distance*, 674.2 *contest*, 674.4 *race*

marathon group 61.3 *psychiatric treatment*

marathon race 21.1 *track events*

marathon racing 21.1 *track events*

marathon runner 21.3, 237.5 *athlete*

marathon running 18 *Sporting Activities*

maraud 679.38 *conquer*

marauder 679.6 *militarist*, 734.6 *taker*, 736.9 *plunderer*

marauding 734.3 *taking away*, 736.17 *stolen*

marble 54 *Common Rocks*, 43.4 *building material*, 50.12 *sculpture*, 50.14 *sculptor's materials*, 63.26 *masonry*, 315.3 *round thing*, 373.1 *hard*, 373.7 *hard substance*, 376.8 *smooth thing*, 446.1 *white*, 446.9 *white thing*, 456.11 *variegate*, 604.2 *building material*

marbled 456.9 *striped*

marbled paper 456.5 *variegated thing*

marbled ware 44.1 *ceramics*

marble-hearted 832.12 *callous*

marbles 42 *Children's Games and Party Games*

marblewood 85 *Trees and Shrubs*

marbling 50.4 *treatment*, 456.3 *striping*

marbly 456.9 *striped*

marcasite 54 *Minerals*

marcato 49 *Musical Terms*

march 28.3 *fencing movements*, 28.5 *fence*, 249.6 *regions*, 324.12 *gait*, 324.15 *walk*, 327.2 *route*, 336.11 *course*, 475.6 *mass demonstration*, 475.19 *protest*, 668.3 *act of defiance*, 668.6 *be insubordinate*, 676.6 *art of war*, 676.13 *be at war*, 811.27 *show*

march against 670.1 *attack*

march away 345.5 *set out*

marcher 668.4 *defiant person*, 693.7, 713.4 *protester*

marches 249.3 *regional boundary*

Marches 249.9 *regions of Britain*

march for 475.19 *protest*

Marchigiana 68 *Breeds of Cattle*

marching 324.1 *motion*, 475.14 *demonstrating*

marching and countermarching 652.9 *tactics*

marching band 49.26 *musical group*

marching orders 252.4 *relegation*, 692.1 *command*, 704.2 *termination*, 727.1 *dismissal*

march in lock step 198.7 *synchronize*

march in slow-time 328.1 *move slowly*

marchioness 802.1 *nobleman*

march off 345.5 *set out*

march of time 188.2 *time*, 336.11 *course*

march on 336, 219.4 *protract*

march out 345.3 *quit*, 347.9 *exit*

march out of step 117.13 *not conform*

march past 159.8 *procession*, 159.17 *line up*, 811.27 *show*, 813.3 *formal occasion*

march-past 811.13 *ceremonial*, 812.8 *salute*

march to a different drum 168.19 *be independent*

march to a different drummer 117.13 *not conform*, 666.8 *be different*

march to war 676.13 *be at war*

marcia 49 *Musical Terms*

Marconi 52 *Scientists*, 36.10 *sailing*

Marconi rig 36.3 *parts of a sailing boat*

Marconi-rigged 36.10 *sailing*

Marcopole 534.7 *satellite communication*

Marcuse 4 *Philosophers*

Mardi Gras 10.15 *holy day*, 811.14 *show*, 812.1 *celebration*

Marduk 8 *Deities*

mare 32.1 *horse*, 53.17 *moon*, 77.18 *female mammal*, 402.14 *female animal*

Mare Anguis 53 *Seas*

Mare Australe 53 *Seas*

Mare Cognitum 53 *Seas*

Mare Crisium 53 *Seas*

Maree 94 *Lakes*

Mare Fecunditatis 53 *Seas*

Mare Frigoris 53 *Seas*

Mare Humboldtianum 53 *Seas*

Mare Humorum 53 *Seas*

Mare Imbrium 53 *Seas*

Mare Ingenii 53 *Seas*

Mare Marginis 53 *Seas*

Maremmana 32 *Breeds of Horse and Pony*

Mare Moscoviense 53 *Seas*

Mare Nectaris 53 *Seas*

Marengo 32.3 *warhorse*

Mare Nubium 53 *Seas*

Mare Orientale 53 *Seas*

mares 161 *Collective Names by Animal*

Mare Serenitatis 53 *Seas*

mare's milk 351.5 *milk*

Mare Smythii 53 *Seas*

Mare Spumans 53 *Seas*

mare's-tail 55.20 *cloud appearance*

Mare Tranquillitatis 53 *Seas*

Mare Undarum 53 *Seas*

Mare Vaporum 53 *Seas*

Margaret Smith 40.7 *famous tennis players*

margarine 45.7 *basic ingredient*, 395.8 *fat*

margarita 351.8 *mixed drink*

margarite 54 *Minerals*

margay 77 *Placental Mammals*

margin 132.3 *difference*, 248.6 *available space*, 265.1 *interval*, 299.3, 300.1 *edge*, 302.3 *furthest point*, 610.3 *superfluity*, 752.1 *discount*, 814.4 *freedom*

marginal 36.7, 36.13 *windsurfing*, 299.6 *outlined*, 300.8 *edging*, 335.19 *deviant person*

marginal constituency 580.12 *election*

marginal costs 13.7 *corporation*

marginalia 130.3 *additional item*, 524.2 *annotation*, 545.3 *notes*

marginalize 300.6 *edge*

marginally 300, 173.7 *fractionally*, 299.7 *essentially*

marginal note 130.3 *additional item*

margin notes 545.3 *notes*

margin of profit 878.5 *turnover*

Margot Fonteyn 46.14 *famous ballet dancers*

margrave 802.1 *nobleman*

margravine 802.1 *nobleman*

marguerite 84 *Flowers and Flowering Plants*

Marianas Trench 277.4 *deep thing*

Mariana Trench 54.16 *ocean floor*, 97.1 *sea*

Maria Taglioni 46.14 *famous ballet dancers*

Maria Tallchief 46.14 *famous ballet dancers*

Marie Rambert 46.14 *famous ballet dancers*

marigold 84 *Flowers and Flowering Plants*, 451.3 *orange thing*

marijuana 631.11 *intoxicant*, 875.6 *drug*

marina 301.2 *enclosed place*, 303.1 *front*, 634.2 *shelter*

marinade 413.2 *seasoning*, 637.2 *preserver*

marinate 355.17 *obtain an extract*, 374.13 *soften*, 413.12 *season*, 637.5 *preserve*

marinated 637.7 *preserved*

marinating 355.7 *obtaining an extract*, 594.17 *developing*

marination 637.1 *preservation*

marine 54.51 *oceanic*, 74.7 *nautical person*, 74.11 *nautical*, 76.15 *of animals*, 97.7 *oceanic*, 676.11 *recruit*, 679.28 *marines*

marine animal 76.5 *aquatic animal*

marine archaeology 3.2 *archaeology*

marine biologist 59.19 *life scientist*, 76.11 *zoologist*, 97.6 *oceanographer*

marine biology 59.1 *life science*, 76.9 *animal science*, 97.5 *oceanography*

marine chronometer 191 *Timepieces and Timers*

marine engineering 63.3 *mechanical engineering*

marine fish 80.1 *fishes*

marine geology 54.1 *earth science*

marine mammal 77, 76.5 *aquatic animal*

marine painter 50.16 *artist*

marine painting 50.10 *art subject*

marine park 256.12 *stall*

mariner 74.7 *nautical person*, 653.13 *director*, 679.27 *naval man*

Mariner 53.33 *planetary probe*

marine reptile 79.6 *extinct reptile*

Mariner's Compass 53 *The Constellations*

marines 679, 17.2 *the military*,

679.14 *armed forces,* 718.4 *security forces*
marine scientist 74.7 *nautical person*
marine sextant 74.5 *navigation*
marine's uniform 544.5 *uniform*
Mariology 7.13 *theology*
marionette 547.6 *image*
marionette show 51.5 *show*
Marist 7 Members of Religious Orders
Maritain 4 Philosophers
marital 823.20 *matrimonial*
marital infidelity 877.4 *illicit love*
maritally 823.24 *matrimonially*
marital relations 821.5 *desire*
maritime 54.51, 97.7 *oceanic*
maritime climate 55.38 *climate*
maritime meteorology 55.1 *meteorology*
Maritsa 96 Rivers
Marius Hills 53 Mountains
Marivaux 48 Dramatists
marjoram 45 Herbs and Spices, 413.5 *herbs*
mark 5.47 *word,* 44.11 *make ceramics,* 103.11 *characterize,* 121.3 *gradation,* 121.5 *measure,* 149.2 *impurity,* 163.4 *type,* 165.3 *characteristic,* 165.22 *characterize,* 216.8 *cause change,* 227.2 *visible effect,* 227.6 *have a visible effect,* 309.3 *deformity,* 309.11 *deform,* 318.1 *prominence,* 467.11 *take note of,* 483.4 *indication,* 543.1 *sign,* 543.9 *use signs,* 544.3 *means of identification,* 544.10 *identify,* 545.12 *vestige,* 588.6 *objective,* 611.1 *importance,* 620.7 *defect,* 622.4 *dirt,* 628.5 *hurt,* 667.2, 667.7 *contract,* 708.2 *permit,* 741.11 *national coins,* 793.1 *spot,* 800.1 *estimation,* 812.16 *commemorate*
Markab 53 Named Stars
mark as one's prey 590.12 *aim at*
mark down 495.3 *underestimate,* 545.14 *inscribe,* 580.4 *pick,* 752.3 *discount*
markdown 754.1 *cheapness,* 754.9 *cheap*
mark down 754.13 *make cheap*
mark down for 588.9 *intend for*
marked 793, 126.15 *excellent,* 165.15 *characteristic,* 237.10 *potent,* 309.7 *deformed,* 327.15 *accessible,* 526.14 *manifest,* 544.12 *identified,* 554.4 *emphasized,* 620.1 *imperfect*
marked down 752.6 *discounted,* 754.9 *cheap*
markedly 165.30 *characteristically*
marked man 856.4 *accused person*
marked out for destruction 244.15 *destroyed*
marked trail 41.1 *skiing*
marker 24.7 *billiards player,* 25.3 *bowls player,* 29.6 *golfer,* 543.1 *sign,* 543.8 *signer*
marker's box 40.5 *real tennis*
market 739, 740, 13.6 *economic factors,* 13.10 *trade with,* 14.2 *stock exchange,* 93.7 *city district,* 223.2 *place of exchange,* 350.17 *food shop,* 526.6 *display,* 627.1 *improve,* 737.1 *trade,* 738.2 *shop,* 739.1 *sell*
Market 740
marketability 739.7 *market*
marketable 13.13 *economic,* 737.13 *mercantile,* 739.15 *saleable*
marketably 739
market cross 740.6 *marketplace*
marketer 737.10 *trader,* 739.12 *wholesaler*
market garden 69.2 *garden,* 69.14 *practise horticulture*
market gardener 69.13 *horticulturist*
market gardening 68.4 *arable farming,* 69.1 *horticulture,* 86.4 *fruit eating,* 243.2 *manufacture*
marketing 13.2 *economy,* 738.14 *buying,* 739.3 *selling*

marketing board 68.2 *Common Agricultural Policy*
market maker 14.3 *stockbroker,* 737.10 *trader,* 739.12 *wholesaler*
marketplace 740, 93.7 *city district,* 223.2 *place of exchange,* 291.4 *centre of activity,* 642.6 *business*
market price 751.1 *price*
market research 477.2 *questioning,* 739.7 *market*
market researcher 477.9 *questioner*
market square 93.7 *city district*
market town 93.9 *town,* 249.11 *settlement,* 291.4 *centre of activity,* 740.6 *marketplace*
market trader 739.11 *pedlar,* 739.14 *street trader*
markhor 77 Placental Mammals
marking 457.3 *external appearance*
marking one's territory 723.1 *possession*
markings 544.4 *insignia,* 560.8 *name*
marking the occasion 812.2 *commemoration*
markka 741.11 *national coins*
mark of authority 544.4 *insignia*
mark off 268.10 *measure,* 544.10 *identify*
mark of recognition 817.3 *courtesies*
mark of respect 849
mark out 136.10 *set apart,* 543.9 *use signs,* 560.17 *describe a circle,* 580.4 *pick*
mark out a course 592.10 *plan out*
Markov 52 Scientists
Markovian chain 52 Named Concepts
Markovnikoff's rules 57 Named Reactions
mark paid 749.7 *receive*
marksman 338.15 *shooter,* 590.6 *hunter*
markswoman 338.15 *shooter,* 590.6 *hunter*
mark the cards 539.30 *be fraudulent*
mark the occasion 511.14, 812.16 *commemorate*
mark the way 543.9 *use signs*
mark time 185.16 *time,* 192.16 *measure time,* 248.21 *space,* 325.8 *be motionless*
mark up 753.10 *overcharge*
marl 54 Common Rocks, 44.2 *raw material,* 246.3 *fertilizer,* 246.7 *make fertile*
Marlborough 92 New Zealand Regions and Territories
marlin 80 Fishes, 20.4 *American game fish*
marlinespike 380.8 *sharp-pointed thing*
marlin fishing 590.2 *chase*
Marlowe 48 Dramatists
marm 402.3 *female title of address*
marmalade 45.42 *preserve,* 414.2 *sweetener,* 451.3 *orange thing,* 637.3 *preserved thing*
marmalade tree 85 Trees and Shrubs
Marmara 97 Oceans and Seas
marmoreal 50.25 *sculptural*
marmoset 77 Placental Mammals
marmot 77 Placental Mammals, 815.10 *social animal*
Marne 96 Rivers
Maronism 7 Christian Movements
maroon 136.11 *divide,* 449.1 *brown,* 450.1 *red,* 455.6 *purple,* 727.9 *dispose of*
marooned 98.11 *continental*
marooned person 816.6 *unsocial person*
marplot 656.10 *unskilled person,* 661.7 *hinderer*
Marquand 48 Writers
marque 163.4 *type,* 544.3 *means of identification*

marquee 293.7 *overhead covering*
marquess 802.1 *nobleman*
Marquess of Queensberry rules 26.2 *boxing*
marquetried 47.14 *wooden*
marquetried furniture 47.1 *furniture*
marquetry 42 Hobbies and Pastimes, 47.1 *furniture,* 47.9 *decorative woodwork,* 456.2 *check*
marquetry worker 47.13 *carpenter*
marquis 802.1 *nobleman*
marquise 45.35 *dessert,* 802.1 *nobleman*
marquisette 67 Natural Fabrics
Marrakech 93 Cities
marram grass 87 Grasses
married 127.17 *defective,* 145.4 *incomplete*
marriage 777 Phobias by Topic, **823,** 2.3 *social environment,* 10.5 *Christian rite,* 133.2 *mixed thing,* 135.4 *sexual union,* 140.2 *cooperation,* 180.3 *companionship*
Marriage 823
marriageability 823
marriageable 823
marriageable age 823.4 *marriageability*
marriageableness 823.4 *marriageability*
marriage act 821.5 *desire*
marriage adviser 654.4 *adviser,* 678.3 *mediator,* 823.13 *matchmaker*
marriage banns 543.6 *word*
marriage bed 823.1 *marriage*
marriage broker 678.3 *mediator,* 823.13 *matchmaker*
marriage bureau 823.13 *matchmaker*
marriage by proxy 823.3 *types of marriage*
marriage by the justice of the peace 823.5 *wedding*
marriage certificate 544.3 *means of identification,* 545.2 *certificate*
marriage contract 714.1 *promise,* 715.1 *contract*
marriage counsellor 678.3 *mediator*
marriage encounter 61.3 *psychiatric treatment*
marriage feast 823.6 *general terms*
marriage guidance 61.3 *psychiatric treatment*
marriage guidance counsellor 654.4 *adviser,* 678.3 *mediator,* 823.13 *matchmaker*
marriage licence 823.6 *general terms*
marriage lines 823.6 *general terms*
marriage of convenience 823.3 *types of marriage*
marriage on the rocks 824.1 *divorce*
marriage partner 823.8 *spouse*
marriage portion 725.6 *marriage settlement*
marriage procession 823.6 *general terms*
marriage relationship 107.1 *relatedness*
marriage service 10.5 *Christian rite*
marriage settlement 725
marriage song 823.6 *general terms*
marriage tie 823.1 *marriage*
marriage toast 823.6 *general terms*
marriage vows 823.5 *wedding*
married 823, 135.12 *united,* 180.19 *associated*
married couple 823
married love 821.2 *romantic love*
married man 823, 401.13 *man in the family*
married name 560.8 *name*
married state 823.1 *marriage*
married status 823.1 *marriage*
married woman 823, 402.12 *woman in the family*
marron 86 Nuts

marrow 45 Vegetables, 103.2 *essential content,* 158.2 *core,* 257.3 *insides,* 290.5 *inner nature,* 291.1 *centre*
marrow squash 45 Vegetables
marry 823, 135.8 *unite,* 135.11 *make love,* 140.6 *come together,* 480.13 *really,* 514.14 *good heavens,* 715.5 *contract,* 821.28 *win the love of*
marry in haste, repent at leisure 823.15 *marry*
marry into money 823.15 *marry*
marry off 727.9 *dispose of,* 823.16 *join in marriage*
marry well 823.15 *marry*
Mars 8 Deities, **53** Planets and their Satellites, 53.16 *planet,* 450.7 *red thing,* 676.3 *god of war*
marsala 351.9 *wine*
marseille 67 Natural Fabrics
Marseilles 93 Cities
marsh 98, 391, 94.2 *small lake,* 374.11 *soft thing,* 635.1 *trap*
Marsh 48 Writers
marshal 150.18 *order,* 152.12 *arrange,* 161.42 *call together,* 180.8 *usher,* 180.15 *escort,* 544.10 *identify,* 653.16 *official,* 688.10 *person of authority,* 696.3 *leader*
marshalled 152.20 *arranged,* 180.20 *accompanied*
marshalling 152.1 *arrangement,* 161.2 *herding,* 544.8 *heraldic device,* 594.11 *fitting out*
marshalling yard 72.8 *railway station,* 327.10 *railway*
Marshal of the Royal Air Force 17 British Military Ranks
marshal of the Royal Air Force 679.32 *airman*
marsh bird 78.3 *water bird*
Marsh Daisy 68 Breeds of Fowl
marsh fern 88 Ferns
marsh gas 57 Common Chemical Compounds
marsh harrier 78 Birds
marshiness 374.10 *compressibility,* 391.7 *bogginess*
marshland 98.3 *marsh*
marshlight 439.9 *firefly*
marsh mallow 84 Flowers and Flowering Plants
marshmallow 45.41 *sweet*
marsh marigold 84 Flowers and Flowering Plants
marshy 391, 94.9 *lakelike,* 98.11 *continental,* 374.4 *compressible,* 393.17 *muddy,* 626.5 *unhygienic*
Marsilius of Padua 4 Philosophers
Mars orange 451.2 *orangeness*
marsupial 77.4 *pouched mammal,* 77.25 *mammalian*
marsupial characteristic 77.4 *pouched mammal*
Marsupialia 77.4 *pouched mammal*
marsupialian 77.25 *mammalian*
marsupial mole 77 Marsupials
marsupial mouse 77 Marsupials
marsupial rat 77 Marsupials
marsupium 77.4 *pouched mammal*
mart 93.7 *city district,* 291.4 *centre of activity,* 740.1 *market*
martagon 84 Flowers and Flowering Plants
Martello tower 275.6 *tall thing,* 671.12 *fort*
marten 77 Placental Mammals
Martha Graham 46.14 *famous ballet dancers*
Martha's Vineyard 98 Islands
Mar Thoma 7 Christian Movements
martial 679, 17.8 *military,* 670.12 *militant,* 676.17 *military,* 778.11 *militant*
Martial 48 Poets
martial art 26.1 *combat sports*
martial arts 671.5 *self-defence*
martial law 12.1 *government,* 688.7 *type of rule,* 690.1 *severity*

martially 679, 17.11 *militarily*

martial music 676.2 *glory of war*

martial race 679.7 *militarist nation*

Martian 11.11 *ghost,* 53.36 *astronomical,* 104.6 *outsider,* 149.5 *extraterrestrial*

Martian poets 48 Literary Groups and Movements

martin 78 Birds

Martin 94 Lakes

Martina Navratilova 40.7 *famous tennis players*

Martineau 48 Writers

martinet 690.4 *strict person,* 696.4 *absolute ruler*

martingale 74 Rigging

martini 351.8 *mixed drink*

Martini 351.9 *wine*

Martinique 48 Islands

Martin Luther King 675.4 *Nobel Peace Prize*

Martinmas 10.15 *holy day*

martlet 78.9 *fabulous bird,* 544.8 *heraldic device*

martyr 710, 7.3 *religious person,* 8.10 *deified person,* 398.20 *kill ritually,* 406.11 *inflict pain,* 481.8 *victim of discrimination,* 668.4 *defiant person,* 687.5 *person in adversity,* 863.4 *virtuous person,* 879.4 *torture*

martyrdom 397.4 *death sentence,* 398.6 *ritual killing,* 406.1 *pain,* 710.6 *offering,* 859.2 *unselfishness,* 879.13 *capital punishment*

martyred 8.15 *deified,* 397.19 *dead,* 406.7 *feeling pain,* 710.19 *sacrificial,* 859.5 *unselfish*

martyrization 398.6 *ritual killing,* 879.13 *capital punishment*

martyrize 398.20 *kill ritually,* 879.4 *torture*

martyrology 397.12 *death count*

martyr to ill health 624.19 *sick person*

Marumda 8 Deities

marvel 457.4 *something that appears,* 786.4, 786.9 *wonder*

Marvell 48 Poets

marvelling 514.7 *amazed,* 786.6 *wondering*

marvellous 617.1 *worthy,* 762.5 *delightful,* 786.8 *wonderful*

marvellously 682.16 *successfully,* 786.13 *wonderfully*

marvel-of-Peru 84 Flowers and Flowering Plants

Marwari 32 Breeds of Horse and Pony

Marx 4 Philosophers

Marxism 2.7 *social stratification,* 4.7 *school of thought,* 627.11 *reformism,* 688.7 *type of rule*

Marxism-Leninism 12.1 *government*

Marxist 2.11 *sociologist,* 2.14 *socioeconomic,* 4.11 *follower of a doctrine,* 4.14 *of a philosophy,* 12.9 *governmental,* 367.3 *materialist,* 498.5 *disbeliever,* 627.12 *reformer,* 688.14 *governmental*

Marxist history 3.1 *history*

Marxists 12.6 *political party*

Mary Ann 875.6 *drug*

Mary Jane 875.6 *drug*

Maryknoll Father 7 Members of Religious Orders

Maryknoll Sister 7 Members of Religious Orders

Maryland 92 American States

Maryland Hunt Cup 32.7 *horseracing*

Mary Warner 875.6 *drug*

Mary Whitehouse 134.6 *prude*

marzipan 45.41 *sweet,* 414.3 *dessert*

Masai 1 Peoples, **5** Languages and Groups of Languages

masala dosa 45.49 *Indian dish*

mascara 791.4 *cosmetics*

Mascarpone 45 Cheeses

mascon 53.17 *moon*

mascot 11.6 *talisman,* 517.6 *good-luck sign,* 637.2 *preserver*

masculine 5.44 *grammatical,* 401.17 *male*

masculine gender 401.1 *male sex*

masculine rhyme 48.11 *rhyme*

masculinity 401.1 *male sex*

Masefield 48 Poets

masenqo 49 Musical Instruments

maser 56.26 *laser,* 64.21 *rectifier*

mash 133.8 *mix,* 136.9 *separate,* 374.13 *soften,* 384.27 *beat,* 393.8, 393.24 *pulp,* 412.3 *tasteless items*

MASH 630.14 *hospital*

mashed 133.12 *mixed*

mashed potato 46.2 *dance*

masher 384.11 *pulverizer,* 393.15 *pulper,* 821.9 *lover*

mashie 29.4 *golf club*

mashie iron 29.4 *golf club*

mashie niblick 29.4 *golf club*

mashiness 393.4 *pulpiness*

mashing 384.4 *pulverization*

mash tun 258.11 *vessel*

mashy 374.4 *compressible*

masjid 10.11 *place of worship*

mask 540, 293.16 *disguise,* 293.31 *hide,* 295.5 *fancy dress,* 303.3 *show,* 436.15 *blind,* 438.6 *that which makes invisible,* 438.8 *make invisible,* 474.11 *practise sophistry,* 531.3 *covering up,* 531.8 *conceal,* 539.12, 539.32 *disguise,* 540.12 *facade,* 632.4 *safety device,* 790.5 *make ugly*

masked 293.37 *protected,* 438.3 *private,* 527.2, 531.14 *concealed,* 539.41 *disguised,* 793.4 *blemished*

masked ball 46.1 *dancing,* 531.3 *covering up,* 815.5 *party*

masker 293.17 *coverer*

masking 436.11 *blinding,* 531.3 *covering up*

masking tape 138.3 *adhesive,* 438.6 *that which makes invisible*

masochism 673.1 *submission*

masochist 673.2 *appeaser*

masochistic 673.5 *submitting*

mason 43.2 *architect,* 646.2 *artisan*

mason bee 82 Insects

Mason-Dixon Line 136.6 *boundary*

Mason-Dixon Line 298.1 *interface*

masonry 63, 604.2 *building material*

Masorah 7.12 *religious text*

masque 51.2 *play,* 539.12 *disguise,* 815.5 *party*

masquerade 46.1 *dancing,* 293.16 *disguise,* 293.31 *hide,* 295.5 *fancy dress,* 474.12 *deceive,* 531.9, 539.12 *disguise,* 539.32 *disguise,* 540.12 *facade,* 540.24 *mask,* 547.3 *acting,* 547.10 *act,* 815.5 *party*

masquerader 293.17 *coverer,* 531.7 *concealer,* 539.15 *deceiver*

masquerading 539.41 *disguised,* 540.30 *pretending*

mass 56, 161, 259, 49.5 *sacred music,* 75.5 *dimension,* 120.1 *quantity,* 120.2 *certain amount,* 135.8 *unite,* 143.5 *largest part,* 143.7 *piece,* 161.20 *crowd,* 161.37 *assemble,* 161.40 *crowd,* 175.3 *majority,* 181.4 *throng,* 181.11 *crowd,* 259.1 *size,* 273.5 *thickness,* 367.4 *matter,* 369.4 *heaviness,* 371.1 *density,* 371.4 *solid body,* 371.9 *make dense,* 605.1 *store,* 679.18 *army of people,* 719.2 *religious observance*

Mass 10.5 *Christian rite,* 10.6 *Eucharist*

Massachuset 5 Languages and Groups of Languages

Massachusetts 92 American States

massacre 244.2 *destroying,* 244.8 *destroy,* 398.4, 398.18 *slaughter,* 679.38 *conquer,* 832.7 *act of malevolence,* 832.17 *kill,* 879.5 *execute,* 879.13 *capital punishment*

massacred 397.19 *dead*

Massacre of the Innocents 398.4 *slaughter*

mass action 664.4 *joint operation*

massage 385, 385, 374.13 *soften,* 374.14 *ease,* 407.11 *touch,* 630.13 *therapy,* 630.20 *doctor*

massage parlour 877.6 *brothel*

massager 407.5 *toucher*

massage the accounts 750.7 *account*

massaging 385.6 *massage,* 407.2 *touching*

massagist 407.5 *toucher*

mass book 10.10 *religious manual*

mass burial 399.1 *burial*

mass communication 528, 533, 532.2 *mass media,* 534.1 *communications*

mass demonstration 475

mass destruction 244.2 *destroying*

massed 161.47 *collected,* 181.10 *crowded,* 371.6 *dense*

massed attack 670.12 *military attack*

mass energy 235.4 *energy*

Massenet 49 Musicians and Composers

masses 124.7 *average person,* 164.11 *general public*

massé shot 24.2 *billiards play*

masses of 181.4 *throng*

masseur 385, 407.5 *toucher,* 630.15 *healer,* 697.4 *personal attendant*

masseuse 385.8 *masseur,* 407.5 *toucher,* 630.15 *healer,* 697.4 *personal attendant*

mass execution 879.13 *capital punishment*

mass grave 399.6 *grave*

massicot 54 Minerals, 452.7 *yellow pigment*

massif 95.1 *mountain,* 275.4 *mountain range*

Massinger 48 Dramatists

massive 85.15 *woody,* 120.6 *quantitative,* 259.15 *big,* 273.1 *thick,* 367.7 *material,* 369.1 *heavy,* 371.6 *dense,* 617.1 *worthy*

massively 120.7 *quantitatively,* 259.20 *largely,* 369.16 *heavily,* 371.10 *densely*

massiveness 259.2 *bigness,* 273.5 *thickness,* 369.4 *heaviness*

mass media 532, 528.4, 533.5 *mass communication,* 534.1 *communications*

mass meeting 161.4 *rally*

mass movement 54, 642.5 *activism*

mass murder 244.2 *destroying,* 398.2 *murder,* 832.7 *act of malevolence,* 879.13 *capital punishment*

mass murderer 241.4 *violent person or animal,* 398.11 *murderer,* 832.8 *malefactor,* 862.6 *evil person*

mass number 56.69 *isotope*

mass of 181.4 *throng*

massotherapist 385.8 *masseur*

massotherapy 385.6 *massage*

mass-produce 110.8 *make the same,* 112.10 *conform,* 243.10 *produce,* 245.9 *reproduce*

mass-produced 112.6 *conforming,* 243.12 *produced*

mass production 110.6 *regularity,* 112.2 *conformity,* 243.2 *manufacture,* 245.1 *reproduction,* 246.2 *productiveness*

mass screening 60.7 *diagnosis*

mass spectrograph 56.91 *spectrometer*

mass spectrometer 56.91 *spectrometer*

mass spectrometry 57.17 *analysis*

mass strike 15.4 *industrial dispute*

mass suicide 398.7 *suicide*

mass together 135.8 *unite*

mass X-ray 60.7 *diagnosis*

massy 259.15 *big,* 367.7 *material,* 369.1 *heavy,* 371.6 *dense*

mast 36.3 *parts of a sailing boat,* 275.6 *tall thing*

mastaba 399.6 *grave*

mastectomy 60 Surgical Operations, 630.12 *surgery*

master 696, 696, 6.4 *educator,* 6.24 *know,* 50.16 *artist,* 74.7 *nautical person,* 126.5 *superior,* 126.15 *excellent,* 165.14 *specialist,* 233.10 *be a prevailing influence,* 401.3 *male title of address,* 459.8 *intellectual person,* 501.11 *know,* 522.6 *understand,* 619.4 *perfectionist,* 646.2 *artisan,* 653.13 *director,* 655.4 *skilled person,* 682.11 *overmaster,* 696.9 *educational leader,* 696.10 *expert,* 696.13 *excellent,* 701.7 *defeat,* 723.6 *lord,* 861.19 *be good at*

Master 696

master aircrew 679.32 *airman*

master builder 43.2 *architect*

MasterCard 733.4 *credit,* 744.2 *credit card*

master carpenter 696.10 *expert*

masterful 696, 166.12 *ruling,* 485.9 *qualified,* 655.6 *skilful,* 688.12 *authoritative,* 861.5 *proficient*

masterfully 696, 485.17 *capably,* 861.25 *skillfully*

masterfulness 688.2 *authoritativeness,* 861.12 *proficiency*

master key 322.2 *opener*

masterliness 861.12 *proficiency*

masterly 126.16 *superiorly,* 619.1 *perfect,* 655.6 *skilful,* 682.13 *successful,* 688.17 *expert,* 688.26 *expertly,* 696.13 *excellent,* 861.5 *proficient*

master mariner 74.7 *nautical person*

master mason 43.2 *architect,* 646.2 *artisan*

mastermind 126.6 *paragon,* 501.6 *knowledgeable person,* 592.8 *planner,* 652.11 *conduct oneself,* 652.14 *behave towards,* 653.1 *manage,* 655.4 *skilled person*

masterminding 652.8 *treatment*

Master of Arts 485 Educational Qualifications

Master of Business Administration 485 Educational Qualifications

master of ceremonies 51.25 *producer,* 526.12 *displayer,* 534.29 *broadcaster,* 653.14 *leader*

Master of Divinity 485 Educational Qualifications

Master of Fine Arts 485 Educational Qualifications

master of hounds 431.9 *crier,* 653.15 *manager*

Master of Library Science 485 Educational Qualifications

Master of Philosophy 485 Educational Qualifications

Master of Science 485 Educational Qualifications

master of the house 696.1 *master*

Master of the Rolls 16.25 *British judge*

master of the violin 688.11, 696.10 *expert*

master painter 619.4 *perfectionist*

masterpiece 655, 696, 50.6 *work of art,* 243.6 *great work,* 617.8 *exceller,* 619.3 *perfection,* 640.2 *deed,* 786.4 *wonder,* 789.2 *beautiful thing,* 789.3 *attractive female,* 861.17 *good thing*

master plan 592.1 *plan*

Masters 48 Poets

mastership 126.2 *leadership,* 655.1 *skill*

master spirit 611.4 *bigwig*

masterstroke 592.3 *expedient plan,* 655.3 *masterpiece,* 786.4 *wonder,* 861.17 *good thing*

master thief 619.4 *perfectionist,* 696.10 *expert*

masterwork 50.6 *work of art,*

243.6 *great work*, 655.3, 696.11
masterpiece
mastery 12.3 *governance*, 50.5
artistry, 166.8 *authority*, 485.2
ability, 501.1 *knowledge*, 501.3
learning, 522.12 *understanding*,
619.3 *perfection*, 655.1 *skill*,
682.1 *success*, 688.1, 692.3 *authority*, 701.2 *domination*
masthead 275.8 *high thing*,
279.2 *head*, 533.12 *headline*,
544.3 *means of identification*,
879.1 *punish*
masthead light 439.6 *electric light*
masthead sloop 36.2 *sailing boat*
mastic 85 Tree Products, 394.2
adhesive
masticate 350.21 *eat*, 374.13
soften
mastication 350.1 *eating*, 393.5
pulping
masticic 395.14 *resinous*
mastiff 77 Breeds of Dogs
Mastigomycotina 89.3 *fungi*
mastigophobia 777 Phobias by
Name
Mastigophora 81.9 *protozoan*
mastigophoran 81.9 *protozoan*
mastodon 77 Placental Mammals, 202.8 *prehistoric animal*,
259.9 *big thing*
mastoid 382 Bones
mastoidectomy 60 Surgical Operations
mastoidotomy 60 Surgical Operations
masturbation 405.1 *physical
pleasure*
Masuren 32 Breeds of Horse
and Pony
mat 25.1 *green bowling*, 44.10 *ceramic*, 63.28 *substructure*, 67.14
weave, 90.1 *alga*, 293.9 *floor
covering*, 621.11 *cleaning cloth*
Matabele 5 Languages and
Groups of Languages
matador 398.13 *animal killer*,
679.3 *athlete*
Mata Hari 586.13 *tempter*
matai 85 Trees and Shrubs
Matamoros 93 Cities
match 18.1 *sport*, 40.4 *tennis
terms*, 42.2 *contest*, 107.8 *be
proportionate to*, 109.3 *correlation*, 109.9 *correlate*, 110.3
lookalike, 110.7 *be the same*,
110.10 *be equal*, 114.10 *be similar*, 116.5 *conformity*, 116.25
conform, 122.5 *equal*, 135.8
unite, 137.13 *intercommunicate*,
167.7 *conform*, 176.14 *pair*,
259.18 *measure*, 410.2 *lighter*,
433.8 *harmonize*, 439.8 *fire*,
457.5 *impression*, 457.11 *appear*, 478.8 *correspondence*,
478.21 *answer to*, 663.18 *counteract*, 667.8 *be compatible*,
670.20 *bout*, 674.2 *contest*,
823.1 *marriage*, 823.17
matchmake
match abandoned 27.1 *cricket
match*
match against 663.16 *confront*
matchbox 258.6 *box*, 410.2 *lighter*
matched 110.14 *lookalike*, 122.8
on equal terms, 176.9 *two*,
823.21 *married*
matched in age 198.9 *simultaneous*
matched pair 114.6 *couple*
matchet 680.8 *sharp weapon*
match fishing 18 Sporting Activities, 20.1 *angling*
match in cunning 657.5 *be cunning*
matching 109.6 *correlative*,
110.14 *lookalike*, 114.7 *similar*,
116.14 *conforming*, 295.31
styled, 433.7 *harmonious*,
444.11 *colourful*, 478.15 *correspondent*, 667.12 *compatible*
matching set 114.6 *couple*
matchless 115.4 *dissimilar*,
126.14, 617.2 *best*, 861.2 *best*
matchlessly 126.17 *supremely*

matchlock 680.10 *historical gun*
matchlockman 679.13 *historical
soldiery*
matchmake 823, 176.14 *pair*,
716.7 *act as a go-between*
matchmaker 823, 135.7 *joiner*,
678.3 *mediator*, 707.3 *agent*,
716.4 *negotiator*
match oneself 674.11 *contend*
match play 29.1 *golf*
match point 106.3 *critical moment*
match poorly 666.8 *be different*
matchstick 238.5 *weak thing*
matchstick man 299.1 *outline*
match up with 122.10 *be equal*
match-winning 682.15 *victorious*
matchwood 238.5 *weak thing*,
379.3 *brittle thing*
mate 42.4 *chess terms*, 114.5
counterpart, 122.5 *equal*,
135.11 *make love*, 140.6 *come
together*, 176.14 *pair*, 180.11
companion, 351.3 *tea*, 401.3
male title of address, 646.5 *partner*, 662.11 *helper*, 784.4 *likable
person*, 815.6 *social person*,
819.5 *friend*, 821.29 *make love*,
823.17 *matchmake*
maté 85 Trees and Shrubs
mated 176.9 *two*, 823.21 *married*
mateless 825.6 *celibate*
matelot 74.7 *nautical person*
mater 402.12 *woman in the family*
materfamilias 402.12 *woman in
the family*
material 367, 67.3 *fabric*, 99.11
intrinsic, 101.6 *real*, 103.1 *essence*, 253.7 *present*, 257.1 *contents*, 257.10 *containing*, 288.4
textile, 367.4 *matter*, 383.5 *textile*, 407.8 *touchable*, 437.1 *visible*, 457.7 *appearing*, 602.2 *supplies*, 604.1 *materials*, 611.5 *important*
material existence 101.1 *reality*,
367.1 *material world*
materialism 4.7 *school of
thought*, 367.2 *materialization*,
860.1 *selfishness*
materialist 367, 4.11 *follower of
a doctrine*, 4.14 *of a philosophy*,
498.5 *disbeliever*
materialistic 367.7 *material*,
860.4 *selfish*
materialistically 860.8 *selfishly*
materiality 99.3 *nature*, 101.1 *reality*, 253.1 *presence*, 367.1 *material world*, 367.4 *matter*,
611.1 *importance*
materialization 367, 8.8 *divine
manifestation*, 11.11 *ghost*, 99.8
creation, 457.1 *appearance*,
526.10 *manifestation*
materialize 99.18 *come to be*,
101.11 *make real*, 253.11 *be
present*, 367.8 *be material*,
437.9 *appear*, 457.12 *become
visible*, 475.18 *appear*, 526.4
show oneself
materialized 99.15 *created*, 367.7
material
materially 367, 103.13 *in essence*, 253.14 *in person*, 257.13
structurally, 611.9 *importantly*
materialness 253.1 *presence*,
367.1 *material world*, 611.1 *importance*
materials 604, 367.4 *matter*,
382.2 *fabric*, 602.2 *supplies*
Materials 604
materials budget 750.2 *budgeting*
material things 725.4 *possessions*
material world 367
Material World 367
materia medica 62.1 *pharmacology*, 630.2 *medicine*
maternal 831.6 *benevolent*
maternal love 821.1 *love*
maternally 831.10 *benevolently*
maternity 245.4 *development*,
402.12 *woman in the family*
maternity allowance 662.4 *social
assistance*
maternity benefit 662.4 *social assistance*

maternity dress 295.7 *frock*
maternity grant 662.4 *social assistance*
maternity hospital 60.10 *hospital*
maternity wear 295.1 *dress*
matey 815.15 *sociable*, 819.8
friendly
mateyness 180.3 *companionship*,
819.1 *friendship*
math 52.1 *mathematics*
math co-processor 65.5 *processor*
mathematical 52, 170, 56.99
theoretical, 537.21 *accurate*,
750.10 *accounting*
mathematical addition 130
mathematical biology 52.3 *applied mathematics*
mathematical biophysics 52.3 *applied mathematics*
mathematical computing 52.3 *applied mathematics*
mathematical ecology 52.3 *applied mathematics*
mathematical exactness 537.8 *accuracy*
mathematical function 52
mathematical geography 52.3 *applied mathematics*
mathematical logic 52, 52.1
mathematics
mathematically 52, 170, 120.7
quantitatively
mathematically exact 537.21 *accurate*
mathematical model 52.65 *theory*
mathematical notation 543.1
sign, 547.1 *representation*
mathematical physics 52.3 *applied mathematics*
mathematical precision 503.1 *accuracy*
mathematical probability 52.62
probability, 488.5 *probability
theory*, 589.7 *calculation of
chance*
mathematical reasoning 52.64
reasoning
mathematical result 169
mathematical symbol 52
mathematical theorem 518.1 *supposition*
mathematician 52, 170, 478.10
answerer
mathematics 52
Mathematics 52
mathimazole 62 Medication
maths 52.1 *mathematics*
matin 204.5 *morning*
matinal 204.5 *morning*
matinée 51.11 *theatrical performance*, 204.4 *afternoon*
matinée coat 295.23 *children's
clothes*
matinée idol 51.22 *actor*, 821.11
loved one
mating 135.4 *sexual union*,
821.5 *desire*
mating call 432.1 *animal cry*
matins 10.4 *public worship*,
204.1 *morning*
Matlock 93 Cities
Matopo 95 Mountains
matriarch 402.12 *woman in the
family*, 696.1 *master*
matriarchal 12.9 *governmental*,
207.14 *aged*, 688.14 *governmental*, 696.12 *masterful*
matriarchate 12.1 *government*
matriarchy 12.1 *government*,
402.1 *female sex*
matricide 398.3 *homicide*,
398.11 *murderer*, 832.7 *act of
malevolence*
matriculate 171.9 *enlist*
matrimonial 823, 10.21 *ritualistic*, 715.7 *contractual*
matrimonial agent 823.13 *matchmaker*
matrimonial cause 824.3 *divorce
court*
matrimonially 823, 715.8 *contractually*
matrimony 42 Card Games,
715.1 *contract*, 823.1 *marriage*
matrix 52, 306.2 *prototype*

matrix mechanics 56.3 *modern
physics*, 56.80 *quantum theory*
matrix printer 65.7 *peripheral*
matron 60.16 *nurse*, 207.9
woman, 402.2 *female*, 653.15
manager, 696.1 *master*, 823.11
married woman
matronage 402.13 *womenfolk*
matronliness 207.2 *adulthood*
matronly 207.13 *middle-aged*,
402.15 *female*, 696.12 *masterful*, 823.20 *matrimonial*
matronymic 560.8 *name*
Matsuo Basho 48 Poets
Matsya 8 Deities
matt 441.7 *dimmed*, 443.2
shady, 444.13 *soft-hued*
matted 371.7 *condensed*, 375.3
barbed, 622.7 *dirty*
matted hair 375.7 *rough thing*
matter 367, 101.1 *reality*, 103.1
essence, 120.1 *quantity*, 226.6
undertaking, 230.3 *business*,
257.1 *contents*, 353.7 *pus*,
353.18 *fester*, 387.3 *body fluid*,
393.10, 394.5 *mucus*, 472.1
topic, 520.1 *meaning*, 604.1 *materials*, 611.1 *importance*, 611.7
be important, 622.4 *dirt*, 624.15
ulcer
matter for discussion 472.2 *issue*
matter for judgment 16.5 *litigation*
Matterhorn 95 Mountains, 95.6
*other major mountains and
ranges*, 275.3 *mountain*
mattering 353.7 *pus*, 353.27 *purulent*
matter in hand 597.2 *undertaking*
matter of course 584.1 *habit*
matter of fact 3.14 *historicalness*,
99.5 *fact*, 101.1 *reality*
matter-of-fact 4.15 *rational*,
101.8 *practical*, 556.1 *simple*,
658.1 *naive*, 783.7 *indifferent*
matter-of-factly 556.8 *simply*,
658.5 *naively*, 783.17 *indifferently*
matter-of-factness 556.4 *simplicity*, 658.2 *naivety*
matter of indifference 612.8 *trifle*
matter of interest 472
matter of life and death 571.1 *necessity*, 593.3 *needfulness*,
611.2 *important matter*
matter of priority 194
matt finish 66.12 *development*,
441.2 *murk*
matt glaze 44.3 *glaze*
Matthews 18 Sporting Personalities
Matthew Walker 74 Knots
matting 67 Natural Fabrics,
293.9 *floor covering*
mattock 380.9 *sharp-edged thing*,
603.2 *garden tool*
mattress 284.4 *rest*, 531.2 *hiding
place*, 741.20 *money store*
mattress cover 293.10 *bed covering*
maturation 207.2 *adulthood*,
261.1 *growth*, 584.7 *habituation*, 594.13 *development*, 684.1
completion
mature 207, 144.7 *complete*,
202.11 *old*, 203.7 *season*,
206.18 *grow*, 207.11 *adult*,
207.13 *middle-aged*, 207.17
age, 220.8 *be transformed*,
261.7 *bigger*, 374.13 *soften*,
594.7 *develop*, 594.20 *developed*, 619.1, 619.5 *perfect*,
627.1 *improve*, 627.2 *get better*,
684.4 *complete*, 684.7 *completed*, 845.18 *be due*
matured 203.15 *seasoned*,
594.20 *developed*, 619.1 *perfect*,
655.8 *expert*, 684.7 *completed*
mature into 220.7 *convert into*
maturely 207, 202.18 *venerably*,
684.9 *completely*
matureness 207.3 *maturity*
Maturine 7 Members of Religious Orders
maturing 206, 220.14 *converting*, 584.7 *habituation*, 594.17
developing, 684.7 *completed*

maturity 207, 202.1 *oldness,* 207.2 *adulthood,* 207.4 *middle age,* 210.1 *timeliness,* 594.14 *preparedness,* 619.3 *perfection,* 684.1 *completion*

matutinal 204.5 *morning*

maudlin 759.12 *sensitive,* 874.2 *slightly drunk*

Maudslay 52 Scientists

Maugham 48 Writers

Maui 18 Deities

maul 35.3 *rugby play,* 35.5 *play rugby,* 406.11 *inflict pain,* 407.4 *kiss,* 407.11 *touch,* 618.14 *ill-treat,* 628.4 *impair,* 670.5 *strike*

mauling 406.3 *injury*

maulstick 50.11 *artist's materials*

Mauna Kea 95 Mountains

Mauna Kea Observatory 53.23 *observatory*

maund 75 Some Foreign Units

maunder 553.6 *be circuitous*

Maundy money 729.3 *offering*

Maundy Thursday 10.15 *holy day*

Maupassant 48 Writers

Maupertuis 52 Scientists

Maureen Connolly 40.7 *famous tennis players*

Mauriac 48 Writers

Mauritania 91 Countries

Mauritius 91 Countries, **98** Islands

Mauritius hurricane 55.16 *wind vortex*

mausoleum 243.8 *construction,* 325.3 *resting place,* 399.6 *grave,* 545.11 *monument*

mauve 455.6 *purple*

mauveine 67.6 *dye,* 455.2 *purple pigment*

maverick 104.5 *nonconformist,* 117.6 *misfit,* 117.9 *nonconforming,* 139.4 *individualist,* 168.7 *nonconformist,* 168.13 *unconventional,* 693.6 *nonconformist,* 698.10 *independent*

mavis 78 Birds

maw 322.4 *body orifice,* 350.16 *eating utensil*

mawashi-geri 26.8 *karate*

mawkish 759.12 *sensitive*

mawkishly 759.21 *emotionally*

mawkishness 759.7 *emotionalism*

max 126.14 *best*

maxidress 295.7 *frock*

maxilla 382 Bones

maxillary 382 Bones

maxim 505, 4.1 *philosophy,* 5.21 *catchword,* 166.4 *guide,* 535.2 *statement,* 537.4 *truism,* 552.2 *outline,* 654.3 *precept,* 847.6 *ethics,* 876.7 *moral*

Maxim 52 Scientists, **505**

maximal 52.75 *equal,* 126.14 *best,* 279.5 *top*

Maxim gun 680.12 *historical guns*

maximization 541.2 *enlargement*

maximize 52.94 *order,* 128.5 *make bigger,* 494.4 *overestimate,* 541.8 *enlarge,* 599.3 *exploit*

maximized 541.13 *enlarged*

maximum 126.14 *best,* 144.2 *fullness,* 279.1 *summit,* 279.5 *top*

maximum-acceleration 33.11 *racing*

maximum-acceleration event 33.1 *motor racing*

maximum and minimun thermometer 56.89 *thermometer*

maximum likelihood 52.62 *probability*

maximum pressure 644.4 *exertion*

maximum-security prison 702.1 *prison,* 816.4 *place of confinement*

maximum speed 329.8 *speed*

maximum-speed 33.11 *racing*

maximum-speed event 33.1 *motor racing*

maxiskirt 295.4 *skirt*

maxwell 75 Scientific and Technical Units

Maxwell 52 Scientists

Maxwell–Boltzmann statistics 56 Named Laws

Maxwell distribution 56 Named Laws

Maxwell's equation 56 Named Laws

may 84 Flowers and Flowering Plants

maya 11.10 *psychic phenomenon*

Maya 1 Peoples, **5** Languages and Groups of Languages

Mayakovskii 48 Poets

Mayan 5 Languages and Groups of Languages, **7** Non-Christian Religions

Maya Plisetskaya 46.14 *famous ballet dancers*

May apple 86 Fruits

Mayas 200.6 *people of the past*

maybe 486.9 *possibly*

may blossom 84.1 *flower*

mayday 636.2 *danger signal*

Mayday 543.6 *word*

May Day 203.2 *spring,* 214.6 *annually celebrated day*

Mayer 52 Scientists

Mayfair 93.5 *London*

mayfly 82 Insects, 20.1 *angling*

mayhem 244.5 *havoc*

Maynard Smith 52 Scientists

Mayo 92 Counties

mayonnaise 45.15 *sauce,* 413.2 *seasoning*

mayor 16.10 *law officer,* 126.5 *superior,* 633.16 *official,* 688.10 *person of authority,* 696.3 *leader*

mayoralty 16.2 *jurisdiction,* 688.5 *position of authority*

mayor-council system 653.9 *US administrative council*

mayoress 688.10 *person of authority,* 696.3 *leader*

maypole 275.6 *tall thing*

maypole dance 46.4 *historic dancing*

May Queen 617.8 *exceller*

Maytime 203.2 *spring*

may tree 85 Trees and Shrubs

mayuri 49 Musical Instruments

Mazdaism 7 Non-Christian Religions

maze 151.7 *tangle,* 314.3 *convoluted thing,* 529.4 *brain-teaser,* 659.4 *problem*

mazindol 62 Medication

mazurka 46.4 *historic dancing*

mazy 335.21 *indirect*

mazzard 85 Trees and Shrubs

Mbabane 93 Cities

mbaqanga 49.10 *world music*

mbila 49 Musical Instruments

MC 51.25 *producer*

MCC 27.2 *ground*

MD 49.24 *musician,* 611.4 *bigwig*

me 165.12 *I,* 368.6 *internal world,* 529.15 *in secret*

ME 624.6 *infection*

mead 68.11 *farmland,* 87.2 *grassland,* 98.6 *lowland,* 414.5 *sweet drink*

meadow 68.11 *farmland,* 87.2 *grassland,* 98.6 *lowland,* 322.8 *open space*

meadow fescue 87 Grasses

meadow foxtail 87 Grasses

meadow grass 87 Grasses, 87.1 *grass*

meadow land 87.2 *grassland*

meadowlark 78 Birds

meadow mushroom 89 Fungi

meadow saffron 84 Flowers and Flowering Plants

meadowsweet 84 Flowers and Flowering Plants

meadowy 87.9 *grassy*

Meads 18 Sporting Personalities

meads of asphodel 397.14 *the spiritual world*

meagre 145.4 *incomplete,* 182.6 *sparse,* 260.7 *little,* 274.6 *scant,* 555.1 *unemphatic,* 609.1 *insufficient,* 743.4 *inadequate,* 756.4 *thrifty*

meagre diet 350.10 *scarcity*

meagrely 182.11 *sparsely,* 274.17 *thin,* 743.17 *inadequately*

meagreness 127.3 *inferior numbers,* 182.3 *fewness,* 260.1 *little-*

ness, 274.12 *thinning,* 555.2 *lack of emphasis,* 609.8 *insufficiency,* 743.9 *inadequacy*

meagre resources 743.5 *poverty*

meal 350, 384, 45.7 *basic ingredient*

mealiness 384.3 *graininess*

meal ticket 729.3 *offering*

mealtime 45.6 *culinary*

mealworm 82 Insects, 82.5 *larva*

mealy 384, 445.8 *drained of colour*

mealy bug 82 Insects, 69.12 *pests and diseases*

mealy-mouth 538.12 *cheat,* 539.19 *hypocrite,* 808.3 *sycophant*

mealy-mouthed 238.12 *weak-willed,* 538.18 *pretentious,* 539.37, 540.27 *hypocritical,* 808.7 *sycophantic,* 876.10 *moralistic*

mealy-mouthedly 540.38 *hypocritically*

mealy-mouthedness 538.9, 539.3 *hypocrisy,* 540.3 *hypocrisy,* 876.4 *self-righteousness*

mealymouthing 808.2 *sycophancy*

mean 520, 758, 52.60 *parameter,* 120.5 *numbers,* 124.2, 124.5 *medium,* 146.4 *include,* 158.3, 158.13 *median,* 291.1 *centre,* 291.6 *central,* 471.19 *epitomize,* 527.14 *imply,* 543.10 *signify,* 547.12 *stand for,* 588.7 *intend,* 609.1 *insufficient,* 611.7 *be important,* 612.2 *obscure,* 618.4 *poor,* 743.3 *beggarly,* 747.13 *nonpaying,* 754.10 *shoddy,* 764.2 *objectionable,* 806.2 *lowly,* 829.4 *irascible,* 832.14 *hostile,* 860.4 *selfish,* 862.7 *evil*

mean business 574.6 *be resolute*

meander 96.2 *channel,* 96.7 *flow,* 286.6 *be oblique,* 314.6 *convolute,* 335.5 *twist,* 363.8 *detour*

meandering 96.10 *fluvial,* 286.1 *obliqueness,* 286.4 *oblique,* 314.2 *coil,* 314.4 *convolutional,* 334.2 *detour,* 334.7 *circuitous,* 335.21 *indirect,* 363.2 *circuitousness,* 363.9 *orbital*

meandering river 96.1 *river*

mean deviation 52.60 *parameter*

me and you 176.1 *two*

mean error 52.60 *parameter*

meanie 758.5 *miser,* 758.6 *nasty person*

meaning 520, 5.1 *linguistics,* 5.17 *word,* 227.4 *significance,* 471.4 *purpose,* 524.1 *interpretation,* 543.1 *sign,* 588.1 *intention,* 611.3 *chief thing*

Meaning 520

meaningful 520, 5.42 *worded,* 471.12 *purposive,* 522.1 *intelligible,* 543.14 *signifying,* 611.5 *important*

meaningful look 563.6 *voiceless speech*

meaningful looks 564.4 *articulation*

meaningfully 520, 5.50 *lexically,* 471.21 *purposively,* 543.18 *indicatively*

meaningfulness 520.1 *meaning,* 520.4 *type of meaning,* 522.9 *intelligibility*

meaning harm 832.10 *malevolent*

meaningless 521, 278.2 *superficial,* 506.5 *nonsensical,* 520.6 *meaningful,* 523.1 *unintelligible*

meaningless act 640.2 *deed*

meaningless gesture 521.3 *meaningless thing*

meaninglessly 521, 506.9 *nonsensically,* 523.13 *unintelligibly*

meaninglessness 521.1 *lack of meaning,* 523.11 *unintelligibility*

meaningless noise 521.1 *lack of meaning*

meaningless thing 521

meaningly 520.13 *meaningfully*

mean life 56.70 *radioactivity*

mean little 612.11 *be unimportant*

meanly 743, 758, 829.9 *irascibly,* 832.20 *malevolently,* 860.8 *selfishly*

mean-minded 860.4 *selfish*

mean-mindedness 860.1 *selfishness*

meanness 127.3 *inferior numbers,* 609.8 *insufficiency,* 612.6 *obscurity,* 618.10 *poverty,* 743.7 *beggary,* 754.3 *shoddiness,* 764.6 *objectionability,* 806.8 *lowliness,* 829.1 *irascibility,* 832.1 *malevolence,* 860.1 *selfishness,* 862.1 *evil*

Meanness 758

mean no harm 675.5 *be at peace,* 865.8 *be innocent*

mean nothing 521, 506.7 *be nonsense,* 523.7 *be unintelligible*

mean old stick 758.5 *miser*

means 602, 106.1 *circumstances,* 232.1 *instrumentality,* 232.2 *instrument,* 327.1 *way,* 604.1 *materials,* 615.5 *convenience,* 725.5 *personal estate,* 741.6 *funds,* 742.5 *wealth*

Means 602

means-ends analysis 65.16 *artificial intelligence*

mean seriously 518.6 *propound*

means of access 327.2 *route*

means of ascent 359

means of communication 534.1 *communications*

means of connection 137

means of entry 346

means of escape 638, 602.1 *means,* 632.1 *safety,* 632.4 *safety device*

means of identification 544

means of protection 632.2 *protection*

means of restraint 699

means of safety 632.4 *safety device*

means of transport 326

mean something 520.10 *mean*

mean something else 520.10 *mean*

mean-spirited 860.4 *selfish*

mean-spiritedness 860.1 *selfishness*

means to an end 662.1 *help*

meant 518, 520, 527.4 *unsaid,* 588.12 *intended,* 592.14 *planned*

mean the opposite 520.10 *mean*

mean the reverse 520.10 *mean*

mean the same thing 520.10 *mean*

meantime 185.6 *interval,* 189.9 *for the time being*

mean to 199.8 *intend,* 588.8 *resolve*

mean to say 520.10 *mean,* 527.14 *imply*

mean-value theorem 52 Theorems and Laws

mean well 831.8 *be benevolent*

mean what one says 312.11 *be straight,* 535.22 *emphasize*

meanwhile 158.20 *in the middle,* 185.26 *all the time,* 189.9 *for the time being,* 196.10 *for the present*

measles 624.6 *infection*

measly 182.6 *sparse,* 612.2 *obscure,* 618.4 *poor,* 747.13 *nonpaying*

measure 214.1 *regularity*

measurability 268

measurable 268, 52.73 *numerable,* 170.14 *calculable*

measurably 268, 170.16 *mathematically*

measure 121, 259, 268, 48.8 *part of poem,* 48.9 *metre,* 49.17 *notation,* 49.19 *tempo,* 52.90 *enumerate,* 75.1 *unit,* 120.1 *quantity,* 120.8 *quantify,* 121.1 *degree,* 124.4 *average,* 170.11 *number,* 230.1 *operation,* 248.1 *space,* 259.1 *size,* 268.1 *measurement,* 269.4 *length,* 269.5 *piece,* 277.2 *intensity,* 295.35

make clothing, 302.2 *limiting factor,* 369.15 *weigh,* 433.1 *melody,* 478.6 *solution,* 478.20 *solve,* 490.18 *particularity,* 490.22 *specify,* 602.1 *means,* 606.1 *provision,* 640.2 *deed,* 731.2 *portion,* 731.4 *allot*
measured 268, 48.20 *metrical,* 120.6 *quantitative,* 121.7 *gradational,* 214.11 *regular,* 242.6 *moderate,* 478.14 *solved,* 582.4 *deliberate,* 608.1 *sufficient,* 869.9 *moderate*
measured quantity 56.82 *measuring instrument,* 120.1 *quantity*
measured value 56.82 *measuring instrument*
measure for measure 109.1 *interchange,* 125.2 *counterbalance,* 223.1 *exchange,* 672.1 *retaliation,* 840.1 *atonement*
Measure for Measure 48 Shakespeare's plays
measureless 181.8 *numberless,* 184.2 *immeasurable*
measurelessly 184.11 *immeasurably*
measurelessness 184.5 *immeasurability*
measurement 1, 268, 52.12 *numeration,* 56.82 *measuring instrument,* 120.1 *quantity,* 121.3 *gradation,* 259.1 *size*
Measurement 268
measurement ton 75 Scientific and Technical Units
measure off 268.10 *measure*
measure of length 269
measure of time 269
measure one's length 360.11 *trip*
measure out 268, 248.21 *space,* 268.10 *measure,* 302.7 *limit,* 729.5 *give*
measure public opinion 580.5 *vote*
measurer 268, 25.3 *bowls player*
measures 592.2 *policy,* 594.10 *preparations,* 602.1 *means,* 640.1 *action*
measure swords 674.12 *fight*
measure time 192, 185.16 *time*
measure up 268.10 *measure*
measure up to 110.10, 122.10 *be equal,* 235.10 *be powerful,* 608.4 *suffice*
measuring 120.1 *quantity,* 120.6 *quantitative,* 268.1 *measurement,* 268.12 *metrical*
measuring cylinder 57 Laboratory Apparatus
measuring device 56.82 *measuring instrument*
measuring instrument 56, 268, 365, 389
measuring jug 45.6 *kitchen equipment*
measuring rod 268.6 *measuring instrument*
measuring system 268
measuring tape 21.2 *field events*
meat 45, 86.3 *fruit structure,* 103.2 *essential content,* 243.7 *produce,* 257.1 *contents,* 350.7 *food,* 472.1 *topic,* 604.1 *materials*
meat-and-bone meal 68.9 *animal feedstuff,* 68.13 *fertilizer*
meatballs 45.20 *meat*
meat compartment 45.4 *kitchen container*
meat dish 45
meat-eater 76.4 *type of animal,* 350.18 *eater*
meat-eating 350.5 *eating habit,* 350.26 *eating*
Meath 92 Counties
meathead 237.6 *muscleman,* 508.3 *foolish person,* 761.5 *insensitive person*
meathooks 726.3 *tools for gripping*
meatiness 259.6 *squatness*
meat juice 387.2 *juice*
meatless day 871.3 *fast day*
meat market 740.1 *market*
meatpacker 646.1 *worker*
meat safe 45.4 *kitchen container*

meat substitute 45
meaty 259.17 *stocky,* 520.7 *significant,* 554.3 *emphatic*
mecamylamine 62 Medication
mecanopsis 84 Flowers and Flowering Plants
Mecca 93 Cities, 10.13 *shrine,* 291.4 *centre of activity,* 588.6 *objective*
Meccano 148.3 *unit*
mechanic 63.4 *mechanical engineer,* 71.21 *miscellaneous motoring terms,* 230.5 *operator,* 603.7 *machinist,* 629.12 *repairer,* 646.2 *artisan*
mechanical 603, 56.98 *physical,* 63.32 *structural,* 112.6 *conforming,* 232.8 *practical,* 235.16 *charged,* 571.13 *involuntary*
mechanical advantage 63.10 *work,* 603.5 *mechanics*
mechanical aid 603.1 *tool*
mechanical device 63.5 *dynamic structure,* 603.1 *tool,* 603.4 *machine*
mechanical digger 355.10 *excavator*
mechanical drawing 50.3 *drawing,* 547.2 *reproduction,* 560.9 *representation*
mechanical energy 235.4 *energy*
mechanical engineer 63, 63.2 *engineer,* 646.2 *artisan*
mechanical engineering 63, 63.1 *engineering,* 603.5 *mechanics*
mechanical instrument 49.25 *musical instrument*
mechanically 56.100 *physically,* 63.33 *structurally,* 112.13 *uniformly,* 232.9 *instrumentally,* 584.19 *habitually,* 603.10 *instrumentally*
mechanically precise 537.21 *accurate*
mechanical malfunction 683.4 *unsuccessful thing*
mechanical means 232.1 *instrumentality*
mechanical oscillation 56.14 *sound wave*
mechanical power 603.5 *mechanics*
mechanical precision 537.8 *accuracy*
mechanical solidarity 2.5 *society*
mechanical strength 237.1 *strength*
mechanical wave 365.5 *wave*
mechanical weathering 44.35 *weathering*
mechanician 603.7 *machinist*
mechanics 603, 330.11 *impulsion,* 367.6 *natural science*
mechanism 4.7 *school of thought,* 57.14 *chemical reaction,* 63.5 *dynamic structure,* 148.4 *components,* 232.2 *instrument,* 603.4 *machine*
mechanist 4.11 *follower of a doctrine,* 603.7 *machinist*
mechanistic 4.14 *of a philosophy,* 603.8 *mechanical*
mechanization 232.1 *instrumentality*
mechanize 243.10 *produce,* 603.9 *use tools*
mechanized 235.16 *charged,* 243.11 *productive,* 603.8 *mechanical*
mechanized battalion 17.4 *military organization*
mechanized division 17.4 *military organization*
mechanophobia 777 Phobias by Name
Mecklenburg 32 Breeds of Horse and Pony
meclozine 62 Medication
Mecoptera 82 Orders of Insects
mecopteran 82.10 *insectan*
medal 21.5 *competition,* 50.13 *relief-carving,* 544.4 *insignia,* 545.11 *monument,* 681.1 *trophy,* 792.3 *honour,* 804.3 *honours,* 878.2 *prize*
medalist 21.3 *athlete*
medallion 43 Architectural Dec-

oration, 11.6 *talisman,* 50.13 *relief-carving,* 681.1 *trophy,* 792.6 *jewellery*
medallist 682.5 *victorious person*
Medal of Honor 17 US Military Medals and Decorations
medal play 29.1 *golf*
Medan 93 Cities
meddle 642, 465.7 *be curious,* 628.4 *impair,* 640.4 *act,* 656.7 *be clumsy,* 661.8 *hinder,* 678.1 *mediate*
meddler 465, 642, 654.4 *adviser,* 661.7 *hinderer,* 678.3 *mediator*
meddlesome 465.6 *prying,* 642.21 *meddling*
meddlesomeness 642.9 *overactivity*
meddle with 133.8 *mix,* 216.8 *cause change*
meddling 642, 233.11 *influential,* 465.2, 465.6 *prying,* 642.9 *overactivity,* 661.1 *hindrance,* 661.13 *hindering,* 678.2 *mediation*
meddling person 642.11 *meddler*
Medea 11.4 *witch*
Medellín 93 Cities
media blitz 532.8 *public relations*
media event 532.8 *public relations*
media hype 532.8 *public relations*, 533.9 *news story*
medial 124.2 *medium,* 158.10 *middle,* 158.13 *median,* 333.4 *middle*
medially 333, 124.12 *mediumly,* 158.20 *in the middle*
median 158, 158, 52.43 *triangle,* 52.60 *parameter,* 124.2, 124.5 *medium,* 167.15 *everyday,* 291.1 *centre,* 291.6 *central,* 333.1 *middle way,* 617.5 *not bad,* 620.4 *ordinary*
medianly 124.12 *mediumly*
mediant 49.16 *musical note*
median triangle 52.43 *triangle*
media personality 534.29 *broadcaster*
mediate 158, 678, 15.12 *have an industrial dispute,* 232.4 *be an instrument,* 242.4 *moderate,* 675.6 *make peace,* 677.4 *pacify,* 707.5 *represent*
mediated 15.10 *unionized,* 716.8 *negotiated*
mediately 678.7 *mediatorially*
mediating 15.10 *unionized*
mediation 678, 15.4 *industrial dispute,* 158.6 *middle ground,* 232.1 *instrumentality,* 677.1 *pacification,* 715.1 *contract,* 716.1 *negotiation*
Mediation 678
mediative 232.7 *causal*
mediator 678, 15.6 *employer,* 158.9 *middleman,* 232.3 *assistant,* 242.2 *moderator,* 298.3 *interfacer,* 492.5 *judge,* 564.10 *speaker,* 646.3 *agent,* 675.3, 677.3 *pacifist,* 707.3 *agent,* 715.4 *contractor,* 716.4 *negotiator,* 823.13 *matchmaker*
mediatorial 678.6 *mediatory*
mediatorially 678, 677.7 *pacifically*
mediatory 158, 678, 677.6 *pacificatory*
medic 60.11 *doctor,* 630.15 *healer,* 767.5 *helper*
medicable 629.14 *repairable,* 630.18 *medical*
Medicaid 60.1 *medicine,* 632.1 *safety*
medical 60, 630, 60.6 *health care*
medical advice 630.11 *medical art*
medical adviser 654.4 *adviser*
medical art 630
medical assistance 662
medical assistant 60.17 *paramedic*
medical attendant 60.17 *paramedic*

medical auxiliary 60.17 *paramedic*
medical care 60.1 *medicine,* 60.8 *treatment,* 630.13 *therapy*
medical centre 291.4 *centre of activity*
medical consultation 60.6 *health care*
medical corps 17.4 *military organization,* 679.16 *army unit*
medical covering 293
medical doctor 60.11 *doctor*
medical ethics 4.6 *branch of philosophy,* 60.1 *medicine*
medical examination 60.6 *health care*
medical examiner 60.13 *medical specialist*
medical genetics 60.3 *medical specialty*
medical history 60.6 *health care*
medical insurance 60.1 *medicine*
medical intervention 60.8 *treatment*
medical jurisprudence 60.1 *medicine*
medically 60, 630.21 *remedially*
medical officer 60.11 *doctor,* 625.3 *hygienist*
medical physics 56.4 *experimental physics*
medical practice 60.1 *medicine,* 630.11 *medical art*
medical practitioner 60.11 *doctor*
medical profession 60.1 *medicine*
medical registrar 60.11 *doctor*
medical report 528.3 *document*
medical school 6.12 *educational institution*
medical science 60.3 *medical specialty*
medical service 17.4 *military organization*
medical specialist 60
medical specialty 60
medical student 60.11 *doctor*
medical technician 60.17 *paramedic*
medical test 60.7 *diagnosis*
medical treatment 60.8 *treatment,* 630.13 *therapy*
medicament 630.2 *medicine*
Medicare 60.1 *medicine,* 632.1 *safety,* 718.1 *protection*
medicate 60.19 *practise medicine,* 629.6 *cure,* 630.20 *doctor*
medicated 629.16 *restorative*
medication 60.8 *treatment,* 62.3 *drug,* 630.2 *medicine*
medicinal 60.25 *therapeutic,* 62.3 *drug,* 413.10 *stimulating,* 629.16 *restorative,* 630.17 *remedial*
medicinal compound 133.2 *mixed thing*
medicinal drink 413.6 *cordial*
medicinal herb 83.2 *plant,* 630.2 *medicine*
medicinal leech 81.6 *worm*
medicinally 413.15 *piquantly,* 630.21 *remedially*
medicinal plant 83.2 *plant*
medicinal value 630.1 *remedy*
medicine 60, 630, 62.3 *drug,* 630.11 *medical art,* 662.5 *medical assistance*
Medicine 60
medicine bottle 630.2 *medicine*
medicine cabinet 630.2 *medicine*
medicine chest 630.2 *medicine*
medicine man 11.4 *witch,* 630.15 *healer,* 636.4 *warner*
medicine show 51.5 *show,* 532.8 *public relations*
medick 84 Flowers and Flowering Plants
medico 630.15 *healer*
medicopsychology 61.2 *psychiatry*
medieval 43 Architectural Styles, 202.14 *historic*
Medieval 3.15 *historic*
medieval art 50 Western Art Styles and Movements
medieval costume 295.5 *fancy dress*

medieval dance 46.4 *historic dancing*
medieval government 12.1 *government*
Medieval Greek 5 Languages and Groups of Languages
medievalism 48 Literary Groups and Movements, 3.12 *historicism*, 200.9, 202.4 *antiquarianism*
medievalist 200.11, 202.9 *antiquarian*
Medieval Latin 5 Languages and Groups of Languages
medieval ownership 723
Medieval times 3.10 *past age*
Medina 93 Cities, **96** Rivers
mediocre 124, 783, 127.16 *ordinary*, 158.15 *middling*, 242.6 *moderate*, 612.4 *trivial*, 617.5 *not bad*, 620.4 *ordinary*
mediocreness 124.6 *mediocrity*
mediocrity 124, 783, 127.5 *inferior state*, 278.5 *shallow person*, 612.7 *triviality*, 612.10 *nonentity*, 620.8 *ordinariness*
meditate 9.7 *worship*, 461.12 *think*, 588.7 *intend*, 786.12 *wonder whether*
meditation 9.1 *worship*, 61.14 *trance*, 461.3 *thoughtfulness*
meditational 9.9 *worshipful*
meditative 4.17 *thoughtful*, 9.9 *worshipful*, 461.10 *speculative*
meditatively 4.28 *thoughtfully*, 9.12 *worshipfully*
meditativeness 461.3 *thoughtfulness*
meditative trance 512.1 *oblivion*
Mediterranean 97 Oceans and Seas, 408.8 *hot place*
Mediterranean climate 55.38 *climate*
medium 124, 124, 259, 11.12 *occultist*, 50.11 *artist's materials*, 51.18 *stage lighting*, 103.1 *essence*, 158.3 *median*, 158.9 *middleman*, 158.13 *median*, 232.1 *instrumentality*, 232.2 *instrument*, 242.6 *moderate*, 333.1 *middle way*, 368.7 *believer in a nonmaterial world*, 444.5 *paint*, 464.5 *intuitive person*, 517.8 *oracle*, 524.6 *interpreter*, 602.1 *means*
medium-grained texture 54.28 *rock*
mediumism 11.1 *occultism*
mediumistic 11.16 *psychic*
mediumistic trance 11.10 *psychic phenomenon*
mediumly 124
medium of conversion 220
medium of exchange 741.1 *money*
medium-pace bowler 27.4 *team*
medium-range 70.5 *transportable*
medium shot 66.4 *portrait*
medium-size 259.14 *medium*
medium steel 74.4 *shipbuilding*
medium-term forecast 55.4 *weather forecast*
medium wave 212.6 *radio frequency*, 534.14 *radio transmission*
medlar 86 Fruits
medley 39.11 *swimming*, 113.2 *assortment*, 133.3, 161.32 *miscellany*
medley of colour 456.1 *variegation*
medley race 39.1 *swimming*
medley relay 21.6 *track*
medley relay race 21.1 *track events*
medroxyprogesterone 62 Medication
medulla 83.5 *stem*
medullary 374.4 *compressible*
medusa 81.7 *coelenterate*
Medusa 11.4 *witch*
medusoid 81.21 *coelenterate*
Medway 96 Rivers
meed 125.1 *compensation*, 878.1 *reward*
meek 236.11 *unprotected*, 673.5

submitting, 694.7 *obedient*, 806.1 *humble*, 810.8 *modest*
meekly 673.6 *with humility*, 694.10 *obediently*, 806.27 *humbly*, 810.17 *modestly*
meekness 236.3 *helplessness*, 694.1 *obedience*, 806.7 *humility*, 810.1 *modesty*
meerkat 77 Placental Mammals
meerschaum 54 Minerals, 413.7 *tobacco*
Meerut 93 Cities
meet 267, 344, 18.1 *sport*, 32.7 *horseracing*, 32.8 *hunting*, 135.8 *unite*, 137.13 *intercommunicate*, 161.3 *meeting*, 161.39 *come together*, 167.7 *conform*, 298.4 *interface*, 330.2 *collide*, 342.10 *come together*, 407.12 *abut*, 496.1 *discover*, 674.12 *fight*, 719.6 *perform*, 746.7 *pay off*, 765.10 *suffice*
meet a crosscurrent 111.8 *be opposite*
meet a deadline 648.2 *make haste*
meet a demand 606.5 *provision*, 739.2 *be sold*
meet adversity 687.9 *be in trouble*
meet a headwind 111.8 *be opposite*
meet an obligation 845.19 *pay*
meet an order 606.5 *provision*
meet around a conference table 568.11 *confer*
meet a sticky end 397.16 *meet one's fate*
meet by accident 589.11 *chance upon*
meet by chance 344.8 *meet*
meet contractual obligations 15.11 *conduct industrial relations*
meet God 7.19 *be religious*
meet halfway 158.19 *mediate*, 333.7 *be halfway*, 576.10 *compromise*, 677.5 *make peace*, 717.4 *compromise*
meet head-on 111.8 *be opposite*, 663.16 *confront*
meeting 161, 267, 267, 344, 815, 18.1 *sport*, 135.1 *union*, 137.1 *connection*, 298.6 *interfacial*, 330.12 *collision*, 342.1 *convergence*, 342.7 *convergent*, 407.6 *contiguity*, 407.9 *touching*, 496.6 *discovery*, 568.4 *conference*, 653.7 *council*, 674.2 *contest*
meeting halfway 717.1 *compromise*
meetinghouse 10.11 *place of worship*
meeting in camera 529.1 *secrecy*
meeting of minds 116.1 *accord*, 499.1 *assent*, 654.2 *consultation*
meeting one's friends 815.3 *meeting*
meeting place 342, 815, 135.6 *point of union*, 344.14 *meeting*, 407.6 *contiguity*
meeting point 135.6 *point of union*, 298.1 *interface*, 407.6 *contiguity*
meeting the cost 746.1 *payment*
meeting with God 8.8 *divine manifestation*
meet one at every turn 253.11 *be present*, 610.4 *be excessive*
meet one's death 397.15 *die*
meet one's end 397.15 *die*
meet one's fate 397, 397.15 *die*
meet one's Maker 397.15 *die*
meet one's match 672.4 *serve one right*
meet on the battlefield 676.14 *battle*
meet requirements 608.4 *suffice*
meet reward 879.9 *retribution*
meet Saint Peter 397.15 *die*
meet the cost 746.8 *defray*, 748.1 *expend*
meet the eye 437.9 *appear*
meet the needs of 765.10 *suffice*
meet unexpectedly 229.5 *happen by chance*

meet with 496.1 *discover*, 654.6 *consult*
meet with a loss 722.9 *lose*
meet with approbation 851.17 *meet with approval*
meet with approval 851
meet with disapproval 852.24 *be open to criticism*
meet with success 682.6 *be successful*
mefanamic acid 62 Medication
mega 75 SI Units, 259.15 *big*
megabucks 741.3 *fortune*, 742.6 *money*
megabyte 65.17 *computing term*
Megaera 828.7 *gods and goddesses of anger*
megahertz 212.6 *radio frequency*
megalith 3.11 *relic*, 200.7 *thing of the past*, 545.11 *monument*
megalithic 259.15 *big*
Megaloceros 77 Placental Mammals
megalomania 61.15 *compulsion*, 494.1 *overestimation*, 510.4 *delusion*, 809.1 *vanity*
megalomaniac 494.3 *optimist*, 510.7 *insane person*, 695.5 *compulsive person*, 809.8 *vain*
megalopolis 93.1 *city*, 249.10 *urban area*
Megaloptera 82 Orders of Insects
megalopteran 82.10 *insectan*
megalosaur 79 Fossil Reptiles
meganucleus 59.9 *cell nucleus*
megaphone 56.18 *source of sound*, 420.9 *audio device*, 423.4 *sound maker*
megaphyll 83.6 *leaf*
megapode 78 Birds
megastar 9.4 *idolized person*, 800.2 *person of repute*
Megatherium 77 Placental Mammals
megaton 75 Scientific and Technical Units
megaton bomb 680.16 *bomb*
megawatt 235.5 *unit of work*
megestrol 62 Medication
megrim 406.2 *painful condition*, 579.3 *whim*
megrims 366.8 *spasm*, 624.18 *veterinary disease*
Mehueret 8 Deities
meibomian gland 352 Exocrine Glands
mein 306.6 *nature*
meiosis 59.10 *cell division*
meiotic 59.25 *genetic*
Meishan 68 Breeds of Pig
me-ism 809.5 *self-interest*
Meissen 93 Cities
Meissen's crossed swords 44.4 *porcelain mark*
Meissen ware 44 Types of Ceramics
Meissner effect 56 Named Laws
Meistersinger 48.14 *author*, 433.5 *melodist*
Meitner 52 Scientists
meke 46.4 *historic dancing*
Meke Meke 8 Deities
Mekong 96 Rivers, 96.5 *other major rivers*
melaleuca 85 Trees and Shrubs
melamine formaldehyde 604.1 *materials*
melancholia 61.10 *neurosis*, 61.13 *depression*, 510.6 *mental breakdown*
melancholic 61.7 *personality type*, 510.7 *insane person*, 510.13 *mentally ill*, 770.4 *depressing person*, 770.6 *depressed*, 771.12 *four humours*, 776.3 *hopeless person*, 776.4 *hopeless*, 830.6 *sullen*
melancholy 454.3 *depressed*, 618.4 *poor*, 618.10 *poverty*, 770.2 *depression*, 776.1 *hopelessness*, 788.1 *boredom*, 788.4 *boring*, 830.1 *sullenness*, 830.6 *sullen*
Melanesian 5 Languages and Groups of Languages, 1.6 *race*,

1.13 *racial*, 5.11 *family of languages*
Melanesian art 50 Non-Western Art
Melanesians 1 Peoples
mélange 133.2 *mixed thing*
melanic 440.10 *dark-coloured*
melanin 447.8 *black pigment*, 449.3 *brownness*
melanism 447.7 *blackness*
melanistic 447.2 *dark*
melanocyte-stimulating hormone 58 Hormones
melanoma 624.12 *cancer*, 624.13 *skin disease*
Melano-Papuan 5 Languages and Groups of Languages
melanosis 447.7 *blackness*
melanous 440.10 *dark-coloured*
melatonin 58 Hormones
Melba 49 Musicians and Composers
Melba toast 45.38 *bread*
Melbourne 93 Cities, 93.6 *other cities*
Melchites 7 Christian Movements
melee 674.6 *fight*
mêlée 151.9 *disorder*
melick 87 Grasses
melifluous 49.30 *harmonic*
melifluously 433.11 *melodiously*
melinite 680.15 *explosive*
meliorable 627.15 *improvable*
meliorate 627.1 *improve*
melioration 6.1 *education*, 627.5 *improvement*
meliorative 627.16 *improving*
meliorism 627.11 *reformism*
meliorist 627.12 *reformer*
melissa 62 Medication
Melitianism 7 Christian Movements
mellifluent 433.6 *melodious*
mellifluous 405.6 *pleasant*, 433.6 *melodious*, 558.3 *elegant*
mellifluously 558.5 *elegantly*
mellophone 49 Musical Instruments
mellow 49.30 *harmonic*, 202.11 *old*, 207.17 *age*, 207.18 *mature*, 220.8 *be transformed*, 374.6 *softhearted*, 374.13 *soften*, 374.14 *ease*, 427.8 *deep*, 433.6 *melodious*, 444.13 *soft-hued*, 444.15 *colour*, 594.7 *develop*, 594.20 *developed*, 627.2 *get better*, 684.7 *completed*, 763.3 *comfortable*
mellow into 220.7 *convert into*
mellowly 202.18 *venerably*
mellowness 202.1 *oldness*, 207.4 *middle age*, 374.12 *gentleness*, 594.14 *preparedness*
melodeon 49 Musical Instruments
melodic 116.13 *harmonious*, 433.6 *melodious*
melodica 49 Musical Instruments
melodically 116.33 *harmoniously*, 433.11 *melodiously*
melodic line 433.1 *melody*
melodics 49.14 *harmonics*
melodic scale 49.20 *key*
melodious 433, 49.30 *harmonic*, 116.13 *harmonious*, 414.7 *pleasant*, 427.8 *deep*
melodiously 433, 414.9 *sweetly*
melodiousness 433, 49.1 *music*, 414.1 *sweetness*
melodist 433
melodize 49.34, 116.24 *harmonize*, 433.9 *set to music*
melodrama 51.2 *play*, 51.9 *tragedy*, 541.1 *exaggeration*
melodramatic 51.37 *dramatic*, 541.12 *exaggerated*, 759.13 *passionate*
melodramatically 51.42 *dramatically*, 403.14 *sensationally*, 541.16 *exaggeratedly*
melodramatics 51.7 *dramaturgy*
melodramatist 51.24 *dramatist*
melodramatize 51.36 *dramatize*
melody 49, 433, 49.1 *music*, 116.4 *harmony*

Melody 433

melon 86 Fruits, 86.5 *figurative usage*

melphalan 62 Medication

Melpomene 51.9 *tragedy*

melt 387, 54.24 *volcanic activity,* 55.30, 55.63 *snow,* 57.3 *phase,* 57.25 *solidify,* 100.13 *cease to exist,* 139.6 *come unstuck,* 141.4 *deconstruct,* 189.4 *be transient,* 220.7 *convert into,* 374.13 *soften,* 408.14 *be hot,* 424.5 *sound faint,* 458.1 *disappear,* 607.1 *waste,* 835.11 *excite pity*

meltable 387.21 *liquefiable*

meltage 55.30 *snow*

melt away 121.6 *change gradually,* 129.4 *decrease,* 189.4 *be transient,* 458.2 *depart,* 607.1 *waste*

meltdown 56.75 *nuclear accident,* 244.4 *ruin*

melt down 355.17 *obtain an extract,* 387.24 *melt,* 408.14 *be hot*

melted 57.32 *solid,* 141.5 *disintegrated,* 387.19 *liquefied*

melted out 743.3 *beggarly*

meltemi 55 Winds

melting 56.37 *temperature,* 57.3 *phase,* 141.2 *deconstruction,* 141.6 *disintegrating,* 220.1 *conversion,* 220.14 *converting,* 224.13 *changeable,* 374.2 *pliant,* 387.8 *fluidification,* 387.20 *liquefying,* 408.5 *hot weather,* 458.4 *disappearance,* 607.3 *waste,* 821.20 *amorous*

melting look 435.6 *look*

melting point 56.37 *temperature,* 408.1 *heat*

melting-point apparatus 57 Laboratory Apparatus

melting pot 133.6 *mixer,* 220.4 *medium of conversion,* 400.11 *nation*

melt into 121.6 *change gradually,* 220.7 *convert into*

melt into thin air 100.13 *cease to exist*

melton 67 Natural Fabrics

melt on the air 424.5 *sound faint*

melts 45.31 *offal*

melt the heart 835.11 *excite pity*

meltwater 54.38 *glacier,* 55.30 *snow,* 389.1 *water*

Melville 48 Writers, **98** Islands

member 148, 665, 52.21 *set,* 143.4 *component,* 146.3 *person included,* 724.3 *participant*

member in good standing 665.5 *member*

member of Congress 12.8 *politician,* 653.16 *official*

member of parliament 699.6 *lawmaker*

member of Parliament 706.1 *delegate*

Member of Parliament 12.8 *politician,* 653.16 *official*

member of society 400

member of staff 148.5 *member*

member of the avant garde 194.6 *person having priority*

member of the establishment 611.4 *bigwig*

member of the legal profession 16.13 *lawyer*

member of the resistance 672.2 *revenger*

member of the smart set 655.5 *expert*

member of the underground 672.2 *revenger*

membership 146.1 *inclusion,* 724.2 *participation,* 815.1 *sociability*

members only 147.4 *exclusiveness*

membrane 266.3 *coat,* 438.6 *that which makes invisible*

membraneously 266.12 *in layers*

membranophone 49.25 *musical instrument*

membranous 266.9 *platelike*

memento 511, 681, 3.11 *relic,* 545.11 *monument,* 729.2 *gift*

memento mori 397.3 *symbol of death*

memo 511.4 *reminder,* 545.1 *record*

memoir 48.4 *non-fiction,* 545.1 *record,* 561.1 *dissertation*

memoirs 3.6 *biography,* 396.11 *life story,* 511.2 *retrospect,* 560.4 *factual account*

memo pad 545.6 *record book*

memorabilia 3.11 *relic,* 132.1 *remainder,* 511.3 *memento,* 545.1 *record*

memorability 611.1 *importance*

memorable 511, 611.6 *notable*

memorably 511, 132.11 *residually,* 611.9 *importantly*

memorandum 511.4 *reminder,* 611.2 *important matter*

memorial 511, 399.4 *funeral objects,* 399.6 *grave,* 399.11 *funeral,* 511.3 *memento,* 545.11 *monument,* 812.11 *commemorative*

memorial arch 545.11 *monument*

Memorial Day 214.6 *annually celebrated day*

memorial inscription 545.11 *monument*

memorialization 190.4 *eternalization*

memorialize 186.4 *perpetuate,* 190.6 *make eternal,* 511.14, 812.16 *commemorate*

memorially 3.25 *reportedly*

memorial service 10.4 *public worship,* 399.2 *funeral,* 812.2 *commemoration*

memorization 511.1 *memory,* 584.7 *habituation,* 726.5 *retentiveness*

memorize 511, 51.35 *rehearse,* 501.12 *know by heart,* 696.15 *learn,* 726.8 *remember*

memorized 511

memorizing 726.5 *retentiveness*

memory 61, 65, 511, 65.4 *computer part,* 132.1 *remainder,* 471.1 *idea,* 511.5 *day to remember,* 605.4 *storage,* 812.2 *commemoration*

Memory 511

memory artist 51.27 *entertainer*

memory gap 546.5 *forgetfulness*

memory trace 61.23 *memory*

Memphis 93 Cities

memsahib 402.3 *female title of address*

men 777 Phobias by Topic, 401.15 *menfolk,* 646.4 *personnel,* 679.14 *armed forces*

Men 727.7 *toilet*

menace 517.11 *predict,* 633.5 *danger,* 633.10 *endanger,* 636.1 *warning,* 636.5 *warn,* 777.13 *frighten,* 822.8 *hated person,* 832.7 *act of malevolence,* 832.18 *torment,* 862.11 *be evil*

menacing 440.11 *benighted,* 633.1 *dangerous,* 636.8 *warning,* 777.10 *frightening,* 832.10 *malevolent*

menacingly 633.11 *dangerously,* 777.16 *frighteningly*

ménage 255.2 *inhabitants*

ménage à trois 877.4 *illicit love*

menagerie 133.3 *miscellany,* 161.31 *exhibition,* 256.12 *stall,* 605.5 *collection*

menaion 10.10 *religious manual*

Menander 48 Dramatists

menarche 246.2 *productiveness,* 353.11 *menstruation*

Mencius 4 Philosophers

mend 125.4 *compensate,* 135.10 *link,* 623.6 *get healthy,* 627.1 *improve,* 627.2 *get better,* 627.3 *rectify,* 629.1, 629.8 *repair,* 630.19 *remedy,* 843.15 *put right*

mendable 629.14 *repairable*

mendaceous 540.25 *false*

mendaceousness 538.3 *lying*

mendacious 309.8 *exaggerated,* 474.10 *hypocritical,* 538.15 *lying,* 538.19 *dishonest*

mendaciously 309.14 *distortedly,*

538.26 *untruthfully,* 540.36 *falsely*

mendaciousness 538.10 *dishonesty,* 540.1 *falsehood*

mendacity 309.4 *distortion of the truth,* 474.5 *hypocrisy,* 538.3 *lying,* 540.1 *falsehood*

mended 629.13 *repaired*

Mendel 52 Scientists

mendelevium 57 Chemical Elements

Mendeleyev 52 Scientists

Mendelian 59.25 *genetic*

Mendelian genetics 59.11 *genetics*

Mendel's laws 59.11 *genetics*

Mendelssohn 4 Philosophers, **49** Musicians and Composers

mender 627.13 *reviser,* 629.12 *repairer*

Menderes 96 Rivers

mendicancy 712.3 *solicitation,* 743.7 *beggary*

mendicant 7.7 *monk,* 712.5 *beggar,* 712.11 *begging,* 743.3 *beggarly,* 743.10 *poor person*

mendicant friar 712.5 *beggar,* 743.10 *poor person*

mending 627.6 *rectification,* 629.8 *repair,* 629.11 *recuperation*

Mendip 95 Mountains

Mendip Hills 95.5 *British mountains*

Mendius reaction 57 Named Reactions

mend one's ways 627.2 *get better*

Mendoza 93 Cities

menfolk 401

menhaden 80 Fishes

menhir 3.11 *relic,* 200.7 *thing of the past,* 399.6 *grave,* 545.11 *monument*

menial 127.6 *inferior,* 646.1 *worker,* 673.2 *appeaser,* 673.5 *submitting,* 697.1 *servant,* 697.9 *serving,* 808.6 *servile*

menially 697.10 *obediently,* 808.16 *with servility*

menialness 808.1 *servility*

Menindee 94 Lakes

meningitis 777 Phobias by Topic, 246.4 *infection*

meningitophobia 777 Phobias by Name

men in white coats 61.30, 510.10 *psychiatrist*

meniscal 311.4 *curved*

meniscectomy 60 Surgical Operations

meniscoid 316.4 *convex*

meniscus 52.42 *circle,* 311.2 *bend,* 316.1 *convexity*

Mennecy ware 44 Types of Ceramics

Mennonite 7.5 *Christian*

Mennonitism 7 Christian Movements

men of today 198.5 *contemporary*

Menomini 5 Languages and Groups of Languages

meno mosso 49 Musical Terms

menopausal 207.13 *middle-aged,* 353.31 *menstrual*

menopause 207.4 *middle age,* 247.1 *infertility,* 353.11 *menstruation*

menorah 10.14 *sacred object*

menorrhagia 353.11 *menstruation*

Menrva 8 Deities

Mensa 53 The Constellations

mensal 45.56 *culinary*

Mensa member 507.4 *intellectual*

men's clothing 295.1 *dress*

menses 214.2 *cycle,* 353.11 *menstruation*

Mensheviks 12.6 *political party*

Menshevist 333.3 *moderate person*

men's magazine 532.5 *journal,* 877.2 *indecency*

Men's Room 727.7 *toilet*

menstrual 353, 214.12 *cyclic*

menstrual cycle 187.5 *recurrent period,* 214.2 *cycle*

menstrual flow 353.11 *menstruation,* 387.3 *body fluid*

menstruate 353, 214.8 *be cyclic*

menstruating 353.31 *menstrual*

menstruation 353, 187.5 *recurrent period,* 214.2 *cycle,* 246.2 *productiveness*

menstruum 387.9 *solvent*

mensurability 268.3 *measurability*

mensurable 52.73 *numerable,* 170.14 *calculable,* 268.14 *measurable*

mensural 268.12 *metrical*

mensuration 56, 268.1 *measurement*

mensurational 268.12 *metrical*

mensurative 268.12 *metrical*

menswear 295.1 *dress*

mental 459, 368.11 *internal,* 461.8 *thoughtful,* 471.11 *ideational,* 510.11 *insane*

mental activity 461.1 *thought*

mental affliction 862.2 *affliction of mind*

mental agility 329.10 *quickness*

mental agitation 366.1 *agitation*

mental and physical distress 650.7 *fatigue*

mental arithmetic 52.12 *numeration*

mental asylum 630.14 *hospital*

mental attitude 652.1 *conduct*

mental block 462, 512.2 *blankness,* 546.5 *forgetfulness*

mental body 11.7 *spirit*

mental breakdown 510, 61.10 *neurosis*

mental case 510.7 *insane person,* 624.19 *sick person*

mental chemistry 61.1 *psychology*

mental cruelty 824.3 *divorce court*

mental decay 236.4 *disability*

mental deficiency 460.1 *lack of intellect,* 510.2 *subnormality*

mental derangement 153.6 *derangement*

mental deterioration 510

mental disorder 61.9 *psychological disorder,* 153.6 *derangement,* 624.4 *disease*

mental entities 4.9 *philosophical problem*

mental equilibrium 509.1 *sanity*

mental fatigue 650.7 *fatigue*

mental fluctuation 365.3 *vacillation*

mental freedom 700.1 *liberation*

mental handicap 236.4 *disability,* 460.1 *lack of intellect,* 510.2 *subnormality*

mental hardness 373

mental health 509.1 *sanity*

mental home 510.8 *mental hospital*

mental hospital 510, 61.31 *psychiatric hospital,* 630.14 *hospital,* 634.2 *shelter*

mental illness 510.1 *insanity,* 862.2 *affliction*

mental image 471.1 *idea,* 519.4 *ideality,* 547.6 *image*

mental impairment 510.2 *subnormality*

mental inertia 466.2 *lack of interest*

mental instability 510.1 *insanity*

mental institution 510.8 *mental hospital*

mentalism 4.7 *school of thought*

mentality 459.1 *mind,* 459.3 *intelligence*

mentally 459, 368.14 *subjectively,* 471.20 *theoretically*

mentally defective personality 61.8 *disordered personality*

mentally deficient 460.5 *lacking intellect,* 460.7 *intellectually subnormal*

mentally deranged 153.16 *deranged*

mentally handicapped 460.5 *lacking intellect,* 460.7 *intellectually subnormal*

mentally hard 373

mentally ill 510

mentally quick 329

mentally retarded 460.5 *lacking intellect*

mentally sharp 380

mentally sound 509.4 *sane*

mentally strong 378.5 *mentally tough*
mentally subnormal 460.7 *intellectually subnormal*
mentally tough 378
mentally weak 460.5 *lacking intellect*
mental object 471.1 *idea*
mental philosophy 4.6 *branch of philosophy*
mental picture 471.1 *idea*, 519.4 *ideality*
mental process 461.1 *thought*
mental product 243
mental quickness 329.10 *quickness of mind*
mental reservation 578.5 *equivocalness*
mental retardation 460.1 *lack of intellect*
mental sharpness 380
mental shock 61.12 *stress*
mental skill 655.1 *skill*
mental specialist 61.30 *psychiatrist*
mental strength 378.9 *mental toughness*
mental stress 61.12 *stress*
mental subnormality 61.9 *psychological disorder*, 510.2 *subnormality*
mental test 61.4 *psychometrics*, 61.5 *psychological test*
mental toughness 378
mental treatment 630.13 *therapy*
mental weakness 460.1 *lack of intellect*
menthol 62 Medication, 58.20 *terpene*, 413.7 *tobacco*
Menthu 8 Deities
mention 165.24 *specify*, 526.3 *reveal*, 528.4 *mass communication*, 532.13 *make public*, 560.16 *define*, 564.11 *speak*
mentionable 876.10 *moralistic*
mentioned 526.13 *displayed*
mentor 4.12 *sage*, 6.4 *educator*, 471.9 *person of ideas*, 632.3 *protector*, 653.13 *director*, 654.4, 662.14 *adviser*, 688.10 *person of authority*, 696.9 *educational leader*
menu 65.17 *computing term*, 171.2 *table*, 171.4 *bill*
Menuhin 49 Musicians and Composers
meow 432.1 *animal cry*, 432.4 *cry*
MEP 653.16 *official*, 688.10 *person of authority*, 696.3 *leader*
mepacrine 62 Medication
meperidine 62 Medication, 630.5 *analgesic*
mephenesin 62 Medication
Mephisto 8.7 *devil*
Mephistophelean 8.16 *devilish*
Mephistopheles 8.7 *devil*, 864.6 *religious sin*
Mephistophelian 864.14 *impious*
mephitic 388.18 *miasmic*, 419.3 *stinking*, 626.7 *toxic*
mephitis 388.3 *miasma*, 419.1 *stench*, 626.1 *lack of hygiene*, 631.9 *pollution*
meprobamate 62 Medication
mepyramine 62 Medication
Merak 53 Named Stars
mercantile 737, 13.13 *economic*
mercantile system 13.6 *economic factors*
mercantile system tariff 699.2 *economic restraint*
mercantilism 699.2 *economic restraint*
mercantilist 699.6 *law-maker*
mercaptan 57 Types of Compounds
mercaptopurine 62 Medication
Mercator 52 Scientists
Mercator projection 299.4 *map*
Mercator's projection 547.7 *map*
mercenaries 679.14 *armed forces*
mercenary 676.11 *recruit*, 676.17 *military*, 679.6 *militarist*, 679.35 *martial*, 703.10 *engaged*
mercenary army 679.15 *army*

mercenary forces 17.2 *the military*
mercer 295.26 *fashion designer*, 739.13 *retailer*
Mercer 48 Dramatists
mercerize 378.11 *make tough*
merchandise 739, 13.10 *trade with*, 243.7 *produce*, 603.6 *equipment*, 605.1 *store*, 725.5 *personal estate*, 737.1 *trade*, 739.1 *sell*
merchandiser 13.9 *economist*, 737.10 *trader*, 739.12 *wholesaler*
merchandising 737.4 *trade*, 739.3 *selling*
merchant 13.9 *economist*, 70.5 *transportable*, 646.3 *agent*, 737.10 *trader*, 739.12 *wholesaler*, 739.13 *retailer*
merchantable 737.13 *mercantile*, 739.15 *saleable*
merchant bank 741.19 *treasury*
merchant class 158.8 *middle class*
merchant jack 544.7 *flag*
merchant-like 737.13 *mercantile*
merchantman 74 Ships and Boats, 74.3 *vessel*
merchant marine 679.22 *navy*
merchant navy 679.22 *navy*
merchant prince 739.12 *wholesaler*
merchant ship 74.3 *vessel*
merchant venturer 739.12 *wholesaler*
merciful 839, 691.4 *lenient*, 835.6 *pitying*
mercifully 16.88 *forgivingly*, 677.7 *pacifically*, 691.6 *leniently*, 835.13 *pitifully*, 839.14 *forgivingly*
mercifulness 691.1 *leniency*, 835.1 *pity*, 835.3 *mercy*, 839.2 *forgivingness*
merciless 832, 574.3 *strong-willed*, 577.3 *unyielding*, 690.8 *severe*
mercilessly 690.11 *severely*, 836.7 *pitilessly*
mercilessness 836.1 *pitilessness*
mercurial 224.14 *irresolute*, 324.16 *moving*, 329.2 *mentally quick*, 491.8 *capricious*, 576.2 *changeable*, 579.1 *capricious*, 759.13 *passionate*
mercurially 324.18 *in motion*
Mercurian 53.36 *astronomical*
mercuric 57.34 *elemental*
Mercurochrome 630.3 *prophylactic*
mercurous 57.34 *elemental*
mercury 57 Chemical Elements, 224.3 *changeable thing*
Mercury 8 Deities, **53** Planets and their Satellites, 53.16 *planet*, 326.8 *messenger*, 329.13 *swift person*
mercury barometer 55.7 *weather instruments*, 56.88 *barometer*
Mercurycard 534.7 *telephone*
mercury thermometer 56.89 *thermometer*
mercury-vapour lamp 56.25 *light source*, 66.20 *electron tube*, 439.6 *electric light*
mercy 835, 8.2 *divine attribute*, 673.7 *I/we surrender*, 677.2 *peace offering*, 691.1 *leniency*, 831.1 *benevolence*
mercy flight 73.1 *aviation*
mercy killer 398.11 *killer*
mercy killing 398.1 *killing*
mercy seat 16.27 *courtroom*
mere 94.2 *small lake*, 134.16 *simple*
Meredith 48 Writers, **48** Poets
mere existence 99, 743.5 *poverty*
mere handful 182.1 *few*
merely exist 99
merengue 49.10 *world music*
mere nothing 612.8 *trifle*
mere notion 518.3 *conjecture*
Mérens pony 32 Breeds of Horse and Pony
mere rhetoric 474.1 *sophistry*
meretricious 538.18 *pretentious*, 540.27 *hypocritical*, 541.14 *extravagant*, 557.4 *ornate*, 559.10

ugly, 795.7 *vulgar*, 797.3 *affected*, 811.19 *flashy*, 877.13 *unchaste*
meretriciously 538.27 *pretentiously*, 811.35 *flashily*
meretriciousness 538.8 *pretence*, 540.3 *hypocrisy*, 811.4 *flashiness*
mere words 521.1 *lack of meaning*
mere wreck 628.9 *dilapidation*
merganser 78 Birds, 360.8 *descender*
merge 823, 110.7 *be the same*, 110.8 *make the same*, 116.24 *harmonize*, 133.8 *mix*, 135.8 *unite*, 137.11 *connect*, 140.5 *combine*, 146.5 *be included*, 174.19 *become one*, 664.16 *join*, 734.7 *take*
merged 107.4 *related*, 110.12 *same*, 116.11 *allied*, 116.13 *harmonious*, 133.12 *mixed*, 135.12 *united*, 137.15 *connected*, 140.9 *assembled*, 146.8 *included*, 734.12 *taking*, 737.19 *corporate*
merge in 148.10 *compose*
merge into 220.7 *convert into*
mergence 110.1 *sameness*
merger 13.7 *corporation*, 107.1 *relatedness*, 133.1 *mixture*, 135.1 *union*, 137.1 *connection*, 140.1 *combination*, 230.2 *joint operation*, 664.7 *association*, 710.3 *business offer*, 734.1 *taking*, 737.9 *bargaining*, 823.2 *alliance*
merge with 664.14 *join with*
merging 110.12 *same*, 664.7 *association*
Mérida 93 Cities
meridian 53.5 *celestial sphere*, 204.3, 204.6 *noon*, 249.2 *geographical region*, 249.16 *regional*, 279.1 *summit*, 279.5 *top*
meridional 279.5 *top*, 332.13 *directional*
Mérimée 48 Writers
meringue 390.10 *air bubble*
merino 288.4 *textile*
Merino 68 Breeds of Sheep
merit 845, 163.9 *distinction*, 485.14 *be qualified*, 611.1 *importance*, 613.6 *usability*, 617.6 *worth*, 617.9 *be worthy*, 843.13 *be right*, 845.1 *entitlement*, 861.8 *good*, 863.3 *worth*
merited 485.9 *qualified*, 845.10 *due*
meritedness 485.1 *qualification*
meriting 845.9 *meritorious*
meritocracy 12.1 *government*, 617.7 *elite*, 688.7 *type of rule*
meritocrat 617.7 *elite*
meritocratic 12.9 *governmental*
meritorious 845, 617.1 *worthy*, 782.8 *desirable*, 804.5 *entitled*, 851.21 *praiseworthy*, 861.1 *good*, 863.7 *worthy*
meritoriously 782.17 *desirably*, 845.21 *deservedly*, 863.11 *worthily*
meritoriousness 782.2 *desirability*
merits 845.2 *due*
Merleau-Ponty 4 Philosophers
Merle Park 46.14 *famous ballet dancers*
merlin 78 Birds
Merlin 11.4 *witch*
merlon 671.11 *fortification*
mermaid 11.4 *witch*, 97.4 *sea god*
merman 97.4 *sea god*
merocrine 352.4 *secretory*
merocrine secretion 352.1 *secretion*
Merodach 8 Deities
merrily 762.9 *joyfully*, 769.9 *cheerfully*, 773.11 *rejoicingly*, 815.18 *sociably*
merriment 762.1 *happiness*, 769.3 *cheerfulness*, 771.2 *amusement*, 773.1 *rejoicing*, 812.1 *celebration*, 815.1 *sociability*
merry 405.7 *pleased*, 506.5 *nonsensical*, 762.4 *happy*, 769.1 *cheerful*, 771.10 *humorous*,

773.9 *rejoicing*, 812.10 *celebrative*, 815.15 *sociable*, 874.1 *drunk*
merry-andrew 51.30 *clown*
merry dancers 439.4 *natural light*
merrymake 812.15 *celebrate*
merrymaker 762.3 *joyful person*, 773.4 *rejoicer*
merrymaking 762.2 *fun*, 769.3 *cheerfulness*, 773.1 *rejoicing*, 812.1 *celebration*, 815.1 *sociability*
merry men 679.17 *army person*
merry widow 51.21 *role*, 824.6 *surviving spouse*
Mersenne numbers 52 Named Concepts
Mersenne prime 52 Named Concepts
Mersey 96 Rivers, 96.4 *British rivers*
Merthyr Tydfil 93 Cities
mesa 98.7 *upland*, 275.2 *heights*
Mesa 93 Cities
mésalliance 823.3 *types of marriage*
mescal 62 Medication
mescaline 62 Medication, 875.6 *drug*
mesembryanthemum 84 Flowers and Flowering Plants
mesh 107.2 *interrelatedness*, 288.2 *braid*, 288.8 *interweave*, 539.13 *snare*, 664.12 *reciprocate*
meshed 539.42 *trapped*
Meshkenit 8 Deities
mesh knot 74 Knots
mesh together 135.8 *unite*, 288.8 *interweave*
mesiad 124.2 *medium*
mesial 124.2 *medium*, 158.13 *median*
mesivta 6.12 *educational institution*
mesmeric 228.11 *motivational*, 233.12 *appealing*, 242.8 *moderating*, 586.19 *persuasive*, 695.9 *compelling*
mesmerically 11.25 *occultly*, 340.13 *attractionally*
mesmerism 11.1 *occultism*, 233.2 *occult influence*, 340.2 *pulling power*
mesmerize 11.21 *bewitch*, 228.10 *manipulate*, 233.10 *be a prevailing influence*, 340.12 *lure*, 404.12 *anaesthetize*
mesmerized 11.19 *bewitched*, 228.12 *motivated*
mesne profits 749.2 *money received*
Mesoamerican art 50 Non-Western Art
mesocarp 86.3 *fruit structure*
mesoderm 59.15 *developmental biology*
mesodermal 59.26 *developmental*
meso-form 57.13 *structure*
Mesolithic 202.15 *primal*
Mesolithic period 200.4 *prehistoric age*
mesomitosis 59.10 *cell division*
mesomorph 1.9 *physical type*, 61.7 *personality type*, 306.6 *nature*
mesomorphic 1.15 *physical*
mesomorphism 61.7 *personality type*
mesomorphy 1.9 *physical type*, 61.7 *personality type*
meson 56.77 *elementary particle*, 260.2 *little thing*, 367.4 *matter*
mesophyll 83.6 *leaf*
Mesopotamian 43 Architectural Styles
Mesopotamian art 50 Non-Western Art
Mesosaurus 79 Fossil Reptiles
mesosome 59.8 *cell organ*
mesosphere 275.8 *high thing*
mesozoan 81.1, 81.16 *invertebrate*
Mesozoic 54 Geological Time Intervals, 202.15 *primal*
Mesozoic era 200.3 *geological period*
mesquite 85 Trees and Shrubs

mess 120.2 *certain amount*, 133.3 *miscellany*, 151.4 *litter*, 151.5 *confusion*, 151.6 *mix-up*, 151.23 *confuse*, 256.7 *room*, 350.24 *have a meal*, 656.9 *bungling*, 659.5 *predicament*, 683.1 *failure*

message 326.10 *transferred thing*, 472.1 *topic*, 520.1 *meaning*, 528.2 *communication*, 543.4 *signal*, 876.7 *moral*

message conveyed 520.1 *meaning*

Messager 49 Musicians and Composers

message-receiver 730.5 *recipient*

messaline 67 Natural Fabrics

Messapian 5 Languages and Groups of Languages

messed up 656.4 *bungled*

messed-up 151.19 *mixed-up*

messenger 74 Rigging, **326**, 154.8 *precursor*, 158.9 *middleman*, 329.13 *swift person*, 517.5 *omen*, 528.9 *informant*, 532.10 *publicizer*, 534.4 *postal worker*, 543.8 *signer*, 697.5 *office assistant*, 703.5 *commissioner*, 706.1 *delegate*, 707.1 *deputy*

messenger of God 8.6 *angel*

messenger of the gods 329.13 *swift person*

messenger RNA 59.13 *genetic material*

messer 350.18 *eater*

Messiaen 49 Musicians and Composers

Messiah 8.4 *God the Son*, 653.14 *leader*

messianic 8.13 *divine*

messianically 8.19 *divinely*

Messianic Judaism 7 Non-Christian Religions

Messier 52 Scientists

Messier Catalogue 53.6 *star catalogue*

messily 622.12 *dirtily*

Messina 93 Cities

messiness 151.3 *untidiness*, 470.2 *indifference*, 622.1 *dirtiness*

messing 350.4 *eating meals*

mess jacket 295.11 *jacket*

mess kit 295.3, 813.4 *formal dress*

messmate 350.18 *eater*, 819.5 *friend*

mess room 256.7 *room*, 350.15 *eating place*

messuage 725.2 *legal terms*

mess up 133.9 *mix up*, 151.24 *make disordered*, 622.11 *dirty*, 628.4 *impair*, 656.7 *be clumsy*

mess with 216.8 *cause change*

messy 151.5 *untidy*, 470.5 *indifferent*, 622.7 *dirty*, 656.4 *bungled*

mestizo 133.5 *hybrid*

mesto 49 Musical Terms

mestranol 62 Medication

metabolic 58.26 *biochemical*, 59.22 *physiological*, 216.13 *transformative*

metabolically 58.27 *biochemically*

metabolic pathway 58.21 *metabolism*

metabolism 58, 59.5 *physiology*, 216.3 *transformation*

metabolite 58.21 *metabolism*

metabolize 58, 216.9 *transform*

metacarpal 382 Bones

metachronism 193.1 *wrong time*

metachronistic 193.4 *mistimed*

metachronistically 193.7 *out of chronological order*

metaethics 4.6 *branch of philosophy*

metafiction 48.2 *fiction*

metage 268.1 *measurement*

metal 777 Phobias by Topic, 41.12 *ski*, 57.6 *chemical element*, 57.23 *metallurgy*, 373.7 *hard substance*, 544.8 *heraldic device*, 604.1 *materials*

metalanguage 5.7 *international language*

metal clip 34.4 *climbing equipment*

metal conductor 56.43 *electrical conduction*

metal detector 496.11 *detector*

metal engraver 50.18 *engraver*

metal engraving 50.15 *engraving*

metal fatigue 63.16 *deformation*

metal furniture 47.1 *furniture*

metal inlay 47.9 *decorative woodwork*

metallic 57.34 *elemental*, 430.7 *strident*

metallic bond 57.11 *chemical bond*

metallic conductor 64.3 *electricity*

metallic currency 741.13 *coinage*

metallic pigment 444.4 *pigment*

metallocene 57 Types of Compounds

metalloid 57.6 *chemical element*, 57.23 *metallurgy*, 57.34 *elemental*

metallophobia 777 Phobias by Name

metallophone 49 Musical Instruments

metalloprotein 58.9 *protein*

metallurgical 57, 57.31 *chemical*

metallurgical engineering 63.1 *engineering*

metallurgically 57.46 *chemically*

metallurgist 57.2 *chemist*

metallurgy 57, 57.1 *chemistry*, 63.1 *engineering*

metal ore 604.1 *materials*

metal poisoning 624.2 *illness*

metals 72.3 *rail*

metal sculptor 50.17 *sculptor*

metal sculpture 50.12 *sculpture*

metal ski 41.5 *ski equipment*

metal spike 34.4 *climbing equipment*

metalwork 50.1 *art*

metalworker 646.2 *artisan*

metalworks 647.1 *workshop*

metamathematics 52.1 *mathematics*

metamitosis 59.10 *cell division*

metamorphic 54.56 *petrographic*, 216.13 *transformative*

metamorphic grade 54.32 *metamorphism*

metamorphic rock 54, 54.28 *rock*

metamorphism 54

metamorphose 82.17 *develop*, 216.9 *transform*, 220.7 *convert into*, 220.9 *transform*, 224.11 *be changeable*

metamorphosed 220.13 *converted*

metamorphosis 54.29 *petrogenesis*, 59.15 *developmental biology*, 79.8 *young amphibian*, 82.5 *larva*, 216.3 *transformation*, 220.1 *conversion*, 224.1 *changeableness*

metamorphous 216.13 *transformative*

metanarrative 4.2 *philosophical system*, 48.3 *aspect of fiction*

metaphase 59.10 *cell division*

metaphor 5.24 *phrasing*, 48.12 *poetic language*, 110.2 *equivalence*, 114.1 *similarity*, 222.3 *substitute thing*, 520.4 *type of meaning*, 524.1 *interpretation*, 527.6 *latency*, 557.1 *mysteriousness*, 557.1 *ornament*, 560.3 *narration*

metaphoric 5.43 *phrasal*, 110.13 *equivalent*

metaphorical 520.6 *meaningful*, 527.5 *mysterious*, 557.4 *ornate*

metaphorically 5.51 *phraseologically*, 110.18 *identically*, 114.13 *similarly*, 520.13 *meaningfully*, 557.6 *ornately*

metaphorical meaning 520.4 *type of meaning*

metaphrastic 524.17 *translational*

metaphysical 4.13 *philosophy*, 7.18 *theological*, 48.16 *literary*, 368.8 *nonmaterial*

metaphysical idealism 368.5 *idealism*

metaphysically 368, 4.24 *philosophically*, 11.25 *occultly*

metaphysical painting 50 Western Art Styles and Movements

metaphysical poet 48.14 *author*

metaphysical poetry 48.6 *poetry*

metaphysical world 368.1 *nonmaterial world*

metaphysician 4.10 *philosopher*, 11.12 *occultist*

metaphysicist 11.12 *occultist*

metaphysics 4.6 *branch of philosophy*, 11.1 *occultism*, 61.1 *psychology*, 99.1 *existence*

metaphysics of presence 99.1 *existence*, 253.1 *presence*

metapsychic 11.16 *psychic*

metapsychical 11.16 *psychic*

metapsychism 11.1 *occultism*

metapsychist 11.12 *occultist*

metapsychology 61.1 *psychology*

metapsychosis 11.8 *psychic power*

metastable 57.35 *combined*

metastable equilibrium 56.10 *force*

metastable state 56.67 *excited atom*

metastasis 326.3 *transmission*

metastasize 326.11 *transfer*

metastatic 326.17 *transferable*

metastatically 326.18 *in transit*

metatarsal 382 Bones

Metatheria 77.4 *pouched mammal*

metatherian 77.4 *pouched mammal*, 77.25 *mammalian*

metathesis 326.1 *transfer*

metathesize 326.11 *transfer*

metathetic 326.17 *transferable*

metazoa 396.9 *classifications of life*

Metazoa 81.1 *invertebrate*

metazoan 81.1, 81.16 *invertebrate*

Metchnikov 52 Scientists

metempsychosis 216.3 *transformation*, 326.1 *transfer*, 367.2 *materialization*

meteor 53, 189.2 *transient thing*, 439.4 *natural light*

meteoric 53.36 *astronomical*, 189.6 *transient*, 329.1 *swift*

meteorically 53.39 *astronomically*, 329.14 *swiftly*

meteorite 53.20 *meteor*

meteorite crater 53.20 *meteor*

meteoritic 53.36 *astronomical*

meteoroid 53.20 *meteor*

meteorologic 55 meteorological 54.49 *geophysical*, 55.41 *meteorologic*

meteorologically 55, 54.66 *geographically*

Meteorological Office 55.4 *weather forecast*

meteorological satellite 53.32 *satellite*

meteorologist 55, 54.4 *geophysicist*, 517.9 *forecaster*

meteorology 55, 54.2 *geophysics*, 56.4 *experimental physics*

Meteorology and Climatology 55

meteor shower 53.20 *meteor*

meteor swarm 53.20 *meteor*

mete out 268.11 *measure out*, 729.5 *give*, 731.4 *allot*

meter 268, 56.82 *measuring instrument*, 268.10 *measure*

meterable 268.14 *measurable*

metered 268.13 *measured*

metered mail 534.2 *postal communication*

metereomancy 11.9 *divination*

metermaid 356.7 *traffic controller*

meter-reader 410.9 *power-worker*

meter reading 56.82 *measuring instrument*

metformin 62 Medication

methadone 62 Medication, 875.6 *drug*

methanderione 62 Medication

methandrione 62 Medication

methane 410.3 *gas*

methapyrilene 62 Medication

methaqualone 62 Medication

methenolone 62 Medication

methicillin 62 Medication

methionine 58 Amino Acids

method 150, 52.66 *proof*, 112.2

conformity, 116.6 *convention*, 152.3 *organization*, 166.6 *custom*, 327.1 *way*, 567.4 *approach*, 602.1 *means*, 652.7 *way*

method act 51.35 *rehearse*

method acting 51.20 *acting*

method actor 51.22 *actor*

methodical 112.8 *monotonous*, 150.14 *well-ordered*, 152.22 *organizational*, 166.10 *customary*, 214.14 *orderly*, 328.5 *unhurried*, 592.14 *planned*, 813.6 *formal*

methodically 150, 112.13 *uniformly*, 152.28 *in place*, 166.19 *to rule*, 592.16 *as planned*

methodicalness 150, 328.8 *slowness*

Methodism 7 Christian Movements

Methodist 7.5 *Christian*

methodization 152.3 *organization*

methodize 150.19 *systematize*, 152.13 *organize*, 592.9 *plan*

methodized 152.21 *organized*

method of operating 652.7 *way*

method of payment 15.2 *industrial negotiations*

method of propulsion 338

methodology 150.6 *methodicalness*, 327.1 *way*

methods 602.1 *means*

methods and resources 602.1 *means*

methoin 62 Medication

methoserpidine 62 Medication

methotrexate 62 Medication

methotrimeprazine 62 Medication

methoxamine 62 Medication

methoxyphenamine 62 Medication

meths 410.6 *oil*

methuselah 258.14 *bottle*

Methuselah 202.2 *old people*, 207.7 *older person*

methylamphetamine 62 Medication

methylated spirits 410.6 *oil*

methylcellulose 62 Medication

methyldopa 62 Medication

methylene blue 62 Medication, 454.5 *blueness*

methyl orange 57.18 *gravimetric analysis*

methyl red 57.18 *gravimetric analysis*

methyltestosterone 62 Medication

methyl violet 455.2 *purple pigment*

methyprylone 62 Medication

methysergide 62 Medication

meticulous 106.10 *detailed*, 150.14 *well-ordered*, 328.5 *unhurried*, 467.8 *diligent*, 469.9 *careful*, 481.9 *discriminating*, 503.5, 537.21 *accurate*, 619.2 *perfectionist*, 690.8 *severe*, 719.7 *observant*, 813.6 *formal*, 857.4 *honourable*

meticulously 106, 467.15 *attentively*, 481.16 *judiciously*, 690.11 *severely*, 719.8 *observantly*, 857.7 *honourably*

meticulousness 150.6 *methodicalness*, 328.8 *slowness*, 467.3, 469.1 *carefulness*, 481.2 *judiciousness*, 503.1, 537.8 *accuracy*, 690.1 *severity*, 857.1 *probity*

métier 165.7 *special skill*, 249.14 *sphere*, 501.2 *information*, 644.3 *job*, 655.1 *skill*, 737.6 *business*

métis 133.5 *hybrid*

Métis Trotter 32 Breeds of Horse and Pony

metolazone 62 Medication

Metonic 214.13 *anniversary*

Metonic cycle 214.12 *cyclic*

metonym 5.17 *word*

metonymy 48.12 *poetic language*

metope 43 Architectural Decoration

metoprolol 62 Medication

metrazol shock therapy 61.3 *psychiatric treatment*
metre 75 SI Units, **75** Scientific and Technical Units, **48,** 49.19 *tempo*, 185.12 *musical time*, 214.5 *regular thing*, 269.7 *measure of length*
metric 268.12 *metrical*
metrical 48, 268, 214.14 *orderly*
metrically 48.22 *poetically*, 268.17 *measurably*
metrical unit 48.9 *metre*
metrics 48.9 *metre*, 564.6 *phonetics*
metric system 75.2 *unit system*, 268.5 *measuring system*
metric ton 75 General Units
metric unit 75.2 *unit system*
metritis 72.1 *railway*
metro 72.1 *railway*, 327.10 *railway*
metrological 268.12 *metrical*
metrologically 268.17 *measurably*
metrology 56.95 *mensuration*, 268.1 *measurement*
metronome 191 Timepieces and Timers, 49.19 *tempo*, 214.5 *regular thing*, 365.7 *oscillator*, 503.3 *accurate thing*
metropolis 92.4 *community*, 93.1 *city*, 249.10 *urban area*
metropolitan 92.6 *administrative*, 93.14 *urban*, 249.17 *national*, 255.4 *townsman*, 255.12 *native*, 256.15 *environmental*
metropolitan area 93.1 *city*, 249.10 *urban area*
metropolitan county 92.1 *administrative area*
metropolitan district 249.5 *state*
Metropolitan Police 16.15 *British police*
mettle 239.1 *vigour*, 574.16 *fortitude*, 778.1 *courage*
mettled 778.9 *courageous*
mettlesome 239.4 *vigorous*, 642.18 *active*, 778.9 *courageous*
Metz 93 Cities
Metztli 8 Deities
Meuse 96 Rivers
Meuse-Rhine-Ijssel 68 Breeds of Cattle
mew 78 Birds, 78.14 *nest*, 432.1 *animal cry*, 432.4 *cry*
mewl 431.13, 432.4 *cry*
mews 327.3 *road*
Mexican GP at Mexico City 33.2 Formula 1 race
Mexican hairless 77 Breeds of Dogs
Mexican mud 875.6 *drug*
Mexican *trajinera* 36.8 *punting*
Mexican War 17 Major Wars
Mexico 91 Countries
Mexico City 93 Cities, 93.6 *other cities*
Meyerhof 52 Scientists
meze 45.52 *Greek dish*
mezuzah 10.14 *sacred object*
mezza 45 Types of Pasta
Mezza-Maiolica 44 Types of Ceramics
mezzanine 51.16 *auditorium*, 158.11 *midway*, 256.7 *room*
mezza voce 49 Musical Terms
mezze 45.12 *hors d'oeuvre*
mezzo 49 Musical Terms
mezzoforte 49 Musical Terms
mezzo relievo 767.6 *profile*
mezzotint 50.15 *engraving*, 444.3 *hue*
mf 49 Musical Terms
MF medium frequency 534 Radio-frequency Bands
mho 75 Scientific and Technical Units
MI5 529.2 *secretiveness*
MI6 529.2 *secretiveness*
Miami 93 Cities, 93.2 *American cities*
mianserin 62 Medication
miasma 388, 419.1 *stench*, 441.2 *murk*, 618.11 *harmful ness*, 624.6 *infection*, 626.1 *lack of hygiene*
miasmal 388.18 *miasmic*, 419.3

stinking, 441.6 *murky*, 618.5 *harmful*, 626.5 *unhygienic*
miasmatic 388.18 *miasmic*
miasmic 388, 398.23 *deadly*, 419.3 *stinking*, 441.6 *murky*
mica 54.34 *mineral*
mica capacitor 64.17 *resistor*
Miccosukee 1 Peoples
mice 777 Phobias by Topic
Michael 8.6 *angel*
Michaelmas 10.15 *holy day*, 203.4 *autumn*
Michaelmas daisy 84 Flowers and Flowering Plants
Michelin 528.5 *reference book*
Michelson 52 Scientists
Michelson—Morley experiment 56 Named Laws
Michigan 92 American States, 94 Lakes, 94.3 US lakes
Mick 91 Names for Inhabitants
Mickey Finn 133.2 *mixed thing*, 404.4 *anaesthetic*, 761.6 *desensitizing substance*
Mickey Mouse 612.4 *trivial*, 614.1 *useless*, 660.9 *easy*
Micmac 5 Languages and Groups of Languages
MICR 65.13 *character recognition*
micro 75 SI Units, 65.3 *computer*
microbe 59.3 *organism*, 260.2 *little thing*, 626.2 *germ*
microbes 777 Phobias by Topic
microbial 59.21 *living*, 260.7 *little*
microbial genetics 59.11 *genetics*
microbic 260.7 *little*
microbiological 59.20 *biological*
microbiologist 59.19 *life scientist*, 60.13 *medical specialist*
microbiology 59.1 *life science*, 60.3 *medical specialty*
microbiophobia 777 Phobias by Name
microcard 545.6 *record book*
microcentrum 59.8 *cell organ*
microchip 64.13 *circuit*, 260.2 *little thing*
microcircuit 64.13 *circuit*, 235.9 *electronics*
microclimate 55.38 *climate*
microcline 54 Minerals
microcomputer 65.3 *computer*
microcopied 110.15 *duplicate*
microcopy 66.6 *microphotograph*, 110.4 *duplicate*
microcosm 142.2 *whole thing*, 260.2 *little thing*
microcosmic 260.7 *little*
microcosmically 260.9 *microscopically*
microcrystal 57.4 *crystal*
microcrystalline 57.33 *crystalline*
microdiskette 65.7 *peripheral*
microdot 260.2 *little thing*
microeconomics 13.1 *economics*
microelectronics 64.1, 235.9 *electronics*
microfibre 67 Synthetic Fibres and Fabrics
microfibril 59.8 *cell organ*
microfiche 66.6 *microphotograph*, 260.2 *little thing*, 545.6 *record book*
microfilaria 81.13 *invertebrate larva*
microfilm 66.6 *microphotograph*, 260.2 *little thing*, 545.6 *record book*
microfilm reader 435.10 *visual aid*
microfloppy 65.7 *peripheral*
micrography 260.1 *littleness*
microgravity 53.31 *space travel*
microhabitat 256.2 *environment*
microlite 73 Types of Aircraft
microlith 3.11 *relic*, 200.7 *thing of the past*
micrometeorite 53.20 *meteor*
micrometeorology 55.1 *meteorology*
micrometer 56.84 *altimeter*, 260.1 *littleness*, 268.8 *meter*, 503.3 *accurate thing*
micrometer calliper 268.8 *meter*
micrometer gauge 268.8 *meter*
micrometre 75 Scientific and Technical Units

micrometric 268
micrometry 268, 537.8 *accuracy*
micromicron 75 Scientific and Technical Units
microminiaturization 260.1 *littleness*
micron 75 Scientific and Technical Units
Micronesian 5 Languages and Groups of Languages, 5.11 *family of languages*
micronization 384.4 *pulverization*
micronize 384.23 *pulverize*
micronucleus 59.9 *cell nucleus*
micronutrient 58.15 *essential element*
microorganism 59.3 *organism*, 260.2 *little thing*, 626.2 *germ*
micropalaeontological 3.17 *archaeological*
micropalaeontologist 3.4 *archaeologist*
micropalaeontology 3.2 *archaeology*
microphobia 777 Phobias by Name
microphone 64.22 *transformer*, 420.9 *audio device*, 423.4 *sound maker*, 534.9 *telephone*
microphotograph 66, 260.2 *little thing*
microphotography 66.1 *photography*
microphyll 83.6 *leaf*
microphyte 59.3 *organism*, 260.2 *little thing*
microprocessor 65.5 *processor*, 235.9 *electronics*
micropyle 83.9 *seed*, 84.3 *flower part*
microreader 435.10 *visual aid*
microscope 56, 56.32 *optical instrument*, 260.1 *littleness*, 435.10 *visual aid*, 437.7 *that which makes visible*
Microscope 53 The Constellations
microscopic 260.7 *little*, 435.20 *visual*, 438.2 *difficult to see*, 537.21 *accurate*
microscopical examination 59.6 *cell biology*
microscopically 260
microscopic detail 537.8 *accuracy*
Microscopium 53 The Constellations
microscopy 56, 260.1 *littleness*, 435.10 *visual aid*
microsecond 185.4 *term*, 187.2 *time period*
microseism 54.22 *seismic activity*
microskirt 295.6 *skirt*, 296.4 *dishabille*
microskirted 296.10 *in dishabille*
Microsoft DOS 65.8 *software*
microsome 59.8 *cell organ*
microspore 384.10 *spore*
microtubule 59.8 *cell organ*
microvillus 59.7 *cell*
microwave 45.5 *cooker*, 45.55 *cook*
microwave amplifier 64.21 *rectifier*
microwave background 53.4 *cosmological model*
microwave cooking 45.1 *cookery*
microwave food 350.7 *food*
microwave generator 64.20 *electron tube*
microwave link 534.14 *radio transmission*
microwave oscillator 64.21 *rectifier*
microwave oven 408.4 *burner*
microwaves 56.13 *electromagnetic radiation*, 534.14 *radio transmission*
microwave spectroscopy 57.17 *analysis*
microwave spectrum 56.68 *emission*
microwhip scorpion 82 Arachnids
microwire 34.4 *climbing equipment*
Mictlancihvatl 8 Deities
Mictlantecuhtli 8 Deities

micturate 353.17 *urinate*
micturation 353.3 *urination*
mid 27.14 *positioned*, 124.5 *medium*, 158.10 *middle*, 176.13 *half*
mid- 124.2 *medium*
Midas 742.10 *wealthy person*
Midas touch 686.2 *good fortune*, 742.5 *wealth*
Mid-Atlantic accent 5.26 *dialect*
Mid-Atlantic Ridge 54.16 *ocean floor*
midchannel 96.2 *channel*
midcourse 158.5 *middle distance*
mid-course 333.1 *middle way*
midday 204.3, 204.6 *noon*
midday sun 408.5 *hot weather*
midden 68.10 *farm tool*, 151.4 *litter*, 614.6 *refuse*, 727.8 *sink*
middle 158, 158, 333, 2.14 *socioeconomic*, 5.32 *voice*, 124.2, 124.5 *medium*, 176.13 *half*, 290.2 *inside*, 291.1 *centre*, 291.6 *central*
Middle 158
middle age 158, 207, 207.2 *adulthood*, 396.5 *life cycle*
middle-aged 207
Middle Ages 3.10 *past age*, 200.5 *historical period*
Middle America 124.8 *middle classes*
Middle American 167.6 *conformist*
Middleback 95 Mountains
middlebrow 124.1 *average*, 164.21 *common*
middle class 158, 2.7 *social stratification*, 400.9 *group*, 815.7 *human society*
middle classes 124
Middle Comedy 51.10 *comedy*
middle course 124.5 *medium*, 333.1 *middle way*, 717.1 *compromise*
middle cut 45.30 *bacon*
middle deck 74 Parts of a Ship
middle distance 158
middle-distance 21.6 *track*, 41.13 *ice-skating*
middle-distance race 21.1 *track events*
middle-distance racing 21.1 *track events*, 41.8 *speed-skating*
middle-distance runner 21.3 *athlete*
middle-distance running 18 Sporting Activities, 21.1 *track events*
Middle Dutch 5 Languages and Groups of Languages
middle ear 420.5 *internal ear*
Middle-earth 519.8 *dreamland*
Middle East 249.7 *regions of the world*
Middle English 5 Languages and Groups of Languages
middle finger 407.7 *sense organ*
middle-finger gesture 543.3 *gesture*
middle ground 158, 124.5 *medium*, 333.2 *middle of the road*, 717.1 *compromise*
Middle High German 5 Languages and Groups of Languages
middle-income earner 124.8 *middle classes*
Middle Jurassic 54 Geological Time Intervals
middle lamella 59.7 *cell*
middle life 158.7, 207.4 *middle age*
Middle Low German 5 Languages and Groups of Languages
middleman 158, 135.7 *joiner*, 298.3 *interfacer*, 606.3 *provider*, 646.3 *agent*, 678.3 *mediator*, 706.1 *delegate*, 707.3 *agent*, 716.4 *negotiator*, 739.12 *wholesaler*, 739.13 *retailer*
middle manager 124.8 *middle classes*
middlemost 124.2 *medium*, 124.12 *mediumly*, 158.10 *middle*

middle name 560.8 *name*
middle neck 45.26 *lamb*
middle of the day 204.3 *noon*
middle of the road **333**, 124.5 *medium*
middle-of-the-road 124.2 *medium*, 158.14 *mediatory*, 164.21 *common*, 242.7 *politically moderate*, 333.4 *middle*, 617.5 *not bad*, 620.4 *ordinary*, 665.10 *political*
middle-of-the-roader 124.8 *middle classes*, 333.3 *moderate person*, 783.6 *indifferent person*
middle position 22.2 *baseball player*
Middlesbrough 93 Cities
middle school 6.12 *educational institution*
middle term 124.5 *medium*
Middleton 48 Dramatists
Middle Triassic 54 Geological Time Intervals
middleware 65.17 *computing term*
middle way **333**, 242.1 *moderation*, 717.1 *compromise*, 783.3 *impartiality*, 869.2 *moderation*
Middle Way **333**
middleweight 26.3 *boxing weight divisions*, 26.4 *boxer*, 26.14 *combat*, 369.1 *heavy*, 369.7 *weighing*, 674.10 *contender*, 679.3 *athlete*
Middle West 249.8 *regions of the US*
Middle White 68 Breeds of Pig
middle years 158.7, 207.4 *middle age*
middling **158**, 124.2 *medium*, 124.3 *mediocre*, 127.16 *ordinary*, 167.15 *everyday*, 242.6 *moderate*, 617.5 *not bad*, 620.4 *ordinary*, 783.10 *mediocre*
middlingly 127.20 *insignificantly*, 783.20 *unexceptionally*
middy blouse 295.8 *shirt*
mideity 158.5 *middle distance*
midfield 38.5 *soccer*, 158.5 *middle distance*
midfield player 31.6 *lacrosse player*
midfield striker 38.3 *football player*
midfield stripe 19.4 *stadium*
midge 82 Insects, 82.1 *insect*, 82.3 *pest*, 270.5 *short person*
midget 260.4 *little person*, 260.7 *little*, 270.5 *short person*
midget-car race 33.1 *motor racing*
midget-car racing 33.1 *motor racing*
Mid Glamorgan 92 Counties
MIDI 65.11 *application*
midicoat 295.11 *jacket*
midinette 402.2 *female*
midiron 29.4 *golf club*
midiskirt 295.6 *skirt*
midland 290.9 *inland*
Midlands 249.9 *regions of Britain*
midlife crisis 158.7 *middle age*, 207.4 *middle age*
midline **158**
mid mashie 29.4 *golf club*
midmost 124.2 *medium*, 124.12 *mediumly*, 158.10 *middle*, 291.6 *central*
midnight **205**
midnight blue 440.3 *dark colour*, 454.1 *blue*
Midnight Mass 10.6 *Eucharist*
midnight sun 53.15 *sun*
midoceanic ridge 54.16 *ocean floor*, 54.19 *plate tectonics*
mid off 27.4 *team*
mid on 27.4 *team*
midpoint 52.36 *point*, 124.5 *medium*, 158.1 *middle*, 291.1 *centre*, 291.6 *central*, 333.1 *middle way*
midpoint theorem 52 Theorems and Laws
mid-range zoom 66.17 *lens*
midriff 158.4 *midline*, 258.18 *stomach*, 291.2 *central thing*
midsection 124.5 *medium*, 158.4 *midline*

midshipman 80 Fishes, 679.27 *naval man*
Midshipman 17 British Military Ranks, 17 US Military Ranks
midships 158.21 *midway*
midst 158.1 *middle*, 158.2 *core*
midst of things 642.1 *activity*
midstream 96.2 *channel*, 158.5 *middle distance*, 158.11, 158.21 *midway*
midsummer 203.3, 203.11 *summer*, 408.5 *hot weather*
Midsummer Day 203.3 *summer*
midterm 124.5 *medium*
midtown 93.7 *city district*, 93.14 *urban*
midway **158, 158,** 124.2 *medium*, 124.12 *mediumly*, 176.13 *half*, 333.1 *middle way*, 333.4 *middle*, 333.8 *medially*
Midwest accent 5.26 *dialect*
midwife 60.16 *nurse*, 60.17 *paramedic*, 232.3 *assistant*, 245.7 *obstetrics*
midwifery 60.6 *health care*, 232.1 *instrumentality*, 245.7 *obstetrics*
midwife toad 79 Amphibians
midwinter 203.5, 203.13 *winter*
mien 289.3 *appearance*, 457.3 *external appearance*, 652.1 *conduct*
Mierzyn 32 Breeds of Horse and Pony
miff 828.2 *offence*, 828.9 *offend*
might 233 *influence*, 235.1 *power*, 237.1 *strength*, 241.1 *violence*, 688.1 *authority*
might and main 644.4 *exertion*
might as well 580.2 *prefer*
might be 486.8 *be possible*
might do worse 580.2 *prefer*
mightily 235.18 *powerfully*, 259.20 *largely*
mightiness 235.1 *influence*, 235.1 *power*, 688.2 *authoritativeness*
might is right 676.5 *bellicosity*
mighty 233.11 *influential*, 235.11 *powerful*, 237.10 *potent*, 241.6 *violent*, 259.15 *big*, 688.12 *authoritative*, 805.18 *prestigious*
mighty effort 644.4 *exertion*
mignonette 84 Flowers and Flowering Plants, 453.1 *green*
migraine 406.2 *painful condition*, 624.3 *symptom*
migrant 78.1 *birds*, 104.10 *foreign*, 149.6, 149.13 *immigrant*, 347.8 *outgoer*
migrant worker 104.7 *new arrival*, 149.6 *immigrant*
migrate 149, 347.13 *emigrate*
migration 324.1 *motion*, 345.7 *departure*, 347.4 *emigration*
migratory bird 78.1 *birds*
migyaun 49 Musical Instruments
mikado 696.2 *sovereign*
mike 420.9 *audio device*, 423.4 *sound maker*
Mike 534 Phonetic Alphabet
Mikhail Baryshnikov 46.14 *famous ballet dancers*
Mikhail Gorbachev 675.4 Nobel Peace Prize
mikvah 10.7 *non-Christian ritual*
mil 75 Scientific and Technical Units, 173.4 *less than one*
milady 402.3 *female title of address*
milah 10.7 *non-Christian ritual*
Milan 93 Cities
milanese sauce 45.15 *sauce*
milch cow 68.8 *livestock*, 246.1 *fertility*, 605.3 *supply*
Milcom 8 Deities
mild 55.50 *warm*, 242.6 *moderate*, 351.7 *alcoholic drink*, 374.6 *softhearted*, 408.9 *hot*, 408.11 *warm*, 412.5 *tasteless*, 675.7 *peaceful*, 691.4 *lenient*, 817.7 *courteous*
mild as milk 242.6 *moderate*
milder 55.45 *fine*
mildew 69.12 *pests and diseases*, 85.10 *tree disease*, 89.1 *fungus*, 89.11 *moulder*, 244.7 *agent of*

destruction, 622.4 *dirt*, 622.10 *be dirty*, 628.2 *decay*, 628.5 *hurt*, 628.9 *dilapidation*, 631.14 *afflict*
mildewed 89.9 *fungal*, 628.13 *dilapidated*, 631.16 *blighting*
mildewy 69.17 *botanical*, 89.9 *fungal*
mildly 55.65 *meteorologically*, 374.18 *softheartedly*, 412.10 *without taste*, 691.6 *leniently*, 817.14 *courteously*
mild manner 817.1 *courtesy*
mild-mannered 675.7 *peaceful*, 817.7 *courteous*
mildness 242.1 *moderation*, 374.12 *gentleness*, 412.1 *tastelessness*, 691.1 *leniency*, 817.1 *courtesy*
mile 75 General Units, 269.7 *measure of length*
mileage 71.21 *miscellaneous motoring terms*, 269.4 *length*
mileometer 71 Motor Vehicle Parts, 268.8 *meter*, 329.8 *speed*, 543.5 *indicator*
milepost 543.5 *indicator*
miler 21.3 *athlete*, 674.10 *contender*
mile race 674.4 *race*
miles away 263.2 *great distance*, 461.10 *speculative*, 512.8 *oblivious*
miles per hour 329.8 *speed*
milestone 103.2 *essential content*, 106.2 *occurrence*, 121.4 *interval*, 268.6 *measuring instrument*, 543.5 *indicator*, 611.2 *important matter*
milfoil 84 Flowers and Flowering Plants
miliaria 624.13 *skin disease*
miliary fever 624.7 *tropical disease*
milieu 106.1 *circumstances*, 297.3 *atmosphere*
militancy 640.1 *action*, 642.5 *activism*, 676.4 *belligerency*, 676.5 *bellicosity*
militant **670, 778,** 7.15 *religious*, 17.8 *military*, 241.4 *violent person or animal*, 640.3 *doer*, 640.5 *acting*, 642.10 *busy person*, 642.18 *active*, 666.9 *disagreeing*, 668.4 *defiant person*, 668.8 *defying*, 670.19 *attacker*, 676.15 *warring*, 676.16 *warlike*, 679.6 *militarist*, 679.33 *combative*, 820.9 *aggressive*
militant Christian 7.5 *Christian*, 679.6 *militarist*
militantly 668.10 *in defiance*, 676.18 *to war*, 679.41 *aggressively*
militant scene 642.5 *activism*
militarily **17,** 2.16 *sociologically*, 676.18 *to war*
militarism 17.7 *miscellaneous terms*, 676.5 *bellicosity*, 690.2 *suppression*
militarist **679**, 679.1 *combatant*, 690.4 *strict person*
militaristic 670.22 *militant*, 676.16 *warlike*, 679.33 *combative*, 690.8 *severe*
militaristically 676.18 *to war*, 679.41 *aggressively*
militarist nation **679**
militarize 676.12 *go to war*
military **17, 676,** 2.12 *sociological*
military academy 6.12 *educational institution*, 17.3 *military training*, 676.6 *art of war*
military action 674.6 *fight*
military affairs **17**
Military Affairs **17**
military aircraft **679**
military architect 43.2 *architect*
military architecture 43.1 *architecture*
military arm 17.2 *the military*
military attack **670**
military band 17.7 *miscellaneous terms*, 49.26 *musical group*, 676.2 *glory of war*

military base 688.6 *place of authority*
military bearing 17.7 *miscellaneous terms*
military branch 17.2 *the military*
military burial 399.1 *burial*
military canteen 350.15 *eating place*
military cap 295.15 *headgear*
military cemetery 399.5 *cemetery*
military citation 681.1 *trophy*
military conduct 584.5 *tradition*
military conflict 674.1 *contention*, 674.6 *fight*, 676.1 *war*
military court 16.7 *legal trial*
Military Cross 17 British Military Medals and Decorations
military decoration 681.1 *trophy*
military defeat 683.2 *defeat*
military defences **671**
military discharge 675.1 *peace*
military discipline 584.5 *tradition*
military duty 676.7 *war measures*
military encounter 674.6 *fight*
military equipment 17.1 *military affairs*
military evolutions 676.6 *art of war*
military experience 676.6 *art of war*
military flag 544.7 *flag*
military forces 17.2 *the military*, 679.14 *armed forces*
military government 12.1 *government*, 17.7 *miscellaneous terms*, 688.7 *type of rule*
military governor 688.10 *person of authority*, 696.3 *leader*
military headquarters staff 17.5 *military staff*
military honours 17.7 *miscellaneous terms*
military–industrial complex 17.2 *the military*
military insignia 544.4 *insignia*
military installations 17.1 *military affairs*
military judge 16.23 *judge*
military justice 16.7 *legal trial*
military law **17**
military leader **696**
military leadership 676.6 *art of war*
military man 679.8 *soldier*
military markings 544.4 *insignia*
military medal 681.1 *trophy*
Military Medal 17 British Military Medals and Decorations
military mess 350.15 *eating place*
military music 17.7 *miscellaneous terms*
military officer 688.10 *person of authority*, 696.7 *military leader*
military operation 676.1 *war*
military orders 676.8 *warfare*
military organization **17**
military police 16.14 *police*, 17.6 *military law*
Military Police 17.6 *military law*
military police corps 17.4 *military organization*, 17.6 *military law*
military prison 702.1 *prison*
military radar 534.28 *radar*
military rank 121.2 *rank*, 688.5 *position of authority*
military rations 871.2 *short rations*
military ribbon 681.1 *trophy*
military salute 17.7 *miscellaneous terms*
military sanctions 676.8 *warfare*
military schottische 46.4 *historic dancing*
military science 17.1 *military affairs*
military service 17.1 *military affairs*, 676.8 *warfare*
military service number 544.3 *means of identification*
military spirit 17.7 *miscellaneous terms*, 676.5 *bellicosity*
military staff **17**
military strategy 17.1 *military affairs*
military tactics 17.1 *military affairs*

military tradition 17.7 *miscellaneous terms*, 676.5 *bellicosity*
military training 17, 112.4 *monotony*
military two-step 46.2 *dance*
military uniform 295.3 *formal dress*, 544.5 *uniform*
military unit 17.4 *military organization*, 688.6 *place of authority*
military victory 682.2 *victory*
militate against 111.9 *oppose*, 231.3 *counteract*, 233.9 *change*, 616.5 *be inconvenient*, 640.4 *act*, 663.13 *be contrary*
militate for 640.4 *act*
militia 17.2 *the military*, 632.3 *protector*, 679.15 *army*
militiaman 679.8 *soldier*
milk **351**, 68.18 *practise livestock farming*, 77.2 *mammalian characteristic*, 77.36 *lactate*, 243.7 *produce*, 352.2 *secreted substance*, 355.14 *suck*, 387.2 *juice*, 387.3 *body fluid*, 446.9 *white thing*, 599.3 *exploit*, 606.5 *provision*, 734.10 *take away*
milk and honey 350.9 *plenty*, 686.1 *prosperity*
milk and water 238.5 *weak thing*
milk-and-water 238.13 *insufficient*, 242.6 *moderate*, 412.5 *tasteless*
milk bar 350.15 *eating place*
milk bottle 258.14 *bottle*
milk bottles 599.7 *reused product*
milk cap 89 *Fungi*
milk chocolate 414.4 *confectionery*
milk dry 607.1 *waste*
milked 68.21 *domesticated*
milker 68.8 *livestock*
milk float **71** *Motor Vehicles*
milkiness 387.7 *juiciness*, 442.7 *semitransparency*, 443.6 *opaqueness*, 446.7 *whiteness*
milking 355.4 *sucking*
milking machine 68.10 *farm tool*
milking parlour 68.7 *farm building*
milking stool 47.2 *chair*
milk it 51.33 *overact*
milkmaid 68.16 *farm worker*
milkman 350.20 *food provider*, 606.3 *provider*, 739.12 *wholesaler*
milk of human kindness 831.1 *benevolence*
milk of magnesia 630.6 *purgative*
Milk of Magnesia **62** *Medication*
milk punch 351.7 *alcoholic drink*
milk shake 351.5 *milk*
milk snake **79** *Reptiles*
milksop 238.4 *weakling*, 779.2 *coward*
milk tank 68.10 *farm tool*
milk tooth 380.11 *tooth*
milk train 72.7 *train*
milkweed **84** Flowers and Flowering Plants
milkweed butterfly **82** *Insects*
milk-white 446.1 *white*
milkwort **84** Flowers and Flowering Plants
milky **387**, 351.17 *drinkable*, 393.19 *juicy*, 395.11 *oily*, 441.6 *murky*, 442.3 *semitransparent*, 443.2 *shady*, 445.7 *colourless*, 446.1 *white*
milky drink 351.5 *milk*
Milky Way 439.4 *natural light*
Milky Way System **53** *Galaxies*
mill 161.40, 181.11 *crowd*, 243.10 *produce*, 375.12 *make rough*, 384.11 *pulverizer*, 384.25 *grind*, 647.1 *workshop*
Mill **4** Philosophers, **4** Philosophers
mill around 161.40 *crowd*, 364.10 *swirl*, 366.21 *be agitated*
Millay **48** Poets
millboard 604.4 *board*
Mille Lacs **94** Lakes
Mille Miglia 674.4 *race*
millenarian 179.21 *thousandth*, 627.12 *reformer*, 627.16 *improving*

millenarianism 627.11 *reformism*
millenary 179.10 *thousand*, 179.21 *thousandth*, 187.8 *periodical*
millenial 179.21 *thousandth*
millenium 269.8 *measure of time*
millennial 187.8 *periodical*, 190.9 *agelong*, 214.13 *anniversary*
millennially 214.16 *cyclically*
millennium 179.9 *treble figures*, 179.10 *thousand*, 185.4 *term*, 187.2 *time period*, 190.2 *a long time*, 214.3 *anniversary*, 492.4 *judgment day*, 519.7 *idealism*
miller **82** Insects, **89** Fungi
Miller **48** Writers, **48** Dramatists
millerite **54** Minerals
miller's thumb **80** Fishes
millet **87** Grasses, 68.12 *crop*
milli **75** SI Units
milliard 169.3 *large number*, 179.11 *million*
milliardaire 179.11 *million*
millibar **75** Scientific and Technical Units
milligram 179.10 *thousand*, 369.9 *avoirdupois weight*
Millikan **52** Scientists
millilitre 179.10 *thousand*
millimetre 179.10 *thousand*, 264.2 *short distance*, 269.7 *measure of length*
millimicron **75** Scientific and Technical Units
milline **75** General Units
milliner 295.26 *fashion designer*, 739.13 *retailer*
millinery 295.2 *dressing*, 295.15 *headgear*
milling 161.50 *crowded*, 384.4 *pulverization*
milling machine 63.9 *machine tool*
million **179**, 169.3 *large number*, 181.7 *myriad*
millionaire 179.11 *million*, 686.4 *prosperous person*, 721.7 *gainer*, 742.10 *wealthy person*, 786.5 *person of wonder*
millionairess 742.10 *wealthy person*
million million 179.11 *million*
millions 181.2 *multitude*, 741.3 *fortune*
millionth **179**, 173.4 *less than one*
million-to-one chance 489.4 *improbability*
millipede 179.10 *thousand*
millisecond 185.4 *term*, 187.2 *time period*, 269.8 *measure of time*
millpond 94.2 *small lake*, 376.8 *smooth thing*
millrace 96.6 *river flow*
Mills & Boon 48.2 *fiction*, 532.6 *book publishing*
millstone 369.8 *weighing down*, 384.11 *pulverizer*, 631.3 *burden*
millstone round one's neck 631.3, 661.6 *burden*
millstream 96.1 *river*, 96.6 *river flow*
mill wheel 364.6 *rotator*
Milne **48** Writers
Milo **18** Sporting Personalities
Miosz **48** Poets
milquetoast 779.2 *coward*
Milton **48** Poets
Miltonic 48.19 *narrative*
Milton Keynes **93** Cities
Milwaukee **93** Cities
mimamsa 4.7 *school of thought*
mime 51.2 *play*, 51.32 *act*, 118.3 *mockery*, 118.9 *imitate*, 543.11 *gesture*, 547.3 *acting*, 547.5 *performer*, 547.10 *act*, 811.14 *show*
mime artist 547.5 *performer*
Mimeograph 110.4, 110.9 *duplicate*, 114.2 *copy*, 114.12 *imitate*, 118.5 *duplicate*, 118.10 *copy*
Mimeographed 110.15 *duplicate*
mimesis 51.20 *acting*, 118.1 *imitation*

mimetic 51.37 *dramatic*, 118.12 *imitative*
mimetite **54** Minerals
mimic 51.27 *entertainer*, 51.32 *act*, 114.4 *person who copies*, 114.12 *imitate*, 118.7 *imitator*, 118.9 *imitate*, 183.8 *creature of habit*, 183.16 *repeat*, 224.8 *person who changes costume*, 543.11 *gesture*, 547.5 *performer*, 547.10 *act*, 799.3 *derider*
mimicked 114.8 *simulated*
mimicking 51.20 *acting*, 114.1 *similarity*
mimicry 51.20 *acting*, 118.3 *mockery*, 118.4 *camouflage*, 547.3 *acting*
miming 51.20 *acting*
mimographer 51.24 *dramatist*
mimosa **84** Flowers and Flowering Plants
Mimosa **53** Named Stars
Mimoseano **32** Breeds of Horse and Pony
Min **8** Deities
mina **75** Some Foreign Units
minacciando **49** Musical Terms
minaret 275.6 *tall thing*
minatory 636.8 *warning*
mince 45.20 *meat*, 45.55 *cook*, 136.9 *separate*, 324.15 *walk*, 328.1 *move slowly*, 384.25 *grind*
minced 45.56 *culinary*, 143.11 *partial*
minced meat 45.20 *meat*
mince no words 556.7 *be simple*
mince pie 45.36 *cake*
mincer 45.6 *kitchen equipment*
minchah 10.4 *public worship*
mincing no words 556.6 *naturalness*
mincing steps 328.10 *slow motion*
mind **459**, 11.7 *spirit*, 61.21 *psyche*, 180.15 *escort*, 368.6 *internal world*, 420.1 *hearing*, 420.15 *hear*, 459.3 *intelligence*, 463.1 *reason*, 469.10 *be careful*, 501.4 *intellect*, 507.2 *intelligence*, 570.1 *will*, 632.9 *protect*, 694.5 *obey*, 784.2 *inclination*, 785.5 *dislike*, 828.10 *be offended*
Mindanao **98** Islands
mind-blowing 786.8 *wonderful*, 875.9 *addictive*
mind-body problem 4.9 *philosophical problem*
mind boggler 477.4 *difficult question*
mind-boggling 184.2 *immeasurable*, 786.8 *wonderful*
mind cure 61.3 *psychiatric treatment*
minded 180.20 *accompanied*
minder 180.7 *attendant*, 603.7 *machinist*, 632.3 *protector*, 679.2 *defender*
mindful 467.9 *solicitous*, 469.9 *careful*, 501.8 *knowledgeable*, 511.8 *remembering*, 781.4 *cautious*, 831.6 *benevolent*
mindfully 467.15 *attentively*, 831.10 *benevolently*
mindfulness 467.1 *attention*, 469.1 *carefulness*, 469.2 *consideration*, 831.1 *benevolence*, 837.1 *gratitude*
mindful of obligations 837.4 *grateful*
mindless 460.5 *lacking intellect*, 462.8 *thoughtless*
mindlessly 460.11 *unintelligently*, 462.14 *thoughtlessly*
mindlessness 460.1 *lack of intellect*, 462.1 *lack of thought*
mind like a sieve 512.3 *poor memory*
mind made up 493.4 *prejudgment*, 574.12 *resolution*
mind of one's own 577.5 *obstinacy*
mind one's health 623.5 *be healthy*
mind one's manners 306.8 *be formal*, 817.11 *have good manners*
mind one's own business 139.7 *be aloof*, 466.6 *be incurious*,

783.12 *be indifferent*, 859.6 *be disinterested*
mind one's p's and q's 166.17 *obey orders*, 306.8 *be formal*, 652.12 *behave well*, 817.11 *have good manners*
Mindoro **98** Islands
mind over matter 570.2 *willpower*, 630.5 *analgesic*
mind reader 11.12 *occultist*, 51.27 *entertainer*, 368.7 *believer in a nonmaterial world*
mind reading 11.1 *occultism*
mind set 234.2 *attitude*
mind's eye 435.4 *visualization*, 511.1 *memory*
mind the gap 636.10 *look out*
mind your step 636.10 *look out*
mine 54.65 *map*, 226.2 *source*, 243.10 *produce*, 244.9 *demolish*, 277.4 *deep thing*, 277.14 *deepen*, 317.2 *concave land*, 317.7 *make concave*, 322.5 *hole*, 355.13 *dig out*, 360.15 *tunnel*, 539.13, 539.33 *snare*, 605.2 *resource*, 628.5 *hurt*, 635.1 *trap*, 647.1 *workshop*, 671.8 *military defences*, 671.18 *fence*, 680.16 *bomb*, 734.10 *take away*, 742.5 *wealth*
mine coal 410.11 *fuel*
mined 539.42 *trapped*
minefield 635.1 *trap*
mine host 606.4 *caterer*, 815.6 *social person*
minelayer 679.24 *warship*
mine of information 501.6 *knowledgeable person*
miner 243.9 *producer*, 277.5 *submariner*, 317.4 *digger*, 322.3 *person who opens*, 323.6 *closed-in person*, 355.10 *excavator*, 646.2 *artisan*, 679.13 *historical soldiery*
mineral **54**, 367.4 *matter*, 460.8 *nonhuman*, 604.1 *materials*
mineral acid 57.8 *acid*
mineral aggregate 54.28 *rock*
mineral deposit 605.2 *resource*
mineral dye 67.6 *dye*
mineralization 54.43 *fossil*
mineralize 54.62 *lithify*
mineralized 54.61 *fossilized*
mineralized bone 54.43 *fossil*
mineralized shell 54.43 *fossil*
mineralocorticoid 58.16 *hormone*
mineralogical 54.48 *geological*
mineralogically 54.66 *geographically*
mineralogist 54.3 *geologist*
mineralogy 54.1 *earth science*
mineral oil 395.7, 410.6 *oil*
mineral rights 723.1 *possession*
minerals 350.11 *food content*
mineral water 351.6 *soft drink*, 389.1 *water*, 389.2 *drinking water*
miner's lamp 439.7 *lantern*
Minerva **8** Deities
mineshaft 322.5 *hole*
minestrone 45.13 *soup*, 45.47 *Italian dish*
minesweeper 679.24 *warship*
mine-thrower 680.11 *guns*
Ming dynasty art **50** Non-Western Art
minginess 758.3 *parsimony*
mingle 2.15 *socialize*, 133.8 *mix*, 140.5 *combine*, 642.16 *be sociable*
mingled 133.12 *mixed*, 140.7 *combined*
mingle with 815.11 *be sociable*
mingling 133.1 *mixture*, 140.1 *combination*, 642.2 *social activity*
Mingrelian **5** Languages and Groups of Languages
Ming ware **44** Types of Ceramics
mingy 758.1 *mean*
Minho **32** Breeds of Horse and Pony
mini **71** Motor Vehicles, 65.3 *computer*, 260.2 *little thing*, 260.7 *little*
miniature 50.7 *picture*, 50.8

painting, 260.2 *little thing*, 260.7 *little*
miniature camera 66.16 *camera*
miniaturist 50.16 *artist*
miniaturization 260.1 *littleness*, 262.1 *contraction*
miniaturize 262.5 *make smaller*
miniaturized 260.7 *little*, 262.7 *smaller*
minibike 71.12 *bicycle*
minicab 71.18 *cab*
minicomputer 65.3 *computer*
minidiskette 65.7 *peripheral*
minidress 295.7 *frock*
minifloppy 65.7 *peripheral*
minim **75** *General Units*, 49.17 *notation*, 260.3 *little piece*
Minim **7** *Members of Religious Orders*
minimal 52.75 *equal*, 127.13 *insignificant*, 182.6 *sparse*, 182.7 *fewer*, 260.7 *little*, 542.14 *simple*
minimal art **50** *Western Art Styles and Movements*
minimalism **48** *Literary Groups and Movements*, 542.4 *simplicity*
minimalist 49.32 *instrumental*, 50.29 *realist*, 333.3 *moderate person*
minimalist music 49.3 *classical music*
minimally 50.30 *pictorially*, 127.19 *inferiorly*, 260.8 *in a small way*, 542.24 *simply*
minimal sculpture 50.12 *sculpture*
minimization 495.1 *underestimation*, 542.1 *understatement*
minimize 52.94 *order*, 129.5 *make smaller*, 495.3 *underestimate*, 542.20 *understate*, 854.10 *disparage*
minimized 542.12 *understated*
minimizer 495.2 *pessimist*
minimizing 495.4 *underestimating*, 854.10 *disparaging*
minimum 127.5 *inferior state*, 127.13 *insignificant*, 182.2 *least*, 182.7 *fewer*, 608.7 *sufficiency*
minimum allowance 609.8 *insufficiency*
minimum hours 15.2 *industrial negotiations*
minimum lending rate 14.1, 741.7 *finance*, 745.3 *loan*
minimum requirement 608.7 *sufficiency*, 620.5 *imperfection*
minimum-security prison 702.1 *prison*
minimum wages 15.2 *industrial negotiations*
mining 277.1 *depth*, 355.3 *digging out*, 360.7 *tunnelling*
mining engineer 646.2 *artisan*
mining engineering 63.1 *engineering*
minion 697.1 *servant*, 701.3 *subordinate*, 808.3 *sycophant*, 826.6 *object of endearment*
minipill 247.3 *birth control*
miniseries 534.25 *broadcast material*
miniskirt 270.4 *short thing*, 295.6 *skirt*, 296.4 *dishabille*
miniskirted 296.10 *in dishabille*
minister 7.8 *priest*, 10.18 *perform rites*, 12.8 *politician*, 220.5 *converter*, 399.3 *funeral director*, 646.3 *agent*, 653.1 *manage*, 653.16 *official*, 662.14 *adviser*, 696.3 *leader*, 706.1 *delegate*, 707.3 *agent*, 710.15 *offer worship*
minister designate 580.13 *electorate*
ministerial 7.17 *priestly*, 12.9, 688.14 *governmental*, 706.6 *delegated*, 707.7 *deputizing*
ministerially **688**, 12.14 *politically*, 706.8 *representatively*, 707.8 *by proxy*
ministering 662.32 *supportive*, 697.9 *serving*
ministering angel 60.16 *nurse*, 662.13 *supporter*
ministering spirits 8.6 *angel*

minister of state 688.10 *person of authority*, 696.3 *leader*
minister plenipotentiary 707.3 *agent*
minister to 60.19 *practise medicine*, 232.4 *be an instrument*, 630.20 *doctor*, 644.7 *work for*, 662.19 *support*, 694.5 *obey*, 697.8 *serve*
ministrant 662.32 *supportive*
ministration 662.2 *support*
ministrative 662.32 *supportive*
ministress 7.8 *priest*
ministry 653.3 *management*, 662.2 *support*
Ministry of Defence 17.4 *military organization*
minium 450.6 *red pigment*
minivet **78** *Birds*
mink **77** *Placental Mammals*, 293.14 *animal covering*, 295.12 *coat*
mink farming 68.3 *livestock farming*
mink hunting **18** *Sporting Activities*
Minneapolis **93** *Cities*
minneola **84** *Fruits*
minnesinger 48.14 *author*, 433.5 *melodist*
Minnesota **92** *American States*
Minnesota multiphasic personality inventory 61.5 *psychological test*
Minnesota preschool scale 61.6 *intelligence test*
Minnie 680.11 *guns*
minnow **80** *Fishes*, 20.1 *angling*, 260.4 *little person*
Miño **96** *Rivers*
Minoan art **50** *Non-Western Art*
minor 127.6 *inferior*, 127.15 *subordinate*, 206.6 *young person*, 206.11 *young*, 612.3 *secondary*
minor axis 52.42 *circle*
Minorca **68** *Breeds of Fowl*
minor-counties cricket 27.1 *cricket match*
minor deity 8.5 *deity*
minor detail 106.6 *aspect*
minor earthquake 54.22 *seismic activity*
Minorite **7** *Members of Religious Orders*
minority 2.14 *socioeconomic*, 120.2 *certain amount*, 121.4 *interval*, 121.7 *gradational*, 127.3 *inferior numbers*, 143.1 *part*, 182.2 *least*, 182.7 *fewer*, 206.1 *youth*, 500.6 *dissenters*, 663.8 *the opposition*
minority group 182.2 *least*
minority rights 700.2 *equal opportunity*
minority rule 12.1 *government*
minority voice 475.8 *protester*
minority whip 12.8 *politician*, 653.15 *manager*
minor key 49.20 *key*
minor league baseball 22.1 *baseball*
minor offence 864.3 *venial sin*
minor planet 53.16 *planet*
minor poet 48.14 *author*
minor role 51.21 *role*
minor scale 49.20 *key*
minor surgery 60.9 *surgery*
minor term 4.8 *philosophical term*
minor third 177.6 *third*
minotaur 76.7 *legendary beast*
Minsk **93** *Cities*
minster 10.11 *place of worship*
minstrel 48.14 *author*, 49.24 *musician*, 51.27 *entertainer*, 433.5 *melodist*
minstrel show 51.5 *show*
mint **45** *Herbs and Spices*, 243.10 *produce*, 306.7 *form*, 413.5 *herbs*, 647.1 *workshop*, 741.24 *monetize*
mint condition 201.1 *newness*, 201.10 *new*, 600.9 *newness*, 619.3 *perfection*
minted 741.22 *monetary*
minted coinage 741.13 *coinage*
minter 741.17 *financier*, 741.18 *treasurer*

minting 741.13 *coinage*
mint julep 351.8 *mixed drink*
mint master 741.17 *financier*, 741.18 *treasurer*
mint money 742.13 *get rich*
mint of money 741.3 *fortune*, 742.6 *money*
mint sauce 45.15 *sauce*, 413.2 *seasoning*
minty 413.9 *piquant*
minuend 52.16 *subtraction*, 131.2 *subtracted item*
minuet 46.4 *historic dancing*
minus 52.88 *equal to*, 100.9 *non-existent*, 127.19 *inferiorly*, 131.1 *subtraction*, 131.7 *reduced*, 131.8 *by subtraction*, 145.6 *incompletely*, 254.12 *missing*, 358.6 *shortcoming*, 358.7 *short*, 745.9 *in debt*
minuscule 5.15 *type style*, 5.41 *lettered*, 260.7 *little*
minus sign 52.13 *mathematical symbol*, 543.1 *sign*
minute **75** *General Units*, 3.20 *chronicle*, 106.10 *detailed*, 185.4 *term*, 187.2 *time period*, 260.7 *little*, 269.8 *measure of time*, 553.3 *diffuse*
minute book 3.5 *chronicle*, 545.6 *record book*
minuted 3.19 *chronicled*
minute gun 192.10, 543.4 *signal*
minute hand 543.5 *indicator*
minutely 106.19 *meticulously*, 260.8 *in a small way*, 553.7 *diffusely*
minuteness 260.1 *littleness*, 367.4 *matter*, 553.1 *diffuseness*
minutes 3.5 *chronicle*, 545.1 *record*
minutia 106.6 *aspect*, 260.3 *little piece*
minutiae 165.4 *specifications*, 612.8 *trifle*
minx 206.8 *young woman*, 402.8 *nasty woman*, 807.12 *impudent person*
minyn 10.17 *worshipper*
Miocene **54** *Geological Time Intervals*
Miocene period 200.3 *geological period*
Mir 53.30 *spacecraft*
Mira **53** *Named Stars*
Mirach **53** *Named Stars*
miracidium 81.13 *invertebrate larva*
miracle 51.2 *play*, 213.4 *rare things*, 457.4 *something that appears*, 489.5 *unexpectedness*, 786.4 *wonder*
miracle drug 630.8 *drug*
miracle-monger 541.6 *exaggerator*
miracle play 51.2 *play*
miracle worker 514.5 *surpriser*
miracle-worker 786.5 *person of wonder*
miracle-working 786.3 *wonder-working*
miraculous 487.2 *unbelievable*, 786.8 *wonderful*
miraculously 786.13 *wonderfully*
miraculousness 11.2 *the occult*, 489.5 *unexpectedness*
mirador 435.9 *viewpoint*
mirage **515**, 102.2 *illusion*, 435.5 *imagination*, 457.4 *something that appears*, 519.5 *fantasy*, 539.5 *falseness*, 540.14 *false thing*
Miranda **68** *Breeds of Cattle*
MIRANDA **65** *Programming Languages*
Mira variable 53.12 *variable star*
mire 98.3, 391.8 *marsh*, 393.13 *mud*, 622.4 *dirt*
Mirfak **53** *Named Stars*
mireness 393.3 *muddiness*, 622.1 *dirtiness*
mirliton **49** *Musical Instruments*
mirror 56.29 *optical element*, 114.10 *be similar*, 116.25 *conform*, 118.1 *imitation*, 118.9 *imitate*, 176.15 *double*, 183.16 *repeat*, 331.1 *recoil*, 331.5 *reflector*, 376.8 *smooth thing*, 435.8

reflection, 435.18 *make visible*, 457.11 *appear*, 517.10 *cards*, 547.9 *represent*
mirror aperture 56.31 *lens element*
mirrored 183.9 *repeated*, 443.3 *mirror-like*, 457.8 *outer*
mirror image 52.48 *transformation*, 435.8 *reflection*, 457.5 *impression*, 547.1 *representation*, 547.6 *image*
mirroring 118.1 *imitation*, 443.3 *mirror-like*, 443.6 *opaqueness*, 457.8 *outer*
mirror lens 66.17 *lens*
mirror-like **443**, 376.4 *polished*, 435.20 *visual*
mirror plane 308.2 *symmetry operation*
mirrors **777** *Phobias by Topic*
mirror symmetry 52.41 *geometric figure*
mirror system 56.30 *lens system*
mirth 769.3 *cheerfulness*, 771.2 *amusement*
miru 90.5 *algal product*
miry 98.11 *continental*, 393.17 *muddy*, 622.7 *dirty*
Mirzam **53** *Named Stars*
misaddress 335.7 *misdirect*
misadventure 211.4 *mishap*, 229.3 *coincidence*, 687.1 *adversity*
misalign 117.12 *be disparate*, 666.8 *be different*
misaligned 666.10 *different*
misaligning 666.3 *difference*
misalliance 108.5 *misconnection*, 117.2 *contradiction*, 823.3 *types of marriage*
misallied 117.8 *contradictory*
misally 117.12 *be disparate*
misandrist 481.7 *bigot*, 481.10 *discriminatory*, 820.5 *hostile person*, 822.9 *hater*, 825.5 *single person*, 834.2 *misanthrope*
misandrous 481.10 *discriminatory*, 825.6 *celibate*, 834.3 *misanthropic*
misandry 481.4 *social discrimination*, 825.1 *celibacy*, 832.1 *malevolence*, 834.1 *misanthropy*
misanthrope **834**, 758.5 *miser*, 820.5 *hostile person*, 822.9 *hater*
misanthropic **834**
misanthropically **834**
misanthropism 834.1 *misanthropy*
misanthropist 820.5 *hostile person*, 822.9 *hater*, 834.2 *misanthrope*
misanthropy **834**, 832.1 *malevolence*
Misanthropy **834**
misapplication 108.5 *misconnection*, 474.1 *sophistry*, 525.2 *misinterpretation*, 601.2 *misuse*, 607.3 *waste*, 656.9 *bungling*
misapplied 108.9 *misconnected*, 474.7 *sophistic*, 616.1 *inconvenient*, 656.4 *bungled*
misapply 474.11 *practise sophistry*, 601.1 *misuse*, 607.1 *waste*, 656.5 *be unskilful*
misapprehend 504.18 *be in error*, 525.1 *misinterpret*
misapprehension 504.1 *mistake*, 525.2 *misinterpretation*
misappropriate 601.1 *misuse*
misappropriated 601.4 *misused*, 736.18 *fraudulent*
misappropriation 601.2 *misuse*, 736.6 *illegal borrowing*
misappropriation of funds 736.7 *dishonesty*
misbegotten 790.4 *ugly*
misbehave 652.13 *behave badly*, 693.15 *be disobedient*, 864.16 *be wicked*
misbehaved 693.13 *disobedient*, 864.11 *wicked*
misbehaving 864.11 *wicked*
misbehaviour 652.4 *bad conduct*, 693.1 *disobedience*, 864.1 *wickedness*, 866.3 *sin*
misbelief 498.4 *unbelief*
miscalculate 493.10 *misjudge*,

494.4 *overestimate*, 495.3 *underestimate*, 504.19 *make a mistake*, 515.4 *be disappointed*
miscalculated 495.5 *underestimated*
miscalculation 493.1 *misjudgment*, 494.1 *overestimation*, 495.1 *underestimation*, 504.1 *mistake*, 514.1 *surprise*, 515.1 *disappointment*
miscarriage 247.1 *infertility*, 683.4 *unsuccessful thing*
miscarriage of justice 16.4 *bad law*, 493.3 *injustice*
miscarried 515.11 *disappointing*, 683.10 *failed*
miscarry 683, 100.14 *cause not to exist*, 247.7 *be infertile*, 358.4 *miss*, 656.7 *be clumsy*, 687.9 *be in trouble*
miscarrying 683.10 *failed*
miscast 51.38 *tragic*, 117.12 *be disparate*
miscegenate 823.15 *marry*
miscegenation 133.1 *mixture*, 823.3 *types of marriage*
miscegenetic 133.12 *mixed*, 823.23 *monogamous*
miscellanea 113.3 *diverse thing*, 133.3 *miscellany*, 143.8 *bits and pieces*, 161.32 *miscellany*, 562.3 *compendium*
miscellaneous 72, 98, 113.6 *assorted*, 133.12 *mixed*, 164.15 *general*, 482.3 *indiscriminate*
miscellaneous architectural features 43
miscellaneous aviation terms 73
miscellaneous collection 133.3 *miscellany*
miscellaneous euphemisms 827
miscellaneous expenses 748.5 *expense*
miscellaneously 113.10 *diversely*, 133.14 *in the midst*
miscellaneous motoring terms 71
miscellaneous swearwords 827
miscellaneous terms 17, 19
miscellany 133, 161, 113.1 *diversity*, 113.2 *assortment*, 562.3 *compendium*
mischance 211.3 *lost chance*, 687.3 *bad fortune*
mischief 579.2 *caprice*, 618.11 *harmfulness*, 628.11 *hurt*, 652.4 *bad conduct*, 832.7 *act of malevolence*, 844.8 *wrong-doing*, 862.1 *evil*
mischief-maker 500.5 *dissenter*, 635.2 *troublemaker*, 661.7 *hinderer*, 693.5 *troublemaker*, 713.4 *protester*, 764.9 *unpleasant person*, 862.6 *evil person*
mischief-making 618.5 *harmful*, 693.1 *disobedience*, 693.15 *disobedient*
mischievous 244.14 *destructive*, 579.1 *capricious*, 618.5 *harmful*, 652.18 *badly behaved*, 844.16 *in the wrong*, 862.7 *evil*
mischievously 862.12 *evilly*
mischievousness 618.11 *harmfulness*, 862.1 *evil*
misch metal 57 *Alloys*
miscibility 133.1 *mixture*
miscible 133.12 *mixed*
miscite 540.22 *falsify*
misciting 540.9 *falsification*
miscomputate 525.1 *misinterpret*
miscomputation 525.2 *misinterpretation*
misconceive 309.12 *distort the truth*, 493.10 *misjudge*, 525.1 *misinterpret*
misconceived 525.3 *misinterpreted*
misconception 102.3 *delusion*, 493.1 *misjudgment*, 504.1 *mistake*, 525.2 *misinterpretation*, 539.5 *falseness*
misconduct 31.8 *hockey*, 652.4 *bad conduct*, 656.5 *be unskilful*, 656.9 *bungling*, 818.2 *bad manners*, 866.3 *sin*
misconduct penalty 31.3 *ice hockey*
misconnected 108

misconnection 108
misconstructed 538.13 *untrue*
misconstruction 309.4 *distortion of the truth*, 493.1 *misjudgment*, 504.1 *mistake*, 525.2 *misinterpretation*, 538.1 *untruth*
misconstrue 309.12 *distort the truth*, 474.11 *practise sophistry*, 493.10 *misjudge*, 504.19 *make a mistake*, 525.1 *misinterpret*
misconstrued 493.9 *misjudged*, 525.3 *misinterpreted*
miscreant 16.40 *lawbreaker*, 832.8 *malefactor*, 844.10 *wrongdoer*, 864.9 *wicked person*, 864.11 *wicked*
miscue 24.2 *billiards play*, 24.8 *play billiards*, 504.9 *trivial error*, 504.13 *sporting error*, 504.19 *make a mistake*
miscued 24.9 *billiard*
misdate 197.4 *be a different time*
misdated 193.4 *mistimed*, 197.2 *occurring at a different time*, 211.11 *anachronistic*
misdating 193.1 *wrong time*, 197.1 *different time*, 211.2 *anachronism*
misdeal 42.3 *card game terms*, 42.10 *play*
misdeed 16.39 *crime*, 504.8 *moral error*, 844.8 *wrong-doing*, 866.3 *sin*
misdemeanour 16.39 *crime*, 844.8 *wrong-doing*, 864.7 *criminality*, 866.3 *sin*
misdiagnose 525.1 *misinterpret*
misdiagnosis 525.2 *misinterpretation*
misdirect 335, 228.10 *manipulate*, 539.27 *be false*, 601.1 *misuse*, 656.5 *be unskilful*
misdirected 335.20 *deviant*, 539.36 *deceived*, 601.4 *misused*
misdirection 19.9 *play*, 335.13 *deviation*, 539.5 *falseness*, 601.2 *misuse*
misdoing 844.8 *wrong-doing*, 866.3 *sin*
misdoubt 841.2, 841.8 *distrust*
misdoubtful 841.5 *distrustful*
mise 715.1 *contract*
miseducate 525.1 *misinterpret*
misemploy 601.1 *misuse*
misemployed 601.4 *misused*
misemployment 601.2 *misuse*
miser 758, 161.36 *hoarder*, 469.6 *careful person*, 747.6 *nonpayer*, 754.8 *bargain hunter*
miserable 406.5 *painful*, 612.2 *obscure*, 618.4 *poor*, 687.6 *adverse*, 770.5 *sad*, 774.4 *lamenting*, 862.8 *afflicted*
miserably 687.12 *in adversity*, 770.11 *sadly*, 862.13 *destructively*
misericord 680.8 *sharp weapon*
miserliness 758.3 *parsimony*, 860.1 *selfishness*
miserly 609.1 *insufficient*, 747.13 *nonpaying*, 758.1 *mean*, 860.4 *selfish*
misery 406.1 *pain*, 618.10 *poverty*, 634.2, 687.1 *adversity*, 770.1 *sorrow*, 770.4 *depressing person*, 788.3 *boring person*, 852.13 *pessimist*, 862.2 *affliction*
miseryguts 770.4 *depressing person*
misevaluate 548.5 *misinform*
misevaluation 548.2 *misinformation*
misfeasance 16.39 *crime*
misfield 504.19 *make a mistake*
misfire 358.4 *miss*, 656.9 *bungling*, 683.9 *malfunction*
misfiring 71.21 *miscellaneous motoring terms*
misfit 117, 149, 108.3 *unconnected person*, 115.2 *unlikeness*, 117.2 *contradiction*, 117.12 *be disparate*, 168.7 *nonconformist*, 335.19 *deviant person*, 666.4 *dissenter*, 666.8 *be different*, 666.10 *different*, 683.5 *failing person*, 816.6 *unsocial person*

misfitting 666.3 *difference*
misform 307.3 *make shapeless*
misfortunate 229.7 *adventurous*
misfortune 835, 211.3 *lost chance*, 229.2 *chance*, 515.2 *bad outcome*, 628.7 *deterioration*, 683.1 *failure*, 687.1 *adversity*, 687.3 *bad fortune*, 832.7 *act of malevolence*, 862.3 *bad luck*
misgiving 477.6 *uncertainty*, 498.1 *disbelief*
misgivings 777.2 *fearfulness*
misgovern 689, 601.1 *misuse*, 656.5 *be unskilful*, 690.6 *suppress*
misgovernment 12.1 *government*, 656.9 *bungling*, 689.1 *anarchy*
misguidance 539.5 *falseness*
misguide 309.12 *distort the truth*, 539.27 *be false*
misguided 309.8 *exaggerated*, 493.7 *misjudging*, 539.36 *deceived*, 656.4 *bungled*
misguidedly 493
mishandle 601.1 *misuse*, 618.14 *ill-treat*, 656.5 *be unskilful*, 690.6 *suppress*
mishandled 601.4 *misused*, 656.4 *bungled*
mishandling 601.2 *misuse*, 656.9 *bungling*
mishap 211, 468.5 *inattentive act*, 661.2 *obstacle*, 687.1 *adversity*
Mishima 48 *Writers*
mishit 504.13 *sporting error*, 504.19 *make a mistake*, 656.7 *be clumsy*, 656.9 *bungling*
mishmash 133.3 *miscellany*, 151.4 *litter*
Mishmi 5 Languages and Groups of Languages
Mishnah 1.8 *tradition*, 7.12 *religious text*
Misima 5 Languages and Groups of Languages
misinform 548, 309.12 *distort the truth*, 335.7 *misdirect*, 474.11 *practise sophistry*, 502.11 *make ignorant*, 539.27 *be false*
misinformation 548, 309.4 *distortion of the truth*, 474.2 *sophism*, 531.5 *evasion*, 538.1 *untruth*, 539.5 *falseness*
misinformed 538, 548, 309.8 *exaggerated*, 474.7 *sophistic*, 502.6 *ignorant*, 539.36 *deceived*, 844.12 *incorrect*
misinterpret 525, 220.9 *transform*, 493.10 *misjudge*, 504.19 *make a mistake*, 521.8 *not understand*, 538.21 *lie*, 540.22 *falsify*, 548.5 *misinform*
misinterpretation 525, 220.1 *conversion*, 493.1 *misjudgment*, 504.1 *mistake*, 538.5 *half-truth*, 540.9 *falsification*, 548.2 *misinformation*
Misinterpretation 525
misinterpreted 525, 493.9 *misjudged*, 521.12 *unmeant*, 548.7 *misinformed*
misjoin 117.12 *be disparate*
misjoinder 117.2 *contradiction*
misjoined 117.8 *contradictory*
misjudge 493, 211.5 *take untimely action*, 211.8 *make a mistake*, 494.4 *overestimate*, 495.3 *underestimate*, 504.19 *make a mistake*, 515.4 *be disappointed*, 523.9 *find unintelligible*, 525.1 *misinterpret*, 601.1 *misuse*
misjudged 493, 494.6 *overestimated*, 495.5 *underestimated*
misjudged person 493
misjudging 493, 211.13 *mistaken*
misjudging person 493
misjudgment 493, 16.4 *bad law*, 211.3 *lost chance*, 494.1 *overestimation*, 495.1 *underestimation*, 504.1 *mistake*, 508.2 *act of folly*, 514.1 *surprise*, 515.1 *disappointment*, 525.2 *misinter-*

pretation, 601.2 *misuse*, 656.9 *bungling*
Misjudgment 493
Miskolc 93 Cities
mislaid 252.13 *misplaced*, 254.12 *missing*, 722.16 *losing*
mislay 252.19 *misplace*, 722.9 *lose*
mislaying 252.6 *misplacement*, 722.1 *loss*
mislead 102.16 *delude*, 228.10 *manipulate*, 309.12 *distort the truth*, 335.7 *misdirect*, 474.11 *practise sophistry*, 502.11 *make ignorant*, 515.8 *be dishonest*, 531.9 *disguise*, 539.27 *be false*, 578.1 *be equivocal*, 864.17 *make wicked*
misleader 539.15 *deceiver*
misleading 309.8 *exaggerated*, 436.11 *blinding*, 474.7 *sophistic*, 515.12 *deceptive*, 539.5 *falseness*, 539.34 *deceiving*, 539.35 *deceptive*, 578.10 *equivocal*
misleadingly 515.13 *disappointingly*
misled 493.7 *misjudging*, 502.6 *ignorant*, 515.10 *deceived*, 538.16 *misinformed*, 539.36 *deceived*
mislike 785.5 *dislike*
mislocate 252.19 *misplace*
mislocated 252.13 *misplaced*
mislocation 252.6 *misplacement*
mismanage 601.1 *misuse*, 656.5 *be unskilful*, 689.5 *misgovern*
mismanaged 656.4 *bungled*
mismanagement 601.2 *misuse*, 656.9 *bungling*
mismanager 656.10 *unskilled person*
mismarry 823.15 *marry*
mismatch 117.2 *contradiction*, 117.12 *be disparate*, 666.8 *be different*
mismatched 117.8 *contradictory*, 123.3 *unequal*, 666.10 *different*
mismatching 666.3 *difference*
mismate 117.12 *be disparate*
mismated 117.8 *contradictory*
misnaming 560.7 *nomenclature*
misogamic 825.6 *celibate*
misogamist 820.5 *hostile person*, 822.9 *hater*, 825.5 *single person*
misogamy 825.1 *celibacy*
misogynist 481.7 *bigot*, 481.10 *discriminatory*, 820.5 *hostile person*, 822.9 *hater*, 825.5 *single person*, 834.2 *misanthrope*
misogynous 481.10 *discriminatory*, 825.6 *celibate*, 834.3 *misanthropic*
misogyny 401.1 *male sex*, 481.4 *social discrimination*, 825.1 *celibacy*, 832.1 *malevolence*, 834.1 *misanthropy*
misperception 656.9 *bungling*
mispickel 57 Common Metal Ores
misplace 252, 722.9 *lose*
misplaced 252, 151.12 *disordered*, 168.15 *irregular*, 722.16 *losing*
misplacement 252
misplacing 722.1 *loss*
misprint 504.12 *typing error*, 504.19 *make a mistake*
misprision 16.39 *crime*
misprize 495.3 *underestimate*, 850.19 *disrespect*
mispronounce 504.19 *make a mistake*
mispronunciation 559, 504.11 *grammatical error*, 564.3 *mode of speech*
misput 252.13 *misplaced*, 252.19 *misplace*
misputting 252.6 *misplacement*
misquotation 504.5 *misrepresentation*, 525.2 *misinterpretation*, 548.2 *misinformation*
misquote 474.11 *practise sophistry*, 504.19 *make a mistake*, 525.1 *misinterpret*, 540.9 *falsification*, 540.22 *falsify*, 548.5 *misinform*

misquoted 525.3 *misinterpreted,*
548.7 *misinformed*

misread 493.10 *misjudge,*
521.12 *unmeant,* 525.1 *misinterpret,* 525.3 *misinterpreted*

misreading 525.2 *misinterpretation*

misreckon 493.10 *misjudge*

misreference 108.5 *misconnection*

misreferred 108.9 *misconnected*

misrelation 108.5 *misconnection*

misremember 512.14 *be forgetful*

misreport 540.22 *falsify*

misreporting 540.9 *falsification*

misrepresent 548, 102.16 *delude,* 115.6 *falsification,* 309.12
distort the truth, 474.11 *practise
sophistry,* 504.19 *make a mistake,* 525.1 *misinterpret,* 538.21
lie, 540.22 *falsify,* 856.6 *accuse
falsely*

misrepresentation 504, 548,
115.3 *disguise,* 309.4 *distortion
of the truth,* 521.1 *lack of meaning,* 525.2 *misinterpretation,*
538.1 *untruth,* 540.9 *falsification,* 547.1 *representation,*
856.2 *false accusation*

Misrepresentation 548

misrepresented 548, 309.8 *exaggerated,* 521.12 *unmeant,* 525.3
misinterpreted, 538.13 *untrue,*
540.32 *falsified,* 856.9 *perjurious*

misrepresentedly 525

misrepresenting 548.6 *misrepresented*

misrule 601.1, 601.2 *misuse,*
656.5 *be unskilful,* 656.9 *bungling,* 689.1 *anarchy,* 689.5 *misgovern,* 690.6 *suppress*

miss 358, 593, 24.2 *billiards
play,* 24.8 *play billiards,* 38.2
football play, 38.4 *play soccer,*
123.5 *be unequal,* 145.5 *be incomplete,* 147.7 *exclude,* 206.8
young woman, 358.1 *fall short,*
421.8 *be deaf,* 493.10 *misjudge,*
504.13 *sporting error,* 512.13
forget, 609.6 *be unsatisfied,*
638.6 *elude,* 656.9 *bungling,*
683.1 *failure,* 683.6 *fail,* 685.5
not complete, 722.9 *lose,* 782.12
desire

Miss 402.3 *female title of address*

missal 10.10 *religious manual*

Miss America 617.8 *exceller*

miss an opportunity 683.6 *fail,*
722.9 *lose*

Miss Clever 809.7 *vain person*

missed 24.9 *billiard,* 38.5 *soccer,*
145.4 *incomplete*

missed chance 656.9 *bungling,*
687.3 *bad fortune*

missed opportunity 211.3 *lost
chance*

missed out 147.11 *excluded*

missed third strike 22.5 *batting
terms*

misshape 307.3 *make shapeless,*
309.9 *distort,* 620.6 *imperfect
item,* 790.5 *make ugly,* 793.7
blemish

misshapen 151.14 *irregular,*
309.6 *distorted,* 790.4 *ugly*

misshapenly 309.13 *asymmetrically*

misshapenness 151.2 *irregular
order,* 309.3 *deformity*

missile 338, 329.11 *swift thing,*
338.18 *projectile,* 680.5 *missile
weapon,* 680.13 *ammunition*

missile battalion 17.4 *military organization*

missilery 680.2 *arms*

missile strike 670.13 *air attack*

missile weapon 680

missing 254, 100.9 *nonexistent,*
145.4 *incomplete,* 147.11 *excluded,* 172.7 *null,* 252.13 *misplaced,* 254.9 *away,* 358.7
short, 458.7 *disappeared,* 593.4
required, 685.4 *uncompleted,*
722.16 *losing*

missing link 145.2 *omission,*
160.1 *broken thread,* 620.6 *imperfect item,* 685.1 *noncompletion*

missing part 685.1 *noncompletion*

missing person 254.6 *absentee,*
458.4 *disappearance,* 590.7 *the
hunted*

mission 10.11 *place of worship,*
597.2, 597.2 *undertaking,*
644.3 *job,* 654.3 *precept,* 676.8
warfare, 703.2 *engagement,*
703.4 *council,* 706.2 *representative body,* 847.2 *task*

missionary 7.4 *religionist,* 7.15 *religious,* 220.5 *converter,* 703.5
commissioner, 710.8 *volunteer,*
833.3 *philanthropist*

missionary spirit 7.2 *religiousness*

mission worker 833.3 *philanthropist*

missis 823.11 *married woman*

Mississippi 92 *American States,*
96 *Rivers,* 96.3 *US rivers*

Mississippi mud pie 45.35 *dessert*

miss nothing 467.11 *take note of*

miss one's cue 51.34 *underact,*
656.5 *be unskilful*

miss one's deadline 648.2 *make
haste*

miss one's footing 360.11 *trip*

miss one's mooring 358.4 *miss*

Missouri 92 *American States,*
96 *Rivers,* 96.3 *US rivers*

miss out 145.5 *be incomplete,*
147.7 *exclude,* 358.4 *miss*

misspell 5.47 *word,* 504.19
make a mistake, 525.1 *misinterpret*

misspelling 5.27 *spelling,* 504.11
grammatical error, 525.2 *misinterpretation*

misspelt 525.3 *misinterpreted*

misspend 607.1, 757.7 *waste*

misspent youth 722.8 *lost thing*

miss stays 36.15 *sail*

misstate 504.19 *make a mistake,*
538.21 *lie,* 540.22 *falsify,*
548.5 *misinform*

misstated 538.13 *untrue,* 548.7
misinformed

misstatement 504.5 *misrepresentation,* 538.1 *untruth,* 540.9 *falsification,* 548.2 *misinformation*

miss the boat 209.7 *wait,* 211.6
lose one's chance, 683.6 *fail*

miss the bus 211.6 *lose one's
chance,* 358.4 *miss*

miss the mark 358.1 *fall short,*
358.4 *miss*

miss the meaning of 521.8 *not
understand*

miss the point 104.13 *be extraneous,* 108.10 *be unrelated,* 334.4
detour, 335.4 *lose track of*

miss the point of 521.8 *not understand*

Miss Universe 617.8 *exceller*

missus 402.3 *female title of address*

missy 206.8 *young woman*

mist 55, 55.64 *fog,* 57.3 *phase,*
388.4 *water vapour,* 389.3 *wateriness,* 389.12 *sprinkler,*
389.33 *sprinkle,* 438.4 *invisibility,* 438.6 *that which makes invisible,* 441.2 *murk,* 441.10
make dim, 442.8 *transparent
thing,* 443.7 *opaque thing,*
443.10 *be opaque*

mistake 493, 504, 133.9 *mix
up,* 211.3 *lost chance,* 468.5 *inattentive act,* 493.10 *misjudge,*
508.2 *act of folly,* 525.1 *misinterpret,* 525.2 *misinterpretation,*
620.7 *defect,* 656.9 *bungling,*
683.1 *failure,* 798.4 *joke,* 844.2
incorrectness, 844.8 *wrong-
doing,* 866.3 *sin*

mistaken 211, 504, 133.13
mixed-up, 493.7 *misjudging,*
493.9 *misjudged,* 521.12 *unmeant,* 525.3 *misinterpreted,*
844.12 *incorrect*

mistakenly 211, 525, 493.13
misguidedly, 504.21 *erroneously,*
844.26 *wrong*

mistakenness 844.2 *incorrectness*

mistake of law 16.4 *bad law*

mistake the date 193.2 *be untimely*

mistake the day 193.2 *be untimely*

mistake the time 193.2 *be untimely*

mistaking 211.13 *mistaken*

mistaught 548.7 *misinformed*

misteach 525.1 *misinterpret,*
548.5 *misinform,* 628.6 *pervert*

misteaching 525.2 *misinterpretation,* 548.2 *misinformation*

misted 443.2 *shady*

mister 401.3 *male title of address*

Mister Charlie 401.3 *male title of
address*

mister fix-it 646.2 *artisan,* 697.1
servant

misthrow 656.7 *be clumsy,* 656.9
bungling

mistily 55.65 *meteorologically,*
307.6 *shapelessly,* 388.30 *smokily,* 441.12 *dimly,* 442.13 *transparently,* 443.13 *opaquely,*
448.9 *greyly,* 491.25 *indeterminately*

mistime 193, 117.12 *be disparate,* 197.4 *be a different time,*
211.5 *take untimely action,*
493.10 *misjudge,* 666.8 *be different*

mistimed 193, 197.2 *occurring
at a different time,* 211.10 *untimely,* 666.10 *different*

mistiming 193.1 *wrong time,*
197.1 *different time,* 211.1 *untimeliness,* 666.3 *difference*

mistiness 391, 55.35 *visibility,*
307.1 *shapelessness,* 438.4 *invisibility,* 441.2 *murk,* 442.7 *semitransparency,* 491.14 *indeterminacy*

mistle 78 *Birds*

mist over 441.9 *be dim*

mistral 55 *Winds*

mistranslate 525.1 *misinterpret*

mistranslated 521.12 *unmeant,*
525.3 *misinterpreted*

mistranslation 525.2 *misinterpretation*

mistreat 601.1 *misuse,* 618.14 *ill-
treat,* 862.11 *be evil*

mistreatment 601.2 *misuse*

mistress 6.4 *educator,* 402.3 *female title of address,* 402.4
girlfriend, 405.3 *pleasure-seeker,*
696.1 *master,* 723.6 *lord,* 821.9
lover, 821.11 *loved one*

mistress of the house 696.1 *master*

mistrial 493.3 *injustice*

mistrust 477.6 *uncertainty,*
477.20 *doubt,* 491.10 *suspicion,*
491.18 *be uncertain,* 498.1 *disbelief,* 498.8 *disbelieve,* 841.2,
841.8 *distrust*

mistrustful 491.1 *uncertain,*
498.6 *disbelieving,* 841.5 *distrustful*

mistrustfully 498.10 *disbelievingly,* 841.9 *jealously*

mistrustfulness 841.2 *distrust*

misty 391, 55.56 *foggy,* 307.5
shapeless, 388.19 *smoky,* 438.2
difficult to see, 441.6 *murky,*
442.3 *semitransparent,* 443.2
shady, 448.3 *dull,* 491.6 *indeterminate,* 523.4 *difficult*

misunderstand 133.11 *be mixed
up,* 493.10 *misjudge,* 504.18 *be
in error,* 523.9 *find unintelligible,* 525.1 *misinterpret,* 666.5
disagree

misunderstanding 473.1 *argument,* 493.1 *misjudgment,*
504.1 *mistake,* 525.2 *misinterpretation,* 666.1 *disagreement*

misunderstood 473.10 *arguable,*
493.9 *misjudged,* 521.12 *unmeant,* 525.3 *misinterpreted*

misusage 504.11 *grammatical
error*

misuse 601, 601, 599.3 *exploit,*
599.6 *use,* 607.1, 607.3 *waste,*
618.14 *ill-treat,* 628.6 *pervert,*
628.8 *perversion,* 656.5 *be unskilful,* 656.9 *bungling,* 722.3
waste, 722.13 *destroy,* 832.7 *act
of malevolence*

Misuse 601

misused 601

misuse of words 525.2 *misinterpretation,* 601.2 *misuse*

misuse power 601.1 *misuse*

misuse words 601.1 *misuse*

mitch 591.9 *play truant*

Mitchell 48 *Writers,* 52 *Scientists*

mite 82 *Arachnids,* 82.2 *arachnid,* 82.3 *pest,* 206.9 *child,*
260.4 *little person,* 609.8 *insufficiency*

mite box 729.3 *offering*

mitelike 82.11 *arachnidan*

mites 777 *Phobias by Topic*

Mithraism 7 *Non-Christian Religions*

mithramycin 62 *Medication*

mithridate 630.4 *antidote*

mitigate 203, 129.5 *make
smaller,* 242.4 *moderate,* 302.7
limit, 374.14 *ease,* 376.13
smooth over, 485.15 *modify,*
627.1 *improve,* 767.9 *relieve,*
855.8 *justify*

mitigated 203, 485.11 *modified*

mitigating 855.11 *vindicatory*

mitigating circumstances 855.2
defence

mitigation 129.1 *decrease,* 242.1
moderation, 302.1 *limitation,*
485.5 *modification,* 627.5 *improvement,* 767.1 *ease,* 835.3
mercy, 855.2 *defence*

mitigative 855.11 *vindicatory*

mitigatory 485.11 *modified*

Mitla 10.13 *shrine*

mitochondrial 59.23 *cellular*

mitochondrion 59.8 *cell organ*

mitosis 59.10 *cell division*

mitotic 59.25 *genetic*

mitraille 680.14 *historical ammunition*

mitrailleuse 680.12 *historical
guns*

mitral stenosis 624.10 *cardiovascular disease*

mitre 7.11 *vestment,* 47.17 *carpenter,* 135.10 *link,* 310.11
angle

mitred 47.16 *joined,* 310.7 *angular*

mitre joint 47.10 *carpenter's
term,* 135.5 *joint,* 310.1 *angle*

mitre shell 81 *Molluscs*

mitts 295.25 *accessories*

mittens 34.4 *climbing equipment,*
295.25 *accessories*

mittimus 692.2 *demand*

mitts 295.25 *accessories,* 726.3
tools for gripping

mitzvah 831.4 *benevolent act*

mix 133, 44.11 *make ceramics,*
45.55 *cook,* 113.8 *be diverse,*
133.2 *mixed thing,* 135.8 *unite,*
140.1 *combination,* 140.5 *combine,* 364.10 *swirl,* 366.22 *agitate,* 482.11 *not discriminate,*
642.16 *be sociable*

Mixacoatl 8 *Deities*

mix and match 133.8 *mix*

mixed 133, 1.13 *racial,* 113.6 *assorted,* 140.7 *combined,* 482.3
indiscriminate

mixed bag 113.3 *diverse thing,*
161.32 *miscellany*

mixed blessing 124.6 *mediocrity,*
616.3 *inconvenience*

mixed cloud 55.18 *cloud*

mixed drink 351, 351.2 *drink*

mixed economy 13.1 *economics*

mixed farm 68.6 *farm*

mixed farming 68.1 *agriculture*

mixed foursome 29.1 *golf*

mixed glyceride 58.7 *fat*

mixed grill 45.32 *meat dish,*
45.44 *British dish*

mixed herbs 413.5 *herbs*

mixed indicator 57.18 *gravimetric
analysis*

mixed lot 161.32 *miscellany*

mixed marriage 823.3 *types of
marriage*

mixed meeting 32.7 *horseracing*

mixed number 52.6 *complex
number*

mixed party 815.5 *party*
mixed race 1.6 *race*
mixed salad 45.14 *salad*
mixed set 33.6 *motor racing terms*
mixed thing 133
mixed-up **133, 151,** 133.12 *mixed,* 482.3 *indiscriminate*
mixer **133,** 133.7 *person who mixes,* 351.6 *soft drink,* 351.8 *mixed drink,* 635.2 *troublemaker,* 815.6 *social person*
mix in 130.6 *add*
mixing 133.1 *mixture,* 140.1 *combination,* 642.2 *social activity*
mixing bowl 45.6 *kitchen equipment,* 133.6 *mixer,* 258.16 *crockery*
mixing it up 26.14 *combat*
mixing tank 44.6 *ceramic workshop*
mix it 674.12 *fight,* 822.16 *cause hate*
mixologist 133.7 *person who mixes*
mixolydian 49.20 *key*
Mixtec **1** *Peoples,* **5** *Languages and Groups of Languages*
mixte frame 71.11 *bicycle part*
mix together 133.10 *become mixed,* 140.5 *combine*
mixture **133,** 57.3 *phase,* 113.2 *assortment,* 133.2 *mixed thing,* 140.1 *combination,* 140.4 *compound,* 161.32 *miscellany,* 482.8 *indiscriminateness,* 628.10 *impairment,* 630.2 *medicine*
Mixture 133
mix up **133,** 133.8 *mix,* 151.21 *disorder,* 151.23 *confuse,* 551.3 *make obscure,* 661.8 *hinder*
mix-up **151,** 661.2 *obstacle*
mix-up in dates 193.1 *wrong time*
mix with 130.6 *add,* 130.7 *support,* 135.8 *unite,* 815.11 *be sociable*
mix with water 140.5 *combine*
Miya-zaki-jingu 10.13 *shrine*
Mizrachi **7** *Non-Christian Religions*
mizzen **74** *Sails,* 304.4 *rear*
mizzenmast **74** *Rigging,* 304.5 *parts of a sailing boat,* 304.1 *rear*
mizzentop **74** *Parts of a Ship*
mizzle 55.62 *rain,* 391.2 *mistiness,* 391.15 *be moist*
mizzly 391.10 *misty*
MKSA system 75.2 *unit system*
MK skates 41.6 *ice-skating*
m.k.s. system 75.2 *unit system*
m.k.s. unit 75.2 *unit system*
ML **65** *Programming Languages*
mmHg **75** *Scientific and Technical Units*
MMR vaccine 630.3 *prophylactic*
mnemonic 511.4 *reminder,* 511.7 *memorable*
mnemonically 511.16 *memorably*
Mnemosyne 511.1 *memory*
mo 191.3 *instant*
moa **78** *Birds,* 78.8 *extinct bird*
moan 55.58 *blow,* 406.12 *express pain,* 424.1 *faintness,* 424.5 *sound faint,* 428.4 *faint sound,* 428.8 *sound faint,* 431.6 *cry of pain,* 431.13 *cry,* 543.3, 543.11 *gesture,* 663.15 *object,* 713.7 *complain,* 766.7 *be dissatisfied,* 770.8 *grieve,* 774.2 *lament,* 830.2 *sign of sullenness,* 830.9 *be sullen*
moaner 713.7 *protester,* 766.3 *dissatisfied person,* 852.13 *pessimist*
moaning 431.18 *crying,* 543.15 *gestural*
moaning Minnie 713.4 *protester*
moat 147.3 *exclusion zone,* 265.2 *crack,* 301.3 *enclosing thing,* 301.5 *enclose,* 317.2 *concave land,* 632.2 *protection,* 661.3 *barrier,* 671.8 *military defences,* 671.12 *fort,* 671.18 *fence*
moated 671.30 *defended*
mob 116.2 *alliance,* 135.1

union, 151.26 *be disorderly,* 161.20 *crowd,* 164.11 *general public,* 181.4 *throng,* 181.11 *crowd,* 590.12 *aim at,* 610.1 *excess,* 665.1 *party,* 679.18 *army of people,* 812.18 *salute,* 852.23 *show disapproval*
mobbed 181.10 *crowded*
mobcap 295.15 *headgear*
mobile 2.14 *socioeconomic,* 50.12 *sculpture,* 57.41 *analytic,* 224.13 *changeable,* 324.16 *moving,* 491.8 *capricious*
Mobile 93 *Cities*
Mobile Army Surgical Hospital 17.4 *military organization*
mobile belt 54.20 *earth movement*
mobile camera 534.21 *television*
mobile crane 63.29 *construction equipment*
mobile home **71** *Motor Vehicles,* **256**
mobile library **71** *Motor Vehicles*
mobile phase 57.17 *analysis*
mobile phone 420.9 *audio device,* 534.16 *transmitter*
mobile radio 534.18 *radio*
mobile radio station 534.20 *radio broadcasting*
mobile station 534.24 *television broadcasting*
mobile telephone 534.9 *telephone*
mobile unit 534.20 *radio broadcasting*
mobile warfare 676.8 *warfare*
mobility 2.7 *social stratification,* 224.1 *changeableness,* 324.1 *motion,* 491.16 *capriciousness*
mobilization 17.1 *military affairs,* 161.1 *assembly,* 324.2 *momentum,* 594.9 *preparation,* 676.7 *war measures*
mobilize 17.10 *enlist,* 135.8 *unite,* 161.42 *call together,* 324.14 *set in motion,* 594.4 *prepare for action,* 676.12 *go to war*
mobilized 161.46 *assembled,* 594.18 *prepared,* 676.15 *warring*
Möbius strip **52** *Named Concepts,* 52.47 *topology,* 159.6 *continuum*
mob law 12.1 *government,* 16.41 *lawlessness,* 688.7 *type of rule,* 689.1 *anarchy*
mob member 736.11 *dishonest person*
mobocracy 12.1 *government,* 688.7 *type of rule,* 689.2 *anarchism*
mobocrat 689.3 *anarchist*
mobocratic 689.7 *anarchistic*
mob rule 12.1 *government,* 151.9 *disorder,* 688.7 *type of rule,* 689.1 *anarchy*
mobs 777 *Phobias by Topic*
mobster 693.9 *criminal,* 736.11 *dishonest person,* 832.8 *malefactor,* 858.4 *dishonourable person,* 862.6 *evil person,* 864.10 *bad person*
Mobutu 94 *Lakes*
moccasin 79 *Reptiles*
moccasin flower 84 *Flowers and Flowering Plants*
moccasins 295.19 *footwear*
Moccus 8 *Deities*
mocha 449.1 *brown*
mock 102.12 *not the real thing,* 114.8 *simulated,* 118.9 *imitate,* 118.13 *imitation,* 479.8 *experimental,* 498.8 *disbelieve,* 539.27 *be false,* 539.28 *trick,* 539.39 *imitative,* 540.10 *fake,* 540.18 *be hypocritical,* 540.33 *fake,* 581.3 *exclude,* 612.13 *make unimportant,* 771.13 *be humorous,* 799.6, 799.6 *deride,* 850.6 *taunt,* 850.24 *ridicule,* 850.25 *taunt,* 854.14 *ridicule*
mocked 114.8 *simulated,* 539.36 *deceived*
mocker 498.5 *disbeliever,* 854.9 *ridiculer*
mockernut 86 *Nuts*
mockery **118, 799,** 539.5 *false-*

ness, 540.3 *hypocrisy,* 799.2 *act of derision,* 818.1 *discourtesy,* 850.4 *ridicule*
mock-heroic 48.19 *narrative*
mock-heroic poetry 48.6 *poetry*
mocking 540.27 *hypocritical,* 850.14 *ridiculing,* 850.15 *taunting,* 854.17 *scornful*
mockingbird 78 *Birds*
mockingly **850,** 118.14 *imitatively,* 818.10 *rudely*
mock orange 84 *Flowers and Flowering Plants*
mock up 479.12 *rehearse*
mock-up 118.2 *copy,* 375.10 *rough idea,* 375.13 *be unfinished,* 479.2 *rehearsal,* 526.7 *showpiece*
modal 105.8 *in a state of*
modality 4.8 *philosophical term,* 105.1 *state*
modal logic 4.6 *branch of philosophy*
modal scale 49.20 *key*
mode 49.20 *key,* 52.60 *parameter,* 105.1 *state,* 327.1 *way,* 549.1 *style,* 567.4 *approach,* 602.1 *means,* 796.1 *fashion,* 796.4 *design*
model **295, 517,** 50.11 *artist's materials,* 50.12 *sculpture,* 50.21 *sculpt,* 56.6 *law,* 110.4 *duplicate,* 118.2 *copy,* 118.5 *duplicate,* 119.2 *original,* 124.4 *average,* 154.4, 166.5 *precedent,* 260.2 *little thing,* 260.7 *little,* 268.7 *standard,* 306.2 *prototype,* 306.7 *form,* 306.10 *prototypical,* 457.5 *impression,* 471.6, 471.13 *ideal,* 471.19 *epitomize,* 475.3 *explanation,* 479.2 *rehearsal,* 479.8 *experimental,* 479.12 *rehearse,* 518.1 *supposition,* 526.1 *display,* 526.7 *showpiece,* 526.12 *display,* 544.3 *means of identification,* 547.6 *image,* 592.6 *outline,* 619.1 *perfect,* 619.3 *perfection,* 796.5 *fashion model,* 796.8 *fashion*
model after 118.9 *imitate*
model builder 518.4 *theorist*
modelled 50.28 *sculpted,* 306.9 *formed*
modeller 50.17 *sculptor,* 547.4 *person who makes a representation*
modelling 50.12 *sculpture,* 61.3 *psychiatric treatment,* 306.4 *forming*
modelling clay 50.14 *sculptor's materials,* 374.11 *soft thing*
modelling tool 50.14 *sculptor's materials*
model maker 547.4 *person who makes a representation*
model making 42 *Hobbies and Pastimes*
model oneself upon 118.9 *imitate*
model railways 42 *Hobbies and Pastimes*
modem 65.7 *peripheral,* 65.12 *electronic office,* 65.14 *data transfer*
mode of behaviour 652.1 *conduct*
mode of expression 520.1 *meaning,* 549.4 *literary style*
mode of operation 327.1 *way*
mode of speech **564**
mode of use 599.6 *use*
moderate **242, 242, 869, 869,** 4.18 *detached,* 12.6 *political party,* 55.50 *warm,* 124.2 *medium,* 124.3 *mediocre,* 124.8 *middle classes,* 129.4 *decrease,* 158.14 *mediatory,* 203.8 *mitigate,* 231.3 *counteract,* 302.7 *limit,* 312.4 *traditional,* 312.9 *straight person,* 328.3 *slow down,* 328.5 *unhurried,* 333.3 *moderate person,* 333.4 *middle,* 482.10 *impartial person,* 485.15 *modify,* 494.5 *underestimating,* 542.22 *play down,* 591.3 *abstain,* 591.19 *abstaining,* 620.4 *ordinary,* 627.1 *improve,* 627.12 *reformer,* 649.3 *ease,* 660.9

easy, 665.6 *political party member,* 678.1 *mediate,* 691.3 *be lenient,* 691.4 *lenient,* 698.7 *free person,* 698.9 *free,* 699.14 *self-restrained,* 754.9 *cheap,* 767.9 *relieve,* 783.6 *indifferent person,* 783.9 *impartial*
moderate breeze 55.13 *wind strength*
moderate climate 55.38 *climate*
moderated 203.16 *mitigated,* 485.11 *modified,* 542.19 *down-played*
moderate drinker 873.8 *sober person*
moderate frost 55.36 *frost*
moderately **242, 542, 869,** 4.27 *stoically,* 124.12 *mediumly,* 143.12 *partly,* 328.16 *slowly,* 333.8 *medially,* 495.6 *pessimistically,* 591.21 *away,* 677.7 *pacifically,* 691.6 *leniently,* 698.20 *freely,* 699.17 *with self-restraint,* 754.15 *cheaply*
moderateness 124.5 *medium,* 242.1 *moderation,* 333.2 *middle of the road,* 869.2 *moderation*
moderate one's hunger 242
moderate one's language 242.4 *moderate*
moderate person 333
moderating 242, 231.4 *counteracting*
moderating influence 678.3 *mediator*
moderation **242, 869,** 4.3 *detachment,* 124.5 *medium,* 129.1 *decrease,* 129.6 *decreasing,* 231.1 *counteraction,* 302.1 *limitation,* 333.2 *middle of the road,* 542.9 *down-playing,* 591.11 *abstinence,* 627.5 *improvement,* 629.11 *recuperation,* 677.1 *pacification,* 678.2 *mediation,* 691.1 *leniency,* 699.3 *self-restraint,* 783.3 *impartiality*
Moderation 242
moderato 49 *Musical Terms*
moderator 242, 56.73 *nuclear reactor,* 158.9 *middleman,* 235.8 *nuclear power,* 630.1 *remedy,* 630.9 *balm,* 653.13 *director,* 678.3 *mediator,* 859.3 *impartial person*
modern 43 *Architectural Styles,* 47.7 *furniture style,* 196.6 *present,* 201.10 *new,* 479.9 *original*
modern ballet 46.8 *ballet*
modern dance 46.1 *dancing,* 46.8 *ballet*
modern dance music 49.7 *dance music*
modern-dress production 51.12 *production*
moderne 43 *Architectural Styles*
Modern English 5 *Languages and Groups of Languages*
Modern Game 68 *Breeds of Fowl*
Modern Greek 5 *Languages and Groups of Languages*
Modern Hebrew 5 *Languages and Groups of Languages*
modernism 48 *Literary Groups and Movements,* 4.7 *school of thought,* 196.4 *up-to-dateness,* 201.1 *newness,* 201.2 *trendiness,* 479.4 *originality*
modernist 43 *Architectural Styles,* 4.11 *follower of a doctrine,* 48.14 *author,* 201.9 *modern person,* 479.9 *original*
modernistic 201.10 *new*
modernistically 201.21 *newly*
modernity 196.4 *up-to-dateness,* 201.1 *newness*
modernization 15.2 *industrial negotiations,* 201.5 *fresh start,* 216.1 *change,* 627.5 *improvement*
modernize 15.11 *conduct industrial relations,* 196.5 *be present,* 201.20 *make new,* 216.7 *be changed,* 216.8 *cause change,* 336.8 *further,* 627.1 *improve,* 629.2 *refurbish*
modernized 15.9 *negotiated,*

201.14 *renewed*, 216.12
changed, 627.14 *improved*
modernizing 15.9 *negotiated*
modern jazz 49.8 *jazz*
Modern Langshan 68 Breeds of
Fowl
modern man 201.9 *modern person*, 400.4 *civilized human*
modern master 50.16 *artist*
modern music 49.3 *classical
music*
modern pentathlon 18 Sporting
Activities
modern person 201
modern physics 56
modern poet 48.14 *author*
modern production 51.12 *production*
modern times 196.2 *the present
day*
modern warfare 676.1 *war*
modern woman 400.4 *civilized
human*, 402.11 *liberated woman*
modest 810, 134.12 *morally
pure*, 242.6 *moderate*, 495.4 *underestimating*, 542.14 *simple*,
542.15 *reserved*, 556.1 *simple*,
573.3 *cautious*, 658.1 *naive*,
699.14 *self-restrained*, 754.9
cheap, 806.1 *humble*, 859.5 *unselfish*, 876.9 *pure*
modestly 810, 134.18 *virtuously*, 495.6 *pessimistically*,
542.25 *reservedly*, 699.17 *with
self-restraint*, 754.15 *cheaply*,
806.27 *humbly*, 859.9 *unselfishly*
Modesto 93 Cities
modest person 542, 810
modesty 810, 134.1 *purity*,
495.1 *underestimation*, 542.4
simplicity, 542.5 *reserve*, 556.4
simplicity, 573.13 *dissociation*,
658.2 *naivety*, 699.3 *self-restraint*, 806.7 *humility*, 816.2
shyness, 859.2 *unselfishness*,
876.3 *moral purity*
Modesty 810
modicum 133.4 *admixture*
modifiability 113.1 *diversity*
modification 485, 216.1 *change*,
220.1 *conversion*
modified 485, 216.12 *changed*
modified leaf 63.46 *leaf*
modifier 5.35 *part of speech*,
216.5 *changer*
modify 485, 115.6 *differentiate*,
216.7 *be changed*, 216.8 *cause
change*, 220.9 *transform*
modifying 5.44 *grammatical*
modillion 43 Architectural Decoration
modish 201.16 *avant-garde*,
295.30 *dressed up*, 584.12 *established*, 813.7 *dressed up*
modishly 201.23 *trendily*,
295.36 *dressily*
modiste 295.26 *fashion designer*
Modula 65 Programming Languages
modular 148
modular arithmetic 52.4 *simple
arithmetic*
modulate 116.24 *harmonize*,
187.11 *make periodical*, 216.8
cause change, 242.4 *moderate*,
485.15 *modify*, 534.30 *communicate*
modulated 116.13 *harmonious*,
485.11 *modified*, 534.34 *communicated*
modulated carrier 534.14 *radio
transmission*
modulating 116.13 *harmonious*
modulation 49.20 *key*, 116.4 *harmony*, 216.1 *change*, 242.1 *moderation*, 485.5 *modification*,
534.14 *radio transmission*,
564.3 *mode of speech*
modulator 534.14 *radio transmission*
module 6.3 *subject*, 43.9 *miscellaneous architectural features*,
53.30 *spacecraft*, 69.4 *nursery*,
148.3 *unit*, 174.1 *one*
modulus 52.6 *complex number*

modulus of elasticity 63.15
strength of materials
modus operandi 105.1 *state*
modus vivendi 105.1 *state*,
222.1 *substitution*, 717.1 *compromise*
Moelwyn 95 Mountains
mog 77.10 *cat*
Mogadishu 93 Cities
Mogadon 62 Medication
mogul 41.1 *skiing*, 41.12 *ski*,
611.4 *bigwig*
Mogul 400.4 *civilized human*,
696.2 *sovereign*
Mogul art 50 Non-Western Art
moguled 41.12 *ski*
moguled piste 41.1 *skiing*
Mogul Empire 91.3 *dominion*
mogul skiing 41.1 *skiing*
mohair 67 Natural Fabrics,
288.4 *textile*
Mohammedan 7.6 *non-Christian*
Mohammedanism 7 Non-Christian Religions
Mohave 5 Languages and
Groups of Languages
Mohawk 1 Peoples, **5** Languages and Groups of Languages
mohican 791.8 *hair cut*
Mohican 1 Peoples
Mohorovičić discontinuity 54.18
earth's crust
moiety 143.1 *part*, 158.5 *middle
distance*, 174.8 *half*
moil 364.10 *swirl*, 366.2 *tumult*,
644.6 *work*
moiler 646.1 *worker*
Moine Thrust 54.20 *earth movement*
moiré 67 Natural Fabrics, 456.1
variegation, 456.5 *variegated
thing*, 456.7 *iridescent*
moist 391, 387.15 *flowing*,
389.21 *watery*, 395.13 *lubricant*
moist air 55.10 *air movement*
moisten 391, 362.6 *throw down*,
389.29 *water*, 395.17 *oil*
moistening 389.26 *wetting*
moistiness 391.1 *moisture*
moistly 391, 55.65 *meteorologically*, 387.26 *fluidly*, 389.35
wetly, 395.20 *oilily*
moistness 389.3 *wateriness*,
391.1 *moisture*
moisture 391, 55.6 *weather
data*, 387.7 *juiciness*, 389.1
water
Moisture 391
moistureless 392.1 *dry*
moistureproof 392.10 *waterproof*
moisturizer 630.9 *balm*
moisty 391.9 *moist*
Mojave 98 Deserts
mojo 11.6 *talisman*, 543.1 *sign*,
618.11 *harmfulness*
moke 326.6 *beast of burden*
mokugyo 49 Musical Instruments
Moksho 7 Non-Christian Religions
molar 13.11 *tooth*
molar gas constant 56.97 *fundamental constant*
molar heat capacity 56.36 *heat
flow*
molasses 68.9 *animal feedstuff*,
138.4 *adherent*, 393.9 *jelly*,
414.2 *sweetener*
Moldavia 91 Countries
mole 75 SI Units, **75** Scientific
and Technical Units, **77** Placental Mammals, 63.24 *water
system*, 301.3 *enclosing thing*,
318.2 *projection*, 436.4 *blind
people*, 449.3 *brownness*, 465.4
meddler, 483.7 *person who gives
evidence*, 496.12 *discoverer*,
528.10 *informer*, 529.2 *secretiveness*, 624.13 *skin disease*, 632.4
safety device, 636.4 *warner*,
661.3 *barrier*
mole-catcher 398.13 *animal
killer*, 590.6 *hunter*
mole-catching 77.23 *mammal
hunting*, 590.2 *chase*
Molech 8 Deities

mole cricket 82 Insects
molecular 57.35 *combined*,
143.11 *partial*, 148.7 *modular*,
260.7 *little*
molecular biologist 59.19 *life scientist*
molecular biology 59, 59.1 *life
science*
molecular cloud 53.11 *stellar
birth*
molecular formula 57.13 *structure*
molecular genetics 59.11 *genetics*, 59.12 *molecular biology*
molecular orbital 57.12 *valence*
molecular-orbital theory 57.12 *valence*
molecular weight 369.9 *avoirdupois weight*
molecule 143.4 *component*,
148.3 *unit*, 260.2 *little thing*,
367.4 *matter*
molehill 276.2 *lowland*
molehole 322.7 *passageway*,
634.3 *animal shelter*
mole poblano 45.50 *Central
American dish*
mole rat 77 Placental Mammals
moles 161 Collective Names
by Animal
moleskin 67 Natural Fabrics,
288.4 *textile*
molest 153.10 *disrupt*, 601.1
misuse, 618.14 *ill-treat*, 832.18
torment, 862.11 *be evil*
molestation 153.4 *disruption*,
601.2 *misuse*, 618.11 *harmfulness*
molested 153.15 *disrupted*
molester 832.8 *malefactor*
mole trap 68.14 *pest control*
moletrap 539.13 *snare*
Molewyn Mountains 95.5 *British
mountains*
Molière 48 Dramatists
Molisch's test 58.5 *sugar test*
moll 402.9 *woman considered as
a sex object*
mollification 242.1 *moderation*,
374.12 *gentleness*, 677.1 *pacification*, 767.1 *ease*
mollified 203.16 *mitigated*,
374.7 *impressionable*, 767.7 *relieved*
mollifier 242.2 *moderator*, 767.3
reliever
mollify 203.8 *mitigate*, 242.4
moderate, 374.14 *ease*, 677.4
pacify, 767.9 *relieve*
mollifying 374.7 *impressionable*,
374.12 *gentleness*
mollusc 81, 76.4 *type of animal*
Mollusca 81.5 *mollusc*
molluscan 81
molluscicide 68.14 *pest control*
mollusc-like invertebrate 81.5
mollusc
molly 80 Fishes
mollycoddle 405.10 *comfort*
mollycoddled 405.7 *pleased*
Molnár 48 Dramatists
moloch 79 Reptiles
Molotov cocktail 680.16 *bomb*
molten 54.55 *volcanic*, 57.32
solid, 141.5 *disintegrated*,
387.19 *liquefied*, 408.9 *hot*,
408.13 *heated*
molto 49 Musical Terms
molybdenite 54 Minerals
molybdenous 57.34 *elemental*
molybdenum 57 Chemical Elements, 58.15 *essential element*
molybdic 57.34 *elemental*
molybdous 57.34 *elemental*
mom 402.12 *woman in the family*
mom and pop store 740.8 *store*
Mombasa 93 Cities
mombin 86 Fruits
moment 56.10 *force*, 106.2 *occurrence*, 185.11 *date*, 187.2 *time
period*, 189.3 *short duration*,
191.3 *instant*, 191.4 *point in
time*, 330.11 *impulsion*, 611.1,
772.6 *importance*
momentarily 189.8 *transiently*
momentariness 189.1 *transience*
momentary 189.6 *transient*

momentary success 682.1 *success*
moment of force 330.11 *impulsion*
moment of inertia 56.9 *mass*
moment of truth 210.3 *critical
time*
momentous 210.7 *critical*,
233.11 *influential*, 611.5, 772.3
important
momentously 210.10 *critically*,
233.14 *influentially*
momentousness 772.6 *importance*
momentum 324, 56.9 *mass*,
235.4 *energy*, 330.11 *impulsion*,
337.29 *in reverse*
Mon 1 Peoples, **5** Languages
and Groups of Languages
monachal 825.8 *monastic*
Monaco 91 Countries
Monaco Gr at Monte Carlo 33.2
Formula 1 race
Monaco-Ville 93 Cities
monad 59.3 *organism*, 99.2
thing, 174.1 *one*, 260.2 *little
thing*, 367.4 *matter*
Monadhliath 95 Mountains
95.5 *British mountains*
monadic 4.16 *dialectical*, 174.11
one
monadism 99.1 *existence*
Monaghan 92 Counties, **93** Cities
mona monkey 77 Placental
Mammals
Monan 8 Deities
monandry 823.3 *types of marriage*
monarch 688.10 *person of authority*, 696.2 *sovereign*
monarchal 688.14 *governmental*
monarch butterfly 82 Insects
monarchical 12.9 *governmental*,
12.10 *governing*
monarchical absolutism 12.1 *government*
monarchical government 12.1 *government*
monarchist 693.12 *reactionary*
monarchy 12.1 *government*, 91.1
country, 688.7 *type of rule*
monastery 7.10 *priestly dwelling*,
301.2 *enclosed place*, 531.6 *privacy*, 634.1 *refuge*
monastic 825, 7.7 *monk*, 7.15 *religious*, 301.7 *enclosed*, 825.4
celibate person
monastically 301.8 *confinedly*,
825.12 *celibately*
monasticism 825
monastic order 825.3 *monasticism*
monatomic 57.35 *combined*
monazite 54 Minerals
monclinic 57.33 *crystalline*
Monel metal 57 Alloys
monetarism 4.7 *school of thought*
monetarist 4.11 *follower of a doctrine*, 4.14 *of a philosophy*,
699.6 *law-maker*
monetary 741, 12.13 *economic*,
14.6 *financial*, 737.14 *commercial*
monetary aid 662.6 *financial assistance*
monetary denomination 741.1
money
monetary policy 13.1 *economics*
monetary unit 741.1 *money*
monetary value 751.2 *value*
monetize 741
money 777 Phobias by Topic,
741, 742, 223.3 *something in
exchange*, 228.5 *positive stimulus*, 602.4 *financial resources*,
742.5 *wealth*, 746.1 *payment*
Money 741
money back 125.1 *compensation*
moneybag 605.4 *storage*, 741.20
money store
moneybags 742.10 *wealthy person*
money belt 258.9 *baggage*,
741.20 *money store*
moneybox 258.6 *box*, 605.4 *storage*, 741.20 *money store*
moneybroker 732.3 *lender*
moneychanger 223.4 *person who*

exchanges, 739.12 *wholesaler,* 741.17 *financier*

money coming in 721.4 *earnings,* 749.2 *money received*

money cowrie 81 Molluscs

money-dealer 741.17 *financier*

money dealings 14.1, 741.7 *finance*

money drawer 605.4 *storage*

moneyed 742.1 *wealthy*

moneyed class 742.11 *the rich*

moneyer 741.17 *financier*

money for a rainy day 721.5 *profit,* 749.3 *income*

money-grubber 721.7 *gainer,* 758.5 *miser,* 860.3 *selfish person*

money-grubbing 721.1 *gain,* 721.16 *greedy,* 758.1 *mean,* 860.4 *selfish*

money in the bank 741.6 *funds*

moneylender 606.3 *provider,* 732.3 *lender,* 739.12 *wholesaler,* 741.17 *financier*

moneylending 732.1 *lending*

moneyless 743.1 *poor*

moneymaker 721.7 *gainer,* 742.10 *wealthy person*

moneymaking 721.1 *gain,* 721.15 *gainful,* 742.5 *wealth,* 746.18 *profitable,* 878.15 *rewarding*

money man 741.17 *financier*

money management 14.1 *finance*

money market 14.1, 741.7 *finance*

money of account 741.1 *money*

money order 534.3 *correspondence,* 741.14 *paper money*

money power 14.1, 741.7 *finance*

money-raising 733.1 *borrowing,* 733.11 *borrowed*

money received 749, 730.2 *something received*

money-saving 756.4 *thrifty*

money spider 82 Arachnids

money-spinner 721.7 *gainer,* 742.10 *wealthy person*

money-spinning 721.15 *gainful*

money store 741

money supply 13.6 *economic factors*

money's worth 751.2 *value,* 754.1 *cheapness*

money to burn 610.3 *superfluity*

moneywort 84 Flowers and Flowering Plants

Monge 52 Scientists

monger 739.13 *retailer*

Mongol 5 Languages and Groups of Languages

Mongolia 91 Countries

Mongolian 68 Breeds of Cattle

Mongolic 5 Languages and Groups of Languages, 5.11 *family of languages*

Mongoloid 1.13 *racial*

Mongoloid race 1.6 *race*

mongoose 77 Placental Mammals

mongrel 77.9 *dog,* 133.5 *hybrid,* 133.12 *mixed*

mongrelism 133.1 *mixture*

mongrelize 133.8 *mix*

Monica Seles 40.7 *famous tennis players*

monies 741.6 *funds*

moniker 560.8 *name*

moniliasis 89.5 *fungal association*

monism 4.7 *school of thought*

monist 4.11 *follower of a doctrine,* 4.14 *of a philosophy*

monition 636.1 *warning*

monitor 65.7 *peripheral,* 79.2 *lizard,* 185.16 *time,* 192.14 *keep time,* 420.2 *hearer,* 420.15 *hear,* 435.11 *observer,* 435.15 *watch,* 632.9 *protect,* 653.16 *official,* 654.4 *adviser*

monitor lizard 79 Reptiles

monitory 517.13 *predicting,* 528.16 *informative,* 587.9 *dissuasive,* 636.8 *warning,* 654.7 *advising*

monk 7, 131.5 *pure person,* 139.14 *individualist,* 497.5 *believer,* 816.6 *unsocial person,* 825.4 *celibate person,* 861.15

good person, 863.4 *virtuous person,* 876.5 *pure person*

monkey 77 Placental Mammals, 179.9 *treble figures,* 330.15 *ram,* 539.22 *dupe,* 579.4 *capricious person,* 741.9 *British money,* 850.9 *butt*

monkey about with 657.5 *be cunning*

monkey around 506.8 *fool*

monkey business 539.7 *tricking,* 657.1 *cunning*

monkeyflower 84 Flowers and Flowering Plants

monkey jacket 295.11 *jacket*

monkey nut 86 Nuts

monkey on one's back 661.6 *burden*

monkey puzzle 85 Trees and Shrubs

monkey rail 74 Parts of a Ship

monkeys 77.16 *primate*

monkey's cousin 179.7 *double figures*

monkey shines 693.1 *disobedience*

monkey tricks 693.1 *disobedience*

monkey up 359.14 *climb*

monkey with 628.4 *impair*

monkfish 80 Fishes

Mon-Khmer 5 Languages and Groups of Languages

monkish 825.8 *monastic*

monkshood 84 Flowers and Flowering Plants, 631.12 *poisonous plant*

Monmouth 93 Cities

mono 174.11 *one,* 624.6 *infection*

monoacidic 57.36 *acid*

monoacidic base 57.9 *base*

monobasic 57.36 *acid*

monobasic acid 57.8 *acid*

monocarpellary 86.9 *of a fruit*

monocarpic 86.9 *of a fruit*

Monoceros 53 The Constellations

monochasial cyme 84.4 *flower head*

monochasium 84.4 *flower head*

monochromatic 174.12 *one-sided,* 444.10 *coloured*

monochromatic light 439.1 *light*

monochromatic radiation 56.26 *laser*

monochromator 56.91 *spectrometer*

monochrome 50.8 *painting,* 56.98 *physical,* 444.1 *colour*

monochrome television 534.21 *television*

monocle 174.10 *single thing,* 435.10 *visual aid*

monoclinic crystal 57.4 *crystal*

monoclonal antibody 630.4 *antidote*

monocoque 71 Motor Vehicle Parts, **73** Aircraft Parts

monocotyledon 83.3 *seed plant*

Monocotyledoneae 83.3 *seed plant*

monocotyledonous 83.16 *taxonomic*

monocropping 68.4 *arable farming*

monoculture 68.4 *arable farming*

monocycle 71.12 *bicycle*

Monod 52 Scientists

monodic 433.7 *harmonious*

monodist 569.2 *soliloquist*

monodrama 51.2 *play,* 569.1 *soliloquy*

monodramatic 569.5 *soliloquizing*

monody 48.7 *poem,* 49.13 *melody,* 433.3 *melodiousness,* 569.1 *soliloquy*

monoecious 84.12 *of flowers*

monofilament 67.1 *fibre*

monogamist 823.10 *married man*

monogamous 823

monogamously 823.24 *matrimonially*

monogamy 823.3 *types of marriage*

monoglot 564.19 *speaking*

monoglyceride 58.7 *fat*

monogram 5.13 *letter,* 44.4 *porcelain mark,* 44.11 *make ceramics,* 544.3 *means of identification*

monogrammatic 5.41 *lettered*

monograph 561.1 *dissertation*

monogynist 823.10 *married man*

monogyny 823.3 *types of marriage*

monohull 74 Sailing Ships and Boats, 174.10 *single thing*

monohydrate 57.10 *salt*

monokini 39.8 *swimwear,* 295.21 *beachwear*

monolingual 174.12 *one-sided,* 564.19 *speaking*

monolingual dictionary 5.28 *dictionary*

monolith 3.11 *relic,* 545.11 *monument*

monolithic 112.6 *conforming,* 134.16 *simple,* 371.6 *dense*

monolithic column 43.8 *column*

monologic 569.5 *soliloquizing*

monological 569.5 *soliloquizing*

monologist 51.27 *entertainer,* 174.9 *soloist,* 564.10 *speaker,* 569.2 *soliloquist*

monologize 564.15 *talk to oneself,* 569.3 *soliloquize*

monologue 51.2 *play,* 51.6 *scene,* 51.7 *dramaturgy,* 174.9 *soloist,* 564.8 *speech,* 569.1 *soliloquy*

monology 569.1 *soliloquy*

monomania 61.15 *compulsion,* 510.4 *delusion*

monomaniac 510.7 *insane person,* 695.5 *compulsive person*

monomer 57.21 *polymer*

monomeric 57.44 *polymeric*

monometallism 741.7 *finance*

monometer 57.20 *surface chemistry*

monomolecular 57.38 *reactive*

monophobia 777 Phobias by Name

monophonic 433.7 *harmonious*

monophonic sound 420.10 *sound quality*

monophony 433.3 *melodiousness*

monopolist 699.6 *law-maker,* 739.12 *wholesaler,* 860.3 *selfish person*

monopolistic 233.13 *dominant,* 665.8 *leagued,* 699.13 *restraining,* 723.8 *possessing,* 860.4 *selfish*

monopolistically 665.18 *cliquishly,* 723.10 *possessively*

monopolization 723.1 *possession*

monopolize 13.10 *trade with,* 233.10 *be a prevailing influence,* 302.7 *limit,* 699.9 *economize,* 723.7 *possess,* 726.7 *detain,* 738.1 *purchase,* 860.6 *be selfish*

monopolized by 723.9 *possessed*

monopolizer 723.5 *possessor*

monopolize the conversation 569, 565.8 *talk too much*

monopoly 13.6 *economic factors,* 147.4 *exclusiveness,* 302.2 *limiting factor,* 665.1 *party,* 699.2 *economic restraint,* 723.1 *possession,* 739.3 *selling*

Monopoly 42 Board Games

monorail 70.5 *transportable,* 72.1 **railway,** 327.12 *cableway*

monosaccharide 58.3 *carbohydrate*

monosemous 520.6 *meaningful*

monosemy 520.3 *comprehension*

monosodium glutamate 350.11 *food content,* 411.4 *flavour*

monostich 48.8 *part of poem,* 552.2 *outline*

monosyllabic 5.39 *of language,* 552.3 *concise,* 566.3 *sparing with words*

monosyllabically 5.48 *linguistically*

monosyllabic language 5.10 *language type*

monosyllabism 552.1 *conciseness*

monosyllable 5.17 *word*

monoterpene 58.20 *terpene*

monotone 49.21 *tone,* 66.3 *photograph,* 112.4 *monotony,* 112.8, 183.13 *monotonous*

monotonous 112, **183,** 110.17 *regular,* 116.14 *conforming,* 122.6 *equal,* 159.11 *continuous,*

412.5 *tasteless,* 426.16 *humming,* 555.1 *unemphatic,* 650.4 *fatiguing,* 788.4 *boring*

monotonous job 788.2 *boring thing*

monotonous life 112.4 *monotony*

monotonously 112, 110.20 *regularly,* 122.13 *equitably,* 183.23 *repeatedly,* 412.10 *without taste,* 426.19 *repeatedly,* 650.9 *tiringly,* 788.8 *boringly*

monotonousness 110.6 *regularity,* 112.4 *monotony*

monotony 112, 110.6 *regularity,* 159.5 *continuity,* 183.3 *repetitiveness,* 412.1 *tastelessness,* 555.2 *lack of emphasis,* 788.1 *boredom*

Monotremata 77.3 *egg-laying mammal*

monotrematous 77.25 *mammalian*

monotreme 77.3 *egg-laying mammal*

monounsaturated fat 58.7 *fat*

monovalent 57.35 *combined*

Monrovia 93 Cities

Monsarrat 48 Writers

monsieur 401.3 *male title of address*

monsignor 7.8 *priest*

monsoon 55 Winds, 55.17 *wind system,* 390.4 *air flow*

monsoon season 55.26 *raininess*

monster 168.10 *eccentric,* 241.4 *violent person or animal,* 259.9 *big thing,* 259.15 *big,* 786.5 *person of wonder,* 790.2 *ugly person,* 864.9 *wicked person*

Monster 53 The Constellations

monster man 259.10 *big person*

Monster Raving Loony Party 665.3 *political grouping*

monsters 777 Phobias by Topic

monstrance 10.14 *sacred object*

monstrosity 786.5 *person of wonder*

monstrous 168.14 *eccentric,* 259.15 *big,* 618.5 *harmful,* 786.8 *wonderful,* 790.4 *ugly,* 832.11 *cruel*

monstrous lie 538.4 *lie*

monstrously 259.20 *largely*

monstrousness 168.4 *unusualness,* 832.2 *cruelness*

montage 50.7 *picture,* 161.33 *putting together*

Montaigne 48 Writers

Montale 48 Poets

Montana 92 American States

Montanism 7 Christian Movements

Mont Blanc 95.6 *other major mountains and ranges,* 275.3 *mountain*

montbretia 84 Flowers and Flowering Plants

monte 42 Card Games

Monte Carlo 93 Cities, 33.4 *motor rally*

Monte Carlo method 52 Named Concepts

Monte Carlo rally 33.1 *motor racing,* 674.4 *race*

Montélimar 93 Cities

Monterey 45 Cheeses

Monterey Jack 45 Cheeses

Monterrey 93 Cities

Montesquieu 4 Philosophers

Montessori system 6.2 *educational system*

Monteverdi 49 Musicians and Composers

Montevideo 93 Cities

Montezuma pie 45.50 *Central American dish*

Montezuma's revenge 353.2 *defecation,* 624.8 *indigestion*

Montgolfier 52 Scientists

Montgomery 93 Cities, **93** Cities with 185.4 *term,* 187.2 *time period,* 269.8 *measure of time*

Montherlant 48 Writers, **48** Dramatists

monthlies 353.11 *menstruation*

monthly 110.17 *regular,* 110.20

regularly, 185.22 periodic, 187.7, 187.8 periodical, 187.13 for specified periods, 214.12 cyclic, 214.16 cyclically, 353.31 menstrual, 532.5 journal, 584.9 habitual

monthly bills 748.5 expense

monthly discharge 353.11 menstruation

months of the year 214.5 regular thing

monticule 95.1, 275.3 mountain

monticulous 95.7 mountainous

montmorillonite 54 Minerals

Montpelier 93 Cities

Montpellier 93 Cities

Montreal 93 Cities

Montrose 93 Cities

Montserrat 95 Mountains

montura 32.1 horse

monument 545, 200.7 thing of the past, 243.8 construction, 275.6 tall thing, 399.4 funeral objects, 511.3 memento, 543.5 indicator

monumental 3.15 historic, 50.25 sculptural, 95.7 mountainous, 259.15 big, 275.12 tall, 611.6 notable

monumentally 3.25 reportedly

monumental mason 50.17 sculptor

monumental sculptor 50.17 sculptor

monumental sculpture 50.12 sculpture

monument mason 399.3 funeral director

Monza 1,000 kilometres 33.3 sports car race

monzonite 54 Common Rocks, 54 Minerals

moo 432.1 animal cry, 432.4 cry

mooch 643.12 be inactive, 712.8 solicit money, 734.7 take

mooch around 328.1 move slowly

moocher 712.5 beggar

mooching 20.1 angling, 712.3 solicitation, 712.11 begging, 734.1 taking

mood 5, 5.30 syntax, 48.3 aspect of fiction, 103.4 nature, 105.4 state of mind, 234.2 attitude, 579.3 whim, 652.1 conduct, 759.4 emotion

moodily 215.9 unusually, 224.15 changeably, 830.13 sullenly

moodiness 215.2 unusualness, 224.2 irresolution, 830.1 sullenness

moody 215.5 unusual, 224.14 irresolute, 579.1 capricious, 659.14 troublesome, 770.6 depressed, 830.6 sullen

moody person 224.5 changeable person

Moog synthesizer 49 Musical Instruments

moolah 741.2 cash

moon 53, 53.18 satellite, 224.3 changeable thing, 294.11 uncover, 296.14 undress, 363.4 orbiting body, 439.4 natural light, 850.26 cock a snook

moon base 53.31 space travel

moonbeam 439.4 natural light

Moon Child 53 The Constellations

mooner 294.4 exposer

moon-faced 259.16 fat

moonfish 80 Fishes

moonflower 84 Flowers and Flowering Plants

moon goddess 8.5 deity

Moonie 7.5 Christian

mooning 294.3 nakedness, 296.1 undress, 296.11 exposed, 821.20 amorous, 850.7 sign of disrespect, 877.7 sexual assault

moonless 440.8 dark

moonlight 53.17 moon, 56.23 light, 439.4 natural light, 638.6 elude, 644.6 work

moonlight flit 345.7 departure, 638.1 escape

moonlighting 638.1 escape

moonlit 439.18 lit

moonraker 74 Sails

moon rat 77 Placental Mammals

moonrise 205.1 evening, 359.3 sun rise, 439.4 natural light

moonset 205.1 evening

moonshine 351.7 alcoholic drink, 439.4 natural light, 474.1 sophistry, 521.5 empty talk, 538.6, 540.13 nonsense, 874.12 alcohol

moonwort 88 Ferns

moor 74.10 sail, 87.2 grassland, 98.3 marsh, 98.6 lowland, 137.12 bind, 275.2 heights, 344.4 land

Moore 4 Philosophers, **18** Sporting Personalities, **48** Poets, **48** Poets

moored 225.10 stabilized

Moore turn 30.6 pommel horse

moorhen 78 Birds

Moorhouse 18 Sporting Personalities

mooring 36.10 sailing, 344.11 landing

mooring line 36.3 parts of a sailing boat

moorings 74 Rigging, 137.6 line

moorish 98.11 continental

Moorish 43 Architectural Styles

Moorish idol 80 Fishes

moorland 87.2 grassland, 98.6 lowland, 248.3 geographical space, 275.2 heights

moor to 135.10 link

moose 77 Placental Mammals, 37.5 game

Moosehead 94 Lakes

Moose Jaw 93 Cities

moot 117.10 disagreeing, 472.8 problematic, 473.10 arguable, 473.14 discuss, 477.14 questionable, 477.20 doubt, 491.1 uncertain, 491.18 be uncertain, 518.6 propound, 518.7 suppositional, 653.7 council, 716.3 discussion

mooted 472.8 problematic, 518.8 supposed, 594.17 developing

mooter 875.6 drug

moot point 472.2 issue, 477.4 difficult question

mop 392.15 dryer , 392.20 absorb, 621.10 cleaning object, 621.13 clean

mopboard 280.2 foot

mope 770.9 despair, 830.9 be sullen

moped 71.13 motorcycle

moper 766.3 dissatisfied person, 770.4 depressing person, 776.3 hopeless person, 788.3 boring person

mopiness 830.1 sullenness

moping 770.6 depressed, 821.20 amorous

mopishness 816.1 unsociability

mop one's brow 651.2 be refreshed

mopped up 684.7 completed

moppet 206.9 child

mopping up 621.2 cleaning, 684.3 elaboration

mopping-up 392.13 drying

mop up 392.20 absorb, 621.13 clean, 684.4 complete

mopy 816.8 unsociable

moquette 67 Natural Fabrics

morainal 54.60 glaciated

moraine 54.38 glacier, 132.2 residue, 143.8 bits and pieces, 275.4 mountain range, 326.10 transferred thing

morainic 54.60 glaciated

moral 843, 876, 876, 4.13 of philosophy, 5.21 catchword, 134.12 morally pure, 473.4 gist, 505.1 maxim, 654.3 precept, 654.7 advising, 847.8 dutiful, 857.4 honourable, 861.3 kind, 863.5 virtuous

moral badness 877.1 immorality

moral climate 876.1 morality

moral code 4.2 philosophical system, 7.1 religion

moral delinquency 877.1 immorality

moral dilemma 477.4 difficult question

morale 17.7 miscellaneous terms, 105.4 state of mind, 664.2 fellowship

morale-boosting 662.32 supportive

moral education 6.2 educational system

moral error 504

moral fibre 574.16 fortitude, 857.1 probity

moral goodness 863.1 virtue

moral guardian 134.6 prude

moral guideline 654.3 precept

moral imperative 847.4 sense of duty

moral injunction 654.1 advice

moralist 876, 4.10 philosopher, 652.3 well-behaved person

moralistic 876, 492.8 judging, 505.2 proverbial, 843.10 moral

moralistically 4.25 theoretically, 876.13 morally

morality 876, 51.2 play, 134.1 purity, 857.1 probity, 861.10 kindness, 863.1 virtue, 865.1 innocence

Morality 876

morality play 51.2 play

moralize 876, 4.22 propound a philosophy, 505.3 aphorize, 654.5 advise

moralizing 505.2 proverbial, 654.1 advice, 654.7 advising, 876.10 moralistic

moral laws 863.2 virtues

morally 876, 4.25 theoretically, 134.18 virtuously, 654.9 advisably, 847.18 on duty, 857.7 honourably, 861.23 nicely, 863.9 virtuously

morally pure 134

morally weak 864.13 venial

morally wrong 877.11 immoral

Moral Majority 876.6 moralist

moralness 876.1 morality

moral obligation 847.4 sense of duty

moral philosophy 4.6 branch of philosophy

moral purity 876, 134.1 purity

Moral Rearmament 7 Christian Movements, 876.2 good morals

moral rectitude 134.1 purity, 863.1 virtue

moral relativism 4.9 philosophical problem

moral rule 654.3 precept

morals 4.2 philosophical system, 7.1 religion, 134.1 purity, 471.5 ideology, 652.6 way of life, 847.6 ethics, 857.1 probity, 863.2 virtues, 876.1 morality

moral sense 847.4 sense of duty

moral sensibility 396.1 life, 519.3 insight

morals of an alley cat 877.3 sexual immorality

moral standards 876.1 morality

moral strength 863.1 virtue

moral support 284, 662.2 support

moral tone 863.1 virtue

moral turpitude 858.1 improbity, 864.2 vice, 877.1 immorality

moral virtues 863.2 virtues

moral weakness 864.3 venial sin

morass 98.3 marsh, 659.6 critical situation

moratorium 209.3 delayed action, 218.3 pause, 283.6 interruption, 677.1 pacification, 747.2 stoppage

moratorium on nuclear testing 677.1 pacification

Moravia 48 Writers

Moravian Church 7 Christian Movements

moray eel 80 Fishes

morbid 618.4 poor, 624.23 diseased

morbid curiosity 465.2 prying

morbidity 618.10 poverty, 624.1 ill health

morbidly 624.25 unhealthily, 626.8 unhygienically

morbido 49 Musical Terms

morbid psychology 61.1 psychology

morbific 624.23 diseased, 626.6 contagious

mordacious 832.14 hostile

mordacity 832.4 bitterness

mordancy 554.1 emphasis, 832.4 bitterness

mordant 67.6 dye, 237.12 strong to the senses, 444.4 pigment, 554.3 emphatic, 832.14 hostile

mordent 49.16 musical note

Mordvin 5 Languages and Groups of Languages

more 120.2 certain amount, 130.8 additional, 130.10 additionally, 175.1 plurality, 175.3 majority, 175.6 plural, 175.11 in majority, 851.27 bravo

More 4 Philosophers

more and more 121.10 by degrees, 128.8 increasingly

more bricks than bouquets 581.5 rejection

more convenient time 197.1 different time

more dead than alive 650.1 fatigued

more detail 612.8 trifle

moreish 350.27 edible, 411.7 tasty

more kicks than ha'pence 581.5 rejection

morel 89 Fungi, 45.33 vegetable

morello 86 Fruits

more of a hindrance than a help 661.13 hindering

more often than not 166.18 as a rule, 212.1 frequently

more or less 120.6 quantitative, 120.7 quantitatively, 124.11 on average, 264.7 nearly

moreover 130.10 additionally

mores 2.3 social environment, 584.4 custom, 652.6 way of life, 813.5 etiquette, 863.2 virtues, 876.1 morality

more so 126.12 superior, 128.8 increasingly

Moresque 43 Architectural Styles

more than a match for 126.12 superior, 235.13 powerful

more than enough 608.2 plentiful, 608.8 plenty, 608.9 enough, 610.2 overdoing it, 755.3 abundant

more than ever 126.17 supremely

more than half 175.3 majority

more than is fair 610.1 excess

more than is needed 610.3 superfluity

more than meets the eye 438.5 invisible thing, 527.6 latency

more than one 175.1 plurality, 175.6 plural

more than one bargained for 489.5 unexpectedness

more than one can afford 753.7 dear, 753.12 dearly

more than one's pocket can stand 753.7 dear

more than satisfy 608.4 suffice

more than the truth 538.1 untruth

more than you can shake a stick at 181.8 numberless

more that one can eat 608.8 plenty

more where it came from 608.8 plenty

Morgan 32 Breeds of Horse and Pony, **52** Scientists

morganatic 823.23 monogamous

morganatically 823.24 matrimonially

morganatic marriage 823.3 types of marriage

morganite 54 Gemstones

morgen 75 Some Foreign Units, **75** Some Foreign Units

morgue 397.8 after death, 399.1 burial

moribund 207.12 ageing, 207.14 aged, 397.18 dying, 624.22 sick

moribundly 207.16 maturely, 397.23 fatally

morin-chur 49 Musical Instruments
morion 54 Gemstones, 671.7 armour
Moriori 5 Languages and Groups of Languages
MORI poll 580.10 vote
Mormon 7.5 Christian, 823.10 married man
Mormonism 7 Christian Movements, 823.3 types of marriage
morn 204.1 morning, 359.3 sun rise
morning 204, 204, 156.2 creation
morning 212.1 frequently
morning 359.3 sun rise
morning after 155.6 aftermath, 874.15 crapulence
morning-after pill 247.3 birth control
morning coat 295.3 formal dress, 295.11 jacket
morning dress 295.3, 813.4 formal dress
morning-fresh 204.5 morning
morning glory 84 Flowers and Flowering Plants, 204.2 morning thing
morning light 204.1 morning
morning paper 532.4 newspaper
morning prayers 10.4 public worship
mornings 110.20 regularly, 204.8 in the morning
morning service 10.4 public worship
morning sickness 204.2 morning thing
morning star 53.10 star, 204.2 morning thing
morning thing 204
morning time 204.1 morning
Moro 5 Languages and Groups of Languages
morocco 293.14 animal covering
Morocco 91 Countries
moron 460.3 unintelligent person, 508.3 foolish person, 510.7 insane person
moronic 460.5 lacking intellect, 460.7 intellectually subnormal, 508.5 foolish
moronically 460.11 unintelligently
moropi 49 Musical Instruments
morose 415.7 splenetic, 770.6 depressed, 816.8 unsociable, 830.6 sullen
morosely 415.11 splenetically, 816.14 unsocially, 830.13 sullenly
moroseness 415.4 spleen, 816.1 unsociability, 830.1 sullenness
Morpeth 93 Cities
morph 875.6 drug
morpheme 5.17 word, 5.35 part of speech
morphemeic 5.44 grammatical
morphemically 5.52 grammatically
Morpheus 643.9 sleep
morphia 630.5 analgesic
morphine 62 Medication, 58.19 alkaloid, 630.5 analgesic, 630.8 drug, 643.10 soporific, 875.6 drug
morphogenesis 306.4 forming
morphogenetic resonance 427.1 resonance
morphogenic 306.9 formed
morphologic 5.38 linguistic, 306.9 formed, 382.12 organic
morphological 5.42 worded, 59.20 biological
morphologically 5.50 lexically, 59.29 biologically, 306.13 formatively, 382.18 structurally
morphological unit 5.17 word
morphologist 5.2 linguist, 59.19 life scientist, 382.10 anatomist
morphology 5.1 linguistics, 59.1 life science, 59.4 anatomy, 306.1, 382.3 form, 382 8 science of structure
morphophonemic 5.38 linguistic
morphophonemics 5.1 linguistics
morphophonology 5.1 linguistics

Morphy 18 Sporting Personalities
Morrigu 8 Deities
Morris chair 47.2 chair
morris dance 46.4 historic dancing
morris dancing 46.1 dancing
morrow 204.1 morning
Mors 8 Deities
Morse 52 Scientists
Morse code 5.8 artificial language, 534.8 data transmission, 534.27 signalling, 543.4 signal
morsel 143.7 piece, 173.3 fragment, 260.3 little piece, 350.14 mouthful, 411.3 appetizer
mortal 189.7 impermanent, 244.14 destructive, 397.20, 398.23 deadly, 400.7 person, 400.12 human, 862.9 detrimental, 866.7 sinful
mortal blow 157.13 ender, 862.2 affliction
mortal fear 777.1 fear
mortal horror 785.1 dislike
mortal illness 397.5 ways of dying
mortality 397.1 death, 397.12 death count, 400.2 human nature
mortality rate 397.12 death count
mortality table 397.12 death count
mortally 398.25 lethally, 400.15 humanly, 862.13 destructively, 864.20 immorally
mortally ill 624.22 sick
mortal remains 132.1 remainder, 397.11 dead person
mortal sin 683.3 personal fault, 864.4 sin
mortar 57 Laboratory Apparatus, 63.25 construction material, 63.26 masonry, 138.3 adhesive, 293.8 wall covering, 293.28 face, 338.8 missile, 604.2 building material, 680.12 historical guns
mortar attack 670.12 military attack
mortarboard 295.15 headgear, 544.5 uniform
mortgage 661.6 burden, 718.2 promise, 718.12 certify, 733.5 loan, 744.1 credit, 744.9 acquire credit, 745.3 loan
mortgage arrears 687.2 economic adversity
mortgage company 732.4 lending institution
mortgaged 718.7 guaranteed, 733.11 borrowed, 745.9 in debt
mortgage deed 715.2 purchase contract
mortgaged to the hilt 745.9 in debt
mortgagee 723.5 possessor, 732.3, 744.5 lender
mortgage holder 732.3 lender
mortgage one's house 661.12 burden, 733.7 borrow
mortgage repayment 745.3 loan
mortgage shark 539.17 cheat
mortgaging 733.1 borrowing
mortgagor 733.6 borrower, 745.6 debtor
mortician 397.9 person dealing with the dead, 399.3 funeral director
mortification 141.1 disintegration, 397.1 death, 515.1 disappointment, 806.9 humiliation, 806.13 disrepute, 840.2 apology, 850.8 indignity, 867.2 type of penance
mortification of the flesh 867.2 type of penance
mortified 515.9 disappointed, 806.3 humbled
mortify 141.3 disintegrate, 622.10 be dirty, 806.17 humiliate, 806.22 shame
mortifying 806.6, 850.16 humiliating
mortify oneself 840.6 apologize
mortify one's flesh 840.6 apologize, 867.5 do penance

mortify the flesh 869.5 be self-restrained
mortise 47.10 carpenter's term, 47.17 carpenter, 135.10 link
mortise and tenon 47.10 carpenter's term
mortise and tenon joint 135.5 joint
mortised 47.16 joined
mortise lock 137.8 fastening
mortiser 47.11 woodworking tool
mortmain 725.2 legal terms
mortuary 397.8 after death, 399.1 burial, 399.11 funeral
morula 59.15 developmental biology
mosaic 44.8 ceramic object, 50.7 picture, 50.24 pictorial, 69.12 pests and diseases, 85.10 tree disease, 113.3 diverse thing, 133.3 miscellany, 140.2 cooperation, 456.2 check, 792.2 pattern
mosaic gold 539.6 imitation
mosaics 42 Hobbies and Pastimes
mosasaur 79 Fossil Reptiles, 79.6 extinct reptile
moschatel 84 Flowers and Flowering Plants
Moscow 93 Cities, 93.6 other cities
Moseley 52 Scientists
Moseley's law 56 Named Laws, **57** Named Reactions
Moselle 96 Rivers, 96.5 other major rivers, 351.9 wine
Moses 136.8 person who separates
Moses basket 258.7 basket
mosey along 328.1 move slowly, 345.1 depart
MOSFET 64.19 transistor
moshupiane 49 Musical Instruments
mosiacs 50.1 art
mosque 10.11 place of worship
mosquito 82 Insects, 82.1 insect, 82.3 pest
mosquito boat 74 Ships and Boats
mosquito-infested 626.5 unhygienic
mosquito net 322.6 porous thing
mosquito netting 293.7 overhead covering
moss 88, 98.3 marsh, 453.8 greenness
Moss 18 Sporting Personalities
moss agate 54 Gemstones
moss ally 88.3 moss
moss-covered 88.6 mosslike
moss-grown 88.6 mosslike
Mossi 5 Languages and Groups of Languages
moss killer 69.8 weedkiller
mosslike 88
mosslike plant 88.3 moss
mosso 49 Musical Terms
moss pink 84 Flowers and Flowering Plants
moss plant 88
moss rose 84 Flowers and Flowering Plants
moss stitch 67.5 knitting
mosstrooper 679.9 guerrilla, 736.9 plunderer
mossy 69.17 botanical, 88.6 mosslike, 374.4 compressible
most 120.2 certain amount, 120.6 quantitative, 126.14 best, 175.3 majority, 175.6 plural, 175.11 in majority, 610.1 excess
most certainly 480.12 assuredly
most desirable 617.1 worthy
most important 611.5 important
most likely 488.11 probably
mostly 103.13 in essence, 124.11 on average, 142.13 on the whole, 164.31 overall, 166.18 as a rule
MOS transistor 64.19 transistor
most recent 201.10 new
Mosul 93 Cities
mot 505.1 maxim
Mot 8 Deities
MOT 71.21 miscellaneous motoring terms

MOT certificate 708.2 permit
mote 260.3 little piece, 370.7 light thing, 384.7 grain, 622.4 dirt
motel 71.21 miscellaneous motoring terms, 218.5 resting place, 256.10 hotel
motet 10.8 hymn, 49.5 sacred music
moth 82.1 insect, 244.7 agent of destruction
moth and rust 628.9 dilapidation
mothball 209.8 delay, 600.6 stop using, 605.6 store, 637.2 preserver
mothballed 209.10 held up, 236.10 powerless, 600.4 disused, 637.7 preserved
mothball fleet 679.22 navy
mothballing 209.3 delayed action
moth-eaten 82.12 verminous, 200.19 antiquarian, 202.12 olden, 628.13 dilapidated, 793.6 seedy
mother 5.39 of language, 156.26 produce, 207.9 woman, 226.7 Prime Mover, 243.9 producer, 245.5 propagator, 402.12 woman in the family, 405.10 comfort, 632.9 protect, 637.5 preserve, 662.20 sustain, 826.7 show endearment for, 831.8 be benevolent
Mother Carey's chicken 78 Birds
Mother Carey's chickens 636.1 warning
mother complex 61.18 complex
mother country 91.6 native land, 249.4 territorial division
mother earth 54.5 earth
Mother Earth 246.1 fertility
mothered 396.15 born
mother figure 61.25 surrogate, 222.2 substitute person
mother fixation 61.17 fixation
motherhood 245.4 development, 396.4 biological function, 402.12 woman in the family
Mother Hubbard 295.7 frock
mothering 662.3 sustenance
motherland 91.6 native land, 249.4 territorial division, 256.3 home
motherly 207.13 middle-aged, 821.17 loving, 831.6 benevolent
Mother Nature 8.3 God, 243.9 producer
mother of all battles 676.1 war
Mother of God 8.10 deified person
Mother of Parliaments 12.4 governing body, 653.11 British government
mother-of-pearl 456.5 variegated thing
mother-of-pearl inlay 47.9 decorative woodwork
Mother of the Muses 511.1 memory
mothers and fathers 42 Children's Games and Party Games
mother's darling 826.6 object of endearment
Mother's Day 214.6 annually celebrated day
mother's milk 351.5 milk, 387.3 body fluid
mother's ruin 351.7 alcoholic drink
mother's skirt 531.2 hiding place
mother substitute 222.2 substitute person
mother superior 7.7 monk, 696.1 master
mother surrogate 61.25 surrogate
mother symbol 61.24 symbolism
Mother Teresa 675.4 Nobel Peace Prize, 831.5 benevolent person
mother-to-be 245.7 obstetrics, 513.4 expectant person
mother tongue 5.4 parent language, 510.3 simplicity, 564.1 faculty of speech
Motherwell 93 Cities
mother wit 459.5 common sense, 507.2 intelligence

motherwort 84 Flowers and Flowering Plants
mothproof 632.6 *invulnerable*
mothy 82.12 *verminous*
motif 48.3 *aspect of fiction*, 433.1 *melody*, 472.1 *topic*
motile 90.7 *algal*, 324.16 *moving*
motility 324.1 *motion*
motion 777 Phobias by Topic, **324,** 56.8 *time*, 230.1 *operation*, 252.1 *displacement*, 324.15 *walk*, 353.2 *defecation*, 353.5 *faeces*, 472.2 *issue*, 543.11 *gesture*, 592.1 *plan*, 640.1 *action*, 642.1 *activity*, 652.1 *conduct*, 654.1 *advice*, 710.2 *tentative offer*, 712.1 *request*
Motion 324
motion after 324.10 *regular movement*
motional 324.16 *moving*
motion from 337.11 *retreat*
motion in front 324.10 *regular movement*
motion into 324.3 *motion towards*
motionless 325, 240.5 *inert*, 641.3, 643.1 *inactive*
motionlessly 325, 240.7 *inertly*, 643.15 *inactively*
motionlessness 325, 240.1 *inertness*, 641.1 *inaction*
Motionlessness 325
motion out of 324.4 *backward motion*
motion picture 526.9 *production*
Motion Picture Association of America 704.5 *abrogator*
motion-picture film 545.7 *recording*
motion-picture rating 709.2 *censorship*
motion round 324.5 *circuition*
motion sickness 71.21 *miscellaneous motoring terms*
motion towards 324
motivate 228, 226.10 *awaken*, 230.8 *activate*, 233.8 *influence*, 324.14 *set in motion*, 330.1 *impel*, 518.6 *propound*, 586.15 *persuade*, 599.5 *dispose of*, 640.4 *act*, 653.1 *manage*, 782.15 *cause desire*
motivated 228, 6.17 *educatable*, 586.20 *persuadable*
motivates 611.7 *be important*
motivating 228.11 *motivational*, 233.12 *appealing*, 586.19 *persuasive*
motivation 6.10 *educatability*, 226.1 *cause*, 228.1 *motive*, 233 *influence*, 324.2 *momentum*, 586.11 *motive*, 653.3 *management*
motivational 228, 324.16 *moving*
motivationally 324.18 *in motion*
motivator 228, 586, 226.7 *Prime Mover*, 496.12 *discoverer*, 640.3 *doer*, 653.13 *director*, 654.4 *adviser*
motive 228, 310, 586, 226.5 *reason*, 233 *influence*, 235.15 *full of energy*, 324.16 *moving*, 330.17 *impelling*, 338.17 *propulsive*, 463.4 *explanation*, 588.1 *intention*, 642.4 *energy*
Motive 228
motive force 61.22 *libido*
motiveless 229, 579.1 *capricious*
motiveless murder 521.3 *meaningless thing*
motivelessness 579.2 *caprice*
motive power 71 Motor Vehicle Parts, 235.4 *energy*, 324.1 *motion*, 330.11 *impulsion*, 337.29 *in reverse*
motivity 324.1 *motion*
motley 51.10 *comedy*, 51.30 *clown*, 113.2 *assortment*, 113.6 *assorted*, 133.3 *miscellany*, 133.12 *mixed*, 295.5 *fancy dress*, 456.1 *variegation*, 456.5 *variegated thing*, 456.6 *variegated*, 482.3 *indiscriminate*
motley collection 113.3 *diverse thing*
motley crew 133.3 *miscellany*

motmot 78 Birds
moto 49 Musical Terms
motocross 33.5 *motorcycle racing*, 674.4 *race*
motocrosser 33.8 *driver*
motocross racer 71.14 *cyclist*
motor 33.11 *racing*, 63.5 *dynamic structure*, 71.16 *car*, 235.6 *source of energy*, 324.16 *moving*, 603.4 *machine*
motorbicycle 71.13 *motorcycle*
motorbike 33.5 *motorcycle racing*, 33.11 *racing*, 71.13 *motorcycle*
motorbike and sidecar 71.13 *motorcycle*
motorbike race 33.5 *motorcycle racing*
motorbike racing 33.5 *motorcycle racing*
motorboat 74 Ships and Boats
motorcade 71.21 *miscellaneous motoring terms*, 159.8 *procession*
motorcar 71.16 *car*, 72.5 *locomotive part*
motor caravan 71 Motor Vehicles
motor coach 71.19 *bus*
motorcycle 71, 33.5 *motorcycle racing*, 33.11 *racing*, 326.5 *means of transport*
motorcycle class 33.5 *motorcycle racing*
motorcycle courier 71.14 *cyclist*
motorcycle race 33.5 *motorcycle racing*
motorcycle racer 33.8 *driver*
motorcycle racing 18 Sporting Activities, **33,** 674.4 *race*
motorcycling 71.1 *road transport*
motorcycling association 33.7 *racing governing body*
motorcyclist 33.8 *driver*, 71.14 *cyclist*
motordrive 66.18 *exposure time*
motor haulage 71.1 *road transport*
motor inn 256.10 *hotel*
motorized 603.8 *mechanical*
motorized division 17.4 *military organization*
motorized sled 71.10 *sled*
motorman 72.9 *railway worker*
motor-mouth 565.4 *talker*
motor mower 603.2 *garden tool*
motor neurone disease 624.17 *nervous disorder*
motor oil 386.4 *lubricant*, 395.9 *petroleum*
motor race 33.1 *motor racing*, 33.9 *race*
motor racer 33.8 *driver*
motor racing 18 Sporting Activities, **33,** 674.4 *race*
Motor Racing 33
motor-racing terms 33
motor rally 33, 33.1 *motor racing*, 674.4 *race*
motorscooter 71.13 *motorcycle*
motor show 526.6 *display*, 740.2 *fair*
motor sport 33.1 *motor racing*
motor torpedo boat 679.24 *warship*
motor transport 71, 71.1 *road transport*
motor trial 33.1 *motor racing*
motorway 41.1 *skiing*, 70.5 *transportable*, 71.2, 137.5 *road*, 327.3 *road*, 356.2 *passing along*
motorway restaurant 350.15 *eating place*
motorway services 218.4 *stopping place*
motorway sign 543.1 *sign*, 543.3 *indicator*
motory 324.16 *moving*
motte 275.3 *mountain*
mottle 85.10 *tree disease*, 456.4 *maculation*, 456.11 *variegate*
mottled 456, 133.12 *mixed*, 446.3 *white-haired*
mottled effect 133.3 *miscellany*
mottlement 456.4 *maculation*
mottling 456.4 *maculation*
motto 5.21 *catchword*, 505.1

maxim, 544.8 *heraldic device*, 876.7 *moral*
Motu 5 Languages and Groups of Languages
motzi 10.9 *prayer*
moue 543.3, 543.11 *gesture*
mouflon 77 Placental Mammals
mould 6.22 *educate*, 43.19 *decorate*, 44.11 *make ceramics*, 45.6 *kitchen equipment*, 50.21 *sculpt*, 54.43 *fossil*, 89.1 *fungus*, 103.4 *nature*, 105.1 *state*, 110.4, 110.9 *duplicate*, 112.10 *conform*, 119.2 *original*, 141.1 *disintegration*, 163.4 *type*, 165.3 *characteristic*, 167.9 *make conform*, 220.9 *transform*, 243.10 *produce*, 293.8 *wall covering*, 293.28 *face*, 306.2 *prototype*, 306.7 *form*, 374.13 *soften*, 382.3 *form*, 382.15 *shape*, 415.2 *unpalatability*, 547.11 *paint*, 599.1 *use*, 622.4 *dirt*, 626.1 *lack of hygiene*, 628.9 *dilapidation*, 631.14 *afflict*, 796.4 *design*, 796.8 *fashion*
mouldable 374.2 *pliant*
mould-breaking 201.11 *unfamiliar*
mould clay 44.11 *make ceramics*
moulded 36.10 *sailing*, 43.17 *structured*, 50.25 *sculptural*, 50.28 *sculpted*, 110.15 *duplicate*, 306.9 *formed*
moulded hull 36.3 *parts of a sailing boat*
moulder 89, 50.17 *sculptor*, 141.3 *disintegrate*, 202.17 *grow old*, 415.8 *sour*, 622.10 *be dirty*, 628.2 *decay*
mouldering 141.1 *disintegration*, 141.5 *disintegrated*, 202.12 *olden*, 628.13 *dilapidated*
mouldiness 618.10 *poverty*, 622.1 *dirtiness*, 628.9 *dilapidation*
moulding 43 Architectural Decoration, 50.12 *sculpture*, 110.4 *duplicate*, 138.9 *adhesive*, 243.1 *production*, 306.4 *forming*, 382.5 *structuring*, 792.2 *pattern*
mould the figure 138.6 *adhere*
mouldy 69.17 *botanical*, 89.9 *fungal*, 202.12 *olden*, 415.6 *unpalatable*, 618.4 *poor*, 622.7 *dirty*, 626.5 *unhygienic*, 631.16 *blighting*
Moulmein 93 Cities
moult 294.5 *shedding*, 294.12 *shed*, 296.6 *peeling*, 296.16 *peel*, 353.23 *cast*
moulted 294.9 *shed*, 296.12 *peeling*
moulter 294.7 *shedder*
moulting 294.5 *shedding*, 296.6, 296.12 *peeling*, 353.12 *dead tissue*, 353.32 *cast-off*
mound 161.26 *mass*, 161.37 *assemble*, 275.3 *mountain*, 316.3 *dome*, 396.9 *grave*, 545.11 *monument*, 671.8 *military defences*
mount 359, 32.1 *horse*, 32.4 *saddle horse*, 32.16 *ride*, 95.1 *mountain*, 95.10 *climb a mountain*, 128.4 *increase*, 135.11 *make love*, 275.3 *mountain*, 275.16 *rise*, 324.13 *be in motion*, 345.5 *set out*, 346.9 *enter*, 354.5 *inset*, 359.6 *mounting*, 359.13 *ascend*, 359.14 *climb*, 361.1 *raise*, 753.9 *be dear*
mountain 95, 275, 34.8 *mountaineering*, 41.12 *ski*, 54.7 *landform*, 120.2 *certain amount*, 161.26 *mass*, 225.4 *stable thing*, 259.7 *mass*, 318.2 *projection*, 375.8 *rough ground*, 721.3 *acquisition*
mountain artillery 680.11 *guns*
mountain ash 85 Trees and Shrubs
mountain beaver 77 Placental Mammals
mountain belt 54.20 *earth movement*
mountain bike 71.12 *bicycle*

mountain biking 18 Sporting Activities
mountain building 54
mountain cat 77 Placental Mammals
mountain circuit 33.6 *motor racing terms*
mountain climate 55.38 *climate*
mountain-climb 34.9 *mountaineer*
mountain climber 95.3 *mountaineer*, 359.11 *ascender*
mountain climbing 34.1 *mountaineering*, 95.1 *mountain*
Mountain Daylight Time 185.9 *time zone*
mountain dew 351.7 *alcoholic drink*
mountain-dweller 95.3 *mountaineer*
mountain-dwelling 95.7, 275.13 *mountainous*
mountained 95.7 *mountainous*
mountaineer 34, 34, 95, 95.10 *climb a mountain*, 359.11 *ascender*
mountaineering 18 Sporting Activities, **34, 34,** 95.1 *mountain*, 359.6 *mounting*
Mountaineering 34
mountaineering association 34
mountain goat 77 Placental Mammals
mountain hypothermia 34.2 *climbing dangers*
mountain infantry 679.16 *army unit*
mountain lake 94.1 *lake*
mountain lion 77 Placental Mammals, 37.5 *game*
mountain man 95.3 *mountaineer*
mountain mist 55.34 *mist*
mountain of money 741.3 *fortune*, 742.6 *money*
mountainous 95, 275, 120.6 *quantitative*, 259.15 *big*, 721.18 *acquisitional*
mountain range 275, 95.1 *mountain*, 215.3 *irregular thing*
mountain running 18 Sporting Activities
Mountains 95
mountain sheep 77 Placental Mammals
mountain skiing 41.1 *skiing*
mountain ski touring 41.2 *cross-country skiing*
Mountain Standard Time 185.9 *time zone*
mountain stream 96.1 *river*
mountaintop 34.5 *rock face*, 95.1 *mountain*, 275.2 *heights*, 279.1 *summit*, 531.6 *privacy*
mountain torrent 96.6 *river flow*
mountain warfare 676.8 *warfare*
mountain wind 55.12 *wind*
Mount Cook 95.6 *other major mountains and ranges*
mountebank 51.27 *entertainer*, 118.7 *imitator*, 474.6 *sophist*, 538.12 *cheat*, 539.15 *deceiver*, 656.10 *unskilled person*
mountebankery 474.5 *hypocrisy*, 540.4 *spuriousness*
mounted 32.17 *equine*, 361.11 *raised*
mounted band 49.26 *musical group*
mounted infantry 679.19 *cavalry*
mounted infantryman 679.20 *cavalryman*
mounted police 16.14 *police*, 32.15 *horse person*, 679.19 *cavalry*
mounted rifles 32.15 *horse person*, 679.19 *cavalry*
mounted soldier 679.20 *cavalryman*
mounted troops 32.15 *horse person*, 679.19 *cavalry*
Mount Elbert 95 Mountains
mount guard 632.9 *protect*
Mountie 16.17 *police officer*, 32.15 *horse person*
Mounties 16.14 *police*
mounting 53, 359, 51.12 *production*, 95.7 *mountainous*, 275.9 *high*, 284.2 *supporting part*,

324.7 *ascending motion*, 324.17 *directional*, 359.23 *rising*, 753.7 *dear*

mounting costs 753.3 *inflationary price*

Mount Logan 95.6 *other major mountains and ranges*

Mount McKinley 95.4 *US mountains*

mount money 32.12 *rodeo*

Mount Olympus 95.6 *other major mountains and ranges*

Mount Omei 10.13 *shrine*

Mount Palomar 95.4 *US mountains*

Mount Tai 10.13 *shrine*

mount the barricades 693.16 *be subversive*

mount the throne 12.12, 688.20 *take authority*

Mount Whitney 95.4 *US mountains*

Mount Wilson 95.4 *US mountains*

mourn 397.17, 399.8 *bury*, 770.8 *grieve*, 774.6 *lament*

Mourne 95 *Mountains*

mourner 399.3 *funeral director*, 774.3 *lamenter*, 835.4 *pitying person*

mourn for 774.6 *lament*

mournful 399.11 *funeral*, 440.11 *benighted*, 447.6, 770.5 *sad*, 774.4 *lamenting*

mournfully 774.4, 440.15 *darkly*, 770.11 *sadly*

mournfulness 774.1 *lamentation*

mourning 397.8 *after death*, 399.2, 399.11 *funeral*, 447.6 *sad*, 770.1 *sorrow*, 774.1 *lamentation*, 774.4 *lamenting*, 835.2 *condolence*

mourning black 813.4 *formal dress*

mourning clothes 295.3 *formal dress*, 440.4 *dark thing*, 447.9 *black thing*, 544.5 *uniform*

mourning colour 455.1 *purpleness*

mourning dove 78 *Birds*

mourn one's husband 824.10 *be widowed*

mouse 74 *Rigging*, 77 *Placental Mammals*, 65.7 *peripheral*, 260.4 *little person*, 542.11 *modest person*, 590.11 *hunt*, 673.2 *appeaser*, 760.9 *oversensitive person*, 777.6 *frightened person*, 779.2 *coward*, 806.16 *humble person*, 810.7 *modest person*

mousebird 78 *Birds*

mouse-coloured 448.1 *grey*

mouse deer 77 *Placental Mammals*

mousehole 322.7 *passageway*

mouselike 77.30 *rodent-like*, 806.1 *humble*, 810.11 *shy*

mouse nest 634.3 *animal shelter*

mouse opossum 77 *Marsupials*

mouser 77.10 *cat*, 590.6 *hunter*

mousetrap 68.14 *pest control*, 539.13 *snare*

moussaka 45.52 *Greek dish*

mousse 45.35 *dessert*, 370.7 *light thing*, 374.11 *soft thing*, 390.10 *air bubble*, 393.8 *pulp*

mousseline 67 *Natural Fabrics*

mousseline de laine 67 *Natural Fabrics*

mousseline de soie 67 *Natural Fabrics*

moustache 375.7 *rough thing*, 380.8 *sharp-pointed thing*

moustached 375.3 *barbed*

mousy 77.30 *rodent-like*, 445.7 *colourless*, 445.8 *drained of colour*, 448.1 *grey*, 559.10 *ugly*

mouth 98.9 *inlet*, 322.4 *body orifice*, 346.5 *entrance*, 350.16 *eating utensil*, 350.21 *eat*, 457.3 *external appearance*, 540.18 *be hypocritical*, 564.5 *organ of speech*, 807.2 *cheek*

mouthbrooder 80.2 *fish*

mouthful 350, 120.3 *container*, 411.3 *appetizer*, 564.8 *speech*, 567.1 *address*

mouthguard 19.3 *uniform*

mouthing 540.3 *hypocrisy*

mouth off 478.18 *answer back*

mouth organ 49 *Musical Instruments*

mouthpiece 26.2 *boxing*, 158.9 *middleman*, 524.7 *news interpreter*, 528.9 *informant*, 534.9 *telephone*, 678.4 *representative*

mouth-to-mouth 39.11 *swimming*

mouth-to-mouth resuscitation 39.3 *survival swimming*

mouthwash 62.11 *linctus*, 134.3 *purifier*, 417.2 *deodorant*, 621.9 *cleaning agent*, 630.3 *prophylactic*

mouthwatering 411.7, 763.4 *tasty*

mouth-watering 350.27 *edible*, 405.6 *pleasant*, 782.8 *desirable*

mouthwateringly 411.11 *tastily*

mouthy 565.6 *effusive*, 797.3 *affected*, 807.14 *cheeky*

movability 324.1 *motion*

movable 70.5 *transportable*, 324.16 *moving*, 326.17 *transferable*, 725.8 *propertied*

movable bridge 63.21 *bridge*

movableness 324.1 *motion*

movables 725.2 *legal terms*

movably 324.18 *in motion*

move 42.10 *play*, 70.4 *transport*, 216.8 *cause change*, 220.7 *convert into*, 228.9 *motivate*, 230.9 *take action*, 250.10 *settle*, 252.1 *displacement*, 252.14 *displace*, 324.13 *be in motion*, 324.14 *set in motion*, 326.15 *take away*, 330.1 *impel*, 336.1 *go forward*, 338.20 *propel*, 340.11 *attract*, 353.16 *defecate*, 366.22 *agitate*, 491.21 *change*, 518.6 *propound*, 586.15 *persuade*, 596.5 *attempt*, 640.1 *action*, 640.2 *deed*, 640.4 *act*, 642.12 *be active*, 652.9 *tactics*, 654.5 *advise*, 657.2 *stratagem*, 712.6 *request*, 835.11 *excite pity*

mourning black —

move across 356.11 *cross*

move along 356.9 *proceed*

move apart 343, 162.9 *be dispersed*

move at the speed of light 329.4 *be swift*

move at the speed of sound 329.4 *be swift*

move back 337.2 *retreat*

move close 264.9 *near*

moved 228.12 *motivated*, 252.8 *displaced*

move fast 329.4 *be swift*, 336.9 *maintain progress*, 345.4 *hurry off*, 642.12 *be active*, 648.2 *make haste*

move forward 338

move freely 698.14 *be free*

move heaven and earth 575.6 *persevere*, 644.8 *exert oneself*

move house 250.10 *settle*, 324.15 *walk*, 345.3 *quit*

move in 250.10, 255.15 *settle*, 256.18 *take up residence*

move in a circle 334.3 *circuit*

move into 723.7 *possess*

move it 324.19 *go*, 648.8 *hurry up*

move lock 252.14 *displace*

movement 664, 7.1 *religion*, 30.8 *floor exercises*, 51.7 *dramaturgy*, 161.16 *party*, 220.1 *conversion*, 230.1 *operation*, 252.1 *displacement*, 324.1 *motion*, 326.1 *transfer*, 353.2 *defecation*, 356.1 *passage*, 640.1 *action*, 642.1 *activity*, 665.3 *political grouping*

move off 345.5 *set out*

move on 188.7 *go on*, 338.21 *move forward*

move one's bowels 353.16 *defecate*

move out 598.2 *withdraw*

move over 324.13 *be in motion*, 324.15 *walk*

mover 586.14 *motivator*, 640.3 *doer*, 643.4 *adviser*

mover and shaker 640.3 *doer*

move round 315

movers and shakers 586.14 *motivator*

move sideways 305

move slowly 328, 645.4 *have leisure*, 788.6 *be boring*

move the goal posts 224.12 *be irresolute*

move the goalposts 578.2 *equivocate*

move through 356.8 *pass*

move to and fro 365.8 *oscillate*

move to compassion 835.11 *excite pity*

move together 34.9 *mountaineer*

move to tears 835.11 *excite pity*

move up 264.9 *near*

move with the times 201.18 *be trendy*, 208.11 *get ahead*, 216.7 *be changed*, 336.5 *develop*

movie 243.5 *work of art*

movie theatre 51.14 *theatre*

moving 324, 233.12 *appealing*, 235.15 *full of energy*, 252.8 *displaced*, 324.1 *motion*, 326.1 *transfer*, 330.17 *impelling*, 336.18 *ongoing*, 356.12 *passing*, 560.11 *descriptive*, 642.18 *active*, 759.14 *emotive*, 835.7 *pitiful*

moving apart 136.1 *separation*, 343.2 *parting*

moving pavement 71.4 *personal transport*, 326.5 *means of transport*

moving spirit 228.7 *motivator*

moving staircase 361.10 *elevator*

moving target 588.6 *objective*

moving together 34.3 *climbing technique*

moving van 71 *Motor Vehicles*

moving with the times 208.6 *getting ahead*

mow 68.17 *farm*, 69.15 *cultivate*, 87.12 *manage grassland*, 270.10 *shorten*, 376.11 *smooth*, 603.9 *use tools*, 605.1, 605.6 *store*, 830.4 *sign of irritableness*

mow down 244.9 *demolish*, 362.2 *flatten*, 398.18 *slaughter*, 676.13 *be at war*

mowed 270.8 *shortened*

mower 68.10 *farm tool*, 87.5 *grass-cutter*

mowing 270.2 *shortening*

mowing grass 87.1 *grass*

mowing machine 68.10 *farm tool*, 87.5 *grass-cutter*

mown 270.8 *shortened*

moxie 574.16 *fortitude*, 575.4 *stamina*, 642.4 *energy*

Mozambique 91 *Countries*

Mozarabic 43 *Architectural Styles*

mozarabic art 50 *Western Art Styles and Movements*

mozarella 45 *Cheeses*

Mozart 49 *Musicians and Composers*

mozzy 82.1 *insect*

MP 688.10 *person of authority*, 696.3 *leader*

Mr 401.3 *male title of address*

Mr and Mrs 823.9 *married couple*

Mr Average 124.7 *average person*, 164.9 *everyman*

Mr Big 126.5 *superior*, 611.4 *bigwig*

MRCA 73 *Types of Aircraft*

Mr Clever 809.7 *vain person*

MRI 60.7 *diagnosis*

mridanga 49 *Musical Instruments*

mRNA 58.10 *nucleoside*

Mr Nobody 502.4 *unknown person*, 803.1 *plebeian*

Mr Normal 509.3 *sane person*

Mrs 402.3 *female title of address*

MR scanner 630.14 *hospital*

Mrs Grundy 134.6 *prude*, 167.6 *conformist*, 788.3 *boring person*, 876.6 *moralist*

Mrs Mary Whitehouse 876.6 *moralist*

Mrs Mop 621.12 *cleaner*, 662.16 *home help*, 697.6 *domestic servant*

Mrs Spend Spend Spend 757.6 *spendthrift*

Mrs Warren's profession 877.5 *prostitution*

Mru 5 *Languages and Groups of Languages*

Mr Universe 237.6 *muscleman*

Mr X 502.4 *unknown person*

Ms 402.3 *female title of address*

MSDOS 65.8 *software*

M star 53.13 *luminosity*

MTI switch 534.28 *radar*

MTU 65.7 *peripheral*

Mtwaran 7 *Non-Christian Religions*

much ado 642.1 *activity*

Much Ado About Nothing 48 *Shakespeare's plays*

much ado about nothing 494.2 *overestimate*, 656.9 *bungling*

much greater than 52.88 *equal to*

much later on 209.17 *later*

much less than 52.88 *equal to*

much-married man 823.10 *married man*

much obliged 837.4 *grateful*, 837.9 *thank you*

much of a muchness 114.7 *similar*, 620.4 *ordinary*

much the same 114.7 *similar*, 122.6 *equal*

much up 622.11 *dirty*

mucilage 386.4 *lubricant*, 393.10 *mucus*, 395.5 *lubricant*

mucilaginous 393, 394.8 *viscous*

mucilaginously 393.27 *slimily*

mucilaginousness 394.1 *viscosity*

mucin 58.9 *protein*

muck 68.13 *fertilizer*, 68.17 *farm*, 69.15 *cultivate*, 353.5 *faeces*, 393.13 *mud*, 614.6 *refuse*, 622.4 *dirt*

mucked-up 151.19 *mixed-up*

muckfork 68.10 *farm tool*

muckheap 68.10 *farm tool*

muckhole 393.14 *puddle*

muckiness 622.1 *dirtiness*

mucking about 506.3 *tomfoolery*

mucking out 32.14 *horse-riding terms*

muck out 32.16 *ride*, 68.18 *practise livestock farming*, 621.13 *clean*

muckrake 854.12 *defame*

muckraker 533.4 *journalist*, 854.8 *defamer*

muckraking 68.5 *cultivation*, 533.3 *reporting*, 854.3 *defamation*

muckspreader 68.10 *farm tool*

muckspreading 68.5 *cultivation*

muck up 628.4 *impair*

mucky 622.7 *dirty*

mucoid 352.5 *of a secretion*, 386.10, 395.11 *oily*

mucopolysaccharide 58.4 *polysaccharide*

mucoprotein 58.9 *protein*

mucopus 353.7 *pus*

mucor 89 *Fungi*, 387.3 *body fluid*

mucous 352.5 *of a secretion*, 353.29 *salivating*, 393.22 *muci-laginous*

mucronate 380.1 *sharp*

mucronation 380.6 *sharpness*

mucus 393, 394, 352.2 *secreted substance*, 353.9 *saliva*, 386.4 *lubricant*, 387.3 *body fluid*, 395.5 *lubricant*, 622.4 *dirt*

mud 393, 54.27 *sediment*, 98.3 *marsh*, 374.11 *soft thing*, 391.8 *marsh*, 622.4 *dirt*

muda 9.1 *worship*, 10.3 *rite of worship*

mudbank 278.4 *shallow thing*

mud brick 44.9 *industrial ceramics*

mudder 32.7 *horseracing*

muddied 443.2 *shady*

muddily 94.10 *limnologically*, 98.13 *continentally*

muddiness 393, 391.7 *bogginess*, 443.6 *opaqueness*, 551.1 *obscurity*, 622.1 *dirtiness*

muddle 133.1 *mixture*, 133.3 *miscellany*, 133.9 *mix up*, 151.4 *litter*, 151.5 *confusion*, 151.21 *disorder*, 151.23 *confuse*, 153.2

disarrangement, 153.8 *disarrange*, 307.4 *disorder*, 460.10 *bemuse*, 482.8 *indiscriminateness*, 531.9 *disguise*, 551.1 *obscurity*, 551.3 *make obscure*, 659.5 *predicament*
muddled 151, 133.13 *mixed-up*, 151.12 *disordered*, 153.13 *disarranged*, 482.3 *indiscriminate*, 493.7 *misjudging*, 551.2 *obscure*, 874.2 *slightly drunk*
muddleheaded 151.16 *confused*
muddle through 336.7 *make one's way*, 682.7 *overcome obstacles*
muddle up 482.11 *not discriminate*
muddling 153.17 *disturbing*
mud-dried 622.7 *dirty*
muddy 393, 94.9 *lakelike*, 98.11 *continental*, 374.4 *compressible*, 391.11 *marshy*, 441.11 *tarnish*, 443.2 *shady*, 443.11 *make opaque*, 523.4 *difficult*, 551.2 *obscure*, 551.3 *make obscure*, 622.7, 622.11 *dirty*
muddy pool 94.2 *small lake*
muddy the waters 366.22 *agitate*, 531.9 *disguise*, 657.5 *be cunning*
muddy water 443.7 *opaque thing*
muddy waters 438.6 *that which makes invisible*
Mudéjar 43 Architectural Styles
mudfish 80 Fishes
mud flap 71.11 *bicycle part*
mud flat 98.3 *marsh*, 278.4 *shallow thing*
mudflow 54.26 *mass movement*
mudguard 71.11 *bicycle part*, 634.2 *shelter*
mud hen 78.3 *water bird*
mudhole 98.3 *marsh*, 393.14 *puddle*
mudlark 622.6 *dirty person*
mudpuppy 79 Amphibians
mud shoe 36.8 *punting*
mudskipper 80 Fishes
mudslinger 674.10 *contender*, 854.8 *defamer*
mudslinging 674.1 *contention*, 854.3 *defamation*, 854.16 *defamatory*
mudstone 54 Common Rocks
mud-wrestler 622.6 *dirty person*
muesli 45.40 *breakfast cereal*
muezzin 7.8 *priest*, 543.8 *signer*
muezzin's call 543.6 *word*
muezzin's cry 10.4 *public worship*
muff 295.25 *accessories*, 504.10 *blunder*, 504.19 *make a mistake*, 656.7 *be clumsy*, 656.9 *bungling*, 656.10 *unskilled person*
muffer 656.10 *unskilled person*
muffin 45.39 *loaf*
muffle 421, 238.7 *weaken*, 244.8 *destroy*, 422.2 *silence*, 424.6, 428.7 *mute*, 531.8 *conceal*, 563.15 *strike dumb*
muffled 238.13 *insufficient*, 424.4 *faint*, 428.1 *faint-sounding*, 428.2 *nonresonant*, 527.2 *concealed*, 563.10 *low-voiced*
muffled drum 399.2 *funeral*, 543.4 *signal*
muffled sound 424.1 *faintness*
muffled tones 424.1 *faintness*
muffled voice 563.4 *whispering*
muffle kiln 44.6 *ceramic workshop*
muffler 71 Motor Vehicle Parts, 295.14 *neckwear*
muffuletta 45.11 *sandwich*
mufti 295.4, 814.6 *informal dress*
mug 44.8 *ceramic object*, 241.8 *use violence*, 258.13 *drinking vessel*, 303.2 *face*, 351.10 *drink container*, 539.22 *dupe*, 670.5 *strike*, 736.12 *steal*, 767.14 *take away*, 850.9 *butt*
MUGA scan 60.7 *diagnosis*
mugger 79 Reptiles, 16.40 *lawbreaker*, 241.4 *violent person or animal*, 670.19 *attacker*, 693.9 *criminal*, 695.4 *coercive person*, 734.6 *taker*, 736.8 *thief*, 832.8 *malefactor*

mugginess 391.3 *humidity*
mugging 670.16 *terrorist attack*, 736.1 *stealing*
muggles 875.6 *drug*
muggy 55.52 *humid*, 391.9 *moist*, 408.11 *warm*, 626.5 *unhygienic*
muggy spell 55.23 *heat*
muggy weather 55.23 *heat*
mughlai 45.49 *Indian dish*
mug shot 66.4 *portrait*, 303.2 *face*
mug up 51.35 *rehearse*
mugwump 333.3 *moderate person*, 482.10 *impartial person*, 698.7 *free person*
mugwumpish 242.7 *politically moderate*, 482.2 *impartial*
mugwumpism 482.7 *impartiality*
Muharram 10.16 *religious festival*
Muir 48 Poets
mujtahid 7.8 *priest*
mukdam 7.8 *priest*
mulatto 1.6 *race*, 1.13 *racial*, 133.5 *hybrid*
mulberry 86 Fruits, 450.7 *red thing*, 455.6 *purple*
mulch 68.17 *farm*, 69.7 *fertilizer*, 69.15 *cultivate*, 246.3 *fertilizer*, 246.7 *make fertile*, 293.2 *cover*
mulct 879.1 *punish*, 879.7 *punishment*
mulctable 879.22 *punishable*
mule 77 Placental Mammals, 133.5 *hybrid*, 577.8 *obstinate person*, 642.10 *busy person*
mule deer 77 Placental Mammals
mules 161 Collective Names by Animal, 295.19 *footwear*
mule train 71.9 *animal transport*
muliebrity 402.1 *female sex*
mulish 77.33 *ungulate*, 570.8 *wilful*, 577.1 *obstinate*
mulishly 577.9 *be obstinate*
mulishness 570.3 *wilfulness*, 577.5 *obstinacy*
mull 98.5 *peninsula*, 414.8 *sweeten*
mullah 6.4 *educator*, 7.8 *priest*
mulled wine 351.7 *alcoholic drink*, 414.5 *sweet drink*
mullein 84 Flowers and Flowering Plants
muller 384.11 *pulverizer*
Müller 52 Scientists
Müller 52 Scientists
mullet 80 Fishes, 45.18 *sea fish*, 544.8 *heraldic device*
mulligatawny 45.13 *soup*
Mulliken 52 Scientists
Mullingar 93 Cities
mullion 43 Architectural Decoration
mullite 54 Minerals
mullock 614.6 *refuse*, 622.4 *dirt*
mull over 461.13 *concentrate*
multiangular 52.82 *polygonal*
multicellular 59.23 *cellular*
multicentre bond 57.11 *chemical bond*
multicolour 444.2 *colourfulness*
multicoloured 113.6 *assorted*, 444.10 *coloured*, 456.6 *variegated*
multicolour yawn 349.23 *vomiting*
multicultural 133.12 *mixed*
multiemployer agreement 15.1 *industrial relations*
multifaceted 113.6 *assorted*, 175.7 *various*, 305.6 *side*
multifacial 52.84 *cubic*
multifarious 113.6 *assorted*, 175.7 *various*, 181.5 *multitudinous*
multifariously 175.10 *plurally*, 181.13 *numerously*
multifariousness 175.2 *multiplicity*
multiflagellate 90.7 *algal*
multiflorous 69.16 *horticultural*
multifold 175.8 *multiplicative*, 181.5 *multitudinous*
multifoldness 181.1 *multiplicity*
multiform 113.6 *assorted*, 115.4 *dissimilar*, 175.7 *various*
multiformity 113.2 *assortment*,

115.1 *dissimilarity*, 175.2 *multiplicity*
multigravida 245.7 *obstetrics*
multihull 74 Sailing Ships and Boats, 36.10 *sailing*
multihull racing 36.1 *sailing*
multilateral 175.7 *various*, 715.7 *contractual*
multilateralism 175.2 *multiplicity*
multilateralist 175.5 *pluralist*
multilaterally 175.10 *plurally*, 715.8 *contractually*
multilingual 5.2 *linguist*, 5.38 *linguistic*, 175.7 *various*, 524.17 *translational*, 564.19 *speaking*
multilingual dictionary 5.28 *dictionary*
multilingualism 5.1 *linguistics*
multilingually 5.48 *linguistically*
multiloquence 565.1 *talkativeness*
multiloquent 565.5 *talkative*
multiloquy 565.1 *talkativeness*
multimillion 179.11 *million*
multimillionaire 179.11 *million*, 686.4 *prosperous person*, 742.10 *wealthy person*
multinational 175.7 *various*, 233.13 *dominant*
multinational company 233.6 *group influence*
multinomial 52.76 *functional*
multinucleate 59.24 *nuclear*
multiparous 246.5 *fertile*
multipartite 136.15 *separate*
multiplane 73 Types of Aircraft
multiple 52.17, 175.4 *multiplication*, 175.6 *plural*, 175.8 *multiplicative*, 181.5 *multitudinous*
multiple collision 330.12 *collision*
multiple fruit 86.2 *botanical fruit*
multiple image 66.4 *portrait*
multiple independently targeted re-entry vehicle 680.5 *missile weapon*
multiple personality 61.8 *disordered personality*, 61.16 *dissociation*, 175.2 *multiplicity*
multiple sclerosis 373.6 *solidification*, 624.17 *nervous disorder*
multiple span 63.21 *bridge*
multiple star 53.9 *constellation*
multiple store 740.8 *store*
multiplexing 65.14 *data transfer*, 65.17 *computing term*
multiplex transmission 534.14 *radio transmission*
multipliable 261.9 *enlargeable*
multiplicand 52.17, 175.4 *multiplication*
multiplication 52, 175, 128.1 *increase*, 170.1 *calculation*, 245.1 *reproduction*, 261.1 *growth*
multiplication sign 52.13 *mathematical symbol*, 543.1 *sign*
multiplication table 170.5 *computer*, 175.4 *multiplication*
multiplication tables 52.17 *multiplication*
multiplicative 175
multiplicity 175, 181, 113.1 *diversity*, 113.2 *assortment*
multiplied 175.8 *multiplicative*
multiplied by 52.88 *equal to*
multiplier 52.17, 175.4 *multiplication*
multiplier reel 20.3 *fishing tackle*
multiply 245, 52.91 *add*, 89.12 *mushroom*, 128.4 *increase*, 128.5 *make bigger*, 170.9 *add*, 175.9 *pluralize*, 175.10 *plurally*, 181.13 *numerously*, 243.10 *produce*, 246.6 *be fertile*, 261.6 *become bigger*
multiply by four 178.11 *quadruple*
multiply by three 177.10 *triple*
multiply by two 176.15 *double*
multiplying 261.8 *growing*
multiplying by three 177.4 *triplication*
multiply out 52.91 *add*
multipoint tool 63.9 *machine tool*
multipurpose 113.6 *assorted*, 175.7 *various*, 613.1 *useful*
multiracial 133.12 *mixed*, 175.7 *various*
multiracial state 400.11 *nation*

multirole 175.7 *various*
multisonous 423.6 *loud*
multistage 266.7 *layered*
multistage rocket 53.35 *rocketry*
multistorey 43.12 *structural*, 256.16 *manorial*, 275.9 *high*
multistorey building 43.3, 63.20 *building*
multistorey car park 275.6 *tall thing*
multistranded wire 64.27 *wire*
multitasking 65.15 *network*
multitude 181, 120.1 *quantity*, 161.20 *crowd*, 164.11 *general public*, 175.2 *multiplicity*, 181.4 *throng*, 679.18 *army of people*
Multitude 181
multitudinal 181.5 *multitudinous*
multitudinous 181, 175.6 *plural*, 212.3 *frequent*, 608.3 *filled*
multitudinously 175.10 *plurally*, 181.13 *numerously*, 212.1 *frequently*
multitudinousness 175.2, 181.1 *multiplicity*, 212.4 *frequency*
multivariate analysis 52.55 *statistical methods*
multivocal 520.3 *comprehension*, 520.6 *meaningful*
multiwire cable 534.6 *telecommunication*
multure 384.4 *pulverization*
mum 402.12 *woman in the family*, 422.3 *silent*, 563.11 *speechless*, 566.1 *taciturn*
mumble 428.4 *faint sound*, 428.8 *sound faint*, 563.4 *whispering*, 563.16 *speak in a low voice*, 564.13 *speak in a particular way*
mumbled 428.1 *faint-sounding*
mumbling 428.4 *faint sound*, 523.11 *unintelligibility*, 563.10 *low-voiced*
mumbo jumbo 11.5 *spell*, 521.1 *lack of meaning*, 539.9 *sleight of hand*, 551.1 *obscurity*
Mumbo Jumbo 8 Deities
mumbo-jumbo 539.40 *illusory*, 551.2 *obscure*
Mu metal 56.59 *ferromagnetism*
mummer 51.22 *actor*, 539.15 *deceiver*
mummers' play 51.2 *play*
mummery 51.20 *acting*, 539.12 *disguise*, 540.1 *hypocrisy*, 812.3 *ceremony*
mummification 392.13 *drying*, 399.1 *burial*, 637.1 *preservation*
mummified 392.3 *dried-up*, 397.22 *post-mortem*, 399.10 *buried*, 637.7 *preserved*
mummifier 637.4 *preservationist*
mummify 392.21 *dry up*, 399.8 *bury*, 637.5 *preserve*
mummy 397.11 *dead person*, 402.12 *woman in the family*, 637.3 *preserved thing*
mummy-case 399.1 *burial*
mummy chamber 399.6 *grave*
mummy's boy 238.4 *weakling*, 401.9 *offensive terms for homosexual*
mummy wrapping 399.4 *funeral objects*
mumpish 830.7 *irritable*
mumpishness 830.1 *sullenness*
mumps 624.6 *infection*
mum's the word 566.11 *hush*
munch 350.21 *eat*
muncheel 71.6 *litter*
munching 350.1 *eating*
Munda 1 Peoples, **5** Languages and Groups of Languages
mundane 110.17 *regular*, 116.15 *conventional*, 183.13 *monotonous*, 556.1, 556.1 *simple*
mundaneness 556.4 *simplicity*, 860.1 *selfishness*
mundanugu 11.4 *witch*
mung bean 45 Vegetables
Munich 93 Cities
municipal 16.48 *jurisdictional*, 92.6 *administrative*, 93.14 *urban*, 249.17 *national*
municipal building 93

municipal council 653.8 *British administrative council*
municipal court 16.21 *US court*
municipal court judge 16.24 *US judge*
municipal garden 69.2 *garden*
municipal hospital 60.10 *hospital*
municipality 16.2 *jurisdiction,* 92.4 *community,* 93.1 *city,* 249.11 *settlement*
municipally 93, 16.86 *jurisdictionally,* 92.8 *administratively,* 249.20 *nationally*
municipal tax 751.7 *tax*
munificence 755.5 *generosity,* 833.1 *philanthropy,* 859.2 *unselfishness*
munificent 755.1 *generous,* 833.6 *philanthropic,* 859.5 *unselfish*
munificently 833.8 *philanthropically,* 859.9 *unselfishly*
munificentness 833.1 *philanthropy*
muniments 545.2 *certificate*
munitions 602.2 *supplies,* 680.2 *arms*
Munster 92 Counties
munt 91 Names for Inhabitants
Munt 8 Deities
Munthe 48 Writers
muntjac 77 Placental Mammals
Muntz metal 57 Alloys
muon 56.77 *elementary particle,* 260.2 *little thing*
Muong 5 Languages and Groups of Languages
Murakōz 32 Breeds of Horse and Pony
mural 50.8 *painting*
mural painter 50.16 *artist*
murder 161 Collective Names for Birds and Animals, **398, 398,** 16.39 *crime,* 78.13 *assemblage of birds,* 100.14 *cause not to exist,* 218.8 *cause to cease,* 241.2 *physical violence,* 241.3 *instance of violence,* 244.2 *destroying,* 244.8 *destroy,* 397.6, 398.1 *killing,* 398.16 *kill,* 607.2 *lay waste,* 693.2 *violation of the law,* 693.15 *be disobedient,* 832.7 *act of malevolence,* 832.17 *kill,* 862.5 *evil thing,* 864.7 *criminality,* 866.10 *sin,* 879.5 *execute*
murdered 397.19 *dead*
murderer 398, 16.40 *lawbreaker,* 241.4 *violent person or animal,* 244.6 *destroyer,* 398.10 *killer,* 607.7 *destroyer,* 631.13 *oppressor,* 670.19 *attacker,* 693.9 *criminal,* 822.8 *hated person,* 832.8 *malefactor,* 862.6 *evil person,* 864.9 *wicked person,* 879.17 *punisher*
murderers' row 22.5 *batting terms*
murderess 398.11 *murderer*
murdering the Queen's English 504.11 *grammatical error*
murder in the dark 42 Children's Games and Party Games
murder most foul 398.2 *murder*
murderous 398, 241.6 *violent,* 397.20 *deadly,* 832.11 *cruel,* 866.7 *sinful*
murderously 398.25 *lethally*
murderousness 241.1 *violence*
murder weapon 398.2 *murder*
Murdoch 4 Philosophers, **48** Writers
murex 81 Molluscs, 450.6 *red pigment*
Murgese 32 Breeds of Horse and Pony
muricate 375.1 *rough,* 380.4 *toothed*
Murigen 8 Deities
murine 77.30 *rodent-like*
murk 441, 440.1 *darkness,* 440.7 *spiritual darkness,* 448.7 *dullness*
murkily 448.9 *greyly,* 551.4 *obscurely*
murkiness 440.1 *darkness,* 441.2 *murk,* 443.6 *opaqueness,* 551.1 *obscurity*

murky 441, 371.7 *condensed,* 440.8 *dark,* 440.11 *benighted,* 443.2 *shady,* 447.2 *dark,* 448.3 *dull,* 523.4 *difficult,* 527.2 *concealed,* 551.2 *obscure,* 622.7 *dirty*
Murmi 5 Languages and Groups of Languages
murmur 55.58 *blow,* 96.7 *flow,* 424.1 *faintness,* 424.5 *sound faint,* 426.2 *humming,* 426.9 *hum,* 428.4 *faint sound,* 428.8 *sound faint,* 527.14 *imply,* 563.4 *whispering,* 563.16 *speak in a low voice,* 564.7 *utterance,* 564.13 *speak in a particular way*
murmuration 161 Collective Names for Birds and Animals, 428.4 *faint sound*
murmured 428.1 *faint-sounding*
murmuring 424.4 *faint,* 563.10 *low-voiced*
murmur of discontent 636.1 *warning*
Murphy's law 166.3 *rule of nature*
murrain 624.18 *veterinary disease*
Murray 96 Rivers
Murray cod 80 Fishes
Murray Grey 68 Breeds of Cattle
murre 78 Birds
murrey 450.1 *red,* 455.6 *purple,* 544.8 *heraldic device,* 544.13 *heraldic*
Murrumbidgee 96 Rivers
Murugan 8 Deities
murumbu 49 Musical Instruments
musaph 10.4 *public worship*
Musca 53 The Constellations
Muscadet 351.9 *wine*
muscadine 86 Fruits
muscat 86 Fruits
Muscat 93 Cities
muscatel 414.5 *sweet drink*
Musci 88.3 *moss*
muscle 137.6 *line,* 180.7 *attendant,* 235.1 *power,* 237.1 *strength,* 316.2 *bulge,* 644.4 *exertion*
muscle-bound 373.2 *tough*
muscle cell 59.7 *cell*
muscle in 235.10 *be powerful,* 346.10 *invade*
muscleman 237, 401.6 *macho man*
muscle power 235.4 *energy,* 644.4 *exertion*
muscle relaxant 62.4 *drug type,* 630.4 *antidote*
muscles 378.8 *physical strength*
muscovado 449.5 *brown thing*
muscovite 54 Minerals
Muscovy 68 Breeds of Fowl
Muscovy duck 78 Birds
muscular 237.9 *physically strong,* 373.2 *tough,* 378.4 *powerful,* 401.17 *male*
muscular dystrophy 624.17 *nervous disorder*
muscularity 237.1 *strength,* 378.8 *physical strength*
muscularly 378.13 *powerfully*
muscular rheumatism 624.16 *rheumatism*
musculature 237.1 *strength*
musculoskeletal disease 624.4 *disease*
muse 4.20 *philosophize,* 8.5 *deity,* 519.2 *inspiration,* 519.15 *fantasize,* 786.12 *wonder whether*
muse of dancing 46.1 *dancing*
musette 49 Musical Instruments, **49** Musical Instruments
museum 161.31 *exhibition,* 526.8 *showplace,* 605.5 *collection*
museum piece 3.11 *relic,* 50.6 *work of art,* 200.7 *thing of the past,* 202.5 *old thing,* 526.7 *showpiece,* 617.8 *exceller*
Musgrave 95 Mountains
mush 45.40 *breakfast cereal,* 393.8 *pulp,* 821.2 *romantic love*
mushiness 393.4 *pulpiness*
mushroom 89, **89,** 45.33, 69.11

vegetable, 89.4 *fungal body,* 128.4 *increase,* 246.6 *be fertile,* 261.6 *become bigger,* 446.1 *white,* 449.1 *brown,* 721.10 *augment*
mushroom bulb 439.6 *electric light*
mushroom cloud 89.2 *mushroom,* 680.1 *weapon,* 680.16 *bomb*
mushroom eating 89.8 *study of fungi*
mushroom farm 68.6 *farm,* 89.8 *study of fungi*
mushroom farmer 89.8 *study of fungi*
mushroom grower 69.13 *horticulturist,* 89.8 *study of fungi*
mushroom growing 69.1 *horticulture*
mushrooming 261.8 *growing,* 359.4 *taking off*
mushroom soup 45.13 *soup*
mushy 393.18 *pulpy*
music 777 Phobias by Topic, **49,** 32.8 *hunting,* 56.17 *sound,* 140.2 *cooperation*
Music 49
musica ficta 433.3 *melodiousness*
musical 49, 51.3 *musical drama,* 51.37 *dramatic,* 420.11 *aural,* 433.6 *melodious,* 526.9 *production*
musical arrangement 152
musical chairs 42 Children's Games and Party Games
musical comedy 51.3 *musical drama,* 771.4 *entertainment*
musical composition 243.1 *production,* 243.5 *work of art*
musical cry 431
musical director 49.24 *musician*
musical dissonance 434
musical drama 51
musical ear 420.1 *hearing*
musical genius 688.11, 696.10 *expert*
musical group 49
musical instrument 49, 56.18 *source of sound*
musical interval 56.20 *musical note*
musicality 49.1 *music,* 420.1 *hearing,* 433.3 *melodiousness*
musicalness 49.1 *music,* 433.3 *melodiousness*
musical notation 543.1 *sign,* 547.1 *representation*
musical note 49, 56, 49.17 *notation*
musical quality 433.3 *melodiousness*
musical repetition 426
musical scale 56.20 *musical note*
musical structure 382.9 *artistic structure*
musical texture 433.3 *melodiousness*
musical time 185
music drama 49.4 *opera,* 51.3 *musical drama*
music hall 51.4 *show business,* 51.5 *show,* 51.14 *theatre*
musician 49, 243.9 *producer,* 646.1 *worker,* 655.4 *skilled person*
musicianly 49.29 *musical*
musicianship 49.1 *music,* 243.1 *production*
music loving 49.29 *musical*
music making 49
music master 49.24 *musician*
musicography 49.14 *harmonics*
musicology 49.14 *harmonics*
musicophile 49.29 *musical*
musicophobia 777 Phobias by Name
music review 524.3 *criticism*
music room 6.15 *schoolroom,* 420.3 *auditorium*
music school 6.12 *educational institution*
music stand 284.2 *supporting part*
music teacher 49.24 *musician*
music theory 49.14 *harmonics*
Musil 48 Writers
musing 4.4 *philosophical investi-*

gation, 4.17 *thoughtful,* 461.3 *thoughtfulness,* 461.10 *speculative*
musique concrète 49.3 *classical music*
musi-yaki 45.54 *other dishes*
musk 352.2 *secreted substance,* 418.1 *fragrance,* 418.3 *incense*
musk deer 77 Placental Mammals
muskellunge 80 Fishes, 20.4 *American game fish*
musket 338.9 *firearm,* 680.10 *historical gun*
musketeer 338.15 *shooter,* 679.13 *historical soldiery*
musketry 338.6 *shooting,* 670.15 *firing,* 680.2 *arms*
musketry practice 676.6 *art of war*
musk gland 77.2 *mammalian characteristic*
muskily 418.7 *fragrantly*
muskiness 418.1 *fragrance*
muskmelon 86 Fruits
Muskogean 5 Languages and Groups of Languages
musk ox 77 Placental Mammals
muskrat 77 Placental Mammals
musk rose 84 Flowers and Flowering Plants
musky 418.4 *fragrant*
Muslim 7.6 *non-Christian,* 7.16 *denominational*
muslin 67 Natural Fabrics, 274.11 *fineness,* 288.4 *textile,* 441.2 *murk,* 442.8 *transparent thing*
musophobia 777 Phobias by Name
mussel 81 Molluscs, 45.19 *shellfish*
mussel shrimp 81.4 *arthropod*
Musset 48 Poets, **48** Dramatists
Mussorgski 49 Musicians and Composers
Mussulman 7.6 *non-Christian*
must 89.1 *fungus,* 571.1 *necessity,* 695.8 *be compelled,* 847.14 *be the duty of*
mustang 32.1 *horse,* 32.4 *saddle horse*
Mustang 32 Breeds of Horse and Pony
mustard 45 Herbs and Spices, 68.12 *crop,* 413.5 *herbs,* 452.1 *yellow,* 452.8 *yellow thing*
mustard and cress 45 Vegetables, 83.9 *seed*
mustard family 83.3 *seed plant*
mustard gas 631.10 *warfare*
mustard plaster 630.10 *surgical dressing*
mustard seed 260.2 *little thing*
mustard-yellow 452.1 *yellow*
mustelid 77.8 *flesh-eating mammal*
Mustelidae 77.8 *flesh-eating mammal*
musteline 77.28 *carnivorous*
muster 161 Collective Names for Birds and Animals, 161.1 *assembly,* 161.42 *call together*
mustered 161.46 *assembled*
muster out 162.13 *dismiss*
muster roll 171.6 *list of names*
must have 593.9 *find necessary*
mustily 202.18 *venerably,* 419.6 *stinkingly,* 622.12 *dirtily*
mustine 62 Medication
mustiness 419.1 *stench,* 622.1 *dirtiness*
musty 89.9 *fungal,* 202.12 *olden,* 419.3 *stinking,* 622.7 *dirty,* 626.5 *unhygienic*
mutability 216.1 *change,* 224.1 *changeableness,* 491.16 *capriciousness*
mutable 216.11, 224.13 *changeable,* 491.8 *capricious*
mutably 216.15 *changeably*
mutant 59.25 *genetic,* 117.8 *contradictory,* 168.10 *eccentric,* 168.17 *abnormal*
mutate 113.8 *be diverse,* 117.12 *be disparate,* 216.9 *transform,*

220.7 *convert into,* 491.21 *change*
mutated 220.13 *converted*
mutating 220.14 *converting*
mutation 113.1 *diversity,* 117.2 *contradiction,* 168.6 *deviation,* 216.3 *transformation,* 220.1 *conversion,* 309.3 *deformity*
mutational 59.25 *genetic*
mutative 216.13 *transformative*
mutchkin 75 Some Foreign Units
mute 161 Collective Names for Birds and Animals, **424, 428, 563,** 238.7 *weaken,* 399.3 *funeral director,* 421.3 *inaudibility,* 421.10 *muffle,* 422.2 *silence,* 422.3 *silent,* 424.2 *sound reducer,* 428.6 *silencer,* 563.7 *voiceless person,* 563.11 *speechless,* 563.15 *strike dumb,* 566.2 *silent,* 620.3 *deformed*
mute button 421.3 *inaudibility*
muted 238.13 *insufficient,* 421.7 *unheard,* 422.3 *silent,* 424.4 *faint,* 428.1 *faint-sounding,* 428.2 *nonresonant,* 441.6 *murky,* 444.13 *soft-hued,* 523.1 *unintelligible,* 563.10 *low-voiced*
mutedness 428, 422.4 *silence,* 424.1 *faintness*
Mutedness 428
muted sound 424.1 *faintness*
muteness 422.4 *silence,* 523.11 *unintelligibility,* 527.10 *quietness,* 563.5 *mutism,* 566.5 *silence*
mute swan 78 Birds
mutilate 131.3 *subtract,* 244.11 *ruin,* 628.5 *hurt,* 790.5 *make ugly,* 793.7 *blemish,* 879.4 *torture*
mutilated 131.7 *reduced,* 145.4 *incomplete,* 620.3 *deformed,* 790.4 *ugly*
mutilation 131.1 *subtraction,* 145.1 *incompleteness,* 628.11 *hurt,* 790.1 *hideousness*
mutineer 689.3 *anarchist,* 693.11 *rebel*
mutineering 693.1 *disobedience*
mutinous 16.61 *lawless,* 151.20 *disorderly,* 669.12 *resisting,* 689.6 *anarchic,* 693.13 *disobedient,* 693.14 *subversive,* 713.10 *law-breaking,* 720.13 *noncompliant*
mutinously 669.14 *resistingly,* 689.8 *anarchically,* 693.17 *disobediently,* 693.18 *subversively,* 713.11 *disapprovingly,* 720.16 *disobediently*
mutinousness 693.1 *disobedience,* 693.4 *revolution,* 720.3 *disregard of orders*
mutiny 16.41 *lawlessness,* 669.3 *resistance movement,* 669.8 *revolt,* 689.1 *anarchy,* 689.4 *be anarchic,* 693.1 *disobedience,* 693.4 *revolution,* 693.16 *be subversive,* 713.1 *protest,* 713.2 *disorder,* 713.6 *protest,* 713.8 *cause mischief,* 720.3 *disregard of orders,* 720.9 *disregard orders*
mutism 563
mutt 77.9 *dog*
mutter 424.5 *sound faint,* 426.2 *humming,* 426.9 *hum,* 428.4 *faint sound,* 428.8 *sound faint,* 527.10 *quietness,* 563.4 *whispering,* 563.16 *speak in a low voice,* 564.7 *utterance,* 564.13 *speak in a particular way,* 830.11 *be irritable*
muttered 428.1 *faint-sounding*
muttering 563.10 *low-voiced,* 636.1 *warning*
muttiness 798.1 *ludicrousness*
muttle furnace 57 Laboratory Apparatus
mutton 45.20 *meat,* 45.44 *British dish*
muttonbird 78 Birds
muttonchops 375.7 *rough thing*
mutual 107.5 *interrelated,* 109.5 *interconnected,* 223.6 *in ex-*

change, 664.18 *joint,* 724.5 *jointly possessing*
mutual affection 821.1 *love*
mutual affinity 784.1 *liking*
mutual agreement 715.1 *contract*
mutual approach 342.1 *convergence*
mutual assistance 664.3 *mutual relationship*
mutual attraction 340.1 *attraction,* 821.1 *love*
mutual concession 242.1 *moderation,* 717.1 *compromise*
mutual concessions 333.2 *middle of the road*
mutual conductance 56.53, 64.12 *resistance*
mutual consultation 654.2 *consultation*
mutual-defence treaty 715.3 *alliance*
mutual dependence 109.2 *interconnection,* 701.1 *subjection*
mutual friend 819.5 *friend*
mutual friends 819.6 *close friend*
mutual good will 819.2 *friendly relations*
mutual hatred 785.1 *dislike*
mutual inductance 56.53, 64.12 *resistance*
mutual induction 56.63 *magnetic phenomenon*
mutual influence 109.2 *interconnection*
mutualism 59.18 *ecology,* 109.2 *interconnection,* 664.3 *mutual relationship,* 724.2 *participation*
mutuality 107.1 *relatedness,* 107.2 *interrelatedness,* 109.2 *interconnection,* 116.1 *accord,* 223.1 *exchange,* 333.2 *middle of the road,* 664.3 *mutual relationship*
mutualization 109.2 *interconnection*
mutual love 784.1 *liking,* 821.1 *love*
mutual lovers 821.10 *lovers*
mutually 107.10 *relevantly,* 109.10 *reciprocally,* 223.8 *in exchange,* 342.12 *convergently*
mutually approaching 342.8 *advancing*
mutually assured destruction 122.2 *equilibrium,* 675.1 *peace*
mutualness 664.3 *mutual relationship*
mutual pledge 714.1 *promise*
mutual regard 819.2 *friendly relations*
mutual relationship 664, 109.2 *interconnection*
mutual repulsion 341.5 *repulsion*
mutual respect 819.2 *friendly relations*
mutual support 667.1 *agreement,* 819.2 *friendly relations*
mutual transfer 326.1 *transfer*
mutual understanding 116.1 *accord,* 667.1 *agreement,* 821.1 *love*
mutule 43 Architectural Decoration
muu-muu 295.7 *frock*
mu yü 49 Musical Instruments
muzzily 441.12 *dimly*
muzzle 236.8 *overpower,* 244.8 *destroy,* 323.3 *restrainer,* 323.11 *restrain,* 422.2 *silence,* 680.9 *firearm,* 699.5 *means of restraint,* 699.12 *gag*
muzzled 699.15 *detained*
muzzleloader 680.10 *historical gun*
muzzy 441.6 *murky,* 874.2 *slightly drunk*
mvet 49 Musical Instruments
MVP 682.4 *successful person*
Mwari 8 Deities
MW transmitter 534.16 *transmitter*
myalgia 406.2 *painful condition,* 624.16 *rheumatism*
myalisma 497.2 *religious belief*
myasthenia 624.17 *nervous disorder*

myasthenia gravis 624.17 *nervous disorder*
mycelial 89.10 *of fungi*
mycelium 89.4 *fungal body*
Mycenean art 50 Non-Western Art
mycetoma 89.5 *fungal association*
mycobiont 89.5 *fungal association,* 90.6 *lichen*
mycologic 89.10 *of fungi*
mycologist 83.12 *plant scientist,* 89.8 *study of fungi*
mycology 83.10 *plant science,* 89.8 *study of fungi*
mycomycin 62 Medication
mycophagist 89.8 *study of fungi*
mycophagy 89.8 *study of fungi*
mycoplasma 59.3 *organism*
mycorrhiza 89.5 *fungal association*
mycosis 89.5 *fungal association*
mycotic 89.10 *of fungi*
my country right or wrong 676.5 *bellicosity*
my dear man 401.3 *male title of address*
my dear woman 402.3 *female title of address*
myectomy 60 Surgical Operations
my good lady 402.3 *female title of address*
my good man 401.3 *male title of address*
my humble self 165.12 *I*
Mylai 398.15 *slaughterhouse*
My Lai 93 Cities
Mylitta 8 Deities
Mylodon 77 Placental Mammals
my lord 401.3 *male title of address*
mylorite 54 Common Rocks
my lud 16.23 *judge*
my man 819.5 *friend*
mynah 78 Birds
mynah bird 78.7 *cagebird*
myocardial infarction 624.10 *cardiovascular disease*
myocarditis 624.10 *cardiovascular disease*
myoglobin 58.9 *protein,* 58.24 *respiration*
myology 382.8 *science of structure*
myomectomy 60 Surgical Operations
myomorphs 77.12 *gnawing mammal*
myopia 436.2 *poor sight*
myopic 436.9 *weak-sighted*
myoplasty 60 Surgical Operations
Myoskinji 10.13 *shrine*
myotomy 60 Surgical Operations
myriad 181, 179.10 *thousand,* 184.2 *immeasurable*
myriads 181.2 *multitude*
myriapod 81.4 *arthropod*
Myriapoda 81.4 *arthropod*
myringoplasty 60 Surgical Operations
myringotomy 60 Surgical Operations
myristic 58 Common Fatty Acids
myrmidon 679.6 *militarist*
myrobalan 86 Fruits
myrrh 85 Tree Products, 399.1 *burial,* 413.5 *herbs,* 418.3 *incense*
myrrhy 395.14 *resinous*
myrtle 85 Trees and Shrubs
myself 165.12 *I,* 368.6 *internal world*
mysophobia 777 Phobias by Name
Mysore 93 Cities
mystagogue 11.12 *occultist,* 653.14 *leader*
mysterious 527, 529, 11.14 *occult,* 440.11 *benighted,* 477.13 *problematic,* 487.2 *unbelievable,* 502.8 *unknown,* 523.1 *unintelligible,* 523.4 *difficult,* 551.2 *obscure,* 786.8 *wonderful*
mysteriously 9.12 *worshipfully,* 11.25 *occultly,* 440.15 *darkly,*

523.13 *unintelligibly,* 551.4 *obscurely,* 786.13 *wonderfully*
mysterious message 523.12 *unintelligible thing*
mysteriousness 527, 11.2 *the occult,* 551.1 *obscurity*
mysterious stranger 529.8 *anonymity*
mystery 11.1 *occultism,* 11.2 *the occult,* 51.2 *play,* 477.4 *difficult question,* 502.3 *unknown thing,* 523.11 *unintelligibility,* 523.12 *unintelligible thing,* 527.11 *mysteriousness,* 529.3 *mystification,* 529.7 *esotericism*
mystery man 527.6 *latency*
mystery play 51.2 *play*
mystery story 48.2 *fiction*
mystery tour 502.3 *unknown thing*
mystic 4.11 *follower of a doctrine,* 4.14 *of a philosophy,* 7.3 *religious person,* 7.15 *religious,* 11.12 *occultist,* 440.11 *benighted,* 497.5 *believer,* 523.1 *unintelligible,* 527.5 *mysterious*
mystical 8.13 *divine,* 487.2 *unbelievable,* 523.1 *unintelligible*
mystical experience 8.8 *divine manifestation*
mystical intuition 8.8 *divine manifestation*
mystically 8.19 *divinely,* 9.12 *worshipfully,* 11.25 *occultly*
mysticism 4.7 *school of thought,* 7.2 *religiousness,* 11.1 *occultism,* 523.11 *unintelligibility,* 527.11 *mysteriousness*
mystification 529, 11.1 *occultism,* 474.3 *cunning,* 521.1 *lack of meaning,* 523.11 *unintelligibility,* 531.5 *evasion*
mystified 523.6 *confused,* 659.16 *troubled*
mystify 529, 11.20 *occult,* 443.12 *obscure,* 460.10 *bemuse,* 474.11 *practise sophistry,* 477.21 *confuse,* 491.20 *make uncertain,* 502.11 *make ignorant,* 523.7 *be unintelligible,* 659.23 *cause difficulties*
mystifying 443.4 *inscrutable,* 474.8 *cunning,* 521.10 *meaningless,* 529.11 *mysterious*
myth 1.8 *tradition,* 3.7 *narrative,* 48.2 *fiction,* 202.6 *tradition,* 519.7 *idealism,* 538.2 *unrealness,* 540.9 *falsification,* 560.3 *narration*
mythical 3.19 *chronicled,* 48.17 *fictional,* 102.10 *theoretical,* 519.12 *imaginary,* 538.14 *unreal*
mythical hero 237.6 *muscleman*
mythically 1.18 *societally,* 3.25 *reportedly,* 538.26 *untruthfully*
mythical seaman 74.7 *nautical person*
mythic heaven 397.14 *the spiritual world*
mythic hell 397.14 *the spiritual world*
myth-maker 519.9 *visionary*
mythological 1.14 *societal,* 48.17 *fictional,* 519.12 *imaginary,* 538.14 *unreal,* 560.12 *narrative*
mythological bird 78.9 *fabulous bird*
mythologically 1.18 *societally,* 538.26 *untruthfully*
mythologist 48.14 *author,* 400.6 *studier of mankind*
mythologize 538.22 *make unreal,* 540.22 *falsify,* 560.15 *recount*
mythologized 540.32 *falsified*
mythology 1.8 *tradition,* 48.2 *fiction,* 202.6 *tradition,* 400.5 *study of mankind,* 538.2 *unrealness*
mythomania 540.6 *lying*
mythomaniac 539.16 *liar*
mythopoeia 48.2 *fiction*
myxomatosis 624.18 *veterinary disease*
myxomycetes 89.3 *fungi*
Myxomycota 89.3 *fungi*
myxophobia 777 Phobias by Name

N

Naafi 350.15 *eating place*
Naas 93 Cities
Naasene 7 Non-Christian Religions
nab 407.11 *touch*, 539.33 *snare*, 699.11 *detain*, 734.10 *take away*
nabbing 734.2 *taking back*
Nabeshima ware 44 Types of Ceramics
Nabis 50 Schools and Groups of Artists
nabla 52.50 *scalar quantity*
nabob 696.2 *sovereign*, 742.10 *wealthy person*
Nabokov 48 Writers
nabothian gland 352 Exocrine Glands
nacelle 73 Aircraft Parts
nacho 45.50 *Central American dish*
nacre 456.5 *variegated thing*
nacreous 456.7 *iridescent*
nacreously 456.12 *variedly*
NAD 58.12 *coenzyme*
Na-Dene 5 Languages and Groups of Languages
nadir 53.5 *celestial sphere*, 53.21 *orbit*, 127.5 *inferior state*, 172.4 *zero level*, 276.3 *lowest point*, 277.4 *deep thing*, 280.1 *base*
NADP 58.12 *coenzyme*
nadrolone 62 Medication
naevus 149.2 *impurity*
naff 614.1 *useless*, 618.2 *inferior*
naff off 218.12 *stop*, 345.15 *go*, 349.33 *go away*
nag 32.1 *horse*, 32.4 *saddle horse*, 183.18 *harp*, 228.10 *manipulate*, 402.8 *nasty woman*, 764.11 *quarrel*, 829.3 *irascible person*, 852.18 *find fault*
Naga 5 Languages and Groups of Languages
Nagari 5.13 *letter*
Nagasaki 93 Cities, 398.15 *slaughterhouse*
Nagel 4 Philosophers
nage-waza 26.7 *judo*
nagging 852.6, 852.28 *fault-finding*
nag into 586.15 *persuade*
Nagoya 93 Cities
Nagpur 93 Cities
nagual 8.5 *deity*
Nahuatl 5 Languages and Groups of Languages
naiad 8.5 *deity*
naif 201.12, 206.12 *immature*, 658.1 *naive*
nail 75 General Units, 135.10 *link*, 137.8 *fastening*, 137.11 *connect*, 283.4 *hanger*, 373.7 *hard substance*, 380.8 *sharp-pointed thing*, 603.1 *tool*, 603.9 *use tools*
nailbomb 680.16 *bomb*
nailbrush 375.7 *rough thing*, 621.10 *cleaning object*
nail down 101.12 *establish reality*, 718.14 *make fast*
nailed 137.15 *connected*
nailfile 376.9 *smoother*, 384.12 *abrasive*, 385.7 *eraser*
nail in one's coffin 683.1 *failure*
nail one's colours to the mast 574.8 *brace oneself*
nail polish 450.6 *red pigment*, 791.4 *cosmetics*
nails 680.1 *weapon*, 726.3 *tools for gripping*
nail varnish 791.4 *cosmetics*
nainsook 67 Natural Fabrics
Naipaul 48 Writers
naira 741.11 *national coins*
Nairobi 93 Cities
naive 658, 865, 50.29 *realist*, 201.12, 206.12 *immature*, 322.16 *open*, 453.3 *raw*, 497.12 *gullible*, 502.9 *ignorant*, 537.18 *truthful*, 560.13 *representing*, 585.1 *unaccustomed*, 633.3 *vulnerable*

naive art 50 Western Art Styles and Movements
naively 658, 865, 322.26 *openly*, 585.6 *unaccustomedly*, 633.11 *dangerously*
naive person 658
naivety 658, 865, 201.3, 206.3 *immaturity*, 322.9 *openness*, 502.1 *ignorance*, 537.5 *truthfulness*, 633.7 *vulnerability*
Naivety 658
naked 134.17 *direct*, 294.8 *uncovered*, 296.9 *undressed*, 437.2 *clear*, 526.15 *open*, 556.1 *simple*, 633.3 *vulnerable*
naked as a jaybird 294.8 *uncovered*, 296.9 *undressed*
naked as the day one was born 294.8 *uncovered*, 296.9 *undressed*
naked eye 437.3 *visibility*
naked force 690.2 *suppression*
naked lady 296.8 *nude person*
nakedly 296
nakedness 294, 294.1 *uncovering*, 296.2 *nudity*, 556.4 *simplicity*, 633.7 *vulnerability*
naked person 296.8 *nude person*
naked steel 680.8 *sharp weapon*
nakers 49 Musical Instruments
Naknek 94 Lakes
nalidixic acid 62 Medication
Nama 5 Languages and Groups of Languages
namby-pamby 238.4 *weakling*, 238.12 *weak-willed*, 779.3 *cowardly*
name 560, 5.17 *word*, 165.24 *specify*, 544.2 *identity*, 544.3 *means of identification*, 544.10 *identify*, 560.16 *define*, 682.1 *success*, 703.6 *commission*, 804.1 *right*
name and address 534.3 *correspondence*, 544.3 *means of identification*
name badge 544.3 *means of identification*
name calling 473.1 *argument*
namechild 5.2 *linguist*
named 5.42 *worded*, 490.7 *particular*, 544.12 *identified*
name day 185.11 *date*
name-day 812.5 *anniversary*
namegiver 5.2 *linguist*
name in lights 532.8 *public relations*
namely 165, 524.18 *in other words*
name names 165.24 *specify*, 530.7 *betray*
name of the game 103.2 *essential content*
name part 51.21 *role*
nameplate 544.3 *means of identification*
namer 5.2 *linguist*
name recognition 682.1 *success*
names 777 Phobias by Topic
namesake 560.8 *name*
name tag 543.1 *sign*
nametape 544.3 *means of identification*
name up in lights 682.1 *success*
Namib 98 Deserts
Namibia 91 Countries
naming 544.1 *identification*, 560.7 *nomenclature*
naming ceremony 560.7 *nomenclature*
namtar 8.7 *devil*
Namur 93 Cities
nan 45.38 *bread*
Nana 8 Deities
nan bread 45.49 *Indian dish*
nancy 401.9 *offensive terms for homosexual*
Nancy 93 Cities
Nanda 8 Deities
Nanfan 32 Breeds of Horse and Pony
Nanjing 93 Cities
nankeen 67 Natural Fabrics
Nankin 68 Breeds of Fowl
Nanking ware 44 Types of Ceramics
Nanna 8 Deities

Nannar 8 Deities
nanny 632.3 *protector*, 697.4 *personal attendant*,697.6 *domestic servant*
nanny goat 68.8 *livestock*, 77.18 *female mammal*, 402.14 *female animal*
nanny state 632.1 *safety*, 833.4 *welfare state*
nano 75 SI Units
nanosecond 185.4 *term*, 187.2 *time period*
Nantes 93 Cities
Nantucket 98 Islands
naos 10.13 *shrine*, 43.9 *miscellaneous architectural features*
Naos 53 Named Stars
nap 42 Card Games, **383**, 67.4 *weaving*, 67.14 *weave*, 218.3, 218.9 *pause*, 404.2 *unconsciousness*, 643.9, 643.13 *sleep*, 649.1 *ease*, 649.2 *take it easy*, 674.10 *contender*
napalm bomb 680.16 *bomb*
naphazoline 62 Medication
naphtha 410.6 *oil*
naphthalene 57 Common Chemical Compounds
Napier 52 Scientists, 93 Cities
Napierian logarithm 52 Named Concepts, 52.19 *logarithm*
Napier's bones 52.67 *calculator*, 65.3, 170.5 *computer*
Naples 93 Cities
Naples yellow 452.7 *yellow pigment*
Napoleon and Josephine 821.10 *lovers*
Napoleonic code 16.1 *the law*
Napoleonic Wars 17 Major Wars
nappe 96.2 *channel*, 360.3 *downflow*
napped 67.10 *woven*
nappy 295.23 *children's clothes*
naproxen 62 Medication
naqara 49 Musical Instruments
Naraka 8.11 *heaven*
narcism 809.4 *self-admiration*
narcissism 809.4 *self-admiration*, 821.1 *love*, 860.2 *egoism*, 870.4 *self-absorption*
narcissist 860.3 *selfish person*, 870.5 *self-indulgent person*
narcissistic 809.10 *self-admiring*, 860.5 *egoistic*, 870.9 *self-absorbed*
narcissus 84 Flowers and Flowering Plants
Narcissus 809.7 *vain person*
narcoanalysis 61.3 *psychiatric treatment*
narcohypnosis 61.3 *psychiatric treatment*
narcosis 236.4 *disability*, 512.1 *oblivion*, 761.4 *desensitization*
narcotherapist 61.30 *psychiatrist*
narcotherapy 61.3 *psychiatric treatment*
narcotic 62.4 *drug type*, 62.15 *sedative*, 242.8 *moderating*, 404.4, 404.9 *anaesthetic*, 630.8 *drug*, 630.17 *remedial*, 631.11 *intoxicant*, 643.10 *soporific*, 761.6 *desensitizing substance*, 875.6 *drug*, 875.9 *addictive*
narcotically 875.11 *in a trance*
narcotics 875.6 *drug*
narcotization 761.4 *desensitization*
narcotize 404.12 *anaesthetize*, 643.14 *make inactive*, 761.7 *render insensitive*
narcotized 643.4 *not awake*
nard 386.5, 395.6 *ointment*
narghile 413.7 *tobacco*
naris 416.2 *sense of smell*
nark 480.7 *verifier*, 483.7 *person who gives evidence*, 483.13 *turn Queen's evidence*, 528.10 *informer*, 856.3 *accuser*, 856.5 *accuse*
Narnia 519.8 *dreamland*
Narraganset 1 Peoples, 5 Languages and Groups of Languages
Narragansett 68 Breeds of Fowl

narrate 3.20 *chronicle*, 528.12 *communicate*, 545.13 *record*, 560.15 *recount*
narrated 3.19 *chronicled*
narration 560, 3.7 *narrative*, 528.2 *communication*
narrative 3, **48**, **560**, 48.3 *aspect of fiction*, 545.1 *record*, 560.3 *narration*, 640.2 *deed*
narrative fiction 48.2 *fiction*
narrative poem 48.7 *poem*, 560.3 *narration*
narrative poetry 48.6 *poetry*
narrative voice 48.3 *aspect of fiction*
narrative writing 560.3 *narration*
narratology 48.3 *aspect of fiction*
narrator 51.22 *actor*, 528.9 *informant*, 564.10 *speaker*
narrow 272, **272**, 41.10 *curling*, 135.8 *unite*, 147.10 *excluding*, 262.5 *make smaller*, 262.6 *become smaller*, 262.7 *smaller*, 302.5 *limited*, 493.8 *unjust*, 699.13 *restraining*
narrow-beaked 272.4 *narrow-leaved*
narrow boat 74 Ships and Boats, 74.3 *vessel*
narrowcast 532.13 *make public*
narrowcasting 532.2 *mass media*
narrow defeat 683.2 *defeat*
narrowed 262.7 *smaller*
narrow escape 633.5 *danger*, 638.1 *escape*
narrow gauge 72.3 *rail*, 272.8 *narrow thing*
narrow-gauge 272.4 *narrow-leaved*
narrow-gauged 272.4 *narrow-leaved*
narrow house 399.6 *grave*
narrowing 272, **342**, 262.1 *contraction*, 262.8 *contracting*, 342.7 *convergent*
narrowing gap 342.2 *approach*, 342.6 *narrowing*
narrow-leaved 272
narrowly 272, 147.12 *exclusively*
narrow means 743.5 *poverty*
narrow mind 493.3 *injustice*
narrow-minded 481.10 *discriminatory*, 490.2 *convinced*, 493.8 *unjust*, 876.10 *moralistic*
narrow-mindedly 481.17 *prejudicially*, 493.14 *unjustly*
narrow-mindedness 481.3 *prejudice*, 490.10 *conviction*, 493.3 *injustice*, 577.7 *opinionatedness*, 876.4 *self-righteousness*
narrowness 777 Phobias by Topic, **272**, 481.3 *prejudice*
Narrowness 272
narrow-nosed 272.4 *narrow-leaved*
narrow outlook 302.2 *limiting factor*
narrow-petalled 272.4 *narrow-leaved*
narrow place 272
narrows 272.6 *narrow place*
narrow-skulled 272.4 *narrow-leaved*
narrow squeak 264.2 *short distance*, 638.1 *escape*
narrow the gap 342.9 *converge*
narrow thing 272
narrow victory 682.2 *victory*
narrow waist 274.7 *thinness*
narrow-waisted 274.1 *thin*
Narsinh 8 Deities
narthex 43.10 *church architecture*
narwhal 77 Placental Mammals
nary a one 100.6 *absence*
NASA 53.31 *space travel*
nasal 5.16 *spoken letter*, 5.41 *lettered*, 416.6 *olfactory*, 564.18 *phonetic*
nasal bone 382 Bones
nasal cavity 322.4 *body orifice*, 416.2 *sense of smell*, 564.5 *organ of speech*
nasal congestion 417.1 *odourlessness*
nasality 430.2 *hoarseness*, 564.3 *mode of speech*
nasally 416.10 *odorously*

nasal mucus 622.4 *dirt*
nasal tone 430.2 *hoarseness*
nascent 156.32 *embryonic*
nascent hydrogen **57** Chemical Elements
Nash **48** Poets
nashi **86** Fruits
Nashville **93** Cities, 49.12 *Tin Pan Alley*, 93.2 *American cities*
Nassau **93** Cities, **93** Cities
Nassau scoring 29.2 *golfing terms*
Nasser **94** Lakes
nastily 618.15 *worthlessly*, 764.13 *unpleasantly*, 818.9 *discourteously*
nastiness 618.9 *badness*, 758.4, 764.5 *unpleasantness*, 818.1 *discourtesy*, 832.1 *malevolence*, 862.1 *evil*, 877.2 *indecency*
nasturtium **84** Flowers and Flowering Plants
nasty 415.6 *unpalatable*, 618.3 *bad*, 622.8 *unclean*, 626.5 *unhygienic*, 633.1 *dangerous*, 758.2, 764.1 *unpleasant*, 818.5 *discourteous*, 822.12 *hated*, 832.14 *hostile*, 862.7 *evil*
nasty person **758**
nasty piece of work 832.8 *malefactor*
nasty taste 415.2 *unpalatability*
nasty type 864.9 *wicked person*
nasty woman **402**
Nat **8** Deities
natality 245.3 *propagation*
natation 39.1 *swimming*
natational 39.11 *swimming*
natatorium 39.7 *swimming pool*, 621.6 *bath*
natatory 39.11 *swimming*, 74.11 *nautical*
Natchez **1** Peoples
nation **400**, 1.7 *society*, 91.1 *country*, 249.4 *territorial division*, 665.2 *society*, 688.8 *governmental organization*
national **91, 249, 255, 400**, 1.14 *societal*, 5.39 *of language*, 91.13 *native*, 92.6 *administrative*, 164.16 *universal*, 290.8 *internal*, 665.9 *societal*, 688.14 *governmental*, 698.9 *free*
National Anglers Council 20.1 *angling*
national anthem 433.2 *song*
National Assembly 653.10 *legislative body*
National Association for Stock Car Auto Racing 33.7 *racing governing body*
National Baseball Hall of Fame and Museum 22.1 *baseball*
National Basketball Association 23.1 *basketball*
national capital 92.5 *administrative headquarters*
national code 534.11 *dialling*
national coins **741**
national colours 544.7 *flag*
national consciousness 91.4 *nationalism*, 400.11 *nation*
national costume 295.3 *formal dress*
national credit 745.2 *national debt*
National Curriculum 6.3 *subject*
national debt **745**, 13.3 *economic statistics*
national defence 17.2 *the military*, 718.4 *security forces*
national defence headquarters 17.4 *military organization*
national device 544.6 *national emblem*
national dress 295.3 *formal dress*, 544.5 *uniform*
national election 580.12 *election*
national emblem **544**
national entity 400.11 *nation*
national flag 544.7 *flag*
National Front 12.6 *political party*
National Front member 679.1 *combatant*, 693.10 *seditionist*
national government 12.1 *government*

national grid 64.33 *power distribution*, 235.7 *electrical power*, 410.4 *electricity*
National Health Service 60.1 *medicine*, 632.1 *safety*, 662.4 *social assistance*, 718.1 *protection*
National Hockey League 31.3 *ice hockey*
National Hot Rod Association 33.7 *racing governing body*
National Hunt racing 32.7 *horseracing*
national income 721.4 *earnings*, 749.3 *income*
national insurance 662.4 *social assistance*, 718.1 *protection*
National Insurance 751.7 *tax*
National Insurance number 544.3 *means of identification*
nationalism 91, 4.7 *school of thought*, 136.3 *separateness*, 249.15 *regionalism*, 400.11 *nation*
nationalist **91**, 4.11 *follower of a doctrine*, 4.14 *of a philosophy*
nationalistic 91.16 *national*, 665.10 *political*
nationalistically 91.19, 249.20 *nationally*
Nationalists 12.6 *political party*
nationality 1.7 *society*, 91.4 *nationalism*, 400.11 *nation*
nationalization 13.1 *economics*, 724.1 *joint possession*, 728.1 *transfer of property*, 734.1 *taking*, 737.5 *commercial trade*
nationalize 13.10 *trade with*, 724.4 *have joint possession*, 728.3 *transfer property*, 734.7 *take*, 737.1 *trade*
nationalized 13.13 *economic*, 737.19 *corporate*
National Labor Relations Act 15.5 *labour law*
National Labor Relations Board 15.5 *labour law*
national language 5.4 *parent language*
National League 22.1 *baseball*
nationally **91, 249**, 1.18 *societally*, 164.32 *universally*, 400.15 *humanly*, 665.18 *cliquishly*, 688.24 *ministerially*
national military college 17.3 *military training*
national monument 545.11 *monument*
national newspaper 533.5 *mass communication*
national official 15.7 *employee*
national paper 532.4 *newspaper*
national planning 592.1 *plan*
National Public Radio 534.20 *radio broadcasting*
national security 531.4 *silence*
national service 676.7 *war measures*
National Socialism 12.1 *government*, 688.7 *type of rule*
national status 698.3 *independence*
national union organization 15.3 *organized labour*
National Vocational Qualification **485** Educational Qualifications
nationhood 91.1 *country*, 698.3 *independence*
nation in arms 679.7 *militarist nation*
nation state 12.5 *political organization*, 249.4 *territorial division*, 400.11 *nation*
nationwide 164.16 *universal*
nationwide circulation 532.7 *publicity*
native **91, 255**, 1.6 *race*, 1.13 *racial*, 5.39 *of language*, 57.34 *elemental*, 83.15 *wild*, 255.1 *inhabitant*, 658.1 *naive*
native accent 564.3 *mode of speech*
native American 1.6 *race*
native custom 584.4 *custom*
native land **91**, 249.4 *territorial division*, 256.3 *home*

native language 5.4 *parent language*
native people 1.6 *race*
native population 255.2 *inhabitants*
native quarter 816.4 *place of confinement*
native soil 91.6 *native land*
native state 595.11 *natural state*
native tongue 5.4 *parent language*, 564.1 *faculty of speech*
native wit 235.2 *ability*, 459.5 *common sense*
nativity 50.10 *art subject*, 156.4 *conception*, 245.3 *propagation*, 396.4 *biological function*
Nativity 10.16 *religious festival*
natriuretic 62.4 *drug type*, 62.17 *stimulating*
natrolite **54** Minerals
natron **54** Minerals, 399.1 *burial*
Natron **94** Lakes
Natta process **57** Named Reactions
natter 564.1 *faculty of speech*, 565.7 *be talkative*, 568.2, 568.10 *chat*
natterer 568.8 *chatterer*
natterjack **79** Amphibians
nattily 295.36 *dressily*
natty 295.30 *dressed up*, 295.31 *styled*, 621.16 *clean*
natural **67, 556**, 20.8 *angling*, 49.16 *musical note*, 59.21 *living*, 99.11 *intrinsic*, 101.7 *realistic*, 114.9 *lifelike*, 119.6 *authentic*, 168.10 *eccentric*, 367.7 *material*, 558.3 *elegant*, 583.2 *spontaneous*, 584.11 *normal*, 595.4 *untrained*, 658.1 *naive*, 814.9 *familiar*, 865.7 *naive*
natural affection 821.1 *love*
natural bent 655.2 *aptitude*
natural cement 44.9 *industrial ceramics*
natural childbirth 245.7 *obstetrics*
natural colour 444.1 *colour*, 444.9 *complexion*
natural death 397.5 *ways of dying*
natural deposit 605.2 *resource*
natural disaster 244.7 *agent of destruction*, 687.1 *adversity*
natural dye 67.6 *dye*, 444.4 *pigment*
natural fabric 67.3 *fabric*
natural feature 54.7 *landform*
natural fibre 67.1 *fibre*
natural fly 20.1 *angling*
natural fly-fishing 20.1 *angling*
natural gas 235.6 *source of energy*, 410.3 *gas*, 604.1 *materials*
natural harbour 98.9 *inlet*
natural history 59.1 *life science*
natural idiom 556.4 *simplicity*
naturalism **48** Literary Groups and Movements, **50** Western Art Styles and Movements, 4.7 *school of thought*, 51.8 *theatre movements*, 101.3 *realism*, 503.2 *correctness*, 537.12 *true to life*
naturalist 4.11 *follower of a doctrine*, 50.29 *realist*, 51.40 *activist*, 59.19 *life scientist*, 83.12 *plant scientist*
naturalistic 4.14 *of a philosophy*, 48.16 *literary*, 101.7 *realistic*, 503.6 *correct*, 537.25 *lifelike*, 547.13 *representational*, 560.11 *descriptive*
naturalistically 50.30 *pictorially*
naturalization 167.3 *pliancy*, 220.2 *evolution*, 348.3 *introduction*, 584.7 *habituation*
naturalize 220, 167.10 *assimilate*, 220.8 *be transformed*, 348.9 *welcome*, 584.18 *habituate*
naturalized 220, 83.15 *wild*, 220.13 *converted*, 255.13 *resident*, 584.14 *habituated*
naturalized citizen 255.8 *national*
natural lake 94.1 *lake*
natural language 5.3 *spoken language*

natural-language understanding 65.16 *artificial intelligence*
natural law 16.1 *the law*, 166.3 *rule of nature*
natural light **439**, 66.15 *lighting*
natural logarithm 52.19, 52.19 *logarithm*, 169.6 *power*
naturally **814**, 20.9 *on the water*, 114.14 *comparably*, 119.8 *originally*, 227.12 *with the effect of*, 367.9 *materially*, 490.26 *certainly*, 537.37 *authentically*, 558.5 *elegantly*, 655.12 *skilfully*, 865.12 *naively*
naturally gifted 655.7 *gifted*
naturally-occurring 57.40 *synthetic*
natural magic 11.3 *witchcraft*
natural medicine **60**
natural mystery **529**
naturalness **556**, 537.12 *true to life*, 558.1 *elegance*, 658.2 *naivety*, 814.3 *familiarity*, 865.3 *naivety*
natural number **52**
natural philosophy 4.6 *branch of philosophy*, 56.1 *physics*
natural politeness 813.5 *etiquette*
natural power 485.2 *ability*
natural resource 605.2 *resource*
natural resources 13.4 *economic development*, 602.2 *supplies*
natural rubber 377.4 *rubber*
natural satellite 53.18 *satellite*
natural science **57**, 56.1 *physics*, 59.1 *life science*, 501.5 *science*
natural scientist 59.19 *life scientist*
natural selection 59.16 *evolution*
natural state **595**
natural talent 234.3, 655.2 *aptitude*
natural theology 7.13 *theology*
natural virtues 863.2 *virtues*
natural weapon 680.1 *weapon*
natural world 59.2 *living world*, 101.2 *real world*
nature **99, 103, 306**, 59.2 *living world*, 163.4 *type*, 165.2 *personality*, 367.1 *material world*
Nature 243.9 *producer*
nature cure 630.11 *medical art*, 630.13 *therapy*
nature of meaning 4.9 *philosophical problem*
nature of the beast 103.4 *nature*
nature of time 4.9 *philosophical problem*
nature reserve 637.1 *preservation*
nature's bounty 246.1 *fertility*
nature topic 472.5 *educational topic*
naturism 294.1 *uncovering*, 296.1 *undress*
naturist 294.4 *exposer*, 296.8 *nude person*
naturistic 296.9 *undressed*
naturopath 60.12, 630.15 *healer*
naturopathy 60.2 *natural medicine*, 60.8 *treatment*, 630.11 *medical art*
naught 100.2 *nothingness*, 172.2 *nothing*
naught beside 174.1 *one*
naughtily 652.20 *badly*, 693.17 *disobediently*, 827.12 *swearingly*, 858.11 *dishonourably*
naughtiness 652.4 *bad conduct*, 693.1 *disobedience*, 864.1 *wickedness*, 866.3 *sin*
naughty 652.18 *badly behaved*, 659.14 *troublesome*, 693.13 *disobedient*, 827.8 *cursing*, 864.11 *wicked*, 877.12 *indecent*, 877.13 *unchaste*
naughty child 652.5 *badly behaved person*, 693.5 *troublemaker*
naughty story 877.2 *indecency*
naughty word 5.19 *swearword*, 827.1 *curse*
nauplius 81.13 *invertebrate larva*
Nauru **91** Countries

nausea 349.23 *vomiting*, 543.1 *sign*, 624.3 *symptom*, 624.8 *indigestion*, 785.4 *sign of dislike*

nauseant 134.4, 406.6 *purgative*

nauseate 341.4 *be repulsive*, 415.9 *disgust*, 764.10 *displease*, 785.7 *cause dislike*, 822.16 *cause hate*

nauseated 349.30 *vomiting*, 453.6, 624.22 *sick*, 785.8 *disliking*

nauseating 341.8 *repulsive*, 415.6 *unpalatable*, 610.6 *excessive*, 618.4 *poor*, 622.8 *unclean*, 764.1 *unpleasant*, 785.9 *disliked*, 822.12 *hated*

nauseatingly 415.10 *sourly*

nauseous 618.4 *poor*, 622.8 *unclean*, 785.8 *disliking*, 822.12 *hated*

nautch 46.4 *historic dancing*

nautch-girl 51.28 *dancer*

nautical 74, 97.7 *oceanic*

nautical almanac 74.5 *navigation*, 528.5 *reference book*

nautically 74, 97

nautical mile 75 General Units, 269.7 *measure of length*

nautical mile per hour 74.6 *nautical speed*

nautical person 74

nautical speed 74

nautilus 81 Molluscs, 314.3 *convoluted thing*

Navajo 1 Peoples, 5 Languages and Groups of Languages, 7 Non-Christian Religions

naval 17.8 *military*, 74.11 *nautical*, 676.17 *military*, 679.35 *martial*

naval airman 679.27 *naval man*

naval architect 74.7 *nautical person*

naval architecture 74.4 *shipbuilding*

naval armament 679.22 *navy*

naval engagement 676.9 *battle*

naval engineering 63.1 *engineering*, 74.4 *shipbuilding*

naval man 679, 74.7 *nautical person*

naval mine 679

naval officer 74.7 *nautical person*, 679.27 *naval man*

naval operations 676.8 *warfare*

naval reservist 679.27 *naval man*

naval service 676.8 *warfare*, 679.22 *navy*

naval unit 679

naval warfare 676.8 *warfare*

navar 73.6 *flight control*

nave 10.12 *church*, 291.2 *central thing*, 327.7 *arcade*, 364.4 *vortex*

navel 291.2 *central thing*

navel orange 86 Fruits

navigable 70.5 *transportable*

navigable river 96.1 *river*, 327.11 *channel*

navigable water 74.2 *waterway*

navigate 74, 250.11 *find*, 332.7 *take a direction*, 335.1 *deviate*, 652.15 *conduct*, 653.2 *direct*

navigated 70.5 *transportable*

navigation 74, 74.1 *water travel*, 250.5 *topography*, 332.1 *direction*

navigational 70.5 *transportable*, 250.8 *locational*, 653.17 *managerial*

navigational aid 74.5 *navigation*, 653.5 *guide*

navigational beacon 534.27 *signalling*

navigational instrument 74.5 *navigation*

navigational radar 74.5 *navigation*

navigational satellite 53.32 *satellite*, 74.5 *navigation*

navigation laws 74.5 *navigation*

navigation lights 439.6 *electric light*

navigator 73.3 *aircraft personnel*, 74.7 *nautical person*, 653.13 *director*, 679.32 *airman*

navvy 646.1 *worker*

navy 679, 17.2 *the military*, 161.14 *force*, 454.1 *blue*, 679.14 *armed forces*, 718.4 *security forces*

navy blue 440.3 *dark colour*, 454.1 *blue*

Navy Cross 17 US Military Medals and Decorations

navy man 74.7 *nautical person*, 676.11 *recruit*, 679.27 *naval man*

navy staff 17.5 *military staff*

navy uniform 544.5 *uniform*

nay 476.13 *no*, 500.2 *disapproval*, 536.1 *negation*, 536.16 *no*, 580.10 *vote*, 713.1 *protest*

naysay 476.9 *deny*, 536.7 *be negative*

naysayer 476.5 *refuter*, 663.9 *opposer*

naysaying 476.1 *refutation*, 536.1 *negation*

Nazarenes 50 Schools and Groups of Artists

Nazarite 7 Non-Christian Religions

Nazi 12.9 *governmental*, 481.7 *bigot*, 481.10 *discriminatory*, 493.5 *misjudging person*, 688.14 *governmental*

Nazis 12.6 *political party*

Nazi SA 679.14 *armed forces*

Nazism 12.1 *government*, 481.4 *social discrimination*, 688.7 *type of rule*, 690.2 *suppression*

Nazi swastika 544.6 *national emblem*

NBA Championship 23.1 *basketball*

NBA Most Valuable Player 23.2 *basketball player*

NBA Rookie of the Year 23.2 *basketball player*

NBC 534.24 *television broadcasting*

NBS 75.4 *standard*

NCAA swimming 39.5 *swimming association*

NCAA wrestler 26.6 *wrestler*

NCCA Baseball Championship 22.1 *baseball*

NCCA Basketball Championship 23.1 *basketball*

NCK 65.14 *data transfer*

N'Dama 68 Breeds of Cattle

Ndebele 5 Languages and Groups of Languages

n-dimensional space 52.35 *space*

Ndola 93 Cities

Neagh 94 Lakes

Neanderthal 241.4 *violent person or animal*

Neanderthaler 200.6 *people of the past*

Neanderthal man 200.6 *people of the past*, 202.7 *ancient people*, 400.3 *uncivilized human*

neap 97.7 *oceanic*

neap tide 54.15, 97.2 *tide*, 129.3 *decreasing thing*, 214.5 *regular thing*, 276.3 *lowest point*

near 264, 264, 264, 114.7 *similar*, 155.17 *next*, 195.12 *succeeding*, 199.11 *future*, 253.10 *available*, 267.5 *juxtaposed*, 305.6 *side*, 758.1 *mean*, 819.10 *familiar*

near and far 248.16 *extensively*

near at hand 199.11 *future*, 208.13 *imminent*, 253.16 *on the spot*, 264.6 *near*

near beer 351.6 *soft drink*

nearby 615, 615, 196.8 *available*, 249.18 *local*, 249.20 *nationally*, 253.10 *available*, 264.5 *near*, 264.6 *near*, 472.9 *local*

near death 624.22 *sick*

near enough 264.7 *nearly*

nearer 264.5 *near*

nearest 253.10 *available*, 264.5 *near*

nearest the top 275.10 *higher*

near extinction 182.6 *sparse*

near failure 515.1 *disappointment*

near gale 55.13 *wind strength*

near infrared 56.13 *electromagnetic radiation*

nearing 264.5 *near*, 344.19 *approaching*

near likeness 114.1 *similarity*

nearly 264, 114.14 *comparably*, 120.7 *quantitatively*, 142.13 *on the whole*, 272.11 *narrowly*

nearly all 143.5 *largest part*

nearly the same 114.7 *similar*

near miss 264.2 *short distance*, 633.5 *danger*, 638.1 *escape*, 683.1 *failure*

nearness 264, 615, 114.1 *similarity*, 135.1 *union*, 191.2 *closeness*, 253.4 *availability*, 267.1 *juxtaposition*, 819.3 *familiarity*

Nearness 264

near place 264

near rhyme 48.11 *rhyme*

nearside 71.21 *miscellaneous motoring terms*

near side 305.3 *side direction*

near sight 435.1 *vision*, 436.2 *poor sight*

near-sighted 435.22 *bespectacled*, 436.9 *weak-sighted*

near-sightedness 436.2 *poor sight*

near the bone 877.12 *indecent*

near the knuckle 454.4 *indecent*, 622.9 *obscene*, 877.12 *indecent*

near the surface 278.8 *shallowly*

near the wind 332.11 *in all directions*

near thing 264.2 *short distance*, 633.5 *danger*, 638.1 *escape*

near tragedy 633.5 *danger*

near-truth 538.5 *half-truth*

near ultraviolet 56.13 *electromagnetic radiation*

near vacuum 372.5 *gas*

neat 134.13 *pure*, 150.13 *orderly*, 152.27 *tidied*, 237.12 *strong to the senses*, 407.10 *handed*, 469.9 *careful*, 556.1 *simple*, 558.3 *elegant*, 617.1 *worthy*, 621.16 *clean*, 655.6 *skilful*, 874.6 *intoxicating*

neat and tidy 150.13 *orderly*

neat as a button 150.13 *orderly*

neaten 150.21, 152.19 *tidy*, 312.10 *straighten*, 621.13 *clean*, 627.1 *improve*

neatened 152.27 *tidied*

neath 276.10 *low*

neatly 150.26 *orderly*, 152.28 *in place*, 558.5 *elegantly*, 621.19 *cleanly*, 655.12 *skilfully*

neatly put 558.3 *elegant*

neatly wrought 558.3 *elegant*

neatness 150.5 *orderliness*, 469.4 *fastidiousness*, 556.4 *simplicity*, 558.1 *elegance*, 567.3, 655.1 *skill*

neat weight 369.7 *weighing*

Nebo 8 Deities

Nebraska 92 American States

nebula 53.8 *interstellar medium*, 161.28 *cluster*

nebulizer 62.10 *inhalant*

nebulous 55.56 *foggy*, 102.8 *unreal*, 164.20 *generalized*, 441.6 *murky*, 523.4 *difficult*

nebulous star 53.10 *star*

necessaries 593.1 *requirement*

necessarily 99.22 *really*, 103.13 *in essence*, 227.12 *with the effect of*, 593.12 *in need*, 695.11 *compellingly*

necessary 571, 52.86 *logical*, 99.10 *existing*, 103.5 *essential*, 490.1 *certain*, 490.5 *inevitable*, 571.1 *necessity*, 593.1 *requirement*, 593.4 *required*, 611.5 *important*, 695.9 *compelling*, 695.10 *compulsory*, 782.7 *desired*

necessary and sufficient condition 52.64 *reasoning*

necessary truth 4.8 *philosophical term*

necessitarian 571, 571.12 *inevitable*

necessitarianism 571

necessitate 571, 593, 695.6 *compel*

necessities 593.1 *requirement*

necessitous 593, 571.11 *needy*, 743.1 *poor*

necessitousness 593.3 *needfulness*, 743.5 *poverty*

necessity 571, 4.8 *philosophical term*, 99.4 *demonstrable existence*, 490.9 *certainty*, 490.16 *inevitability*, 593.1 *requirement*, 593.3 *needfulness*, 695.1 *compulsion*, 743.5 *poverty*

Necessity 571

neck 29.4 *golf club*, 30.6 *pommel horse*, 43.9 *miscellaneous architectural features*, 45.22 *beef*, 98.5 *peninsula*, 137.4 *means of connection*, 262.3 *contracted thing*, 272.8 *narrow thing*, 295.24 *part of garment*, 821.27 *kiss*, 826.7 *show endearment for*

neck and crop 144.9 *completely*, 241.10 *violently*

neck and neck 110.19, 122.12 *equally*, 198.4 *equal race*, 198.14 *equal with*

neck-and-neck 110.16 *equal*, 122.8 *on equal terms*, 198.11 *equal*, 264.5 *near*

neck-and-neck finish 674.2 *contest*

neck-and-neck race 110.5 *equality*, 122.2 *equilibrium*

Neckar 96 Rivers

neckband 137.10 *band*, 295.14 *neckwear*, 313.3 *circular thing*

neckcloth 295.14 *neckwear*

neckerchief 295.14 *neckwear*

necking 43 Architectural Decoration, 279.3 *architectural summit*, 821.6 *courtship*, 821.14 *communication of love*, 826.1 *endearment*

necklace 295.14 *neckwear*, 313.3 *circular thing*, 792.6 *jewellery*, 879.5 *execute*, 879.16 *instrument of execution*

neckmould 43 Architectural Decoration

neck of the womb 245.8 *organs of reproduction*

neck of the woods 249.13 *locality*, 250.1 *location*

neck or nothing 574.17 *resolutely*

neckpiece 295.14 *neckwear*

neck slice 45.27 *lamb*

neckstrap 32.14 *horse-riding terms*

neck sweetbread 45.31 *offal*

necktie 295.14 *neckwear*

neckwear 295

necrolater 9.6 *idolater*

necrolatrous 9.10 *idolatrous*

necrolatry 9.2 *idolatry*

necrological 399.11 *funeral*

necrologically 399.12 *funereally*

necrologist 399.3 *funeral director*

necrology 397.12 *death count*

necromancer 11.4 *witch*, 11.13 *diviner*

necromancy 11.3 *witchcraft*, 11.9, 517.2 *divination*

necromania 510.4 *delusion*

necromantic 11.15 *witchlike*

necromantically 11.26 *magically*

necrophobia 777 Phobias by Name

necropolis 399.5 *cemetery*

necropsy 397.8 *after death*, 399.7 *inquest*

necrose 141.3 *disintegrate*

necrosis 141.1 *disintegration*, 397.1 *death*

necrotic 141.6 *disintegrating*

necrotically 141.8 *destructively*

nectar 84.8 *flower product*, 351.2 *drink*, 352.2 *secreted substance*, 405.4 *pleasurable things*, 414.2 *sweetener*

nectared 414.6 *sweet*

nectareous 414.6 *sweet*

nectarine 86 Fruits, 451.3 *orange thing*

nectary 84.3 *flower part*, 352.3 *gland*

need 571, 593, 145.1 *incompleteness*, 145.2 *omission*, 145.5 *be incomplete*, 358.1 *fall short*, 358.5 *shortfall*, 513.11 *demand*, 571.1 *necessity*, 571.14 *necessitate*, 593.7 *require*, 599.6 *use*,

609.5 *be insufficient*, 609.6 *be unsatisfied*, 609.9 *scarcity*, 620.5 *imperfection*, 662.27 *find useful*, 687.2 *economic adversity*, 695.1 *compulsion*, 743.5 *poverty*, 743.12 *be poor*, 782.1, 782.12 *desire*

need a break 650.5 *be fatigued*
need a change 650.5 *be fatigued*
need a holiday 650.5 *be fatigued*
need an interpreter 523.7 *be unintelligible*
need a rest 650.5 *be fatigued*
need a vacation 650.5 *be fatigued*
need badly 593.8 *miss*
needed 571.9 *necessary*, 593.4 *required*, 782.7 *desired*
need few words 552.4 *be concise*
need for 593.3 *needfulness*
needful 571.11 *needy*, 593.4 *required*
needfulness **593,** 571.2 *indispensability*
need help 105.7 *be in a predicament*
neediness 593.3 *needfulness*, 743.5 *poverty*
needing 145.4 *incomplete*, 593.5 *necessitous*, 609.2 *unprovided*, 782.9 *desirous*
needing water 392.1 *dry*
need kid-glove treatment 760.11 *be sensitive*
needle 50.15 *engraving*, 56.82 *measuring instrument*, 67.5 *knitting*, 74.5 *navigation*, 83.6 *leaf*, 85.2 *tree part*, 228.10 *manipulate*, 322.2 *opener*, 380.8 *sharppointed thing*, 380.14 *be sharp*, 543.5 *indicator*, 653.5 *guide*, 828.9 *offend*
needle bath 389.11 *wash*
needle bearing 364.4 *vortex*
needle bush 85 Trees and Shrubs
needle candy 875.6 *drug*
needle cast 85.10 *tree disease*
needlefish 80 Fishes
needlegun 680.10 *historical gun*
needle-like 380.1 *sharp*
needle match 674.2 *contest*
needle-pointed 380.1 *sharp*
needles 777 Phobias by Topic
needle-sharp 380.1 *sharp*
needless 610.7 *superfluous*
needlessly 610.8 *excessively*
needless risk 780.2 *rash move*
needlewoman 295.26 *fashion designer*, 646.2 *artisan*
needlework 792.2 *pattern*
needleworker 295.26 *fashion designer*
need money 687
needs 593.1 *requirement*
need training 595.12 *be unprepared*
needy 571, 358.7 *short*, 593.5 *necessitous*, 743.1 *poor*
needy person 743.10 *poor person*
Néel temperature 56 Named Laws
neem 85 Trees and Shrubs
neep 45 Vegetables
ne'er 186.9 *never*
ne'er a one 100.6 *absence*
ne'er-do-well 722.6 *loser*, 801.2 *disreputable character*, 864.9 *wicked person*
nefarious 16.60 *offending*, 447.5 *black-hearted*, 801.4 *disreputable*, 858.5 *dishonourable*, 862.7 *evil*, 864.11 *wicked*
nefariously 862.12 *evilly*
Nefud 98 Deserts
negate 4.23 *discuss philosophically*, 100.14 *cause not to exist*, 117.12 *be disparate*, 231.3 - *counteract*, 244.8 *destroy*, 476.8 *refute*, 484.7 *counter*, 487.8 *make impossible*, 498.8 *disbelieve*, 500.9 *refuse*, 536.7 *be negative*, 578.4 *recant*, 581.4 *revoke*, 663.15 *object*, 704.6 *cancel*, 711.5 *refuse*, 727.9 *dispose of*
negated 484.6 *countered*, 536.12 *rejected*, 704.10 *cancelled*

negating 476.7 *refuting*, 711.8 *refused*, 713.9 *protesting*
negation 536, 4.8 *philosophical term*, 52.63 *mathematical logic*, 61.19 *defence mechanism*, 100.3 *negativeness*, 117.2 *contradiction*, 231.1 *counteraction*, 476.1 *refutation*, 476.2 *denial*, 484.1 *counterevidence*, 500.2 *disapproval*, 578.8 *recantation*, 581.7 *abrogation*, 704.1 *cancellation*, 711.1 *refusal*, 713.1 *protest*
Negation 536
negative 536, 52.71 *numerical*, 64.36 *electronic*, 66.12 *development*, 100.9 *nonexistent*, 110.4, 110.15 *duplicate*, 118.5 *duplicate*, 169.8 *odd*, 235.7 *electrical power*, 244.14 *destructive*, 442.8 *transparent thing*, 500.2 *disapproval*, 536.1 *negation*, 661.15 *inhibitive*, 663.22 *uncooperative*, 669.10 *resistant*, 711.8 *refused*, 713.9 *protesting*, 776.4 *hopeless*
negative acceleration 328.9 *deceleration*
negative answer 711.1 *refusal*
negative attitude 536.1 *negation*
negative balance of payments 745.2 *national debt*
negative charge 56.50 *electric charge*
negative command 692.1 *command*
negative correlation 52.61 *correlation*
negative electrode 235.7 *electrical power*
negative equity 687.2 *economic adversity*
negative feedback 64.15 *circuit function*, 672.1 *retaliation*
negative ion 56.66 *ion*
negatively 536, 52.87 *mathematically*, 64.37 *electronically*, 476.11 *in reply*, 661.18 *inhibitively*, 669.14 *resistingly*, 711.11 *uncooperatively*, 713.11 *disapprovingly*, 776.11 *hopelessly*
negativeness 100, 536.1 *negation*, 663.4 *uncooperativeness*, 669.1 *resistance*
negative number 52.5 *number*
negative outlook 495.1 *underestimation*
negative reaction 672.1 *retaliation*
negative reinforcement 61.20 *conditioning*
negative resistance 64.15 *circuit function*
negative result 683.1 *failure*
negative review 524.3 *criticism*
negative stimulus 228
negative transference 61.27 *association of ideas*
negative veto 852.3 *nonacceptance*
negative vote 580.10 *vote*
negativism 61.19 *defence mechanism*, 536.1 *negation*, 661.5 *inhibition*, 776.1 *hopelessness*
negativist 536, 661.7 *hinderer*, 663.9 *opposer*, 776.3 *hopeless person*
negativistic 776.4 *hopeless*
negativity 100.3 *negativeness*, 476.1 *refutation*, 536.1 *negation*, 663.4 *uncooperativeness*, 713.1 *protest*
negator 476.5 *refuter*
Negev 98 Deserts
neglect 145.5 *be incomplete*, 151.3 *untidiness*, 462.4 *inconsideration*, 470.6 *be neglectful*, 512.4 *unthinkingness*, 512.13 *forget*, 573.7 *refuse*, 573.15 *delay*, 595.8 *lack of preparation*, 600.5 *not use*, 600.8 *nonuse*, 628.9 *dilapidation*, 641.1 *inaction*, 641.4 *not act*, 683.1 *failure*, 685.1 *noncompletion*, 685.5 *not complete*, 720.1 *nonobservance*, 720.7 *not observe*, 783.2 *carelessness*, 838.6 *be ungrate-

ful, 850.2 *disesteem*, 850.21 *disregard*
neglected 145.4 *incomplete*, 600.4 *disused*, 612.2 *obscure*, 656.4 *bungled*, 685.4 *uncompleted*, 838.4 *unthanked*, 850.18 *undervalued*
neglectful 151.15 *untidy*, 462.10 *inconsiderate*, 468.10 *careless*, 470.4 *negligent*, 512.10 *unthinking*, 573.4 *procrastinating*, 641.3 *inactive*, 683.10 *failed*, 685.4 *uncompleted*, 720.11 *nonobservant*, 850.12 *disregardful*
neglectfully 145.6 *incompletely*, 470.7 *negligently*, 683.12 *unsuccessfully*, 685.7 *incompletely*
neglectfulness 470.1 *negligence*, 720.1 *nonobservance*
neglect one's obligations 720.7 *not observe*
neglect one's vows 720.7 *not observe*
neglect to finish 685.5 *not complete*
négligée 295.16 *robe*, 295.22 *nightwear*
negligence 470, 145.1 *incompleteness*, 151.3 *untidiness*, 482.6 *lack of discrimination*, 504.2 *inaccuracy*, 573.15 *delay*, 595.8 *lack of preparation*, 600.8 *nonuse*, 628.9 *dilapidation*, 641.1 *inaction*, 648.5 *hastiness*, 683.1 *failure*, 685.1 *noncompletion*, 720.1 *nonobservance*, 780.1 *rashness*, 783.2 *carelessness*, 866.3 *sin*
Negligence 470
negligent 470, 151.15 *untidy*, 468.10 *careless*, 482.1 *undiscriminating*, 512.10 *unthinking*, 573.4 *procrastinating*, 595.3 *without preparation*, 641.3 *inactive*, 648.3 *hasty*, 656.3 *clumsy*, 683.10 *failed*, 720.11 *nonobservant*, 780.4 *rash*, 783.8 *careless*, 850.12 *disregardful*
negligent dress 296.4 *dishabille*
negligently 470, 145.6 *incompletely*, 512.16 *obliviously*, 595.14 *unreadily*, 641.5 *without action*, 656.11 *unskilfully*, 683.12 *unsuccessfully*, 720.15 *inattentively*, 783.18 *carelessly*
negligently dressed 296.10 *in dishabille*
negligent person 470
negligible 260.7 *little*, 612.1 *unimportant*
negligibly 260.8 *in a small way*, 612.14 *unimportantly*
negotiability 717.1 *compromise*
negotiable 15.9 *negotiated*, 230.11 *workable*, 326.17 *transferable*, 715.7 *contractual*, 716.8 *negotiated*, 717.6 *compromising*, 728.5 *transferring*
negotiable instrument 741.14 *paper money*
negotiate 13.11 *deal*, 15.12 *have an industrial dispute*, 116.23 *arrange*, 158.19 *mediate*, 356.11 *cross*, 568.11 *confer*, 654.6 *consult*, 678.1 *mediate*, 707.5 *represent*, 710.10 *offer to buy*, 715.5 *contract*, 717.4 *compromise*, 737.3 *bargain*
negotiate a loan 732.5 *lend*, 733.7 *borrow*
negotiate a trade-off 746.6 *pay*
negotiate a treaty 715.5 *contract*
negotiated 15, 716, 116.12 *arranged*, 677.6 *pacificatory*, 715.7, 737.18 *contractual*
negotiated points 15.2 *industrial negotiations*
negotiated release 632.1 *safety*
negotiate for 707.4 *substitute for*
negotiate peace 678.1 *mediate*
negotiating 15.9 *negotiated*, 116.12 *arranged*, 715.7 *contractual*
negotiating body 706.2 *representative body*

negotiating rights 15.2 *industrial negotiations*
negotiation 716, 15.1 **industrial relations**, 678.2 *mediation*, 715.1 *contract*, 717.1 *compromise*, 737.9 *bargaining*
Negotiation 716
negotiations 15.4 *industrial dispute*, 568.5 *talks*, 654.2 *consultation*, 716.1 *negotiation*
negotiation session 654.2 *consultation*
negotiator 716, 158.9 *middleman*, 298.3 *interfacer*, 677.3 *pacifist*, 678.3 *mediator*, 706.1 *delegate*, 707.3 *agent*, 715.4 *contractor*, 728.2 *person transferring property*, 737.10 *trader*
Negrillo 1.6 *race*
Negrito 5 Languages and Groups of Languages, 1.6 *race*
Negro 1.6 *race*, 447.2 *dark*
Negroes 777 Phobias by Topic
Negroid 1.13 *racial*, 447.2 *dark*
Negroid race 1.6 *race*
Negroism 447.7 *blackness*
Negrophobia 777 Phobias by Name
Negros 98 Islands
negro spiritual 49.5 *sacred music*
negus 351.7 *alcoholic drink*
Nehru jacket 295.1 *jacket*
Neiderviller ware 44 Types of Ceramics
neigh 432.1 *animal cry*, 432.4 *cry*
neighbour 264, 267.3 *juxtapose*
neighbourhood 249.13 *locality*, 253.4 *availability*, 255.2 *inhabitants*, 256.2 *environment*, 256.15 *environmental*, 264.3 *near place*, 297.1 *surroundings*, 297.4 *surrounding*, 400.9 *group*
neighbourhood watch 16.17 *police officer*, 469.5 *watchfulness*
Neighbourhood Watch 632.3 *protector*, 718.4 *security forces*
neighbourhood watchman 469.8 *watchful person*
neighbouring 249.18 *local*, 264.5 *near*, 615.2 *nearby*
neighbourliness 815.1 *sociability*, 819.1 *friendship*
neighbourly 662.35 *benevolent*, 815.15 *sociable*, 819.8 *friendly*, 831.6 *benevolent*
Neisse 96 Rivers
neither confirm nor deny 529.12 *keep secret*, 566.8 *be taciturn*
neither good nor bad 124.3 *mediocre*, 617.5 *not bad*
neither here nor there 100.17 *nowhere*, 104.18 *extraneously*, 108.7 *illogical*, 124.12 *mediumly*, 158.22 *half and half*, 254.21 *away*
neither hide nor hair 100.7 *not any*
neither hot nor cold 333.4 *middle*
neither more no less 122.6 *equal*
neither more nor less 110.16 *equal*, 537.39 *accurately*
neither one thing nor the other 158.22 *half and half*, 333.4 *middle*, 491.14 *indeterminacy*, 717.6 *compromising*
Nekhebit 8 Deities
Nekhen 8 Deities
nekton 76.5 *aquatic animal*
nelson 27.10 *score*
Nelson 93 Cities
Nelson Bays 92 New Zealand Regions and Territories
Nematoda 81.6 *worm*
nematode 81 Worms, 81.6 *worm*
nematomorph 81.6 *worm*
Nematomorpha 81.6 *worm*
nembutsu 10.9 *prayer*
Nemertea 81.6 *worm*
nemertean 81.6 *worm*
Nemertina 81 Worms
nemesia 84 Flowers and Flowering Plants
nemesis 571.5 *inevitability*
Nemesis 8 Deities, 635.2 *troublemaker*, 672.1 *retaliation*, 828.7

gods and goddesses of anger, 855.6 *avenger,* 879.9 *retribution*
Nemi 94 Lakes
Nemon 8 Deities
Nemu 8 Deities
Neneh 8 Deities
neoclassical 43 Architectural Styles, 50.29 *realist*
neoclassic costume 295.5 *fancy dress*
neoclassicism 48 Literary Groups and Movements, **50** Western Art Styles and Movements
neocolonialism 12.3 *governance*
neo-Darwinian 59.27 *evolutionary*
neo-Darwinism 59.16 *evolution*
Neo-Darwinist 59.19 *life scientist*
neodymium 57 Chemical Elements
neodymium-glass laser 56.26 *laser*
neoexpressionism 50 Western Art Styles and Movements
neoexpressionist 50.29 *realist*
Neogene 54 Geological Time Intervals
Neo-Gothic 43 Architectural Styles
neoimpressionism 50 Western Art Styles and Movements
neoimpressionist 50.29 *realist*
neo-Lamarckian 59.27 *evolutionary*
neo-Lamarckism 59.16 *evolution*
Neo-Latin 5 Languages and Groups of Languages
neolith 3.11 *relic*
Neolithic 202.15 *primal*
Neolithic period 200.4 *prehistoric age*
neological 201.10 *new*
neologically 201.21 *newly*
neologism 5.17 *word,* 201.1 *newness*
neologist 5.2 *linguist,* 201.9 *modern person*
neologistic 5.42 *worded,* 201.10 *new*
neologistical 201.10 *new*
neologistically 5.50 *lexically,* 201.21 *newly*
neologize 5.45 *use language*
neology 201.1 *newness*
Neo-Melanesian 5 Languages and Groups of Languages
neomycin 62 Medication, 89.6 *fungal antibiotic*
neon 57 Chemical Elements
neo-Nazi 635.2 *troublemaker,* 679.1 *combatant*
neon lamp 56.25 *light source*
neon light 64.20 *electron tube,* 439.6 *electric light*
neon lighting 439.6 *electric light*
neophilia 201.1 *newness*
neophiliac 201.9 *modern person*
neophobia 777 Phobias by Name
neophyte 6.7 *learner,* 7.3 *religious person,* 156.14 *beginner,* 201.8 *new arrival,* 220.6 *convert*
neophytic 201.10 *new*
neoplasm 624.12 *cancer*
neoplastic disease 624.4 *disease*
Neo-Platonic 368.10 *idealistic*
Neo-Platonically 368.14 *subjectively*
Neo-Platonism 4.7 *school of thought,* 368.5 *idealism*
Neo-Platonist 4.11 *follower of a doctrine,* 4.14 *of a philosophy,* 368.7 *believer in a nonmaterial world*
neoprene 377.4 *rubber*
neorealism 48 Literary Groups and Movements
neoromantic 50.29 *realist*
neoromanticism 50 Western Art Styles and Movements
neosilicate 54.34 *mineral*
neotenous 59.26 *developmental,* 79.13 *amphibian*
neotenous amphibian 79.8 *young amphibian*
neoteny 59.15 *developmental biology,* 79.8 *young amphibian*

neoteric 201.9 *modern person*
Nepal 91 Countries
Nepali 5 Languages and Groups of Languages
nepenthe 630.5 *analgesic,* 643.10 *soporific*
nepenthes 761.6 *desensitizing substance*
neper 75 Scientific and Technical Units
nephanalysis 55.1 *meteorology*
nepheline 54 Minerals
nephew 401.13 *man in the family*
nephological 55.49 *cloudy*
nephology 55.1 *meteorology*
nephophobia 777 Phobias by Name, **777** Phobias by Name
nephrectomy 60 Surgical Operations
nephrite 54 Minerals
nephrologist 60.13 *medical specialist*
nephrology 60.3 *medical specialty*
nephrostomy 60 Surgical Operations
nephrotomy 60 Surgical Operations
nephroureterectomy 60 Surgical Operations
Nephthys 8 Deities
nepotism 481.5 *favouritism,* 493.3 *injustice*
nepotistic 481.10 *discriminatory*
Neptune 8 Deities, **53** Planets and their Satellites, 53.16 *planet,* 74.7 *nautical person,* 97.4 *sea god*
Neptunian 53.36 *astronomical*
neptunium 57 Chemical Elements
nerd 238.4 *weakling,* 502.5 *ignorant person,* 656.10 *unskilled person,* 788.3 *boring person,* 818.4 *discourteous person*
nerdy 502.6 *ignorant*
Nereid 8.5 *deity,* 97.4 *sea god*
Nereus 97.4 *sea god*
Nergal 8 Deities
neritic 54.52 *coastal*
Nernst 52 Scientists
Nernst calorimeter 56 Named Laws
Nerthus 8 Deities
Neruda 48 Poets
nerval 403.10 *sensory*
nerve 225.2 *determination,* 237.1 *strength,* 303.5 *boldness,* 403.4 *someone or something that feels,* 407.7 *sense organ,* 668.1 *defiance,* 778.1 *courage,* 807.2 *cheek*
nerve cell 403.4 *someone or something that feels*
nerve centre 291.4 *centre of activity,* 403.4 *someone or something that feels*
nerved 225.11 *determined*
nerve-end 403.4 *someone or something that feels*
nerve-ending 407.7 *sense organ*
nerve fibre 403.4 *someone or something that feels*
nerve gas 631.10 *warfare*
nerveless 236.12 *impotent,* 238.12 *weak-willed,* 404.6 *unfeeling,* 576.3 *timid*
nervelessness 238.2 *indecisiveness*
nerve oneself 237.8 *strengthen*
nerve-racking 633.2 *unsafe*
nerves 61.12 *stress,* 510.6 *mental breakdown,* 624.1 *ill health,* 642.7 *restlessness,* 777.2 *fearfulness*
nerves of steel 225.2 *determination,* 778.1 *courage*
nervily 668.9 *defiantly*
nerviness 366.1 *agitation,* 576.13 *timidity,* 668.1 *defiance*
nervosity 366.1 *agitation*
nervous 61.36 *psychologically disturbed,* 238.12 *weak-willed,* 366.15 *agitated,* 403.10 *sensory,* 642.18 *active,* 777.8 *fearful,* 781.4 *cautious,* 810.9 *blushing,* 829.4 *irascible*

nervous breakdown 61.10 *neurosis,* 510.6 *mental breakdown,* 624.17 *nervous disorder*
nervous disease 624.4 *disease*
nervous disorder 624, 61.9 *psychological disorder*
nervously 153.19 *distractedly,* 238.14 *weakly,* 242.9 *moderately,* 366.27 *agitatedly,* 576.16 *irresolutely,* 777.15 *fearfully,* 829.9 *irascibly*
nervousness 238.2 *indecisiveness,* 366.1 *agitation,* 576.13 *timidity,* 633.5 *danger,* 642.7 *restlessness,* 671.4 *defensiveness,* 777.2 *fearfulness*
nervous person 777.6 *frightened person*
nervous system 403.4 *someone or something that feels*
nervous tic 61.12 *stress,* 366.8 *spasm,* 510.6 *mental breakdown*
nervous wreck 777.6 *frightened person*
nervy 366.15 *agitated,* 576.3 *timid,* 642.18 *active,* 668.7 *defiant,* 760.2 *oversensitive,* 777.8 *fearful,* 807.14 *cheeky*
nescience 462.2, 502.1 *ignorance,* 658.2 *naivety*
nescient 502.6 *ignorant*
ness 318.2 *projection*
Ness 94 Lakes
nest 78, 78, 82.5 *larva,* 156.3 *source,* 181.4 *throng,* 256.3 *home,* 256.13 *lair,* 256.18 *take up residence,* 634.3 *animal shelter*
nestbox 78.14 *nest,* 78.19 *ornithology*
nest building 78.14 *nest*
nest egg 594.10 *preparations,* 602.5 *reserves,* 605.1 *store,* 632.2 *protection,* 742.5 *wealth,* 781.2 *insurance*
nesting 65.17 *computing term*
nestle 256.18 *take up residence,* 405.8 *feel pleasure,* 821.27 *kiss,* 826.7 *show endearment for*
nestling 78.12 *young bird,* 156.15 *baby,* 206.4 *young animal*
nest of tables 266.5 *layered thing*
Nestor 4.12 *sage,* 202.2 *old people,* 654.4 *adviser*
Nestorian Church 7 Christian Movements
nest site 78.14 *nest*
net 67 Natural Fabrics, 20.7 *angle,* 23.3 *basketball equipment,* 38.1 *soccer,* 40.3 *tennis equipment,* 40.5, 40.5 *real tennis,* 80.15 *fish,* 132.10 *surplus,* 135.1 *union,* 288.2 *braid,* 288.8 *interweave,* 295.15 *headgear,* 301.4 *wrapper,* 301.6 *wrap,* 442.8 *transparent thing,* 539.13, 539.33 *snare,* 590.11 *hunt,* 635.3 *trap,* 657.2 *stratagem,* 721.5 *profit,* 721.15 *gainful,* 725.8 *propertied,* 730.9, 749.7 *receive*
Net 8 Deities, **53** The Constellations
net assets 725.5 *personal estate*
netball 18 Sporting Activities
Neter 8 Deities
nether 276.6 *lower*
Netherlands 91 Countries
nethermost 280.3 *base*
nether regions 276.4 *low thing,* 368.1 *nonmaterial world,* 397.14 *the spiritual world*
nether world 8.11 *heaven,* 368.1 *nonmaterial world,* 397.14 *the spiritual world*
net player 40.6 *tennis player*
net position 40.4 *tennis terms*
net post 40.5 *real tennis*
net posts 40.11 *badminton equipment*
net profit 13.7 *corporation,* 878.5 *turnover*
net profits 721.5 *profit,* 749.2 *money received*

net receipts 721.4 *earnings,* 730.2 *something received,* 749.2 *money received*
net result 195.9 *sequel,* 227.1 *effect*
net return 721.4 *earnings*
net revenue 721.4 *earnings*
net score 29.2 *golfing terms*
nett 120.4 *total*
netted 67.10 *woven,* 539.42 *trapped*
netting 67 Natural Fabrics, 288.2 *braid*
nettle 84 Flowers and Flowering Plants, 380.8 *sharp-pointed thing,* 631.6 *source of trouble,* 828.9 *offend,* 829.8 *make irascible*
nettled 828.15 *resentful,* 829.4 *irascible*
nettle family 83.3 *seed plant*
nettle rash 624.13 *skin disease*
net ton 75 General Units
net weight 369.7 *weighing*
network 65, 56.55, 64.13 *circuit,* 135.1 *union,* 135.10 *link,* 137.2 *association,* 137.13 *intercommunicate,* 140.5 *combine,* 232.5 *find means,* 288.2 *braid,* 383.4 *weave,* 534.6 *telecommunication*
network architecture 65.15 *network*
network database 65.11 *application*
networked 140.7 *combined*
networking 664.3 *mutual relationship*
network television 534.24 *television broadcasting*
net worth 725.5 *personal estate*
Neuburg an der Donau 93 Cities
Neue Sachlichkeit 50 Western Art Styles and Movements
Neufchâtel 45 Cheeses
Neumann 52 Scientists
Neumann's law 56 Named Laws
neural computer 65.16 *artificial intelligence*
neuralgia 406.2 *painful condition,* 624.17 *nervous disorder*
neural net 65.16 *artificial intelligence*
neurasthenia 510.6 *mental breakdown*
neurectomy 60 Surgical Operations
neurilemma 624.17 *nervous disorder*
neurocomputer 65.16 *artificial intelligence*
neurohormone 58.16 *hormone*
neurohumour 58.16 *hormone*
neuroleptic 62.4 *drug type,* 62.15 *sedative*
neurological 60.22 *medical,* 403.10 *sensory*
neurological disease 624.4 *disease*
neurologist 60.13 *medical specialist*
neurology 60.3 *medical specialty,* 382.8 *science of structure*
neurone 403.4 *someone or something that feels*
neuronoplasty 60 Surgical Operations
neuropath 61.8 *disordered personality,* 624.19 *sick person*
neuropsychiatric 61.32 *psychological*
neuropsychiatrist 61.30 *psychiatrist*
neuropsychiatry 61.2 *psychiatry*
neuropsychology 61.1 *psychology*
Neuroptera 82 Orders of Insects
neuropteran 82.10 *insectan*
neuroscience 59.1 *life science*
neurosis 61, 61.9 *psychological disorder,* 510.6 *mental breakdown,* 624.1 *ill health*
neurosurgeon 60.13 *medical specialist*
neurosurgery 60.9 *surgery*
neurotic 61.8 *disordered personality,* 61.36 *psychologically disturbed,* 153.16 *deranged,*

510.7 *insane person*, 510.13
mentally ill, 760.9 *oversensitive
person*
neurotically 61.39 *psychologically*, 153.19 *distractedly*,
510.17 *insanely*
neurotic-depressive reaction
61.10 *neurosis*
neurotic disorder 61.10 *neurosis*
neuroticism 61.10 *neurosis*,
510.6 *mental breakdown*
neurotic personality 61.8 *disordered personality*
neurotomy 60 Surgical Operations
Neusiedl 94 Lakes
neuter 5.44 *grammatical*, 236.9
make impotent, 247.8 *make infertile*, 367.7 *material*
neutered 236.13 *unsexed*, 247.5
rendered infertile
neutering 247.2 *making infertile*
neutral 31.8 *hockey*, 56.52 *electric potential*, 57.36 *acid*, 64.36
electronic, 136.17 *unjoined*,
158.14 *mediatory*, 242.7 *politically moderate*, 333.4 *middle*,
445.7 *colourless*, 448.1 *grey*,
482.2 *impartial*, 591.18 *avoiding*, 641.3 *inactive*, 675.3 *pacifist*, 675.7 *peaceful*, 698.7 *free
person*, 698.9 *free*, 717.8 *irresolute*, 783.6 *indifferent person*,
783.9 *impartial*, 843.7 *right*,
859.4 *disinterested*
neutral colour 444.1 *colour*
neutral-density filter 66.20 *filter*
neutral ground 333.2 *middle of
the road*
neutral hue 445.1 *colourlessness*
neutralist 333.3 *moderate person*,
783.6 *indifferent person*
neutrality 108.1 *unrelatedness*,
242.1 *moderation*, 333.2 *middle
of the road*, 400.11 *nation*,
482.7 *impartiality*, 591.12 *shyness*, 675.1 *peace*, 698.1 *freedom*, 717.3 *irresolution*, 783.3
impartiality, 859.1 *disinterestedness*
neutralization 57 Types of
Chemical Reaction, 57.14
chemical reaction, 125.2 *counterbalance*, 231.1 *counteraction*,
236.1 *powerlessness*, 238.1
weakness, 704.4 *cancelling out*
neutralize 57.26 *react*, 109.8 *interrelate*, 125.5 *counterbalance*,
231.3 *counteract*, 236.7 *remove
power from*, 242.4 *moderate*,
244.8 *destroy*, 630.19 *remedy*,
643.14 *make inactive*, 704.9
cancel out
neutralized 57.41 *analytic*,
125.10 *counterbalancing*,
704.10 *cancelled*
neutralizer 231.1 *counteraction*
neutralizing 125.10 *counterbalancing*, 231.4 *counteracting*,
704.4 *cancelling out*
neutrally 136.22 *in isolation*,
333.8 *medially*, 445.9
colourlessly, 482.15 *impartially*,
698.20 *freely*, 717.10 *irresolutely*, 859.8 *disinterestedly*
neutral nation 91.1 *country*
neutral person 333.3 *moderate
person*
neutral stick 31.3 *ice hockey*
neutral tint 445.1 *colourlessness*,
448.4 *greyness*
neutral zone 31.3 *ice hockey*
neutrino 56.77 *elementary particle*, 260.2 *little thing*
neutron 56.65 *atom*, 56.77 *elementary particle*, 260.2 *little
thing*, 367.4 *matter*
neutron bomb 235.8 *nuclear
power*, 680.16 *bomb*
neutron number 56.69 *isotope*
neutron star 53.11 *stellar birth*
neutrophil 387.4 *blood*
Nevada 92 American States
neve 34.5 *rock face*
never 186
never! 536

never 100.16 *not ever*, 711.12
no, 786.14 *wonderful*
never again 157.28 *conclusively*,
174.24 *once*
never a one 100.6 *absence*
never cease 184.9 *be infinite*,
190.5 *be eternal*
never darken my door again
345.15 *go*
never despair 574.11 *persist*,
575.8 *hold out*
never die 184.9 *be infinite*
never end 184.9 *be infinite*,
553.5 *be diffuse*, 788.6 *be boring*
neverending 190.8 *eternal*
never-ending 159.11 *continuous*,
184.3 *eternal*, 553.3 *diffuse*,
685.4 *uncompleted*
never-ending story 685.1 *noncompletion*
never-ending task 685
never-failing 682.13 *successful*
never full 872.6 *gluttonous*
never give up hope 575.8 *hold
out*
never hear the last of 183.18 *hold
harp*
never ill 623.1 *healthy*
never in a million years 186.9
never
never in a month of Sundays
489.9 *unexpectedly*
never learn 500.8 *be foolish*
never let go 726.6 *retain*
never let liquor pass one's lips
873.3 *be sober*
never look back 336.9 *maintain
progress*
never mind 612.15 *no matter*
never mind! 783
neverness 186.1 *timelessness*
never-never land 519.8 *dreamland*
never on time 209.9 *late*
never out of date 186.5 *timeless*
never out of fashion 186.5 *timeless*
never-resting 642.20 *industrious*
never say die 219.8 *go on*, 237.7
be strong, 574.11 *persist*, 575.8
hold out, 775.9 *be hopeful*
never say die! nil desperandum!
where there's life **775**
never-slacking 642.20 *industrious*
never-sleeping 642.20 *industrious*
never sober 874.5 *drunken*
never solved 523.2 *unexplained*
never stop 329.2 *be full of vigour*, 642.15 *try*
never surrender 574.11 *persist*
nevertheless 327.16 *how*
never the same 113.5 *diverse*,
224.13 *changeable*
never the twain shall meet
136.21 *apart*
never-tiring 642.20 *industrious*
never touch 869.5 *be self-restrained*
never touch a drop 873.3 *be sober*
never vary 584.16 *have a habit*
Nevis 95 Mountains
new 201, 600, 115.4 *dissimilar*,
119.5 *novel*, 130.9 *extra*,
156.32 *embryonic*, 201.21
newly, 453.4 *fresh*, 479.9 *original*, 585.1 *unaccustomed*
New Age 201.2 *trendiness*
New-Age traveller 104.5, 168.7
nonconformist, 224.7 *person
who moves around*
New American Bible 201.7 *new
thing*
Newara 5 Languages and
Groups of Languages
Newark 93 Cities, **93** Cities
new arrival 104, **201**, 149.7
newcomer, 195.5 *successor*
new-baked bread 418.2 *fragrant
thing*
new ball 27.7 *bat*
New Bedford 93 Cities
new beginning 704, 221.2 *restoration*
new beginnings 156
new birth 396.5 *life cycle*,
629.10 *revival*

new blood 195.5 *successor*
newborn 156.15 *baby*, 156.32
embryonic, 201.12 *immature*,
322.17 *beginning*, 396.15 *born*
newborn babe 865.4 *innocent
person*
newborn baby 201.8 *new arrival*
new boy 104.7 *new arrival*,
149.7 *newcomer*, 156.14 *beginner*, 195.5 *successor*, 201.8 *new
arrival*, 346.7 *entrant*
New Britain 98 Islands
new broom 155.13 *replacement*,
195.5 *successor*, 201.8 *new arrival*, 642.10 *busy person*, 704.5
abrogator
New Brunswick 92 Canadian
Provinces and Territories, **93**
Cities
new-brutalist 43 Architectural
Styles
new business 592.1 *plan*
New Caledonia 98 Islands
Newcastle 93 Cities, **93** Cities
Newcastle-upon-Tyne 93 Cities,
93.4 *British cities*
new chapter 156.13 *new beginnings*
new city 249.10 *urban area*
Newcombe 18 Sporting Personalities
New Comedy 51.10 *comedy*
newcomer 149, 104.7 *new arrival*, 195.5 *successor*, 201.8
new arrival, 346.7 *entrant*,
865.4 *innocent person*
New Consciousness 61.3 *psychiatric treatment*
new convert 201.8 *new arrival*
New Critic 48.15 *literary person*
New Criticism 524.3 *criticism*
New Deal 201.7 *new thing*,
627.11 *reformism*
New Dealer 627.12 *reformer*
New Delhi 93 Cities
New Democratic Party 12.6 *political party*
new departure 119.1 *originality*,
156.13 *new beginnings*
New Drama 51.8 *theatre movements*
new edition 183.5 *repeat*, 245.2
print, 627.8 *better thing*
newel 281.3 *vertical thing*
newel post 281.3 *vertical thing*
new energy 629.10 *revival*
New England clam chowder
45.43 *US dish*
New England dialect 5.26 *dialect*
New Englander 255.10 *US inhabitant*
New English Art Club 50 Schools
and Groups of Artists
New English Bible 7.12 *religious
text*
new face 104.7 *new arrival*,
149.7 *newcomer*, 346.7 *entrant*
new-fallen snow 446.9 *white
thing*
newfangled 5.42 *worded*, 201.11
unfamiliar
newfangled expression 5.17 *word*
newfangledness 201.1 *newness*
new-fledged 206.11 *young*
New Forest pony 32 Breeds of
Horse and Pony
Newfoundland 77 Breeds of
Dogs, 92 Canadian Provinces
and Territories, **98** Islands
new franc 741.11 *national coins*
New General Catalogue 53.6 *star
catalogue*
new generation 201.6 *avant-
garde*
new girl 149.7 *newcomer*,
156.14 *beginner*, 346.7 *entrant*
New Guinea 98 Islands
New Hampshire 92 American
States
New Hampshire Red 68 Breeds
of Fowl
New Haven 93 Cities
new high 126.4 *summit*
new hope 629.10 *revival*
new idea 627.8 *better thing*
New Ireland 98 Islands
New Jersey 92 American States

new kid 149.7 *newcomer*
new kid on the block 104.7 *new
arrival*, 195.5 *successor*, 201.8
new arrival
New Kingdom art 50 Non-Western Art
New Kirgiz 32 Breeds of Horse
and Pony
new-laid 396.15 *born*
new lamps for old 223.3 *something in exchange*
Newlands 52 Scientists
Newland's law 57 Named Reactions
Newland's octaves 57.6 *chemical
element*
new leaf 156.13 *new beginnings*,
201.5 *fresh start*, 627.5 *improvement*, 704.3 *new beginning*
new life 629.10 *revival*, 651.5 *refreshment*
New London 93 Cities
new look 201.5 *fresh start*, 629.8
repair, 796.1 *fashion*
New Look 201.2 *trendiness*
new-look 201.14 *renewed*
newly 201, 600, 119.8 *originally*, 201.10 *new*
newly born 396.15 *born*
newly fledged 78.24 *newly
hatched*
newly hatched 78
newly opened 156.37 *enrolled*
newly produced 201.10 *new*
newlywed 823.21 *married*
newlyweds 823.9 *married couple*
new-made 201.10 *new*
new man 201.9 *modern person*,
220.6 *convert*, 401.14 *liberated
man*, 760.8 *sensitive person*
Newmarket 42 Card Games, **93**
Cities
new mathematics 52.1 *mathematics*
new maths 201.7 *new thing*
new member 201.8 *new arrival*,
346.7 *entrant*
New Mexico 92 American States
new money 742.6 *money*
new moon 53.17 *moon*, 201.7
new thing
new-mown hay 418.2 *fragrant
thing*
newness 201, 600, 119.1,
479.4 *originality*, 595.10 *immaturity*
Newness 201
New Orleans 93 Cities, 93.2
American cities
new page 156.13 *new beginnings*
new penny 741.9 *British money*
new poor 743.11 *the poor*
Newport 93 Cities, **93** Cities,
93 Cities
Newport News 93 Cities
new production 51.12 *production*, 201.1 *newness*
New Providence 93 Cities
new recruit 201.8 *new arrival*
new resident 104.7 *new arrival*
new resolution 627.5 *improvement*
Newry 93 Cities
news 533, 472.3 *matter of interest*, 528.1 *information*, 528.4
mass communication, 534.25
broadcast material, 611.2 *important matter*, 636.1 *warning*,
654.1 *advice*
News 533
news account 533.2 *news event*
news agency 528.8 *source of information*, 533.7 *press agency*
newsagent 533.11 *news source*,
739.13 *retailer*
news analysis 533.9 *news story*
news article 533.9 *news story*
news beat 533.11 *news source*
news blackout 709.2 *censorship*
newsboy 533.11 *news source*
news brief 533.9 *news story*
news bulletin 533.9 *news story*
news bureau chief 533.4 *journalist*
news camera crew 533.4 *journalist*
news cameraman 533.4 *journalist*

newscast 528.4 *mass communication,* 533.6 *radio news*
newscaster 528.9 *informant,* 533.4 *journalist,* 534.29 *broadcaster,* 646.1 *worker*
newscasting 533.3 *reporting*
news commentator 528.9 *informant,* 533.4 *journalist*
news conference 528.4 *mass communication,* 532.8 *public relations ,* 533.2 *news event*
news coverage 293.20 *fixing,* 528.4 *mass communication*
news crew 533.4 *journalist*
newsdealer 533.11 *news source*
news desk 533.8 *newsroom*
news dispatch 533.9 *news story*
news documentary 534.25 *broadcast material*
news editor 532.11 *newspaper man*
news event 533
news flash 533.9 *news story*
news gathering 533.3 *reporting*
news happening 533.2 *news event*
newshound 528.9 *informant,* 533.4 *journalist*
newsie 533.11 *news source*
news interpreter 524
news item 293.20 *fixing,* 528.4 *mass communication,* 533.9 *news story,* 561.2 *article*
newsletter 187.7 *periodical,* 532.5 *journal,* 533.11 *news source*
newsmagazine 532.5 *journal,* 533.5 *mass communication*
newsman 532.11 *newspaper man,* 533.4 *journalist,* 534.29 *broadcaster,* 545.9 *recorder,* 646.1 *worker*
news media 533.5 *mass communication*
newsmonger 528.10 *informer*
news organization 533.5 *mass communication*
New South Wales 92 *Australian States and Territories*
news outlet 533.5 *mass communication*
newspaper 532, 533.5 *mass communication*
newspapering 532.3 *journalism,* 533.3 *reporting*
newspaperman 532, 533.4 *journalist*
newspaper proprietor 532.11 *newspaperman*
newspaperwoman 532.11 *newspaperman*
newspaper world 532.3 *journalism*
newspeak 5.20 *jargon word,* 578.5 *equivocalness*
news photographer 533.4 *journalist*
news pool 533.4 *journalist*
newsprint 533.11 *news source,* 604.3 *paper*
newsprint ink 447.8 *black pigment*
news programme 533.9 *news story*
newsreader 528.9 *informant,* 533.4 *journalist,* 534.29 *broadcaster*
newsreel 533.6 *radio news*
news release 528.4 *mass communication,* 533.9 *news story*
news report 533.9 *news story,* 534.25 *broadcast material*
news reporter 532.11 *newspaper man,* 533.4 *journalist*
news reporting 533.3 *reporting*
news review 533.9 *news story*
newsroom 533
news roundup 534.25 *broadcast material*
news service 533.7 *press agency*
newssheet 533.11 *news source*
news-sheet 532.5 *journal*
news source 533, 524.7 *news interpreter*
newsspeak 564.1 *faculty of speech*
news staff 533.4 *journalist*

news stall 533.11 *news source*
newsstand 533.11 *news source,* 740.9 *stall*
news story 533
news style 533.9 *news story*
news summary 534.25 *broadcast material*
news syndicate 528.8 *source of information*
new start 201.5 *fresh start*
news update 533.9 *news story*
new supply 629.10 *revival*
news vendor 533.11 *news source*
newswoman 532.11 *newspaper man,* 534.29 *broadcaster*
newsworthy 528, 533.14 *journalistic,* 611.6 *notable*
newsy 528.17 *newsworthy,* 533.14 *journalistic,* 568.14 *conversational*
newt 79 *Amphibians*
new tack 156.13 *new beginnings*
new technology 243.2 *manufacture,* 602.1 *means*
new term 5.17 *word*
New Testament 7.12 *religious text*
new thing 201
new things 777 *Phobias by Topic*
New Thought 201.2 *trendiness*
newtlike 79.13 *amphibian*
new to 585.1 *unaccustomed*
newton 75 *SI Units*
Newton 52 *Scientists*
Newtonian mechanics 56.2 *classical physics,* 367.6 *natural science*
Newtonian telescope 53.24 *telescope*
Newton St Boswells 93 *Cities*
Newton's law of cooling 56 *Named Laws*
Newton's law of gravitation 56 *Named Laws*
Newton's laws of motion 56 *Named Laws*
Newton's method 52 *Named Concepts*
Newton's rings 56 *Named Laws*
new to the job 201.12 *immature*
new town 93.9 *town,* 201.7 *new thing,* 249.11 *settlement*
Newtown 93 *Cities*
Newtownabbey 93 *Cities*
New Wave 49.9 *popular music,* 201.2 *trendiness*
new way 652.7 *way*
new word 5.17 *word*
New World 249.7 *regions of the world*
New World monkey 77 *Placental Mammals*
New World monkeys 77.16 *primate*
new wrinkle 201.1 *newness,* 201.7 *new thing*
New Year 201.7 *new thing*
New Year Honours 878.1 *reward*
New Year party 665.7 *social gathering*
New Year's Day 214.6 *annually celebrated day*
New York 45 *Cheeses,* 92 *American States,* 93 *Cities,* 93.2 *American cities,* 249.10 *urban area*
New York City Ballet 46.12 *ballet companies*
New Yorker 255.10 *US inhabitant*
New York school 50 *Western Art Styles and Movements*
New Zealand 91 *Countries,* 98 *Islands*
New Zealand greenstone 54 *Gemstones*
next 155, 155.28 *after,* 195.12 *succeeding,* 264.5 *near*
next door 264.6 *near,* 615.2 *nearby*
next-door 249.18 *local,* 264.5 *near*
next-door neighbour 264.4 *neighbour*
next generation 201.6 *avant-garde*
next-generation 227.10 *caused*
next in line 195.5 *successor,* 730.6, 845.7 *beneficiary*

next instalment 155.4 *sequel*
next man in 195.5 *successor*
next month 199.1 *future time,* 199.14 *in the future*
next of kin 513.4 *expectant person*
next step 336.14 *development*
next to 615.8 *nearby*
next week 199.1 *future time,* 199.14 *in the future*
next world 397.14 *the spiritual world*
next year 199.1 *future time,* 199.14 *in the future*
nexus 137.2 *association,* 137.4 *means of connection,* 159.2 *consecution,* 210.3 *critical time,* 407.6 *contiguity,* 611.3 *chief thing*
Nez Percé 1 *Peoples,* 5 *Languages and Groups of Languages*
NFC 19.1 *football*
NFL 19.1 *football*
ngaio 85 *Trees and Shrubs*
ngoma 49 *Musical Instruments*
Nguni 1 *Peoples,* 5 *Languages and Groups of Languages,* 68 *Breeds of Cattle*
nguru 49 *Musical Instruments*
Nguruhe 8 *Deities*
NHR 57.17 *analysis*
NHS hospital 60.10 *hospital*
NHS trust hospital 60.10 *hospital*
Niagara Falls 93 *Cities,* 93 *Cities*
nialamide 62 *Medication*
Niasese 5 *Languages and Groups of Languages*
nib 380.8 *sharp-pointed thing*
nibble 65.17 *computing term,* 350.14 *mouthful,* 350.21 *eat,* 350.23 *taste,* 411.3 *appetizer,* 411.9 *taste,* 821.14 *communication of love,* 826.1 *endearment*
nibbler 350.18 *eater,* 411.5 *taster*
nibbles 45.10 *snack*
nibbling 350.3 *delicate eating*
Nibelung 260.4 *little person*
niblick 29.4 *golf club*
Nicaragua 91 *Countries,* 94 *Lakes,* 94.5 *other major lakes*
niccolite 54 *Minerals*
nice 134.14 *purified,* 405.6 *pleasant,* 469.9 *careful,* 503.5, 537.21 *accurate,* 617.5 *not bad,* 621.16 *clean,* 763.1 *pleasant,* 817.7 *courteous,* 831.6 *benevolent,* 861.3 *kind*
Nice 93 *Cities*
nice distinction 503.3 *accurate thing*
nice little earner 742.5 *wealth*
nicely **861,** 817.14 *courteously*
niceness 469.4 *fastidiousness,* 537.8 *accuracy,* 763.6 *pleasantness,* 817.1 *courtesy,* 831.1 *benevolence,* 861.10 *kindness*
nice point 654.3 *precept*
nice predicament 659.5 *predicament*
nicety 503.1, 537.8 *accuracy*
Nichant 8 *Deities*
niche 34.5 *rock face,* 59.18 *ecology,* 152.6 *category,* 163.2 *class,* 256.2 *environment,* 288.5 *compartment,* 317.3 *cavity,* 531.2 *hiding place*
Nichiren 7 *Non-Christian Religions*
Nicholas 68 *Breeds of Fowl*
Nichrome 57 *Alloys*
nick 265.2, 265.5 *crack,* 319.1, 319.5 *notch,* 323.4 *closed place,* 539.33 *snare,* 699.11 *detain,* 702.2 *the inside ,* 734.3 *taking away,* 734.10 *take away,* 736.12 *steal*
nicked 16.59 *stolen*
nickel 57 *Chemical Elements,* 56.59 *ferromagnetism,* 741.8 *American money*
nickel bronze 57 *Alloys*
nickel coinage 741.13 *coinage*
nickel defence 19.10 *defence*
nickelic 57.34 *elemental*
nickeliferous 57.34 *elemental*
nickelous 57.34 *elemental*

nickel silver 57 *Alloys,* 539.6 *imitation*
nicker 432.4 *cry,* 741.9 *British money*
nicking 734.2 *taking back,* 736.1 *stealing*
Nicklaus 18 *Sporting Personalities*
nickles and dimes 741.4 *change*
nickname 560.8 *name*
nicknames for lovers 821
nicknaming 560.7 *nomenclature*
nick of time 210.3 *critical time*
nick someone for 539.30 *be fraudulent*
Nicobarese 5 *Languages and Groups of Languages*
Nicol prism 56 *Named Laws*
Nicosia 93 *Cities*
nicotiana 84 *Flowers and Flowering Plants*
nicotine 413.7 *tobacco,* 630.7 *tonic,* 631.11 *intoxicant*
nicotinic acid 58.13 *vitamin*
nicotinyl 62 *Medication*
nictitation 436.2 *poor sight*
nidicolous 78.24 *newly hatched*
nidification 78.14 *nest*
nidifugous 78.24 *newly hatched*
nidify 78.26 *nest*
nidus 82.5 *larva*
niece 402.12 *woman in the family*
niello 447.8 *black pigment,* 447.11 *blacken*
Nielsen 49 *Musicians and Composers*
niente 49 *Musical Terms*
Nietzsche 4 *Philosophers*
Nietzschean 4.11 *follower of a doctrine,* 4.14 *of a philosophy*
Nietzscheanism 4.7 *school of thought*
NIFE cell 57.19 *electrochemistry*
niff 419.1 *stench,* 419.5 *stink*
niffy 419.3 *stinking*
Niflheim 8.11 *heaven*
niftily 329.14 *swiftly*
nifty 329.1 *swift*
nifty pace 329.8 *speed*
nifuratel 62 *Medication*
Niger 91 *Countries,* 96 *Rivers,* 96.5 *other major rivers*
Niger-Congo 5 *Languages and Groups of Languages*
Nigeria 91 *Countries*
niggard 161.36 *hoarder,* 758.5 *miser*
niggardliness 758.3 *parsimony,* 860.1 *selfishness*
niggardly 182.6 *sparse,* 609.1 *insufficient,* 758.1 *mean,* 758.9 *meanly,* 860.4 *selfish*
nigger in the woodpile 635.2 *troublemaker,* 661.2 *obstacle*
nigger-rig 609.5 *be insufficient*
nigger-rigging 614.5 *waste of effort*
niggertown 93.7 *city district*
niggle 852.18 *find fault*
niggling 612.4 *trivial,* 852.6, 852.28 *fault-finding*
niggun 10.8 *hymn*
nigh 199.11 *future,* 264.5, 264.6 *near*
night 777 *Phobias by Topic,* **205,** 438.6 *that which makes invisible,* 447.7 *blackness*
night and day 111.2 *opposites,* 159.19 *continuously,* 212.1 *frequently,* 365.1 *oscillation*
night attack 670.12 *military attack*
night-blind 436.9 *weak-sighted*
night blindness 58.14 *vitamin deficiency disease,* 436.2 *poor sight*
night-blindness 440.1 *darkness*
nightcap 422 *moderator,* 295.22 *nightwear,* 345.9 *parting,* 643.10 *soporific*
nightclothes 295.22 *nightwear*
nightclub 51.14 *theatre,* 205.5 *night thing*
night court 16.21 *US court*
night court judge 16.24 *US judge*
night dew 391.6 *dew*

nightdress 295.22 *nightwear,* 296.4 *dishabille*
nightfall 205.1 *evening,* 360.4 *fall*
night falls 440.13 *become dark*
night fighter 73 *Types of Aircraft,* 679.31 *military aircraft*
night glasses 435.10 *visual aid*
nightgown 296.4 *dishabille*
night hawk 78 *Birds*
night heron 78 *Birds*
nightie 295.22 *nightwear,* 296.4 *dishabille*
nightingale 78 *Birds,* 78.6 *songbird,* 433.5 *melodist*
nightjar 78 *Birds*
night lamping 37.2 *hunting*
nightlife 205.5 *night thing*
nightlight 439.7 *lantern*
nightly 205.6, 205.7 *evening,* 214.12 *cyclic,* 214.16 *cyclically*
night mail 72.7 *train*
nightmare 102.2 *illusion,* 205.5 *night thing,* 519.5 *fantasy,* 636.3 *false alarm,* 777.5 *frightener*
night nurse 60.16 *nurse*
Night of the Long Knives 398.4 *slaughter*
night patrol 679.14 *armed forces*
nightpiece 50.10 *art subject*
nights 110.20 *regularly,* 205.7 *evening*
night safe 605.4 *storage*
night-scented stock 84 *Flowers and Flowering Plants*
night school 6.12 *educational institution,* 205.5 *night thing*
night shift 205.5 *night thing*
night-shift 15.9 *negotiated*
night-shift work 15.2 *industrial negotiations*
nightshirt 295.22 *nightwear*
night sister 60.16 *nurse*
night soil 353.5 *faeces,* 622.4 *dirt*
night sounds 633.6 *danger signal*
nightspot 51.14 *theatre*
night thing 205
night-time 205.2 *night,* 205.6 *evening,* 209.2 *late hour*
Night-time 205
night vision 435.1 *vision*
night watch 205.3 *midnight,* 671.14 *guard,* 679.14 *armed forces*
night watchman 27.4 *team,* 323.5 *person who closes,* 435.11 *observer,* 632.3 *protector,* 671.14 *guard,* 718.3 *security officer*
nightwear 295, 296.4 *dishabille*
nigrescence 447.7 *blackness*
nigrescent 447.1 *black*
nigritude 447.7 *blackness*
nigrosine 447.8 *black pigment*
nihilism 4.7 *school of thought,* 151.8 *lawlessness,* 689.2 *anarchism*
nihilist 4.11 *follower of a doctrine,* 4.14 *of a philosophy,* 151.11 *troublemaker,* 244.6 *destroyer,* 641.2 *nonacting person,* 689.3 *anarchist,* 713.5 *seditionist,* 713.10 *law-breaking,* 832.8 *malefactor*
nihilistic 151.20 *disorderly,* 689.7 *anarchistic*
nihility 100.2, 172.3 *nothingness,* 254.1 *absence*
nihil obstat 708.2 *permit*
Nihongi 7.12 *religious text*
nikau 85 *Trees and Shrubs*
Nikaya 7.12 *religious text*
Nike 8 *Deities*
nikethamide 62 *Medication*
Nikkal 8 *Deities*
Nikkei Dow Index 14.2 *stock exchange*
nikkyo 26.10 *aikido*
nil 100.2 *nothingness,* 172.1, 172.6 *zero*
Nile 96 *Rivers,* 96.5 *other major rivers*
Nile green 453.1 *green*
nilgai 77 *Placental Mammals*
nill 52.10 *zero*
Nilometer 389.12 *measuring instrument*

Nilo-Saharan 5 *Languages and Groups of Languages*
Nilotic 5 *Languages and Groups of Languages,* 1.13 *racial*
Nilotic type 1.6 *race*
Nilsson 49 *Musicians and Composers*
nimble 329.1 *swift,* 642.18 *active,* 655.6 *skilful*
nimble-fingered 655.6 *skilful*
nimble-footed 329.1 *swift*
nimbleness 642, 329.8 *speed*
nimblewit 771.6 *humorist*
nimblewitted 771.10 *humorous*
nimble-witted 329.2 *mentally quick*
nimbly 329.14 *swiftly,* 642.22 *actively*
nimbostratous 55.49 *cloudy*
nimbostratus 55.18 *cloud*
nimbus 55.18 *cloud,* 439.12 *highlight*
Nîmes 93 *Cities*
nimiety 610.1 *excess*
Nimrod 37.4 *hunter,* 338.16 *archer,* 590.6 *hunter*
Nina from Carolina 179.5 *nine*
nincompoop 460.3 *unintelligent person,* 508.3 *foolish person*
nine 179, 52.9 *numeral,* 179.16 *ninth*
nine-bob note 540.14 *false thing*
nine-card brag 42 *Card Games*
nine centuries 179.9 *treble figures*
nine-day wonder 179.5 *nine,* 189.2 *transient thing,* 270.4 *short thing,* 786.5 *person of wonder*
ninefold 179.16 *ninth*
nine-hole course 29.1 *golf*
Ninella 8 *Deities*
ninepins 25.4 *bowling,* 42.7 *other games*
nine points of the law 723.1 *possession*
niner 179.5 *nine*
nineteenth 173.4 *less than one*
nineteenth hole 29.2 *golfing terms,* 651.7 *refreshments*
nine tenths of the law 723.1 *possession*
ninetieth 173.4 *less than one,* 179.19 *twentieth*
Ninette de Valois 46.14 *famous ballet dancers*
ninety 179.18 *twenty and over*
ninety-nine per cent 143.5 *largest part*
ninety-pound weakling 238.4 *weakling*
Ningal 8 *Deities*
Ningirsu 8 *Deities*
Ninib 8 *Deities,* **8** *Deities*
ninny 460.3 *unintelligent person,* 508.3 *foolish person,* 658.3 *naive person*
ninth 179, 49.16 *musical note,* 52.75 *equal,* 173.4 *less than one,* 179.5 *nine*
ninth part 179.5 *nine*
niobic 57.34 *elemental*
niobium 57 *Chemical Elements*
niobous 57.34 *elemental*
nip 342.9 *converge,* 345.4 *hurry off,* 351.13 *drink,* 380.16 *use a sharp tool* , 406.11 *inflict pain,* 407.3 *press,* 407.11 *touch,* 411.3 *appetizer,* 413.6 *cordial,* 821.14 *communication of love,* 826.1 *endearment,* 874.13 *drink*
Nip 91 *Names for Inhabitants*
nipa 85 *Trees and Shrubs,* **86** *Fruits*
nip along 329.4 *be swift*
nip and tuck 122.12 *equally,* 198.4 *equal race,* 198.14 *equal with,* 791.2 *plastic surgery*
nip-and-tuck 122.8 *on equal terms,* 198.11 *equal*
nip-and-tuck race 122.2 *equilibrium*
Nipigon 94 *Lakes,* 94.5 *other major lakes*
nip in the air 409.7 *cold weather*
nip in the bud 208.9 *prepare,* 244.11 *ruin,* 398.16 *kill,* 587.3 *deflect,* 661.8 *hinder*

nip off 345.4 *hurry off*
nipper 206.9 *child,* 245.6 *progeny*
nippers 380.8 *sharp-pointed thing,* 603.1 *tool,* 726.3 *tools for gripping*
nippiness 409.1 *coldness,* 409.7 *cold weather*
nipping 351.1 *drinking*
nipple 77.2 *mammalian characteristic,* 316.2 *bulge*
nippy 55.55 *cool,* 239.4 *vigorous,* 409.8 *cold,* 642.18 *active*
Nirenberg 52 *Scientists*
Nirmalin 7 *Non-Christian Religions*
nirvana 8.1 *divinity,* 199.3 *future condition,* 325.2 *repose,* 512.5 *death,* 649.1 *ease*
nirvanic 512.9 *blank*
nishmat 10.9 *prayer*
nisi prius 16.6 *legal process*
Nisroch 8 *Deities*
Nisus and Euryalus 819.7 *famous friendships*
nit 75 *Scientific and Technical Units,* 82.3 *pest,* 622.4 *dirt,* 656.10 *unskilled person*
NIT Championship 23.1 *basketball*
nit-pick 115.6 *differentiate,* 467.12 *scrutinize,* 474.13 *quibble,* 852.18 *find fault,* 854.11 *criticize*
nit-picker 474.6 *sophist,* 503.4 *accurate person,* 852.12 *critic*
nit-picking 106.10 *detailed,* 467.2 *close attention,* 474.4, 474.9 *quibbling,* 503.5 *accurate,* 612.4 *trivial,* 644.11 *laborious,* 659.14 *troublesome,* 852.6, 852.28 *fault-finding,* 854.1 *disparagement,* 854.15 *disparaging*
nitrate 57.26 *react,* 68.13 *fertilizer*
nitrates 246.3 *fertilizer*
nitration 57 *Types of Chemical Reaction*
nitrazapam 62 *Medication*
nitric acid 57 *Common Chemical Compounds*
nitric oxide 57 *Common Chemical Compounds*
nitrile 57 *Types of Compounds,* 377.4 *rubber*
nitrite 57 *Types of Compounds*
nitro compound 57 *Types of Compounds*
nitrofurantoin 62 *Medication*
nitrogen 57 *Chemical Elements,* 58.15 *essential element*
nitrogen mustard 62 *Medication*
nitrogenous 57.34 *elemental*
nitrogenous base 58.10 *nucleoside,* 59.12 *molecular biology*
nitroglycerine 244.7 *agent of destruction,* 680.15 *explosive*
nitrometer 268.8 *meter*
nitrometric 268.16 *micrometric*
nitrous acid 57 *Common Chemical Compounds*
nitrous oxide 57 *Common Chemical Compounds,* **62** *Medication,* 630.5 *analgesic*
nitty gritty 99.5 *fact,* 103.2 *essential content,* 143.5 *largest part,* 165.4 *specifications,* 290.5 *inner nature,* 520.1 *meaning,* 611.3 *chief thing*
nitwit 460.3 *unintelligent person,* 508.3 *foolish person,* 656.10 *unskilled person*
Niue 5 *Languages and Groups of Languages,* **92** *New Zealand Regions and Territories*
nix 172.2 *nothing,* 536.1 *negation,* 536.16, 711.12 *no*
nixed 536.12 *rejected*
Njord 8 *Deities*
nkui 45.53 *African dish*
NMR scan 60.7 *diagnosis*
no! 476, 500, 536, 711
no 172.6 *zero,* 172.11 *none,* 500.2 *disapproval,* 536.1 *negation,* 580.10 *vote,* 709.1 *veto,* 713.1 *protest*
no. 169.1 *number*
No. 8 35.4 *rugby player*
no-account 612.2 *obscure*

no Adonis 790.2 *ugly person*
no aggro 675.1 *peace*
no allegiance 698.3 *independence*
no alternative 571.3 *lack of choice*
no answer 683.1 *failure*
no apologies 868.1 *impenitence*
no appeal 690.1 *severity*
no attributable cause 229.1 *lack of motive*
no authority 689.1 *anarchy*
nob 802.1 *nobleman*
no backbone 576.13 *timidity*
no-ball 27.8 *delivery,* 27.10 *score,* 504.13 *sporting error*
nobble 236.8 *overpower,* 540.21 *be fraudulent,* 736.12 *steal*
nobbling 628.11 *hurt*
no bearing 521.1 *lack of meaning*
no beauty 790.2 *ugly person*
Nobel 52 *Scientists*
nobelium 57 *Chemical Elements*
Nobel Peace Prize 675
Nobel Prize 878.2 *prize*
no better 628.12 *deteriorated*
no better and no worse 110.16 *equal*
Nob Hill 126.4 *summit*
no bid 42.3 *card game terms*
nobile 49 *Musical Terms*
nobility 126.7 *the best people,* 400.9 *group,* 617.6 *worth,* 617.7 *elite,* 688.1 *authority,* 789.1 *gorgeousness,* 802.2 *aristocracy,* 802.3 *nobleness,* 805.5 *stateliness,* 815.7 *human society,* 876.2 *good morals*
nobilmente 49 *Musical Terms*
noble 134.12 *morally pure,* 611.4 *bigwig,* 611.5 *important,* 617.1 *worthy,* 688.12 *authoritative,* 696.12 *masterful,* 741.10 *former British money,* 802.1 *nobleman,* 802.4 *aristocratic,* 805.19 *stately,* 857.4 *honourable,* 859.5 *unselfish,* 863.5 *virtuous,* 876.8 *moral*
noble art of self-defence 26.2, 674.7 *boxing*
noble family 802.3 *nobleness*
noble gas 57.6 *chemical element*
nobleman 802, 400.10 *member of society,* 696.1 *master*
nobleness 802, 857.1 *probity,* 859.2 *unselfishness,* 863.1 *virtue*
noble savage 658.3 *naive person*
noblesse oblige 817.1 *courtesy*
noblewoman 400.10 *member of society,* 802.1 *nobleman*
no bloody good 614.1 *useless*
nobly 134.18 *virtuously,* 617.11 *worthily,* 688.23 *authoritatively,* 696.16 *masterfully,* 805.33 *with dignity,* 805.36 *majestically,* 857.7 *honourably,* 859.9 *unselfishly,* 863.9 *virtuously*
no boaster 806.16 *humble person*
nobody 254, 100.6 *absence,* 172.2 *nothing,* 172.5 *nonentity,* 278.5 *shallow person,* 612.10 *nonentity*
nobody else 174.1 *one*
nobody present 254.7 *nobody*
nobody's darling 822.8 *hated person*
nobody's fool 4.12 *sage*
nobody there 254.7 *nobody*
no break 642.6 *business*
nobs 126.7 *the best people,* 802.2 *aristocracy*
no buts 537.35 *truly*
no buts about it 101.14 *certainly*
no can do 487.13 *impossible*
no case 16.42 *acquittal*
no catch 698.12 *unconditional*
no chance 229.2 *chance,* 487.13 *impossible,* 589.6 *poor chance,* 711.11 *uncooperatively*
no change 110.6 *regularity,* 217.1 *permanence*
no change of pace 788.2 *boring thing*
no change of scenery 788.2 *boring thing*
no chicken 207.13 *middle-aged*
no choice 571.3 *lack of choice,* 580.8 *choice,* 695.1 *compulsion*
nock 319.1, 319.5 *notch*

no-claims bonus 71.21 *miscellaneous motoring terms*
no comment 566.11 *hush*
no common ground 115.2 *unlikeness*, 136.4 *disunity*
no comparison 115.2 *unlikeness*
no compromise 577.6 *determination*, 690.1 *severity*
no connection 108.5 *misconnection*
no context 521.1 *lack of meaning*
no-count 612.2 *obscure*
no courage 641.1 *inaction*
noctilucent cloud 55.18 *cloud*
noctuid moth 82 Insects
noctule 77 Placental Mammals
nocturnal 76.15 *of animals*, 205.6 *evening*, 440.8 *dark*
nocturnal enuresis. urinalysis 353.3 *urination*
nocturnally 205.7 *evening*, 440.15 *darkly*
nocturne 50.10 *art subject*
nod 116.28 *consent*, 362.9 *bow*, 362.16 *courtesy*, 365.11 *rock*, 499.4 *assent*, 528.7 *advice*, 650.5 *be fatigued*, 817.13 *defer to*, 849.4 *mark of respect*, 849.19 *take off one's hat to*, 851.1 *approval*, 851.12 *accept*
nod and a wink 540.9 *falsification*
nodding 628.12 *deteriorated*, 650.1 *fatigued*, 817.4 *deference*, 817.9 *deferential*, 849.11 *in a respectful stance*
nodding donkey 410.6 *oil*
nodding off 643.14 *not awake*
noddle 459.7 *brain*
noddy 78 Birds
node 52.39 *angle*, 56.12 *wave*, 65.15 *network*, 83.5 *stem*, 135.5 *joint*, 365.5 *wave*, 371.4 *solid body*, 373.7 *hard substance*, 407.6 *contiguity*
Nodens 8 Deities
no desire for 783.1 *indifference*
no difference 110.1 *sameness*
no dilution 134.8 *simplicity*
no discipline 611.8 *lawlessness*
no distance 264.2 *short distance*
nod of approval 499.2 *yes*, 708.1 *permission*, 851.1 *approval*
nod off 240.4 *be inert*, 404.11 *be unfeeling*, 643.13 *sleep*
nod of the head 543.3 *gesture*
nod one's head 543.11 *gesture*
nodose 375.2 *coarse*
nodosity 373.5 *hardness*, 375.6 *roughness*
nodular 375.2 *coarse*
nodularity 373.5 *hardness*
nodule 371.4 *solid body*, 373.7 *hard substance*
nodus 659.4 *problem*
no easy task 659.3 *difficult task*
Noel 10.16 *religious festival*
no encouragement 587.6 *dissuasion*
no end 181.13 *numerously*, 757.9 *extravagantly*
no end of 181.8 *numberless*, 184.3 *eternal*
no end to 269.1 *long*
no entry 147.1 *exclusion*
noetic 459.7 *mental*
no exception 146.1 *inclusion*
no execution 685.1 *noncompletion*
no fear 487.1.1 *impossible*, 711.11 *uncooperatively*
no fixed abode 108.1 *unrelatedness*, 567.5 *place of residence*
no flies on 657.4 *cunning*
no friend 820.5 *hostile person*
no frills 134.16 *simple*
no-frills 101.8 *practical*
no fun 788.2 *boring thing*
Nogai 5 Languages and Groups of Languages
no gentleman 818.4 *discourteous person*
noggin 75 General Units, 258.13 *drinking vessel*, 459.7 *brain*
no gift for 656.8 *unskilfulness*
no go 358.5 *shortfall*

no-go 93.14 *urban*, 302.5 *limited*, 614.1 *useless*
no-go area 93.7 *city district*, 136.2 *setting apart*, 147.3 *exclusion zone*, 249.10 *urban area*, 302.2 *limiting factor*, 487.7 *obstacle*, 659.8 *snag*, 699.1 *restraint*
no going back 868.1 *impenitence*
no good 614.1 *useless*, 618.2 *inferior*, 776.8 *bad*
no-good 722.6 *loser*
no good reason 229.1 *lack of motive*
no great matter 612.8 *trifle*
no great shakes 124.3 *mediocre*, 612.4 *trivial*, 612.8 *trifle*, 620.8 *ordinariness*, 783.10 *mediocre*
no grit 576.13 *timidity*
no hangover 873.6 *sobriety*
no harm done 619.1 *perfect*
no hassle 675.1 *peace*
no holding back 572.2 *eager*
no holds barred 530.3 *openness*, 674.1 *contention*, 674.8 *wrestling*, 674.1 *war*, 698.6 *liberality*, 698.12 *unconditional*
no-holds-barred 26.15 *wrestling*
no-holds-barred wrestling 26.5 *wrestling*
no hope 776.1 *hopelessness*
no-hoper 127.6 *inferior*, 195.8 *follower*, 337.21 *backslider*, 581.9 *rejected person*, 683.5 *failing person*, 687.5 *person in adversity*, 722.6 *loser*, 776.3 *hopeless person*
no hurry 328.8 *slowness*, 645.1 *leisure*
no ifs or buts 99.22 *really*
no illusion 537.6 *authenticity*
no imitation 537.6 *authenticity*
no inclination for 785.1 *dislike*
noise 56.17 *sound*, 64.14 *terminal*, 155.5 *commotion*, 420.8 *something heard*, 423.1 *loudness*, 423.3 *audibility*, 434.2 *dissonant noise*, 534.19 *radio reception*, 534.23 *television reception*
noise abatement 424.1 *faintness*
noise abroad 532.13 *make public*
noiseless 422.3 *silent*
noiselessly 422.5 *silently*
noiselessness 422.4 *silence*
noisily 423.9 *loudly*, 431.20 *vociferously*
noisiness 423.2 *outcry*
noisome 341.8 *repulsive*, 416.5 *odorous*, 419.3 *stinking*, 618.3 *bad*, 618.4 *poor*, 618.5 *harmful*, 622.8 *unclean*, 631.16 *blighting*
noisomely 341.11 *repulsively*
noisy 423.6 *loud*, 431.16 *vociferous*
no joke 611.2 *important matter*, 772.4 *solemnity*
no laughing matter 611.2 *important matter*, 772.4 *solemnity*
no less 608.7 *sufficiency*
no life 397.1 *death*
nolle prosequi 704.2 *termination*
no longer 200.23 *before now*
no longer among us 254.9 *away*
no longer law 16.57 *null*
no longer made 160.9 *discontinued*
no longer present 200.20 *former*
no longer serving 200.20 *former*
no loss of time 329.8 *speed*
no love lost 820.3 *ill feeling*
no luck 683.1 *failure*, 687.3 *bad fortune*
nomad 104.5 *nonconformist*
nomadic 104.10 *foreign*, 168.13 *unconventional*, 324.16 *moving*
nomadically 104.18 *extraneously*, 324.18 *in motion*
no man 254.7 *nobody*
no manners 818.2 *bad manners*
no-man's-land 147.3 *exclusion zone*, 158.6 *middle ground*
no marksman 656.10 *unskilled person*
no marriage 824.1 *divorce*
no match 115.2 *unlikeness*
no matter! 612

no matter 612.8 *trifle*
no matter how 327.16 *how*
no matter what 164.14 *whatever*
no matter who 164.13 *whoever*
nombril point 544.8 *heraldic device*
nom de plume 529.8 *anonymity*, 531.7 *concealer*
no meaning 521.1 *lack of meaning*
nomen 560.8 *name*
nomenclator 5.2 *linguist*
nomenclature 560, 5.1 *linguistics*, 171.3 *dictionary*
nominal 543.14 *signifying*, 612.4 *trivial*, 754.9 *cheap*
nominalism 4.7 *school of thought*, 306.1 *form*
nominalist 4.11 *follower of a doctrine*, 4.14 *of a philosophy*
nominally 540.37 *spuriously*, 754.15 *cheaply*
nominal price 754.1 *cheapness*
nominal scale 52.56 *nonparametric methods*
nominate 7.21 *ordain*, 580.4 *pick*, 703.6 *commission*, 706.4 *delegate*, 706.7 *deputize*
nominated 24.9 *billiard*, 703.9 *commissioned*, 706.6 *delegated*
nominated ball 24.5 *snooker*
nomination 7.9 *priesthood*, 580.6 *selection*, 703.1 *commission*, 706.3 *delegation*
nominative 5.31 *case*
nominee 580.13 *electorate*, 703.5 *commissioner*, 706.1 *delegate*
no mixture 134.8 *simplicity*
nomological 16.45 *legislative*
nomology 16.31 *legislation*, 16.32 *jurisprudence*
no money 687.2 *economic adversity*
no morals 864.2 *vice*, 877.3 *sexual immorality*
no more 100, 3.18 *in the past*, 397.19 *dead*
no more work 645.3 *unemployment*
nomothetic 4.13 *of philosophy*, 16.45 *legislative*, 653.17 *managerial*
nonacceptance 852, 536.2, 581.5 *rejection*, 663.4 *uncooperativeness*, 711.1 *refusal*
nonaccepted 536.12 *rejected*
nonaccepting 711.8 *refusal*
nonaccomplishment 685.1 *noncompletion*
nonachievement 685.1 *noncompletion*
nonacknowledgment 838.1 *ingratitude*
nonacting person 641
nonaction 641.1 *inaction*
nonactive 641.3 *inactive*
nonactivist 573.16 *reluctant person*
nonaddict 873.8 *sober person*
nonadherence 720.1, 814.5 *nonobservance*
nonadherent 139.3 *nonadhesive thing*, 720.11 *nonobservant*
nonadhering 139.8 *nonadhesive*
nonadhesion 139
Nonadhesion 139
nonadhesive 139
nonadhesive thing 139
nonadmission 147.1 *exclusion*
nonadult 595.5 *immature*
nonage 206.1 *youth*
nonagenarian 179.8 *twenty and over*, 207.7 *older person*
nonaggression 675.1 *peace*
nonaggression pact 675.1 *peace*, 677.1 *pacification*, 715.3 *alliance*
nonaggressive 675.7 *peaceful*
nonagon 52.44 *polygon*, 179.5 *nine*
nonagonal 179.16 *ninth*
nonagreeing 117.10 *disagreeing*
nonagreement 117.4 *disagreement*
nonahydrate 57.10 *salt*
nonalcoholic 873, 351.17 *drinkable*, 873.8 *sober person*

nonalcoholic beverage 351.6 *soft drink*
nonaligned 91.16 *national*, 136.17 *unjoined*, 333.4 *middle*, 482.2 *impartial*, 675.7 *peaceful*, 698.9 *free*, 859.4 *disinterested*
nonaligned country 91.1 *country*
nonaligned nations 675.1 *peace*
nonalignment 136.2 *setting apart*, 482.7 *impartiality*, 675.1 *peace*, 698.1 *freedom*, 859.1 *disinterestedness*
no name 527.6 *latency*, 529.8 *anonymity*, 531.7 *concealer*
nonappearance 254.4 *absenteeism*, 438.4 *invisibility*, 458.4 *disappearance*
nonapproval 581.5 *rejection*
nonary 179.5 *nine*, 179.16 *ninth*
nonassimilate 104.11 *separate*
nonassimilation 104.3 *separateness*
nonassociation 536.2 *rejection*, 573.13 *dissociation*
nonassociative 536.11 *negative*
nonattached 136.17 *unjoined*
nonattachment 136.2 *setting apart*
nonattendance 254.4 *absenteeism*
nonattendant 254.8 *absent*
nonbearing wall 43.9 *miscellaneous architectural features*
nonbeing 100.1 *nonexistence*, 172.3 *nothingness*, 254.1 *absence*
nonbelief 498.3 *incredulity*, 536.2 *rejection*
nonbeliever 498.5 *disbeliever*, 573.16 *reluctant person*, 698.8 *free-thinker*, 720.5 *nonobserver*
nonbelieving 698.10 *independent*, 720.11 *nonobservant*
nonbelligerent 675.3 *pacifist*
nonbenzenoid aromatic 57.7 *chemical compound*
nonbreakable 378.1 *tough*
noncausal 229.6 *motiveless*, 589.8 *chance*
nonce word 5.17 *word*
nonchalance 466.2 *lack of interest*, 470.1 *negligence*, 660.4 *ease of manner*, 783.1 *indifference*, 787.1 *lack of wonder*
nonchalant 466.4 *uninterested*, 470.4 *negligent*, 783.7 *indifferent*, 787.3 *unmoved*
nonchalantly 783.17 *indifferently*, 787.9 *without wonder*
nonchordate invertebrate 81.1 *invertebrate*
non-Christian 7
non-Christian ritual 10
nonclassically 56.100 *physically*
nonclastic rock 54.31 *sedimentary rock*
noncoagulation 387.5 *fluidity*
noncoercion 698.1 *freedom*
noncoherence 139.1 *nonadhesion*
noncoherent 139.8 *nonadhesive*
noncoherently 139.10 *noncohesively*
noncohesion 139.1 *nonadhesion*
noncohesive 139.8 *nonadhesive*
noncohesively 139
noncombatant 17.9 *enlisted*, 675.3 *pacifist*, 675.7 *peaceful*
noncombination 139.1 *nonadhesion*
noncommissioned 17.9 *enlisted*
noncommissioned officer 17.5 *military staff*, 679.17 *army person*
noncommittal 531,158.14 *mediatory*, 242.7 *politically moderate*, 333.2 *middle of the road*, 333.4 *middle*, 717.8 *irresolute*, 576.1 *vacillating*, 591.18 *avoiding*, 598.6 *apathetic*, 783.7 *indifferent*
noncommittally 576.16, 717.10 *irresolutely*
noncommitted 591.18 *avoiding*
noncompetitive 664.19 *associating*
noncompletion 685, 145.1 *incompleteness*, 358.5 *shortfall*, 515.1 *disappointment*, 609.8 *insufficiency*, 656.9 *bungling*,

683.1 *failure,* 720.2 *nonperformance*
Noncompletion 685
noncompliance 168.2 *dissent,*
573.14, 693.1 *disobedience,*
711.1 *refusal,* 713.1 *protest,*
720.1 *nonobservance,* 720.3 *disregard of orders*
noncompliant 720, 693.13 *disobedient,* 711.8 *refused,* 713.9
protesting, 720.11 *nonobservant*
noncomplying 711.8 *refused*
nonconcurrence 168.2 *dissent*
nonconductor 64, 56.48 *insulation,* 235.7 *electrical power*
nonconformability 117.3 *nonconformity*
nonconformance 168.1 *nonconformity,* 720.1 *nonobservance*
nonconformant 720.11 *nonobservant*
nonconformer 168.7 *nonconformist*
nonconforming 117, 168,
104.11 *separate,* 215.5 *unusual,*
698.10 *independent,* 720.11
nonobservant
nonconformism 168, 335.13 *deviation,* 500.3 *dissentience*
**nonconformist 104, 168, 168,
693,** 117.6 *misfit,* 117.9 *nonconforming,* 139.4 *individualist,*
335.19 *deviant person,* 335.20
deviant, 498.5 *disbeliever,* 500.5
dissenter, 500.7 *dissenting,*
585.2 *not customary,* 668.4 *defiant person,* 698.8 *free-thinker,*
698.10 *independent,* 713.4 *protester,* 713.9 *protesting,* 720.5
nonobserver, 720.11 *nonobservant,* 814.7 *informal*
Nonconformist 7.5 *Christian,*
7.16 *denominational*
nonconformity 117, 168, 104.3
separateness, 108.1 *unrelatedness,* 113.1 *diversity,* 215.2 *unusualness,* 500.3 *dissentience,*
585.3 *unaccustomedness,* 666.3
difference, 693.1 *disobedience,*
698.1 *freedom,* 720.1 *nonobservance,* 814.1 *informality*
Nonconformity 168
nonconsummation of marriage
824.1 *divorce*
noncontinuation 685.1 *noncompletion*
noncontinuous 52.70 *universal,*
160.8 *discontinuous*
noncontributory benefit 662.4 *social assistance*
nonconvergence 285.1 *parallelism*
nonconvergent 285.3 *parallel*
nonconvertible 600.1 *unused*
nonconvulsive electric treatment
61.3 *psychiatric treatment*
noncooperation 500.3 *dissentience,* 573.12 *opposition,* 591.15
evasiveness, 663.4 *uncooperativeness,* 666.1 *disagreement,* 669.1
resistance, 693.1 *disobedience,*
711.1 *refusal,* 713.1 *protest,*
720.1 *nonobservance*
noncooperative 591.18 *avoiding,*
663.22 *uncooperative,* 666.9 *disagreeing,* 669.10 *resistant,*
693.13 *disobedient,* 711.8 *refused,* 713.9 *protesting,* 720.11
nonobservant
noncooperatively 666.11 *in disagreement,* 669.14 *resistingly*
noncooperator 666.4 *dissenter*
noncorroboration 536.1 *negation*
noncrystalline 57.33 *crystalline*
noncrystalline mineral 54.34 *mineral*
nondescript 412.5 *tasteless,*
612.1 *unimportant*
nondeviation 333.1 *middle way*
nondirective therapy 61.3 *psychiatric treatment*
nondiscriminatory 146.7 *including*
nondivergence 285.1 *parallelism*
nondivergent 285.3 *parallel*
nondrinker 591.17 *avoider,*
873.8 *sober person*
nondrinking 873.1 *sober*

non-drying oil 395.7 *oil*
nondurable 189.7 *impermanent*
nondutiable 751.15 *chargeable*
none 172, 100.6 *absence,* 172.1
zero, 172.2 *nothing*
nonelastic 378.3 *hard*
nonelastic fluid 387.1 *fluid*
nonelection 581.6 *discarding*
nonemployment 641.1 *inaction*
nonentitlement 846.1 *lack of entitlement*
nonentity 172, 612, 100.1 *nonexistence,* 102.5 *insubstantial
person,* 127.6 *inferior,* 254.1 *absence,* 278.5 *shallow person,*
536.5 *nonexistence,* 536.6 *negativist*
none other 110.1 *sameness*
nones 10.4 *public worship*
Nones 185.11 *date*
**none so deaf as those who will
not hear** 421.7 *unheard*
nonessential 108.7 *illogical,*
610.3 *superfluity,* 610.7 *superfluous,* 612.1 *unimportant,*
612.8 *trifle*
nonessential amino acid 58.8
amino acid
nonesuch 617.8 *exceller,* 861.16
superior person
nonet 49.26 *musical group,*
140.3 *assembly,* 179.5 *nine,*
664.9 *team*
nonetheless 372.16 *how*
none the worse 629.15 *cured*
none too soon 209.16 *at a late
hour*
non-Euclidean geometry 52.34 *geometry*
nonexclusive 146.7 *including,*
164.15 *general*
nonexistence 100, 536, 102.1
unreality, 172.3 *nothingness,*
254.1 *absence,* 458.4 *disappearance,* 487.5 *impossibility*
Nonexistence 100
nonexistent 100, 536, 102.8 *unreal,* 172.7 *null,* 254.8 *absent,*
458.7 *disappeared,* 519.12 *imaginary,* 538.14 *unreal,* 609.4
scarce
nonexternal 368.11 *internal*
nonexternality 368.6 *internal
world*
nonexternally 368.14 *subjectively*
nonextreme 242.7 *politically
moderate,* 333.4 *middle*
nonextremist 124.2 *medium,*
124.8 *middle classes,* 333.3
moderate person
nonfeasance 720.2 *nonperformance*
nonfiction 48, 560.4 *factual account*
nonflammable 632.5 *safe*
nonfriction 386.1 *lubrication*
nonfrictional 376.1 *smooth*
nonfulfiling 720.12 *nonperforming*
nonfulfilment 145.1 *incompleteness,* 358.6 *shortcoming,* 515.1
disappointment, 609.8 *insufficiency,* 683.1 *failure,* 685.1 *noncompletion,* 720.2 *nonperformance*
nonfunctional 614.1 *useless*
non-functional 792.8 *decorated*
nonfunctioning 614.1 *useless*
nonhappening 100.1 *nonexistence*
nonhuman 460
nonhuman existence 460
nonhumanly 460
nonillion 169.3 *large number,*
179.11 *million*
nonimitation 119.1 *originality*
nonimmunity 633.7 *vulnerability*
noninclusion 147.1 *exclusion*
nonindustrial 243.11 *productive*
noninfectious 625.4 *hygienic*
noninjurious 625.4 *hygienic*
nonintention 229.1 *lack of motive*
noninterference 641.1 *inaction,*
698.1 *freedom*
nonintervention 591.12 *shyness,*
641.1 *inaction,* 675.1 *peace,*
698.1 *freedom*
noninterventional 698.9 *free*

noninterventionist 641.2 *nonacting person*
nonintimidation 698.1 *freedom*
noninvolved 698.9 *free*
noninvolvement 104.3 *separateness,* 400.11 *nation,* 591.12 *shyness,* 698.1 *freedom,* 783.1 *indifference,* 859.1 *disinterestedness*
noninvolvment 675.1 *peace*
nonirritant 242.8 *moderating*
Nonius 32 Breeds of Horse and
Pony
nonjudgmental 482.2 *impartial*
nonliability 16.42 *acquittal,*
698.1 *freedom,* 708.1 *permission,* 727.1 *disposal,* 848.1 *exemption*
nonliable 16.63 *acquitted,* 698.9
free, 848.5 *exempt*
nonlinear 160.11 *digressive*
nonlinear circuit 64.13 *circuit*
nonlinearity 160.7 *broken thread*
nonmalignant 625.4 *hygienic*
nonmanual 15.8 *industrial*
nonmanual worker 15.7 *employee*
nonmaterial 368, 11.18 *spiritual*
nonmaterial world 368
Nonmaterial World 368
nonmember 147.5 *excluded person*
non-meritorious 846.11 *undeserving*
nonmetal 57.6 *chemical element*
non-negative 52.71 *numerical*
non-negative number 52.5 *number*
no-no 487.7 *obstacle,* 827.1 *curse*
nonobservance 720, 814, 168.2
dissent, 468.1 *inattention,*
536.2 *rejection,* 573.14, 693.1
disobedience
Nonobservance 720
nonobservant 720, 585.1 *unaccustomed,* 693.13 *disobedient*
nonobserved 536.12 *rejected*
nonobserver 720
nonoccurrence 100.1 *nonexistence,* 254.1 *absence*
nonoccurrent 254.8 *absent*
no-nonsense 4.15 *rational,*
101.8 *practical,* 526.15 *open,*
658.1 *naive*
no novice 655.5 *expert*
nonparametric methods 52
nonparametric statistics 52.53
statistics
nonpareil 115.4 *dissimilar,* 126.6
paragon, 617.8 *exceller,* 861.2
best, 861.9 *the best*
nonpartisan 333.3 *moderate person,* 333.4 *middle,* 482.2 *impartial,* 665.10 *political,* 698.7 *free
person,* 698.9 *free,* 859.4 *disinterested*
nonpayer 747, 683.5 *failing person,* 685.3 *quitter,* 745.6 *debtor*
nonpaying 747, 722.17 *unprofitable,* 745.10 *unable to pay*
nonpaying person 683.5 *failing
person*
nonpayment 747, 638.1 *escape,*
711.1 *refusal,* 713.1 *protest*
Nonpayment 747
nonperformance 720, 683.1 *failure*
nonperforming 720
nonperseverance 576.11 *vacillation*
nonperson 102.5 *insubstantial
person,* 254.6 *absentee,* 612.10
nonentity
nonphysical 11.18 *spiritual,*
368.8 *nonmaterial*
nonphysical world 368.1 *nonmaterial world*
nonplus 491.20 *make uncertain,*
659.4 *problem,* 659.23 *cause difficulties*
nonplussed 491.3, 523.6 *confused,* 659.16 *troubled*
nonpolar 57.35 *combined*
nonpolar compound 57.7 *chemical compound*
nonpolar solvent 57.3 *phase*
nonporous 323.12 *closed*
nonporously 323.16 *impermeably*

nonpractice 720.2 *nonperformance*
nonpractising 720.11 *nonobservant,* 720.12 *nonperforming*
nonpractising person 720.5 *nonobserver*
nonpreparation 595.8 *lack of
preparation,* 648.4 *haste*
nonprescription drug 62.3 *drug*
nonpresence 254.1 *absence*
non-presence 438.4 *invisibility*
nonprevalent 585.2 *not customary*
nonprintable character 65.10
character
nonprofessional 656.2 *unskilled*
nonprofessional army 17.2 *the
military*
non-profit-making 722.17 *unprofitable,* 737.16 *unprofitable*
nonprosecution 16.42 *acquittal*
nonprovision 595.8 *lack of preparation*
non-radical 242.7 *politically moderate*
non-reactionary 242.7 *politically
moderate*
nonrealism 548.1 *misrepresentation*
nonrealist 591.17 *avoider*
nonreality 100
nonrecognition 502.1 *ignorance,*
838.1 *ingratitude*
nonrecovery 722.1 *loss*
nonrecurrent 160.9 *discontinued*
nonrecyclable 722.16 *losing*
nonreflective 442.1 *transparent*
nonrenewable energy source
410.1 *fuel*
nonrepentance 868.1 *impenitence*
nonrepresentational 547.13 *representational,* 548.6 *misrepresented*
nonrepresentational art 50 Western Art Styles and Movements
nonresident 254
nonresistance 673.1 *submission,*
694.1 *obedience*
nonresisting 673.5 *submitting,*
694.7 *obedient*
nonresistive 374.7 *impressionable*
nonresonance 424.1 *faintness,*
428.3 *muteness*
nonresonant 428, 424.4 *faint,*
430.8 *hoarse*
nonresponsibility 848.1 *exemption*
nonrestoration 722.1 *loss*
non-restriction 346.4 *right of
entry*
nonresumption 683.1 *failure*
nonretention 727.1 *disposal*
nonreturnable 600.1 *unused*
nonrigid 374.1 *soft*
nonrigidity 374.8 *softness*
nonsaponifiable lipid 58.6 *lipid*
nonsatisfaction 145.1 *incompleteness,* 609.8 *insufficiency*
nonseed-bearing 83.16 *taxonomic*
nonseed-bearing plant 83.4 *lower
plant*
nonsense 506
nonsense! 521
nonsense 538, 540, 476.13 *no,*
520.4 *type of meaning,* 521.1
lack of meaning, 521.4 *senseless
talk,* 521.10 *meaningless,*
523.11 *unintelligibility*
Nonsense 506
nonsense poetry 48.6 *poetry*
nonsense verse 506.1 *nonsense*
nonsensical 506, 508.5 *foolish,*
520.6 *meaningful,* 521.10 *meaningless,* 538.13 *untrue,* 540.27
hypocritical
nonsensicality 521.1 *lack of
meaning*
nonsensically 506, 508.8 *foolishly,* 521.13 *meaninglessly,*
538.26 *untruthfully*
nonsensical talk 538.6 *nonsense*
nonsensical writing 521.1 *lack of
meaning*
nonsequential 160.11 *digressive*
non sequitur 4.8 *philosophical
term,* 108.2 *unrelated thing,*

117.2 *contradiction*, 160.7 *broken thread*, 685.1 *noncompletion*
nonserial 160.11 *digressive*
nonseriality 160.7 *broken thread*
nonsignificance 521.1 *lack of meaning*
nonsignificant 521.10 *meaningless*
nonsingle 175.6 *plural*
nonsinusoidal wave 56.16 *waveform*
nonsmoker 413.8 *smoking*, 869.4 *self-restrained person*
nonspecialist 656.2 *unskilled*
nonspecific 164.20 *generalized*
nonspecificness 164
nonspiritual 367.7 *material*
nonstandard 5.39 *of language*, 168.15 *irregular*
nonstandard language 5
nonstarter 683.4 *unsuccessful thing*, 683.5 *failing person*
nonsterile 622.8 *unclean*, 626.6 *contagious*
nonstick 139.8 *nonadhesive*
nonstick frying pan 139.3 *nonadhesive thing*
nonstoichiometric 57.35 *combined*
nonstoichiometric compound 57.7 *chemical compound*
nonstop 159.11 *continuous*, 159.19 *continuously*, 183.14 *recurrent*, 190.10 *continuing forever*, 212.3 *frequent*, 219.6 *protracted*, 219.7 *continually*, 312.3 *continuous*, 553.3 *diffuse*
nonstop talker 565.4 *talker*
nonstop talking 553.1 *diffuseness*
nonstriker 693.12 *reactionary*, 713.4 *protester*, 720.5 *nonobserver*
nonsubsistence 100.1 *nonexistence*
nonsuit 16.42 *acquittal*
nonsuited 16.64 *convicted*
nonsymmetrical 151.14 *irregular*
nonsymmetry 151.2 *irregular order*
nontaxable 751.15 *chargeable*
nontoxic 632.5 *safe*
nontraditional 201.11 *unfamiliar*
nontraditionally 201.21 *newly*
nontranslucent 443.1 *opaque*
nontransparent 443.1 *opaque*
non-U 585.2 *not customary*, 795.7 *vulgar*, 803.4 *common*
nonuniform 113.5 *diverse*, 115.4 *dissimilar*, 117.7 *disparate*, 133.12 *mixed*, 151.14 *irregular*, 160.8 *discontinuous*, 215.4 *irregular*, 375.1 *rough*
nonuniformity 113.1 *diversity*, 115.1 *dissimilarity*, 117.1 *disparity*, 123.1 *inequality*, 133.1 *mixture*, 139.1 *nonadhesion*, 151.2 *irregular order*, 160.1 *discontinuity*, 215.1 *irregularity*, 375.6 *roughness*
nonuniformly 113.10 *diversely*, 123.7 *unequally*
nonunion labour 15.1 *industrial relations*
nonuple 179.16 *ninth*
nonuplet 179.5 *nine*
nonuse 600, 581.6 *discarding*, 598.3 *relinquishment*, 641.1 *inaction*, 656.8 *unskilfulness*
Nonuse 600
nonuser of drugs 872.9 *straight person*
nonvenomous snake 79.3 *snake*
non-verbal glossolalia 5.5 *nonstandard language*
nonviolence 242.1 *moderation*, 675.1 *peace*, 677.1 *pacification*
nonviolent 242.6 *moderate*, 675.7 *peaceful*
nonviolent resistance 669.3 *resistance movement*
nonviscosity 387.5 *fluidity*
nonvolatile memory 65.6 *memory*
nonvolatile oil 395.7 *oil*
nonwage demands 15.2 *industrial negotiations*
nonwilling 711.8 *refused*
nonwillingness 711.1 *refusal*
nonworker 643

non-working 645.7 *leisurely*
noodle 459.7 *brain*, 508.3 *foolish person*
noodles 45 Types of Pasta
no oil painting 124.6 *mediocrity*, 790.2 *ugly person*
nook 258.2 *compartment*, 317.3 *cavity*, 531.2 *hiding place*
nooky 821.5 *desire*
no omission 146.1 *inclusion*
noon 204, 204
noonday 204.3 *noon*
no one 172.2 *nothing*, 254.7 *nobody*
no-one 100.6 *absence*
noontide 204.3 *noon*
noontime 204.3 *noon*
no option 571.3 *lack of choice*
no orator 566.7 *taciturn person*
noose 137.9 *yoke*, 313.3 *circular thing*, 879.16 *instrument of execution*
noosphere 390.2 *aerosphere*
no other 110.1 *sameness*, 174.1 *one*
Nootka 1 Peoples, **5** Languages and Groups of Languages
no pattern 151.2 *irregular order*
nope 536.16 *no*
no performance 685.1 *noncompletion*
no picnic 659.3 *difficult task*
no place 254.21 *away*
no preference 783.3 *impartiality*
no prejudice 783.3 *impartiality*
no priority 195.3 *subordination*
no prisoners taken 674.1 *contention*, 676.1 *war*
no problem 660.21 *easily*
no progress 683.1 *failure*
no quarter! 398
no quorum 609.8 *insufficiency*
nor' 332.4 *compass point*
noradrenalin 58 Hormones
nordic 41.12 *ski*
Nordic 1.13 *racial*, 446.3 *white-haired*
Nordic combined event 18 Sporting Activities
nordic skiing 41.1 *skiing*
Nordic type 1.6 *race*
no real alternative 580.8 *choice*
no reason 229.1 *lack of motive*
no regrets 868.1 *impenitence*
no relation 108.5 *misconnection*
no remorse 868.1 *impenitence*
no rest for the wicked 642.6 *business*
no result 683.1 *failure*, 685.1 *noncompletion*
norethandrolone 62 Medication
norethisterone 62 Medication
no reward 838.1 *ingratitude*
Norfold Roadster 32 Breeds of Horse and Pony
Norfolk 92 Counties, **93** Cities
Norfolk Grey 68 Breeds of Fowl
Norfolk Horn 68 Breeds of Sheep
Norfolk jacket 295.11 *jacket*
Norfolk terrier 77 Breeds of Dogs
no rhyme or reason 151.2 *irregular order*
no right 846.1 *lack of entitlement*
norimon 71.6 *litter*
norito 10.9 *prayer*
norm 116.6 *convention*, 124.4 *average*, 164.4 *guide*, 268.7 *standard*, 654.3 *precept*
Norma 53 The Constellations
normal 584, 52.37 *line*, 52.70 *universal*, 52.80 *linear*, 112.6 *conforming*, 116.15 *conventional*, 124.1 *average*, 164.21 *common*, 166.10 *customary*, 167.15 *everyday*, 214.14 *orderly*, 281.3 *vertical thing*, 281.10 *perpendicular*, 509.4 *sane*
normal behaviour 513.3 *the expected thing*
normalcy 124.4 *average*
normal distribution 52.59 *probability distribution*
normal fault 54.20 *earth movement*
normality 124.4 *average*, 214.4 *orderliness*, 509.1 *sanity*

normalization 112.2 *conformity*
normalize 52.94 *order*, 112.10 *conform*, 116.26 *make uniform*, 124.10 *make average*, 152.13 *organize*, 166.14 *regulate*, 214.10 *make regular*
normalized 112.6 *conforming*
normally 112.13 *uniformly*, 116.37 *conventionally*, 124.11 *on average*, 164.30 *usually*, 166.18 *as a rule*, 214.17 *orderly*
normal sight 435.1 *vision*
normal stress 63.14 *load*
normal temperature and pressure 56.38 *thermodynamics*
normal use 599.6 *use*
normal vision 435.1 *vision*
Norman 32 Breeds of Horse and Pony, **43** Architectural Styles, 202.14 *historic*
Norman arch 43.5 *arch*
Normandy 68 Breeds of Cattle
normative 4.13 *of philosophy*, 124.1 *average*
Norn 5 Languages and Groups of Languages
no room to spare 144.8 *full*
no room to swing a cat 144.8 *full*, 260.7 *little*
no room to turn round 144.8 *full*
Norse 5 Languages and Groups of Languages, **7** Non-Christian Religions
north 332, 332.4 *compass point*, 332.13 *directional*
North 97 Oceans and Seas
North America 98.1 *continent*
North American Nebula 53 Nebulae
Northampton 93 Cities
Northamptonshire 92 Counties
north and south 111.2 *opposites*
North and South 249.7 *regions of the world*
northbound 332.13 *directional*
North Carolina 92 American States
North Country Cheviot 68 Breeds of Sheep
North Dakota 92 American States
northeast 332.4 *compass point*, 332.12 *north*, 332.13 *directional*
northeast by east 332.12 *north*
northeast by north 332.12 *north*
northeaster 55.15 *wind direction*
northeasterly 55.15 *wind direction*, 55.47 *windy*, 332.12 *north*, 332.13 *directional*
northeastern 332.13 *directional*
northeast trades 55.17 *wind system*
northeastwards 332.12 *north*
northeast wind 55.15 *wind direction*
norther 55.15 *wind direction*
northerly 55.15 *wind direction*, 55.47 *windy*, 332.12 *north*, 332.13 *directional*
northern 249.16 *regional*, 305.6 *side*, 332.13 *directional*
Northern Crown 53 The Constellations
Northerner 91.9 *England*, 255.9 *British inhabitant*, 255.10 *US inhabitant*
Northern Ireland 91.10 *Ireland*
northern lights 54.46 *aurora*, 439.4 *natural light*
northernmost 332.13 *directional*
northern pike 20.4 *American game fish*
Northern Sotho 5 Languages and Groups of Languages
North Germanic 5 Languages and Groups of Languages
North Holland Blue 68 Breeds of Fowl
northing 332.4 *compass point*
Northland 92 New Zealand Regions and Territories
Northlands Pony 32 Breeds of Horse and Pony
north light 439.10 *window*
north magnetic pole 54.45 *magnetic pole*
north-northeast 332.12 *north*

north-northwest 332.12 *north*
north of Watford 249.9 *regions of Britain*
North Pole 409.6 *Arctic*
North Ronaldsay 68 Breeds of Sheep
North Sea gas 410.3 *gas*
North Sea oil 410.6 *oil*
north side 305.3 *side direction*
North-South divide 249.7 *regions of the world*
North Star 53 Named Stars, 439.4 *natural light*, 543.5 *indicator*
North Swedish 32 Breeds of Horse and Pony
Northumberland 92 Counties
North Wales 91.12 *Wales*
North Walian 91.12 *Wales*
northward 332.4 *compass point*, 332.13 *directional*
northwardly 332.12 *north*
northwards 332.12 *north*
northwest 332.4 *compass point*, 332.12 *north*, 332.13 *directional*
northwest by north 332.12 *north*
northwest by west 332.12 *north*
northwester 55.15 *wind direction*
northwesterly 55.15 *wind direction*, 55.47 *windy*, 332.12 *north*, 332.13 *directional*
northwestern 332.13 *directional*
North West Highlands 95 Mountains, 95.5 *British mountains*
Northwest Territories 92 Canadian Provinces and Territories
northwestwardly 332.12 *north*
northwestwards 332.12 *north*
northwest wind 55.15 *wind direction*
north wind 55.15 *wind direction*
North Wind 409.7 *cold weather*
North Yorkshire 92 Counties
Nortia 8 Deities
nortryptyline 62 Medication
Norway 91 Countries
Norway maple 85 Trees and Shrubs
Norway spruce 85 Trees and Shrubs
Norwegian 5 Languages and Groups of Languages
Norwegian Racing Trotter 32 Breeds of Horse and Pony
nor'wester 55 Winds
Norwich 93 Cities
Norwich school 50 Schools and Groups of Artists
Norwich terrier 77 Breeds of Dogs
no score 172.1 *zero*
nose 73 Aircraft Parts, 34.5 *rock face*, 283.5 *projecting object*, 316.2 *bulge*, 318.3 *protuberance*, 322.4 *body orifice*, 400.7 *person*, 416.1 *odour*, 416.2 *sense of smell*, 416.7 *smell*, 457.3 *external appearance*, 528.10 *informer*
nose around 465.7 *be curious*
nosebag 258.8 *bag*
noseband 32.14 *horse-riding terms*
nosebleed 353.10 *bleeding*
nose candy 875.6 *drug*
no secret 501.10 *known*
nose-dive 73.5 *flight*, 129.2 *decline*, 360.12 *drop*, 360.5 *dive*
nose-diving 360.18 *falling*
nosedown 360.19 *down*
nose drops 62.8 *drops*
nosegay 84.1 *flower*, 161.29 *bunch*, 418.2 *fragrant thing*
nose guard 19.3 *uniform*
nose-in-the-air 805.17 *conceited*
nose job 791.2 *plastic surgery*
noseless 417.3 *odourless*
no sense 520.4 *type of meaning*
nose out 416.7 *smell*
nose-ring 792.6 *jewellery*
nose to nose 111.6 *oppositely*, 267.7 *beside*
nose-to-nose 111.4 *opposite*, 267.5 *juxtaposed*, 674.15 *contentious*
nose-to-nose confrontation 674.9 *duel*

nose to tail 159.20 *in a line*, 267.7 *beside*

nose-to-tail 267.5 *juxtaposed*

nose wheel 73 Aircraft Parts

nosh 350.7 *food*, 350.22 *eat well*, 606.2 *provisions*

no shining knight 818.4 *discourteous person*

no-show 254.6 *absentee*

nosh-up 350.13 *feast*, 872.3 *act of gluttony*

nosily 465.9 *officiously*

no sinecure 642.6 *business*

nosiness 465.2 *prying*

nosing 412.5 *sense of smell*

no sirree 536.17 *never*

no slave 698.7 *free person*

no slouch 642.10 *busy person*

no-smoking area 417.1 *odourlessness*

no-smoking section 625.2 *salubrity*

nosologist 60.13 *medical specialist*

nosology 60.3 *medical specialty*, 624.20 *pathology*

no sooner said than done 660.9 *easy*

no speaker 566.7 *taciturn person*

no spring chicken 207.7 *older person*, 207.13 *middle-aged*

nostalgia 3.13, 337.15 *looking back*, 511.1 *memory*, 759.7 *emotionalism*, 782.1 *desire*

nostalgic 337.24 *retroactive*, 511.7 *memorable*, 759.12 *sensitive*, 782.9 *desirous*

nostalgically 3.25 *reportedly*

nostoc 90 Algae

nostologist 60.13 *medical specialist*

nostology 60.3 *medical specialty*

no stomach for 573.13 *dissociation*, 785.1 *dislike*

no stone unturned 248.16 *extensively*

Nostradamus 517.8 *oracle*, 636.4 *warner*

no stranger to 501.8 *knowledgeable*

no strike-no lockout agreement 15.1 *industrial relations*

nostril 322.4 *body orifice*, 412.2 *sense of smell*

no strings attached 698.12 *unconditional*

no strong feelings 576.14 *apathy*

nostrum 592.3 *expedient plan*, 630.1 *remedy*

no success 685.1 *noncompletion*, 687.3 *bad fortune*

no such thing 100.2 *nothingness*, 115.4 *dissimilar*

no surplus 608.7 *sufficiency*

no surrender 669.16 *fight on*

no sweat 660.6 *easy thing*, 660.21 *easily*

nosy 465.6 *prying*, 642.21 *meddling*

nosy parker 435.11 *observer*, 465.4, 642.11 *meddler*

not 620.1 *imperfect*

not abide 663.14 *be against*

notability 611.1 *importance*, 611.4 *bigwig*

not a bit 100.7 *not any*

not a bit alike 115.4 *dissimilar*

not a bit of it 115.4 *dissimilar*

notable 611, 165.17 *exceptional*

not able 236.10 *powerless*

notable 511.7 *memorable*, 526.14 *manifest*, 611.4 *bigwig*, 617.1 *worthy*, 800.2 *person of repute*

notable point 611.2 *important matter*

not a blessed one 100.6 *absence*, 172.2 *nothing*

notably 611.9 *importantly*, 617.11 *worthily*

not above temptation 864.13 *venial*

not a breath of air 325.2 *repose*

not accept 536.7 *be negative*, 581.1 *reject*, 600.5 *not use*, 711.5 *refuse*, 720.7 *not observe*

not accepted 581.10 *rejected*

not accomplish 685.5 *not complete*

not accomplished 685.4 *uncompleted*

not according to law 16.55 *illegal*

not accountable 848.5 *exempt*

not achieve 685.5 *not complete*

not acknowledge 816.13 *ignore*

not act 641

not activate 600.5 *not use*

not activated 600.1 *unused*

not adhere 720.7 *not observe*

not admire 787.5 *not wonder about*, 852.14 *disapprove*

not admit 536.7 *be negative*

not a fake 537.6 *authenticity*

not a few 181.6 *many*

not affordable 753.7 *dear*

not a full deck 609.8 *insufficiency*

not a full team 609.8 *insufficiency*

not a great talker 566.7 *taciturn person*

not a hair out of place 150.13 *orderly*

not a hint 100.7 *not any*

not a hope in hell 487.13 *impossible*

not airtight 620.1 *imperfect*

not a jot 100.7 *not any*, 172.2 *nothing*

not a lick 100.7 *not any*, 172.2 *nothing*

not a lick or smell 100.7 *not any*

not a living thing 254.7 *nobody*

not allied 108.9 *misconnected*

not all it's cracked up to be 494.6 *overestimated*, 540.33 *fake*

not allow 711.6 *dissent*

not allowed 709.5 *vetoed*, 711.9 *dissenting*

not allowed visitors 624.22 *sick*

not allow out of one's sight 841.8 *distrust*

not allow to deviate 537.31 *be accurate*

not allow to forget 511.13 *remind*

not all there 145.4 *incomplete*, 460.6 *unintelligent*

not alter 373.11 *be stubborn*

not alter things 236.6 *be powerless*

not a mite 100.7 *not any*, 172.2 *nothing*

not a mouse stirring 325.2 *repose*

not amused 828.15 *resentful*

not an iota 100.7 *not any*, 172.2 *nothing*

not answer 358.1 *fall short*

not answerable 848.5 *exempt*

not anxious to please 818.5 *discourteous*

not any 100, 172.2 *nothing*, 172.6 *zero*

not any more 200.23 *before now*

not a one 100.6 *absence*, 172.2 *nothing*

not a pair 115.2 *unlikeness*

not a particle 100.7 *not any*

not a patch on 127.18 *outclassed*

not apparent 438.1 *invisible*

not apply 104.13 *be extraneous*

not approve 581.1 *reject*, 852.14 *disapprove*

not apropos 612.1 *unimportant*

notarized statement 545.2 *certificate*

not arouse 787.7 *not cause wonder*

notary 545.9 *recorder*

not a sausage 172.2 *nothing*

not a scrap 100.7 *not any*

not a shadow of a suspicion 100.7 *not any*

not a single person 254.7 *nobody*

not ask 466

not a smell 172.2 *nothing*

not a smidgen 100.7 *not any*

not a soul 172.2 *nothing*, 254.7 *nobody*

not a sound 422.4 *silence*

not a speck 100.7 *not any*

not a squeak 422.4 *silence*

not associate 536.7 *be negative*

not associated 108.9 *misconnected*

no taste 795.1 *tastelessness*

not a stitch on 294.8 *uncovered*, 296.2 *nudity*

not a stitch to one's name 296.2 *nudity*

not a suspicion 100.7 *not any*

not as young as one was 207.13 *middle-aged*

not at all 100, 172.11 *none*, 476.13 *no*, 536.15 *negatively*, 536.16 *no*, 711.11 *uncooperatively*

not at any time 100.16 *not ever*

not at home 254.10 *nonresident*

notation 49, 49.18 *written music*, 121.3 *gradation*, 169.1 *number*, 547.1 *representation*

not a trace 100.7 *not any*

not at risk 632.5 *safe*

not a true picture 548.1 *misrepresentation*

not attempt 591.4 *shy*

not at the moment 197.3 *another time*

not at war 675.7 *peaceful*

not at work 254.10 *nonresident*

not available 600.1 *unused*

not awake 643

not a whit 100.7 *not any*, 172.2 *nothing*

not bad 617, 124.3 *mediocre*, 284.10 *supportable*, 623.1 *healthy*, 765.6 *satisfactory*

not balance 123.5 *be unequal*

not bat an eye 641.4 *not act*

not bat an eyelid 225.8 *show determination*

not be 536.10 *be nothing*

not be able to bear 785.5 *dislike*, 828.8 *resent*

not be able to cut the mustard 236.6 *be powerless*

not be able to find 722.9 *lose*

not be able to stomach 828.8 *resent*

not be absent 196.5 *be present*

not be affected by 783.12 *be indifferent*

not bear inspection 620.9 *be imperfect*

not beat about the bush 552.4 *be concise*

not be caught flatfooted 210.5 *take the opportunity*

not be conducive to 231.3 *counteract*

not be entitled 846

not believe 536.7 *be negative*, 720.7 *not observe*

not believe one's eyes 786.9 *wonder*

not belong 147.9 *be excluded*

not belonging 136.17 *unjoined*

not be moved 836.6 *be pitiless*

not bend 373.11 *be stubborn*, 669.7 *be obstinate*

not bending 669.2 *obstinacy*

not be one's business 108.11 *be unconcerned*

not be tempted by 669.6 *resist*

not be thought of 581.10 *rejected*

not be too hard on 835.10 *show mercy*

not be up to it 127.8 *be inferior*

not be willing to 711.5 *refuse*

not blessed with this world's goods 743.1 *poor*

not blink an eye 787.5 *not wonder about*

not blow one's own trumpet 810.14 *be modest*

not born yesterday 657.4 *cunning*

not bothered 859.4 *disinterested*

not breathe 325.8 *be motionless*

not breathe a word 529.12 *keep secret*, 563.13 *be voiceless*

not broken 585.1 *unaccustomed*

not budge 225.8 *show determination*, 325.8 *be motionless*, 574.10 *insist*, 575.8 *hold out*, 577.9 *be obstinate*, 641.4 *not act*

not butt in 698.15 *set free*

not buy 711.5 *refuse*

not by a long chalk 536.17 *never*

not by a long shot 536.17 *never*

not by any stretch of the imagination 100.15 *not at all*

not care 466.6 *be incurious*, 783.12 *be indifferent*

not care a straw about 783.12 *be indifferent*

not care for 470.6 *be neglectful*, 785.5 *dislike*

not cater for 581.3 *exclude*

not cause a stir 124.9 *be average*

not cause wonder 787

notch 319, 319, 36.4 *rowing*, 121.3 *gradation*, 265.2, 265.5 *crack*, 319.3 *rung*, 375.12 *make rough*, 380.7 *sharp point*, 380.15 *make sharp*, 544.10 *identify*

Notch 319

not change 225.6 *be stable*

not change anything 236.6 *be powerless*

not change one's mind 577.9 *be obstinate*

not charge 729.5 *give*

not charged for 754.11 *free of charge*

not charmed 785.8 *disliking*

notched 319, 375.3 *barbed*, 380.4 *toothed*

notched thing 319

notched wood 375.7 *rough thing*

not chickenfeed 611.2 *important matter*

not choose 132.8 *leave*, 785.6 *react against*, 822.14 *hate*

notch up 319, 169.10 *number*, 170.8 *calculate*, 545.15 *register*

notchy 319.4 *notched*

not clean 622.7 *dirty*

not cleared up 685.4 *uncompleted*

not clear up 685.5 *not complete*

not closely packed 139.8 *nonadhesive*

not come 254.15 *be absent*

not come amiss 615.6 *be convenient*, 662.26 *be useful*

not come off 683.6 *fail*, 683.8 *miscarry*

not come to the point 104.13 *be extraneous*, 553.6 *be circuitous*

not come up to 127.8 *be inferior*

not come up to expectations 515.6 *disappoint*, 683.6 *fail*

not come up to scratch 127.8 *be inferior*, 358.2 *fail*, 515.6 *disappoint*, 683.6 *fail*

not come up to standard 127.8 *be inferior*

not come up to the mark 127.8 *be inferior*

not come up with the goods 683.6 *fail*

not compare with 115.5 *be dissimilar*

not complete 685, 145.5 *be incomplete*, 470.6 *be neglectful*, 656.5 *be unskilful*, 685.4 *uncompleted*, 685.6 *drop out*, 720.8 *not perform*

not comply 711.5 *refuse*, 713.6 *protest*, 720.7 *not observe*, 720.9 *disregard orders*

not comply with 693.15 *be disobedient*, 711.6 *dissent*

not compromise 574.10 *insist*

not concentrating 468.7 *inattentive*

not concern 108.10 *be unrelated*

not confess 868.5 *be impenitent*

not confessing 868.3 *impenitent*

not conform 104, 117, 168, 693.15 *be disobedient*, 720.7 *not observe*

not connected 108.9 *misconnected*

not connect with 108.10 *be unrelated*

not consider 581.1 *reject*

not considered 147.11 *excluded*, 612.2 *obscure*

not contemporary 197.2 *occurring at a different time*

not contest 673.3 *submit*

not cooperate 573, 666.5 *disagree*, 669.6 *resist*, 693.15 *be disobedient*, 711.5 *refuse*, 713.6 *protest*, 720.7 *not observe*

not corroborate 536.7 *be negative*
not count 581.3 *exclude,* 612.11 *be unimportant*
not counted 147.11 *excluded*
not counting 147.12 *exclusively*
not covered by law 16.56 *unauthorized*
not cramp one's style 698.15 *set free*
not cramp someone's style 708.4 *be permissive*
not cricket 168.15 *irregular,* 481.3 *prejudice,* 493.3 *injustice,* 844.11 *wrong,* 858.5 *dishonourable*
not cross one's bridges before one comes to them 775.8 *be optimistic*
not current 585.2 *not customary*
not customary 585
not dangerous 632.5 *safe*
not dare to show one's face 806.24 *be humiliated*
not dead 396.12 *alive*
not deep 278.1 *shallow*
not defend 783.12 *be indifferent*
not de rigueur 585.2 *not customary*
not despair 575.8 *hold out*
not deviate 312.11 *be straight,* 333.6 *be in the middle*
not die 396.16 *live*
not difficult 660.9 *easy*
not dilute 134.11 *simplify*
not dirty 621.16 *clean*
not discriminate 482
not dispose of 726.7 *detain*
not dispute 535.22 *emphasize*
not do 236.6 *be powerless,* 616.5 *be inconvenient*
not do as one is told 693.15 *be disobedient,* 720.9 *disregard orders*
not do by halves 684.4 *complete*
not doing well 687.6 *adverse*
not do justice to 495.3 *underestimate*
not done 168.15 *irregular,* 585.2 *not customary,* 844.13 *improper*
not do one's part 573.9 *not cooperate*
not drink 873.3 *be sober*
not drunk 873.1 *sober*
not dry behind the ears 658.1 *naive*
note 49.16 *musical note,* 171.8 *list,* 299.5 *outline,* 432.2 *bird song,* 467.10 *be attentive,* 511.4 *reminder,* 524.2 *annotation,* 544.10 *identify,* 545.1 *record,* 545.14 *inscribe,* 611.1 *importance,* 741.14 *paper money,* 804.1 *right*
not easy 659.10 *difficult,* 661.14 *blocked*
not eating 871.6 *fasting*
notebook 3.5 *chronicle,* 6.14 *school book,* 545.6 *record book*
noted 146.8 *included,* 171.11 *listed,* 545.16 *recorded*
note down 545.14 *inscribe*
not empowered 236.10 *powerless*
not enabled 236.10 *powerless*
not enclose 322.19 *open up*
not endure 785.5 *dislike*
not enough 358, 609.1 *insufficient,* 609.8 *insufficiency,* 609.10 *insufficiently*
not enough to count 182.1 *few*
not enough work 645.1 *leisure*
not entertain 147.7 *exclude*
not entire 620.2 *incomplete*
note of explanation 524.2 *annotation*
note of hand 741.14 *paper money*
note of interrogation 477.11 *question mark*
note of warning 636.1 *warning*
notepad 545.6 *record book*
notepaper 604.3 *paper*
not equal to 52.88 *equal to*
not equate 123.5 *be unequal*
not equivocate 535.22 *emphasize*
note row 434.4 *atonality*
notes 545, 3.5 *chronicle,* 299.1 *outline*
not ever 100, 186.9 *never*

noteworthiness 611.1 *importance*
noteworthy 165.17 *exceptional,* 511.7 *memorable,* 611.6 *notable,* 617.1 *worthy,* 786.8 *wonderful*
not excessive 242.6 *moderate,* 869.8 *self-restrained*
not exist 100, 172, 536.10 *be nothing*
not expect 514.12 *be surprised,* 656.5 *be unskilful,* 786.9 *wonder*
not extreme 242.6 *moderate*
not face 573.7 *refuse*
not fall from grace 865.8 *be innocent*
not far 264.6 *near*
not feeling like 573.1 *unwilling*
not feel well 624.24 *be unhealthy*
not fill the bill 358.1 *fall short*
not finalize 685.5 *not complete*
not finalized 685.4 *uncompleted*
not find 722.9 *lose*
not find one's way to first base 460.9 *lack intellect*
not finish 685.5 *not complete*
not finished 145.4 *incomplete,* 685.4 *uncompleted*
not finish the job 656.5 *be unskilful*
not fit 104.13 *be extraneous,* 616.5 *be inconvenient*
not fit in 168.19 *be independent*
not fit in with 666.8 *be different*
not fit to be seen 790.4 *ugly*
not fit to hold a candle to 127.18 *outclassed*
not fit to live with 816.10 *lonely*
not follow 720.7 *not observe*
not follow through 685.5 *not complete*
not follow up 685.5 *not complete*
not for all the tea in China 711.11 *uncooperatively*
not forget 726.8 *remember*
not forgetting 130.10 *additionally,* 726.5 *retentiveness*
not forgive 836.6 *be pitiless*
not for long 196.10 *for the present*
not for the life of me 536.16 *no*
not for the love of money 536.16 *no*
not for the world 536.16 *no*
not free 808.6 *servile*
not fresh 618.4 *poor,* 626.5 *unhygienic*
not fulfil 685.5 *not complete,* 720.8 *not perform*
not fully 143.12 *partly*
not function 614.7 *be useless*
not functioning 628.13 *dilapidated*
not get along 666.5 *disagree*
not get it 523.9 *find unintelligible*
not get started 328.2 *hesitate*
not getting it 523.6 *confused*
not give 373.11 *be stubborn*
not give a damn 783.12 *be indifferent*
not give a fig 807.29 *ridicule*
not give a fig for 783.12 *be indifferent*
not give a hoot 783.12 *be indifferent*
not give a monkey's 108.11 *be unconcerned*
not give an inch 574.10 *insist*
not give another thought to 512.13 *forget*
not give a toss 108.11 *be unconcerned*
not give it another thought 839.9 *forgive*
not give offence 817.11 *have good manners*
not give the time of day 591.1 *avoid*
not give way 669.6 *resist*
not go 614.7 *be useless*
not go amiss 615.6 *be convenient*
not go near 591.1 *avoid*
not good enough 358.8 *defective,* 618.2 *inferior,* 620.1 *imperfect,* 852.32 *unsatisfactory*
not go out 325.8 *be motionless*
not go well 683.8 *miscarry*
not granted 711.9 *dissenting*

not grasp it 523.9 *find unintelligible*
not grow 129.4 *decrease*
not guilty 16.7 *legal trial,* 16.63 *acquitted,* 855.12, 865.5 *innocent*
no thanks 838.1 *ingratitude*
not hard 660.9 *easy*
not have 593.7 *require*
not have a clue 502.9 *be ignorant,* 656.5 *be unskilful*
not have a dry thread 391.15 *be moist*
not have a good word to say for oneself 806.24 *be humiliated*
not have a leg to stand on 236.6 *be powerless,* 846.13 *not be entitled*
not have a moment to spare 642.13 *be busy*
not have anything to do with 663.14 *be against*
not have a penny 743.12 *be poor*
not have enough sense to come in out of the rain 460.9 *lack intellect*
not have one's heart in it 783.12 *be indifferent*
not have the first idea 523.9 *find unintelligible*
not have the foggiest idea 502.9 *be ignorant*
not have the heart to 573.6 *be unwilling*
not have the sense one was born with 508.6 *be foolish*
not have the skills 656.5 *be unskilful*
not have time 211.7 *be busy*
not have two halfpennies to rub together 743.12 *be poor*
not having time 211.12 *busy*
not hear of 852.15 *withhold approval*
not heed 470.6 *be neglectful,* 693.15 *be disobedient*
not held against one 839.8 *overlooked*
not held together 139.8 *nonadhesive*
not help 236.6 *be powerless,* 614.7 *be useless,* 616.5 *be inconvenient*
not here 254.21 *away*
nothing 172, 52.10 *zero,* 100.2 *nothingness,* 172.1 *zero,* 172.5 *nonentity,* 254.3 *emptiness,* 536.5 *nonexistence,* 612.8 *trifle,* 612.10 *nonentity*
nothing at all 100.2 *nothingness,* 172.2 *nothing*
nothing but 134.16 *simple*
nothing daunted 574.4 *undaunted,* 596.8 *attempting*
nothing doing 536.16, 711.12 *no*
nothing earthshattering 620.8 *ordinariness*
nothing else 174.1 *one*
nothing else but 101.14 *certainly,* 537.37 *authentically*
nothing for it but 580.8 *choice*
nothing happening 641.1 *inaction*
nothing in common 115.2 *unlikeness*
nothing in excess 869.2 *moderation*
nothing in it 110.5, 122.1 *equality,* 674.2 *contest*
nothing in one's way 698.6 *liberality*
nothing in particular 612.8 *trifle*
nothing in the kitty 747.5 *insolvency*
nothing lacking 144.1 *completeness*
nothing left out 146.1 *inclusion*
nothing like 115.4 *dissimilar*
nothing like it 617.2 *best*
nothing missing 144.1 *completeness*
nothingness 100, 172, 248.2 *empty space,* 254.3 *emptiness,* 536.5 *nonexistence,* 612.5 *unimportance*
nothing of note 612.8 *trifle*
nothing of the kind 536.16 *no*

nothing of the sort 115.4 *dissimilar,* 536.16 *no*
nothing on earth 100.2 *nothingness*
nothing out of the ordinary 127.12 *inferior*
nothing special 124.6 *mediocrity,* 127.12 *inferior*
nothing stirring 325.2 *repose*
nothing to add 144.1 *completeness*
nothing to boast about 124.6 *mediocrity*
nothing to boast of 612.8 *trifle*
nothing to choose between 110.5, 122.1 *equality*
nothing to confess 865.1 *innocence*
nothing to declare 865.1 *innocence*
nothing to do with 108.7 *illogical*
nothing to it 612.8 *trifle,* 660.9 *easy,* 787.4 *predictable*
nothing to it! 787.11 *naturally!*
nothing to shout about 127.12 *inferior*
nothing to sneeze at 611.2 *important matter*
nothing to spare 609.9 *scarcity*
nothing to speak of 612.8 *trifle,* 620.8 *ordinariness*
nothing to wonder about 787.4 *predictable*
nothing to worry about 612.8 *trifle*
nothing to write home about 124.3 *mediocre,* 124.6 *mediocrity,* 127.12 *inferior,* 612.8 *trifle,* 620.8 *ordinariness,* 787.4 *predictable*
nothing ventured 479.4 *originality*
nothing ventured, nothing gained 596.11 *here goes give it a shot*
nothing whatever 100.2 *nothingness*
nothing wonderful 787.4 *predictable*
not hold a candle to 127.9 *yield to*
not hold one's liquor 874.7 *be drunk*
not hold water 620.9 *be imperfect*
not hold with 663.14 *be against,* 766.7 *be dissatisfied*
nothosaur 79 Fossil Reptiles, 79.6 *extinct reptile*
no thought for others 860.2 *egoism*
not hurt 617.10 *do good*
notice 435.12 *see,* 467.1 *attention,* 467.10 *be attentive,* 492.1 *judgment,* 496.1 *discover,* 517.3 *plan,* 524.3 *criticism,* 528.2 *communication,* 532.3 *journalism,* 532.9 *advertisement,* 561.2 *article,* 636.1 *warning,* 712.2 *demand*
noticeable 403.8 *sensate,* 435.23, 437.1 *visible,* 526.14 *manifest*
noticeably 268.17 *measurably,* 435.25, 437.11 *visibly*
notice board 526.8 *showplace,* 532.9 *advertisement*
notice of resignation 705.1 *resignation*
noticing 435.21 *seeing*
notifiable disease 624.4 *disease*
not if I can help it 536.16 *no*
notification 528.2 *communication,* 532.1 *publication,* 636.1 *warning,* 654.1 *advice*
notificatory 532.21 *publishing*
notifier 528.9 *informant,* 532.10 *publicizer*
notify 6.22 *educate,* 517.11 *predict,* 528.11 *inform,* 532.14 *proclaim,* 636.5 *warn,* 654.5 *advise*
notifying 636.8 *warning*
not imbibe 873.3 *be sober*
no time 186.1 *timelessness*
no time to lose 648.4 *haste*
not immune 633.3 *vulnerable*
not impress 620.9 *be imperfect*
not improve 628.1 *deteriorate,* 628.5 *hurt*

not improved 628.12 *deterio-rated*, 768.4 *aggravated*
not in a million years 100.16 *not ever*
not in a month of Sundays 186.9 *never*
not in a state of grace 864.14 *impious*
not include 147.7 *exclude*
not included 147.11 *excluded*, 254.12 *missing*
not in contention 147.11 *excluded*
not increase 129.4 *decrease*
not in danger 632.5 *safe*
not independent 701.9 *subject*
not indigenous 149.14 *imported*
not indulge 591.1 *abstain*, 873.3 *be sober*
not indulging 873.1 *sober*
not in error 537.15 *true*
not in good health 624.22 *sick*
not in proper condition 628.13 *dilapidated*
not in residence 254.10 *nonresident*
not insist 673.3 *submit*, 814.11 *not stand on ceremony*
not interest 787.7 *not cause wonder*
not interfere 219.3 *continue*, 698.15 *set free*
not in the habit of 585.1 *unaccustomed*
not in the mood 573.1 *unwilling*
not in the pink 620.1 *imperfect*
not in the same league 127.18 *outclassed*, 147.11 *excluded*
not in time 211.10 *untimely*
not in vogue 585.2 *not customary*
not involve 108.10 *be unrelated*
not involved 591.18 *avoiding*, 783.7 *indifferent*
notion 4.1 *philosophy*, 461.6, 471.1 *idea*, 497.1 *belief*, 518.1 *supposition*, 519.4 *ideality*, 579.3 *whim*, 592.3 *expedient plan*, 759.2 *impression*
notional 4.13 *of philosophy*, 461.10 *speculative*, 471.10 *theoretical*, 518.7 *suppositional*, 519.12 *imaginary*
notionally 4.25, 471.20 *theoretically*
not just stand there 596.1 *attempt*
not just this minute 197.3 *another time*
not kept 727.12 *disposed*
not know 502.9 *be ignorant*, 523.9 *find unintelligible*, 656.5 *be unskilful*
not know how 656.5 *be unskilful*
not knowing which way to turn 743.2 *insolvent*
not know oneself 220.8 *be transformed*
not know one's own business 656.6 *act foolishly*
not know one's own mind 576.7 *be irresolute*
not know the meaning of failure 682.7 *overcome obstacles*
not know what one is about 523.9 *find unintelligible*, 656.6 *act foolishly*
not know what to do 576.7 *be irresolute*
not know what to make of 523.9 *find unintelligible*
not know what to say 786.9 *wonder*
not know when one is beaten 682.7 *overcome obstacles*
not know when to stop 541.9 *be extravagant*, 870.11 *overindulge*
not know which way is up 642.13 *be busy*
not know which way to turn 642.13 *be busy*, 659.20 *be in difficulty*, 687.9 *be in trouble*
not lawful 236.10 *powerless*
not leave a leg to stand on 476.8 *refute*
not legal 16.55 *illegal*
not let anyone get a word in edgeways 565.8 *talk too much*

not let go 575.8 *hold out*, 637.5 *preserve*, 726.6 *retain*, 826.7 *show endearment for*
not let grass grow under one's feet 596.1 *attempt*
not let out of one's sight 437.10 *make visible*
not let the grass grow under one's feet 642.13 *be busy*
not liable 848.5 *exempt*
not likely 500.11, 536.16 *no*, 711.12 *no*
not like the look of 785.5 *dislike*
not like the rest 126.15 *excellent*
not liking 785.8 *disliking*
not listen 421.8 *be deaf*, 468.12 *be inattentive*, 577.9 *be obstinate*
not listen to 693.15 *be disobedient*
not live up to expectations 620.9 *fall short*
not long 189.8 *transiently*
not long ago 201.21 *newly*
not long for this world 207.14 *aged*, 244.15 *destroyed*, 397.18 *dying*
not long in the telling 552.3 *concise*
not long to go 397.18 *dying*
not look a day older 217.5 *be permanent*
not look for praise 810.14 *be modest*
not look like 115.5 *be dissimilar*
not look where one is going 656.7 *be clumsy*
not lose any sleep over 783.12 *be indifferent*
not lucky 687.8 *unlucky*
not mad 509.4 *sane*
not maintain one's position 628.1 *deteriorate*
not make 358.1 *fall short*
not make a peep 422.1 *be silent*
not make a sound 422.1 *be silent*
not make ends meet 722.10 *have a financial loss*
not make it 358.2 *fail*
not make out 523.9 *find unintelligible*
not make sense 523.7 *be unintelligible*
not make the grade 127.8 *be inferior*, 236.6 *be powerless*, 358.2 *fail*, 620.9 *be imperfect*, 683.6 *fail*
not making ends meet 722.2 *financial loss*
not many 182.1, 182.5 *few*
not match 123.5 *be unequal*
not matter 612.11 *be unimportant*
not mean what one says 521.9 *talk nonsense*
not measure up 358.1 *fall short*
not meddle 698.15 *set free*
not meet expectations 609.5 *be insufficient*
not meet requirements 609.5 *be insufficient*
not memorized 595.2 *spontaneous*
not mention 566.9 *lapse into silence*
not mince one's words 658.4 *be naive*
not mind 466.6 *be incurious*, 667.6 *agree with*, 783.12 *be indifferent*
not mind one's own business 642.11 *meddle*
not missed 512.11 *forgotten*
not mix 134.11 *simplify*
not modern 197.2 *occurring at a different time*
not move 641.4 *not act*
not much 182.5 *few*
not natural 551.2 *obscure*
not needed 614.1 *useless*
not negative 535.14 *assertive*
not nice 618.3 *bad*, 822.12 *hated*
not notice 468.12 *be inattentive*
not now 197.3 *another time*, 199.14 *in the future*
not obey 689.4 *be anarchic*, 693.15 *be disobedient*
not observe 720, 536.7 *be negative*

not observed 585.2 *not customary*
not obstruct 322.19 *open up*
not occur 172.8 *not exist*
not offered 711.8 *refused*
not often 213.1 *infrequently*
not of this world 104.12 *external*, 149.12 *extraterrestrial*, 519.12 *imaginary*
not one 172.6 *zero*, 254.7 *nobody*
not one of us 816.6 *unsocial person*
not one's best 620.6 *imperfect item*
not one's cup of tea 785.9 *disliked*
not one's sort 785.9 *disliked*
not one's type 785.3 *disliked person*, 790.2 *ugly person*, 822.8 *hated person*
not on guard 633.3 *vulnerable*, 658.1 *naive*
not on speaking terms 820.8 *estranged*
not on the level 801.4 *disreputable*
not on this earth 100.17 *nowhere*
not on time 209.9 *late*
not on your life 487.13 *impossible*, 500.11 *no*, 711.11 *uncooperatively*
not on your nelly 487.13 *impossible*, 711.11 *uncooperatively*
not open one's mouth 422.1 *be silent*
not open to new ideas 443.5 *unintelligent*
not operate 236.6 *be powerless*
not oppose 667.6 *agree with*
notoriety 511.5 *day to remember*, 532.7 *publicity*, 801.1 *disrespect*
notorious 501.10 *known*, 526.14 *manifest*, 532.20 *well-known*, 801.4 *disreputable*
notoriously 526.16 *manifestly*
not out 219.5 *continual*
not out of the wood 633.4 *endangered*
not overdoing it 869.8 *self-restrained*
not over one's dead body 711.11 *uncooperatively*
not participating 643
not part with 726.7 *detain*
not pass 127.8 *be inferior*, 581.1 *reject*, 683.6 *fail*
not pass muster 620.9 *be imperfect*
not pass the test 127.8 *be inferior*
not pay 745, 747
not paying 614.2 *futile*
not peanuts 611.2 *important matter*
not perfect 620.1 *imperfect*, 864.13 *venial*
not perform 720
not permitted 711.9 *dissenting*
not persevere 576.10 *compromise*
not plain sailing 661.2 *obstacle*
not play 573.9 *not cooperate*
not play ball 117.13 *not conform*, 573.9 *not cooperate*, 666.5 *disagree*
not playing the ball 35.3 *rugby play*
not playing the game 844.11 *wrong*, 858.1 *improbity*
not playing with a full deck 460.6 *unintelligent*
not play the ball 35.5 *play rugby*
not play the game 844.21 *do wrong*
not possible 487.1 *impossible*
not practise 720.8 *not perform*
not prepared 573.1 *unwilling*
not present 254.8 *absent*, 458.7 *disappeared*
not press 691.3 *be lenient*
not press charges 16.78 *acquit*
not proceed with 598.1 *relinquish*, 600.5 *not use*
not prosecute 16.78 *acquit*
not proud 806.1 *humble*
not proud of 806.3 *humbled*
not proven 16.63 *acquitted*
not public 527.2 *concealed*

not pull one's weight 573.9 *not cooperate*
not push oneself forward 591.4 *shy*, 810.14 *be modest*
not put a foot wrong 655.10 *be skilful*, 682.6 *be successful*
not put it past 488.10 *think likely*
not put up with 663.14 *be against*
not question 466.5 *not ask*, 535.22 *emphasize*
not quite 264.7 *nearly*, 620.11 *imperfectly*
not raise a finger 641.4 *not act*
not raise an eyebrow 787.5 *not wonder about*
not reach to 358.1 *fall short*
not react 641.4 *not act*
not ready 573.1 *unwilling*, 595.1 *unprepared*
not real 518.8 *supposed*, 519.12 *imaginary*
not realize one's expectations 515.4 *be disappointed*
not really 536.16 *no*
not recommended 616.1 *inconvenient*
Notre Dame Cathedral 43 *Noted Buildings*
not redeemable 868.3 *impenitent*
not redeemed 868.3 *impenitent*
not reform 868.5 *be impenitent*
not register 523.9 *find unintelligible*
not relate 104.13 *be extraneous*
not related 108.9 *misconnected*, 612.1 *unimportant*
not relate to 108.10 *be unrelated*
not remember 512.13 *forget*
not remembered 512.11 *forgotten*
not representative 548.6 *misrepresented*
not required 600.3 *not wanted*
not resemble 115.5 *be dissimilar*
not resident 254.10 *nonresident*
not resist 673.3 *submit*, 694.5 *obey*
not respect 818.7 *be discourteous*
not respond 783.12 *be indifferent*
not responsible 848.5 *exempt*
not retain 727.9 *dispose of*
not retained 727.12 *disposed*
not right 616.1 *inconvenient*, 844.12 *incorrect*
not ring true 540.16 *be false*
no trouble 660.6 *easy thing*
not rusty 386.8 *lubricated*
not safe 633.2 *unsafe*
not satisfying 609.1 *insufficient*
not say a word 422.1 *be silent*
not secure 633.3 *vulnerable*
not see 436.14 *be blind*
not see an inch beyond one's nose 460.9 *lack intellect*
not see beyond one's nose 481.13 *prejudge*
not seen before 201.11 *unfamiliar*
not see the wood for the trees 659.18 *find difficult*
not select 581.1 *reject*
not serious 612.4 *trivial*
not set the world on fire 783.16 *be mediocre*
not show up 254.15 *be absent*
not signposted 438.1 *invisible*
not singular 175.6 *plural*
not sixteen annas to the rupee 460.6 *unintelligent*
not sixteen ounces to the pound 145.2 *omission*, 460.6 *unintelligent*
not sleep 642.14 *push*
not so 536.16 *no*
not so minded 573.1 *unwilling*
not sorry 868.3 *impenitent*
not speak 422.1 *be silent*, 563.13 *be voiceless*
not speak the truth 540.16 *be false*
not stand a chance 487.9 *be impossible*
not stand for 711.6 *dissent*
not stand in the way of 660.16 *make easy*, 708.3 *permit*, 708.4 *be permissive*
not stand on ceremony 814
not start 683.9 *malfunction*

not stay the course 358.1 *fall short*, 685.6 *drop out*
not sticky 139.8 *nonadhesive*
not stir 240.4 *be inert*, 325.8 *be motionless*, 641.4 *not act*
not stirring 641.3 *inactive*
not stop 159.14, 219.3 *continue*
not stop and think 462.12 *lack thought*
not stop at trifles 574.6 *be resolute*
not straight 858.7 *criminal*
not stretch 358.1 *fall short*
not strike 720.7 *not observe*
not strong 238.8 *weak*
not stuck on 139.8 *nonadhesive*
not subject to 848.5 *exempt*
not succeed 683.6 *fail*
not suffice 123.5 *be unequal*, 358.1 *fall short*, 609.5 *be insufficient*, 620.9 *be imperfect*
not sufficient 609.1 *insufficient*
not support 663.14 *be against*
not surprising 787.4 *predictable*
not swerve 333.6 *be in the middle*
not take a joke 828.10 *be offended*
not take it lying down 642.14 *push*, 669.8 *revolt*, 672.3 *retaliate*
not take no for an answer 574.10 *insist*, 575.8 *hold out*, 577.9 *be obstinate*, 695.6 *compel*
not take offence 817.10 *be courteous*
not take sides 783.15 *be impartial*
not tamper 698.15 *set free*
not tell apart 114.11 *make similar*
not tell one from the other 114.11 *make similar*
not tell the truth 862.11 *be evil*
not the done thing 844.13 *improper*
not the end of the world 612.8 *trifle*
not the full pound note 145.2 *omission*, 460.6 *unintelligent*
not there 254.21 *away*
not the real thing 102
not the thing 844.13 *improper*
not think much of 766.7 *be dissatisfied*
not think twice about 783.12 *be indifferent*
not thought through 685.4 *uncompleted*
Nottingham 93 Cities
Nottinghamshire 92 Counties
not to be caught napping 657.4 *cunning*
not to be despised 611.5 *important*
not to be drawn 566.1 *taciturn*, 657.4 *cunning*
not to be had 609.4 *scarce*
not to be had at any price 609.4 *scarce*
not to be had for love or money 609.4 *scarce*, 753.8 *valuable*
not to be overlooked 611.5 *important*
not to be pinned down 576.2 *changeable*
not to be recommended 852.32 *unsatisfactory*
not to be sneezed at 580.15 *chosen*, 611.5 *important*
not to be sniffed at 580.15 *chosen*
not to be spared 593.4 *required*
not to be thought of 487.1 *impossible*
not to be trusted 858.6 *faithless*
not today 197.3 *another time*
not tolerate 663.14 *be against*, 690.5 *be severe*, 709.3 *veto*
not tolerated 785.9 *disliked*
not tolerating 785.8 *disliking*
not to mention 130.10 *additionally*
not to mince words 537.36 *truthfully*, 857.7 *honourably*
not too little 608.1 *sufficient*
not too much 608.1 *sufficient*
not to one's taste 785.9 *disliked*

not to put too fine a point upon it 556.8 *simply*
not touch 591.3 *abstain*, 600.5 *not use*, 669.9 *desist*
not touching 669.4 *desisting*
not touch with a bargepole 591.1 *avoid*
not transparent 551.2 *obscure*
not trouble oneself 466.6 *be incurious*
not true 540.25 *false*
not true to life 115.4 *dissimilar*
not try 591.4 *shy*
not try to hide 526.4 *show oneself*
not turn a hair 783.12 *be indifferent*, 787.5 *not wonder about*
not turn up 254.15 *be absent*
not understand 521, 133.11 *be mixed up*, 523.9 *find unintelligible*
not understandable 523.1 *unintelligible*
not univocal 578.10 *equivocal*
not unlike 114.7 *similar*
not up 40.5 *real tennis*
not up to date 145.4 *incomplete*
not up to expectations 515.11 *disappointing*, 620.1 *imperfect*
not up to it 609.1 *insufficient*
not up to much 127.12 *inferior*
not up to scratch 358.8 *defective*, 656.1 *unskilful*, 766.5 *unsatisfactory*
not up to snuff 127.17 *defective*, 609.1 *insufficient*
not up to the mark 620.1 *imperfect*
not use 600, 607.1 *waste*
not used 600.1 *unused*
not used to 585.1 *unaccustomed*
not useful 614.1 *useless*
not using drugs 312.4 *traditional*
not utilize 600.5 *not use*
not utilized 600.1 *unused*
not utter a squeak 422.1 *be silent*
not vital 612.1 *unimportant*
not vote for 581.1 *reject*
not wait to be asked 710.11 *volunteer*
not walk straight 874.7 *be drunk*
not want 581.3 *exclude*
not want anything to do with 711.5 *refuse*
not wanted 600
not waterproof 620.1 *imperfect*
not weaken 237.7 *be strong*
not wear 711.5 *refuse*
not weigh 612.11 *be unimportant*
not well 624.22 *sick*
not well inclined 820.8 *estranged*
not what one had expected 515.2 *bad outcome*
not what one had hoped for 515.2 *bad outcome*
not whole 143.11 *partial*
not wholly 143.12 *partly*
not willing to hear of 711.8 *refused*
not with it 468.8 *absent-minded*
notwithstanding 231.5 *counter*
not wonder 783.12 *be indifferent*
not wonder about 787
not work 236.6 *be powerless*, 614.7 *be useless*, 683.9 *malfunction*
not worked out 685.4 *uncompleted*
not working 643, 236.10 *powerless*, 614.1 *useless*, 628.13 *dilapidated*, 844.18 *gone wrong*
not worth a bean 618.1 *worthless*
not worth a bucket of warm spit 618.1 *worthless*
not worth a bumper 618.1 *worthless*
not worth a hill of beans 618.1 *worthless*
not worth a light 618.1 *worthless*
not worth a piss in the snow 618.1 *worthless*
not worth a plugged nickel 618.1 *worthless*
not worth a second thought 612.4 *trivial*, 618.1 *worthless*
not worth a thought 612.4 *trivial*
not worth considering 612.1 *unimportant*

not worth powder and shot 618.1 *worthless*
not worth the effort 614.2 *futile*, 618.1 *worthless*
not worth the paper it's written on 614.1 *useless*, 618.1 *worthless*
not worthwhile 612.4 *trivial*, 614.2 *futile*
not worth worrying about 612.1 *unimportant*
no two ways about it 480.12 *assuredly*
not yield 373.11 *be stubborn*, 574.10 *insist*, 669.7 *be obstinate*
not yielding 669.2 *obstinacy*
Nouakchott 93 Cities
nought 52.10 *zero*, 100.2 *nothingness*, 172.1 *zero*
noughts and crosses 42 Children's Games and Party Games
noumenon 4.8 *philosophical term*, 471.1 *idea*
noun 5.35 *part of speech*, 560.8 *name*
noun phrase 5.23 *phrase*
nourish 350.25 *provide food*, 396.20 *support life*, 662.20 *sustain*
nourishing 350.27 *edible*, 623.2 *healthful*, 625.4 *hygienic*
nourishment 350.7 *food*, 396.3 *life requirements*, 662.3 *sustenance*
nous 6.9 *learnedness*, 459.3 *intelligence*, 459.5 *common sense*, 507.2 *intelligence*, 655.1 *skill*
nouveau riche 201.8 *new arrival*, 201.12 *immature*, 686.4 *prosperous person*, 795.5 *vulgar person*, 795.8 *discourteous*
nouveaux riches 742.11 *the rich*
nouvelle cuisine 45.1 *cookery*
nova 53.12 *variable star*, 439.4 *natural light*
Nova Scotia 92 Canadian Provinces and Territories
Novaya Zemlya 98 Islands
Novecento Italiano 50 Schools and Groups of Artists
novel 119, 48.2 *fiction*, 115.4 *dissimilar*, 201.11 *unfamiliar*, 243.5 *work of art*, 479.9 *original*, 519.4 *ideality*, 532.6 *book publishing*, 560.5 *fiction*
novelette 48.2 *fiction*
novelettist 48.14 *author*
novel idea 461.6 *idea*
novelist 48.14 *author*, 532.12 *publisher*, 560.10 *descriptive writer*
novella 48.2 *fiction*, 243.5 *work of art*, 560.5 *fiction*
novel of ideas 48.2 *fiction*
novel of sensibility 48.2 *fiction*
novel sequence 48.2 *fiction*
novelty 119.1 *originality*, 201.1 *newness*, 479.4 *originality*, 612.9 *bauble*, 754.5 *cheap item*
novelty costume 295.5 *fancy dress*
November 534 Phonetic Alphabet
Novembergruppe 50 Schools and Groups of Artists
novemdecillion 169.3 *large number*, 179.11 *million*
novena 179.5 *nine*
novenary 179.16 *ninth*
Novgorod 93 Cities
novice 6.7 *learner*, 7.7 *monk*, 156.14 *beginner*, 201.8 *new arrival*, 201.12 *immature*, 502.5 *ignorant person*, 656.10 *unskilled person*, 658.3 *naive person*
novitiate 594.12 *briefing*
novobiocin 62 Medication
novocaine 404.4 *anaesthetic*
no voice 563.1 *voicelessness*
Novokirghiz 32 Breeds of Horse and Pony
now 99, 185.27 *at what time*, 191.8 *immediately*, 196.9 *at present*, 198.2 *present time*
nowadays 196.9 *at present*

now and again 185.28 *sometimes*, 187.14 *for short periods*, 212.2 *sometimes*, 265.8 *apart*
now and then 160.17 *discontinuously*, 185.28 *sometimes*, 187.14 *for short periods*, 212.2 *sometimes*, 215.8 *irregularly*, 265.8 *apart*
no way 100.15 *not at all*, 325.11 *stop*, 476.13 *no*, 487.13 *impossible*, 500.11 *no*
noway 536.16 *no*
no way 711.11 *uncooperatively*, 711.12 *no*
nowhere 100
now here 224.15 *changeably*
nowhere 254.21 *away*, 618.2 *inferior*
nowhere city 249.10 *urban area*
nowhere to be found 254.9 *away*, 722.16 *losing*
nowhere to turn 659.6 *critical situation*
no will of one's own 576.14 *apathy*
no-win situation 659.5 *predicament*
no woman 254.7 *nobody*
no words wasted 552.1 *conciseness*
no work 641.1 *inaction*, 645.1 *leisure*
no worse 623.1 *healthy*
nowt 100.2 *nothingness*
now this 224.15 *changeably*
now this, now that 579.6 *capriciously*
now you see it now you don't 438.7 *become invisible*, 458.6 *disappearing*
Nox 8 Deities
noxious 244.14 *destructive*, 416.5 *odorous*, 618.3 *bad*, 618.5 *harmful*, 626.5 *unhygienic*, 631.16 *blighting*, 862.9 *detrimental*
noxiously 626.8 *unhygienically*
noxiousness 618.11 *harmfulness*, 862.1 *evil*
noyade 398.4 *slaughter*, 879.13 *capital punishment*
nozzle 69.6 *garden tool*, 389.12 *sprinkler*
NPL 75.4 *standard*
npn transistor 64.19 *transistor*
NSU 624.14 *venereal disease*
ntenga 49 Musical Instruments
n-type conductivity 56.44, 64.4 *semiconductor*
n-type semiconductor 56.44, 64.4 *semiconductor*
nuance 121.4 *interval*, 527.10 *quietness*, 759.2 *impression*
nub 103.2 *essential content*, 158.2 *core*, 257.1 *contents*, 291.1 *centre*, 383.3 *nap*, 473.4 *gist*, 611.3 *chief thing*
Nuba 5 Languages and Groups of Languages
nubbiness 375.6 *roughness*
nubbliness 375.6 *roughness*
nubby 375.2 *coarse*
Nubian 7 Non-Christian Religions, 98 Deserts
nubile 823.22 *marriageable*
nubility 594.14 *preparedness*, 823.4 *marriageability*
nuclear 59.24 *nuclear*
nuclear 59, 158.12 *core*, 235.17 *powered*, 291.6 *central*, 410.10 *powered*
nuclear accident 56, 410.7 *nuclear power*
nuclear blast 671.8 *havoc*
nuclear bomb 680.16 *bomb*
nuclear cardiology 60.3 *medical specialty*
nuclear chemistry 57.1 *chemistry*
nuclear contamination 56.75 *nuclear accident*
nuclear deterrent 680.1 *weapon*
nuclear disarmament 675.1 *peace*
nuclear energy 56.11 *energy*, 56.72 *nuclear fission*, 235.4 *energy*, 410.7 *nuclear power*
nuclear engineering 56.72 *nuclear fission*, 63.1 *engineering*

nuclear envelope 59.9 *cell nucleus*
nuclear fallout 244.7 *agent of destruction*
nuclear family 161.17 *family*, 665.2 *society*
nuclear fission 56, 136.1 *separation*, 141.2 *deconstruction*, 410.7 *nuclear power*
nuclear-free zone 677.1 *pacification*
nuclear fuel 56.73 *nuclear reactor*, 235.6 *source of energy*, 338.13 *fuel*, 410.7 *nuclear power*
nuclear fusion 56.72 *nuclear fission*, 135.1 *union*, 410.7 *nuclear power*
nuclear generating station 410.7 *nuclear power*
nuclear interaction 56.79 *fundamental interaction*
nuclear medicine 60.3 *medical specialty*
nuclear membrane 59.9 *cell nucleus*
nuclear missile 235.8 *nuclear power*, 244.7 *agent of destruction*
nuclear physics 56.3 *modern physics*, 235.8 *nuclear power*, 367.6 *natural science*
nuclear pore 59.9 *cell nucleus*
nuclear power 235, 410, 56.11 *energy*, 56.72 *nuclear fission*, 235.4 *energy*, 235.6 *source of energy*, 410.1 *fuel*
nuclear-powered 410.10 *powered*
nuclear power station 56.72 *nuclear fission*, 64.32 *power station*
nuclear reaction 56
nuclear reactor 56, 235.8, 410.7 *nuclear power*
Nuclear Regulatory Commission 235.8 *nuclear power*
nuclear reprocessing plant 727.5 *wasteyard*
nuclear sap 59.9 *cell nucleus*
nuclear submarine 679.24 *warship*, 680.5 *missile weapon*
nuclear war 676.1 *war*
nuclear warfare 678.8 *warfare*
nuclear warhead 235.8 *nuclear power*, 244.7 *agent of destruction*
nuclear waste 56, 410.7 *nuclear power*
nuclear weapon 235.8 *nuclear power*, 244.7 *agent of destruction*, 631.10 *warfare*, 680.1 *weapon*
nuclear winter 244.5 *havoc*
nucleary 59.24 *nuclear*
nucleate 59.24 *nuclear*, 291.6 *central*, 291.9 *centre*, 371.8 *be dense*
nucleation 371.2 *concentration*
nucleic 59.24 *nuclear*
nucleic acid 58.10 *nucleoside*, 59.9 *cell nucleus*, 59.12 *molecular biology*
nucleic-acid structure 59.12 *molecular biology*
nucleolar 59.24 *nuclear*
nucleolate 59.24 *nuclear*
nucleolus 59.9 *cell nucleus*
nucleon 56.65 *atom*, 56.77 *elementary particle*, 367.4 *matter*
nucleonics 56.72 *nuclear fission*, 235.8 *nuclear power*, 367.6 *natural science*
nucleon number 56.69 *isotope*
nucleopeptide 59.9 *cell nucleus*
nucleophile 57.14 *chemical reaction*
nucleophilic 57.38 *reactive*
nucleophilic reaction 57.14 *chemical reaction*
nucleoplasm 59.9 *cell nucleus*
nucleoprotein 58.9 *protein*, 59.9 *cell nucleus*
nucleoside 58, 59.12 *molecular biology*
nucleosome 59.9 *cell nucleus*
nucleotide 58.10 *nucleoside*, 59.12 *molecular biology*
nucleus 53.7 *galaxy*, 56.65 *atom*, 59.8 *cell organ*, 103.2 *essential content*, 156.3 *source*, 158.2 *core*, 226.3 *rudiment*, 260.2 *little thing*, 291.1 *centre*,

367.4 *matter*, 371.4 *solid body*, 611.3 *chief thing*, 646.4 *personnel*
nuclide 56.69 *isotope*
nuddy 294.8 *uncovered*, 296.9 *undressed*
nude 50.10 *art subject*, 294.4 *exposer*, 294.8 *uncovered*, 296.8 *nude person*, 296.9 *undressed*
nude figure 296.8 *nude person*
nude model 294.4 *exposer*, 296.8 *nude person*
nude painting 296.3 *pornography*
nude person 296
nudge 267.2 *meeting*, 267.4 *meet*, 324.14 *set in motion*, 330.2 *collide*, 330.12 *collision*, 330.13 *blow*, 366.9 *jolt*, 407.3 *press*, 407.11 *touch*, 528.7 *advice*, 543.3, 543.11 *gesture*, 586.8 *incentive*, 636.1 *warning*, 636.5 *warn*
nudibranch 81 Molluscs
nudie 296.2 *nudity*
nudie show 51.5 *show*
nudism 294.1 *uncovering*, 296.1 *undress*
nudist 294.4 *exposer*, 296.8 *nude person*, 296.9 *undressed*, 408.5 *hot weather*
nudity 296, 294.1 *uncovering*, 294.3 *nakedness*
nugatory 612.4 *trivial*
nuggar 74 Ships and Boats, **74** Sailing Ships and Boats
nugget 371.4 *solid body*, 741.16 *bullion*
nuisance 768, 151.11 *troublemaker*, 153.1 *disturbance*, 462.7 *inconsiderate person*, 616.3 *inconvenience*, 642.3 *nimbleness*, 642.11 *meddler*, 693.5 *troublemaker*, 764.9 *unpleasant person*
nuisance call 534.10 *telephone call*
Nu Jiang 94 Lakes
nuke 100.14 *cause not to exist*, 607.2 *lay waste*, 670.3 *bomb*, 676.13 *be at war*
null 16, 172, 100.9 *nonexistent*, 254.8 *absent*, 521.10 *meaningless*, 614.1 *useless*
null and void 16.57 *null*, 236.10 *powerless*, 247.6 *having no effect*, 536.14 *nonexistent*, 614.1 *useless*, 704.10 *cancelled*, 709.5 *vetoed*
null hypothesis 52.54 *hypothesis testing*
nullification 125.2 *counterbalance*, 231.1 *counteraction*, 244.1 *destruction*, 476.1 *refutation*, 484.1 *counterevidence*, 536.4 *renunciation*, 704.1 *cancellation*
nullified 16.57 *null*, 125.10 *counterbalancing*, 536.12 *rejected*, 704.10 *cancelled*
nullifier 476.5 *refuter*
nullify 16.57 *annul*, 125.5 *counterbalance*, 172.9 *annihilate*, 231.3 *counteract*, 244.8 *destroy*, 476.8 *refute*, 484.7 *counter*, 536.9 *renounce*, 704.6 *cancel*, 711.6 *dissent*
nullifying 231.4 *counteracting*
nullipore 90 Algae
nullity 100.2, 172.3 *nothingness*, 254.1 *absence*, 521.1 *lack of meaning*, 536.5 *nonexistence*, 612.5 *unimportance*
null matrix 52.22 *matrix*
null set 52.21 *set*
numb 236.8 *overpower*, 240.5 *inert*, 325.5 *sedentary*, 381.3 *dull*, 404.7 *anaesthetized*, 466.4 *uninterested*, 761.2 *desensitized*, 761.7 *render insensitive*, 783.7 *indifferent*, 783.13 *make indifferent*
numbat 77 Marsupials
number 52, 169, 169, 170, 5.30 *syntax*, 51.6 *score*, 52.90 *enumerate*, 120.4 *total*, 120.8 *quantify*, 142.9 *be whole*, 143.2 *particular*, 146.4 *include*, 295.1 *dress*, 490.18 *particularity*,

544.10 *identify*, 567.5 *place of residence*
Number 169
numberable 170.14 *calculable*
number among one's possessions 723.7 *possess*
numbercruncher 170.5 *computer*
numbercrunching 170.4 *computing*
numbered 24.9 *billiard*, 120.6 *quantitative*, 544.12 *identified*
numbered ball 24.1 *billiards*
numbered with the dead 397.19 *dead*
number five 36.9 *sailor*
number four 36.9 *sailor*
numbering 52.12 *numeration*, 170.3 *count*
numberless 181, 184.2 *immeasurable*
numberlessness 184.5 *immeasurability*
number one 36.9 *sailor*, 126.6 *paragon*, 165.12 *I*, 682.3 *successful thing*, 682.4 *successful person*, 861.16 *superior person*
number-one 126.14, 617.2 *best*, 619.1 *perfect*
number-one driver 33.8 *driver*
number-one ranking 682.3 *successful thing*
number ones 353.6 *urine*
numberplate 71 Motor Vehicle Parts
numberplate registration number 544.3 *means of identification*
numbers 120, 48.6 *poetry*, 48.9 *metre*, 52.1 *mathematics*
number six 36.9 *sailor*
number system 52
Number Ten 688.6 *place of authority*
number theory 52 Mathematical Theories, 52.4 *simple arithmetic*
number three 36.9 *sailor*
number two 36.9 *sailor*, 707.1 *deputy*
number-two driver 33.8 *driver*
number twos 353.5 *faeces*
number with 146.6 *subsume*
number work 52.4 *simple arithmetic*, 170.1 *calculation*
numbing 404.9 *anaesthetic*
numbly 240.7 *inertly*, 381.13 *obtusely*, 466.8 *disinterestedly*, 783.17 *indifferently*
numbness 240.1 *inertness*, 325.1 *motionlessness*, 381.7 *dullness*, 404.2 *unconsciousness*, 466.2 *lack of interest*, 624.3 *symptom*, 624.17 *nervous disorder*, 761.4 *desensitization*, 783.1 *indifference*
numbskull 460.3 *unintelligent person*
numen 8.5 *deity*
numerable 52, 170.14 *calculable*
numeracy 52.1 *mathematics*, 501.3 *learning*
numeral 52, 169.1 *number*
numerary 169.7 *numerical*
numerate 6.18 *educated*, 169.7 *numerical*, 170.11 *number*, 501.9 *literate*
numeration 52, 170.1 *calculation*
numerative 169.7 *numerical*, 170.13 *calculative*
numerator 52.18 *division*, 169.5 *ratio*
numeric 169.7 *numerical*
numerical 52, 169, 150.12 *hierarchical*, 170.13 *calculative*
numerical analysis 52.1 *mathematics*
numerical analyst 52.2 *mathematician*
numerical coefficient 52.25 *algebraic expression*
numerical forecast 55.4 *weather forecast*
numerically 169, 52.87 *mathematically*, 150.25 *in order*, 170.16 *mathematically*, 171.13 *inventorially*
numerical order 150.3 *hierarchy*
numerical result 478

numerical taxonomy 59.17 *taxonomy*
numerologist 11.13 *diviner*
numerology 11.9 *divination*
numero uno 126.6 *paragon*, 861.16 *superior person*
numerous 175.6 *plural*, 181.5 *multitudinous*, 212.3 *frequent*
numerously 181, 212.1 *frequently*
numerousness 175.2, 181.1 *multiplicity*, 212.4 *frequency*
numinous 8.13 *divine*
numinously 8.19 *divinely*
numinousness 8.1 *divinity*, 11.2 *the occult*
numismatic 741.22 *monetary*
numismatically 741.28 *financially*
numismatics 741.13 *coinage*
numismatist 161.35 *collector*, 741.17 *financier*
numismatology 741.13 *coinage*
nummary 741.22 *monetary*
nummular 741.22 *monetary*
numnah 32.14 *horse-riding terms*
nun 7.7 *monk*, 134.5 *pure person*, 139.4 *individualist*, 497.5 *believer*, 825.4 *celibate person*, 861.15 *good person*, 863.4 *virtuous person*, 876.5 *pure person*
Nun 8 Deities
Nunc Dimittis 10.9 *prayer*
nuncio 707.1 *deputy*
nuncupative 564.17 *oral*
nunnery 7.10 *priestly dwelling*, 531.6 *privacy*, 634.1 *refuge*
nunnish 825.8 *monastic*
nun's habit 295.3 *formal dress*
Nupe 5 Languages and Groups of Languages
nuptial 10.21 *ritualistic*, 715.7 *contractual*, 823.20 *matrimonial*
nuptial benediction 823.5 *wedding*
nuptial bond 715.1 *contract*, 823.1 *marriage*
nuptial chamber 821.13 *abode of love*
nuptially 715.8 *contractually*, 823.24 *matrimonially*
nuptial Mass 10.5 *Christian rite*, 823.5 *wedding*
nuptial ode 823.6 *general terms*
nuptials 823.5 *wedding*
nuptial song 823.6 *general terms*
nuptial vows 823.5 *wedding*
Nuremberg 93 Cities
Nuri 5 Languages and Groups of Languages
Nurmi 18 Sporting Personalities
Nurrundere 8 Deities
nurse 60, 60.17 *paramedic*, 60.19 *practise medicine*, 77.36 *lactate*, 350.25 *provide food*, 351.15 *provide drink*, 469.7 *caring person*, 469.11 *care for*, 594.7 *develop*, 629.6 *cure*, 630.15 *healer*, 630.20 *doctor*, 632.3 *protector*, 632.9 *protect*, 637.5 *preserve*, 653.1 *manage*, 653.15 *manager*, 662.19 *support*, 697.4 *personal attendant*, 697.6 *domestic servant*, 767.5 *helper*, 831.8 *be benevolent*
nurse corps 17.4 *military organization*
nurse cow 68.8 *livestock*
nursed 351.16 *drinking*
nursemaid 632.3 *protector*, 697.4 *personal attendant*, 697.6 *domestic servant*
nurse practitioner 60.16 *nurse*
nurse resentment 828.8 *resent*
nursery 69, 41.12 *ski*, 226.2 *source*, 246.1 *fertility*, 256.7 *room*, 647.1 *workshop*
nursery education 6.2 *educational system*
nurseryman 69.13 *horticulturist*
nursery rhyme 48.7 *poem*
nursery school 6.12 *educational institution*
nursery slope 41.1 *skiing*, 276.2 *lowland*
nurse shark 80 Fishes

nurse's uniform 295.3 *formal dress*, 544.5 *uniform*
nurse through 629.6 *cure*
nursing 60.8 *treatment*, 60.25 *therapeutic*, 594.13 *development*, 630.13 *therapy*
nursing auxiliary 60.17 *paramedic*
nursing care 60.8 *treatment*
nursing chair 47.2 *chair*
nursing home 60.10 *hospital*, 218.5 *resting place*, 630.14 *hospital*, 634.2 *shelter*
nursing home patient 624.19 *sick person*
nursing officer 60.16 *nurse*
nursling 206.9 *child*
nurture 304, 6.1 *education*, 6.22 *educate*, 68.18 *practise livestock farming*, 350.7 *food*, 350.25 *provide food*, 594.7 *develop*, 594.13 *development*, 662.3 *sustenance*, 662.20 *sustain*
nurtured 6.20 *refined*
nurturing 662.32 *supportive*
nusach 10.8 *hymn*
Nusku 8 Deities
nut 34.4 *climbing equipment*, 86.2 *botanical fruit*, 137.8 *fastening*, 168.10 *eccentric*, 378.7 *tough thing*, 510.7 *insane person*, 603.1 *tool*, 798.3 *object of ridicule*
Nut 8 Deities
nutate 365.8 *oscillate*
nutation 365.1 *oscillation*
nutational 365.13 *oscillating*
nut bread 45.38 *bread*
nutbrown 449.1 *brown*
nutcase 168.10 *eccentric*, 510.7 *insane person*
nut college 510.8 *mental hospital*
nutcracker 78 Birds, 396.6 *things brought to life*
nut cutlet 45.34 *vegetarian dish*
nut farm 510.8 *mental hospital*
nuthatch 78 Birds
nut hatch 510.8 *mental hospital*
nuthouse 510.8 *mental hospital*
nut key 34.4 *climbing equipment*
nutlet 86.3 *fruit structure*
nutmeg 45 Herbs and Spices, 413.5 *herbs*
nutmeg grater 384.13 *grater*
nut pine 85 Trees and Shrubs
nut protein 45.21 *meat substitute*
Nutrasweet 414.2 *sweetener*
nutriment 350.7 *food*
nutrition 350, 59.5 *physiology*, 60.6 *health care*, 350.7 *food*
nutritional 350.27 *edible*, 630.17 *remedial*
nutritionally 45.57 *culinarily*
nutrition expert 350.19 *dietitian*
nutritionist 60.17 *paramedic*, 350.19 *dietitian*, 625.3 *hygienist*, 630.15 *healer*
nutritious 350.27 *edible*, 623.2 *healthful*, 625.4 *hygienic*
nutritiously 45.57 *culinarily*, 350.29 *edibly*, 623.8 *healthily*
nutritiousness 623.4 *healthfulness*, 625.2 *salubrity*
nutritive 350.27 *edible*, 630.17 *remedial*
nut roast 45.34 *vegetarian dish*
nuts 45.10 *snack*, 85.9 *tree product*, 86.1 *fruits*, 245.8 *organs of reproduction*, 350.8 *animal food*, 510.11 *insane*
nuts about 821.18 *in love*
nuts and bolts 99.5 *fact*, 103.2 *essential content*, 143.5 *largest part*, 165.4 *specifications*, 226.3 *rudiment*, 367.4 *matter*, 520.1 *meaning*, 602.2 *supplies*, 603.1 *tool*, 603.4 *machine*, 611.3 *chief thing*
nutshell 293.13 *casing*, 552.1 *conciseness*
nutter 510.7 *insane person*
nuttiness 510.1 *insanity*
nutty 117.9 *nonconforming*, 460.6 *unintelligent*, 508.5 *foolish*, 510.11 *insane*, 798.5 *ridiculous*
nutty as a fruitcake 510.11 *insane*
nux vomica 62 Medication, 85

Trees and Shrubs, 631.12 *poisonous plant*
nuzzle 407.4 *kiss*, 407.11 *touch*, 821.14 *communication of love*, 821.27 *kiss*, 826.7 *show endearment for*
nuzzling 821.14 *communication of love*
nyala 77 Placental Mammals
Nyanja 5 Languages and Groups of Languages
Nyasa 94 Lakes
Nyaya 4.7 *school of thought*
nyckelharpa 49 Musical Instruments
nyctalopia 436.2 *poor sight*
nyctalopic 436.9 *weak-sighted*
nyctophobia 777 Phobias by Name
Nyigma-pa 7 Non-Christian Religions
nylon 67 Synthetic Fibres and Fabrics, 57.21 *polymer*, 604.1 *materials*
nylon line 20.3 *fishing tackle*
nylons 295.20 *legwear*
nylon stockings 322.6 *porous thing*
nylon webbing 34.4 *climbing equipment*
nymph 8.5 *deity*, 59.15 *developmental biology*, 82.5 *larva*, 206.4 *young animal*, 206.8 *young woman*, 402.6 *loose woman*
nymphalid butterfly 82 Insects
nymphet 206.8 *young woman*, 402.6 *loose woman*
nympho 402.6 *loose woman*, 877.9 *immoral woman*
nymphomania 61.15 *compulsion*, 510.4 *delusion*, 782.4 *sexual desire*, 877.3 *sexual immorality*
nymphomaniac 402.6 *loose woman*, 405.3 *pleasure-seeker*, 405.7 *pleased*, 482.9 *undiscriminating person*, 510.7 *insane person*, 877.9 *immoral woman*, 877.13 *unchaste*
Nyoro 1 Peoples, 5 Languages and Groups of Languages
nystagmatic 436.9 *weak-sighted*
nystagmus 436.2 *poor sight*

O

oaf 460.3 *unintelligent person*, 656.10 *unskilled person*, 764.9 *unpleasant person*
oafish 460.6 *unintelligent*
oafishness 460.2 *unintelligence*
Oahu 98 Islands
oak 85 Trees and Shrubs, 373.7 *hard substance*
oak apple 85.10 *tree disease*
oaken 85.15 *woody*
oak fern 88 Ferns
oak gall 85.10 *tree disease*
Oakland 93 Cities
Oak Leaf Cluster 17 US Military Medals and Decorations
oak moss 88.3 *moss*, 90.6 *lichen*
Oak Ridge 93 Cities
Oannes 8 Deities
oar 74 Parts of a Ship, 36.4 *rowing*, 338.11 *propeller*
oarfish 80 Fishes
oarlock 364.4 *vortex*
oarsman 36.9 *sailor*, 74.8 *boatman*
oarweed 90 Algae
oasis 389.13 *irrigator*
oast house 68.7 *farm building*, 408.6 *fire*
oatcake 45.39 *loaf*
oaten 87.8 *grasslike*
oat grass 87 Grasses
oath 535.3 *vow*, 714.1 *promise*, 827.1 *curse*, 847.7 *commitment*
oath administrator 535.9 *affirmer*
oath of allegiance 535.3 *vow*
oath of office 535.3 *vow*
oath-taker 535.9 *affirmer*

oatmeal 45.40 *breakfast cereal*, 449.1 *brown*
oats 87 Grasses, 68.12 *crop*, 350.8 *animal food*
oat straw 68.9 *animal feedstuff*
Ob 96 Rivers
Obaku-shu 7 Non-Christian Religions
Oban 93 Cities
Obatalla 8 Deities
obbligato 49 Musical Terms
obduracy 225.2 *determination*, 373.8 *mental hardness*, 570.3 *wilfulness*, 577.5, 669.2 *obstinacy*, 832.3 *callousness*, 868.1 *impenitence*
obdurate 225.11 *determined*, 373.4 *mentally hard*, 378.5 *mentally tough*, 570.8 *wilful*, 577.1 *obstinate*, 577.3 *unyielding*, 659.14 *troublesome*, 669.11 *obstinate*, 832.12 *callous*, 836.4 *pitiless*, 868.3 *impenitent*
obdurately 225.13 *determinedly*, 378.14 *single-mindedly*, 577.9 *be obstinate*, 836.7 *pitilessly*
obdurateness 378.9 *mental toughness*, 577.5 *obstinacy*, 832.3 *callousness*
obeah 497.2 *religious belief*
obeah doctor 11.4 *witch*
obedience 694, 9.1 *worship*, 167.2 *compliance*, 374.12 *gentleness*, 572.8 *acquiescence*, 673.1 *submission*, 701.1 *subjection*, 719.1 *observance*, 806.12 *submissiveness*, 847.3 *allegiance*, 861.11 *good behaviour*, 863.2 *virtues*
Obedience 694
obedient 694, 16.50 *law-abiding*, 150.17 *disciplined*, 167.13 *compliant*, 572.3 *amenable*, 673.5 *submitting*, 697.9 *serving*, 701.9 *subject*, 719.7 *observant*, 806.5 *submissive*, 847.9 *loyal*, 861.4 *well-behaved*, 863.6 *ethical*
obediently 694, 697, 861, 167.16 *adaptably*, 673.6 *with humility*, 719.8 *observantly*, 863.10 *ethically*
obedient person 694
obeisance 694, 362.16 *courtesy*, 673.1 *submission*, 808.2 *sycophancy*, 817.4 *deference*, 849.2 *admiration*, 849.4 *mark of respect*, 849.6 *greeting*
obeisant 694, 808.7 *sycophantic*, 817.9 *deferential*, 849.9 *showing respect*
obeisantly 817.16 *deferentially*
obelise 543.13 *punctuate*
obelisk 275.6 *tall thing*, 545.11 *monument*
obelize 543.13 *punctuate*
obelus 543.7 *punctuation*
Oberammergau 51.2 *play*
OBERON 65 Programming Languages
obese 259.16 *fat*, 273.1 *thick*, 315.10 *well-rounded*, 369.1 *heavy*
obesely 259.20 *largely*
obesity 259.5 *fatness*, 273.5 *thickness*, 315.2 *round body*, 369.4 *heaviness*, 610.2 *overdoing it*
obey 694, 7.19 *be religious*, 9.7 *worship*, 167.8 *comply*, 374.16 *yield*, 673.3 *submit*, 697.8 *serve*, 701.8 *be subject to*, 847.16 *do one's duty*, 849.18 *show respect*, 861.18 *be good*
obeying the law 719.1 *observance*
obey one's conscience 586.18 *be persuaded*
obey orders 166, 694.5 *obey*
obey regulations 167.8 *comply*
obey the law 719.4 *observe*
obfuscate 307.4 *disorder*, 440.14 *make dark*, 441.10 *make dim*, 443.11 *make opaque*, 474.11 *practise sophistry*, 529.14 *make mysterious*, 531.9 *disguise*, 551.3 *make obscure*, 555.4 *de-emphasize*

obfuscated 440.11 *benighted*, 443.2 *shady*, 474.8 *cunning*
obfuscating 659.12 *problematic*
obfuscation 440.2 *darkening*, 443.6 *opaqueness*, 474.3 *cunning*, 531.5 *evasion*, 551.1 *obscurity*
obfuscatory 551.2 *obscure*
obi 9.2 *idolatry*, 11.3 *witchcraft*, 11.6 *talisman*, 295.25 *accessories*, 497.2 *religious belief*
Obi 8 Deities
obiism 9.2 *idolatry*
obit 399.2 *funeral*
obituarist 399.3 *funeral director*
obituary 345.9 *parting*, 397.12 *death count*, 399.2, 399.11 *funeral*, 528.4 *mass communication*, 545.1 *record*, 560.4 *factual account*
obituary writer 399.3 *funeral director*
object 367, 663, 5.35 *part of speech*, 16.71 *try a case*, 99.2 *thing*, 117.14 *disagree*, 157.14 *aim*, 226.5 *reason*, 228.1 *motive*, 243.3 *product*, 471.4 *purpose*, 475.19 *protest*, 476.10 *countercharge*, 477.20 *doubt*, 478.18 *answer back*, 500.9 *refuse*, 520.5 *point*, 536.8 *rebut*, 588.6 *objective*, 711.6 *dissent*, 713.6 *protest*
object ball 24.3 English billiards
object code 65.9 *programming language*
object distance 56.31 *lens element*
objectification 519.1 *imagination*
objectify 367.8 *be material*, 519.14 *imagine*
objecting 16.53 *litigating*, 475.14 *demonstrating*, 478.13 *retaliatory*, 536.13 *rebutting*, 669.10 *resistant*, 852.26 *disagreeing*
objecting to 711.9 *dissenting*
objection 663, 16.5 *litigation*, 32.7 *horseracing*, 476.3 *countercharge*, 477.1 *question*, 478.5 *counterstatement*, 500.2 *disapproval*, 536.3 *rebuttal*, 573.11 *unwillingness*, 587.6 *dissuasion*, 669.1 *resistance*, 711.2 *dissent*, 713.1 *protest*, 852.4 *disagreement*
objectionability 764
objectionable 764, 476.6 *refutable*, 478.13 *retaliatory*, 616.1 *inconvenient*, 618.3 *bad*, 844.17 *unforgivable*, 852.36 *blameworthy*
objection overruled 16.7 *legal trial*
objection sustained 16.7 *legal trial*
objective 588, 4.15 *rational*, 5.44 *grammatical*, 56.30 *lens system*, 157.14 *aim*, 228.1 *motive*, 332.1 *direction*, 344.15 *destination*, 367.7 *material*, 471.4 *purpose*, 507.5 *wise*, 537.18 *truthful*, 586.11 *motive*, 596.6 *venture*, 782.5 *object of desire*, 783.9 *impartial*, 843.7 *right*, 859.4 *disinterested*
objective existence 101.1 *reality*
objective lens 53.25 *mounting*
objectively 4.26 *rationally*, 5.52 *grammatically*, 367.9 *materially*, 507.9 *wisely*, 537.36 *truthfully*, 783.19 *impartially*, 859.8 *disinterested*
objective observer 333.3 *moderate person*
objective psychology 61.1 *psychology*
objective reporting 533.3 *reporting*
objectivism 4.7 *school of thought*
objectivist 4.11 *follower of a doctrine*, 4.14 *of a philosophy*
objectivity 4.3 *detachment*, 507.1 *wisdom*, 537.5 *truthfulness*, 783.3 *impartiality*, 859.1 *disinterestedness*
object lesson 636.1 *warning*

object of admiration 786.4 *wonder*
object of charity 730.5 *recipient*
object of desire 782
object of dislike 785.2 *disliked thing*
object of endearment 826
object of one's affections 821.11 *loved one*
object of pride 805
object of ridicule 798
object of scorn 612.10 *nonentity*
object of virtu 50.6 *work of art*
object of wonder 786.4 *wonder*
object of worship 8.5 *deity*
objector 16.8 *litigant*, 475.8 *protester*, 478.10 *answerer*, 536.6 *negativist*, 573.16 *reluctant person*, 663.9 *opposer*, 666.4 *dissenter*, 713.4 *protester*, 852.11 *disapprover*
object-relations theory 61.1 *psychology*
object to 663.14 *be against*, 666.5 *disagree*, 669.6 *resist*, 766.7 *be dissatisfied*, 785.5 *dislike*, 822.14 *hate*, 852.16 *disagree*
oblast 92.3 *other*
oblate 10.18 *perform rites*, 52.83 *spherical*
oblation 9.1 *worship*, 10.3 *rite of worship*, 349.22 *disgorgement*, 351.2 *drink*, 710.6, 729.3 *offering*, 840.2 *apology*
oblational 10.21 *ritualistic*, 710.19 *sacrificial*
oblatory 729.9 *as a gift*
oblatory 710.19 *sacrificial*, 729.7 *given*, 840.12 *atoning*
obligate 667.7 *contract*, 847.17 *impose a duty*
obligated 714.13 *guaranteeing*, 837.4 *grateful*, 847.11 *duty-bound*
obligation 478.9 *answerability*, 485.7 *condition*, 571.3 *lack of choice*, 593.3 *needfulness*, 597.3, 667.2 *contract*, 695.1 *compulsion*, 715.1 *contract*, 745.1 *debt*, 804.2 *entitlement*, 837.1 *gratitude*, 845.4, 847.1 *duty*, 847.7 *commitment*
obligatorily 667.15 *contractually*, 692.16 *commandingly*, 695.11 *compellingly*
obligatory 571, 847, 103.5 *essential*, 166.9 *legal*, 478.16 *answerable*, 485.12 *conditional*, 593.4 *required*, 667.17 *contractual*, 692.14 *commanding*, 695.10 *compulsory*
oblige 478.21 *answer to*, 485.16 *specify*, 571.15 *compel*, 593.10 *necessitate*, 662.22 *improve*, 691.3 *be lenient*, 695.6 *compel*, 697.8 *serve*, 810.10 *be courteous*, 831.8 *be benevolent*, 847.17 *impose a duty*
obliged 478.16 *answerable*, 518.9 *meant*, 745.9 *in debt*, 837.4 *grateful*, 847.11 *duty-bound*
obliging 662.35 *benevolent*, 664.17 *cooperative*, 817.7 *courteous*, 831.6 *benevolent*
obligingly 662.38 *benevolently*, 817.14 *courteously*, 831.10 *benevolently*
obligingness 817.1 *courtesy*
obligor 714.5 *promise-maker*, 745.6 *debtor*, 853.7 *sycophant*
oblique 283, 310, 335, 52.80 *linear*, 286.2 *oblique line*, 286.6 *be oblique*, 305.6 *side*, 324.17 *directional*, 332.14 *directed*, 334.7 *circuitous*, 363.9 *orbital*, 527.5 *mysterious*, 553.4 *circumlocutory*
oblique angle 52.39 *angle*, 286.2 *oblique line*, 310.1 *angle*
oblique-angled 310.9 *angled*
oblique light 441.1 *dimness*
oblique line 286
obliquely 286, 305.10 *laterally*, 310.12 *askew*, 334.8 *circuitously*, 335.28 *indirectly*, 363.12, 553.8 *circuitously*

oblique motion 324.5 *circuition*
obliqueness 286, 335.13 *deviation*
Obliqueness 286
obliquity 310, 123.1 *inequality*, 286.1 *obliqueness*, 335.13 *deviation*
obliterate 546, 131.3 *subtract*, 147.8 *eject*, 244.8 *destroy*, 349.10 *exterminate*, 385.14 *erode*, 458.3 *cause to disappear*, 607.2 *lay waste*, 614.8 *make useless*, 621.13 *clean*, 704.6 *cancel*
obliterated 546, 100.11 *no more*, 131.5 *subtracted*
obliteration 546, 100.8 *extinction*, 131.1 *subtraction*, 147.2 *ejection*, 244.1 *destruction*, 385.2 *wearing away*, 458.5 *disguise*, 512.5 *death*, 704.1 *cancellation*
Obliteration 546
oblivion 512, 100.8 *extinction*, 421.1 *deafness*, 440.7 *spiritual darkness*, 462.1 *lack of thought*, 470.1 *negligence*, 546.3 *obliteration*, 643.9 *sleep*
Oblivion 512
oblivious 512, 404.6 *unfeeling*, 421.5 *unhearing*, 436.12 *blind to*, 440.11 *benighted*, 462.8 *thoughtless*, 468.7 *inattentive*, 470.4 *negligent*, 502.6 *ignorant*, 720.11 *nonobservant*, 783.7 *indifferent*
obliviously 512, 404.13 *insensibly*, 462.14 *thoughtlessly*, 468.14, 720.15 *inattentively*, 783.17 *indifferently*
obliviousness 436.7 *figurative blindness*, 468.1 *inattention*, 512.1 *oblivion*, 720.1 *nonobservance*
oblivious to 462.10 *inconsiderate*
oblong 269, 52.44 *polygon*, 52.82 *polygonal*, 52.84 *cubic*, 178.2 *quadrilateral*, 269.2 *elongated*
O blood groups 387.4 *blood*
obloquy 564.8 *speech*, 827.3 *vilification*, 850.1 *disrespect*, 854.3, 854.3 *defamation*
obnoxious 341.8 *repulsive*, 618.3 *bad*, 652.18 *badly behaved*, 764.2 *objectionable*, 822.12 *hated*, 862.7 *evil*
obnoxiously 341.11 *repulsively*, 652.20 *badly*, 822.18 *hatefully*, 862.12 *evilly*
obnoxiousness 618.9 *badness*, 801.1 *disrespect*, 822.4 *hatefulness*, 862.1 *evil*
obnoxious person 652.5 *badly-behaved person*
oboe 49 Musical Instruments
obolus 75 Some Foreign Units, 741.12 *ancient coins*
O'Brien 48 Writers
obscene 622, 5.39 *of language*, 341.8 *repulsive*, 412.6 *coarse*, 454.4 *indecent*, 618.4 *poor*, 795.9 *ribald*, 827.8 *cursing*, 864.12 *immoral*, 877.12 *indecent*
obscene language 5.19 *swearword*, 827.2 *offensive language*
obscene literature 877.2 *indecency*
obscenely 5.49 *colloquially*, 271.7 *broadly*, 341.11 *repulsively*, 412.11 *tastelessly*, 622.12 *dirtily*, 827.12 *swearingly*, 864.20 *immorally*
obscene person 622.6 *dirty person*
obscenity 622, 412.4 *bad taste*, 618.10 *poverty*, 827.1 *curse*, 877.2 *indecency*
obscurantism 577.7 *opinionatedness*
obscurantist 577.4 *set*, 577.8 *obstinate person*
obscuration 440.2 *darkening*, 447.7 *blackness*, 458.5 *disguise*, 551.1 *obscurity*
obscure 443, 551, 612, 11.14,

11.20 *occult*, 102.8 *unreal*, 293.31 *hide*, 307.3 *make shapeless*, 307.5 *shapeless*, 436.13 *hidden*, 436.15 *blind*, 438.3 *private*, 438.8 *make invisible*, 440.11 *benighted*, 440.14 *make dark*, 441.6 *murky*, 441.10 *make dim*, 443.2 *shady*, 443.11 *make opaque*, 458.3 *cause to disappear*, 460.10 *bemuse*, 491.6 *indeterminate*, 491.20 *make uncertain*, 502.8 *unknown*, 520.6 *meaningful*, 523.1 *unintelligible*, 523.4 *difficult*, 523.8 *make unintelligible*, 527.2 *concealed*, 529.14 *make mysterious*, 531.9 *disguise*, 551.3 *make obscure*, 659.12 *problematic*
obscured 293.37 *protected*, 438.2 *difficult to see*, 438.3 *private*, 441.6 *murky*, 531.14 *concealed*
obscurely 551, 11.25 *occultly*, 307.6 *shapelessly*, 440.15 *darkly*, 441.12 *dimly*, 443.13 *opaquely*, 447.12 *blackly*, 491.25 *indeterminately*, 659.27 *problematically*
obscureness 307.1 *shapelessness*
obscure person 612.10 *nonentity*
obscure point 523.12 *unintelligible thing*
obscuring 293.1 *covering*, 436.11 *blinding*, 440.9 *darkening*, 458.5 *disguise*
obscurity 443, 551, 612, 11.2 *the occult*, 127.1 *inferiority*, 307.1 *shapelessness*, 438.4 *invisibility*, 440.1 *darkness*, 440.7 *spiritual darkness*, 441.2 *murk*, 491.14 *indeterminacy*, 523.11 *unintelligibility*, 527.8 *concealment*, 529.7 *esotericism*, 531.5 *evasion*, 659.1 *difficulty*
Obscurity 551
obsequial 399.11 *funeral*
obsequies 5.25 *inscription*, 397.7 *dying day*, 399.2 *funeral*, 564.8 *speech*, 774.2 *lament*
obsequious 694.7 *obedient*, 808.7 *sycophantic*, 849.9 *showing respect*, 853.16 *sycophantic*
obsequiously 5.51 *phraseologically*, 694.10 *obediently*, 808.17 *sycophantically*, 849.22 *respectfully*, 853.17 *flatteringly*
obsequiousness 694.1 *obedience*, 808.2 *sycophancy*
obsequy 694.3 *obeisance*, 849.6 *greeting*
observability 437.3 *visibility*
observable 435.23, 437.1 *visible*
observably 435.25 *visibly*
observance 719, 7.2 *religiousness*, 10.1 *ritual*, 167.2 *compliance*, 584.4 *custom*, 652.1 *conduct*, 694.1 *obedience*, 812.1 *celebration*, 812.2 *commemoration*, 847.5 *discharge of duty*
Observance 719
observant 719, 10.22 *worshipping*, 380.5 *mentally sharp*, 435.21 *seeing*, 467.7 *watchful*, 469.9 *careful*, 694.7 *obedient*
observantly 719, 10.23 *ritually*, 435.26 *watchfully*, 467.15 *attentively*, 694.10 *obediently*
observation 435, 53.23 *observatory*, 56.82 *measuring instrument*, 471.1 *idea*, 496.6 *discovery*, 505.1 *maxim*, 564.7 *utterance*, 719.1 *observance*
observational 52.69 *theoretic*
observational astronomy 53.1 *astronomy*
observational error 56.83 *sensitivity*
observation balloon 679.31 *military aircraft*
observation car 72.6 *rolling stock*, 435.9 *viewpoint*
observation point 435.9 *viewpoint*
observation post 692.8 *vantage point*
observation tower 275.6 *tall thing*
observatory 53, 435.9 *viewpoint*
observe 53, 719, 4.20 *philoso-*

phize, 7.19 *be religious*, 10.18 *perform rites*, 167.8 *comply*, 253.12 *attend*, 435.15 *watch*, 467.11 *take note of*, 496.1 *discover*, 505.3 *aphorize*, 511.14 *commemorate*, 640.4 *act*, 812.16 *commemorate*
observe a limit 869.6 *moderate*
observe a practice 719.6 *perform*
observe a ritual 306.8 *be formal*, 719.5 *observe religious ceremony*
observe etiquette 817.11 *have good manners*
observe neutrality 675.5 *be at peace*
observe protocol 817.11 *have good manners*
observer 435, 29.6 *golfer*, 53.2 *astronomer*, 73.3 *aircraft personnel*, 253.5 *someone present*, 496.12 *discoverer*, 679.32 *airman*
observe religious ceremony 719
observe routine 584.16 *have a habit*
observe the formalities 811.31 *put on a show*, 813.11 *be formal*
observe the rule of business 719.6 *perform*
observe the rules 694.5 *obey*
observe tradition 584.16 *have a habit*
observing 719.7 *observant*
obsessed 11.19 *bewitched*, 467.8 *diligent*, 574.1 *resolute*, 577.4 *set*, 759.13 *passionate*
obsessed with jealousy 841.4 *jealous*
obsession 61.15 *compulsion*, 467.4 *diligence*, 493.4 *prejudgment*, 510.4 *delusion*, 577.7 *opinionatedness*, 584.1 *habit*, 695.1 *compulsion*, 759.4 *emotion*
obsessional neurosis 61.10 *neurosis*
obsessive 510.7 *insane person*, 584.15 *habit-forming*
obsessive behaviour 510.4 *delusion*
obsessive-compulsive neurosis 61.10 *neurosis*
obsessive dieter 695.5 *compulsive person*
obsessive need 695.1 *compulsion*
obsessiveness 695.1 *compulsion*
obsidian 54 Common Rocks, 440.4 *dark thing*, 447.9 *black thing*, 551.1 *obscurity*, 551.2 *obscure*
obsolescence 100.8 *extinction*, 600.10 *disuse*
obsolescent 200.20 *former*, 458.6 *disappearing*
obsolescently 600.12 *out of use*
obsolete 3.18 *in the past*, 5.42 *worded*, 100.11 *no more*, 200.19 *antiquarian*, 458.7 *disappeared*, 600.4 *disused*, 614.1 *useless*
obsolete coinage 741.15 *false money*
obsoletely 5.50 *lexically*, 600.12 *out of use*
obsoleteness 600.10 *disuse*
obstacle 487, 661, 21.1 *track events*, 32.9 *jumping*, 231.1 *counteraction*, 371.4 *solid body*, 515.2 *bad outcome*, 616.3 *inconvenience*, 620.7 *defect*, 635.1 *trap*, 659.8 *snag*, 699.1 *restraint*, 709.1 *veto*
obstacle course 676.6 *art of war*
obstacle race 674.4 *race*
obstetric 60.22 *medical*, 245.16 *reproductive*, 620.18 *medical*
obstetrical 630.18 *medical*
obstetrician 60.13 *medical specialist*, 245.7 *obstetrics*
obstetrics 245, 60.3 *medical specialty*, 402.1 *female sex*
obstinacy 161 Collective Names for Birds and Animals, **577, 669,** 138.2 *tenacity*, 217.2 *conservatism*, 225.2 *determination*, 373.8 *mental hardness*, 378.9 *mental toughness*,

490.10 *conviction,* 570.3 *wilfulness,* 574.14 *tenacity,* 575.1 *perseverance,* 663.5 *contrariness,*
690.1 *severity,* 693.1 *disobedience,* 805.2 *unapproachability,*
868.1 *impenitence*
Obstinacy 577
obstinate 577, 669, 138.10 *tenacious,* 217.8 *conservative,*
225.11 *determined,* 373.4 *mentally hard,* 378.5 *mentally
tough,* 490.2 *convinced,* 570.8
wilful, 574.3 *strong-willed,*
575.10 *persevering,* 659.14 *troublesome,* 663.22 *uncooperative,*
668.7 *defiant,* 668.8 *defying,*
690.8 *severe,* 693.13 *disobedient,* 805.15 *unapproachable,*
868.3 *impenitent*
obstinately 577, 138.12 *tenaciously,* 217.10 *conservatively,*
225.13 *determinedly,* 378.14
single-mindedly, 490.24 *with
certainty,* 659.29 *perversely,*
668.9 *defiantly,* 668.10 *in defiance,* 669.14 *resistingly,* 690.11
severely, 693.17 *disobediently*
obstinate person 577, 217.3 *conservative person*
obstreperous 151.20 *disorderly,*
431.16 *vociferous,* 659.14 *troublesome,* 693.13 *disobedient,*
818.6 *bad-mannered*
obstreperously 431.20 *vociferously,* 693.17 *disobediently,*
818.10 *rudely*
obstreperousness 693.1 *disobedience*
obstruct 111.9 *oppose,* 153.10
disrupt, 209.8 *delay,* 231.3 *counteract,* 323.8 *stop,* 328.3 *slow
down,* 536.8 *rebut,* 573.9 *not cooperate,* 591.2 *avert,* 614.8
make useless, 616.5 *be inconvenient,* 659.23 *cause difficulties,*
661.8 *hinder,* 663.17 *withstand,*
669.6 *resist,* 671.18 *fence,*
671.25 *stall,* 693.15 *be disobedient,* 709.3 *veto*
obstruct a river 96.9 *stop the flow*
obstructed 111.5 *opposing,*
153.16 *disrupted,* 209.10 *held
up,* 323.13 *stopped,* 328.7 *delayed,* 438.3 *private,* 536.12 *rejected*
obstructer 661.7 *hinderer*
obstructing 111.5 *opposing,*
209.12 *delaying,* 536.13 *rebutting*
obstruction 27.11 *dismissal,* 29.1
golf, 111.3 *opposition,* 153.4 *disruption,* 209.3 *delayed action,*
231.1 *counteraction,* 323.1 *closure,* 328.12 *hesitation,* 536.3 *rebuttal,* 591.1 *avoidance,* 659.8
snag, 661.1 *hindrance,* 663.4
uncooperativeness, 693.1 *disobedience,* 709.1 *veto*
obstructionism 693.1 *disobedience*
obstructionist 661.7 *hinderer,*
663.9 *opposer*
obstructive 111.5 *opposing,*
209.12 *delaying,* 231.4 *counteracting,* 536.11 *negative,* 661.13
hindering, 663.9 *opposer,*
663.22 *uncooperative,* 669.10 *resistant,* 693.13 *disobedient,*
709.5 *vetoed*
obstructively 153.18 *disturbingly,* 209.15 *late,* 536.15 *negatively,* 591.22 *evasively,* 661.16
with delay, 709.7 *by veto*
obstructiveness 661.1 *hindrance,*
663.4 *uncooperativeness*
obtain 164.28 *prevail,* 326.14
bring back, 355.15 *draw out,*
584.17 *become a habit,* 721.9
gain, 730.9 *receive,* 734.7 *take,*
738.1 *purchase*
obtainable 721.15 *gainful*
obtain a divorce 824.7 *divorce*
obtain an extract 355
obtain assistance 232.5 *find
means*
obtainer 730.5 *recipient*
obtaining 355.5 *drawing out,*
584.10 *familiar,* 734.1 *taking*

obtaining an extract 355
obtainment 721.1 *gain*
obtain one's objective 682.6 *be
successful*
obtain under false pretenses
539.30 *be fraudulent*
obtrude 349.14 *let out*
obtrusion 349.22 *disgorgement*
obtrusive 526.14 *manifest,*
807.15 *audacious,* 809.11
cocky, 811.21 *blatant*
obtrusively 807.32 *audaciously,*
809.21 *cockily,* 811.37
blantantly
obtrusiveness 809.3 *cockiness,*
811.6 *blatancy*
obtund 242.4 *moderate,* 381.10
blunt
obtundity 381.7 *dullness*
obtuse 273.3 *thick-witted,* 381.3
dull, 441.8 *stupid,* 443.5, 460.6
unintelligent, 761.1 *insensitive*
obtuse angle 52.39, 310.1 *angle*
obtuse-angled 310.9 *angled*
obtuse-angled triangle 52.43 *triangle*
obtusely 381, 460.11 *unintelligently*
obtuseness 381.7 *dullness,*
441.4 *stupidity,* 460.2 *unintelligence*
obukano 49 Musical Instruments
obverse 111.1 *oppositeness,*
111.4 *opposite,* 303.6 *front*
obversely 111.6 *oppositely*
obviate 231.3 *counteract,* 660.18
disentangle, 661.8 *hinder*
obviation 661.1 *hindrance*
obvious 99.10 *existing,* 318.7
conspicuous, 322.13 *opened up,*
435.23, 437.1 *visible,* 442.4 *easily seen through,* 457.7 *appearing,* 475.9 *demonstrated,*
475.12 *demonstrable,* 483.9 *evident,* 490.1 *certain,* 522.2 *simple,* 526.14 *manifest,* 530.10
disclosed, 550.3 *clear*
obviously 322, 318.10 *protuberantly,* 435.25, 437.11 *visibly,*
442.13 *transparently,* 457.15 *apparently,* 475.20 *manifestly,*
483.15 *evidently,* 496.16 *originally,* 526.16 *manifestly,* 550.4
clearly
obviousness 318.4 *conspicuousness,* 437.4 *clarity,* 442.10 *openness,* 483.3 *evidentness,* 490.9
certainty, 522.10 *simplicity,*
526.11 *openness,* 550.1 *clarity*
ocarina 49 Musical Instruments
O'Casey 48 Dramatists
occasion 106.2 *occurrence,*
185.11 *date,* 191.4 *point in
time,* 226.1 *cause,* 226.5 *reason,*
226.9 *be the cause of,* 232.1 *instrumentality,* 322.10 *opportunity,* 589.5 *good chance,* 593.3
needfulness, 812.1 *celebration*
occasional 185, 196, 182.6
sparse, 213.2 *infrequent*
occasional help 697.1 *servant*
occasionally 160.17 *discontinuously,* 182.11 *sparsely,* 185.28
sometimes, 187.14 *for short periods,* 212.2 *sometimes*
occasional showers 55.25 *rain*
occasional verse 48.6 *poetry*
Occident 249.7 *regions of the
world*
Occidental 249.16 *regional,*
332.13 *directional*
occipital bone 382 Bones
occlude 323.8 *stop*
occluded 323.13 *stopped*
occluded front 55.10 *air movement*
occlusion 55.10 *air movement,*
323.1 *closure*
occult 11, 11, 368.9 *parapsychological,* 440.11 *benighted,*
440.14 *make dark,* 523.1 *unintelligible,* 523.4 *difficult,* 527.5,
529.11 *mysterious,* 531.15 *disguised*
occultation 53.21 *orbit,* 440.2

darkening, 458.5 *disguise,* 531.1
concealment
occulted 458.7 *disappeared*
occult influence 233
occulting 439.15 *lucent*
occulting light 439.6 *electric light*
occultism 11, 517.2 *divination,*
523.11 *unintelligibility,* 526.10
manifestation, 527.11 *mysteriousness,* 529.7 *esotericism*
Occultism 11
occultist 11, 368.7 *believer in a
nonmaterial world,* 517.8 *oracle*
occultly 11, 368.13 *metaphysically*
occult meaning 527.11 *mysteriousness*
occultness 11.2 *the occult,*
527.11 *mysteriousness*
occult phenomena 368.3 *spiritual
world*
occult power 235.1 *power*
occupancy 253.3 *residence,*
723.1 *possession*
occupant 255.1 *inhabitant,*
723.5 *possessor*
occupation 251.4 *employment,*
475.6 *mass demonstration,*
588.3 *future intention,* 590.4 *activity,* 597.2 *undertaking,* 640.1
action, 642.2 *social activity,*
644.3 *job,* 670.14 *siege,* 723.1
possession, 737.6 *business*
occupational 2.14 *socioeconomic,*
251.6 *situated,* 584.9 *habitual,*
640.5 *acting,* 737.17 *professional*
occupational disease 624.4 *disease*
occupational-health nurse 60.16
nurse
occupationally 584.19 *habitually*
occupational medicine 60.1 *medicine*
occupational neurosis 61.10 *neurosis*
occupational power 12.3 *governance*
occupational prestige 2.7 *social
stratification*
occupational therapist 60.17 *paramedic*
occupational therapy 60.8 *treatment,* 61.3 *psychiatric treatment,* 630.13 *therapy*
occupation troops 679.14 *armed
forces*
occupied 255.11 *inhabited,*
599.9 *used,* 642.19 *busy*
occupied by 255.11 *inhabited*
occupied country 91.3 *dominion*
occupier 255.1 *inhabitant,* 723.5
possessor
occupy 91.18 *exert sovereignty,*
144.6 *fill,* 253.13 *reside,*
255.14, 256.17 *inhabit,* 475.19
protest, 723.7 *possess*
occupy 10 Downing Street 12.11
govern
occupy a certain social position
105.6 *be in a state of*
occupy a certain standing 105.6
be in a state of
occupy a certain walk of life
105.6 *be in a state of*
occupy a freehold 725.9 *own
property*
occupy a post 12.11 *govern*
occupy illegally 846.14 *arrogate*
occupying 253.9 *resident,* 723.1
possession, 723.8 *possessing*
occupying force 679.14 *armed
forces*
occupy oneself 640.4 *act*
occupy the centre 333.7 *be halfway*
occupy the White House 12.11
govern
occur 457, 99.17 *exist,* 101.10
be real, 227.9 *take effect,*
253.11 *be present,* 589.10
chance
occur annually 214.8 *be cyclic*
occur monthly 214.8 *be cyclic*
occur periodically 212.7 *be frequent*
occur regularly 212.7 *be frequent*

occurrence 106, 52.58 *frequency
distribution,* 99.1 *existence,*
101.1 *reality,* 457.2 *being in
view*
occurring 99.10 *existing,* 101.6
real
occurring at a different time 197
occur to one 471.14 *have an idea*
ocean 54, 70.5 *transportable,*
97.1 *sea,* 271.5 *broad thing*
ocean basin 54.16 *ocean floor*
ocean blue 97.1 *sea*
ocean-bottom 277.4 *deep thing*
ocean-cruising 36.10 *sailing*
ocean-cruising yacht 36.2 *sailing
boat*
ocean current 54
ocean depths 54.12 *ocean,* 97.1
sea, 277.4 *deep thing*
ocean floor 54, 97.1 *sea*
ocean-floor 277.4 *deep thing,*
280.1 *base*
ocean-going 70.5 *transportable,*
74.11 *nautical,* 97.7 *oceanic*
Oceania 98.1 *continent*
oceanic 54, 97
Oceanic 5 Languages and
Groups of Languages
oceanic bird 78.3 *water bird*
oceanic climate 55.38 *climate*
oceanic crust 54.18 *earth's crust*
oceanic ridge 54.16 *ocean floor,*
54.21 *mountain building*
oceanic rise 54.21 *mountain
building*
oceanic sediment 54.27 *sediment*
oceanic trench 54.16 *ocean floor,*
54.19 *plate tectonics*
Oceanid 97.4 *sea god*
oceanographer 97, 54.4 *geophysicist,* 268.9 *measurer*
oceanographic 54.49 *geophysical,*
268.12 *metrical,* 277.13 *bathymetric*
oceanographic(al 97
oceanographically 97, 268.17
measurably
oceanography 97, 56.4 *experimental physics,* 268.1 *measurement,* 277.6 *bathymetry*
ocean racer 74 Sailing Ships
and Boats
ocean racing 36.1 *sailing*
ocean-racing 36.10 *sailing*
ocean-racing yacht 36.2 *sailing
boat*
ocean radar station ship 679.24
warship
ocean research vessel 54
ocean shore 98.4 *coast*
ocean track 74.2 *waterway*
Oceanus 97.4 *sea god*
Oceanus Procellarum 53 Seas
oceanwards 97.11 *nautically*
ocean water 54.12 *ocean*
ocean wave 54.14 *wave*
ocelot 77 Placental Mammals
oche 42.6 *darts*
ochlocracy 12.1 *government,*
688.7 *type of rule,* 689.2 *anarchism*
ochlocrat 689.3 *anarchist*
ochlocratic 689.7 *anarchistic*
ochlophobia 777 Phobias by
Name
ochophobia 777 Phobias by
Name
ochre 449.4 *brown pigment,*
451.2 *orangeness*
ochreous 451.1 *orange*
Ockham's razor 4.8 *philosophical
term*
o'clock 192.18 *horologically*
ocotillo 85 Trees and Shrubs
OCR 65.13 *character recognition*
octad 179.6 *eight*
octadic 179.15 *eighth*
octagon 52.44 *polygon,* 179.4
eight, 310.3 *angled figure*
octagonal 52.82 *polygonal,*
179.15 *eighth,* 310.9 *angled*
octahedral 52.84 *cubic,* 179.15
eighth
octahedron 52.46 *polyhedron,*
179.4 *eight*
octahydrate 57.10 *salt*
octal code 65.10 *character*

offer counsel 654.5 *advise*
offer criticism 524.11 *criticize*
offer easy terms 754.13 *make cheap*
offered 710, 572.5 *voluntary*, 606.8 *provisional*, 712.9 *requesting*
offered for arbitration 16.54 *litigated*
offerer 738.12 *purchaser*
offer factual evidence 537.30 *prove true*
offer financial assistance 710.11 *volunteer*
offer for approval 526.1 *display*
offer for sale 13.10 *trade with*, 710.9 *offer*, 739.1 *sell*
offer help 710.11 *volunteer*
offer homage 694.6 *show obeisance to*
offer hospitality 710.11 *volunteer*
offer in defence 476.10 *countercharge*
offering 710, 729, 9.1 *worship*, 10.3 *rite of worship*, 572.5 *voluntary*, 710.17 *offered*, 729.1 *giving*, 746.1 *payment*, 840.2 *apology*, 840.4 *atoning*, 878.18 *giving*
offering homage 694.9 *obeisant*
offering no advantage 614.2 *futile*
offering no benefit 614.2 *futile*
offer no apologies 868.5 *be impenitent*
offer no compromise 690.5 *be severe*
offer no surprises 787.8 *be predictable*
offer of a lifetime 586.10 *bribe*
offer of marriage 826.2 *courtship*
offer of public service 710
offer one cannot refuse 228.5 *positive stimulus*, 586.10 *bribe*, 710.1 *offer*
offer one's apologies 710.14 *offer reparation*, 840.6 *apologize*
offer oneself 710.13 *be a candidate*
offer one's hand 826.8 *court*
offer one's heart 826.8 *court*
offer one's heart to 821.26 *court*
offer one's intercession 678.1 *mediate*
offer one's life 710
offer one's resignation 705.5 *resign*
offer price 751.1 *price*
offer readability 522.4 *be intelligible*
offer refuge 718.10 *secure*
offer reparation 710
offer resistance 669.6 *resist*
offer sacrifice 840.6 *apologize*
offer satisfaction 710.14 *offer reparation*
offer shelter 718.10 *secure*
offer sympathy to 405.10 *comfort*
offer to buy 710
offer to run for Congress 710.5 *offer of public service*
offer to stand for Parliament 710.5 *offer of public service*
offer up 398.20 *kill ritually*, 729.5 *give*
offer value for money 754.13 *make cheap*
offer worship 10, 710
off familiar territory 722.18 *at a loss*, 722.21 *out of place*
off food 871.6 *fasting*
off form 620.1 *imperfect*, 656.3 *clumsy*
off guard 514.6 *surprised*, 514.13 *surprisingly*
offhand 583.1 *improvised*, 583.7 *extempore*, 595.15 *spontaneously*, 814.7 *informal*, 814.13 *casually*
offhanded 470.5 *indifferent*, 583.1 *improvised*, 818.5 *discourteous*
offhandedly 814.13 *casually*, 818.9 *discourteously*
offhandedness 470.2 *indiffer-*

ence, 583.4 *improvisation*, 814.1 *informality*
offical 302.9 *commissioned*
offically 688.25 *authentically*
office 10.1 *ritual*, 16.2 *jurisdiction*, 185.3 *duration*, 230.3 *business*, 251.4 *employment*, 256.7 *room*, 647.1 *workshop*, 703.2 *engagement*, 812.3 *ceremony*, 847.2 *task*
office assistant 697
office bearer 653.16 *official*
office block 243.8 *construction*, 275.6 *tall thing*
office boy 697.5 *office assistant*
office building 63.20 *building*
office-holder 653.16 *official*
office manager 653.15 *manager*
office memorandum 545.1 *record*
office of power 688.5 *position of authority*
officer 646.3 *agent*, 653.16 *official*, 679.8 *soldier*, 696.3 *leader*, 703.5 *commissioner*
officer of state 653.16 *official*
officer-training school 6.12 *educational institution*
offices 647.1 *workshop*, 662.2 *support*, 831.4 *benevolent act*
office shirt 295.8 *shirt*
office supplies 751.6 *business costs*
office worker 646.1 *worker*, 697.5 *office assistant*
official 27, 653, 5.39 *of language*, 10.21 *ritualistic*, 12.9 *governmental*, 15.10 *unionized*, 16.10 *law officer*, 23.2 *basketball player*, 166.9 *legal*, 537.19 *authentic*, 545.16 *recorded*, 584.12 *established*, 646.3 *agent*, 653.17 *managerial*, 688.10 *person of authority*, 688.12 *authoritative*, 688.14 *governmental*, 688.15 *true*, 696.3 *leader*, 703.5 *commissioner*, 813.6 *formal*
official body 706.2 *representative body*
official documents 528.3 *document*
officialdom 688.4 *governance*, 696.8 *the power structure*
officialese 5.20 *jargon word*
officialism 12.3, 688.4 *governance*
official language 5
officially 10.23 *ritually*, 15.13 *industrially*, 537.37 *authentically*, 545.17 *on the record*, 653.19 *managerially*, 688.23 *authoritatively*, 703.11 *under commission*, 813.12 *formally*
officialness 537.6 *authenticity*
official notice 532.1 *publication*
official oath 535.3 *vow*
official procedure 584.6 *procedure*
official publication 545.1 *record*
official punishment 879.8 *penalty*
official receiver 730.7 *collector*
official record 545.1 *record*
official reply 478.2 *acknowledgment*
official report 545.1 *record*
official representative 703.5 *commissioner*, 706.1 *delegate*
official residence 256
official scorer 22.2 *baseball player*
Official Secrets Act 529.1 *secrecy*, 531.4 *silence*, 690.2 *suppression*, 699.1 *restraint*, 709.2 *censorship*
official stamp 544.3 *means of identification*
officials' time out 19.5 *game time*
official strike 15.4 *industrial dispute*
official visit 815.3 *meeting*
officiate 10.18 *perform rites*, 640.4 *act*, 678.1 *mediate*, 710.15 *offer worship*, 719.5 *observe religious ceremony*
officious 465.6 *prying*, 642.21 *meddling*, 653.17 *managerial*
officiously 465
officiousness 465.2 *prying*, 610.2 *overdoing it*, 642.9 *overactivity*
officious person 642.11 *meddler*
offing 263.3 *distant place*

off-key 434.9 *unmelodious*
of flesh and blood 367.7 *material*
off-limits 302.5 *limited*, 302.8 *within limits*, 709.5 *vetoed*
off-limits area 136.2 *setting apart*, 302.2 *limiting factor*, 699.1 *restraint*
off-line 65.20, 65.21 *on-line*
off-load 70.4 *transport*, 349.12 *unload*, 370.10 *lighten*
off-loaded 370.3 *lightening*
off-loading 70.1 *transport*, 349.20 *eviction*
of flowers 84
off-off-Broadway 51.1 *drama*, 51.4 *show business*
off one's block 510.11 *insane*
off one's chump 510.11 *insane*
off one's crust 510.11 *insane*
off one's food 624.22 *sick*
off one's guard 633.3 *vulnerable*
off one's head 153.16 *deranged*, 510.11 *insane*
off one's nuts 510.11 *insane*
off one's onion 510.11 *insane*
off one's own bat 572.18 *voluntarily*, 710.18 *voluntary*
off one's rocker 510.11 *insane*
off one's stride 656.3 *clumsy*
off one's timing 656.3 *clumsy*
off one's trolley 510.11 *insane*
off-peak 754.9 *cheap*
off-peak fare 754.4 *bargain*
off-peak supply 64.34 *power supply*
off-piste 41.12 *ski*
off-piste skiing 18 *Sporting Activities*, 41.1 *skiing*
off-pitch 434.9 *unmelodious*
offprint 110.4, 110.9 *duplicate*, 118.5 *duplicate*, 183.5 *repeat*, 245.2 *print*
offprinted 110.15 *duplicate*
off-putting 153.17 *disturbing*, 341.8 *repulsive*, 661.13 *hindering*
offscourings 132.2 *residue*, 614.6 *refuse*, 622.4 *dirt*
off-season 754.9 *cheap*
off-season fare 754.4 *bargain*
off-season traveller 754.8 *bargain hunter*
offset 69.5 *gardening*, 122.3 *equalization*, 122.11 *equalize*, 125.2, 125.5 *counterbalance*, 131.1 *subtraction*, 131.3 *subtract*, 231.1 *counteraction*, 663.18 *counteract*, 704.9 *cancel out*
offset lithography 245.1 *reproduction*
offsetting 125.10 *counterbalancing*, 231.4 *counteracting*
offshoot 83.5 *stem*, 143.6 *branch*, 206.5 *young plant*, 243.3 *product*, 343.5 *fork*, 665.3 *political grouping*
offshore 36, 36.10 *sailing*, 97.11 *nautically*, 263.8 *distant*
offshore fishing 590.2 *chase*
offshore racing 36.1 *sailing*
offshore rig 410.6 *oil*
offshore rights 249.3 *regional boundary*
offshore wind 55.12 *wind*
offshore yacht racing 18 *Sporting Activities*
offside 19.13 *penalty*, 27.14 *positioned*, 31.5 *lacrosse*, 31.8 *hockey*, 35.3 *rugby play*, 35.6 *rugger*, 38.2 *football play*, 38.5 *soccer*, 71.21 *miscellaneous motoring terms*, 305.3 *side direction*
offside fielder 27.4 *team*
offside pass 31.3 *ice hockey*
offsides 31.3 *ice hockey*
off soundings 97.11 *nautically*
offspring 132.6 *person remaining*, 155.11 *progeny*, 243.7 *produce*, 245.6 *progeny*
offstage 51.41 *onstage*
offstreet parking 356.2 *passing along*
off stride 620.1 *imperfect*
off target 335.21 *indirect*, 844.12 *incorrect*

off-target 286.4 *oblique*, 286.8 *obliquely*, 309.6 *distorted*
off the active list 240.6 *suspended*
off the agenda 598.7 *on hold*
off the air 421.7 *unheard*
off the back of a lorry 16.59 *stolen*
off the beam 335.21 *indirect*
off the beaten track 168.22 *out of step*, 816.11 *secluded*
off the bottle 873.1 *sober*
off the cuff 583.1 *improvised*, 583.7 *extempore*, 595.15 *spontaneous*, 595.15 *spontaneously*
off the fairway 335.21 *indirect*
off the hard stuff 873.1 *sober*
off the hook 848.6 *acquitted*
off-the-lip 36.13 *windsurfing*
off-the-lip turn 36.7 *windsurfing*
off the mark 335.21 *indirect*, 335.27 *astray*
off the market 609.4 *scarce*
off the menu 609.4 *scarce*
off the peg 191.7 *prepared for immediate use*, 306.10 *prototypical*, 594.21 *ready-made*
off-the-peg 112.6 *conforming*, 295.31 *styled*
off-the-peg clothes 295.1 *dress*
off the point 108.12 *irrelevantly*, 335.25 *wandering*, 612.1 *unimportant*
off the premises 254.21 *away*
off the rack 306.10 *prototypical*
off the rails 151.28 *anyhow*, 153.18 *disturbingly*
off the record 529.15 *in secret*, 568.15 *conversationally*
off-the-record 526.15 *open*, 526.17 *frankly*, 527.2 *concealed*, 529.9 *secret*
off-the-shoulder 296.10 *in dishabille*
off the side 510.11 *insane*
off the subject 108.7 *illogical*, 335.25 *wandering*
off the top of one's head 331.10 *on the rebound*, 583.7 *extempore*, 595.2 *spontaneous*
off the track 504.17 *mistaken*
off the wagon 351.16 *drinking*
off the wall 168.13 *unconventional*, 510.11 *insane*
off-track 41.12 *ski*
off-track touring 41.2 *cross-country skiing*
of fungi 89
off-white 439.14 *light colour*, 446.1 *white*
off-whiteness 446.7 *whiteness*
off-width 34.8 *mountaineering*
off-width crack 34.5 *rock face*
offwind 36.10 *sailing*
off with his head 879.24 *string him up*
off with you 349.33 *go away*
off work 643.2 *not working*
off you go 349.33 *go away*
of good constitution 623.1 *healthy*
of good family 802.4 *aristocratic*
of good omen 517.15 *presageful*
of help 613.1 *useful*, 662.30 *helping*
of historical interest 202.14 *historic*
of humble birth 803.3 *common*
of ill omen 517.15 *presageful*
of importance 611.5 *important*
of known date 185
O'Flaherty 48 *Writers*
of language 5
of late 201.21 *newly*
of leaves 83
of like mind 667.10 *agreeing*
of little value 612.1 *unimportant*, 618.1 *worthless*
of many kinds 113.6 *assorted*
of many parts 655.7 *gifted*
of many words 553.3 *diffuse*
of mark 611.6 *notable*
of material 367.9 *materially*
of mature years 207.13 *middle-aged*
of mixed blood 133.12 *mixed*
of moment 520.7 *significant*
of necessity 571.19 *necessarily*,

593.12 *in need,* 695.9 *compelling,* 695.11 *compellingly*
of no account 850.17 *unrespected*
of no consequence 612.1 *unimportant*
of no effect 683.10 *failed*
of no fixed abode 224.13 *changeable,* 252.10 *replaced*
of no fixed address 252.10 *replaced*
of no great weight 612.1 *unimportant*
of no use 614.1 *useless*
of no value 850.17 *unrespected*
of old 3.24 *historically,* 200.22 *in the past,* 202.19 *anciently*
of one mind 116.31 *in accord,* 667.10 *agreeing*
of one's own accord 572.18 *voluntarily,* 698.20 *freely*
of one's own free will 572.18 *voluntarily,* 698.20 *freely,* 710.18 *voluntary*
of one's own volition 698.20 *freely*
of opposite polarity 341.9 *abducent*
of philosophy 4
of plants 83
of poor quality 618.2 *inferior*
of repute 800.3 *reputable*
of roots 83
of second rank 612.3 *secondary*
of service 613.1 *useful,* 662.30 *helping*
of sound mind 509.4 *sane*
of stems 83
oft 212.1 *frequently*
often 121.9 *differentially,* 183.23 *repeatedly,* 185.28 *sometimes,* 212.1 *frequently*
often encountered 212.3 *frequent*
oftenness 212.4 *frequency*
oftentimes 212.1 *frequently*
of that ilk 110.12 *same*
of that order 259.13 *this size*
of the deepest dye 447.2 *dark*
of the essence 103.5 *essential*
of the first water 617.1 *worthy*
of the opposing party 663.24 *in opposition*
of the opposite camp 663.24 *in opposition*
of the people 803.3 *common*
of the same age 198.9 *simultaneous*
of the same generation 198.9 *simultaneous*
of the same kidney 110.12 *same*
of the same vintage 198.9 *simultaneous*
of the same year 198.9 *simultaneous*
of this date 196.6 *present*
of today 196.6 *present*
of today's date 196.6 *present*
of two minds 576.1 *vacillating*
of unsound mind 510.11 *insane*
of use 613.1 *useful*
of value 617.3 *valuable*
of weak constitution 624.21 *unhealthy*
of weight 611.5 *important*
of yore 3.24 *historically,* 202.19 *anciently*
Ogdon 49 Musicians and Composers
ogee 43 Architectural Decoration
ogee arch 43.5 *arch*
ogham 5.41 *lettered*
ogham alphabet 5.14 *alphabet*
ogle 435.6, 435.13 *look,* 543.3, 543.11 *gesture,* 818.7 *be discourteous,* 821.6 *courtship,* 821.14 *communication of love,* 821.26 *court,* 826.2 *courtship,* 826.8 *court*
ogonek 5.36 *accent*
ogre 259.10 *big person,* 864.9 *wicked person*
ogress 259.10 *big person*
O'Hara 48 Writers
oharai 10.7 *non-Christian ritual*
Ohio 92 American States, **96** Rivers
ohm 75 SI Units, **75** Scientific

and Technical Units, 235.5 *unit of work*
Ohm 52 Scientists
Ohm's law 56 Named Laws
oikophobia 777 Phobias by Name
oil 395, **395**, **410**, 45.7 *basic ingredient,* 50.8 *painting,* 58.6 *lipid,* 62.7 *ointment,* 70.5 *transportable,* 85.9 *tree product,* 200.10 *fossilization,* 235.6 *source of energy,* 338.13 *fuel,* 350.11 *food content,* 374.13 *soften,* 376.10 *polish,* 376.11 *smooth,* 386.4 *lubricant,* 386.13 *lubricate,* 410.1 *fuel,* 424.2 *sound reducer,* 547.2 *reproduction,* 586.17 *bribe,* 604.1 *materials,* 630.9 *balm,* 660.16 *make easy,* 853.9 *blarney*
oil and water 111.2 *opposites,* 136.3 *separateness*
oil beetle 82 Insects
oilbird 78 Birds
oilcan 376.10 *polish,* 386.7 *lubricator,* 395.5 *lubricant,* 410.6 *oil*
oil crisis 609.9 *scarcity*
oil drum 410.6 *oil*
oiled 376.4 *polished,* 386.8 *lubricated,* 395.15 *basted,* 395.16 *lubricated*
oiler 74 Ships and Boats
oil field 410.6 *oil*
oilfield 605.2 *resource*
oil filter 621.10 *cleaning object*
oil-fired 408.13 *heated,* 410.10 *powered*
oil gauge 71 Motor Vehicle Parts
oil gland 352.3 *gland*
oilily 386, **395**
oiliness 386, **395**, 376.7 *smoothness,* 540.3 *hypocrisy,* 817.4 *deference,* 853.4 *unctuousness*
Oiliness 395
oiling 386.3 *anointment,* 395.3 *lubrication*
oil lamp 439.5 *incandescent light*
oilman 410.9 *power-worker*
oil of lavender 84.8 *flower product*
oil of vitriol 57 Common Chemical Compounds
oil one's tongue 565.8 *talk too much*
oil on troubled waters 242.2 *moderator,* 630.1 *remedy,* 767.3 *reliever*
oil paint 50.11 *artist's materials*
oil painter 50.16 *artist*
oil painting 50.8 *painting,* 547.2 *reproduction*
oil paints 444.5 *paint*
oil palm 85 Trees and Shrubs
oil pipeline 410.6 *oil*
oil platform 410.6 *oil*
oil refinery 410.6 *oil*
oil refining 57.22 *industrial chemistry*
oil reserves 410.6 *oil*
oil rig 410.6 *oil*
oils 50.11 *artist's materials*
oilseed rape 68.12 *crop*
oil shale 410.6 *oil*
oil silk 67 Natural Fabrics
oilskin 634.2 *shelter*
oilskins 295.12 *coat*
oil slick 410.6 *oil*
oilstone 380.12 *sharpener,* 380.15 *make sharp*
oil tanker 410.6 *oil,* 679.24 *warship*
oil-tempered 373.3 *hardened*
oil the hand 586.17 *bribe*
oil the tongue 853.9 *blarney*
oil the wheels 386.15 *ease*
oil well 410.6 *oil,* 605.2 *resource*
oil-worker 410.9 *power-worker*
oily 386, **395**, 376.4 *polished,* 395.16 *lubricated,* 540.27 *hypocritical,* 622.7 *dirty,* 771.11 *humouring,* 808.7 *sycophantic,* 817.9 *deferential,* 853.15 *unctuous*
oink 432.5 *sing*

ointment 62, **386**, **395**, 630.9 *balm*
Oireachtas 12.4 *governing body*
Oise 96 Rivers
Oistrakh 49 Musicians and Composers
OJ 610.2 *overdoing it,* 610.4 *be excessive*
Ojibwa 1 Peoples, **5** Languages and Groups of Languages
Ojos del Salado 95 Mountains
OK 29.5 *golf ball,* 116.28 *consent,* 499.9 *yes,* 537.21 *accurate,* 617.5 *not bad,* 617.11 *worthily,* 765.6 *satisfactory,* 843.12 *all right,* 851.1 *approval,* 851.12 *accept*
oka 75 Some Foreign Units
Oka 45 Cheeses
Okanagan 5 Languages and Groups of Languages
okapi 77 Placental Mammals, 77.15 *hoofed mammal*
okay 116.7 *consent,* 124.3 *mediocre,* 617.5 *not bad*
oke 617.5 *not bad*
okedo 49 Musical Instruments
Okeechobee 94 Lakes
okey-doke 617.5 *not bad*
Okhotsk 97 Oceans and Seas
Okinawa 98 Islands
Oklahoma 92 American States
Oklahoma City 93 Cities
Oklahoma City All-American Finals 32.12 *rodeo*
okra 45 Vegetables, 68.12 *crop*
okta 75 Scientific and Technical Units
olam 54.41 *geological time,* 187.3 *geological period,* 190.2 *a long time*
Olbers 52 Scientists, **53** Comets
old 202, 3.15 *historic,* 200.17 *past,* 207.14 *aged,* 209.14 *dead,* 396.12 *alive,* 448.2 *grey-haired,* 584.11 *normal*
old age 207, 202.1 *oldness,* 207.2 *adulthood,* 396.5 *life cycle,* 628.9 *dilapidation*
old-age death 397.5 *ways of dying*
old-age insurance 729.2 *gift*
old age pension 662.4 *social assistance*
old-age pensioner 207.7 *older person,* 730.5 *recipient*
old-age security 718.1 *protection*
old and grey 202.11 *old,* 207.14 *aged*
old as Methuselah 207.14 *aged*
old as the hills 207.14 *aged*
old bachelor 207.8 *man*
old bag 207.9 *woman*
Old Bailey 16.20 *British court*
old ball 27.7 *bat*
old bat 207.9 *woman*
Old Bill 16.14 *police,* 718.3 *security officer*
old bone 379.3 *brittle thing*
old boy 207.8 *man*
old boy network 527.9 *backstage manipulator,* 657.1 *cunning*
old buffer 207.8 *man*
old business 592.1 *plan*
old campaigner 679.11 *former soldier*
old chestnut 505.1 *maxim,* 771.5 *joke,* 788.2 *boring thing*
Old Church Slavonic 5 Languages and Groups of Languages
Old Clootie 8.7 *devil*
old clothes 295.1 *dress,* 614.6 *refuse*
old codger 207.8 *man*
Old Comedy 51.10 *comedy*
old country 249.4 *territorial division*
old custom 584.4 *custom*
Old Delhi 93 Cities
old dog 655.5 *expert*
old duffer 207.8 *man*
old dutch 823.11 *married woman*
Old Dutch 5 Languages and Groups of Languages
olden 202, 200.17 *past*

Oldenburg 32 Breeds of Horse and Pony
olden days 3.8, 200.1 *past time*
olden days 202.3 *antiquity*
Old English 5 Languages and Groups of Languages, 5.41 *lettered*
Old English Game 68 Breeds of Fowl, **68** Breeds of Fowl
Old English Pheasant Fowl 68 Breeds of Fowl
Old English sheepdog 77 Breeds of Dogs
Old English type 5.15 *type style*
olden times 202.3 *antiquity*
older 202.11 *old*
older generation 202.2 *old people*
older man 207.8 *man*
older person 207
older woman 207.9 *woman*
oldest profession 877.5 *prostitution*
olde-worlde 202.12 *olden*
Old Faithful 98.10 *miscellaneous,* 214.5 *regular thing,* 408.8 *hot place*
Old Fashioned 351.8 *mixed drink*
old-fashioned 167.14 *conformist,* 200.19 *antiquarian,* 217.8 *conservative,* 312.4 *traditional,* 584.11 *normal,* 585.2 *not customary,* 600.4 *disused,* 614.1 *useless,* 628.12 *deteriorated,* 817.7 *courteous*
old-fashioned look 435.6 *look*
old-fashionedly 217.10 *conservatively*
Old Father Thames 96.4 *British rivers*
old fogy 207.7 *older person,* 490.11 *opinionist,* 577.8 *obstinate person,* 584.8 *creature of habit*
Old French 5 Languages and Groups of Languages
Old Frisian 5 Languages and Groups of Languages
old gal 207.9 *woman*
old geezer 207.8 *man*
old girl 821.9 *lover*
old git 207.8 *man*
Old Glory 544.7 *flag*
Old Gloucestershire 68 Breeds of Cattle
old-gold 451.1 *orange,* 452.1 *yellow*
Old Grey Whistle Test 448.6 *figurative usage*
old guard 575.5 *tenacious person,* 584.8 *creature of habit*
old guy 207.8 *man*
Oldham 93 Cities
old hand 485.8 *qualified person,* 655.5, 688.11 *expert,* 696.10 *expert*
Old Harry 8.7 *devil*
old hat 3.18 *in the past,* 200.19 *antiquarian,* 585.2 *not customary*
Old High German 5 Languages and Groups of Languages
Old Hornie 8.7 *devil*
old horse 32.1 *horse*
Old Icelandic 5 Languages and Groups of Languages
oldie 207.7 *older person*
Old Irish 5 Languages and Groups of Languages
old ivory 452.8 *yellow thing*
old joke 183.3 *repetitiveness*
Old Kingdom art 50 Non-Western Art
old lady 402.12 *woman in the family,* 821.9 *lover,* 823.11 *married woman*
Old Lady of Threadneedle Street 741.19 *treasury*
old lag 699.7 *charge,* 702.5 *prisoner,* 866.4 *guilty person*
Old Latin 5 Languages and Groups of Languages
old-line 584.11 *normal*
old maid 42 Card Games, 134.5 *pure person,* 402.5 *single girl,* 825.5 *single person*
old-maidish 825.6 *celibate,* 876.10 *moralistic*

old man 207.8 *man*, 401.2 *mule*, 401.3 *male title of address*, 401.13 *man in the family*, 821.9 *lover*, 823.10 *married man*
old man cactus 84 Flowers and Flowering Plants
Old Man River 96.3 *US rivers*
old man's beard 84 Flowers and Flowering Plants
old master 50.6 *work of art*, 50.16 *artist*, 688.11, 696.10 *expert*
old money 742.6 *money*
oldness 202, 207.2 *adulthood*
Oldness 202
old newspaper 614.6 *refuse*
Old Nick 8.7 *devil*, 862.6 *evil person*
Old Norse 5 Languages and Groups of Languages
old paper 379.3 *brittle thing*
old penny 741.10 *former British money*
old people 202, 207.10 *the old*
old people's home 634.2 *shelter*
Old Persian 5 Languages and Groups of Languages
old person 207.7 *older person*
old pillow 307.2 *shapeless thing*
Old Prussian 5 Languages and Groups of Languages
old salt 74.7 *nautical person*
old school 577.7 *opinionatedness*, 584.6 *procedure*
old school tie 544.5 *uniform*
Old Scratchy 8.7 *devil*
Old Slavonic 5 Languages and Groups of Languages
old softy 691.2 *lenient person*
old soldier 655.5 *expert*, 676.11 *recruit*, 679.11 *former soldier*
old spinster 207.9 *woman*
old stager 655.5 *expert*
oldster 207.7 *older person*
old story 3.18 *in the past*
Old Testament 7.12 *religious text*
old thing 202
old-time dancing 46.1 *dancing*
old-timer 207.8 *man*
old times 3.8 *past time*
old trick 657.2 *stratagem*
old trooper 679.11 *former soldier*
old witch 207.9 *woman*, 790.2 *ugly person*
old wives' medicine 60.2 *natural medicine*
old wives' tale 497.2 *religious belief*, 504.6 *fallibility*, 538.5 *half-truth*
old woman 207.9 *woman*, 402.2 *female*, 402.12 *woman in the family*
Old Worcester ware 44 Types of Ceramics
Old World 249.7 *regions of the world*
old-world 202.12 *olden*, 584.11 *normal*, 817.7 *courteous*
old-worldly 202.21 *archaically*, 817.14 *courteously*
Old World monkey 77 Placental Mammals
Old World monkeys 77.16 *primate*
oleaginize 395.17 *oil*
oleaginous 386.10, 395.11 *oily*
oleander 84 Flowers and Flowering Plants
oleandomycin 62 Medication
oleic 386.10, 395.11 *oily*
olent 416.5 *odorous*
oleoresin 395.10 *resin*
olfactible 416.5 *odorous*
olfactive 416.6 *olfactory*
olfactologist 416.1 *odour*
olfactology 416.1 *odour*
olfactometry 416.1 *odour*
olfactophobia 777 Phobias by Name
olfactorily 416.10 *odorously*
olfactory 416
olfactory nerve 416.2 *sense of smell*
olfactronics 416.1 *odour*
olibanum 418.3 *incense*
olid 419.3 *stinking*

oligarch 696.5 *company leader*
oligarchic 12.9, 688.14 *governmental*, 696.12 *masterful*
oligarchy 12.1 *government*, 91.1 *country*, 688.7 *type of rule*
Oligocene 54 Geological Time Intervals
Oligocene period 200.3 *geological period*
Oligochaeta 81.6 *worm*
oligochaete 81.6 *worm*
oligochaetous 81.20 *wormlike*
oligoclase 54.34 *mineral*
oligomenorrhoea 353.11 *menstruation*
oligomeric protein 58.9 *protein*
oligopeptide 58.8 *amino acid*
oligophrenia 510.2 *subnormality*
oligopolist 739.12 *wholesaler*
oligopoly 739.3 *selling*
oligosaccharide 58.3 *carbohydrate*
olingo 77 Placental Mammals
oliphant 49 Musical Instruments
Oliphant 52 Scientists
olive 86 Fruits
olive branch 85.12 *figurative usage*, 675.2 *symbol of peace*, 677.2 *peace offering*
olive-drab shirt 295.8 *shirt*
olive-green 453.1 *green*
olive grove 69.2 *garden*
olivenite 54 Minerals
olive oil 62 Medication, 45.7 *basic ingredient*
olives 45.10 *snack*
Olives 95 Mountains
olive shell 81 Molluscs
Olivetan 7 Members of Religious Orders
olivine 54.34 *mineral*, 453.11 *green thing*
olla podrida 45.50 *Central American dish*, 133.2 *mixed thing*
olm 79 Amphibians
Olmec 1 Peoples
ology 501.5 *science*
Olorun 8 Deities
Olympia 93 Cities
olympiad 185.4 *term*
Olympiad 75 Some Foreign Units
Olympian 8.14 *heavenly*, 95.7 *mountainous*, 275.12 *tall*, 816.8 *unsociable*
Olympic 95 Mountains, 21.6 *track*, 26.14 *combat*, 30.11 *gymnastic*, 31.8 *hockey*, 36.10 *sailing*, 41.12 *ski*
Olympic athlete 21.3 *athlete*
Olympic boxer 26.4 *boxer*
Olympic canoeing 36.6 *canoeing*
Olympic champion 655.4 *skilled person*, 682.5 *victorious person*, 786.5 *person of wonder*
Olympic class 36.2 *sailing boat*
Olympic French shooting 18 Sporting Activities
Olympic Games 21.5 *competition*, 674.2 *contest*
Olympic Gold Medal 878.2 *prize*
Olympic gymnastics 30.1 *gymnastics*
Olympic hockey 31.1 *hockey*
Olympic ice-dancing 41.7 *ice-dancing*
Olympic lugeing 41.9 *bobsledding*
Olympic Mountains 95.4 *US mountains*
Olympic regatta 36.4 *rowing*
Olympic rowing 36.4 *rowing*
Olympics 674.2 *contest*
Olympic-size 39.11 *swimming*
Olympic-size pool 39.7 *swimming pool*
Olympic skating 41.6 *ice-skating*
Olympic skiing 41.1 *skiing*
Olympic wrestler 26.6 *wrestler*
Olympic wrestling 26.5 *wrestling*
Olympic yacht classes 18 Sporting Activities
Olympus 95 Mountains, 275.3 *mountain*, 368.1 *nonmaterial world*
om 10.9 *prayer*
Omacatl 8 Deities
Omagh 93 Cities

Omaha 1 Peoples, **93** Cities
Oman 91 Countries
Omar Khayyam 48 Poets
ombgwe 49 Musical Instruments
ombre 42 Card Games
ombudsman 16.23 *judge*, 158.9 *middleman*, 664.4 *adviser*, 678.4 *representative*
Omdurman 93 Cities
Omeciuatl 8 Deities
Omega Nebula 53 Nebulae
omelette 45.34 *vegetarian dish*
omelette pan 45.6 *kitchen equipment*
omen 517, 154.6 *preview*, 513.4 *expectant person*, 516.3 *foresight*, 526.10 *manifestation*, 543.1 *sign*, 636.1 *warning*, 786.4 *wonder*
omentectomy 60 Surgical Operations
omer 75 Some Foreign Units
Ometecuhtli 8 Deities
Omicle 8 Deities
ominous 211.10 *untimely*, 440.11 *benighted*, 517.15 *presageful*, 543.14 *signifying*, 618.5 *harmful*, 633.1 *dangerous*, 636.8 *warning*, 687.6 *adverse*, 772.3 *important*, 776.6, 862.10 *inauspicious*
ominously 211.15 *at the wrong time*, 440.15 *darkly*, 517.16 *predictively*, 543.18 *indicatively*, 633.11 *dangerously*, 687.12 *in adversity*, 862.14 *inauspiciously*
ominousness 211.1 *untimeliness*, 517.5 *omen*, 862.3 *bad luck*
omission 145, 147.1 *exclusion*, 504.9 *trivial error*, 525.2 *misinterpretation*, 683.1 *failure*, 685.1 *noncompletion*, 720.2 *nonperformance*
omission mark 543.7 *punctuation*
omissive 720.12 *nonperforming*
omit 131.3 *subtract*, 145.5 *be incomplete*, 147.7 *exclude*, 248.21 *space*, 504.19 *make a mistake*, 512.13 *forget*, 525.1 *misinterpret*, 720.8 *not perform*
omitted 145.4 *incomplete*, 147.11 *excluded*, 254.12 *missing*
omitting 145.4 *incomplete*, 147.12 *exclusively*
ommataphobia 777 Phobias by Name
omnibus 71.19 *bus*
omnidirectional antenna 534.17 *antenna*
omnifarious 113.6 *assorted*
omnifariously 113.10 *diversely*
omnifariousness 113.2 *assortment*
omnipotence 8.2 *divine attribute*, 235.1 *power*
omnipotent 8.13 *divine*, 235.13 *powerful*
omnipotently 8.19 *divinely*, 235.18 *powerfully*
omnipresence 253, 8.2 *divine attribute*, 164.4 *widespreadness*
omnipresent 8.13 *divine*, 164.17 *widespread*, 253.7 *present*
omniscience 8.2 *divine attribute*, 501.3 *learning*
omniscient 8.13 *divine*, 501.8 *knowledgeable*
omnisciently 8.19 *divinely*
omniscient narrator 48.3 *aspect of fiction*
omnium-gatherum 133.3 *miscellany*
omnivore 76.4 *type of animal*, 350.18 *eater*, 482.9 *undiscriminating person*, 872.4 *glutton*
omnivorous 76.15 *of animals*, 350.26 *eating*, 482.1 *undiscriminating*, 872.6 *gluttonous*
omnivorously 350.28 *carnivorously*
omnivorousness 350.5 *eating habit*
omophagic 350.26 *eating*
omophagically 350.28 *carnivorously*
omophagous 350.26 *eating*

omophagously 350.28 *carnivorously*
omophagy 350.5 *eating habit*
omote 26.10 *aikido*
omphalic 291.6 *central*
omphalos 291.1 *centre*
Omsk 93 Cities
on 27.14 *positioned*, 253.10 *available*, 327.17 *via*, 336.19 *forward*, 353.31 *menstrual*, 526.13 *displayed*, 784.7 *like*
on a back burner 598.7 *on hold*
on account 750, 744.14 *on credit*
on a cliff edge 777.8 *fearful*
on a climb 34
on a climbing expedition 34.10 *on a climb*
on a crash diet 871.6 *fasting*
on active duty 676.15 *warring*
on a declining scale 129.8 *decreasingly*
on a demo 475.23 *in protest*
on a diet 871.6 *fasting*
on a downer 129.6 *decreasing*
on advance 732.7 *on loan*
on a fact-finding mission 477.23 *questioningly*
on a firm basis 225.12 *stably*
on a firm footing 225.12 *stably*, 237.13 *strengthened*
on a firm foundation 237.13 *strengthened*
on a first-name basis 819.10 *familiar*
on again off again 215.8 *irregularly*
on-again-off-again 215.4 *irregular*
onager 77 Placental Mammals
on a good footing 819.9 *friends with*
on a hiding to nothing 614.10 *uselessly*
on a high 405.7 *pleased*
on a large scale 259.20 *largely*
on a leash 694.7 *obedient*
on a level 110.20 *regularly*
on a liquid diet 871.6 *fasting*
on all counts 144.9 *completely*
on all cylinders 642.22 *actively*, 644.12 *laboriously*
on all fours 178.14 *in fours*, 806.28 *subserviently*
on all sides 293.42 *inclusively*, 297.5 *surrounded*, 297.8 *round*
on a mission 477.23 *questioningly*
on a motorcycle 33.12 *in a race*
on analysis 141.7 *to pieces*
on an artificial slope 41.17 *on a ski run*
on and off 185.28 *sometimes*, 187.14 *for short periods*, 215.4 *irregular*, 215.8 *irregularly*, 216.15, 224.15 *changeably*
on and on 190.11 *eternally*, 219.7 *continually*, 553.7 *diffusely*
on an even keel 122.12 *equally*, 376.14 *smoothly*
on a par 110.16 *equal*, 110.19 *equally*, 122.8 *on equal terms*
on a par with 198.11 *equal*
on a pension 705.7 *resigning*
on appro 596.9 *tentative*
on approval 580.15 *chosen*, 596.9 *tentative*
on a quest 477.23 *questioningly*
on a racetrack 33.12 *in a race*
on arrival 344
on a shoestring 758.9 *meanly*
on a ski jump 41.17 *on a ski run*
on a ski run 41
on a small scale 260.8 *in a small way*
on a starvation diet 871.6 *fasting*
on a string 283.13 *pendulously*
on a strong foundation 225.12 *stably*
on a tangent 553.8 *circuitously*
on a tightrope 659.16 *troubled*
on auction 710.17 *offered*
on average 164, 164.31 *overall*, 488.11 *probably*
on a whim 491.27 *capriciously*
on a wild-goose chase 614.10 *uselessly*
on bad terms 820.8 *estranged*

on balance 124.11 *on average,* 164.31 *overall*
on behalf of 222.9 *instead,* 293.43 *alternatively,* 662.37 *in aid of*
on bended knee 673.5 *submitting,* 806.28 *subserviently,* 808.7 *sycophantic,* 849.11 *in a respectful stance*
on board 74.11 *nautical,* 74.12 *nautically*
on borrowed time 207.16 *maturely*
on bread and water 871.6 *fasting,* 871.7 *abstemiously*
on call 253.16 *on the spot,* 593.4 *required,* 594.18 *prepared,* 613.1 *useful,* 662.31 *supplementary,* 847.13 *on duty*
once **174,** 3.24 *historically,* 213.1 *infrequently*
once again 183.24 *again*
once and for all 157.28 *conclusively,* 174.24 *once,* 213.1 *infrequently,* 217.9 *permanently,* 574.17 *resolutely*
once bitten 636.9 *warned*
once bitten twice shy 781.4 *cautious*
once in a blue moon 186.10 *seldom,* 213.1 *infrequently,* 489.10 *rarely*
once in a coon's age 213.1 *infrequently*
once in a lifetime 489.10 *rarely*
once-in-a-lifetime 174.14 *singular*
once in a month of Sundays 213.1 *infrequently*
once in a while 160.17 *discontinuously,* 185.28, 212.2 *sometimes,* 213.1 *infrequently,* 215.8 *irregularly*
once more 176.19 *twice,* 183.24, 201.22 *again*
once more unto the breach 574.18 *here goes*
once only 174.24 *once*
once or twice 213.1 *infrequently*
once-over 278.8 *shallowly,* 435.3 *observation*
oncer 741.9 *British money*
once removed 335.24 *diverging*
once upon a time 185.29 *one day,* 197.3 *another time,* 200.22 *in the past*
onchocerciasis 81.11 *helminthic disease,* 436.1 *blindness,* 624.7 *tropical disease*
onchosphere 81.13 *invertebrate larva*
on civvy street 675.7 *peaceful*
on cloud nine 279.8 *on top,* 762.4 *happy*
oncogenic 624.23 *diseased*
oncogenous 624.23 *diseased*
on collateral 732.6 *loaned,* 732.7 *on loan*
oncologist 60.13 *medical specialist*
oncology 60.3 *medical specialty*
oncoming 111.4 *opposite,* 199.11 *future,* 336.18 *ongoing,* 342.8 *advancing,* 344.19 *approaching*
on compassionate leave 254.10 *nonresident*
on compulsion 695.11 *compellingly*
on course 332.9 *directly*
on credit **744,** 732.6 *loaned,* 732.7 *on loan,* 745.11 *insolvently,* 750.12 *on account*
on dangerous ground 633.4 *endangered*
on death row 633.4 *endangered*
on deck 74.12 *nautically*
on-deck circle 22.1 *baseball*
on demand 608.9 *enough,* 746.21 *cash down*
on display 437.2 *clear,* 475.9 *demonstrated,* 483.15 *evidently,* 526.13 *displayed*
on double time 644.12 *laboriously*
on drive 27.9 *stroke,* 330.14 *sporting hit*
on duty **847, 847**
one **174, 174,** 27.10 *score,* 52.9

numeral, 110.12 *same,* 134.16 *simple,* 142.6 *whole,* 400.7 *person,* 823.21 *married*
One **174**
one-act play 51.2 *play*
one after another 159.18 *consecutively,* 195.14 *in succession*
one after the other 155.27 *in sequence,* 159.18 *consecutively,* 195.14 *in succession*
on eagle's wings 329.14 *swiftly*
one and all **142,** 142.4 *all,* 164.10 *everyone*
one and nine balls 24.6 *pool*
one and only 119.5 *novel,* 174.1 *one,* 174.14 *singular*
one and the same 110.1 *sameness,* 110.12 *same,* 174.11 *one*
one another 109.2 *interconnection*
one-arm 36.14 *punting*
one-armed 145.4 *incomplete*
one-arm punting 36.8 *punting*
on Easy Street 686.8 *prosperous,* 686.9 *prosperously,* 742.1 *wealthy*
one at a time 136.20 *separately,* 174.22 *one by one*
one at the receiving end 730.5 *recipient*
one behind the other 159.18 *consecutively,* 195.14 *in succession,* 269.12 *longitudinally*
one bill 741.8 *American money*
one bone and one flesh 823.21 *married*
one by one **174,** 136.20 *separately,* 165.32 *severally*
one C 179.9 *treble figures*
one cent 741.8 *American money*
one chance in a million 229.3 *coincidence*
onecroid psychosis 61.11 *psychosis*
one day **185**
one-day event 32.11 *eventing*
one-design 36.10 *sailing*
one-design boat 36.2 *sailing boat*
one-design racing 36.7 *windsurfing*
on edge 777.8 *fearful*
one-dimensional 278.2 *superficial*
one-dimensional wave 365.5 *wave*
one-dollar bill 741.8 *American money*
one eighth 179.4 *eight*
one eye 42.3 *card game terms*
one-eyed 145.4 *incomplete,* 436.9 *weak-sighted*
one-eyed jack 42.3 *card game terms*
one fifth 179.1 *five*
one fine day 199.14 *in the future*
one flesh 823.1 *marriage,* 823.9 *married couple*
one foot in the grave 628.9 *dilapidation*
one-foot upright spin 41.6 *ice-skating*
one for the book 786.4 *wonder*
one for the road 345.9 *parting,* 651.7 *refreshments,* 874.13 *drink*
one fourth 178.6 *quarter*
Onega **94** Lakes, 94.5 *other major lakes*
one-handed 656.3 *clumsy*
one-hand shot 23.4 *playing terms*
one-hit wonder 270.4 *short thing*
one-hop 312.3 *continuous*
one-horse 127.13 *insignificant,* 260.7 *little,* 612.4 *trivial*
one-horse carriage **71** Carriages and Carts
one-horse town 93.10 *village,* 127.7 *inferior thing,* 249.11 *settlement*
one hundred 179.9 *treble figures*
one hundred and eighty 42.6 *darts*
one hundredfold 179.9 *treble figures*
one hundred per cent 142.4 *all,* 142.11 *wholly,* 619.1 *perfect,* 619.3 *perfection*

Oneida 1 Peoples, **5** Languages and Groups of Languages
O'Neill 48 Dramatists
one in a hundred 589.6 *poor chance*
one in a million 335.19 *deviant person,* 617.8 *exceller*
one in a thousand 617.8 *exceller,* 786.4 *wonder*
one in the eye for 515.2 *bad outcome*
oneirocritic 524.6 *interpreter*
oneiromancer 11.13 *diviner*
oneiromancy 11.9, 517.2 *divination*
one-legged 145.4 *incomplete*
one-liner 771.5 *joke*
one-man 174.15 *solo*
one-man band 49.26 *musical group,* 174.9 *soloist*
one-man canoe race 36.6 *canoeing*
one man one vote 12.1 *government*
one-man show 51.2 *play,* 174.9 *soloist,* 569.1 *soliloquy*
one-many 52.76 *functional*
one-metre springboard 39.6 *diving*
one-mile 21.6 *track*
one-mile race 21.1 *track events*
one mind 116.1 *accord*
one-minute suspension 31.5 *lacrosse*
on end 281.11 *vertically*
oneness **174,** 110.1 *sameness,* 116.5 *conformity,* 134.8 *simplicity,* 142.1 *whole*
oneness with 110.1 *sameness*
one-night stand 51.13 *engagement*
one ninth 179.5 *nine*
one of 148.5 *member,* 148.8 *belonging*
one of a kind 117.6 *misfit,* 119.5 *novel,* 165.17 *exceptional,* 213.2 *infrequent*
one-off 113.1 *diversity,* 119.5 *novel,* 165.6 *exception,* 165.20 *personalized,* 168.10 *eccentric,* 174.14 *singular,* 189.7 *impermanent*
one of the best 617.8 *exceller*
one of the boys 198.5 *contemporary*
one of the family 815.6 *social person*
one of the gang 198.5 *contemporary*
one of the girls 198.5 *contemporary*
one of the lads 198.5 *contemporary*
one of the lasses 198.5 *contemporary*
one of these days 197.3 *another time*
one of those days 656.9 *bungling*
one of us 146.3 *person included,* 148.5 *member*
one-one 52.76 *functional*
one-on-one 31.8 *hockey,* 674.9 *duel*
one-on-one assignment 31.3 *ice hockey*
one or two 182.1 *few*
one over the eight 179.4 *eight,* 610.6 *excessive,* 874.1 *drunk,* 874.13 *drink*
one-parent family 815.7 *human society*
one-piece 39.11 *swimming,* 174.12 *one-sided,* 295.31 *styled*
one-piece suit 295.10 *suit*
one-piece swimsuit 39.8 *swimwear,* 295.21 *beachwear*
one-pointer 23.4 *playing terms*
on equal terms **122,** 107.10 *relevantly,* 110.16 *equal,* 110.19, 122.12 *equally*
onerous 369.3 *ponderous,* 616.1 *inconvenient,* 618.3 *bad,* 659.10 *difficult*
onerously 369.17 *burdensomely*
onerousness 369.8 *weighing down,* 618.9 *badness*
one's adieus 345.9 *parting*

one's age 207.1 *age*
one's all 725.4 *possessions*
one's betrothed 823.8 *spouse*
one's betters 126.7 *the best people*
one's bit 564.7 *utterance*
one's born days 396.5 *life cycle*
one's cards 252.4 *relegation,* 349.18 *dismissal,* 704.2 *termination*
one's club 815.7 *human society*
one's contemporaries 196.2 *the present day,* 198.5 *contemporary*
one's cut 752.1 *discount*
one's despair 656.10 *unskilled person*
one's due 845.2 *due*
one's duty 847.1 *duty*
one-seater toboggan 41.9 *bobsledding*
oneself 165.11 *identity*
oneself again 629.15 *cured,* 651.4 *refreshed*
oneself to 734.10 *take away*
one seventh 179.3 *seven*
one's fault 866.1 *guilt*
one's fill 608.7 *sufficiency*
one's fortune 725.5 *personal estate*
one's gang 815.7 *human society*
one's group 815.7 *human society*
one's heart's desire 782.5 *object of desire*
one's hour having come 397.18 *dying*
one-sided **174,** 481.10 *discriminatory,* 493.8 *unjust,* 844.11 *wrong*
one-sidedness 481.3 *prejudice,* 493.3 *injustice,* 844.1 *unfairness*
one sixth 179.2 *six*
one-size 174.12 *one-sided*
one's level best 596.5 *attempt*
one's lot 571.5 *inevitability,* 589.2 *luck*
one's marching orders 349.18 *dismissal*
one's money 725.5 *personal estate*
one's money's worth 738.6 *purchase*
one's name in lights 439.6 *electric light*
one's native ground 91.6 *native land*
one's number being up 397.18 *dying*
one's own 723.9 *possessed*
one's own boss 698.10 *independent*
one's own devices 698.6 *liberality*
one's own generation 198.5 *contemporary*
one's own hand 119.2 *original*
one's own man 139.4 *individualist,* 698.10 *independent*
one's own master 698.10 *independent*
one's own sweet will 570.3 *wilfulness*
one's own way 698.6 *liberality*
one's peers 198.5 *contemporary*
one's piece 564.7 *utterance*
one's prime 207.4 *middle age*
one's promised 823.8 *spouse*
one's set 815.7 *human society*
one's teeth chatter 409.10 *be cold*
one-step 46.2 *dance*
one's time being up 397.18 *dying*
one's time of life 207.1 *age*
one's two cents' worth 564.7 *utterance*
one's two-pennyworth 564.7 *utterance*
one's walking papers 349.18 *dismissal*
one's word 714.1 *promise*
one's worth 725.5 *personal estate*
one-syllable word 5.17 *word*
one-tailed test 52.54 *hypothesis testing*
one tenth 179.6 *ten*
one thing after another 159.2 *consecution*
one third 177.6 *third*

one-time 154.11 *prior*, 202.13
former, 705.7 *resigning*
one-time offer 213.3 *infrequency*
one too many 610.2 *overdoing it*,
610.6 *excessive*
one-to-one 52.76 *functional*,
122.8 *on equal terms*
one-track mind 493.3 *injustice*
one-two-three 170.3 *count*
one-up 126.12 *superior*
one-upmanship 126.3 *advantage*,
652.9 *tactics*
one up on 357.14 *surpassing*
on everyone's lips 532.20 *well-
known*
on every side 332.11 *in all directions*
one voice 116.1 *accord*
one-way 174.12 *one-sided*,
332.15 *direct*
one-way communication 534.6
telecommunication
one-way street 327.3 *road*
one-way system 71.3 *carriageway*
one-woman 174.15 *solo*
one-woman show 174.9 *soloist*,
569.1 *soliloquy*
on exhibition 526.16 *manifestly*
one you can hang the wash on
22.5 *batting terms*
on familiar terms 819.10 *familiar*, 826.10 *endearingly*
on file 152.24 *categorized*
on film 545.16 *recorded*
on fire 408
on foot 594.17 *developing*
on form 306, 105.8 *in a state of*,
623.1 *healthy*
on full volume 423.6 *loud*
on furlough 254.10 *nonresident*,
254.21 *away*, 645.7 *leisurely*,
649.6 *with ease*
ongo 336.11 *course*
ongoing 336, 159.9 *consecutive*,
219.5 *continual*, 336.11 *course*,
396.12 *alive*
on good grounds 483.14 *as evidence*
on good terms 667.10 *agreeing*,
667.14 *agreeably*
on good terms with 819.9 *friends
with*
on guard 28, 28.3 *fencing movements*, 467.7 *watchful*, 469.9
careful, 671.29 *defending*,
671.32 *defensively*
on hand 253.8 *attendant*, 723.9
possessed
on heat 245.16 *reproductive*
on high 8.14 *heavenly*, 95.11 *on
the mountain*, 275.19 *high*,
361.12 *exalted*, 361.13 *highly*
on hire 710.17 *offered*
on hold 598, 209.10 *held up*,
218.10 *finished*, 240.6 *suspended*, 240.7 *inertly*
on holiday 254.10 *nonresident*,
254.21 *away*, 645.7 *leisurely*,
649.6 *with ease*
on home ground 632.5 *safe*
on hunger strike 871.6 *fasting*
on ice 209.10 *held up*, 218.10
finished, 240.6 *suspended*,
240.7 *inertly*, 409.8 *cold*, 637.7
preserved, 702.8 *imprisoned*
on impulse 579.6 *capriciously*
on information received 528.19
reportedly
on intimate terms 819.10 *familiar*
onion 45 *Vegetables*, 266.5 *layered thing*, 413.2 *seasoning*
onion fly 69.12 *pests and diseases*
onion hoe 69.6 *garden tool*
onion sauce 45.13 *sauce*
onion soup 45.13 *soup*, 45.45
French dish
on its hindlegs 281.11 *vertically*
on its last legs 238.9, 628.13 *dilapidated*
on its own 174.21 *alone*
on its side 282.11 *horizontally*
on land 98.13 *continentally*
on leave 254.10 *nonresident*,
254.21 *away*, 645.7 *leisurely*,
649.6 *with ease*
onlie begetter 243.9 *producer*

on-line 65, 65, 235.15 *full of energy*, 613.1 *useful*
on loan 732, 733, 732.6 *loaned*,
745.11 *insolvently*
on location 250.12 *where*,
251.11 *geographically*, 253.16
on the spot, 254.10 *nonresident*,
254.21 *away*
onlooker 253.5 *someone present*,
264.4 *neighbour*, 435.11 *observer*
only 174.11 *one*, 174.24 *once*
only a few 182.1 *few*
only a step 264.6 *near*
only begetter 226.7 *Prime Mover*
only-begotten 174.14 *singular*
only chance 210.2 *opportunity*
only child 174.8 *loner*
only choice 580.8 *choice*
only exception 174.2 *item*
only for oneself 860.8 *selfishly*
only human 864.15 *venial*
only just 272.11 *narrowly*
only just enough 608.1 *sufficient*
only just win 682.9 *be victorious*
only occasionally 213.1 *infrequently*
only once 213.1 *infrequently*
only passable 620.4 *ordinary*
only sometimes 213.1 *infrequently*
only yesterday 200.22 *in the
past*, 201.21 *newly*
on meagre rations 871.6 *fasting*
on mortgage 718.7 *guaranteed*
on my mother's life 535.26 *as
God is my witness*
on my word of honour 535.26 *as
God is my witness*
Onnion 8 *Deities*
on no account 100.15 *not at all*,
711.11 *uncooperatively*
on oath 535.12 *vowed*, 714.12
promised, 714.16 *as promised*
on occasion 187.14 *for short periods*
on-off 160.8 *discontinuous*
on offer 710.17 *offered*
onomasiological 5.38 *linguistic*
onomasiologist 5.2 *linguist*
onomastic 5.38 *linguistic*
onomastics 5.1 *linguistics*, 560.7
nomenclature
onomatology 560.7 *nomenclature*
onomatomania 510.4 *delusion*
onomatophobia 777 *Phobias by
Name*
onomatopoeia 48.12 *poetic language*, 118.1 *imitation*
onomatopoeic 5.42 *worded*,
48.20 *metrical*, 118.12 *imitative*
onomatopoeically 118.14 *imitatively*
onomatopoeic word 5.17 *word*
onomatopoetically 118.14 *imitatively*
Onondaga 1 *Peoples*, 5 *Languages and Groups of Lan-
guages*
on one 729.9 *as a gift*
on one's back 236.12 *impotent*,
325.5 *sedentary*, 362.25 *courteously*
on one's beam-ends 127.18 *outclassed*, 236.12 *impotent*,
683.10 *failed*, 687.7 *unprosperous*, 743.2 *insolvent*
on one's best behaviour 652.17
well-behaved
on one's credit account 733.13
on loan
on one's deathbed 209.16 *at a
late hour*, 210.11 *in time*,
397.18 *dying*
on one's dignity 805.17 *conceited*
on one's doorstep 264.6 *near*
on one's feet 281.11 *vertically*,
849.11 *in a respectful stance*
on one's guard 781.4 *cautious*
on one's head 866.5 *guilty*
on one's high horse 805.17 *conceited*
on one's hind legs 361.13 *highly*
on one's Jack 174.21 *alone*
on one's knees 362.25 *courteously*, 806.3 *humbled*, 806.28
subserviently, 808.7 *sychophan-

tic*, 808.17 *sycophantically*,
849.11 *in a respectful stance*
on one's last legs 238.11 *weakened*, 238.14 *weakly*, 397.18
dying, 650.1 *fatigued*, 687.6 *adverse*
on one's legs 623.1 *healthy*
on one's lonesome 174.21 *alone*
on one's marks 594.18 *prepared*
on one's own 174.15 *solo*,
174.21 *alone*, 816.10 *lonely*
on one's own accord 710.18 *voluntary*
on one's own account 698.20
freely
on one's own initiative 572.18
voluntarily, 698.20 *freely*
on one's own responsibility
698.20 *freely*
on one's own say-so 698.20
freely
on one's own volition 572.18 *voluntarily*
on one's scent 590.15 *pursuing*
on one's shitlist 820.8 *estranged*
on one's tail 590.15 *pursuing*
on one's tod 174.21 *alone*,
816.10 *lonely*
on one's toes 642.18 *active*,
642.22 *actively*
on one's travels 104.18 *extraneously*, 149.19 *abroad*
on one's uppers 743.2 *insolvent*,
743.15 *poorly*
on one's way 331.19 *forward*
on one's word 714.12 *promised*
on order 593.4 *required*
on overtime 644.12 *laboriously*
on paper 545.16 *recorded*,
545.17 *on the record*
on par 110.16 *equal*
on parade 475.14 *demonstrating*,
475.23 *in protest*
on parole 700.7 *liberated*
on pins and needles 777.8 *fearful*
on probation 479.14 *experimentally*, 594.17 *developing*
on purpose 471.21 *purposively*,
588.13 *intentionally*
on Queer Street 659.16 *troubled*
on reconsideration 461.18
thoughtfully
on record 152.24 *categorized*,
545.16 *recorded*
on remand 699.15 *detained*,
702.8 *imprisoned*
on route to 327.17 *via*
onrush 96.6 *river flow*, 241.3 *instance of violence*, 324.2 *momentum*
on sabbatical 254.10 *nonresident*, 254.21 *away*, 645.7 *leisurely*, 649.6 *with ease*
Onsager 52 *Scientists*
on sale 739
on schedule 208.17 *early*
on second thoughts 461.18
thoughtfully
on security 732.7 *on loan*
onset 156.1 *beginning*, 344.10
arrival, 457.1 *appearance*,
670.12 *military attack*
on several levels 266.12 *in layers*
on shaky foundations 633.2 *unsafe*
onshore wind 55.12 *wind*
on short commons 609.3 *underfed*
onshot 25.2 *grip*
on show 437.2 *clear*, 457.7 *appearing*, 475.9 *demonstrated*,
526.13 *displayed*
on sick leave 254.10 *nonresident*
onside 27.14 *positioned*, 38.2
football play, 38.5 *soccer*
onside fielder 27.4 *team*
onside kick 19.12 *special team*
on sight 457.15 *apparently*
on site 250.12 *where*, 251.11
geographically, 253.16 *on the
spot*
on-site broadcast 534.25 *broadcast material*
onslaught 670.12 *military attack*, 827.3 *vilification*, 852.8
berating
on slippery ground 633.4 *endangered*

on social security benefits 705.7
resigning
on soft drinks 873.1 *sober*
on someone's shitlist 822.12
hated
on spec 479.14 *experimentally*
on special offer 710.17 *offered*,
752.7 *at a discount*
onstage 51
on stage 532.22 *publicly*
on stand-by 513.5 *expecting*
on stilts 275.19 *high*, 361.13
highly
on stream 235.15 *full of energy*
on-stream 613.1 *useful*
on strike 643.2 *not working*
on sure ground 632.5 *safe*
on tap 253.10 *available*, 253.16
on the spot, 606.7 *provisioning*,
608.9 *enough*, 613.1 *useful*
on tape 545.16 *recorded*
Ontario 92 *Canadian Provinces
and Territories*, 94 *Lakes*, 94.3
US lakes
on tenterhooks 513.5 *expecting*,
513.12 *expectantly*, 777.8 *fearful*
on terra firma 632.5 *safe*
on that ground 116.36 *accordingly*
on the active list 230.10 *operational*
on the agenda 472.8 *problematic*, 472.13 *problematically*
on the air 420.17 *aurally*,
532.19 *published*
on the alert 642.18 *active*
on the anvil 594.17 *developing*
on the assumption that 4.25 *theoretically*, 518.11 *supposing*
on the attack 670.26 *aggresively*
on the back burner 209.10 *held
up*
on the back of 361.13 *highly*
on the ball 507.6 *intelligent*
on the beam 312.12 *straight*
on the beat 198.10 *synchronized*,
198.13 *synchronously*
on the beaten track 788.8 *boringly*
on the bias 286.8 *obliquely*,
310.12 *askew*
on the Bible 535.24 *truthfully*
on the bill 750.12 *on account*
on the black market 16.83 *dishonestly*
on the blind side 438.9 *invisibly*
on the blink 600.1 *unused*,
844.18 *gone wrong*
on the block 727.16 *disposably*,
739.18 *on sale*
on the boil 408.9 *hot*
on the books 545.16 *recorded*
on the border 300.11 *marginally*
on the borderline 477.24 *questionably*
on the bottle 874.5 *drunken*
on the bottom 362.24 *down*
on the bounce 331.10 *on the rebound*, 478.24 *in answer*
on the brain 472.12 *topically*
on the breadline 593.5 *necessitous*, 743.1 *poor*, 743.15 *poorly*
on the bridge 74.12 *nautically*,
653.19 *managerially*
on the brink 302.6 *furthest*,
633.2 *unsafe*, 633.11 *dangerously*
on the brink of 264.6 *near*
on the button 503.5, 537.21 *accurate*, 843.8 *correct*
on the cards 488.6 *probable*,
513.7 *expected*, 513.23 *predetermined*
on the cause list 16.54 *litigated*
on the cheap 754.15 *cheaply*
on the chin 26.16 *professionally*
on the coast 54.66 *geographically*
on the contrary 473.18 *arguably*,
484.9 *to the contrary*
on the council 16.86 *jurisdictionally*
on the credit side 721.15 *gainful*
on the crest 95.11 *on the mountain*, 126.17 *supremely*
on the crest of the wave 279.8
on top

on the cuff 744.14 *on credit*
on the cutting edge 653.19 *managerially*
on the danger list 397.18 *dying*, 624.22 *sick*
on the decline 628.12 *deteriorated*
on the defensive 591.18 *avoiding*, 671.29 *defending*, 671.32 *defensively*, 676.15 *warring*
on the descendant 360.16 *descending*
on the diagonal 286.4 *oblique*
on the dole 641.3 *inactive*, 743.1 *poor*, 743.15 *poorly*
on the doorstep 344.22 *on arrival*
on the dot 746.21 *cash down*
on the double 329.14 *swiftly*
on the downgrade 360.17 *drooping*, 628.12 *deteriorated*, 687.6 *adverse*
on the downward path 628.12 *deteriorated*
on the drawing board 592.14 *planned*, 594.17 *developing*
on the edge 300.11 *marginally*, 633.2 *unsafe*
on the face of it 289.15 *externally*, 457.15 *apparently*, 526.16 *manifestly*
on the face of the earth 248.16 *extensively*
on the fiddle 736.18 *fraudulent*, 858.5 *dishonourable*
on the field 31
on the floor 362.24 *down*
on the fritz 600.1 *unused*, 628.13 *dilapidated*
on the front line 679.42 *martially*
on the game 877.13 *unchaste*
on the go 324.18 *in motion*, 642.19 *busy*, 642.22 *actively*, 644.10 *working*
on the gravy train 742.16 *wealthily*
on the ground 253.16 *on the spot*, 362.24 *down*
on the heavy side 123.7 *unequally*
on the high seas 74.11 *nautical*, 74.12, 97.11 *nautically*
on the home stretch 632.5 *safe*
on the hop 324.18 *in motion*
on the horizon 199.14 *in the future*, 263.10 *distantly*
on the horns of a dilemma 477.11 *problematic*, 477.24 *questioningly*, 491.24 *confusingly*, 659.16 *troubled*
on the house 729.9 *as a gift*, 754.11 *free of charge*, 754.15 *cheaply*
on the increase 128.6 *increasing*
on the inside 702.11 *captively*
on the instant 191.9 *in the shortest possible time*
on the international scene 724.6 *in common*
on the job 15.13 *industrially*
on-the-job 15.9 *negotiated*
on-the-job relations 15.1 *industrial relations*
on-the-job training 6.2 *educational system*, 15.2 *industrial negotiations*
on the lam 591.18 *avoiding*
on the level 658.1 *naive*, 857.4 *honourable*
on the light side 123.7 *unequally*
on the lines of 327.16 *how*
on the list 146.8 *included*, 545.16 *recorded*
on the lookout 435.21 *seeing*, 513.5 *expecting*
on the lookout for 590.18 *pursuant to*
on the loose 698.9 *free*
on the losing team 683.11 *defeated*
on the make 596.10 *ambitiously*, 642.19 *busy*, 686.8 *prosperous*, 721.16 *greedy*, 860.4 *selfish*, 860.8 *selfishly*
on the march 324.18 *in motion*
on the mark 332.14 *directed*, 503.8 *accurately*

on the market 710.17 *offered*, 739.18 *on sale*
on the mend 623.1 *healthy*, 627.14 *improved*, 629.15 *cured*
on the menu 606.7 *provisioning*
on the money 332.14 *directed*
on the morrow 199.14 *in the future*
on the mountain 95
on the move 252.20 *out of place*, 324.18 *in motion*, 642.19 *busy*
on the nail 746.21 *cash down*
on the never-never 744.14 *on credit*, 745.11 *insolvently*
on the nod 708.9 *with permission*
on the nose 26.16 *professionally*, 36.20 *offshore*, 332.14 *directed*, 537.21 *accurate*, 608.9 *enough*
on the occasion of 812.21 *in honour of*
on the off chance 486.9 *possibly*
on the offensive 670.22 *militant*, 670.26 *aggresively*, 676.15 *warring*
on the one hand and on the other 308.8 *equally*
on the other hand 473.18 *arguably*, 484.9 *to the contrary*
on the other side 111.6 *oppositely*, 357.17 *ahead*, 397.19 *dead*, 663.24 *in opposition*
on the other side of the fence 111.6 *oppositely*
on the outside 104.18 *extraneously*, 289.15 *externally*
on the payroll 697.9 *serving*
on the peak 95.11 *on the mountain*
on the pill 247.5 *rendered infertile*
on the pinnacle 95.11 *on the mountain*
on the poverty line 743.15 *poorly*
on the premises 253.9 *resident*, 253.17 *at home*
on the q.t. 529.16 *stealthily*
on the quarter 36.20 *offshore*
on the quarterdeck 74.12 *nautically*
on the quiet 529.16 *stealthily*
on the radio 420.17 *aurally*
on the rag 353.31 *menstrual*
on the rail 36.20 *offshore*
on the rampage 151.29 *riotously*, 241.6 *violent*
on the razor's edge 633.4 *endangered*
on the rebound 331, 478.24 *in answer*
on the receiving end 730.11 *receiving*
on the record 545
on the return 331.10 *on the rebound*
on the right side of 819.9 *friends with*
on the right track 332.9 *directly*, 496.13 *discovering*
on the rim 31.10 *on the field*
on the road 254.10 *nonresident*, 324.18 *in motion*, 326.18 *in transit*, 327.17 *via*, 336.19 *forward*
on the road to ruin 687.7 *unprosperous*
on the rocks 409.8 *cold*, 633.4 *endangered*, 683.10 *failed*, 743.2 *insolvent*, 824.11 *divorced*
on the ropes 26.14 *combat*
on the run 159.18 *consecutively*, 252.20 *out of place*, 324.18 *in motion*, 583.7 *extempore*, 633.4 *endangered*
on the safe side 632.5 *safe*, 781.4 *cautious*
on the same footing 110.16 *equal*, 110.19 *equally*, 122.8 *on equal terms*
on the same level 122.8 *on equal terms*
on the same plane 122.8 *on equal terms*
on the same wavelength 140.8 *cooperative*, 667.14 *agreeably*
on the scent 37.9 *on the trail*, 590.18 *pursuant to*
on the scrap heap 598.7 *on hold*

on the sea 97.11 *nautically*, 326.18 *in transit*
on the shelf 132.10 *surplus*, 132.12 *with a remainder*, 598.7 *on hold*, 600.4 *disused*, 656.3 *clumsy*, 825.6 *celibate*
on the shelves 739.18 *on sale*
on the shoulders of 361.13 *highly*
on the sick list 624.22 *sick*, 624.25 *unhealthily*
on the side 130.10 *additionally*
on the side of the angels 134.12 *morally pure*, 843.11 *rightminded*, 863.5 *virtuous*
on the slab 479.14 *experimentally*
on the slate 744.14 *on credit*, 745.11 *insolvently*, 750.12 *on account*
on the slide 129.6 *decreasing*
on the slippery slope 687.6 *adverse*
on the slope 286.4 *oblique*
on the sly 474.15 *hypocritically*, 529.16 *stealthily*, 657.6 *cunningly*
on the spot 253, 191.8 *immediately*, 250.12 *where*, 253.9 *resident*, 264.5 *near*, 659.16 *troubled*
on-the-spot 191.5 *immediate*
on-the-spot purchase 738.7 *purchasing*
on the spur of the moment 331.10 *on the rebound*, 583.7 *extempore*, 595.2 *spontaneous*, 595.15 *spontaneously*, 648.6 *hastily*
on the staff 697.9 *serving*
on the stage 526.16 *manifestly*
on the stocks 145.4 *incomplete*, 592.14 *planned*, 594.17 *developing*, 594.22 *in preparation*
on the street 743.3 *beggarly*
on the streets 743.15 *poorly*
on the summit 95.11 *on the mountain*
on the surface 20.9 *on the water*, 278.8 *shallowly*, 289.15 *externally*, 383.15 *texturally*, 437.11 *visibly*, 457.15 *apparently*, 526.14 *manifest*, 526.16 *manifestly*
on the tab 745.11 *insolvently*, 750.12 *on account*
on the table 472.13 *problematically*
on the tail 36.20 *offshore*
on the threshold 298.7 *interfacially*, 300.11 *marginally*
on the throne 12.10 *governing*, 688.12 *authoritative*, 688.23 *authoritatively*
on the tilt 286.4 *oblique*
on the tip of one's tongue 264.6 *near*, 512.11 *forgotten*, 615.8 *nearby*
on the top 279.8 *on top*
on the track 37.9 *on the trail*, 590.18 *pursuant to*
on the trail 37, 590.15 *pursuing*, 590.18 *pursuant to*
on the trail of 496.13 *discovering*
on the treadmill 644.12 *laboriously*
on the trot 155.27 *in sequence*, 159.18 *consecutively*, 195.14 *in succession*, 642.19 *busy*
on the turn 415.6 *unpalatable*
on the up 27.20 *in*
on the up and up 128.6 *increasing*, 233.13 *dominant*, 359.23 *rising*, 623.1 *healthy*, 658.1 *naive*, 682.13 *successful*, 686.8 *prosperous*, 857.4 *honourable*
on the up-grade 623.1 *healthy*
on the verge 633.2 *unsafe*
on the verge of 264.6 *near*
on the wagon 591.19 *abstaining*, 869.8 *self-restrained*, 873.1 *sober*
on the waiting list 513.5 *expecting*, 545.16 *recorded*
on the wane 129.8 *decreasingly*, 207.12 *ageing*, 238.11 *weakened*, 687.6 *adverse*
on the warpath 241.6 *violent*,

670.22 *militant*, 670.26 *aggresively*, 676.15 *warring*
on the water 20
on the way 70.6 *commercially*, 326.18 *in transit*
on the way out 628.12 *deteriorated*
on the way to 220.18 *convertibly*, 327.17 *via*, 336.19 *forward*
on the way to the breaker's yard 244.15 *destroyed*
on the whole 142, 124.11 *on average*, 164.31 *overall*, 166.18 *as a rule*, 271.7 *broadly*
on the wing 324.18 *in motion*, 326.18 *in transit*
on the wrong foot 595.1 *unprepared*
on the wrong side of the law 16.55 *illegal*
on the wrong track 153.18 *disturbingly*
on thin ice 633.4 *endangered*
on this side of the grave 396.12 *alive*
on this spot 250.12 *where*
on tick 744.14 *on credit*, 745.11 *insolvently*
on time 208.12, 208.17 *early*, 210.8, 210.11 *in time*
on tiptoe 275.19 *high*, 361.13 *highly*
ontogenic 59.26 *developmental*
ontogeny 59.15 *developmental biology*, 99.8 *creation*
ontological 99.11 *intrinsic*
ontologically 4.24 *philosophically*
ontological time 185.1 *time*
ontology 4.6 *branch of philosophy*, 99.3 *nature*, 253.1 *presence*
on top 279, 275.19 *high*, 682.15 *victorious*
on top of 130.10 *additionally*
on top of each other 281.11 *vertically*
on top of the heap 682.15 *victorious*
on top of the world 95.1 *mountain*, 279.8 *on top*
ontotheological 7.18 *theological*
ontotheology 4.6 *branch of philosophy*, 7.13 *theology*
on tour 254.10 *nonresident*, 254.21 *away*
on trial 16.54 *litigated*, 479.14 *experimentally*, 492.10 *judged*
onus 847.1 *duty*
onus of guilt 866.2 *signs of guilt*
on vacation 254.10 *nonresident*, 254.21 *away*, 645.7 *leisurely*, 649.6 *with ease*
on velvet 686.8 *prosperous*, 686.9 *prosperously*
on view 457.7 *appearing*, 526.13 *displayed*
on visiting terms 819.10 *familiar*
onward 336.18 *ongoing*, 336.19, 338.34 *forward*
onward and upward 219.8 *go on*, 359.26 *up*
onward course 96.6 *river flow*, 336.11 *course*
onward march 627.5 *improvement*
onwards 336.19 *forward*
on welfare 743.1 *poor*, 743.15 *poorly*
Onychophora 81.4 *arthropod*, 81.6 *worm*
onychophoran 81.4 *arthropod*, 81.6 *worm*
on your way 349.33 *go away*
onyx 54 *Gemstones*
oodles 181.3 *profuseness*, 608.8 *plenty*
oogamy 90.4 *reproductive body*
oogonium 90.4 *reproductive body*
oolite 54 *Common Rocks*
oomph 239.1 *vigour*, 535.6 *assertiveness*, 554.1 *emphasis*
Oonawieh Unggi 8 *Deities*
oophorectomy 60 *Surgical Operations*
Oort cloud 53.19 *comet*
oose 370.7 *light thing*
oosperm 59.15 *developmental biology*
oosphere 90.4 *reproductive body*

ooze 54.27 *sediment,* 54.63 *ebb,* 98.3 *marsh,* 328.1 *move slowly,* 347.3 *leakage,* 347.12 *leak,* 349.14 *let out,* 387.25 *flow,* 389.32 *seep,* 391.8 *marsh,* 391.16 *seep,* 393.13 *mud,* 622.4 *dirt*
ooze at every pore 610.4 *be excessive*
ooze out 347.12 *leak*
oozily 387.26 *fluidly,* 389.35 *wetly,* 391.17 *moistly,* 393.27 *slimily*
ooziness 393.3 *muddiness*
oozing 144.8 *full,* 347.3 *leakage,* 389.25 *seeping*
oozy 98.11 *continental,* 347.17 *leaky,* 391.11 *marshy,* 393.17 *muddy*
op 60.9, 630.12 *surgery*
opacity 66.10 *graininess,* 443.6 *opaqueness,* 443.8, 551.1 *obscurity*
opah 80 Fishes
opal 54 Minerals, 54 Gemstones, 456.5 *variegated thing*
opalescence 439.2 *quality of light,* 442.7 *semitransparency,* 456.1 *variegation*
opalescent 439.17 *lustrous,* 442.3 *semitransparent,* 456.7 *iridescent*
opal glass 442.9 *glass*
opaline 442.3 *semitransparent,* 443.2 *shady,* 456.7 *iridescent*
opaque 443, 44.10 *ceramic,* 441.6 *murky,* 551.2 *obscure*
opaquely 443, 44.12 *ornamentally*
opaqueness 443, 441.2 *murk*
Opaqueness 443
opaque pigment 444.4 *pigment*
opaque thing 443
opaque white glaze 44.3 *glaze*
op art 50 Western Art Styles and Movements
open 156, 322, 322, 322, 526, 15.10 *unionized,* 36.12 *canoeing,* 37.8 *shooting,* 41.12 *ski,* 42.10 *play,* 51.36 *dramatize,* 98.11 *continental,* 136.15 *separate,* 156.17, 201.19 *begin,* 226.11 *inaugurate,* 261.5 *make bigger,* 261.7 *bigger,* 265.5 *crack,* 265.7 *cracked,* 271.1 *broad,* 271.3 *broad-minded,* 271.11 *broaden,* 289.7 *outside,* 289.9 *externalized,* 294.11 *uncover,* 312.5 *honourable,* 348.15 *receptive,* 437.1 *visible,* 437.2 *clear,* 437.9 *appear,* 437.10 *make visible,* 442.4 *easily seen through,* 442.12 *make transparent,* 475.10 *demonstrative,* 526.14 *manifest,* 530.5 *disclose,* 530.10 *disclosed,* 530.11 *disclosing,* 532.19 *published,* 537.18 *truthful,* 556.3 *natural,* 658.1 *naive,* 698.9 *free,* 698.13 *informal,* 727.9 *dispose of,* 730.12 *receptive,* 857.4 *honourable,* 859.4 *disinterested*
open a campaign 676.13 *be at war*
open a charge account 744.9 *acquire credit*
open a credit account 733.10 *buy on credit*
open air 390, 289.2 *outside,* 625.2 *salubrity*
open-air 390, 289.7 *outside*
open-air theatre 51.14 *theatre*
open an account with 737.1 *trade*
open and above-board 526.16 *manifestly*
open and shut 490.3 *decided*
open-and-shut 526.14 *manifest*
open-and-shut case 490.12 *something certain,* 526.11 *openness,* 582.6 *premeditation*
open arms 819.14 *act of friendship*
open a trade 13.10 *trade with,* 737.1 *trade*
open a way 356.10 *enter*
open a window 417.5 *deodorize*
open bidding 710.9 *offer*
open canoe 36.6 *canoeing*

open circuit 64.13 *circuit*
open-class racing 36.7 *windsurfing*
open-classroom school 6.12 *educational institution*
open cluster 53.9 *constellation*
open competition 674.2 *contest*
open conflict 666.2 *argument*
open country 98.6 *lowland,* 248.3 *geographical space,* 322.8 *open space*
open court 16.19 *lawcourt*
open cruising race 36.6 *canoeing*
open day 815.5 *party*
open door 322.10 *opportunity,* 348.2 *receptivity*
open-door 322.13 *opened up*
open-door policy 346.4 *right of entry,* 740.4 *free market*
opened 156.37 *enrolled,* 201.13 *inaugurated,* 294.8 *uncovered*
opened up 322
open-ended 184.3 *eternal*
opener 322, 27.4 *team,* 154.5 *preface,* 156.10 *introduction*
open event 36.4 *rowing*
open exchange 654.2 *consultation*
open-face 322.9 *openness*
open-face 20.8 *angling*
open-faced 322.16 *open*
open-face reel 20.3 *fishing tackle*
open fire 338.28 *shoot,* 408.6, 670.2 *fire,* 674.12 *fight,* 676.14 *battle*
open for bid 710.17 *offered*
open forum 568.4 *conference*
open gate 41.3 *ski racing*
open grave 399.6 *grave*
open hand 879.14 *instrument of punishment*
open-handed 608.2 *plentiful,* 729.8 *giving,* 755.1 *generous,* 831.7 *charitable,* 859.5 *unselfish,* 878.18 *giving*
open-handedly 831.11 *charitably,* 859.9 *unselfishly*
open-handedness 755.5 *generosity,* 831.2 *charity,* 833.1 *philanthropy,* 859.2 *unselfishness*
open heart 322.9 *openness*
open-hearted 322.16 *open,* 442.4 *easily seen through,* 537.18 *truthful,* 831.6 *benevolent*
open-heartedness 442.10 *openness,* 537.5 *truthfulness,* 831.1 *benevolence*
open hearth 44.6 *ceramic workshop*
open-heart surgery 60.9, 630.12 *surgery*
open hostilities 6/6.12 *go to war*
open house 164.3 *nonspecificness,* 815.5 *party*
opening 322, 42.4 *chess terms,* 136.3 *separateness,* 154.5 *preface,* 156.1 *beginning,* 156.9 *premiere,* 156.11 *starting point,* 156.29, 201.4 *beginning,* 210.2 *opportunity,* 261.1 *growth,* 261.8 *growing,* 265.2 *crack,* 271.4 *breadth,* 294.1 *uncovering,* 295.2 *part of garment,* 322.10 *opportunity,* 346.5 *entrance,* 347.7 *outlet,* 457.1 *appearance,* 486.3 *strong possibility,* 710.2 *tentative offer*
Opening 322
opening an umbrella indoors 517.7 *bad-luck sign*
opening batsman 27.4 *team*
opening bowler 27.4 *team*
opening ceremony 156.9 *premiere*
opening gambit 156.10 *introduction*
opening line 156.10 *introduction*
opening meet 32.8 *hunting*
opening night 457.1 *appearance*
opening one's doors 734.4 *taking in*
opening scene 51.6 *scene*
opening up 322.9 *openness,* 457.1 *appearance*
open letter 164.3 *nonspecificness,* 532.3 *journalism*
openly 322, 530, 98.13 *conti-*

nentally, 271.7 *broadly,* 312.13 *straightforwardly,* 437.11 *visibly,* 442.13 *transparently,* 475.21 *demonstratively,* 526.16 *manifestly,* 532.22 *publicly,* 537.36 *truthfully,* 556.8 *simply,* 658.5 *naively,* 698.22 *informally,* 857.7 *honourably,* 859.8 *disinterestedly*
openly happen 526.5 *be visible*
open market 698.1 *freedom,* 737.5 *commercial trade,* 740.1 *market,* 740.4 *free market*
open mind 491.9 *uncertainty,* 783.3 *impartiality*
open-minded 271.3 *broadminded,* 491.1 *uncertain,* 698.9 *free,* 730.12 *receptive,* 783.9 *impartial,* 843.7 *right,* 859.4 *disinterested*
open-mindedly 698.20 *freely,* 783.19 *impartially,* 859.8 *disinterestedly*
open-mindedness 271.6 *broadmindedness,* 698.1 *freedom,* 859.1 *disinterestedness*
open mouth 636.2 *danger signal,* 786.2 *sign of wonderment*
open-mouthed 322.12 *open,* 786.7 *wide-eyed*
openness 322, 442, 526, 530, 271.4 *breadth,* 271.6 *broadmindedness,* 289.4 *externalization,* 348.2 *receptivity,* 475.2 *demonstrativeness,* 532.7 *publicity,* 537.5 *truthfulness,* 556.6 *naturalness,* 565.2 *effusiveness,* 633.7 *vulnerability,* 658.2 *naivety,* 698.4 *informality,* 857.1 *probity*
open one's doors to 730.10 *receive someone,* 734.11 *be hospitable*
open one's eyes 522.4 *be intelligible*
open one's eyes wide 786.9 *wonder*
open one's heart 322.22 *be open,* 537.29 *be truthful*
open one's heart to 530.8 *admit*
open one's mind to 859.6 *be disinterested*
open one's mouth 786.9 *wonder*
open one's pocket 748.1 *expend*
open one's purse 729.6 *give to charity*
open one's wallet 746.6 *pay*
open out 322.18 *open,* 442.12 *make transparent*
open Pandora's box 659.22 *cause trouble*
open places 777 Phobias by Topic
open-plan 322.13 *opened up*
open primary 580.12 *election*
open quarrel 674.1 *contention*
open sandwich 45.11 *sandwich*
open sea 322.8 *open space*
open season 37.2 *hunting,* 203.1 *season*
open sesame 11.5 *spell,* 322.2 *opener*
open sewer 96.1 *river,* 626.1 *lack of hygiene*
open shop 15.3 *organized labour,* 15.5 *labour law*
open space 322, 248.3 *geographical space,* 322.1 *opening*
open table 24.6 *pool*
open texture 442.6 *translucency*
open-textured 442.2 *translucent*
open the books 530.6 *divulge*
open the door 346.9 *enter*
open the door to 226.11 *inaugurate,* 348.7 *admit,* 660.16 *make easy*
open the floodgates 349.14 *let out,* 708.4 *be permissive,* 748.1 *expend*
open the hatches 348.7 *admit*
open the shutters 439.29 *clarify*
open the sluice gates 96.8 *cause to flow*
open the throttle 329.6 *accelerate*
open the windows 530.5 *disclose*
open to 633.3 *vulnerable*

open to criticism 852.36 *blameworthy*
open to debate 477.14 *questionable*
open-toed sandals 295.19 *footwear*
open to offers 710.17 *offered*
open to question 473.10 *arguable,* 477.14 *questionable*
open to suggestion 586.20 *persuadable*
open to the public 437.2 *clear*
open to view 437.2 *clear*
open universe 53.4 *cosmological model*
Open University 6.2 *educational system,* 534.25 *broadcast material*
open up 322, 66.21 *photograph,* 156.21 *pioneer,* 261.6 *become bigger,* 294.11 *uncover,* 322.18 *open,* 322.22 *be open,* 329.6 *accelerate,* 526.3 *reveal,* 530.5 *disclose,* 537.29 *be truthful,* 627.1 *improve,* 660.16 *make easy*
open verdict 491.9 *uncertainty*
open vote 580.10 *vote*
open war 676.8 *warfare*
open-water 39.11 *swimming*
open-water swimming 39.1 *swimming*
open-weave 67.10 *woven*
open windows 651.1 *refresh*
Opéra 43 Noted Buildings
operability 486.2 *possibleness*
operable 230.11 *workable,* 486.5 *possible,* 629.14 *repairable,* 630.18 *medical*
opéra bouffe 49.4 *opera*
opera buff 51.31 *theatregoer*
opera buffa 49.4 *opera*
opéra comique 49.4 *opera*
opera glasses 56.32 *optical instrument,* 435.10 *visual aid*
operagoer 51.31 *theatregoer*
opera house 49.27 *performance,* 51.14 *theatre,* 420.3 *auditorium*
operand 52.13 *mathematical symbol*
operant conditioning 61.20 *conditioning*
opera semi-seria 49.4 *opera*
opera seria 49.4 *opera*
opera singer 51.22 *actor,* 423.5 *loud person,* 646.1 *worker,* 811.15 *showman*
operate 60.20 *practise surgery,* 150.23 *be in order,* 230.7 *be operational,* 232.4 *be an instrument,* 599.1 *use,* 613.9 *be useful,* 629.6 *cure,* 630.20 *doctor,* 640.4 *act,* 652.14 *behave towards,* 737.2 *speculate*
operate a closed shop 699.9 *economize*
operate at a loss 722.10 *have a financial loss*
operate in the corridors of power 696.14 *master*
operate on 228.10 *manipulate*
operate on the black market 737.1 *trade*
operatic 49.32 *instrumental,* 51.37 *dramatic*
operatic music 49.3 *classical music*
operating 230.10 *operational,* 232.8 *practical*
operating at a loss 722.2 *financial loss*
operating room 630.14 *hospital*
operating system 65.8 *software*
operating table 630.14 *hospital*
operating theatre 60.10, 630.14 *hospital*
operation 52, 230, 60.9 *surgery,* 232.1 *instrumentality,* 327.1 *way,* 596.6 *venture,* 597.2 *undertaking,* 599.6 *use,* 630.12 *surgery,* 640.1 *action,* 640.2 *deed,* 644.2 *task,* 652.8 *treatment,* 676.8 *warfare*
Operation 230
operational 230, 232.8 *practical,*

594.19 *in hand*, 640.6 *effective*, 676.17 *military*
operational command 17.4 *military organization*
operational fleet 17.4 *military organization*
operationally 230
operational research 592.2 *policy*, 653.3 *management*
operations 17.1 *military affairs*, 676.8 *warfare*
operations room 592.7 *planning*
operative 230, 230, 235, 101.8, 232.8 *practical*, 603.7 *machinist*, 613.1 *useful*, 640.3 *doer*, 640.5 *acting*, 642.18 *active*, 646.1 *worker*, 646.3 *agent*
operator 65, 230, 4.8 *philosophical term*, 52.13 *mathematical symbol*, 52.63 *mathematical logic*, 534.13 *telephoner*, 599.8 *user*, 603.7 *machinist*, 640.3 *doer*, 646.3 *agent*, 715.4 *contractor*, 739.12 *wholesaler*
operator gene 59.13 *genetic material*
operculum 80.5 *fish anatomy*, 293.14 *animal covering*
operetta 49.4 *opera*, 51.3 *musical drama*
operon 59.13 *genetic material*
operoseness 644.4 *exertion*
Ophian 7 Non-Christian Religions
ophiciophobia 777 Phobias by Name
ophicleide 49 Musical Instruments
Ophidia 79.3 *snake*
ophidian 79.3 *snake*, 79.11 *reptilian*, 79.12 *snakelike*
ophiolater 9.6 *idolater*
ophiolatrous 9.10 *idolatrous*
ophiolatry 9.2 *idolatry*
ophiological 79.14 *herpetological*
ophiologist 79.10 *herpetologist*
ophiology 79.9 *herpetology*
ophiomancer 11.13 *diviner*
ophiomancy 11.9 *divination*
ophiomorphic 79.12 *snakelike*
Ophiuchids 53 Meteor Showers
Ophiuchus 53 The Constellations
Ophiuchus Nebula 53 Nebulae
ophiuroid 81.3 *echinoderm*, 81.17 *echinodermal*
ophresiophobia 777 Phobias by Name
ophthalmectomy 60 Surgical Operations
ophthalmia 436.2 *poor sight*
ophthalmic 435.20 *visual*
ophthalmitis 436.2 *poor sight*
ophthalmological 60.22 *medical*
ophthalmologist 60.13 *medical specialist*, 436.3 *aid for poor sight*
ophthalmology 60.3 *medical specialty*, 436.3 *aid for poor sight*
ophthalmoscope 60.7 *diagnosis*
ophthalmotomy 60 Surgical Operations
opiate 62.4 *drug type*, 242.2 *moderator*, 643.10 *soporific*, 767.3 *reliever*
opilionid 82.2 *arachnid*
opine 4.22 *propound a philosophy*, 471.17 *theorize*, 497.8 *be of the opinion*, 518.5 *suppose*, 759.19 *believe*
opiniativeness 577.7 *opinionatedness*
opinion 4.1 *philosophy*, 471.5 *ideology*, 473.3 *line of argument*, 492.1 *judgment*, 497.1 *belief*, 518.1 *supposition*, 564.7 *utterance*, 652.1 *conduct*, 654.1 *advice*, 759.3 *feelings*
opinionated 809, 490.2 *convinced*, 497.11 *believing*, 577.4 *set*, 809.13 *boastful*
opinionatedness 577
opinion column 533.9 *news story*
opinionist 490
opinion poll 170.3 *count*, 580.10 *vote*
opium 62 Medication, 242.2

moderator, 404.4 *anaesthetic*, 630.8 *drug*, 631.11 *intoxicant*, 643.10 *soporific*, 875.6 *drug*
opium den 864.8 *wicked place*
opium poppy 84 Flowers and Flowering Plants
Opium Wars 17 Major Wars
Oporto 93 Cities
opossum 77 Marsupials
opossum shrimp 81.4 *arthropod*
Oppenheimer 52 Scientists
oppidan 93.11 *urbanite*, 93.14 *urban*, 255.4 *townsman*
oppo 122.5 *equal*
opponent 663, 18.3 *sportsman* , 500.5 *dissenter*, 668.4 *defiant person*, 669.5 *resister*, 674.10 *contender*, 679.1 *combatant*, 693.6 *nonconformist*, 820.5 *hostile person*, 852.11 *disapprover*
opportune 106.9 *comfortable*, 203.14 *seasonable*, 210.6 *timely*, 615.1 *convenient*
opportunely 210, 106.18 *comfortably*, 615.7 *conveniently*
opportuneness 210.1 *timeliness*
opportunism 615.3 *convenience*, 652.9 *tactics*, 858.1 *improbity*, 860.1 *selfishness*
opportunist 578.9 *equivocator*, 597.6 *enterprising*, 860.3 *selfish person*
opportunistic 858.5 *dishonourable*, 860.4 *selfish*
opportunity 210, 322, 106.2 *occurrence*, 226.5 *reason*, 232.1 *instrumentality*, 486.1 *possibility*, 589.5 *good chance*, 615.3 *convenience*, 645.1 *leisure*, 710.2 *tentative offer*
oppose 111, 663, 820, 111.8 *be opposite*, 117.14, 136.12 *disagree*, 231.3 *counteract*, 473.13 *argue*, 475.19 *protest*, 476.9 *deny*, 484.7 *counter*, 500.9 *refuse*, 661.8 *hinder*, 668.5 *defy*, 668.6 *be insubordinate*, 669.6 *resist*, 670.8 *counterattack*, 674.11 *contend*, 679.39 *defend*, 693.15 *be disobedient*, 711.6 *dissent*, 713.6 *protest*, 852.16 *disagree*
oppose change 217.6 *make permanent*
opposed 111.4 *opposite*, 136.18 *disagreeable*, 573.2 *refusing*, 663.19 *oppositional*, 669.10 *resistant*, 687.6 *adverse*, 820.9 *aggressive*, 852.31 *disapproved*
opposed to 663, 231.4 *counteracting*
opposer 663, 669.5 *resister*, 852.11 *disapprover*
opposing 111, 111.4 *opposite*, 231.4 *counteracting*, 475.14 *demonstrating*, 500.7 *dissenting*, 536.13 *rebutting*, 663.19 *oppositional*, 669.10 *resistant*, 670.24 *counterattacking*, 679.33 *combative*, 687.6 *adverse*, 693.13 *disobedient*, 711.9 *dissenting*, 713.9 *protesting*, 820.9 *aggressive*, 852.26 *disagreeing*
opposing action 231.1 *counteraction*
opposing force 231.1 *counteraction*, 663.8 *the opposition*
opposingly 663, 536.15 *negatively*
opposing party 663.8 *the opposition*
opposing side 111.1 *oppositeness*, 305.5 *team*
opposite 111, 52.43 *triangle*, 107.5 *interrelated*, 109.5 *interconnected*, 117.8 *contradictory*, 117.10 *disagreeing*, 136.18 *disagreeable*, 287.1 *inversion*, 520.4 *type of meaning*, 520.6 *meaningful*, 536.3 *rebuttal*, 663.21 *contrary*, 711.9 *dissenting*
opposite angles 52.39 *angle*
opposite camp 663.8 *the opposition*
oppositely 111, 107.10 *relevantly*, 109.10 *reciprocally*,

117.15 *dissimilarly*, 136.23 *disagreeably*, 711.11 *uncooperatively*
opposite meaning 520.4 *type of meaning*
oppositeness 111, 117.2 *contradiction*, 663.6 *contrariety*
Oppositeness 111
opposite number 109.2 *interconnection*, 111.1 *oppositeness*, 122.5 *equal*
opposite pole 111.1 *oppositeness*
opposites 111
opposite side 111.1 *oppositeness*, 305.5 *team*
opposite tide 97.2 *tide*
opposition 111, 573, 663, 53.16 *planet*, 111.1 *oppositeness*, 117.4 *disagreement*, 136.4 *disunity*, 231.1 *counteraction*, 310.4 *angular measurement*, 484.1 *counterevidence*, 500.3 *dissentience*, 587.6 *dissuasion*, 661.1 *hindrance*, 668.2 *disobedience*, 669.1 *resistance*, 687.1 *adversity*, 693.1 *disobedience*, 711.2 *dissent*, 713.1 *protest*, 820.1 *enmity*, 852.4 *disagreement*
Opposition 663
oppositional 663, 111.4 *opposite*, 231.4 *counteracting*, 484.5 *countering*
oppositionist 663.9 *opposer*
opposition party 663.8 *the opposition*
opposition rally 668.3 *act of defiance*
opposure 111.1 *oppositeness*
oppress 807, 12.11 *govern*, 369.13 *weigh on*, 369.14 *make heavy*, 481.14 *discriminate against*, 590.8 *pursue*, 601.1 *misuse*, 618.14 *ill-treat*, 642.17 *meddle*, 687.11 *cause adversity*, 688.19 *be authoritarian*, 690.6 *suppress*, 695.6 *compel*, 696.14 *master*, 699.8 *restrain*, 701.7 *defeat*, 820.12 *oppose*, 832.18 *torment*, 844.20 *wrong*
oppressed 362.22 *overthrown*, 369.3 *ponderous*, 481.11 *judged*, 601.4 *misused*, 690.9 *suppressed*
oppressing 701.10 *dominating*
oppression 362.13 *submergence*, 369.8 *weighing down*, 601.2 *misuse*, 618.11 *harmfulness*, 690.2 *suppression*, 701.2 *domination*
oppressive 805, 16.62 *above the law*, 55.52 *humid*, 369.3 *ponderous*, 601.5 *abusive*, 618.5 *harmful*, 659.10 *difficult*, 690.8 *severe*, 695.9 *compelling*, 696.12 *masterful*, 699.13 *restraining*, 701.10 *dominating*, 820.7 *intolerant*, 832.10 *malevolent*
oppressively 362.24 *down*, 369.17 *burdensomely*, 601.6 *abusively*, 690.11 *severely*, 695.11 *compellingly*, 696.16 *masterfully*, 820.14 *hostilely*
oppressiveness 369.8 *weighing down*
oppressive person 690.4 *strict person*
oppressor 631, 690.4 *strict person*, 696.4 *absolute ruler*
opprobrious 827.9 *vituperative*, 850.11 *insulting*
opprobriously 827.13 *vituperatively*
opprobrium 827.3 *vilification*, 850.1 *disrespect*
oppugn 663.15 *object*
oppugnancy 663.5 *contrariness*
oppugnant 663.22 *uncooperative*
Ops 8 Deities
opsonin 387.4 *blood*
opt 580.1 *select*
optative 5.33 *mood*
opt for 570.12 *choose*, 580.1 *select*
optic 56.98 *physical*, 435.2 *eye*, 435.20 *visual*, 439.23 *photoelectric*

optical 44.10 *ceramic*, 50.24 *pictorial*, 56.98 *physical*, 435.20 *visual*
optical aberration 56.31 *lens element*
optical activity 56.33 *photosensitivity*, 57.13 *structure*
optical astronomy 53.1 *astronomy*
optical disk 65.7 *peripheral*
optical double 53.9 *constellation*
optical element 56
optical fibre 56.29 *optical element*
optical glass 44.9 *industrial ceramics*
optical illusion 102.3 *delusion*, 435.5 *imagination*, 436.5 *visual distortion*, 519.5 *fantasy*
optical instrument 56, 435.10 *visual aid*, 437.7 *that which makes visible*
optical isomer 57.13 *structure*
optically 44.12 *ornamentally*, 50.30 *pictorially*, 56.100 *physically*, 435.24 *visually*
optical microscope 56.85 *microscope*
optical observatory 53.23 *observatory*
optical perspective 50.4 *treatment*
optical rotation 56.33 *photosensitivity*, 57.13 *structure*
optical spectrum 56.68 *emission*
optical telescope 53.24 *telescope*, 56.85 *microscope*
optic axis 56.31 *lens element*
optician 436.3 *aid for poor sight*, 630.15 *healer*
optic nerve 435.2 *eye*
optics 56.2 *classical physics*, 235.9 *electronics*, 435.10 *visual aid*
optimate 800.2 *person of repute*, 802.1 *nobleman*
optimism 471.7 *idealism*, 513.1 *expectation*, 769.3 *cheerfulness*, 775.1 *hope*
optimist 494, 471.9 *person of ideas*, 769.4 *cheerful person*, 775.5 *hoper*
optimistic 471.13 *ideal*, 513.5 *expecting*, 714.14 *auspicious*, 769.1 *cheerful*, 775.11 *hopeful*
optimistically 471.22 *imaginatively*, 513.12 *expectantly*, 714.17 *auspiciously*, 775.15 *hopefully*
optimum 617.2 *best*
opting out 573.2 *refusing*
option 19.15 *play offence*, 570.1 *will*, 580.8 *choice*, 698.1 *freedom*
optional 30.11 *gymnastic*, 570.10 *free*, 580.14 *selecting*
optional exercise 30.1 *gymnastics*
optionally 30.12 *competitively*, 580.17 *selectively*
option pass 19.9 *play*
option run 19.9 *play*
optoelectronics 64.1 *electronics*
optometer 268.8 *meter*
optometric 268.16 *micrometric*
optometrist 436.3 *aid for poor sight*
optometry 268.2 *micrometry*, 436.3 *aid for poor sight*
opt out 168.19 *be independent*, 573.9 *not cooperate*
opt-out 573.12 *opposition*
opt-out clause 632.1 *safety*
opulence 742, 405.1 *physical pleasure*
opulent 742, 405.6 *pleasant*, 608.2 *plentiful*, 686.8 *prosperous*
opulently 686.9 *prosperously*, 742.16 *wealthily*
opuntia 84 Flowers and Flowering Plants
opus 49.15 *composition*, 243.5 *work of art*
or 451.1 *orange*, 452.1 *yellow*, 544.8 *heraldic device*, 544.13 *heraldic*
oracle 517, 11.13 *diviner*, 199.5 *predictor*, 459.8 *intellectual person*, 505.1 *maxim*, 507.3 *wise man*, 527.11 *mysteriousness*, 578.5 *equivocalness*, 654.4 *adviser*

Oracle 534.25 *broadcast material*
oracular 8.13 *divine,* 11.17 *divinatory,* 505.2 *proverbial,* 507.5 *wise,* 517.13 *predicting,* 523.1 *unintelligible,* 523.4 *difficult,* 578.10 *equivocal*
oracular utterance 578.5 *equivocalness*
oral 564, 1.14 *societal,* 60.23 *dental,* 534.33 *communicational*
oral administration 62.13 *administration*
oral cavity 322.4 *body orifice,* 564.5 *organ of speech*
oral communication 564.1 *faculty of speech*
oral contraceptive 58.16 *hormone,* 62.4 *drug type*
oral examination 477.3 *questionnaire*
oral hygiene 621.5 *ablutions*
oral literature 48.1 *literature*
orally 564
oral pathologist 60.14 *dentist*
oral pathology 60.4 *dentistry*
oral surgeon 60.14 *dentist*
oral surgery 60.4 *dentistry*
oral tobacco 413.7 *tobacco*
oral tradition 1.8 *tradition*
Oran 93 Cities
orange 86 Fruits, 451, 56.28 *colour,* 451.3 *orange thing,* 875.6 *drug*
Orange 96 Rivers
orangeade 351.6 *soft drink,* 414.5 *sweet drink,* 451.3 *orange thing*
orange blossom 84.1 *flower,* 418.2 *fragrant thing,* 451.4 *figurative usage*
Orange Bowl 19.1 *football*
orange-brown 449.1 *brown*
orange colour 451.2 *orangeness*
orange-flower water 451.4 *figurative usage*
Orange Free State 451.4 *figurative usage*
orange grove 69.2 *garden*
orange hawkweed 451.3 *orange thing*
orange juice 351.6 *soft drink,* 451.3 *orange thing*
Orangeman 49.26 *musical group*
Orangeman's Day 451.4 *figurative usage*
Orange March 451.4 *figurative usage*
orangeness 451
Orangeness 451
orange peel 614.6 *refuse*
orange-peel fungus 89 Fungi
orange pekoe 351.3 *tea,* 451.4 *figurative usage*
orange pigment 451.2 *orangeness*
orange-pink 450.1 *red*
orangery 69.4 *nursery,* 85.4 *trees,* 256.7 *room,* 451.4 *figurative usage*
orange squash 451.3 *orange thing*
orange stick 451.4 *figurative usage*
orange sunshine 451.3 *orange thing,* 875.6 *drug*
orange thing 451
orangewood 451.4 *figurative usage*
orang-utan 77 Placental Mammals
Oraon 5 Languages and Groups of Languages
orate 553.5 *be diffuse,* 561.4 *dissertate,* 564.14 *speak to,* 567.7 *address*
oration 553.1 *diffuseness,* 561.1 *dissertation,* 564.8 *speech,* 567.1 *address*
orator 228.7 *motivator,* 549.5 *stylist,* 557.3 *phrasemonger,* 561.3 *dissertator,* 564.10 *speaker,* 567.6 *public speaker,* 586.12 *persuader*
Oratorian 7 Members of Religious Orders
oratorical 567, 557.4 *ornate*
oratorio 49.5 *sacred music*
oratorium 10.11 *place of worship*

oratory 4.5 *philosophical argument,* 10.11 *place of worship,* 549.4 *literary style,* 564.9 *art of public speaking*
oratrix 564.10 *speaker*
orb 53.10 *star,* 313.2 *circle,* 315.3 *round thing,* 435.2 *eye,* 544.4 *insignia*
orbicular 83.18 *of leaves,* 313.5 *circular,* 315.9 *round*
orbicularity 313.1 *circularity,* 315.1 *roundness*
orbicularly 313.8 *circularly,* 315.13 *roundly*
orbit 53, 363, 363, 53.35 *rocketry,* 53.37 *observe,* 214.2 *cycle,* 214.8 *be cyclic,* 233.7 *sphere of influence,* 249.13 *locality,* 313.2, 313.6 *circle,* 315.3 *round thing,* 315.6 *round,* 315.12 *move round,* 327.2 *route,* 327.13 *flight path,* 327.14 *find one's way,* 334.1, 334.3 *circuit,* 356.2 *passing along,* 363.1 *orbital motion,* 364.1 *rotation,* 364.8 *rotate,* 435.2 *eye*
orbital 363, 57.12 *valence,* 214.12 *cyclic,* 313.5, 334.6 *circular,* 363.5 *ringroad,* 364.12 *rotary*
orbitally 214.16 *cyclically,* 313.8 *circularly*
orbital motion 363, 214.2 *cycle,* 364.1 *rotation*
Orbital Motion 363
orbital period 53.21 *orbit*
orbiter 53.33 *planetary probe*
orbiting 363, 363.1 *orbital motion,* 364.1 *rotation,* 364.11 *rotating*
orbiting body 363
orbiting observatory 53.32 *satellite*
orbitotomy 60 Surgical Operations
orb weaver 82 Arachnids
orc 11.11 *ghost,* 76.7 *legendary beast*
orchard 69.2 *garden,* 85.4 *trees*
orchard grass 87 Grasses
orchardist 69.13 *horticulturist*
Orchard Street 740.1 *market*
orchestra 49.26 *musical group,* 51.15 *stage,* 140.3 *assembly,* 161.12 *team*
orchestra conductor 646.1 *worker*
orchestra director 646.1 *worker*
orchestral music 49.3 *classical music*
orchestra pit 51.15 *stage*
orchestra stalls 51.16 *auditorium*
orchestrate 49.35 *compose,* 116.24 *harmonize,* 152.16 *adapt,* 433.9 *set to music,* 652.14 *behave towards,* 653.1 *manage*
orchestrated 49.31 *composed,* 116.13 *harmonious,* 140.8 *cooperative*
orchestration 49.2 *music making,* 116.4 *harmony,* 140.2 *cooperation,* 152.9 *musical arrangement,* 433.3 *melodiousness,* 652.8 *treatment,* 653.3 *management*
orchestrator 49.24 *musician*
orchid 84 Flowers and Flowering Plants
orchidaceous 83.16 *taxonomic*
orchidectomy 60 Surgical Operations
orchidotomy 60 Surgical Operations
orchids 83.3 *seed plant*
orciprenaline 62 Medication
Orcus 8.11 *heaven*
ORD 57.13 *structure*
ordain 7, 16.68 *legislate,* 150.18 *order,* 156.25 *enrol,* 166.13 *rule,* 348.10 *introduce,* 354.7 *install,* 570.15 *impose one's will,* 571.17 *preordain,* 703.6 *commission*
ordained 7.17 *priestly,* 10.21 *ritualistic,* 16.46 *legislated,* 150.10 *ordered,* 571.12 *inevitable,* 582.3 *predetermined*

ordainment 7.9 *priesthood,* 703.1 *commission*
ordeal 406.1 *pain*
order 52, 150, 150, 7.1 *religion,* 10.1 *ritual,* 16.3 *law,* 16.6 *legal process,* 16.68 *legislate,* 52.22 *matrix,* 59.17 *taxonomy,* 105.1 *state,* 107.3 *relative position,* 112.2 *conformity,* 112.10 *conform,* 116.6 *convention,* 116.26 *make uniform,* 121.2 *rank,* 121.5 *measure,* 152.1 *arrangement,* 152.6 *category,* 152.12 *arrange,* 159.2 *consecution,* 163.2 *class,* 163.3 *kingdom,* 163.5 *social class,* 163.14 *sort,* 166.1 *rule,* 166.14 *regulate,* 195.1 *succession,* 208.9 *prepare,* 214.4 *orderliness,* 214.10 *make regular,* 248.21 *space,* 306.1 *form,* 306.3 *kind,* 306.7 *form,* 327.1 *way,* 492.2 *verdict,* 505.1 *maxim,* 528.2 *communication,* 570.15 *impose one's will,* 592.7 *planning,* 592.9 *plan,* 593.1 *requirement,* 593.10 *necessitate,* 594.4 *prepare for action,* 654.3 *precept,* 665.1 *party,* 675.1 *peace,* 676.8 *warfare,* 692.1, 692.9 *command,* 695.2 *coercion,* 695.6 *compel,* 712.2, 712.7 *demand,* 718.15 *reserve,* 738.1 *purchase,* 741.14 *paper money,* 792.3 *honour,* 804.1 *right,* 847.17 *impose a duty*
Order 150
order by telephone 593.10 *necessitate,* 738.1 *purchase*
ordered 150, 16.46 *legislated,* 52.75 *equal,* 107.6 *ranked,* 112.6 *conforming,* 152.20 *arranged,* 163.12 *classed,* 195.12 *succeeding,* 593.4 *required*
ordered arrangement 52.21 *set*
ordered set 52.21 *set*
ordering 52.56 *nonparametric methods,* 126.13 *dominant,* 152.1 *arrangement,* 163.1 *classification,* 692.14 *commanding*
ordering relation 52.63 *mathematical logic*
orderless 133.12 *mixed,* 151.12 *disordered,* 595.1 *unprepared*
orderliness 150, 214, 112.2 *conformity,* 469.4 *fastidiousness*
orderly 150, 150, 214, 214, 60.17 *paramedic,* 112.6, 116.14 *conforming,* 152.20 *arranged,* 166.10 *customary,* 306.9 *formed,* 469.9 *careful,* 592.14 *planned,* 621.16 *clean,* 697.1 *servant,* 813.6 *formal*
order number 52.56 *nonparametric methods*
order of battle 676.9 *battle*
order of business 171.5 *list of appointments*
order of chivalry 681.1 *trophy*
order off 349.6 *send away*
order of magnitude 259.1 *size*
order of merit 681.1 *trophy*
order of service 10.4 *public worship,* 10.6 *Eucharist,* 192.2 *timetable*
order of the day 167.5 *convention,* 192.2 *timetable,* 582.6 *premeditation,* 584.5 *tradition,* 592.1 *plan,* 692.1 *command*
order of things 166.6 *custom*
order of worship 10.1 *ritual*
order one's life 594.8 *prepare oneself*
order paper 582.6 *premeditation*
order through a catalogue 738.1 *purchase*
order up 692.10 *demand*
ordinal 10.10 *religious manual,* 52.7 *natural number,* 52.75 *equal,* 159.9 *consecutive,* 169.8 *odd*
ordinal number 52.7 *natural number,* 169.2 *kind of number*
ordinal scale 52.56 *nonparametric methods*
ordinance 10.1 *ritual,* 16.3 *law,* 166.1 *rule,* 654.3 *precept,* 692.1 *command*

ordinand 7.8 *priest*
ordinarily 116.37 *conventionally,* 124.11 *on average,* 127.20 *insignificantly,* 164.30 *usually,* 166.18 *as a rule,* 212.1 *frequently,* 214.17 *orderly,* 787.10 *predictably*
ordinariness 620, 124.4 *average,* 127.1 *inferiority,* 164.5 *averageness,* 214.4 *orderliness,* 556.4 *simplicity,* 783.4 *mediocrity,* 787.2 *predictability*
ordinary 127, 620, 116.15 *conventional,* 124.1 *average,* 158.15 *middling,* 164.21 *common,* 167.15 *everyday,* 214.14 *orderly,* 242.6 *moderate,* 544.8 *heraldic device,* 556.1 *simple,* 584.10 *familiar,* 599.9 *used,* 612.4 *trivial,* 617.5 *not bad,* 783.10 *mediocre,* 787.4 *predictable*
ordinary differential equation 52.31 *differentiation*
ordinary joe 124.7 *average person,* 164.9 *everyman*
Ordinary level 485 Educational Qualifications
ordinary matter 612.8 *trifle*
ordinary person 400.7 *person*
ordinary rating 679.27 *naval man*
ordinary run 164.6 *average*
ordinary seaman 679.27 *naval man*
ordinate 52.33 *coordinates,* 268.4 *size*
ordination 7.9 *priesthood,* 10.5 *Christian rite,* 156.8 *enrolment,* 348.3 *introduction,* 703.1 *commission*
ordnance 680.11 *guns*
Ordnance Survey map 547.7 *map*
Ordovician 54 Geological Time Intervals
Ordovician period 200.3 *geological period*
ordure 353.5 *faeces,* 622.4 *dirt*
ore 57, 604.1 *materials*
oread 8.5 *deity*
orecchiette 45 Types of Pasta
oregano 45 Herbs and Spices, 413.5 *herbs*
Oregon 92 American States
ore roaster 44.6 *ceramic workshop*
orfe 80 Fishes
Orff 49 Musicians and Composers
organ 49 Musical Instruments, 143.4 *component,* 232.2 *instrument,* 532.5 *journal*
organdie 442.8 *transparent thing*
organ donor 729.4 *giver*
organdy 67 Natural Fabrics
organelle 59.8 *cell organ*
organic 382, 2.13 *communal,* 57.31 *chemical,* 57.35 *combined,* 59.21 *living,* 103.8 *quintessential*
organic acid 57.8 *acid*
organically 68.22 *agriculturally,* 382.18 *structurally*
organic base 57.9 *base*
organic being 59.3 *organism*
organic chemist 57.2 *chemist*
organic chemistry 57.1 *chemistry,* 367.6 *natural science*
organic compound 57.7 *chemical compound*
organic disease 624.4 *disease*
organic farm 68.6 *farm*
organic farming 68.1 *agriculture*
organic fertilizer 246.3 *fertilizer*
organic food 350.7 *food*
organic manure 68.13 *fertilizer*
organic matter 367.4 *matter*
organic pigment 444.4 *pigment*
organic psychosis 61.11 *psychosis*
organic remains 59.3 *organism*
organic sediment 54.27 *sediment*
organic solidarity 2.5 *society*
organic structure 382.1 *structure*
organism 59, 367.4 *matter,* 396.2 *living matter*
organismal 382.12 *organic*
organization 152, 135.3 *unification,* 150.1 *order,* 150.7 *method,*

161.15 *association*, 243.1 *production*, 382.1 *structure*, 592.7 *planning*, 594.9 *preparation*, 646.4 *personnel*, 652.8 *treatment*, 653.3 *management*
organizational 152, 382.11 *structural*, 653.17 *managerial*
organization man 167.6 *conformist*
Organization of Petroleum-Exporting Countries 13.5 *international trade*, 737.5 *commercial trade*, 740.4 *free market*
organize 152, 2.15 *socialize*, 92.7 *administer*, 150.18 *order*, 152.18 *make arrangements*, 163.14 *sort*, 166.14 *regulate*, 243.10 *produce*, 248.21 *space*, 382.14 *structure*, 592.9 *plan*, 594.2 *do the groundwork*, 652.14 *behave towards*, 653.1 *manage*
organize a dragnet 590.8 *pursue*
organize a search party 590.8 *pursue*
organize a vigilante committee 590.8 *pursue*
organized 152, 15.10 *unionized*, 150.10 *ordered*, 592.14 *planned*, 594.18 *prepared*
organized crime 864.7 *criminality*
organized labour 15.4 *industrial dispute*
organized society 400.9 *group*
organized strike 15.4 *industrial dispute*
organizer 135.7 *joiner*, 592.8 *planner*
organ music 49.3 *classical music*
organ notes 423.1 *loudness*
organ of speech 564
organological 382.12 *organic*
organology 382.8 *science of structure*
organometallic 57.35 *combined*
organometallic compound 57.7 *chemical compound*
organ-pipe cactus 84 *Flowers and Flowering Plants*
organs of reproduction 245
organza 67 *Natural Fabrics*, 442.8 *transparent thing*
orgasm 366.8 *spasm*, 405.1 *physical pleasure*
orgasmic 366.19 *convulsive*
orgone theory 61.1 *psychology*
orgy 350.13 *feast*, 405.4 *pleasurable things*, 608.8 *plenty*, 665.7 *social gathering*, 812.1 *celebration*, 870.2 *dissipation*
orgy of drinking 874.14 *drinking bout*
oribi 77 *Placental Mammals*
Oriel window 43.9 *miscellaneous architectural features*
orient 332, 584.18 *habituate*
Orient 249.7 *regions of the world*
Oriental 1.6 *race*, 1.13 *racial*, 249.16 *regional*, 332.13 *directional*
Oriental almandine 54 *Gemstones*
Orientale 32.13 *breeding*
Oriental emerald 54 *Gemstones*
orientalize 220.12 *naturalize*
orientalized 220.17 *naturalized*
Oriental topaz 54 *Gemstones*
orientate 251.10 *situate*, 584.18 *habituate*
orientated 251.6 *situated*
orientated towards 332.14 *directed*
orientation 332, 52.37 *line*, 251.1 *situation*, 518.1 *supposition*, 584.7 *habituation*
orienteering 18 *Sporting Activities*, 250.5 *topography*, 674.4 *race*
Orient Express 72.10 *miscellaneous*
orient onself 332.8 *orient*
orifice 265.2 *crack*, 322.1 *opening*, 346.5 *entrance*, 347.7 *outlet*
oriflamme 544.7 *flag*
origami 42 *Hobbies and Pastimes*
origin 52.32 *graph*, 156.2 *creation*, 156.3 *source*, 156.5 *inven-*

tion, 367.4 *matter*, 396.4 *biological function*
original 119, 119, 479, 16.49 *judicatory*, 41.13 *ice-skating*, 115.4 *dissimilar*, 156.31 *prime*, 156.33 *inventive*, 165.15 *special*, 168.10, 168.14 *eccentric*, 201.10 *new*, 226.13 *causal*, 243.11 *productive*, 306.10 *prototypical*, 471.11 *ideational*, 519.10 *imaginative*, 537.19 *authentic*, 585.2 *not customary*
originality 119, 479, 30.1 *gymnastics*, 41.7 *ice-dancing*, 165.1 *speciality*, 168.4 *unusualness*, 201.1 *newness*, 243.1 *production*, 461.5 *creative thought*, 471.8, 519.1 *imagination*, 537.6 *authenticity*
Originality 119
originally 119, 496, 156.38 *in the beginning*, 201.21 *newly*, 202.21 *archaically*, 226.14 *causally*, 306.13 *formatively*, 471.22 *imaginatively*, 585.8 *unusually*
original meaning 520.4 *type of meaning*
original model 594.10 *preparations*
original sin 864.4, 866.3 *sin*
original thought 119.1 *originality*
original title 723.1 *possession*
original work 243.1 *production*
originate 119, 156.17 *begin*, 156.22 *invent*, 156.27 *emerge*, 201.18 *be trendy*, 226.9 *be the cause of*, 243.10 *produce*, 461.16 *have an idea*, 471.15 *imagine*, 496.4 *invent*, 519.14 *imagine*
originate in 227.7 *follow from*
origination 156.2 *creation*, 156.5 *invention*, 226.1 *cause*, 243.1 *production*, 496.9 *invention*
originative 245.16 *reproductive*
originator 119, 156, 226.7 *Prime Mover*, 243.9 *producer*, 496.12 *discoverer*, 592.8 *planner*
oriole 78 *Birds*, 78.6 *songbird*
Orion 53 The Constellations, **53** The Constellations
Orionids 53 *Meteor Showers*
Orion nebula 53.8 *interstellar medium*
Orion's Belt 53 *Other Groups of Stars*
Orion's Sword 53 *Other Groups of Stars*
Orishako 8 *Deities*
orismology 560.7 *nomenclature*
orison 10.9 *prayer*
Oriya 5 *Languages and Groups of Languages*
Orkney 92 *Counties*
Orko 8 *Deities*
Orlando 93 *Cities*
Orléans 93 *Cities*
Orloff 68 *Breeds of Fowl*
Orlon 67 *Synthetic Fibres and Fabrics*
orlop 74 *Parts of a Ship*
Orlov Trotter 32 *Breeds of Horse and Pony*
ormolu 539.6 *imitation*, 792.2 *pattern*
ornament 557, 557, 43.19 *decorate*, 49.16 *musical note*, 130.6 *add*, 180.4 *concomitant*, 551.1 *obscurity*, 557.1 *elegance*, 558.4 *be elegant*, 627.1 *improve*, 627.5 *improvement*, 789.2 *beautiful thing*, 792.10 *decorate*
Ornament 557
ornamental 69, 43.17 *structured*, 44.10 *ceramic*, 85.1 *tree*, 130.9 *extra*, 456.6 *variegated*, 551.2 *obscure*, 557.4 *ornate*, 614.1 *useless*, 789.5 *beautiful*, 792.8 *decorated*
ornamental garden 69, 69.2 *garden*
ornamental grass 87.1 *grass*
ornamentally 44, 43.20 *architecturally*, 69.20 *horticulturally*, 456.12 *variedly*, 551.4 *obscurely*
ornamental ware 44.1 *ceramics*
ornamentation 130.3 *additional*

item, 557.1 *ornament*, 627.5 *improvement*, 792.1 *adornment*
ornamented 43.17 *structured*, 557.4 *ornate*, 558.3 *elegant*, 792.8 *decorated*
ornate 557, 84.10 *floral*, 553.3 *diffuse*, 792.8 *decorated*
ornately 557, 549.10 *stylistically*
ornateness 792.1 *adornment*
orneriness 693.1 *disobedience*, 829.1 *irascibility*
ornery 693.13 *disobedient*, 829.4 *irascible*
ornithine 58 Amino Acids
ornithischian 79.6 *extinct reptile*
Ornitholestes 79 Fossil Reptiles
ornithological 78
ornithologist 78, 76.11 *zoologist*
ornithology 78, 76.9 *animal science*
ornithophobia 777 Phobias by Name
ornithopod 79.6 *extinct reptile*
Oro 8 Deities
orogenesis 54.21 *mountain building*
orogenetic 95.8 *orogenic*, 275.13 *mountainous*
orogenic 95, 54.54 *tectonic*, 275.13 *mountainous*
orogeny 54.21 *mountain building*
orographic 95.8 *orogenic*, 275.14 *altimetric*
orography 275.5 *height measure*
orological 95.8 *orogenic*
orologist 95.2 *orology*
orology 95
orometer 95.2 *orology*
orometric 95.8 *orogenic*
Orontes 96 Rivers
orotund 427.8 *deep*, 557.4 *ornate*
orotundity 557.2 *affectation*, 564.2 *power of speech*
orphan 132.6 *person remaining*, 132.9 *remaining*, 701.4 *dependent*, 816.7 *outsider*
orphanage 632.2 *protection*, 634.2 *shelter*
orphaned 132.9 *remaining*, 236.11 *unprotected*
orphan's home 632.2 *protection*
orpharion 49 Musical Instruments
Orphean 433.6 *melodious*
orphenadrine 62 Medication
orphica 49 Musical Instruments
orphism 50 Western Art Styles and Movements
Orphism 7 Non-Christian Religions
Orphistic 50.29 *realist*
orphrey 7.11 *vestment*
orpiment 54 Minerals, 452.7 *yellow pigment*
orpine 84 Flowers and Flowering Plants
Orpington 68 Breeds of Fowl, **68** Breeds of Fowl
orrery 53.23 *observatory*
Ortega y Gasset 4 Philosophers
orthocentre 52.43 *triangle*
orthoclase 54.34 *mineral*
orthodontic 60.23 *dental*
orthodontics 60.4 *dentistry*
orthodontist 60.14 *dentist*
orthodox 7.15 *religious*, 116.15 *conventional*, 124.1 *average*, 167.14 *conformist*, 490.2 *convinced*, 497.11 *believing*, 584.11 *normal*, 690.8 *severe*, 719.7 *observant*
Orthodox 7.16 *denominational*
Orthodox Church 7 Christian Movements
Orthodox Jew 7.6 *non-Christian*
Orthodox Judaism 7 Non-Christian Religions
orthodoxly 719.8 *observantly*
orthodox medicine 60.1 *medicine*
orthodoxy 116.6 *convention*, 167.4 *conventionalism*, 490.10 *conviction*, 690.1 *severity*
orthoepic 5.38 *linguistic*
orthoepist 5.2 *linguist*
orthoepy 5.1 *linguistics*, 564.6 *phonetics*

orthogonal 52.80 *linear*, 281.10 *perpendicular*
orthogonal projection 52.48 *transformation*
orthographer 5.2 *linguist*
orthographic 5.38 *linguistic*, 52.80 *linear*
orthographically 5.48 *linguistically*
orthographic convention 5.27 *spelling*
orthographic projection 547.7 *map*
orthography 5.27 *spelling*
orthohydrogen 57 Chemical Elements
orthologist 543.8 *signer*
orthontics 60.8 *treatment*
orthopaedic 630.18 *medical*
orthopaedics 60.3 *medical speciality*, 630.13 *therapy*
orthopaedist 60.13 *medical specialist*
orthopsychiatry 61.2 *psychiatry*
Orthoptera 82 Orders of Insects
orthopteran 82.10 *insectan*
orthoptist 630.15 *healer*
orthopyroxene 54.34 *mineral*
orthorhombic 57.33 *crystalline*
orthotic 630.18 *medical*
ortolan 78 Birds
Orton 48 Dramatists
Orwell 48 Writers
oryx 77 Placental Mammals
os 275.4 *mountain range*
OS/2 65.8 *software*
Osage 1 Peoples, **5** Languages and Groups of Languages
Osage orange 86 Fruits
Osaka 93 Cities
Osborne 48 Dramatists
Oscan 5 Languages and Groups of Languages
Oscar 534 Phonetic Alphabet, 878.2 *prize*
oscillate 365, 64.35 *conduct*, 183.22 *resound*, 214.7 *be regular*, 215.6 *be irregular*, 224.11 *be changeable*, 324.13 *be in motion*, 331.1 *recoil*, 335.10 *slide*, 427.9 *resonate*, 576.5 *vacillate*
oscillating 365, 214.11 *regular*, 215.4 *irregular*, 224.13 *changeable*, 324.17 *directional*
oscillating current 56.14 *sound wave*
oscillating universe 53.4 *cosmological model*
oscillation 365, 56.12 *wave*, 64.15 *circuit function*, 183.6 *reverberation*, 214.1 *regularity*, 215.1 *irregularity*, 224.1 *changeableness*, 235.7 *electrical power*, 324.5 *circuition*, 331.4 *recoil*, 427.1 *resonance*
Oscillation 365
oscillator 365, 56.55 *circuit*, 64.21 *rectifier*, 64.30 *generator*, 235.6 *source of energy*
oscillatory 183.15 *reverberatory*, 214.11 *regular*, 215.4 *irregular*, 365.13 *oscillating*
oscillograph 365.6 *measuring instrument*
oscillometer 365.6 *measuring instrument*
oscilloscope 56.90 *ammeter*, 64.23 *electrical instrument*, 365.6 *measuring instrument*
oscine 78.23 *avian*
oscitancy 643.9 *sleep*
oscitate 783.12 *be indifferent*
oscitation 783.1 *indifference*
Osco-Umbrian 5 Languages and Groups of Languages
osculate 821.27 *kiss*, 826.7 *show endearment for*
osculation 821.14 *communication of love*, 826.1 *endearment*
osculatory 10.14 *sacred object*
Oseretsky test 61.5 *psychological test*
O-shaped 334.6, 363.10 *circular*
osier 85 Trees and Shrubs, 137.6 *line*
Osijek 93 Cities
Osiris 8 Deities

Oslo 93 Cities
Osmanli 5 Languages and Groups of Languages
osmic 57.34 *elemental*
osmidrosis 419.1 *stench*
osmious 57.34 *elemental*
osmiridium 57 Alloys
osmium 57 Chemical Elements
osmophobia 777 Phobias by Name
osmoregulation 59.5 *physiology*
osmose 348.13 *absorb*, 356.10 *enter*
osmosis 56.10 *force*, 326.3 *transmission*, 348.5 *absorption*, 356.3 *passage into*
osmotic 348.17 *absorbent*, 356.13 *penetrating*
osmous 57.34 *elemental*
osmunda 88 Ferns
o.s.p. 247.12 *without issue*
osprey 78 Birds, 78.5 *bird of prey*, 80.11 *fishing animal*
Ossa 95 Mountains
osseous 373.1 *hard*, 382.13 *skeletal*
Ossetic 5 Languages and Groups of Languages
ossicle 371.4 *solid body*, 382.7 *skeleton*
ossicular 382.13 *skeletal*
ossiferous 382.13 *skeletal*
ossific 373.1 *hard*
ossification 371.2 *concentration*, 373.6 *solidification*, 382.7 *skeleton*
ossified 373.3 *hardened*, 382.13 *skeletal*
ossify 371.8 *be dense*, 373.10 *solidify*
ossuary 399.4 *funeral objects*
O star 53.13 *luminosity*
osteal 382.13 *skeletal*
ostectomy 60 Surgical Operations
Ostend 93 Cities
ostensibility 540.7 *pretence*
ostensible 457, 289.8 *apparent*, 483.9 *evident*, 488.6 *probable*, 490.1 *certain*, 526.14 *manifest*, 540.30 *pretending*
ostensibly 102.19 *apparently*, 437.11 *visibly*, 457.15 *apparently*, 483.15 *evidently*, 488.11 *probably*, 540.37 *spuriously*
ostensorium 10.14 *sacred object*
ostentation 805, 475.2 *demonstrativeness*, 526.10 *manifestation*, 532.8 *public relations* , 540.12 *facade*, 541.3 *extravagance*, 557.2 *affectation*, 809.6 *boastfulness*, 811.1 *showiness*
ostentatious 805, 475.10 *demonstrative*, 526.14 *manifest*, 540.27 *hypocritical*, 541.14 *extravagant*, 557.4 *ornate*, 757.2 *unrestrained*, 795.7 *vulgar*, 809.13 *boastful*, 811.16 *showy*
ostentatiously 805, 475.21 *demonstratively*, 541.17 *excessively*, 557.6 *ornately*, 809.23 *boastfully*, 811.32 *showily*
ostentatiousness 540.3 *hypocrisy*, 811.1 *showiness*
osteoarthritis 624.16 *rheumatism*
osteoblast 382.7 *skeleton*
osteoclast 382.7 *skeleton*
osteocyte 382.7 *skeleton*
osteography 382.8 *science of structure*
Osteolepis 80.4 *fossil fish*
osteologist 60.13 *medical specialist*
osteology 1.10 *measurement*, 60.3 *medical specialty*, 382.8 *science of structure*
osteomalacia 58.14 *vitamin deficiency disease*
osteometric 1.11 *anthropological*
osteopath 60.12 *healer*, 407.5 *toucher*, 629.12 *repairer*, 630.15 *healer*
osteopathic 60.22 *medical*
osteopathy 60.2 *natural medicine*, 60.8 *treatment*, 630.13 *therapy*
osteopothy 407.2 *touching*

osteotherapy 630.13 *therapy*
osteotomy 60 Surgical Operations
ostler 32.15 *horse person*, 68.16 *farm worker*
ostracism 349, 147.1 *exclusion*, 709.1 *veto*, 816.3 *separation*, 852.3 *nonacceptance*, 879.7 *punishment*
ostracization 349.19 *ostracism*
ostracize 349, 136.10 *set apart*, 147.7 *exclude*, 252.16 *replace*, 709.3 *veto*, 816.13 *ignore*, 852.15 *withhold approval*, 879.1 *punish*
ostracized 252.10 *replaced*, 816.10 *lonely*, 852.31 *disapproved*
ostracod 81.4 *arthropod*
ostracoderm 80.4 *fossil fish*
Ostrava 93 Cities
ostrich 78 Birds, 78.2 *flightless bird*, 329.12 *swift animal*, 519.9 *visionary*, 591.17 *avoider*
ostrich feathers 295.1 *dress*
ostrich-like 78.23 *avian*, 641.3 *inactive*
Ostrovskii 48 Dramatists
Ostwald 52 Scientists
Ostwald's dilution law 57 Named Reactions
Ostyak 5 Languages and Groups of Languages
Otago 92 New Zealand Regions and Territories
otalgia 420.6 *otology*
otalgic 420.13 *otological*
Othello 48 Shakespeare's plays
other 92, 104.10 *foreign*, 108.6 *unrelated*, 111.4 *opposite*, 114.5 *counterpart*, 368.8 *nonmaterial*
other cities 93
other-directedness 61.7 *personality type*
other dishes 45
other games 42
Other Geographical Features 98
other half 114.5 *counterpart*
other major lakes 94
other major mountains and ranges 95
other major rivers 96
other minds 4.9 *philosophical problem*
otherness 104.2 *foreignness*
other place 368.1 *nonmaterial world*
other ranks 127.6 *inferior*, 612.10 *nonentity*
others 289.5 *extraneousness*
other self 110.3 *lookalike*, 165.11 *identity*, 819.6 *close friend*
other side 111.1 *oppositeness*, 305.3 *side direction*
other side of the coin 111.1 *oppositeness*, 287.1 *inversion*
other side of the fence 111.1 *oppositeness*
other side of the picture 111.1 *oppositeness*
other things being equal 122.12 *equally*
other times 197.1 *different time*
otherwise engaged 512.8 *oblivious*
other world 368.1 *nonmaterial world*
otherworldliness 11.2 *the occult*
otherworldliness 289.5 *extraneousness*, 368.2 *unworldliness*
otherworldly 7.15 *religious*, 11.18 *spiritual*, 289.10 *extraneous*, 368.8 *nonmaterial*, 519.11 *fantastical*
otiose 132.10 *surplus*, 183.12 *repetitious*, 600.3 *not wanted*, 610.7 *superfluous*
Otis 52 Scientists
otitis 420.6 *otology*
otolaryngological 420.13 *otological*
otolaryngologist 60.13 *medical specialist*, 420.6 *otology*
otolaryngology 60.3 *medical specialty*, 420.6 *otology*
otological 420

otologist 60.13 *medical specialist*, 420.6 *otology*
otology 420, 60.3 *medical specialty*
otoplasty 60 Surgical Operations
otorhinolaryngological 420.13 *otological*
otorhinolaryngologist 60.13 *medical specialist*, 420.6 *otology*
otorhinolaryngology 60.3 *medical specialty*, 420.6 *otology*
otoscope 60.7 *diagnosis*
otoscopic 420.13 *otological*
o-tsuzumi 49 Musical Instruments
OTT 759.13 *passionate*
ottava rima 48.10 *verse form*
ottavino 49 Musical Instruments
Ottawa 1 Peoples, **93** Cities
otter 77 Placental Mammals, 80.11 *fishing animal*
otterhound 77 Breeds of Dogs, 590.6 *hunter*
otter hunting 18 Sporting Activities, 77.23 *mammal hunting*
otter shrew 77 Placental Mammals
otto 418.3 *incense*
Otto 52 Scientists
Otto cycle 56 Named Laws, 56.38 *thermodynamics*, 63.13 *engine cycle*
ottoman 284.4 *rest*
Ottoman 5 Languages and Groups of Languages, 202.14 *historic*
Ottoman art 50 Non-Western Art
Ottoman Empire 91.3 *dominion*
Otway 48 Dramatists
ouabain 85 *Tree Products*
Ouachita 96 Rivers
oubain 62 Medication
oubliette 323.4 *closed place*, 702.1 *prison*
ouch 431.6 *cry of pain*
oud 49 Musical Instruments
Oughtred 52 Scientists
ought to 847.14 *be the duty of*
Ouija 11.10 *psychic phenomenon*
Ouija board 517.10 *cards*
Oulton Broad 94 Lakes, 94.4 *British lakes*
ounce 75 General Units, **77** Placental Mammals, 369.9 *avoirdupois weight*
ouranophobia 777 Phobias by Name
Ouranos 8 Deities
our day 196.2 *the present day*
Our Father 10.9 *prayer*
Our Lady 8.10 *deified person*
our own day 196.2 *the present day*
ourselves 165.12 *I*, 400.1 *humankind*
our side 305.5 *team*
Ouse 96 Rivers, 96.4 *British rivers*
Ouspensky 4 Philosophers
oust 147.8 *eject*, 222.4 *be a substitute*, 252.16 *replace*, 349.8 *evict*, 581.2 *discard*, 704.7 *terminate*
ouster 349.26 *ejector*
ousting 349.20 *eviction*
out 22.6 *fielding terms*, 27.12 *cricketing*, 27.20 *in*, 40.4 *tennis terms*, 42.6 *darts*, 254.9 *away*, 347.18 *forth*, 487.3 *hopeless*, 493.9 *misjudged*, 609.4 *scarce*, 643.2 *not working*, 722.17 *unprofitable*, 855.2 *defence*, 874.3 *dead drunk*
out-and-out 144.7 *complete*
out at elbows 743.3 *beggarly*
out-at-elbows 296.10 *in dishabille*
outback 248.3 *geographical space*, 249.6 *regions*, 263.3 *distant place*, 289.2 *outside*
outbalance 369.12 *be heavy*
outbid 126.9 *outdo*, 357.3 *exceed*, 357.14 *surpassing*, 737.3 *bargain*
outboard 74 Ships and Boats, **74** Parts of a Ship

outbound 347.15 *outgoing*
outbrake 33.10 *be on the track*
outbraking 33.6 *motor racing terms*
outbreak 156.1 *beginning*, 241.3 *instance of violence*, 347.1 *exit*
outbreak of rain 55.25 *rain*
outbreak of war 676.4 *belligerency*
outburst 153.5 *commotion*, 241.3 *instance of violence*, 347.1 *exit*, 349.22 *disgorgement*, 431.1 *cry*, 828.4 *anger*
outcast 132.10 *surplus*, 147.5 *excluded person*, 147.11 *excluded*, 149.9 *misfit*, 252.7 *displaced person*, 252.10 *replaced*, 335.19 *deviant person*, 349.27 *expellee*, 816.7 *outsider*, 864.9 *wicked person*
outcaste 349.27 *expellee*, 816.7 *outsider*
outclass 123.5 *be unequal*, 329.6 *accelerate*, 357.3 *exceed*, 682.11 *overmaster*
outclassed 127, 147.11 *excluded*, 357.14 *surpassing*, 683.11 *defeated*
outclassing 126.12 *superior*
out cold 404.8 *unconscious*, 643.4 *not awake*, 874.3 *dead drunk*
outcome 155.5 *consequence*, 157.12 *end result*, 195.9 *sequel*, 227.1 *effect*, 243.3 *product*, 347.1 *exit*, 478.6 *solution*
outcoming 347.1 *exit*
outcrop 34.5 *rock face*, 318.2 *projection*, 437.6 *visible thing*
outcropping 34.8 *mountaineering*
outcry 423, 153.5 *commotion*, 431.1 *cry*, 713.1 *protest*, 852.9 *show of disapproval*
outdated 200.19 *antiquarian*, 202.12 *olden*, 628.12 *deteriorated*
out-directed 61.35 *extroverted*
outdistance 126.8 *be superior*, 126.9 *outdo*, 263.5 *be distant*, 329.6 *accelerate*, 336.9 *maintain progress*, 357.3 *exceed*
outdo 126, 806, 123.5 *be unequal*, 329.6 *accelerate*, 357.3 *exceed*, 633.10 *endanger*, 657.5 *be cunning*, 674.11 *contend*
outdoing 674.14 *contending*
outdone 357.14 *surpassing*
outdoor 39.11 *swimming*, 289.7 *outside*, 390.16 *open-air*
outdoor game 42.1 *game*
outdoors 625.2 *salubrity*
outdoor sport 18.4 *sporting activity*
outdoor swimming pool 39.7 *swimming pool*
outdoor theatre 51.14 *theatre*
outdrive 329.6 *accelerate*
outer 457, 104.12 *external*, 289.6 *exterior*
outer atmosphere 390.3 *atmospheric layers*
outer block 26.9 *tae kwon do*
outer darkness 147.3 *exclusion zone*
outer ear 420.4 *ear*
outer face 289.1 *exterior*
outer layer 289.1 *exterior*
outer limit 249.3 *regional boundary*
Outer Mongolia 263.3 *distant place*
outermost 289.7 *outside*
outer product 52.50 *scalar quantity*
outer self 165.11 *identity*
outer side 289.1 *exterior*
outer skin 293.14 *animal covering*
outer space 53.3 *universe*, 184.6 *vastness*, 248.2 *empty space*, 263.3 *distant place*
outer wall 289.1 *exterior*
outface 574.8 *brace oneself*, 778.15 *be courageous*, 807.27, 807.27 *dare*
outfall 347.2 *outflow*, 347.7 *outlet*

outfield 22.1 *baseball*
outfielder 22.2 *baseball player*
outfielder's glove 22.3 *baseball equipment*
outfield fence 22.1 *baseball*
outfit 17.4 *military organization*, 51.23 *cast*, 142.5 *unit*, 161.12 *team*, 251.2 *circumstances*, 295.1 *dress*, 295.5 *fancy dress*, 295.10 *suit*, 295.35 *make clothing*, 594.5 *equip*, 594.11 *fitting out*, 603.6 *equipment*, 606.5 *provision*, 665.1 *party*
outfitter 295.26 *fashion designer*
outfitting 606.1 *provision*
outflank 357.3 *exceed*, 682.11 *overmaster*
outflanking 652.9 *tactics*
outflow 347, 96.6 *river flow*, 347.11 *run out*, 607.3 *waste*, 610.1 *excess*, 638.4 *leak*, 722.4 *lessening*, 727.1 *disposal*
outflowing 347, 347.2 *outflow*
outflux 347.2 *outflow*
out for 588.11 *intending*, 596.10 *ambitiously*
out for the count 404.8 *unconscious*
out front 532.22 *publicly*
outgas 57.29 *absorb*
outgassed 57.43 *absorbed*
outgassing 57.20 *surface chemistry*
outgate 347.6 *way out*
outgo 126.9 *outdo*, 347.1 *exit*
outgoer 347
outgoing 345, 347, 61.35 *extroverted*, 239.4 *vigorous*, 347.1 *exit*, 705.7 *resigning*, 815.15 *sociable*
outgoingness 61.7 *personality type*
outgoings 347.5 *export*, 748.5 *expense*
outgrow 261.6 *become bigger*
outgrown 585.2 *not customary*
outgrowth 227.3 *growth*
outgunned 683.11 *defeated*
out-handle 41.13 *ice-skating*
out-handle turn 41.10 *curling*
outhaul 36.3 *parts of a sailing boat*
out-Herod Herod 126.8 *be superior*, 541.10 *boast*
outhouse 130.3 *additional item*, 256.7 *room*, 256.8 *shelter*, 353.13 *lavatory*, 727.7 *toilet*
outi 49 *Musical Instruments*
out in front 123.7 *unequally*
out in left field 147.11 *excluded*
out in the cold 147.11 *excluded*
out in the open 526.16 *manifestly*, 658.1 *naive*
outjump 126.9 *outdo*
outland 289.2 *outside*
outlander 104.6 *outsider*, 149.4 *foreigner*
outlandish 104.10 *foreign*, 117.9 *nonconforming*, 149.11 *foreign*, 168.14 *eccentric*, 519.11 *fantastical*, 786.8 *wonderful*
outlandishly 104.18 *extraneously*, 117.15 *dissimilarly*, 168.21 *unconformably*
outlandishness 168.4 *unusualness*
outlandish notion 579.3 *whim*
outlast 188.6 *last*, 190.5 *be eternal*, 378.10 *be tough*
outlaw 16.75 *make illegal*, 16.79 *convict*, 32.1 *horse*, 104.5 *nonconformist*, 147.5 *excluded person*, 147.8 *eject*, 149.8 *exile*, 168.8 *dissenter*, 335.19 *deviant person*, 349.4 *ostracize*, 349.27 *expellee*, 635.2 *troublemaker*, 659.9 *difficult person*, 709.3 *veto*, 736.11 *dishonest person*, 816.7 *outsider*, 816.13 *ignore*, 832.8 *malefactor*, 864.9 *wicked person*, 879.1 *punish*
outlawed 16.55 *illegal*, 16.64 *convicted*, 816.10 *lonely*
outlawing 349.19 *ostracism*, 879.7 *punishment*
outlawry 16.41 *lawlessness*,

16.43 *conviction*, 349.19 *ostracism*, 736.5 *plundering*
outlay 347.5 *export*, 607.3 *waste*, 746.1 *payment*, 748.5 *expense*, 751.5 *cost*
outleap 126.9 *outdo*
out-Lear Lear 828.12 *become angry*
outlet 347, 98.9 *inlet*, 327.11 *channel*
outlie 263.5 *be distant*, 297.7 *surround*
outline 299, 299, 552, 562, 592, 50.9 *drawing*, 50.20 *draw*, 270.3 *shortened version*, 289.1 *exterior*, 289.11 *be exterior*, 306.1, 306.7 *form*, 457.3 *external appearance*, 457.14 *present*, 473.4 *gist*, 518.5 *suppose*, 518.6 *propound*, 544.1 *identification*, 547.1 *representation*, 547.11 *paint*, 552.4 *be concise*, 560.2 *brief description*, 560.14 *describe*, 562.8 *summarize*, 594.2 *do the groundwork*, 594.10 *preparations*, 685.5 *not complete*, 767.6 *profile*
Outline 299
outlined 299, 50.27 *painted*, 552.3 *concise*
outlining 50.3 *drawing*
outlive 188.6 *last*, 190.5 *be eternal*, 217.5 *be permanent*
outlive one's spouse 824.10 *be widowed*
outlook 4.1 *philosophy*, 7.1 *religion*, 55.4 *weather forecast*, 199.4 *looking to the future*, 435.7 *view*, 488.1 *probability*, 513.2 *expectations*, 652.1 *conduct*, 807.27 *dare*
out loud 420.17 *aurally*
outlying 263.8 *distant*, 289.7 *outside*, 297.4 *surrounding*
outmanoeuvre 74.9 *navigate*, 126.9 *outdo*, 300.7 *have an advantage*, 357.3 *exceed*, 539.28 *trick*, 682.11 *overmaster*
outmanoeuvred 357.14 *surpassing*, 539.4 *deceived*, 683.11 *defeated*
outmanoeuvring 539.7 *tricking*
outmarch 126.9 *outdo*, 329.6 *accelerate*
outmatch 237.7 *be strong*
outmatched 683.11 *defeated*
outmigrant 347.8 *outgoer*
outmigrate 347.13 *emigrate*
outmigration 347.4 *emigration*
outmoded 200.19 *antiquarian*, 202.12 *olden*, 614.1 *useless*
outnumber 181.12 *overcrowd*, 610.4 *be excessive*
outnumbered 610.6 *excessive*
out of 347, 227.10 *caused*, 396.15 *born*
out of account 147.11 *excluded*
out of action 236.10 *powerless*, 614.1 *useless*, 643.2 *not working*
out of a job 252.11 *relegated*
out of balance 309.6 *distorted*
out-of-body experience 11.10 *psychic phenomenon*
out of bounds 16.55 *illegal*, 29.1 *golf*, 263.10 *distantly*, 302.8 *within limits*, 357.15 *out of reach*, 709.5 *vetoed*
out of breath 503.9 *panting*
out of character 117.8 *contradictory*
out of chronological order 193
out of circulation 236.10 *powerless*
out of commission 325.5 *sedentary*, 600.4 *disused*, 643.2 *not working*, 844.18 *gone wrong*
out of context 309.6 *distorted*
out of control 151.20 *disorderly*, 236.12 *impotent*, 241.6 *violent*, 693.13 *disobedient*
out of countenance 806.3 *humbled*
out of danger 632.5 *safe*, 632.10 *safely*
out of date 193.6 *too late*, 193.7 *out of chronological order*, 197.2

occurring at a different time, 200.19 *antiquarian*
out of debt 742.2 *solvent*, 746.16 *paid*
out of doors 289.2 *outside*, 289.15 *externally*
out-of-doors 390, 289.7 *outside*, 390.5 *open air*, 390.16 *open-air*, 625.2 *salubrity*
out of earshot 263.10 *distantly*, 421.7 *unheard*, 421.12 *deafly*, 424.7, 428.10 *faintly*
out of fashion 193.7 *out of chronological order*, 585.2 *not customary*, 754.10 *shoddy*
out of favour 785.9 *disliked*, 822.12 *hated*
out of focus 438.2 *difficult to see*
out of hand 659.14 *troublesome*
out of harm's way 632.5 *safe*, 632.10 *safely*
out of harness 698.13 *informal*
out of hearing 263.10 *distantly*
out of hiding 437.11 *visibly*
out of house 254.21 *away*
out of house and home 872.7 *gluttonously*
out of humour 830.7 *irritable*
out of it 523.6 *confused*, 650.1 *fatigued*
out of joint 117.11 *unfit*, 151.12 *disordered*, 252.12 *disconnected*
out of keeping 117.8 *contradictory*, 168.22 *out of step*
out of kilter 105.8 *in a state of*, 309.6 *distorted*, 624.22 *sick*, 628.13 *dilapidated*, 656.3 *clumsy*
out of kindness 831.10 *benevolently*
out of line 117.11 *unfit*, 117.15 *dissimilarly*, 168.15 *irregular*, 168.22 *out of step*, 844.11 *wrong*
out of luck 687.8 *unlucky*
out of mind 722.16 *losing*
out of one's depth 277.16 *deep*, 358.8 *defective*, 523.6 *confused*, 659.16 *troubled*, 722.18 *at a loss*, 722.21 *out of place*
out of one's element 117.11 *unfit*, 168.15 *irregular*, 252.10 *replaced*, 722.18 *at a loss*, 722.21 *out of place*
out of one's head 510.11 *insane*
out of one's league 236.14 *powerlessly*
out of one's mind 510.11 *insane*
out of one's misery 397.19 *dead*
out of one's skull 510.11 *insane*
out of one's tree 510.11 *insane*
out of operation 600.12 *out of use*
out of orbit 335.20 *deviant*
out of order 105.8 *in a state of*, 117.11 *unfit*, 117.15 *dissimilarly*, 133.12 *mixed*, 133.14 *in the midst*, 151.12 *disordered*, 211.10 *untimely*, 236.10 *powerless*, 600.1 *unused*, 614.1 *useless*, 628.13 *dilapidated*, 844.18 *gone wrong*
out of phase 117.11 *unfit*, 117.15 *dissimilarly*, 365.5 *wave*
out of place 252, 722, 117.11 *unfit*, 117.15 *dissimilarly*, 149.11 *foreign*, 151.12 *disordered*, 168.15 *irregular*, 252.10 *replaced*, 616.1 *inconvenient*, 722.18 *at a loss*, 816.10 *lonely*
out-of-play wall 40.9 *squash terms*
out of pocket 722.20 *at a loss*, 743.2 *insolvent*
out-of-pocket 722.17 *unprofitable*, 748.10 *expending*
out-of-pocket expenses 748.5 *expense*
out of practice 656.3 *clumsy*
out of print 546.6 *obliterated*, 609.4 *scarce*
out of proportion 108.8 *distorted*, 117.7 *disparate*
out of range 263.8 *distant*, 263.10 *distantly*, 421.7 *unheard*, 421.12 *deafly*, 438.1 *invisible*, 438.9 *invisibly*, 458.7 *disappeared*, 638.9 *fugitively*

out of reach 357, 119.5 *novel*, 263.8 *distant*, 263.10 *distantly*
out of season 117.11 *unfit*, 203.9 *seasonal*, 211.11 *anachronistic*, 609.4 *scarce*
out of sequence 193.7 *out of chronological order*
out of service 600.1 *unused*
out of shape 309.6 *distorted*
out of sight 254.9 *away*, 263.8 *distant*, 263.10 *distantly*, 438.1 *invisible*, 438.9 *invisibly*, 458.7 *disappeared*, 617.1 *worthy*, 722.16 *losing*, 722.21 *out of place*, 753.12 *dearly*
out-of-sight 753.7 *dear*
out of sight, out of mind 438.1 *invisible*, 512.11 *forgotten*
out of sorts 105.8 *in a state of*, 624.22 *sick*, 770.6 *depressed*
out of soundings 97.11 *nautically*
out of spite 832.20 *malevolently*
out of step 168, 113.5 *diverse*, 113.10 *diversely*, 117.11 *unfit*, 117.15 *dissimilarly*, 168.15 *irregular*, 585.2 *not customary*
out of stock 609.4 *scarce*
out of sympathy 785.8 *disliking*
out of sync 197.2 *occurring at a different time*, 656.3 *clumsy*
out of temper 830.7 *irritable*
out of the Ark 202.12 *olden*
out of the black 744.15 *into the black*
out of the blue 489.9 *unexpectedly*, 514.13 *surprisingly*
out of the common 168.14 *eccentric*
out of the common run 126.16 *superiorly*
out of the corner of one's eye 435.26 *watchfully*
out of the frying pan into the fire 768.9 *from bad to worse*
out of the habit 585.1 *unaccustomed*
out of the ordinary 115.4 *dissimilar*, 165.16 *characteristic*, 168.14 *eccentric*, 201.11 *unfamiliar*, 514.8 *surprising*, 585.2 *not customary*
out of the picture 458.7 *disappeared*
out of the question 487.1 *impossible*, 536.17 *never*, 581.10 *rejected*
out of the red 744.15 *into the black*, 746.16 *paid*
out of the running 236.12 *impotent*, 612.1 *unimportant*, 683.11 *defeated*
out of the top drawer 126.16 *superiorly*
out of the way 168.22 *out of step*, 263.10 *distantly*, 334.7 *circuitous*, 616.2 *distant*, 816.11 *secluded*
out-of-the-way 108.7 *illogical*, 263.8 *distant*, 335.21 *indirect*
out of the window 722.16 *losing*
out of the wood 632.5 *safe*
out of thin air 583.7 *extempore*
out of this world 126.14 *best*, 126.17 *supremely*, 168.14 *eccentric*, 263.8 *distant*, 263.10 *distantly*, 397.19 *dead*, 617.1 *worthy*, 762.5 *delightful*, 763.1 *pleasant*
out of time 117.11 *unfit*, 117.15 *dissimilarly*, 186.7 *beyond time*, 585.2 *not customary*
out of touch 656.3 *clumsy*
out-of-touch 531.14 *concealed*
out of town 254.10 *nonresident*, 254.21 *away*
out of training 656.3 *clumsy*
out of true 504.22 *wrongly*
out of true alignment 309.6 *distorted*
out of tune 117.11 *unfit*, 168.15 *irregular*, 434.9 *unmelodious*
out of turn 211.10 *untimely*
out of use 600, 600.4 *disused*
out of view 438.9 *invisibly*, 722.16 *losing*, 722.21 *out of place*

out of whack 117.8 *contradictory*, 628.13 *dilapidated*
out of work 600.3 *not wanted*, 641.3 *inactive*, 643.2 *not working*, 645.7 *leisurely*
out on a limb 168.14 *eccentric*, 168.22 *out of step*, 633.3 *vulnerable*, 659.16 *troubled*
out on bail 700.7 *liberated*
out on one's arse 252.11 *relegated*
out on one's ear 252.11 *relegated*
outpace 126.9 *outdo*, 329.6 *accelerate*
out-patient 60.18 *patient*, 624.19 *sick person*
out-patient clinic 60.10 *hospital*
outperform 126.9 *outdo*
outplay 126.9 *outdo*, 682.11 *overmaster*
outplayed 683.11 *defeated*
outpoint 682.11 *overmaster*
outpost 249.6 *regions*, 263.3 *distant place*, 302.3 *furthest place*
outposts 297.1 *surroundings*
outpour 347.2 *outflow*, 347.11 *run out*, 349.14 *let out*, 349.22 *disgorgement*
outpouring 347.2 *outflow*, 347.16 *outflowing*, 553.1 *diffuseness*, 608.8 *plenty*
output 64.35 *conduct*, 65.17 *computing term*, 65.19 *abort*, 243.1 *production*, 243.3 *product*, 243.10 *produce*, 553.1 *diffuseness*, 721.6 *yield*
output signal 64.14 *terminal*
output terminal 64.14 *terminal*
outrace 126.9 *outdo*
outrage 241.3 *instance of violence*, 601.2 *misuse*, 618.14 *illtreat*, 628.10 *impairment*, 690.1 *severity*, 818.7 *be discourteous*, 828.9 *offend*, 832.7 *act of malevolence*, 864.1 *wickedness*, 866.3 *sin*
outrageous 241.6 *violent*, 541.14 *extravagant*, 601.5 *abusive*, 618.5 *harmful*, 757.2 *unrestrained*, 832.11 *cruel*, 850.11 *insulting*, 864.11 *wicked*, 864.12 *immoral*
outrageously 541.17 *excessively*, 601.6 *abusively*, 753.12 *dearly*
outrageousness 541.3 *extravagance*
outrange 126.9 *outdo*, 263.5 *be distant*
outrank 123.5 *be unequal*, 126.9 *outdo*, 154.16 *take precedence*
outré 786.8 *wonderful*
outreach 126.9 *outdo*, 263.7 *reach*, 269.9 *be long*
outride 126.9 *outdo*, 357.3 *exceed*
outrider 180.7 *attendant*
outrigger 74 Ships and Boats, **74** Sailing Ships and Boats, **74** Parts of a Ship, 36.4 *rowing*, 36.6 *canoeing*
outright 144.9 *completely*, 530.13 *openly*
outright gift 729.2 *gift*
outright purchase 738.7 *purchasing*
outrival 357.3 *exceed*, 674.11 *contend*
outrun 126.9 *outdo*, 329.6 *accelerate*, 357.3 *exceed*, 648.2 *make haste*, 722.15 *lose someone*
outrun the constable 745.8, 747.7 *not pay*
outsail 329.6 *accelerate*
outset 156.1 *beginning*, 345.8 *start*, 345.10 *place of departure*
outshine 126.9 *outdo*, 300.7 *have an advantage*
outshone 127.18 *outclassed*, 683.11 *defeated*
outside 52.35 *space*, 104.4 *externality*, 104.12 *external*, 117.11 *unfit*, 147.12 *exclusively*, 289.15 *externally*, 390.26 *out-of-doors*, 437.6 *visible thing*, 457.3 *external appearance*
outside agency 29.6 *golfer*

outside broadcast 534.25 *broadcast material*
outside chance 229.2 *chance*, 486.4 *remote possibility*, 489.4 *improbability*
outside edge 299.3 *edge*, 302.3 *furthest point*
outside home 31.6 *lacrosse player*
outside hope 486.4 *remote possibility*
outside left 38.3 *football player*
outside of 147.12 *exclusively*
outsider 104, 816, 32.7 *horseracing*, 117.6 *misfit*, 147.5 *excluded person*, 149.4 *foreigner*, 168.7 *nonconformist*, 335.19 *deviant person*, 666.4 *dissenter*, 816.6 *unsocial person*
outside right 38.3 *football player*
outsiders 289.5 *extraneousness*
outside run 19.9 *play*
outside ski 41.5 *ski equipment*
outside the law 16.55 *illegal*
outside time 186.7 *beyond time*
outsize 259.3 *large scale*, 259.15 *big*
outsized 248.13 *spacious*
outskirts 49.8 *suburb*, 249.11 *settlement*, 263.3 *distant place*, 297.1 *surroundings*
outsmart 476.8 *refute*, 539.28 *trick*, 657.5 *be cunning*, 734.10 *take away*
outsmarted 538.16 *misinformed*, 539.36 *deceived*
outsmarting 539.7 *tricking*
out-speaking 564.19 *speaking*
outspoken 381, 526.15 *open*, 530.11 *disclosing*, 535.14 *assertive*, 537.18 *truthful*, 564.19 *speaking*, 658.1 *naive*, 668.7 *defiant*
outspokenness 381, 530.3 *openness*, 535.6 *assertiveness*, 537.5 *truthfulness*, 658.2 *naivety*
outspread 261.5 *make bigger*, 261.6 *become bigger*, 261.7 *bigger*, 343.11 *move apart*
outspreading 261.1 *growth*
outstanding 126.15 *excellent*, 132.10 *surplus*, 437.2 *clear*, 611.6 *notable*, 617.1 *worthy*, 733.11 *borrowed*, 845.12 *owed*
outstanding balance 733.5 *loan*, 744.1 *credit*
outstandingly 126.16 *superiorly*, 132.12 *with a remainder*
outstare 668.5 *defy*, 806.26 *outdo*
outstay one's welcome 346.10 *invade*, 788.6 *be boring*
outstep 126.9 *outdo*
outstretch 261.5 *make bigger*, 263.7 *reach*, 269.9 *be long*
outstretched 261.7 *bigger*, 269.1 *long*
outstretched hand 677.2 *peace offering*
outstretching 261.1 *growth*
outstrip 123.5 *be unequal*, 126.9 *outdo*, 300.7 *have an advantage*, 329.6 *accelerate*, 336.9 *maintain progress*, 357.3 *exceed*, 648.2 *make haste*, 722.15 *lose someone*
outswinger 27.8 *delivery*
out-talk 565
outthink 300.7 *have an advantage*
out to 588.11 *intending*
out to lunch 153.16 *deranged*, 460.6 *unintelligent*, 468.8 *absent-minded*, 512.8 *oblivious*
outtrump 126.9 *outdo*
out-turn 41.16 *bobsled*
outvie 126.9 *outdo*
outvote 123.5 *be unequal*
outvoted 683.11 *defeated*
outward 303, 104.12 *external*, 289.7 *outside*, 289.8 *apparent*, 289.9 *externalized*, 347.18 *forth*, 437.1 *visible*, 437.11 *visibly*, 457.8 *outer*
outward appearance 289.3 *appearance*, 303.3 *show*
outward-bound 345.13, 347.15 *outgoing*
outward form 457.3 *external appearance*

outwardly 104.18 *extraneously*, 289.15 *externally*, 347.18 *forth*, 437.11 *visibly*, 457.15 *apparently*
outwardness 104.4 *externality*, 289.2 *outside*, 289.4 *externalization*
outwards 289.15 *externally*
outward self 165.11 *identity*
outward show 539.3 *hypocrisy*, 540.12 *facade*
outweigh 123.5 *be unequal*, 233.10 *be a prevailing influence*, 369.12 *be heavy*
out-wick 41.16 *bobsled*
outwit 126.9 *outdo*, 300.7 *have an advantage*, 476.8 *refute*, 539.28 *trick*, 657.5 *be cunning*, 734.10 *take away*
outwith the law 16.55 *illegal*
outwitted 539.36 *deceived*, 683.11 *defeated*
outwitting 539.7 *tricking*
outwork 644.1 *work*, 671.8 *military defences*, 671.11 *fortification*
outworn 200.19 *antiquarian*
ouzel 78 Birds
ouzo 351.7 *alcoholic drink*
oval 33.6 *motor racing terms*, 52.42 *circle*, 52.81 *curvilinear*, 52.83 *spherical*, 311.2 *bend*, 311.4 *curved*, 313.2 *circle*, 313.5 *circular*, 334.1 *circuit*, 334.6 *circular*
ovally 313.8 *circularly*
Ovambo 5 Languages and Groups of Languages
ovarian 245.16 *reproductive*, 352.5 *of a secretion*
ovariotomy 60 Surgical Operations
ovary 352 Endocrine Glands, 84.3 *flower part*, 245.8 *organs of reproduction*
ovate 83.18 *of leaves*, 313.5, 334.6 *circular*
ovately 313.8 *circularly*
ovation 51.6 *scene*, 773.2 *fanfare*, 812.3 *ceremony*, 812.9 *rejoicing*, 851.5 *acclaim*
oven 57 Laboratory Apparatus, 44.6 *ceramic workshop*, 408.4 *burner*
ovenbird 78 Birds
oven-fresh 201.10 *new*
oven gloves 45.6 *kitchen equipment*
ovenproof dish 45.6 *kitchen equipment*
oven-ready 45.56 *culinary*, 594.21 *ready-made*
oven-roasting 45.8 *cooking technique*
ovenware 44.1 *ceramics*
over 200, 3.18 *in the past*, 27.8 *delivery*, 126.12 *superior*, 132.10 *surplus*, 144.7 *complete*, 157.21 *ended*, 218.10 *finished*, 275.19 *high*, 293.42 *inclusively*, 323.17 *finally*, 327.17 *via*, 487.3 *hopeless*
overabundance 132.4 *surplus*
overabundant 132.10 *surplus*
overabundantly 132.11 *residually*
overact 51, 357.4, 541.7 *exaggerate*, 610.4 *be excessive*, 656.5 *be unskilful*
overacted 541.12 *exaggerated*, 610.6 *excessive*
overacting 51.20 *acting*, 357.9 *excessiveness*, 541.1 *exaggeration*
overactive 642.18 *active*
overactivity 642, 610.2 *overdoing it*, 644.4 *exertion*
over again 176.19 *twice*
over against 111.6 *oppositely*, 327.17 *via*
overall 164, 124.11 *on average*, 146.7 *including*, 164.15 *general*, 295.25 *accessories*
overall design 588.5 *final intention*
overall length 269.4 *length*
overall picture 164.7 *global view*
overall plan 592.1 *plan*
overalls 295.9 **trousers**

overambition 642.9 *overactivity*
overambitious 597, 357.13 *exaggerated*, 780.4 *rash*
overambitiously 597.9 *enterprisingly*
overambitiousness 805.3 *conceit*
over and above 130.10 *additionally*, 610.8 *excessively*
over and done with 3.18 *in the past*, 157.21 *ended*, 200.18 *over*
over and over 183.23 *repeatedly*, 212.1 *frequently*
over and over again 183.23, 426.19 *repeatedly*
overappreciative 851.18 *approving*
overarch 275.15 *be high*, 279.7 *top*, 293.26 *overlie*
overarching 293.1 *covering*
overarm 27.13 *bowling*
overattentive 808.7 *sycophantic*
overawe 233.10 *be a prevailing influence*, 849.21 *command respect*
overbalance 123.1 *inequality*, 123.5 *be unequal*, 360.11 *trip*, 369.8 *weighing down*, 369.12 *be heavy*
overbalanced 123.3 *unequal*, 369.3 *ponderous*
overbear 233.10 *be a prevailing influence*
overbearance 688.1 *authority*
overbearing 688.12 *authoritative*, 690.8 *severe*, 805.16 *oppressive*
overbid 357.3 *exceed*, 357.4 *exaggerate*, 737.3 *bargain*
overblouse 295.8 *shirt*
overblown 207.13 *middle-aged*
over-blunt 818.5 *discourteous*
overbridge 327.9 *bridge*
overburden 369.14 *make heavy*, 610.4 *be excessive*, 618.14 *illtreat*, 650.6 *fatigue*, 687.11 *cause adversity*
overburdened 369.3 *ponderous*, 610.6 *excessive*, 661.14 *blocked*
overburdening 369.8 *weighing down*
overbusy 642.21 *meddling*
overcall one's hand 357.4 *exaggerate*
overcast 830, 55.49 *cloudy*, 440.8 *dark*, 441.5 *dim*, 448.3 *dull*
overcast sky 55.19 *cloud cover*
overcaution 779.1 *cowardice*, 781.1 *caution*
overcautious 781.4 *cautious*
overcautiously 781.7 *cautiously*
overcautiousness 781.1 *caution*
overcharge 753, 61.28 *cathexis*, 494.4 *overestimate*, 610.4 *be excessive*, 750.9 *settle accounts*, 751.3 *fee*, 753.2 *unfair price*
overcharged 610.6 *excessive*, 753.7 *dear*
overcharger 753
overcharging 753.2 *unfair price*, 753.7 *dear*
overclever 809.11 *cocky*
overclouded 55.49 *cloudy*
overcoat 295.12 *coat*, 408.3 *heater*
overcolour 541.7 *exaggerate*
overcoloured 541.12 *exaggerated*
overcolouring 541.1 *exaggeration*
overcome 126.8 *be superior*, 233.10 *be a prevailing influence*, 670.9 *attack successfully*, 679.38 *conquer*, 682.11 *overmaster*, 696.14 *master*, 701.7 *defeat*, 759.12 *sensitive*
overcome difficulties 682.7 *overcome obstacles*
overcome obstacles 682
overcoming 701.2 *domination*, 701.10 *dominating*
overcommend 853.8 *flatter*
overcommendation 853.1 *flattery*
overcommunicative 528.16 *informative*
overcompensate 123.5 *be unequal*, 125.4 *compensate*, 541.7 *exaggerate*

overcompensated 125.7 *compensated*, 541.12 *exaggerated*
overcompensation 61.19 *defence mechanism*, 123.1 *inequality*, 125.1 *compensation*, 541.1 *exaggeration*
overcompressed 551.2 *obscure*
overcompression 551.1 *obscurity*
overconfidence 490.10 *conviction*, 494.1 *overestimation*, 780.1 *rashness*, 805.3 *conceit*
overconfident 303.9 *arrogant*, 490.2 *convinced*, 494.5 *overestimating*, 780.4 *rash*
overconfidently 494.7 *overoptimistically*, 780.6 *rashly*
overconfident person 490.11 *opinionist*
overcooked 45.56 *culinary*
overcritical 659.14 *troublesome*, 852.28 *fault-finding*
overcriticalness 852.6 *fault-finding*
overcrop 607.1 *waste*, 609.7 *make insufficient*
overcropping 601.2 *misuse*
overcrossing 327.9 *bridge*, 356.5 *crossing point*
overcrowd 181
overcrowded 181.10 *crowded*, 327.15 *accessible*
overdaring 633.5 *danger*
over-decorated 792.8 *decorated*
overdelicate 876.10 *moralistic*
overdevelop 261.5 *make bigger*, 261.6 *become bigger*
overdeveloped 261.7 *bigger*
overdevelopment 261.1 *growth*
overdevout 7.15 *religious*
overdiversification 642.9 *overactivity*
overdo 144.4 *complete*, 357.4 *exaggerate*, 540.24 *mask*, 541.7 *exaggerate*, 541.9 *be extravagant*, 610.4 *be excessive*, 870.11 *overindulge*
overdoing 541.1 *exaggeration*, 870.3 *overindulgence*
overdoing it 610, 525.2 *misinterpretation*, 541.3 *extravagance*, 644.4 *exertion*, 650.7 *fatigue*
overdo it 541.9 *be extravagant*, 608.4 *suffice*, 642.15 *try*, 644.6 *work*, 650.5 *be fatigued*, 853.8 *flatter*
overdone 357.13 *exaggerated*, 378.3 *hard*, 540.35 *disguised*, 541.12 *exaggerated*, 541.14 *extravagant*, 594.20 *developed*, 610.6 *excessive*, 620.2 *incomplete*
overdose 610.2 *overdoing it*, 610.4 *be excessive*, 631.11 *intoxicant*
overdose of sleeping pills 398.7 *suicide*
overdraft 602.4 *financial resources*, 722.2 *financial loss*, 733.5 *loan*, 744.1 *credit*, 745.1 *debt*, 745.5 *amount owing*, 747.5 *insolvency*
overdramatization 548.1 *misrepresentation*
overdramatize 548.4 *misrepresent*
overdraw 541.7 *exaggerate*, 548.4 *misrepresent*, 722.10 *have a financial loss*, 744.9 *acquire credit*, 745.7 *be in debt*, 757.8 *overspend*
overdrawing 541.1 *exaggeration*
overdrawn 541.12 *exaggerated*, 722.17 *unprofitable*, 744.12 *charged*, 745.9 *in debt*
overdrawn account 747.5 *insolvency*
overdress 295.7 *frock*
overdressed 559.10 *ugly*
overdressing 295.2 *dressing*
overdrink 610.4 *be excessive*
overdrinking 610.2 *overdoing it*
overdrive 71.21 *miscellaneous motoring terms*, 235.1 *power*, 650.6 *fatigue*
overdue 193.6 *too late*, 209.9 *late*
overdue account 744.1 *credit*
overdue amount 745.5 *amount owing*

overdue payment 745.5 *amount owing*, 746.1 *payment*
overeager 572.2 *eager*
overeagerness 572.7 *eagerness*
overeat 350.22 *eat well*, 608.4 *suffice*, 610.4 *be excessive*, 872.5 *be greedy*
overeating 350.2 *appetite*, 610.2 *overdoing it*, 870.3 *overindulgence*, 872.1 *gluttony*, 872.6 *gluttonous*
overelaborate 549.8 *inelegant*, 557.5 *ornament*
overelaborated 620.2 *incomplete*
overelaboration 549.3 *inelegance*
overembellish 548.4 *misrepresent*
overemotional 759.12 *sensitive*
overemotionalism 475.2 *demonstrativeness*, 759.7 *emotionalism*
overemphasis 541.1 *exaggeration*, 548.1 *misrepresentation*
overemphasize 541.7 *exaggerate*, 548.4 *misrepresent*
overemphasized 541.12 *exaggerated*
overemphatic 541.12 *exaggerated*
overemphatically 541.16 *exaggeratedly*
overemployed 610.7 *superfluous*, 642.19 *busy*
overemployment 610.3 *superfluity*
overenlargement 128.1 *increase*
overenthuse 541.7 *exaggerate*
overenthusiasm 541.1 *exaggeration*, 572.7 *eagerness*, 780.1 *rashness*
overenthusiastic 494.5 *overestimating*, 541.12 *exaggerated*, 572.2 *eager*, 780.4 *rash*
overenthusiastically 494.7 *overoptimistically*, 541.16 *exaggeratedly*
overesteem 853.8 *flatter*
overestimate 494, 494, 357.4 *exaggerate*, 493.10 *misjudge*, 525.1 *misinterpret*, 541.7 *exaggerate*, 611.8 *make important*, 851.14 *praise*, 853.8 *flatter*
overestimated 494, 493.9 *misjudged*, 538.13 *untrue*, 541.12 *exaggerated*
overestimating 494
overestimation 494, 357.9 *excessiveness*, 493.1 *misjudgment*, 515.1 *disappointment*, 525.2 *misinterpretation*, 538.1 *untruth*, 541.1 *exaggeration*, 610.2 *overdoing it*, 851.3 *praise*
Overestimation 494
overexcited 403.7 *susceptible*, 610.6 *excessive*
overexert 650.5 *be fatigued*
overexertion 642.9 *overactivity*, 644.4 *exertion*, 650.7 *fatigue*
overexpand 610.4 *be excessive*
overexpansion 642.9 *overactivity*
overexpose 439.28 *bleach*, 541.7 *exaggerate*
overexposed 439.21 *light*, 445.7 *colourless*, 541.12 *exaggerated*
overexposed negative 445.3 *pen-and-ink sketch*
overexposed photograph 445.3 *pen-and-ink sketch*
overexposure 66.8 *composition*, 439.3 *lightening*, 445.3 *pen-and-ink sketch*, 541.1 *exaggeration*
overexpression 610.2 *overdoing it*
overextend 609.7 *make insufficient*, 610.4 *be excessive*
overextended 357.14 *surpassing*, 597.7 *overambitious*, 722.17 *unprofitable*
overextension 357.10 *expansionism*, 610.2 *overdoing it*, 642.9 *overactivity*
overfall 97.3 *wave*
overfatigued 650.1 *fatigued*
overfed 259.16 *fat*, 610.6 *excessive*
overfeed 610.4 *be excessive*
overfeeding 610.2 *overdoing it*
overfill 144.6 *fill*
overfilled 144.8 *full*
overfilling 144.2 *fullness*
overfish 247.10 *waste*, 601.1 *misuse*, 607.1 *waste*, 609.7

make insufficient, 614.8 *make useless*
overfishing 601.2 *misuse*
overflight 73.5 *flight*
overflow 96.2 *channel*, 96.6 *river flow*, 96.7 *flow*, 144.2 *fullness*, 144.5 *be complete*, 181.11 *crowd*, 347.7 *outlet*, 347.11 *run out*, 357.1 *overstep*, 360.13 *drip*, 553.5 *be diffuse*, 608.5 *about*, 610.1 *excess*, 610.4 *be excessive*
overflowed 389.24 *flooded*
overflowing 96.6 *river flow*, 144.2 *fullness*, 144.8 *full*, 357.6 *overstepping*, 357.11 *overrun*, 553.3 *diffuse*, 608.2 *plentiful*, 608.3 *filled*, 610.6 *excessive*, 755.3 *abundant*
overfly 356.11 *cross*
over-frank 818.5 *discourteous*
overfulfil 144.4 *complete*, 610.4 *be excessive*
overfulfilment 144.2 *fullness*, 357.9 *excessiveness*, 610.3 *superfluity*
overfull 144.8 *full*, 610.6 *excessive*
overglaze 44.3 *glaze*, 44.11 *make ceramics*
overglazed 44.10 *ceramic*
overglaze decoration 44.3 *glaze*
overglazing 44.10 *ceramic*
overgo 357.1 *overstep*
overgorged 872.6 *gluttonous*
overgorging 872.6 *gluttonous*
overgraze 247.10 *waste*, 601.1 *misuse*, 607.1 *waste*, 609.7 *make insufficient*
overgrazing 601.2 *misuse*
overground railway 72.1 *railway*
overgrow 83.21 *vegetate*, 261.6 *become bigger*, 357.1 *overstep*
overgrown 83.13 *plantlike*, 259.15 *big*, 261.7 *bigger*, 357.11 *overrun*
overgrowth 132.4 *surplus*, 259.3 *large scale*, 261.1 *growth*, 357.6 *overstepping*, 375.8 *rough ground*
overhand knot 74 Knots
overhang 34.5 *rock face*, 199.7 *be in the future*, 275.15 *be high*, 283.2 *projection*, 283.11 *project*, 293.26 *overlie*, 318.2 *projection*, 318.8 *protrude*
overhanging 34.8 *mountaineering*, 199.11 *future*, 275.9 *high*, 283.8 *projecting*
overhaste 642.3 *nimbleness*, 648.5 *hastiness*, 780.1 *rashness*
overhastily 208.20 *prematurely*, 648.7 *rashly*
overhasty 193.5 *too early*, 208.16 *premature*, 648.3 *hasty*, 780.4 *rash*
overhaul 329.6 *accelerate*, 629.1 *repair*, 629.3 *restore*, 629.8 *repair*
overhauling 629.8 *repair*
overhead 40.14 *forehand*, 275.19 *high*, 293.7 *overhead covering*
overhead beam 293.7 *overhead covering*
overhead covering 293
overhead locker 258.10 *cart*
overhead projector 66.12 *development*
overheads 748.5 *expense*, 751.6 *business costs*
overhead smash 40.2 *tennis strokes*
overhead wire 64.33 *power distribution*
overhear 420.15 *hear*, 528.15 *be informed*
overheat 683.9 *malfunction*
overheated 408.9 *hot*, 626.5 *unhygienic*
overheating 408.1 *heat*
overhot 55.51 *hot*
overindulge 870, 350.22 *eat well*, 357.4 *exaggerate*, 541.9 *be extravagant*, 610.4 *be excessive*, 872.5 *be greedy*
overindulgence 870, 350.2 *appetite*, 357.9 *excessiveness*, 541.3 *extravagance*, 610.2 *overdoing it*, 872.1 *gluttony*

overindulgent 870, 357.13 *exaggerated*, 541.14 *extravagant*, 708.8 *permitting*, 872.6 *gluttonous*
overindulgently 357.16 *excessively*
overindulge oneself 610.4 *be excessive*
overindulging 872.1 *gluttony*
overjolt 610.2 *overdoing it*, 610.4 *be excessive*
overjoyed 762.4 *happy*
overjump 126.8 *be superior*, 357.1 *overstep*
overkeen 572.2 *eager*
overkill 123.1 *inequality*, 541.1 *exaggeration*, 541.7 *exaggerate*, 610.3 *superfluity*
overladen 369.2 *loaded*, 369.3 *ponderous*
overlaid 293.2 *projection*
overlap 266.1, 266.10 *layer*, 293.26 *overlie*, 320.1, 320.7 *fold*, 407.6 *contiguity*, 407.12 *abut*, 610.3 *superfluity*, 610.4 *be excessive*
overlap integral 57.12 *valence*
overlapped 266.8 *coated*
overlapping 266.8 *coated*, 293.1 *covering*, 407.9 *touching*
overlarge 259.15 *big*
overlaud 853.8 *flatter*
overlaudation 853.1 *flattery*
overlay 130.6 *add*, 266.3 *coat*, 266.10 *layer*, 293.24 *coat*, 376.11 *smooth*, 531.8 *conceal*, 557.5 *ornament*
overlayer 266.1 *layer*
overlaying 266.8 *coated*, 293.1, 293.38 *covering*
overleaf 111.6 *oppositely*
overleap 126.8 *be superior*, 357.1 *overstep*
overlie 293, 283.2 *projection*, 283.11 *project*, 289.11 *be exterior*
overload 123.1 *inequality*, 130.6 *add*, 132.4 *surplus*, 369.6 *displacement*, 369.14 *make heavy*, 557.5 *ornament*, 610.2 *overdoing it*, 610.4 *be excessive*, 650.6 *fatigue*, 661.6, 661.12 *burden*, 687.11 *cause adversity*
overloaded 123.3 *unequal*, 132.10 *surplus*, 144.8 *full*, 369.2 *loaded*, 369.3 *ponderous*, 557.4 *ornate*, 597.7 *overambitious*, 610.6 *excessive*, 661.14 *blocked*
overloading 369.6 *displacement*
overlong 269.1 *long*, 357.14 *surpassing*, 788.4 *boring*
overlook 95.9 *tower*, 126.8 *be superior*, 275.15 *be high*, 436.16 *be blind to*, 468.12 *be inattentive*, 504.19 *make a mistake*, 512.13 *forget*, 600.5 *not use*, 612.12 *think unimportant*, 673.3 *submit*, 720.7 *not observe*, 839.11 *condone*
overlooked 839, 612.2 *obscure*, 720.11 *nonobservant*
overlooking 275.9 *high*, 720.1 *nonobservance*, 720.11 *nonobservant*, 839.2 *forgivingness*
overlord 696.1 *master*, 723.6 *lord*
overlordship 12.3 *governance*
overly 610.8 *excessively*
overlying 293.38 *covering*
overman 181.12 *overcrowd*
overmanned 181.10 *crowded*, 610.7 *superfluous*
overmanning 610.3 *superfluity*
overmaster 682, 233.10 *be a prevailing influence*, 237.7 *be strong*, 670.9 *attack successfully*
overmature 594.20 *developed*
overmeasure 610.2 *overdoing it*
overmighty 16.62 *above the law*
overmodest 876.10 *moralistic*
overmodesty 876.4 *self-righteousness*
overmuch 610.6 *excessive*, 610.8 *excessively*
over my dead body 500.11 *no*, 536.11 *never*, 711.12 *no*
overnight 205.7 *evening*

overnight bag 258.8 *bag*, 258.9 *baggage*
overnight sensation 682.1 *success*
over one's head 523.4 *difficult*
over one's head in debt 745.9 *in debt*, 747.13 *nonpaying*
overoptimism 494.1 *overestimation*, 610.2 *overdoing it*
overoptimistic 494.5 *overestimating*
overoptimistically 494
overorthodoxy 7.2 *religiousness*
overpaint 50.19 *paint*
overpainting 50.2 *painting*
overpass 63.21 *bridge*, 327.3 *road*, 327.9 *bridge*, 356.5 *crossing point*, 357.1 *overstep*
overpassing 357.6 *overstepping*
overpay 753
overpayment 610.2 *overdoing it*, 846.6 *excessiveness*
overpiety 7.2 *religiousness*
overplay 51.33 *overact*, 126.8 *be superior*, 357.4 *exaggerate*, 610.4 *be excessive*
overplayed 610.6 *excessive*
overplaying 357.9 *excessiveness*
overplus 610.3 *superfluity*
overpolite 610.6 *excessive*
overpoliteness 610.2 *overdoing it*
overpopulate 181.12 *overcrowd*, 246.6 *be fertile*, 610.4 *be excessive*
overpopulated 181.10 *crowded*, 610.6 *excessive*
overpopulation 610.1 *excess*
overpossessive 841.4 *jealous*
overpotential 57.19 *electrochemistry*
overpower 236, 237.7 *be strong*, 670.9 *attack successfully*, 682.11 *overmaster*, 696.14 *master*, 701.7 *defeat*
overpowering 237.10 *potent*, 419.3 *stinking*, 670.23 *attacking*, 701.2 *domination*, 701.10 *dominating*
overpraise 494.4 *overestimate*, 525.1 *misinterpret*, 541.4 *bombast*, 541.10 *boast*, 610.2 *overdoing it*, 610.4 *be excessive*, 851.3, 851.14 *praise*, 853.1 *flattery*, 853.8 *flatter*
overpraised 494.6 *overestimated*, 541.12 *exaggerated*
overpraising 851.18 *approving*
over-preciseness 813.2 *formalism*
overprice 494.4 *overestimate*, 753.10 *overcharge*
overpriced 494.6 *overestimated*, 753.7 *dear*, 757.3 *costly*
overpricing 753.2 *unfair price*
overprint 544.10 *identify*, 546.1 *obliterate*
overprinted 531.14 *concealed*
overprinting 546.3 *obliteration*
overprize 494.4 *overestimate*
overproduce 610.4 *be excessive*
overproduction 607.3 *waste*
overproductiveness 246.2 *productiveness*
overproof 874.6 *intoxicating*
overproud 809.8 *vain*
overproudness 805.3 *conceit*, 809.1 *vanity*
overqualified 501.9 *literate*
overrate 128.5 *make bigger*, 357.4 *exaggerate*, 493.10 *misjudge*, 494.4 *overestimate*, 525.1 *misinterpret*, 532.16 *publicize*, 541.10 *boast*, 611.8 *make important*
overrated 357.13 *exaggerated*, 493.9 *misjudged*, 494.6 *overestimated*, 541.12 *exaggerated*
overrating 357.9 *excessiveness*, 494.1 *overestimation*, 541.4 *bombast*
overreach 357.1 *overstep*, 471.18 *aim*, 657.5 *be cunning*
overreaching 357.12 *excessive*
overreact 541.7 *exaggerate*, 601.1 *misuse*
overreaction 541.1 *exaggeration*
over-refinement 813.2 *formalism*
overreligious 7.15 *religious*

over-rev 33.6 *motor racing terms*, 33.10 *be on the track*
override 126.8 *be superior*, 228.10 *manipulate*, 233.10 *be a prevailing influence*, 682.11 *overmaster*
overrider 71 Motor Vehicle Parts
overriding 126.13 *dominant*, 611.5 *important*, 695.9 *compelling*
overrighteous 7.15 *religious*
overripe 374.4 *compressible*, 393.11 *juicy*, 415.6 *unpalatable*, 594.20 *developed*, 620.1 *imperfect*
overripen 374.13 *soften*
overripeness 202.10 *staleness*, 393.4 *pulpiness*, 620.5 *imperfection*
overrule 704.6 *cancel*
overruled verdict 16.4 *bad law*
overruling 126.13 *dominant*, 611.5 *important*, 688.12 *authoritative*
overrun 357, 83.21 *vegetate*, 96.7 *flow*, 144.6 *fill*, 144.8 *full*, 181.10 *crowded*, 181.12 *overcrowd*, 253.11 *be present*, 357.1 *overstep*, 357.5 *transgress*, 357.6 *overstepping*, 628.5 *hurt*, 670.9 *attack successfully*, 734.7 *take*
overrun brake 71 Motor Vehicle Parts
overrunning 96.6 *river flow*, 357.6 *overstepping*, 670.14 *siege*, 682.2 *victory*
oversatisfy 610.4 *be excessive*
oversea 97.11 *nautically*, 149.19 *abroad*
overseas 97.11 *nautically*, 104.10 *foreign*, 104.18 *extraneously*, 149.19 *abroad*, 263.8 *distant*, 263.10 *distantly*
overseas call 534.10 *telephone call*
overseas mail 534.2 *postal communication*
overseas telegram 534.8 *data transmission*
oversee 166.16 *direct*, 435.15 *watch*, 653.1 *manage*
overseer 15.6 *employer*, 435.11 *observer*, 653.13 *director*, 653.15 *manager*
oversell 541.10 *boast*, 610.4 *be excessive*, 753.10 *overcharge*
overselling 541.1 *exaggeration*
oversensitive 760, 403.7 *susceptible*, 829.4 *irascible*
oversensitively 760
oversensitive person 760
oversensitivity 760, 403.2 *ability to sense*
overset 362.3 *bring down*, 362.12 *downthrow*, 362.22 *overthrown*
oversexed 877.14 *lecherous*
overshadow 95.9 *tower*, 126.8 *be superior*, 275.15 *be high*, 293.26 *overlie*, 440.14 *make dark*
overshadowing 275.9 *high*, 293.1 *covering*, 441.3 *dimming*
overshift 19.10 *defence*, 19.16 *play defence*
overshoes 295.19 *footwear*
overshoot 73.5 *flight*, 123.5 *be unequal*, 541.9 *be extravagant*, 656.7 *be clumsy*
overshooting 541.3 *extravagance*
overshot 123.3 *unequal*, 541.14 *extravagant*
overshy 810.11 *shy*
oversight 468.5 *inattentive act*, 504.9 *trivial error*, 685.1 *noncompletion*, 720.1 *nonobservance*
oversize 259.3 *large scale*
oversized 248.13 *spacious*, 259.15 *big*
overskirt 295.6 *skirt*
oversleep 209.6 *be late*
oversman 41.11 *skier*
oversold 541.12 *exaggerated*
oversoul 8.3 *God*
overspecialization 493.3 *injustice*
overspecialized 659.12 *problematic*

overspend 757, 541.9 *be extravagant*, 607.1 *waste*, 610.4 *be excessive*, 722.10 *have a financial loss*, 745.7 *be in debt*, 748.1 *expend*, 753.11 *overpay*
overspender 722.6 *loser*
overspending 541.3 *extravagance*, 541.14 *extravagant*, 607.3 *waste*, 722.2 *financial loss*
overspent 722.17 *unprofitable*
overspill 610.1 *excess*, 610.4 *be excessive*
overspread 357.1 *overstep*, 357.11 *overrun*
overspreading 357.6 *overstepping*
overstaff 181.12 *overcrowd*
overstaffed 181.10 *crowded*, 610.7 *superfluous*
overstate 494.4 *overestimate*, 535.22 *emphasize*, 540.22 *falsify*, 541.7 *exaggerate*, 557.5 *ornament*
overstated 444.12 *gaudy*, 535.15 *emphasized*, 538.13 *untrue*, 541.12 *exaggerated*, 557.4 *ornate*
overstatement 494.1 *overestimation*, 535.7 *emphasis*, 538.1 *untruth*, 540.9 *falsification*, 541.1 *exaggeration*, 557.2 *affectation*
oversteer 71.21 *miscellaneous motoring terms*
overstep 357, 126.8 *be superior*, 610.4 *be excessive*, 656.7 *be clumsy*, 846.15 *presume*
overstep oneself 471.18 *aim*
overstepped 541.14 *extravagant*
overstepping 357, 16.38 *lawbreaking*, 336.15 *improvement*, 670.14 *siege*
Overstepping 357
overstepping the mark 541.3 *extravagance*
overstep the mark 357.1 *overstep*, 541.9 *be extravagant*, 610.4 *be excessive*, 846.15 *presume*
overstock 610.4 *be excessive*
overstrain 650.6 *fatigue*
overstrained 650.1 *fatigued*
overstress 541.1 *exaggeration*, 541.7 *exaggerate*
overstressed 541.12 *exaggerated*
overstretched 610.6 *excessive*
overstretching oneself 610.2 *overdoing it*
overstrict 7.15 *religious*
overstride 357.1 *overstep*
oversubscribe 610.4 *be excessive*
oversubtlety 474.4 *quibbling*
oversupplied 754.9 *cheap*
oversupply 132.4 *surplus*, 610.3 *superfluity*, 642.9 *overactivity*, 754.2 *declining prices*
oversupply of food 350.9 *plenty*
overswarm 253.11 *be present*
overt 312.5 *honourable*, 437.1 *visible*, 526.14 *manifest*
overt act 640.2 *deed*
overtake 329.6 *accelerate*, 336.9 *maintain progress*, 356.8 *pass*, 357.3 *exceed*, 633.10 *endanger*, 648.2 *make haste*, 721.10 *augment*
overtaken 357.14 *surpassing*
overtaking 71.21 *miscellaneous motoring terms*, 329.3 *accelerating*, 329.9 *acceleration*, 336.15 *improvement*, 356.12 *passing*, 357.6 *overstepping*, 721.2 *augmentation*
overtask 601.1 *misuse*, 650.6 *fatigue*
overtax 369.14 *make heavy*, 601.1 *misuse*, 609.7 *make insufficient*, 650.6 *fatigue*, 734.8 *take back*
overtaxed 369.3 *ponderous*
overtaxing 369.3 *ponderous*, 369.8 *weighing down*
overtax one's strength 650.5 *be fatigued*
overtechnical 659.12 *problematic*
over the border 357.17 *ahead*
over the counter 727.16 *disposably*
over-the-counter drug 62.3 *drug*

over-the-counter market 740.3 *sellers' market*
over-the-counter medication 630.2 *medicine*
over the hill 202.11 *old*, 614.1 *useless*
over the hills and far away 263.10 *distantly*, 357.17 *ahead*, 638.9 *fugitively*
over the horizon 438.1 *invisible*
over-the-knee socks 295.20 *legwear*
over the moon 610.6 *excessive*, 762.4 *happy*
over-the-rim shot 23.4 *playing terms*
over the top 144.10 *fully*, 610.6 *excessive*, 759.13 *passionate*, 811.21 *blatant*
over-the-top 357.13 *exaggerated*, 780.4 *rash*
over the water 97.11 *nautically*
over the way 111.6 *oppositely*
overthrow 27.10 *score*, 244.1 *destruction*, 244.8 *destroy*, 244.9 *demolish*, 252.3 *replacement*, 252.16 *replace*, 362.3 *bring down*, 362.12 *downthrow*, 476.1 *refutation*, 476.8 *refute*, 628.4 *impair*, 640.2 *deed*, 656.7 *be clumsy*, 656.9 *bungling*, 676.12 *go to war*, 682.11 *overmaster*, 688.20 *take authority*, 689.1 *anarchy*, 689.4 *be anarchic*, 693.16 *be subversive*
overthrowing 688.5 *acquisition of power*
overthrown 362, 252.10 *replaced*, 683.11 *defeated*
overtime 15.9 *negotiated*, 19.5 *game time*, 23.1 *basketball*, 187.4 *period of activity*, 644.2 *task*
overtime ban 15.4 *industrial dispute*
overtime pay 746.3 *pay*, 878.4 *reward for service*
overtime victory 682.2 *victory*
overtime work 15.2 *industrial negotiations*
overtired 628.12 *deteriorated*, 650.1 *fatigued*
overtiredness 650.7 *fatigue*
overtly 526.16 *manifestly*, 640.7 *actively*
overtness 437.3 *visibility*
overtone 49.16 *musical note*, 49.21 *tone*, 56.20 *musical note*, 297.3 *atmosphere*
overtop 95.9 *tower*, 123.5 *be unequal*, 126.8 *be superior*, 275.15 *be high*, 279.7 *top*, 617.9 *be worthy*
overtopping 126.12 *superior*, 275.9 *high*
overture 49.4 *opera*, 51.6 *scene*, 154.5 *preface*, 710.2 *tentative offer*
overturn 74.10 *sail*, 244.8 *destroy*, 244.9 *demolish*, 288.7 *invert*, 360.11 *trip*, 362.3 *bring down*, 362.12 *downthrow*, 476.8 *refute*, 682.11 *overmaster*
overturned 362.22 *overthrown*
overturned conviction 638.1 *escape*
overturned fold 54.20 *earth movement*
overturned verdict 16.4 *bad law*
overturning 244.1 *destruction*, 287.1 *inversion*, 360.4 *fall*, 476.7 *refuting*
overuse 601.1, 601.2 *misuse*
overused 164.22 *commonplace*
overvaluation 493.1 *misjudgment*, 494.1 *overestimation*, 541.1 *exaggeration*
overvalue 493.10 *misjudge*, 494.4 *overestimate*, 541.7 *exaggerate*
overvalued 493.9 *misjudged*, 494.6 *overestimated*, 541.12 *exaggerated*
overview 692, 142.3 *whole situation*, 164.7 *global view*, 435.7 *view*, 562.1 *summary*, 653.3 *management*

overwarm 55.51 *hot*
overween 805.28 *disdain*
overweening 805.16 *oppressive*, 807.3 *audacity*, 807.16 *arrogant*
overweening pride 494.1 *overestimation*, 805.3 *conceit*
overweigh 369.12 *be heavy*, 369.14 *make heavy*
overweighed 369.2 *loaded*
overweight 123.1 *inequality*, 123.3 *unequal*, 259.5 *fatness*, 259.16 *fat*, 261.7 *bigger*, 273.1 *thick*, 315.10 *well-rounded*, 369.1 *heavy*, 369.7 *weighing*, 610.2 *overdoing it*
overweighted 369.2 *loaded*
overweighting 369.6 *displacement*
overwhelm 144.6 *fill*, 181.12 *overcrowd*, 237.7 *be strong*, 244.12 *consume*, 610.4 *be excessive*, 670.9 *attack successfully*, 682.10 *defeat heavily*, 849.21 *command respect*
overwhelmed 144.8 *full*, 610.6 *excessive*, 759.12 *sensitive*
overwhelming 237.10 *potent*, 241.6 *violent*, 244.14 *destructive*, 610.6 *excessive*, 670.23 *attacking*, 759.14 *emotive*, 786.8 *wonderful*
overwinter 83.22 *be dormant*, 203.6 *spend the season*
overwise 809.13 *boastful*
over with 323.17 *finally*
overwork 599.1 *use*, 601.1 *misuse*, 607.1, 607.3 *waste*, 609.7 *make insufficient*, 614.8 *make useless*, 642.15 *try*, 644.4 *exertion*, 644.6 *work*, 650.5 *be fatigued*, 650.6, 650.7 *fatigue*
overworked 164.22 *commonplace*, 642.19 *busy*, 650.1 *fatigued*
overwrite 541.7 *exaggerate*, 549.9 *style*
overwriting 541.1 *exaggeration*
overwritten 541.12 *exaggerated*
overwrought 594.20 *developed*, 620.2 *incomplete*, 642.18 *active*, 650.1 *fatigued*, 759.12 *sensitive*
overzealous 572.2 *eager*, 780.4 *rash*
overzealousness 572.7 *eagerness*
Ovid 48 *Poets*
ovine 77.33 *ungulate*
oviparous 245.16 *reproductive*
ovipositor 245.8 *organs of reproduction*
ovoid 52.83 *spherical*, 313.5 *circular*, 315.9 *round*
ovolo 43 Architectural Decoration
ovule 83.9 *seed*, 84.3 *flower part*
ovum 245.8 *organs of reproduction*
ow 431.6 *cry of pain*
owe 132.8 *leave*, 745.7 *be in debt*
owe a grudge 820.11 *be hostile*
owe allegiance 12.13 *be governed*
owed 845, 132.10 *surplus*, 746.17 *payable*
owe everything to 227.7 *follow from*
owe fealty 12.13 *be governed*
owe loyalty 12.13 *be governed*
owe loyalty to 701.8 *be subject to*
owe money 745.7 *be in debt*
Owen 48 *Poets*
owe nothing to 108.11 *be unconcerned*
Owens 18 Sporting Personalities
owe obedience 12.13 *be governed*
ower 733.6 *borrower*
owing 615.1 *convenient*, 743.2 *insolvent*, 745.1 *debt*, 745.9 *in debt*, 746.17 *payable*, 845.12 *owed*
owing a favour 837.4 *grateful*
owing nothing 746.16 *paid*
owing nothing to 108.6 *unrelated*
owing to 227.10 *caused*
owl 78 Birds, 78.5 *bird of prey*, 205.5 *night thing*, 517.7 *bad-luck sign*
owlet 78.12 *young bird*
owlet frogmouth 78 Birds

owlet moth 82 Insects
owlhead 32.1 *horse*
owlish 78.23 *avian*
owl-like 78.23 *avian*
Owl Nebula 53 Nebulae
owls 161 Collective Names by Animal
own 530.8 *admit*, 723.7 *possess*
own account 698.1 *freedom*
own assets 725.9 *own property*
own authority 698.3 *independence*
own back yard 256.2 *environment*
owned 723.9 *possessed*
owned by 723.9 *possessed*
owned property 723.4 *possession*
owner 32.15 *horse person*, 599.8 *user*, 696.1 *master*, 723.5 *possessor*, 725.7 *property man*, 804.4 *titleholder*, 845.7 *beneficiary*
owner-occupier 255.3 *householder*, 723.5 *possessor*
ownership 723.1 *possession*
ownership papers 545.2 *certificate*
own free will 698.1 *freedom*
own goal 504.13 *sporting error*, 656.9 *bungling*
owning 723.1 *possession*, 723.8 *possessing*
own initiative 698.1 *freedom*
own personal effects 725.9 *own property*
own property 725
own responsibility 698.1 *freedom*
own stocks and shares 725.9 *own property*
own up 530.8, 535.20 *admit*
own volition 698.1 *freedom*
own way 698.3 *independence*
owzat 27.21 *how's that*
ox 77 Placental Mammals, 326.6 *beast of burden*, 401.16 *male animal*
oxacillin 62 Medication
oxalic 58 Common Fatty Acids
oxazepam 62 Medication
oxblood 450.1 *red*
oxbow lake 94.1 *lake*
Oxbridge 6.13 *university*
oxcart 71 Carriages and Carts
ox cheek 45.31 *offal*
oxeye daisy 84 Flowers and Flowering Plants
OXFAM 712.3 *solicitation*, 729.3 *offering*, 831.2, 833.5 *charity*
Oxford 93 Cities, 93.4 *British cities*
Oxford accent 5.26 *dialect*
Oxford bags 295.9 *trousers*
Oxford blue 454.1 *blue*
Oxford-Cambridge boat race 674.4 *race*
Oxford-Cambridge race 36.4 *rowing*
Oxford Down 68 Breeds of Sheep
Oxford English 5.6 *official language*
Oxford Movement 7 Christian Movements
Oxfords 295.19 *footwear*
Oxford Sandy-and-Black 68 Breeds of Pig
Oxfordshire 45 Cheeses, 92 Counties
oxidation 57 Types of Chemical Reaction
oxidimetric 268.16 *micrometric*
oxidimetry 268.2 *micrometry*
oxidization 628.9 *dilapidation*
oxidize 57.26 *react*
oxidoreductase 58.11 *enzyme*
oxime 57 Types of Compounds
oxlike 77.33 *ungulate*
oxlip 84 Flowers and Flowering Plants
Oxnard 93 Cities
oxolinic acid 62 Medication
oxpecker 78 Birds
oxprenolol 62 Medication
oxtail 45.31 *offal*
oxtail soup 45.13 *soup*
ox tongue 45.31 *offal*
Oxus 96.5 *other major rivers*
oxyacetylene burner 408.6 *fire*
oxychromatin 59.9 *cell nucleus*
oxygen 57 Chemical Elements, 58.15 *essential element*, 372.5

gas, 390.1 *air*, 396.3 *life requirements*, 651.6 *refresher*
oxygenate 388.26, 390.20 *aerate*
oxygenated 57.34 *elemental*
oxygenation 390.6 *ventilation*
oxygen depletion 631.9 *pollution*
oxygenic 388.24 *oxygenous*
oxygenization 390.6 *ventilation*
oxygenized 57.34 *elemental*
oxygenous 388
oxygen tank 34.4 *climbing equipment*
oxygen tent 630.14 *hospital*, 632.4 *safety device*
oxymesterone 62 Medication
oxymoron 117.2 *contradiction*
oxymoronic 117.8 *contradictory*
oxypertine 62 Medication
oxyphenbutazone 62 Medication
oxytetracycline 62 Medication
oxythiazine 62 Medication
oxytocin 58 Hormones
Oyomei 7 Non-Christian Religions
oyster 81 Molluscs, 45.19 *shellfish*, 448.4 *greyness*
oystercatcher 78 Birds, 78.3 *water bird*
oyster crab 74 Ships and Boats
oyster-like 81.19 *molluscan*
oyster loaf 45.11 *sandwich*
oysterman 90.6 *hunter*
oyster mushroom 89 Fungi
oyster pieces 47.9 *decorative woodwork*
oyster plant 45 Vegetables
oyster shell 293.14 *animal covering*
oysters Rockefeller 45.43 *US dish*
oyster-white 446.1 *white*
oysterwood marquetry 47.9 *decorative woodwork*
Oz 519.8 *dreamland*
OZ 875.6 *drug*
Ozark 93 Cities
ozocerite 54 Minerals
ozone 57 Chemical Elements, 390.1 *air*, 390.5 *open air*
ozone depletion 631.9 *pollution*
ozone-friendly 388.24 *oxygenous*, 453.7 *environmental*
ozone layer 54.47 *radiation belt*, 55.8 *atmosphere*, 390.3 *atmospheric layers*
ozonic 388.24 *oxygenous*
ozonide 57 Types of Compounds
ozonize 57.26 *react*
ozonolysis 57 Types of Chemical Reaction
ozonosphere 54.47 *radiation belt*, 55.8 *atmosphere*
ozonous 388.24 *oxygenous*

P

p 49 Musical Terms
PA 423.4 *sound maker*
Pablum 350.7 *food*
pabulum 350.7 *food*
paca 77 Placental Mammals
pace 27.8 *delivery*, 43.9 *miscellaneous architectural features*, 324.12 *gait*, 328.10 *slow motion*
pace bowler 27.4 *team*
pacemaker 32.7 *horseracing*, 222.3 *substitute thing*, 653.14 *leader*
pace off 268.10 *measure*
pacer 32.2 *thoroughbred*
pacesetter 653.14 *leader*
pacey 27.13 *bowling*
pachyderm 77, 404.5 *unfeeling person*
pachydermatous 77, 273.1 *thick*
pacifiable 677.6 *pacificatory*
pacific 4.18 *detached*, 240.5 *inert*, 242.6 *moderate*, 325.6 *quiescent*, 675.7 *peaceful*
Pacific 97 Oceans and Seas
pacifically 677, 675.8 *peacefully*
pacification 677, 675.1 *peace*,

678.2 *mediation*, 839.3 *absolution*, 840.1 *atonement*
Pacification 677
pacificatory 677, 242.8 *moderating*, 678.6 *mediatory*
Pacific Daylight Time 185.9 *time zone*
Pacific Ocean 271.5 *broad thing*
Pacific salmon 20.4 American game fish, 45.17 *freshwater fish*
Pacific Standard Time 185.9 *time zone*
pacified 677.6 *pacificatory*, 839.6 *forgiven*
pacifier 242.2 *moderator*, 675.3, 677.3 *pacifist*, 678.3 *mediator*
pacifism 675.1 *peace*
pacifist 675, 677, 4.11 *follower of a doctrine*, 4.14 *of a philosophy*, 669.5 *resister*, 675.7 *peaceful*
pacify 150, 677, 242.4 *moderate*, 325.9 *make motionless*, 376.13 *smooth over*, 586.15 *persuade*, 675.6 *make peace*, 678.1 *mediate*, 710.14 *offer reparation*, 710.15 *offer worship*, 765.9 *comfort*, 767.9 *relieve*, 840.5 *atone*
pacifying 677.1 *pacification*, 677.6 *pacificatory*, 765.5 *satisfying*, 839.4 *forgiving*, 840.4 *atoning*
pack 77 Placental Mammals, 161 Collective Names for Birds and Animals, 71, 42.3 *card game terms*, 70.5 *transportable*, 77.21 *assemblage of mammals*, 120.2 *certain amount*, 120.8 *quantify*, 135.8 *unite*, 142.5 *unit*, 144.6 *fill*, 161.11 *group*, 161.23 *flock*, 161.40 *crowd*, 181.4 *throng*, 181.11 *crowd*, 257.7 *stuff*, 258.5 *packet*, 258.21 *put in a container*, 292.4 *fill*, 293.25 *wrap*, 326.10 *transferred thing*, 326.12 *transport*, 371.9 *make dense*, 540.21 *be fraudulent*, 590.6 *hunter*, 594.4 *prepare for action*, 605.6 *store*
package 43.18 *be an architect*, 65.8 *software*, 146.1 *inclusion*, 161.27 *bundle*, 161.38 *group*, 257.6 *contain*, 258.21 *put in a container*, 292.4 *fill*, 293.25 *wrap*
packaged 161.49 *grouped*, 293.37 *protected*
package deal 146.1 *inclusion*
packaged food 350.7 *food*
packager 293.17 *coverer*
packaging 258.5 *packet*, 292.2 *filling*, 293.4 *wrapping*, 437.6 *visible thing*, 637.1 *preservation*
pack a jury 582.2 *premeditate*
pack animal 71.9 *animal transport*, 76.3 *domesticated animal*, 326.6 *beast of burden*
pack a punch 237.7 *be strong*
pack a scrum 35.5 *play rugby*
pack away 600.6 *stop using*, 605.6 *store*
packed 120.6 *quantitative*, 144.8 *full*, 160.50, 181.10 *crowded*, 257.11 *loaded*, 258.20 *containing*, 273.2 *dense*, 323.13 *stopped*, 582.4 *deliberate*, 605.7 *stored*
packed house 51.31 *theatregoer*
packed jury 493.3 *injustice*, 540.8 *fraud*, 582.6 *premeditation*
packed like sardines 144.8 *full*
packed like sardines in a can 181.10 *crowded*
packed lunch 350.12 *meal*
packed with meaning 520.6 *meaningful*
packer 594.15 *preparer*, 646.1 *worker*
packet 74 Ships and Boats, 258, 65.17 *computing term*, 120.2 *certain amount*, 413.7 *tobacco*, 534.3 *correspondence*, 605.1 *store*, 742.6 *money*
packet of money 741.3 *fortune*

packet switching 65.14 *data transfer*
packhorse 32.1 *horse,* 71.9 *animal transport,* 326.6 *beast of burden*
pack ice 54.39 *iceberg,* 409.5 *ice*
pack in 144.6 *fill,* 257.7 *stuff,* 346.12 *flood in,* 354.3 *impact*
packing 257.4 *stuffing,* 258.20 *containing,* 292.2 *filling,* 637.1 *preservation*
packing box 258.6 *box*
packing case 605.4 *storage*
pack it in 160.12 *discontinue,* 218.12 *stop*
pack-lunch 350.12 *meal*
pack mule 326.6 *beast of burden*
pack off 341.2 *eject,* 349.6 *send away*
pack of lies 538.3 *lying*
pack of troubles 687.1 *adversity*
pack up 650.5 *be fatigued*
pact 116.3 *arrangement,* 667.2, 715.1 *contract*
pad 27, 27.17 *bat,* 31.3 *ice hockey,* 32.4 *saddle horse,* 237.8 *strengthen,* 256.1 *habitat,* 257.7 *stuff,* 261.5 *make bigger,* 273.8 *fatten,* 292.4 *fill,* 374.11 *soft thing,* 374.13 *soften,* 408.14 *be hot,* 424.1 *faintness,* 553.5 *be diffuse,* 671.19 *buffer*
Padarn 94 *Lakes*
padded 28.6 *fencing,* 130.9 *extra,* 257.11 *loaded,* 261.7 *bigger,* 273.1 *thick,* 374.4 *compressible,* 408.13 *heated,* 553.3 *diffuse*
padded cell 510.8 *mental hospital,* 634.2 *shelter*
padded glove 31.3 *ice hockey*
padded gloves 28.2 *fencing equipment*
padded out 553.3 *diffuse*
padded text 610.3 *superfluity*
padding 130.3 *additional item,* 183.2 *iteration,* 257.4 *stuffing,* 261.1 *growth,* 261.4 *enlarger,* 273.5 *thickness,* 292.2 *filling,* 374.11 *soft thing,* 553.1 *diffuseness*
Paddington 93.5 *London*
paddle 36.6 *canoeing,* 36.16 *row,* 36.21 *avast,* 39.1 *swimming,* 366.14 *agitator,* 366.22 *agitate,* 389.33 *sprinkle,* 879.3 *hit*
paddle a canoe 36.17 *canoe*
paddle a kayak 36.17 *canoe*
paddle boat 74 *Ships and Boats*
paddled 36.12 *canoeing*
paddlefish 80 *Fishes*
paddle one's own canoe 174.18 *be one,* 652.11 *conduct oneself,* 698.16 *be independent*
paddler 74.8 *boatman*
paddle wheel 74 *Parts of a Ship,* 338.11 *propeller,* 364.6 *rotator*
paddleworm 81 *Worms*
paddling 161 *Collective Names for Birds and Animals,* 36.4, 36.11 *rowing,* 36.12 *canoeing,* 39.1, 39.11 *swimming,* 330.12 *collision,* 879.12 *corporal punishment*
paddling canoe 36.6 *canoeing*
paddock 32.7 *horseracing,* 68.11 *farmland,* 79.7 *amphibian,* 301.2 *enclosed place,* 301.5 *enclose,* 323.4 *closed place*
paddock grazing 68.3 *livestock farming*
paddy 87 *Grasses,* 68.11 *farmland,* 828.4 *anger*
Paddy 91 *Names for Inhabitants*
paddy field 68.11 *farmland*
paddy wagon 71.17 *police car*
pademelon 77 *Marsupials*
Paderewski 49 *Musicians and Composers*
pad-lid 41.10 *curling*
padlock 137.8 *fastening,* 137.12 *bind,* 323.3 *restrainer,* 323.7 *close*

padlocked 137.16 *bound,* 323.12 *closed*
pad-nag 32.4 *saddle horse*
pad out 128.5 *make bigger,* 553.5 *be diffuse*
padre 7.8 *priest*
pads 19.3 *uniform,* 31.1 *hockey*
Padua 93 *Cities*
pad up to 27.17 *bat*
paean 10.8 *hymn,* 431.3 *cry of praise,* 837.2 *thanks,* 851.4 *compliment*
paediatric 60.22, 630.18 *medical*
paediatrician 60.13 *medical specialist*
paediatric patient 624.19 *sick person*
paediatrics 60.3 *medical specialty*
paedogenesis 59.15 *developmental biology,* 79.8 *young amphibian*
paedogenetic 59.26 *developmental*
paedophile 864.9 *wicked person*
paedophobia 777 *Phobias by Name*
paella 45.54 *other dishes*
paeon 48.9 *metre*
pagan 9.6 *idolater,* 9.10 *idolatrous,* 498.5 *disbeliever,* 498.6 *disbelieving*
Paganini 49 *Musicians and Composers*
paganism 9.2 *idolatry,* 498.4 *unbelief*
Paganism 7 *Non-Christian Religions*
paganize 9.8 *idolatrize*
pagano-Christian 9.6 *idolater*
pagano-Christianism 9.2 *idolatry*
paganry 9.2 *idolatry*
pagans 400.3 *uncivilized human*
page 143.2 *particular,* 326.7 *transferor ,* 534.30 *communicate,* 544.10 *identify,* 697.3 *attendant,* 823.7 *bridal party*
page 3 girl 877.2 *indecency*
pageant 51.5 *show,* 159.8 *procession,* 435.7 *view,* 475.6 *mass demonstration,* 526.10 *manifestation,* 811.14 *show,* 813.3 *formal occasion*
pageantry 526.10 *manifestation,* 811.7 *pomp*
pageboy 823.7 *bridal party*
Pagemaker 65.11 *application*
pager 420.9 *audio device,* 534.18 *radio*
paginate 544.10 *identify*
paglia e fieno 45 *Types of Pasta*
pagoda 10.11 *place of worship,* 275.6 *tall thing*
Pagoda 43 *Notable Buildings*
pagoda tree 85 *Trees and Shrubs*
Pago Pago 263.3 *distant place*
Pahari 5 *Languages and Groups of Languages*
Pahlavan 32 *Breeds of Horse and Pony*
Pahlavi 5 *Languages and Groups of Languages*
pahoehoe 54.25 *eruption*
paid 746, 703.10 *engaged,* 721.15 *gainful,* 730.11 *receiving,* 748.12 *expended,* 749.6 *received*
paid back 125.7 *compensated*
paid for 738.13 *bought*
paid helper 697.1 *servant*
paid in advance 746.19 *receiving pay*
paid in full 746.16 *paid*
paid off 125.7 *compensated*
paid out 748.12 *expended*
p'ai hsiao 49 *Musical Instruments*
pail 258.11 *vessel*
paimensarvi 49 *Musical Instruments*
pain 777 *Phobias by Topic,* 406, 631, 406.11 *inflict pain,* 543.1 *sign,* 616.3 *inconvenience,* 618.11 *harmfulness,* 624.3 *symptom,* 628.11 *hurt,* 687.1 *adversity,* 764.5 *unpleasantness,* 764.9 *unpleasant person,* 770.1 *sorrow,* 788.3 *boring*

person, 788.6 *be boring,* 862.2 *affliction*
Paine 4 *Philosophers*
pained 406.7 *feeling pain,* 828.15 *resentful*
painfree 660.14 *relaxed*
painful 406, 764, 406.8 *inflicting pain,* 624.23 *diseased,* 644.11 *laborious,* 760.3 *sore,* 764.1 *unpleasant,* 770.7 *distressing,* 879.21 *punishing*
painful condition 406
painfully 406, 862.13 *destructively*
painfulness 406.1 *pain,* 618.11 *harmfulness,* 862.2 *affliction*
pain in the arse 693.5 *troublemaker,* 764.9 *unpleasant person,* 788.3 *boring person*
pain in the neck 151.11, 693.5 *troublemaker,* 764.9 *unpleasant person,* 788.3 *boring person*
painkiller 62.4 *drug type,* 242.2 *moderator,* 404.4 *anaesthetic,* 630.5 *analgesic,* 761.6 *desensitizing substance,* 767.3 *reliever*
pain-killing 242.8 *moderating*
painless 660.9 *easy*
painlessly 405.11 *pleasingly*
pain relief 406, 630.5 *analgesic*
pain-reliever 630.5 *analgesic*
pains 644.4 *exertion*
pains and penalties 879.8 *penalty*
painstaking 467.8 *diligent,* 469.9 *careful,* 642.8 *assiduity,* 644.10 *working,* 644.11 *laborious*
paint 50, 444, 547, 47.18 *work wood,* 56.28 *colour,* 62.7 *ointment,* 130.6 *add,* 243.10 *produce,* 293.3 *coating,* 293.8 *wall covering,* 293.24 *coat,* 293.28 *face,* 376.11 *smooth,* 444.4 *pigment,* 444.15 *colour,* 519.14 *imagine,* 539.12, 539.32 *disguise,* 545.13 *record,* 560.14 *describe,* 621.9 *cleaning agent,* 637.2 *preserver,* 637.5 *preserve,* 791.4 *cosmetics,* 791.16 *make up,* 792.10 *decorate*
paintable 547.13 *representational*
paint a masterpiece 696.14 *master*
paint and decorate 792
paintbox 50.11 *artist's materials*
paint box 791.5 *make-up box*
paintbrush 50.11 *artist's materials*
paint china 44.11 *make ceramics*
painted 50, 47.14 *wooden,* 293.36 *covered,* 444.10 *coloured,* 539.41 *disguised,* 811.19 *flashy*
Painted 98 *Deserts*
painted furniture 47.1 *furniture*
painted image 547.6 *image*
painted lady 82 *Insects*
painter 74 *Parts of a Ship,* **444,** 36.3 *parts of a sailing boat,* 50.16, 50.16 *artist,* 114.4 *person who copies,* 118.8 *copier,* 137.6 *line,* 243.9 *producer,* 293.17 *coverer,* 547.4 *person who makes a representation,* 629.12 *repairer,* 646.2 *artisan,* 792.7 *decorator*
Painter 53 *The Constellations*
painterliness 50.4 *treatment*
painterly 50.26 *artistic,* 547.13 *representational*
painterly values 50.4 *treatment*
Painters Eleven 50 *Schools and Groups of Artists*
painting 42 *Hobbies and Pastimes,* **50, 50,** 47.1 *furniture,* 50.1 *art,* 50.7 *picture,* 243.1 *production,* 435.7 *view,* 547.2 *reproduction,* 637.1 *preservation*
painting and decorating 792.4 *decorating*
Painting and Sculpture 50
painting over 546.3 *obliteration*
painting the Forth Bridge 685.2 *never-ending task*
paint in words 519.14 *imagine*
paint locker 74 *Parts of a Ship*
paint majolica 44.11 *make ceramics*

paint oneself into a corner 656.6 *act foolishly,* 659.20 *be in difficulty*
paint over 130.6 *add,* 220.9 *transform,* 531.8 *conceal,* 546.1 *obliterate*
paints 50.11 *artist's materials*
paint-stripper 546.4 *eraser*
paint the town red 405.8 *feel pleasure,* 773.5 *rejoice,* 815.11 *be sociable*
paint tile 44.11 *make ceramics*
paint tube 50.11 *artist's materials*
paint with a broad brush 164.27 *make a generalization*
p'ai pan 49 *Musical Instruments*
pair 176, 27.10 *score,* 40.4 *tennis terms,* 41.13 *ice-skating,* 42.3 *card game terms,* 109.8 *interrelate,* 110.3 *lookalike,* 110.8 *make the same,* 114.6 *couple,* 135.8 *unite,* 135.11 *make love,* 161.24 *brace,* 169.8 *odd,* 176.1 *two*
pair bond 57.11 *chemical bond*
pair-bond 135.11 *make love*
pair-bonding 135.4 *sexual union*
paired 107.4 *related,* 110.14 *lookalike,* 116.14 *conforming,* 176.9 *two,* 180.19 *associated,* 823.21 *married*
paired cable 64.27 *wire*
paired with 180.24 *with*
pairing 135.4 *sexual union,* 176.4 *doubling,* 821.5 *desire*
pair of compasses 52.49 *geometric construction*
pair off 135.8 *unite,* 158.17 *average,* 176.14 *pair*
pair of scales 369.10 *scales*
pair of spectacles 435.10 *visual aid*
pairs 42 *Card Games,* 25.9 *bowls,* 36.4 *rowing,* 41.6 *ice-skating*
pair-skating 41.6, 41.13 *ice-skating*
pair-skating movement 41.6 *ice-skating*
pairs match 25.1 *green bowling*
pairs sit spin 41.6 *ice-skating*
pair up 135.8 *unite,* 137.13 *intercommunicate,* 180.14 *keep company with*
pair up with 107.7 *relate to*
paisa 741.4 *change*
paisley 67 *Natural Fabrics*
Paisley 93 *Cities*
Paiute 1 *Peoples,* **5** *Languages and Groups of Languages*
pak-choi cabbage 45 *Vegetables*
Paki 91 *Names for Inhabitants*
Paki-bash 481.14 *discriminate against*
Paki-basher 481.7 *bigot*
Paki-bashing 481.4 *social discrimination,* 865.11 *prejudice*
Pakistan 91 *Countries*
pakora 45.12 *hors d'oeuvre,* 45.49 *Indian dish*
pal 401.3 *male title of address,* 784.4 *likable person,* 815.6 *social person,* 819.5 *friend*
palace 243.8 *construction,* 256.4 *official residence,* 688.6 *place of authority*
paladin 671.13 *defender,* 679.1 *combatant*
palaeethnologist 200.11 *antiquarian*
palaeethnology 200.9 *antiquarianism*
palaeoanthropographic 1.12 *palaeoanthropological*
palaeoanthropographical 1.12 *palaeoanthropological*
palaeoanthropographically 1.17 *palaeoanthropologically*
palaeoanthropography 1.2 *palaeoanthropology*
palaeoanthropological 1
palaeoanthropologically 1
palaeoanthropologist 1, 200.11 *antiquarian*
palaeoanthropology 1, 200.9 *antiquarianism*

palaeobiogeographer 3.4 *archaeologist*
palaeobiogeographical 3.17 *archaeological*
palaeobiogeography 3.2 *archaeology*
palaeobiological 3.17 *archaeological*
palaeobiologist 3.4 *archaeologist*
palaeobiology 3.2 *archaeology*
palaeobotanical 3.17 *archaeological*
palaeobotanist 3.4 *archaeologist*, 83.12 *plant scientist*
palaeobotany 3.2 *archaeology*, 59.1 *life science*, 83.10 *plant science*
palaeoceanography 3.2 *archaeology*
Palaeocene 54 Geological Time Intervals
Palaeocene period 200.3 *geological period*
palaeoclimatological 3.17 *archaeological*
palaeoclimatologist 3.4 *archaeologist*, 54.3 *geologist*, 200.11 *antiquarian*
palaeoclimatology 3.2 *archaeology*, 54.1 *earth science*, 200.9 *antiquarianism*
palaeocosmological 3.17 *archaeological*
palaeocosmologist 3.4 *archaeologist*
palaeocosmology 3.2 *archaeology*
palaeodendrology 3.2 *archaeology*
palaeoecological 3.17 *archaeological*
palaeoecologist 3.4 *archaeologist*
palaeoecology 3.2 *archaeology*
palaeoeremological 3.17 *archaeological*
palaeoeremology 3.2 *archaeology*
palaeoethnobotany 83.10 *plant science*
palaeoethnographer 1.4 *palaeoanthropologist*
palaeoethnographic 1.12 *palaeoanthropological*
palaeoethnographically 1.17 *palaeoanthropologically*
palaeoethnography 1.2 *palaeoanthropology*
palaeoethnological 1.12 *palaeoanthropological*
palaeoethnologically 1.17 *palaeoanthropologically*
palaeoethnologist 1.4 *palaeoanthropologist*
palaeoethnology 1.2 *palaeoanthropology*
Palaeogene 54 Geological Time Intervals
palaeogeographer 3.4 *archaeologist*, 54.3 *geologist*, 200.11 *antiquarian*
palaeogeographical 3.17 *archaeological*
palaeogeographically 54.66 *geographically*
palaeogeography 3.2 *archaeology*, 54.1 *earth science*, 200.9 *antiquarianism*
palaeoglaciology 3.2 *archaeology*
palaeographer 3.4 *archaeologist*, 5.2 *linguist*, 200.11 *antiquarian*, 524.6 *interpreter*
palaeographic 5.38 *linguistic*
palaeographical 3.17 *archaeological*
palaeography 3.2 *archaeology*, 5.1 *linguistics*, 5.12 *translation*, 200.9 *antiquarianism*, 524.5 *science of interpretation*
palaeoherpetology 3.2 *archaeology*
palaeohistological 3.17 *archaeological*
palaeohistologist 3.4 *archaeologist*
palaeohistology 3.2 *archaeology*
palaeohydrographer 3.4 *archaeologist*
palaeohydrographical 3.17 *archaeological*

palaeohydrography 3.2 *archaeology*
palaeolimnological 3.17 *archaeological*
palaeolimnologist 3.4 *archaeologist*
palaeolimnology 3.2 *archaeology*
Palaeolithic 202.15 *primal*
Palaeolithic art 50 Non-Western Art
Palaeolithic period 200.4 *prehistoric age*
palaeolithy 3.2 *archaeology*
palaeological 3.17 *archaeological*, 5.38 *linguistic*
palaeologist 3.4 *archaeologist*
palaeology 3.2 *archaeology*, 5.1 *linguistics*
palaeomagnetic 54.49 *geophysical*
palaeomagnetism 54.44, 56.58 *geomagnetism*
palaeomammology 3.2 *archaeology*
palaeometeorological 3.17 *archaeological*
palaeometeorologist 3.4 *archaeologist*, 200.11 *antiquarian*
palaeometeorology 3.2 *archaeology*, 200.9 *antiquarianism*
palaeontographer 3.4 *archaeologist*, 200.11 *antiquarian*
palaeontographical 3.17 *archaeological*
palaeontography 3.2 *archaeology*, 200.9 *antiquarianism*
palaeontological 3.17 *archaeological*, 54.48 *geological*, 59.20 *biological*
palaeontologist 3.4 *archaeologist*, 54.3 *geologist*, 59.19 *life scientist*, 200.11 *antiquarian*
palaeontology 3.2 *archaeology*, 54.1 *earth science*, 59.1 *life science*, 59.16 *evolution*, 76.9 *animal science*, 200.9 *antiquarianism*
palaeopathological 3.17 *archaeological*
palaeopathologist 3.4 *archaeologist*
palaeopathology 3.2 *archaeology*
palaeophysiography 3.2 *archaeology*
palaeophysiological 3.17 *archaeological*
palaeophysiologist 3.4 *archaeologist*
palaeophysiology 3.2 *archaeology*
palaeophytologist 3.4 *archaeologist*
palaeophytology 3.2 *archaeology*
palaeopotamological 3.17 *archaeological*
palaeopotamologist 3.4 *archaeologist*
palaeopotamology 3.2 *archaeology*
palaeopsychological 1.12 *palaeoanthropological*
palaeopsychologically 1.17 *palaeoanthropologically*
palaeopsychologist 1.4 *palaeoanthropologist*
palaeopsychology 1.2 *palaeoanthropology*
palaeornithological 3.17 *archaeological*
palaeornithologist 3.4 *archaeologist*
palaeornithology 3.2 *archaeology*
Palaeozoic 54 Geological Time Intervals
Palaeozoic era 200.3 *geological period*
palaeozoological 3.17 *archaeological*, 76.16 *zoological*
palaeozoologist 3.4 *archaeologist*, 76.11 *zoologist*, 200.11 *antiquarian*
palaeozoology 3.2 *archaeology*, 76.9 *animal science*, 200.9 *antiquarianism*
palais de danse 46.6 *famous dancers*
Palais Glide 46.2 *dance*
palanquin 71.6 *litter*

palatability 411.1 *taste*, 763.9 *tastiness*
palatable 350.27 *edible*, 405.6 *pleasant*, 411.7, 763.4 *tasty*
palatably 45.57 *culinarily*, 411.11 *tastily*
palate 411.1 *taste*, 481.2 *judiciousness*
palate-tickling 350.3 *delicate eating*, 350.27 *edible*
palatial 256.16 *manorial*, 742.3 *opulent*, 811.22 *majestic*
palatinate 12.5 *political organization*, 91.3 *dominion*, 688.8 *governmental organization*
palatoplasty 60 Surgical Operations
Palau 5 Languages and Groups of Languages
Palaung 5 Languages and Groups of Languages
palaver 565.3 *talk*
Palawan 98 Islands
pale 446, 137.8 *fastening*, 147.3 *exclusion zone*, 238.10 *ill*, 249.3 *regional boundary*, 249.14 *sphere*, 301.3 *enclosing thing*, 301.5 *enclose*, 397.21 *deathly*, 438.2 *difficult to see*, 439.21 *light*, 439.28 *bleach*, 441.6 *murky*, 441.9 *be dim*, 444.13 *soft-hued*, 444.16 *make up*, 445.5 *lose colour*, 445.6 *decolour*, 445.8 *drained of colour*, 446.13 *whiten*, 544.8 *heraldic device*, 624.21 *unhealthy*, 650.1 *fatigued*
palea 87.3 *grass plant*
pale ale 351.7 *alcoholic drink*
pale as a ghost 624.21 *unhealthy*, 777.7 *frightened*
pale as ashes 445.8 *drained of colour*
pale as death 445.8 *drained of colour*
pale blue 454.1 *blue*
pale brown 449.1 *brown*
pale colour 439.14 *light colour*
pale-grey 448.1 *grey*
pale imitation 656.9 *bungling*
palely 439.30 *lightly*, 446.14 *whitely*
Palembang 93 Cities
paleness 445, 238.3 *poor health*, 438.4 *invisibility*, 439.14 *light colour*, 441.1 *dimness*, 444.3 *hue*, 444.9 *complexion*, 446.7 *whiteness*, 636.2 *danger signal*
Paleo-Asiatic 5.11 *family of languages*
pale purple 455.6 *purple*
Palermo 93 Cities
pales 671.9 *barrier*
Palestinians 1 Peoples
paletot 295.12 *coat*
palette 50.11 *artist's materials*
palette knife 50.11 *artist's materials*, 381.9 *blunt instrument*
pale with anger 828.16 *angry*
pale yellow 452.1 *yellow*
palfrey 32.4 *saddle horse*
Pali 5 Languages and Groups of Languages
Pali Canon 7.12 *religious text*
palimony 721.4 *earnings*, 725.6 *marriage settlement*, 729.2 *gift*, 730.2 *something received*, 749.3 *income*
palimpsest 599.7 *reused product*
palindrome 5.17 *word*, 287.1 *inversion*
palindromic 5.42 *worded*
paling 301.3 *enclosing thing*, 671.9 *barrier*
palingenesis 245.1 *reproduction*, 629.10 *revival*
palinode 48.7 *poem*
palinody 484.2 *reversal*
palisade 83.6 *leaf*, 281.3 *vertical thing*, 301.2 *enclosed place*, 632.2 *protection*, 671.9 *barrier*, 671.18 *fence*
palisaded 671.30 *defended*
Palissy ware 44 Types of Ceramics
pall 293.2 *cover*, 399.4 *funeral*

objects, 412.7 *be tasteless*, 785.7 *cause dislike*, 788.6 *be boring*
Palladian 43 Architectural Styles
palladium 57 Chemical Elements
Pallas 53 Minor Planets
Pallas's cat 77 Placental Mammals
pallbearer 326.7 *transferor* , 399.3 *funeral director*
pallet 70.2 *thing transported*, 71.6 *litter*
palletization 70.1 *transport*
palliate 60.19 *practise medicine*, 242.4 *moderate*, 485.15 *modify*, 627.1 *improve*, 630.19 *remedy*, 767.9 *relieve*, 855.8 *justify*
palliated 485.11 *modified*
palliation 485.5 *modification*, 627.5 *improvement*, 767.1 *ease*, 855.2 *defence*
palliative 62.4 *drug type*, 242.2 *moderator*, 485.11 *modified*, 630.5 *analgesic*, 630.17 *remedial*, 767.3 *reliever*, 767.8 *relieving*, 855.11 *vindicatory*
palliatively 855.15 *in vindication*
palliator 855.5 *vindicator*
pallid 238.10 *ill*, 397.21 *deathly*, 439.21 *light*, 445.8 *drained of colour*, 446.4 *pale*, 542.17 *insipid*
pallidectomy 60 Surgical Operations
pallidity 445.2 *paleness*
pallidly 446.14 *whitely*, 542.26 *insipidly*
pallidness 542.8 *insipidness*
palliness 819.1 *friendship*
pallium 7.11 *vestment*, 295.16 *robe*
pall on 785.7 *cause dislike*
pallor 439.14 *light colour*, 444.9 *complexion*, 445.2 *paleness*, 446.7 *whiteness*
pally 815.15 *sociable*, 819.8 *friendly*
palm 85.1 *tree*, 517.10 *cards*, 681.1 *trophy*
palmaceous 85.14 *treelike*
palmate 83.18 *of leaves*, 85.14 *treelike*, 343.8 *fanlike*
palm civet 77 Placental Mammals
palmelloid 90.7 *algal*
palmer 7.3 *religious person*, 7.7 *monk*
Palmer 18 Sporting Personalities
palm frond 85.2 *tree part*
palm grease 741.2 *cash*
palmist 11.13 *diviner*, 516.5 *predictor*, 517.9 *forecaster*
palmistry 11.9 *divination*, 516.3 *foresight*, 517.2 *divination*
palmitic 58 Common Fatty Acids
palm-kernel meal 68.9 *animal feedstuff*
palm leaf 85.2 *tree part*
palm nut 86 Nuts
palm off 222.6 *give a substitute*
palm oil 85.9 *tree product*, 729.2 *gift*, 741.2 *cash*
palmreader 11.13 *diviner*
palm-reader 516.5 *predictor*, 517.9 *forecaster*
palm-reading 11.9 *divination*, 516.3 *foresight*
palms 83.3 *seed plant*
Palm Springs 93 Cities
Palm Sunday 10.15 *holy day*
palmy 675.7 *peaceful*, 686.8 *prosperous*
palmy days 185.5 *indefinite period*, 675.1 *peace*, 686.3 *time of plenty*
palmyra 85 Trees and Shrubs
Palmyra 93 Cities
Palo Alto 93 Cities
palolo worm 81 Worms
Palomar 95 Mountains
Palomar Observatory 53.23 *observatory*
palomino 32.1 *horse*
Palomino 32 Breeds of Horse and Pony
palp 407.7 *sense organ*

palpability 367.1 *material world,* 407.1 *touch*
palpable 367.7 *material,* 403.8 *sensate,* 407.8 *touchable,* 437.1 *visible,* 526.11 *manifest*
palpably 407, 367.9 *materially,* 526.16 *manifestly*
palpate 407.11 *touch*
palpating 407.2 *touching*
palpitant 365.14 *vibrating*
palpitate 365.9 *vibrate,* 366.24 *shake,* 777.12 *be fearful*
palpitating 365.14 *vibrating*
palpitation 365.2 *vibration,* 366.10 *beat,* 426.1 *drumming,* 624.10 *cardiovascular disease*
palpitations 650.7 *fatigue,* 777.2 *fearfulness*
palpus 407.7 *sense organ*
palsied 366.19 *convulsive,* 624.23 *diseased*
palsy 624.17 *nervous disorder*
palsy-walsy 819.8 *friendly*
palter 474.13 *quibble,* 538.21 *lie,* 576.5 *vacillate*
palterer 538.11 *liar*
paltering 474.4 *quibbling,* 538.15 *lying*
paltriness 260.1 *littleness,* 612.6 *obscurity,* 754.3 *shoddiness*
paltry 260.7 *little,* 612.2 *obscure,* 618.1 *worthless,* 754.10 *shoddy*
paltry sum 741.4 *change*
paludal 98.11 *continental*
pal up with 815.13 *fraternize*
Palus Epidemiarum 53 Seas
Palus Nebularum 53 Seas
Palus Putredinis 53 Seas
Palus Somnii 53 Seas
paly 544.13 *heraldic*
palynology 83.10 *plant science*
Pama-Nyungan 5 Languages and Groups of Languages
Pamirs 95 Mountains
Pampango 5 Languages and Groups of Languages
pampas 87.2 *grassland,* 98.6 *lowland,* 282.3 *flat thing*
pampas cat 77 Placental Mammals
pampas grass 87 Grasses
pamper 405.10 *comfort,* 610.4 *be excessive,* 662.20 *sustain,* 708.4 *be permissive,* 771.15 *humour,* 826.7 *show endearment for*
pampered 405.7 *pleased*
pampering 771.11 *humouring*
pamper oneself 610.4 *be excessive*
pamphlet 243.5 *work of art,* 532.5 *journal,* 532.9 *advertisement*
pamphleteer 532.10 *publicizer,* 532.16 *publicize,* 561.3 *dissertator*
pamphleteering 586.5 *propaganda*
Pamplona 93 Cities
pan 45.6 *kitchen equipment,* 45.39 *loaf,* 66.21 *photograph,* 258.15 *pot,* 303.2 *face,* 524.11 *criticize,* 727.7 *toilet,* 850.24 *ridicule,* 852.17, 854.11 *criticize*
Pan 8 Deities
panacea 62.3 *drug,* 630.1 *remedy*
panacean 630.17 *remedial*
panache 549.2 *stylishness,* 554.1 *emphasis,* 811.4 *flashiness*
panaeolus 89 Fungi
Pan-Africanism 400.11 *nation*
panama 295.15 *headgear*
Panama 68 Breeds of Sheep, **91** Countries
Panama City 93 Cities
Pan-American Games 21.5 *competition*
Pan-American Three-Day Event 32.11 *eventing*
panatella 413.7 *tobacco,* 875.6 *drug*
Panathenea 10.16 *religious festival*
Panay 98 Islands
pancake 32.14 *horse-riding terms,* 45.39 *loaf,* 282.3 *flat thing*
Pancake Day 10.15 *holy day*

pancake house 350.15 *eating place*
pancake landing 73.5 *flight*
pancake race 674.4 *race*
pancakes and maple syrup 45.43 *US dish*
Pancharatra 7 Non-Christian Religions
Panchen Lama 7.8 *priest*
panchromatic film 66.9 *film*
pancreas 352 Exocrine Glands
pancreatectomy 60 Surgical Operations
pancreatic 352.5 *of a secretion*
pancreatic juice 352.2 *secreted substance*
pancreatotomy 60 Surgical Operations
pancreozymin 58 Hormones
panda 77 Placental Mammals
panda car 71.17 *police car*
panda crossing 71.3 *carriageway,* 327.5 *crossing*
Pandarus 678.3 *mediator*
pandect 16.1 *the law*
Pandects of Justinian 16.1 *the law*
pandemic 164.12 *widespread,* 624.5 *plague,* 626.6 *contagious*
pandemonium 8.16 *devilish*
pandemonium 161 Collective Names for Birds and Animals, 133.3 *miscellany,* 151.5 *confusion,* 423.2 *outcry,* 434.2 *dissonant noise*
pander 135.7 *joiner,* 232.3 *assistant,* 232.4 *be an instrument,* 606.3 *provider,* 606.5 *provision,* 678.3 *mediator,* 707.3 *agent,* 877.8 *immoral man,* 877.18 *prostitute*
panderer 158.9 *middleman,* 606.3 *provider,* 678.3 *mediator*
pandering 606.1 *provision,* 877.5 *prostitution*
pander to 808, 232.4 *be an instrument,* 586.16 *tempt,* 662.25, 697.8 *serve*
pandora 49 Musical Instruments
Pandora 322.3 *person who opens*
Pandora's box 631.6 *source of trouble,* 635.1 *trap,* 862.5 *evil thing*
pane 266.4 *slice,* 442.9 *glass*
paned 456.3 *striped*
panegyric 494.2 *overestimate,* 564.8 *speech,* 851.4 *compliment,* 851.18 *approving,* 853.1 *flattery*
panegyrist 851.9 *praiser*
panegyrize 494.4 *overestimate,* 851.15 *compliment*
panel 47.17 *carpenter,* 161.7 *committee,* 171.6 *list of names,* 266.4 *slice,* 292.3 *line,* 293.28 *face,* 492.5 *judge,* 653.7 *council,* 706.2 *representative body*
panel-back 47.14 *wooden*
panel-back chair 47.2 *chair*
panel beater 71.21 *miscellaneous motoring terms*
panelboard 47.12 *wood*
panelled 47.14 *wooden,* 293.36 *covered,* 456.9 *striped*
panelled bed 47.6 *bed*
panelling 47.12 *wood,* 292.1 *lining,* 293.8 *wall covering*
panel of judges 16.18 *tribunal,* 492.5 *judge*
panel saw 47.11 *woodworking tool*
panel show 51.5 *show*
panelwork 47.12 *wood*
pan fish 80.8 *food fish*
pang 366.8 *spasm,* 406.1 *pain,* 618.11 *harmfulness,* 631.5 *pain*
panga 380.10 *knife,* 680.8 *sharp weapon*
Pangaea 54.19 *plate tectonics*
Pangasinan 5 Languages and Groups of Languages
pangolin 77 Placental Mammals, 77.6 *insect-eating mammal*
pangs 406.1 *pain,* 867.1 *penitence*

pangs of conscience 867.1 *penitence*
pangs of jealousy 841.1 *jealousy*
panhandle 249.6 *regions,* 712.8 *solicit money*
panhandler 712.5 *beggar,* 730.5 *recipient*
panhandling 712.3 *solicitation*
panhuéhuetl 49 Musical Instruments
panic 648.4 *haste,* 777.1 *fear,* 777.11 *be afraid,* 777.13 *frighten*
panic attack 61.12 *stress*
panic button 636.2 *danger signal*
panic buy 605.6 *store*
panicky 576.3 *timid,* 777.8 *fearful,* 779.3 *cowardly*
panicle 84.4 *flower head,* 87.3 *grass plant*
panic-stricken 777.7 *frightened*
panjandrum 494.3 *optimist,* 541.6 *exaggerator*
pan loaf 45.39 *loaf*
panned 852.33 *criticized*
panne velvet 67 Natural Fabrics
pannier 71.11 *bicycle part,* 258.7 *basket,* 295.18 *underwear*
pannikin 258.13 *drinking vessel*
panning 66.13 *framing,* 524.3, 852.5 *criticism,* 854.2 *criticism*
panoplied 632.6 *invulnerable,* 671.30 *defended*
panoply 295.1 *dress,* 632.2 *protection,* 671.7 *armour*
panoply of war 676.2 *glory of war*
panorama 50.10 *art subject,* 142.3 *whole situation,* 164.7 *global view,* 435.7 *view*
panoramic 164.15 *general,* 435.20 *visual*
pan out 227.9 *take effect*
panphobia 777 Phobias by Name
panpipe 49 Musical Instruments
panpsychic 11.16 *psychic*
panpsychism 4.7 *school of thought*
panpsychist 4.11 *follower of a doctrine,* 11.12 *occultist*
pansy 84 Flowers and Flowering Plants, 238.4 *weakling,* 401.9 *offensive terms for homosexual,* 453.3 *purple thing*
pant 365.9 *vibrate,* 564.13 *speak in a particular way,* 650.5 *be fatigued*
Pantagruel 259.10 *big person*
pantalets 295.18 *underwear*
Pantalone 51.30 *clown*
Pantaloon 51.21 *role,* 51.30 *clown*
pantaloons 295.9 *trousers*
pant for 782.12 *desire*
pantheism 4.7 *school of thought*
pantheist 4.11 *follower of a doctrine*
pantheistic 4.14 *of a philosophy*
pantheon 10.11 *place of worship,* 399.6 *grave*
Pantheon 43 Noted Buildings
panther 77 Placental Mammals
panther cap 89 Fungi
panties 295.18 *underwear*
pantile 44.9 *industrial ceramics*
panting 650, 366.16 *restless,* 650.7 *fatigue*
pantisocracy 12.1 *government*
pantograph 72.5 *locomotive part,* 118.5 *duplicate*
pantomime 51.2 *play,* 118.3 *mockery,* 543.11 *gesture*
pantomime dame 51.21 *role*
pantomimic 543.15 *gestural*
pantomiming 51.20 *acting*
pantomimist 51.22 *actor*
pantothenic acid 58.13 *vitamin*
pantry 45.3 *kitchen,* 256.7 *room,* 605.4 *storage*
pants 295.9 *trousers,* 295.18 *underwear*
pantsuit 295.10 *suit*
panty girdle 295.18 *underwear*
pantyhose 295.20 *legwear*
panurgic 655.6 *skilful*
Panzer 679.21 *armoured cavalry*

panzer division 679.16 *army unit*
pap 77.2 *mammalian characteristic,* 350.7 *food,* 393.8 *pulp,* 412.3 *tasteless items*
papa 7.8 *priest*
Papa 534 Phonetic Alphabet
papacy 7.9 *priesthood*
Papago 1 Peoples
papain 58.11 *enzyme*
papal 7.17 *priestly,* 692.14 *commanding,* 696.12 *masterful*
Papal Court 16.22 *ecclesiastical court*
papal decree 692.1 *command*
papaloi 7.8 *priest*
papal rule 12.1 *government,* 688.7 *type of rule*
papaphobia 777 Phobias by Name
papaveretum 62 Medication
papaverine 62 Medication, 58.19 *alkaloid*
papaw 86 Fruits
papaya 86 Fruits
paper 604, 49.18 *written music,* 50.11 *artist's materials,* 238.5 *weak thing,* 274.11 *fineness,* 292.3 *line,* 293.28 *face,* 446.9 *white thing,* 528.3 *document,* 532.4 *newspaper,* 561.1 *dissertation,* 754.6 *absence of charge*
paperback 532.6 *book publishing*
paper bag 258.8 *bag*
paper-bag job 790.2 *ugly person*
paper chase 590.2 *chase*
paper chromatography 57.17 *analysis*
paperclip 135.5 *joint,* 726.3 *tools for gripping*
papered 293.36 *covered*
paper handkerchief 621.11 *cleaning cloth*
paperiness 274.11 *fineness*
paper mill 647.1 *workshop*
paper money 741, 741.1 *money*
paper mulberry 85 Trees and Shrubs
paper nautilus 81 Molluscs
paper over 220.9 *transform,* 531.8 *conceal,* 629.1 *repair*
paper over the cracks 220.9 *transform,* 609.5 *be insufficient,* 614.9 *waste effort,* 656.5 *be unskilful,* 685.5 *not complete,* 811.31 *put on a show*
paper reed 87 Grasses
papers 356.6 *passport,* 483.6 *documentation,* 545.1 *record*
paper sculpture 50.12 *sculpture*
paper tape 65.7 *peripheral*
paper tiger 102.5 *insubstantial person*
paper war 676.1 *war*
paper warfare 674.1 *contention*
papery 274.4 *fine,* 379.1 *brittle*
Paphian 877.14 *lecherous*
papier-mâché 604.3 *paper*
papier mâché mask 295.5 *fancy dress*
papilionid butterfly 82 Insects
papilla 77.2 *mammalian characteristic,* 316.2 *bulge*
papillon 77 Breeds of Dogs
papillotomy 60 Surgical Operations
papish 7.16 *denominational*
papist 7.5 *Christian,* 7.16 *denominational*
pappardelle 45 Types of Pasta
Pappus of Alexandria 52 Scientists
paprika 45 Herbs and Spices, 413.5 *herbs*
Pap test 60.7 *diagnosis*
Papuan 5 Languages and Groups of Languages
Papua New Guinea 91 Countries
papyrus 87 Grasses
par 14.1 *finance,* 29.2 *golfing terms,* 110.5 *equality,* 110.16 *equal,* 122.1 *equality,* 122.8 *on equal terms,* 124.1, 124.4 *average,* 158.3 *median,* 741.7 *finance*
para 679.32 *airman*

para-aminosalicylic acid 62 Medication
parabaloid 52.83 *spherical*
parable 48.2 *fiction*, 114.1 *similarity*, 473.4 *gist*, 560.3 *narration*, 578.5 *equivocalness*
parablock 41.5 *ski equipment*
parabola 52.42 *circle*, 311.2 *bend*
parabolic 43.13 *arched*, 43.17 *structured*, 52.81 *curvilinear*, 311.4 *curved*
parabolically 311.7 *curvedly*
parabolic arch 43.5 *arch*
parabolic orbit 53.21 *orbit*
parabolic vault 43.7 *vault*
paraboloid 52.45 *curved surface*
paraboloid mirror 56.29 *optical element*
paracentesis 349.22 *disgorgement*
paracetamol 62 Medication, 630.5 *analgesic*, 630.8 *drug*
parachronism 193.1 *wrong time*, 197.1 *different time*, 211.2 *anachronism*
parachronistic 193.6 *too late*, 197.2 *occurring at a different time*, 211.11 *anachronistic*
parachronistically 193.7 *out of chronological order*, 211.16 *anachronistically*
parachute 360.12 *drop*, 632.4 *safety device*
parachute division 17.4 *military organization*
parachute troops 679.14 *armed forces*, 679.32 *airman*
parachuting 18 Sporting Activities
parachutist 360.8 *descender*
parade 161 Collective Names for Birds and Animals, 159.8 *procession*, 159.17 *line up*, 327.7 *arcade*, 457.2 *being in view*, 475.6 *mass demonstration*, 475.19 *protest*, 526.1, 526.6 *display*, 811.7 *pomp*, 811.14, 811.27 *show*, 817.12 *greet*
paraded 526.13 *displayed*
parade of honour 849.5 *presenting arms*
parade one's wares 811.31 *put on a show*
paradigm 5.30 *syntax*, 119.2 *original*, 154.4 *precedent*, 306.2 *prototype*, 471.6 *ideal*
paradigmatic 306.10 *prototypical*, 471.13 *ideal*
paradigmatically 306.13 *formatively*, 471.24 *ideologically*
parading 475.14 *demonstrating*
paradise 51.16 *auditorium*, 190.3 *life without end*, 199.3 *future condition*, 325.3 *resting place*, 396.5 *life cycle*, 397.14 *the spiritual world*, 762.2 *fun*
paradisiac 8.14 *heavenly*
paradisiacal 405.6 *pleasant*
paradisial 8.14 *heavenly*
paradisical 8.14 *heavenly*
parados 671.8 *military defences*
paradox 4.8 *philosophical term*, 52.64 *reasoning*, 117.2 *contradiction*, 474.2 *sophism*, 487.5 *impossibility*, 523.12 *unintelligible thing*
paradoxical 52.86 *logical*, 117.8 *contradictory*, 474.7 *sophistic*, 487.1 *impossible*, 523.4 *difficult*
paradoxically 117.15 *dissimilarly*, 474.14 *sophistically*, 487.11 *impossibly*
paradox of the unexpected hanging 4.9 *philosophical problem*
paradrop 73.1 *aviation*
paraffin 57 Types of Compounds, 395.9 *petroleum*, 410.6 *oil*
paraffinic 395.11 *oily*
paraffin lamp 439.5 *incandescent light*
paraffin stove 408.6 *fire*
paraformaldehyde 62 Medication
paragliding 18 Sporting Activities
paragon 126, 134.5 *pure person*,

471.6 *ideal*, 617.8 *exceller*, 619.3 *perfection*, 655.4 *skilled person*, 786.5 *person of wonder*, 805.13 *proud person*, 861.9 *the best*, 861.16 *superior person*, 863.4 *virtuous person*
paragon of virtue 134.5 *pure person*, 863.4 *virtuous person*
paragraph 41.13 *ice-skating*, 143.2 *particular*, 543.7 *punctuation*
paragraph bracket 41.6 *ice-skating*
paragraph double three 41.6 *ice-skating*
paragraph loop 41.6 *ice-skating*
Paraguay 91 Countries, **96** Rivers
parahydrogen 57 Chemical Elements
parakeet 78 Birds, 78.7 *cagebird*
paraldehyde 57 Common Chemical Compounds, **62** Medication
parallax 53.13 *luminosity*
parallel 285, 285, 30.11 *gymnastic*, 41.12 *ski*, 52.80 *linear*, 107.1 *relatedness*, 107.5 *interrelated*, 107.8 *be proportionate to*, 109.6 *correlative*, 109.9 *correlate*, 110.8 *make the same*, 110.13 *equivalent*, 114.1 *similarity*, 114.7 *similar*, 114.10 *be similar*, 116.14 *conforming*, 116.25 *conform*, 122.5, 122.6 *equal*, 122.8 *on equal terms*, 122.10 *be equal*, 180.18 *concurrent*, 249.2 *geographical region*, 285.1 *parallelism*, 332.14 *directed*, 478.15 *correspondent*, 478.21 *answer to*, 667.12 *compatible*
parallel access 65.17 *computing term*
parallel bars 18 Sporting Activities, 30.3 *gymnastic apparatus*, 30.5 *horizontal bar*, 32.9 *jumping*, 32.11 *eventing*, 285.2 *parallel thing*
parallel christie 41.4 *skiing technique*
parallel computer 65.3 *computer*
parallel connection 64.16 *circuit element*
parallelepiped 52.46 *polyhedron*, 285.2 *parallel thing*
parallel evolution 59.16 *evolution*
parallelism 285, 48.12 *poetic language*, 109.3 *correlation*, 110.2 *equivalence*, 114.1 *similarity*, 116.5 *conformity*, 122.1 *equality*, 308.1 *symmetry*, 478.8 *correspondence*, 667.3 *compatibility*
Parallelism 285
parallelize 109.9 *correlate*
parallel lines 52.37 *line*
parallelogram 52.44 *polygon*, 178.2 *quadrilateral*, 285.2 *parallel thing*, 310.3 *angled figure*
parallelogram of forces 52.50 *scalar quantity*
parallel sailing 74.5 *navigation*
parallel swing 41.4 *skiing technique*
parallel thing 285
parallel turn 41.2 *cross-country skiing*
paralogism 474.2 *sophism*
paralogist 474.6 *sophist*
paralogistic 474.7 *sophistic*
paralyse 236.8 *overpower*, 460.10 *bemuse*, 761.7 *render insensitive*
paralysed 236.12 *impotent*, 240.5 *inert*, 325.4 *motionless*, 624.23 *diseased*, 641.3 *inactive*, 761.2 *desensitized*
paralysed with fear 777.7 *frightened*
paralysis 236.4 *disability*, 240.1 *inertness*, 404.1 *lack of feeling*, 624.3 *symptom*, 624.17 *nervous disorder*, 641.1 *inaction*, 761.4 *desensitization*

paralysis agitans 624.17 *nervous disorder*
paralytic 236.12 *impotent*, 624.19 *sick person*, 624.23 *diseased*, 874.3 *dead drunk*
paramagnet 340.3 *magnet*
paramagnetism 56.59 *ferromagnetism*
Paramatman 8.3 *God*
paramedic 60, 767.5 *helper*
paramedical 60.17 *paramedic*
parameter 52, 52.25 *algebraic expression*, 485.7 *condition*
paramethadione 62 Medication
parametric 52.77 *given*, 485.12 *conditional*
parametric statistics 52.53 *statistics*
paramilitary 676.17 *military*
paramount 103.5 *essential*, 126.14 *best*, 279.5 *top*, 611.5 *important*
paramountcy 126.1 *superiority*, 611.1 *importance*
paramountly 126.16 *superiorly*
paramour 821.9 *lover*
paramylum 90.3 *plant body*
Paraná 96 Rivers
Paraná pine 85 Trees and Shrubs
parang 380.10 *knife*, 680.8 *sharp weapon*
paranoia 61.15 *compulsion*, 61.16 *dissociation*, 510.4 *delusion*
paranoiac 510.7 *insane person*
paranoid 61.36 *psychologically disturbed*, 510.13 *mentally ill*
paranoid personality 61.8 *disordered personality*, 61.16 *dissociation*
paranormal 11.14 *occult*, 104.12 *external*
paranormally 11.25 *occultly*
paransitologist 76.11 *zoologist*
parapet 634.1 *refuge*, 661.3 *barrier*, 671.11 *fortification*
paraph 544.3 *means of identification*, 544.11 *identify oneself*
paraphasia 563.3 *speech defect*
paraphasic 563.12 *inarticulate*
paraphernalia 133.3 *miscellany*, 295.25 *accessories*, 603.6 *equipment*, 725.4 *possessions*
paraphrase 5.12 *translation*, 5.24 *phrasing*, 5.46 *translate*, 520.10 *mean*, 524.4 *translation*, 524.12 *translate*
paraphrased 5.40 *translated*, 5.43 *phrasal*
paraphraser 524.6 *interpreter*
paraphrasing 5.40 *translated*, 5.43 *phrasal*
paraphrast 524.6 *interpreter*
paraphrastic 5.43 *phrasal*, 520.6 *meaningful*, 524.17 *translational*
paraphrenia 510.4 *delusion*
paraplegia 236.4 *disability*, 624.17 *nervous disorder*
paraplegic 236.12 *impotent*, 624.19 *sick person*
parapsychological 368, 11.16 *psychic*
parapsychologically 11.25 *occultly*
parapsychologist 11.12 *occultist*, 368.7 *believer in a nonmaterial world*
parapsychology 368, 11.1 *occultism*, 61.1 *psychology*
Paraquat 68.14 *pest control*, 631.8 *poison*
pararhyme 48.11 *rhyme*
parasang 75 Some Foreign Units
parascending 18 Sporting Activities
parasite 81, 59.18 *ecology*, 76.4 *type of animal*, 82.3 *pest*, 83.2 *plant*, 83.4 *lower plant*, 89.5 *fungal association*, 138.4 *adherent*, 138.5, 180.9 *follower*, 610.3 *superfluity*, 624.6 *infection*, 643.8 *nonworker*, 701.4 *dependent*, 734.6 *taker*, 808.3 *sycophant*, 815.6 *social person*
parasite drag 73.7 *miscellaneous aviation terms*

parasites 777 Phobias by Topic
parasitic 76.15 *of animals*, 83.14 *of plants*, 89.10 *of fungi*, 138.10 *tenacious*, 643.3 *not participating*, 808.7 *sycophantic*
parasitically 808, 89.13 *saprophytically*, 138.12 *tenaciously*
parasitic flatworm 81.6 *worm*
parasitic fungus 89.5 *fungal association*
parasiticide 62.4 *drug type*
parasitic worm 81.6 *worm*
parasitism 59.18 *ecology*, 89.5 *fungal association*, 808.2 *sycophancy*
parasitize 82.16 *infest*, 808.15 *sponge*
parasitological 59.20 *biological*
parasitologist 59.19 *life scientist*, 60.13 *medical specialist*, 81.15 *invertebrate zoologist*
parasitology 59.1 *life science*, 60.3 *medical specialty*, 76.9 *animal science*, 81.14 *invertebrate zoology*, 624.20 *pathology*
parasitophobia 777 Phobias by Name
parasol 293.12 *protective covering*, 440.6 *shade*, 634.2 *shelter*
parasol mushroom 89 Fungi
parasuicide 398.7 *suicide*
parasympatholytic 62.4 *drug type*, 62.14 *counteracting*
parasympathomimetic 62.4 *drug type*, 62.17 *stimulating*
parataxis 5.30 *syntax*
paratha 45.49 *Indian dish*
parathion 68.14 *pest control*
parathyroidectomy 60 Surgical Operations
parathyroid gland 352 Endocrine Glands
parathyroid hormone 58 Hormones
paratrooper 360.8 *descender*, 679.32 *airman*
paratrooper boots 295.19 *footwear*
paratroops 679.14 *armed forces*
paratyphoid 624.6 *infection*
paraxial ray 56.31 *lens element*
parazoa 396.9 *classifications of life*
Parazoa 81.8 *sponge*
parazoan 81.1 *invertebrate*, 81.8 *sponge*
parboil 45.55 *cook*, 408.14 *be hot*
parboiling 45.8 *cooking technique*
parcel 161 Collective Names for Birds and Animals, 68.11 *farmland*, 120.2 *certain amount*, 120.8 *quantify*, 143.7 *piece*, 161.27 *bundle*, 161.38 *group*, 257.6 *contain*, 258.5 *packet*, 534.3 *correspondence*, 725.1 *property*
parcel bomb 539.13 *snare*
Parcel Force 534.2 *postal communication*
parcelled 161.49 *grouped*
parcelling out 731.1 *allocation*
parcel of land 249.12 *plot*
parcel out 731.4 *allot*
parcel post 534.2 *postal communication*
parch 392.18 *thirst*, 392.21 *dry up*, 408.14 *be hot*
parched 392.2 *thirsty*, 392.8 *baked*, 782.10 *hungry*
parchedness 392.11 *dryness*
parchment 379.3 *brittle thing*, 604.1 *materials*
parchment-like 392.3 *dried-up*
parchment worm 81 Worms
pardon 16.42 *acquittal*, 16.78 *acquit*, 512.6 *amnesty*, 675.1 *peace*, 677.2 *peace offering*, 691.1 *leniency*, 691.3 *be lenient*, 700.4 *liberate*, 835.3 *mercy*, 835.10 *show mercy*, 839.1 *forgiveness*, 839.9 *forgive*, 848.2 *acquittal*, 848.10 *acquit*, 855.1 *vindication*, 855.9 *vindicate*
pardonable 839.7 *forgivable*, 855.13 *vindicable*
pardonably 16.88 *forgivingly*
pardoned 16.63 *acquitted*, 691.5

given consideration, 839.6 forgiven, 848.6 acquitted, 855.12 innocent
pardoning 700.1 liberation, 839.4 forgiving
pare 121.6 change gradually, 136.10 set apart, 296.15 make nude, 542.22 play down
pared 542.19 downplayed
pared-down 542.19 downplayed
pare down 129.5 make smaller, 182.8 reduce, 542.22 play down
paregoric 62.4 drug type, 630.17 remedial
parenchymatous 90.7 algal
parent 5.39 of language, 226.7 Prime Mover, 233.5 influential person, 243.9 producer, 245.5 propagator, 496.12 discoverer
parentage 245.4 development
parental love 821.1 love
parent complex 61.18 complex
parenteral administration 62.13 administration
parent fixation 61.17 fixation
parentheses 52.25 algebraic expression, 543.7 punctuation
parenthesis 137.4 means of connection, 160.7 broken thread, 335.13 deviation, 354.8 insertion
parenthesize 543.13 punctuate
parenthetic 160.11 digressive
parenthetical 354.12 inserted
parenthetically 354.15 in
parenthood 245.4 development, 396.4 biological function
parent language 5
parent nuclide 56.70 radioactivity
parent rock 54.33 metamorphic rock
parent surrogate 61.25 surrogate
paresis 624.17 nervous disorder
Paressi 7 Non-Christian Religions
parget 293.8 wall covering, 293.28 face
parhelic circle 55.22 sun
parhelion 55.22 sun
pariah 147.5 excluded person, 149.9 misfit, 335.19 deviant person, 816.7 outsider
pariah dog 77.9 dog
Parian porcelain 44 Types of Ceramics
parietal bone 382 Bones
paring 266.4 slice
paring down 542.9 down-playing
paring knife 380.10 knife
parings 143.8 bits and pieces
Paris 93 Cities, 93.6 other cities
Paris and Helen 821.10 lovers
Paris fashion 295.2 dressing
Paris green 453.10 green pigment
parish 7.9 priesthood, 92.1 administrative area, 143.1 part, 249.5 state
parish council 16.2 jurisdiction, 653.8 British administrative council, 706.2 representative body
parishioner 10.17 worshipper, 93.11 urbanite, 255.5 countryman
parish-pump 612.4 trivial
Paris Opera Ballet 46.12 ballet companies
Paris white 446.8 whitener
parity 14.1 finance, 56.78 quantum, 65.17 computing term, 110.5 equality, 114.1 similarity, 116.5 conformity, 122.1 equality, 741.7 finance
Parjana 8 Deities
park 87.2 grassland, 301.2 enclosed place, 453.8 greenness, 637.1 preservation
parka 34.4 climbing equipment, 295.11 jacket, 408.3 heater
Parker 48 Writers
parkin 45.36 cake
parking 71.21 miscellaneous motoring terms, 356.2 passing along
parking light 71 Motor Vehicle Parts, 439.6 electric light
parking meter 71.21 miscellaneous motoring terms

parking orbit 53.35 rocketry, 327.13 flight path
parking place 356.2 passing along
parking space 71.21 miscellaneous motoring terms, 248.5 reserved space
parkinsonism 366.7 shake
Parkinson's disease 624.17 nervous disorder
Parkinson's law 12.3 governance, 166.3 rule of nature, 642.9 overactivity
park keeper 632.3, 671.15 protector
parkland 87.2 grassland
park one's carcass 256.18 take up residence
park oneself 362.8 sit
parkway 327.3 road
parky 55.55 cool, 409.8 cold
parlance 5.3 spoken language, 564.1 faculty of speech
parley 568.4 conference, 568.9 converse, 568.11 confer, 654.2 consultation, 654.6 consult, 678.5 conference
parley with 567.9 approach
parliament 161 Collective Names for Birds and Animals, 653.10 legislative body
Parliament 12.4 governing body, 653.11 British government, 688.6 place of authority, 706.2 representative body
Parliamentarian 12.8 politician, 653.16 official, 706.1 delegate
parliamentary 653, 12.9, 688.14 governmental, 696.12 masterful
Parliamentary 706.6 delegated
parliamentary committee 654.4 adviser
parliamentary democracy 91.1 country
parliamentary government 12.1 government, 688.7 type of rule
parliamentary offices 647.1 workshop
parliamentary reporting 533.3 reporting
parliamentary system 580.11 franchise
Parliament House 43 Noted Buildings
PARLOG 65 Programming Languages
parlor 72.6 rolling stock
parlour 256.7 room
parlourmaid 697.6 domestic servant
parlous state 633.5 danger
Parma 93 Cities
Parma violet 455.2 purple pigment
Parmenides 4 Philosophers
Parmesan 45 Cheeses
Parnassian 48.19 narrative
Parnassians 48 Literary Groups and Movements
Parnassus 95 Mountains, 48.13 poetic genius
parochial 7.17 priestly, 10.22 worshipping, 93.14 urban, 249.18 local, 481.10 discriminatory, 493.8 unjust, 612.4 trivial
parochialism 249.15 regionalism, 481.3 prejudice, 493.3 injustice
parochially 16.86 jurisdictionally, 92.8 administratively, 93.16 municipally, 481.17 prejudicially, 493.14 unjustly
parodic 850.14 ridiculing
parodied 118.12 imitative, 309.8 exaggerated, 548.6 misrepresented
parody 118.1 imitation, 118.3 mockery, 118.9 imitate, 309.4 distortion of the truth, 504.5 misrepresentation, 504.19 make a mistake, 525.1 misinterpret, 525.2 misinterpretation, 548.1 misrepresentation, 548.4 misrepresent, 733.9 borrow illegally, 771.4 entertainment, 771.13 be humorous, 799.2 act of derision, 850.4 ridicule
parodying 733.3 illegal borrowing

parol 564.17 oral
parole 5.5 nonstandard language, 564.1 faculty of speech, 700.1 liberation, 700.4 liberate, 708.2 permit
paroled 700.7 liberated
parolee 700.3 liberator
paromomycin 62 Medication
paronomasia 48.12 poetic language, 578.5 equivocalness
paronym 5.17 word
paronymic 5.42 worded
parotid 352.5 of a secretion
parotid gland 352 Exocrine Glands
paroxysm 241.3 instance of violence, 366.8 spasm, 510.3 mental deterioration, 670.20 bout, 828.4 anger
paroxysmic 366.19 convulsive
parquet 51.16 auditorium, 280.1 base, 293.9 floor covering, 293.24 coat
parquet circle 51.16 auditorium
parquet floor 293.9 floor covering, 456.5 variegated thing
parquetried 47.14 wooden
parquetried furniture 47.1 furniture
parquetry 47.1 furniture, 456.2 check
parr 80.3 young fish
parricide 398.3 homicide, 398.11 murderer
parried 28.6 fencing
parrot 78 Birds, 78.7 cagebird, 118.7 imitator, 118.9 imitate, 167.6 conformist, 183.8 creature of habit, 183.16 repeat
parrot-fashion 118.14 imitatively
parrot fever 624.18 veterinary disease
parrot fish 80 Fishes
parroting 118.12 imitative
parrot-like 78.23 avian, 118.12 imitative, 183.9 repeated
parrotry 118.3 mockery, 167.1 conformity
parrots 161 Collective Names by Animal
parry 671, 26.2 boxing, 26.11 do a combat sport, 28.3 fencing movements, 28.5 fence, 38.4 play soccer, 341.3 fend off, 341.7 deflection, 476.10 countercharge, 591.6 evade, 591.14 evasion, 671.1 defence, 672.3 retaliate
Parry 49 Musicians and Composers
parrying 26.2 boxing, 26.14 combat, 28.6 fencing, 38.2 football play
parse 141.4 deconstruct
parsec 75 Scientific and Technical Units, 53.22 astronomical unit, 269.7 measure of length
Parsee 7 Non-Christian Religions
parser 65.8 software
Parshuram 8 Deities
parsimonious 609.1 insufficient, 726.9 retentive, 758.1 mean, 860.4 selfish, 869.8 self-restrained
parsimoniously 609.10 insufficiently, 726.11 tenaciously, 758.9 meanly, 860.8 selfishly, 869.11 with self-restraint
parsimoniousness 758.3 parsimony
parsimony 758, 609.8 insufficiency, 860.1 selfishness, 869.1 self-restraint
parsing 5.30 syntax, 141.2 deconstruction
parsley 45 Herbs and Spices, 413.5 herbs
parsley family 83.3 seed plant
parsnip 45 Vegetables
parson 7.8 priest
parsonage 7.10 priestly dwelling, 256.4 official residence
Parsons 52 Scientists
person's nose 45.28 poultry
part 143, 143, 345, 51.21 role, 120.2 certain amount, 121.4 in-

terval, 136.9 separate, 136.13 diverge, 143.2 particular, 143.11 partial, 145.3 incomplete thing, 146.2 thing included, 148.1 component, 148.2 piece, 162.9 be dispersed, 162.12 disperse, 173.2 fractional part, 173.5 fractional, 173.7 fractionally, 173.8 divide, 265.4 space, 343.11 move apart, 603.4 machine, 824.7 divorce
Part 143
partake 350.24 have a meal
partake of 724.4 have joint possession
partaker 350.18 eater, 724.3 participant
partaking 350.4 eating meals, 724.2 participation, 724.5 jointly possessing, 815.1 sociability
part and parcel 148.1 component
part and parcel of 146.8 included
Partbred Arabian 32 Breeds of Horse and Pony
part by part 143.12 partly
part company 136.13 diverge, 162.9 be dispersed, 343.12 separate, 345.6 part, 591.8 run away
part company with 666.5 disagree
parted 265.6 spaced
parterre 51.16 auditorium, 69.2 garden
parterre box 51.16 auditorium
part for part 143.12 partly
parthenocarpic 86.9 of a fruit
parthenogenesis 245.3 propagation
parthenogenetic 245.16 reproductive
Parthenon 43 Noted Buildings
parthenophobia 777 Phobias by Name
Parthians 200.6 people of the past
Parthian shot 157.10 ending, 657.2 stratagem
partiable 136.19 separable
partial 143, 49.16, 56.20 musical note, 123.4 unjust, 145.4 incomplete, 173.5 fractional, 234.5 tending to, 481.10 discriminatory, 493.8 unjust, 620.2 incomplete, 844.11 wrong
partial deafness 421.1 deafness
partial derivative 52.31 differentiation
partial differential equation 52.31 differentiation
partial eclipse 441.1 dimness
partial excuse 855.2 defence
partial fraction 52.18 division
partiality 123.2 injustice, 145.1 incompleteness, 234.2 attitude, 493.3 injustice, 580.7 preference, 665.4 partisanship, 782.1 desire, 784.2 inclination, 819.1 friendship, 844.1 unfairness, 858.1 impropriety
partial knowledge 501.2 information
partially 143.12 partly, 145.6 incompletely, 173.7 fractionally, 493.14 unjustly
partially deaf 421.4 deaf
partially ordered 52.75 equal
partially sighted 436.9 weaksighted
partially sighted register 436.3 aid for poor sight
partialness 145.1 incompleteness
partial paralysis 624.17 nervous disorder
partial payment 746.1 payment
partial success 515.1 disappointment
partial to 782.9 desirous, 784.6 liking
partial truth 538.5 half-truth
participant 724, 146.3 person included, 253.5 someone present, 674.10 contender
participate 18, 2.15 socialize, 109.8 interrelate, 146.5 be included, 253.12 attend, 640.4 act, 642.16 be sociable, 652.11 conduct oneself, 664.13 work together, 724.4 have joint posses-

sion, 729.6 *give to charity*, 815.11 *be sociable*
participate actively 642.16 *be sociable*
participate in 148.10 *compose*
participating 253.8 *attendant*, 642.21 *meddling*, 724.5 *jointly possessing*
participation 143, 724, 146.1 *inclusion*, 253.2 *omnipresence*, 642.2 *social activity*, 664.3 *mutual relationship*, 815.1 *sociability*
participative 724.5 *jointly possessing*
participator 642.10 *busy person*, 646.1 *worker*, 724.3 *participant*
participator sport 18.4 *sporting activity*
participatory 664.17 *cooperative*, 724.5 *jointly possessing*
participatory democracy 724.1 *joint possession*
participial 5.44 *grammatical*
participle 5.35 *part of speech*
particle 5.35 *part of speech*, 56.77 *elementary particle*, 143.1 *part*, 143.4 *component*, 148.3 *unit*, 173.1 *fragment*, 260.2 *little thing*, 384.7 *grain*
particle accelerator 56, 235.8 *nuclear power*
particle collider 56.94 *particle accelerator*
particle counter 56.93 *radiation detector*
particle detector 56.93 *radiation detector*
particle physics 56.3 *modern physics*
particle–wave duality 56.13 *electromagnetic radiation*
parti-coloured 456.6 *variegated*
particular 143, 490, 103.9 *characteristic*, 106.6 *aspect*, 106.10 *detailed*, 148.1 *component*, 148.8 *belonging*, 163.11 *typical*, 165.15 *special*, 174.14 *singular*, 469.9 *careful*, 579.1 *capricious*, 580.14 *selecting*, 619.2 *perfectionist*, 659.14 *troublesome*, 665.10 *political*
particular instance 52.58 *frequency distribution*
particular interpretation 524.1 *interpretation*
particularism 665.4 *partisanship*
particularity 490, 165.1 *speciality*, 174.4 *singularity*, 469.4 *fastidiousness*, 544.2 *identity*
particularization 165.8 *specialization*, 490.18 *particularity*, 537.8 *accuracy*
particularize 165, 106.11 *circumstantiate*, 475.16 *explain*, 490.22 *specify*, 503.7, 537.31 *be accurate*, 553.5 *be diffuse*, 560.16 *define*
particularized 537.21 *accurate*
particularly 106.19 *meticulously*, 165.28 *specially*
particulars 165.4 *specifications*, 560.1 *description*
particulate radiation 56.70 *radioactivity*
parting 343, 345, 136.1 *separation*, 162.5 *divergence*, 345.11 *departing*
parting gift 837.3 *recognition*
parting of the ways 343.4 *branching*, 500.4 *faction*, 666.1 *disagreement*
parting shot 155.9 *conclusion*, 157.10 *ending*, 345.9 *parting*, 478.5 *counterstatement*
parting with 727.1 *disposal*
partisan 481.7 *bigot*, 481.10 *discriminatory*, 490.2 *convinced*, 490.11 *opinionist*, 493.5 *misjudging person*, 493.8 *unjust*, 500.5 *dissenter*, 500.7 *dissenting*, 665.10 *political*, 679.9 *guerrilla*, 680.8 *sharp weapon*, 693.10, 713.5 *seditionist*, 844.11 *wrong*
partisanism 665.4 *partisanship*
partisanship 665, 481.3 *preju-*

dice, 481.5 *favouritism*, 490.10 *conviction*, 493.3 *injustice*, 819.1 *friendship*, 844.1 *unfairness*
partition 136.3 *separateness*, 136.5 *separator*, 136.11 *divide*, 141.2 *deconstruction*, 141.4 *deconstruct*, 143.1, 143.10 *part*, 147.3 *exclusion zone*, 438.6 *that which makes invisible*, 731.1 *allocation*
partitioned 136.15 *separate*
partition wall 302.4 *boundary marker*
partitive 143.11 *partial*
partitively 141.7 *to pieces*
partly 143, 145.6 *incompletely*, 173.7 *fractionally*
partly visible 438.2 *difficult to see*
part missing 145.2 *omission*
partner 180, 646, 823, 109.8 *interrelate*, 116.22 *form an alliance*, 135.8 *unite*, 140.6 *come together*, 180.11 *companion*, 180.14 *keep company with*, 401.4 *boyfriend*, 662.11 *helper*, 664.10 *cooperator*, 724.3 *participant*, 823.8 *spouse*
partnered 135.12 *united*, 180.19 *associated*, 823.21 *married*
partnered with 180.24 *with*
partners 664.9 *team*
partnership 107.1 *relatedness*, 109.2 *interconnection*, 116.2 *alliance*, 180.3 *companionship*, 664.5 *joint control*, 665.1 *party*, 715.1 *contract*, 724.1 *joint possession*, 823.2 *alliance*
part of 146.1 *included*, 148.8 *belonging*, 724.5 *jointly possessing*
part of garment 295
part of poem 48
part of speech 5, 143.2 *particular*
part of the bargain 716.2 *basis for negotiations*
part of the furniture 217.7 *permanent*
parton 260.2 *little thing*
part ownership 724.1 *joint possession*
part payment 143.2 *particular*
part payment instalment 145.3 *incomplete thing*
partridge 78 *Birds*, 37.5 *game*, 45.20 *meat*, 78.4 *table bird*
partridges 161 Collective Names by Animal
partridge-wood 85 Trees and Shrubs
parts 250.1 *location*, 257.1 *contents*
parts of a canoe 36.6 *canoeing*
parts of a circle 313
parts of a punt 36.8 *punting*
parts of a racing boat 36.4 *rowing*
parts of a sailboard 36.7 *windsurfing*
parts of a sailing boat 36
part song 376.3 *round*, 433.2 *song*
part-time worker 15.7 *employee*
parturient 156.32 *embryonic*, 245.16 *reproductive*, 246.5 *fertile*
parturition 156.4 *conception*, 245.3 *propagation*
part with 727.9 *dispose of*, 729.5 *give*
part work 532.5 *journal*
party 161, 665, 815, 16.8 *litigant*, 140.3 *assembly*, 161.9 *social gathering*, 161.11 *group*, 350.13 *feast*, 400.7 *person*, 568.3 *social gathering*, 665.17 *socialize*, 679.14 *armed forces*, 679.16 *army unit*, 703.4 *council*, 714.5 *promise-maker*, 724.3 *participant*, 762.2 *fun*, 773.1 *rejoicing*, 812.1 *celebration*, 812.15 *celebrate*
Party 665
party chairman 12.8 *politician*, 653.15 *manager*
party dress 295.3 *formal dress*
party-goer 762.3 *joyful person*
party hack 167.6 *conformist*

party line 167.5 *convention*, 534.12 *public telephone system*, 592.2 *policy*, 652.9 *tactics*, 654.3 *precept*
party man 665.6 *political party member*
party manager 12.8 *politician*, 653.15 *manager*
party member 12.6 *political party*, 665.6 *political party member*, 724.3 *participant*
party-minded 500.7 *dissenting*, 665.10 *political*, 815.15 *sociable*
party official 653.16 *official*, 688.10 *person of authority*, 696.3 *leader*
party pooper 587.8 *cautionary person*
party-pooper 641.2 *nonacting person*, 661.7 *hinderer*
party rule 12.1 *government*
party system 12.1 *government*
party ticket 654.3 *precept*
party to a suit 16.8 *litigant*, 856.3 *accuser*
party whip 12.8 *politician*, 653.15 *manager*, 688.10 *person of authority*
party worker 12.6 *political party*, 665.6 *political party member*
par value 751.2 *value*
Parvati 8 Deities
parvenu 201.8 *new arrival*, 201.12 *immature*, 686.4 *prosperous person*, 721.7 *gainer*, 742.10 *wealthy person*, 795.5 *vulgar person*, 795.8 *discourteous*, 803.4 *common*, 805.13 *proud person*
Pasadena 93 Cities
pascal 75 SI Units, **75** Scientific and Technical Units
Pascal 4 Philosophers, **52** Scientists, **65** Programming Languages
Pascal-Plus 65 Programming Languages
Pascal's triangle 52 Named Concepts
paschal candle 10.14 *sacred object*
Paschen series 56 Named Laws
pas de chat 46.9 *ballet steps*
pas de deux 46.9 *ballet steps*
pash 821.2 *romantic love*
pasha 696.3 *leader*
Pashto 5 Languages and Groups of Languages
Pashtuns 1 Peoples
paso doble 41.7 *ice-dancing*, 46.2 *dance*
Paso Fino 32 Breeds of Horse and Pony
pasquinade 854.6 *ridicule*
Pasquino 51.30 *clown*
pass 185, 200, 356, 16.68 *legislate*, 19.9 *play*, 19.15 *play offence*, 23.4 *playing terms*, 23.6 *play basketball*, 31.1 *hockey*, 31.3 *ice hockey*, 31.9 *play hockey*, 35.3 *rugby play*, 38.2 *football play*, 38.4 *play soccer*, 42.3 *card game terms*, 42.10 *play*, 116.29 *permit*, 126.8 *be superior*, 188.7 *go on*, 189.4 *be transient*, 265.3 *gulf*, 272.6 *narrow place*, 317.2 *concave land*, 322.1 *opening*, 322.7 *passageway*, 329.6 *accelerate*, 338.5, 338.23 *throw*, 338.27 *kick*, 346.4 *right of entry*, 353.15 *excrete*, 353.16 *defecate*, 356.4 *access*, 356.6 *passport*, 397.15 *die*, 458.1 *disappear*, 485.13 *qualify*, 539.8, 539.28 *trick*, 580.4 *pick*, 608.4 *suffice*, 608.7 *sufficiency*, 617.9 *be worthy*, 632.2 *protection*, 645.4 *have leisure*, 670.18 *hit*, 682.6 *be successful*, 708.2 *permit*, 710.4 *illegal offer*, 741.24 *monetize*, 754.6 *absence of charge*, 783.16 *be mediocre*, 826.2 *courtship*, 851.12 *accept*, 851.17 *meet with approval*, 861.19 *be good at*
pass a bad check 741.24 *monetize*

passable 124.3 *mediocre*, 242.6 *moderate*, 284.10 *supportable*, 617.5 *not bad*, 765.6 *satisfactory*, 783.10 *mediocre*, 851.22 *approvable*
passableness 124.6, 783.4 *mediocrity*
passably 783.20 *unexceptionally*, 851.26 *approvably*
passacaglia 433.3 *melodiousness*
pass a decree 692.9 *command*
passado 670.18 *hit*
passage 356, 32.10 *dressage*, 74.1 *water travel*, 143.2 *particular*, 216.1 *change*, 256.7 *room*, 265.1 *interval*, 272.6 *narrow place*, 322.1 *opening*, 324.2 *momentum*, 326.2 *transportation*, 327.2 *route*, 335.8 *sidestep*, 336.11 *course*, 346.5 *entrance*, 433.3 *melodiousness*
Passage 356
passage into 356
passage of arms 674.6 *fight*
passage of time 185, 188.2 *time*
passage right 10.7 *non-Christian ritual*
passageway 322, 322.1 *opening*, 356.4 *access*
Passamaquoddy 1 Peoples
pass and repass 365.8 *oscillate*
passant 544.13 *heraldic*
pass around the hat 712.8 *solicit money*
pass as 547.12 *stand for*
pass away 100.13 *cease to exist*, 129.4 *decrease*, 157.19 *expire*, 189.4 *be transient*, 200.14 *pass*, 345.2 *withdraw*, 397.15 *die*, 458.1 *disappear*
pass back 31.9 *play hockey*
pass-back 31.1, 31.8 *hockey*
passbook 750.5 *account book*
pass by 185.15, 356.8 *pass*
passé 3.18 *in the past*, 200.19 *antiquarian*
passed 16.46 *legislated*, 31.8 *hockey*, 38.5 *soccer*, 116.18 *permitting*, 329.3 *accelerating*, 397.19 *dead*, 655.8 *expert*, 708.7 *permitted*, 851.23 *approved*
passed away 100.11 *no more*, 397.19 *dead*
passed over 132.10 *surplus*, 397.19 *dead*
passenger 70.5 *transportable*, 326.10 *transferred thing*, 643.8 *nonworker*
passenger pigeon 78 Birds, 78.8 *extinct bird*
passenger ship 74.3 *vessel*
passenger train 72.7 *train*
passenger transport 70.1 *transport*
passer 19.7 *offence*, 23.2 *basketball player*
passer-by 253.5 *someone present*, 480.7 *verifier*, 483.7 *person who gives evidence*
passeriform 78.23 *avian*
passerine 78.6 *songbird*, 78.23 *avian*
pas seul 46.2 *dance*
pass for 547.12 *stand for*
pass from hand to hand 728.4 *be transferred*
pass holder 51.31 *theatregoer*, 754.8 *bargain hunter*
passing 356, 23.4 *playing terms*, 31.1 *hockey*, 31.3 *ice hockey*, 31.5 *lacrosse*, 31.8 *hockey*, 35.3 *rugby play*, 35.6 *rugger*, 38.2 *football play*, 38.5 *soccer*, 157.3 *death*, 189.6 *transient*, 196.7 *occasional*, 293.41 *progressing*, 324.16 *moving*, 329.3 *accelerating*, 329.9 *acceleration*, 356.1 *passage*, 397.1 *death*, 458.4 *disappearance*, 458.6 *disappearing*
passing along 356
passing away 397.1 *death*, 458.4 *disappearance*
passing back 31.1 *hockey*
passing bell 397.7 *dying day*, 399.2 *funeral*

passing by 327.17 *via*
passing fancy 579.3 *whim*,
821.2 *romantic love*
passing fashion 189.2 *transient thing*
passing game 19.9 *play*
passing grade 620.5 *imperfection*
passing into law 16.31 *legislation*
passing knell 543.4 *signal*
passing the buck 591.13 *shirking*, 848.3 *self-exemption*
passing through 293.22 *progression*, 356.1 *passage*
passing up 869.1 *self-restraint*
passing word 528.7 *advice*
pass interference 19.13 *penalty*
pass into 220.7 *convert into*
pass into history 129.4 *decrease*, 200.14 *pass*
pass into oblivion 129.4 *decrease*
pass into one's hand 730.9 *receive*
passion 49.5 *sacred music*, 61.15 *compulsion*, 241.1 *violence*, 406.1 *pain*, 510.4 *delusion*, 554.1 *emphasis*, 759.4 *emotion*, 782.1 *desire*, 782.4 *sexual desire*, 784.1 *liking*, 821.5 *desire*, 828.4 *anger*
passionate 759, 241.6 *violent*, 408.12 *warm-hearted*, 554.3 *emphatic*, 782.9 *desirous*, 784.6 *liking*, 821.20 *amorous*
passionate friendship 819.3 *familiarity*
passionately 554.7 *emphatically*, 759.20 *with feeling*, 784.11 *admiringly*, 821.30 *lovingly*
passionflower 84 Flowers and Flowering Plants
passion fruit 86 Fruits
passionless 783.7 *indifferent*
passion play 51.2 *play*
passive 5.32 *voice*, 57.38 *reactive*, 167.13 *compliant*, 240.5 *inert*, 325.5 *sedentary*, 527.1 *latent*, 591.18 *avoiding*, 641.3, 643.1 *inactive*, 675.7 *peaceful*, 694.7 *obedient*
passively 4.27 *stoically*, 167.16 *adaptably*, 240.7 *inertly*, 325.10 *motionlessly*, 527.15 *latently*, 591.23 *shyly*, 643.15 *inactively*, 694.10 *obediently*
passiveness 240.1 *inertness*, 325.1 *motionlessness*, 673.1 *submission*, 694.1 *obedience*, 783.1 *indifference*
passive resistance 641.1 *inaction*, 669.3 *resistance movement*, 671.1 *defence*, 693.1 *disobedience*
passive resister 500.5 *dissenter*, 675.3, 677.3 *pacifist*
passive sex 673.1 *submission*
passive smoking 413.8 *smoking*, 631.9 *pollution*
passive suspension system 33.6 *motor racing terms*
passivity 4.3 *detachment*, 240.1 *inertness*, 325.1 *motionlessness*, 527.6 *latency*, 576.14 *apathy*, 591.3 *shirking*, 641.1 *inaction*, 643.5 *inactivity*, 673.1 *submission*, 694.1 *obedience*, 783.1 *indifference*
pass judgment 16.76, 492.11 *judge*, 692.11 *have authority over*
passkey 322.2 *opener*
pass laws 653.1 *manage*
pass marks 608.7 *sufficiency*
pass muster 608.4 *suffice*, 617.9 *be worthy*, 851.17 *meet with approval*
pass on 157.19 *expire*, 326.14 *bring back*, 336.1 *go forward*, 570.16 *bequeath*, 728.3 *transfer property*, 728.4 *be transferred*
pass oneself off as 540.20 *pretend*
pass one's prime 207.17 *age*
pass on the information 560.15 *recount*
pass on to the next 598.2 *withdraw*
pass out 236.6 *be powerless*, 347.9 *exit*, 404.11 *be unfeeling*,

812.20 *come out*, 874.7 *be drunk*
pass out of the picture 100.13 *cease to exist*
pass over 147.7 *exclude*, 345.2 *withdraw*, 347.9 *exit*, 566.9 *lapse into silence*, 581.1 *reject*, 612.12 *think unimportant*, 720.7 *not observe*, 839.11 *condone*
Passover 10.16 *religious festival*
pass over one's head 521.8 *not understand*
passport 356, 346.4 *right of entry*, 480.6 *evidence*, 483.6 *documentation*, 544.3 *means of identification*, 545.2 *certificate*, 632.2 *protection*, 703.3 *authority*, 708.2 *permit*, 718.2 *promise*
passport photograph 544.3 *means of identification*
pass reception 19.9 *play*
pass round 532.13 *make public*, 532.17 *be published*
pass round the hat 729.6 *give to charity*
pass rush 19.11 *defensive huddle*, 19.16 *play defence*
pass sentence 16.76 *judge*
pass the buck 591.5 *shirk*, 641.4 *not act*, 848.12 *exempt oneself*, 858.8 *be dishonourable*
pass the crisis 216.7 *be changed*, 627.2 *get better*
pass the parcel 42 Children's Games and Party Games
pass the point of no return 357.2 *cross*
pass the summer aestivate 203.6 *spend the season*
pass the test 851.17 *meet with approval*
pass the time of day 568.9 *converse*
pass the time of day with 567.9 *approach*
pass the winter 203.6 *spend the season*
pass through 293.35 *progress*, 356.8 *pass*
pass to another 728.4 *be transferred*
pass up 591.3 *abstain*, 641.4 *not act*, 673.3 *submit*, 711.5 *refuse*, 869.5 *be self-restrained*
pass water 353.17 *urinate*, 389.32 *seep*
pass with flying colours 682.11 *overmaster*
password 65.17 *computing term*, 322.2 *opener*, 543.1 *sign*, 560.8 *means of identification*, 560.8 *name*, 676.8 *warfare*, 708.2 *permit*
past 200, 3.6 *biography*, 100.11 *no more*, 209.14 *dead*, 458.7 *disappeared*, 512.11 *forgotten*, 585.2 *not customary*, 705.7 *resigning*
pasta 45.47 *Italian dish*
past age 3
past and gone 200.18 *over*, 458.7 *disappeared*
past behaviour 652.1 *conduct*
paste 394, 133.2 *mixed thing*, 138.3 *adhesive*, 138.7 *cause to adhere*, 330.3 *hit*, 374.11 *soft thing*, 393.1 *semiliquid*, 393.8 *pulp*, 393.11 *thickener*, 394.2 *adhesive*, 394.10 *stick*, 539.6 *imitation*, 540.10 *fake*, 726.3 *tools for gripping*, 726.6 *retain*
pasteboard 604.3 *paper*
paste gem 540.14 *false thing*
pastel 50.8 *painting*, 50.11 *artist's materials*, 439.21 *light*, 444.13 *soft-hued*, 542.13 *subtle*
pastel colour 439.14 *light colour*
pastel drawing 50.9 *drawing*
pasteles 45.51 *West Indian dish*
pastellist 50.16 *artist*
Pasternak 48 Writers, 48 Poets
Pasteur 52 Scientists
pasteurization 621.2 *cleaning*, 625.1 *hygiene*
pasteurize 134.10, 621.15 *pu-*

rify, 625.6 *make hygienic*, 630.20 *doctor*, 632.9 *protect*
pasteurized 621.17 *cleaned*, 625.4 *hygienic*
pasteurized milk 351.5 *milk*
past historic 5.34 *tense*
past hope 776
pasticcio 49.4 *opera*, 133.2 *mixed thing*
pastiche 118.2 *copy*, 133.2 *mixed thing*, 733.3 *illegal borrowing*
pastille 62.6 *pill*, 418.2 *fragrant thing*, 630.2 *medicine*
pastime 42, 590.4 *activity*, 642.2 *social activity*
pastiness 393.4 *pulpiness*, 394.1 *viscosity*, 439.14 *light colour*
past it 202.11 *old*, 207.14 *aged*, 614.1 *useless*, 628.12 *deteriorated*
past its prime 620.1 *imperfect*
past its sell-by date 200.19 *antiquarian*, 620.1 *imperfect*, 754.10 *shoddy*
past master 655.4 *skilled person*, 688.11, 696.10 *expert*
past one's best 202.11 *old*, 628.12 *deteriorated*
past one's prime 202.11 *old*, 207.14 *aged*, 207.16 *maturely*
pastor 7.8 *priest*, 662.14 *adviser*
pastorage 7.9 *priesthood*
pastoral 7.17 *priestly*, 48.7 *poem*, 48.19 *narrative*, 50.10 *art subject*, 51.2 *play*, 68.19 *agricultural*
pastoral care 7.9 *priesthood*
pastoral counselling 61.3 *psychiatric treatment*
pastoral elegy 48.7 *poem*
pastorally 68.22 *agriculturally*
pastoral poet 48.14 *author*
pastoral poetry 48.6 *poetry*
pastoral staff 544.4 *insignia*
pastorate 7.9 *priesthood*
pastoress 7.8 *priest*
pastorship 7.9 *priesthood*
past participle 5.35 *part of speech*
pastrami sandwich 45.11 *sandwich*
pastry 45, 379.3 *brittle thing*, 414.3 *dessert*
pastry bag 45.6 *kitchen equipment*
pastrycook 606.4 *caterer*
pastry cutter 45.6 *kitchen equipment*
pastry shell 293.13 *casing*
past time 3, 200, 197.1 *different time*
Past Time 200
past times 200.1 *past time*
pasturage 87.2 *grassland*, 350.8 *animal food*
pasture 68.11 *farmland*, 87.11 *eat grass*, 350.8 *animal food*, 350.21 *eat*, 350.25 *provide food*, 453.8 *greenness*
pasture grass 87.1 *grass*
pasture land 87.2 *grassland*
pastures new 156.13 *new beginnings*
pasturing 350.5 *eating habit*
pasty 45.32 *meat dish*, 374.2 *pliant*, 393.16 *semiliquid*, 393.18 *pulpy*, 439.21 *light*, 445.8 *drained of colour*
Pasupati 8 Deities
pat 330.6 *tap*, 330.13 *blow*, 407.11 *touch*, 543.11 *gesture*, 821.14 *communication of love*, 826.1 *endearment*, 826.7 *show endearment for*
PAT 19.6 *scoring*
Patagonian 98 Deserts
patas monkey 77 Placental Mammals
patch 62.12 *injection*, 65.17 *computing term*, 65.19 *abort*, 68.11 *farmland*, 130.3 *additional item*, 135.10 *link*, 143.7 *piece*, 249.12 *plot*, 249.13 *locality*, 250.1 *location*, 436.6 *blinder*, 456.2 *check*, 456.11 *variegate*, 622.4 *dirt*, 622.11 *dirty*, 627.3 *rectify*, 629.1, 629.8 *repair*, 630.10 *surgical dressing*

patched 133.12 *mixed*, 135.12 *united*, 456.8 *checked*, 743.3 *beggarly*
patched up 629.13 *repaired*
patcher 629.12 *repairer*
patchily 133.14 *in the midst*, 456.12 *variedly*
patchiness 123.1 *inequality*, 133.1 *mixture*, 215.1 *irregularity*, 456.2 *check*, 620.5 *imperfection*
patchiness patch 456.4 *maculation*
patching 629.8 *repair*
patching up 629.8 *repair*
patchouli 84 Flowers and Flowering Plants, 418.3 *incense*
patch pocket 295.24 *part of garment*
patch test 60.7 *diagnosis*
patch together 382.17 *assemble*
patch up 627.1 *improve*, 629.1 *repair*
patch up a quarrel 677.5 *make peace*
patchwork 42 Hobbies and Pastimes, 133.3 *miscellany*, 140.2 *cooperation*, 456.2 *check*, 792.2 *pattern*
patchwork quilt 113.3 *diverse thing*, 293.10 *bed covering*, 456.5 *variegated thing*
patchy 123.3 *unequal*, 127.14 *poor*, 133.12 *mixed*, 160.8 *discontinuous*, 215.4 *irregular*, 456.8 *checked*, 620.1 *imperfect*
patchy cloud 55.19 *cloud cover*
pâté 45.12 *hors d'oeuvre*, 45.29 *sausage*, 45.45 *French dish*
patella 382 Bones
patent 116.8, 116.29 *permit*, 119.7 *originate*, 302.2 *limiting factor*, 302.7 *limit*, 322.13 *opened up*, 435.23, 437.1 *visible*, 442.4 *easily seen through*, 457.7 *appearing*, 526.14 *manifest*, 708.2 *permit*, 708.7 *permitted*, 725.1 *property*, 845.6 *bond*, 845.16 *entitle*, 848.4 *licence*
patented 119.6 *authentic*, 302.5 *limited*, 725.8 *propertied*
patented invention 119.2 *original*
patently 322.25 *obviously*, 435.25, 437.11 *visibly*
patent medicine 133.2 *mixed thing*, 630.1 *remedy*, 630.2 *medicine*
pater 401.13 *man in the family*
paterfamilias 401.13 *man in the family*
paternal 821.17 *loving*, 831.6 *benevolent*
paternalism 12.1 *government*, 12.3 *governance*
paternal love 821.1 *love*
paternally 831.10 *benevolently*
paternity 245.4 *development*, 401.13 *man in the family*
paternoster 11.5 *spell*, 71.4 *personal transport*
Paternoster 10.9 *prayer*
path 327, 25.2 *grip*, 52.36 *point*, 137.5 *road*, 327.2 *route*, 327.13 *flight path*, 332.2 *bearing*, 347.6 *way out*, 356.2 *passing along*, 356.4 *access*
pathetic 238.15 *insufficient*, 612.2 *obscure*, 618.2 *inferior*, 776.8 *bad*, 835.7 *pitiful*
pathetically 238.14 *weakly*
pathetic fallacy 48.12 *poetic language*
pathfinder 73.3 *aircraft personnel*, 154.8 *precursor*, 194.6 *person having priority*, 496.12 *discoverer*
pathia 45.49 *Indian dish*
Pathian marble 50.14 *sculptor's materials*
path of least resistance 327.2 *route*
pathogen 89.5 *fungal association*, 624.6 *infection*
pathogenic 624.23 *diseased*, 626.6 *contagious*
pathological 60.22 *medical*,

398.23 *deadly,* 624.23 *diseased,* 630.18 *medical*
pathological dieting 350.3 *delicate eating*
pathological drunk 874.17 *drunkard*
pathological killer 398.11 *murderer*
pathological liar 538.11, 539.16 *liar*
pathologically 624.25 *unhealthily,* 630.21 *remedially*
pathological lying 538.3, 540.6 *lying*
pathologist 60.13 *medical specialist*
pathology 624, 60.3 *medical specialty*
pathoneurosis 61.10 *neurosis*
pathophobia 777 *Phobias by Name*
pathway 327.6 *path,* 356.4 *access*
patience 42 Card Games, 4.3 *detachment,* 174.10 *single thing,* 328.8 *slowness,* 575.1 *perseverance,* 691.1 *leniency,* 839.2 *forgivingness*
patient 60, 4.18 *detached,* 328.5 *unhurried,* 479.7 *experimentee,* 575.10 *persevering,* 624.19 *sick person,* 626.4 *infectious person,* 691.4 *lenient,* 699.7 *charge,* 839.5 *merciful*
patiently 4.27 *stoically,* 328.16 *slowly,* 575.13 *persistently,* 691.6 *leniently,* 839.14 *forgivingly*
patina 266.3 *coat,* 376.10 *polish,* 439.2 *quality of light,* 444.3 *hue,* 453.11 *green thing,* 628.9 *dilapidation*
patinated 444.13 *soft-hued*
patio 69.3 *ornamental garden,* 256.7 *room,* 301.2 *enclosed place*
patio door 346.6 *means of entry*
patio set 69.3 *ornamental garden*
patisserie 414.3 *dessert*
Patna 93 Cities
pato 18 Sporting Activities
patois 5.3 *spoken language,* 5.26 *dialect,* 165.10 *specialized language,* 564.1 *faculty of speech*
pat oneself on the back 805.29 *feel pride*
pat on the back 851.4, 851.15 *compliment,* 878.9 *reward*
pat on the head 826.7 *show endearment for*
Patras 93 Cities
patriarch 7.8 *priest,* 401.13 *man in the family,* 696.1 *master*
patriarchal 12.9 *governmental,* 202.11 *old,* 207.14 *aged,* 688.14 *governmental,* 696.12 *masterful*
patriarchally 202.18 *venerably,* 207.16 *maturely*
patriarchy 12.1 *government,* 401.1 *male sex*
patrician 400.10 *member of society,* 688.10 *person of authority,* 802.1 *nobleman,* 802.4 *aristocratic*
patricide 398.3 *homicide,* 398.11 *murderer,* 832.7 *act of malevolence*
patrimonial 132.9 *remaining,* 725.8 *propertied,* 749.6 *received*
patrimonially 725.10 *proprietarily,* 749.8 *profitably*
patrimony 132.5 *estate,* 723.1 *possession,* 730.1 *receiving,* 749.4 *legacy*
patriot 91.14 *nationalist*
Patriot 680.5 *missile weapon*
patriotic 249.17 *national,* 821.17 *loving*
patriotically 91.19, 249.20 *nationally*
patriotism 91.4 *nationalism,* 249.15 *regionalism,* 676.5 *bellicosity,* 784.1 *liking,* 821.1 *love*
patristic 7.18 *theological*
patristics 7.13 *theology*
patristic theology 7.13 *theology*
patroiophobia 777 *Phobias by Name*

patrol 356.1 *passage,* 356.9 *proceed,* 632.3 *protector,* 632.9 *protect,* 671.14 *guard,* 679.14 *armed forces,* 699.8 *restrain,* 718.10 *secure*
patrol boat 679.24 *warship*
patrol car 71.17 *police car*
patrolman 16.17 *police officer,* 435.11 *observer,* 632.3 *protector,* 671.14 *guard*
patrol plane 679.31 *military aircraft*
patrolwoman 671.14 *guard*
patron 13.9 *economist,* 51.25 *producer,* 207.8 *man,* 253.5 *someone present,* 284.8 *supporter,* 535.9 *affirmer,* 632.3 *protector,* 662.15 *benefactor,* 671.13 *defender,* 729.4 *giver,* 737.12 *custom,* 738.12 *purchaser,* 831.5 *benevolent person,* 851.7 *advocate*
patronage 662, 233.4 *indirect influence,* 284.7 *financial support,* 632.2 *protection,* 653.3 *management,* 688.1 *authority,* 692.4 *authorization,* 703.1 *commission,* 737.12, 738.11 *custom,* 831.2 *charity,* 851.1 *approval*
patronal 284.9 *supportive*
patroness 632.3 *protector*
patronize 116.30 *grant,* 212.8 *frequent,* 284.13 *support financially,* 632.9 *protect,* 662.23 *advise,* 688.21 *grant authority,* 703.6 *commission,* 771.15 *humour,* 805.28 *disdain,* 806.18 *condescend,* 831.9 *be charitable*
patronized 632.5 *safe*
patronizing 212.5 *frequenting,* 688.12 *authoritative,* 805.18 *prestigious*
patron saint 8.10 *deified person,* 632.3 *protector,* 662.15 *benefactor*
patronymic 560.8 *name*
pat someone's bottom 543.11 *gesture*
pat someone's head 543.11 *gesture*
patsy 222.2 *substitute person,* 236.5 *powerless person,* 238.4 *weakling,* 539.22 *dupe,* 683.5 *failing person*
pattens 295.19 *footwear*
patter 5.5 *nonstandard language,* 5.20 *jargon word,* 5.45 *use language,* 55.62 *rain,* 228.2 *inducement,* 324.15 *walk,* 360.13 *drip,* 424.1 *faintness,* 424.5 *sound faint,* 426.11 *knock,* 521.5 *empty talk,* 564.1 *faculty of speech,* 586.1 *persuasion*
pattering 424.4 *faint*
pattern 792, 55.3 *weather,* 61.26 *gestalt,* 67.4 *weaving,* 67.5 *knitting,* 103.4 *nature,* 109.3 *correlation,* 112.2 *conformity,* 112.10 *conform,* 116.6 *convention,* 119.2 *original,* 150.1 *order,* 150.7 *method,* 152.2 *array,* 154.4, 166.5 *precedent,* 214.1 *regularity,* 268.7 *standard,* 306.1 *form,* 306.2 *prototype,* 306.7 *form,* 382.1, 382.14 *structure,* 456.11 *variegate,* 471.6 *ideal,* 471.19 *epitomize,* 584.1 *habit,* 592.6 *outline,* 619.1 *perfect,* 619.3 *perfection*
pattern after 118.9 *imitate*
patterned 109.6 *correlative,* 112.6 *conforming,* 456.6 *variegated,* 544.12 *identified,* 792.8 *decorated*
patterning 67.7 *dyeing,* 306.1 *form,* 382.5 *structuring*
pattern poetry 48.6 *poetry*
pattern settlement 15.4 *industrial dispute*
pat the bottom 821.27 *kiss*
pat the cheek 821.27 *kiss*
pat the head 821.27 *kiss*
patting 543.15 *gestural*
patulous 261.8 *growing,* 271.1 *broad*

paucity 182.3 *fewness,* 213.3 *infrequency,* 254.2 *disappearance,* 274.12 *thinning,* 609.9 *scarcity,* 743.9 *inadequacy*
Pauli 52 Scientists
Paulicianism 7 Christian Movements
Pauli exclusion principle 57 Named Reactions
Pauling 52 Scientists
Paul Jones 46.2 *dance*
paulownia 85 Trees and Shrubs
Paul Pry 465.4 *meddler*
paunch 258.18 *stomach,* 259.8 *fat,* 290.4 *insides,* 350.16 *eating utensil*
paunchiness 259.5 *fatness*
paunchiness podginess 315.2 *round body*
paunchy 259.16 *fat,* 315.10 *well-rounded*
pauper 743.10 *poor person*
pauperism 743.5 *poverty*
pauperize 743.1 *impoverish*
pauperized 743.2 *insolvent*
pauropod 81.4 *arthropod*
pause 160, 218, 218, 49.17 *notation,* 160.3 *interval,* 160.5 *caesura,* 185.6 *interval,* 187.1 *period,* 209.3 *delayed action,* 209.7 *wait,* 248.8 *intervening space,* 248.21 *space,* 283.6 *interruption,* 283.12 *interrupt,* 325.1 *motionlessness,* 325.8 *be motionless,* 328.2 *hesitate,* 344.6 *stop at,* 641.4 *not act,* 649.1 *ease*
pause for breath 185.6 *interval,* 218.9 *pause*
pause for thought 160.3 *interval,* 160.13 *pause*
Pautiwa 8 Deities
pavane 46.4 *historic dancing*
Pavarotti 49 Musicians and Composers
pave 293.29 *surface,* 376.11 *smooth*
paved 327.15 *accessible*
paved road 327.3 *road*
pavement 280.1 *base,* 293.11 *paving,* 327.6 *path*
pavement artist 50.16 *artist*
pavement pizza 349.23 *vomiting*
paver 293.17 *coverer,* 594.15 *preparer*
Pavese 48 Writers, 48 Poets
pave the way 154.18 *forerun,* 594.1 *prepare,* 660.16 *make easy*
pavilion 27.2 *ground,* 51.14 *theatre,* 256.9 *mobile home*
paving 293, 63.29 *construction equipment,* 69.3 *ornamental garden,* 280.1 *base,* 293.1 *covering,* 376.8 *smooth thing,* 604.2 *building material*
paving material 604.2 *building material*
paving stone 327.4 *road surface,* 604.2 *building material*
pavior 63.26 *masonry*
paviour 594.15 *preparer*
pavis 671.7 *armour*
Pavlov 61.29 *psychologist*
pavlova 45.35 *dessert*
Pavlovian 61.33 *Freudian,* 464.8 *instinctive*
Pavlovian conditioning 61.20 *conditioning*
Pavlovian psychology 61.1 *psychology*
Pavlovian reaction 462.3 *instinct,* 571.8 *involuntariness*
Pavlovian response 464.4 *instinct*
Pavo 53 The Constellations
pavonine 456.7 *iridescent*
paw 407.4 *kiss,* 407.7 *sense organ,* 407.11 *touch,* 726.3 *tools for gripping,* 826.7 *show endearment for*
pawkiness 771.1 *humorousness*
pawky 67.4 *cunning,* 771.10 *humorous*
pawn 42.4 *chess terms,* 127.6 *inferior,* 223.5 *exchange,* 232.3 *assistant,* 539.22 *dupe,* 612.10 *nonentity,* 733.7 *borrow*
pawnbroker 223.4 *person who exchanges,* 728.2 *person transfer-*

ring property, 732.3, 744.5 *lender*
pawnbroker's 744.4 *bank*
pawnbroking 732.1 *lending*
pawned 223.7 *exchanged,* 718.7 *guaranteed,* 733.11 *borrowed*
Pawnee 1 Peoples, 5 Languages and Groups of Languages
pawner 733.6 *borrower*
pawning 223.1 *exchange,* 733.1 *borrowing*
pawn in the game 612.10 *nonentity*
pawnshop 223.2 *place of exchange,* 744.4 *bank*
pawn shop's three balls 544.3 *means of identification*
pawn ticket 223.3 *something in exchange,* 714.2 *guarantee,* 718.2 *promise*
paw the ground 543.11 *gesture,* 828.11 *be angry*
Pax 10.9 *prayer*
Pax Americana 675.1 *peace*
Pax Britannica 675.1 *peace*
Pax Romana 675.1 *peace*
pay 746, 746, 845, 878, 228.5 *positive stimulus,* 613.10 *benefit,* 721.4 *earnings,* 721.13 *be profitable,* 729.5 *give,* 730.2 *something received,* 741.26 *bank,* 748.1 *expend,* 749.3 *income,* 749.7 *receive,* 878.4 *reward for service*
payable 746, 845.12 *owed*
payable on demand 746.17 *payable*
pay a call 353.15 *excrete*
pay a compliment 851.15 *compliment*
pay addresses to 819.14 *seek the friendship of*
pay a dividend 721.13 *be profitable*
pay an exorbitant price 746.6 *pay*
pay a pretty penny 753.11 *overpay*
pay a salary 746.11 *remunerate*
pay as you earn 751.7 *tax*
pay attention 420.15 *hear*
pay attentions to 826.8 *court*
pay attention to 293.33 *fix,* 467.10 *be attentive,* 467.14 *be solicitous,* 469.10 *be careful*
pay a visit 815.12 *visit*
pay back 746, 125.4 *compensate,* 629.3 *restore,* 735.5 *compensate,* 746.13 *retaliate,* 840.5 *atone,* 878.11 *pay,* 879.2 *penalize*
pay back in his own coin 878.11 *pay*
pay back taxes 735.5 *compensate*
pay by cashier's check 746.6 *pay*
pay by cheque 738.1 *purchase,* 746.6 *pay*
pay by credit card 738.1 *purchase*
pay by standing order 746.6 *pay*
pay cash 746.6 *pay*
pay cash for 738.1 *purchase*
pay cheque 721.4 *earnings,* 746.3 *pay*
pay commission 746.11 *remunerate*
pay conscious money 735.5 *compensate*
pay court to 808.9, 808.9 *fawn,* 819.14 *seek the friendship of,* 821.26, 826.8 *court*
pay damages 735.5 *compensate*
pay dearly 746.6 *pay,* 753.11 *overpay*
pay differential 15.2 *industrial negotiations*
pay dividends 682.8 *be effective,* 721.14 *profit*
pay double indemnity 735.5 *compensate*
payee 730.5 *recipient*
payer 746, 741.18 *treasurer*
pay for 284.13 *support financially,* 738.1 *purchase,* 738.5 *defray,* 746.6 *pay,* 746.8 *defray,* 748.3 *donate*
pay for it with one's head 879.6 *be punished*

pay freeze 699.2 *economic restraint*
pay homage 694.6 *show obeisance to*, 817.13 *defer to*
pay homage to 9.7 *worship*, 701.8 *be subject to*, 719.4 *observe*, 861.18 *be good*
pay in advance 718.15 *reserve*, 746.6 *pay*
pay increase 228.5 *positive stimulus*, 721.2 *augmentation*
pay increases 13.6 *economic factors*
pay in full 746.7 *pay off*
paying 746, 243.11 *productive*, 246.5 *fertile*, 613.4 *profitable*, 682.14 *rewarding*, 721.15 *gainful*, 746.1 *payment*, 878.15 *rewarding*
paying back 735.2 *compensation*
paying for 746.1 *payment*
paying guest 255.5 *householder*, 723.5 *possessor*
paying in return 746
paying off 744.1 *credit*, 746.1 *payment*
paying out 746.1 *payment*
paying respect to 719.1 *observance*
pay in kind 109.7 *reciprocate*, 223.5 *exchange*, 746.6 *pay*
pay interest 721.13 *be profitable*, 745.7 *be in debt*
pay lip service 539.26 *be a hypocrite*
payload 53.35 *rocketry*, 70.2 *thing transported*, 73.1 *aviation*, 257.2 *load*, 326.10 *transferred thing*
paymaster 741.17 *financier*, 741.18 *treasurer*, 746.5 *payer*, 750.6 *accountant*
payment 746, 228.5 *positive stimulus*, 729.2 *gift*, 741.6 *funds*, 748.4 *expenditure*, 840.1 *atonement*, 845.5 *dues*, 878.4 *reward for service*, 879.8 *penalty*
Payment 746
payment in kind 109.1 *interchange*, 737.4 *trade*, 746.1 *payment*, 878.4 *reward for service*
payment-in-lieu 746.2 *repayment*, 746.3 *pay*
payment refused 745.5 *amount owing*
payments and receipts 750.1 *accounts*
pay more than it's worth 753.11 *overpay*
Payne's grey 448.4 *greyness*
pay no attention 468.12 *be inattentive*
pay no attention to 693.15 *be disobedient*
pay no heed to 468.12 *be inattentive*, 720.7 *not observe*
pay no regard to 720.7 *not observe*
pay off 746, 74.9 *navigate*, 125.4 *compensate*
payoff 125.1 *compensation*, 155.5 *consequence*, 157.12 *end result*, 195.9 *sequel*, 227.1 *effect*, 684.2 *conclusion*, 746.1 *payment*, 746.3 *pay*, 746.4 *grant*, 878.4 *reward for service*, 878.8 *secret money*
pay off 227.5 *show an effect*, 600.7 *stop work*, 613.10 *benefit*, 672.4 *serve one right*, 682.8 *be effective*, 738.4 *buy off*, 746.11 *remunerate*, 746.13 *retaliate*, 749.7 *receive*, 878.11 *pay*
pay off a debt 700.4 *liberate*
pay off a loan 735.5 *compensate*
pay off a mortgage 700.4 *liberate*
pay off old scores 672.3, 746.13 *retaliate*
payola 746.4 *grant*
pay on call 746.6 *pay*
pay on delivery 746.6 *pay*
pay on demand 746.6 *pay*
pay one back 672.3 *retaliate*
pay one in his own coin 672.3 *retaliate*
pay one out 672.3 *retaliate*

pay one's addresses to 826.8 *court*
pay one's dues 840.5 *atone*
pay one's last respects 399.8 *bury*
pay one's respects 812.16 *commemorate*, 835.9 *sorrow*, 849.18 *show respect*
pay one's share 769.4 *give to charity*, 746.9 *pay one's way*
pay one's way 746
pay one's whack 729.5 *give*
pay on sight 746.6 *pay*
pay on the dot 746.6 *pay*
pay on the nail 746.6 *pay*
pay on the spot 738.1 *purchase*
pay out 36.15 *sail*
payout 746.1 *payment*, 746.3 *pay*
pay out 746.6 *pay*, 748.1 *expend*
pay packet 721.4 *earnings*, 746.3 *pay*
payphone 534.9 *telephone*
pay respect 849.18 *show respect*
pay respects 362.9 *bow*, 817.13 *defer to*
pay respects to 773.6 *fête*
pay respect to 719.4 *observe*
payroll 171.6 *list of names*, 646.4 *personnel*, 746.3 *pay*
pay slip 746.3 *pay*
pay station 534.9 *telephone*
pay suit to 826.8 *court*
pay taxes 729.5 *give*
pay television 534.21 *television*
pay the debt of nature 397.15 *die*
pay the forfeit 840.5 *atone*
pay the freight 746.8 *defray*
pay the penalty 840.5 *atone*
pay the piper 746.8 *defray*
pay the ultimate price 879.6 *be punished*
pay through the nose 746.6 *pay*, 753.11 *overpay*
pay too much 753.11 *overpay*
pay towards 729.5 *give*, 755.10 *be generous*
pay tribute 694.6 *show obeisance to*, 729.5 *give*, 837.6 *be grateful*, 878.9 *reward*
pay tribute to 511.14 *commemorate*, 701.8 *be subject to*, 812.17 *congratulate*, 849.18 *show respect*, 851.15 *compliment*
pay tribute to mammon 742.14 *seek riches*
pay under the table 586.17 *bribe*, 878.11 *pay*
pay up 125.4 *compensate*, 746.7 *pay off*, 750.9 *settle accounts*
pay wages 746.11 *remunerate*
pay well 721.13 *be profitable*
p-block 57.6 *chemical element*
pbow 413.7 *tobacco*
PBS 534.24 *television broadcasting*
PC 65.3 *computer*, 632.3 *protector*
PCP 875.6 *drug*
pdq 329.14 *swiftly*
p.d.q. 648.6 *hastily*
PE 6.3 *subject*, 644.5 *exercise*
pea 45 Vegetables, 315.3 *round thing*
pea bean 45 Vegetables
peabody 46.2 *dance*
peabrain 460.3 *unintelligent person*
peace 675, 116.1 *accord*, 135.2 *agreement*, 150.8 *harmony*, 325.2 *repose*, 422.4 *silence*, 645.2 *time off*, 649.1 *ease*, 667.1 *agreement*
Peace 675
peace! 675
peaceable 150.17 *disciplined*, 242.6 *moderate*, 675.7 *peaceful*, 819.8 *friendly*
peaceable kingdom 675.1 *peace*
peaceableness 675.1 *peace*
peaceably 675.8 *peacefully*, 819.17 *in friendship*
peace advocate 627.12 *reformer*
peace agreement 675.1 *peace*
peace and quiet 150.8 *harmony*, 649.1 *ease*, 675.1 *peace*
peace at any price 673.1 *submission*, 675.1 *peace*, 677.1 *pacification*

peace be with you! 675.9 *peace!*
peace camp 675.1 *peace*, 677.1 *pacification*
peace conference 678.5 *conference*
Peace Corps 675.2 *symbol of peace*, 710.8 *volunteer*
peaceful 675, 135.13 *agreeable*, 150.16 *harmonious*, 240.5 *inert*, 242.6 *moderate*, 325.6 *quiescent*, 376.3 *soothing*, 422.3 *silent*, 649.4 *at ease*, 667.10 *agreeing*, 673.5 *submitting*
peaceful approach 677.2 *peace offering*
peacefully 675, 135.17 *agreeably*, 240.7 *inertly*, 325.10 *motionlessly*, 376.15 *soothingly*, 422.5 *silently*, 649.6 *with ease*, 667.14 *agreeably*, 677.7 *pacifically*
peacefulness 240.1 *inertness*, 325.2 *repose*, 376.7 *smoothness*, 675.1 *peace*
peaceful protest 713.3 *gesture of protest*
peace in our time 675.1 *peace*, 677.1 *pacification*
peacekeeper 675.3 *pacifist*
peacelike 675.7 *peaceful*
peace-lover 675.3 *pacifist*
peace-loving 675.7 *peaceful*, 677.6 *pacificatory*
peacemaker 242.2 *moderator*, 667.5 *assenter*, 675.3 *pacifist*, 677.3 *pacifist*, 678.3 *mediator*, 678.4 *representative*, 715.4 *contractor*
peacemaking 675.1 *peace*, 675.7 *peaceful*, 677.1 *pacification*, 677.6 *pacificatory*
peacemonger 675.3 *pacifist*
peace movement 627.11 *reformism*, 675.1 *peace*, 677.1 *pacification*
peace negotiator 675.3, 677.3 *pacifist*
peacenik 627.12 *reformer*, 675.3 *pacifist*
peace offering 677, 675.1 *peace*, 710.6, 729.3 *offering*, 840.2 *apology*
peace of mind 4.3 *detachment*, 675.1 *peace*, 765.1 *satisfaction*
peace overture 677.2 *peace offering*
peace party 675.1 *peace*
peace pipe 675.1 *peace*, 675.2 *symbol of peace*, 677.2 *peace offering*
peace proposal 675.1 *peace*
peace protester 677.3 *pacifist*
peace sign 675.2 *symbol of peace*
peace talks 675.1 *peace*
peace that passeth all understanding 675.1 *peace*
peacetime 675.1 *peace*, 675.7 *peaceful*
peace treaty 667.2 *contract*, 675.1 *peace*, 677.1 *pacification*, 715.3 *alliance*
peace with honour 657.1 *cunning*
peach 86 Fruits, 450.7 *red thing*, 451.1 *orange*, 451.3 *orange thing*, 528.13 *inform on*, 530.7 *betray*, 861.17 *good thing*
peach cobbler 45.36 *cake*
peach-coloured 450.1 *red*
peacher 530.4 *discloser*
peachiness 383.2 *grain*
peachlike 376.1 *smooth*
peach melba 45.35 *dessert*
peachy 617.1 *worthy*, 789.6 *personable*
peacock 78 Birds, 78.10 *male bird*, 456.5 *variegated thing*, 526.12 *displayer*, 805.13 *proud person*, 809.7 *vain person*, 811.15 *showman*, 811.29 *show off*
Peacock 48 Writers, 53 The Constellations
peacock blue 454.1 *blue*
peacock butterfly 82 Insects
peacock feather 517.7 *bad-luck sign*
peacockish 809.13 *boastful*

peacockry 811.10 *exhibitionism*
peacocks 161 Collective Names by Animal
peacock sitar 49 Musical Instruments
peacock's tail 90 Algae, 456.5 *variegated thing*
peacock worm 81 Worms
pea crab 81.4 *arthropod*
pea family 83.3 *seed plant*
peafowl 78 Birds
pea-green 453.1 *green*
peahen 78.11 *female bird*
pea jacket 295.12 *coat*
peak 34.5 *rock face*, 95.1 *mountain*, 97.3 *wave*, 97.10 *billow*, 126.4 *summit*, 126.8 *be superior*, 144.1 *completeness*, 157.7 *limit*, 272.8 *narrow thing*, 275.2 *heights*, 275.16 *rise*, 279.1 *summit*, 279.7 *top*, 318.2 *projection*, 380.8 *sharp-pointed thing*, 380.14 *be sharp*, 445.5 *lose colour*, 594.14 *preparedness*, 619.3 *perfection*, 624.24 *be unhealthy*, 684.4 *complete*
Peak District 95 Mountains, 95.5 *British mountains*
Peake 48 Writers
peaked 272.3 *tapered*, 274.2 *emaciated*, 445.8 *drained of colour*, 624.21 *unhealthy*
peakish 445.8 *drained of colour*
peak load 64.34 *power supply*
peak of perfection 619.3 *perfection*
peaky 445.8 *drained of colour*, 624.21 *unhealthy*, 624.22 *sick*
peal 49.6 *campanology*, 423.1 *loudness*, 423.8 *be loud*, 425.1, 425.5 *bang*, 426.12 *ring*, 427.2 *ringing*, 427.10 *ring*
pealing 426, 423.6 *loud*, 426.5, 427.7 *ringing*
pea moth 69.12 *pests and diseases*
pean 544.8 *heraldic device*
peanut 86 Nuts
peanut butter 875.6 *drug*
peanut butter and jelly sandwich 45.11 *sandwich*
peanut gallery 51.16 *auditorium*
peanuts 45.10 *snack*, 68.12 *crop*, 86.5 *figurative usage*, 612.8 *trifle*, 741.4 *change*
peanut worm 81 Worms, 81.6 *worm*
pear 86 Fruits
pearl 446.9 *white thing*, 789.3 *attractive female*
pearl bulb 439.6 *electric light*
pearler 74 Ships and Boats
pearlfish 80 Fishes
Pearl Grey 68 Breeds of Fowl
pearl-grey 448.1 *grey*
Pearl Harbor 398.15 *slaughterhouse*
pearlies 295.3 *formal dress*
pearl in an oyster 213.4 *rare things*
pearliness 442.7 *semitransparency*, 446.7 *whiteness*, 456.1 *variegation*
pearlized 439.17 *lustrous*
pearl pearl of price 617.8 *exceller*
pearls 380.11 *tooth*
pearls of wisdom 654.1 *advice*
pearly 439.17 *lustrous*, 442.3 *semitransparent*, 444.13 *soft-hued*, 446.1 *white*, 448.1 *grey*, 456.7 *iridescent*
pearly nautilus 81 Molluscs
Pears 49 Musicians and Composers
pear shape 315.2 *round body*
pear-shaped 311.5, 315.10 *well-rounded*
peas 68.12 *crop*
peasant 68.19 *agricultural*, 255.5 *countryman*, 803.1 *plebeian*
peasant farmer 68.15 *agriculturist*
pease pudding 45.34 *vegetarian dish*
peashooter 338.9 *firearm*
pea soup 55.33 *fog*
peasouper 55.33 *fog*, 438.6 *that*

which makes invisible, 441.2
murk, 443.7 *opaque thing*
peastick 69.6 *garden tool*
peat 69.7 *fertilizer,* 200.10 *fossilization,* 338.13, 410.1 *fuel*
peat bog 98.3 *marsh,* 410.1 *fuel*
peat-brown 449.1 *brown*
peat cutter 410.9 *power-worker*
peat moss 88.3 *moss,* 410.1 *fuel*
pea viner 68.10 *farm tool*
pebble 373.7 *hard substance*
pebbled 98.11 *continental,* 384.18 *grainy*
pebble dash 293.8 *wall covering*
pebble-dash 293.28 *face*
pebble glasses 435.10 *visual aid*
pebble hand-axe 603.3 *prehistoric tool*
pebbles 54.27 *sediment,* 98.4 *coast*
pebbly 54.58 *earthy,* 373.1 *hard,* 384.18 *grainy*
pecan 86 *Nuts*
pecan pie 45.36 *cake*
peccability 620.5 *imperfection,* 864.1 *wickedness*
peccable 620.1 *imperfect*
peccadillo 612.8 *trifle,* 620.5 *imperfection,* 683.3 *personal fault,* 864.3 *venial sin,* 866.3 *sin*
peccancy 618.10 *poverty,* 866.1 *guilt*
peccant 618.4 *poor,* 624.23 *diseased,* 866.5 *guilty*
peccary 77 *Placental Mammals*
peccatiphobia 777 *Phobias by Name*
Pechorsky 32 *Breeds of Horse and Pony*
peck 75 *General Units,* 78.26 *nest,* 330.6 *tap,* 330.13 *blow,* 350.21 *eat,* 821.13 *communication of love,* 826.1 *endearment*
peck at 350.23 *taste*
pecker 245.8 *organs of reproduction,* 350.18 *eater*
pecking 350.3 *delicate eating*
pecking order 150.3 *hierarchy,* 163.5 *social class,* 195.1 *succession*
peckings 350.7 *food*
peckish 782.10 *hungry*
peck on the cheek 815.9 *welcome,* 819.9 *act of friendship,* 821.14 *communication of love,* 826.1 *endearment*
pecks 316.2 *bulge*
Pecksniff 538.12 *cheat,* 539.19 *hypocrite*
Pecksniffery 538.9, 539.3 *hypocrisy,* 540.3 *hypocrisy*
Pecksniffian 538.18 *pretentious,* 539.37, 540.27 *hypocritical*
Pecos 96 *Rivers*
Pécs 93 *Cities*
pectic substance 58.4 *polysaccharide*
pectin 58.4 *polysaccharide,* 637.2 *preserver*
pectinate 380.4 *toothed*
pectoral 316.2 *bulge*
pectoral fin 80.5 *fish anatomy*
pectorals 237.1 *strength*
peculation 601.2 *misuse*
peculator 736.11 *dishonest person*
peculiar 103.9 *characteristic,* 115.4 *dissimilar,* 117.9 *nonconforming,* 163.11 *typical,* 165.16 *characteristic,* 168.14 *eccentric,* 215.5 *unusual,* 510.11 *insane,* 514.8 *surprising,* 786.8 *wonderful*
peculiarity 117.3 *nonconformity,* 165.3 *characteristic,* 165.6 *exception,* 168.4 *unusualness,* 168.5 *idiosyncrasy,* 215.2 *unusualness,* 519.1 *style,* 579.3 *whim*
peculiarize 117.13 *not conform*
peculiarly 115.7, 117.15 *dissimilarly,* 165.30 *characteristically,* 168.21 *unconformably,* 215.9 *unusually*
peculiar trait 168.5 *idiosyncrasy*
pecuniary 13.13 *economic,* 741.22 *monetary*

pecuniary assistance 284.7 *financial support*
pecuniously 741.28 *financially*
ped 49 *Musical Terms*
pedagogical 6.16 *educational*
pedagogically 6.25 *educationally*
pedagogue 6.4 *educator,* 696.9 *educational leader*
pedagogy 6.1 *education*
pedal 71.11 *bicycle part,* 338.11 *propeller,* 338.20 *propel,* 603.1 *tool*
pedalfer 54.36 *soil*
pedal note 427.3 *deepness*
pedal point 49.16 *musical note*
pedal power 235.4 *energy*
pedal pushers 295.9 *trousers*
pedal wheel 44.6 *ceramic workshop*
pedant 167.6 *conformist,* 469.6 *careful person,* 481.6 *discriminating person,* 501.6 *knowledgeable person,* 503.4 *accurate person,* 577.8 *obstinate person,* 619.4 *perfectionist,* 690.4 *strict person*
pedantic 537, 167.14 *conformist,* 467.8 *diligent,* 469.9 *careful,* 481.9 *discriminating,* 493.8 *unjust,* 501.9 *literate,* 503.5 *accurate,* 557.4 *ornate,* 577.4 *set,* 619.2 *perfectionist,* 659.14 *troublesome,* 690.8 *severe,* 719.7 *observant,* 813.6 *formal*
pedantically 467.15 *attentively,* 481.16 *judiciously,* 501.15 *knowledgeably,* 537.38 *literally,* 557.6 *ornately,* 690.11 *severely,* 719.8 *observantly*
pedantry 537, 467.4 *diligence,* 469.4 *fastidiousness,* 503.1 *accuracy,* 690.1 *severity,* 813.2 *formalism*
peddle 727.11 *dispose of property,* 737.1 *trade,* 739.1 *sell*
peddler 739.11 *pedlar*
peddling 612.4 *trivial,* 739.3 *selling*
pederast 877.10 *sex offender*
pederasty 877.7 *sexual assault*
pedestal 43.8 *column,* 280.2 *foot,* 284.2 *supporting part*
pedestal table 47.4 *table*
pedestrian 124.3 *mediocre,* 164.21 *common,* 788.4 *boring*
pedestrian bridge 63.21 *bridge*
pedestrian crossing 71.3 *carriageway,* 327.5 *crossing,* 356.5 *crossing point,* 634.1 *refuge*
pedestrianism 324.1 *motion*
pedestrian lights 439.6 *electric light*
pedestrian precinct 740.7 *emporium*
pedicel 83.5 *stem*
pediculicide 62.4 *drug type*
pediculophobia 777 *Phobias by Name*
pediculosis 622.2 *uncleanness*
pediculous 622.8 *unclean*
pedicure 791.3 *beauty treatment*
pedicurist 630.15 *healer,* 791.13 *beautician*
pedigree 32.13 *breeding,* 134.7 *purebred,* 159.3 *line,* 163.8, 200.12 *genealogy,* 802.3 *nobleness*
pedigreed 134.13 *pure*
pediment 279.3 *architectural summit*
pedlar 739
pedocal 54.36 *soil*
pedological 54.48 *geological*
pedologist 54.3 *geologist*
pedology 54.1 *earth science*
pedometer 268.8 *meter*
Pedrolino 51.30 *clown*
peduncle 83.5 *stem*
pedunculate oak 85 *Trees and Shrubs*
pee 353.3 *urination,* 353.6 *urine,* 353.17 *urinate,* 387.3 *body fluid,* 389.4 *exudate,* 389.32 *seep,* 767.13 *relieve oneself*
peek 435.6, 435.13 *look*
peel 296, 86.3 *fruit structure,*

131.4 *take off,* 132.2 *residue,* 136.10 *set apart,* 266.3 *coat,* 266.11 *scale,* 293.13 *casing,* 294.11 *uncover,* 296.15 *make nude,* 408.16 *feel hot,* 614.6 *refuse*
Peel 96 *Rivers*
peeled 296.11 *exposed,* 296.12 *peeling*
peeler 296.8 *nude person*
peeling 296, 296, 35.6 *rugger,* 294.2 *undressing,* 408.5 *hot weather*
peeling off 33.6 *motor racing terms,* 35.3 *rugby play,* 139.8 *nonadhesive*
peelings 132.2 *residue,* 143.8 *bits and pieces*
peel off 31.9 *play hockey,* 33.10 *be on the track,* 35.5 *play rugby,* 139.5 *unstick,* 139.6 *come unstuck,* 266.11 *scale,* 294.11 *uncover,* 296.14 *undress*
peel-off 31.3 *ice hockey,* 31.8 *hockey*
peen 330.15 *ram*
pee oneself 353.17 *urinate*
peep 78.18 *birdsong,* 78.28, 432.5 *sing,* 435.6, 435.13 *look,* 457.12 *become visible*
pee-pee 353.6 *urine,* 353.17 *urinate*
peepers 435.2 *eye*
peephole 322.5 *hole,* 435.9 *viewpoint*
peeping Tom 435.11 *observer*
Peeping Tom 465.4 *meddler*
peep out 457.12 *become visible*
peepshow 51.5 *show,* 435.7 *view*
peep sight 435.10 *visual aid*
peepul 85 *Trees and Shrubs*
peer 12.8 *politician,* 122.5 *equal,* 653.16 *official,* 802.1 *nobleman*
peerage 802.2 *aristocracy,* 878.1 *reward*
peerer 435.11 *observer*
peer group 2.6 *social group,* 161.17 *family,* 161.18 *generation,* 198.5 *contemporary,* 815.7 *human society*
peering 435.3 *observation*
peerless 103.8 *quintessential,* 115.4 *dissimilar,* 126.14, 617.2 *best,* 619.1 *perfect,* 861.2 *best*
peerlessly 126.17 *supremely,* 861.22 *well*
peeve 768.8 *annoy,* 829.8 *make irascible*
peeved 828.15 *resentful*
peevish 473.8 *argumentative,* 818.5 *discourteous,* 820.6 *hostile,* 829.4 *irascible,* 830.7 *irritable*
peevishly 818.9 *discourteously,* 820.14 *hostilely,* 829.9 *irascibly,* 830.14 *irritably*
peevishness 820.3 *ill feeling,* 828.1 *resentment,* 829.1 *irascibility,* 830.3 *irritableness*
peewee 78 *Birds,* 206.9 *child,* 260.4 *little person,* 270.5 *short person*
peewit 78 *Birds*
peg 34.4 *climbing equipment,* 34.8 *mountaineering,* 121.3 *gradation,* 121.5 *measure,* 137.8 *fastening,* 137.11 *connect,* 283.4 *hanger,* 319.3 *rung,* 323.2 *stopper,* 338.5, 338.23 *throw,* 603.1 *tool*
Pegasus 53 *The Constellations,* 53 *The Constellations,* 32.1 *horse,* 48.13 *poetic genius,* 76.7 *legendary beast*
peg away 219.4 *protract,* 328.1 *move slowly,* 575.6 *persevere,* 644.6 *work*
pegboard 526.8 *showplace*
pegged 137.15 *connected*
pegged pants 295.9 *trousers*
pegged trousers 295.9 *trousers*
peg hammer 34.4 *climbing equipment*
peg it 397.15 *die*
pegmatite 54 *Common Rocks,*

44.2 *raw material,* 54.34 *mineral*
peg out 392.23 *drip-dry,* 397.15 *die*
peg top 364.6 *rotator*
Péguy 48 *Poets*
peignoir 295.16 *robe,* 814.6 *informal dress*
Peipus 94 *Lakes*
Peirce 4 *Philosophers*
pejorate 612.12 *think unimportant*
pejorative 5.17 *word,* 5.42 *worded,* 850.11 *insulting,* 850.13 *contemptuous,* 854.15 *disparaging*
pejoratively 5.50 *lexically,* 854.18 *disparagingly*
Pekin 68 *Breeds of Fowl,* 68 *Breeds of Fowl*
Peking duck 45.48 *Chinese dish*
pekingese 77 *Breeds of Dogs*
Pekingese 5 *Languages and Groups of Languages*
Peking man 200.6 *people of the past,* 202.7 *ancient people,* 400.3 *uncivilized human*
pekoe 351.3 *tea*
pelage 77.2 *mammalian characteristic*
pelagian 97.7 *oceanic*
pelagic 54.51 *oceanic,* 76.15 *of animals,* 97.7 *oceanic*
pelagic ooze 54.27 *sediment*
pelargonic 58 *Common Fatty Acids*
pelargonium 84 *Flowers and Flowering Plants*
Pele 8 *Deities*
Pelé 18 *Sporting Personalities*
p-electron 56.65 *atom*
pelf 721.5 *profit,* 741.2 *cash,* 742.6 *money*
pelican 78 *Birds,* 78.3 *water bird*
pelican crossing 71.3 *carriageway,* 327.5 *crossing,* 356.5 *crossing point,* 634.1 *refuge*
pellagra 350.10 *scarcity,* 624.4 *disease*
pellet 62.12 *injection,* 315.3 *round thing,* 338.8 *missile,* 680.5 *missile weapon,* 680.13 *ammunition*
pellicle 266.3 *coat*
pellicular 266.9 *platelike*
pell-mell 151.28 *anyhow,* 648.6 *hastily*
pellucid 442.1 *transparent,* 522.2 *simple,* 550.3 *clear*
pellucidity 442.5 *transparency,* 522.10 *simplicity,* 550.1 *clarity*
pellucidly 442.13 *transparently,* 550.4 *clearly*
pellucidness 442.5 *transparency*
pelmanism 42 *Card Games*
Peloponnesian Wars 17 *Major Wars*
pelt 55.62 *rain,* 293.14 *animal covering,* 330.3 *hit,* 330.13 *blow,* 338.23 *throw,* 338.29 *riddle,* 670.7 *stone*
peltate 83.18 *of leaves*
Peltier effect 56 *Named Laws*
pelting 55.53 *rainy,* 329.1 *swift,* 338.3 *throwing*
pelt with rotten eggs 852.23 *show disapproval*
pelvic fin 80.5 *fish anatomy*
pelvis 382 *Bones*
pelycosaur 79 *Fossil Reptiles*
Pembroke 68 *Breeds of Cattle,* 93 *Cities*
Pembroke table 47.4 *table*
pemmican 350.7 *food*
pen 50.11 *artist's materials,* 68.7 *farm building,* 68.18 *practise livestock farming,* 77.20 *abode of mammals,* 78.11 *female bird,* 301.2 *enclosed place,* 301.5 *enclose,* 323.4 *closed place,* 323.10 *enclose,* 402.14 *female animal,* 634.3 *animal shelter,* 702.2 *the inside ,* 816.4 *place of confinement*
penal 879.19 *punitive*
penal code 16.1 *the law,* 654.3 *precept,* 879.18 *penology*

penal colony 816.4 *place of confinement,* 879.7 *punishment*
penal institution 816.4 *place of confinement*
penalization 879.7 *punishment*
penalize 879, 616.5 *be inconvenient*
penalizing 879.19 *punitive*
penally 879.23 *punitively*
penal servitude 879.7 *punishment*
penal settlement 816.4 *place of confinement*
penalties 23
penalty 19, 879, 31.8 *hockey,* 32.7 *horseracing,* 35.3 *rugby play,* 35.6 *rugger,* 38.2 *football play,* 125.1 *compensation,* 644.1 *work,* 699.1 *restraint,* 722.1 *loss,* 735.2 *compensation,* 746.4 *grant,* 751.8 *levy*
penalty area 38.1 *soccer*
penalty award 31.1 *hockey,* 31.3 *ice hockey,* 31.3 *ice hockey*
penalty box 31.3 *ice hockey*
penalty clause 695.3 *coercive methods*
penalty corner 31.1 *hockey*
penalty flag 19.13 *penalty*
penalty goal 35.3 *rugby play*
penalty kick 35.3 *rugby play,* 330.13 *blow*
penalty-kick 330.7 *kick*
penalty marker 19.13 *penalty*
penalty play 31.5 *lacrosse*
penalty plays 31.1 *hockey,* 31.3 *ice hockey*
penalty shot 23.4 *playing terms,* 31.3 *ice hockey*
penalty spot 31.1 *hockey,* 38.1 *soccer*
penalty stroke 29.3 *golf shots,* 31.1 *hockey*
penalty try 35.3 *rugby play*
penal work 644.1 *work*
penance 879, 10.5 *Christian rite,* 125.1 *compensation,* 840.2 *apology*
pen-and-ink 50.9 *drawing*
pen-and-ink sketch 445
Penang 98 Islands
Penates 8 Deities
penchant 234.2 *attitude,* 782.1 *desire,* 784.2 *inclination*
pencil 50.11 *artist's materials,* 50.20 *draw*
pencil cedar 85 Trees and Shrubs
pencil drawing 50.9 *drawing*
pencil of light 56.24 *light emission*
pencil point 380.7 *sharp point*
pencil sharpener 380.12 *sharpener*
pendant 43 Architectural Decoration, **74** Rigging, 114.5 *counterpart,* 283.3 *suspended object*
pendency 283.1 *suspension*
pendent 283.7 *suspended*
pendente lite 16.87 *in litigation*
pendentive 43.14 *roofed,* 43.17 *structured*
pendentive dome 43.6 *roof*
pendently 283.13 *pendulously*
pending 185.21 *lasting through time,* 199.11 *future,* 218.10 *finished,* 240.6 *suspended,* 283.9 *interrupted*
Pendleton Round Up 32.12 *rodeo*
Pend Oreille 94 Lakes
pendular motion 365.1 *oscillation*
pendulate 365.8 *oscillate*
pendulation 365.1 *oscillation*
pendule 34.3 *climbing technique*
pendulous 139.8 *nonadhesive,* 283.7 *suspended*
pendulously 283, 139.10 *noncohesively*
pendulousness 283.1 *suspension*
pendulum 34.3 *climbing technique,* 56.87 *clock,* 214.5 *regular thing,* 283.3 *suspended object,* 331.5 *reflector,* 365.7 *oscillator*
pendulum clock 191 Timepieces and Timers

pendulum movement 214.1 *regularity*
pendulum wheel 365.7 *oscillator*
Penelope's web 614.5 *waste of effort,* 685.2 *never-ending task*
penetrability 522.9 *intelligibility*
penetrable 522.1 *intelligible*
penetrate 19.16 *play defence,* 133.10 *become mixed,* 253.11 *be present,* 322.20 *hole,* 346.11 *infiltrate,* 354.2 *inject,* 356.10 *enter,* 522.4 *be intelligible,* 522.6 *understand,* 554.6 *emphasize*
penetrated 322.14 *holed*
penetrating 356, 253.7 *present,* 346.16 *invasive,* 430.7 *strident,* 554.3 *emphatic,* 832.14 *hostile*
penetrating eye 435.2 *eye*
penetration 19.10 *defence,* 133.1 *mixture,* 277.3 *profundity,* 346.3 *inroad,* 354.9 *injection,* 356.3 *passage into,* 507.1 *wisdom,* 554.1 *emphasis*
pen friend 534.5 *correspondent*
penguin 78 Birds, 78.2 *flightless bird*
penguins 161 Collective Names by Animal
peniaphobia 777 Phobias by Name
penicillamine 62 Medication
penicillin 62 Medication, 62.4 *drug type,* 89.6 *fungal antibiotic,* 630.8 *drug*
penicillium 89 Fungi
penile 245.16 *reproductive*
peninsula 98, 54.11 *coast,* 249.1 *region,* 272.6 *narrow place,* 318.2 *projection*
peninsular 98.11 *continental,* 249.16 *regional*
penis 245.8 *organs of reproduction*
penitence 867, 9.1 *worship,* 10.3 *rite of worship,* 627.5 *improvement,* 840.2 *apology,* 866.2 *signs of guilt*
Penitence 867
penitent 867, 9.5 *worshipper,* 9.9 *worshipful,* 10.17 *worshipper,* 840.3 *atoner,* 840.4 *atoning,* 867.3 *penitent person*
penitential 867, 10.21 *ritualistic,* 125.9 *compensatory,* 840.4 *atoning*
penitential act 840.2 *apology*
penitential exercise 840.2 *apology*
penitentially 9.12 *worshipfully,* 125.11 *in compensation,* 867.8 *penitently*
penitential rites 10.5 *Christian rite*
penitentiary 125.9 *compensatory,* 816.4 *place of confinement,* 840.4 *atoning,* 867.7 *penitential*
penitently 840, 867
penitent person 867
penknife 380.10 *knife*
penman 48.14 *author*
pen name 529.8 *anonymity,* 531.7 *concealer,* 560.8 *name*
pennant 36.3 *parts of a sailing boat,* 544.7 *flag*
pennant winner 22.1 *baseball*
penne 45 Types of Pasta
penned 301.7 *enclosed,* 726.10 *retained*
penne lisce 45 Types of Pasta
penne rigate 45 Types of Pasta
pennette rigate 45 Types of Pasta
penniless 593.5 *necessitous,* 687.7 *unprosperous,* 743.1 *poor*
pennilessness 743.5 *poverty*
Pennines 95 Mountains, 95.5 *British mountains*
pennon 544.7 *flag*
Pennsylvania 92 American States
Pennsylvania Dutch ware 44 Types of Ceramics
Pennsylvania Station 43 Noted Buildings
penny 741.8 *American money,* 741.9 *British money,* 741.10 *former British money*

penny ante 42 Card Games
penny dreadful 48.2 *fiction*
penny-farthing 71.12 *bicycle*
penny-pincher 161.36 *hoarder,* 754.8 *bargain hunter,* 758.5 *miser*
penny-pinching 758.1 *mean*
pennyroyal 84 Flowers and Flowering Plants
pennyweight 75 General Units, 369.9 *avoirdupois weight*
penny whistle 430.3 *shrillness*
penny-wise 758.1 *mean*
penny wise and pound foolish 607.8 *wasteful*
Penobscot 1 Peoples
penological 879.19 *punitive*
penologically 879.23 *punitively*
penologist 879.18 *penology*
penology 879, 16.37 *criminology*
penorcon 49 Musical Instruments
pen pal 534.5 *correspondent*
pen pusher 560.10 *descriptive writer*
pensile 283.7 *suspended*
pensileness 283.1 *suspension*
pension 13.8 *industrial relations,* 14.4 *personal finance,* 284.7 *financial support,* 284.13 *support financially,* 662.4 *social assistance,* 721.4 *earnings,* 729.2 *gift,* 730.2 *something received,* 749.3 *pay,* 749.3 *income,* 831.3 *welfare,* 878.4 *reward for service*
pensionable age 207.5 *old age*
pensionary 729.7 *given,* 730.14 *receivable*
pensioned 705.7 *resigning,* 730.11 *receiving*
pensioned-off 705.7 *resigning,* 730.11 *receiving*
pensioner 207.7 *older person,* 705.3 *resigner,* 730.5 *recipient*
pensioners 202.2 *old people*
pension fund 749.3 *income*
pension off 349.2 *dismiss,* 600.7 *stop work,* 727.10 *dismiss*
pension programme 15.2 *industrial negotiations*
pensive 4.17 *thoughtful,* 461.9 *concentrating,* 772.1 *solemn*
pensively 4.28 *thoughtfully*
pensiveness 461.3 *thoughtfulness,* 462.6 *daydream*
pent 272.1 *narrow*
pentachord 179.1 *five*
pentacle 52.44 *polygon,* 179.1 *five*
pentadic 179.12 *fifth*
pentaerythritol 62 Medication
pentagon 52.44 *polygon,* 179.1 *five,* 310.3 *angled figure*
pentagonal 52.82 *polygonal,* 179.12 *fifth,* 310.9 *angled*
Pentagonese 5.20 *jargon word,* 578.5 *equivocalness*
pentagram 11.5 *spell,* 52.44 *polygon,* 179.1 *five*
pentahedral 179.12 *fifth*
pentahedron 52.46 *polyhedron,* 179.1 *five*
pentahydrate 57.10 *salt*
pentameter 48.9 *metre,* 179.1 *five*
pentane 57 Common Chemical Compounds
pentangle 52.44 *polygon*
pentangular 179.12 *fifth*
pentaprism 66.17 *lens*
pentarchy 179.1 *five*
pentastich 48.8 *part of poem,* 179.1 *five*
pentastomid 81.4 *arthropod*
Pentastomida 81.4 *arthropod*
Pentateuch 16.1 *the law,* 179.1 *five*
pentathlete 21.3 *athlete*
pentathlon 21.2 *field events,* 179.1, 179.1 *five,* 674.2 *contest*
pentatonic 179.12 *fifth*
pentavalent 57.35 *combined*
pentazocine 62 Medication
Pentecostalism 7 Christian Movements
penthouse 256.5 *house,* 275.8 *high thing,* 279.3 *architectural summit,* 725.1 *property*

pentlandite 54 Minerals
pentobarbitone 62 Medication
pentode 64.20 *electron tube*
pentose 58.3 *carbohydrate*
pentothal interview 61.3 *psychiatric treatment*
pent up 699.14 *self-restrained*
pent-up 272.1 *narrow,* 301.7 *enclosed*
penumbra 56.24 *light emission,* 441.1 *dimness*
pen up 301.5 *enclose*
penurious 687.7 *unprosperous,* 743.1 *poor,* 758.1 *mean*
penuriously 743.15 *poorly*
penury 571.4 *need,* 743.5 *poverty*
Penutian 5 Languages and Groups of Languages
Penzance 93 Cities
peon 679.17 *army person,* 697.5 *office assistant,* 701.5 *subjected person,* 808.3 *sycophant*
peonage 701.1 *subjection,* 808.1 *servility*
peony 84 Flowers and Flowering Plants, 450.7 *red thing*
people 777 Phobias by Topic, 1.7 *society,* 124.7 *average person,* 161.17 *family,* 255.2 *inhabitants,* 255.15 *settle,* 256.17 *inhabit,* 400.9 *group,* 400.11 *nation*
people at large 255.2 *inhabitants*
people mover 71.4 *personal transport*
people of antiquity 200.6 *people of the past*
people of the past 200
people of today 198.5 *contemporary*
people's choice 12.1 *government*
people's front 665.3 *political grouping*
peoples of the earth 400.1 *humankind*
People's Party 12.6 *political party*
people's republic 91.1 *country,* 249.4 *territorial division*
Peoria 93 Cities
pep 235.3 *vitality,* 239.1 *vigour,* 642.4 *energy*
PEP 14.4 *personal finance*
pepe supi 45.53 *African dish*
peplum 295.24 *part of garment*
pepo 86.2 *botanical fruit*
pepper 45 Vegetables, 45.7 *basic ingredient,* 162.18 *sprinkle,* 239.1 *vigour,* 338.29 *riddle,* 413.2 *seasoning,* 413.12 *season,* 456.11 *variegate,* 670.2 *fire*
pepper-and-salt 446.3 *white-haired,* 448.2 *grey-haired,* 456.10 *mottled*
peppercorn 413.2 *seasoning*
peppercorn rent 754.1 *cheapness*
peppered 162.23 *sprinkled,* 456.10 *mottled*
peppered with shot 322.14 *holed*
pepperiness 829.1 *irascibility*
peppering 162.4 *sprinkling*
pepper mill 384.11 *pulverizer*
peppermint 45 Herbs and Spices, 45.41 *sweet,* 413.5 *herbs,* 414.4 *confectionery*
peppermint tea 351.3 *tea*
pepper tree 85 Trees and Shrubs
pepper with shot 322.20 *hole*
pepperwort 88 Ferns
peppery 413.9 *piquant,* 829.4 *irascible*
pep pill 630.7 *tonic,* 875.6 *drug*
peppy 239.4 *vigorous,* 554.3 *emphatic*
pep rally 19.14 *miscellaneous terms,* 586.4 *exhortation*
Pepsi 91 Names for Inhabitants, 351.6 *soft drink*
pepsin 58.11 *enzyme,* 371.5 *condenser*
pep squad 19.14 *miscellaneous terms*
pep talk 567.2 *salutation,* 586.4 *exhortation*
peptic 630.17 *remedial*
peptic ulcer 624.8 *indigestion*

peptidase 58.11 *enzyme*
peptide 57 *Types of Compounds*, 58.8 *amino acid*
peptide bond 58.8 *amino acid*
peptidoglycan 58.9 *protein*
pep up 133.8 *mix*, 239.3, 239.3 *invigorate*
Pequot 1 *Peoples*, **5** *Languages and Groups of Languages*
per 232.9 *instrumentally*
peradventure 486.9 *possibly*
perambulation 324.1 *motion*, 356.1 *passage*
perambulator 71.8 *baby carriage*
per annum 214.16 *cyclically*
peraphrasis 48.12 *poetic language*
percale 67 *Natural Fabrics*
per capita 731.8 *proportionately*
perceivability 437.3 *visibility*
perceivable 435.23, 437.1 *visible*
perceive 6.24 *know*, 403.11 *sense*, 420.15 *hear*, 435.12 *see*, 435.16 *visualize*, 459.12 *think*, 463.11 *reason*, 464.9 *be intuitive*, 471.14 *have an idea*, 496.1 *discover*, 501.11 *know*, 519.14 *imagine*, 522.7 *recognize*, 759.15 *feel*
perceived 501.10 *known*
perceived noise decibel 75 *Scientific and Technical Units*
per cent 52.87 *mathematically*
percent 169.5 *ratio*
percentage 52.18 *division*, 143.1 *part*, 169.5 *ratio*, 173.2 *fractional part*, 721.5 *profit*, 752.1 *discount*
percentile 52.60 *parameter*, 52.74 *divisible*
perceptibility 437.3 *visibility*
perceptible 268.14 *measurable*, 403.8 *sensate*, 407.8 *touchable*, 435.23, 437.1 *visible*, 496.15 *discoverable*
perceptibly 268.17 *measurably*, 407.16 *sensitively*, 435.25, 437.11 *visibly*
perception 6.11 *refinement*, 403.1 *sensation*, 435.4 *visualization*, 459.1 *mind*, 463.1 *reason*, 464.1 *intuition*, 471.1 *idea*, 471.8 *imagination*, 481.2 *judiciousness*, 496.6 *discovery*, 501.1 *knowledge*, 507.1 *wisdom*, 519.1 *imagination*, 522.12 *understanding*, 759.1 *feeling*
perceptive 6.20 *refined*, 380.5 *mentally sharp*, 403.7 *susceptible*, 435.21 *seeing*, 463.7 *reasoning*, 464.6 *intuitive*, 481.9 *discriminating*, 501.8 *knowledgeable*, 507.5 *wise*, 519.10 *imaginative*, 759.10 *feeling*, 760.1 *sensitive*
perceptively 6.27 *discerningly*, 471.22 *imaginatively*, 481.16 *judiciously*, 760.12 *sensitively*
perceptiveness 6.11 *refinement*, 459.1 *mind*
perceptual 471.10 *theoretical*
perceptual computing 65.16 *artificial intelligence*
perceptual concept 61.26 *gestalt*
perch 75 *General Units*, **80** *Fishes*, **20.5** *British game fish*, 45.17 *freshwater fish*, 78.14, 78.26 *nest*, 256.13 *lair*, 256.18 *take up residence*, 325.8 *be motionless*, 344.4 *land*, 360.12 *drop*, 362.8 *sit*, 649.2 *take it easy*
perchance 589, 229.8 *by chance*, 486.9 *possibly*
Percheron 32 *Breeds of Horse and Pony*
perching 78.23 *avian*
perching bird 78.6 *songbird*
perching duck 78.3 *water bird*
perchlike 80.13 *fishlike*
perchloric acid 57 *Common Chemical Compounds*
Perchta 8 *Deities*
percipience 459.1 *mind*
percipient 403.5 *sensible*
percoid 80.13 *fishlike*
percolate 54.63 *ebb*, 134.10 *pu-*

rify, 346.11 *infiltrate*, 347.12 *leak*, 348.13 *absorb*, 356.10 *enter*, 387.23 *dissolve*, 389.29 *water*, 389.32, 391.16 *seep*, 621.15 *purify*
percolating 347.3 *leakage*, 356.13 *penetrating*, 391.12 *seeping*
percolation 54.10 *water cycle*, 346.3 *inroad*, 347.3 *leakage*, 348.5 *absorption*, 356.3 *passage into*, 387.8 *fluidification*, 389.9 *soaking*, 391.4 *seepage*, 621.2 *cleaning*
percolator 258.15 *pot*
percuss 330.2 *collide*
percussion 49.25 *musical instrument*, 330.12 *collision*
percussion cap 410.2 *lighter*
percussively 330.18 *dynamically*
perdendosi 49 *Musical Terms*
per diem 214.16 *cyclically*
perdition 8.11 *heaven*, 244.4 *ruin*, 722.1 *loss*
perdurability 188.4 *long-lastingness*
Perec 48 *Writers*
Père David's deer 77 *Placental Mammals*
peregrine falcon 78 *Birds*
pereira bark 85 *Tree Products*
Perelman 48 *Writers*
peremptoriness 535.6 *assertiveness*, 688.2 *authoritativeness*
peremptory 535.14 *assertive*, 688.12 *authoritative*, 847.12 *obligatory*
perennate 83.22 *be dormant*
perennial 69.9 *garden plant*, 69.17 *botanical*, 83.2 *plant*, 83.14 *of plants*, 84.2 *flowering plant*, 188.9 *permanent*, 214.12 *cyclic*, 217.7 *permanent*, 225.9 *stable*
perennially 69.20 *horticulturally*, 83.24 *herbaceously*, 185.30 *chronologically*, 188.12 *everlastingly*, 214.16 *cyclically*, 217.9 *permanently*, 225.12 *stably*
pererrate 335.3 *go astray*
pereration 335.16 *wandering*
perfect 619, 619, 5.34 *tense*, 8.13 *divine*, 84.12 *of flowers*, 126.14 *best*, 134.12 *morally pure*, 142.7 *uncut*, 142.10, 144.4 *complete*, 144.7 *complete*, 469.4 *careful*, 503.5, 537.21 *accurate*, 537.31 *be accurate*, 558.4 *be elegant*, 617.1 *worthy*, 617.2 *best*, 621.16 *clean*, 627.1 *improve*, 637.7 *preserved*, 655.6 *skilful*, 684.6 *elaborate*, 684.7 *completed*, 861.2 *best*, 863.5 *virtuous*, 865.5 *innocent*, 876.9 *pure*
perfecta 32.7 *horseracing*
perfect cadence 49.13 *melody*, 433.3 *melodiousness*
perfect candidate 485.8 *qualified person*, 667.5 *assenter*
perfect condition 619.3 *perfection*
perfected 144.7 *complete*, 594.20 *developed*, 619.1 *perfect*, 684.7 *completed*
perfecter 619.4 *perfectionist*
perfect fit 667.3 *compatibility*
perfect game 22.4 *pitching terms*
perfect gentleman 857.3 *honourable person*
perfectibility 336.15 *improvement*, 620.5 *imperfection*
perfectible 620.1 *imperfect*, 627.15 *improvable*
perfection 619, 8.1 *divinity*, 126.1 *superiority*, 134.1 *purity*, 144.1 *completeness*, 469.4 *fastidiousness*, 537.8 *accuracy*, 617.6 *worth*, 627.5 *improvement*, 655.1 *skill*, 696.11 *masterpiece*, 861.9 *the best*, 863.1 *virtue*, 865.1 *innocence*, 876.3 *moral purity*
Perfection 619
perfectionism 469.4 *fastidiousness*, 481.2 *judiciousness*, 596.6 *venture*, 627.5 *improvement*,

627.11 *reformism*, 642.8 *assiduity*
perfectionist 619, 619, 469.6 *careful person*, 469.9 *careful*, 481.6 *discriminating person*, 481.9 *discriminating*, 596.7 *attempter*, 627.12 *reformer*, 627.16 *improving*
perfective 684.7 *completed*
perfectly 8.19 *divinely*, 102.18 *ideally*, 126.17 *supremely*, 134.18 *virtuously*, 144.9 *completely*, 469.12 *carefully*, 471.23 *ideally*, 537.39 *accurately*, 684.9 *completely*, 861.22 *well*, 863.9 *virtuously*, 865.11 *innocently*
perfectly dreadful 618.3 *bad*
perfect moment 210.1 *timeliness*
perfectness 619.3 *perfection*
perfect number 52.5 *number*
perfect participle 5.35 *part of speech*
perfect pitch 49.21 *tone*, 420.1 *hearing*, 503.1 *accuracy*
perfect sacrifice 22.5 *batting terms*
perfect silence 422.4 *silence*
perfect style 558.1 *elegance*
perfect touch 549.2 *stylishness*
perfect treasure 617.8 *exceller*
perfect vision 435.1 *vision*
perfect wreck 628.9 *dilapidation*
perfervid 642.18 *active*
perfidious 309.8 *exaggerated*, 474.8 *cunning*, 491.7 *unreliable*, 527.5 *mysterious*, 538.15 *lying*, 539.38 *treacherous*, 540.29 *deceitful*, 578.11 *equivocating*, 657.4 *cunning*, 693.13 *disobedient*, 858.6 *faithless*
perfidiously 578, 309.14 *distortedly*, 474.15 *hypocritically*, 538.28 *dishonestly*, 693.17 *disobediently*
perfidiousness 693.1 *disobedience*, 858.2 *faithlessness*
perfidy 309.4 *distortion of the truth*, 538.3 *lying*, 539.4 *falseheartedness*, 540.6 *lying*, 578.7 *apostasy*, 693.1 *disobedience*, 858.2 *faithlessness*
perflation 390.6 *ventilation*
perforate 322.20 *hole*, 380.16 *use a sharp tool*
perforated 322.14 *holed*
perforation 322.1 *opening*
perforator 380.8 *sharp-pointed thing*, 603.1 *tool*
perforce 571.19 *necessarily*, 695.11 *compellingly*
perform 719, 49.36 *play*, 51.32 *act*, 144.4 *complete*, 230.7 *be operational*, 232.4 *be an instrument*, 243.10 *produce*, 457.13 *occur*, 475.15 *demonstrate*, 475.18 *appear*, 526.1 *display*, 547.10 *act*, 590.14 *carry on*, 640.4 *act*, 694.5 *obey*, 811.27 *show*, 812.16 *commemorate*
performable 486.5 *possible*
perform a combined movement 30.10 *compete in gymnastics*
perform a function 613.9 *be useful*
perform a gymnastic routine 30.10 *compete in gymnastics*
perform a miracle 629.6 *cure*
performance 49, 719, 49.2 *music making*, 51.11 *theatrical performance*, 51.20 *acting*, 230.1 *operation*, 232.1 *instrumentality*, 243.1 *production*, 243.5 *work of art*, 435.7 *view*, 437.5 *manifestation*, 457.2 *being in view*, 475.1 *demonstration*, 526.9 *production*, 547.3 *acting*, 640.1 *action*, 684.1 *completion*, 812.1 *celebration*, 847.5 *discharge of duty*
performance art 50 *Western Art Styles and Movements*
performance gain 721.2 *augmentation*
performance-oriented 232.6 *instrumental*
performance poetry 48.6 *poetry*

perform a somersault 30.10 *compete in gymnastics*
perform a stunt 640.4 *act*
perform better 721.10 *augment*
perform do 613.9 *be useful*
performed 51.37 *dramatic*
performer 547, 49.24 *musician*, 51.27 *entertainer*, 475.7 *demonstrator*, 640.3 *doer*, 646.1 *worker*
performing 51.20, 547.3 *acting*, 640.5 *acting*
performing area 51.15 *stage*
Performing Arts 51
perform magic 216.8 *cause change*
perform one's ablutions 389.34 *hose*
perform rites 10
perform skilfully 861.19 *be good at*
perform the hajj 7.19 *be religious*
perform the rites 719.5 *observe religious ceremony*
perform vivisection on 398.22 *kill animals*
perfrication 385.1 *friction*
perfume 418, 349.14 *let out*, 388.26 *aerate*, 389.14 *lavender water*, 416.1 *odour*, 416.9 *impart odour to*, 418.1 *fragrance*, 418.2 *fragrant thing*, 791.6 *toiletries*, 791.16 *make up*
perfume bottle 418.2 *fragrant thing*
perfumed 405.6 *pleasant*, 416.5 *odorous*, 418.4 *fragrant*
perfume dynamics 418.1 *fragrance*
perfume oil 791.6 *toiletries*
perfumer 418.2 *fragrant thing*
perfumery 418.2 *fragrant thing*
perfume spray 418.2 *fragrant thing*
perfunctorily 685.7 *incompletely*
perfunctoriness 145.1 *incompleteness*, 358.5 *shortfall*, 573.14 *disobedience*, 620.5 *imperfection*, 685.1 *noncompletion*, 720.1 *nonobservance*, 783.1 *indifference*
perfunctory 468, 145.4 *incomplete*, 358.8 *defective*, 482.1 *undiscriminating*, 620.2 *incomplete*, 648.3 *hasty*, 656.4 *bungled*, 685.4 *uncompleted*, 720.11 *nonobservant*, 783.7 *indifferent*
perfuse 60.20 *practise surgery*, 62.19 *administer*, 326.11 *transfer*, 354.2 *inject*, 630.20 *doctor*
perfused 354.13 *injected*
perfusion 60.9 *surgery*, 326.3 *transmission*, 354.9 *injection*, 630.12 *surgery*
Pergamene school 50 *Western Art Styles and Movements*
pergola 69.3 *ornamental garden*
perhaps 486.9 *possibly*, 589.14 *perchance*
per head 731.8 *proportionately*
perianth 84.3 *flower part*
periapt 11.6 *talisman*
pericardiectomy 60 *Surgical Operations*
pericardiostomy 60 *Surgical Operations*
pericardiotomy 60 *Surgical Operations*
pericarditis 624.10 *cardiovascular disease*
pericarp 86.3 *fruit structure*
periclase 54 *Minerals*
Pericles 48 *Shakespeare's plays*
peridotite 54 *Common Rocks*, 54.30 *igneous rock*
perigee 53.35 *rocketry*, 264.1 *nearness*
perigynous 84.12 *of flowers*
perihelion 53.21 *orbit*, 264.1 *nearness*
peril 633.5 *danger*
perilous 491.7 *unreliable*, 633.1 *dangerous*, 772.3 *important*
perilously 491.26 *unreliably*, 633.11 *dangerously*
perilousness 633.5 *danger*

perilous state 633.5 *danger*
perimeter 38.1 *soccer*, 52.37 *line*, 297.1 *surroundings*, 299.3 *edge*
perimetric 297.4 *surrounding*
perinatal 245.16 *reproductive*
perineoplasty 60 *Surgical Operations*
period **187**, 54.41 *geological time*, 55.3 *weather*, 56.8 *time*, 57.6 *chemical element*, 121.4 *interval*, 136.5 *separator*, 185.3, 188.1 *duration*, 203.1 *season*, 214.2 *cycle*, 248.8 *intervening space*, 353.11 *menstruation*, 365.5 *wave*, 543.7 *punctuation*, 731.3 *allotted task*
Period 187
periodic **185, 187**, 52.85 *cyclic*, 159.12 *cyclical*, 160.8 *discontinuous*, 183.14 *recurrent*, 212.3 *frequent*, 214.11 *regular*, 324.17 *directional*, 365.13 *oscillating*
periodical **187, 187**, 185.22 *periodic*, 214.11 *regular*, 532.5 *journal*
periodically **187**, 160.17 *discontinuously*, 212.1 *frequently*, 214.15 *regularly*
periodical publication 187.7 *periodical*
periodic function 52.29 *mathematical function*, 187.5 *recurrent period*
periodicity **187**, 159.6 *continuum*, 212.4 *frequency*, 214.1 *regularity*, 365.1 *oscillation*
periodic table 57.6 *chemical element*
period of activity **187**
period of detention 702.4 *prison sentence*
period of work 644.2 *task*
periodontal 60.23 *dental*
periodontic 60.23 *dental*
periodontics 60.4 *dentistry*
periodontist 60.14 *dentist*
periodontologist 60.14 *dentist*
periodontology 60.4 *dentistry*
period pains 406.2 *painful condition*
peripatetic 4.11 *follower of a doctrine*, 4.14 *of a philosophy*, 324.16 *moving*
peripatetically 324.18 *in motion*
peripatetic philosophy 4.7 *school of thought*
peripatus 81.6 *worm*
peripeteia 48.3 *aspect of fiction*
peripheral **65**, 65.4 *computer part*, 104.12 *external*, 130.4 *extra*, 147.11 *excluded*, 263.8 *distant*, 297.4 *surrounding*, 299.6 *outlined*, 300.8 *edging*, 612.3 *secondary*
peripherally 104.18 *extraneously*, 299.7 *essentially*, 300.11 *marginally*
peripherals 136.7 *separates*
periphery 104.4 *externality*, 263.3 *distant place*, 289.1 *exterior*, 297.1 *surroundings*, 300.1 *edge*
periphrasis 5.24 *phrasing*, 285.3 *deviousness*, 334.2 *detour*, 553.2 *circumlocution*
periphrastic 5.43 *phrasal*, 286.5 *devious*, 334.7 *circuitous*, 553.4 *circumlocutory*
periphrastically 5.51 *phraseologically*, 286.9 *deviously*, 334.8, 553.8 *circuitously*
periscope 56.32 *optical instrument*
perish 141.3 *disintegrate*, 244.13 *be destroyed*, 397.15 *die*, 409.10 *be cold*, 458.1 *disappear*, 628.1 *deteriorate*
perishability 397.1 *death*
perishable 189.6 *transient*, 397.20 *deadly*
perishable goods 13.6 *economic factors*, 739.8 *merchandise*
perishables 13.6 *economic factors*, 739.8 *merchandise*
perishing 55.55 *cool*, 409.8 *cold*
perissodactyl 77.15 *hoofed mammal*, 77.33 *ungulate*

Perissodactyla 77.15 *hoofed mammal*
peristyle 43.8 *column*
periwig 295.15 *headgear*
periwinkle **81** *Molluscs*, **84** Flowers and Flowering Plants
perjorate 766.7 *be dissatisfied*, 850.19 *disrespect*
perjorative 766.4 *dissatisfied*
perjure 538.21 *lie*
perjured 856.9 *perjurious*
perjured testimony 856.2 *false accusation*
perjure oneself 856.6 *accuse falsely*, 858.8 *be dishonourable*
perjurer 538.11, 539.16 *liar*, 540.15 *false person*, 856.3 *accuser*
perjuring 538.15 *lying*, 540.29 *deceitful*
perjurious 856, 538.13 *untrue*, 540.32 *falsified*
perjuriously 538.26 *untruthfully*, 856.10 *accusingly*
perjury 531.5 *evasion*, 538.1 *untruth*, 538.3, 540.6 *lying*, 856.2 *false accusation*
perk 116.9 *grant*, 130.4 *extra*, 228.5 *positive stimulus*, 361.3 *promote*, 610.3 *superfluity*, 721.5 *profit*, 729.2 *gift*, 730.2 *something received*, 754.6 *absence of charge*, 878.4 *reward for service*
perked up 651.4 *refreshed*
perkily 769.9 *cheerfully*, 809.21 *cockily*
Perkin 52 *Scientists*
perkiness 809.3 *cockiness*
perking up 629.11 *recuperation*, 651.5 *refreshment*
perknite 54.30 *igneous rock*
Perkunas 8 *Deities*
perk up 361.1 *raise*, 361.3 *promote*, 651.2 *be refreshed*, 769.6 *bring cheer*
perky 769.1 *cheerful*, 809.11 *cocky*
perm 791.8 *hair cut*
permafrost 55.36 *frost*, 409.6 *Arctic*
permalloy 57 *Alloys*
Permalloy 56.59 *ferromagnetism*
permanence **217**, 112.1 *uniformity*, 186.3 *immutability*, 188.4 *long-lastingness*, 190.1 *eternity*, 225.1 *stability*, 575.3 *constancy*, 637.1 *preservation*
Permanence **217**
permanency 188.4 *long-lastingness*, 217.1 *permanence*
permanent **188, 217**, 112.5 *uniform*, 186.6 *changeless*, 190.8 *eternal*, 225.9 *stable*, 584.11 *normal*
permanently 217, 112.13 *uniformly*, 188.12 *everlastingly*, 225.12 *stably*
permanent magenta 455.2 *purple pigment*
permanent magnet 56.60 *magnet*
permanent pasture 87.2 *grassland*
permanent post 632.1 *safety*
permanent secretary 653.16 *official*
permanent stoppage 218.2 *stop*
permanent tooth 380.11 *tooth*
permanent way 72.3 *rail*
permanganate 57 *Types of Compounds*
permeability 56.61 *magnetic quantity*
permeability of vacuum 56.97 *fundamental constant*
permeable 347.17 *leaky*
permeate 133.10 *become mixed*, 233.10 *be a prevailing influence*, 253.11 *be present*, 298.5 *cooperate*, 322.20 *hole*, 346.11 *infiltrate*, 348.13 *absorb*, 356.10 *enter*, 389.29 *water*
permeated 298.6 *interfacial*, 322.14 *holed*, 584.13 *fixed*
permeating 253.7 *present*, 356.13 *penetrating*
permeation 133.1 *mixture*, 253.2 *omnipresence*, 298.2 *interaction*,

356.3 *passage into*, 389.9 *soaking*, 391.4 *seepage*
permeative 253.7 *present*
Permian **5** Languages and Groups of Languages, **54** Geological Time Intervals
Permian period 200.3 *geological period*
perminvar 57 *Alloys*
permissible 16.44 *legal*, 708.8 *permitting*, 851.22 *approvable*
permissibly 708.9 *with permission*
permission **485, 688, 708**, 16.29 *legalization*, 116.8 *permit*, 346.4 *right of entry*, 453.15 *green light*, 499.1 *assent*, 667.1 *agreement*, 691.1 *leniency*, 703.3 *authority*, 848.4 *licence*, 851.1 *approval*
Permission **708**
permissive 660.13 *easygoing*, 691.4 *lenient*, 698.12 *unconditional*, 708.8 *permitting*, 814.10 *free*
permissively 691.6 *leniently*, 698.21 *excessively*, 708.9 *with permission*
permissiveness 691.1 *leniency*, 698.6 *liberality*, 708.1 *permission*, 814.4 *freedom*
permissive parent 691.2 *lenient person*
permissive society 698.6 *liberality*, 708.1 *permission*, 814.4 *freedom*, 877.3 *sexual immorality*
permit **116, 116, 708, 708**, 16.65 *make legal*, 346.4 *right of entry*, 356.6 *passport*, 480.6 *evidence*, 483.6 *documentation*, 485.3 *qualifications*, 485.13 *qualify*, 486.7 *make possible*, 499.4 *assent*, 544.3 *means of identification*, 632.2 *protection*, 660.16 *make easy*, 688.9 *permission*, 688.21 *grant authority*, 691.3 *be lenient*, 692.4 *authorization*, 692.13 *authorize*, 703.3 *authority*, 703.8 *authorize*, 718.2 *promise*, 845.6 *bond*, 845.16 *entitle*, 848.4 *licence*
permit oneself 698.19 *liberalize*
permitted **708**, 16.44 *legal*, 116.18 *permitting*, 485.10, 688.16 *authorized*, 691.5 *given consideration*, 845.8 *entitled*
permitting **116, 708**
permittivity 56.54, 64.11 *electric field*
permittivity of vacuum 56.97 *fundamental constant*
permutable 216.14 *exchangeable*
permutation 52.21 *set*, 170.1 *calculation*, 216.4, 223.1 *exchange*
permute 216.10 *exchange*
pernicious 244.14 *destructive*, 618.5 *harmful*, 832.10 *malevolent*, 862.9 *detrimental*
pernicious anaemia 58.14 *vitamin deficiency disease*, 624.11 *blood disease*
perniciously 832.20 *malevolently*, 862.13 *destructively*
perniciousness 618.11 *harmfulness*
pernicketiness 469.4 *fastidiousness*
pernickety 106.10 *detailed*, 469.9 *careful*, 659.12 *problematic*, 659.14 *troublesome*
peroral administration 62.13 *administration*
perorate 183.17 *iterate*, 561.4 *dissertate*, 564.14 *speak to*, 567.7 *address*
peroration 183.2 *iteration*, 561.1 *dissertation*, 564.8 *speech*, 567.2 *salutation*
perovskite **54** *Minerals*
peroxide **57** *Types of Compounds*, **62** Medication, 439.3 *lightening*, 439.28 *bleach*, 445.4 *colour remover*, 445.6 *decolour*
peroxided 439.21 *light*
peroxisome 59.8 *cell organ*
perpendicular **281**, 52.37 *line*, 52.80 *linear*, 281.3 *vertical*

thing, 310.1 *angle*, 310.9 *angled*, 312.1 *straight*, 312.7 *straight line*
Perpendicular **43** Architectural Styles
perpendicularity 281.1 *verticality*, 312.6 *straightness*
perpendicular lines 52.37 *line*
perpendicularly **281**
perpetrate 640.4 *act*
perpetration 640.1 *action*
perpetrator 640.3 *doer*, 646.3 *agent*
perpetual 99.12 *lasting*, 159.11 *continuous*, 184.3 *eternal*, 185.21 *lasting through time*, 186.5 *timeless*, 188.9 *permanent*, 190.8 *eternal*, 217.7 *permanent*, 219.6 *protracted*, 225.9 *stable*, 368.8 *nonmaterial*, 584.14 *habituated*
perpetual calendar 185.13 *timer*
perpetually 159.19 *continuously*, 184.12 *eternally*, 185.30 *chronologically*, 212.1 *frequently*, 217.9 *permanently*, 219.7 *continually*, 225.12 *stably*, 368.13 *metaphysically*
perpetual motion 184.7 *eternity*, 225.4 *stable thing*
perpetuate 186, 184.9 *be infinite*, 190.6 *make eternal*, 217.6 *make permanent*, 219.4 *protract*, 637.5 *preserve*
perpetuation 186.3 *immutability*, 190.4 *eternalization*, 219.2 *protraction*, 637.1 *preservation*
perpetuity 99.6 *continuing existence*, 184.7 *eternity*, 186.3 *immutability*, 190.1 *eternity*, 217.1 *permanence*, 219.2 *protraction*, 368.1 *nonmaterial world*
perphenazine 62 *Medication*
Perpignan **93** *Cities*
perplex 443.1 *obscure*, 460.10 *bemuse*, 491.20 *make uncertain*, 523.7 *be unintelligible*, 529.13 *mystify*, 659.23 *cause difficulties*
perplexed 491.3, 523.6 *confused*, 659.16 *troubled*
perplexing 491.3 *confused*, 523.4 *difficult*, 529.11 *mysterious*, 659.12 *problematic*
perplexing question 523.12 *unintelligible thing*
perplexity 491.12 *confusion*, 498.3 *incredulity*, 523.11 *unintelligibility*, 659.4 *problem*
per pro 222.9 *instead*, 293.43 *alternatively*, 703.11 *under commission*
perquisite 116.9 *grant*, 130.4 *extra*, 610.3 *superfluity*, 721.5 *profit*, 729.2 *gift*, 730.2 *something received*, 754.6 *absence of charge*, 878.4 *reward for service*
Perrier 351.6 *soft drink*
Perrin 52 *Scientists*
perron 359.7 *means of ascent*
Perry 18 *Sporting Personalities*
per se 103.13 *in essence*
perse 454.1 *blue*
persecute 7.20 *preach*, 231.3 *counteract*, 481.14 *discriminate against*, 590.8 *pursue*, 618.14 *ill-treat*, 642.17 *meddle*, 690.6 *suppress*, 820.12 *oppose*, 832.18 *torment*, 862.11 *be evil*, 879.1 *punish*, 879.4 *torture*
persecuted 481.11 *judged*, 690.9 *suppressed*
persecuting 618.5 *harmful*, 820.7 *intolerant*, 832.10 *malevolent*
persecution 7.2 *religiousness*, 231.1 *counteraction*, 590.1 *pursuit*, 618.11 *harmfulness*, 690.2 *suppression*, 820.1 *enmity*, 832.5 *intolerance*, 879.7 *punishment*
persecution complex 61.18 *complex*
persecution mania 510.4 *delusion*
persecution to the death 879.13 *capital punishment*
persecutor 7.4 *religionist*, 481.7

bigot, 577.8 *obstinate person,* 690.4 *strict person,* 879.17 *punisher*
Perseids 53 Meteor Showers
Persephone 8 Deities
Perseus 53 The Constellations, **53** The Constellations
perseverance 575, 138.2 *tenacity,* 217.1 *permanence,* 219.2 *protraction,* 574.14 *tenacity,* 577.6 *determination,* 590.1 *pursuit,* 642.8 *assiduity,* 778.3 *steadfastness*
Perseverance 575
persevere 575, 138.8 *be tenacious,* 217.5 *be permanent,* 219.4 *protract,* 225.8 *show determination,* 574.11 *persist,* 577.9 *be obstinate,* 590.13 *follow up,* 642.15 *try,* 644.6 *work,* 644.8 *exert oneself,* 682.7 *overcome obstacles,* 778.16 *take courage*
persevering 575, 138.10 *tenacious,* 217.7 *permanent,* 574.2 *tenacious,* 577.3 *unyielding,* 642.20 *industrious,* 644.10 *working,* 778.12 *self-reliant*
perseveringly 217.9 *permanently,* 575.13 *persistently*
Persian Languages and Groups of Languages, **43** Architectural Styles, **77** Breeds of Cats, 202.14 *historic,* 400.4 *civilized human*
Persian Arab 32 Breeds of Horse and Pony
Persian carpet 293.9 *floor covering*
Persian Gulf 98.9 *inlet*
Persian melon 86 Fruits
Persians 200.6 *people of the past*
Persian wheel 355.10 *excavator,* 389.13 *irrigator*
persimmon 86 Fruits
persist 574, 99.19 *continue to be,* 110.11 *be regular,* 112.9 *be uniform,* 112.12 *be monotonous,* 217.5 *be permanent,* 219.4 *protract,* 225.8 *show determination,* 396.16 *live,* 575.6 *persevere,* 577.9 *be obstinate,* 590.13 *follow up,* 642.15 *try*
persistence 99.6 *continuing existence,* 112.1 *uniformity,* 138.2 *tenacity,* 212.4 *frequency,* 217.1 *permanence,* 219.2 *protraction,* 574.14 *tenacity,* 575.1 *perseverance,* 590.1 *pursuit,* 726.1 *retention*
persistent 55.53 *rainy,* 99.12 *lasting,* 112.5 *uniform,* 138.10 *tenacious,* 212.3 *frequent,* 217.7 *permanent,* 219.6 *protracted,* 426.15 *drumming,* 427.6 *resonant,* 574.2 *tenacious,* 575.10 *persevering,* 577.3 *unyielding*
persistently 575, 112.13 *uniformly,* 138.12 *tenaciously,* 212.1 *frequently,* 217.9 *permanently,* 219.7 *continually,* 426.19 *repeatedly,* 574.17 *resolutely*
persistent rain 55.25 *rain*
persist in 219.4 *protract*
persisting 99.12 *lasting,* 217.7 *permanent,* 427.6 *resonant*
person 165, 400, 51.21 *role,* 174.1 *one,* 367.5 *object,* 396.1 *life*
persona 61.21 *psyche,* 165.2 *personality,* 174.1 *one,* 303.3 *show*
personable 789
personage 51.21 *role,* 400.7 *person,* 611.4 *bigwig*
personal 165, 5.39 *of language,* 31.8 *hockey,* 119.5 *novel,* 165.16 *characteristic,* 290.12 *internalized,* 368.11 *internal,* 400.12 *human*
personal account 560.4 *factual account*
personal aims 860.1 *selfishness*
personal alarm 671.5 *self-defence*
personal allowance 749.3 *income,* 751.7 *tax*

personal appearance 51.11 *theatrical performance*
personal assistant 646.1 *worker,* 697.5 *office assistant*
personal attack 670
personal attendance 253.2 *omnipresence*
personal attendant 697
personal bearing 652.1 *conduct*
personal belongings 326.10 *transferred thing*
personal benefit 721.1 *gain*
personal borrower 745.6 *debtor*
personal call 534.10 *telephone call*
personal column 532.3 *journalism*
personal conflict 820
personal correspondence 560.4 *factual account*
personal criticism 524.3 *criticism*
personal desires 860.1 *selfishness*
personal effects 227.2 *visible effect,* 723.4 *possession,* 725.4 *possessions*
personal error 56.83 *sensitivity*
personal estate 725
personal fault 683
personal feeling 524.1 *interpretation*
personal file 545.1 *record*
personal finance 14
personal foul 19.13 *penalty,* 23.4 *playing terms,* 31.5 *lacrosse*
personal freedom 570.4 *free will*
personal history 545.1 *record*
personal honour 863.1 *virtue*
personal identification number 741.21 *till*
personal identity 4.9 *philosophical problem*
personal influence 233
personal initiative 698.1 *freedom*
personality 165, 61.21 *psyche,* 233.3 *personal influence,* 291.5 *focus,* 367.1 *material world,* 544.2 *identity,* 611.4 *bigwig*
personality adjustment test 61.5 *psychological test*
personality disorder 61.8 *disordered personality,* 510.4 *delusion*
personality inventory 61.5 *psychological test*
personality research form 61.5 *psychological test*
personality tendency 61.7 *personality type*
personality test 61.5 *psychological test*
personality type 61
personalize 165
personalized 165
personalized numberplate 544.3 *means of identification*
personal language 5.5 *nonstandard language*
personal law 16.1 *the law*
personal liberty 698.1 *freedom*
personal loan 732.2, 733.5 *loan,* 745.3 *loan*
personally 165, 119.8 *originally,* 253.14 *in person,* 368.14 *subjectively,* 400.15, 400.15 *humanly*
personal motive 310.6 *motive*
personal note 545.4 *inscription*
personal organizer 65.3 *computer*
personal property 725.4 *possessions*
personal question 477.4 *difficult question*
personal reasons 586.11 *motive*
personal recognizance 16.6 *legal process*
personal reward 878.1 *reward*
personals 532.3 *journalism*
personal sector 13.2 *economy*
personal servant 697.4 *personal attendant*
personal stereo 420.9 *audio device,* 534.18 *radio*
personal style 549.1 *style*
personal transport 71, 70.1 *transport*
personalty 725.2 *legal terms*
personal violence 832.7 *act of malevolence*
personate 547.9 *represent*

personation 51.20 *acting*
person dealing with the dead 397
person having priority 194
personification 48.12 *poetic language,* 103.3 *quintessence,* 526.10 *manifestation,* 547.1 *representation*
personified 526.14 *manifest*
personify 51.32 *act,* 103.12 *embody,* 367.8 *be material,* 547.9 *represent*
person in adversity 687
person in authority 696.3 *leader*
person in charge 653.15 *manager*
person included 146
person in command 692
person in office 696.3 *leader*
person in responsibility 653.15 *manager*
person keeping time 192
person left 132.6 *person remaining*
personnel 646, 146.3 *person included,* 161.13 *workforce,* 235.1 *power,* 400.7 *person,* 602.3 *human resources,* 679.14 *armed forces*
personnel manager 15.6 *employer*
personnel officer 15.6 *employer*
personnel staff 17.5 *military staff*
person of active habits 642.10 *busy person*
person of authority 688
person of few words 566.7 *taciturn person*
person of ideas 471
person of many parts 655.4 *skilled person*
person of note 400.7 *person*
person of repute 800, 686.4 *prosperous person*
person of wonder 786
person questioned 477
person remaining 132
persons of the drama 51.23 *cast*
person-to-person call 534.10 *telephone call*
person-to-person interaction 642.2 *social activity*
person transferring property 728
person unknown 502.4 *unknown person*
person who changes costume 224
person who changes sex 224
person who closes 323
person who copies 114
person who exchanges 223
person who gives evidence 483
person who humours 771
person who is exchanged 224
person who makes a representation 547
person who mixes 133
person who moves around 224
person who opens 322
person who separates 136
perspective 7.1 *religion,* 43.1 *architecture,* 50.4 *treatment,* 66.8 *composition,* 263.1 *distance,* 342.3 *convergent view,* 435.9 *viewpoint*
perspective projection 52.48 *transformation*
Perspex 57.21 *polymer,* 442.8 *transparent thing*
perspicacious 277.11 *wise,* 380.5 *mentally sharp,* 435.21 *seeing,* 507.5 *wise,* 558.3 *elegant*
perspicaciously 380.18 *sharply,* 507.9 *wisely,* 558.5 *elegantly*
perspicaciousness 380.13 *mental sharpness*
perspicacity 277.3 *profundity,* 380.13 *mental sharpness,* 435.4 *visualization,* 507.1 *wisdom,* 516.4 *prudence*
perspicuity 435.4 *visualization,* 522.10 *simplicity,* 550.1 *clarity,* 558.1 *elegance*
perspicuous 475.12 *demonstrable,* 520.6 *meaningful,* 522.2 *simple,* 550.3 *clear*
perspicuously 550.4 *clearly*
perspicuousness 550.1 *clarity*
perspiration 347.2 *outflow,*

352.1 *secretion,* 353.8 *sweat,* 387.3 *body fluid,* 389.4 *exudate,* 408.1 *heat*
perspire 347.12 *leak,* 349.14 *let out,* 352.7 *secrete,* 353.19 *sweat,* 389.32, 391.16 *seep,* 408.16 *feel hot*
perspiring 353.8 *sweat,* 353.28 *sweaty,* 391.12 *seeping*
persuadability 586
persuadable 586, 220.15 *convertible,* 572.3 *amenable*
persuade 220, 586, 228.9 *motivate,* 233.8 *influence,* 340.11 *attract,* 473.16 *plead,* 497.9 *make someone believe,* 518.6 *propound,* 710.9 *offer,* 712.6 *request,* 765.9 *comfort*
persuade against 587.1 *dissuade*
persuaded 220.16 *influenced,* 228.12 *motivated,* 490.2 *convinced*
persuade oneself 518.5 *suppose*
persuader 586, 228.7 *motivator*
persuasability 572.8 *acquiescence*
persuasible 586.20 *persuadable*
persuasion 220, 586, 7.1 *religion,* 163.4 *type,* 228.2 *inducement,* 233 *influence,* 235.1 *power,* 497.1 *belief,* 497.2 *religious belief,* 712.1 *request*
Persuasion 586
persuasive 586, 228.11 *motivational,* 233.11 *influential,* 237.10 *potent,* 488.7 *plausible,* 497.13 *believable,* 654.7 *advising,* 695.9 *compelling,* 710.17 *offered*
persuasively 586, 710, 228.14, 233.14 *influentially,* 237.15 *acutely,* 497.16 *believably,* 695.11 *compellingly*
persuasiveness 228.2 *inducement,* 586.1 *persuasion*
pert 668.7 *defiant,* 807.21 *impudent,* 809.11 *cocky,* 850.10 *disrespectful*
pertain 107.7 *relate to,* 116.27 *fit,* 478.22 *be the answer*
pertaining 116.16 *fitting,* 146.8 *included*
pertain to 107.7 *relate to,* 146.5 *be included,* 847.14 *be the duty of*
Perth 93 Cities, **93** Cities
pertinacious 138.2 *tenacity,* 138.10 *tenacious,* 577.1 *obstinate*
pertinaciously 138.12 *tenaciously*
pertinaciousness 575.1 *perseverance,* 577.5 *obstinacy*
pertinacity 575.1 *perseverance,* 577.5 *obstinacy*
pertinence 107.1 *relatedness,* 667.4 *suitability*
pertinent 107.4 *related,* 116.16 *fitting,* 146.8 *included,* 667.13 *suitable*
pertinently 107.10 *relevantly,* 116.38 *fittingly,* 146.9 *inclusively,* 667.17 *suitably*
pertly 668.9 *defiantly,* 807.30 *insolently,* 809.21 *cockily*
pertness 668.1 *defiance,* 807.11 *sauciness,* 809.3 *cockiness*
perturb 151.22 *discompose,* 153.7 *disturb,* 366.22 *agitate,* 659.23 *cause difficulties*
perturbate 366.22 *agitate*
perturbation 153.1 *disturbance,* 252.1 *displacement,* 366.1 *agitation,* 777.2 *fearfulness*
perturbed 151.17 *discomposed,* 153.12 *disturbed,* 366.15 *agitated,* 659.16 *troubled*
pertussis 624.6 *infection,* 624.9 *respiratory disease*
Peru 91 Countries
peruke 295.15 *headgear*
perusal 6.8 *learning,* 435.3 *observation*
peruse 6.23 *learn,* 435.14 *inspect*
Perutz 52 Scientists
Peruvian 7 Non-Christian Religions
Peruvian marching powder 875.6 *drug*

Peruvian Stepping Horse 32 Breeds of Horse and Pony
pervade 133.10 *become mixed,* 144.6 *fill,* 233.10 *be a prevailing influence,* 253.11 *be present*
pervading 253.7 *present*
pervasion 133.1 *mixture,* 253.2 *omnipresence*
pervasive 133.12 *mixed,* 164.17 *widespread,* 233.13 *dominant,* 253.7 *present*
pervasively 133.14 *in the midst,* 233.14 *influentially*
pervasiveness 164.4 *widespreadness,* 253.2 *omnipresence*
perverse 216.11 *changeable,* 504.16 *errant,* 577.2 *refractory,* 579.1 *capricious,* 659.14 *troublesome,* 663.22 *uncooperative,* 864.12 *immoral*
perversely 659, 153.18 *disturbingly,* 309.14 *distortedly,* 663.23 *opposingly*
perverseness 663.5 *contrariness*
perverse personality 61.8 *disordered personality*
perversion 628, 153.4 *disruption,* 168.6 *deviation,* 216.1 *change,* 220.2 *evolution,* 309.4 *distortion of the truth,* 504.7 *errancy,* 525.2 *misinterpretation,* 538.1 *untruth,* 540.9 *falsification,* 548.1 *misrepresentation,* 601.2 *misuse,* 844.4 *abnormality,* 864.2 *vice*
perversity 577.5 *obstinacy,* 663.5 *contrariness*
pervert 628, 102.16 *delude,* 153.10 *disrupt,* 216.8 *cause change,* 220.9 *transform,* 309.5 *defacer,* 309.12 *distort the truth,* 335.19 *deviant person,* 493.5 *misjudging person,* 525.1 *misinterpret,* 538.21 *lie,* 540.22 *falsify,* 548.4 *misrepresent,* 601.1 *misuse,* 618.13 *be worthless,* 862.6 *evil person,* 862.11 *be evil,* 864.9 *wicked person,* 864.17 *make wicked,* 877.10 *sex offender,* 877.19 *corrupt*
perverted 309.8 *exaggerated,* 504.16 *errant,* 538.13 *untrue,* 548.6 *misrepresented,* 601.4 *misused,* 844.14 *abnormal,* 864.12 *immoral,* 877.15 *unlawful*
pervertedly 538.26 *untruthfully,* 601.6 *abusively*
PES 57.17 *analysis*
Pesach 10.16 *religious festival*
pesante 49 Musical Terms
peseta 741.11 *national coins*
Peshawar 93 Cities
peso 741.11 *national coins*
pessary 62, 630.10 *surgical dressing*
pessimism 495.1 *underestimation,* 513.1 *expectation,* 536.1 *negation,* 776.1 *hopelessness*
pessimist 495, 852, 536.6 *negativist,* 641.2 *nonacting person,* 776.3 *hopeless person*
pessimistic 495.4 *underestimating,* 513.5 *expecting,* 536.11 *negative,* 776.4 *hopeless*
pessimistically 495, 513.12 *expectantly,* 536.15 *negatively,* 776.11 *hopelessly*
pest 82, 151.11 *troublemaker,* 462.7 *inconsiderate person,* 624.5 *plague,* 631.1 *affliction,* 693.5 *troublemaker,* 764.9 *unpleasant person,* 788.3 *boring person,* 822.8 *hated person*
pest control 68
pester 151.22 *discompose,* 153.7 *disturb,* 462.13 *be inconsiderate,* 616.5 *be inconvenient,* 642.17 *meddle,* 659.17 *be difficult,* 712.6 *request,* 828.9 *offend,* 852.18 *find fault*
pesterer 462.7 *inconsiderate person*
pestering 462.10 *inconsiderate,* 712.1 *request,* 852.6 *fault-finding*

pest exterminator 398.13 *animal killer*
pesticidal 69.18 *herbicidal*
pesticide 68.14 *pest control,* 69.8 *weedkiller,* 244.7 *agent of destruction,* 398.13 *animal killer*
pestiferous 626.6 *contagious*
pestilence 244.7 *agent of destruction,* 618.10 *poverty,* 624.5 *plague,* 631.1 *affliction*
pestilent 626.6 *contagious,* 626.7 *toxic,* 631.16 *blighting*
pestilential 626.7 *toxic*
pestilentially 626.8 *unhygienically*
pestle 57 Laboratory Apparatus, 384.11 *pulverizer,* 384.23 *pulverize*
pestle and mortar 384.11 *pulverizer*
pestled 384.19 *pulverized*
pests and diseases 69
pet 9.4 *idolized person,* 76.3 *domesticated animal,* 385.16 *massage,* 405.9 *give pleasure,* 405.10 *comfort,* 407.4 *kiss,* 407.11 *touch,* 580.15 *chosen,* 821.12 *nicknames for lovers,* 821.21 *beloved,* 821.27 *kiss,* 826.4 *terms of endearment,* 826.7 *show endearment for*
peta 75 SI Units
petal 83.6 *leaf,* 84.3 *flower part,* 143.6 *branch,* 826.4 *terms of endearment*
pet animal 76.3 *domesticated animal*
petard 680.12 *historical guns*
pet aversion 785.2 *disliked thing,* 822.7 *hated thing*
pet cemetery 399.5 *cemetery*
petechia 353.10 *bleeding*
Peterborough 93 Cities
peterman 736.8 *thief*
peter out 100.13 *cease to exist,* 129.4 *decrease,* 157.18 *come to an end,* 218.6 *cease,* 458.1 *disappear*
Peter Pan collar 295.14 *neckwear*
Peter Schaufuss 46.14 *famous ballet dancers*
Peter's pence 729.3 *offering,* 751.7 *tax*
Peters' projection 299.4 *map*
pet food 350.8 *animal food*
pet hate 777.5 *frightener,* 822.7 *hated thing*
pet hated 785.2 *disliked thing*
pethidine 62 Medication, 404.4 *anaesthetic,* 630.5 *analgesic*
petiole 83.5 *stem,* 83.6 *leaf*
petit allegro 46.9 *ballet steps*
petite 260.7 *little*
petiteness 260.1 *littleness*
petition 9.1 *worship,* 10.3 *rite of worship,* 10.9 *prayer,* 10.20 *pray,* 16.5 *litigation,* 16.70 *litigate,* 567.8 *appeal to,* 708.6 *ask permission,* 712.1, 712.6 *request*
petitionary 10.21 *ritualistic*
petitionary prayer 10.9 *prayer*
petitioned 712.9 *requesting*
petitioner 9.5, 10.17 *worshipper,* 16.8 *litigant,* 545.9 *recorder,* 712.4 *requester,* 856.3, 856.3 *accuser*
petit jury 16.26 *jury*
petit larceny 736.1 *stealing*
petit mal 510.3 *mental deterioration,* 624.17 *nervous disorder*
petit pois 45 Vegetables
petits battements 46.10 *positions at the barre*
petits pois 45.45 *French dish*
petkins 821.12 *nicknames for lovers,* 826.4 *terms of endearment*
Pet Milk 351.5 *milk*
pet name 560.8 *name,* 826.1 *endearment*
pet names 821.14 *communication of love*
pet owner 76.10 *animal welfarist*
pet peeve 785.2 *disliked thing,* 822.7 *hated thing*
Petrarch 48 Poets
Petrarchan 48.19 *narrative*
Petrarchan sonnet 48.7 *poem*

petrea 84 Flowers and Flowering Plants
petrel 78 Birds, 78.3 *water bird*
petrifaction 371.2 *concentration,* 373.6 *solidification*
petrifactive 373.1 *hard*
petrification 54.43 *fossil,* 200.10 *fossilization*
petrified 54.61 *fossilized,* 325.4 *motionless,* 373.3 *hardened,* 777.7 *frightened*
petrified forest 200.10 *fossilization*
petrified wood 54.43 *fossil,* 202.5 *old thing*
petrify 54.62 *lithify,* 371.8 *be dense,* 373.10 *solidify,* 777.13 *frighten,* 786.10 *be wonderful*
petrifying 373.1 *hard,* 777.10 *frightening*
petrochemical 57 Types of Compounds, 604.1 *materials*
petrochemicals 57.22 *industrial chemistry*
petrodollar diesel 410.6 *oil*
petrogenesis 54
petrogenic 54.56 *petrographic*
petroglyph 50.12 *sculpture*
petrographic 54
petrographical 54.56 *petrographic*
petrographically 54.66 *geographically*
petrol 338.13 *fuel,* 395.9 *petroleum,* 410.6 *oil*
petrol can 410.6 *oil*
petrol-driven 410.10 *powered*
petrol engine 63.11 *engine*
petroleum 395, 200.10 *fossilization,* 410.6 *oil,* 604.1 *materials*
petroleum jelly 630.9 *balm*
petrological 54.48 *geological,* 54.56 *petrographic*
petrologically 54.66 *geographically*
petrologist 54.3 *geologist*
petrology 54.1 *earth science*
petrol-propelled 338.19 *propelled*
petrol propulsion 338.2 *method of propulsion*
petrol pump 410.6 *oil,* 605.4 *storage*
petrol station 218.4 *stopping place,* 410.6 *oil,* 605.4 *storage*
petrol tank 605.4 *storage*
petronel 680.10 *historical gun*
Petrosian 18 Sporting Personalities
pe-tsai cabbage 45 Vegetables
PET scan 60.7 *diagnosis*
pet subject 165.8 *specialization*
petticoat 292.1 *lining,* 295.18 *underwear*
Petticoat Lane 740.1 *market*
pettifog 474.13 *quibble*
pettifogger 474.6 *sophist,* 539.17 *cheat,* 852.12 *critic*
pettifoggery 474.4 *quibbling,* 852.6 *fault-finding*
pettifogging 474.9 *quibbling,* 612.4 *trivial,* 852.28 *fault-finding*
pettiness 260.1 *littleness,* 481.3 *prejudice,* 612.7 *triviality,* 754.3 *shoddiness,* 758.4 *unpleasantness*
petting 407.2 *touching,* 821.6 *courtship,* 821.14 *communication of love,* 826.1 *endearment*
pettishness 579.2 *caprice*
petty 260.7 *little,* 278.2 *superficial,* 481.10 *discriminatory,* 612.4 *trivial,* 758.2 *unpleasant*
petty bureaucracy 642.9 *overactivity*
petty cash 741.2 *cash*
petty-cash book 750.5 *account book*
petty criminal 693.9 *criminal*
petty detail 612.8 *trifle*
petty officer 679.27 *naval man*
petty official 653.16 *official*
petty officialdom 12.3 *governance,* 584.6 *procedure,* 642.9 *overactivity*

petty sessions 16.19 *lawcourt,* 492.3 *place of judgment*
petty sin 612.8 *trifle*
petty theft 736.1 *stealing*
petty thief 736.8 *thief*
petty tyrant 690.4 *strict person,* 696.4 *absolute ruler*
petulance 807.9 *discourtesy,* 829.1 *irascibility,* 830.3 *irritableness*
petulant 473.8 *argumentative,* 807.20 *discourteous,* 829.4 *irascible,* 830.7 *irritable*
petulantly 473.17 *argumentatively,* 807.36 *discourteously,* 829.9 *irascibly,* 830.14 *irritably*
petunia 84 Flowers and Flowering Plants
petuntse 54 Minerals, 44.2 *raw material*
pew 10.12 *church,* 258.2 *compartment*
pewee 78 Birds
pewter 57 Alloys, 133.2 *mixed thing,* 446.9 *white thing,* 448.5 *grey thing*
peyote 84 Flowers and Flowering Plants, 875.6 *drug*
Pfannkuchen 45.46 *German dish*
pfennig 741.11 *national coins*
pH 57.19 *electrochemistry*
Phaedrus 48 Writers
Phaeophyta 90.2 *algae*
phaeophyte 90.2 *algae*
phaeton 71 Carriages and Carts, 71 Motor Vehicles
phage 59.3 *organism*
phagocyte 387.4 *blood*
phagophobia 777 Phobias by Name
phalangectomy 60 Surgical Operations
phalanger 77 Marsupials
phalangid 82.2 *arachnid*
phalanx 382 Bones, 679.16 *army unit*
phalarope 78 Birds
phallic 9.10 *idolatrous,* 245.16 *reproductive*
phallicism 9.2 *idolatry*
phallicist 9.6 *idolater*
phallic symbol 61.24 *symbolism,* 246.4 *fertility cult*
phalloplasty 60 Surgical Operations
phallus 245.8 *organs of reproduction,* 246.4 *fertility cult*
phanerogam 83.3 *seed plant*
phanerogamic 83.16 *taxonomic*
Phanerozoic 54 Geological Time Intervals
phansigar 679.1 *combatant,* 832.8 *malefactor*
phantasm 11.11 *ghost,* 102.2 *illusion,* 435.5 *imagination,* 539.5 *falseness*
phantasmagoria 102.2 *illusion,* 133.3 *miscellany,* 435.5 *imagination*
phantasmagoric 133.12 *mixed*
phantasmagorical 102.9 *illusory*
phantasmagorically 133.14 *in the midst*
phantasmal 11.18 *spiritual,* 102.8 *unreal*
phantasmic 11.18 *spiritual,* 539.40 *illusory*
phantom 11.11 *ghost,* 11.18 *spiritual,* 102.2 *illusion,* 253.6 *ghostly presence,* 368.3 *spiritual world,* 368.9 *parapsychological,* 435.5 *imagination,* 457.4 *something that appears,* 519.5 *fantasy*
phantoms 397.14 *the spiritual world*
Pharaoh 696.2 *sovereign*
pharaoh hound 77 Breeds of Dogs
Pharisaic 7.15 *religious,* 474.10 *hypocritical,* 538.18 *pretentious,* 539.37, 540.27 *hypocritical*
Pharisaism 7 Non-Christian Religions, 474.5, 538.9 *hypocrisy,* 539.3, 540.3 *hypocrisy*
pharisee 539.19 *hypocrite*
Pharisee 7.6 *non-Christian,*

538.12 *cheat*, 540.15 *false person*
pharmaceutic 62.18 *pharmacological*
pharmaceutical 62.3 *drug*, 630.2 *medicine*
pharmaceuticals 57.22 *industrial chemistry*
pharmaceutics 62.1 *pharmacology*
pharmaceutist 62.2 *pharmacologist*
pharmacist 62.2 *pharmacologist*, 630.16 *druggist*
pharmacodynamic 62.18 *pharmacological*
pharmacodynamics 62.1 *pharmacology*
pharmacognostic 62.18 *pharmacological*
pharmacognosy 630.2 *medicine*
pharmacokinetic 62.18 *pharmacological*
pharmacokinetics 62.1 *pharmacology*
pharmacological 62
pharmacologist 62, 630.16 *druggist*
pharmacology 62
Pharmacology 62
pharmacophobia 777 Phobias by Name
pharmacopoeia 62.1 *pharmacology*, 630.2 *medicine*
pharmacy 62.1 *pharmacology*, 630.16 *druggist*
pharmocognosy 62.1 *pharmacology*
pharos 74.5 *navigation*, 439.6 *electric light*
pharyngectomy 60 Surgical Operations
pharyngitis 624.9 *respiratory disease*
pharynx 564.5 *organ of speech*
phase 57, 53.17 *moon*, 56.8 *time*, 56.51, 64.9 *electric current*, 105.1 *state*, 110.8 *make the same*, 143.3 *stage*, 187.4 *period of activity*, 420.10 *sound quality*, 592.10 *plan out*, 784.3 *likes*
phaseal 214.11 *regular*
phase angle 64.9 *electric current*
phase change 56.37 *temperature*, 57.3 *phase*
phase-contrast microscope 56.85 *microscope*
phase-contrast microscopy 59.6 *cell biology*
phased 198.10 *synchronized*, 214.11 *regular*
phase diagram 57.3 *phase*
phase difference 64.9 *electric current*
phase modulation 534.14 *radio transmission*
phases of the moon 224.3 *changeable thing*
phase speed 56.16 *waveform*
phasic 214.11 *regular*
phasing 214.1 *regularity*
phasmid 82.10 *insectan*
Phasmida 82 Orders of Insects
phasmophobia 777 Phobias by Name
pheasant 78 Birds, 45.20 *meat*, 78.4 *table bird*
pheasants 161 Collective Names by Animal
pheasant season 203.1 *season*
pheasant shoot 590.2 *chase*
pheasant shooter 398.13 *animal killer*
pheasant shooting 18 Sporting Activities, 37.2 *hunting*, 398.9 *animal killing*
Phecda 53 Named Stars
phellem 85.3 *timber*
phenacetin 62 Medication, **62** Medication
phenacite 54 Minerals
phenazocine 62 Medication
phenazone 62 Medication
phenazopyridine 62 Medication
phenelzine 62 Medication
phenethicillin 62 Medication
phenetoin 62 Medication

pheneturide 62 Medication
phenindione 62 Medication
pheniramine 62 Medication
phenmetrazine 62 Medication
phenol 57 Types of Compounds, 621.9 *cleaning agent*
phenolate 621.13 *clean*
phenolphthalein 62 Medication, 57.18 *gravimetric analysis*
phenomenal 99.13 *real*, 457.7 *appearing*, 786.8 *wonderful*
phenomenalism 4.7 *school of thought*
phenomenalist 4.11 *follower of a doctrine*, 4.14 *of a philosophy*
phenomenologically 4.24 *philosophically*
phenomenological psychology 61.1 *psychology*
phenomenological theology 7.13 *theology*
phenomenology 4.6 *branch of philosophy*
phenomenon 99.2 *thing*, 457.2 *being in view*, 786.4 *wonder*
phenol formaldehyde 604.1 *materials*
phenothiazine 62 Medication
phenotype 59.11 *genetics*, 59.12 *molecular biology*
phenoxybenzamine 62 Medication
phenoxymethylpenicillin 62 Medication
phensuximide 62 Medication
phentermine 62 Medication
phentolamine 62 Medication
phenylalanine 58 Amino Acids
phenylbutazone 62 Medication
phenylephrine 62 Medication
phenylpropanolamine 62 Medication
pheromonal 416.5 *odorous*
pheromone 58.16 *hormone*, 352.2 *secreted substance*, 416.3 *scent*
phial 258.14 *bottle*
Philadelphia 93 Cities, 93.2 *American cities*
Philadelphia lawyer 463.6 *arguer*
philadelphus 84 Flowers and Flowering Plants
philander 821.26, 826.8 *court*, 877.17 *be sexually immoral*
philanderer 224.6 *fickle person*, 401.7 *libertine*, 405.3 *pleasure-seeker*, 821.9 *lover*, 826.5 *courting person*, 877.8 *immoral man*
philandering 538.20 *unfaithful*, 826.2 *courtship*, 826.9 *endearing*
philanthropic 833, 572.4 *helpful*, 662.35 *benevolent*, 710.18 *voluntary*, 729.8 *giving*, 755.2 *magnanimous*, 819.8 *friendly*, 831.7 *charitable*, 863.5 *virtuous*
philanthropical 833.6 *philanthropic*
philanthropically 833, 710.20 *persuasively*, 831.11 *charitably*
philanthropism 833.1 *philanthropy*
philanthropist 572, 833, 519.9 *visionary*, 627.12 *reformer*, 646.1 *worker*, 662.15 *benefactor*, 691.2 *lenient person*, 710.8 *volunteer*, 729.4 *giver*, 755.9 *generous person*, 831.5 *benevolent person*, 861.15 *good person*
philanthropize 729.6 *give to charity*
philanthropize 833.7 *be charitable*
philanthropy 833, 729.1 *giving*, 755.6 *magnanimity*, 819.1 *friendship*, 831.2 *charity*, 863.1 *virtue*
Philanthropy 833
philatelist 161.35 *collector*
philately 42 Hobbies and Pastimes
Philemon 48 Dramatists
Philemon and Baucis 823.9 *married couple*
philharmonic 49.29 *musical*
philippic 567.1 *address*
Philippine 97 Oceans and Seas
Philippine eagle 78 Birds

Philippines 91 Countries
philistine 482.9 *undiscriminating person*
Philistine 167.6 *conformist*, 502.5 *ignorant person*, 502.6 *ignorant*, 658.1 *naive*, 658.3 *naive person*, 761.5 *insensitive person*, 795.5 *vulgar person*
Philistinism 658.2 *naivety*, 761.3 *insensitiveness*
Phillip's process 57 Named Reactions
philocarpine 62 Medication
Philo Judaeus 4 Philosophers
philological 5.38 *linguistic*, 520.8 *semantic*
philologically 5.48 *linguistically*
philologist 5.2 *linguist*
philology 5.1 *linguistics*, 5.30 *syntax*
philoprogenitive 246.5 *fertile*
philosopher 48 Literary Groups and Movements, **4**, 368.7 *believer in a nonmaterial world*, 461.7 *thinker*, 463.5 *reasoner*, 471.9 *person of ideas*, 477.9 *questioner*, 507.3 *wise man*, 518.4 *theorist*, 654.4 *adviser*, 696.9 *educational leader*
philosopher's stone 588.6 *objective*, 630.1 *remedy*, 742.5 *wealth*
philosophical 4.13 *of philosophy*, 4.15 *rational*, 461.8 *thoughtful*, 461.11 *reasoning*, 471.10 *theoretical*, 477.15 *sceptical*, 696.13 *excellent*
philosophical argument 4
philosophical doctrine 4.1 *philosophy*
philosophical idealism 368.5 *idealism*
philosophical inquiry 4.4 *philosophical investigation*, 477.2 *questioning*
philosophical investigation 4
philosophical linguistics 5.1 *linguistics*
philosophically 4, 4.26 *rationally*, 4.27 *stoically*, 461.18 *thoughtfully*, 471.20 *theoretically*, 477.23 *questioningly*, 696.16 *masterfully*
philosophical problem 4
philosophical speculation 4.1 *philosophy*
philosophical system 4
philosophical term 4
philosophical theology 7.13 *theology*
philosophical theory 4.1 *philosophy*
philosophism 474.1 *sophistry*
philosophist 474.6 *sophist*
philosophize 4, 461, 4.21 *rationalize*, 7.22 *theologize*, 463.14 *premise*
philosophobia 777 Phobias by Name
philosophy 777 Phobias by Topic, **4**, 471.5 *ideology*, 497.2 *religious belief*
Philosophy 4
philosophy of commonsense 4.6 *branch of philosophy*
philosophy of history 3.1 *history*, 4.6 *branch of philosophy*
philosophy of language 4.6 *branch of philosophy*
philosophy of law 4.6 *branch of philosophy*
philosophy of life 7.1 *religion*
philosophy of mind 4.6 *branch of philosophy*
philosophy of psychology 4.6 *branch of philosophy*
philosophy of religion 4.6 *branch of philosophy*
philosophy of science 4.6 *branch of philosophy*
philosophy of signs 4.6 *branch of philosophy*
philtre 11.5 *spell*, 405.4 *pleasurable things*
phiz 303.2 *face*
phlebectomy 60 Surgical Operations

phlebitis 624.10 *cardiovascular disease*
phlebotomize 630.20 *doctor*
phlebotomy 60 Surgical Operations, 349.22 *disgorgement*, 355.4 *sucking*, 630.12 *surgery*
phlegm 352.2 *secreted substance*, 353.9 *saliva*, 387.3 *body fluid*, 393.10, 394.5 *mucus*, 643.7 *idleness*, 705.2 *stoicism*, 783.1 *indifference*
phlegmatic 61.7 *personality type*, 325.5 *sedentary*, 328.5 *unhurried*, 466.4 *uninterested*, 641.3 *inactive*, 643.3 *not participating*, 705.8 *resigned*, 771.12 *four humours*, 783.7 *indifferent*, 787.3 *unmoved*
phlegmatically 325.10 *motionlessly*, 705.9 *stoically*, 783.17 *indifferently*, 787.9 *without wonder*
phlegmaticalness 783.1 *indifference*, 787.1 *lack of wonder*
phlegmy 387.16 *rheumy*
phloem 83.5 *stem*
phlox 84 Flowers and Flowering Plants
Phnom Penh 93 Cities
phobia 61.10 *neurosis*, 510.4 *delusion*, 777.1 *fear*, 785.1 *dislike*, 820.3 *ill feeling*, 822.7 *hated thing*
phobic 822.9 *hater*, 822.11 *racist*
phobophobia 777 Phobias by Name
phoebe 78 Birds
Phoebe 8 Deities
Phoebus 8 Deities
Phoenician 5 Languages and Groups of Languages, **7** Non-Christian Religions, 400.4 *civilized human*
Phoenicians 1 Peoples, 200.6 *people of the past*
Phoenicids 53 Meteor Showers
phoenix 76.7 *legendary beast*, 78.9 *fabulous bird*, 213.4 *rare things*
Phoenix 53 The Constellations, **53** The Constellations, **68** Breeds of Fowl, **93** Cities
phoenix-like 629.13 *repaired*
Phoenix-like 245.15 *reproduced*
pholcodine 62 Medication
pholidote 77.6 *insect-eating mammal*, 77.26 *insectivorous*
phon 75 Scientific and Technical Units
phonation 564.4 *articulation*
phone 5.16 *spoken letter*, 420.9 *audio device*, 528.12 *communicate*, 534.9, 534.32 *telephone*
phone book 171.3 *dictionary*, 528.5 *reference book*, 534.11 *dialling*
phone call 534.10 *telephone call*
phonecard 56.64 *magnetic recording*, 534.9 *telephone*, 733.4 *credit*, 744.2 *credit card*
phone-in 534.25 *broadcast material*
phoneme 5.16 *spoken letter*, 564.7 *utterance*
phonemic 5.38 *linguistic*
phonemicist 5.2 *linguist*
phonemics 5.1 *linguistics*
phone number 534.11 *dialling*
phoner 534.13 *telephoner*
phonetic 564, 5.38 *linguistic*
phonetically 5.48 *linguistically*, 564.21 *orally*
phonetic alphabet 5.14 *alphabet*
phonetician 5.2 *linguist*
phonetics 564, 5.1 *linguistics*, 56.2 *classical physics*
phonetic spelling 5.27 *spelling*
phonetic symbol 5.14 *alphabet*
phonetist 5.2 *linguist*
phoney 114.8 *simulated*, 118.2 *copy*, 118.7 *imitator*, 118.13 *imitation*, 474.10 *hypocritical*, 538.11 *liar*, 538.12 *cheat*, 538.14 *unreal*, 538.18 *pretentious*, 539.15 *deceiver*, 539.19 *hypocrite*, 539.37 *hypocritical*, 539.39 *imitative*, 540.10 *fake*, 540.28 *spurious*, 540.33 *fake*

phoney war 676.1 *war*
phonic 564.18 *phonetic*
phonily 538.28 *dishonestly*
phoniness 538.2 *unrealness,*
540.4 *spuriousness*
phonogram 5.16 *spoken letter*
phonogramic 5.41 *lettered*
phonographic 5.41 *lettered*
phonograph record 545.7 *recording*
phonography 5.1 *linguistics*
phonological 5.38 *linguistic*
phonologist 5.2 *linguist*
phonology 5.1 *linguistics,* 564.6
phonetics
phonometer 268.8 *meter*
phonometric 268.16 *micrometric*
phony 102.12 *not the real thing*
phoronid 81.6 *worm*
Phoronida 81.6 *worm*
phosgene 631.10 *warfare*
phosgenite 54 Minerals
phosphagen 58.22 *bioenergetics*
phosphate 68.13 *fertilizer*
phosphate bond 58.22 *bioenergetics*
phosphates 246.3 *fertilizer,*
631.9 *pollution*
phosphatide 58.6 *lipid*
phosphine 57 Common Chemical Compounds
phosphoglyceride 58.6 *lipid*
phospholipid 58.6 *lipid*
phosphoprotein 58.9 *protein*
phosphor bronze 57 Alloys
phosphoresce 439.25 *light up*
phosphorescence 56.24 *light emission,* 439.1 *light*
phosphorescent 439.15 *lucent*
phosphoric 57.34 *elemental*
phosphorite 57 Minerals
phosphorous 57.34 *elemental*
phosphorus 57 Chemical Elements, 58.15 *essential element*
phosphorylation 58.22 *bioenergetics*
phot 75 Scientific and Technical Units
photic 439.23 *photoelectric*
photo 66.3, 66.21 *photograph*
photobiography 66.4 *portrait*
photo booth 66.16 *camera*
photocall 532.8 *public relations*
photocathode 64.24 *electron emission*
photocell 64.25 *photoconductivity,* 235.7 *electrical power*
photochemical 57.31 *chemical*
photochemically 57.46 *chemically*
photochemical reaction 57.14
chemical reaction
photochemist 57.2 *chemist*
photochemistry 57.1 *chemistry*
photochromic 444.14 *chromolithographic*
photochromic glass 44.1 *ceramics*
photochromic lenses 56.29 *optical element*
photoconduction 439.11 *photoelectricity*
photoconductive 439.23 *photoelectric*
photoconductivity 64, 56.33 *photosensitivity,* 56.49 *electromagnetic induction*
photocopied 110.15 *duplicate,*
176.12 *double,* 545.16 *recorded*
photocopier 118, 114.3 *copier,*
545.10 *recording instrument*
photocopy 66, 110.4, 110.9 *duplicate,* 114.2, 118.2 *copy,*
118.5 *duplicate,* 118.10 *copy,*
176.5 *twin,* 183.7 *replica,* 245.1 *reproduction,* 245.2 *print,* 245.9 *reproduce,* 326.16 *translate,*
545.5 *copy,* 545.13 *record,*
547.2 *reproduction,* 560.9 *representation*
photocopying 66.2 *photoreproduction,* 245.1 *reproduction,* 326.4 *translation*
photocurrent 64.25 *photoconductivity*
photodetector 64.25 *photoconductivity*
photodiode 64.18 *diode,* 64.25 *photoconductivity*

photoelastic modelling 63.17
civil engineering
photoelectric 439, 64.36 *electronic*
photoelectrically 64.37 *electronically*
photoelectric cell 235.7 *electrical power,* 439.11 *photoelectricity*
photoelectric effect 56.33 *photosensitivity,* 56.49 *electromagnetic induction,* 64.24 *electron emission*
photoelectric emission 64.24 *electron emission*
photoelectricity 439, 56.42 *electricity,* 235.7 *electrical power*
photoelectron 64.24 *electron emission*
photoemission 439.11 *photoelectricity*
photoemissive 439.23 *photoelectric*
photo finish 32.7 *horseracing,*
122.2 *equilibrium,* 198.1 *same time,* 264.2 *short distance,*
344.15 *destination,* 674.2 *contest*
photo-finish 198.9 *simultaneous*
Photofit 66.4 *portrait,* 547.2 *reproduction*
photoflood 66.15 *lighting,* 439.7 *lantern*
photogenic 66.22 *photographic,*
547.13 *representational*
photogenically 66.23 *photographically*
photogrammetric 268.16
micrometric
photogrammetry 63.17 *civil engineering,* 66.2 *photoreproduction,*
268.2 *micrometry*
photograph 66, 66, 110.4,
110.9 *duplicate,* 118.5 *duplicate,* 435.7 *view,* 457.5 *impression,* 544.3 *means of identification,* 544.10 *identify,* 545.1,
545.13 *record,* 547.2 *reproduction,* 547.6 *image,* 547.9 *represent*
photograph album 66.3 *photograph,* 511.4 *reminder*
photographed 110.15 *duplicate,*
544.12 *identified,* 545.16 *recorded*
photographer 114.4 *person who copies,* 118.8 *copier,* 545.9 *recorder,* 547.4 *person who makes a representation*
photographic 66, 50.24 *pictorial,*
110.15 *duplicate,* 114.9 *lifelike,*
503.6 *correct,* 547.13 *representational,* 560.11 *descriptive,*
560.13 *representing*
photographically 66, 50.30 *pictorially,* 110.18 *identically,*
114.14 *comparably*
photographic density 66.10 *graininess*
photographic likeness 547.1 *representation*
photographic memory 503.3 *accurate thing,* 511.1 *memory,* 726.5 *retentiveness*
photographic paper 66.9 *film*
photographic plate 66.9 *film*
photographic realism 537.12 *true to life*
photography 42 Hobbies and Pastimes, 66, 50.1 *art,* 56.34
photometry
Photography 66
photogravure 50.7 *picture,* 66.2
photoreproduction
photointaglio 66.2 *photoreproduction*
photojournalism 66.1 *photography*
photolithography 56.34 *photometry,* 66.2 *photoreproduction*
photolysis 141.2 *deconstruction*
photolytically 141.7 *to pieces*
photomechanical transfer 114.2
copy
photometer 53.27 *imaging,*
56.32 *optical instrument,* 56.92 *light meter,* 268.8 *meter,* 439.11 *photoelectricity*
photometric 53.36 *astronomical,*

268.16 *micrometric,* 439.23 *photoelectric*
photometry 56, 53.27 *imaging,*
56.96 *microscopy,* 268.2 *micrometry*
photomicrograph 66.7 *photocopy*
photomontage 50.7 *picture,* 66.4
portrait
photomultiplier 64.24 *electron emission*
photomural 66.4 *portrait*
photon 56.13 *electromagnetic radiation,* 56.78 *quantum,* 367.4
matter, 439.1 *light*
photo-opportunity 532.8 *public relations*
photoperiodism 187.5 *recurrent period*
photophobia 777 Phobias by Name
photophobic 439.23 *photoelectric*
photophosphorylation 58.23 *photosynthesis*
photoprint 50.7 *picture*
photorealism 50 Western Art Styles and Movements
photorealist 50.29 *realist*
photoreproduction 66, 245.1 *reproduction*
photorespiration 58.24 *respiration*
photosensitive 44.10 *ceramic,*
66.22 *photographic,* 439.23 *photoelectric*
photosensitive glass 44.9 *industrial ceramics*
photosensitive material 56.33
photosensitivity
photosensitivity 56, 66.10 *graininess,* 439.11 *photoelectricity*
photosensor 439.11 *photoelectricity*
photosphere 53.15 *sun,* 390.3 *atmospheric layers*
Photostat 66.7 *photocopy,* 110.4,
110.9 *duplicate,* 114.3 *copier,*
114.12 *imitate,* 118.5, 118.5 *duplicate*
Photostated 110.15 *duplicate*
photosynthesis 58, 59.5 *physiology*
photosynthesize 58.25 *metabolize,* 83.21 *vegetate*
photosynthetic 58.26 *biochemical,* 59.22 *physiological,* 83.14
of plants
photosynthetically 58.27 *biochemically,* 83.24 *herbaceously*
photosynthetic pigment 58.18
pigment
phototherapy 630.13 *therapy*
phototopography 66.1 *photography*
phototropic 439.23 *photoelectric*
photovoltaic cell 64.25 *photoconductivity,* 410.8 *renewable energy*
photovoltaic effect 56.33 *photosensitivity,* 56.49 *electromagnetic induction,* 64.25 *photoconductivity*
phrasal 5
phrase 5, 49, 5.45 *use language,*
143.2 *particular,* 433.3
melodiousness, 549.4 *literary style,* 549.9 *style,* 564.7 *utterance*
phrased 5.43 *phrasal,* 549.6
styled
phrasegraph 5.24 *phrasing*
phrasemaker 5.2 *linguist*
phrasemonger 557, 5.2 *linguist,*
549.5 *stylist*
phraseogram 5.24 *phrasing*
phraseographic 5.43 *phrasal*
phraseological 5.43 *phrasal*
phraseologically 5
phraseology 5.3 *spoken language,* 5.24 *phrasing,* 549.4 *literary style*
phrase-structure grammar 5.29
grammar
phrasing 5, 5.43 *phrasal,* 433.3
melodiousness, 549.4 *literary style*
phrenic 459.9 *mental*
phrenicectomy 60 Surgical Operations
phrenologist 11.12 *occultist*

phrenology 11.1 *occultism,*
524.5 *science of interpretation*
phronemophobia 777 Phobias by Name
Phrygian 5 Languages and Groups of Languages
Phrygian mode 49.20 *key*
phthalocyanine blue zaffre 454.5
blueness
phthalocyanine dye 67.6 *dye*
phthalylsulphathiazole 62 Medication
phthiriasis 622.2 *uncleanness*
phthisic 1.15 *physical*
phthisic build 1.9 *physical type*
phthisiophobia 777 Phobias by Name
phthistic 624.23 *diseased*
phycobilin 58.18 *pigment*
phycobiont 90.1 *alga,* 90.6 *lichen*
phycocyanin 90.3 *plant body*
phycoerythrin 90.3 *plant body*
phycological 90.7 *algal*
phycologist 83.12 *plant scientist,*
90.2 *algae*
phycology 83.10 *plant science,*
90.2 *algae*
phycomycetes 89.3 *fungi*
phycomycosis 89.5 *fungal association*
phylactery 10.14 *sacred object,*
11.6 *talisman*
phyllite 54 Common Rocks
phylloclade 83.6 *leaf*
phyllode 83.6 *leaf*
phyllosilicate 54.34 *mineral*
phylloxera 82 Insects
phylogenetic 59.27 *evolutionary*
phylogeny 59.16 *evolution*
phylum 59.17 *taxonomy,* 143.1
part, 163.3 *kingdom*
physic 629.6 *cure,* 630.2 *medicine,* 630.20 *doctor*
physical 1, 56, 60.6 *health care,*
367.7 *material*
physical abuse 241.2 *physical violence,* 832.7 *act of malevolence*
physical anthropology 1.1 *anthropology*
physical attack 670.16 *terrorist attack*
physical being 367.1 *material world*
physical change 220.1 *conversion*
physical chemist 57.2 *chemist*
physical chemistry 56.4 *experimental physics,* 57.1 *chemistry,*
367.6 *natural science*
physical condition 105.5 *physical state,* 367.1 *material world*
physical constant 56.97 *fundamental constant*
physical contact 407.2 *touching*
physical cruelty 241.2 *physical violence*
physical disability 236.4 *disability*
physical element 367.4 *matter*
physical energy 239.1 *vigour*
physical examination 60.6 *health care*
physical existence 367.1 *material world*
physical fatigue 650.7 *fatigue*
physical fitness 237.2 *healthiness*
physical force 237.1 *strength,*
695.2 *coercion*
physical form 105.5 *physical state*
physical geography 54.1 *earth science*
physical geology 54.1 *earth science*
physical handicap 236.4 *disability*
physical improvement 627
physicalism 4.7 *school of thought*
physicalist 4.11 *follower of a doctrine,* 4.14 *of a philosophy*
physically 56, 367.9 *materially*
physically demanding 650.4 *fatiguing,* 659.10 *difficult*
physically strong 237
physical medicine 60.3 *medical specialty*
physical oceanography 54.2 *geophysics*

physical optics 56.2 *classical physics*
Physical Pain **406**
physical pleasure **405**
Physical Pleasure **405**
physical power 378.8 *physical strength*
physical presence 253.1 *presence*, 367.5 *object*
physical punishment 406.1 *pain*
physical quantity 75.5 *dimension*
physical roughness 378.8 *physical strength*
physical science 56.1 *physics*, 367.6 *natural science*
physical state **105**
physical strength **378**, 237.1 *strength*
physical type **1**, 457.3 *external appearance*
physical violence **241**, 670.16 *terrorist attack*
physical weakness 236.4 *disability*
physical well-being 623.3 *health*
physical world 101.2 *real world*, 367.1 *material world*
physical wreck 628.9 *dilapidation*
physician 60.11 *doctor*, 630.15 *healer*, 688.11 *expert*
physicist 56.1 *physics*, 367.3 *materialist*
physicotheological 7.18 *theological*
physicotheology 7.13 *theology*
physics **56**, 367.6 *natural science*
Physics **56**
physiochemical 57.31 *chemical*
physiochemist 57.2 *chemist*
physiocracy 12.1 *government*
physiocratic school 13.6 *economic factors*
physiognomic 303.6 *front*
physiognomical 303.6 *front*
physiognomy 303.2 *face*, 306.6 *nature*, 457.3 *external appearance*, 524.5 *science of interpretation*
physiographer 54.3 *geologist*
physiography 54.1 *earth science*
physiological **59**, 59.20 *biological*
physiologically 59.29 *biologically*
physiological psychology 61.1 *psychology*
physiologist 59.19 *life scientist*
physiology **59**, 59.1 *life science*
physiotherapist 60.17 *paramedic*
physiotherapy 60.8 *treatment*, 630.13 *therapy*
physique 1.9 *physical type*, 306.6 *nature*, 382.3 *form*
physisorb 57.29 *absorb*
physisorbed 57.43 *absorbed*
physisorption 57.20 *surface chemistry*
physostigmine **62** Medication
phytobiology 59.1 *life science*
phytochemical 83.20 *botanical*
phytochemist 83.12 *plant scientist*
phytochemistry 59.1 *life science*, 83.10 *plant science*
phytochrome 58.18 *pigment*
phytoecology 59.1 *life science*, 59.18 *ecology*
phytogenesis 83.10 *plant science*
phytogenetically 83.25 *botanically*
phytogeneticist 83.12 *plant scientist*
phytogeographer 83.12 *plant scientist*
phytogeographic 83.20 *botanical*
phytogeography 83.10 *plant science*
phytographer 83.12 *plant scientist*
phytographic 83.20 *botanical*
phytography 59.1 *life science*, 83.10 *plant science*
phytohormone 58.17 *plant hormone*
phytol 58.20 *terpene*
phytological 83.20 *botanical*
phytologically 83.25 *botanically*
phytologist 83.12 *plant scientist*

phytology 59.1 *life science*, 83.10 *plant science*
phytopathological 83.20 *botanical*
phytopathologist 83.12 *plant scientist*
phytopathology 83.10 *plant science*
phytoplankton 90.1 *alga*
phytosaur 79 Fossil Reptiles
phytosociological 83.20 *botanical*
phytosociologically 83.25 *botanically*
phytosociologist 83.12 *plant scientist*
phytosociology 83.10 *plant science*
piacular 125.9 *compensatory*, 840.4 *atoning*
piaculum 840.2 *apology*
piaffe 32.10 *dressage*
piaffer 328.10 *slow motion*
Piaget 61.29 *psychologist*
pianino **49** Musical Instruments
pianissimo **49** Musical Terms, 424.7 *faintly*, 428.1 *faint-sounding*, 428.10 *faintly*
piano **49** Musical Instruments, **49** Musical Terms, 424.4 *faint*, 424.7 *faintly*, 428.1 *faint-sounding*, 428.10 *faintly*
pianoforte **49** Musical Instruments
pianola **49** Musical Instruments
piastre 741.4 *change*
Piave **96** Rivers
piazza 256.7 *room*
pibcorn **49** Musical Instruments
pica **75** General Units
picador 398.13 *animal killer*, 679.3 *athlete*
picaresque 560.12 *narrative*
picaresque novel 48.2, 560.5 *fiction*
Piccadilly Circus 291.4 *centre of activity*
piccalilli 413.2 *seasoning*
piccolo **49** Musical Instruments
picco pipe **49** Musical Instruments
pick **580**, 49.38 *sound*, 131.3 *subtract*, 322.2 *opener*, 330.6 *tap*, 355.10 *excavator*, 380.8 *sharp-pointed thing*, 481.12 *discriminate*, 580.6 *selection*, 580.9 *chosen thing*, 605.6 *store*, 611.3 *chief thing*, 617.7 *elite*, 805.12 *object of pride*, 861.9 *the best*
pick a bone with 666.7 *pick a fight*
pick a fight **666**
pick and choose 481.12 *discriminate*, 579.5 *be capricious*, 580.4 *pick*
pick a pocket 131.3 *subtract*
pick a quarrel 666.7 *pick a fight*
pick at 350.23 *taste*
pickaxe 322.2 *opener*, 355.10 *excavator*, 380.8 *sharp-pointed thing*, 603.2 *garden tool*
pick clean 621.13 *clean*
picked 580.15 *chosen*, 617.1 *worthy*
picked man 655.4 *skilled person*
picked out 136.17 *unjoined*, 437.2 *clear*, 792.8 *decorated*
picked troops 679.14 *armed forces*
picker 350.18 *eater*, 621.12 *cleaner*
pickerel **80** Fishes
picket 15.4 *industrial dispute*, 475.6 *mass demonstration*, 475.8 *protester*, 475.19 *protest*, 632.3 *protector*, 636.4 *warner*, 661.9 *block*, 671.14 *guard*, 679.14 *armed forces*, 679.39 *defend*, 713.8 *cause mischief*, 879.1 *punish*
picketed 15.10 *unionized*
picketer 693.7, 713.4 *protester*
picket fence 726.4 *wall*
picketing 15.4 *industrial dispute*, 15.10 *unionized*, 475.14 *demonstrating*, 713.3 *gesture of protest*
picket line 15.4 *industrial dis-*

pute, 147.1 *exclusion*, 661.2 *obstacle*
pick holes 852.18 *find fault*
pick holes in 766.7 *be dissatisfied*
picking and choosing 580.6 *selection*
picking at one's food 350.3 *delicate eating*
picking out 580.6 *selection*
pickings 580.9 *chosen thing*, 721.4 *earnings*, 734.5 *takings*, 736.4 *stolen goods*
picking up 36.8 *punting*, 361.6 *raising*
pickle 45.42 *preserve*, 105.2 *predicament*, 106.4 *difficult circumstances*, 151.4 *litter*, 251.3 *difficult circumstances*, 389.31 *steep*, 413.2 *seasoning*, 413.12 *season*, 605.6 *store*, 637.2 *preserver*, 637.5 *preserve*, 659.5 *predicament*
pickled 413.9 *piquant*, 605.7 *stored*, 637.7 *preserved*, 874.1 *drunk*
pickled herring 45.16 *fish dish*
pickled onion 413.2 *seasoning*
pickle-herring 51.30 *clown*
pickles 637.3 *preserved thing*
pickling 45.8 *cooking technique*, 637.1 *preservation*
picklock 346.8 *intruder*, 736.8 *thief*
pick-me-up 351.2 *drink*, 413.6 *cordial*, 630.7 *tonic*, 651.7 *refreshments*
pick off 338.31 *snipe*, 398.17 *murder*, 670.2 *fire*
pick of the bunch 617.7 *elite*, 805.12 *object of pride*, 861.16 *superior person*
pick on 481.14 *discriminate against*
pick oneself up 629.4 *be restored*
pick one's pockets 736.12 *steal*
pick one's way 324.13 *be in motion*, 659.20 *be in difficulty*
pick out 131.3 *subtract*, 136.10 *set apart*, 165.22 *characterize*, 174.20 *single out*, 355.11 *extract*, 435.12 *see*, 481.12 *discriminate*, 580.4 *pick*
pickpocket 736.8 *thief*, 736.12 *steal*
pickpocketing 736.1 *stealing*
Pick's disease 510.3 *mental deterioration*
pick someone's brains 599.4 *resort to*
pick the best 580.4 *pick*
pick the brains of 477.17 *question*
pick the lock 346.10 *invade*
pick them up and lay them down 648.2 *make haste*
pick the seam 27.18 *bowl*
pick to pieces 244.9 *demolish*, 852.18 *find fault*
pickup 22.6 *fielding terms*, 64.22 *transformer*, 329.8 *speed*, 420.9 *audio device*, 656.2 *unskilled*
pick up 36.19 *punt*, 219.4 *protract*, 326.14 *bring back*, 361.4 *gather up*, 407.11 *touch*, 420.15 *hear*, 627.2 *get better*, 629.4 *be restored*
pick up cheap 752.5 *buy at a discount*
pick up for nothing 754.14 *buy cheaply*
pick up speed 329.6 *accelerate*
pick up the bill 746.8 *defray*
pick up the gauntlet 674.11 *contend*
pick up the pace 648.2 *make haste*
pick up the pieces 629.1 *repair*
pick up where one left off 219.4 *protract*
Pickwickian 521.10 *meaningless*
picky 481.9 *discriminating*, 580.14 *selecting*
picky eater 350.18 *eater*
picnic 289.12 *be outside*, 350.13 *feast*, 660.6 *easy thing*, 812.1 *celebration*

picnic hamper 258.7 *basket*
picnicker 350.18 *eater*
pico **75** SI Units
Pico della Mirandola **4** Philosophers
picrite 54.30 *igneous rock*
picrotoxin **62** Medication
Pictish **5** Languages and Groups of Languages
pictogram 5.13 *letter*, 547.1 *representation*
pictograph 5.13 *letter*
pictographic 5.41 *lettered*, 50.24 *pictorial*
Pictor **53** The Constellations
pictorial **50**, **52**, 547.13 *representational*, 560.13 *representing*
pictorial equivalent 50.7 *picture*
pictorially **50**, 547.14 *representationally*
Picts **1** Peoples, 200.6 *people of the past*
picture **50**, 66.3 *photograph*, 118.2 *copy*, 251.2 *circumstances*, 283.3 *suspended object*, 299.1, 299.5 *outline*, 435.7 *view*, 435.16 *visualize*, 457.5 *impression*, 471.15 *imagine*, 519.4 *ideality*, 519.14 *imagine*, 544.10 *identify*, 545.1 *record*, 547.2 *reproduction*, 547.11 *paint*, 560.1 *description*, 560.9 *representation*, 560.14 *describe*
picture card 42.3 *card game terms*
picture clarity 534.23 *television reception*
pictured 544.12 *identified*
picture frame 50.11 *artist's materials*, 382.4 *framework*
picture-frame stage 51.15 *stage*
picture gallery 50.11 *artist's materials*
picture hat 295.15 *headgear*
picture hook 283.4 *hanger*
picture house 51.14 *theatre*
picture magazine 532.5 *journal*
picture marriage 823.3 *types of marriage*
picture of 110.3 *lookalike*
picture postcard 50.7 *picture*
picture quality 534.23 *television reception*
picture rail 279.3 *architectural summit*
picturesque 50.26 *artistic*, 560.11 *descriptive*, 789.5 *beautiful*, 792.8 *decorated*
picturesquely 50.31 *artistically*
picture taking 66.1 *photography*
picture to oneself 519.14 *imagine*
picture window 435.9 *viewpoint*
picture writing 543.1 *sign*, 547.1 *representation*
picul **75** Some Foreign Units
piddle 353.6 *urine*, 353.17 *urinate*, 767.13 *relieve oneself*
piddling 260.7 *little*, 612.4 *trivial*
piddock **81** Molluscs
pidgin 5.10 *language type*
pidgin English 5.26 *dialect*
pi-dog 77.9 *dog*
pie 45.32 *meat dish*, 45.35, 414.3 *dessert*, 660.6 *easy thing*
piebald 32.1 *horse*, 456.8 *checked*
piece **143**, **148**, **269**, 42.4 *chess terms*, 49.15 *composition*, 50.6 *work of art*, 51.2 *play*, 51.6 *scene*, 68.11 *farmland*, 120.2 *certain amount*, 120.8 *quantify*, 132.1 *remainder*, 146.2 *thing included*, 173.2 *fractional part*, 174.2 *item*, 243.5 *work of art*, 350.14 *mouthful*, 680.9 *firearm*, 680.11 *guns*, 741.13 *coinage*
piece by piece 136.20 *separately*
piecemeal 15.8 *industrial*, 121.10 *by degrees*, 136.20 *separately*, 143.11 *partial*, 143.12 *partly*
piecemeal agreement 15.1 *industrial relations*
piece of advice 654.1 *advice*
piece of architecture 243.8 *construction*

piece of cake 477.5 *easy question*, 660.6 *easy thing*, 682.2 *victory*
piece of eight 179.4 *eight*, 741.12 *ancient coins*
piece of evidence 526.7 *showpiece*
piece of fluff 402.9 *woman considered as a sex object*
piece of good luck 686.2 *good fortune*
piece of land 143.7 *piece*
piece of luck 210.2 *opportunity*, 721.5 *profit*, 729.2 *gift*
piece of nonsense 798.4 *joke*
piece of one's mind 852.7 *blame*
piece of the action 731.2 *portion*
piece of the pie 731.2 *portion*
piece of virtu 50.6 *work of art*
piece of writing 243.5 *work of art*
piece on the board 612.10 *nonentity*
piece rate 751.3 *fee*
piece to eat 350.12 *meal*
piece together 135.8 *unite*, 144.4 *complete*, 148.13 *make*, 382.17 *assemble*, 524.9 *decipher*, 629.1 *repair*
piecework 644.1 *work*
pieceworker 646.1 *worker*
pie chart 52.32 *graph*, 152.8 *chart*
piecrust 293.2 *cover*, 379.3 *brittle thing*
pied 456.6 *variegated*, 456.8 *checked*
piedmont 276.7 *lowland*
piedmontite 54 Minerals
pie-eyed 874.2 *slightly drunk*
pie in the sky 102.4 *theorization*, 519.7 *idealism*
Piemontese 68 Breeds of Cattle
pien ch'ing 49 Musical Instruments
pie plate 45.6 *kitchen equipment*
pier 43.8 *column*, 43.9 *miscellaneous architectural features*, 63.21 *bridge*, 63.24 *water system*, 63.27 *superstructure*, 283.5 *projecting object*, 284.2 *supporting part*, 318.2 *projection*
pierce 322.20 *hole*, 346.11 *infiltrate*, 354.2 *inject*, 380.14 *be sharp*, 544.10 *identify*, 618.14 *ill-treat*, 670.6 *stab*
pierced 322.14 *holed*
pierced ears 420.4 *ear*
piercing 55.47 *windy*, 322.1 *opening*, 421.6 *deafening*, 423.6 *loud*, 430.9 *shrill*, 832.14 *hostile*
pier glass 435.8 *reflection*
Pierian Spring 48.13 *poetic genius*
Pierre 93 Cities
Pierrot 51.21 *role*, 51.30 *clown*
pier table 47.4 *table*
pietà 50.10 *art subject*
Pietermaritzburg 93 Cities
pietism 876.4 *self-righteousness*
pietist 7.3 *religious person*
pietistic 876.10 *moralistic*
Pietrain 68 Breeds of Pig
piety 7.2 *religiousness*, 9.1 *worship*, 134.1 *purity*
piezoelectric 64.36 *electronic*
piezoelectric effect 56.49 *electromagnetic induction*
piezoelectricity 235.7 *electrical power*
piezoelectric oscillator 64.21 *rectifier*
piezometer 268.8 *meter*
piezometric 268.16 *micrometric*
piezometry 268.2 *micrometry*
piffaro 49 Musical Instruments
piffle 506.1 *nonsense*, 521.4 *senseless talk*
piffling 506.5 *nonsensical*, 521.10 *meaningless*, 612.4 *trivial*
pig 42 Children's Games and Party Games, 77 Placental Mammals, 16.17 *police officer*, 68.8 *livestock*, 350.18 *eater*, 481.7 *bigot*, 622.6 *dirty person*, 626.3 *unhygienic person*, 718.3 *security officer*, 818.4 *discourteous person*, 872.4 *glutton*

pig ark 68.7 *farm building*
pig breeder 68.15 *agriculturist*
pigeon 78 Birds, 45.20 *meat*, 78.4 *table bird*, 249.14 *sphere*, 539.22 *dupe*
pigeon box 534.3 *correspondence*
pigeon fancier 78.21 *ornithologist*
pigeon hawk 78 Birds
pigeonhole 150.19 *systematize*, 152.6 *category*, 152.15 *categorize*, 163.2, 163.13 *class*, 171.8 *list*, 209.8 *delay*, 260.5 *little space*, 534.3 *correspondence*
pigeonholed 150.11 *grouped*, 152.24 *categorized*, 163.12 *classed*, 600.1 *unused*
pigeonholing 150.2 *grouping*, 152.5 *categorization*, 209.3 *delayed action*
pigeon-like 78.23 *avian*
pigeon loft 78.19 *ornithology*, 256.12 *stall*
pigeon racing 18 Sporting Activities
pigeon shooting 18 Sporting Activities
pig farmer 68.15 *agriculturist*
pig farming 68.3 *livestock farming*
piggery 68.7 *farm building*
piggish 77.33 *ungulate*, 872.6 *gluttonous*
piggishly 872.7 *gluttonously*
piggishness 872.1 *gluttony*
Piggott 18 Sporting Personalities
piggy 77.33 *ungulate*
piggyback 70.5 *transportable*
piggy bank 741.20 *money store*
pigheaded 570.8 *wilful*, 577.1 *obstinate*
pig-headedly 577.9 *be obstinate*
pig-headedness 570.3 *wilfulness*, 577.5 *obstinacy*
pighide 604.1 *materials*
pig ignorant 502.6 *ignorant*
pig in a poke 502.3 *unknown thing*, 659.5 *predicament*
pig-in-the-middle 158.9 *middleman*
pig iron 57 Alloys, 604.1 *materials*
pig Latin 5.18 *slang*
pig lead 57 Alloys
piglet 68.8 *livestock*, 77.19 *young mammal*, 206.4 *young animal*
piglike 77.33 *ungulate*
pigman 68.16 *farm worker*
pigment 58, **444**, 56.28, 444.15 *colour*, 447.7 *blackness*
pigmentation 444.1 *colour*, 447.7 *blackness*
pigment cell 59.7 *cell*
pigment chart 444.2 *colourfulness*
pigment deficiency 445.2 *paleness*
pigmented 444.10 *coloured*, 447.2 *dark*
pigments 50.11 *artist's materials*
pig netting 68.11 *farmland*
pignut 86 Nuts
pigout 350.2 *appetite*
pig out 350.22 *eat well*
pigout 872.3 *act of gluttony*
pig out 872.5 *be greedy*
pigpen 68.7 *farm building*, 256.8 *shelter*, 301.2 *enclosed place*, 727.8 *sink*
pig racing 674.4 *race*
pigs 161 Collective Names by Animal
pig's breakfast 656.9 *bungling*
pig's ear 151.6 *mix-up*, 559.6 *blunder*, 656.9 *bungling*
pig's feet 45.31 *offal*
pig's fry 45.31 *offal*
pig's head 45.31 *offal*
pigskin 19.1 *football*, 293.14 *animal covering*, 604.1 *materials*
pig's knuckles 45.31 *offal*
pig-sticker 680.8 *sharp weapon*
pigsticking 77.23 *mammal hunting*, 590.2 *chase*
pigsty 68.7 *farm building*, 151.4 *litter*, 256.8 *shelter*, 256.12 *stall*, 301.2 *enclosed place*,

323.4 *closed place*, 634.3 *animal shelter*, 727.8 *sink*
pigswill 350.8 *animal food*
pig-swill 622.5 *swill*
pigtail 283.3 *suspended object*, 288.2 *braid*, 304.1 *rear*, 375.7 *rough thing*
pigtailed 375.3 *barbed*
pigweed 84 Flowers and Flowering Plants
pika 77 Placental Mammals
pike 80 Fishes, 20.5 *British game fish*, 39.11 *swimming*, 45.17 *freshwater fish*, 95.1, 275.3 *mountain*, 380.8 *sharp-pointed thing*, 680.8 *sharp weapon*
pikelet 45.39 *loaf*
pikeman 679.13 *historical soldiery*
pikeperch 80 Fishes
pike position 39.6 *diving*
Pikes Peak 95 Mountains, 95.4 *US mountains*
Pikes Peak climb 33.1 *motor racing*
pikle 68.10 *farm tool*
Pilan 8 Deities
pilaster 43.8 *column*, 275.6 *tall thing*, 284.2 *supporting part*
pilastered 43.16 *columned*
pilau rice 45.49 *Indian dish*
pilchard 80 Fishes, 45.18 *sea fish*
pile 43.3 *building*, 63.28 *substructure*, 137.8 *fastening*, 161.26 *mass*, 161.37 *assemble*, 243.8 *construction*, 256.4 *official residence*, 275.6 *tall thing*, 284.2 *supporting part*, 382.6 *construction*, 383.3 *nap*, 544.8 *heraldic device*, 605.1 *store*, 721.3 *acquisition*, 721.11 *acquire*
pile builder 94.6 *lake dweller*
pile carpet 293.9 *floor covering*
piled 161.47 *collected*
piled-on 144.10 *extravagant*
pile-drive 330.2 *collide*
pile-driver 63.29 *construction equipment*, 330.15 *ram*
piled up 605.7 *stored*
pile dweller 94.6 *lake dweller*
pile hammer 63.29 *construction equipment*
pile house 94.7 *lake dwelling*
pile in 144.6 *fill*, 359.15 *mount*
pile it on 541.9 *be extravagant*, 541.10 *boast*, 610.4 *be excessive*
pile of money 741.3 *fortune*, 742.6 *money*
pile on 19.18 *be penalized*, 130.6 *add*, 144.6 *fill*
pile Ossa upon Pelion 541.9 *be extravagant*
pile up 71.21 *miscellaneous motoring terms*, 330.2 *collide*, 605.6 *store*, 610.4 *be excessive*, 721.11 *acquire*
pile-up 35.3 *rugby play*, 330.12 *collision*
pileus 89.4 *fungal body*
pilfer 734.10 *take away*, 736.12 *steal*, 858.10 *be criminal*
pilferage 736.1 *stealing*
pilfered 736.17 *stolen*
pilferer 736.8 *thief*
pilfering 736.1 *stealing*
pilgrim 7.3 *religious person*, 7.7 *monk*, 9.5 *worshipper*, 497.5 *believer*
Pilgrim 68 Breeds of Fowl
pilgrimage 9.1 *worship*, 597.2 *undertaking*
piling it on 541.3 *extravagance*
piling on 19.13 *penalty*
piling Ossa upon Pelion 541.3 *extravagance*
pili nut 86 Nuts
pill 62, 315.3 *round thing*, 630.2 *medicine*, 879.10 *affliction*
pillage 244.5 *havoc*, 244.10, 607.2 *lay waste*, 607.4 *destruction*, 670.14 *siege*, 681.2 *spoils*, 734.10 *take away*, 736.4 *stolen goods*, 736.5 *plundering*, 736.14 *plunder*

pillager 244.6 *destroyer*, 734.6 *taker*, 736.9 *plunderer*
pillaging 734.3 *taking away*, 736.5 *plundering*, 736.17 *stolen*
pillar 34.5 *rock face*, 43.8 *column*, 63.27 *superstructure*, 225.4 *stable thing*, 275.6 *tall thing*, 281.3 *vertical thing*, 284.2 *supporting part*, 545.11 *monument*, 634.1 *refuge*
pillarbox 450.7 *red thing*, 534.3 *correspondence*
pillarbox red 450.1 *red*
pillarist 7.7 *monk*
pillar of society 225.5 *stable person*, 611.4 *bigwig*
pillar of strength 718.1 *protection*
pillar of the church 225.5 *stable person*
pillar of the community 225.5 *stable person*, 611.4 *bigwig*, 694.4 *obedient person*, 800.2 *person of repute*
Pillars of Hercules 263.3 *distant place*
pillary 799.6 *deride*
pillbox 295.15 *headgear*, 671.12 *fort*
pill bug 81.4 *arthropod*
pilliwinks 879.15 *instrument of torture*
pillock 508.3 *foolish person*
pillory 699.5 *means of restraint*, 879.1 *punish*, 879.14 *instrument of punishment*
pillow 284.4 *rest*, 325.3 *resting place*, 374.11 *soft thing*
pillowcase 293.10 *bed covering*
pillowed 374.4 *compressible*, 649.4 *at ease*
pillow lava 54.25 *eruption*
pillow sham 293.10 *bed covering*
pill-popping 875.1 *drug-taking*
pillwort 88 Ferns
pilot 74 Ships and Boats, 73.3 *aircraft personnel*, 74.7 *nautical person*, 119.2 *original*, 154.8 *precursor*, 154.15 *precede*, 156.21 *pioneer*, 180.8 *usher*, 180.15 *escort*, 596.9 *tentative*, 632.4 *safety device*, 652.10 *conductor*, 652.15 *conduct*, 653.2 *direct*, 653.13 *director*
pilotage 73.1 *aviation*, 74.5 *navigation*, 653.4 *directorship*
pilot a ship 74.9 *navigate*
pilot fish 80 Fishes
pilot house 74 Parts of a Ship
piloting 73.1 *aviation*, 74.5 *navigation*, 154.14 *preparatory*, 332.1 *direction*
pilot jack 544.7 *flag*
pilot light 408.6 *fire*
pilot officer 679.32 *airman*
Pilot Officer 17 British Military Ranks
pilot run 479.2 *rehearsal*
pilot scheme 592.6 *outline*, 594.10 *preparations*
pilotship 74.5 *navigation*
pilot whale 77 Placental Mammals
Piltdown Man 539.11 *hoax*
Piltzintecuhtli 8 Deities
pilum 59.8 *cell organ*
Pima 1 Peoples
pimento 45 Herbs and Spices
pi meson 56.77 *elementary particle*
pimiento 45 Vegetables
Pimms 351.8 *mixed drink*
pimozide 62 Medication
pimp 135.7 *joiner*, 158.9 *middleman*, 158.19 *mediate*, 232.3 *assistant*, 232.4 *be an instrument*, 606.3 *provider*, 606.5 *provision*, 707.3 *agent*, 864.9 *wicked person*, 877.8 *immoral man*, 877.18 *prostitute*
pimpernel 84 Flowers and Flowering Plants
pimping 877.5 *prostitution*
pimple **793**, 149.2 *impurity*, 309.3 *deformity*, 456.4 *maculation*, 624.13 *skin disease*
pimply 375.2 *coarse*, 456.10 *mottled*

pin 26.5 *wrestling*, 29.2 *golfing terms*, 42.4 *chess terms*, 135.10 *link*, 137.11 *connect*, 322.2 *opener*, 323.2 *stopper*, 364.4 *vortex*, 380.8 *sharp-pointed thing*, 612.8 *trifle*, 792.6 *jewellery*, 821.15 *love item*, 821.26, 826.8 *court*

PIN 65.12 *electronic office*

pina colada 351.8 *mixed drink*

pinafore 295.25 *accessories*

pinafore dress 295.7 *frock*

pi nai 49 *Musical Instruments*

pinaster 85 Trees and Shrubs

pin back one's ears 420.15 *hear*

pince-nez 435.10 *visual aid*

pincer movement 670.12 *military attack*, 726.2 *detention*

pincers 355.10 *excavator*, 603.1 *tool*, 726.3 *tools for gripping*

pinch 19.10 *defence*, 19.16 *play defence*, 36.19 *punt*, 106.4 *difficult circumstances*, 133.4 *admixture*, 210.3 *critical time*, 260.5 *little space*, 262.1 *contraction*, 262.5 *make smaller*, 272.10 *narrow*, 342.9 *converge*, 406.11 *inflict pain*, 407.3 *press*, 407.11 *touch*, 528.7 *advice*, 593.3 *needfulness*, 636.1 *warning*, 636.5 *warn*, 659.5 *predicament*, 699.11 *detain*, 734.3 *taking away*, 734.10 *take away*, 736.3 *theft*, 736.12 *steal*, 743.6 *insolvency*, 743.12 *be poor*, 821.14 *communication of love*, 826.1 *endearment*, 826.7 *show endearment for*

pinchbeck 57 Alloys, 612.4 *trivial*

pinched 16.59 *stolen*, 36.14 *punting*, 262.7 *smaller*, 272.1 *narrow*, 274.2 *emaciated*, 409.8 *cold*, 593.5 *necessitous*, 743.2 *insolvent*

pinch hit 222.4 *be a substitute*

pinch-hit for 707.4 *substitute for*

pinch hitter 22.2 *baseball player*, 222.2 *substitute person*, 707.2 *alternative*

pinching 36.8 *punting*, 262.1 *contraction*, 262.8 *contracting*, 593.6 *demanding*, 736.1 *stealing*

pinching out 69.5 *gardening*

pinch of snuff 413.7 *tobacco*

pinch pennies 743.12 *be poor*

pinch someone's bottom 543.11 *gesture*

pincoffin 67.6 *dye*

pin connection 63.27 *superstructure*

Pindar 48 Poets

Pindaric 48.19 *narrative*

Pindaric ode 48.7 *poem*

pindling 260.7 *little*

pin down 165.24 *specify*, 250.11 *find*, 490.21 *make certain*, 695.6 *compel*

pin dropping 424.3 *faint-sounding thing*

Pindus 95 Mountains

pine 85 Trees and Shrubs, 624.24 *be unhealthy*, 770.8 *grieve*

pineal 352.5 *of a secretion*

pineal gland 352 Endocrine Glands

pineapple 86 Fruits, 680.16 *bomb*

pineapple family 83.3 *seed plant*

pineapple juice 351.6 *soft drink*

pine cone 85.2 *tree part*

pine drape 397.8 *after death*, 399.4 *funeral objects*

pine for 782.12 *desire*

pine furniture 47.1 *furniture*

pine marten 77 Placental Mammals, 85.11 *tree-related animal*

pinene 58.20 *terpene*

pine needle 85.2 *tree part*, 380.8 *sharp-pointed thing*

pine nut 86 Nuts

pine resin 395.10 *resin*

Pinero 48 Dramatists

pinery 85.4 *trees*

pine tar 85.9 *tree product*

pinetum 85.4 *trees*

pinewood oil 85.9 *tree product*

pinfold 68.7 *farm building*, 634.3 *animal shelter*

ping 426.5 *ringing*, 426.12 *ring*, 427.2 *ringing*, 427.10 *ring*

pinging 426.5, 427.7 *ringing*

ping pong 40.1 *tennis*

pinguedinous 395.11 *oily*

pinguescence 395.1 *oiliness*

pinguescent 386.10, 395.11 *oily*

pinguid 386.10, 395.11 *oily*

pinguidinous 386.10 *oily*

pinguidity 386.2, 395.1 *oiliness*

pinguidly 395.20 *oilily*

pinhead 260.2 *little thing*, 279.2 *head*, 460.3 *unintelligent person*, 508.3 *foolish person*

pinhole 322.5 *hole*

pinhole camera 66.16 *camera*

pining 624.22 *sick*, 770.5 *sad*, 782.1 *desire*, 782.9 *desirous*

pinion 63.7 *gear*, 135.10 *link*, 628.5 *hurt*

pinioned 726.10 *retained*

pinite 54 Minerals

pink 74 Sailing Ships and Boats, **84** Flowers and Flowering Plants, 319.5 *notch*, 450.1 *red*, 595.6 *uncooked*, 665.6 *political party member*, 665.10 *political*

Pinkafelder 32 Breeds of Horse and Pony

pink ball 24.5 *snooker*

pinked 319.4 *notched*

pink elephant 435.5 *imagination*

pink elephants 874.16 *alcoholism*

pink eye 436.2 *poor sight*

pink gin 351.8 *mixed drink*

pinkie 407.7 *sense organ*

pinking shears 319.2 *notched thing*, 380.9 *sharp-edged thing*

pinko 12.6 *political party*, 665.6 *political party member*, 693.11 *rebel*

pink of condition 623.3 *health*

pink salmon 80 Fishes

pink slip 349.18 *dismissal*

pin money 721.5 *profit*, 725.6 *marriage settlement*, 730.2 *something received*, 741.4 *change*, 749.3 *income*

pin mould 89 Fungi

pinna 88.2 *fern plant*

pinnace 74 Ships and Boats, **74** Sailing Ships and Boats

pinnacle 34.5 *rock face*, 95.1 *mountain*, 126.4 *summit*, 275.2 *heights*, 279.1 *summit*, 619.3 *perfection*

pinnate 83.18 *of leaves*

pinned 137.15 *connected*, 726.10 *retained*, 826.9 *endearing*

pinned down 225.10 *stabilized*, 250.7 *found*, 490.7 *particular*

pinning down 250.3 *locating*, 490.18 *particularity*

pinniped 77.11 *marine mammal*, 77.29 *cetacean*

Pinnipedia 77.11 *marine mammal*

pinnipedian 77.29 *cetacean*

pinny 295.25 *accessories*, 621.11 *cleaning cloth*

Pinocchio 260.4 *little person*, 396.6 *things brought to life*

pinochle 42 Card Games

pin on 135.10 *link*

pin on to 808.14 *follow*

pinpoint 165.22 *characterize*, 250.2 *exact location*, 250.11 *find*, 260.2 *little thing*, 291.9 *centre*, 503.5 *accurate*, 532.16 *publicize*, 537.21 *accurate*, 537.31 *be accurate*, 544.10 *identify*

pinpoint accuracy 503.1, 537.8 *accuracy*, 760.10 *accuracy*

pinpointed 250.7 *found*, 291.7 *centralized*, 537.21 *accurate*

pinpointing 250.3 *locating*, 291.3 *centrality*, 291.7 *centralized*, 544.1 *identification*

pinprick 278.4 *shallow thing*, 406.1 *pain*, 612.8 *trifle*, 828.3 *cause of offence*, 828.9 *offend*

pins 777 Phobias by Topic

pins and needles 403.3 *stimulus*, 406.1 *pain*

Pinsk 93 Cities

pin someone 26.12 *wrestle*

pin someone's shoulders 26.12 *wrestle*

pin spot 25.4 *bowling*

pinstripes 295.9 **trousers**

pinstripe suit 295.10 *suit*

pint 75 General Units, 351.2 *drink*

pinta 351.5 *milk*

pintail 78 Birds

Pinter 48 Dramatists

pint glass 258.13 *drinking vessel*

pin the tail on the donkey 42 Children's Games and Party Games

pintle 71 Motor Vehicle Parts, **74** Parts of a Ship, 364.4 *vortex*

pinto 32.1 *horse*

pin to 130.6 *add*, 135.10 *link*

pinto 456.8 *checked*

Pinto 32 Breeds of Horse and Pony

pinto bean 45 Vegetables

pint of milk 351.5 *milk*

pint-size 260.7 *little*

Pintubi 5 Languages and Groups of Languages

pin-up 66.4 *portrait*

pin-up girl 789.3 *attractive female*

pinwheel 364.6 *rotator*, 439.8 *fire*

pinworm 81 Worms, 81.10 *parasite*

piny 85.14 *treelike*

Pinyin 5.13 *letter*

Pinzgauer 68 Breeds of Cattle

Pinzgauer Noriker 32 Breeds of Horse and Pony

pion 56.77 *elementary particle*

pioneer 156, 119.7 *originate*, 154.8 *precursor*, 154.18 *forerun*, 255.7 *settler*, 255.15 *settle*, 298.3 *interfacer*, 496.4 *invent*, 496.12 *discoverer*, 594.1 *prepare*, 594.15 *preparer*, 597.1 *undertake*, 597.4 *volunteer*, 653.2 *direct*, 660.16 *make easy*, 679.17 *army person*

Pioneer 53.33 *planetary probe*

pioneering 119.4 *original*, 154.3 *preparation*, 154.14 *preparatory*, 496.9 *invention*, 496.13 *discovering*, 594.9 *preparation*, 597.6 *enterprising*

piononos 45.51 *West Indian dish*

pious 7.15 *religious*, 10.22 *worshipping*, 857.5 *pure*, 876.10 *moralistic*

pious fraud 539.10 *fraud*

piously 7.23 *religiously*, 857.8 *purely*, 876.13 *morally*

piousness 7.2 *religiousness*, 876.2 *good morals*

pip 83.9 *seed*, 86.3 *fruit structure*, 426.5 *ringing*, 544.4 *insignia*, 830.10 *make sullen*

pipa 79 Amphibians

p'i p'a 49 Musical Instruments

pip at the post 657.5 *be cunning*, 682.9 *be victorious*

pipe 49 Musical Instruments, **75** General Units, 49.39 *sing*, 65.8 *software*, 258.11 *vessel*, 272.8 *narrow thing*, 300.6 *edge*, 315.4 *cylinder*, 322.7 *passageway*, 322.21 *provide passage for*, 430.6 *be shrill*, 432.5 *sing*, 564.13 *speak in a particular way*, 605.2 *resource*

pipe band 49.26 *musical group*

pipeclay 44.2 *raw material*, 446.8 *whitener*, 446.13 *whiten*

pipe cleaner 621.10 *cleaning object*

piped 70.5 *transportable*

pipe down 218.6 *cease*, 325.11 *stop*, 422.1 *be silent*, 422.6 *hush sh silence quiet shut up that's enough peace soft mum's the word whist*, 566.9 *lapse into silence*

pipe dream 102.2 *illusion*, 435.5 *imagination*, 471.15 *imagine*,

489.4 *improbability*, 494.2 *overestimate*, 519.6 *reverie*, 775.3 *aspiration*

pipefish 80 Fishes

pipeline 322.7 *passageway*, 605.3 *supply*, 606.1 *provision*

pipe of peace 413.7 *tobacco*

piperazine 62 Medication

piperidolate 62 Medication

piperocaine 62 Medication

Pipe rolls 3.11 *relic*

pipe tobacco 413.7 *tobacco*

pipette 45 Types of Pasta, **57** Laboratory Apparatus, 355.9 *extractor*, 355.14 *suck*

pipetting 355.4 *sucking*

pipe vein 605.2 *resource*

pipe wrench 603.1 *tool*

piping 70.5 *transportable*, 300.2 *edging*, 430.3 *shrillness*, 430.9 *shrill*, 675.7 *peaceful*

piping down 218.2 *stop*

piping hot 408.9 *hot*

piping times of peace 675.1 *peace*

pipistrelle 77 Placental Mammals

pipit 78 Birds, 78.6 *songbird*

pipkin 44.8 *ceramic object*

pipped 683.11 *defeated*

pippin 86 Fruits

pips 543.4 *signal*, 792.3 *honour*

pipsqueak 260.4 *little person*, 612.10 *nonentity*

piquancy 413, 554.1 *emphasis*

Piquancy 413

piquant 413, 237.12 *strong to the senses*, 554.3 *emphatic*

piquantly 413

pique 413.13 *be piquant*, 828.1 *resentment*, 828.9 *offend*

piqué 67 Natural Fabrics

piqued 828.15 *resentful*

piquet 42 Card Games

piquet pack 42.3 *card game terms*

piracy 733.3 *illegal borrowing*, 734.3 *taking away*, 736.1 *stealing*, 736.6 *illegal borrowing*

Piraeus 93 Cities

piragua 74 Sailing Ships and Boats

Pirandello 48 Dramatists

piranha 80 Fishes

Pirani gauge 57.20 *surface chemistry*

pirate 74.7 *nautical person*, 118.10 *copy*, 679.6 *militarist*, 733.6 *borrower*, 736.10 *infringer*, 736.15 *infringe*

pirate a record 733.9 *borrow illegally*, 736.15 *infringe*

pirate a video 733.9 *borrow illegally*, 736.15 *infringe*

pirated 733.11 *borrowed*, 736.18 *fraudulent*

pirated record 114.2 *copy*

pirate flag 544.7 *flag*

piratelike 736.17 *stolen*

pirate radio 534.20 *radio broadcasting*

pirate ship 679.25 *historical naval ships*

piratess 74.7 *nautical person*

piratic 736.18 *fraudulent*

piratical 679.33 *combative*

piratically 736.19 *thievishly*

pirating 733.3, 736.6 *illegal borrowing*

pirogue 74 Sailing Ships and Boats

piroplasm 81.10 *parasite*

piroplasmosis 81.12 *protozoal disease*

pirouette 30.5 *horizontal bar*, 30.10 *compete in gymnastics*, 32.10 *dressage*, 41.7 *ice-dancing*, 41.15 *ice-skate*, 46.9 *ballet steps*, 364.3 *reel*, 364.8 *rotate*

pirouetting 364.2 *turning*

Pisa 93 Cities

Pisacha 8.7 *devil*

piscary 80.7 *fishing*

piscatology 80.7 *fishing*

piscator 80.10 *fisher*, 590.6 *hunter*

piscatorial 20.8 *angling*, 80.13 *fishlike*, 80.14 *ichthyological*, 590.16 *hunting*

piscatorially 20.9 *on the water*
Pisces 53 The Constellations, **53** Zodiac Constellations, 80.1 *fishes*
piscicultural 80.14 *ichthyological*
pisciculturalist 80.10 *fisher*
pisciculturally 68.22 *agriculturally*
pisciculture 68.3 *livestock farming*, 80.7 *fishing*
pisciform 80.13 *fishlike*
piscine 80.13 *fishlike*
Piscis Austrinus 53 The Constellations
Piscis Volans 53 The Constellations
pishogue 497.2 *religious belief*, 822.2 *curse*
piskie 11.11 *ghost*
pismire 82.4 *social insect*
piss 353.3 *urination*, 353.6 *urine*, 353.17 *urinate*, 387.3 *body fluid*, 389.4 *exudate*, 389.32 *seep*, 767.13 *relieve oneself*
piss and vinegar 239.1 *vigour*
piss-ant 576.15 *indecisive person*
piss-artist 874.17 *drunkard*
piss away 607.1 *waste*
piss down 55.62 *rain*
pissed 874.1 *drunk*
pissed as a newt 874.1 *drunk*
pissed off 650.2 *bored*, 828.16 *angry*
pisshead 351.12 *drinker*, 874.17 *drunkard*
pissing down 55.53 *rainy*
piss off 345.1 *depart*, 345.15 *go*, 349.33 *go away*, 827.15 *miscellaneous swearwords*
piss one off 828.14 *make angry*
pisspot 353.14 *toilet*
piss-take 799.2 *act of derision*
pistachio 86 Nuts
piste 28.1 *fencing*, 41.1 *skiing*, 545.12 *vestige*
pistil 84.3 *flower part*
pistillate 84.12 *of flowers*
pistol 338.9 *firearm*, 338.28 *shoot*, 398.17 *murder*, 680.9 *firearm*
pistole 741.12 *ancient coins*
pistoleer 338.15 *shooter*, 679.13 *historical soldiery*
pistolet 680.10 *historical gun*
pistols 295.9 *trousers*
pistols for two and coffee for one 674.9 *duel*
pistol shooting 18 Sporting Activities, 37.1 *target shooting*
pistol-shot 425.1 *bang*
piston 71 Motor Vehicle Parts, 63.11 *engine*, 72.5 *locomotive part*, 323.2 *stopper*, 338.11 *propeller*
piston movement 214.1 *regularity*
piston slap 71.21 *miscellaneous motoring terms*
pit 25.4 *bowling*, 33.6 *motor racing terms*, 51.15 *stage*, 51.16 *auditorium*, 51.31 *theatregoer*, 71.21 *miscellaneous motoring terms*, 86.3 *fruit structure*, 277.4 *deep thing*, 309.11 *deform*, 317.2 *concave land*, 383.3 *nap*, 410.5 *coal*, 435.9 *viewpoint*, 539.13 *snare*, 634.1 *refuge*, 635.1 *trap*, 647.1 *workshop*, 657.2 *stratagem*
pit against 663.16 *confront*
Pitaka 7.12 *religious text*
pitapat 365.2 *vibration*, 366.10 *beat*, 424.1 *faintness*
pit-a-pat 426.4 *knocking*
pit bull terrier 77 Breeds of Dogs, 679.4 *fighting animal*
pitch 366, 5.16 *spoken letter*, 22.7 *play baseball*, 29.1, 29.7 *golf*, 34.5 *rock face*, 43.6 *roof*, 49.16 *musical note*, 49.21 *tone*, 56.20 *musical note*, 121.1 *degree*, 224.11 *be changeable*, 250.1 *location*, 275.1 *height*, 279.1 *summit*, 281.6 *make vertical*, 286.1 *obliqueness*, 286.6 *be oblique*, 330.4 *throw*, 335.14 *deviating course*, 335.15 *deviating motion*, 338.5, 338.23 *throw*,

360.11 *trip*, 360.12 *drop*, 362.6 *throw down*, 365.4, 365.11 *rock*, 366.11 *stagger*, 440.4 *dark thing*, 447.9 *black thing*, 564.3 *mode of speech*, 674.3 *stadium*, 739.6 *salesmanship*
pitch a bitch 532.14 *proclaim*
pitch and plunge 366.25 *pitch*
pitch-and-run approach 29.1 *golf*
pitch and toss 338.5 *throw*
pitch a perfect game 22.7 *play baseball*
pitch a shut-out 22.7 *play baseball*
pitch-black 440.10 *dark-coloured*, 447.1 *black*
pitchblende 54 Minerals, **57** Common Metal Ores
pitch-dark 440.8 *dark*
pitch-darkness 440.1 *darkness*
pitch diameter 63.7 *gear*
pitched 43.14 *roofed*, 286.4 *oblique*, 564.18 *phonetic*
pitched battle 674.1 *contention*, 674.6 *fight*, 676.9 *battle*
pitched roof 293.7 *overhead covering*
pitcher 22.2 *baseball player*, 44.8 *ceramic object*, 120.3 *container*, 258.11 *vessel*, 338.14 *thrower*, 389.16 *water carrier*
pitcher plant 539.13 *snare*
pitcher's mound 22.1 *baseball*
pitcher's plate 22.1 *baseball*
pitchfork 68.10 *farm tool*, 338.24 *push*, 380.8 *sharp-pointed thing*, 603.2 *garden tool*
pitch forward 338.24 *push*
pitch in 156.18 *make a beginning*, 350.22 *eat well*, 662.22 *improve*, 662.29 *finance*, 664.13 *work together*
pitching 73.5 *flight*, 74.11 *nautical*, 338.3 *throwing*, 365.16 *rocking*, 366.3 *turbulence*, 366.17 *turbulent*
pitching coach 22.2 *baseball player*
pitching into 852.8 *berating*
pitching niblick 29.4 *golf club*
pitching terms 22
pitch into 670.5 *strike*, 674.12 *fight*, 852.1 *berate*
pitch of perfection 594.14 *preparedness*
pitch one's tent 256.18 *take up residence*
pitchout 19.9 *play*, 19.15 *play of-fence*
pitchpole 36.15 *sail*
pitch upon 344.2 *reach*
pitchy 395.14 *resinous*, 440.10 *dark-coloured*, 447.1 *black*
piteous 835.7 *pitiful*
piteously 835.13 *pitifully*
pitfall 539.13 *snare*, 631.6 *source of trouble*, 633.5 *danger*, 635.1 *trap*, 657.2 *stratagem*, 659.8 *snag*
pith 83.5 *stem*, 86.3 *fruit structure*, 103.2 *essential content*, 257.3 *insides*, 290.5 *inner nature*, 291.1 *centre*, 393.8 *pulp*, 472.1 *topic*, 520.1 *meaning*, 520.2 *significance*, 611.1 *importance*
Pithecanthropus 202.7 *ancient people*, 400.3 *uncivilized human*
pith helmet 293.12 *protective covering*, 295.15 *headgear*, 634.2 *shelter*
pithily 552.5 *concisely*, 562.11 *summarily*
pithiness 393.4 *pulpiness*, 552.1 *conciseness*, 562.4 *summariness*
pithy 374.4 *compressible*, 505.2 *proverbial*, 520.7 *significant*, 552.3 *concise*, 554.3 *emphatic*, 562.6 *summary*
pithy saying 552.1 *conciseness*
pitiable 612.2 *obscure*, 618.4 *poor*, 835.7 *pitiful*
pitiably 691.5 *given consideration*
pitied 691.5 *given consideration*
pitiful 835, 612.2 *obscure*, 618.4 *poor*, 774.5 *lamentable*
pitifully 835

pitifulness 618.10 *poverty*
pitiless 836, 574.3 *strong-willed*, 577.3 *unyielding*, 690.8 *severe*, 832.13 *merciless*
pitilessly 836
pitilessness 836, 574.14 *tenacity*, 690.1 *severity*, 868.1 *impenitence*
Pitilessness 836
pitiless person 836
Pitjantjatjara 5 Languages and Groups of Languages
pit lane 33.6 *motor racing terms*
pit mechanic 33.8 *driver*
pit of Acheron 8.11 *heaven*
pit of one's stomach 759.8 *seat of feelings*
piton 34.4 *climbing equipment*
Piton 53 Mountains
pit pony 32.2 *thoroughbred*
pitressin 58 Hormones
pit stop 33.6 *motor racing terms*
pitta bread 45.38 *bread*
pittance 120.2 *certain amount*, 609.8 *insufficiency*, 731.2 *portion*
pitted 309.7 *deformed*, 317.5 *concave*, 375.2 *coarse*, 793.5 *marked*
pitter-patter 365.2 *vibration*, 366.10 *beat*, 424.1 *faintness*, 426.4 *knocking*
pittite 51.31 *theatregoer*
Pittsburgh 93 Cities, 93.2 *American cities*
pituita 393.10 *mucus*
pituitary 352.5 *of a secretion*
pituitary gland 352 Endocrine Glands
pit viper 79 Reptiles
pit wall 33.6 *motor racing terms*
pity 835, 835, 691.1 *leniency*, 691.3 *be lenient*, 759.18 *feel for*, 760.5 *sensitivity*, 760.11 *be sensitive*, 831.1 *benevolence*, 859.2 *unselfishness*, 859.7 *be unselfish*
Pity 835
pitying 835, 691.4 *lenient*
pitying person 835
più 49 Musical Terms
piuttosto 49 Musical Terms
pivot 23.6 *play basketball*, 29.3 *golf shots*, 41.7 *ice-dancing*, 41.15 *ice-skate*, 46.3 *ballroom dance steps*, 103.2 *essential content*, 135.5 *joint*, 158.2 *core*, 158.16 *place in the middle*, 291.1 *centre*, 337.9 *turn round*, 342.5 *focus*, 364.4 *vortex*, 364.8 *rotate*, 603.1 *tool*, 611.3 *chief thing*
pivotal 106.8 *difficult*, 158.12 *core*, 210.7 *critical*, 226.13 *causal*, 291.6 *central*, 364.12 *rotary*, 611.5 *important*
pivotally 210.10 *critically*, 226.14 *causally*
pivotal point 210.3 *critical time*, 221.3 *turning point*
pivot cartwheel 30.6 *pommel horse*
pivoting 23.4 *playing terms*, 364.2 *turning*, 364.11 *rotating*
pivot man 23.2 *basketball player*
pivot on 227.7 *follow from*, 291.9 *centre*
pixel 65.17 *computing term*, 260.2 *little thing*
pixie 11.11 *ghost*
pixilated 874.1 *drunk*
piz 49 Musical Terms
pizza 45.47 *Italian dish*
pizzazz 239.1 *vigour*
pizzeria 350.15 *eating place*
pizzicato 49 Musical Terms
PJs 295.22 *nightwear*
placability 839.2 *forgivingness*
placable 839.5 *merciful*
placableness 839.2 *forgivingness*
placali 45.53 *African dish*
placard 526.8 *showplace*, 532.9 *advertisement*, 532.16 *publicize*, 543.1 *sign*
placate 677.4 *pacify*, 765.9 *comfort*, 771.15 *humour*
placating 771.11 *humouring*

placatory 675.7 *peaceful*, 677.6 *pacificatory*
place 32.7 *horseracing*, 105.1 *state*, 121.2 *rank*, 121.4 *interval*, 121.5 *measure*, 150.4 *position*, 150.19 *systematize*, 152.6 *category*, 152.12 *arrange*, 152.15 *categorize*, 163.13 *class*, 248.5 *reserved space*, 249.1 *region*, 250.1 *location*, 250.9 *locate*, 251.1 *situation*, 251.2 *circumstances*, 251.4 *employment*, 251.10 *situate*, 256.1 *habitat*, 327.3 *road*, 496.1 *discover*, 847.2 *task*
place an advertisement 532.16 *publicize*
place an obstacle in someone's path 709.3 *veto*
place at intervals 248.21, 265.4 *space*
placebo 62.3 *drug*, 630.2 *medicine*
place card 544.3 *means of identification*
placed 105.8 *in a state of*, 106.7 *circumstantial*, 152.20 *arranged*, 152.24 *categorized*, 163.12 *classed*, 250.6 *located*, 251.6 *situated*
placed at intervals 265.6 *spaced*
place in a shop window 526.2 *display something*
place in a situation 251.10 *situate*
place in history 3.7 *narrative*, 511.5 *day to remember*, 682.1 *success*
place in one's account 744.10 *deposit*
place in order 152.15 *categorize*
place in the foreground 526.3 *reveal*, 611.8 *make important*
place in the middle 158
place in the spotlight 526.3 *reveal*
place in the sun 686.1 *prosperity*
place kick 19.17 *kick*, 35.3 *rugby play*, 330.13 *blow*
place-kick 330.7 *kick*
place kicker 19.12 *special team*
placemat 293.12 *protective covering*
place mat 621.11 *cleaning cloth*
placement 152.1 *arrangement*, 152.5 *categorization*, 250.4 *placing*
place name 560.8 *name*
placenta 352 Endocrine Glands, 77.5 *placental mammal*, 245.7 *obstetrics*
placental 77.25 *mammalian*, 352.5 *of a secretion*
placental mammal 77
place of authority 688
place of confinement 816
place of confrontation 298.1 *interface*
place of contact 298.1 *interface*
place of departure 345
place of embarkation 345.10 *place of departure*
place of exchange 223
place of experimentation 479
place of interaction 298.1 *interface*
place of judgment 492
place of pilgrimage 291.4 *centre of activity*, 588.6 *objective*
place of residence 567, 256.1 *habitat*
place of safety 634.1 *refuge*
place of the damned 368.1 *nonmaterial world*
place of the dead 8.11 *heaven*
place of trade 223.2 *place of exchange*
place of work 647.1 *workshop*
place of worship 10
place on 130.6 *add*
place oneself 150.24 *line up*
placer 57.24 *ore*
places 777 Phobias by Topic
place side by side 267.3 *juxtapose*
place strictures on 302.7 *limit*
place to one's credit 744.10 *deposit*
place under 146.6 *subsume*

place under an embargo 147.7 *exclude*
place under oath 535.18 *vow*
place-value notation 52.8 *number system*
place where one hangs one's hat 256.3 *home*
place where one lives 256.1 *habitat*
placid 4.18 *detached*, 325.6 *quiescent*
placidity 4.3 *detachment*, 325.2 *repose*
placidly 4.27 *stoically*, 325.10 *motionlessly*
placidness 325.2 *repose*
placing 250, 152.1 *arrangement*, 152.5 *categorization*
placket 295.24 *part of garment*
placoderm 80.4 *fossil fish*
placoid 266.9 *platelike*
placoid scale 80.5 *fish anatomy*
plagiarism 118.2 *copy*, 183.1 *repetition*, 183.2 *iteration*, 326.4 *translation*, 733.3 *illegal borrowing*, 734.1 *taking*, 734.3 *taking away*, 736.6 *illegal borrowing*
plagiarist 114.4 *person who copies*, 118.8 *copier*, 733.6 *borrower*, 734.6 *taker*, 736.10 *infringer*
plagiarize 118.10 *copy*, 183.16 *repeat*, 326.16 *translate*, 733.9 *borrow illegally*, 734.7 *take*, 734.10 *take away*, 736.15 *infringe*
plagiarized 118.13 *imitation*, 183.9 *repeated*, 733.11 *borrowed*, 736.18 *fraudulent*
plagiarized book 540.14 *false thing*
plagiarizing 736.6 *illegal borrowing*
plagiary 736.6 *illegal borrowing*
plagioclase 54.34 *mineral*
plague 624, 82.4 *social insect*, 82.16 *infest*, 244.7 *agent of destruction*, 357.8 *transgression*, 618.10 *poverty*, 618.13 *be worthless*, 628.5 *hurt*, 631.1 *affliction*, 631.14 *afflict*, 687.1 *adversity*, 777.14 *worry*, 862.2 *affliction*, 862.11 *be evil*
plagued 357.11 *overrun*, 659.16 *troubled*, 777.9 *worried*, 862.8 *afflicted*
plagued by conscience 867.6 *penitent*
plague pit 399.6 *grave*
plague spot 624.6 *infection*
plague-stricken 624.23 *diseased*, 626.6 *contagious*
plaguey 659.13 *inconvenient*
plaguy 618.4 *poor*
plaice 80 *Fishes*, 20.5 *British game fish*, 45.18 *sea fish*, 80.8 *food fish*
plaid 67 *Natural Fabrics*, 375.7 *rough thing*, 375.12 *make rough*, 456.2 *check*, 456.8 *checked*
Plaid Cymru 12.6 *political party*
plain 24.3 *English billiards*, 39.11 *swimming*, 54.7 *landform*, 87.2 *grassland*, 98.6 *lowland*, 98.11 *continental*, 112.6 *conforming*, 127.5 *inferior state*, 144.7 *complete*, 144.9 *completely*, 248.3 *geographical space*, 276.2 *lowland*, 282.3 *flat thing*, 282.8 *horizontal*, 312.2 *straightforward*, 312.5 *honourable*, 322.16 *open*, 376.8 *smooth thing*, 412.5 *tasteless*, 435.23, 437.1 *visible*, 437.2 *clear*, 442.4 *easily seen through*, 444.13 *soft-hued*, 457.10 *aspectual*, 475.9 *demonstrated*, 520.6 *meaningful*, 522.2 *simple*, 526.15 *open*, 535.14 *assertive*, 537.18 *truthful*, 542.14 *simple*, 549.8 *inelegant*, 550.3 *clear*, 556.1 *simple*, 558.3 *elegant*, 559.10 *ugly*, 658.1 *naive*, 660.9 *easy*, 690.10 *unadorned*, 698.13 *informal*, 787.4 *predictable*, 788.4 *boring*, 790.4 *ugly*, 814.9 *familiar*, 857.4 *honourable*, 869.8 *self-restrained*
plain as a pikestaff 437.2 *clear*
plain as day 787.4 *predictable*
plain as the nose on one's face 437.2 *clear*, 526.15 *open*
plainchant 10.8 *hymn*, 433.2 *song*
plain clothes 295.4 *informal dress*
plain-clothes officer 16.17 *police officer*
plain English 522.10, 556.4 *simplicity*
plain flour 45.7 *basic ingredient*
plain Jane 124.7 *average person*
plain jump 39.6 *diving*
plain living 869.1 *self-restraint*
plainly 690, 112.15 *monotonously*, 312.13 *straightforwardly*, 322.25 *obviously*, 322.26 *openly*, 381.12 *bluntly*, 435.25, 437.11 *visibly*, 442.13 *transparently*, 457.15 *apparently*, 475.20 *manifestly*, 520.13 *meaningfully*, 522.13 *intelligibly*, 524.18 *in other words*, 526.16 *manifestly*, 530.13 *openly*, 535.25 *explicitly*, 542.24 *simply*, 549.10 *stylistically*, 550.4 *clearly*, 555.3 *unemphatically*, 556.8 *simply*, 558.5 *elegantly*, 698.22 *informally*, 787.10 *predictably*, 788.8 *boringly*, 814.14 *naturally*, 857.7 *honourably*, 869.11 *with self-restraint*
plainly stated 522.2 *simple*
plainly visible 318.7 *conspicuous*
plain man 658.3 *naive person*
plainness 112.2 *conformity*, 282.1 *horizontality*, 312.8 *directness*, 412.1 *tastelessness*, 437.4 *clarity*, 442.10 *openness*, 520.3 *comprehension*, 520.4 *type of meaning*, 522.10 *simplicity*, 526.11 *openness*, 535.6 *assertiveness*, 537.5 *truthfulness*, 542.4 *simplicity*, 549.3 *inelegance*, 550.1 *clarity*, 555.2 *lack of emphasis*, 556.4 *simplicity*, 558.1 *elegance*, 559.3 *ugliness*, 658.2 *naivety*, 660.2 *simplicity*, 690.3 *unadornment*, 787.2 *predictability*, 788.1 *boredom*, 790.1 *hideousness*, 814.3 *familiarity*, 857.1 *probity*, 869.1 *self-restraint*
plain prose 556.4 *simplicity*
plain reason 463.2 *reasoning*
plain sailing 74.5 *navigation*, 660.6 *easy thing*
plainsong 10.8 *hymn*
plain speaking 312.8 *directness*, 522.10 *simplicity*, 530.3 *openness*, 556.6 *naturalness*
plain-speaking 526.15 *open*, 556.3 *natural*, 564.19 *speaking*
plain speech 522.10 *simplicity*, 526.11 *openness*, 556.6 *naturalness*
plain-spoken 381.2 *outspoken*, 526.15 *open*, 528.16 *informative*, 564.19 *speaking*, 698.13 *informal*, 857.4 *honourable*
plain-spokenness 381.6 *outspokenness*
plain stitch 67.5 *knitting*
plains-wanderer 78 *Birds*
plaint 856.1 *accusation*
plaintiff 16.8 *litigant*, 463.6 *arguer*, 477.10 *person questioned*, 483.7 *person who gives evidence*, 663.9 *opposer*, 856.3 *accuser*
plaintive 774.4 *lamenting*
plaintively 774.8 *mournfully*
plain to see 437.2 *clear*
plain weave 67.4 *weaving*
plain words 322.9 *openness*, 522.10, 556.4 *simplicity*
plain wrapper 438.6 *that which makes invisible*
plait 45.39 *loaf*, 67.2 *spinning*, 67.13 *spin*, 133.8 *mix*, 135.10 *link*, 137.6 *line*, 137.11 *connect*, 288.2 *braid*, 288.8 *interweave*, 320.2 *pleat*, 791.8 *hair cut*

plaited 67.9 *spun*, 133.12 *mixed*, 135.15 *tied*, 137.15 *connected*, 288.6 *interwoven*
plaiting 67.2 *spinning*, 288.1 *interweaving*
plan 471, 517, 592, 592, 48.3 *aspect of fiction*, 50.23 *design*, 54.65 *map*, 63.30 *engineer*, 150.7 *method*, 152.8 *chart*, 152.13 *organize*, 152.18 *make arrangements*, 226.10 *awaken*, 243.10 *produce*, 250.2 *exact location*, 299.1, 299.5 *outline*, 382.1, 382.14 *structure*, 435.16 *visualize*, 471.18 *aim*, 478.6 *solution*, 478.20 *solve*, 513.8 *expect*, 516.2 *show prudence*, 516.4 *prudence*, 518.5 *suppose*, 520.5 *point*, 520.12 *intend*, 528.5 *reference book*, 547.2 *reproduction*, 547.11 *paint*, 562.2 *outline*, 570.13 *intend*, 582.2 *premeditate*, 582.6 *premeditation*, 583.3 *future intention*, 588.7 *intend*, 592.5 *map*, 594.2 *do the groundwork*, 594.10 *preparations*, 597.2 *undertaking*, 602.6 *find means*, 652.9 *tactics*, 652.14 *behave towards*, 657.5 *be cunning*, 676.6 *art of war*
Plan 592
plan ahead 592, 516.2 *show prudence*
planar 52.79 *spatial*, 282.8 *horizontal*
planarian 81 *Worms*, 81.6 *worm*
plan beforehand 582.2 *premeditate*
planchette 11.10 *psychic phenomenon*
Planck 52 *Scientists*
Planck constant 56.97 *fundamental constant*
Planck's radiation law 56 *Named Laws*
plane 73 *Aircraft Parts*, 85 *Trees and Shrubs*, 36.15 *sail*, 36.18 *windsurf*, 47.11 *woodworking tool*, 47.17 *carpenter*, 52.38 *surface*, 52.79 *spatial*, 121.4 *interval*, 282.2 *horizontal surface*, 282.4 *flattener*, 282.7 *make horizontal*, 282.8 *horizontal*, 282.11 *horizontally*, 359.19 *take off*, 376.2 *uniform*, 376.9 *smoother*, 376.11 *smooth*, 380.9 *sharp-edged thing*, 380.16 *use a sharp tool* , 385.15 *grind*, 679.31 *military aircraft*
plane angle 52.39 *angle*, 56.7 *space*
plane figure 52.41 *geometric figure*
plane geometry 52.34 *geometry*
plane mirror 56.29 *optical element*
planeness 282.1 *horizontality*
plane of symmetry 52.41 *geometric figure*
plane polarization 56.15 *wave property*
plane-polarized light 56.27 *polarized light*
planer 47.11 *woodworking tool*, 63.9 *machine tool*
plane sailing 74.5 *navigation*
plane surface 52.38 *surface*, 282.2 *horizontal surface*
planet 53, 363.4 *orbiting body*
planetarium 53.23 *observatory*, 435.9 *viewpoint*
planetary 53.36 *astronomical*, 164.16 *universal*
planetary atmosphere 53.16 *planet*
planetary influence 226.4 *contributing factor*, 233.2 *occult influence*
planetary meteorology 55.1 *meteorology*
planetary nebula 53.8 *interstellar medium*
planetary probe 53
planetary system 53.14 *solar system*
planet earth 54.5 *earth*
planetesimal 363.4 *orbiting body*

planetoid 53.16 *planet*, 363.4 *orbiting body*
planetologist 54.3 *geologist*
planetology 54.1 *earth science*
plane trigonometry 52.51 *trigonometry*
plan for 588.7 *intend*
plangency 423.1 *loudness*, 427.3 *deepness*, 774.1 *lamentation*
plangent 423.6 *loud*, 427.8 *deep*, 774.4 *lamenting*
plangently 427.11 *resonantly*, 774.8 *mournfully*
planigale 77 *Marsupials*
planimeter 268.8 *meter*, 282.5 *planometer*
planimetric 268.16 *micrometric*
planimetry 268.2 *micrometry*
planing 36.7 *windsurfing*, 36.10 *sailing*, 36.13 *windsurfing*
planing keelboat 36.2 *sailing boat*
planish 376.11 *smooth*
planisphere 53.23 *observatory*
plank 47.12 *wood*, 47.17 *carpenter*, 266.4 *slice*, 293.28 *face*, 604.1 *materials*, 632.4 *safety device*
planking 74 *Parts of a Ship*, 47.12 *wood*, 293.8 *wall covering*, 604.1 *materials*
plank road 327.3 *road*
planks 32.9 *jumping*
plankton 76.5 *aquatic animal*, 260.2 *little thing*
planktonic 76.15 *of animals*
planned 592, 112.8 *monotonous*, 152.21 *organized*, 268.15 *deliberate*, 471.12 *purposive*, 478.14 *solved*, 520.9 *meant*, 582.4 *deliberate*, 588.12 *intended*, 594.17 *developing*
planned event 597.2 *undertaking*
planned parenthood 247.3 *birth control*
planner 592, 243.9 *producer*, 478.10 *answerer*, 516.5 *predictor*, 518.4 *theorist*, 586.14 *motivator*, 642.11 *meddler*, 655.5 *expert*
planning 592, 592, 152.3 *organization*, 152.11 *arrangements*, 243.1 *production*, 435.4 *visualization*, 517.3 *plan*, 594.9 *preparation*, 657.4 *cunning*, 676.6 *art of war*
planning ahead 516.6 *foreseeing*
planning office 592.7 *planning*
planoconvex lens 56.29 *optical element*
plan of action 592.2 *policy*
plan of attack 652.9 *tactics*
plan of battle 676.6 *art of war*
plan of campaign 652.9 *tactics*
plan of the day 592.1 *plan*
planometer 282
plan one's family 247.9 *practise birth control*
plan out 592
plan-position indicator 534.28 *radar*
plans 152.11 *arrangements*
plans and operations staff 17.5 *military staff*
plant 83, 354, 21.2 *field events*, 25.2 *grip*, 51.31 *theatregoer*, 59.3 *organism*, 59.21 *living*, 68.17 *farm*, 69.15 *cultivate*, 83.20 *botanical*, 243.2 *manufacture*, 246.7 *make fertile*, 250.9 *locate*, 397.17, 399.8 *bury*, 539.18 *decoy*, 540.9 *falsification*, 540.22 *falsify*, 647.1 *workshop*, 725.5 *personal estate*, 856.2 *false accusation*
plant a car bomb 539.33 *snare*
Plantae 83.1 *plants*
plant a flag on the summit 34.9 *mountaineer*
planta genista 544.8 *heraldic device*
plantain 84 *Flowers and Flowering Plants*, 86 *Fruits*
plant anatomy 83.10 *plant science*
plant and animal life 59.2 *living world*
plantation 68.6 *farm*, 85.4 *trees*, 723.4 *possession*, 725.1 *property*

plantation rubber 377.4 rubber
plant biochemist 58.2 biochemist
plant biochemistry 83.10 plant science
plant body 90, 88.2 fern plant, 88.4 moss plant
plant breeding 68.4 arable farming, 69.5 gardening
plant bug 82 Insects, 82.3 pest
plant cell 59.7 cell
plant-covered 83.13 plantlike
plant cytology 83.10 plant science
plant disease 89.5 fungal association
plant ecology 59.18 ecology, 83.10 plant science
planted 83.13 plantlike, 85.16 wooded, 250.6 located, 354.12 inserted, 856.9 perjurious
planter 68.15 agriculturist, 69.4 nursery, 243.9 producer, 255.7 settler, 594.15 preparer
plant evidence 856.6 accuse falsely
plant geography 83.10 plant science
plant gland 352.3 gland
plant hopper 82 Insects
plant hormone 58
plant hunter 83.12 plant scientist
planting 68.5 cultivation, 69.5 gardening, 354.8 insertion, 594.13 development
plant killer 398
plant kingdom 83.1 plants
plant life 83.1 plants, 396.1 life
plantlike 83
plant mines 679.37 fight
plan to 199.8 intend
plant out 69.15 cultivate, 354.6 plant
plant pathology 83.10 plant science
plant physiology 83.10 plant science
plant pigment 58.18 pigment
plant products 243.7 produce
plants 83, 396.9 classifications of life
plant science 83
plant scientist 83
plant secretion 352.2 secreted substance
Plants (General) 83
plantsman 69.13 horticulturist, 243.9 producer
plantswoman 243.9 producer
plant taxonomy 83.10 plant science
plan urban renewal 2.15 socialize
plaque 266.4 slice, 511.3 memento, 545.11 monument, 622.4 dirt
plash 55.62 rain, 96.6 river flow, 96.7 flow, 424.1 faintness, 424.5 sound faint, 429.1, 429.4 hiss
plasher 68.10 farm tool
plashing 68.5 cultivation
plasma 54 Gemstones, 56.76 fusion reactor, 367.4 matter, 387.3 body fluid
plasma confinement 56.76 fusion reactor
plasma containment 56.76 fusion reactor
plasmagene 59.13 genetic material
plasmajet propulsion 338.2 method of propulsion
plasmalemma 59.7 cell
plasma membrane 59.7 cell
plasma physics 56.3 modern physics
plasma substitute 387.4 blood
plasmic 59.23 cellular
plasmid 59.3 organism, 59.13 genetic material
plasmodesma 59.7 cell
plasmodium 89.4 fungal body
plasmosome 59.9 cell nucleus
plaster 50.14 sculptor's materials, 63.26 masonry, 130.6 add, 138.3 adhesive, 293.6 medical covering, 293.8 wall covering, 293.24 coat, 293.27 roof, 293.28 face, 393.12 poultice,

604.2 building material, 629.1 repair, 630.2 medicine, 630.10 surgical dressing, 630.20 doctor, 670.3 bomb
plasterboard 604.4 board
plaster cast 50.12 sculpture, 293.6 medical covering
plaster casting 50.12 sculpture
plaster down 376.11 smooth
plastered 874.3 dead drunk
plasterer 293.17 coverer, 646.2 artisan
plastering 293.3 coating
plaster of Paris 51 Common Chemical Compounds, 630.10 surgical dressing
plaster work 293.8 wall covering
plastic 41.12 ski, 50.25 sculptural, 57.21 polymer, 63.25 construction material, 167.11 conformable, 224.13 changeable, 306.9 formed, 374.2 pliant, 377.6 elastic, 395.10 resin, 539.39 imitative, 604.1 materials, 637.2 preserver, 733.4 credit, 733.11 borrowed, 744.2 credit card
plastically 306.13 formatively, 377.11 elastically
plastic art 50.1 art, 50.12 sculpture
plastic bag 258.8 bag
plastic bullet 680.13 ammunition
plastic container 258.15 pot
plastic deformation 63.16 deformation
plastic explosive 680.15 explosive
plastic flow 54.26 mass movement
plastic furniture 47.1 furniture
Plasticiens 50 Schools and Groups of Artists
Plasticine 50.14 sculptor's materials, 374.11 soft thing
plasticity 167.3 pliancy, 224.1 changeableness, 374.8 softness, 377.1 elasticity
plasticize 377.9 make elastic
plasticizer 57.21 polymer
plastic mixing 44.5 ceramic process
plastic money 744.2 credit card
plastics 57.22 industrial chemistry
plastic shuttle 40.11 badminton equipment
plastic ski 41.5 ski equipment
plastic spoon 539.6 imitation
plastic strain 63.14 load
plastic surgeon 60.13 medical specialist, 629.12 repairer, 791.13 beautician
plastic surgery 791, 60.9, 630.12 surgery
plastic wrap 45.6 kitchen equipment, 293.4 wrapping, 442.8 transparent thing
plastid 59.8 cell organ
plastometer 268.8 meter
plastometric 268.16 micrometric
plastometry 268.2 micrometry
plastosome 59.8 cell organ
plastron 671.7 armour
plate 44.8 ceramic object, 50.7 picture, 50.15 engraving, 54.19 plate tectonics, 120.3 container, 258.16 crockery, 266.3 coat, 266.10 layer, 282.3 flat thing, 293.3 coating, 293.24 coat, 313.3 circular thing, 350.16 eating utensil, 544.3 means of identification, 680.1 weapon, 681.1 trophy
plateau 54.7 landform, 98.7 upland, 121.4 interval, 275.2 heights, 282.3 flat thing
Plateau Persian 32 Breeds of Horse and Pony
plate boundary 54.19 plate tectonics
plate camera 66.16 camera
plated 266.8 coated
plate engraving 50.15 engraving
plate girder 63.27 superstructure
plate-girder bridge 63.21 bridge
plate glass 44.9 industrial ceramics, 442.9 glass

platelayer 72.9 railway worker
plate-layer 646.1 worker
platelike 266
plate margin 54.19 plate tectonics
plate steel 63.25 construction material
plate tectonics 54, 54.2 geophysics, 382.8 science of structure
platform 39.6 diving, 39.11 swimming, 72.8 railway station, 282.3 flat thing, 327.10 railway, 532.7 publicity, 592.2 policy
platform diving 39.6 diving
platform heels 295.19 footwear
platform scale 369.10 scales
platform soles 275.8 high thing
Plath 48 Poets
plating 266.3 coat
platinic 57.34 elemental
platiniferous 57.34 elemental
platiniridium 57 Alloys
platinized 57.34 elemental
platinoid 57.34 elemental
platinous 57.34 elemental
platinum 57 Chemical Elements, 446.9 white thing, 617.2 best, 741.16 bullion
platinum black 57.15 catalysis
platinum-blond 446.3 white-haired, 452.3 yellow-haired
platinum metal 57.6 chemical element
platinum resistance thermometer 56.89 thermometer
platinum wire 57 Laboratory Apparatus
platitude 164.8 generalization, 505.1 maxim, 521.1 lack of meaning, 537.4 truism, 555.2 lack of emphasis
platitudinous 164.22 commonplace, 505.2 proverbial, 521.10 meaningless, 537.17 truistic, 555.1 unemphatic
platitudinously 505.4 proverbially, 555.3 unemphatically
Plato 4 Philosophers, 53 Lunar Features
platonic 821.17 loving
Platonic 4.14 of a philosophy, 306.9 formed, 368.10 idealistic, 876.9 pure
Platonically 306.13 formatively, 368.14 subjectively
Platonic form 306.1 form
Platonic Idea 471.1 idea
Platonic love 821.1 love
Platonic solid 52.46 polyhedron
Platonism 4.7 school of thought, 306.1 form, 368.5 idealism
Platonist 4.11 follower of a doctrine, 368.7 believer in a nonmaterial world
platoon 17.4 military organization, 161.14 force, 679.16 army unit
platoon commander 17.5 military staff
Platte 96 Rivers
platter 258.16 crockery, 282.3 flat thing
platyhelminth 81 Worms, 81.6 worm
Platyhelminthes 81.6 worm
platyhelminthic 81.20 wormlike
plaudit 851.5 acclaim
plausibility 488, 486.1 possibility, 497.4 believability
plausible 488, 4.15 rational, 101.9 realizable, 497.13 believable
plausibly 4.26 rationally, 473.18 arguably, 486.11 potentially, 497.16 believably, 540.37 spuriously
Plautus 48 Dramatists
play 19, 27, 42, 49, 51, 18.6 participate, 27.17 bat, 51.32 act, 230.1 operation, 230.7 be operational, 233 influence, 243.5 work of art, 248.6 available space, 359.17 spring up, 457.13 occur, 458.2 depart, 526.9 production, 540.20 pretend, 547.10 act, 640.1 action,

640.2 deed, 674.11 contend, 698.5 scope, 811.14 show
playa 98.3 marsh
play about 640.4 act
play above par 123.5 be unequal
play a character 547.10 act
play a confidence trick 539.28 trick
play-act 51.32 act, 538.24, 540.20 pretend, 797.4 be affected
play-acting 51.20 acting, 538.9 hypocrisy, 538.18 pretentious, 540.7 pretence, 540.30 pretending
play-action 19.9 play
play-actor 51.22 actor
play a dangerous game 657.5 be cunning
play a double role 540.17 double-deal
play a frame 24.8 play billiards, 25.8 bowl
play against 674.11 contend
play a game of chance 229.4 chance
play a joke on 539.31 hoax, 771.13 be humorous
play along with 673.3 submit
play an April fool joke on 539.31 hoax
play a part 540.20 pretend
play a part in 640.4 act
play a practical joke on 539.31 hoax
play a role 105.6 be in a state of
play a role in 233.8 influence
play around 576.9 change sides, 821.26 court
play a trick 515.8 be dishonest
play a trick on 539.28 trick
play back 19.16 play defence, 183.20 renew
play ball 664.11 cooperate
play baseball 22
play basketball 23
play below par 123.5 be unequal
play billiards 24
play both ends against the middle 540.17 double-deal
playboy 405.3 pleasure-seeker, 815.6 social person, 877.8 immoral man
playbroker 51.25 producer
play by ear 49.36 play
play by the rules 857.6 be honourable
play cat and mouse 590.11 hunt
play close to one's chest 529.12 keep secret
play construction 51.7 dramaturgy
play defence 19
play devil's advocate 484.7 counter
play dirty pool 858.8 be dishonourable
play doctor 51.24 dramatist
play dough 374.11 soft thing
play down 542, 129.5 make smaller, 242.4 moderate, 422.2 silence, 495.3 underestimate, 854.10 disparage
play down the table 24.8 play billiards
play ducks and drakes with 244.12 consume
played 24.9 billiard
played down 556.1 simple
played-down 542.19 downplayed
played out 157.22 cancelled
play English billiards 24.8 play billiards
player 18.3 sportsman , 27.4 team, 49.24 musician, 51.22 actor, 547.5 performer, 640.3 doer, 646.1 worker, 663.10 competitor, 674.10 contender
play fake 19.9 play
play false 515.8 be dishonest
play fast and loose 224.12 be irresolute, 826.8 court
play field hockey 31.9 play hockey
play fixer 51.24 dramatist
play flat 434.10 lack harmony

play follow-my-leader 118.11 *emulate*
play follow-the-leader 118.11 *emulate*
play football 38.4 *play soccer*
play footsie 543.11 *gesture,* 821.27 *kiss,* 826.7 *show endearment for*
play for a draw 671.26 *act on the defensive*
play for time 209.8 *delay,* 657.5 *be cunning,* 661.9 *block*
playful 579.1 *capricious,* 865.5 *innocent*
playfully 865.11 *innocently*
playfulness 579.2 *caprice,* 865.1 *innocence*
play god 688.19 *be authoritarian*
playgoer 51.31 *theatregoer*
play golf 29.7 *golf*
playground 6.15 *schoolroom*
playgroup 6.12 *educational institution*
play havoc with 628.4 *impair*
play hell 659.22 *cause trouble*
play hell with 244.11 *ruin*
play hide-and-seek 438.7 *become invisible,* 531.11 *conceal oneself,* 591.6 *evade*
play hob 659.22 *cause trouble*
play hockey **31**
play hookey 458.2 *depart*
play hookey 591.9 *play truant*
play hooky 254.18 *abscond,* 598.2 *withdraw,* 638.5 *escape*
playhouse 51.14 *theatre*
play ice hockey 31.9 *play hockey*
playing 49.2 *music making,* 51.20, 547.3 *acting*
playing a character 547.3 *acting*
playing area 51.15 *stage*
playing card 42.3 *card game terms*
playing court 23.1 *basketball*
playing dead 118.4 *camouflage*
playing down 542.9 *down-playing*
playing down the table 24.3 *English billiards*
playing engagement 51.13 *engagement*
playing field 6.15 *schoolroom*
playing for time 652.9 *tactics*
playing from hand 24.3 *English billiards*
playing one's cards close to one's chest 566.3 *sparing with words*
playing possum 118.4 *camouflage*
playing short-handed 31.3 *ice hockey*
playing terms **23**
playing the part of 547.3 *acting*
playing the stock market 737.8 *speculation*
playing up 652.18 *badly behaved*
playing up the table 24.3 *English billiards*
playing with fire 780.1 *rashness*
playing with one's food 350.3 *delicate eating*
play into the hands of 656.7 *be clumsy*
play it by ear 781.5 *be cautious*
play it cool 675.5 *be at peace*
play it low-key 673.3 *submit*
play lacrosse 31.9 *play hockey*
playland 51.1 *drama*
playlet 51.2 *play*
play man-to-man 23.6 *play basketball*
play match point 106.12 *come to a juncture*
playmate 819.5 *friend*
play merry hell with 244.11 *ruin*
play no part in 591.1 *avoid*
play of colour 456.1 *variegation*
play off 599.3 *exploit*
play off against 599.3 *exploit*
play of fancy 519.4 *ideality*
play offence **19**
playoff game 19.1 *football*
play on 228.10 *manipulate,* 599.3 *exploit*
play one's cards right 861.19 *be good at*

play one's cards well 655.10 *be skilful*
play one's part 652.11 *conduct oneself*
play on words 506.2 *solecism,* 506.6 *talk nonsense,* 578.1 *be equivocal*
play piano 424.5 *sound faint*
play politics 717.4 *compromise*
play pool 24.8 *play billiards*
play possum 540.20 *pretend*
play producer 243.9 *producer*
playroom 256.7 *room*
play rugby **35**
play run-and-shoot 23.6 *play basketball*
play Russian roulette 633.9 *face danger*
play safe 632.8 *be safe,* 781.5 *be cautious*
play school 6.12 *educational institution*
play second fiddle 124.9 *be average,* 127.10 *follow,* 806.19 *be humble,* 810.14 *be modest*
play sharp 434.10 *lack harmony*
play short-handed 31.9 *play hockey*
play silly buggers 508.7 *play the fool*
play soccer **38**
playsuit 295.23 *children's clothes*
play the ball 35.5 *play rugby*
play-the-ball 35.3 *rugby play*
play the devil's advocate 668.6 *be insubordinate*
play the devil with 244.11 *ruin*
play the fool 508, 51.33 *overact,* 460.9 *lack intellect,* 506.8 *fool,* 771.13 *be humorous,* 798.6 *be ridiculous*
play the fop 809.17 *be affected*
play the fox 657.5 *be cunning*
play the futures market 14.5 *invest,* 737.2 *speculate*
play the game 167.8 *comply,* 652.12 *behave well,* 843.14 *be fair*
play the lead 51.32 *act,* 126.10 *lead*
play the market 741.27 *invest*
play the part of 547.10 *act*
play therapy 61.3 *psychiatric treatment*
play the same old record 183.18 *harp*
play the same old tune 788.6 *be boring*
play the stock exchange 14.5 *invest*
play the stock market 737.2 *speculate*
play the waiting game 209.8 *delay*
plaything 539.22 *dupe,* 612.9 *bauble,* 754.5 *cheap item*
plaything of the gods 687.5 *person in adversity*
play to the gallery 51.33 *overact,* 475.18 *appear,* 797.4 *be affected,* 811.29 *show off*
play tricks with 657.5 *be cunning*
play truant 591, 254.18 *abscond,* 458.2 *depart,* 591.8 *run away,* 598.2 *withdraw,* 638.5 *escape*
play up 652.13 *behave badly*
play upon 230.9 *take action*
play upon words 525.1 *misinterpret,* 578.5 *equivocalness*
play up the table 24.8 *play billiards*
play up to 808.9 *fawn,* 819.14 *seek the friendship of*
play with 407.11 *touch,* 655.11 *be expert,* 826.7 *show endearment for*
play with dynamite 633.8 *be in danger*
play with fire 508.6 *be foolish,* 633.8 *be in danger,* 780.5 *be rash*
play with one's food 350.23 *taste*
play with one's thoughts 519.14 *imagine*
playwright 48.14 *author,* 51.24

dramatist, 243.9 *producer,* 560.10 *descriptive writer*
play writer 51.24 *dramatist*
play writing 51.7 *dramaturgy*
plaza 93.7 *city district*
plea **473,** 16.5 *litigation,* 477.1 *question,* 478.5 *counterstatement,* 855.2 *defence*
plea-bargaining 16.7 *legal trial*
pleach 288.8 *interweave*
pleached 288.6 *interwoven*
pleaching 68.5 *cultivation,* 288.1 *interweaving*
plead **473,** 16.70 *litigate,* 477.17 *question,* 478.18 *answer back,* 855.8 *justify*
plead a case 518.6 *propound*
pleader 473.6 *arguer,* 586.12 *persuader,* 678.4 *representative,* 855.5 *vindicator*
plead for **671**
plead for forgiveness 835.12 *ask for mercy,* 839.13 *ask forgiveness*
plead for mercy 835.12 *ask for mercy*
plead for one's life 835.12 *ask for mercy*
plead guilty 16.72 *stand trial,* 16.80 *convict oneself,* 530.8 *admit,* 866.8 *be guilty*
pleading 16.5 *litigation,* 228.2 *inducement,* 473.5 *plea,* 473.12 *apologetic,* 477.12 *questioning,* 478.13 *retaliatory,* 586.2 *flattery*
pleadings 16.7 *legal trial*
plead nolo contendere 16.72 *stand trial*
plead not guilty 16.72 *stand trial*
plead one's own cause 855.8 *justify*
plead to the charge 16.72 *stand trial*
plead with 835.12 *ask for mercy*
plea for peace 677.2 *peace offering*
pleasant **405, 414, 763,** 55.50 *warm,* 392.5 *rainless,* 782.8 *desirable,* 819.8 *friendly*
pleasantly **763,** 414.9 *sweetly,* 782.17 *desirably,* 819.17 *in friendship*
pleasantness **763,** 405.1 *physical pleasure,* 414.1 *sweetness*
Pleasantness **763**
pleasant person **763**
pleasant remark 763.10 *pleasant thing*
pleasantries 817.3 *courtesies*
pleasantry 763.10 *pleasant thing,* 771.5 *joke*
pleasant sensation 405.1 *physical pleasure*
pleasant taste 411.1 *taste*
pleasant thing **763**
please 405.9 *give pleasure,* 762.8 *cause joy,* 763.13 *give pleasure,* 765.8 *satisfy,* 771.15 *humour*
pleased **405,** 762.4 *happy,* 765.4 *satisfied,* 837.4 *grateful*
pleased as a dog with two tails 805.14 *proud*
pleased as punch 837.4 *grateful*
pleased as Punch 762.4 *happy,* 805.14 *proud*
pleased with oneself 805.17 *conceited*
please oneself 16.74 *be lawless,* 405.8 *feel pleasure,* 570.14 *follow one's own will,* 689.4 *be anarchic,* 698.16 *be independent,* 860.6 *be selfish*
pleasing 405.6, 763.1 *pleasant,* 765.5 *satisfying,* 771.11 *humouring,* 784.5 *likable,* 821.22 *lovable*
pleasingly **405,** 784.10 *with great liking*
pleasing qualities 821.4 *lovability*
pleasurable 405.6, 763.1 *pleasant,* 782.8 *desirable*
pleasurableness 763.6 *pleasantness*
pleasurable things **405**
pleasure **777** Phobias by Topic, **763,** 36.14 *punting,* 570.1 *will,* 762.1 *happiness,* 763.11 *pleas-*

ant person, 765.1 *satisfaction,* 784.3 *likes*
pleasure boat 74.3 *vessel*
pleasure-bound 870.6 *self-indulgent*
pleasure garden 69.2 *garden*
pleasure-giving 405.6 *pleasant*
pleasure-loving **763**
pleasure-loving person **763**
pleasure principle 61.22 *libido,* 405.1 *physical pleasure*
pleasure punt 36.8 *punting*
pleasure punting 36.8 *punting*
pleasure-seeker **405,** 870.5 *self-indulgent person*
pleasure seeking 870.1 *self-indulgence*
pleasure-seeking 405.7 *pleased,* 763.5 *pleasure-loving,* 870.6 *self-indulgent*
pleat **320, 320,** 266.1 *layer,* 295.24 *part of garment,* 295.35 *make clothing*
pleated 295.31 *styled,* 320.5 *folded*
pleated dress 321.3 *furrowed thing*
pleated skirt 295.6 *skirt*
pleb 795.5 *vulgar person,* 803.1 *plebeian*
plebby 795.5 *vulgar,* 803.3 *common*
plebeian **803,** 127.16 *ordinary,* 164.21 *common,* 795.7 *vulgar,* 803.3 *common,* 806.2 *lowly*
plebeians 803.2 *the common people*
plebiscite 492.1 *judgment,* 580.10 *vote*
plebs 400.9 *group,* 803.2 *the common people*
Plecoptera **82** Orders of Insects
plecopteran 82.10 *insectan*
pledge 116.3 *arrangement,* 116.23 *arrange,* 326.10 *transferred thing,* 351.14 *drink to,* 490.14 *guarantee,* 490.21 *make certain,* 497.3 *believing,* 535.3, 535.18 *vow,* 597.1 *undertake,* 597.3, 667.2 *contract,* 667.7 *contract,* 714.1, 714.7 *promise,* 715.1 *contract,* 718.2, 718.11 *promise,* 718.12 *certify,* 733.7 *borrow,* 815.11 *be sociable,* 847.7 *commitment,* 847.17 *impose a duty*
pledged 116.12 *arranged,* 490.4 *guaranteed,* 535.12 *vowed,* 667.11 *contractual,* 714.12 *promised,* 714.13 *guaranteeing,* 718.7 *guaranteed,* 745.9 *in debt,* 847.11 *duty-bound*
pledgee 744.5 *lender*
pledge oneself 714.7 *promise,* 847.15 *be liable*
pledge one's honour 714.7 *promise*
pledge one's word 714.7 *promise*
pledger 490.15 *guarantor,* 535.9 *affirmer,* 667.3 *assenter,* 733.6 *borrower*
pledget 630.10 *surgical dressing*
pledging 714.13 *guaranteeing,* 733.1 *borrowing*
pledgor 745.6 *debtor*
Pléiade **48** Literary Groups and Movements
Pleiades **53** Other Groups of Stars
plein air painting **50** Western Art Styles and Movements
Pleistocene **54** Geological Time Intervals
plenary 144.7 *complete*
plenipotentiary 235.13 *powerful,* 703.5 *commissioner,* 703.9 *commissioned,* 707.7 *deputizing*
plenitude 144.2 *fullness,* 246.1 *fertility,* 606.1 *provision,* 608.8 *plenty,* 610.1 *excess*
plenteous 181.9 *ample,* 246.5 *fertile,* 371.6 *dense,* 608.2 *plentiful,* 742.4 *lush*
plenteously 371.10 *densely,* 608.9 *enough*
plenteousness 608.8 *plenty,* 755.8 *abundance*

plentiful 608, 181.9 *ample,* 246.5 *fertile,* 605.7 *stored,* 610.6 *excessive,* 742.4 *lush,* 755.3 *abundant*

plentifully 608.9 *enough,* 755.12 *generously*

plentifulness 608.8 *plenty*

plenty 350, 608, 181.3 *profuseness,* 246.1 *fertility,* 253.4 *availability,* 253.10 *available,* 605.3 *supply,* 610.1 *excess,* 682.1 *success,* 686.1 *prosperity,* 742.7 *opulence,* 754.2 *declining prices,* 755.8 *abundance*

plenty of rope 698.6 *liberality*

plenty to do 642.6 *business*

pleonasm 5.22 *many words,* 104.1 *extraneousness,* 132.4 *surplus,* 553.1 *diffuseness,* 610.3 *superfluity*

pleonastic 5.42 *worded,* 104.8 *intruder,* 132.10 *surplus,* 183.12 *repetitious,* 553.3 *diffuse,* 610.7 *superfluous*

pleonastically 5.50 *lexically,* 132.11 *residually*

plesiosaur 79 Fossil Reptiles, 79.6 *extinct reptile*

plethora 610.1 *excess*

plethoric 610.6 *excessive*

pleurectomy 60 Surgical Operations

pleurisy 624.9 *respiratory disease*

pleurotomy 60 Surgical Operations

Pleven 32 Breeds of Horse and Pony

Plexiglass 57.21 *polymer,* 442.8 *transparent thing*

PL/I 65 Programming Languages

pliability 6.10 *educatability,* 374.8 *softness,* 377.1 *elasticity,* 572.8 *acquiescence,* 586.7 *persuadability,* 660.3 *wieldiness*

pliable 6.17 *educatable,* 374.2 *pliant,* 377.6 *elastic,* 572.3 *amenable,* 660.12 *wieldy*

pliableness 374.8 *softness*

pliably 6.26 *studiously*

pliance 694.1 *obedience*

pliancy 167, 224.1 *changeableness,* 374.8 *softness,* 377.1 *elasticity,* 572.8 *acquiescence,* 576.14 *apathy,* 586.7 *persuadability,* 660.3 *wieldiness,* 808.1 *servility*

pliant 374, 167.11 *conformable,* 224.1 *changeable,* 377.6 *elastic,* 572.3 *amenable,* 576.4 *unsteady,* 660.12 *wieldy,* 673.5 *submitting,* 694.7 *obedient,* 808.6 *servile*

pliantly 167.16 *adaptably,* 224.15 *changeably,* 374.17 *softly,* 377.11 *elastically,* 694.10 *obediently*

plica 320.1 *fold*

plical 320.5 *folded*

plicate 320.5 *folded*

plicately 320.11 *doubly*

plication 320.1 *fold*

plicature 320.1 *fold*

plié 46.10 *positions at the barre*

pliers 355.10 *excavator,* 603.1 *tool,* 726.3 *tools for gripping*

plight 105.2 *predicament,* 106.4, 251.3 *difficult circumstances,* 659.5 *predicament,* 687.1 *adversity*

plighted 823.22 *marriageable*

plight one's troth 477.22 *pop the question,* 714.7 *promise,* 821.28 *win the love of,* 823.15 *marry,* 826.8 *court*

Plimsoll line 74 Parts of a Ship, 268.6 *measuring instrument,* 543.5 *indicator*

plimsolls 295.19 *footwear*

plinth 280.2 *foot*

Pliny the Younger 48 Writers

Pliocene 54 Geological Time Intervals

Pliocene period 200.3 *geological period*

pliosaur 79 Fossil Reptiles

Plistocene period 200.3 *geological period*

PLO 679.14 *armed forces*

plod 328.1 *move slowly,* 328.10 *slow motion,* 575.6 *persevere,* 644.6 *work*

plod along 328.1 *move slowly*

plodder 328.15 *slow person*

plodding 328.4 *slow,* 575.1 *perseverance,* 575.10 *persevering,* 642.20 *industrious,* 644.10 *working*

ploddy 718.3 *security officer*

plod on 219.4 *protract*

PLO member 679.9 *guerrilla*

plonk 351.9 *wine,* 424.1 *faintness,* 424.5 *sound faint,* 425.6 *crack,* 428.5 *dull sound,* 428.9 *be nonresonant,* 874.12 *alcohol*

plonker 460.3 *unintelligent person,* 502.5 *ignorant person*

plop 332.9 *directly,* 360.10 *droop,* 424.1 *faintness,* 424.5 *sound faint,* 425.2, 425.6 *crack,* 428.5 *dull sound,* 428.9 *be nonresonant*

plop down 360.10 *droop*

plot 249, 592, 592, 48.3 *aspect of fiction,* 51.7 *dramaturgy,* 52.32 *graph,* 52.96 *represent,* 68.11 *farmland,* 74.9 *navigate,* 140.2 *cooperation,* 140.6 *come together,* 399.5 *cemetery,* 471.18 *aim,* 472.1 *topic,* 473.4 *gist,* 527.8 *concealment,* 529.2 *secretiveness,* 547.11 *paint,* 560.3 *narration,* 582.6 *premeditation,* 594.2 *do the groundwork,* 642.9 *overactivity,* 657.1 *cunning,* 657.2 *stratagem,* 657.5 *be cunning,* 693.3 *subversion,* 693.16 *be subversive,* 725.1 *property,* 731.2 *portion*

plot horoscopes 11.23 *divine*

Plotinus 4 Philosophers

plot of land 68.11 *farmland,* 249.12 *plot*

plot-spinner 592.8 *planner*

plotted 268.13 *measured*

plotter 539, 65.7 *peripheral,* 540.15 *false person,* 592.8 *planner,* 657.3 *cunning person*

plotting 74.5 *navigation,* 592.15 *planning,* 657.4 *cunning*

plotzed 874.3 *dead drunk*

plough 68.10 *farm tool,* 68.17 *farm,* 321.6 *furrow,* 380.16 *use a sharp tool* , 683.6 *fail*

Plough 53 Other Groups of Stars

ploughable 68.20 *farmable*

plough a lonely furrow 174.18 *be one*

ploughed 68.20 *farmable,* 321.4 *furrowed,* 683.10 *failed*

ploughed field 321.3 *furrowed thing*

ploughed land 68.11 *farmland*

plough horse 32.2 *thoroughbred*

ploughing 68.5 *cultivation*

ploughman 68.16 *farm worker,* 594.15 *preparer*

ploughman's lunch 45.44 *British dish,* 350.12 *meal*

ploughshare 380.9 *sharp-edged thing*

Plovdiv 93 Cities

plover 78 Birds, 45.20 *meat,* 78.3 *water bird*

plowed under 874.3 *dead drunk*

ploy 539.8 *trick,* 592.3 *expedient plan,* 657.2 *stratagem*

pluck 49.38 *sound,* 131.4 *take off,* 136.10 *set apart,* 237.1 *strength,* 239.1 *vigour,* 294.13 *remove,* 296.15 *make nude,* 339.3 *jerk,* 339.13 *pull at,* 407.11 *touch,* 574.6 *fortitude,* 575.4 *stamina,* 778.1 *courage*

pluck at one's heartstrings 340.11 *attract*

plucked 252.9 *removed,* 296.12 *peeling*

plucking 296.7 *depilation*

plucking out 252.2 *removal*

pluck out 252.15 *remove,* 355.11 *extract*

pluck up 361.4 *gather up*

pluck up courage 778.16 *take courage*

plucky 237.11 *strong in spirit,* 575.12 *indomitable,* 778.9 *courageous*

plug 64, 20.2 *artificial fly,* 32.1 *horse,* 132.1 *remainder,* 183.18 *harp,* 293.2, 293.23 *cover,* 323.2 *stopper,* 323.8 *stop,* 338.28 *shoot,* 413.7 *tobacco,* 532.9 *advertisement,* 532.16 *publicize,* 539.13 *snare,* 554.6 *emphasize,* 629.1 *repair,* 726.2 *detention,* 726.7 *detain*

plug a hole 629.1 *repair*

plug along 328.1 *move slowly*

plug away 575.6 *persevere,* 642.15 *try*

plugged 323.13 *stopped*

plugged nickel 612.8 *trifle*

plug hat 295.15 *headgear*

plug in 64.35 *conduct,* 135.10 *link,* 230.8 *activate,* 235.11 *give power,* 410.11 *fuel*

plug the gap 671.21 *entrench*

plug ugly 790.4 *ugly*

plug up 629.1 *repair*

plum 86 Fruits, 450.7 *red thing,* 455.3 *purple thing,* 455.6 *purple,* 617.1 *worthy,* 617.7 *elite,* 721.5 *profit,* 734.5 *takings,* 861.17 *good thing*

plumage 78, 293.14 *animal covering*

plumb 144.7 *complete,* 144.9 *completely,* 268.10 *measure,* 277.4 *deep thing,* 277.14 *deepen,* 281.3 *vertical thing,* 281.4 *plumb line,* 281.6 *make vertical,* 281.8 *vertical,* 281.12 *perpendicularly,* 312.1 *straight,* 332.9 *directly,* 369.11 *weight,* 503.8, 537.39 *accurately*

plumbago 84 Flowers and Flowering Plants, 386.4, 395.5 *lubricant*

plumbane 57 Common Chemical Compounds

plumb bob 283.3 *suspended object,* 369.11 *weight*

plumber 322.3 *person who opens,* 629.12 *repairer,* 646.2 *artisan*

plumbic 57.34 *elemental*

plumbiferous 57.34 *elemental*

plumbing 621.2 *cleaning*

plumb line 281, 268.6 *measuring instrument,* 277.4 *deep thing*

plumbline 312.7 *straight line*

plumb on 503.8 *accurately*

plumb the depths 277.11 *become inferior,* 277.14 *deepen*

plumb the ocean depths 97.9 *sail the high seas*

plumb wicket 376.8 *smooth thing*

plum-coloured 455.6 *purple*

plume 78.17 *plumage,* 295.5 *fancy dress*

plumed 805.21 *ostentatious*

plumes 295.15 *headgear*

plummet 281.7 *fall vertically,* 360.12 *drop,* 369.11 *weight,* 754.12 *be cheap*

plummeting 360.4 *fall,* 360.18 *falling*

plummet lead 20.3 *fishing tackle*

plummy 617.1 *worthy*

plump 259.16 *fat,* 261.5 *make bigger,* 261.6 *become bigger,* 273.1 *thick,* 315.10 *well-rounded,* 332.9 *directly,* 360.10 *droop,* 374.13 *soften,* 428.5 *dull sound,* 428.9 *be nonresonant*

plump as a dumpling 259.16 *fat*

plump as a partridge 259.16 *fat*

plump down 360.10 *droop*

plump for 570.12 *choose,* 580.1 *select,* 662.23 *advise*

plumpishness 259.5 *fatness*

plumply 259.20 *largely*

plumpness 259.5 *fatness,* 273.5 *thickness,* 315.2 *round thing*

plump out 261.6 *become bigger*

plum pudding 45.35 *dessert*

plump up 261.5 *make bigger,* 374.13 *soften*

plum sawfly 69.12 *pests and diseases*

plum tomato 45 Vegetables

plumulae 78.17 *plumage*

plumule 83.5 *stem,* 83.9 *seed*

plunder 736, 244.10, 607.2 *lay waste,* 628.4 *impair,* 679.38 *conquer,* 681.2 *spoils,* 721.5, 721.14 *profit,* 734.5 *takings,* 734.10 *take away,* 736.4 *stolen goods,* 736.5 *plundering*

plundered 734.12 *taking*

plunderer 736, 679.6 *militarist,* 721.7 *gainer*

plundering 736, 721.16 *greedy,* 734.3 *taking away,* 734.12 *taking,* 736.17 *stolen*

plunderous 736.17 *stolen*

plunge 39.10 *dive,* 74.10 *sail,* 127.11 *become inferior,* 129.2 *decline,* 129.4 *decrease,* 244.13 *be destroyed,* 277.14 *deepen,* 281.1 *verticality,* 281.7 *fall vertically,* 324.13 *be in motion,* 329.4 *be swift,* 354.4 *immerse,* 354.10 *immersion,* 360.5 *dive,* 360.12 *drop,* 362.3 *bring down,* 366.11 *stagger,* 366.25 *pitch,* 621.5 *ablutions,* 754.2 *declining prices,* 754.12 *be cheap*

plunge bath 621.6 *bath*

plunge in 354.3 *impact*

plunge into 156.18 *make a beginning,* 346.13 *fall into,* 597.1 *undertake*

plunging 277.8 *deep,* 281.8 *vertical,* 324.6 *descending motion,* 324.17 *directional,* 360.4 *fall,* 360.18 *falling,* 362.13 *submergence*

plunging fire 670.15 *firing*

plunging neckline 296.4 *dishabille*

plunk 330.3 *hit,* 330.13 *blow,* 332.9 *directly,* 424.1 *faintness,* 424.5 *sound faint,* 425.2, 425.6 *crack,* 428.5 *dull sound,* 428.9 *be nonresonant*

pluperfect 5.34 *tense*

plural 175, 5.44 *grammatical,* 120.6 *quantitative*

pluralism 4.7 *school of thought,* 12.1 *government,* 175.2 *multiplicity,* 688.7 *type of rule*

pluralist 175, 4.11 *follower of a doctrine,* 4.14 *of a philosophy*

plurality 175, 120.5 *numbers*

Plurality 175

pluralize 175

plurally 175, 5.52 *grammatically*

pluralness 175.1 *plurality*

plural number 175.1 *plurality*

plurify 175.9 *pluralize*

plus 52.88 *equal to,* 130.4 *extra,* 130.10 *additionally*

plus fours 295.9 *trousers*

plush 67 Natural Fabrics, 374.3 *smooth,* 374.11 *soft thing,* 742.3 *opulent,* 811.24 *grand*

plushiness 374.9 *smoothness*

plushness 742.7 *opulence,* 811.9 *grandeur*

plushy 374.3 *smooth,* 742.3 *opulent*

plus sign 52.13 *mathematical symbol,* 543.1 *sign*

Plutarch 48 Writers

pluteus 89 Fungi

Pluto 8 Deities, **8** Deities, **53** Planets and their Satellites, 53.16 *planet*

plutocracy 742, 12.1 *government,* 688.7 *type of rule*

plutocrat 14.3 *stockbroker,* 686.4 *prosperous person,* 696.5 *company leader,* 742.10 *wealthy person*

plutocratic 12.9, 688.14 *governmental,* 696.12 *masterful*

pluton 54.30 *igneous rock*

Plutonian 8.16 *devilish,* 53.36 *astronomical*

plutonic 54.56 *petrographic*

plutonic intrusion 54.30 *igneous rock*

plutonic rock 54.30 *igneous rock*

plutonium 57 Chemical Ele-

ments, 56.73 *nuclear reactor*,
410.7 *nuclear power*, 631.10
warfare
Plutus 8 Deities, 742.10 *wealthy
person*
pluvial 55
pluviometer 55.7 *weather instruments*, 389.19 *measuring instrument*
pluviometric 55.42 *barometric*
pluviosity 55.26 *raininess*, 391.2
mistiness
pluvious 55.54 *pluvial*
ply 214.7 *be regular*, 266.1 *layer*,
599.1 *use*, 640.4 *act*
plying 74.11 *nautical*
Plymouth 93 Cities, **93** Cities,
93.4 *British cities*
Plymouth Brethren 7 Christian
Movements
Plymouth Rock 68 Breeds of
Fowl
Plymouth Sound 98.9 *inlet*
ply one's trade 640.4 *act*
ply the oar 644.6 *work*
plywood 47.12 *wood*, 63.25 *construction material*, 266.5 *layered
thing*, 293.8 *wall covering*,
604.1 *materials*
p.m. 192.18 *horologically*, 204.4
afternoon, 205.1 *evening*
PMT 66.7 *photocopy*, 110.4 *duplicate*, 245.1 *reproduction*
pneuma 11.7 *spirit*, 61.21 *psyche*
pneumatic 374.4 *compressible*,
388.22 *aerostatic*, 390.14 *aerial*
pneumatically 374.17 *softly*,
388.29 *aerostatically*, 390.25
airily
pneumatics 388.12 *aerostatics*
pneumatic trough 57 Laboratory
Apparatus
pneumatic tyre 71 Motor Vehicle Parts
pneumatometer 268.8 *meter*,
388.15 *vaporimeter*
pneumatometry 268.2 *micrometry*
pneumatophobia 777 Phobias
by Name
pneumatostatics 388.12 *aerostatics*
pneumoconiosis 624.9 *respiratory
disease*
pneumodynamically 388.29 *aerostatically*
pneumodynamics 388.12 *aerostatics*
pneumonectomy 60 Surgical Operations
pneumonia 409.3 *chill*, 624.6 *infection*, 624.9 *respiratory disease*
pneumonic 390.19 *respiratory*
pneumonic plague 624.5 *plague*
pnigophobia 777 Phobias by
Name
p−n junction 56.44, 64.4 *semiconductor*
p−n junction diode 64.18 *diode*
pnp transistor 64.19 *transistor*
po 353.14 *toilet*
Po 96 Rivers, 96.5 *other major
rivers*
Poaceae 87.1 *grass*
poaceous 87.8 *grasslike*
poach 37.7 *shoot*, 45.55 *cook*,
357.5 *transgress*, 590.11 *hunt*,
736.12 *steal*
poached 45.56 *culinary*, 98.11
continental
poached fish 45.16 *fish dish*
poacher 37.4 *hunter*, 45.6
kitchen equipment, 590.6
hunter, 736.8 *thief*
poaching 45.8 *cooking technique*,
736.1 *stealing*, 736.17 *stolen*
po-boy 45.11 *sandwich*
pochard 78 Birds
pochette 49 Musical Instruments
pock 383.3 *nap*
pocked 317.5 *concave*, 375.2
coarse, 456.10 *mottled*
pocket 19.9 *play*, 24.1 *billiards*,
24.3 *English billiards*, 34.8
mountaineering, 163.2 *class*,
260.7 *little*, 295.24 *part of garment*, 676.10 *battleground*,

730.9 *receive*, 741.20 *money
store*
pocket billiard table 24.5 *snooker*
pocketbook 741.20 *money store*
pocket borough 580.12 *election*
pocket calculator 170.5 *computer*
pocket comb 621.10 *cleaning object*
pocketed 24.9 *billiard*
pocket edition 260.2 *little thing*
pocketful 120.3 *container*
pocket gopher 77 Placental
Mammals
pocket hold 34.5 *rock face*
pocketing the ball 24.2 *billiards
play*
pocketknife 380.10 *knife*
pocketless table 24.4 *carom*
pocket money 721.5 *profit*,
729.2 *gift*, 730.2 *something received*, 741.4 *change*, 749.3 *income*
pocket mouse 77 Placental
Mammals
pocket rot 85.10 *tree disease*
pocket-size 260.7 *little*
pocket the affront 839.12 *show
mercy*
pocket the ball 24.8 *play billiards*
pocket the insult 673.4 *succumb*
pocket torch 197.7 *lantern*
pocket veto 709.1 *veto*
pocket watch 191 Timepieces
and Timers, 192.7 *watch*
pockmark 309.3 *deformity*,
309.11 *deform*, 317.3 *cavity*,
317.7 *make concave*, 624.13
skin disease, 793.1 *spot*
pockmarked 309.7 *deformed*,
317.5 *concave*, 375.2 *coarse*,
456.10 *mottled*, 793.5 *marked*
pocky 375.2 *coarse*
pococurante 783.6 *indifferent person*, 783.7 *indifferent*
pococurantism 466.2 *lack of interest*
pod 73 Aircraft Parts, **161** Collective Names for Birds and
Animals, 86.2 *botanical fruit*,
289.1 *exterior*, 293.13 *casing*
PO'd 828.11 *angry*
podded 289.6 *exterior*
podetium 90.6 *lichen*
podginess 259.5 *fatness*, 273.5
thickness
podgy 259.16 *fat*, 273.1 *thick*,
315.10 *well-rounded*, 374.4 *compressible*
podiatrist 630.15 *healer*
podiatry 60.6 *health care*,
630.12 *surgery*
podium 43.9 *miscellaneous architectural features*, 51.15 *stage*
podophylline 62 Medication
Podunk 816.5 *solitary place*
podzol 54.36 *soil*
poem 48, 243.5 *work of art*
poesy 48.6 *poetry*, 48.13 *poetic
genius*
poet 5.2 *linguist*, 48.14 *author*,
243.9 *producer*, 519.9 *visionary*,
560.10 *descriptive writer*
poetaster 48.14 *author*
poetess 48.14 *author*
poetic 48.19 *narrative*, 519.10
imaginative
poetical 48.19 *narrative*
poetically 48
poetic diction 48.12 *poetic language*
poetic drama 51.2 *play*
poetic frenzy 519.2 *inspiration*
poetic genius 48
poetic imagination 519.1 *imagination*
poeticism 48.12 *poetic language*
poeticize 519.15 *fantasize*
poetic justice 855.4 *revenge*,
879.9 *retribution*
poetic language 48
poetic licence 48.12 *poetic language*, 519.4 *ideality*, 698.1 *freedom*
poetic prose 48.5 *prose*
poetics 48.6 *poetry*
poetic truth 309.4 *distortion of
the truth*

poetize 48.21 *write*
poet laureate 48.14 *author*,
126.6 *paragon*
poetry 48, 48.21 *write*, 519.4
ideality
pogonophobia 777 Phobias by
Name
Pogonophora 81.6 *worm*
pogonophoran 81 Worms, 81.6
worm
pogo stick 377.3 *elastic thing*
pogrom 398.4 *slaughter*, 481.4
social discrimination
pohutukawa 85 Trees and
Shrubs
poignancy 413.1 *piquancy*,
413.4 *stimulation*, 554.1 *emphasis*
poignant 403.9 *exciting*, 413.10
stimulating, 554.3 *emphatic*,
560.11 *descriptive*
poignantly 413.16 *stimulatingly*
poikilotherm 79.1 *reptile*
poikilothermic 79.11 *reptilian*,
80.13 *fishlike*
poilu 679.8 *soldier*
Poincaré 52 Scientists
poinciana 85 Trees and Shrubs
poinephobia 777 Phobias by
Name
poinsettia 84 Flowers and Flowering Plants
point 75 General Units, **75**
General Units, **52**, **520**, 20.3
fishing tackle, 27.4 *team*, 31.3
ice hockey, 31.6 *lacrosse player*,
37.7 *shoot*, 50.14 *sculptor's materials*, 50.15 *engraving*, 98.5
peninsula, 106.2 *occurrence*,
106.6 *aspect*, 121.4 *interval*,
157.7 *limit*, 174.1 *one*, 185.11
date, 191.4 *point in time*, 250.2
exact location, 251.1 *situation*,
260.2 *little thing*, 272.8 *narrow
thing*, 279.1 *summit*, 318.2 *projection*, 332.6 *direct*, 332.7 *take
a direction*, 380.7 *sharp point*,
380.15 *make sharp*, 471.4 *purpose*, 472.1 *topic*, 472.2 *issue*,
473.3 *line of argument*, 473.4
gist, 477.1 *question*, 543.3 *gesture*, 543.7 *punctuation*, 543.11
gesture, 599.6 *use*, 613.5 *usefulness*, 653.2 *direct*, 876.7 *moral*
point a moral 876.12 *moralize*
point at 543.11 *gesture*, 588.10
aim
point at infinity 52.36 *point*
point at issue 472.2 *issue*
point-blank 332.9 *directly*
point-blank 503.5 *accurate*,
537.39 *accurately*, 556.8 *simply*
point-blank refusal 711.1 *refusal*
pointed 52.80 *linear*, 251.6 *situated*, 272.3 *tapered*, 310.7 *angular*, 342.7 *convergent*, 380.1
sharp, 472.7 *focused*, 520.6
meaningful, 535.14 *assertive*,
535.15 *emphasized*, 552.3 *concise*, 554.3 *emphatic*, 562.6 *summary*
pointed for 332.14 *directed*
pointedly 380.18 *sharply*,
472.14 *thematically*, 535.25 *explicitly*, 552.5 *concisely*, 562.11
summarily, 588.13 *intentionally*
pointedness 380.6 *sharpness*,
535.6 *assertiveness*, 552.1 *conciseness*, 562.4 *summariness*
pointed out 554.4 *emphasized*
pointed shoes 295.19 *footwear*
pointed up 554.4 *emphasized*
Pointe-Noire 93 Cities
pointer 77 Breeds of Dogs, 37.6
sporting dog, 56.82 *measuring
instrument*, 437.7 *that which
makes visible*, 483.4 *indication*,
528.7 *advice*, 543.5 *indicator*
Pointers 53 Other Groups of
Stars
pointillism 50 Western Art
Styles and Movements, 456.4
maculation
pointillist 50.29 *realist*
point in common 114.1 *similarity*
pointing 50.12 *sculpture*, 332.5

directions, 483.8 *evidential*,
543.3 *gesture*, 543.14 *signifying*
pointing machine 50.14 *sculptor's
materials*
pointing out 437.5 *manifestation*, 543.1 *sign*, 544.1 *identification*
pointing to 234.5 *tending to*,
856.8 *accusatory*
point in time 191
pointless 104.8 *intruder*, 381.1
blunt, 508.5 *foolish*, 521.11
aimless, 553.4 *circumlocutory*,
555.1 *unemphatic*, 614.2, 776.7
futile
pointlessly 104.18 *extraneously*,
381.11 *smoothly*
pointlessness 104.1 *extraneousness*, 108.1 *unrelatedness*, 508.1
folly, 521.2, 521.6 *aimlessness*,
553.2 *circumlocution*, 555.2
lack of emphasis, 614.4 *futility*
point of action 300.3 *cutting edge*
point of Aries 203.2 *spring*
point of arrival 344.15 *destination*
point of departure 156.11 *starting point*
point of etiquette 813.5 *etiquette*
point of inflection 52.36 *point*
point of land 98.5 *peninsula*
point of Libra 203.4 *autumn*
point of no return 106.3 *critical
moment*, 210.3 *critical time*
point of union 135
point of view 4.1 *philosophy*, 7.1
religion, 48.3 *aspect of fiction*,
435.9 *viewpoint*, 457.3 *external
appearance*, 461.6 *idea*, 497.1
belief, 518.1 *supposition*
point one's finger 543.11 *gesture*
point out 165.22 *characterize*,
435.18, 437.10 *make visible*,
457.14 *present*, 471.11 *raise the
point*, 475.15 *demonstrate*,
526.1 *display*, 526.3 *reveal*,
528.11 *inform*, 543.9 *use signs*,
544.10 *identify*, 554.6 *emphasize*
point out to 332.6 *direct*
point Percy at the porcelain
353.17 *urinate*, 767.13 *relieve
oneself*
points 72.3 *rail*, 126.3 *advantage*, 327.10 *railway*
points game 41.10 *curling*
pointsman 72.9 *railway worker*
points table 33.1 *motor racing*
point system 26.2 *boxing*
point the finger at 856.5 *accuse*
point the way 154.15 *precede*,
332.6 *direct*, 543.9 *use signs*
point to 165.24 *specify*, 234.4
tend, 332.6 *direct*, 471.18 *aim*,
472.10 *focus on*, 517.11 *predict*,
520.10 *mean*, 543.9 *use signs*,
653.2 *direct*
point-to-point 18 Sporting Activities, 674.4 *race*
point-to-point racing 32.6
horsemanship, 32.7 *horseracing*
point up 457.14 *present*, 526.3
reveal, 554.6 *emphasize*
pointy 380.1 *sharp*
poise 75 Scientific and Technical Units, 122.2 *equilibrium*,
122.11 *equalize*, 325.1 *motionlessness*, 359.20 *hover*, 652.2
good conduct, 660.4 *ease of manner*
poised 325.4 *motionless*
poison 777 Phobias by Topic,
631, **631**, 57.15 *catalysis*,
57.26 *react*, 57.39 *catalytic*,
244.7 *agent of destruction*,
351.7 *alcoholic drink*, 398.13
animal killer, 398.17 *murder*,
398.22 *kill animals*, 618.10 *poverty*, 622.11 *dirty*, 624.6 *infection*, 628.3 *make worse*, 630.3
prophylactic, 822.16 *cause hate*,
828.14 *make angry*, 862.5 *evil
thing*, 862.11 *be evil*, 879.13
capital punishment, 879.16 *instrument of execution*
poisoned 618.4 *poor*, 626.7 *toxic*
poisoned apple 539.14 *fatal gift*

poisoned arrow 680.6 *historical missile weapon*
poisoner 398.11 *murderer*, 631.13 *oppressor*, 862.6 *evil person*
poison gas 631.10 *warfare*
poisoning 631, 397.6 *killing*, 398.2 *murder*, 624.2 *illness*, 624.6 *infection*, 628.10 *impairment*
poison ivy 631.12 *poisonous plant*
poison oak 85 *Trees and Shrubs*
poisonous 398.23 *deadly*, 415.6 *unpalatable*, 618.5 *harmful*, 622.8 *unclean*, 624.23 *diseased*, 626.5 *unhygienic*, 626.7 *toxic*, 631.16 *blighting*, 633.1 *dangerous*, 822.10 *hating*, 832.14 *hostile*
poisonous fumes 626.1 *lack of hygiene*
poisonous gas 388.3 *miasma*
poisonously 626.8 *unhygienically*, 822.18 *hatefully*
poisonousness 618.11 *harmfulness*, 624.6 *infection*, 626.1 *lack of hygiene*, 631.7 *poisoning*
poisonous plant 631
poisonous snake 398.10 *killer*
poison-pen letter 854.4 *aspersion*
poison sumac 85 *Trees and Shrubs*
Poisson 52 *Scientists*
Poisson distribution 52 *Named Concepts*, 52.59 *probability distribution*
Poisson ratio 56 *Named Laws*
Poitevin 32 *Breeds of Horse and Pony*
poke 258.8 *bag*, 330.1 *impel*, 330.3 *hit*, 330.13 *blow*, 407.3 *press*, 407.11 *touch*, 543.11 *gesture*, 670.5 *strike*, 821.14 *communication of love*, 826.7 *show endearment for*
poke along 328.1 *move slowly*
poke bonnet 295.15 *headgear*
pokecheck 31.3 *ice hockey*, 31.9 *play hockey*
pokechecking 31.3 *ice hockey*
poke fun at 771.13 *be humorous*, 799.6 *deride*, 850.24, 854.14 *ridicule*
poke in 354.2 *inject*
poke one's nose in 465.7 *be curious*, 642.17 *meddle*
poke out 318.8 *protrude*
poker 42 *Card Games*
poker face 523.11 *unintelligibility*
poker-faced 523.1 *unintelligible*, 531.17 *noncommittal*, 772.1 *solemn*
pokerlike 373.2 *round*
pokerwork 42 *Hobbies and Pastimes*, 792.2 *pattern*
poke someone in the ribs 543.11 *gesture*
pokily 328.17 *in slow motion*
pokiness 260.1 *littleness*, 754.3 *shoddiness*
poking 328.4 *slow*
pokingly 328.17 *in slow motion*
poking out 318.5 *protuberant*
poking someone in the ribs 543.3 *gesture*
pokunt 8.5 *deity*
poky 260.7 *little*, 328.4 *slow*, 702.2 *the inside* , 754.10 *shoddy*
pol 12.8 *politician*, 653.15 *manager*
polacre 74 *Sailing Ships and Boats*
polak 91 *Names for Inhabitants*
Poland 68 *Breeds of Fowl*, **91** *Countries*
Poland-China 68 *Breeds of Pig*
polar 57.35 *combined*, 111.4 *opposite*, 157.24 *limiting*, 279.5 *top*, 409.8 *cold*
polar air 55.10 *air movement*
polar bear 77 *Placental Mammals*, 80.11 *fishing animal*
polar bond 57.11 *chemical bond*
polar climate 55.38 *climate*
polar compound 57.7 *chemical compound*

polar coordinates 52.33 *coordinates*
polar front 55.10 *air movement*
polarimeter 56.92 *light meter*, 268.8 *meter*
polarimetric 268.16 *micrometric*
polarimetry 57.13 *structure*, 268.2 *micrometry*
Polaris 53 *Named Stars*, 439.4 *natural light*, 543.5 *indicator*, 680.5 *missile weapon*
polarity 111.1 *oppositeness*, 231.1 *counteraction*, 235.4 *energy*, 663.6 *contrariety*
polarity reversal 54.44 *geomagnetism*
polarization 56.15 *wave property*, 57.19 *electrochemistry*, 111.1 *oppositeness*, 231.1 *counteraction*, 341.5 *repulsion*, 666.1 *disagreement*
polarize 111.8 *be opposite*, 231.3 *counteract*, 666.5 *disagree*
polarized 111.4 *opposite*, 231.4 *counteracting*, 235.16 *charged*, 663.21 *contrary*
polarized light 56
polarizing 666.9 *disagreeing*
polarizing filter 66.20 *filter*
polarizing microscope 56.85 *microscope*
polar lights 54.46 *aurora*
polarogram 57.17 *analysis*
polarographic 57.41 *analytic*
polarography 57.17 *analysis*
Polaroid 56.27 *polarized light*, 66.16 *camera*
Polaroid film 66.9 *film*
polaroid glasses 435.10 *visual aid*
polar opposition 111.1 *oppositeness*
polar solvent 57.3 *phase*
polar wandering 54.45 *magnetic pole*
polar zone 55.39 *climatic zone*
polder 98.6 *lowland*
pole 74 *Rigging*, **75** *General Units*, 21.2 *field events*, 47.12 *wood*, 85.3 *timber*, 157.7 *limit*, 263.3 *distant place*, 275.6 *tall thing*, 279.1 *summit*, 281.3 *vertical thing*, 338.20 *propel*, 364.4 *vortex*, 603.1 *tool*
pole a canoe 36.19 *punt*
poleaxe 398.17 *murder*, 398.18 *slaughter*, 680.8 *sharp weapon*
pole-body-foot 36.14 *punting*
pole-body-foot movement 36.8 *punting*
polecat 77 *Placental Mammals*, 419.2 *something that makes an unpleasant smell*, 864.10 *bad person*
pole-jump 359.5 *jump*
polemic 4.5 *philosophical argument*, 48.4 *non-fiction*, 463.9 *argumentative*, 473.2 *logical argument*, 666.2 *argument*, 666.9 *disagreeing*, 676.1 *war*
polemical 473.9 *hostile*
polemically 4.24 *philosophically*, 473.17 *argumentatively*
polemicist 463.6, 473.6 *arguer*
polemicize 4.23 *discuss philosophically*, 473.13 *argue*
polemics 463.3 *debate*, 568.4 *conference*, 674.1 *contention*
polemist 473.6 *arguer*
polenta 45.40 *breakfast cereal*
pole plant 41.4 *skiing technique*
pole position 33.6 *motor racing terms*, 126.3 *advantage*, 154.2 *priority*
Poles 1 *Peoples*
poles apart 111.1 *oppositeness*, 111.4 *opposite*, 111.6 *oppositely*, 115.4 *dissimilar*, 136.4 *disunity*
poles asunder 111.6 *oppositely*
Pole Star 340.3 *magnet*, 653.5 *guide*, 439.4 *natural light*, 543.5 *indicator*
pole-vault 21.2 *field events*, 359.5 *jump*
pole-vaulter 21.3, 237.5 *athlete*

pole-vaulting 18 *Sporting Activities*, 21.2 *field events*
police 16, 12.11 *govern*, 150.22 *pacify*, 397.9 *person dealing with the dead*, 632.3 *protector*, 632.9 *protect*, 653.1 *manage*, 679.39 *defend*, 688.18 *have authority*, 699.8 *restrain*, 718.10 *secure*
police barrier 632.4 *safety device*
police car 71
police commissioner 16.17 *police officer*
police constable 632.3 *protector*, 718.3 *security officer*
police court 16.19 *lawcourt*, 492.3 *place of judgment*
police dog 77.9 *dog*, 632.3 *protector*
police force 16.14 *police*, 718.4 *security forces*
police inspector 16.17 *police officer*
police lieutenant 16.17 *police officer*
police magistrate 16.23 *judge*
policeman 16.17 *police officer*, 543.8 *signer*, 632.3 *protector*, 679.2 *defender*, 688.10 *person of authority*, 692.6 *person in command*, 699.6 *law-maker*, 718.3 *security officer*
policeman's uniform 295.3 *formal dress*
Police Motu 5 *Languages and Groups of Languages*
police officer 16, 632.3 *protector*, 718.3 *security officer*
police protection 634.2 *shelter*
police rank 688.5 *position of authority*
police record 545.1 *record*
police report 528.3 *document*
police sergeant 16.17 *police officer*, 632.3 *protector*
police siren 543.4 *signal*
police state 688.7 *type of rule*
police station 93.13 *municipal building*, 688.6 *place of authority*
police superintendent 16.17 *police officer*
police van 71.17 *police car*
police whistle 543.4 *signal*, 636.2 *danger signal*
policewoman 632.3 *protector*, 688.10 *person of authority*, 718.3 *security officer*
Polichinelle 51.30 *clown*
policy 592, 166.6 *custom*, 167.5 *convention*, 584.6 *procedure*, 640.1 *action*, 640.2 *deed*, 652.1 *conduct*, 652.9 *tactics*, 653.3 *management*, 657.1 *cunning*
polio 624.6 *infection*, 624.17 *nervous disorder*
poliomyelitis 624.6 *infection*, 624.17 *nervous disorder*
polis 12.5 *political organization*
polish 376, 27.18 *bowl*, 60.21 *practise dentistry*, 293.24 *coat*, 376.11 *smooth*, 385.12 *rub*, 439.2 *quality of light*, 439.27 *glaze*, 558.1 *elegance*, 558.4 *be elegant*, 619.3 *perfection*, 619.5 *perfect*, 621.1 *cleanness*, 621.9 *cleaning agent*, 621.13 *clean*, 627.1 *improve*, 627.5 *improvement*, 660.4 *ease of manner*, 794.1 *elegance*, 817.2 *good manners*
Polish 5 *Languages and Groups of Languages*
polished 376, 6.20 *refined*, 34.8 *mountaineering*, 48.16 *literary*, 134.14 *purified*, 439.17 *lustrous*, 558.3 *elegant*, 619.1 *perfect*, 621.17 *cleaned*, 684.7 *completed*, 696.13 *excellent*, 794.5 *refined*, 817.8 *good-mannered*
polished hold 34.5 *rock face*
polishing 385, 60.4 *dentistry*, 621.2 *cleaning*
polish off 142.10 *complete*, 157.16 *cease*, 350.22 *eat well*, 642.15 *try*, 684.5 *conclude*
polish the apple 808.9 *fawn*
polish up 6.23 *learn*

polite 558.3 *elegant*, 652.17 *well-behaved*, 763.2 *likable*, 817.7 *courteous*, 849.9 *showing respect*
polite listener 652.3 *well-behaved person*
polite literature 48.1 *literature*
politely 652.19 *well*, 763.15 *pleasantly*, 817.14 *courteously*, 817.15 *genteelly*, 849.22 *respectfully*
politeness 558.1 *elegance*, 652.2 *good conduct*, 763.8 *amiability*, 813.5 *etiquette*, 817.1 *courtesy*
polite regard 849.3 *respectfulness*
politic 507.5 *wise*, 615.1 *convenient*, 654.8 *advisable*, 655.6 *skilful*, 781.4 *cautious*
political 665, 2.12 *sociological*, 12.9 *governmental*, 652.16 *behaving*, 653.17 *managerial*, 688.14 *governmental*
political action 15.4 *industrial dispute*
political activism 642.5 *activism*
political activist 475.8 *protester*, 640.3 *doer*
political administration 12.1 *government*
political animal 400.4 *civilized human*
political association 586.14 *motivator*
political authority 12.1 *government*
political behaviour 2.1 *sociology*
political border 298.1 *interface*
political campaign 580.12 *election*
political cartoonist 50.16 *artist*
political economist 653.13 *director*
political economy 653.3 *management*
political entity 249.4 *territorial division*, 400.11 *nation*
political favours 228.5 *positive stimulus*
political grouping 665
political history 3.1 *history*
political institution 2.8 *human institution*
political line 592.2 *policy*
politically 2, 2.16 *sociologically*, 249.20 *nationally*, 653.19 *managerially*, 665.18 *cliquishly*, 688.24 *ministerially*
politically correct 5.39 *of language*
politically moderate 242
political machine 665.3 *political grouping*
political map 299.4 *map*
political movement 642.5 *activism*
political organization 12, 2.4 *social organization*, 12.1 *government*
political party 12, 2.8 *human institution*, 665.3 *political grouping*
political party member 665
political party platform 592.2 *policy*
political party ticket 592.2 *policy*
political persecution 481.4 *social discrimination*
political philosophy 4.6 *branch of philosophy*
political plank 592.2 *policy*
political possession 725.1 *property*
political prisoner 702.5 *prisoner*
political refugee 104.7 *new arrival*
political reporting 533.3 *reporting*
political representative 706.1 *delegate*
political rule 12.1 *government*
political science 12.2 *politics*, 652.9 *tactics*
political sociology 2.1 *sociology*
political symbol 543.1 *sign*
political system 12.1 *government*
political trick 657.2 *stratagem*
politician 12, 228.7 *motivator*, 557.3 *phrasemonger*, 592.8 *planner*, 653.15 *manager*, 665.6 *political party member*, 697.2 *public servant*
politicize 665

politicized 665.10 *political*
politicking 12.1 *government*
politico 12.8 *politician*, 665.6 *political party member*
politicophobia 777 Phobias by Name
politics 777 Phobias by Topic, **12,** 652.9 *tactics*, 688.4 *governance*
politics in a smoke-filled room 657.1 *cunning*
polity 12.1 *government*, 400.11 *nation*
polka 46.2 *dance*, 46.4 *historic dancing*
polka dot 456.4 *maculation*
poll 170.3 *count*, 170.11 *number*, 171.6 *list of names*, 270.10 *shorten*, 477.2 *questioning*, 477.3 *questionnaire*, 477.17 *question*, 580.5, 580.10 *vote*
pollack 80 Fishes, 20.5 *British game fish*
pollard 85.1 *tree*, 85.18 *manage trees*
pollarding 85.6 *tree management*
polled 270.8 *shortened*, 477.16 *questioned*
Polled Dorset 68 Breeds of Sheep
Polled Hereford 68 Breeds of Cattle
Polled Welsh Black 68 Breeds of Cattle
pollen 84.3 *flower part*, 245.8 *organs of reproduction*, 384.10 *spore*
pollen analysis 83.10 *plant science*
pollen grain 84.3 *flower part*, 384.10 *spore*
pollen tube 84.3 *flower part*
pollinate 69.15 *cultivate*, 245.13 *propagate*, 246.7 *make fertile*
pollination 84, 245.3 *propagation*, 246.2 *productiveness*
pollinator 245.5 *propagator*
polling 580.12 *election*
polling booth 580.12 *election*
polling day 580.12 *election*
polling district 580.12 *election*
polling place 580.12 *election*
polling station 580.12 *election*
polliwog 79.8 *young amphibian*, 206.4 *young animal*
polls 580.12 *election*
pollster 170.6 *calculator*, 170.7 *mathematician*, 477.9 *questioner*
poll tax 751.7 *tax*
pollucite 54 Minerals
pollutant 55.8 *atmosphere*, 149.2 *impurity*, 631.9 *pollution*, 862.5 *evil thing*
pollute 133.10 *become mixed*, 601.1 *misuse*, 607.1 *waste*, 614.8 *make useless*, 618.13 *be worthless*, 622.11 *dirty*, 628.3 *make worse*, 631.15 *poison*, 862.11 *be evil*
polluted 601.4 *misused*, 622.7 *dirty*, 626.5 *unhygienic*, 793.4 *blemished*
polluted area 647.1 *workshop*
polluted river 96.1 *river*
polluter 601.3 *abuser*, 607.7 *destroyer*, 722.6 *loser*
polluting 618.5 *harmful*, 626.5 *unhygienic*
pollution 631, 55.8 *atmosphere*, 59.18 *ecology*, 133.1 *mixture*, 601.2 *misuse*, 618.11 *harmfulness*, 622.1 *dirtiness*, 624.6 *infection*, 626.1 *lack of hygiene*, 628.10 *impairment*, 862.5 *evil thing*
Pollux 8 Deities, **53** Named Stars
poll watcher 580.13 *electorate*
Pollyanna 775.5 *hoper*
polo 18 Sporting Activities, 32.6 *horsemanship*
polonaise 46.4 *historic dancing*
polo-neck 295.13 *sweater*
polonium 57 Chemical Elements
polony 45.29 *sausage*
polo pony 32.5 *pony*

Polo Pony 32 Breeds of Horse and Pony
polo shirt 295.8 *shirt*
poltergeist 11.11 *ghost*, 618.11 *harmfulness*, 661.7 *hinderer*
poltergeistism 11.1 *occultism*
poltroon 779.2 *coward*
poltroonery 779.1 *cowardice*
Polwarth 68 Breeds of Sheep
polyacetate 67 Synthetic Fibres and Fabrics
polyadic 4.16 *dialectical*
polyamide 67 Synthetic Fibres and Fabrics, 604.1 *materials*
polyandrous 823.23 *monogamous*
polyandry 175.2 *multiplicity*, 823.3 *types of marriage*
polyanthus 84 Flowers and Flowering Plants
polyatomic 57.35 *combined*
polybasite 54 Minerals
polycarbonate 57.21 *polymer*
polycarpellary 86.9 *of a fruit*
Polychaeta 81.6 *worm*
polychaete 81.6 *worm*
polychaetous 81.20 *wormlike*
polychromatic 444.10 *coloured*, 456.6 *variegated*
polychromatically 444.18 *colourfully*, 456.12 *variedly*
polychromatism 444.2 *colourfulness*, 456.1 *variegation*
polychrome 50.8 *painting*, 56.98 *physical*, 444.2 *colourfulness*, 444.10 *coloured*, 456.6 *variegated*
polychromy 43 Architectural Decoration, 456.1 *variegation*
polyclinic 60.10 *hospital*
polyester 67 Synthetic Fibres and Fabrics, 57.21 *polymer*, 604.1 *materials*
polyethylene 604.1 *materials*
polygamist 175.5 *pluralist*, 823.10 *married man*
polygamous 823.23 *monogamous*
polygamously 823.24 *matrimonially*
polygamy 175.2 *multiplicity*, 823.3 *types of marriage*
polyglot 5.2 *linguist*, 5.38 *linguistic*, 175.5 *pluralist*, 175.7 *various*, 524.17 *translational*, 564.19 *speaking*
polyglot dictionary 5.28 *dictionary*
polyglot medley 5.5 *nonstandard language*
polyglottism 5.1 *linguistics*
polygon 52, 175.2 *multiplicity*
polygonal 52, 175.7 *various*, 310.9 *angled*
polygraph 61.4 *psychometrics*
polygynist 823.10 *married man*
polygynous 823.23 *monogamous*
polygyny 175.2 *multiplicity*, 823.3 *types of marriage*
polyhedral 52.84 *cubic*, 310.9 *angled*
polyhedron 52, 175.2 *multiplicity*, 310.3 *angled figure*
polyline 52.44 *polygon*
polymath 175.5 *pluralist*, 459.8 *intellectual person*, 655.5 *expert*
polymathic 6.18 *educated*, 501.8 *knowledgeable*
polymathy 6.9 *learnedness*, 501.3 *learning*
polymer 57 Types of Compounds, **57**
polymer chemist 57.2 *chemist*
polymer chemistry 57.1 *chemistry*
polymeric 57, 57.38 *reactive*
polymerization 57.14 *chemical reaction*, 57.21 *polymer*
polymerize 57.26 *react*
polymers 604.1 *materials*
polymethylmethacrylate 57.21 *polymer*
polymixin 62 Medication
polymorphous 113.6 *assorted*, 175.7 *various*
Polynesian 5 Languages and Groups of Languages, 1.6 *race*, 1.13 *racial*
Polynesians 1 Peoples

polynomial 52.25 *algebraic expression*, 52.76 *functional*
polynomial expression 52.25 *algebraic expression*
polynucleotide 59.12 *molecular biology*
polyp 81.7 *coelenterate*
polypectomy 60 Surgical Operations
polypeptide 58.8 *amino acid*
polypeptide chain 59.12 *molecular biology*
polyphagia 872.1 *gluttony*
polyphagous 872.6 *gluttonous*
Polyphemus 259.10 *big person*
polyphone 5.16 *spoken letter*
polyphonic 5.41 *lettered*, 433.7 *harmonious*
polyphonically 5.48 *linguistically*
polyphonic prose 48.5 *prose*
polyphonous 5.41 *lettered*
polyphonously 5.48 *linguistically*
polyphony 433.3 *melodiousness*
polyploid 59.25 *genetic*, 69.5 *gardening*
polyploidy 59.14 *chromosome*
polypody 86 Ferns
polypoid 81.21 *coelenterate*
polypoid invertebrate 81.7 *coelenterate*
polypore 89 Fungi
polypropylene 57.21 *polymer*, 604.1 *materials*
polyrhythm 185.12 *musical time*
polysaccharide 58
polysemous 520.6 *meaningful*
polysemy 520.3 *comprehension*, 578.5 *equivocalness*
polysome 59.8 *cell organ*
polystyrene 57.21 *polymer*, 292.2 *filling*, 408.3 *heater*, 604.1 *materials*
polysyllabic 5.39 *of language*, 269.1 *long*, 553.3 *diffuse*
polysyllabically 5.48 *linguistically*
polysyllabic language 5.10 *language type*
polysyllable 5.17 *word*
polysynthetic 5.39 *of language*
polysynthetic language 5.10 *language type*
polytechnic 6.13 *university*
polytheism 175.2 *multiplicity*
polytheist 175.5 *pluralist*
polythene 57.21 *polymer*, 293.4 *wrapping*, 604.1 *materials*
polythene bag 258.8 *bag*
polytonic 5.39 *of language*
polytonic language 5.10 *language type*
polytunnel 69.4 *nursery*
polyunsaturated fat 58.7, 395.8 *fat*
polyunsaturates 350.11 *food content*
polyurethane 57.21 *polymer*, 604.1 *materials*
polyurethane rubber 377.4 *rubber*
pom 91 Names for Inhabitants
Pom 255.9 *British inhabitant*
poma 41.1 *skiing*
pomade 386, 386.14 *anoint*, 395.4 *ointment*, 395.18 *anoint*, 418.2 *fragrant thing*
pomander 418.2 *fragrant thing*
pomatum 386.6 *pomade*, 395.6 *ointment*
pome 86.2 *botanical fruit*
pomegranate 86 Fruits
pomelo 86 Fruits
Pomeranian 77 Breeds of Dogs
pomiculture 69.1 *horticulture*
pomiferous 86.6 *fruiting*
pomme 544.13 *heraldic*
pommel 30.6 *pommel horse*
pommel horse 18 Sporting Activities, 30
pommer 49 Musical Instruments
Pomo 7 Non-Christian Religions
pomological 69.16 *horticultural*
pomologically 69.20 *horticulturally*
pomologist 69.13 *horticulturist*, 83.12 *plant scientist*

pomology 59.1 *life science*, 83.10 *plant science*
pomp 811, 526.10 *manifestation*, 805.6 *majesty*, 813.1 *formality*
pomp and circumstance 805.6 *majesty*
pomp and circumstance of war 676.2 *glory of war*
pompano 80 Fishes
Pompeian art 50 Western Art Styles and Movements
Pompidou Centre 43 Noted Buildings
pom-pom 680.11 *guns*, 680.12 *historical guns*
pomposity 811, 541.4 *bombast*, 557.2 *affectation*, 559.4 *inelegance of speech*, 805.6 *majesty*
pompous 811, 541.15 *bombastic*, 557.4 *ornate*, 559.9 *inelegant*, 805.17 *conceited*, 805.19 *stately*, 809.11 *cocky*, 809.13 *boastful*, 813.6 *formal*, 813.8 *ceremonious*
pompously 809, 811, 541.16 *exaggeratedly*, 557.6 *ornately*
pompousness 809.3 *cockiness*, 811.5 *pomposity*
pompous twit 809.7 *vain person*
poncho 295.25 *accessories*
pond 39.7 *swimming pool*, 69.3 *ornamental garden*, 94.2 *small lake*
ponder 4.20 *philosophize*, 461.12 *think*, 461.15 *think about*, 588.7 *intend*, 786.12 *wonder whether*
ponderable 367.7 *material*
pondered 461.10 *speculative*
pondering 4.4 *philosophical investigation*, 461.4 *deliberation*, 461.10 *speculative*
ponderosity 369.8 *weighing down*
ponderous 369, 557.4 *ornate*, 656.3, 659.15 *clumsy*, 788.4 *boring*
ponderously 369.17 *burdensomely*, 557.6 *ornately*, 659.28 *awkwardly*, 788.8 *boringly*
ponderousness 369.8 *weighing down*, 559.4 *inelegance of speech*, 788.1 *boredom*
ponder over 492.12 *estimate*
ponder the nature of God 7.22 *theologize*
pondlike 94.9 *lakelike*
Pondo 1 Peoples, **5** Languages and Groups of Languages
pond scum 90.1 *alga*
pond skater 82 Insects
pond turtle 79 Reptiles
pong 416.8 *have odour*, 419.1 *stench*, 419.5 *stink*, 628.2 *decay*
ponga 88 Ferns
pongee 67 Natural Fabrics
pongid 77.34 *primate*
Pongidae 77.16 *primate*
pongids 77.16 *primate*
ponging 622.8 *unclean*
pongy 419.3 *stinking*, 622.8 *unclean*
poniard 680.8 *sharp weapon*
ponies 161 Collective Names by Animal
pons asinorum 635.1 *trap*
Pons—Brooks 53 Comets
Pons—Winnecke 53 Comets
Pont-Aven school 50 Schools and Groups of Artists
Pontchartrain 94 Lakes
pontentilla 84 Flowers and Flowering Plants
pontif 7.8 *priest*
pontifex maximus 7.8 *priest*
pontiff 696.6 *religious leader*
pontifical 7.17 *priestly*, 10.10 *religious manual*, 535.14 *assertive*, 692.14 *commanding*, 696.12 *masterful*
pontificalia 7.11 *vestment*
pontificals 7.11 *vestment*
pontificate 7.9 *priesthood*, 490.20 *be certain*, 561.4 *dissertate*, 567.7 *address*, 692.9 *command*, 811.30 *put on airs*, 876.12 *moralize*

pontificating 811.20 *pompous*

pontificatingly 811.36 *pompously*

pontification 811.5 *pomposity*

pontificator 567.6 *public speaker*

pontoon 42 Card Games, **74** Ships and Boats, 356.5 *crossing point*

pontoon bridge 63.21, 327.9 *bridge*

Pontus 8 Deities, **8** Deities

Pontypool 93 Cities

Pontypridd 93 Cities

pony **32**, 32.1 *horse*, 118.2 *copy*, 179.8 *twenty and over*, 258.13 *drinking vessel*, 524.4 *translation*, 741.9 *British money*

pony express 71.9 *animal transport*, 329.11 *swift thing*

Pony Express 326.8 *messenger*, 534.2 *postal communication*

Pony of the Americas **32** Breeds of Horse and Pony

ponytail 283.3 *suspended object*, 375.7 *rough thing*, 791.8 *hair cut*

ponytailed 375.3 *barbed*

pony trekking 32.6 *horsemanship*

poo 353.5 *faeces*, 353.16 *defecate*

pooch 77.9 *dog*

pood **75** Some Foreign Units

poodle **77** Breeds of Dogs, 808.3 *sycophant*

poodle-faking 821.6 *courtship*

pooh-pooh 495.3 *underestimate*

pooh-pooh theory 5.37 *linguistic theory*

pool **18** Sporting Activities, **24**, 24.1 *billiards*, 94.2 *small lake*, 140.5 *combine*, 278.4, 278.4 *shallow thing*, 605.1, 605.6 *store*, 721.3 *acquisition*, 721.11 *acquire*, 724.1 *joint possession*

pool ball 24.1 *billiards*

Poole 93 Cities

pooled 664.18 *joint*

pool hall 24.1 *billiards*

pooling of resources 664.4 *joint operation*

pool interests 664.14 *join with*

pool of labour 602.3 *human resources*

pool player 24.7 *billiards player*

pool resources 664.14 *join with*

pool table 24.6 *pool*

pool together 721.11 *acquire*

Poona 93 Cities, 40.10 *badminton*

poonghie 7.8 *priest*

poop **74** Parts of a Ship, 353.5 *faeces*, 683.6 *fail*

Poop 53 The Constellations

poop deck **74** Parts of a Ship, 304.1 *rear*

pooped 650.1 *fatigued*

poo-poo 353.5 *faeces*

poop-scoop 621.10 *cleaning object*

poor **127**, **618**, **743**, 145.4 *incomplete*, 238.13 *insufficient*, 242.6 *moderate*, 247.3 *birth control*, 358.8 *defective*, 515.11 *disappointing*, 571.11 *needy*, 593.5 *necessitous*, 609.1 *insufficient*, 609.2 *unprovided*, 612.2 *obscure*, 612.4 *trivial*, 620.1 *imperfect*, 628.12 *deteriorated*, 687.7 *unprosperous*, 722.17 *unprofitable*, 747.13 *nonpaying*, 754.10 *shoddy*, 776.8 *bad*, 806.2 *lowly*, 852.27 *critical*

poor as a church mouse 743.1 *poor*

poor as dirt 743.1 *poor*

poor as Job 743.1 *poor*

poor as Lazarus 743.1 *poor*

poor as Mother Hubbard 743.1 *poor*

poor-boy 45.11 *sandwich*

poor chance 589

Poor Clare 7 Members of Religious Orders, 743.10 *poor person*

poor dab 238.4 *weakling*

poor definition 438.4 *invisibility*

poor diction 559.5 *mispronunciation*

poor dress 296.4 *dishabille*

poor ear 420.1 *hearing*

poor effort 620.6 *imperfect item*

poor hand 656.10 *unskilled person*

poor health 238, 624.1 *ill health*, 687.1 *adversity*

poor hearing 421.1 *deafness*

poorhouse 634.2 *shelter*, 743.7 *beggary*

poor imitation 115.3 *disguise*

poor judgment 493.1 *misjudgment*

poor light 439.10 *window*, 440.1 *darkness*, 441.1 *dimness*

poor likeness 548.1 *misrepresentation*

poorly **743**, 127.21 *badly*, 145.6 *incompletely*, 238.10 *ill*, 238.14 *weakly*, 609.10 *insufficiently*, 624.22 *sick*, 628.14 *worse*, 687.12 *in adversity*

poorly defined 523.3 *unrecognizable*

poorly disciplined 693.13 *disobedient*

poorly done 555.1 *unemphatic*

poorly dressed 296.10 *in dishabille*

poorly fed 871.6 *fasting*

poorly off 743.1 *poor*

poorly planned 595.3 *without preparation*

poorly timed 211.10 *untimely*, 616.1 *inconvenient*

poor memory 512

poorness 743.5 *poverty*, 754.3 *shoddiness*, 806.8 *lowliness*

poor opinion 852.2 *disrespect*

poor performance 656.9 *bungling*

poor person **743**, 687.5 *person in adversity*

poor prospect 484.4 *remote possibility*, 489.4 *improbability*

poor quality **127**, 612.4 *trivial*, 618.8 *inferiority*

poor-quality 127.14 *poor*

poor reception 421.3 *inaudibility*

poor relation 127.6 *inferior*, 195.8 *follower*, 612.10 *nonentity*, 620.6 *imperfect item*, 743.10 *poor person*

poor relief 2.10 *social services*, 767.4 *charity*, 833.4 *welfare state*

poor representation 547.1 *representation*

poor return 247.1 *infertility*, 722.2 *financial loss*

poor risk 687.5 *person in adversity*

poor second 127.6 *inferior*

poor shot 656.10 *unskilled person*

poor show 656.9 *bungling*

poor sight **436**, 441.2 *murk*

poor table 350.10 *scarcity*

poor third 127.6 *inferior*

poor timing 211.1 *untimeliness*, 616.3 *inconvenience*

poor turnout 182.1 *few*

poor visibility 55.35 *visibility*, 438.4 *invisibility*, 441.2 *murk*

poor vision 436.2 *poor sight*

poor white 743.11 *the poor*

poor white trash 816.7 *outsider*

poor White trash 612.10 *nonentity*

poor wretch 687.5 *person in adversity*, 770.3 *sad person*

Pooter 124.8 *middle classes*

pop 49.9 *popular music*, 49.33 *jazz*, 351.6 *soft drink*, 401.3 *male title of address*, 401.13 *man in the family*, 424.1 *faintness*, 425.2, 425.6 *crack*, 733.7 *borrow*

POP 65 Programming Languages

pop art 50 Western Art Styles and Movements

pop at 670.2 *fire*

pope 7.8 *priest*, 126.5 *superior*, 688.10 *person of authority*, 696.6 *religious leader*

Pope 48 Poets, **777** Phobias by Topic

popedom 7.9 *priesthood*

Pope Joan 42 Card Games

pop-eyed 435.21 *seeing*, 786.7 *wide-eyed*

pop fan 821.9 *lover*

pop group 49.26 *musical group*, 140.3 *assembly*, 161.12 *team*

pop gun 338.9 *firearm*, 425.3 *banger*

pop in 346.9 *enter*, 354.2 *inject*

pop into one's head 471.14 *have an idea*

popish 7.16 *denominational*

poplar 85 Trees and Shrubs

poplin 67 Natural Fabrics, 288.4 *textile*

POPLOG 65 Programming Languages

pop music 49.9 *popular music*

Popocatepetl 95 Mountains

pop off 397.15 *die*

pop one's clogs 397.15 *die*

pop out 347.9 *exit*, 437.9 *appear*

pop-out 36.13 *windsurfing*

pop-out board 36.7 *windsurfing*

Popov 52 Scientists

popover 45.39 *loaf*

poppadom 45.38 *bread*, 45.49 *Indian dish*

popper 20.2 *artificial fly*, 137.8 *fastening*

Popper 4 Philosophers

poppet 206.9 *child*, 821.12 *nicknames for lovers*, 826.4 *terms of endearment*

popping 425.9 *crackling*, 732.1 *lending*, 733.1 *borrowing*

popping crease 27.5 *wicket*

popping eyes 786.2 *sign of wonderment*

popple 97.10 *billow*

poppy 84 Flowers and Flowering Plants, 450.7 *red thing*, 643.10 *soporific*, 741.2 *cash*

poppycock 506.1 *nonsense*, 521.5 *empty talk*, 521.14 *nonsense*

poppy day 812.5 *anniversary*

Poppy Day 84.9 *figurative usage*, 214.6 *annually celebrated day*

poppy head 43 Architectural Decoration

pop shop 732.4 *lending institution*

pop single 22.5 *batting terms*

pop song 49.9 *popular music*

pop star 126.6 *paragon*, 617.8 *exceller*, 821.11 *loved one*

popster 49.24 *musician*

pop the question **477**, 712.6 *request*, 821.28 *win the love of*, 826.8 *court*

populace 164.11 *general public*, 255.2 *inhabitants*, 400.9 *group*

popular **815**, 12.9 *governmental*, 124.1 *average*, 164.19 *prevailing*, 522.2 *simple*, 532.20 *well-known*, 665.10 *political*, 688.14 *governmental*, 739.16 *sold*, 782.7 *desired*, 784.5 *likable*, 800.3 *reputable*, 821.22 *lovable*, 851.24 *admired*

popular belief 497.1 *belief*

Popular Coalition 12.6 *political party*

popular front 12.6 *political party*, 665.3 *political grouping*

popularity 124.4 *average*, 815.2 *social ambition*, 821.1 *love*, 851.2 *admiration*

popularization 522.10 *simplicity*

popularize **164**, 522.5 *simplify*, 524.8 *interpret*, 660.16 *make easy*

popularized 522.2 *simple*

popularizer 524.6 *interpreter*

popular literature 48.1 *literature*

popularly 784.10 *with great liking*

popular melody 433.1 *melody*

popular misconception 504.6 *fallibility*

popular movement 642.5 *activism*

popular music 49

popular newspaper 533.5 *mass communication*

popular press 532.3 *journalism*, 533.5 *mass communication*

popular price 754.1 *cheapness*

popular psychology 61.1 *psychology*

popular regard 821.1 *love*

popular song 49.9 *popular music*, 433.2 *song*

popular will 12.1 *government*

populate 246.6 *be fertile*, 255.15 *settle*, 256.17 *inhabit*

populated 255.11 *inhabited*

population **52**, 1.7 *society*, 59.18 *ecology*, 255.2 *inhabitants*

population drift 162.7 *sprawl*

population explosion 246.2 *productiveness*

population genetics 59.11 *genetics*

population growth 13.4 *economic development*

population inversion 56.26 *laser*

population study 2.2 *sociological research*

populist 12.6 *political party*

pop up 22.7 *play baseball*, 183.21 *be repeated*, 344.1 *arrive*, 359.17 *spring up*, 437.9 *appear*, 457.12 *become visible*, 589.10 *chance*

pop-up 22.5 *batting terms*

porbeagle 80 Fishes

porcelain 44.1 *ceramics*, 243.7 *produce*, 379.3 *brittle thing*

porcelain clay 44.2 *raw material*

porcelain enamel 44.1 *ceramics*

porcelain insulation 44.9 *industrial ceramics*

porcelain mark 44

porch 256.7 *room*, 322.7 *passageway*, 327.2 *route*, 346.6 *means of entry*

porcine 77.33 *ungulate*

porcupine **77** Placental Mammals, 380.8 *sharp-pointed thing*

porcupine fish 80 Fishes

pore 322.4 *body orifice*, 347.7 *outlet*

pore fungi 89.3 *fungi*

pore over 435.14 *inspect*

porgy 80 Fishes

Porifera 81.8 *sponge*

poriferan 81.8 *sponge*, 81.22 *spongelike*

poriferous 81.22 *spongelike*

pork 45.20 *meat*

pork barrel 228.5 *positive stimulus*, 586.10 *bribe*

pork: blade shoulder **45**

porker 68.8 *livestock*, 872.4 *glutton*

pork pie 309.4 *distortion of the truth*

pork-pie hat 295.15 *headgear*

pork sausage 45.29 *sausage*

pork: spare rib **45**

porky 309.4 *distortion of the truth*, 489.6 *implausibility*

porn 622.3 *obscenity*, 877.2 *indecency*

pornographer 862.6 *evil person*, 877.10 *sex offender*

pornographic 296.11 *exposed*, 618.4 *poor*, 622.9 *obscene*, 877.12 *indecent*

pornographically 296.17 *nakedly*

pornographic film 296.3 *pornography*

pornographic magazine 296.3 *pornography*

pornographic novel 48.2 *fiction*

pornographic picture 296.3 *pornography*

pornography **296**, 618.10 *poverty*, 622.3 *obscenity*, 862.5 *evil thing*, 877.2 *indecency*

porous 317.5 *concave*, 322.14 *holed*, 347.17 *leaky*

porously 322.27 *cavernously*

porous pottery 44.1 *ceramics*

porous thing 322

porphyrite **54** Common Rocks

porphyritic texture 54.28 *rock*

porphyry **54** Common Rocks

Porphyry 4 Philosophers

porpoise **77** Placental Mammals

porpoises 161 Collective Names by Animal

porridge 41.1 *skiing*, 45.40 *breakfast cereal*, 45.44 *British dish*,

393.7 *soup,* 699.4 *detention,* 702.4 *prison sentence,* 702.7 *imprisonment*
Porrima 53 Named Stars
porringer 258.16 *crockery*
Porsche 52 Scientists
port 74 Parts of a Ship, 63.24 *water system,* 65.7 *peripheral,* 98.9 *inlet,* 218.4 *stopping place,* 305.1 *side,* 344.15 *destination,* 345.10 *place of departure,* 347.6 *way out,* 351.9 *wine,* 450.7 *red thing,* 634.2 *shelter,* 652.1 *conduct*
portability 260.1 *littleness,* 370.5 *lightness*
portable 70.5 *transportable,* 260.7 *little,* 326.17 *transferable,* 370.1 *light*
portable radio 34.4 *climbing equipment,* 1338.14 *radio*
portable stereo player 423.4 *sound maker*
portable television 534.22 *television set*
portable toilet 727.7 *toilet*
Portadown 93 Cities
portage 70.1, 70.4 *transport,* 326.2 *transportation*
portal 322.7 *passageway,* 346.6 *means of entry*
portamento 49 Musical Terms
portando 49 Musical Terms
portative 326.17 *transferable*
Port-au-Prince 93 Cities
portcullis 544.8 *heraldic device,* 661.3 *barrier,* 671.12 *fort*
porte-cochere 346.6 *means of entry*
Port Elizabeth 93 Cities
portend 516.1 *foresee,* 517.11 *predict,* 520.12 *intend*
portent 513.4 *expectant person,* 516.3 *foresight,* 517.5 *omen,* 636.1 *warning,* 786.4 *wonder*
portentous 517.15 *presageful*
portentously 517.16 *predictively*
portentousness 517.5 *omen*
porter 34.7 *mountaineer,* 72.9 *railway worker,* 323.5 *person who closes,* 326.7 *transferor,* 646.1 *worker,* 697.3 *attendant*
Porter 48 Writers, **52** Scientists
porterage 326.2 *transportation*
porterhouse steak 45.43 *US dish*
Porterhouse steak 45.23 *beef*
porterwhisky 351.7 *alcoholic drink*
portfolio 16.2 *jurisdiction,* 258.9 *baggage,* 545.1 *record,* 605.5 *collection,* 725.5 *personal estate*
porthole 74 Parts of a Ship, 322.5 *hole*
portico 43.9 *miscellaneous architectural features,* 256.7 *room,* 327.7 *arcade,* 346.6 *means of entry*
port in a storm 344.16 *stopover*
portion 731, 120.2 *certain amount,* 120.8 *quantify,* 121.4 *interval,* 143.1 *part,* 143.7, 148.2 *piece,* 173.2 *fractional part,* 269.5 *piece,* 350.14 *mouthful,* 606.1 *provision,* 725.6 *marriage settlement*
portioned 121.7 *gradational*
portionless 743.2 *insolvent*
portion out 731.4 *allot*
Portland 68 Breeds of Sheep, **93** Cities
Portland Bill 98.5 *peninsula*
Portland cement 44.9 *industrial ceramics,* 63.26 *masonry,* 293.11 *paving,* 604.2 *building material*
Portlaoise 93 Cities
portliness 259.5 *fatness,* 273.5 *thickness,* 315.2 *round body*
Port Louis 93 Cities
portly 259.16 *fat,* 273.1 *thick,* 315.10 *well-rounded*
portmanteau 5.42 *worded,* 258.9 *baggage,* 552.3 *concise,* 605.4 *storage*
portmanteau word 5.21 *catchword,* 140.4 *compound,* 552.1 *conciseness*

Porto Alegre 93 Cities
Portobello Road 740.1 *market*
port of call 218.4 *stopping place*
Port of Spain 93 Cities
portrait 66, 50.10 *art subject,* 110.3 *lookalike,* 118.2 *copy,* 545.1 *record,* 547.2 *reproduction,* 560.1 *description,* 560.9 *representation*
portraitist 50.16 *artist*
portrait painter 50.16 *artist*
portrait sculpture 50.12 *sculpture*
portraiture 66.1 *photography,* 547.2 *reproduction*
portray 48.21 *write,* 50.20 *draw,* 103.11 *characterize,* 114.12 *imitate,* 299.5 *outline,* 547.9 *represent,* 547.10 *act,* 560.14 *describe*
portrayal 51.20 *acting,* 114.1 *similarity,* 299.1 *outline,* 547.1 *representation,* 547.3 *acting,* 560.1 *description*
portraying 547.3 *acting,* 547.13 *representational*
Portrush 93 Cities
Port Said 93 Cities
Port Salut 45 Cheeses
portside 74 Parts of a Ship
Portsmouth 93 Cities, 93.4 *British cities*
Port Sudan 93 Cities
port tack 36.15 *sail*
port tacking 36.1 *sailing*
Port Talbot 93 Cities
Portugal 91 Countries
Portuguese 5 Languages and Groups of Languages
Portuguese GP at Estoril 33.2 *Formula 1 race*
portulaca 84 Flowers and Flowering Plants
pose 4.22 *propound a philosophy,* 457.4 *something that appears,* 477.21 *confuse,* 538.8 *pretence,* 538.24 *pretend,* 540.7 *pretence,* 540.20 *pretend,* 652.1 *conduct,* 652.11 *conduct oneself,* 797.1 *affectedness,* 797.4 *be affected*
pose as 540.20 *pretend,* 547.10 *act*
Poseidon 8 Deities, 74.7 *nautical person,* 97.4 *sea god*
pose problems 659.17 *be difficult*
poser 295.27 *model,* 475.7 *demonstrator,* 477.4 *difficult question,* 529.3 *mystification,* 538.12 *cheat,* 539.15 *deceiver,* 659.4 *problem,* 797.2 *pretender*
poset 52.23 *algebra*
poseur 118.7 *imitator,* 538.12 *cheat,* 539.15 *deceiver,* 797.2 *pretender*
posh 796.7 *fashionable,* 811.24 *grand*
poshness 811.9 *grandeure*
Posidonius 53 Rills and Valleys
Posidonius of Apamea 4 Philosophers
posing 118.12 *imitative,* 538.8 *pretence,* 538.18 *pretentious,* 540.7 *pretence,* 540.30 *pretending,* 547.3 *acting*
posing pouch 296.4 *dishabille*
posit 4.22 *propound a philosophy,* 518.5 *suppose*
position 150, 4.2 *philosophical system,* 52.36 *point,* 56.7 *space,* 105.1 *state,* 106.1 *circumstances,* 121.2 *rank,* 121.5 *measure,* 150.19 *systematize,* 152.6 *category,* 152.12 *arrange,* 163.5 *social class,* 230.3 *business,* 250.1 *location,* 250.9 *locate,* 251.1 *situation,* 251.2 *circumstances,* 251.4 *employment,* 251.5 *rank,* 251.10 *situate,* 318.1 *prominence,* 322.10 *opportunity,* 332.1 *direction,* 471.5 *ideology,* 473.3 *line of argument,* 497.1 *belief,* 518.1 *supposition,* 535.2 *statement*
positional 250.8 *locational*
positional notation 52.8 *number system*
positioned 27, 250.6 *located,* 251.6 *situated*

position in society 251.5 *rank*
position of authority 688
position of power 235.1 *power*
position of strength 235.1 *power*
position paper 535.2 *statement*
positions at the barre 46
position vector 52.50 *scalar quantity*
positive 52.71 *numerical,* 64.36 *electronic,* 99.13 *real,* 110.4, 110.15 *duplicate,* 169.8 *odd,* 235.7 *electrical power,* 475.12 *demonstrable,* 490.2 *convinced,* 497.11 *believing,* 522.1 *intelligible,* 535.14 *assertive,* 554.3 *emphatic,* 662.33 *helpful,* 688.15 *true,* 775.11 *hopeful*
positive charge 56.50 *electric charge*
positive correlation 52.61 *correlation*
positive declaration 535.2 *statement*
positive discrimination 122.3 *equalization,* 481.5 *favouritism*
positive electrode 235.7 *electrical power*
positive feedback 64.15 *circuit function*
positive ion 56.66 *ion*
positively 52.87 *mathematically,* 64.37 *electronically,* 99.22 *really,* 490.23 *certainly,* 497.15 *believingly,* 535.23 *affirmatively,* 554.7 *emphatically,* 662.36 *helpfully,* 688.25 *authentically,* 775.15 *hopefully*
positiveness 490.10 *conviction,* 522.9 *intelligibility,* 535.6 *assertiveness*
positive number 52.5 *number*
positive outlook 554.1 *emphasis*
positive reinforcement 61.20 *conditioning*
positive stimulus 228
positive thinking 775.1 *hope*
positive vetting 632.2 *protection*
positive vote 580.10 *vote*
positivism 4.7 *school of thought,* 367.2 *materialization,* 490.10 *conviction*
positivist 4.11 *follower of a doctrine,* 4.14 *of a philosophy,* 367.3 *materialist,* 490.11 *opinionist*
positron 56.77 *elementary particle*
posologist 60.13 *medical specialist,* 630.16 *druggist*
posology 60.3 *medical specialty,* 62.1 *pharmacology*
posse 16.17 *police officer,* 116.2 *alliance,* 161.11 *group,* 665.1 *party*
posse comitatus 16.17 *police officer*
possess 723, 8.18 *devilize,* 11.21 *bewitch,* 135.11 *make love,* 599.5 *dispose of,* 725.9 *own property,* 734.7 *take,* 860.6 *be selfish*
possess an even temper 817.10 *be courteous*
possessed 723, 11.19 *bewitched,* 135.14 *conjunctive,* 725.8 *propertied*
possessed of 723.8 *possessing*
possessing 723, 723.1 *possession,* 725.8 *propertied*
possessing narcotics 875.2 *drug pushing*
possession 723, 723, 11.3 *witchcraft,* 19.7 *offence,* 23.4 *playing terms,* 35.3 *rugby play,* 249.4 *territorial division,* 599.6 *use,* 725.1 *property,* 734.1 *taking*
Possession 723
possession ball 23.4 *playing terms*
possession in common 724.1 *joint possession*
possessions 725, 742.5 *wealth*
possessive 135.14 *conjunctive,* 734.12 *taking,* 782.9 *desirous,* 821.20 *amorous,* 841.4 *jealous,* 860.4 *selfish*
possessive love 821.2 *romantic love*

possessively 723, 135.16 *as one,* 734.13 *avariciously,* 841.9 *jealously,* 860.8 *selfishly*
possessiveness 147.4 *exclusiveness,* 821.2 *romantic love,* 841.1 *jealousy,* 841.2 *distrust,* 860.1 *selfishness*
possess magical power 235.10 *be powerful*
possess narcotics 875.10 *drug oneself*
possessor 723, 804.4 *titleholder*
possessorship 723.1 *possession*
possessory 723.8 *possessing*
possess power 688.18 *have authority*
possess special power 235.10 *be powerful*
possess spirit 235.10 *be powerful*
possess strength 237.7 *be strong*
possess with 725.9 *own property*
posset 351.7 *alcoholic drink*
possibilities 714.3 *potential*
possibility 486, 322.10 *opportunity,* 488.3 *plausibility,* 513.1 *expectation,* 513.2 *expectations,* 518.2 *basis of supposition,* 527.6 *latency,* 660.3 *wieldiness*
Possibility 486
possibility of perfection 620.5 *imperfection*
possible 486, 101.9 *realizable,* 199.12 *predictable,* 235.13 *powerful,* 486.6 *potential,* 488.7 *plausible,* 497.13 *believable,* 527.1 *latent,* 660.10 *feasible,* 714.14 *auspicious,* 714.15 *future*
possible choice 580.8 *choice*
possible need 606.1 *provision*
possibleness 486
possible outcome 52.62 *probability*
possible worlds 4.9 *philosophical problem*
possibly 486, 199.16 *predictably,* 229.8 *by chance,* 235.18 *powerfully,* 518.10 *supposedly,* 589.14 *perchance,* 714.17 *auspiciously,* 714.18 *potentially*
possum 591.17 *avoider*
possuming 590.2 *chase*
post 326, 32.7 *horseracing,* 43.8 *column,* 47.12 *wood,* 47.17 *carpenter,* 68.11 *farmland,* 137.8 *fastening,* 171.8 *list,* 230.3 *business,* 250.1 *location,* 250.9 *locate,* 251.4 *employment,* 251.10 *situate,* 275.6 *tall thing,* 281.3 *vertical thing,* 284.2 *supporting part,* 284.11 *support,* 326.10 *transferred thing,* 528.12 *communicate,* 534.3 *correspondence,* 534.31 *correspond,* 567.10 *send,* 703.7 *engage,* 750.7 *account*
postage 751.6 *business costs*
postage meter 534.3 *correspondence*
postage stamp 534.3 *correspondence*
postal 534.33 *communicational*
postal address 250.2 *exact location*
postal card 534.3 *correspondence*
postal communication 534
postal district 250.2 *exact location*
post a letter bomb 539.33 *snare*
postal order 534.3 *correspondence,* 741.14 *paper money*
postal service 534.2 *postal communication*
Postal Union 534.2 *postal communication*
postal vote 580.10 *vote*
postal worker 534
post and rail 301.3 *enclosing thing*
post and rails 32.9 *jumping*
post a parcel bomb 539.33 *snare*
postbag 534.3 *correspondence*
postbellum 675.7 *peaceful*
post bills 532.16 *publicize*
post boat 74 Ships and Boats
postbox 534.3 *correspondence*
postboy 32.15 *horse person*
postbus 71 Motor Vehicles, 326.5 *means of transport*

postcard 326.10 *transferred thing,* 534.3 *correspondence*

post chaise **71** Carriages and Carts

postcode 250.2 *exact location,* 534.3 *correspondence,* 567.5 *place of residence*

postdate 193.3 *mistime*

postdated 193.6 *too late*

posted 250.6 *located,* 251.6 *situated,* 528.18 *informed,* 534.34 *communicated*

poster 50.7 *picture,* 526.8 *showplace,* 532.9 *advertisement,* 543.1 *sign*

poster artist 50.16 *artist*

poste restante 534.2 *postal communication*

posterior 155.10, 155.20 *rear,* 304.2 *rear end,* 304.4 *rear*

posterity **195,** 199.2 *future generation*

postern 304.1, 304.4 *rear,* 322.7 *passageway,* 346.6 *means of entry ,* 671.12 *fort*

poster paint 444.5 *paint*

post-existence 199.3 *future condition*

post-free 754.11 *free of charge,* 848.8 *tax-free*

postglacial 54.60 *glaciated,* 55.40 *climatic change*

postglaciation 55.40 *climatic change*

postgraduate 6.7 *learner,* 6.21 *curricular,* 485.8 *qualified person*

Postgraduate Certificate **485** Educational Qualifications

Postgraduate Certificate of Education **485** Educational Qualifications

posthaste 191.9 *in the shortest possible time,* 329.14 *swiftly,* 648.6 *hastily*

post horse 32.2 *thoroughbred*

posthumous 209.14 *dead,* 397.22 *post-mortem*

posthumously 209.18 *formerly,* 325.10 *motionlessly,* 397.23 *fatally*

post-hypnotic suggestion 61.3 *psychiatric treatment*

postilion 32.15 *horse person*

postimpressionism **50** Western Art Styles and Movements

postimpressionist 50.29 *realist*

postindustrial 243.11 *productive*

posting 250.4 *placing,* 326.2 *transportation*

postlude 155.8 *addition,* 195.9 *sequel*

postman 326.8 *messenger,* 534.4 *postal worker*

postman's knock **42** Children's Games and Party Games

postmark 534.3 *correspondence*

postmaster 534.4 *postal worker*

postmaster general 534.4 *postal worker*

postmerldlan 204.7 *afternoon,* 205.6 *evening*

post meridiem 205.7 *evening*

postmistress 534.4 *postal worker*

postmodern 201.10 *new*

postmodernism **48** Literary Groups and Movements, **50** Western Art Styles and Movements, 201.2 *trendiness*

postmodernist **43** Architectural Styles, 50.29 *realist,* 201.9 *modern person*

postmortem 60.7 *diagnosis*

post mortem 195.9 *sequel*

post-mortem **397,** 397.8 *after death,* 397.23 *fatally,* 399.7 *inquest,* 399.12 *funereally*

post-mortem examination 397.8 *after death,* 399.7 *inquest*

postnatal 245.16 *reproductive*

post-obit 397.22 *post-mortem*

post-obitum 399.12 *funereally*

post office 534.2 *postal communication*

Post Office 534.2 *postal communication*

post-office box 534.3 *correspondence*

Post Office savings bank 741.19 *treasury*

post-paid 534.34 *communicated,* 746.19 *receiving pay,* 754.11 *free of charge*

post-painterly abstraction **50** Western Art Styles and Movements

post pattern 19.9 *play*

postpone 209.8 *delay,* 283.12 *interrupt,* 573.8 *hold back,* 591.7 *be evasive,* 598.2 *withdraw,* 685.5 *not complete*

postponed 209.10 *held up,* 283.9 *interrupted*

postponement 209.3 *delayed action,* 283.6 *interruption,* 573.15 *delay*

postponing 573.4 *procrastinating*

postposition 155.8 *addition*

postpositional 155.19 *additional*

postpositive 155.19 *additional*

post-prandial 45.56 *culinary,* 649.4 *at ease*

posts 40.3 *tennis equipment*

postscript 130.3 *additional item,* 155.8 *addition,* 157.10 *ending,* 195.9 *sequel,* 219.1 *continuity,* 304.1 *rear*

post-structuralism **48** Literary Groups and Movements, 4.7 *school of thought,* 382.9 *artistic structure*

post-structuralist 4.11 *follower of a doctrine,* 485.13 *literary person*

post the banns 714.1 *promise*

post-traumatic stress disorder 61.12 *stress*

postulant 7.7 *monk*

postulate 4.1 *philosophy,* 4.8 *philosophical term,* 4.20 *philosophize,* 4.22 *propound a philosophy,* 52.65 *theory,* 52.89 *theorize,* 463.14 *premise,* 473.3 *line of argument,* 473.15 *state,* 518.1 *supposition,* 518.5 *suppose*

postulated 473.11 *logical,* 518.8 *supposed*

postulation 518.1 *supposition*

postulatory 518.7 *suppositional*

posture 105.1 *state,* 106.1 *circumstances,* 306.6 *nature,* 457.3 *external appearance,* 538.8 *pretence,* 538.24 *pretend,* 540.7 *pretence,* 540.20 *pretend,* 640.2 *deed,* 652.1 *conduct,* 652.11 *conduct oneself,* 797.1 *affectedness,* 797.4 *be affected*

posturing 538.18 *pretentious,* 540.30 *pretending*

postwar 675.7 *peaceful*

postwoman 534.4 *postal worker*

posy 84.1 *flower,* 161.29 *bunch,* 418.2 *fragrant thing*

pot **258,** 42.3 *card game terms,* 44.8 *ceramic object,* 44.11 *make ceramics,* 69.15 *cultivate,* 120.3 *container,* 258.21 *put in a container,* 338.31 *snipe,* 354.1 *insert,* 407.3 *press,* 562.8 *summarize,* 637.2 *preserver,* 637.5 *preserve,* 681.1 *trophy,* 875.6 *drug,* 878.2 *prize*

pot a ball 24.8 *play billiards*

potable 351.17 *drinkable,* 411.7 *tasty,* 632.5 *safe*

potamophobia **777** Phobias by Name

potash 68.13, 246.3 *fertilizer*

potassium **57** Chemical Elements, 58.15 *essential element*

potassium–argon dating 54.42 *dating,* 56.70 *radioactivity*

potassium chloride **57** Common Chemical Compounds

potassium permanganate **57** Common Chemical Compounds

potate 351.13 *drink*

potation 351.1 *drinking,* 351.2, 874.13 *drink*

potations 874.12 *alcohol*

potato **45** Vegetables

potato beetle **82** Insects

potato blight **89** Fungi, 244.7 *agent of destruction*

potato chips 45.10 *snack*

potatoes 68.12 *crop*

potato field 68.11 *farmland*

potato harvester 68.10 *farm tool*

potato masher 393.15 *pulper*

potato picker 68.16 *farm worker*

potato planter 68.10 *farm tool*

potato salad 45.14 *salad*

Potawatomi **1** Peoples

potbellied 273.1 *thick,* 259.16 *fat,* 315.10 *well-rounded*

pot belly 258.18 *stomach*

potbelly 259.8 *fat,* 273.5 *thickness*

pot-belly 315.2 *round body*

potboiler 560.5 *fiction*

potboiling 612.4 *trivial*

potboy 697.3 *attendant*

pot cheese **45** Cheeses

poteen 351.7 *alcoholic drink*

potence 688.1 *authority*

potency 233 *influence,* 235.1 *power,* 237.1 *strength,* 613.7 *instrumentality,* 688.1 *authority*

potent **237,** 233.11 *influential,* 235.13 *powerful,* 544.8 *heraldic device,* 688.22 *authoritative,* 874.6 *intoxicating*

potentate 696.3 *leader*

potential **486, 714,** 56.52, 64.10 *electric potential,* 199.12 *predictable,* 235.2 *ability,* 235.4 *energy,* 235.13 *powerful,* 486.1 *possibility,* 486.5 *possible,* 527.1 *latent,* 714.14 *auspicious,* 714.15 *future*

potential difference 56.52, 64.10 *electric potential,* 235.4 *energy*

potential energy 56.11, 235.4 *energy*

potentiality 233 *influence,* 235.2 *ability,* 485.1 *qualification,* 486.1 *possibility,* 527.6 *latency*

potentially **486, 714,** 199.16 *predictably,* 235.18 *powerfully,* 527.15 *latently,* 714.17 *auspiciously*

potentiometer 56.90 *ammeter,* 64.17 *resistor,* 64.23 *electrical instrument,* 268.8 *meter*

potentiometry 268.2 *micrometry*

potently 233.14 *influentially,* 235.18 *powerfully,* 237.15 *acutely,* 688.23 *authoritatively*

pother 151.9 *disorder,* 541.1 *exaggeration,* 541.7 *exaggerate*

potherb **45** Vegetables, 69.11 *vegetable,* 83.2 *plant*

pothole 277.4 *deep thing,* 290.1 *interior,* 317.2 *concave land,* 375.12 *make rough*

potholed 375.2 *coarse*

potholed road 375.8 *rough ground*

potholer 277.5 *submariner*

potholing **18** Sporting Activities, 277.1 *depth,* 360.7 *tunnelling*

pothunter 674.10 *contender*

potion 62.3 *drug,* 133.2 *mixed thing,* 351.2 *drink,* 630.2 *medicine*

potlatch 10.3 *rite of worship,* 10.7 *non-Christian ritual*

potluck 229.2 *chance,* 350.12 *meal,* 589.2 *luck,* 595.8 *lack of preparation*

potluck dinner 815.5 *party*

pot magnet 56.60 *magnet*

pot marigold **84** Flowers and Flowering Plants

pot of gold 714.4 *promised land,* 742.5 *wealth*

pot of gold at the end of the rainbow 588.6 *objective*

Potomac **96** Rivers, 96.3 *US rivers*

pot on 69.15 *cultivate*

potophobia **777** Phobias by Name

pot plant 83.2 *plant,* 84.1 *flower*

potpourri 133.2 *mixed thing,* 133.3, 161.32 *miscellany,* 418.2 *fragrant thing*

pot-roast 45.32 *meat dish,* 45.55 *cook*

pot-roasting 45.8 *cooking technique*

pots and pans 258.15 *pot*

Potsdam **93** Cities

potsherd 143.7 *piece*

potshoot 338.31 *snipe*

pot shot 338.7 *shot,* 338.31 *snipe*

pots of money 742.6 *money*

potted 258.20 *containing,* 562.7 *shortened,* 637.7 *preserved,* 874.1 *drunk*

potted version 562.2 *outline*

potter **44,** 324.15 *walk,* 646.2 *artisan*

Potter **48** Writers

pottering 324.9 *slow motion,* 324.17 *directional,* 642.7 *restlessness,* 642.19 *busy*

potter's clay 44.2 *raw material,* 604.1 *materials*

potter's earth 44.2 *raw material*

potter's wheel 44.6 *ceramic workshop,* 220.4 *medium of conversion,* 364.6 *rotator*

potter's workplace 44.6 *ceramic workshop*

potter wasp **82** Insects

pottery **42** Hobbies and Pastimes, 44.1 *ceramics,* 44.6 *ceramic workshop,* 243.7 *produce,* 258.16 *crockery,* 379.3 *brittle thing*

pottery factory 44.6 *ceramic workshop*

potting 258.20 *containing*

potting a ball 24.5 *snooker*

potting compost 69.7 *fertilizer*

potting on 69.5 *gardening*

potting shed 69.4 *nursery*

potto **77** Placental Mammals

potty 258.15 *pot,* 353.14 *toilet,* 508.5 *foolish,* 727.7 *toilet*

potty-trained 353.26 *urinary*

pot-valiant 874.1 *drunk*

pouch 77.4 *pouched mammal,* 258.8 *bag*

pouched mammal **77**

pouched rat **77** Placental Mammals

Poughkeepsie **93** Cities

Poujadism 12.1 *government*

poult 68.8 *livestock,* 78.12 *young bird*

poulterer 606.3 *provider*

poultice **393,** 62.7 *ointment,* 408.3 *heater,* 630.10 *surgical dressing,* 630.20 *doctor*

poulticing 630.13 *therapy*

poultry **45,** 45.20 *meat,* 68.8 *livestock*

poultry farm 68.6 *farm*

poultry farmer 68.15 *agriculturist*

poultry farming 68.3 *livestock farming*

pounce 329.4 *be swift,* 329.9 *acceleration,* 360.5 *dive,* 360.12 *drop,* 384.5 *powder*

pounce on 514.10 *ambush*

pounce upon 670.5 *strike*

pound **75** General Units, 49.38 *sound,* 77.20 *abode of mammals,* 133.8 *mix,* 183.22 *resound,* 256.12 *stall,* 301.2 *enclosed place,* 330.3 *hit,* 330.5 *beat,* 330.13 *blow,* 369.9 *avoirdupois weight,* 384.27 *beat,* 406.10 *be painful,* 426.8 *drum,* 634.3 *animal shelter,* 670.1 *attack,* 702.1 *prison*

Pound **48** Poets

poundage 369.4 *heaviness,* 752.1 *discount*

poundal **75** Scientific and Technical Units, 235.5 *unit of work*

pound coin 741.9 *British money*

pounder 384.11 *pulverizer*

pound-foolish 541.14 *extravagant*

pound-foolishness 541.3 *extravagance*

pound for pound 142.11 *wholly*

pound in 354.3 *impact*

pounding 384.4 *pulverization,* 406.5 *painful,* 426.1, 426.15 *drumming*

pound net 539.13 *snare*

pound note 741.9 *British money*

pound of flesh 690.1 *severity,* 745.4 *interest,* 836.1 *pitilessness*

pound sterling 741.1 *money*

pour 55.62 *rain,* 96.7 *flow,*

161.40, 181.11 *crowd*, 347.11
run out, 360.3 *downflow*,
360.13 *drip*, 362.6 *throw down*,
387.25 *flow*, 608.5 *about*
pour a broadside into 670.2 *fire*
pour balm into one's wounds
677.4 *pacify*
pour cold water on 770.10 *depress*
pour down 360.13 *drip*
pour down the drain 607.1
waste, 722.11 *be wasteful*,
757.7 *waste*
pour in 257.7 *stuff*, 258.21 *put
in a container*, 342.10 *come together*, 346.12 *flood in*, 354.2 *inject*
pouring 55.53 *rainy*, 246.5 *fertile*, 360.16 *descending*
pouring oil on troubled waters
840.1 *atonement*
pour it on 329.5 *run like a shot*
pour money down the drain
722.10 *have a financial loss*
pour oil on 395.18 *anoint*
pour oil on troubled water
150.22 *pacify*
pour oil on troubled waters
242.4 *moderate*, 386.15 *ease*,
677.4 *pacify*, 840.5 *atone*
pour oil upon 386.14 *anoint*
pour on 389.29 *water*
pour out 347.11 *run out*, 349.14
let out, 362.6 *throw down*,
553.5 *be diffuse*, 729.5 *give*
pour vitriol 852.22 *vituperate*
pour vitriol upon 827.6 *vilify*
pour wrath onto 828.13 *vent
one's anger*
pout 309.2 *facial distortion*,
309.10 *make faces*, 543.3,
543.11 *gesture*, 818.8 *get angry*,
829.7 *frown*, 830.2 *sign of sullenness*, 830.9 *be sullen*
pouting 829.5 *showing irascibility*, 830.6 *sullen*
poverty 777 *Phobias by Topic*,
618, 743, 127.2 *deficiency*,
145.1 *incompleteness*, 571.4
need, 593.3 *needfulness*, 609.9
scarcity, 628.7 *deterioration*,
687.2 *economic adversity*
Poverty 743
poverty level 593.3 *needfulness*,
609.8 *insufficiency*
poverty line 743.5 *poverty*
poverty of intellect 460.1 *lack of
intellect*
poverty-stricken 687.7 *unprosperous*, 743.1 *poor*
poverty-stricken 571.11 *needy*
poverty trap 593.3 *needfulness*,
743.5 *poverty*
POW 701.5 *subjected person*,
702.5 *prisoner*, 816.7 *outsider*
powan 80 *Fishes*
POW camp 816.4 *place of confinement*
powder 384, 384, 41.12 *ski*,
62.6 *pill*, 132.2 *residue*, 162.18
sprinkle, 295.5 *fancy dress*,
295.35 *make clothing*, 384.23
pulverize, 444.16 *make up*,
456.11 *variegate*, 630.2 *medicine*, 680.15 *explosive*, 791.4
cosmetics
powder and shot 680.13 *ammunition*
powder barrel 680.4 *arsenal*
powder blue 454.1 *blue*
powder box 258.6 *box*
powder boy 679.27 *naval man*
powdered 162.23 *sprinkled*,
384.19 *pulverized*, 456.10 *mottled*
powdered milk 351.5 *milk*
powdered sugar 414.2 *sweetener*
powdered wig 295.15 *headgear*
powder flask 680.4 *arsenal*
powder-grey 448.1 *grey*
powder horn 680.4 *arsenal*
powderiness 384
Powderiness 384
powdering 162.4 *sprinkling*,
384.4 *pulverization*
powder keg 635.1 *trap*, 680.4 *arsenal*

powder magazine 680.4 *arsenal*
powder monkey 679.27 *naval
man*
powder room 353.13 *lavatory*,
727.7 *toilet*
powder snow 41.1 *skiing*, 409.5
ice
powdery 384, 379.1 *brittle*,
392.6 *desert*
powdery mildew 89 *Fungi*,
69.12 *pests and diseases*
powdery snow 55.30 *snow*
Powell 48 *Writers*, **52** *Scientists*
power 169, 235, 8.2 *divine attribute*, 52.17 *multiplication*,
56.11 *energy*, 91.1 *country*,
126.2 *leadership*, 166.8 *authority*, 230.1 *operation*, 230.9 *take
action*, 232.1 *instrumentality*,
233 *influence*, 235.11 *give
power*, 235.12 *generate power*,
237.1 *strength*, 239.1 *vigour*,
241.1 *violence*, 249.4 *territorial
division*, 330.1 *impel*, 330.11
impulsion, 410.11 *fuel*, 554.1
emphasis, 599.6 *use*, 602.1
means, 611.1 *importance*, 613.7
instrumentality, 640.1 *action*,
644.4 *exertion*, 653.3 *management*, 688.1 *authority*, 688.21
grant authority, 690.1 *severity*,
692.3 *authority*, 703.1 *commission*, 845.3 *prerogative*
Power 235
power abuse 601.2 *misuse*
power amplifier 64.21 *rectifier*
powerband 33.6 *motor racing
terms*
power behind the throne 226.8
contributor, 233.4 *indirect influence*, 527.9 *backstage manipulator*, 531.7 *concealer*, 688.1 *authority*, 707.1 *deputy*
powerboat 74 *Ships and Boats*
powerboat racing 18 *Sporting
Activities*
power brakes 71 *Motor Vehicle
Parts*
power broker 233.4 *indirect influence*
power cable 410.4 *electricity*
power conversion 64.34 *power
supply*
power cord 235.7 *electrical power*
power cut 64.34 *power supply*,
410.4 *electricity*, 440.2 *darkening*, 609.9 *scarcity*
power distribution 64
power dive 329.9 *acceleration*
powerdive 360.5 *dive*, 360.12
drop
power down 236.8 *overpower*
power-driven 603.8 *mechanical*
power-driven saw 47.11 *woodworking tool*
powered 235, 410, 603.8 *mechanical*
powered up 235.15 *full of energy*
power factor 64.26 *electrical energy*
power failure 236.1 *powerlessness*
powerful 235, 378, 166.12 *ruling*, 232.7 *causal*, 233.11 *influential*, 237.9 *physically strong*,
237.10 *potent*, 239.4 *vigorous*,
241.6 *violent*, 300.10 *advantaged*, 423.6 *loud*, 554.3 *emphatic*, 611.6 *notable*, 613.3 *instrumental*, 640.6 *effective*,
688.12 *authoritative*, 692.15
self-assured
powerful build 378.8 *physical
strength*
powerful influence 233 *influence*
powerfully 235, 378, 410,
232.9 *instrumentally*, 233.14 *influentially*, 237.14 *strongly*,
241.10 *violently*, 300.12 *at an
advantage*, 338.34 *forward*,
599.11 *usefully*, 640.8 *effectively*, 688.23 *authoritatively*,
692.16 *commandingly*
powerfulness 235.1 *power*, 688.2
authoritativeness
powerful person 611.4 *bigwig*
power generation 64.32 *power
station*

power harrow 68.10 *farm tool*
powerhead 36.7 *windsurfing*
power hitter 22.2 *baseball player*
powerhouse 64.32 *power station*,
235.6 *source of energy*, 642.10
busy person, 647.1 *workshop*
powerless 236, 238.8 *weak*,
240.6 *suspended*, 612.2 *obscure*,
614.1 *useless*, 641.3 *inactive*
powerlessly 236, 641.5 *without
action*
powerlessness 236, 612.6 *obscurity*, 614.3 *uselessness*, 689.1 *anarchy*
Powerlessness 236
powerless person 236
power line 64.33 *power distribution*, 235.7 *electrical power*
power mower 69.6 *garden tool*
power of attorney 222.1 *substitution*, 703.1 *commission*
power of conception 463.1 *reason*
power of imagination 519.1 *imagination*
power of reason 463.1 *reason*
power of seeing 435.1 *vision*
power of speech 564
power of the purse 14.1, 741.7
finance
power of three 177.1 *three*
power of two 176.1 *two*
power pack 64.34 *power supply*,
235.7 *electrical power*, 410.4
electricity
power plant 64.32 *power station*,
235.6 *source of energy*, 647.1
workshop
power-plant worker 646.2 *artisan*
power play 31.3 *ice hockey*
power point 64.28 *plug*, 410.4
electricity
power production 64.32 *power
station*
power regulation 64.34 *power
supply*
powers 8.6 *angel*
power-saw 85.7 *timber production*
power series 52.20 *sequence*
power shovel 63.29 *construction
equipment*
powers of darkness 8.7 *devil*
power source 64
power station 64, 56.11 *energy*,
56.56 *electrical energy*, 235.6
source of energy, 410.4 *electricity*, 647.1 *workshop*
power steering 71 *Motor Vehicle Parts*
power structure 121.2 *rank*
power supply 64, 56.56 *electrical energy*
power sweep 19.9 *play*
power to act 703.1 *commission*
power transistor 64.19 *transistor*
power up 235.11 *give power*
power vacuum 236.1 *powerlessness*, 689.1 *anarchy*
power wheel 44.6 *ceramic workshop*
power-worker 410
Powhatan 1 *Peoples*
powwow 568.4 *conference*,
568.11 *confer*, 654.2 *consultation*, 716.3 *discussion*, 716.4 *negotiator*
Powys 48 *Writers*, **92** *Counties*
Poyang 94 *Lakes*
Poynting vector 56 *Named Laws*
Poznań 93 *Cities*
pp 49 *Musical Terms*, 703.11
under commission
PPS 130.3 *additional item*
practicability 486.2 *possibleness*,
615.3 *convenience*
practicable 101.9 *realizable*,
230.11 *workable*, 486.5 *possible*, 613.1 *useful*, 615.1 *convenient*, 660.10 *feasible*, 716.8 *negotiated*
practicableness 615.3 *convenience*, 660.3 *wieldiness*
practical 101, 232, 4.15 *rational*, 230.11 *workable*, 486.5 *possible*, 599.9 *used*, 613.1 *useful*,
615.1 *convenient*, 654.8 *advisable*, 660.10 *feasible*, 660.12

wieldy, 662.33 *helpful*, 716.8 *negotiated*
practical ability 655.1 *skill*
practical compromise 717.1 *compromise*
practical criticism 524.3 *criticism*
practical experience 501.3 *learning*
practicality 101.1 *reality*, 232.1
instrumentality, 486.2 *possibleness*, 599.6 *use*, 613.5 *usefulness*, 615.3 *convenience*, 660.3
wieldiness
practical joke 506.3 *tomfoolery*,
539.11 *hoax*, 612.8 *trifle*, 771.5
joke
practical joker 506.4 *buffoon*,
539.15 *deceiver*
practical knowledge 655.1 *skill*
practically 486, 4.26 *rationally*,
57.46 *chemically*, 142.13 *on the
whole*, 230.13 *operationally*,
264.7 *nearly*, 599.11, 613.12
usefully, 615.7 *conveniently*,
662.36 *helpfully*
practical person 640.3 *doer*
practice 60.1 *medicine*, 166.6
custom, 167.5 *convention*,
183.1 *repetition*, 306.5 *formality*, 327.1 *way*, 479.2 *rehearsal*,
479.8 *experimental*, 501.3 *learning*, 520.4 *type of meaning*,
584.6 *procedure*, 594.10 *preparations*, 594.12 *briefing*, 599.6
use, 630.11 *medical art*, 640.1
action, 644.5 *exercise*, 652.7
way, 654.3 *precept*, 719.3 *performance*, 813.3 *formal occasion*
practice run 479.2 *rehearsal*
practise 183.16 *repeat*, 479.12 *rehearse*, 584.18 *habituate*,
590.14 *carry on*, 594.8 *prepare
oneself*, 599.1 *use*, 630.20 *doctor*, 640.4 *act*, 644.9 *exercise*,
719.6 *perform*
practise abstinence 876.11 *be
moral*
practise artifice 538.25 *be dishonest*
practise at 696.15 *learn*
practise atheism 536.7 *be negative*
practise birth control 247
practise celibacy 825.9 *be celibate*
practise creative accounting
750.7 *account*
practised 6.19 *knowledgeable*,
485.9 *qualified*, 501.8 *knowledgeable*, 584.12 *established*,
584.14 *habituated*, 594.18 *prepared*, 655.8 *expert*
practise dentistry 60
practised eye 655.5 *expert*
practised hand 655.5 *expert*
practise etiquette 306.8 *be formal*
practise forestry 85.18 *manage
trees*
practise horticulture 69
practise hygiene 625.5 *by hygienic*
practise judo 26.13 *do martial
arts*
practise livestock farming 68
practise magic 539.29 *juggle*
practise medicine 60, 630.20
doctor
practise one's religion 368.12
enter a nonmaterial world
practise philanthropy 831.9 *be
charitable*
practise self-defence 26.11 *do a
combat sport*
practise sophistry 474
practise sorcery 539.28 *trick*
practise spiritualism 11.22 *conjure*
practise subversion 689.4 *be anarchic*
practise surgery 60
practise tae kwon do 26.13 *do
martial arts*
practise tax evasion 747.7 *not
pay*
practise the golden rule 831.8 *be
benevolent*
practise usury 732.5 *lend*
practise virtue 863.8 *be virtuous*

practise witchcraft 11.21 *bewitch,*
233.10 *be a prevailing influence,*
235.10 *be powerful,* 539.28 *trick*
practising 7.15 *religious,* 183.1
repetition, 644.10 *working,*
657.4 *cunning*
practising Christian 7.5 *Christian,* 497.5 *believer*
practitioner 640.3 *doer,* 646.3
agent, 655.5, 688.11 *expert,*
696.10 *expert*
praedial 68.19 *agricultural,*
725.8 *propertied*
praenomen 560.8 *name*
praetor 653.16 *official*
Praetorian Guard 679.12 *ceremonial troops*
pragmatic 4.15 *rational,* 4.18 *detached,* 101.8 *practical,* 479.8
experimental, 599.9 *used,* 613.1
useful, 615.1 *convenient,* 716.8
negotiated
pragmatically 2.16 *sociologically,*
4.26 *rationally,* 599.11 *usefully,*
716.9 *feasibly*
pragmatic sociology 2.1 *sociology*
pragmatism 4.7 *school of
thought,* 101.3 *realism,* 479.3
experimentation, 615.3 *convenience*
pragmatist 101.4 *realist*
Prague 93 Cities, 93.6 *other cities*
prairie 87.2 *grassland,* 98.6 *lowland,* 248.3 *geographical space,*
282.3 *flat thing*
prairie dog 77 Placental Mammals
prairie schooner 71 Carriages
and Carts
prairie wolf 77 Placental Mammals
praise 849, 851, 851, 9.1, 9.7
worship, 10.3 *rite of worship,*
10.19 *offer worship,* 284.14 *give
moral support,* 763.10 *pleasant
thing,* 773.2 *fanfare,* 773.6 *fête,*
812.17 *congratulate,* 837.2
thanks, 837.3 *recognition,* 837.6
be grateful, 851.4, 851.15 *compliment,* 853.1 *flattery,* 853.8
flatter, 878.1, 878.9 *reward*
praised 9.11 *worshipped,* 878.16
rewarded
praise heaven 837.7 *give thanks*
praise oneself 860.7 *be egoistic*
praiser 851
praise-singer 9.5 *worshipper*
praise to the skies 851.15 *compliment*
praiseworthiness 617.6 *worth,*
861.8 *good*
praiseworthy 851, 617.1 *worthy,*
782.8 *desirable,* 849.13 *respectable,* 861.1 *good,* 863.7 *worthy*
praising 9.9 *worshipful,* 837.5
thanking, 853.12 *flattering*
Prajapati 8 Deities
Prakrit 5 Languages and
Groups of Languages
praline 45.41 *sweet*
pram 71.8 *baby carriage*
prance 46.15 *dance,* 811.29
show off
prancing 359.24 *leaping*
prandial 45.56 *culinary*
prang 360.12 *drop,* 670.3 *bomb*
prank 506.3 *tomfoolery,* 579.3
whim, 771.5 *joke*
prankish 579.1 *capricious*
prankster 506.4 *buffoon,* 579.4
capricious person
praseodymium 57 Chemical Elements
prat 460.3 *unintelligent person,*
508.3 *foolish person*
prate 521.5 *empty talk,* 521.9
talk nonsense, 565.7 *be talkative,* 568.10 *chat*
pratfall 360.4 *fall*
pratincole 78 Birds
prating 565.3 *talk,* 565.6 *effusive*
prattle 521.5 *empty talk,* 521.9
talk nonsense, 565.3 *talk,*
568.2, 568.10 *chat*
prattle on 565.7 *be talkative*
prattler 564.10 *speaker*

prattling 521.10 *meaningless,*
565.6 *effusive*
prawn 45.19 *shellfish,* 81.4 *arthropod*
prawn cocktail 45.12 *hors
d'oeuvre*
praxis 1.8 *tradition,* 10.1 *ritual,*
116.6 *convention,* 166.6 *custom,* 584.1 *habit,* 640.1 *action,*
652.6 *way of life*
pray 10, 9.7 *worship,* 712.6 *request,* 840.6 *apologize*
prayer 10, 10.3 *rite of worship,*
662.2 *support,* 712.1 *request,*
837.2 *thanks*
prayer book 10.10 *religious manual*
prayer cap 7.11 *vestment*
prayer for the dead 10.9 *prayer*
prayerful 7.15 *religious,* 9.9 *worshipful,* 10.22 *worshipping*
prayerfully 10.23 *ritually*
prayerfulness 7.2 *religiousness*
prayermat 10.14 *sacred object*
prayer meeting 10.4 *public worship*
prayer of thanks 837.2 *thanks*
prayers 10.4 *public worship*
prayer shawl 10.14 *sacred object*
prayerwheel 10.14 *sacred object*
prayer wheel 364.6 *rotator*
pray for 712.6 *request,* 782.12 *desire*
praying 9.1 *worship,* 10.3 *rite of
worship*
praying gesture 543.3 *gesture*
praying mantis 82 Insects
pray to 567.8 *appeal to*
preach 7, 4.22 *propound a philosophy,* 220.11 *persuade,* 561.4
dissertate, 876.12 *moralize*
preach at 567.7 *address*
preacher 6.4 *educator,* 7.4 *religionist,* 220.5 *converter,* 228.7
motivator, 233.5 *influential person,* 561.3 *dissertator,* 564.10
speaker, 567.6 *public speaker*
preachify 7.20 *preach*
preachiness 7.2 *religiousness*
preach to 564.14 *speak to*
preach to the converted 614.9
waste effort
preachy 6.16 *educational,* 7.15
religious
Preakness 32.7 *horseracing*
preamble 156.10 *introduction,*
564.8 *speech*
prearrange 152.18 *make arrangements,* 194.9 *do before,* 582.2
premeditate, 592.12 *plan ahead,*
594.2 *do the groundwork*
prearranged 152.21 *organized,*
582.4 *deliberate*
prearrangement 582.6 *premeditation,* 594.9 *preparation*
Precambrian 54 Geological
Time Intervals
Precambrian era 200.3 *geological
period*
Precambrian Palaeozoic 202.15
primal
precarious 224.13 *changeable,*
491.7 *unreliable,* 633.2 *unsafe*
precariously 224.15 *changeably,*
491.26 *unreliably,* 633.11 *dangerously*
precariousness 491.15 *unreliability,* 633.5 *danger*
precast 63.32 *structural*
precast concrete 63.25 *construction material*
precaution 516.4 *prudence,*
606.1 *provision,* 632.2 *protection,* 781.2 *insurance*
precautionary 594.16 *preparatory*
precautionary steps 632.4 *safety
device*
precautions 632.4 *safety device*
precede 154, 208, 121.5 *measure,* 194.8 *be before,* 194.9 *do
before,* 611.7 *be important,*
653.2 *direct*
precede in time 208.8 *precede*
precedence 154, 119.1 *originality,* 121.2 *rank,* 126.1 *superiority,* 194.1 *priority,* 611.1 *importance*

Precedence 154
precedent 154, 166, 16.7 *legal
trial,* 119.2 *original,* 154.10 *preceding,* 654.3 *precept*
preceding 154, 121.8 *ranked,*
154.1 *precedence,* 200.19 *antiquarian,* 208.15 *precursory,*
303.6 *front*
precentor 7.8 *priest,* 653.14
leader
precept 654, 4.1 *philosophy,*
16.3 *law,* 166.4 *guide,* 461.6
idea, 505.1 *maxim,* 537.4 *truism,* 654.1 *advice,* 692.1 *command,* 847.6 *ethics,* 876.7 *moral*
preceptive 505.2 *proverbial,*
537.17 *instructive*
preceptor 6.4 *educator*
preceptress 6.4 *educator*
precession 53.13 *luminosity,*
53.21 *orbit,* 154.1 *precedence,*
324.10 *regular movement*
precessional 154.10 *preceding*
pre-Christian 3.15 *historic*
precinct 93.7 *city district,* 249.5
state, 249.10 *urban area,* 264.3
near place, 301.2 *enclosed place,*
580.12 *election*
precincts 297.1 *surroundings*
precinct station 93.13 *municipal
building*
preciosity 557.1 *ornament,*
813.2 *formalism*
precious 557.4 *ornate,* 617.3,
753.8 *valuable,* 797.3 *affected,*
813.6 *formal,* 821.12 *nicknames for lovers,* 826.4 *terms of
endearment*
precious few 182.5 *few*
precious heart 821.12 *nicknames
for lovers,* 826.4 *terms of endearment*
precious little 182.5 *few*
preciously 557.6 *ornately,*
753.13 *valuably*
precious metal 741.1 *money,*
741.16 *bullion*
preciousness 557.1 *ornament,*
753.6 *value,* 813.2 *formalism*
precipice 95.1, 275.3 *mountain,*
281.3 *vertical thing,* 360.3
downflow, 360.6 *slide,* 635.1
trap
precipices 777 Phobias by Topic
precipitation 208.5 *prematurity,*
468.2 *impetuosity,* 595.8 *lack of
preparation,* 648.5 *hastiness,*
780.1 *rashness*
precipitancy 780.1 *rashness*
precipitant 595.3 *without preparation,* 648.3 *hasty,* 780.4 *rash*
precipitately 648.6 *hastily*
precipitate 54.63 *ebb,* 55.62
rain, 57.3 *phase,* 57.25 *solidify,*
131.3 *subtract,* 132.2 *residue,*
193.5 *too early,* 208.9 *prepare,*
208.16 *premature,* 226.10
awaken, 227.1 *effect,* 227.5
show an effect, 244.8 *destroy,*
329.1 *swift,* 329.4 *be swift,*
349.13 *throw away,* 360.13
drip, 371.4 *solid body,* 371.8 *be
dense,* 622.4 *dirt,* 648.1 *hasten,*
648.3 *hasty,* 780.4 *rash*
precipitated 57.32 *solid,* 132.9 *remaining*
precipitately 208.20 *prematurely,*
241.10 *violently,* 648.6 *hastily*
precipitateness 648.5 *hastiness,*
780.1 *rashness*
precipitation 55, 54.10 *water
cycle,* 57.3 *phase,* 57.5 *process,*
131.1 *subtraction,* 244.1 *destruction,* 329.8 *speed,* 338.3 *throwing,* 349.20 *eviction,* 362.12
downthrow, 371.2 *concentration*
precipitative 208.16 *premature*
precipitous 208.16 *premature,*
281.8 *vertical,* 329.1 *swift,*
362.20 *falling,* 468.10 *careless,*
595.3 *without preparation*
precipitously 208.20 *prematurely*
precipitousness 281.1 *verticality*
precis 129.1 *decrease,* 129.5
make smaller, 270.3 *shortened
version,* 299.1, 299.5 *outline,*
552.2 *outline,* 552.4 *be concise,*

562.1 *summary,* 562.8 *summarize*
precise 106.10 *detailed,* 165.15
special, 469.9 *careful,* 503.5 *accurate,* 522.1 *intelligible,*
537.21 *accurate,* 619.1 *perfect,*
619.2 *perfectionist,* 760.4 *accurate,* 813.6, 813.6 *formal,* 843.8
correct
precisely 106.19 *meticulously,*
165.28 *specially,* 332.9 *directly,*
469.12 *carefully,* 503.8, 537.39
accurately, 619.7 *perfectly,*
813.12 *formally,* 843.20 *correctly*
precise measurement 503.3 *accurate thing*
preciseness 503.1 *accuracy,*
522.9 *intelligibility,* 537.8 *accuracy,* 619.3 *perfection,* 660.2
simplicity, 813.1 *formality,*
813.2 *formalism,* 843.2 *correctness*
precisian 7.4 *religionist,* 167.6
conformist
precision 52.8 *number system,*
56.83 *sensitivity,* 469.1 *carefulness,* 503.1 *accuracy,* 522.9 *intelligibility,* 537.8 *accuracy,*
660.2 *simplicity,* 760.10 *accuracy,* 843.2 *correctness*
precision bombing 670.13 *air attack*
precision instrument 503.3 *accurate thing*
precisionism 50 Western Art
Styles and Movements, 813.2
formalism
precisionist 50.29 *realist*
precision tool 603.1 *tool*
precis writer 562.5 *summarizer*
pre-classical 3.15 *historic*
preclude 147.7 *exclude,* 661.8
hinder
precluded 147.11 *excluded*
preclusion 147.1 *exclusion,*
661.1 *hindrance*
preclusive 147.10 *excluding,*
661.13 *hindering*
preclusively 661.16 *with delay*
precocial 78.24 *newly hatched*
precocious 208.16 *premature,*
595.5 *immature,* 807.15 *audacious*
precociously 208.20 *prematurely,*
807.30 *insolently,* 807.32 *audaciously*
precociousness 208.5 *prematurity*
precocity 208.5 *prematurity,*
595.10 *immaturity*
precognition 464, 11.8 *psychic
power,* 11.9 *divination,* 368.4
parapsychology, 516.3 *foresight*
precognitive 464, 11.17 *divinatory,* 368.9 *parapsychological,*
516.6 *foreseeing*
preconceive 493.11 *be unjust,*
582.2 *premeditate*
preconceived 493.8 *unjust*
preconceived idea 493.4 *prejudgment*
preconceived opinion 582.6 *premeditation*
preconception 493.4 *prejudgment*
preconcert 582.2 *premeditate*
precondemn 481.13 *prejudge*
precondition 571.1 *necessity,*
593.1 *requirement*
preconscious 61.21 *psyche*
preconsultation 594.9 *preparation*
precooked 191.7 *prepared for immediate use,* 594.21 *ready-made*
precursive 208.15 *precursory*
precursor 154, 194.6 *person having priority,* 194.7 *foretaste,*
208.4 *early comer,* 255.7 *settler,*
517.5 *omen,* 653.13 *director*
precursors 397.13 *the dead*
precursory 154, 208, 156.36 *introductory,* 517.13 *predicting*
predacious 76.15 *of animals,*
736.17 *stolen*
predate 154.15, 208.8 *precede*
predator 76.4 *type of animal,*
398.13 *animal killer,* 734.6
taker, 832.8 *malefactor*

predatorily 734.13 *avariciously*, 736.19 *thievishly*

predatory 78.23 *avian*, 734.12 *taking*, 736.17 *stolen*

predecease 194.9 *do before*, 397.15 *die*

predecessor 154, 194.6 *person having priority*, 208.4 *early comer*

pre-decimal coinage 741.10 *former British money*

predeliberation 582.6 *premeditation*

predestinate 582.1 *predetermine*

predestination 4.9 *philosophical problem*, 490.16 *inevitability*, 516.4 *prudence*, 571.6 *necessitarianism*, 582.5 *predetermination*

predestine 516.1 *foresee*, 520.12 *intend*, 571.17 *preordain*, 582.1 *predetermine*, 588.9 *intend for*

predestined 490.5 *inevitable*, 520.9 *meant*, 571.12 *inevitable*, 582.3 *predetermined*

predetermination 582, 490.16 *inevitability*, 493.4 *prejudgment*, 516.4 *prudence*, 571.6 *necessitarianism*, 588.2 *intentionality*, 594.9 *preparation*

Predetermination 582

predetermine 582, 228.10 *manipulate*, 516.1 *foresee*, 571.17 *preordain*, 588.8 *resolve*, 592.12 *plan ahead*, 594.2 *do the groundwork*

predetermined 582, 490.5 *inevitable*, 588.12 *intended*

predeterminist 571.7 *necessitarian*

predicament 105, 659, 106.4, 251.3 *difficult circumstances*, 491.12 *confusion*, 593.3 *needfulness*, 633.5 *danger*, 687.1 *adversity*, 776.2 *hopeless situation*

predicate 5.35 *part of speech*, 5.44 *grammatical*, 518.5 *suppose*, 535.17 *affirm*

predicate calculus 52.63 *mathematical logic*

predication 535.2 *statement*

predicational 535.10 *affirmative*

predicative 535.10 *affirmative*

predict 513, 517, 11.23 *divine*, 55.57, 154.19 *forecast*, 199.9 *look ahead*, 488.10 *think likely*, 516.1 *foresee*, 592.12 *plan ahead*, 636.5 *warn*

predictability 787, 488.1 *probability*, 490.17 *infallibility*

predictable 199, 787, 11.17 *divinatory*, 225.9 *stable*, 488.6 *probable*, 490.6 *infallible*, 513.7 *expected*, 516.7 *foreseeable*, 517.14 *predicted*, 584.9 *habitual*, 714.15 *future*

predictable response 331.6 *response*

predictably 199, 787, 225.12 *stably*, 488.11 *probably*, 513.13 *expectedly*, 517.16 *predictively*, 714.18 *potentially*

predicted 517, 11.17 *divinatory*, 199.13 *foreseen*, 513.7 *expected*, 516.7 *foreseeable*, 714.15 *future*

predicting 517, 516.6 *foreseeing*, 636.8 *warning*

prediction 517, 11.9 *divination*, 194.7 *foretaste*, 199.4 *looking to the future*, 488.1 *probability*, 513.2 *expectations*, 516.3 *foresight*, 592.2 *policy*, 636.1 *warning*

Prediction 517

predictive 11.17 *divinatory*, 488.6 *probable*, 516.6 *foreseeing*, 517.13 *predicting*

predictively 517

predictor 199, 516, 11.13 *diviner*

predigest 522.5 *simplify*

predigested 350.27 *edible*, 594.21 *ready-made*

predilection 234.2 *attitude*, 411.2 *taste of life*, 493.3 *injustice*, 580.7 *preference*, 782.1 *de-*

sire, 784.2 *inclination*, 821.7 *choice*

predispose 228.10 *manipulate*, 233.8 *influence*, 493.12 *bias*, 594.2 *do the groundwork*

predisposed 493.8 *unjust*, 784.6 *liking*

predispose oneself 784.8 *prefer*

predisposition 234.2 *attitude*, 493.3 *injustice*, 784.2 *inclination*

prednisolone 62 Medication

prednisone 62 Medication

predominance 124.4 *average*, 126.1 *superiority*, 233 *influence*, 235.1 *power*, 688.1 *authority*

predominant 124.1 *average*, 126.14 *best*, 164.19 *prevailing*, 233.13 *dominant*, 235.13 *powerful*, 688.12 *authoritative*

predominantly 124.11 *on average*, 126.16 *superiorly*, 142.13 *on the whole*, 164.32 *universally*, 233.14 *influentially*, 235.18 *powerfully*

predominate 124.9 *be average*, 126.8 *be superior*, 164.28 *prevail*, 166.15 *be the rule*, 233.10 *be a prevailing influence*, 235.10 *be powerful*, 611.7 *be important*, 688.18 *have authority*

predominating 164.19 *prevailing*

predomination 126.1 *superiority*

pre-eminence 126.1 *superiority*, 154.2 *priority*, 194.2 *greater importance*, 611.1 *importance*, 617.6 *worth*

preeminent 688.12 *authoritative*

pre-eminent 126.14 *best*, 154.12 *primary*, 611.5 *important*

pre-eminently 154.23 *primarily*, 611.9 *importantly*

pre-empt 42.10 *play*, 147.7 *exclude*, 154.16 *take precedence*, 193.3 *mistime*, 194.9 *do before*, 208.7 *be early*, 208.9 *prepare*, 737.3 *bargain*, 738.1 *purchase*

pre-empted 147.11 *excluded*

pre-emption 147.1 *exclusion*, 154.1 *precedence*, 193.1 *wrong time*, 208.5 *prematurity*, 723.2 *legal terms*, 738.7 *purchasing*

pre-emptive 17.8 *military*, 147.10 *excluding*, 154.10 *preceding*, 193.5 *too early*, 208.16 *premature*, 738.14 *buying*

pre-emptive bid 42.3 *card game terms*

pre-emptively 17.11 *militarily*, 154.23 *primarily*, 193.7 *out of chronological order*, 738.17 *acquisitively*

pre-emptive strike 670.12 *military attack*

pre-emptor 738.12 *purchaser*

preen 78.26 *nest*

preen oneself 805.29 *feel pride*, 809.16 *show off*

pre-established 582.4 *deliberate*

pre-existence 194.1 *priority*

prefab 382.6 *construction*

prefabricate 43.18 *be an architect*, 194.9 *do before*, 243.10 *produce*

prefabricated 594.21 *ready-made*

prefabrication 382.6 *construction*

preface 154, 130.6 *add*, 156.10 *introduction*, 194.7 *foretaste*, 194.9 *do before*, 303.1 *front*, 303.10 *be in front*

prefatorial 154.13 *precursory*

prefatory 154.13 *precursory*, 156.36 *introductory*

prefect 653.16 *official*

prefecture 92.3 *other*, 688.5 *position of authority*

prefer 580, 784, 481.12 *discriminate*, 662.28 *further*, 782.12 *desire*

preferability 580.7 *preference*

preferable 580.15 *chosen*, 617.1 *worthy*

preferably 580.17 *selectively*

prefer charges 16.70 *litigate*

preference 580, 154.2 *priority*, 411.2 *taste of life*, 570.1 *will*,

782.1 *desire*, 784.2 *inclination*, 821.7 *choice*, 821.11 *loved one*

preferential 284.9 *supportive*, 481.10 *discriminatory*, 493.8 *unjust*, 580.14 *selecting*

preferentially 481.17 *prejudicially*, 493.14 *unjustly*, 580.17 *selectively*

preferential treatment 284.6 *moral support*, 481.5 *favouritism*, 493.3 *injustice*

preferment 7.9 *priesthood*, 336.12 *advance*, 662.8 *furtherance*

prefer not to 785.5 *dislike*

preferred 126.12 *superior*, 580.15 *chosen*, 821.21 *beloved*

preferring 784.6 *liking*

prefer soft drinks 873.3 *be sober*

prefiguration 517.1 *prediction*

prefigure 517.11 *predict*

prefigurement 517.1 *prediction*, 517.5 *omen*

prefiguring 517.13 *predicting*

prefix 154, 5.35 *part of speech*, 130.3 *additional item*, 130.6 *add*, 135.10 *link*, 303.1 *front*, 303.10 *be in front*

prefixation 154.7 *prefix*

prefixed 130.8 *additional*, 156.36 *introductory*

prefixion 130.1 *addition*, 154.7 *prefix*

prefrontal leucotomy 61.3 *psychiatric treatment*

preggers 245.16 *reproductive*

preglacial 202.15 *primal*

pregnability 633.7 *vulnerability*

pregnable 236.11 *unprotected*, 633.3 *vulnerable*

pregnancy 144.2 *fullness*, 156.4 *conception*, 245.3 *propagation*, 316.2 *bulge*, 396.4 *biological function*

pregnancy test 60.7 *diagnosis*

pregnant 156.32 *embryonic*, 245.16 *reproductive*, 246.5 *fertile*, 513.6 *expectant*, 611.5 *important*

pregnant moment 210.3 *critical time*

pregnant with doom 517.15 *presageful*

pregnant with meaning 520.6 *meaningful*

pregnant woman 245.7 *obstetrics*

preheated 408.13 *heated*

prehensile 726.9 *retentive*

prehensility 726.1 *retention*

prehension 726.1 *retention*

prehistoric 3.15 *historic*, 200.17 *past*, 202.15 *primal*

prehistoric age 200

prehistorical 3.16 *historical*, 200.17 *past*

prehistorically 3.24 *historically*

prehistoric animal 202

prehistoric anthropologist 200.11 *antiquarian*

prehistoric anthropology 1.2 *palaeoanthropology*, 200.9 *antiquarianism*

prehistoric archaeologist 200.11 *antiquarian*

prehistoric archaeology 3.2 *archaeology*, 200.9 *antiquarianism*

prehistoric man 202.7 *ancient people*

prehistoric people 200.6 *people of the past*

prehistoric tool 603

prehistory 3.10 *past age*, 200.1 *past time*

prejudge 481, 493.11 *be unjust*

prejudged 493.8 *unjust*

prejudgment 493, 481.3 *prejudice*

prejudice 481, 805, 123.2 *injustice*, 228.10 *manipulate*, 233.8 *influence*, 234.2 *attitude*, 436.7 *figurative blindness*, 481.13 *prejudge*, 493.3 *injustice*, 493.12 *bias*, 504.6 *fallibility*, 577.7 *opinionatedness*, 580.7 *preference*, 784.2 *inclination*, 785.1 *dislike*, 819.1 *friendship*, 820.1 *enmity*, 822.3 *race hatred*,

844.1 *unfairness*, 858.1 *improbity*

prejudiced 805, 123.4 *unjust*, 234.5 *tending to*, 481.10 *discriminatory*, 493.8 *unjust*, 504.17 *mistaken*, 784.6 *liking*, 820.7 *intolerant*, 822.11 *racist*, 844.11 *wrong*, 858.5 *dishonourable*

prejudiced against 785.8 *disliking*

prejudices 471.5 *ideology*

prejudicial 234.5 *tending to*, 481.10 *discriminatory*, 493.8 *unjust*, 618.5 *harmful*, 862.7 *evil*

prejudicially 481, 123.8 *unjustly*, 234.6 *probably*, 862.12 *evilly*

prejudicial treatment 493.3 *injustice*

prelapsarian 202.15 *primal*, 865.5 *innocent*, 865.7 *naive*

prelapsarian innocence 865.3 *naivety*

prelate 7.8 *priest*

prelatic 7.17 *priestly*

prelature 7.9 *priesthood*

preliminaries 154.5 *preface*, 156.10 *introduction*, 303.1 *front*, 594.10 *preparations*

preliminarily 375.15 *incompletely*, 594.23 *preparatorily*

preliminary 154.13 *precursory*, 156.36 *introductory*, 375.5 *unfinished*, 594.16 *preparatory*

preliminary course 594.10 *preparations*

preliminary race 21.1 *track events*

preliminary sketch 375.10 *rough idea*

preliminary step 594.10 *preparations*

preliminary swing 21.2 *field events*

preliminary warning 517.3 *plan*

prelims 154.5 *preface*, 156.10 *introduction*, 303.1 *front*

prelude 49.4 *opera*, 154.5 *preface*, 156.10 *introduction*, 194.7 *foretaste*, 303.10 *be in front*

preludial 156.36 *introductory*

premarital 823.20 *matrimonial*

premature 208, 211.10 *untimely*, 595.5 *immature*

premature baby 208.4 *early comer*

premature baldness 296.5 *baldness*

prematurely 208, 211.15 *at the wrong time*, 595.16 *immaturely*

prematureness 208.5 *prematurity*

prematurity 208, 211.1 *untimeliness*, 595.10 *immaturity*

premed 60.9 *surgery*

premedication 60.9 *surgery*, 62.3 *drug*

premeditate 582, 588.8 *resolve*

premeditated 582.4 *deliberate*, 588.12 *intended*, 592.14 *planned*

premeditated murder 398.2 *murder*

premeditation 582, 516.4 *prudence*, 588.2 *intentionality*, 594.9 *preparation*

pre-menstrual syndrome 61.12 *stress*

premier 12.7 *governor*, 126.5 *superior*, 233.5 *influential person*, 653.13 *director*, 688.10 *person of authority*, 692.6 *person in command*, 696.3 *leader*

premiere 156, 51.11 *theatrical performance*, 51.36 *dramatize*, 201.4 *beginning*, 201.13 *inaugurated*, 201.19 *begin*, 457.1 *appearance*

premiered 156.37 *enrolled*, 201.13 *inaugurated*

premiere performance 51.11 *theatrical performance*

premiership 126.2 *leadership*, 653.4 *directorship*, 688.5 *position of authority*

premise 463, 4.1 *philosophy*, 4.22 *propound a philosophy*, 52.63 *mathematical logic*, 52.64

reasoning, 52.65 *theory*, 56.6 *law*, 310.5 *viewpoint*, 461.6 *idea*, 461.16 *have an idea*, 463.4 *explanation*, 473.3 *line of argument*, 497.1 *belief*, 518.1 *supposition*, 518.5 *suppose*
premised 518.8 *supposed*
premises 483.1 *evidence*, 602.4 *financial resources*
premium 68.2 *Common Agricultural Policy* , 745.4 *interest*, 746.1 *payment*, 749.2 *money received*, 751.2 *value*, 878.7 *bounty*
premium bond 589.3 *equal chance*, 741.14 *paper money*
premium gas 395.9 *petroleum*
Premium Savings Bond 741.14 *paper money*
premolar 380.11 *tooth*
premonition 11.8 *psychic power*, 11.9 *divination*, 11.10 *psychic phenomenon*, 154.6 *preview*, 199.4 *looking to the future*, 516.3 *foresight*, 517.1 *prediction*, 636.1 *warning*
premonition of disaster 636.1 *warning*
premonitory 11.17 *divinatory*, 517.13 *predicting*, 636.8 *warning*
Premonstratensian 7 Members of Religious Orders
prenatal clinic 60.10 *hospital*
prenatal diagnosis 60.7 *diagnosis*
prenylamine 62 Medication
preoccupation 61.13 *depression*, 467.4 *diligence*, 588.3 *future intention*, 695.1 *compulsion*
preoccupied 4.17 *thoughtful*, 467.8 *diligent*, 512.8 *oblivious*
preordain 571, 582.1 *predetermine*
preordained 571.12 *inevitable*, 582.3 *predetermined*
preordination 582.5 *predetermination*
pre-owned 599.9 *used*
prep 60.20 *practise surgery*
prepaid 746.19 *receiving pay*
preparation 154, 594, 6.1 *education*, 62.3 *drug*, 156.7 *rudiments*, 199.4 *looking to the future*, 208.5 *prematurity*, 243.1 *production*, 434.4 *atonality*, 469.3 *circumspection*, 516.4 *prudence*, 582.6 *premeditation*, 606.1 *provision*, 630.2 *medicine*, 644.5 *exercise*
Preparation 594
preparations 594, 152.11 *arrangements*
preparative 594.16 *preparatory*
preparatively 594.23 *preparatorily*
preparatorily 594, 154.22 *in anticipation*, 208.20 *prematurely*
preparatory 154, 594, 156.36 *introductory*, 208.16 *premature*
preparatory school 6.12 *educational institution*
preparatory work 594.10 *preparations*
prepare 208, 594, 6.22 *educate*, 152.18 *make arrangements*, 234.4 *tend*, 382.14 *structure*, 469.10 *be careful*, 516.2 *show prudence*, 592.12 *plan ahead*, 602.6 *find means*, 605.5 *provision*, 636.5 *warn*, 644.9 *exercise*
prepare a balance sheet 750.7 *account*
prepare a brief 16.70 *litigate*
prepare a budget 750.7 *account*
prepare a case 16.70 *litigate*
prepare a cash-flow forecast 750.7 *account*
prepare a meal 45.55 *cook*
prepare a statement 750.9 *settle accounts*
prepare beforehand 194.9 *do before*
prepared 594, 45.56 *culinary*, 207.11 *adult*, 234.5 *tending to*, 469.9 *careful*, 485.9 *qualified*, 513.5 *expecting*, 572.1 *willing*, 592.14 *planned*, 606.8 *provi-*

sional, 636.9 *warned*, 671.30 *defended*
prepared for immediate use 191
preparedly 207.16 *maturely*
preparedness 594, 207.3 *maturity*, 234.2 *attitude*, 485.1 *qualification*
prepared speech 567.1 *address*
prepared text 535.2 *statement*
prepare for 199.10 *expect*, 588.7 *intend*, 594.3 *be prepared*
prepare for action 594
prepare for a rainy day 594.3 *be prepared*, 605.6 *store*
prepare for blastoff 594.4 *prepare for action*
prepare for burial 399.8 *bury*
prepare for publication 532.15 *publish*
prepare for surgery 60.20 *practise surgery*
prepare for takeoff 594.4 *prepare for action*
prepare for the future 516.2 *show prudence*
prepare for use 599.1 *use*
prepare for war 676.12 *go to war*
prepare oneself 594, 605.6 *store*
prepare oneself 597.1 *undertake*
preparer 594, 516.5 *predictor*
prepare the ground 594.2 *do the groundwork*
prepare the way 660.16 *make easy*
prepare to dive 594.4 *prepare for action*
preparing 152.11 *arrangements*, 594.9 *preparation*, 594.16 *preparatory*
prepatella bursitis 624.16 *rheumatism*
prep book 6.14 *school book*
prepense 582.4 *deliberate*
preplanned 582.4 *deliberate*
preponderance 123.1 *inequality*, 126.1 *superiority*, 175.3 *majority*
preponderant 126.14 *best*
preponderantly 126.16 *superiorly*
preponderate 123.5 *be unequal*
preposition 5.35 *part of speech*
prepositional 5.44 *grammatical*
prepositionally 5.52 *grammatically*
prepositional phrase 5.23 *phrase*
prepositive 156.36 *introductory*
preposterous 487.1 *impossible*, 506.5 *nonsensical*, 508.5 *foolish*, 519.11 *fantastical*, 757.2 *unrestrained*, 798.5 *ridiculous*
preposterously 506.9 *nonsensically*
prepotence 126.1 *superiority*
prepotency 126.1 *superiority*
pre-prandial 45.56 *culinary*
prep school 6.12 *educational institution*
prepublication 517.3 *plan*
preputial gland 352 Exocrine Glands
prequel 194.7 *foretaste*
Pre-Raphaelite Brotherhood 50 Schools and Groups of Artists
Pre-Raphaelitism 48 Literary Groups and Movements, **50** Western Art Styles and Movements
prerelease 194.7 *foretaste*
prerequisite 103.5 *essential*, 485.7 *condition*, 571.1 *necessity*, 593.1 *requirement*, 593.4 *required*, 695.1 *compulsion*, 695.10 *compulsory*
prerogative 845, 126.1 *superiority*, 154.2 *priority*, 194.4 *claim to priority*, 688.1 *authority*, 698.1 *freedom*, 843.6 *right*
preromanticism 48 Literary Groups and Movements
presage 154.19 *forecast*, 194.7 *foretaste*, 199.9 *look ahead*, 516.1 *foresee*, 517.1 *prediction*, 517.5 *omen*, 517.11 *predict*, 520.12 *intend*
presageful 517, 543.14 *signifying*, 636.8 *warning*
presbyopia 436.2 *poor sight*
presbyopic 436.9 *weak-sighted*

presbyteral 7.17 *priestly*
Presbyterian 7.5 *Christian*
Presbyterianism 7 Christian Movements
presbytery 7.10 *priestly dwelling*, 10.12 *church*
pre-school 206.11 *young*
pre-school education 6.2 *educational system*
pre-school playgroup 6.12 *educational institution*
prescience 199.4 *looking to the future*, 516.3 *foresight*
prescient 8.13 *divine*, 516.6 *foreseeing*, 517.13 *predicting*
prescribe 60.19 *practise medicine*, 166.13 *rule*, 485.16 *specify*, 630.20 *doctor*, 653.1 *manage*, 654.5 *advise*, 692.9 *command*
prescribed 30.11 *gymnastic*, 485.12 *conditional*
prescribed diet 871.1 *fasting*
prescribed exercise 30.1 *gymnastics*
prescribed form 10.1 *ritual*, 813.5 *etiquette*
prescribed punishment 879.8 *penalty*
prescribed remedy 630.1 *remedy*
prescribe medication 629.6 *cure*
prescriber 654.4 *adviser*
prescript 654.3 *precept*, 692.1 *command*
prescription 62, 60.8 *treatment*, 166.1 *rule*, 166.4 *guide*, 485.6 *specification*, 584.5 *tradition*, 630.1 *remedy*, 630.2 *medicine*, 654.1 *advice*, 654.3 *precept*, 692.1 *command*, 723.2 *legal terms*
prescription drug 62.3 *drug*
prescriptive 4.13 *of philosophy*, 124.1 *average*, 166.9 *legal*, 485.12 *conditional*, 654.7 *advising*, 692.14 *commanding*
prescriptively 485.18 *with qualification*, 692.16 *commandingly*
prescriptive right 225.4 *stable thing*
preselect 580.4 *pick*
presence 253, 11.11 *ghost*, 99.1 *existence*, 101.1 *reality*, 146.1 *inclusion*, 163.9 *distinction*, 253.6 *ghostly presence*, 344.10 *arrival*, 437.3 *visibility*, 457.2 *being in view*, 652.2 *good conduct*, 692.5 *self-assurance*
Presence 253
presenile dementia 510.3 *mental deterioration*
present 196, 253, 457, 5.3a *tense*, 51.36 *dramatize*, 99.10 *existing*, 116.9, 116.30 *grant*, 156.23 *inaugurate*, 243.10 *produce*, 332.6 *direct*, 437.1 *visible*, 457.7 *appearing*, 472.6 *topical*, 526.1 *display*, 547.9 *represent*, 547.10 *act*, 549.9 *style*, 606.5 *provision*, 710.6 *offering*, 710.11 *volunteer*, 729.2 *gift*, 729.5 *give*, 811.27 *show*, 812.19 *install*, 819.15 *be hospitable*, 878.9 *reward*
present a bold front 668.5 *defy*
present a brave face 668.5 *defy*
present a false air 540.24 *mask*
present age 198.2 *present time*
present an account 750.9 *settle accounts*
present and correct 196.8 *available*
present a puzzle 523.7 *be unintelligible*
present arms 817.12 *greet*, 849.20 *salute*
presentation 51.11 *theatrical performance*, 156.9 *premiere*, 163.7 *lecture*, 457.1 *appearance*, 475.1 *demonstration*, 526.6 *display*, 526.9 *production*, 547.1 *representation*, 567.1 *address*, 710.2 *tentative offer*, 729.1 *giving*, 729.2 *gift*, 815.5 *party*, 817.3 *courtesies*
present day 198.2 *present time*

present difficulties 659.17 *be difficult*
presented 116.19 *granted*, 156.37 *enrolled*, 526.13 *displayed*
presenter 51.22 *actor*, 51.27 *entertainer*, 475.7 *demonstrator*, 526.12 *displayer*, 534.29 *broadcaster*, 564.10 *speaker*, 646.1 *worker*, 729.4 *giver*
presentient 464.7 *precognitive*, 517.13 *predicting*
presentiment 194.7 *foretaste*, 464.2 *precognition*, 516.3 *foresight*, 517.1 *prediction*, 759.2 *impression*
presenting arms 849
present itself 457.12 *become visible*
presently 99.23 *now*, 196.9 *at present*, 208.18 *soon*
presentment 51.11 *theatrical performance*, 116.9 *grant*, 475.1 *demonstration*, 547.1 *representation*, 729.1 *giving*
present moment 198.2 *present time*
present no difficulties 660.15 *be easy*
present oneself 253.12 *attend*
present participle 5.35 *part of speech*
present problems 659.17 *be difficult*
present tense 196.3 *actuality*
present the facts 537.30 *prove true*
present the main points 299.5 *outline*
present throughout 253.7 *present*
present time 196, 198
Present Time 196
present with an ultimatum 692.10 *demand*
preservation 637, 136.2 *setting apart*, 217.1 *permanence*, 219.1 *continuity*, 605.4 *storage*, 671.1 *defence*, 726.2 *detention*
Preservation 637
preservationism 453.16 *green politics*
preservationist 637
preservation order 637.2 *preserver*
preservative 350.11 *food content*, 637.2 *preserver*, 637.6 *preserving*
preservatively 637
preserve 45, 637, 136.10 *set apart*, 186.4 *perpetuate*, 217.6 *make permanent*, 219.3 *continue*, 392.21 *dry up*, 414.2 *sweetener*, 605.6 *store*, 625.6 *make hygienic*, 632.9 *protect*, 726.7 *detain*
preserve a balance 333.7 *be halfway*
preserved 637, 217.7 *permanent*, 600.1 *unused*, 605.7 *stored*, 632.5 *safe*, 726.10 *retained*
preserved fish 80.8 *food fish*
preserved thing 637
preserve for posterity 545.13 *record*
preserve one's dignity 805.31 *save face*
preserve one's honour 805.31 *save face*, 857.6 *be honourable*
preserve one's reputation 805.31 *save face*
preserver 637, 632.3 *protector*, 632.4 *safety device*
preserves 637.3 *preserved thing*
preserving 637, 632.7 *tutelary*, 671.1 *defence*
preserving pan 45.6 *kitchen equipment*
preset 582.2 *premeditate*, 582.4 *deliberate*
preset tuning 534.18 *radio*, 534.22 *television set*
preshrink 67.15 *treat*, 262.5 *make smaller*
preshrinkage 262.1 *contraction*
preshrinking 67.8 *fabric treatment*, 262.1 *contraction*
preshrunk 67.11 *treated*, 262.7 *smaller*

preside 16.76 *judge*, 242.4 *moderate*, 653.2 *direct*, 815.11 *be sociable*
presidency 12.3 *governance*, 126.2 *leadership*, 688.5 *position of authority*
president 12.7 *governor*, 126.5 *superior*, 233.5 *influential person*, 653.13 *director*, 688.10 *person of authority*, 692.6 *person in command*, 696.3 *leader*
president-elect 580.13 *electorate*
presidential 12.9 *governmental*, 256.16 *manorial*, 653.17 *managerial*, 688.14 *governmental*
presidentially 12.14 *politically*, 688.24 *ministerially*
presidential palace 256.4 *official residence*
preside over 166.16 *direct*, 688.18 *have authority*
presidium 653.7 *council*
pre-Socratic philosophy 4.7 *school of thought*
press 407, 23.6 *play basketball*, 47.5 *cabinet*, 114.3 *copier*, 161.21 *scrum*, 167.9 *make conform*, 181.4 *throng*, 181.11 *crowd*, 228.10 *manipulate*, 262.4 *contractor*, 262.5 *make smaller*, 274.16 *make thin*, 282.4 *flattener*, 282.7 *make horizontal*, 317.7 *make concave*, 330.1 *impel*, 330.13 *blow*, 355.9 *extractor*, 355.17 *obtain an extract*, 362.5 *bear down on*, 376.9 *smoother*, 376.11, 383.13 *smooth*, 407.11 *touch*, 533.5 *mass communication*, 574.10 *insist*, 642.6 *business*, 648.1 *hasten*, 654.5 *advise*, 695.6 *compel*, 826.7 *show endearment for*, 879.4 *torture*
press a claim 712.7 *demand*
press agency 533
press agent 51.25 *producer*, 228.7 *motivator*, 524.7 *news interpreter*, 526.12 *displayer*, 528.9 *informant*, 532.10 *publicizer*, 533.4 *journalist*, 678.4 *representative*
press announcement 532.8 *public relations*, 535.2 *statement*
Press Association 528.8 *source of information*, 533.7 *press agency*
press baron 532.11 *newspaper man*
press box 19.4 *stadium*
press charges 16.70 *litigate*
press conference 526.10 *manifestation*, 528.4 *mass communication*, 532.8 *public relations* , 533.2 *news event*
press cutting 545.1 *record*
press drill 63.9 *machine tool*
pressed 181.10 *crowded*, 262.7 *smaller*, 274.5 *thinned*, 282.9 *flattened*, 242.3 *insolvent*
pressed duck 45.45 *French dish*
pressed flower 84.1 *flower*
pressed for time 648.3 *hasty*
pressed man 679.8 *soldier*, 679.27 *naval man*
press forward 336.3 *press on*
press gang 695.3 *coercive methods*
pressgang 695.7 *force*
press home 554.6 *emphasize*
press in 346.12 *flood in*, 354.3 *impact*
pressing 237.10 *potent*, 262.1 *contraction*, 330.13 *blow*, 355.7 *obtaining an extract*, 369.3 *ponderous*, 545.7 *recording*, 574.2 *tenacious*, 593.6 *demanding*, 695.9 *compelling*
pressing defence 23.4 *playing terms*
pressing one's suit 821.6, 826.2 *courtship*
press into service 599.4 *resort to*
press inwards 317.7 *make concave*
press laws 699.1 *restraint*
press notice 533.9 *news story*
press of business 642.6 *business*
press office 528.8 *source of infor-*

mation, 532.8 *public relations* , 533.8 *newsroom*
press officer 51.25 *producer*, 524.7 *news interpreter*, 533.4 *journalist*
press of sail 329.8 *speed*
press on 336, 330.1 *impel*, 362.5 *bear down on*, 590.13 *follow up*
press one's suit 821.26, 826.8 *court*
pressor 62.4 *drug type*
press photographer 532.11 *newspaper man*, 545.9 *recorder*
press release 528.4 *mass communication*, 532.8 *public relations* , 533.9 *news story*
press room 533.8 *newsroom*
press secretary 533.4 *journalist*
press service 528.8 *source of information*
press stud 137.8 *fastening*
press the button 230.8 *activate*, 676.13 *be at war*
press the emergency button 636.7 *raise the alarm*
press to one's bosom 821.27 *kiss*, 826.7 *show endearment for*
press upon 369.13 *weigh on*
pressure 41.12 *ski*, 56.10 *force*, 56.38 *thermodynamics*, 228.2 *inducement*, 232.1 *instrumentality*, 232.4 *be an instrument*, 233 *influence*, 235.4 *energy*, 237.3 *intensity*, 262.1 *contraction*, 330.13 *blow*, 369.8 *weighing down*, 388.7 *gaseousness*, 574.14 *tenacity*, 586.1 *persuasion*, 586.15 *persuade*, 631.4 *strain*, 640.1 *action*, 644.4 *exertion*, 648.4 *haste*, 687.1 *adversity*, 688.1 *authority*, 688.18 *have authority*, 695.2 *coercion*, 695.6 *compel*, 699.1 *restraint*, 699.8 *restrain*, 712.1, 712.6 *request*
pressure cabin 73 *Aircraft Parts*
pressure-cook 45.55 *cook*
pressure cooker 45.6 *kitchen equipment*
pressure cooking 45.1 *cookery*
pressured 228.12 *motivated*, 586.20 *persuadable*
pressure gauge 56.88 *barometer*, 268.8 *meter*, 388.15 *vaporimeter*
pressure gradient 55.6 *weather data*
pressure group 140.3 *assembly*, 228.7 *motivator*, 233.6 *group influence*, 586.14 *motivator*
pressure of deadlines 642.6 *business*
pressure of work 642.6 *business*
pressure system 55.11 *weather system*
pressure tendency 55.6 *weather data*
pressure turn 41.4 *skiing technique*
pressuring 232.7 *causal*
pressurize 233.8 *influence*, 631.14 *afflict*
pressurized 369.3 *ponderous*, 699.13 *restraining*
pressurized water reactor 235.8 *nuclear power*
pressurized-water reactor 56.73 *nuclear reactor*, 410.7 *nuclear power*
Prestel 534.25 *broadcast material*
prestidigitation 539.9 *sleight of hand*
prestidigitator 51.27 *entertainer*
prestige 805, 27.9 *social stratification*, 126.1 *superiority*, 163.9 *distinction*, 233.3 *personal influence*, 318.1 *prominence*, 611.1 *importance*, 686.1 *prosperity*, 744.7 *repute*, 800.1 *estimation*, 849.1 *respect*, 851.2 *admiration*
prestigious 805, 126.15 *excellent*, 233.11 *influential*, 611.6 *notable*, 811.17 *lofty*, 849.12 *respected*
prestigiously 126.16 *superiorly*, 233.14 *influentially*, 811.33 *loftily*

prestissimo 329.14 *swiftly*
presto 329.14 *swiftly*, 648.3 *hasty*
Preston 93 *Cities*
prestressed 63.32 *structural*
prestressed concrete 43.4 *building material*, 63.25 *construction material*, 604.2 *building material*
presumable 488.6 *probable*, 518.8 *supposed*
presumably 488.11 *probably*
presume 846, 4.22 *propound a philosophy*, 471.17 *theorize*, 488.10 *think likely*, 497.8 *be of the opinion*, 513.9 *predict*, 516.1 *foresee*, 518.5 *suppose*, 668.5 *defy*, 698.19 *liberalize*, 775.6 *hope*, 807.22 *be rude*, 807.23 *be proud*, 807.27 *dare*, 807.28 *get above oneself*
presumed 106.7 *circumstantial*, 471.10 *theoretical*, 488.6 *probable*, 518.8 *supposed*
presume on 599.4 *resort to*
presumingly 4.25 *theoretically*
presumption 471.1 *idea*, 488.1 *probability*, 513.1 *expectation*, 518.1 *supposition*, 668.1 *defiance*, 775.2 *expectation*, 780.1 *rashness*, 807.5 *bravado*, 846.3 *arrogation*
presumptuousness 807.3 *audacity*
presumptive 846, 488.6 *probable*, 518.7 *suppositional*
presumptively 4.25 *theoretically*
presumptuous 668.7 *defiant*, 807.16 *arrogant*, 846.9 *presumptive*
presumptuously 668.9 *defiantly*, 807.33 *arrogantly*, 846.18 *unduly*
presumptuousness 846
presuppose 52.89 *theorize*, 518.5 *suppose*
presupposition 4.1 *philosophy*, 52.65 *theory*, 493.4 *prejudgment*, 518.1 *supposition*
presurmise 518.5 *suppose*
pre-tax profit 878.5 *turnover*
preteens 206.1 *youth*
pretence 538, 540, 457.4 *something that appears*, 474.5 *hypocrisy*, 518.1 *supposition*, 539.3 *hypocrisy*, 640.2 *deed*, 797.1 *affectedness*
pretend 538, 540, 102.12 *not the real thing*, 117.12 *be disparate*, 474.12 *deceive*, 518.5 *suppose*, 519.12 *imaginary*, 519.14 *imagine*, 538.18 *pretentious*, 539.26 *be a hypocrite*, 640.4 *act*, 797.4 *be affected*
pretended 102.12 *not the real thing*, 474.10 *hypocritical*, 518.8 *supposed*
pretender 797, 117.6 *misfit*, 538.12 *cheat*, 539.15 *deceiver*, 540.15 *false person*, 846.7 *usurper*
pretending 540, 117.11 *unfit*, 518.1 *supposition*, 538.8 *pretence*, 538.18 *pretentious*, 538.19 *dishonest*, 539.37 *hypocritical*, 540.7 *pretence*
pretend it never happened 677.5 *make peace*
pretend not to see 641.4 *not act*
pretend to be 547.9 *represent*
pretension 538.8, 540.7 *pretence*, 557.2 *affectation*, 656.8 *unskilfulness*, 797.1 *affectedness*, 805.3 *conceit*, 811.1 *showiness*
pretentious 538, 5.42 *worded*, 357.13 *exaggerated*, 540.30 *pretending*, 553.3 *diffuse*, 557.4 *ornate*, 656.2 *unskilled*, 797.3 *affected*, 809.11 *cocky*, 809.13 *boastful*, 811.16 *showy*
pretentiously 538, 5.50 *lexically*, 557.6 *ornately*, 809.21 *cockily*, 811.32 *showily*
pretentiousness 557.2 *affectation*, 797.1 *affectedness*, 811.1 *showiness*
preternatural 11.14 *occult*
preternaturalism 11.1 *occultism*
pretext 226.5 *reason*, 228.1 *mo-*

tive, 463.4 *explanation*, 473.3 *line of argument*, 538.8, 540.7 *pretence*, 657.2 *stratagem*
Pretoria 93 *Cities*, 93.6 *other cities*
prettify 457.14 *present*, 789.8 *beautify*
prettily 791.15 *beautify*
prettiness 789.1 *gorgeousness*
pretty 121.11 *to a degree*, 242.9 *moderately*, 789.3 *attractive female*, 789.5 *beautiful*
pretty boy 401.9 *offensive terms for homosexual*
pretty good 617.5 *not bad*, 623.1 *healthy*
pretty much the same 114.7 *similar*
pretty name 826.1 *endearment*
pretty names 821.14 *communication of love*
pretty pass 106.4 *difficult circumstances*, 659.5 *predicament*
pretty penny 753.1 *high price*
pretty pickle 659.5 *predicament*
pretty-pretty 792.8 *decorated*
pretty printing 65.7 *peripheral*
pretzels 45.10 *snack*
prevail 164, 99.19 *continue to be*, 124.9 *be average*, 126.8 *be superior*, 166.15 *be the rule*, 212.7 *be frequent*, 233.10 *be a prevailing influence*, 235.10 *be powerful*, 584.17 *become a habit*, 682.7 *overcome obstacles*, 682.9 *be victorious*
prevailing 164, 55.47 *windy*, 124.1 *average*, 126.14 *best*, 233.13 *dominant*, 235.13 *powerful*
prevailingly 124.11 *on average*, 235.18 *powerfully*
prevailing wind 55.15 *wind direction*
prevail over 701.7 *defeat*
prevail upon 228.9 *motivate*, 228.10 *manipulate*, 473.16 *plead*, 586.15 *persuade*
prevalence 124.4 *average*, 212.4 *frequency*, 233 *influence*, 235.1 *power*
prevalent 99.10 *existing*, 124.1 *average*, 164.19 *prevailing*, 212.3 *frequent*, 233.13 *dominant*, 235.13 *powerful*, 584.10 *familiar*
prevalently 212.1 *frequently*, 235.18 *powerfully*
prevaricate 286.7 *deviate*, 474.13 *quibble*, 491.19 *hesitate*, 531.13 *equivocate*, 538.21 *lie*, 578.1 *be equivocal*, 591.7 *be evasive*, 858.8 *be dishonourable*
prevaricating 474.9 *quibbling*, 538.15 *lying*, 540.29 *deceitful*, 578.10 *equivocal*
prevarication 286.3 *deviousness*, 474.4 *quibbling*, 531.5 *evasion*, 538.1 *untruth*, 578.5 *equivocalness*, 591.15 *evasiveness*
prevaricator 474.6 *sophist*, 538.11, 539.16 *liar*
prevenience 208.5 *prematurity*
prevenient 208.16 *premature*
preveniently 208.20 *prematurely*
prevent 147.7 *exclude*, 208.9 *prepare*, 209.8 *delay*, 231.3 *counteract*, 587.3 *deflect*, 591.2 *avert*, 661.8 *hinder*, 663.18 *counteract*, 699.8 *restrain*, 709.3 *veto*
preventable 591.20 *avoidable*
preventably 591.22 *evasively*
preventative 231.1 *counteraction*, 231.4 *counteracting*, 630.3 *prophylactic*, 630.17 *remedial*, 637.6 *preserving*, 709.5 *vetoed*
prevent defence 19.10 *defence*
prevent disease 625.5 *by hygienic*
prevented 147.11 *excluded*
preventer 74 *Rigging*
prevent from falling 361.1 *raise*
prevention 147.1 *exclusion*, 209.3 *delayed action*, 231.1 *counteraction*, 591.10 *avoidance*, 661.1 *hindrance*, 663.4 *uncooperativeness*, 699.1 *restraint*, 709.1 *veto*

preventive 60.25 *therapeutic,* 147.10 *excluding,* 231.1 *counteraction,* 231.4 *counteracting,* 591.18 *avoiding,* 630.3 *prophylactic,* 630.17 *remedial,* 637.6 *preserving,* 661.13 *hindering,* 699.13 *restraining,* 709.5 *vetoed*
preventive action 592.2 *policy*
preventively 231.5 *counter,* 591.22 *evasively,* 637.8 *preservatively,* 661.16 *with delay,* 699.16 *under restraints,* 709.7 *by veto*
preventive measure 632.2 *protection*
preventive medicine 60.1 *medicine,* 60.6 *health care,* 625.1 *hygiene,* 630.11 *medical art,* 637.1 *preservation*
preview 154, 51.11 *theatrical performance,* 51.36 *dramatize,* 143.2 *particular,* 194.7 *foretaste,* 194.9 *do before,* 457.1 *appearance,* 517.3 *plan,* 526.9 *production*
Previn 49 Musicians and Composers
previous 154.11 *prior,* 193.5 *too early,* 194.10 *prior,* 202.13 *former,* 209.14 *dead*
previously 154.20 *before,* 197.3 *another time,* 202.20 *formerly*
previously owned 599.9 *used*
previousness 194.1 *priority*
prevision 435.4 *visualization,* 516.3 *foresight*
Prévost's theory of exchanges 56 Named Laws
prewar 202.12 *olden,* 675.7 *peaceful*
prey 37.5 *game,* 76.4 *type of animal,* 481.8 *victim of discrimination,* 493.6 *misjudged person,* 588.6 *objective,* 590.7 *the hunted,* 687.5 *person in adversity,* 722.6 *loser*
prey on 350.22 *eat well*
prey upon 618.14 *ill-treat,* 736.14 *plunder*
prial 42.3 *card game terms*
priapic 877.14 *lecherous*
priapism 877.3 *sexual immorality*
price 751, 751, 32.7 *horseracing,* 617.6 *worth,* 748.5 *expense*
Price 751
price charged 751.1 *price*
price control 699.2 *economic restraint,* 751.1 *price*
price controls 13.2 *economy*
price cut 131.2 *subtracted item,* 751.1 *price,* 754.1 *cheapness*
price cutting 131.1 *subtraction*
priced 751
price fall 754.2 *declining prices*
price fixing 699.2 *economic restraint*
price-fixing 751.3 *fee*
price freeze 302.2 *limiting factor,* 699.2 *economic restraint*
price increase 721.2 *augmentation*
price index 13.3 *economic statistics*
price itself out of the market 753.9 *be dear*
pricelessness 798.1 *ludicrousness*
priceless 613.4 *profitable,* 617.3, 753.8 *valuable,* 798.5 *ridiculous*
pricelessly 753.13 *valuably*
pricelessness 617.6 *worth,* 753.6 *value*
price list 171.4 *bill,* 751.1 *price*
price oneself out of the market 494.4 *overestimate*
price on one's head 16.43 *conviction*
price range 751.1 *price*
price reduction 752.1 *discount*
prices 13.3 *economic statistics*
prices going through the ceiling 753.3 *inflationary price*
price support 13.6 *economic factors,* 729.2 *gift*
price-wage spiral 13.6 *economic factors*
price war 751.1 *price*
pricey 753.7 *dear*

pricing 13.6 *economic factors*
prick 228.9 *motivate,* 245.8 *organs of reproduction,* 322.20 *hole,* 380.8 *sharp-pointed thing,* 380.14 *be sharp,* 401.2 *male,* 403.3 *stimulus,* 406.1 *pain,* 406.11 *inflict pain*
prick a punt 36.19 *punt*
pricked 322.14 *holed*
pricked by conscience 867.6 *penitent*
pricked up 281.9 *unbowed*
pricking 322.1 *opening,* 380.2 *spiked*
pricking of conscience 867.1 *penitence*
prickle 375.7 *rough thing,* 375.11 *be rough,* 380.8 *sharp-pointed thing,* 380.14 *be sharp,* 403.3 *stimulus,* 403.11 *sense*
prickliness 380.6 *sharpness,* 385.9 *irritation,* 403.2 *ability to sense,* 666.1 *disagreement,* 829.1 *irascibility*
prickly 375.3 *barbed,* 380.2 *spiked,* 403.9 *exciting,* 666.9 *disagreeing,* 805.15 *unapproachable,* 829.4 *irascible*
prickly ash 85 Trees and Shrubs
prickly heat 624.13 *skin disease*
prickly pear 84 Flowers and Flowering Plants, **86** Fruits
prickly poppy 84 Flowers and Flowering Plants
prick out 69.15 *cultivate*
prick up 281.6 *make vertical*
prick up one's ears 420.15 *hear,* 465.7 *be curious,* 467.11 *take note of*
pricky 380.2 *spiked*
pride 161 Collective Names for Birds and Animals, **805,** 77.21 *assemblage of mammals,* 526.7 *showpiece,* 807.4 *arrogance,* 809.6 *boastfulness,* 811.7 *pomp,* 813.1 *formality,* 861.17 *good thing,* 864.5 *seven deadly sins*
Pride 805
pride and joy 805.12 *object of pride,* 861.17 *good thing*
prideful 805.14 *proud,* 809.13 *boastful*
pridefully 805.32 *proudly*
pridefulness 805.1 *pride*
pride of place 126.1 *superiority,* 154.2 *priority,* 805.12 *object of pride*
prier 435.11 *observer,* 465.4 *meddler*
priest 7, 220.5 *converter,* 233.5 *influential person,* 399.3 *funeral director,* 654.4 *adviser,* 696.6 *religious leader,* 825.4 *celibate person,* 861.15 *good person,* 863.4 *virtuous person*
priestcraft 9.2 *idolatry*
priestess 7.8 *priest*
priest hole 634.1 *refuge*
priesthood 7
Priestley 52 Scientists
priestly 7, 825.8 *monastic*
priestly dwelling 7
priestly government 12.1 *government*
priest-ridden 7.15 *religious*
priests 777 Phobias by Topic
priest's cap 7.11 *vestment*
priestship 7.9 *priesthood*
prig 134.6 *prude,* 876.6 *moralist*
priggish 134.12 *morally pure,* 876.10 *moralistic*
priggishly 134.18 *virtuously*
priggishness 134.1 *purity,* 876.4 *self-righteousness*
prill 68.13 *fertilizer*
prim 134.12 *morally pure,* 167.14 *conformist,* 813.6 *formal,* 876.10 *moralistic*
prima ballerina 46.13 *ballet dancer,* 51.28 *dancer,* 619.4 *perfectionist,* 655.4 *skilled person*
prima donna 49.24 *musician,* 51.22 *actor,* 126.6 *paragon,*

611.4 *bigwig,* 655.4 *skilled person,* 805.13 *proud person*
prima facie 104.18 *extraneously,* 435.24 *visually,* 480.9 *verificatory,* 483.8 *evidential*
prima-facie evidence 483.5 *legal evidence*
primal 202, 3.15 *historic,* 156.31 *prime,* 194.10 *prior,* 200.17 *past,* 226.13 *causal*
primal therapy 61.3 *psychiatric treatment,* 630.13 *therapy*
primaquine 62 Medication
primarily 154, 103.13 *in essence,* 126.16 *superiorly,* 156.40 *first,* 156.42 *principally,* 202.21 *archaically,* 226.14 *causally,* 611.9 *importantly*
primary 154, 78.17 *plumage,* 103.6 *intrinsic,* 126.14 *best,* 156.29 *beginning,* 174.11 *one,* 226.13 *causal,* 291.8 *focal,* 318.6 *eminent,* 537.17 *truistic,* 580.12 *election,* 611.5 *important*
primary cell 56.43 *electrical conduction,* 64.5 *electrolytic conduction,* 64.29 *power source*
primary character 54.33 *metamorphic rock*
primary chord 49.16 *musical note*
primary clay 44.2 *raw material*
primary coil 64.22 *transformer*
primary colour 444.1 *colour*
primary colours 56.28 *colour*
primary consumer 59.18 *ecology*
primary education 6.2 *educational system*
primary election 580.12 *election*
primary evidence 483.5 *legal evidence*
primary group 2.6 *social group*
primary growth 624.12 *cancer*
primary health care 60.1 *medicine*
primary issue 194.3 *matter of priority*
primary memory 65.6 *memory*
primary mirror 53.25 *mounting*
primary premise 537.4 *truism*
primary producer 59.18 *ecology*
primary quality 4.9 *philosophical problem*
primary radar 534.28 *radar*
primary rainbow 55.27 *rainbow*
primary school 6.12 *educational institution*
primary source 291.5 *focus*
primary structure 58.9 *protein*
primary triads 444.1 *colour*
primary wave 54.23 *seismic wave*
primate 77, 77, 7.8 *priest,* 688.10 *person of authority*
Primates 77.16 *primate*
primatial 77.34 *primate*
primatologist 77.22 *mammologist*
primatology 77.16 *primate*
prime 156, 6.22 *educate,* 10.4 *public worship,* 52.74 *divisible,* 126.14 *best,* 169.8 *odd,* 204.1 *morning,* 338.32 *load,* 501.14 *cause to know,* 594.4 *prepare for action,* 611.5 *important,* 617.1 *worthy,* 617.7 *elite,* 686.3 *time of plenty*
prime a witness 582.2 *premeditate*
prime beef 401.4 *boyfriend*
prime condition 594.14 *preparedness*
prime cut 617.7 *elite*
primed 6.19 *knowledgeable,* 582.4 *deliberate,* 594.18 *prepared*
primed *au fait* 501.8 *knowledgeable*
primed witness 582.6 *premeditation*
prime factor 52.17 *multiplication*
prime lending rate 741.7 *finance*
prime matter 367.4 *matter*
prime meridian 249.2 *geographical region*
prime minister 12.7 *governor,* 126.5 *superior,* 233.5 *influential person,* 653.13 *director,* 688.10 *person of authority,* 692.6 *person in command,* 696.3 *leader*

prime ministership 126.2 *leadership*
prime mover 63.11 *engine,* 156.16 *originator,* 228.7 *motivator,* 243.9 *producer,* 586.14 *motivator*
Prime Mover 226, 8.3 *God*
prime number 52.5 *number,* 169.2 *kind of number*
prime of life 207.2 *adulthood*
primer 6.14 *school book,* 444.5 *paint*
prime rate 745.3 *loan*
primero 42 Card Games
prime-time programme 534.25 *broadcast material*
primeval 208, 156.31 *prime,* 200.17 *past,* 202.15 *primal*
primeval forest 85.4 *trees*
primeval humanity 400.3 *uncivilized human*
primevally 208, 202.21 *archaically*
primeval man 400.3 *uncivilized human*
primeval stage 208.3 *early stage*
primicarb 69.8 *weedkiller*
primidone 62 Medication
primigravida 245.7 *obstetrics*
priming 594.9 *preparation,* 680.15 *explosive*
primitive 50.29 *realist,* 156.31 *prime,* 200.17 *past,* 202.15 *primal,* 208.4 *early comer,* 208.14 *primeval,* 226.13 *causal,* 560.13 *representing,* 658.1 *naive,* 803.4 *common*
primitive art 50 Western Art Styles and Movements
primitive human 400.3 *uncivilized human*
primitive humanity 400.3 *uncivilized human*
primitively 50.30 *pictorially,* 202.21 *archaically,* 208.19 *primevally,* 226.14 *causally*
primitive man 202.7 *ancient people*
primitiveness 202.3 *antiquity,* 208.3 *early stage,* 658.2 *naivety*
primitive self 61.21 *psyche*
primitive society 400.9 *group*
primitive stage 208.3 *early stage*
primitivism 48 Literary Groups and Movements
primly 134.18 *virtuously,* 813.12 *formally*
primness 134.1 *purity,* 167.4 *conventionalism,* 813.1 *formality,* 876.4 *self-righteousness*
primogenitary 730.14 *receivable*
primogeniture 194.4 *claim to priority,* 730.1 *receiving*
primordial 3.15 *historic,* 59.26 *developmental,* 156.31 *prime,* 202.15 *primal,* 226.13 *causal*
primordial fireball 53.4 *cosmological model*
primordially 3.24 *historically,* 202.21 *archaically,* 226.14 *causally*
primordial soup 156.3 *source*
primordium 59.15 *developmental biology*
primp 295.33 *dress up,* 627.1 *improve,* 789.8, 791.15 *beautify*
primrose 84 Flowers and Flowering Plants, 452.8 *yellow thing*
primrose path 84.9 *figurative usage,* 327.2 *route,* 628.7 *deterioration*
primrose-yellow 452.1 *yellow*
primula 84 Flowers and Flowering Plants
prince 696.2 *sovereign*
Prince Albert 295.12 *coat*
Prince Edward Island 92 Canadian Provinces and Territories, **98** Islands
princeliness 805.6 *majesty*
princely 12.10 *governing,* 688.14 *governmental,* 755.1 *generous,* 802.4 *aristocratic,* 804.6 *worshipful,* 805.19 *stately,* 811.22 *majestic*
Prince of Darkness 8.7 *devil*
Prince of Peace 8.4 *God the Son*

Prince of Wales 98 Islands, 696.2 sovereign
Prince of Wales chequer 456.2 check
Prince Philip Cup 36.5 Henley trophies
prince regent 696.2 sovereign
princess 696.2 sovereign
Princess Elizabeth Cup 36.5 Henley trophies
princess-line 295.31 styled
Princeton 9 Cities
principal 6.4 educator, 126.5 superior, 126.14 best, 291.5 focus, 291.8 focal, 617.2 best, 653.13 director, 688.10 person of authority, 696.9 educational leader, 696.12 masterful
principal boy 51.21 role
principal character 51.21 role
principal girl 51.21 role
principalities and powers 696.8 the power structure
principality 8.6 angel, 12.5 political organization, 91.3 dominion, 249.4 territorial division, 688.8 governmental organization
principally 156, 126.16 superiorly
principal nursing officer 60.16 nurse
principal part 143.5 largest part
principate 91.3 dominion
principle 4.1 philosophy, 52.65 theory, 56.6 law, 103.2 essential content, 166.4 guide, 226.3 rudiment, 226.6 undertaking, 367.4 matter, 461.6 idea, 497.1 belief, 497.2 religious belief, 505.1 maxim, 537.4 truism, 654.3 precept
principle component analysis 52.55 statistical methods
principled 537.17 truistic, 847.8 dutiful, 857.4 honourable, 863.6 ethical, 876.8 moral
principles 4.2 philosophical system, 156.7 rudiments, 471.5 ideology, 652.6 way of life, 857.1 probity, 863.2 virtues, 876.1 morality
prink 295.33 dress up, 627.1 improve, 791.15 beautify
print 245, 5.13 letter, 50.7 picture, 50.22 engrave, 66.12 development, 66.21 photograph, 67.3 fabric, 110.4, 110.9 duplicate, 118.5 duplicate, 183.7 replica, 225.7 make visible, 227.2 visible effect, 227.6 have a visible effect, 245.9 reproduce, 532.15 publish, 545.12 vestige, 545.13 record, 547.2 reproduction, 547.9 represent, 547.11 paint, 741.24 monetize
printable 708.8 permitting, 876.10 moralistic
printable character 65.10 character
printed 5.41 lettered, 110.15 duplicate, 245.15 reproduced, 532.19 published, 545.16 recorded
printed circuit 64.13 circuit
printed circuit board 64.13 circuit
printer 50.18 engraver, 65.7 peripheral, 114.3 copier, 114.4 person who copies, 118.8 copier, 532.12 publisher
printer's ink 447.8 black pigment
printing 66.12 development, 67.7 dyeing, 245.1 reproduction, 545.8 registration
printing error 504.12 typing error
printing mark 543.7 punctuation
printing over 546.3 obliteration
print journalism 533.1 news
printmaker 547.1 person who makes a representation
print media 533.5 mass communication
print off 245.9 reproduce
printout 65.7 peripheral
print over 546.1 obliterate
prion 78 Birds
prior 154, 194, 3.15 historic, 7.7 monk, 202.13 former

prior conditions 593.1 requirement
prior consideration 517.1 prediction
prioress 7.7 monk
prioritization 150.1 order
prioritize 150.19 systematize, 154.17 give priority
priority 154, 194, 126.1 superiority, 554.1 emphasis, 611.1 importance, 611.3 chief thing
Priority 194
priority mail 534.2 postal communication
prior to 154.20, 194.11 before
priory 7.10 priestly dwelling
prism 52.46 polyhedron, 56.29 optical element, 66.17 lens, 310.3 angled figure, 436.5 visual distortion, 444.2 colourfulness, 456.5 variegated thing
prismatic 52.84 cubic, 310.9 angled, 444.10 coloured, 456.6 variegated
prismatoid 52.46 polyhedron
prismoid 52.46 polyhedron
prison 702, 63.20 building, 136.2 setting apart, 218.5 resting place, 290.2 inside, 301.2 enclosed place, 323.4 closed place, 688.6 place of authority, 816.4 place of confinement, 879.14 instrument of punishment
Prison 702
prison camp 702.1 prison, 816.4 place of confinement
prison cell 702, 218.5 resting place
prison clothes 544.5 uniform
prison colony 702.1 prison
prisoner 702, 323.6 closed-in person, 699.7 charge, 701.5 subjected person, 816.7 outsider, 856.4 accused person, 866.4 guilty person
prisoner at the bar 16.8 litigant
prisoner before the court 16.8 litigant
prisoner behind bars 702.5 prisoner
prisoner of conscience 702.5 prisoner
prisoner's broad arrow 544.3 means of identification
prison fare 871.2 short rations
prison farm 702.1 prison
prison governor 702.6 prison officer
prison guard 699.6 law-maker, 702.6 prison officer
prison house 879.14 instrument of punishment
prison inmate 866.4 guilty person
prison officer 702
prison sentence 702, 16.43 conviction, 879.7 punishment
prison term 16.7 legal trial
pristine 156.31 prime, 865.5 innocent
Pritchett 48 Writers
Prithivi 8 Deities, **8** Deities
privacy 531, 139.2 aloofness, 174.5 aloneness, 290.6 internalization, 438.4 invisibility, 523.11 unintelligibility, 527.8 concealment, 529.1 secrecy, 531.4 silence, 634.1 refuge, 816.1, 816.1 unsociability
private 438, 70.5 transportable, 127.6 inferior, 139.9 aloof, 147.10 excluding, 165.19 personal, 290.12 internalized, 523.1 unintelligible, 527.2 concealed, 529.9 secret, 531.14 concealed, 679.8 soldier, 679.17 army person, 737.19 corporate, 816.8 unsociable, 816.11 secluded
private automatic branch exchange 534.12 public telephone system
private box 534.3 correspondence
private branch exchange 534.12 public telephone system
private car 71.16 car
private caterer 606.4 caterer

private club 147.4 exclusiveness, 531.6 privacy
private company 737.7 company
private detective 16.17 police officer, 496.12 discoverer, 632.3 protector
private enterprise 13.1 economics, 13.6 economic factors, 737.5 commercial trade
private enterprise economy 13.1 economics
privateer 74.7 nautical person, 679.6 militarist, 679.25 historical naval ships, 736.9 plunderer
privateering 736.5 plundering, 736.17 stolen
private exchange 534.12 public telephone system
private eye 16.17 police officer, 496.12 discoverer, 632.3 protector
private garden 531.6 privacy
private hospital 60.10 hospital
private income 721.4 earnings, 749.3 income
private investigator 632.3 protector
private language 564.1 faculty of speech
private law 16.1 the law
privately 531, 139.11 aloofly, 165.29 personally, 529.15 in secret, 810.17 modestly, 816.14 unsocially
private manual branch exchange 534.12 public telephone system
private means 698.3 independence
private medicine 60.1 medicine
private meeting 529.1 secrecy
private nurse 60.16 nurse
private parts 143.4 component, 245.8 organs of reproduction
private police 16.17 police officer
private quarters 816.5 solitary place
private road 327.3 road
privates 143.4 component, 245.8 organs of reproduction
private sale 739.3 selling
private school 6.12 educational institution
private sector 13.1 economics, 13.2 economy, 737.5 commercial trade
private security company 718.4 security forces
private soldier 679.8 soldier
private space 634.1 refuge
private tuition 6.1 education
private tutor 6.4 educator
private world 816.1 unsociability
privation 571.4 need, 722.1 loss, 743.5 poverty
privatization 13.1 economics, 728.1 transfer of property, 737.5 commercial trade
privatize 13.10 trade with, 728.3 transfer property, 737.1 trade
privatized 13.13 economic, 737.19 corporate
privet 85 Trees and Shrubs
privilege 116.9, 116.30 grant, 126.1 superiority, 154.2 priority, 194.4 claim to priority, 698.1 freedom, 845.3 prerogative, 848.1 exemption, 848.4 licence, 848.9 exempt
privileged 2.14 socioeconomic, 116.19 granted, 698.9 free, 848.5 exempt
privileged class 2.7 social stratification, 742.11 the rich
privileged will 570.5 will
privvy member 245.8 organs of reproduction
privy 353.13 lavatory, 529.9 secret, 727.7 toilet
Privy Council 653.7 council
Privy Councillor's oath 531.4 silence
privy purse 721.4 earnings, 749.3 income
privy seal 544.3 means of identification
Prix des Nations 32.9 jumping
prize 878, 545.11 monument,

588.6 objective, 617.7 elite, 681.1 trophy, 721.5 profit, 729.2 gift, 730.2 something received, 734.5 takings, 736.4 stolen goods, 749.5 winnings, 751.2 value, 782.5 object of desire, 784.7 like, 804.3 honours, 821.23 love, 849.15 respect, 851.11 approve, 861.17 good thing
prize competition 674.2 contest
prized 617.3 valuable, 821.21 beloved, 849.12 respected
prizefight 26.2 boxing, 26.11 do a combat sport, 674.7 boxing
prizefighter 26.4 boxer, 674.10 contender, 679.3 athlete
prizefighting 26.2, 674.7 boxing
prize-giver 729.4 giver
prize-giving 729.1 giving
prize money 878.2 prize
prizewinner 126.6 paragon, 617.8 exceller, 655.4 skilled person, 682.5 victorious person, 730.5 recipient
prizewinning 682.15 victorious
PR line 521.5 empty talk
PR man 532.10 publicizer, 586.12 persuader
pro 655.5, 688.11 expert, 696.10 expert, 851.19 supporting
proa 74 Sailing Ships and Boats
pro-active 235.15 full of energy
pro-am 674.2 contest
probabilism 488.5 probability theory
probability 52, 488, 4.8 philosophical term, 56.81 causality, 234.2 attitude, 475.5 demonstrability, 488.3 plausibility, 513.1 expectation, 518.2 basis of supposition, 589.5 good chance, 589.7 calculation of chance
Probability 488
probability curve 488.5 probability theory
probability density function 52.59 probability distribution, 488.5 probability theory
probability distribution 52, 488.5 probability theory
probability function 488.5 probability theory
probability theory 488, 52.53 statistics
probable 488, 101.9 realizable, 199.12 predictable, 234.5 tending to, 488.7 plausible, 497.13 believable, 513.7 expected, 516.7 foreseeable, 714.15 future
probable error 52.60 parameter, 56.83 sensitivity
probably 234, 488, 199.16 predictably, 475.22 demonstrably, 714.18 potentially
probate court 16.19 lawcourt
probation 479.1 experiment
probational 479.8 experimental
probationary 15.9 negotiated, 479.8 experimental, 594.17 developing, 596.9 tentative
probationary period 15.2 industrial negotiations, 594.12 briefing
probationer 60.16 nurse, 156.14 beginner, 656.10 unskilled person
probative 475.13 proven, 480.9 verificatory, 483.8 evidential
probatory 475.13 proven
probe 268.10 measure, 277.4 deep thing, 277.14 deepen, 322.2 opener, 322.20 hole, 477.2 questioning, 477.17 question, 479.1, 479.11 experiment, 496.11 detector
probed 322.14 holed, 477.16 questioned
probenecid 62 Medication
prober 477.9 questioner
probing 277.6 bathymetry, 277.13 bathymetric, 477.8 curiosity, 477.12 questioning
probingly 477.23 questioningly
probity 857, 537.5 truthfulness, 658.2 naivety, 744.7 repute, 843.3 properness, 843.4 righ-

teousness, 863.1 *virtue*, 865.1 *innocence*, 876.2 *good morals*
Probity 857
problem 659, 105.2 *predicament*, 472.2 *issue*, 477.1 *question*, 487.7 *obstacle*, 523.12 *unintelligible thing*, 529.3 *mystification*
problematic 472, 477, 659, 473.10 *arguable*, 491.3 *confused*, 529.11 *mysterious*
problematically 472, 659, 477.24 *questionably*, 491.24 *confusingly*
problem child 659.9 *difficult person*
problem drinker 874.17 *drunkard*
problem novel 48.2 *fiction*
problem play 51.2 *play*
Proboscidea 77.14 *pachyderm*
proboscidean 77.14 *pachyderm*, 77.32 *pachydermatous*
proboscis 318.3 *protuberance*, 403.4 *someone or something that feels*, 407.7 *sense organ*, 416.2 *sense of smell*
proboscis monkey 77 Placental Mammals
proboscis worm 81 Worms
Pro Bowl 19.1 *football*
procacity 807.1 *insolence*
procaine 62 Medication
procaine penicillin 62 Medication
procarbazine 62 Medication
procedural 166.9 *legal*, 306.11 *formal*, 640.6 *effective*, 813.6 *formal*
procedurally 306.14 *conventionally*, 813.12 *formally*
procedure 584, 10.1 *ritual*, 16.34 *legal formality*, 52.66 *proof*, 166.6 *custom*, 230.1 *operation*, 306.5 *formality*, 327.1 *way*, 592.2 *policy*, 640.1 *action*, 652.7 *way*, 719.3 *performance*, 813.3 *formal occasion*
proceed 356, 188.7 *go on*, 219.3 *continue*, 324.13 *be in motion*, 336.1 *go forward*, 640.4 *act*
proceed from 227.7 *follow from*
proceeding 327.1 *way*, 336.18 *ongoing*, 356.12 *passing*, 640.1 *action*, 640.2 *deed*
proceedings 16.6 *legal process*, 472.3 *matter of interest*
proceeds 721.4 *earnings*, 721.6 *yield*, 730.2 *something received*, 734.5 *takings*, 749.2 *money received*
proceed to 597.1 *undertake*
proceed with 640.4 *act*
proceed with caution 781.5 *be cautious*
process 57, 57.14 *chemical reaction*, 66.21 *photograph*, 152.15 *categorize*, 188.3 *continuity*, 195.1 *succession*, 216.1 *change*, 216.8 *cause change*, 220.7 *convert into*, 220.9 *transform*, 230.1 *operation*, 230.9 *take action*, 243.10 *produce*, 327.1 *way*, 547.9 *represent*, 602.1 *means*, 637.5 *preserve*, 640.1 *action*, 652.7 *way*, 692.2 *demand*
process data 152.15 *categorize*
processed 152.24 *categorized*, 243.12 *produced*, 594.21 *ready-made*
processed cheese 45 Cheeses
processed food 350.7 *food*, 637.3 *preserved thing*
processing 66.12 *development*, 220.1 *conversion*, 220.14 *converting*, 243.2 *manufacture*, 637.1 *preservation*
procession 159, 155.1 *sequence*, 155.14 *follower*, 159.1 *consecutiveness*, 195.1 *succession*, 811.13 *ceremonial*
processionally 10.23 *ritually*
process of death 397.1 *death*
processor 65, 65.4 *computer part*
process-server 16.10 *law officer*, 692.6 *person in command*
prochlorperazine 62 Medication

prochronism 193.1 *wrong time*, 197.1 *different time*, 211.2 *anachronism*
prochronistic 193.5 *too early*, 197.2 *occurring at a different time*, 211.11 *anachronistic*
prochronistically 193.7 *out of chronological order*, 211.16 *anachronistically*
proclaim 532, 4.22 *propound a philosophy*, 526.3 *reveal*, 535.17 *affirm*, 543.12 *signal*, 564.11 *speak*, 611.8 *make important*, 692.9 *command*, 811.28 *flourish*
proclaimed 532.19 *published*, 535.11 *stated*
proclaimer 532.10 *publicizer*, 535.9 *affirmer*, 543.8 *signer*
proclaiming 543.16 *signalling*
proclamation 526.10 *manifestation*, 532.1 *publication*, 535.2 *statement*, 543.6 *word*, 692.1 *command*
proclamatory 535.10 *affirmative*
proclivity 234.2 *attitude*, 464.4 *instinct*, 584.2 *tendency*, 784.2 *inclination*
Proclus 4 Philosophers, **53** Lunar Features
proconsul 653.16 *official*, 688.10 *person of authority*, 696.3 *leader*, 707.1 *deputy*
Proconsul 77 Placental Mammals
proconsular 707.7 *deputizing*
proconsulate 688.5 *position of authority*
procrastinate 209.8 *delay*, 283.12 *interrupt*, 470.6 *be neglectful*, 573.8 *hold back*, 576.7 *be irresolute*, 591.7 *be evasive*, 641.4 *not act*, 643.12 *be inactive*, 685.5 *not complete*, 720.7 *not observe*
procrastinating 573, 209.12 *delaying*, 328.6 *hesitant*, 470.5 *indifferent*, 641.3 *inactive*, 643.3 *not participating*, 685.4 *uncompleted*, 720.11 *nonobservant*
procrastination 209.3 *delayed action*, 224.2 *irresolution*, 283.6 *interruption*, 328.12 *hesitation*, 470.2 *indifference*, 573.15 *delay*, 591.15 *evasiveness*, 641.1 *inaction*, 643.7 *idleness*, 685.1 *noncompletion*, 720.1 *nonobservance*
procrastinator 209.5 *delayer*, 328.15 *slow person*, 470.3 *negligent person*, 573.16 *reluctant person*, 685.3 *quitter*, 720.6 *evader*
procreant 245.16 *reproductive*, 246.5 *fertile*
procreate 245.13 *propagate*, 246.7 *make fertile*, 261.6 *become bigger*, 396.19 *give birth to*
procreation 135.4 *sexual union*, 245.3 *propagation*, 246.2 *productiveness*, 261.1 *growth*, 396.4 *biological function*
procreative 245.16 *reproductive*, 246.5 *fertile*
procreatively 261.10 *largely*
procreator 245.5 *propagator*
Procrustean law 166.3 *rule of nature*
proctectomy 60 Surgical Operations
proctocolectomy 60 Surgical Operations
proctor 653.1 *manage*, 653.15 *manager*
proctorship 653.3 *management*
proctotomy 60 Surgical Operations
procumbent 282.10 *lying*
procurable 721.15 *gainful*
procural 721.1 *gain*
procurance 721.1 *gain*
procuration 721.1 *gain*
procurator 653.15 *manager*
procurator fiscal 16.10 *law officer*, 492.6 *justice*
procure 226.10 *awaken*, 228.9 *motivate*, 230.9 *take action*,

232.4 *be an instrument*, 326.14 *bring back*, 355.15 *draw out*, 586.15 *persuade*, 606.5 *provision*, 721.9 *gain*, 738.1 *purchase*, 877.18 *prostitute*
procurement 721.1 *gain*
procurer 232.3 *assistant*, 606.3 *provider*, 721.7 *gainer*, 730.5 *recipient*, 739.12 *wholesaler*, 877.8 *immoral man*
procuring 606.1 *provision*, 877.5 *prostitution*
procyclidine 62 Medication
Procyon 53 Named Stars
procyonid 77.8 *flesh-eating mammal*
Procyonidae 77.8 *flesh-eating mammal*
prod 228.3 *stimulus*, 228.10 *manipulate*, 330.1 *impel*, 330.13 *blow*, 380.8 *sharp-pointed thing*, 380.16 *use a sharp tool* , 407.3 *press*, 407.11 *touch*, 543.11 *gesture*, 586.8 *incentive*
prodded 228.12 *motivated*
prodder 34.4 *climbing equipment*
prodigal 508.5 *foolish*, 607.6 *waster*, 607.8 *wasteful*, 608.2 *plentiful*, 722.17 *unprofitable*, 748.11 *spendthrift*, 757.1 *extravagant*, 757.6 *spendthrift*, 870.8 *overindulgent*
prodigality 541.1 *exaggeration*, 607.3 *waste*, 608.8 *plenty*, 748.6, 757.4 *extravagance*, 870.3 *overindulgence*
prodigally 607.10 *wastefully*, 722.20 *at a loss*, 748.14 *generously*
prodigal returned 867.3 *penitent person*
prodigal son 757.6 *spendthrift*, 864.9 *wicked person*, 867.3 *penitent person*
prodigal's return 344.13 *return*
prodigious 259.15 *big*, 541.12 *exaggerated*, 617.1 *worthy*
prodigiously 541.17 *excessively*
prodigiousness 259.2 *bigness*
prodigous 786.8 *wonderful*
prodigy 126.6 *paragon*, 457.4 *something that appears*, 489.5 *unexpectedness*, 617.8 *exceller*, 655.4 *skilled person*, 786.5 *person of wonder*, 861.16 *superior person*
produce 156, 243, 243, 2.15 *socialize*, 51.36 *dramatize*, 52.97 *align*, 86.1 *fruits*, 226.9 *be the cause of*, 227.3 *growth*, 227.5 *show an effect*, 227.8 *grow*, 245.13 *propagate*, 246.7 *make fertile*, 269.10 *lengthen*, 306.7 *form*, 352.7, 352.7 *secrete*, 475.15 *demonstrate*, 519.14 *imagine*, 526.3 *reveal*, 594.7 *develop*, 606.1, 606.5 *provision*, 721.6 *yield*, 721.13 *be profitable*, 796.8 *fashion*
produced 243, 306.9 *formed*, 396.15 *born*, 526.13 *displayed*
produce market 740.1 *market*
produce offspring 245.13 *propagate*
produce power 235.12 *generate power*
producer 51, 243, 59.18 *ecology*, 226.7 *Prime Mover*, 475.7 *demonstrator*, 496.12 *discoverer*, 646.3 *agent*
produce results 615.6 *be convenient*, 662.26 *be useful*
producer gas 410.3 *gas*
producer goods 13.2 *economy*
produce secretion 352.7 *secrete*
produce seeds 246.6 *be fertile*
producible 526.13 *displayed*
producing 243.1 *production*
product 243, 52.17 *multiplication*, 57.14 *chemical reaction*, 155.5 *consequence*, 169.4 *mathematical result*, 175.4 *multiplication*, 227.1 *effect*, 478.7 *numerical result*, 606.1 *provision*, 721.6 *yield*, 739.8 *merchandise*
product dumping 610.3 *superfluity*

production 51, 243, 526, 13.6 *economic factors*, 51.11 *theatrical performance*, 226.1 *cause*, 230.3 *business*, 243.5 *work of art*, 306.4 *forming*, 382.5 *structuring*, 594.13 *development*, 640.1 *action*, 721.6 *yield*
Production 243
production budget 750.2 *budgeting*
production car racing 33.1 *motor racing*
production cost budget 750.2 *budgeting*
production costs 13.6 *economic factors*
production efficiency 13.6 *economic factors*
production engineering 63.1 *engineering*
production line 161.33 *putting together*, 243.2 *manufacture*, 647.1 *workshop*
production manager 15.6 *employer*
production metallurgy 57.23 *metallurgy*
productive 243, 2.14 *socioeconomic*, 68.20 *farmable*, 86.6 *fruiting*, 226.13 *causal*, 246.5 *fertile*, 519.10 *imaginative*, 613.4 *profitable*, 640.6 *effective*, 721.19 *yielding*, 742.4 *lush*
productive capacity 246.2 *productiveness*
productively 243, 2.16 *sociologically*, 68.22 *agriculturally*, 86.11 *fructiferously*, 226.14 *causally*, 246.8 *fruitfully*, 306.13 *formatively*, 640.8 *effectively*, 721.20 *gainfully*
productiveness 246, 243.1 *production*, 553.1 *diffuseness*, 608.8 *plenty*, 613.8 *benefit*
productivity 13.6 *economic factors*, 243.1 *production*, 246.2 *productiveness*, 553.1 *diffuseness*, 608.8 *plenty*, 613.8 *benefit*
product testing 739.7 *market*
proem 154.5 *preface*, 564.8 *speech*
proemial 154.13 *precursory*, 156.36 *introductory*
profanation 601.2 *misuse*, 827.1 *curse*
profane 601.1 *misuse*, 601.5 *abusive*, 622.8 *unclean*, 622.11 *dirty*, 628.3 *make worse*, 822.13 *angry*, 827.8 *cursing*, 850.27 *desecrate*, 864.14 *impious*
profane language 827.2 *offensive language*
profanely 601.6 *abusively*, 827.12 *swearingly*, 864.20 *immorally*
profaneness 864.6 *religious sin*
profaner 864.9 *wicked person*
profanity 622.2 *uncleanness*, 822.6 *swearing*, 827.1 *curse*
profess 4.22 *propound a philosophy*, 497.7 *believe*, 535.17 *affirm*
professed 535.11 *stated*, 714.12 *promised*
professedly 102.19 *apparently*
profession 535.2 *statement*, 644.3 *job*, 714.1 *promise*, 737.6 *business*, 847.2 *task*
professional 737, 19.19 *varsity*, 26.14 *combat*, 38.5 *soccer*, 124.8 *middle classes*, 165.14 *specialist*, 165.21 *specialized*, 485.8 *qualified person*, 485.9 *qualified*, 520.6 *meaningful*, 584.9 *habitual*, 640.3 *doer*, 640.6 *effective*, 642.20 *industrious*, 655.5, 655.8 *expert*, 655.9 *well-made*, 688.11, 688.17 *expert*, 696.10 *expert*, 696.13 *excellent*
professional army 17.2 *the military*, 679.15 *army*
professional athlete 237.5 *athlete*
professional baseball 22.1 *baseball*
professional basketball 23.1 *basketball*

professional bowler 25.6 *bowler*
professional boxer 26.4 *boxer*
professional boxing 26.1 *combat sports*
professional class 158.8 *middle class*
professional code 847.6 *ethics*
professional consultant 654.4 *adviser*
professional football 19.1 *football*, 38.1 *soccer*
professional footballer 38.3 *football player*
Professional Golfers Association 29.1 *golf*
professional ice hockey 31.3 *ice hockey*
professionalism 207.3 *maturity*, 655.1 *skill*
professional journal 532.5 *journal*
professional killer 398.11 *murderer*
professionally 26, 485.17 *capably*, 584.19 *habitually*, 655.12 *skilfully*, 688.26 *expertly*, 696.16 *masterfully*
professional murderer 398.11 *murderer*
professional person 646.1 *worker*
Professional Punting Championship 36.8 *punting*
professional skill 655.1 *skill*
professional soldier 679.6 *militarist*, 679.8 *soldier*
professional team 31.3 *ice hockey*
professional wrestler 26.6 *wrestler*
professional wrestling 26.1 *combat sports*, 26.5 *wrestling*
professor 6.4 *educator*, 461.7 *thinker*, 485.8 *qualified person*, 535.9 *affirmer*, 646.1 *worker*, 653.13 *director*, 654.4 *adviser*, 655.5, 688.11 *expert*, 696.9 *educational leader*
professorate 6.6 *instructorship*
professor emeritus 6.4 *educator*
professorhood 6.6 *instructorship*
professorial 461.11 *reasoning*
professorship 6.6 *instructorship*
proffer 710.1, 710.9 *offer*, 714.7 *promise*
proffer aid 662.17 *help*
proffer one's good offices 678.1 *mediate*
proficiency 861, 235.2 *ability*, 485.1 *qualification*, 501.3 *learning*, 619.3 *perfection*, 655.1 *skill*, 660.1 *easiness*
proficient 861, 235.13 *powerful*, 485.9 *qualified*, 501.8 *knowledgeable*, 619.1 *perfect*, 655.6 *skilful*, 655.8 *expert*, 696.13 *excellent*
proficiently 235.18 *powerfully*, 485.17 *capably*, 501.15 *knowledgeably*, 655.12 *skilfully*, 696.16 *masterfully*
proficient person 646.2 *artisan*, 655.4 *skilled person*, 786.5 *person of wonder*
profile 767, 48.4 *non-fiction*, 50.10 *art subject*, 299.1 *outline*, 299.2 *shadow*, 299.5 *outline*, 303.2 *face*, 305.1 *side*, 306.1 *form*, 457.3 *external appearance*, 560.1 *description*
profit 721, 721, 13.6 *economic factors*, 13.7 *corporation*, 128.4 *increase*, 132.3 *difference*, 227.3 *growth*, 227.8 *grow*, 228.5 *positive stimulus*, 243.7 *produce*, 599.6 *use*, 613.8, 613.10 *benefit*, 615.3 *convenience*, 615.6 *be convenient*, 662.21 *be helpful*, 686.5 *be prosperous*, 721.9 *gain*, 737.1 *trade*, 742.5 *wealth*, 819.16 *be favourable*, 861.13 *benefit*, 861.20 *do good*, 878.5 *turnover*
profitability 128.1 *increase*, 613.8 *benefit*, 662.10 *helpfulness*, 721.1 *gain*, 861.13 *benefit*
profitable 613, 737, 746, 13.13 *economic*, 243.11 *productive*, 246.5 *fertile*, 599.10 *usable*, 615.1 *convenient*, 617.4 *worthwhile*, 662.34 *beneficial*, 682.14

rewarding, 721.15 *gainful*, 749.6 *received*, 782.8 *desirable*, 819.12 *favourable*, 861.1 *good*, 861.6 *beneficial*, 878.15 *rewarding*
profitableness 721.1 *gain*
profitable return 878.5 *turnover*
profitable transaction 721.1 *gain*
profitably 749, 878, 13.14 *economically*, 243.13 *productively*, 246.8 *fruitfully*, 599.11, 613.12 *usefully*, 617.11 *worthily*, 662.36 *helpfully*, 682.16 *successfully*, 721.20 *gainfully*, 738.17 *acquisitively*, 739.17 *marketably*, 819.20 *favourably*, 861.26 *usefully*
profit after tax 878.5 *turnover*
profit-and-loss account 13.7 *corporation*, 750.1 *accounts*
profit by 210.5 *take the opportunity*, 599.3 *exploit*, 613.11 *find useful*, 627.2 *get better*, 642.14 *push*, 655.10 *be skilful*
profit by example 636.6 *be warned*
profit by one's mistakes 636.6 *be warned*
profiteer 13.9 *economist*, 721.7 *gainer*, 721.9 *gain*, 737.1 *trade*, 737.10 *trader*, 753.10 *overcharge*
profiteering 686.8 *prosperous*, 721.1 *gain*, 737.4 *trade*, 753.4 *extortion*, 753.7 *dear*
profit from 627.1 *improve*
profitless 614.2 *futile*, 683.10 *failed*, 722.17 *unprofitable*
profitlessness 614.4 *futility*
profit-making 721.1 *gain*, 721.15 *gainful*, 737.4 *trade*, 737.15 *profitable*
profit margin 13.6 *economic factors*, 878.5 *turnover*
profit motive 13.6 *economic factors*
profits 721.5 *profit*, 730.2 *something received*, 742.5 *wealth*, 749.2 *money received*
profit-sharing 15.2 *industrial negotiations*, 15.9 *negotiated*, 724.1 *joint possession*, 724.5 *jointly possessing*
profit-taking 721.1 *gain*, 721.15 *gainful*, 734.1 *taking*
profligacy 405.1 *physical pleasure*, 757.4 *extravagance*, 864.2 *vice*, 870.2 *dissipation*, 877.3 *sexual immorality*
profligate 405.7 *pleased*, 748.11 *spendthrift*, 757.1 *extravagant*, 757.6 *spendthrift*, 864.9 *wicked person*, 864.12 *immoral*, 870.7 *dissipated*, 877.14 *lecherous*
profligately 748.14 *generously*
profluence 96.6 *river flow*
profluent 96.10 *fluvial*, 336.18 *ongoing*
pro forma 813.12 *formally*
profound 4.19 *learned*, 277.9 *deep-seated*, 277.11 *wise*, 459.11 *thoughtful*, 461.10 *speculative*, 507.5 *wise*, 523.1 *unintelligible*, 551.2 *obscure*
profoundly 277, 4.29 *wisely*, 427.11 *resonantly*, 459.15 *intelligently*, 551.4 *obscurely*
profoundness 277.3 *profundity*, 459.6 *thoughtfulness*, 523.11 *unintelligibility*
profound thought 461.2 *intellectual exercise*
profundity 277, 277.7 *deep thinking*, 427.3 *deepness*, 459.6 *thoughtfulness*, 461.4 *deliberation*, 507.1 *wisdom*, 551.1 *obscurity*
profuse 181.9 *ample*, 246.5 *fertile*, 541.14 *extravagant*, 553.3 *diffuse*, 608.2 *plentiful*, 610.6 *excessive*, 755.3 *abundant*, 757.2 *unrestrained*
profusely 541.17 *excessively*, 553.7 *diffusely*, 608.9 *enough*
profuseness 181, 541.3 *extravagance*, 553.1 *diffuseness*
profusion 181.3 *profuseness*, 246.1 *fertility*, 541.3 *extrava-*

gance, 608.8 *plenty*, 610.1 *excess*, 742.7 *opulence*, 755.8 *abundance*, 757.5 *unrestrainedness*
progenitor 226.7 *Prime Mover*
progeny 155, 245
progesterone 58 Hormones, 630.8 *drug*
progestogen 58 Hormones, 62 Medication
prognosis 60.6 *health care*, 60.7 *diagnosis*, 488.1 *probability*, 513.2 *expectations*, 516.3 *foresight*, 517.1 *prediction*, 624.20 *pathology*
prognostic 60.24 *diagnostic*, 513.5 *expecting*, 516.6 *foreseeing*, 517.5 *omen*, 636.8 *warning*
prognosticate 60.19 *practise medicine*, 488.10 *think likely*, 517.11 *predict*
prognostication 516.3 *foresight*, 517.1 *prediction*, 517.5 *omen*
prognosticator 516.5 *predictor*, 517.9 *forecaster*
program 65.8 *software*, 152.15 *categorize*
programmable calculator 65.3 *computer*
programme 152.8 *chart*, 171.5 *list of appointments*, 192.2 *timetable*, 257.9 *itemize*, 472.1 *topic*, 516.4 *prudence*, 517.3 *plan*, 534.25 *broadcast material*, 592.1, 592.9 *plan*, 592.10 *plan out*, 597.2 *undertaking*, 640.1 *action*, 652.9 *tactics*, 652.14 *behave towards*
programmed 171.11 *listed*, 257.12 *itemized*, 472.7 *focused*
programme-maker 243.9 *producer*
programmer 65.2 *operator*
programme-seller 51.26 *stagehand*
programming 65.1 *computing*
programming language 65, 65.8 *software*
progress 293, 6.1 *education*, 128.1, 128.4 *increase*, 159.13 *be consecutive*, 188.3 *continuity*, 188.7 *go on*, 195.1 *succession*, 219.1 *continuity*, 219.3 *continue*, 220.2 *evolution*, 220.8 *be transformed*, 324.3 *motion towards*, 324.13 *be in motion*, 327.1 *way*, 336.1 *go forward*, 336.10 *forward motion*, 356.2 *passing along*, 356.10 *enter*, 590.13 *follow up*, 627.2 *get better*, 627.5 *improvement*, 642.13 *be busy*, 682.6 *be successful*, 686.5 *be prosperous*
progressing 293, 128.6 *increasing*, 220.14 *converting*, 324.17 *directional*, 336.17 *forward*
progression 293, 52.20 *sequence*, 150.3 *hierarchy*, 155.1 *sequence*, 159.1 *consecutiveness*, 188.3 *continuity*, 195.1 *succession*, 219.1 *continuity*, 324.3 *motion towards*, 327.1 *way*, 336.10 *forward motion*, 627.5 *improvement*
progressionist 627.12 *reformer*
progressive 6.16 *educational*, 121.7 *gradational*, 128.6 *increasing*, 150.12 *hierarchical*, 155.15 *sequential*, 159.9 *consecutive*, 219.5 *continual*, 324.17 *directional*, 336.16 *progressive person*, 336.17 *forward*, 597.6 *enterprising*, 627.12 *reformer*, 627.16 *improving*
Progressive Conservative Party 12.6 *political party*
Progressive Democrats 12.6 *political party*
progressive jazz 49.8 *jazz*
progressively 6.25 *educationally*, 121.10 *by degrees*, 128.8 *increasingly*, 150.25 *in order*, 159.18 *consecutively*, 219.7 *continually*, 324.18 *in motion*, 336.20 *in progress*, 338.34 *forward*, 597.9 *enterprisingly*, 627.17 *better*
progressiveness 336.10 *forward motion*

progressive person 336
progressive tax 751.7 *tax*
progressive taxation 13.6 *economic factors*
progressivism 627.11 *reformism*
progressivist 627.12 *reformer*
progress report 528.3 *document*
prohibit 16.75 *make illegal*, 147.7 *exclude*, 231.3 *counteract*, 302.7 *limit*, 325.9 *make motionless*, 349.4 *ostracize*, 487.8 *make impossible*, 536.7 *be negative*, 661.8 *hinder*, 692.9 *command*, 699.8 *restrain*, 709.3 *veto*, 709.4 *censor*, 711.6 *dissent*, 816.13 *ignore*, 846.17 *criminalize*, 852.15 *withhold approval*
prohibit drinking 869.5 *be self-restrained*
prohibited 16.55 *illegal*, 147.11 *excluded*, 487.4 *forbidden*, 536.12 *rejected*, 699.13 *restraining*, 709.5 *vetoed*, 711.9 *dissenting*, 816.10 *lonely*, 846.12 *disentitled*, 869.8 *self-restrained*
prohibiting 536.13 *rebutting*, 661.13 *hindering*, 709.5 *vetoed*, 711.9 *dissenting*
prohibition 873, 16.35 *illegality*, 147.1 *exclusion*, 302.2 *limiting factor*, 487.7 *obstacle*, 536.2 *rejection*, 661.1 *hindrance*, 692.1 *command*, 699.1 *restraint*, 709.1 *veto*, 711.2 *dissent*, 869.1 *self-restraint*
Prohibition 3.10 *past age*, 627.11 *reformism*, 873.7 *prohibition*, 876.4 *self-righteousness*
prohibitionary 711.9 *dissenting*
prohibitionism 627.11 *reformism*
prohibitionist 627.12 *reformer*, 869.4 *self-restrained person*, 873.1 *sober*, 873.8 *sober person*, 876.6 *moralist*
Prohibitionist 627.12 *reformer*
prohibition of alcohol 709.1 *veto*
prohibitive 147.10 *excluding*, 302.5 *limited*, 661.13 *hindering*, 692.14 *commanding*, 699.13 *restraining*, 709.5 *vetoed*, 753.7 *dear*, 757.3 *costly*
prohibitively 536.15 *negatively*, 661.16 *with delay*, 692.16 *commandingly*, 699.16 *under restraints*, 709.7 *by veto*, 753.12 *dearly*
prohibitory 709.5 *vetoed*
project 283, 51.32 *act*, 52.96 *represent*, 66.21 *photograph*, 104.16 *be external*, 243.1 *production*, 289.14 *externalize*, 299.5 *outline*, 318.8 *protrude*, 330.1 *impel*, 338.20 *propel*, 347.10 *emerge*, 471.3 *plan*, 472.5 *educational topic*, 547.9 *represent*, 582.6 *premeditation*, 588.3 *future intention*, 588.8 *resolve*, 592.1, 592.9 *plan*, 597.2 *undertaking*, 644.2 *task*
projected 104.12 *external*, 289.9 *externalized*, 303.7 *outward*
projected image 303.3 *show*
projectile 338, 338.8 *missile*, 680.13 *ammunition*
projecting 283, 104.12 *external*
projecting object 283
projecting part 283.2 *projection*
projection 283, 318, 51.20 *acting*, 52.48 *transformation*, 61.19 *defence mechanism*, 98.5 *peninsula*, 104.4 *externality*, 289.4 *externalization*, 299.1 *outline*, 318.2 *projection*, 338.3 *throwing*, 380.8 *sharp-pointed thing*, 519.4 *ideality*, 526.10 *manifestation*, 547.6 *image*, 547.7 *map*, 767.6 *profile*
projectional 299.6 *outlined*
projection map 299.4 *map*
projective geometry 52.34 *geometry*
projective test 61.5 *psychological test*
projector 51.18 *stage lighting*, 66.14 *cine film*, 435.8 *reflection*, 592.8 *planner*

prokaryote 59.3 *organism*

prokaryotic 59.23 *cellular*

prokaryotic cell 59.7 *cell*

prolactin 58 Hormones

prolapse 360.10 *droop*

prolate 52.83 *spherical*

prole 795.5 *vulgar person,* 803.1 *plebeian*

prolegomenon 561.1 *dissertation*

prolepsis 193.1 *wrong time*

proleptic 193.5 *too early*

proletarian 803.1 *plebeian,* 803.3 *common*

proletarianism 12.1 *government*

proletariat 124.7 *average person,* 646.4 *personnel,* 803.2 *the common people*

proliferate 89.12 *mushroom,* 128.4 *increase,* 175.9 *pluralize,* 245.12 *multiply,* 246.6 *be fertile,* 608.5 *about,* 721.10 *augment*

proliferated 175.8 *multiplicative*

proliferating 175.8 *multiplicative*

proliferation 128.1 *increase,* 175.4 *multiplication,* 245.1 *reproduction,* 608.8 *plenty*

proliferative 175.8 *multiplicative*

prolific 128.6 *increasing,* 243.11 *productive,* 246.5 *fertile,* 553.3 *diffuse,* 608.2 *plentiful,* 721.19 *yielding,* 742.4 *lush*

prolificacy 608.8 *plenty*

prolifically 128.8 *increasingly,* 243.13 *productively,* 246.8 *fruitfully,* 553.7 *diffusely,* 608.9 *enough,* 721.20 *gainfully*

prolificness 608.8 *plenty*

proline 58 Amino Acids

prolix 183.12 *repetitious,* 553.3 *diffuse,* 555.1 *unemphatic,* 565.5 *talkative,* 788.4 *boring*

prolixity 553.1 *diffuseness,* 564.2 *power of speech,* 565.1 *talkativeness,* 788.1 *boredom*

Prolog 65 Programming Languages

prologue 51.6 *scene,* 51.22 *actor,* 154.5 *preface,* 194.7 *foretaste,* 303.1 *front,* 564.8 *speech*

prolong 128.5 *make bigger,* 209.8 *delay,* 219.4 *protract,* 269.10 *lengthen,* 637.5 *preserve*

prolongation 128.1 *increase,* 130.1 *addition,* 155.3 *continuity,* 209.3 *delayed action,* 219.2 *protraction,* 269.4 *length,* 637.1 *preservation*

prolonged 209.10 *held up,* 219.6 *protracted,* 269.1 *long*

prolonged noise 423.1 *loudness*

prolonged note 49.19 *tempo*

prom 46.1 *dancing,* 49.27 *performance,* 161.10 *dance*

promazine 62 Medication

promenade 46.1 *dancing,* 159.8 *procession,* 159.17 *line up,* 303.1 *front,* 327.7 *arcade,* 811.27 *show,* 811.29 *show off*

promenade concert 49.27 *performance*

promenade deck 74 Parts of a Ship

promenader 51.31 *theatregoer*

promethazine 62 Medication

Promethean 396.12 *alive*

promethium 57 Chemical Elements

prominence 318, 53.15 *sun,* 126.1 *superiority,* 275.1 *height,* 316.1 *convexity,* 361.8 *height,* 437.4 *clarity,* 483.3 *evidentness,* 554.2 *seriousness,* 611.1 *importance*

Prominence 318

prominent 126.15 *excellent,* 275.11 *exalted,* 316.4 *convex,* 318.6 *eminent,* 361.12 *exalted,* 437.2 *clear,* 457.7 *appearing,* 483.9 *evident,* 526.14 *manifest,* 611.5 *important,* 611.6 *notable*

prominent feature 318.3 *protuberance*

prominently 126.16 *superiorly,* 316.6 *convexly,* 318.11 *eminently,* 483.15 *evidently,* 611.9 *importantly*

promiscuity 482.6 *lack of discrimination,* 628.8 *perversion,* 683.3 *personal fault,* 708.1 *permission,* 877.3 *sexual immorality*

promiscuous 482.1 *undiscriminating,* 538.20 *unfaithful,* 783.8 *careless,* 877.13 *unchaste*

promiscuously 482.13 *unselectively,* 783.18 *carelessly*

promiscuousness 783.2 *carelessness*

promise 714, 714, 718, 718, 116.3 *arrangement,* 116.23 *arrange,* 486.1 *possibility,* 488.8 *be probable,* 490.14 *guarantee,* 490.21 *make certain,* 516.1 *foresee,* 517.11 *predict,* 535.3, 535.18 *vow,* 588.4 *formulated intention,* 588.8 *resolve,* 597.1 *undertake,* 597.3 *contract,* 632.9 *protect,* 667.2, 667.7 *contract,* 715.1 *contract,* 718.12 *certify,* 775.4 *comfort,* 775.10 *inspire hope,* 819.16 *be favourable,* 847.7 *commitment*

Promise 714

promised 714, 116.12 *arranged,* 135.12 *united,* 199.13 *foreseen,* 490.4 *guaranteed,* 513.7 *expected,* 535.12 *vowed,* 597.5 *undertaken,* 667.11, 715.7 *contractual,* 718.7 *guaranteed,* 823.22 *marriageable*

promised land 714, 519.8 *dreamland,* 775.3 *aspiration*

Promised Land 588.6 *objective*

promise-maker 714

promise-making 714.1 *promise*

promise oneself 714

promiser 490.15 *guarantor,* 714.5 *promise-maker*

promises 228.2 *inducement*

promise to pay 714.8 *guarantee,* 745.1 *debt*

promise well 686.7, 714.9 *be auspicious*

promising 486.6 *potential,* 517.15 *presageful,* 686.8 *prosperous,* 714.14 *auspicious,* 775.14 *cheering,* 819.12 *favourable*

promisingly 517.16 *predictively,* 686.9 *prosperously,* 714.17 *auspiciously,* 775.15 *hopefully,* 819.20 *favourably*

promissory 714.13 *guaranteeing*

promissory note 714.2 *guarantee,* 715.2 *purchase contract,* 741.14 *paper money*

promitosis 59.10 *cell division*

promo 532.8 *public relations*

promontory 98.5 *peninsula,* 98.11 *continental,* 318.2 *projection*

promorphology 382.8 *science of structure*

promote 361, 15.11 *conduct industrial relations,* 57.26 *react,* 226.12 *determine,* 232.4 *be an instrument,* 233.8 *influence,* 336.8 *further,* 526.3 *reveal,* 532.16 *publicize,* 602.6 *find means,* 611.8 *make important,* 613.9 *be useful,* 615.6 *be convenient,* 627.1 *improve,* 660.16 *make easy,* 662.28 *further,* 737.1 *trade,* 739.1 *sell*

promoted 15.9 *negotiated,* 361.12 *exalted,* 526.13 *displayed*

promoter 51.25 *producer,* 494.3 *optimist,* 528.9 *informant,* 532.10 *publicizer,* 535.9 *affirmer,* 586.12 *persuader,* 592.8 *planner,* 662.15 *benefactor*

promoting 232.6 *instrumental,* 662.30 *helping,* 662.33 *helpful*

promotion 15.2 *industrial negotiations,* 195.4 *accession,* 232.1 *instrumentality,* 336.12 *advance,* 361.7 *lift,* 526.10 *manifestation,* 586.5 *propaganda,* 594.9 *preparation,* 627.5 *improvement,* 662.8 *furtherance,* 739.3 *selling*

promotional 232.6 *instrumental*

promotional literature 586.6 *advertising*

promotional manager 526.12 *displayer*

promotion tour 532.6 *book publishing*

promotive 232.6 *instrumental*

prompt 51.36 *dramatize,* 156.20 *activate,* 191.5 *immediate,* 208.12 *early,* 228.9 *motivate,* 329.1 *swift,* 511.4 *reminder,* 511.13 *remind,* 528.7 *advice,* 572.2 *eager,* 586.15 *persuade,* 642.18 *active,* 648.3 *hasty,* 654.5 *advise*

prompt book 51.2 *play*

prompted 51.37 *dramatic,* 228.12 *motivated*

prompter 51.26 *stagehand,* 228.7 *motivator,* 511.4 *reminder,* 586.14 *motivator,* 654.4 *adviser*

prompter's box 51.15 *stage*

prompting 586.1 *persuasion*

promptitude 191.1 *immediacy,* 208.1 *earliness,* 329.8 *speed,* 642.3 *nimbleness*

promptly 191.8 *immediately,* 208.17 *early,* 329.14 *swiftly,* 642.22 *actively,* 648.6 *hastily*

promptness 191.1 *immediacy,* 208.1 *earliness,* 329.8 *speed,* 572.7 *eagerness,* 648.4 *haste*

promulgate 532.13 *make public,* 692.9 *command*

promulgation 532.1 *publication*

pronate 28.5 *fence*

pronated 28.6 *fencing*

pronation 28.3 *fencing movements*

prone 276.5 *low,* 282.10 *lying,* 362.8 *sit,* 488.6 *probable,* 572.1 *willing*

proneness 234.2 *attitude,* 276.1 *lowness,* 282.1 *horizontality,* 488.1 *probability*

prone to 234.5 *tending to*

prone to sickness 624.21 *unhealthy*

prong 176.8 *half,* 343.5 *fork,* 380.7 *sharp point*

pronged 343.9 *branched*

pronghorn 77 Placental Mammals

pronominal 5.44 *grammatical*

pronoun 5.35 *part of speech*

pronounce 4.22 *propound a philosophy,* 5.45 *use language,* 16.76 *judge,* 166.13 *rule,* 505.3 *aphorize,* 532.14 *proclaim,* 535.17 *affirm,* 692.9 *command*

pronounced 5.38 *linguistic,* 526.14 *manifest,* 535.11 *stated,* 554.4 *emphasized,* 564.16 *speech*

pronounce guilty 16.79 *convict*

pronounce man and wife 823.16 *join in marriage*

pronouncement 492.2 *verdict,* 532.1 *publication,* 535.2 *statement,* 564.7 *utterance,* 692.1 *command*

pronounce sentence 16.71 *try a case,* 492.11 *judge*

pronto 329.14 *swiftly,* 648.6 *hastily*

Pronuba 823.14 *gods and goddesses of marriage*

pronunciamento 532.1 *publication*

pronunciation 5.1 *linguistics,* 564.3 *mode of speech,* 564.6 *phonetics*

proof 52, 475, 480, 483, 16.7 *legal trial,* 392.10 *waterproof,* 490.9 *certainty,* 490.13 *confirmation,* 526.10 *manifestation,* 535.4, 537.7 *confirmation,* 592.6 *outline,* 632.6 *invulnerable,* 874.6 *intoxicating*

proof against 761.1 *insensitive*

proof copy 592.6 *outline*

proofed 373.3 *hardened*

proof of purchase 718.2 *promise,* 749.1 *receipt*

proof of regard 878.1 *reward*

proofread 627.3 *rectify*

proofreader 532.12 *publisher,* 627.13 *reviser,* 627.12 *repairer*

proofreading 627.6 *rectification*

prop 73 Aircraft Parts, 35.4 *rugby player,* 51.19 *stage requi-*

site, 225.3 *stabilizer,* 284.2 *supporting part,* 284.11 *support,* 338.11 *propeller,* 364.6 *rotator,* 603.1 *tool,* 634.1 *refuge,* 662.13 *supporter,* 662.19 *support*

propaganda 586, 228.2 *inducement,* 309.4 *distortion of the truth,* 474.2 *sophism,* 532.8 *public relations ,* 538.5 *half-truth,* 676.7 *war measures*

propaganda machine 538.5 *half-truth*

propagandist 228.7 *motivator,* 309.5 *defacer,* 474.6 *sophist,* 532.10 *publicizer,* 538.11 *liar,* 561.3 *dissertator,* 586.12 *persuader*

propagandize 309.12 *distort the truth,* 474.11 *practise sophistry,* 497.9 *make someone believe,* 532.16 *publicize,* 538.21 *lie,* 628.6 *pervert*

propagandizing 538.15 *lying*

propagate 245, 69.15 *cultivate,* 128.5 *make bigger,* 162.16 *distribute,* 175.9 *pluralize,* 226.9 *be the cause of,* 243.10 *produce,* 246.7 *make fertile,* 532.13 *make public,* 534.30 *communicate*

propagated 162.22 *distributed,* 534.34 *communicated*

propagation 245, 69.5 *gardening,* 88.4 *moss plant,* 90.6 *lichen,* 128.1 *increase,* 135.4 *sexual union,* 162.1 *dispersion,* 226.1 *cause,* 246.2 *productiveness,* 396.4 *biological function,* 534.6 *telecommunication*

propagator 245, 69.4 *nursery,* 226.2 *source,* 226.7 *Prime Mover,* 246.1 *fertility*

propagatory 246.5 *fertile*

propagule 90.4 *reproductive body*

propane 57 Common Chemical Compounds, 410.3 *gas*

propanidid 62 Medication

propanolol 62 Medication

propantheline 62 Medication

propel 338, 324.14 *set in motion,* 326.12 *transport,* 330.1 *impel,* 330.4 *throw,* 361.2 *send up,* 648.1 *hasten*

propellant 338, 349, 53.35 *rocketry,* 324.16 *moving,* 338.11 *propeller,* 337.17 *propulsive,* 388.11 *vaporizer,* 680.15 *explosive*

propelled 338

propeller 73 Aircraft Parts, 74 Parts of a Ship, 338, 364.6 *rotator*

propeller shaft 71 Motor Vehicle Parts, 74 Parts of a Ship

propelling 324.16 *moving,* 337.29 *in reverse,* 338.17 *propulsive*

propelment 337.29 *in reverse*

propensity 234.2 *attitude,* 488.2, 584.2 *tendency,* 655.2 *aptitude,* 784.2 *inclination*

proper 16.44 *legal,* 167.14 *conformist,* 615.1 *convenient,* 782.8 *desirable,* 845.13 *fit,* 863.5 *virtuous,* 876.8 *moral*

proper eating 350.6 *nutrition*

proper fraction 52.18 *division,* 169.5 *ratio,* 173.1 *fraction*

proper gentleman 817.6 *courteous person*

properly 843, 16.81 *legally,* 485.17 *capably,* 537.39 *accurately,* 652.19 *well,* 843.17 *by rights,* 863.9 *virtuously*

proper match 823.4 *marriageability*

proper motion 53.13 *luminosity*

properness 843, 863.1 *virtue*

proper noun 5.35 *part of speech,* 560.8 *name*

proper observance 719.1 *observance*

propertied 725, 723.8 *possessing,* 742.1 *wealthy*

propertied class 742.11 *the rich*

proper time 210.1 *timeliness,* 615.3 *convenience*

proper treatment 599.6 *use*

property 725, 51.19 *stage requisite,* 103.4 *nature,* 165.3 *characteristic,* 227.2 *visible effect,* 235.2 *ability,* 602.4 *financial resources,* 603.6 *equipment,* 605.1 *store,* 723.4 *possession,* 742.5 *wealth*

Property 725

property man 725

property owner 696.1 *master,* 723.5 *possessor,* 725.7 *property man*

property-owning 723.8 *possessing*

property rights 723.1 *possession*

property roll 171.6 *list of names*

property tax 749.2 *money received,* 751.7 *tax*

prop forward 35.4 *rugby player*

prophase 59.10 *cell division*

prophecy 11.11 *occultism,* 11.9 *divination,* 199.4 *looking to the future,* 516.3 *foresight,* 517.1 *prediction,* 524.5 *science of interpretation*

prophesy 11.23 *divine,* 199.9 *look ahead,* 516.1 *foresee,* 517.11 *predict*

prophet 11.13 *diviner,* 126.5 *superior,* 199.5 *predictor,* 208.4 *early comer,* 464.5 *intuitive person,* 507.3 *wise man,* 516.5 *predictor,* 517.8 *oracle,* 636.4 *warner,* 654.4 *adviser*

prophetess 199.5 *predictor,* 517.8 *oracle*

prophetic 11.17 *divinatory,* 208.16 *premature,* 516.6 *foreseeing,* 517.13 *predicting,* 543.14 *signifying*

prophetically 11.25 *occultly,* 208.20 *prematurely,* 516.8 *foresightedly,* 517.16 *predictively,* 543.18 *indicatively*

prophet of doom 517.8 *oracle,* 776.3 *hopeless person*

prophylactic 630, 60.25 *therapeutic,* 62.4 *drug type,* 231.2 *counteracting thing,* 247.3 *birth control,* 625.1 *hygiene,* 625.4 *hygienic,* 630.17 *remedial,* 632.7 *tutelary,* 637.6 *preserving,* 661.13 *hindering*

prophylactically 637.8 *preservatively*

prophylactic psychiatry 61.2 *psychiatry*

prophylaxis 60.6 *health care,* 625.1 *hygiene,* 630.3 *prophylactic,* 632.2 *protection,* 661.3 *barrier*

propinquity 107.1 *relatedness,* 253.4 *availability,* 264.1 *nearness*

propionic 58 Common Fatty Acids

propitiable 125.8 *compensable*

propitiate 9.7 *worship,* 10.19 *offer worship,* 125.4 *compensate,* 677.4 *pacify,* 678.1 *mediate,* 710.14 *offer reparation,* 710.15 *offer worship,* 765.11 *recompense,* 840.5 *atone*

propitiated 125.7 *compensated*

propitiating 125.9 *compensatory*

propitiation 9.1 *worship,* 10.5 *Christian rite,* 125.1 *compensation,* 677.1 *pacification,* 678.2 *mediation,* 710.6 *offering,* 765.2 *reparation,* 840.1 *atonement*

propitiatious 125.9 *compensatory*

propitiative 125.9 *compensatory*

propitiator 125.3 *compensator,* 678.3 *mediator,* 678.4 *representative*

propitiatorily 125.11 *in compensation*

propitiatory 677.6 *pacificatory,* 678.6 *mediatory,* 710.19 *sacrificial,* 840.4 *atoning*

propitious 210.6 *timely,* 517.15 *presageful,* 617.4 *worthwhile,* 662.34 *beneficial,* 686.8 *prosperous,* 714.14 *auspicious,* 775.14 *cheering,* 819.12 *favourable,* 861.1 *good*

propitiously 210.9 *opportunely,* 686.9 *prosperously,* 714.17 *aus-*

piciously, 775.15 *hopefully,* 819.20 *favourably*

propitiousness 210.1 *timeliness,* 775.4 *comfort,* 861.8 *good*

proponent 463.6 *arguer,* 855.5 *vindicator*

proportion 52.18 *division,* 52.91 *add,* 107.2 *interrelatedness,* 107.8 *be proportionate to,* 109.3 *correlation,* 109.9 *correlate,* 121.3 *gradation,* 122.2 *equilibrium,* 122.11 *equalize,* 124.10 *make average,* 143.1 *part,* 145.3 *incomplete thing,* 150.7 *method,* 169.5 *ratio,* 173.2 *fractional part,* 248.1, 248.21 *space,* 259.1 *size,* 259.18 *measure,* 308.1 *symmetry,* 308.6 *symmetrize,* 558.1 *elegance,* 731.2 *portion*

proportionable 121.7 *gradational*

proportional 52.74 *divisible,* 107.5 *interrelated,* 109.6 *correlative,* 121.7 *gradational,* 143.11 *partial,* 173.5 *fractional,* 248.11 *spatial,* 308.4 *symmetrical,* 558.3 *elegant*

proportionality 107.2 *interrelatedness,* 109.3 *correlation,* 114.1 *similarity,* 308.1 *symmetry*

proportionally 107.10 *relevantly,* 109.10 *reciprocally,* 109.11 *correlatively,* 121.9 *differentially,* 143.12 *partly,* 308.7 *symmetrically*

proportional notation 49.18 *written music*

proportional representation 12.1 *government,* 580.11 *franchise,* 688.7 *type of rule*

proportional tax 751.7 *tax*

proportional taxation 13.6 *economic factors*

proportional to 52.88 *equal to*

proportionate 109.6 *correlative,* 122.6 *equal,* 143.11 *partial,* 308.4 *symmetrical*

proportionately 731, 107.10 *relevantly,* 109.10 *reciprocally,* 109.11 *correlatively,* 143.12 *partly,* 308.7 *symmetrically*

proportioned 109.6 *correlative,* 308.4 *symmetrical*

proportionment 109.3 *correlation*

proportions 120.1 *quantity*

proposable 712.9 *requesting*

proposal 471.3 *plan,* 518.1 *supposition,* 588.3 *future intention,* 592.1 *plan,* 654.1 *advice,* 710.1 *offer,* 712.1 *request,* 821.6, 826.2 *courtship*

propose 4.22 *propound a philosophy,* 284.14 *give moral support,* 336.8 *further,* 471.18 *aim,* 472.10 *focus on,* 473.15 *state,* 477.20 *doubt,* 477.22 *pop the question,* 505.3 *aphorize,* 518.6 *propound,* 535.17 *affirm,* 580.4 *pick,* 588.7 *intend,* 592.9 *plan,* 654.5, 662.23 *advise,* 710.9 *offer,* 712.6 *request,* 821.28 *win the love of,* 826.8 *court*

propose a merger 737.3 *bargain*

propose a motion 518.6 *propound*

propose conditions 485.16 *specify*

proposed 471.12 *purposive,* 472.7 *focused,* 473.11 *logical,* 518.8 *supposed,* 712.9 *requesting*

proposed action 592.1 *plan*

proposed conduct 652.1 *conduct*

proposed line of action 592.1 *plan*

proposer 284.8 *supporter,* 592.8 *planner*

proposing 821.6 *courtship*

proposition 4.1 *philosophy,* 52.63 *mathematical logic,* 52.65 *theory,* 56.6 *law,* 472.1 *topic,* 473.3 *line of argument,* 477.1 *question,* 497.1 *belief,* 518.1 *supposition,* 535.2 *statement,* 592.1 *plan,* 654.1 *advice,* 710.1 *offer,* 712.1 *712.6 request,* 826.8 *court*

propositional 52.69 *theoretic,* 471.10 *theoretical,* 473.11 *logical,* 518.7 *suppositional,* 535.10

affirmative, 710.17 *offered,* 712.9 *requesting*

propositional calculus 4.6 *branch of philosophy,* 52.63 *mathematical logic*

propound 518, 654.5 *advise*

propound a philosophy 4

propping up 284.1 *support*

propraetor 707.1 *deputy*

proprietarily 725

proprietary 725.8 *propertied*

proprietary drug 630.2 *medicine*

proprietary name 62.3 *drug*

proprietary rights 723.1 *possession*

proprieties 813.5 *etiquette*

proprietor 696.1 *master,* 723.5 *possessor*

proprietorial 723.8 *possessing*

proprietorship 723.1 *possession*

propriety 134.1 *purity,* 485.1 *qualification,* 558.1 *elegance,* 615.3 *convenience,* 794.1 *elegance,* 813.1 *formality,* 843.3 *properness,* 876.2 *good morals*

prop root 83.7 *root*

propulsion 338, 324.2 *momentum,* 330.11 *impulsion,* 349.17 *expulsion*

Propulsion 338

propulsive 338, 235.15 *full of energy*

propulsor 338.11 *propeller*

propulsory 338.17 *propulsive*

prop up 237.8 *strengthen,* 284.11 *support,* 361.1 *raise,* 637.5 *preserve,* 662.19 *support*

propylaeum 43.9 *miscellaneous architectural features,* 346.6 *means of entry*

propylene 57 Common Chemical Compounds

proquanil 62 Medication

pro rata 143.12 *partly,* 731.8 *proportionately*

prorate 731.4 *allot*

prorogation 209.3 *delayed action*

prorogue 209.8 *delay*

prorogued 209.10 *held up*

proruption 347.1 *exit*

prosaic 124.3 *mediocre,* 555.1 *unemphatic,* 556.1 *simple,* 658.1 *naive,* 788.4 *boring*

prosaically 555.3 *unemphatically,* 556.8 *simply,* 788.8 *boringly*

prosaicness 788.1 *boredom*

proscenium 51.15 *stage,* 303.1 *front*

proscenium arch 51.15 *stage*

proscenium box 51.16 *auditorium*

proscenium stage 51.15 *stage*

proscribe 16.75 *make illegal,* 16.79 *convict,* 147.7 *exclude,* 302.7 *limit,* 349.4 *ostracize,* 485.16 *specify,* 692.9 *command,* 709.4 *censor,* 827.7 *wish ill,* 879.1 *punish*

proscribed 16.55 *illegal,* 16.64 *convicted,* 485.12 *conditional,* 709.6 *censored,* 827.10 *maledictive*

proscripted 302.5 *limited*

proscription 16.35 *illegality,* 16.43 *conviction,* 147.1 *exclusion,* 302.1 *limitation,* 349.19 *ostracism,* 485.6 *specification,* 692.1 *command,* 709.2 *censorship,* 827.4 *malediction,* 879.7 *punishment*

proscriptive 485.12 *conditional,* 692.14 *commanding,* 709.6 *censored*

proscriptively 485.18 *with qualification,* 692.16 *commandingly,* 709.8 *under censorship*

prose 48, 48.21 *write,* 556.4 *simplicity*

prosecute 16.70 *litigate,* 590.14 *carry on,* 640.4 *act,* 856.5 *accuse*

prosecuted 856.8 *accusatory*

prosecution 16.5 *litigation,* 16.7 *legal trial,* 590.1 *pursuit,* 856.1 *accusation*

prosecutor 16.8 *litigant,* 856.3 *accuser*

prose fiction 48.2 *fiction,* 48.5 *prose*

proselyte 220.6 *convert,* 561.3 *dissertator,* 578.9 *equivocator*

proselyter 220.5 *converter*

proselytization 220.3 *persuasion*

proselytize 7.20 *preach,* 220.11 *persuade,* 497.9 *make someone believe,* 561.4 *dissertate*

proselytized 220.13 *converted,* 220.16 *influenced*

proselytizer 220.5 *converter,* 561.3 *dissertator*

proselytizing 220.3 *persuasion*

prose poetry 48.5 *prose*

prose rhythm 48.5 *prose*

Proserpina 8 Deities

prose style 48.5 *prose*

prosify 48.21 *write*

prosimian 77.34 *primate*

prosimians 77.16 *primate*

prosiness 555.2 *lack of emphasis,* 788.1 *boredom*

prosodics 564.6 *phonetics*

prosody 48.9 *metre,* 49.19 *tempo,* 564.6 *phonetics*

prosopopoeia 48.12 *poetic language*

prospect 50.10 *art subject,* 199.4 *looking to the future,* 435.7 *view,* 479.11 *experiment,* 486.1 *possibility,* 488.1 *probability,* 513.1 *expectation,* 517.1 *prediction,* 588.3 *future intention*

prospective 486.6 *potential,* 488.6 *probable,* 513.7 *expected,* 516.6 *foreseeing,* 588.11 *intending,* 714.15 *future*

prospectively 486.11, 714.18 *potentially*

prospective parents 513.4 *expectant person*

prospector 243.9 *producer,* 496.12 *discoverer*

prospects 199.4 *looking to the future,* 513.2 *expectations,* 775.4 *comfort*

prospectus 171.5 *list of appointments,* 516.4 *prudence,* 517.3 *plan,* 562.2 *outline,* 592.2 *policy*

prosper 106.14 *be comfortable,* 128.4 *increase,* 246.6 *be fertile,* 336.5 *develop,* 344.9 *achieve,* 627.2 *get better,* 642.13 *be busy,* 682.6 *be successful,* 686.5 *be prosperous,* 721.14 *profit,* 742.13 *get rich,* 861.21 *do well*

prospering 686.8 *prosperous*

prosperity 686, 106.5 *comfortable circumstances,* 128.1 *increase,* 246.2 *productiveness,* 336.12 *advance,* 627.5 *improvement,* 629.10 *revival,* 682.1 *success,* 721.5 *profit,* 742.5 *wealth,* 861.13 *benefit*

Prosperity 686

prosperous 686, 106.9 *comfortable,* 246.5 *fertile,* 517.15 *presageful,* 682.13 *successful,* 721.17 *well-off,* 742.1 *wealthy*

prosperously 686, 106.18 *comfortably,* 682.16 *successfully,* 721.20 *gainfully,* 742.16 *wealthily*

prosperousness 686.1 *prosperity*

prosperous person 686

prostaglandin 58.16 *hormone*

prostate 245.8 *organs of reproduction*

prostate cancer 624.12 *cancer*

prostatectomy 60 Surgical Operations

prostate gland 352 Exocrine Glands, 245.8 *organs of reproduction*

prostatic 352.5 *of a secretion*

prosthesis 222.3 *substitute thing,* 630.12 *surgery*

prosthetic dentistry 60.4 *dentistry*

prosthetic group 58.9 *protein,* 58.11 *enzyme*

prosthetics 630.12 *surgery*

prosthodontic 60.23 *dental*

prosthodontics 60.4 *dentistry*

prosthodontist 60.14 *dentist*

prostitute 402, 877, 601.1 *mis-*

use, 628.6 pervert, 877.9 immoral woman
prostituted 877.13 unchaste
prostitution 877, 601.2 misuse, 628.8 perversion, 737.4 trade
prostrate 7.15 religious, 9.9 worshipful, 83.14 of plants, 236.8 overpower, 236.4 impotent, 276.5 low, 282.7 make horizontal, 282.10 lying, 362.8 sit, 362.23 sedentary, 624.22 sick, 650.1 fatigued, 650.6 fatigue, 673.5 submitting, 808.7 sycophantic, 849.11 in a respectful stance
prostrate oneself 7.19 be religious, 9.7 worship, 276.8 be low, 282.6 be horizontal, 362.9 bow, 694.6 show obeisance to, 808.10 knuckle under, 817.13 defer to, 849.19 take off one's hat to, 867.5 do penance
prostration 7.2 religiousness, 9.1 worship, 236.4 disability, 244.1 destruction, 276.1 lowness, 282.1 horizontality, 362.16 courtesy, 624.3 symptom, 650.7 fatigue, 673.1 submission, 694.3 obeisance, 808.2 sycophancy, 849.4 mark of respect, 867.2 type of penance
prostyle 43.9 miscellaneous architectural features
prosy 553.3 diffuse, 555.1 unemphatic, 788.4 boring
protactinium 57 Chemical Elements
protagonist 51.21 role
protagonistic 51.37 dramatic
protagonistically 51.42 dramatically
Protagoras 4 Philosophers
Protagorean 4.11 follower of a doctrine, 4.14 of a philosophy
protanopia 436.2 poor sight
protanopic 436.9 weak-sighted
protasis 5.23 phrase
protea 84 Flowers and Flowering Plants
protean 224.13 changeable
protease 58.11 enzyme
protect 293, 632, 19.15 play of fence, 180.15 escort, 237.8 strengthen, 348.9 welcome, 637.5 preserve, 662.20 sustain, 671.17, 679.39 defend, 699.9 economize, 699.11 detain, 718.10 secure
protected 293, 180.20 accompanied, 625.4 hygienic, 632.5 safe, 637.7 preserved, 671.30 defended, 718.6 secure, 848.5 exempt
protected area 637.1 preservation
protected building 637.3 preserved thing
protected from wet 392.10 waterproof
protected species 637.3 preserved thing
protecting 237.4 strengthening, 632.7 tutelary, 637.6 preserving
protection 632, 718, 19.9 play, 231.2 counteracting thing, 237.1 strength, 284.6 moral support, 293.15 shelter, 348.2 receptivity, 467.5 solicitude, 605.4 storage, 625.1 hygiene, 632.1 safety, 632.4 safety device, 637.1 preservation, 653.3 management, 662.4 social assistance, 671.2 safeguard, 737.5 commercial trade, 781.1 caution
protectionism 13.6 economic factors, 91.4 nationalism, 699.2 economic restraint, 737.5 commercial trade
protectionist 91.14 nationalist, 699.6 law-maker
protection money 751.8 levy, 878.8 secret money
protection quota 13.6 economic factors
protection racket 699.2 economic restraint, 734.3 taking away, 736.7 dishonesty
protective 237.13 strengthened,

467.9 solicitous, 625.4 hygienic, 632.7 tutelary, 637.6 preserving, 671.29 defending, 699.13 restraining, 718.6 secure
protective belt 671.6 protective clothing
protective clothing 671, 632.4 safety device
protective coloration 458.5, 539.12 disguise
protective colouration 118.4 camouflage
protective colouring 293.16 disguise, 438.6 that which makes invisible, 671.4 defensiveness
protective covering 293
protective custody 632.2 protection, 699.4 detention
protective duty 737.5 commercial trade
protective glasses 435.10 visual aid
protectively 632.10 safely, 637.8 preservatively, 671.32 defensively, 699.16 under restraints, 718.16 surely
protective quota 737.5 commercial trade
protective shoulder 31.3 ice hockey
protective tariff 699.2 economic restraint, 737.5 commercial trade
protect oneself 632.8 be safe
protector 632, 671, 180.7 attendant, 284.8 supporter, 636.4 warner, 653.15 manager, 679.2 defender, 679.12 ceremonial troops, 679.14 armed forces, 696.3 leader, 718.3 security of officer
protectorate 12.5 political organization, 91.3 dominion, 249.4 territorial division, 632.2 protection, 688.8 governmental organization, 723.4 possession
protectress 632.3 protector
protect the ball 35.5 play rugby
protect the interests of 671.22 plead for
protégé 701.4 dependent
protein 57 Types of Compounds, **59.12** molecular biology, 350.11 food content
protein diet 350.6 nutrition
protein-rich 350.27 edible
protein sequencing 59.12 molecular biology
protein structure 58.9 protein, 59.12 molecular biology
protein synthesis 59.13 genetic material
pro tem 196.7 occasional
proteoglycan 58.9 protein
proteolysis 58.11 enzyme
proteolytic enzyme 58.11 enzyme
Proterozoic 54 Geological Time Intervals
protest 475, 713, 713, 111.9 oppose, 168.2 dissent, 168.18 not conform, 475.6 mass demonstration, 484.1 counterevidence, 484.7 counter, 500.2 disapproval, 500.9 refuse, 536.3 rebuttal, 536.8 rebut, 573.6 be unwilling, 573.11 unwillingness, 587.6 dissuasion, 636.1 warning, 636.5 warn, 642.14 push, 663.2 objection, 663.15 object, 668.5 defy, 669.1 resistance, 669.6 resist, 679.39 defend, 747.1 nonpayment, 852.9 show of disapproval
Protest 713
protest a bill 747.8 stop payment
protest against 587.1 dissuade, 663.12 oppose
protestant 500.5 dissenter, 500.7 dissenting, 536.6 negativist, 536.11 negative, 693.6 nonconformist, 713.4 protester, 713.9 protesting
Protestant 7.5 Christian, 7.16 denominational
Protestantism 7 Christian Movements
protestation 713.1 protest
protested bill 747.3 bad payment

protester 475, 693, 713, 168.8, 500.5 dissenter, 536.6 negativist, 573.16 reluctant person, 663.9 opposer, 666.4 dissenter
protesting 713, 475.14 demonstrating, 500.7 dissenting, 573.5 reluctant, 636.8 warning, 669.10 resistant, 711.9 dissenting, 852.26 disagreeing
protestingly 669.14 resistingly
protest march 475.6 mass demonstration, 713.3 gesture of protest
protest meeting 161.4 rally, 713.3 gesture of protest
protestor 668.4 defiant person
protest sign 543.1 sign
protest song 713.3 gesture of protest
proteus 224.3 changeable thing
Proteus 113.2 assortment
prothalamion 48.7 poem
prothalamium 823.6 general terms
prothallus 88.2 fern plant
prothesis 154.7 prefix
prothionamide 62 Medication
prothipendyl 62 Medication, **62** Medication
protist 59.3 organism, 76.4 type of animal, 81.1 invertebrate
Protoceratops 79 Fossil Reptiles
protochordate 81, 81.1, 81.16 invertebrate
protocol 65.14 data transfer, 65.17 computing term, 306.5 formality, 306.11 formal, 584.5 tradition, 652.2 good conduct, 794.3 etiquette, 796.4 design, 811.11 ritual, 813.1 formality, 813.5 etiquette, 817.2 good manners
Proto-Germanic 5 Languages and Groups of Languages
protohistoric 3.15 historic, 200.17 past
protohistorical 3.16 historical
protohistorically 3.24 historically
protohistory 3.10 past age, 200.1 past time
protohuman 202.7 ancient people
Proto-Indo-European 5 Languages and Groups of Languages, 5.11 family of languages
proto-martyr 710.7 martyr
protomer 58.9 protein
proton 56.50 electric charge, 56.65 atom, 56.97 elementary particle, 260.2 little thing, 367.4 matter
protonema 90.3 plant body
protonic 57.36 acid
protonic acid 57.8 acid
proton mass 56.97 fundamental constant
proton number 56.69 isotope
Proto-Norse 5 Languages and Groups of Languages
proton synchrotron 56.94 particle accelerator
protoplasm 59.7 cell, 156.3 source, 367.4 matter, 396.2 living matter
protoplasmatic 396.14 biotic
protoplasmic 59.23 cellular, 396.14 biotic
protoplast 59.7 cell
protoplastic 396.14 biotic
Protosemitic 5 Languages and Groups of Languages
protostar 53.11 stellar birth
Prototheria 77.3 egg-laying mammal
prototherian 77.3 egg-laying mammal, 77.25 mammalian
prototypal 119.4 original
prototype 306, 119.2 original, 154.4, 166.5 precedent, 268.7 standard, 471.6 ideal, 517.4 model, 592.6 outline, 594.10 preparations
prototypical 306, 471.13 ideal
prototypically 306.13 formatively
protozoa 396.9 classifications of life
Protozoa 81.9 protozoan
protozoal disease 81
protozoan 81, 81, 76.4 type of

animal, 81.1 invertebrate, 81.10 parasite, 81.16 invertebrate, 260.2 little thing, 260.7 little thing
protozoic 81.23 protozoan
protozoological 81.23 protozoan
protozoologist 76.11 zoologist, 81.15 invertebrate zoologist
protozoology 76.9 animal science, 81.14 invertebrate zoology
protract 219, 209.8 delay, 269.10 lengthen, 553.5 be diffuse, 661.9 block
protracted 219, 209.10 held up, 269.1 long, 553.3 diffuse
protractedly 209.15 late, 219.7 continually
protraction 219, 128.1 increase, 155.3 continuity, 209.3 delayed action, 269.4 length, 553.1 diffuseness
protractor 52.49 geometric construction, 268.6 measuring instrument, 310.4 angular measurement
proteptic 586.19 persuasive
protriptyline 62 Medication
protruberance 283.2 projection
protrude 318, 316.5 be convex, 347.10 emerge
protrudent 318.5 protuberant
protruding 316.4 convex
protrusion 316.1 convexity, 318.3 protuberance
protuberance 318, 316.1 convexity, 383.3 nap
protuberant 318
protuberantly 318, 316.6 convexly
Protura 82 Orders of Insects
proturan 82.10 insectan
proud 805, 318.5 protuberant, 807.16 arrogant, 809.13 boastful, 811.22 majestic, 813.6 formal
proud as a peacock 805.14 proud
proud bearing 805.5 stateliness
Proudhon 4 Philosophers
proud-looking 805.14 proud
proudly 805, 318.11 eminently, 807.33 arrogantly, 809.23 boastfully, 811.38 majestically
proudness 805.1 pride
proud person 805
proud-spirited 805.14 proud
Proust 48 Writers, **52** Scientists
proustite 54 Minerals
Prout 52 Scientists
provability 475.5 demonstrability
provable 99.13 real, 475.12 demonstrable
prove 475, 480, 483, 52.89 theorize, 101.12 establish reality, 473.15 state, 479.11 experiment, 490.21 make certain, 535.19 confirm, 855.8 justify
prove acceptable 608.4 suffice
prove adequate 608.4 suffice
prove a fiasco 683.8 miscarry
proved 537, 480.8 verifiable, 483.8 evidential, 490.1 certain, 501.10 known
proved guilty 866.5 guilty
prove false 858
prove fruitful 714.10 show potential
prove guilty 16.79 convict
prove helpful 613.9 be useful
prove infertile 247.7 be infertile
prove innocent 16.78 acquit
prove itself 615.6 be convenient
prove just as one thought 787.8 be predictable
proven 475, 537.20 proved
provenance 156.3 source
Provençal 5 Languages and Groups of Languages
provender 350.7 food, 350.8 animal food, 606.2 provisions
proven fact 503.3 accurate thing
proven way 652.7 way
prove one's point 101.12 establish reality, 475.17 prove
proverb 5.21 catchword, 505.1 maxim, 505.3 aphorize, 537.4 truism, 876.7 moral
proverbial 505, 5.42 worded, 537.17 truistic

proverbialist 5.2 *linguist*
proverbially 505, 4.25 *theoretically,* 5.51 *phraseologically*
prove real 537.30 *prove true*
prove the contrary 476.8 *refute*
prove the truth of 855.8 *justify*
prove too much for 126.8 *be superior*
prove true 537
prove unreliable 720.8 *not perform*
provide 116.30 *grant,* 243.10 *produce,* 594.5 *equip,* 602.6 *find means,* 605.6 *store,* 606.5 *provision,* 637.5 *preserve,* 710.11 *volunteer,* 729.5 *give*
provide a background 107.7 *relate to*
provide a benefit 819.16 *be favourable*
provide a chance 210.4 *be timely*
provide against 516.2 *show prudence*
provide aid 831.9 *be charitable*
provide a living for 396.20 *support life*
provide an alibi for 632.9 *protect*
provide an opportunity 710.9 *offer*
provide a role model 652.11 *conduct oneself*
provide a sweetener 746.11 *remunerate*
provide collateral 733.7 *borrow*
provided 606.8 *provisional*
provide drink 351
provided that 106.15 *under the circumstances*
provide firepower 594.5 *equip*
provide food 350
provide for 284.13 *support financially,* 396.20 *support life,* 606.5 *provision,* 608.4 *suffice,* 662.20 *sustain,* 729.5 *give*
provide for oneself 606.5 *provision*
provide money 742.15 *make rich*
provide more oxygen 651.1 *refresh*
providence 210.1 *timeliness,* 516.4 *prudence,* 589.2 *luck,* 781.1 *caution*
Providence 93 Cities, 8.3 *God*
provide needed funds 831.9 *be charitable*
provide no enjoyment 788.6 *be boring*
provident 516.6 *foreseeing,* 781.4 *cautious*
providential 8.13 *divine,* 203.14 *seasonable,* 210.6 *timely*
providentiality 210.1 *timeliness*
providentially 8.19 *divinely,* 210.9 *opportunely*
providently 516.8 *foresightedly,* 781.7 *cautiously*
provide on-the-job training 15.11 *conduct industrial relations*
provide passage for 322
provider 606, 594.15 *preparer,* 729.4 *giver*
provide shade 85.19 *grow*
provide the basis 594.2 *do the groundwork*
provide the means 662.29 *finance*
provide the wherewithal 602.6 *find means*
provide with arms 594.5 *equip*
provide with teeth 594.5 *equip*
providing 606.1 *provision,* 606.7 *provisioning*
providing passage 322
province 6.3 *subject,* 7.9 *priesthood,* 12.5 *political organization,* 91.3 *dominion,* 92.1 *administrative area,* 249.5 *state,* 249.14 *sphere,* 688.8 *governmental organization*
provinces 249.6 *regions*
provincial 92.6 *administrative,* 167.14 *conformist,* 249.17 *national,* 249.18 *local,* 255.5 *countryman,* 255.12 *native,* 493.8 *unjust,* 658.3 *naive person,* 803.3 *common*

provincial capital 92.5 *administrative headquarters*
provincialism 5.26 *dialect,* 249.15 *regionalism,* 493.3 *injustice*
provincially 92.8 *administratively,* 249.20 *nationally*
provincial newspaper 533.5 *mass communication*
provincial paper 532.4 *newspaper*
proving 480.5 *proof*
proving ground 479.6 *place of experimentation*
provirus 59.3 *organism*
provision 606, 606, 116.9 *grant,* 284.7 *financial support,* 350.25 *provide food,* 485.7 *condition,* 516.4 *prudence,* 593.1 *requirement,* 594.11 *fitting out,* 605.1, 605.6 *store,* 629.9 *restoration,* 632.2 *protection,* 637.1 *preservation,* 637.5 *preserve,* 662.3 *sustenance,* 716.2 *basis for negotiations,* 729.1 *giving,* 741.6 *funds*
Provision 606
provisional 606, 106.7 *circumstantial,* 196.7 *occasional,* 222.7 *substitute,* 479.8 *experimental,* 485.12 *conditional,* 491.1 *uncertain,* 594.16 *preparatory,* 599.9 *used,* 608.1 *sufficient,* 620.2 *incomplete,* 707.7 *deputizing,* 716.8 *negotiated*
Provisional 693.10 *seditionist*
provisionally 105.9 *conditionally,* 106.16 *relatively,* 196.10 *for the present,* 222.9 *instead,* 479.14 *experimentally,* 485.18 *with qualification,* 594.23 *preparatorily,* 716.9 *feasibly*
provisioner 594.15 *preparer,* 739.13 *retailer*
provisioning 606, 45.1 *cookery,* 594.11 *fitting out,* 606.1 *provision*
provision merchant 606.3 *provider,* 739.13 *retailer*
provision oneself 606.5 *provision*
provisions 606, 130.4 *extra,* 350.7 *food,* 602.2 *supplies*
proviso 485.7 *condition,* 593.1 *requirement,* 716.2 *basis for negotiations*
provisory 485.12 *conditional,* 716.8 *negotiated*
Provo 693.10 *seditionist*
provocation 226.1 *cause,* 228.2 *inducement,* 674.1 *contention,* 768.2 *annoyance,* 828.3 *cause of offence*
provocative 228.11 *motivational,* 413.10 *stimulating,* 473.9 *hostile,* 586.19 *persuasive,* 666.9 *disagreeing,* 668.8 *defying,* 670.21 *aggressive,* 782.11 *lustful,* 795.9 *ribald,* 877.12 *indecent*
provocatively 228.14 *influentially,* 413.16 *stimulatingly,* 473.17 *argumentatively,* 535.25 *explicitly,* 586.21 *persuasively,* 666.11 *in disagreement,* 668.10 *in defiance,* 782.20 *lustfully*
provocativeness 666.1 *disagreement,* 668.1 *defiance*
provoke 156.20 *activate,* 226.10 *awaken,* 228.9 *motivate,* 413.13 *be piquant,* 478.18 *answer back,* 666.5 *disagree,* 666.7 *pick a fight,* 668.5 *defy,* 768.8 *annoy,* 807.25 *answer back,* 820.13 *antagonize,* 828.9 *offend*
provoke action 636.5 *warn*
provoke an engagement 676.14 *battle*
provoked 228.12 *motivated,* 828.15 *resentful*
provoke disbelief 787.7 *not cause wonder*
provoke thought 554.6 *emphasize*
provoking 228.11 *motivational,* 768.5 *aggravating*
provost 688.10 *person of authority,* 696.6 *religious leader,* 696.9 *educational leader*
provost general 16.10 *law officer*

provost marshal 16.17 *police officer*
prow 74 Parts of a Ship, 34.5 *rock face,* 36.3 *parts of a sailing boat,* 303.1 *front*
prowess 655.1 *skill,* 778.2 *heroism,* 778.8 *courageous act*
prowl after 590.9 *follow*
prowl car 71.17 *police car*
prowler 736.8 *thief*
Proxima Centauri 53 Named Stars
proximal 155.17 *next,* 264.5 *near*
proximate 155.17 *next,* 195.12 *succeeding,* 264.5 *near*
proximity 191.2 *closeness,* 253.4 *availability,* 264.1, 615.4 *nearness*
proxy 222.2 *substitute person,* 222.7 *substitute,* 293.21 *substitution,* 547.8 *representative,* 646.3 *agent,* 703.3 *authority,* 703.5 *commissioner,* 707.2 *alternative,* 716.7 *act as a go-between*
PR person 532.10 *publicizer*
PR representative 524.7 *news interpreter*
prude 134, 167.6 *conformist,* 852.11 *disapprover,* 876.6 *moralist*
prudence 516, 469.3 *circumspection,* 507.1 *wisdom,* 615.3 *convenience,* 756.1 *thrift,* 781.1 *caution,* 863.2 *virtues,* 869.2 *moderation*
prudent 469.9 *careful,* 507.5 *wise,* 516.6 *foreseeing,* 615.1 *convenient,* 654.8 *advisable,* 756.4 *thrifty,* 781.4 *cautious,* 863.6 *ethical,* 869.9 *moderate*
prudently 507.9 *wisely,* 516.8 *foresightedly,* 654.9 *advisably,* 756.7 *economically,* 781.7 *cautiously,* 863.10 *ethically,* 869.12 *moderately*
prudery 134.1 *purity,* 167.4 *conventionalism,* 690.3 *unadornment,* 876.4 *self-righteousness*
prudish 134.12 *morally pure,* 167.14 *conformist,* 690.10 *unadorned,* 810.10 *bashful,* 876.10 *moralistic*
prudishly 134.18 *virtuously,* 690.12 *plainly*
prudishness 134.1 *purity,* 810.3 *bashfulness,* 876.4 *self-righteousness*
prune 45.42 *preserve,* 69.15 *cultivate,* 85.18 *manage trees,* 129.5 *make smaller,* 131.4 *take off,* 136.10 *set apart,* 182.8 *reduce,* 262.5 *make smaller,* 270.10 *shorten,* 355.12 *displace,* 380.16 *use a sharp tool*
pruned 69.19 *ornamental,* 262.7 *smaller,* 270.8, 562.7 *shortened*
pruner 69.6 *garden tool,* 380.9 *sharp-edged thing*
pruning 69.5 *gardening,* 85.6 *tree management,* 262.1 *contraction,* 270.2 *shortening,* 355.2 *displacement,* 562.2 *outline*
pruning saw 603.2 *garden tool*
pruning shears 380.9 *sharp-edged thing*
prurience 465.2 *prying,* 622.3 *obscenity,* 821.5 *desire,* 877.2 *indecency*
prurient 465.6 *prying,* 622.9 *obscene,* 877.12 *indecent*
pruriently 465.9 *officiously,* 622.12 *dirtily*
prurigo 624.13 *skin disease*
pruritis 624.13 *skin disease*
pruritus 366.5 *restlessness*
prusik 74 Knots, 34.9 *mountaineer*
prusiking 34.3 *climbing technique,* 34.8 *mountaineering*
Prussian blue 454.5 *blueness*
prussic acid 631.8 *poison*
PR woman 532.10 *publicizer*
pry 465.4 *meddler,* 465.7 *be curious,* 477.17 *question,* 642.17 *meddle*
prying 465, 465, 435.3 *observa-*

tion, 477.8 *curiosity,* 477.12 *questioning,* 642.21 *meddling*
prying person 642.11 *meddler*
pry into 642.17 *meddle*
Przemyśl 93 Cities
Przevalski's Horse 32 Breeds of Horse and Pony
PS 130.3 *additional item*
psalm 10.8 *hymn,* 48.7 *poem,* 49.5 *sacred music,* 433.2 *song*
psalmic 49.32 *instrumental*
psalmist 49.24 *musician,* 433.5 *melodist*
psalmodic 49.32 *instrumental*
psalmody 10.8 *hymn,* 49.5 *sacred music*
psalm-singing 9.1 *worship,* 10.3 *rite of worship,* 10.8 *hymn*
psalter 10.8 *hymn*
psaltery 49 Musical Instruments
psathyrella 89 Fungi
psephological 170.13 *calculative,* 580.16 *elective*
psephologist 170.7 *mathematician,* 580.13 *electorate*
psephology 170.2 *statistics,* 580.12 *election*
psephomancer 11.13 *diviner*
psephomancy 11.9 *divination*
pseud 539.15 *deceiver,* 540.10 *fake,* 540.15 *false person*
pseudo 102.12 *not the real thing,* 114.8 *simulated,* 118.13 *imitation,* 474.10 *hypocritical,* 540.10 *fake*
pseudoaromatic 57.7 *chemical compound,* 57.35 *combined*
pseudocoelomate 81.16 *invertebrate*
pseudohalogen 57 Types of Compounds
pseudolanguage 65.9 *programming language*
pseudologist 538.11 *liar*
pseudologue 539.16 *liar*
pseudology 538.3, 540.6 *lying*
pseudonym 529.8 *anonymity,* 531.7 *concealer,* 560.8 *name*
pseudonymity 560.7 *nomenclature*
pseudoparenchymatous 90.7 *alga*
pseudopsychological 11.16 *psychic*
pseudopsychology 11.1 *occultism*
pseudoscorpion 82 Arachnids, 82.2 *arachnid*
pseudostatement 48.12 *poetic language*
pseudosyllogism 474.2 *sophism*
pseudosyllogistic 474.7 *sophistic*
psi faculty 11.8 *psychic power*
psilocybe 89 Fungi
psilocyloin 62 Medication
psilomelane 54 Minerals
psittaciform 78.23 *avian*
psittacine 78.23 *avian*
psittacosis 624.18 *veterinary disease*
Pskov 93 Cities
Psocoptera 82 Orders of Insects
psocopteran 82.10 *insectan*
PSV 71 Motor Vehicles
psychalgia 61.12 *stress*
psyche 61, 11.7 *spirit,* 165.2 *personality,* 165.11 *identity,* 368.6 *internal world*
psychedelic 62.17 *stimulating,* 875.9 *addictive*
psychedelically 875.11 *in a trance*
psychedelic drug 62.4 *drug type*
psyched up 594.18 *prepared*
psychiatric 61.32 *psychological*
psychiatrically 61.39 *psychologically*
psychiatric care 61.3 *psychiatric treatment,* 510.9 *treatment*
psychiatric hospital 61, 510.8 *mental hospital*
psychiatric social worker 61.30 *psychiatrist*
psychiatric treatment 61
psychiatric unit 61.31 *psychiatric hospital,* 510.8 *mental hospital*
psychiatric ward 61.31 *psychiatric hospital,* 510.8 *mental hospital*

sychiatrist 61, 510, 60.11 *doctor*, 61.29 *psychologist*, 629.12 *repairer*, 630.15 *healer*, 654.4 *adviser*
sychiatry 61, 60.3 *medical specialty*, 630.13 *therapy*
sychic 11, 11.12 *occultist*, 11.13 *diviner*, 368.7 *believer in a nonmaterial world*, 368.8 *nonmaterial*, 368.9 *parapsychological*
sychical 11.16 *psychic*
sychically 11.25 *occultly*, 368.13 *metaphysically*
sychic apparatus 61.21 *psyche*
sychic combat 674.6 *fight*
sychic determinism 61.1 *psychology*
sychic energy 61.22 *libido*
sychicist 11.12 *occultist*
sychic phenomena 368.4 *parapsychology*
sychic phenomenon 11
sychic power 11
sychic research 11.1 *occultism*, 368.4 *parapsychology*
sychics 11.1 *occultism*
sychism 11.1 *occultism*
sychist 11.12 *occultist*
sycho 61.8 *disordered personality*, 398.11 *murderer*, 510.7 *insane person*
sychoacoustics 61.1 *psychology*
sychoanalyse 61.38 *psychologize*, 368.12 *enter a nonmaterial world*
sychoanalysis 61.1 *psychology*, 61.3 *psychiatric treatment*, 368.6 *internal world*, 510.9 *treatment*, 630.13 *therapy*
sychoanalyst 61.29 *psychologist*, 368.7 *believer in a nonmaterial world*, 510.10 *psychiatrist*, 629.12 *repairer*, 630.15 *healer*, 654.4 *adviser*
sychoanalytic 368.11 *internal*
sychoanalytical 61.32 *psychological*
sychoanalytically 368.14 *subjectively*
sychoanalytic method 61.3 *psychiatric treatment*
sychoanalytic theory 61.1 *psychology*
sychobabble 5.5 *nonstandard language*, 5.20 *jargon word*, 65.10 *specialized language*, 521.5 *empty talk*, 521.9 *talk nonsense*, 564.1 *faculty of speech*
sychobiochemistry 61.1 *psychology*
sychobiological 61.32 *psychological*
sychobiologist 61.29 *psychologist*
sychobiology 61.1 *psychology*
sychocatharsis 61.3 *psychiatric treatment*
sychochemist 61.29 *psychologist*
sychodiagnosis 61.2 *psychiatry*
sychodiagnostic 61.32 *psychological*
sychodiagnostics 61.2 *psychiatry*
sychodrama 51.2 *play*, 61.3 *psychiatric treatment*
sychodynamics 61.1 *psychology*
sychogalvanic response 61.4 *psychometrics*
sychogalvanic skin response 61.4 *psychometrics*
sychogalvanometer 61.4 *psychometrics*
sychogenesis 61.1 *psychology*
sychogenetic 61.32 *psychological*
sychogenetics 61.1 *psychology*
sychogenic 61.32 *psychological*
sychogenic disorder 61.9 *psychological disorder*
sychogeriatric 61.32 *psychological*
sychogeriatrician 61.30 *psychiatrist*
sychogeriatrics 61.2 *psychiatry*
sychognosis 61.1 *psychology*
sychogony 61.20 *conditioning*
sychogram 61.4 *psychometrics*

psychographer 61.29 *psychologist*
psychographist 11.12 *occultist*
psychography 11.1 *occultism*, 61.1 *psychology*, 61.4 *psychometrics*
psychokinesis 11.1 *occultism*, 61.1 *psychology*, 368.4 *parapsychology*
psychokinetic 11.16 *psychic*, 368.9 *parapsychological*
psycholinguist 5.2 *linguist*
psycholinguistics 5.1 *linguistics*, 61.1 *psychology*
psycholinguistic 5.38 *linguistic*
psychological 61, 1.11 *anthropological*, 459.9 *mental*
psychological counselling 61.3 *psychiatric treatment*
psychological cure 629.11 *recuperation*
psychological disorder 61
psychological drama 51.2 *play*
psychologically 61
psychologically disturbed 61
psychological me 61.21 *psyche*
psychological medicine 61.2 *psychiatry*
psychological novel 48.2 *fiction*
psychological screening 61.4 *psychometrics*
psychological stress 61.12 *stress*
psychological test 61
psychological thriller 48.2 *fiction*
psychological time 185.1 *time*
psychological warfare 61.1 *psychology*, 676.1 *war*, 676.8 *warfare*, 777.4 *intimidation*
psychologism 61.1 *psychology*
psychologist 61
psychologize 61
psychologue 61.29 *psychologist*
psychology 61, 630.13 *therapy*, 652.1 *conduct*
Psychology and Psychiatry 61
psychomachia 674.6 *fight*
psychomancer 11.13 *diviner*
psychomancy 11.1 *divination*
psychometer 11.12 *occultist*, 61.4 *psychometrics*
psychometric 61.32 *psychological*, 268.16 *micrometric*
psychometrics 61, 61.1 *psychology*
psychometrist 11.12 *occultist*
psychometry 11.8 *psychic power*, 61.1 *psychology*, 61.4 *psychometrics*, 268.2 *micrometry*
psych oneself up 594.8 *prepare oneself*
psychoneurological 61.32 *psychological*
psychoneurosis 61.1 *psychology*, 61.10 *neurosis*, 510.6 *mental breakdown*
psychoneurotic 61.8 *disordered personality*
psychopath 61.8 *disordered personality*, 241.4 *violent person or animal*, 398.11 *murderer*, 510.7 *insane person*
psychopathia martialis 61.10 *neurosis*
psychopathic 61.36 *psychologically disturbed*, 398.24 *murderous*, 510.13 *mentally ill*
psychopathic killer 398.11 *murderer*
psychopathic personality 61.8 *disordered personality*
psychopathological 61.32 *psychological*
psychopathologist 61.29 *psychologist*
psychopathology 61.1 *psychology*
psychopathy 61.11, 510.5 *psychosis*
psychopharmacological 61.32 *psychological*
psychopharmacology 61.1 *psychology*
psychophysical 61.32 *psychological*
psychophysicist 61.29 *psychologist*
psychophysics 61.1 *psychology*
psychophysiologist 61.29 *psychologist*

psychophysiology 61.1 *psychology*
psychorrhagy 11.1 *occultism*
psychosensory 11.16 *psychic*
psychosexual 61.32 *psychological*
psychosexual development 61.1 *psychology*
psychosexuality 61.1 *psychology*
psychosis 61, 510, 61.9 *psychological disorder*
psychosocial 61.32 *psychological*
psychosocial medicine 61.2 *psychiatry*
psychosociologist 61.29 *psychologist*
psychosociology 61.1 *psychology*
psychosomatic 61.32 *psychological*, 624.23 *diseased*
psychosomatic medicine 61.2 *psychiatry*
psychosomatics 61.1 *psychology*
psychosophical 11.16 *psychic*
psychosophy 11.1 *occultism*
psychosurgery 60.9 *surgery*, 61.3 *psychiatric treatment*
psychotechnical 61.32 *psychological*
psychotechnics 61.1 *psychology*
psychotechnologist 61.29 *psychologist*
psychotechnology 61.1 *psychology*
psychotherapeutic 61.32 *psychological*
psychotherapeutics 61.3 *psychiatric treatment*
psychotherapeutist 61.30 *psychiatrist*
psychotherapist 61.29 *psychologist*, 61.30, 510.10 *psychiatrist*, 629.12 *repairer*, 630.15 *healer*, 654.4 *adviser*
psychotherapy 61.3 *psychiatric treatment*, 510.9 *treatment*, 629.11 *recuperation*, 630.13 *therapy*
psychotic 61.8 *disordered personality*, 61.36 *psychologically disturbed*, 153.16 *deranged*, 510.7 *insane person*, 510.13 *mentally ill*
psychotically 153.19 *distractedly*, 510.17 *insanely*
psychotic personality 61.8 *disordered personality*
psychotropic drug 61.3 *psychiatric treatment*
psychrometer 55.7 *weather instruments*, 389.19 *measuring instrument*
psychrometric 55.42 *barometric*
psych up 239.3 *invigorate*
PT 6.3 *subject*, 644.5 *exercise*
Ptah 8 Deities
ptarmigan 78 Birds
P. T. Barnum 532.8 *public relations*
PT boat 74 Ships and Boats, 679.24 *warship*
pteranodon 79 Fossil Reptiles
Pteraspis 80.4 *fossil fish*
pteridological 88.5 *fernlike*
pteridologist 83.12 *plant scientist*, 88.2 *fern plant*
pteridology 83.10 *plant science*, 88.2 *fern plant*
Pteridophyta 83.4 *lower plant*
pteridophyte 83.4 *lower plant*, 88.1 *fern*, 88.5 *fernlike*
pteridophytes 396.9 *classifications of life*
pteridophytic 88.5 *fernlike*
pteridophytous 88.5 *fernlike*
pteridosperm 88.1 *fern*
pterodactyl 202.8 *prehistoric animal*
pteronophobia 777 Phobias by Name
pterosaur 79 Fossil Reptiles, 79.6 *extinct reptile*
pteryla 78.17 *plumage*
PTFE 57.21 *polymer*, 604.1 *materials*
Ptolemaeus 53 Lunar Features
Ptolemaic universe 53.4 *cosmological model*
Ptolemy 52 Scientists

ptomaine poisoning 624.6 *infection*, 624.8 *indigestion*, 631.7 *poisoning*
ptyalism 353.9 *saliva*
p-type conductivity 56.44, 64.4 *semiconductor*
p-type semiconductor 56.44, 64.4 *semiconductor*
pub 256.10 *hotel*, 815.4 *meeting place*
pub circuit 51.13 *engagement*
pub-crawl 874.8 *get drunk*, 874.14 *drinking bout*
pub-crawler 874.17 *drunkard*
pub-crawling 874.5 *drunken*
puberty 206.1 *youth*, 245.4 *development*, 594.14 *preparedness*
pubescence 206.1 *youth*
pubescent 206.11 *young*
pubiotomy 60 Surgical Operations
pubis 382 Bones
public 12.9 *governmental*, 93.14 *urban*, 164.19 *prevailing*, 255.2 *inhabitants*, 322.13 *opened up*, 400.9 *group*, 400.13 *national*, 437.1 *visible*, 501.10 *known*, 526.14 *manifest*, 532.19 *published*, 724.5 *jointly possessing*, 737.19 *corporate*, 811.21 *blatant*, 815.7 *human society*, 815.15 *sociable*
public-address system 420.9 *audio device*, 532.1 *publication*
public-address system 56.18 *source of sound*, 423.4 *sound maker*
public affairs 12.2 *politics*
publican 606.4 *caterer*
public assistance 662.4 *social assistance*
publication 532, 6.14 *school book*, 162.1 *dispersion*, 457.1 *appearance*, 475.1 *demonstration*, 517.3 *plan*, 526.10 *manifestation*, 528.2 *communication*, 530.2 *divulgence* , 543.6 *word*, 636.1 *warning*
Publication 532
public baths 621.6 *bath*
public benefit 613.8 *benefit*
public broadcasting 534.24 *television broadcasting*
public building 63.20 *building*
public comment 532.3 *journalism*
public company 724.1 *joint possession*, 737.7 *company*
public convenience 353.13 *lavatory*, 727.7 *toilet*
public corporation 724.1 *joint possession*
public debt 13.4 *economic development*
public discussion 532.7 *publicity*
public domain 724.1 *joint possession*
public enemy 820.5 *hostile person*, 822.8 *hated person*
public enterprise 13.1 *economics*
public entertainer 51.27 *entertainer*
public expenditure 13.6 *economic factors*
public eye 532.7 *publicity*
public file 545.1 *record*
public forum 532.7 *publicity*
public garden 69.2 *garden*
public good 613.8 *benefit*
public hall 815.4 *meeting place*
public-health inspector 625.3 *hygienist*
public-health medicine 60.1 *medicine*, 60.6 *health care*
public-health physican 60.11 *doctor*
public house 351.11 *drink provider*
public image 457.5 *impression*
public information officer 524.7 *news interpreter*
public inquiry 654.4 *adviser*
publicist 228.7 *motivator*, 293.18 *fixer*, 526.12 *displayer*, 528.9 *informant*, 532.10 *publicizer*, 561.3 *dissertator*, 586.12 *persuader*, 678.4 *representative*

publicity 532, 293.20 *fixing,* 437.4 *clarity,* 526.10 *manifestation,* 528.4 *mass communication,* 586.5 *propaganda,* 586.6 *advertising*
publicity agent 528.9 *informant,* 532.10 *publicizer,* 586.12 *persuader*
publicity man 51.25 *producer*
publicity manager 51.25 *producer*
publicity woman 51.25 *producer*
publicize 532, 293.33 *fix,* 526.3 *reveal,* 528.12 *communicate,* 530.6 *divulge,* 533.13 *report,* 611.8 *make important*
publicized 475.9 *demonstrated,* 526.13 *displayed*
publicizer 532, 524.7 *news interpreter,* 526.12 *displayer,* 528.9 *informant,* 530.4 *discloser,* 561.3 *dissertator,* 586.12 *persuader*
public-key cryptography 529.4 *brain-teaser*
public knowledge 532.7 *publicity*
public land 724.1 *joint possession*
Public Lending Right 532.6 *book publishing*
public limited company 13.7 *corporation,* 737.7 *company*
publicly 532, 93.16 *municipally,* 322.25 *obviously,* 475.20, 526.16 *manifestly,* 811.37 *blatantly*
public money 741.19 *treasury*
publicness 532.7 *publicity*
public notice 532.1 *publication*
public nuisance 822.8 *hated person*
public office holder 697.2 *public servant*
public official 697.2 *public servant*
public opinion 12.1 *government,* 16.18 *tribunal,* 233.6 *group influence,* 492.1 *judgment*
public opinion poll 580.10 *vote*
public ownership 13.1 *economics,* 724.1 *joint possession*
public persona 289.3 *appearance,* 457.5 *impression*
public property 725.1 *property*
public prosecutor 16.10 *law officer,* 492.6 *justice,* 856.3 *accuser*
public provision 662.4 *social assistance*
public purse 741.19 *treasury*
public recognition 532.7 *publicity,* 878.1 *reward*
public record 3.5 *chronicle,* 545.1 *record*
public relations 532, 533.1 *news,* 586.6 *advertising,* 653.3 *management*
public relations man 293.18 *fixer,* 524.7 *news interpreter,* 526.12 *displayer,* 535.9 *affirmer,* 707.1 *deputy*
public relations officer 528.9 *informant,* 532.10 *publicizer,* 586.12 *persuader,* 678.4 *representative*
public relations person 228.7 *motivator*
public relations practitioner 533.4 *journalist*
public relations release 535.2 *statement*
public sale 739.4 *sale*
public school 6.12 *educational institution*
public sector 13.1 *economics,* 13.2 *economy,* 15.10 *unionized,* 737.5 *commercial trade*
public sector borrowing 745.2 *national debt*
public sector borrowing requirement 745.2 *national debt*
public sector union 15.3 *organized labour*
public servant 697, 653.16 *official,* 703.5 *commissioner,* 710.8 *volunteer*
public service 703.4 *council*
public service announcement 534.25 *broadcast material*

public speaker 567, 564.10 *speaker*
public speech 567.1 *address*
public spirit 833.2 *public spiritedness*
public spirited 833.6 *philanthropic*
public spiritedness 833
public telephone 534.9 *telephone,* 534.12 *public telephone system*
public telephone system 534
public transport 326.5 *means of transport*
public utilities 13.1 *economics*
public utility 613.8 *benefit*
public warning 636.1 *warning*
public weal 861.13 *benefit*
public welfare 729.2 *gift,* 831.3 *welfare*
public worship 10
publish 532, 162.16 *distribute,* 457.14 *present,* 475.15 *demonstrate,* 526.1 *display,* 526.3 *reveal,* 528.12 *communicate,* 530.6 *divulge,* 532.14 *proclaim,* 533.13 *report,* 543.12 *signal*
publishable 876.10 *moralistic*
published 532, 162.22 *distributed,* 475.9 *demonstrated,* 526.13 *displayed*
publisher 532, 528.9 *informant,* 543.8 *signer*
publisher's catalogue 171.2 *table*
publish freely 698.14 *be free*
publishing 532, 245.1 *reproduction,* 532.1 *publication,* 532.6 *book publishing,* 543.16 *signalling*
publishing contract 715.2 *purchase contract*
publish the banns 821.28 *win the love of,* 823.15 *marry,* 826.8 *court*
pub sign 544.3 *means of identification*
pub theatre 51.1 *drama*
púcán 74 *Sailing Ships and Boats*
Puccini 49 *Musicians and Composers*
puce 449.1 *brown,* 455.6 *purple*
puck 31.3 *ice hockey,* 338.10 *ball*
Puck 11.11 *ghost,* 539.15 *deceiver*
puck-carrier 31.4 *ice hockey player*
pucker 262.5 *make smaller,* 262.6 *become smaller,* 320.2, 320.8 *pleat,* 321.2, 321.7 *wrinkle*
puckered 262.7 *smaller,* 321.5 *wrinkly*
puckered up 262.7 *smaller*
puckering 262.1 *contraction,* 262.8 *contracting*
puckering up 262.1 *contraction*
pucker up 262.5 *make smaller,* 262.6 *become smaller*
puckish 618.5 *harmful*
puck possession 31.3 *ice hockey*
pud 45.9 *dish*
pudding 45.9 *dish,* 45.35 *dessert,* 350.14 *mouthful,* 393.8 *pulp,* 414.3 *dessert*
pudding basin 45.6 *kitchen equipment*
puddle 393, 278.4, 278.4 *shallow thing*
puddle in 69.15 *cultivate*
pudency 134.1 *purity,* 876.3 *moral purity*
pudenda 245.8 *organs of reproduction*
pudgy 374.4 *compressible*
Puebla 93 *Cities*
Pueblo 1 *Peoples*
puerile 460.6 *unintelligent,* 508.5 *foolish,* 595.5 *immature,* 612.4 *trivial*
puerilely 460.11 *unintelligently*
puerility 206.1 *youth,* 460.2 *unintelligence,* 508.1 *folly*
puerperal 245.16 *reproductive*
puerperal psychosis 61.11 *psychosis*
Puerto Rico 98 *Islands*
puff 349.14 *let out,* 374.11 *soft thing,* 390.22 *blow,* 413.8 *smok-*

ing, 413.14 *smoke,* 524.3 *criticism,* 524.11 *criticize,* 532.8 *public relations* , 532.16 *publicize,* 561.2 *article,* 650.5 *be fatigued,* 851.15 *compliment,* 853.8 *flatter*
puff adder 79 *Reptiles*
puff away 338.28 *shoot*
puffball 89 *Fungi*
puffball mushroom 45.33 *vegetable*
puffed 541.12 *exaggerated*
puffed-out chest 805.10 *boastfulness*
puffed up 797.3 *affected,* 805.22, 809.13 *boastful*
puffed-up 261.7 *bigger,* 541.13 *enlarged*
puffer 80 *Fishes,* 72.4 *locomotive*
puffery 541.1 *exaggeration,* 797.1 *affectedness*
puffily 261.10 *largely*
puffin 78 *Birds,* 78.3 *water bird*
puffiness 259.5 *fatness,* 261.1 *growth*
puffing 650.3 *panting*
puffing and blowing 650.3 *panting*
Puffing Billy 72.10 *miscellaneous*
puffing up 541.2 *enlargement*
puff job 532.9 *advertisement*
puff of wind 55.14 *windiness*
puff pastry 45.37 *pastry*
puff piece 532.9 *advertisement*
puff puff 72.4 *locomotive*
puff sleeve 295.24 *part of garment*
puff up 261.5 *make bigger,* 261.6 *become bigger,* 361.2 *send up,* 541.8 *enlarge,* 851.15 *compliment*
puff up with pride 809.18 *make conceited*
puffy 259.16 *fat,* 261.7 *bigger,* 797.3 *affected*
pug 77 *Breeds of Dogs,* 26.4 *boxer,* 44.6 *ceramic workshop,* 44.11 *make ceramics,* 679.3 *athlete*
pugging 44.5 *ceramic process,* 44.10 *ceramic*
pugilism 26.2, 674.7 *boxing*
pugilist 26.4 *boxer,* 674.10 *contender,* 679.3 *athlete*
pugilistic 26.14 *combat,* 674.15 *contentious,* 676.16 *warlike,* 679.35 *martial*
pugilistically 679.42 *martially*
pug mill 44.6 *ceramic workshop*
pugnacious 17.8 *military,* 473.9 *hostile,* 670.21 *aggressive,* 674.15 *contentious,* 676.16 *warlike,* 679.33 *combative*
pugnaciously 674.17 *contentiously,* 679.41 *aggressively*
pugnaciousness 676.5 *bellicosity*
pugnacity 670.11 *attack,* 676.5 *bellicosity*
pug-nosed 270.7 *short*
pu-liu 49 *Musical Instruments*
puissance 18 *Sporting Activities,* 235.1 *power,* 688.1 *authority*
puissant 235.13 *powerful,* 237.10 *potent,* 688.12 *authoritative*
puja 7.2 *religiousness,* 9.1 *worship,* 10.3 *rite of worship*
puke 349.15 *vomit,* 349.23 *vomiting*
pukey 349.30 *vomiting,* 618.4 *poor*
puking 349.23 *vomiting*
pukish 618.4 *poor*
pukka 537.19 *authentic*
pulchritude 789.1, 789.1 *gorgeousness*
pulchritudinous 789.5 *beautiful*
Pulcinella 51.30 *clown*
pule 431.13 *cry,* 432.5 *sing*
puli 77 *Breeds of Dogs*
pulicide 62.4 *drug type*
Pulitzer Prize 532.6 *book publishing,* 878.2 *prize*
pull 339, 339, 29.3 *golf shots,* 29.7 *golf,* 60.21 *practise dentistry,* 126.1 *superiority,* 228.9

motivate, 233 *influence,* 233.4 *indirect influence,* 233.10 *be a prevailing influence,* 241.8 *use violence,* 324.14 *set in motion,* 330.10 *bat,* 330.14 *sporting hit* 335.2 *divert,* 335.5 *twist,* 338.9 *throw,* 338.26 *bat,* 340.1 *attraction,* 340.4 *allurement,* 340.11 *attract,* 355.1 *extraction,* 407.3 *press,* 407.11 *touch,* 630.20 *door,* 644.4 *exertion,* 644.6 *work,* 656.7 *be clumsy*
pull a bonehead play 628.4 *imp air*
pull a boner 628.4 *impair*
pull a fast one 539.23 *deceive,* 657.5 *be cunning*
pull a long face 772.8 *be serious*
pull apart 139.5 *unstick,* 141.4 *deconstruct,* 244.9 *demolish*
pull aside 335.2 *divert*
pull at 339
pull back 331.2 *respond,* 337.2 *retreat*
pullback 337.11 *retreat*
pull back 339.14 *draw in,* 699.8 *restrain*
pull down 141.4 *deconstruct,* 244.9 *demolish,* 362.2 *flatten,* 362.3 *bring down,* 721.9 *gain*
pull down about one's ears 362.2 *flatten*
pull down the blind 440.14 *make dark*
pulled 252.9 *removed*
pulled muscle 624.16 *rheumatism,* 628.11 *hurt*
pulled open 322.12 *open*
pulled out by the roots 252.9 *removed*
pulled through a hedge backwards 151.15 *untidy*
puller 339.6 *towline*
puller of strings 527.9 *backstage manipulator*
pullet 68.8 *livestock,* 78.12 *young bird*
pulley 63.6 *simple machine,* 63. *machine element,* 603.1 *tool*
pull faces 543.11 *gesture*
pull for 431.12 *cheer*
pull hair 26.12 *wrestle*
pull hard 596.2 *try hard*
pull in 71.21 *miscellaneous motoring terms,* 339.14 *draw in,* 344.6 *stop at*
pull-in 350.15 *eating place*
pulling 66.13 *framing,* 235.15 *full of energy,* 339.1 *traction,* 339.8 *tractional,* 340.8 *attracting,* 351.1 *drinking*
pulling back 337.11 *retreat,* 339.1 *traction,* 339.8 *tractiona*
pulling down 721.1 *gain*
pulling no punches 554.3 *emphatic*
pulling off 139.8 *nonadhesive*
pulling one's leg 539.11 *hoax*
pulling out 331.6 *response,* 345. *departure,* 355.1 *extraction*
pulling out by the roots 252.2 *r moval*
pulling power 340, 235.4 *energy,* 339.1 *traction*
pulling the goalie 31.3 *ice hocke*
pulling the wool over someone's eyes 474.3 *cunning*
pulling together 664.4 *joint operation*
pulling towards 339.5 *magnetis*
pulling up 252.2 *removal*
pull it off 682.6 *be successful,* 718.13 *secure one's objective*
Pullman 72.6 *rolling stock,* 326. *means of transport*
pull no punches 552.4 *be concise,* 554.6 *emphasize,* 690.6 *suppress*
pull off 139.5 *unstick,* 682.6 *be successful*
pull off a coup d'état 713.8 *cau: mischief*
pull off a robbery in broad daylight 736.12 *steal*
pull off someone's clothes 296.15 *make nude*
pull on 295.34 *wear*

pull-on 295.31 *styled*
pull oneself up 361.5 *arise*
pull oneself up by one's boot-straps 682.6 *be successful*
pull one's finger out 156.18 *make a beginning*
pull one's leg 539.31 *hoax,* 850.24 *ridicule*
pull one's punches 591.3 *abstain,* 691.3 *be lenient*
pull open 322.18 *open*
pullout 331.6 *response,* 337.11 *retreat*
pull out 131.3 *subtract,* 252.15 *remove,* 337.2 *retreat,* 339.13 *pull at,* 345.2 *withdraw,* 355.11 *extract,* 673.3 *submit*
pull out all the stops 239.2 *be full of vigour,* 644.8 *exert oneself,* 698.19 *liberalize,* 811.31 *put on a show*
pull out of the station 345.5 *set out*
pullover 295.13 *sweater*
pullover shirt 295.8 *shirt*
pull rank 805.28 *disdain*
pull someone's chestnuts out of the fire 232.4 *be an instrument*
pull someone's leg 771.13 *be humorous*
pull strings 232.4 *be an instrument,* 233.8 *influence,* 592.13 *plot,* 688.18 *have authority*
pull the blankets over one's head 634.4 *shelter*
pull the emergency handle 636.7 *raise the alarm*
pull the goalie out 31.9 *play hockey*
pull the plug on 157.16 *cease*
pull the rug from under one's feet 661.8 *hinder*
pull the strings 527.13 *hide,* 653.1 *manage*
pull the trigger 37.7, 338.28 *shoot,* 670.2 *fire,* 679.37 *fight*
pull the wool over someone's eyes 474.11 *practise sophistry,* 531.9 *disguise,* 539.23 *deceive,* 858.8 *be dishonourable*
pull through 629.4 *be restored*
pull-through 621.10 *cleaning object*
pull tight 135.8 *unite*
pull together 116.22 *form an alliance,* 664.13 *work together,* 667.6 *agree with*
pull to pieces 141.4 *deconstruct,* 244.9 *demolish,* 854.11 *criticize*
pull towards 339, 340.11 *attract*
pullulate 156.26 *produce,* 181.11 *crowd,* 206.18 *grow,* 246.6 *be fertile,* 261.6 *become bigger*
pullulating 206.13 *maturing,* 261.8 *growing*
pullulation 156.4 *conception,* 261.1 *growth*
pull up 218.6 *cease,* 252.15 *remove,* 325.8 *be motionless*
pull up by the roots 131.3 *subtract,* 252.15 *remove*
pull up stakes 345.3 *quit*
pull wires 233.8 *influence,* 592.13 *plot,* 688.18 *have authority*
pulmonary 290.10 *visceral,* 390.19 *respiratory*
pulmonary phthisis 624.9 *respiratory disease*
pulp 393, 393, 86.3 *fruit structure,* 244.9 *demolish,* 374.11 *soft thing,* 374.13 *soften,* 412.3 *tasteless items,* 604.3 *paper,* 612.4 *trivial*
pulped 244.15 *destroyed*
pulpefaction 393.5 *pulping*
pulp engine 393.15 *pulper*
pulper 393
pulp fiction 48.2 *fiction,* 532.6 *book publishing,* 560.5 *fiction*
pulpification 393.5 *pulping*
pulpifier 393.15 *pulper*
pulpiness 393, 374.10 *compressibility,* 387.5 *fluidity*
pulping 393, 389.10 *steeping*

pulpiteer 7.4 *religionist,* 567.6 *public speaker*
pulp magazine 532.5 *journal*
pulpousness 393.4 *pulpiness*
pulpwood 85.3 *timber*
pulpy 393, 374.4 *compressible*
pulsar 53.11 *stellar birth*
pulsate 183.22 *resound,* 214.7 *be regular,* 365.9 *vibrate,* 366.24 *shake,* 426.8 *drum*
pulsatile 214.11 *regular,* 365.14 *vibrating*
pulsating 183.15 *reverberatory,* 214.11 *regular,* 365.14 *vibrating,* 366.18 *shaky,* 427.6 *resonant*
pulsatingly 214.15 *regularly*
pulsating variable 53.12 *variable star*
pulsation 183.6 *reverberation,* 214.1 *regularity,* 365.2 *vibration,* 426.1 *drumming*
pulsative 365.14 *vibrating*
pulsatory 214.11 *regular,* 365.14 *vibrating*
pulse 45.33 *vegetable,* 49.19 *tempo,* 56.16 *waveform,* 56.51 *electric current,* 69.11 *vegetable,* 183.6 *reverberation,* 183.22 *resound,* 185.12 *musical time,* 212.4 *frequency,* 214.5 *regular thing,* 214.7 *be regular,* 235.7 *electrical power,* 365.2 *vibration,* 365.9 *vibrate,* 366.24 *shake,* 426.1 *drumming,* 426.8 *drum*
pulsebeat 214.5 *regular thing*
pulse code modulation 534.14 *radio transmission*
pulsed signal 534.14 *radio transmission*
pulsejet propulsion 338.2 *method of propulsion*
pulse radar 534.28 *radar*
pulse train 56.16 *waveform,* 64.14 *terminal*
pulsimeter 268.8 *meter*
pulsing 183.15 *reverberatory,* 365.14 *vibrating*
pulsion 337.29 *in reverse*
pulsive 330.17 *impelling,* 338.17 *propulsive*
pulverable 384.21 *pulverizable*
pulverableness 384.2 *crumbliness*
pulverizable 384
pulverization 384, 244.2 *destroying*
pulverize 384, 133.8 *mix,* 136.9 *separate,* 244.9 *demolish,* 330.5 *beat,* 374.13 *soften,* 385.16 *massage,* 393.24 *pulp,* 404.3 *impair*
pulverized 384, 244.15 *destroyed*
pulverizer 384
pulverous 384.16 *powdery*
pulverulence 384.1 *powderiness*
pulverulent 384.16 *powdery,* 384.21 *pulverizable*
pulvinate frieze 43 *Architectural Decoration*
pulvule 62 *Medication*
puma 77 *Placental Mammals*
pumice 54.25 *eruption,* 385.7 *eraser,* 621.9 *cleaning agent*
pumice stone 621.9 *cleaning agent*
pummel 26.11 *do a combat sport,* 330.5 *beat,* 674.12 *fight*
pummelling 26.2, 330.12 *collision,* 674.7 *boxing*
pump 36.18 *windsurf,* 235.12 *generate power,* 261.4 *enlarger,* 261.5 *make bigger,* 355.9 *extractor,* 355.14 *suck,* 389.13 *irrigator,* 477.18 *interrogate*
Pump 53 *The Constellations*
pump a fish 20.7 *angle*
pump bilge 353.17 *urinate*
pumped 70.5 *transportable,* 477.16 *questioned*
pumped storage scheme 235.6 *source of energy*
pumped-up 261.7 *bigger*
pumpernickel 45.38 *bread*
pump full of lead 338.29 *riddle*
pump in 606.5 *provision*
pumping 36.7, 36.13 *windsurf-*

ing, 70.5 *transportable,* 355.4 *sucking,* 477.2 *questioning*
pumping iron 644.5 *exercise*
pumpkin 45 Vegetables, 451.3 *orange thing*
pumpkin bread 45.38 *bread*
pumpkin lantern 439.7 *lantern*
pumpkin pie 45.36 *cake*
pump oil 410.11 *fuel*
pump one's hand 817.12 *greet*
pump out 349.11 *void,* 355.14 *suck,* 372.6 *make sparse*
pump petrol 410.11 *fuel*
pump room 630.14 *hospital*
pumps 295.19 *footwear*
pump up 261.5 *make bigger*
pun 48.12 *poetic language,* 506.2 *solecism,* 506.6 *talk nonsense,* 578.1 *be equivocal,* 578.5 *equivocalness,* 771.5 *joke,* 771.13 *be humorous*
punch 32.2 *thoroughbred,* 50.14 *sculptor's materials,* 133.2 *mixed thing,* 239.1 *vigour,* 306.2 *prototype,* 322.2 *opener,* 330.3 *hit,* 330.13 *blow,* 330.14 *sporting hit,* 330.15 *ram,* 351.7 *alcoholic drink,* 407.3 *press,* 407.11 *touch,* 414.5 *sweet drink,* 544.1 *identify,* 554.1 *emphasis,* 603.1 *tool,* 603.9 *use tools,* 670.5 *strike,* 670.18 *hit,* 674.12, 679.37 *fight*
Punch 51.30 *clown*
Punch-and-Judy show 51.5 *show*
Punchau 5 Deities
punch bowl 258.16 *crockery*
punch cattle 68.18 *practise livestock farming*
punched card 65.7 *peripheral*
punched full of holes 322.14 *holed*
punched open 322.12 *open*
puncheon 75 General Units, 47.12 *wood,* 258.11 *vessel*
puncher 26.4 *boxer,* 68.16 *farm worker,* 330.15 *ram,* 674.10 *contender,* 679.3 *athlete*
punch full of holes 322.20 *hole*
punch in 317.7 *make concave,* 344.5 *get in,* 644.6 *work*
Punchinello 51.30 *clown*
punching 26.15 *wrestling,* 670.23 *attacking,* 674.7 *boxing*
punch line 157.10 *ending*
punch open 322.18 *open*
punch out 306.7 *form,* 345.2 *withdraw,* 644.6 *work*
punch-up 151.9 *disorder,* 241.3 *instance of violence,* 674.6 *fight*
punchy 239.4 *vigorous,* 554.3 *emphatic*
punctilio 813.5 *etiquette*
punctilious 150.14 *well-ordered,* 537.21 *accurate,* 619.2 *perfectionist,* 719.7 *observant,* 811.26 *ritualistic,* 813.6 *formal,* 847.8 *dutiful*
punctiliously 719.8 *observantly,* 811.42 *ritualistically*
punctiliousness 150.6 *methodicalness,* 537.8 *accuracy,* 813.2 *formalism*
punctual 208.12 *early,* 210.8 *in time,* 719.7 *observant*
punctuality 208.1 *earliness,* 642.3 *nimbleness*
punctually 208.17 *early,* 210.11 *in time,* 719.8 *observantly*
punctualness 208.1 *earliness*
punctuate 543
punctuated 543
punctuation 543, 5.30 *syntax*
punctuation mark 137.4 *means of connection,* 543.7 *punctuation*
puncture 60.7 *diagnosis,* 322.1 *opening,* 322.20 *hole,* 346.11 *infiltrate,* 406.3 *injury,* 406.11 *inflict pain,* 542.21 *detract from,* 661.2 *obstacle*
punctured 322.14 *holed,* 406.6 *injured,* 542.18 *deflated*
punctured tyre 129.3 *decreasing thing*
puncturing 542.10 *deflation*
pundit 4.12 *sage,* 6.4 *educator,*

7.8 *priest,* 459.8 *intellectual person,* 655.5 *expert*
pung 71.10 *sled*
pungency 413.1 *piquancy,* 416.1 *odour,* 554.1 *emphasis*
pungent 237.12 *strong to the senses,* 300.10 *advantaged,* 411.7 *tasty,* 413.9 *piquant,* 415.5 *acid,* 416.5 *odorous,* 418.4 *fragrant,* 554.3 *emphatic*
pungently 237.15 *acutely,* 300.12 *at an advantage,* 411.11 *tastily,* 413.15 *piquantly,* 415.10 *sourly,* 418.7 *fragrantly*
pungent taste 411.1 *taste*
Punic 5 Languages and Groups of Languages
Punic War 17 Major Wars
punily 260.8 *in a small way*
puniness 238.1 *weakness,* 260.1 *littleness,* 274.7 *thinness*
punish 879, 16.75 *make illegal,* 406.11 *inflict pain,* 672.3 *retaliate,* 690.5 *be severe,* 699.8 *restrain,* 855.10 *avenge*
punishable 879, 16.5 *unjust*
punishable offence 16.39 *crime*
punishably 879.23 *punitively*
punished 879, 699.13 *restraining*
punisher 879, 398.10 *killer,* 855.6 *avenger*
punishing 879, 644.11 *laborious,* 650.4 *fatiguing,* 659.10 *difficult,* 855.14 *vindictive,* 879.19 *punitive*
punishing experience 879.10 *affliction*
punishingly 659.26 *arduously,* 855.16 *vindictively,* 879.23 *punitively*
punishing work 644.1 *work*
punishment 777 Phobias by Topic, **879,** 16.33 *litigation,* 16.43 *conviction,* 406.1 *pain,* 672.1 *retaliation,* 699.1 *restraint,* 845.2 *due,* 855.4 *revenge*
Punishment 879
punish oneself 866.9 *appear guilty,* 867.5 *do penance*
punish with death 879.5 *execute*
punitive 879, 672.5 *retaliatory,* 855.14 *vindictive*
punitively 879, 855.16 *vindictively*
punitive tax 751.7 *tax*
punitory 879.19 *punitive*
Punjabi 5 Languages and Groups of Languages
punk 49.33 *jazz,* 168.8 *dissenter,* 410.2 *lighter,* 618.2 *inferior,* 720.5 *nonobserver,* 832.8 *malefactor*
punk band 49.26 *musical group*
punk rock 49.9 *popular music*
punnet 258.6 *box,* 258.7 *basket*
punt 74 Ships and Boats, **36,** 19.12 *special team,* 36.8 *punting,* 330.7 *kick,* 330.13 *blow,* 338.5 *throw,* 338.27 *kick*
punter 32.15 *horse person,* 36.9 *sailor,* 74.8 *boatman*
punt for pleasure 36.19 *punt*
punting 36, 36
punting techniques 36.8 *punting*
punt pole 36.8 *punting*
punt-race 36.19 *punt*
punt-racing 36.8 *punting*
punt with one arm 36.19 *punt*
puny 238.8 *weak,* 260.7 *little,* 274.1 *thin,* 612.2 *obscure*
pup 77.9 *dog,* 77.19 *young mammal,* 77.35 *give birth,* 206.4 *young animal,* 206.7 *young man,* 245.11 *have young*
pupa 59.15 *developmental biology,* 82.5 *larva,* 206.4 *young animal,* 226.3 *rudiment*
pupal 59.26 *developmental,* 82.13 *immature*
pupate 82.17 *develop*
pupil 6.7 *learner,* 156.14 *beginner,* 291.2 *central thing,* 435.2 *eye*
pupilage 206.1 *youth*
pupils 163.6 *students*
puppet 91.16 *national,* 102.5 *in-*

substantial person, 232.3 *assistant*, 260.2 *little thing*, 539.22 *dupe*, 547.6 *image*, 701.5 *non-entity*, 701.5 *subjected person*, 808.3 *sycophant*

puppeteer 527.9 *backstage manipulator*

puppet government 12.1 *government*, 688.7 *type of rule*

puppet regime 91.3 *dominion*

puppetry 51.5 *show*

puppet show 51.5 *show*

Puppis 53 The Constellations

puppy 77.9 *dog*, 206.4 *young animal*

puppy-dog 77.9 *dog*

puppyish 77.28 *carnivorous*

puppy love 821.2 *romantic love*

Purana 7.12 *religious text*

purblind 436.9 *weak-sighted*

purblindness 436.2 *poor sight*

Purcell 49 Musicians and Composers, **52** Scientists

purchasable 738.13 *bought*

purchase 738, 738, 36.3 *parts of a sailing boat*, 339.4 *friction*, 361.9 *lifter*, 639.1 *deliver*, 639.2 *deliverance*, 748.1 *expend*, 748.4 *expenditure*

Purchase 730

purchase by mail order 738.1 *purchase*

purchase contract 715

purchased 738.13 *bought*

purchase of premises 751.6 *business costs*

purchase on account 738.7 *purchasing*

purchase on credit 738.7 *purchasing*

purchase price 751.5 *cost*

purchaser 738, 13.9 *economist*, 723.5 *possessor*, 730.5 *recipient*, 737.10 *trader*, 748.8 *spender*

purchases 738.6 *purchase*

purchase tax 751.7 *tax*

purchasing 738, 738.14 *buying*

purchasing power 13.2 *economy*

purdah 402.13 *womenfolk*, 438.6 *that which makes invisible*, 531.3 *covering up*, 816.3 *separation*

pure 134, 446, 857, 876, 5.39 *of language*, 7.15 *religious*, 56.99 *theoretical*, 57.32 *solid*, 134.12 *morally pure*, 142.7 *uncut*, 144.7 *complete*, 237.12 *strong to the senses*, 442.1 *transparent*, 537.19 *authentic*, 550.3 *clear*, 556.1 *simple*, 558.3 *elegant*, 600.2 *new*, 617.1 *worthy*, 619.1 *perfect*, 621.16 *clean*, 625.4 *hygienic*, 810.10 *bashful*, 825.7 *virginal*, 843.10 *moral*, 863.6 *ethical*, 865.5 *innocent*, 869.8 *self-restrained*

pure and simple 134.16 *simple*

pure as driven snow 863.5 *virtuous*

pure as the driven snow 134.14 *purified*, 857.5, 876.9 *pure*

purebred 134, 32.2 *thoroughbred*, 32.13 *breeding*, 32.17 *equine*, 68.21 *domesticated*, 134.13 *pure*

pure colour 56.28 *colour*

purée 45.13 *soup*, 393.8, 393.24 *pulp*

pure gold 617.8 *exceller*

pure heart 658.3 *naive person*, 857.2 *purity*

purely 134, 857, 174.24 *once*, 537.37 *authentically*, 550.4 *clearly*, 556.8 *simply*, 600.13 *newly*, 619.8 *completely*, 825.12 *celibately*, 863.10 *ethically*, 865.11 *innocently*, 869.11 *with self-restraint*, 876.13 *morally*

pure mathematics 52.1 *mathematics*

pureness 134.1 *purity*

pure of heart 865.5 *innocent*

pure person 134, 876

pure physics 56.4 *experimental physics*

pure speculation 518.3 *conjecture*

---

pure-white 446.1 *white*

purgation 134.2 *purification*, 349.21 *removal*, 353.2 *defecation*, 621.3 *religious cleansing*, 840.2 *apology*, 855.1 *vindication*, 867.2 *type of penance*

purgative 134, 630, 62.4 *drug type*, 62.17 *stimulating*, 134.15 *purifying*, 349.28 *propellant*, 349.29 *expulsive*, 353.25 *faecal*, 621.2 *cleaning*, 621.18 *cleansing*, 840.4 *atoning*

purgative agent 134.4 *purgative*

purgatively 134.19 *purely*, 840.8 *penitently*

purgatorial 8.16 *devilish*, 406.5 *painful*, 840.4 *atoning*

purgatorially 840.8 *penitently*

purgatory 8.11 *heaven*, 134.15 *purifying*, 406.1 *pain*, 621.18 *cleansing*, 840.2 *apology*

Purgatory 621.3 *religious cleansing*

purge 134.4 *purgative*, 134.10 *purify*, 349.10 *exterminate*, 349.11 *void*, 353.2 *defecation*, 353.16 *defecate*, 398.4, 398.18 *slaughter*, 546.1 *obliterate*, 546.3 *obliteration*, 621.15 *purify*, 630.6 *purgative*, 630.20 *doctor*, 855.7 *vindicate*, 879.5 *execute*, 879.13 *capital punishment*

purged 621.17 *cleaned*

purging 62.17 *stimulating*, 134.2 *purification*, 134.15 *purifying*, 349.21 *removal*, 621.2 *cleaning*, 630.17 *remedial*, 855.1 *vindication*

puri 45.38 *bread*, 45.49 *Indian dish*

purification 134, 10.5 *Christian rite*, 355.7 *obtaining an extract*, 621.2 *cleaning*, 621.3 *religious cleansing*, 625.1 *hygiene*, 627.5 *improvement*, 840.2 *apology*, 867.2 *type of penance*

Purification 10.15 *holy day*

purificatory 134.15 *purifying*, 621.18 *cleansing*

purified 134, 134.13 *pure*, 621.17 *cleaned*, 876.9 *pure*

purifier 134, 621.9 *cleaning agent*

purify 134, 621, 57.30 *extract*, 355.17 *obtain an extract*, 442.12 *make transparent*, 625.6 *make hygienic*, 627.1 *improve*, 794.6 *refine*

purifying 134, 840.4 *atoning*

purify oneself 134.10, 621.15 *purify*, 840.6 *apologize*

Purim 10.16 *religious festival*

purine base 58.10 *nucleoside*

puriri 85 Trees and Shrubs

purism 50 Western Art Styles and Movements, 467.4 *diligence*, 813.2 *formalism*

purist 50.29 *realist*, 467.8 *diligent*, 481.6 *discriminating person*, 558.2 *stylist*, 619.2, 619.4 *perfectionist*, 690.4 *strict person*, 690.10 *unadorned*

puristic 813.6 *formal*

puritan 690.4 *strict person*, 852.11 *disapprover*, 869.4 *self-restrained person*, 876.6 *moralist*, 876.10 *moralistic*

Puritan 7.5 *Christian*, 134.5 *pure person*

puritanic 869.8 *self-restrained*

puritanical 690.10 *unadorned*

Puritanical 134.12 *morally pure*, 869.11 *with self-restraint*

Puritanically 134.18 *virtuously*

puritanism 690.3 *unadornment*, 869.1 *self-restraint*, 876.4 *self-righteousness*

Puritanism 7 Christian Movements, 134.1 *purity*

purity 134, 446, 857, 442.5 *transparency*, 444.3 *hue*, 537.6 *authenticity*, 550.1 *clarity*, 556.4 *simplicity*, 558.1 *elegance*, 600.9 *newness*, 619.3 *perfection*, 621.1 *cleanness*,

---

825.2 *virginity*, 863.2 *virtues*, 865.1 *innocence*, 869.1 *self-restraint*, 876.3 *moral purity*

Purity 134

purity of heart 865.1 *innocence*

purl 96.7 *flow*, 424.1 *faintness*, 424.5 *sound faint*

purlieus 264.3 *near place*

purling 96.10 *fluvial*

purloin 734.10 *take away*, 736.12 *steal*

purloined 736.17 *stolen*

purloiner 736.8 *thief*

purloining 734.3 *taking away*, 736.1 *stealing*

purl stitch 67.5 *knitting*

purohita 7.8 *priest*

purple 455, 455.9 *empurple*, 551.2 *obscure*

purple-blue 455.6 *purple*

purple-brown 449.1 *brown*

purple colour 455.1 *purpleness*

purpled 455.6 *purple*

purple dye 444.4 *pigment*, 455.2 *purple pigment*

purple emperor 455.3 *purple thing*

purple-fringed orchid 455.3 *purple thing*

purple gallinule 455.3 *purple thing*

purple grackle 455.3 *purple thing*

purple haze 455.3 *purple thing*, 875.6 *drug*

purple heart 455.3 *purple thing*, 875.6 *drug*

Purple Heart 17 US Military Medals and Decorations, 455.3 *purple thing*

purple martin 455.3 *purple thing*

purpleness 455

Purpleness 455

purple passage 455.4 *figurative usage*, 564.2 *power of speech*

purple passages 557.1 *ornament*

purple patch 455.4 *figurative usage*, 541.1 *exaggeration*

purple-patch 541.12 *exaggerated*

purple pigment 455

purple prose 455.4 *figurative usage*, 541.4 *bombast*, 551.1 *obscurity*

purple-red 450.1 *red*, 455.6 *purple*

purple thing 455

purple with rage 455.8 *furious*

purplish 455.6 *purple*

purplish-blue 454.1 *blue*

purplishness 455.1 *purpleness*

purply 455.6 *purple*

purpore 544.8 *heraldic device*

purport 227.4 *significance*, 520.1 *meaning*, 520.10 *mean*

purportedly 4.25 *theoretically*, 102.19 *apparently*

purporting 520.6 *meaningful*

purpose 471, 157.14 *aim*, 226.5 *reason*, 226.6 *undertaking*, 228.1, 310.6 *motive*, 520.5 *point*, 520.12 *intend*, 570.1 *will*, 570.13 *intend*, 574.7 *resolve*, 574.12 *resolution*, 588.1 *intention*, 588.7 *intend*, 599.6 *use*, 613.5 *usefulness*

purposed 588.12 *intended*

purposeful 570.7 *iron-willed*, 574.1 *resolute*, 588.12 *intended*, 592.15 *planning*, 772.2 *earnest*

purposefully 574.17 *resolutely*, 592.16 *as planned*

purposefulness 574.12 *resolution*

purposeless 229.6 *motiveless*, 521.11 *aimless*, 579.1 *capricious*, 614.2 *futile*

purposelessly 229.8 *by chance*, 521.13 *meaninglessly*

purposelessness 229.1 *lack of motive*, 521.2, 521.6 *aimlessness*, 579.2 *caprice*, 614.4 *futility*

purposely 588.13 *intentionally*

purposive 471, 574.1 *resolute*, 588.11 *intending*

purposively 471

purpure 455.6 *purple*, 544.13 *heraldic*

purr 405.8 *feel pleasure*, 424.1 *faintness*, 424.5 *sound faint*,

---

426.2 *humming*, 426.9 *hum*, 428.8 *sound faint*, 432.1 *animal cry*, 432.4 *cry*, 762.7 *show joy*, 765.7 *be satisfied*

purring 424.4 *faint*, 428.4 *faint sound*

purse 258.8 *bag*, 262.5 *make smaller*, 741.6 *funds*, 741.20 *money store*

pursed 262.7 *smaller*

pursed lips 543.3 *gesture*

purse of Fortunatus 742.5 *wealth*

purse one's lips 543.11 *gesture*

purse-pride 805.3 *conceit*

purse-proud 805.17 *conceited*

purser 73.3 *aircraft personnel*, 606.3 *provider*, 741.17 *financier*, 741.18 *treasurer*, 746.5 *payer*, 750.6 *accountant*

purse seine 539.13 *snare*

purse-snatching 736.1 *stealing*

purse strings 14.1 *finance*, 688.1 *authority*, 741.7 *finance*

pursing 262.1 *contraction*, 262.8 *contracting*

pursuance 590.1 *pursuit*

pursuant 195.12 *succeeding*, 590.15 *pursuing*

pursuant to 590, 588.14 *for*

pursue 590, 165.27 *specialize*, 219.4 *protract*, 477.17 *question*, 574.9 *undertake*, 640.4 *act*, 652.11 *conduct oneself*, 782.13 *like*, 821.26, 826.8 *court*

pursued 590

pursue one's course 219.4 *protract*

pursue one's ends 590.12 *aim at*

pursue one's goals 590.12 *aim at*

pursue one's interest 590.12 *aim at*

pursue one's interests 860.6 *be selfish*

pursuer 590, 16.8 *litigant*, 821.9 *lover*, 826.5 *courting person*

pursuing 590, 590.1 *pursuit*, 826.9 *endearing*

pursuit 590, 165.8 *specialization*, 219.2 *protraction*, 324.10 *regular movement*, 496.7 *detection*, 588.3 *future intention*, 590.2 *chase*, 642.2 *social activity*

Pursuit 590

pursuit of a loved one 821.6, 826.2 *courtship*

pursuit of love 821.6, 826.2 *courtship*

pursuivant 544.9 *herald*

purulence 353.7 *pus*, 387.3 *body fluid*, 624.6 *infection*, 624.15 *ulcer*, 626.1 *lack of hygiene*

purulent 353, 387.16 *rheumy*, 624.23 *diseased*, 626.7 *toxic*

purulently 387.26 *fluidly*

purvey 350.25 *provide food*, 606.5 *provision*

purveyance 606.1 *provision*

purveying 606.1 *provision*

purveyor 606.4 *caterer*

purveyor of filth 622.6 *dirty person*

purview 588.3 *future intention*

pus 353, 387.3 *body fluid*, 393.10, 394.5 *mucus*, 622.4 *dirt*, 624.15 *ulcer*

Pusan 93 Cities

push 338, 642, 31.8 *hockey*, 31.9 *play hockey*, 38.4 *play soccer*, 128.2 *spread*, 228.10 *manipulate*, 233 *influence*, 239.2 *be full of vigour*, 324.14 *set in motion*, 326.12 *transport*, 330.1 *impel*, 330.13 *blow*, 336.3 *press on*, 336.8 *further*, 337.29 *in reverse*, 338.20 *propel*, 407.3 *press*, 532.16 *publicize*, 535.6 *assertiveness*, 535.21 *be assertive*, 543.3, 543.11 *gesture*, 642.4 *energy*, 644.4 *exertion*, 644.6 *work*, 648.1 *hasten*, 648.4 *haste*, 670.1 *attack*, 670.5 *strike*, 670.12 *military attack*, 727.11 *dispose of property*, 737.1 *trade*, 739.1 *sell*

Pushan 8 Deities

push around 330.1 *impel*
push-bike 71.12 *bicycle*
pushbutton 232.8 *practical*
pushbutton telephone 534.9 *telephone*
pushbutton war 676.1 *war*
push car 71.7 *handcart*
pushcart 71.7 *handcart*, 258.10 *cart*
pushchair 71.8 *baby carriage*
push down 362.5 *bear down on*
pushed 31.8 *hockey*, 38.5 *soccer*, 743.2 *insolvent*
pushed open 322.12 *open*
pushed through 648.3 *hasty*
pusher 73 Types of Aircraft, **73** Aircraft Parts, 330.15 *ram*, 535.9 *affirmer*, 642.10 *busy person*, 875.5 *drug pusher*
push forward 648.1 *hasten*
push hard 596.2 *try hard*
pushily 338.34 *forward*, 807.33 *arrogantly*
push in 31.9 *play hockey*, 354.3 *impact*
push-in 31.1, 31.8 *hockey*
pushiness 535.6 *assertiveness*, 807.4 *arrogance*
pushing 31.1 *hockey*, 31.5 *lacrosse*, 31.8 *hockey*, 38.2 *football play*, 38.5 *soccer*, 66.13 *framing*, 338.17 *propulsive*, 543.15 *gestural*, 642.18 *active*, 648.3 *hasty*
pushing down 362.13 *submergence*
pushing power 235.4 *energy*
pushing under 362.13 *submergence*
pushing up daisies 399.10 *buried*
push in the right direction 332.6 *direct*
push into 586.15 *persuade*
push into a corner 571.15 *compel*
Pushkin 48 Poets, **48** Dramatists
push off 74.9 *navigate*, 345.1 *depart*, 345.5 *set out*, 345.15 *go*, 349.33 *go away*
push on 336.3 *press on*
push oneself forward 809.16 *show off*
push one's way 590.13 *follow up*
push on with 640.4 *act*
push open 322.18 *open*
push out 349.7 *drive out*
push out of the way 330.1 *impel*
pushover 36.12 *canoeing*, 236.5 *powerless person*, 238.4 *weakling*, 477.5 *easy question*, 539.22 *dupe*, 660.6 *easy thing*, 673.2 *appeaser*, 682.2 *victory*
pushover stroke 36.6 *canoeing*
pushpin 137.8 *fastening*, 380.8 *sharp-pointed thing*
pushpit 36.3 *parts of a sailing boat*
push shot 24.4 *carom*
push stroke 24.3 *English billiards*, 31.1 *hockey*
push to extremes 574.6 *be resolute*
push too far 828.14 *make angry*
push up 359.18 *jump*, 737.3 *bargain*
push up daisies 397.15 *die*
pushy 239.4 *vigorous*, 535.14 *assertive*, 642.21 *meddling*, 807.16 *arrogant*
pusillanimity 238.2 *indecisiveness*, 576.13 *timidity*, 779.1 *cowardice*
pusillanimous 238.12 *weak-willed*, 576.3 *timid*, 779.3 *cowardly*
pusillanimously 576.16 *irresolutely*, 779.5 *cravenly*
puss 77.10 *cat*, 303.2 *face*
pussies 384.5 *powder*
pussiness 353.7 *pus*
puss moth 82 Insects
pussy 245.8 *organs of reproduction*, 353.27 *purulent*, 387.16 *rheumy*, 393.22 *mucilaginous*, 626.7 *toxic*
pussyfoot 474.13 *quibble*, 578.1

be equivocal, 591.7 *be evasive*, 673.3 *submit*, 781.5 *be cautious*
pussyfooter 474.6 *sophist*
pussyfooting 474.4, 474.9 *quibbling*, 591.15 *evasiveness*
pussy willow 85 Trees and Shrubs
pustulate 793.7 *blemish*
pustule 353.7 *pus*, 624.13 *skin disease*, 793.2 *pimple*
put 258, 250.9 *locate*, 251.10 *situate*, 338.5, 338.23 *throw*, 524.8 *interpret*, 549.6 *styled*, 549.9 *style*
put a ball and chain on 699.12 *gag*
put a bomb under 329.7 *hurry someone up*
put about 74.9 *navigate*, 532.13 *make public*
put a case 518.6 *propound*
put a construction on 524.8 *interpret*
put a crimp in 661.8 *hinder*
put across one's knee 879.3 *hit*
put a curse on 827.7 *wish ill*
put a damper on 242.4 *moderate*, 699.8 *restrain*
put a D-notice on 529.12 *keep secret*
put a false construction on 525.1 *misinterpret*, 540.22 *falsify*
put a false sense on 525.1 *misinterpret*
put ahead 336.8 *further*
put a hex on 827.7 *wish ill*
put a jinx on 827.7 *wish ill*
put a lid on 293.12 *cover*, 362.5 *bear down on*, 438.8 *make invisible*
put all one's eggs in one basket 656.6 *act foolishly*
put a mark on 544.10 *identify*
put a match to 408.15 *burn*, 410.11 *fuel*
put among 146.6 *subsume*
Putana 8.7 *devil*
put an edge on 380.15 *make sharp*
put an embargo on 147.7 *exclude*
put an end to 157.16 *cease*, 160.12 *discontinue*, 172.9 *annihilate*, 189.5 *make transient*, 244.8 *destroy*
put an end to one's life 398.21 *commit suicide*
put an idea into one's head 518.6 *propound*
put another way 520.10 *mean*
put a person's nose out of joint 806.22 *shame*, 866.5 *deflate*
put a plaster on 629.6 *cure*, 630.20 *doctor*
put a point on 380.15 *make sharp*
put a price on one's head 16.79 *convict*
put aside 136.10 *set apart*, 147.7 *exclude*, 600.6 *stop using*, 605.6 *store*, 605.7 *stored*
put aside for 588.9 *intend for*
put a spanner in the works 487.8 *make impossible*
put a spell on 827.7 *wish ill*
put a spoke in one's wheel 614.8 *make useless*
put a spoke in someone's wheel 236.8 *overpower*
put a stop to 157.16 *cease*, 218.8 *cause to cease*, 302.7 *limit*, 325.9 *make motionless*, 690.5 *be severe*, 699.8 *restrain*, 869.5 *be self-restrained*
put asunder 136.14 *come between*, 824.7 *divorce*
put a tax on 751.12 *charge*
putative 102.10, 471.10 *theoretical*, 497.14 *believed*, 518.7 *suppositional*, 518.8 *supposed*
putatively 102.19 *apparently*, 471.20 *theoretically*
put a toe in the water 781.5 *be cautious*
put at rest 225.7 *make stable*
put at risk 633.10 *endanger*
put a tuck in one's tail 806.25 *deflate*

put away 244.8 *destroy*, 350.22 *eat well*, 351.13 *drink*, 510.16 *certify*, 605.6 *store*, 702.9 *imprison*, 824.7 *divorce*, 879.1 *punish*
put a wet blanket on 770.10 *depress*
put a wrong construction on 525.1 *misinterpret*
put back 337.5 *turn back*, 629.3 *restore*
put back into operation 629.1 *repair*
put back together 161.45 *reassemble*, 629.1 *repair*
put between 160.16 *interrupt*, 354.1 *insert*
put body into 237.8 *strengthen*
put by 605.6 *store*, 605.7 *stored*
put by for a rainy day 199.10 *expect*
put down 171.8 *list*, 244.8 *destroy*, 362.1 *lower*, 362.4 *debase*, 398.16 *kill*, 398.22 *kill animals*, 545.14 *inscribe*, 612.13 *make unimportant*, 682.9 *be victorious*, 699.8 *restrain*, 746.6 *pay*, 799.6 *deride*, 806.3 *humbled*
putdown 806.10 *abasement*
put down 806.23 *abase*, 850.23 *insult*, 854.10 *disparage*, 854.11 *criticize*
put-down 799.2 *act of derision*, 850.5 *insult*
put down for hearing 16.71 *try a case*
put down one's gun 677.5 *make peace*
put dynamite under 329.7 *hurry someone up*, 338.30 *blow up*
put English on the ball 24.8 *play billiards*
put first 154.17 *give priority*
put for 332.7 *take a direction*
put forth 345.5 *set out*, 518.6 *propound*
put forward 4.22 *propound a philosophy*, 336.8 *further*, 457.14 *present*, 472.11 *raise the point*, 475.15 *demonstrate*, 518.6 *propound*, 535.17 *affirm*, 572.15 *volunteer*
put forward a counterargument 4.23 *discuss philosophically*
put forward an argument about 561.4 *dissertate*
put forward a notion 518.6 *propound*
put heads together 140.6 *come together*, 654.6 *consult*, 664.13 *work together*, 716.4 *negotiator*
put heart into 239.3 *invigorate*
put in 69.15 *cultivate*, 146.6 *subsume*, 344.6 *stop at*, 346.9 *enter*, 354.1 *insert*
put-in 35.3 *rugby play*
put in a bad humour 830.12 *make irritable*
put in a bad temper 830.12 *make irritable*
put in a claim 712.7 *demand*
put in a claim for 593.8 *miss*
put in advance 303.10 *be in front*
put in a false light 525.1 *misinterpret*, 540.24 *mask*, 548.4 *misrepresent*
put in a good word for 851.13 *support*
put in an appearance 253.12 *attend*, 437.9 *appear*
put in a nutshell 552.4 *be concise*
put in a safe place 632.9 *protect*
put in bold relief 526.1 *display*
put in bondage 699.11 *detain*
put in bright lights 611.8 *make important*
put in capital letters 611.8 *make important*
put in check 682.9 *be victorious*
put in clauses 716.6 *make conditions*
put in cold storage 209.8 *delay*
put in commission 594.4 *prepare for action*, 703.8 *authorize*
put in contact with 135.10 *link*

put in context 106.11 *circumstantiate*
put in danger 633.10 *endanger*
put in detention 879.1 *punish*
put in double jeopardy 633.10 *endanger*
put in front 336.8 *further*
put in front of a firing squad 879.5 *execute*
put in headlines 532.16 *publicize*
put in inverted order 287.3 *invert*
put in italics 554.6 *emphasize*
put in its context 107.7 *relate to*
put in jeopardy 633.10 *endanger*
put in limbo 600.6 *stop using*
put in mothballs 600.6 *stop using*, 605.6 *store*
put in one's debt 617.10 *do good*
put in one's defence 16.72 *stand trial*
put in one's hands 703.6 *commission*
put in one's will 728.3 *transfer property*
put in order 150.18 *order*, 152.12 *arrange*, 152.15 *categorize*, 629.1 *repair*
put in place 250.9 *locate*
put in place of 222.6 *give a substitute*
put in plain words 522.5 *simplify*
put in possession 725.9 *own property*, 728.3 *transfer property*
put in quarantine 625.6 *make hygienic*
put in quotes 543.13 *punctuate*
put in readiness 594.4 *prepare for action*
put in reserve 600.6 *stop using*
put in solitary 702.9 *imprison*
put in solitary confinement 702.9 *imprison*
put in splints 630.20 *doctor*
put in the big house 702.9 *imprison*
put in the clear 855.7 *vindicate*
put in the corner 879.1 *punish*
put in the dock 856.5 *accuse*
put in the gas chamber 879.5 *execute*
put in the kitty 605.6 *store*
put in the microwave 45.55 *cook*
put in the minutes 545.13 *record*
put in the oven 45.55 *cook*
put in the picture 528.11 *inform*
put in the shade 440.14 *make dark*, 806.22 *shame*
put in the slot 354.1 *insert*
put in the stocks 879.1 *punish*
put in the bottom drawer 605.6 *store*
put in the wrong place 252.19 *misplace*
put into 524.12 *translate*
put into circulation 162.16 *distribute*
put into code 524.12 *translate*
put into disorder 307.4 *disorder*
put into effect 652.14 *behave towards*, 684.4 *complete*
put into legal effect 16.46 *legislated*
put into one's hands 710.11 *volunteer*
put into operation 599.1 *use*
put into port 344.4 *land*
put into practice 599.1 *use*, 640.4 *act*, 652.14 *behave towards*
put into quarantine 699.11 *detain*
put into shape 152.12 *arrange*, 306.7 *form*
put into the hands of 729.5 *give*
put in touch 135.10 *link*
put into use 640.4 *act*
put into verse 48.21 *write*
put into words 5.47 *word*, 306.7 *form*, 564.11 *speak*
put into working order 629.1 *repair*
put in trim 152.19 *tidy*
put in working order 594.4 *prepare for action*
put it bluntly 535.21 *be assertive*, 552.4 *be concise*
put itself right 629.6 *cure*

put life into 237.8 *strengthen,* 239.3 *invigorate*
put money up front 746.6 *pay*
put new life into 396.21 *invigorate*
put new wine into old bottles 656.6 *act foolishly*
put off 587, 153.10 *disrupt,* 209.8 *delay,* 233.9 *change,* 283.9 *interrupted,* 283.12 *interrupt,* 296.14 *undress,* 341.3 *fend off,* 573.8 *hold back,* 576.7 *be irresolute,* 587.1 *dissuade,* 598.2 *withdraw,* 641.4 *not act,* 685.5 *not complete,* 764.10 *displease,* 785.7 *cause dislike,* 785.8 *disliking*
put off a decision 576.7 *be irresolute*
put off the scent 335.7 *misdirect,* 417.5 *deodorize*
put off until tomorrow 470.6 *be neglectful*
put of of commission 614.8 *make useless*
put on 51.36 *dramatize,* 295.34 *wear,* 361.1 *raise,* 439.24 *light,* 526.1 *display,* 538.24, 540.20 *pretend,* 540.21 *be fraudulent,* 811.30 *put on airs*
put-on 102.12 *not the real thing,* 538.8 *pretence,* 539.8 *trick,* 540.8 *fraud,* 540.30 *pretending,* 540.31 *fraudulent*
put on a brave face 769.7 *be cheerful,* 778.16 *take courage*
put on a business footing 737.1 *trade*
put on a front 540.20 *pretend*
put on airs 811, 797.4 *be affected,* 807.23 *be proud,* 809.16 *show off*
put on airs and graces 797.4 *be affected*
put on alert 594.4 *prepare for action*
put on an act 474.12 *deceive*
put on a pedestal 9.8 *idolatrize,* 361.3 *promote,* 849.16 *revere*
put on a show 811
put on a spurt 239.2 *be full of vigour*
put on a uniform 676.12 *go to war*
put on a war footing 676.12 *go to war*
put on blinkers 481.13 *prejudge*
put on display 437.10 *make visible,* 526.1 *display*
put one in mind 636.5 *warn*
put one in mind of 114.10 *be similar*
put one over 657.5 *be cunning*
put one's back into 237.8 *strengthen*
put one's back into it 644.8 *exert oneself*
put one's back up 785.7 *cause dislike*
put one's best foot forward 597.1 *undertake,* 644.8 *exert oneself*
put one's bristles up 828.9 *offend*
put one's cards on the table 526.4 *show oneself,* 530.6 *divulge,* 857.6 *be honourable*
put one's case 473.16 *plead*
put one's cross on 544.11 *identify oneself*
put oneself at one's service 694.5 *obey*
put oneself between 678.1 *mediate*
put oneself first 860.6 *be selfish,* 870.10 *indulge oneself*
put oneself forward 811.29 *show off*
put oneself in a spot 659.20 *be in difficulty*
put oneself in the firing line 572.15 *volunteer*
put oneself last 859.7 *be unselfish*
put oneself out 644.8 *exert oneself*

put oneself through hell 840.6 *apologize*
put one's faith in 497.7 *believe*
put one's feet up 470.6 *be neglectful,* 649.2, 660.20 *take it easy*
put one's finger on 165.22 *characterize*
put one's fingers in one's ears 421.10 *muffle*
put one's fingers in the till 736.12 *steal*
put one's foot down 225.8 *show determination,* 329.6 *accelerate,* 574.10 *insist,* 690.5 *be severe,* 692.10 *demand*
put one's foot in it 211.8 *make a mistake,* 346.10 *invade,* 656.5 *be unskilful,* 656.7 *be clumsy,* 659.23 *cause difficulties*
put one's foot in one's mouth 211.8 *make a mistake,* 656.7 *be clumsy*
put one's fur up 828.9 *offend*
put one's hand in one's pocket 729.6 *give to charity*
put one's hand to 544.11 *identify oneself*
put one's hand to the plough 156.18 *make a beginning*
put one's hand to the tiller 642.15 *try*
put one's head in the lion's mouth 633.8 *be in danger,* 633.9 *face danger*
put one's head in the oven 398.21 *commit suicide*
put one's heart and soul into it 644.8 *exert oneself*
put one's heart into 574.9 *undertake*
put one's house in order 594.8 *prepare oneself*
put one's mark on 544.11 *identify oneself*
put one's mark upon 165.26 *personalize*
put one's mind to 642.15 *try*
put one's money to work 14.5 *invest,* 737.2 *speculate*
put one's name down 665.13 *be a member*
put one's name on the list 665.13 *be a member*
put one's nose in the air 807.23 *be proud*
put one's nose out of joint 515.7 *thwart*
put one's oar in 160.16 *interrupt,* 642.17 *meddle*
put one's pride in one's pocket 806.21 *humble oneself*
put one's shoulder to the wheel 156.18 *make a beginning,* 574.9 *undertake,* 642.15 *try*
put one's signature to 543.9 *use signs*
put one's tongue in one's cheek 540.18 *be hypocritical*
put one's tongue out 807.29 *ridicule*
put one's trust in 775.6 *hope*
put one's two cents in 642.17 *meddle*
put one under the table 874.9 *be intoxicating*
put on half rations 609.7 *make insufficient*
put on hold 209.8 *delay,* 283.12 *interrupt*
put on ice 209.8 *delay*
put on layaway 588.9 *intend for,* 744.9 *acquire credit*
put on one's boxing globes 679.37 *fight*
put on one's calendar 652.14 *behave towards*
put on one's guard 636.5 *warn*
put on one side 131.3 *subtract,* 335.9 *shove aside*
put on one's robe and slippers 649.2 *take it easy*
put on one's running shoes 329.6 *accelerate*
put on paper 545.14 *inscribe*
put on parole 700.4 *liberate*

put on radio 526.2 *display something*
put on record 545.13 *record*
put on sackcloth and ashes 840.6 *apologize*
put on sale 739.1 *sell*
put on short commons 609.7 *make insufficient*
put on show 526.1 *display*
put on side 809.16 *show off,* 811.30 *put on airs*
put on speed 329.6 *accelerate*
put on television 526.2 *display something*
put on the agenda 472.11 *raise the point,* 518.6 *propound*
put on the back burner 209.8 *delay,* 573.8 *hold back*
put on the black cap 16.79 *convict*
put on the block 727.11 *dispose of property*
put on the brake 218.6 *cease*
put on the drag 328.3 *slow down*
put on the feedbag 350.22 *eat well*
put on the finishing touch 619.5 *perfect*
put on the Index 709.4 *censor*
put on the list 545.15 *register*
put on the map 532.16 *publicize,* 611.8 *make important*
put on the market 727.11 *dispose of property*
put on the rack 879.4 *torture*
put on the right track 332.6 *direct*
put on the scales 369.15 *weigh*
put on the shelf 600.6 *stop using*
put on the sick list 630.20 *doctor*
put on the waiting list 545.15 *register*
put onto paper 50.23 *design*
put on trial 16.70 *litigate,* 479.11 *experiment,* 856.5 *accuse*
put on view 437.10 *make visible,* 526.1 *display*
put on weight 128.4 *increase,* 261.6 *become bigger,* 273.8 *fatten,* 369.12 *be heavy,* 721.10 *augment*
put on widow's weeds 824.10 *be widowed*
putorino 49 *Musical Instruments*
put others first 806.19 *be humble*
put out 153.10 *disrupt,* 244.8 *destroy,* 349.1 *expel,* 349.8 *evict,* 532.13 *make public,* 532.15 *publish,* 616.5 *be inconvenient,* 659.16 *troubled,* 659.23 *cause difficulties,* 806.17 *humiliate,* 828.14 *make angry,* 830.7 *irritable*
put-out 22.6 *fielding terms,* 828.15 *resentful*
put out a contract on 715.5 *contract*
put out a feeler 596.4 *test,* 710.9 *offer*
put out for the count 682.10 *defeat heavily*
put out of action 236.8 *overpower,* 628.4 *impair*
put out of bounds 709.3 *veto*
put out of commission 236.8 *overpower,* 600.6 *stop using*
put out of countenance 806.17 *humiliate*
put out of gear 153.8 *disarrange*
put out of his misery 244.8 *destroy*
put out of joint 252.18 *disconnect*
put out of kilter 309.9 *distort*
put out of mind 468.12 *be inattentive*
put out of one's misery 398.16 *kill,* 835.10 *show mercy*
put out of reach 487.8 *make impossible*
put out of sight 438.8 *make invisible*
put outside the law 709.3 *veto*
put out the bunting 849.20 *salute*
put out the fire 677.4 *pacify*
put out the welcome mat 815.11 *be sociable*

put out to grass 87.11 *eat grass,* 350.25 *provide food,* 600.7 *stop work,* 727.10 *dismiss*
put out to pasture 727.10 *dismiss*
put over 522.5 *simplify*
put paid to 157.16 *cease*
put pressure on 233.8 *influence,* 695.6 *compel*
put put 71.16 *car*
putrefaction 141.1 *disintegration,* 397.1 *death,* 419.2 *something that makes an unpleasant smell,* 618.10 *poverty,* 622.2 *uncleanness,* 628.9 *dilapidation*
putrefy 89.11 *moulder,* 141.3 *disintegrate,* 622.10 *be dirty,* 628.2 *decay*
putrefying 618.4 *poor*
putrescence 419.2 *something that makes an unpleasant smell,* 622.2 *uncleanness*
putrescent 419.4 *putrid*
putrid 419, 141.5 *disintegrated,* 618.4 *poor*
putridly 141.8 *destructively*
putridness 618.10 *poverty*
put right 843, 125.4 *compensate,* 332.6 *direct,* 528.11 *inform,* 627.3 *rectify,* 629.1 *repair,* 629.13 *repaired,* 630.19 *remedy*
put rudder on 335.2 *divert*
putsch 693.4 *revolution,* 713.2 *disorder*
put screw on 335.2 *divert*
put side on the ball 24.8 *play billiards*
put someone in a melancholy mood 830.10 *make sullen*
put someone in fear of his life 633.10 *endanger*
put someone's eyes out 436.15 *blind*
put someone's mind at rest 765.9 *comfort*
put someone's nose out of joint 828.9 *offend,* 841.7 *arouse jealousy*
put something aside 594.3 *be prepared*
put something in the pot 729.5 *give*
put store by 611.8 *make important*
put straight 125.4 *compensate*
putt 29.3 *golf shots,* 29.7 *golf*
puttees 295.20 *legwear*
putter 29.4 *golf club*
puttering 642.7 *restlessness,* 642.19 *busy*
put that in your pipe and smoke it 672.7 *revenge*
put the bite on someone 712.7 *demand*
put the brakes on 699.8 *restrain*
put the cart before the horse 287.3 *invert,* 656.6 *act foolishly*
put the cat among the pigeons 117.14 *disagree*
put the clock back 3.23 *turn back time,* 192.14 *keep time,* 200.15 *look back*
put the clock forward 192.14 *keep time*
put the clocks back 185.18 *adjust the clock*
put the clocks forward 185.18 *adjust the clock*
put the colour back in one's cheeks 623.7 *make healthy*
put the double whammy on 687.11 *cause adversity,* 862.11 *be evil*
put the evil eye on 11.21 *bewitch,* 687.11 *cause adversity*
put the fear of God into 777.13 *frighten*
put the finger on 543.9 *use signs,* 856.5 *accuse*
put the finishing touches on 142.10 *complete*
put the finishing touch to 130.6 *add,* 144.4 *complete*
put the flags out 348.9 *welcome*
put the frighteners on 690.6 *sup-*

press, 777.13 *frighten*, 832.18 *torment*
put the hammer down 235.11 *give power*, 329.4 *be swift*
put the helm down 74.9 *navigate*
put the helm up 74.9 *navigate*
put the horns on 877.17 *be sexually immoral*
put the icing on the cake 142.10, 144.4 *complete*, 684.6 *elaborate*
put the jinx on 687.11 *cause adversity*
put the kibosh on 236.8 *overpower*, 244.11 *ruin*
put the lid on 157.16 *cease*, 323.7 *close*, 422.2 *silence*, 529.12 *keep secret*, 699.8 *restrain*
put the phone down 218.6 *cease*
put the screws on 586.15 *persuade*, 690.6 *suppress*, 695.7 *force*
put the shot 338.23 *throw*
put the skids under 244.11 *ruin*, 628.5 *hurt*, 687.11 *cause adversity*
put the squeeze on 712.8 *solicit money*
put the squeeze on someone 712.7 *demand*
put the stoppers on 157.16 *cease*
put the touch on 712.8 *solicit money*
put the whammy on 687.11 *cause adversity*, 862.11 *be evil*
put the wind up 777.13 *frighten*, 832.18 *torment*
put through the hoop 477.18 *interrogate*
put through the shredder 598.1 *relinquish*
put through to 135.10 *link*
putting 29.3 *golf shots*
putting aside 136.2 *setting apart*
putting back 629.9 *restoration*
putting down 699.1 *restraint*, 854.1 *disparagement*
putting green 29.1 *golf*
putting in cold storage 209.3 *delayed action*
putting in mint condition 629.8 *repair*
putting in order 150.1 *order*, 152.1 *arrangement*
putting into effect 640.1 *action*
putting off 209.3 *delayed action*, 283.6 *interruption*, 573.15 *delay*
putting off till tomorrow 641.1 *inaction*
putting on 51.12 *production*, 539.7 *tricking*
putting on airs 557.2 *affectation*, 809.13 *boastful*
putting one's fingers in the till 736.1 *stealing*
putting one's heads together 568.4 *conference*
putting on hold 209.3 *delayed action*
putting on ice 209.3 *delayed action*
putting on the back burner 209.3 *delayed action*, 573.15 *delay*
putting on the market 727.2 *disposal of property*
putting out of joint 252.5 *disconnection*
putting right 627.6 *rectification*, 629.8 *repair*
putting the boot in 652.8 *treatment*
putting together 161
putto 43 Architectural Decoration
put to 654.5 *advise*
put to a lot of trouble 659.23 *cause difficulties*
put to auction 739.1 *sell*
put to bad use 601.1 *misuse*
put to bed 532.15 *publish*, 630.20 *doctor*
put to bed with a shovel 399.8 *bury*
put to death 398.19, 879.5 *execute*
put to flight 162.13 *dismiss*,

338.21 *move forward*, 682.10 *defeat heavily*, 683.11 *defeated*
put together 161, 135.8 *unite*, 140.5 *combine*, 148.13 *make*, 161.47 *collected*, 243.10 *produce*, 257.8 *embody*, 382.17 *assemble*, 594.4 *prepare for action*
put-together 135.12 *united*
put to good use 599.3 *exploit*
put to inconvenience 616.5 *be inconvenient*
put to it 659.23 *cause difficulties*
put to one's shifts 743.2 *insolvent*
put to rights 150.21, 152.19 *tidy*
put to sea 74.9 *navigate*, 345.5 *set out*
put to shame 126.8 *be superior*, 801.4 *disreputable*, 806.22 *shame*, 850.21 *disregard*
put to silence 422.2 *silence*
put to sleep 398.16 *kill*, 398.22 *kill animals*, 404.12 *anaesthetize*, 650.6 *fatigue*
put to the block 739.1 *sell*
put to the sword 244.10 *lay waste*, 398.17 *murder*, 398.18 *slaughter*, 676.13 *be at war*, 690.6 *suppress*
put to the test 479.11 *experiment*
put to the vote 500.5 *vote*
put to the wrong use 607.1 *waste*
put to torture 879.4 *torture*
put to trouble 616.5 *be inconvenient*
put to use 599.1 *use*, 599.9 *used*
put to work 644.7 *work for*
putty 138.3 *adhesive*, 374.11 *soft thing*, 393.12 *poultice*
putty in one's hands 228.6 *suggestibility*, 576.14 *apathy*, 586.7 *persuadability*
putty-like 374.2 *pliant*, 576.4 *unsteady*, 808.6 *servile*
put under 404.12 *anaesthetize*
put under an obligation 847.17 *impose a duty*
put under arrest 699.11 *detain*
put under duress 695.6 *compel*
put under the hammer 727.11 *dispose of property*
put under wraps 438.8 *make invisible*
put up 275.18 *erect*, 283.10 *suspend*, 361.1 *raise*, 382.16 *construct*, 580.4 *pick*, 606.5 *provision*
put-up 540.31 *fraudulent*, 582.4 *deliberate*, 592.4 *plot*, 856.2 *false accusation*, 856.9 *perjurious*
put up a brave front 669.6 *resist*
put up a fight 674.11 *contend*
put up a front 474.12 *deceive*, 540.24 *mask*, 811.30 *put on airs*
put up at 256.18 *take up residence*
put up collateral 725.9 *own property*
put up for sale 710.9 *offer*, 727.11 *dispose of property*, 739.1 *sell*
put up front 303.10 *be in front*
put-up job 538.10 *dishonesty*, 540.8 *fraud*, 582.6 *premeditation*, 592.4 *plot*, 856.2 *false accusation*
put up money 746.8 *defray*
put upon 130.6 *add*, 618.14 *illtreat*
put up one's fists 674.12 *fight*
put up one's sword 677.5 *make peace*
put up one's umbrella 634.4 *shelter*
put up prices 753.10 *overcharge*
put up the banns 714.7 *promise*
put up the shutters 218.7 *stop working*
put up to 228.10 *manipulate*
put up with 222.5 *take a substitute*, 284.12 *bear*, 499.5 *assent to*, 667.6 *agree with*, 673.4 *succumb*, 839.12 *show mercy*
put wise 528.11 *inform*
put zest into 396.21 *invigorate*
puzzle 133.9 *mix up*, 443.12 *obscure*, 477.1 *question*, 477.21

confuse, 491.20 *make uncertain*, 521.8 *not understand*, 523.7 *be unintelligible*, 523.9 *find unintelligible*, 523.12 *unintelligible thing*, 523.12 *unintelligible thing*, 529.13 *mystification*, 529.13 *mystify*, 659.4 *problem*, 659.23 *cause difficulties*, 786.5 *person of wonder*, 786.10 *be wonderful*
puzzled 133.13 *mixed-up*, 491.3, 523.6 *confused*, 659.16 *troubled*, 786.6 *wondering*
puzzlement 477.8 *curiosity*, 491.12 *confusion*, 786.1 *wonder*
puzzle out 524.9 *decipher*
puzzle over 133.11 *be mixed up*
puzzler 523.12 *unintelligible thing*
puzzling 477.13 *problematic*, 491.3 *confused*, 523.4 *difficult*, 529.11 *mysterious*, 659.12 *problematic*, 786.8 *wonderful*
puzzlingly 477.24 *questionably*, 491.24 *confusingly*
PVC 67 Synthetic Fibres and Fabrics, 57.21 *polymer*
PVS 99.9 *mere existence*, 604.1 *materials*
Pwllheli 93 Cities
pyaemia 624.6 *infection*
pycnogonid 81.4 *arthropod*
Pycnogonida 81.4 *arthropod*
pyelogram 60.7 *diagnosis*
pyelography 60.7 *diagnosis*
pyeloplasty 60 Surgical Operations
pyelotomy 60 Surgical Operations
Pygmalion's statue 396.6 *things brought to life*
Pygmies 1 Peoples
pygmy 260.4 *little person*, 260.7 *little*, 270.5 *short person*
pygmy hippopotamus 77 Placental Mammals
pygmy owl 78 Birds
pyinkado 85 Trees and Shrubs
pyjama party 665.7 *social gathering*
pyjamas 295.22 *nightwear*, 296.4 *dishabille*
pylon 73 Aircraft Parts, 63.19 *structure*, 64.33 *power distribution*, 235.7 *electrical power*, 275.6 *tall thing*, 281.3 *vertical thing*, 410.4 *electricity*
Pylon Poets 48 Literary Groups and Movements
pylorectomy 60 Surgical Operations
pyloric 352.5 *of a secretion*
pyloromyotomy 60 Surgical Operations
pyloroplasty 60 Surgical Operations
Pynchon 48 Writers
pyocyanase 62 Medication
pyocyanin 62 Medication
Pyongyang 93 Cities
pyracantha 84 Flowers and Flowering Plants
pyralid moth 82 Insects
pyramid 52.46 *polyhedron*, 200.7 *thing of the past*, 225.4 *stable thing*, 243.8 *construction*, 310.3 *angled figure*, 380.8 *sharp-pointed thing*, 382.6 *construction*, 399.6 *grave*, 545.11 *monument*
Pyramid 94 Lakes
pyramidal 52.84 *cubic*, 310.9 *angled*, 342.7 *convergent*, 380.1 *sharp*
pyramidologist 11.12 *occultist*
pyramidology 11.1 *occultism*
Pyramids 43 Noted Buildings
pyramid spot 24.3 *English billiards*, 24.5 *snooker*
Pyramus and Thisbe 821.10 *lovers*
pyranometer 268.8 *meter*
pyranose 58.3 *carbohydrate*
pyrargyrite 54 Minerals
pyrazinamide 62 Medication
pyre 399.1 *burial*, 408.6 *fire*
Pyrenees 53 Mountains, 95

Mountains, 95.6 *other major mountains and ranges*
Pyrennean mountain dog 77 Breeds of Dogs
pyrenoid 90.3 *plant body*
pyrethrum 84 Flowers and Flowering Plants, 69.8 *weedkiller*
pyretic 624.23 *diseased*
pyrexia 408.1 *heat*, 624.3 *symptom*
pyrexial 408.12 *warm-hearted*
pyridine 57 Common Chemical Compounds
pyridoxal phosphate 58.12 *coenzyme*
pyrimidine base 58.10 *nucleoside*
pyrite 54 Minerals
pyroclastic 54.55 *volcanic*, 54.56 *petrographic*
pyroclastic material 54.25 *eruption*
pyroclastic rock 54.30 *igneous rock*
pyrogen 62.4 *drug type*
pyrogenic 408.10 *on fire*
pyroglaze 44.11 *make ceramics*
pyroglazer 44.7 *potter*
pyrographer 47.13 *carpenter*, 792.7 *decorator*
pyrographic 47.15 *woodcrafted*
pyrography 47.8 *woodwork*, 792.2 *pattern*
pyrogravure 47.8 *woodwork*
pyrolater 9.6 *idolater*
pyrolatrous 9.10 *idolatrous*
pyrolatry 9.2 *idolatry*
pyrolusite 54 Minerals
pyrolyse 57.26 *react*
pyrolysis 57.14 *chemical reaction*
pyromancer 11.13 *diviner*
pyromancy 11.9, 517.2 *divination*
pyromania 408.6 *fire*, 510.4 *delusion*
pyromaniac 241.4 *violent person or animal*, 244.6 *destroyer*, 408.7 *fireman*
pyrometer 44.6 *ceramic workshop*, 56.89 *thermometer*, 268.8 *meter*
pyrometric 44.10 *ceramic*, 268.16 *micrometric*
pyrometrically 44.12 *ornamentally*
pyrometric cone 44.6 *ceramic workshop*
pyrometry 56.41 *thermometry*, 56.96 *microscopy*, 268.2 *micrometry*
pyromorphite 54 Minerals
pyrophobia 777 Phobias by Name
pyrophoric alloy 439.8 *fire*
pyrophosphate 58.12 *coenzyme*
pyrophyllite 54 Minerals
pyrosis 406.2 *painful condition*, 624.8 *indigestion*
pyrotechnics 439.8 *fire*, 811.14 *show*
pyroxene 54.34 *mineral*
pyroxenite 54 Minerals
pyrrhic 46.4 *historic dancing*, 48.9 *metre*
Pyrrhic victory 616.3 *inconvenience*, 682.2 *victory*
Pyrrho 4 Philosophers
Pyrrhonism 477.6 *uncertainty*
Pyrrhonist 4.11 *follower of a doctrine*, 4.14 *of a philosophy*, 477.15 *sceptical*
pyrrhotite 54 Minerals
Pythagoras 4 Philosophers
Pythagoras's theorem 52 Named Concepts
Pythagorean 4.11 *follower of a doctrine*, 4.14 *of a philosophy*
Pythagoreanism 4.7 *school of thought*
Pythia 517.8 *oracle*
Pythian oracle 517.8 *oracle*
python 79 Reptiles, 79.3 *snake*
pythoness 11.13 *diviner*, 517.8 *oracle*
pythonism 11.9 *divination*
pythonist 11.13 *diviner*
pyx 10.14 *sacred object*
pyxidium 86.2 *botanical fruit*
Pyxis 53 The Constellations

Q

Qacentina 93 Cities
Qadarite 7 Non-Christian Religions
Qadesh 8 Deities
qadi 7.8 *priest*
qanun 49 Musical Instruments
qasisha 7.8 *priest*
Qatar 91 Countries
qawwali 49.10 *world music*
QED 52.66 *proof*
Qinghai Hu 94 Lakes
Q-ship 74 Ships and Boats, 679.24 *warship*
quack 60.11 *doctor*, 432.2 *bird song*, 432.5 *sing*, 474.6 *sophist*, 502.5 *ignorant person*, 502.7 *semi-skilled*, 538.12 *cheat*, 539.15 *deceiver*, 539.39 *imitative*, 630.15 *healer*, 656.2 *unskilled*, 656.10 *unskilled person*
quacker 565.4 *talker*
quackery 474.5 *hypocrisy*, 502.2 *half-knowledge*, 539.7 *tricking*, 540.4 *spuriousness*, 656.8 *unskilfulness*
quack grass 87 Grasses
quacking 41.10 *curling*
quackish 540.28 *spurious*, 656.2 *unskilled*
quackishness 540.4 *spuriousness*
quackism 540.4 *spuriousness*
quack remedy 630.1 *remedy*
quacksalver 539.15 *deceiver*
quackster 538.12 *cheat*, 539.15 *deceiver*
quad 178.1 *four*, 301.2 *enclosed place*
quadragenarian 179.8 *twenty and over*
Quadragesima 10.15 *holy day*
Quadragesimal 871.6 *fasting*
Quadragesimal fare 871.1 *fasting*
quadrangle 52.44, 52.44 *polygon*, 178.2 *quadrilateral*, 301.2 *enclosed place*, 310.3 *angled figure*, 323.4 *closed place*
quadrangular 310.9 *angled*
quadrant 52.42 *circle*, 74.5 *navigation*, 178.6 *quarter*, 268.6 *measuring instrument*, 310.4 *angular measurement*, 313.4 *parts of a circle*
quadrantal 52.81 *curvilinear*
Quadrantids 53 Meteor Showers
quadraphonic 178.9 *tetramerous*
quadraphonic sound 420.10 *sound quality*
quadrate 178.8 *quadrilateral*, 178.11 *quadruple*
quadratic 52.76 *functional*, 178.7 *four*
quadratic equation 52.27 *equation*
quadrega 43 Architectural Decoration
quadrennial 178.3 *foursome*, 178.9 *tetramerous*
quadrennially 178.13 *four times*
quadrennium 178.3 *foursome*
quadricycle 71.12 *bicycle*
quadrifid 178.10 *quartered*
quadrihydrate 57.10 *salt*
quadrilateral 178, 178, 52.44 *polygon*, 52.82 *polygonal*, 305.6 *side*, 310.3 *angled figure*, 310.9 *angled*
quadrille 42 Card Games, 32.10 *dressage*, 46.4 *historic dancing*, 178.3 *foursome*
quadrillion 169.3 *large number*, 179.11 *million*
quadripartite 178.10 *quartered*
quadripartite vault 43.7 *vault*
quadripartition 178.5 *quadrisection*
quadriplegia 236.4 *disability*, 624.17 *nervous disorder*
quadriplegic 236.12 *impotent*, 624.19 *sick person*
quadrisect 178
quadrisected 178.10 *quartered*
quadrisection 178

quadrivalent 57.35 *combined*, 178.9 *tetramerous*
quadroon 1.6 *race*, 1.13 *racial*, 133.5 *hybrid*
quadruped 32.1 *horse*, 76.4 *type of animal*, 178.3 *foursome*, 178.9 *tetramerous*
quadrupedal 76.15 *of animals*
quadruple 178, 36.11 *rowing*, 128.5 *make bigger*, 178.1, 178.7 *four*
quadruple sculling 36.4 *rowing*
quadruple sculls 36.4 *rowing*
quadruplet 178.1 *four*
quadruplex 178.7 *four*
quadruplicate 178.7 *four*, 178.11 *quadruple*
quadruplicating 178.4 *quadruplication*
quadruplication 178, 128.1 *increase*
quadruplicature 178.4 *quadruplication*
quadruplicity 178.4 *quadruplication*
quadrupling 178.4 *quadruplication*
quadruply 178.13 *four times*
quadrupole 56.50 *electric charge*
quaestor 653.16 *official*, 741.17 *financier*, 741.18 *treasurer*
quaff 351.13 *drink*, 874.8 *get drunk*
quaffer 351.12 *drinker*
quaffing 351.1 *drinking*
quag 98.3 *marsh*
quagga 77 Placental Mammals
quaggy 98.11 *continental*
quagmire 98.3, 391.8 *marsh*, 622.4 *dirt*, 635.1 *trap*, 659.6 *critical situation*
quahog 81 Molluscs
quail 78 Birds, 37.5 *game*, 45.20 *meat*, 78.4 *table bird*, 331.2 *respond*, 777.11 *be afraid*, 779.4 *be a coward*
quails 161 Collective Names by Animal
quaint 523.5 *strange*
quake 54.22 *seismic activity*, 54.64 *fold*, 241.3 *instance of violence*, 366.24 *shake*
quake in one's boots 777.11 *be afraid*
Quaker 7.5 *Christian*, 134.5 *pure person*, 675.3 *pacifist*
Quakerism 7 Christian Movements
quakily 366.28 *shakily*
quaking 366.6 *shaking*, 366.18 *shaky*, 777.2 *fearfulness*, 777.8 *fearful*
quaking grass 87 Grasses
quaky 366.18 *shaky*
qualification 485, 133.1 *mixture*, 216.1 *change*, 235.2 *ability*, 485.5 *modification*, 485.6 *specification*, 485.7 *condition*, 608.7 *sufficiency*, 615.3 *convenience*, 655.2 *aptitude*, 699.1 *restraint*, 716.2 *basis for negotiations*, 845.6 *bond*, 855.2 *defence*
Qualification 485
qualifications 485, 165.4 *specifications*
qualificatory 485.12 *conditional*
qualified 485, 6.19 *knowledgeable*, 133.12 *mixed*, 216.12 *changed*, 235.13 *powerful*, 501.8 *knowledgeable*, 594.18 *prepared*, 615.1 *convenient*, 655.8 *expert*, 696.13 *excellent*, 845.8 *entitled*
qualified for 116.16 *fitting*
qualifiedness 485.1 *qualification*
qualified person 485
qualify 485, 133.8 *mix*, 216.8 *cause change*, 235.10 *be powerful*, 242.4 *moderate*, 485.15 *modify*, 485.16 *specify*, 608.4 *suffice*, 617.9 *be worthy*, 682.6 *be successful*, 845.16 *entitle*, 855.8 *justify*
qualify for 116.27 *fit*, 615.6 *be convenient*, 861.19 *be good at*
qualifying 855.11 *vindicatory*

qualitative analysis 57.17 *analysis*
qualities 863.2 *virtues*
quality 103.4 *nature*, 126.1 *superiority*, 165.3 *characteristic*, 234.2 *attitude*, 485.2 *ability*, 549.1 *style*, 617.1 *worthy*, 617.6 *worth*, 794.1 *elegance*, 802.3 *nobleness*, 861.8 *good*
quality daily 532.4 *newspaper*
quality of light 439
quality press 533.5 *mass communication*
qualm 498.1 *disbelief*, 573.13 *dissociation*
qualms 777.2 *fearfulness*, 866.2 *signs of guilt*, 867.1 *penitence*
Quamta 8 Deities
quandary 106.4 *difficult circumstances*, 491.12 *confusion*, 659.4 *problem*, 776.2 *hopeless situation*
quandong 86 Fruits, **86** Nuts
quango 653.6 *governing body*, 665.3 *political grouping*
quantifiability 268.3 *measurability*
quantifiable 52.73 *numerable*, 170.14 *calculable*, 268.14 *measurable*
quantifiably 170.16 *mathematically*
quantification 52.12 *numeration*, 268.1 *measurement*
quantified 120.6 *quantitative*, 268.13 *measured*
quantifier 4.8 *philosophical term*, 268.9 *measurer*
quantify 120, 52.90 *enumerate*, 121.5 *measure*, 165.24 *specify*, 170.11 *number*, 268.10 *measure*, 490.22 *specify*
quantifying 52.12 *numeration*, 170.13 *calculative*
quantitation 268.1 *measurement*
quantitative 120, 57.41 *analytic*, 268.12 *metrical*
quantitative analysis 57.17 *analysis*
quantitatively 120, 268.17 *measurably*
quantitative metre 48.9 *metre*
quantity 120, 48.9 *metre*, 121.1 *degree*, 169.4 *mathematical result*, 268.4 *size*, 490.18 *particularity*, 605.1 *store*
Quantity 120
quantity of electricity 56.50 *electric charge*
quantity of heat 56.35 *heat*
quantity surveyor 63.18 *civil engineer*
quantize 120.8 *quantify*, 170.11 *number*
quantized 56.98 *physical*, 120.6 *quantitative*
quantized property 56.78 *quantum*
quantum 56, 56.98 *physical*, 120.2 *certain amount*, 367.4 *matter*
quantum chemistry 57.1 *chemistry*
quantum chromodynamics 56.80 *quantum theory*
quantum electrodynamics 56.80 *quantum theory*
quantum electrothermodynamics 56.3 *modern physics*
quantum field theory 56.5 *theory*
quantum gravity 56.3 *modern physics*
quantum jump 56.67 *excited atom*, 56.80 *quantum theory*
quantum leap 56.80 *quantum theory*, 359.5 *jump*, 459.2 *ways of thinking*, 461.6 *idea*
quantum mathematics 4.6 *branch of philosophy*
quantum mechanical 56.98 *physical*
quantum mechanically 56.100 *physically*
quantum mechanics 56.3 *modern physics*, 56.80 *quantum theory*, 57.1 *chemistry*, 367.6 *natural science*

quantum number 56.78 *quantum*
quantum of radiation 56.78 *quantum*
quantum physics 4.6 *branch of philosophy*
quantum statistics 56.3 *modern physics*
quantum theory 56, 56.3 *modern physics*, 56.5 *theory*
quantum uncertainty 56.80 *quantum theory*
quarantine 136.2 *setting apart*, 136.11 *divide*, 147.3 *exclusion zone*, 147.7 *exclude*, 625.1 *hygiene*, 625.6 *make hygienic*, 630.3 *prophylactic*, 632.2 *protection*, 637.1 *preservation*, 699.4 *detention*, 699.11 *detain*, 727.8 *sink*, 816.3 *separation*, 816.13 *ignore*
quarantined 624.22 *sick*, 699.15 *detained*
quarantined house 727.8 *sink*
quarantine flag 544.7 *flag*, 727.8 *sink*
quark 56.77 *elementary particle*, 260.2 *little thing*, 367.4 *matter*
quark colour 56.77 *elementary particle*
quark flavour 56.77 *elementary particle*
Quark Xpress 65.11 *application*
quarrel 764, 764, 828, 16.5 *litigation*, 117.4 *disagreement*, 117.14 *disagree*, 338.10 *ball*, 380.8 *sharp-pointed thing*, 434.6 *disagreement*, 434.11 *disagree*, 473.1 *argument*, 473.13 *argue*, 500.1, 500.8 *dissent*, 642.1 *activity*, 666.2 *argument*, 666.5 *disagree*, 666.6 *argue*, 674.1 *contention*, 674.6 *fight*, 674.13 *conflict*, 676.1 *war*, 679.40 *argue*, 680.6 *historical missile weapon*, 820.12 *oppose*, 828.11 *be angry*, 829.6 *be irascible*
quarreller 473.6 *arguer*, 666.4 *dissenter*, 674.10 *contender*, 679.5 *arguer*, 764.9 *unpleasant person*
quarrelling 16.53 *litigating*, 117.4 *disagreement*, 117.10 *disagreeing*, 473.7 *arguing*, 500.7 *dissenting*, 666.9 *disagreeing*, 674.15 *contentious*, 764.2 *objectionable*, 820.1 *enmity*
quarrelsome 16.53 *litigating*, 117.10 *disagreeing*, 473.8 *argumentative*, 666.9 *disagreeing*, 670.21 *aggressive*, 674.15 *contentious*, 679.34 *argumentative*, 764.2 *objectionable*, 820.9 *aggressive*, 829.4 *irascible*, 830.7 *irritable*
quarrelsomeness 16.5 *litigation*, 500.3 *dissentience*, 666.1 *disagreement*, 820.1 *enmity*, 829.1 *irascibility*
quarrel with one's bread and butter 656.6 *act foolishly*
quarrier 355.10 *excavator*
quarry 37.5 *game*, 54.65 *map*, 226.2 *source*, 243.10 *produce*, 317.2 *concave land*, 355.13 *dig out*, 588.6 *objective*, 590.7 *the hunted*, 605.2 *resource*, 647.1 *workshop*
quarrying 355.3 *digging out*
quarryman 317.4 *digger*
quarry tile 44.9 *industrial ceramics*
quart 75 General Units
quarte and tierce 670.18 *hit*
quarter 75 General Units, **178,** 19.5 *game time*, 23.1 *basketball*, 36.3 *parts of a sailing boat*, 36.15 *sail*, 92.4 *community*, 93.7 *city district*, 136.11 *divide*, 143.1 *part*, 173.4 *less than one*, 173.5 *fractional*, 178.12 *quadrisect*, 185.4 *term*, 187.2 *time period*, 250.9 *locate*, 256.18 *take up residence*, 332.1 *direction*, 528.8 *source of information*, 544.8 *heraldic device*, 544.10 *identify*, 691.1 *leniency*, 741.8

422.4 *silence,* 527.6 *latency,* 641.1 *inaction,* 643.5 *inactivity,* 649.1 *ease,* 675.1 *peace,* 761.4 *desensitization*
quiescency 325.2 *repose*
quiescent 325, 240.5 *inert,* 376.3 *soothing,* 422.3 *silent,* 527.1 *latent,* 641.3, 643.1 *inactive,* 649.4 *at ease,* 675.7 *peaceful,* 761.2 *desensitized*
quiescently 376.15 *soothingly,* 527.15 *latently*
quiet 150.8 *harmony,* 150.16 *harmonious,* 225.1 *stability,* 225.9 *stable,* 238.13 *insufficient,* 240.5 *inert,* 242.4, 242.6 *moderate,* 325.2 *repose,* 325.6 *quiescent,* 376.3 *soothing,* 422.2 *silence,* 422.3 *silent,* 422.4 *silence,* 424.4 *faint,* 428.1 *faintsounding,* 428.7 *mute,* 444.13 *soft-hued,* 542.15 *reserved,* 566.1 *taciturn,* 587.5 *discourage,* 641.1 *inaction,* 641.3, 643.1 *inactive,* 643.5 *inactivity,* 645.2 *time off,* 649.1 *ease,* 649.4 *at ease,* 673.5 *submitting,* 675.7 *peaceful,* 699.14 *selfrestrained,* 767.9 *relieve,* 810.13 *reserved,* 816.11 *secluded*
quiet as a lamb 422.3 *silent,* 675.7 *peaceful*
quiet as a mouse 325.4 *motionless,* 422.3 *silent*
quiet as death 325.6 *quiescent*
quieten 129.5 *make smaller,* 225.7 *make stable,* 242.4 *moderate,* 422.2 *silence,* 428.7 *mute*
quiet end 397.5 *ways of dying*
quieten down 218.8 *cause to cease,* 225.6 *be stable,* 225.7 *make stable*
quietening 242.1 *moderation*
quietism 325.2 *repose*
quiet life 675.1 *peace*
quietly 4.27 *stoically,* 225.12 *stably,* 238.14 *weakly,* 240.7 *inertly,* 325.10 *motionlessly,* 376.15 *soothingly,* 422.5 *silently,* 424.7, 428.10 *faintly,* 542.25 *reservedly,* 566.10 *taciturnly,* 641.5 *without action,* 649.6 *with ease,* 675.8 *peacefully,* 810.17 *modestly,* 816.14 *unsocially*
quietly spoken 564.19 *speaking*
quietness 527, 150.8 *harmony,* 242.1 *moderation,* 325.2 *repose,* 422.4 *silence,* 542.5 *reserve,* 566.4 *taciturnity,* 641.1 *inaction,* 643.5 *inactivity,* 699.3 *selfrestraint*
quiet person 542.11 *modest person*
quiet sun 53.15 *sun*
quiet tone 424.1 *faintness*
quietude 4.3 *detachment,* 150.8 *harmony,* 225.1 *stability,* 325.2 *repose,* 397.1 *death,* 422.4 *silence*
quietus 16.42 *acquittal,* 157.3 *death,* 397.4 *death sentence,* 398.5 *execution*
quiet wedding 823.5 *wedding*
quiff 791.8 *hair cut*
quill 78.17 *plumage,* 380.8 *sharppointed thing,* 875.1 *drug-taking*
quillwort 88.1 *fern*
quilt 292.4 *fill,* 293.10 *bed covering,* 408.3 *heater*
quilted 41.12 *ski*
quilted clothing 41.5 *ski equipment*
quilter 293.17 *coverer*
quilting 42 Hobbies and Pastimes, 292.2 *filling*
quim 245.8 *organs of reproduction*
quin 179.1 *five*
quinary 179.12 *fifth*
quince 86 Fruits
quincentenary 179.9 *treble figures,* 511.5 *day to remember*
quincunx 179.1 *five,* 310.4 *angular measurement*
quindecagon 179.7 *double figures*
quindecagonal 179.18 *eleventh*

quindecaplet 179.7 *double figures*
quindecennial 179.7 *double figures,* 179.18 *eleventh*
quindecillion 169.3 *large number,* 179.11 *million*
Quine 4 Philosophers
quinidine 62 Medication
quinine 62 Medication, 58.19 *alkaloid,* 630.3 *prophylactic,* 630.4 *antidote*
quinquagenarian 179.8 *twenty and over*
quinquennial 179.1 *five,* 179.12 *fifth,* 187.8 *periodical*
quinquennially 179.24 *fivefold,* 187.13 *for specified periods*
quinquennium 179.1 *five,* 187.2 *time period*
quinquepartite 179.12 *fifth*
quinquereme 179.1 *five,* 679.25 *historical naval ships*
quinquevalent 57.35 *combined*
quint 179.1 *five*
quintain 588.6 *objective*
quintal 75 General Units
quintessence 103, 257.1 *contents,* 355.8 *extract,* 471.6 *ideal,* 547.1 *representation,* 617.6 *worth,* 619.3 *perfection,* 861.9 *the best*
quintessential 103, 116.15 *conventional,* 165.15 *special,* 257.10 *containing,* 471.13 *ideal,* 547.13 *representational,* 861.2 *best*
quintessentially 257.13 *structurally*
quintet 49.26 *musical group,* 140.3 *assembly,* 179.1 *five,* 664.9 *team*
quintic 179.12 *fifth*
quintile 310.4 *angular measurement*
quintillion 169.3 *large number,* 179.11 *million*
quinton 49 Musical Instruments
quintuple 179, 179.1 *five,* 179.12 *fifth*
quintuplet 179.1 *five*
quintuplicate 179.1 *five,* 179.12 *fifth,* 179.23 *quintuple*
quinze 42 Card Games
quip 474.2 *sophism,* 506.2 *solecism,* 506.6 *talk nonsense,* 771.5 *joke,* 771.13 *be humorous*
quipping 771.3 *wit*
quire 604.3 *paper*
quirk 43 Architectural Decoration, 165.3 *characteristic,* 168.5 *idiosyncrasy,* 474.2 *sophism,* 579.3 *whim,* 620.7 *defect*
quirkiness 168.4 *unusualness,* 229.1 *lack of motive,* 579.2 *caprice*
quirky 165.16 *characteristic,* 168.14 *eccentric,* 229.6 *motiveless,* 579.1 *capricious,* 771.10 *humorous*
quirt 879.14 *instrument of punishment*
quisling 539.21 *traitor,* 578.9 *equivocator,* 664.10 *cooperator,* 693.10 *seditionist,* 864.9 *wicked person*
quit 345, 136.13 *diverge,* 160.12 *discontinue,* 218.6 *cease,* 591.8 *run away,* 598.2 *withdraw,* 590.9 *forget it,* 641.4 *not act,* 705.5 *resign*
quitch grass 87 Grasses
quitclaim 700.1 *liberation*
quite 121.11 *to a degree,* 142.13 *on the whole,* 144.9 *completely,* 242.9 *moderately,* 619.8 *completely,* 621.20 *clean*
quite a few 181.2 *multitude*
quite another thing 115.4 *dissimilar*
quite some 181.6 *many*
quite something 786.4 *wonder*
quite the contrary 536.16 *no*
quit it 218.12 *stop,* 397.15 *die*
Quito 93 Cities
quit one's hold 598.1 *relinquish*
quit one's post 598.2 *withdraw*
quitrent 751.3 *fee*

quits 110.5 *equality,* 110.16 *equal,* 122.1 *equality,* 840.1 *atonement*
quittance 700.1 *liberation,* 718.2 *promise,* 746.1 *payment,* 840.1 *atonement*
quitter 685, 578.9 *equivocator,* 591.17 *avoider,* 673.2 *appeaser,* 705.3 *resigner*
quit the saddle 344.4 *land*
quit the scene 345.3 *quit,* 397.15 *die,* 591.9 *play truant*
quit the single state 823.15 *marry*
quitting 705.1 *resignation*
quitting work 705.1 *resignation*
quit work 600.7 *stop work,* 644.6 *work,* 705.5 *resign*
quiver 161.27 *bundle,* 365.9 *vibrate,* 366.7 *shake,* 366.12 *flicker,* 366.24 *shake,* 409.10 *be cold,* 605.4 *storage,* 680.4 *arsenal,* 777.11 *be afraid*
quivering 365.2 *vibration,* 365.14 *vibrating,* 366.6 *shaking,* 366.18 *shaky*
quiveringly 366.28 *shakily*
quiver with rage 828.11 *be angry*
quivery 366.18 *shaky*
quixotic 519.11 *fantastical*
quixotry 519.4 *ideality*
quiz 465.7 *be curious,* 477.3 *questionnaire,* 477.17 *question*
quiz master 477.9 *questioner*
quiz show 51.5 *show,* 534.25 *broadcast material*
quiz-show host 51.27 *entertainer*
quizzed 477.16 *questioned*
quizzical 477.13 *problematic,* 799.5 *derisive*
quizzically 477.23 *questioningly*
quizzing glass 435.10 *visual aid*
quod 702.2 *the inside*
quoin 43 Architectural Decoration, 279.3 *architectural summit*
quoit 338.10 *ball*
quokka 77 Marsupials
quondam 200.20, 202.13 *former*
quorate 144.7 *complete*
Quorn 45.21 *meat substitute*
quorum 120.2 *certain amount,* 144.2 *fullness,* 608.7 *sufficiency,* 653.10 *legislative body,* 706.2 *representative body*
quota 52.18 *division,* 68.2 Common Agricultural Policy , 120.2 *certain amount,* 143.1 *part,* 144.2 *fullness,* 302.2 *limiting factor,* 731.2 *portion*
quotable 876.10 *moralistic*
quotation 5.21 *catchword,* 143.2 *particular,* 183.2 *iteration,* 751.1 *price*
quotation mark 543.7 *punctuation*
quote 5.21 *catchword,* 110.7 *be the same,* 143.2 *particular,* 165.24 *specify,* 183.17 *iterate,* 475.16 *explain,* 526.3 *reveal,* 564.11 *speak*
quote a price 751.11 *price*
quote chapter and verse 106.11 *circumstantiate*
quoted 183.10 *iterated,* 526.13 *displayed,* 543.17 *punctuated*
quoted price 751.1 *price*
quote oneself 183.17 *iterate*
quotes 543.7 *punctuation*
quotidian 167.15 *everyday,* 214.12 *cyclic,* 556.1 *simple,* 584.9 *habitual*
quotient 52.18 *division,* 143.1 *part*
Quran 7.12 *religious text*

R

R18 certificate 709.2 *censorship*
Ra 8 Deities
RA 50.16 *artist*
Rabat 93 Cities
rabato 295.14 *neckwear*
rabbet 135.10 *link*

rabbi 7.8 *priest,* 126.5 *superior,* 688.10 *person of authority,* 696.6 *religious leader*
rabbic 696.12 *masterful*
rabbinate 7.9 *priesthood*
rabbinic 7.17 *priestly*
Rabbinic 5 Languages and Groups of Languages
rabbinical 696.12 *masterful*
rabbinically 7.23 *religiously*
Rabbinism 7 Non-Christian Religions
rabbit 77 Placental Mammals, 37.5 *game,* 45.20 *meat,* 564.1 *faculty of speech,* 777.6 *frightened person,* 779.2 *coward*
rabbit farming 68.3 *livestock farming*
rabbitfish 80 Fishes
rabbit food 350.8 *animal food*
rabbit guard 69.6 *garden tool*
rabbithole 322.7 *passageway*
rabbit hunter 398.13 *animal killer*
rabbit hunting 37.2 *hunting,* 398.9 *animal killing*
rabbiting 77.23 *mammal hunting,* 590.2 *chase*
rabbit-like 77
rabbit on 553.5 *be diffuse,* 565.7 *be talkative,* 569.4 *monopolize the conversation*
rabbit punch 26.2 *boxing*
rabbits 161 Collective Names by Animal, 77.12 *gnawing mammal*
rabbit's foot 11.6 *talisman,* 517.6 *good-luck sign*
rabbity 77.31 *rabbit-like*
rabble 127.6 *inferior,* 161.20 *crowd,* 164.11 *general public,* 795.6 *vulgar herd*
rabble-rouse 567.7 *address,* 679.36 *combat*
rabble-rouser 228.7 *motivator,* 567.6 *public speaker,* 586.14 *motivator,* 653.14 *leader,* 679.5 *arguer,* 693.8 *agitator,* 713.4 *protester*
rabble-rousing 679.34 *argumentative*
Rabelais 48 Writers
Rabelaisian 795.9 *ribald,* 827.8 *cursing,* 877.12 *indecent*
Rabi 52 Scientists
rabid 241.6 *violent,* 510.12 *manic,* 828.16 *angry*
rabid animal 398.10 *killer*
rabidly 828.18 *angrily*
rabies 777 Phobias by Topic, 510.3 *mental deterioration,* 624.6 *infection,* 624.18 *veterinary disease*
raccoon 77 Placental Mammals
raccoon dog 77 Placental Mammals
race 1, 21, 33, 674, 1.7 *society,* 21.1 *track events,* 32.16 *ride,* 33.1 *motor racing,* 36.16 *row,* 41.3 *ski racing,* 59.17 *taxonomy,* 68.10 *farm tool,* 74.9 *navigate,* 96.6 *river flow,* 96.7 *flow,* 163.8 *genealogy,* 195.2 *descent,* 329.4 *be swift,* 329.11 *swift thing,* 357.3 *exceed,* 400.9 *group,* 590.2 *chase,* 642.3 *nimbleness,* 642.12 *be active,* 648.2 *make haste,* 652.1 *conduct,* 665.2 *society,* 674.11 *contend*
race a canoe 36.17 *canoe*
race against a deadline 648.4 *haste*
race against time 648.4 *haste*
race a punt 36.19 *punt*
race at a speedway 33.9 *race*
race bangers 33.9 *race*
race card 32.7 *horseracing*
race consciousness 400.11 *nation*
racecourse 674, 32.7 *horseracing,* 313.2 *circle,* 327.6 *path*
race hatred 822, 481.4 *social discrimination*
racehorse 32.2 *thoroughbred,* 329.12 *swift animal*
race hot rods 33.9 *race*
race internationally 33.9 *race*
racemate 57.13 *structure*

raceme 84.4 *flower head*
race meeting 32.7 *horseracing*
race memory 511.1 *memory*
racemic mixture 57.13 *structure*
race midget cars 33.9 *race*
racemization 57.13 *structure*
racemize 57.26 *react*
racemized 57.37 *structural*
racemose 84.12 *of flowers*
racemose inflorescence 84.4 *flower head*
race motorbikes 33.9 *race*
race motorcycles 33.9 *race*
race neck-and-neck 110.10 *be equal*
Race of the Year 33.5 *motorcycle racing*
race on skis 41.14 *ski*
race psychology 61.1 *psychology*
racer 79 Reptiles, 21.3 *athlete*, 32.2 *thoroughbred*, 33.8 *driver*, 329.12 *swift animal*, 329.13 *swift person*, 674.10 *contender*
races 644.5 *exercise*, 674.4 *race*
race sports cars 33.9 *race*
race stock cars 33.9 *race*
racetrack 33.1 *motor racing*, 674.5 *racecourse*
racewalker 21.3 *athlete*
racewalking 21.1 *track events*
raceway 33.1 *motor racing*
rachial 83.17 *of stems*
rachilla 83.5 *stem*, 87.3 *grass plant*
rachiotomy 60 Surgical Operations
rachis 382 Bones, 78.17 *plumage*, 83.5 *stem*, 88.2 *fern plant*
Rachmaninov 49 Musicians and Composers
Rachmanism 690.2 *suppression*
racial 1, 1.14 *societal*, 2.14 *socioeconomic*, 400.12 *human*, 665.9 *societal*
racial class hatred 805.11 *prejudice*
racial discrimination 147.4 *exclusiveness*, 481.4 *social discrimination*
racial group 2.6 *social group*, 400.9 *group*
racial harassment 832.5 *intolerance*
racial hatred 832.5 *intolerance*
racial intolerance 493.3 *injustice*
racialism 481.4 *social discrimination*, 493.3 *injustice*, 832.5 *intolerance*
racialist 481.7 *bigot*, 481.10 *discriminatory*, 493.5 *misjudging person*
racially 1.18 *societally*, 2.16 *sociologically*, 400.15 *humanly*, 481.17 *prejudicially*, 665.18 *cliquishly*
racially prejudiced 805.23 *prejudiced*, 844.11 *wrong*
racial memory 1.8 *tradition*
racial phobia 822.3 *race hatred*
racial prejudice 493.3 *injustice*, 805.11 *prejudice*
racial unconscious 61.21 *psyche*
racily 412.11 *tastelessly*
Racine 48 Dramatists
raciness 412.4 *bad taste*, 413.1 *piquancy*, 554.1 *emphasis*
racing 33, 21.1 *track events*, 21.6 *track*, 32.6 *horsemanship*, 32.7 *horseracing*, 32.17 *equine*, 36.4 *rowing*, 36.14 *punting*, 41.3 *ski racing*, 96.10 *fluvial*, 329.1 *swift*, 329.8 *speed*, 590.2 *chase*, 648.3 *hasty*, 674.4 *race*, 674.14 *contending*
racing bicycle 71.12 *bicycle*
racing boat 36.4 *rowing*
racing canoe 36.6 *canoeing*
racing car 71 Motor Vehicles, 329.11 *swift thing*
racing circuit 33.1 *motor racing*
racing driver 329.13 *swift person*
racing forecaster 517.9 *forecaster*
racing governing body 33
racing handlebars 71.11 *bicycle part*
racing oar 36.4 *rowing*
racing pole 36.8 *punting*

racing punt 36.8 *punting*
racing river 96.1 *river*
racing saddle 32.14 *horse-riding terms*
racing shell 74 Ships and Boats
racing ski 41.2 *cross-country skiing*
racing-step turn 41.4 *skiing technique*
racing steward 32.15 *horse person*
racing suit 41.5 *ski equipment*
racing track 32.7 *horseracing*, 327.6 *path*
racing tyre 33.1 *motor racing*
racism 91.4 *nationalism*, 481.4 *social discrimination*, 493.3 *injustice*, 820.1 *enmity*, 822.3 *race hatred*, 832.5 *intolerance*
racist 822, 91.14 *nationalist*, 147.10 *excluding*, 481.7 *bigot*, 481.10 *discriminatory*, 493.5 *misjudging person*, 493.8 *unjust*, 820.5 *hostile person*, 820.7 *intolerant*, 822.9 *hater*, 832.8 *malefactor*, 832.10 *malevolent*
rack 258, 24.1 *billiards*, 134.10 *purify*, 328.10 *slow motion*, 382.4 *framework*, 406.11 *inflict pain*, 618.14 *ill-treat*, 621.15 *purify*, 879.4 *torture*, 879.15 *instrument of torture*
rack and pinion 71 Motor Vehicle Parts, 63.7 *gear*, 71.21 *miscellaneous motoring terms*
rack-and-pinion railway 327.10 *railway*
rack and ruin 244.4 *ruin*, 628.9 *dilapidation*
racket 49 Musical Instruments, 40.11 *badminton equipment*, 151.5 *confusion*, 153.5 *commotion*, 366.2 *tumult*, 377.3 *elastic thing*, 423.2 *outcry*, 426.3 *rattle*, 434.2 *dissonant noise*, 538.10 *dishonesty*, 539.10 *fraud*, 592.4 *plot*, 642.1 *activity*, 644.3 *job*, 858.3 *criminality*
racketeer 734.6 *taker*, 736.11 *dishonest person*, 737.1 *trade*, 737.10 *trader*, 858.4 *dishonourable person*, 858.10 *be criminal*, 864.9 *wicked person*
racketeering 737.4 *trade*, 858.3 *criminality*
rackety 423.6 *loud*
racking 406.5 *painful*, 879.12 *corporal punishment*
rack of equipment 34.4 *climbing equipment*
rack one's brains 461.12 *think*, 523.9 *find unintelligible*
rack railway 72.1 *railway*, 327.10 *railway*
rack-rent 753.4 *extortion*, 753.10 *overcharge*
rack-renter 753.5 *overcharger*
raconteur 560.10 *descriptive writer*
racquetball 18 Sporting Activities
racy 412.6 *coarse*, 413.9 *piquant*, 554.3 *emphatic*, 877.12 *indecent*
rad 75 Scientific and Technical Units, 617.1 *worthy*, 861.1 *good*, 861.27 *great super*
radar 534, 56.13 *electromagnetic radiation*, 74.5 *navigation*, 420.9 *audio device*, 496.11 *detector*, 543.5 *indicator*, 653.5 *guide*
radar astronomy 53.1 *astronomy*, 534.28 *radar*
radar beacon 73.6 *flight control*
radar beam 534.28 *radar*
radar guidance 534.28 *radar*
radar indicator 534.28 *radar*
radar navigation 534.28 *radar*
radar receiver 730.8 *receiver*
radarscope 534.28 *radar*
radar screen 534.28 *radar*
radar surveillance 534.28 *radar*
radar tracking 534.28 *radar*
radar trap 329.8 *speed*
raddle 450.9 *redden*
radiaesthesia 11.9 *divination*
radiaesthetic 11.16 *psychic*

radial 52.81 *curvilinear*, 248.11 *spatial*, 324.17 *directional*, 342.7 *convergent*, 343.7 *radiating*
radial-arm saw 47.11 *woodworking tool*
radially 343.16 *divergently*
radial motion 324.5 *circuition*
radial energy 235.4 *energy*
radial tyre 71 Motor Vehicle Parts
radial velocity 53.13 *luminosity*
radian 75 SI Units, 75 Scientific and Technical Units
radiance 343.3 *radiation*, 439.1 *light*, 789.1 *gorgeousness*
radiant 53.20 *meteor*, 343.7 *radiating*, 364.4 *vortex*, 439.15 *lucent*, 769.1 *cheerful*
radiant energy 235.4 *energy*
radiant heat 408.1 *heat*
radiantly 343.16 *divergently*, 439.30 *lightly*, 769.9 *cheerfully*
radiata pine 85 Trees and Shrubs
radiate 343, 55.37 *observe*, 55.61 *shine*, 162.10 *diverge*, 235.12 *generate power*, 326.11 *transfer*, 343.7 *radiating*, 349.14 *let out*, 439.25 *light up*
radiate light 439.25 *light up*
radiating 343, 136.16 *apart*, 162.24 *divergent*, 342.7 *convergent*, 349.29 *expulsive*
radiation 343, 55.9 *atmospheric process*, 56.12 *wave*, 56.36 *heat flow*, 162.5 *divergence*, 244.7 *agent of destruction*, 349.25 *emission*, 365.5 *wave*, 439.1 *light*, 680.1 *weapon*, 680.16 *bomb*
radiation balance 55.9 *atmospheric process*
radiation belt 54, 53.16 *planet*
radiation detector 56
radiation exposure 56.75 *nuclear accident*
radiation fog 55.33 *fog*
radiation frost 55.36 *frost*
radiation physics 56.3 *modern physics*
radiative 55.43 *atmospheric*
radiator 71 Motor Vehicle Parts, 349.28 *propellant*, 408.3 *heater*, 534.17 *antenna*
radical 83.19 *of roots*, 168.8 *dissenter*, 168.12 *nonconformist*, 169.9 *fractional*, 226.3 *rudiment*, 226.13 *causal*, 280.3 *base*, 290.11 *intrinsic*, 541.6 *exaggerator*, 611.5 *important*, 617.1 *worthy*, 627.12 *reformer*, 627.16 *improving*, 663.9 *opposer*, 665.6 *political party member*, 665.15 *political*, 693.6 *nonconformist*, 861.1 *good*
radicalism 627.11 *reformism*
radically 103.14 *at heart*, 226.14 *causally*, 627.17 *better*, 665.18 *cliquishly*
radical mastectomy 630.12 *surgery*
radical reform 627.5 *improvement*
Radicals 12.6 *political party*
radical sign 52.13 *mathematical symbol*
radical therapy 61.3 *psychiatric treatment*
radical treatment 60.8 *treatment*
radicle 83.7 *root*, 83.9 *seed*
radicular 83.19 *of roots*
radio 534, 56.13 *electromagnetic radiation*, 235.9 *electronics*, 420.9 *audio device*, 420.11 *aural*, 528.4 *mass communication*, 532.2 *mass media*, 532.13 *make public*, 534.1 *communications*, 534.30 *communicate*
Radio 1 534.20 *radio broadcasting*
Radio 2 534.20 *radio broadcasting*
Radio 3 534.20 *radio broadcasting*
Radio 4 534.20 *radio broadcasting*
Radio 5 534.20 *radio broadcasting*

radioactive 618.5 *harmful*, 633.1 *dangerous*
radioactive cloud 680.1 *weapon*, 680.16 *bomb*
radioactive dating 54.42 *dating*
radioactive decay 56.70 *radioactivity*
radioactive series 56.70 *radioactivity*
radioactive substance 56.70 *radioactivity*
radioactive waste 56.74 *nuclear waste*, 235.8 *nuclear power*
radioactivity 56, 235.8 *nuclear power*, 349.25 *emission*, 626.1 *lack of hygiene*, 631.10 *warfare*, 680.1 *weapon*, 680.16 *bomb*
radio amplifier 64.21 *rectifier*
radio astronomy 53.1 *astronomy*, 534.27 *signalling*
radio audience measurement 532.2 *mass media*
radiobeacon 534.27 *signalling*
radio-beacon station 74.5 *navigation*
radio beam 534.14 *radio transmission*
radio bearing 534.27 *signalling*
radiobiology 59.1 *life science*
radio broadcaster 534.29 *broadcaster*
radio broadcasting 534
radio car 534.20 *radio broadcasting*
radiocarbon dating 54.42 *dating*, 56.70 *radioactivity*, 192.3 *chronology*
radio channel 534.14 *radio transmission*
radiochemical 57.31 *chemical*
radiochemical reaction 57.14 *chemical reaction*
radiochemist 57.2 *chemist*
radiochemistry 57.1 *chemistry*
Radio City Rockettes 46.5 *dancer*
radio communication 534.1 *communications*
radio compass 534.27 *signalling*
radio control 534.27 *signalling*
radio direction-finding 534.27 *signalling*
radio dish 53.26 *radio telescope*
radio drama 51.2 *play*
radio dramatist 51.24 *dramatist*
radioed 534.34 *communicated*
radio engineer 646.2 *artisan*
radio engineering 534.6 *telecommunication*
radio frequency 212, 534.14 *radio transmission*
radio-frequency band 212.6 *radio frequency*
radio galaxy 53.7 *galaxy*
radiogoniometer 534.27 *signalling*
radiograph 60.7 *diagnosis*, 66.3 *photograph*
radiographer 60.17 *paramedic*
radiography 56.70 *radioactivity*, 60.7 *diagnosis*, 66.1 *photography*
radio ham 534.29 *broadcaster*
radio interferometer 53.26 *radio telescope*, 56.85 *microscope*
radioisotope 56.70 *radioactivity*
radio link 534.14 *radio transmission*
radiological 60.22 *medical*
radiologist 60.13 *medical specialist*
radiology 56.70 *radioactivity*, 60.3 *medical specialty*
radioluminescence 56.24 *light emission*
radio marker 534.27 *signalling*
radio mast 275.6 *tall thing*, 534.20 *radio broadcasting*
radiometer 53.27 *imaging*, 56.92 *light meter*, 268.8 *meter*
radiometric 268.16 *micrometric*
radiometric dating 54.42 *dating*, 56.70 *radioactivity*, 185.8 *dating*
radiometry 268.2 *micrometry*
radio microphone 534.16 *transmitter*
radiomobile 534.20 *radio broadcasting*
radio navigation 534.27 *signalling*

radio news 533
radionuclide 56.70 *radioactivity*
radio observatory 53.23 *observatory*
radio operator 534.29 *broadcaster*
radio oscillator 64.21 *rectifier*
radiopager 420.9 *audio device*, 534.18 *radio*
radiopaging 420.9 *audio device*
radio personality 51.27 *entertainer*
radiophone 420.9 *audio device*, 534.9 *telephone*
radio phone 534.16 *transmitter*
radiophonic 420.11 *aural*
radiophonics 420.1 *hearing*
radio play 51.2 *play*
radio producer 243.9 *producer*
radio programme 526.9 *production*
radio receiver 420.9 *audio device*, 534.18 *radio*, 730.8 *receiver*
radio reception 534
radio room 74 *Parts of a Ship*
radio set 534.18 *radio*
radio signal 534.14 *radio transmission*
radio signalling 534.27 *signalling*
radiosonde 55.5 *weather station*
radio spectrum 56.13 *electromagnetic radiation*, 534.14 *radio transmission*
radio station 534.20 *radio broadcasting*
radiotelegraph 534.8 *data transmission*
radiotelegraphy 534.6 *telecommunication*
radiotelephone 420.9 *audio device*, 534.9 *telephone*
radiotelephony 420.9 *audio device*, 534.6 *telecommunication*
radio telescope 53, 56.85 *microscope*
radiotherapist 60.13 *medical specialist*
radiotherapy 56.70 *radioactivity*, 60.8 *treatment*, 630.13 *therapy*
radio tower 534.20 *radio broadcasting*
radio transmission 534
radio transmitter 534.16 *transmitter*
radio wave 365.5 *wave*, 534.14 *radio transmission*
radio waves 56.13 *electromagnetic radiation*
radish 45 *Vegetables*
radium 57 *Chemical Elements*
radius 382 *Bones*, 52.37 *line*, 52.42 *circle*, 56.7 *space*, 122.7 *dividing line*, 248.7 *range*, 259.1 *size*, 271.4 *breadth*, 313.4 *parts of a circle*, 333.1 *middle way*, 342.5 *focus*, 343.3 *radiation*
radius rod 71 *Motor Vehicle Parts*
radius vector 52.50 *scalar quantity*
radix 83.7 *root*, 226.3 *rudiment*
radix point 52.8 *number system*
Radnor 68 *Breeds of Sheep*
radon 57 *Chemical Elements*
RAF 36.7, 36.13 *windsurfing*
raffia 137.6 *line*
raffia work 42 *Hobbies and Pastimes*
raffinose 58 *Common Sugars*
raffle 229.2, 229.4 *chance*, 589.3 *equal chance*, 749.5 *winnings*
raffle ticket 544.3 *means of identification*
raft 63.28 *substructure*, 326.12 *transport*
rafter 161 *Collective Names for Birds and Animals*, 47.12 *wood*, 284.2 *supporting part*, 604.1 *materials*
rafters 293.7 *overhead covering*
rag 51.17 *stage set*, 67.3 *fabric*, 143.7 *piece*, 295.1 *dress*, 532.4 *newspaper*, 539.11, 539.31 *hoax*, 771.13 *be humorous*, 850.24 *ridicule*
raga 49.20 *key*

ragamuffin 49.9 *popular music*, 622.6 *dirty person*
rag and bone man 727.6 *rubbish collector*
rag-and-bone man 739.11 *pedlar*
ragbag 113.3 *diverse thing*, 133.3 *miscellany*
rag doll 547.6 *image*
rage 233.10 *be a prevailing influence*, 241.7 *be violent*, 642.12 *be active*, 665.17 *socialize*, 759.6 *bad feeling*, 796.1 *fashion*, 822.5, 822.17 *anger*, 828.4 *anger*, 828.11 *be angry*
ragga 49.9 *popular music*
ragged 151.15 *untidy*, 296.10 *in dishabille*, 375.1 *rough*, 539.36 *deceived*, 743.3 *beggarly*
ragged edge 300.1 *edge*
raggedness 113.1 *diversity*, 375.6 *roughness*, 743.7 *beggary*
ragged robin 84 *Flowers and Flowering Plants*
ragger 539.15 *deceiver*
raging 55.48 *stormy*, 241.6 *violent*, 244.14 *destructive*, 670.23 *attacking*, 759.13 *passionate*, 828.4 *anger*, 828.16 *angry*
raging fury 822.5 *anger*
raglan 295.12 *coat*
raglan sleeve 295.24 *part of garment*
ragout 133.2 *mixed thing*
rag paper 604.3 *paper*
rag-picker 743.10 *poor person*
rags 143.8 *bits and pieces*, 295.1 *dress*, 296.4 *dishabille* , 743.7 *beggary*
rags and bones 614.6 *refuse*
ragtime 49.8 *jazz*
ragtime band 49.26 *musical group*
ragworm 81 *Worms*
ragwort 84 *Flowers and Flowering Plants*
raid 244.5 *havoc*, 244.10 *lay waste*, 346.3 *inroad*, 346.10 *invade*, 670.1 *attack*, 670.12 *military attack*, 676.8 *warfare*, 676.13 *be at war*, 679.38 *conquer*, 734.3 *taking away*, 734.10 *take away*, 736.5 *plundering*, 736.14 *plunder*
Raiden 8 *Deities*
raider 244.6 *destroyer*, 346.8 *intruder*, 670.19 *attacker*, 679.6 *militarist*, 679.9 *guerrilla*, 679.25 *historical naval ships*, 734.6 *taker*, 736.9 *plunderer*
raiding 244.5 *havoc*, 734.3 *taking away*, 736.5 *plundering*, 736.17 *stolen*
raiding party 679.14 *armed forces*
rail 74 *Parts of a Ship*, **78** *Birds*, 72.6 *railway*, 36.17 *windsurfing*, 36.18 *windsurf*, 68.11 *farmland*, 70.1 *transport*, 70.5 *transportable*, 78.3 *water bird*, 301.5 *enclose*, 564.14 *speak to*, 852.21 *berate*
rail against 827.6 *vilify*, 852.21 *berate*
rail at 850.25 *taunt*
railcar 72.6 *rolling stock*
railcard 754.4 *bargain*
railhead 72.8 *railway station*
railing 36.7 *windsurfing*, 301.3 *enclosing thing*, 632.4 *safety device*, 852.8 *berating*
raillery 807.9, 818.1 *discourtesy*
railroad 72.1 *railway*, 327.10 *railway*, 648.1 *hasten*, 695.7 *force*, 701.6 *subject*
railroaded 648.3 *hasty*
railroad yard 327.10 *railway*
rails 72.3 *rail*, 327.10 *railway*
rail station 72.8 *railway station*
rail transport 326.5 *means of transport*
Rail Transport 72
railway 72, 327, 63.19 *structure*, 70.5 *transportable*
railway bridge 63.21, 327.9 *bridge*
railway engineering 63.17 *civil engineering*

railway express 326.2 *transportation*
railway halt 218.4 *stopping place*
railway line 327.10 *railway*
railwayman 72.9 *railway worker*
railway signal 543.4 *signal*
railway signals 534.27 *signalling*
railway station 72, 218.4 *stopping place*, 344.15 *destination*, 345.10 *place of departure*
railway system 72.1 *railway*
railway tracks 285.2 *parallel thing*
railway tunnel 63.22, 327.8 *tunnel*
railway worker 72
rain 55, 55, 55.24 *precipitation*, 360.3 *downflow*, 360.13 *drip*, 389.1 *water*, 391.2 *mistiness*, 608.5 *about*
rain-bearing cloud 55.18 *cloud*
rain blows down on 330.5 *beat*
rainbow 55, 56.28 *colour*, 113.3 *diverse thing*, 159.2 *consecution*, 311.3 *curved things*, 439.12 *highlight*, 444.2 *colourfulness*, 456.5 *variegated thing*
rainbow-coloured 456.6 *variegated*
rainbow effect 456.1 *variegation*
rainbow's end 55.27 *rainbow*
rainbow trout 80 *Fishes*, 20.4 *American game fish*, 45.17 *freshwater fish*
rain cats and dogs 55.62 *rain*, 360.13 *drip*, 608.5 *about*
rain cloud 55.18 *cloud*
raincoat 295.12 *coat*, 634.2 *shelter*
rain damage 55.26 *raininess*
rain dance 10.7 *non-Christian ritual*, 46.4 *historic dancing*, 55.26 *raininess*
rain day 55.24 *precipitation*
rain dew 391.6 *dew*
raindrop 55.24 *precipitation*
raindrops 424.3 *faint-sounding thing*
rain erosion 54.35 *weathering*
rainfall 55.24 *precipitation*, 55.25 *rain*, 362.11 *lowering*, 389.3 *wateriness*, 391.2 *mistiness*
rainforest 85.4 *trees*
rain forest 408.8 *hot place*
rainforest climate 55.38 *climate*
rain gauge 55.7 *weather instruments*, 389.19 *measuring instrument*
rain god 8.5 *deity*
rain hat 295.15 *headgear*
rainier 55.53 *rainy*
Rainier 95 *Mountains*
rainily 55.65 *meteorologically*
raininess 55, 389.3 *wateriness*, 391.2 *mistiness*
raining 330.12 *collision*
raining cats and dogs 55.53 *rainy*
rainless 392, 55.45 *fine*
rainmaking 55.26 *raininess*
rainproof 392.10 *waterproof*
rain stopped play 27.1 *cricket match*
rainstorm 55.25 *rain*, 241.5 *violent weather*
rain tree 85 *Trees and Shrubs*
rainwater 55.25 *rain*
rain water 389.1 *water*
rainy 55, 391.10 *misty*
Rainy 94 *Lakes*
rainy day 687.4 *time of adversity*
rainy day policy 781.2 *insurance*
rainy season 55.26 *raininess*, 203.1 *season*
raise 275, 361, 6.22 *educate*, 42.3 *card game terms*, 42.10 *play*, 52.91 *add*, 68.18 *practise livestock farming*, 128.5 *make bigger*, 228.5 *positive stimulus*, 243.10 *produce*, 245.13 *propagate*, 248.20 *extend*, 261.5 *make bigger*, 281.6 *make vertical*, 304.8 *nurture*, 336.8 *further*, 336.12 *advance*, 370.10 *lighten*, 382.15 *shape*, 594.7 *develop*, 627.1 *improve*, 721.2 *augmentation*, 878.4 *reward for service*

raise a cry 431.10 *cry out*
raise a finger 640.4 *act*
raise a hue and cry 532.14 *proclaim*, 636.7 *raise the alarm*
raise all hell 423.8 *be loud*
raise an embargo 727.9 *dispose of*
raise an objection 713.6 *protest*
raise a rafter 47.17 *carpenter*
raise a rumpus 151.26 *be disorderly*
raise a storm 241.7 *be violent*
raise Cain 423.8 *be loud*, 659.22 *cause trouble*, 828.11 *be angry*
raise children 304.8 *nurture*
raised 361, 6.20 *refined*, 68.21 *domesticated*, 243.12 *produced*, 261.7 *bigger*, 281.9 *unbowed*
raised expectations 515.1 *disappointment*
raised eyebrow 852.10 *disapproving look*
raised eyebrows 543.3 *gesture*, 713.3 *gesture of protest*
raised fist 713.3 *gesture of protest*
raise difficulties 659.23 *cause difficulties*, 659.24 *create difficulties*
raise doubts about 476.9 *deny*
raised seam 27.7 *bat*
raised temperature 408.1 *heat*
raise expectations 517.11 *predict*
raise from cuttings 128.5 *make bigger*
raise from seed 128.5 *make bigger*, 245.13 *propagate*
raise from the dead 396.19 *give birth to*
raise funds 712.8 *solicit money*, 721.9 *gain*
raise ghosts 11.22 *conjure*
raise hell 151.26 *be disorderly*, 532.14 *proclaim*, 659.22 *cause trouble*, 828.11 *be angry*
raise hob 659.22 *cause trouble*
raise money 602.6 *find means*, 733.7 *borrow*
raise money for 831.9 *be charitable*
raise objections 663.15 *object*
raise one's banner 674.12 *fight*, 676.12 *go to war*
raise one's consciousness 403.13 *arouse sensation*
raise one's expectations 515.6 *disappoint*
raise one's eyebrows 543.11 *gesture*, 852.23 *show disapproval*
raise one's fist 713.6 *protest*
raise one's glass 351.14 *drink to*, 812.17 *congratulate*
raise one's hackles 828.12 *become angry*
raise one's hand 543.11 *gesture*, 580.5 *vote*
raise one's hand against 670.5 *strike*
raise one's hat 294.11 *uncover*, 817.12 *greet*
raise one's hopes 775.10 *inspire hope*
raise one's sights 128.5 *make bigger*, 336.7 *make one's way*
raise one's voice 423.8 *be loud*, 431.10 *cry out*, 475.18 *appear*, 526.4 *show oneself*, 554.6 *emphasize*
raise one's voice against 713.6 *protest*
raiser 68.15 *agriculturist*, 361.10 *elevator*
raise someone's hackles 828.9 *offend*
raise steam 74.9 *navigate*, 594.4 *prepare for action*
raise suspicions 498.5 *cause disbelief*
raise taxes 734.8 *take back*
raise the alarm 636, 543.12 *signal*
raise the bid 13.11 *deal*, 753.11 *overpay*
raise the curtain 51.36 *dramatize*, 530.5 *disclose*
raise the curtain on 437.10 *make visible*
raise the devil 151.26 *be disorderly*, 659.22 *cause trouble*,

828.11 *be angry*
raise the drawbridge 634.4 *shelter*
raise the dust 642.12 *be active*
raise the flag 849.20 *salute*
raise the hue and cry 590.10 *chase*
raise the hunt 590.10 *chase*
raise the issue 472.11 *raise the point*, 477.20 *doubt*
raise the point 472
raise the pressure 239.2 *be full of vigour*
raise the price 753.10 *overcharge*
raise the rafters 423.8 *be loud*
raise the roof 423.8 *be loud*, 532.14 *proclaim*, 659.22 *cause trouble*, 828.11 *be angry*, 851.16 *acclaim*
raise the roof over 713.6 *protest*
raise the stakes 128.5 *make bigger*
raise the tempo 329.6 *accelerate*
raise to the peerage 802.5 *make noble*
raise to the power of 128.5 *make bigger*
raise trade barriers 737.1 *trade*
raise up 281.6 *make vertical*, 361.1 *raise*, 396.19 *give birth to*
raisin 45.42 *preserve*
raisin bread 45.38 *bread*
raising 361, 6.1 *origination*, 261.1 *growth*, 281.2 *making vertical*, 281.9 *unbowed*, 370.4 *leavening*
Raising 361
raising agent 361.10 *elevator*, 370.8 *leavening*, 390.11 *aeration*
raitha 45.12 *hors d'oeuvre*, 45.49 *Indian dish*
raj 12.3 *governance*
rajah 696.2 *sovereign*, 696.3 *leader*
Rajasthani 5 Languages and Groups of Languages
Rajput 679.6 *militarist*
rake 68.17 *farm*, 69.6 *garden tool*, 69.15 *cultivate*, 72.7 *train*, 73.7 *miscellaneous aviation terms*, 339.12 *drag*, 355.10 *excavator*, 376.9 *smoother*, 376.11 *smooth*, 380.8 *sharp-pointed thing*, 380.16 *use a sharp tool* , 401.7 *libertine*, 405.3 *pleasure-seeker*, 586.13 *tempter*, 603.2 *garden tool*, 603.9 *use tools*, 621.10 *cleaning object*, 670.2 *fire*, 864.9 *wicked person*, 877.8 *immoral man*
raked 69.19 *ornamental*
rakehell 877.8 *immoral man*
rake in 339.12 *drag*
rake in the cash 742.13 *get rich*
rake it in 721.14 *profit*, 742.12 *be rich*, 742.13 *get rich*
rake off 710.9 *offer*, 721.14 *profit*, 752.4 *take a discount*
rake-off 131.2 *subtracted item*, 710.4 *illegal offer*, 721.5 *profit*, 729.2 *gift*, 749.5 *winnings*, 751.3 *fee*, 752.1 *discount*, 878.8 *secret money*
rake out 339.12 *drag*, 355.11 *extract*, 621.13 *clean*
rake up the past 511.12 *remember*
raki 351.7 *alcoholic drink*
rakily 811.35 *flashily*
raking arch 43.5 *arch*
raking fire 670.15 *firing*
raking it in 721.1 *gain*, 742.1 *wealthy*
rakish 811.19 *flashy*, 877.14 *lecherous*
rakish angle 286.2 *oblique line*
raku firing 44.5 *ceramic process*
raku kiln 44.6 *ceramic workshop*
rale 429.1 *hiss*
Raleigh 93 Cities
rall 49 Musical Terms
rallentando 49 Musical Terms, 49.19 *tempo*
rally 161, 40.4 *tennis terms*, 140.5 *combine*, 161.1 *assembly*, 161.42 *call together*, 228.9 *motivate*, 237.7 *be strong*, 338.5

throw, 475.6 *mass demonstration*, 475.19 *protest*, 543.6 *word*, 627.2 *get better*, 629.3 *restore*, 629.4 *be restored*, 629.10 *revival*, 629.11 *recuperation*, 662.19 *support*, 674.2 *contest*, 676.7 *war measures*, 676.12 *go to war*, 676.14 *battle*
rally car 71 Motor Vehicles
rally cross 18 Sporting Activities
rallycross 33.5 *motorcycle racing*, 674.4 *race*
rallying 14.1 *finance*, 33.1 *motor racing*, 475.14 *demonstrating*, 629.11 *recuperation*
rallying cry 431.1 *cry*, 543.6 *word*, 586.4 *exhortation*, 636.2 *danger signal*, 676.2 *glory of war*
rallying symbol 543.1 *sign*
rally round 161.39 *come together*, 664.13 *work together*
rally round the flag 676.12 *go to war*
ram 330, 68.8 *livestock*, 77.17 *male mammal*, 244.9 *demolish*, 330.2 *collide*, 384.14 *hammer*, 401.16 *male animal*, 603.1 *tool*, 603.9 *use tools*, 670.1 *attack*, 680.7 *blunt weapon*
Ram 53 The Constellations
RAM 65.6 *memory*, 511.6 *artificial memory*
Rama 8 Deities
Ramadan 10.16 *religious festival*, 871.3 *fast day*
ram-air turbine 73 Aircraft Parts
Rama Krishna 7 Non-Christian Religions
Raman 52 Scientists
Ramanandi 7 Non-Christian Religions
Ramanuja 4 Philosophers
Ramapithecus 400.3 *uncivilized human*
ramble 104.13 *be extraneous*, 104.14 *be foreign*, 108.10 *be unrelated*, 160.15 *lose one's train of thought*, 335.3 *go astray*, 510.14 *become insane*, 523.7 *be unintelligible*, 553.6 *be circuitous*
ramble on 553.5 *be diffuse*, 565.7 *be talkative*
rambler 69.9 *garden plant*
rambling 104.10 *foreign*, 224.13 *changeable*, 335.16, 335.25 *wandering*, 523.1 *unintelligible*, 553.2 *circumlocution*, 553.4 *circumlocutory*, 555.1 *unemphatic*, 610.7 *superfluous*
rambling speech 610.3 *superfluity*
rambling wreck 628.9 *dilapidation*
Rambo 237.6 *muscleman*
Ramboesque 676.16 *warlike*
Ramboism 676.5 *bellicosity*
Rambouillet 68 Breeds of Sheep
rambunctious 423.6 *loud*
rambutan 86 Fruits
ram down 144.6 *fill*, 330.2 *collide*, 371.9 *make dense*
ram down one's throat 695.7 *force*
ramekin 258.16 *crockery*
ramification 137.4 *means of connection*, 143.6 *branch*, 162.5 *divergence*, 176.7 *halving*, 261.1 *growth*, 343.4 *branching*
ramified 176.13 *half*
ramiform 162.24 *divergent*
ramify 162.10 *diverge*, 176.16 *halve*, 261.5 *make bigger*, 261.6 *become bigger*, 343.14 *branch*
ram in 144.6 *fill*, 354.3 *impact*
ramjet 73 Types of Aircraft, **73** Aircraft Parts
ramjet propulsion 338.2 *method of propulsion*
ramkie 49 Musical Instruments
rammer 330.15 *ram*
ramming 330.12 *collision*, 330.17 *impelling*
ramose 343.9 *branched*
ramosely 343.16 *divergently*
ramous 343.9 *branched*
ramously 343.16 *divergently*
ramp 34.5 *rock face*, 286.1 *obliqueness*, 310.2 *obliquity*,

359.2 *upturn*, 359.14 *climb*, 359.16 *stand up*, 539.10 *fraud*
rampage 151.9 *disorder*, 151.26 *be disorderly*, 241.7 *be violent*, 423.8 *be loud*, 642.12 *be active*, 828.11 *be angry*
rampageous 151.20 *disorderly*
rampaging 244.14 *destructive*, 828.16 *angry*
rampant 164.17 *widespread*, 241.6 *violent*, 281.9 *unbowed*, 359.23 *rising*, 544.13 *heraldic*, 689.6 *anarchic*, 877.14 *lecherous*
rampant arch 43.5 *arch*
rampantness 164.4 *widespreadness*
rampart 147.3 *exclusion zone*, 284.2 *supporting part*, 284.11 *support*, 634.1 *refuge*, 661.3 *barrier*, 671.2 *safeguard*, 671.11 *fortification*, 671.12 *fort*
ramped 34.8 *mountaineering*
Rampur 93 Cities
ram raid 736.3 *theft*
ram-raid 736.12 *steal*
ram-raiding 736.1 *stealing*
ramrod 330.15 *ram*, 680.9 *firearm*
Ramsay 52 Scientists
Ramsey 18 Sporting Personalities
ramshackle 628.13 *dilapidated*, 633.2 *unsafe*
Ramus 4 Philosophers
ranasringa 49 Musical Instruments
ranch 68.6 *farm*, 68.18 *practise livestock farming*, 725.1 *property*
rancher 68.15 *agriculturist*, 243.9 *producer*, 350.20 *food provider*
ranchero 68.15 *agriculturist*
ranch foreman 653.14 *leader*
ranch house 43.3 *building*, 256.5 *house*
ranch-house cook 45.2 *cook*
ranching 68.3 *livestock farming*
ranchman 68.15 *agriculturist*
rancho 68.6 *farm*
rancid 141.5 *disintegrated*, 415.6 *unpalatable*, 419.4 *putrid*, 764.3 *unpalatable*
rancidity 419.2 *something that makes an unpleasant smell*
rancidness 415.2 *unpalatability*
rancorous 415.7 *splenetic*, 820.6 *hostile*, 822.10 *hating*, 832.14 *hostile*
rancorously 415.11 *splenetically*, 820.14 *hostilely*, 822.18 *hatefully*
rancour 415.4 *spleen*, 618.11 *harmfulness*, 820.3 *ill feeling*, 822.1 *hate*, 828.1 *resentment*, 832.4 *bitterness*
rand 741.11 *national coins*
randan 74 Ships and Boats
R and D worker 479.5 *experimenter*
randem 71 Carriages and Carts
randiness 782.4 *sexual desire*, 821.5 *desire*
random 108.7 *illogical*, 133.12 *mixed*, 151.14 *in the midst*, 151.27 *in disorder*, 215.8 *irregularly*, 229.8 *by chance*, 482.14 *indiscriminately*, 491.27 *capriciously*, 589.13 *by chance*
random access 65.17 *computing term*
random chance 589.1 *chance*
randomly 133.14 *in the midst*, 151.27 *in disorder*, 215.8 *irregularly*, 229.8 *by chance*, 482.14 *indiscriminately*, 491.27 *capriciously*, 504.2 *inaccuracy*, 589.1 *chance*, 642.7 *restlessness*

randomness of recurrence 215.1 *irregularity*
random number 52.7 *natural number*, 224.3 *changeable thing*
random sample 52.57 *population*, 229.2 *chance*, 299.1 *outline*, 589.3 *equal chance*
random sampling 52.57 *population*
random variable 52.57 *population*
R and R 651.5 *refreshment*
randy 782.11 *lustful*, 821.20 *amorous*, 877.14 *lecherous*
Raney nickel 57 Named Reactions, 57.15 *catalysis*
range 248, 52.29 *mathematical function*, 52.60 *parameter*, 87.2 *grassland*, 95.1 *mountain*, 98.6 *lowland*, 121.1 *degree*, 152.12 *arrange*, 159.16 *arrange consecutively*, 163.14 *sort*, 235.2 *ability*, 248.20 *extend*, 256.2 *environment*, 259.1, 268.4 *size*, 271.4 *breadth*, 420.1 *hearing*, 420.10 *sound quality*, 435.9 *viewpoint*, 437.3 *visibility*, 580.6 *selection*, 605.3 *supply*, 698.18 *have scope*, 739.8 *merchandise*
ranged 152.20 *arranged*
range finder 25.4 *bowling*
rangefinder 66.18 *exposure time*, 332.3 *orientation*, 437.7 *that which makes visible*
range horse 32.1 *horse*
range of choice 580.6 *selection*
range of colour 444.2 *colourfulness*
ranger 85.8 *forester*
range with 664.14 *join with*
ranginess 274.7 *thinness*, 275.1 *height*
ranging 698
ranging freely 698.11 *ranging*
rangiora 85 Trees and Shrubs
Rangoon 93 Cities
rangy 274.1 *thin*, 275.12 *tall*
rani 696.2 *sovereign*
Ranjitsinhji Vibhaji 18 Sporting Personalities
rank 121, 251, 17.1 *military affairs*, 17.4 *military organization*, 52.56 *nonparametric methods*, 52.94 *order*, 83.13 *plantlike*, 105.1 *state*, 107.3 *relative position*, 107.9 *have a relative position*, 121.5 *measure*, 126.10 *lead*, 150.4 *position*, 150.19 *systematize*, 152.6 *category*, 152.15 *categorize*, 159.16 *arrange consecutively*, 163.5 *social class*, 163.14 *sort*, 248.21 *space*, 259.18 *measure*, 419.3 *stinking*, 608.2 *plentiful*, 611.1 *importance*, 618.4 *poor*, 679.16 *army unit*, 877.12 *indecent*
rank air fume 388.3 *miasma*
rank and file 124.7 *average person*, 164.11 *general public*, 679.17 *army person*, 795.6 *vulgar herd*, 803.2 *the common people*
ranked 107, 121, 52.75 *equal*, 105.8 *in a state of*, 150.12 *hierarchical*, 152.24 *categorized*, 163.12 *classed*
rank first 126.10 *lead*
rank high 849.15 *respect*, 849.21 *command respect*
Rankine cycle 63.13 *engine cycle*
Rankine scale 75.3 *scale*
ranking 52.56 *nonparametric methods*, 105.1 *state*, 105.8 *in a state of*, 121.3 *gradation*, 150.4 *position*, 152.5 *categorization*, 163.1 *classification*, 611.6 *notable*
rankle 353.18 *fester*, 628.2 *decay*, 828.9 *offend*
rankling 353.7 *pus*, 828.1 *resentment*
rank low 850.19 *disrespect*
rankly 419.6 *stinkingly*
rankness 202.10 *staleness*, 415.2 *unpalatability*, 618.10 *poverty*
Rannoch 94 Lakes

ransack 244.10 *lay waste,*
736.14 *plunder*
ransacker 734.6 *taker,* 736.9
plunderer
ransacking 736.5 *plundering*
ransom 125.1 *compensation,*
223.1 *exchange,* 629.3 *restore,*
629.9 *restoration,* 639.1 *deliver,*
639.2 *deliverance,* 735.1 *giving
back,* 735.4 *give back,* 738.3
buy back, 738.9 *repurchase,*
746.4 *grant,* 751.8 *levy,* 879.8
penalty
Ransom 48 Poets
Ransome 48 Writers
ransomed 223.7 *exchanged,*
738.13 *bought*
ransomer 738.12 *purchaser*
rant 51.33 *overact,* 506.6, 521.9
talk nonsense, 541.10 *boast,*
553.5 *be diffuse,* 557.2 *affectation,* 557.5 *ornament,* 564.9 *art
of public speaking,* 564.14 *speak
to,* 567.1, 567.7 *address,* 713.7
complain, 818.8 *get angry,*
828.11 *be angry*
rant and rave 521.9 *talk nonsense,* 553.5 *be diffuse,* 828.11
be angry
ranter 564.10 *speaker,* 565.4
talker, 567.6 *public speaker,*
713.4 *protester*
ranting 510.12 *manic,* 521.10
meaningless, 541.4 *bombast,*
557.4 *ornate,* 564.9 *art of public
speaking,* 564.20 *eloquent*
ranunculaceous 83.16 *taxonomic*
ranunculus 84 Flowers and
Flowering Plants
Raoult's law 57 Named Reactions
rap 49.9 *popular music,* 330.3
hit, 330.6 *tap,* 330.13 *blow,*
425.2, 425.6 *crack,* 564.1 *faculty of speech,* 565.3 *talk,*
741.15 *false money,* 852.5 *criticism,* 852.17 *criticize,* 879.12
corporal punishment
rapacious 734.12 *taking,* 872.6
gluttonous
rapaciously 734.13 *avariciously*
rapacity 734.1 *taking,* 872.1 *gluttony*
rap across the knuckles 879.1
punish, 879.7 *punishment*
rape 84 Flowers and Flowering
Plants, 16.39 *crime,* 68.12 *crop,*
241.2 *physical violence,* 241.8
use violence, 244.5 *havoc,*
244.10 *lay waste,* 618.14 *ill-
treat,* 628.4 *impair,* 670.9 *attack successfully,* 670.14 *siege,*
670.16 *terrorist attack,* 676.13
be at war, 734.1 *taking,* 734.7
take, 736.5 *plundering,* 736.14
plunder, 832.7 *act of malevolence,* 832.18 *torment,* 864.7
criminality, 877.7 *sexual assault,* 877.20 *seduce*
rape alarm 671.5 *self-defence*
raped 734.12 *taking*
rapeseed 83.9 *seed*
Raphael 8.6 *angel*
rapid 191.5 *immediate,* 324.17
directional, 329.1 *swift,* 412.5
tasteless, 648.3 *hasty*
rapid fire 670.15 *firing*
rapid-fire 329.1 *swift*
rapid-fire pistol shooting 18
Sporting Activities
rapidity 324.8 *rapid motion,*
329.8 *speed,* 648.4 *haste*
rapidly 191.8 *immediately,*
324.18 *in motion,* 329.14
swiftly, 648.6 *hastily*
rapid motion 324
rapids 96.2 *channel,* 96.6 *river
flow,* 360.3 *downflow,* 635.1
trap
rapid slalom pole 41.3 *ski racing*
rapid tempo 329.8 *speed*
rapid-transit system 72.1 *railway*
rapier 380.8 *sharp-pointed thing,*
680.8 *sharp weapon*
rapine 244.5 *havoc*
raping 736.5 *plundering*

rapist 16.40 *lawbreaker,* 241.4 *violent person or animal,* 670.19
attacker, 693.9 *criminal,* 734.6
taker, 736.9 *plunderer,* 832.8
malefactor, 862.6 *evil person,*
864.9 *wicked person,* 877.10 *sex
offender*
rap on the knuckles 828.5 *quarrel*
rap over the knuckles 852.7
blame, 852.20 *censure,* 879.3
hit, 879.12 *corporal punishment*
rapparee 679.9 *guerrilla*
rappel 34.3 *climbing technique,*
34.9 *mountaineer,* 360.9 *descend*
rapper 46.4 *historic dancing*
rapping 330.12 *collision*
rap poet 48.14 *author*
rap poetry 48.6 *poetry*
rapport 107.1 *relatedness,* 116.1
accord, 667.1 *agreement,* 819.2
friendly relations
rapportage 532.3 *journalism*
rapprochement 677.1 *pacification*
rapscallion 864.9 *wicked person*
rapt 467.8 *diligent,* 786.6 *wondering*
raptness 786.1 *wonder*
raptor 78.5 *bird of prey*
raptorial 78.23 *avian*
rapture 512.1 *oblivion,* 759.4
emotion, 762.1 *happiness*
rapturous 512.8 *oblivious,*
759.13 *passionate,* 821.19 *enamoured*
rapturously 759.20 *with feeling*
rara avis 213.4 *rare things*
rare 45.56 *culinary,* 126.15 *excellent,* 168.14 *eccentric,* 182.6
sparse, 213.2 *infrequent,* 274.5
thinned, 370.2 *insubstantial,*
372.1 *sparse,* 390.12 *airy,*
489.3 *unexpected,* 595.6 *uncooked,* 609.4 *scarce,* 617.1 *worthy,* 617.3, 753.8 *valuable,*
786.8 *wonderful*
rare as hen's teeth 213.2 *infrequent*
rare bird 213.4 *rare things*
rare chance 589.6 *poor chance*
rare-earth element 57.6 *chemical
element*
raree show 51.5 *show*
rarefaction 372, 274.12 *thinning*
rarefactional 372.2 *rarefied*
rarefied 372, 274.5 *thinned*
rarefy 182.8 *reduce,* 274.16
make thin, 372.6 *make sparse*
rare gas 57.6 *chemical element,*
388.1 *gas*
rarely 489, 126.16 *superiorly,*
182.11 *sparsely,* 186.10 *seldom,*
213.1 *infrequently,* 609.10 *insufficiently,* 753.13 *valuably*
rareness 168.4 *unusualness,*
182.4 *rarity,* 213.3 *infrequency,*
372.3 *sparseness,* 753.6 *value*
rare occurrence 213.3 *infrequency*
rare things 213
rarified 390.12 *airy*
raring to go 572.2 *eager,* 594.18
prepared
rarity 182, 168.4 *unusualness,*
213.3 *infrequency,* 370.5 *lightness,* 372.3 *sparseness,* 390.1
air, 489.5 *unexpectedness,*
617.6 *worth,* 753.6 *value*
Ras Algethi 53 Named Stars
rascal 693.5 *troublemaker,* 801.2
disreputable character, 858.4 *dishonourable person,* 864.9 *wicked
person*
rascally 657.4 *cunning,* 864.11
wicked
rase 362.2 *flatten*
rash 780, 329.2 *mentally quick,*
468.10 *careless,* 494.5 *overestimating,* 508.5 *foolish,* 583.2
spontaneous, 595.3 *without preparation,* 597.7 *overambitious,*
624.3 *symptom,* 624.13 *skin disease,* 648.3 *hasty,* 689.6 *anarchic,* 778.13 *adventurous,* 783.8
careless
rasher 45.30 *bacon,* 143.7 *piece,*
266.4 *slice*
Rashig process 57 Named Reactions

rashly 648, 780, 468.14 *inattentively,* 494.7 *overoptimistically,*
508.8 *foolishly,* 595.14 *unreadily,* 597.9 *enterprisingly,* 633.11
dangerously, 689.8 *anarchically,*
778.18 *courageously,* 783.18
carelessly
rash move 780
rashness 780, 237.3 *intensity,*
329.8 *speed,* 468.1 *inattention,*
468.2 *impetuosity,* 494.1 *overestimation,* 508.1 *folly,* 595.8 *lack
of preparation,* 633.5 *danger,*
648.5 *hastiness,* 668.1 *defiance,*
778.4 *adventurousness,* 783.2
carelessness
Rashness 780
Rashnu 8.6 *angel*
rash person 508, 780
rashy 624.23 *diseased*
rasorial 78.23 *avian*
rasp 384.26 *grate,* 385.7 *eraser,*
385.15 *grind,* 429.4 *hiss,* 430.4
be strident, 430.5 *sound hoarse,*
432.6 *buzz,* 434.10 *lack harmony*
raspa 49 Musical Instruments
raspberry 86 Fruits, 86.5 *figurative usage,* 429.2 *catcall,* 431.7
cry of disapproval, 450.7 *red
thing,* 543.3 *gesture,* 751.3 *gesture of protest,* 850.6 *taunt,*
852.9 *show of disapproval*
raspberry beetle 69.12 *pests and
diseases*
raspberry midge 69.12 *pests and
diseases*
rasping 385.3 *grinding,* 385.11
rough, 424.4 *faint,* 430.8
hoarse, 434.7 *dissonant*
raspingly 385.17 *abrasively,*
430.10 *stridently,* 434.12 *dissonantly*
raspings 384.6 *crumb*
rasping sound 430.2 *hoarseness*
Rasputin 228.7 *motivator*
Rasta 7.6 *non-Christian*
Rastafarian 7.6 *non-Christian*
Rastafarianism 7 Non-Christian
Religions
Ras Tafari Makonnen 8 Deities
raster 65.17 *computing term*
rat 77 Placental Mammals,
480.3 *testify,* 480.7 *verifier,*
483.7 *person who gives evidence,*
483.13 *turn Queen's evidence,*
528.10 *informer,* 528.13 *inform
on* , 530.7 *betray,* 539.21 *traitor,* 578.3 *apostatize,* 578.9
equivocator, 598.2 *withdraw,*
598.4 *deserter,* 636.4 *warner,*
779.2 *coward,* 864.10 *bad person*
rataplan 365.2 *vibration*
rat-arsed 874.1 *drunk*
rat-a-tat 365.2 *vibration,* 426.4
knocking
ratatouille 45.45 *French dish*
rat-catcher 77.24 *hunter,* 398.13
animal killer, 590.6 *hunter*
ratchet 380.8 *sharp-pointed thing*
ratchet wheel 364.6 *rotator*
rate 52.18 *division,* 107.9 *have a
relative position,* 120.8 *quantify,*
121.3 *degree,* 121.5 *measure,*
152.15 *categorize,* 163.14 *sort,*
268.10 *measure,* 492.12 *estimate,* 748.5 *expense,* 751.3 *fee,*
751.11 *price,* 845.15 *merit*
rateable 751.15 *chargeable*
rateable value 751.7 *tax*
rate a movie 709.4 *censor*
rate-capped 699.2 *restraining*
rate-capping 699.2 *economic restraint*
rate constant 57.14 *chemical reaction*
rated 107.6 *ranked,* 121.7 *gradational,* 152.24 *categorized,*
163.12 *classed,* 268.13 *measured,* 751.14 *priced*
rate-determining step 57.14
chemical reaction
rate for the job 751.3 *fee*
ratel 77 Placental Mammals
rate of change 52.31 *differentiation*

rate of interest 745.4 *interest*
rate of speed 329.8 *speed*
rate of striking 36.4 *rowing*
ratepayer 751.10 *taxpayer*
rates 749.2 *money received,*
751.7 *tax*
rat-faced 874.1 *drunk*
ratfish 80 Fishes
rat flea 82.3 *pest*
ratha 71 Carriages and Carts
rather 121.11 *to a degree,* 242.9
moderately, 580.17 *selectively*
Rati 8 Deities
ratification 16.31 *legislation,*
116.7 *consent,* 475.4 *proof,*
480.4 *verification,* 499.2 *yes,*
535.4 *confirmation,* 667.2 *contract,* 708.1 *permission,* 715.1
contract
ratificatory 116.17 *consenting,*
480.9 *verificatory*
ratified 16.46 *legislated,* 116.17
consenting, 475.13 *proven,*
480.10 *verified,* 499.7 *agreed,*
535.13 *supported,* 667.11,
715.7 *contractual*
ratifier 535.9 *affirmer,* 667.5 *assenter,* 715.4 *contractor*
ratify 16.68 *legislate,* 101.12 *establish reality,* 116.28 *consent,*
225.7 *make stable,* 475.17
prove, 480.1 *verify,* 499.4 *assent,* 535.19 *confirm,* 544.11
identify oneself, 667.7 *contract,*
708.3 *permit,* 715.5 *contract,*
851.12 *accept*
ratifying 116.17 *consenting*
rat-infested 626.5 *unhygienic,*
628.13 *dilapidated*
rating 107.3 *relative position,*
121.3 *gradation,* 152.5 *categorization,* 163.5 *social class,* 268.1
measurement, 492.1 *judgment,*
611.1 *importance,* 679.27 *naval
man,* 751.7 *tax*
ratings 532.2 *mass media*
ratio 169, 52.18 *division,* 107.2
interrelatedness, 121.3 *gradation,* 731.2 *portion*
ratiocinate 4.20 *philosophize,*
459.12, 461.12 *think,* 463.11
reason, 473.14 *discuss,* 509.6 *be
sane*
ratiocination 4.4 *philosophical investigation,* 459.1 *mind,* 459.2
ways of thinking, 461.1 *thought,*
463.2 *reasoning,* 473.2 *logical
argument*
ratiocinative 4.15, 463.8 *rational*
ration 68.9 *animal feedstuff,*
120.2 *certain amount,* 120.8
quantify, 121.3 *gradation,*
173.2 *fractional part,* 302.7
limit, 606.1 *provision,* 609.7
make insufficient, 699.2 *economic restraint,* 699.9 *economize,* 731.2 *portion,* 731.4 *allot*
rational 4, 463, 509, 52.6 *complex number,* 52.72 *complex,*
52.74 *divisible,* 152.22 *organizational,* 169.8 *odd,* 242.6 *moderate,* 459.9 *mental,* 461.11,
463.7 *reasoning,* 473.12 *apologetic,* 507.5 *wise,* 592.14
planned
rationale 226.5 *reason,* 228.1 *motive,* 459.2 *ways of thinking,*
473.3 *line of argument,* 586.11
motive
rational-emotive therapy 61.3 *psychiatric treatment*
rationalism 4.7 *school of thought,*
7.13 *theology,* 463.2 *reasoning*
rationalist 4.11 *follower of a doctrine,* 4.14 *of a philosophy,*
463.5 *reasoner,* 498.5 *disbeliever,* 698.8 *free-thinker,*
698.10 *independent*
rationalistic 463.8 *rational,*
698.10 *independent*
rationalistically 698.20 *freely*
rationality 509, 4.3 *detachment,*
459.1 *mind,* 463.1 *reason,*
463.2 *reasoning*
rationalization 4.1 *philosophy,*
13.6 *economic factors,* 61.19 *defence mechanism,* 129.1 *de-*

crease, 152.3 *organization,* 220.1 *conversion,* 463.2 *reasoning,* 473.5 *plea,* 592.7 *planning,* 627.5 *improvement*

rationalize 4, 129.5 *make smaller,* 150.19 *systematize,* 152.13 *organize,* 182.8 *reduce,* 214.10 *make regular,* 220.9 *transform,* 459.12 *think,* 463.11 *reason,* 473.16 *plead,* 592.9 *plan,* 627.1 *improve,* 627.3 *rectify*

rationalized 152.21 *organized*
rationalized units 75.2 *unit system*
rationalizing 463.2 *reasoning*
rationally 4, 152.28 *in place,* 459.15 *intelligently,* 461.18 *thoughtfully,* 463.15 *reasonably,* 473.20 *apologetically,* 507.9 *wisely,* 509.7 *sanely*
rational number 52.6 *complex number,* 1069.2 *kind of number*
rational person 461.7 *thinker*
rational psychology 61.1 *psychology*
rationed 120.6 *quantitative,* 609.2 *unprovided,* 699.13 *restraining*
rationing 302.2 *limiting factor,* 676.7 *war measures,* 699.2 *economic restraint*
ration oneself 810.14 *be modest,* 869.5 *be self-restrained*
rations 350.7 *food,* 606.1 *provision*
ratio scale 52.56 *nonparametric methods*
ratite 78.2 *flightless bird,* 78.23 *avian*
rat kangaroo 77 Marsupials
ratlike 77.30 *rodent-like*
ratlin 359.9 *ladder*
ratline 36.3 *parts of a sailing boat,* 137.7 *tackle*
rat opossum 77 Marsupials
rat poison 68.14 *pest control,* 631.8 *poison*
rat race 364.3 *reel,* 642.3 *nimbleness,* 674.1 *contention*
rat run 71.2 *road*
ratsbane 398.13 *animal killer,* 631.8 *poison*
rat snake 79 Reptiles
rat's nest 151.4 *litter*
rattan 87 Grasses, 879.14 *instrument of punishment*
rat-tat-tat 425.2 *crack,* 426.4 *knocking*
ratted 874.1 *drunk*
ratter 77.10 *cat,* 578.9 *equivocator*
Rattigan 48 Dramatists
ratting 77.23 *mammal hunting,* 578.7 *apostasy,* 590.2 *chase*
rattish 77.30 *rodent-like*
rattle 49 Musical Instruments, **426, 426,** 153.7 *disturb,* 238.7 *weaken,* 365.9 *vibrate,* 423.1 *loudness,* 423.4 *sound maker,* 423.8 *be loud,* 425.6 *crack,* 587.2 *deter,* 612.9 *bauble,* 670.2 *fire*
rattle along 329.4 *be swift*
rattled 153.12 *disturbed,* 576.3 *timid,* 779.3 *cowardly*
rattle on 565.7 *be talkative*
rattler 79.3 *snake*
rattlesnake 79 Reptiles, 79.3 *snake*
rattle the windows 423.8 *be loud*
rattletrap 71.16 *car*
rattling 426, 329.1 *swift,* 423.6 *loud,* 425.9 *crackling*
rattling pace 329.8 *speed*
rattling thunder 423.1 *loudness*
rat trap 68.14 *pest control,* 71.11 *bicycle part,* 539.13 *snare,* 628.9 *dilapidation,* 743.7 *beggary*
ratty 77.30 *rodent-like,* 828.16 *angry*
Ratushinskaya 48 Poets
raucous 430.7 *strident,* 434.7 *dissonant*
raucously 434.12 *dissonantly*

raucousness 430.1 *stridency ,* 563.2 *inarticulation*
rauschpfeife 49 Musical Instruments
rauwolfia 85 Tree Products
ravage 244.10, 607.2 *lay waste,* 628.4 *impair,* 670.9 *attack successfully,* 676.13 *be at war,* 736.14 *plunder*
ravager 244.6 *destroyer,* 736.9 *plunderer*
ravages of time 185.2 *passage of time,* 628.9 *dilapidation*
ravaging 736.5 *plundering,* 736.17 *stolen*
Ravana 8.7 *devil*
rave 46.1 *dancing,* 161.10 *dance,* 506.6 *talk nonsense,* 510.14 *become insane,* 521.9 *talk nonsense,* 541.10 *boast,* 557.5 *ornament,* 665.17 *socialize,* 773.1 *rejoicing,* 773.5 *rejoice,* 815.5 *party,* 828.11 *be angry*
rave about 532.16 *publicize,* 851.15 *compliment*
Ravel 49 Musicians and Composers
ravelin 671.11 *fortification*
raven 78 Birds, 78.6 *songbird,* 350.22 *eat well,* 440.4 *dark thing,* 447.1 *black,* 447.9 *black thing,* 517.7 *bad-luck sign,* 782.14 *be hungry*
raven-haired 447.4 *black-haired*
ravening 241.6 *violent,* 609.3 *underfed*
Ravenna 93 Cities
ravenous 350.26 *eating,* 609.3 *underfed,* 782.10 *hungry,* 871.6 *fasting,* 872.6 *gluttonous*
ravenously 350.28 *carnivorously,* 782.19 *hungrily,* 871.7 *abstemiously,* 872.7 *gluttonously*
ravenousness 872.1 *gluttony*
ravens 161 Collective Names by Animal
Ravensburger waltz 41.7 *ice-dancing*
rave on 569.4 *monopolize the conversation*
raver 762.3 *joyful person,* 773.4 *rejoicer,* 815.6 *social person*
rave review 524.3 *criticism,* 851.4 *compliment*
rave reviews 682.3 *successful thing*
Ravi 96 Rivers
ravine 54.7 *landform,* 98.8 *valley,* 265.3 *gulf,* 272.6 *narrow place,* 277.4 *deep thing,* 317.2 *concave land*
raving 510.12 *manic,* 521.1 *lack of meaning,* 521.10 *meaningless,* 541.4 *bombast,* 541.15 *bombastic,* 569.5 *soliloquizing,* 759.13 *passionate*
raving beauty 789.3 *attractive female*
raving mad 510.11 *insane*
ravings 510.4 *delusion,* 569.1 *soliloquy*
ravioli 45 Types of Pasta
ravish 241.8 *use violence,* 734.7 *take,* 736.14 *plunder,* 877.20 *seduce*
ravisher 736.9 *plunderer*
ravishment 734.1 *taking,* 736.5 *plundering,* 877.7 *sexual assault*
ravvivando 49 Musical Terms
raw 453, 45.56 *culinary,* 55.47 *windy,* 55.55 *cool,* 145.4 *incomplete,* 156.32 *embryonic,* 201.12, 206.12 *immature,* 296.9 *undressed,* 307.5 *shapeless,* 375.5 *unfinished,* 406.5 *painful,* 406.7 *feeling pain,* 409.8 *cold,* 410.10 *powered,* 444.12 *gaudy,* 585.1 *unaccustomed,* 595.5 *immature,* 595.6 *uncooked,* 620.2 *incomplete,* 656.2 *unskilful,* 760.3 *sore,* 827.8 *cursing*
raw deal 687.1 *adversity,* 844.7 *sense of wrong*
rawboned 274.1 *thin*

raw feelings 760.6 *oversensitivity*
raw glaze 44.3 *glaze*
rawhide 293.14 *animal covering,* 604.1 *materials*
rawly 201.24, 206.15 *immaturely*
raw material 44, 226.3 *rudiment,* 367.4 *matter,* 595.11 *natural state,* 602.2 *supplies*
raw materials 604.1 *materials*
raw nerve 403.4 *someone or something that feels,* 828.3 *cause of offence*
rawness 145.1 *incompleteness,* 201.3, 206.3 *immaturity,* 307.1 *shapelessness,* 595.10 *immaturity,* 620.5 *imperfection,* 656.8 *unskilfulness,* 760.7 *soreness*
raw recruit 156.14 *beginner,* 201.8 *new arrival,* 656.10 *unskilled person*
raw sienna 449.4 *brown pigment,* 451.2 *orangeness*
raw umber 449.4 *brown pigment*
ray 80 Fishes, 52.37 *line,* 343.3 *radiation,* 343.13 *radiate,* 365.5 *wave,* 439.1 *light*
Ray 52 Scientists
rayed 343.7 *radiating*
ray-finned fish 80.2 *fish*
ray floret 84.4 *flower head*
Rayleigh 52 Scientists
Rayleigh scattering 56 Named Laws
ray of hope 775.1 *hope*
ray of light 56.24 *light emission*
ray of sunshine 767.3 *reliever,* 769.4 *cheerful person*
rayon 67 Synthetic Fibres and Fabrics, 67.12 *natural,* 604.1 *materials*
rayonism 50 Western Art Styles and Movements
rayonist 50.29 *realist*
rays of the sun 439.1 *light,* 439.4 *natural light*
razamatazz 811.4 *flashiness*
raze 244.9 *demolish,* 282.7 *make horizontal,* 362.2 *flatten,* 385.13 *abrade,* 546.1 *obliterate,* 607.2 *lay waste*
razed to the ground 282.10 *lying,* 546.6 *obliterated*
razee 74 Sailing Ships and Boats
raze to the ground 244.9 *demolish,* 282.7 *make horizontal,* 362.2 *flatten*
razing 244.2 *destroying*
razor 296.7 *depilation,* 380.9 *sharp-edged thing,* 380.16 *use a sharp tool*
razorbill 78 Birds
razor blade 380.9 *sharp-edged thing*
razor edge 380.7 *sharp point*
razor-edged 380.3 *sharp-edged*
razor's edge 272.8 *narrow thing,* 300.3 *cutting edge,* 633.5 *danger*
razor-sharp 380.3 *sharp-edged,* 380.5 *mentally sharp*
razor shell 81 Molluscs
razor wire 671.9 *barrier*
RBI leader 22.2 *baseball player*
RC 7.16 *denominational*
RE 6.3 *subject*
reabsorb 348.13 *absorb*
reach 71 Motor Vehicle Parts, **263, 344,** 12.3 *governance,* 36.15 *sail,* 36.19 *punt,* 121.1 *degree,* 235.2 *ability,* 248.3 *geographical space,* 248.7 *range,* 248.20 *extend,* 259.1 *size,* 269.4 *length,* 407.12 *abut,* 420.16 *be heard,* 608.4 *suffice,* 721.10 *augment,* 835.11 *excite pity*
reach a better world 397.15 *die*
reachable 407.8 *touchable,* 420.14 *hearable,* 486.5 *possible*
reach a climax 684.5 *conclude*
reach a compromise 717.4 *compromise*
reach a consensus 112.11 *agree*
reach a crescendo 721.10 *augment*
reach a crisis 106.13 *get into difficulties*

reach a gentleman's agreement 667.7 *contract*
reach a lower level 360.9 *descend*
reach a mass audience 522.5 *simplify*
reach a milestone 106.12 *come to a juncture*
reach an accord 112.11, 135.9 *agree,* 667.6 *agree with*
reach an agreement 135.9 *agree*
reach an all-time low 172.10 *hit rock bottom*
reach a new high 126.8 *be superior*
reach an impasse 661.9 *block*
reach an international agreement 667.7 *contract*
reach a stage 106.12 *come to a juncture,* 220.8 *be transformed*
reach a stalemate 661.9 *block*
reach a unanimous decision 667.6 *agree with*
reach boiling point 828.12 *become angry*
reach full growth 144.5 *be complete*
reach home 634.4 *shelter*
reaching 25.9 *bowls,* 36.1 *sailing,* 36.8, 36.14 *punting,* 121.7 *gradational,* 344.17 *achievement*
reaching a mass audience 522.2 *simple*
reaching shot 25.2 *grip*
reach its peak 684.4 *complete*
reach manhood 207.18 *mature*
reach maturity 144.5 *be complete*
reach-me-down 295.1 *dress*
reach new heights 126.8 *be superior*
reach one's destination 327.14 *find one's way,* 344.2 *reach*
reach one's goal 142.10 *complete,* 718.13 *secure one's objective*
reach one's majority 207.18 *mature*
reach one's nadir 127.11 *become inferior,* 360.10 *droop*
reach one's threshold 302.7 *limit*
reach out 263.7 *reach,* 269.9 *be long,* 336.7 *make one's way*
reach perfection 144.5 *be complete*
reach safety 632.8 *be safe,* 634.4 *shelter*
reach the boiling point 684.4 *complete*
reach the bottom 277.14 *deepen*
reach the depths 360.10 *droop*
reach the limit 684.4 *complete*
reach the mountaintop 34.9 *mountaineer*
reach the other side 356.11 *cross*
reach the prime of one's life 207.18 *mature*
reach there 344.2 *reach*
reach the top 344.9 *achieve,* 359.13 *ascend,* 696.14 *master*
reach the turning point 106.12 *come to a juncture*
reach the zenith 359.13 *ascend,* 684.4 *complete*
reach to 263.7 *reach*
reach to the far ends of the earth 610.4 *be excessive*
reach to the four corners of the earth 610.4 *be excessive*
reach towards 336.7 *make one's way*
react 57, 478, 109.7 *reciprocate,* 221.6 *reverse,* 227.5 *show an effect,* 231.3 *counteract,* 331.2 *respond,* 403.11 *sense,* 642.14 *push,* 672.3 *retaliate*
react against 785, 231.3 *counteract*
reactance 56.53, 64.12 *resistance*
reactant 57.14 *chemical reaction*
react automatically 464.10 *be instinctive*
reacted 221.11 *reversed*
reacting 109.4 *reciprocal,* 227.10 *caused,* 331.9 *reactive*
reacting to 227.10 *caused*
reaction 478, 109.1 *interchange,* 221.1 *reversion,* 227.1 *effect,* 231.1 *counteraction,* 331.6 *re-*

sponse, 403.1 *sensation,* 471.1
idea, 629.9 *restoration,* 663.5
contrariness, 759.1 *feeling*
reactionarily 217.10 *conserva-*
tively
reactionary 693, 12.6 *political*
party, 217.3 *conservative person,*
217.8 *conservative,* 221.10 *re-*
gressive, 231.4 *counteracting,*
331.7 *responder,* 331.9 *reactive,*
337.24 *retroactive,* 577.4 *set,*
577.8 *obstinate person,* 663.9
opposer, 663.22 *uncooperative,*
669.5, 669.5 *resister,* 669.12 *re-*
sisting
reaction formation 61.19 *defence*
mechanism
reactionist 331.7 *responder,*
663.22 *uncooperative*
reaction order 57.14 *chemical re-*
action
reaction propulsion 338.2
method of propulsion
reactions 592.2 *policy*
reaction turbine 63.12 *turbine*
reaction wood 85.3 *timber*
reactivate 629.1 *repair*
reactivation 629.8 *repair,* 629.10
revival
reactive 57, 331, 478, 221.10
regressive, 231.4 *counteracting*
reactive depression 61.13 *depres-*
sion
reactively 221.13 *reversibly,*
231.5 *counter,* 331.10 *on the re-*
bound, 478.24 *in answer*
reactive neurosis 61.10 *neurosis*
reactive power 64.26 *electrical en-*
ergy
reactology 61.1 *psychology*
reactor 56.73 *nuclear reactor*
reactor core 56.73 *nuclear reactor*
react sharply 642.14 *push*
read 4.21 *rationalize,* 5.46 *trans-*
late, 6.23 *learn,* 19.8 *huddle,*
65.19 *abort,* 293.35 *progress,*
435.14 *inspect,* 524.8 *interpret,*
524.9 *decipher,* 534.34 *commu-*
nicated, 535.11 *stated,* 652.14
behave towards, 730.1 *received*
Read 48 Texts
readability 522.10 *simplicity,*
558.1 *elegance*
readable 522.2 *simple,* 558.3 *ele-*
gant
readably 558.5 *elegantly*
read a liturgy 719.5 *observe reli-*
gious ceremony
read between the lines 524.8 *in-*
terpret
readdress 326.13 *post,* 567.10
send
read easily 522.4 *be intelligible*
reader 6.4 *educator,* 6.14 *school*
book, 65.7 *peripheral,* 293.22
progression, 567.6 *public*
speaker, 696.9 *educational*
leader, 730.5 *register*
readership 6.6 *instructorship,*
532.2 *mass media*
read hieroglyphics 524.9 *decipher*
readied 594.18 *prepared*
readies 602.4 *financial resources,*
741.2 *cash*
readily 208.17 *early,* 230.13 *oper-*
ationally, 234.6 *probably,*
485.17 *capably,* 572.16 *will-*
ingly, 594.22 *in preparation,*
660.21 *easily,* 694.10 *obedi-*
ently, 784.11 *admiringly*
read in 7.21 *ordain*
readiness 6.10 *educatability,*
207.3 *maturity,* 208.1 *earliness,*
210.1 *timeliness,* 234.2 *attitude,*
253.4 *availability,* 469.3 *circum-*
spection, 485.1 *qualification,*
516.4 *prudence,* 572.6 *willing-*
ness, 594.14 *preparedness,*
613.5 *usefulness,* 619.3 *perfec-*
tion, 642.3 *nimbleness,* 660.1
easiness, 684.1 *completion,*
694.1 *obedience,* 784.2 *inclina-*
tion
readiness to take offence 829.1
irascibility
reading 42 Hobbies and Pastimes, 6.8 *learning,* 56.82 *mea-*

suring instrument, 268.1 *mea-*
surement, 524.1 *interpretation,*
564.8 *speech,* 567.1 *address*
Reading 93 Cities, **93** Cities
reading cards 517.2 *divination*
reading desk 47.4 *table*
reading glass 435.10 *visual aid*
reading glasses 435.10 *visual aid*
reading in 7.9 *priesthood*
reading lamp 439.6 *electric light*
reading list 171.2 *table*
reading of the verdict 16.7 *legal*
trial
read into 524.8 *interpret,* 525.1
misinterpret
readjust 122.11 *equalize,* 125.5
counterbalance, 717.4 *compro-*
mise
readjusted 125.10 *counterbalanc-*
ing
readjustment 122.3 *equalization,*
125.2 *counterbalance,* 629.9 *res-*
toration
read lips 524.12 *translate*
read minds 11.24 *experience psy-*
chic phenomena
readmission 348.1 *admittance*
readmit 348.7 *admit*
read one's astrology chart 516.1
foresee
read one's hand 517.12 *divine*
read one's palm 516.1 *foresee,*
517.12 *divine*
read-only 65.20 *on-line*
readout 56.82 *measuring instru-*
ment
read-out 268.1 *measurement*
read palms 11.23 *divine*
read sign language 524.12 *trans-*
late
read signs 11.23 *divine*
read something into it 309.12 *dis-*
tort the truth
read tea leaves 11.23 *divine,*
199.9 *look ahead,* 516.1 *foresee*
read the banns 714.1 *promise*
read the cards 516.1 *foresee,*
517.12 *divine*
read the chart 74.9 *navigate*
read the defence 19.15 *play of-*
fence
read the entrails 517.12 *divine*
read the future 516.1 *foresee,*
517.12 *divine*
read the riot act 852.21 *berate*
read the runes 516.1 *foresee,*
517.12 *divine*
read the signs 517.12 *divine*
read the stars 517.12 *divine*
read the Tarot 11.23 *divine*
read the wedding service 823.16
join in marriage
read the wedding vows 823.16
join in marriage
readthrough 51.12 *production*
read through 51.35 *rehearse*
read up on 6.23 *learn*
ready 6.17 *educatable,* 196.8
available, 208.12 *early,* 234.5
tending to, 253.10 *available,*
469.9 *careful,* 485.9 *qualified,*
513.5 *expecting,* 572.1 *willing,*
594.4 *prepare for action,* 594.18
prepared, 606.8 *provisional,*
613.1 *useful,* 615.2 *nearby,*
619.1 *perfect,* 642.18 *active,*
655.6 *skilful,* 694.7 *obedient,*
784.6 *liking*
ready and willing 572.2 *eager*
ready cash 746.1 *payment*
ready for another round 651.4 *re-*
freshed
ready for anything 594.19 *in*
hand, 655.6 *skilful*
ready for bed 650.1 *fatigued*
ready for hearing 16.54 *litigated*
ready-formed 594.21 *ready-made*
ready for more 651.4 *refreshed*
ready for sleep 650.1 *fatigued*
ready for use 594.19 *in hand,*
613.1 *useful*
ready-furnished 594.21 *ready-*
made
ready-made 594, 50.12 *sculp-*
ture, 243.12 *produced,* 295.31
styled, 306.10 *prototypical*

ready-made verdict 582.6 *pre-*
meditation
ready-mixed 594.21 *ready-made*
ready money 741.2 *cash,* 741.6
funds
ready oneself 594.8 *prepare one-*
self
ready reckoner 170.5 *computer*
ready to 234.5 *tending to*
ready to break 379.1 *brittle*
ready to burst 379.1 *brittle,*
608.3 *filled,* 610.6 *excessive*
ready-to-cook 45.56 *culinary,*
594.21 *ready-made*
ready to crack 379.1 *brittle*
ready to die for 859.5 *unselfish*
ready to eat 191.7 *prepared for*
immediate use
ready to go 594.18 *prepared*
ready to hand 196.8 *available,*
594.19 *in hand*
ready to rest 650.1 *fatigued*
ready-to-serve 45.56 *culinary,*
594.21 *ready-made*
ready to split 379.1 *brittle*
ready to use 594.21 *ready-made*
ready to wear 191.7 *prepared for*
immediate use
ready-to-wear 112.6 *conforming,*
295.31 *styled,* 594.21 *ready-*
made
ready-to-wear clothes 295.1 *dress*
ready wit 771.3 *wit*
reaffirm 554.6 *emphasize*
reafforest 629.3 *restore*
reafforestation 629.9 *restoration*
reafforested 85.16 *wooded*
reagent 57.14 *chemical reaction*
reagent bottle 57 Laboratory
Apparatus
real 99, 101, 3.19 *chronicled,*
16.51 *legitimate,* 52.6 *complex*
number, 52.72 *complex,* 119.6
authentic, 169.8 *odd,* 253.7 *pres-*
ent, 367.7 *material,* 407.8 *touch-*
able, 490.1 *certain,* 537.16 *exist-*
ing, 537.19 *authentic,* 725.8
propertied
real ale 351.7 *alcoholic drink*
real analysis 52.30 *calculus*
real bargain 738.6 *purchase*
real bastard 659.3 *difficult task*
real bitch 659.3 *difficult task*
real bugger 659.3 *difficult task*
real estate 725.1 *property*
real-estate agent 725.7 *property*
man
realgar 54 Minerals
real George 617.1 *worthy*
realign 152.14 *rearrange*
realigned 152.23 *rearranged*
realignment 152.4 *rearrangement*
real image 56.31 *lens element*
realism 48 Literary Groups and
Movements, **50** Western Art
Styles and Movements, **101,**
4.7 *school of thought,* 51.8 *thea-*
tre movements, 503.2 *correct-*
ness, 537.12 *true to life,* 547.1
representation
realist 50, 101, 4.11 *follower of*
a doctrine, 4.14 *of a philosophy,*
51.40 *activist,* 367.3 *material-*
ist, 640.3 *doer*
realistic 101, 4.15 *rational,*
48.16 *literary,* 101.8 *practical,*
114.9 *lifelike,* 490.1 *certain,*
497.13 *believable,* 503.6 *correct,*
537.25 *lifelike,* 547.13 *represen-*
tational, 560.11 *descriptive,*
560.13 *representing*
realistically 4.26 *rationally,*
50.30 *pictorially,* 51.42 *dramati-*
cally, 114.14 *comparably,*
547.14 *representationally,*
560.18 *descriptively*
realistic comedy 51.10 *comedy*
realistic representation 537.12
true to life
realities 101
reality 101, 537, 3.14 *historical-*
ness, 99.4 *demonstrable exis-*
tence, 253.1 *presence,* 407.1
touch, 490.9 *certainty,* 611.3
chief thing
Reality 101

reality therapy 61.3 *psychiatric*
treatment
realizable 101, 486.5 *possible,*
522.1 *intelligible*
realization 144.3 *completion,*
367.2 *materialization,* 457.1 *ap-*
pearance, 496.8 *finding out,*
501.1 *knowledge,* 522.12 *under-*
standing, 547.1 *representation,*
684.1 *completion,* 721.1 *gain,*
759.1 *feeling*
realize 4.21 *rationalize,* 99.20
bring into being, 101.11 *make*
real, 144.4 *complete,* 367.8 *be*
material, 403.11 *sense,* 457.14
present, 471.14 *have an idea,*
496.3 *find out,* 501.11 *know,*
519.14 *imagine,* 522.6 *under-*
stand, 528.15 *be informed,*
547.9 *represent,* 619.5 *perfect,*
684.4 *complete,* 721.9 *gain,*
739.1 *sell,* 741.26 *bank,* 759.15
feel
realized 367.7 *material,* 457.7
appearing, 684.7 *completed*
realize one's capital 13.10 *trade*
with
realize one's potential 144.5 *be*
complete
realizing 759.10 *feeling*
real life 101.3 *realism*
real-life 101.7 *realistic,* 560.11
descriptive
real-life story 560.4 *factual ac-*
count
really 99, 101
really! 480
really 3.25 *reportedly,* 253.14 *in*
person, 480.12 *assuredly,*
490.23 *certainly,* 537.35 *truly,*
537.37 *authentically,* 772.11
earnestly, 772.12 *indeed,*
786.14 *wonderful*
really mean 520.10 *mean,* 588.8
resolve
really move 329.4 *be swift*
really-truly 101.14 *certainly,*
537.35 *truly*
realm 6.3 *subject,* 12.5 *political*
organization, 91.3 *dominion,*
163.4 *type,* 249.4 *territorial divi-*
sion, 249.11 *sphere,* 400.11 *na-*
tion, 688.8 *governmental organi-*
zation
realm of light 8.11 *heaven*
realm of Pluto 8.11 *heaven*
realness 3.14 *historicalness,*
537.6 *authenticity*
real number 52.6 *complex num-*
ber, 169.2 *kind of number*
real part 52.6 *complex number*
real person 367.5 *object*
realpolitik 652.9 *tactics,* 657.1
cunning
real presence 10.6 *Eucharist*
real property 725.1 *property*
real saint 7.3 *religious person*
real self 165.11 *identity*
real sod 659.3 *difficult task*
real sweat 674.2 *contest*
real tennis 40, 40.1 *tennis*
real time 65.17 *computing term,*
185.7 *time measurement*
realtor 725.7 *property man*
realty 725.1 *property*
real wages 13.6 *economic factors*
real war 676.1 *war*
real world 101, 367.1 *material*
world
ream 322.20 *hole,* 604.3 *paper*
reamed 322.14 *holed*
reamer 322.2 *opener,* 621.10
cleaning object
reanimate 396.21 *invigorate,*
629.5 *revive,* 651.1 *refresh*
reanimation 245.1 *reproduction,*
396.5 *life cycle,* 629.10 *revival,*
651.5 *refreshment*
reap 68.17 *farm,* 270.10
shorten, 605.6 *store,* 878.14 *gain*
reap a profit 721.14 *profit,*
878.14 *gain*
reaper 161.35 *collector*
reaping hook 183.21 *farm tool*
reappear 183.21 *be repeated,*
187.10 *be periodical,* 457.13
occur, 629.4 *be restored*

reappearance 457, 183.4 *return,* 629.10 *revival*

reappearing 183.14 *recurrent,* 245.15 *reproduced*

reappoint 629.3 *restore,* 735.4 *give back*

reappointment 735.1 *giving back*

reap the benefit of 613.11 *find useful*

reap the fruits 682.6 *be successful,* 845.15 *merit,* 878.14 *gain*

reap the harvest 682.6 *be successful*

reap the profit from 613.11 *find useful*

rear 155, 155, 304, 304, 6.22 *educate,* 68.18 *practise livestock farming,* 111.1 *oppositeness,* 128.5 *make bigger,* 157.25 *hindmost,* 243.10 *produce,* 245.13 *propagate,* 275.16 *rise,* 281.5 *be vertical,* 304.8 *nurture,* 359.16 *stand up,* 361.5 *arise,* 679.14 *armed forces*

Rear 304

Rear Admiral 17 British Military Ranks, **17** US Military Ranks

rear-admiral 679.27 *naval man*

rear cushion 25.4 *bowling*

rear-dump truck 63.29 *construction equipment*

reared 6.20 *refined,* 68.21 *domesticated,* 243.12 *produced,* 281.9 *unbowed*

rear end 304

rear entrance 304.1 *rear*

rearguard 636.4 *warner,* 671.14 *guard,* 679.14 *armed forces*

rearing 6.1 *education,* 281.2 *making vertical,* 281.9 *unbowed,* 359.23 *rising,* 361.6 *raising*

rearing up 304

rear its head 457.12 *become visible*

rear light 71 Motor Vehicle Parts, 439.6 *electric light*

rear mast 304.1 *rear*

rear one's head 526.4 *show oneself*

rear part 304.1 *rear*

rearrange 152, 57.26 *react,* 152.19 *tidy,* 216.8 *cause change*

rearranged 152, 216.12 *changed*

rearrangement 152, 57.14 *chemical reaction,* 216.1 *change*

rearrange the deckchairs on the Titanic 614.9 *waste effort*

rear sentry 636.4 *warner*

rear up 304, 275.16 *rise,* 281.5 *be vertical,* 359.16 *stand up*

rear-view mirror 71 Motor Vehicle Parts, 56.29 *optical element,* 435.8 *reflection*

rearward 155.30 *behind,* 304.4 *rear,* 304.9 *in the rear,* 337.28 *backward*

reason 226, 463, 463, 4.21 *rationalize,* 52.89 *theorize,* 157.14 *aim,* 228.1 *motive,* 459.3 *intelligence,* 459.12 *think,* 461.1 *thought,* 461.12 *think,* 471.4 *purpose,* 473.14 *discuss,* 478.6 *solution,* 478.20 *solve,* 492.12 *estimate,* 507.1 *wisdom,* 509.2 *rationality,* 518.5 *suppose,* 524.8 *interpret,* 586.11 *motive,* 642.4 *energy,* 855.2 *defence*

Reason 463

reasonability 488.3 *plausibility*

reasonable 4.15 *rational,* 242.6 *moderate,* 459.11 *thoughtful,* 463.7 *reasoning,* 471.12 *purposive,* 488.5 *possible,* 488.7 *plausible,* 497.13 *believable,* 509.5 *rational,* 691.4 *lenient,* 754.9 *cheap,* 855.13 *vindicable,* 869.9 *moderate*

reasonable charge 754.1 *cheapness*

reasonableness 4.3 *detachment,* 242.1 *moderation,* 509.2 *rationality,* 691.1 *leniency,* 754.1 *cheapness,* 869.2 *moderation*

reasonable person 509.3 *sane person*

reasonably 463, 4.26 *rationally,* 242.9 *moderately,* 459.15 *intelli-*

gently, 471.21 *purposively,* 473.20 *apologetically,* 478.26 *correspondingly,* 486.10 *practically,* 497.16 *believably,* 509.7 *sanely,* 691.6 *leniently,* 754.15 *cheaply,* 869.12 *moderately*

reason behind 226.5 *reason*

reasoned 4.15 *rational,* 471.12 *purposive,* 478.21 *solved*

reasoner 463, 679.5 *arguer*

reasoning 52, 461, 463, 463, 4.4 *philosophical investigation,* 16.7 *legal trial,* 459.2 *ways of thinking,* 459.9 *mental,* 461.1 *thought,* 461.8 *thoughtful,* 473.2 *logical argument,* 473.3 *line of argument,* 492.1 *judgment,* 507.5 *wise,* 586.11 *motive*

reasons 483.1 *evidence*

reason why 226.5 *reason*

reassemble 161, 629.1 *repair,* 629.3 *restore*

reassembling 629.8 *repair*

reassert 554.6 *emphasize*

reassurance 767.1 *ease,* 775.4 *comfort,* 778.6 *encouragement*

reassure 765.9 *comfort,* 767.9 *relieve,* 775.10 *inspire hope,* 778.17 *give courage*

reassured 767.7 *relieved*

reassuring 284.9, 662.32 *supportive,* 767.8 *relieving,* 775.14 *cheering,* 778.14 *encouraging*

reassuringly 767.15 *comfortingly*

Réaumur 52 Scientists

Réaumur scale 75.3 *scale,* 408.2 *heat measurement*

reawaken 629.4 *be restored,* 629.5 *revive*

reawakening 629.10 *revival*

rebab 49 Musical Instruments

rebarbative 764.1 *unpleasant,* 785.9 *disliked*

rebarbatively 785.11 *disgustingly*

rebate 131.2 *subtracted item,* 752.1, 752.3 *discount*

rebated 752.6 *discounted*

rebec 49 Musical Instruments

rebel 693, 104.5 *nonconformist,* 117.6 *misfit,* 117.14 *disagree,* 168.8 *dissenter,* 168.18 *not conform,* 241.7 *be violent,* 335.19 *deviant person,* 500.5 *dissenter,* 500.7 *dissenting,* 500.8 *dissent,* 663.9 *opposer,* 668.4 *defiant person,* 668.6 *be insubordinate,* 670.8 *counterattack,* 676.12 *go to war,* 689.3 *anarchist,* 689.4 *be anarchic,* 693.16 *be subversive,* 713.4 *protester,* 713.8 *cause mischief,* 720.5 *nonobserver,* 720.7 *not observe*

rebel angel 8.7 *devil*

rebellion 16.41 *lawlessness,* 117.4 *disagreement,* 168.2 *dissent,* 500.3 *dissentience,* 668.2 *disobedience,* 670.14 *siege,* 689.1 *anarchy,* 693.4 *revolution,* 713.2 *disorder,* 858.2 *faithlessness*

rebellious 16.61 *lawless,* 104.11 *separate,* 117.9 *nonconforming,* 151.20 *disorderly,* 168.12 *nonconformist,* 500.7 *dissenting,* 668.8 *defying,* 669.12 *resisting,* 670.24 *counterattacking,* 689.6 *anarchic,* 693.14 *subversive,* 713.10 *law-breaking,* 858.6 *faithless*

rebelliously 16.84 *lawlessly,* 117.16 *disagreeably,* 151.29 *riotously,* 168.21 *unconformably,* 500.10 *dissentiently,* 668.10 *in defiance,* 669.14 *resistingly,* 689.8 *anarchically,* 693.18 *subversively,* 713.11 *disapprovingly,* 858.11 *dishonourably*

rebelliousness 151.8 *lawlessness,* 668.2 *disobedience,* 693.4 *revolution*

rebel yell 543.6 *word,* 668.3 *act of defiance,* 676.2 *glory of war*

rebirth 183.4 *return,* 220.2 *evolution,* 245.1 *reproduction,* 629.10 *revival,* 704.3 *new beginning*

reboant 427.6 *resonant*

reborn 183.11 *reprinted,* 220.16 *influenced,* 245.15 *reproduced,* 396.12 *alive,* 629.13 *repaired,* 704.10 *cancelled*

rebound 23.4 *playing terms,* 23.6 *play basketball,* 30.6 *pommel horse,* 30.10 *compete in gymnastics,* 35.3 *rugby play,* 221.8 *return,* 331.1, 331.4 *recoil,* 377.1 *elasticity,* 377.8 *be elastic,* 427.9 *resonate*

rebounder 23.2 *basketball player*

rebounding 23.4 *playing terms,* 331.8 *recoiling,* 377.6 *elastic,* 427.1 *resonance,* 427.6 *resonant*

rebuff 331.2 *respond,* 331.6 *response,* 341.1 *repel,* 341.6 *repulse,* 478.4 *reaction,* 478.19 *react,* 573.12 *opposition,* 581.1 *reject,* 581.5 *rejection,* 669.1 *resistance,* 669.6 *resist,* 687.1 *adversity,* 709.1, 709.3 *veto,* 711.2, 711.6 *dissent,* 816.13 *ignore,* 818.3 *act of discourtesy,* 850.5, 850.23 *insult*

rebuffed 478.12 *reactive,* 711.9 *dissenting*

rebuffer 331.7 *responder*

rebuffing 669.10 *resistant,* 850.11 *insulting*

rebuild 201.20 *make new,* 629.3 *restore*

rebuildable 201.15 *renewable*

rebuilder 629.12 *repairer*

rebuilding 201.5 *fresh start,* 629.9 *restoration,* 791.1 *transfiguration*

rebuilt 201.14 *renewed,* 629.13 *repaired*

rebuke 806, 766.2 *expression of dissatisfaction,* 766.7 *be dissatisfied,* 827.6 *vilify,* 852.7 *blame,* 852.20 *censure,* 879.1 *punish,* 879.7 *punishment*

rebuked 806.3 *humbled,* 852.34 *censured*

rebuking 852.30 *censuring*

rebus 529.4 *brain-teaser,* 544.8 *heraldic device*

rebut 536, 476.10 *counter-charge,* 478.18 *answer back,* 484.7 *counter,* 663.15 *object,* 711.6 *dissent,* 855.8 *justify*

rebuttable 855.13 *vindicable*

rebuttal 536, 16.7 *legal trial,* 476.2 *denial,* 476.3 *counter-charge,* 478.5 *counterstatement,* 484.1 *counterevidence,* 663.2 *objection,* 711.2 *dissent,* 855.2 *defence*

rebutted 478.13 *retaliatory,* 536.12 *rejected*

rebutter 16.7 *legal trial,* 484.3 *counterclaimant,* 536.6 *negativist*

rebut the charge 855.8 *justify*

rebutting 536, 476.7 *refuting,* 484.5 *countering,* 855.11 *vindicatory*

recalcitrance 168.2 *dissent,* 231.1 *counteraction,* 573.12 *opposition,* 663.5 *contrariness,* 669.2 *obstinacy,* 693.1 *disobedience,* 711.1 *refusal,* 713.1 *protest*

recalcitrant 168.12 *nonconformist,* 231.4 *counteracting,* 331.7 *responder,* 331.9 *react,* 478.12 *reactive,* 577.2 *refractory,* 663.22 *uncooperative,* 668.8 *defying,* 669.11 *obstinate,* 693.7 *protester,* 693.13 *disobedient,* 711.8 *refused,* 713.9 *protesting,* 720.5 *nonobserver*

recalcitrantly 331.10 *on the rebound,* 478.24 *in answer*

recalcitrate 478.19 *react*

recalcitration 478.4 *reaction*

recall 3.22 *remember,* 61.23 *memory,* 183.19 *return to,* 511.1 *memory,* 511.12 *remember,* 578.4 *recant,* 578.8 *recantation,* 629.3 *restore,* 629.9 *restoration,* 704.1 *cancellation,* 704.2 *termination,* 704.6 *cancel,* 726.5 *retentiveness,* 726.8 *remember*

recalled 3.19 *chronicled,* 704.10 *cancelled*

recall from the grave 629.10 *revival*

recalling 3.13 *looking back,* 726.5 *retentiveness*

recall of ambassadors 666.1 *disagreement*

recall one's words 578.4 *recant*

recall to life 629.5 *revive*

recant 578, 7.19 *be religious,* 221.6 *reverse,* 221.9 *reply,* 476.9 *deny,* 484.8 *reverse,* 536.9 *renounce,* 581.4 *revoke,* 598.1 *relinquish,* 704.6 *cancel,* 727.9 *dispose of,* 734.9 *withdraw a statement,* 867.4 *be penitent*

recantation 578, 221.1 *reversion,* 476.2 *denial,* 484.2 *reversal,* 536.4 *renunciation,* 581.7 *abrogation,* 598.3 *relinquishment,* 704.1 *cancellation,* 867.1 *penitence*

recanted 221.11 *reversed,* 536.12 *rejected*

recanter 476.5 *refuter,* 536.6 *negativist,* 578.9 *equivocator,* 598.4 *deserter,* 704.5 *abrogator*

recanting 578.11 *equivocating,* 734.2 *taking back*

recant one's errors 867.4 *be penitent*

recap 183.2 *iteration,* 183.17 *iterate,* 562.1 *summary,* 562.8 *summarize*

recapitulate 183.17 *iterate,* 511.13 *remind,* 522.5 *simplify,* 560.15 *recount,* 562.8 *summarize*

recapitulation 59.16 *evolution,* 183.2 *iteration,* 492.2 *verdict,* 562.1 *summary*

recapitulative 183.12 *repetitious*

recapture 511.12 *remember,* 519.14 *imagine,* 734.2 *taking back,* 734.8 *take back*

recapturing 734.2 *taking back*

recast 592.10 *plan out,* 627.3 *rectify*

recce 435.3 *observation*

recede 221.6 *reverse,* 294.12 *shed,* 458.1 *disappear*

recede into the distance 337.2 *retreat*

receding 337, 294.10 *bald*

receding hair 294.6 *baldness*

receipt 749, 348.1 *admittance,* 478.2 *acknowledgment,* 483.6 *documentation,* 545.1 *record,* 654.3 *precept,* 718.2 *promise,* 725.1 *property,* 730.9 *receive,* 746.1 *payment,* 749.7 *receive*

Receipt 749

receipted 749.6 *received*

receipted payment 746.1 *payment*

receipt for payment 746.1 *payment*

receipt in full 746.1 *payment*

receipt of custom 730.3 *acknowledgment of payment*

receipts 26.2 *boxing,* 602.4 *financial resources,* 721.4 *earnings,* 730.2 *something received,* 734.5 *takings,* 744.3 *deposit,* 749.2 *money received*

receipts and expenditures 750.1 *accounts*

receivable 730, 348.14 *admissive*

receivables 745, 745.5 *amount owing,* 746.1 *payment*

receive 730, 749, 27.17 *bat,* 40.13 *serve,* 146.4 *include,* 348.7 *admit,* 534.30 *communicate,* 817.10 *be courteous*

receive a benefit 721.9 *gain*

receive a bequest 721.14 *profit,* 730.9 *receive*

receive a bonus 721.14 *profit*

receive absolution 10.18 *perform rites,* 840.7 *be punished*

receive a death sentence 397.16 *meet one's fate*

receive a final notice 712.7 *demand*

receive a free gift 721.14 *profit*

receive a fringe benefit 721.14 *profit*
receive a golden handshake 345.2 *withdraw*, 721.14 *profit*
receive a good omen 714.10 *show potential*
receive a legacy 721.14 *profit*
receive a letter from Uncle Sam 676.12 *go to war*
receive alimony 721.12 *earn*
receive an advance 721.12 *earn*
receive an honorary degree 878.12 *be rewarded*
receive an injunction 712.7 *demand*
receive a pawn ticket 714.8 *guarantee*
receive a pay increase 721.10 *augment*
receive a pension 721.12 *earn*
receive a raise 721.10 *augment*
receive a rise 721.10 *augment*
receive a stipend 721.12 *earn*
receive a summons 856.7 *be accused*
receive a sweetener 878.13 *get paid*
receive a tip 721.14 *profit*
receive a title 878.12 *be rewarded*
receive a voucher 714.8 *guarantee*
receive a windfall profit 721.14 *profit*
receive Christ 7.19 *be religious*
receive communion 7.19 *be religious*
received 730, 749, 1.14 *societal*, 497.14 *believed*, 534.34 *communicated*, 584.12 *established*, 750.11 *accounted*
received idea 167.5 *convention*
received into the church 730.13 *received*
received meaning 520.4 *type of meaning*
Received Pronunciation 5.6 *official language*
Received Standard 5.6 *official language*
receive forgiveness 840.7 *be punished*
receive guests 730.10 *receive someone*
receive help 662
receive immunity 638.5 *escape*
receive into the church 7.20 *preach*, 730.10 *receive someone*
receive maintenance 721.12 *earn*
receive no proposals 825.9 *be celibate*
receive notice 636.6 *be warned*
receive one's death warrant 397.16 *meet one's fate*
receive one's due 878.12 *be rewarded*
receive one's marriage lines 823.15 *marry*
receive palimony 721.12 *earn*
receive permission 708.5 *be permitted*
receiver 57 Laboratory Apparatus, 730, 19.7 *offence*, 40.6 *tennis player*, 40.12 *badminton terms*, 53.26 *radio telescope*, 534.9 *telephone*, 534.18 *radio*, 534.22 *television set*, 730.5 *recipient*, 730.7 *collector*, 734.6 *taker*
receiver of honours 730.5 *recipient*
receiver of stolen property 730.5 *recipient*, 736.11 *dishonest person*
receive royalties 721.12 *earn*
receivership 13.7 *corporation*, 730.1 *receiving*
receive satisfaction 125.6 *be compensated*
receive social security 730.9 *receive*
receive social security payments 721.12 *earn*
receive someone 730
receive the sacrament 10.18 *perform rites*
receive welfare payments 662.18 *receive help*

receive with grateful thanks 837.6 *be grateful*
receive with open arms 837.6 *be grateful*
receiving 730, 730, 348.1 *admittance*, 721.1 *gain*
Receiving 730
receiving antenna 534.17 *antenna*
receiving family friends 399.2 *funeral*
receiving pay 746
receiving team 19.12 *special team*
recency 201.1 *newness*
recension 627.6 *rectification*
recent 201.10 *new*
Recent 54 Geological Time Intervals
recently 200.22 *in the past*, 201.21 *newly*
recentness 201.1 *newness*
recent occurrence 201.1 *newness*
recent past 200.1 *past time*
receptacle 84.3 *flower part*, 258.1 *container*, 605.4 *storage*
receptible 348.14 *admissive*
reception 344, 730, 812, 146.1 *inclusion*, 161.9 *social gathering*, 346.1 *entry*, 348.1 *admittance*, 350.13 *feast*, 420.10 *sound quality*, 534.19 *radio reception*, 534.23 *television reception*, 665.7 *social gathering*, 730.1 *receiving*, 730.4 *reception*, 815.3 *meeting*, 817.3 *courtesies*
reception committee 812.4 *reception*
receptionist 545.9 *recorder*
reception room 256.7 *room*, 730.4 *reception*
receptive 348, 730, 6.17 *educatable*, 228.13 *suggestible*, 572.1 *willing*, 586.20 *persuadable*, 730.11 *receiving*, 760.1 *sensitive*, 819.8 *friendly*
receptively 348, 730, 6.26 *studiously*, 228.14 *influentially*, 819.17 *in friendship*
receptiveness 348.2 *receptivity*, 403.1 *sensation*, 572.6 *willingness*
receptivity 348, 6.10 *educatability*, 228.6 *suggestibility*, 403.1 *sensation*, 760.5 *sensitivity*
recess 218.9 *pause*, 258.2 *compartment*, 317.3 *cavity*, 337.11 *retreat*, 645.2 *time off*, 649.1 *ease*, 651.6 *refresher*
recesses 290.2 *inside*
recession 13.2 *economy*, 129.3 *decreasing thing*, 221.1 *reversion*, 247.1 *infertility*, 324.4, 337.10 *backward motion*, 628.7 *deterioration*, 643.6 *unemployment*, 687.2 *economic adversity*, 739.5 *sales*, 743.6 *insolvency*, 754.2 *declining prices*
recessional 10.5 *Christian rite*, 49.5 *sacred music*
recessionary 247.3 *birth control*
recessive 59.25 *genetic*, 221.10 *regressive*, 337.23 *receding*
recessiveness 59.11 *genetics*
Rechabite 869.4 *self-restrained person*, 873.8 *sober person*
Rechabitism 869.1 *self-restraint*
rechargeable battery 64.29 *power source*
recharge 410.11 *fuel*
rechargeable 64.36 *electronic*
recheck 480.1 *verify*
recherché 580.15 *chosen*, 617.1 *worthy*
recidivate 221.6 *reverse*, 337.1 *go backward*
recidivation 337.19 *backsliding*
recidivism 221.1 *reversion*, 337.19 *backsliding*, 628.7 *deterioration*, 864.1 *wickedness*
recidivist 16.40 *lawbreaker*, 221.10 *regressive*, 337.21 *backslider*, 578.9 *equivocator*, 578.11 *equivocating*, 628.12 *deteriorated*, 866.4 *guilty person*
recidivistic 221.10 *regressive*
recidivous 221.10 *regressive*, 864.11 *wicked*

Recife 93 Cities
recipe 45.1 *cookery*, 592.3 *expedient plan*, 630.1 *remedy*, 654.3 *precept*
recipience 348.2 *receptivity*, 730.1 *receiving*
recipiency 348.2 *receptivity*
recipient 662, 730, 348.15 *receptive*, 513.4 *expectant person*, 730.11 *receiving*
reciprocal 109, 52.18 *division*, 52.74 *divisible*, 107.5 *interrelated*, 110.13 *equivalent*, 114.5 *counterpart*, 116.14 *conforming*, 214.11 *regular*, 223.6 *in exchange*, 308.4 *symmetrical*, 365.13 *oscillating*, 478.15 *correspondent*, 664.18 *joint*, 667.10 *agreeing*, 672.5 *retaliatory*
reciprocally 109, 107.10 *relevantly*, 214.15 *regularly*, 223.8 *in exchange*, 308.8 *equally*, 478.24 *in answer*, 667.14 *agreeably*
reciprocal manners 652.1 *conduct*
reciprocate 109, 664, 110.7 *be the same*, 116.25 *conform*, 214.7 *be regular*, 223.5 *exchange*, 365.8 *oscillate*, 478.21 *answer to*, 667.6 *agree with*, 672.3, 746.13 *retaliate*
reciprocated 223.7 *exchanged*
reciprocating 109.4 *reciprocal*
reciprocating engine 63.11 *engine*
reciprocation 107.2 *interrelatedness*, 109.1 *interchange*, 110.2 *equivalence*, 116.5 *conformity*, 122.3 *equalization*, 223.1 *exchange*, 308.1 *symmetry*, 365.1 *oscillation*, 672.1 *retaliation*
reciprocative 109.4 *reciprocal*, 223.6 *in exchange*, 365.13 *oscillating*
reciprocatory 109.4 *reciprocal*
reciprocity 107.2 *interrelatedness*, 214.1 *regularity*, 223.1 *exchange*, 308.1 *symmetry*, 333.2 *middle of the road*, 664.3 *mutual relationship*, 667.1 *agreement*
Reciprocity 109
reciprocity failure 66.10 *graininess*
recital 49.27 *performance*, 183.1 *repetition*, 564.8 *speech*, 567.1 *address*
recitation 567.1 *address*
recitation of rights 16.6 *legal process*
recitative 49.4 *opera*
recite 51.35 *rehearse*, 183.17 *iterate*, 545.13 *record*, 560.15 *recount*, 564.11 *speak*
reciter 51.27 *entertainer*
recite the creed 7.19 *be religious*
recite the rosary 10.20 *pray*
reckless 329.2 *mentally quick*, 479.9 *original*, 508.5 *foolish*, 595.3 *without preparation*, 648.3 *hasty*, 668.7 *defiant*, 780.4 *rash*, 783.8 *careless*
recklessly 468.14 *inattentively*, 479.15 *inventively*, 508.8 *foolishly*, 633.11 *dangerously*, 648.7 *rashly*, 668.9 *defiantly*, 780.6 *rashly*, 783.18 *carelessly*
recklessness 468.2 *impetuosity*, 479.4 *originality*, 508.1 *folly*, 648.5 *hastiness*, 780.1 *rashness*, 783.2 *carelessness*
reckless speed 329.8 *speed*
reckon 169.10 *number*, 170.8 *calculate*, 268.10 *measure*, 471.17 *theorize*, 488.10 *think likely*, 492.12 *estimate*, 513.9 *predict*
reckonable 170.14 *calculable*
reckon among 146.6 *subsume*
reckoned 268.13 *measured*
reckoner 170.6 *calculator*
reckoning 52.1 *mathematics*, 52.12 *numeration*, 169.4 *mathematical result*, 170.1 *calculation*, 170.3 *count*, 268.1 *measurement*, 750.3, 750.10 *accounting*, 751.4 *bill*, 879.9 *retribution*

reckon on 588.7 *intend*
reckon up 52.90 *enumerate*
reckon without one's host 656.5 *be unskilful*
reclaim 125.6 *be compensated*, 599.3 *exploit*, 627.1 *improve*, 629.3 *restore*, 734.8 *take back*
reclaimable 125.8 *compensable*
reclaimed 599.9 *used*, 629.13 *repaired*, 867.6 *penitent*
reclaimed land 599.7 *reused product*
reclaimed rubber 377.4 *rubber*
reclaiming 734.2 *taking back*
reclamation 599.6 *use*, 629.9 *restoration*
reclination 282.1 *horizontality*
recline 276.8 *be low*, 282.6 *be horizontal*, 362.8 *sit*, 649.2 *take it easy*
recliner 47.2 *chair*
reclining 47.14 *wooden*, 276.1 *lowness*, 276.5 *low*, 282.1 *horizontality*, 282.10 *lying*
reclining chair 47.2 *chair*
recluse 108.3 *unconnected person*, 168.9 *hermit*, 174.8 *loner*, 531.7 *concealer*, 816.6 *unsocial person*, 825.4 *celibate person*
reclusion 598.3 *relinquishment*
reclusive 108.6 *unrelated*, 136.17 *unjoined*, 168.16 *solitary*, 174.16 *alone*, 531.14 *concealed*, 816.8 *unsociable*
reclusive life 825.3 *monasticism*
reclusiveness 816.1 *unsociability*
recognition 837, 48.3 *aspect of fiction*, 61.23 *memory*, 116.7 *consent*, 496.6 *discovery*, 497.10 *assent*, 511.1 *memory*, 522.12 *understanding*, 544.1 *identification*, 719.1 *observance*, 817.3 *courtesies*, 845.2 *due*, 849.1 *respect*, 851.2 *admiration*, 878.1 *reward*
recognition of one's services 837.3 *recognition*
recognition scene 51.6 *scene*
recognizability 522, 437.3 *visibility*
recognizable 522, 435.23, 437.1 *visible*, 496.15 *discoverable*, 526.14 *manifest*, 544.12 *identified*
recognizably 435.25 *visibly*, 496.16 *originally*
recognizance 16.6 *legal process*, 718.2 *promise*
recognize 522, 744, 116.28 *consent*, 146.4 *include*, 435.12 *see*, 496.1 *discover*, 499.4 *assent*, 501.11 *know*, 511.12 *remember*, 544.10 *identify*, 719.4 *observe*, 817.10 *be courteous*, 837.6 *be grateful*, 845.17 *credit*, 878.9 *reward*
recognized 116.17 *consenting*, 501.10 *known*, 544.12 *identified*, 584.12 *established*, 878.16 *rewarded*
recognized procedure 584.6 *procedure*
recoil 331, 331, 337, 109.1 *interchange*, 109.7 *reciprocate*, 221.1 *reversion*, 221.6 *reverse*, 221.8 *return*, 231.1 *counteraction*, 231.3 *counteract*, 331.2 *respond*, 331.6 *response*, 337.17 *resilience*, 341.5 *repulsion*, 359.5 *jump*, 377.1 *elasticity*, 377.8 *be elastic*, 478.4 *reaction*, 478.19 *react*, 573.7 *refuse*, 573.13 *dissociation*, 591.12 *shyness*, 672.3 *retaliate*, 777.11 *be afraid*, 779.4 *be a coward*, 785.6 *react against*
Recoil 331
recoil at 822.14 *hate*
recoiled 221.11 *reversed*
recoiling 331, 109.4 *reciprocal*, 337.25 *reversed*, 377.6 *elastic*, 478.12 *reactive*
recollect 3.20 *chronicle*, 511.12, 726.8 *remember*
Recollect 7 Members of Religious Orders
recollected 3.19 *chronicled*

recollection 3.5 *chronicle*, 61.23, 511.1 *memory*, 726.5 *retentiveness*

recombinant DNA technology 59.12 *molecular biology*

recommence 156.28 *begin again*, 219.4 *protract*, 221.7 *restore*

recommencement 219.2 *protraction*, 221.2 *restoration*

recommend 228.9 *motivate*, 284.14 *give moral support*, 580.4 *pick*, 654.5 *advise*, 851.13 *support*

recommendable 654.8 *advisable*

recommendation 851, 480.6 *evidence*, 483.6 *documentation*, 654.1 *advice*, 708.2 *permit*, 851.1 *approval*

recommendatory 654.7 *advising*

recommended 654.8 *advisable*, 851.23 *approved*

recommended diet 350.6 *nutrition*

recommended for leniency 16.63 *acquitted*

recommended for mercy 16.63 *acquitted*

recommender 654.5 *adviser*, 851.7 *advocate*

recommend for leniency 16.78 *acquit*

recommend for mercy 16.78 *acquit*

recommending 851.19 *supporting*

recompense 765, 125.1 *compensation*, 125.4 *compensate*, 223.1, 223.5 *exchange*, 735.2 *compensation*, 735.5 *compensate*, 746.2 *repayment*, 746.10 *pay back*, 765.2 *reparation*, 840.1 *atonement*, 878.1, 878.9 *reward*

recompensed 125.7 *compensated*

recompensing 840.4 *atoning*

reconcilable 116.10 *in accord*, 667.10 *agreeing*

reconcilably 667.14 *agreeably*

reconcile 107.7 *relate to*, 485.15 *modify*, 667.6 *agree with*, 677.4 *pacify*, 678.1 *mediate*, 765.11 *recompense*, 839.9 *forgive*, 840.5 *atone*

reconciled 485.11 *modified*, 839.6 *forgiven*

reconcilement 677.1 *pacification*

reconciliation 116.1 *accord*, 485.5 *modification*, 667.1 *agreement*, 677.1 *pacification*, 678.2 *mediation*, 705.4 *resignedness*, 765.2 *reparation*, 839.3 *absolution*, 840.1 *atonement*

reconciliatory 667.10 *agreeing*, 840.4 *atoning*

reconciling 116.10 *in accord*, 839.4 *forgiving*

recondite 438.3 *private*, 443.4 *inscrutable*, 523.4 *difficult*, 531.14 *concealed*, 551.2 *obscure*, 659.12 *problematic*

reconditeness 531.1 *concealment*, 659.1 *difficulty*

recondition 627.1 *improve*, 629.2 *refurbish*

reconditioned 629.13 *repaired*

reconditioning 627.5 *improvement*, 629.8 *repair*

reconnaisance party 154.8 *precursor*

reconnaissance 435.3 *observation*

reconnaissance battalion 17.4 *military organization*

reconnaissance party 679.14 *armed forces*

reconnoitre 154.18 *forerun*, 435.14 *inspect*

reconnoitring 154.14 *preparatory*

reconsider 627, 461.14 *have second thoughts*

reconsideration 627

reconstitute 629.3 *restore*

reconstituted 629.13 *repaired*

reconstitution 629.9 *restoration*

reconstruct 3.23 *turn back time*, 201.20 *make new*, 629.3 *restore*

reconstructed 201.14 *renewed*, 629.13 *repaired*

reconstructible 201.15 *renewable*

---

reconstruction 201.5 *fresh start*, 245.1 *reproduction*, 518.3 *conjecture*, 629.9 *restoration*

Reconstruction 3.10 *past age*

Reconstructionism 7 *Non-Christian Religions*

reconvene 629.3 *restore*

reconversion 221.2, 629.9 *restoration*

reconvert 221.7 *restore*

record 545, 545, 3.5, 3.20 *chronicle*, 16.7 *legal trial*, 21.5 *competition*, 48.4 *non-fiction*, 65.17 *computing term*, 126.14 *best*, 132.1 *remainder*, 152.7 *catalogue*, 152.15 *categorize*, 171.8 *list*, 185.16 *time*, 192.15 *chronologize*, 420.9 *audio device*, 480.1 *verify*, 483.1 *evidence*, 483.6 *documentation*, 485.3 *qualifications*, 511.4 *reminder*, 528.3 *document*, 534.30 *communicate*, 544.10 *identify*, 545.7 *recording*, 547.9 *represent*, 560.1 *description*, 560.3 *narration*, 560.15 *recount*, 605.5 *collection*, 617.2 *best*, 652.1 *conduct*, 750.7 *account*

Record 545

record book 545

record-breaker 126.6 *paragon*, 617.8 *exceller*, 682.4 *successful person*, 861.17 *good thing*

record-breaking 21.6 *track*, 126.14, 617.2 *best*, 786.8 *wonderful*, 861.2 *best*

record collection 605.5 *collection*

recorded 545, 3.19 *chronicled*, 146.8 *included*, 171.11 *listed*, 480.8 *verifiable*, 483.8 *evidential*, 534.34 *communicated*, 750.11 *accounted*

recorded delivery 534.2 *postal communication*

recorded material 545.1 *record*

recorded proceedings 545.1 *record*

recorded sunshine 55.22 *sun*

recorder 545, 3.3 *historian*, 16.13 *lawyer*, 16.23, 16.23 *judge*, 26.7 *judo*, 192.13 *chronicler*, 492.6 *justice*, 545.10 *recording instrument*, 560.10 *descriptive writer*

record high 126.4 *summit*

record-holder 126.6 *paragon*

record-holding 126.14 *best*

recording 534, 545, 3.5 *chronicle*, 56.82 *measuring instrument*, 534.25 *broadcast material*, 545.1 *record*, 545.8 *registration*

Recording Angel 16.23 *judge*

recording device 56.82 *measuring instrument*

recording instrument 545, 56.82 *measuring instrument*

recording of evidence 16.7 *legal trial*

recording system 53.27 *imaging*

record-keeper 545.9 *recorder*

record-keeping 545.8 *registration*

record low 127.5 *inferior state*

record piracy 736.6 *illegal borrowing*

record pirate 114.4 *person who copies*, 118.8 *copier*, 736.10 *infringer*

records 750.5 *account book*

record size 259.3 *large scale*

record-size 259.15 *big*

recount 560, 183.17 *iterate*, 528.12 *communicate*, 545.13 *record*

recounted 183.10 *iterated*

recounter 344.14 *meeting*

recounting 183.2 *iteration*

recoup 125.6 *be compensated*, 336.4 *make good time*, 672.3 *retaliate*, 734.8 *take back*

recoupable 125.8 *compensable*

recouped 125.7 *compensated*

recoupment 125.1 *compensation*, 734.2 *taking back*, 735.2 *compensation*

---

recourse 599.6 *use*, 602.1 *means*, 634.1 *refuge*

recover 28.5 *fence*, 29.7 *golf*, 36.16 *row*, 36.19 *punt*, 125.6 *be compensated*, 221.7 *restore*, 231.3 *counteract*, 237.7 *be strong*, 623.6 *get healthy*, 627.2 *get better*, 629.1 *repair*, 629.4 *be restored*, 639.1 *deliver*, 651.2 *be refreshed*, 734.8 *take back*

recoverable 125.8 *compensable*, 221.12 *reversible*, 629.14 *repairable*

recoverably 629.17 *repairably*

recovered 125.7 *compensated*, 142.8 *sound*, 221.11 *reversed*, 629.13 *repaired*, 651.4 *refreshed*

recover from the lunge 28.5 *fence*

recovering 36.11 *rowing*, 627.14 *improved*

recover lost ground 336.4 *make good time*, 721.10 *augment*

recover one's costs 734.8 *take back*

recover one's health 623.6 *get healthy*

recover one's losses 734.8 *take back*

recovery 36.4 *rowing*, 36.8 *punting*, 39.11 *swimming*, 125.1 *compensation*, 221.2 *restoration*, 627.5 *improvement*, 629.9 *restoration*, 629.10 *revival*, 629.11 *recuperation*, 630.1 *remedy*, 639.2 *deliverance*, 651.5 *refreshment*, 734.2 *taking back*

recovery shot 29.3 *golf shots*

recovery stroke 39.2 *swimming technique*

recreancy 578.7 *apostasy*

recreant 578.9 *equivocator*, 779.3 *cowardly*, 864.9 *wicked person*

re-create 245.12 *multiply*, 627.3 *rectify*, 651.1 *refresh*

re-created 245.15 *reproduced*

re-creating 245.15 *reproduced*

recreation 42.8 *pastime*, 590.4 *activity*, 645.2 *time off*, 651.5 *refreshment*

recreational 42, 26.15 *wrestling*, 39.11 *swimming*, 645.6 *leisure*, 651.3 *refreshing*

recreational architecture 43.1 *architecture*

recreational canoeing 36.6 *canoeing*

recreational diving 39.6 *diving*

recreational education 6.2 *educational system*

recreational karate 26.8 *karate*

recreationally 42

recreational swimming 39.1 *swimming*

recreational therapy 61.3 *psychiatric treatment*

recreation room 256.7 *room*

recreative 651.3 *refreshing*

recriminate 852.19 *blame*, 855.8 *justify*, 856.5 *accuse*

recriminated 856.8 *accusatory*

recrimination 500.3 *dissentience*, 852.7 *blame*, 855.2 *defence*, 856.1 *accusation*

recriminative 852.29 *blaming*

recriminatory 672.5 *retaliatory*, 856.8 *accusatory*

recruit 6.7 *learner*, 17.10 *enlist*, 128.5 *make bigger*, 130.7 *support*, 156.14 *beginner*, 228.9 *motivate*, 627.1 *improve*, 629.5 *revive*, 651.1 *refresh*, 676.12 *go to war*, 679.8 *soldier*, 703.7 *engage*

recruited 679.35 *martial*

recruiting 17.1 *military affairs*

recruitment 627.5 *improvement*, 629.9 *restoration*, 629.10 *revival*, 651.5 *refreshment*, 676.7 *war measures*, 703.2 *engagement*

recruits 679.14 *armed forces*

recrystallization 54.29 *petrogenesis*

recrystallize 54.62 *lithify*

rectal 290.10 *visceral*

rectal administration 62.13 *administration*

---

rectangle 52.44 *polygon*, 178.2 *quadrilateral*, 269.6 *oblong*, 310.3 *angled figure*

rectangular 52.82 *polygonal*, 178.8 *quadrilateral*, 269.2 *elongated*, 281.10 *perpendicular*, 310.9 *angled*

rectangular backboard 23.3 *basketball equipment*

rectangular coordinates 52.33 *coordinates*

rectangular pulse 56.16 *waveform*

rectifiable 125.8 *compensable*, 629.14 *repairable*

rectification 627, 64.15 *circuit function*, 125.1 *compensation*, 627.5 *improvement*, 629.8 *repair*, 840.1 *atonement*, 843.5 *righting wrong*

rectified 125.7 *compensated*, 629.13 *repaired*

rectifier 64, 56.55 *circuit*, 64.34 *power supply*, 629.12 *repairer*

rectify 627, 125.4 *compensate*, 619.5 *perfect*, 627.1 *improve*, 629.1 *repair*, 840.5 *atone*, 843.15 *put right*

rectifying 840.4 *atoning*

rectilinear 52.80 *linear*, 312.1 *straight*

rectilinearity 312.6 *straightness*

rectitude 843.4 *righteousness*, 857.2 *purity*, 861.10 *kindness*, 863.1 *virtue*, 876.2 *good morals*

rectophobia 777 *Phobias by Name*

rector 7.8 *priest*, 653.13 *director*

rectorate 7.9 *priesthood*

rectorship 7.9 *priesthood*

rectory 7.10 *priestly dwelling*, 256.4 *official residence*

rectrix 78.17 *plumage*

rectum 777 *Phobias by Topic*, 290.4 *insides*

recumbency 276.1 *lowness*, 282.1 *horizontality*

recumbent 276.5 *low*, 282.10 *lying*

recumbent fold 54.20 *earth movement*

recuperate 623.6 *get healthy*, 627.2 *get better*, 629.4 *be restored*, 651.2 *be refreshed*

recuperating 627.14 *improved*

recuperation 629, 623.3 *health*, 627.5 *improvement*, 630.1 *remedy*, 630.11 *medical art*, 651.5 *refreshment*

recuperative 629.16 *restorative*

recur 183.21 *be repeated*, 184.9 *be infinite*, 187.10 *be periodical*, 212.7 *be frequent*, 214.7 *be regular*, 219.3 *continue*, 427.9 *resonate*, 457.13 *occur*, 511.15 *be remembered*

recurrence 159.6 *continuum*, 183.1 *repetition*, 184.3 *return*, 187.6 *periodicity*, 212.4 *frequency*, 214.1 *regularity*, 219.1 *continuity*, 427.1 *resonance*, 457.6 *reappearance*, 629.10 *revival*

recurrent 183, 159.12 *cyclical*, 187.8 *periodical*, 212.3 *frequent*, 214.11 *regular*, 219.5 *continual*, 584.14 *habituated*

recurrently 183.23 *repeatedly*, 187.12 *periodically*, 212.1 *frequently*, 219.7 *continually*, 427.11 *resonantly*

recurrent nova 53.12 *variable star*

recurrent pattern 187.5 *recurrent period*

recurrent period 187

recurring 183.14 *recurrent*, 184.1 *infinite*, 212.3 *frequent*, 214.11 *regular*, 324.17 *directional*, 457.7 *appearing*

recurring decimal 52.18 *division*

recurring movement 324.10 *regular movement*

recursion 52.28 *algorithm*, 344.13 *return*

recursive procedure 52.28 *algorithm*

recusance 168.2 *dissent*, 476.2 *denial*, 536.2 *rejection*, 713.1

protest

recusancy 536.2 *rejection*

recusant 168.8 *dissenter*, 168.12 *nonconformist*, 476.5 *refuter*, 484.4 *tergiversator*, 500.5 *dissenter*, 500.7 *dissenting*, 536.11 *negative*, 693.7 *protester*, 693.13 *disobedient*, 713.9 *protesting*

recyclable 141.5 *disintegrated*, 221.12 *reversible*, 599.10, 613.2 *usable*

recycle 183.20 *renew*, 221.7 *restore*, 599.3 *exploit*, 629.3 *restore*, 735.4 *give back*

recycled 183.11 *reprinted*, 221.11 *reversed*, 599.9 *used*

recycled paper 735.1 *giving back*

recycled substance 599.7 *reused product*

recycler 735.3 *returner*

recycling 183.4 *return*, 221.2 *restoration*, 599.6 *use*, 629.9 *restoration*, 735.1 *giving back*

red 80 Fishes, **450**, 31.8 *hockey*, 45.56 *culinary*, 56.28, 56.28 *colour*, 595.6 *uncooked*, 665.10 *political*, 810.9 *blushing*

Red 96 Rivers, **97** Oceans and Seas, 12.6 *political party*, 96.3 *US rivers*, 450.8 *figurative usage*, 627.12 *reformer*, 665.6 *political party member*, 693.11 *rebel*

red Abyssinian 77 Breeds of Cats

redact 5.46 *translate*, 627.3 *rectify*

redacted 5.40 *translated*

redaction 5.12 *translation*, 627.6 *rectification*

red admiral 82 Insects, 450.7 *red thing*

red alert 450.8 *figurative usage*, 636.2 *danger signal*

red algae 90.2 *algae*

redan 671.8 *military defences*

red-and-white 26.15 *wrestling*

Red-and-White Friesian 68 Breeds of Cattle

red ant 82 Insects, 82.4 *social insect*

red as a beetroot 450.2 *red-faced*

red as a lobster 450.2 *red-faced*

red-bait 481.14 *discriminate against*

red-baiter 481.7 *bigot*

red-baiting 481.4 *social discrimination*

red ball 24.3 *English billiards*, 24.4 *carom*, 24.5 *snooker*

red bean 45 Vegetables

red beans with rice 45.43 *US dish*

red beet 45 Vegetables

red bird 450.7 *red thing*

red-blind 436.9 *weak-sighted*

red-blindness 436.2 *poor sight*

red blood cell 387.4 *blood*, 450.7 *red thing*

red-blooded 237.9 *physically strong*, 239.4 *vigorous*

red brass 57 Alloys

redbrick university 6.13 *university*

redbud 85 Trees and Shrubs

red bug 82 Insects, 82.3 *pest*

redbug 450.7 *red thing*

red cabbage 45 Vegetables

redcap 326.7 *transferor* , 697.3 *attendant*

Redcap 68 Breeds of Fowl

red card 450.7 *red thing*

red carpet 450.8 *figurative usage*, 811.13 *ceremonial*, 813.1 *formality*, 849.5 *presenting arms*

red-carpet treatment 812.4 *reception*

red caviar 45.16 *fish dish*

red cedar 85 Trees and Shrubs

red-cheeked 450.2 *red-faced*

red cheeks 450.7 *red thing*

red clover 68.12 *crop*, 450.7 *red thing*

redcoat 450.8 *figurative usage*, 679.8 *soldier*

red coats 676.2 *glory of war*

red colour 450.5 *redness*

red complexion 450.5 *redness*

red cosmetic 450.6 *red pigment*

Red Crescent 450.8 *figurative usage*

Red Cross 450.8 *figurative usage*, 729.3 *offering*, 831.2, 833.5 *charity*

redcurrant 86 Fruits, 450.7 *red thing*

red deal 47.12 *wood*

red deer 77 Placental Mammals, 37.5 *game*, 450.7 *red thing*

red demand 692.2 *demand*

redden 450, 444.15 *colour*, 444.16 *make up*, 828.12 *become angry*

reddened 450.2 *red-faced*

reddening 53.21 *orbit*, 450.5 *redness*, 810.2, 810.9 *blushing*

red devils 761.6 *desensitizing substance*

reddish-brown 449.1 *brown*

reddish-yellow 451.1 *orange*

red-dog 19.16 *play defence*

red duster 544.7 *flag*

red dwarf 450.7 *red thing*

red dye 444.4 *pigment*, 450.6 *red pigment*

rede 654.1 *advice*

Rede 96 Rivers

redecorate 216.8 *cause change*, 220.9 *transform*, 629.2 *refurbish*

redecorated 216.12 *changed*, 629.13 *repaired*

redecoration 216.1 *change*

redeem 125.4 *compensate*, 125.6 *be compensated*, 627.1 *improve*, 629.3 *restore*, 639.1 *deliver*, 700.4 *liberate*, 735.4 *give back*, 738.3 *buy back*, 746.7 *pay off*, 839.9 *forgive*, 840.5 *atone*, 845.19 *pay*

redeemability 125.1 *compensation*

redeemable 125.8 *compensable*, 629.14 *repairable*, 639.4 *deliverable*, 746.17 *payable*, 845.12 *owed*

redeemably 125.11 *in compensation*, 629.17 *repairably*, 639.6 *extricably*

redeemed 8.15 *deified*, 125.7 *compensated*, 629.13 *repaired*, 735.6 *restoring*, 738.13 *bought*, 839.6 *forgiven*

redeemed soul 8.10 *deified person*

redeemer 125.3 *compensator*, 639.3 *deliverer*, 700.3 *liberator*, 735.3 *returner*, 738.12 *purchaser*

redeeming 125.9 *compensatory*, 735.6 *restoring*, 839.4 *forgiving*

redeeming feature 617.6 *worth*

redeem one's pledge 719.6 *perform*

redemptible 125.8 *compensable*

redemption 125.1 *compensation*, 223.1 *exchange*, 627.5 *improvement*, 629.9 *restoration*, 637.1 *preservation*, 639.2 *deliverance*, 700.1 *liberation*, 735.1 *giving back*, 738.9 *repurchase*, 839.3 *absolution*, 840.1 *atonement*

redemptional 735.6 *restoring*

redemptive 125.9 *compensatory*, 629.16 *restorative*, 637.6 *preserving*, 700.7 *liberated*, 735.6 *restoring*, 738.14 *buying*, 746.20 *paying in return*

redemptively 735, 125.11 *in compensation*, 738.17 *acquisitively*

Redemptorism 7 Christian Movements

redemptory 125.9 *compensatory*

Red Ensign 544.7 *flag*

redesign 201.5 *fresh start*, 201.20 *make new*

redesignable 201.15 *renewable*

redesigned 201.14 *renewed*

red eye 351.8 *mixed drink*

red-eye 66.8 *composition*

red-eyed 436.9 *weak-sighted*, 774.4 *lamenting*

red-eye flight 450.8 *figurative usage*

red eyes 436.2 *poor sight*

red face 810.2 *blushing*

red-faced 450

---

red face-off spot 31.3 *ice hockey*

redfin 80 Fishes

red fir 85 Trees and Shrubs

redfish 80 Fishes

red flag 543.4 *signal*, 544.7 *flag*, 636.2 *danger signal*

red fox 77 Placental Mammals, 450.7 *red thing*

red giant 53.11 *stellar birth*, 450.7 *red thing*

red glow 439.8 *fire*

red goal line 31.3 *ice hockey*

red grouse 78 Birds, 450.7 *red thing*

red gum 85 Trees and Shrubs

red hair 450.7 *red thing*

red-haired 450

red-handed 398.24 *murderous*, 640.5 *acting*, 640.7 *actively*, 866.6 *appearing guilty*, 866.11 *guiltily*

red-handedly 866.11 *guiltily*

red-handedness 866.1 *guilt*

red hands 866.2 *signs of guilt*

redhead 78 Birds, 450.7 *red thing*

red heat 439.8 *fire*

red herring 108.2 *unrelated thing*, 450.8 *figurative usage*, 474.2 *sophism*, 539.12 *disguise*, 591.14 *evasion*, 612.8 *trifle*, 614.5 *waste of effort*, 657.2 *stratagem*

red-hot 241.6 *violent*, 408.9 *hot*, 450.2 *red-faced*

red-hot mama 450.8 *figurative usage*

red-hot poker 84 Flowers and Flowering Plants

redia 81.13 *invertebrate larva*

redingote 295.12 *coat*

red ink 450.7 *red thing*

redintegrate 629.3 *restore*

redintegration 629.8 *repair*

redirect 567.10 *send*

rediscover 496.4 *invent*

rediscovery 496.9 *invention*

redivivus 629.13 *repaired*

red lead 57 Common Chemical Compounds, 450.6 *red pigment*

redleg 91 Names for Inhabitants

Red Leicester 45 Cheeses

red-letter day 185.11 *date*, 450.8 *figurative usage*, 611.2 *important matter*, 813.3 *formal occasion*

red light 439.6 *electric light*, 450.7 *red thing*, 500.3 *disapproval*, 543.4 *signal*, 587.6 *dissuasion*, 636.2 *danger signal*, 709.1 *veto*, 711.1 *refusal*, 852.3 *nonacceptance*

red-light 93.14 *urban*

red-light district 93.7 *city district*, 450.8 *figurative usage*, 877.6 *brothel*

red meat 45.20 *meat*, 450.7 *red thing*

red menace 635.2 *troublemaker*

red mite 82 Arachnids

red mullet 80 Fishes

redneck 255.5 *countryman*, 450.8 *figurative usage*, 481.7 *bigot*, 761.5 *insensitive person*

redness 450, 408.5 *hot weather*

Redness 450

red nose 874.16 *alcoholism*

red-nosed 874.5 *drunken*

redo 183.16 *repeat*, 592.10 *plan out*, 627.4 *reconsider*, 629.3 *restore*

red oak 85 Trees and Shrubs

red ochre 450.6 *red pigment*

redolence 416.1 *odour*

redolent 416.5 *odorous*

redone 629.13 *repaired*

redouble 128.5 *make bigger*, 183.16 *repeat*, 239.3 *invigorate*

redoubled 183.9 *repeated*

redoublement 28.3 *fencing movements*

redoubling 128.1 *increase*, 183.1 *repetition*, 183.12 *repetitious*

redoubt 671.8 *military defences*

redoubtable 237.10 *potent*

---

redound 234.4 *tend*

red pepper 45 Vegetables, 450.7 *red thing*

red phosphorus 57 Chemical Elements

red pigment 450

red pine 85 Trees and Shrubs

red planet 450.7 *red thing*

red-pointed Siamese 77 Breeds of Cats

redpoll 78 Birds

Red Poll 68 Breeds of Cattle

redraft 627.3 *rectify*

red rag to a bull 828.3 *cause of offence*

red rash 450.5 *redness*

redress 125.1 *compensation*, 125.4 *compensate*, 629.9 *restoration*, 630.1 *remedy*, 672.1 *retaliation*, 672.3 *retaliate*, 840.1 *atonement*, 840.5 *atone*, 843.15 *put right*

redressed 125.7 *compensated*

redressing 840.4 *atoning*

redress the balance 122.11 *equalize*, 672.3 *retaliate*

red roses 826.3 *love token*

Red Ruby Devon 68 Breeds of Cattle

reds 761.6 *desensitizing substance*

red salmon 450.7 *red thing*

Red Sea 450.8 *figurative usage*

red self 77 Breeds of Cats

redshank 78 Birds

redshift 53.21 *orbit*

redshirt 19.2 *football player*, 707.2 *alternative*

Red Sindhu 68 Breeds of Cattle

red snapper 450.7 *red thing*

red spider mite 69.12 *pests and diseases*

red squirrel 77 Placental Mammals, 450.7 *red thing*

Red Star delivery 534.2 *postal communication*

redstart 78 Birds

Red Steppe 68 Breeds of Cattle

reds under the bed 635.2 *troublemaker*

red tabby 77 Breeds of Cats

red tape 12.3 *governance*, 209.3 *delayed action*, 450.8 *figurative usage*, 584.6 *procedure*, 610.2 *overdoing it*, 642.9 *overactivity*, 661.2 *obstacle*, 688.4 *governance*

Red Tarn 94 Lakes

red thing 450

red tide 90.1 *alga*

redtop 87 Grasses

reduce 182, 57.26 *react*, 66.21 *photograph*, 120.8 *quantify*, 129.5 *make smaller*, 141.4 *deconstruct*, 220.7 *convert into*, 220.9 *transform*, 238.7 *weaken*, 242.4 *moderate*, 262.5 *make smaller*, 262.6 *become smaller*, 270.10 *shorten*, 273.7 *thicken*, 274.14 *become thin*, 299.5 *outline*, 350.23 *taste*, 362.1 *lower*, 542.22 *play down*, 562.8 *summarize*, 628.5 *hurt*, 649.3 *ease*, 739.1 *sell*, 752.3 *discount*, 806.23 *abase*, 871.5 *fast*

reduced 131, 182.7 *fewer*, 262.7 *smaller*, 273.2 *dense*, 362.17 *lowered*, 542.19 *downplayed*, 710.17 *offered*, 754.9 *cheap*, 806.3 *humbled*

reduced circumstances 127.5 *inferior state*, 743.5 *poverty*

reduced payment 747.2 *stoppage*

reduced pressure 372.3 *sparseness*

reduced price 754.1 *cheapness*

reduced price rate 751.1 *price*

reduced rate 754.1 *cheapness*

reduced to a jelly 777.7 *frightened*

reduced to clear 754.9 *cheap*

reduced to poverty 743.2 *insolvent*

reduced to slavery 701.9 *subject*

reduced to the last extremity 633.4 *endangered*

reduce in number 238.7 *weaken*

action
reflux condenser 57 Laboratory Apparatus
refluxing 57.5 *process*
reforest 629.3 *restore*
reforestation 85.5 *forestry*, 629.9 *restoration*
reform 2.15 *socialize*, 201.17 *become new*, 216.7 *be changed*, 216.8 *cause change*, 220.8 *be transformed*, 220.9 *transform*, 336.15 *improvement*, 585.5 *disaccustom*, 627.1 *improve*, 627.2 *get better*, 627.3 *rectify*, 627.5 *improvement*, 629.2 *refurbish*, 629.3 *restore*, 704.8 *be reborn*, 831.8 *be benevolent*, 843.5 *righting wrong*, 843.15 *put right*, 867.4 *be penitent*
Reform 7.16 *denominational*
reformable 627.15 *improvable*
reformation 216.1 *change*, 220.2 *evolution*, 627.5 *improvement*, 629.9 *restoration*, 704.3 *new beginning*, 843.5 *righting wrong*, 867.1 *penitence*
reformational 216.11 *changeable*
reformative 216.11 *changeable*, 627.16 *improving*, 704.10 *cancelled*
reformatory 627, 323.4 *closed place*, 627.16 *improving*, 702.1 *prison*, 816.4 *place of confinement*
reformed 627.14 *improved*, 704.10 *cancelled*, 867.6 *penitent*
reformed character 867.3 *penitent person*
reformed prostitute 867.3 *penitent person*
reformer 627, 216.6, 224.4 *editor*, 336.16 *progressive person*, 596.7 *attempter*, 629.12 *repairer*, 704.5 *abrogator*, 831.5 *benevolent person*
reforming 627.16 *improving*, 833.6 *philanthropic*
reformism 627, 833.2 *public spiritedness*
reformist 336.17 *forward*, 627.12 *reformer*, 627.16 *improving*, 629.12 *repairer*
Reform Judaism 7 Non-Christian Religions
reform school 627.10 *reformatory*, 702.1 *prison*
reformulate 629.3 *restore*
reformulation 629.9 *restoration*
refound 629.3 *restore*
refract 335.12 *deflect*, 439.27 *glaze*
refracted 335.26 *diffractive*
refracted colour 444.2 *colourfulness*
refractile 335.26 *diffractive*
refraction 56.15 *wave property*, 56.29 *optical element*, 335.18 *diffraction*, 436.5 *visual distortion*
refractive 335.26 *diffractive*, 442.1 *transparent*
refractive index 56.29 *optical element*
refractivity 56.29 *optical element*
refractometer 268.8 *meter*
refractometric 268.16 *micrometric*
refractometry 268.2 *micrometry*
refractor 53.24 *telescope*
refractorily 44.12 *ornamentally*
refractoriness 573.14 *disobedience*, 663.5 *contrariness*, 669.2 *obstinacy*, 693.1 *disobedience*, 713.1 *protest*
refractory 577, 44.10 *ceramic*, 57.7 *chemical compound*, 579.1 *capricious*, 659.14 *troublesome*, 663.22 *uncooperative*, 668.8 *defying*, 669.11 *obstinate*, 713.9 *protesting*
refractory brick 44.9 *industrial ceramics*
refractory clay 44.2 *raw material*
refractory ware 44.1 *ceramics*
refrain 48.8 *part of poem*, 155.8 *addition*, 426.6 *musical repetition*, 433.1 *melody*, 591.3 *abstain*, 641.4 *not act*, 869.5 *be*

self-restrained
refrainer 669.5 *resister*
refrain from 160.12 *discontinue*, 218.6 *cease*, 669.9 *desist*
refraining 591.11 *abstinence*, 641.1 *inaction*, 641.3 *inactive*, 669.4, 669.13 *desisting*, 869.8 *self-restrained*
refrainment 869.1 *self-restraint*
refrangible 335.26 *diffractive*
refresh 651, 201.20 *make new*, 237.8 *strengthen*, 239.3 *invigorate*, 405.10 *comfort*, 606.6 *replenish*, 627.1 *improve*, 629.5 *revive*
refreshed 651, 201.14 *renewed*, 767.7 *relieved*
refresher 651, 630.7 *tonic*, 751.3 *fee*
refreshing 651, 237.4 *strengthening*, 239.5 *invigorating*, 405.6 *pleasant*, 617.4 *worthwhile*, 625.4 *hygienic*, 767.8 *relieving*
refreshingly 651, 767.15 *comfortingly*
refreshment 651, 237.4 *strengthening*, 239.1 *vigour*, 350.12 *meal*, 390.6 *ventilation*, 627.5 *improvement*, 629.10 *revival*, 649.1 *ease*
Refreshment 651
refreshment room 350.15 *eating place*
refreshments 651
refresh oneself 651.2 *be refreshed*
refresh one's memory 511.13 *remind*
refrigerant 409.4 *cooler*, 409.9 *heat-resistant*
refrigerate 373.9 *harden*, 409.12 *make cold*, 637.5 *preserve*, 651.1 *refresh*
refrigerated 409.9 *heat-resistant*
refrigeration 56.35 *heat*, 390.6 *ventilation*, 637.1 *preservation*, 651.5 *refreshment*
refrigeration ship 74 Ships and Boats
refrigerator 71 Motor Vehicles, 45.4 *kitchen container*, 56.35 *heat*, 258.3 *cabinet*, 409.4 *cooler*, 605.4 *storage*, 637.2 *preserver*
refuel 410.11 *fuel*, 605.6 *store*, 606.6 *replenish*
refuge 634, 256.11 *retreat*, 293.15 *shelter*, 325.3 *resting place*, 348.2 *receptivity*, 531.2 *hiding place*, 632.2 *protection*, 671.12 *fort*, 718.1 *protection*
Refuge 634
refugee 104.7 *new arrival*, 108.3 *unconnected person*, 149.6 *immigrant*, 149.8 *exile*, 252.7 *displaced person*, 252.10 *replaced*, 349.27 *expellee*, 591.17 *avoider*, 638.3 *escaper*, 816.7 *outsider*
refulgence 439.1 *light*
refulgent 439.15 *lucent*
refund 125.1 *compensation*, 125.4 *compensate*, 131.2 *subtracted item*, 735.2 *compensation*, 735.5 *compensate*, 746.2 *repayment*, 746.10 *pay back*, 752.1, 752.3 *discount*
refundable 746.17 *payable*
refunded 125.7 *compensated*, 735.6 *restoring*
refunder 735.3 *returner*
refunding 735.6 *restoring*
refurbish 629, 201.20 *make new*, 627.1 *improve*, 792.11 *paint and decorate*
refurbished 201.14 *renewed*, 629.13 *repaired*
refurbisher 629.12 *repairer*
refurbishment 201.5 *fresh start*, 627.5 *improvement*, 791.1 *transfiguration*
refusal 711, 32.9 *jumping*, 100.3 *negativeness*, 147.1 *exclusion*, 341.6 *repulse*, 500.2 *disapproval*, 536.2 *rejection*, 573.12 *opposition*, 581.5 *rejection*, 591.12 *shyness*, 661.1 *hindrance*, 663.2 *objection*, 668.2 *disobedience*, 669.1 *resistance*,

669.4 *desisting*, 709.1 *veto*, 852.3 *nonacceptance*
Refusal 711
refusal of bail 699.4 *detention*
refusal of belief 536.2 *rejection*
refusal of consent 536.2 *rejection*, 711.1 *refusal*
refusal to act 641.1 *inaction*
refusal to be impressed 787.1 *lack of wonder*
refusal to mix 816.1 *unsociability*
refusal to obey orders 693.1 *disobedience*, 713.1 *protest*
refusal to pay 711.1 *refusal*, 713.1 *protest*, 747.1 *nonpayment*
refusal to recant 868.1 *impenitence*
refusal to work 669.1 *resistance*, 711.1 *refusal*
refuse 500, 573, 614, 711, 132.2 *residue*, 147.7 *exclude*, 341.1 *repel*, 515.7 *thwart*, 536.7 *be negative*, 581.1 *reject*, 591.4 *shy*, 600.5 *not use*, 607.5 *waste product*, 622.4 *dirt*, 661.8 *hinder*, 663.17 *withstand*, 668.6 *be insubordinate*, 669.6 *resist*, 709.3 *veto*, 726.7 *detain*, 822.14 *hate*, 852.15 *withhold approval*
refuse bail 699.11 *detain*
refuse collector 621.12 *cleaner*
refuse consent 536.7 *be negative*
refuse credence 536.8 *rebut*
refused 711, 515.9 *disappointed*, 536.12 *rejected*, 709.5 *vetoed*, 726.10 *retained*, 852.31 *disapproved*
refuse dump 605.4 *storage*, 614.6 *refuse*, 727.8 *sink*
refuse flatly 711.5 *refuse*
refuse food 722.9 *lose*, 871.5 *fast*
refuse heap 727.5 *wasteyard*
refusenik 669.5 *resister*, 711.4 *refuser*
refuse oneself 711, 669.9 *desist*
refuse payment 747.8 *stop payment*
refuse permission 709.3 *veto*, 711.5 *refuse*
refuse point-blank 711.5 *refuse*
refuser 711, 536.6 *negativist*, 669.5 *resister*
refuse to accept 536.7 *be negative*
refuse to act 641.4 *not act*
refuse to be impressed 787.5 *not wonder about*
refuse to believe 498.8 *disbelieve*
refuse to bow down 669.6 *resist*
refuse to bow to 669.5 *defy*
refuse to budge 217.5 *be permanent*, 663.17 *withstand*, 669.7 *be obstinate*
refuse to comment 566.8 *be taciturn*
refuse to cooperate 693.15 *be disobedient*
refuse to judge 482.12 *be fair*
refuse to obey orders 693.15 *be disobedient*, 713.6 *protest*
refuse to pay 711.5 *refuse*, 747.7 *not pay*
refuse to recant 868.5 *be impenitent*
refuse to say sorry 818.7 *be discourteous*
refuse to say thank you 818.7 *be discourteous*
refuse to see the error of one's ways 868.5 *be impenitent*
refuse to stoop 805.24 *be proud*
refuse to work 711.5 *refuse*
refuse to yield 378.10 *be tough*
refusing 573, 536.13 *rebutting*, 669.10 *resistant*, 711.8 *refused*
refusing oneself 669.4 *desisting*, 711.3 *abnegation*
refusing to eat 624.22 *sick*
refutability 476
refutable 476, 221.12 *reversible*, 473.10 *arguable*, 855.13 *vindicable*
refutably 476, 221.13 *reversibly*
refutation 476, 221.5 *reply*, 476.2 *denial*, 476.3 *countercharge*, 478.5 *counterstatement*, 484.1 *counterevidence*, 536.3 *re-*

buttal, 663.2 *objection*, 704.4 *cancelling out*, 711.2 *dissent*, 713.1 *protest*, 855.2 *defence*
Refutation 476
refutative 476.7 *refuting*, 478.13 *retaliatory*, 484.5 *countering*
refutatory 476.7 *refuting*, 478.13 *retaliatory*, 484.5 *countering*
refute 476, 4.23 *discuss philosophically*, 221.9 *reply*, 476.9 *deny*, 477.20 *doubt*, 478.18 *answer back*, 484.7 *counter*, 536.8 *rebut*, 578.4 *recant*, 663.15 *object*, 704.9 *cancel out*, 711.6 *dissent*, 855.8 *justify*
refuted 221.11 *reversed*, 484.6 *countered*, 536.12 *rejected*
refuter 476, 484.3 *counterclaimant*, 704.5 *abrogator*
refuting 476, 536.13 *rebutting*, 711.9 *dissenting*, 855.11 *vindicatory*
regain 125.6 *be compensated*, 734.8 *take back*
regain consciousness 396.16 *live*, 403.12 *awake*
regained safety 632.1 *safety*
regaining 734.2 *taking back*
regaining one's figure 350.6 *nutrition*
regain one's breath 651.2 *be refreshed*
regain one's freedom 824.7 *divorce*
regain one's strength 629.4 *be restored*
regal 12.10 *governing*, 688.12 *authoritative*, 688.14 *governmental*, 805.19 *stately*
regale 350.13 *feast*, 350.24 *have a meal*, 350.25 *provide food*, 405.9 *give pleasure*, 665.16 *host*, 771.13 *be humorous*
regalement 350.4 *eating meals*
regalia 7.11 *vestment*, 295.1 *dress*, 544.4 *insignia*, 813.4 *formal dress*
regality 688.1 *authority*
regally 805.36 *majestically*
regard 416.4 *reputation*, 435.13 *look*, 467.1 *attention*, 467.10 *be attentive*, 492.12 *estimate*, 497.8 *be of the opinion*, 611.8 *make important*, 719.1 *observance*, 719.4 *observe*, 800.1 *estimation*, 819.1 *friendship*, 821.1 *love*, 849.1, 849.15 *respect*, 851.2 *admiration*
regardant 544.13 *heraldic*
regard as 222.5 *take a substitute*
regarded 821.21 *beloved*
regarded highly by 819.9 *friends with*
regardful 719.7 *observant*, 849.8 *respectful*
regard highly 849.15 *respect*, 851.11 *approve*
regarding 107.10 *relevantly*, 719.7 *observant*
regardless 327.16 *how*, 720.11 *nonobservant*, 780.4 *rash*
regardlessness 780.1 *rashness*
regards 817.3 *courtesies*, 849.7 *respects*
regatta 36.1 *sailing*, 36.4 *rowing*, 674.4 *race*
regency 12.1 *government*, 12.3 *governance*, 688.7 *type of rule*, 703.4 *council*
Regency 43 Architectural Styles, 47.7 *furniture style*
regeneracy 629.1 *revival*
regenerate 201.20 *make new*, 220.8 *be transformed*, 627.1 *improve*, 629.5 *revive*, 867.6 *penitent*
regenerated 201.14 *renewed*, 220.13 *converted*
regenerating 220.14 *converting*
regeneration 201.5 *fresh start*, 220.2 *evolution*, 245.1 *reproduction*, 627.5 *improvement*, 629.10 *revival*
regenerative 246.5 *fertile*
regent 696.9 *educational leader*, 703.5 *commissioner*
regentship 703.4 *council*

Regent's Park 93.5 *London*
reggae 49.9 *popular music,*
49.10 *world music*
Reggiano 45 Cheeses
Reggio di Calabria 93 Cities
regicidal 713.10 *law-breaking*
regicide 398.3 *homicide,* 398.11
murderer, 693.2 *violation of the*
law, 713.2 *disorder*
regime 12.3 *governance,* 350.6
nutrition, 653.3 *management,*
688.8 *governmental organization*
regimen 12.3 *governance,* 350.6
nutrition, 630.13 *therapy,* 653.3
management
regiment 12.3 *governance,* 17.4
military organization, 112.10
conform, 140.3 *assembly,*
161.14 *force,* 679.16 *army unit,*
690.5 *be severe,* 695.6 *compel,*
701.6 *subject*
regimental colours 544.7 *flag*
regimental commander 17.5 *mili-*
tary staff
regimentals 295.3 *formal dress,*
544.5 *uniform,* 813.4 *formal*
dress
regimentation 110.6 *regularity,*
112.2 *conformity,* 690.1 *severity*
regimented 110.17 *regular,*
112.6 *conforming,* 690.8 *severe,*
694.7 *obedient*
Regina 93 Cities, 696.2 *sovereign*
Regiomontanus 52 Scientists
region 249, 12.5 *political organi-*
zation, 92.1 *administrative area,*
143.1 *part,* 248.3 *geographical*
space, 249.5 *state*
Region 249
regional 249, 5.39 *of language,*
16.48 *jurisdictional,* 248.12 *ex-*
tensive
regional accent 564.3 *mode of*
speech
regional boundary 249
regional climate 55.38 *climate*
regional council 16.2 *jurisdiction,*
653.8 *British administrative*
council
regional enteritis 624.8 *indiges-*
tion
regional forecast 55.4 *weather*
forecast
regionalism 50 Western Art
Styles and Movements, **249**
regionalist 50.29 *realist*
regionalization 141.2 *deconstruc-*
tion, 162.6 *decentralization*
regionalize 141.4 *deconstruct,*
162.15 *decentralize*
regionalized 162.26 *decentralized*
regional language 5.4 *parent lan-*
guage
regionally 16.86 *jurisdictionally,*
92.8 *administratively,* 249.19
geographically
regional metamorphism 54.32
metamorphism
regional novel 48.2 *fiction*
regional official 653.16 *official*
regional pronunciation 5.26 *dia-*
lect
regionism 5.26 *dialect*
regions 249
regions of Britain 249
regions of the US 249
regions of the world 249
register 545, 3.20 *chronicle,*
49.21 *tone,* 65.6 *memory,* 121.1
degree, 152.7 *catalogue,* 152.15
categorize, 171.1 *list,* 171.6 *list*
of names, 171.8 *list,* 257.5 *divi-*
sions, 257.9 *itemize,* 348.10 *in-*
troduce, 467.11 *take note of,*
522.4 *be intelligible,* 544.10
identify, 545.6 *record book,*
545.13 *record,* 547.9 *represent,*
750.5 *account book,* 750.7 *ac-*
count
registered 3.19 *chronicled,*
171.11 *listed,* 257.12 *itemized,*
534.34 *communicated,* 545.16
recorded, 750.11 *accounted*
registered blind 436.8 *blind*
Registered General Nurse 60.16
nurse

registered historic building 637.3
preserved thing
registered letter 534.3
correspondence
registered mail 534.2 *postal com-*
munication
Registered Nurse 60.16 *nurse*
registered voter 580.13 *electorate*
register one's vote 580.5 *vote*
registrar 60.11 *doctor,* 545.9 *re-*
corder
registration 545, 71.21 *miscella-*
neous motoring terms, 171.7 *list-*
ing, 348.3 *introduction*
registration document 71.21 *mis-*
cellaneous motoring terms,
545.2 *certificate*
registration number 71.21 *miscel-*
laneous motoring terms
registry 171.1 *list,* 545.6 *record*
book, 545.8 *registration*
registry office wedding 823.5
wedding
reglet 43 Architectural Decoration
regma 86.2 *botanical fruit*
regnal 12.10 *governing*
regnancy 12.3 *governance,* 688.7
type of rule
regnant 12.10 *governing,* 233.11
influential
Regnault's apparatus 56 Named
Laws
Regnault's method 57 Named
Reactions
regolith 54.36 *soil*
regrater 739.13 *retailer*
regress 74.9 *navigate,* 183.19 *re-*
turn to, 200.15 *look back,* 221.6
reverse, 324.13 *be in motion,*
328.3 *slow down,* 337.1 *go back-*
ward, 337.10 *backward motion,*
358.1 *fall short,* 628.1 *deterio-*
rate
regressed 221.11 *reversed*
regression 61.19 *defence mecha-*
nism, 129.1 *decrease,* 221.1 *re-*
version, 324.4, 337.10 *back-*
ward motion, 628.7 *deterioration*
regression analysis 13.3 *eco-*
nomic statistics, 52.55 *statisti-*
cal methods
regression neurosis 61.10 *neuro-*
sis
regression therapy 61.3 *psychiat-*
ric treatment
regressive 221, 129.7 *decres-*
cent, 324.17 *directional,* 337.23
receding, 628.12 *deteriorated*
regressively 221.13 *reversibly,*
324.18 *in motion*
regressive tax 751.7 *tax*
regressive taxation 13.6 *eco-*
nomic factors
regret 397.17 *bury,* 515.1 *disap-*
pointment, 515.4 *be disap-*
pointed, 687.9 *be in trouble,*
770.1 *sorrow,* 774.6 *lament,*
835.2 *condolence,* 835.5
misfortune, 866.2 *signs of guilt,*
867.1 *penitence,* 867.4 *be peni-*
tent
regretful 866.6 *appearing guilty,*
867.6 *penitent*
regretfully 573.17 *unwillingly,*
866.11 *guiltily,* 867.8 *penitently*
regretfulness 867.1 *penitence*
regret it 879.6 *be punished*
regretless 868.3 *impenitent*
regrets 515.1 *disappointment,*
840.2 *apology,* 867.1 *penitence*
regrettable 774.5 *lamentable*
regretted 397.19 *dead*
regretting 840.4 *atoning,* 867.1
penitence, 867.6 *penitent*
regroup 140.5 *combine*
regrouping 152.4 *rearrangement*
regular 110, 214, 5.44 *gram-*
matical, 17.9 *enlisted,* 52.79
spatial, 84.12 *of flowers,* 112.5
uniform, 116.13 *harmonious,*
116.15 *conventional,* 121.7 *gra-*
dational, 122.6 *equal,* 124.1
average, 150.14 *well-ordered,*
150.15 *habitual,* 164.21 *com-*
mon, 166.11 *uniform,* 183.14 *re-*
current, 187.8 *periodical,* 212.3

frequent, 214.14 *orderly,* 253.5
someone present, 253.8 *atten-*
dant, 259.14 *medium,* 308.5
even, 324.17 *directional,* 376.2
uniform, 395.9 *petroleum,*
490.6 *infallible,* 537.22 *uni-*
form, 584.8 *creature of habit,*
584.9 *habitual,* 679.8 *soldier*
regular army 679.15 *army*
regular customer 253.5 *someone*
present, 584.8 *creature of habit,*
738.12 *purchaser*
regular feature 528.4 *mass com-*
munication
regular features 308.3 *evenness*
regular forces 17.2 *the military*
regular guy 803.1 *plebeian*
regular income 749.3 *income*
regularity 110, 214, 112.1 *uni-*
formity, 116.4 *harmony,* 124.4
average, 150.7 *method,* 166.7
uniformity, 183.3 *repetitiveness,*
187.6 *periodicity,* 212.4 *fre-*
quency, 214.4 *orderliness,* 308.3
evenness, 376.7 *smoothness,*
490.17 *infallibility,* 537.9 *uni-*
formity, 584.1 *habit,* 719.1 *ob-*
servance
Regularity 214
regularize 110.8 *make the same,*
112.9 *be uniform,* 116.26 *make*
uniform, 124.10 *make average,*
150.20 *harmonize,* 187.11
make periodical, 214.11 *make*
regular, 308.6 *symmetrize,*
537.31 *be accurate,* 627.3 *rectify*
regularly 110, 214, 5.52 *gram-*
matically, 112.13 *uniformly,*
116.35 *consistently,* 121.9 *differ-*
entially, 122.13 *equitably,*
150.27 *methodically,* 187.12 *pe-*
riodically, 212.1 *frequently,*
214.17 *orderly,* 376.14
smoothly, 584.19 *habitually*
regular motion 353.2 *defecation*
regular movement 324
regular occurrence 212.4 *fre-*
quency, 214.1 *regularity*
regular petrol 395.9 *petroleum*
regular polygon 52.44 *polygon*
regular polyhedron 52.46 *polyhe-*
dron
regular practice 644.5 *exercise*
regular recurrence 214.1 *regular-*
ity, 219.1 *continuity*
regular return 214.2 *cycle*
regular thing 214
regulate 166, 110.8 *make the*
same, 112.9 *be uniform,*
116.24, 150.20 *harmonize,*
166.16 *direct,* 187.11 *make peri-*
odical, 214.10 *make regular,*
242.4 *moderate,* 485.15 *modify,*
653.1 *manage,* 692.9 *command,*
699.8 *restrain*
regulated 116.13 *harmonious,*
116.15 *conventional,* 124.1 *aver-*
age, 166.10 *customary,* 485.11
modified
regulated diet 350.6 *nutrition*
regulation 16.31 *legislation,*
124.1 *average,* 166.1 *rule,*
166.10 *customary,* 214.4 *orderli-*
ness, 242.1 *moderation,* 485.5
modification, 652.8 *treatment,*
653.3 *management,* 654.3 *pre-*
cept, 692.1 *command*
regulation by law 16.31 *legisla-*
tion
regulation by statute 16.31 *legis-*
lation
regulations 661.2 *obstacle,* 847.6
ethics
regulator gene 59.13 *genetic ma-*
terial
regulatory 15.8 *industrial,* 166.9
legal, 661.14 *blocked,* 692.14
commanding
Regulus 53 Named Stars
regurgitate 337.3 *reverse,* 349.15
vomit
regurgitation 337.12 *reversal,*
349.23 *vomiting*
rehabilitate 60.19 *practise medi-*
cine, 167.10 *assimilate,* 220.9
transform, 627.1 *improve,* 629.3
restore, 735.4 *give back,* 855.7

vindicate
rehabilitated 839.6 *forgiven,*
855.12 *innocent*
rehabilitating 839.4 *forgiving*
rehabilitation 60.8 *treatment,*
167.3 *pliancy,* 220.2 *evolution,*
627.5 *improvement,* 629.9 *resto-*
ration, 735.1 *giving back,* 839.3
absolution, 855.1 *vindication*
rehash 183.5 *repeat,* 183.20
renew, 216.8 *cause change,*
524.12 *translate*
rehashed 183.11 *reprinted*
rehearsal 479, 51.12 *production,*
183.1 *repetition,* 594.10 *prepara-*
tions
rehearse 51, 479, 183.16 *re-*
peat, 560.15 *recount,* 594.6
brief, 594.8 *prepare oneself*
reheat 45.55 *cook,* 183.20
renew, 408.14 *be hot*
reheated 183.11 *reprinted,*
408.13 *heated*
reheating 73.7 *miscellaneous avi-*
ation terms
rehoboam 258.14 *bottle*
Rehschnitzel 45.46 *German dish*
Reich 61.29 *psychologist*
Reichian 61.33 *Freudian*
Reichian psychology 61.1 *psy-*
chology
Reid 4 Philosophers
reify 99.20 *bring into being,*
101.11 *make real,* 367.8 *be ma-*
terial
reign 12.3 *governance,* 12.11 *gov-*
ern, 164.28 *prevail,* 166.8 *au-*
thority, 166.16 *direct,* 185.3 *du-*
ration, 233.3 *personal influence,*
688.4 *governance,* 688.18 *have*
authority
reigning 12.10 *governing,* 166.12
ruling, 233.11 *influential,*
688.12 *authoritative*
reigning champion 682.5 *victori-*
ous person
reign of terror 689.1 *anarchy,*
777.4 *intimidation,* 832.7 *act of*
malevolence
reign supreme 12.11 *govern,*
233.10 *be a prevailing influence,*
688.18 *have authority*
reimburse 125.4, 735.5 *compens-*
ate, 746.10 *pay back,* 840.5
atone
reimbursed 125.7 *compensated*
reimbursement 125.1, 735.2 *com-*
pensation, 746.2 *repayment,*
840.1 *atonement*
Reims 93 Cities
Reims Cathedral 43 Noted Buildings
rein 661.4 *restraint,* 661.10 *re-*
strain
reincarnate 367.8 *be material*
reincarnated 183.11 *reprinted,*
367.7 *material*
reincarnation 183.4 *return,* 245.1
reproduction, 367.2 *materializa-*
tion, 396.5 *life cycle,* 396.8 *theo-*
ries of life
reincarnationism 11.1 *occultism*
reindeer 77 Placental Mammals, 326.6 *beast of burden*
Reindeer 94 Lakes
reindeer moss 88.3 *moss,* 90.6 *li-*
chen
Reiner 53 Lunar Features
reinforce 671, 101.12 *establish*
reality, 128.5 *make bigger,*
130.7 *support,* 237.8 *strengthen,*
284.11 *support,* 373.9 *harden,*
535.19 *confirm,* 606.6 *replen-*
ish, 629.3 *restore,* 662.19 *sup-*
port
reinforced 130.8 *additional,*
237.13 *strengthened,* 373.3 *har-*
dened, 535.13 *supported,*
629.13 *repaired*
reinforced concrete 43.4 *building*
material, 63.25 *construction ma-*
terial, 74.4 *shipbuilding,* 373.7
hard substance, 604.2 *building*
material
reinforced glass 442.9 *glass*
reinforced plastic 63.25 *construc-*
tion material

275.5 *height measure,* 293.21 *substitution,* 293.40 *substitutive,* 299.2 *shadow,* 306.1 *form,* 370.6 *lightening,* 457.3 *external appearance,* 629.11 *recuperation,* 630.1 *remedy,* 638.1 *escape,* 639.2 *deliverance,* 645.2 *time off,* 651.5 *refreshment,* 662.2 *support,* 662.4 *social assistance,* 700.1 *liberation,* 729.2 *gift,* 767.4 *charity,* 831.4 *benevolent act,* 833.5 *charity,* 835.3 *mercy*
Relief 767
relief-carving 50
relief map 299.4, 547.7 *map*
relief pitcher 22.2 *baseball player*
relief printing 47.8 *woodwork*
relief worker 707.1 *deputy*
relieve 767, 60.19 *practise medicine,* 131.3 *subtract,* 155.22 *succeed,* 222.4 *be a substitute,* 242.4 *moderate,* 293.34 *cover for,* 370.10 *lighten,* 405.10 *comfort,* 630.19 *remedy,* 639.1 *deliver,* 649.3 *ease,* 651.1 *refresh,* 662.19 *support,* 700.4 *liberate,* 831.8 *be benevolent*
relieved 767, 638.8 *escaping*
relieve from duty 767
relieve one of 736.12 *steal*
relieve oneself 767, 353.15 *excrete*
reliever 767
relieving 767, 62.16 *soothing,* 370.3 *lightening,* 651.3 *refreshing*
relievo 50.13 *relief-carving,* 767.6 *profile*
religion 7, 163.8 *genealogy,* 368.2 *unworldliness,* 497.2 *religious belief,* 584.4 *custom*
Religion 7
religionist 7
religiose 540.27 *hypocritical*
religiosity 7.2 *religiousness,* 540.3 *hypocrisy*
religious 7, 2.12 *sociological,* 7.3 *religious person,* 7.7 *monk,* 7.18 *theological,* 10.22 *worshipping,* 368.8 *nonmaterial,* 719.7 *observant,* 857.5 *pure*
religious architecture 43.1 *architecture*
religious belief 497
religious believer 368.7 *believer in a nonmaterial world*
religious broadcasting 534.25 *broadcast material*
religious celibate 134.5 *pure person,* 825.4 *celibate person,* 876.5 *pure person*
religious ceremony 813.3 *formal occasion*
religious cleansing 621
religious conversion 220.3 *persuasion*
religious disobedience 693.1 *disobedience*
religious ecstasy 61.14 *trance*
religious education 7.13 *theology*
religious fasting 871.1 *fasting*
religious feeling 497.2 *religious belief*
religious festival 10
religious group 7.1 *religion*
religious history 3.1 *history*
religious institution 2.8 *human institution*
religious instruction 7.13 *theology*
religious leader 696
religiously 7, 2.16 *sociologically,* 368.13 *metaphysically,* 719.8 *observantly,* 857.8 *purely*
religious mania 510.4 *delusion*
religious manual 10
religious movement 7.1 *religion*
religiousness 7
religious observance 719, 10.1 *ritual,* 584.4 *custom*
religious organization 2.4 *social organization*
religious painter 50.16 *artist*
religious persecution 481.4 *social discrimination*
religious person 7
religious practice 10.1 *ritual*

religious rite 389.15 *holy water*
religious sacrifice 398.6 *ritual killing*
religious sin 864
religious studies 7.13 *theology*
religious symbol 543.1 *sign*
religious teacher 524.6 *interpreter*
religious text 7
religious war 676.1 *war*
reline 629.1 *repair*
relinquish 598, 136.13 *diverge,* 218.6 *cease,* 345.2 *withdraw,* 536.9 *renounce,* 600.6 *stop using,* 673.3 *submit,* 705.5 *resign,* 722.9 *lose,* 727.9 *dispose of,* 869.5 *be self-restrained*
relinquish authority 708.4 *be permissive*
relinquish control 600.7 *stop work*
relinquished 598, 536.12 *rejected,* 711.10 *abnegating,* 727.12 *disposed ,* 869.8 *self-restrained*
relinquisher 705.3 *resigner*
relinquishing 711.10 *abnegating*
relinquishment 598, 218.1 *cessation,* 536.4 *renunciation,* 673.1 *submission,* 705.1 *resignation,* 711.3 *abnegation,* 727.1 *disposal,* 869.1 *self-restraint*
Relinquishment 598
relinquish one's life 397.16 *meet one's fate*
reliquary 10.13 *shrine*
relish 350.23 *taste,* 405.8 *feel pleasure,* 411.4 *flavour,* 411.9 *taste,* 413.2 *seasoning,* 762.6 *enjoy,* 763.14 *like,* 784.3 *likes,* 784.7 *like,* 821.23 *love*
relishable 411.7 *tasty*
relishing 350.3 *delicate eating*
relive 200.15 *look back*
reload 606.6 *replenish*
relocate 216.7 *be changed,* 250.10 *settle,* 252.14 *displace,* 326.15 *take away,* 345.3 *quit*
relocated 252.8 *displaced,* 252.10 *replaced*
relocation 216.1 *change,* 252.1 *displacement,* 252.3 *replacement,* 326.1 *transfer*
reluctance 328.12 *hesitation,* 573.11 *unwillingness,* 591.12 *shyness,* 669.1 *resistance,* 781.1 *caution,* 785.1 *dislike,* 810.6 *reserve*
reluctant 573, 328.6 *hesitant,* 573.1 *unwilling,* 587.10 *dissuaded,* 591.18 *avoiding,* 669.10 *resistant,* 781.4 *cautious,* 785.8 *disliking,* 810.13 *reserved*
reluctantly 328.16 *slowly,* 573.17 *unwillingly,* 591.23 *shyly,* 669.14 *resistingly,* 781.7 *cautiously,* 785.10 *discontentedly*
reluctant person 573
rely on 490.20 *be certain,* 497.7 *believe,* 599.4 *resort to,* 775.6 *hope*
rely on supposition 518.5 *suppose*
remade 183.11 *reprinted,* 201.14 *renewed,* 629.13 *repaired*
remain 99.19 *continue to be,* 132.7 *be left,* 188.6 *last,* 219.4 *protract,* 325.8 *be motionless,* 575.9 *endure*
remain at a distance 263.6 *keep away*
remain at anchor 325.8 *be motionless*
remain at rest 217.5 *be permanent*
remain a virgin 825.10 *be continent,* 876.11 *be moral*
remain celibate 876.11 *be moral*
remainder 132, 3.11 *relic,* 52.18 *division,* 143.1 *part,* 169.4 *mathematical result,* 200.7 *thing of the past,* 227.1 *effect,* 478.7 *numerical result,* 600.11 *unused thing,* 610.3 *superfluity,* 725.2 *legal terms,* 739.1 *sell*
Remainder 132
remaindered 600.3 *not wanted*
remainder theorem 52 *Theorems and Laws*

remain fixed 225.6 *be stable*
remain forever 190.5 *be eternal*
remain good-humoured 817.10 *be courteous*
remaining 132, 3.15 *historic,* 600.3 *not wanted,* 610.7 *superfluous,* 727.15 *unclaimed*
remain in situ 325.8 *be motionless*
remain intransigent 373.11 *be stubborn*
remain neutral 482.12 *be fair,* 698.16 *be independent*
remain neutral about 783.15 *be impartial*
remain obstinate 868.5 *be impenitent*
remain on one's best behaviour 817.11 *have good manners*
remain on one's hands 610.5 *be superfluous*
remain pure 876.11 *be moral*
remain raw 307.3 *make shapeless*
remains 3.11 *relic,* 127.7 *inferior thing,* 132.1 *remainder,* 200.7 *thing of the past,* 397.11 *dead person,* 483.4 *indication,* 545.12 *vestige,* 600.11 *unused thing*
remain sceptical 720.7 *not observe*
remain seated 325.8 *be motionless,* 850.22 *show disrespect*
remain steadfast 112.9 *be uniform*
remain the same 217.5 *be permanent*
remain unchanged 112.12 *be monotonous,* 217.5 *be permanent*
remain unmarried 825.9 *be celibate*
remain unmoved 783.12 *be indifferent*
remain unrepentant 868.5 *be impenitent*
remain unsolved 523.10 *be unexplained*
remake 183.5 *repeat,* 183.20 *renew,* 201.5 *fresh start,* 201.20 *make new,* 221.7, 629.3 *restore*
remand 209.3 *delayed action,* 209.8 *delay,* 699.4 *detention,* 699.11 *detain*
remanded 209.10 *held up*
remanence 56.63 *magnetic phenomenon*
remark 492.1 *judgment,* 505.3 *aphorize,* 564.7 *utterance*
remarkable 165.17 *exceptional,* 437.2 *clear,* 611.6 *notable,* 786.8 *wonderful*
remarkably 165.30 *characteristically,* 611.9 *importantly,* 786.13 *wonderfully*
Remarque 48 Writers
remarriage 823.3 *types of marriage*
remarried 823.21 *married*
remarry 823.15 *marry*
remediably 125.11 *in compensation*
remedial 630, 6.16 *educational,* 60.25 *therapeutic,* 125.9 *compensatory,* 231.4 *counteracting,* 478.14 *solved,* 625.4 *hygienic,* 627.16 *improving,* 629.16 *restorative,* 662.34 *beneficial,* 767.8 *relieving*
remedial education 6.2 *educational system*
remedially 630, 6.25 *educationally,* 125.11 *in compensation,* 231.5 *counter,* 478.26 *correspondingly,* 627.17 *better,* 629.17 *repairably*
remedial measure 630.1 *remedy*
remedied 125.7 *compensated*
remedy 630, 125.1 *compensation,* 125.4 *compensate,* 231.1 *counteraction,* 231.2 *counteracting thing,* 478.6 *solution,* 478.20 *solve,* 592.3 *expedient plan,* 602.1 *means,* 627.3 *rectify,* 627.5 *improvement,* 629.1 *repair,* 629.8 *repair,* 629.11 *recuperation,* 630.2 *medicine,* 654.3 *precept,* 662.2 *support,* 662.5 *medical assistance,* 662.19 *support,*

767.3 *reliever*
Remedy 630
remember 3, 511, 726, 183.19 *return to,* 200.15 *look back,* 471.14 *have an idea,* 511.11 *memorize,* 511.14 *commemorate,* 522.6 *understand,* 696.15 *learn,* 812.16 *commemorate,* 831.8 *be benevolent*
remembered 511.7 *memorable*
remember forever 190.6 *make eternal*
remembering 511, 3.13 *looking back,* 200.21 *retrospective,* 511.1 *memory*
remember wrongly 512.14 *be forgetful*
remembrance 3.13 *looking back,* 132.1 *remainder,* 190.4 *eternalization,* 200.2 *retrospection,* 511.1 *memory,* 726.5 *retentiveness,* 812.2 *commemoration*
remembrancer 654.4 *adviser*
remembrance service 812.2 *commemoration*
Remembrance Sunday 214.6 *annually celebrated day,* 812.5 *anniversary*
remex 78.17 *plumage*
remigrate 337.5 *turn back*
remigrating 337.27 *returning*
remigration 345.7 *departure*
remind 511, 636.5 *warn*
reminder 511, 132.1 *remainder,* 528.7 *advice,* 545.1 *record,* 611.2 *important matter,* 654.4 *adviser*
reminding 511.7 *memorable*
remind oneself 511.13 *remind*
Remington 52 Scientists
reminisce 3.22 *remember,* 200.15, 337.8 *look back,* 511.12 *remember,* 560.15 *recount*
reminiscence 3.13 *looking back,* 200.2 *retrospection,* 337.15 *looking back,* 511.1 *memory,* 560.3 *narration*
reminiscence therapy 61.3 *psychiatric treatment*
reminiscent 511.7 *memorable*
reminiscently 3.25 *reportedly,* 511.16 *memorably*
reminiscing 200.21 *retrospective,* 337.15 *looking back*
remise 28.3 *fencing movements*
remiss 468.10 *careless,* 470.4 *negligent,* 573.4 *procrastinating,* 720.11 *nonobservant*
remissible 855.13 *vindicable*
remission 131.2 *subtracted item,* 242.1 *moderation,* 767.1 *ease,* 839.1 *forgiveness,* 855.1 *vindication*
remission of sin 839.1 *forgiveness*
remissive 720.11 *nonobservant,* 855.11 *vindicatory*
remissively 855.15 *in vindication*
remissness 470.1 *negligence,* 573.15 *delay,* 720.1 *nonobservance*
remit 125.4 *compensate,* 242.3 *be moderate,* 326.12 *transport,* 746.6 *pay,* 839.10 *absolve,* 855.7 *vindicate*
remittable 125.8 *compensable,* 746.17 *payable*
remittal 125.1 *compensation,* 855.1 *vindication*
remittance 125.1 *compensation,* 741.6 *funds,* 746.1 *payment*
remittance man 347.8 *outgoer*
remitted 125.7 *compensated,* 839.6 *forgiven*
remitter 125.3 *compensator*
remit the penalty 16.78 *acquit*
remnant 132.1 *remainder*
remnants 132.2 *residue*
remodel 216.8 *cause change,* 220.9 *transform,* 627.3 *rectify,* 629.2 *refurbish*
remodelled 216.12 *changed*
remodelling 216.1 *change,* 629.9 *restoration*
remonstrance 587.6 *dissuasion*
remonstrate 473.13 *argue,* 587.1 *dissuade,* 636.5 *warn,* 663.15

object, 852.16 *disagree*
remonstration 663.2 *objection,* 766.2 *expression of dissatisfaction*
remora 80 *Fishes,* 138.4 *adherent*
remorse 835.2 *condolence,* 840.2 *apology,* 866.2 *signs of guilt,* 867.1 *penitence*
remorseful 866.6 *appearing guilty,* 867.6 *penitent*
remorsefully 866.11 *guiltily,* 867.8 *penitently*
remorsefulness 867.1 *penitence*
remorseless 836.4 *pitiless,* 868.3 *impenitent*
remorselessly 836.7 *pitilessly,* 868.6 *impenitently*
remorselessness 836.1 *pitilessness,* 868.1 *impenitence*
remorsing 867.6 *penitent*
remortgage 744.1 *credit,* 745.3 *loan*
remote 108.7 *illogical,* 263.8 *distant,* 438.2 *difficult to see,* 441.6 *murky,* 489.1 *improbable,* 616.2 *distant,* 816.8 *unsociable,* 816.11 *secluded*
remote age 3.9 *distant past*
remote ages 200.1 *past time*
remote chance 229.2 *chance*
remote control 534.22 *television set,* 653.5 *guide*
remotely 263.10 *distantly,* 816.14 *unsocially*
remoteness 263.1 *distance,* 438.6 *that which makes invisible,* 441.2 *murk,* 616.4 *distance,* 816.1 *unsociability*
remote possibility 486, 489.4 *improbability*
remote sensing 56.95 *mensuration*
remould 216.8 *cause change,* 627.3 *rectify*
remoulded 216.12 *changed*
remoulding 216.1 *change*
remount 32.3 *warhorse,* 222.3 *substitute thing*
removable 131.6 *subtractive,* 326.17 *transferable,* 355.18 *extractive*
removably 131.9 *decreasingly,* 355.21 *away*
removal 252, 349, 131.1 *subtraction,* 136.2 *setting apart,* 147.2 *ejection,* 252.1 *displacement,* 252.3 *replacement,* 263.1 *distance,* 326.1 *transfer,* 349.20 *eviction,* 355.1 *extraction,* 546.3 *obliteration,* 704.1 *cancellation,* 704.2 *termination,* 727.1 *disposal,* 734.3 *taking away*
removal of the body 399.7 *inquest*
removal van 71 *Motor Vehicles,* 258.10 *cart*
remove 252, 294, 45.9 *dish,* 70.4 *transport,* 104.15 *separate,* 121.3 *gradation,* 131.3 *subtract,* 136.10 *set apart,* 147.8 *eject,* 248.8 *intervening space,* 296.14 *undress,* 324.15 *walk,* 326.15 *take away,* 345.3 *quit,* 349.8 *evict,* 349.11 *void,* 350.14 *mouthful,* 355.11 *extract,* 458.3 *cause to disappear,* 546.1 *obliterate,* 704.6 *cancel,* 704.7 *terminate,* 734.10 *take away*
remove all doubt 475.17 *prove*
remove all obstacles 708.3 *permit*
remove all signs of 704.6 *cancel*
remove any trace 546.1 *obliterate*
remove authority from 236.7 *remove power from*
removed 252, 104.11 *separate,* 108.6 *unrelated,* 131.5 *subtracted,* 252.8 *displaced,* 252.10 *replaced,* 265.6 *spaced,* 816.8 *unsociable*
removed from the record 839.8 *overlooked*
remove doubt 480.1 *verify*
remove errors 627.3 *rectify*
remove friction 376.11 *smooth*
removement 326.1 *transfer*
remove one's name from 598.2 *withdraw*

remove power from 236
remover 734.6 *taker*
remove the dirt 621.13 *clean*
remunerate 746, 125.4 *compensate,* 878.9 *reward,* 878.11 *pay*
remunerated 125.7 *compensated*
remuneration 125.1 *compensation,* 721.4 *earnings,* 746.3 *pay,* 749.3 *income,* 878.1 *reward,* 878.4 *reward for service*
remunerative 243.11 *productive,* 246.5 *fertile,* 613.4 *profitable,* 682.14 *rewarding,* 721.15 *gainful,* 746.18 *profitable,* 878.15 *rewarding*
remuneratively 243.13 *productively,* 721.20 *gainfully,* 749.8, 878.20 *profitably*
remunerativeness 721.1 *gain*
renaissance 183.4 *return,* 396.5 *life cycle,* 629.10 *revival,* 704.3 *new beginning*
Renaissance 43 Architectural Styles, 3.10 *past age,* 3.15 *historic,* 50.29 *realist,* 200.5 *historical period*
Renaissance art 50 Western Art Styles and Movements
Renaissance humanism 48 Literary Groups and Movements
Renaissance man 175.5 *pluralist,* 655.4 *skilled person*
Renaissance perspective 50.4 *treatment*
Renaissance tragedy 51.9 *tragedy*
renal 290.10 *visceral*
renal graft 630.12 *surgery*
renascent 245.15 *reproduced,* 629.13 *repaired*
rend 116.30 *grant,* 136.9 *separate,* 265.5 *crack,* 350.21 *eat*
rend asunder 244.9 *demolish*
render 537, 49.36 *play,* 116.30 *grant,* 220.9 *transform,* 293.28 *face,* 355.17 *obtain an extract,* 387.24 *melt,* 524.8 *interpret,* 524.12 *translate,* 547.9 *represent,* 729.5 *give*
render assistance 833.7 *be charitable*
render averse 587.4 *put off*
rendered 116.19 *granted,* 524.15 *interpreted*
rendered infertile 247
render faithfully 537.34 *render*
render good 735.5 *compensate*
render hard 373.9 *harden*
render harmless 614.8 *make useless*
render incorrectly 525.1 *misinterpret*
rendering 5.12 *translation,* 5.40 *translated,* 43.1 *architecture,* 293.8 *wall covering,* 355.7 *obtaining an extract,* 524.1 *interpretation,* 524.4 *translation,* 547.1 *representation*
render insensible 404.12 *anaesthetize*
render insensitive 761
render lip service 540.18 *be hypocritical*
render necessary 593.10 *necessitate*
render soft 374.13 *soften*
render thanks 837.6 *be grateful*
render unconscious 404.12 *anaesthetize*
render unfit 614.8 *make useless*
rendezvous 161, 53.35 *rocketry,* 135.1 *union,* 135.6 *point of union,* 161.39 *come together,* 344.8 *meet,* 344.14, 815.3 *meeting*
rendition 355.7 *obtaining an extract,* 524.1 *interpretation*
rend the eardrums 423.8 *be loud*
rend the skies 423.8 *be loud*
renegade 168.8 *dissenter,* 168.12 *nonconformist,* 220.6 *convert,* 335.19 *deviant person,* 484.4 *tergiversator,* 578.9 *equivocator,* 591.17 *avoider,* 864.9 *wicked person*
renege 220.10 *be converted,* 221.6, 484.8 *reverse,* 578.4 *re-*

cant, 704.6 *cancel*
reneged 484.6 *countered*
renege on 720.7 *not observe*
reneger 578.9 *equivocator,* 704.5 *abrogator*
reneging 484.2 *reversal,* 704.1 *cancellation*
renew 183, 201.20 *make new,* 216.8 *cause change,* 627.1 *improve,* 629.2 *refurbish,* 629.5 *revive,* 651.1 *refresh*
renewable 201
renewable energy 410, 56.11 *energy*
renewable energy source 235.6 *source of energy,* 410.1 *fuel*
renewable gas-guzzling 410.10 *powered*
renewal 183.4 *return,* 201.5 *fresh start,* 216.1 *change,* 245.1 *reproduction,* 627.5 *improvement,* 629.8 *repair,* 629.10 *revival,* 651.5 *refreshment*
renewed 201, 183.11 *reprinted,* 216.12 *changed,* 245.15 *reproduced,* 575.11 *steady,* 629.13 *repaired*
renewing 245.15 *reproduced*
renew one's efforts 575.6 *persevere*
renew oneself 201.17 *become new,* 651.2 *be refreshed*
renitency 573.12 *opposition,* 669.1 *resistance*
renitent 669.10 *resistant*
rennet 371.5 *condenser,* 393.11 *thickener*
Rennie 52 Scientists
rennin 58.11 *enzyme*
Reno 93 Cities
renounce 536, 476.9 *deny,* 484.8 *reverse,* 578.4 *recant,* 581.2 *discard,* 598.1 *relinquish,* 704.6 *cancel,* 711.7 *refuse oneself,* 713.6 *protest,* 727.9 *dispose of,* 869.5 *be self-restrained*
renounce authority 673.3 *submit*
renounced 484.6 *countered,* 536.12 *rejected*
renounce drinking 869.5 *be self-restrained*
renouncement 705.1 *resignation*
renouncer 705.3 *resigner*
renounce the throne 705.5 *resign*
renouncing 476.7 *refuting*
renovate 201.20 *make new,* 627.1 *improve,* 629.2 *refurbish,* 651.1 *refresh*
renovated 201.14 *renewed,* 627.14 *improved,* 629.13 *repaired*
renovation 201.5 *fresh start,* 245.1 *reproduction,* 627.5 *improvement,* 629.8 *repair,* 651.5 *refreshment*
renovator 629.12 *repairer*
renown 532.7 *publicity,* 682.13 *successful,* 804.1 *right*
renowned 501.10 *known,* 532.20 *well-known,* 800.3 *reputable,* 804.5 *entitled*
Renpet 8 Deities
rent 136.3 *separateness,* 136.16 *apart,* 255.14 *inhabit,* 265.2 *crack,* 265.7 *cracked,* 723.7 *possess,* 728.3 *transfer property,* 749.2 *money received,* 751.3 *fee*
rental 728.1 *transfer of property,* 751.3 *fee*
rental contract 715.2 *purchase contract*
rent arrears 687.2 *economic adversity*
rent boy 401.7 *libertine,* 877.8 *immoral man*
rent collector 161.35, 730.7 *collector*
rented 255.11 *inhabited*
renter 255.3 *householder,* 728.2 *person transferring property*
rent-free 754.11 *free of charge*
rent-payer 255.3 *possessor*
rent-roll 725.1 *property,* 749.2 *money received*
renunciate 536.7 *be negative,* 705.5 *resign,* 711.6 *dissent*

renunciation 536, 476.2 *denial,* 484.2 *reversal,* 536.2 *rejection,* 578.8 *recantation,* 598.3 *relinquishment,* 705.1 *resignation,* 711.2 *dissent,* 713.1 *protest,* 727.1 *disposal,* 869.1 *self-restraint*
renunciation of wealth 743
renunciative 536.11 *negative,* 711.9 *dissenting,* 869.8 *self-restrained*
renunciatory 536.11 *negative,* 705.7 *resigning,* 711.9 *dissenting*
renvers 32.10 *dressage*
reoccur 183.21 *be repeated,* 212.7 *be frequent,* 214.7 *be regular*
reoccur constantly 214.7 *be regular*
reoccurring 183.14 *recurrent*
reorder 152.14 *rearrange,* 216.8 *cause change*
reordered 152.23 *rearranged,* 216.12 *changed*
reordering 152.4 *rearrangement,* 216.1 *change*
reorganization 152.4 *rearrangement,* 201.5 *fresh start,* 216.1 *change,* 220.1 *conversion,* 627.6 *rectification,* 629.7 *restoration*
reorganize 152.14 *rearrange,* 201.20 *make new,* 216.7 *be changed,* 216.8 *cause change,* 220.9 *transform,* 627.3 *rectify,* 629.3 *restore*
reorganized 152.23 *rearranged,* 201.14 *renewed,* 216.12 *changed*
reorient 629.3 *restore*
reorientation 61.20 *conditioning,* 629.9 *restoration*
rep 67 Natural Fabrics, 32.15 *horse person,* 51.1 *drama,* 51.13 *engagement,* 564.10 *speaker,* 646.3 *agent,* 678.4 *representative,* 739.10 *salesman*
repaid 125.7 *compensated*
repaint 201.20 *make new,* 629.2 *refurbish*
repainted 201.14 *renewed*
repainting 201.5 *fresh start*
repair 629, 629, 105.1 *state,* 216.1 *change,* 216.8 *cause change,* 627.1 *improve,* 627.3 *rectify,* 627.5 *improvement,* 627.6 *rectification,* 651.1 *refresh,* 651.5 *refreshment,* 840.5 *atone,* 843.15 *put right*
Repair 629
repairable 629
repairably 629
repaired 629, 216.12 *changed,* 627.14 *improved*
repairer 629, 627.13 *reviser*
repairing 216.1 *change*
repairman 629.12 *repairer,* 646.2 *artisan*
repairs 629.8 *repair*
repair ship 679.24 *warship*
repaper 629.2 *refurbish*
reparable 629.14 *repairable*
reparably 629.17 *repairably*
reparation 765, 125.1 *compensation,* 629.8 *repair,* 629.9 *restoration,* 672.1 *retaliation,* 677.2 *peace offering,* 735.2 *compensation,* 840.1 *atonement,* 862.1 *type of penance,* 878.6 *compensation*
reparations 629.9 *restoration*
reparative 125.9 *compensatory,* 629.16 *restorative,* 735.6 *restoring,* 840.4 *atoning*
reparatory 125.9 *compensatory,* 735.6 *restoring,* 840.4 *atoning,* 878.17 *compensatory*
repartee 223.1 *exchange,* 478.1 *answer,* 568.2 *chat,* 771.3 *wit*
repast 350.12 *meal*
repatriate 349.4 *ostracize,* 629.3 *restore,* 735.4 *give back*
repatriation 349.19 *ostracism,* 629.9 *restoration,* 735.1 *giving back*
repay 125.4 *compensate,* 664.12 *reciprocate,* 672.3 *retaliate,* 735.5 *compensate,* 746.10 *pay back,* 840.5 *atone,* 878.11 *pay*

repayable 733.11 *borrowed*
repayable amount 733.5 *loan*
repaying 840.4 *atoning*
repayment **746,** 125.1 *compensation,* 672.1 *retaliation,* 735.2 *compensation,* 840.1 *atonement,* 879.9 *retribution*
repayment plan 733.1 *borrowing*
repay with interest 128.5 *make bigger*
repeal 536.4 *renunciation,* 536.9 *renounce,* 704.1 *cancellation,* 704.6 *cancel,* 709.3 *veto*
repealed 536.12 *rejected,* 704.10 *cancelled*
repealer 536.6 *negativist*
repealing 704.1 *cancellation,* 709.1 *veto*
repeat **183, 183, 426,** 110.7 *be the same,* 110.11 *be regular,* 112.9 *be uniform,* 112.12 *be monotonous,* 119.9 *imitate,* 176.12, 176.15 *double,* 183.17 *iterate,* 187.10 *be periodical,* 214.7 *be regular,* 219.3 *continue,* 245.9 *reproduce,* 457.6 *reappearance,* 520.10 *mean,* 522.5 *simplify,* 534.25 *broadcast material,* 534.30 *communicate,* 553.5 *be diffuse,* 554.6 *emphasize,* 560.15 *recount,* 575.6 *persevere,* 788.6 *be boring*
repeatable 876.10 *moralistic*
repeated **183,** 110.12 *same,* 176.12 *double,* 212.3 *frequent,* 245.15 *reproduced,* 426.15 *drumming,* 457.7 *appearing,* 520.6 *meaningful,* 534.34 *communicated,* 553.3 *diffuse,* 575.11 *steady,* 788.4 *boring*
repeated decimal 52.18 *division*
repeated efforts 575.2 *commitment*
repeatedly **183, 245, 426,** 187.12 *periodically,* 212.1 *frequently,* 214.15 *regularly,* 219.7, 575.14 *continually,* 788.8 *boringly*
Repeated Sound 426
repeated word 426
repeater **191** Timepieces and Timers, 192.7 *watch,* 680.9 *firearm*
repeating 183.1 *repetition,* 183.2 *iteration,* 183.12 *repetitious,* 214.11 *regular,* 426.18 *pealing*
repeating rifle 680.9 *firearm*
repeat itself 212.7 *be frequent*
repeat old wives' tales 538.21 *lie*
repeat oneself 183.17 *iterate,* 212.7 *be frequent,* 553.5 *be diffuse,* 788.6 *be boring*
repeat order 183.5 *repeat*
repeat performance 183.5 *repeat*
repeat wrongly 525.1 *misinterpret*
repel **341,** 233.9 *change,* 341.4 *be repulsive,* 581.1 *reject,* 587.4 *put off,* 669.6 *resist,* 671.26 *act on the determined,* 711.5 *refuse,* 764.10 *displease,* 785.7, 785.7 *cause dislike,* 816.13 *ignore,* 822.16 *cause hate*
repelled 785.8 *disliking*
repellence 341.5 *repulsion,* 669.1 *resistance*
repellency 341.5 *repulsion*
repellent 341.8 *repulsive,* 669.10 *resistant*
repellently 341.11 *repulsively,* 669.14 *resistingly*
repellent quality 341.5 *repulsion*
repeller 669.5 *resister*
repelling 341.5 *repulsion*
repelling 341.9 *abducent*
repelling 669.10 *resistant,* 822.12 *hated*
repent 7.19 *be religious,* 221.9 *reply,* 484.8 *reverse,* 840.6 *apologize,* 867.4 *be penitent*
repentance 221.1 *reversion,* 484.2 *reversal,* 840.2 *apology,* 867.1 *penitence*
repentant 840.4 *atoning,* 867 6 *penitent*
repentantly 840.8, 867.8 *penitently*
repenter 840.3 *atoner*

repenting 867.6 *penitent*
repent in sackcloth and ashes 867.5 *do penance*
repercussion 159, 227.1 *effect,* 231.1 *counteraction,* 331.4 *recoil,* 331.6 *response,* 478.4 *reaction*
repercussive **159,** 331.8 *recoiling,* 478.12 *reactive*
repertoire 605.3 *supply,* 605.5 *collection,* 739.8 *merchandise*
repertory 51.1 *drama,* 171.1 *list,* 605.5 *collection*
repertory circuit 51.13 *engagement*
repertory company 51.23 *cast*
repertory player 51.22 *actor*
repertory show 51.5 *show*
repetiteur 49.24 *musician,* 180.6 *accompanier*
repetition 110.8, 48.12 *poetic language,* 110.1 *sameness,* 110.6 *regularity,* 112.1 *uniformity,* 112.4 *monotony,* 118.1 *imitation,* 176.4 *doubling,* 183.3 *repetitiveness,* 183.5 *repeat,* 187.6 *periodicity,* 212.4 *frequency,* 214.1 *regularity,* 219.1 *continuity,* 245.1 *reproduction,* 553.1 *diffuseness,* 554.1 *emphasis,* 575.3 *constancy,* 788.1 *boredom*
Repetition 183
repetitional 183.12 *repetitious*
repetitious **183,** 110.12 *same,* 110.17 *regular,* 112.5 *uniform,* 112.8 *monotonous,* 187.8 *periodical,* 212.3 *frequent,* 788.4 *boring*
repetitiously 110.18 *identically,* 112.13 *uniformly,* 183.23 *repeatedly,* 187.12 *periodically,* 214.15 *regularly,* 788.8 *boringly*
repetitiousness 183.3 *repetitiveness,* 788.1 *boredom*
repetitive 110.12 *same,* 110.17 *regular,* 112.8 *monotonous,* 159.12 *cyclical,* 183.12 *repetitious,* 185.22 *periodic,* 187.8 *periodical,* 212.3 *frequent,* 214.11 *regular,* 219.5 *continual,* 426.16 *humming,* 553.3 *diffuse,* 554.3 *emphatic,* 788.4 *boring*
repetitive job 584.3 *way*
repetitively 110.18 *identically,* 110.20 *regularly,* 112.13 *uniformly,* 183.23 *repeatedly,* 187.12 *periodically,* 212.1 *frequently,* 219.7 *continually,* 426.19 *regularly,* 553.7 *diffusely,* 788.8 *boringly*
repetitiveness **183,** 187.6 *periodicity,* 214.1 *regularity,* 553.2 *diffuseness,* 564.2 *power of speech,* 788.1 *boredom*
rephrase 5.47 *word,* 520.10 *mean,* 524.12 *translate*
replace 252, 125.4 *compensate,* 155.22 *succeed,* 195.11 *follow in office,* 216.10 *exchange,* 222.4 *be a substitute,* 293.34 *cover for,* 349.5 *take the place of,* 478.23 *answer for,* 547.12 *stand for,* 600.6 *stop using,* 629.3 *restore,* 707.4 *substitute for,* 716.7 *act as a go-between,* 727.9 *dispose of,* 735.4 *give back,* 767.11 *assist*
replaceable 216.14 *exchangeable*
replaced 252, 125.7 *compensated,* 222.8 *substituted*
replacement 155, 252, 125.1 *compensation,* 195.5 *successor,* 216.4 *exchange,* 222.1 *substitution,* 222.2 *substitute person,* 222.7 *substitute,* 293.21 *substitution,* 547.8 *representative,* 629.9 *restoration,* 707.2 *alternative,* 735.1 *giving back,* 767.5 *helper*
replacements 679.14 *armed forces*
replacer 224.4 *editor*
replant 629.3 *restore*
replanting 629.9 *restoration*
replay 183.5 *repeat,* 183.20 *renew*
replayed 183.11 *reprinted*
replaying 183.5 *repeat*

replenish **606,** 144.6 *fill,* 605.6 *store,* 608.4 *suffice,* 629.3 *restore*
replenished 144.8 *full*
replenishment 144.2 *fullness,* 606.1 *provision,* 629.9 *restoration*
replete 144.8 *full,* 608.3 *filled,* 610.6 *excessive*
replete with meaning 520.6 *meaningful*
repletion 144.2 *fullness,* 608.7 *sufficiency*
repleviable 125.8 *compensable*
replevin 125.1 *compensation*
replevy 125.4 *compensate*
replica **183,** 110.4 *duplicate,* 118.2 *copy,* 118.5 *duplicate,* 245.2 *print,* 457.5 *impression,* 547.1 *representation,* 547.6 *image*
replicate 110.9 *duplicate,* 114.12 *imitate,* 118.10 *copy,* 175.9 *pluralize,* 176.15 *double,* 183.16 *repeat,* 245.9 *reproduce*
replicated 110.15 *duplicate,* 114.8 *simulated,* 183.9 *repeated*
replication 110.4 *duplicate,* 183.1 *repetition,* 245.1 *reproduction,* 478.1 *answer*
replied 221.11 *reversed*
replier 478.10 *answerer*
reply **221, 221,** 331.2 *respond,* 331.6 *response,* 476.3, 476.10 *countercharge,* 478.1, 478.17 *answer,* 534.31 *correspond,* 564.7 *utterance,* 564.11 *speak*
reply for the defence 855.2 *defence*
replying 478.11 *answering*
report **533,** 3.5, 3.20 *chronicle,* 6.22 *educate,* 55.4 *weather forecast,* 253.12 *attend,* 293.33 *fix,* 420.8 *something heard,* 423.1 *loudness,* 425.1 *bang,* 483.1 *evidence,* 492.1 *judgment,* 524.13 *interpret news,* 528.2 *communication,* 528.3 *document,* 528.12 *communicate,* 532.1 *publication,* 532.3 *journalism,* 532.15 *publish,* 545.1 *record,* 560.1 *description,* 560.4 *factual account,* 560.15 *recount,* 800.1 *estimation*
reportable 533.14 *journalistic*
reportage 3.5 *chronicle,* 533.3 *reporting,* 560.3 *narration*
report card 545.1 *record*
reported 3.19 *chronicled,* 483.8 *evidential,* 533.14 *journalistic*
reportedly 3, **528,** 483.14 *as evidence,* 533.15 *journalistically*
reported speech 5.23 *phrase*
reporter 492.5 *judge,* 524.7 *news interpreter,* 528.9 *informant,* 530.4 *discloser,* 532.11 *newspaper man,* 533.4 *journalist,* 545.9 *recorder,* 560.10 *descriptive writer*
report for duty 253.12 *attend*
reporting **533,** 532.3 *journalism*
reportorial 533.14 *journalistic*
reportorially 533.15 *journalistically*
repose **325,** 325.8 *be motionless,* 641.1 *inaction,* 641.4 *not act,* 643.9 *sleep,* 645.1 *leisure,* 645.4 *have leisure,* 649.1 *ease,* 649.2 *take it easy,* 651.2 *be refreshed,* 651.5 *refreshment,* 651.6 *refresher*
reposeful 325.6 *quiescent,* 645.7 *leisurely,* 649.4 *at ease,* 649.5 *labour-saving*
reposefully 649.6 *with ease*
reposing 325.6 *quiescent*
repository 258.1 *container,* 605.5 *collection*
repossess 125.6 *be compensated,* 349.8 *evict,* 734.8 *take back*
repossessed 745.10 *unable to pay*
repossession 349.20 *eviction,* 734.2 *taking back,* 745.5 *amount owing*
repot a ball 24.8 *play billiards*
repotting 69.5 *gardening*
reprehend 852.20 *censure*

reprehensibility 866.1 *guilt*
reprehensible 618.4 *poor,* 844.17 *unforgivable,* 852.36 *blameworthy,* 862.7 *evil,* 864.11 *wicked,* 866.5 *guilty*
reprehensibly 862.12 *evilly,* 866.11 *guiltily*
reprehension 852.7 *blame*
reprehensive 866.5 *guilty*
reprehensively 866.11 *guiltily*
represent **52, 547, 706, 707,** 48.21 *write,* 50.20 *draw,* 51.32 *act,* 103.11 *characterize,* 222.4 *be a substitute,* 299.5 *outline,* 471.19 *epitomize,* 478.23 *answer for,* 483.10 *make evident,* 517.11 *predict,* 519.14 *imagine,* 520.10 *mean,* 537.34 *render,* 538.24, 540.20 *pretend,* 543.10 *signify,* 545.13 *record,* 560.14 *describe,* 611.7 *be important*
representation **547, 560,** 50.7 *picture,* 51.20 *acting,* 110.2 *equivalence,* 110.4 *duplicate,* 118.1 *imitation,* 222.1 *substitution,* 222.3 *substitute thing,* 299.1 *outline,* 435.8 *reflection,* 457.5 *impression,* 526.10 *manifestation,* 538.9 *hypocrisy,* 540.7 *pretence,* 543.1 *sign,* 545.1 *record,* 703.1 *commission*
Representation 547
representational **547,** 560.11 *descriptive,* 560.13 *representing,* 703.9 *commissioned*
representational art 50 Western Art Styles and Movements
representationalism 537.12 *true to life*
representational **547,** 538.27 *pretentiously*
representative **547, 678,** 110.13 *equivalent,* 124.1 *average,* 163.11 *typical,* 222.2 *substitute person,* 299.6 *outlined,* 475.11 *explanatory,* 526.14 *manifest,* 537.25 *lifelike,* 543.14 *signifying,* 547.13 *representational,* 560.13 *representing,* 564.10 *speaker,* 646.3 *agent,* 653.16 *official,* 688.10 *person of authority,* 696.3 *leader,* 703.5 *commissioner,* 706.1 *delegate,* 706.6 *delegated,* 707.3 *agent,* 739.10 *salesman*
Representative 12.8 *politician,* 653.16 *official,* 706.1 *delegate*
representative body 706
representative government 12.1 *government,* 688.7 *type of rule*
representatively 706, 478.27 *answerably,* 543.18 *indicatively,* 547.14 *representationally*
representative sample 299.1 *outline*
representing **560,** 543.14 *signifying,* 547.13 *representational,* 707.7 *deputizing*
represent the interests of 706.5 *represent*
represent to oneself 519.14 *imagine*
represent unfairly 548.4 *misrepresent*
repress 231.3 *counteract,* 242.4 *moderate,* 244.8 *destroy,* 302.7 *limit,* 546.2 *forget,* 591.7 *be evasive,* 661.8 *hinder,* 690.6 *suppress,* 699.8 *restrain,* 701.7 *defeat,* 709.4 *censor,* 726.7 *detain,* 869.5 *be self-restrained*
repress a smile 772.8 *be serious*
repressed 61.37 *subconscious,* 690.9 *suppressed,* 869.8 *self-restrained*
repressing 701.10 *dominating*
repression 61.19 *defence mechanism,* 231.1 *counteraction,* 244.1 *destruction,* 302.2 *limiting factor,* 546.5 *forgetfulness,* 591.15 *evasiveness,* 661.1 *hindrance,* 690.2 *suppression,* 699.1 *restraint,* 701.2 *domination,* 709.1 *veto,* 726.2 *detention,* 869.1 *self-restraint*
repressive 231.4 *counteracting,* 302.5 *limited,* 591.18 *avoiding,*

661.13 *hindering,* 690.8 *severe,* 701.10 *dominating,* 709.5 *vetoed,* 869.8 *self-restrained*
repressively 231.5 *counter,* 661.16 *with delay,* 690.11 *severely,* 709.7 *by veto,* 869.11 *with self-restraint*
repressive regime 709.1 *veto*
repress one's desires 869.5 *be self-restrained*
reprieval 639.2 *deliverance*
reprieve 16.42 *acquittal,* 16.78 *acquit,* 209.3 *delayed action,* 209.8 *delay,* 638.1 *escape,* 639.1 *deliver,* 639.2 *deliverance,* 700.1 *liberation,* 700.4 *liberate,* 704.1 *cancellation,* 704.6 *cancel,* 767.10 *save,* 835.3 *mercy,* 835.10 *show mercy,* 839.1 *forgiveness,* 839.9 *forgive*
reprieved 16.63 *acquitted,* 638.8 *escaping,* 704.10 *cancelled,* 839.6 *forgiven*
reprieved prisoner 638.3 *escaper*
repriever 704.5 *abrogator*
reprieving 839.4 *forgiving*
reprimand 636.1 *warning,* 766.2 *expression of dissatisfaction,* 806.14 *rebuke,* 852.7 *blame,* 852.20 *censure,* 879.1 *punish,* 879.7 *punishment*
reprimanded 852.34 *censured*
reprimanding 852.30 *censuring*
reprint 66.12 *development,* 110.4, 110.9 *duplicate,* 183.5 *repeat,* 183.20 *renew,* 245.2 *print,* 245.9 *reproduce*
reprinted 183, 110.15 *duplicate*
reprisal 125.2 *counterbalance,* 221.2 *restoration,* 672.1 *retaliation,* 855.4 *revenge,* 879.9 *retribution*
reprise 183.4 *return,* 200.2 *retrospection,* 200.15 *look back,* 433.1 *melody*
reproach 827.1 *vilification,* 827.6, 827.6 *vilify,* 852.7 *blame,* 852.20 *censure,* 856.1 *accusation,* 856.5 *accuse,* 866.1 *guilt*
reproachable 866.5 *guilty*
reproached 852.34 *censured*
reproachful 827.9 *vituperative,* 828.15 *resentful,* 852.30 *censuring,* 866.5 *guilty*
reproachfully 827.13 *vituperatively,* 828.17 *resentfully,* 852.37 *disapprovingly,* 866.11 *guiltily*
reproachfulness 866.1 *guilt*
reproaching 852.30 *censuring*
reproachless 865.5 *innocent*
reproach oneself 867.4 *be penitent*
reprobate 852.19 *blame,* 864.9 *wicked person,* 864.14 *impious,* 866.4 *guilty person*
reprobation 766.1 *dissatisfaction,* 852.7 *blame*
reprocess 183.20 *renew,* 629.3 *restore*
reprocessed 183.11 *reprinted*
reprocessing 629.9 *restoration*
reproduce 245, 110.9 *duplicate,* 114.12 *imitate,* 118.10 *copy,* 128.5 *make bigger,* 183.16 *repeat,* 243.10 *produce,* 261.6 *become bigger,* 396.19 *give birth to,* 547.9 *represent*
reproduced 245, 110.15 *duplicate,* 183.9 *repeated*
reproduce oneself 245
reproduction 245, 547, 50.7 *picture,* 59.5 *physiology,* 61.23 *memory,* 110.4 *duplicate,* 114.2, 118.2 *copy,* 128.1 *increase,* 135.4 *sexual union,* 176.4 *doubling,* 183.1 *repetition,* 246.2 *productiveness,* 261.1 *growth,* 396.4 *biological function*
Reproduction 245
reproductive 245, 59.22 *physiological,* 82.4 *social insect,* 183.12 *repetitious*
reproductive body 90, 89.4 *fungal body*
reproductive cell 59.7 *cell*

reproductively 245, 261.10 *largely*
reproductive organ 88.2 *fern plant,* 88.4 *moss plant*
reproductive organs 245.8 *organs of reproduction*
reprogramme 629.3 *restore*
reprogramming 629.9 *restoration*
reproof 587.6 *dissuasion,* 766.2 *expression of dissatisfaction,* 852.7 *blame,* 879.7 *punishment*
reprovable 866.5 *guilty*
reprove 587.1 *dissuade,* 636.5 *warn,* 766.7 *be dissatisfied,* 852.20 *censure,* 879.1 *punish*
reprove oneself 867.4 *be penitent*
reprover 766.3 *dissatisfied person*
reproving look 852.10 *disapproving look*
rep show 51.5 *show*
reptant 79.11 *reptilian*
reptilarium 79.9 *herpetology*
reptile 79, 76.4 *type of animal*
reptile house 79.9 *herpetology*
reptilelike 79.11 *reptilian*
reptiles 777 Phobias by Topic
Reptiles and Amphibians 79
Reptilia 79.1 *reptile*
reptilian 79, 79.1 *reptile*
reptiliary 79.9 *herpetology*
reptiliform 79.11 *reptilian*
reptiloid 79.11 *reptilian*
republic 12.5 *political organization,* 91.1 *country,* 249.4 *territorial division,* 400.11 *nation,* 688.8 *governmental organization*
republican 12.9 *governmental,* 91.16, 249.17 *national,* 400.13 *national,* 688.14 *governmental*
Republican 217.3 *conservative person,* 665.6 *political party member,* 665.10 *political*
republicanism 12.1 *government,* 665.3 *political grouping,* 688.7 *type of rule*
Republican Party 12.6 *political party,* 665.3 *political grouping*
republican state 400.11 *nation*
Republican whip 688.10 *person of authority,* 696.3 *leader*
republication 457.6 *reappearance*
Republic Day 825.3 *anniversary*
republic of letters 48.1 *literature*
repudiate 476.9 *deny,* 484.8 *reverse,* 536.7 *be negative,* 536.9 *renounce,* 578.4 *recant,* 581.4 *revoke,* 598.1 *relinquish,* 704.6 *cancel,* 711.6 *dissent,* 713.6 *protest,* 720.7 *not observe,* 747.8 *stop payment*
repudiated 484.6 *countered,* 536.12 *rejected,* 713.9 *protesting*
repudiating 476.7 *refuting,* 711.9 *dissenting,* 720.11 *nonobservant*
repudiation 476.2 *denial,* 484.2 *reversal,* 536.2 *rejection,* 536.4 *renunciation,* 578.8 *recantation,* 581.7 *abrogation,* 704.1 *cancellation,* 711.2 *dissent,* 713.1 *protest,* 720.1 *nonobservance*
repudiation of debts 747.1 *nonpayment*
repudiative 536.11 *negative*
repudiator 476.5 *refuter,* 704.5 *abrogator*
repugn 476.9 *deny*
repugnance 573.13 *dissociation,* 663.1 *opposition,* 785.1 *dislike,* 820.1 *enmity,* 822.1 *hate*
repugnancy 663.1 *opposition*
repugnant 341.8 *repulsive,* 663.19 *oppositional,* 663.21 *contrary,* 785.9 *disliked,* 820.9 *aggressive,* 822.12 *hated*
repugnantly 341.11 *repulsively,* 785.11 *disgustingly*
repulse 341, 233.9 *change,* 341.1 *repel,* 581.1 *reject,* 581.5 *rejection,* 669.1 *resistance,* 669.6 *resist,* 671.24 *parry,* 671.26 *act on the defensive,* 711.1 *refusal,* 711.5 *refuse,* 850.5, 850.23 *insult*
repulsing 669.10 *resistant,* 850.11 *insulting*
repulsion 341, 233 *influence,* 235.4 *energy,* 669.1 *resistance,*

711.1 *refusal,* 785.1 *dislike,* 822.1 *hate*
Repulsion 341
repulsive 341, 622.8 *unclean,* 764.1 *unpleasant,* 785.9 *disliked,* 790.4 *ugly,* 822.12 *hated*
repulsive force 341.5 *repulsion*
repulsively 341, 764.13 *unpleasantly,* 785.11 *disgustingly*
repulsiveness 341.5 *repulsion,* 764.5 *unpleasantness,* 790.1 *hideousness*
repurchase 738, 738.3 *buy back*
reputable 800, 318.6 *eminent,* 849.13 *respectable,* 857.4 *honourable*
reputably 857.7 *honourably*
reputation 416, 233.3 *personal influence,* 611.1 *importance,* 744.7 *repute,* 800.1 *estimation,* 805.4 *prestige*
repute 744, 233.3 *personal influence,* 318.1 *prominence,* 416.4 *reputation,* 611.1 *importance,* 849.1 *respect,* 857.1 *probity*
Repute 800
reputed 800, 518.8 *supposed*
reputedly 4.25 *theoretically,* 518.10 *supposedly*
request 712, 712, 10.9 *prayer,* 10.20 *pray,* 16.5 *litigation,* 16.70 *litigate,* 473.5 *plea,* 473.16 *plead,* 477.1, 477.17 *question,* 518.6 *propound,* 532.16 *publicize,* 593.1 *requirement,* 593.10 *necessitate,* 708.6 *ask permission,* 782.5 *object of desire,* 782.12 *desire*
Request 712
request aid 634.4 *shelter*
request credit 733.7 *borrow*
requested 593.4 *required,* 710.17 *offered,* 712.9 *requesting,* 782.7 *desired*
requester 712
request euthanasia 398.21 *commit suicide*
request for credit 733.1 *borrowing*
request for money 733.1 *borrowing*
request for support 710.5 *offer of public service*
requesting 712, 477.12 *questioning*
request money 733.7 *borrow*
request one's hand in marriage 712.6 *request*
request stop 218.4 *stopping place*
request support 710.13 *be a candidate*
request the pleasure of one's company 712.6 *request*
requiem 49.5 *sacred music,* 399.2 *funeral,* 774.2 *lament*
requiem mass 49.5 *sacred music*
Requiem Mass 10.5 *Christian rite*
requiem shark 80 Fishes
require 593, 358.1 *fall short,* 478.21 *answer to,* 485.16 *specify,* 513.11 *demand,* 571.14 *necessitate,* 609.5 *be insufficient,* 609.6 *be unsatisfied,* 692.10 *demand,* 695.6 *compel,* 712.6 *request,* 738.2 *shop,* 782.12 *desire,* 847.17 *impose a duty*
required 593, 478.16 *answerable,* 518.9 *meant,* 571.9 *necessary,* 611.5 *important,* 695.10 *compulsory,* 699.13 *restraining,* 712.9 *requesting,* 782.7 *desired*
required giving 729.2 *gift*
required number 608.7 *sufficiency*
require explanation 523.10 *be unexplained*
requirement 593, 358.5 *shortfall,* 478.9 *answerability,* 571.1 *necessity,* 608.7 *sufficiency,* 611.3 *chief thing,* 620.5 *imperfection,* 695.1 *compulsion,* 699.1 *restraint,* 712.1 *request,* 716.2 *basis for negotiations,* 738.8 *shopping,* 782.1 *desire,* 782.5 *object of desire*
Requirement 593
require no explanation 526.5 *be visible*

require qualifications 699.8 *restrain*
require some effort 659.17 *be difficult*
requiring 145.4 *incomplete*
requiring effort 659.10 *difficult*
requiring great effort 644.11 *laborious*
requisite 103.5 *essential,* 485.7 *condition,* 571.1 *necessity,* 571.9 *necessary,* 593.1 *requirement,* 593.4 *required,* 695.10 *compulsory*
requisite number 144.2 *fullness*
requisition 593.1 *requirement,* 593.10 *necessitate,* 599.5 *dispose of,* 692.2, 692.10 *demand,* 695.7 *force,* 712.2, 712.7 *demand,* 734.1 *taking,* 734.7 *take*
requisitional 485.12 *conditional*
requisitionary 712.10 *demanding,* 734.12 *taking*
requitable 109.4 *reciprocal,* 125.8 *compensable*
requital 109.1 *interchange,* 125.1 *compensation,* 735.1 *giving back,* 840.1 *atonement,* 855.4 *revenge,* 878.6 *compensation,* 879.9 *retribution*
requite 109.7 *reciprocate,* 125.4 *compensate,* 223.5 *exchange,* 664.12 *reciprocate,* 672.3 *retaliate,* 735.4 *give back,* 746.13 *retaliate,* 840.5 *atone,* 855.10 *avenge,* 878.11 *pay*
requited 109.4 *reciprocal,* 125.7 *compensated,* 223.7 *exchanged*
requitement 125.1 *compensation*
requiter 125.3 *compensator*
requiting 855.14 *vindictive*
reredos 50.8 *painting*
Reret 8 Deities
rerun 183.5 *repeat,* 183.20 *renew,* 534.25 *broadcast material,* 534.30 *communicate*
reschedule one's debts 745.8 *not pay*
rescind 536.9 *renounce,* 578.4 *recant,* 704.6 *cancel*
rescindable 704.10 *cancelled*
rescinded 536.12 *rejected,* 704.10 *cancelled*
rescinder 704.5 *abrogator*
rescinding 704.1 *cancellation*
rescindment 536.4 *renunciation,* 704.1 *cancellation*
rescript 16.3 *law,* 478.2 *acknowledgment,* 634.3 *precept*
rescuable 639.4 *deliverable*
rescue 671, 629.3 *restore,* 629.9 *restoration,* 632.1 *safety,* 632.9 *protect,* 637.5 *preserve,* 638.1 *escape,* 639.1 *deliver,* 639.2 *deliverance,* 662.2 *support,* 662.17 *help,* 698.15 *set free,* 700.1 *liberation,* 700.4 *liberate,* 735.1 *giving back,* 735.4 *give back,* 767.2 *aid,* 767.10 *save,* 831.4 *benevolent act*
rescue at the eleventh hour 639.1 *deliver*
rescued 639.4 *deliverable,* 700.7 *liberated*
rescue device 637.2 *preserver*
rescuer 671, 637.4 *preservationist,* 639.3 *deliverer,* 700.3 *liberator,* 784.4 *likable person,* 861.15 *good person*
rescue team 639.3 *deliverer*
research 4.4 *philosophical investigation,* 4.20 *philosophize,* 6.23 *learn,* 477.2 *questioning,* 477.17 *question,* 479.3 *experimentation,* 479.11 *experiment,* 594.2 *do the groundwork,* 652.14 *behave towards*
research and development 13.6 *economic factors,* 479.3 *experimentation*
research data 518.2 *basis of supposition*
researched 477.16 *questioned,* 479.10 *tested*
researcher 4.10 *philosopher,* 6.7 *learner,* 268.9 *measurer,* 477.9 *questioner,* 479.5 *experimenter,* 518.4 *theorist,* 530.4 *discloser,*

590.5 *pursuer*, 596.7 *attempter*, 688.11 *expert*
research establishment 479.6 *place of experimentation*
research fellowship 6.6 *instructorship*
researching 477.12 *questioning*, 479.8 *experimental*
research into 696.15 *learn*
research laboratory 647.1 *workshop*
research satellite 53.32 *satellite*
research scientist 479.5 *experimenter*
research worker 479.5 *experimenter*, 518.4 *theorist*
resection 60.9 *surgery*, 136.3 *separateness*
reseda 453.1 *green*
resell 739.1 *sell*
resemblance 114.1 *similarity*
resemble 109.9 *correlate*, 114.10 *be similar*, 116.25 *conform*, 457.11 *appear*, 547.9 *represent*
resembling 114.7 *similar*, 116.14 *conforming*
resene 395.10 *resin*
resent 828, 758.8 *grudge*, 766.7 *be dissatisfied*, 785.5 *dislike*, 820.11 *be hostile*, 822.14 *hate*, 829.6 *be irascible*, 841.6 *be jealous*, 842.3 *be envious of*
resent competition 841.6 *be jealous*
resentful 828, 453.5 *green-eyed*, 785.8 *disliking*, 820.6 *hostile*, 822.10 *hating*, 829.4 *irascible*, 830.7 *irritable*, 832.14 *hostile*, 841.4 *jealous*, 842.2 *envious*
resentfully 828, 785.10 *discontentedly*, 820.14 *hostilely*, 822.18 *hatefully*, 829.9 *irascibly*, 830.14 *irritably*, 841.9 *jealously*, 842.4 *enviously*
resentfulness 828.1 *resentment*, 829.1 *irascibility*, 842.1 *envy*
resentment 828, 759.6 *bad feeling*, 785.1 *dislike*, 820.3 *ill feeling*, 822.1 *hate*, 832.4 *bitterness*, 841.1 *jealousy*, 842.1 *envy*
Resentment; Anger 828
reservation 136.2 *setting apart*, 477.1 *question*, 485.7 *condition*, 498.1 *disbelief*, 545.8 *registration*, 637.1 *preservation*, 716.2 *basis for negotiations*, 816.4 *place of confinement*
reserve 263, 542, 718, 810, 17.9 *enlisted man*, 38.3 *football player*, 136.10 *set apart*, 208.9 *prepare*, 209.8 *delay*, 222.2 *substitute person*, 222.7 *substitute*, 258.21 *put in a container*, 293.21 *substitution*, 293.40 *substitutive*, 301.2 *enclosed place*, 301.5 *enclose*, 323.4 *closed place*, 485.16 *specify*, 531.4 *silence*, 545.15 *register*, 566.4 *taciturnity*, 580.4 *pick*, 593.10 *necessitate*, 600.5 *not use*, 600.8 *nonuse*, 602.5 *reserves*, 605.6 *store*, 637.5 *preserve*, 699.3 *self-restraint*, 707.2 *alternative*, 767.5 *helper*, 816.1 *unsociability*, 816.4 *place of confinement*
reserved 263, 542, 810, 258.20 *containing*, 485.12 *conditional*, 531.16 *silent*, 566.1 *taciturn*, 593.4 *required*, 600.1 *unused*, 657.4 *cunning*, 699.14 *self-restrained*
reservedly 263, 542
reserved nature 699.3 *self-restraint*
reserved section 301.2 *enclosed place*
reserved space 248
reserve equipment 130.4 *extra*
reserve fleet 17.4 *military organization*
reserve for 588.9 *intend for*
reserve forces 17.2 *the military*
reserve fund 605.1 *store*
reserve liability 741.6 *funds*
reserves 602, 17.2 *the military*, 130.4 *extra*, 594.10 *preparations*, 605.1 *store*, 606.1 *provi-*

sion, 662.11 *helper*, 679.14 *armed forces*, 741.6 *funds*, 741.19 *treasury*
reservist 222.2 *substitute person*, 679.8 *soldier*
reservoir 63.23 *dam*, 94.1 *lake*, 258.1 *container*, 389.16 *water carrier*, 605.1 *store*, 605.4 *storage*
reset 216.8 *cause change*
reshape 216.8 *cause change*, 220.9 *transform*, 309.12 *distort the truth*
reshaped 216.12 *changed*
reshaping 216.1 *change*
reship 70.4 *transport*
reshoto 49 Musical Instruments
reshowing 183.5 *repeat*
reshown 183.11 *reprinted*
reside 253, 255.14 *inhabit*
reside at 396.17 *dwell*
reside in 148.12 *be one of*, 250.10 *settle*, 256.17 *inhabit*
residence 253, 256.1 *habitat*, 567.5 *place of residence*
resident 253, 255, 60.11 *doctor*, 255.1 *inhabitant*, 256.14 *inhabiting*, 723.5 *possessor*
residential 93.14 *urban*, 253.9 *resident*, 255.11 *inhabited*, 256.14 *inhabiting*
residential area 93.7 *city district*
residential building 63.20 *building*
residential zone 93.7 *city district*
residentiary 255.1 *inhabitant*, 256.14 *inhabiting*
residents 255.2 *inhabitants*
resider 255.1 *inhabitant*
residing 255.13 *resident*, 256.14 *inhabiting*
residual 132.2 *residue*, 132.9 *remaining*, 169.4 *mathematical result*
residual insecticide 68.14 *pest control*
residually 132
residual magnetization 56.63 *magnetic phenomenon*
residuary 132.9 *remaining*
residue 132, 52.18 *division*, 227.1 *effect*, 622.4 *dirt*
residuum 132.2 *residue*, 622.4 *dirt*
resign 705, 218.7 *stop working*, 337.2 *retreat*, 345.2 *withdraw*, 347.14 *be dismissed*, 578.2 *equivocate*, 598.1 *relinquish*, 598.2 *withdraw*, 600.7 *stop work*, 645.4 *have leisure*, 673.3 *submit*, 704.7 *terminate*
resignation 705, 4.3 *detachment*, 136.2 *setting apart*, 218.2 *stop*, 337.11 *retreat*, 598.3 *relinquishment*, 600.10 *disuse*, 645.3 *unemployment*, 673.1, 673.1 *submission*, 704.2 *termination*, 806.12 *submissiveness*
Resignation 705
resigned 705, 4.18 *detached*, 598.6 *apathetic*, 673.5 *submitting*, 694.7 *obedient*, 705.7 *resigning*, 806.5 *submissive*
resignedly 4.27 *stoically*, 598.8 *apathetically*
resignedness 705
resigned to one's fate 705.4 *resignedness*
resigner 705
resigning 705, 337.11 *retreat*
resign oneself 705, 673.3 *submit*, 806.21 *humble oneself*
resign oneself to 708.4 *be permissive*
resign one's membership 139.7 *be aloof*
resign under pressure 705.5 *resign*
resilience 337, 237.1 *strength*, 331.4 *recoil*, 377.1 *elasticity*, 377.2 *adaptability*, 378.8 *physical strength*
resilient 337, 237.11 *strong in spirit*, 331.8 *recoiling*, 377.6 *elastic*, 377.7 *adaptive*, 378.4 *powerful*

resiliently 331.10 *on the rebound*, 377.12 *adaptably*, 378.13 *powerfully*
resin 395, 57.21 *polymer*, 85.9 *tree product*, 352.2 *secreted substance*, 394.2 *adhesive*, 395.19 *resinify*, 418.3 *incense*
resina 395.10 *resin*
resinaceous 395.14 *resinous*
resinate 395.10 *resin*, 395.19 *resinify*
resinic 395.14 *resinous*
resiniferous 395.14 *resinous*
resiniform 395.14 *resinous*
resinify 395
resinize 395.19 *resinify*
resinoid 395.10 *resin*, 395.14 *resinous*
resinous 395, 85.14 *treelike*
resinously 395.20 *oilily*
resiny 395.14 *resinous*
resist 669, 111.9 *oppose*, 231.3 *counteract*, 378.10 *be tough*, 484.7 *counter*, 573.6 *be unwilling*, 661.8 *hinder*, 663.12 *oppose*, 663.17 *withstand*, 668.6 *be insubordinate*, 669.16 *fight on*, 670.8 *counterattack*, 671.26 *act on the defensive*, 672.3 *retaliate*, 674.11 *contend*, 676.14 *battle*, 679.39 *defend*, 711.5 *refuse*, 713.6 *protest*
resistance 56, 64, 669, 61.19 *defence mechanism*, 111.3 *opposition*, 231.1 *counteraction*, 235.4 *energy*, 235.7 *electrical power*, 237.1 *strength*, 341.7 *deflection*, 373.5 *hardness*, 378.6 *toughness*, 385.1 *friction*, 484.1 *counterevidence*, 573.12 *opposition*, 577.5 *obstinacy*, 587.6 *dissuasion*, 661.1 *hindrance*, 663.1 *opposition*, 668.2 *disobedience*, 671.1 *defence*, 679.14 *armed forces*, 693.1 *disobedience*, 693.4 *revolution*, 711.1 *refusal*
Resistance 669
resistance fighter 679.9 *guerrilla*, 713.5 *seditionist*
resistance movement 669, 693.4 *revolution*
resistance to compaction 63.15 *strength of materials*
resistance to sliding 63.15 *strength of materials*
resistant 669, 111.5 *opposing*, 231.4 *counteracting*, 237.13 *strengthened*, 341.10 *defensive*, 373.2, 378.1 *tough*, 500.7 *dissenting*, 573.5 *reluctant*, 663.22 *uncooperative*, 711.8 *refused*
resistantly 231.5 *counter*, 341.12 *defensively*, 373.12, 378.12 *toughly*, 669.14 *resistingly*, 711.11 *uncooperatively*
resist authority 689.4 *be anarchic*
resist breaking 378.10 *be tough*
resist change 217.5 *be permanent*
resist control 689.4 *be anarchic*
resisted 111.5 *opposing*
resister 669, 573.16 *reluctant person*, 663.9 *opposer*
resist incursions 676.13 *be at war*
resisting 669, 111.5 *opposing*, 231.4 *counteracting*, 378.1 *tough*, 669.10 *resistant*, 670.24 *counterattacking*, 671.29 *defending*, 711.8 *refused*
resistingly 669, 231.5 *counter*, 378.12 *toughly*, 711.11 *uncooperatively*
resistive 64.36 *electronic*
resistivity 56.53, 64.12 *resistance*
resistor 64, 56.55 *circuit*
resist temptation 134.9 *be pure*, 863.8 *be virtuous*
resojet propulsion 338.2 *method of propulsion*
resole 629.1 *repair*
resoling 629.8 *repair*
resolute 574, 225.11 *determined*, 237.11 *strong in spirit*, 570.7 *iron-willed*, 575.10 *persevering*, 577.3 *unyielding*, 588.11 *intending*, 642.18 *active*, 772.2 *earnest*, 778.12 *self-reliant*

resolutely 574, 225.13 *determinedly*, 237.15 *acutely*, 575.13 *persistently*
resoluteness 570.2 *willpower*, 574.12 *resolution*, 778.3 *steadfastness*
resolution 53, 574, 49.13 *melody*, 51.6 *scene*, 56.32 *optical instrument*, 57.13 *structure*, 116.4 *harmony*, 136.1 *separation*, 141.2 *deconstruction*, 220.1 *conversion*, 225.2 *determination*, 237.1 *strength*, 323.1 *closure*, 433.3 *melodiousness*, 478.6 *solution*, 524.1 *interpretation*, 530.1 *disclosure*, 570.2 *willpower*, 575.1 *perseverance*, 577.6 *determination*, 588.2 *intentionality*, 592.1 *plan*, 642.8 *assiduity*, 684.2 *conclusion*, 772.5 *earnestness*
Resolution 574
resolutive 387.9 *solvent*
resolvable 136.19 *separable*, 220.15 *convertible*
resolve 574, 588, 4.21 *rationalize*, 52.90 *enumerate*, 116.24 *harmonize*, 136.10 *set apart*, 141.4 *deconstruct*, 157.15 *end*, 166.13 *rule*, 220.7 *convert into*, 225.2 *determination*, 323.9 *close down*, 378.9 *mental toughness*, 387.23 *dissolve*, 478.20 *solve*, 524.9 *decipher*, 570.2 *willpower*, 574.12 *resolution*, 582.6 *premeditation*, 588.2 *intentionality*, 592.9 *plan*
resolve beforehand 582.2 *premeditate*
resolved 225.11 *determined*, 323.14 *closed down*, 378.5 *mentally tough*, 478.14 *solved*, 574.1 *resolute*
resolve into 220.9 *transform*
resolvent 387.9 *solvent*
resolve problems 677.4 *pacify*
resolving 478.6 *solution*
resolving power 53.28 *resolution*, 56.32 *optical instrument*, 136.1 *separation*
resonance 427, 49.21 *tone*, 56.14 *sound wave*, 116.4 *harmony*, 183.6 *reverberation*, 331.4 *recoil*, 365.2 *vibration*, 365.5 *wave*, 423.1 *loudness*
Resonance 427
resonant 427, 116.13 *harmonious*, 183.15 *reverberatory*, 331.8 *recoiling*, 365.14 *vibrating*, 420.14 *hearable*, 423.6 *loud*, 426.15 *drumming*, 433.6 *melodious*, 557.4 *ornate*
resonant circuit 64.13 *circuit*
resonant frequency 56.14 *sound wave*, 64.13 *circuit*, 365.5 *wave*
resonantly 427, 116.33 *harmoniously*, 331.10 *on the rebound*, 426.19 *repeatedly*, 433.11 *melodiously*
resonate 427, 116.24 *harmonize*, 365.9 *vibrate*, 426.8 *drum*
resonating 116.13 *harmonious*, 427.6 *resonant*
resonating chamber 427.5 *resonator*
resonation 427.1 *resonance*
resonator 427
resorb 348.13 *absorb*
resorbence 348.5 *absorption*
resorcinol 62 Medication
resorption 348.5 *absorption*
resort 629, 592.3 *expedient plan*, 599.6 *use*, 602.1 *means*, 634.1 *refuge*, 657.2 *stratagem*
resort to 599
resort to arms 676.4 *belligerency*
resort to fisticuffs 241.7 *be violent*
resort to greenmail 737.3 *bargain*
resort to violence 241.7 *be violent*
resort to war 676.12 *go to war*
resound 183, 116.24 *harmonize*, 331.1 *recoil*, 420.16 *be heard*, 423.8 *be loud*, 425.5 *bang*, 426.8 *drum*, 427.9 *resonate*
resounding 116.13 *harmonious*, 423.6 *loud*, 427.1 *resonance*,

427.6 *resonant*
resoundingly 116.33 *harmoniously*, 427.11 *resonantly*
resource 605, 478.6 *solution*, 592.3 *expedient plan*, 657.2 *stratagem*
resourceful 237.11 *strong in spirit*, 246.5 *fertile*, 519.10 *imaginative*, 592.15 *planning*, 597.6 *enterprising*, 655.6 *skilful*, 657.4 *cunning*
resourcefully 246.8 *fruitfully*, 519.17 *imaginatively*, 592.17 *conspiratorially*, 655.12 *skilfully*
resourcefulness 237.1 *strength*, 246.2 *productiveness*, 519.1 *imagination*, 655.1 *skill*, 657.1 *cunning*
resource management 606.1 *provision*
resources 106.1 *circumstances*, 602.2 *supplies*, 604.1 *materials*, 725.5 *personal estate*, 742.5 *wealth*
respect 849, 849, 9.7 *worship*, 167.2 *compliance*, 167.8 *comply*, 362.16 *courtesy*, 611.8 *make important*, 617.6 *worth*, 694.3 *obeisance*, 719.1 *observance*, 817.3 *courtesies*, 821.1 *love*, 831.8 *be benevolent*, 847.3 *allegiance*, 851.2 *admiration*, 851.11 *approve*
Respect 849
respectability 124.8 *middle classes*, 857.1 *probity*
respectable 849, 617.5 *not bad*, 800.3 *reputable*, 857.4 *honourable*
respectably 857.7 *honourably*
respected 849, 617.1 *worthy*, 800.3 *reputable*, 821.21 *beloved*, 851.24 *admired*
respect for legal principles 16.28 *legality*
respect for the law 16.28 *legality*
respectful 849, 694.9 *obeisant*, 817.8 *good-mannered*, 847.9 *loyal*, 851.18 *approving*
respectfully 849, 694.10 *obediently*, 817.15 *genteelly*, 847.18 *on duty*
respectfulness 849, 817.3 *courtesies*
respective 165.15 *special*
respectively 107.10 *relevantly*, 165.32 *severally*, 731.8 *proportionately*
respects 849
respect the law 16.67 *follow the law*
Respighi 49 Musicians and Composers
respiration 58, 390, 59.5 *physiology*, 348.4 *intake*, 396.4 *biological function*, 651.5 *refreshment*
respirator 630.14 *hospital*, 632.4 *safety device*, 637.2 *preserver*
respiratory 390, 59.22 *physiological*
respiratory chain 58.24 *respiration*
respiratory disease 624, 624.4 *disease*
respiratory organ 390.8 *respiration*
respiratory pigment 58.18 *pigment*
respire 390, 348.12 *draw in*, 349.14 *let out*, 396.16 *live*, 651.2 *be refreshed*
respiring 390.19 *respiratory*
respite 16.78 *acquit*, 185.6 *interval*, 209.3 *delayed action*, 218.3 *pause*, 639.2 *deliverance*, 645.2 *time off*, 649.1, 767.1 *ease*
resplendence 439.1 *light*, 811.9 *grandeur*
resplendent 439.16 *bright*, 811.24 *grand*
resplendently 811.40 *grandly*
respond 43 Architectural Decoration, **331,** 4.23 *discuss philosophically*, 43.9 *miscellaneous architectural features*, 221.9 *reply*, 403.11 *sense*, 476.10

word
counter-charge, 478.17 *answer*, 564.11 *speak*, 642.14 *push*, 664.12 *reciprocate*
responded 221.11 *reversed*
respondence 478.1 *answer*
respondent 16.8 *litigant*, 331.9 *reactive*, 478.10 *answerer*, 478.11 *answering*, 568.7 *conversationalist*, 856.4 *accused person*
responder 331, 476.5 *refuter*
respond favourably 667.6 *agree with*
responding 331.9 *reactive*, 377.7 *adaptive*, 476.7 *refuting*, 478.11 *answering*
respond quickly 377.10 *be adaptable*
respond to treatment 623.6 *get healthy*, 629.4 *be restored*
response 331, 10.8 *hymn*, 56.83 *sensitivity*, 221.5 *reply*, 403.1 *sensation*, 476.3 *counter-charge*, 478.1 *answer*, 478.4 *reaction*, 564.7 *utterance*
response to therapy 629.11 *recuperation*
response to treatment 629.11 *recuperation*
responsibility 777 Phobias by Topic, 143.9 *participation*, 230.4 *management*, 232.1 *instrumentality*, 478.9 *answerability*, 513.2 *expectations*, 653.4 *directorship*, 703.1 *commission*, 745.1 *debt*, 845.4, 847.1 *duty*, 866.1 *guilt*
responsible 226.13, 232.7 *causal*, 478.16 *answerable*, 597.6 *enterprising*, 671.29 *defending*, 703.9 *commissioned*, 719.7 *observant*, 745.9 *in debt*, 847.10 *liable*, 852.36 *blameworthy*, 857.4 *honourable*, 866.5 *guilty*
responsibleness 847.1 *duty*
responsible person 653.15 *manager*
responsibly 597, 226.14 *causally*, 478.27 *answerably*, 703.11 *under commission*, 719.8 *observantly*, 847.18 *on duty*, 857.7 *honourably*
responsive 331.9 *reactive*, 377.7 *adaptive*, 403.7 *susceptible*, 478.11 *answering*, 759.10 *feeling*, 760.1 *sensitive*
responsively 377.12 *adaptably*, 478.24 *in answer*
responsiveness 377.2 *adaptability*, 759.5 *good feeling*, 760.5 *sensitivity*
responsory 478.4 *reaction*
rest 284, 24.3 *English billiards*, 49.17 *notation*, 83.22 *be dormant*, 132.1 *remainder*, 132.7 *be left*, 160.3 *interval*, 160.5 *caesura*, 160.13, 218.3 *pause*, 218.9 *pause*, 225.1 *stability*, 225.6 *be stable*, 251.9 *be situated*, 325.2 *repose*, 325.8 *be motionless*, 359.10 *step*, 397.1 *death*, 442.4 *silence*, 641.1 *inaction*, 641.4 *not act*, 643.9, 643.13 *sleep*, 645.1 *leisure*, 645.4 *have leisure*, 649.1 *ease*, 649.2 *take it easy*, 651.2 *be refreshed*, 651.5 *refreshment*, 651.6 *refresher*, 675.1 *peace*
rest and be thankful 325.8 *be motionless*, 649.2 *take it easy*
rest and recreation 209.3 *delayed action*
restart 33.6 *motor racing terms*, 33.10 *be on the track*, 183.20 *renew*, 219.4 *protract*, 221.7 *restore*
rest assured 497.7 *believe*, 775.6 *hope*
restate 5.46 *translate*, 183.17 *iterate*, 426.14 *repeat*, 524.12 *translate*
restated 5.40 *translated*, 183.10 *iterated*
restatement 5.12 *translation*, 183.2 *iteration*, 426.7 *repeated*

word
restating 5.40 *translated*
restaurant 256.7 *room*, 350.15 *eating place*, 815.4 *meeting place*
restaurant car 72.6 *rolling stock*
restaurateur 350.20 *food provider*, 606.4 *caterer*
rested 651.4 *refreshed*
rest energy 235.4 *energy*
rest from one's labours 649.1 *ease*, 649.2 *take it easy*
restful 225.9 *stable*, 325.6 *quiescent*, 405.6 *pleasant*, 649.4 *at ease*, 649.5 *labour-saving*, 763.3 *comfortable*
restfully 225.12 *stably*, 325.10 *motionlessly*, 649.6 *with ease*, 651.8 *refreshingly*
restfulness 325.2 *repose*, 649.1 *ease*
rest home 60.10, 630.14 *hospital*
resting 132.9 *remaining*, 325.6 *quiescent*, 600.3 *not wanted*, 643.2 *not working*, 643.4 *not awake*, 645.7 *leisurely*, 649.4 *at ease*
resting bud 83.8 *bud*
resting place 218, 325
Rest in Peace 399.4 *funeral objects*
restitute 125.4 *compensate*, 629.3 *restore*, 672.4 *serve one right*, 746.10 *pay back*, 878.11 *pay*
restituted 125.7 *compensated*
restitution 125.1 *compensation*, 221.2, 629.9 *restoration*, 630.1 *remedy*, 677.2 *peace offering*, 735.1 *giving back*, 746.2 *repayment*, 840.1 *atonement*, 855.1 *vindication*, 878.6 *compensation*, 879.8 *penalty*
restitutional 840.4 *atoning*
restitutive 125.9 *compensatory*, 221.10 *regressive*, 735.6 *restoring*, 840.4 *atoning*
restitutory 125.9 *compensatory*, 221.10 *regressive*, 735.6 *restoring*, 840.4 *atoning*
restive 577.2 *refractory*, 693.13 *disobedient*
restively 693.17 *disobediently*
restiveness 693.1 *disobedience*
restless 366, 215.4 *irregular*, 224.14 *irresolute*, 324.16 *moving*, 576.2 *changeable*, 642.18 *active*, 693.13 *disobedient*
restlessly 215.8 *irregularly*, 324.18 *in motion*, 366.27 *agitatedly*, 642.22 *actively*, 693.17 *disobediently*
restlessness 366, 642, 215.1 *irregularity*, 224.2 *irresolution*, 324.2 *momentum*, 693.1 *disobedience*
restock 606.6 *replenish*, 629.3 *restore*
rest on one's laurels 218.9 *pause*, 641.4 *not act*, 649.2 *take it easy*
rest on one's oars 218.9 *pause*, 325.8 *be motionless*, 641.4 *not act*, 649.2 *take it easy*
rest on the shoulders of 847.14 *be the duty of*
restorable 125.8 *compensable*, 201.15 *renewable*, 221.12 *reversible*, 629.14 *repairable*, 735.6 *restoring*
restoration 221, 629, 125.1 *compensation*, 183.4 *return*, 201.5 *fresh start*, 216.1 *change*, 237.4 *strengthening*, 245.1 *reproduction*, 627.5 *improvement*, 629.8 *repair*, 639.2 *deliverance*, 651.5 *refreshment*, 735.1 *giving back*, 791.1 *transfiguration*, 855.1 *vindication*, 879.8 *penalty*
Restoration 51.40 *activist*
Restoration comedy 51.10 *comedy*
restoration to health 629.11 *recuperation*
restorative 629, 125.9 *compensatory*, 413.6 *cordial*, 413.10 *stimulating*, 625.4 *hygienic*, 627.16 *improving*, 630.7 *tonic*, 630.17 *remedial*, 651.3 *refreshing*,

651.6 *refresher*, 767.8 *relieving*
restoratively 627.17 *better*
restore 221, 629, 60.19 *practise medicine*, 125.4 *compensate*, 183.20 *renew*, 201.20 *make new*, 216.8 *cause change*, 239.3, 396.21 *invigorate*, 413.13 *be piquant*, 623.7 *make healthy*, 627.1 *improve*, 629.2 *refurbish*, 630.19 *remedy*, 639.1 *deliver*, 651.1 *refresh*, 662.19 *support*, 677.4 *pacify*, 735.4 *give back*, 855.7 *vindicate*
restored 125.7 *compensated*, 183.11 *reprinted*, 201.14 *renewed*, 216.12 *changed*, 221.11 *reversed*, 237.13 *strengthened*, 396.12 *alive*, 627.14 *improved*, 629.13 *repaired*, 651.4 *refreshed*, 735.6 *restoring*, 767.7 *relieved*, 839.6 *forgiven*, 855.12 *innocent*
restored to health 623.1 *healthy*
restore harmony 677.4 *pacify*
restore one to favour 735.4 *give back*
restore order 150.22 *pacify*
restore peace 677.4 *pacify*
restorer 125.3 *compensator*, 216.6 *editor*, 627.13 *reviser*, 629.12 *repairer*, 735.3 *returner*
restore the status quo 221.7 *restore*
restore to consciousness 396.19 *give birth to*
restore to equilibrium 125.5 *counterbalance*
restore to health 623.7 *make healthy*, 629.6 *cure*
restore to sanity 509.6 *be sane*
restore vitality 629.5 *revive*
restoring 735, 125.9 *compensatory*, 237.4 *strengthening*, 239.5 *invigorating*, 735.1 *giving back*
restrain 323, 661, 699, 209.8 *delay*, 218.8 *cause to cease*, 231.3 *counteract*, 242.4 *moderate*, 302.7 *limit*, 485.16 *specify*, 542.22 *play down*, 587.3 *deflect*, 609.5 *be insufficient*, 661.8 *hinder*, 695.6 *be severe*, 695.6 *compel*, 701.7 *defeat*, 709.4 *censor*, 726.7 *detain*
restrained 4.18 *detached*, 61.37 *subconscious*, 150.17 *disciplined*, 209.10 *held up*, 242.6 *moderate*, 328.5 *unhurried*, 328.7 *delayed*, 542.13 *subtle*, 542.15 *reserved*, 542.19 *downplayed*, 556.1 *simple*, 558.3 *elegant*, 661.14 *blocked*, 690.10 *unadorned*, 699.13 *restraining*, 810.13 *reserved*, 869.8 *self-restrained*
restrainedly 4.27 *stoically*
restrainedness 542.3 *subtlety*
restrainer 323
restrain from 669.9 *desist*
restraining 699, 209.12 *delaying*, 231.4 *counteracting*, 661.14 *blocked*, 695.9 *compelling*, 726.9 *retentive*
restraining hand 242.2 *moderator*, 699.5 *means of restraint*
restraining line 19.4 *stadium*
restrain oneself 699, 690.7 *be unadorned*, 869.5 *be self-restrained*
restraint 661, 699, 16.6 *legal process*, 209.3 *delayed action*, 231.1 *counteraction*, 242.1 *moderation*, 242.2 *moderator*, 302.1 *limitation*, 328.8 *slowness*, 328.9 *deceleration*, 542.3 *subtlety*, 542.5 *reserve*, 542.9 *downplaying*, 556.4 *simplicity*, 558.1 *elegance*, 587.7 *deterrence*, 661.1 *hindrance*, 690.1 *severity*, 690.3 *unadornment*, 695.2 *coercion*, 699.1 *restraint*, 701.2 *domination*, 709.1 *veto*, 810.6 *reserve*, 869.1 *self-restraint*
Restraint 699
restraint of trade 13.5 *international trade*, 699.2 *economic restraint*
restrain trade 699.9 *economize*

restrict 129.5 *make smaller*, 242.4 *moderate*, 262.5 *make smaller*, 272.10 *narrow*, 302.7 *limit*, 485.16 *specify*, 529.12 *keep secret*, 609.5 *be insufficient*, 661.8 *hinder*, 699.8 *restrain*, 709.3 *veto*, 709.4 *censor*

restrict consumption 699.9 *economize*

restricted 147.10 *excluding*, 242.6 *moderate*, 260.7 *little*, 262.7 *smaller*, 272.1 *narrow*, 302.5 *limited*, 485.12 *conditional*, 527.2 *concealed*, 529.9 *secret*, 617.1 *worthy*, 699.13 *restraining*, 702.8 *imprisoned*, 709.6 *censored*, 869.8 *self-restrained*

restricted area 302.2 *limiting factor*, 699.1 *restraint*

restricted information 709.2 *censorship*

restrict imports 699.9 *economize*

restricting 262.8 *contracting*, 699.13 *restraining*

restriction 52.64 *reasoning*, 129.1 *decrease*, 131.2 *subtracted item*, 262.1 *contraction*, 272.5 *narrowness*, 302.1 *limitation*, 485.6 *specification*, 527.8 *concealment*, 661.1 *hindrance*, 699.1 *restraint*, 709.1 *veto*, 869.1 *self-restraint*

restriction endonuclease 58.11 *enzyme*

restriction enzyme 58.11 *enzyme*, 59.12 *molecular biology*

restrictionist 699.6 *law-maker*

restriction on movement 699.4 *detention*

restrictive 147.10 *excluding*, 262.8 *contracting*, 302.5 *limited*, 485.12 *conditional*, 661.13 *hindering*, 699.13 *restraining*, 709.5 *vetoed*, 709.6 *censored*, 869.8 *self-restrained*

restrictively 485.18 *with qualification*, 661.16 *with delay*, 699.15 *under restraints*, 709.8 *under censorship*, 869.11 *with self-restraint*

restrictiveness 147.4 *exclusiveness*

restrictive practice 302.2 *limiting factor*, 699.2 *economic restraint*

restrictive trade agreement 13.5 *international trade*

restrict oneself 869.5 *be self-restrained*

restrict one's movement 699.11 *detain*

restrict supplies 699.9 *economize*

rest room 353.13 *lavatory*, 727.7 *toilet*

restructure 152.14 *rearrange*, 201.5 *fresh start*, 201.20 *make new*, 216.8 *cause change*, 220.9 *transform*

restructured 152.23 *rearranged*, 201.14 *renewed*, 216.12 *changed*

restructuring 152.4 *rearrangement*, 216.1 *change*

restructuring of industry 13.4 *economic development*

rest with 847.14 *be the duty of*

restyle 216.8 *cause change*

restyled 216.12 *changed*

restyling 216.1 *change*

result 155, 52.14 *operation*, 132.1 *remainder*, 132.7 *be left*, 155.5 *consequence*, 157.12 *end result*, 159.4 *repercussion*, 195.9 *sequel*, 195.10 *succeed*, 227.1 *effect*, 227.7 *follow from*, 232.1 *instrumentality*, 243.3 *product*, 478.6 *solution*, 684.2 *conclusion*

resultant 52.50 *scalar quantity*, 132.9 *remaining*, 159.10 *repercussive*, 227.10 *caused*, 478.14 *solved*

result from 195.10 *succeed*, 227.7 *follow from*

result in 226.9 *be the cause of*, 227.5 *show an effect*, 520.12 *intend*

resulting 155.18 *consequent*, 227.10 *caused*

resulting from 227.10 *caused*

results 52.14 *operation*

resume 183.17 *iterate*, 183.20 *renew*, 219.4 *protract*, 221.7 *restore*, 562.8 *summarize*, 629.4 *be restored*

résumé 3.6 *biography*, 183.2 *iteration*, 270.3 *shortened version*, 483.6 *documentation*

resumé 545.1 *record*

resumé 552.2 *outline*, 560.4 *factual account*, 562.1 *summary*

resumed 221.11 *reversed*

resumption 219.2 *protraction*, 221.2, 629.9 *restoration*

resupply 606.6 *replenish*

resurface 619.1 *repair*

resurfacing 629.8 *repair*

resurgence 245.1 *reproduction*, 629.10 *revival*

resurgent 245.15 *reproduced*, 629.13 *repaired*

resurrect 201.20 *make new*, 396.21 *invigorate*, 629.5 *revive*

resurrected 201.14 *renewed*

resurrection 201.5 *fresh start*, 245.1 *reproduction*, 396.5 *life cycle*, 629.10 *revival*

resurrectional 245.15 *reproduced*

resurrectionary 245.15 *reproduced*

resurrection day 492.4 *judgment day*, 629.10 *revival*

resuscitate 396.19 *give birth to*, 629.5 *revive*, 651.1 *refresh*

resuscitated 629.13 *repaired*

resuscitation 39.3 *survival swimming*, 245.1 *reproduction*, 629.10 *revival*, 651.5 *refreshment*

retable 50.8 *painting*

retail 13.13 *economic*, 532.13 *make public*, 737.13 *mercantile*, 739.1 *sell*, 739.3 *selling*

retailer 739, 606.3 *provider*, 737.10 *trader*

retailer's 740.8 *store*

retailing 13.2 *economy*

retail outlet 740.8 *store*

retail price 751.1 *price*

retail price index 13.3 *economic statistics*

retain 726, 326.14 *bring back*, 501.11 *know*, 511.11 *memorize*, 522.6 *understand*, 605.6 *store*, 637.5 *preserve*, 696.15 *learn*, 711.5 *refuse*, 726.7 *detain*

retained 726, 711.8 *refused*

retainer 127.6 *inferior*, 155.14 *follower*, 326.7 *transferor*, 697.1 *servant*, 808.5 *adherent*, 878.4 *reward for service*

retainers 180.10 *attendance*

retaining 284.9 *supportive*, 726.9 *retentive*

retaining wall 63.19 *structure*, 284.2 *supporting part*, 726.4 *wall*

retainment 726.1 *retention*

retake 125.6 *be compensated*

retaliate 671, 672, 746, 109.7 *reciprocate*, 125.5 *counterbalance*, 221.7 *restore*, 331.2 *respond*, 476.10 *countercharge*, 484.7 *counter*, 663.15 *object*, 670.8 *counterattack*, 878.11 *pay*, 879.2 *penalize*

retaliating 125.10 *counterbalancing*

retaliation 672, 109.1 *interchange*, 125.2 *counterbalance*, 221.2 *restoration*, 223.1 *exchange*, 476.3 *countercharge*, 478.5 *counterstatement*, 484.1 *counterevidence*, 670.14 *siege*, 878.6 *compensation*, 879.9 *retribution*

Retaliation 672

retaliative 672.5 *retaliatory*

retaliator 855.6 *avenger*, 879.17 *punisher*

retaliatory 478, 672, 109.4 *reciprocal*, 125.10 *counterbalancing*, 223.6 *in exchange*, 476.7 *refuting*, 484.5 *countering*, 670.24 *counterattacking*, 878.17 *compensatory*, 879.19 *punitive*

retard 129.5 *make smaller*, 209.8 *delay*, 328.3 *slow down*, 661.8 *hinder*, 699.8 *restrain*, 869.5 *be self-restrained*

retardation 129.1 *decrease*, 209.1 *lateness*, 328.9 *deceleration*, 661.1 *hindrance*, 699.1 *restraint*

retarded 328.7 *delayed*, 460.7 *intellectually subnormal*, 595.5 *immature*

retarding 209.12 *delaying*

retardment 328.9 *deceleration*

retch 349.15 *vomit*

retching 349.23 *vomiting*, 624.8 *indigestion*

retell 183.17 *iterate*, 560.15 *recount*, 627.3 *rectify*

retelling 183.2 *iteration*

retention 726, 61.23, 511.1 *memory*, 637.1 *preservation*, 711.1 *refusal*, 723.1 *possession*, 726.5 *retentiveness*

Retention 726

retentive 726

retentiveness 726, 511.1 *memory*

retenu 49 *Musical Terms*

rethink 461.14 *have second thoughts*

retiarius 679.3 *athlete*

reticence 531.4 *silence*, 542.5 *reserve*, 563.5 *mutism*, 566.4 *taciturnity*, 781.1 *caution*, 810.6 *reserve*, 816.1 *unsociability*

reticent 529.10 *secretive*, 531.16 *silent*, 542.15 *reserved*, 563.11 *speechless*, 566.1 *taciturn*, 657.4 *cunning*, 781.4 *cautious*, 810.13 *reserved*, 816.8 *unsociable*

reticently 542.25 *reservedly*, 566.10 *taciturnly*, 816.14 *unsocially*

reticular 59.23 *cellular*

reticulate 89.10 *of fungi*, 288.6 *interwoven*, 288.8 *interweave*, 456.9 *striped*

reticulately 456.12 *variedly*

reticulation 288.1 *interweaving*, 456.3 *striping*

reticulum 59.7 *cell*

Reticulum 53 The Constellations

retina 435.2 *eye*

retinopathy 436.2 *poor sight*

retinue 155.14 *follower*, 180.10 *attendance*, 195.1 *succession*

retiral 705.1 *resignation*

retire 218.7 *stop working*, 221.6 *reverse*, 254.16 *absent oneself*, 325.8 *be motionless*, 337.2 *retreat*, 345.2 *withdraw*, 347.14 *be dismissed*, 349.2 *dismiss*, 458.2 *depart*, 591.8 *run away*, 598.2 *withdraw*, 600.7 *stop work*, 645.4 *have leisure*, 671.28 *survive*, 673.3 *submit*, 705.5 *resign*, 810.15 *escape notice*, 816.12 *be unsocial*

retired 15.9 *negotiated*, 200.20, 202.13 *former*, 221.11 *reversed*, 598.6 *apathetic*, 600.3 *not wanted*, 600.4 *disused*, 645.7 *leisurely*, 698.13 *informal*, 705.7 *resigning*

retired list 171.6 *list of names*

retired person 207.7 *older person*

retiree 207.7 *older person*, 598.4 *deserter*, 705.3 *resigner*

retire from the world 816.12 *be unsocial*

retirement 15.2 *industrial negotiations*, 136.2 *setting apart*, 202.1 *oldness*, 218.2 *stop*, 221.1 *reversion*, 337.11 *retreat*, 345.7 *departure*, 591.12 *shyness*, 598.3 *relinquishment*, 600.10 *disuse*, 645.3 *unemployment*, 705.1 *resignation*, 816.1 *unsociability*

retirement age 207.5 *old age*

retirement benefit 729.2 *gift*, 749.3 *income*

retirement benefits 13.8 *industrial relations*, 718.1 *protection*, 831.3 *welfare*

retirement gift 837.3 *recognition*

retirement home 218.5 *resting place*, 634.2 *shelter*

retirement pay 721.4 *earnings*

retirement pension 662.4 *social assistance*, 746.3 *pay*, 878.4 *reward for service*

retiring 15.9 *negotiated*, 542.15 *reserved*, 705.7 *resigning*, 810.4 *shyness*, 810.11 *shy*, 810.13 *reserved*, 816.8 *unsociable*

retiring disposition 542.5, 810.6 *reserve*

retold 183.10 *iterated*

retort 109.1 *interchange*, 109.7 *reciprocate*, 220.4 *medium of conversion*, 221.5, 221.9 *reply*, 223.5 *exchange*, 331.2 *respond*, 331.6 *response*, 388.11 *vaporizer*, 423.1 *loudness*, 476.3, 476.10 *countercharge*, 478.1, 478.17 *answer*, 484.1 *counterevidence*, 484.7 *counter*, 536.3 *rebuttal*, 536.8 *rebut*, 672.1 *retaliation*, 672.3 *retaliate*, 806.14 *rebuke*, 807.25 *answer back*, 855.2 *defence*, 855.8 *justify*

retorted 221.11 *reversed*, 478.11 *answering*, 484.6 *countered*

retorting 331.9 *reactive*, 536.13 *rebutting*, 855.11 *vindicatory*

retortion 221.5 *reply*, 536.3 *rebuttal*

retortive 331.9 *reactive*

retouch 540.22 *falsify*, 629.2 *refurbish*

retouching 540.9 *falsification*

retrace 511.12 *remember*

retrace one's steps 183.19 *return to*, 337.3 *reverse*, 337.5 *turn back*

retract 221.6 *reverse*, 339.14 *draw in*, 484.8 *reverse*, 536.9 *renounce*, 578.4 *recant*, 704.6 *cancel*, 720.7 *not observe*, 734.9 *withdraw a statement*

retractability 339.1 *traction*

retractable 339.9 *retractive*

retractably 339.16 *magnetically*

retractation 536.4 *renunciation*, 578.8 *recantation*, 704.1 *cancellation*

retracted 221.11 *reversed*, 484.6 *countered*, 536.12 *rejected*

retractile 337.23 *receding*, 339.9 *retractive*

retractility 339.1 *traction*

retracting 734.2 *taking back*

retraction 221.1 *reversion*, 339.1 *traction*, 484.2 *reversal*, 536.4 *renunciation*, 578.8 *recantation*, 704.1 *cancellation*

retractive 339

retractiveness 339.1 *traction*

retractor 536.6 *negativist*, 704.5 *abrogator*, 720.5 *nonobserver*

retrain 15.11 *conduct industrial relations*

retrained 15.9 *negotiated*

retraining 15.2 *industrial negotiations*, 15.9 *negotiated*

retrally 337.28 *backward*

retread 629.1 *repair*

retreat 256, 337, 337, 7.10 *priestly dwelling*, 174.18 *be one*, 221.1 *reversion*, 221.6 *reverse*, 254.16 *absent oneself*, 290.2 *inside*, 293.15 *shelter*, 293.30 *protect*, 324.4 *backward motion*, 324.19 *go*, 331.2 *respond*, 331.6 *response*, 345.2 *withdraw*, 345.7 *departure*, 438.7 *become invisible*, 458.2 *depart*, 458.4 *disappearance*, 531.6 *privacy*, 543.6 *word*, 591.4 *shy*, 591.8 *run away*, 591.12 *shyness*, 634.1 *refuge*, 634.4 *shelter*, 638.1, 638.5 *escape*, 673.3 *submit*, 683.2 *defeat*, 683.7 *be defeated*, 687.1 *adversity*, 779.4 *be a coward*, 816.3 *separation*, 816.5 *solitary place*

retreated 221.11 *reversed*

retreater 638.3 *escaper*

retreating 337.23 *receding*

retreat into 290.14 *go inside*

retreat into one's shell 531.11 *conceal oneself*
retrench 129.5 *make smaller*, 270.10 *shorten*, 699.8 *restrain*, 756.6 *save*
retrenchment 129.1 *decrease*, 131.1 *subtraction*, 136.3 *separateness*, 270.2 *shortening*, 699.1 *restraint*, 756.2 *act of thrift*
retrial 16.7 *legal trial*
retribution 879, 672.1 *retaliation*, 855.4 *revenge*
retributive 125.9 *compensatory*, 672.5 *retaliatory*, 746.20 *paying in return*, 855.14 *vindictive*, 878.17 *compensatory*, 879.19 *punitive*
retributive justice 879.9 *retribution*
retributively 855.16 *vindictively*, 879.23 *punitively*
retrievable 221.12 *reversible*, 629.14 *repairable*, 734.12 *taking*
retrievably 221.13 *reversibly*, 734.13 *avariciously*
retrieval 125.1 *compensation*, 221.2, 629.9 *restoration*, 639.2 *deliverance*, 734.2 *taking back*
retrieve 37.7 *shoot*, 125.6 *be compensated*, 221.7 *restore*, 231.3 *counteract*, 326.14 *bring back*, 639.1 *deliver*, 734.8 *take back*
retrieved 221.11 *reversed*
retriever 77 *Breeds of Dogs*, 37.6 *sporting dog*
retroact 478.19 *react*
retroaction 125.2 *counterbalance*, 221.1 *reversion*, 231.1 *counteraction*, 331.6 *response*, 337.10 *backward motion*, 478.4 *reaction*
retroactive 337, 3.18 *in the past*, 125.10 *counterbalancing*, 200.21 *retrospective*, 221.10 *regressive*, 231.4 *counteracting*, 331.9, 478.12 *reactive*
retroactively 3.24 *historically*, 221.13 *reversibly*, 231.5 *counter*, 331.10 *on the rebound*, 478.24 *in answer*
retroactive pay 746.3 *pay*
retrocede 337.1 *go backward*, 629.3 *restore*, 735.4 *give back*
retrocession 337.10 *backward motion*, 629.9 *restoration*, 735.1 *giving back*
retrocessive 337.22 *backward*
retroflex 337.1 *go backward*
retroflexion 221.1 *reversion*, 337.10 *backward motion*
retrogradation 337.10 *backward motion*, 628.7 *deterioration*
retrograde 221.10 *regressive*, 337.1 *go backward*, 337.22 *backward*, 628.1 *deteriorate*, 628.12 *deteriorated*
retrograde metamorphism 54.32 *metamorphism*
retrograde state 221.1 *reversion*
retrogress 221.6 *reverse*, 324.13 *be in motion*, 337.1 *go backward*, 628.1 *deteriorate*
retrogression 221.1 *reversion*, 337.10 *backward motion*, 628.7 *deterioration*
retrogressive 324.17 *directional*, 337.22 *backward*, 628.12 *deteriorated*
retrorocket 53.35 *rocketry*
retrospect 511
retrospection 200, 221.1 *reversion*, 461.3 *thoughtfulness*, 511.1 *memory*
retrospective 200, 200.2 *retrospection*, 221.10 *regressive*, 337.24 *retroactive*, 511.2 *retrospect*, 511.8 *remembering*, 526.6 *display*
retrospective action 221.1 *reversion*
retrospectively 200, 3.24 *historically*, 221.13 *reversibly*, 511.16 *memorably*
retroussé 270.7 *short*, 359.22 *ascending*
retroverse 221.10 *regressive*

retroversion 221.1 *reversion*, 287.1 *inversion*
retrovert 287.3 *invert*
retrovirus 59.3 *organism*, 624.6 *infection*
retrovirus disease 624.4 *disease*
retsina 351.9 *wine*
return 183, 221, 221, 337, 344, 19.12 *special team*, 19.17 *kick*, 109.1 *interchange*, 109.7 *reciprocate*, 125.10 *counterbalancing*, 183.21 *be repeated*, 187.6 *periodicity*, 187.10 *be periodical*, 214.1 *regularity*, 214.2 *cycle*, 214.8 *be cyclic*, 219.2 *protraction*, 221.1 *reversion*, 221.6 *reverse*, 243.7 *produce*, 331.1, 331.4 *recoil*, 335.11 *turn round*, 337.1 *go backward*, 337.5 *turn back*, 338.5, 338.23 *throw*, 344.4 *land*, 345.7 *departure*, 457.6 *reappearance*, 478.4 *reaction*, 478.17 *answer*, 478.19 *react*, 528.3 *document*, 545.1 *record*, 580.5 *vote*, 581.1 *reject*, 606.1 *provision*, 613.8 *benefit*, 629.3 *restore*, 672.3 *retaliate*, 721.4 *earnings*, 735.1 *giving back*, 735.4 *give back*, 749.2 *money received*, 878.5 *turnover*
returnable 221.12 *reversible*
return action 125.2, 125.5 *counterbalance*, 231.1 *counteraction*
return a favour 837.6 *be grateful*
return a soft answer 677.4 *pacify*
return a verdict 16.76 *judge*
return blow for blow 670.8 *counterattack*
return correspondence 478.2 *acknowledgement*
returned 221.11 *reversed*, 478.11 *answering*, 580.15 *chosen*, 581.10 *rejected*
returned-letter office 534.2 *postal communication*
returned to health 629.15 *cured*
return empty-handed 683.6 *fail*
returner 735
return from the grave 629.4 *be restored*
return good for evil 672.3 *retaliate*, 831.8 *be benevolent*, 839.12 *show mercy*
return home 221.8 *return*
returning 337, 183.14 *recurrent*, 187.8 *periodical*, 214.11 *regular*, 478.12 *reactive*, 629.9 *restoration*, 735.1 *giving back*
returning good for evil 672.1 *retaliation*
returning home 221.4 *return*
return like for like 672.3 *retaliate*
return match 183.5 *repeat*
return once again 214.8 *be cyclic*
return receipt 534.2 *postal communication*
returns 580.12 *election*, 721.4 *earnings*, 730.2 *something received*
return signal 534.28 *radar*
return thanks 837.6 *be grateful*
return the compliment 223.5 *exchange*, 664.12 *reciprocate*, 672.3 *retaliate*
return ticket 221.4 *return*
return to 183, 219.4 *protract*
return to base 337.17 *resilience*
return to fashion 629.10 *revival*
return to go 156.28 *begin again*
return to health 623.6 *get healthy*, 629.11 *recuperation*
return to mint condition 629.3 *restore*
return to normal 629.4 *be restored*, 629.9 *restoration*, 629.11 *recuperation*
return to the land of the living 629.4 *be restored*, 629.10 *revival*
return to the past 200.15 *look back*
return to the starting point 334.3 *circuit*, 363.6 *orbit*
return to the straight and narrow 867.4 *be penitent*
Reuben sandwich 45.11 *sandwich*
reunion 135.1 *union*, 161.9 *social gathering*

reupholster 629.1 *repair*
reusable 599.10, 613.2 *usable*
reusably 599.11 *usefully*
reuse 599.3 *exploit*, 599.6 *use*
reused 599.9 *used*
reused product 599
Reuters 528.8 *source of information*, 533.7 *press agency*
revalidate 629.3 *restore*
revamp 216.8 *cause change*, 629.2 *refurbish*
rev counter 268.8 *meter*
reveal 526, 6.22 *educate*, 43.9 *miscellaneous architectural features*, 243.10 *produce*, 289.14 *externalize*, 296.14 *undress*, 322.18 *open*, 435.18, 437.10 *make visible*, 442.11 *be transparent*, 457.14 *present*, 475.15 *demonstrate*, 496.2 *detect*, 517.11 *predict*, 530.5 *disclose*, 532.13 *make public*, 543.10 *signify*
revealed 457.7 *appearing*, 475.9 *demonstrated*, 496.14 *discovered*, 526.14 *manifest*, 530.10 *disclosed*, 532.19 *published*, 537.15 *true*
revealer 530.4 *discloser*
revealing 6.16 *educational*, 296.1 *undress*, 442.2 *translucent*, 496.13 *discovering*, 528.16 *informative*, 530.11 *disclosing*, 543.14 *signifying*
revealing dress 296.4 *dishabille*
revealingly 6.25 *educationally*, 296.17 *nakedly*, 496.16 *originally*, 543.18 *indicatively*
reveal itself 457.12 *become visible*
reveal oneself 526.4 *show oneself*
reveal one's mind 526.4 *show oneself*
reveal one's opinions 526.4 *show oneself*
reveal one's thoughts 526.4 *show oneself*
reveal to the public 526.1 *display*
reveille 543.6 *word*
revel 350.24 *have a meal*, 773.1 *rejoicing*, 773.5 *rejoice*, 812.1 *celebration*, 812.15 *celebrate*, 874.14 *drinking bout*
revelation 437.3 *visibility*, 457.1 *appearance*, 457.4 *something that appears*, 475.1 *demonstration*, 496.7 *detection*, 514.4 *surprising thing*, 517.1 *prediction*, 526.10 *manifestation*, 530.1 *disclosure*, 537.3 *the truth*
revelatory 530, 6.16 *educational*, 475.9 *demonstrated*, 496.13 *discovering*
revel in 405.8 *feel pleasure*
reveller 762.3 *joyful person*, 773.4 *rejoicer*, 874.17 *drunkard*
revelling 773.9 *rejoicing*
revelry 405.4 *pleasurable things*, 762.2 *fun*, 812.1 *celebration*, 815.1 *sociability*
revels 812.1 *celebration*
revenge! 672
revenge 855, 125.2, 125.5 *counterbalance*, 672.1 *retaliation*, 672.3 *retaliate*, 855.10 *avenge*, 879.9 *retribution*
revenged 125.7 *compensated*
revengeful 672.5 *retaliatory*, 832.13 *merciless*, 836.4 *pitiless*, 855.14 *vindictive*, 862.7 *evil*, 879.19 *punitive*
revengefully 855.16 *vindictively*, 862.12 *evilly*
revengefulness 836.1 *pitilessness*, 862.1 *evil*
revenge killing 398.1 *killing*
revenge match 674.2 *contest*
revenge oneself 746.13 *retaliate*, 879.2 *penalize*
revenger 672, 635.2 *troublemaker*, 879.17 *punisher*
revenge tragedy 51.9 *tragedy*
revenue 13.6 *economic factors*, 243.7 *produce*, 602.4 *financial resources*, 721.4 *earnings*, 725.5 *personal estate*, 730.2 *something received*, 734.5 *takings*, 749.2 *money received*

revenue cutter 74 *Ships and Boats*
reverb 420.10 *sound quality*
reverberant 426.15 *drumming*
reverberantly 427.11 *resonantly*, 478.24 *in answer*
reverberate 183.22 *resound*, 331.1 *recoil*, 420.16 *be heard*, 423.8 *be loud*, 426.8 *drum*, 427.9 *resonate*, 478.19 *react*
reverberating 427.6 *resonant*
reverberation 183, 56.21 *architectural acoustics*, 159.4 *repercussion*, 331.4 *recoil*, 420.8 *something heard*, 423.1 *loudness*, 426.1 *drumming*, 427.1 *resonance*, 478.4 *reaction*
reverberation chamber 56.21 *architectural acoustics*
reverberation time 56.21 *architectural acoustics*
reverberative 331.8 *recoiling*, 426.15 *drumming*, 427.6 *resonant*
reverberatory 183, 44.6 *ceramic workshop*, 44.10 *ceramic*, 159.10 *repercussive*, 478.12 *reactive*
reverberatory kiln 44.6 *ceramic workshop*
reverdie 48.7 *poem*
revere 849, 7.19 *be religious*, 9.7 *worship*, 10.19 *offer worship*, 362.9 *bow*, 821.3 *love*
revered 9.11 *worshipped*, 821.21 *beloved*, 849.12 *respected*
reverence 7.2 *religiousness*, 9.1, 9.7 *worship*, 10.3 *rite of worship*, 10.19 *offer worship*, 362.16 *courtesy*, 694.3 *obeisance*, 847.3 *allegiance*, 849.2 *admiration*, 849.16 *revere*
reverenced 849.12 *respected*
reverend father 7.7 *monk*
reverend mother 7.7 *monk*
reverent 849, 7.15 *religious*, 9.9 *worshipful*, 10.22 *worshipping*, 804.6 *worshipful*
reverential 7.15 *religious*, 9.9 *worshipful*, 694.9 *obeisant*, 847.9 *loyal*, 849.10 *reverent*
reverentially 7.23 *religiously*, 9.12 *worshipfully*, 694.10 *obediently*, 849.22 *respectfully*
reverently 849.22 *respectfully*
reverie 519, 61.14 *trance*, 461.3 *thoughtfulness*, 462.6 *daydream*
reversal 337, 484, 111.1 *oppositeness*, 216.1 *change*, 221.1 *reversion*, 287.1 *inversion*, 476.1 *refutation*, 476.2 *denial*, 514.4 *surprising thing*, 578.6 *equivocation*, 683.2 *defeat*, 704.1 *cancellation*, 722.1 *loss*
reverse 42 *Card Games,* **71** *Motor Vehicle Parts,* **221, 337, 484,** 19.9 *play*, 34.3 *climbing technique*, 34.9 *mountaineer*, 39.11 *swimming*, 111.1 *oppositeness*, 111.4 *opposite*, 111.8 *be opposite*, 216.7 *be changed*, 216.11 *changeable*, 287.1 *inversion*, 287.3 *invert*, 328.3 *slow down*, 335.11 *turn round*, 337.12 *reversal*, 337.25 *reversed*, 476.9 *deny*, 536.3 *rebuttal*, 536.8 *rebut*, 663.21 *contrary*, 704.6 *cancel*, 722.1 *loss*
reverse-charge call 534.10 *telephone call*
reverse curve 22.4 *pitching terms*
reversed 221, 337, 111.4 *opposite*, 287.2 *inverted*, 536.12 *rejected*
reverse direction 335.11 *turn round*, 337.10 *backward motion*
reverse dive 39.6 *diving*
reversed-phase 57.41 *analytic*
reverse fault 54.20 *earth movement*
reverse killian hold 41.7 *ice-dancing*
reverse of the truth 538.1 *untruth*
reverse one's field 337.3 *reverse*
reverse order 150.3 *hierarchy*
reverse punch 26.9 *tae kwon do*
reverser 704.5 *abrogator*

reverse snowplough 41.4 *skiing technique*
reverse sweep 27.9 *stroke*
reverse twist 40.2 *tennis strokes*
reverse word dictionary 5.28 *dictionary*
reversible 221, 57.38 *reactive,* 337.25 *reversed*
reversible reaction 57.14 *chemical reaction*
reversibly 221
reversing 337.12 *reversal*
reversing light 71 Motor Vehicle Parts, 439.6 *electric light*
reversion 221, 61.19 *defence mechanism,* 127.2 *deficiency,* 287.1 *inversion,* 331.4 *recoil,* 337.12 *reversal,* 337.16 *countermotion,* 704.1 *cancellation,* 725.2 *legal terms,* 728.1 *transfer of property,* 735.1 *giving back*
Reversion 221
reversional 221.10 *regressive*
reversionary 221.10 *regressive*
reversion to type 628.7 *deterioration*
revert 183.19 *return to,* 216.7 *be changed,* 221.6 *reverse,* 331.1 *recoil,* 335.11 *turn round,* 337.1 *go backward,* 628.1 *deteriorate*
reverted 221.11 *reversed*
revert to bachelorhood 824.7 *divorce*
revert to the single state 824.7 *divorce*
revet 293.28 *face*
revetment 293.8 *wall covering*
revictual 606.6 *replenish*
review 3.22 *remember,* 6.8 *learning,* 48.4 *non-fiction,* 51.5 *show,* 183.2 *iteration,* 183.17 *iterate,* 200.2 *retrospection,* 200.15 *look back,* 477.2 *questioning,* 477.17 *question,* 492.1 *judgment,* 492.12 *estimate,* 511.2 *retrospect,* 511.12 *remember,* 511.13 *remind,* 524.3 *criticism,* 524.11 *criticize,* 528.2 *communication,* 528.3 *document,* 532.5 *journal,* 560.15 *recount,* 561.2 *article,* 562.1 *summary,* 568.6 *interview,* 627.3 *rectify,* 627.7 *reconsideration,* 811.13 *ceremonial,* 813.3 *formal occasion*
reviewed 477.16 *questioned*
reviewer 51.31 *theatregoer,* 477.9 *questioner,* 492.5 *judge,* 524.6 *interpreter,* 561.3 *dissertator*
reviewing 3.13 *looking back*
revile 670.10 *criticize,* 766.7 *be dissatisfied,* 827.6 *vilify,* 852.22 *vituperate,* 854.13 *vilify*
revilement 670.16 *terrorist attack,* 827.3 *vilification,* 852.8 *berating,* 854.5 *scorn*
reviling 827.9 *vituperative*
revisable 201.15 *renewable*
revisal 201.5 *fresh start,* 627.6 *rectification*
revise 201.20 *make new,* 216.8 *cause change,* 592.6 *outline,* 592.10 *plan out,* 627.3 *rectify,* 627.6 *rectification*
revised 201.14 *renewed,* 216.12 *changed,* 627.14 *improved*
revised copy 592.6 *outline*
revised edition 245.2 *print,* 627.8 *better thing*
Revised Version 7.12 *religious text*
reviser 627, 216.6 *editor*
revision 216.1 *change,* 592.6 *outline,* 627.6 *rectification*
revisionism 168.3 *nonconformism*
revisionist 224.4 *editor*
revisionist history 3.1 *history*
revitalization 239.1 *vigour,* 629.10 *revival,* 651.5 *refreshment*
revitalize 239.3, 396.21 *invigorate,* 606.6 *replenish,* 629.5 *revive,* 651.1 *refresh*
revitalized 651.4 *refreshed*
revitalizing 239.5 *invigorating,* 651.3 *refreshing*

revival 629, 51.12 *production,* 183.4 *return,* 201.5 *fresh start,* 216.1 *change,* 220.3 *persuasion,* 221.2 *restoration,* 237.4 *strengthening,* 245.1 *reproduction,* 396.5 *life cycle,* 627.5 *improvement,* 651.5 *refreshment*
revivalism 220.3 *persuasion,* 629.10 *revival*
revivalist 7.5 *Christian*
revive 629, 183.20 *renew,* 201.20 *make new,* 216.8 *cause change,* 220.11 *persuade,* 221.7 *restore,* 237.7 *be strong,* 237.8 *strengthen,* 239.3 *invigorate,* 396.16 *live,* 396.19 *give birth to,* 413.13 *be piquant,* 623.7 *make healthy,* 627.1 *improve,* 627.2 *get better,* 629.3 *restore,* 629.4 *be restored,* 630.20 *doctor,* 651.1 *refresh,* 651.2 *be refreshed,* 662.19 *support,* 769.6 *bring cheer*
revived 183.11 *reprinted,* 201.14 *renewed,* 216.12 *changed,* 220.16 *influenced,* 221.11 *reversed,* 237.13 *strengthened,* 396.12 *alive,* 629.13 *repaired,* 651.4 *refreshed*
reviver 413.6 *cordial,* 630.7 *tonic,* 651.6 *refresher*
revivescence 629.10 *revival*
revive the spirit 396.21 *invigorate*
revivification 201.5 *fresh start,* 237.4 *strengthening,* 396.5 *life cycle,* 629.10 *revival*
revivified 201.14 *renewed*
revivify 201.20 *make new,* 237.8 *strengthen,* 629.5 *revive*
revivifying 237.4 *strengthening,* 239.5 *invigorating*
reviving 237.4 *strengthening,* 239.5 *invigorating,* 629.16 *restorative,* 651.3 *refreshing,* 769.2 *cheering*
rev limiter 33.6 *motor racing terms*
revocation 484.2 *reversal,* 536.4 *renunciation,* 578.8 *recantation,* 704.1 *cancellation*
revocatory 536.11 *negative,* 711.9 *dissenting*
revoke 581, 244.8 *destroy,* 484.8 *reverse,* 536.9 *renounce,* 578.4 *recant,* 704.6 *cancel,* 709.3 *veto,* 727.9 *dispose of*
revoked 484.6 *countered,* 704.10 *cancelled*
revoker 704.5 *abrogator*
revoking 578.8 *recantation,* 711.9 *dissenting*
revolt 669, 16.41 *lawlessness,* 168.2 *dissent,* 168.18 *not conform,* 216.1 *change,* 216.7 *be changed,* 216.8 *cause change,* 220.8 *be transformed,* 341.4 *be repulsive,* 669.3 *resistance movement,* 676.1 *war,* 676.12 *go to war,* 689.4 *be anarchic,* 693.4 *revolution,* 693.16 *be subversive,* 713.2 *disorder,* 713.8 *cause mischief,* 764.10 *displease,* 766.6 *dissatisfy,* 785.7 *cause dislike*
revolter 12.6 *political party,* 693.11 *rebel,* 713.5 *seditionist*
revolting 618.4 *poor,* 764.1 *unpleasant,* 785.9 *disliked,* 822.12 *hated*
revolution 693, 53.21 *orbit,* 151.8 *lawlessness,* 214.2 *cycle,* 216.1 *change,* 220.2 *evolution,* 334.1 *circuit,* 362.12 *downthrow,* 363.1 *orbital motion,* 364.1 *rotation,* 627.11 *reformism,* 668.3 *act of defiance,* 669.3 *resistance movement,* 676.1 *war,* 688.3 *acquisition of power,* 689.1 *anarchy*
revolutionarily 201.21 *newly*
revolutionary 119.5 *novel,* 168.8 *dissenter,* 168.12 *nonconformist,* 201.10 *new,* 216.6 *editor,* 216.11 *changeable,* 224.4 *editor,* 241.4 *violent person or animal,* 244.6 *destroyer,* 244.14 *destructive,* 362.22 *overthrown,* 363.9 *orbital,* 500.5 *dissenter,*

627.12 *reformer,* 635.2 *troublemaker,* 663.9 *opposer,* 669.5 *resister,* 669.12 *resisting,* 689.3 *anarchist,* 689.6 *anarchic,* 693.11 *rebel,* 693.14 *subversive,* 713.5 *seditionist,* 713.10 *lawbreaking*
revolutionist 244.6 *destroyer,* 693.11 *rebel*
revolutionize 119.7 *originate,* 216.8 *cause change*
revolutions 364.1 *rotation*
revolutions per minute 364.1 *rotation*
revolve 53.37 *observe,* 214.8 *be cyclic,* 313.6 *circle,* 334.3 *circuit,* 363.6 *orbit,* 364.8 *rotate*
revolver 338.9, 680.9 *firearm*
revolving 214.11 *regular,* 214.12 *cyclic,* 364.1 *rotation,* 364.11 *rotating*
revolving door 364.6 *rotator*
revolving fund 14.1, 741.7 *finance*
revolving stage 51.15 *stage*
revs 364.1 *rotation*
revue 51.5 *show*
revulsion 331.6 *response,* 591.12 *shyness,* 822.1 *hate*
revulsive 331.9 *reactive*
rev up 230.8 *activate,* 426.10 *rattle,* 594.4 *prepare for action*
reward 878, 878, 125.1 *compensation,* 125.4 *compensate,* 586.17 *bribe,* 681.1 *trophy,* 721.5 *profit,* 729.2 *gift,* 729.5 *give,* 746.3 *pay,* 746.11 *remunerate,* 751.2 *value,* 812.17 *congratulate,* 837.3 *recognition,* 837.6 *be grateful,* 845.2 *due*
Reward 878
rewarded 878, 125.7 *compensated,* 730.11 *receiving*
rewarder 125.3 *compensator,* 729.4 *giver*
reward for service 878
rewarding 682, 878, 721.15 *gainful,* 746.18 *profitable*
rewardingly 878, 682.16 *successfully*
reward of conduct 652.1 *conduct*
rewa-rewa 85 Trees and Shrubs
rewed 823.15 *marry*
reword 5.46 *translate,* 5.47 *word,* 524.12 *translate*
reworded 5.40 *translated*
rewording 5.12 *translation,* 5.40 *translated,* 524.4 *translation*
rewritable 65.20 *on-line*
rewrite 5.47 *word,* 558.4 *be elegant,* 627.3 *rectify*
rewriter 627.13 *reviser*
rewritten 627.14 *improved*
rex 77 Breeds of Cats
Rex 696.2 *sovereign*
Reykjavik 93 Cities
Reynard 657.3 *cunning person*
Reynolds number 56 Named Laws
RFC 35.1 *rugger*
R-form 57.13 *structure*
RFU 35.1 *rugger*
rfz 49 Musical Terms
RGA 57.20 *surface chemistry*
rhabdophobia 777 Phobias by Name
Rhadamanthine 16.49 *judicatory*
Rhadamanthus 16.23 *judge*
Rhaetian 5 Languages and Groups of Languages
Rhaeto-Romanic 5 Languages and Groups of Languages
rhamnose 58 Common Sugars
rhapsodic 48.19 *narrative,* 519.10 *imaginative*
rhapsodist 48.14 *author,* 519.9 *visionary*
rhapsodize 506.6 *talk nonsense,* 519.15 *fantasize*
rhapsody 519.4 *ideality*
rhea 78 Birds, 78.2 *flightless bird*
Rhea 8 Deities
Rheita Valley 53 Rills and Valleys
rhenium 57 Chemical Elements
rheometer 268.8 *meter*
rheometric 268.16 *micrometric*

rheometry 268.2 *micrometry*
rheostat 64.17 *resistor*
Rhesus factor 387.4 *blood*
rhesus monkey 77 Placental Mammals
Rheticus 52 Scientists
rhetoric 4.5 *philosophical argument,* 549.4 *literary style,* 553.1 *diffuseness,* 557.1 *ornament,* 557.2 *affectation,* 564.9 *art of public speaking*
rhetorical 474.7 *sophistic,* 553.3 *diffuse,* 557.4 *ornate,* 559.9 *inelegant,* 564.20 *eloquent,* 567.13 *oratorical*
rhetorically 4.24 *philosophically,* 474.14 *sophistically,* 549.10 *stylistically,* 564.21 *orally*
rhetorical question 477.5 *easy question*
rhetorician 228.7 *motivator,* 549.5 *stylist,* 557.3 *phrasemonger,* 564.10 *speaker,* 567.6 *public speaker,* 586.12 *persuader*
rheum 352.2 *secreted substance,* 353.9 *saliva,* 387.3 *body fluid*
rheumatic 624.23 *diseased*
rheumatic fever 624.16 *rheumatism*
rheumatic heart disease 624.10 *cardiovascular disease*
rheumaticky 624.23 *diseased*
rheumatics 624.16 *rheumatism*
rheumatism 624, 406.2 *painful condition*
rheumatoid 624.23 *diseased*
rheumatoid arthritis 624.16 *rheumatism*
rheumatologist 60.13 *medical specialist*
rheumatology 60.3 *medical specialty*
rheuminess 387.5 *fluidity*
rheumy 387, 353.29 *salivating*
Rh factor 387.4 *blood*
Rhine 52 Scientists, **96** Rivers, 96.5 *other major rivers*
Rhineland Heavy Draught 32 Breeds of Horse and Pony
Rhine wine 351.9 *wine*
rhinitis 624.9 *respiratory disease*
rhino 741.2 *cash*
rhinoceros 77 Placental Mammals, **161** Collective Names by Animal, 77.14 *pachyderm*
rhinoceros beetle 82 Insects
rhinoceroses 77.15 *hoofed mammal*
rhinocerotic 77.32 *pachydermatous*
Rhinog Fawr 95 Mountains
rhino-hided 761.1 *insensitive*
rhinological 416.6 *olfactory*
rhinoplastic 630.18 *medical*
rhinoplasty 60 Surgical Operations, 630.12 *surgery*
rhinorrhoea 624.9 *respiratory disease*
Rhiw Hill 68 Breeds of Sheep
rhizine 90.6 *lichen*
rhizoid 83.7 *root,* 83.19 *of roots,* 88.4 *moss plant,* 89.4 *fungal body,* 90.3 *plant body*
rhizome 69.9 *garden plant,* 83.5 *stem*
rhizomorph 83.7 *root,* 89.4 *fungal body*
rhizopus 89 Fungi
rhizotomy 60 Surgical Operations
Rh-negative 387.4 *blood*
rhodamine dye 67.6 *dye*
Rhode Island 92 American States
Rhode Island Red 68 Breeds of Fowl
Rhodes 18 Sporting Personalities, **98** Islands
Rhodesian ridgeback 77 Breeds of Dogs
rhodic 57.34 *elemental*
rhodium 57 Chemical Elements
rhodochrosite 50 Minerals
rhododendron 84 Flowers and Flowering Plants, 455.3 *purple thing*
rhodolite 54 Gemstones

rhodonite 54 Minerals
Rhodophyta 90.2 *algae*
rhodophyte 90.2 *algae*
rhodous 57.34 *elemental*
rhomb 52.44 *polygon*
rhombic 52.82 *polygonal*, 57.33 *crystalline*
rhombic crystal 57.4 *crystal*
rhombohedron 52.46 *polyhedron*
rhomboid 52.44 *polygon*, 286.2 *oblique line*, 310.3 *angled figure*
rhomboidal 52.82 *polygonal*, 310.9 *angled*
rhombus 52.44 *polygon*, 178.2 *quadrilateral*, 310.3 *angled figure*
rhonchus 429.1 *hiss*
Rhondda 93 Cities
Rhône 96.5 *other major rivers*
Rh-positive 387.4 *blood*
rhubarb 86 Fruits, 5.5 *nonstandard language*, 666.2 *argument*, 674.1 *contention*
rhubarb! rhubarb! 565
rhumb line 332.3 *orientation*
Rhyl 93 Cities
rhyme 48, 5.45 *use language*, 48.6 *poetry*, 48.7 *poem*, 48.21 *write*, 114.12 *imitate*, 116.4 *harmony*, 116.24 *harmonize*, 183.6 *reverberation*, 183.22 *resound*, 308.1 *symmetry*, 426.7 *repeated word*, 433.8 *harmonize*
rhymed 183.15 *reverberatory*
rhymer 48.14 *author*
rhyme royal 48.10 *verse form*
rhyme scheme 48.11 *rhyme*
rhymester 48.14 *author*
rhyming 5.42 *worded*, 48.20 *metrical*, 114.7 *similar*, 116.13 *harmonious*, 183.15 *reverberatory*, 433.7 *harmonious*
rhyming couplet 48.8 *part of poem*
rhyming dictionary 5.28 *dictionary*
rhyming slang 5.18 *slang*, 5.26 *dialect*
rhyming word 5.17 *word*
Rhynocephalia 79.1 *reptile*
rhynocephalian 79.2 *lizard*
rhyolite 54 Common Rocks
Rhys 93 Writers
rhythm 30.8 *floor exercises*, 48.9 *metre*, 49.19 *tempo*, 183.6 *reverberation*, 185.12 *musical time*, 214.1 *regularity*, 214.5 *regular thing*, 324.10 *regular movement*, 365.2 *vibration*, 382.9 *artistic structure*, 426.6 *musical repetition*, 433.3 *melodiousness*, 558.1 *elegance*
rhythmic 30.11 *gymnastic*, 159.12 *cyclical*, 183.15 *reverberatory*, 214.11 *regular*, 324.17 *directional*, 365.14 *vibrating*, 558.3 *elegant*
rhythmical 48.20 *metrical*, 183.15 *reverberatory*, 214.11 *regular*, 365.14 *vibrating*
rhythmically 21.7 *fast*, 48.22 *poetically*, 214.15 *regularly*, 426.19 *repeatedly*, 558.5 *elegantly*
rhythmic gymnastics 18 Sporting Activities, 30.1 *gymnastics*
rhythmic pattern 564.6 *phonetics*
rhythmics 49.14 *harmonics*
rhythm method 247.3 *birth control*
rhythm 'n' blues 49.9 *popular music*
rhythm section 180.6 *accompanier*
RI 6.3 *subject*
rialto 223.2 *place of exchange*
Rialto 740.5 *stock market*
rib 382 Bones, 34.5 *rock face*, 43.9 *miscellaneous architectural features*, 43.19 *decorate*, 45.23 *beef*, 45.27 *lamb*, 63.27 *superstructure*, 771.13 *be humorous*
ribald 795, 622.9 *obscene*, 827.8 *cursing*, 877.12 *indecent*
ribaldly 827.12 *swearingly*
ribaldry 622.3 *obscenity*, 827.1 *curse*, 877.2 *indecency*
ribband 137.6 *line*

ribbed 43.15 *vaulted*, 43.17 *structured*, 383.8 *rough*
Ribble 96 Rivers
ribbon 137.10 *band*, 295.15 *headgear*, 544.4 *insignia*, 545.11 *monument*, 681.1 *trophy*, 792.5 *decorative articles*, 804.3 *honours*, 821.15 *love item*
ribbon development 162.7 *sprawl*, 357.10 *expansionism*
ribbonfish 80 Fishes
ribbons 137.9 *yoke*
ribbonwood 85 Trees and Shrubs
ribbonworm 81 Worms
ribbon worm 81.6 *worm*
riblets 45.27 *lamb*
ribonucleotide 58.10 *nucleoside*
ribose 58 Common Sugars
ribosomal 59.23 *cellular*
ribosomal RNA 59.13 *genetic material*
ribosome 59.8 *cell organ*
ribs 44.6 *ceramic workshop*, 284.2 *supporting part*, 305.1 *side*
rib-tickling 798.5 *ridiculous*
rib vault 43.7 *vault*
rice 87 Grasses, 68.12 *crop*
ricebird 78 Birds
rice paddy 68.11 *farmland*
rice pancake 45.49 *Indian dish*
rice paper 379.3 *brittle thing*, 604.3 *paper*
rice pudding 45.35 *dessert*
rich 243.11 *productive*, 246.5 *fertile*, 350.27 *edible*, 386.10, 395.11 *oily*, 427.8 *deep*, 433.6 *melodious*, 444.11 *colourful*, 553.3 *diffuse*, 557.4 *ornate*, 608.2 *plentiful*, 617.3 *valuable*, 686.8 *prosperous*, 721.17 *well-off*, 741.23 *solvent*, 742.1 *wealthy*, 792.8 *decorated*
rich and poor 111.2 *opposites*
Richard II 48 Shakespeare's plays
Richard III 48 Shakespeare's plays
Richards 18 Sporting Personalities
Richardson 48 Writers
Richard's paradox 4.9 *philosophical problem*
rich as Croesus 721.17 *well-off*, 742.1 *wealthy*
rich as King Midas 721.17 *well-off*
rich as Rockefeller 742.1 *wealthy*
rich as Solomon 742.1 *wealthy*
rich earth 246.1 *fertility*
riches 608.8 *plenty*, 682.1 *success*, 741.3 *fortune*, 742.6 *money*
riches of Solomon 742.6 *money*
rich food 350.7 *food*
rich harvest 246.1 *fertility*, 608.8 *plenty*
rich in 608.3 *filled*
Richler 48 Writers
richly 395.20 *oilily*, 427.11 *resonantly*, 686.9 *prosperously*, 721.20 *gainfully*, 742.16 *wealthily*
richly decorated 557.4 *ornate*
richly deserve 845.15 *merit*
richly-deserved 845.10 *due*
richly furnished 742.3 *opulent*
Richmond 93 Cities, 93 Cities, 93.3 New York
richness 246.1 *fertility*, 395.1 *oiliness*, 411.4 *flavour*, 427.2 *deepness*, 553.1 *diffuseness*, 608.8 *plenty*, 610.1 *excess*, 742.5 *wealth*, 792.1 *adornment*
rich person 686.4 *prosperous person*, 721.7 *gainer*, 742.10 *wealthy person*
rich pickings 734.5 *takings*, 736.4 *stolen goods*
rich soil 246.1 *fertility*
Richter scale 54.22 *seismic activity*
rich uncle 729.4 *giver*
rich vein 605.2 *resource*, 608.8 *plenty*
rich vocabulary 553.1 *diffuseness*, 564.2 *power of speech*
rick 68.10 *farm tool*, 161.27 *bundle*

rickets 58.14 *vitamin deficiency disease*, 350.10 *scarcity*, 624.4 *disease*
rickettsia 59.3 *organism*
rickettsial 59.21 *living*
rickety 238.8 *weak*, 620.1 *imperfect*, 624.23 *diseased*, 628.13 *dilapidated*, 633.2 *unsafe*
rickshaw 71 Carriages and Carts
ricky-tick 612.4 *trivial*
ricochet 221.1 *reversion*, 221.6 *reverse*, 331.1, 331.4 *recoil*
Ricoeur 4 Philosophers
rictus 309.2 *facial distortion*, 366.8 *spasm*
rid 767.10 *save*
riddance 134.2 *purification*, 147.2 *ejection*, 638.1 *escape*, 639.2 *deliverance*, 722.1 *loss*, 727.1 *disposal*
riddle 338, 477.4 *difficult question*, 506.2 *solecism*, 523.12 *unintelligible thing*, 529.4 *brainteaser*, 578.5 *equivocalness*, 603.2 *garden tool*, 603.9 *use tools*, 621.10 *cleaning object*
riddled with holes 322.14 *holed*
riddle-me-ree 529.4 *brain-teaser*
riddle of the Sphinx 527.11 *mysteriousness*
riddle of the sphinx 529.5 *difficult problem*
riddle with holes 322.20 *hole*
riddling 477.13 *problematic*
ride 32, 70.4 *transport*, 74.10 *sail*
ride a broomstick 11.21 *bewitch*
ride against 670.1 *attack*
ride and tie 365.8 *oscillate*, 365.18 *to and fro*
ride a tiger 633.8 *be in danger*
ride a wave 36.18 *windsurf*
ride bareback 32.16 *ride*
ride down 590.10 *chase*, 670.9 *attack successfully*
ride full tilt at 590.10 *chase*, 670.1 *attack*
ride hard 329.4 *be swift*
ride height 33.6 *motor racing terms*
ride it out 632.8 *be safe*
ride on an even keel 74.10 *sail*
ride on a rail 349.7 *drive out*
ride on the crest of a wave 686.5 *be prosperous*
ride out a storm 36.15 *sail*
ride out the storm 74.10 *sail*
rider 32.15 *horse person*, 130.3 *additional item*, 679.20 *cavalryman*
ride roughshod over 330.7 *kick*, 688.19 *be authoritarian*, 690.6 *suppress*, 720.10 *violate the law*, 807.26 *oppress*, 850.22 *show disrespect*
ride shotgun 632.9 *protect*
ride side-saddle 32.16 *ride*
ride the tiger 780.5 *be rash*
ride to hounds 590.11 *hunt*
ridge 34.5 *rock face*, 41.1 *skiing*, 55.11 *weather system*, 68.11 *farmland*, 95.1 *mountain*, 137.4 *means of connection*, 272.6 *narrow place*, 275.4 *mountain range*, 279.1 *summit*
ridged 34.8 *mountaineering*, 41.12 *ski*, 375.2 *coarse*
ridgepole 279.3 *architectural summit*
ridger 68.10 *farm tool*
ridgetree 85.12 *figurative usage*
ridicule 777 Phobias by Topic, 807, 850, 854, 498.8 *disbelieve*, 525.1 *misinterpret*, 539.28 *trick*, 581.3 *exclude*, 807.8 *rudeness*, 818.1 *discourtesy*, 852.9 *show of disapproval*, 852.23 *show disapproval*
ridiculed 539.36 *deceived*, 852.35 *hissed*
ridiculer 854
ridiculing 850, 525.2 *misinterpretation*, 799.5 *derisive*, 854.17 *scornful*
ridiculous 798, 487.1 *impossible*, 506.5 *nonsensical*, 508.5 *foolish*

ridiculously 487.11 *impossibly*, 506.9 *nonsensically*, 508.8 *foolishly*
ridiculousness 508.1 *folly*
Ridiculousness 798
riding 32.6 *horsemanship*, 32.17 *equine*, 71.9 *animal transport*, 92.2 *former British divisions*, 249.5 *state*, 324.2 *momentum*, 324.16 *moving*, 356.2 *passing along*
riding at anchor 225.9 *stable*
riding boots 295.19 *footwear*
riding breeches 295.9 *trousers*
riding habit 295.3 *formal dress*, 295.6 *skirt*
riding horse 32.4 *saddle horse*
riding jacket 295.11 *jacket*
riding lamp 74 Parts of a Ship
riding lights 439.6 *electric light*
riding pants 295.9 *trousers*
riding pony 32.5 *pony*
riding school 6.12 *educational institution*, 32.14 *horse-riding terms*
rid of 639.1 *deliver*
rid oneself of 129.5 *make smaller*, 349.13 *throw away*, 638.6 *elude*
Riemann 52 Scientists
Riemannian geometry 52 Named Concepts
riesling 351.9 *wine*
Rif 1 Peoples
rifampicin 62 Medication
rifamycin 62 Medication
rife 164.17 *widespread*, 181.9 *ample*, 246.5 *fertile*
rifeness 164.4 *widespreadness*, 181.3 *profuseness*
riff 49.37 *syncopate*
riffle 96.6 *river flow*, 96.7 *flow*, 97.3 *wave*, 97.10 *billow*
riff-raff 795.6 *vulgar herd*
rifle 338.9 *firearm*, 425.3 *banger*, 590.3 *hunting and fishing equipment*, 680.9 *firearm*, 680.11 *guns*
riflebird 78 Birds
rifle brigade 679.16 *army unit*
rifle fire 679.15 *firing*
rifled bore 680.9 *firearm*
rifleman 78 Birds, 338.15 *shooter*, 679.13 *historical soldiery*
rifle practice 676.6 *art of war*
rifle shooting 18 Sporting Activities, 37.1 *target shooting*
rifle sling 37.3 *hunting equipment*
rift 136.3 *separateness*, 265.2 *crack*, 500.4 *faction*, 620.7 *defect*, 666.2 *argument*
rift valley 54.7 *landform*
rig 71 Carriages and Carts, 74 Sails, 36.3 *parts of a sailing boat*, 36.15 *sail*, 137.7 *tackle*, 295.1 *dress*, 295.5 *fancy dress*, 309.12 *distort the truth*, 474.11 *practise sophistry*, 540.22 *falsify*
Riga 93 Cities
rigadoon 46.4 *historic dancing*
rigatoni 45 Types of Pasta
Rigel 53 Named Stars
rigged 295.29 *dressed*, 594.18 *prepared*
rigged out 594.18 *prepared*
rigger 74 Sailing Ships and Boats, 74 Parts of a Ship
rigging 36.3 *parts of a sailing boat*, 137.7 *tackle*, 540.9 *falsification*
right! 537
right 804, 843, 12.6 *political party*, 16.28 *legality*, 16.44 *legal*, 26.14 *combat*, 38.5 *soccer*, 56.78 *quantum*, 126.1 *superiority*, 305.6 *side*, 312.1 *straight*, 332.9 *directly*, 492.9 *judicious*, 503.8 *accurately*, 537.15 *true*, 537.21 *accurate*, 615.1 *convenient*, 620.1 *imperfect*, 629.1 *repair*, 629.13 *repaired*, 688.1 *authority*, 725.1 *property*, 845.3 *prerogative*, 845.13 *fit*, 861.1 *good*, 876.2 *good morals*, 876.8 *moral*
Right 843

right-about 337.13 *about-turn*
right-about-face 337.9 *turn round*, 337.13 *about-turn*
right about turn 221.1 *reversion*
right amount 608.7 *sufficiency*
right and left 297.8 *round*
right angle 52.39 *angle*, 281.3 *vertical thing*, 310.1 *angle*
right-angled 281.10 *perpendicular*, 310.9 *angled*
right-angled triangle 52.43 *triangle*, 310.3 *angled figure*
right arm 235.1 *power*
right as a trivet 619.1 *perfect*
right ascension 53.5 *celestial sphere*, 268.4 *size*
right as rain 619.1 *perfect*
right as right can be 619.1 *perfect*
right away 191.8 *immediately*, 208.17 *early*, 648.8 *hastily*
right a wrong 843.15 *put right*
right centre three-quarter 35.4 *rugby player*
right Charlie 508.3 *foolish person*
right cross 26.2 *boxing*
right defence 31.4 *ice hockey player*
righteous 134.12 *morally pure*, 843.10 *moral*, 857.5 *pure*, 861.3 *kind*, 863.5 *virtuous*, 876.8 *moral*
righteously 134.18 *virtuously*, 857.8 *purely*, 863.9 *virtuously*
righteousness 843, 857.2 *purity*, 861.10 *kindness*, 863.1 *virtue*, 876.2 *good morals*
right field 22.1 *baseball*
right fielder 22.2 *baseball player*
right form 811.11 *ritual*, 813.5 *etiquette*
rightful 16.51 *legitimate*, 537.19 *authentic*, 688.12 *authoritative*, 843.9 *in the right*, 845.8 *entitled*, 845.13 *fit*
rightful authority 688.1 *authority*
rightfully 537.37 *authentically*, 688.23 *authoritatively*, 843.16 *right*, 845.20 *duly*
rightfulness 16.30 *legitimacy*, 537.6 *authenticity*
rightful possession 723.1 *possession*
right half 38.3 *football player*
right hand 235.1 *power*, 305.1 *side*
right-hand 33.11 *racing*
right-handed 407.5 *toucher*, 407.10 *handed*
right-handed hitter 22.2 *baseball player*
right-handedness 407.7 *sense organ*
right-hand entry 744.3 *deposit*
right-hander 33.6 *motor racing terms*
right-hand kink 33.6 *motor racing terms*
right hand man 195.7 *subordinate*
right-hand man 662.11 *helper*, 697.5 *office assistant*, 701.3 *subordinate*, 707.1 *deputy*, 765.5 *helper*
right-hand side 305.3 *side direction*
right honourable 804.6 *worshipful*
right hook 26.2 *boxing*
right idea 592.3 *expedient plan*
righting 840.4 *atoning*
righting wrong 843
right in the head 509.4 *sane*
rightism 217.2 *conservatism*
rightist 12.6 *political party*, 217.8 *conservative*, 665.6 *political party member*, 665.10 *political*
right itself 629.6 *cure*
rightly 16.81 *legally*, 537.39 *accurately*, 843.16 *right*
rightly served 672.5 *retaliatory*
right man for the job 485.8 *qualified person*
right-minded 843, 876.8 *moral*
right moment 185.11 *date*, 210.1 *timeliness*
right mood 572.9 *goodwill*

rightness 537.1 *truth*, 537.8 *accuracy*, 843.1 *fairness*, 861.8 *good*
right now 191.8 *immediately*, 196.9 *at present*, 648.8 *hurry up*
righto 537.40 *right*
right of centre 665.3 *political grouping*
right of choice 580.6 *selection*
right of entry 346
right of possession 723.1 *possession*
right of purchase 738.7 *purchasing*
right of representation 580.11 *franchise*
right of way 327.2 *route*, 356.4 *access*
right-on 813.7 *dressed up*
right oneself 122.11 *equalize*
right person for the job 655.5 *expert*
right qualities 608.7 *sufficiency*
rights 698.2 *free speech*
right side 305.3 *side direction*
rights of man 845.3 *prerogative*
right stick 31.3 *ice hockey*
rights under law 225.4 *stable thing*
right time 106.2 *occurrence*, 185.7 *time measurement*, 185.11 *date*, 210.1 *timeliness*, 615.3 *convenience*
right time and place 615.3 *convenience*
right to a hair 537.39 *accurately*
right to an inch 537.39 *accurately*
right to a T 537.39 *accurately*
right to a turn 537.39 *accurately*
right to bear arms 698.2 *free speech*
right to left 365.18 *to and fro*
right-to-work law 15.5 *labour law*
right triangle 52.43 *triangle*
right up one's alley 615.1 *convenient*
right up one's street 615.1 *convenient*
right uppercut 26.2 *boxing*, 330.14 *sporting hit*
rightward 332.10 *clockwise*
right whale 77 *Placental Mammals*
right wing 31.4 *ice hockey player*, 31.6 *lacrosse player*
right-wing 217.8 *conservative*, 665.10 *political*
right-winger 12.6 *political party*, 217.3 *conservative person*, 665.6 *political party member*
right-wing politics 217.2 *conservatism*
right wing three-quarter 35.4 *rugby player*
right you are 537.40 *right*
Rigi 95 *Mountains*
rigid 217.7 *permanent*, 312.1 *straight*, 371.6 *dense*, 373.2 *tough*, 378.3 *hard*, 379.1 *brittle*, 537.24 *pedantic*, 577.3 *unyielding*, 669.11 *obstinate*, 690.8 *severe*, 813.6 *formal*
rigid control 61.19 *defence mechanism*
rigidity 217.1 *permanence*, 325.1 *motionlessness*, 373.5 *hardness*, 503.1 *accuracy*, 537.11 *pedantry*, 669.2 *obstinacy*, 690.1 *severity*
rigidly 217.9 *permanently*, 371.10 *densely*, 373.12, 378.12 *toughly*, 379.5 *fragilely*, 669.14 *resistingly*, 690.11 *severely*, 813.12 *formally*
rigidness 373.5 *hardness*, 378.6 *toughness*, 379.2 *brittleness*, 813.1 *formality*
rigid with fear 777.7 *frightened*
Rigil Kent 53 *Named Stars*
rigmarole 521.4 *senseless talk*, 553.1 *diffuseness*
Rigoberta Menchú 675.4 *Nobel Peace Prize*
rigor 366.7 *shake*
rigorism 577.7 *opinionatedness*
rigorist 577.8 *obstinate person*
rigor mortis 397.8 *after death*

rigorous 503.5, 537.21 *accurate*, 537.24 *pedantic*, 690.8 *severe*
rigorously 537.38 *literally*, 690.11 *severely*
rigorousness 503.1, 537.8 *accuracy*, 537.11 *pedantry*, 690.1 *severity*
rigorous proof 52.66 *proof*
rigour 52.64 *reasoning*, 373.5 *hardness*, 503.1, 537.8 *accuracy*, 537.11 *pedantry*, 690.1 *severity*
rigout 295.1 *dress*
rig out 295.33 *dress up*, 295.35 *make clothing*, 594.5 *equip*
rig the market 737.2 *speculate*
Rigveda 7.12 *religious text*, 10.8 *hymn*
Riksmål 5 *Languages and Groups of Languages*
rile 366.22 *agitate*, 622.11 *dirty*, 828.9 *offend*, 829.8 *make irascible*
riled 828.15 *resentful*, 829.4 *irascible*
Rilke 48 *Poets*
rill 96.1 *river*
rille 53.17 *moon*
rillet 96.1 *river*
rillettes 45.45 *French dish*
rim 23.3 *basketball equipment*, 157.7 *limit*, 299.3, 300.1 *edge*, 300.5 *border*
rimaye 34.5 *rock face*
Rimbaud 48 *Poets*
rime 35.36 *frost*, 409.5 *ice*
rimiterol 62 *Medication*
Rimman 5 *Deities*
rimose 265.7 *cracked*, 321.4 *furrowed*
rimosely 321.8 *ruttily*
Rimsky-Korsakov 49 *Musicians and Composers*
rinchik 49 *Musical Instruments*
rind 86.3 *fruit structure*, 289.1 *exterior*, 293.13 *casing*
rinderpest 624.18 *veterinary disease*
rind, pips, and all 142.5 *unit*, 142.11 *wholly*, 144.9 *completely*
rinforzando 49 *Musical Terms*
ring 363, 426, 427, 18.2 *sportsground*, 49.38 *sound*, 52.21 *set*, 52.23 *algebra*, 52.42 *circle*, 65.15 *network*, 137.8 *fastening*, 161.11 *group*, 313.2 *circle*, 313.3 *circular thing*, 334.1, 334.3 *circuit*, 423.8 *be loud*, 534.32 *telephone*, 557.5 *ornament*, 636.2 *danger signal*, 665.1 *party*, 792.6 *jewellery*, 823.6 *general terms*, 826.3 *love token*
ring a bell 331.3 *get a response*, 511.13 *remind*
ring closure 57.14 *chemical reaction*
ringdove 78 *Birds*
ring down the curtain 157.16 *cease*, 218.7 *stop working*, 397.15 *die*, 684.5 *conclude*
ringer 32.7 *horseracing*, 78.21 *ornithologist*, 176.5 *twin*, 222.2 *substitute person*, 457.5 *impression*, 538.12 *cheat*, 539.15 *deceiver*
ring false 540.16 *be false*
ring finger 407.7 *sense organ*
ringhals 79 *Reptiles*
ring in 154.19 *forecast*, 344.5 *get in*
ringing 426, 427, 427, 78.19 *ornithology*, 423.6 *loud*, 543.16 *signalling*, 557.4 *ornate*
ringing gold 741.1 *money*
ringing in the ears 420.8 *something heard*
ringing off 218.2 *stop*
ringing round 301.1 *enclosure*
ringing tones 423.1 *loudness*
ringing true 537.25 *lifelike*
ringing-up 130.2 *mathematical addition*
ring in the ear 423.8 *be loud*, 427.10 *ring*
ringleader 228.7, 586.14 *motivator*, 653.14 *leader*, 693.8 *agitator*

ringlet 82 *Insects*, 314.2 *coil*
ringlike 52.81 *curvilinear*
ring main 64.34 *power supply*
ringmaster 51.25 *producer*, 51.29 *circus performer*, 653.14 *leader*, 811.15 *showman*
ring nebula 53.8 *interstellar medium*
Ring Nebula 53 *Nebulae*
ring-necked pheasant 78 *Birds*, 37.5 *game*
ring off 218.6 *cease*, 534.32 *telephone*
ring of invisibility 11.6 *talisman*
ring of truth 537.12 *true to life*
ring opening 57.14 *chemical reaction*
ring ouzel 78 *Birds*
ring-ring 426.5 *ringing*
ringroad 363
ring road 327.3 *road*, 334.2 *detour*
rings 18 *Sporting Activities*, 30.3 *gymnastic apparatus*
ring-shaped 52.81 *curvilinear*, 313.5 *circular*
ringside seat 264.3 *near place*, 435.9 *viewpoint*
ring spot 69.12 *pests and diseases*, 85.10 *tree disease*
ring the bell 636.7 *raise the alarm*, 682.6 *be successful*, 682.8 *be effective*
ring the changes 113.8 *be diverse*, 216.8 *cause change*, 224.11 *be changeable*
ring the church bells 543.12 *signal*
ring tone 534.11 *dialling*
ring true 537.33 *seem lifelike*
ringworm 89.5 *fungal association*, 624.13 *skin disease*
rink 25.1 *green bowling*, 31.3 *ice hockey*
rinky-dink 612.4 *trivial*
rinse 389.11 *wash*, 389.34 *hose*, 621.14 *bathe*
rinsing 389.11 *wash*, 621.5 *ablutions*
Rio de Janeiro 93 *Cities*, 93.6 *other cities*
Río de la Plata 96 *Rivers*
Rio Grande 96 *Rivers*, 96.3 *US rivers*
rioja 351.9 *wine*
riot 16.41 *lawlessness*, 151.9 *disorder*, 151.26 *be disorderly*, 153.5 *commotion*, 241.3 *instance of violence*, 241.7 *be violent*, 246.1 *fertility*, 608.5 *about*, 608.8 *plenty*, 610.1 *excess*, 610.4 *be excessive*, 674.6 *fight*, 693.2 *violation of the law*, 693.15 *be disobedient*, 713.2 *disorder*, 713.8 *cause mischief*
rioter 151.11 *troublemaker*, 693.10 *seditionist*
rioting 16.41 *lawlessness*, 693.2 *violation of the law*, 713.2 *disorder*
riot of colour 442.2 *colourfulness*, 456.1 *variegation*
riotous 16.61 *lawless*, 151.20 *disorderly*, 241.6 *violent*, 608.2 *plentiful*, 610.6 *excessive*, 689.6 *anarchic*, 693.13 *disobedient*, 713.10 *law-breaking*, 870.7 *dissipated*
riotous living 870.2 *dissipation*
riotously 151, 16.84 *lawlessly*, 693.17 *disobediently*
riot policeman 632.3 *protector*
rip 47.17 *carpenter*, 136.3 *separateness*, 136.9 *separate*
rip along 329.4 *be swift*
ripcord 137.6 *line*
ripe 86.9 *of a fruit*, 202.11 *old*, 207.11 *adult*, 594.20 *developed*, 619.1 *perfect*, 684.7 *completed*
ripe for marriage 823.22 *marriageable*
ripely 202.18 *venerably*, 207.16 *maturely*, 684.9 *completely*
ripen 86.10 *fruit*, 207.17 *age*, 207.18 *mature*, 220.8 *be transformed*, 374.13 *soften*, 594.7 *develop*, 619.5 *perfect*, 627.2 *get*

better, 684.4 *complete*

ripened 594.20 *developed*, 619.1 *perfect*

ripeness 207.2 *adulthood*, 207.4 *middle age*, 210.1 *timeliness*, 594.14 *preparedness*, 619.3 *perfection*, 684.1 *completion*, 823.4 *marriageability*

ripening 594.13 *development*

ripen into 220.7 *convert into*

ripe old age 202.1 *oldness*, 207.5 *old age*, 623.3 *health*

Riphaeus 53 *Mountains*

rip off 13.12 *cheat*, 458.3 *cause to disappear*, 539.28 *trick*, 539.30, 540.21 *be fraudulent*, 734.10 *take away*, 753.10 *overcharge*

rip-off 118.2 *copy*, 539.8 *trick*, 539.10, 540.8 *fraud*, 540.31 *fraudulent*, 734.3 *taking away*, 734.12 *taking*, 736.4 *stolen goods*, 736.7 *dishonesty*, 736.17 *stolen*, 738.6 *purchase*, 751.3 *fee*, 753.4 *extortion*

rip-off artist 753.5 *overcharger*

riposte 28.3 *fencing movements*, 28.5 *fence*, 331.2 *respond*, 331.6 *response*, 476.3 *countercharge*, 478.1, 478.17 *answer*, 672.1 *retaliation*, 672.3 *retaliate*

rip out 131.3 *subtract*, 252.15 *remove*, 355.11 *extract*, 355.16 *extort*

ripped 252.9 *removed*

ripping 355.6 *extorsion*, 617.1 *worthy*

ripping out 252.2 *removal*, 355.1 *extraction*

ripple 33.6 *motor racing terms*, 56.14 *sound wave*, 96.6 *river flow*, 96.7 *flow*, 97.3 *wave*, 97.10 *billow*, 320.2, 320.8 *pleat*, 366.21 *be agitated*, 375.9 *broken water*, 375.11 *be rough*, 424.1 *faintness*, 424.5 *sound faint*

ripple bed 630.14 *hospital*

rippled 375.1 *rough*

rippled lake 321.3 *furrowed thing*

rippling 96.10 *fluvial*, 375.1 *rough*

ripplingly 320.11 *doubly*, 321.8 *ruttily*

ripply 96.10 *fluvial*, 375.1 *rough*

rip saw 47.11 *woodworking tool*

ripsote 671.24 *parry*

riptide 97.2 *tide*

Rip van Winkle 643.11 *sleeper*

rise 275, 95.9 *tower*, 97.3 *wave*, 97.10 *billow*, 128.2 *spread*, 128.4 *increase*, 228.5 *positive stimulus*, 261.6 *become bigger*, 275.1 *height*, 281.5 *be vertical*, 324.13 *be in motion*, 336.3 *press on*, 336.12 *advance*, 359.1 *ascent*, 359.13 *ascend*, 361.5 *arise*, 370.9 *be light*, 457.1 *appearance*, 457.12 *become visible*, 627.2 *get better*, 627.5 *improvement*, 642.12 *be active*, 676.12 *go to war*, 721.2 *augmentation*, 849.19 *take off one's hat to*

rise above 95.9 *tower*, 126.8 *be superior*, 357.3 *exceed*

rise above oneself 859.7 *be unselfish*

rise above one's station 807.28 *get above oneself*

rise above temptation 863.8 *be virtuous*

rise and fall 97.10 *billow*

rise and shine 642.12 *be active*

rise and shine! wakey wakey! **642**

rise at the crack of dawn 208.7 *be early*

rise early 642.13 *be busy*

rise from the dead 629.4 *be restored*

rise higher 336.3 *press on*

rise in arms 693.16 *be subversive*

rise in price 128.4 *increase*, 721.10 *augment*, 753.9 *be dear*

rise in the world 627.2 *get better*, 682.6 *be successful*, 686.5 *be prosperous*

rise like a phoenix from the ashes 629.4 *be restored*

riser 359.10 *step*

rise to a maximum 128.4 *increase*

rise to a peak 126.8 *be superior*, 128.4 *increase*

rise to fame 686.5 *be prosperous*

rise to one's feet 281.5 *be vertical*, 359.16 *stand up*, 849.19 *take off one's hat to*

rise to the occasion 478.22 *be the answer*, 574.8 *brace oneself*, 583.3 *improvise*, 608.4 *suffice*, 642.15 *try*, 682.7 *overcome obstacles*

rise up 275.16 *rise*, 281.5 *be vertical*, 304.7 *rear up*, 359.13 *ascend*, 361.5 *arise*, 669.8 *revolt*, 669.16 *fight on*

rishi 7.8 *priest*

risible 771.9 *funny*, 798.5 *ridiculous*

rising 359, 14.6 *financial*, 233.11 *influential*, 261.1 *growth*, 261.8 *growing*, 275.9 *high*, 281.2 *making vertical*, 324.7 *ascending motion*, 324.17 *directional*, 359.1 *ascent*, 627.14 *improved*, 682.13 *successful*, 686.8 *prosperous*, 753.7 *dear*, 849.11 *in a respectful stance*

rising air 359.2 *upturn*

rising current 359.2 *upturn*

rising damp 391.4 *seepage*

rising exchange rate 14.1, 741.7 *finance*

rising from the dead 629.10 *revival*

rising ground 275.2 *heights*, 359.2 *upturn*

rising of the curtain 51.6 *scene*

rising pressure 55.6 *weather data*

rising price 128.3 *increasing thing*

rising prices 753.3 *inflationary price*

rising river 633.6 *danger signal*, 636.1 *warning*

rising star 682.4 *successful person*

rising tide 97.2 *tide*, 128.3 *increasing thing*

rising up 304.3 *rearing up*

rising water 635.1 *trap*

risk 491, 54.5 *invest*, 229.2, 229.4 *chance*, 477.7 *questionableness*, 477.20 *doubt*, 479.1 *experiment*, 479.4 *originality*, 479.13 *invent*, 488.10 *think likely*, 491.15 *unreliability*, 589.1 *chance*, 589.12 *take a chance*, 618.11 *harmfulness*, 633.5 *danger*, 633.9 *face danger*, 633.10 *endanger*, 737.2 *speculate*, 780.2 *rash move*

risked 479.10 *tested*

risk-free 632.5 *safe*

riskily 229.8 *by chance*, 477.24 *questionably*, 479.15 *inventively*, 491.26 *unreliably*, 633.11 *dangerously*

riskiness 477.7 *questionableness*, 633.5 *danger*

risk it 229.4 *chance*, 589.12 *take a chance*

risk-taking 589.7 *calculation of chance*, 780.4 *rash*

risky 229.6 *motiveless*, 477.14 *questionable*, 479.9 *original*, 491.7 *unreliable*, 589.8 *chance*, 618.5 *harmful*, 633.1 *dangerous*, 633.2 *unsafe*, 737.15 *profitable*

risky venture 633.5 *danger*

risoni 45 *Types of Pasta*

Risorgimento 3.10 *past age*

risotto 45.47 *Italian dish*

risqué 622.9 *obscene*, 827.8 *cursing*

risqué 454.4, 877.12 *indecent*

rissole 45.32 *meat dish*

rissoles 45.32 *meat*

rit 49 *Musical Terms*

ritardando 49 *Musical Terms*, 328.17 *in slow motion*

rite 1.8 *tradition*, 10.1 *ritual*, 16.34 *legal formality*, 584.4 *custom*, 719.2 *religious observance*,

812.3 *ceremony*, 813.3 *formal occasion*

ritenuto 49 *Musical Terms*, 328.17 *in slow motion*

rite of passage 348.3 *introduction*, 812.3 *ceremony*, 813.3 *formal occasion*

rite of spring 10.7 *non-Christian ritual*

rite of worship 10

rites 817.3 *courtesies*

ritual 10, 811, 1.8 *tradition*, 306.5 *formality*, 306.11 *formal*, 584.4 *custom*, 584.11 *normal*, 719.2 *religious observance*, 812.3 *ceremony*, 812.12 *ceremonial*, 813.3 *formal*, 813.8 *ceremonious*

Ritual 10

ritual act 10.5 *Christian rite*

ritual dance 46.4 *historic dancing*

ritual drama 51.8 *theatre movements*

ritualism 10, 7.2 *religiousness*, 813.2 *formalism*

ritualistic 10, 811, 7.15 *religious*, 306.11 *formal*, 813.8 *ceremonious*

rituality 10.2 *ritualism*

ritualization 10.2 *ritualism*

ritualize 10.18 *perform rites*, 813.9 *formalize*

ritual killing 398, 398.1 *killing*

ritually 10, 1.18 *sociably*, 306.14 *conventionally*, 813.12 *formally*

ritually clean 134.14 *purified*, 621.16 *clean*

ritually prepared 621.16 *clean*

ritual mutilation 10.7 *non-Christian ritual*

ritual observance 812.3 *ceremony*

ritual practice 10.1 *ritual*

ritual prostitution 10.7 *non-Christian ritual*

rituals 817.3 *courtesies*

ritzily 811.40 *grandly*

ritziness 811.9 *grandeur*

ritz it 811.30 *put on airs*

ritzy 742.3 *opulent*, 753.7 *dear*, 811.24 *grand*, 813.7 *dressed up*

ritzy price 753.1 *high price*

rival 491, 111.5 *opposing*, 617.9 *be worthy*, 663.10 *competitor*, 663.16 *confront*, 663.20 *discordant*, 674.10 *contender*, 674.11 *contend*, 674.14 *contending*, 820.5 *hostile person*, 841.4 *jealous*

rival in love 841.3 *rival*

rivalling 674.14 *contending*

rivalry 111.3 *opposition*, 663.3 *conflict*, 674.1 *contention*, 841.1 *jealousy*

rive 136.9 *separate*, 265.5 *crack*

riven 136.16 *apart*, 265.7 *cracked*

river 96, 39.7 *swimming pool*, 70.5 *transportable*, 74.2 *waterway*, 74.11 *nautical*, 302.4 *boundary marker*, 327.11 *channel*

River 53 *The Constellations*

river bed 280.1 *base*

river blindness 81.11 *helminthic disease*, 436.1 *blindness*, 624.7 *tropical disease*

river crossing 96.2 *channel*

river engineering 63.17 *civil engineering*

river erosion 54.35 *weathering*

river flow 96

river fog 55.33 *fog*

River Ganges 10.13 *shrine*

River Godavari 10.13 *shrine*

riverhead 96.2 *channel*

river horse 77.14 *pachyderm*

riverine 54.52 *coastal*

river island 98.2 *island*

River Kistna 10.13 *shrine*

River Narbada 10.13 *shrine*

river network 54.8 *drainage*

river of time 188.2 *time*

river running to the sea 96.1 *river*

rivers 777 *Phobias by Topic*

Rivers 96

riverscape 50.10 *art subject*

river's end 96.2 *channel*

riverside 96.2 *channel*, 300.1 *edge*, 300.8 *edging*

Riverside 93 *Cities*

river's mouth 96.2 *channel*

river system 96.1 *river*

river travel 74.1 *water travel*

rivet 63.27 *superstructure*, 135.5 *joint*, 135.10 *link*, 137.8 *fastening*, 137.11 *connect*

riveted 137.15 *connected*

riveter 135.7 *joiner*

rivulet 96.1 *river*

Riyadh 93 *Cities*

riyal 741.11 *national coins*

rkan-dung 49 *Musical Instruments*

rkan-ling 49 *Musical Instruments*

RNA 58.10 *nucleoside*, 59.9 *cell nucleus*, 59.13 *genetic material*

road 71, 137, 327, 63.19 *structure*, 70.1 *transport*, 70.5 *transportable*, 327.2 *route*, 356.2 *passing along*, 356.4 *access*

roadbed 72.3 *rail*, 327.10 *railway*

road block 323.4 *closed place*

roadblock 587.6 *dissuasion*, 661.2 *obstacle*

road block 671.9 *barrier*

road bridge 63.21 *bridge*

road circuit 33.6 *motor racing terms*

road fatality 397.5 *ways of dying*

road-fund licence 71.21 *miscellaneous motoring terms*

road haulage 71.15 *motor transport*

road hog 462.7 *inconsiderate person*, 860.3 *selfish person*

roadholding 71.21 *miscellaneous motoring terms*

road junction 288.5 *crossroads*

roadman 646.1 *worker*

road map 299.4, 547.7 *map*, 592.5 *map*

road metal 327.4 *road surface*

road name 567.5 *place of residence*

road patrol 356.7 *traffic controller*

road race 33.1 *motor racing*, 674.4 *race*

road-race 33.9 *race*

road racing 33.1 *motor racing*

road report 55.4 *weather forecast*

roadroller 71 *Motor Vehicles*

roadrunner 78 *Birds*, 329.12 *swift animal*

road show 51.5 *show*

roadside 264.5 *near*, 300.1 *edge*, 300.8 *edging*

roadside cafe 350.15 *eating place*

road sign 543.1 *sign*

roadsign 543.5 *indicator*

roadster 32.4 *saddle horse*, 71.12 *bicycle*, 71.16 *car*

road surface 327, 293.11 *paving*

roadsweeper 621.10 *cleaning object*

road system 71.2 *road*

road tax 71.21 *miscellaneous motoring terms*

road test 71.21 *miscellaneous motoring terms*, 479.2 *rehearsal*

road-test 479.12 *rehearse*

road to hell 864.8 *wicked place*

road to ruin 244.4 *ruin*, 633.5 *danger*

road transport 71, 71.15 *motor transport*, 326.5 *means of transport*

Road Transport 71

road transportation 71.1 *road transport*

road tunnel 63.22 *tunnel*

roadway 327.3 *road*

road worker 646.1 *worker*

roadworthy 70.5 *transportable*, 326.17 *transferable*

roam 104.14 *be foreign*, 149.16 *migrate*, 324.15 *walk*, 698.16 *be independent*

roaming 104.10 *foreign*

roller hockey 18 Sporting Activities, **18** Sporting Activities
roller-reefed 36.10 sailing
rollers 137.8 fastening
roller-skate 376.12 go smoothly
roller skates 326.5 means of transport
roller skating 18 Sporting Activities
roller skiing 18 Sporting Activities
roll film 66.9 film
rollick 773.7 dance
roll in 342.10 come together, 608.5 about, 610.4 be excessive, 721.13 be profitable
rolling 73.5 flight, 74.11 nautical, 95.7 mountainous, 97.7 oceanic, 98.11 continental, 275.13 mountainous, 364.2 turning, 364.11 rotating, 365.16 rocking, 366.3 turbulence, 366.17 turbulent, 426.15 drumming, 742.1 wealthy
rolling friction 56.10 force, 385.1 friction
rolling hitch 74 Knots
rolling in 144.8 full
rolling in it 686.8 prosperous, 721.17 well-off, 742.1 wealthy
rolling in money 742.1 wealthy
rolling on 336.10 forward motion
rolling pin 45.6 kitchen equipment, 282.4 flattener, 364.6 rotator, 376.9 smoother
rolling-pin 315.4 cylinder
rolling stock 72
rolling the jack 25.1 green bowling
rolling tobacco 413.7 tobacco
roll in money 742.12 be rich
roll in the aisles 771.14, 773.8 laugh
roll in the dirt 622.10 be dirty
roll into one 135.8 unite, 482.11 not discriminate
rollmop 45.16 fish dish, 80.8 food fish
Roll of Arms 544.9 herald
roll of cloud 55.20 cloud appearance
roll on 185.15 pass, 219.4 protract, 336.1 go forward, 336.6 march on
roll-on 295.18 underwear, 417.2 deodorant
roll one's own 174.18 be one
roll one's sleeves up 574.9 undertake
roll-on/roll-off 74 Ships and Boats
rollout 19.9 play, 19.15 play-offence
roll out 274.16 make thin, 282.7 make horizontal, 475.15 demonstrate
roll out the red carpet 812.18, 849.20 salute
roll over 362.7 lean
roll over and play dead 540.20 pretend
roll the jack 25.7 bowl
roll-top 47.14 wooden
roll-top desk 47.4 table
roll up 262.5 make smaller, 262.6 become smaller, 315.11 make round, 320.7 fold, 342.10 come together, 344.1 arrive, 364.9 roll, 605.6 store
roll up in 295.32 dress
roll up one's sleeves 594.8 prepare oneself, 644.6 work
roll up the blind 439.29 clarify
roll-your-own 413.7, 413.11 tobacco
roly-poly 45.35 dessert, 259.12 fat person, 259.16 fat
ROM 65.6 memory, 511.6 artificial memory
Romagnola 68 Breeds of Cattle
Romaic 5 Languages and Groups of Languages
romaine lettuce 45 Vegetables
Romains 48 Poets
Roman 7 Non-Christian Religions, **43** Architectural Styles, **68** Breeds of Fowl, 5.41 let-

tered, 202.14 historic, 400.4 civilized human
Roman alphabet 5.14 alphabet
Roman balance 369.10 scales
Roman candle 439.8 fire
Roman Catholic 7.5 Christian, 7.16 denominational
Roman Catholicism 7 Christian Movements
romance 48.2 fiction, 506.6 talk nonsense, 519.4 ideality, 519.6 reverie, 560.5 fiction, 821.8 love affair
Romance 5 Languages and Groups of Languages, 5.11 family of languages
romancer 48.14 author, 519.9 visionary, 538.11 liar
romancing 519.10 imaginative
Roman comedy 51.10 comedy
Roman eagle 544.6 national emblem
Roman Empire 3.10 past age, 91.3 dominion
Romanes 5 Languages and Groups of Languages
Romanesque 43 Architectural Styles, 202.14 historic
romanesque art 50 Western Art Styles and Movements
Roman holiday 398.4 slaughter
Romania 91 Countries
Romanian 5 Languages and Groups of Languages
Roman mile 75 Some Foreign Units
Roman numeral 52.9 numeral, 169.1 number
Roman orgy 350.13 feast
Romanov 68 Breeds of Sheep
Roman pace 75 Some Foreign Units
Roman Republic 3.10 past age
Romansch 5 Languages and Groups of Languages
Roman school 50 Western Art Styles and Movements
romantic 48.16 literary, 48.17 fictional, 49.32 instrumental, 50.29 realist, 51.38 tragic, 102.6 unrealistic person, 102.11 unrealistic, 471.9 person of ideas, 471.13 ideal, 519.9 visionary, 519.10 imaginative, 560.12 narrative, 759.12 sensitive, 821.20 amorous
romantically 51.42 dramatically, 471.22, 519.17 imaginatively, 821.30 lovingly
romantic ballet 46.8 ballet
romantic classical 43 Architectural Styles
romantic comedy 51.10 comedy
romanticism 50 Western Art Styles and Movements, 471.7 idealism, 519.6 reverie, 759.7 emotionalism, 821.3 lovingness
Romanticism 48 Literary Groups and Movements
romanticist 519.9 visionary
romanticize 102.15 idealize, 471.15 imagine, 519.15 fantasize, 538.21 lie, 560.15 recount
romanticized 538.13 untrue
romanticized version 538.1 untruth
romantic lighting 441.1 dimness
romantic love 821
romantic music 49.3, 49.3 classical music
romantic novel 532.6 book publishing
romantic poet 48.14 author
romantic tie 821.8 love affair
romantic tragedy 51.9 tragedy
romany 11.13 diviner
Romany 5 Languages and Groups of Languages
Rome 93 Cities, 12.5 political organization, 93.6 other cities
Romeldale 68 Breeds of Sheep
Romeo 534 Phonetic Alphabet, 586.13 tempter, 821.9 lover
Romeo and Juliet 48 Shakespeare's plays, 821.10 lovers

rommelpot 49 Musical Instruments
Romney Marsh 68 Breeds of Sheep
rompers 295.23 children's clothes
romp home 329.6 accelerate, 682.10 defeat heavily
Ronaldsay 93 Cities
rondeau 48.7 poem, 48.10 verse form
rondel 48.7 poem
ronds de jambes à terre 46.10 positions at the barre
ronds de jambes en l'air 46.10 positions at the barre
rondure 311.2 bend
ronéat-ek 49 Musical Instruments
Ronga 5 Languages and Groups of Languages
rood 75 General Units, 10.14 sacred object
rood screen 10.12 church
roof 43, 293, 34.5 rock face, 275.8 high thing, 279.3 architectural summit, 279.7 top, 293.7 overhead covering, 634.2 shelter
roofed 43, 256.14 inhabiting, 279.6 topped, 293.36 covered
roofed in 293.36 covered
roofer 293.17 coverer
roof garden 69.2 garden
roof in 293.27 roof
roofing 293.7 overhead covering
roofing material 604.2 building material
roofing tile 44.9 industrial ceramics
roof ladder 359.9 ladder
roof over one's head 256.1 habitat, 634.2 shelter
roof rack 71 Motor Vehicle Parts
rooftop 279.3 architectural summit, 293.7 overhead covering
rooftree 85.12 figurative usage
rook 78 Birds, 4.24 chess terms, 78.6 songbird, 815.10 social animal
Rook 53 Mountains
rookery 161 Collective Names for Birds and Animals, 78.14 nest
rookie 6.7 learner, 19.2 football player, 23.2 basketball player, 149.7 newcomer, 156.14 beginner, 201.8 new arrival, 201.12 immature, 656.10 unskilled person, 679.8 soldier
Rookie of the Year 22.2 baseball player
rooks 161 Collective Names by Animal
rool up into a ball 262.5 make smaller, 262.6 become smaller
room 256, 146.1 inclusion, 248.5 reserved space, 248.6 available space, 256.18 take up residence, 259.1 size, 265.1 interval, 290.2 inside, 605.4 storage, 698.5 scope
roomer 255.3 householder
roomette 72.6 rolling stock
room for improvement 620.5 imperfection
roomful 120.3 container
room freshener 621.9 cleaning agent
roominess 248.4 spaciousness, 259.2 bigness, 271.4 breadth
roommate 255.3 householder, 724.3 participant, 819.5 friend
room overhead 248.6 available space
rooms 256.1 habitat
room temperature 408.1 heat
room to manoeuvre 248.6 available space
room to spare 248.6 available space
room to swing a cat 248.6 available space, 698.6 liberality
roomy 248.13 spacious, 259.15 big, 271.1 broad, 390.12 airy, 755.4 big
roost 78.14 nest, 256.13 lair, 256.18 take up residence, 649.2 take it easy

rooster 68.8 livestock, 78.10 male bird, 401.16 male animal
root 83, 5.17 word, 5.35 part of speech, 5.42 worded, 52.27 equation, 69.11 vegetable, 83.21 vegetate, 88.4 moss plant, 90.6 lichen, 156.3 source, 169.6 power, 225.7 make stable, 226.3 rudiment, 280.1, 280.4 base
root and branch 142.11 wholly, 144.9 completely, 244.16 destructively
root aphid 69.12 pests and diseases
root beer 351.6 soft drink
root canal work 60.4 dentistry
root cap 83.7 root
root crop 68.12 crop
rooted 83.19 of roots, 135.15 tied, 202.12 olden, 225.10 stabilized, 584.13 fixed
rootedness 225.1 stability
rooted to the spot 225.10 stabilized, 325.4 motionless, 777.7 frightened, 786.7 wide-eyed
rooter 431.9 crier, 851.8 admirer
root for 228.9 motivate, 239.3 invigorate, 431.12 cheer, 851.16 acclaim
root hair 83.7 root
rooting out 355.1 extraction
rootless 108.6 unrelated, 224.13 changeable, 252.10 replaced
rootlessness 108.1 unrelatedness
rootlet 83.7 root
rootlike 83.19 of roots
rootlike part 83.7 root
root mean square 52.17 multiplication
root nodule 83.7 root
root of all evil 741.2 cash
root of dissension 674.1 contention
root out 131.3 subtract, 252.15 remove, 349.10 exterminate, 355.11 extract
root rot 69.12 pests and diseases
roots 86.1 fruits
root sign 52.25 algebraic expression
rootstock 69.5 gardening, 83.5 stem, 83.7 root, 226.3 rudiment
root tuber 83.7 root
root up 244.8 destroy
root vegetable 45.33, 69.11 vegetable
root vegetables 86.1 fruits
rope 26.5 wrestling, 34.4 climbing equipment, 36.3 parts of a sailing boat, 137.6 line, 137.7 tackle, 323.3 restrainer, 323.11 restrain, 398.2 murder, 398.5 execution, 603.1 tool, 604.1 materials, 632.4 safety device, 875.6 drug, 879.16 instrument of execution
rope and pulley 361.9 lifter
rope bridge 63.21, 327.9 bridge
roped 135.15 tied
rope horse 32.12 rodeo
rope ladder 359.9 ladder
rope off 34.9 mountaineer
rope out 699.8 restrain
ropes 26.2 boxing
rope's end 879.14 instrument of punishment
rope together 135.10 link
ropewalker 51.29 circus performer
ropiness 394.1 viscosity
roping off 34.3 climbing technique
ropy 371.7 condensed, 394.8 viscous, 618.2 inferior
Roquefort 45 Cheeses
roric 391.10 misty
rorqual 77 Placental Mammals
Rorschach test 61.5 psychological test
Rorty 4 Philosophers
rosaceous 83.16 taxonomic
rosaniline 450.6 red pigment
rosarian 69.13 horticulturist
Rosario 93 Cities
rosarium 69.3 ornamental garden
rosary 10.9 prayer
rosary beads 10.14 sacred object
Roscelin 4 Philosophers

Roscius 51.22 *actor*
Roscommon 92 Counties, **93** Cities
rose 84 Flowers and Flowering Plants, 69.6 *garden tool*, 389.12 *sprinkler*, 418.2 *fragrant thing*, 450.7 *red thing*
rosé 351.9 *wine*
rose apple 86 Fruits
roseate 450.1 *red*
rose bed 69.3 *ornamental garden*
rose bowl 258.16 *crockery*
Rose Bowl 19.1 *football*
rose-coloured 450.1 *red*, 775.14 *cheering*
rose-coloured glasses 775.1 *hope*
Rosecomb 68 Breeds of Fowl
rose family 83.3 *seed plant*
rose garden 69.2 *garden*, 418.2 *fragrant thing*
rose grower 69.13 *horticulturist*
rose growing 69.1 *horticulture*
rosella 78 Birds
rose madder 450.6 *red pigment*
rosemary 45 Herbs and Spices, 413.5 *herbs*
rose of China 84 Flowers and Flowering Plants
rose of Jericho 84 Flowers and Flowering Plants
rose of Sharon 84 Flowers and Flowering Plants
rose oil 84.8 *flower product*
roseola 624.6 *infection*
rose-pink 450.1 *red*
rose-red 450.1 *red*
rosery 69.3 *ornamental garden*
Rose's metal 57 Alloys
rose-tinted 775.14 *cheering*
rose-tinted view 775.1 *hope*
rosette 84.9 *figurative usage*, 544.4 *insignia*
Rosette Nebula 53 Nebulae
rose water 84.8 *flower product*
rosewater 242.2 *moderator*
rose water 389.14 *lavender water*, 418.2 *fragrant thing*
rose window 84.9 *figurative usage*, 439.10 *window*
rosewood 85 Trees and Shrubs
Rosh Chodesh 10.15 *holy day*
Rosh Hashanah 10.15 *holy day*
Rosicrucian 11.12 *occultist*, 11.14 *occult*
Rosicrucianism 7 Christian Movements, 11.1 *occultism*
rosily 450.10 *ruddily*, 714.17 *auspiciously*
rosin 395.10 *resin*, 395.19 *resinify*
Rosinante 32.1 *horse*
rosiness 450.5 *redness*, 623.3 *health*
rosiny 395.14 *resinous*
Ross 53 Named Stars, **97** Oceans and Seas
Rossini 49 Musicians and Composers
roster 171.6 *list of names*
Rostock 93 Cities
rostrum 51.15 *stage*, 532.7 *publicity*
rosy 450.1 *red*, 450.2 *red-faced*, 623.1 *healthy*, 686.8 *prosperous*, 714.14 *auspicious*, 775.14 *cheering*, 789.6 *personable*
rosy-cheeked 450.2 *red-faced*, 623.1 *healthy*
rosy cheeks 444.9 *complexion*, 450.7 *red thing*, 623.3 *health*
rosy-fingered dawn 204.1 *morning*
rot 89.1 *fungus*, 89.11 *moulder*, 141.1 *disintegration*, 141.3 *disintegrate*, 189.4 *be transient*, 202.17 *grow old*, 247.7 *be infertile*, 506.1 *nonsense*, 521.4 *senseless talk*, 521.14 *nonsense*, 618.13 *be worthless*, 622.2 *uncleanness*, 622.4 *dirt*, 622.10 *be dirty*, 624.11 *ulcer*, 628.2 *decay*, 628.5 *hurt*, 628.9 *dilapidation*, 631.14 *afflict*
rota 171.6 *list of names*, 195.1 *succession*, 214.2 *cycle*
rotaplane 73 Types of Aircraft

rotary 364, 324.17 *directional*, 334.6 *circular*, 363.9 *orbital*
rotary beater 45.6 *kitchen equipment*
rotary drill 364.6 *rotator*
rotary engine 603.4 *machine*
rotary mower 68.10 *farm tool*, 69.6 *garden tool*
rotary pump 57.20 *surface chemistry*
rotate 364, 46.15 *dance*, 52.96 *represent*, 53.37 *observe*, 96.7 *flow*, 214.8 *be cyclic*, 313.6 *circle*, 324.13 *be in motion*
rotating 364, 214.12 *cyclic*
rotating air mass 55.16 *wind vortex*
rotation 364, 21.2 *field events*, 41.12 *ski*, 52.48 *transformation*, 53.21 *orbit*, 155.2 *series*, 159.6 *continuum*, 214.2 *cycle*, 308.2 *symmetry operation*, 324.5 *circuition*, 363.1 *orbital motion*
Rotation 364
rotational 36.13 *windsurfing*, 214.12 *cyclic*, 324.17 *directional*, 364.12 *rotary*
rotational axis 53.21 *orbit*
rotational motion 364.1 *rotation*
rotational period 53.21 *orbit*
rotational sail 36.7 *windsurfing*
rotational symmetry 52.41 *geometric figure*, 308.2 *symmetry operation*
rotation turn 41.4 *skiing technique*
rotative 214.12 *cyclic*, 364.12 *rotary*
rotator 364
rotatory 324.17 *directional*, 363.9 *orbital*, 364.12 *rotary*
rotavate 68.17 *farm*, 69.15 *cultivate*
Rotavator 68.10 *farm tool*, 69.6, 603.2 *garden tool*
rot down 141.3 *disintegrate*
rote 49 Musical Instruments, 584.7 *habituation*
rotelle 45 Types of Pasta
rotenone 631.8 *poison*
rotgut 351.7 *alcoholic drink*, 874.12 *alcohol*
Roth 48 Writers
rotifer 81.6 *worm*
Rotifera 81.6 *worm*
rotisserie 350.15 *eating place*
Rotkohl 45.46 *German dish*
rotl 75 Some Foreign Units
rotor 64.31 *electric motor*, 338.11 *propeller*, 364.6 *rotator*
Rottaler 32 Breeds of Horse and Pony
rotted 141.5 *disintegrated*, 622.8 *unclean*
rotten 69.17 *botanical*, 89.9 *fungal*, 141.5 *disintegrated*, 238.9 *dilapidated*, 415.6 *unpalatable*, 419.4 *putrid*, 618.4 *poor*, 624.23 *diseased*, 626.5 *unhygienic*, 628.12 *deteriorated*, 631.16 *blighting*, 858.5 *dishonourable*, 862.7 *evil*, 864.11 *wicked*
rotten apple 864.10 *bad person*
rotten borough 580.12 *election*
rotten egg 419.2 *something that makes an unpleasant smell*
rotten luck 589.2 *luck*, 687.3 *bad fortune*
rottenness 202.10 *staleness*, 415.2 *unpalatability*, 618.10 *poverty*, 628.9 *dilapidation*, 862.1 *evil*
rotten to the core 618.4 *poor*, 864.11 *wicked*, 868.3 *impenitent*
rotter 864.10 *bad person*
Rotterdam 93 Cities
Rotter incomplete sentences blank 61.5 *psychological test*
rotting 141.1 *disintegration*, 141.6 *disintegrating*, 419.4 *putrid*, 622.8 *unclean*, 624.23 *diseased*, 631.16 *blighting*
rotting vegetables 419.2 *something that makes an unpleasant smell*
Rottweiler 77 Breeds of Dogs
rotund 259.16 *fat*, 273.1 *thick*, 313.5 *circular*, 315.9 *round*

rotunda 43.9 *miscellaneous architectural features*
rotundity 259.5 *fatness*, 273.5 *thickness*, 313.1 *circularity*, 315.1 *roundness*
rotundly 313.8 *circularly*, 315.13 *roundly*
rouble 741.11 *national coins*
roué 405.3 *pleasure-seeker*, 877.8 *immoral man*
Rouen 68 Breeds of Fowl, **93** Cities
rouge 444.9 *complexion*, 444.15 *colour*, 444.16 *make up*, 450.6 *red pigment*, 450.9 *redden*, 791.4 *cosmetics*
Rouge Croix 544.9 *herald*
rouged 450.2 *red-faced*
Rouge Dragon 544.9 *herald*
rouge et noir 42 Card Games
rough 375, 383, 385, 659, 29.1 *golf*, 31.9 *play hockey*, 40.5 *real tennis*, 55.48 *stormy*, 145.3 *incomplete thing*, 145.4 *incomplete*, 145.5 *be incomplete*, 160.8 *discontinuous*, 215.4 *irregular*, 241.4 *violent person or animal*, 241.6 *violent*, 366.17 *turbulent*, 375.10 *rough idea*, 375.12 *make rough*, 375.14 *roughly*, 378.4 *powerful*, 380.4 *toothed*, 415.6 *unpalatable*, 430.8 *hoarse*, 479.8 *experimental*, 559.10 *ugly*, 592.6 *outline*, 594.10 *preparations*, 595.5 *immature*, 618.5 *harmful*, 679.1 *combatant*, 679.33 *combative*, 818.5 *discourteous*, 832.8 *malefactor*, 832.12 *callous*
roughage 68.9 *animal feedstuff*, 350.11 *food content*
rough air 375.6 *roughness*
rough and ready 613.1 *useful*, 620.2 *incomplete*, 648.3 *hasty*, 656.4 *bungled*
rough-and-ready 375.5 *unfinished*
rough and tumble 151.9 *disorder*, 674.6 *fight*
rough-and-tumble 648.3 *hasty*
rough approximation 375.10 *rough idea*
rough book 6.14 *school book*
roughcast 375.1 *rough*, 375.7 *rough thing*, 375.12 *make rough*, 592.6 *outline*
rough copy 50.9 *drawing*, 375.10 *rough idea*
rough diamond 595.11 *natural state*, 658.3 *naive person*
rough draft 50.9 *drawing*, 479.2 *rehearsal*, 547.2 *reproduction*
rough edge 375.6 *roughness*
rough-edged 375.2 *coarse*
rough edge of one's tongue 852.8 *berating*
rough edges 685.1 *noncompletion*
roughen 375.12 *make rough*, 383.12 *coarsen*
rough endoplasmic reticulum 59.8 *cell organ*
roughened 375.1 *rough*
roughen up 375.12 *make rough*
Rough Fell 68 Breeds of Sheep
rough fibre 375.6 *roughness*
rough going 375.6 *roughness*, 659.3 *difficult task*
rough-going 659.11 *rough*
rough-grained 375.2 *coarse*
rough grazing 68.11 *farmland*
rough ground 375, 375.6 *roughness*, 659.3 *difficult task*
rough guess 518.3 *conjecture*
rough hair 375.6 *roughness*
rough handling 241.1 *violence*, 652.8 *treatment*
rough-hew 306.7 *form*, 375.12 *make rough*, 594.2 *do the groundwork*
rough-hewn 145.4 *incomplete*, 375.1 *rough*, 595.5 *immature*
roughhouse 151.9 *disorder*, 241.3 *instance of violence*, 241.7 *be violent*, 674.6 *fight*
rough idea 375

roughing 31.3 *ice hockey*, 31.8 *hockey*
roughing the kicker 19.13 *penalty*
roughing the passer 19.13 *penalty*
roughly 375, 124.11 *on average*, 145.6 *incompletely*, 215.8 *irregularly*, 264.7 *nearly*, 378.13 *powerfully*, 383.15 *texturally*, 385.17 *abrasively*, 818.9 *discourteously*
roughly speaking 124.11 *on average*
rough measure 268.1 *measurement*
roughneck 832.8 *malefactor*
roughness 375, 123.1 *inequality*, 145.1 *incompleteness*, 160.1 *discontinuity*, 215.1 *irregularity*, 241.1 *violence*, 383.2 *grain*, 385.1 *friction*, 413.4 *stimulation*, 430.2 *hoarseness*, 559.2 *impropriety*, 818.1 *discourtesy*, 832.3 *callousness*
Roughness 375
rough out 299.5 *outline*, 306.7 *form*, 375.13 *be unfinished*, 547.11 *paint*, 560.14 *describe*
rough outline 50.9 *drawing*
rough patch 687.4 *time of adversity*
rough puff pastry 45.37 *pastry*
roughride 33.10 *be on the track*
roughrider 32.15 *horse person*
rough-rider 32.15 *horse person*, 679.20 *cavalryman*
roughriding 33.6 *motor racing terms*
rough road 375.8 *rough ground*
rough sea 97.3 *wave*
rough shooting 18 Sporting Activities, 37.2 *hunting*
rough sketch 594.10 *preparations*, 685.1 *noncompletion*
rough skin 375.6 *roughness*
rough surface 375.6 *roughness*
rough terrain 659.3 *difficult task*
rough texture 375.6 *roughness*
rough the kicker 19.18 *be penalized*
rough the passer 19.18 *be penalized*
rough thing 375
rough up 375.12 *make rough*, 383.12 *coarsen*
rough water 97.3 *wave*, 375.6 *roughness*
rough weather 241.5 *violent weather*
rough working 375.10 *rough idea*
roulette 42.7 *other games*
roulette wheel 364.6 *rotator*
round 297, 315, 315, 315, 364, 18.1 *sport*, 26.2 *boxing*, 26.5 *wrestling*, 42.2 *contest*, 45.23 *beef*, 52.81 *curvilinear*, 112.4 *monotony*, 112.5 *uniform*, 122.6 *equal*, 122.11 *equalize*, 142.3 *whole situation*, 143.3 *stage*, 159.6 *continuum*, 169.8 *odd*, 183.4 *return*, 214.2 *cycle*, 249.13 *locality*, 259.16 *fat*, 273.1 *thick*, 306.7 *form*, 311.4 *curved*, 313.5 *circular*, 313.7 *make circular*, 315.10 *well-rounded*, 329.1 *swift*, 334.1 *circuit*, 334.6 *circular*, 356.1 *passage*, 359.10 *step*, 363.10 *circular*, 364.3 *reel*, 381.10 *blunt*, 425.1 *bang*, 426.6 *musical repetition*, 433.2 *song*, 558.3 *elegant*, 584.3 *way*, 670.20 *bout*, 674.7 *boxing*, 680.13 *ammunition*, 796.8 *fashion*, 874.13 *drink*
roundabout 5.43 *phrasal*, 71.3 *carriageway*, 286.5 *devious*, 297.5 *surrounded*, 313.2 *circle*, 327.3 *road*, 334.1 *circuit*, 334.7 *circuitous*, 335.21 *indirect*, 356.5 *crossing point*, 363.9 *orbital*, 363.12 *circuitously*, 553.4 *circumlocutory*, 578.10 *equivocal*
round about 124.11 *on average*, 251.11 *geographically*, 297.8 *round*, 327.17 *via*, 334.8 *circuitously*, 335.27 *astray*

roundaboutness 334.2 *detour,* 363.2 *circuitousness*

roundabout phrase 5.24 *phrasing,* 553.2 *circumlocution*

roundabout way 313.2 *circle,* 327.2 *route,* 334.2 *detour,* 363.5 *ringroad*

round a cape 98.12 *be marooned*

round and about 297.5 *surrounded,* 332.11 *in all directions*

round and round 214.16 *cyclically,* 224.15 *changeably,* 364.13 *round,* 365.18 *to and fro*

round angle 52.39 *angle*

round-arm blow 330.14 *sporting hit*

round as a ball 315.9 *round*

round ball 23.3 *basketball equipment*

roundboard 36.7 *windsurfing*

round body 315

round-bottomed flask 57 Laboratory Apparatus

round down 52.91 *add*

rounded 5.43 *phrasal,* 43.13 *arched,* 52.81 *curvilinear,* 122.6 *equal,* 306.9 *formed,* 311.5 *well-rounded,* 313.5 *circular,* 376.2 *uniform,* 381.1 *blunt,* 427.8 *deep*

rounded arch 43.5 *arch*

rounded out 315.10 *well-rounded*

rounded phrase 5.24 *phrasing*

rounded up 161.46 *assembled*

roundel 48.7 *poem*

roundelay 48.7 *poem,* 433.2 *song*

rounders 18 Sporting Activities

rounders bat 330.15 *ram*

round-eyed 786.7 *wide-eyed*

round-faced 259.16 *fat*

round here 251.11 *geographically*

round house 74 Parts of a Ship, 330.14 *sporting hit*

rounding 363.1 *orbital motion*

rounding down 52.18 *division*

rounding off 684.3 *elaboration*

rounding out 206.13 *maturing*

rounding up 52.18 *division,* 122.3 *equalization*

roundly 315, 122.13 *equitably,* 259.20 *largely,* 311.7 *curvedly,* 313.8 *circularly,* 329.14 *swiftly,* 381.11 *smoothly*

roundness 315, 112.1 *uniformity,* 259.5 *fatness,* 273.5 *thickness,* 311.2 *bend,* 313.1 *circularity,* 381.2 *bluntness*

Roundness 315

round of ammunition 680.13 *ammunition*

round of applause 837.3 *recognition,* 851.5 *acclaim*

round of drinks 874.13 *drink*

round off 112.9 *be uniform,* 142.10, 144.4 *complete,* 157.15 *end,* 315.11 *make round*

round-off 30.8 *floor exercises,* 30.10 *compete in gymnastics*

round of visits 815.3 *meeting*

round on 670.5 *strike,* 672.3 *retaliate*

round out 206.18 *grow,* 315.11 *make round,* 316.5 *be convex*

round pace 329.8 *speed*

round robin 712.1 *request*

round-robin 712.9 *requesting*

rounds 36.8 *punting,* 363.3 *orbit*

round shot 680.14 *historical ammunition*

roundsman 739.12 *wholesaler*

round steak 45.23 *beef*

round sum 741.5 *sum*

round table 653.7 *council,* 654.2 *consultation,* 706.2 *representative body*

round-table conference 568.4 *conference*

round-table discussion 716.3 *discussion*

round the bend 153.16 *deranged*

round the clock 42.6 *darts,* 159.19 *continuously*

round thing 315

round trip 221.4 *return,* 313.2 *circle,* 315.6 *round,* 334.1 *circuit,* 363.3 *orbit*

round turn and two half hitches 74 Knots

roundup 161.30 *compilation*

round up 52.91 *add,* 68.18 *practise livestock farming,* 122.11 *equalize,* 161.43 *herd,* 721.11 *acquire*

round-up 161.2 *herding*

round upon 827.6 *vilify*

roundworm 81 Worms, 81.6 *worm*

roup 739.4 *sale*

rouse 228.9 *motivate,* 239.3 *invigorate,* 355.15 *draw out,* 821.25 *be loved,* 829.8 *make irascible*

roused 228.12 *motivated*

rouse easily 829.6 *be irascible*

rouse oneself 642.12 *be active*

rousing 228.11 *motivational,* 239.5 *invigorating,* 431.17 *cheering,* 586.19 *persuasive*

rousingly 228.14 *influentially*

Rousseau 2 Philosophers

rout 162.13 *dismiss,* 181.4 *throng,* 366.2 *tumult,* 682.2 *victory,* 682.10 *defeat heavily,* 683.2 *defeat*

route 162.13 *dismiss,* 34.1 *mountaineering,* 71.2 *road,* 332.2 *bearing,* 356.2 *passing along,* 653.2 *direct*

routed 683.11 *defeated*

router 47.11, 47.11 *woodworking tool*

routine 10.1 *ritual,* 51.6 *scene,* 110.6 *regularity,* 110.17 *regular,* 112.1 *uniformity,* 112.4 *monotony,* 112.5 *uniform,* 112.8 *monotonous,* 116.6 *convention,* 124.1 *average,* 150.7 *method,* 150.15 *habitual,* 159.7 *stability,* 164.5 *averageness,* 164.21 *common,* 166.6 *custom,* 166.10 *customary,* 183.3 *repetitiveness,* 183.13 *monotonous,* 214.2 *cycle,* 214.4 *orderliness,* 214.12 *cyclic,* 214.14 *orderly,* 306.5 *formality,* 306.11 *formal,* 327.1, 584.3 *way,* 584.6 *procedure,* 584.9 *habitual,* 640.1 *action,* 652.7 *way,* 719.3 *performance,* 813.3 *formal occasion*

routinely 110.20 *regularly,* 112.13 *uniformly,* 116.37 *conventionally,* 122.19 *differentially,* 124.11 *on average,* 150.27 *methodically,* 164.30 *usually,* 212.1 *frequently,* 214.16 *cyclically,* 214.17 *orderly,* 306.14 *conventionally*

routineness 164.5 *averageness*

routine procedure 652.7 *way*

routine work 584.3 *way*

routinization 152.3 *organization*

rout out 349.7 *drive out*

roux 45.15 *sauce*

rove 335.3 *go astray*

rove beetle 82 Insects

roving 224.13 *changeable*

roving eye 435.6 *look,* 877.3 *sexual immorality*

row 36, 36.11 *rowing,* 52.22 *matrix,* 68.11 *farmland,* 151.9 *disorder,* 241.3 *instance of violence,* 266.2 *level,* 312.7 *straight line,* 327.3 *road,* 338.20 *prod,* 366.4 *fuss,* 423.2 *outcry,* 434.2 *dissonant noise,* 473.1 *argument,* 642.1 *activity,* 666.2 *argument,* 666.6 *argue,* 674.6, 674.12 *fight,* 674.13 *conflict,* 764.8 *quarrel*

rowan 85 Trees and Shrubs

rowboat 36.4 *rowing,* 74.3 *vessel*

rowdily 679.41 *aggressively*

rowdiness 151.8 *lawlessness*

rowdy 151.20 *disorderly,* 423.6 *loud,* 679.1 *combatant,* 679.33 *combative,* 693.9 *criminal*

Rowe 48 Dramatists

rowel 380.8 *sharp-pointed thing*

rower 36.9 *sailor,* 74.8 *boatman*

row house 43.3 *building,* 256.5 *house*

rowing 18 Sporting Activities, **36, 36,** 74.1 *water travel,* 74.11 *nautical,* 339.2 *pull,* 473.7 *arguing,* 644.5 *exercise*

Rowing 36

rowing association 36.4 *rowing*

rowing boat 74 Ships and Boats, 74.3 *vessel*

rowing race 36.4 *rowing*

rowing technique 36.4 *rowing*

rowlack arch 43.5 *arch*

rowlock 74 Parts of a Ship, 36.4 *rowing,* 364.4 *vortex*

rows of nodding plumes 676.2 *glory of war*

royal 74 Sails, 12.10 *governing,* 126.13 *dominant,* 688.12 *authoritative,* 688.14 *governmental,* 696.12 *masterful,* 805.19 *stately,* 811.22 *majestic,* 813.6 *formal*

Royal Air Force 679.29 *air force*

Royal Air Force Academy 17.3 *military training*

Royal Air Force Volunteer Reserve 679.29 *air force*

royal antelope 77 Placental Mammals

Royal Automobile Club 33.7 *racing governing body*

Royal Ballet 46.12 *ballet companies*

royal blue 454.1 *blue*

royal box 51.16 *auditorium*

Royal Caledonian Curling Club 41.10 *curling*

Royal Canadian Henley 36.4 *rowing*

Royal Canadian Mounted Police 16.14 *police*

Royal Canoe Club 36.6 *canoeing*

royal command 692.1 *command*

Royal Commission 653.7 *council*

Royal Crescent 43 Noted Buildings

Royal Danish Ballet 46.12 *ballet companies*

Royal Doulton porcelain 44 Types of Ceramics

royal enclosure 301.2 *enclosed place*

royal fern 88 Ferns

Royal Festival Ballet 46.12 *ballet companies*

royal flush 42.3 *card game terms*

Royal Greenwich Observatory 53.23 *observatory*

royal jelly 630.7 *tonic*

royally 126.13 *superiorly,* 688.23 *authoritatively,* 696.16 *masterfully,* 805.36, 811.38 *majestically,* 813.12 *formally*

Royal Mail 326.8 *messenger,* 534.2 *postal communication*

Royal Marine Commandos 679.28 *marines*

Royal Marines 679.28 *marines*

Royal Military Academy 17.3 *military training,* 676.6 *art of war*

Royal Military College 17.3 *military training*

Royal Military College of Canada 17.3 *military training*

Royal Military Police 17.6 *military law*

Royal Naval College 17.3 *military training*

Royal Naval Reserve 679.22 *navy*

Royal Naval Reservist 679.27 *naval man*

Royal Naval Volunteer Reserve 679.22 *navy*

Royal Naval Volunteer Reservist gob 679.27 *naval man*

Royal Navy 679.22 *navy*

Royal Observatory Edinburgh 53.23 *observatory*

Royal Pavilion 43 Noted Buildings

royal poinciana 85 Trees and Shrubs

royal prerogative 688.1 *authority*

royal road 327.3 *road,* 660.6 *easy thing*

Royal Society for the Prevention of Cruelty to Animals 76.8 *animal welfare*

royal tennis 40.1 *tennis,* 40.5 *real tennis*

royalties 749.2 *money received*

royalty 688.1 *authority,* 721.4 *earnings,* 746.3 *pay,* 749.2

money received

royal we 813.1 *formality*

Royal Yachting Association 36.1 *sailing*

rozzer 16.17 *police officer,* 718.3 *security officer*

rpm 329.8 *speed*

RR Lyrae star 53.12 *variable star*

RSI 624.16 *rheumatism*

RSJ 63.27 *superstructure*

RS-ski 41.5 *ski equipment*

RSVP 478.2 *acknowledgment*

ruan 49 Musical Instruments

rub 385, 210.3 *critical time,* 267.4 *meet,* 376.11 *smooth,* 385.1 *friction,* 392.20 *absorb,* 407.4 *kiss,* 407.11 *touch,* 408.14 *be hot,* 458.3 *cause to disappear,* 621.13 *clean,* 630.20 *doctor,* 644.4 *exertion,* 644.6 *work,* 661.2 *obstacle*

rub-a-dub 426.4 *knocking*

rub against 385.13 *abrade*

Rub' al Khali 98 Deserts

rubbed out 131.5 *subtracted,* 546.6 *obliterated*

rubbed the wrong way 828.16 *angry*

rubber 85 Tree Products, **377,** 42.3 *card game terms,* 85.9 *tree product,* 244.6 *destroyer,* 247.3 *birth control,* 377.6 *elastic,* 377.9 *make elastic,* 385.7 *eraser,* 438.6 *that which makes invisible,* 546.4 *eraser,* 621.10 *cleaning object,* 674.2 *contest*

rubber ball 377.3 *elastic thing*

rubber band 377.3 *elastic thing*

rubber bridge 42 Card Games

rubber bullet 680.13 *ammunition*

rubber cheque 741.15 *false money,* 747.3 *bad payment*

rubber-chicken circuit 51.13 *engagement*

rubber dinghy 632.4 *safety device*

rubber heel 424.2 *sound reducer*

rubber hose 879.14 *instrument of punishment*

rubberiness 374.8 *softness,* 377.1 *elasticity,* 378.6 *toughness*

rubberize 67.15 *treat,* 377.9 *make elastic*

rubberized 67.11 *treated,* 377.6 *elastic*

rubber-legged 656.3 *clumsy*

rubberlike 377.6 *elastic*

rubber mask 295.5 *fancy dress*

rubberneck 435.12 *see,* 465.7 *be curious*

rubbernecker 435.11 *observer,* 465.4 *meddler*

rubbernecking 465.2 *prying*

rubber plant 85 Trees and Shrubs, 377.4 *rubber*

rubber plantation 377.4 *rubber*

rubber ring 39.3 *survival swimming*

rubbers 295.19 *footwear*

rubber-soled shoes 295.19 *footwear*

rubber soles 424.2 *sound reducer*

rubberstamp 116.28 *consent*

rubber stamp 499.2 *yes,* 708.2 *permit,* 851.1 *approval*

rubber-stamp 499.4 *assent,* 667.6 *agree with,* 851.12 *accept*

rubberstamped 116.17 *consenting*

rubber tapping 85.6 *tree management*

rubber tree 85 Trees and Shrubs, 377.4 *rubber*

rubbery 374.1 *soft,* 377.6 *elastic,* 378.3 *hard*

rubbing 41.10 *curling,* 118.5 *duplicate,* 267.6 *meeting,* 385.1 *friction,* 385.5 *polishing,* 385.10 *frictional,* 407.2 *touching*

rubbing against 385.2 *wearing away*

rubbing noses 819.4 *act of friendship*

rubbing out 131.1 *subtraction,* 385.2 *wearing away,* 398.2 *murder,* 546.3 *obliteration,* 734.3 *taking away*

rubbing together 385.2 *wearing away*

rubbish 132.2 *residue*, 151.4 *litter*, 506.1 *nonsense*, 521.4 *senseless talk*, 521.14 *nonsense*, 539.6 *imitation*, 540.10 *fake*, 607.5 *waste product*, 614.6 *refuse*, 618.8 *inferiority*, 622.4 *dirt*, 727.3 *disposable things*
rubbish bin 258.11 *vessel*, 621.10 *cleaning object*, 727.4 *wastebin*
rubbish collector 727
rubbish dump 605.4 *storage*, 614.6 *refuse*, 727.8 *sink*
rubbish heap 614.6 *refuse*, 727.5 *wasteyard*, 727.8 *sink*
rubbish pile 614.6 *refuse*, 727.8 *sink*
rubbish scow 727.4 *wastebin*
rubbish truck 727.4 *wastebin*
rubbishy 521.10 *meaninglessness*, 539.39 *imitative*, 540.33 *fake*, 612.4 *trivial*, 614.1 *useless*, 618.2 *inferior*
rubble 143.8 *bits and pieces*
rubby-dubby 20.1 *angling*
rubdown 385.6 *massage*
rub down 68.18 *practise livestock farming*, 376.11 *smooth*, 384.26 *grate*, 385.16 *massage*
rube 93.12 *rural dweller*, 656.10 *unskilled person*, 658.3 *naive person*
rubefacient 62.4 *drug type*, 62.17 *stimulating*, 450.5 *redness*
rubefaction 450.5 *redness*
rubefy 450.9 *redden*
Rube Goldberg 519.11 *fantastical*
rubella 624.6 *infection*
rubellite 54 *Gemstones*
rubeola 624.6 *infection*
rubescence 450.5 *redness*
rubescent 450.2 *red-faced*
rube town 93.10 *village*
rub gently 385.16 *massage*
Rubicon 106.3 *critical moment*
rubicund 450.2 *red-faced*
rubicundity 450.5 *redness*
rubidium 57 *Chemical Elements*
rubidium–strontium dating 54.42 *dating*
rubiginous 449.1 *brown*
Rubik Cube 529.4 *brain-teaser*
rub in 554.6 *emphasize*
Rubinstein 49 *Musicians and Composers*, 49 *Musicians and Composers*
rub it in 768.6 *aggravate*
rub noses 407.11 *touch*
rub off 296.15 *make nude*, 546.1 *obliterate*
rub of the green 29.1 *golf*
rub on 336.6 *march on*
rub one's eyes 786.9 *wonder*
rub one's nose in it 768.6 *aggravate*, 806.17 *humiliate*
rub out 131.3 *subtract*, 147.8 *eject*, 244.8 *destroy*, 349.10 *exterminate*, 385.14 *erode*, 398.17 *murder*, 438.8 *make invisible*, 458.3 *cause to disappear*, 546.1 *obliterate*, 621.13 *clean*, 734.10 *take away*
rubric 10.10 *religious manual*, 472.1 *topic*, 654.3 *precept*
rubricate 450.9 *redden*
rub salt in the wound 768.6 *aggravate*
rub shoulders with 267.4 *meet*, 815.11 *be sociable*
rub the sleep from one's eyes 642.12 *be active*
rub the wrong way 383.14 *go against the grain*, 666.7 *pick a fight*, 785.7 *cause dislike*, 830.12 *make irritable*
rub up 6.23 *learn*, 385.12 *rub*, 439.27 *glaze*
rub up the right way 808.9 *fawn*
rub up the wrong way 375.12 *make rough*, 385.15 *grind*, 828.9 *offend*
ruby 54 *Gemstones*, 450.1 *red*, 450.7 *red thing*, 617.8 *exceller*
ruby laser 56.26 *laser*
ruby port 351.9 *wine*
ruby spinel 54 *Gemstones*
ruby wedding 812.5 *anniversary*

ruby wedding anniversary 214.6 *annually celebrated day*
ruche 320.2 *pleat*
ruched 295.31 *styled*, 320.5 *folded*
ruck 35.3 *rugby play*, 35.5 *play rugby*, 124.7 *average person*, 161.20 *crowd*, 164.6 *average*, 181.4 *throng*, 320.2, 320.8 *pleat*
rucked 295.31 *styled*
rucked up 320.5 *folded*
rucksack 34.4 *climbing equipment*, 258.9 *baggage*, 326.10 *transferred thing*
ruckus 151.9 *disorder*, 241.3 *instance of violence*, 666.2 *argument*
ructation 349.24, 388.5 *belch*
ruction 151.9 *disorder*, 153.5 *commotion*, 666.2 *argument*, 674.6 *fight*
rudbeckia 84 Flowers and Flowering Plants
rudd 80 *Fishes*, 20.5 *British game fish*
rudder 73 Aircraft Parts, **74** Parts of a Ship, 36.3 *parts of a sailing boat*, 74.5 *navigation*, 122.4 *equilizer*, 603.1 *tool*, 653.5 *guide*
rudderless 236.12 *impotent*
rudderpost 74 Parts of a Ship, 36.3 *parts of a sailing boat*
ruddily 450
ruddiness 444.9 *complexion*, 450.5 *redness*
ruddle 450.6 *red pigment*, 450.9 *redden*
ruddy 450.2 *red-faced*, 623.1 *healthy*, 810.9 *blushing*, 827.11 *miscellaneous euphemisms*
ruddy complexion 623.3 *health*
ruddy duck 78 *Birds*
rude 807, 5.36 *accent*, 5.39 *of language*, 145.4 *incomplete*, 241.6 *violent*, 270.9 *abrupt*, 559.8 *indecorous*, 595.5 *immature*, 622.9 *obscene*, 652.18 *badly behaved*, 656.3 *clumsy*, 764.2 *objectionable*, 816.8 *unsociable*, 816.6 *bad-mannered*, 838.3 *ungrateful*, 850.10 *disrespectful*
rude gesture 818.3 *act of discourtesy*, 850.7 *sign of disrespect*
rude health 623.3 *health*
rudely 807, 818, 241.10 *violently*, 622.12 *dirtily*, 652.20 *badly*, 816.14 *unsociably*, 838.7 *ungratefully*, 850.28 *disrespectfully*
rudeness 807, 270.6 *abruptness*, 559.2 *impropriety*, 622.3 *obscenity*, 652.4 *bad conduct*, 764.6 *objectionability*, 807.1 *insolence*, 818.2 *bad manners*, 838.1 *ingratitude*, 850.1 *disrespect*
rude person 652.5 *badly behaved person*, 785.3 *disliked person*, 818.4 *discourteous person*
rude remark 668.3 *act of defiance*
rude word 5.19 *swearword*
rude words 818.3 *act of discourtesy*
rudiment 226, 59.15 *developmental biology*, 375.10 *rough idea*
rudimental 156.35 *rudimentary*, 260.7 *little*
rudimentary 156, 59.26 *developmental*, 226.13 *causal*, 260.7 *little*, 280.3 *base*, 375.5 *unfinished*, 595.5 *immature*
rudiments 156
Rudolf 94 Lakes
Rudolf Nureyev 46.14 *famous ballet dancers*
Rudra 8 Deities
rue 45 Herbs and Spices, 413.5 *herbs*, 774.6 *lament*
rueful 867.6 *penitent*
ruefully 867.8 *penitently*
rue the day 867.4 *be penitent*
rufescence 450.5 *redness*
rufescent 450.1 *red*
ruff 78 *Birds*, 42.10 *play*, 78.17 *plumage*, 295.14 *neckwear*

ruffed grouse 78 *Birds*
ruffian 241.4 *violent person or animal*, 398.11 *murderer*, 635.2 *troublemaker*, 679.1 *combatant*, 693.9 *criminal*, 832.8 *malefactor*
ruffianism 16.41 *lawlessness*
ruffle 151.24 *make disordered*, 153.7 *disturb*, 320.2, 320.8 *pleat*, 366.22 *agitate*, 375.12 *make rough*, 792.5 *decorative articles*, 828.9 *offend*
ruffled 151.15 *untidy*, 153.12 *disturbed*, 366.15 *agitated*, 375.1 *rough*
ruffle feelings 818.7 *be discourteous*
ruffle one's feathers 828.9 *offend*
ruffle one's temper 828.14 *make angry*
ruffle the dignity 828.9 *offend*
rufous 450.1 *red*
rug 19.4 *stadium*, 280.1 *base*, 293.5 *body covering*, 293.9 *floor covering*, 295.15 *headgear*, 791.10 *wig*
rugby 35.1, 35.6 *rugger*
Rugby 93 Cities
rugby ball 35.1 *rugger*, 338.10 *ball*
rugby boots 295.19 *footwear*
rugby coach 35.4 *rugby player*
rugby fives 18 Sporting Activities
rugby football 35.1 *rugger*
Rugby Football 35
rugby ground 35.1 *rugger*
rugby league 18 Sporting Activities
Rugby League 35.1 *rugger*
rugby match 35.1 *rugger*
rugby pack 35.1 *rugger*
rugby pitch 35.1 *rugger*
rugby play 35
rugby player 35
rugby referee 35.4 *rugby player*
rugby side 35.1 *rugger*
rugby stadium 35.1 *rugger*
rugby union 18 Sporting Activities
Rugby Union 35.1 *rugger*
Rugby World Cup 35.2 *championship*
rugged 375.1 *rough*, 378.1 *tough*, 659.11 *rough*, 690.8 *severe*, 818.5 *discourteous*, 832.12 *callous*
rugged individualist 698.7 *free person*
ruggedly 237.14 *strongly*, 375.14 *roughly*, 378.12 *toughly*
ruggedness 375.6 *roughness*, 378.6 *toughness*, 659.1 *difficulty*, 690.1 *severity*
rugger 35, 35
rug making 42 Hobbies and Pastimes
rugose 375.1 *rough*
rugosely 375.14 *roughly*
rugosity 375.6 *roughness*
rugrat 59.15 *baby*, 206.9 *child*
Ruhr 96 *Rivers*
ruin 777 Phobias by Topic, **244**, **244**, 3.11 *relic*, 157.4 *annihilation*, 200.7 *thing of the past*, 233.9 *change*, 360.4 *fall*, 607.2 *lay waste*, 607.4 *destruction*, 618.11 *harmfulness*, 618.13 *be worthless*, 618.14 *illtreat*, 628.4 *impair*, 628.6 *pervert*, 628.8 *perversion*, 628.9 *dilapidation*, 631.1 *affliction*, 683.1 *failure*, 687.1 *adversity*, 722.5 *destruction*, 722.13 *destroy*, 743.6 *insolvency*, 743.14 *impoverish*, 747.5 *insolvency*, 862.2 *affliction*, 877.19 *corrupt*
ruination 244.4 *ruin*, 628.9 *dilapidation*, 628.10 *impairment*
ruined 127.18 *outclassed*, 141.5 *disintegrated*, 157.23 *annihilated*, 244.15 *destroyed*, 618.2 *inferior*, 628.13 *deteriorated*, 628.13 *dilapidated*, 722.16 *losing*, 722.17 *unprofitable*, 743.2 *insolvent*, 747.13 *nonpaying*, 864.12 *immoral*

ruin oneself 628.1 *deteriorate*, 753.11 *overpay*
ruin one's name 864.16 *be wicked*
ruin one's plans 515.6 *disappoint*, 587.3 *deflect*
ruinous 241.6 *violent*, 244.14 *destructive*, 618.5 *harmful*, 628.13 *dilapidated*, 687.6 *adverse*, 722.17 *unprofitable*
ruinously 244.16 *destructively*
ruins 132.1 *remainder*, 244.4 *ruin*
rule 166, **166**, **166**, 12.3 *governance*, 12.11 *govern*, 16.3 *law*, 16.71 *try a case*, 52.49 *geometric construction*, 52.65 *theory*, 56.6 *law*, 91.18 *exert sovereignty*, 92.7 *administer*, 124.4 *average*, 126.2 *leadership*, 150.7 *method*, 164.5 *averageness*, 164.28 *prevail*, 166.16 *direct*, 167.5 *convention*, 170.5 *computer*, 214.4 *orderliness*, 214.10 *make regular*, 233.10 *be a prevailing influence*, 268.6 *measuring instrument*, 282.5 *planometer*, 492.11 *judge*, 505.1 *maxim*, 592.2 *policy*, 652.1 *conduct*, 653.1 *manage*, 654.3 *precept*, 688.4 *governance*, 688.18 *have authority*, 692.1 *command*, 692.3 *authority*, 692.9 *command*, 692.11 *have authority over*, 696.14 *master*
Rule 53 The Constellations, **166**
rule absolutely 12.11 *govern*, 688.18 *have authority*
rule a territory 725.9 *own property*
rulebook 166.2 *canon*
ruled out 487.4 *forbidden*
rule of business 719.3 *performance*
rule of conduct 847.6 *ethics*
rule of custom 654.3 *precept*
rule of expediency 615.3 *convenience*
rule of law 12.1 *government*, 150.9 *discipline*, 688.7 *type of rule*
rule of terror 688.7 *type of rule*
rule of thumb 166.3 *rule of nature*, 268.7 *standard*, 479.3 *experimentation*
rule of wealth 12.1 *government*
rule out 147.7 *exclude*, 487.8 *make impossible*, 546.1 *obliterate*
rule over 166.16 *direct*, 692.11 *have authority over*
ruler 52.49 *geometric construction*, 126.5 *superior*, 170.5 *computer*, 268.6 *measuring instrument*, 282.5 *planometer*, 688.10 *person of authority*, 696.3 *leader*, 879.14 *instrument of punishment*
rules 584.5 *tradition*, 652.1 *conduct*, 847.6 *ethics*
rules and regulations 584.5 *tradition*
rules of business 584.5 *tradition*, 652.1 *conduct*
rules of conduct 813.5 *etiquette*
rules of inference 52.64 *reasoning*
rules of life 652.1 *conduct*
rules of the game 652.9 *tactics*
rules of the road 652.1 *conduct*
rules of the sea 74.5 *navigation*
rule the roost 166.16 *direct*, 688.18 *have authority*, 688.19 *be authoritarian*
rule with an iron hand 690.6 *suppress*
rule with an iron rod 688.19 *be authoritarian*
ruling 166, 2.14 *socioeconomic*, 12.10 *governing*, 16.7 *legal trial*, 126.13 *dominant*, 166.1 *rule*, 233.11 *influential*, 492.2 *verdict*, 688.12 *authoritative*, 692.1 *command*, 692.14 *commanding*
ruling class 2.7 *social stratification*
ruling party 696.8 *the power structure*

ruling passion 577.7 *opinionatedness*
rum 168.14 *eccentric*, 351.7 *alcoholic drink*, 798.5 *ridiculous*
rum and black 351.8 *mixed drink*
rum and Coke 351.8 *mixed drink*
rum and pep 351.8 *mixed drink*
rumba 41.7 *ice-dancing*, 46.2, 46.15 *dance*
rumble 423.1 *loudness*, 425.5 *bang*, 426.1 *drumming*, 426.8 *drum*, 522.6 *understand*, 666.2 *argument*, 674.6 *fight*
rumble seat 71 Motor Vehicle Parts
rumbling 426.1 *drumming*
rumbling thunder 423.1 *loudness*
rumbustious 423.6 *loud*
Rum Collins 351.8 *mixed drink*
Rumford 52 Scientists
ruminant 4.17 *thoughtful*, 77.15 *hoofed mammal*, 77.33 *ungulate*
Ruminantia 77.15 *hoofed mammal*
ruminate 4.20 *philosophize*, 77.37 *graze*, 87.11 *eat grass*, 350.21 *eat*, 461.12 *think*
rumination 350.5 *eating habit*, 461.1 *thought*
ruminative 4.17, 461.8 *thoughtful*
ruminatively 4.28 *thoughtfully*
Rümker Hills 53 Mountains
rummage sale 727.2 *disposal of property*, 739.4 *sale*, 740.10 *bazaar*, 752.2 *bargain*, 754.7 *discounter*
rummer 258.13 *drinking vessel*, 351.10 *drink container*
rummy 42 Card Games
rum one 168.10 *eccentric*
rumour 420.8 *something heard*, 472.3 *matter of interest*, 528.7 *advice*, 532.1 *publication*, 532.13 *make public*, 538.21 *lie*
rump 45.22 *beef* , 132.1 *remainder*, 304.2 *rear end*
rumple 151.24 *make disordered*, 320.2, 320.8 *pleat*, 366.22 *agitate*, 375.12 *make rough*, 383.14 *go against the grain*
Rumpless 68 Breeds of Fowl
rum punch 351.7 *alcoholic drink*
rumpus 151.9 *disorder*, 153.5 *commotion*, 241.3 *instance of violence*, 423.2 *outcry*, 666.2 *argument*, 674.6 *fight*
rumpus room 256.7 *room*
rumpy-pumpy 135.4 *sexual union*, 821.5 *desire*
run 19.9 *play*, 21.1 *track events*, 21.6 *race*, 27.10 *score*, 30.6 *pommel horse*, 35.3 *rugby play*, 36.15 *sail*, 36.19 *punt*, 41.1 *skiing*, 41.9 *bobsledding* , 42.3 *card game terms*, 51.13 *engagement*, 68.18 *practise livestock farming*, 77.20 *abode of mammals*, 96.1 *river*, 96.6 *river flow*, 96.7 *flow*, 124.4 *average*, 126.10 *lead*, 136.3 *separateness*, 136.9 *separate*, 139.6 *come unstuck*, 155.2 *series*, 159.2 *consecution*, 159.14 *continue*, 164.6 *average*, 166.16 *direct*, 188.7 *go on*, 195.1 *succession*, 219.1 *continuity*, 230.7 *be operational*, 233.10 *be a prevailing influence*, 256.12 *stall*, 269.5 *piece*, 324.2 *momentum*, 324.12 *gait*, 324.15 *walk*, 327.2 *route*, 329.4 *be swift*, 329.6 *accelerate*, 329.9 *acceleration*, 330.1 *impel*, 332.2 *bearing*, 353.18 *fester*, 387.24 *melt*, 387.25 *flow*, 445.5 *lose colour*, 458.2 *depart*, 580.5 *vote*, 584.3 *way*, 590.2 *chase*, 591.8 *run away*, 596.5 *attempt*, 642.12 *be active*, 644.9 *exercise*, 648.2 *make haste*, 652.14 *behave towards*, 653.1 *manage*, 670.12 *military attack*
runabout 71 Motor Vehicles, 74 Ships and Boats, 71.16 *car*
run abreast 122.10 *be equal*, 285.5 *parallel*
run across 229.5 *happen by chance*, 589.11 *chance upon*

run a dead heat 198.8 *run equally*
run a deficit 722.10 *have a financial loss*
run after 326.14 *bring back*, 590.10 *chase*, 782.13 *like*, 808.11 *pander to*, 819.14 *seek the friendship of*, 826.8 *court*
run aground 74.10 *sail*, 344.4 *land*, 687.9 *be in trouble*
run a lap 214.8 *be cyclic*
run along 349.33 *go away*
run amok 151.26 *be disorderly*, 241.7 *be violent*, 244.10 *lay waste*, 510.14 *become insane*, 670.5 *strike*, 759.17 *feel deeply*
run and run 159.14 *continue*
run-and-bump 33.11 *racing*
run-and-bump tactic 33.6 *motor racing terms*
run-and-shoot offence 19.8 *huddle*
run a pattern 19.15 *play offence*
run a protection racket 734.10 *take away*
run a punt 36.19 *punt*
run a race 674.11 *contend*
run around 821.26 *court*
run as a candidate 710.13 *be a candidate*
run a second edition 110.9 *duplicate*
run a stone 41.16 *bobsled*
run at 670.11 *attack*
run at a loss 722.10 *have a financial loss*
run a temperature 408.16 *feel hot*
run a tight ship 690.5 *be severe*
runaway 254.6 *absentee*, 324.16 *moving*, 329.1 *swift*, 458.4 *disappearance*, 578.9 *equivocator*, 591.17 *avoider*, 591.18 *avoiding*, 598.4 *deserter*, 638.3 *escaper*, 638.8 *escaping*, 720.6 *evader*, 720.12 *nonperforming*
run away 591, 254.18 *abscond*, 329.6 *accelerate*, 337.2 *retreat*, 345.4 *hurry off*, 458.2 *depart*, 632.8 *be safe*, 638.5 *escape*, 683.7 *be defeated*, 720.8 *not perform*, 779.4 *be a coward*, 823.15 *marry*
runaway success 682.1 *success*
runaway tongue 565.1 *talkativeness*
runaway victory 682.2 *victory*
runaway wedding 638.1 *escape*
run away with 734.10, 767.14 *take away*
run back 19.12 *special team*, 19.17 *kick*, 337.2 *retreat*, 337.3 *reverse*
run bases 22.7 *play baseball*
run before a gale 74.9 *navigate*
run before the wind 74.9 *navigate*
run counter 111.8 *be opposite*
run counter to 231.3 *counteract*, 663.13 *be contrary*
rundle 359.10 *step*
run down 129.4 *decrease*, 129.5 *make smaller*, 218.6 *cease*, 238.8 *weak*, 496.2 *detect*
rundown 562.1 *summary*
run down 590.10 *chase*, 600.4 *disused*, 609.7 *make insufficient*, 624.21 *unhealthy*, 670.9 *attack successfully*, 766.7 *be dissatisfied*, 850.20 *scorn*, 852.17 *criticize*, 852.33 *criticized*, 854.10 *disparage*
run-down 22.6 *fielding terms*, 628.12 *deteriorated*, 628.13 *dilapidated*
run down one's account 748.1 *expend*
rune 5.13 *letter*, 11.5 *spell*, 543.1 *sign*
run equally 198
runes 517.10 *cards*, 547.1 *representation*
run faster 721.10 *augment*
run for 332.7 *take a direction*
run for it 591.8 *run away*, 591.24 *hands off*
run for office 710.13 *be a candidate*

run for one's life 345.4 *hurry off*, 591.8 *run away*
run for port 74.10 *sail*, 632.8 *be safe*
run for your life 591.24 *hands off*
run full stride 21.6 *race*
run foul of 330.2 *collide*
rung 319, 121.4 *interval*, 315.4 *cylinder*, 359.10 *step*
run helter-skelter 648.2 *make haste*
runic 5.41 *lettered*, 11.14 *occult*
runic alphabet 5.14 *alphabet*
runic letter 5.14 *alphabet*
runic verse 48.6 *poetry*
run in 27.18 *bowl*, 354.3 *impact*, 699.11 *detain*, 734.10 *take away*
run-in 666.2 *argument*
run interference for 662.24 *back*
run into 344.8 *meet*, 407.12 *abut*, 589.11 *chance upon*
run into danger 633.8 *be in danger*
run into debt 745.7 *be in debt*
run into money 753.9 *be dear*
run into the ground 599.3 *exploit*
run into trouble 105.7 *be in a predicament*, 659.20 *be in difficulty*
run its course 188.7 *go on*, 200.14 *pass*
run level 36.16 *row*, 122.10 *be equal*
run like a bat out of hell 329.5 *run like a shot*
run like a blue-streak 329.5 *run like a shot*
run like a flash 329.5 *run like a shot*
run like a hare 329.5 *run like a shot*
run like a house on fire 329.5 *run like a shot*
run like a scared rabbit 329.5 *run like a shot*
run like a shot 329
run like a streak 329.5 *run like a shot*
run like a streak of lightning 329.5 *run like a shot*
run like crazy 329.5 *run like a shot*
run like greased lightning 329.5 *run like a shot*
run like hell 648.2 *make haste*
run like lightning 329.5 *run like a shot*
run like mad 329.5 *run like a shot*
run like sin 329.5 *run like a shot*
run like sixty 329.5 *run like a shot*
run like the clappers 329.5 *run like a shot*
run like the devil 329.5 *run like a shot*, 648.2 *make haste*
run like the wind 329.5 *run like a shot*
run like wildfire 329.5 *run like a shot*
run low 129.4 *decrease*, 607.1 *waste*
run messages for 678.1 *mediate*
run neck and neck 122.10 *be equal*, 198.8 *run equally*
runnel 96.1 *river*
runner 19.7 *offence*, 21.3 *athlete*, 22.2 *baseball player*, 27.4 *team*, 32.7 *horseracing*, 34.4 *climbing equipment*, 41.9 *bobsledding* , 69.5 *gardening*, 83.5 *stem*, 237.5 *athlete*, 293.9 *floor covering*, 329.13 *swift person*, 674.10 *contender*, 697.5 *office assistant*
runner bean 45 Vegetables
runner-up 237.5 *athlete*, 674.10 *contender*
runner-up prize 878.2 *prize*
runnily 387.26 *fluidly*, 389.35 *wetly*
runniness 139.1 *nonadhesion*, 274.12 *thinning*, 387.5 *fluidity*, 389.3 *wateriness*
running 21.1 *track events*, 25.9 *bowls*, 30.6 *pommel horse*, 35.3 *rugby play*, 35.6 *rugger*, 36.8, 36.14 *punting*, 51.39 *stagestruck*, 96.10 *fluvial*, 139.8 *nonadhesive*, 155.27 *in sequence*, 159.9

consecutive, 195.14 *in succession*, 219.5 *continual*, 230.10 *operational*, 324.1 *motion*, 324.16 *moving*, 329.1 *swift*, 353.7 *pus*, 353.27 *purulent*, 387.8 *fluidification*, 625.1 *hygiene*, 642.18 *active*, 644.5 *exercise*, 653.3 *management*, 674.4 *race*, 674.14 *contending*
running account 750.1 *accounts*
running around 538.20 *unfaithful*, 877.3 *sexual immorality*
running a stone 41.10 *curling*
running at a loss 722.2 *financial loss*
running attack 28.3 *fencing movements*
running away 458.4 *disappearance*
running back 19.7 *offence*
running battle 674.1 *contention*
running belay 34.3 *climbing technique*
running board 71 Motor Vehicle Parts
running bowline 74 Knots
running changes 49.20 *key*
running costs 751.6 *business costs*
running dog 167.6 *conformist*
running down 854.1 *disparagement*
running fight 674.6 *fight*
running flush 42.3 *card game terms*
running game 19.9 *play*
running game target shooting 18 Sporting Activities
running hop 21.2 *field events*
running lights 439.6 *electric light*
running offence 23.4 *playing terms*
running on 565.5 *talkative*
running out 32.9 *jumping*
running over 144.8 *full*, 610.6 *excessive*
running repairs 629.8 *repair*
running rigging 36.3 *parts of a sailing boat*
running riot 541.3 *extravagance*
running shoes 21.4 *sports equipment*, 295.19 *footwear*
running short 358.8 *defective*
running shorts 21.4 *sports equipment*
running shot 25.2 *grip*
running sore 347.2 *outflow*, 631.1, 862.2 *affliction*
running start 126.3 *advantage*
running steps 46.3 *ballroom dance steps*
running story 533.9 *news story*
running the gauntlet 879.12 *corporal punishment*
running to earth 250.3 *locating*
running to seed 207.12 *ageing*
running total 169.4 *mathematical result*
running vest 21.4 *sports equipment*
running water 96.1 *river*, 387.2 *juice*, 389.1 *water*
running with the ball 23.5 *penalties*
running with the hare and hunting with the hounds 858.2 *faithlessness*
run nip and tuck 122.10 *be equal*, 198.8 *run equally*
runny 139.8 *nonadhesive*, 238.11 *insufficient*, 274.5 *thinned*, 347.17 *leaky*, 387.15 *flowing*, 393.19 *juicy*
runny nose 347.2 *outflow*, 624.9 *respiratory disease*
run of bad luck 589.2 *luck*
runoff 54.10 *water cycle*
run off 54.63 *ebb*, 345.4 *hurry off*, 591.8 *run away*
run-off 674.2 *contest*
run off at the mouth 565.7 *be talkative*, 569.4 *monopolize the conversation*
run off with 734.10 *take away*
run of good luck 589.2 *luck*
run of luck 682.1 *success*, 686.2 *good fortune*

run-of-the-mill 124.3 *mediocre*, 158.15 *middling*, 164.21 *common*, 164.6 *average*, 212.3 *frequent*, 787.4 *predictable*
run on 159.13 *be consecutive*, 219.3 *continue*, 593.2 *need*
run one hard 633.10 *endanger*
run one's head against 330.2 *collide*
run one's mouth 610.4 *be excessive*
run on in order 214.7 *be regular*
run on rails 376.12 *go smoothly*
run on savings 748.6 *extravagance*
run on the rocks 633.10 *endanger*
run out 347, 27.11 *dismissal*, 27.19 *dismiss*, 157.18 *come to an end*, 200.14 *pass*, 218.6 *cease*, 330.1 *impel*, 347.9 *exit*, 607.1 *waste*, 609.5 *be insufficient*
run out of gas 218.6 *cease*
run out of luck 687.9 *be in trouble*
run out of steam 328.2 *hesitate*
run out of time 157.18 *come to an end*
run out on 598.2 *withdraw*
run over 144.5 *be complete*
run parallel 285.5 *parallel*, 667.8 *be compatible*
run pell-mell 648.2 *make haste*
run rings around 126.8 *be superior*
run riot 151.26 *be disorderly*, 241.7 *be violent*, 541.9 *be extravagant*, 610.4 *be excessive*, 642.12 *be active*
run round in circles 642.13 *be busy*
runs batted in 22.5 *batting terms*
runs-batted-in leader 22.2 *baseball player*
run short 358.1 *fall short*
run smoothly 660.19 *go easily*
runt 260.4 *little person*, 270.5 *short person*, 274.9 *thin person*
run the gauntlet 633.9 *face danger*, 668.5 *defy*
run the hurry-up offence 19.15 *play offence*
run the offence 19.15 *play offence*
run the power sweep 19.15 *play offence*
run the quarterback sneak 19.15 *play offence*
run the risk of 633.8 *be in danger*
runthrough 51.12 *production*
run through 51.35 *rehearse*, 133.10 *become mixed*, 233.10 *be a prevailing influence*, 244.12 *consume*, 253.11 *be present*, 322.20 *hole*, 398.17 *murder*, 406.11 *inflict pain*, 607.1 *waste*, 670.6 *stab*, 748.2 *consume*
run-through 24.2 *billiards play*, 25.9 *bowls*
run-through shot 25.2 *grip*
runtiness 260.1 *littleness*
run to 263.7 *reach*, 599.4 *resort to*
run to beat the band 329.5 *run like a shot*
run to earth 250.11 *find*, 496.2 *detect*
run together 140.5 *combine*, 342.10 *come together*
run to ground 590.9 *follow*
run to seed 83.21 *vegetate*, 207.13 *middle-aged*, 247.7 *be infertile*, 607.1 *waste*
run to waste 607.1 *waste*
run true to form 167.7 *conform*
run true to type 112.10 *conform*
runty 260.7 *little*
run up 243.10 *produce*
run-up 21.2 *field events*
run up a bill 744.9 *acquire credit*, 745.7 *be in debt*
run up a debt 733.10 *buy on credit*
run up against a brick wall 330.2 *collide*
run up an account 733.10 *buy on credit*, 744.9 *acquire credit*,

745.7 *be in debt*
run up an overdraft 722.10 *have a financial loss*
runway 63.19 *structure*, 73.4 *airport*, 327.13 *flight path*
runway lights 439.6 *electric light*
run wild 151.26 *be disorderly*, 241.7 *be violent*, 698.19 *liberalize*
run with 180.14 *keep company with*
run with the hare and hunt with the hounds 158.18 *stand in the middle*, 540.17 *double-deal*, 578.2 *equivocate*, 808.14 *follow*, 858.9 *prove false*
run with the pack 167.8 *comply*
Runyon 48 *Writers*
rupee 741.11 *national coins*
rupture 63.16 *deformation*, 63.31 *load*, 117.4 *disagreement*, 117.14 *disagree*, 136.3 *separateness*, 136.9 *separate*, 265.2, 265.5 *crack*, 322.1 *opening*, 322.18 *open*, 406.2 *painful condition*, 500.4 *faction*, 666.2 *argument*, 666.6 *argue*
ruptured 136.15 *separate*, 265.7 *cracked*, 322.12 *open*
rural 2.13 *communal*, 68.19 *agricultural*, 70.5 *transportable*, 92.6 *administrative*, 93.14 *urban*, 249.17 *national*, 453.2 *verdant*
rural area 249.6 *regions*
rural district 92.1 *administrative area*
rural dweller 93
rural economics 68.1 *agriculture*
rural economist 68.15 *agriculturist*
ruralism 2.5 *society*
ruralist 255.5 *countryman*
rurally 68.22 *agriculturally*, 93.16 *municipally*
rural road 71.2 *road*
rural sector 2.5 *society*
rural society 2.5 *society*
rural sociology 2.1 *sociology*, 2.5 *society*
rural-urban 2.13 *communal*
rural-urban migration 2.5 *society*
rural village 93.10 *village*
Ruritania 519.8 *dreamland*
RURP 34.4 *climbing equipment*
ruse 474.2 *sophism*, 539.8 *trick*, 592.3 *expedient plan*, 635.1 *trap*, 657.2 *stratagem*
rush 87 *Grasses*, 19.11 *defensive huddle*, 19.16 *play defence*, 87.1 *grass*, 96.6 *river flow*, 96.7 *flow*, 161.40 *crowd*, 241.3 *instance of violence*, 324.2 *momentum*, 324.15 *walk*, 329.4 *be swift*, 329.9 *acceleration*, 366.2 *tumult*, 366.21 *be agitated*, 595.8 *lack of preparation*, 612.8 *trifle*, 642.12 *be active*, 648.1 *hasten*, 648.2 *make haste*, 648.3 *hasty*, 648.4 *haste*, 670.1 *attack*, 670.12 *military attack*
rush about 241.7 *be violent*
rush along 648.1 *hasten*
rush around 239.2 *be full of vigour*
rush around like a chicken with its head cut off 239.2 *be full of vigour*
rush at 590.10 *chase*, 670.1 *attack*
rush basket 258.7 *basket*
rushed 31.8 *hockey*, 595.3 *without preparation*, 648.3 *hasty*
rushed into 648.3 *hasty*
rushed off one's feet 642.19 *busy*
rush family 83.3 *seed plant*
rush headlong 241.7 *be violent*, 648.2 *make haste*
rush hour 204.2 *morning thing*, 205.4 *evening thing*
rush in 346.10 *invade*, 346.12 *flood in*
rushing 31.8 *hockey*, 96.10 *fluvial*, 324.1 *motion*, 324.16 *moving*, 648.3 *hasty*
rushing the puck 31.3 *ice hockey*
rushing to and fro 642.19 *busy*

rush into 780.5 *be rash*
rush in where angels fear to tread 462.12 *lack thought*, 780.5 *be rash*
rush job 648.4 *haste*
rush light 439.5 *incandescent light*
rush off 345.4 *hurry off*, 648.2 *make haste*
rush one's fences 648.2 *make haste*, 780.5 *be rash*
rush the passer 19.16 *play defence*
rush the puck 31.9 *play hockey*
rush through 648.2 *make haste*
rush to and fro 642.12 *be active*, 648.2 *make haste*
rush to the assistance of 662.17 *help*
rushy 87.9 *grassy*
rusk 45.38 *bread*
Ruskie 91 *Names for Inhabitants*
Russ 32 *Breeds of Horse and Pony*
Russell 4 *Philosophers*, **48** *Dramatists*
Russell's paradox 52 *Named Concepts*, 4.9 *philosophical problem*
Russell's viper 79 *Reptiles*
russet 67 *Natural Fabrics*, **86** *Fruits*, 449.1 *brown*, 450.1 *red*
Russia 91 *Countries*
Russian 5 *Languages and Groups of Languages*
Russian ballet 46.8 *ballet*
Russian bear 544.6 *national emblem*
Russian blue 77 *Breeds of Cats*
Russian brag 42 *Card Games*
Russian dance 46.4 *historic dancing*
Russian doll 266.5 *layered thing*
Russian Formalists 48 *Literary Groups and Movements*
Russian Heavy Draught 32 *Breeds of Horse and Pony*
Russian Orthodox Church 7 *Christian Movements*
Russians 777 *Phobias by Topic*
Russian salad 45.14 *salad*
Russian tea 351.3 *tea*
Russian Trotter 32 *Breeds of Horse and Pony*
Russify 220.12 *naturalize*
Russo-Japanese War 17 *Major Wars*
Russophobia 777 *Phobias by Name*
russula 89 *Fungi*
rust 89 *Fungi*, 69.12 *pests and diseases*, 85.10 *tree disease*, 141.1 *disintegration*, 141.3 *disintegrate*, 202.3 *antiquity*, 202.17 *grow old*, 238.1 *weakness*, 244.7 *agent of destruction*, 247.7 *be infertile*, 384.29 *weather*, 441.11 *tarnish*, 450.7 *red thing*, 595.12 *be unprepared*, 622.4 *dirt*, 622.10 *be dirty*, 628.2 *decay*, 628.5 *hurt*, 628.9 *dilapidation*, 631.14 *afflict*, 641.4 *not act*
Rust Belt 647.1 *workshop*
rust-coloured 449.1 *brown*, 450.1 *red*
rusted 238.9 *dilapidated*
rustic 68.19 *agricultural*, 93.12 *rural dweller*, 255.5 *countryman*, 255.12 *native*, 658.3 *naive person*, 803.1 *plebeian*
rustically 68.22 *agriculturally*
rusticate 43.19 *decorate*, 349.3 *disbar*, 349.4 *ostracize*
rusticated 43.17 *structured*
rustication 43 *Architectural Decoration*, 43.9 *miscellaneous architectural features*, 349.19 *ostracism*
rustic brick 43.4 *building material*
rustic fence 69.3 *ornamental garden*
rustiness 430.2 *hoarseness*, 585.3 *unaccustomedness*, 595.8 *lack of preparation*, 628.9 *dilapidation*, 656.8 *unskilfulness*

rusting 57.19 *electrochemistry*, 600.4 *disused*
rustle 424.1 *faintness*, 424.5 *sound faint*, 428.4 *faint sound*, 428.8 *sound faint*, 429.1, 429.4 *hiss*
rustle cattle 736.12 *steal*
rustle of spring 203.2 *spring*
rustler 736.8 *thief*
rustle up 594.2 *do the groundwork*
rustling 424.4 *faint*, 428.4 *faint sound*, 429.1 *hiss*, 429.6 *hissing*
rustling leaves 424.3 *faint-sounding thing*
rustproof 632.6 *invulnerable*
rustre 544.8 *heraldic device*
rusts 89.3 *fungi*
rusty 141.5 *disintegrated*, 141.6 *disintegrating*, 430.8 *hoarse*, 441.7 *dimmed*, 449.1 *brown*, 585.1 *unaccustomed*, 628.13 *dilapidated*, 656.3 *clumsy*
rusty-dusty 304.2 *rear end*
rusty hinge 430.3 *shrillness*
rut 41.1 *skiing*, 112.4 *monotony*, 159.7 *stability*, 166.6 *custom*, 183.3 *repetitiveness*, 315.6 *round*, 321.1, 321.6 *furrow*, 327.6 *path*, 375.8 *rough ground*, 584.3 *way*, 788.2 *boring thing*
rutabaga 45 *Vegetables*
ruth 835.2 *condolence*
ruthenium 57 *Chemical Elements*
rutherford 75 *Scientific and Technical Units*
Rutherford 52 *Scientists*
rutherfordium 57 *Chemical Elements*
ruthful 835.7 *pitiful*
ruthless 574.3 *strong-willed*, 832.13 *merciless*, 836.4 *pitiless*
ruthlessly 588.13 *intentionally*
ruthlessness 574.14 *tenacity*, 832.3 *callousness*, 836.1 *pitilessness*
rutile 54 *Minerals*
Rutland 94 *Lakes*
Rutland Water 94.4 *British lakes*
rutted 41.12 *ski*, 321.4 *furrowed*, 375.2 *coarse*
ruttily 321
rutting 203.17 *in season*, 877.14 *lecherous*
ruttish 877.14 *lecherous*
rutty 321.4 *furrowed*, 375.2 *coarse*
RV 71 *Motor Vehicles*
Rwanda 5 *Languages and Groups of Languages*, **91** *Countries*
Rydal Water 94 *Lakes*, 94.4 *British lakes*
Rydberg constant 56 *Named Laws*, 56.97 *fundamental constant*
rye 87 *Grasses*, 68.12 *crop*, 351.7 *alcoholic drink*
rye bread 45.38 *bread*
rye-brome 87 *Grasses*
ryegrass 87 *Grasses*, 68.12 *crop*
Ryeland 68 *Breeds of Sheep*
rye whiskey 351.7 *alcoholic drink*
Ryle 4 *Philosophers*, **52** *Scientists*
rypophobia 777 *Phobias by Name*

S

Saar 96 *Rivers*
Saarbrücken 93 *Cities*
sab 661.9 *block*
Sabaean 5 *Languages and Groups of Languages*
Sabaic 9.10 *idolatrous*
Sabaism 7 *Non-Christian Religions*, 9.2 *idolatry*
Sabaist 9.6 *idolater*
Sabatier 52 *Scientists*
Sabazios 8 *Deities*

Sabbatarian 7.4 *religionist*
Sabbatarianism 10.2 *ritualism*
Sabbath 10.15 *holy day*, 649.1 *ease*
sabbatical 254.5 *leave of absence*, 645.2 *time off*, 649.1 *ease*, 649.4 *at ease*, 708.2 *permit*
sabbatical leave 254.5 *leave of absence*
Sabbatism 10.2 *ritualism*
sabbing 661.2 *obstacle*
Sabellian 5 Languages and Groups of Languages, 5.11 *family of languages*
sabin 75 Scientific and Technical Units
Sabine 5 Languages and Groups of Languages
Sabine women 677.3 *pacifist*
sable 77 Placental Mammals, 293.14 *animal covering*, 440.10 *dark-coloured*, 447.1 *black*, 447.9 *black thing*, 544.8 *heraldic device*, 544.13 *heraldic*
sable antelope 77 Placental Mammals
Sable Island 32 Breeds of Horse and Pony
sabot 74 Ships and Boats, **74** Sailing Ships and Boats
sabotage 153.4 *disruption*, 153.10 *disrupt*, 244.3 *destructiveness*, 607.2 *lay waste*, 607.4 *destruction*, 614.8 *make useless*, 628.10 *impairment*, 661.2 *obstacle*, 661.9 *block*, 693.3 *subversion*, 693.16 *be subversive*, 722.5 *destruction*, 722.13 *destroy*
sabotaged 153.15 *disrupted*
saboteur 244.6 *destroyer*, 539.20 *plotter*, 540.15 *false person*, 661.7 *hinderer*, 672.2 *revenger*, 693.10 *seditionist*
sabots 295.19 *footwear*
sabre 28.2 *fencing equipment*, 28.6 *fencing*, 398.17 *murder*, 680.8 *sharp weapon*
sabre-fence 28.5 *fence*
sabre fencing 28.1 *fencing*
sabre leg 47.3 *chair leg*
sabre-rattling 670.22 *militant*, 676.1 *war*, 676.5 *bellicosity*
sabres 679.19 *cavalry*
sabre-toothed tiger 77 Placental Mammals, 202.8 *prehistoric animal*
sabreur 679.1 *combatant*
sabulosity 384.3 *graininess*
sabulous 384.18 *grainy*
sac 258.19 *inflatable*
saccharic acid 58.3 *carbohydrate*
saccharide 57 Types of Compounds, 58.3 *carbohydrate*
saccharimeter 268.8 *meter*
saccharimetry 268.2 *micrometry*
saccharine 414.2 *sweetener*, 414.6 *sweet*, 853.13 *honeyed*
saccharine sweet 853.13 *honeyed*
saccharinity 414.1 *sweetness*
saccharometer 268.8 *meter*
sacerdotal 7.17 *priestly*
sacerdotalism 7.9 *priesthood*
sac fungi 89.3 *fungi*
Sachse reaction 57 Named Reactions
sack 15.11 *conduct industrial relations*, 19.11 *defensive huddle*, 19.16 *play defence*, 120.3 *container*, 147.8 *eject*, 218.8 *cause to cease*, 244.10 *lay waste*, 252.17 *relegate*, 258.8 *bag*, 295.7 *frock*, 341.2 *eject*, 349.2 *dismiss*, 351.9 *wine*, 600.7 *stop work*, 607.2 *lay waste*, 643.14, 643.14 *make inactive*, 645.5 *dismiss*, 704.7 *terminate*, 727.10 *dismiss*, 734.3 *taking away*, 734.10 *take away*, 736.5 *plundering*, 736.14 *plunder*, 767.12 *relieve from duty*
sackbut 49 Musical Instruments
sackcloth 67 Natural Fabrics, 288.4 *textile*, 375.7 *rough thing*
sackcloth and ashes 774.1 *lamentation*, 840.2 *apology*, 867.2 *type of penance*

sack coat 295.11 *jacket*
sack dress 307.2 *shapeless thing*
sacked 15.9 *negotiated*, 218.10 *finished*, 252.11 *relegated*, 600.3 *not wanted*, 645.7 *leisurely*, 704.10 *cancelled*, 727.13 *dismissed*
sacked out 650.1 *fatigued*
sacker 734.6 *taker*, 736.9 *plunderer*
sacking 67 Natural Fabrics, 15.2 *industrial negotiations*, 147.2 *ejection*, 218.2 *stop*, 288.4 *textile*, 349.18 *dismissal*, 727.1 *disposal*, 734.3 *taking away*, 736.5 *plundering*
sack out 651.2 *be refreshed*
sack race 674.4 *race*
sacral 10.21 *ritualistic*
sacrament 10.1 *ritual*, 10.5 *Christian rite*
sacramental 10.21 *ritualistic*
sacramentalism 10.2 *ritualism*
sacramentally 10.23 *ritually*
sacramentarianism 10.2 *ritualism*
Sacramento 93 Cities
sacrament of marriage 823.1 *marriage*
sacrarium 10.13 *shrine*
sacred 8.13 *divine*
sacred dance 46.4 *historic dancing*
sacred ibis 78 Birds
sacredly 8.19 *divinely*
sacred music 49
sacredness 8.1 *divinity*
sacred object 10
sacred place 10.13 *shrine*
sacred symbol 543.1 *sign*
sacred text 7.12 *religious text*
sacred writings 7.12 *religious text*
sacrifice 9.1, 9.7 *worship*, 10.3 *rite of worship*, 10.19 *offer worship*, 22.5 *batting terms*, 22.7 *play baseball*, 131.2 *subtracted item*, 222.3 *substitute thing*, 244.8 *destroy*, 398.6 *ritual killing*, 398.20 *kill ritually*, 710.6 *offering*, 722.1 *loss*, 722.9 *lose*, 729.3 *offering*, 729.5 *give*, 754.13 *make cheap*, 840.2 *apology*, 859.7 *be unselfish*
sacrificed 397.19 *dead*, 710.19 *sacrificial*
sacrifice fly 22.5 *batting terms*
sacrifice oneself 572.15 *volunteer*, 710.12 *offer one's life*, 859.7 *be unselfish*
sacrifice one's life 710.12 *offer one's life*
sacrificer 729.4 *giver*
sacrifice the interests of others 860.6 *be selfish*
sacrifice to 840.6 *apologize*
sacrifice to Bacchus 874.8 *get drunk*
sacrificial 710, 10.21 *ritualistic*, 244.14 *destructive*, 729.7 *given*, 754.9 *cheap*, 840.4 *atoning*
sacrificial anode 57.19 *electrochemistry*
sacrificial knife 10.14 *sacred object*
sacrificial lamb 710.6 *offering*, 710.7 *martyr*
sacrificially 9.12 *worshipfully*, 710.20 *persuasively*, 729.9 *as a gift*, 840.8 *penitently*
sacrificial offering 710.6 *offering*
sacrilege 827.1 *curse*, 864.6 *religious sin*
sacrilegious 827.8 *cursing*, 844.15 *immoral*, 864.14 *impious*
sacrilegiously 827.12 *swearingly*, 864.20 *immorally*
sacring bell 10.14 *sacred object*, 543.4 *signal*
sacristy 10.12 *church*
sacrosanct 8.13 *divine*, 632.6 *invulnerable*
sacrosanctity 8.1 *divinity*
sacrum 382 Bones
sad 447, 770, 399.11 *funeral*, 454.3 *depressed*, 515.9 *disappointed*, 616.1 *inconvenient*, 618.4 *poor*, 774.4 *lamenting*, 835.7 *pitiful*, 862.8 *afflicted*

sadden 515.6 *disappoint*, 770.8 *grieve*
saddened 770.5 *sad*
sadder but wiser man 867.3 *penitent person*
saddle 30.6 *pommel horse*, 32.14 *horse-riding terms*, 32.16 *ride*, 71.11 *bicycle part*, 95.1 *mountain*, 275.4 *mountain range*, 284.4 *rest*, 369.14 *make heavy*
saddleback 78 Birds, 275.4 *mountain range*
saddlebag 71.5 *pack*, 71.11 *bicycle part*, 258.8 *bag*
Saddlebred 32 Breeds of Horse and Pony
saddle-bronc-riding 32.12 *rodeo*
saddlecloth 293.14 *animal covering*
saddled 369.3 *ponderous*, 594.18 *prepared*, 847.11 *duty-bound*
saddled with 661.14 *blocked*
saddle horse 32
saddler 32.15 *horse person*
saddle tank 72.5 *locomotive part*
saddletree 85.12 *figurative usage*
saddle with 130.6 *add*, 661.12 *burden*, 847.17 *impose a duty*
saddling 369.8 *weighing down*
Sadducee 7.6 *non-Christian*
Sadduceeism 7 Non-Christian Religions
Sade 48 Writers
sad ending 862.2 *affliction*
sadhearted 770.5 *sad*
sadheartedness 770.1 *sorrow*
sadhu 7.3 *religious person*
sadism 832.2 *cruelness*, 877.7 *sexual assault*
sadist 832.8 *malefactor*, 864.9 *wicked person*, 877.10 *sex offender*
sadistic 406.8 *inflicting pain*, 832.11 *cruel*, 836.4 *pitiless*, 877.15 *unlawful*
sadistically 832.20 *malevolently*, 836.7 *pitilessly*
sadistic cruelty 832.2 *cruelness*
sadistic tyrant 836.3 *pitiless person*
Sadler's Wells Ballet 46.12 *ballet companies*
sadly 770, 687.12 *in adversity*, 774.8 *mournfully*, 862.13 *destructively*
sadness 618.10 *poverty*, 687.1 *adversity*, 770.1 *sorrow*, 774.1 *lamentation*
sado-masochism 877.7 *sexual assault*
sado-masochistic 877.15 *unlawful*
sad person 770
sad sack 687.5 *person in adversity*
SAD syndrome 61.13 *depression*
safari hunt 590.2 *chase*
safari hunter 590.6 *hunter*
safari park 76.8 *animal welfare*
safe 161 Collective Names for Birds and Animals, **632**, **718**, 258.6 *box*, 490.1 *certain*, 531.2 *hiding place*, 605.4 *storage*, 637.7 *preserved*, 718.6 *secure*, 741.20 *money store*, 765.4 *satisfied*, 865.5 *innocent*
safe and sound 619.1 *perfect*, 623.1 *healthy*, 632.5 *safe*, 718.6 *secure*, 718.16 *surely*
safe as houses 632.5 *safe*, 718.6 *secure*
safe as the Bank of England 718.6 *secure*
safe bet 229.2 *chance*, 490.12 *something certain*, 589.5 *good chance*
safe-blower 736.8 *thief*
safe-blowing 736.1 *stealing*
safe-breaker 736.8 *thief*
safe-breaking 736.1 *stealing*
safe conduct 356.6 *passport*, 632.2 *protection*
safe-conduct pass 708.2 *permit*
safe-cracker 736.8 *thief*
safe-cracking 736.1 *stealing*
safe deposit 605.4 *storage*

safe-deposit 531.2 *hiding place*, 741.20 *money store*
safe-deposit box 741.20 *money store*
safe distance 591.10 *avoidance*, 632.1 *safety*
safeguard 671, 180.15 *escort*, 348.9 *welcome*, 469.11 *care for*, 602.5 *reserves*, 632.2 *protection*, 632.4 *safety device*, 632.9 *protect*, 637.5 *preserve*, 662.7 *convenience*, 671.17 *defend*, 718.1 *protection*, 718.10 *secure*, 718.11 *promise*, 781.2 *insurance*
safeguarded 718.6 *secure*
safeguarding 671.1 *defence*
safeguard oneself 781.5 *be cautious*
safe hands 632.2 *protection*
safe house 293.15 *shelter*, 531.2 *hiding place*, 632.2 *protection*, 634.2 *shelter*
safe job 632.1 *safety*
safekeep 718.10 *secure*
safekeeping 632.2 *protection*, 637.1 *preservation*, 671.1 *defence*, 718.1 *protection*
safelight 66.12 *development*
safely 632, 106.18 *comfortably*, 675.8 *peacefully*, 718.16 *surely*
safeness 632.1 *safety*, 718.1 *protection*
safe place 632.1 *safety*, 634.1 *refuge*
safe retreat 634.1 *refuge*
safety 632, 19.6 *scoring*, 19.10 *defence*, 24.2 *billiards play*, 24.4 *carom*, 34.8 *mountaineering*, 41.12 *ski*, 718.1 *protection*
Safety 632
safety and health 15.2 *industrial negotiations*
safety barrier 33.6 *motor racing terms*
safety belt 632.4 *safety device*, 637.2 *preserver*
safety bicycle 71.12 *bicycle*
safety catch 137.8 *fastening*, 323.3 *restrainer*, 632.4 *safety device*
safety chain 632.4 *safety device*
safety curtain 51.17 *stage set*
safety deposit box 718.5 *safe*
safety device 632, 637.2 *preserver*
safety first 781.2 *insurance*
safety glass 44.9 *industrial ceramics*, 266.5 *layered thing*, 442.9 *glass*
safety goggles 632.4 *safety device*
safety harness 632.4 *safety device*
safety hat 295.15 *headgear*
safety helmet 632.4 *safety device*
safety in numbers 632.1 *safety*
safety lamp 439.7 *lantern*
safety lock 632.4 *safety device*
safety match 410.2 *lighter*, 439.8 *fire*, 632.4 *safety device*
safety net 632.4 *safety device*
safety pin 137.8 *fastening*, 632.4 *safety device*
safety razor 632.4 *safety device*
safety rope 34.4 *climbing equipment*
safety ski stick 41.5 *ski equipment*
safety strap 41.5 *ski equipment*
safety valve 632.1 *safety*, 632.4 *safety device*, 638.2 *means of escape*
safety zone 634.1 *refuge*
safflower 84 Flowers and Flowering Plants
saffron 45 Herbs and Spices, 413.5 *herbs*, 451.1 *orange*, 451.3 *orange thing*
saffron robe 823.6 *general terms*
saffron veil 823.6 *general terms*
sag 238.6 *be weak*, 283.1 *suspension*, 360.2 *sinkage*, 360.10 *droop*, 374.13 *soften*, 673.4 *succumb*, 754.12 *be cheap*
saga 48.7 *poem*, 155.4 *sequel*, 534.25 *broadcast material*, 560.3 *narration*
sagacious 4.19 *learned*, 6.18 *educated*, 459.10 *intelligent*, 501.8

knowledgeable, 507.5 wise, 516.6 foreseeing, 655.6 skilful
sagaciously 6.25 educationally, 459.15 intelligently, 507.9 wisely
sagaciousness 507.1 wisdom
sagacity 277.3 profundity, 459.4 cleverness, 501.3 learning, 507.1 wisdom, 516.4 prudence, 655.1 skill
Sagan 48 Writers
sage 45 Herbs and Spices, **4,** 277.7 deep thinking, 413.5 herbs, 459.8 intellectual person, 459.10 intelligent, 501.6 knowledgeable person, 507.3 wise man, 517.8 oracle, 611.4 big-wig, 654.4 adviser, 655.4 skilful person, 688.10 person of authority, 696.9 educational leader, 849.14 awe-inspiring
Sage Derby 45 Cheeses
sage-green 453.1 green
sage grouse 78 Birds
sagging 238.8 weak, 283.7 suspended, 360.2 sinkage, 360.17 drooping
Saginaw 93 Cities
Sagitta 53 The Constellations
sagittal 380.1 sharp
Sagittarius 53 The Constellations, **53** Zodiac Constellations, 338.16 archer
sagittate 83.18 of leaves, 380.1 sharp
sago palm 85 Trees and Shrubs
saguaro 84 Flowers and Flowering Plants
Sahaptin 5 Languages and Groups of Languages
Sahara 98 Deserts, 271.5 broad thing, 392.14 desert, 408.8 hot place
Saharan 5 Languages and Groups of Languages, 392.6 desert
sahib 401.3 male title of address, 696.1 master
said 564.16 speech
said again 183.10 iterated
said before 183.10 iterated
saiga 77 Placental Mammals
sail 36, 74, 36.3 parts of a sailing boat, 36.7 windsurfing, 36.18 windsurf, 74.9 navigate, 660.19 go easily, 679.22 navy
sail a canoe 36.17 canoe
sail against 670.1 attack
sailboard 74 Sailing Ships and Boats, 36.7 windsurfing, 36.18 windsurf
Sailboard class 36.2 sailing boat
sailboat 74.3 vessel
sailboat on calm waters 240.3 inert thing
sail by the lee 36.15 sail
sail close-hauled 36.15 sail
sail close to the wind 36.15 sail, 74.9 navigate, 633.8 be in danger
sailcloth 67 Natural Fabrics
sailcloth jacket 28.2 fencing equipment
sail downwind 36.15 sail
sailer 74 Sailing Ships and Boats
sailfish 80 Fishes, 20.4 American game fish
sail for 332.7 take a direction
sail home 660.17 do easily
sailing 36, 36, 36.7 windsurfing, 36.12 canoeing, 74.1 water travel, 74.11 nautical, 356.2 passing along
sailing aid 74.5 navigation
sailing boat 74 Ships and Boats, **74** Sailing Ships and Boats, **36,** 74.3 vessel
sailing boat designer 36.9 sailor
sailing canoe 36.6 canoeing
sailing dinghy 74 Sailing Ships and Boats
sailing master 74.7 nautical person, 696.10 expert
Sailing, Rowing, Etc. 36
sailing ship 74 Ships and Boats
sailing techniques 36.1 sailing

sailing trophy 36.1 sailing
sailing wind 36.1 sailing
sail in the same boat 664.13 work together
sail into 670.5 strike, 674.12 fight
sail on a run 36.15 sail
sailor 36, 74.7 nautical person, 679.27 naval man
sailor-like 74.11 nautical
sailorly 74.11 nautical
sailorman 74.7 nautical person
sailor's dance 46.4 historic dancing
sailplaning 18 Sporting Activities
Sails 53 The Constellations
sail the high seas 97
sail the ocean 97.9 sail the high seas
sail under false colours 540.20 pretend
Saimaa 94 Lakes
sainfoin 84 Flowers and Flowering Plants, 68.12 crop
saint 7.3 religious person, 8.10 deified person, 134.5 pure person, 652.3 well-behaved person, 729.4 giver, 861.15 good person, 863.4 virtuous person, 865.4 innocent person, 876.5 pure person
St Andrews 93 Cities
St Andrew's 29.1 golf
St Andrew's cross 544.7 flag
St Anthony's fire 624.13 skin disease
St Bartholomew's Day Massacre 398.4 slaughter
Saint Basil's Cathedral 43 Noted Buildings
St Bernard 77 Breeds of Dogs, 46.2 dance
St Christopher 11.6 talisman
St Christopher and Nevis 91 Countries
Saint Christopher's medal 517.6 good-luck sign
St Clair 94 Lakes
Sainte-Chapelle 43 Noted Buildings
sainted 397.19 dead
St Elias 95 Mountains
St Elmo's fire 439.9 firefly
St Étienne 93 Cities
Saint-Exupéry 48 Writers
St George's cross 544.7 flag
St George's mushroom 89 Fungi
sainthood 876.3 moral purity
sainting 8.9 deification
St Ives 93 Cities
St James's Park Lake 94 Lakes
St John 96 Rivers
St John's 93 Cities
St John's wort 84 Flowers and Flowering Plants
St Lawrence 96 Rivers, 96.5 other major rivers
saintlike 863.5 virtuous
saintliness 863.1 virtue, 865.1 innocence, 876.2 good morals
St Louis 93 Cities, 93.2 American cities
St Lucia 91 Countries, **98** Islands
St Luke's summer 408.5 hot weather
saintly 7.15 religious, 8.14 heavenly, 619.1 perfect, 857.5 pure, 863.5 virtuous, 865.5 innocent, 876.8 moral
St Malo 93 Cities
Saint Mark's Cathedral 43 Noted Buildings
St Martin's summer 203.3 summer, 408.5 hot weather
St Moritz 93 Cities
St Patrick's cross 43 Noted Buildings, 544.7 flag
St Paul 93 Cities
St Paul's Cathedral 43 Noted Buildings
St Peter's 43 Noted Buildings
St Petersburg 93 Cities, **93** Cities
saints 777 Phobias by Topic, 397.14 the spiritual world
Saint-Saëns 49 Musicians and

Composers
saints and sinners 111.2 opposites
saint's day 185.11 date, 214.6 annually celebrated day, 812.5 anniversary
Saint-Simon 4 Philosophers
St Swithin's day 55.3 weather
St Tropez 93 Cities
St Valentine's Day murder 398.2 murder
St Vincent 98 Islands
St Vincent and the Grenadines 91 Countries
St Vitus's dance 366.7 shake, 624.17 nervous disorder
Saiph 53 Named Stars
saithe 80 Fishes
Saivism 7 Non-Christian Religions
Sakai 5 Languages and Groups of Languages
Sakhalin 98 Islands
Sakharov 52 Scientists
saki 77 Placental Mammals
Saki 48 Writers
Saktism 7 Non-Christian Religions
salaam 362.9 bow, 362.16 courtesy, 567.2 salutation, 694.3 obeisance, 694.6 show obeisance to, 817.13 defer to, 849.4 mark of respect, 849.19 take off one's hat to
salaaming 817.4 deference
salacious 622.9 obscene, 877.12 indecent
salaciously 622.12 dirtily, 877.21 immorally
salaciousness 622.3 obscenity, 877.2 indecency, 877.3 sexual immorality
salad 45, 45.9 dish, 180.5 side dish
salad bowl 258.16 crockery
salad cream 45.15 sauce
salad days 185.5 indefinite period, 206.1 youth, 686.3 time of plenty, 865.3 naivety
salad dressing 45.15 sauce, 413.2 seasoning
salad fork 350.16 eating utensil
salad niçoise 45.14 salad
salad vegetable 45.33, 69.11 vegetable
salad vegetables 86.1 fruits
salamander 79 Amphibians
salamandrian 79.13 amphibian
salami 45.29 sausage
salaried 730.11 receiving, 746.19 receiving pay, 749.6 received
salary 228.5 positive stimulus, 721.4 earnings, 730.2 something received, 746.3 pay, 749.3 income, 878.4 reward for service
salary bill 751.6 business costs
salary earner 646.1 worker
salary negotiations 15.1 industrial relations
salbutamol 62 Medication
salchow jump 41.6 ice-skating
sale 739, 710.3 business offer, 727.2 disposal of property, 728.1 transfer of property, 739.3 selling, 752.2 bargain, 754.9 cheap
Sale 739
saleability 727.2 disposal of property, 739.7 market
saleable 739, 727.14 for sale, 729.7 given, 737.13 mercantile
saleable commodity 739.8 merchandise
saleableness 727.2 disposal of property
saleably 739.17 marketably
sale and lease back 727.2 disposal of property
sale by auction 739.4 sale
sale goods 754.4 bargain
Salem 93 Cities
sale merchandise 754.4 bargain
sale of office 739.3 selling
sale of the century 586.9 enticement, 739.4 sale, 752.2 bargain
sale of work 739.4 sale, 740.10 bazaar

sale price 751.1 price, 754.1 cheapness
sale-price 710.17 offered, 754.9 cheap
Salerno 32 Breeds of Horse and Pony, **93** Cities
saleroom 740.1 market
Salers 68 Breeds of Cattle
sales 739
sales blandishment 521.5 empty talk
salesclerk 697.3 attendant
sales conference 739.6 salesmanship
sales coverage 739.3 selling
sales force 739.10 salesman
sales forecasting 739.6 salesmanship
salesgirl 739.10 salesman
Salesian 7 Members of Religious Orders
salesman 739, 228.7 motivator, 564.10 speaker, 586.12 persuader
salesman of the month 655.5 expert
salesmanship 739, 586.1 persuasion
sales patter 521.5 empty talk, 739.6 salesmanship
salesperson 564.10 speaker, 739.10 salesman
sales pitch 586.1 persuasion
sales promotion 586.6 advertising
sales representative 739.10 salesman
sales revenue 13.6 economic factors, 749.2 money received
sales talk 228.2 inducement, 521.5 empty talk, 586.1 persuasion, 739.6 salesmanship
sales tax 13.6 economic factors, 749.2 money received, 751.7 tax
sales volume 749.2 money received
saleswoman 564.10 speaker, 739.10 salesman
salicylamide 62 Medication
salicylic acid 62 Medication
salience 318.1 prominence
salient 318.6 eminent, 437.2 clear, 457.7 appearing, 526.14 manifest, 676.10 battleground
salient angle 52.39 angle
Salienta 79.7 amphibian
salientian 79.7, 79.13 amphibian
salient point 611.3 chief thing
salimeter 268.8 meter
salimetric 268.16 micrometric
salimetry 268.2 micrometry
salina 94.1 lake, 98.3 marsh
saline 57.36 acid
Salinger 48 Writers
salinity 54.12 ocean
salinometer 268.8 meter
salinometric 268.16 micrometric
salinometry 268.2 micrometry
Salisbury 93 Cities
Salish 5 Languages and Groups of Languages
saliva 353, 352.2 secreted substance, 386.4 lubricant, 387.3 body fluid, 389.4 exudate, 395.5 lubricant
salivant 349.29 expulsive
salivary 349.29 expulsive, 352.5 of a secretion
salivary gland 352 Exocrine Glands, 353.9 saliva
salivate 353, 347.12 leak, 350.22 eat well, 352.7 secrete, 389.32, 391.16 seep, 782.14 be hungry
salivating 353, 352.4 secretory
salivation 352.1 secretion, 353.9 saliva
sallee 85 Trees and Shrubs
sallet 671.7 armour
sallow 85 Trees and Shrubs, 445.8 drained of colour, 446.4 pale, 452.4 yellow-faced, 624.21 unhealthy
sallowness 446.7 whiteness
sally 347.10 emerge, 670.8 counterattack, 670.14 siege
sally forth 156.19 start off, 345.5 set out, 347.10 emerge

sally port 671.12 *fort*
salmagundi 133.2 *mixed thing*
salmon 80 Fishes, 20.4 *American game fish*, 20.5 *British game fish*, 45.17 *freshwater fish*, 80.8 *food fish*
salmonberry 86 Fruits
salmonella 631.7 *poisoning*
salmonellosis 631.7 *poisoning*
salmon fishing 590.2 *chase*
salmon-pink 450.1 *red*
salmon sandwich 45.11 *sandwich*
salmon trout 80 Fishes, 45.17 *freshwater fish*
sal nut 86 Nuts
Salomonic column 43.8 *column*
salon 49.27 *performance*, 50.11 *artist's materials*, 256.7 *room*, 815.4 *meeting place*
Salonika 93 Cities
saloon 71 Motor Vehicles, 36.8 *punting*, 71.16 *car*
salp 81.2 *protochordate*
salpingectomy 60 Surgical Operations
salpingostomy 60 Surgical Operations
salpinx 49 Musical Instruments
salsa 49.10 *world music*
salsify 45 Vegetables
salt 57, 45.7 *basic ingredient*, 74.7 *nautical person*, 350.11 *food content*, 413.2 *seasoning*, 413.12 *season*, 540.21 *be fraudulent*, 594.7 *develop*, 637.2 *preserver*, 637.5 *preserve*
SALT 715.3 *alliance*
salt a mine 540.21 *be fraudulent*
saltant 359.24 *leaping*
saltation 359.5 *jump*
saltatorial 359.24 *leaping*
saltatorily 366.29 *jerkily*
saltatory 359.24 *leaping*, 366.19 *convulsive*
salt away 605.6 *store*
salted 637.7 *preserved*
salted mine 540.8 *fraud*
salted nuts 45.10 *snack*
salt flat 98.3 *marsh*, 392.14 *desert*
salt-free diet 350.6 *nutrition*
salt gland 352.3 *gland*
salt-glaze 44.3 *glaze*
salt-glazed 44.10 *ceramic*
salt-glazed porcelain 44.1 *ceramics*
saltiness 411.4 *flavour*
saltire 544.8 *heraldic device*
SALT I Treaty 677.1 *pacification*
salt lake 94.1 *lake*
Salt Lake City 93 Cities
saltlick 350.8 *animal food*
salt marsh 98.3, 391.8 *marsh*
Salto 93 Cities
salt of the earth 611.4 *bigwig*, 617.7 *elite*, 857.3 *honourable person*
Salton Sea 94 Lakes
saltpan 98.3 *marsh*
saltpetre 57 Common Chemical Compounds, 680.15 *explosive*
salt pork 45.30 *bacon*, 350.7 *food*
salt sea 97.1 *sea*
salt tax 751.9 *historical taxes*
salt water 97.1 *sea*, 389.1 *water*
saltwater bait fishing 20.1 *angling*
saltwater fish 45.18 *sea fish*, 80.1 *fishes*
saltwater fisherman 20.6 *angler*
saltwater fishing 20.1 *angling*
saltwater trolling 20.1 *angling*
salty 74.11 *nautical*, 97.7 *oceanic*, 411.7 *tasty*, 413.9 *piquant*
salty taste 411.1 *taste*
salubrious 306.12 *on form*, 617.4 *worthwhile*, 621.16 *clean*, 623.2 *healthful*, 625.4 *hygienic*, 630.17 *remedial*, 632.5 *safe*, 637.6 *preserving*, 861.1 *good*
salubriously 623.8 *healthily*, 625.7 *hygienically*
salubriousness 623.4 *healthfulness*, 625.2 *salubrity*
salubrity 625, 623.4 *healthfulness*

Saluki 77 Breeds of Dogs
salutary 613.4 *profitable*, 617.4 *worthwhile*, 623.2 *healthful*, 625.4 *hygienic*, 662.34 *beneficial*, 861.1 *good*
salutation 567, 431.4 *cry of greeting*, 817.5 *sign of courtesy*, 849.6 *greeting*
salutations 849.7 *respects*
salutatory 567.14 *vocative*
salutatory address 567.2 *salutation*
salute 812, 812, 849, 351.14 *drink to*, 543.11 *gesture*, 567.9 *approach*, 773.2 *fanfare*, 773.6 *fête*, 817.5 *sign of courtesy*, 817.12 *greet*, 849.4 *mark of respect*, 849.6 *greeting*
salutiferous 630.17 *remedial*
saluting 849.11 *in a respectful stance*
salvable 639.4 *deliverable*
salvably 639.6 *extricably*
salvage 3.23 *turn back time*, 629.3 *restore*, 629.9 *restoration*, 639.1 *deliver*, 639.2 *deliverance*, 751.6 *business costs*, 767.2 *aid*
salvageable 639.4 *deliverable*
salvage company 639.3 *deliverer*
salvaged 629.13 *repaired*
salvager 629.12 *repairer*
salvation 629.9 *restoration*, 637.1 *preservation*, 639.2 *deliverance*, 700.1 *liberation*, 704.1 *cancellation*, 767.2 *aid*
Salvation Army 7 Christian Movements, 831.2 *charity*
Salvation Army bonnet 7.11 *vestment*
salvationism 7.2 *religiousness*
salvationist 7.4 *religionist*
salva veritate 4.8 *philosophical term*
salve 62.7, 386.5 *ointment*, 386.14 *anoint*, 395.6 *ointment*, 395.18 *anoint*, 405.10 *comfort*, 630.5 *analgesic*, 630.9 *balm*, 853.2 *blarney*
salve one's conscience 865.8 *be innocent*, 867.5 *do penance*
salver 258.16 *crockery*
salvia 84 Flowers and Flowering Plants
salvo 338.7 *shot*, 425.1 *bang*, 670.15 *firing*, 812.8 *salute*
sal volatile 413.6 *cordial*, 630.7 *tonic*
salvor 629.12 *repairer*
Salyut 53.30 *spacecraft*
Salzburg 93 Cities
samadhi 11.10 *psychic phenomenon*
Samar 93 Islands
samara 86.2 *botanical fruit*
Samaritan 833.3 *philanthropist*
samarium 57 Chemical Elements
Samarkand 93 Cities
samarskite 54 Minerals
Samas 8 Deities
Samaveda 7.12 *religious text*, 10.8 *hymn*
samba 46.2 *dance*
sambar 77 Placental Mammals
Sam Brown belt 137.10 *band*
same 110, 112.5 *uniform*, 112.8 *monotonous*, 114.7 *similar*, 116.14 *conforming*, 122.6 *equal*, 298.6 *interfacial*
same damn thing 788.2 *boring thing*
same date 198.1 *same time*
same day 198.1 *same time*
same degree 122.1 *equality*
same meaning 520.4 *type of meaning*
sameness 110, 112.1 *uniformity*, 112.4 *monotony*, 114.1 *similarity*, 116.5 *conformity*, 122.1 *equality*, 127.5 *inferior state*, 159.5 *continuity*, 788.1 *lack of emphasis*, 788.1 *boredom*
Sameness 110
same old round 183.3 *repetitiveness*
same old story 110.6 *regularity*, 112.4 *monotony*, 183.3 *repeti-*

tiveness, 788.2 *boring thing*
same old thing 110.6 *regularity*, 788.2 *boring thing*
same quantity 122.1 *equality*
same time 198
Same Time 198
Samhain 10.16 *religious festival*
samisen 49 Musical Instruments
samite 67 Natural Fabrics
samizdat 117.4 *disagreement*
Samkhat 8 Deities
Sammael 8.7 *devil*
Samnite Wars 17 Major Wars
Samoan 5 Languages and Groups of Languages
samosa 45.12 *hors d'oeuvre*, 45.49 *Indian dish*
Samoyed 1 Peoples, **5** Languages and Groups of Languages, **77** Breeds of Dogs
sampan 74 Ships and Boats
samphire 84 Flowers and Flowering Plants, 45.33 *vegetable*
sample 52.57 *population*, 52.93 *equate*, 60.7 *diagnosis*, 143.2 *particular*, 299.1, 299.5 *outline*, 299.6 *outlined*, 350.23 *taste*, 411.3 *appetizer*, 411.9 *taste*, 475.3 *explanation*, 479.2 *rehearsal*, 479.11 *experiment*, 526.7 *showpiece*, 547.8 *representative*, 733.9 *borrow illegally*
sample freedom 698.14 *be free*
sampler 411.3 *appetizer*, 411.5 *taster*
sample size 52.57 *population*
sample statistic 52.57 *population*
sampling 52.57 *population*, 411.3 *appetizer*
samsara 396.8 *theories of life*
Samson 237.6 *muscleman*
samurai 679.6 *militarist*
San 5 Languages and Groups of Languages
San'a 93 Cities
San Andreas fault 54.20 *earth movement*
San Andreas Fault 98.10 *miscellaneous*
San Antonio 93 Cities
sanative 625.4 *hygienic*, 629.16 *restorative*
sanatorium 6.15 *schoolroom*, 60.10 *hospital*, 625.1 *hygiene*, 630.14 *hospital*
sanatory 625.4 *hygienic*
San Cristóbal 93 Cities
sanctification 804.1 *right*
sanctified 8.15 *deified*, 857.5 *pure*, 863.5 *virtuous*
sanctify 8.17 *deify*, 812.16 *commemorate*
sanctimonious 7.15 *religious*, 134.12 *morally pure*, 538.18 *pretentious*, 539.37, 540.27 *hypocritical*, 797.3 *affected*, 876.10 *moralistic*
sanctimonious fraud 539.19 *hypocrite*
sanctimoniously 134.18 *virtuously*, 876.13 *morally*
sanctimoniousness 7.2 *religiousness*, 134.1 *purity*, 540.3 *hypocrisy*, 797.1 *affectedness*, 876.4 *self-righteousness*
sanctimony 7.2 *religiousness*, 134.1 *purity*, 540.3 *hypocrisy*, 797.1 *affectedness*, 876.4 *self-righteousness*
sanction 13.6 *economic factors*, 16.29 *legalization*, 16.65 *make legal*, 116.8, 116.29 *permit*, 499.1, 499.4 *assent*, 662.23 *advise*, 667.2, 667.7 *contract*, 688.9 *permission*, 688.21 *grant authority*, 708.1 *permission*, 708.3 *permit*, 851.1 *approval*, 851.12 *accept*
sanctioned 16.44 *legal*, 116.18 *permitting*, 688.16 *authorized*, 708.7 *permitted*, 845.8 *entitled*
sanctions 676.8 *warfare*, 695.3 *coercive methods*
sanctitude 8.1 *divinity*
sanctity 8.1 *divinity*, 857.2 *pu-*

rity, 863.1 *virtue*
sanctuary 10.12 *church*, 10.13 *shrine*, 256.11 *retreat*, 290.2 *inside*, 323.4 *closed place*, 348.2 *receptivity*, 531.2 *hiding place*, 632.2 *protection*, 634.1 *refuge*, 718.1 *protection*, 734.4 *taking in*, 816.5 *solitary place*
sanctum 10.13 *shrine*, 531.6 *privacy*, 634.1 *refuge*, 816.5 *solitary place*
sanctum sanctorum 10.13 *shrine*, 301.2 *enclosed place*, 634.1 *refuge*
Sanctus 10.8 *hymn*
sanctus bell 10.14 *sacred object*
sand 47.17 *carpenter*, 54.27 *sediment*, 54.36 *soil*, 63.26 *masonry*, 98.4 *coast*, 376.11 *smooth*, 384.9 *grit*, 384.22 *powder*, 385.12 *rub*, 451.3 *orange thing*, 604.1 *materials*
Sand 48 Writers
Sandage 52 Scientists
sandals 295.19 *footwear*
sandalwood 85 Trees and Shrubs, 418.3 *incense*
Sandalwood Pony 32 Breeds of Horse and Pony
sandarac 85 Trees and Shrubs
sandbag 330.8 *club*, 398.17 *murder*, 671.8 *military defences*, 680.7 *blunt weapon*, 879.14 *instrument of punishment*
sandbank 54.11 *coast*, 96.2 *channel*, 98.2 *island*, 161.26 *mass*, 278.4 *shallow thing*, 635.1 *trap*
sand bar 54.11 *coast*
sandbar 98.2 *island*
sand bar 278.4 *shallow thing*
sandbar 635.1 *trap*
sandblast 385.12 *rub*, 621.13 *clean*
sandblasting 385.2 *wearing away*
sand-blind 436.9 *weak-sighted*
sand-blindness 436.2 *poor sight*
sandbox 72.5 *locomotive part*
sandbox tree 85 Trees and Shrubs
Sandburg 48 Poets
sand casting 50.12 *sculpture*
sand castle 238.5 *weak thing*, 379.3 *brittle thing*
sand column 55.16 *wind vortex*
sand dance 46.2 *dance*
sand dollar 81.3 *echinoderm*
sand dune 54.11 *coast*, 54.37 *dune*, 275.3 *mountain*, 392.14 *desert*
sand dunes 247.1 *infertility*
sander 47.11 *woodworking tool*, 376.9 *smoother*, 385.7 *eraser*
sanderling 78 Birds
s and f 48.2 *fiction*
sand flea 82 Insects, 82.3 *pest*
sandfly 82 Insects
sandglass 191 Timepieces and Timers, 192.9 *hourglass*
sandgrouse 78 Birds
sand hopper 81.4 *arthropod*, 81.10 *parasite*
Sandhurst 676.6 *art of war*
San Diego 93 Cities
sandiness 384.3 *graininess*
sanding 385.5 *polishing*
sanding disc 385.7 *eraser*
sand lizard 79 Reptiles
s and m 877.7 *sexual assault*
sandman 643.9 *sleep*
sand martin 78 Birds
sandpaper 47.11 *woodworking tool*, 375.7 *rough thing*, 375.12 *make rough*, 376.9 *smoother*, 376.11 *smooth*, 380.12 *sharpener*, 380.15 *make sharp*, 384.12 *abrasive*, 385.7 *eraser*, 385.12 *rub*
sandpiper 78 Birds, 78.3 *water bird*
sand pit 21.2 *field events*
sands 98.10 *miscellaneous*
sand shot 29.3 *golf shots*
sands of time running out 397.18 *dying*
sandspit 98.5 *peninsula*
sandstone 54 Common Rocks, 43.4 *building material*, 63.26

masonry
sandstorm 55.12 *wind*, 241.5 *violent weather*, 441.2 *murk*, 443.7 *opaque thing*
sand trap 29.1 *golf*
sand wave 54.11 *coast*
sandwich 45, 158.16 *place in the middle*, 266.5 *layered thing*, 266.10 *layer*
sandwich bar 350.15 *eating place*
sandwich board 532.9 *advertisement*
sandwich boards 526.8 *showplace*
sandwich compound 57.7 *chemical compound*
sandwich course 6.2 *educational system*
sandwich-maker 45.5 *cooker*, 408.4 *burner*
sandwichman 532.10 *publicizer*
sandy 54.58 *earthy*, 98.11 *continental*, 384.18 *grainy*, 392.6 *desert*, 450.3 *red-haired*
sane 509, 463.7 *reasoning*, 522.1 *intelligible*
sanely 509, 463.15 *reasonably*
saneness 463.1 *reason*, 509.1 *sanity*
sane person 509
Sanforize 67.15 *treat*, 262.5 *make smaller*
Sanforized 67.11 *treated*, 262.7 *smaller*
Sanforizing 67.8 *fabric treatment*
San Francisco 93 Cities, 93.2 *American cities*
Sanger 52 Scientists
sang-froid 4.3 *detachment*, 242.1 *moderation*, 660.4 *ease of manner*, 869.3 *calmness*
sangha 10.17 *worshipper*
Sangha 7 Non-Christian Religions
Sango 5 Languages and Groups of Languages
Sangreal 10.14 *sacred object*, 714.4 *promised land*
sangria 351.8 *mixed drink*
sanguinarily 387.26 *fluidly*, 450.10 *ruddily*
sanguinary 398.24 *murderous*, 450.4 *bloody*
sanguine 61.7 *personality type*, 450.2 *red-faced*, 513.5 *expecting*, 705.8 *resigned*, 771.12 *four humours*, 775.11 *hopeful*, 787.3 *unmoved*
sanguinely 387.26 *fluidly*, 705.9 *stoically*
sanguineous 387.18, 450.4 *bloody*
sanguineously 450.10 *ruddily*
sanguinity 705.2 *stoicism*, 787.1 *lack of wonder*
Sanhedrin 653.7 *council*
Sanhedrist 653.16 *official*
san hsien 49 Musical Instruments
sanicle 84 Flowers and Flowering Plants
sanies 353.7 *pus*, 387.3 *body fluid*
sanious 387.16 *rheumy*
sanitarian 625.3 *hygienist*
sanitarily 625.7 *hygienically*
sanitary 134.15 *purifying*, 621.16 *clean*, 621.18 *cleansing*, 623.2 *healthful*, 625.4 *hygienic*, 630.17 *remedial*
sanitary engineer 621.12 *cleaner*, 625.3 *hygienist*
sanitary inspector 625.3 *hygienist*
sanitary precaution 630.3 *prophylactic*, 632.2 *protection*
sanitate 134.10 *purify*, 625.6 *make hygienic*, 630.20 *doctor*, 632.9 *protect*
sanitation 134.2 *purification*, 621.2 *cleaning*, 625.1 *hygiene*, 630.3 *prophylactic*
sanitize 134.10, 621.15 *purify*, 625.6 *make hygienic*, 632.9 *protect*
sanity 509, 463.1 *reason*
Sanity 509
San Jose 93 Cities
San José 93 Cities

Sankar 7 Non-Christian Religions
Sankara 4 Philosophers
Sankhya 7 Non-Christian Religions, 4.7 *school of thought*
sankyo 26.10 *aikido*
San Marino 91 Countries
San Marino GP at Imola 33.2 *Formula 1 race*
sannyasi 7.3 *religious person*, 816.6 *unsocial person*
San Pedro Sula 93 Cities
San Remo 93 Cities
sansa 49 Musical Instruments
San Salvador 93 Cities
sans-culotte 693.11 *rebel*
sans-culottism 693.4 *revolution*
San Sebastián 93 Cities
Sanskrit 5 Languages and Groups of Languages
Sanskritic 5 Languages and Groups of Languages
sans serif 5.41 *lettered*
sans serif type 5.15 *type style*
Santa Ana 93 Cities, **93** Cities
Santa Barbara 93 Cities
Santa Catalina 98 Islands
Santa Claus 729.4 *giver*, 755.9 *generous person*
Santa Cruz 93 Cities
Santa Fe 93 Cities
Santa Gertrudis 68 Breeds of Cattle
Santali 5 Languages and Groups of Languages
Santayana 4 Philosophers
Santiago 93 Cities
Santiago de Compostela 93 Cities
Santiago de Cuba 93 Cities
santification 8.9 *deification*
santir 49 Musical Instruments
Santo Domingo 93 Cities
santon 816.6 *unsocial person*
santoor 49 Musical Instruments
Sanusi 7 Non-Christian Religions
sanyasin 497.5 *believer*
São Paulo 93 Cities
São Tomé e Principe 91 Countries
sap 103.2 *essential content*, 236.7 *remove power from*, 238.7 *weaken*, 317.2 *concave land*, 360.15 *tunnel*, 387.2 *juice*, 539.22 *dupe*, 628.5 *hurt*
sapele 85 Trees and Shrubs
sapid 411.7 *tasty*
sapidity 411.1 *taste*
sapience 459.4 *cleverness*, 507.1 *wisdom*
sapient 459.11 *thoughtful*, 507.5 *wise*
Sapir-Whorf hypothesis 5.37 *linguistic theory*
sapless 392.3 *dried-up*
sapling 83.2 *plant*, 85.1 *tree*, 206.5 *young plant*
sapodilla 86 Fruits
saponaceous 386.10, 395.11 *oily*
saponacity 386.2, 395.1 *oiliness*
saponifiable lipid 58.6 *lipid*
saponification 57 Types of Chemical Reaction, 57.5 *process*, 58.7 *fat*
saponify 57.26 *react*
saponite 54 Minerals
sappan 85 Trees and Shrubs
sapped 238.11 *weakened*, 628.12 *deteriorated*
sapper 317.4 *digger*, 679.17 *army person*
Sapphic 48.19 *narrative*, 402.10 *homosexual*
Sapphic ode 48.7 *poem*
Sapphics 48.10 *verse form*
sapphire 54 Gemstones, 454.1 *blue*, 454.6 *blue thing*
sapphirine 54 Minerals
Sappho 48 Poets
sappiness 206.2 *youthfulness*, 387.5 *fluidity*, 387.7 *juiciness*, 393.4 *pulpiness*
sapping 360.7 *tunnelling*
Sapporo 93 Cities
sappy 203.10 *spring*, 387.15 *flowing*, 393.19 *juicy*, 453.4

fresh
saprophyte 83.4 *lower plant*, 89.5 *fungal association*
saprophytic 83.14 *of plants*, 89.10 *of fungi*
saprophytically 89, 83.24 *herbaceously*
sapsucker 78 Birds
sap the foundations of 244.9 *demolish*
sapwood 47.12 *wood*, 85.3 *timber*
saraband 46.4 *historic dancing*
Saracen 43 Architectural Styles
Saragossa 93 Cities
Sarajevo 93 Cities
sarangi 49 Musical Instruments
Saranyu 8 Deities
Sarasvati 8 Deities
sarcasm 771.3 *wit*, 799.1 *mockery*, 850.4 *ridicule*
sarcastic 415.7 *splenetic*, 771.10 *humorous*, 799.5 *derisive*, 832.14 *hostile*, 850.14 *ridiculing*, 854.17 *scornful*
sarcastically 415.11 *splenetically*, 771.16 *humorously*, 850.29 *mockingly*
sarcenet 67 Natural Fabrics
Sarcodina 81.9 *protozoan*
sarcoma 624.12 *cancer*
sarcophagus 258.6 *box*, 399.1 *burial*
sard 54 Gemstones
sardine 80 Fishes, 45.18 *sea fish*, 80.8 *food fish*
sardines 42 Children's Games and Party Games
Sardinia 98 Islands
Sardinian 5 Languages and Groups of Languages, **32** Breeds of Horse and Pony
sardonic 799.5 *derisive*
sardonyx 54 Gemstones
Sargasso 97 Oceans and Seas
sargassum 90 Algae
Sargent 49 Musicians and Composers
sari 295.16 *robe*
sarinda 49 Musical Instruments
sark 295.8 *shirt*
Sark 98 Islands
Sarnath 10.13 *shrine*
sarnie 45.11 *sandwich*
saron 49 Musical Instruments
saron demong 49 Musical Instruments
sarong 295.6 *skirt*
Saroyan 48 Writers, **48** Dramatists
Sarraute 48 Writers
sarrusophone 49 Musical Instruments
sarsaparilla 351.6 *soft drink*
sartor 295.26 *fashion designer*
sartorial 295.31 *styled*
Sartre 4 Philosophers, **48** Writers
Sartrism 4.7 *school of thought*
Sartrist 4.11 *follower of a doctrine*
SAS 617.7 *elite*, 679.14 *armed forces*
sash 137.10 *band*, 295.25 *accessories*, 313.3 *circular thing*, 544.4 *insignia*
sash weight 704.4 *cancelling out*
Saskatchewan 92 Canadian Provinces and Territories, **96** Rivers
saskatoon 85 Trees and Shrubs
Saskatoon 93 Cities
Sasquatch 76.7 *legendary beast*, 95.3 *mountaineer*
sass 303.5 *boldness*, 668.3 *act of defiance*, 668.5 *defy*, 807.2 *cheek*, 807.25 *answer back*
sassafras 85 Trees and Shrubs, **85** Tree Products
sassafras oil 85 Tree Products
Sassak 5 Languages and Groups of Languages
sassily 807.31 *cheekily*, 850.28 *disrespectfully*
sassiness 807.11 *sauciness*
sassy 85 Trees and Shrubs, 303.9 *arrogant*, 668.7 *defiant*,

807.14 *cheeky*, 818.6 *bad-mannered*, 850.10 *disrespectful*
Satan 777 Phobias by Topic, 8.7 *devil*, 538.11, 539.16 *liar*, 586.13 *tempter*, 618.12 *bad person*, 862.6 *evil person*, 864.6 *religious sin*
satanic 8.16 *devilish*, 832.11 *cruel*, 864.14 *impious*
Satanic 9.10 *idolatrous*, 11.15 *witchlike*
satanically 8.20 *devilishly*, 864.20 *immorally*
Satanism 9.2 *idolatry*, 864.6 *religious sin*
Satanist 9.6 *idolater*, 864.9 *wicked person*
Satanophobia 777 Phobias by Name
Satan's 89 Fungi
satchel 258.8 *bag*
sate 144.6 *fill*, 350.22 *eat well*, 405.9 *give pleasure*, 608.4 *suffice*, 610.4 *be excessive*, 765.8 *satisfy*, 785.7 *cause dislike*, 788.6 *be boring*
sated 144.8 *full*, 350.26 *eating*, 608.3 *filled*, 610.6 *excessive*, 650.2 *bored*, 785.8 *disliking*, 788.5 *bored*
sateen 67 Natural Fabrics
satellite 53, 53, 91.16 *national*, 127.6 *inferior*, 138.5, 180.9 *follower*, 363.4 *orbiting body*, 701.4 *dependent*, 808.5 *adherent*
satellite communication 534
satellite link 137.2 *association*
satellite nation 91.3 *dominion*
satellite radio 534.20 *radio broadcasting*
satellite status 701.1 *subjection*
satellite television 534.21 *television*, 534.24 *television broadcasting*
satellite tracking 53.32 *satellite*
satiate 405.9 *give pleasure*, 608.4 *suffice*, 610.4 *be excessive*, 765.8 *satisfy*, 788.6 *be boring*
satiated 144.8 *full*, 608.3 *filled*, 610.6 *excessive*, 650.2 *bored*, 765.4 *satisfied*, 788.5 *bored*
satiating 610.6 *excessive*, 765.5 *satisfying*, 788.4 *boring*
satiation 765.1 *satisfaction*
Satie 49 Musicians and Composers
satiety 144.2 *fullness*, 608.7 *sufficiency*, 610.2 *overdoing it*, 610.3 *superfluity*, 765.1 *satisfaction*, 788.1 *boredom*
satin 67 Natural Fabrics, 288.4 *textile*, 374.11 *soft thing*, 376.8 *smooth thing*, 383.2 *grain*, 383.9 *smooth*
satininess 374.9, 376.7 *smoothness*, 383.2 *grain*
satinlike 374.3 *smooth*
satin-smooth 376.5 *smooth as a peach*
satin walnut 85 Trees and Shrubs
satinwood 85 Trees and Shrubs
satiny 374.3, 376.1 *smooth*, 383.9 *smooth*
satire 48.7 *poem*, 51.10 *comedy*, 118.3 *mockery*, 771.4 *entertainment*, 799.2 *act of derision*, 850.4, 854.6 *ridicule*
satirical 771.10 *humorous*, 799.5 *derisive*, 850.14 *ridiculing*
satirical comedy 51.10 *comedy*
satirically 771.16 *humorously*, 850.29 *mockingly*
satirical poetry 48.6 *poetry*
satirist 48.14 *author*, 771.6 *humorist*, 799.3 *derider*, 854.9 *ridiculer*
satirize 118.9 *imitate*, 771.13 *be humorous*, 799.6 *deride*, 850.24, 854.14 *ridicule*
satisfaction 765, 125.1 *compensation*, 405.1 *physical pleasure*, 608.7 *sufficiency*, 719.3 *performance*, 746.1 *payment*, 763.7 *pleasure*, 805.7 *fulfilment*, 840.1 *atonement*, 851.1 *ap-*

proval, 878.1 *reward*, 878.6 *compensation*
Satisfaction 765
satisfactorily 765, 608.9 *enough*, 843.18 *properly*, 851.26 *approvably*
satisfactoriness 765
satisfactory 765, 608.1 *sufficient*, 617.5 *not bad*, 851.22 *approvable*
satisfactory amount 608.7 *sufficiency*
satisfiable 125.8 *compensable*
satisfied 765, 125.7 *compensated*, 144.8 *full*, 405.7 *pleased*, 490.2 *convinced*, 608.3 *filled*, 677.6 *pacificatory*, 805.20 *fulfilled*, 851.18 *approving*
satisfier 125.3 *compensator*
satisfy 765, 52.89 *theorize*, 125.4 *compensate*, 144.6 *fill*, 405.9 *give pleasure*, 608.4 *suffice*, 677.4 *pacify*, 719.6 *perform*, 746.7 *pay off*, 763.13 *give pleasure*, 840.5 *atone*, 851.17 *meet with approval*, 878.9 *reward*
satisfying 765, 405.6 *pleasant*, 608.1 *sufficient*, 677.6 *pacificatory*, 763.1 *pleasant*, 840.4 *atoning*, 878.15 *rewarding*
satisfyingly 405.11 *pleasingly*, 878.19 *rewardingly*
satisfy one's appetite 242.5 *moderate one's hunger*
Satnami 7 Non-Christian Religions
satori 325.2 *repose*
satrap 696.4 *absolute ruler*
satsuma 86 Fruits, 451.3 *orange thing*
Satsuma porcelain 44 Types of Ceramics
saturate 57.25 *solidify*, 144.6 *fill*, 253.11 *be present*, 389.29 *water*, 610.4 *be excessive*
saturated 55.43 *atmospheric*, 57.32 *solid*, 57.35 *combined*, 144.8 *full*, 389.22 *diluted*, 389.23 *wet*, 610.6 *excessive*
saturated compound 57.7 *chemical compound*
saturated fat 58.7, 395.8 *fat*
saturated fats 350.11 *food content*
saturated solution 57.3 *phase*
saturation 55.9 *atmospheric process*, 133.1 *mixture*, 144.2 *fullness*, 389.5 *dilution*, 389.9 *soaking*, 391.3 *humidity*, 444.3 *hue*, 610.1 *excess*
saturation bombing 670.13 *air attack*, 676.8 *warfare*
saturation level 66.10 *graininess*
saturation point 144.2 *fullness*, 391.3 *humidity*, 610.1 *excess*
Saturday 10.15 *holy day*
Saturday night special 680.9 *firearm*
Saturn 8 Deities, 53 Planets and their Satellites, 53.16 *planet*
saturnalia 812.1 *celebration*, 870.2 *dissipation*
Saturnalia 10.16 *religious festival*
Saturnian 53.36 *astronomical*
saturniid moth 82 Insects
saturnine 830.6 *sullen*
saturninely 830.13 *sullenly*
Saturn Nebula 53 Nebulae
Saturn V 53.35 *rocketry*
satyagraha 4.7 *school of thought*, 677.1 *pacification*
satyr 8.5 *deity*, 482.9 *undiscriminating person*, 877.8 *immoral man*
satyriasis 61.15 *compulsion*, 510.4 *delusion*, 782.4 *sexual desire*, 877.3 *sexual immorality*
satyrid butterfly 82 Insects
satyr play 51.10 *comedy*
sauce 45, 45.55 *cook*, 130.3 *additional item*, 180.5 *side dish*, 303.5 *boldness*, 887.2 *juice*, 411.10 *make taste*, 413.2 *seasoning*, 668.1 *defiance*, 818.2 *bad manners*

saucebox 807.12 *impudent person*
sauce espagnole 45.15 *sauce*
saucepan 45.6 *kitchen equipment*, 258.15 *pot*
saucer 44.8 *ceramic object*, 258.16 *crockery*, 282.3 *flat thing*, 313.3 *circular thing*
saucer dome 43.6 *roof*
sauce suprême 45.15 *sauce*
saucily 668.9 *defiantly*, 807.31 *cheekily*, 818.10 *rudely*
sauciness 807, 668.1 *defiance*
saucy 668.7 *defiant*, 807.14 *cheeky*, 818.6 *bad-mannered*, 850.10 *disrespectful*
Saudi Arabia 91 Countries
Sauerbraten 45.46 *German dish*
Sauerkraut 45.46 *German dish*
sault 96.2 *channel*
sauna 408.8 *hot place*, 621.6 *bath*
saunter 324.12 *gait*, 324.15 *walk*, 328.1 *move slowly*, 328.10 *slow motion*
sauntering 328.4 *slow*
Sauria 79.2 *lizard*
saurian 79.2 *lizard*, 79.11 *reptilian*
saurischian 79.6 *extinct reptile*
sauropod 79.6 *extinct reptile*
sauropterygian 79.6 *extinct reptile*
saury 80 Fishes
sausage 45
sausagemeat 45.29 *sausage*
sauté 45.55 *cook*
sautéed 45.56 *culinary*
sautéing 45.8 *cooking technique*
Sauternes 351.9 *wine*, 414.5 *sweet drink*
savage 241.4 *violent person or animal*, 241.6 *violent*, 398.24 *murderous*, 406.11 *inflict pain*, 595.5 *immature*, 618.14 *ill-treat*, 658.1 *naive*, 658.3 *naive person*, 670.5 *strike*, 670.23 *attacking*, 795.5 *vulgar person*, 803.4 *common*, 818.4 *discourteous person*, 818.6 *bad-mannered*, 832.11 *cruel*, 832.17 *kill*, 864.9 *wicked person*
savage beast 241.4 *violent person or animal*
savagely 818.10 *rudely*, 832.20 *malevolently*
savageness 832.2 *cruelness*
savagery 241.2 *physical violence*, 658.2 *naivety*, 832.2 *cruelness*
savages 400.3 *uncivilized human*
savaging 406.3 *injury*
savanna 83.1 *plants*, 87.2 *grassland*, 98.6 *lowland*
Savannah 93 Cities, 96 Rivers
savant 4.12 *sage*, 459.8 *intellectual person*, 501.6 *knowledgeable person*, 655.5 *expert*
Savara 5 Languages and Groups of Languages
save 756, 767, 22.4 *pitching terms*, 38.2 *football play*, 38.4 *play soccer*, 131.8 *by subtraction*, 147.12 *exclusively*, 220.11 *persuade*, 594.3 *be prepared*, 600.5 *not use*, 605.6 *store*, 629.3 *restore*, 632.9 *protect*, 637.5 *preserve*, 639.1 *deliver*, 662.17 *help*, 671.23 *rescue*, 700.4 *liberate*, 721.11 *acquire*, 721.14 *profit*, 726.7 *detain*, 741.27 *invest*, 758.7 *hoard*, 781.5 *be cautious*
saveable 639.4 *deliverable*
save and except 131.8 *by subtraction*
save at the last second 639.1 *deliver*
save by the bell 26.11 *do a combat sport*, 639.1 *deliver*
saved 8.15 *deified*, 220.16 *influenced*, 600.1 *unused*, 605.7 *stored*, 629.13 *repaired*, 637.7 *preserved*, 639.4 *deliverable*, 700.7 *liberated*, 726.10 *retained*, 750.11 *accounted*
saved by the bell 639.4 *deliverable*
save face 805

save from 639.1 *deliver*
saveloy 45.29 *sausage*
save one's ass 632.8 *be safe*
save one's bacon 632.8 *be safe*, 638.5 *escape*
save one's breath 566.9 *lapse into silence*
save oneself 638.5 *escape*
save oneself the trouble 660.20 *take it easy*
save one's face 805.31 *save face*
save one's own skin 483.13 *turn Queen's evidence*
save one's skin 632.8 *be safe*, 638.5 *escape*
saver 756, 721.7 *gainer*, 744.6 *depositor*
savernake horn 49 Musical Instruments
Savery 52 Scientists
save someone's bacon 232.4 *be an instrument*
Save the Children 833.5 *charity*
save the life of 396.20 *support life*
save up 605.6 *store*, 637.5 *preserve*, 721.11 *acquire*, 758.7 *hoard*
Savile Row 295.2 *dressing*
savin 85 Trees and Shrubs
saving 637.1 *preservation*, 639.2 *deliverance*, 639.4 *deliverable*, 726.2 *detention*, 756.4 *thrifty*
saving clause 485.7 *condition*
saving grace 863.2 *virtues*
saving qualities 863.2 *virtues*
savings 14.4 *personal finance*, 594.10 *preparations*, 600.11 *unused thing*, 605.1 *store*, 632.2 *protection*, 721.5 *profit*, 734.5 *takings*, 742.5 *wealth*, 781.2 *insurance*
savings account 605.1 *store*, 632.2 *protection*, 741.6 *funds*, 742.5 *wealth*, 750.1 *accounts*
savings account deposit 744.3 *deposit*
savings and loan association 732.4 *lending institution*, 741.19 *treasury*
savings bank 741.19 *treasury*, 744.4 *bank*
saving up 637.1 *preservation*
saving your grace 849
saving your reverence 849.23 *saving your grace*
saviour 637.4 *preservationist*, 639.3 *deliverer*, 671.15 *protector*, 700.3 *liberator*, 729.4 *giver*, 784.4 *likable person*
Savitri 8 Deities
savoir-faire 6.11 *refinement*, 501.1 *knowledge*, 652.2 *good conduct*, 655.1 *skill*, 817.2 *good manners*
savoir-vivre 817.2 *good manners*
savorous 411.7 *tasty*, 416.5 *odorous*
savory 45 Herbs and Spices, 413.5 *herbs*
savour 165.3 *characteristic*, 350.23 *taste*, 411.4 *flavour*, 411.9 *taste*, 416.1 *odour*, 416.4 *reputation*, 763.14, 784.7 *like*
savouries 45.9 *dish*
savouring 350.3 *delicate eating*
savour of 114.10 *be similar*, 520.10 *mean*
savoury 350.27 *edible*, 411.7 *tasty*, 413.9 *piquant*, 763.4 *tasty*
savoury food 350.7 *food*
savoy cabbage 45 Vegetables
savvy 6.9 *learnedness*, 459.5 *common sense*, 501.1 *knowledge*, 501.11 *know*, 522.6 *understand*
saw 47.11 *woodworking tool*, 47.17 *carpenter*, 63.9 *machine tool*, 85.7 *timber production*, 136.9 *separate*, 322.2 *opener*, 322.18 *open*, 380.9 *sharp-edged thing*, 380.16 *use a sharp tool*, 430.5 *sound hoarse*, 434.10 *lack harmony*, 505.1 *maxim*, 603.1 *tool*, 603.9 *use tools*, 876.7 *moral*
sawbench 85.7 *timber production*

saw blade 319.2 *notched thing*
sawbones 60.11 *doctor*, 630.15 *healer*
sawbuck 741.8 *American money*
sawdust 132.2 *residue*, 384.5 *powder*
sawed 322.12 *open*
saw edge 375.6 *roughness*
saw-edge 380.7 *sharp point*
saw-edged 380.3 *sharp-edged*
sawfish 80 Fishes
sawfly 82 Insects
sawlike 319.4 *notched*
sawmill 85.7 *timber production*, 647.1 *workshop*
Sawney 91 Names for Inhabitants
sawn-off 270.8 *shortened*
sawn-off shotgun 680.9 *firearm*
saw off the limb one sits on 656.6 *act foolishly*
sawt 161 Collective Names for Birds and Animals
saw-thai 49 Musical Instruments
saw-toothed 319.4 *notched*
sawtooth wave 365.5 *wave*
sawyer 47.13 *carpenter*, 646.2 *artisan*
saxe blue 454.1 *blue*
saxhorn 49 Musical Instruments
saxicolous 90.8 *lichenoid*
saxifrage 84 Flowers and Flowering Plants
Saxon 202.14 *historic*
Saxon blue 454.5 *blueness*
Saxons 1 Peoples, 200.6 *people of the past*
saxophone 49 Musical Instruments
saxotromba 49 Musical Instruments
saxtuba 49 Musical Instruments
say 67 Natural Fabrics, 126.1 *superiority*, 264.7 *nearly*, 473.15 *state*, 535.2 *statement*, 535.17 *affirm*, 564.7 *utterance*, 564.11 *speak*
sayable 708.8 *permitting*
say again 183.17 *iterate*
Sayan 95 Mountains
say a prayer of thanks 837.7 *give thanks*
say aye 116.28 *consent*
say clearly 520.10 *mean*
say directly 520.10 *mean*
say ditto to 499.4 *assent*
sayer 564.10 *speaker*
Sayers 48 Writers
say farewell 345.6 *part*
say goodbye to 722.9 *lose*
say good morning to 567.9 *approach*
say grace 10.20 *pray*, 837.7 *give thanks*
say hear hear 116.28 *consent*
say hello 817.12 *greet*
say "I do" 714.7 *promise*, 823.15 *marry*
saying 505.1 *maxim*, 535.2 *statement*, 876.7 *moral*
saying again 183.2 *iteration*
saying little 566.3 *sparing with words*
say in other words 520.10 *mean*
say it again 426.14 *repeat*
say it all 144.5 *be complete*
say magic words 11.21 *bewitch*
say no 500.9 *refuse*, 536.7 *be negative*, 711.5 *refuse*, 713.6 *protest*
say no more 566.11 *hush*
say nothing 566.8 *be taciturn*, 699.10 *restrain oneself*
say no to 341.1 *repel*, 581.1 *reject*, 709.3 *veto*, 852.15 *withhold approval*
say office 719.5 *observe religious ceremony*
say one is sorry 840.6 *apologize*, 867.4 *be penitent*
say one's prayers 10.20 *pray*
say one thing and mean another 540.18 *be hypocritical*
say one will 714.7 *promise*
say 'Our Father' 10.20 *pray*
say outright 556.7 *be simple*

say over again 183.17 *iterate*
say over and over 183.18 *harp*
say plainly 520.10 *mean*
say prayers 9.7 *worship*, 10.19 *offer worship*
say so 535.21 *be assertive*, 692.9 *command*
say-so 535.2 *statement*, 688.9 *permission*, 698.1 *freedom*
say sotto voce 424.5 *sound faint*
say thank you 837.6 *be grateful*
say the Lord's Prayer 10.20 *pray*
say the magic word 708.3 *permit*
say the prayers 710.15 *offer worship*
say the same as 499.4 *assent*
say the word 116.28 *consent*
say together 198.7 *synchronize*
say to oneself 569.3 *soliloquize*
say whatever comes into one's mind 583.3 *improvise*
say whatever pops into one's head 583.3 *improvise*
say what is in one's mind 658.4 *be naive*
say yes 499.4 *assent*
say yes to 667.6 *agree with*, 708.3 *permit*, 714.7 *promise*
saz 49 Musical Instruments
SBA 73.6 *flight control*
S-bend 33.6 *motor racing terms*, 71.3 *carriageway*
s-block 57.6 *chemical element*
sc 165.31 *namely*
scab 15.7 *employee*, 69.12 *pests and diseases*, 293.14 *animal covering*, 335.19 *deviant person*, 375.7 *rough thing*, 500.5 *dissenter*, 578.9 *equivocator*, 666.4 *dissenter*, 693.12 *reactionary*, 711.4 *refuser*, 713.4 *protester*, 720.5 *nonobserver*, 822.8 *hated person*
scabbard 680.4 *arsenal*
scabbing over 629.11 *recuperation*
scabby 375.2 *coarse*, 622.8 *unclean*
scab formation 629.11 *recuperation*
scabicide 62.4 *drug type*
scabies 777 Phobias by Topic, 624.13 *skin disease*
scabiophobia 777 Phobias by Name
scabious 84 Flowers and Flowering Plants
scab over 629.6 *cure*
scabrid 793.5 *marked*
scabrous 375.2 *coarse*, 622.9 *obscene*, 793.5 *marked*, 877.12 *indecent*
scabrousness 375.6 *roughness*
scads 181.2 *multitude*
scads of money 741.3 *fortune*, 742.6 *money*
Scafell Pike 95 Mountains
scaffold 284.11 *support*, 382.4 *framework*, 398.5 *execution*, 594.10 *preparations*, 879.16 *instrument of execution*
scaffolding 284.2 *supporting part*, 594.10 *preparations*
scag 875.6 *drug*
scag jones 875.4 *drug taker*
scalable 359.25 *ladder-like*
scalar 52.50 *scalar quantity*, 359.25 *ladder-like*
scalariform 359.25 *ladder-like*
scalar product 52.50 *scalar quantity*
scalar quantity 52
scald 45.55 *cook*, 69.12 *pests and diseases*, 406.3 *injury*, 406.11 *inflict pain*, 408.14 *be hot*
scalding 406.5 *painful*, 408.9 *hot*
scale 75, 266, 30.6 *pommel horse*, 49.16 *musical note*, 49.20 *key*, 56.82 *measuring instrument*, 80.5 *fish anatomy*, 82.3 *pest*, 95.10 *climb a mountain*, 107.2 *interrelatedness*, 121.1 *degree*, 121.5 *measure*, 143.7 *piece*, 159.2 *consecution*, 259.1 *size*, 266.4 *slice*, 268.6 *measuring instrument*, 293.14

animal covering, 296.16 *peel*, 359.9 *ladder*, 359.10 *step*, 359.14 *climb*, 369.10 *scales*, 375.7 *rough thing*, 375.11 *be rough*
scale a peak 34.9 *mountaineer*
scale armour 671.7 *armour*
scaled 121.7 *gradational*
scaled-down 262.7 *smaller*
scale down 129.5 *make smaller*, 182.8 *reduce*, 262.5 *make smaller*
scale drawing 592.5 *map*
scale insect 82 Insects, 69.12 *pests and diseases*, 82.3 *pest*
scale leaf 83.6 *leaf*
scalene 123.3 *unequal*, 310.9 *angled*
scalene triangle 52.43 *triangle*, 310.3 *angled figure*
scale off 296.16 *peel*
scales 369, 45.6 *kitchen equipment*, 56.86 *weighing instrument*, 268.7 *standard*, 622.4 *dirt*
Scales 53 The Constellations
scale the heights 359.14 *climb*, 684.4 *complete*
scaleworm 81 Worms
scaliness 266.6 *layering*, 375.6 *roughness*
scaling 60.4 *dentistry*, 359.6 *mounting*
scaling-down 262.1 *contraction*
scaling the heights 359.6 *mounting*
scallion 45 Vegetables
scallop 81 Molluscs, 45.19 *shellfish*, 293.14 *animal covering*, 314.6 *convolute*, 319.2 *notched thing*
scalloped 319.4 *notched*
scalloped edge 375.6 *roughness*
scallop shell 314.3 *convoluted thing*
scallywag 693.5 *troublemaker*, 801.2 *disreputable character*
scalp 293.14 *animal covering*, 294.13 *remove*, 296.15 *make nude*, 681.2 *spoils*
scalped 294.9 *shed*
scalpel 380.10 *knife*
scalper 294.7 *shedder*
scalping 294.5 *shedding*
scaly 79.11 *reptilian*, 80.14 *ichthyological*, 266.9 *platelike*, 375.2 *coarse*, 384.20 *crumbly*
scaly anteater 77 Placental Mammals, 77.6 *insect-eating mammal*
scaly-tailed squirrel 77 Placental Mammals
scam 474.2 *sophism*, 539.10 *fraud*, 539.30 *be fraudulent*, 657.2 *stratagem*, 736.7 *dishonesty*, 747.1 *nonpayment*, 801.3 *disreputable action*, 858.3 *criminality*, 858.10 *be criminal*
scamp 693.5 *troublemaker*, 864.9 *wicked person*
scamper 324.12 *gait*, 329.4 *be swift*, 329.6 *accelerate*, 329.9 *acceleration*, 648.2 *make haste*
scamper away 345.4 *hurry off*
scampering 648.3 *hasty*
scampi-and-chips circuit 51.13 *engagement*
scan 60.7 *diagnosis*, 60.19 *practise medicine*, 435.3 *observation*, 435.14 *inspect*, 477.17 *question*, 492.12 *estimate*, 534.28 *radar*, 547.9 *represent*
scandal 618.10 *poverty*, 801.1 *disrespect*, 844.9 *dishonour*, 854.3 *defamation*, 856.2 *false accusation*
scandalize 785.7 *cause dislike*, 786.10 *be wonderful*
scandalized 786.6 *wondering*
scandalizing 786.8 *wonderful*, 864.13 *venial*
scandalmonger 465.4 *meddler*, 533.4 *journalist*, 854.8 *defamer*
scandalous 618.4 *poor*, 801.4 *disreputable*, 844.15 *immoral*, 854.16 *defamatory*, 864.13 *venial*
scandalously 864.18 *wickedly*

scandal sheet 533.5 *mass communication*
scandent 359.22 *ascending*
scandic 57.34 *elemental*
Scandinavian 5 Languages and Groups of Languages, 5.11 *family of languages*, 47.7 *furniture style*
scandium 57 Chemical Elements
scanned 48.20 *metrical*
scanner 65.7 *peripheral*, 65.13 *character recognition*, 65.17 *computing term*, 435.11 *observer*, 630.14 *hospital*
scanning 48.20 *metrical*, 60.7 *diagnosis*, 435.3 *observation*
scanning electron microscope 56.85 *microscope*
scanning transmission electron microscope 56.85 *microscope*
scansion 57 metre
scansorial 359.22 *ascending*
scant 274, 145.4 *incomplete*, 182.6 *sparse*, 260.7 *little*, 609.1 *insufficient*, 743.4 *inadequate*
scant courtesy 818.2 *bad manners*
scanties 295.18 *underwear*
scantily 145.6 *incompletely*, 182.11 *sparsely*, 274.17 *thin*, 609.10 *insufficiently*, 743.17 *inadequately*
scantiness 145.1 *incompleteness*, 182.3 *fewness*, 254.2 *disappearance*, 260.1 *littleness*, 270.1 *shortness*, 274.12 *thinning*, 609.8 *insufficiency*, 685.1 *noncompletion*, 743.9 *inadequacy*
scantling 259.1 *size*
scantly 609.10 *insufficiently*, 743.17 *inadequately*
scantness 145.1 *incompleteness*, 260.1 *littleness*, 609.8 *insufficiency*, 743.9 *inadequacy*
scanty 145.4 *incomplete*, 182.6 *sparse*, 260.7 *little*, 270.7 *short*, 272.2 *fine*, 274.6 *scant*, 609.1 *insufficient*, 685.4 *uncompleted*, 743.4 *inadequate*
scapegoat 222.2 *substitute person*, 481.8 *victim of discrimination*, 493.6 *misjudged person*, 687.5 *person in adversity*, 722.6 *loser*, 730.5 *recipient*, 840.3 *atoner*
scaphoid 382 Bones
scaphopod 81.5 *mollusc*
Scaphopoda 81.5 *mollusc*
scapolite 54 Minerals
scapula 382 Bones
scapular 7.11 *vestment*
scar 275.3 *mountain*, 281.3 *vertical thing*, 293.14 *animal covering*, 309.3 *deformity*, 544.3 *means of identification*, 544.10 *identify*, 628.5 *hurt*, 790.5 *make ugly*, 793.1 *mar*
scarab 11.6 *talisman*
scarab beetle 82 Insects
Scaramouch 51.21 *role*, 51.30 *clown*
Scarborough 93 Cities
scarce 609, 182.6 *sparse*, 213.2 *infrequent*, 358.7 *short*, 372.1 *sparse*, 743.4 *inadequate*, 753.8 *valuable*
scarce as hen's teeth 609.4 *scarce*
scarcely 121.11 *to a degree*, 182.11 *sparsely*, 186.10 *seldom*, 213.1 *infrequently*, 609.10 *insufficiently*, 620.11 *imperfectly*, 753.13 *valuably*
scarcely any 182.5 *few*
scarcely ever 186.10 *seldom*, 213.1 *infrequently*
scarcely like 115.4 *dissimilar*
scarcely to be expected 489.1 *improbable*
scarceness 182.3 *fewness*, 213.3 *infrequency*, 372.3 *sparseness*, 609.9 *scarcity*
scarcity 350, 609, 129.1 *decrease*, 182.3 *fewness*, 213.3 *infrequency*, 254.2 *disappearance*, 358.5 *shortfall*, 372.3 *sparseness*, 605.3 *supply*, 743.9 *inade-*

quacy, 753.6 *value*
scarcity value 751.2, 753.6 *value*
scare 636.3 *false alarm*, 636.7 *raise the alarm*, 777.13 *frighten*, 832.18 *torment*
scarebaby 777.6 *frightened person*
scarecrow 68.14 *pest control*, 274.9 *thin person*, 547.6 *image*, 790.2 *ugly person*
scarecrow and tin man in *The Wizard of Oz* 396.6 *things brought to life*
scared 238.12 *weak-willed*, 777.7 *frightened*, 779.3 *cowardly*
scared rabbit 329.12 *swift animal*
scared shitless 777.7 *frightened*
scared stiff 777.7 *frightened*
scaredy-cat 777.6 *frightened person*, 779.2 *coward*
scaremonger 636.4 *warner*, 777.5 *frightener*
scarer 777.5 *frightener*
scare shitless 777.13 *frighten*
scare someone half to death 777.13 *frighten*
scare the living daylights out of 777.13 *frighten*
scare the pants off 777.13 *frighten*
scare up 721.11 *acquire*
scarf 293.5 *body covering*, 295.14 *neckwear*, 295.15 *headgear*, 301.4 *wrapper*
scarf joint 47.10 *carpenter's term*
scarf up 350.22 *eat well*
scaring 777.10 *frightening*
scarlatina 624.6 *infection*
Scarlatti 49 Musicians and Composers
scarlet 450.1 *red*, 864.12 *immoral*, 877.13 *unchaste*
scarlet fever 450.5 *redness*, 624.6 *infection*
scarlet runner 45 Vegetables
Scarlett and Rhett 821.10 *lovers*
scarlet woman 877.9 *immoral woman*
scarp 54.7 *landform*, 281.3 *vertical thing*, 310.2 *obliquity*, 671.11 *fortification*
scarper 345.4 *hurry off*, 458.2 *depart*
scarred 309.7 *deformed*, 544.12 *identified*, 793.5 *marked*
scary 777.10 *frightening*
scat 591.9 *play truant*, 648.2 *make haste*
scathe 618.13 *be worthless*, 628.5 *hurt*
scatheless 619.1 *perfect*
scatological 353.25 *faecal*, 827.8 *cursing*
scatologic 5.39 *of language*, 353.25 *faecal*, 622.9 *obscene*, 795.9 *ribald*, 877.12 *indecent*
scatologically 353, 5.49 *colloquially*
scatologize 827.5 *curse*
scatology 5.19 *swearword*, 622.3 *obscenity*, 827.1 *curse*
scatter 182, 136.9 *separate*, 136.13 *diverge*, 141.4 *deconstruct*, 151.21 *disorder*, 162.9 *be dispersed*, 162.12 *disperse*, 244.8 *destroy*, 324.14 *set in motion*, 326.14 *bring back*, 335.12 *deflect*, 335.18 *diffraction*, 343.13 *radiate*, 362.6 *throw down*, 384.22 *powder*, 389.33 *sprinkle*, 458.3 *cause to disappear*, 607.1 *waste*, 682.10 *defeat heavily*
scatter around 162.17 *sow*
scatterbrain 460.3 *unintelligent person*, 468.6 *inattentive person*, 512.7 *forgetful person*
scatterbrained 151.16 *confused*, 224.14 *irresolute*, 656.1 *unskilful*
scatter diagram 52.32 *graph*, 152.8 *chart*
scattered 136.16 *apart*, 162.19 *dispersed*, 182.6 *sparse*, 335.26 *diffractive*
scattered showers 55.25 *rain*
scattergram 52.32 *graph*
scattering 55.9 *atmospheric pro-*

cess, 56.15 *wave property*, 56.71 *nuclear reaction*, 136.1 *separation*, 141.2 *deconstruction*, 162.1 *dispersion*, 162.28 *dispersive*, 182.1 *few*, 343.3 *radiation*, 362.20 *falling*, 458.4 *disappearance*
scattering of the ashes 399.1 *burial*
scatterment 162.1 *dispersion*
scatter seed 68.17 *farm*
scatter to the winds 162.17 *sow*, 722.14 *go to waste*
scatty 224.14 *irresolute*
scaup 78 *Birds*
scavenger 76.4 *type of animal*, 621.12 *cleaner*, 622.6 *dirty person*
scavenger bird 621.12 *cleaner*
Scavenger's Daughter 879.15 *instrument of torture*
scenario 48.3 *aspect of fiction*, 51.2 *play*, 251.2 *circumstances*, 473.4 *gist*, 560.3 *narration*, 592.2 *policy*
scenarioist 51.24 *dramatist*
scenario writer 51.24 *dramatist*
scenarist 51.24 *dramatist*
scend 97.10 *billow*
scene 51, 50.10 *art subject*, 51.17 *stage set*, 165.8 *specialization*, 251.1 *situation*, 251.2 *circumstances*, 297.1 *surroundings*, 435.7 *view*, 526.8 *showplace*, 640.2 *deed*, 811.14 *show*, 813.3 *formal occasion*, 828.4 *anger*
scene bay 51.15 *stage*
scene dock 51.15 *stage*
scene of desolation 244.5 *havoc*
scene of destruction 244.5 *havoc*, 607.4 *destruction*
scene painter 50.16 *artist*, 51.26 *stagehand*
scene painting 50.2 *painting*
scenery 51.17 *stage set*, 251.1 *situation*, 297.1 *surroundings*, 435.7 *view*
scene shifter 51.26 *stagehand*
scenic 50.26 *artistic*, 435.20 *visual*, 789.5 *beautiful*, 792.8 *decorated*, 811.24 *grand*
scenic railway 72.1 *railway*
scenic route 363.5 *ringroad*
scent 416, 32.8 *hunting*, 348.12 *draw in*, 349.14 *let out*, 389.14 *lavender water*, 416.1 *odour*, 416.9 *impart odour to*, 418.1 *fragrance*, 418.2 *fragrant thing*, 418.6 *perfume*, 483.4 *indication*, 516.1 *foresee*, 528.15 *be informed*, 543.1 *sign*, 545.12 *vestige*, 791.6 *toiletries*
scent bottle 418.2 *fragrant thing*
scented 416.5 *odorous*, 418.4 *fragrant*
scented soap 395.8 *fat*, 418.2 *fragrant thing*, 621.9 *cleaning agent*
scent from afar 516.1 *foresee*
scent game 37.7 *shoot*
scent gland 77.2 *mammalian characteristic*, 352.3 *gland*, 416.3 *scent*
scentless 417.3 *odourless*
scentlessness 417.1 *odourlessness*
scent out 37.7 *shoot*, 348.12 *draw in*, 590.9 *follow*
sceptic 4.11 *follower of a doctrine*, 477.9 *questioner*, 491.17 *uncertain person*, 498.5 *disbeliever*, 573.16 *reluctant person*, 720.5 *nonobserver*, 720.11 *nonobservant*, 781.4 *cautious*
sceptical 477, 4.14 *of a philosophy*, 491.1 *uncertain*, 498.6 *disbelieving*, 500.7 *dissenting*, 573.5 *reluctant*, 776.4 *hopeless*
sceptically 477.23 *questioningly*, 491.23 *uncertainly*, 498.10 *disbelievingly*, 720.16 *disobediently*, 781.7 *cautiously*
scepticism 4.7 *school of thought*, 477.6 *uncertainty*, 491.10 *suspicion*, 498.1 *disbelief*, 776.1 *hopelessness*, 781.1 *caution*
sceptre 544.4 *insignia*

Schaumasse 53 Comets
Scheat 53 Named Stars
Schedar 53 Named Stars
schedule 150.1 *order*, 152.8 *chart*, 152.18 *make arrangements*, 171.5 *list of appointments*, 171.8 *list*, 185.16 *time*, 192.2 *timetable*, 192.14 *keep time*, 257.5 *divisions*, 257.9 *itemize*, 517.3, 592.1 *plan*, 592.10 *plan out*
scheduled 171.11 *listed*, 257.12 *itemized*
scheduled event 199.6 *future event*
scheduled flight 73.1 *aviation*
schedule of events 592.1 *plan*
scheduling 192.1 *timekeeping*
Scheele 52 Scientists
scheelite 54 Minerals
Schelling 4 Philosophers
Schellingian 4.11 *follower of a doctrine*, 4.14 *of a philosophy*
schema 152.8 *chart*
schematic 150.10 *ordered*, 152.22 *organizational*, 152.26 *diagrammatic*, 257.12 *itemized*, 471.12 *purposive*, 592.14 *planned*
schematically 152.28 *in place*, 257.15 *thematically*, 471.21 *purposively*, 592.16 *as planned*
schematize 152.13 *organize*, 257.9 *itemize*
scheme 48.3 *aspect of fiction*, 150.1 *order*, 150.7 *method*, 152.8 *chart*, 257.5 *divisions*, 471.3 *plan*, 471.18 *aim*, 474.2 *sophism*, 474.11 *practise sophistry*, 539.8, 539.28 *trick*, 592.1 *plan*, 592.4 *plot*, 592.9 *plan*, 592.13 *plot*, 657.5 *be cunning*
SCHEME 65 Programming Languages
schemer 474.6 *sophist*, 539.20 *plotter*, 540.15 *false person*, 592.8 *planner*, 657.3 *cunning person*
scheming 539.34 *deceiving*, 592.7, 592.15 *planning*, 657.4 *cunning*, 858.5 *dishonourable*
Schenectady 93 Cities
scherzando 49 Musical Terms
scherzo 46.4 *historic dancing*
Schickard 53 Lunar Features
Schiff's base 57 Types of Compounds, **57** Named Reactions
Schiff's reagent 57 Named Reactions, 58.5 *sugar test*
Schiller 4 Philosophers, **48** Poets, **48** Dramatists, **53** Lunar Features
schilling 741.11 *national coins*
schipperke 77 Breeds of Dogs
schism 117.4 *disagreement*, 136.1 *separation*, 168.3 *nonconformism*, 500.4 *faction*, 598.3 *relinquishment*, 666.2 *argument*, 693.4 *revolution*
schismatic 117.10 *disagreeing*, 168.8 *dissenter*, 168.12 *nonconformist*, 500.5 *dissenter*, 500.7 *dissenting*, 666.9 *disagreeing*, 693.14 *subversive*
schismatical 168.12 *nonconformist*, 500.7 *dissenting*
schismatically 117.16 *disagreeably*, 666.11 *in disagreement*, 693.18 *subversively*
schismatize 117.14 *disagree*, 500.8 *dissent*, 598.2 *withdraw*
schist 54 Common Rocks
schistose 54.57 *chalky*
schistosity 54.33 *metamorphic rock*
schistosome 81 Worms
schistosomiasis 81.11 *helminthic disease*, 624.7 *tropical disease*
schizo 61.8 *disordered personality*, 510.13 *mentally ill*
schizoaffective psychosis 61.11 *psychosis*
schizocarp 86.2 *botanical fruit*
schizocarpic 86.9 *of a fruit*
schizocarpic fruit 86.2 *botanical fruit*
schizoid 61.8 *disordered personal-*

ity, 61.36 *psychologically disturbed*, 136.16 *apart*, 510.7 *insane person*, 510.13 *mentally ill*
schizoidism 61.16 *dissociation*
schizoid personality 61.8 *disordered personality*, 61.16 *dissociation*, 510.5 *psychosis*
schizophrenia 61.11 *psychosis*, 61.16 *dissociation*, 510.5 *psychosis*
schizophrenic 224.5 *changeable person*, 510.7 *insane person*, 510.13 *mentally ill*
schizothyme 61.8 *disordered personality*
schizothymia 61.16 *dissociation*
schizothymic personality 61.8 *disordered personality*
Schlegel 4 Philosophers
Schleiermacher 4 Philosophers
schlemiel 539.22 *dupe*
schlep 326.12 *transport*
schleppend 49 Musical Terms
Schleswig 32 Breeds of Horse and Pony
Schlick 4 Philosophers
schlock 618.8 *inferiority*
schlocky 618.2 *inferior*
schmaltz 555.2 *lack of emphasis*
schmaltzy 555.1 *unemphatic*
schmear 729.2 *gift*
Schmeling 18 Sporting Personalities
Schmidt telescope 53.24 *telescope*
schmuck 539.22 *dupe*
schmutter business 796.3 *fashion business*
schnauzer 77 Breeds of Dogs
schnell 49 Musical Terms
schneller 49 Musical Terms
schnook 236.5 *powerless person*, 539.22 *dupe*
schnozzle 318.3 *protuberance*, 416.2 *sense of smell*
Schoenberg 49 Musicians and Composers
Schoffen–Baumann reagent 57 Named Reactions
schola cantorum 6.12 *educational institution*
scholar 6.7 *learner*, 165.14 *specialist*, 459.8 *intellectual person*, 461.7 *thinker*, 467.6 *attentive person*, 501.6 *knowledgeable person*, 507.4 *intellectual*, 655.5, 688.11 *expert*, 696.9 *educational leader*, 730.5 *recipient*
scholarliness 6.9 *learnedness*
scholarly 4.19 *learned*, 6.18 *educated*, 48.16 *literary*, 165.21 *specialized*, 461.11 *reasoning*, 501.9 *literate*, 696.13 *excellent*
scholarship 6.8 *learning*, 6.9 *learnedness*, 501.3 *learning*, 662.6 *financial assistance*, 721.5 *profit*, 729.2 *gift*, 730.2 *something received*, 749.3 *income*, 878.3 *grant*
scholarship winner 730.5 *recipient*
scholastic 6.16 *educational*, 6.18 *educated*, 7.14 *theologian*
Scholastic 4.11 *follower of a doctrine*
scholastically 6.26 *studiously*
scholasticism 4.7 *school of thought*
scholastic theology 7.13 *theology*
scholiast 524.6 *interpreter*
scholiastic 524.16 *annotative*
scholium 524.2 *annotation*
school 161 Collective Names for Birds and Animals, 2.8 *human institution*, 6.12 *educational institution*, 6.22 *educate*, 7.1 *religion*, 63.20 *building*, 77.21 *assemblage of mammals*, 80.1 *fishes*, 161.23 *flock*, 165.8 *specialization*, 167.10 *assimilate*, 220.4 *medium of conversion*, 243.8 *construction*, 497.2 *religious belief*, 501.14 *cause to know*
schoolable 6.17 *educatable*
school age 206.1 *youth*
school-age 206.11 *young*
School Attendance Officer 6.5 *edu-*

cationalist
school bag 258.8 *bag*
school board 6.5 *educationalist*
school book 6
schoolboy 6.7 *learner*, 206.7 *young man*
schoolchildren 206.10 *the young*
schooldays 206.1 *youth*
school dictionary 5.28 *dictionary*
schooled 501.9 *literate*
schoolfellow 819.5 *friend*
schoolgirl 6.7 *learner*, 206.8 *young woman*
school grammar 5.29 *grammar*
schoolhouse 6.15 *schoolroom*
schooling 6.1 *education*, 501.3 *learning*
school letter 544.4 *insignia*
schoolman 6.4 *educator*
schoolmarm 696.9 *educational leader*
schoolmarmish 6.16 *educational*
schoolmaster 6.4 *educator*, 696.9 *educational leader*
schoolmastery 6.6 *instructorship*
schoolmate 784.4 *likable person*, 819.5 *friend*
schoolmistress 6.4 *educator*, 696.9 *educational leader*
school notes 545.3 *notes*
school nurse 60.16 *nurse*
School of Paris 50 Western Art Styles and Movements
school of thought 4, 4.2 *philosophical system*
school prefect 653.16 *official*
school report 545.1 *record*
school ring 544.5 *uniform*
schoolroom 6
school ship 74 Ships and Boats
school teacher 6.4 *educator*
school term 187.4 *period of activity*
school uniform 295.3 *formal dress*, 544.5 *uniform*, 813.4 *formal dress*
school work 644.1 *work*
schoolyard 6.15 *schoolroom*
schooner 74 Sailing Ships and Boats, 36.2 *sailing boat*, 258.13 *drinking vessel*
Schopenhauer 4 Philosophers
Schottky diode 64.18 *diode*
schrillpfeife 49 Musical Instruments
Schrödinger 52 Scientists
Schrödinger Canyon 53 Rills and Valleys
Schrödinger equation 365.5 *wave*
Schrödinger's cat 56 Named Laws, 4.9 *philosophical problem*, 56.80 *quantum theory*
Schrödinger's wave equation 56 Named Laws
Schröter's Valley 53 Rills and Valleys
Schubert 49 Musicians and Composers
Schumann 49 Musicians and Composers, **49** Musicians and Composers
schuss 41.14 *ski*
schussing 41.12 *ski*
schussing position 41.4 *skiing technique*
Schwann 52 Scientists
Schwarzkopf 49 Musicians and Composers
Schwarzwald Heavy Horse 32 Breeds of Horse and Pony
Schweitzer 4 Philosophers
schyzothymia 61.8 *disordered personality*
sciamachy 519.4 *ideality*
Sciascia 48 Writers
sciatica 406.2 *painful condition*, 624.17 *nervous disorder*
science 501, 367.6 *natural science*
science fiction 519.4 *ideality*, 560.5 *fiction*
science-fiction novel 48.2 *fiction*
science of colour 444.8 *chromatics*
science of forces 330.11 *impulsion*
science of human and animal

behaviour 61.1 *psychology*
science of interpretation 524, 5.12 *translation*
science of language 5.1 *linguistics*
science of law 16.32 *jurisprudence*
science of man 1.1 *anthropology*
science of matter 367.6 *natural science*
science of physical properties 367.6 *natural science*
science of rotation 364
science of structure 382
science of the mind 61.1 *psychology*
science park 647.1 *workshop*
science subject 6.3 *subject*
science topic 472.5 *educational topic*
scientific 150.14 *well-ordered*, 477.15 *sceptical*, 479.8 *experimental*, 537.21 *accurate*
scientifically 477.23 *questioningly*, 479.14 *experimentally*, 655.12 *skilfully*
scientific aptitude test 61.5 *psychological test*
scientific exactness 537.8 *accuracy*
scientific investigation 477.2 *questioning*
scientific man 400.4 *civilized human*
scientific perspective 50.4 *treatment*
scientific researcher 518.4 *theorist*
scientism 367.2 *materialization*
scientist 268.9 *measurer*, 367.3 *materialist*, 477.9 *questioner*, 479.5 *experimenter*, 501.6 *knowledgeable person*, 518.4 *theorist*, 646.1 *worker*, 655.5, 688.11 *expert*
scientological 11.16 *psychic*
scientology 11.1 *occultism*
Scientology 7 Non-Christian Religions
sci-fi 48.2, 560.5 *fiction*
scil. 165.31 *namely*
scimitar 380.10 *knife*, 680.8 *sharp weapon*
scintilla 410.2 *lighter*, 439.8 *fire*
scintillate 439.25 *light up*, 507.8 *be intelligent*
scintillating 439.16 *bright*
scintillatingly 439.30 *lightly*
scintillation 53.21 *orbit*, 439.2 *quality of light*
scintillation counter 56.93 *radiation detector*
sciolism 502.2 *half-knowledge*
scion 69.5 *gardening*, 83.5 *stem*, 143.6 *branch*, 206.5 *young plant*
sciophobia 777 Phobias by Name
sciopticon 51.18 *stage lighting*
scissile 136.19 *separable*, 379.1 *brittle*
scission 136.3 *separateness*, 379.2 *brittleness*
scissor 36.10 *sailing*, 380.16 *use a sharp tool*
scissor gybe 36.1 *sailing*, 36.15 *sail*
scissors 30.6 *pommel horse*, 41.12 *ski*, 380.9 *sharp-edged thing*
scissors block 19.9 *play*
scissors kick 39.2 *swimming technique*
scissors style 21.2 *field events*
scissors turn 41.4 *skiing technique*
scissure 265.2 *crack*
sciurine 77.30 *rodent-like*
sciuromorphs 77.12 *gnawing mammal*
sclaff 29.3 *golf shots*, 29.7 *golf*
sclera 435.2 *eye*
sclerectomy 60 Surgical Operations
scleroprotein 58.9 *protein*
sclerosis 373.6 *solidification*
sclerotic 373.1 *hard*
sclerotization 58.9 *protein*
sclerotomy 60 Surgical Opera-

tions
scobicula 384.16 *powdery*
scobiform 384.16 *powdery*
scoff 350.7 *food*, 350.22 *eat well*, 771.13 *be humorous*, 807.29 *ridicule*, 850.6, 850.25 *taunt*, 854.14 *ridicule*
scoff at 498.8 *disbelieve*, 799.6 *deride*
scoff at virtue 864.16 *be wicked*
scoffing 799.1 *mockery*, 818.1 *discourtesy*, 850.15 *taunting*, 854.17 *scornful*
scoffingly 818.10 *rudely*
scold 500.5 *dissenter*, 827.6 *vilify*, 829.3 *irascible person*, 852.20 *censure*, 879.1 *punish*
scolded 852.34 *censured*
scolding 852.7 *blame*, 852.30 *censuring*, 879.7 *punishment*
scolecite 54 Minerals
sconce 439.6 *electric light*
scone 45.39 *loaf*
scoop 31.8 *hockey*, 31.9 *play hockey*, 34.5 *rock face*, 258.17 *ladle*, 326.15 *take away*, 355.10 *excavator*, 528.4 *mass communication*, 532.3 *journalism*, 532.15 *publish*, 533.3 *reporting*, 533.9 *news story*, 533.13 *report*
scooped 31.8 *hockey*, 258.20 *containing*
scooping 31.1, 31.8 *hockey*
scoop out 317.7 *make concave*
scoop stroke 31.1 *hockey*
scoot 71.10 *sled*, 329.4 *be swift*, 591.8 *run away*
scooter 71.13 *motorcycle*
scop 48.14 *author*
scope 698, 121.1 *degree*, 210.2 *opportunity*, 235.2 *ability*, 248.6 *available space*, 248.7 *range*, 249.14 *sphere*, 259.1, 268.4 *size*, 271.4 *breadth*, 435.9 *viewpoint*, 520.1 *meaning*
scope sight 37.3 *hunting equipment*
scops owl 78 Birds
scorch 329.4 *be swift*, 392.19 *bake*, 408.15 *burn*, 628.4 *impair*, 670.9 *attack successfully*, 676.13 *be at war*
scorched 392.8 *baked*, 408.13 *heated*
scorched earth 244.5 *havoc*
scorched earth policy 247.1 *infertility*, 676.8 *warfare*
scorcher 55.23 *heat*, 329.13 *swift person*, 408.5 *hot weather*
scorching 241.6 *violent*, 329.1 *swift*, 329.8 *speed*, 408.9 *hot*, 408.11 *warm*
score 27, 171, 19.15 *play offence*, 22.7 *play baseball*, 27.17 *bat*, 35.5 *play rugby*, 38.2 *football play*, 38.4 *play soccer*, 49.18 *written music*, 49.35 *compose*, 52.12 *numeration*, 121.3 *gradation*, 121.5 *measure*, 152.9 *musical arrangement*, 152.16 *adapt*, 169.4 *mathematical result*, 170.8 *calculate*, 179.8 *twenty and over*, 319.1, 319.5 *notch*, 319.6 *notch up*, 321.1, 321.6 *furrow*, 433.9 *set to music*, 478.7 *numerical result*, 478.20 *solve*, 545.15 *register*, 682.3 *successful thing*, 744.1 *credit*, 745.5 *amount owing*, 750.3 *accounting*
score 300 25.8 *bowl*
score a bull's-eye 503.7, 537.31 *be accurate*
score a goal 31.9 *play hockey*
score an own goal 656.7 *be clumsy*
score a perfect game 25.8 *bowl*
score a point 682.11 *overmaster*
score a run 22.7 *play baseball*
score a spare 25.8 *bowl*
score a strike 25.8 *bowl*
score a success 682.6 *be successful*
score a try 35.5 *play rugby*
scoreboard 19.4 *stadium*, 27.2 *ground*, 38.1 *soccer*, 545.1 *record*
scoreboard clock 19.4 *stadium*

score card 29.2 *golfing terms*, 52.67 *calculator*
scored 38.5 *soccer*, 321.4 *furrowed*
scorekeeper 26.8 *karate*, 545.9 *recorder*
score one hundred per cent 619.6 *be perfect*
score out 546.1 *obliterate*
score points against 476.8 *refute*
scorer 23.2 *basketball player*, 27.3 *official*, 49.24 *musician*
scores 181.2 *multitude*
scoresheet 545.1 *record*
score ten out of ten 619.6 *be perfect*
score through 546.1 *obliterate*
scoria 132.2 *residue*, 614.6 *refuse*, 622.4 *dirt*
scoring 19, 38.2 *football play*
scoring a bull's-eye 537.8 *accuracy*
scoring desk 23.3 *basketball equipment*
scorn 850, 854, 495.3 *underestimate*, 498.1 *disbelief*, 498.8 *disbelieve*, 581.3 *exclude*, 612.13 *make unimportant*, 668.6 *be insubordinate*, 766.1 *dissatisfaction*, 766.7 *be dissatisfied*, 807.29 *ridicule*, 820.11 *be hostile*, 850.3 *contempt*, 854.14 *ridicule*
scorned 806.3 *humbled*, 820.10, 822.12 *hated*
scorned person 612.10 *nonentity*
scornful 854, 429.7 *catcalling*, 495.4 *underestimating*, 498.6 *disbelieving*, 766.4 *dissatisfied*, 850.13 *contemptuous*
scornfully 495.6 *pessimistically*, 766.8 *discontentedly*, 850.30 *contemptuously*, 854.18 *disparagingly*
scornfulness 850.3 *contempt*
scorning 850.15 *taunting*
Scorpio 53 Zodiac Constellations
scorplon 82 Arachnids, 82.2 *arachnid*
Scorpion 53 The Constellations
scorpion fish 80 Fishes
scorpion fly 82 Insects
scorpion spider 82 Arachnids
Scorpius 53 The Constellations
scorrevole 49 Musical Terms
Scot 91.11 *Scotland*, 255.9 *British inhabitant*
scot and lot 751.9 *historical taxes*
scotch 157.16 *cease*, 628.5 *hurt*, 661.8 *hinder*
Scotch 351.7 *alcoholic drink*
Scotch broth 45.13 *soup*, 45.44 *British dish*
Scotch mist 55.34 *mist*, 391.2 *mistiness*
Scotch tape 138.3 *adhesive*
Scotch whisky 351.7 *alcoholic drink*
scot-free 638.8 *escaping*, 698.9 *free*, 700.7 *liberated*, 700.8 *free*, 754.11 *free of charge*
scotia 43 Architectural Decoration
Scotland 91
Scotland Yard 16.15 *British police*
scotophobia 777 Phobias by Name
scotopia 435.1 *vision*
Scots 1 Peoples
Scots Dumpy 68 Breeds of Fowl
Scots Grey 68 Breeds of Fowl
Scots Guard 679.12 *ceremonial troops*
Scotsman 91.11 *Scotland*
Scots pine 85 Trees and Shrubs
Scott 48 Writers, **48** Writers
Scotticism 5.26 *dialect*
Scottish 5 Languages and Groups of Languages, **77** Breeds of Dogs
Scottish accent 5.26 *dialect*
Scottish Blackface 68 Breeds of Sheep
Scottish Certificate of Education 485 Educational Qualifications

Scottish Chaucerians 48 Literary Groups and Movements
Scottish Colourists 50 Schools and Groups of Artists
Scottish country dancing 46.1 *dancing*
Scottish Enlightenment 48 Literary Groups and Movements
Scottish Gaelic 5 Languages and Groups of Languages
Scottish Grand Committee 12.4 *governing body*
Scottish hockey 31.7 *hurling*
Scottish Mountaineering Club 34.6 *mountaineering association*
Scottish mountains 95.5 *British mountains*
Scottish National Party 12.6 *political party*, 665.3 *political grouping*
Scottishness 91.11 *Scotland*
Scottish reel 46.4 *historic dancing*
Scottish Six-Days trial 33.1 *motor racing*
Scottish thistle 544.6 *national emblem*
scoundrel 801.2 *disreputable character*, 832.8 *malefactor*, 858.4 *dishonourable person*, 862.6 *evil person*, 864.9 *wicked person*
scour 329.4 *be swift*, 385.12 *rub*, 621.13 *clean*
scoured 54.59 *weathered*, 621.17 *cleaned*
scourer 621.10 *cleaning object*
scourge 607.7 *destroyer*, 618.10 *poverty*, 624.5 *plague*, 631.1 *affliction*, 687.1 *adversity*, 879.3 *hit*, 879.14 *instrument of punishment*
scourge oneself 867.5 *do penance*
scourger 879.17 *punisher*
scourging 879.12 *corporal punishment*
scouring 385.4 *scraping*
scouring out 349.21 *removal*
scouring pad 621.9 *cleaning agent*
scouring powder 621.9 *cleaning agent*
scouring rush 87 Grasses
scourings 132.2 *residue*, 614.6 *refuse*, 622.4 *dirt*
Scouse 255.9 *British inhabitant*
scout 154.8 *precursor*, 208.4 *early comer*, 435.11 *observer*, 435.14 *inspect*, 496.12 *discoverer*, 581.3 *exclude*, 636.4 *warner*, 679.31 *military aircraft*
scout ahead 208.8 *precede*
scout car 71 Motor Vehicles
scout's honour 535.26 *as God is my witness*
scout signs 543.1 *sign*
scout the territory 594.1 *prepare*
scow 74 Ships and Boats, **74** Sailing Ships and Boats
scowl 309.2 *facial distortion*, 309.10 *make faces*, 435.6, 435.13 *look*, 543.3, 543.11 *gesture*, 785.4 *sign of dislike*, 818.3 *act of discourtesy*, 818.8 *get angry*, 828.6 *sign of anger*, 828.11 *be angry*, 829.2 *sign of irascibility*, 829.7 *frown*, 830.4 *sign of irritableness*, 830.11 *be irritable*, 852.10 *disapproving look*, 852.23 *show disapproval*
scowling 829.5 *showing irascibility*, 830.7 *irritable*
Scrabble 42 Board Games
scrabble up 359.14 *climb*
scrag end 45.26 *lamb*, 132.1 *remainder*, 157.8 *tail*
scragginess 260.1 *littleness*, 274.7 *thinness*
scraggliness 375.6 *roughness*
scraggly 375.2 *coarse*
scraggy 260.7 *little*, 274.1 *thin*, 375.2 *coarse*, 609.3 *underfed*
scram 345.4 *hurry off*, 345.15 *go*, 389.3 *go away*, 591.9 *play truant*, 591.24 *hands off*
scramble 33.9 *race*, 33.10 *be on the track*, 34.9 *mountaineer*, 45.55 *cook*, 113.8 *be diverse*,

133.1 *mixture*, 133.9 *mix up*, 151.21 *disorder*, 324.12 *gait*, 359.14 *climb*, 523.8 *make unintelligible*, 642.3 *nimbleness*, 642.12 *be active*, 648.4 *haste*, 674.6 *fight*

scrambled 45.56 *culinary*, 133.12 *mixed*, 133.13 *mixed-up*, 151.18 *muddled*, 482.3 *indiscriminate*, 523.1 *unintelligible*, 524.15 *interpreted*, 659.12 *problematic*

scrambled pork brains 45.43 *US dish*

scrambler 133.6 *mixer*

scrambling 33.5 *motorcycle racing*, 33.6 *motor racing terms*, 34.3 *climbing technique*, 34.8 *mountaineering*, 45.8 *cooking technique*

scrap 143.7 *piece*, 157.16 *cease*, 173.3 *fragment*, 260.3 *little piece*, 349.13 *throw away*, 473.1 *argument*, 500.1 *dissent*, 581.2 *discard*, 598.1 *relinquish*, 600.6 *stop using*, 614.6 *refuse*, 666.2 *argument*, 666.6 *argue*, 674.12 *fight*, 676.9 *battle*, 727.9 *dispose of*, 764.8, 764.11 *quarrel*

scrapbook 511.4 *reminder*, 545.6 *record book*, 562.3 *compendium*

scrape 50.22 *engrave*, 129.5 *make smaller*, 267.4 *meet*, 278.6 *be shallow*, 330.12 *collision*, 380.16 *use a sharp tool*, 384.26 *grate*, 385.4 *scraping*, 385.13 *abrade*, 406.3 *injury*, 406.11 *inflict pain*, 430.2 *hoarseness*, 430.5 *sound hoarse*, 434.10 *lack harmony*, 506.3 *tomfoolery*, 621.13 *clean*, 659.5 *predicament*, 694.6 *show obeisance to*, 756.6 *save*, 806.21 *humble oneself*, 849.4 *mark of respect*

scrape and save 747.11 *be parsimonious*

scrape by 685.5 *not complete*

scraped 406.6 *injured*

scrape home 682.9 *be victorious*

scrape off 296.15 *make nude*

scrape one's feet 543.11 *gesture*

scraper 63.29 *construction equipment*, 380.9 *sharp-edged thing*, 385.7 *eraser*

scrape through 620.9 *be imperfect*, 638.5 *escape*, 671.28 *survive*, 682.9 *be victorious*

scrape together 721.11 *acquire*

scrapie 624.18 *veterinary disease*

scraping 385, 430.8 *hoarse*, 434.7 *dissonant*, 808.7 *sycophantic*

scraping by 609.2 *unprovided*

scrapings 132.2 *residue*

scrapped 157.22 *cancelled*, 598.5 *relinquished*, 600.4 *disused*

scrapper 674.10 *contender*

scrappily 143.12 *partly*, 145.6 *incompletely*

scrappiness 145.1 *incompleteness*, 685.1 *noncompletion*

scrapping 473.7 *arguing*, 600.10 *disuse*, 727.1 *disposal*

scrappy 143.11 *partial*, 145.4 *incomplete*, 160.8 *discontinuous*, 685.4 *uncompleted*

scraps 132.2 *residue*, 607.5 *waste product*, 614.6 *refuse*

scrap with 674.12 *fight*

scrapyard 727.5 *wasteyard*

scratch 24.2 *billiards play*, 24.6 *pool*, 32.7 *horseracing*, 127.14 *poor*, 157.16 *cease*, 278.4 *shallow thing*, 321.1, 321.6 *furrow*, 380.16 *use a sharp tool*, 385.4 *scraping*, 385.13 *abrade*, 406.3 *injury*, 406.11 *inflict pain*, 424.1 *faintness*, 430.2 *hoarseness*, 430.5 *sound hoarse*, 521.7 *mean nothing*, 595.4 *untrained*, 598.2 *withdraw*, 612.8 *trifle*, 618.14 *ill-treat*, 620.2 *incomplete*, 620.7 *defect*, 656.2 *unskilled*, 674.12 *fight*

scratch a living 743.12 *be poor*

scratch each other's back 223.5 *exchange*

scratched 321.4 *furrowed*, 620.11 *imperfect*

scratchiness 375.6 *roughness*

scratching 385.4 *scraping*

scratch line 21.2 *field events*

scratch out 244.8 *destroy*, 546.1 *obliterate*

scratchpad 6.14 *school book*, 50.11 *artist's materials*, 65.6 *memory*

scratch pad 545.6 *record book*

scratch player 29.6 *golfer*

scratch the surface 278.6 *be shallow*

scratch through 546.1 *obliterate*

scratchy 375.3 *barbed*, 430.8 *hoarse*

scrawl 521.1 *lack of meaning*, 523.7 *be unintelligible*, 523.8 *make unintelligible*, 523.12 *unintelligible thing*

scrawly 523.1 *unintelligible*

scrawniness 260.1 *littleness*, 274.7 *thinness*

scrawny 260.7 *little*, 274.1 *thin*

scream 55.58 *blow*, 406.12 *express pain*, 423.2 *outcry*, 423.8 *be loud*, 430.3 *shrillness*, 430.6 *be shrill*, 431.1 *cry*, 431.6 *cry of pain*, 431.10 *cry out*, 506.2 *solecism*, 532.14 *proclaim*, 564.12 *speak loudly*, 633.6 *danger signal*, 636.7 *raise the alarm*

screamer 78 *Birds*, 504.10 *blunder*, 532.3 *journalism*

screaming 423.2 *outcry*, 423.6 *loud*, 431.16 *vociferous*, 444.12 *gaudy*, 811.21 *blatant*

screamingly 811.37 *blantantly*

scream therapy 61.3 *psychiatric treatment*

scree 326.10 *transferred thing*

screech 55.58 *blow*, 406.12 *express pain*, 430.3 *shrillness*, 430.6 *be shrill*, 431.1 *cry*, 432.2 *bird song*, 432.5 *sing*, 564.12 *speak loudly*

screech owl 78 *Birds*, 78.5 *bird of prey*

screed 561.1 *dissertation*, 567.1 *address*

screen 23.4 *playing terms*, 23.6 *play basketball*, 31.9 *play hockey*, 44.11 *make ceramics*, 60.19 *practise medicine*, 66.12 *development*, 66.14 *cine film*, 136.6 *boundary*, 147.3 *exclusion zone*, 152.15 *categorize*, 293.12 *protective covering*, 293.15 *shelter*, 293.30 *protect*, 322.6 *porous thing*, 322.21 *provide passage for*, 436.6 *blinder*, 436.15 *blind*, 438.6 *that which makes invisible*, 438.8 *make invisible*, 443.7 *opaque thing*, 443.11 *make opaque*, 457.14 *present*, 526.2 *display something*, 531.3 *covering up*, 531.8 *conceal*, 534.22 *television set*, 621.10 *cleaning object*, 632.2 *protection*, 632.9 *protect*, 634.2 *shelter*, 671.2 *safeguard*, 671.19 *buffer*

screened 31.8 *hockey*, 44.10 *ceramic*, 152.24 *categorized*, 293.17 *protected*, 438.3 *private*, 527.2, 531.14 *concealed*, 632.5 *safe*, 816.11 *secluded*

screen idol 340.6 *charmer*

screening 23.4 *playing terms*, 31.3 *ice hockey*, 31.8 *hockey*, 44.5 *ceramic process*, 44.10 *ceramic*, 60.7 *diagnosis*, 152.5 *categorization*, 293.1 *covering*, 440.9 *darkening*, 531.3 *covering up*

screening test 60.7 *diagnosis*

screen off 136.11 *divide*, 147.7 *exclude*

screen pass 19.9 *play*

screenplay 51.2 *play*

screen print 67.3 *fabric*

screen printing 50.1 *art*, 67.7 *dyeing*

screenwriter 48.14 *author*, 51.24 *dramatist*

screw 24.2 *billiards play*, 32.1 *horse*, 47.17 *carpenter*, 63.6 *simple machine*, 135.5 *joint*, 135.10 *link*, 135.11 *make love*, 137.8 *fastening*, 137.11 *connect*, 245.14 *have sex*, 323.5 *person who closes*, 335.6 *distort*, 338.11 *propeller*, 364.6 *rotator*, 364.9 *roll*, 539.30 *be fraudulent*, 603.1 *tool*, 603.9 *use tools*, 699.6 *law-maker*, 702.6 *prison officer*, 753.10 *overcharge*, 821.29 *make love*

screw around 877.17 *be sexually immoral*

screw around with 628.4 *impair*

screwball 22.4 *pitching terms*, 168.10 *eccentric*, 510.7 *insane person*

screw down 718.14 *make fast*

screwdriver 351.8 *mixed drink*, 355.10 *excavator*, 603.1 *tool*

screwed 135.14 *conjunctive*, 137.15 *connected*

screwed up 656.4 *bungled*

screwed-up 151.19 *mixed-up*, 614.1 *useless*

screw factory 510.8 *mental hospital*

screwgate 34.4 *climbing equipment*

screwing 135.4 *sexual union*, 821.5 *desire*

screwing around 877.3 *sexual immorality*

screw loose 145.2 *omission*, 153.6 *derangement*, 510.1 *insanity*

screw one's courage to the sticking place 778.15 *be courageous*

screw pine 85 *Trees and Shrubs*

screw propeller 338.11 *propeller*

screwthread 314.2 *coil*

screw up 135.10 *link*, 151.23 *confuse*, 504.19 *make a mistake*, 594.4 *prepare for action*, 601.1 *misuse*, 628.4 *impair*, 656.7 *be clumsy*

screw-up 151.6 *mix-up*, 504.10 *blunder*, 661.2 *obstacle*

screw up one's courage 237.8 *strengthen*, 778.16 *take courage*

screw up one's eyes 436.14 *be blind*

screwworm 82 *Insects*, 82.3 *pest*, 82.5 *larva*

screwy 510.7 *insane*

scribble 50.9 *drawing*, 521.1 *lack of meaning*, 521.7 *mean nothing*, 523.7 *be unintelligible*, 523.8 *make unintelligible*, 523.12 *unintelligible thing*, 560.14 *describe*

scribbled 523.1 *unintelligible*

scribbled out 546.6 *obliterated*

scribble out 546.1 *obliterate*, 704.6 *cancel*

scribbler 560.10 *descriptive writer*, 656.10 *unskilled person*

scribbling 521.1 *lack of meaning*

scribe 7.8 *priest*, 48.14 *author*, 192.13 *chronicler*, 545.9 *recorder*

scrim 67 *Natural Fabrics*, 51.17 *stage set*, 442.8 *transparent thing*

scrimmage 473.1, 666.2 *argument*, 674.6, 674.12 *fight*

scrimp 685.5 *not complete*, 747.11 *be parsimonious*, 756.6 *save*, 758.7 *hoard*

scrimper 756.3 *saver*

scrimping 758.1 *mean*

scrimpy 756.4 *thrifty*

scrimshank 591.5 *shirk*

scrimshanker 591.17 *avoider*

scrimshaw 50.12 *sculpture*

scrip 741.14 *paper money*

scrip certificate 741.14 *paper money*

script 51.2 *play*, 51.36 *dramatize*

scripted 51.37 *dramatic*

scriptural 7.18 *theological*

scripture 7.12 *religious text*, 7.13 *theology*

script writer 51.24 *dramatist*, 560.10 *descriptive writer*

script writing 51.7 *dramaturgy*

scrobis 10.14 *sacred object*

scrofulous 877.12 *indecent*

scroll 43 *Architectural Decoration*, 3.11 *relic*, 65.19 *abort*, 171.6 *list of names*, 364.9 *roll*

scrolled 43.17 *structured*

scrolling 43 *Architectural Decoration*

scroll leg 47.3 *chair leg*

scrollwork 792.2 *pattern*

scroll worker 792.7 *decorator*

scrooch down 362.8 *sit*

scrooge 754.8 *bargain hunter*

Scrooge 161.36 *hoarder*, 469.6 *careful person*, 758.5 *miser*

scrotal 245.16 *reproductive*

scrotomy 60 *Surgical Operations*

scrotum 245.8 *organs of reproduction*

scrounge 712.8 *solicit money*, 733.7 *borrow*, 734.7 *take*, 736.12 *steal*

scrounger 643.8 *nonworker*, 712.5 *beggar*, 736.8 *thief*

scrounging 712.3 *solicitation*, 712.11 *begging*, 734.1 *taking*, 736.1 *stealing*, 736.18 *fraudulent*

scrub 83.1 *plants*, 385.4 *scraping*, 385.12 *rub*, 458.3 *cause to disappear*, 546.1 *obliterate*, 621.13 *clean*, 644.4 *exertion*, 644.6 *work*, 707.2 *alternative*

scrubbed 134.14 *purified*, 621.17 *cleaned*

scrubber 621.12 *cleaner*

scrubbiness 260.1 *littleness*

scrubbing 385.4 *scraping*, 621.2 *cleaning*

scrubbing brush 375.7 *rough thing*, 621.10 *cleaning object*

scrub bird 78 *Birds*

scrubby 69.17 *botanical*, 260.7 *little*

scrubmite 82 *Arachnids*

scrub out 704.6 *cancel*

scruffily 743.16 *meanly*

scruffiness 151.3 *untidiness*, 618.10 *poverty*, 622.2 *uncleanness*, 743.7 *beggary*, 754.3 *shoddiness*

scruffy 151.15 *untidy*, 612.2 *obscure*, 618.4 *poor*, 622.8 *unclean*, 743.3 *beggarly*, 754.10 *shoddy*

scrum 161, 35.3 *rugby play*, 674.6 *fight*

scrum half 35.4 *rugby player*

scrummage 161.21 *scrum*, 674.6 *fight*

scrumping 736.1 *stealing*

scrumptious 350.27 *edible*, 405.6 *pleasant*, 411.7 *tasty*, 617.1 *worthy*

scrumptiously 411.11 *tastily*

scrunch 350.21 *eat*, 384.27 *beat*, 430.5 *sound hoarse*

scrungy 618.4 *poor*

scruple 75 *General Units*, 369.9 *avoirdupois weight*, 498.1 *disbelief*, 573.13 *dissociation*

scruples 469.3 *circumspection*, 857.1 *probity*, 867.1 *penitence*, 876.1 *morality*

scrupulous 469.9 *careful*, 503.5 *accurate*, 619.2 *perfectionist*, 719.7 *observant*, 813.6 *formal*, 847.8 *dutiful*, 857.4 *honourable*, 876.8 *moral*

scrupulously 719.8 *observantly*, 857.7 *honourably*

scrupulousness 312.8 *directness*, 469.3 *circumspection*, 503.1 *accuracy*, 813.2 *formalism*, 857.1 *probity*

scrutability 522.9 *intelligibility*

scrutable 522.1 *intelligible*

scrutator 435.11 *observer*

scrutineer 435.11 *observer*, 477.5 *questioner*

scrutinize 467, 4.20 *philosophize*, 435.14 *inspect*, 477.17 *question*

scrutinized 477.16 *questioned*

scrutinizer 435.11 *observer*

scrutinizing 467.7 *watchful*

scrutiny 4.4 *philosophical investigution*, 435.3 *observation*, 467.3 *carefulness*, 477.2 *questioning*

scry 435.17 *imagine*

scrying 435.5 *imagination*

scuba-dive 39.10 *dive*

scuba-diver 39.4 *swimmer*

scuba diving 18 Sporting Activities, 39.1 *swimming*

scubbin 68.10 *farm tool*

scud 55.12 *wind*, 55.18, 55.60 *cloud*, 74.9 *navigate*

Scud 338.8 *missile*, 680.5 *missile weapon*

Scudamore 18 Sporting Personalities

scuff 328.1 *move slowly*, 385.4 *scraping*, 385.13 *abrade*

scuffing 385.4 *scraping*

scuffle 153.5 *commotion*, 473.1 *argument*, 473.12 *argue*, 674.6, 674.12 *fight*, 764.8 *quarrel*

scuffling 473.7 *arguing*

scuffs 295.1 *footwear*

scull 74 Ships and Boats, 36.4, 36.11 *rowing*, 36.16 *row*

sculler 36.9 *sailor*, 74.8 *boatman*

scullery 256.7 *room*

sculling 18 Sporting Activities, 36.4 *rowing*

scullion 621.12 *cleaner*

scull racing 36.4 *rowing*

sculls 36.4 *rowing*

sculpin 80 Fishes

sculpt 50, 243.10 *produce*, 306.7 *form*, 547.11 *paint*, 796.8 *fashion*

sculpted 50

sculptor 50, 243.9 *producer*, 547.4 *person who makes a representation*

Sculptor 53 The Constellations, 53 The Constellations

sculptor's materials 50

sculptor's tools 220.4 *medium of conversion*

sculptor's wax 50.14 *sculptor's materials*

sculptress 547.4 *person who makes a representation*

sculptural 50

sculpturally 50.30 *pictorially*

sculpture 50, 50.1 *art*, 243.1 *production*, 547.6 *image*

sculptured 50.28 *sculpted*, 306.9 *formed*

sculpturing 50.12 *sculpture*

sculpt wood 47.18 *work wood*

scum 127.6 *inferior*, 132.2 *residue*, 134.10 *purify*, 266.3 *coat*, 612.10 *nonentity*, 614.6 *refuse*, 621.15 *purify*, 622.4 *dirt*, 795.6 *vulgar herd*

scumble 50.19 *paint*

scumbling 50.4 *treatment*

scummy 266.9 *platelike*, 622.7 *dirty*, 754.10 *shoddy*

scum of the earth 612.10 *nonentity*, 864.9 *wicked person*

scup 80 Fishes

scupper 74 Parts of a Ship, 244.11 *ruin*, 487.8 *make impossible*

scurf 132.2 *residue*, 266.4 *slice*, 384.6 *crumb*, 622.4 *dirt*

scurfy 266.9 *platelike*, 384.20 *crumbly*, 622.8 *unclean*

scurrility 827.1 *curse*, 827.3 *vilification*, 850.1 *disrespect*, 854.5 *scorn*

scurrilous 827.8 *cursing*, 850.1 *disrespectful*, 854.16 *defamatory*

scurrilously 827.12 *swearingly*

scurry 329.4 *be swift*, 642.12 *be active*, 648.2 *make haste*, 648.4 *haste*

scurrying 324.16 *moving*

S-curve 311.2 *bend*

scurvy 58.14 *vitamin deficiency disease*, 350.10 *scarcity*, 609.3 *underfed*, 624.4 *disease*

scutage 751.9 *historical taxes*

scutch 87 Grasses

scute 293.14 *animal covering*

scuttle 258.11 *vessel*, 329.4 *be swift*, 346.6 *means of entry* ,

362.3 *bring down*, 648.2 *make haste*, 779.4 *be a coward*

scuttlebutt 528.7 *advice*

scutum 671.7 *armour*

Scutum 53 The Constellations

Scyphozoa 81.7 *coelenterate*

scyphozoan 81.7, 81.21 *coelenterate*

scythe 68.10 *farm tool*, 87.5 *grass-cutter*, 87.12 *manage grassland*, 380.9 *sharp-edged thing*, 380.16 *use a sharp tool*, 603.2 *garden tool*

Scythian 5 Languages and Groups of Languages

sea 777 Phobias by Topic, **97**, 53.17 *moon*, 74.11 *nautical*, 97.7 *oceanic*, 454.6 *blue thing*

sea air 390.5 *open air*, 418.2 *fragrant thing*, 625.2 *salubrity*

sea angler 20.6 *angler*

sea area 55.4 *weather forecast*

sea attack 670.12 *military attack*

sea bass 80 Fishes

sea battles 676.8 *warfare*

sea bed 97.1 *sea*

sea-bed 277.4 *deep thing*, 280.1 *base*

Seabee 69.27 *naval man*

seabird 78.3 *water bird*

sea biscuit 81.3 *echinoderm*

seaboard 98.4 *coast*

sea bombardment 676.8 *warfare*

Seaborg 52 Scientists

seaborne 74.11 *nautical*

sea bottom 97.1 *sea*

sea-bottom 277.4 *deep thing*

sea bream 80 Fishes

sea breeze 36.1 *sailing*, 55.12 *wind*

sea butterfly 81 Molluscs

sea cadet 74.7 *nautical person*

sea change 216.1 *change*, 627.5 *improvement*

sea cliff 98.4 *coast*

sea cow 77 Placental Mammals

sea cucumber 81.3 *echinoderm*

sea dog 74.7 *nautical person*, 655.5 *expert*

sea duck 78.3 *water bird*

sea eagle 78 Birds

sea elephant 77 Placental Mammals

seafarer 74.7 *nautical person*

seafaring 74.1 *water travel*, 74.11 *nautical*, 97.7 *oceanic*

seafaring man 74.7 *nautical person*

sea fight 676.9 *battle*

sea fish 95, 80.1 *fishes*

sea fishing 18 Sporting Activities, 80.7 *fishing*, 590.2 *chase*

seafloor 54.16 *ocean floor*

sea-floor 277.4 *deep thing*, 280.1 *base*

seafloor spreading 54.19 *plate tectonics*

sea fog 55.33 *fog*

seafood 45.19 *shellfish*, 81.4 *arthropod*

seafront 303.1 *front*, 327.7 *arcade*

Sea Goat 53 The Constellations

sea god 97, 74.7 *nautical person*

sea-going 74.11 *nautical*, 97.7 *oceanic*

sea-green 453.1 *green*

seagull 78 Birds, 78.3 *water bird*

sea hare 81 Molluscs

sea horse 80 Fishes

sea ice 54.39 *iceberg*

sea kale 45 Vegetables

sea king 74.7 *nautical person*

seal 77 Placental Mammals, 44.4 *porcelain mark*, 44.11 *make ceramics*, 76.5 *aquatic animal*, 110.4 *duplicate*, 116.28 *consent*, 165.3 *characteristic*, 323.2 *stopper*, 323.7 *close*, 480.6 *evidence*, 529.12 *keep secret*, 544.3 *means of identification*, 544.10 *identify*, 567.10 *send*, 574.7 *resolve*, 629.1 *re pair*, 667.2, 667.7 *contract*, 708.2 *permit*, 715.1, 715.5 *contract*, 718.2, 718.11 *promise*

sea lace 90 Algae

sea ladder 74 Parts of a Ship

sea lane 74.2 *waterway*, 97.1 *sea*, 327.2 *route*, 327.6 *path*, 356.2 *passing along*

sea lavender 84 Flowers and Flowering Plants

sealed 116.17 *consenting*, 323.12 *closed*, 499.7 *agreed*, 529.9 *secret*, 667.11 *contractual*

sealed book 11.2 *the occult*

sealed lips 527.10 *quietness*

sealed off 626.5 *unhygienic*

sealed orders 529.1 *secrecy*

sea lemon 81 Molluscs

sealer 74 Ships and Boats

sea lettuce 90 Algae

sea level 54.12 *ocean*, 276.2 *lowland*, 280.1 *base*, 282.2 *horizontal surface*

sea lily 81.3 *echinoderm*

sealing off 323.1 *closure*

sealing wax 138.3 *adhesive*

sea lion 77 Placental Mammals

seal-like 77.29 *cetacean*

sea loch 94.1 *lake*

seal of approval 499.2 *yes*, 851.1 *approval*

seal off 323.7 *close*

seal of the confessional 529.1 *secrecy*

Sea Lord 74.7 *nautical person*

seal-point 449.5 *brown thing*

seal-pointed Siamese 77 Breeds of Cats

seals 161 Collective Names by Animal

seal up 135.10 *link*, 531.8 *conceal*

Sealyham terrier 77 Breeds of Dogs

seam 27.7 *bat*, 27.18 *bowl*, 135.5 *joint*, 135.10 *link*, 266.1 *layer*, 295.35 *make clothing*, 321.1, 321.6 *furrow*, 407.6 *contiguity*, 605.2 *resource*

sea mail 534.2 *postal communication*

seaman 74.7 *nautical person*, 676.11 *recruit*, 679.27 *naval man*

seaman-like 74.11 *nautical*

seamanship 74.5 *navigation*, 652.9 *tactics*, 676.6 *art of war*

sea mark 74.5 *navigation*, 543.5 *indicator*

seam bowler 27.4 *team*

seamed 135.12 *united*, 321.5 *wrinkly*

seamed stockings 295.20 *legwear*

seamer 27.4 *team*, 27.8 *delivery*

sea mile 75 General Units

sea mist 441.2 *murk*

seamless 159.11 *continuous*

seamless stockings 295.20 *legwear*

seamount 54.16 *ocean floor*

sea mouse 81 Worms

seamstress 135.7 *joiner*, 295.26 *fashion designer*, 629.12 *repairer*

Seanad Éireann 12.4 *governing body*, 653.10 *legislative body*

seance 11.10 *psychic phenomenon*, 526.10 *manifestation*

sea nymph 81.8 *deity*, 97.4 *sea god*

sea of 181.4 *throng*

sea of flames 408.6 *fire*

sea operations 676.8 *warfare*

sea otter 77 Placental Mammals, 80.11 *fishing animal*

sea path 327.2 *route*, 327.6 *path*

sea perch 80 Fishes

seaplane 73 Types of Aircraft

sea power 679.22 *navy*

sear 262.5 *make smaller*, 262.7 *smaller*, 406.10 *be painful*, 408.15 *burn*

sea raiding 676.8 *warfare*

search 4.4 *philosophical investigation*, 4.20 *philosophize*, 477.2 *questioning*, 477.17 *question*, 496.7 *detection*, 590.1 *pursuit*, 597.2 *undertaking*

searcher 4.10 *philosopher*, 590.5 *pursuer*, 596.7 *attempter*

search for 465.7 *be curious*, 590.8 *pursue*

search for the end of the rainbow

614.9 *waste effort*

searching 477.12 *questioning*, 590.15 *pursuing*, 596.9 *tentative*

searchingly 477.23 *questioningly*

searchlight 439.6 *electric light*

search me 502.13 *who knows?*

search one's soul 867.4 *be penitent*

search out 477.17 *question*

search party member 590.5 *pursuer*

search warrant 16.6 *legal process*, 692.2 *demand*

seared 262.7 *smaller*

seared conscience 868.1 *impenitence*

searing 262.1 *contraction*, 262.8 *contracting*, 392.13 *drying*, 406.5 *painful*, 408.9 *hot*

Searle's bar 56 Named Laws

sea robin 80 Fishes

sea room 248.6 *available space*

sea rover 74.7 *nautical person*

Sears Tower 43 Noted Buildings

Seas 97

sea salt 45.7 *basic ingredient*, 413.2 *seasoning*

seascape 50.10 *art subject*, 435.7 *view*

sea scout 74.7 *nautical person*

sea serpent 97.4 *sea god*

seashore 98.4 *coast*

seasick 74.11 *nautical*, 349.30 *vomiting*

seaside 54.11, 98.4 *coast*, 300.1 *edge*, 300.8 *edging*

sea slug 81 Molluscs

sea snake 79 Reptiles

season 203, 203, 403, 413, 45.55 *cook*, 130.6 *add*, 133.8 *mix*, 185.4 *term*, 187.5 *recurrent period*, 584.18 *habituate*, 594.7 *develop*, 637.5 *preserve*

Season 203

seasonable 203, 210.6 *timely*, 615.1 *convenient*

seasonably 210.9 *opportunely*

seasonal 55, 203, 187.8 *periodical*, 214.12 *cyclic*, 532.5 *journal*

seasonally 203, 214.16 *cyclically*

seasoned 203, 413.9 *piquant*, 584.14 *habituated*, 594.20 *developed*, 655.8 *expert*, 684.7 *completed*

seasoning 413, 45.7 *basic ingredient*, 130.3 *additional item*, 133.4 *admixture*, 411.4 *flavour*, 584.7 *habituation*, 594.13 *development*

season of the year 203.1 *season*

season skiing ticket 41.1 *skiing*

seasons of the year 214.5 *regular thing*

season ticket 754.4 *bargain*

sea squirt 81.2 *protochordate*

sea star 81.3 *echinoderm*

sea survey 97.5 *oceanography*

sea swivel 20.1 *angling*

seat 36.4 *rowing*, 36.6 *canoeing*, 248.5 *reserved space*, 250.1 *location*, 251.1 *situation*

sea tangle 90 Algae

seat belt 71 Motor Vehicle Parts, 73 Aircraft Parts, 632.4 *safety device*, 637.2 *preserver*

seat connection 63.27 *superstructure*

seated 251.6 *situated*

seating 51.16 *auditorium*, 248.5 *reserved space*

seating capacity 248.5 *reserved space*

SEATO 715.3 *alliance*

seat of feelings 759

seat of government 92.5 *administrative headquarters*, 93.1 *city*, 688.5 *position of authority*

seat of justice 16.18 *tribunal*, 492.3 *place of judgment*

seat of life 396.1 *life*

seat of thought 459.7 *brain*

seat oneself 362.8 *sit*

sea transport 326.5 *means of transport*

sea travel 74.1 *water travel*

sea trip 74.1 *water travel*

sea trout 80 Fishes, 20.4 *Ameri-*

can game fish, 20.5 *British game fish*, 45.17 *freshwater fish*
Seattle 93 *Cities*, 93.2 *American cities*
sea urchin 81.3 *echinoderm*
seawall 63.24 *water system*
sea wall 98.4 *coast*
seawall 64.3 *safety device*
sea wall 661.3 *barrier*
seaward 332.10 *clockwise*
seawards 97.11 *nautically*
seaware 90 *Algae*
seawater 54.12 *ocean*
sea water 97.1 *sea*, 389.1 *water*
seawave 54.14 *wave*
seaway 74.2 *waterway*, 248.6 *available space*
seaweed 45.33 *vegetable*, 83.4 *lower plant*, 90.1 *alga*
seaweed marquetry 47.9 *decorative woodwork*
seaweed meal 68.13 *fertilizer*
seaworthy 70.5 *transportable*, 74.11 *nautical*, 97.7 *oceanic*, 326.17 *transferable*, 619.1 *perfect*, 632.6 *invulnerable*
sea wrack 90 *Algae*
sea zoo 256.12 *stall*
Seb 8 *Deities*
sebaceous 352.4 *secretory*, 352.5 *of a secretion*, 386.10, 395.11 *oily*
sebaceous gland 352 *Exocrine Glands*, 77.2 *mammalian characteristic*
sebaceousness 395.1 *oiliness*
Se-baptism 7 *Christian Movements*
Sebastian 710.7 *martyr*
Sebastopol 68 *Breeds of Fowl*
Sebek 8 *Deities*
sebiferous 352.4 *secretory*
Sebright 68 *Breeds of Fowl*
Sebring 12-hour race 33.3 *sports car race*
sebum 352.2 *secreted substance*, 395.8 *fat*
secant 52.52 *trigonometric function*
secateurs 69.6 *garden tool*, 380.9 *sharp-edged thing*, 603.2 *garden tool*
secede 500.8 *dissent*, 598.2 *withdraw*, 693.16 *be subversive*
seceder 578.9 *equivocator*, 693.11 *rebel*
seceding 500.7 *dissenting*
secern 352.7 *secrete*
secernment 352.1 *secretion*
secession 500.3 *dissentience*, 598.3 *relinquishment*, 693.4 *revolution*
secessionist 500.7 *dissenting*, 578.9 *equivocator*, 693.11 *rebel*
seclude 136.11 *divide*, 147.7 *exclude*, 349.4 *ostracize*, 531.8 *conceal*, 816.13 *ignore*
secluded 816, 136.17 *unjoined*, 139.9 *aloof*, 357.15 *out of reach*, 527.2 *concealed*, 529.9 *secret*, 531.14 *concealed*, 698.9 *free*, 816.10 *lonely*
seclude oneself 290.14 *go inside*, 816.12 *be unsocial*
seclusion 136.2 *setting apart*, 139.2 *aloofness*, 147.1 *exclusion*, 174.5 *aloneness*, 290.2 *inside*, 349.19 *ostracism*, 527.8 *concealment*, 531.6 *privacy*, 598.3 *relinquishment*, 632.2 *protection*, 698.1 *freedom*, 816.3 *separation*
seclusionist 168.9 *hermit*, 174.8 *loner*
seclusive 816.8 *unsociable*
seclusiveness 816.1 *unsociability*
second 75 *SI Units*, **75** *General Units*, **176**, 25.3 *bowls player*, 26.4 *boxer*, 49.16 *musical note*, 52.75 *equal*, 116.28 *consent*, 127.6 *inferior*, 176.9 *two*, 176.12 *double*, 185.4 *term*, 187.2 *time period*, 191.3 *instant*, 195.12 *succeeding*, 222.7 *substitute*, 269.8 *measure of time*, 284.14 *give moral support*, 480.1 *verify*, 499.4 *assent*,

535.4 *confirmation*, 535.19 *confirm*, 580.4 *pick*, 620.6 *imperfect item*, 662.11 *helper*, 662.23 *advise*, 667.7 *contract*
secondarily 104.18 *extraneously*, 176.21 *second*, 227.12 *with the effect of*, 612.14 *unimportantly*
secondariness 104.1 *extraneousness*, 127.1 *inferiority*, 612.5 *unimportance*
secondary 612, 19.10 *defence*, 78.17 *plumage*, 104.8 *intruder*, 127.12 *inferior*, 176.9 *two*, 227.10 *caused*
secondary battery 64.29 *power source*
secondary cell 56.43 *electrical conduction*, 64.5 *electrolytic conduction*, 64.29 *power source*
secondary character 54.33 *metamorphic rock*
secondary chord 49.16 *musical note*
secondary clay 44.2 *raw material*
secondary coil 64.22 *transformer*
secondary colour 444.1 *colour*
secondary colours 56.28 *colour*
secondary consumer 59.18 *ecology*
secondary education 6.2 *educational system*
secondary electron 64.24 *electron emission*
secondary emission 64.24 *electron emission*
secondary evidence 483.5 *legal evidence*
secondary growth 624.12 *cancer*
secondary matter 612.8 *trifle*
secondary picketing 15.4 *industrial dispute*
secondary quality 4.9 *philosophical problem*
secondary radar 534.28 *radar*
secondary rainbow 55.27 *rainbow*
secondary road 327.3 *road*
secondary school 6.12 *educational institution*
secondary structure 58.9 *protein*
secondary triads 444.1 *colour*
secondary wave 54.23 *seismic wave*
second banana 771.6 *humorist*
second base 22.1 *baseball*
second-baseman 22.2 *baseball player*
second best 124.6 *mediocrity*, 127.1 *inferiority*, 222.1 *substitution*, 620.6 *imperfect item*, 717.2 *half-measure*
second-best 124.3 *mediocre*, 127.12 *inferior*, 515.11 *disappointing*, 620.1 *imperfect*, 707.7 *deputizing*, 717.7 *half-measure*
second birth 629.10 *revival*
second bite at the cherry 155.7 *afterthought*
second chance 155.7 *afterthought*, 629.10 *revival*, 835.3 *mercy*
second childhood 207.5 *old age*, 629.10 *revival*
second class 127.1 *inferiority*, 195.3 *subordination*, 620.5 *imperfection*
second-class 124.3 *mediocre*, 127.12 *inferior*, 195.13 *subordinate*, 618.2 *inferior*, 620.1 *imperfect*, 754.9 *cheap*, 803.3 *common*
second-class citizens 803.2 *the common people*
second-class fare 754.4 *bargain*
second-class mail 534.2 *postal communication*
second-class stamp 534.3 *correspondence*
second coming 457.6 *reappearance*
second crop 246.1 *fertility*, 721.6 *yield*
second-degree burn 408.1 *heat*
second-degree murder 398.2 *murder*
second derivative 52.31 *differentiation*
second division 124.6 *medioc-*

rity, 195.3 *subordination*
second-division 124.3 *mediocre*, 195.13 *subordinate*
second early 68.12 *crop*
second echelon 679.14 *armed forces*
seconded 116.17 *consenting*, 480.8 *verifiable*
second edition 110.4 *duplicate*
second eleven 127.1 *inferiority*, 195.3 *subordination*
seconder 284.8 *supporter*, 499.3 *assenter*, 535.9 *affirmer*
second fiddle 127.1 *inferiority*, 195.7 *subordinate*, 612.10 *non-entity*
second finger 407.7 *sense organ*
second gallery 40.5 *real tennis*
second-generation 227.10 *caused*
second guard 28.3 *fencing movements*
second hand 543.5 *indicator*
second-hand 599.9 *used*
second-hand clothes 295.1 *dress*, 296.4 *dishabille*, 599.7 *reused product*
second-hand sale 739.4 *sale*
second-hand shop 754.7 *discounter*
second helping 183.5 *repeat*, 350.14 *mouthful*
second honeymoon 629.10 *revival*
second house 51.11 *theatrical performance*
second husband 823.10 *married man*
second-in-command 707.1 *deputy*
seconding 662.9 *patronage*
second law 56.38 *thermodynamics*
second lieutenant 679.17 *army person*
Second Lieutenant 17 *British Military Ranks*, **17** *US Military Ranks*
second line 662.11 *helper*
secondly 176.21 *second*, 195.15 *as follows*
second marriage 823.3 *types of marriage*
second mortgage 744.1 *credit*, 745.3 *loan*
second name 560.8 *name*
second nature 584.1 *habit*
second opinion 492.1 *judgment*
second-opinion 60.6 *health care*
second-order 57.38 *reactive*
second place 195.3 *subordination*
second printing 110.4 *duplicate*
second prize 878.2 *prize*
second rank 127.1 *inferiority*
second rate 620.5 *imperfection*
second-rate 124.3 *mediocre*, 127.12 *inferior*, 515.11 *disappointing*, 612.4 *trivial*, 618.2 *inferior*, 620.1 *imperfect*, 754.10 *shoddy*
second-ratedness 754.3 *shoddiness*
second-rater 124.7 *average person*, 127.6 *inferior*, 683.5 *failing person*
second row 35.4 *rugby player*
second-row forward 35.4 *rugby player*
seconds 127.7 *inferior thing*, 295.1 *dress*, 350.14 *mouthful*, 754.4 *bargain*
second self 114.5 *counterpart*
second sex 402.1 *female sex*
second showing 457.6 *reappearance*
second sight 11.8 *psychic power*, 199.4 *looking to the future*, 403.11 *sensation*, 435.5 *imagination*, 464.2 *precognition*, 516.3 *foresight*
second-sighted 464.7 *precognitive*, 516.6 *foreseeing*
second slip 27.4 *team*
seconds out 674.9 *duel*
second spring 629.10 *revival*
second string 127.1 *inferiority*
second-stringer 127.6 *inferior*
second thought 627.8 *better thing*
second thoughts 155.7 *after-*

thought, 484.2 *reversal*, 578.6 *equivocation*, 781.1 *caution*
second to none 126.17 *supremely*, 617.2 *best*
second try 155.7 *afterthought*
second wife 823.11 *married woman*
second wind 126.3 *advantage*
Second World War 676.1 *war*
second youth 629.10 *revival*
secrecy 529, 11.2 *the occult*, 290.6 *internalization*, 293.15 *shelter*, 438.4 *invisibility*, 523.11 *unintelligibility*, 527.8 *concealment*, 529.7 *esotericism*, 566.4 *taciturnity*, 592.4 *plot*
Secrecy 529
secret 529, 10.9 *prayer*, 11.14 *occult*, 290.12 *internalized*, 293.37 *protected*, 438.3 *private*, 440.11 *benighted*, 502.3 *unknown thing*, 502.8 *unknown*, 523.12 *unintelligible thing*, 527.2 *concealed*, 527.5 *mysterious*, 527.11 *mysteriousness*, 529.1 *secrecy*, 531.15 *disguised*, 611.5 *important*, 657.4 *cunning*, 709.6 *censored*
secret agent 529.2 *secretiveness*
secretaire 47.4 *table*, 258.3 *cabinet*
secretarial college 6.12 *educational institution*
secretariat 16.2 *jurisdiction*, 647.1 *workshop*, 653.3 *management*, 688.5 *position of authority*
secret art 529.7 *esotericism*
secretary 12.8 *politician*, 545.9 *recorder*, 646.1 *worker*, 653.16 *official*, 696.3 *leader*, 697.5 *official assistant*, 701.3 *subordinate*, 707.1 *deputy*
secretary bird 78 *Birds*
secretary-general 653.16 *official*
secretary of state 696.3 *leader*
Secretary of the Treasury 741.18 *treasurer*
secret ballot 580.10 *vote*
secret book 523.12 *unintelligible thing*
secret compartment 531.2 *hiding place*
secret document 527.8 *concealment*, 709.2 *censorship*
secret drawer 293.15 *shelter*, 539.12 *disguise*
secret drinker 874.17 *drunkard*
secrete 352, 347.12 *leak*, 349.14 *let out*, 353.15 *excrete*, 531.8 *conceal*, 605.6 *store*
secreted substance 352
secret enemy 820.5 *hostile person*
secret formula 529.7 *esotericism*
secret garden 816.5 *solitary place*
secretin 58 *Hormones*
secret influence 233.4 *indirect influence*, 592.4 *plot*, 657.1 *cunning*
secret influencer 527.9 *backstage manipulator*
secreting 352.4 *secretory*
secretion 352, 77.2 *physiology*, 347.2 *outflow*, 349.22 *disgorgement*, 352.2 *secreted substance*, 353.1 *excretion*, 387.6 *flow*, 531.1 *concealment*
Secretion 352
secretionary 352.4 *secretory*
secretive 529, 290.12 *internalized*, 352.4 *secretory*, 531.17 *noncommittal*, 566.3 *sparing with words*, 709.6 *censored*, 781.4 *cautious*
secretively 11.25 *occultly*, 290.16 *inwardly*, 709.8 *under censorship*
secretiveness 529, 290.6 *internalization*
secret language 523.12 *unintelligible thing*
secret lore 529.7 *esotericism*
secretly 11.25 *occultly*, 438.9 *invisibly*, 527.15 *latently*, 529.15 *in secret*, 531.18 *privately*, 657.6 *cunningly*
secretly cause 527.13 *hide*
secret meeting 529.1 *secrecy*

secret money 878
secretory 352, 59.22 *physiological*, 349.29 *expulsive*, 353.24 *excretory*
secretory mechanism 352.1 *secretion*
secret panel 531.2 *hiding place*
secret passage 531.2 *hiding place*, 539.12 *disguise*, 638.2 *means of escape*
secret passageway 293.15 *shelter*
secret place 290.2 *inside*, 634.1 *refuge*
secret places 759.8 *seat of feelings*
secret plan 592.4 *plot*
secret plot 642.9 *overactivity*
secret service 529.2 *secretiveness*
Secret Service 632.3 *protector*
Secret Service member 679.2 *defender*
secret sign 543.1 *sign*
secret signal 544.3 *means of identification*
secret society 527.6 *latency*, 529.7 *esotericism*, 665.1 *party*, 693.3 *subversion*
secret surveillance system 438.5 *invisible thing*
secret symbol 543.1 *sign*
secret weapon 611.3 *chief thing*, 680.1 *weapon*
secret word 544.3 *means of identification*
sect 7.1 *religion*, 163.8 *genealogy*, 665.1 *party*
sectarian 7.16 *denominational*, 493.8 *unjust*, 500.5 *dissenter*, 500.7 *dissenting*, 665.6 *political party member*, 665.8 *leagued*, 665.10 *political*, 713.4 *protester*
sectarianism 493.3 *injustice*, 500.3 *dissentience*, 665.4 *partisanship*
section 17.4 *military organization*, 52.41 *geometric figure*, 59.17 *taxonomy*, 60.9 *surgery*, 72.2 *track*, 136.3 *separateness*, 143.2 *particular*, 143.7, 148.2 *piece*, 152.6 *category*, 163.2 *class*, 173.2 *fractional part*, 249.1 *region*, 249.12 *plot*, 257.9 *itemize*, 269.5 *piece*, 457.3 *external appearance*, 510.16 *certify*, 679.16 *army unit*
sectional 143.11 *partial*, 173.5 *fractional*, 249.17 *national*, 665.10 *political*
sectionalism 665.4 *partisanship*
sectionalize 136.11 *divide*, 143.10 *part*
sectionalized 143.11 *partial*
sectionally 92.8 *administratively*, 257.15 *thematically*
Section d'Or 50 Schools and Groups of Artists
sectioned 257.12 *itemized*
sectioning 59.6 *cell biology*
sections 257.5 *divisions*
sector 52.41 *geometric figure*, 52.42 *circle*, 65.17 *computing term*, 143.1 *part*, 148.2 *piece*, 249.1 *region*, 313.4 *parts of a circle*, 676.10 *battleground*
secular 214.13 *anniversary*
secularism 7.13 *theology*
secularist 498.5 *disbeliever*
secularly 214.16 *cyclically*
secure 718, 718, 106.9 *comfortable*, 135.15 *tied*, 137.12 *bind*, 225.7 *make stable*, 225.9 *stable*, 323.7 *close*, 326.14 *bring back*, 355.15 *draw out*, 490.1 *certain*, 490.6 *infallible*, 490.21 *make certain*, 632.5 *safe*, 632.9 *protect*, 671.17 *defend*, 714.8 *guarantee*, 721.9 *gain*, 730.9 *receive*, 765.4 *satisfied*
secure a fail 26.12 *wrestle*
secure a loan 733.7 *borrow*
secure an acquittal 638.5 *escape*
secure a personal loan 733.7 *borrow*
secured 135.15 *tied*, 137.16 *bound*, 323.12 *closed*, 671.30 *defended*, 684.7 *completed*, 714.13 *guaranteeing*, 725.8

propertied, 730.13 *received*, 732.6 *loaned*, 733.11 *borrowed*
secured debt 745.1 *debt*
secured loan 732.2, 733.5 *loan*, 745.3 *loan*
secure exemption 638.5 *escape*
securely 106.18 *comfortably*, 135.18 *inextricably*, 137.17 *in connection with*, 225.12 *stably*, 632.10 *safely*
securement 721.1 *gain*
secureness 225.1 *stability*
secure one's object 682.6 *be successful*
secure one's objective 718
secure position 632.1 *safety*, 718.1 *protection*
secure the basics 602.6 *find means*
secure to 718.14 *make fast*
Securicor 718.4 *security forces*
securing 714.13 *guaranteeing*, 733.11 *borrowed*
securities 725.5 *personal estate*
securities market 740.5 *stock market*
security 16.6 *legal process*, 106.5 *comfortable circumstances*, 326.10 *transferred thing*, 490.17 *infallibility*, 632.1 *safety*, 671.5 *self-defence*, 686.1 *prosperity*, 714.2 *guarantee*, 715.1 *contract*, 775.4 *comfort*, 845.6 *bond*
Security 718
security alarm 636.2 *danger signal*
security blanket 284.6 *moral support*
security camera 66.16 *camera*
security check 632.2 *protection*
security clearance 708.1 *permission*
Security Council 653.7 *council*
security forces 718, 632.3 *protector*
security guard 632.3 *protector*, 636.4 *warner*, 671.14 *guard*
security man 435.11 *observer*, 632.3 *protector*, 636.4 *warner*
security officer 718, 16.17 *police officer*
security pass 483.6 *documentation*
security risk 539.20 *plotter*
security system 632.2, 718.1 *protection*
sedan 71 Motor Vehicles, 71.6 *litter*
sedani 45 Types of Pasta
sedanini 45 Types of Pasta
sedate 60.20 *practise surgery*, 242.4 *moderate*, 643.14 *make inactive*, 767.9 *relieve*, 772.1 *solemn*, 805.19 *stately*, 813.6 *formal*
sedated 643.4 *not awake*, 767.7 *relieved*
sedately 805.33 *with dignity*
sedateness 242.1 *moderation*, 805.6 *majesty*, 813.1 *formality*
sedation 60.9 *surgery*, 242.1 *moderation*, 767.1 *ease*
sedative 62, 62.4 *drug type*, 242.2 *moderator*, 242.8 *moderating*, 630.4 *antidote*, 630.8 *drug*, 631.11 *intoxicant*, 643.10 *soporific*, 767.3 *reliever*, 767.8 *relieving*
sedentary 325, 362, 325.4 *motionless*, 643.1 *inactive*
sedentary person 325
sedge 87 Grasses, 87.1 *grass*
sedge family 83.3 *seed plant*
sedgy 87.9 *grassy*
sediment 54, 132.2 *residue*, 161.26 *mass*, 326.10 *transferred thing*, 371.4 *solid body*, 393.13 *mud*, 622.4 *dirt*
sedimentary 54.56 *petrographic*, 132.9 *remaining*, 393.17 *muddy*
sedimentary rock 54, 54.28 *rock*
sedimentation 54, 54.29 *petrogenesis*, 54.35 *weathering*, 131.1 *subtraction*, 371.2 *concentration*, 622.4 *dirt*
sedition 16.41 *lawlessness*,

500.3 *dissentience*, 642.5 *activism*, 689.1 *anarchy*, 693.3 *subversion*, 693.4 *revolution*, 713.2 *disorder*, 858.2 *faithlessness*
seditionary 689.3 *anarchist*, 693.10 *seditionist*
seditionist 693, 713, 586.14 *motivator*
seditious 16.61 *lawless*, 500.7 *dissenting*, 689.6 *anarchic*, 693.14 *subversive*, 713.10 *law-breaking*, 858.6 *faithless*
seditiously 689.8 *anarchically*, 693.18 *subversively*, 713.11 *disapprovingly*, 858.11 *dishonourably*
seditiousness 693.3 *subversion*
Sedna 8 Deities
seduce 877, 228.10 *manipulate*, 340.12 *lure*, 586.16 *tempt*, 864.17 *make wicked*
seduced 228.12 *motivated*, 877.13 *unchaste*
seducer 228.7 *motivator*, 340.6 *charmer*, 405.3 *pleasure-seeker*, 539.15 *deceiver*, 540.15 *false person*, 586.13 *tempter*, 821.9 *lover*, 826.5 *courting person*
seduction 228.2 *inducement*, 340.4 *allurement*, 586.3 *incentive*, 821.8 *love affair*, 877.3 *sexual immorality*
seductive 233.12 *appealing*, 340.9 *attractive*, 405.6 *pleasant*, 782.11 *lustful*, 821.20 *amorous*, 821.22 *lovable*
seductively 228.14, 233.14 *influentially*, 340.14 *attractively*, 782.20 *lustfully*, 821.30, 821.30 *lovingly*
seductiveness 228.2 *inducement*, 340.4 *allurement*, 586.3 *incentive*
seductress 228.7 *motivator*, 340.6 *charmer*, 405.3 *pleasure-seeker*, 586.13 *tempter*
sedulity 575.2 *commitment*, 642.8 *assiduity*
sedulous 467.8 *diligent*, 575.10 *persevering*, 642.20 *industrious*
sedulously 106.19 *meticulously*, 467.15 *attentively*, 857.7 *honourably*
sedulousness 467.3 *carefulness*, 575.2 *commitment*
sedum 84 Flowers and Flowering Plants
see 435, 7.9 *priesthood*, 253.12 *attend*, 403.11 *sense*, 471.14 *have an idea*, 501.11 *know*, 519.14 *imagine*, 522.7 *recognize*, 815.12 *visit*
seeable 437.1 *visible*
see again 344.8 *meet*
see ahead 516.1 *foresee*
see another woman 877.17 *be sexually immoral*
see at a glance 522.7 *recognize*
see auras 11.24 *experience psychic phenomena*
see badly 436.14 *be blind*
see both sides 482.12 *be fair*
see coming 513.8 *expect*
seed 83, 69.15 *cultivate*, 86.3 *fruit structure*, 87.12 *manage grassland*, 152.15 *categorize*, 155.11 *progeny*, 156.3 *source*, 162.17 *sow*, 226.3 *rudiment*, 243.7 *produce*, 245.8 *organs of reproduction*, 246.3 *fertilizer*, 260.2 *little thing*, 655.4 *skilled person*, 674.10 *contender*
seed bank 83.11 *herbarium*
seed-bearing 83.16 *taxonomic*
seedbed 68.11 *farmland*, 156.3, 226.2 *source*, 246.1 *fertility*
seed cake 45.36 *cake*
seed capsule 83.9 *seed*, 86.3 *fruit structure*
seedcase 83.9 *seed*
seed coat 83.9 *seed*, 293.13 *casing*
seed drill 68.10 *farm tool*, 69.6 *garden tool*
seeded 152.24 *categorized*, 580.15 *chosen*

seeded player 655.4 *skilled person*
seeded position 126.3 *advantage*
seed fern 88.1 *fern*
seedily 743.16 *meanly*
seediness 624.1 *ill health*, 743.7 *beggary*
seeding 152.5 *categorization*, 162.1 *dispersion*
seed itself 246.6 *be fertile*
seed leaf 83.6 *leaf*, 83.9 *seed*
seedling 69.9 *garden plant*, 83.2 *plant*, 83.9 *seed*, 206.5 *young plant*
seed oneself 245.11 *have young*
see double 436.14 *be blind*, 874.7 *be drunk*
seed plant 83
seed pod 83.9 *seed*, 86.3 *fruit structure*
seeds 86.1 *fruits*, 614.6 *refuse*
seed shrimp 81.4 *arthropod*
seedsman 69.13 *horticulturist*
seed stalk 83.5 *stem*, 83.9 *seed*
seedtime 203.2 *spring*
seed tray 69.4 *nursery*
seedy 793, 238.8 *weak*, 559.10 *ugly*, 624.22 *sick*, 628.13 *dilapidated*, 743.3 *beggarly*
see eye to eye 116.21 *be in accord*, 499.4 *assent*, 667.6 *agree with*
see fair play 843.14 *be fair*
see fit 570.12 *choose*, 580.2 *prefer*
see how it feels 672.7 *revenge*
see how it goes 106.11 *circumstantiate*
see how the cat jumps 516.2 *show prudence*
see how the land lies 781.5 *be cautious*
see how the wind blows 516.2 *show prudence*, 781.5 *be cautious*
seeing 435, 53.23 *observatory*, 435.1 *vision*
seeing a bride 517.6 *good-luck sign*
seeing a chimney sweep 517.6 *good-luck sign*
seeing double 436.2 *poor sight*, 436.9 *weak-sighted*, 874.2 *slightly drunk*, 874.10 *drunkenness*
seeing one's family 815.3 *meeting*
seeing red 828.16 *angry*
seeing to 768.3 *nuisance*
see in the mind's eye 435.16 *visualize*, 519.14 *imagine*
see into the future 516.1 *foresee*
see it all 522.6 *understand*
see it coming 199.10 *expect*, 787.5 *not wonder about*
see it through 575.9 *endure*, 632.8 *be safe*, 684.4 *complete*
see justice done 843.14 *be fair*
seek 4.20 *philosophize*, 477.17 *question*, 496.2 *detect*, 590.8 *pursue*, 596.1 *attempt*
seek acquaintance 815.13 *fraternize*
seek advice 654.6 *consult*
seek a favour 708.6 *ask permission*
seek a second opinion 60.19 *practise medicine*
seek asylum 634.4 *shelter*
seek a verdict 16.70 *litigate*
seeker 4.10 *philosopher*, 477.9 *questioner*, 590.5 *pursuer*, 712.4 *requester*
seek help 708.6 *ask permission*
seeking 588.11 *intending*, 590.1 *pursuit*, 590.15 *pursuing*, 596.6 *venture*, 596.8 *attempting*
seeking advice 654.2 *consultation*
seeking a verdict 16.5 *litigation*
seeking justice 16.5 *litigation*
seeking legal protection 16.5 *litigation*
seek justice 16.70 *litigate*
seek legal protection 16.70 *litigate*
seek opinion 654.6 *consult*
seek out 465.7 *be curious*

seek payment 744.8 *credit*
seek political asylum 149.16 *migrate*
seek privacy 139.7 *be aloof*
seek refuge 634.4 *shelter*
seek riches **742**
seek safety 632.8 *be safe*, 634.4 *shelter*
seek sanctuary 634.4 *shelter*
seek seclusion 598.2 *withdraw*
seek shelter 634.4 *shelter*
seek solitude 139.7 *be aloof*
seek the company of 819.14 *seek the friendship of*
seek the end of the rainbow 487.10 *attempt the impossible*
seek the friendship of **819**
seek to 596.1 *attempt*
see light at the end of the tunnel 775.9 *be hopeful*
seem 289.13 *appear outwardly*, 457.11 *appear*, 540.24 *mask*
seem guilty 866.9 *appear guilty*
seeming 114.1 *similarity*, 289.8 *apparent*, 457.4 *something that appears*, 457.9 *ostensible*, 540.12 *facade*, 540.30 *pretending*, 540.35 *disguised*
seemingly 4.25 *theoretically*, 102.19 *apparently*, 289.15 *externally*, 437.11 *visibly*, 457.15 *apparently*, 518.10 *supposedly*, 540.37 *spuriously*
seemingness 289.3 *appearance*
seeming real 537.25 *lifelike*
seem lifelike **537**
seem like 114.10 *be similar*, 457.11 *appear*
seem likely 488.8 *be probable*
seemliness 794.1 *elegance*, 843.3 *properness*
seemly 615.1 *convenient*
seem propitious 819.16 *be favourable*
seem real 537.33 *seem lifelike*
seem to be 457.11 *appear*
seem true to life 537.33 *seem lifelike*
seem true to nature 537.33 *seem lifelike*
seen 496.14 *discovered*, 501.10 *known*, 534.34 *communicated*, 730.13 *received*
see no cause for haste 645.4 *have leisure*
see no difference 114.11 *make similar*
see no difference between 482.11 *not discriminate*
see no one 816.12 *be unsocial*
see no reason to thank 838.6 *be ungrateful*
see nothing remarkable 787.5 *not wonder about*
see nothing wonderful 783.12 *be indifferent*
see no way out 105.7 *be in a predicament*
see off 218.8 *cause to cease*, 349.6 *send away*
see oneself in print 532.17 *be published*
see one's name in lights 51.32 *act*
see one's summer 207.17 *age*
seep 389, 391, 346.11 *infiltrate*, 347.3 *leakage*, 347.12 *leak*, 360.9 *descend*, 387.25 *flow*
seepage 391, 346.3 *inroad*, 347.3 *leakage*, 638.4 *leak*
seep away 722.12 *lessen*
seep down 360.9 *descend*
seep in 348.13 *absorb*
seeping 389, 391, 347.3 *leakage*, 348.5 *absorption*
seeping away 722.4 *lessening*
see pink elephants 874.7 *be drunk*
seep out 347.12, 638.7 *leak*
seer 11.13 *diviner*, 199.5 *predictor*, 435.11 *observer*, 464.5 *intuitive person*, 507.3 *wise man*, 517.8 *oracle*, 519.9 *visionary*
see red 241.7 *be violent*, 759.17 *feel deeply*, 828.12 *become angry*
seeress 435.11 *observer*
see round corners 435.12 *see*,

442.12 *make transparent*
seersucker 67 Natural Fabrics, 288.4 *textile*
seesaw 107.2 *interrelatedness*, 109.4 *reciprocal*, 109.7 *reciprocate*, 224.12 *be irresolute*, 365.7 *oscillator*, 365.8 *oscillate*, 365.13 *oscillating*, 365.18 *to and fro*, 576.5 *vacillate*
seesawing 224.14 *irresolute*
see signs 11.24 *experience psychic phenomena*
seethe 45.55 *cook*, 161.40, 181.11 *crowd*, 364.10 *swirl*, 366.3 *turbulence*, 366.21 *be agitated*, 389.31 *steep*, 828.11 *be angry*
see the catch 657.5 *be cunning*
see the end of 219.4 *protract*
see the error of one's ways 867.4 *be penitent*
see the last of 218.8 *cause to cease*
see the lay of the land 516.2 *show prudence*, 522.6 *understand*, 594.1 *prepare*
see the light 457.12 *become visible*, 496.3 *find out*, 522.6 *understand*, 867.4 *be penitent*
see the light of day 156.27 *emerge*
see the little people 11.24 *experience psychic phenomena*
see the sights 435.12 *see*
see the whole picture 106.11 *circumstantiate*
seething 161.50 *crowded*, 366.3 *turbulence*, 366.17 *turbulent*, 389.10 *steeping*, 408.12 *warmhearted*
seething mob 642.6 *business*
see things 102.13, 435.17 *imagine*
see things as they are 537.28 *bring into existence*
seething with 144.8 *full*
see through 442.12 *make transparent*, 507.7 *be wise*, 522.6 *understand*, 574.6 *be resolute*, 662.29 *finance*, 684.4 *complete*, 787.5 *not wonder about*
see-through 442.2 *translucent*
see through a brick wall 435.12 *see*, 442.12 *make transparent*
see through a glass darkly 438.7 *become invisible*
see through rose-coloured glasses 102.15 *idealize*, 471.15 *imagine*, 519.15 *fantasize*
see to 652.14 *behave towards*
see visions 519.15 *fantasize*
see which way the land lies 332.8 *orient*
see which way the wind blows 332.8 *orient*
see with half an eye 435.12 *see*, 522.7 *recognize*
see with the naked eye 435.12 *see*
see you 345.14 *goodbye*
see you later 345.14 *goodbye*
Seger cone 44.6 *ceramic workshop*
segment 52.41 *geometric figure*, 136.11 *divide*, 143.1 *part*, 143.7 *piece*, 143.10 *part*, 148.2 *piece*, 173.2 *fractional part*, 313.4 *parts of a circle*
segmental 43.13 *arched*, 43.17 *structured*, 143.11 *partial*, 148.6 *component*, 173.5 *fractional*
segmental arch 43.5 *arch*
segmental vault 43.7 *vault*
segmentation 136.3 *separateness*
segmented 81.20 *wormlike*
segmented worm 81.6 *worm*
segment stage 51.15 *stage*
segno 49 Musical Terms
Segomo 8 Deities
Segrè 52 Scientists
segregate 104.5 *separate*, 136.11 *divide*, 147.7 *exclude*, 481.12 *discriminate*, 816.13 *ignore*
segregated 104.11 *separate*, 108.6 *unrelated*, 481.11 *judged*

segregation 104.3 *separateness*, 136.2 *setting apart*, 147.1 *exclusion*, 481.1 *discrimination*, 481.4 *social discrimination*, 632.2 *protection*, 805.11 *prejudice*, 816.3 *separation*, 820.1 *enmity*, 822.3 *race hatred*
segregationist 136.8 *person who separates*
segue 155.3 *continuity*, 155.21 *follow in sequence*
Sehanakavasi 7 Non-Christian Religions
seiche 54.14 *wave*
Seidlitz powder 62 Medication
seif 54.37 *dune*
seigneur 696.1 *master*
seigneury 725.3 *historic property terms*
seignorial 725.8 *propertied*
seine 80.7 *fishing*, 80.15 *fish*, 539.13, 539.33 *snare*
Seine 96 Rivers, 96.5 *other major rivers*
seisin 723.2 *legal terms*
seism 54.22 *seismic activity*
seismatical 365.17 *waving*
seismic 54.55 *volcanic*, 241.6 *violent*, 365.17 *waving*, 611.6 *notable*
seismic activity 54
seismic event 54.22 *seismic activity*
seismicity 54.22 *seismic activity*, 365.5 *wave*
seismic seawave 54.14 *wave*
seismic wave 54, 54.16 *sound wave*, 365.5 *wave*
seismograph 54.23 *seismic wave*, 365.6 *measuring instrument*, 545.10 *recording instrument*
seismographic 54.49 *geophysical*, 365.17 *waving*
seismography 54.2 *geophysics*
seismological 54.49 *geophysical*, 365.17 *waving*
seismologically 54.66 *geographically*
seismologist 54.4 *geophysicist*
seismology 54.2 *geophysics*
seismometer 268.8 *meter*, 365.6 *measuring instrument*
seismometric 54.49 *geophysical*, 365.17 *waving*
seismoscope 365.6 *measuring instrument*
sei whale 77 Placental Mammals
seize 407.11 *touch*, 522.6 *understand*, 699.11 *detain*, 726.6 *retain*, 734.7 *take*, 734.8 *take back*, 846.14 *arrogate*
seized 624.22 *sick*
seize on 611.8 *make important*
seize one's chance 208.11 *get ahead*, 210.5 *take the opportunity*
seize one's opportunity 210.5 *take the opportunity*
seize power 12.12, 688.20 *take authority*, 734.7 *take*
seizer 734.6 *taker*
seize the crown 689.4 *be anarchic*
seize the day 210.5 *take the opportunity*
seize the moment 208.11 *get ahead*
seize the occasion 208.11 *get ahead*
seize the opportunity 642.14 *push*
seize up 683.9 *malfunction*
seizing one's chance 208.6 *getting ahead*
seizing the moment 208.6 *getting ahead*
seizing the occasion 208.6 *getting ahead*
seizure 366.8 *spasm*, 510.3 *mental deterioration*, 624.2 *illness*, 624.17 *nervous disorder*, 670.20 *bout*, 726.1 *retention*, 734.1 *taking*, 734.2 *taking back*, 846.3 *arrogation*
seizure of power 688.3 *acquisition of power*, 734.1 *taking*
sejant 544.13 *heraldic*

Seker 8 Deities
Sekhmet 8 Deities
selachian 80.2 *fish*, 80.13 *fishlike*
seldom 186, 182.11 *sparsely*, 213.1 *infrequently*
seldom if ever 489.10 *rarely*
seldom met with 182.6 *sparse*, 213.2 *infrequent*
seldomness 213.3 *infrequency*
seldom seen 182.6 *sparse*, 213.2 *infrequent*
select 580, 136.10 *set apart*, 147.10 *excluding*, 152.15 *categorize*, 165.22 *characterize*, 481.12 *discriminate*, 562.9 *compile*, 570.12 *choose*, 580.15 *chosen*, 617.1 *worthy*, 688.21 *grant authority*, 784.8 *prefer*
select building materials 43.18 *be an architect*
select committee 653.6 *governing body*, 654.4 *adviser*
selected 41.13 *ice-skating*, 152.24 *categorized*, 481.11 *judged*, 580.15 *chosen*, 617.1 *worthy*, 688.13 *elected*
select few 126.7 *the best people*
selecting 580, 492.8 *judging*
selection 580, 136.2 *setting apart*, 152.5 *categorization*, 481.1 *discrimination*, 492.1 *judgment*, 562.3 *compendium*, 580.9 *chosen thing*, 688.3 *acquisition of power*, 784.2 *inclination*, 784.3 *likes*
Selection 580
selection of music 41.7 *ice-dancing*
selective 136.17 *unjoined*, 481.9 *discriminating*, 492.8 *judging*, 580.14 *selecting*
selective facts 309.4 *distortion of the truth*
selective killing 398.9 *animal killing*
selectively 580, 136.22 *in isolation*, 481.15 *discriminatingly*, 492.13 *judicially*
selectiveness 481.1 *discrimination*
selectivity 481.1 *discrimination*
selector 136.8 *person who separates*, 481.6 *discriminating person*
s-electron 56.65 *atom*
Selene 8 Deities, 53.17 *moon*
selenic 57.34 *elemental*
selenious 57.34 *elemental*
selenium 57 Chemical Elements, 58.15 *essential element*
selenium meter 66.18 *exposure time*
selenous 57.34 *elemental*
Seles 18 Sporting Personalities
self 61.21 *psyche*, 165.11 *identity*, 368.6 *internal world*, 544.2 *identity*
self-abasement 806
self-abasing 806
self-abnegating 806.4 *self-abasing*, 859.5 *unselfish*
self-abnegation 806.11 *self-abasement*, 859.2 *unselfishness*, 869.1 *self-restraint*
self-absorbed 870, 290.12 *internalized*, 860.5 *egoistic*
self-absorption 870, 290.6 *internalization*, 512.1 *oblivion*, 860.2 *egoism*
self-accusation 866.2 *signs of guilt*, 867.1 *penitence*
self-accusing 867.6 *penitent*
self-accusingly 867.8 *penitently*
self-adhesive film 45.6 *kitchen equipment*
self-admiration 809, 805.3 *conceit*
self-admirer 809.7 *vain person*
self-admiring 809, 805.17 *conceited*
self-applause 809.4 *self-admiration*
self-appointed 572.5 *voluntary*
self-appointed task 572.10 *voluntary work*
self-approbation 809.2 *self-satisfaction*

self-approving 809.10 *self-admir-*
ing
self-assertion 535.6 *assertive-*
ness, 668.1 *defiance*, 688.2 *au-*
thoritativeness
self-assertive 237.11 *strong in*
spirit, 535.14 *assertive*, 688.12
authoritative, 809.11 *cocky*
self-assertively 809.21 *cockily*
self-assertiveness 809.3 *cockiness*
self-assurance 692, 303.4 *assur-*
ance, 490.10 *conviction*, 668.1
defiance, 809.2 *self-satisfaction*
self-assured 692, 303.8 *assured*,
490.2 *convinced*, 668.7 *defiant*,
809.9 *self-satisfied*
self-assuredly 668.9 *defiantly*,
692.16 *commandingly*, 809.20
smugly
self-centred 165.18 *subjective*,
809.12 *self-interested*, 860.5 *ego-*
istic, 870.9 *self-absorbed*
self-centredness 809.5 *self-inter-*
est, 860.2 *egoism*, 870.4 *self-ab-*
sorption
self-certification 848.3 *self-exemp-*
tion
self-command 574.15 *will*
self-commiseration 835.1 *pity*
self-compassion 835.1 *pity*
self-conceit 809.6 *boastfulness*
self-conceited 809.13 *boastful*
self-concern 860.1 *selfishness*
self-concerned 860.4 *selfish*
self-condemnation 867.1 *peni-*
tence
self-condemning 867.6 *penitent*
self-confidence 303.4 *assurance*,
490.10 *conviction*, 692.5 *self-as-*
surance, 805.1 *pride*, 809.3 *cock-*
iness
self-confident 303.8 *assured*,
490.2 *convinced*, 692.15 *self-as-*
sured, 805.14 *proud*, 809.11
cocky
self-confidently 692.16 *com-*
mandingly, 805.32 *proudly*,
809.21 *cockily*
self-congratulation 809.2 *self-sat-*
isfaction
self-congratulatory 809.9 *self-sat-*
isfied, 809.20 *smugly*
self-conscious 797.3 *affected*,
810.11 *shy*
self-consciousness 810.4 *shyness*
self-consideration 860.1 *selfish-*
ness
self-contained 144.7 *complete*,
566.1 *taciturn*, 698.10 *indepen-*
dent, 816.8 *unsociable*
self-containment 816.1 *unsocia-*
bility
self-content 809.2 *self-satisfac-*
tion
self-contented 809.9 *self-satisfied*
self-contentedly 809.20 *smugly*
self-contradicting 117.8 *contradic-*
tory, 504.17 *mistaken*
self-contradiction 117.2 *contradic-*
tion, 484.2 *reversal*, 487.5 *im-*
possibility, 504.4 *faulty reason-*
ing
self-contradictory 117.8 *contradic-*
tory, 484.5 *countering*, 487.1 *im-*
possible, 504.15 *erroneous*
self-control 4.3 *detachment*,
242.1 *moderation*, 302.2 *limit-*
ing factor, 570.2 *willpower*,
574.15 *will*, 699.3 *self-restraint*,
859.1 *disinterestedness*, 863.2
virtues, 869.1 *self-restraint*
self-controlled 4.18 *detached*,
242.6 *moderate*, 570.7 *iron-*
willed, 574.5 *steady*, 699.14 *self-*
restrained, 859.4 *disinterested*,
863.6 *ethical*, 869.8 *self-re-*
strained
self-convicted 16.64 *convicted*
self-correcting 125.10 *counterbal-*
ancing
self-correction 125.2 *counterbal-*
ance
self-deceived 539.36 *deceived*
self-deception 539, 102.3 *delu-*
sion, 493.1 *misjudgment*, 504.6
fallibility
self-defeating 487.1 *impossible*

self-defence 671, 26.1 *combat*
sports, 669.3 *resistance move-*
ment
self-defensive 26.14 *combat*,
669.12 *resisting*
self-defensively 671.32 *defen-*
sively
self-denial 591.11 *abstinence*,
669.4 *desisting*, 690.3 *unadorn-*
ment, 711.3 *abnegation*, 825.2
virginity, 859.2 *unselfishness*,
869.1 *self-restraint*
self-denying 669.13 *desisting*,
711.10 *abnegating*, 859.5 *unself-*
ish, 869.8 *self-restrained*
self-deprecating 810, 806.4 *self-*
abasing
self-deprecation 810, 495.1 *un-*
derestimation
self-depreciation 495.1 *underesti-*
mation
self-destruct 244.13 *be destroyed*,
628.1 *deteriorate*
self-destruction 398.7 *suicide*
self-destructive 398.24 *murderous*
self-determination 91.1 *country*,
570.4 *free will*, 698.3 *indepen-*
dence
self-determined 570.10 *free*
self-determining 91.16 *national*,
698.9 *free*
self-devoted 870.9 *self-absorbed*
self-devotion 574.13 *concentra-*
tion, 860.2 *egoism*, 870.4 *self-*
absorption
self-discipline 699.3, 869.1 *self-*
restraint, 879.11 *penance*
self-disciplined 699.14, 869.8
self-restrained
self-display 809.6 *boastfulness*
self-distrustful 810.12 *self-depre-*
cating
self-doubt 776.1 *hopelessness*,
810.5 *self-depreciation*
self-doubting 806.4 *self-abasing*,
810.12 *self-deprecating*
self-education 6.2 *educational*
system, 501.3 *learning*
self-effacement 495.1 *underesti-*
mation, 806.11 *self-abasement*,
810.5 *self-depreciation*, 859.2 *un-*
selfishness
self-effacing 806.4 *self-abasing*,
810.12 *self-deprecating*, 859.5
unselfish
self-employed 698.10 *indepen-*
dent
self-employed person 646.1
worker
self-endearing 809.10 *self-admir-*
ing
self-endearment 809.4 *self-admi-*
ration
self-esteem 805.1 *pride*, 809.4
self-admiration
self-esteeming 805.14 *proud*
self-evidence 483.3 *evidentness*,
522.10 *simplicity*
self-evident 52.69 *theoretic*,
475.12 *demonstrable*, 483.9 *evi-*
dent, 490.1 *certain*, 522.2 *sim-*
ple, 526.14 *manifest*
self-evidently 483.15 *evidently*
self-examination 4.4 *philosophi-*
cal investigation
self-exemption 848
self-existence 99
self-existent 99
self-existing 99.14 *self-existent*
self-explanatory 522.2 *simple*
self-expression 698.3 *indepen-*
dence
self-expressive 698.13 *informal*
self-flagellation 867.2 *type of pen-*
ance
self-flattery 809.4 *self-admiration*
self-glorification 541.4 *bombast*,
805.10 *boastfulness*
self-glorify 541.10 *boast*
self-glorifying 541.15 *bombastic*,
805.22 *boastful*, 809.10 *self-ad-*
miring
self-governing 12.9 *governmen-*
tal, 91.16 *national*, 688.14 *gov-*
ernmental, 698.9 *free*
self-governing state 91.1 *country*
self-government 12.1 *govern-*

ment, 688.7 *type of rule*, 698.3
independence
self-gratification 405.1 *physical*
pleasure, 870.1 *self-indulgence*
self-gratifying 870.6 *self-indul-*
gent
self heal 84 Flowers and Flowering Plants
self-help 662.5 *medical assist-*
ance
self-help group 233.6 *group influ-*
ence
selfhood 368.6 *internal world*
self-humiliation 867.2 *type of pen-*
ance
self-hypnosis 61.3 *psychiatric*
treatment
self-immolation 398.7 *suicide*,
710.6 *offering*
self-importance 805.1 *pride*,
809.1 *vanity*, 811.5 *pomposity*,
811.6 *blatancy*
self-important 805.14 *proud*,
809.8 *vain*, 811.20 *pompous*
self-importantly 809.19 *vainly*,
811.36 *pompously*
self-imposed 597.5 *undertaken*
self-imposed task 597.2 *under-*
taking
self-improvement 627.5 *improve-*
ment, 662.4 *social assistance*
self-inductance 56.53, 64.12 *re-*
sistance
self-induction 56.63 *magnetic*
phenomenon
self-indulge 872.5 *be greedy*
self-indulgence 870, 405.1 *physi-*
cal pleasure, 763.7 *pleasure*,
860.1 *selfishness*, 872.1 *gluttony*
Self-Indulgence 870
self-indulgent 870, 405.7
pleased, 763.5 *pleasure-loving*,
860.4 *selfish*, 872.6 *gluttonous*
self-indulgently 870, 860.8 *self-*
ishly, 872.7 *gluttonously*
self-indulgent person 870
self-infatuated 809.10 *self-admir-*
ing
self-infatuation 809.4 *self-admira-*
tion
selfing 84.6 *pollination*
self-instruction 501.3 *learning*
self-interest 809, 860.1 *selfish-*
ness
self-interested 809, 860.4 *selfish*
selfish 860, 165.18 *subjective*,
462.10 *inconsiderate*, 468.9
thoughtless, 512.10 *unthinking*,
652.18 *badly behaved*, 809.12
self-interested, 834.3 *misan-*
thropic, 838.3 *ungrateful*, 870.9
self-absorbed
selfishly 809, 860, 462.14
thoughtlessly, 468.14 *inatten-*
tively, 652.20 *badly*, 834.5 *mis-*
anthropically, 838.7 *ungratefully*
selfish motive 228.1 *motive*
selfishness 860, 462.4 *inconsid-*
eration, 468.4 *thoughtlessness*,
512.4 *unthinkingness*, 637.1
preservation, 652.4 *bad conduct*,
809.5 *self-interest*, 834.1 *misan-*
thropy, 838.1 *ingratitude*, 870.4
self-absorption
Selfishness 860
selfish person 860
selfless 859.5 *unselfish*
selflessly 859.9 *unselfishly*
selflessness 831.2 *charity*, 859.2
unselfishness
self-loss 512.1 *oblivion*
self-love 809.4 *self-admiration*,
821.1 *love*, 860.2 *egoism*, 870.4
self-absorption
self-loving 809.10 *self-admiring*,
860.5 *egoistic*, 870.9 *self-ab-*
sorbed
self-lovingly 860.9 *egoistically*
self-made 656.2 *unskilled*, 658.1
naive
self-made man 682.4 *successful*
person, 686.4 *prosperous person*,
742.10 *wealthy person*
self-mastered 574.5 *steady*
self-mastery 574.15 *will*, 869.1
self-restraint
self-mortification 690.3 *unadorn-*

ment, 879.11 *penance*
self-motivated 228.12 *motivated*,
698.10 *independent*
self-obsessed 870.9 *self-absorbed*
self-obsession 870.4 *self-absorp-*
tion
self-opinion 577.7 *opinionated-*
ness
self-opinionated 809.13 *boastful*
self-pity 835.1 *pity*, 860.1 *selfish-*
ness
self-pitying 835.7 *pitiful*
self-pleaser 860.3 *selfish person*
self-pleasing 860.1 *selfishness*
self-pollination 84.6 *pollination*
self-possessed 4.18 *detached*,
574.5 *steady*
self-possession 4.3 *detachment*,
242.1 *moderation*, 574.15 *will*
self-praise 805.3 *conceit*, 809.4
self-admiration, 860.2 *egoism*
self-praising 805.17 *conceited*
self-preservation 637.1 *preserva-*
tion, 781.1 *caution*, 860.1 *self-*
ishness
self-promotion 586.5 *propaganda*
self-propelled 324.16 *moving*,
338.19 *propelled*
self-protection 781.1 *caution*
self psychology 61.1 *psychology*
self-punishing 867.7 *penitential*
self-punishment 867.2 *type of*
penance, 879.11 *penance*
self-raising 370.4 *leavening*
self-raising flour 45.7 *basic ingre-*
dient, 370.8 *leavening*
self-regard 805.1 *pride*
self-regarding 805.14 *proud*
self-regulating 122.6 *equal*,
698.9 *free*
self-regulating market 698.1 *free-*
dom
self-regulatory 698.9 *free*
self-reliance 698.3 *independence*,
778.3 *steadfastness*
self-reliant 778, 698.10 *indepen-*
dent
self-reliantly 805.32 *proudly*
self-remorse 867.1 *penitence*
self-renunciation 711.3 *abnega-*
tion
self-renunciatory 711.10 *abnegat-*
ing
self-reproach 866.2 *signs of guilt*,
867.1 *penitence*
self-reproachful 867.6 *penitent*
self-reproaching 867.6 *penitent*
self-respect 805.1 *pride*
self-respecting 809.10 *self-admir-*
ing
self-restrained 699, 869, 4.18
detached, 574.5 *steady*, 690.10
unadorned
self-restrained person 869
self-restraint 699, 869, 4.3 *de-*
tachment, 302.2 *limiting factor*,
574.15 *will*, 669.4 *desisting*,
690.3 *unadornment*, 711.3 *abne-*
gation, 859.1 *disinterestedness*
Self-Restraint 869
self-righteous 7.15 *religious*,
876.10 *moralistic*
self-righteousness 876
self-rule 12.1 *government*, 12.3
governance, 698.3 *independence*
self-ruling 12.9 *governmental*,
698.9 *free*
self-sacrifice 7.2 *religiousness*,
711.3 *abnegation*, 729.3 *offer-*
ing, 859.2 *unselfishness*
self-sacrificing 7.15 *religious*,
711.10 *abnegating*, 859.5 *unself-*
ish
selfsame 110.12 *same*
selfsameness 110.1 *sameness*
self-satisfaction 809, 765.1 *satis-*
faction
self-satisfied 809, 765.4 *satisfied*
self-scourging 867.2 *type of pen-*
ance
self-seeker 860.3 *selfish person*
self-seeking 860.1 *selfishness*,
860.4 *selfish*
self-server 860.3 *selfish person*
self-service 606.1 *provision*,
606.7 *provisioning*
self-service restaurant 350.15 *eat-*

ing place
self-serving 860.1 *selfishness*
self-serving politician 657.3 *cunning person*
self-slaughter 398.7 *suicide*
self-starter 640.3 *doer*
self-styled 498.7 *disbelieved*, 809.12 *self-interested*
self-submission 806.11 *self-abasement*
self-submitting 806.4 *self-abasing*
self-sufficiency 144.1 *completeness*, 608.7 *sufficiency*, 698.3 *independence*, 742.8 *solvency*, 805.2 *unapproachability*, 809.2 *self-satisfaction*, 869.1 *self-restraint*
self-sufficient 136.17 *unjoined*, 144.7 *complete*, 608.1 *sufficient*, 698.10 *independent*, 805.15 *unapproachable*, 809.9 *self-satisfied*, 816.8 *unsociable*, 869.8 *self-restrained*
self-sufficiently 136.22 *in isolation*, 809.20 *smugly*, 816.14 *unsociably*, 869.11 *with self-restraint*
self-support 662.4 *social assistance*
self-supporting 698.10 *independent*
self-surrender 7.2 *religiousness*
self-surrendering 7.15 *religious*
self-taught 6.17 *educatable*, 656.2 *unskilled*, 658.1 *naive*
self-timer 66.18 *exposure time*
self-will 570.3 *wilfulness*, 577.5 *obstinacy*
self-willed 570.8 *wilful*, 577.1 *obstinate*, 689.6 *anarchic*
self-worship 809.4 *self-admiration*, 870.4 *self-absorption*
self-worshipping 809.10 *self-admiring*, 870.9 *self-absorbed*
Seliwanoff's test 58.5 *sugar test*
Selkirk 93 *Cities*
sell 739, 532.16 *publicize*, 539.10 *fraud*, 539.30 *be fraudulent*, 605.5 *provision*, 727.11 *dispose of property*, 728.3 *transfer property*, 737.1 *trade*, 739.2 *be sold*
Sellafield 410.7 *nuclear power*
sell again 739.1 *sell*
sell a gold brick 539.28 *trick*
sell a pig in a poke 13.12 *cheat*
sell at a loss 722.10 *have a financial loss*, 739.1 *sell*
sell at a profit 13.10 *trade with*, 721.14 *profit*, 739.1 *sell*
sell at a sacrifice 739.1 *sell*
sell badly 739.2 *be sold*
sell by auction 739.1 *sell*
sell dear 753.10 *overcharge*
sell down the river 528.13 *inform on*, 858.9 *prove false*
seller 739, 13.9 *economist*, 646.1 *worker*, 728.2 *person transferring property*, 737.10 *trader*, 739.11 *pedlar*
sellers' market 740, 13.6 *economic factors*, 593.2 *need*, 609.9 *scarcity*, 753.3 *inflationary price*
sell for 751.13 *cost*
sell forward 739.1 *sell*
selling 739, 13.2 *economy*, 727.2 *disposal of property*
selling line 739.8 *merchandise*
selling off 727.2 *disposal of property*
selling party 665.7 *social gathering*
selling price 751.1 *price*
sell like hotcakes 532.18 *become famous*
sell like hot cakes 739.2 *be sold*
sell off 727.11 *dispose of property*, 739.1 *sell*
sell on credit 744.8 *credit*
sell on the black economy 739.1 *sell*
sell on the black market 727.11 *dispose of property*, 739.1 *sell*
Sellotape 138.3 *adhesive*
sell out 576.9 *change sides*, 598.2 *withdraw*, 673.3 *submit*

sellout 682.3 *successful thing*
sell out 739.1 *sell*, 739.2 *be sold*
sellout 858.2 *faithlessness*
sell out 858.9 *prove false*
sell-out 51.11 *theatrical performance*, 673.1 *submission*, 739.4 *sale*
sell over the counter 727.11 *dispose of property*, 739.1 *sell*
sell property 727.11 *dispose of property*
sell short 542.20 *understate*, 739.1 *sell*, 854.10 *disparage*
sell someone a bill of goods 539.23 *deceive*
sell the family silver 743.13 *lose one's money*
sell to 737.1 *trade*
sell to the highest bidder 727.11 *dispose of property*, 739.1 *sell*
sell under the counter 727.11 *dispose of property*, 739.1 *sell*
sell up 739.1 *sell*
sell well 532.18 *become famous*, 739.2 *be sold*
Selma 93 *Cities*
seltzer water 62 *Medication*
Selu 8 *Deities*
selvage 67.4 *weaving*, 300.2 *edging*
Semang 5 Languages and Groups of Languages
semanteme 5.35 *part of speech*
semantic 520, 5.38 *linguistic*
semantically 4.24 *philosophically*, 5.48 *linguistically*
semantic content 520.1 *meaning*
semantic field 520.4 *type of meaning*
semantic flow 520.1 *meaning*
semanticist 5.2 *linguist*
semantic net 65.16 *artificial intelligence*
semantics 4.6 *branch of philosophy*, 5.1 *linguistics*, 65.9 *programming language*, 520.1 *meaning*
semantic shift 520.4 *type of meaning*
semaphore 5.8 *artificial language*, 72.2 *track*, 421.1 *deafness*, 534.27 *signalling*, 543.4, 543.12 *signal*
semaphoric 543.16 *signalling*
semaphorically 543.18 *indicatively*
semasiological 5.38 *linguistic*, 520.8 *semantic*
semasiologist 5.2 *linguist*
semasiology 5.1 *linguistics*, 520.1 *meaning*
sematology 520.1 *meaning*
semblance 114.1 *similarity*, 435.5 *imagination*, 457.4 *something that appears*, 540.12 *facade*, 547.1 *representation*
seme 544.13 *heraldic*
semeiology 60.3 *medical specialty*
sememe 5.17 *word*
semen 245.8 *organs of reproduction*, 246.3 *fertilizer*, 352.2 *secreted substance*, 387.3 *body fluid*
semen sample 60.7 *diagnosis*
semester 185.4 *term*, 187.4 *period of activity*
semi 256.5 *house*
semiannual 214.12 *cyclic*
semiannually 214.16 *cyclically*
semiarid climate 55.38 *climate*
semiautomatic 680.9 *firearm*
Semi-Bantu 5 Languages and Groups of Languages
semibreve 49.17 *notation*
semicarbazone 57 *Types of Compounds*
semicircle 28.3 *fencing movements*, 52.42 *circle*, 143.1 *part*, 176.8 *half*, 311.2 *bend*, 313.2 *circle*
semicircular 52.81 *curvilinear*, 311.4 *curved*, 313.5 *circular*
semicircular apse 43.10 *church architecture*
semicircular arch 43.5 *arch*
semicircular canals 420.5 *internal ear*

semicolon 543.7 *punctuation*
semiconductor 56, 64, 56.43 *electrical conduction*, 235.7 *electrical power*
semiconductor device 56.44 *semiconductor*, 64.16 *circuit element*
semiconductor laser 56.26 *laser*
semiconductor memory 65.6 *memory*
semidark 441.5 *dim*
semidarkness 441.1 *dimness*
semidetached 43.12 *structural*, 256.16 *manorial*
semidetached house 43.3 *building*, 124.8 *middle classes*, 256.5 *house*
semifinal 674.2 *contest*
semifinalist 674.10 *contender*
semi-final race 21.1 *track events*
semifluid 393.1, 393.16 *semiliquid*
semifluidity 393.2 *semiliquidity*
semihumid climate 55.38 *climate*
semiliquid 393, 393, 273.2 *dense*
Semiliquid 393
semiliquidity 393, 374.10 *compressibility*, 387.5 *fluidity*
semi-literacy 502.2 *half-knowledge*
semi-literate 502.7 *semi-skilled*
semimajor axis 53.21 *orbit*
semimatt finish 66.12 *development*
semimetal 57.6 *chemical element*
semimonthly 214.12 *cyclic*, 214.16 *cyclically*, 532.5 *journal*
seminal 119.4 *original*, 226.13 *causal*, 245.16 *reproductive*, 352.5 *of a secretion*
seminal fluid 245.8 *organs of reproduction*, 352.2 *secreted substance*
seminally 119.8 *originally*
seminar 163.7 *lecture*, 568.4 *conference*
seminary 6.12 *educational institution*
Seminole 1 Peoples, 5 Languages and Groups of Languages
semiological 520.8 *semantic*, 524.14 *interpretive*, 543.14 *signifying*
semiologically 543.18 *indicatively*
semiologist 543.8 *signer*
semiology 520.1 *meaning*, 524.5 *science of interpretation*, 543.2 *symbolism*
semiopaque 44.10 *ceramic*, 442.3 *semitransparent*, 443.2 *shady*
semiopaque glaze 44.3 *glaze*
semiopaquely 44.12 *ornamentally*
semiotic 520.8 *semantic*, 543.14 *signifying*
semiotician 543.8 *signer*
semiotics 4.6 *branch of philosophy*, 520.1 *meaning*, 543.2 *symbolism*
semipolar bond 57.11 *chemical bond*
semiprofessional 124.8 *middle classes*
semiquaver 49.17 *notation*
semi-schooled 502.7 *semi-skilled*
semi-sextile 310.4 *angular measurement*
semiskilled 15.8 *industrial*, 656.2 *unskilled*
semi-skilled 502
semiskilled worker 15.7 *employee*, 124.7 *average person*, 230.6 *operative*
semi-skilled worker 646.2 *artisan*
semi-skimmed milk 351.5 *milk*
Semite 5 Languages and Groups of Languages
Semites 1 Peoples
Semitic 5 Languages and Groups of Languages, 5.11 *family of languages*
Semito-Hamitic 5 Languages and Groups of Languages
semitone 49.16 *musical note*
semitrailer 71 *Motor Vehicles*

semitransparency 442, 441.2 *murk*, 446.7 *whiteness*
semitransparent 442, 446.2 *whitened*, 456.7 *iridescent*
semitransparently 446.14 *whitely*
semi-transparent pigment 444.4 *pigment*
semiweekly 214.12 *cyclic*, 214.16 *cyclically*
semmit 295.18 *underwear*
semolina 45.35 *dessert*
sempiternal 186.5 *timeless*, 190.8 *eternal*, 217.7 *permanent*
sempiternally 217.9 *permanently*
sempiternity 186.1 *timelessness*, 190.1 *eternity*
sempre 49 *Musical Terms*
Semtex 244.7 *agent of destruction*, 680.15 *explosive*
senarmontite 54 *Minerals*
senate 653.10 *legislative body*
Senate 12.4 *governing body*, 653.12 *US government*, 706.2 *representative body*
Senate majority leader 12.8 *politician*, 653.14 *leader*
Senate minority leader 12.8 *politician*, 653.14 *leader*
senator 653.16 *official*
Senator 12.8 *politician*, 653.16 *official*, 688.10 *person of authority*, 696.3 *leader*, 706.1 *delegate*
senatorial 12.9 *governmental*, 653.18 *parliamentary*, 696.12 *masterful*
Senatorial 706.6 *delegated*
senatorial government 12.1 *government*
Senatorially 706.8 *representatively*
senatus 653.10 *legislative body*
Senatus Populusque Romanus 12.1 *government*
send 567, 70.4 *transport*, 324.14 *set in motion*, 326.12 *transport*, 326.14 *bring back*, 534.31 *correspond*, 729.5 *give*, 762.8 *cause joy*
send about one's business 349.6 *send away*
send abroad 347.13 *emigrate*
send after 590.8 *pursue*
send a letter to 534.31 *correspond*
send a message 543.12 *signal*
send an order for 593.10 *necessitate*
send an SOS 543.12 *signal*
send a signal 543.12 *signal*
send a telegram 534.31 *correspond*
send away 349, 162.13 *dismiss*, 349.4 *ostracize*, 458.3 *cause to disappear*
send away with a flea in one's ear 349.6 *send away*
send away with a flea in the ear 806.17 *humiliate*
send back 581.1 *reject*, 735.4 *give back*
send before the beak 856.5 *accuse*
send before the judge 856.5 *accuse*
send by hand 326.13 *post*
send down 323.10 *enclose*, 349.3 *disbar*, 702.9 *imprison*, 879.1, 879.1 *punish*
send flying 326.12 *transport*, 338.24 *push*
send for 590.8 *pursue*
send forth 326.12 *transport*, 349.14 *let out*
send headlong 338.24 *push*, 362.3 *bring down*
send home 162.13 *dismiss*, 700.4 *liberate*
send in 348.8 *show in*
sending 70.1 *transport*, 326.2 *transportation*
sending back 735.1 *giving back*
sending home 162.2 *disbandment*
sending one to Coventry 816.3 *separation*
sending someone to Coventry 816.1 *unsociability*
sending to Coventry 349.19 *ostra-*

cism, 852.3 nonacceptance, 879.7 punishment
send in one's papers 705.5 resign
send off 162.13 dismiss, 326.12 transport, 338.28 shoot, 338.32 load
sendoff 345.9 parting
send off 349.6 send away
send on 534.31 correspond, 567.10 send
send on an errand 703.7 engage
send on a wild goose chase 539.27 be false, 591.6 evade
send one's apologies 711.5 refuse
send one's condolences 835.9 sorrow
send one's regrets 817.10 be courteous
send one's respects 817.10 be courteous
send one to sleep 788.6 be boring
send out 349.14 let out, 388.27 give off
send out a distress call 543.12 signal
send out a search party 590.8 pursue
send out of the room 879.1 punish
send out of the world 398.16 kill
send over the edge 510.15 make insane
send packing 147.8, 341.2 eject, 349.6 send away
send Season's greetings 203.6 spend the season
send smoke signals 543.12 signal
send someone about his business 341.2 eject
send someone off with a flea in his ear 341.3 fend off
send the marines 679.36 combat
send to blazes 807.29 ridicule, 827.6 vilify
send to Coventry 136.10 set apart, 147.7 exclude, 349.4 ostracize, 709.3 veto, 816.13 ignore, 852.15 withhold approval, 879.1 punish
send to one's account 398.16 kill
send to one's Maker 398.16 kill
send to prison 699.11 detain
send to the big house 323.10 enclose
send to the block 879.5 execute
send to the bottom 362.3 bring down
send to the chair 879.5 execute
send to the devil 827.6 vilify
send to the gallows 879.5 execute
send to the gas chamber 398.18 slaughter
send to the hot seat 879.5 execute
send to the scaffold 398.19, 879.5 execute
send to the showers 349.6 send away
send to the stake 398.19, 879.5 execute
send up 361, 51.33 overact, 118.9 imitate, 702.9 imprison, 771.13 be humorous, 799.6 deride, 850.24, 854.14 ridicule
send-up 118.3 mockery, 771.4 entertainment, 850.4, 854.6 ridicule
send up a trial balloon 516.2 show prudence
send up the river 699.11 detain, 702.9 imprison
Seneca 1 Peoples, 5 Languages and Groups of Languages
Senecan 4.11 follower of a doctrine, 4.14 of a philosophy
Senecan tragedy 51.9 tragedy
Seneca the Elder 4 Philosophers
Senegal 91 Countries
senescence 207.5 old age
senescent 202.11 old, 207.12 ageing, 628.12 deteriorated
seneschal 688.10 person of authority
Sengen 8 Deities
senhor 401.3 male title of address
senile 202.11 old, 207.14 aged, 236.12 impotent, 460.5 lacking

intellect, 460.7 intellectually subnormal, 508.5 foolish, 628.12 deteriorated
senile dementia 236.4 disability, 510.3 mental deterioration
senilely 202.18 venerably, 207.16 maturely, 460.11 unintelligently
senility 202.1 oldness, 207.5 old age, 236.4 disability, 238.3 poor health, 460.1 lack of intellect, 508.1 folly, 628.9 dilapidation
senior 126.5 superior, 126.15 excellent, 154.9 predecessor, 154.12 primary, 202.11 old, 207.7 older person, 207.11 adult, 688.12 authoritative, 696.5 company leader
senior aircraftman 679.32 airman
senior citizen 207.7 older person
senior citizens 202.2 old people
senior commander 17.5 military staff
senior high 6.12 educational institution
senior house officer 60.11 doctor
seniority 15.2 industrial negotiations, 126.1 superiority, 154.2 priority, 194.2 greater importance, 202.1 oldness, 207.2 adulthood, 207.5 old age, 688.1 authority
senior nursing officer 60.16 nurse, 653.15 manager
senior officer 17.5 military staff
senior registrar 60.11 doctor
senior service 679.22 navy
Senior Service 17.2 the military
senmurv 78.9 fabulous bird
senna 62 Medication
Senna 18 Sporting Personalities
senna pods 85 Tree Products, 630.6 purgative
sennet 49.22 phrase, 543.6 word
señor 401.3 male title of address
señora 402.3 female title of address
señorita 402.3 female title of address
sensate 403
sensation 403, 59.5 physiology, 383.1 texture, 396.1 life, 407.1 touch, 541.1 exaggeration, 682.1 success, 759.1 feeling, 786.4 wonder
Sensation 403
sensational 51.38 tragic, 403.9 exciting, 532.20 well-known, 617.1 worthy, 786.8 wonderful, 811.18 dramatic, 811.21 blatant
sensationalism 4.7 school of thought, 374.1 dramaturgy, 532.8 public relations , 541.1 exaggeration, 811.3 dramatics, 811.6 blatancy
sensationalist 541.6 exaggerator
sensationalize 541.7 exaggerate, 811.31 put on a show
sensationalized 541.12 exaggerated
sensationally 403, 541.16 exaggeratedly, 811.34 dramatically, 811.37 blatantly
sense 403, 4.8 philosophical term, 6.24 know, 227.4 significance, 459.3 intelligence, 459.5 common sense, 463.1 reason, 492.1 judgment, 507.2 intelligence, 520.1 meaning, 522.9 intelligibility, 759.1 feeling, 759.15 feel, 759.16 feel in one's bones
sense data 4.8 philosophical term
sense-datum 403.1 sensation
senseless 404.6 unfeeling, 460.5 lacking intellect, 506.5 nonsensical, 508.5 foolish, 512.8 oblivious, 521.10 meaningless
senseless killing 398.1 killing, 521.3 meaningless thing
senselessly 460.11 unintelligently, 508.8 foolishly, 512.16 obliviously, 521.13 meaninglessly
senselessness 460.1 lack of intellect, 506.1 nonsense, 508.1 folly, 512.1 oblivion, 798.1 ludi-

crousness
senseless talk 521
sense of community 2.5 society
sense of danger 633.5 danger
sense of duty 847, 857.1 probity
sense of hearing 420.1 hearing
sense of indebtedness 837.1 gratitude
sense of language 549.4 literary style
sense of mystery 786.1 wonder
sense of obligation 837.1 gratitude
sense of responsibility 719.1 observance, 857.1 probity
sense of right and wrong 876.2 good morals
sense of security 632.1 safety, 718.1 protection
sense of sight 435.1 vision
sense of smell 416
sense of taste 411.1 taste
sense of time 185.1 time
sense of touch 407.1 touch
sense of wonder 786.1 wonder
sense of wrong 844
sense organ 407, 403.4 someone or something that feels
sense perception 407.1 touch
sense-perception 403.1 sensation
sense vibrations 11.24 experience psychic phenomena
sensibilia 4.8 philosophical term
sensibilities 759.3 feelings
sensibility 6.11 refinement, 396.1 life, 481.2 judiciousness, 492.1 judgment, 760.5 sensitivity
sensible 403, 4.15 rational, 6.20 refined, 101.8 practical, 242.6 moderate, 367.7 material, 459.11 thoughtful, 463.7 reasoning, 507.5 wise, 509.5 rational, 613.1 useful, 654.8 advisable, 754.9 cheap, 759.10 feeling
sensibleness 459.5 common sense
sensible price 754.1 cheapness
sensibly 4.26 rationally, 367.9 materially, 459.15 intelligently, 463.15 reasonably, 507.9 wisely
sensing 464.6 intuitive, 759.10 feeling
sensitive 759, 760, 6.20 refined, 374.7 impressionable, 403.5 sensible, 407.8 touchable, 464.6 intuitive, 481.9 discriminating, 492.9 judicious, 558.3 elegant, 759.10 feeling, 794.5 refined
sensitively 407, 760, 6.27 discerningly, 374.18 softheartedly, 481.16 judiciously
sensitive man 401.14 liberated man
sensitiveness 374.12 gentleness, 760.5 sensitivity
sensitive payment 729.2 gift
sensitive person 760, 759.9 feeling person
sensitive plant 403.4 someone or something that feels, 760.9 oversensitive person
sensitive to touch 407.8 touchable
sensitivity 56, 760, 6.11 refinement, 66.10 graininess, 403.2 ability to sense, 407.1 touch, 481.2 judiciousness, 519.3 insight, 586.7 persuadability
Sensitivity 760
sensitivity training 61.3 psychiatric treatment
sensitivity training group 61.3 psychiatric treatment
sensitized 760.3 sore
sensitometer 268.8 meter
sensitometry 268.2 micrometry
sensor 496.11 detector
sensorial 403.10 sensory
sensorium 403.4 someone or something that feels
sensory 403, 407.8 touchable
sensory awareness training 61.3 psychiatric treatment
sensory pattern 61.26 gestalt
sensual 367.7 material, 405.6

pleasant, 405.7 pleased, 870.6 self-indulgent
sensualism 367.2 materialization, 405.1 physical pleasure
sensualist 405.3 pleasure-seeker, 870.5 self-indulgent person
sensuality 367.2 materialization, 403.2 ability to sense, 870.1 self-indulgence
sensually 367.9 materially
sensual pleasure 405.1 physical pleasure
sensum 403.1 sensation
sensuous 403.7 susceptible, 407.8 touchable
sensuousness 403.2 ability to sense, 405.1 physical pleasure
sent 534.34 communicated
sent after 590.15 pursuing
sent back 581.10 rejected
sentence 5.23 phrase, 16.7 legal trial, 16.33 litigation, 16.43 conviction, 16.79 convict, 143.2 particular, 187.4 period of activity, 492.2 verdict, 564.7 utterance, 699.4 detention, 699.11 detain, 879.2 penalize, 879.8 penalty
sentenced 16.64 convicted, 699.15 detained
sentenced to death 16.64 convicted, 397.18 dying
sentencer 879.17 punisher
sentence structure 549.4 literary style
sentence to death 16.79 convict, 879.5 execute
sentencing 879.8 penalty
sentential 5.43 phrasal
sententious 492.8 judging, 505.2 proverbial, 552.3 concise, 554.3 emphatic
sententiously 552.5 concisely
sententiousness 552.1 conciseness
sentience 396.1 life, 403.1 sensation
sentient 403.5 sensible, 759.10 feeling, 760.1 sensitive
sentiment 4.1 philosophy, 403.1 sensation, 471.1 idea, 497.1 belief, 821.1 love, 821.3 lovingness
sentimental 471.13 ideal, 759.12, 760.1 sensitive, 821.17 loving, 821.20 amorous, 826.9 endearing
sentimental attachment 784.1 liking, 821.3 lovingness
sentimental comedy 51.10 comedy
sentimentalism 48 Literary Groups and Movements
sentimentality 759.7 emotionalism, 760.5 sensitivity, 821.3 lovingness
sentimentally 471.22 imaginatively, 555.3 unemphatically, 759.21 emotionally, 821.30 lovingly, 826.10 endearingly
sentiments 759.3 feelings
sentinel 323.5 person who closes, 435.11 observer, 469.8 watchful person, 632.3 protector, 636.4 warner, 671.14 guard, 679.14 armed forces, 718.3 security officer
sentry 323.5 person who closes, 435.11 observer, 469.8 watchful person, 632.3 protector, 636.4 warner, 671.14 guard, 679.14 armed forces, 718.3 security officer
sent to Coventry 816.10 lonely
senza 49 Musical Terms
Seoul 93 Cities
sepak takrow 18 Sporting Activities
sepal 83.6 leaf, 84.3 flower part, 143.6 branch
separability 136.1 separation, 136.3 separateness, 139.1 nonadhesion
separable 136
separate 104, 104, 136, 136, 343, 57.25 solidify, 108.6 unrelated, 110.4 duplicate, 139.5 unstick, 139.9 aloof, 141.4

deconstruct, 143.10 part, 160.14 disconnect, 162.9 be dispersed, 162.12 disperse, 162.20 separated, 174.16 alone, 174.20 single out, 252.18 disconnect, 263.6 keep away, 265.4 space, 265.6 spaced, 343.6 divergent, 345.6 part, 355.17 obtain an extract, 481.11 judged, 481.12 discriminate, 500.8 dissent, 580.4 pick, 824.7 divorce
separated 162, 104.11 separate, 108.6 unrelated, 136.15 separate, 141.5 disintegrated, 174.16 alone, 174.17 single, 252.12 disconnected, 263.8 distant, 265.6 spaced, 343.6 divergent, 816.10 lonely, 820.8 estranged, 824.11 divorced
separate from 139.7 be aloof
separately 136, 104.18 extraneously, 108.12 irrelevantly, 139.11 aloofly, 141.8 destructively, 174.22 one by one, 252.21 disconnectedly, 265.8 apart, 343.6 divergently, 481.15 discriminatingly
separateness 104, 136, 108.1 unrelatedness, 139.2 aloofness, 174.5 aloneness
separate out 141.4 deconstruct
separates 136, 295.10 suit
separate the sheep from the goats 115.6 differentiate, 136.11 divide
separate the wheat from the chaff 136.11 divide
separating 136.1 separation, 481.9 discriminating
separating funnel 57 Laboratory Apparatus
separation 136, 816, 824, 57.5 process, 139.1 nonadhesion, 141.2 deconstruction, 162.5 divergence, 174.6 singleness, 252.5 disconnection, 265.1 distance, 265.1 interval, 343.2, 345.9 parting, 355.7 obtaining an extract, 481.1 discrimination, 500.4 faction, 820.2 personal conflict
Separation 136
separatism 136.3 separateness, 174.5 aloneness, 500.3 dissentience, 665.4 partisanship
separatist 136.8 person who separates, 139.4 individualist, 174.16 alone, 500.5 dissenter, 500.7 dissenting, 665.10 political, 713.4 protester
separatists 500.5 dissenters
separative 57.40 synthetic, 136.17 unjoined
separatively 136.22 in isolation
separator 136, 355.9 extractor
separatrix 286.2 oblique line
Sephardic 7.16 denominational
Sephardim 7 Non-Christian Religions
sepia 66.12 development, 449.4 brown pigment
sepoy 679.6 militarist
seppuku 879.11 penance
seppuku 398.7 suicide
sepsis 622.2 uncleanness, 624.6 infection, 626.1 lack of hygiene
septenary 179.3 seven, 179.14 seventh
septendecillion 169.3 large number, 179.11 million
septennial 179.14 seventh
septennially 179.24 fivefold
septet 48.8 part of poem, 49.26 musical group, 140.3 assembly, 179.3 seven, 664.9 team
septic 618.4 poor, 622.8 unclean, 626.6 contagious, 626.7 toxic, 727.8 sink
septicaemia 624.6 infection
septically 626.8 unhygienically
septic tank 605.4 storage, 614.6 refuse, 727.5 wasteyard, 727.8 sink
septillion 169.3 large number, 179.11 million
septivalent 57.35 combined
septuagenarian 179.8 twenty and

over, 207.7 older person
Septuagesima 10.15 holy day
Septuagint 7.12 religious text
septuple 179.3 seven, 179.14 seventh, 179.23 quintuple
septuplet 179.3 seven
septuplicate 179.3 seven, 179.14 seventh
sepulchral 399.11 funeral, 427.8 deep
sepulchrally 399.12 funereally
sepulchral monument 399.4 funeral objects
sepulchre 323.4 closed place, 399.6 grave
sepulture 399.1 burial
sequacious 155.15 sequential
sequel 155, 195, 155.5 consequence, 219.1 continuity, 227.1 effect, 627.8 better thing
sequence 52, 155, 150.3 hierarchy, 159.2 consecution, 195.1 succession, 219.1 continuity, 433.3 melodiousness
Sequence 155
sequence dancing 46.1 dancing
sequent 155.15 sequential, 219.5 continual
sequential 155, 150.12 hierarchical, 159.9 consecutive, 195.12 succeeding, 219.5 continual, 227.10 caused
sequential access 65.17 computing term
sequentially 150.25 in order, 155.27 in sequence, 159.18 consecutively, 219.7 continually
sequential scanning 534.21 television
sequester 136.11 divide, 147.7 exclude, 734.8 take back, 747.7 not pay, 816.13 ignore
sequestered 325.6 quiescent, 527.2, 531.14 concealed, 816.11 secluded
sequestered nook 816.5 solitary place
sequestering of the jury 16.7 legal trial
sequester the jury 16.71 try a case
sequestrate 767.14 take away, 879.1 punish
sequestration 147.1 exclusion, 527.8 concealment, 734.2 taking back, 879.7 punishment
sequestrator 730.7 collector, 734.6 taker
sequestrectomy 60 Surgical Operations
sequin 439.2 quality of light, 456.5 variegated thing
sequined 439.16 bright
sequoia 85 Trees and Shrubs, 275.6 tall thing
ser 75 Some Foreign Units
sérac 34.5 rock face, 54.38 glacier
seraglio 402.13 womenfolk, 821.13 abode of love
Seram 98 Islands
seraph 8.6 angel
seraphic 7.15 religious, 8.14 heavenly, 821.22 lovable, 863.5 virtuous
seraphically 8.19 divinely
Serbia 91 Countries
Serbo-Croat 5 Languages and Groups of Languages
Serbs 1 Peoples
sere 59.18 ecology, 392.3 dried-up, 628.12 deteriorated
serenade 433.2 song, 821.15 love item, 821.26 court
serenader 433.5 melodist
serendipitous 229.6 motiveless, 514.8 surprising, 589.8 chance
serendipitously 589.13 by chance
serendipity 130.4 extra, 229.3 coincidence, 496.6 discovery, 514.4 surprising thing, 589.2 luck
serene 4.18 detached, 325.6 quiescent, 660.13 easygoing, 675.7 peaceful, 765.4 satisfied, 787.3 unmoved
serenely 4.27 stoically, 675.8 peacefully, 765.13 with satisfac-

tion, 787.9 without wonder
serenity 4.3 detachment, 325.2 repose, 376.7 smoothness, 649.1 ease, 765.1 satisfaction, 787.1 lack of wonder
serf 697.7 slave, 701.5 subjected person, 803.1 plebeian, 808.3 sycophant
serfdom 701.1 subjection, 808.1 servility
serge 67 Natural Fabrics, 161 Collective Names for Birds and Animals
sergeant 679.17 army person
sergeant aircrew 679.32 airman
sergeant fish 80 Fishes
sergeant major 690.4 strict person
serial 51.2 play, 150.12 hierarchical, 155.15 sequential, 159.9 consecutive, 214.5 regular thing, 214.11 regular, 434.9 unmelodious, 532.5 journal, 534.25 broadcast material, 560.3 narration
serialism 434.4 atonality
serialization 155.1 sequence, 214.1 regularity
serialize 214.10 make regular, 532.15 publish
serialized 214.11 regular
serial killer 241.4 violent person or animal, 398.11 murderer, 832.8 malefactor, 862.6 evil person
serial killing 832.7 act of malevolence
serially 159.18 consecutively, 214.15 regularly
serial order 150.3 hierarchy
serial printer 65.7 peripheral
seriate 159.18 consecutive
sericultural 82.14 entomological
sericulturalist 82.8 entomologist
sericulture 82.7 study
seriema 78 Birds
series 155, 49.20 key, 52.20 sequence, 54.41 geological time, 59.17 taxonomy, 142.5 unit, 150.3 hierarchy, 155.4 sequel, 159.2 consecution, 171.1 list, 187.5 recurrent period, 195.1 succession, 434.4 atonality, 532.5 journal, 534.25 broadcast material
series connection 64.16 circuit element
serin 78 Birds
serine 58 Amino Acids
seringa 85 Trees and Shrubs
serious 554, 277.9 deep-seated, 520.7 significant, 556.1 simple, 574.2 tenacious, 588.11 intending, 611.5 important, 624.22 sick, 633.1 dangerous, 772.1 solemn, 772.3 important, 830.6 sullen, 876.10 moralistic
serious climbing 34.1 mountaineering
Serious Crime Squad 16.15 British police
serious literature 48.1 literature
seriously 535.24 truthfully, 574.17 resolutely, 611.9 importantly, 772.10 solemnly, 772.12 indeed, 830.13 sullenly
serious-minded 588.11 intending
seriousness 554, 520.2 significance, 554.4 simplicity, 574.13 concentration, 611.1 importance, 876.4 self-righteousness
Seriousness 772
serious person 772
serious press 528.4 mass communication, 532.3 journalism
sermon 532.1 publication, 553.1 diffuseness, 561.1 dissertation, 564.8 speech, 567.1 address, 852.7 blame
sermoner 567.6 public speaker
sermonist 567.6 public speaker
sermonize 4.22 propound a philosophy, 7.20 preach, 561.4 dissertate, 564.14 speak to, 567.7 address, 876.12 moralize
sermonizer 7.4 religionist, 564.10 speaker, 567.6 public speaker

serologist 60.13 medical specialist
serology 60.3 medical specialty
seropus 353.7 pus
serosity 387.7 juiciness
serotest 60.7 diagnosis
serotine bat 77 Placental Mammals
serous 387.16 rheumy
serous fluid 387.3 body fluid
serow 77 Placental Mammals
Serpens 53 The Constellations
serpent 49 Musical Instruments, 79.3 snake, 127.6 inferior, 429.3 hisser, 539.21 traitor, 631.6 source of trouble, 657.3 cunning person
Serpent 53 The Constellations
Serpent Bearer 53 The Constellations
Serpentes 79.3 snake
serpentiform 79.12 snakelike
serpentine 54 Common Rocks, 54 Minerals, 79.12 snakelike, 96.10 fluvial, 314.4 convolutional, 335.21 indirect, 456.5 variegated thing, 657.4 cunning
Serpentine 94 Lakes
serpenting 32.10 dressage
serpent's tooth 631.6 source of trouble
serpigo 624.13 skin disease
serpulid 81 Worms
serrate 83.18 of leaves, 319.5 notch, 375.12 make rough, 380.15 make sharp
serrated 319.4 notched, 375.2 coarse, 380.4 toothed
serration 319.1 notch, 375.6 roughness, 380.6 sharpness
serried 159.11 continuous, 161.50 crowded, 371.6 dense
serriform 319.4 notched
serrulation 319.1 notch
Sertanejo 32 Breeds of Horse and Pony
serum 387.3 body fluid
serval 77 Placental Mammals
servant 697, 127.6 inferior, 232.3 assistant, 612.10 nonentity, 646.1, 646.1 worker, 653.16 official, 662.16 home help, 673.2 appeaser, 694.4 obedient person, 701.3 subordinate, 808.5 adherent
Servant 697
servant girl 697.6 domestic servant
servant's uniform 295.3 formal dress
serve 40, 662, 697, 40.2 tennis strokes, 116.27 fit, 135.11 make love, 230.7 be operational, 232.4 be an instrument, 338.23 throw, 606.5 provision, 608.4 suffice, 613.9 be useful, 615.6 be convenient, 644.7 work for, 662.21 be helpful, 694.5 obey, 701.8 be subject to, 765.10 suffice, 782.16 be desirable, 808.11 pander to, 819.15 be hospitable, 861.20 do good
serve a citation 856.5 accuse
serve an apprenticeship 6.23 learn, 594.8 prepare oneself
serve as a doormat for 701.8 be subject to
serve as a makeshift 608.4 suffice
serve as a model 233.8 influence
serve as an example 107.7 relate to
serve as a representative 706.5 represent
serve a sentence 702.10 be in prison
serve as host 819.15 be hospitable
serve as press officer for 534.13 interpret news
serve as proxy 222.4 be a substitute
serve a stretch 699.11 detain, 702.10 be in prison
serve a summons 856.5 accuse
serve a use 819.16 be favourable
serve badly 515.6 disappoint
serve involuntarily 701.8 be sub-

ject to
serve notice on 16.70 *litigate*
serve on a working party 706.5 *represent*
serve one right **672**, 845.15 *merit*
serve one's country 676.12 *go to war*
serve one's king 676.12 *go to war*
serve one's turn 613.9 *be useful*
serve one well 613.10 *benefit*
server 40.5 *real tennis*, 40.6 *tennis player*, 40.12 *badminton terms*, 65.15 *network*, 338.14 *thrower*, 697.3 *attendant*
serve the time 615.6 *be convenient*
serve the times 808.13 *conform*
serve time 699.11 *detain*
serve up 606.5 *provision*
serve with a writ 856.5 *accuse*
service 74 *Rigging*, 10.1 *ritual*, 17.8 *military*, 40.2 *tennis strokes*, 230.4 *management*, 230.9 *take action*, 232.1 *instrumentality*, 251.4 *employment*, 338.5 *throw*, 599.6 *use*, 606.1, 606.5 *provision*, 613.5 *usefulness*, 629.1 *repair*, 629.3 *restore*, 629.8 *repair*, 637.1 *preservation*, 637.5 *preserve*, 662.2 *support*, 694.2 *loyalty*, 701.1 *subjection*, 719.2 *religious observance*, 729.1 *giving*, 739.6 *salesmanship*, 812.3 *ceremony*, 813.3 *formal occasion*, 831.4 *benevolent act*, 847.2 *task*
serviceability 232.1 *instrumentality*, 599.6 *use*, 613.6 *usability*
serviceable 101.8, 232.8 *practical*, 613.2 *usable*, 662.33 *helpful*
serviceably 613.12 *usefully*, 662.36 *helpfully*
service an order 606.5 *provision*
serviceberry 85 *Trees and Shrubs*, 86 *Fruits*
service box 40.9 *squash terms*
service ceiling 73.5 *flight*
service charge 751.3 *fee*
service contract 715.2 *purchase contract*
service court line 40.8 *squash*
service fee 751.3 *fee*
service line 40.4 *tennis terms*, 40.5 *real tennis*, 40.8 *squash*
serviceman 679.8 *soldier*
service penthouse 40.5 *real tennis*
service road 137.5 *road*
services 13.6 *economic factors*, 679.14 *armed forces*
service side 40.5 *real tennis*
services no longer required 704.2 *termination*
service station 218.4 *stopping place*
service tree 85 *Trees and Shrubs*
servicewoman 679.8 *soldier*, 679.10 *woman soldier*
servicing 232.8 *practical*, 629.8 *repair*, 637.1 *preservation*
serviette 621.11 *cleaning cloth*
servile **808**, 673.5 *submitting*, 694.7 *obedient*, 697.9 *serving*, 701.9 *subject*, 771.11 *humouring*, 849.9 *showing respect*, 853.16 *sycophantic*
servilely 694.10, 697.10 *obediently*, 701.11 *under subjection*
servility **808**, 694.1 *obedience*, 701.1 *subjection*, 853.5 *sycophancy*
Servility 808
serving **697**, 350.14 *mouthful*, 662.30 *helping*, 701.9 *subject*
serving a sentence 699.15 *detained*, 702.8 *imprisoned*
serving girl 697.6 *domestic servant*
serving maid 697.6 *domestic servant*
serving man 697.6 *domestic servant*
serving one's country 676.8 *warfare*
serving the purpose 116.16 *fitting*
Servite 7 *Members of Religious*

Orders
servitor 697.1 *servant*
servitude 576.14 *apathy*, 673.1 *submission*, 699.4 *detention*, 701.1 *subjection*
servomechanism 63.5 *dynamic structure*, 603.4 *machine*
servomotor 603.4 *machine*
sesame **45** *Herbs and Spices*
sesame seeds 413.5 *herbs*
sesamoid bones 382 *Bones*
Sesha 8 *Deities*
Sesheta 8 *Deities*
Sesotho 5 *Languages and Groups of Languages*
sesquicentenary 812.5 *anniversary*
sesquicentennial 214.3, 214.13 *anniversary*, 812.14 *centennial*
sesquicentennially 214.16 *cyclically*
sesquihydrate 57.10 *salt*
sesquipedal 269.1 *long*
sesquipedalian 5.17 *word*, 5.42 *worded*, 269.1 *long*, 553.3 *diffuse*, 557.4 *ornate*
sesquipedalianism 269.4 *length*, 559.4 *inelegance of speech*
sesquiterpene 58.20 *terpene*
sessile 83.18 *of leaves*, 89.10 *of fungi*, 90.7 *algal*, 138.9 *adhesive*
session 42.2 *contest*, 161.6 *sitting*, 187.4 *period of activity*, 653.7 *council*
sessions 16.7 *legal trial*, 16.19 *lawcourt*
sessions judge 16.23 *judge*, 492.6 *justice*
sestet 48.8 *part of poem*
sestina 48.7 *poem*, 48.10 *verse form*
set **52**, **577**, 5.43 *phrasal*, 18.1 *sport*, 19.8 *huddle*, 35.6 *rugger*, 40.4 *tennis terms*, 51.17 *stage set*, 52.23 *algebra*, 69.15 *cultivate*, 112.2 *conformity*, 124.1 *average*, 135.10 *link*, 140.3 *assembly*, 142.5 *unit*, 146.1 *inclusion*, 152.6 *category*, 152.12 *arrange*, 161.19 *clique*, 161.23 *flock*, 161.25 *assemblage*, 163.2 *class*, 163.5 *social class*, 165.24 *specify*, 185.16 *time*, 206.5 *young plant*, 214.10 *make regular*, 225.7 *make stable*, 250.6 *located*, 251.6 *situated*, 251.10 *situate*, 273.7 *thicken*, 306.6 *nature*, 324.2 *momentum*, 332.1 *direction*, 332.2 *bearing*, 332.6 *direct*, 332.7 *take a direction*, 332.14 *directed*, 360.9 *descend*, 371.7 *condensed*, 371.8 *be dense*, 373.3 *hardened*, 373.10 *solidify*, 400.9 *group*, 490.5 *inevitable*, 532.15 *publish*, 537.21 *accurate*, 537.31 *be accurate*, 582.4 *deliberate*, 584.13 *fixed*, 594.18 *prepared*, 596.5 *attempt*, 605.5 *collection*, 629.6 *cure*, 630.20 *doctor*, 665.1 *party*, 674.2 *contest*, 796.1 *fashion*, 796.4 *design*
Set 8 *Deities*, 8.7 *devil*
seta 83.5 *stem*, 88.4 *moss plant*
set a bad example 652.13 *behave badly*, 864.17 *make wicked*
set a booby trap 539.33 *snare*
set about 597.1 *undertake*, 644.6 *work*
set a ceiling 120.8 *quantify*
set a course 74.9 *navigate*
set a curfew 302.7 *limit*
set a date for 185.16 *time*, 192.14 *keep time*
set adrift 136.13 *diverge*
set afloat 226.11 *inaugurate*, 338.33 *start*
set a floor 120.8 *quantify*
set against 111.8 *be opposite*, 136.11 *divide*, 587.4 *put off*, 663.16 *confront*, 785.7 *cause dislike*, 820.13 *antagonize*, 822.10 *hating*
set a good example 652.12 *behave well*, 863.8 *be virtuous*
set a gun 539.33 *snare*
set a high value on oneself

809.15 *be vain*
set algebra 52.23 *algebra*
set alight 408.15 *burn*, 439.24 *light*
set a lower limit 120.8 *quantify*
set a new record 126.8 *be superior*
set an example 471.19 *epitomize*, 652.11 *conduct oneself*
set an upper limit 120.8 *quantify*
set apart **136**, 136.17 *unjoined*, 165.22 *characterize*, 265.4 *space*, 265.6 *spaced*, 485.15 *modify*, 580.4 *pick*, 848.9 *exempt*
set a precedent 156.21 *pioneer*
set a price 751.11 *price*
set a quota 120.8 *quantify*, 302.7 *limit*
set a record 21.6 *compete in athletics*, 126.8 *be superior*
set a riddle 477.21 *confuse*
set a sail 36.15 *sail*
set aside 136.10 *set apart*, 326.15 *take away*, 580.4 *pick*, 581.2 *discard*, 593.10 *necessitate*, 600.6 *stop using*, 605.6 *store*, 605.7 *stored*, 704.6 *cancel*, 704.10 *cancelled*
set-aside 68.2 *Common Agricultural Policy*
set aside the sentence 16.78 *acquit*
set at each other's throats 820.13 *antagonize*
set at ease 765.9 *comfort*
set a time for 185.16 *time*, 192.14 *keep time*
set at large 639.1 *deliver*, 700.4 *liberate*
set at liberty 700.4 *liberate*, 848.10 *acquit*
set at loggerheads 828.14 *make angry*
set at odds 117.14 *disagree*, 666.7 *pick a fight*, 785.7 *cause dislike*, 820.13 *antagonize*
set a trap for 496.2 *detect*, 592.13 *plot*
set a trend 154.18 *forerun*, 201.18 *be trendy*, 228.9 *motivate*
set at rest 101.12 *establish reality*
setback 337
set back 209.8 *delay*, 328.3 *slow down*, 328.7 *delayed*
setback 328.12 *hesitation*, 515.2 *bad outcome*, 587.6 *dissuasion*, 628.7 *deterioration*, 683.1 *failure*, 687.1 *adversity*, 722.1 *loss*
set before someone's eyes 526.1 *display*
set by the ear 828.14 *make angry*
set by the ears 822.16 *cause hate*
set dance 46.4 *historic dancing*
set designer 51.25 *producer*
set difference 52.21 *set*
set down 171.8 *list*, 362.1 *lower*, 535.17 *affirm*, 806.3 *humbled*
setdown 806.10 *abasement*
set down 806.23 *abase*, 852.20 *censure*
set-down 852.7 *blame*
set down in black and white 545.14 *inscribe*
set eyes on 496.1 *discover*
set fair 392.5 *rainless*
set fire to 408.15 *burn*, 439.24 *light*
set foot in 344.5 *get in*, 346.9 *enter*
set foot on dry land 344.4 *land*
set form 813.5 *etiquette*
set forth 4.22 *propound a philosophy*, 345.5 *set out*
set forward 597.1 *undertake*
set free **698**, 136.9 *separate*, 639.1 *deliver*, 700.4 *liberate*, 767.10 *save*, 839.10 *absolve*, 848.10 *acquit*, 855.7 *vindicate*
set going 226.11 *inaugurate*, 230.8 *activate*, 338.33 *start*, 597.1 *undertake*, 599.5 *dispose of*
set gun 539.13 *snare*
SETI 53

setiform 375.3 *barbed*
set in 55.59 *storm*, 217.5 *be permanent*, 225.6 *be stable*, 354.5 *inset*
set in action 599.5 *dispose of*
set in concrete 225.7 *make stable*
set in granite 225.7 *make stable*
set in motion 324, 156.20 *activate*, 226.11 *inaugurate*, 228.9 *motivate*, 243.10 *produce*, 330.1 *impel*, 338.33 *start*, 599.5 *dispose of*
set in one's ways 577.4 *set*, 584.13 *fixed*
set in opposition 663.18 *counteract*
set in order 150.18 *order*, 594.4 *prepare for action*
set in stone 225.7 *make stable*
set in towards 332.7 *take a direction*
set no store by 495.3 *underestimate*, 542.22 *play down*
set of beliefs 4.2 *philosophical system*, 7.1 *religion*
set off 122.11 *equalize*, 125.2 *counterbalance*, 131.3 *subtract*, 156.19 *start off*, 226.10 *awaken*, 410.11 *fuel*
set off against 663.18 *counteract*
set off an alarm 543.12 *signal*
set off at a run 329.6 *accelerate*
set of four 178.1 *four*
set of points 52.36 *point*
set of rules 654.3 *precept*
set of teeth 380.11 *tooth*
set of terms 716.2 *basis for negotiations*
set of three 177.1 *three*
set of two 176.1 *two*
set on 670.5 *strike*, 821.18 *in love*
set on an even keel 125.5 *counterbalance*
set one a problem 659.17 *be difficult*
set one back 751.13 *cost*
set on edge 375.12 *make rough*
set one off 798.7 *make one laugh*
set one's cap at 821.26 *court*
set one's cap for 590.12 *aim at*, 826.8 *court*
set one's compass for 332.7 *take a direction*
set one's course 590.12 *aim at*
set one's course for 332.7 *take a direction*
set one's dignity aside 806.21 *humble oneself*
set oneself against 852.16 *disagree*
set one's face 574.8 *brace oneself against*, 852.16 *disagree*
set one's face against 663.14 *be against*, 852.16 *disagree*
set one's hand to the plough 597.1 *undertake*
set one's heart on 574.9 *undertake*, 714.11 *promise oneself*, 782.12 *desire*, 784.7 *like*
set one's shoulder to the wheel 597.1 *undertake*
set one's sights higher 128.5 *make bigger*
set one's sights on 332.7 *take a direction*, 471.18, 588.10 *aim*, 782.12 *desire*
set one's teeth on edge 415.8 *sour*, 430.4 *be strident*
set on foot 408.15 *burn*
set on foot 226.11 *inaugurate*
set on its feet 225.7 *make stable*
set on one's feet 662.29 *finance*
set on one's feet again 629.6 *cure*
setose 375.3 *barbed*
set out **345**, 152.12 *arrange*, 248.21 *space*, 526.1 *display*, 549.9 *style*
set out for 332.7 *take a direction*
set out on foot 338.33 *start*
Seto ware **44** *Types of Ceramics*
set parameters 302.7 *limit*
set pattern dancing 41.7 *ice-dancing*
set phrase 5.24 *phrasing*
set piece 51.6 *scene*, 811.14 *show*, 813.3 *formal occasion*
set position 21.1 *track events*

set purpose 588.1 *intention*
set requirements 593.10 *necessitate*
set right 627.3 *rectify*, 843.15 *put right*, 855.7 *vindicate*
set rolling 364.9 *roll*
set sail 74.9 *navigate*, 74.10 *sail*, 156.19 *start off*, 345.5 *set out*
set scrum 35.3 *rugby play*
set shot 23.4 *playing terms*
set snares 590.11 *hunt*
set someone on his feet 237.8 *strengthen*
set someone up properly 237.8 *strengthen*
set speech 567.1 *address*
set square 52.49 *geometric construction*, 268.6 *measuring instrument*, 281.4 *plumb line*, 310.4 *angular measurement*
set store by 849.15 *respect*
set straight 332.6 *direct*, 530.6 *divulge*
sett 77.20 *abode of mammals*, 256.13 *lair*
settee 47.2 *chair*
setter 77 *Breeds of Dogs*
set terms 5.24 *phrasing*
set the alarm 185.18 *adjust the clock*, 192.14 *keep time*, 594.4 *prepare for action*
set the ball rolling 156.20 *activate*
set the example 154.18 *forerun*
set the fashion 154.18 *forerun*, 228.9 *motivate*, 233.8 *influence*
set the law in motion 16.70 *litigate*
set theory 52 Mathematical Theories
set the pace 228.9 *motivate*
set the price tag too high 753.10 *overcharge*
set the record straight 530.6 *divulge*
set the stage 594.2 *do the groundwork*
set the trend 233.8 *influence*
set the world on fire 682.6 *be successful*
setting 49.15 *composition*, 51.17 *stage set*, 106.1 *circumstances*, 250.1 *location*, 251.1 *situation*, 251.2 *circumstances*, 297.1 *surroundings*, 371.7 *condensed*, 373.6 *solidification*, 473.4 *gist*, 537.8 *accuracy*
setting apart 136
setting aside 136.2 *setting apart*, 704.1 *cancellation*, 731.1 *allocation*
setting circle 53.25 *mounting*
setting free 638.1 *escape*, 700.1 *liberation*
setting in motion 156.6 *inauguration*
setting lotion 386.6 *pomade*
setting of court date 16.7 *legal trial*
setting of the sun 205.1 *evening*
setting up 156.6 *inauguration*, 243.2 *manufacture*
settle 250, 255, 47.2 *chair*, 54.63 *ebb*, 91.18 *exert sovereignty*, 116.23 *arrange*, 125.4 *compensate*, 149.16 *migrate*, 152.12 *arrange*, 152.17 *come to an arrangement*, 157.15 *end*, 166.13 *rule*, 208.8 *precede*, 242.3 *be moderate*, 256.17 *inhabit*, 317.6 *be concave*, 325.8 *be motionless*, 346.14 *enrol*, 360.9 *descend*, 369.12 *be heavy*, 475.17 *prove*, 490.21 *make certain*, 492.11 *judge*, 574.7 *resolve*, 584.17 *become a habit*, 662.29 *finance*, 667.7 *contract*, 684.5 *conclude*, 715.5 *contract*, 728.3 *transfer property*, 746.7 *pay off*, 765.10 *suffice*, 879.2 *penalize*
settle accounts 750, 125.4 *compensate*
settle an account 746.7 *pay off*
settle a score 746.13 *retaliate*
settle a strike 15.12 *have an industrial dispute*

settled 55.45 *fine*, 116.12 *arranged*, 157.21 *ended*, 225.10 *stabilized*, 250.6 *located*, 255.13 *resident*, 475.13 *proven*, 490.3 *decided*, 717.6 *compromising*, 746.16 *paid*, 750.11 *accounted*
settle differences 677.4 *pacify*, 678.1 *mediate*
settle down 225.6 *be stable*, 242.3 *be moderate*, 325.8 *be motionless*
settled purpose 588.1 *intention*
settle for 737.3 *bargain*
settle in 225.6 *be stable*, 346.14 *enrol*
settlement 249, 91.3 *dominion*, 116.3 *arrangement*, 125.1 *compensation*, 152.10 *agreement*, 475.4 *proof*, 662.6 *financial assistance*, 667.2, 715.1 *contract*, 717.1 *compromise*, 728.1 *transfer of property*, 729.1 *giving*, 746.1 *payment*
settlement on account 746.1 *payment*
settlement out of court 16.7 *legal trial*
settle on 360.12 *drop*, 580.1 *select*
settle on a date 185.16 *time*
settle on a time 185.16 *time*
settle one's differences 675.6 *make peace*
settler 255, 104.7 *new arrival*, 149.6 *immigrant*, 157.13 *ender*, 346.7 *entrant*, 347.8 *outgoer*
settle the matter 101.12 *establish reality*, 492.11 *judge*
settle the score 125.4 *compensate*
settle up 878.11 *pay*
settle with 879.2 *penalize*
settling 250.4 *placing*, 728.1 *transfer of property*
settlor 729.2 *giver*
set to 156.18 *make a beginning*, 350.22 *eat well*, 473.1 *argument*, 574.9, 597.1 *undertake*, 644.6 *work*, 674.12 *fight*, 872.5 *be greedy*
set-to 151.9 *disorder*, 500.1 *dissent*, 666.2 *argument*, 674.6 *fight*, 764.8 *quarrel*
set to music 433, 49.35 *compose*
set to rights 629.1 *repair*, 843.15 *put right*
set to work 156.18 *make a beginning*
set to work on 594.2 *do the groundwork*
set two 40.9 *squash terms*
set up 33.10 *be on the track*
setup 106.1 *circumstances*
set up 148.13 *make*
setup 150.1 *order*
set up 150.18 *order*, 156.23 *inaugurate*, 190.7 *make permanent*, 225.7 *make stable*, 226.11 *inaugurate*, 243.10 *produce*, 250.9 *locate*, 251.10 *situate*, 281.6 *make vertical*
setup 304.4 *forming*
set up 361.1 *raise*, 361.11 *raised*
setup 382.3 *form*
set up 382.16 *construct*, 582.2 *premeditate*, 629.6 *cure*
setup 660.6 *easy thing*
set up 662.29 *finance*
set-up 33.6 *motor racing terms*, 251.2 *circumstances*, 306.9 *formed*, 582.4 *deliberate*
set up a kangaroo court 590.8 *pursue*
set up house 255.15 *settle*
set up house together 823.15 *marry*
set upon 574.1 *resolute*
set up one's standard 676.12 *go to war*
set up shop 597.1 *undertake*
Sevastopol 93 Cities
seven 179, 52.9 *numeral*, 179.14 *seventh*
seven ages of man 396.5 *life cycle*
seven-card brag 42 Card Games
seven centuries 179.9 *treble fig-*

ures
seven days 179.3 *seven*
seven deadly sins 864, 179.3 *seven*
sevener 179.3 *seven*
sevenfold 179.14 *seventh*, 179.24 *fivefold*
seven-footer 275.7 *tall person*
seven-league boots 11.6 *talisman*, 329.11 *swift thing*
seven lean years 609.9 *scarcity*
seven sacraments 10.5 *Christian rite*
seven seas 97.1 *sea*
seven-sided 52.82 *polygonal*
seven-stone weakling 238.4 *weakling*
seventeenth 173.4 *less than one*
seventeen-year locust 82 Insects, 82.3 *pest*
seventh 179, 49.16 *musical note*, 52.75 *equal*, 173.4 *less than one*, 179.3 *seven*, 179.24 *fivefold*
Seventh-Day Adventist 7.5 *Christian*
seventh guard 28.3 *fencing movements*
seventh heaven 279.1 *summit*
seventhly 179.24 *fivefold*
seventh part 179.3 *seven*
seventieth 173.4 *less than one*, 179.19 *twentieth*
seventy 179.8 *twenty and over*
seventy-four 680.12 *historical guns*
seven up 42 Card Games
Seven Wonders of the World 179.3 *seven*, 786.4 *wonder*
seven years of plenty 608.8 *plenty*
Seven Years' War 17 Major Wars
sever 131.4 *take off*, 136.9 *separate*, 143.10 *part*, 160.14 *disconnect*, 824.7 *divorce*
severable 136.19 *separable*
several 175.1 *plurality*, 175.6 *plural*, 490.8 *unspecified*
several irons in the fire 642.6 *business*
severally 165, 136.20 *separately*, 175.10 *plurally*
severalty 136.3 *separateness*
severance 131.1 *subtraction*, 136.1 *separation*, 136.2 *setting apart*
severance of cordial relations 666.1 *disagreement*
severance of relations 500.4 *faction*
severance pay 746.3 *pay*, 878.4 *reward for service*
severe 690, 237.10 *potent*, 241.6 *violent*, 409.8 *cold*, 537.24 *pedantic*, 556.1 *simple*, 659.10 *difficult*, 699.13 *restraining*, 772.1 *solemn*, 818.5 *discourteous*, 832.12 *callous*, 836.4 *pitiless*, 876.10 *moralistic*
severed 131.7 *reduced*, 136.15 *separate*
severe frost 55.36 *frost*
severely 690, 241.10 *violently*, 699.16 *under restraints*, 772.10 *solemnly*, 818.9 *discourteously*, 832.20 *malevolently*, 836.7 *pitilessly*
severe weather 409.7 *cold weather*
severity 690, 167.4 *conventionalism*, 237.3 *intensity*, 241.1 *violence*, 537.11 *pedantry*, 556.4 *simplicity*, 618.11 *harmfulness*, 652.8 *treatment*, 659.1 *difficulty*, 699.1 *restraint*, 772.4 *solemnity*, 772.6 *importance*, 818.1 *discourtesy*, 832.3 *callousness*, 836.1 *pitilessness*
Severity 690
Severn 96 Rivers, 96.4 *British rivers*
sever relations 666.5 *disagree*
sever ties 136.9 *separate*
Seville 93 Cities
Seville orange 86 Fruits
Sèvres 44 Types of Ceramics
Sèvres' royal monogram 44.4 *por-*

celain mark
sew 135.10 *link*, 137.11 *connect*, 243.10 *produce*, 288.8 *interweave*, 295.35 *make clothing*
sewage 68.13 *fertilizer*, 132.2 *residue*, 353.4 *excrement*, 419.2 *something that makes an unpleasant smell*, 622.5 *swill*
sewage farm 727.5 *wasteyard*
sewage system 63.24 *water system*
sewage works 605.4 *storage*, 614.6 *refuse*
sewer 63.22 *tunnel*, 295.26 *fashion designer*, 322.7 *passageway*, 327.11 *channel*, 419.2 *something that makes an unpleasant smell*, 618.10 *poverty*, 621.10 *cleaning object*, 727.4 *wastebin*, 727.8 *sink*
sewerage 353.4 *excrement*, 621.2 *cleaning*, 622.5 *swill*
sewer gas 419.2 *something that makes an unpleasant smell*
sewing 135.3 *unification*
sewing machine 288.3 *weaving*
sewing room 547.1 *workshop*
sewn 135.12 *united*, 135.15 *tied*, 137.15 *connected*
sewn up 718.8 *accomplished*
sew up 718.13 *secure one's objective*
sex 777 Phobias by Topic, 135.4 *sexual union*, 163.3 *kingdom*, 245.3 *propagation*, 396.4 *biological function*, 821.5 *desire*
sex act 821.5 *desire*
sexagenarian 179.8 *twenty and over*, 207.7 *older person*
sexagenary 179.8 *twenty and over*
sex appeal 340.4 *allurement*, 586.3 *incentive*, 821.4 *lovability*
sexcentenary 179.9 *treble figures*, 511.5 *day to remember*
sex chromosome 59.14 *chromosome*
sex comedy 51.10 *comedy*
sex-crazy 877.14 *lecherous*
sex criminal 877.10 *sex offender*
sexdecillion 169.3 *large number*, 179.11 *million*
sex drive 61.22 *libido*
sex education 6.3 *subject*
sexennial 179.13 *sixth*
sexennially 179.24 *fivefold*
sex fiend 877.10 *sex offender*
sex hormone 58.16 *hormone*
sexily 340.14 *attractively*, 782.20 *lustfully*, 821.30 *lovingly*
sexiness 821.4 *lovability*, 821.5 *desire*, 877.3 *sexual immorality*
sex instinct 61.22 *libido*
sexism 481.4 *social discrimination*, 493.3 *injustice*, 805.11 *prejudice*
sexist 147.10 *excluding*, 481.7 *bigot*, 481.10 *discriminatory*, 493.5 *misjudging person*, 493.8 *unjust*, 805.23 *prejudiced*, 834.3 *misanthropic*
sexist loner 834.2 *misanthrope*
sexivalent 57.35 *combined*
sexless 236.13 *unsexed*, 876.9 *pure*
sex-mad 877.13 *unchaste*, 877.14 *lecherous*
sex maniac 510.7 *insane person*
sex murderer 241.4 *violent person or animal*
sex offender 877
sexpartite 179.13 *sixth*
sexpartite vault 43.7 *vault*
sexploitation 877.2 *indecency*
sexpot 228.7 *motivator*, 405.3 *pleasure-seeker*
sex role 2.3 *social environment*
sex scene 51.6 *scene*
sex show 51.5 *show*
sex symbol 340.6 *charmer*
sext 10.4 *public worship*
Sextans 53 The Constellations
sextant 56.32 *optical instrument*, 56.84 *altimeter*, 74.5 *navigation*, 268.6 *measuring instrument*, 310.4 *angular measurement*, 313.4 *parts of a circle*

Sextant 53 The Constellations
sex test 21.5 *competition*
sextet 49.26 *musical group*, 140.3 *assembly*, 179.2 *six*, 664.9 *team*
sex therapy 61.3 *psychiatric treatment*
sextile 179.2 *six*, 310.4 *angular measurement*
sextillion 169.3 *large number*, 179.11 *million*
sexton 82 Insects, 7.8 *priest*, 399.3 *funeral director*
sextuple 179.2 *six*, 179.13 *sixth*, 179.23 *quintuple*
sextuplet 179.2 *six*
sextuplicate 179.2 *six*, 179.13 *sixth*, 179.23 *quintuple*
Sextus Empiricus 4 Philosophers
sexual 245.16 *conjunctive*, 245.16 *reproductive*, 821.20 *amorous*
sexual abstinence 869.1 *self-restraint*
sexual abuse 618.11 *harmfulness*, 832.7 *act of malevolence*, 877.7 *sexual assault*
sexual abuser 693.9 *criminal*
sexual activity 396.4 *biological function*
sexual appetite 782.4 *sexual desire*
sexual assault 877, 241.2 *physical violence*, 734.1 *taking*, 832.7 *act of malevolence*
sexual awakening 245.4 *development*
sexual delinquency 877.3 *sexual immorality*
sexual desire 782
sexual deviancy 877.7 *sexual assault*
sexual deviant 335.19 *deviant person*
sexual discrimination 147.4 *exclusiveness*, 481.4 *social discrimination*
sexual disease 624.14 *venereal disease*
sexual harassment 618.11 *harmfulness*, 832.5 *intolerance*
sexual immorality 877
sexual impotence 236.4 *disability*
sexual indulgence 877.3 *sexual immorality*
sexual intercourse 135.4 *sexual union*, 245.3 *propagation*, 396.4 *biological function*, 405.1 *physical pleasure*, 821.5 *desire*
sexuality 782.4 *sexual desire*, 877.3 *sexual immorality*
sexual jealousy 841.1 *jealousy*
sexual licence 877.3 *sexual immorality*
sexual love 821.2 *romantic love*, 821.5 *desire*
sexually 135.16 *as one*, 245.18 *reproductively*
sexually abstinent 869.8 *self-restrained*
sexually abuse 832.18 *torment*, 877.20 *seduce*
sexually assault 877.20 *seduce*
sexually attractive 340.9 *attractive*
sexually desirable 782.11 *lustful*
sexually enslaving 821.20 *amorous*
sexually explicit literature 877.2 *indecency*
sexually transmitted disease 624.4 *disease*, 624.14 *venereal disease*
sexual offence 877.7 *sexual assault*
sexual perversion 877.7 *sexual assault*
sexual pleasure 405.1 *physical pleasure*
sexual possession 734.1 *taking*
sexual relations 821.5 *desire*
sexual reproduction 90.4 *reproductive body*, 396.4 *biological function*
sexual submission 673.1 *submission*
sexual union 135, 821.5 *desire*

sexual urge 782.4 *sexual desire*, 821.5 *desire*
sex-worker 402.7 *prostitute*
sexy 340.9 *attractive*, 405.6 *pleasant*, 586.19 *persuasive*, 782.11 *lustful*, 821.20 *amorous*, 877.14 *lecherous*
Seychelles 91 Countries
Seyfert galaxy 53.7 *galaxy*
sf 49 Musical Terms
sfogato 49 Musical Terms
S-form 57.13 *structure*
sforzando 49 Musical Terms
sfz 49 Musical Terms
sgian-dhu 680.8 *sharp weapon*
sgraffito 44.1 *ceramics*
sh! 429
shabbily 559.11 *inelegantly*, 743.16 *meanly*
shabbiness 127.4 *poor quality*, 151.3 *untidiness*, 559.3 *ugliness*, 618.10 *poverty*, 622.2 *uncleanness*, 628.9 *dilapidation*, 743.7 *beggary*, 754.3 *shoddiness*, 758.4 *unpleasantness*
shabby 151.15 *untidy*, 559.10 *ugly*, 599.9 *used*, 612.2 *obscure*, 618.4 *poor*, 622.8 *unclean*, 628.13 *dilapidated*, 743.3 *beggarly*, 754.10 *shoddy*, 758.2 *unpleasant*, 793.6 *seedy*
Shabuoth 10.15 *holy day*
shack 256.8 *shelter*
shacking up 823.1 *marriage*
shackle 135.10 *link*, 137.4 *means of connection*, 137.12 *bind*, 323.11, 661.10 *restrain*, 699.12 *gag*
shackled 137.16 *bound*, 661.14 *blocked*
shackles 661.4 *restraint*, 699.5 *means of restraint*
shack up with 823.18 *live together*
shad 80 Fishes
shade 440, 11.11 *ghost*, 50.19 *paint*, 56.28 *colour*, 102.2 *illusion*, 121.4 *interval*, 121.5 *measure*, 293.12 *protective covering*, 293.30 *protect*, 438.6 *that which makes invisible*, 440.1 *darkness*, 440.14 *make dark*, 441.1 *dimness*, 441.10 *make dim*, 444.3 *hue*, 444.15 *colour*, 542.6 *suggestion*, 632.9 *protect*, 634.2 *shelter*, 651.1 *refresh*, 651.5 *refreshment*
shaded 50.27 *painted*, 85.16 *wooded*, 440.8 *dark*, 444.10 *coloured*
shade in 440.14 *make dark*
shade off 121.6 *change gradually*
shade of feeling 759.2 *impression*
shades 293.12 *protective covering*, 295.21 *beachwear*, 295.25 *accessories*, 435.10 *visual aid*, 440.6 *shade*
shades of death 397.1 *death*
shade tree 85.1 *tree*
shadily 440.15 *darkly*, 858.11 *dishonourably*
shadiness 16.38 *lawbreaking*, 286.3 *deviousness*, 441.1 *dimness*, 858.3 *criminality*
shading 50.4 *treatment*, 121.3 *gradation*, 440.2, 440.9 *darkening*, 441.3 *dimming*
shading-in 440.2 *darkening*
shading off 121.7 *gradational*
shadoof 355.10 *excavator*, 389.13 *irrigator*
shadow 299, 41.13 *ice-skating*, 50.4 *treatment*, 56.24 *light emission*, 102.2 *illusion*, 102.7 *artificiality*, 110.2 *equivalence*, 110.7 *be the same*, 114.5 *counterpart*, 121.4 *interval*, 122.5 *equal*, 155.23 *follow close*, 180.9 *follower*, 180.16 *attend*, 264.10 *stay near*, 274.9 *thin person*, 440.1 *darkness*, 440.4 *dark thing*, 440.7 *spiritual darkness*, 440.14 *make dark*, 441.1 *dimness*, 441.10 *make dim*, 447.9 *black thing*, 519.5 *fantasy*, 590.5 *pursuer*, 590.9 *follow*, 808.5 *adherent*, 819.6 *close*

friend
shadow box 26.11 *do a combat sport*
shadow boxing 26.2, 674.7 *boxing*
shadow-boxing 519.4 *ideality*
shadowed 307.5 *shapeless*
shadow figure 547.6 *image*
shadow forth 517.11 *predict*
shadowgraph 66.3 *photograph*
shadowiness 368.2 *unworldliness*, 527.11 *mysteriousness*, 542.7 *imperceptibility*
shadowing 110.13 *equivalent*, 440.9 *darkening*, 441.3 *dimming*, 590.1 *pursuit*
shadow of death 397.1 *death*, 633.5 *danger*
shadow of one's former self 628.9 *dilapidation*
shadow play 51.5 *show*
shadows 777 Phobias by Topic, 440.1 *darkness*
shadow show 51.5 *show*
shadow-skate 41.15 *ice-skate*
shadow-skating 41.6 *ice-skating*
shadowy 11.18 *spiritual*, 102.8 *unreal*, 368.8 *nonmaterial*, 438.2 *difficult to see*, 440.11 *benighted*, 441.5 *dim*, 441.6 *murky*, 519.12 *imaginary*, 523.4 *difficult*, 542.16 *imperceptible*
Shadwell 48 Dramatists
shady 443, 16.60 *offending*, 85.16 *wooded*, 286.5 *devious*, 440.8 *dark*, 440.11 *benighted*, 441.5 *dim*, 477.14 *questionable*, 801.4 *disreputable*, 858.5 *dishonourable*, 858.7 *criminal*
shady business 736.7 *dishonesty*
shady character 858.4 *dishonourable person*
shady past 801.1 *disrespect*
Shaffer 48 Dramatists
shaft 71 Motor Vehicle Parts, 29.4 *golf club*, 43.8 *column*, 63.8 *machine element*, 245.14 *have sex*, 275.6 *tall thing*, 277.4 *deep thing*, 284.2 *supporting part*, 322.5 *hole*, 338.8 *missile*, 364.4 *vortex*, 603.1 *tool*, 605.2 *resource*, 680.6 *historical missile weapon*
shaft horse 32.2 *thoroughbred*
shafting 43.9 *miscellaneous architectural features*
shaft tomb 399.6 *grave*
shag 78 Birds, 78.3 *water bird*, 135.11 *make love*, 245.14 *have sex*, 375.7 *rough thing*, 383.3 *nap*, 413.7 *tobacco*
shag ass 329.4 *be swift*
shagbark 85 Trees and Shrubs
shagged 375.3 *barbed*
shagginess 375.6 *roughness*
shagging 135.4 *sexual union*
shaggy 375.3 *barbed*
shaggy dog story 538.4 *lie*, 541.5 *tall story*, 771.5 *joke*
shaggy inkcap 89 Fungi
Shagya 32 Breeds of Horse and Pony
shah 696.2 *sovereign*
shaing 49 Musical Instruments
Shaitan 8.7 *devil*
shake 366, 366, 36.15 *sail*, 47.12 *wood*, 49.16 *musical note*, 54.64 *fold*, 133.8 *mix*, 153.7 *disturb*, 215.1 *irregularity*, 215.6 *be irregular*, 224.11 *be changeable*, 238.6 *be weak*, 238.7 *weaken*, 241.8 *use violence*, 365.4 *rock*, 365.9 *vibrate*, 365.11 *rock*, 365.12 *wave*, 366.22 *agitate*, 491.21 *change*, 587.2 *deter*, 628.5 *hurt*, 700.5 *be liberated*, 777.11 *be afraid*, 777.13 *frighten*
shakedown 734.3 *taking away*
shake down 734.10 *take away*
shakedown artist 734.6 *taker*
shake free 700.5 *be liberated*
shake hands 407.12 *abut*, 677.5 *make peace*, 817.12 *greet*, 819.15 *be hospitable*, 839.9 *forgive*

shake hands on 116.23 *arrange*, 737.3 *bargain*
shake hands with 730.10 *receive someone*, 815.14 *welcome*
shake in one's shoes 366.24 *shake*
shake like a leaf 366.24 *shake*, 777.11 *be afraid*
shaken 133.12 *mixed*, 153.12 *disturbed*, 366.15 *agitated*, 576.3 *timid*, 628.12 *deteriorated*
shaken up 366.15 *agitated*
shake off 139.5 *unstick*, 329.6 *accelerate*, 349.6 *send away*, 349.10 *exterminate*, 638.6 *elude*, 700.5 *be liberated*, 722.15 *lose someone*
shake of the head 543.3 *gesture*
shake on 737.3 *bargain*
shake on a deal 715.5 *contract*
shake one's head 500.9 *refuse*, 536.7 *be negative*, 543.11 *gesture*, 711.5 *refuse*
shake on it 667.7 *contract*, 677.5 *make peace*, 714.7 *promise*, 839.9 *forgive*
shake out 36.17 *canoe*
shaker 49 Musical Instruments, 133.6 *mixer*, 366.14 *agitator*
Shaker 47.7 *furniture style*
Shaker chair 47.2 *chair*
Shakers 7 Christian Movements
shakes 624.3 *symptom*
Shakespeare 48 Dramatists
Shakespearean 48.19 *narrative*
Shakespearean actor 423.5 *loud person*
Shakespearean comedy 51.10 *comedy*
Shakespearean sonnet 48.7 *poem*
Shakespearean tragedy 51.9 *tragedy*
shake the dust from one's feet 591.8 *run away*
shake to pieces 244.9 *demolish*
shake up 113.8 *be diverse*, 152.14 *rearrange*, 238.7 *weaken*, 374.13 *soften*
shake-up 152.4 *rearrangement*, 627.6 *rectification*
shake with passion 828.11 *be angry*
shakily 366, 215.8 *irregularly*, 224.15 *changeably*, 491.26 *unreliably*, 858.11 *dishonourably*
shakiness 215.1 *irregularity*, 224.1 *changeableness*, 238.3 *poor health*, 491.15 *unreliability*, 633.5 *danger*
shaking 366, 133.1 *mixture*, 215.4 *irregular*, 365.2 *vibration*, 365.4 *rock*, 365.14 *vibrating*, 365.16 *rocking*, 365.17 *waving*, 366.18 *shaky*, 777.2 *fearfulness*, 777.8 *fearful*
shaking like a leaf 777.8 *fearful*
shaking out 36.6 *canoeing*
shaking palsy 366.7 *shake*
shako 295.15 *headgear*, 671.7 *armour*
shakuhachi 49 Musical Instruments
shaky 366, 215.4 *irregular*, 224.13 *changeable*, 238.10 *ill*, 491.7 *unreliable*, 620.1 *imperfect*, 628.13 *dilapidated*, 633.2 *unsafe*, 777.8 *fearful*, 858.6 *faithless*
shale 54 Common Rocks, 379.3 *brittle thing*
shale oil 395.9 *petroleum*
shall 199.8 *intend*
shalloon 67 Natural Fabrics
shallop 74 Ships and Boats, **74** Sailing Ships and Boats
shallot 45 Vegetables
shallow 278, 238.13 *insufficient*, 247.3 *birth control*, 276.5 *low*, 278.4 *shallow thing*, 278.7 *make shallow*, 289.8 *apparent*, 470.5 *indifferent*, 502.7 *semi-skilled*, 612.4 *trivial*
shallow-bottomed 278.1 *shallow*
shallow-bottomed boat 278.4 *shallow thing*
shallow cut 278.4 *shallow thing*
shallow depression 55.11

weather system
shallow-fry 45.55 *cook*
shallow groove 34.5 *rock face*
shallowly 278
shallowness 278, 276.1 *lowness,*
289.3 *appearance,* 470.2 *indifference,* 609.9 *scarcity,* 612.7
triviality
Shallowness 278
shallow person 278
shallow-rooted 278.1 *shallow*
shallows 278.4 *shallow thing,*
635.1 *trap*
shallow structure 5.29 *grammar*
shallow thing 278
shallow water 278.4 *shallow
thing,* 635.1 *trap*
shaly 54.57 *chalky*
sham 102.7 *artificiality,* 102.12
not the real thing, 117.6 *misfit,*
117.11 *unfit,* 117.12 *be disparate,* 118.2 *copy,* 118.13 *imitation,* 474.10 *hypocritical,* 538.8
pretence, 538.12 *cheat,* 538.14
unreal, 538.25 *be dishonest,*
539.3 *hypocrisy,* 539.11 *hoax,*
539.15 *deceiver,* 539.19 *hypocrite,* 539.28 *trick,* 539.39 *imitative,* 540.10 *fake,* 540.12 *facade,* 540.33 *fake,* 540.35 *disguised,* 657.2 *stratagem*
shaman 11.4 *witch,* 507.3 *wise
man,* 636.4 *warner*
shamaness 11.4 *witch*
shamanic 11.15 *witchlike*
shamanism 11.1 *occultism,* 11.3
witchcraft
Shamanism 7 Non-Christian Religions
shamanist 11.4 *witch*
shamanize 11.21 *bewitch*
shamble 328.1 *move slowly,*
328.10 *slow motion*
shambles 151.4 *litter,* 244.5
havoc, 398.15 *slaughterhouse,*
656.9 *bungling,* 727.8 *sink*
shambling 328.4 *slow,* 656.3
clumsy
shambolic 151.15 *untidy*
shame 806, 618.10 *poverty,*
717.3 *irresolution,* 801.1 *disrespect,* 801.4 *disreputable,*
806.13 *disreputable,* 844.9 *dishonour,* 850.21 *disregard,* 858.1 *improbity,* 864.17 *make wicked,*
866.2 *signs of guilt,* 867.1 *penitence,* 876.3 *moral purity,*
877.19 *corrupt,* 879.1 *punish,*
879.7 *punishment*
shamed 806.3 *humbled*
shamefaced 806.3 *humbled,*
810.9 *blushing,* 810.10 *bashful,*
844.15 *immoral,* 866.6 *appearing guilty,* 867.6 *penitent*
shamefaced look 806.13 *disrepute*
shamefacedly 810.18 *shyly,*
866.11 *guiltily,* 867.8 *penitently*
shamefacedness 806.13 *disrepute,* 810.3 *bashfulness*
shamefastly 810.18 *shyly*
shamefastness 806.13 *disrepute,*
810.3 *bashfulness*
shameful 618.4 *poor,* 844.15 *immoral,* 850.12 *disregardful,*
858.5 *dishonourable,* 866.6 *appearing guilty,* 867.6 *penitent*
shamefully 618.15 *worthlessly,*
858.11 *dishonourably,* 866.11
guiltily, 867.8 *penitently*
shamefulness 867.1 *penitence*
shameless 526.15 *open,* 668.7
defiant, 801.4 *disreputable,*
807.16 *arrogant,* 807.21 *impudent,* 811.16 *showy,* 811.21 *blatant,* 844.15 *immoral,* 864.11
wicked, 868.3 *impenitent,*
877.13 *unchaste*
shameless hussy 868.2 *impenitent person*
shameless lie 538.4 *lie*
shamelessly 668.9 *defiantly,*
807.33 *arrogantly,* 811.32 *showily,* 811.37 *blatantly,* 868.6 *impenitently*
shameless lying 538.3, 540.6
lying
shamelessness 668.1 *defiance,*

807.4 *arrogance,* 811.6 *blatancy,* 864.1 *wickedness,* 868.1
impenitence, 877.3 *sexual immorality*
shame oneself 864.16 *be wicked*
shame the devil 863.8 *be virtuous*
shammer 538.12 *cheat,* 539.15
deceiver, 657.3 *cunning person*
shamming 538.19 *dishonest,*
539.7 *tricking*
shammy 621.11 *cleaning cloth*
shampoo 134.3 *purifier,* 385.6,
385.16 *massage,* 621.5 *ablutions,* 621.9 *cleaning agent,*
621.14 *bathe*
shampooer 385.8 *masseur*
shamrock 84 Flowers and Flowering Plants, 11.6 *talisman,*
177.2 *trident*
Shan 5 Languages and Groups
of Languages, **32** Breeds of
Horse and Pony
shanai 49 Musical Instruments
shanghai 42.6 *darts,* 539.33
snare, 734.10 *take away,*
736.13 *kidnap*
Shanghai 93 Cities
shanghaier 736.8 *thief*
shanghaiing 539.13 *snare,* 736.2
kidnapping
Shangri-la 519.8 *dreamland,*
588.6 *objective,* 714.4 *promised
land*
shank 20.3 *fishing tackle,*
338.26 *bat*
shanks's pony 71.4 *personal
transport*
Shannon 93 Cities, **96** Rivers,
96.5 *other major rivers*
shantung 67 Natural Fabrics,
288.4 *textile*
shanty 256.8 *shelter,* 433.2 *song*
shanty town 249.11 *settlement*
shapable 374.2 *pliant*
shape 382, 6.22 *educate,* 44.11
make ceramics, 47.17 *carpenter,*
50.21 *sculpt,* 105.1 *state,* 105.5
physical state, 116.24 *harmonize,* 163.4 *type,* 165.3 *characteristic,* 167.9 *make conform,*
220.9 *transform,* 243.10 *produce,* 299.2 *shadow,* 306.1
form, 306.6 *nature,* 306.7 *form,*
374.13 *soften,* 382.3 *form,*
457.3 *external appearance,*
544.1 *identification,* 547.11
paint, 560.14 *describe,* 592.10
plan out, 623.3 *health,* 796.8,
796.8 *fashion*
SHAPE 17.5 *military staff*
shape a course 592.10 *plan out*
shaped 116.13 *harmonious,*
306.9 *formed*
shapeless 307, 151.14 *irregular,*
375.5 *unfinished,* 551.2 *obscure,* 555.1 *unemphatic*
shapelessly 307, 375.15 *incompletely*
shapelessness 307, 151.2 *irregular order,* 375.10 *rough idea,*
551.1 *obscurity*
Shapelessness 307
shapeless thing 307
shapeliness 308.3 *evenness,*
315.2 *round body,* 789.1 *gorgeousness*
shapely 308.5 *even,* 315.10 *well-
rounded,* 789.5 *beautiful*
shape of things to come 517.4
model
shape one's career 652.11 *conduct oneself*
shaper 47.17 *woodworking tool,*
63.9 *machine tool*
shape up 105.6 *be in a state of,*
627.1 *improve*
shaping 243.1 *production,* 306.1
form, 306.4 *forming,* 382.5
structuring
shard 132.1 *remainder,* 143.7
piece, 173.3 *fragment,* 384.23
pulverize
sharded 384.19 *pulverized*
sharding 384.4 *pulverization*
share 109.8 *interrelate,* 120.2 *certain amount,* 120.8 *quantify,*
143.1, 143.10 *part,* 146.5 *be in-*

cluded, 173.2 *fractional part,*
173.8 *divide,* 176.17 *go halves,*
268.11 *measure out,* 298.4 *interface,* 380.9 *sharp-edged thing,*
605.6 *store,* 606.1 *provision,*
664.13 *work together,* 718.2
promise, 724.1 *joint possession,*
724.4 *have joint possession,*
729.5 *give,* 731.2 *portion,* 731.4
allot, 815.11 *be sociable*
share a common hatred 785.5
dislike
share and share alike 724.4 *have
joint possession,* 724.5 *jointly
possessing*
share-buyer 738.12 *purchaser*
sharecrop 68.17 *farm*
sharecropper 68.15 *agriculturist,*
724.3 *participant*
sharecropping 68.1 *agriculture,*
724.1 *joint possession*
shared 298.6 *interfacial,* 664.18
joint, 706.7 *decentralized*
shared delusions 510.4 *delusion*
shared feelings 724.2 *participation*
shared frontier 298.1 *interface*
shared grief 835.2 *condolence*
shared out 731.7 *allocated*
shared ownership 724.1 *joint possession*
shared responsibility 706.3 *delegation*
shared sorrow 835.2 *condolence*
shared suffering 835.2 *condolence*
share expenses 724.4 *have joint
possession,* 746.9 *pay one's way*
sharefarmer 724.3 *participant*
share farming 68.1 *agriculture*
share grief 835.9 *sorrow*
shareholder 724.3 *participant,*
725.7 *property man*
share one's bed and board
823.15 *marry*
share one's sorrow 835.9 *sorrow*
share out 124.10 *make average,*
136.11 *divide,* 268.11 *measure
out,* 729.5 *give,* 731.4 *allot*
share-pusher 739.12 *wholesaler*
share-pushing 737.4 *trade*
sharer 724.3 *participant*
share-seller 739.9 *seller*
share shop 740.5 *stock market*
share the work 706.4 *delegate*
share with 729.5 *give*
sharing 109.2 *interconnection,*
122.1 *equality,* 122.6 *equal,*
664.3 *mutual relationship,*
717.1 *compromise,* 724.2 *participation,* 731.1 *allocation,* 815.1
sociability
sharing out 731.1 *allocation*
shark 80 Fishes, 20.4 *American
game fish,* 398.10 *killer,*
538.12, 539.17 *cheat,* 734.6
taker, 736.11 *dishonest person,*
753.5 *overcharger*
shark fishing 80.7 *fishing*
sharkish 80.13 *fishlike*
sharklike 80.13 *fishlike*
shark net 80.7 *fishing*
sharkskin 67 Natural Fabrics
sharon fruit 86 Fruits
sharp 380, 6.20 *refined,* 49.16
musical note, 55.47 *windy,*
237.12 *strong to the senses,*
241.6 *violent,* 300.10 *advantaged,* 375.2 *coarse,* 409.8 *cold,*
411.7 *tasty,* 413.9 *piquant,*
415.5 *acid,* 430.9 *shrill,* 434.9
unmelodious, 437.2 *clear,*
459.10, 507.6 *intelligent,*
539.34 *deceiving,* 554.3 *emphatic,* 655.5 *expert,* 657.3 *cunning person,* 657.4 *cunning,*
818.5 *discourteous,* 822.10 *hating,* 828.15 *resentful,* 829.4 *irascible,* 832.14 *hostile*
sharp as a needle 380.1 *sharp*
sharp as a razor 380.3 *sharp-
edged*
sharp as a tack 380.5 *mentally
sharp*
sharp as broken glass 380.2
spiked
sharp corner 310.1 *angle*
sharp-cornered 310.7 *angular*

sharp ear 420.1 *hearing*
sharp edge 300.3 *cutting edge,*
375.6 *roughness,* 380.7 *sharp
point*
sharp-edged 380
sharp-edged thing 380
sharpen 239.3 *invigorate,* 241.9
make violent, 380.15 *make
sharp,* 409.12 *make cold,* 415.8
sour
sharpened 380.1 *sharp*
sharpener 380
sharper 657.3 *cunning person,*
736.11 *dishonest person*
Sharpeville 93 Cities
sharp eye 435.2 *eye*
sharp-eyed 380.5 *mentally
sharp,* 435.21 *seeing,* 467.7
watchful
sharp fellow 642.10 *busy person*
sharp flavouring 415.1 *sourness*
sharp frost 55.36 *frost*
sharpie 642.10 *busy person*
sharply 380, 237.15 *acutely,*
300.12 *at an advantage,* 375.14
roughly, 380.19 *suddenly,*
413.15 *piquantly,* 415.10
sourly, 818.9 *discourteously,*
822.18 *hatefully,* 828.17 *resentfully,* 829.9 *irascibly*
sharpness 777 Phobias by
Topic, **380,** 66.8 *composition,*
300.3 *cutting edge,* 415.1 *sourness,* 434.3 *musical dissonance,*
437.4 *clarity,* 459.4 *cleverness,*
554.1 *emphasis,* 655.1 *skill,*
657.1 *cunning,* 818.1 *discourtesy,* 829.1 *irascibility,* 832.4 *bitterness*
Sharpness 380
sharp-nosed 416.5 *odorous*
sharp note 430.3 *shrillness*
sharp point 380
sharp-pointed 380.1 *sharp*
sharp-pointed thing 380
sharp practice 539.7 *tricking,*
540.8 *fraud,* 540.9 *falsification,*
657.1 *cunning,* 801.3 *disreputable action,* 858.3 *criminality*
sharp-set 380.3 *sharp-edged*
sharpshooter 670.19 *attacker,*
679.8 *soldier*
sharpshooting 18 Sporting Activities, 670.15 *firing*
sharp taste 411.1 *taste*
sharp temper 829.1 *irascibility*
sharp tongue 832.4 *bitterness*
sharp-tongued 380.5 *mentally
sharp,* 818.5 *discourteous,* 829.4
irascible
sharp weapon 680
sharp-witted 380.5 *mentally
sharp,* 507.1 *intelligent*
sharp-wittedness 380.13 *mental
sharpness*
shastra 7.12 *religious text*
shatter 136.9 *separate,* 141.3 *disintegrate,* 189.4 *be transient,*
244.9 *demolish,* 379.4 *be brittle*
shatterable 379.1 *brittle*
shattered 136.16 *apart,* 141.5
disintegrated, 244.15 *destroyed,*
375.2 *coarse,* 379.1 *brittle*
shattered silence 123.1 *loudness*
shattered surface 375.6 *roughness*
shattering 136.1 *separation,*
244.2 *destroying,* 379.1 *brittle,*
611.6 *notable,* 786.8 *wonderful*
shatter one's hopes 776.10 *disappoint*
shatterproof 373.2, 378.1 *tough,*
378.11 *make tough,* 632.6 *invulnerable*
shatterproof glass 632.4 *safety
device*
shatter the dreams of 189.5
make transient
shatter the eardrums 423.8 *be
loud*
shatter the peace 423.8 *be loud,*
679.36 *combat*
Shaula 53 Named Stars
shave 791, 129.5, 262.5 *make
smaller,* 266.11 *scale,* 267.4
meet, 270.10 *shorten,* 294.13 *re*
move, 296.7 *depilation,* 296.15
make nude, 376.11 *smooth,*

407.11 *touch*, 621.13 *clean*
shaved 270.8 *shortened*, 294.9 *shed*, 296.13 *hairless*
shaven 270.8 *shortened*, 294.9 *shed*, 296.13 *hairless*, 621.17 *cleaned*
shaver 294.7 *shedder*
shaving 260.3 *little piece*, 266.4 *slice*, 270.2 *shortening*, 274.11 *fineness*, 294.5 *shedding*, 296.7 *depilation*, 791.9 *shave*
shaving mirror 56.29 *optical element*, 435.8 *reflection*
shavings 132.2 *residue*, 143.8 *bits and pieces*, 614.6 *refuse*, 622.4 *dirt*
Shaw 48 Dramatists
shawl 295.14 *neckwear*, 295.25 *accessories*
shawl collar 295.14 *neckwear*
shawm 49 Musical Instruments
Shawnee 5 Languages and Groups of Languages
she 402.2 *female*
shea 85 Trees and Shrubs
sheading 92.1 *administrative area*
sheaf 161.27 *bundle*
shear 52.48 *transformation*, 63.31 *load*, 136.10 *set apart*, 262.5 *make smaller*, 270.10 *shorten*, 296.7 *depilation*, 296.15 *make nude*, 380.16 *use a sharp tool*
sheared 270.8 *shortened*
shearing 270.2 *shortening*, 296.7 *depilation*
shearing shaving 262.1 *contraction*
shears 69.6 *garden tool*, 380.9 *sharp-edged thing*, 603.2 *garden tool*
shear strain 63.14 *load*
shear stress 63.14 *load*
shearwater 78 Birds, 78.3 *water bird*
sheath 87.3 *grass plant*, 247.3 *birth control*, 258.5 *packet*, 258.21 *put in a container*, 293.4 *wrapping*, 301.4 *wrapper*, 301.6 *wrap*, 680.4 *arsenal*
sheathbill 78 Birds
sheath dress 295.7 *frock*
sheathe 266.3 *coat*, 293.25 *wrap*, 295.32 *dress*, 339.14 *draw in*, 354.5 *inset*
sheathed 258.20 *containing*, 266.8 *coated*, 293.37 *protected*
sheathe the sword 677.5 *make peace*
sheathing 47.12 *wood*, 293.4 *wrapping*
sheathing board 47.12 *wood*
sheath knife 380.10 *knife*
sheave 36.3 *parts of a sailing boat*, 603.1 *tool*
shed 75 Scientific and Technical Units, 294, 294, 72.8 *railway station*, 129.4 *decrease*, 130.3 *additional item*, 256.8 *shelter*, 296.12 *peeling*, 296.16 *peel*, 349.10 *exterminate*, 353.32 *cast-off*, 362.6 *throw down*, 585.5 *disaccustom*, 598.1 *relinquish*, 605.4 *storage*
shed a layer 294.12 *shed*
shed blessings on 686.7 *be auspicious*
shed blood 398.16 *kill*, 674.12 *fight*, 676.13 *be at war*, 690.6 *suppress*
shed crocodile tears 540.18 *be hypocritical*, 858.8 *be dishonourable*
shedder 294
shedding 294, 296.6, 296.12 *peeling*, 349.22 *disgorgement*
shedding light 439.3 *lightening*
shedding light on 439.15 *lucent*
shedding of daylight on 526.10 *manifestation*
she-devil 829.3 *irascible person*, 832.9 *vixen*
Shedir 53 Named Stars
shed leaves 93.12 *be dormant*
shed light on 439.29 *clarify*
shed one's skin 353.23 *cast*

shed seeds 83.21 *vegetate*
shed skin 294.12 *shed*
shed tears 391.16 *seep*
shed tears over 774.7 *weep*
shedu 8.7 *devil*
sheen 439.2 *quality of light*
sheeny 91 Names for Inhabitants
sheep 77 Placental Mammals, **161** Collective Names by Animal, 10.17 *worshipper*, 68.8 *livestock*, 118.7 *imitator*, 167.6 *conformist*
sheep and goats 111.2 *opposites*
sheep breeder 68.15 *agriculturist*
sheep-dip 68.14 *pest control*
sheepdog 77.9 *dog*, 161.34 *assembler*
sheep farm 68.6 *farm*
sheep farmer 68.15 *agriculturist*, 243.9 *producer*
sheep farming 68.3 *livestock farming*
sheepfold 68.7 *farm building*, 634.3 *animal shelter*
sheephide 604.1 *materials*
sheepish 238.12 *weak-willed*, 806.3 *humbled*, 810.9 *blushing*, 866.6 *appearing guilty*
sheepishly 238.14 *weakly*, 810.18 *shyly*, 866.11 *guiltily*
sheepishness 238.2 *indecisiveness*
sheep ked 82 Insects
sheeplike 77.33 *ungulate*
sheep-like 167.13 *compliant*, 694.7 *obedient*
sheep netting 68.11 *farmland*
sheep ranch 68.6 *farm*
sheeprot 624.18 *veterinary disease*
sheep's currants 353.5 *faeces*
sheep's eyes 435.6 *look*, 821.6 *courtship*, 821.14 *communication of love*, 826.2 *courtship*
sheep's fescue 87 Grasses
sheepshank 74 Knots
sheepskin 604.1 *materials*
sheep tick 82 Arachnids, 82.3 *pest*
sheeptrack 375.8 *rough ground*
sheer 67 Natural Fabrics, 36.8 *punting*, 67.10 *woven*, 134.16 *simple*, 274.4 *fine*, 281.8 *vertical*, 281.12 *perpendicularly*, 335.1 *deviate*, 335.14 *deviating course*, 442.2 *translucent*
sheer drop 360.6 *slide*
sheer fabric 441.2 *murk*, 442.8 *transparent thing*
sheerness 274.11 *fineness*, 281.1 *verticality*, 442.6 *translucency*
sheer off 331.2 *respond*
sheer perfection 619.3 *perfection*
sheer stockings 295.20 *legwear*
sheet 36.3 *parts of a sailing boat*, 47.17 *carpenter*, 143.2 *particular*, 266.3 *coat*, 293.10 *bed covering*, 532.4 *newspaper*, 604.3 *paper*
sheet anchor 137.9 *yoke*, 632.2 *protection*, 632.4 *safety device*
sheet bend 74 Knots
sheet glass 442.9 *glass*
sheet in 36.15 *sail*
sheeting 47.12 *wood*
sheeting in 36.1 *sailing*
sheeting out 36.1 *sailing*
sheet lightning 55.21 *thunderstorm*, 439.4 *natural light*
sheet music 49.18 *written music*
sheet of cloud 55.20 *cloud appearance*
sheet of fire 408.6 *fire*
sheet of rain 55.25 *rain*
sheet out 36.15 *sail*
sheets 137.7 *tackle*
sheet steel 63.25 *construction material*
sheet winch 36.3 *parts of a sailing boat*
Sheffield 93 Cities
she-goat 402.14 *female animal*
sheik 126.5 *superior*, 696.3 *leader*, 821.9 *lover*
sheikh 7.8 *priest*

sheila 402.2 *female*
shekel 741.12 *ancient coins*
shekels 741.2 *cash*
Shekinah 8.2 *divine attribute*
Sheldon scale 1.10 *measurement*
shelduck 78 Birds
shelf 258.3 *cabinet*, 258.4 *rack*, 266.2 *level*, 278.4 *shallow thing*, 284.2 *supporting part*, 318.2 *projection*, 605.4 *storage*
shelf room 605.4 *storage*
shelf space 605.4 *storage*
shell 74 Ships and Boats, 63.27 *superstructure*, 78.15 *eggs*, 86.3 *fruit structure*, 132.1 *remainder*, 289.1 *exterior*, 293.13 *casing*, 293.14 *animal covering*, 319.2 *notched thing*, 338.8 *missile*, 355.14 *suck*, 373.7 *hard substance*, 382.4 *framework*, 399.4 *funeral objects*, 670.2 *fire*, 680.5 *missile weapon*, 680.13 *ammunition*, 680.16 *bomb*
shellback 655.5 *expert*
shell burst 423.1 *loudness*
shell collecting 42 Hobbies and Pastimes
Shelley 48 Poets
shellfish 45, 76.5 *aquatic animal*, 81.4 *arthropod*
shelling 355.4 *sucking*
shell jacket 295.11 *jacket*
shell-like 420.4 *ear*
shell money 741.1 *money*
shell on brass 47.9 *decorative woodwork*
shell out 729.5 *give*, 746.6 *pay*, 748.1 *expend*
shell-pink 450.1 *red*
shell shock 61.10 *neurosis*, 510.6 *mental breakdown*
shell-shocked 236.12 *impotent*, 676.17 *military*
shell suit 21.4 *sports equipment*, 295.4 *informal dress*, 295.10 *suit*
shellsuits 814.6 *informal dress*
shelly 289.6 *exterior*
Shelta 5 Languages and Groups of Languages
shelter 256, 293, 634, 634, **671**, 258.21 *put in a container*, 325.3 *resting place*, 344.16 *stop-over*, 348.2 *receptivity*, 348.9 *welcome*, 531.2 *hiding place*, 632.2, 632.2 *protection*, 632.9 *protect*, 637.5 *preserve*, 718.1 *protection*, 734.4 *taking in*, 734.11 *be hospitable*
shelter belt 85.4 *trees*
sheltered 256.14 *inhabiting*, 258.20 *containing*, 632.5 *safe*, 718.6 *secure*
sheltered housing 256.11 *retreat*, 634.2 *shelter*
sheltered workshop 634.2 *shelter*
sheltering 258.20 *containing*
shelterless 633.3 *vulnerable*, 743.3 *beggarly*
shelter under the wing of 634.4 *shelter*
sheltie 32.5 *pony*
shelve 209.8 *delay*, 283.12 *interrupt*, 573.8 *hold back*, 591.7 *be evasive*, 598.2 *withdraw*
shelved 258.20 *containing*, 283.9 *interrupted*
shelves 47.5 *cabinet*
shelving 258.4 *rack*, 283.6 *interruption*, 573.15 *delay*
shemozzle 153.5 *commotion*, 423.2 *outcry*
Shenandoah 96 Rivers
shenanigan 539.7 *tricking*
shenanigans 506.3 *tomfoolery*
sheng 49 Musical Instruments
Shenstone 48 Poets
Shenyang 93 Cities
sheol 8.11 *heaven*
Sheol 397.14 *the spiritual world*
Shepard 52 Scientists
shepherd 68.16 *farm worker*, 68.18 *practise livestock farming*, 161.34 *assembler*, 161.43 *herd*, 180.8 *usher*, 180.15 *escort*, 632.3 *protector*, 632.9 *protect*, 653.2 *direct*, 653.14 *leader*

shepherded 161.46 *assembled*, 180.20 *accompanied*
shepherdess 68.16 *farm worker*
shepherding 161.2 *herding*
shepherdlike 632.7 *tutelary*
shepherd's pie 45.44 *British dish*
Sheraton 47.7 *furniture style*
Sheraton chair 47.2 *chair*
sherbet 351.6 *soft drink*, 414.5 *sweet drink*
sherd 143.7 *piece*, 173.3 *fragment*
Sheridan 48 Dramatists
sheriff 16.10 *law officer*, 16.25 *British judge*, 632.3 *protector*, 688.10 *person of authority*, 696.3 *leader*
sheriff court 16.19 *lawcourt*, 16.20 *British court*
Sherpa guide 34.7 *mountaineer*
Sherpas 1 Peoples
sherry 351.9 *wine*
sherry glass 258.13 *drinking vessel*, 351.10 *drink container*
sherry party 815.5 *party*
Shetland 68 Breeds of Cattle, **68** Breeds of Sheep, **92** Counties
Shetland pony 32 Breeds of Horse and Pony
Shetland sheepdog 77 Breeds of Dogs
she-wolf 241.4 *violent person or animal*
SHF 534 Radio-frequency Bands
SHF transmitter 534.16 *transmitter*
Shiah 7 Non-Christian Religions
shiatsu 60.2 *natural medicine*
shibboleth 543.1 *sign*, 543.6 *word*, 544.3 *means of identification*
shield 49 Musical Instruments, 54.7 *landform*, 56.73 *nuclear reactor*, 293.12 *protective covering*, 293.30 *protect*, 544.8 *heraldic device*, 632.2 *protection*, 632.9 *protect*, 634.2 *shelter*, 671.7 *armour*, 671.19 *buffer*, 718.1 *protection*, 718.10 *secure*, 878.2 *prize*
Shield 53 The Constellations
shield-bearer 326.7 *transferor*
shield bug 82 Insects
shielded 293.37 *protected*, 632.5 *safe*, 718.6 *secure*, 848.5 *exempt*
shield fern 88 Ferns
shielding 293.1 *covering*
shield volcano 54.24 *volcanic activity*
shift 71 Motor Vehicle Parts, 19.8 *huddle*, 121.4 *interval*, 131.3 *subtract*, 185.3 *duration*, 187.4 *period of activity*, 214.2 *cycle*, 216.1 *change*, 216.7 *be changed*, 216.8 *cause change*, 220.1 *conversion*, 220.7 *convert into*, 252.1 *displacement*, 252.14 *displace*, 295.18 *underwear*, 324.13 *be in motion*, 324.15 *walk*, 326.1 *transfer*, 326.15 *take away*, 329.4 *be swift*, 335.15 *deviating motion*, 491.21 *change*, 538.8 *pretence*, 538.24 *pretend*, 539.8, 539.28 *trick*, 592.3 *expedient plan*, 644.2 *task*, 644.6 *work*, 652.9 *tactics*, 657.2 *stratagem*, 657.5 *be cunning*, 731.3 *allotted task*, 847.2 *task*
shifted 252.8 *displaced*
shift for oneself 652.11 *conduct oneself*, 698.16 *be independent*
shift gears 573.8 *equivocate*
shiftily 216.15, 224.15 *changeably*, 491.26 *unreliably*, 538.27 *pretentiously*
shiftiness 224.2 *irresolution*, 474.3 *cunning*, 491.15 *unreliability*, 539.1 *deception*, 540.11 *evasion*, 657.1 *cunning*
shifting 216.11, 224.13 *changeable*, 252.8 *displaced*, 324.16 *moving*, 326.1 *transfer*, 326.17 *transferable*, 335.21 *indirect*

shifting one's ground 578.6 *equivocation*
shifting sands 224.3 *changeable thing*
shift into 220.7 *convert into*
shift lens 66.17 *lens*
shiftless 595.3 *without preparation*
shift one's ground 576.9 *change sides*, 578.2 *equivocate*
shift the blame 848.12 *exempt oneself*, 858.8 *be dishonourable*
shift the responsibility 848.12 *exempt oneself*
shifty 216.11 *changeable*, 224.14 *irresolute*, 474.8 *cunning*, 491.7 *unreliable*, 538.15 *lying*, 539.34 *deceiving*, 540.34 *evasive*, 576.1 *vacillating*, 657.4 *cunning*
shiho nage 26.10 *aikido*
shih tzu 77 *Breeds of Dogs*
Shiite 7.6 *non-Christian*
Shikoku 98 *Islands*
shiksa 91 *Names for Inhabitants*
Shilha 5 *Languages and Groups of Languages*
shill 532.10 *publicizer*, 532.16 *publicize*, 539.18 *decoy*
shillelagh 680.7 *blunt weapon*
Shillelagh 93 *Cities*
shilling 741.10 *former British money*
Shillong 93 *Cities*
shillyshally 224.12 *be irresolute*, 328.2 *hesitate*, 576.5 *vacillate*, 578.1 *be equivocal*
shillyshallying 328.7 *delayed*, 328.11 *lingering*
shime-waza 26.7 *judo*
shimmer 55.61 *shine*, 439.2 *quality of light*
shimmering 439.2 *quality of light*, 439.17 *lustrous*
shimmery 439.17 *lustrous*
shimmy 46.2 *dance*, 71.21 *miscellaneous motoring terms*, 314.2 *coil*, 314.6 *convolute*
shin 45.22 *beef*
Shina 5 *Languages and Groups of Languages*
shinbone 382 *Bones*
shindig 46.1 *dancing*, 151.9 *disorder*, 161.9, 665.7 *social gathering*, 674.6 *fight*, 815.5 *party*
shindy 161.9 *social gathering*, 666.2 *argument*, 674.6 *fight*, 815.5 *party*
shine 55, 27.7 *bat*, 27.18 *bowl*, 53.37 *observe*, 163.15 *be in a class of one's own*, 165.25 *excel*, 376.7 *smoothness*, 376.11 *smooth*, 439.2 *quality of light*, 439.25 *light up*, 507.8 *be intelligent*, 621.1 *cleanness*, 621.13 *clean*, 655.10 *be skilful*, 784.3 *likes*, 789.7 *be beautiful*, 821.2 *romantic love*
shine brightly 55.61 *shine*
shine like a new pin 439.27 *glaze*
shine on 686.7 *be auspicious*
shiner 406.3 *injury*
shine some light on 530.5 *disclose*
shine through 437.9 *appear*, 442.11 *be transparent*
shine up to 819.14 *seek the friendship of*
shingle 47.12 *wood*, 47.17 *carpenter*, 54.11 *coast*, 54.27 *sediment*, 98.4 *coast*, 266.10 *layer*, 293.26 *overlie*, 384.9 *grit*, 604.2 *building material*
shingled 98.11 *continental*, 384.18 *grainy*
shingled roof 266.5 *layered thing*
shingles 293.7 *overhead covering*, 624.13 *skin disease*
shingly 384.18 *grainy*
shin guard 31.1 *hockey*, 31.3 *ice hockey*
shin guards 22.3 *baseball equipment*
shininess 376.7 *smoothness*, 439.2 *quality of light*
shining 134.14 *purified*, 385.5

---

polishing, 439.2 *quality of light*, 439.15 *lucent*, 439.16 *bright*, 621.16 *clean*
shining armour 676.2 *glory of war*
shining light 439.13 *enlightenment*
shinny up 359.14 *climb*
shin pad 671.6 *protective clothing*
shinpads 38.1 *soccer*
shinplaster 741.14 *paper money*
Shinto text 7.12 *religious text*
shinty 18 *Sporting Activities*, 31.7 *hurling*
shinty stick 31.7 *hurling*
shin up 359.14 *climb*
shiny 134.14 *purified*, 376.4 *polished*, 439.17 *lustrous*, 443.3 *mirror-like*
ship 70.4 *transport*, 74.3 *vessel*, 326.12, 326.12 *transport*
shipbuilder 74.7 *nautical person*, 646.2 *artisan*
shipbuilding 74, 74.11 *nautical*
shipbuilding contract 74.4 *shipbuilding*
shipbuilding skill 74.4 *shipbuilding*
shipbuilding yard 74.4 *shipbuilding*
ship chandler 606.3 *provider*
ship design 74.4 *shipbuilding*
ship designer 74.7 *nautical person*
ship halfpenny 741.10 *former British money*
shipmate 74.7 *nautical person*, 819.5 *friend*
ship materials 74.4 *shipbuilding*
shipment 70.1 *transport*, 70.2 *thing transported*, 257.2 *load*, 326.2 *transportation*, 326.10 *transferred thing*
ship of the line 679.24 *warship*
ship out 74.9 *navigate*, 676.13 *be at war*
shipped 70.5 *transportable*
shipper 70.3 *transporter*
shipping 70.5 *transportable*, 74.1 *water travel*, 74.11 *nautical*, 326.2 *transportation*
shipping forecast 55.4 *weather forecast*
shipping lane 97.1 *sea*, 327.6 *path*
ship's boat 74 *Ships and Boats*
ship's chronometer 74.5 *navigation*
ship's colours 544.7 *flag*
ship's compass 74.5 *navigation*
shipshape 150.13 *orderly*, 655.9 *well-made*
shipshape condition 594.14 *preparedness*
ship's log 74.5 *navigation*
ship's master 74.7 *nautical person*
ship specifications 74.4 *shipbuilding*
ship's speed 74.6 *nautical speed*
ship's steering 74.5 *navigation*
ship's steward 74.7 *nautical person*
ship's timekeeper 74.5 *navigation*
ship-to-shore telephone 534.9 *telephone*
shipworm 81 *Molluscs*
shipwreck 244.4, 244.11 *ruin*
shipwright 646.2 *artisan*
shipyard 647.1 *workshop*
Shiraz 93 *Cities*
shire 92.2 *former British divisions*, 249.5 *state*
Shire Horse 32 *Breeds of Horse and Pony*
shire town 93.4 *British cities*
shirk 591, 573.7 *refuse*, 576.6 *hesitate*, 720.8 *not perform*
shirker 470.3 *negligent person*, 573.16 *reluctant person*, 591.17 *avoider*, 641.2 *nonacting person*, 643.8 *nonworker*, 685.3 *quitter*, 720.6 *evader*
shirking 591, 573.3 *cautious*
shirr 320.2, 320.8 *pleat*
shirt 295
shirtdress 295.7 *frock*
shirt-front 295.24 *part of garment*

---

shirtsleeves 814.6 *informal dress*
shirtwaist 295.7 *frock*
shirtwaister 295.7 *frock*
shirty 828.15 *resentful*, 830.7 *irritable*
shish kebab 45.54 *other dishes*
shit 353.5 *faeces*, 353.16 *defecate*, 387.3 *body fluid*, 449.5 *brown thing*, 506.1 *nonsense*, 622.4 *dirt*, 764.9 *unpleasant person*, 801.2 *disreputable character*, 827.15 *miscellaneous swearwords*
shitbag 764.9 *unpleasant person*
shitfaced 874.3 *dead drunk*
shithouse 353.13 *lavatory*, 818.4 *discourteous person*
shitlist 822.4 *hatefulness*
shit oneself 353.16 *defecate*, 777.11 *be afraid*
shit scared 777.7 *frightened*
shittily 353.33 *scatologically*
shitty 353.25 *faecal*, 614.1 *useless*, 624.22 *sick*
shitwork 644.1 *work*
shiver 136.9 *separate*, 244.9 *demolish*, 365.9 *vibrate*, 366.24 *shake*, 379.4 *be brittle*, 409.10 *be cold*, 777.11 *be afraid*
shivering 365.2 *vibration*, 365.14 *vibrating*, 366.6 *shaking*, 366.18 *shaky*, 624.23 *diseased*
shivers 366.7 *shake*, 624.3 *symptom*, 777.2 *fearfulness*
shivers up and down the spine 777.2 *fearfulness*
shivery 366.18 *shaky*, 409.8 *cold*
shiwaya 49 *Musical Instruments*
shô 49 *Musical Instruments*
shoal 161 *Collective Names for Birds and Animals*, 80.1 *fishes*, 161.23 *flock*, 181.4 *throng*, 278.1 *shallow*, 278.4 *shallow thing*, 278.7 *make shallow*, 635.1 *trap*
shoaliness 278.3 *shallowness*
shoals 278.4 *shallow thing*
shoal water 635.1 *trap*
shoaly 278.1 *shallow*
shock 777 *Phobias by Topic*, **514**, 54.22 *seismic activity*, 61.12 *stress*, 241.3 *instance of violence*, 241.8 *use violence*, 330.12 *collision*, 366.9, 366.23 *jolt*, 514.11 *amaze*, 515.2 *bad outcome*, 624.2 *illness*, 670.12 *military attack*, 777.13 *frighten*, 785.7 *cause dislike*, 786.1 *wonder*, 786.10 *be wonderful*, 864.16 *be wicked*
shockability 876.4 *self-righteousness*
shockable 810.10 *bashful*, 876.10 *moralistic*
shock absorber 71 *Motor Vehicle Parts*, 242.2 *moderator*, 377.5 *spring*
shock cord 36.3 *parts of a sailing boat*
shocked 366.15 *agitated*, 514.7 *amazed*, 786.6 *wondering*
shocked silence 786.2 *sign of wonderment*
shockheaded 375.3 *barbed*
shocking 514.8 *surprising*, 618.4 *poor*, 777.10 *frightening*, 786.8 *wonderful*, 864.12 *immoral*, 877.12 *indecent*
shockingly 330.18 *dynamically*
shocking manners 818.2 *bad manners*
shocking pink 450.1 *red*
shocking temper 830.3 *irritableness*
Shockley 52 *Scientists*
shockproof 378.1 *tough*
shock reaction 61.12 *stress*
shock stall 73.5 *flight*
shock tactics 670.12 *military attack*
shock therapy 61.3 *psychiatric treatment*, 510.9 *treatment*
shock treatment 61.3 *psychiatric treatment*, 630.13 *therapy*
shock trooper 679.1 *combatant*

---

shock troops 679.14 *armed forces*
shock wave 56.14 *sound wave*, 365.5 *wave*
shod 295.29 *dressed*
shoddily 127.21 *badly*, 379.5 *fragilely*
shoddiness 754, 127.4 *poor quality*, 151.3 *untidiness*, 470.2 *indifference*, 618.8 *inferiority*, 795.2 *tawdriness*
shoddy 67 *Natural Fabrics*, **754**, 127.4 *poor*, 151.15 *untidy*, 238.8 *weak*, 379.1 *brittle*, 470.5 *indifferent*, 539.39 *imitative*, 612.4 *trivial*, 618.2 *inferior*, 633.2 *unsafe*
shoe 36.8 *punting*, 42.3 *card game terms*, 63.27 *superstructure*, 295.32 *dress*
shoebill 78 *Birds*
shoeblack 621.12 *cleaner*, 697.3 *attendant*
shoe box 258.6 *box*
shoe brush 621.10 *cleaning object*
shoed 295.29 *dressed*
shoelace 137.6 *line*
shoemaker 295.26 *fashion designer*
shoemaking 295.2 *dressing*
shoe polish 376.10 *polish*, 621.9 *cleaning agent*
shoe-repairer 629.12 *repairer*
shoes 295.19 *footwear*
shoe seller 739.13 *retailer*
shoeshine boy 621.12 *cleaner*, 697.3 *attendant*
shoeshiner 621.12 *cleaner*
shoetree 85.12 *figurative usage*
shofar 49 *Musical Instruments*
shogun 696.4 *absolute ruler*
Sholes 52 *Scientists*
Sholokhov 48 *Writers*
Shona 5 *Languages and Groups of Languages*
Shoney 8 *Deities*
shonin 7.7 *monk*
shoo 345.15 *go*
shoo-in 682.5 *victorious person*
shoo off 349.6 *send away*
shooping 431.17 *cheering*
shoot 37, 338, 23.6 *play basketball*, 37.2 *hunting*, 38.2 *football play*, 38.4 *play soccer*, 66.21 *photograph*, 67.4 *weaving*, 83.5 *stem*, 83.9 *seed*, 83.21 *vegetate*, 96.2 *channel*, 110.9 *duplicate*, 143.6 *branch*, 206.5 *young plant*, 261.6 *become bigger*, 322.20 *hole*, 354.2 *inject*, 398.17 *murder*, 398.19 *execute*, 398.22 *kill animals*, 406.10 *be painful*, 406.11 *inflict pain*, 547.9 *represent*, 590.11 *hunt*, 590.19 *after him*, 670.2 *fire*, 676.14 *battle*
shoot 679.37 *fight*
shoot 879.5 *execute*
shoot a cat 349.15 *vomit*
shoot a free-throw 23.6 *play basketball*
shoot ahead 357.3 *exceed*
shoot ahead of 126.8 *be superior*
shoot a line 811.31 *put on a show*
shoot an air ball 23.6 *play basketball*
shoot an arrow 380.16 *use a sharp tool*
shoot-and-run offence 23.4 *playing terms*
shoot an eagle 29.7 *golf*
shoot a picture 547.9 *represent*
shoot at 338.28 *shoot*, 670.2 *fire*
shoot back 672.3 *retaliate*
shoot down 157.17 *kill*, 338.28 *shoot*, 362.3 *bring down*, 398.17 *murder*, 398.18 *slaughter*, 670.2 *fire*
shoot down in flames 157.17 *kill*, 244.11 *ruin*, 362.3 *bring down*
shoot 'em up 65.18 *computer game*
shooter 338, 23.2 *basketball player*, 27.8 *delivery*, 37.4 *hunter*, 338.9 *firearm*, 679.8 *sol-*

dier

shoot game 37.7 *shoot*
shoot gravy 875.10 *drug oneself*
shooting 37, 338, 23.4 *playing terms,* 31.8 *hockey,* 38.2 *football play,* 38.5 *soccer,* 261.1 *growth,* 261.8 *growing,* 338.7 *shot,* 397.6 *killing,* 398.2 *murder,* 398.5 *execution,* 398.9 *animal killing,* 406.5 *painful,* 590.2 *chase,* 590.16 *hunting,* 670.15 *firing,* 879.13 *capital punishment*
Shooting 37
shooting association 37.2 *hunting*
shooting box 37.2 *hunting*
shooting brake 71 *Motor Vehicles,* 71.16 *car*
shooting circle 31.1 *hockey*
shooting gallery 875.1 *drug-taking*
shooting in the dark 504.2 *inaccuracy*
shooting iron 680.9 *firearm*
shooting jacket 295.11 *jacket*
shooting kit 37.3 *hunting equipment*
shooting oneself 398.7 *suicide*
shooting party 37.2 *hunting*
shooting script 51.2 *play*
shooting season 203.1 *season*
shooting star 53.20 *meteor,* 189.2 *transient thing,* 439.4 *natural light,* 517.6 *good-luck sign*
shooting stick 37.3 *hunting equipment,* 284.4 *rest*
shooting the rapids 36.6 *canoeing*
shooting up 359.4 *taking off,* 875.1 *drug-taking*
shoot off one's mouth 530.7 *betray*
shoot one's cookies 349.15 *vomit*
shoot oneself 398.21 *commit suicide*
shoot oneself in the foot 656.6 *act foolishly*
shoot one's mouth off 565.8 *talk too much*
shoot-out 674.6 *fight,* 676.9 *battle*
shoot par 29.7 *golf*
shoot straight 857.6 *be honourable*
shoot the rapids 36.17 *canoe*
shoot through 356.8 *pass,* 591.8 *run away*
shoot to kill 674.12 *fight*
shoot up 83.21 *vegetate,* 128.4 *increase,* 261.6 *become bigger,* 275.16 *rise,* 359.17 *spring up,* 361.2 *send up,* 875.10 *drug oneself*
shoot with an arrow 380.16 *use a sharp tool*
shop 738, 63.20 *building,* 528.13 *inform on,* 647.1 *workshop,* 740.8 *store,* 748.1 *expend*
shopaholic 748.9 *spendthrift*
shop around 754.14 *buy cheaply*
shop assistant 646.1 *worker,* 697.3 *attendant,* 739.10 *salesman*
shop at 599.2 *frequent*
shop floor 161.13 *workforce,* 647.1 *workshop*
shop for 738.2 *shop*
shop girl 739.10 *salesman*
shop goods 739.8 *merchandise*
shopkeeper 606.3 *provider,* 739.13 *retailer*
shoplift 734.10 *take away,* 736.12 *steal,* 858.10 *be criminal*
shoplifter 695.5 *compulsive person,* 736.8 *thief*
shoplifting 736.1 *stealing,* 864.7 *criminality*
shop manager 653.15 *manager*
shop owner 646.3 *agent,* 739.13 *retailer*
shopper 599.8 *user,* 738.12 *purchaser,* 748.8 *spender*
shopping 738, 738.6 *purchase,* 738.14 *buying,* 748.4 *expenditure*
shopping and fucking novel 48.2 *fiction*
shopping arcade 93.7 *city district*

shopping area 93.7 *city district*
shopping bag 258.8 *bag,* 326.10 *transferred thing*
shopping basket 258.7 *basket*
shopping by mail order 738.8 *shopping*
shopping centre 93.7 *city district,* 291.4 *centre of activity,* 740.7 *emporium*
shopping list 171.4 *bill,* 593.1 *requirement,* 738.8 *shopping*
shopping mall 93.7 *city district,* 291.4 *centre of activity,* 740.7 *emporium*
shopping precinct 93.7 *city district*
shopping spree 738.8 *shopping*
shopping trolley 71.7 *handcart,* 258.10 *cart*
Shops Act 15.5 *labour law*
shopsoiled 127.17 *defective,* 599.9 *used,* 620.1 *imperfect,* 628.13 *dilapidated*
shop soiled 752.6 *discounted*
shopsoiled 754.10 *shoddy*
shop-soiled 358.8 *defective,* 793.4 *blemished*
shopsoiled item 620.6 *imperfect item*
shop steward 15.7 *employee,* 653.16 *official,* 737.11 *chamber of commerce member*
shop till one drops 738.2 *shop,* 748.1 *expend*
shopwalker 739.10 *salesman*
shop window 435.9 *viewpoint,* 437.7 *that which makes visible,* 442.8 *transparent thing,* 526.8 *showplace,* 740.2 *fair,* 740.9 *stall*
shopworn 127.17 *defective,* 752.6 *discounted,* 754.10 *shoddy*
shore 54.11, 98.4 *coast,* 249.3 *regional boundary,* 300.1 *edge,* 303.1 *front,* 373.9 *harden,* 662.19 *support*
shore bird 78.3 *water bird*
shore direction-finding station 74.5 *navigation*
shoreline 54.11, 98.4 *coast,* 300.1 *edge*
shore patrol 16.14 *police*
shore up 284.11 *support,* 373.9 *harden,* 637.5 *preserve,* 662.19 *support*
shorn 262.7 *smaller,* 270.8 *shortened*
shorn of 722.16 *losing*
short 270, 270, 358, 41.12 *ski,* 131.7 *reduced,* 145.4 *incomplete,* 189.6 *transient,* 243.5 *work of art,* 254.12 *missing,* 260.7 *little,* 276.5 *low,* 351.2 *drink,* 379.1 *brittle,* 552.3 *concise,* 562.6 *summary,* 566.3 *sparing with words,* 609.4 *scarce,* 685.4 *uncompleted,* 743.2 *insolvent,* 818.5 *discourteous,* 829.4 *irascible*
shortage 123.1 *inequality,* 129.1 *decrease,* 182.3 *fewness,* 254.2 *disappearance,* 358.5 *shortfall,* 593.2 *need,* 609.9 *scarcity,* 683.1 *failure,* 743.9 *inadequacy*
shortage of cash 743.6 *insolvency*
shortage of funds 743.6 *insolvency*
short allowance 609.8 *insufficiency*
shortan 73.6 *flight control*
short and sweet 270.7 *short,* 552.3 *concise,* 562.6 *summary*
short and to the point 562.6 *summary*
short answer 478.1 *answer,* 818.3 *act of discourtesy*
short-arm blow 330.14 *sporting hit*
short-back-and-sides 791.8 *hair cut*
short board sailing 18 *Sporting Activities*
shortbread 45.39 *loaf*
short-change 539.30 *be fraudulent*
short-changer 539.17 *cheat*
short circuit 33.6 *motor racing*

terms, 64.13 *circuit,* 235.7 *electrical power,* 333.1 *middle way*
short-circuit 334.4 *detour*
shortcoming 358, 620.7 *defect,* 720.2 *nonperformance,* 864.3 *venial sin*
short commons 609.8 *insufficiency,* 871.2 *short rations*
short-course 39.11 *swimming*
short-course pool 39.7 *swimming pool*
shortcrust pastry 45.37 *pastry*
short cut 264.2 *short distance,* 270.4 *short thing,* 327.2 *route,* 332.2 *bearing,* 333.1 *middle way*
short-cut 270
short distance 264
short-distance 41.13 *ice-skating*
short-distance racing 41.8 *speedskating*
short division 52.18 *division*
short drink 351.2 *drink*
short duration 189
shorten 270, 129.5 *make smaller,* 131.4 *take off,* 262.5 *make smaller,* 262.6 *become smaller,* 376.11 *smooth,* 552.4 *be concise,* 562.8 *summarize,* 628.5 *hurt*
shortened 270, 562, 131.7 *reduced,* 145.4 *incomplete,* 262.7 *smaller,* 552.3 *concise*
shortened version 270
shortener 562.5 *summarizer*
shortening 270, 45.7 *basic ingredient,* 129.1 *decrease,* 131.1 *subtraction,* 262.1 *contraction,* 262.8 *contracting,* 552.1 *conciseness,* 562.2 *outline*
shorten sail 328.3 *slow down,* 632.8 *be safe*
shorten someone's life 398.16 *kill*
shorten the life of 189.5 *make transient*
shortfall 358, 123.1 *inequality,* 127.2 *deficiency,* 131.2 *subtracted item,* 145.2 *omission,* 593.2 *need,* 609.8 *insufficiency,* 620.5 *imperfection,* 620.7 *defect,* 683.1 *failure,* 685.1 *noncompletion,* 722.2 *financial loss*
Shortfall 358
short fuse 829.1 *irascibility,* 830.4 *sign of irritableness*
shorthand 270.4 *short thing*
short-handed 31.8 *hockey,* 609.2 *unprovided,* 620.2 *incomplete*
Shorthorn 68 *Breeds of Cattle*
short hundredweight 75 *General Units*
short legs 270.4 *short thing*
short list 171.6 *list of names*
shortlist 580.6 *selection*
short-list 171.8 *list*
shortlived 189.6 *transient*
short loin 45.23 *beef*
shortly 189.8 *transiently,* 208.18 *soon,* 270.12 *short,* 562.11 *summarily*
short measure 358.5 *shortfall*
shortness 270, 260.1 *littleness,* 276.1 *lowness,* 552.1 *conciseness,* 562.4 *summariness,* 566.4 *taciturnity,* 818.1 *discourtesy*
Shortness 270
shortness of breath 650.7 *fatigue*
short note 49.19 *tempo*
short novel 243.5 *work of art*
short odds 229.2 *chance*
short of 127.19 *inferiorly,* 131.8 *by subtraction,* 145.4 *incomplete,* 147.12 *exclusively,* 358.7 *short*
short of breath 650.3 *panting*
short of cash 743.2 *insolvent*
short of funds 743.2 *insolvent*
short one 351.2 *drink*
short-order cook 45.2 *cook*
short-order food 350.7 *food*
short pants 295.9 *trousers*
short period 57.6 *chemical element*
short person 270
short plate 45.23 *beef*
short-range 70.5 *transportable*
short rations 871

short run 51.11 *theatrical performance*
shorts 23.3 *basketball equipment,* 38.1 *soccer,* 270.4 *short thing,* 295.9 *trousers,* 295.18 *underwear,* 296.4 *dishabille*
short service line 40.12 *badminton terms*
short shorts 295.9 *trousers*
short shrift 836.1 *pitilessness*
short sight 435.1 *vision,* 436.2 *poor sight*
short-sighted 435.22 *bespectacled,* 436.9 *weak-sighted*
short-sightedness 436.2 *poor sight*
short ski 41.5 *ski equipment*
short sleeve 295.24 *part of garment*
short-sleeved 295.21 *styled*
short-sleeved shirt 295.8 *shirt*
short space of time 189.3 *short duration*
short-staffed 620.2 *incomplete*
short stop 22.2 *baseball player*
short story 48.2 *fiction,* 243.5 *work of art,* 560.5 *fiction*
short-story writer 48.14 *author*
short stuff 270.5 *short person*
short supply 609.9 *scarcity*
short sword 680.8 *sharp weapon*
short temper 829.1 *irascibility*
short-tempered 270.9 *abrupt,* 829.4, 829.4 *irascible*
short tennis 18 *Sporting Activities*
short-term 189.6 *transient*
short-term debt 745.1 *debt*
short-term forecast 55.4 *weather forecast*
short-term loan 732.2 *loan*
short thing 270
short time 189.3 *short duration*
short ton 75 *General Units*
short-track 41.13 *ice-skating*
short-track racing 41.8 *speed-skating*
short-track speed skating 18 *Sporting Activities*
short wave 212.6 *radio frequency,* 534.14 *radio transmission*
short-wave radio 534.16 *transmitter*
short way 264.2 *short distance*
short word 5.17 *word*
short words 522.10 *simplicity*
shorty 270.5 *short person*
short zoom 66.17 *lens*
Shoshone 5 *Languages and Groups of Languages*
Shoshoni 1 *Peoples*
shot 75 *General Units,* **338,** 20.3 *fishing tackle,* 21.2 *field events,* 23.4 *playing terms,* 25.2 *grip,* 40.12 *badminton terms,* 41.10 *curling,* 66.3 *photograph,* 133.12 *mixed,* 322.14 *holed,* 338.8 *missile,* 338.10 *ball,* 338.15 *shooter,* 354.9 *injection,* 425.1 *bang,* 456.7 *iridescent,* 479.1 *experiment,* 518.3 *conjecture,* 590.6 *hunter,* 596.5 *attempt,* 630.2 *medicine,* 680.6 *historical missile weapon,* 680.13 *ammunition,* 874.3 *dead drunk,* 875.6 *drug*
shot across the bows 636.2 *danger signal,* 670.15 *firing*
shot bowl 25.2 *grip*
shot-clock 23.3 *basketball equipment*
shotgun 37.3 *hunting equipment,* 338.9 *firearm*
shot gun 425.3 *banger*
shotgun 590.3 *hunting and fishing equipment,* 680.9 *firearm*
shotgun formation 19.7 *offence*
shotgun patrol 16.16 *US police*
shotgun wedding 823.5 *wedding*
shot in the dark 229.3 *coincidence,* 518.3 *conjecture,* 589.6 *poor chance*
shot put 21.2 *field events*
shot-put 338.5 *throw*

shot-putter 21.3 *athlete,* 338.14 *thrower*
shot putting 18 Sporting Activities
shot-putting 21.2 *field events*
shots down 25.2 *grip*
shot silk 67 Natural Fabrics, 456.5 *variegated thing*
shots up 25.2 *grip*
shot through with 133.12 *mixed,* 456.7 *iridescent*
shot to pieces 136.16 *apart*
shot up 361.11 *raised*
shot velocity 21.2 *field events*
should 695.8 *be compelled,* 847.14 *be the duty of*
shoulder 45.25 *pork* , 45.26, 45.27 *lamb* , 135.5 *joint,* 330.1 *impel,* 330.2 *collide,* 338.24 *push,* 361.1 *raise,* 361.3 *promote,* 588.8 *resolve,* 597.1 *undertake,* 640.4 *act*
shoulder a musket 676.13 *be at war*
shoulder arms 594.8 *prepare oneself*
shoulder bag 258.8 *bag*
shoulder belt 137.10 *band*
shoulder blade 382 Bones
shoulder clasping 543.3 *gesture*
shouldered arch 43.5 *arch*
shoulder-guard 31.3 *ice hockey*
shoulder harness 632.4 *safety device*
shoulder harp 49 Musical Instruments
shoulder-high 275.12 *tall*
shouldering 330.12 *collision*
shouldering responsibility 597.6 *enterprising*
shoulder-length 269.1 *long*
shoulder one's responsibilities 847.16 *do one's duty*
shoulder pad 295.25 *accessories,* 671.6 *protective clothing*
shoulder-pad 31.5 *lacrosse*
shoulder responsibility 222.4 *be a substitute*
shoulder sling 34.4 *climbing equipment*
shoulder to shoulder 116.32 *in alliance,* 464.20 *cooperatively*
shoulder-to-shoulder 138.9 *adhesive,* 138.11 *cohesively,* 264.5 *near*
should it be that 106.15 *under the circumstances*
should it so happen 106.15 *under the circumstances*
shout 423.2 *outcry,* 423.8 *be loud,* 431.1 *cry,* 431.10 *cry out,* 532.14 *proclaim,* 543.6 *word,* 543.12 *signal,* 554.6 *emphasize,* 564.12 *speak loudly,* 636.2 *danger signal,* 769.5, 769.8 *cheer,* 773.2 *fanfare,* 773.7 *dance*
shout at the top of one's voice 431.10 *cry out*
shout bravo 851.16 *acclaim*
shout down 431.14 *hiss,* 476.8 *refute,* 563.15 *strike dumb,* 565.9 *out-talk,* 699.12 *gag,* 807.25 *answer back,* 818.8 *get angry,* 852.23 *show disapproval*
shouter 431.9 *crier,* 543.8 *signer*
shout for 431.12 *cheer*
shout for more 851.16 *acclaim*
shout from the rooftops 532.14 *proclaim*
shouting 423.2 *outcry,* 423.6 *loud,* 431.16 *vociferous,* 543.16 *signalling,* 822.6 *swearing,* 828.4 *anger*
shouting from the rooftops 526.14 *manifest*
shout oneself hoarse 431.10 *cry out*
shout out 431.10 *cry out*
shove 35.3 *rugby play,* 35.5 *play rugby,* 36.8 *punting,* 36.19 *punt,* 324.14 *set in motion,* 330.1 *impel,* 330.13 *blow,* 337.29 *in reverse,* 338.20 *propel,* 338.24 *push,* 543.3, 543.11 *gesture,* 642.14 *push,* 644.6 *work*
shove around 690.5 *be severe*
shove around a punt 36.19 *punt*

shove aside 335, 850.22 *show disrespect*
shovel 68.10 *farm tool,* 120.3 *container,* 258.17 *ladle,* 326.15 *take away,* 355.10 *excavator,* 380.9 *sharp-edged thing,* 380.16 *use a sharp tool* , 603.2 *garden tool,* 603.9 *use tools*
shoveler duck 78 Birds
shovel hat 295.15 *headgear*
shovelhead 80 Fishes
shovel in 350.22 *eat well*
shovelled 258.20 *containing*
shovelnose 80 Fishes
shove off 345.15 *go,* 349.33 *go away*
shover 330.15 *ram*
shove shot 24.4 *carom*
shoving 338.17 *propulsive,* 648.3 *hasty*
show 51, 303, 811, 811, 4.21 *rationalize,* 4.22 *propound a philosophy,* 32.7 *horseracing,* 49.27 *performance,* 51.2 *play,* 51.3 *musical drama,* 51.11 *theatrical performance,* 161.31 *exhibition,* 243.10 *produce,* 322.18 *open,* 435.7 *view,* 435.18 *make visible,* 435.19 *be visible,* 437.5 *manifestation,* 437.8 *be visible,* 437.10 *make visible,* 457.2 *being in view,* 457.11 *appear,* 457.12 *become visible,* 457.14 *present,* 473.15 *state,* 475.1 *demonstration,* 475.15 *demonstrate,* 480.2 *prove,* 483.10 *make evident,* 524.8 *interpret,* 526.1 *display,* 526.3 *reveal,* 526.6 *display,* 526.9 *production,* 530.5 *disclose,* 538.8 *pretence,* 538.24 *pretend,* 539.3 *hypocrisy,* 539.26 *be a hypocrite,* 540.12 *facade,* 540.24 *mask,* 544.10 *identify,* 547.12 *stand for,* 653.2 *direct,* 740.2 *fair,* 805.9 *ostentation,* 813.3 *formal occasion*
showable 526.13 *displayed*
show a clean pair of heels 329.4 *be swift,* 591.8 *run away*
show acuteness 380.17 *be mentally sharp*
show a false face 539.26 *be a hypocrite*
show a false front 539.26 *be a hypocrite,* 540.24 *mask*
show an affinity 234.4 *tend*
show an effect 227
show anger 543.11 *gesture*
show apathy for 673.3 *submit*
show appreciation 837.6 *be grateful*
show approval for 784.8 *prefer*
show a profit 721.13 *be profitable*
show aptitude 655.10 *be skilful*
show aptitude for 784.8 *prefer*
show arena 32.9 *jumping*
show a sense of duty 857.6 *be honourable*
show a talent for 655.10 *be skilful*
show a tendency 234.4 *tend,* 488.8 *be probable*
show a trend 234.4 *tend*
show authority 692.11 *have authority over*
show a weakness for 784.7 *like*
show bad faith 538.25 *be dishonest,* 540.16 *be false*
show benevolence 819.13 *befriend,* 833.7 *be charitable*
show bias 123.6 *be unjust*
showbiz 51.4 *show business*
showboat 51.14 *theatre*
show business 51
show candour 698.17 *be informal*
showcase 437.7 *that which makes visible,* 442.8 *transparent thing,* 526.8 *showplace*
show caution 328.2 *hesitate*
show compassion 839.12 *show mercy*
show compassion for 859.7 *be unselfish*
show compunction 867.4 *be penitent*
show concern 831.8 *be benevolent*

show consideration 691.3 *be lenient,* 831.8 *be benevolent*
show consideration for 467.14 *be solicitous*
show contempt 668.6 *be insubordinate*
show courage 668.5 *defy*
show courtesies 817.10 *be courteous*
show courtesy 694.6 *show obeisance to*
show determination 225
show devotion to 694.5 *obey*
show diligence 719.4 *observe*
show disapproval 852, 713.6 *protest*
show discontent 713.6 *protest*
show disdain 720.7 *not observe*
show disloyalty 720.9 *disregard orders*
show displeasure 822.14 *hate*
show disrespect 850, 720.9 *disregard orders*
show dissatisfaction 713.6 *protest*
show dog 77.9 *dog*
showdown 496.7 *detection,* 530.1 *disclosure,* 674.6 *fight*
show empathy 784.7 *like*
show endearment for 826
show enterprise 597.1 *undertake*
shower 55.25, 55.62 *rain,* 161.22 *flood,* 162.18 *sprinkle,* 338.23 *throw,* 360.3 *downflow,* 360.13 *drip,* 362.6 *throw down,* 362.11 *lowering,* 389.11 *wash,* 389.33 *sprinkle,* 608.5 *about,* 608.8 *plenty,* 621.6 *bath,* 621.14 *bathe,* 651.6 *refresher*
shower attention on 467.14 *be solicitous*
shower bath 389.11 *wash*
shower gel 418.2 *fragrant thing,* 621.9 *cleaning agent*
shower head 389.11 *wash*
showeriness 55.26 *raininess,* 391.2 *mistiness*
showering 362.20 *falling,* 389.11 *wash*
showerproof 67.11 *treated,* 67.15 *treat,* 392.10 *waterproof,* 632.6 *invulnerable*
shower room 256.7 *room*
shower upon 729.5 *give*
shower with arrows 338.28 *shoot*
showery 55.53 *rainy,* 391.10 *misty*
show false colours 539.32 *disguise*
show falsely 538.24 *pretend*
show favour 729.5 *give*
show favouritism 844.22 *discriminate*
show fear 777.11 *be afraid*
show feelings 760.11 *be sensitive*
show fickleness 579.5 *be capricious*
show fight 642.14 *push,* 671.26 *act on the defensive*
show fortitude 406.9 *feel pain*
show for what it is 530.5 *disclose*
show friendship for 667.6 *agree with*
show genius 461.17 *philosophize*
show gentleness 374.15 *be kind*
show girl 51.27 *entertainer,* 51.28 *dancer*
show good faith 694.5 *obey*
show good grounds 855.8 *justify*
show gratitude 837.6 *be grateful*
show greed 734.7 *take*
show hostility 111.9 *oppose,* 136.12, 666.5 *disagree,* 852.16 *disagree*
show how 475.16 *explain*
show humility 694.6 *show obeisance to*
show ignorance 460.9 *lack intellect*
show ill will 832.16 *be malevolent*
showily 811, 805.35 *ostentatiously*
show impatience 829.6 *be irascible*
show in 348
show inconsideration for 468.13 *be thoughtless*

show indifference 412.7 *be tasteless*
show indifference towards 859.6 *be disinterested*
showiness 811, 437.4 *clarity,* 475.2 *demonstrativeness,* 557.2 *affectation,* 795.1 *tastelessness*
Showiness 811
showing 51.39 *stagestruck,* 435.7 *view,* 437.1 *visible,* 457.2 *being in view,* 457.7 *appearing,* 475.1 *demonstration,* 526.6 *display,* 530.10 *disclosed*
showing irascibility 829
showing leniency 374.7 *impressionable*
showing off 475.2 *demonstrativeness,* 494.1 *overestimation,* 526.10 *manifestation,* 809.6 *boastfulness,* 811.10 *exhibitionism*
showing preference 580.14 *selecting*
showing respect 849
showing signs of 624.22 *sick*
showing symptoms of 624.22 *sick*
show in one's true colours 496.2 *detect*
show insolence 668.5 *defy*
show insubordination 693.15 *be disobedient*
show intelligence 380.17 *be mentally sharp*
show interest 465.7 *be curious,* 642.16 *be sociable*
show interest in 465.7 *be curious*
show ire 822.17 *anger*
show irreverence 787.5 *not wonder about*
show its face 530.9 *be disclosed*
show its true colours 530.9 *be disclosed*
show joy 762
showjumper 32.15 *horse person*
showjumping 18 Sporting Activities, 32.6 *horsemanship,* 32.9 *jumping,* 32.11 *eventing,* 32.17 *equine,* 674.2 *contest*
show kindness 817.10 *be courteous*
show leniency 374.15 *be kind,* 691.3 *be lenient*
show love 817.10 *be courteous*
show loyalty to 138.8 *be tenacious*
showman 811, 51.25 *producer,* 475.7 *demonstrator,* 526.12 *display player*
showmanship 51.7 *dramaturgy,* 51.20 *acting,* 532.8 *public relations* , 797.1 *affectedness,* 811.1 *showiness*
show mercy 835, 839, 632.9 *protect,* 677.4 *pacify,* 691.3 *be lenient,* 831.8 *be benevolent,* 848.10 *acquit*
show moderation 333.7 *be halfway,* 810.14 *be modest*
shown 475.13 *proven,* 526.13 *displayed,* 530.10 *disclosed,* 544.12 *identified*
show no concern for 783.12 *be indifferent*
show no excitement 783.12 *be indifferent,* 787.5 *not wonder about*
shown off 526.13 *displayed*
show no fight 673.4 *succumb*
show no flexibility 669.7 *be obstinate,* 836.6 *be pitiless*
show no interest in 859.6 *be disinterested*
show no leniency 836.6 *be pitiless*
show no mercy 690.5 *be severe,* 836.6 *be pitiless*
show no pity 690.5 *be severe,* 836.6 *be pitiless*
show no regard for someone's feelings 818.7 *be discourteous*
show no respect 850.22 *show disrespect*
show no respect for 720.9 *disregard orders,* 814.11 *not stand on ceremony*
show no sign of life 641.4 *not act*
show no surprise 783.12 *be indif-*

ferent
show no sympathy 836.6 *be pitiless*
shown up 544.12 *identified*
show obeisance to 694
show of disapproval 852
show off 809, 811, 475.18 *appear*, 526.1 *display*, 526.3 *reveal*, 640.4 *act*, 655.11 *be expert*, 797.4 *be affected*, 805.27 *be ostentatious*
show-off 475.7 *demonstrator*, 490.11 *opinionist*, 809.7 *vain person*
show of force 690.2 *suppression*
show of hands 580.10 *vote*
show of respect 849.4 *mark of respect*
show one's Achilles' heel 620.9 *be imperfect*
show one's cards 530.6 *divulge*
show one's colours 574.8 *brace oneself*, 676.12 *go to war*
show one's distaste 573.10 *grudge*
show oneself 526, 457.12 *become visible*
show oneself in one's true colours 530.5 *disclose*
show oneself up 801.4 *disreputable*
show one's face 253.12 *attend*, 526.4 *show oneself*
show one's fangs 830.11 *be irritable*
show one's gratitude 878.9 *reward*
show one's hand 530.6 *divulge*
show one's heels 648.2 *make haste*
show one's ignorance 656.5 *be unskilful*
show one's mettle 671.26 *act on the defensive*, 778.15 *be courageous*
show one's paces 809.16, 811.29 *show off*
show one's true colours 526.4 *show oneself*
show one's years 207.17 *age*
show partiality 123.6 *be unjust*, 844.22 *discriminate*
show phases 224.11 *be changeable*
show photographs 526.2 *display something*
showpiece 526
show pity 835.8 *pity*
showplace 526
show poor attention 783.14 *be careless*
show potential 714, 235.10 *be powerful*
show prejudice 123.6 *be unjust*, 234.4 *tend*
show promise 336.5 *develop*, 714.10 *show potential*
show prudence 516
show readiness 208.7 *be early*
show refinement 817.11 *have good manners*
show reluctance 669.6 *resist*
show resentment 785.5 *dislike*
show resilience 377.8 *be elastic*
show respect 849, 611.8 *make important*, 694.6 *show obeisance to*, 719.4 *observe*, 857.6 *be honourable*, 861.18 *be good*
show results 682.6 *be successful*, 682.8 *be effective*
show-ring 674.3 *stadium*
showroom 526.8 *showplace*
show round 526.1 *display*
show self-restraint 690.7 *be unadorned*, 699.10 *restrain oneself*
show signs of 483.10 *make evident*, 488.8 *be probable*, 543.10 *signify*
show signs of emotion 759.17 *feel deeply*
show sincerity 537.29 *be truthful*
show skill for 861.19 *be good at*
show someone the door 341.1 *repel*, 349.1 *expel*
show stamina 378.10 *be tough*
show strength 378.10 *be tough*
show stubbornness 225.8 *show*

determination
show style 549.9 *style*, 558.4 *be elegant*
show sufficient grounds for 4.21 *rationalize*
show talent 234.4 *tend*, 235.10 *be powerful*
show taste 558.4 *be elegant*
show tenaciousness 726.6 *retain*
show tenderness 374.15 *be kind*
show the door 252.17 *relegate*, 818.7 *be discourteous*
show the flag 526.4 *show oneself*, 676.12 *go to war*
show them what's what 476.8 *refute*
show the red light to 711.5 *refuse*
show the ropes 348.10 *introduce*
show the way 154.15 *precede*, 543.9 *use signs*, 594.1 *prepare*, 653.2 *direct*
show the white feather 779.4 *be a coward*
show the white flag 673.3 *submit*
show through 435.19 *be visible*, 437.9 *appear*, 442.11 *be transparent*, 530.9 *be disclosed*
show tolerance 839.12 *show mercy*
show treachery 540.19 *be deceitful*, 720.9 *disregard orders*
show unconcern 468.12 *be inattentive*
show understanding 835.8 *pity*
show up 253.12 *attend*, 344.1 *arrive*, 437.9, 457.11 *appear*, 457.12 *become visible*, 457.14 *present*, 476.8 *refute*, 496.2 *detect*, 496.5 *be discovered*, 526.4 *show oneself*, 526.5 *be visible*, 530.5 *disclose*
show up again 183.21 *be repeated*
show up well 526.5 *be visible*
show variety 224.11 *be changeable*
show willing 572.13 *be willing*, 664.13 *work together*
show willingness 642.14 *push*, 667.6 *agree with*
show wisdom 463.12 *be reasonable*
showy 811, 437.2 *clear*, 444.12 *gaudy*, 475.10 *demonstrative*, 526.14 *manifest*, 538.18 *pretentious*, 557.4 *ornate*, 757.2 *unrestrained*, 795.7 *vulgar*, 797.3 *affected*, 805.23 *ostentatious*
show zeal 642.14 *push*
shrapnel 680.5 *missile weapon*, 680.13 *ammunition*
Shrapnel 52 Scientists
shred 45.55 *cook*, 136.9 *separate*, 143.7 *piece*, 173.3 *fragment*, 244.9 *demolish*, 384.26 *grate*, 598.1 *relinquish*
shredded 143.11 *partial*, 244.15 *destroyed*, 384.19 *pulverized*
shredder 384.13 *grater*
shredding 244.2 *destroying*, 384.4 *pulverization*
Shreveport 93 Cities
shrew 77 Placental Mammals, 241.4 *violent person or animal*, 402.8 *nasty woman*, 500.5 *dissenter*, 759.9 *feeling person*, 764.9 *unpleasant person*, 822.8 *hated person*, 829.3 *irascible person*, 832.9 *vixen*
shrewd 6.20 *refined*, 380.5 *mentally sharp*, 459.10 *intelligent*, 492.9 *judicious*, 501.8 *knowledgeable*, 507.6 *intelligent*, 655.6 *skilful*, 657.4 *cunning*
shrewd businessman 469.6 *careful person*
shrewd idea 518.3 *conjecture*
shrewdly 380.18 *sharply*, 459.15, 507.10 *intelligently*, 655.12 *skilfully*, 657.6 *cunningly*
shrewdness 380.13 *mental sharpness*, 459.4 *cleverness*, 507.1 *wisdom*, 657.1 *cunning*
shrewish 829.4 *irascible*, 830.7 *irritable*
shrewishness 829.1, 829.1 *irasci-*

bility
Shrewsbury 93 Cities
shriek 55.58 *blow*, 406.12 *express pain*, 423.2 *outcry*, 423.8 *be loud*, 430.3 *shrillness*, 430.6 *be shrill*, 431.1 *cry*, 431.6 *cry of pain*, 431.10 *cry out*, 564.12 *speak loudly*
shrieking 444.12 *gaudy*
shrievalty 16.2 *jurisdiction*
shrift 839.1 *forgiveness*, 840.2 *apology*
shrike 78 Birds, 78.6 *songbird*
shrill 430, 423.6 *loud*, 423.8 *be loud*, 434.7 *dissonant*
shrillness 430, 423.1 *loudness*
shrilly 430.10 *stridently*
shrimp 45.19 *shellfish*, 80.15 *fish*, 81.4 *arthropod*, 260.4 *little person*, 270.5 *short person*, 590.11 *hunt*
shrimp balls 45.48 Chinese dish
shrimper 80.7 *fishing*, 590.6 *hunter*
shrimplike 81.18 *arthropodous*
shrimp loaf 45.11 *sandwich*
shrimp plant 84 Flowers and Flowering Plants
shrine 10, 10.11 *place of worship*, 399.6 *grave*, 545.11 *monument*
shrink 61.30 *psychiatrist*, 129.4 *decrease*, 262.5 *make smaller*, 262.6 *become smaller*, 331.2 *respond*, 337.6 *shrink back*, 510.10 *psychiatrist*, 591.4 *shy*, 628.1 *deteriorate*, 630.15 *healer*, 722.12 *lessen*, 777.11 *be afraid*, 777.12 *be fearful*, 779.4 *be a coward*
shrinkability 262.2 *contractibility*
shrinkable 262.9 *contractible*
shrinkage 129.1 *decrease*, 131.1 *subtraction*, 262.1 *contraction*, 722.4 *lessening*
shrink back 337, 810.15 *escape notice*
shrinker 591.17 *avolder*
shrink from 573.7, 711.5 *refuse*, 785.6 *react against*, 822.14 *hate*
shrink from public gaze 810.15 *escape notice*
shrinking 129.1 *decrease*, 262.1 *contraction*, 262.8 *contracting*, 272.9 *narrowing*, 573.3 *cautious*, 573.13 *dissociation*, 591.12 *shyness*, 591.18 *avoiding*, 810.11 *shy*
shrinking violet 84.9 *figurative usage*, 403.4 *someone or something that feels*, 542.11 *modest person*, 760.9 *oversensitive person*, 806.16 *humble person*, 810.7 *modest person*
shrink-wrapped 632.6 *invulnerable*
shrive 10.18 *perform rites*, 839.9 *forgive*
shrivel 129.4 *decrease*, 207.17 *age*, 262.5 *make smaller*, 262.6 *become smaller*, 392.21 *dry up*, 408.14 *be hot*, 607.1 *waste*, 628.1 *deteriorate*, 631.14 *afflict*
shrivelled 207.14 *aged*, 247.3 *birth control*, 260.7 *little*, 262.7 *smaller*, 274.2 *emaciated*, 392.3 *dried-up*
shrivelled-up 262.7 *smaller*
shrivelling 262.1 *contraction*, 262.8 *contracting*
shrivel up 262.6 *become smaller*
shriven 839.6 *forgiven*
shrive oneself 840.6 *apologize*
shriving 839.4 *forgiving*
Shropshire 68 Breeds of Sheep, **92** Counties, **95** Mountains
Shropshire Hills 95.5 British mountains
shroud 74 Rigging, 36.3 *parts of a sailing boat*, 137.7 *tackle*, 293.2 *cover*, 293.4 *wrapping*, 293.5 *body covering*, 293.25 *wrap*, 293.31 *hide*, 295.17 *grave clothes*, 295.32 *dress*, 399.4 *funeral objects*, 438.6 *that which makes invisible*, 440.6 *shade*, 440.14 *make dark*, 441.10

make dim, 531.8 *conceal*, 632.9 *protect*
shrouded 293.37 *protected*
shrouded in mystery 523.1 *unintelligible*, 523.2 *unexplained*
shroud in mystery 523.8 *make unintelligible*
shroud knot 74 Knots
Shrove Tuesday 10.15 *holy day*
shrub 69.9 *garden plant*, 83.2 *plant*, 85.1 *tree*
shrubbery 69.3 *ornamental garden*
shrubby 69.17 *botanical*, 85.14 *treelike*
shrug 543.11 *gesture*
shrugged-off 542.19 *downplayed*
shrugging off 542.9 *down-playing*
shrug off 495.3 *underestimate*, 542.22 *play down*, 612.12 *think unimportant*, 783.12 *be indifferent*, 848.12 *exempt oneself*
shrug one's shoulders 502.9 *be ignorant*, 673.3 *submit*
shrunk 260.7 *little*, 262.7 *smaller*
shrunken 260.7 *little*, 262.7 *smaller*
shrunken head 681.2 *spoils*
shrunkenness 260.1 *littleness*, 262.1 *contraction*
shruti 7.12 *religious text*
shtoom 563.11 *speechless*, 566.1 *taciturn*
Shu 8 Deities
shuck 86.3 *fruit structure*, 293.13 *casing*
shudder 366.7 *shake*, 366.23 *jolt*, 366.24 *shake*, 409.10 *be cold*, 777.11 *be afraid*, 785.6 *react against*
shudder at 820.11 *be hostile*, 822.14 *hate*
shuddering 366.6 *shaking*, 366.18 *shaky*, 785.4 *sign of dislike*
shuffle 42.3 *card game terms*, 42.10 *play*, 46.2, 46.15 *dance*, 113.8 *be diverse*, 133.9 *mix up*, 151.21 *disorder*, 222.1 *substitution*, 222.6 *give a substitute*, 223.1, 223.5 *exchange*, 324.12 *gait*, 324.15 *walk*, 326.11 *transfer*, 328.10 *slow motion*, 335.9 *shove aside*, 474.2 *sophism*, 474.13 *quibble*, 538.8 *pretence*, 538.24 *pretend*, 540.23 *evade*, 543.11 *gesture*, 576.5 *vacillate*, 578.2 *equivocate*
shuffle along 328.1 *move slowly*
shuffled 133.12 *mixed*, 151.12 *disordered*
shuffle off 591.8 *run away*
shuffle off this mortal coil 397.15 *die*
shuffler 46.5 *dancer*
shuffle the cards 216.10 *exchange*, 594.4 *prepare for action*
shuffling 223.1 *exchange*, 328.4 *slow*, 474.4, 474.9 *quibbling*, 540.11 *evasion*, 540.34 *evasive*, 578.11 *equivocating*
shufty 435.6 *look*
Shukokai 26.8 *karate*
shul 10.11 *place of worship*
shun 147.7 *exclude*, 531.11 *conceal oneself*, 591.1 *avoid*, 785.6 *react against*, 816.13 *ignore*
shun alcohol 869.5 *be self-restrained*
shun company 816.12 *be unsocial*
shunned 147.11 *excluded*, 600.3 *not wanted*, 816.10 *lonely*
shunning 147.1 *exclusion*, 591.10 *avoidance*, 591.19 *abstaining*
shunt 71.21 *miscellaneous motoring terms*, 252.1 *displacement*, 252.14 *displace*, 326.15 *take away*, 335.9 *shove aside*, 337.29 *in reverse*, 338.21 *move forward*
shunted 252.8 *displaced*
shunter 72.4 *locomotive*
shun the limelight 810.15 *escape notice*
shunting engine 72.4 *locomotive*
shunting yard 327.10 *railway*

665.14 *be a party member*
Sidgwick 4 Philosophers
siding 47.12 *wood,* 72.2 *track,*
305.1 *side,* 327.10 *railway*
Siding Spring 95 Mountains
sidle 305.8 *move sideways,*
335.8 *sidestep*
Sidney 48 Poets
siege 670, 699.4 *detention,*
699.11 *detain*
siege cap 671.7 *armour*
siegecraft 17.1 *military affairs,*
676.6 *art of war*
siege gun 680.11 *guns*
sieges 676.8 *warfare*
Siegfried Line 298.1 *interface,*
671.9 *barrier*
siemens 75 SI Units, **75** Scientific and Technical Units
Siemens 52 Scientists
Siena 93 Cities
Sienese school 50 Western Art
Styles and Movements
sierra 95.1 *mountain,* 275.4
mountain range, 375.8 *rough
ground*
Sierra 534 Phonetic Alphabet
Sierra Leone 91 Countries
Sierra Madre 95 Mountains
Sierra Morena 95 Mountains
Sierra Nevada 95 Mountains,
95.4 *US mountains*
siesta 204.4 *afternoon,* 643.9
sleep
sieve 134.10 *purify,* 152.15 *categorize,* 322.6 *porous thing,*
322.21 *provide passage for,*
621.10 *cleaning object,* 621.15
purify
sievelike 322.14 *holed*
sievert 75 SI Units, **75** Scientific and Technical Units
Sif 8 Deities
sifaka 77 Placental Mammals
sift 134.10 *purify,* 150.19 *systematize,* 152.15 *categorize,* 580.4
pick, 621.15 *purify*
sifted 152.24 *categorized,*
384.19 *pulverized*
sifting 152.5 *categorization*
sift out 152.15 *categorize*
Siger of Brabant 4 Philosophers
sigh 55.58 *blow,* 424.1 *faintness,* 424.5 *sound faint,* 428.4
faint sound, 428.8 *sound faint,*
431.6 *cry of pain,* 431.13 *cry,*
543.3, 543.11 *gesture,* 563.4
whispering, 563.16 *speak in a
low voice,* 564.13 *speak in a particular way,* 770.8 *grieve,* 774.2
lament, 774.7 *weep,* 821.26
court, 830.2 *sign of sullenness*
sighing 424.4 *faint,* 431.18 *crying,* 543.15 *gestural,* 563.12 *inarticulate,* 821.6 *courtship*
sight 344.5 *approach,* 396.4 *biological function,* 403.1 *sensation,* 435.1 *vision,* 435.7, 435.7
view, 435.12 *see,* 437.6 *visible
thing,* 457.4 *something that appears,* 496.1 *discover,* 496.6 *discovery,* 680.9 *firearm,* 786.4
wonder
sight a coastline 98.12 *be
marooned*
sighted 435.21 *seeing*
sight for sore eyes 435.7 *view*
sight hole 435.9 *viewpoint*
sight in 37.7 *shoot*
sighting 496.6 *discovery*
sighting-in 37.2 *hunting*
sight land 74.10 *sail*
sightless 436.8 *blind*
sightlessness 436.1 *blindness*
sightline 437.3 *visibility*
sightly 457.10 *aspectual*
sight on 332.7 *take a direction*
sight quarry 37.7 *shoot*
sight screen 27.2 *ground*
sightscreen 435.10 *visual aid*
sightsee 435.12 *see,* 465.7 *be curious*
sightseeing 465.5 *curious*
sightseer 435.11 *observer,* 465.3
curious person
sight unseen 438.9 *invisibly*
sigil 544.3 *means of identification*

tion
sigillary 544.12 *identified*
sigla 543.1 *sign*
sigma 429.3 *hisser*
sigmoidectomy 60 Surgical Operations
sign 543, 5.13 *letter,* 5.47 *word,*
116.28 *consent,* 169.1 *number,*
180.4 *concomitant,* 421.8 *be
deaf,* 437.6 *visible thing,* 437.7
that which makes visible,
437.10 *make visible,* 480.1 *verify,* 517.5 *omen,* 524.12 *translate,* 526.8 *showplace,* 526.10
manifestation, 543.9 *use signs,*
543.11 *gesture,* 544.3 *means of
identification,* 544.11 *identify
oneself,* 563.14 *have difficulty
speaking,* 624.3 *symptom,* 636.1
warning, 667.7 *contract,* 692.1
command, 708.3 *permit,* 715.5
contract, 786.4 *wonder*
Sign 543
sign a confession 16.80 *convict
oneself*
sign a deal 667.7 *contract*
sign a decree 692.9 *command*
signal 192, 543, 543, 5.5 *nonstandard language,* 64.14 *terminal,* 72.2 *track,* 327.10 *railway,*
437.6 *visible thing,* 437.10
make visible, 526.10 *manifestation,* 526.14 *manifest,* 528.7 *advice,* 528.14 *tip,* 534.27 *signalling,* 534.30 *communicate,*
543.1 *sign,* 543.9 *use signs,*
611.6 *notable,* 636.1 *warning,*
692.1, 692.9 *command*
signal battalion 17.4 *military organization*
signal box 72.2 *track,* 327.10
railway
signal-caller 19.7 *offence*
signal fire 439.8 *fire*
signalize 543.10 *signify,* 812.16
commemorate
signalizing 543.14 *signifying*
signal lamp 543.4, 543.4 *signal*
signalled 327.15 *accessible,*
534.34 *communicated*
signaller 543.8 *signer,* 636.4
warner
signalling 534, 543, 534.1 *communications,* 543.4 *signal,*
543.14 *signifying*
signalman 72.9 *railway worker*
sign a loan agreement 733.7 *borrow*
signal rocket 543.4 *signal*
signals 19.8 *huddle*
signal-to-noise ratio 64.14 *terminal*
sign an affidavit 535.18 *vow*
sign a pact 667.7, 715.5 *contract*
sign a petition 712.6 *request*
sign a promissory note 714.8
guarantee
signatory 480.7 *verifier,* 499.3 *assenter,* 543.8 *signer,* 544.12
identified, 714.5 *promise-maker,*
715.4 *contractor*
sign a round robin 712.6 *request*
sign a treaty 667.7, 715.5 *contract*
sign a truce 677.5 *make peace*
signature 49.17 *notation,* 49.20
key, 119.2 *original,* 480.6 *evidence,* 543.1 *sign,* 544.3 *means
of identification,* 545.4 *inscription,* 560.8 *name,* 708.2 *permit,*
715.1 *contract,* 718.2 *promise*
signature tune 433.1 *melody*
sign away 728.3 *transfer property*
signboard 437.6 *visible thing,*
544.3 *means of identification*
signed 52.71 *numerical,* 116.17
consenting, 437.2 *clear,* 499.7
agreed, 543.12 *identified,*
667.11, 667.11 *contractual,*
714.13 *guaranteeing,* 715.7 *contractual*
signed agreement 597.3 *contract*
signed number 52.5 *number*
signed sealed and delivered
715.7 *contractual*
signed up 679.35 *martial*
signer 543, 714.5 *promise-*

maker, 715.4 *contractor*
signet 544.3 *means of identification,* 715.1 *contract*
signet ring 544.5 *uniform*
significantly 543.18 *indicatively*
significance 227, 520, 52.61 *correlation,* 232.1 *instrumentality,*
233 *influence,* 471.4 *purpose,*
554.2 *seriousness,* 611.1, 772.6
importance
significance level 52.54 *hypothesis testing*
significance test 52.54 *hypothesis
testing*
significant 520, 226.13 *causal,*
230.12 *operative,* 232.7 *causal,*
233.11 *influential,* 471.12 *purposive,* 483.8 *evidential,* 517.15
presageful, 554.5 *serious,* 611.5,
772.3 *important*
significant digits 52.8 *number
system*
significant figures 52.8 *number
system*
significant form 50.4 *treatment,*
306.1 *form*
significantly 226.14 *causally,*
230.13 *operationally,* 232.9 *instrumentally,* 233.14 *influentially,* 471.21 *purposively,*
483.14 *as evidence,* 517.16 *predictively,* 520.13 *meaningfully,*
611.9 *importantly*
signification 520.1 *meaning,*
543.1 *sign*
significative 520.6 *meaningful,*
543.14 *signifying*
signify 543, 165.24 *specify,*
471.19 *epitomize,* 473.15 *state,*
517.11 *predict,* 520.10 *mean,*
611.7 *be important*
signifying 543, 517.13 *predicting*
signify little 612.11 *be unimportant*
sign in 344.5 *get in*
signing 421.1 *deafness,* 543.3
gesture, 543.15 *gestural*
signing on 641.3 *inactive,* 643.2
not working
sign language 5.8 *artificial language,* 421.1 *deafness,* 543.3
gesture, 563.6 *voiceless speech,*
564.4 *articulation*
sign-language reader 524.6 *interpreter*
sign-language reading 524.4
translation
sign-maker 543.8 *signer*
sign of alarm 636.2 *danger signal*
sign of anger 828
sign of courtesy 817
sign of dislike 785
sign of disrespect 850
sign off 345.2 *withdraw*
sign of illness 543.1 *sign,* 624.3
symptom
sign of irascibility 829
sign of irritableness 830
sign of politeness 817.5 *sign of
courtesy*
sign of sullenness 830
sign of the Cross 10.5 *Christian
rite*
sign of the times 234.1 *tendency,*
543.1 *sign*
sign of wonderment 786
sign on 346.14 *enrol,* 354.7 *install,* 665.13 *be a member,*
665.14 *be a party member,*
743.12 *be poor*
sign one's death warrant 16.79
convict
sign one's name 543.9 *use signs*
sign one's score card 29.7 *golf*
sign on the dotted line 499.5 *assent to,* 543.9 *use signs,* 714.7
promise, 737.3 *bargain*
signor 401.3 *male title of address*
signora 402.3 *female title of address*
signorina 402.3 *female title of address*
sign out 345.2 *withdraw*
sign over 728.3 *transfer property*
sign painter 50.16 *artist*
sign painting 50.2 *painting*
signpost 332.3 *orientation,*

332.6 *direct,* 437.6 *visible thing,*
437.7 *that which makes visible,*
437.10 *make visible,* 543.1 *sign,*
543.5 *indicator,* 543.9 *use signs*
signposted 327.15 *accessible,*
332.14 *directed,* 437.2 *clear*
signs 490.13 *confirmation,*
543.1 *sign*
signs of guilt 866
signs of the times 517.5 *omen,*
636.1 *warning*
sign the death warrant 398.19 *execute*
sign the pledge 873.4 *give up alcohol*
sign up 171.9 *enlist,* 354.7 *install,* 597.1 *undertake,* 665.13
be a member
sika 77 Placental Mammals
sike 96.1 *river*
Sikh 7.6 *non-Christian*
Sikorsky 52 Scientists
silage 68.9 *animal feedstuff,*
350.8 *animal food,* 605.4 *storage*
silage clamp 68.10 *farm tool*
silaging 68.5 *cultivation*
silane 57 Types of Compounds
sild 45.18 *sea fish*
silence 422, 422, 531, 566,
236.8 *overpower,* 244.8 *destroy,*
325.2 *repose,* 421.10 *muffle,*
424.6, 428.7 *mute,* 476.8 *refute,* 529.1 *secrecy,* 546.1 *obliterate,* 563.5 *mutism,* 563.15
strike dumb, 643.5 *inactivity,*
699.12 *gag,* 786.2 *sign of wonderment*
Silence 422
silenced 428.2 *nonresonant,*
563.11 *speechless,* 786.7 *wideeyed*
silencer 71 Motor Vehicle
Parts, **428,** 421.3 *inaudibility,*
424.2 *sound reducer*
silencing 244.1 *destruction*
silent 422, 531, 566, 325.6 *quiescent,* 386.8 *lubricated,* 529.10
secretive, 563.9 *voiceless,*
563.11 *speechless,* 786.7 *wideeyed,* 816.8 *unsociable,* 816.9
shy
silent about 147.10 *excluding*
silent as the grave 422.3 *silent*
silent as the tomb 422.3 *silent*
silent discharge 64.6 *electric discharge*
silently 422, 563.17 *voicelessly,*
566.10 *taciturnly,* 816.14 *unsocially*
silent reproach 852.10 *disapproving look*
silent service 679.22 *navy*
Silenus 874.17 *drunkard*
Siletz 1 Peoples
silhouette 50.9 *drawing,* 50.20
draw, 46.4 *portrait,* 299.2
shadow, 306.1, 306.7 *form,*
440.4 *dark thing,* 440.14 *make
dark,* 447.9 *black thing,* 457.3
external appearance, 457.14
present, 547.6 *image,* 767.6 *profile*
silica 57 Common Chemical
Compounds, 44.2 *raw material,* 373.7 *hard substance*
silicate 57 Types of Compounds, 54.34 *mineral*
silicic 57.34 *elemental*
silicide 57 Types of Compounds
silicon 57 Chemical Elements,
58.15 *essential element,* 64.4
semiconductor
silicon bronze 57 Alloys
silicon chip 64.13 *circuit,* 260.2
little thing
silicone 57 Types of Compounds, 386.4, 395.5 *lubricant*
silicone rubber 377.4 *rubber*
silicone steel 57 Alloys
Silicon Valley 249.8 *regions of
the US*
silicosis 624.9 *respiratory disease*
silicula 86.2 *botanical fruit*
siliqua 86.2 *botanical fruit*
silk 67 Natural Fabrics, 67.12
natural, 82.6 *spinner,* 288.4 *textile,* 374.11 *soft thing,* 376.8

smooth thing, 383.2 grain, 604.1 materials
silk-cotton tree 85 Trees and Shrubs
silken 67.12 natural, 374.3, 376.1 smooth, 405.6 pleasant
silken repose 325.2 repose
silk gland 82.6 spinner
silk hat 295.15 headgear
Silkie 68 Breeds of Fowl
silkily 374.17 softly, 383.15 texturally
silkiness 374.9, 376.7 smoothness, 383.2 grain
silks 32.7 horseracing, 295.5 fancy dress
silk-screen printing 50.1 art
silk stockings 295.20 legwear
silkworm 81.6 worm, 82.5 larva, 82.6 spinner
silkworm moth 82 Insects
silky 67.12 natural, 374.3, 376.1 smooth, 383.9 smooth
silky oak 85 Trees and Shrubs
silky terrier 77 Breeds of Dogs
sill 54.30 igneous rock, 280.2 foot
siller 741.1 money
sillimanite 54 Minerals
silliness 506.3 tomfoolery, 508.1 folly
Sillitoe 48 Writers
silly 27.14 positioned, 278.2 superficial, 460.6 unintelligent, 506.5 nonsensical, 508.5 foolish, 656.1 unskilful
silly idiot 460.3 unintelligent person
silly mid on 27.4 team
silly point 27.4 team
silly question 477.5 easy question
silly season 203.1 season, 506.3 tomfoolery
silly talk 521.4 senseless talk
silo 68.7 farm building, 258.11 vessel, 605.4 storage, 637.2 preserver, 680.5 missile weapon
siloxane 57 Types of Compounds
silt 54.27 sediment, 54.36 soil, 132.2 residue, 326.10 transferred thing, 393.13 mud
siltstone 54 Common Rocks
silt up 278.7 make shallow
silty 54.58 earthy, 393.17 muddy
Silurian 54 Geological Time Intervals
Silurian period 200.3 geological period
silver 57 Chemical Elements, 21.6 track, 293.24 coat, 444.15 colour, 446.1 white, 446.9 white thing, 446.13 whiten, 448.1 grey, 448.5 grey thing, 448.8 grey, 741.1 money, 741.4 change, 741.16 bullion
Silver 32.1 horse
silver beet 85 Vegetables
silver birch 85 Trees and Shrubs
silver bullet 11.6 talisman
silver coating 56.29 optical element
silver coinage 741.13 coinage
silver cup 544.4 insignia, 588.6 objective, 681.1 trophy
silver dollar 741.8 American money
silvered 446.1 white, 448.1 grey
silver fir 85 Trees and Shrubs
silverfish 82 Insects
silver fox 77 Placental Mammals
silver frost 55.29 hail
Silver Goblets 36.5 Henley trophies
silver-grey 448.1 grey
silver halide 66.11 emulsion
silveriness 446.7 whiteness
silver inlay 47.9 decorative woodwork
silver jubilee 179.8 twenty and over, 214.6 annually celebrated day, 812.5 anniversary
silver leaf 69.12 pests and diseases
silver lining 775.1 hope
silver maple 85 Trees and Shrubs

silver medal 21.5 competition, 30.1 gymnastics, 544.4 insignia, 681.1 trophy
silver-medal 611.6 notable
silver-medallist 21.3 athlete, 237.5 athlete, 655.4 skilled person
silver plate 293.3 coating, 544.4 insignia, 588.6 objective
silver-plate 293.24 coat
silverpoint drawing 50.9 drawing
silver polish 376.10 polish
silver print 66.12 development
silver salmon 20.4 American game fish
silverside 80 Fishes, 45.22 beef
silversmith 646.2 artisan
silver solder 57 Alloys
silver tabby 77 Breeds of Cats
silver-toned 433.6 melodious
silver-tongued 564.20 eloquent
silver-tongued orator 567.6 public speaker
silver vault 605.4 storage
silver wedding 812.5 anniversary
silver wedding anniversary 214.6 annually celebrated day
silvery 433.6 melodious, 446.1 white, 448.1 grey
silvical 85.17 arboricultural
silvicultural 69.16 horticultural, 85.17 arboricultural
silviculturally 85.20 arboriculturally
silviculture 69.1 horticulture, 83.10 plant science, 85.5 forestry
silviculturist 85.8 forester
sima 54.18 earth's crust
simarouba 85 Trees and Shrubs
Simenon 48 Writers
simian 77.34 primate
similar 114, 107.5 interrelated, 109.6 correlative, 110.13 equivalent, 116.14 conforming, 122.6 equal, 520.6 meaningful, 547.13 representational, 667.12 compatible
similarity 114, 107.1 relatedness, 107.2 interrelatedness, 109.3 correlation, 110.2 equivalence, 112.1 uniformity, 116.1 accord, 116.5, 167.1 conformity, 457.5 impression, 547.1 representation, 667.3 compatibility
Similarity 114
similar look 114.1 similarity
similarly 114, 106.15 under the circumstances, 107.10 relevantly, 109.11 correlatively, 116.34 uniformly, 122.12 equally, 667.16 compatibly
similar relation 107.2 interrelatedness
similar triangles 52.43 triangle
similation 114.1 similarity
simile 48.12 poetic language, 110.2 equivalence, 114.1 similarity, 557.1 ornament, 560.3 narration
similitude 52.48 transformation, 114.1 similarity
simious 77.34 primate
Simla 93 Cities
Simmental 68 Breeds of Cattle
simmer 45.55 cook, 366.21 be agitated, 390.24 bubble, 408.14 be hot, 828.11 be angry
simmer down 374.14 ease
simmering 45.8 cooking technique, 408.9 hot
Simon 48 Dramatists
Simon Legree 618.12 bad person
Simonov 48 Writers, 48 Dramatists
Simon says 42 Children's Games and Party Games
simony 739.3 selling
simoom 55 Winds
simpatico 819.8 friendly
simple 134, 522, 542, 556, 52.70 universal, 83.18 of leaves, 312.2 straightforward, 444.13 soft-hued, 460.5 lacking intellect, 460.7 intellectually subnormal, 502.6 ignorant, 508.5 foolish, 537.18 truthful, 550.3 clear, 558.3 elegant, 595.4 un-

trained, 630.2 medicine, 658.1 naive, 660.9 easy, 690.10 unadorned, 814.9 familiar, 865.7 naive
simple arithmetic 52
simple as ABC 660.9 easy
simple eloquence 522.10 simplicity
simple fraction 52.18 division, 169.5 ratio, 173.1 fraction
simple fruit 86.2 botanical fruit
simple glyceride 58.7 fat
simple harmonic motion 56.8 time, 214.1 regularity
simple-hearted 556.3 natural
simple interest 128.3 increasing thing, 721.5 profit, 745.4 interest
simple language 522.10 simplicity
simple life 869.1 self-restraint
simple lipid 58.6 lipid
simple machine 63
simple melody 433.1 melody
simple microscope 56.85 microscope
simple-minded 460.5 lacking intellect, 460.7 intellectually subnormal, 658.1 naive
simple-mindedly 460.11 unintelligently
simple-mindedness 460.1 lack of intellect, 658.2 naivety
simpleness 134.8 simplicity, 537.5 truthfulness, 542.4, 556.4 simplicity, 660.2 simplicity
simple picture 299.1 outline
simple reflex 61.20 conditioning
Simple Simon 460.3 unintelligent person
simple soul 658.3 naive person
simple sugar 58.3 carbohydrate
simpleton 460.3 unintelligent person, 502.5 ignorant person, 508.3 foolish person, 658.3 naive person
simple truth 526.11 openness
simple twist of the wrist 660.6 easy thing
simplex 52.41 geometric figure
simplicity 134, 522, 542, 556, 660, 134.1 purity, 312.8 directness, 550.1 clarity, 558.1 elegance, 658.2 naivety, 690.3 unadornment, 806.7 humility, 814.3 familiarity, 865.3 naivety
Simplicity 56
Simplicius of Cilicia 4 Philosophers
simplification 52.24 evaluation, 141.2 deconstruction, 152.4 rearrangement, 522.10 simplicity, 524.1 interpretation, 524.4 translation, 660.7 easing
simplified 134.16 simple, 152.23 rearranged, 522.2 simple, 524.15 interpreted, 660.11 made easy
simplifier 524.6 interpreter
simplify 134, 522, 52.92 manipulate, 141.4 deconstruct, 152.14 rearrange, 524.8 interpret, 524.12 translate, 556.7 be simple, 660.16 make easy
simplifying 660.7 easing
simplistic 134.17 direct
simplistically 134.20 homogenously, 660.21 easily
simply 542, 556, 174.24 once, 522.13 intelligibly, 537.36 truthfully, 550.4 clearly, 558.5 elegantly, 660.21 easily, 690.12 plainly, 814.14 naturally, 865.12 naively
Simpson 98 Deserts
Simpson's rule 52 Named Concepts
SIMULA 65 Programming Languages
simulacrum 102.2 illusion, 540.12 facade
simulate 102.17 fabricate, 114.12 imitate, 479.12 rehearse, 540.24 mask
simulated 114, 102.12 not the real thing, 479.8 experimental, 519.12 imaginary, 539.39 imita-

tive, 540.35 disguised
simulated wood 539.6 imitation, 540.14 false thing
simulation 52.65 theory, 102.7 artificiality, 118.1 imitation, 118.2 copy, 118.4 camouflage, 540.12 facade
simulcast 534.25 broadcast material
simultaneity 180.2 synchronism, 198.1 same time
simultaneous 198, 180.18 concurrent
simultaneous equations 52.27 equation
simultaneously 198, 180.23 concurrently
simurg 78.9 fabulous bird
sin 777 Phobias by Topic, **844, 864, 866, 866,** 16.38 lawbreaking, 504.8 moral error, 504.20 transgress, 618.9 badness, 683.3 personal fault, 693.1 disobedience, 693.15 be disobedient, 844.8 wrong-doing, 862.1 evil, 864.1 wickedness, 864.16 be wicked, 877.16 do wrong
Sina 8 Deities
Sinai 392.14 desert
sin'al fine 49 Musical Terms
Sinbad the Sailor 74.7 nautical person
sin-bin 31.3 ice hockey
since Adam was a lad 202.19 anciently
since before the Flood 202.19 anciently
since days of yore 202.19 anciently
since God knows when 202.19 anciently
since long ago 202.19 anciently
sincere 119.6 authentic, 134.17 direct, 277.9 deep-seated, 322.16 open, 537.18 truthful, 658.1 naive, 772.2 earnest, 857.4 honourable
sincerely 119.8 originally, 134.20 homogenously, 322.26 openly, 537.36 truthfully, 658.5 naively, 772.11 earnestly, 857.7 honourably
sincere thanks 837.2 thanks
sincerity 322.9 openness, 537.5 truthfulness, 658.2 naivety, 772.5 earnestness, 857.1 probity
since the big bang 202.19 anciently
since the world was new 202.19 anciently
since the world was young 202.19 anciently
since the year one 202.19 anciently
Sinclair 48 Writers
Sindhi 5 Languages and Groups of Languages
sine 52.52 trigonometric function
sinecure 641.1 inaction, 645.1 leisure, 660.6 easy thing
sinecurist 643.8 nonworker
sine curve 52.40 curve
sine rule 52.51 trigonometry
sine wave 56.16 waveform, 311.3 curved things, 365.5 wave
sinews 237.1 strength, 378.8 physical strength
sinewy 237.9 physically strong, 378.4 powerful
sinfonia 49.4 opera
sinfonietta 49.26 musical group
sinful 866, 504.16 errant, 618.3 bad, 844.16 in the wrong, 862.7 evil, 864.11 wicked
sinfully 844.28 immorally, 862.12 evilly, 864.18 wickedly
sinfulness 618.9 badness, 693.1 disobedience, 844.5 unrighteousness, 864.1 wickedness, 866.3 sin
sing 49, 78, 432, 433, 480.3 testify, 483.13 turn Queen's evidence, 528.13 inform on , 530.7 betray, 557.5 ornament, 762.7 show joy, 856.5 accuse
singable 49.30 harmonic, 433.6

melodious

sing a different tune 216.7 *be changed*

Singapore 91 Countries, **93** Cities, **98** Islands

Singapore sling 351.8 *mixed drink*

sing a requiem 399.8 *bury*

singe 408.15 *burn*, 447.11 *blacken*, 449.7 *brown*

singed 408.13 *heated*, 447.3 *blackened*, 449.2 *browned*

singer 49, 49.24 *musician*, 433.5 *melodist*, 646.1 *worker*

Singer 48 Writers, **52** Scientists

sing for one's supper 743.12 *be poor*

sing Happy Birthday 812.17 *congratulate*

sing hymns 9.7 *worship*, 10.19 *offer worship*

sing in a round 426.13 *trill*

singing 432, 78.23 *avian*, 557.4 *ornate*

sing in unison 112.9 *be uniform*

single 174, 22.5 *batting terms*, 22.7 *play baseball*, 29.1 *golf*, 36.11 *rowing*, 42.6 *darts*, 134.16 *simple*, 142.6 *whole*, 165.15 *special*, 174.1 *one*, 174.7 *single person*, 174.11 *one*, 490.7 *particular*, 545.7 *recording*, 658.1 *naive*, 816.10 *lonely*, 825.5 *single person*, 825.6 *celibate*

single-action 20.8 *angling*

single-action reel 20.3 *fishing tackle*

single aspect 299.1 *outline*

single-barrelled gun 680.9 *firearm*

single bed 47.6 *bed*

single-bladed 36.12 *canoeing*

single-bladed paddle 36.6 *canoeing*

single-blade race 36.6 *canoeing*

single-blind trial 479.2 *rehearsal*

single-breasted 295.31 *styled*

single-celled 59.23 *cellular*

single-celled invertebrate 81.1 *invertebrate*

single combat 674.9 *duel*

single coverage 19.10 *defence*

single cream 174.10 *single thing*, 395.8 *fat*

single crystal 57.4 *crystal*

single decker 71.19 *bus*, 174.10 *single thing*

single entry 750.1 *accounts*

single European market 740.4 *free market*

single file 174.10 *single thing*, 269.5 *piece*

single-foot 328.10 *slow motion*

single girl 402, 825.5 *single person*

single-handed 20.8 *angling*, 36.10 *sailing*, 174.15 *solo*

single-handed dinghy 36.2 *sailing boat*

single-handedly 174.21 *alone*

single-handed racing 36.1 *sailing*

single-handed rod 20.3 *fishing tackle*

Single-handed Transatlantic Race 36.1 *sailing*

single-hearted 658.1 *naive*

single instance 174.2 *item*

single kayak race 36.6 *canoeing*

single lane 71.3 *carriageway*

single-leg 30.11 *gymnastic*

single-leg circle 30.6 *pommel horse*

single-lens reflex 66.16 *camera*

single-loop goniometer 74.5 *navigation*

single man 401, 825.5 *single person*

single market 740.4 *free market*

single-masted boat 36.2 *sailing boat*

single meaning 520.3 *comprehension*

single-minded 134.17 *direct*, 378.5 *mentally tough*, 467.8 *diligent*, S70.7 *iron-willed*, 574.1

---

resolute

single-mindedly 378, 134.20 *homogenously*, 574.17 *resolutely*

single-mindedness 378.9 *mental toughness*, 467.4 *diligence*, 570.2 *willpower*, 574.13 *concentration*, 575.2 *commitment*, 577.6 *determination*

singleness 174, 174.3 *oneness*, 816.1 *unsociability*, 825.1 *celibacy*

singleness of purpose 575.2 *commitment*

single-oar 36.11 *rowing*

single-oar rowing 36.4 *rowing*

single out 174, 136.10 *set apart*, 165.22 *characterize*, 580.4 *pick*

single overarm 39.2 *swimming technique*

single paddle 36.17 *canoe*

single-paddle 36.12 *canoeing*

single-paddle canoeing 36.6 *canoeing*

single parent 174.7 *single person*

single person 174, 825

single-phase supply 64.34 *power supply*

single-point tool 63.9 *machine tool*

single quotes 543.7 *punctuation*

single rhyme 48.11 *rhyme*

single-rhythm crawl 39.2 *swimming technique*

singles 25.9 *bowls*, 40.4 *tennis terms*, 40.14 *forehand*

singles court 40.3 *tennis equipment*

single sculling 36.4 *rowing*

single sculls 36.4 *rowing*

single-sex school 6.12 *educational institution*

single-shot 37.8 *shooting*

single-shot rifle 37.3 *hunting equipment*

single sideband transmission 534.14 *radio transmission*

single-sided 41.12 *ski*

single-sided skating 41.3 *ski racing*

singles match 25.1 *green bowling*

single space 265.1 *interval*

singles player 40.6 *tennis player*

single span 63.21 *bridge*

single state 825.1 *celibacy*

singlestick 28.1 *fencing*, 674.9 *duel*

single storey 43.12 *structural*

single-storey 256.16 *manorial*, 276.5 *low*

single-storey building 43.3 *building*

single-support phase 21.2 *field events*

singlet 295.18 *underwear*

single tenoner 47.11 *woodworking tool*

single thing 174

single ticket 174.10 *single thing*

singleton 174.1 *one*, 174.10 *single thing*

single track 71.2 *road*, 174.10 *single thing*, 272.8 *narrow thing*

single-track 272.4 *narrow-leaved*

single-use 189.7 *impermanent*

single voice 499.1 *assent*

single woman 402.5 *single girl*

sing like a bird 432.5 *sing*

sing like a canary 530.7 *betray*

sing low 424.5 *sound faint*

singly 136.20 *separately*, 165.32 *severally*, 174.22 *one by one*, 825.12 *celibately*

sing out 431, 564.13 *speak in a particular way*

sing praises 9.7 *worship*

Sing Sing 702.1 *prison*

sing small 806.20 *submit*

sing softly 424.5 *sound faint*

singsong 112.4 *monotony*, 112.8, 183.13 *monotonous*, 434.9 *unmelodious*

singspiel 49.4 *opera*

sing the praises of 431.12 *cheer*, 773.6 *fête*, 812.17 *congratulate*, 849.17 *praise*, 851.15 *compli-*

---

ment

sing the same old song 183.18 *harp*

sing together 49.39 *sing*, 198.7 *synchronize*

singular 174, 5.44 *grammatical*, 103.8 *quintessential*, 108.6 *unrelated*, 115.4 *dissimilar*, 117.9 *nonconforming*, 126.15 *excellent*, 165.15 *special*, 168.14 *eccentric*, 490.7 *particular*

singularity 174, 53.11 *stellar birth*, 108.1 *unrelatedness*, 117.3 *nonconformity*, 165.3 *characteristic*, 168.4 *unusualness*, 490.18 *particularity*

singularly 5.52 *grammatically*, 108.12 *irrelevantly*, 115.7, 117.15 *dissimilarly*, 126.17 *supremely*, 165.30 *characteristically*, 168.21 *unconformably*

Sinhalese 1 Peoples, **5** Languages and Groups of Languages

sinister 440.11 *benighted*, 517.15 *presageful*, 544.13 *heraldic*, 618.5 *harmful*, 687.6 *adverse*, 862.7 *evil*

sinisterly 687.12 *in adversity*, 862.12 *evilly*

sinister side 305.1 *side*

sinistral 407.10 *handed*

sinistrality 407.7 *sense organ*

Sinitic 5 Languages and Groups of Languages

sink 727, 127.11 *become inferior*, 129.4 *decrease*, 207.17 *age*, 244.11 *ruin*, 244.13 *be destroyed*, 258.12 *bath*, 277.14 *deepen*, 317.6 *be concave*, 324.13 *be in motion*, 360.9 *descend*, 362.3 *bring down*, 369.12 *be heavy*, 624.24 *be unhealthy*, 628.1 *deteriorate*, 650.5 *be fatigued*, 683.6 *fail*, 687.9 *be in trouble*, 687.11 *cause adversity*, 747.9 *be unable to pay*, 877.16 *do wrong*

sinkable 360.16 *descending*

sinkage 360, 277.1 *depth*, 369.6 *displacement*

sink a mineshaft 322.20 *hole*

sink a shaft 317.7 *make concave*

sink below the horizon 458.1 *disappear*

sink down 360.9 *descend*

sinker 20.3 *fishing tackle*, 36.7, 36.13 *windsurfing*, 45.36 *cake*, 338.5 *throw*, 369.11 *weight*

sinkhole 362.14 *depression*

sink in 522.4 *be intelligible*

sinking 20.8 *angling*, 129.2 *decline*, 129.6 *decreasing*, 207.12 *ageing*, 244.4 *ruin*, 277.1 *depth*, 317.1 *concavity*, 324.6 *descending motion*, 324.17 *directional*, 360.16 *descending*, 362.11 *lowering*, 362.13 *submergence*, 397.18 *dying*

sinking fast 244.15 *destroyed*, 397.18 *dying*

sinking fund 14.1, 741.7 *finance*

sinking plug 20.2 *artificial fly*

sinking stomach 777.2 *fearfulness*

sink into 220.7 *convert into*, 346.13 *fall into*

sink into oblivion 512.12 *be forgotten*

sink into obscurity 127.10 *follow*

sink into silence 424.5 *sound faint*

sink into the earth 360.15 *tunnel*

sink low 127.11 *become inferior*

sink money 748.1 *expend*

sink one's capital in 14.5 *invest*, 737.2 *speculate*

sink one's money in 738.1 *purchase*

sink one's teeth into 350.22 *eat well*

sink or swim 575.8 *hold out*

sink-or-swim 589.8 *chance*

sink or swim together 664.13 *work together*

sink through the floor 806.24 *be humiliated*

sink to the bottom 277.14

---

deepen, 360.10 *droop*

sink without trace 100.13 *cease to exist*, 127.11 *become inferior*, 244.13 *be destroyed*, 438.7 *become invisible*, 458.1 *disappear*, 512.12 *be forgotten*, 546.1 *obliterate*

sinless 134.12 *morally pure*, 619.1 *perfect*, 863.5 *virtuous*, 865.5 *innocent*, 876.9 *pure*

sinlessly 863.9 *virtuously*

sinlessness 134.1 *purity*, 863.1 *virtue*, 865.1 *innocence*, 876.3 *moral purity*

sinner 722.6 *loser*, 832.8 *malefactor*, 844.10 *wrongdoer*, 864.9 *wicked person*

Sinn Fein 12.6 *political party*

sinning 16.60 *offending*, 693.13 *disobedient*, 864.11 *wicked*, 866.3 *sin*

sino 49 Musical Terms

sin of omission 866.3 *sin*

Sino-Japanese War 17 Major Wars

Sinophobia 777 Phobias by Name

Sino-Tibetan 5 Languages and Groups of Languages, 5.11 *family of languages*

sinter 57.30 *extract*, 326.10 *transferred thing*

sintered-glass crucible 57 Laboratory Apparatus

sinuous 79.12 *snakelike*, 311.5 *well-rounded*, 314.4 *convolutional*, 365.17 *waving*

sinuousity 311.1 *curvature*

sinuously 311.7 *curvedly*, 314.8 *circularly*

sinuousness 314.1 *convolution*

Sinurc 8 Deities

Sinus Aestuum 53 Seas

Sinus Amoris 53 Seas

Sinus Iridum 53 Seas

sinusitis 624.9 *respiratory disease*

Sinus Medii 53 Seas

sinusoid 52.40 *curve*

sinusoidal 52.85 *cyclic*, 311.4 *curved*, 365.17 *waving*

sinusoidally 311.7 *curvedly*

sinusoidal wave 56.16 *waveform*

Sinus Roris 53 Seas

Siouan 5 Languages and Groups of Languages

Sioux 1 Peoples, **5** Languages and Groups of Languages, **7** Non-Christian Religions

sip 351.2, 351.13 *drink*

siphon 326.11 *transfer*, 355.9 *extractor*, 355.14 *suck*

siphonaceous 90.7 *algal*

Siphonaptera 82 Orders of Insects

siphonapteran 82.10 *insectan*

siphoning 355.4 *sucking*

siphon off 349.11 *void*, 355.14 *suck*

siphon the python 353.17 *urinate*

sipper 351.12 *drinker*

sipping 351.1 *drinking*

sipunculid 81 Worms, 81.6 *worm*

Sipunculida 81.6 *worm*

Sipunculida 81.6 *worm*

sir 696.1 *master*

Sir 401.3 *male title of address*

sire 32.1 *horse*, 32.13 *breeding*, 156.26 *produce*, 226.7 *Prime Mover*, 245.5 *propagator*, 245.13 *propagate*

sired 396.15 *born*

siren 79 Amphibians, 11.4 *witch*, 76.7 *legendary beast*, 97.4 *sea god*, 192.10 *signal*, 228.7 *motivator*, 340.5 *lure*, 340.6 *charmer*, 423.1 *loudness*, 423.4 *sound maker*, 543.4 *signal*, 586.13 *tempter*, 636.2 *danger signal*, 832.9 *vixen*

Sirenia 77.11 *marine mammal*

sirenian 77.11 *marine mammal*, 77.29 *cetacean*

siren song 340.5 *lure*, 586.3 *incentive*

Sir Galahad 876.5 *pure person*

Sirius 53 Named Stars

Sir John Mandeville 538.11,

539.16 *liar*
sirloin 45.22, 45.23 *beef*
sirocco 55 Winds, 241.5 *violent weather*, 408.8 *hot place*
Sir Roger de Coverley 46.4 *historic dancing*
Sirsalis 53 Rills and Valleys
sis 402.12 *woman in the family*
siskin 78 Birds
sissy 238.4 *weakling*, 238.12 *weak-willed*, 401.9 *offensive terms for homosexual*, 779.2 *coward*, 779.3 *cowardly*
sister 7.7 *monk*, 60.16 *nurse*, 116.5 *conformity*, 122.5 *equal*, 146.3 *person included*, 198.5 *contemporary*, 402.3 *female title of address*, 402.11 *liberated woman*, 402.12 *woman in the family*, 653.15 *manager*, 665.5 *member*, 819.6 *close friend*
sister city 93.1 *city*
sisterhood 135.2 *agreement*, 161.15 *association*, 664.9 *team*, 665.1 *party*, 819.1 *friendship*
sisterly 665.8 *leagued*, 819.8 *friendly*, 831.6 *benevolent*
sisterly interest 819.1 *friendship*
Sister Moon 53.17 *moon*
sistrum 49 Musical Instruments
Sisyphean 614.2 *futile*
Sisyphean labour 685.2 *never-ending task*
Sisyphean task 487.7 *obstacle*
sit 362, 30.10 *compete in gymnastics*, 105.6 *be in a state of*, 251.9 *be situated*, 325.8 *be motionless*
Sita 8 Deities
Sitala 8 Deities
sit and watch the world go by 783.16 *be mediocre*
sit an examination 477.19 *be questioned*
sitar 49 Musical Instruments
sitatunga 77 Placental Mammals
sit back 573.8 *hold back*, 641.4 *not act*, 649.2 *take it easy*
sit cheek by jowl 138.6 *adhere*
sitcom 51.10 *comedy*, 534.25 *broadcast material*, 771.4 *entertainment*
sit down 15.12 *have an industrial dispute*, 325.8 *be motionless*, 360.10 *droop*, 362.8 *sit*, 649.2 *take it easy*
sit-down 15.10 *unionized*, 711.8 *refused*
sit-down meal 350.12 *meal*
sit-down strike 15.4 *industrial dispute*, 711.1 *refusal*, 713.3 *gesture of protest*
sit down together 568.11 *confer*
site 250.1 *location*, 250.9 *locate*, 251.1 *situation*, 251.10 *situate*
sited 250.6 *located*, 251.6 *situated*
sit-harness 34.4 *climbing equipment*
sit in 15.12 *have an industrial dispute*, 475.19 *protest*, 713.8 *cause mischief*
sit-in 15.4 *industrial dispute*, 15.10 *unionized*, 161.4 *rally*, 475.6 *mass demonstration*, 668.3 *act of defiance*, 711.8 *refused*, 713.3 *gesture of protest*
sit in committee 568.11 *confer*
sit in conclave 654.6 *consult*
sit in council 568.11 *confer*, 654.6 *consult*
siting 250.4 *placing*
sit in judgment 16.69 *have jurisdiction over*, 16.71 *try a case*, 16.76, 492.11 *judge*
sit in on 253.12 *attend*
sit it out 219.4 *protract*
sitka spruce 85 Trees and Shrubs
sit on 244.8 *destroy*, 699.8 *restrain*, 701.6 *subject*, 806.17 *humiliate*
sit on a goldmine 742.12 *be rich*
sit on a powder keg 633.8 *be in danger*
sit on one's hands 641.4 *not act*

sit on one's tail 590.9 *follow*
sit on someone's tail 155.23 *follow close*
sit on the bench 16.69 *have jurisdiction over*, 16.76 *judge*
sit on the board 696.14 *master*
sit on the fence 124.9 *be average*, 158.18 *stand in the middle*, 333.7 *be halfway*, 482.12 *be fair*, 491.19 *hesitate*, 576.7 *be irresolute*, 578.1 *be equivocal*, 641.4 *not act*, 717.4 *compromise*, 783.15 *be impartial*
sit on the shelf 825.9 *be celibate*
sit on the tail of 264.10 *stay near*
sit on the throne 12.11 *govern*, 166.16 *direct*, 688.18 *have authority*
sitophobia 777 Phobias by Name
sit round a table 654.6 *consult*
sit-sling 34.4 *climbing equipment*
sit spin 41.6 *ice-skating*
Sittar 7 Non-Christian Religions
sitter 36.9 *sailor*, 50.11 *artist's materials*, 304.2 *rear end*, 632.3 *protector*
sit tight 325.8 *be motionless*, 573.8 *hold back*, 577.9 *be obstinate*, 641.4 *not act*
sitting 161, 11.10 *psychic phenomenon*, 30.6 *pommel horse*, 37.2 *hunting*, 362.23 *sedentary*, 653.7 *council*
sitting duck 539.22 *dupe*, 633.7 *vulnerability*, 660.6 *easy thing*
sitting on the fence 124.2 *medium*, 333.4 *middle*, 858.2 *faithlessness*
sitting pretty 682.13 *successful*
sitting room 256.7 *room*, 730.4 *reception*
sitting target 633.7 *vulnerability*
sitting tenant 255.3 *householder*, 723.5 *possessor*, 725.7 *property man*
situate 251, 250.9 *locate*
situated 251, 105.8 *in a state of*, 106.7 *circumstantial*, 250.6 *located*, 250.8 *locational*
situating 250.4 *placing*
situation 251, 105.1 *state*, 106.1 *circumstances*, 250.1 *location*, 297.3 *atmosphere*, 332.1 *direction*, 659.5 *predicament*
Situation 251
situational 251, 106.7 *circumstantial*, 297.6 *atmospheric*
situational neurosis 61.10 *neurosis*
situation comedy 51.10 *comedy*, 534.25 *broadcast material*
situations vacant 251.4 *employment*
sit up 281.5 *be vertical*
sit-up-and-beg 71.12 *bicycle*
sit up late 209.8 *be late*
sit-upon 304.2 *rear end*
sitvac column 251.4 *employment*
Sitwell 48 Writers
sitzbath 258.12 *bath*
SI unit 75.2 *unit system*
Siva 8 Deities
Siwash 91 Names for Inhabitants
six 179, 27.10 *score*, 52.9 *numeral*, 179.13 *sixth*, 397.8 *after death*, 399.6 *grave*, 682.3 *successful thing*
sixain 179.2 *six*
six and two threes 110.5 *equality*
six-beat crawl 39.2 *swimming technique*
six centuries 179.9 *treble figures*
Six Day War 17 Major Wars
sixer 179.2 *six*
six feet deep 399.12 *funereally*
six feet under 397.19 *dead*, 399.10 *buried*
six-figure 179.21 *thousandth*
sixfold 179.13 *sixth*, 179.24 *fivefold*
six footer 259.11 *tall person*
six-footer 179.2 *six*, 275.7 *tall person*
six-gear straight 33.6 *motor racing terms*

six of one and half a dozen of the other 110.5, 122.1 *equality*
sixpence 741.10 *former British money*
six-pocket table 24.3 *English billiards*
six-shooter 179.2 *six*, 338.9, 680.9 *firearm*
six-sided 52.82 *polygonal*
sixteen 179.7 *double figures*
sixteenth 173.4 *less than one*, 179.18 *eleventh*
sixteenth note 49.17 *notation*
sixth 179, 49.16 *musical note*, 52.75 *equal*, 173.4 *less than one*, 179.2 *six*, 179.24 *fivefold*
sixth form 179.2 *six*
sixth-form 6.21 *curricular*
sixth-form college 6.12 *educational institution*
sixth-former 6.7 *learner*
sixth guard 28.3 *fencing movements*
sixthly 179.24 *fivefold*
sixth part 179.2 *six*
sixth sense 11.8 *psychic power*, 179.2 *six*, 368.3 *spiritual world*, 403.1 *sensation*, 459.2 *ways of thinking*, 464.2 *precognition*, 759.22 *impression*
Sixth Year Studies 485 Educational Qualifications
sixtieth 173.4 *less than one*, 179.19 *twentieth*
sixty 179.8 *twenty and over*
sixty-four dollar question 477.4 *difficult question*
sixty-fourth note 49.17 *notation*
six ways from Sunday 248.16 *extensively*
six-wheeler 33.5 *motorcycle racing*
six-yard 38.5 *soccer*
six-yard box 38.1 *soccer*
sizable 259.15 *big*
sizableness 259.2 *bigness*
size 259, 268, 50.11 *artist's materials*, 52.35 *space*, 112.10 *conform*, 120.1 *quantity*, 120.8 *quantify*, 121.1 *degree*, 138.3 *adhesive*, 248.1 *space*, 259.18 *measure*, 293.8 *wall covering*, 293.28 *face*, 393.10 *mucus*, 394.2 *adhesive*, 394.3 *paste*, 544.1 *identification*, 611.1 *importance*
Size 259
sizeable 248.13 *spacious*
sizeably 248.15 *spaciously*
sized 120.6 *quantitative*, 121.7 *gradational*
size up 268.10 *measure*, 492.12 *estimate*
sizzle 424.1 *faintness*, 424.5 *sound faint*, 425.6 *crack*, 429.1, 429.4 *hiss*, 828.11 *be angry*
sizzler 55.23 *heat*, 408.5 *hot weather*
sizzling 55.51, 408.9 *hot*, 408.11 *warm*, 425.2 *crack*, 425.9 *crackling*, 429.1 *hiss*, 429.6 *hissing*, 828.16 *angry*
sjambok 879.14 *instrument of punishment*
ska 49.9 *popular music*, 49.10 *world music*
skald 48.14 *author*
skat 42 Card Games
skate 80 Fishes, 20.5 *British game fish*, 32.1 *horse*, 41.6 *ice-skating*, 45.18 *sea fish*, 376.12 *go smoothly*
skateboard 326.5 *means of transport*
skateboarding 18 Sporting Activities
skate on thin ice 633.8 *be in danger*
skating association 41.6 *ice-skating*
skating boot 41.6 *ice-skating*
skating equipment 41.6 *ice-skating*
skean 680.8 *sharp weapon*
skedaddle 329.4 *be swift*, 345.4 *hurry off*, 349.33 *go away*, 591.9 *play truant*, 632.8 *be*

safe, 648.2 *make haste*, 648.4 *haste*
skeet 338.6 *shooting*
skeeter 82.1 *insect*
skeet shooting 18 Sporting Activities, 37.1 *target shooting*, 338.6 *shooting*
skeg 74 Parts of a Ship, 36.7 *windsurfing*
skein 161 Collective Names for Birds and Animals, 78.13 *assemblage of birds*, 161.27 *bundle*, 288.2 *braid*
skeletal 382, 63.32 *structural*, 238.10 *ill*, 274.2 *emaciated*, 299.6 *outlined*, 397.18 *dying*, 397.21 *deathly*
skeletal frame 63.27 *superstructure*
skeletally 299.7 *essentially*, 382.18 *structurally*
skeleton 382, 41.9 *bobsledding*, 132.1 *remainder*, 274.9 *thin person*, 284.2 *supporting part*, 299.1 *outline*, 382.4 *framework*, 397.11 *dead person*, 562.2, 592.6 *outline*
skeleton in the cupboard 529.1 *secrecy*, 801.1 *disrespect*, 862.5 *evil thing*
skeleton key 322.2 *opener*
skeleton shrimp 81.4 *arthropod*
skeleton staff 182.3 *fewness*
Skelton 48 Poets
skep 258.7 *basket*
skepping out 32.14 *horse-riding terms*
skerry 98.2 *island*
sketch 48.2 *fiction*, 50.9 *drawing*, 50.20 *draw*, 51.2 *play*, 51.6 *scene*, 145.3 *incomplete thing*, 145.5 *be incomplete*, 243.5 *work of art*, 299.1, 299.5 *outline*, 306.7 *form*, 375.13 *be unfinished*, 479.2 *rehearsal*, 479.12 *rehearse*, 518.5 *suppose*, 545.1 *record*, 547.2 *reproduction*, 547.11 *paint*, 552.4 *be concise*, 560.9 *representation*, 560.14 *describe*, 562.1 *summary*, 562.8 *summarize*, 592.6 *outline*, 592.10 *plan out*, 594.2 *do the groundwork*, 594.10 *preparations*
sketchbook 50.11 *artist's materials*
sketched 50.27 *painted*
sketcher 50.16 *artist*, 114.4 *person who copies*, 118.8 *copier*, 547.4 *person who makes a representation*
sketchily 145.6, 375.15 *incompletely*, 609.10 *insufficiently*
sketch in 107.7 *relate to*
sketchiness 145.1 *incompleteness*, 375.10 *rough idea*, 685.1 *noncompletion*
sketching 50.3 *drawing*
sketch map 299.4, 547.7 *map*
sketch out 299.5 *outline*, 547.11 *paint*, 560.14 *describe*, 562.8 *summarize*, 592.10 *plan out*, 685.5 *not complete*
sketchpad 50.11 *artist's materials*
sketchy 145.4 *incomplete*, 375.5 *unfinished*, 609.1 *insufficient*, 685.4 *uncompleted*
skew 52.80 *linear*, 123.5 *be unequal*, 286.6 *be oblique*, 310.8 *oblique*, 335.6 *distort*, 335.13 *deviation*
skew arch 43.5 *arch*
skewball 32.1 *horse*, 456.8 *checked*
skew distribution 52.59 *probability distribution*
skewed 286.4, 310.8 *oblique*, 335.23 *oblique*
skewed bridge 63.21 *bridge*
skewer 137.8 *fastening*, 137.11 *connect*, 380.8 *sharp-pointed thing*, 380.16 *use a sharp tool*
skew gear 63.7 *gear*
skew lines 52.37 *line*
skewness 52.59 *probability distribution*, 123.1 *inequality*, 286.1 *obliqueness*, 309.1 *distortion*, 310.2 *obliquity*

skewwhiff 123.3 *unequal*, 286.4 *oblique*, 309.6 *distorted*, 310.8 *oblique*
ski 41, **41**, 41.5 *ski equipment*, 376.12 *go smoothly*
skiagraphy 43.1 *architecture*
skibob racing 18 Sporting Activities
ski boots 295.19 *footwear*
ski championship 41.3 *ski racing*
ski clothes 41.5 *ski equipment*
ski competitively 41.14 *ski*
ski cross-country 41.14 *ski*
skid 71.21 *miscellaneous motoring terms*, 335.10 *slide*, 335.15 *deviating motion*, 360.14 *slide*, 376.12 *go smoothly*
skidder 85.7 *timber production*
skidding 73.5 *flight*, 360.18 *falling*
skiddy 376.4 *polished*
skid lid 295.15 *headgear*
skidoo 349.33 *go away*
skidpan 33.6 *motor racing terms*, 71.21 *miscellaneous motoring terms*
skid-proof 327.15 *accessible*
skid row 93.7 *city district*, 249.10 *urban area*
skid-row 93.14 *urban*
ski equipment 41
skier 41
skiff 74 Sailing Ships and Boats, 36.4, 36.11 *rowing*
skiffle 49.11 *folk music*
skiffle group 49.26 *musical group*
skiff-race 36.16 *row*
skiff racing 36.4 *rowing*
ski freestyle 41.14 *ski*
skiing 41, 41.12 *ski*
skiing association 41.1 *skiing*
skiing on ice 41.1 *skiing*
skiing posture 41.4 *skiing technique*
skiing snow 41.1 *skiing*
skiing technique 41
ski jacket 41.5 *ski equipment*
ski jump 41.1 *skiing*, 286.2 *oblique line*
ski-jump 41.14 *ski*, 359.5 *jump*
ski jumping 18 Sporting Activities
ski-jumping 41.1 *skiing*
skilful 655, 6.19 *knowledgeable*, 407.10 *handed*, 485.9 *qualified*, 507.6 *intelligent*, 519.10 *imaginative*, 619.1 *perfect*, 657.4 *cunning*, 696.13 *excellent*, 861.5 *proficient*
skilfully 655, **861**, 6.26 *studiously*, 485.17 *capably*, 688.26 *expertly*, 696.16 *masterfully*
skilfulness 655.1 *skill*, 660.1 *easiness*, 861.12 *proficiency*
skilful person 655.4 *skilled person*
skilful use 655.1 *skill*
ski lift 41.1 *skiing*, 327.12 *cableway*, 361.10 *elevator*
ski-lift 359.8 *lift*
skill 567, 655, 165.7 *special skill*, 235.2 *ability*, 243.1 *production*, 327.1 *way*, 485.2 *ability*, 501.2 *information*, 519.1 *imagination*, 602.1 *means*, 617.6 *worth*, 619.3 *perfection*, 640.2 *deed*, 652.9 *tactics*, 653.3 *management*, 657.1 *cunning*, 660.1 *easiness*
Skill 655
skilled 4.19 *learned*, 6.19 *knowledgeable*, 15.8 *industrial*, 485.9 *qualified*, 501.8 *knowledgeable*, 507.6 *intelligent*, 619.1 *perfect*, 655.6 *skilful*, 655.8 *expert*, 659.12 *problematic*, 688.17 *expert*, 696.13 *excellent*, 861.5 *proficient*
skilled person 655
skilled worker 15.7 *employee*, 124.8 *middle classes*, 230.5 *operator*, 485.8 *qualified person*, 603.7 *machinist*, 646.2 *artisan*, 655.5, 696.10 *expert*
skillet 45 Vegetables, 45.6 *kitchen equipment*, 258.15 *pot*
skills 485.3 *qualifications*
skilly 45.40 *breakfast cereal*,

412.3 *tasteless items*
skim 134.10 *purify*, 267.4 *meet*, 278.6 *be shallow*, 360.14 *slide*, 407.3 *press*, 407.11 *touch*, 407.12 *abut*, 580.4 *pick*, 621.15 *purify*, 628.5 *hurt*
skimmed milk 351.5 *milk*
skimmer 78 Birds, 45.6 *kitchen equipment*
skimmings 132.2 *residue*
Skimobile 71.10 *sled*
skim off 580.4 *pick*
skim off the cream 580.4 *pick*
ski mountaineering 18 Sporting Activities
ski-mountaineering 41.1 *skiing*
ski move 41.4 *skiing technique*
skim over 278.6 *be shallow*
skimp 270.10 *shorten*, 609.7 *make insufficient*, 685.5 *not complete*, 758.7 *hoard*
skimped 609.2 *unprovided*
skimpily 609.10 *insufficiently*, 685.7 *incompletely*, 743.17 *inadequately*
skimpiness 182.3 *fewness*, 260.1 *littleness*, 270.1 *shortness*, 609.8 *insufficiency*, 685.1 *non-completion*, 743.9 *inadequacy*
skimp on 145.5 *be incomplete*
skimpy 145.4 *incomplete*, 260.7 *little*, 270.7 *short*, 609.1 *insufficient*, 685.4 *uncompleted*, 743.4 *inadequate*
skin 777 Phobias by Topic, 86.3 *fruit structure*, 131.4 *take off*, 132.2 *residue*, 136.10 *set apart*, 243.7 *produce*, 266.3 *coat*, 278.4 *shallow thing*, 289.1 *exterior*, 293.13 *casing*, 293.14 *animal covering*, 294.13 *remove*, 385.14 *erode*, 437.6 *visible thing*, 457.3 *external appearance*, 604.1 *materials*, 753.10 *overcharge*
skin alive 852.21 *berate*
skin and bone 609.3 *underfed*
skin-and-bone 238.10 *ill*
skin and bones 274.2 *emaciated*
skin cancer 624.4 *disease*, 624.12 *cancer*, 624.13 *skin disease*
skin colour 457.3 *external appearance*
skin-deep 278.2 *superficial*
skin disease 777 Phobias by Topic, **624**
skin-dive 39.10 *dive*
skin-diver 39.4 *swimmer*
skin diving 39.1 *swimming*
skin flick 296.3 *pornography*, 877.2 *indecency*
skinflint 747.6 *nonpayer*, 747.13 *nonpaying*, 754.8 *bargain hunter*, 758.5 *miser*
skinfold 1.10 *measurement*
skin friction 385.1 *friction*
skinful 144.2 *fullness*
skin fungi 89.3 *fungi*
skin game 736.7 *dishonesty*
skin graft 630.12 *surgery*
skinhead 296.5 *baldness*, 635.2 *troublemaker*, 679.1 *combatant*, 791.8 *hair cut*, 832.8 *malefactor*
skink 79 Reptiles, 79.2 *lizard*
skin lesion 624.13 *skin disease*
skin magazine 296.3 *pornography*
skinned 294.9 *shed*
skinned alive 852.34 *censured*
skinner 294.7 *shedder*
Skinner 61.29 *psychologist*
Skinnerian 61.33 *Freudian*
Skinnerian psychology 61.1 *psychology*
skinniness 274.7 *thinness*
skinning 294.5 *shedding*
skinning alive 852.8 *berating*
skinny 238.10 *ill*, 274.1 *thin*, 609.3 *underfed*
skinny-dip 296.14 *undress*
skinny-dipper 294.4 *exposer*, 296.8 *nude person*
skinny-dipping 296.1 *undress*, 296.11 *exposed*
skin over 289.11 *be exterior*
skin-popping 875.1 *drug-taking*
skint 593.5 *necessitous*, 687.7

unprosperous, 743.2 *insolvent*
skin test 60.7 *diagnosis*
skintight 138.9 *adhesive*, 295.31 *styled*
ski on ice 41.14 *ski*
ski orienteering 41.3 *ski racing*
skip 25.3 *bowls player*, 41.11 *skier*, 46.15 *dance*, 254.18 *abscond*, 324.12 *gait*, 345.4 *hurry off*, 359.5, 359.18 *jump*, 366.29 *jerkily*, 638.5 *escape*, 720.7 *not observe*, 727.4 *wastebin*, 773.7 *dance*
ski pants 41.5 *ski equipment*, 295.9 *trousers*
skipjack 74 Sailing Ships and Boats, **80** Fishes
skip off 345.4 *hurry off*
ski pole 41.5 *ski equipment*
skipper 82 Insects, 36.9 *sailor*, 36.15 *sail*, 74.7 *nautical person*, 653.2 *direct*, 653.13 *director*
skipping 359.24 *leaping*
skip town 531.11 *conceal oneself*
ski race 41.3 *ski racing*
ski racer 41.11 *skier*
ski racing 41
ski rambling 41.2 *cross-country skiing*
skirl 423.8 *be loud*, 430.1 *stridency*, 430.4 *be strident*
skirmish 674.1 *contention*, 674.6, 674.12 *fight*, 676.9, 676.14 *battle*
skirmisher 679.8 *soldier*
skirmishes 676.8 *warfare*
skirmishing 674.6 *fight*
skirr 329.4 *be swift*
skirt 295, 264.10 *stay near*, 300.1 *edge*, 300.5 *border*, 305.7 *be alongside*, 334.3 *circuit*, 334.5 *encircle*, 356.8 *pass*, 363.7 *ring*, 402.9 *woman considered as a sex object*
skirt around 313.6 *circle*
skirt-chaser 821.9 *lover*, 826.5 *courting person*
skirted 300.9 *skirting*
skirting 300, 305.6 *side*
skirting board 280.2 *foot*
skirt round 591.7 *be evasive*
ski run 41.1 *skiing*
skis 34.4 *climbing equipment*
skish 20.1 *angling*
ski slope 41.1 *skiing*
ski socks 295.20 *legwear*
ski stick 41.5 *ski equipment*
ski stopper 41.5 *ski equipment*
skisuit 41.5 *ski equipment*
ski sweater 295.13 *sweater*
skit 51.2 *play*, 854.6 *ridicule*
ski teaching method 41.1 *skiing*
ski touring 41.2 *cross-country skiing*
ski-tow 41.1 *skiing*
ski trail 41.1 *skiing*
skittish 491.8, 579.1 *capricious*
skittishness 810.3 *bashfulness*
skittles 18 Sporting Activities, 25.4 *bowling*, 42.7 *other games*
ski turn 41.4 *skiing technique*
skive 380.16 *use a sharp tool*, 591.5 *shirk*, 591.9 *play truant*, 643.12 *be inactive*
skive off 254.18 *abscond*, 638.5 *escape*, 720.8 *not perform*
skiver 254.6 *absentee*, 380.10 *knife*, 591.17 *avoider*, 643.8 *nonworker*, 720.6 *evader*
skiving 591.13 *shirking*, 720.12 *nonperforming*
skivvies 295.18 *underwear*
skivvy 697.6 *domestic servant*
skivvy shirt 295.18 *underwear*
ski wax 41.5 *ski equipment*
skol 351.18 *cheers*
skua 78 Birds, 78.3 *water bird*
Skuld 8 Deities
skulduggery 539.7 *tricking*, 801.3 *disreputable action*, 858.3 *criminality*
skulk 161 Collective Names for Birds and Animals, 527.13 *hide*, 591.6 *evade*, 657.5 *be cunning*, 779.4 *be a coward*
skulker 591.17 *avoider*
skulking 527.2 *concealed*, 527.8

concealment, 591.14 *evasion*, 591.18 *avoiding*
skull 382 Bones, 74.3 *vessel*, 397.3 *symbol of death*, 671.7 *armour*
skull and crossbones 397.3 *symbol of death*, 544.7 *flag*
skullcap 7.11 *vestment*, 295.15 *headgear*
skunk 77 Placental Mammals, 419.2 *something that makes an unpleasant smell*, 682.2 *victory*, 864.10 *bad person*
sky 8.11 *heaven*, 53.3 *universe*, 248.2 *empty space*, 275.8 *high thing*, 279.1 *summit*, 361.2 *send up*, 454.6 *blue thing*
Sky 534.24 *television broadcasting*
sky blue 454.1 *blue*
skycap 326.7 *transferor*, 697.3 *attendant*
skydive 360.12 *drop*
sky-diver 360.8 *descender*
skydiving 18 Sporting Activities
Skye 98 Islands
Skye terrier 77 Breeds of Dogs
sky-high 275.9 *high*, 753.7 *dear*, 757.3 *costly*
skyhook 34.4 *climbing equipment*
skyjack 73.1 *aviation*, 734.10 *take away*, 736.12 *steal*
skyjacker 734.6 *taker*, 736.8 *thief*
skyjacking 734.3 *taking away*, 736.1 *stealing*, 736.17 *stolen*
Skylab 53.30 *spacecraft*
skylark 78 Birds, 359.11 *ascender*, 359.14 *climb*, 506.8 *fool*, 640.4 *act*
skylarking 359.6 *mounting*, 506.3 *tomfoolery*, 812.1 *celebration*
skylight 322.7 *passageway*, 439.10 *window*
skylight filter 66.20 *filter*
skyline 263.3 *distant place*, 282.3 *flat thing*, 299.3 *edge*, 437.3 *visibility*
Sky Pilot 7.8 *priest*
skyrocket 128.4 *increase*, 359.11 *ascender*, 359.19 *take off*
skyrocketing 359.24 *leaping*, 753.7 *dear*
skyrocketing price 753.3 *inflationary price*
Skyros pony 32 Breeds of Horse and Pony
skysail 74 Sails
skyscape 50.10 *art subject*
skyscraper 43.3, 63.20 *building*, 243.8 *construction*, 275.6 *tall thing*, 281.3 *vertical thing*, 382.6 *construction*
skyscraping 275.9 *high*
sky survey 53.6 *star catalogue*
Skytext 534.25 *broadcast material*
skyward 275.20 *higher*, 359.26 *up*
sky wave 365.5 *wave*, 534.15 *transmitted wave*
skyway 327.13 *flight path*
skywriting 73.1 *aviation*
slab 34.5 *rock face*, 47.12 *wood*, 63.28 *substructure*, 143.7 *piece*, 266.4 *slice*, 273.5 *thickness*, 282.3 *flat thing*, 545.11 *monument*
slabber 353.9 *saliva*, 353.20 *salivate*
slabbiness 393.3 *muddiness*
slabbinness 394.1 *viscosity*
slabby 393.17 *muddy*, 394.8 *viscous*
slab method 44.5 *ceramic process*
slack 139.8 *nonadhesive*, 151.15 *untidy*, 238.8 *weak*, 240.5 *inert*, 325.5 *sedentary*, 328.5 *unhurried*, 328.7 *delayed*, 374.1 *soft*, 410.5 *coal*, 468.10 *careless*, 470.5 *indifferent*, 643.3 *not participating*
slacken 129.4 *decrease*, 136.9 *separate*, 238.7 *weaken*, 242.4 *moderate*, 374.13 *soften*, 649.3 *ease*
slackening 129.1 *decrease*, 328.9

deceleration
slacken off 218.6 *cease,* 328.3
slow down
slacker 328.15 *slow person,*
591.17 *avoider,* 643.8 *non-worker,* 685.3 *quitter,* 720.6
evader, 783.6 *indifferent person*
slackly 374.17 *softly*
slackness 238.1 *weakness,* 240.1
inertness, 328.8 *slowness,* 374.8
softness, 470.2 *indifference*
slack off 649.2 *take it easy*
slack-rope artist 51.29 *circus performer*
slacks 295.4 *informal dress,*
295.9 *trousers,* 814.6 *informal
dress*
slack suit 295.4 *informal dress,*
295.10 *suit*
slag 132.2 *residue,* 151.10 *slattern,* 243.3 *product,* 401.7 *libertine,* 402.6 *loose woman,* 614.6
refuse, 622.4 *dirt*
slag heap 614.6 *refuse*
slag off 766.7 *be dissatisfied,*
854.11 *criticize*
sláinte 351.18 *cheers*
slake 405.10 *comfort,* 765.8 *satisfy*
slaked lime 68.13 *fertilizer*
slake one's thirst 242.5 *moderate
one's hunger,* 351.13 *drink*
slalom 18 Sporting Activities,
41.12 *ski,* 674.4 *race*
slalom course 36.7 *windsurfing,*
335.14 *deviating course*
slalomer 41.11 *skier*
slalom pole 41.3 *ski racing*
slalom race 41.3 *ski racing*
slalom racer 41.11 *skier*
slalom racing 36.6 *canoeing,*
36.7 *windsurfing,* 41.3 *ski racing*
slalom ski 41.5 *ski equipment*
slam 36.10 *sailing,* 42.3 *card
game terms,* 330.3 *hit,* 330.13
blow, 338.26 *bat,* 423.1 *loudness,* 423.8 *be loud,* 425.1,
425.5 *bang,* 852.5 *criticism,*
852.17 *criticize,* 854.2 *criticism,*
854.11 *criticize*
slam dunk 23.6 *play basketball*
slam gybe 36.1 *sailing,* 36.15
sail
slam into 330.2 *collide*
slammer 323.4 *closed place,*
702.2 *the inside*
slamming 423.2 *outcry,* 425.8
banging
slammock 622.6 *dirty person*
slander 525.1 *misinterpret,*
525.2 *misinterpretation,* 538.1
untruth, 538.3 *lying,* 538.21 *lie,*
540.6 *lying,* 618.11 *harmfulness,* 618.14 *ill-treat,* 670.10
criticize, 670.16 *terrorist attack,*
827.3 *vilification,* 827.6 *vilify,*
854.3 *defamation,* 854.12 *defame,* 856.2 *false accusation,*
856.6 *accuse falsely*
slandered 856.9 *perjurious*
slanderer 854.8 *defamer*
slandering 538.15 *lying,* 540.29
deceitful
slanderous 525.3 *misinterpreted,*
538.13 *untrue,* 540.32 *falsified,*
670.25 *critical,* 827.9 *vituperative,* 854.16 *defamatory,* 856.9
perjurious
slanderously 525.5
misrepresentedly, 538.26 *untruthfully,* 827.13 *vituperatively,*
854.18 *disparagingly,* 856.10 *accusingly*
slang 5, 5.3 *spoken language,*
5.39 *of language,* 564.1 *faculty
of speech,* 827.6 *vilify*
slanging match 473.1, 666.2 *argument,* 827.3 *vilification*
slang term 5.18 *slang*
slang word 5.18 *slang*
slangy 5.39 *of language*
slant 19.10 *defence,* 19.16 *play
defence,* 286.1 *obliqueness,*
286.6 *be oblique,* 310.2 *obliquity,* 310.5 *viewpoint,* 335.13
deviation, 335.14 *deviating
course,* 474.11 *practise soph-*

istry, 524.13 *interpret news,*
540.9 *falsification,* 540.22 *falsify,* 548.4 *misrepresent*
slanted 52.80 *linear,* 286.4
oblique, 310.10 *biased,* 335.23
oblique, 548.6 *misrepresented*
slanting 286.4, 310.8 *oblique,*
540.9 *falsification*
slant-in pass 19.9 *play*
slant-top 47.14 *wooden*
slant-top desk 47.4 *table*
slap 330.13 *blow,* 407.3 *press,*
407.11 *touch,* 425.2, 425.6
crack, 543.3, 543.11 *gesture,*
586.8 *incentive,* 618.14 *ill-treat,*
674.12 *fight,* 791.4 *cosmetics,*
879.3 *hit,* 879.12 *corporal punishment*
slapdash 468.10 *careless,* 470.5
indifferent, 648.3 *hasty,* 656.3
clumsy, 656.4 *bungled,* 780.4
rash
slaphead 296.5 *baldness*
slap in the face 806.10 *abasement,* 828.5 *quarrel,* 850.5,
850.23 *insult*
slap one's thighs 771.14 *laugh*
slap on the wrist 879.3 *hit,*
879.12 *corporal punishment*
slapped down 806.3 *humbled*
slapped in the face 806.3 *humbled*
slapping 543.15 *gestural,* 879.12
corporal punishment
slapstick 51.10 *comedy,* 51.30
clown, 51.38 *tragic,* 771.4 *entertainment,* 771.10 *humorous,*
798.5 *ridiculous*
slapstick comedian 51.30 *clown*
slapstick comedy 798, 51.10
comedy
slap-up 742.3 *opulent*
slash 31.9 *play hockey,* 129.5
make smaller, 136.5 *separator,*
136.9 *separate,* 137.4 *means of
connection,* 270.10 *shorten,*
286.2 *oblique line,* 322.20 *hole,*
353.3 *urination,* 406.3 *injury,*
406.11 *inflict pain,* 670.6 *stab,*
752.3 *discount,* 754.13 *make
cheap*
slash-and-burn 68.4 *arable farming*
slashed 31.8 *hockey,* 322.14
holed, 754.9 *cheap*
slashed price 754.1 *cheapness*
slashing 31.3 *ice hockey,* 31.5 *lacrosse,* 31.8 *hockey,* 554.3 *emphatic,* 670.23 *attacking*
slashing one's wrists 398.7 *suicide*
slash one's wrists 398.21 *commit suicide*
slat 47.12 *wood,* 47.17 *carpenter,* 266.4 *slice,* 274.11 *fineness*
slate 54 Common Rocks, 43.4
building material, 63.26 *masonry,* 192.14 *keep time,* 266.4
slice, 379.3 *brittle thing,* 448.5
grey thing, 524.11 *criticize,*
592.2 *policy,* 602.4 *building material,* 766.7 *be dissatisfied,*
852.17, 854.11 *criticize*
slate blue 454.1 *blue*
slate-coloured 448.1 *grey*
slated 852.33 *criticized*
slate grey 440.3 *dark colour*
slate-grey 448.1 *grey*
slate loose 510.1 *insanity*
slater 81.4 *arthropod*
slates 293.7 *overhead covering*
slating 852.5, 854.2 *criticism*
slatted 47.16 *joined*
slattern 151, 622.6 *dirty person*
slatternliness 151.3 *untidiness*
slatternly 151.15 *untidy,* 622.7
dirty, 656.3 *clumsy*
slaty 54.57 *chalky*
slaty cleavage 54.28 *rock*
slaughter 398, 398, 241.2 *physical violence,* 244.2 *destroying,*
244.8 *destroy,* 244.9 *demolish,*
670.9 *attack successfully,*
670.14 *siege,* 676.13 *be at war,*
832.7 *act of malevolence,*
832.11 *kill,* 879.5 *execute,*
879.13 *capital punishment*

slaughtered 397.19 *dead*
slaughterer 241.4 *violent person
or animal,* 398.10 *killer*
slaughterhouse 398, 244.5
havoc, 727.8 *sink*
slaughtering 398.9 *animal killing*
slaughterman 398.13 *animal
killer*
slaughterous 398.24 *murderous*
slave 697, 127.6 *inferior,* 232.3
assistant, 481.8 *victim of discrimination,* 642.10 *busy person,* 642.15 *try,* 644.6 *work,*
646.1 *worker,* 673.2 *appeaser,*
694.4 *obedient person,* 701.5
subjected person, 808.3 *sycophant*
slave 96 Rivers
slave away 644.6 *work*
slave-driver 690.4 *strict person*
slave-girl 697.7 *slave*
slave-making ant 82 Insects
slave of the lamp 232.3 *assistant*
slaver 74 Ships and Boats,
347.12 *leak,* 349.14 *let out,*
353.9 *saliva,* 353.20 *salivate,*
622.11 *dirty*
slave-raider 736.9 *plunderer*
slavering 353.29 *salivating*
slavery 644.1 *work,* 695.3 *coercive methods,* 699.4 *detention,*
701.1 *subjection,* 734.3 *taking
away,* 808.1 *servility*
slave ship 74 Ships and Boats
slave to drink 874.17 *drunkard*
slave to fashion 118.7 *imitator*
slave trade 737.4 *trade*
slave unit 66.19 *flash*
slavey 697.6 *domestic servant*
slavish 118.1 *imitation,* 673.5
submitting, 694.7 *obedient,*
808.6 *servile*
slavishly 694.10 *obediently,*
808.16 *with servility*
slavishness 118.1 *imitation,*
673.1 *submission,* 694.1 *obedience,* 808.1 *servility*
Slavonic 5 Languages and
Groups of Languages, **7** Non-Christian Religions, 5.11 *family of languages*
Slavs 1 Peoples
slay 100.14 *cause not to exist,*
398.16 *kill,* 676.13 *be at war*
slay en masse 398.18 *slaughter*
slayer 398.10 *killer*
slaying 398.1 *killing*
sleaze 618.10 *poverty*
sleaziness 618.10 *poverty,* 622.1
dirtiness
sleazo 618.4 *poor*
sleazoid 618.4 *poor*
sleazy 618.4 *poor,* 622.7 *dirty*
sled 71, 326.5 *means of transport,* 326.12 *transport*
sled-dog racing 18 Sporting Activities
sledge 71.10 *sled,* 326.5 *means
of transport,* 326.12 *transport,*
330.15 *ram,* 384.14 *hammer*
sledge dog 326.6 *beast of burden*
sledgehammer 330.2 *collide,*
330.15 *ram*
sledge hammer 384.14 *hammer*
sledgehammering 330.12 *collision*
sleek 150.13 *orderly,* 376.1
smooth, 376.6 *smooth-mannered,* 386.12 *smooth,* 395.11
oily
sleekly 376.14 *smoothly,* 376.16
suavely, 395.20 *oilily*
sleekness 376.7 *smoothness,*
386.1 *lubrication,* 395.2 *smoothness*
sleep 777 Phobias by Topic,
643, 643, 205.5 *night thing,*
218.3, 218.9 *pause,* 240.4 *be
inert,* 325.2 *repose,* 325.8 *be motionless,* 404.2 *unconsciousness,*
404.11 *be unfeeling,* 527.6 *latency,* 527.12 *be latent,* 649.1
ease, 649.2 *take it easy,* 650.5
be fatigued
sleep around 821.29 *make love,*
877.17 *be sexually immoral*
sleeper 643, 32.7 *horseracing,*

72.3 *rail,* 72.6 *rolling stock,*
327.10 *railway,* 641.2 *nonacting person*
sleepily 643, 240.7 *inertly,*
404.13 *insensibly,* 650.8 *tiredly*
sleep-in 475.6 *mass demonstration*
sleep-inducing 788.4 *boring*
sleepiness 240.1 *inertness,*
404.2 *unconsciousness,* 643.9
sleep, 650.7 *fatigue*
sleeping 325.5 *sedentary,* 527.1
latent, 643.4 *not awake*
sleeping around 821.5 *desire,*
877.3 *sexual immorality*
sleeping baby 527.7 *latent things*
sleeping bag 34.4 *climbing equipment*
Sleeping Beauty 404.5 *unfeeling
person,* 643.11 *sleeper*
sleeping car 72.6 *rolling stock*
sleeping dog 527.7 *latent things,*
635.1 *trap*
sleeping draught 404.4 *anaesthetic,* 761.6 *desensitizing substance,* 767.3 *reliever*
sleeping giant 527.7 *latent things*
sleeping partner 612.10 *nonentity,* 643.8 *nonworker*
sleeping pill 62.4 *drug type,*
242.2 *moderator,* 404.4 *anaesthetic,* 630.8 *drug,* 631.11 *intoxicant,* 643.10 *soporific,* 761.6 *desensitizing substance,* 767.3 *reliever*
sleeping place 256.1 *habitat*
sleeping room 256.7 *room*
sleeping sickness 81.12 *protozoal disease,* 624.6 *infection*
sleeping together 821.5 *desire*
sleeping with 135.4 *sexual
union,* 821.5 *desire*
sleep it off 651.2 *be refreshed,*
873.5 *sober up*
sleepless 403.6 *conscious,*
575.11 *steady,* 642.18 *active*
sleeplessness 642.7 *restlessness*
sleep like a log 643.13 *sleep*
sleep off 629.4 *be restored*
sleep on a volcano 633.8 *be in
danger*
sleep one's last sleep 397.15 *die*
sleep on it 209.8 *delay,* 461.14
have second thoughts
sleepsuit 295.23 *children's
clothes*
sleep therapy 61.3 *psychiatric
treatment*
sleep through 629.4 *be restored*
sleep together 821.29 *make love*
sleep treatment 61.3 *psychiatric
treatment*
sleepwalk 404.11 *be unfeeling*
sleepwalker 404.5 *unfeeling person*
sleepwalking 61.14 *trance,* 519.6
reverie
sleepwear 295.22 *nightwear*
sleep with 135.11, 821.29 *make
love*
sleepy 404, 240.5 *inert,* 325.6
quiescent, 643.4 *not awake,*
650.1 *fatigued*
sleepyhead 328.15 *slow person,*
643.11 *sleeper*
sleepy sickness 624.7 *tropical
disease*
sleet 55.24 *precipitation,* 55.29
hail, 55.63 *snow,* 409.5 *ice*
sleety 55.55 *cool,* 409.8 *cold*
sleeve 295.24 *part of garment,*
544.7 *flag*
sleigh 71.10 *sled,* 326.5 *means
of transport*
sleigh bells 49 Musical Instruments
sleight 474.1 *sophistry,* 539.7
tricking, 539.8 *trick,* 657.1 *cunning*
sleight of hand 539, 102.3 *delusion*
sleight-of-hand 539.40 *illusory*
sleight-of-hand artist 51.27 *entertainer*
slender 85.14 *treelike,* 272.1 *narrow,* 274.1 *thin,* 609.1 *insufficient*

slenderize 274.14 *become thin*
slenderizing 274.3 *slimming*
slender means 743.5 *poverty*
slenderness 272.5 *narrowness*, 274.7 *thinness*
slentando 49 *Musical Terms*
sleuth 590.5 *pursuer*, 590.9 *follow*
slew 36.15 *sail*
slice 266, 29.3 *golf shots*, 29.7 *golf*, 136.9 *separate*, 143.7 *piece*, 330.10 *bat*, 330.14 *sporting hit*, 335.2 *divert*, 338.5, 338.23 *throw*, 338.26 *bat*, 350.14 *mouthful*, 380.16 *use a sharp tool*, 656.7 *be clumsy*, 656.9 *bungling*, 731.2 *portion*
sliced 143.11 *partial*
sliced bread 45.38 *bread*
slice of life 51.2 *play*, 101.3 *realism*
slice of the cake 731.2 *portion*
slicer 380.10 *knife*
slice service 40.2 *tennis strokes*
slick 150.13 *orderly*, 376.1 *smooth*, 376.4 *polished*, 376.6 *smooth-mannered*, 376.11, 386.12 *smooth*, 395.11 *oily*, 395.18 *anoint*, 539.34 *deceiving*, 655.6 *skilful*, 657.4 *cunning*
slick down 376.11 *smooth*
slicked up 295.30 *dressed up*
slicker 255.4 *townsman*, 295.12 *coat*
slickly 376.14 *smoothly*, 386.16, 395.20 *oilily*
slickness 376.7 *smoothness*, 386.1 *lubrication*, 395.2 *smoothness*
slick on 395.18 *anoint*
slick tyre 139.3 *nonadhesive thing*
slid 360.6 *slide*
slidder 360.14 *slide*
slide 335, 360, 360, 36.16 *row*, 54.26 *mass movement*, 63.31 *load*, 66.3 *photograph*, 66.12 *development*, 96.7 *flow*, 286.1 *obliqueness*, 286.2 *oblique line*, 376.8 *smooth thing*, 376.12 *go smoothly*, 435.8 *reflection*, 442.8 *transparent thing*, 628.1 *deteriorate*, 633.8 *be in danger*, 641.4 *not act*, 660.19 *go easily*
slide back 221.6 *reverse*
slide carrier 66.12 *development*
slide down 360.14 *slide*
slide down the slippery slope 337.1 *go backward*
slide home 22.7 *play baseball*
slide in 354.5 *inset*
slide into 220.7 *convert into*
slide off 33.10 *be on the track*
slide projector 66.12 *development*
slider 22.4 *pitching terms*, 338.5 *throw*
slide rule 170.5 *computer*
slide show 51.5 *show*
slide trombone 49 *Musical Instruments*
sliding 63.16 *deformation*, 360.6 *slide*, 360.18 *falling*, 628.12 *deteriorated*, 864.11 *wicked*
sliding down the slippery slope 337.19 *backsliding*
sliding friction 385.1 *friction*
sliding off 33.6 *motor racing terms*
sliding outrigger seat 36.6 *canoeing*
sliding pads 22.3 *baseball equipment*
sliding panel 539.12 *disguise*
sliding-scale 15.9 *negotiated*
sliding-scale rates 15.2 *industrial negotiations*
sliding seat 36.4 *rowing*
slight 127.17 *defective*, 238.13 *insufficient*, 260.7 *little*, 274.1 *thin*, 278.2 *superficial*, 341.1 *repel*, 372.1 *sparse*, 468.13 *be thoughtless*, 542.16 *imperceptible*, 581.5 *exclude*, 581.5 *rejection*, 612.1 *unimportant*, 668.6 *be insubordinate*, 720.1 *nonobservance*, 720.7 *not observe*,

806.17 *humiliate*, 850.5, 850.23 *insult*, 854.10 *disparage*
slight build 274.7 *thinness*
slighting 850.11 *insulting*, 854.1 *disparagement*, 854.15 *disparaging*
slightingly 854.18 *disparagingly*
slighting remark 854.4 *aspersion*
slightly 120.7 *quantitatively*, 121.11 *to a degree*, 127.21 *badly*, 143.12 *partly*, 173.7 *fractionally*, 238.14 *weakly*, 242.9 *moderately*, 260.8 *in a small way*
slightly built 274.1 *thin*
slightly drunk 874
slightness 260.1 *littleness*, 274.7 *thinness*, 278.3 *shallowness*, 372.3 *sparseness*
slight smell 416.1 *odour*
slight transgression 864.3 *venial sin*
Sligo 92 *Counties*, 93 *Cities*
slim 262.5 *make smaller*, 262.6 *become smaller*, 262.7 *smaller*, 274.1 *thin*, 274.14 *become thin*, 699.10 *restrain oneself*, 722.9 *lose*, 871.5 *fast*
slim chance 486.4 *remote possibility*, 489.4 *improbability*
slim down 274.14 *become thin*
slime 777 *Phobias by Topic*, 394, 391.8 *marsh*, 393.1 *semiliquid*, 393.13 *mud*, 622.4 *dirt*
slime moulds 89.3 *fungi*
slimily 393
sliminess 622.1 *dirtiness*, 853.4 *unctuousness*
slimmer 274.9 *thin person*, 350.18 *eater*, 722.7 *dieter*
slimming 274, 262.1 *contraction*, 262.8 *contracting*, 274.10 *diet*, 350.6 *nutrition*, 350.27 *edible*, 722.1 *loss*, 871.1, 871.6 *fasting*
slimming diet 350.6 *nutrition*, 871.1 *fasting*
slimming pills 274.10 *diet*
slimness 274.7 *thinness*
slimy 386.12 *smooth*, 393.16 *semiliquid*, 393.17 *muddy*, 393.22 *mucilaginous*, 622.7 *dirty*, 771.11 *humouring*, 808.7 *sycophantic*, 817.9 *deferential*, 853.15 *unctuous*
sling 74 *Rigging*, 284.3 *body support*, 338.5 *throw*, 338.9 *firearm*, 338.23 *throw*, 351.8 *mixed drink*, 630.10 *surgical dressing*, 670.7 *stone*, 680.6 *historical missile weapon*
slinger 338.14 *thrower*
slinger ring 73 *Aircraft Parts*
slinging 338.3 *throwing*
sling mud 854.12 *defame*
sling one's hook 345.3 *quit*
sling out 581.2 *discard*
sling psychrometer 389.19 *measuring instrument*
slings and arrows 862.3 *bad luck*
sling shoes 295.19 *footwear*
slingshot 244.7 *agent of destruction*, 338.8 *missile*, 377.3 *elastic thing*
slingstone 338.8 *missile*
slink 527.13 *hide*, 531.11 *conceal oneself*
slink in 346.11 *infiltrate*
slink off 345.1 *depart*, 591.8 *run away*
slinky 295.31 *styled*
slip 27.4 *team*, 44.2 *raw material*, 44.3 *glaze*, 71.21 *miscellaneous motoring terms*, 143.6 *branch*, 260.4 *little person*, 272.6 *narrow place*, 274.9 *thin person*, 292.1 *lining*, 295.18 *underwear*, 335.10, 360.6 *slide*, 360.11 *trip*, 360.14 *slide*, 376.12 *go smoothly*, 393.12 *poultice*, 393.13 *mud*, 468.5 *inattentive act*, 491.21 *change*, 493.10 *misjudge*, 504.9 *trivial error*, 504.19 *make a mistake*, 585.4 *be unaccustomed*, 628.1 *deteriorate*, 633.8 *be in danger*, 687.9 *be in trouble*, 864.16 *be*

wicked, 866.3 *sin*
slip anchor 36.15 *sail*
slip away 254.16 *absent oneself*, 345.3 *quit*
slip back 337, 221.6 *reverse*, 337.1 *go backward*, 358.1 *fall short*, 628.1 *deteriorate*
slip by 531.11 *conceal oneself*
slip casting 44.5 *ceramic process*
slipcover 293.12 *protective covering*
slip friction 385.1 *friction*
slip in 346.11 *infiltrate*, 354.5 *inset*
slip into 295.34 *wear*
slipknot 74 *Knots*, 137.6 *line*
slip money to 729.5 *give*
slip of a girl 206.8 *young woman*
slip off 296.14 *undress*
slip of the pen 504.9 *trivial error*
slip of the tongue 504.9 *trivial error*
slip on 295.34 *wear*
slip one's collar 638.5 *escape*
slip one's lead 638.5 *escape*
slip one's mind 512.12 *be forgotten*
slip-ons 295.19 *footwear*
slip out 254.16 *absent oneself*
slip out of 296.14 *undress*
slipover 295.13 *sweater*
slippage 145.2 *omission*, 360.6 *slide*, 593.2 *need*, 609.8 *insufficiency*
slipped disc 624.16 *rheumatism*
slipper 879.3 *hit*
slippered 649.4 *at ease*
slipperiness 139.1 *nonadhesion*, 224.2 *irresolution*, 376.7 *smoothness*, 386.1 *lubrication*, 395.2 *smoothness*, 474.3 *cunning*, 633.5 *danger*, 657.1 *cunning*
slipper orchid 84 *Flowers and Flowering Plants*
slipper pad 41.5 *ski equipment*
slippers 295.4 *informal dress*, 295.19 *footwear*, 814.6 *informal dress*
slipper shell 81 *Molluscs*
slipperwort 84 *Flowers and Flowering Plants*
slippery 139.8 *nonadhesive*, 376.4 *polished*, 386.10 *oily*, 386.12 *smooth*, 395.11 *oily*, 395.16 *lubricated*, 491.7 *unreliable*, 539.34 *deceiving*, 578.11 *equivocating*, 591.18 *avoiding*, 633.2 *unsafe*, 657.4 *cunning*, 858.5 *dishonourable*
slippery as a greased pig 376.5 *smooth as a peach*
slippery as an eel 376.5 *smooth as a peach*
slippery customer 578.9 *equivocator*, 858.4 *dishonourable person*
slippery elm 85 *Trees and Shrubs*
slippery slope 244.4 *ruin*, 633.5 *danger*, 659.6 *critical situation*
slipping 360.18 *falling*, 397.18 *dying*, 628.12 *deteriorated*, 633.4 *endangered*, 656.3 *clumsy*, 864.11 *wicked*
slipping away 397.18 *dying*
slipping back 628.7 *deterioration*
slip-ring rotor 64.31 *electric motor*
slip road 71.3 *carriageway*, 137.5 *road*
slips 647.1 *workshop*
slipshod 151.15 *untidy*, 468.10 *careless*, 470.5 *indifferent*, 482.1 *undiscriminating*, 555.1 *unemphatic*
slipshodness 151.3 *untidiness*
slip stage 51.15 *stage*
slipstream 33.10 *be on the track*, 73.7 *miscellaneous aviation terms*
slipstreaming 33.6 *motor racing terms*
slip-strike fault 54.20 *earth movement*
slip the cable 591.8 *run away*
slip the collar 700.5 *be liberated*
slip through 638.5 *escape*

slip through one's fingers 362.6 *throw down*
slip through someone's fingers 638.5 *escape*
slip 'twixt the cup and the lip 515.2 *bad outcome*
slip up 360.11 *trip*, 504.19 *make a mistake*, 683.6 *fail*, 844.19 *be wrong*
slip-up 468.5 *inattentive act*, 504.9 *trivial error*, 683.4 *unsuccessful thing*
slipware 44.1 *ceramics*
slipway 376.8 *smooth thing*
slit 136.3 *separateness*, 136.9 *separate*, 245.8 *organs of reproduction*, 265.2, 265.5 *crack*, 265.7 *cracked*, 319.1 *notch*, 319.4 *notched*, 319.5 *notch*, 321.1, 321.6 *furrow*
slit drum 49 *Musical Instruments*
slither 360.6, 360.14 *slide*
slitheriness 376.7 *smoothness*
slithering 79.11 *reptilian*, 360.18 *falling*
slithery 376.4 *polished*, 386.10 *oily*, 386.12 *smooth*, 395.11 *oily*
slit shell 81 *Molluscs*
slit skirt 295.6 *skirt*
sliver 143.7 *piece*, 149.2 *impurity*, 173.3 *fragment*, 260.3 *little piece*, 266.4 *slice*, 350.14 *mouthful*
Sloane 52 *Scientists*
Sloane Ranger 617.7 *elite*, 684.4 *prosperous person*, 796.6 *fashionable élite*, 802.1 *nobleman*
slob 151.10 *slattern*, 393.13 *mud*, 470.3 *negligent person*, 626.3 *unhygienic person*, 656.10 *unskilled person*, 795.5 *vulgar person*
slobber 347.12 *leak*, 349.14 *let out*, 353.9 *saliva*, 353.20 *salivate*, 389.33 *sprinkle*, 391.16 *seep*, 622.11 *dirty*
slobbering 353.29 *salivating*
slobber over 821.27 *kiss*
slobbiness 393.3 *muddiness*
slobbish 151.15 *untidy*
slobbishness 151.3 *untidiness*
sloe 86 *Fruits*, 415.3 *sour thing*, 447.9 *black thing*
sloe-black 447.1 *black*
sloe-eyed 447.4 *black-haired*
sloe gin 415.3 *sour thing*
slog 27.17 *bat*, 330.3 *hit*, 330.13 *blow*, 338.26 *bat*, 575.6 *persevere*, 642.15 *try*, 644.6 *work*
slogan 5.21 *catchword*, 426.7 *repeated word*, 505.1 *maxim*, 543.6 *word*
slog at 644.8 *exert oneself*
slog away 575.6 *persevere*
slogger 642.10 *busy person*, 679.3 *athlete*
slogging 642.19 *busy*, 642.20 *industrious*, 644.10 *working*
slogging away 575.10 *persevering*
sloop 74 *Sailing Ships and Boats*, 36.2 *sailing boat*, 679.24 *warship*
sloop of war 74 *Sailing Ships and Boats*
slop 347.11 *run out*, 362.6 *throw down*, 389.33 *sprinkle*, 393.13 *mud*, 412.3 *tasteless items*, 607.1 *waste*, 656.7 *be clumsy*
slope 41.1 *skiing*, 52.37 *line*, 52.97 *align*, 286.1 *obliqueness*, 286.6 *be oblique*, 310.2 *obliquity*, 310.11 *angle*, 335.14 *deviating course*, 359.2 *upturn*, 360.6, 360.14 *slide*
sloped 286.4, 310.8 *oblique*, 311.4 *curved*
slope off 345.1 *depart*, 591.9 *play truant*
slope up 359.21 *upturn*
sloping 52.80 *linear*, 286.4, 310.8 *oblique*, 311.4 *curved*
slop over 144.5 *be complete*, 347.11 *run out*
sloppily 393.27 *slimily*, 470.7 *negligently*, 685.7 *incompletely*,

720.15 *inattentively*
sloppiness 151.3 *untidiness*, 393.3 *muddiness*, 470.2 *indifference*, 504.2 *inaccuracy*, 555.2 *lack of emphasis*, 685.1 *noncompletion*, 720.1 *nonobservance*
slopping over 144.8 *full*
sloppy 295.31 *styled*, 393.17 *muddy*, 468.10 *careless*, 470.5 *indifferent*, 482.1 *undiscriminating*, 555.1 *unemphatic*, 685.4 *uncompleted*, 720.11 *nonobservant*, 759.12 *sensitive*, 826.9 *endearing*
sloppy joe 295.13 *sweater*
sloppy sweater 307.2 *shapeless thing*
sloppy thinking 504.4 *faulty reasoning*
slops 238.5 *weak thing*, 295.1 *dress*, 393.7 *soup*, 622.5 *swill*
slosh 96.6 *river flow*, 96.7 *flow*, 391.14 *sprinkle*, 393.13 *mud*, 622.5 *swill*
sloshed 874.3 *dead drunk*
sloshiness 393.3 *muddiness*
sloshy 393.17 *muddy*
slot 31.3 *ice hockey*, 136.3 *separateness*, 152.6 *category*, 163.2 *class*, 265.2, 265.5 *crack*, 321.1, 321.6 *furrow*, 322.1 *opening*, 322.20 *hole*
slot formation 19.7 *offence*
sloth 77 Placental Mammals, **161** Collective Names for Birds and Animals, 99.9 *mere existence*, 240.1 *inertness*, 328.8 *slowness*, 328.14 *slow creature*, 328.15 *slow person*, 643.7 *idleness*, 864.5 *seven deadly sins*
sloth bear 77 Placental Mammals
slothful 99.16 *vegetating*, 240.5 *inert*, 328.5 *unhurried*, 643.3 *not participating*
slothfully 643.16 *impassively*
slothfulness 643.7 *idleness*
slot machine 741.21 *till*
slotted 321.4 *furrowed*
slouch 276.8 *be low*, 328.10 *slow motion*, 360.10 *droop*, 643.12 *be inactive*
sloucher 328.15 *slow person*
slouch hat 295.15 *headgear*
slouching 328.4 *slow*
slough 98.3 *marsh*, 132.2 *residue*, 296.16 *peel*, 353.12 *dead tissue*, 353.23 *cast*, 393.13 *mud*, 598.1 *relinquish*, 600.6 *stop using*, 622.4 *dirt*, 622.5 *swill*, 727.8 *sink*
Slough of Despond 770.2 *depression*
slough off 294.12 *shed*, 585.5 *disaccustom*, 598.1 *relinquish*
sloughy 296.12 *peeling*
Slovak 5 Languages and Groups of Languages
Slovakia 91 Countries
sloven 151.10 *slattern*, 470.3 *negligent person*, 622.6 *dirty person*
Slovene 5 Languages and Groups of Languages
Slovenia 91 Countries
slovenliness 151.3 *untidiness*, 470.2 *indifference*, 622.1 *dirtiness*
slovenly 151.15 *untidy*, 470.5 *indifferent*, 555.1 *unemphatic*, 622.7 *dirty*, 656.3 *clumsy*
slovenly person 626.3 *unhygienic person*
slow 328, 325.9 *bowls*, 27.13 *bowling*, 57.38 *reactive*, 209.9 *late*, 238.10 *ill*, 240.5 *inert*, 268.15 *deliberate*, 324.17 *directional*, 328.3 *slow down*, 328.16 *slowly*, 381.3 *dull*, 460.5 *lacking intellect*, 466.4 *uninterested*, 502.6 *ignorant*, 508.5 *foolish*, 595.1 *unprepared*, 643.3 *not participating*, 645.7 *leisurely*, 649.4 *at ease*, 699.8 *restrain*, 699.13 *restraining*, 781.1 *cautious*, 788.4 *boring*
slow as death 328.4 *slow*

slow-as-slow 328.4 *slow*
slow bowler 27.4 *team*
slow burn 828.1 *resentment*
slow-changing 121.7 *gradational*
slow clock 328.13 *slow thing*
slowcoach 209.4 *latecomer*, 328.15 *slow person*
slow creature 328
slow delivery 27.8 *delivery*
slow development 209.1 *lateness*
slow down 328, 15.12 *have an industrial dispute*
slowdown 129.1 *decrease*
slow down 129.4 *decrease*, 129.5 *make smaller*, 325.8 *be motionless*
slowdown 328.12 *hesitation*
slow down 628.1 *deteriorate*, 649.2 *take it easy*
slow-down 15.4 *industrial dispute*, 15.10 *unionized*
slowed down 328.7 *delayed*
slow film 66.10 *graininess*
slow-footed 328.4 *slow*
slow foxtrot 46.2 *dance*
slow-goer 328.15 *slow person*
slow green 25.1 *green bowling*
slow handclap 713.3 *gesture of protest*, 852.9 *show of disapproval*
slowing 209.12 *delaying*
slowing down 328.9 *deceleration*, 628.7 *deterioration*, 699.1 *restraint*
slow lane 71.3 *carriageway*
slow learner 209.4 *latecomer*, 683.5 *failing person*
slowly 328, 121.10 *by degrees*, 209.15 *late*, 240.7 *inertly*, 324.18 *in motion*, 699.16 *under restraints*, 788.8 *boringly*
slowly but surely 121.10 *by degrees*
slow motion 324, 328
slow-moving 328.4 *slow*
slowness 328, 121.1 *degree*, 209.1 *lateness*, 238.2 *indecisiveness*, 240.1 *inertness*, 324.9 *slow motion*, 460.1 *lack of intellect*, 466.2 *lack of interest*, 573.13 *dissociation*, 643.7 *idleness*, 656.8 *unskilfulness*, 699.1 *restraint*, 781.1 *caution*, 788.1 *boredom*
Slowness 328
slow off the mark 328.6 *hesitant*
slow-paced 328.4 *slow*
slow person 328
slowpoke 209.4 *latecomer*, 328.15 *slow person*
slow progress 643.7 *idleness*
slow-ranging 121.7 *gradational*
slow reaction 57.14 *chemical reaction*
slow-running 328.4 *slow*
slow start 328.12 *hesitation*
slow starter 209.4 *latecomer*, 328.15 *slow person*, 781.3 *cautious person*
slow thing 328
slow train 72.7 *train*, 328.13 *slow thing*
slow up 328.3 *slow down*
slow wheel 44.6 *ceramic workshop*
slow wicket 27.5 *wicket*
slow-witted 273.3 *thick-witted*, 502.6 *ignorant*
slow worm 79.2 *lizard*
slow-worm 79 Reptiles
slubbed 375.2 *coarse*
sludge 68.13 *fertilizer*, 132.2 *residue*, 391.8 *marsh*, 393.13 *mud*, 622.4 *dirt*
sludgeball 626.3 *unhygienic person*
sludgy 55.55 *cool*, 391.11 *marshy*, 393.17 *muddy*
slug 75 Scientific and Technical Units, **81** Molluscs, 26.11 *do a combat sport*, 69.12 *pests and diseases*, 328.14 *slow creature*, 328.15 *slow person*, 330.3 *hit*, 330.13 *blow*, 338.8 *missile*, 680.13 *ammunition*
slugabed 209.4 *latecomer*
sluggard 209.4 *latecomer*, 325.7

sedentary person, 328.15 *slow person*, 643.8 *nonworker*
sluggardly 328.5 *unhurried*
slugged 26.14 *combat*
slugger 26.4 *boxer*, 674.10 *contender*
slugging 26.2 *boxing*, 26.14 *combat*, 674.7 *boxing*
sluggish 96.10 *fluvial*, 209.9 *late*, 240.5 *inert*, 325.5 *sedentary*, 328.5 *unhurried*, 466.4 *uninterested*, 573.4 *procrastinating*, 641.3 *inactive*, 643.3 *not participating*, 649.4 *at ease*, 761.2 *desensitized*, 783.7 *indifferent*
sluggishly 96.13 *fluently*, 209.15 *late*, 240.7 *inertly*, 325.10 *motionlessly*, 328.16 *slowly*, 643.16 *impassively*, 783.17 *indifferently*
sluggish market 754.2 *declining prices*
sluggishness 240.1 *inertness*, 328.8 *slowness*, 466.2 *lack of interest*, 573.15 *delay*, 643.7 *idleness*, 761.4 *desensitization*, 783.1 *indifference*
slug it out with 674.11 *contend*
sluglike 81.19 *molluscan*
slug pellet 68.14 *pest control*, 69.8 *weedkiller*
sluice 347.7 *outlet*, 389.29 *water*, 621.14 *bathe*
sluicegate 63.24 *water system*
sluiceway 96.2 *channel*
slum 93.7 *city district*, 151.4 *litter*, 256.8 *shelter*, 626.1 *lack of hygiene*, 628.9 *dilapidation*, 727.8 *sink*, 743.7 *beggary*, 790.3 *ugly place*
slumber 240.4 *be inert*, 325.2 *repose*, 325.8 *be motionless*, 643.9, 643.13 *sleep*
slumberer 643.11 *sleeper*
slumbering 325.5 *sedentary*
slumberous 240.5 *inert*, 643.4 *not awake*
slumber party 665.7 *social gathering*
slum-dweller 93.11 *urbanite*, 743.10 *poor person*
slum hustler 612.10 *nonentity*
slumminess 622.1 *dirtiness*
slummy 249.18 *local*, 622.7 *dirty*, 628.13 *dilapidated*, 743.3 *beggarly*
slump 13.2 *economy*, 54.26 *mass movement*, 129.2 *decline*, 129.3 *decreasing thing*, 129.4 *decrease*, 247.1 *infertility*, 337.14 *decline*, 358.3 *fall through*, 358.6 *shortcoming*, 360.2 *sinkage*, 360.10 *droop*, 628.1 *deteriorate*, 628.7 *deterioration*, 643.6 *unemployment*, 687.2 *economic adversity*, 743.6 *insolvency*, 754.2 *declining prices*, 754.12 *be cheap*
slump down 360.10 *droop*
slumping 360.16 *descending*, 754.9 *cheap*
slumping market 687.2 *economic adversity*
slums 249.10 *urban area*
slur 618.10 *poverty*, 670.10 *criticize*, 670.16 *terrorist attack*, 801.1 *disrespect*, 844.9 *dishonour*, 854.4 *aspersion*, 854.13 *vilify*
slur one's words 874.7 *be drunk*
slurp 348.4 *intake*, 348.11 *ingest*, 350.21 *eat*
slurping 348.4 *intake*, 350.1 *eating*
slurred speech 874.10 *drunkenness*
slurry 68.13, 246.3 *fertilizer*
slurry pit 68.10 *farm tool*
slurry scraper 68.10 *farm tool*
slurry tank 68.10 *farm tool*
slurry turbine 68.10 *farm tool*
slush 41.1 *skiing*, 55.30 *snow*, 393.13 *mud*, 409.5 *ice*
slush fund 228.5 *positive stimulus*, 586.10 *bribe*, 710.4 *illegal offer*, 729.2 *gift*, 878.8 *secret money*

slushily 393.27 *slimily*
slushiness 393.3 *muddiness*
slushy 55.55 *cool*, 391.11 *marshy*, 393.17 *muddy*, 393.23 *thawing*
slut 151.10 *slattern*, 470.3 *negligent person*, 622.6 *dirty person*, 877.9 *immoral woman*
slut's wool 384.5 *powder*
sluttish 151.15 *untidy*, 470.5 *indifferent*, 622.7 *dirty*
sluttishly 622.12 *dirtily*
sluttishness 151.3 *untidiness*, 470.2 *indifference*, 622.1 *dirtiness*
sly 474.8 *cunning*, 529.10 *secretive*, 538.19 *dishonest*, 657.4 *cunning*
slyboots 655.5 *expert*, 657.3 *cunning person*
sly looks 821.6 *courtship*
slyly 474.15 *hypocritically*, 657.6 *cunningly*
slyness 474.3, 657.1 *cunning*
SM 51.25 *producer*
smack 74 Sailing Ships and Boats, **161** Collective Names for Birds and Animals, 133.4 *admixture*, 330.3 *hit*, 330.13 *blow*, 332.9 *directly*, 411.9 *taste*, 425.2, 425.6 *crack*, 542.6 *suggestion*, 821.14 *communication of love*, 821.27 *kiss*, 826.1 *endearment*, 826.7 *show endearment for*, 875.6 *drug*, 879.3 *hit*, 879.12 *corporal punishment*
smack-dab 332.9 *directly*
smacker 741.8 *American money*, 741.9 *British money*, 821.14 *communication of love*, 826.1 *endearment*
smacking 879.12 *corporal punishment*
smack in the middle 158.21 *midway*
smack of 114.10 *be similar*, 543.10 *signify*
smack on the lips 821.14 *communication of love*
smack on the wrist 879.1 *punish*, 879.7 *punishment*
small 173, 120.6 *quantitative*, 127.13 *insignificant*, 238.8 *weak*, 238.13 *insufficient*, 260.7 *little*, 612.1 *unimportant*, 612.4 *trivial*, 758.2 *unpleasant*, 806.2 *lowly*
small ad 528.4 *mass communication*, 532.9 *advertisement*
small ads 754.7 *discounter*
small amount 120.2 *certain amount*, 182.1 *few*, 609.8 *insufficiency*
small-animal practice 60.5 *veterinary medicine*
small arms 680.2 *arms*
small beer 124.6 *mediocrity*, 127.6 *inferior*, 612.8 *trifle*, 612.10 *nonentity*
small calorie 75 Scientific and Technical Units
small chance 229.2 *chance*, 486.4 *remote possibility*, 489.4 *improbability*, 589.6 *poor chance*
small change 124.6 *mediocrity*, 223.3 *something in exchange*, 612.8 *trifle*, 612.10 *nonentity*, 741.4 *change*
small circle 52.42 *circle*
small claims court 16.19 *lawcourt*
small consideration 223.1 *exchange*
small eater 350.18 *eater*
smaller 262, 120.6 *quantitative*, 127.13 *insignificant*
smallest 52.75 *equal*, 127.13 *insignificant*
smallest room 256.7 *room*, 727.7 *toilet*
small fault 864.3 *venial sin*
small fragment 143.1 *part*
small frame 274.7 *thinness*
small-framed 274.1 *thin*
small fry 124.6 *mediocrity*, 127.6 *inferior*, 238.4 *weakling*, 260.4 *little person*, 270.5 *short person*, 612.10 *nonentity*

small game 37.5 *game*, 76.1 *animals*, 612.10 *nonentity*
small-game 37.8 *shooting*
small-game hunting 37.2 *hunting*
small gap 272.6 *narrow place*
small group 2.6 *social group*
smallholder 68.15 *agriculturist*, 255.5 *countryman*
smallholding 68.6 *farm*
small holding 725.1 *property*
small hours 205.3 *midnight*, 209.2 *late hour*
smallish 260.7 *little*
smallishness 260.1 *littleness*
small lake 94
small letter 5.15 *type style*
small-lettered 5.41 *lettered*
Small Magellanic Cloud 53 Galaxies
small-minded 481.10 *discriminatory*, 758.2 *unpleasant*
small-mindedly 481.17 *prejudicially*
small-mindedness 481.3 *prejudice*
smallmouth black bass 20.4 *American game fish*
smallness 127.3 *inferior numbers*, 238.1 *weakness*, 260.1 *littleness*, 612.7 *triviality*, 806.8 *lowliness*
small number 182.1 *few*
small office 647.1 *workshop*
small potatoes 124.6 *mediocrity*, 127.6 *inferior*, 612.8 *trifle*, 612.10 *nonentity*
smallpox 624.6 *infection*, 624.13 *skin disease*
small print 485.7 *condition*, 716.2 *basis for negotiations*
small quantity 120.2 *certain amount*, 182.1 *few*, 609.8 *insufficiency*
small risk 589.5 *good chance*
smalls 295.18 *underwear*
small scale 260.1 *littleness*
small-scale 260.7 *little*
small screen 534.21 *television*, 534.22 *television set*
small shot 338.8 *missile*, 680.13 *ammunition*
small slam 423.1 *card game terms*
small stream 96.1 *river*
small talk 565.3 *talk*, 568.2 *chat*
Smalltalk 65 Programming Languages
small things 777 Phobias by Topic
small-time 124.3 *mediocre*, 127.13 *insignificant*, 612.4 *trivial*
small town 124.8 *middle classes*, 249.11 *settlement*
small-town 127.13 *insignificant*, 249.18 *local*
small toy 612.9 *bauble*
smalt 454.5 *blueness*
smaltite 54 Minerals
smaragdite 54 Minerals
smarm 771.15 *humour*, 853.4 *unctuousness*, 853.9 *blarney*
smarmily 376.16 *suavely*, 853.17 *flatteringly*
smarminess 853.4 *unctuousness*
smarmy 376.6 *smooth-mannered*, 771.11 *humouring*, 808.7 *sycophantic*, 853.15 *unctuous*
smart 150.13 *orderly*, 295.30 *dressed up*, 295.31 *styled*, 329.1 *swift*, 380.5 *mentally sharp*, 406.9 *feel pain*, 406.10 *be painful*, 459.10 *intelligent*, 501.8 *knowledgeable*, 507.6 *intelligent*, 558.3 *elegant*, 642.18 *active*, 655.6 *skilful*, 657.4 *cunning*, 764.12 *be painful*, 771.10 *humorous*, 796.7 *fashionable*, 811.26 *ritualistic*, 813.6 *formal*
Smart 48 Poets
smart aleck 459.8 *intellectual person*, 501.6 *knowledgeable person*, 507.4 *intellectual*, 807.12 *impudent person*, 809.7 *vain person*
smart aleck answer 478.1 *answer*
smart-alecky 807.14 *cheeky*, 809.13 *boastful*
smartarse 459.8 *intellectual per-*

son, 501.6 *knowledgeable person*, 507.4 *intellectual*, 507.6 *intelligent*
smart arse 807.12 *impudent person*, 809.7 *vain person*
smart-arsed 807.14 *cheeky*, 809.13 *boastful*
smart card 56.64 *magnetic recording*, 65.3 *computer*, 65.12 *electronic office*, 322.2 *opener*
smart cookie 655.5 *expert*
smart customer 655.5 *expert*
smarten up 150.21 *tidy*, 627.1 *improve*, 629.2 *refurbish*, 791.15 *beautify*, 792.11 *paint and decorate*
smart for it 879.6 *be punished*
smart guy 655.5 *expert*
smarting 406.1 *pain*, 406.5, 764.4 *painful*, 828.15 *resentful*
smartly 295.36 *dressily*, 329.14 *swiftly*, 380.18 *sharply*, 459.15 *intelligently*, 558.5 *elegantly*, 813.12 *formally*
smart money 878.8 *secret money*
smartness 380.13 *mental sharpness*, 507.2 *intelligence*, 657.1 *cunning*, 811.11 *ritual*, 813.1 *formality*
smart pace 329.8 *speed*
smarts 501.4 *intellect*
smart under 828.8 *resent*
smarty pants 459.8 *intellectual person*, 807.12 *impudent person*, 809.7 *vain person*
smarty-pants 501.6 *knowledgeable person*
smash 40.2 *tennis strokes*, 40.12 *badminton terms*, 40.13 *serve*, 136.9 *separate*, 141.4 *deconstruct*, 241.8 *use violence*, 244.4 *ruin*, 244.9 *demolish*, 330.2 *collide*, 330.10 *bat*, 330.12 *collision*, 338.5, 338.23 *throw*, 384.27 *beat*, 406.11 *inflict pain*, 407.3 *press*, 407.11 *touch*, 682.1 *success*, 699.8 *restrain*, 861.17 *good thing*
smash and grab raid 736.3 *theft*
smashed 141.5 *disintegrated*, 874.3 *dead drunk*
smasher 617.8 *exceller*, 789.3 *attractive female*
smash hit 51.11 *theatrical performance*, 617.8 *exceller*, 655.3 *masterpiece*, 682.1 *success*, 861.17 *good thing*
smashing 330.17 *collision*, 330.17 *impelling*, 384.4 *pulverization*, 617.1 *worthy*, 699.1 *restraint*, 786.14 *wonderful*, 861.1 *good*
smash to matchwood 244.9 *demolish*
smash to pieces 141.3 *disintegrate*
smash to smithereens 244.9 *demolish*
smash up 244.9 *demolish*, 330.2 *collide*
smash-up 244.4 *ruin*, 330.12 *collision*
smatter 162.18 *sprinkle*
smattered 162.23 *sprinkled*
smatterer 612.10 *nonentity*
smattering 162.4 *sprinkling*, 501.2 *information*, 542.6 *suggestion*
smattering of knowledge 502.2 *half-knowledge*
smear 34.9 *mountaineer*, 386.14, 395.18 *anoint*, 441.10 *make dim*, 622.4 *dirt*, 622.11 *dirty*, 670.10 *criticize*, 670.16 *terrorist attack*, 793.1 *spot*, 793.7 *blemish*, 854.4 *aspersion*, 854.12 *defame*
smear campaign 854.3 *defamation*
smearer 854.8 *defamer*
smear glaze 44.3 *glaze*
smearing 34.3 *climbing technique*, 854.16 *defamatory*
smear test 59.6 *cell biology*, 60.7 *diagnosis*
smectite 54 Minerals
smeghead 502.5 *ignorant person*

smell 777 Phobias by Topic, **416**, 165.3 *characteristic*, 348.12 *draw in*, 396.4 *biological function*, 403.1 *sensation*, 403.11 *sense*, 416.1 *odour*, 416.8 *have odour*, 419.5 *stink*, 622.10 *be dirty*, 628.2 *decay*
smell a rat 498.8 *disbelieve*
smell at 416.7 *smell*
smell bad 419.5 *stink*
smeller 416.2 *sense of smell*
smell fishy 858.8 *be dishonourable*
smell foul 419.5 *stink*
smellies 791.6 *toiletries*
smellily 419.6 *stinkingly*
smelliness 416.1 *odour*, 419.1 *stench*
smelling 416.2 *sense of smell*, 416.5 *odorous*
smelling bottle 416.2 *sense of smell*
smelling of drink 874.5 *drunken*
smelling salts 413.6 *cordial*, 416.2 *sense of smell*, 630.7 *tonic*
smell-less 417.3 *odourless*
smell like a drain 419.5 *stink*
smell like a flower garden 418.5 *be fragrant*
smell like a midden 419.5 *stink*
smell of 416.8 *have odour*, 543.10 *signify*
smell of drains 419.2 *something that makes an unpleasant smell*
smell of rotten eggs 419.5 *stink*
smell of success 416.4 *reputation*
smell out 416.7 *smell*, 496.2 *detect*
smell powder 676.13 *be at war*
smell sweet 418.5 *be fragrant*
smell trap 417.2 *deodorant*
smelly 416.5 *odorous*, 419.3 *stinking*
smelly feet 419.2 *something that makes an unpleasant smell*
smelt 80 Fishes, 387.24 *melt*, 408.14 *be hot*
smelter 44.6 *ceramic workshop*, 408.6 *fire*, 647.1 *workshop*
Smetana 49 Musicians and Composers
smew 78 Birds
smidgen 133.4 *admixture*, 182.1 *few*, 542.6 *suggestion*
smidgin 143.7 *piece*
smile 543.3, 543.11 *gesture*, 762.7 *show joy*, 769.7 *be cheerful*, 817.5 *sign of courtesy*, 817.12 *greet*
smile on 686.7 *be auspicious*
smiler 769.4 *cheerful person*
smiles of fortune 686.2 *good fortune*
smiling 543.15 *gestural*, 769.1 *cheerful*, 815.15 *sociable*
smiling reception 815.9 *welcome*
Smilodon 77 Placental Mammals
sminthopsis 77 Marsupials
smir 55.25 *rain*
smirch 447.11 *blacken*, 622.11 *dirty*, 854.12 *defame*, 877.19 *corrupt*
smircher 854.8 *defamer*
smite 398.17 *murder*
smite hip and thigh 398.18 *slaughter*
smith 306.7 *form*, 646.2 *artisan*
Smith 4 Philosophers, 18 Sporting Personalities, 18 Poets
smithereens 384.6 *crumb*
Smithfield 68.1 *agriculture*, 740.1 *market*
smithsonite 54 Minerals, 57 Common Metal Ores
smithy 647.1 *workshop*
smitten 821.18 *in love*, 821.19 *enamoured*
smock 262.5 *make smaller*, 295.8 *shirt*, 295.18 *underwear*, 792.10 *decorate*
smocked 262.7 *smaller*
smocker 792.7 *decorator*
smocking 792.2 *pattern*
smog 55.33 *fog*, 384.5 *powder*, 388.3 *miasma*, 441.2 *murk*, 626.1 *lack of hygiene*, 631.9 *pol-*

lution
smoggy 55.56 *foggy*, 388.19 *smoky*, 441.6 *murky*
smog-laden 441.6 *murky*
smoke 77 Breeds of Cats, **413**, 57.3 *phase*, 349.14 *let out*, 388.3 *miasma*, 388.27 *give off*, 392.17 *dry*, 408.6 *fire*, 408.15 *burn*, 413.12 *season*, 416.1 *odour*, 436.6 *blinder*, 438.6 *that which makes invisible*, 441.2 *murk*, 442.8 *transparent thing*, 443.7 *opaque thing*, 443.11 *make opaque*, 527.12 *be latent*, 594.7 *develop*, 622.4 *dirt*, 626.1 *lack of hygiene*, 631.9 *pollution*, 637.5 *preserve*, 828.11 *be angry*, 875.10 *drug oneself*
smoke alarm 632.4 *safety device*
smoke a pipe 413.14 *smoke*
smoke blue 454.1 *blue*
smoke cigarettes 413.14 *smoke*
smoke cigars 413.14 *smoke*
smoked 413.9 *piquant*, 441.6 *murky*, 442.3 *semitransparent*, 443.2 *shady*, 637.7 *preserved*
smoked bacon 45.30 *bacon*
smoked fish 45.16 *fish dish*, 80.8 *food fish*
smoked glass 440.6 *shade*, 441.2 *murk*
smoked haddock 45.16 *fish dish*, 80.8 *food fish*
smoked mackerel 45.16 *fish dish*
smoke-dry 392.17 *dry*
smoked salmon 45.16 *fish dish*, 45.44 *British dish*
smoked trout 45.16 *fish dish*
smoke-filled 441.6 *murky*, 626.5 *unhygienic*
smoke-free 413.11 *tobacco*, 417.3 *odourless*
smoke-free area 413.8 *smoking*
smoke-free zone 417.1 *odourlessness*
smokehole 322.7 *passageway*
smokehouse 68.7 *farm building*
smoke-laden 441.6 *murky*
smokeless 417.3 *odourless*
smokeless area 625.2 *salubrity*
smokeless zone 417.1 *odourlessness*
smoke out 349.7 *drive out*, 355.12 *displace*
smoker 413.8 *smoking*, 665.7 *social gathering*, 695.5 *compulsive person*, 815.5 *party*
smoker's cough 413.8 *smoking*, 624.9 *respiratory disease*
smoker's requisites 413.8 *smoking*
smoke screen 293.2 *cover*
smokescreen 436.6 *blinder*, 438.6 *that which makes invisible*, 443.7 *opaque thing*
smoke screen 531.3 *covering up*, 539.12 *disguise*, 657.2 *stratagem*
smokescreen 671.10 *shelter*
smoke signal 543.4 *signal*
smoke signals 421.1 *deafness*, 534.27 *signalling*
smokestack 275.6 *tall thing*, 322.7 *passageway*
smoke the peace pipe 675.5 *be at peace*, 677.5 *make peace*, 839.9 *forgive*
smoke tree 85 Trees and Shrubs
Smokey 688.10 *person of authority*, 718.3 *security officer*
Smokey Bear 16.17 *police officer*
smokily 388, 442.13 *transparently*, 448.9 *greyly*
smokiness 413.1 *piquancy*, 442.7 *semitransparency*
smoking **413**, 44.5 *ceramic process*, 45.8 *cooking technique*, 388.10 *vaporization*, 388.19 *smoky*, 408.9 *hot*, 413.3 *curing*, 413.11 *tobacco*, 637.1 *preservation*, 875.1 *drug-taking*
smoking area 413.8 *smoking*
smoking compartment 413.8 *smoking*
smoking jacket 295.4, 811.6 *informal dress*
smoking-related 413.11 *tobacco*
smoking-room story 877.2 *inde-*

cency

smoky 388, 45.16 *fish dish,*
371.7 *condensed,* 413.9 *pi-*
quant, 441.6 *murky,* 442.3 *semi-*
transparent, 443.2 *shady,* 447.2
dark, 448.1 *grey,* 622.7 *dirty,*
626.5 *unhygienic*

Smoky 95 Mountains

Smoky Mountains 95.4 *US moun-*
tains

Smolensk 93 Cities

Smollett 48 Writers

smolt 80.3 *young fish*

smooch 821.27 *kiss,* 826.7 *show*
endearment for

smooching 821.6 *courtship,*
821.14 *communication of love,*
826.1 *endearment*

smoodge 821.27 *kiss,* 826.1 *en-*
dearment, 826.7 *show endear-*
ment for

smoodging 821.6 *courtship,*
821.14 *communication of love*

smooth 374, 376, 376, 383,
383, 386, 25.9 *bowls,* 40.5
real tennis, 110.8 *make the*
same, 110.17 *regular,* 112.5 *uni-*
form, 112.9 *be uniform,* 122.11
equalize, 139.8 *nonadhesive,*
150.13 *orderly,* 150.21, 152.19
tidy, 159.11 *continuous,* 242.8
moderating, 282.7 *make horizon-*
tal, 282.8 *horizontal,* 296.13
hairless, 315.11 *make round,*
325.6 *quiescent,* 327.15 *accessi-*
ble, 381.1, 381.10 *blunt,*
385.12 *rub,* 385.16 *massage,*
395.11 *oily,* 395.17 *oil,* 405.6,
414.7 *pleasant,* 433.6 *melodi-*
ous, 539.34 *deceiving,* 555.1 *un-*
emphatic, 558.3 *elegant,* 660.9
easy, 660.16 *make easy,* 817.8
good-mannered

smooth as a baby's bottom
376.5 *smooth as a peach*

smooth as a peach 376

smooth as glass 376.5 *smooth as*
a peach

smooth as marble 376.5 *smooth*
as a peach

smooth as satin 376.5 *smooth as*
a peach

smooth as velvet 376.5 *smooth*
as a peach

smoothbore 680.9 *firearm*

smooth delivery 25.2 *grip*

smooth down 282.7 *make hori-*
zontal, 376.11 *smooth*

smoothed 282.9 *flattened,* 376.1
smooth, 381.1 *blunt*

smoothen 282.7 *make horizon-*
tal, 376.11 *smooth*

smooth endoplasmic reticulum
59.8 *cell organ*

smoothened 282.9 *flattened*

smoother 376

smooth-faced 294.9 *shed,* 296.13
hairless

smooth-haired 376.1 *smooth*

smoothie 657.3 *cunning person,*
808.3 *sycophant*

smoothing 376.1 *smooth,* 385.5
polishing, 660.7 *easing*

smoothing iron 376.9 *smoother*

smoothing plane 47.11 *wood-*
working tool

smoothly 376, 381, 110.20 *regu-*
larly, 112.13 *uniformly,* 282.11
horizontally, 325.10 *motion-*
lessly, 374.17 *softly,* 383.15 *tex-*
turally, 395.20 *oilily,* 414.9
sweetly, 558.5 *elegantly,* 660.21
easily, 817.15 *genteelly*

smooth-mannered 376

smoothness 374, 376, 395,
660, 110.6 *regularity,* 112.1
uniformity, 150.5 *orderliness,*
282.1 *horizontality,* 381.5 *blunt-*
ness, 383.2 *grain,* 386.1 *lubrica-*
tion, 405.1 *physical pleasure,*
414.1 *sweetness,* 558.1 *ele-*
gance, 657.1 *cunning,* 817.1
courtesy

Smoothness 376

smooth one's ruffled feathers
677.4 *pacify*

smooth out 124.10 *make aver-*

age, 282.7 *make horizontal,*
312.10 *straighten,* 374.13
soften, 376.11, 383.13 *smooth*

smooth over 376, 242.4 *moder-*
ate, 386.15 *ease,* 677.4 *pacify*

smooth over the differences
482.11 *not discriminate*

smooth road 660.6 *easy thing*

smooth-running 386.8, 395.16 *lu-*
bricated, 660.12 *wieldy*

smooth-shaven 294.9 *shed,*
296.13 *hairless*

smooth-skinned 376.1 *smooth*

smooth snake 79 Reptiles

smooth-spoken 376.6 *smooth-*
mannered, 853.13 *honeyed*

smooth surface 376.7 *smoothness*

smooth-surfaced 376.1 *smooth*

smooth talker 657.3 *cunning per-*
son, 853.6 *flatterer*

smooth-talker 564.10 *speaker*

smooth-talking 564.20 *eloquent*

smooth texture 376.7 *smoothness*

smooth-textured 376.1 *smooth*

smooth the way 386.15 *ease,*
395.17 *oil,* 660.16 *make easy*

smooth the way for 488.9 *make*
probable

smooth thing 376

smooth-tongued 853.13 *honeyed*

smooth water 376.8 *smooth thing*

smorgasbord 45.12 *hors*
d'oeuvre, 161.32 *miscellany*

smother 38.4 *play soccer,* 236.8
overpower, 244.8 *destroy,*
398.17 *murder,* 422.2 *silence,*
531.8 *conceal,* 699.8 *restrain,*
826.7 *show endearment for*

smothered 428.2 *nonresonant,*
531.14 *concealed*

smothering 777 Phobias by
Topic, 244.1 *destruction,* 699.1
restraint

smoulder 240.4 *be inert,* 408.15
burn, 527.12 *be latent,* 828.11
be angry, 830.11 *be irritable*

smouldering 240.5 *inert,* 325.5
sedentary, 408.9 *hot,* 828.16
angry, 830.7 *irritable*

smriti 7.12 *religious text*

smudge 447.11 *blacken,* 620.7
defect, 622.4 *dirt,* 622.11 *dirty,*
793.1 *spot,* 793.7 *blemish*

smudged 622.7 *dirty*

smudgy 447.2 *dark*

smug 765.4 *satisfied,* 805.17
conceited, 809.9 *self-satisfied,*
809.10 *self-admiring,* 817.9 *def-*
erential, 876.10 *moralistic*

smuggle 737.1 *trade,* 858.10 *be*
criminal

smuggled 16.59 *stolen*

smuggler 737.10 *trader*

smuggling 737.4 *trade*

smugly 809

smugness 765.1 *satisfaction,*
809.2 *self-satisfaction,* 876.4
self-righteousness

smur 793.3 *blot on the landscape*

smut 89 Fungi, 384.5 *powder,*
440.4 *dark thing,* 447.9 *black*
thing, 622.4 *dirt,* 877.2 *inde-*
cency

smuts 89.3 *fungi*

smuttiness 622.3 *obscenity*

smutty 454.4 *indecent,* 622.9 *ob-*
scene, 795.9 *ribald,* 877.12 *inde-*
cent

snack 45, 350.12 *meal,* 350.24
have a meal, 651.7 *refreshments*

snack bar 350.15 *eating place*

snacking 350.4 *eating meals*

snacks 350.7 *food*

snaffle 736.12 *steal*

snafu 151.6 *mix-up,* 151.19
mixed-up, 659.5 *predicament,*
661.8 *hinder*

snag 659, 85.2 *tree part,* 620.7
defect, 633.5 *danger,* 635.1 *trap,*
661.2 *obstacle,* 661.9 *block*

snagged 375.2 *coarse,* 380.4
toothed

snaggled 375.2 *coarse*

snaggletooth 380.11 *tooth*

snaggle-toothed 380.4 *toothed*

snaggy 375.2 *coarse,* 380.4
toothed, 633.1 *dangerous*

snail 81 Molluscs, 45.19 *shell-*
fish, 69.12 *pests and diseases,*
328.14 *slow creature,* 328.15
slow person

snail-like 81.19 *molluscan,*
328.4 *slow*

snail-paced 328.4 *slow*

snail shell 293.14 *animal cover-*
ing

snailshell 314.3 *convoluted thing*

snail's pace 328.10 *slow motion*

snake 79 Reptiles, **79,** 14.1 *fi-*
nance, 314.3 *convoluted thing,*
314.6 *convolute,* 335.5 *twist,*
339.12 *drag,* 429.3 *hisser,*
539.21 *traitor,* 631.6 *source of*
trouble, 657.3 *cunning person,*
832.8 *malefactor,* 864.9 *wicked*
person

Snake 96 Rivers

snake and mongoose 679.4 *fight-*
ing animal

snakebird 78 Birds

snakebite 351.8 *mixed drink*

snake charmer 51.29 *circus per-*
former, 79.10 *herpetologist*

snake eyes 42.5 *dice*

snakefly 82 Insects

snake in the grass 527.7 *latent*
things, 539.21 *traitor,* 618.12
bad person, 631.6 *source of trou-*
ble, 635.2 *troublemaker,* 657.3
cunning person, 661.7 *hinderer,*
832.8 *malefactor,* 858.4 *dis-*
honourable person, 862.6 *evil*
person, 864.9 *wicked person*

snakelike 79, 79.11 *reptilian*

snake-necked turtle 79 Reptiles

snake pit 634.3 *animal shelter*

snakeroot 84 Flowers and Flowering Plants

snakes 777 Phobias by Topic

snakes and ladders 42 Board
Games, **42** Children's Games
and Party Games

snake's head 84 Flowers and
Flowering Plants

snake worship 9.2 *idolatry*

snake worshipper 9.6 *idolater*

snake-worshipping 9.10 *idola-*
trous

snaking 96.10 *fluvial,* 335.21 *in-*
direct

snaky 79.12 *snakelike*

snap 42 Card Games, 19.8 *hud-*
dle, 66.3, 66.21 *photograph,*
136.9 *separate,* 137.11 *connect,*
239.1 *vigour,* 338.23 *throw,*
377.1 *elasticity,* 377.8 *be elas-*
tic, 379.4 *be brittle,* 425.2,
425.6 *crack,* 432.1 *animal cry,*
432.4 *cry,* 543.11 *gesture,* 547.9
represent, 564.13 *speak in a par-*
ticular way, 583.2, 595.2 *spon-*
taneous, 660.6 *easy thing,*
828.6 *sign of anger,* 828.11 *be*
angry, 829.2 *sign of irascibility,*
830.4 *sign of irritableness,*
830.11 *be irritable*

snap answer 595.8 *lack of prepa-*
ration

snap at 828.13 *vent one's anger,*
829.6 *be irascible*

snap back 331.2 *respond*

snapback 377.1 *elasticity*

snap back 377.8 *be elastic*

snap count 19.8 *huddle*

snap decision 583.5 *spontaneity*

snapdragon 84 Flowers and
Flowering Plants

snaplink 34.4 *climbing equipment*

snap off 379.4 *be brittle*

snap of the fingers 612.7 *trivial-*
ity

snap one's fingers at 612.12
think unimportant, 668.6 *be in-*
subordinate, 693.15 *be disobedi-*
ent, 720.7 *not observe,* 807.29
ridicule

snap one's head off 829.6 *be ir-*
ascible

snap out of it 629.4 *be restored,*
651.2 *be refreshed*

snapper 80 Fishes, 20.4 *Ameri-*
can game fish

snappily 329.14 *swiftly,* 811.35
flashily

snapping 117.10 *disagreeing,*
377.6 *elastic,* 828.16 *angry,*
830.7 *irritable*

snapping turtle 79 Reptiles

snappish 829.4 *irascible,* 830.7
irritable

snappishness 828.4 *anger*

snappy 239.4 *vigorous,* 329.1
swift, 811.19 *flashy,* 818.5 *dis-*
courteous, 829.4 *irascible*

snappy dresser 295.27 *model,*
796.5 *fashion model*

snappy pace 329.8 *speed*

snap ring 34.4 *climbing equip-*
ment

snap roll 73.5 *flight*

snaps 137.8 *fastening*

snapshot 66.3 *photograph,* 545.1
record

snap up 350.22 *eat well,* 738.1
purchase, 872.5 *be greedy*

snare 539, 539, 68.14 *pest con-*
trol, 340.5 *lure,* 635.1, 635.3
trap

snared 539.42 *trapped*

snark 76.7 *legendary beast*

snarl 151.7 *tangle,* 151.24 *make*
disordered, 309.2 *facial distor-*
tion, 309.10 *make faces,* 432.1
animal cry, 432.4 *cry,* 564.13
speak in a particular way, 659.5
predicament, 828.6 *sign of*
anger, 828.11 *be angry,* 829.2
sign of irascibility, 829.7 *frown,*
830.4 *sign of irritableness,*
830.11 *be irritable*

snarled-up 151.19 *mixed-up*

snarling 829.5 *showing irascibil-*
ity, 830.7 *irritable*

snarling dog 633.6 *danger signal*

snarl up 151.23 *confuse*

snarl-up 151.6 *mix-up,* 659.5 *pre-*
dicament

snatch 339.3 *jerk,* 339.13 *pull*
at, 407.11 *touch,* 734.7 *take,*
736.3 *theft,* 736.12 *steal,*
767.14 *take away*

snatch a bag 736.12 *steal*

snatch a purse 736.12 *steal*

snatch at 339.13 *pull at,* 590.10
chase

snatch block 36.3 *parts of a sail-*
ing boat

snatcher 734.6 *taker*

snatch from the grave 629.6 *cure*

snatch from the jaws of death
639.1 *deliver*

snatch from under one's nose
657.5 *be cunning*

snatching 734.1 *taking,* 736.1
stealing

snazzily 295.36 *dressily,* 811.35
flashily

snazzy 295.31 *styled,* 796.7
fashionable, 811.19 *flashy*

sneak 19.15 *play offence,* 539.23
deceive, 540.19 *be deceitful,*
779.4 *be a coward*

sneak after 590.9 *follow*

sneakers 23.3 *basketball equip-*
ment, 30.2 *gymnastic clothing,*
295.19 *footwear*

sneakily 474.15 *hypocritically*

sneak in 346.11 *infiltrate*

sneakiness 474.3 *cunning,* 539.1
deception, 540.5 *deceitfulness*

sneaking 808.7 *sycophantic*

sneaking around 538.20 *unfaith-*
ful

sneaking suspicion 518.2 *basis*
of supposition

sneak off 591.8 *run away,* 638.5
escape

sneak off with 736.12 *steal*

sneak out 254.16 *absent oneself,*
638.5 *escape*

sneak thief 736.8 *thief*

sneaky 474.8 *cunning,* 539.34
deceiving, 540.29 *deceitful*

sneck 135.5 *joint*

sneer 309.2 *facial distortion,*
309.10 *make faces,* 807.6 *con-*
tempt, 807.29 *ridicule,* 850.6,
850.25 *taunt,* 852.9 *show of dis-*
approval, 854.14 *ridicule*

sneer at 785.6 *react against*

sneered at 852.35 *hissed*
sneering 807.6 *contempt*, 807.17 *contemptuous*, 850.15 *taunting*, 854.17 *scornful*
sneeringly 807.34 *contemptuously*
sneeze 429.1, 429.4 *hiss*
sneeze at 581.3 *exclude*
sneezer 702.2 *the inside*
sneezewood 85 Trees and Shrubs
sneezing 429.1 *hiss*, 429.6 *hissing*
snick 27.9 *stroke*, 27.17 *bat*
snicker 771.14 *laugh*
snickersnee 680.8 *sharp weapon*
snide 618.5 *harmful*, 741.15 *false money*, 832.14 *hostile*, 854.16 *defamatory*
snideness 832.4 *bitterness*
sniff 348.4 *intake*, 348.12 *draw in*, 416.2 *sense of smell*, 416.7 *smell*, 850.6, 850.25 *taunt*
sniff at 350.23 *taste*, 416.7 *smell*, 581.3 *exclude*, 785.6 *react against*
sniffer dog 77.9 *dog*, 416.2 *sense of smell*, 496.12 *discoverer*, 632.3 *protector*
sniffing 348.4 *intake*, 416.2 *sense of smell*, 875.1 *drug-taking*
sniffle 348.4 *intake*, 348.12 *draw in*, 416.2 *sense of smell*, 416.7 *smell*
sniffly 624.23 *diseased*
sniff out 416.7 *smell*, 465.7 *be curious*, 496.2 *detect*, 590.9 *follow*
snifter 351.2, 874.13 *drink*
snigger 431.2 *cry of joy*, 431.11, 771.14 *laugh*, 771.3 *laughter*
snigger about 799.6 *deride*
sniggle 539.13, 539.33 *snare*
snip 143.7 *piece*, 260.4 *little person*, 754.4 *bargain*
snipe 78 Birds, **338**, 45.20 *meat*, 78.3 *water bird*, 78.4 *table bird*
snipe at 670.2 *fire*, 852.17 *criticize*
sniper 338.15 *shooter*, 670.19 *attacker*, 679.8 *soldier*
sniping 670.15 *firing*, 670.16 *terrorist attack*, 676.8 *warfare*
snippet 143.7 *piece*, 260.3 *little piece*
snippets 133.3 *miscellany*
snipsnapsnorum 42 Card Games
snitch 528.10 *informer*, 528.13 *inform on*, 736.12 *steal*, 856.3 *accuser*, 856.5 *accuse*
snitcher 856.3 *accuser*
snitching 736.1 *stealing*
snivel 774.7 *weep*
sniveller 774.3 *lamenter*
snivelling 808.7 *sycophantic*
snob 805.13 *proud person*
snobbery 794.3 *etiquette*, 805.3 *conceit*
snobbish 493.8 *unjust*, 805.17 *conceited*, 850.13 *contemptuous*
SNOBOL 65 Programming Languages
Sno-Cat 71.10 *sled*
snog 826.7 *show endearment for*
snood 295.15 *headgear*
snook 80 Fishes, 20.4 *American game fish*, 807.7 *insult*, 850.7 *sign of disrespect*
snooker 18 Sporting Activities, **24**, 659.23 *cause difficulties*, 661.8 *hinder*
snookered 24.9 *billiard*, 659.16 *troubled*
snooker player 24.7 *billiards player*
snooker table 24.5 *snooker*
snookums 821.12 *nicknames for lovers*
snoop 465.4 *meddler*, 465.7 *be curious*
snooping 465.2, 465.6 *prying*
snoopy 465.6 *prying*
snoot 318.3 *protuberance*, 416.2 *sense of smell*
snooty 805.17 *conceited*, 809.8 *vain*, 850.13 *contemptuous*

snooze 240.4 *be inert*, 404.2 *unconsciousness*, 643.9, 643.13 *sleep*, 649.1 *ease*, 649.2 *take it easy*
snore 423.8 *be loud*, 430.2 *hoarseness*, 430.5 *sound hoarse*
snoring 423.1 *loudness*, 430.8 *hoarse*
snorkel 39.1 *swimming*, 39.9 *swim*
snorkeler 39.4 *swimmer*
snorkeling 39.1 *swimming*
snorkelling 18 Sporting Activities
snort 430.2 *hoarseness*, 430.5 *sound hoarse*, 432.4 *cry*, 807.29 *ridicule*, 830.4 *sign of irritableness*, 850.6, 850.25 *taunt*, 874.13 *drink*, 875.6 *drug*, 875.10 *drug oneself*
snorting 430.8 *hoarse*, 650.3 *panting*, 875.1 *drug-taking*
snot 353.9 *saliva*, 387.3 *body fluid*, 394.5 *mucus*, 622.4 *dirt*
snotty 393.22 *mucilaginous*, 850.13 *contemptuous*
snout 54.38 *glacier*, 318.3 *protuberance*, 416.2 *sense of smell*, 480.7 *verifier*, 483.7 *person who gives evidence*
snout beetle 82 Insects
snow 777 Phobias by Topic, **55, 55**, 55.24 *precipitation*, 360.13 *drip*, 374.11 *soft thing*, 409.5 *ice*, 438.6 *that which makes invisible*, 446.9 *white thing*, 534.23 *television reception*, 539.28 *trick*, 608.5 *about*, 875.4 *drug*
snow and ice climbing 34.1 *mountaineering*
snowball 46.2 *dance*, 128.3 *increasing thing*, 128.4 *increase*, 261.6 *become bigger*, 338.10 *ball*, 338.23 *throw*, 351.8 *mixed drink*, 409.5 *ice*, 721.10 *augment*
snowball effect 159.4 *repercussion*
snowballer 338.14 *thrower*
snowballing 128.6 *increasing*, 261.8 *growing*
snowballing effect 128.1 *increase*
snowball's chance in hell 589.6 *poor chance*
snowball tree 85 Trees and Shrubs
snow bed 55.30 *snow*
snow-blind 436.8 *blind*, 436.10 *blinded*
snow-blinded 436.10 *blinded*
snow blindness 436.1 *blindness*
snowboard 71.10 *sled*
snow bollard belay 34.3 *climbing technique*
snowbound 409.8 *cold*, 699.15 *detained*
snow bunting 78 Birds
snow-capped 95.7 *mountainous*, 446.2 *whitened*
snow-capped mountain 95.1 *mountain*
snow-clad 55.55 *cool*, 95.7 *mountainous*
snow-clad peak 95.1 *mountain*
snow cover 55.30 *snow*
snow-covered 55.55 *cool*, 446.2 *whitened*
snow crystal 409.5 *ice*
Snowdon 95 Mountains, 95.5 *British mountains*
Snowdonia 95.5 *British mountains*, 275.4 *mountain range*
snowdrift 55.30 *snow*, 161.26 *mass*, 409.5 *ice*
snowdrop 84 Flowers and Flowering Plants
snowdrop tree 85 Trees and Shrubs
snowed in 409.8 *cold*
snowed under 597.7 *overambitious*
snowfall 55.24 *precipitation*, 55.30 *snow*, 409.5 *ice*
snowflake 55.24 *precipitation*, 370.7 *light thing*, 374.11 *soft thing*, 384.6 *crumb*, 409.5 *ice*
snow flurry 409.5 *ice*

snow-forest climate 55.38 *climate*
snowglasses 34.4 *climbing equipment*
snow goose 78 Birds
snow house 409.6 *Arctic*
snowily 55.65 *meteorologically*
snowiness 446.7 *whiteness*
snow job 539.7 *tricking*
snow leopard 77 Placental Mammals
snowline 409.6 *Arctic*
snowman 379.3 *brittle thing*, 409.5 *ice*, 547.6 *image*
snowmobile 71 Motor Vehicles, 71.10 *sled*
snow-on-the-mountain 84 Flowers and Flowering Plants
snowplough 71 Motor Vehicles, 41.4 *skiing technique*, 41.12, 41.14 *ski*, 621.10 *cleaning object*
snowplough brake 41.2 *cross-country skiing*
snowplough glide 41.2 *cross-country skiing*
snowploughing 41.4 *skiing technique*, 41.12 *ski*
snowplough turn 41.2 *cross-country skiing*, 41.4 *skiing technique*
snowplough wedeln 41.4 *skiing technique*
Snow Queen 409.5 *ice*
snow season 203.1 *season*
snow shed 72.8 *railway station*
snowshoe hare 77 Placental Mammals
snowshoes 295.19 *footwear*
snow shower 55.30 *snow*
snow ski 41.14 *ski*
snow-skiing 41.1 *skiing*
snowslide 360.3 *downflow*
snowslip 360.3 *downflow*
snow storm 55.30 *snow*
snowstorm 241.5 *violent weather*, 409.5 *ice*
snow suit 601.2 *shelter*
snow under 181.12 *overcrowd*
snow-white 134.14 *purified*, 446.1 *white*
snowy 55.55 *cool*, 134.14 *purified*, 409.8 *cold*, 446.1 *white*, 621.16 *clean*, 876.9 *pure*
Snowy 95 Mountains
snowy owl 78 Birds
snowy picture 534.23 *television reception*
snub 74 Rigging, 270.7 *short*, 341.1 *repel*, 341.6 *repulse*, 349.4 *ostracize*, 362.4 *debase*, 381.1 *blunt*, 581.3 *exclude*, 581.5 *rejection*, 591.1 *avoid*, 591.10 *avoidance*, 711.6 *dissent*, 766.2 *expression of dissatisfaction*, 806.17 *humiliate*, 816.13 *ignore*, 818.3 *act of discourtesy*, 818.7 *be discourteous*, 850.5, 850.23 *insult*
snubbed 581.10 *rejected*
snubbing 850.11 *insulting*
snubness 270.1 *shortness*
snub-nosed 270.7 *short*
snuff 348.4 *intake*, 348.12 *draw in*, 398.16 *kill*, 413.7 *tobacco*, 416.7 *smell*, 440.14 *make dark*
snuff box 258.6 *box*
snuffbox 413.7 *tobacco*
snuff-coloured 449.1 *brown*
snuff it 100.13 *cease to exist*, 397.15 *die*
snuffle 348.4 *intake*, 348.12 *draw in*, 416.7 *smell*, 429.4 *hiss*
snuffler 416.2 *sense of smell*, 539.19 *hypocrite*
snuffly 624.23 *diseased*
snuff movie 877.2 *indecency*
snuff out 100.14 *cause not to exist*, 244.8 *destroy*, 440.14 *make dark*
snuff out like a candle 397.16 *meet one's fate*
snug 256.7 *room*, 260.7 *little*, 392.10 *waterproof*, 405.6 *pleasant*, 405.7 *pleased*, 408.9 *hot*, 632.5 *safe*, 632.6 *invulnerable*, 649.4 *at ease*, 763.3 *comfortable*
snug as a bug in a rug 405.7 *pleased*
snuggery 256.5 *house*, 256.7

room, 258.2 *compartment*, 405.4 *pleasurable things*
snuggle 405.8 *feel pleasure*, 821.27 *kiss*, 826.7 *show endearment for*
snuggling 821.14 *communication of love*
snugness 260.1 *littleness*
so 106.15 *under the circumstances*, 114.13 *similarly*, 116.36 *accordingly*, 327.16 *how*
soak 114.6 *fill*, 253.11 *be present*, 348.13 *absorb*, 355.17 *obtain an extract*, 389.9 *soaking*, 389.29 *water*, 621.14 *bathe*, 753.10 *overcharge*, 874.8 *get drunk*
soakage 389.9 *soaking*
soakaway 727.8 *sink*
soaked 389.23 *wet*, 584.13 *fixed*, 610.6 *excessive*, 874.3 *dead drunk*
soaked to the skin 389.23 *wet*
soaker 874.17 *drunkard*
soak in 346.11 *infiltrate*, 348.13 *absorb*, 360.9 *descend*
soaking 389, 44.5 *ceramic process*, 348.17 *absorbent*, 351.1 *drinking*, 355.7 *obtaining an extract*, 621.5 *ablutions*, 874.11 *drinking*
soaking wet 389.23 *wet*
soak through 356.10 *enter*
soak up 140.5 *combine*, 348.13 *absorb*, 351.13 *drink*, 392.20 *absorb*
so and so 400.7 *person*
soap 57 Types of Compounds, 51.2 *play*, 134.3 *purifier*, 374.11 *soft thing*, 386.4 *lubricant*, 386.13 *lubricate*, 395.5 *lubricant*, 395.8 *fat*, 395.17 *oil*, 534.25 *broadcast material*, 560.3 *narration*, 621.9 *cleaning agent*, 621.14 *bathe*
soap and water 134.3 *purifier*, 389.11 *wash*, 621.9 *cleaning agent*
soapbark 85 Trees and Shrubs
soapbox 51.15 *stage*, 532.7 *publicity*
soapbox orator 567.6 *public speaker*, 693.8 *agitator*
soap-box orator 564.10 *speaker*
soap-box oratory 564.9 *art of public speaking*
soapflakes 134.3 *purifier*, 395.8 *fat*
soap flakes 621.9 *cleaning agent*
soapily 386.16, 395.20 *oilily*
soapiness 386.2, 395.1 *oiliness*
soaping 621.5 *ablutions*
soap opera 51.2 *play*, 155.4 *sequel*, 534.25 *broadcast material*, 560.3 *narration*
soap pad 621.9 *cleaning agent*
soap powder 395.8 *fat*, 621.9 *cleaning agent*
soap the ways 386.15 *ease*, 395.17 *oil*, 660.16 *make easy*
soapwort 84 Flowers and Flowering Plants
soapy 376.4 *polished*, 386.10, 395.11 *oily*, 446.2 *whitened*, 808.7 *sycophantic*, 817.9 *deferential*
soar 78.27 *fly*, 95.9 *tower*, 128.4 *increase*, 259.19 *be big*, 275.15 *be high*, 324.13 *be in motion*, 359.13 *ascend*, 359.19 *take off*, 370.9 *be light*, 753.9 *be dear*
soarer 359.11 *ascender*
soaring 73.5 *flight*, 95.7 *mountainous*, 275.9 *high*, 324.7 *ascending motion*, 324.17 *directional*, 359.4 *taking off*, 359.23 *rising*, 753.7 *dear*
soaring prices 753.3 *inflationary price*
soave 49 Musical Terms
Soay 68 Breeds of Sheep
sob 431.6 *cry of pain*, 431.13 *cry*, 561.13 *speak in a particular way*, 770.8 *grieve*, 774.7 *weep*
sobbing 431.18 *crying*, 774.1 *lamentation*
so be it 499.9 *yes*

place, 351.6 *soft drink*
soda jerk 697.3 *attendant*
sodalite 54 Minerals
sodality 664.2 *fellowship*, 819.1 *friendship*
sod all 172.2 *nothing*
sodamide 57 Common Chemical Compounds
soda water 351.6 *soft drink*, 389.2 *drinking water*
sodden 389.23 *wet*, 391.9 *moist*, 391.11 *marshy*, 874.5 *drunken*
soddenness 391.1 *moisture*
Soddy 52 Scientists
sodium 57 Chemical Elements, 58.15 *essential element*
sodium bicarbonate 57 Common Chemical Compounds, **62** Medication
sodium cyanide 631.8 *poison*
sodium hypochlorite 62 Medication
sodium lamp 439.6 *electric light*
sodium sulphate 62 Medication
sod off 345.1 *depart*, 345.15 *go*
sodomy 877.7 *sexual assault*
sod's law 166.3 *rule of nature*
sofa 47.2 *chair*, 284.4 *rest*, 374.11 *soft thing*
sofa bed 47.6 *bed*
Sofia 93 Cities
soft 374, 41.12 *ski*, 44.10 *ceramic*, 167.11 *conformable*, 224.13 *changeable*, 238.8 *weak*, 238.13 *insufficient*, 242.8 *moderating*, 351.17 *drinkable*, 370.2 *insubstantial*, 372.1 *sparse*, 376.1 *smooth*, 393.18 *pulpy*, 405.6 *pleasant*, 420.14 *hearable*, 422.3 *silent*, 424.4 *faint*, 428.1 *faint-sounding*, 433.6 *melodious*, 444.13 *soft-hued*, 460.6 *unintelligent*, 673.5 *submitting*, 691.4 *lenient*, 694.7 *obedient*, 779.3 *cowardly*, 821.20 *amorous*, 835.6 *pitying*, 873.2 *nonalcoholic*
soft as a baby's bottom 374.5 *soft as butter*
soft as a kiss 374.5 *soft as butter*
soft as a sigh 374.5 *soft as butter*
soft as a whisper 374.5 *soft as butter*
soft as butter 374
soft as dough 374.5 *soft as butter*
soft as down 374.5 *soft as butter*
soft as putty 374.5 *soft as butter*
soft as silk 374.5 *soft as butter*
soft as soap 374.5 *soft as butter*
soft as velvet 374.5 *soft as butter*
soft as wax 374.5 *soft as butter*
softball 18 Sporting Activities
soft-core pornography 877.2 *indecency*
soft corn 424.15 *ulcer*
soft currency 741.1 *money*
soft damp snow 41.1 *skiing*
soft drink 351, 414.5 *sweet drink*
soft drug 875.6 *drug*
soften 374, 238.7 *weaken*, 242.4 *moderate*, 405.10 *comfort*, 424.6, 428.7 *mute*, 485.15 *modify*, 627.1 *improve*, 767.9 *relieve*, 835.11 *excite pity*, 839.12 *show mercy*, 855.8 *justify*
softened 374.1 *soft*, 485.11 *modified*
softening 129.6 *decreasing*, 374.1 *soft*, 374.8 *softness*, 485.5 *modification*
softening of the brain 236.4 *disability*, 510.3 *mental deterioration*
softening-up 374.8 *softness*
soften the blow 591.3 *abstain*
soften the tone 374.14 *ease*
soften up 238.7 *weaken*, 374.13 *soften*, 594.2 *do the groundwork*, 853.9 *blarney*
soft-fire 44.11 *make ceramics*
soft firing 44.5 *ceramic process*
soft focus 441.2 *murk*
soft-focus 441.6 *murky*
soft focusing 66.13 *framing*
soft football 424.1 *faintness*
soft fruit 69.10 *fruit tree*, 86.1

fruits
soft-fruit growing 69.1 *horticulture*
soft furnishing 67.3 *fabric*
soft furnishings 47.1 *furniture*, 293.8 *wall covering*
soft glaze 44.3 *glaze*
soft-grained 85.15 *woody*
soft hail 55.29 *hail*
soft heart 620.7 *defect*, 835.1 *pity*
softhearted 374, 835.6 *pitying*
soft-hearted 759.12, 760.1 *sensitive*, 831.6 *benevolent*
softheartedly 374
soft-heartedly 831.10 *benevolently*
softheartedness 835.1 *pity*
soft-heartedness 831.1 *benevolence*
soft-hued 444
soft in the head 460.6 *unintelligent*
soft landing 53.35 *rocketry*
soft light 66.15 *lighting*, 439.2 *quality of light*
softly 374, 224.15 *changeably*, 238.14 *weakly*, 370.11 *lightly*, 376.15 *soothingly*, 422.5 *silently*, 424.7, 428.10 *faintly*, 675.8 *peacefully*, 691.6 *leniently*, 694.10 *obediently*
softly-softly 328.6 *hesitant*, 328.17 *in slow motion*
softness 374, 167.3 *pliancy*, 224.1 *changeableness*, 236.3 *helplessness*, 238.1 *weakness*, 370.5 *lightness*, 372.3 *sparseness*, 376.7 *smoothness*, 383.2 *grain*, 393.4 *pulpiness*, 405.1 *physical pleasure*, 422.4 *silence*, 424.1 *faintness*, 428.3 *mutedness*, 444.3 *hue*, 586.7 *persuadability*, 691.1 *leniency*, 694.1 *obedience*
Softness 374
soft-nosed bullet 680.13 *ammunition*
soft option 660.6 *easy thing*
soft palate 564.5 *organ of speech*
soft-paste 44.10 *ceramic*
soft-paste porcelain 44.1 *ceramics*
soft pedal 421.3 *inaudibility*, 424.2 *sound reducer*, 428.6 *silencer*, 563.8 *mute*
soft-pedal 242.4 *moderate*, 422.2 *silence*, 424.6, 428.7 *mute*, 495.3 *underestimate*
soft-pedalled 424.4 *faint*
soft pitch 72.4 *pitching terms*
soft porn 296.3 *pornography*, 877.2 *indecency*
soft return 65.17 *computing term*
soft rock 49.9 *popular music*
soft roe 45.16 *fish dish*, 80.5 *fish anatomy*
soft rot 69.12 *pests and diseases*, 85.10 *tree disease*
soft sector 65.17 *computing term*
soft sell 22.2 *inducement*, 586.6 *advertising*, 739.6 *salesmanship*
soft-shell clam 81 Molluscs
soft-shelled turtle 79 Reptiles
soft-shoe shuffle 46.2 *dance*
soft shoulder 71.3 *carriageway*, 300.1 *edge*
soft ski 41.5 *ski equipment*
soft soap 538.9, 539.3 *hypocrisy*, 540.3 *hypocrisy*, 586.2 *flattery*, 817.1 *courtesy*, 853.2 *blarney*
soft-soap 538.24 *pretend*, 539.26 *be a hypocrite*, 540.18 *be hypocritical*, 771.15 *humour*, 808.9 *fawn*, 817.10 *be courteous*, 853.9 *blarney*
soft-soaping 540.27 *hypocritical*, 808.2 *sycophancy*, 808.7 *sycophantic*, 853.13 *honeyed*
soft sound 424.1 *faintness*, 428.4 *faint sound*
soft-speaking 564.19 *speaking*
soft-spoken 564.19 *speaking*
soft spot 620.7 *defect*, 633.7 *vulnerability*, 784.3 *likes*
soft thing 374
soft tick 82.2 *arachnid*
soft tongue 817.1 *courtesy*

soft-tongued 817.8 *good-mannered*
soft touch 539.22 *dupe*, 660.6 *easy thing*
soft toy 547.6 *image*
soft underbelly 403.2 *ability to sense*, 620.7 *defect*, 633.7 *vulnerability*
soft vacuum 57.20 *surface chemistry*
soft voice 424.1 *faintness*
software 65, 65.4 *computer part*
soft water 389.1 *water*
softwood 36.12 *canoeing*, 47.12 *wood*, 85.1 *tree*, 85.15 *woody*
softwood paddle 36.6 *canoeing*
soft words 817.1 *courtesy*, 821.14 *communication of love*, 826.1 *endearment*
softy 238.4 *weakling*
Sogdian 5 Languages and Groups of Languages
soggily 98.13 *continentally*, 374.17 *softly*, 391.17 *moistly*
sogginess 374.10 *compressibility*, 391.1 *moisture*, 393.4 *pulpiness*
soggy 98.11 *continental*, 374.4 *compressible*, 389.23 *wet*, 391.9 *moist*, 391.11 *marshy*, 393.18 *pulpy*
so happen 589.10 *chance*
Soho 93.5 London
soigné 6.20 *refined*, 558.3 *elegant*
soignée 813.7 *dressed up*
soil 54, 353.16 *defecate*, 604.1 *materials*, 622.11 *dirty*, 622.4 *dirt*, 628.5 *hurt*, 793.7 *blemish*, 854.12 *defame*, 877.19 *corrupt*
soiled 620.1 *imperfect*, 622.7 *dirty*, 793.4 *blemished*
soil erosion 54.36 *soil*, 247.1 *infertility*
soil horizon 54.36 *soil*
soiling 777 Phobias by Topic, 622.1 *dirtiness*
soil mechanics 63.17 *civil engineering*
soil one's hands 644.6 *work*
soil profile 54.36 *soil*
soil structure 54.36 *soil*
soil texture 54.36 *soil*
so inclined 588.11 *intending*
soiree 205.4 *evening thing*, 815.3 *meeting*
soirée 161.9, 568.3 *social gathering*, 665.7 *social gathering*, 815.3 *meeting*
so it seems 471.24 *ideologically*
sojourn 255.14, 256.17 *inhabit*, 815.12 *visit*
soke 92.2 *former British divisions*, 249.5 *state*
sol 57.3 *phase*
Sol 8 Deities, 53.15 *sun*
solace 767.1 *ease*, 767.9 *relieve*
solan 78 Birds
solar 53.36 *astronomical*, 97.7 *oceanic*, 235.17, 410.10 *powered*
solar activity 53.15 *sun*
solar battery 64.29 *power source*, 235.6 *source of energy*, 410.8 *renewable energy*
solar cell 53.32 *satellite*, 64.25 *photoconductivity*, 64.29 *power source*, 235.6 *source of energy*
solar cycle 53.15 *sun*
solar eclipse 53.15 *sun*, 440.1 *darkness*
solar energy 56.11, 56.11 *energy*, 64.29 *power source*, 235.6 *source of energy*, 410.8 *renewable energy*, 439.11 *photoelectricity*
solar flare 53.15 *sun*
solar heating 408.3 *heater*
solarimeter 268.8 *meter*
solarium 256.7 *room*, 408.5 *hot weather*, 630.14 *hospital*
solarization 66.13 *framing*
solar mass 53.22 *astronomical unit*
solar panel 53.32 *satellite*, 64.29 *power source*, 235.6 *source of energy*, 408.3 *heater*
solar power 55.22 *sun*, 235.6 *source of energy*, 410.8 *renew-*

able energy
solar-powered 410.10 *powered*
solar radiation 55.22 *sun*
solar spectrum 53.15 *sun*
solar system 53
solar telescope 53.24 *telescope*
solar tide 97.2 *tide*
solar time 185.9 *time zone*, 192.3 *chronology*
solar wind 53.14 *solar system*
solatium 878.6 *compensation*
sold 739
sold a pig in a poke 539.36 *deceived*
sold a pup 539.36 *deceived*
solder 57 Alloys, 50.14 *sculptor's materials*, 135.10 *link*, 138.3 *adhesive*, 138.7 *cause to adhere*, 408.14 *be hot*
soldering 138.1 *adhesion*
soldering iron 50.14 *sculptor's materials*, 408.3 *heater*
soldier 679, 82.4 *social insect*, 398.10 *killer*, 676.14 *contender*, 676.11 *recruit*, 676.13 *be at war*, 679.1 *combatant*, 694.4 *obedient person*
soldier ant 82.4 *social insect*
soldier beetle 82 Insects
soldiering 676.8 *warfare*
soldierlike 676.17 *military*, 679.35 *martial*
soldierly 17.8, 676.17 *military*, 679.35 *martial*, 778.10 *chivalrous*
soldier of fortune 679.6 *militarist*
soldier on 574.11 *persist*
soldiership 676.6 *art of war*
sold into slavery 701.9 *subject*
soldo 741.12 *ancient coins*
sold off 727.14 *for sale*
sold on 821.18 *in love*
sold out 144.8 *full*, 609.4 *scarce*, 739.16 *sold*
sole 80 Fishes, 29.4 *golf club*, 80.8 *food fish*, 147.10 *excluding*, 174.11 *one*, 280.2 *foot*, 629.1 *repair*, 825.6 *celibate*
solecism 506, 5.29 *grammar*, 474.1 *sophistry*, 474.2 *sophism*, 504.11 *grammatical error*, 525.2 *misinterpretation*, 559.4 *inelegance of speech*, 601.2 *misuse*, 795.4 *inelegance*
solecist 474.6 *sophist*
solecistic 474.7 *sophistic*, 525.3 *misinterpreted*, 559.9 *inelegant*, 601.5 *abusive*
solecistically 474.14 *sophistically*, 601.6 *abusively*
solely 174.24 *once*
solemn 772, 7.15 *religious*, 10.22 *worshipping*, 306.11 *formal*, 422.3 *silent*, 554.5 *serious*, 611.5 *important*, 805.19 *stately*, 811.22 *majestic*, 812.11 *commemorative*, 812.12 *ceremonial*, 813.6 *formal*, 813.8 *ceremonious*
solemn affirmation 535.3 *vow*
solemn entreaty 712.1 *request*
solemness 813.1 *formality*
solemnity 772, 10.1 *ritual*, 306.5 *formality*, 422.4 *silence*, 554.2 *seriousness*, 611.1 *importance*, 805.6 *majesty*, 811.7 *pomp*, 813.1 *formality*
solemnization 10.2 *ritualism*, 812.2 *commemoration*
solemnize 10.18 *perform rites*, 306.8 *be formal*, 640.4 *act*, 812.16 *commemorate*, 813.9 *formalize*
solemnly 772, 7.23 *religiously*, 10.23 *ritually*, 306.14 *conventionally*, 554.7 *emphatically*, 805.33 *with dignity*, 811.38 *majestically*, 813.12 *formally*
solemnly promise 714.7 *promise*
solemnness 422.4 *silence*
solemn oath 535.3 *vow*
solemn observance 10.1 *ritual*, 812.3 *ceremony*
solemn promise 714.1 *promise*
solemn silence 422.4 *silence*
solemn wedding 823.5 *wedding*
solemn word 535.3 *vow*
solenodon 77 Placental Mam-

mals
solenoid 71 Motor Vehicle Parts, 56.60, 340.3 *magnet*
sole possession 723.1 *possession*
sole rights 147.4 *exclusiveness*
sole survivor 132.6 *person remaining*
solfege 49.17 *notation*
solfeggio 49.17 *notation*
solferino 450.6 *red pigment*
solicit 712.6 *request*, 739.1 *sell*, 877.18 *prostitute*
solicitation 712, 228.2 *inducement*, 586.2 *flattery*, 712.1 *request*
solicitation of votes 710.5 *offer of public service*
solicit business 737.1 *trade*
soliciting 712.1 *request*, 739.3 *selling*, 877.5 *prostitution*
soliciting money 712.3 *solicitation*
solicit money 712
solicitor 16.13 *lawyer*, 654.4 *adviser*, 707.3 *agent*, 712.4 *requester*, 716.4 *negotiator*
Solicitor General 16.11 *British law officer*, 16.12 *US law officer*
solicitous 467, 777.9 *worried*, 817.7 *courteous*, 831.6 *benevolent*, 841.5 *distrustful*
solicitously 817.14 *courteously*, 817.15 *genteelly*, 831.10 *benevolently*, 841.9 *jealously*
solicitousness 817.1 *courtesy*, 841.2 *distrust*
solicitude 467, 469.2 *consideration*, 777.3 *worry*, 817.1 *courtesy*
solicit votes 665.14 *be a party member*, 710.13 *be a candidate*
solid 57, 52.41 *geometric figure*, 52.79 *spatial*, 57.3 *phase*, 85.15 *woody*, 101.6 *real*, 110.12 *same*, 112.7 *agreeing*, 135.13 *agreeable*, 138.9 *adhesive*, 144.8 *full*, 159.11 *continuous*, 174.13 *whole*, 217.7 *permanent*, 225.9 *stable*, 253.7 *present*, 273.1 *thick*, 306.9 *formed*, 367.7 *material*, 369.1 *heavy*, 371.4 *solid body*, 371.6 *dense*, 373.2, 378.1 *tough*, 407.8 *touchable*, 443.1 *opaque*, 490.6 *infallible*, 499.6 *assenting*, 537.19 *authentic*, 554.5 *serious*, 574.5 *steady*, 617.3 *valuable*, 742.2 *solvent*
solid angle 52.39 *angle*, 56.7 *space*
solidarity 110.1 *sameness*, 112.3 *agreement*, 116.1 *accord*, 135.2 *agreement*, 144.1 *completeness*, 174.3 *oneness*, 664.2 *fellowship*, 819.1 *friendship*
solid body 371, 369.4 *heaviness*
solid-coloured ball 24.6 *pool*
solid-earth 54
solid-earth geophysics 54.2 *geophysics*
solid figure 52.41 *geometric figure*
solid footing 225.4 *stable thing*
solid foundations 225.4 *stable thing*
solid fuel 53.35 *rocketry*, 338.13, 410.1 *fuel*
solid geometry 52.34 *geometry*
solid gold 741.16 *bullion*
solidification 373, 135.1 *union*, 371.2 *concentration*
solidified 371.7 *condensed*, 373.3 *hardened*
solidify 57, 373, 138.6 *adhere*, 253.11 *be present*, 273.7 *thicken*, 371.8 *be dense*, 490.21 *make certain*
solidifying 135.14 *conjunctive*, 371.7 *condensed*
solidity 101.1 *reality*, 144.1 *completeness*, 174.3 *oneness*, 217.1 *permanence*, 225.1 *stability*, 253.1 *presence*, 273.5 *thickness*, 367.1 *material world*, 371.1 *density*, 373.5 *hardness*, 407.1 *touch*, 443.6 *opaqueness*, 490.7 *infallibility*, 537.6 *authenticity*, 742.8 *solvency*
solidly 112.14 *equanimously*,

116.31 *in accord*, 135.17 *agreeably*, 138.11 *cohesively*, 144.9 *completely*, 217.9 *permanently*, 225.12 *stably*, 253.14 *in person*, 306.13 *formatively*, 367.9 *materially*, 371.10 *densely*, 378.12 *toughly*, 407.14 *palpably*, 443.13 *opaquely*
solid mass 371.4 *solid body*
solidness 371.1 *density*, 378.6 *toughness*
solid of revolution 52.45 *curved surface*
solid rocket booster 53.35 *rocketry*
solid silver 741.16 *bullion*
solid-state 56.98 *physical*, 64.36 *electronic*
solid-state device 64.16 *circuit element*
solid-state memory 65.6 *memory*
solid-state physics 56.3 *modern physics*
solid substance 367.4 *matter*
solid surface 52.38 *surface*
solidus 136.5 *separator*, 137.4 *means of connection*, 286.2 *oblique line*, 543.7 *punctuation*
soliloquist 569, 174.9 *soloist*, 564.10 *speaker*
soliloquize 569, 564.15 *talk to oneself*
soliloquizer 564.10 *speaker*, 569.2 *soliloquist*
soliloquizing 569
soliloquy 569, 51.6 *scene*, 51.7 *dramaturgy*, 174.9 *soloist*, 564.8 *speech*
Soliloquy 569
soling 629.8 *repair*
Soling class 36.2 *sailing boat*
solipsism 4.7 *school of thought*, 368.6 *internal world*, 809.2 *self-satisfaction*
solipsist 4.11 *follower of a doctrine*, 4.14 *of a philosophy*, 368.7 *believer in a nonmaterial world*, 368.11 *internal*, 641.2 *nonacting person*
solipsistic 165.18 *subjective*, 368.11 *internal*, 809.12 *self-interested*
solipsistically 809.22 *smugly*
solitaire 42 Card Games, 168.9 *hermit*, 174.10 *single thing*
solitarily 139.11 *aloofly*, 825.12 *celibately*
solitariness 174.5 *aloneness*, 816.3 *separation*
solitary 168, 76.15 *of animals*, 139.9 *aloof*, 168.9 *hermit*, 174.8 *loner*, 174.11 *one*, 174.16 *alone*, 335.19 *deviant person*, 702.3 *prison cell*, 702.7 *imprisonment*, 816.10 *lonely*, 834.2 *misanthrope*
solitary confinement 290.2 *inside*, 699.4 *detention*, 702.3 *prison cell*, 702.7 *imprisonment*
solitary person 816.6 *unsocial person*
solitary place 816
solitary state 825.3 *monasticism*
solitude 139.2 *aloofness*, 174.5 *aloneness*, 816.3 *separation*
solitudinarian 168.9 *hermit*
solmization 49.17 *notation*
solo 174, 34.9 *mountaineer*, 46.8 *ballet*, 174.9 *soloist*, 174.11 *one*, 174.21 *alone*, 431.8 *musical cry*, 433.1 *melody*
solo dance 46.2 *dance*
solo effort 174.9 *soloist*
soloing 34.3 *climbing technique*, 34.8 *mountaineering*
soloist 174, 49.24 *musician*, 433.5 *melodist*
soloistic 569.5 *soliloquizing*
Solomon 4.12 *sage*, 16.23 *judge*, 136.8 *person who separates*, 507.3 *wise man*, 823.10 *married man*
Solomon Islands 91 Countries
Solomon's seal 84 Flowers and Flowering Plants
Solon 4.12 *sage*
so long 345.14 *goodbye*

so long as 185.26 *all the time*
Soloviov 4 Philosophers
solo whist 42 Card Games
solstice 53.5 *celestial sphere*
solstitial 203.9 *seasonal*
Solti 49 Musicians and Composers
solubility 133.1 *mixture*, 387.8 *fluidification*
solubilization 387.8 *fluidification*
solubilize 387.23 *dissolve*
soluble 52.73 *numerable*, 133.12 *mixed*, 387.21 *liquefiable*, 478.14 *solved*
soluble dye 67.6 *dye*
solubleness 387.5 *fluidity*
solubly 478.25 *conclusively*
solute 57.3 *phase*
solution 387, 478, 52.14 *operation*, 52.27 *equation*, 57.3 *phase*, 133.2 *mixed thing*, 140.4 *compound*, 387.8 *fluidification*, 389.5 *dilution*, 478.7 *numerical result*, 524.1 *interpretation*, 630.1 *remedy*, 684.2 *conclusion*
solution set 52.27 *equation*
solvable 52.73 *numerable*
solvate 57.26 *react*
solvation 57 Types of Chemical Reaction
solve 478, 4.21 *rationalize*, 52.90 *enumerate*, 170.8 *calculate*, 387.23 *dissolve*, 524.9 *decipher*, 526.3 *reveal*
solved 478
solvency 742
solvent 387, 741, 742, 50.11 *artist's materials*, 57.3 *phase*, 274.13 *thinner*, 387.19 *liquefied*, 721.17 *well-off*
solvent front 57.17 *analysis*
solvently 741.28 *financially*
solver 478.10 *answerer*
solvolysis 57 Types of Chemical Reaction
Solzhenitsyn 48 Writers
Somali 1 Peoples, **5** Languages and Groups of Languages
Somalia 91 Countries
so many 120.6 *quantitative*
somatic 367.7 *material*
somatic cell 59.7 *cell*
somatology 400.5 *study of mankind*
somatotrophin 58 Hormones
somatype 1.9 *physical type*
sombre 399.11 *funeral*, 440.11 *benighted*, 441.5 *dim*, 444.13 *soft-hued*, 447.6 *sad*, 448.3 *dull*, 772.1 *solemn*, 805.19 *stately*, 830.6 *sullen*
sombrely 399.12 *funereally*, 440.15 *darkly*, 448.9 *greyly*, 830.13 *sullenly*
sombreness 440.1 *darkness*, 440.7 *spiritual darkness*
sombrero 295.15 *headgear*
Sombrero Galaxy 53 Galaxies
some 120.2 *certain amount*, 120.6 *quantitative*, 120.7 *quantitatively*, 175.1 *plurality*, 175.6 *plural*, 182.1, 182.5 *few*
somebody 400.7 *person*, 611.4 *bigwig*, 800.2 *person of repute*
someday 185.27 *at what time*, 197.3 *another time*, 199.14 *in the future*
somehow 327.16 *how*, 486.11 *potentially*, 602.7 *by means of*
somehow or other 327.16 *how*
someone 400.7 *person*
someone in a hurry 642.10 *busy person*
someone or something that feels 403
someone present 253
someone promised 714
someone's undoing 244.4 *ruin*
some other time 197.1 *different time*, 197.3 *another time*, 199.14 *in the future*
somersault 30.8 *floor exercises*, 30.10 *compete in gymnastics*, 39.6 *diving*, 41.14 *ski*, 287.1 *inversion*, 287.3 *invert*
somersaulting 41.1 *skiing*, 41.12 *ski*

Somerset 92 Counties, **98** Islands
something 99.2 *thing*, 367.5 *object*
something between them 821.8 *love affair*
something certain 490
something else 108.7 *illogical*, 115.4 *dissimilar*
something extra 126.3 *advantage*, 610.3 *superfluity*, 729.2 *gift*
something for a rainy day 14.4 *personal finance*, 132.4 *surplus*, 632.2 *protection*
something for nothing 721.5 *profit*, 754.6 *absence of charge*
something heard 420
something in common 107.1 *relatedness*
something incredible 786.4 *wonder*
something in exchange 223
something in hand 126.3 *advantage*, 605.1 *store*
something in reserve 126.3 *advantage*, 602.5 *reserves*, 605.1 *store*
something in the air 516.3 *foresight*
something like 114.7 *similar*
something missing 358.6 *shortcoming*
something new 119.1 *originality*
something off 752.1 *discount*
something over 610.3 *superfluity*
something owing 745.1 *debt*
something received 730
something that appears 457
something that makes an unpleasant smell 419
something the cat brought in 790.2 *ugly person*
something the cat sicked up 790.2 *ugly person*
some time 185.5 *indefinite period*
sometime 185.27 *at what time*, 197.3 *another time*, 200.20, 202.13 *former*, 209.14 *dead*, 705.7 *resigning*
some time ago 3.24 *historically*, 200.22 *in the past*
sometimes 185, 212
somewhat 120.2 *certain amount*, 121.11 *to a degree*, 143.12 *partly*, 242.9 *moderately*
somewhere 253.15 *here*
somewhere else 254.21 *away*
some while back 200.22 *in the past*
so minded 588.11 *intending*
Somme 96 Rivers
sommelier 697.3 *attendant*
Sommerfeld 52 Scientists
somnabulate 404.11 *be unfeeling*
somnambulism 61.14 *trance*, 519.6 *reverie*
somnambulist 404.5 *unfeeling person*, 519.9 *visionary*
somnifacient 62.4 *drug type*, 643.10 *soporific*
somnifer 404.4 *anaesthetic*
somniferous 404.9 *anaesthetic*
somnific 404.9 *anaesthetic*
somnolence 404.2 *unconsciousness*, 643.9 *sleep*
somnolent 404.10 *sleepy*, 643.4 *not awake*
somnolently 404.13 *insensibly*, 643.17 *sleepily*
Somnus 8 Deities
so much 120.6 *quantitative*
so much nonsense 523.1 *unintelligible*
son 49.10 *world music*, 401.3 *male title of address*, 401.13 *man in the family*
sona 49 Musical Instruments
sonajero 49 Musical Instruments
Son and Holy Ghost 8.3 *God*
sonant 5.16 *spoken letter*, 5.41 *lettered*
sonar 56.22 *sounding*, 74.5 *navigation*, 277.6 *bathymetry*, 420.9 *audio device*, 496.11 *detector*
sonata 49.3 *classical music*, 243.5 *work of art*

sonata form 306.3 *kind*

so near and yet so far 515.13 *disappointingly*

son et lumière 811.14 *show*, 813.3 *formal occasion*

song 433, 48.6 *poetry*, 48.7 *poem*, 49.13 *melody*, 431.8 *musical cry*, 433.1 *melody*

song and dance 51.4 *show business*, 51.5 *show*, 366.4 *fuss*, 423.2 *outcry*, 642.9 *overactivity*

song and dance man 51.27 *entertainer*

songbird 78, 433.5 *melodist*

Song dynasty art 50 Non-Western Art

Songhai 5 Languages and Groups of Languages

Songhua 96 Rivers

songster 49.23 *singer*, 49.24 *musician*, 78.7 *cagebird*, 433.5 *melodist*

song thrush 78 Birds

song writer 49.24 *musician*

songwriter 433.5 *melodist*

sonic boom 56.19 *sound propagation*, 423.1 *loudness*, 425.1 *bang*

sonic depth finder 420.9 *audio device*

sonic speed 329.8 *speed*

sonnet 48.7 *poem*, 48.10 *verse form*

sonneteer 48.14 *poet*

sonnet sequence 48.7 *poem*

sonny 401.3 *male title of address*

sonobuoy 420.9 *audio device*

son of a bitch 864.10 *bad person*

Son of God 8.4 *God the Son*

Son of Man 8.4 *God the Son*

sonority 423.1 *loudness*, 427.3 *deepness*

sonorous 420.14 *hearable*, 423.6 *loud*, 427.8 *deep*, 557.4 *ornate*

sonorously 423.9 *loudly*, 427.11 *resonantly*

sonorousness 423.1 *loudness*, 427.3 *deepness*

Sonotan 98 Deserts

soon 208, 197.3 *another time*, 199.14 *in the future*, 208.17 *early*

soon counted 182.5 *few*

sooner 580.17 *selectively*

sooner or later 197.3 *another time*

sooping 41.10 *curling*

soot 384.5 *powder*, 440.4 *dark thing*, 447.9 *black thing*, 622.4 *dirt*

soothe 242.4 *moderate*, 325.9 *make motionless*, 374.14 *ease*, 376.13 *smooth over*, 405.10 *comfort*, 630.19 *remedy*, 677.4 *pacify*, 763.13 *give pleasure*, 767.9 *relieve*, 835.9 *sorrow*

soothed 767.7 *relieved*

soothing 6, 376, 242.8 *moderating*, 386.9, 395.13 *lubricant*, 405.6 *pleasant*, 630.17 *remedial*, 677.6 *pacificatory*, 763.3 *comfortable*, 767.8 *relieving*

soothing influence 242.2 *moderator*

soothingly 376, 677.7 *pacifically*, 767.15 *comfortingly*

soothing syrup 386.5, 395.6 *ointment*, 630.9 *balm*

soothsay 11.23, 517.12 *divine*

soothsayer 11.13 *diviner*, 199.5, 516.5 *predictor*, 517.8 *oracle*

soothsaying 11.9, 517.2 *divination*

sooty 384.16 *powdery*, 447.1 *black*, 622.7 *dirty*

sooty mould 89 Fungi, 69.12 *pests and diseases*

sop 228.3 *stimulus*, 586.8 *incentive*, 691.1 *leniency*

sophism 474

sophist 474, 4.10 *philosopher*, 4.11 *follower of a doctrine*, 473.6 *arguer*, 657.3 *cunning person*

sophister 474.6 *sophist*

sophistic 474, 473.11 *logical*, 521.10 *meaningless*, 540.28 *spurious*

sophistical 4.14 *of a philosophy*, 474.7 *sophistic*, 657.4 *cunning*

sophistically 474, 4.24 *philosophically*

sophisticate 133.8 *mix*, 628.3 *make worse*, 655.5 *expert*

sophisticated 6.20 *refined*, 133.12 *mixed*, 376.6 *smooth-mannered*, 474.8 *cunning*, 501.9 *literate*, 549.7 *stylish*, 558.3 *elegant*, 655.9 *well-made*, 657.4 *cunning*, 794.5 *refined*

sophisticatedly 6.27 *discerningly*, 376.16 *suavely*

sophistication 6.11 *refinement*, 133.1 *mixture*, 474.3 *cunning*, 558.1 *elegance*, 628.10 *impairment*, 655.1 *skill*, 657.1 *cunning*, 794.1 *elegance*, 817.2 *good manners*

sophisticator 474.6 *sophist*

sophistry 474, 473.2 *logical argument*, 504.4 *faulty reasoning*, 519.6 *reverie*, 521.1 *lack of meaning*, 540.4 *spuriousness*, 578.5 *equivocalness*, 657.1 *cunning*

Sophistry 474

Sophoclean tragedy 51.9 *tragedy*

Sophocles 48 Dramatists

sophomore 6.7 *learner*

sopile 49 Musical Instruments

soporific 643, 62.4 *drug type*, 62.15 *sedative*, 242.8 *moderator*, 242.8 *moderating*, 404.9 *anaesthetic*, 630.8 *drug*, 643.4 *not awake*, 761.6 *desensitizing substance*, 767.3 *reliever*, 788.4 *boring*

soporifically 643.17 *sleepily*, 788.8 *boringly*

soppiness 391.1 *moisture*

sopping 389.23 *wet*

sopping wet 389.23 *wet*

soprano 49.32 *instrumental*, 433.5 *melodist*

sorb 85 Trees and Shrubs, 57.29, 348.13 *absorb*

sorb apple 86 Fruits

sorbed 57.43 *absorbed*

sorbent 348.17 *absorbent*

sorbet 45.35 *dessert*

Sorbian 5 Languages and Groups of Languages

sorbitol 58.3 *carbohydrate*

sorbose 58 Common Sugars

sorcerer 11.4 *witch*, 216.6 *editor*, 517.8 *oracle*, 630.15 *healer*, 786.5 *person of wonder*

sorceress 11.4 *witch*

sorcerize 11.21 *bewitch*

sorcerous 11.15 *witchlike*, 539.35 *deceptive*

sorcery 11.3 *witchcraft*, 233.2 *occult influence*, 235.1 *power*, 539.7 *tricking*, 618.11 *harmfulness*, 786.3 *wonder-working*, 864.6 *religious sin*

sordid 151.15 *untidy*, 618.4 *poor*, 622.8 *unclean*, 626.5 *unhygienic*, 758.2 *unpleasant*

sordidly 622.12 *dirtily*

sordidness 151.3 *untidiness*, 618.10 *poverty*

sordine 49 Musical Instruments

sordino 49 Musical Terms, 421.3 *inaudibility*, 428.6 *silencer*

sordone 49 Musical Instruments

sore 760, 406.5 *painful*, 406.7 *feeling pain*, 618.4 *poor*, 624.3 *symptom*, 624.15 *ulcer*, 624.23 *diseased*, 650.1 *fatigued*, 764.4 *painful*, 820.6 *hostile*, 828.15 *resentful*, 829.4 *irascible*, 862.2 *affliction*, 862.8 *afflicted*

soredium 90.6 *lichen*

sorehead 829.3 *irascible person*, 830.5 *sullen person*

Sorel 4 Philosophers

soreness 760, 406.1, 631.5 *pain*, 820.3 *ill feeling*, 828.1 *resentment*

sore point 666.1 *disagreement*, 760.6 *oversensitivity*, 828.3 *cause of offence*

sore spot 403.3 *stimulus*, 406.1 *pain*

sore throat 406.2 *painful condition*, 624.3 *symptom*, 624.9 *respiratory disease*

sorghum 87 Grasses, 68.12 *crop*

sororicide 398.3 *homicide*, 398.11 *murderer*

sorority 161.15 *association*, 400.9 *group*, 664.2 *fellowship*, 664.9 *team*, 665.1 *party*, 819.1 *friendship*

sorority house 6.15 *schoolroom*

sorosilicate 54.34 *mineral*

sorosis 86.2 *botanical fruit*

sorption 57.20 *surface chemistry*, 348.5 *absorption*

Sorraia 32 Breeds of Horse and Pony

sorrel 45 Herbs and Spices, **45** Vegetables, **84** Flowers and Flowering Plants, 32.1 *horse*, 413.5 *herbs*, 449.1 *brown*

sorrel tree 85 Trees and Shrubs

sorrily 866.11 *guiltily*

sorriness 867.1 *penitence*

sorrow 770, 835, 631.2, 687.1 *adversity*, 687.9 *be in trouble*, 770.8 *grieve*, 774.1 *lamentation*, 774.6 *lament*, 835.2 *condolence*, 862.2 *affliction*

Sorrow 770

sorrowful 770.5 *sad*, 774.4 *lamenting*, 862.8 *afflicted*, 867.6 *penitent*

sorrowfully 862.13 *destructively*, 867.8 *penitently*

sorrowfulness 770.1 *sorrow*, 774.1 *lamentation*

sorry! 867

sorry 612.2 *obscure*, 770.7 *distressing*, 840.4 *atoning*, 866.6 *appearing guilty*, 867.6 *penitent*

sorry for 835.6 *pitying*

sorry for oneself 835.7 *pitiful*

sorry plight 659.5 *predicament*

sort 163, 560, 121.5 *measure*, 136.10 *set apart*, 150.19 *systematize*, 152.15 *categorize*, 163.4 *type*, 259.18 *measure*, 306.3 *kind*, 481.12 *discriminate*, 534.31 *correspond*

sorted 121.7 *gradational*, 152.24 *categorized*, 163.12 *classed*, 481.11 *judged*, 580.15 *chosen*

sorted out 152.24 *categorized*, 478.14 *solved*

sorter 534.4 *postal worker*

sortie 73.1 *aviation*, 241.3 *instance of violence*, 670.14 *siege*

sortilege 11.3 *witchcraft*, 11.9, 517.2 *divination*

sorting 152.5 *categorization*, 481.1 *discrimination*

sorting office 534.2 *postal communication*

sorting out 152.5 *categorization*, 478.6 *solution*

sortkey 65.17 *computing term*

sort of 121.11 *to a degree*

sort out 134.11 *simplify*, 150.19 *systematize*, 152.15 *categorize*, 478.20 *solve*, 524.9 *decipher*, 621.15 *purify*, 843.15 *put right*

sort the grain from the chaff 481.12 *discriminate*

sort the sheep from the goats 481.12 *discriminate*

sorus 88.2 *fern plant*

SOS 543.4 *signal*, 543.6 *word*, 636.2 *danger signal*

SOSENET 65.15 *network*

Sosigenes of Alexandria 52 Scientists

so silent one could hear a pin drop 422.3 *silent*

so-so 124.3 *mediocre*, 158.15 *middling*, 242.6 *moderate*, 284.10 *supportable*, 617.5 *not bad*, 620.4 *ordinary*, 765.6 *satisfactory*, 783.10 *mediocre*, 783.20 *unexceptionally*

sostenuto 49 Musical Terms

sot 874.17 *drunkard*

sotalol 62 Medication

soteriological 7.18 *theological*

soteriology 7.13 *theology*

Sotheby's 740.1 *market*

Sotho 1 Peoples, **5** Languages

and Groups of Languages

so to speak 114.13 *similarly*, 520.13 *meaningfully*

soto-ude-uke 26.8 *karate*

sottish 874.5 *drunken*

sottishness 874.11 *drinking*

sotto voce 49 Musical Terms, 424.7, 428.10 *faintly*

sou 741.4 *change*, 741.12 *ancient coins*

souari nut 86 Nuts

soubresauté 46.9 *ballet steps*

soubrette 51.21 *role*

soufflé 45.35 *dessert*, 45.45 French dish, 370.7 *light thing*, 390.10 *air bubble*

soufflé dish 45.6 *kitchen equipment*

sough 55.58 *blow*, 424.1 *faintness*, 424.5 *sound faint*

sought 477.16 *questioned*, 590.17 *pursued*

sought after 739.16 *sold*, 815.16 *popular*

sought-after 782.7 *desired*

soul 11.7 *spirit*, 49.9 *popular music*, 49.10 *world music*, 49.33 *jazz*, 61.21 *psyche*, 103.3 *quintessence*, 165.11 *identity*, 174.1 *one*, 290.5 *inner nature*, 368.6 *internal world*, 396.1 *life*, 400.7 *person*, 759.8 *seat of feelings*

soul body 11.7 *spirit*

soul food 45.43 US dish, 350.7 *food*

soul in bliss 8.10 *deified person*

soul in glory 8.10 *deified person*

soulless 836.4 *pitiless*

soul mate 114.5 *counterpart*, 821.11 *loved one*, 823.8 *spouse*

soul mates 821.10 *lovers*

soul of wit 552.1 *conciseness*

souls 397.14 *the spiritual world*

soul-search 4.20 *philosophize*, 477.17 *question*

soul-searching 477.8 *curiosity*, 867.1 *penitence*

sound 777 Phobias by Topic, **49, 56, 142,** 4.15 *rational*, 52.86 *logical*, 56.2 *classical physics*, 98.9 *inlet*, 101.8 *practical*, 116.24 *harmonize*, 225.9 *stable*, 237.9 *physically strong*, 268.10 *measure*, 277.4 *deep thing*, 277.14 *deepen*, 327.11 *channel*, 420.8 *something heard*, 420.15 *hear*, 420.16 *be heard*, 423.3 *audibility*, 423.8 *be loud*, 427.10 *ring*, 459.11 *thoughtful*, 479.1 *experiment*, 490.6 *infallible*, 509.5 *rational*, 537.19 *authentic*, 617.3 *valuable*, 617.4 *worthwhile*, 617.5 *not bad*, 619.1 *perfect*, 623.1 *healthy*, 632.5 *safe*, 655.6 *skilful*, 718.9 *fast*, 741.23, 742.2 *solvent*, 857.4 *honourable*, 861.1 *good*

soundalike 222.2 *substitute person*, 222.7 *substitute*

sound a retreat 337.2 *retreat*

sound argument 52.64 *reasoning*

sound as a bell 237.9 *physically strong*, 619.1 *perfect*, 623.1 *healthy*

sound a siren 636.7 *raise the alarm*

sound asleep 643.4 *not awake*

sound a warning 636.7 *raise the alarm*

sound barrier 56.19 *sound propagation*, 329.8 *speed*

sound bite 143.2 *particular*

sound box 427.5 *resonator*

sound currency 741.1 *money*

sound dead 424.5 *sound faint*, 428.9 *be nonresonant*

sounddesk 51.15 *stage*

sounder 277.4 *deep thing*, 479.1 *experiment*

sound faint 424, 428, 563.16 *speak in a low voice*

sound generator 56.18 *source of sound*

sound hoarse 430

sounding 56, 116.13 *harmonious*, 277.6 *bathymetry*, 277.13

bathymetric, 420.1 *hearing*, 427.7 *ringing*
sounding board 331.5 *reflector*, 427.5 *resonator*
sounding brass 427.2 *ringing*, 521.1 *lack of meaning*
sounding line 277.4 *deep thing*
soundingly 116.33 *harmoniously*
sounding out 479.1 *experiment*
sounding true 537.25 *lifelike*
sound insulation 56.21 *architectural acoustics*, 421.3 *inaudibility*
sound in wind and limb 142.8 *sound*, 237.9 *physically strong*, 623.1 *healthy*
sound judgment 459.5 *common sense*
soundless 277.8 *deep*, 325.6 *quiescent*, 422.3 *silent*
soundlessly 422.5 *silently*
soundlessness 277.1 *depth*, 422.4 *silence*
sound level 56.19 *sound propagation*
sound like 116.25 *conform*
sound like a broken record 788.6 *be boring*
soundly 4.26 *rationally*, 225.12 *stably*, 237.14 *strongly*, 718.17 *fastly*
sound maker 423
sound man 51.26 *stagehand*
sound mind 509.1 *sanity*
soundness 52.64 *reasoning*, 225.1 *stability*, 237.2 *healthiness*, 306.6 *nature*, 490.17 *infallibility*, 537.6 *authenticity*, 617.6 *worth*, 619.3 *perfection*, 623.3 *health*, 742.8 *solvency*, 857.1 *probity*, 861.8 *good*
soundness of mind 507.1 *wisdom*, 509.1 *sanity*
sound one's horn 636.7 *raise the alarm*
sound out 477.10 *question*, 479.1 *experiment*
sound-power level 56.19 *sound propagation*
sound-pressure level 56.19 *sound propagation*
soundproof 292.3 *line*, 421.7 *unheard*, 421.10 *muffle*, 422.3 *silent*, 423.14 *faint*, 424.6 *mute*, 428.2 *nonresonant*
soundproofed 424.4 *faint*
soundproofing 56.21 *architectural acoustics*, 292.1 *lining*, 421.3 *inaudibility*, 424.1 *faintness*, 424.2 *sound reducer*
sound propagation 56
sound proposition 744.1 *credit*
sound quality 420, 534.23 *television reception*
sound receiver 420.9 *audio device*
sound recordist 51.26 *stagehand*
sound reducer 424
sound reduction 424.1 *faintness*
sound the alarm 636.7 *raise the alarm*
sound the charge 670.1 *attack*, 676.14 *battle*
sound the depth 36.15 *sail*
sound the fire alarm 636.7 *raise the alarm*
sound the last post 399.8 *bury*
sound the praises of 851.15 *compliment*
sound the trumpet 228.9 *motivate*
sound the trumpets 543.12 *signal*
sound true 537.33 *seem lifelike*
sound wave 56, 365.5 *wave*
soup 45, 393, 45.9 *dish*, 133.2 *mixed thing*, 350.14 *mouthful*, 387.2 *juice*
soup and fish 295.3 *formal dress*
soup bowl 258.16 *crockery*
soupçon 182.1 *few*, 411.3 *appetizer*
souped-up 235.16 *charged*, 329.1 *swift*
soup of the day 45.9 *dish*
soup's on 45.58 *grub's on*
soupspoon 258.17 *ladle*
soup spoon 350.16 *eating utensil*
soup up 235.11 *give power*,

237.8 *strengthen*, 239.3 *invigorate*
soupy 393.18 *pulpy*
sour 415, 141.5 *disintegrated*, 411.7 *tasty*, 413.9 *piquant*, 415.5 *acid*, 419.4 *putrid*, 515.7 *thwart*, 764.3 *unpalatable*, 820.6 *hostile*, 822.10 *hating*, 822.16 *cause hate*, 829.4 *irascible*, 830.6 *sullen*, 830.10 *make sullen*, 832.14 *hostile*, 841.4 *jealous*
source 156, 226, 64.19 *transistor*, 119.2 *original*, 119.3 *originator*, 528.8 *source of information*, 528.10 *informer*, 530.4 *discloser*, 605.2 *resource*, 606.1 *provision*
source code 65.9 *programming language*
source electrode 64.19 *transistor*
source of a river 96.2 *channel*
source of energy 235
source of information 528
source of pride 805.12 *object of pride*
source of sound 56
source of trouble 631, 635.1 *trap*
sources of resonance 427
sour cherry 86 Fruits
sour cream 415.3 *sour thing*
sourdine 49 Musical Terms, 421.3 *inaudibility*
sourdough *biscuit* 45.39 *loaf*
sourdough bread 45.38 *bread*
soured 515.9 *disappointed*
soured cream 415.3 *sour thing*
sour gourd 86 Fruits
sour grapes 415.4 *spleen*, 841.1 *jealousy*
sour gum 85 Trees and Shrubs
sour look 818.3 *act of discourtesy*
sourly 415, 419.6 *stinkingly*, 820.14 *hostilely*, 822.18 *hatefully*, 829.9 *irascibly*, 830.13 *sullenly*
sour milk 415.3 *sour thing*, 419.2 *something that makes an unpleasant smell*
sourness 777 Phobias by Topic, 415, 202.10 *staleness*, 411.4 *flavour*, 413.1 *piquancy*, 631.4 *strain*, 785.1 *dislike*, 820.3 *ill feeling*, 829.1 *irascibility*, 830.1 *sullenness*, 832.4 *bitterness*
Sourness 415
sourpuss 415.4 *spleen*, 770.4 *depressing person*, 852.13 *pessimist*
soursop 86 Fruits
sour taste 411.1 *taste*, 411.2 *taste of life*, 415.1 *sourness*
sour thing 415
sour wine 415.3 *sour thing*
sourwood 85 Trees and Shrubs
Sousa 49 Musicians and Composers
sousaphone 49 Musical Instruments
sous chef 45.2 *cook*
souse 354.4 *immerse*, 362.3 *bring down*, 389.9 *soaking*, 389.29 *water*, 411.12 *season*, 637.5 *preserve*, 874.8 *get drunk*, 874.17 *drunkard*
soused 362.19 *fallen*, 389.23 *wet*, 413.9 *piquant*, 637.7 *preserved*, 874.3 *dead drunk*
sousing 362.13 *submergence*, 389.9 *soaking*
souslik 77 Placental Mammals
soutane 7.11 *vestment*
souter 295.26 *fashion designer*
south 332.4 *compass point*, 332.12 *north*, 332.13 *directional*
South Africa 91 Countries
South America 98.1 *continent*
Southampton 93 Cities, 98 Islands
South Australia 92 Australian States and Territories
southbound 332.13 *directional*
South Carolina 92 American States
South China 97 Oceans and Seas
South Dakota 92 American States
South Devon 68 Breeds of Cat-

tle, **68** Breeds of Sheep
Southdown 68 Breeds of Sheep
southeast 332.4 *compass point*, 332.12 *north*, 332.13 *directional*
southeast by east 332.12 *north*
southeast by south 332.12 *north*
southeaster 55.15 *wind direction*
southeasterly 55.15 *wind direction*, 55.47 *windy*, 332.12 *north*, 332.13 *directional*
southeastern 332.13 *directional*
southeast trades 55.17 *wind system*
southeastwardly 332.12 *north*
southeastwards 332.12 *north*
southeast wind 55.15 *wind direction*
southerly 55.15 *wind direction*, 55.47 *windy*, 332.12 *north*, 332.13 *directional*
southerly buster 55 Winds
southern 249.16 *regional*, 305.6 *side*, 332.13 *directional*
Southern accent 5.26 *dialect*
Southern Cross 53 The Constellations, 543.5 *indicator*
Southern Crown 53 The Constellations
Southerner 91.9 *England*, 255.9 *British inhabitant*
Southern Fish 53 The Constellations
Southern fried chicken 45.43 *US dish*
southern lights 54.46 *aurora*, 439.4 *natural light*
southernmost 332.13 *directional*
Southern Triangle 53 The Constellations
Southey 48 Poets
South Georgia 98 Islands
South Glamorgan 92 Counties
southing 332.4 *compass point*
South Kensington 93.5 *London*
Southland 92 New Zealand Regions and Territories
south magnetic pole 54.45 *magnetic pole*
South Pacific 408.8 *hot place*
southpaw 26.4 *boxer*
South Pole 409.6 *Arctic*
Southport 93 Cities
Southron 5 Languages and Groups of Languages
South Seas hurricane 55.16 *wind vortex*
south side 305.3 *side direction*
south-southeast 332.12 *north*
south-southwest 332.12 *north*
South Wales 91.12 *Wales*
South Wales Mountain 68 Breeds of Sheep
South Walian 91.12 *Wales*
southward 332.4 *compass point*, 332.13 *directional*
southwardly 332.12 *north*
southwards 332.12 *north*
Southwark 93.5 *London*
southwest 332.4 *compass point*, 332.12 *north*, 332.13 *directional*
southwest by south 332.12 *north*
southwest by west 332.12 *north*
southwester 55.15 *wind direction*, 295.12 *coat*, 295.15 *headgear*
southwesterly 55.15 *wind direction*, 55.47 *windy*, 332.12 *north*, 332.13 *directional*
southwestern 332.13 *directional*
southwestwardly 332.12 *north*
southwestwards 332.12 *north*
southwest wind 55.15 *wind direction*
south wind 55.15 *wind direction*, 408.8 *hot place*
South Yemen 91 Countries
South Yorkshire 92 Counties
souvenir 3.11 *relic*, 132.1 *remainder*, 511.3 *memento*, 545.11 *monument*, 681.3 *memento*, 729.2 *gift*
souvlaki 45.52 *Greek dish*
sou'wester 634.2 *shelter*
sov 741.9 *British money*
sovereign 696, 8.13 *divine*, 12.10 *governing*, 91.16 *national*, 126.13 *dominant*,

166.12 *ruling*, 235.13 *powerful*, 630.17 *remedial*, 688.10 *person of authority*, 688.14 *governmental*, 696.12 *masterful*, 741.10 *former British money*
sovereign remedy 630.1 *remedy*
sovereign state 91.1 *country*, 249.4 *territorial division*
sovereignty 8.2 *divine attribute*, 12.3 *governance*, 91.1 *country*, 126.2 *leadership*, 166.8 *authority*, 235.1 *power*, 688.4 *governance*, 692.3 *authority*, 723.1 *possession*
soviet 653.7 *council*
Soviet bloc 91.2 *union of nations*
Soviet hammer and sickle 544.6 *national emblem*
Soviet Heavy Draught 32 Breeds of Horse and Pony
sovietism 12.1 *government*
sow 162, 68.8 *livestock*, 68.17 *farm*, 69.15 *cultivate*, 77.18 *female mammal*, 164.25 *broadcast*, 243.10 *produce*, 362.6 *throw down*, 402.14 *female animal*
sow above 357.3 *exceed*
sowar 32.15 *horse person*, 679.6 *militarist*, 679.20 *cavalryman*
sowbelly 45.30 *bacon*
sow bug 81.4 *arthropod*
sow dissension 666.7 *pick a fight*, 822.16 *cause hate*
sower 594.15 *preparer*
Soweto 93 Cities
so what 612.15 *no matter*
sowing 68.5 *cultivation*, 162.1 *dispersion*, 594.13 *development*
sown 162.22 *distributed*, 243.12 *produced*
sow one's oats 864.16 *be wicked*
sow one's wild oats 698.19 *liberalize*, 870.11 *overindulge*
sowse 161 Collective Names for Birds and Animals
sow seed 87.12 *manage grassland*
sow the seed 594.2 *do the groundwork*
sow the seeds 156.22 *invent*
sow the seeds of 226.11 *inaugurate*
sow the wind and reap the whirlwind 659.22 *cause trouble*
sow thistle 84 Flowers and Flowering Plants
soya 45.21 *meat substitute*
soya bean 45 Vegetables
soyabean meal 68.9 *animal feedstuff*
soyabeans 68.12 *crop*
Soyot 5 Languages and Groups of Languages
soy sauce 45.15 *sauce*, 413.2 *seasoning*
Soyuz 53.31 *space travel*
sozzled 874.3 *dead drunk*
spa 625.1 *hygiene*, 630.14 *hospital*
space 52, 56, 248, 248, 265, 49.17 *notation*, 53.3 *universe*, 100.4 *emptiness*, 120.1 *quantity*, 121.4 *interval*, 146.1 *inclusion*, 152.12 *arrange*, 184.6 *vastness*, 185.3 *duration*, 187.1 *period*, 248.11 *spatial*, 249.1 *region*, 259.1 *size*, 265.1 *interval*, 322.1 *opening*, 605.4 *storage*
Space 248
space age 53.31 *space travel*
space between 265.1 *interval*
space biologist 59.19 *life scientist*
space biology 59.1 *life science*
space cadet 510.7 *insane person*
space capsule 53.30 *spacecraft*
space-case 510.7 *insane person*
space coordinates 56.7 *space*
spacecraft 53
spaced 265
spaced out 265.6 *spaced*, 875.7 *drugged*
spaced-out 508.5 *foolish*, 512.8 *oblivious*
space engineering 53.29 *astronautics*
space exploration 53.29 *astronau-*

tics
spaceflight 53.31 *space travel*
space frame 63.27 *superstructure*, 382.4 *framework*
space heater 408.3 *heater*
space heating 408.3 *heater*
space helmet 53.31 *space travel*
space invader 104.6 *outsider*
Space Invaders 65.18 *computer game*
spacelab 53.30 *spacecraft*
space laboratory 53.30 *spacecraft*
spaceman 248, 53.31 *space travel*
space medicine 53.29 *astronautics*, 60.3 *medical specialty*
space navigation 53.29 *astronautics*
space observatory 53.32 *satellite*
space out 152.12 *arrange*, 182.9 *scatter*, 248.2 *space*, 263.6 *keep away*, 265.4 *space*
space platform 53.30 *spacecraft*
space port 53.31 *space travel*
space probe 53.30 *spacecraft*
space research 53.29 *astronautics*
space science 53.29 *astronautics*
spaceship 53.30 *spacecraft*, 363.4 *orbiting body*
space shuttle 53.30 *spacecraft*
space station 53.30 *spacecraft*
spacesuit 53.31 *space travel*, 295.10 *suit*
space technology 53.29 *astronautics*
space the final frontier 248.2 *empty space*
space-time 56.7 *space*, 185.1 *time*, 248.9 *fourth dimension*, 248.11 *spatial*
space-time continuum 56.7 *space*, 185.1 *time*, 248.9 *fourth dimension*
space travel 53
space traveller 248.10 *spaceman*
spacewalk 53.31 *space travel*
space wave 534.15 *transmitted wave*
spacewoman 53.31 *space travel*, 248.10 *spaceman*
spacial 248.11 *spatial*, 322.14 *holed*
spacing 265.1 *interval*
spacious 248, 259.15, 755.4 *big*
spaciously 248, 259.20 *largely*
spaciousness 248, 259.2 *bigness*, 271.4 *breadth*
spade 91 Names for Inhabitants, 29.4 *golf club*, 36.11 *rowing*, 42.3 *card game terms*, 68.17 *farm*, 69.6 *garden tool*, 69.15 *cultivate*, 258.17 *ladle*, 317.7 *make concave*, 326.15 *take away*, 380.9 *sharp-edged thing*, 380.16 *use a sharp tool*, 603.2 *garden tool*, 644.6 *work*
spadefoot toad 79 Amphibians
spade mashie 29.4 *golf club*
spade oar 36.4 *rowing*
spadework 156.7 *rudiments*, 226.3 *rudiment*, 594.10 *preparations*, 644.1 *work*
spadix 84.4 *flower head*
spagane 49 Musical Instruments
spaghetti 45 Types of Pasta
spaghetti house 350.15 *eating place*
spaghetti junction 71.3 *carriageway*, 137.5 *road*, 288.5 *crossroads*, 327.3 *road*
Spaghetti Junction 356.5 *crossing point*
spahi 679.20 *cavalryman*
Spain 91 Countries
Spallanzani 52 Scientists
span 75 General Units, **161** Collective Names for Birds and Animals, **271,** 63.21 *bridge*, 135.10 *link*, 137.5 *road*, 176.1 *two*, 176.14 *pair*, 185.3 *duration*, 187.1 *period*, 248.8 *intervening space*, 248.20 *extend*, 269.4 *length*, 271.4 *breadth*, 293.26 *overlie*, 327.9 *bridge*, 356.11 *cross*
Spandau 93 Cities

spandex 377.3 *elastic thing*
spandrel 43.9 *miscellaneous architectural features*
spang 332.9 *directly*
spangle 439.2 *quality of light*, 439.25 *light up*, 456.5 *variegated thing*, 456.11 *variegate*
spangles 792.5 *decorative articles*
spangly 439.16 *bright*
spaniel 77 Breeds of Dogs, 808.3 *sycophant*, 808.9 *fawn*
Spanish 5 Languages and Groups of Languages, **43** Architectural Styles, **68** Breeds of Fowl
Spanish-American War 17 Major Wars
Spanish bayonet 380.8 *sharp-pointed thing*
Spanish cedar 85 Trees and Shrubs
Spanish Civil War 17 Major Wars
Spanish fly 82 Insects
Spanish GP at Jerez 33.2 *Formula 1 race*
Spanish mackerel 20.4 *American game fish*
Spanish moss 88.3 *moss*, 90.6 *lichen*
Spanish Riding School 32.10 *dressage*
Spanish topaz 54 Gemstones
spank 330.5 *beat*, 330.13 *blow*, 879.12 *corporal punishment*
spanker 74 Sails, 259.9 *big thing*
spanking 259.15 *big*, 329.1 *swift*, 330.12 *collision*, 879.12 *corporal punishment*
spanking rate 329.8 *speed*
spanking wind 55.14 *windiness*
spanned 327.15 *accessible*
spanner 603.1 *tool*, 726.3 *tools for gripping*
spanner in the works 661.2 *obstacle*
spanning 293.1, 293.38 *covering*
spar 26.11 *do a combat sport*, 36.3 *parts of a sailing boat*, 63.27 *superstructure*, 473.13 *argue*, 674.7 *boxing*, 674.12, 679.37 *fight*
spare 25.5 *bowling delivery*, 130.9 *extra*, 132.10 *surplus*, 274.1 *thin*, 556.1 *simple*, 591.3 *abstain*, 599.5 *dispose of*, 600.1 *unused*, 600.5 *not use*, 600.11 *unused thing*, 605.7 *stored*, 609.3 *underfed*, 610.3 *superfluity*, 610.7 *superfluous*, 632.4 *safety device*, 632.9 *protect*, 637.5 *preserve*, 639.1 *deliver*, 645.6 *leisure*, 691.3 *be lenient*, 727.9 *dispose of*, 835.10 *show mercy*, 839.9 *forgive*, 848.10 *acquit*
spare cash 610.3 *superfluity*
spare copy 545.5 *copy*
spared 632.5 *safe*, 839.6 *forgiven*, 848.6 *acquitted*
spare hours 645.1 *leisure*, 649.1 *ease*
sparely 132.12 *with a remainder*
spareness 274.7 *thinness*, 556.4 *simplicity*
spare no effort 644.8 *exert oneself*
spare no expense 729.5 *give*, 748.1 *expend*, 755.10 *be generous*
spare none 398.18 *slaughter*
spare one's blushes 542.22 *play down*
spare one's words 566.8 *be taciturn*
spare part 148.3 *unit*, 632.4 *safety device*
spare parts 130.4 *extra*
spare rib 45.24, 45.25 *pork*
spares 130.4 *extra*, 132.4 *surplus*
spare the rod 691.3 *be lenient*
spare time 645.1 *leisure*, 649.1 *ease*
spare tyre 71 Motor Vehicle Parts, 258.18 *stomach*, 259.8 *fat*, 610.3 *superfluity*
spare wheel 71 Motor Vehicle Parts, 610.3 *superfluity*
sparge 389.12 *sprinkler*, 389.33,

391.5 *sprinkle*
spargefaction 389.8 *watering*
sparger 389.12 *sprinkler*
sparging 389.8 *watering*
sparing 756.4 *thrifty*, 839.1 *forgiveness*, 839.4 *forgiving*, 869.8 *self-restrained*
sparingly 869.11 *with self-restraint*
sparing of words 552.3 *concise*
sparing with words 566
spark 56.46, 64.6 *electric discharge*, 226.1 *cause*, 410.2 *lighter*, 439.2 *quality of light*, 439.8 *fire*, 439.25 *light up*
Spark 48 Writers
spark discharge 56.46, 64.6 *electric discharge*
sparking 439.16 *bright*
sparking plug 410.2 *lighter*
sparkle 239.1 *vigour*, 390.24 *bubble*, 439.2 *quality of light*, 439.25 *light up*, 554.1 *emphasis*, 554.6 *emphasize*, 769.7 *be cheerful*, 789.7 *be beautiful*
sparkler 439.8 *fire*
sparklers 435.2 *eye*, 792.5 *decorative articles*
sparkling 351.17 *drinkable*, 370.2 *insubstantial*, 370.5 *lightness*, 388.21 *gassy*, 439.16 *bright*, 554.3 *emphatic*, 769.1 *cheerful*
sparkling burgundy 351.9 *wine*
sparkling water 351.6 *soft drink*
sparkling wine 351.9 *wine*
spark off 156.20 *activate*, 226.10 *awaken*
spark plug 71 Motor Vehicle Parts
sparky 439.22 *enlightened*
sparring 26.2 *boxing*, 26.14 *combat*, 674.7 *boxing*
sparring helmet 26.2 *boxing*
sparring partner 26.4 *boxer*, 679.3 *athlete*
sparrow 78 Birds, 78.6 *songbird*
sparrowhawk 78 Birds
sparse 182, 372, 120.6 *quantitative*, 162.19 *dispersed*, 213.2 *infrequent*, 247.3 *birth control*, 274.6 *scant*, 609.4 *scarce*
sparsely 182, 372, 120.7 *quantitatively*, 162.30 *diffusely*, 213.1 *infrequently*, 274.17 *thin*, 609.10 *insufficiently*
sparseness 372, 182.3 *fewness*, 274.12 *thinning*
Sparseness 372
sparsity 182.3 *fewness*, 213.3 *infrequency*
Sparta 12.5 *political organization*
spartan 690.4 *strict person*, 690.10 *unadorned*, 699.14 *self-restrained*, 756.4 *thrifty*
Spartan 556.1 *simple*, 699.6 *lawmaker*, 869.4 *self-restrained person*, 869.8 *self-restrained*, 871.6 *fasting*
Spartan fare 609.8 *insufficiency*, 871.2 *short rations*
spartanism 4.3 *detachment*, 699.3 *self-restraint*
Spartanism 690.3 *unadornment*, 869.1 *self-restraint*
Spartan race 679.7 *militarist nation*
Spartan simplicity 542.4 *simplicity*
spasm 366, 241.3 *instance of violence*, 406.1 *pain*, 624.2 *illness*, 624.3 *symptom*, 624.17 *nervous disorder*, 642.3 *nimbleness*, 670.20 *bout*
spasmodic 113.5 *diverse*, 151.14 *irregular*, 160.8 *discontinuous*, 215.4 *irregular*, 224.13 *changeable*, 241.6 *violent*, 366.19 *convulsive*
spasmodically 113.11 *irregularly*, 151.27 *in disorder*, 160.17 *discontinuously*, 215.8 *irregularly*, 224.15 *changeably*, 366.29 *jerkily*
spasmodicalness 160.1 *discontinuity*
Spasmodic School 48 Literary

Groups and Movements
spasmolytic 62.4 *drug type*, 62.14 *counteracting*
Spassky 18 Sporting Personalities
spastic 366.19 *convulsive*, 624.19 *sick person*, 624.23 *diseased*
spat 473.1 *argument*, 500.1 *dissent*, 666.2 *argument*, 666.6 *argue*, 674.1 *contention*
spatchcock 45.55 *cook*
spate 55.25 *rain*, 96.6 *river flow*, 161.22 *flood*, 608.8 *plenty*, 610.1 *excess*
spathe 84.3 *flower part*
spatial 52, 248, 249.16 *regional*
spatial extension 52.35, 248.1 *space*
spatialism 50 Western Art Styles and Movements
spatially 248, 52.87 *mathematically*, 248.15 *spaciously*, 249.19 *geographically*
spatiotemporal 248.11 *spatial*, 367.7 *material*
spatiotemporally 248.14 *spatially*, 248.15 *spaciously*
spats 295.20 *legwear*
spatter 55.62 *rain*, 162.18 *sprinkle*, 366.26 *flicker*, 389.33, 391.5 *sprinkle*, 391.14 *sprinkle*, 622.11 *dirty*
spatterdashes 295.20 *legwear*
spattered 162.23 *sprinkled*, 391.12 *seeping*
spattering 162.4 *sprinkling*, 389.8 *watering*
spatula 57 Laboratory Apparatus, 45.6 *kitchen equipment*, 50.11 *artist's materials*, 50.14 *sculptor's materials*, 258.17 *ladle*, 381.9 *blunt instrument*
spavin 624.18 *veterinary disease*
spavined 624.23 *diseased*
spa water 389.2 *drinking water*
spawn 128.4 *increase*, 206.4 *young animal*, 243.7, 243.10 *produce*, 245.11 *have young*, 245.13 *propagate*, 396.19 *give birth to*
spawned 396.15 *born*
spawning 245.3 *propagation*
spay 131.4 *take off*, 236.9 *make impotent*, 247.8 *make infertile*
spayed 236.13 *unsexed*, 247.5 *rendered infertile*
spaying 247.2 *making infertile*
speak 564, 5.45 *use language*, 423.8 *be loud*, 530.6 *divulge*, 534.30 *communicate*, 535.17 *affirm*, 568.9 *converse*
speak about 561.4 *dissertate*
speak badly 523.7 *be unintelligible*
speak clearly 522.5 *simplify*
speak directly 271.12 *be broad-minded*
speak empty words 538.24 *pretend*
speaker 564, 51.22 *actor*, 56.18 *source of sound*, 420.9 *audio device*, 423.4 *sound maker*, 534.18 *radio*, 557.3 *phrasemonger*, 561.3 *dissertator*, 565.4 *talker*, 653.13 *director*
speak ex cathedra 535.21 *be assertive*
speak for 158.19 *mediate*, 478.23 *answer for*, 706.5, 707.5 *represent*
speak for itself 483.10 *make evident*, 522.4 *be intelligible*, 526.5 *be visible*
speak freely 698.14 *be free*
speak gobbledegook 523.7 *be unintelligible*
speak highly of 851.13 *support*
speak ill of 854.13 *vilify*
speak in a low voice 563
speak in a particular way 564
speaking 564, 114.9 *lifelike*, 564.1 *faculty of speech*
speaking clock 192.6 *clock*
speaking in tongues 7.2 *religiousness*, 564.2 *power of speech*
speaking likeness 547.1 *represen-*

tation
speaking part 51.21 *role*
speaking straight from the shoulder 556.6 *naturalness*
speaking voice 564.1 *faculty of speech*
speak in muted tones 563.16 *speak in a low voice*
speak in tongues 7.20 *preach,* 523.7 *be unintelligible*
speak loudly 564
speak low 424.5 *sound faint*
speak of 520.10 *mean*
speak one's mind 312.11 *be straight,* 475.18 *appear,* 658.4 *be naive*
speak oracles 578.1 *be equivocal*
speak out 475.18 *appear,* 526.4 *show oneself,* 530.6 *divulge,* 535.21 *be assertive,* 663.15 *object*
speak out against 713.6 *protest*
speak plainly 526.4 *show oneself,* 556.7 *be simple,* 658.4 *be naive,* 857.6 *be honourable*
speak simply 556.7 *be simple*
speak slowly 328.2 *hesitate*
speak softly 424.5 *sound faint,* 563.16 *speak in a low voice*
speak sotto voce 563.16 *speak in a low voice*
speak straight from the shoulder 322.22 *be open,* 556.7 *be simple*
speak the partial truth 538.21 *lie*
speak the truth 312.11 *be straight,* 537.29 *be truthful,* 857.6 *be honourable*
speak to 567.7 *address*
speak to one's understanding 522.4 *be intelligible*
speak truthfully 857.6 *be honourable*
speak under one's breath 563.16 *speak in a low voice*
speak up 423.8 *be loud,* 526.4 *show oneself,* 564.12 *speak loudly*
speak up for 851.13 *support,* 855.8 *justify*
speak volumes 520.10 *mean,* 522.4 *be intelligible*
speak well of 851.13 *support*
speak with forked tongue 309.12 *distort the truth,* 578.1 *be equivocal*
speak without thinking 462.12 *lack thought*
speak with two voices 117.12 *be disparate,* 578.1 *be equivocal*
spear 31.9 *play hockey,* 87.3 *grass plant,* 380.8 *sharp-pointed thing,* 380.16 *use a sharp tool ,* 398.17 *murder,* 670.6 *stab,* 679.37 *fight*
spear carrier 284.8 *supporter*
spear-carrier 51.22 *actor*
speared 31.8 *hockey*
spear grass 87 Grasses
spearhead 126.10 *lead,* 154.15 *precede,* 156.21 *pioneer,* 303.1 *front,* 303.10 *be in front,* 380.8 *sharp-pointed thing,* 611.3 *chief thing,* 653.14 *leader,* 670.19 *attacker,* 679.14 *armed forces*
spearing 31.3 *ice hockey,* 31.8 *hockey*
spearlike 380.1 *sharp*
spearman 679.13 *historical soldiery*
spearmint 45 Herbs and Spices
spear side 401.15 *menfolk*
special 165, 165, 29.5 *golf ball,* 45.9 *dish,* 106.10 *detailed,* 163.11 *typical,* 165.17 *exceptional,* 174.14 *singular,* 520.6 *meaningful,* 543.14 *signifying,* 580.15 *chosen*
special affinity 819.3 *familiarity*
Special Air Service 17.2 *the military*
special area 301.2 *enclosed place*
Special Boat Service 17.2 *the military*
Special Branch 16.15 *British police*
special case 113.1 *diversity,* 147.1 *exclusion,* 165.6 *excep-*

tion, 168.6 *deviation*
special constable 16.17 *police officer,* 718.3 *security officer*
special correspondent 528.9 *informant,* 532.11 *newspaper man,* 560.10 *descriptive writer*
special court martial 17.6 *military law*
special day 611.2 *important matter,* 773.1 *rejoicing,* 812.5 *anniversary*
special delivery 534.2 *postal communication*
special-delivery messenger 534.4 *postal worker*
special diet 350.6 *nutrition*
special dispensation 147.1 *exclusion*
special edition 532.4 *newspaper,* 533.5 *mass communication*
special effects man 51.26 *stagehand*
special effort 640.2 *deed*
special envoy 653.16 *official*
special faculty 655.1 *skill*
special forces 17.2 *the military*
Special Forces 617.7 *elite,* 679.14 *armed forces*
special gift 235.1 *power*
special handling 534.2 *postal communication*
special hospital 61.31 *psychiatric hospital,* 510.8 *mental hospital*
special interest 165.8 *specialization,* 642.2 *social activity*
special interest group 228.7 *motivator*
special-interest group 586.14 *motivator*
specialism 165.1 *skill*
special issue 533.5 *mass communication*
specialist 165, 19.19 *varsity,* 60.13 *medical specialist,* 126.6 *paragon,* 165.21 *specialized,* 485.8 *qualified person,* 655.5, 688.11 *expert,* 696.10 *expert,* 696.13 *excellent*
specialist publication 532.5 *journal*
specialist source 524.7 *news interpreter*
speciality 165, 6.3 *subject,* 45.9 *dish,* 174.4 *singularity,* 549.1 *style,* 655.1 *skill*
Speciality 165
speciality of the house 45.9 *dish,* 165.9 *special*
specialization 165
specialize 165, 696.14 *master*
specialized 165, 6.21 *curricular,* 520.6 *meaningful,* 655.8 *expert,* 659.12 *problematic*
specialized company 13.7 *corporation*
specialized language 165
specialized meaning 520.4 *type of meaning*
specialize in 165.27 *specialize,* 688.22 *be an authority on,* 696.15 *learn*
special jury 16.26, 492.7 *jury*
Special level 485 Educational Qualifications
specially 165, 106.19 *meticulously,* 543.18 *indicatively*
special meaning 520.4 *type of meaning*
specialness 165.1 *speciality,* 174.4 *singularity*
special nurse 60.16 *nurse*
special offer 228.5 *positive stimulus,* 586.9 *enticement,* 710.3 *business offer,* 752.2, 754.4 *bargain*
Special Olympics 674.2 *contest*
special patrol 16.16 *US police*
special patrol group 16.15 *British police*
special power 235.1 *power*
special prayer 10.9 *prayer*
special price 752.2 *bargain*
special request 712.1 *request*
special sale 710.3 *business offer*
special school 6.12 *educational institution,* 510.8 *mental hospital*

special skill 165
special study 165.8 *specialization*
special subject 165.8 *specialization*
special team 19
special theory of relativity 56.5 *theory*
special topic 472.5 *educational topic*
special treat 514.4 *surprising thing*
special treatment 662.8 *furtherance,* 848.1 *exemption*
special-treatment 74.11 *nautical*
special-treatment steel 74.4 *shipbuilding*
specialty 655.1 *skill*
specialty team 19.12 *special team*
speciarness 797.1 *affectedness*
speciation 59.16 *evolution*
specie 741.1 *money,* 741.13 *coinage*
species 59.17 *taxonomy,* 143.1 *part,* 163.3 *kingdom,* 163.4 *type,* 560.6 *sort*
specific 59.28 *taxonomic,* 103.9 *characteristic,* 106.10 *detailed,* 163.11 *typical,* 165.15 *special,* 490.7 *particular,* 630.1 *remedy,* 630.17 *remedial*
specifically 59.29 *biologically,* 106.19 *meticulously,* 163.16 *taxonomically,* 165.28 *specially*
specification 485, 150.2 *grouping,* 302.2 *limiting factor,* 490.18 *particularity,* 528.3 *document,* 560.1 *description,* 593.1 *requirement*
specifications 165
specific gravity 56.9 *mass,* 369.5 *gravity,* 371.3 *relative density*
specific heat 408.2 *heat measurement*
specific heat capacity 56.36 *heat flow*
specific latent heat 56.38 *thermodynamics*
specificness 490.18 *particularity*
specific quality 165.1 *speciality*
specific remedy 630.1 *remedy*
specified 150.11 *grouped,* 485.12 *conditional,* 490.7 *particular*
specified value 56.83 *sensitivity*
specify 165, 485, 490, 106.11 *circumstantiate,* 302.7 *limit,* 544.10 *identify,* 560.16 *define*
specimen 475.3 *explanation,* 526.7 *showpiece,* 547.8 *representative*
specimen shrub 69.9 *garden plant*
specimen tree 69.9 *garden plant,* 85.1 *tree*
speciosity 797.1 *affectedness*
specious 102.12 *not the real thing,* 457.9 *ostensible,* 474.7 *sophistic,* 540.28 *spurious,* 656.2 *unskilled,* 797.3 *affected*
speciously 474.14 *sophistically,* 538.27 *pretentiously,* 540.37 *spuriously*
speciousness 474.1 *sophistry,* 538.8 *pretence,* 540.4 *spuriousness*
specious reasoning 474.1 *sophistry*
speck 143.7 *piece,* 149.2 *impurity,* 162.18 *sprinkle,* 173.3 *fragment,* 260.3 *little piece,* 384.7 *grain,* 456.4 *maculation,* 793.1 *spot*
speckle 133.8 *mix,* 162.18 *sprinkle,* 456.4 *maculation,* 456.11 *variegate*
speckled 133.12 *mixed,* 162.23 *sprinkled,* 456.10 *mottled*
speckled effect 133.3 *miscellany*
speckledy 456.10 *mottled*
speckling 133.3 *miscellany,* 162.4 *sprinkling*
specs 165.4 *specifications,* 435.10 *visual aid*
spectacle 51.5 *show,* 51.7 *dramaturgy,* 435.7 *view,* 457.4 *something that appears,* 475.6 *mass demonstration,* 526.6 *display,*

526.9 *production,* 786.4 *wonder,* 811.14 *show,* 813.3 *formal occasion*
spectacled bear 77 Placental Mammals
spectacles 56.29 *optical element,* 435.10 *visual aid,* 436.3 *aid for poor sight,* 437.7 *that which makes visible,* 442.8 *transparent thing*
spectacle theatre 51.14 *theatre*
spectacular 51.37 *dramatic,* 435.23 *visible,* 437.2 *clear,* 444.12 *gaudy,* 457.7 *appearing,* 811.24 *grand*
spectacularly 811.40 *grandly*
spectate 253.12 *attend,* 435.12 *see*
spectator 51.31 *theatregoer,* 253.5 *someone present,* 435.11 *observer,* 465.3 *curious person,* 480.7 *verifier,* 483.7 *person who gives evidence,* 730.5 *recipient*
spectator sport 18.4 *sporting activity,* 435.7 *view*
spectinomycin 62 Medication
spectrometer 57.17 *analysis*
spectral 11.18 *spiritual,* 102.8 *unreal,* 253.7 *present,* 439.23 *photoelectric,* 456.6 *variegated*
spectral colour 56.28, 444.1 *colour*
spectral type 53.13 *luminosity*
spectre 11.11 *ghost,* 102.2 *illusion,* 253.6 *ghostly presence,* 435.5 *imagination,* 457.4 *something that appears,* 519.5 *fantasy,* 777.5 *frightener*
spectrograph 53.27 *imaging,* 56.91 *spectrometer,* 57.17 *analysis,* 444.8 *chromatics*
spectrographic 57.41 *analytic,* 444.14 *chromolithographic*
spectrographic analysis 57.17 *analysis*
spectrography 444.8 *chromatics*
spectrometer 56, 53.27 *imaging,* 56.32 *optical instrument,* 268.8 *meter,* 444.8 *chromatics*
spectrometric 53.43 *astronomical,* 56.98 *physical,* 268.16 *micrometric*
spectrometrically 56.100 *physically*
spectrometry 53.27 *imaging,* 56.96 *microscopy,* 57.17 *analysis,* 268.2 *micrometry*
spectrophotometer 56.32 *optical instrument,* 56.91 *spectrometer,* 268.8 *meter,* 444.8 *chromatics*
spectrophotometric 268.16 *micrometric,* 444.14 *chromolithographic*
spectrophotometry 268.2 *micrometry,* 444.8 *chromatics*
spectroscope 56.91 *spectrometer,* 444.8 *chromatics*
spectroscopic 56.98 *physical,* 57.41 *analytic,* 444.10 *coloured*
spectroscopically 56.100 *physically*
spectroscopic binary 53.9 *constellation*
spectroscopy 56.3 *modern physics,* 56.96 *microscopy,* 435.10 *visual aid*
spectrum 57.17 *analysis,* 159.2 *consecution,* 248.7 *range,* 439.12 *highlight,* 444.2 *colourfulness,* 456.1 *variegation,* 456.5 *variegated thing*
spectrum analysis 444.8 *chromatics*
speculate 737, 4.20 *philosophize,* 14.5 *invest,* 461.12 *think,* 461.16 *have an idea,* 479.11 *experiment,* 491.18 *be uncertain,* 491.22 *risk,* 517.11 *predict,* 518.5 *suppose,* 589.12 *take a chance,* 596.3 *tackle,* 738.1 *purchase,* 786.12 *wonder whether*
speculation 42 Card Games, **737,** 4.1 *philosophy,* 4.4 *philosophical investigation,* 102.4 *theorization,* 461.3 *thoughtfulness,* 463.4 *explanation,* 471.2 *theory,* 479.3 *experimentation,*

492.1 *judgment,* 497.1 *belief,* 504.2 *inaccuracy,* 517.2 *divination,* 518.3 *conjecture,* 589.7 *calculation of chance,* 596.6 *venture,* 597.2 *undertaking*
speculative 461, 4.13 *of philosophy,* 4.17 *thoughtful,* 102.10, 471.10 *theoretical,* 479.8 *experimental,* 491.1 *uncertain,* 491.5 *uncertified,* 518.7 *suppositional,* 597.6 *enterprising,* 633.1 *dangerous,* 737.15 *profitable,* 738.14 *buying*
speculatively 4.25 *theoretically,* 479.14 *experimentally,* 491.23 *uncertainly,* 518.10 *supposedly,* 596.10 *ambitiously,* 739.17 *marketably*
speculator 4.10 *philosopher,* 14.3 *stockbroker,* 102.6 *unrealistic person,* 230.5 *operator,* 479.5 *experimenter,* 517.9 *forecaster,* 518.4 *theorist,* 597.4 *volunteer,* 725.7 *property man* , 737.10 *trader,* 738.12 *purchaser,* 739.12 *wholesaler*
speculum 435.8 *reflection*
speculum metal 57 Alloys
speech 777 Phobias by Topic, **564, 564,** 5.3 *spoken language,* 51.6 *scene,* 420.8 *something heard,* 532.1 *publication,* 534.1 *communications,* 567.1 *address*
Speech 564
speech-act theory 4.9 *philosophical problem*
speech community 5.26 *dialect,* 161.17 *family*
speech defect 563, 559.5 *mispronunciation,* 564.3 *mode of speech*
speechifier 564.10 *speaker*
speechify 564.14 *speak to,* 567.7 *address*
speechifying 564.9 *art of public speaking*
speech impediment 559.5 *mispronunciation,* 563.3 *speech defect,* 564.3 *mode of speech*
speechless 563, 422.3 *silent,* 514.7 *amazed,* 566.2 *silent,* 786.7 *wide-eyed*
speechlessness 422.4 *silence,* 563.5 *mutism,* 566.5 *silence*
speechless with rage 828.16 *angry*
speechmaker 567.6 *public speaker*
speech-maker 564.10 *speaker*
speech-making 564.9 *art of public speaking*
speech sound 5.16 *spoken letter,* 564.7 *utterance*
speech therapist 60.17 *paramedic*
speech therapy 60.8 *treatment*
speed 777 Phobias by Topic, **329,** 41.12 *ski,* 56.8 *time,* 63.9 *machine tool,* 121.1 *degree,* 212.4 *frequency,* 324.8 *rapid motion,* 329.4 *be swift,* 642.3 *nimbleness,* 648.2 *make haste,* 648.4 *haste,* 660.1 *easiness,* 660.16 *make easy,* 662.28 *further,* 875.6 *drug*
speed and endurance 32.11 *eventing*
speedball 18 Sporting Activities, 875.6 *drug*
speedboat 329.11 *swift thing*
speed contest 674.4 *race*
speed demon 329.13 *swift person*
speeder 32.2 *thoroughbred,* 329.13 *swift person,* 674.10 *contender*
speed freak 329.13 *swift person*
speedily 191.8 *immediately,* 329.14 *swiftly,* 648.6 *hastily*
speediness 329.8 *speed*
speeding 128.1 *increase,* 324.17 *directional,* 329.1 *swift,* 329 8 *speed,* 648.3 *hasty,* 660.7 *easing,* 674.4 *race*
speeding-up 329.3 *accelerating*
speed limit 71.21 *miscellaneous motoring terms,* 302.2 *limiting factor,* 699.1 *restraint*
speed maniac 329.13 *swift person*
speed measurement 329.8 *speed*

speed of light 56.16 *waveform,* 329.8 *speed*
speed of light gravitational constant 56.97 *fundamental constant*
speed of sound 56.16 *waveform,* 56.19 *sound propagation,* 329.8 *speed*
speed of thought 329.10 *quickness of mind*
speedometer 71 Motor Vehicle Parts, 268.8 *meter,* 329.8 *speed,* 543.5 *indicator,* 545.10 *recording instrument*
speed-skate 41.15 *ice-skate*
speed-skater 41.11 *skier*
speed skating 18 Sporting Activities
speed-skating 41, 41.13 *ice-skating*
speed-skating circuit 41.8 *speed-skating*
speed-skating race 41.8 *speed-skating*
speed-skating track 41.8 *speed-skating*
speed-skiing 41.1 *skiing*
speed sprayer 389.12 *sprinkler*
speed the parting guest 345.6 *part*
speed trap 71.21 *miscellaneous motoring terms,* 329.8 *speed*
speed up 128.5 *make bigger,* 329.6 *accelerate,* 648.1 *hasten,* 648.2 *make haste,* 648.8 *hurry up*
speed-up 329.9 *acceleration*
speedway 33.11 *racing,* 674.4 *race*
speedway race 33.1 *motor racing*
speedway racing 33.1 *motor racing*
speedwell 84 Flowers and Flowering Plants
speedy 191.5 *immediate,* 324.17 *directional,* 329.1 *swift,* 642.18 *active,* 648.3 *hasty*
speleology 360.7 *tunnelling*
spell 11, 5.47 *word,* 55.3 *weather,* 185.3 *duration,* 187.1 *period,* 187.4 *period of activity,* 203.1 *season,* 228.5 *positive stimulus,* 248.8 *intervening space,* 520.10 *mean,* 527.14 *imply,* 618.11 *harmfulness,* 670.20 *bout,* 822.2 *curse,* 827.4 *malediction*
spellbind 11.21 *bewitch,* 339.15 *pull towards,* 786.10 *be wonderful*
spellbinder 11.4 *witch*
spellbinding 11.3 *witchcraft,* 11.15 *witchlike,* 228.11 *motivational,* 786.3 *wonder-working*
spellbound 11.19 *bewitched,* 228.12 *motivated,* 325.4 *motionless,* 586.20 *persuadable,* 786.6 *wondering*
spellcasting 11.3 *witchcraft*
spellcraft 11.3 *witchcraft*
spell danger 636.5 *warn*
spell disaster 636.5 *warn*
spelling 5
spelling bee 5.27 *spelling*
spelling checker 65.11 *application*
spelling game 5.27 *spelling*
spelling mistake 504.11 *grammatical error*
spelling pronunciation 5.27 *spelling*
spell of duty 644.1 *work*
spell of work 644.2 *task,* 731.3 *allotted task*
spell out 4.21 *rationalize,* 5.47 *word,* 106.11 *circumstantiate,* 165.23 *particularize,* 520.10 *mean,* 522.5 *simplify,* 524.8 *interpret,* 524.9 *decipher*
spelt 87 Grasses
spelunker 277.5 *submariner*
spelunking 18 Sporting Activities, 277.1 *depth*
spencer 295.11 *jacket*
Spencer 4 Philosophers
spend 599.1 *use,* 607.1 *waste,* 645.4 *have leisure,* 738.2 *shop,*

746.6 *pay,* 748.1 *expend*
spend a penny 353.17 *urinate*
spender 748, 13.9 *economist,* 738.12 *purchaser,* 757.6 *spendthrift*
Spender 48 Poets
spending 347.5 *export,* 607.3 *waste,* 738.8 *shopping,* 746.15 *paying,* 748.4 *expenditure,* 748.10 *expending*
spending money 721.5 *profit,* 741.4 *change,* 749.3 *income*
spending money as if it grows on trees 748.11 *spendthrift*
spending money like water 748.11 *spendthrift*
spending plan 756.2 *act of thrift*
spending spree 748.6, 757.4 *extravagance*
spend lavishly 738.2 *shop,* 748.1 *expend*
spend like it's going out of style 757.8 *overspend*
spend like water 757.8 *overspend*
spend money as if it grows on trees 748.1 *expend*
spend money like water 607.1 *waste,* 748.1 *expend*
spend on 599.1 *use*
spend, spend, spend 757.8 *overspend*
spend the season 203
spend the summer 203.6 *spend the season*
spend the winter 203.6 *spend the season*
spendthrift 748, 748, 757, 607.6 *waster,* 607.8 *wasteful,* 757.1 *extravagant*
Spengler 4 Philosophers
Spenser 48 Poets
Spenserian 48.19 *narrative*
Spenserian stanza 48.10 *verse form*
spent 200.18 *over,* 238.9 *dilapidated,* 347.16 *outflowing,* 555.1 *unemphatic,* 599.9 *used,* 614.1 *useless,* 650.1 *fatigued,* 722.16 *losing,* 748.12 *expended,* 750.11 *accounted*
spent cartridge 680.13 *ammunition*
sperm 226.3 *rudiment,* 245.8 *organs of reproduction,* 246.3 *fertilizer*
spermatangium 90.4 *reproductive body*
spermatic 245.16 *reproductive*
spermatium 90.4 *reproductive body*
Spermatophyta 83.3 *seed plant*
spermatophyte 83.3 *seed plant*
spermatophytes 396.9 *classifications of life*
spermatozoa 245.8 *organs of reproduction*
spermatozoid 90.4 *reproductive body*
sperm bank 605.4 *storage*
sperm duct 322.7 *passageway*
spermicidal 62.14 *counteracting*
spermicide 62.4 *drug type,* 247.3 *birth control*
spermophobia 777 Phobias by Name
sperm whale 77 Placental Mammals
sperrylite 54 Minerals
spessartite 54 Gemstones
spew 347.11 *run out,* 349.14 *let out,* 349.15 *vomit*
spew out 347.11 *run out,* 387.25 *flow*
Spey 96 Rivers, 96.4 *British rivers*
sphagnum 88.3 *moss*
sphalerite 54 Minerals
sphene 54 Minerals, **54** Gemstones
sphenodon 79 Reptiles
sphenoid 382 Bones
sphenopsid 88.1 *fern*
sphere 249, 472, 6.3 *subject,* 52.45 *curved surface,* 53.10 *star,* 163.4 *type,* 163.5 *social class,* 165.8 *specialization,* 248.7 *range,* 251.5 *rank,* 313.2

circle, 315.3 *round thing*
spherelike 313.5 *circular,* 315.9 *round*
sphere of influence 233, 12.1 *government,* 91.3 *dominion*
spheric 313.5 *circular,* 315.9 *round*
spherical 52, 313.5 *circular,* 315.9 *round*
spherical aberration 53.25 *mounting,* 56.31 *lens element*
spherical coordinates 52.33 *coordinates*
spherical geometry 52.34 *geometry*
spherical lens 56.29 *optical element*
spherically 52.87 *mathematically,* 313.8 *circularly,* 315.13 *roundly*
sphericalness 313.1 *circularity,* 315.1 *roundness*
spherical sailing 74.5 *navigation*
spherical triangle 52.43 *triangle*
spherical trigonometry 52.51 *trigonometry*
sphericity 52.38 *surface,* 315.1 *roundness*
spheroid 52.45 *curved surface,* 315.3 *round thing*
spheroidal 52.83 *spherical,* 313.5 *circular*
spheroidally 313.8 *circularly*
spherosome 59.8 *cell organ*
spherulite 54 Minerals
sphincterectomy 60 Surgical Operations
sphincterotomy 60 Surgical Operations
sphingolipid 58.6 *lipid*
sphingomyelin 58.6 *lipid*
sphinxlike 523.1 *unintelligible,* 523.4 *difficult*
sphragistics 544.5 *uniform*
spic 91 Names for Inhabitants
Spica 53 Named Stars
spice 45.7 *basic ingredient,* 45.55 *cook,* 130.6 *add,* 133.4 *admixture,* 133.8 *mix,* 411.10 *make taste,* 418.1 *fragrance,* 637.2 *preserver*
spiceberry 86 Fruits
spice cake 45.36 *cake*
spiced 413.9 *piquant*
spiced green bananas 45.49 *Indian dish*
spiced wine 351.7 *alcoholic drink,* 414.5 *sweet drink*
spices 399.1 *burial,* 413.5 *herbs,* 416.2 *sense of smell,* 418.2 *fragrant thing*
spicily 418.7 *fragrantly*
spiciness 413.1 *piquancy,* 418.1 *fragrance*
spick and span 150.13 *orderly*
spick-and-span 134.14 *purified,* 201.12 *immature,* 621.16 *clean*
spiculate 380.14 *be sharp*
spicule 380.8 *sharp-pointed thing*
spicy 237.12 *strong to the senses,* 411.7 *tasty,* 413.9 *piquant,* 416.5 *odorous,* 418.4 *fragrant*
spicy taste 411.1 *taste*
spider 74 Rigging, **82** Arachnids, 82.2 *arachnid,* 82.6 *spinner,* 288.3 *weaving*
spider conch 81 Molluscs
spider crab 81.4 *arthropod*
spider flower 84 Flowers and Flowering Plants
spideriness 272.7 *fineness*
spider-like 81.18 *arthropodous,* 82.11 *arachnidan*
spiderling 82.5 *larva*
spider mite 82 Arachnids
spider monkey 77 Placental Mammals
spider phaeton 71 Carriages and Carts
spider plant 84 Flowers and Flowering Plants
spiders 777 Phobias by Topic
spider's web 82.6 *spinner,* 288.2 *braid*
spider wasp 82 Insects
spiderwort 84 Flowers and Flowering Plants

spidery 81.18 *arthropodous,* 82.11 *arachnidan,* 272.2 *fine*
spiegeleisen 57 Alloys
spiel 41.10 *curling,* 521.5 *empty talk,* 521.9 *talk nonsense,* 564.1 *faculty of speech,* 565.1 *talkativeness,* 739.6 *salesmanship*
spieler 532.10 *publicizer*
spiel man 51.29 *circus performer*
spiffed up 295.30, 813.7 *dressed up*
spiffing 617.1 *worthy*
spifflicate 244.11 *ruin*
spiff up 295.33 *dress up*
spiffy 617.1 *worthy,* 861.1 *good*
spigot 323.2 *stopper*
spike 19.14 *miscellaneous terms,* 34.5 *rock face,* 84.4 *flower head,* 87.3 *grass plant,* 133.8 *mix,* 380.16 *use a sharp tool ,* 661.8 *hinder,* 671.9 *barrier*
spiked 380
spiked device 879.15 *instrument of torture*
spiked shoes 21.4 *sports equipment*
spike fiddle 49 Musical Instruments
spike heels 295.19 *footwear*
spikelet 84.4 *flower head,* 87.3 *grass plant*
spikenard 84 Flowers and Flowering Plants, 386.5, 395.6 *ointment,* 418.3 *incense*
spike oil 395.6 *ointment*
spikes 21.4 *sports equipment,* 295.19 *footwear*
spike someone's guns 236.8 *overpower,* 661.8 *hinder*
spiky 380.2 *spiked*
spill 96.7 *flow,* 287.1 *inversion,* 287.3 *invert,* 347.2 *outflow,* 347.11 *run out,* 360.4 *fall,* 362.6 *throw down,* 410.2 *lighter,* 439.8 *fire,* 607.1 *waste,* 656.7 *be clumsy*
spillage 96.6 *river flow,* 362.11 *lowering,* 607.3 *waste*
spill blood 353.21 *bleed*
spilling 349.22 *disgorgement,* 360.18, 362.20 *falling*
spill one's guts 528.13 *inform on*
spillover 96.6 *river flow*
spill over 347.11 *run out,* 357.1 *overstep*
spill the beans 496.2 *detect,* 528.13 *inform on ,* 530.7 *betray*
spill the brains of 398.17 *murder*
spillway 96.2 *channel*
spilt milk 722.3 *waste*
spilt salt 517.7 *bad-luck sign*
spin 67, 27.8 *delivery,* 27.18 *bowl,* 41.6 *ice-skating,* 41.15 *ice-skate,* 56.78 *quantum,* 73.5 *flight,* 214.8 *be cyclic,* 243.10 *produce,* 288.8 *interweave,* 324.13 *be in motion,* 364.1 *rotation,* 364.3 *reel,* 364.8, 364.8 *rotate,* 364.9 *roll,* 524.13 *interpret news*
spina bifida 624.17 *nervous disorder*
spinach 45 Vegetables
spinach beet 45 Vegetables
spin a coin 229.4 *chance*
spinakoturikopita 45.52 *Greek dish*
spinal column 382 Bones
spin a long tale 553.5 *be diffuse*
spin a web 657.5 *be cunning*
spin a wheel 229.4 *chance*
spin a yarn 102.16 *delude,* 489.7 *be improbable,* 541.11 *tell a tall story,* 560.15 *recount*
spin bowler 27.4 *team*
spin-cast 20.7 *angle*
spin-casting 20.1 *angling*
spindle 59.10 *cell division,* 272.8 *narrow thing,* 364.4 *vortex,* 364.6 *rotator*
spindle fibres 59.10 *cell division*
spindle-legged 274.1 *thin*
spindlelegs 274.9 *thin person*
spindle sander 47.11 *woodworking tool*
spindle-shaped 272.2 *fine,* 380.1 *sharp*

spindle tree 85 Trees and Shrubs
spindling 272.2 *fine*
spindly 272.2 *fine*
spin doctor 293.18 *fixer,* 309.5 *defacer,* 524.7 *news interpreter,* 532.10 *publicizer,* 586.12 *persuader*
spindrift 55.30 *snow,* 390.10 *air bubble*
spin-dry 392.23 *drip-dry*
spin-dryer 364.6 *rotator,* 392.15 *dryer*
spine 382 Bones, 77.2 *mammalian characteristic,* 83.6 *leaf,* 275.4 *mountain range,* 284.2 *supporting part,* 373.7 *hard substance,* 380.8 *sharp-pointed thing*
spinel 54.34 *mineral*
spineless 236.12 *impotent,* 238.12 *weak-willed,* 452.5 *cowardly,* 576.3 *timid,* 779.3 *cowardly*
spinelessly 779.5 *cravenly*
spinelessness 238.2 *indecisiveness,* 576.13 *timidity*
spinerette 67.2 *spinning*
spinet 49 Musical Instruments
sping lobster 45.19 *shellfish*
spininess 375.6 *roughness,* 380.6 *sharpness*
spin like a teetotum 364.8 *rotate*
spin money 742.13 *get rich*
spinnaker 74 Sails, 36.3 *parts of a sailing boat*
spinner 73 Aircraft Parts, 82, 20.2 *artificial fly,* 27.4 *team,* 67.2 *spinning,* 288.3 *weaving,* 539.13 *snare,* 646.2 *artisan*
spinneret 82.6 *spinner*
spinney 85.4 *trees*
spinning 42 Hobbies and Pastimes, 67, 20.1, 20.8 *angling,* 334.1 *circuit,* 363.11 *orbiting,* 364.2 *turning,* 364.11 *rotating*
spinning jenny 67.2 *spinning,* 364.6 *rotator*
spinning motion 364.1 *rotation*
spinning mule 67.2 *spinning*
spinning out 33.6 *motor racing terms,* 36.7 *windsurfing,* 269.4 *length*
spinning rod 20.3 *fishing tackle*
spinning top 315.5 *cone,* 364.6 *rotator*
spinning wheel 67.2 *spinning,* 288.3 *weaving,* 364.6 *rotator*
spin off 227.5 *show an effect*
spin-off 155.6 *aftermath,* 227.1 *effect,* 243.3 *product*
spin off from 227.7 *follow from*
spin of the coin 229.2 *chance*
spin of the wheel 229.2 *chance,* 589.3 *equal chance,* 633.5 *danger*
spin one's wheels 614.9 *waste effort*
spinose 380.2 *spiked*
spinosity 380.6 *sharpness*
spinous 380.2 *spiked*
spin out 33.10 *be on the track,* 36.18 *windsurf,* 209.8 *delay,* 219.4 *protract,* 269.10 *lengthen,* 553.5 *be diffuse,* 565.8 *talk too much*
spin-out 33.6 *motor racing terms,* 36.7 *windsurfing*
Spinoza 4 Philosophers
spin round 364.8 *rotate*
spinster 134.5 *pure person,* 174.7 *single person,* 402.5 *single girl,* 825.5 *single person*
spinsterhood 825.1 *celibacy*
spinsterish 825.6 *celibate*
spinsterlike 825.6 *celibate*
spinsterly 825.6 *celibate*
spin the bottle 42 Children's Games and Party Games
spin words 549.9 *style*
spiny 375.2 *coarse,* 380.2 *spiked*
spiny anteater 77.6 *insect-eating mammal*
spin yarn 364.9 *roll*
spin yarns 538.21 *lie*
spiny dormouse 77 Placental Mammals
spiny-headed worm 81.6 *worm*
spiny lobster 81.4 *arthropod*

spiracle 80.5 *fish anatomy,* 347.7 *outlet*
spiraea 84 Flowers and Flowering Plants
spiral 52.40 *curve,* 52.81 *curvilinear,* 73.5 *flight,* 128.2 *spread,* 128.4 *increase,* 129.4 *decrease,* 311.2 *bend,* 311.6 *curve,* 314.2 *coil,* 314.4 *convolutional,* 314.6 *convolute,* 334.3 *circuit,* 334.6 *circular,* 359.2 *upturn,* 359.13 *ascend,* 360.12 *drop,* 363.1 *orbital motion,* 363.6 *orbit,* 363.10 *circular,* 364.2 *turning*
spiral balance 369.10 *scales*
spiral down 360.12 *drop*
spiraled 311.4 *curved*
spiral galaxy 53.7 *galaxy*
spiralling 359.24 *leaping,* 363.1 *orbital motion,* 363.11 *orbiting,* 364.2 *turning,* 753.7 *dear*
spiralling prices 753.3 *inflationary price*
spiralling up 359.4 *taking off*
spirally 314.8 *circularly*
spiral spring 377.5 *spring*
spiral staircase 359.7 *means of ascent*
spirant 5.16 *spoken letter,* 5.41 *lettered*
spire 87.3 *grass plant,* 95.9 *tower,* 272.8 *narrow thing,* 275.4 *tall thing,* 275.15 *be high,* 279.2 *head,* 359.13 *ascend,* 359.19 *take off,* 380.8 *sharp-pointed thing*
spirelet 43.10 *church architecture*
spirillum 59.3 *organism*
spirit 11, 8.5 *deity,* 11.11 *ghost,* 102.2 *illusion,* 103.3 *quintessence,* 165.11 *identity,* 235.3 *vitality,* 239.1 *vigour,* 257.1 *contents,* 355.8 *extract,* 368.3 *spiritual world,* 368.6 *internal world,* 396.1 *life,* 413.4 *stimulation,* 520.1 *meaning,* 554.1 *emphasis,* 574.16 *fortitude,* 642.4 *energy,* 759.8 *seat of feelings,* 778.1 *courage,* 805.1 *pride*
spirit away 458.3 *cause to disappear,* 736.13 *kidnap*
spirited 235.15 *full of energy,* 239.4 *vigorous,* 396.13 *lively,* 413.10 *stimulating,* 554.3 *emphatic,* 642.18 *active,* 778.9 *courageous,* 805.14 *proud*
spiritedly 413.16 *stimulatingly*
spirit gum 51.19 *stage requisite*
spiritism 11.1 *occultism*
spiritist 11.12 *occultist*
spirit lamp 439.5 *incandescent light*
spiritless 783.7 *indifferent,* 787.3 *unmoved*
spiritlessly 783.17 *indifferently*
spiritlessness 783.1 *indifference*
spirit level 282.5 *planometer*
Spirit of God 8.3 *God*
spirit of the age 234.1 *tendency*
spiritous 351.17 *drinkable,* 874.6 *intoxicating*
spirit-raising 11.10 *psychic phenomenon*
spirit rapper 11.12 *occultist*
spirit rapping 11.1 *occultism*
spirits 777 Phobias by Topic, 105.4 *state of mind,* 397.14 *the spiritual world,* 874.12 *alcohol*
spiritual 11, 7.15 *religious,* 49.5 *sacred music,* 368.8 *nonmaterial,* 368.9 *parapsychological,* 433.2 *song,* 863.5 *virtuous*
spiritual body 11.7 *spirit*
spiritual darkness 440
spiritualism 11.1 *occultism,* 368.3 *spiritual world*
Spiritualism 7 Non-Christian Religions
spiritualist 11.12 *occultist,* 368.7 *believer in a nonmaterial world,* 368.9 *parapsychological,* 524.6 *interpreter*
spiritualistic 11.16 *psychic,* 368.9 *parapsychological*
spirituality 7.2 *religiousness,* 11.2 *the occult,* 368.2 *unworldliness,* 863.1 *virtue,* 876.2 *good morals*

spiritualization 368.2 *unworldliness*
spiritualize 11.20 *occult,* 368.12 *enter a nonmaterial world*
spiritual loss 722.1 *loss*
spiritual love 821.1 *love*
spiritually 7.23 *religiously,* 8.19 *divinely,* 11.25 *occultly,* 368.13 *metaphysically,* 863.9 *virtuously*
spiritual marriage 823.3 *types of marriage,* 825.3 *monasticism*
spiritualness 368.2 *unworldliness*
spiritual rebirth 220.3 *persuasion*
spiritual world 368
spirit world 11.2 *the occult,* 368.3 *spiritual world,* 438.5 *invisible thing*
spirit writing 11.1 *occultism*
spirogyra 90 Algae
spirometer 268.8 *meter,* 388.15 *vaporimeter*
spirometric 268.16 *micrometric*
spirometry 268.2 *micrometry*
spissitude 393.2 *semiliquidity,* 394.1 *viscosity*
spit 45.5 *cooker,* 54.11 *coast,* 55.62 *rain,* 98.5 *peninsula,* 110.3 *lookalike,* 114.5 *counterpart,* 137.8 *fastening,* 272.6 *narrow place,* 318.2 *projection,* 349.15 *vomit,* 353.9 *saliva,* 353.20 *salivate,* 364.6 *rotator,* 366.26 *flicker,* 380.8 *sharp-pointed thing,* 386.4 *lubricant,* 389.32 *seep,* 395.5 *lubricant,* 408.4 *burner,* 425.6 *crack,* 830.11 *be irritable*
spit and polish 584.5 *tradition,* 621.1 *cleanness,* 811.11 *ritual,* 813.1 *formality*
spit at 850.26 *cock a snook*
spit ball 22.4 *pitching terms*
spitball 338.5 *throw*
spite 618.11 *harmfulness,* 618.13 *be worthless,* 618.14 *illtreat,* 758.4 *unpleasantness,* 759.6 *bad feeling,* 820.1 *enmity,* 822.1 *hate,* 832.4 *bitterness,* 832.16 *be malevolent,* 842.1 *envy*
spiteful 618.5 *harmful,* 758.2 *unpleasant,* 820.6 *hostile,* 822.10 *hating,* 828.15 *resentful,* 832.14 *hostile,* 842.2 *envious,* 855.14 *vindictive*
spitefully 618.15 *worthlessly,* 820.15 *aggressively,* 822.18 *hatefully,* 828.17 *resentfully,* 832.20 *malevolently,* 842.4 *enviously,* 855.16 *vindictively*
spitefulness 618.11 *harmfulness,* 820.1 *enmity,* 822.1 *hate,* 830.3 *irritableness,* 832.4 *bitterness*
spitfire 241.4 *violent person or animal,* 759.9 *feeling person,* 829.3 *irascible person*
Spiti 32 Breeds of Horse and Pony
spit on one's palms 644.6 *work*
spit out 349.15 *vomit*
spit-roast 45.55 *cook*
spit-roasting 45.8 *cooking technique*
Spitsbergen 98 Islands
spit tacks 366.21 *be agitated,* 822.17 *anger*
spitter 338.5 *throw*
spitting 353.9 *saliva,* 353.29 *salivating,* 425.2 *crack,* 425.9 *crackling*
spitting distance 264.2 *short distance*
spitting image 110.3 *lookalike,* 114.5 *counterpart,* 116.5 *conformity,* 176.5 *twin,* 547.1 *representation,* 547.6 *image,* 560.9 *representation*
spittle 353.9 *saliva,* 386.4 *lubricant,* 387.3 *body fluid,* 389.4 *exudate,* 395.5 *lubricant*
spittlebug 82 Insects
spittoon 727.8 *sink*
spit upon 822.14 *hate*
spitz 77 Breeds of Dogs
Spitz 18 Sporting Personalities
Spitzbergen 53 Mountains

spitzharfe 49 Musical Instruments

spiv 539.17 *cheat*, 858.4 *dishonourable person*

splanchnic 290.10 *visceral*

splanchnography 382.8 *science of structure*

splanchnology 382.8 *science of structure*

splash 96.6 *river flow*, 96.7 *flow*, 162.18 *sprinkle*, 389.11 *wash*, 389.33, 391.5 *sprinkle*, 391.14 *sprinkle*, 424.5 *sound faint*, 429.1, 429.4 *hiss*, 456.4 *maculation*, 526.10 *manifestation*, 532.16 *publicize*, 611.8 *make important*, 622.11 *dirty*, 811.4 *flashiness*

splashboard 71 Motor Vehicle Parts

splashdown 53.35 *rocketry*, 327.13 *flight path*

splash down 327.14 *find one's way*

splashed 391.12 *seeping*

splashing 389.8 *watering*

splash of colour 444.2 *colourfulness*

splash out 748.1 *expend*, 755.10 *be generous*

splash out on 757.8 *overspend*

splashy 391.11 *marshy*

splat 47.12 *wood*

splatter 55.62 *rain*, 162.18, 389.33 *sprinkle*, 391.5 *sprinkle*

splattered 162.23 *sprinkled*

splattering 162.4 *sprinkling*

splay 43 Architectural Decoration, 162.10 *diverge*, 261.1 *growth*, 261.5 *make bigger*, 261.6 *become bigger*, 271.1 *broad*, 271.4 *breadth*, 271.9 *be broad* , 343.12 *separate*

splay apart 343.12 *separate*

splayed 261.7 *bigger*, 271.1 *broad*, 343.8 *fanlike*

splaying 162.5 *divergence*, 261.1 *growth*, 261.8 *growing*, 343.2 *parting*

spleen 415, 290.4 *insides*, 822.1 *hate*, 828.1 *resentment*, 830.3 *irritableness*, 832.4 *bitterness*

spleenful 822.10 *hating*

spleenfully 822.18 *hatefully*

spleenwort 88 Ferns

splendid 439.16 *bright*, 617.1 *worthy*, /42.3 *opulent*, 811.24 *grand*, 861.1 *good*

splendid isolation 816.3 *separation*

splendidly 617.11 *worthily*, 786.13 *wonderfully*, 811.40 *grandly*, 861.22 *well*

splendidness 861.8 *good*

splendiferous 617.1 *worthy*

splendiferousness 811.9 *grandeur*

splendour 439.1 *light*, 789.1 *gorgeousness*, 811.9 *grandeur*

splenectomy 60 Surgical Operations

splenetic 415, 828.15 *resentful*, 832.14 *hostile*

splenetically 415

splice 135.5 *joint*, 135.10 *link*, 407.12 *abut*, 629.1 *repair*

spliced 107.4 *related*, 135.15 *tied*, 823.21 *married*

splice ropes 36.15 *sail*

splicing 629.8 *repair*

spliff 875.6 *drug*

spline 27.7 *bat*

splint 284.3 *body support*, 630.10 *surgical dressing*

splint armour 671.7 *armour*

splinter 136.9 *separate*, 141.3 *disintegrate*, 143.7 *piece*, 149.2 *impurity*, 173.3 *fragment*, 272.8 *narrow thing*, 375.7 *rough thing*, 379.4 *be brittle*

splinter group 500.6 *dissenters*, 665.3 *political grouping*

splintering 379.1 *brittle*, 379.2 *brittleness*

splintery 379.1 *brittle*

split 25.5 *bowling delivery*, 25.8 *bowl*, 25.10 *bowling*, 136.1 *separation*, 136.3 *separateness*, 136.9 *separate*, 136.16 *apart*, 141.4 *deconstruct*, 143.10 *part*, 160.4 *interruption*, 173.8 *divide*, 238.6 *be weak*, 244.13 *be destroyed*, 265.2, 265.5 *crack*, 265.7 *cracked*, 319.1 *notch*, 319.4 *notched*, 319.5 *notch*, 322.1 *opening*, 322.12, 322.18 *open*, 343.12 *separate*, 345.4 *hurry off*, 379.1 *brittle*, 379.2 *brittleness*, 379.4 *be brittle*, 500.4 *faction*, 528.13 *inform on*, 530.7 *betray*, 666.2 *argument*, 666.6 *argue*, 731.4 *allot*, 824.1, 824.7 *divorce*, 824.11 *divorced*

split apart 265.5 *crack*

split down the middle 124.10 *make average*, 158.17 *average*, 176.17 *go halves*, 731.4 *allot*

split four ways 178.12 *quadrisect*

split hairs 115.6 *differentiate*, 474.13 *quibble*, 481.12 *discriminate*, 485.15 *modify*, 503.7 *be accurate*, 852.18 *find fault*

split half-and-half 110.10 *be equal*

split hat trick 27.8 *delivery*

split image 66.4 *portrait*

split infinitive 504.11 *grammatical error*

split in half 176.13 *half*, 176.16 *halve*

split in three 177.11 *trisect*

split in two 158.17 *average*, 176.16 *halve*

split jump 41.6 *ice-skating*

split-level 256.16 *manorial*

split-level house 256.5 *house*

split lutz lift 41.6 *ice-skating*

split off 343.12 *separate*

split one's ears 430.4 *be strident*

split one's sides 431.11, 771.14 *laugh*, 773.8 *laugh*

split pea 45 Vegetables

split personality 61.8 *disordered personality*, 61.16 *dissociation*, 176.3 *duality*, 510.5 *psychosis*

splits 30.8 *floor exercises*

split second 191.3 *instant*

split-second 191.5 *immediate*

split-shot 20.3 *fishing tackle*

splitter 85.7 *timber production*

split the difference 124.10 *make average*, 158.17 *average*, 717.4 *compromise*, 724.4 *have joint possession*

split the ears 423.8 *be loud*

split the uprights 19.17 *kick*

split three ways 177.11 *trisect*

split tin 45.39 *loaf*

splitting 61.19 *defence mechanism*, 136.1 *separation*, 379.1 *brittle*, 379.2 *brittleness*, 406.5 *painful*

splitting headache 406.2 *painful condition*, 624.3 *symptom*

splitting in four 178.5 *quadrisection*

splitting in half 176.7 *halving*

splitting in three 177.5 *trisection*

splitting in two 176.7 *halving*

splitting the atom 56.72 *nuclear fission*

splitting the difference 717.1 *compromise*

split two ways 176.13 *half*, 176.17 *go halves*

split up 136.9 *separate*, 162.9 *be dispersed*, 824.7 *divorce*

split-up 162.5 *divergence*, 162.20 *separated*, 824.1 *divorce*

split up with 666.5 *disagree*

splodge 456.4 *maculation*

splotch 456.4 *maculation*

splurge 405.4 *pleasurable things*, 405.8 *feel pleasure*, 607.1, 607.3 *waste*, 748.1 *expend*, 748.6 *extravagance*, 811.4 *flashiness*

splutter 349.14 *let out*, 353.20 *salivate*, 366.36 *flicker*, 424.5 *sound faint*, 429.1, 429.4 *hiss*

spluttering 353.29 *salivating*, 366.20 *flickering*

Spode ware 44 Types of Ceramics

spodumene 54 Minerals, **54** Gemstones

spoil 33.10 *be on the track*, 133.8 *mix*, 202.17 *grow old*, 216.8 *cause change*, 233.9 *change*, 238.7 *weaken*, 244.11 *ruin*, 405.10 *comfort*, 415.8 *sour*, 467.14 *be solicitous*, 601.1 *misuse*, 610.4 *be excessive*, 618.13 *be worthless*, 628.2 *decay*, 628.4 *impair*, 631.15 *poison*, 656.7 *be clumsy*, 708.4 *be permissive*, 722.13 *destroy*, 771.15 *humour*, 790.5 *make ugly*, 793.7 *blemish*, 826.7 *show endearment for*

spoilage 202.10 *staleness*, 614.6 *refuse*, 628.10 *impairment*

spoiled 145.4 *incomplete*, 405.7 *pleased*, 618.2 *inferior*, 691.5 *given consideration*, 793.4 *blemished*

spoiled child 821.11 *loved one*

spoiled darling 826.6 *object of endearment*

spoiled rotten 691.5 *given consideration*

spoiler 73 Aircraft Parts, 122.4 *equilizer*, 225.3 *stabilizer*, 244.6 *destroyer*, 309.5 *defacer*, 533.3 *reporting*, 734.6 *taker*, 736.9 *plunderer*, 832.8 *malefactor*

spoil for a fight 666.7 *pick a fight*

spoiling 33.6 *motor racing terms*, 467.5 *solicitude*, 628.10 *impairment*, 691.1 *leniency*, 691.4 *lenient*, 722.5 *destruction*, 771.11 *humouring*

spoiling for 572.2 *eager*, 594.18 *prepared*

spoiling for a fight 670.22 *militant*, 674.15 *contentious*

spoil one's chances 211.6 *lose one's chance*

spoil oneself 860.6 *be selfish*

spoil one's pleasure 515.6 *disappoint*

spoil one's reputation 683.6 *fail*

spoils 681, 721.5 *profit*, 734.5 *takings*, 736.4 *stolen goods*

spoils of office 736.4 *stolen goods*

spoils of war 681.2 *spoils*, 721.5 *profit*, 734.5 *takings*, 736.4 *stolen goods*

spoilsport 587.8 *cautionary person*, 642.11 *meddler*, 661.7 *hinderer*, 766.3 *dissatisfied person*, 770.4 *depressing person*, 852.13 *pessimist*

spoils system 228.5 *positive stimulus*

spoilt 127.17 *defective*, 601.4 *misused*, 628.12 *deteriorated*, 793.4 *blemished*

spoil the ship for a ha'p'orth of tar 614.9 *waste effort*, 656.6 *act foolishly*

Spokane 93 Cities

spoke 71.11 *bicycle part*, 343.3 *radiation*, 359.10 *step*

spoked 343.7 *radiating*

spoken 5.39 *of language*, 534.34 *communicated*, 564.16 *speech*

spoken for 714.12 *promised*, 823.22 *marriageable*

spoken language 5, 564.1 *faculty of speech*

spoken letter 5

spoken radio 420.9 *audio device*

spoken unit 5.17 *word*

spoken word 564.7 *utterance*

spokes 342.5 *focus*

spokeshave 47.11 *woodworking tool*, 376.9 *smoother*, 380.9 *sharp-edged thing*

spokesman 524.7 *news interpreter*, 528.9 *informant*, 533.4 *journalist*, 547.8 *representative*, 564.10 *speaker*, 567.6 *public speaker*, 646.3 *agent*, 678.4 *representative*, 707.1 *deputy*

spokesperson 158.9 *middleman*, 528.9 *informant*, 547.8 *representative*, 564.10 *speaker*, 567.6 *public speaker*, 646.3 *agent*,

spokeswoman 564.10 *speaker*, 567.6 *public speaker*, 678.4 *representative*, 707.1 *deputy*

spoliate 722.13 *destroy*, 736.14 *plunder*

spoliation 244.5 *havoc*, 722.5 *destruction*, 734.3 *taking away*, 736.5 *plundering*

spolitory 736.17 *stolen*

spondaic 48.20 *metrical*

spondee 48.9 *metre*

spondulix 741.2 *cash*

sponge 81, 348, 808, 76.5 *aquatic animal*, 322.6 *porous thing*, 348.13 *absorb*, 370.7 *light thing*, 389.34 *hose*, 390.10 *air bubble*, 392.15 *dryer* , 392.20 *absorb*, 546.4 *eraser*, 621.10 *cleaning object*, 621.13 *clean*, 643.12 *be inactive*, 712.8 *solicit money*, 733.7 *borrow*, 754.14 *buy cheaply*, 808.3 *sycophant*, 874.17 *drunkard*

sponge bag 258.8 *bag*

sponge bath 621.6 *bath*

sponge cake 45.36 *cake*, 414.3 *dessert*

spongelike 81

sponge off 546.1 *obliterate*, 621.13 *clean*

sponge on 808.15 *sponge*

spongeous 348.17 *absorbent*

sponge out 546.1 *obliterate*

sponger 808, 138.5 *follower*, 643.8 *nonworker*, 712.5 *beggar*, 733.6 *borrower*, 754.8 *bargain hunter*

sponge rubber 377.4 *rubber*

sponge up 351.13 *drink*

spongeware 44.1 *ceramics*

spongiform encephalopathy 510.3 *mental deterioration*

sponginess 372.3 *sparseness*, 374.10 *compressibility*, 393.4 *pulpiness*

sponging 348.5 *absorption*, 712.3 *solicitation*, 712.11 *begging*, 808.2 *sycophancy*, 808.7 *sycophantic*

spongy 81.22 *spongelike*, 98.11 *continental*, 317.5 *concave*, 322.14 *holed*, 348.17 *absorbent*, 372.1 *sparse*, 374.4 *compressible*, 393.18 *pulpy*

sponsor 284.8 *supporter*, 284.13 *support financially*, 535.9 *affirmer*, 602.6 *find means*, 662.15 *benefactor*, 662.23 *advise*, 662.29 *finance*, 851.7 *advocate*

sponsorship 284.7 *financial support*, 602.4 *financial resources*, 632.2 *protection*, 662.6 *financial assistance*, 662.9 *patronage*

spontaneity 583, 595

spontaneous 583, 595, 15.10 *unionized*, 464.8 *instinctive*, 572.5 *voluntary*, 658.1 *naive*, 698.13 *informal*

spontaneous abortion 247.1 *infertility*

spontaneous combustion 408.6 *fire*

spontaneous generation 245.3 *propagation*

spontaneously 572, 595, 15.13 *industrially*, 464.11 *intuitively*, 583.7 *extempore*, 698.22 *informally*

spontaneous person 583.6 *improviser*

spontaneous response 331.6 *response*

spontaneous strike 15.4 *industrial dispute*

spoof 118.3 *mockery*, 118.9 *imitate*, 539.11 *hoax*, 539.28 *trick*, 539.31 *hoax*

spoofed 539.36 *deceived*

spoofer 539.15 *deceiver*

spook 11.11 *ghost*, 102.2 *illusion*, 153 7 *disturb*, 253.6 *ghostly presence*

spooked 11.19 *bewitched*

spookily 11.26 *magically*

spooky 11.18 *spiritual*, 777.10

frightening
spool 65.19 *abort*, 66.9 *film*, 364.6 *rotator*
spoon 20.2 *artificial fly*, 29.4 *golf club*, 36.11 *rowing*, 120.3 *container*, 133.6 *mixer*, 258.17 *ladle*, 326.15 *take away*, 350.16 *eating utensil*, 355.10 *excavator*, 821.26 *court*, 821.27 *kiss*, 826.8 *court*
spoonbill 78 Birds, 78.3 *water bird*
spoon bread 45.38 *bread*
spooned 258.20 *containing*
spoonerism 5.29 *grammar*, 504.11 *grammatical error*, 506.2 *solecism*, 798.4 *joke*
spoon-feed 826.7 *show endearment for*
spoon in 350.22 *eat well*
spooning 821.6 *courtship*, 821.14 *communication of love*, 826.1 *endearment*
spoon oar 36.4 *rowing*
spoons 49 Musical Instruments
spoor 483.4 *indication*, 545.12 *vestige*, 590.9 *follow*
spooring 590.1 *pursuit*
sporadic 113.5 *diverse*, 151.14 *irregular*, 160.8 *discontinuous*, 162.19 *dispersed*, 182.6 *sparse*, 185.23 *occasional*, 187.9 *periodic*, 213.2 *infrequent*, 215.4 *irregular*, 626.6 *contagious*
sporadically 113.11 *irregularly*, 151.27 *in disorder*, 160.17 *discontinuously*, 162.30 *diffusely*, 185.28 *sometimes*, 215.8 *irregularly*
sporadicalness 160.1 *discontinuity*, 215.1 *irregularity*
sporadicness 182.4 *rarity*
sporangium 88.2 *fern plant*
spore 384, 59.7 *cell*, 88.2 *fern plant*, 89.4 *fungal body*, 226.3 *rudiment*
spore capsule 88.4 *moss plant*
spore case 88.2 *fern plant*
spore-producing protozoan 81.9 *protozoan*
sporicide 62.4 *drug type*
sporophore 89.4 *fungal body*
sporophyte 88.2 *fern plant*
Sporozoa 81.9 *protozoan*
sporozoan 81.9 *protozoan* , 81.23 *protozoan*
sport 18, 26.15 *wrestling*, 401.3 *male title of address*, 526.1 *display*, 539.11 *hoax*, 625.1 *hygiene*, 644.5 *exercise*, 674.1 *contention*, 674.2 *contest*, 811.27 *show*
Sport 18
sported 526.13 *displayed*
sportily 295.36 *dressily*, 811.35 *flashily*
sporting 18, 674.14 *contending*, 843.11 *right-minded*, 857.4 *honourable*
sporting activity 18
sporting chance 229.2 *chance*, 486.3 *strong possibility*, 488.4 *chance*, 589.4 *fair chance*
sporting dog 37
sporting error 504
sporting event 674.2 *contest*
sporting feat 655.3 *masterpiece*
sporting gun 680.9 *firearm*
sporting hit 330
sporting jacket 295.11 *jacket*
sportingly 857.7 *honourably*
sporting rifle 37.3 *hunting equipment*
sportive 18.5 *sporting*
sport karate 26.8 *karate*
sport of kings 32.7 *horseracing*, 674.4 *race*
sports 644.5 *exercise*, 674.1 *contention*
sports aerobics 18 Sporting Activities
sports and recreation 15.2 *industrial negotiations*
sports bag 258.8 *bag*
sports book 532.6 *book publishing*
sports car 71 Motor Vehicles,

71.16 *car*, 329.11 *swift thing*
Sports Car Club of America 33.7 *racing governing body*
sports car race 33
sports-car race 33.1 *motor racing*
sports car racing 33.1 *motor racing*
sportscast 533.6 *radio news*
sportscaster 533.4 *journalist*
sportscasting 533.3 *reporting*
sports coat 295.11 *jacket*
sports correspondent 560.10 *descriptive writer*
sports day 674.2 *contest*
sports desk 533.8 *newsroom*
sports edition 532.4 *newspaper*
sports editor 532.11 *newspaper man*, 533.4 *journalist*
sports equipment 21
sports field 6.15 *schoolroom*
sports forecaster 517.9 *forecaster*
sportsground 18
sports jacket 295.4 *informal dress*, 295.11 *jacket*
sportsman 18, 37.4 *hunter*, 237.5 *athlete*, 590.6 *hunter*, 679.3 *athlete*, 857.3 *honourable person*
sportsmanlike 843.11 *right-minded*, 857.4 *honourable*
sports outfit 544.5 *uniform*
sportsperson 37.4 *hunter*
sports reporter 533.4 *journalist*
sports shirt 295.8 *shirt*
sports skirt 295.6 *skirt*
sports trophy 681.1 *trophy*
sports uniform 544.5 *uniform*
sportswear 295.1 *dress*, 295.4 *informal dress*
sportswoman 37.4, 590.6 *hunter*, 679.3 *athlete*, 857.3 *honourable person*
sporty 18.5 *sporting*, 295.31 *styled*, 811.19 *flashy*
sporty person 237.5 *athlete*
sporty type 18.3 *sportsman*
sporule 384.10 *spore*
spot 793, 51.18 *stage lighting*, 126.2 *leadership*, 149.2 *impurity*, 162.18 *sprinkle*, 250.1 *location*, 250.2 *exact location*, 250.9 *locate*, 251.1 *situation*, 309.3 *deformity*, 309.11 *deform*, 435.12 *see*, 456.4 *maculation*, 456.11 *variegate*, 496.1 *discover*, 522.7 *recognize*, 620.7 *defect*, 622.4 *dirt*, 622.11 *dirty*, 624.13 *skin disease*, 628.5 *hurt*, 659.5 *predicament*, 793.2 *pimple*, 793.7 *blemish*
spot cash 741.2 *cash*
spotless 134.12 *morally pure*, 134.13, 446.5 *pure*, 619.1 *perfect*, 621.16 *clean*, 863.5 *virtuous*, 865.5 *innocent*, 876.9 *pure*
spotlessly 134.19 *purely*, 619.7 *perfectly*, 621.19 *cleanly*, 865.11 *innocently*
spotlessness 134.1, 446.11 *purity*, 619.3 *perfection*, 621.1 *cleanness*, 865.1 *innocence*
spotlight 51.18 *stage lighting*, 66.15 *lighting*, 437.7 *that which makes visible*, 437.10 *make visible*, 439.6 *electric light*, 439.24 *light*, 526.1 *display*, 526.3 *reveal*, 526.10 *manifestation*, 532.7 *publicity*, 532.16 *publicize*, 554.6 *emphasize*
spotlighted 437.2 *clear*
spotlit 439.18 *lit*
spot meter 66.18 *exposure time*
spot of bother 151.9 *disorder*, 153.5 *commotion*, 500.1 *dissent*, 659.7 *awkward situation*, 661.2 *obstacle*, 764.8 *quarrel*, 768.3 *nuisance*
spot of enforcement 19.13 *penalty*
spot of trouble 659.7 *awkward situation*
spot on 503.5 *accurate*, 537.39 *accurately*, 619.1 *perfect*, 843.8 *correct*
spot-on 537.21 *accurate*
spot pass 19.9 *play*
spot putt 29.3 *golf shots*, 29.7

golf
spots 42.5 *dice*, 624.3 *symptom*
spot stroke 24.2 *billiards play*
spotted 24.9 *billiard*, 162.23 *sprinkled*, 456.10 *mottled*, 496.14 *discovered*, 620.1 *imperfect*, 622.7 *dirty*, 793.5 *marked*
spotted dick 45.35 *dessert*
spotted gum 85 Trees and Shrubs
spotted wilt 69.12 *pests and diseases*
spotter 435.11 *observer*, 496.12 *discoverer*
spot the ball 24.8 *play billiards*
spottiness 215.1 *irregularity*, 456.4 *maculation*
spotting 162.4 *sprinkling*, 496.6 *discovery*
spotty 160.8 *discontinuous*, 215.4 *irregular*, 309.7 *deformed*, 456.10 *mottled*, 624.23 *diseased*
spot white ball 24.3 *English billiards*
spousal 823.5 *wedding*, 823.20 *matrimonial*
spouse 823, 180.12 *partner*, 401.13 *man in the family*, 402.12 *woman in the family*
spousehood 823.1 *marriage*
spouseless 825.6 *celibate*
spout 347.7 *outlet*, 347.11 *run out*, 349.14 *let out*, 349.22 *disgorgement*, 359.2 *upturn*, 359.17 *spring up*, 387.25 *flow*, 565.8 *talk too much*
spouter 359.12 *geyser*
spouting 521.5 *empty talk*
spout out 347.11 *run out*
sprag 71 Motor Vehicle Parts
sprain 238.7 *weaken*, 241.3 *instance of violence*, 241.8 *use violence*, 406.3 *injury*, 406.11 *inflict pain*, 628.11 *hurt*
sprained 406.6 *injured*
sprat 80 Fishes, 45.18 *sea fish*, 80.8 *food fish*
sprat to catch a mackerel 539.13 *snare*
sprawl 162, 162.9 *be dispersed*, 261.1 *growth*, 261.5 *make bigger*, 261.6 *become bigger*, 282.1 *horizontality*, 282.6 *be horizontal*, 360.4 *fall*, 360.11 *trip*, 649.2 *take it easy*
sprawled 162, 282.10 *lying*
sprawling 162.25 *sprawled*, 261.1 *growth*, 261.8 *growing*, 282.1 *horizontality*, 282.10 *lying*, 360.18 *falling*
sprawly 261.8 *growing*
spray 62.10 *inhalant*, 68.14 *pest control*, 68.17 *farm*, 69.8 *weedkiller*, 69.15 *cultivate*, 83.5 *stem*, 84.1 *flower*, 87.12 *manage grassland*, 143.6 *branch*, 161.29 *bunch*, 162.18 *sprinkle*, 338.7 *shot*, 388.11 *vaporizer*, 388.26 *aerate*, 389.12 *sprinkler*, 389.33 *sprinkle*, 390.10 *air bubble*, 391.14 *sprinkle*, 418.6 *perfume*, 670.15 *firing*
spray can 389.12 *sprinkler*
spray-can painting 50.8 *painting*
spray deodorant 417.2 *deodorant*
sprayed 162.23 *sprinkled*
sprayer 68.10 *farm tool*, 69.6 *garden tool*, 389.12 *sprinkler*
spraygun 50.11 *artist's materials*
spraying 162.4 *sprinkling*, 389.8 *watering*, 391.5 *sprinkle*
spread 128, 52.60 *parameter*, 68.6 *farm*, 73.7 *miscellaneous aviation terms*, 85.19 *grow*, 128.4 *increase*, 136.1 *separation*, 162.1 *dispersion*, 162.9 *be dispersed*, 162.16 *distribute*, 162.22 *distributed*, 164.24 *broaden*, 233.10 *be a prevailing influence*, 248.20 *extend*, 259.1 *size*, 261.1 *growth*, 261.5 *make bigger*, 261.6 *become bigger*, 261.7 *bigger*, 266.10 *layer*, 271.11 *broaden*, 282.7 *make horizontal*, 282.9 *flattened*, 293.10 *bed covering*, 293.24

coat, 322.19 *open up*, 326.3 *transmission*, 326.11 *transfer*, 343.2 *parting*, 343.11 *move apart*, 350.13 *feast*, 395.18 *anoint*, 405.4 *pleasurable things*, 532.13 *make public*, 532.17 *be published*, 721.2 *augmentation*, 721.10 *augment*, 872.3 *act of gluttony*
spreadability 261.2 *enlargeability*
spreadable 261.9 *enlargeable*
spread abroad 532.13 *make public*, 532.17 *be published*
spread around 532.19 *published*, 731.4 *allot*
spread a rumour 532.13 *make public*, 538.21 *lie*
spread canvas 74.9 *navigate*, 345.5 *set out*
spreadeagle 269.9 *be long*, 360.11 *trip*, 362.3 *bring down*, 362.8 *sit*
spread eagle 544.4 *insignia*, 544.8 *heraldic device*
spread-eagle 282.6 *be horizontal*, 343.14 *branch*, 879.1 *punish*
spread-eagled 282.10 *lying*, 343.8 *fanlike*
spreader 69.6 *garden tool*, 261.4 *enlarger*
spreader of alarm and despondency 777.5 *frightener*
spread far and wide 610.4 *be excessive*
spread fence 32.9 *jumping*
spread formation 19.7 *offence*
spread foundation 63.28 *substructure*
spreading 128.6 *increasing*, 136.1 *separation*, 162.28 *dispersive*, 261.1 *growth*, 261.8 *growing*, 326.3 *transmission*, 721.2 *augmentation*
spreading abroad 532.1 *publication*
spreading like wildfire 128.6 *increasing*
spreading out 261.1 *growth*, 343.2 *parting*
spreading the word 532.1 *publication*
spread like wildfire 233.10 *be a prevailing influence*, 261.6 *become bigger*, 532.17 *be published*
spread on 293.24 *coat*
spread oneself thin 642.13 *be busy*
spread one's wings 113.8 *be diverse*
spread out 162.9 *be dispersed*, 182.6 *sparse*, 182.9 *scatter*, 248.20 *extend*, 248.21 *space*, 261.5 *make bigger*, 261.6 *become bigger*, 343.11 *move apart*, 526.3 *reveal*
spread-out 261.7 *bigger*, 271.1 *broad*
spread over 144.6 *fill*, 293.24 *coat*
spread sail 345.5 *set out*
spreadsheet 65.11 *application*, 152.8 *chart*, 171.12 *table*
spread the bull 521.9 *talk nonsense*
spread the good news 7.20 *preach*
spread the load 706.4 *delegate*
spread the word 497.9 *make someone believe*, 532.13 *make public*
spread the Word 7.20 *preach*
Sprechgesang 49.4 *opera*
spree 405.4 *pleasurable things*, 607.3 *waste*, 748.6 *extravagance*, 874.14 *drinking bout*
sprig 143.6 *branch*, 206.5 *young plant*
sprightliness 396.1 *life*
sprightly 396.13 *lively*, 642.18 *active*
spring 74 Rigging, **161** Collective Names for Birds and Animals, **203**, **203**, **377**, 21.6 *jump*, 36.3 *parts of a sailing boat*, 155.25 *result*, 156.27 *emerge*, 214.5 *regular thing*, 226.2 *source*, 235.4 *energy*,

314.2 *coil*, 329.4 *be swift*, 329.6 *accelerate*, 329.9 *acceleration*, 331.1, 331.4 *recoil*, 347.2 *outflow*, 359.5, 359.18 *jump*, 361.10 *elevator*, 374.13 *soften*, 377.1 *elasticity*, 377.3 *elastic thing*, 377.8 *be elastic*, 389.1 *water*, 603.4 *machine*, 605.2 *resource*
spring apart 136.9 *separate*
spring back 331.1 *recoil*
spring balance 56.86 *weighing instrument*, 369.10 *scales*
spring barley 68.12 *crop*
springboard 30.3 *gymnastic apparatus*, 30.6 *pommel horse*, 39.6 *diving*, 39.11 *swimming*, 331.5 *reflector*, 345.10 *place of departure*, 359.8 *lift*, 361.10 *elevator*, 377.3 *elastic thing*, 662.1 *help*
springboard diving 39.6 *diving*
springbok 77 Placental Mammals
Springbok 93 Cities
spring cabbage 45 Vegetables
spring catch 137.8 *fastening*
spring-clean 621.13 *clean*
spring-cleaning 621.2 *cleaning*
springe 635.1 *trap*
springer 43.9 *miscellaneous architectural features*
springer spaniel 77 Breeds of Dogs
Springfield 93 Cities
spring forward 329.6 *accelerate*
spring from 227.7 *follow from*
spring greens 45.33 *vegetable*, 453.9 *greenstuff*
spring gun 539.13 *snare*
springhaas 77 Placental Mammals
springily 377.11 *elastically*
springiness 235.4 *energy*, 374.8 *softness*, 377.1 *elasticity*
springing 331.8 *recoiling*, 359.24 *leaping*, 374.8 *softness*, 377.6 *elastic*
springlike 55.46 *seasonal*, 203.10 *spring*, 453.4 *fresh*
spring-like 408.11 *warm*
spring oats 68.12 *crop*
spring on 514.9 *surprise*
spring onion 45 Vegetables
spring roll 45.48 *Chinese dish*
spring rounds 10.7 *non-Christian ritual*
springs 284.4 *rest*
spring sale 739.4 *sale*
spring scale 369.10 *scales*
springtail 82 Insects
spring tide 54.15, 97.2 *tide*, 128.3 *increasing thing*
springtide 203.2 *spring*
spring tide 214.5 *regular thing*, 275.8 *high thing*
springtime 203.2 *spring*
springtime of life 206.1 *youth*
spring-tine harrows 68.10 *farm tool*
spring up 359, 54.63 *ebb*, 89.12 *mushroom*, 128.4 *increase*, 156.27 *emerge*, 261.6 *become bigger*
spring up like mushrooms 245.12 *multiply*, 246.6 *be fertile*
spring upon 514.10 *ambush*
spring water 351.6 *soft drink*, 389.1 *water*
spring wheat 68.12 *crop*
spring wood 85.3 *timber*
springy 331.8 *recoiling*, 374.2 *pliant*, 377.6 *elastic*
sprinkle 162, 389, 391, 391, 10.18 *perform rites*, 69.15 *cultivate*, 133.8 *mix*, 182.9 *scatter*, 362.6 *throw down*, 384.22 *powder*, 389.29 *water*, 456.11 *variegate*
sprinkled 162, 182.6 *sparse*, 456.10 *mottled*
sprinkler 389, 69.6 *garden tool*, 621.10 *cleaning object*
sprinkler head 389.12 *sprinkler*
sprinkler system 632.4 *safety device*
sprinkling 162, 10.5 *Christian rite*, 133.4 *admixture*, 182.1

few, 278.3 *shallowness*, 362.20 *falling*, 389.8 *watering*, 391.5 *sprinkle*, 542.6 *suggestion*
sprinkling of water 621.3 *religious cleansing*
sprinkling system 389.12 *sprinkler*
sprint 21.1 *track events*, 21.6 *race*, 33.1 *motor racing*, 41.13 *ice-skating*, 329.6 *accelerate*, 329.9 *acceleration*, 648.2 *make haste*, 674.4 *race*
sprinter 21.3 *athlete*, 32.2 *thoroughbred*, 32.7 *horseracing*, 237.5 *athlete*, 329.13 *swift person*, 674.10 *contender*
sprinting 18 Sporting Activities, 21.1 *track events*, 21.6 *track*, 41.12 *ski*
sprinting race 41.2 *cross-country skiing*
sprint race 21.1 *track events*, 36.4 *rowing*
sprint racing 21.1 *track events*
sprint-skate 41.15 *ice-skate*
sprint-skating 41.8 *speed-skating*
sprit 36.3 *parts of a sailing boat*, 36.8 *punting*
sprite 11.11 *ghost*, 65.17 *computing term*, 260.4 *little person*
spritsail 74 Sails
spritzer 351.8 *mixed drink*
sprocket 380.8 *sharp-pointed thing*
sprocket wheel 364.6 *rotator*
sprog 245.6 *progeny*
sprout 45 Vegetables, 83.5 *stem*, 83.21 *vegetate*, 128.4 *increase*, 156.27 *emerge*, 206.5 *young plant*, 227.8 *grow*, 245.11 *have young*, 261.6 *become bigger*
sprouting 261.1 *growth*, 261.8 *growing*
sprout up 83.21 *vegetate*, 261.6 *become bigger*
spruce 85 Trees and Shrubs, 150.13 *orderly*, 295.30 *dressed up*, 621.13, 621.16 *clean*
spruced up 295.30 *dressed up*
spruce pine 85 Trees and Shrubs
spruce up 150.21 *tidy*, 295.33 *dress up*, 621.13 *clean*, 627.1 *improve*, 651.1 *refresh*, 791.15 *beautify*, 792.11 *paint and decorate*
sprung 374.1 *soft*, 377.6 *elastic*
sprung rhythm 48.9 *metre*
spry 239.4 *vigorous*, 642.18 *active*
spumante 351.9 *wine*
spume 54.14, 97.3 *wave*, 370.7 *light thing*, 390.10 *air bubble*
spumy 446.2 *whitened*
spun 67
spunk 235.5 *vitality*, 237.1 *strength*, 239.1 *vigour*, 410.2 *lighter*, 574.16 *fortitude*, 778.1 *courage*
spunky 239.4 *vigorous*, 778.9 *courageous*
spun out 269.1 *long*, 553.3 *diffuse*
spun-out six-gear 33.11 *racing*
spur 72.2 *track*, 85.2 *tree part*, 95.1 *mountain*, 98.5 *peninsula*, 128.1 *increase*, 143.6 *branch*, 228.3 *stimulus*, 228.9 *motivate*, 275.4 *mountain range*, 329.7 *hurry someone up*, 330.1 *impel*, 380.15 *make sharp*, 586.8 *incentive*, 648.1 *hasten*, 648.4 *haste*, 710.9 *offer*, 769.8 *cheer*
spurge 84 Flowers and Flowering Plants
spur gear 63.7 *gear*, 603.4 *machine*
spurious 540, 102.12 *not the real thing*, 114.8 *simulated*, 286.5 *devious*, 309.8 *exaggerated*, 474.7, 474.7 *sophistic*, 477.14 *questionable*, 538.14 *unreal*, 540.25 *false*, 846.8 *unentitled*
spuriously 540, 114.14 *comparably*, 286.9 *deviously*, 309.14 *distortedly*, 474.14 *sophistically*,

538.28 *dishonestly*
spuriousness 540, 286.3 *deviousness*, 309.4 *distortion of the truth*, 538.2 *unrealness*, 540.1 *falsehood*
spurious signal 64.14 *terminal*
spurn 147.7 *exclude*, 341.1 *repel*, 349.4 *ostracize*, 581.1 *reject*, 581.5 *rejection*, 668.6 *be insubordinate*, 711.6 *dissent*, 822.14 *hate*, 850.5, 850.23 *insult*
spurned 785.9 *disliked*, 822.12 *hated*
spurned lover 581.9 *rejected person*
spurning 341.6 *repulse*, 850.5 *insult*, 850.11 *insulting*
spur of the moment 586.11 *motive*
spur-of-the-moment 583.2 *spontaneous*
spur-of-the-moment response 331.6 *response*
spur on 128.5 *make bigger*, 228.9 *motivate*, 769.8 *cheer*
spurred on 228.12 *motivated*, 586.20 *persuadable*
spurrey 84 Flowers and Flowering Plants
spurs 681.1 *trophy*, 792.3 *honour*
spurt 329.6 *accelerate*, 329.9 *acceleration*, 336.13 *step*, 347.11 *run out*, 349.14 *let out*, 349.22 *disgorgement*, 359.2 *upturn*, 359.17 *spring up*, 638.7 *leak*, 642.3 *nimbleness*, 642.12 *be active*, 648.2 *make haste*, 648.4 *haste*
spurt of activity 583.5 *spontaneity*
spurt out 347.11 *run out*
spur wheel 364.6 *rotator*, 603.4 *machine*
sputnik 53.32 *satellite*
Sputnik 363.4 *orbiting body*
sputter 57.29 *absorb*, 349.14 *let out*, 366.12, 366.26 *flicker*, 424.5 *sound faint*, 426.10 *rattle*, 429.1, 429.4 *hiss*
sputtering 57.20 *surface chemistry*, 366.20 *flickering*, 426.17 *rattling*
sputter-ion pump 57.20 *surface chemistry*
sputtery 366.20 *flickering*
sputum 352.2 *secreted substance*
sputum test 60.7 *diagnosis*
spy 435.12 *see*, 465.4 *meddler*, 483.7 *person who gives evidence*, 496.1 *discover*, 496.12 *discoverer*, 529.2 *secretiveness*, 636.4 *warner*, 642.17 *meddle*, 693.16 *be subversive*, 713.5 *seditionist*
spyglass 435.10 *visual aid*
spyhole 435.9 *viewpoint*
spying 435.3 *observation*, 693.3 *subversion*
spy on 435.15 *watch*
spy plane 679.31 *military aircraft*
spy satellite 53.32 *satellite*
spy story 48.2, 560.5 *fiction*
squab 45.20 *meat*, 78.12 *young bird*, 259.16 *fat*
squabble 117.4 *disagreement*, 117.14 *disagree*, 473.1 *argument*, 473.13 *argue*, 500.1 *dissent*, 642.1 *activity*, 642.12 *be active*, 666.2 *argument*, 666.6 *argue*, 674.1 *contention*, 674.13 *conflict*, 764.8, 764.11 *quarrel*
squabbling 117.4 *disagreement*, 117.10 *disagreeing*, 473.7 *arguing*, 666.9 *disagreeing*, 764.7 *dissension*
squad 17.4 *military organization*, 161.12 *team*, 161.14 *force*, 646.4 *personnel*, 665.1 *party*, 679.16 *army unit*
squad car 717.7 *police car*
squadron 17.4 *military organization*, 140.3 *assembly*, 161.14 *force*, 679.16 *army unit*, 679.23 *naval unit*, 679.30 *air force unit*
squadron leader 679.32 *airman*
Squadron Leader 17 British Military Ranks
squalene 58.20 *terpene*
squalid 151.15 *untidy*, 559.10

ugly, 618.4 *poor*, 622.7 *dirty*, 622.8 *unclean*, 626.5 *unhygienic*, 743.3 *beggarly*, 758.2 *unpleasant*
squalidity 622.1 *dirtiness*
squalidly 626.8 *unhygienically*
squalidness 151.3 *untidiness*, 618.10 *poverty*, 622.1 *dirtiness*
squall 55.12 *wind*, 241.5 *violent weather*, 366.3 *turbulence*, 366.13 *tempest*, 431.10 *cry out*, 635.1 *trap*
squally 55.47 *windy*
squalor 618.10 *poverty*, 622.1 *dirtiness*, 626.1, 626.1 *lack of hygiene*, 743.7 *beggary*, 758.4 *unpleasantness*
squama 266.4 *slice*
Squamata 79.1 *reptile*
squamation 266.6 *layering*
squamose 266.9 *platelike*
squamosely 266.12 *in layers*
squamous 79.11 *reptilian*, 80.14 *ichthyological*, 266.9 *platelike*
squamously 266.12 *in layers*
squamulose 266.9 *platelike*
squander 244.12 *consume*, 599.1 *use*, 601.1 *misuse*, 607.1 *waste*, 609.7 *make insufficient*, 722.11 *be wasteful*, 748.1 *expend*, 757.7 *waste*, 870.11 *overindulge*
squandered 614.2 *futile*, 722.16 *losing*
squanderer 607.6 *waster*, 722.6 *luser*, 748.9, 757.6 *spendthrift*
squandering 607.3, 722.3 *waste*, 722.17 *unprofitable*, 757.4 *extravagance*
square 27.2 *ground*, 27.4 *team*, 27.14 *positioned*, 36.16 *row*, 42.4 *chess terms*, 52.17 *multiplication*, 52.44 *polygon*, 52.82 *polygonal*, 52.91 *add*, 74.9 *navigate*, 93.7 *city district*, 122.6 *equal*, 122.11 *equalize*, 125.5 *counterbalance*, 128.5 *make bigger*, 167.6, 167.14 *conformist*, 170.9 *add*, 176.1 *two*, 176.15 *double*, 178.2, 178.8 *quadrilateral*, 225.5 *stable person*, 259.17 *stocky*, 281.4 *plumb line*, 281.6 *make vertical*, 281.10 *perpendicular*, 306.7 *form*, 310.3 *angled figure*, 310.4 *angular measurement*, 310.9 *angled*, 312.4 *traditional*, 332.9 *directly*, 381.1 *blunt*, 537.31 *be accurate*, 537.39 *accurately*, 586.17 *bribe*, 679.16 *army unit*, 735.5 *compensate*, 738.4 *buy off*, 843.7 *right*, 857.4 *honourable*
square accounts 750.9 *settle accounts*
square bracket 137.4 *means of connection*
square brackets 52.25 *algebraic expression*, 543.7 *punctuation*
square bridge 63.21 *bridge*
square cut 27.9 *stroke*, 27.17 *bat*
squared 36.11 *rowing*, 122.6 *equal*, 176.1, 176.9 *two*, 306.9 *formed*, 537.21 *accurate*
square dance 46.1 *dancing*, 46.4 *historic dancing*, 178.3 *foursome*, 815.5 *party*
square deal 843.1 *fairness*
square-in pass 19.9 *play*
square it 840.5 *atone*
square John 167.6 *conformist*
square knot 74 Knots
square leg 27.4 *team*
square-leg umpire 27.3 *official*
squarely 26.16 *professionally*, 122.13 *equitably*, 178.13 *four times*, 332.9 *directly*, 503.8, 537.39 *accurately*, 843.20 *correctly*, 857.7 *honourably*
square match 29.2 *golfing terms*
square matrix 52.22 *matrix*
square meal 350.12 *meal*
square measure 75.1 *unit*
squareness 259.6 *squatness*, 281.1 *verticality*
square off 117.14 *disagree*
square one 156.1 *beginning*,

156.11 *starting point*
square-out pass 19.9 *play*
square peg 117.6 *misfit*, 816.6
unsocial person
square peg in a round hole
108.2 *unrelated thing*, 149.9
misfit, 168.7 *nonconformist*,
252.7 *displaced person*, 335.19
deviant person, 666.4 *dissenter*
square-rigged 36.10 *sailing*
square rigger 74 Sailing Ships
and Boats
square-rigger 36.2 *sailing boat*
square root 52.17 *multiplication*,
169.6 *power*
square root sign 52.13 *mathematical symbol*
square sail 74 Sails
square shooter 857.3 *honourable
person*
square the account 672.3 *retaliate*
square things 840.5 *atone*
square-toed shoes 295.19 *footwear*
square up 125.5 *counterbalance*
square up to 674.12 *fight*
square wave 56.16 *waveform*,
365.5 *wave*
square with 116.25, 167.7 *conform*
square with facts 537.27 *be true*
square with the evidence 537.27
be true
square with the facts 537.29 *be
truthful*
squaring 36.4, 36.11 *rowing*,
537.8 *accuracy*, 735.2 *compensation*, 840.1 *atonement*, 840.4
atoning
squaring the circle 52.49 *geometric construction*, 529.5 *difficult
problem*
squash 18 Sporting Activities,
45 Vegetables, **40**, 40.8
squash, 244.8 *destroy*, 351.6
soft drink, 362.5 *bear down on*,
374.13 *soften*, 384.27 *beat*,
393.8 *pulp*, 424.1 *faintness*,
424.5 *sound faint*, 429.1, 429.4
hiss, 476.8 *refute*, 618.14 *illtreat*, 806.17 *humiliate*
Squash 40
squash ball 40.9 *squash terms*
squash bug 82 Insects
squash court 40.8 *squash*
squashed 806.3 *humbled*
squashed flat 282.9 *flattened*
squash equipment 40.9 *squash
terms*
squash flat 276.9 *lower*, 282.7
make horizontal
squashily 429.8 *sibilantly*
squashiness 374.10 *compressibility*, 393.4 *pulpiness*
squash racket 40.9 *squash terms*
squash rackets 40.8 *squash*
squash terms 40
squashy 98.11 *continental*,
374.4 *compressible*, 387.15 *flowing*, 391.11 *marshy*, 393.18
pulpy
squat 104.16 *be external*, 149.17
intrude, 255.15 *settle*, 256.1
habitat, 256.8 *shelter*, 256.17
inhabit, 259.17 *stocky*, 260.7 *little*, 270.7 *short*, 276.5 *low*,
276.8 *be low*, 357.5 *transgress*,
362.8 *sit*, 362.16 *courtesy*,
723.7 *possess*, 734.7 *take*,
846.14 *arrogate*
squatness 259, 260.1 *littleness*,
270.1 *shortness*, 276.1 *lowness*
squat on 723.7 *possess*
squatted 255.11 *inhabited*
squatter 104.8, 149.10 *intruder*,
255.6 *illegal occupant*, 723.5
possessor, 743.10 *poor person*,
846.7 *usurper*
squatterism 723.1 *possession*
squatters' rights 723.1 *possession*
squatting 30.11 *gymnastic*,
362.23 *sedentary*, 723.1 *possession*, 723.8 *possessing*
squatting vault 30.6 *pommel
horse*
squaw 402.12 *woman in the family*, 823.11 *married woman*

squawk 406.12 *express pain*,
423.8 *be loud*, 430.1 *stridency ,
430.4 *be strident*, 432.2 *bird
song*, 432.5 *sing*, 713.3 *gesture
of protest*, 713.7 *complain*
squawking 430.7 *strident*
squawky 430.7 *strident*
squeak 424.1 *faintness*, 424.5
sound faint, 430.3 *shrillness*,
430.6 *be shrill*, 432.2 *bird song*,
432.4 *cry*, 564.13 *speak in a particular way*
squeaker 528.10 *informer*
squeakiness 430.3 *shrillness*
squeaking 430.9 *shrill*
squeaky 430.9 *shrill*
squeaky clean 843.11 *rightminded*
squeal 406.12 *express pain*,
430.3 *shrillness*, 430.6 *be shrill*,
431.6 *cry of pain*, 432.4 *cry*,
480.3 *testify*, 483.13 *turn
Queen's evidence*, 528.13 *inform
on* , 530.7 *betray*, 856.5 *accuse*
squealer 480.7 *verifier*, 483.7 *person who gives evidence*, 528.10
informer, 530.4 *discloser*, 578.9
equivocator, 636.4 *warner*,
856.3 *accuser*
squeamish 576.3 *timid*, 624.22
sick, 785.8 *disliking*, 876.10
moralistic
squeamishness 576.13 *timidity*,
876.4 *self-righteousness*
squeegee 621.10 *cleaning object*
squeezable 374.4 *compressible*
squeeze 22.7 *play baseball*,
129.1 *decrease*, 129.5 *make
smaller*, 138.6 *adhere*, 161.21
scrum, 262.1 *contraction*, 262.5
make smaller, 355.17 *obtain an
extract*, 371.9 *make dense*,
644.4 *exertion*, 659.5 *predicament*, 690.5 *be severe*, 695.6
compel, 699.1 *restraint*, 699.8
restrain, 726.1 *retention*, 726.6
retain, 817.12 *greet*, 821.14
communication of love, 821.27
kiss, 826.1 *endearment*, 826.7
show endearment for
squeeze credit 699.9 *economize*
squeezed 257.11 *loaded*, 262.7
smaller
squeezed dry 392.4 *dried-out*
squeeze in 144.6 *fill*, 257.7
stuff, 346.12 *flood in*, 354.3 *impact*, 371.9 *make dense*
squeeze one's hand 817.12 *greet*
squeeze out 355.12 *displace*
squeeze play 22.5 *batting terms*
squeezer 262.4 *contractor*
squeeze someone's hand 543.11
gesture
squeeze the last ounce out of
655.10 *be skilful*
squeeze the trigger 37.7 *shoot*
squeeze together 371.9 *make
dense*
squeezing 262.1 *contraction*,
355.7 *obtaining an extract*,
593.6 *demanding*, 821.14 *communication of love*
squeezing out 355.2 *displacement*
squelch 391.8 *marsh*, 391.15 *be
moist*, 429.1, 429.4 *hiss*, 587.5
discourage, 699.8 *restrain*
squelchiness 374.10 *compressibility*
squelching 699.1 *restraint*
squelchy 374.4 *compressible*,
391.11 *marshy*, 393.17 *muddy*
squib 425.3 *banger*, 854.6 *ridicule*
squib kick 19.12 *special team*
squid 81 Molluscs, 45.18 *sea
fish*, 539.13 *snare*
squiffy 874.2 *slightly drunk*
squiggle 314.2 *coil*, 314.6 *convolute*
squiggly 314.4 *convolutional*
squilgee 621.10 *cleaning object*
squill 84 Flowers and Flowering Plants
squillion 169.3 *large number*,
179.11 *million*
squinch 43.9 *miscellaneous architectural features*

squint 43.9 *miscellaneous architectural features*, 309.2 *facial
distortion*, 435.6 *look*, 435.9
viewpoint, 435.13 *look*, 436.2
poor sight, 436.14 *be blind*
squinting 436.9 *weak-sighted*
squire 180.7 *attendant*, 180.15
escort, 401.3 *male title of address*, 696.1 *master*, 723.6 *lord*,
808.11 *pander to*, 821.9 *lover*,
821.26 *court*
squirearchy 12.1 *government*
squirm 314.2 *coil*, 314.6 *convolute*, 366.7 *shake*, 366.21 *be agitated*, 366.24 *shake*, 406.9 *feel
pain*, 810.16 *be self-conscious*
squirming 314.4 *convolutional*,
366.18 *shaky*
squirmy 366.18 *shaky*
squirrel 77 Placental Mammals,
161.36 *hoarder*
squirrel away 600.6 *stop using*,
605.6 *store*
squirrel hunting 37.2 *hunting*
squirrel-like 77.30 *rodent-like*
squirrel monkey 77 Placental
Mammals
squirrel-tail grass 87 Grasses
squirrel tank 510.8 *mental hospital*
squirt 260.4 *little person*, 270.5
short person, 349.14 *let out*,
349.22 *disgorgement*, 389.34
hose, 612.10 *nonentity*
squirt gun 389.12 *sprinkler*
squirt in 354.2 *inject*
squirting 389.8 *watering*
squish 424.1 *faintness*, 424.5
sound faint, 429.1, 429.4 *hiss*
squishy 98.11 *continental*, 374.4
compressible
squit 260.4 *little person*, 612.10
nonentity
sralay 49 Musical Instruments
Sraosha 8.6 *angel*
Sri 401.3 *male title of address*
Sri Lanka 91 Countries, **98** Islands
Srinagar 93 Cities
sringara 49 Musical Instruments
Staatsgalerie 43 Noted Buildings
stab 670, 38.4 *play soccer*,
136.9 *separate*, 322.20 *hole*,
398.17 *murder*, 406.1 *pain*,
406.3 *injury*, 406.10 *be painful*,
406.11 *inflict pain*, 479.1 *experiment*, 596.5 *attempt*, 618.14 *illtreat*, 670.18 *hit*
stabbed 322.14 *holed*
stabbing 397.6 *killing*, 406.5
painful, 670.18 *hit*, 832.14 *hostile*
stabile 50.12 *sculpture*
stability **159**, **225**, 63.14 *load*,
112.1 *uniformity*, 122.2 *equilibrium*, 150.8 *harmony*, 150.9 *discipline*, 188.4 *long-lastingness*,
217.1 *permanence*, 237.1
strength, 325.1 *motionlessness*,
490.17 *infallibility*, 509.1 *sanity*, 574.15 *will*
Stability 225
stabilization 225.1 *stability*
stabilize 57.25 *solidify*, 112.9 *be
uniform*, 122.11 *equalize*,
150.20 *harmonize*, 217.6 *make
permanent*, 225.6 *be stable*,
225.7 *make stable*, 490.21
make certain, 718.14 *make fast*
stabilized 225, 57.32 *solid*
stabilizer 73 Aircraft Parts, **74**
Parts of a Ship, **225**, 57.3
phase, 57.15 *catalysis*, 57.21
polymer, 122.4 *equilizer*
stab in the back 670.16 *terrorist
attack*, 854.12 *defame*, 858.2
faithlessness, 858.9 *prove false*
stabismic 436.9 *weak-sighted*
stable **225**, 68.7 *farm building*,
68.18 *practise livestock farming*,
77.20 *abode of mammals*,
112.5 *uniform*, 122.6 *equal*,
150.16 *harmonious*, 161.23
flock, 214.11 *regular*, 217.7 *permanent*, 256.12 *stall*, 256.18

take up residence, 258.21 *put in
a container*, 344.16 *stopover*,
490.6 *infallible*, 509.5 *rational*,
605.4 *storage*, 605.6 *store*,
634.3 *animal shelter*, 647.1
workshop, 718.9 *fast*
stableboy 32.15 *horse person*,
68.16 *farm worker*, 697.6 *domestic servant*
stable colours 544.5 *uniform*
stable companion 819.6 *close
friend*
stabled 258.20 *containing*
stable equilibrium 56.10 *force*,
225.1 *stability*
stable horse 32.1 *horse*
stable lad 32.15 *horse person*
stableman 68.16 *farm worker*,
697.6 *domestic servant*
stable management 32.14 *horseriding terms*
stable person 225
stable state 122.2 *equilibrium*
stable thing 225
stabling 258.20 *containing*,
605.4 *storage*
stably 225, 122.13 *equitably*
stab to death 398.17 *murder*
staccato 49 Musical Terms,
365.2 *vibration*, 365.14 *vibrating*, 425.9 *crackling*, 425.10 *explosively*
stack 74 Parts of a Ship, 42.3
card game terms, 42.10 *play*,
54.11 *coast*, 73.6 *flight control*,
161.26 *mass*, 161.37 *assemble*,
281.3 *vertical thing*, 540.21 *be
fraudulent*, 605.1, 605.6 *store*,
721.3 *acquisition*, 721.11 *acquire*
stacked 161.47 *collected*, 582.4
deliberate, 605.7 *stored*
stacked deck 540.8 *fraud*
stacking 73.6 *flight control*
stacks of money 741.3 *fortune*
stack the cards 582.2 *premeditate*
stack the deck 539.30 *be fraudulent*
stack up 105.6 *be in a state of*
stack up with 122.10 *be equal*
stadial 54.40 *glaciation*
stadium 19, **674**, 18.2
sportsground, 51.14 *theatre*,
63.20 *building*, 435.9 *viewpoint*, 815.4 *meeting place*
Staël 48 Writers
staff 6.6 *instructorship*, 7.11 *vestment*, 15.8 *industrial*, 49.17 *notation*, 146.3 *person included*,
161.13 *workforce*, 235.1 *power*,
284.3 *body support*, 544.4 *insignia*, 602.3 *human resources*,
602.6 *find means*, 606.5 *provision*, 646.4 *personnel*, 653.6 *governing body*, 662.11 *helper*,
679.14 *armed forces*, 680.7
blunt weapon
staff college 17.3 *military training*, 676.6 *art of war*
staffed 606.8 *provisional*
staff member 15.7 *employee*,
146.3 *person included*, 697.5 *office assistant*, 701.3 *subordinate*
staff nurse 60.16 *nurse*
staff officers 17.5 *military staff*
staff of life 350.7 *food*, 396.3 *life
requirements*
Stafford 93 Cities
Staffordshire 92 Counties
Staffordshire bull terrier 77
Breeds of Dogs
Staffordshire ware 44 Types of
Ceramics
staff representative 15.7 *employee*
staffroom 6.15 *schoolroom*
staff work 653.3 *management*
staffwork 676.6 *art of war*
stag 14.5 *invest*, 77.17 *male
mammal*, 401.16 *male animal*,
737.2 *speculate*, 738.1 *purchase*,
738.12 *purchaser*
stag beetle 82 Insects
stage **51**, **143**, 54.41 *geological
time*, 106.2 *occurrence*, 121.4 *interval*, 243.10 *produce*, 266.2
level, 297.1 *surroundings*, 319.3
rung, 322.8 *open space*, 344.16

stopover, 526.1 *display*
stage a comeback 183.20 *renew*
stage a coup 252.16 *replace*
stage a coup d'état 12.12 *take authority*
stage a demo 475.19 *protest*
stage a play 526.2 *display something*
stage appearance 457.2 *being in view*
stage a revolt 693.16 *be subversive*
stage a shoot-out 676.14 *battle*
stage a sit-down 713.8 *cause mischief*
stage a sit-in 475.19 *protest,* 668.6 *be insubordinate*
stage a strike 218.7 *stop working*
stage box 51.16 *auditorium*
stage business 51.20 *acting*
stage carpenter 51.26 *stagehand*
stagecoach 71 Carriages and Carts
stagecraft 51.7 *dramaturgy*
staged 51.37 *dramatic*
staged event 532.8 *public relations*
stage director 243.9 *producer*
stagedom 51.1 *drama*
stage door 51.15 *stage*
stage-door Johnny 51.31 *theatregoer*
stage drunk 51.21 *role*
stage fever 51.20 *acting*
stage fright 51.20 *acting,* 777.2 *fearfulness,* 810.4 *shyness*
stagehand 51
stage Irishman 51.21 *role*
stage L 51.15 *stage*
stage land 51.1 *drama*
stage left 51.15 *stage,* 51.41 *onstage*
stage lighting 51
stage-manage 51.36 *dramatize,* 527.13 *hide,* 811.27 *show*
stage management 51.12 *production*
stage manager 51.25 *producer,* 526.12 *displayer*
stage name 529.8 *anonymity,* 531.7 *concealer,* 560.8 *name*
stage performer 51.22 *actor*
stage play 51.2 *play*
stage player 51.22 *actor*
stage presence 51.20 *acting*
stage presentation 51.11 *theatrical performance*
stage property 51.19 *stage requisite*
stage R 51.15 *stage*
stage requisite 51
stage right 51.15 *stage,* 51.41 *onstage*
stage screw 51.17 *stage set*
stage set 51
stage setting 51.17 *stage set*
stage show 51.5, 811.14 *show*
stagestruck 51
stage technician 51.26 *stagehand*
stage villain 51.21 *role*
stage whisper 51.20 *acting,* 429.1 *hiss,* 527.10 *quietness,* 563.4 *whispering,* 563.16 *speak in a low voice*
stage world 51.1 *drama*
stagey 797.3 *affected,* 811.18 *dramatic*
stagflation 13.2 *economy,* 14.1, 741.7 *finance*
stagger 366, 215.1 *irregularity,* 215.6 *be irregular,* 224.11 *be changeable,* 238.6 *be weak,* 324.15 *walk,* 360.11 *trip,* 365.11 *rock,* 366.25 *pitch,* 498.9 *cause disbelief,* 514.11 *amaze,* 587.2 *deter,* 650.5 *be fatigued,* 777.13 *frighten,* 786.10 *be wonderful,* 874.7 *be drunk*
stagger along 328.1 *move slowly,* 345.1 *depart*
stagger belief 786.10 *be wonderful*
staggered 514.7 *amazed*
staggering 215.1 *irregularity,* 215.4 *irregular,* 328.4 *slow,* 365.16 *rocking,* 514.8 *surprising,* 874.2 *slightly drunk,*

874.10 *drunkenness*
staggers 366.8 *spasm,* 624.18 *veterinary disease*
staghorn 88 Ferns
staghound 77 Breeds of Dogs
stag hunt 37.2 *hunting,* 590.2 *chase*
stag hunting 32.8, 37.2 *hunting*
staghunting 77.23 *mammal hunting*
stagily 811.34 *dramatically*
staginess 475.2 *demonstrativeness*
staging 51.7 *dramaturgy,* 51.12 *production*
stagnancy 325.1 *motionlessness*
stagnant 94.9 *lakelike,* 99.16 *vegetating,* 240.5 *inert,* 247.3 *birth control,* 325.4 *motionless,* 626.5 *unhygienic,* 641.3, 643.1 *inactive*
stagnantly 94.10 *limnologically,* 325.10 *motionlessly,* 466.8 *disinterestedly*
stagnant water 94.2 *small lake,* 622.5 *swill,* 626.1 *lack of hygiene*
stagnate 99.21 *merely exist,* 240.4 *be inert,* 247.7 *be infertile,* 325.8 *be motionless,* 641.4 *not act,* 643.12 *be inactive*
stagnating 99.16 *vegetating,* 240.5 *inert,* 247.3 *birth control,* 466.4 *uninterested*
stagnation 13.2 *economy,* 99.9 *mere existence,* 240.1 *inertness,* 247.1 *infertility,* 325.1 *motionlessness,* 466.2 *lack of interest,* 641.1 *inaction,* 741.7 *finance,* 761.4 *desensitization*
stag party 161.9 *social gathering,* 401.15 *menfolk,* 665.7 *social gathering,* 815.5 *party*
stag's-horn fungus 89 Fungi
stagy 51.37 *dramatic,* 475.10 *demonstrative*
Stahl 52 Scientists
staid 167.14 *conformist,* 772.1 *solemn,* 813.6 *formal*
staidness 772.4 *solemnity,* 813.1 *formality*
stain 127.2 *deficiency,* 133.4 *admixture,* 133.10 *become mixed,* 149.2 *impurity,* 293.3 *coating,* 293.24 *coat,* 309.3 *deformity,* 309.11 *deform,* 440.3 *dark colour,* 444.4 *pigment,* 444.15 *colour,* 456.11 *variegate,* 545.12 *vestige,* 620.7 *defect,* 622.4 *dirt,* 622.11 *dirty,* 628.5 *hurt,* 793.1 *spot,* 793.7 *blemish,* 844.9 *dishonour*
stained 145.4 *incomplete,* 293.36 *covered,* 440.10 *dark-coloured,* 442.3 *semitransparent,* 444.10 *coloured,* 620.1 *imperfect,* 622.7 *dirty*
stained glass 50.1 *art,* 439.10 *window,* 442.9 *glass,* 456.5 *variegated thing*
stained-glass window 50.7 *picture,* 113.3 *diverse thing*
staining 59.6 *cell biology,* 67.7 *dyeing*
staining pigment 444.4 *pigment*
stainless 134.13 *pure,* 621.16 *clean,* 863.5 *virtuous,* 865.5 *innocent*
stainlessly 863.9 *virtuously*
stainlessness 134.1 *purity,* 863.1 *virtue,* 865.1 *innocence*
stainless steel 57 Alloys, 63.25 *construction material*
stain removal 67.8 *fabric treatment*
stair 121.4 *interval,* 359.10 *step*
stair carpet 293.9 *floor covering*
staircase 159.2 *consecution,* 327.2 *route,* 359.7 *means of ascent*
stairhead 279.3 *architectural summit*
stairs 137.4 *means of connection,* 159.2 *consecution,* 359.7 *means of ascent*
stairway 137.4 *means of connection,* 359.7 *means of ascent*

stake 68.11 *farmland,* 69.6 *garden tool,* 69.15 *cultivate,* 137.8 *fastening,* 281.3 *vertical thing,* 633.10 *endanger,* 674.11 *contend,* 879.16 *instrument of execution*
stake a claim to 845.14 *be entitled*
stakeholder 741.18 *treasurer*
stake one's claim to 734.7 *take*
stake-out 469.5 *watchfulness*
stakes 671.9 *barrier,* 674.1 *contention,* 674.2 *contest*
Stakhanovite 642.10 *busy person,* 646.1 *worker*
stalactite 281.3 *vertical thing*
stalagmite 281.3 *vertical thing*
stale 183.13 *monotonous,* 200.19 *antiquarian,* 202.12 *olden,* 353.17 *urinate,* 412.5 *tasteless,* 415.6 *unpalatable,* 419.3 *stinking,* 555.1 *unemphatic,* 585.2 *not customary,* 599.9 *used,* 618.4 *poor,* 620.1 *imperfect,* 626.5 *unhygienic,* 628.2 *decay,* 628.12 *deteriorated,* 650.1 *fatigued,* 788.4 *boring*
stale line 32.8 *hunting*
stalely 202.18 *venerably,* 788.8 *boringly*
stalemate 110.5 *equality,* 110.10 *be equal,* 122.2 *equilibrium,* 218.2 *stop,* 218.8 *cause to cease,* 323.1 *closure,* 325.1 *motionlessness,* 325.9 *make motionless,* 641.1 *inaction,* 659.8 *snag,* 661.2 *obstacle,* 671.26 *act on the defensive,* 685.1 *noncompletion*
stalemated 110.16 *equal,* 641.3 *inactive*
staleness 202, 412.1 *tastelessness,* 419.1 *stench,* 555.2 *lack of emphasis,* 585.3 *unaccustomedness,* 618.10 *poverty,* 620.5 *imperfection,* 650.7 *fatigue,* 788.1 *boredom*
stale repetition 183.3 *repetitiveness*
Stalin 618.12 *bad person,* 822.8 *hated person,* 862.6 *evil person*
Stalingrad 398.15 *slaughterhouse*
Stalinism 692.0 *suppression*
stalk 37.7 *shoot,* 83.5 *stem,* 88.4 *moss plant,* 89.4 *fungal body,* 143.6 *branch,* 243.7 *produce,* 315.4 *cylinder,* 324.12 *gait,* 324.15 *walk,* 590.9 *follow,* 590.11 *hunt*
stalked 83.18 *of leaves*
stalked barnacle 81.4 *arthropod*
stalker 37.4, 590.6 *hunter*
stalk game 37.7 *shoot*
stalking 37.2 *hunting,* 37.8 *shooting,* 590.1 *pursuit,* 590.2 *chase*
stalking-horse 657.2 *stratagem*
stalking stick 37.3 *hunting equipment*
stall 256, 671, 740, 10.12 *church,* 47.2 *chair,* 68.7 *farm building,* 71.21 *miscellaneous motoring terms,* 73.5 *flight,* 77.20 *abode of mammals,* 209.8 *delay,* 218.6 *cease,* 258.2 *compartment,* 576.5 *vacillate,* 634.3 *animal shelter,* 661.8 *hinder,* 661.9 *block,* 683.1 *failure,* 683.9 *malfunction*
stalled 209.10 *held up*
staller 576.15 *indecisive person,* 661.7 *hinderer*
stall-holder 739.14 *street trader*
stalling 73.5 *flight,* 576.1 *vacillating,* 683.1 *failure*
stalling for time 652.9 *tactics*
stallion 32.1 *horse,* 77.17 *male mammal,* 401.7 *libertine,* 401.16 *male animal*
stall-keeper 739.11 *pedlar,* 739.14 *street trader*
stalls 51.16 *auditorium,* 51.31 *theatregoer,* 435.9 *viewpoint*
stalwart 237.9 *physically strong,* 378.4 *powerful,* 623.1 *healthy,* 665.6 *political party member*

stalwartly 378.13 *powerfully*
stalwartness 378.8 *physical strength*
stamen 84.3 *flower part,* 143.6 *branch,* 245.8 *organs of reproduction*
Stamford 93 Cities
stamina 575, 235.1 *power,* 237.1 *strength,* 378.8 *physical strength,* 642.8 *assiduity,* 778.1 *courage*
staminate 84.12 *of flowers*
stammel 67 Natural Fabrics
stammer 563.3 *speech defect,* 563.14 *have difficulty speaking,* 564.3 *mode of speech,* 656.7 *be clumsy,* 810.16 *be self-conscious,* 866.2 *signs of guilt,* 866.9 *appear guilty,* 874.7 *be drunk*
stammerer 810.7 *modest person*
stammering 523.11 *unintelligibility,* 563.3 *speech defect,* 563.12 *inarticulate,* 656.3 *clumsy,* 810.11 *shy,* 866.6 *appearing guilty,* 874.10 *drunkenness*
stamp 103.4 *nature,* 103.11 *characterize,* 105.1 *state,* 110.4, 110.9 *duplicate,* 112.2 *conformity,* 112.10 *conform,* 116.28 *consent,* 138.4 *adherent,* 163.4 *type,* 165.3 *characteristic,* 225.7 *make stable,* 306.2 *prototype,* 306.7 *form,* 317.7 *make concave,* 324.12 *gait,* 330.7 *kick,* 330.13 *blow,* 423.8 *be loud,* 534.3 *correspondence,* 534.31 *correspond,* 543.11 *gesture,* 544.10 *identify,* 567.10 *send,* 667.2, 667.7 *contract,* 708.2 *permit,* 718.2, 718.11 *promise,* 741.24 *monetize,* 851.16 *acclaim*
stamp collecting 42 Hobbies and Pastimes
stamp collection 605.5 *collection*
stamp collector 161.35 *collector*
stamped 110.15 *duplicate,* 112.6 *conforming,* 116.17 *consenting,* 741.22 *monetary*
stamped coinage 741.13 *coinage*
stampede 241.7 *be violent,* 329.4 *be swift,* 648.1 *hasten,* 648.4 *haste,* 695.7 *force*
stampeded 648.3 *hasty*
stamped on one's memory 511.7 *memorable*
stamping 423.2 *outcry,* 543.15 *gestural,* 851.5 *acclaim*
stamping foot 543.3 *gesture*
stamping ground 249.13 *locality,* 250.1 *location,* 256.2 *environment*
stamping the foot 828.4 *anger*
stamp of approval 851.1 *approval*
stamp off 345.1 *depart*
stamp on 330.7 *kick,* 690.6 *suppress*
stamp one's feet 236.6 *be powerless,* 408.14 *be hot,* 409.10 *be cold*
stamp one's foot 828.11 *be angry*
stamp out 100.14 *cause not to exist,* 244.8 *destroy*
stamp tax 751.9 *historical taxes*
stamp with impatience 642.12 *be active*
stance 4.2 *philosophical system,* 26.2 *boxing,* 29.3 *golf shots,* 34.5 *rock face,* 306.6 *nature,* 471.5 *ideology,* 473.9 *line of argument,* 497.1 *belief,* 535.2 *statement*
stanchion 74 Parts of a Ship, 38.1 *soccer*
stand 57 Laboratory Apparatus, 51.13 *engagement,* 85.4 *trees,* 99.19 *continue to be,* 105.6 *be in a state of,* 188.6 *last,* 225.6 *be stable,* 251.2 *circumstances,* 251.9 *be situated,* 251.10 *situate,* 280.2 *foot,* 281.5 *be vertical,* 284.2 *supporting part,* 284.12 *bear,* 310.5 *viewpoint,* 325.1 *motionlessness,* 325.8 *be motionless,* 435.9 *viewpoint,* 471.5 *ideology,* 497.1 *belief,*

518.1 *supposition*, 535.2 *statement*, 580.5 *vote*, 608.4 *suffice*, 669.1 *resistance*, 676.9, 676.14 *battle*, 729.5 *give*, 740.9 *stall*, 746.8 *defray*, 748.3 *donate*, 849.19 *take off one's hat to*
stand above suspicion 865.8 *be innocent*
stand above the law 16.74 *be lawless*
stand accused 856.7 *be accused*
stand a chance 229.4 *chance*, 486.8 *be possible*
stand a fair chance 488.8 *be probable*
stand against 663.12 *oppose*, 669.6 *resist*, 670.8 *counterattack*
stand against a wall 879.5 *execute*
stand aghast 777.11 *be afraid*
stand a good chance 486.8 *be possible*, 488.8 *be probable*
stand alone 174.18 *be one*, 698.16 *be independent*
stand aloof 174.18 *be one*, 263.6 *keep away*, 591.1 *avoid*, 816.12 *be unsocial*
stand apart 174.18 *be one*, 591.1 *avoid*
standard 75, 268, 5.39 *of language*, 52.70 *universal*, 69.10 *fruit tree*, 85.1 *tree*, 112.2 *conformity*, 112.6 *conforming*, 116.5 *convention*, 116.15 *conventional*, 121.3 *gradation*, 121.7 *gradational*, 124.1, 124.4 *average*, 154.4 *precedent*, 164.21 *common*, 166.4 *guide*, 166.10 *customary*, 167.15 *everyday*, 259.14 *medium*, 471.6 *ideal*, 482.5 *vague*, 544.7 *flag*, 617.5 *not bad*, 619.1 *perfect*, 619.3 *perfection*
standard atmosphere 56.38 *thermodynamics*
standard-bearer 679.8 *soldier*
Standardbred 32 Breeds of Horse and Pony
standard candle 75 Scientific and Technical Units
standard deviation 52.60 *parameter*, 56.83 *sensitivity*
Standard English 5.29 *grammar*
standard error 52.60 *parameter*, 56.83 *sensitivity*
standard event 32.12 *rodeo*
standard gauge 72.3 *rail*, 327.10 *railway*
Standard grade 485 Educational Qualifications
standardization 57.18 *gravimetric analysis*, 75.4 *standard*, 110.6 *regularity*, 112.2 *conformity*, 152.3 *organization*
standardize 52.94 *order*, 110.8 *make the same*, 112.10 *conform*, 116.26 *make uniform*, 124.10 *make average*, 150.19 *systematize*, 152.13 *organize*, 166.14 *regulate*, 167.9 *make conform*
standardized 57.41 *analytic*, 110.17 *regular*, 112.6 *conforming*, 116.15 *conventional*
standard lamp 439.6 *electric light*
standard language 5.6 *official language*
standard lens 66.17 *lens*
standardly 471.24 *ideologically*
standardness 124.4 *average*, 164.5 *averageness*
standard of living 13.6 *economic factors*
standard palette 444.5 *paint*
standard practice 584.6 *procedure*
standard price 751.1 *price*
standard procedure 584.6 *procedure*
standard rate of taxation 13.6 *economic factors*
standards 4.2 *philosophical system*, 471.5 *ideology*, 593.1 *requirement*, 876.1 *morality*
standard solution 57.18 *gravimetric analysis*
standard temperature and pressure 56.38 *thermodynamics*
standard usage 5.6 *official language*

guage, 584.4 *custom*
standardwing 78 Birds
stand a round 746.9 *pay one's way*
stand as a candidate 710.13 *be a candidate*
stand aside 705.5 *resign*
stand at the door 344.3 *approach*
stand at the head 154.15 *precede*
stand away 263.6 *keep away*
stand back 263.6 *keep away*, 337.2 *retreat*, 591.1 *avoid*
stand back of 662.24 *back*
stand bail 718.11 *promise*
stand bail for 714.8 *guarantee*
stand before the judge 856.7 *be accused*
stand behind 284.14 *give moral support*, 662.24 *back*
standby 51.22 *actor*
stand by 209.8 *delay*, 236.6 *be powerless*, 253.12 *attend*, 284.14 *give moral support*, 513.10 *wait*, 594.8 *prepare oneself*, 641.4 *not act*
standby 662.11 *helper*
stand by 662.24 *back*, 671.21 *entrench*
stand-by 602.5 *reserves*
stand-by fare 754.4 *bargain*
stand by oneself 174.18 *be one*
stand by the letter of the law 836.6 *be pitiless*
stand clear 591.1 *avoid*
stand clear of 263.6 *keep away*
stand close to 264.8 *be near*
stand condemned 866.8 *be guilty*
stand condemned out of one's own mouth 16.80 *convict oneself*
stand defenceless 236.6 *be powerless*
stand down 218.7 *stop working*, 598.2 *withdraw*, 673.3 *submit*, 705.5 *resign*
standee 51.31 *theatregoer*
stand erect 281.5 *be vertical*, 805.24 *be proud*
stand far away 263.5 *be distant*
stand fast 217.5 *be permanent*, 325.8 *be motionless*, 574.10 *insist*
stand firm 217.5 *be permanent*, 225.6 *be stable*, 225.8 *show determination*, 325.8 *be motionless*, 574.10 *insist*, 575.8 *hold out*, 577.9 *be obstinate*, 663.17 *withstand*, 669.7 *be obstinate*, 671.21 *entrench*, 676.13 *be at war*
stand for 547, 520.10 *mean*, 543.10 *signify*, 706.5 *represent*
stand for office 710.13 *be a candidate*
stand guard 469.11 *care for*
stand high 849.21 *command respect*
stand in 222.4 *be a substitute*, 293.34 *cover for*
stand-in 51.22 *actor*, 130.5 *extra person*, 155.13 *replacement*, 222.2 *substitute person*, 293.21 *substitution*, 293.40 *substitutive*, 547.8 *representative*, 707.2 *alternative*, 707.7 *deputizing*, 767.5 *helper*
stand in amazement 786.9 *wonder*
stand in for 478.23 *answer for*, 547.12 *stand for*, 707.4 *substitute for*, 716.7 *act as a go-between*, 767.11 *assist*
stand in front 303.10 *be in front*, 671.21 *entrench*
stand in full view 526.4 *show oneself*
standing 777 Phobias by Topic, 94.9 *lakelike*, 105.1 *state*, 106.1 *circumstances*, 121.2 *rank*, 163.5 *social class*, 217.7 *permanent*, 251.2 *circumstances*, 251.5 *rank*, 281.8 *vertical*, 325.4 *motionless*, 611.1 *importance*, 744.7 *repute*, 849.11 *in a respectful stance*
standing army 17.2 *the military*, 679.15 *army*
standing at attention 849.5 *pre-*

senting arms
standing by 196.8 *available*, 594.18 *prepared*
standing committee 653.6 *governing body*
standing custom 584.4 *custom*
standing firm 669.11 *obstinate*
standing in 707.7 *deputizing*
standing jump 359.5 *jump*
standing on ceremony 811.26 *ritualistic*, 813.6 *formal*
standing order 16.3 *law*, 166.1 *rule*, 746.1 *payment*
standing out 318.5 *protuberant*, 522.3 *recognizable*
standing ovation 51.6 *scene*, 812.9 *rejoicing*, 851.5 *acclaim*
standing rigging 36.3 *parts of a sailing boat*
standing room 51.16 *auditorium*, 248.5 *reserved space*
standing room only 144.8 *full*
standing start 328.12 *hesitation*
standing stone 200.7 *thing of the past*
standing the test 537.15 *true*
standing the test of time 537.15 *true*
standing up 281.2 *making vertical*, 281.8 *vertical*, 537.15 *true*
standing up for one's rights 845.11 *entitled to*
standing water 94.2 *small lake*, 389.1 *water*
standing wave 56.12 *wave*
standing in need of 593.7 *require*, 609.6 *be unsatisfied*
stand in one's own light 656.6 *act foolishly*
stand in relation to 107.7 *relate to*
stand in the breach 633.9 *face danger*
stand in the dock 16.72 *stand trial*, 856.7 *be accused*
stand in the light 656.7 *be clumsy*
stand in the middle 158
stand in the open 526.4 *show oneself*
stand in the stead of 707.4 *substitute for*
stand in the way of 661.9 *block*
stand in with 664.14 *join with*
stand like a post 325.8 *be motionless*
stand no nonsense 574.10 *insist*
standoff 218.2 *stop*
stand off 263.6 *keep away*
stand-off half 35.4 *rugby player*
standoffish 168.16 *solitary*, 263.9 *reserved*, 816.8 *unsociable*
stand-offish 805.15 *unapproachable*
standoffishly 263.11 *reservedly*
standoffishness 263.4 *reserve*, 816.1 *unsociability*
stand on 36.15 *sail*
stand on ceremony 306.8 *be formal*, 811.31 *put on a show*, 813.11 *be formal*
stand one in good stead 613.10 *benefit*
stand on end 281.6 *make vertical*
stand one's ground 217.5 *be permanent*, 225.8 *show determination*, 663.17 *withstand*
stand on middle ground 158.18 *stand in the middle*
stand on one's dignity 805.24 *be proud*
stand on one's head 287.3 *invert*
stand on one's own two feet 174.18 *be one*, 698.16 *be independent*, 700.5 *be liberated*
stand on the opposite side 111.8 *be opposite*
stand on tiptoe 269.9 *be long*, 275.16 *rise*, 361.5 *arise*
stand or fall together 664.13 *work together*
stand out 115.5 *be dissimilar*, 163.15 *be in a class of one's own*, 165.25 *excel*, 318.8 *protrude*, 435.19, 437.8 *be visible*, 522.8 *be recognizable*, 526.5 *be visible*, 544.11 *identify oneself*, 720.7 *not observe*

stand out a mile 526.5 *be visible*
stand out in a crowd 115.5 *be dissimilar*
stand outside the law 16.74 *be lawless*
stand pat 217.5 *be permanent*, 225.8 *show determination*
standpipe 389.13 *irrigator*
standpoint 251.2 *circumstances*, 310.5 *viewpoint*, 497.1 *belief*, 518.1 *supposition*
stand poles apart 136.12 *disagree*
stand ready 594.8 *prepare oneself*, 671.21 *entrench*
stand responsible for 847.15 *be liable*
stand revealed 530.9 *be disclosed*
stand rigid 669.7 *be obstinate*
stands 22.1 *baseball*
stand shoulder to shoulder 138.6 *adhere*, 664.13 *work together*
stand side by side 138.6 *adhere*
stand side-by-side 305.7 *be alongside*
standstill 122.2 *equilibrium*, 218.2 *stop*, 323.1 *closure*, 325.1 *motionlessness*
stand still 325.8 *be motionless*
standstill 639.2 *deliverance*, 641.1 *inaction*, 659.8 *snag*
stand surety 718.11 *promise*
stand surety for 632.9 *protect*
stand the cost 746.8 *defray*
stand the racket 879.6 *be punished*
stand the test 537.27 *be true*, 617.9 *be worthy*
stand the test of time 188.6 *last*, 219.4 *protract*, 537.27 *be true*
stand to attention 281.5 *be vertical*
stand together 664.13 *work together*
stand to reason 526.5 *be visible*
stand trial 16
stand up 359, 281.5 *be vertical*, 361.5 *arise*, 515.7 *thwart*, 526.4 *show oneself*, 537.27 *be true*
stand up and be counted 475.18 *appear*, 526.4 *show oneself*
stand-up collar 295.14 *neckwear*
stand-up comedy 51.10 *comedy*, 771.4 *entertainment*
stand-up comic 51.27 *entertainer*, 771.6 *humorist*
stand-up fight 674.6 *fight*
stand up for 284.14 *give moral support*, 632.9 *protect*, 855.8 *justify*
stand up for one's principles 574.10 *insist*
stand up for one's rights 698.16 *be independent*, 845.14 *be entitled*
stand up in law 16.66 *be legal*
stand-up meal 350.12 *meal*
stand upright 281.5 *be vertical*
stand up straight 281.5 *be vertical*, 805.24 *be proud*
stand up to 536.8 *rebut*, 608.4 *suffice*, 663.17 *withstand*, 668.5 *defy*, 778.15 *be courageous*
stand up well 225.6 *be stable*
Stanford-Binet Intelligence Scale 61.6 *intelligence test*
Stanford-Binet test 61.6 *intelligence test*
Stanford revision 61.6 *intelligence test*
Stanley Cup 31.3 *ice hockey*
Stanley knife 603.1 *tool*
stannane 57 Common Chemical Compounds
stannary 647.1 *workshop*
stannic 57.34 *elemental*
stanniferous 44.10 *ceramic*, 57.34 *elemental*
stanniferous ware 44.1 *ceramics*
stannite 54 Minerals
stannous 57.34 *elemental*
stanolone 62 Medication
stanza 48.8 *part of poem*
Stanzione 41.6 *ice-skating*
stapedectomy 60 Surgical Operations
stapes 382 Bones, 420.5 *inter-*

nal ear
staphylectomy 60 Surgical Operations
staple 135.5 *joint,* 135.10 *link,* 137.8 *fastening,* 137.11 *connect,* 380.8 *sharp-pointed thing,* 383.5 *textile,* 604.1 *materials,* 611.5 *important,* 726.3 *tools for gripping,* 726.6 *retain,* 739.8 *merchandise*
stapled 137.15 *connected,* 726.10 *retained*
staple food 350.7 *food*
stapler 726.3 *tools for gripping*
staple to 130.6 *add*
star 53, 41.12 *ski,* 51.22 *actor,* 51.36 *dramatize,* 65.15 *network,* 126.6 *paragon,* 126.10 *lead,* 126.15 *excellent,* 291.5 *focus,* 363.4 *orbiting body,* 400.7 *person,* 439.4 *natural light,* 439.13 *enlightenment,* 543.5 *indicator,* 543.7 *punctuation,* 544.4 *insignia,* 611.4 *bigwig,* 617.8 *exceller,* 621.13 *clean person,* 682.4 *successful person,* 786.5 *person of wonder,* 792.3 *honour,* 800.2 *person of repute,* 861.16 *superior person*
star-apple 86 Fruits
star atlas 53.6 *star catalogue*
starboard 74 Parts of a Ship, 305.1 *side*
starboard tack 36.15 *sail*
starboard tacking 36.1 *sailing*
starbright 439.20 *starry*
starburst galaxy 53.7 *galaxy*
star catalogue 53
starch 58.4 *polysaccharide,* 90.3 *plant body,* 350.11 *food content,* 373.9 *harden,* 376.11 *smooth,* 393.11 *thickener,* 621.13 *clean*
Star Chamber 16.20 *British court,* 492.3 *place of judgment,* 653.7 *council*
star chart 11.9 *divination*
starched 373.2 *tough,* 621.17 *cleaned*
starched collar 295.14 *neckwear*
starchily 811.38 *majestically,* 813.12 *formally*
starchiness 373.5 *hardness,* 669.2 *obstinacy,* 811.7 *pomp,* 813.1 *formality*
starching 373.5 *hardness*
starchy 373.2 *tough,* 393.18 *pulpy,* 669.11 *obstinate,* 805.15 *unapproachable,* 811.22 *majestic,* 813.6 *formal*
Star class 36.2 *sailing boat*
star-crossed 687.8 *unlucky*
star-crossed lover 722.6 *loser*
star-crossed lovers 821.10 *lovers*
stardom 682.1 *success*
stardust 519.6 *reverie*
stare 161 Collective Names for Birds and Animals, 435.6, 435.13 *look,* 786.9 *wonder,* 818.7 *be discourteous*
stare down 574.8 *brace oneself*
stare one in the face 199.7 *be in the future,* 437.8, 526.5 *be visible*
starer 435.11 *observer*
starfish 76.5 *aquatic animal,* 81.3 *echinoderm*
star fruit 86 Fruits
stargaze 435.17 *imagine,* 468.12 *be inattentive*
star gazer 53.2 *astronomer*
stargazer 435.11 *observer*
star gazing 53.1 *astronomy*
stargazing 435.5 *imagination,* 468.3 *absent-mindedness,* 468.8 *absent-minded*
star grass 87 Grasses
star in 457.13 *occur*
staring 435.21 *seeing*
staring one in the face 437.2 *clear,* 526.14 *manifest*
star in the firmament 682.4 *successful person*
stark 49 Musical Terms, 144.9 *completely,* 237.12 *strong to the senses,* 247.3 *birth control,* 373.2 *tough,* 437.2 *clear,*

444.12 *gaudy,* 542.14 *simple,* 550.3 *clear,* 556.1 *simple*
starkers 294.8 *uncovered,* 296.9 *undressed*
starkly 373.12 *toughly,* 542.24, 556.8 *simply*
stark-naked 294.8 *uncovered,* 296.9 *undressed*
starkness 437.4 *clarity,* 542.4 *simplicity,* 550.1 *clarity,* 556.4 *simplicity*
stark raving mad 510.11 *insane*
stark-staring 526.14 *manifest*
stark staring mad 510.11 *insane*
starless 440.8 *dark*
starlet 51.22 *actor,* 682.4 *successful person*
starlight 439.4 *natural light*
starlight waltz 41.7 *ice-dancing*
starlike 380.2 *spiked*
starling 78 Birds, 78.6 *songbird*
starlings 161 Collective Names by Animal
starlit 439.18 *lit*
star map 547.7 *map*
star of Bethlehem 84 Flowers and Flowering Plants
Star of Bethlehem 439.4 *natural light*
star of stage and screen 51.22 *actor*
star player 655.4 *skilled person*
star-pointed 380.2 *spiked*
star quality 51.20 *acting*
starring 51.39 *stagestruck*
starring role 51.21 *role*
star-rise 359.3 *sun rise*
starry 439, 53.36 *astronomical*
starry-eyed 519.11 *fantastical,* 762.4 *happy,* 775.11 *hopeful*
stars 777 Phobias by Topic, 226.4 *contributing factor,* 233.2 *occult influence*
Stars and Bars 544.7 *flag*
Stars and Stripes 91.7 *United States ,* 544.7 *flag*
star-shaped 380.2 *spiked*
star-shaped figure 52.44 *polygon*
star shell 680.5 *missile weapon*
starshine 439.4 *natural light*
star-spangled 439.20 *starry*
Star-Spangled Banner 544.7 *flag*
starstruck 51.39 *stagestruck*
star-studded 53.36 *astronomical,* 439.20 *starry*
star system 161.28 *cluster*
start 336, 338, 345, 21.1 *track events,* 21.6 *race,* 32.7 *horseracing,* 33.6 *motor racing terms,* 33.10 *be on the track,* 119.7 *originate,* 126.3 *advantage,* 156.1 *beginning,* 156.11 *starting point,* 156.17 *begin,* 201.4 *beginning,* 226.11 *inaugurate,* 228.9 *motivate,* 322.11 *beginning,* 322.24 *begin,* 330.1 *impel,* 339.3 *jerk,* 345.5 *set out,* 366.9 *jolt,* 514.3 *shock,* 514.12 *be surprised,* 597.1 *undertake,* 636.2 *danger signal,* 777.12 *be fearful*
START 2 677.1 *pacification*
start a fight 670.1 *attack*
start afresh 156.28 *begin again,* 183.20 *renew,* 201.17 *become new,* 221.7 *restore,* 839.10 *absolve*
start again 183.20 *renew,* 221.7 *restore,* 629.4 *be restored*
start an action 16.70 *litigate*
start anew 156.28 *begin again,* 201.17 *become new,* 221.7 *restore*
start a prairie fire 98.12 *be marooned*
start a row 642.12 *be active*
start aside 591.4 *shy*
start at the wrong end 656.5 *be unskilful*
start climbing the wall 510.14 *become insane*
start early 208.7 *be early*
starter 71 Motor Vehicle Parts, 21.3 *athlete,* 22.2 *baseball player,* 45.9 *dish,* 45.12 *hors d'oeuvre,* 156.12 *first move,* 156.14 *beginner,* 350.14 *mouth-*

---

ful, 411.3 *appetizer,* 674.10 *contender*
starter motor 71 Motor Vehicle Parts
starter's gun 543.4 *signal,* 636.2 *danger signal*
starter's orders 32.7 *horseracing*
start from the beginning 201.17 *become new*
start game 590.11 *hunt*
start going 156.20 *activate,* 338.33 *start*
starting 156.29, 322.17 *beginning,* 345.8 *start,* 674.14 *contending*
starting afresh 183.4 *return*
starting again 183.4 *return*
starting ahead of the game 652.9 *tactics*
starting block 156.11 *starting point*
starting blocks 21.4 *sports equipment*
starting grid 33.6 *motor racing terms*
starting gun 192.10 *signal*
starting pistol 21.4 *sports equipment,* 156.11 *starting point*
starting point 156, 345.10 *place of departure*
starting position 21.1 *track events*
starting post 156.11 *starting point*
startle 514.9 *surprise,* 636.7 *raise the alarm,* 777.13 *frighten,* 786.10 *be wonderful*
startled 514.6 *surprised*
startling 777.10 *frightening*
start off 156, 338.33 *start*
startoff 345.8 *start*
start out 156.19 *start off,* 345.5 *set out*
start the ball rolling 338.33 *start*
start too soon 208.7 *be early*
start up 156.20 *activate,* 156.23 *inaugurate,* 230.8 *activate,* 359.17 *spring up,* 590.11 *hunt*
start-up capital 602.4 *financial resources*
start-up costs 751.6 *business costs*
star turn 41.2 *cross-country skiing,* 41.4 *skiing technique*
starvation 274.8 *emaciation,* 350.10 *scarcity,* 397.5 *ways of dying,* 609.9 *scarcity,* 782.3 *appetite,* 871.2 *short rations*
starvation diet 609.8 *insufficiency,* 871.1 *fasting*
starvation rations 606.1 *provision,* 609.8 *insufficiency*
starve 238.7 *weaken,* 274.15 *be emaciated,* 350.22 *eat well,* 743.12 *be poor,* 758.7 *hoard,* 782.14 *be hungry,* 869.5 *be self-restrained,* 871.5 *fast*
starved 274.2 *emaciated,* 609.3 *underfed,* 782.10 *hungry,* 871.6 *fasting*
starved of 609.2 *unprovided*
starveling 609.3 *underfed*
starve oneself 722.9 *lose*
starve out 670.4 *besiege,* 676.13 *be at war,* 699.11 *detain*
starve to death 397.16 *meet one's fate,* 398.17 *murder*
starving 274.2 *emaciated,* 350.3 *delicate eating,* 593.5 *necessitous,* 609.3 *underfed,* 743.3 *beggarly,* 782.10 *hungry,* 871.6 *fasting*
starving out 699.4 *detention*
Star Wars 632.4 *safety device,* 676.8 *warfare,* 680.5 *missile weapon*
star watching 53.1 *astronomy*
star worship 9.2 *idolatry*
star worshipper 9.6 *idolater*
star-worshipping 9.10 *idolatrous*
stash 531.2 *hiding place,* 531.8 *conceal*
stash away 605.6 *store*
stasis 122.2 *equilibrium,* 225.1 *stability,* 325.1 *motionlessness*
stasophobia 777 Phobias by Name
statant 544.13 *heraldic*

---

state 105, 249, 473, 4.22 *propound a philosophy,* 5.45 *use language,* 12.5 *political organization,* 12.9 *governmental,* 91.1 *country,* 91.16 *national,* 92.1 *administrative area,* 106.1 *circumstances,* 249.4 *territorial division,* 249.17 *national,* 251.2 *circumstances,* 400.11 *nation,* 400.13 *national,* 472.10 *focus on,* 480.3 *testify,* 483.11 *give evidence,* 535.17 *affirm,* 549.9 *style,* 564.11 *speak,* 623.3 *health,* 688.8 *governmental organization,* 725.5 *personal estate,* 811.7 *pomp,* 813.1 *formality*
State 105
state attorney general 16.12 *US law officer*
state banquet 350.13 *feast*
state capital 92.5 *administrative headquarters,* 93.2 *American cities*
state control 12.3 *governance,* 688.7 *type of rule*
statecraft 12.2 *politics,* 653.3 *management*
state crew 51.26 *stagehand*
stated 535, 473.11 *logical*
state election 580.12 *election*
State Enrolled Nurse 60.16 *nurse*
state enterprise 737.5 *commercial trade*
state farm 68.6 *farm*
state highway 327.3 *road*
state highway patrol 16.16 *US police*
statehood 91.1 *country,* 400.11 *nation,* 698.3 *independence*
state in plain English 522.5 *simplify*
state insurance 662.4 *social assistance*
stateless 104.10 *foreign,* 252.10 *replaced*
stateless person 104.7 *new arrival,* 252.7 *displaced person,* 816.7 *outsider*
statelessness 805, 811.7 *pomp,* 813.1 *formality*
state lottery 589.3 *equal chance*
stately 805, 557.4 *ornate,* 558.3 *elegant,* 811.22 *majestic,* 811.38 *majestically,* 813.6 *formal,* 813.8 *ceremonious*
stately home 243.8 *construction,* 256.4 *official residence*
statement 535, 750, 4.1 *philosophy,* 52.63 *mathematical logic,* 56.6 *law,* 171.4 *bill,* 472.1 *topic,* 473.3 *line of argument,* 480.6 *evidence,* 483.5 *legal evidence,* 528.2 *communication,* 528.3 *document,* 532.1 *publication,* 545.1 *record,* 560.1 *description,* 564.7 *utterance,* 692.1 *command,* 751.4 *bill*
statement of account 528.3 *document,* 750.4 *statement*
statement of belief 497.2 *religious belief*
statement of defence 476.3 *countercharge*
statement of facts 560.1 *description*
statement under oath 535.3 *vow,* 714.1 *promise*
state occasion 811.13 *ceremonial,* 813.1 *formality*
state of affairs 105, 106.1, 251.2 *circumstances*
state of grace 8.1 *divinity,* 865.1 *innocence*
state of health 105.5 *physical state,* 625.2 *salubrity*
state of indebtedness 745.1 *debt*
state of matrimony 823.1 *marriage*
state of mind 105, 759.4 *emotion*
state of nature 296.2 *nudity*
state of order 150.5 *orderliness*
state of peace 675.1 *peace*
state of play 106.1 *circumstances*
state of siege 676.4 *belligerency*
state of sobriety 873.6 *sobriety*
state of the art 201.1 *newness*
state-of-the-art 201.10 *new*

state of war 674.6 *fight*, 676.4 *belligerency*, 820.4 *act of hostility*
state of wonder 786.1 *wonder*
state one's terms 737.3 *bargain*
state-owned industry 13.1 *economics*
state ownership 724.1 *joint possession*
state pension 662.4 *social assistance*
state plainly 522.5 *simplify*
state prison 702.1 *prison*
state prosecuting attorney 16.12 *US law officer*
state prosecutor 16.12 *US law officer*
state provision 662.4 *social assistance*
State Registered Nurse 60.16 *nurse*
stateroom 74 *Parts of a Ship*
state school 6.12 *educational institution*
state secret 529.1 *secrecy*
state's evidence 530.2 *divulgence*
States General 653.10 *legislative body*
Stateside 91.7 *United States*
statesman 12.7 *governor*, 592.8 *planner*, 653.15 *manager*, 678.3 *mediator*
statesmanlike 507.5 *wise*, 652.16 *behaving*, 655.6 *skilful*
statesmanship 12.2 *politics*, 592.2 *policy*, 652.9 *tactics*, 653.3 *management*, 678.2 *mediation*
states' righter 698.7 *free person*
states' rights 698.3 *independence*
state supreme court 16.21 *US court*
state Supreme Court Justice 16.24 *US judge*
stateswoman 12.7 *governor*
state system 12.1 *government*
state tax 751.7 *tax*
state terms 485.16 *specify*
state under oath 535.18 *vow*
static 34.8 *mountaineering*, 56.98 *physical*, 122.6 *equal*, 217.7 *permanent*, 240.5 *inert*, 325.4 *motionless*, 434.5 *atmospheric dissonance*, 534.19 *radio reception*, 643.11 *inactive*
statically 56.100 *physically*, 325.10 *motionlessly*, 643.15 *inactively*
static electrical conduction 64.3 *electricity*
static electricity 56.42, 64.3 *electricity*, 235.7 *electrical power*
static friction 56.10 *force*, 385.1 *friction*
static load 63.14 *load*
static rope 34.4 *climbing equipment*
statics 56.2 *classical physics*
static warfare 676.8 *warfare*
station 68.6 *farm*, 72.8 *railway station*, 92.5 *administrative headquarters*, 121.2 *rank*, 163.5 *social class*, 218.4 *stopping place*, 250.1 *location*, 250.9 *locate*, 251.4 *employment*, 251.5 *rank*, 251.10 *situate*, 327.10 *railway*, 345.10 *place of departure*, 804.1 *right*, 847.2 *task*
stationarily 325.10 *motionlessly*
stationary 30.11 *gymnastic*, 57.41 *analytic*, 217.7 *permanent*, 325.4 *motionless*, 641.3, 643.1 *inactive*
stationary depression 55.11 *weather system*
stationary high 55.11 *weather system*
stationary phase 57.17 *analysis*
stationary point 52.36 *point*
stationary rings 30
stationary target 588.6 *objective*
station break 534.25 *broadcast material*
stationed 250.6 *located*, 251.6 *situated*
stationery 604.3 *paper*
station identification 534.20

radio broadcasting
stationing 250.4 *placing*
station in life 105.1 *state*
station manager 72.9 *railway worker*
stationmaster 72.9 *railway worker*
station wagon 71.16 *car*
statism 12.1 *government*, 12.3 *governance*
statistic 52.57 *population*
statistical 52.68 *mathematical*, 56.98 *physical*, 170.13 *calculative*, 750.10 *accounting*
statistical analysis 52.53 *statistics*
statistical inference 52.53 *statistics*
statistically 56.100 *physically*, 750.13 *financially*
statistically proven 537.20 *proved*
statistical mechanic 57.2 *chemist*
statistical mechanics 56.3 *modern physics*, 57.1 *chemistry*
statistical methods 52
statistical physics 56.3 *modern physics*
statistical probability 488.5 *probability theory*
statistician 52.2, 170.7 *mathematician*, 750.6 *accountant*
statistico-mechanical 57.31 *chemical*
statistics 52, 170, 52.1 *mathematics*, 528.6 *information technology*, 537.7 *confirmation*, 547.7 *map*, 589.7 *calculation of chance*
stator 64.31 *electric motor*
statuary 50.12 *sculpture*, 50.17 *sculptor*
statue 50.12 *sculpture*, 511.3 *memento*, 545.11 *monument*, 547.6 *image*
Statue of Liberty 698.3 *independence*
statuesque 50.26 *artistic*, 275.12 *tall*, 789.5 *beautiful*, 805.19 *stately*
statuette 50.12 *sculpture*, 547.6 *image*, 681.1 *trophy*
stature 275.1 *height*
status 105.1 *state*, 106.1 *circumstances*, 107.3 *relative position*, 121.2 *rank*, 150.4 *position*, 152.6 *category*, 251.5 *rank*, 611.1 *importance*
status group 2.6 *social group*
status quo 106.1 *circumstances*, 122.2 *equilibrium*, 251.2 *circumstances*
status-seeking 815.2 *social ambition*
statute 16.3 *law*, 166.1 *rule*, 654.3 *precept*
statute book 16.1 *the law*, 166.2 *canon*
statute law 16.1 *the law*
statutory 16.46 *legislated*, 166.9 *legal*
staunch 96.9 *stop the flow*, 237.10 *potent*, 323.8 *stop*, 490.6 *infallible*, 574.5 *steady*, 575.10 *persevering*, 584.13 *fixed*, 630.20 *doctor*, 694.8 *loyal*, 819.11 *devoted*
staunched 323.13 *stopped*
staunchly 694.10 *obediently*, 819.19 *devotedly*
staunchness 490.17 *infallibility*, 574.15 *will*, 575.3 *constancy*, 694.2 *loyalty*, 819.3 *familiarity*
staurolite 54 *Minerals*, 54 *Gemstones*
stave 47.12 *wood*, 48.8 *part of poem*, 49.17 *notation*, 359.10 *step*, 604.1 *materials*, 680.7 *blunt weapon*
stave in 317.7 *make concave*, 362.2 *flatten*
stave off 671.24 *parry*
stay 16.6 *legal process*, 99.19 *continue to be*, 132.7 *be left*, 137.4 *means of connection*, 137.7 *tackle*, 188.6 *last*, 209.3 *delayed action*, 209.7 *wait*, 209.8 *delay*, 217.5 *be permanent*, 218.2 *stop*, 218.8 *cause to cease*, 218.9 *pause*, 219.4 *pro-*

tract, 225.6 *be stable*, 255.14, 256.17 *inhabit*, 283.6 *interruption*, 283.12 *interrupt*, 323.8 *stop*, 325.8 *be motionless*, 325.11 *stop*, 328.3 *slow down*, 396.17 *dwell*, 661.2 *obstacle*, 815.3 *meeting*, 815.12 *visit*
stay alert 380.17 *be mentally sharp*, 467.11 *take note of*
stay alone 139.7 *be aloof*
stay at 250.10 *settle*
stay at home 325.8 *be motionless*, 632.8 *be safe*, 816.12 *be unsocial*
stay-at-home 325.5 *sedentary*, 816.6 *unsocial person*, 816.10 *lonely*
stay at one's post 847.16 *do one's duty*
stay at peace 675.5 *be at peace*, 677.4 *pacify*
stay away 254.15 *be absent*, 458.2 *depart*
stay away from 591.1 *avoid*
stay away from the hard stuff 873.3 *be sober*
stay away in droves 254.15 *be absent*
stay behind the scenes 527.13 *hide*
stay cool 699.10 *restrain oneself*
stay devoted to 784.7 *like*
stayed 283.9 *interrupted*
stayer 32.2 *thoroughbred*, 32.7 *horseracing*, 575.5 *tenacious person*, 577.8 *obstinate person*
stay flexible 377.10 *be adaptable*
stay-in 15.10 *unionized*
stay in a rut 112.12 *be monotonous*, 577.9 *be obstinate*, 788.7 *suffer boredom*
stay in control 698.16 *be independent*
stay indoors 325.8 *be motionless*
staying 256.14 *inhabiting*
staying away 458.4 *disappearance*
staying power 188.4 *long-lastingness*, 235.1 *power*, 237.1 *strength*, 575.4 *stamina*
stay in line 167.8 *comply*, 694.5 *obey*
stay innocent 134.9 *be pure*
stay in one place 225.6 *be stable*
stay in one's lane 21.6 *race*
stay in one's shell 783.12 *be indifferent*, 816.12 *be unsocial*
stay-in strike 15.4 *industrial dispute*
stay in the background 124.9 *be average*
stay in the black 744.10 *deposit*
stay in the shadows 531.11 *conceal oneself*
stay in time 198.7 *synchronize*
stay near 264
stay neutral 641.4 *not act*
stay of execution 209.3 *delayed action*
stay on 219.4 *protract*
stay on an even keel 242.3 *be moderate*
stay one's hand 218.9 *pause*
stay on good terms 819.13 *befriend*
stay on one's good behaviour 863.8 *be virtuous*
stay on the beam 332.7 *take a direction*
stay on the right side of the law 16.67 *follow the law*
stay on the shelf 641.4 *not act*, 739.2 *be sold*
stay on the straight and narrow 166.17 *obey orders*
stay out 147.9 *be excluded*
stay out late 209.6 *be late*
stay out of the limelight 531.11 *conceal oneself*
stay outside 147.9 *be excluded*
stay packed away 641.4 *not act*
stay pure 825.10 *be continent*
stay put 225.6 *be stable*, 325.8 *be motionless*, 574.10 *insist*, 577.9 *be obstinate*
stays 295.18 *underwear*
staysail 74 *Sails*, 36.3 *parts of a*

sailing boat
stay silent 566.8 *be taciturn*
stay single 825.9 *be celibate*
stay sober 873.3 *be sober*
stay still 641.4 *not act*
stay the course 188.6 *last*, 378.10 *be tough*
stay the same 112.9 *be uniform*, 112.12 *be monotonous*
stay till the bitter end 575.9 *endure*
stay too long 788.6 *be boring*
stay underground 638.6 *elude*
stay unmarried 698.16 *be independent*
stay up late 209.6 *be late*
stay virtuous 134.9 *be pure*
stay within bounds 242.3 *be moderate*
stay within one's limits 699.10 *restrain oneself*
stay with it 225.8 *show determination*
stay young 206.16 *be young*
steadfast 112.5 *uniform*, 217.7 *permanent*, 225.9 *stable*, 237.11 *strong in spirit*, 490.6 *infallible*, 570.7 *iron-willed*, 574.4 *undaunted*, 694.8 *loyal*, 718.9 *fast*, 778.12 *self-reliant*, 819.11 *devoted*, 857.4 *honourable*
steadfastly 112.13 *uniformly*, 217.9 *permanently*, 225.12 *stably*, 694.10 *obediently*, 718.17 *fastly*, 778.18 *courageously*, 819.19 *devotedly*, 857.7 *honourably*
steadfastness 778, 112.1 *uniformity*, 217.1 *permanence*, 225.1 *stability*, 237.1 *strength*, 490.17 *infallibility*, 570.2 *willpower*, 574.15 *will*, 575.3 *constancy*, 694.2 *loyalty*, 819.3 *familiarity*, 857.1 *probity*
steadily 110.20 *regularly*, 112.13 *uniformly*, 116.35 *consistently*, 122.13 *equitably*, 212.1 *frequently*, 214.15 *regularly*, 214.17 *orderly*, 217.9 *permanently*, 219.7 *continually*, 225.12 *stably*
steadiness 112.1 *uniformity*, 122.2 *equilibrium*, 159.7 *stability*, 212.4 *frequency*, 214.4 *orderliness*, 217.1 *permanence*, 225.1 *stability*, 242.1 *moderation*, 325.1 *motionlessness*, 490.17 *infallibility*, 574.15 *will*
steading 68.6 *farm*
steady 574, 575, 4.18 *detached*, 55.53 *rainy*, 110.17 *regular*, 112.5 *uniform*, 112.9 *be uniform*, 116.14 *conforming*, 122.6 *equal*, 150.16 *harmonious*, 212.3 *frequent*, 214.10 *make regular*, 214.11 *regular*, 214.14 *orderly*, 217.7 *permanent*, 219.5 *continual*, 225.7 *make stable*, 225.9 *stable*, 242.6 *moderate*, 325.4 *motionless*, 490.6 *infallible*, 490.21 *make certain*, 509.5 *rational*, 718.9 *fast*, 718.14 *make fast*, 726.7 *detain*, 821.9 *lover*
steady as a rock 225.9 *stable*
steady drizzle 55.25 *rain*
steady flow 56.8 *time*
steady progress 336.10 *forward motion*
steady state 53.4 *cosmological model*, 122.2 *equilibrium*, 159.7, 225.1 *stability*
steady stream 159.8 *procession*
steak 143.7 *piece*
steak and kidney 45.31 *offal*
steak au poivre 45.45 *French dish*
steakhouse 350.15 *eating place*
steak knife 350.16 *eating utensil*
steak tartare 45.45 *French dish*
steak tenderizer 393.15 *pulper*
steal 736, 458.3 *cause to disappear*, 721.14 *profit*, 733.9 *borrow illegally*, 734.10 *take away*, 736.3 *theft*, 736.4 *stolen goods*, 754.4 *bargain*, 767.14 *take away*, 846.14 *arrogate*, 858.10 *be criminal*, 866.10 *sin*

steal a car 736.12 *steal*
steal a glance 435.13 *look*
steal a march on 126.8 *be superior*, 194.9 *do before*, 208.9 *prepare*, 357.3 *exceed*, 657.5 *be cunning*
steal away 531.11 *conceal oneself*, 591.8 *run away*, 638.5 *escape*
stealer 736.8 *thief*
steal every heart 821.25 *be loved*
stealing 777 Phobias by Topic, **736**, 31.8 *hockey*, 721.5 *profit*, 733.3 *illegal borrowing*, 734.3 *taking away*
Stealing 736
stealings 736.4 *stolen goods*
stealing the puck 31.3 *ice hockey*
steal one's stuff 733.9 *borrow illegally*
steal one's thunder 661.8 *hinder*
steal on the air 424.5 *sound faint*
steal someone's thunder 126.8 *be superior*
stealth 527.8 *concealment*, 529.2 *secretiveness*, 657.1 *cunning*
steal the puck 31.9 *play hockey*
steal the show 51.33 *overact*, 126.8 *be superior*
stealthily 529, 657.6 *cunningly*
stealthiness 529.2 *secretiveness*, 657.1 *cunning*
stealthy 328.5 *unhurried*, 424.4 *faint*, 527.2 *concealed*, 529.10 *secretive*, 657.4 *cunning*
steam 45.55 *cook*, 338.12 *propellant*, 349.14 *let out*, 353.19 *sweat*, 388.4 *water vapour*, 388.27 *give off*, 389.3 *wateriness*, 408.1 *heat*, 408.14 *be hot*, 441.2 *murk*, 443.7 *opaque thing*
steam away 239.2 *be full of vigour*
steam bath 621.6 *bath*
steamboat 74 Ships and Boats, 74.3 *vessel*
steam-distil 57.25 *solidify*
steamed 45.56 *culinary*
steamed pudding 45.35 *dessert*
steamed up 441.6 *murky*, 443.2 *shady*
steam engine 63.11 *engine*, 603.4 *machine*
steamer 74 Ships and Boats, 45.6 *kitchen equipment*, 72.4 *locomotive*, 258.15 *pot*
steamer route 74.2 *waterway*
steamily 388.30 *smokily*
steaminess 408.1 *heat*
steaming 44.5 *ceramic process*, 45.8 *cooking technique*, 74.11 *nautical*, 388.10 *vaporization*, 388.19 *smoky*, 408.9 *hot*, 626.5 *unhygienic*
steam iron 282.4 *flattener*, 408.3 *heater*
steam locomotive 72.4 *locomotive*
steam-operated 235.17, 410.10 *powered*
steam power 235.4 *energy*
steam-powered 235.17 *powered*
steam pressure 235.4 *energy*
steam-propelled 338.19 *propelled*
steam propulsion 338.2 *method of propulsion*
steam radio 420.9 *audio device*
steam reforming 57.22 *industrial chemistry*
steamrolled 376.2 *uniform*
steamroller 71 Motor Vehicles, 244.9 *demolish*, 282.4 *flattener*, 376.9 *smoother*, 384.11 *pulverizer*, 695.4 *coercive person*, 695.7 *force*, 695.9 *compelling*
steamrolling 695.9 *compelling*
steamship 74 Ships and Boats, 74.3 *vessel*
steam turbine 63.12 *turbine*
steam up 441.9 *be dim*, 443.10 *be opaque*
steamy 388.19 *smoky*, 408.11 *warm*, 441.6 *murky*
stearate 57 Types of Compounds
stearic 58 Common Fatty Acids
steatopygic 259.16 *fat*
steatopygous 259.16 *fat*

steed 32.1 *horse*, 32.3 *warhorse*
steel 57 Alloys, 43.4 *building material*, 63.25 *construction material*, 74.4 *shipbuilding*, 133.2 *mixed thing*, 300.3 *cutting edge*, 373.1 *hard*, 373.7 *hard substance*, 373.9 *harden*, 380.12 *sharpener*, 448.5 *grey thing*, 574.16 *fortitude*
steel band 49.26 *musical group*
steel blue 454.1 *blue*
steel-clad 632.6 *invulnerable*
Steele 48 Writers, **48** Dramatists
steeled 373.3 *hardened*, 574.4 *undaunted*
steel engraving 50.15 *engraving*
steel-grey 448.1 *grey*
steelhead 80 Fishes
steel helmet 671.7 *armour*
steeliness 225.2 *determination*, 373.5 *hardness*, 574.14 *tenacity*
steeling 373.6 *solidification*
steel oneself 237.8 *strengthen*, 574.8 *brace oneself*, 778.16 *take courage*, 868.5 *be impenitent*
steel plate 50.15 *engraving*
steel-plate armour 671.7 *armour*, 680.1 *weapon*
steel poles 30.5 *horizontal bar*
steel-rimmed glasses 435.10 *visual aid*
steel rule 268.6 *measuring instrument*
steel wool 375.7 *rough thing*
steelworker 646.2 *artisan*
steelworks 647.1 *workshop*
steely 225.11 *determined*, 373.1 *hard*, 448.1 *grey*, 574.3 *strong-willed*, 832.12 *callous*
steelyard 56.86 *weighing instrument*, 369.10 *scales*, 647.1 *workshop*
steely-eyed 832.12 *callous*
steep 389, 310.8 *oblique*, 354.4 *immerse*, 355.17 *obtain an extract*, 359.22 *ascending*, 374.13 *soften*, 621.14 *bathe*, 635.1 *trap*, 659.10 *difficult*, 753.7 *dear*, 757.3 *costly*
steeped 389.23 *wet*
steeped in poison 626.7 *toxic*
steeped in vice 864.12 *immoral*
steepen 359.21 *upturn*
steeping 389, 355.7 *obtaining an extract*, 393.5 *pulping*
steeple 275.6 *tall thing*, 380.8 *sharp-pointed thing*
steeplechase 21.1 *track events*, 32.7 *horseracing*, 32.16 *ride*, 359.5 *jump*, 590.2 *chase*, 674.4 *race*
steeplechaser 21.3 *athlete*, 32.2 *thoroughbred*, 32.15 *horse person*
steeplechasing 18 Sporting Activities, **18** Sporting Activities, 32.6 *horsemanship*, 32.7 *horseracing*, 359.5 *jump*
steeplejack 359.11 *ascender*
steeply 753.12 *dearly*
steepness 95.1 *mountain*, 281.1 *verticality*, 310.2 *obliquity*
steep one's hands in blood 398.18 *slaughter*
steep price 753.1 *high price*
steer 36.15 *sail*, 36.16 *row*, 41.16 *bobsled*, 68.8 *livestock*, 74.9 *navigate*, 166.16, 332.6 *direct*, 401.16 *male animal*, 652.15 *conduct*, 653.2 *direct*
steerable 332.14 *directed*
steerage 332.1 *direction*, 653.4 *directorship*
steer a middle course 333.6 *be in the middle*, 717.4 *compromise*
steer a straight course 332.7 *take a direction*
steer clear 591.1 *avoid*
steer clear of 263.6 *keep away*, 335.8 *sidestep*
steer for 74.9 *navigate*, 332.7 *take a direction*, 590.12 *aim at*, 652.11 *conduct oneself*
steering 41.9 *bobsledding* , 41.13 *ice-skating*, 74.5 *navigation*, 332.1 *direction*, 332.16 *directing*, 653.4 *directorship*, 653.17

managerial
steering column 71 Motor Vehicle Parts
steering committee 653.6 *governing body*
steering gear 71 Motor Vehicle Parts
steering oar 74.5 *navigation*
steering wheel 71 Motor Vehicle Parts, 364.6 *rotator*
steer one away from 587.3 *deflect*
steer one's career 652.11 *conduct oneself*
steersman 74.7 *nautical person*, 653.13 *director*
steersmanship 653.4 *directorship*
steer towards 332.6 *direct*
steer with the foot 36.18 *windsurf*
steer-wrestling 32.12 *rodeo*
Stefan–Boltzmann constant 56.97 *fundamental constant*
Stefan's law 56 Named Laws
Steffi Graf 40.7 *famous tennis players*
Stegi 93 Cities
stegodon 79 Fossil Reptiles
Stegodon 77 Placental Mammals
stegophilist 359.11 *ascender*
stegosaur 79 Fossil Reptiles
stein 351.10 *drink container*
Stein 48 Writers
Steinbeck 48 Writers
steinbok 77 Placental Mammals
Steiner 4 Philosophers
Steingut 44 Types of Ceramics
Steinmetz 52 Scientists
stellar 53.36 *astronomical*
stellar association 53.9 *constellation*
stellar birth 53
stellar cluster 53.9 *constellation*
stellar evolution 53.11 *stellar birth*
stellar group 53.9 *constellation*
stellar population 53.9 *constellation*
stellar statistics 53.1 *astronomy*
stellate 380.2 *spiked*
stelline 45 Types of Pasta
Stellite 57 Alloys
stellular 380.2 *spiked*
stem 83, 5.17 *word*, 5.35 *part of speech*, 36.3 *parts of a sailing boat*, 41.12, 41.14 *ski*, 87.3 *grass plant*, 88.2 *fern plant*, 90.3 *plant body*, 143.6 *branch*, 218.8 *cause to cease*, 226.3 *rudiment*, 284.2 *supporting part*, 343.5 *fork*, 343.14 *branch*, 413.7 *tobacco*, 663.16 *confront*
stem christie 41.4 *skiing technique*
stem cutting 69.5 *gardening*
stemming 41.4 *skiing technique*
stem rot 69.12 *pests and diseases*
stem the flow 96.9 *stop the flow*
stem the tide 663.17 *withstand*, 682.7 *overcome obstacles*
stem tissue 83.5 *stem*
stem to stern 269.11 *lengthily*
stem tuber 83.5 *stem*
stem turn 41.2 *cross-country skiing*, 41.4 *skiing technique*
stemwinder 191 Timepieces and Timers
stench 419, 416.1 *odour*, 622.2 *uncleanness*
Stench 419
stench trap 417.2 *deodorant*
stencil 50.20 *draw*, 114.2 *copy*, 118.5 *duplicate*, 118.10 *copy*, 306.2 *prototype*
stenciller 114.3 *copier*, 118.6 *photocopier*
stencilling 42 Hobbies and Pastimes
Stendhal 48 Writers
Sten gun 680.11 *guns*
stenographer 545.9 *recorder*
stenopetalous 272.4 *narrow-leaved*
stenophyllous 272.4 *narrow-leaved*
stenosis 262.1 *contraction*, 272.9 *narrowing*

Stentor 423.5 *loud person*
stentorian 423.6 *loud*, 427.6 *resonant*, 431.16 *vociferous*
stentorian tones 423.1 *loudness*
stentorian voice 423.4 *sound maker*
step 336, 359, 41.12 *ski*, 57.14 *chemical reaction*, 121.4 *interval*, 263.2 *great distance*, 264.2 *short distance*, 266.2 *level*, 319.3 *rung*, 324.12 *gait*, 327.2 *route*, 596.5 *attempt*, 606.1 *provision*, 640.2 *deed*
step ashore 344.4 *land*
step aside 305.8 *move sideways*, 673.3 *submit*
step between 136.14 *come between*
step by step 121.10 *by degrees*, 150.25 *in order*, 328.16 *slowly*
step-by-step procedure 52.28 *algorithm*
step-cut 34.9 *mountaineer*
step-cutting 34.3 *climbing technique*, 34.8 *mountaineering*
step dance 46.2 *dance*
step-down transformer 64.22 *transformer*
stepfather 293.21 *substitution*
step forward 336.1 *go forward*
step function 52.29 *mathematical function*
Stephan-Oterma 53 Comets
stephanotis 84 Flowers and Flowering Plants, 418.2 *fragrant thing*
Stephen 710.7 *martyr*
Stephenson 52 Scientists
Stephenson's Rocket 72.10 *miscellaneous*
step in 295.34 *wear*, 678.1 *mediate*
step-in 295.31 *styled*
step-ins 295.18 *underwear*
step into the place of 155.22 *succeed*
step into the shoes of 155.22 *succeed*, 222.4 *be a substitute*, 730.9 *receive*, 767.11 *assist*
stepladder 137.4 *means of connection*, 327.2 *route*, 359.9 *ladder*
stepmother 293.21 *substitution*
step on it 235.11 *give power*, 324.19 *go*, 329.4 *be swift*, 329.6 *accelerate*, 648.8 *hurry up*
step on someone's lines 208.9 *prepare*
step on someone's toes 828.9 *offend*
step on the gas 235.11 *give power*, 239.3 *invigorate*, 329.6 *accelerate*, 410.11 *fuel*
step on the ladder 336.13 *step*
step out of 296.14 *undress*
step out of line 807.28 *get above oneself*
step over 356.11 *cross*
steppe 83.1 *plants*, 87.2 *grassland*, 98.6 *lowland*, 243.3 *geographical space*, 282.3 *flat thing*
stepped 359.25 *ladder-like*
stepper 32.2 *thoroughbred*
stepping a curve 41.2 *cross-country skiing*
stepping-in 678.2 *mediation*
stepping on a crack 517.7 *bad-luck sign*
stepping over end line on throw-in 23.5 *penalties*
stepping over foul line during free throw 23.5 *penalties*
steppingstone 121.4 *interval*
stepping stone 137.4 *means of connection*, 210.2 *opportunity*, 293.11 *paving*
stepping-stone 106.2 *occurrence*, 359.10 *step*
stepping stones 63.21 *bridge*
steppingstones 327.9 *bridge*
stepping stones 356.4 *access*
stepping up 128.1 *increase*
steps 30.6 *pommel horse*, 137.4 *means of connection*, 159.2 *consecution*, 275.8 *high thing*, 359.7 *means of ascent*, 592.2 *policy*, 594.10 *preparations*,

602.1 *means*, 640.1 *action*
stepstool 359.10 *step*
step to the front 811.31 *put on a show*
step turn 41.4 *skiing technique*
step up 128.5 *make bigger*, 239.3 *invigorate*, 336.8 *further*
step up the pace 329.6 *accelerate*
step-up transformer 64.22 *transformer*
step wide 343.14 *branch*
steradian 75 SI Units, **75** Scientific and Technical Units
stercoraceous 353.25 *faecal*, 622.8 *unclean*
stercoral 353.25 *faecal*
stercorous 353.25 *faecal*
stere 75 General Units
stereochemistry 57.13 *structure*
stereoisomer 57.13 *structure*
stereoisomeric 57.37 *structural*
stereometric 268.16 *micrometric*
stereometry 268.2 *micrometry*
stereomicroscope 56.85 *microscope*
stereophonic sound 420.10 *sound quality*
stereophotography 66.1 *photography*
stereoregular 57.44 *polymeric*
stereoregular polymer 57.21 *polymer*
stereoscopic 248.11 *spatial*, 435.20 *visual*
stereoscopic image 66
stereoscopy 435.10 *visual aid*
stereospecific 57.44 *polymeric*
stereospecific polymerization 57.21 *polymer*
stereotaxy 61.3 *psychiatric treatment*
stereotype 51.21 *role*, 110.8 *make the same*, 112.2 *conformity*, 112.10 *conform*, 116.6 *convention*, 116.26 *make uniform*, 167.9 *make conform*, 225.7 *make stable*
stereotyped 112.6 *conforming*, 164.22 *commonplace*, 167.15 *everyday*, 225.10 *stabilized*, 505.2 *proverbial*, 584.11 *normal*
stereotypical 51.38 *tragic*, 116.15 *conventional*, 163.11 *typical*, 164.22 *commonplace*
stereotypically 51.42 *dramatically*
steric 57.37 *structural*
steric effect 57.13 *structure*
steric hindrance 57.13 *structure*
sterigma 89.4 *fungal body*
sterile 134.14 *purified*, 236.13 *unsexed*, 247.3 *birth control*, 621.16 *clean*, 625.4 *hygienic*
sterilely 134.19 *purely*
sterility 236.1 *powerlessness*, 236.4 *disability*, 247.1 *infertility*, 614.4 *futility*
sterilization 134.2 *purification*, 236.1 *powerlessness*, 247.2 *making infertile*, 621.2 *cleaning*, 625.1 *hygiene*, 630.3 *prophylactic*, 637.1 *preservation*
sterilize 134.14 *purify*, 236.9 *make impotent*, 247.8 *make infertile*, 614.8 *make useless*, 621.15 *purify*, 625.6 *make hygienic*, 630.20 *doctor*
sterilized 134.14 *purified*, 236.13 *unsexed*, 247.5 *rendered infertile*, 621.17 *cleaned*, 625.4 *hygienic*
sterilizing 134.15 *purifying*
sterling 537.19 *authentic*, 611.6 *notable*, 617.3 *valuable*, 741.1 *money*
sterling balances 741.6 *funds*
sterling-based 741.22 *monetary*
sterling silver 57 Alloys, 537.6 *authenticity*
stern 74 Parts of a Ship, 36.3 *parts of a sailing boat*, 36.6 *canoeing*, 304.1 *rear*, 304.2 *rear end*, 378.5 *mentally tough*, 574.3 *strong-willed*, 690.8 *severe*, 772.1 *solemn*, 830.6 *sullen*, 832.12 *callous*, 852.30 *censuring*, 876.10 *moralistic*
Stern 49 Musicians and Com-

posers, **53** The Constellations
stern daughter of the voice of God 847.4 *sense of duty*
Sterne 48 Writers
stern ladder 359.9 *ladder*
stern light 439.6 *electric light*
sternly 378.14 *single-mindedly*, 690.11 *severely*, 772.10 *solemnly*, 830.13 *sullenly*
sternmost 304.9 *in the rear*
sternness 378.9 *mental toughness*, 574.14 *tenacity*, 690.1 *severity*, 772.4 *solemnity*, 830.1 *sullenness*, 832.3 *callousness*, 876.4 *self-righteousness*
sternotomy 60 Surgical Operations
sternpost 74 Parts of a Ship
sternum 382 Bones
sternutator 62.4 *drug type*
sternway 324.4 *backward motion*
steroid 58.6 *lipid*, 62.4 *drug type*, 630.8 *drug*
steroid hormone 58.16 *hormone*
sterol 58.6 *lipid*
stertor 430.2 *hoarseness*
stertorous 430.8 *hoarse*
stertorousness 423.1 *loudness*
stethoscope 60.7 *diagnosis*, 420.9 *audio device*
stetson 295.15 *headgear*, 544.5 *uniform*
stevedore 70.3 *transporter*, 326.7 *transferor* , 594.15 *preparer*, 646.1 *worker*
stevedore's knot 74 Knots
Stevens 48 Poets
Stevenson 48 Writers
Stevenson screen 55.7 *weather instruments*
Stevinus 53 Lunar Features
stew 45.32 *meat dish*, 45.55 *cook*, 133.2 *mixed thing*, 393.7 *soup*, 393.24 *pulp*, 408.14 *be hot*, 594.7 *develop*, 828.4 *anger*, 828.11 *be angry*
steward 73.3 *aircraft personnel*, 606.3 *provider*, 653.15 *manager*, 653.16 *official*, 697.3 *attendant*, 697.6 *domestic servant*, 741.18 *treasurer*
stewardess 73.3 *aircraft personnel*, 697.3 *attendant*
Stewards' Cup 36.5 *Henley trophies*
stewardship 653.3 *management*
Stewart 18 Sporting Personalities
stewed 45.56 *culinary*, 874.1 *drunk*
stewed fruit 45.35 *dessert*
stewing 594.17 *developing*
stew in one's own juice 687.9 *be in trouble*, 816.12 *be unsocial*
stew pan 45.6 *kitchen equipment*
Stheno 11.4 *witch*
stibnite 54 Minerals, **57** Common Metal Ores
sticht plate 34.4 *climbing equipment*
stick 71 Motor Vehicle Parts, **74** Rigging, **394**, 47.12 *wood*, 135.10 *link*, 137.11 *connect*, 138.6 *adhere*, 138.7 *cause to adhere*, 218.6 *cease*, 250.9 *locate*, 272.8 *narrow thing*, 284.3 *body support*, 284.12 *bear*, 322.20 *hole*, 325.9 *make motionless*, 380.14 *be sharp*, 380.16 *use a sharp tool* , 385.15 *grind*, 407.11 *touch*, 417.2 *deodorant*, 573.6 *be unwilling*, 584.17 *become a habit*, 604.1 *materials*, 656.10 *unskilled person*, 658.3 *naive person*, 680.7 *blunt weapon*, 764.8 *quarrel*, 875.6 *drug*, 879.14 *instrument of punishment*
stickability 642.8 *assiduity*
stick at it 219.4 *protract*
stick at nothing 574.6 *be resolute*
stick by 662.24 *back*
stickcheck 31.3 *ice hockey*, 31.9 *play hockey*
stickchecking 31.3 *ice hockey*
stick close 138.6 *adhere*
sticker 380.8 *sharp-pointed*

thing, 544.3 *means of identification*
stick fast 225.6 *be stable*, 225.8 *show determination*, 325.8 *be motionless*, 378.10 *be tough*, 574.10 *insist*
stick figure 299.1 *outline*
stick glove 31.3 *ice hockey*
stickily 138.11 *cohesively*, 353.33 *scatologically*, 391.17 *moistly*, 393.27 *slimily*, 394.12 *viscously*, 726.11 *tenaciously*
stick in 130.6 *add*, 354.1 *insert*
stickiness 138.1 *adhesion*, 391.3 *humidity*, 393.2 *semiliquidity*, 394.1 *viscosity*, 726.1 *retention*
sticking 138.1 *adhesion*
sticking one's nose in 642.9 *overactivity*
sticking out 283.8 *projecting*, 318.5 *protuberant*
sticking out one's tongue 818.3 *act of discourtesy*
sticking plaster 138.3 *adhesive*, 222.3 *substitute thing*, 630.10 *surgical dressing*
sticking to 719.7 *observant*
stick in one's craw 828.9 *offend*
stick in one's throat 764.10 *displease*, 785.7 *cause dislike*
stick insect 82 Insects, 82.1 *insect*
stick in the mind 511.15 *be remembered*
stick in the mud 325.5 *sedentary*, 358.1 *fall short*
stick-in-the-mud 167.6 *conformist*, 217.3 *conservative person*, 217.8 *conservative*, 325.7 *sedentary person*, 328.15, 328.15 *slow person*, 490.11 *opinionist*, 577.8 *obstinate person*, 584.8 *creature of habit*, 669.5 *resister*, 788.3 *boring person*
stick it out 225.8 *show determination*, 574.11 *persist*, 575.9 *endure*
stick it out to the bitter end 219.4 *protract*
stickle 573.6 *be unwilling*, 737.3 *bargain*
stickleback 80 Fishes
stickler 577.8 *obstinate person*, 619.4 *perfectionist*, 690.4 *strict person*
stick like a leech 138.6 *adhere*, 726.6 *retain*
stick like a limpet 138.6 *adhere*
stick like glue 138.6 *adhere*, 575.8 *hold out*, 590.9 *follow*
stickling 811.26 *ritualistic*
stick one's neck out 229.4 *chance*, 508.6 *be foolish*, 633.9 *face danger*, 780.5 *be rash*
stick one's nose in 678.1 *mediate*
stick onto 130.6 *add*, 138.6 *adhere*
stick out 316.5 *be convex*, 318.8 *protrude*, 437.8 *be visible*, 544.11 *identify oneself*
stick out a mile 117.12 *be disparate*
stick out for 674.11 *contend*, 737.3 *bargain*
stick out like a sore thumb 115.5 *be dissimilar*, 117.12 *be disparate*, 149.15 *be foreign*, 168.19 *be independent*, 318.8 *protrude*, 437.8 *be visible*
stick out one's tongue 543.11 *gesture*
stick out one's tongue at 850.26 *cock a snook*
stick out over 283.11 *project*
sticks 32.7 *horseracing*, 674.4 *race*
sticks and stones 460.4 *nonhuman existence*
stick shift 71 Motor Vehicle Parts
stick someone up 736.12 *steal*
stick to 130.6 *add*, 138.7 *cause to adhere*, 138.8 *be tenacious*, 219.4 *protract*, 264.10 *stay near*, 719.4 *observe*, 726.6 *retain*
stick together 135.8 *unite*, 137.13 *intercommunicate*,

138.6 *adhere*, 138.7 *cause to adhere*
stick-to-itive 138.10 *tenacious*, 642.20 *industrious*
stick-to-itiveness 138.2 *tenacity*, 642.8 *assiduity*
stick to one's fingers 730.9 *receive*
stick to one's guns 225.8 *show determination*, 490.20 *be certain*, 535.19 *confirm*, 575.8 *hold out*, 577.9, 669.7 *be obstinate*
stick to the facts 503.7 *be accurate*, 537.29 *be truthful*
stick to the ground game 19.15 *play offence*
stick to the letter 503.7 *be accurate*
stick to the letter of the law 690.5 *be severe*
stick to the point 107.7 *relate to*
stick to the rules 166.17 *obey orders*, 167.8 *comply*, 306.8 *be formal*, 857.6 *be honourable*
stick to the truth 312.11 *be straight*, 857.6 *be honourable*
stick up 281.6 *make vertical*, 361.1 *raise*
stick-up 736.3 *theft*
stick up for 284.14 *give moral support*, 662.24 *back*, 855.8 *justify*
stick-up job 736.3 *theft*
stick-up man 736.11 *dishonest person*
stick with it 219.8 *go on*, 225.8 *show determination*
sticky 34.8 *mountaineering*, 55.52 *humid*, 137.14 *connective*, 138.9 *adhesive*, 353.28 *sweaty*, 391.9 *moist*, 393.16 *semiliquid*, 394.8 *viscous*, 408.11 *warm*, 477.13 *problematic*, 633.1 *dangerous*, 659.12 *problematic*, 726.9 *retentive*
sticky boots 34.4 *climbing equipment*
sticky-fingered 736.17 *stolen*
sticky fingers 736.1 *stealing*
sticky label 138.4 *adherent*
sticky moment 477.4 *difficult question*
sticky tape 138.3 *adhesive*
sticky wicket 27.5 *wicket*, 659.7 *awkward situation*
stiff 36.10 *sailing*, 41.12 *ski*, 225.9 *stable*, 325.4 *motionless*, 373.2 *tough*, 378.3 *hard*, 397.11 *dead person*, 397.19 *dead*, 551.2 *obscure*, 557.4 *ornate*, 559.9 *inelegant*, 577.3 *unyielding*, 650.1 *fatigued*, 656.3 *clumsy*, 659.10 *difficult*, 669.11 *obstinate*, 699.14 *self-restrained*, 753.7 *dear*, 805.15 *unapproachable*, 811.22 *majestic*, 813.6 *formal*, 874.3 *dead drunk*
stiff as a board 373.2 *tough*
stiff as a poker 373.2 *tough*
stiff as a ramrod 373.2 *tough*
stiff as buckram 373.2 *tough*
stiff boat 36.2 *sailing boat*
stiff collar 295.14 *neckwear*
stiffen 225.6 *be stable*, 225.8 *show determination*, 237.8 *strengthen*, 373.9 *harden*, 373.10 *solidify*, 378.10 *be tough*
stiffened 373.3 *hardened*
stiffening 225.1 *stability*, 237.4 *strengthening*, 373.5 *hardness*
stiffen one's resolve 237.8 *strengthen*
stiffen the sinews 237.8 *strengthen*
stiffly 225.12 *stably*, 373.12, 378.12 *toughly*, 551.4 *obscurely*, 669.14 *resistingly*, 699.17 *with self-restraint*, 753.12 *dearly*, 811.38 *majestically*, 813.12 *formally*
stiff neck 577.5 *obstinacy*
stiff-necked 577.2 *refractory*, 668.7 *defiant*, 805.15 *unapproachable*
stiff-neckedly 805.32 *proudly*
stiff-neckedness 805.2 *unap-*

proachability, 813.1 *formality*
stiff-necked pride 805.2 *unapproachability*
stiffness 63.15 *strength of materials*, 225.1 *stability*, 325.1 *motionlessness*, 373.5 *hardness*, 378.6 *toughness*, 551.1 *obscurity*, 559.4 *inelegance of speech*, 624.3 *symptom*, 669.2 *obstinacy*, 699.3 *self-restraint*, 811.7 *pomp*, 813.1 *formality*
stiff one 351.2 *drink*
stiff opposition 663.1 *opposition*
stiff price 753.1 *high price*
stiff ski 41.5 *ski equipment*
stiff upper lip 574.16 *fortitude*, 778.2 *heroism*, 787.1 *lack of wonder*
stiff wind 55.14 *windiness*
stiff with 144.8 *full*
stiff with cold 409.8 *cold*
stifle 147.7 *exclude*, 236.8 *overpower*, 244.8 *destroy*, 398.17 *murder*, 422.2 *silence*, 424.6, 428.7 *mute*, 531.8 *conceal*, 661.8 *hinder*, 699.8 *restrain*, 709.4 *censor*
stifled 424.4 *faint*, 428.1 *faint-sounding*, 428.2 *nonresonant*, 531.14 *concealed*
stifling 244.1 *destruction*, 398.23 *deadly*, 408.11 *warm*, 699.1 *restraint*, 699.13 *restraining*
stigma 84.3 *flower part*, 90.3 *plant body*, 245.8 *organs of reproduction*, 544.3 *means of identification*, 793.1 *spot*, 844.9 *dishonour*
stigmatized 544.12 *identified*
stilb 75 Scientific and Technical Units
stilbite 54 Minerals
stilboestrol 62 Medication
stile 346.6 *means of entry*
stiletto 380.8 *sharp-pointed thing*, 680.8 *sharp weapon*
still 57 Laboratory Apparatus, 94.9 *lakelike*, 240.5 *inert*, 242.4, 242.6 *moderate*, 325.2 *repose*, 325.4 *motionless*, 325.6 *quiescent*, 325.10 *motionlessly*, 351.17 *drinkable*, 376.3 *soothing*, 388.11 *vaporizer*, 397.19 *dead*, 422.2 *silence*, 422.3 *silent*, 428.7 *mute*, 641.3, 643.1 *inactive*, 649.4 *at ease*, 675.7 *peaceful*
still as a statue 325.4 *motionless*
still as death 325.4 *motionless*
stillbirth 397.1 *death*, 397.11 *dead person*
stillborn 397.19 *dead*, 683.10 *failed*
still breathing 396.12 *alive*
still feel hungry 609.6 *be unsatisfied*
still fishing 20.1 *angling*
still hunting 37.2 *hunting*
still in full possession of one's faculties 207.14 *aged*
still life 367.5 *object*
still-life 50.10 *art subject*, 66.4 *portrait*
still-life painter 50.16 *artist*
still more 126.17 *supremely*
stillness 150.8 *harmony*, 240.1 *inertness*, 325.1 *motionlessness*, 325.2 *repose*, 376.7 *smoothness*, 422.4 *silence*, 641.1 *inaction*, 643.5 *inactivity*, 649.1 *ease*, 675.1 *peace*
still remaining 132.10 *surplus*
still room 45.3 *kitchen*, 256.7 *room*
stillroom 605.4 *storage*
still small voice 847.4 *sense of duty*
Stillson 603.1 *tool*
still standing 217.7 *permanent*
still the same 217.9 *permanently*
still tired 650.1 *fatigued*
still water 94.2 *small lake*
still wet behind the ears 585.1 *unaccustomed*
still wine 351.9 *wine*
stilly 325.10 *motionlessly*, 376.15 *soothingly*, 422.3 *silent*

stilt 78 Birds
stilted 557.4 *ornate*, 559.9 *inelegant*, 797.3 *affected*, 813.6 *formal*
stilted arch 43.5 *arch*
stiltedly 813.12 *formally*
stiltedness 559.4 *inelegance of speech*
stilt house 94.7 *lake dwelling*
Stilton 45 Cheeses, 454.6 *blue thing*
stilt root 83.7 *root*
stilts 275.8 *high thing*
stilt village 94.7 *lake dwelling*
stimulant 228.3, 403.3 *stimulus*, 413.6 *cordial*, 630.7 *tonic*, 630.8 *drug*, 651.6 *refresher*, 874.6 *intoxicating*, 875.6 *drug*
stimulate 128.5 *make bigger*, 226.10 *awaken*, 228.9 *motivate*, 230.8 *activate*, 239.3 *invigorate*, 355.15 *draw out*, 403.13 *arouse sensation*, 405.9 *give pleasure*, 413.13 *be piquant*, 651.1 *refresh*, 782.15 *cause desire*, 874.9 *be intoxicating*
stimulated 228.12 *motivated*, 651.4 *refreshed*
stimulated emission 56.26 *laser*
stimulating 62, 413, 228.11 *motivational*, 239.5 *invigorating*, 355.18 *extractive*, 403.9 *exciting*, 518.7 *suppositional*, 586.19 *persuasive*, 651.3 *refreshing*
stimulatingly 413, 228.14 *influentially*, 355.22 *expressively*
stimulation 413, 128.1 *increase*, 226.1 *cause*, 228.1 *motive*, 239.1 *vigour*, 355.5 *drawing out*, 403.3 *stimulus*, 642.1 *activity*, 651.5 *refreshment*, 874.10 *drunkenness*
stimulative 630.17 *remedial*
stimulus 228, 403, 128.1 *increase*, 226.4 *contributing factor*, 586.8 *incentive*
stimulus-response psychology 61.1 *psychology*
sting 82.16 *infest*, 380.7 *sharp point*, 380.8 *sharp-pointed thing*, 380.14 *be sharp*, 406.10 *be painful*, 406.11 *inflict pain*, 413.1 *piquancy*, 413.13 *be piquant*, 515.8 *be dishonest*, 539.8 *trick*, 540.8 *fraud*, 540.21 *be fraudulent*, 592.3 *expedient plan*, 618.11 *harmfulness*, 631.6 *source of trouble*, 631.14 *afflict*, 736.7 *dishonesty*, 753.10 *overcharge*, 764.12 *be painful*, 828.9, 828.9 *offend*
stingily 609.10 *insufficiently*, 860.8 *selfishly*
stinginess 609.8 *insufficiency*, 758.3 *parsimony*, 860.1 *selfishness*
stinging 380.2 *spiked*, 406.5 *painful*, 413.9 *piquant*, 764.4 *painful*, 832.14 *hostile*
sting in the tail 157.10 *ending*
stingray 80 Fishes
stingy 380.2 *spiked*, 609.1 *insufficient*, 758.1 *mean*, 860.4 *selfish*
stink 419, 416.1 *odour*, 416.8 *have odour*, 419.1 *stench*, 618.10 *poverty*, 622.2 *uncleanness*, 622.10 *be dirty*, 628.2 *decay*
stinkard 419.2 *something that makes an unpleasant smell*
stink-bomb 419.2 *something that makes an unpleasant smell*
stink bug 82 Insects
stinker 419.2 *something that makes an unpleasant smell*, 864.10 *bad person*
stinkhorn 89 Fungi, 419.2 *something that makes an unpleasant smell*
stinking 419, 416.5 *odorous*, 618.4 *poor*, 622.8 *unclean*, 785.9 *disliked*, 877.12 *indecent*
stinking drunk 874.3 *dead drunk*
stinkingly 419
stinking of liquor 874.5 *drunken*
stinking rich 742.1 *wealthy*

stinking smut 89 Fungi
stinko 874.3 *dead drunk*
stink of 608.5 *about*, 610.4 *be excessive*
stink of money 742.12 *be rich*
stink out 419.5 *stink*
stink to high heaven 419.5 *stink*
stink trap 417.2 *deodorant*
stinkwood 85 Trees and Shrubs
stinky 618.4 *poor*, 622.8 *unclean*
stint 120.2 *certain amount*, 121.1 *degree*, 121.4 *interval*, 185.3 *duration*, 187.4 *period of activity*, 609.7 *make insufficient*, 644.2 *task*, 731.3 *allotted task*, 758.7 *hoard*
stinted 609.2 *unprovided*
stinting 869.8 *self-restrained*
stintingly 869.11 *with self-restraint*
stipe 83.5 *stem*, 89.4 *fungal body*, 90.3 *plant body*
stipend 284.7 *financial support*, 662.6 *financial assistance*, 721.4 *earnings*, 729.2 *gift*, 730.2 *something received*, 746.3 *pay*, 878.3 *grant*
stipendiary 284.9 *supportive*, 729.7 *given*
stipendiary magistrate 492.6 *justice*
stipple 456.11 *variegate*
stippling 456.4 *maculation*
stipulate 165.24, 485.16 *specify*, 490.22 *specify*, 593.10 *necessitate*, 699.8 *restrain*, 716.6 *make conditions*
stipulated 52.77 *given*, 485.12 *conditional*, 490.7 *particular*
stipulation 485.7 *condition*, 490.18 *particularity*, 518.1 *supposition*, 593.1 *requirement*, 699.1 *restraint*, 716.2 *basis for negotiations*
stipulatory 485.12 *conditional*, 716.8 *negotiated*
stipule 83.6 *leaf*
stir 45.55 *cook*, 55.58 *blow*, 113.8 *be diverse*, 133.8 *mix*, 151.9 *disorder*, 153.7 *disturb*, 324.2 *momentum*, 324.13 *be in motion*, 364.10 *swirl*, 366.2 *tumult*, 366.3 *turbulence*, 366.22 *agitate*, 403.13 *arouse sensation*, 413.13 *be piquant*, 642.1 *activity*, 642.12 *be active*, 702.2 *the inside*, 821.25 *be loved*
stir-fried 45.56 *culinary*
stir fry 45.48 *Chinese dish*
stir-fry 45.55 *cook*
stir-frying 45.8 *cooking technique*
stirk 68.8 *livestock*
Stirling 52 Scientists, 93 Cities
Stirling engine 63.11 *engine*
stir one's stumps 642.12 *be active*
stirred 133.12 *mixed*, 403.7 *susceptible*
stirred up 366.15 *agitated*
stirrer 57 Laboratory Apparatus, 133.6 *mixer*, 133.7 *person who mixes*, 151.11 *troublemaker*, 465.4 *meddler*, 635.2 *troublemaker*, 642.11 *meddler*
stirring 133.1 *mixture*, 324.2 *momentum*, 324.16 *moving*, 403.9 *exciting*, 611.6 *notable*, 642.1 *activity*, 642.18 *active*, 642.19 *busy*
stirrup 74 Rigging, **382** Bones, 34.4 *climbing equipment*
stirrup bone 420.5 *internal ear*
stirrup cup 345.9 *parting*, 351.10 *drink container*
stir the blood 828.9 *offend*
stir the possum 574.9 *undertake*
stir up 241.9 *make violent*, 366.22 *agitate*, 443.11 *make opaque*, 828.9 *offend*
stir up a hornet's nest 659.22 *cause trouble*
stir up trouble 666.7 *pick a fight*
stitch 67.5 *knitting*, 135.10 *link*, 137.6 *line*, 137.8 *fastening*, 137.11 *connect*, 295.35 *make clothing*, 406.1 *pain*
stitched 135.12 *united*, 135.15

tied, 137.15 *connected*
stitcher 295.26 *fashion designer*
stitching 27.7 *bat*, 135.3 *unification*, 135.5 *joint*
stitchwort 84 Flowers and Flowering Plants
stithy 647.1 *workshop*
St. Moritz Tobogganing Club 41.9 *bobsledding*
stoat 77 Placental Mammals
stoba 45.51 *West Indian dish*
stochastic 229.6 *motiveless*, 589.8 *chance*
stochastic process 52.57 *population*
stochastics 589.7 *calculation of chance*
stochastic variable 52.57 *population*
stock 84 Flowers and Flowering Plants, 1.7 *society*, 32.8 *hunting*, 45.13 *soup*, 68.8 *livestock*, 69.5 *gardening*, 76.3 *domesticated animal*, 83.5 *stem*, 116.15 *conventional*, 124.1 *average*, 137.6 *line*, 144.6 *fill*, 163.8 *genealogy*, 167.15 *everyday*, 171.1 *list*, 226.3 *rudiment*, 295.14 *neckwear*, 304.8 *nurture*, 387.2 *juice*, 505.2 *proverbial*, 584.10 *familiar*, 602.2 *supplies*, 604.1 *materials*, 605.1, 605.6 *store*, 606.1, 606.5 *provision*, 721.3 *acquisition*, 725.5 *personal estate*, 739.1 *sell*, 739.8 *merchandise*
stockade 301.2 *enclosed place*, 632.2 *protection*, 634.2 *shelter*, 671.9 *barrier*, 671.12 *fort*, 702.1 *prison*
stock-and-horn 49 Musical Instruments
stockbreeder 68.15 *agriculturist*, 243.9 *producer*
stockbreeding 243.2 *manufacture*
stockbroker 14, 223.4 *person who exchanges*, 716.4 *negotiator*, 737.10 *trader*, 739.12 *wholesaler*
stockbroker belt 93.8 *suburb*, 249.11 *settlement*
stock car 71 Motor Vehicles
stock-car 33.11 *racing*
stock-car race 33.1 *motor racing*
stockcar racing 674.4 *race*
stock-car racing 18 Sporting Activities, 33.1 *motor racing*
stock character 51.21 *role*
stock company 51.23 *cast*
stocked 606.8 *provisional*
stock exchange 14, 215.3 *irregular thing*, 223.2 *place of exchange*, 741.7 *finance*
Stock Exchange 740.5 *stock market*
stock farm 68.6 *farm*, 647.1 *workshop*
stock farmer 68.15 *agriculturist*
stockfish 80.8 *food fish*
Stockhausen 49 Musicians and Composers
stockholder 725.7 *property man*
Stockholm 93 Cities
stockhorse 32.4 *saddle horse*
stockiness 259.6 *squatness*, 270.1 *shortness*
stockinet 67 Natural Fabrics
stocking 741.20 *money store*
stocking cap 295.15 *headgear*
stockings 22.3 *baseball equipment*, 295.20 *legwear*
stocking stitch 67.5 *knitting*
stock in trade 602.4 *financial resources*, 725.5 *personal estate*
stock-in-trade 603.6 *equipment*, 605.1 *store*, 739.8 *merchandise*
stock-jobber 14.3 *stockbroker*, 737.10 *trader*, 739.12 *wholesaler*
stock-jobbing 737.4 *trade*
stockkeeper 68.15 *agriculturist*
stockman 68.16 *farm worker*
stock market 740, 14.2 *stock exchange*, 741.7 *finance*
stock market decline 687.2 *economic adversity*
stock of words 5.22 *many words*
stock part 51.21 *role*

saccharide
storage space 248.5 *reserved space*, 605.4 *storage*
storax 85 Tree Products
store 605, 605, 740, 63.20 *building*, 65.6 *memory*, 68.8 *livestock*, 136.10 *set apart*, 140.5 *combine*, 161.25 *assemblage*, 161.37 *assemble*, 258.1 *container*, 258.21 *put in a container*, 531.8 *conceal*, 594.4 *prepare for action*, 594.10 *preparations*, 600.5 *not use*, 600.8 *nonuse*, 600.11 *unused thing*, 602.5 *reserves*, 606.5 *provision*, 632.2 *protection*, 632.9 *protect*, 637.5 *preserve*, 647.1 *workshop*, 721.3 *acquisition*, 724.1 *joint possession*, 726.7 *detain*, 739.8 *merchandise*, 741.6 *funds*, 741.19 *treasury*
Store 605
store away 600.6 *stop using*, 721.11 *acquire*
store-bought 295.31 *styled*
store-bought clothes 295.1 *dress*
store cattle 68.8 *livestock*
store coal 605.6 *store*
stored 605, 258.20 *containing*, 600.1 *unused*, 637.7 *preserved*
store energy 235.12 *generate power*
store fuel 605.6 *store*
storehouse 605.4 *storage*
storehouse of words 5.28 *dictionary*
store in a database 545.13 *record*
store information 3.20 *chronicle*
store in one's heart 511.11 *memorize*
store in the archives 545.13 *record*
store in the barn 605.6 *store*
store in the garage 605.6 *store*
storekeeper 606.3 *provider*, 739.13 *retailer*, 750.6 *accountant*
store manager 653.15 *manager*
store of memories 605.4 *storage*
store owner 646.3 *agent*, 739.13 *retailer*
storeroom 256.7 *room*, 605.4 *storage*
stores 350.7 *food*, 606.1 *provision*
storeship 605.4 *storage*
store ship 679.24 *warship*
store the mind 6.23 *learn*
store window 526.8 *showplace*, 740.9 *stall*
storey 258.4 *rack*, 266.2 *level*
Storey 48 Writers, **48** Dramatists
storified 48.19 *narrative*
storing 258.20 *containing*
storing the mind 6.8 *learning*
stork 78 Birds, 78.3 *water bird*, 245.7 *obstetrics*
storm 78 Birds, **55,** 55.13 *wind strength*, 151.26 *be disorderly*, 161.22 *flood*, 241.5 *violent weather*, 241.7 *be violent*, 244.7 *agent of destruction*, 346.10 *invade*, 366.13 *tempest*, 423.1 *loudness*, 423.8 *be loud*, 635.1 *trap*, 670.9 *attack successfully*, 670.14 *siege*, 679.36 *combat*, 679.38 *conquer*, 682.9 *be victorious*, 828.4 *anger*, 828.11 *be angry*
storm along 329.4 *be swift*
storm blown over 632.1 *safety*
storm brewing 633.6 *danger signal*
storm cloud 55.18 *cloud*
storm clouds 687.1 *adversity*
storm cone 636.2 *danger signal*
storm door 346.6 *means of entry*
stormer 670,19 *attacker*, 679.1 *combatant*
storm-force 55.47 *windy*
storm force ten 55.14 *windiness*
storm glass 55.7 *weather instruments*
storm home 682.10 *defeat heavily*
stormily 55.65 *meteorologically*
storm in 346.10 *invade*

storm in a teacup 494.2 *overestimate*, 541.1 *exaggeration*, 666.2 *argument*
storminess 241.1 *violence*
storming 670.23 *attacking*
storm out 345.1 *depart*
storm petrel 636.1 *warning*
stormproof 392.10 *waterproof*
storm signal 636.2 *danger signal*
storm-tossed 375.4 *bumpy*, 628.13 *dilapidated*
storm trooper 670.19 *attacker*, 679.1 *combatant*
storm troops 679.14 *armed forces*
storm warning 636.1 *warning*
storm wave 54.14 *wave*
stormy 55, 241.6 *violent*, 366.17 *turbulent*, 440.8 *dark*, 441.5 *dim*
stormy sea 215.3 *irregular thing*
Stornoway 93 Cities
Storting 613.10 *legislative body*
story 3.6 *biography*, 48.2 *fiction*, 48.3 *aspect of fiction*, 51.7 *dramaturgy*, 243.5 *work of art*, 472.3 *matter of interest*, 473.4 *gist*, 519.4 *ideality*, 538.4 *lie*, 560.3 *narration*
storybook 519.12 *imaginary*
storyline 48.3 *aspect of fiction*, 560.3 *narration*
story so far 106.1 *circumstances*
storyteller 48.14 *author*, 538.11 *liar*, 539.16 *liar*, 560.10 *descriptive writer*
storytelling 538.15 *lying*
stoup 258.13 *drinking vessel*
Stour 96 Rivers
stout 237.9 *physically strong*, 237.13 *strengthened*, 259.16 *fat*, 259.17 *stocky*, 273.1 *thick*, 315.10 *well-rounded*, 351.7 *alcoholic drink*, 369.1 *heavy*
stouthearted 237.11 *strong in spirit*, 778.9 *courageous*
stoutheartedness 237.1 *strength*, 778.1 *courage*
stoutly 237.14 *strongly*, 259.20 *largely*, 369.16 *heavily*
stoutness 259.5 *fatness*, 273.5 *thickness*, 315.2 *round body*
stout try 596.5 *attempt*
stove 44.6 *ceramic working*, 45.5 *cooker*, 408.4 *burner*
stovepipe hat 295.15 *headgear*
stow 144.6 *fill*, 594.4 *prepare for action*, 605.6 *store*
stowage 248.5 *reserved space*, 257.2 *load*, 259.1 *size*, 605.4 *storage*
stowaway 104.8 *intruder*, 104.16 *be external*, 108.3 *unconnected person*, 149.10 *intruder*
stow away 149.17 *intrude*, 527.13 *hide*, 531.8 *conceal*, 594.4 *prepare for action*, 605.6 *store*
Stowe 48 Writers
stowed 605.7 *stored*
stow it 218.12 *stop*, 422.6 *hush*
STP 875.6 *drug*
Strabane 93 Cities
strabismus 436.2 *poor sight*
straddle 30.5 *horizontal bar*, 135.10 *link*, 158.18 *stand in the middle*, 248.20 *extend*, 271.10 *span*, 343.14 *branch*, 356.11 *cross*, 670.2 *fire*
straddled-leg 30.11 *gymnastic*
straddled-leg vault 30.6 *pommel horse*
straddle style 21.2 *field events*
Stradivari 49 Musicians and Composers
strafe 670.2 *fire*, 670.13 *air attack*, 670.15 *firing*, 879.1 *punish*
straggle 162.9 *be dispersed*, 335.3 *go astray*
straggling 162.25 *sprawled*, 269.1 *long*
straggly 162.25 *sprawled*
straight 312, 312, 26.14 *combat*, 33.6 *motor racing terms*, 42.3 *card game terms*, 47.14 *wooden*, 52.80 *linear*, 116.14 *conforming*, 134.17 *direct*, 150.13 *orderly*, 150.14 *well-or-*

dered, 167.15 *everyday*, 225.5 *stable person*, 281.8 *vertical*, 281.11 *vertically*, 332.9 *directly*, 332.15 *direct*, 333.5 *undeviating*, 537.21 *accurate*, 537.22 *uniform*, 537.39 *accurately*, 843.10 *moral*, 857.4 *honourable*, 874.6 *intoxicating*
Straight 53 Mountains
straight across 332.9 *directly*
straight ahead 332.9 *directly*
straight angle 52.39 *angle*
straight as a dye 332.9 *directly*
straight as an arrow 312.1 *straight*, 332.9 *directly*
straight away 191.8 *immediately*
straightaway 332.15 *direct*
straight away 648.6 *hastily*
straight chair 47.2 *chair*
straight down 281.8 *vertical*
straight down the line 312.5 *honourable*
straight drama 51.1 *drama*
straight drive 330.14 *sporting hit*
straightedge 52.49 *geometric construction*
straight-edged 52.80 *linear*
straighten 312, 150.21, 152.19 *tidy*, 167.9 *make conform*, 281.6 *make vertical*, 537.31 *be accurate*, 627.1 *improve*, 627.3 *rectify*
straightened 152.27 *tidied*, 312.1 *straight*
straightened out 152.27 *tidied*, 312.1 *straight*
straightening 281.2 *making vertical*
straightening out 627.6 *rectification*
straighten out 312.10 *straighten*, 627.1 *improve*, 627.3 *rectify*, 629.1 *repair*
straighten the record 530.6 *divulge*
straighten up 150.21, 152.19 *tidy*, 281.5 *be vertical*
straighten up and fly right 627.2 *get better*
straight face 772.4 *solemnity*
straight-faced 772.1 *solemn*
straight fence 32.9 *jumping*, 32.11 *eventing*
straight fertilizer 68.13 *fertilizer*
straightforward 312, 332.9 *honourable*, 332.9 *directly*, 332.15 *direct*, 381.2 *outspoken*, 442.4 *easily seen through*, 522.2 *simple*, 526.15 *open*, 537.18 *truthful*, 550.3 *clear*, 556.3 *natural*, 658.1 *naive*, 660.9 *easy*, 787.4 *predictable*, 843.10 *moral*, 857.4 *honourable*
straightforwardly 312, 381.12 *bluntly*, 550.4 *clearly*, 658.5 *naively*, 787.10 *predictably*
straightforwardness 312.8 *directness*, 381.6 *outspokenness*, 442.10 *openness*, 522.10 *simplicity*, 537.5 *truthfulness*, 550.1 *clarity*, 556.6 *naturalness*, 658.2 *naivety*, 787.2 *predictability*, 857.1 *probity*
straight from the horse's mouth 472.6 *topical*, 528.19 *reportedly*
straight from the shoulder 134.17 *direct*, 239.6 *with vigour*, 322.26 *openly*, 535.14 *assertive*, 537.18 *truthful*, 857.7 *honourably*
straight glass 258.13 *drinking vessel*
straight handlebars 71.11 *bicycle part*
straight hang 30.7 *stationary rings*
straight left 26.2 *boxing*, 330.14 *sporting hit*
straight line 312, 52.37 *line*, 333.1 *middle way*
straight-line 25.10 *bowling*, 33.10 *be on the track*
straight-lined 52.80 *linear*, 312.1 *straight*
straight-line delivery 25.5 *bowling delivery*
straight-lining 33.6 *motor racing*

terms
straightly 312.12 *straight*, 332.9 *directly*
straight man 51.21 *role*, 51.27 *entertainer*, 771.6 *humorist*
straightness 312, 150.5 *orderliness*, 150.6 *methodicalness*, 281.1 *verticality*, 537.9 *uniformity*
Straightness 312
straight news 533.1 *news*, 533.9 *news story*
straight part 51.21 *role*
straight person 312
straight pin 137.8 *fastening*
straight poker 42 Card Games
straight position 39.6 *diving*
straight punch 26.2 *boxing*
straight-rail 24.9 *billiard*
straight-rail billiards 24.4 *carom*
straight run 41.1 *skiing*
straight-shooter 312.9 *straight person*
straight skirt 295.6 *skirt*
straight talking 312.8 *directness*
straight through 312.3 *continuous*
straight thrust 28.3 *fencing movements*
straight up 95.11 *on the mountain*, 275.20 *higher*, 281.8 *vertical*, 312.5 *honourable*, 537.21 *accurate*, 857.7 *honourably*
straight-up 857.4 *honourable*
straight up and down 281.12 *perpendicularly*
straight-up-and-down 281.8 *vertical*
Straight Wall 53 Rills and Valleys
strain 631, 1.7 *society*, 48.8 *part of poem*, 49.13 *melody*, 54.20 *earth movement*, 54.64 *fold*, 56.10 *force*, 63.14, 63.31 *load*, 69.5 *gardening*, 103.4 *nature*, 108.10 *be unrelated*, 133.4 *admixture*, 134.10 *purify*, 163.4 *type*, 163.8 *genealogy*, 230.1 *operation*, 234.2 *attitude*, 235.1 *power*, 235.10 *be powerful*, 238.7 *weaken*, 241.8 *use violence*, 309.1 *distortion*, 309.9 *distort*, 326.11 *transfer*, 309.2 *pull*, 347.12 *leak*, 357.4 *exaggerate*, 377.1 *elasticity*, 433.1 *melody*, 474.11 *practise sophistry*, 540.22 *falsify*, 541.7 *exaggerate*, 549.1 *style*, 596.2 *try hard*, 596.5 *attempt*, 601.1 *misuse*, 621.15 *purify*, 628.11 *hurt*, 631.14 *afflict*, 644.4 *work*, 644.4 *exertion*, 644.8 *exert oneself*, 650.6, 650.7 *fatigue*, 659.1 *difficulty*, 820.2 *personal conflict*, 829.6 *be irascible*
strain at a gnat and swallow a camel 656.6 *act foolishly*
strained 108.7 *illogical*, 357.13, 541.12 *exaggerated*, 650.1 *fatigued*, 777.8 *fearful*, 820.6 *hostile*, 829.4 *irascible*
strained sense 525.2 *misinterpretation*
strainer 134.3 *purifier*, 621.10 *cleaning object*
strainer arch 43.5 *arch*
strain every nerve 644.8 *exert oneself*
strain gauge 56.88 *barometer*
straining 347.3 *leakage*, 540.9 *falsification*, 541.1 *exaggeration*, 644.4 *exertion*
straining the sense 525.2 *misinterpretation*
strain one's credulity 489.7 *be improbable*
strain oneself 642.15 *try*
strain one's lungs 431.10 *cry out*
strain one's voice 423.8 *be loud*
strain the sense 525.1 *misinterpret*
strain to the utmost 644.8 *exert oneself*
strait 272.1 *narrow*, 272.6 *narrow place*, 327.11 *channel*
straiten 272.10 *narrow*
straitened 272.1 *narrow*, 743.1 *poor*

straitened circumstance 743.5 *poverty*
straitened circumstances 127.5 *inferior state*
straitjacket 323.3 *restrainer*, 323.11 *restrain*, 699.5 *means of restraint*, 699.12 *gag*
strait-laced 167.14 *conformist*, 690.10 *unadorned*, 869.8 *self-restrained*, 876.10 *moralistic*
straitlacedness 813.1 *formality*
straitness 272.5 *narrowness*
Strait of Messina 98.9 *inlet*
straits 98.9 *inlet*, 272.6 *narrow place*
strake 74 Parts of a Ship
stramash 423.2 *outcry*
strand 98.4 *coast*, 272.8 *narrow thing*, 300.1 *edge*, 303.1 *front*
stranded 225.10 *stabilized*, 598.5 *relinquished*, 633.3 *vulnerable*
strange 523, 11.18 *spiritual*, 104.10 *foreign*, 108.6 *unrelated*, 115.4 *dissimilar*, 117.7 *disparate*, 149.11 *foreign*, 168.14 *eccentric*, 289.10 *extraneous*, 479.9 *original*, 502.8 *unknown*, 585.2 *not customary*, 786.8 *wonderful*, 822.12 *hated*
strangely 104.18 *extraneously*, 108.12 *irrelevantly*, 115.7, 117.15 *dissimilarly*, 149.18 *extraneously*, 168.21 *unconformably*, 335.29 *erratically*, 479.15 *inventively*, 585.8 *unusually*
strangeness 56.78 *quantum*, 104.2, 149.3 *foreignness*, 168.4 *unusualness*, 289.5 *extraneousness*, 479.4 *originality*
strange noise 633.6 *danger signal*
stranger 104.6 *outsider*, 108.3 *unconnected person*, 117.6 *misfit*, 149.4 *foreigner*
strangers 289.5 *extraneousness*
strange to say 786.13 *wonderfully*
Strangford Lough 94.4 *British lakes*
strangle 26.12 *wrestle*, 236.8 *overpower*, 244.8 *destroy*, 262.5 *make smaller*, 323.8 *stop*, 398.17 *murder*, 726.6 *retain*, 879.5 *execute*
strangled 262.7 *smaller*, 726.10 *retained*
strangle hold 26.5 *wrestling*
stranglehold 726.1 *retention*
strangler 398.11 *murderer*
strangles 624.18 *veterinary disease*
strangling 26.5 *wrestling*, 262.1 *contraction*, 262.8 *contracting*, 726.9 *retentive*
strangulate 262.5 *make smaller*
strangulated 262.7 *smaller*
strangulation 262.1 *contraction*, 323.1 *closure*, 398.2 *murder*, 879.13 *capital punishment*
strap 30.7 *stationary rings*, 40.3 *tennis equipment*, 135.10 *link*, 137.10 *band*, 380.12 *sharpener*, 380.15 *make sharp*, 879.3 *hit*, 879.14 *instrument of punishment*
strapless 296.10 *in dishabille*
strapless dress 295.7 *frock*
strappado 879.12 *corporal punishment*
strapped 743.2 *insolvent*
strapping 237.9 *physically strong*, 239.4 *vigorous*, 259.17 *stocky*, 378.4 *powerful*, 623.1 *healthy*
Strasbourg 93 Cities
stratagem 657, 474.2 *sophism*, 539.8 *trick*, 592.3 *expedient plan*, 635.1 *trap*, 652.9 *tactics*, 655.1 *skill*
strategic 17.8 *military*, 592.14 *planned*
strategical 652.16 *behaving*, 657.4 *cunning*, 676.17 *military*
strategically 17.11 *militarily*, 474.15 *hypocritically*, 592.16 *as planned*, 657.6 *cunningly*
Strategic Arms Control Treaty

677.1 *pacification*
Strategic Arms Limitation Talks 675.1 *peace*, 677.1 *pacification*
Strategic Arms Reduction Talks 675.1 *peace*
strategic bombing 670.13 *air attack*, 676.8 *warfare*
strategic defence initiative 632.4 *safety device*
Strategic Defense Initiative 676.8 *warfare*, 680.5 *missile weapon*
strategic importance 611.1 *importance*
strategic objectives 17.1 *military affairs*
strategist 228.7, 586.14 *motivator*, 592.8 *planner*, 655.5 *expert*, 657.3 *cunning person*
strategy 592.2 *policy*, 652.9 *tactics*, 676.6 *art of war*
Stratford-on-Avon 93 Cities
strath 98.6 *lowland*
Strathblane 93 Cities
Strathclyde 92 Counties
Strathspey 46.4 *historic dancing*
straticulate 266.7 *layered*
stratification 152.5 *categorization*, 266.6 *layering*, 293.1 *covering*
stratified 54.56 *petrographic*, 152.24 *categorized*, 266.7 *layered*
stratified rock 54.31 *sedimentary rock*
stratified society 400.9 *group*
stratiform 55.49 *cloudy*, 266.7 *layered*
stratify 266.10 *layer*
stratigrapher 54.3 *geologist*
stratigraphical 54.48 *geological*
stratigraphy 54.1 *earth science*
stratocracy 12.1 *government*
stratocumulus 55.18 *cloud*
strato-isothermal region 390.3 *atmospheric layers*
stratopause 55.8 *atmosphere*
stratosphere 55.8 *atmosphere*, 275.8 *high thing*, 390.3 *atmospheric layers*
stratospheric 55.43, 390.13 *atmospheric*
stratous 55.49 *cloudy*
stratum 152.14 *sedimentary rock*, 163.5 *social class*, 266.1 *layer*, 282.3 *flat thing*, 390.3 *atmospheric layers*
stratus 55.18 *cloud*
Strauss 49 Musicians and Composers
Strauss the Younger 49 Musicians and Composers
Stravinsky 49 Musicians and Composers
straw 68.9 *animal feedstuff*, 69.15 *cultivate*, 87.3 *grass plant*, 87.4 *cereal grass*, 370.7 *light thing*, 612.8 *trifle*
strawberry 86 Fruits, 450.7 *red thing*
strawberry-blond 452.3 *yellow-haired*
strawberry bush 85 Trees and Shrubs
strawberry mark 86.5 *figurative usage*, 450.7 *red thing*, 456.4 *maculation*, 544.3 *means of identification*
strawberry roan 32.1 *horse*
strawberry tree 85 Trees and Shrubs
strawboard 604.4 *board*
straw-burning 68.5 *cultivation*
straw-coloured 452.1 *yellow*
strawflower 84 Flowers and Flowering Plants
strawhat 51.4 *show business*
straw hat 295.15 *headgear*
strawhat circuit 51.13 *engagement*
straw man 102.5 *insubstantial person*, 238.4 *weakling*
straw poll 580.10 *vote*
Strawson 4 Philosophers
stray 160.15 *lose one's train of thought*, 162.9 *be dispersed*, 162.25 *sprawled*, 168.15 *irregular*, 229.6 *motiveless*, 252.7 *displaced person*, 324.15 *walk*,

335.3 *go astray*, 335.21 *indirect*, 633.8 *be in danger*, 698.16 *be independent*, 816.7 *outsider*, 864.16 *be wicked*, 877.16 *do wrong*
stray capacitance 64.12 *resistance*
stray from the straight and narrow 844.23 *sin*, 864.16 *be wicked*
stray from the topic 108.10 *be unrelated*
straying 335.16, 335.25 *wandering*
streak 133.4 *admixture*, 269.5 *piece*, 272.8 *narrow thing*, 294.11 *uncover*, 296.14 *undress*, 329.4 *be swift*, 439.4 *natural light*, 456.3 *striping*, 456.11 *variegate*, 622.11 *dirty*
streaked 456.9 *striped*
streaker 294.4 *exposer*, 296.8 *nude person*
streakiness 456.3 *striping*
streaking 294.2 *undressing*, 296.1 *undress*
streak of lightning 329.11 *swift thing*
streak of luck 686.2 *good fortune*
streaky bacon 45.30 *bacon*
stream 55.62 *rain*, 96.1 *river*, 96.6 *river flow*, 96.7 *flow*, 159.8 *procession*, 161.22 *flood*, 161.40 *crowd*, 163.6 *students*, 181.11 *crowd*, 234.1 *tendency*, 324.2 *momentum*, 324.13 *be in motion*, 324.15 *walk*, 327.11 *channel*, 346.2 *influx*, 347.2 *outflow*, 349.14 *let out*, 387.25 *flow*, 605.3 *supply*, 608.5 *about*, 608.8 *plenty*, 610.4 *be excessive*
stream course 54.8 *drainage*
streamer 20.2 *artificial fly*, 532.3 *journalism*, 544.7 *flag*
streamers 439.4 *natural light*, 812.8 *salute*
streaming 55.53 *rainy*, 96.10 *fluvial*, 139.8 *nonadhesive*, 246.5 *fertile*, 324.16 *moving*, 347.2 *outflow*, 389.23 *wet*, 610.6 *excessive*
streaming eyes 347.2 *outflow*
streamlet 96.1 *river*
streamline 152.14 *rearrange*, 376.11 *smooth*, 627.3 *rectify*
streamlined 152.23 *rearranged*, 329.1 *swift*, 376.1 *smooth*
streamlining 152.4 *rearrangement*, 660.7 *easing*
stream of consciousness 48.3 *aspect of fiction*, 61.21 *psyche*, 61.27 *association of ideas*, 461.5 *creative thought*, 560.3 *narration*, 569.1 *soliloquy*
stream-of-consciousness novel 48.2 *fiction*
stream of rain 55.25 *rain*
stream past 159.17 *line up*
streams of sweat 353.8 *sweat*
strecher 74 Parts of a Ship
Strecker synthesis 57 Named Reactions
street 137.5, 327.3 *road*
street Arab 622.6 *dirty person*
streetcar 71 Motor Vehicles, 327.10 *railway*
streetcar line 327.10 *railway*
street cleaner 621.12 *cleaner*
street cred 800.1 *estimation*
street credibility 105.1 *state*, 800.1 *estimation*
street fight 674.6 *fight*, 693.2 *violation of the law*
street-fighter 640.3 *doer*
streetlamp 439.6 *electric light*
streetlight 275.6 *tall thing*, 439.6 *electric light*
street map 592.5 *map*
street market 740.1 *market*
street musician 49.24 *musician*
street name 567.5 *place of residence*
street party 773.1 *rejoicing*
street performer 51.27 *entertainer*
street railway 327.10 *railway*
street riot 693.2 *violation of the law*

streets 777 Phobias by Topic
streets ahead 126.12 *superior*
street seller 739.11 *pedlar*, 739.14 *street trader*
street smarts 235.2 *ability*, 459.5 *common sense*, 501.4 *intellect*
street sweeper 727.6 *rubbish collector*
street theatre 51.1 *drama*
street trader 739, 431.9 *crier*, 754.7 *discounter*
street urchin 206.7 *young man*, 622.6 *dirty person*
street vendor 739.11 *pedlar*, 739.14 *street trader*
streetwalk 877.18 *prostitute*
streetwalker 864.9 *wicked person*, 877.9 *immoral woman*
streetwalking 877.5 *prostitution*
street wise 6.19 *knowledgeable*
streetwise 501.8 *knowledgeable*, 507.6 *intelligent*
strelitzia 84 Flowers and Flowering Plants
strength 237, 225.1 *stability*, 233 *influence*, 235.1 *power*, 239.1 *vigour*, 241.1 *violence*, 277.2 *intensity*, 373.5 *hardness*, 378.6 *toughness*, 554.1 *emphasis*, 575.4 *stamina*, 623.3 *health*, 655.1 *skill*, 688.1 *authority*
Strength 237
strengthen 237, 235.11 *give power*, 284.11 *support*, 284.14 *give moral support*, 373.9 *harden*, 378.11 *make tough*, 629.3 *restore*, 632.9 *protect*, 651.1 *refresh*, 662.19 *support*, 671.20 *reinforce*, 718.14 *make fast*
strengthened 237, 373.3 *hardened*, 378.2 *toughened*, 629.13 *repaired*
strengthening 237, 239.5 *invigorating*, 284.1 *support*, 629.9 *restoration*
strengthen oneself 237.8 *strengthen*
strength exercises 30.1 *gymnastics*
strength of character 574.15 *will*
strength of materials 63
strength of purpose 570.2 *willpower*
strength of will 570.2 *willpower*
strenuous 239.4 *vigorous*, 554.3 *emphatic*, 575.10 *persevering*, 642.18 *active*, 644.11 *laborious*, 659.10 *difficult*, 879.21 *punishing*
strenuous climbing 34.1 *mountaineering*
strenuously 554.7 *emphatically*, 644.12 *laboriously*, 659.26 *arduously*
strenuousness 659.1 *difficulty*
Strepsiptera 82 Orders of Insects
strepsipteran 82.10 *insectan*
streptocarpus 84 Flowers and Flowering Plants
streptomyces 89 Fungi
streptomycin 62 Medication, 89.6 *fungal antibiotic*, 630.8 *drug*
stress 61, 5.16 *spoken letter*, 48.9 *metre*, 56.10 *force*, 63.14, 63.31 *load*, 230.1 *operation*, 235.1 *power*, 235.10 *be powerful*, 237.3 *intensity*, 237.8 *strengthen*, 309.1 *distortion*, 309.9 *distort*, 330.1 *impel*, 330.13 *blow*, 535.7 *emphasis*, 535.22 *emphasize*, 543.13 *punctuate*, 554.1 *emphasis*, 554.6 *emphasize*, 564.3 *mode of speech*, 611.1 *importance*, 611.8 *make important*, 631.4 *strain*, 644.4 *exertion*
stress a point 535.22 *emphasize*
stressed 535.15, 554.4 *emphasized*, 564.18 *phonetic*
stressed point 535.7 *emphasis*
stress reaction 61.12 *stress*
stretch 128.5 *make bigger*, 185.3 *duration*, 187.1 *period*, 248.3 *ge-*

ographical space, 248.7 *range,* 248.8 *intervening space,* 248.20 *extend,* 261.1 *growth,* 261.2 *enlargeability,* 261.5 *make bigger,* 261.6 *become bigger,* 263.7 *reach,* 269.4 *length,* 269.9 *be long,* 269.10 *lengthen,* 272.10 *narrow,* 357.4 *exaggerate,* 377.1 *elasticity,* 377.6 *elastic,* 377.8 *be elastic,* 541.7 *exaggerate,* 644.2 *task,* 644.4 *exertion,* 699.4 *detention,* 702.4 *prison sentence,* 731.3 *allotted task*
stretchability 261.2 *enlargeability,* 377.1 *elasticity*
stretchable 261.9 *enlargeable,* 374.2 *pliant,* 377.6 *elastic*
stretch a point 357.4 *exaggerate,* 691.3 *be lenient,* 717.4 *compromise*
stretched 128.7 *increased,* 261.7 *bigger,* 269.1 *long,* 377.6 *elastic,* 540.32 *falsified,* 541.12 *exaggerated*
stretched out 269.1 *long*
stretched-out 261.7 *bigger*
stretcher 36.4 *rowing,* 50.11 *artist's materials,* 63.26 *masonry,* 71.6 *litter,* 137.4 *means of connection,* 261.4 *enlarger,* 326.5 *means of transport,* 630.14 *hospital*
stretcher-bearer 60.17 *paramedic,* 326.7 *transferor*
stretcher bond 63.26 *masonry*
stretcher case 624.19 *sick person*
stretch fabric 377.3 *elastic thing*
stretchiness 377.1 *elasticity*
stretching 52.47 *topology,* 261.1 *growth,* 261.8 *growing,* 377.1 *elasticity,* 377.6 *elastic,* 541.1 *exaggeration*
stretching out 261.1 *growth,* 269.4 *length*
stretching the meaning 525.2 *misinterpretation*
stretch jeans 377.3 *elastic thing*
stretch limo 71.16 *car*
stretch of the imagination 519.1 *imagination,* 541.5 *tall story*
stretch oneself 269.9 *be long*
stretch one's legs 651.2 *be refreshed*
stretch one's neck 879.5 *execute*
stretch out 261.5 *make bigger,* 261.6 *become bigger,* 263.7 *reach,* 269.9 *be long*
stretch the imagination 541.11 *tell a tall story*
stretch the meaning 525.1 *misinterpret*
stretch the point 708.4 *be permissive*
stretch the truth 309.12 *distort the truth*
stretch to 263.7 *reach*
stretch to the ends of the earth 263.5 *be distant*
stretchy 261.9 *enlargeable,* 377.6 *elastic*
stretto 49 Musical Terms
strew 162.17 *sow*
strewing 162.1 *dispersion*
strewn 162.22 *distributed*
stria 43 Architectural Decoration, 456.3 *striping*
striate 456.9 *striped,* 456.11 *variegate*
striated 54.59 *weathered*
striation 54.35 *weathering,* 456.3 *striping*
Stribog 8 Deities
stricken 624.23 *diseased*
stricken in years 207.14 *aged,* 207.16 *maturely*
strict 7.15 *religious,* 116.15 *conventional,* 537.24 *pedantic,* 690.8 *severe,* 699.13 *restraining,* 869.8 *self-restrained*
strict control 699.1 *restraint*
strict discipline 690.1 *severity*
strictly 7.23 *religiously,* 690.11 *severely,* 699.16 *under restraints,* 869.11 *with self-restraint*
strictly controlled 699.13 *restraining*

strictly speaking 537.38 *literally*
strictly teetotal 873.1 *sober*
strictness 7.2 *religiousness,* 167.4 *conventionalism,* 503.1 *accuracy,* 537.11 *pedantry,* 690.1 *severity,* 699.1 *restraint*
strict observance 7.2 *religiousness,* 10.1 *ritual*
strict person 690
strict teetotaller 873.8 *sober person*
stricture 272.9 *narrowing,* 302.2 *limiting factor,* 852.7 *blame*
stricturoplasty 60 Surgical Operations
stride 324.12 *gait,* 324.15 *walk,* 336.13 *step*
stridency 430, 423.1 *loudness,* 434.1 *dissonance*
strident 430, 423.6 *loud,* 434.7 *dissonant*
stridently 430, 423.9 *loudly,* 434.12 *dissonantly*
striders 295.9 *trousers*
stridor 49.21 *tone,* 423.1 *loudness,* 430.1 *stridency ,* 564.3 *mode of speech*
stridulantly 432.10 *howlingly*
stridulate 432.6 *buzz*
stridulation 432.3 *insect noise*
stridulous 430.7 *strident,* 432.9 *humming*
stridulously 432.10 *howlingly*
strife 473.1 *argument,* 500.1 *dissent,* 663.3 *conflict,* 666.1 *disagreement,* 674.1 *contention,* 764.8 *quarrel*
strigiform 78.23 *avian*
strigil 43 Architectural Decoration, 621.10 *cleaning object*
strigose 375.3 *barbed*
strike 670, 13.8 *industrial relations,* 15.12 *have an industrial dispute,* 20.1 *angling,* 22.4 *pitching terms,* 25.5 *bowling delivery,* 31.1, 31.8 *hockey,* 31.9 *play hockey,* 36.16 *row,* 38.4 *play soccer,* 218.2 *stop,* 218.7 *stop working,* 241.8 *use violence,* 325.1 *motionlessness,* 330.3 *hit,* 330.13 *blow,* 338.26 *bat,* 338.28 *shoot,* 362.10 *lower the flag,* 385.13 *abrade,* 398.17 *murder,* 407.3 *press,* 407.11 *touch,* 410.11 *fuel,* 439.24 *light,* 475.6 *mass demonstration,* 475.19 *protest,* 496.10 *find,* 500.3 *dissentience,* 500.8 *dissent,* 598.2 *withdraw,* 598.3 *relinquishment,* 605.2 *resource,* 618.14 *ill-treat,* 661.2 *obstacle,* 661.9 *block,* 669.1 *resistance,* 669.6 *resist,* 670.1 *attack,* 670.12 *military attack,* 672.6 *fight,* 693.1 *disobedience,* 693.15 *be disobedient,* 711.1 *refusal,* 711.5 *refuse,* 713.3 *gesture of protest,* 713.8 *cause mischief,* 879.3 *hit*
strike a bad patch 659.20 *be in difficulty*
strike a balance 122.11 *equalize,* 124.10 *make average,* 158.17 *average,* 369.15 *weigh,* 717.4 *compromise*
strike a ball 330.10 *bat*
strike a bargain 667.7, 715.5 *contract*
strike a blow for 640.4 *act*
strike a chord 331.3 *get a response*
strike a false note 117.12 *be disparate*
strike a light 439.24 *light*
strike an average 717.4 *compromise*
strike a rich vein 686.6 *be fortunate*
strike at 22.7 *play baseball,* 330.3 *hit,* 670.5 *strike,* 674.11 *contend,* 672.14 *fight*
strike back at 670.8 *counterattack*
strike blind 436.15 *blind*
strike-bound 711.8 *refused*
strikebreaker 15.7 *employee,* 578.9 *equivocator,* 693.12 *reactionary,* 720.5 *nonobserver*

strike breaking 15.4 *industrial dispute*
strike-breaking 15.10 *unionized*
strike camp 345.3 *quit*
strike colours 673.3 *submit*
strike down 631.14 *afflict*
strike dumb 563, 514.11 *amaze,* 786.10 *be wonderful*
strike first 670.1 *attack*
strike force 670.19 *attacker*
strike hard 239.2 *be full of vigour*
strike it lucky 229.5 *chance,* 686.5 *be prosperous,* 686.6 *be fortunate*
strike it rich 686.5 *be prosperous,* 686.6 *be fortunate,* 742.13 *get rich*
strike notice 15.4 *industrial dispute*
strike off 147.8 *eject,* 349.3 *disbar*
strike off the register 704.7 *terminate*
strike off the roll 349.3 *disbar*
strike oil 410.11 *fuel,* 686.6 *be fortunate*
strike one 471.14 *have an idea*
strike one in the face 437.8 *be visible*
strike out 22.4 *pitching terms,* 22.7 *play baseball,* 147.8 *eject,* 244.8 *destroy,* 320.10 *close,* 345.5 *set out,* 546.1 *obliterate,* 704.6 *cancel*
strike out for 332.7 *take a direction*
striker 15.7 *employee,* 24.7 *billiards player,* 27.4 *team,* 31.2 *hockey player,* 38.3 *football player,* 338.14 *thrower,* 475.8 *protester,* 598.4 *deserter,* 693.7 *protester,* 711.4 *refuser,* 713.4 *protester*
strike root 225.6 *be stable*
strike root in 233.8 *influence*
striker-out 40.5 *real tennis*
strike settlement 15.4 *industrial dispute*
strike the first blow 670.1 *attack*
strike through 546.1 *obliterate*
strike up 49.36 *play*
strike up a friendship 819.13 *befriend*
strike up an acquaintance 819.13 *befriend*
strike upon 344.2 *reach*
strike while the iron is hot 210.5 *take the opportunity*
strike with admiration 786.10 *be wonderful*
strike zone 22.4 *pitching terms*
striking 15.4 *industrial dispute,* 15.10 *unionized,* 31.1, 31.8 *hockey,* 36.4, 36.11 *rowing,* 38.2 *football play,* 237.12 *strong to the senses,* 403.9 *exciting,* 437.2 *clear,* 475.14 *demonstrating,* 522.1 *intelligible,* 526.14 *manifest,* 560.11 *descriptive,* 669.10 *resistant,* 670.23 *attacking,* 711.8 *refused,* 786.8 *wonderful,* 879.12 *corporal punishment*
striking circle 31.1 *hockey*
striking distance 264.2 *short distance*
striking force 679.14 *armed forces*
striking likeness 547.1, 560.9 *representation*
striking off 349.18 *dismissal*
striking out 131.1 *subtraction,* 320.4 *closure*
striking the cushion 24.4 *carom*
strim 69.15 *cultivate*
Strimmer 69.6, 603.2 *garden tool*
Strindberg 48 Writers, **48** Dramatists
Strine 5.26 *dialect*
string 161 Collective Names for Birds and Animals, **777** Phobias by Topic, 24.3 *English billiards,* 43.9 *miscellaneous architectural features,* 56.79 *fundamental interaction,* 137.6 *line,* 155.2 *series,* 159.2 *consecution,* 159.15 *concatenate,* 161.23 *flock,* 269.5 *piece,* 359.10 *step,*

383.6 *fibre*
string along 539.27 *be false*
string along with 664.14 *join with*
string bag 258.8 *bag*
string band 49.26 *musical group*
string bean 45 Vegetables
stringed instrument 427.4 *sources of resonance*
stringency 690.1 *severity*
stringendo 49 Musical Terms
stringent 690.8 *severe*
stringently 690.11 *severely*
stringer 74 Parts of a Ship, 43.9 *miscellaneous architectural features,* 63.27 *superstructure,* 528.9 *informant,* 532.11 *newspaper man,* 605.2 *resource*
string him up! 879, 398.26 *no quarter*
stringiness 378.6 *toughness,* 378.8 *physical strength,* 394.1 *viscosity*
stringing 24.5 *snooker*
stringing out 269.4 *length*
string of invectives 827.1 *curse*
string out 159.16 *arrange consecutively,* 182.9 *scatter,* 269.10 *lengthen*
stringpuller 688.10 *person of authority*
string pulling 592.4 *plot*
stringpulling 688.1 *authority*
string quartet 49.26 *musical group,* 140.3 *assembly*
strings 49.25 *musical instrument,* 233.4 *indirect influence,* 716.2 *basis for negotiations*
string section 180.6 *accompanier*
string tie 295.14 *neckwear*
string together 135.10 *link,* 159.15 *concatenate*
string up 398.19, 879.5 *execute*
stringy 378.4 *powerful,* 394.8 *viscous*
strip 68.11 *farmland,* 131.4 *take off,* 136.10 *set apart,* 238.7 *weaken,* 244.10 *lay waste,* 266.1 *layer,* 266.11 *scale,* 269.5 *piece,* 272.8 *narrow thing,* 294.11 *uncover,* 296.14 *undress,* 296.15 *make nude,* 349.3 *disbar,* 621.13 *clean,* 722.9 *lose,* 743.14 *impoverish*
strip bare 136.10 *set apart,* 238.7 *weaken,* 244.10 *lay waste,* 296.14 *undress,* 530.5 *disclose*
strip-casting 20.1 *angling*
strip clean 621.13 *clean*
strip club 296.3 *pornography*
stripe 103.4 *nature,* 163.4 *type,* 269.5 *piece,* 272.8 *narrow thing,* 330.5 *beat,* 330.13 *blow,* 456.3 *striping,* 456.11 *variegate,* 544.4 *insignia,* 879.12 *corporal punishment*
striped 456
striped ball 24.6 *pool*
striped bass 20.4 *American game fish*
stripes 792.3 *honour*
strip grazing 68.3 *livestock farming*
striping 456
strip jack naked 42 Card Games
strip joint 296.3 *pornography*
strip light 56.25 *light source,* 439.6 *electric light*
stripling 206.7 *young man*
strip off 131.4 *take off,* 296.14 *undress*
strip of land 731.2 *portion*
strip-o-gram 296.3 *pornography,* 296.8 *nude person*
stripped 294.8 *uncovered,* 296.9 *undressed,* 296.11 *exposed,* 743.2 *insolvent*
stripped-down 556.1 *simple*
stripped naked 296.9 *undressed*
stripped of 722.16 *losing*
stripped to the buff 296.9 *undressed*
stripper 51.27 *entertainer,* 51.28 *dancer,* 294.4 *exposer,* 296.8 *nude person,* 526.12 *displayer*

stripping 294.2 *undressing,* 296.1 *undress,* 349.18 *dismissal,* 722.1 *loss*
stripping bare 296.1 *undress*
strip poker 42 *Card Games,* 294.2 *undressing,* 296.1 *undress*
strip-search 296.1 *undress,* 296.15 *make nude*
strip-searched 296.9 *undressed*
strip show 51.5 *show*
striptease 51.4 *show business,* 51.5 *show,* 294.2 *undressing,* 296.1 *undress*
striptease artist 51.27 *entertainer,* 51.28 *dancer*
striptease artiste 296.8 *nude person,* 526.12 *displayer*
striptease dancer 294.4 *exposer,* 296.8 *nude person*
stripteaser 294.4 *exposer,* 296.8 *nude person,* 526.12 *displayer*
strip the assets of 734.10 *take away*
Strip the Willow 46.4 *historic dancing*
strip to the buff 296.14 *undress*
stripy 456.8 *checked,* 456.9 *striped*
strive 596.2 *try hard,* 644.8 *exert oneself,* 674.11 *contend*
strive after 588.10 *aim*
strive against 663.12 *oppose*
strive for 590.12 *aim at*
strive in vain 236.6 *be powerless*
striver 479.5 *experimenter,* 596.7 *attempter,* 674.10 *contender*
strive to keep for oneself 841.8 *distrust*
striving 596.8 *attempting*
strobe 51.18 *stage lighting*
strobe lighting 439.6 *electric light*
stroboscope 51.18 *stage lighting,* 56.90 *ammeter,* 439.6 *electric light*
stroboscopic 439.15 *lucent*
stroke 27, 24.3 *English billiards,* 29.3 *golf shots,* 31.1 *hockey,* 31.9 *play hockey,* 36.4 *rowing,* 36.6 *canoeing,* 36.9 *sailor,* 36.11 *rowing,* 36.16 *row,* 39.1 *swimming,* 236.4 *disability,* 286.2 *oblique line,* 330.3 *hit,* 330.13 *blow,* 338.5 *throw,* 366.8 *spasm,* 385.16 *massage,* 407.4 *kiss,* 407.11 *touch,* 510.3 *mental deterioration,* 543.7 *punctuation,* 543.11 *gesture,* 624.2 *illness,* 624.10 *cardiovascular disease,* 640.2 *deed,* 653.2 *direct,* 653.13 *director,* 821.14 *communication of love,* 821.27 *kiss,* 826.1 *endearment,* 826.7 *show endearment for,* 879.12 *corporal punishment*
stroked 24.9 *billiard*
stroke of genius 640.2 *deed,* 655.3 *masterpiece,* 786.3 *wonder-working*
stroke of luck 210.2 *opportunity*
stroke of policy 592.2 *policy*
stroke of work 644.2 *task*
stroke play 29.1 *golf,* 29.2 *golfing terms*
stroke side 36.4 *rowing*
stroking 385.6 *massage,* 407.2 *touching*
stroll 324.12 *gait,* 324.15 *walk,* 328.1 *move slowly,* 328.10 *slow motion*
stroller 71.8 *baby carriage*
strolling 328.4 *slow*
strolling player 51.22 *actor*
stromatolite 90.5 *algal product*
strong 55.47 *windy,* 57.36 *acid,* 142.8 *sound,* 225.9 *stable,* 233.11 *influential,* 235.13 *powerful,* 237.9 *physically strong,* 239.4 *vigorous,* 241.6 *violent,* 351.17 *drinkable,* 371.6 *dense,* 373.2, 378.1 *tough,* 413.9 *piquant,* 444.11 *colourful,* 554.3 *emphatic,* 623.1 *healthy,* 632.6 *invulnerable,* 642.18 *active,* 688.12 *authoritative,* 874.6 *intoxicating,* 877.12 *indecent*
strong acid 57.8 *acid*
strong ale 351.7 *alcoholic drink*

strong alkali 57.9 *base*
strong-arm 695.7 *force,* 695.9 *compelling*
strongarm man 632.3 *protector*
strong-arm man 237.6 *muscleman,* 679.1 *combatant*
strong-arm tactics 241.2 *physical violence,* 695.3 *coercive methods*
strong as a bull 237.9 *physically strong*
strong as a horse 237.9 *physically strong,* 623.1 *healthy*
strong as a lion 237.9 *physically strong*
strong as an ox 237.9 *physically strong,* 623.1 *healthy*
strongbox 605.4 *storage,* 741.20 *money store*
strong breeze 55.13 *wind strength*
strong card 655.1 *skill*
strong cheese 419.2 *something that makes an unpleasant smell*
strong currency 14.1 *finance*
strong drink 874.12 *alcohol*
strong feeling 642.4 *energy,* 759.4 *emotion*
strong flavour 411.4 *flavour,* 413.1 *piquancy*
strong foundation 225.4 *stable thing*
strong gale 55.13 *wind strength*
strong hand 602.1 *means,* 690.1 *severity*
stronghold 634.1 *refuge,* 671.12 *fort*
strong in 6.19 *knowledgeable*
strong in spirit 237
strong interaction 56.79 *fundamental interaction*
strong language 554.1 *emphasis,* 827.2 *offensive language*
strongly 237, 225.12 *stably,* 233.14 *influentially,* 235.18 *powerfully,* 371.10 *densely,* 373.12, 378.12 *toughly,* 554.7 *emphatically,* 688.23 *authoritatively*
strongly worded 535.14 *assertive,* 535.15 *emphasized*
strongly-worded 535.14 *emphatic*
strongman 51.29 *circus performer,* 237.5 *athlete*
strong-minded 574.3 *strong-willed*
strong nuclear interaction 56.79 *fundamental interaction*
strong point 165.7 *special skill,* 617.6 *worth,* 655.1 *skill,* 671.12 *fort*
strong position 235.1 *power*
strong possibility 486, 488.4 *chance*
strong pulse 396.1 *life*
strongroom 605.4 *storage,* 741.20 *money store*
strong safety 19.10 *defence*
strong side 19.7 *offence*
strong silent type 566.7 *taciturn person*
strong smell 416.1 *odour*
strong-smelling 237.12 *strong to the senses*
strong suit 617.6 *worth*
strong sun 55.22 *sun*
strong-tasting 237.12 *strong to the senses*
strong to the senses 237
strong vocational interest test 61.5 *psychological test*
strong-willed 574
strong wind 55.14 *windiness,* 241.5 *violent weather,* 375.6 *roughness*
strong woman 237.6 *muscleman*
strong words 535.6 *assertiveness*
strontia 57 *Common Chemical Compounds*
strontianite 54 *Minerals*
strontium 57 *Chemical Elements*
strontium-90 631.10 *warfare*
strop 380.12 *sharpener,* 380.15 *make sharp*
strophe 48.8 *part of poem*
stroppiness 693.1 *disobedience*
stroppy 151.20 *disorderly,*

659.14 *troublesome*
struck 31.8 *hockey*
struck dumb 514.7 *amazed,* 563.11 *speechless,* 786.7 *wide-eyed*
struck off 147.11 *excluded,* 704.10 *cancelled*
struck out 704.10 *cancelled*
structural 43, 57, 63, 382, 5.38 *linguistic,* 5.44 *grammatical,* 57.33 *crystalline,* 103.8 *quintessential,* 243.11 *productive*
structural connection 63.27 *superstructure*
structural design 74.4 *shipbuilding*
structural engineer 63.18 *civil engineer*
structural engineering 63.17 *civil engineering*
structural formula 57.13 *structure*
structural framework 63.27 *superstructure*
structural-functional 2.14 *socioeconomic*
structural-functionalism 2.2 *sociological research*
structural gene 59.13 *genetic material*
structural geology 54.1 *earth science*
structural glass 44.9 *industrial ceramics*
structural grammar 5.29 *grammar*
structuralism 48 *Literary Groups and Movements,* 1.5 *anthropological concept,* 4.7 *school of thought,* 5.1 *linguistics,* 61.1 *psychology,* 382.9 *artistic structure*
structural isomer 57.13 *structure*
structuralist 1.11 *anthropological,* 4.11 *follower of a doctrine,* 5.2 *linguist,* 48.15 *literary person*
structural linguistics 5.1 *linguistics,* 5.29 *grammar*
structural loading 63.14 *load*
structurally 63, 257, 382, 5.48 *linguistically,* 43.20 *architecturally,* 383.15 *texturally*
structural material 63.25 *construction material*
structural member 63.27 *superstructure*
structural model 74.4 *shipbuilding*
structural polysaccharide 58.4 *polysaccharide*
structural psychology 61.1 *psychology*
structural test 74.4 *shipbuilding*
structure 57, 63, 382, 382, 43.3 *building,* 43.18 *be an architect,* 48.3 *aspect of fiction,* 57.4 *crystal,* 59.4 *anatomy,* 103.1 *essence,* 105.1 *state,* 135.3 *unification,* 148.13 *make,* 150.1 *order,* 150.7 *method,* 150.18 *order,* 152.2 *array,* 152.12 *arrange,* 243.1 *production,* 243.8 *construction,* 243.10 *produce,* 257.1 *contents,* 257.8 *embody,* 306.1, 306.7 *form,* 367.4 *matter,* 383.1 *texture,* 796.4 *design*
Structure 382
structured 43, 150.10 *ordered,* 152.20 *arranged,* 257.10 *containing*
structuring 382, 152.1 *arrangement,* 152.3 *organization*
struggle 366.25 *pitch,* 596.2 *try hard,* 596.5 *attempt,* 597.2 *undertaking,* 644.4 *exertion,* 644.8 *exert oneself,* 659.3 *difficult task,* 659.19 *have difficulty,* 666.2 *argument,* 666.6 *argue,* 674.1 *contention,* 674.2 *contest,* 674.6 *fight,* 674.11 *contend,* 687.1 *adversity*
struggle against 674.11 *contend*
struggler 596.7 *attempter,* 674.10 *contender,* 679.1 *combatant*
struggle up 359.14 *climb*
struggle with 659.18 *find difficult*
struggling 241.6 *violent,* 674.14 *contending*

struggling for breath 397.18 *dying*
strum 49.38 *sound,* 521.7 *mean nothing*
strumento di porco 49 *Musical Instruments*
strumming 521.1 *lack of meaning*
strumpet 402.7 *prostitute,* 821.9 *lover,* 877.9 *immoral woman*
strung out 182.6 *sparse,* 269.1 *long*
strut 47.10 *carpenter's term,* 47.17 *carpenter,* 63.27 *superstructure,* 137.4 *means of connection,* 284.2 *supporting part,* 324.12 *gait,* 324.15 *walk,* 805.27 *be ostentatious,* 809.16, 811.29 *show off*
struthioniform 78.23 *avian*
struthious 78.23 *avian*
strutting 47.10 *carpenter's term,* 805.17 *conceited,* 805.22 *boastful,* 811.10 *exhibitionism,* 811.25 *vain*
struttingly 811.41 *vainly*
Struve 52 *Scientists*
strychnine 62 *Medication,* 58.19 *alkaloid,* 631.8 *poison*
stub 132.1 *remainder,* 381.1 *blunt,* 413.7 *tobacco,* 545.1 *record,* 718.2 *promise,* 730.3 *acknowledgment of payment,* 749.1 *receipt*
stubbily 381.11 *smoothly*
stubbiness 270.1 *shortness,* 381.5 *bluntness*
stubble 68.11 *farmland,* 87.4 *cereal grass,* 132.2 *residue,* 375.7 *rough thing,* 614.6 *refuse*
stubbled 375.3 *barbed*
stubbly 375.3 *barbed*
stubborn 138.10 *tenacious,* 217.8 *conservative,* 225.11 *determined,* 373.4 *mentally hard,* 378.5 *mentally tough,* 490.2 *convinced,* 570.8 *wilful,* 574.3 *strong-willed,* 575.10 *persevering,* 577.1 *obstinate,* 659.14 *troublesome,* 663.22 *uncooperative,* 668.7 *defiant,* 669.11 *obstinate,* 690.8 *severe,* 693.13 *disobedient*
stubborn as a mule 577.1 *obstinate*
stubbornly 138.12 *tenaciously,* 217.10 *conservatively,* 225.13 *determinedly,* 373.13 *inflexibly,* 378.14 *single-mindedly,* 490.24 *with certainty,* 577.9 *be obstinate,* 659.29 *perversely,* 663.23 *opposingly,* 668.9 *defiantly,* 690.11 *severely,* 693.17 *disobediently*
stubbornness 138.2 *tenacity,* 217.2 *conservatism,* 225.2 *determination,* 373.8 *mental hardness,* 378.9 *mental toughness,* 490.10 *conviction,* 570.3 *wilfulness,* 574.14 *tenacity,* 575.1 *perseverance,* 577.5 *obstinacy,* 663.5 *contrariness,* 669.2 *obstinacy,* 690.1 *severity,* 693.1 *disobedience,* 868.1 *impenitence*
stubborn persistence 577.6 *determination*
stubby 270.7 *short,* 381.1 *blunt*
stucco 43 *Architectural Decoration,* 43.19 *decorate,* 50.14 *sculptor's materials,* 293.8 *wall covering,* 293.28 *face*
stuck 135.15 *tied,* 137.15 *connected,* 322.14 *holed,* 325.4 *motionless,* 378.3 *hard,* 659.16 *troubled*
stuck fast 225.9 *stable*
stuck firm 726.10 *retained*
stuck-in-a-groove 183.12 *repetitious*
stuck on 821.18 *in love*
stuck on oneself 809.10 *self-admiring,* 860.5 *egoistic*
stuck-out tongue 543.3 *gesture*
stuck up 805.17 *conceited*
stuck-up 809.8 *vain,* 809.13 *boastful*
stud 161 *Collective Names for Birds and Animals,* 32.1 *horse,*

32.13 *breeding,* 137.8 *fastening,* 162.18 *sprinkle,* 340.6 *charmer,* 375.12 *make rough,* 401.7 *libertine,* 401.16 *male animal,* 456.11 *variegate,* 792.6 *jewellery*
studbook 32.13 *breeding*
studded 162.23 *sprinkled,* 375.2 *coarse,* 456.10 *mottled*
studding 162.4 *sprinkling*
studdingsail 74 Sails
student 6.7 *learner,* 156.14 *beginner,* 293.22 *progression,* 461.7 *thinker,* 477.9 *questioner,* 656.10 *unskilled person,* 701.3 *subordinate*
student council 654.4 *adviser*
student days 206.1 *youth*
student loan 732.2 *loan*
student number 544.3 *means of identification*
student nurse 60.16 *nurse*
student of literature 48.15 *literary person*
students 163
student teacher 6.4 *educator*
stud groom 32.15 *horse person*
studhorse 32.1 *horse*
stud horse 401.16 *male animal*
studied 268.15 *deliberate,* 477.16 *questioned,* 582.4 *deliberate,* 588.12 *intended*
studier of mankind 400
studies of life 396
studio 50.11 *artist's materials,* 256.5 *house,* 256.7 *room,* 479.6 *place of experimentation,* 647.1 *workshop*
studio couch 47.2 *chair*
studio flash 66.15 *lighting*
studio lighting 66.15 *lighting*
studio photograph 66.4 *portrait*
studious 4.17 *thoughtful,* 6.18 *educated,* 293.41 *progressing,* 467.8 *diligent,* 642.20 *industrious*
studiously 6, 4.28 *thoughtfully,* 467.15 *attentively*
studiousness 6.9 *learnedness,* 467.4 *diligence,* 642.8 *assiduity*
Studite 7 Members of Religious Orders
stud poker 42 Card Games
studs 47.10 *carpenter's term*
studwork 47.10 *carpenter's term*
study 82, 4.4 *philosophical investigation,* 4.20 *philosophize,* 4.28 *learning,* 6.23 *learn,* 48.4 *nonfiction,* 50.6 *work of art,* 50.9 *drawing,* 52.1 *mathematics,* 165.27 *specialize,* 256.7 *room,* 293.35 *progress,* 435.3 *observation,* 435.14 *inspect,* 461.13 *concentrate,* 467.12 *scrutinize,* 472.11 *raise the point,* 477.2 *questioning,* 477.17 *question,* 501.13 *get to know,* 531.6 *privacy,* 561.1 *dissertation,* 588.3 *future intention,* 594.8 *prepare oneself,* 594.10 *preparations,* 627.2 *get better,* 647.1 *workshop,* 652.14 *behave towards,* 816.5 *solitary place*
studying 4.17 *thoughtful*
study of algae 90.2 *algae*
study of conduct 652.1 *conduct*
study of ferns 88.2 *fern plant*
study of fish 80
study of fungi 89
study of lichens 90.6 *lichen*
study of mammals 77.1 *mammal*
study of mankind 400
study of mosses 88.4 *moss plant*
study of names 560.7 *nomenclature*
study of place names 560.7 *nomenclature*
study of primates 77.16 *primate*
study on a scholarship 721.14 *profit*
study plants 83
study the Bible 7.22 *theologize*
study theology 7.22 *theologize*
study up on 6.23 *learn*
stuff 257, 45.55 *cook,* 103.1 *essence,* 144.6 *fill,* 237.8 *strengthen,* 257.1 *contents,* 261.5 *make bigger,* 292.4 *fill,*

367.4 *matter,* 383.5 *textile,* 521.4 *senseless talk,* 604.1 *materials,* 610.4 *be excessive,* 614.6 *refuse,* 637.5 *preserve,* 723.4 *possession,* 725.4 *possessions,* 872.5 *be greedy*
stuff and nonsense 506.1 *nonsense,* 521.4 *senseless talk,* 521.14 *nonsense*
stuffed 45.56 *culinary,* 130.9 *extra,* 144.8 *full,* 257.11 *loaded,* 261.7 *bigger,* 323.13 *stopped,* 350.26 *eating,* 608.3 *filled,* 610.6 *excessive,* 637.7 *preserved,* 872.6 *gluttonous*
stuffed animal 637.3 *preserved thing*
stuffed Idaho potato 45.43 *US dish*
stuffed marrow 45.34 *vegetarian dish*
stuffed shirt 809.7 *vain person*
stuffed up 323.13 *stopped*
stuffed vine leaves 45.52 *Greek dish*
stuffily 788.8 *boringly,* 811.36 *pompously*
stuff in 354.3 *impact*
stuffiness 408.1 *heat,* 788.1 *boredom,* 811.5 *pomposity,* 813.1 *formality*
stuffing 257, 130.3 *additional item,* 261.1 *growth,* 261.4 *enlarger,* 292.2 *filling,* 323.2 *stopper,* 354.11 *thing inserted,* 872.6 *gluttonous*
stuffing oneself 350.2 *appetite*
stuff oneself 350.22 *eat well,* 608.4 *suffice,* 872.5 *be greedy*
stuffy 167.14 *conformist,* 371.7 *condensed,* 408.9 *hot,* 626.5 *unhygienic,* 788.4 *boring,* 811.20 *pompous*
stum 566.1 *taciturn*
stumble 360.4 *fall,* 360.11 *trip,* 366.11 *stagger,* 366.25 *pitch,* 493.10 *misjudge,* 656.7 *be clumsy,* 864.16 *be wicked*
stumble into 229.5 *happen by chance*
stumble on 496.1 *discover*
stumble upon 344.2 *reach,* 589.11 *chance upon*
stumbling 360.4 *fall,* 360.18 *falling,* 656.3 *clumsy*
stumbling block 635.1 *trap,* 661.2 *obstacle,* 699.1 *restraint*
stump 27.5 *wicket,* 27.19 *dismiss,* 85.2 *tree part,* 132.1 *remainder,* 143.6 *branch,* 460.10 *bemuse,* 477.21 *confuse,* 491.20 *make uncertain,* 523.7 *be unintelligible,* 529.13 *mystify,* 659.23 *cause difficulties*
stump along 328.1 *move slowly*
stumped 523.6 *confused,* 659.16 *troubled*
stumper 27.4 *team,* 477.4 *difficult question*
stumpie 27.4 *team*
stumpiness 270.1 *shortness,* 276.1 *lowness*
stumping 27.11 *dismissal,* 580.12 *election*
stump orator 567.6 *public speaker*
stump oratory 564.9 *art of public speaking*
stump up 746.6 *pay*
stumpy 270.7 *short,* 276.5 *low*
stun 26.11 *do a combat sport,* 404.12 *anaesthetize,* 421.9 *deafen,* 423.8 *be loud,* 460.10 *bemuse,* 514.11 *amaze,* 786.10 *be wonderful*
stun and stab 24.2 *billiards play*
stung 828.15 *resentful*
stunned 404.8 *unconscious,* 421.4 *deaf,* 514.7 *amazed*
stunned into silence 514.7 *amazed*
stunner 786.5 *person of wonder*
stunning 436.11 *blinding,* 617.1 *worthy*
stunt 19.10 *defence,* 19.16 *play defence,* 41.12 *ski,* 262.5 *make smaller,* 270.10 *shorten,* 592.3 *expedient plan,* 640.2 *deed,*

640.4 *act,* 655.3 *masterpiece,* 655.11 *be expert,* 811.14 *show*
stunted 260.7 *little,* 262.7 *smaller,* 270.7 *short,* 276.5 *low,* 609.3 *underfed*
stuntedness 260.1 *littleness,* 270.1 *shortness,* 276.1 *lowness*
stunting 262.8 *contracting*
stuntman 51.29 *circus performer*
stunt man 114.5 *counterpart*
stuntman 222.2 *substitute person*
stunt man 293.21 *substitution,* 640.3 *doer,* 707.2 *alternative,* 778.7 *courageous person*
stuntman 811.15 *showman*
stunt-skiing 41.1 *skiing*
stupa 10.13 *shrine*
stupefaction 514.2 *amazement,* 761.4 *desensitization,* 786.1 *wonder*
stupefied 514.7 *amazed,* 761.2 *desensitized,* 786.6 *wondering,* 874.3 *dead drunk*
stupefy 404.12 *anaesthetize,* 514.11 *amaze,* 761.7 *render insensitive,* 786.10 *be wonderful,* 874.9 *be intoxicating*
stupendous 259.15 *big,* 786.8 *wonderful*
stupendously 786.13 *wonderfully*
stupid 441, 273.3 *thick-witted,* 443.5, 460.6 *unintelligent,* 502.6 *ignorant,* 508.5 *foolish,* 656.1 *unskilful*
stupidity 441, 443, 460.2 *unintelligence,* 462.2, 502.1 *ignorance,* 508.1 *folly*
stupidly 443.13 *opaquely,* 460.11 *unintelligently,* 502.12 *ignorantly,* 508.8 *foolishly*
stupid question 477.5 *easy question*
stupid with fatigue 650.1 *fatigued*
stupor 61.13 *depression,* 61.14 *trance,* 404.2 *unconsciousness,* 466.2 *lack of interest,* 512.1 *oblivion,* 643.9 *sleep,* 761.4 *desensitization,* 786.1 *wonder*
sturdily 237.14 *strongly,* 378.12 *toughly*
sturdiness 378.6 *toughness*
sturdy 237.9 *physically strong,* 273.1 *thick,* 378.1 *tough,* 623.1 *healthy*
sturgeon 80 Fishes
Sturm und Drang 48 Literary Groups and Movements
Sturt Stony 98 Deserts
stutter 563.3 *speech defect,* 563.14 *have difficulty speaking,* 564.3 *mode of speech,* 656.7 *be clumsy,* 874.7 *be drunk*
stutterer 810.7 *modest person*
stuttering 523.11 *unintelligibility,* 563.3 *speech defect,* 563.12 *inarticulate,* 656.3 *clumsy,* 828.16 *angry,* 874.10 *drunkenness*
Stuttgart 93 Cities
St. Valentine's Day 214.6 *annually celebrated day*
sty 68.7 *farm building,* 77.20 *abode of mammals,* 256.12 *stall,* 634.3 *animal shelter*
Stygian 440.8 *dark*
Stygian darkness 397.14 *the spiritual world*
Stygian gloom 440.1 *darkness*
Stygian shore 397.14 *the spiritual world*
stygiophobia 777 Phobias by Name
style 549, 549, 50.15 *engraving,* 84.3 *flower part,* 105.1 *state,* 114.2 *copy,* 152.2 *array,* 163.4 *type,* 163.9 *distinction,* 167.5 *convention,* 245.8 *organs of reproduction,* 295.35 *make clothing,* 306.5 *formality,* 327.1 *way,* 457.3 *external appearance,* 520.1 *meaning,* 558.1 *elegance,* 564.2 *power of speech,* 567.11 *title,* 652.1 *conduct,* 655.1 *skill,* 791.8 *hair cut,* 796.1 *elegance,* 796.1 *fashion,* 796.4 *design,* 796.8 *fashion,* 805.4 *prestige*
Style 549

styled 295, 549, 306.9 *formed*
style of cooking 45.1 *cookery*
stylet 680.8 *sharp weapon*
styling gel 386.6 *pomade*
styling mousse 386.6 *pomade*
stylish 549, 105.8 *in a state of,* 295.30 *dressed up,* 295.31 *styled,* 306.9 *formed,* 306.11 *formal,* 558.3 *elegant,* 655.9 *well-made,* 796.7 *fashionable,* 805.18 *prestigious,* 813.7 *dressed up*
stylishly 105.9 *conditionally,* 295.36 *dressily,* 306.13 *formatively,* 306.14 *conventionally,* 549.10 *stylistically,* 558.5 *elegantly,* 655.12 *skilfully*
stylishness 549, 558.1 *elegance,* 796.2 *fashionableness*
stylish writer 549.5, 558.2 *stylist*
stylist 549, 558, 557.3 *phrasemonger*
stylistically 549
stylistics 5.1 *linguistics*
stylite 7.7 *monk,* 168.9 *hermit,* 174.8 *loner*
stylization 813.1 *formality*
stylize 813.9 *formalize*
stylized 50.26 *artistic,* 306.9 *formed,* 813.6 *formal*
stylobate 43.8 *column*
stylophone 49 Musical Instruments
stylops 82 Insects
stylus 380.8 *sharp-pointed thing*
stymie 661.8 *hinder*
styptic 262.4 *contractor,* 262.8 *contracting,* 371.6 *dense*
styrax 85 Trees and Shrubs
Styrofoam cup 351.10 *drink container*
Styx 96.5 *other major rivers,* 397.14 *the spiritual world*
suable 16.54 *litigated*
suan pan 170.5 *computer*
Suarez 4 Philosophers
suave 6.20 *refined,* 376.6 *smooth-mannered,* 558.3 *elegant,* 817.8 *good-mannered*
suavely 376, 6.27 *discerningly,* 558.5 *elegantly,* 817.15 *genteelly*
suaveness 558.1 *elegance,* 817.1 *courtesy*
suavity 6.11 *refinement,* 558.1 *elegance,* 817.1 *courtesy*
sub 19.2 *football player,* 23.2 *basketball player,* 155.13 *replacement,* 222.2 *substitute person,* 532.15 *publish,* 533.13 *report,* 707.2 *alternative*
subabdominal 276.6 *lower*
subacid 415.5 *acid*
subacidity 415.1 *sourness*
subalpine 95.7, 275.13 *mountainous,* 276.7 *lowland*
subaltern 4.8 *philosophical term,* 127.6 *inferior,* 195.7 *subordinate,* 697.1 *servant*
subaqua 39.11 *swimming,* 97.7 *oceanic,* 277.12 *under*
subaqua swimmer 39.4 *swimmer*
subaqua swimming 39.1 *swimming*
subaquatic 97.7 *oceanic,* 277.12 *under*
subaqueous 97.7 *oceanic,* 277.12 *under*
subatomic 260.7 *little*
subatomically 260.9 *microscopically*
subatomic particle 56.77 *elementary particle,* 260.2 *little thing*
subaudition 524.1 *interpretation*
subauricular 276.6 *lower*
subaxillary 276.6 *lower*
subbase 276.4 *low thing*
subbasement 256.7 *room*
subbed copy 533.10 *copy*
sub-bottom profiling 54.17 *ocean research vessel*
subbranch 143.6 *branch,* 163.3 *kingdom*
subcartilaginous 276.6 *lower*
subcategory 143.1 *part,* 152.6 *category,* 163.2 *class*
subclass 59.17 *taxonomy,* 143.1 *part,* 152.6 *category,* 163.2

class, 163.3 *kingdom*
subclavian 276.6 *lower*
subcommittee 703.4 *council*
subconscious 61, 11.16 *psychic*, 61.21 *psyche*, 368.6 *internal world*, 368.11 *internal*, 464.4 *instinct*, 527.1 *latent*, 527.6 *latency*
subconsciously 11.25 *occultly*, 61.39 *psychologically*, 527.15 *latently*
subconsciousness 527.6 *latency*
subconscious self 165.11 *identity*
subcontinent 54.6, 98.1 *continent*
subcontinental 98.11 *continental*
subcontinentally 98.13 *continentally*
subcontrary 111.4 *opposite*
subcortex 276.4 *low thing*, 290.1 *interior*
subcortical 276.6 *lower*, 290.7 *interior*
subcranial 276.6 *lower*
subcutaneous 276.6 *lower*, 290.7 *interior*
subcutaneous injection 62.12 *injection*
subdivide 52.91 *add*, 136.11 *divide*, 143.10 *part*, 163.14 *sort*, 173.8 *divide*, 257.9 *itemize*, 731.4 *allot*
subdivided 136.15 *separate*, 257.12 *itemized*
subdivision 59.17 *taxonomy*, 136.3 *separateness*, 143.1 *part*, 148.2 *piece*, 152.6 *category*, 163.2 *class*, 173.2 *fractional part*, 731.1 *allocation*
subdivisional 173.5 *fractional*
subdivisions 257.5 *divisions*
subdominant 49.16 *musical note*
subdorsal 276.6 *lower*
subdual 699.1 *restraint*
subduction zone 54.19 *plate tectonics*
subdue 233.10 *be a prevailing influence*, 242.4 *moderate*, 374.14 *ease*, 422.2 *silence*, 428.7 *mute*, 677.4 *pacify*, 679.38 *conquer*, 682.9 *be victorious*, 696.14 *master*, 699.8 *restrain*, 701.6 *subject*, 734.7 *take*
subdued 242.6 *moderate*, 424.4 *faint*, 428.1 *faint-sounding*, 542.15 *reserved*, 673.5 *submitting*
subduedness 542.5 *reserve*
subdue oneself 673.3 *submit*
subduer 682.5 *victorious person*
subduing 734.1 *taking*
subedit 532.15 *publish*, 533.13 *report*, 627.3 *rectify*
subediting 627.6 *rectification*
subeditor 532.11 *newspaper man*, 533.4 *journalist*, 627.13 *reviser*, 629.12 *repairer*
subfamily 59.17 *taxonomy*, 143.1 *part*, 163.3 *kingdom*
subfloor 276.4 *low thing*
subfusc 295.3 *formal dress*, 440.10 *dark-coloured*, 813.4 *formal dress*
subgenus 143.1 *part*, 163.3 *kingdom*
subgiant 53.13 *luminosity*
subglottal 276.6 *lower*
subgrade 276.4 *low thing*
subgroup 143.1 *part*, 152.6 *category*, 163.2 *class*
subgun 680.11 *guns*
subhuman 76.14 *animalian*, 400.12 *human*, 832.11 *cruel*
subito 49 Musical Terms
subjacency 276.4 *low thing*
subjacent 276.6 *lower*
subject 6, 701, 701, 5.35 *part of speech*, 48.3 *aspect of fiction*, 49.13 *melody*, 50.11 *artist's materials*, 103.1 *essence*, 127.6 *inferior*, 127.15 *subordinate*, 165.8 *specialization*, 226.6 *undertaking*, 236.11 *unprotected*, 255.8 *national*, 382.9 *artistic structure*, 433.1 *melody*, 472.1 *topic*, 472.5 *educational topic*, 473.4 *gist*, 479.7 *experimentee*, 682.9 *be victorious*, 690.6 *suppress*,

697.9 *serving*, 729.4 *giver*, 734.7 *take*
subject and predicate 5.23 *phrase*
subjected 690.9 *suppressed*, 701.9 *subject*
subjected person 701
subject-group 163.6 *students*
subjecting 701.9 *subject*
subjection 701, 12.3 *governance*, 618.11 *harmfulness*, 670.14 *siege*, 690.2 *suppression*, 734.1 *taking*
Subjection 701
subjective 165, 5.44 *grammatical*, 102.9 *illusory*, 368.11 *internal*, 472.7 *focused*, 493.8 *unjust*, 519.12 *imaginary*
subjective existence 102.1 *unreality*
subjectively 368, 5.52 *grammatically*, 493.14 *unjustly*
subjective probability 488.5 *probability theory*
subjectivism 4.7 *school of thought*, 519.6 *reverie*
subjectivist 4.11 *follower of a doctrine*
subjectivistic 4.14 *of a philosophy*
subjectivity 102.1 *unreality*, 368.6 *internal world*, 504.6 *fallibility*
subject matter 103.2 *essential content*, 257.5 *divisions*, 472.1 *topic*, 520.1 *meaning*
subject of investigation 472.4 *sphere*
subject to 227.10 *caused*
subject to jurisdiction 16.48 *jurisdictional*
subject to terms 716.8 *negotiated*
subjoin 130.6 *add*
subjoined 130.8 *additional*
sub judice 16.54 *litigated*, 492.10 *judged*
subjugate 233.10 *be a prevailing influence*, 682.9 *be victorious*, 688.19 *be authoritarian*, 690.6 *suppress*, 696.14 *master*, 701.6 *subject*, 734.7 *take*
subjugated 690.9 *suppressed*, 701.9 *subject*
subjugation 683.2 *defeat*, 690.2 *suppression*, 701.1 *subjection*, 734.1 *taking*
subjugator 682.5 *victorious person*
subjunction 155.8 *addition*
subjunctive 5.33 *mood*
subjunctively 5.52 *grammatically*
subkingdom 59.17 *taxonomy*, 163.3 *kingdom*
sublease 723.1 *possession*
subletly 794
sublevation 361.6 *raising*
Sublieutenant 17 British Military Ranks
sub-lieutenant 679.27 *naval man*
sublimate 8.17 *deify*, 134.10 *purify*, 355.8 *extract*, 361.3 *promote*, 388.25 *gasify*, 621.15 *purify*, 627.1 *improve*
sublimated 55.43 *atmospheric*, 876.9 *pure*
sublimation 55.9 *atmospheric process*, 56.37 *temperature*, 57.3 *phase*, 61.19 *defence mechanism*, 355.7 *obtaining an extract*, 388.10 *vaporization*, 627.3 *improvement*
sublimation point 56.37 *temperature*
sublime 8.13 *divine*, 275.11, 361.12 *exalted*, 370.2 *insubstantial*, 388.25 *gasify*, 554.5 *serious*, 619.1 *perfect*, 763.1 *pleasant*, 859.5 *unselfish*
sublimely 8.19 *divinely*, 275.19 *high*, 361.13 *highly*, 370.11 *lightly*, 859.9 *unselfishly*
subliminal 61.21 *psyche*, 61.37 *subconscious*, 438.2 *difficult to see*, 527.1 *latent*
subliminal advertising 527.7 *latent things*
subliminal influence 527.7 *latent things*
subliminally 61.39 *psychologi-*

cally, 527.15 *latently*
subliminal self 61.21 *psyche*, 165.11 *identity*
sublimity 8.1 *divinity*, 126.1 *superiority*, 275.1, 361.8 *height*, 527.6 *latency*, 554.2 *seriousness*, 859.2 *unselfishness*
sublingual gland 352 Exocrine Glands
sublittoral 97.7 *oceanic*
submachine gun 680.11 *guns*
submandibular gland 352 Exocrine Glands
submarine 54.51, 97.7 *oceanic*, 277.4 *deep thing*, 277.12 *under*, 360.8 *descender*, 679.24 *warship*, 680.5 *missile weapon*
submarine canyon 54.16 *ocean floor*
submarine chaser 679.24 *warship*
submarine division 17.4 *military organization*
submariner 277, 323.6 *closed-in person*, 360.8 *descender*, 679.27 *naval man*
submarine tender 679.24 *warship*
submarine warfare 676.8 *warfare*
submediant 49.16 *musical note*
submental 276.6 *lower*
submerge 96.7 *flow*, 244.8 *destroy*, 277.14 *deepen*, 354.4 *immerse*, 360.9 *descend*, 362.3 *bring down*, 389.29 *water*, 527.13 *hide*, 546.1 *obliterate*
submerged 98.11 *continental*, 276.7 *lowland*, 277.12 *under*, 354.14 *immersed*, 362.19 *fallen*, 389.24 *flooded*, 438.1 *invisible*, 527.1 *latent*
submerged coast 98.4 *coast*
submerged log 74.5 *navigation*
submergence 362, 354.10 *immersion*, 360.2 *sinkage*, 527.8 *concealment*
submerse 389.29 *water*
submersed 354.14 *immersed*, 389.24 *flooded*
submersible 54.17 *ocean research vessel*, 277.4 *deep thing*, 360.16 *descending*
submersion 96.6 *river flow*, 277.1 *depth*, 354.10 *immersion*, 389.9 *soaking*
subminiature 260.7 *little*
submission 673, 167.2 *compliance*, 518.1 *supposition*, 535.2 *statement*, 576.14 *apathy*, 654.1 *advice*, 683.2 *defeat*, 694.1 *obedience*, 710.2 *tentative offer*, 808.1 *servility*, 847.3 *allegiance*
Submission 673
submissive 806, 167.13 *compliant*, 660.13 *easygoing*, 673.5 *submitting*, 675.7 *peaceful*, 694.7 *obedient*, 808.6 *servile*, 847.9 *loyal*, 849.9 *showing respect*
submissively 167.16 *adaptably*, 374.18 *softheartedly*, 694.10 *obediently*, 806.28 *subserviently*, 808.16 *with servility*
submissiveness 806, 576.14 *apathy*, 673.1 *submission*, 694.1 *obedience*, 808.1 *servility*
submit 673, 806, 127.9 *yield to*, 167.8 *comply*, 228.8 *be motivated*, 374.16 *yield*, 499.5 *assent to*, 518.6 *propound*, 535.17 *affirm*, 586.18 *be persuaded*, 598.2 *withdraw*, 654.5 *advise*, 673.4 *succumb*, 694.5 *obey*, 710.9 *offer*
submit a report 560.15 *recount*
submit one's judgment to another's 654.6 *consult*
submitted 535.11 *stated*
submitted for judgment 16.54 *litigated*, 492.10 *judged*
submitter 535.9 *affirmer*
submitting 673, 673.1 *submission*, 675.7 *peaceful*, 694.7 *obedient*, 806.4 *self-abasing*, 849.9 *showing respect*
submit to 284.12 *bear*
submit to a whim 579.5 *be capricious*

submit to fate 571.16 *be compelled*
submit to judgment 16.72 *stand trial*
submontane 276.7 *lowland*
submucosa 276.4 *low thing*
submultiple 52.17 *multiplication*
subnormal 127.14 *poor*, 460.7 *intellectually subnormal*
subnormality 510
subnormally 127.21 *badly*
suboceanic 54.51 *oceanic*, 277.12 *under*
suborbital 276.6 *lower*
suborder 59.17 *taxonomy*, 152.6 *category*, 163.3 *kingdom*
subordinacy 701.1 *subjection*
subordinate 127, 195, 195, 701, 127.6 *inferior*, 232.6 *instrumental*, 612.10 *nonentity*, 662.11 *helper*, 697.1 *servant*, 701.6, 701.9 *subject*
subordinate clause 143.2 *particular*
subordinate judge 16.23 *judge*
subordinately 127.22 *basely*
subordinate position 127.1 *inferiority*, 701.1 *subjection*
subordinate role 701.1 *subjection*
subordinating 5.44 *grammatical*
subordinating conjunction 5.35 *part of speech*
subordination 195, 127.1 *inferiority*, 150.4 *position*, 167.2 *compliance*, 232.1 *instrumentality*, 276.1 *lowness*, 701.1 *subjection*
suborn 586.17 *bribe*, 738.4 *buy off*
subornment 738.10 *bribery*
suboxide 57 Types of Compounds
subpanation 10.6 *Eucharist*
subperiod 54.41 *geological time*
subphylum 59.17 *taxonomy*, 163.3 *kingdom*
sub-plane 36.18 *windsurf*
sub-planing 36.13 *windsurfing*
subplot 48.3 *aspect of fiction*, 51.7 *dramaturgy*, 473.4 *gist*, 560.3 *narration*
subpoena 16.6 *legal process*, 692.2, 692.10 *demand*
subpolar zone 55.39 *climatic zone*
sub rosa 529.15 *in secret*
subscapular 276.6 *lower*
subscribe 544.11 *identify oneself*, 710.16 *make an offering*, 746.6 *pay*, 755.11 *give*
subscriber 499.3 *assenter*, 534.13 *telephoner*, 729.4 *giver*, 755.9 *generous person*
subscriber line 534.12 *public telephone system*
subscriber trunk dialling 534.11 *dialling*
subscribe to 4.22 *propound a philosophy*, 499.4 *assent*, 662.23 *advise*, 665.13 *be a member*, 667.6 *agree with*, 715.5 *contract*, 729.5 *give*
subscript 155.8 *addition*, 276.4 *low thing*, 276.6 *lower*
subscription 710.6 *offering*, 729.1 *giving*, 729.3 *offering*, 746.1 *payment*, 746.4 *grant*, 751.3 *fee*, 755.7 *gift*
subscription list 528.4 *mass communication*
subsection 143.2 *particular*, 163.2 *class*
subsequence 195.1 *succession*
subsequent 195.12 *succeeding*, 227.10 *caused*
subsequently 155.28 *after*, 227.12 *with the effect of*
subserve 613.9 *be useful*, 662.28 *further*
subservience 127.1 *inferiority*, 232.1 *instrumentality*, 673.1 *submission*, 694.1 *obedience*, 701.1 *subjection*, 806.12 *submissiveness*, 808.1 *servility*
subservient 127.15 *subordinate*, 232.6 *instrumental*, 599.9 *used*, 613.3 *instrumental*, 662.31 *supplementary*, 673.5 *submitting*,

694.7 *obedient,* 701.9 *subject,* 806.5 *submissive,* 808.6 *servile*

subserviently 806, 127.22 *basely,* 232.9 *instrumentally,* 694.10 *obediently,* 701.11 *under subjection,* 808.16 *with servility*

subset 52.21 *set,* 163.2 *class*

subshell 56.65 *atom*

subside 54.64 *fold,* 129.4 *decrease,* 324.13 *be in motion,* 325.8 *be motionless,* 360.9 *descend*

subsidence 54.20 *earth movement,* 129.1 *decrease,* 360.2 *sinkage,* 360.3 *downflow*

subsidiarity 162.6 *decentralization*

subsidiary 127.6 *inferior,* 127.15 *subordinate,* 130.8 *additional,* 284.9 *supportive,* 612.3 *secondary,* 613.3 *instrumental,* 662.31 *supplementary*

subsidiary office 647.1 *workshop*

subsiding 129.6 *decreasing,* 324.17 *directional,* 360.16 *descending*

subsiding motion 324.6 *descending motion*

subsidization 662.9 *patronage,* 729.1 *giving*

subsidize 284.13 *support financially,* 602.6 *find means,* 662.29 *finance,* 729.5 *give,* 878.10 *grant*

subsidized 729.7 *given*

subsidy 13.6 *economic factors,* 68.2 *Common Agricultural Policy ,* 284.7 *financial support,* 602.4 *financial resources,* 606.1 *provision,* 662.6 *financial assistance,* 721.5 *profit,* 729.2 *gift,* 746.4, 878.3 *grant*

subsist 99.17 *exist,* 132.7 *be left,* 217.5 *be permanent,* 350.21 *eat,* 396.16 *live*

subsistence 99.1 *existence,* 217.1 *permanence,* 284.7 *financial support,* 396.1 *life,* 396.3 *life requirements,* 662.3 *sustenance*

subsistence farming 68.1 *agriculture,* 608.7 *activity*

subsistence level 593.3 *needfulness,* 609.8 *insufficiency,* 743.5 *poverty*

subsistent 99.10 *existing*

subsisting 217.7 *permanent*

subsoil 54.36 *soil,* 276.4 *low thing,* 290.1 *interior*

subcoiler 68.10 *farm tool*

subsonic 56.98 *physical*

subsonically 56.100 *physically*

subsonic speed 56.19 *sound propagation*

subspecies 59.17 *taxonomy,* 143.1 *part,* 163.3 *kingdom*

subspecific 59.28 *taxonomic*

substance 99.2 *thing,* 101.1 *reality,* 103.1 *essence,* 120.1 *quantity,* 257.1 *contents,* 306.1 *form,* 367.4 *matter,* 382.2 *fabric,* 520.1 *meaning,* 520.2 *significance,* 537.2 *reality,* 602.4 *financial resources,* 604.1 *materials,* 611.1 *importance,* 611.3 *chief thing,* 725.5 *personal estate,* 742.8 *solvency*

substandard 5.39 *of language,* 75.4 *standard,* 127.14 *poor,* 238.13 *insufficient,* 358.8 *defective,* 618.2 *inferior,* 766.5 *unsatisfactory*

substandard housing 743.7 *beggary*

substandard language 5.5 *nonstandard language*

substandard usage 5.5 *nonstandard language*

substantial 99.11 *intrinsic,* 101.6 *real,* 237.13 *strengthened,* 257.10 *containing,* 259.15 *big,* 273.1 *thick,* 367.7 *material,* 407.8 *touchable,* 480.9 *verificatory,* 520.7 *significant,* 537.16 *existing,* 537.19 *authentic,* 861.7 *large*

substantial capital 742.5 *wealth*

substantiality 99.3 *nature,* 101.1 *reality,* 367.1 *material world,* 537.2 *reality,* 537.7 *confirmation,* 611.1 *importance,* 861.14 *largeness*

substantialize 367.8 *be material*

substantially 103.13 *in essence,* 142.13 *on the whole,* 257.13 *structurally,* 259.20 *largely,* 367.9 *materially,* 407.14 *palpably*

substantial resources 742.5 *wealth*

substantiate 101.12 *establish reality,* 106.11 *circumstantiate,* 367.8 *be material,* 475.17 *prove,* 479.11 *experiment,* 480.2 *prove,* 490.21 *make certain,* 535.19 *confirm,* 537.30 *prove true,* 544.10 *identify,* 855.8 *justify*

substantiated 475.13 *proven,* 535.13 *supported,* 537.20 *proved,* 544.12 *identified*

substantiation 475.4, 480.5 *proof,* 483.2 *proof,* 535.4, 537.7 *confirmation,* 544.1 *identification*

substantive 5.35 *part of speech,* 5.44 *grammatical,* 99.11 *intrinsic,* 101.6 *real*

substantivity 101.1 *reality*

substation 64.33 *power distribution*

substitutable 216.14 *exchangeable,* 223.6 *in exchange,* 293.40 *substitutive*

substitute 222, 19.2 *football player,* 22.2 *baseball player,* 23.2 *basketball player,* 38.3 *football player,* 51.22 *actor,* 52.92 *manipulate,* 57.26 *react,* 61.25 *surrogate,* 130.5 *extra person,* 155.13 *replacement,* 155.22 *succeed,* 195.5 *successor,* 216.10 *exchange,* 223.4 *person who exchanges,* 223.5 *exchange,* 252.10 *replaced,* 252.16 *replace,* 284.8 *supporter,* 284.9 *supportive,* 293.21 *substitution,* 293.40 *substitutive,* 349.5 *take the place of,* 349.26 *ejector,* 547.8 *representative,* 600.6 *stop using,* 602.1 *means,* 620.6 *imperfect item,* 646.3 *agent,* 701.3 *subordinate,* 701.9 *subject,* 707.2 *alternative,* 707.7 *deputizing,* 727.9 *dispose of,* 728.3 *transfer property,* 767.5 *helper*

substituted 222, 223.7 *exchanged,* 539.39 *imitative*

substitute for 707, 284.14 *give moral support,* 293.34 *cover for,* 547.12 *stand for,* 706.5 *represent,* 767.11 *assist*

substitute person 222

substitute thing 222

substituting 707.7 *deputizing*

substitution 222, 293, 52.24 *evaluation,* 57.14 *chemical reaction,* 61.19 *defence mechanism,* 216.4, 223.1 *exchange,* 252.3 *replacement,* 727.1 *disposal,* 728.1 *transfer of property,* 746.2 *repayment*

Substitution 222

substitutional 57.38 *reactive,* 222.7 *substitute*

substitutive 293, 222.7 *substitute,* 223.6 *in exchange*

substrate 57.15 *catalysis,* 58.11 *enzyme*

substrative 290.7 *interior*

substratosphere 390.3 *atmospheric layers*

substratum 266.1 *layer,* 276.4 *low thing,* 280.1 *base,* 290.1 *interior*

substructural 63.32, 382.11 *structural*

substructurally 382.18 *structurally*

substructure 63, 280.2 *foot,* 284.2 *supporting part,* 382.6 *construction*

subsume 146, 148.11 *consist of,* 257.8 *embody*

subsuming 257.10 *containing*

subsurface 54.50 *terrestrial*

subsurface water 54.9 *groundwater*

subtend 52.97 *align,* 111.8 *be opposite*

subterfuge 474.1 *sophistry,* 474.2 *sophism,* 531.5 *evasion,* 538.8 *pretence,* 539.1 *deception,* 539.9 *sleight of hand,* 635.1 *trap,* 657.2 *stratagem*

subterranean 8.16 *devilish,* 54.50 *terrestrial,* 277.12 *under,* 527.1 *latent*

subterranean water 54.9 *groundwater*

subterraneity 277.1 *depth*

subterraneous 277.12 *under*

subterrestrial 277.12 *under*

subtilin 62 *Medication*

subtitle 560.2 *brief description*

subtle 542, 383.10 *delicate,* 503.5, 537.21 *accurate,* 657.4 *cunning*

subtle body 11.7 *spirit*

subtleness 537.8 *accuracy*

subtlety 542, 459.4 *cleverness,* 474.4 *quibbling,* 503.1, 537.8 *accuracy,* 657.1 *cunning*

subtle word 528.7 *advice*

subtly 383.15 *texturally,* 474.14 *sophistically*

subtonic 49.16 *musical note*

subtopia 93.8 *suburb*

subtopian 93.14 *urban*

subtract 131, 52.91 *add,* 120.8 *quantify,* 136.10 *set apart,* 170.9 *add,* 525.1 *misinterpret,* 722.9 *lose,* 734.10 *take away,* 752.3 *discount*

subtracted 131, 254.12 *missing*

subtracted item 131

subtraction 52, 131, 120.2 *certain amount,* 123.1 *inequality,* 129.1 *decrease,* 170.1 *calculation,* 525.2 *misinterpretation,* 722.1 *loss,* 734.3 *taking away*

Subtraction 131

subtractive 131

subtractive colour 444.4 *pigment*

subtractive process 56.28 *colour*

subtrahend 52.16 *subtraction,* 131.2 *subtracted item*

subtribe 59.17 *taxonomy*

subtropical 69.19 *ornamental,* 249.16 *regional*

subtropical climate 55.38 *climate*

subtropical dry zone 55.39 *climatic zone*

subtropically 69.20 *horticulturally,* 249.19 *geographically*

subtropical winter rainy zone 55.39 *climatic zone*

subtropics 55.39 *climatic zone,* 249.2 *geographical region,* 408.8 *hot place*

subungulate 77.14 *pachyderm,* 77.32 *pachydermatous*

suburb 93, 124.8 *middle classes,* 297.1 *surroundings*

suburban 93.14 *urban,* 249.17 *national,* 255.12 *native,* 256.15 *environmental,* 297.4 *surrounding,* 788.4 *boring*

suburban dweller 93.11 *urbanite*

suburbanite 93.11 *urbanite,* 124.8 *middle classes,* 255.4 *townsman*

suburbanization 2.5 *society,* 93.1 *city*

suburbanize 93.15 *urbanize*

suburbanized 93.14 *urban*

suburban whine 564.3 *mode of speech*

suburbia 93.8 *suburb,* 124.8 *middle classes,* 158.8 *middle class,* 249.11 *settlement*

suburbs 249.11 *settlement*

subvariety 163.3 *kingdom*

subvene 662.28 *further*

subvention 606.1 *provision,* 662.6 *financial assistance,* 729.1 *giving,* 729.2 *gift,* 746.4, 878.3 *grant*

subventionary 729.7 *given*

subventionize 662.29 *finance*

subversion 693, 216.1 *change,*

244.1 *destruction,* 362.12 *downthrow,* 476.1 *refutation,* 628.8 *perversion,* 689.1 *anarchy*

subversive 693, 216.11 *changeable,* 244.14 *destructive,* 362.22 *overthrown,* 539.20 *plotter,* 689.3 *anarchist,* 693.10 *seditionist*

subversively 693, 216.15 *changeably,* 362.24 *down*

subversiveness 693.3 *subversion*

subvert 216.8 *cause change,* 244.8 *destroy,* 244.9 *demolish,* 362.3 *bring down,* 628.6 *pervert,* 689.4 *be anarchic,* 693.16 *be subversive*

subverted 362.22 *overthrown*

subway 63.22 *tunnel,* 72.1 *railway,* 277.4 *deep thing,* 327.8 *tunnel,* 327.10 *railway*

sub-zero temperature 409.2 *freezing*

succedaneum 222.3 *substitute thing*

succeed 155, 195, 106.14 *be comfortable,* 142.10 *complete,* 155.21 *follow in sequence,* 159.13 *be consecutive,* 195.11 *follow in office,* 214.7 *be regular,* 219.3 *continue,* 222.4 *be a substitute,* 344.9 *achieve,* 615.6 *be convenient,* 627.2 *get better,* 682.6 *be successful,* 682.12 *succeed to,* 684.4 *complete,* 686.5 *be prosperous,* 688.20 *take authority,* 718.13 *secure one's objective,* 767.11 *assist,* 861.21 *do well*

succeeding 195, 155.15 *sequential,* 159.9 *consecutive,* 682.13 *successful*

succeed to 682, 195.11 *follow in office,* 721.14 *profit,* 730.9 *receive*

succeed to the throne 12.12 *take authority*

succentor 7.8 *priest*

success 682, 51.11 *theatrical performance,* 52.58 *frequency distribution,* 106.5 *comfortable circumstances,* 126.1 *superiority,* 336.12 *advance,* 411.2 *taste of life,* 627.5 *improvement,* 682.4 *successful person,* 684.1 *completion,* 686.1 *prosperity,* 686.4 *prosperous person*

Success 682

successful 682, 686.8 *prosperous*

successful attack 682.2 *victory*

successful battle 682.2 *victory*

successful defence 16.42 *acquittal,* 855.2 *defence*

successfully 682, 686.9 *prosperously*

successful person 682, 686.4 *prosperous person*

successful production 51.11 *theatrical performance*

successful prosecution 16.43 *conviction*

successful speculation 721.1 *gain*

successful thing 682

succession 195, 59.18 *ecology,* 155.1 *sequence,* 159.1 *consecutiveness,* 219.1 *continuity,* 688.3 *acquisition of power,* 728.1 *transfer of property,* 730.1 *receiving*

Succession 195

successional 155.15 *sequential,* 195.12 *succeeding,* 688.13 *elected*

successive 155.15 *sequential,* 159.9 *consecutive,* 195.12 *succeeding*

successively 155.27 *in sequence,* 159.18 *consecutively,* 195.14 *in succession*

successiveness 155.1 *sequence,* 159.1 *consecutiveness,* 195.1 *succession*

successor 155, 195, 132.6 *person remaining,* 222.2 *substitute person,* 513.4 *expectant person,* 730.6 *beneficiary*

successors 199.2 *future generation*

ably, 116.38 *fittingly,* 210.9 *opportunely,* 478.26 *correspondingly,* 782.17 *desirably,* 843.18 *properly*
suit at law 16.5 *litigation*
suitcase 258.9 *baggage,* 605.4 *storage*
suite 159.2 *consecution,* 180.10 *attendance,* 195.1 *succession*
suited 210.6 *timely,* 485.9 *qualified*
suited for 655.7 *gifted*
suitedness 485.1 *qualification*
suited to the weather 203.14 *seasonable*
suite of programs 65.17 *computing term*
suiting 288.4 *textile*
suit of cards 159.2 *consecution*
suit of clothes 295.1 *dress*
suit oneself 698.16 *be independent*
suit one's purpose 613.9 *be useful*
suitor 16.8 *litigant,* 138.5 *follower,* 467.6 *attentive person,* 712.4 *requester,* 821.9 *lover*
suit the action to the word 543.11 *gesture*
suit the occasion 210.4 *be timely,* 615.6 *be convenient*
Sukkoth 10.16 *religious festival*
Sulawesi 98 Islands
sulk 573.10 *grudge,* 766.7 *be dissatisfied,* 770.9 *despair,* 830.9 *be sullen*
sulker 573.16 *reluctant person,* 766.3 *dissatisfied person,* 818.4 *discourteous person,* 830.5 *sullen person*
sulkily 818.9 *discourteously,* 830.13 *sullenly*
sulkiness 573.14 *disobedience,* 830.1 *sullenness*
sulking 766.4 *dissatisfied*
sulky 71 Carriages and Carts, 573.5 *reluctant,* 766.4 *dissatisfied,* 830.6 *sullen*
sullen 830, 415.7 *splenetic,* 566.1 *taciturn,* 772.1 *solemn,* 788.5 *bored,* 816.8 *unsociable,* 818.5 *discourteous,* 822.10 *hating,* 829.4 *irascible,* 832.15 *inconsiderate*
sullen look 830.2 *sign of sullenness*
sullenly 830, 415.11 *splenetically,* 772.10 *solemnly,* 816.14 *unsocially,* 818.9 *discourteously,* 822.18 *hatefully,* 829.9 *irascibly*
sullenness 830, 415.4 *spleen,* 566.4 *taciturnity,* 573.14 *disobedience,* 772.4 *solemnity,* 788.1 *boredom,* 816.1 *unsociability,* 818.1 *discourtesy,* 822.1 *hate,* 828.4 *anger,* 829.1 *irascibility*
Sullenness 830
sullen person 830
Sullivan 49 Musicians and Composers
sully 441.11 *tarnish,* 447.11 *blacken,* 622.11 *dirty,* 854.12 *defame,* 877.19 *corrupt*
sulphacetamide 62 Medication
sulphadiazine 62 Medication
sulphadimidine 62 Medication
sulphadoxine 62 Medication
sulpha drug 62.4 *drug type,* 630.8 *drug*
sulphafurazole 62 Medication
sulphamethizole 62 Medication
sulphamethoxazole 62 Medication
sulphaquanidine 62 Medication
sulphate 57 Types of Compounds
sulphates 246.3 *fertilizer*
sulphide 57 Types of Compounds
sulphinpyrazole 62 Medication
sulphisoxazole 62 Medication
sulphite 57 Types of Compounds
sulphonamide 57 Types of Compounds, 62.4 *drug type,* 630.8 *drug*
sulphonate 57.26 *react*

sulphonation 57 Types of Chemical Reaction
sulphone 62.4 *drug type*
sulphonic 57.34 *elemental*
sulphonic acid 57 Types of Compounds
sulphonous 57.34 *elemental*
sulphur 57 Chemical Elements, 58.15 *essential element,* 452.8 *yellow thing*
sulphur dioxide 57 Common Chemical Compounds, 419.2 *something that makes an unpleasant smell,* 631.9 *pollution*
sulphuretted 57.34 *elemental*
sulphuric 57.34 *elemental*
sulphuric acid 57 Common Chemical Compounds, 631.9 *pollution*
sulphurize 57.26 *react*
sulphurous 8.16 *devilish,* 57.34 *elemental,* 419.3 *stinking,* 452.2 *yellowish,* 828.16 *angry*
sulphurous acid 57 Common Chemical Compounds
sulphurously 828.18 *angrily*
sulphuryl 57.34 *elemental*
sultan 126.5 *superior,* 696.2 *sovereign*
Sultan 68 Breeds of Fowl
sultana 45.42 *preserve*
sultanate 91.3 *dominion,* 249.4 *territorial division*
sulthiame 62 Medication
sultriness 408.5 *hot weather*
sultry subtropical 408.11 *warm*
sum 741, 52.15 *addition,* 52.91 *add,* 120.4 *total,* 130.6 *add,* 142.2 *whole thing,* 169.4 *mathematical result,* 170.9 *add,* 478.7 *numerical result,* 478.20 *solve,* 520.1 *meaning*
sumach 85 Trees and Shrubs
sum and substance 520.1 *meaning,* 611.3 *chief thing*
sum asked for 751.1 *price*
Sumatra 98 Islands
Sumatra Game 68 Breeds of Fowl
sum entrusted 745.3 *loan*
Sumerian 5 Languages and Groups of Languages, **7** Non-Christian Religions, 400.4 *civilized human*
Sumerian art 50 Non-Western Art
Sumerians 200.6 *people of the past*
Sumerological 3.17 *archaeological*
Sumerologist 1.4 *palaeoanthropologist,* 3.4 *archaeologist*
Sumerology 1.2 *palaeoanthropology,* 3.2 *archaeology*
summarily 16, 562, 3.25 *reportedly,* 208.17 *early,* 552.5 *concisely*
summariness 562
summarize 562, 3.20 *chronicle,* 183.17 *iterate,* 270.10 *shorten,* 299.5 *outline,* 552.4 *be concise*
summarized 299.6 *outlined,* 552.3 *concise,* 562.7 *shortened*
summarizer 562
summary 562, 562, 3.5 *chronicle,* 143.5 *largest part,* 183.2 *iteration,* 208.12 *early,* 270.3 *shortened version,* 270.7 *short,* 299.1 *outline,* 473.4 *gist,* 552.2 *outline,* 552.3 *concise,* 560.2 *brief description,* 561.1 *dissertation,* 592.6 *outline,* 692.7 *overview*
Summary 562
summary court 16.19 *lawcourt*
summary court-martial 16.19 *lawcourt,* 17.6 *military law*
summation 52.15 *addition,* 130.2 *mathematical addition,* 142.2 *whole thing,* 169.4 *mathematical result*
summer 203, 203, 203.6 *spend the season,* 214.5 *regular thing,* 408.5 *hot weather,* 686.3 *time of plenty,* 815.12 *visit*
summer drought 408.5 *hot weather*
summer holiday 214.5 *regular*

thing
summerhouse 69.3 *ornamental garden*
summer house 256.7 *room*
summer lightning 55.21 *thunderstorm,* 439.4 *natural light*
summerlike 203.11 *summer*
summerly 203.18 *seasonally*
summer monsoon 55.17 *wind system*
Summer Olympics 674.2 *contest*
summer pudding 45.35 *dessert*
summer sale 739.4 *sale*
summer school 6.12 *educational institution*
summer soldier 538.12 *cheat,* 539.19 *hypocrite*
summer solstice 10.15 *holy day,* 203.3 *summer*
summertide 203.3 *summer*
summer time 192.3 *chronology*
summertime 203.3 *summer,* 408.5 *hot weather*
summer tree 85.12 *figurative usage*
summer wood 85.3 *timber*
summery 55.46 *seasonal,* 203.11 *summer,* 408.11 *warm*
summing up 183.2 *iteration,* 492.2 *verdict*
summing-up 16.7 *legal trial*
summit 126, 279, 34.5 *rock face,* 95.1 *mountain,* 144.1 *completeness,* 157.7 *limit,* 275.2 *heights,* 380.8 *sharp-pointed thing,* 568.5 *talks,* 611.5 *important,* 619.3 *perfection,* 653.7 *council,* 684.1 *completion,* 716.3 *discussion*
Summit 279
summital 279.5 *top*
summit conference 716.3 *discussion*
summit meeting 568.5 *talks,* 716.3 *discussion*
summit talks 568.5 *talks*
summon 16.70 *litigate,* 161.42 *call together,* 543.12 *signal,* 712.7 *demand,* 782.12 *desire,* 856.5 *accuse*
summoned 161.46 *assembled,* 856.8 *accusatory*
summoner 16.10 *law officer,* 543.8 *signer,* 692.6 *person in command*
summoning 543.16 *signalling*
summoning sound 543.4 *signal*
summons 16.6 *legal process,* 16.33 *litigation,* 543.6 *word,* 692.2, 712.2 *demand,* 856.1 *accusation*
summon spirits 11.22 *conjure*
summon up 355.15 *draw out,* 511.12 *remember,* 519.14 *imagine*
sum of money 741.5 *sum*
sumo wrestler 237.5, 679.3 *athlete*
sump 280.2 *foot,* 317.3 *cavity,* 605.4 *storage,* 614.6 *refuse,* 727.8 *sink*
sumpter 326.6 *beast of burden*
sumptuary 741.22 *monetary,* 748.10 *expending*
sumptuous 405.6 *pleasant,* 742.3 *opulent,* 811.24 *grand*
sumptuously 811.40 *grandly*
sumptuousness 742.7 *opulence,* 811.9 *grandeur*
sums 52.1 *mathematics,* 52.4 *simple arithmetic,* 170.1 *calculation*
sum total 142.2 *whole thing*
sum up 16.71 *try a case,* 130.6 *add,* 142.9 *be whole,* 169.10 *number,* 170.9 *add,* 183.17 *iterate,* 270.10 *shorten,* 492.11 *judge,* 552.4 *be concise,* 562.8 *summarize*
sun 777 Phobias by Topic, **53, 55,** 291.2 *central thing,* 363.4 *orbiting body,* 392.14 *desert,* 392.19 *bake,* 439.4 *natural light,* 543.1 *sign*
sunbaked 373.3 *hardened,* 392.8 *baked,* 408.11 *warm*
sunbath 408.5 *hot weather*

sunbathe 408.16 *feel hot*
sunbather 408.5 *hot weather*
sunbathing 55.22 *sun,* 408.5 *hot weather*
sunbeam 439.1 *light,* 439.4 *natural light*
sun bear 477 Placental Mammals
sun bed 630.14 *hospital*
sun-bed 408.5 *hot weather*
Sunbelt 249.8 *regions of the US,* 408.8 *hot place*
sunbird 78 Birds
sun bittern 78 Birds
sun block 634.2 *shelter*
sun-block 34.8 *mountaineering*
sun-block cream 34.4 *climbing equipment*
sunbonnet 293.5 *body covering,* 295.15 *headgear*
sunburn 55.22 *sun,* 408.5 *hot weather,* 449.3 *brownness,* 449.7 *brown*
sunburnt 447.3 *blackened,* 449.2 *browned,* 450.2 *red-faced*
sundae 45.35 *dessert*
sun dance 10.7 *non-Christian ritual*
Sunday 10.15 *holy day*
Sunday best 295.1 *dress,* 813.4 *formal dress*
Sunday go-to-meeting clothes 295.1 *dress*
Sunday lunch 350.12 *meal*
Sunday newspaper 533.5 *mass communication*
Sunday-opening laws 876.4 *self-righteousness*
Sunday painter 50.16 *artist*
Sunday paper 532.4 *newspaper*
Sunday school 6.12 *educational institution*
sun deck 408.8 *hot place*
sunder 136.9 *separate,* 136.14 *come between,* 162.12 *disperse,* 176.16 *halve*
sundered 136.16 *apart*
Sunderland 93 Cities
sundew 84 Flowers and Flowering Plants
sundial 191 Timepieces and Timers, 192.9 *hourglass,* 310.4 *angular measurement*
sundown 205.1 *evening*
sundowner 351.2 *drink*
sundress 295.7 *frock,* 295.21 *beachwear*
sun-dried 44.10 *ceramic,* 392.8 *baked,* 637.7 *preserved*
sun-dried brick 44.9 *industrial ceramics*
sundries 130.4 *extra,* 161.32 *miscellany,* 739.8 *merchandise*
sundry 113.6 *assorted,* 175.7 *various*
sun-dry 392.19 *bake,* 637.5 *preserve*
sun-drying 637.1 *preservation*
sunfish 80 Fishes
sunflower 84 Flowers and Flowering Plants, 451.3 *orange thing*
sunflower oil 45.7 *basic ingredient*
sunflower-seed meal 68.9 *animal feedstuff*
Sunflower State 84.9 *figurative usage*
sung 804.5 *entitled*
sunglasses 34.4 *climbing equipment,* 41.5 *ski equipment,* 56.29 *optical element,* 293.12 *protective covering,* 295.21 *beachwear,* 295.25 *accessories,* 435.10 *visual aid,* 440.6 *shade,* 634.2 *shelter*
Sung ware 44 Types of Ceramics
sun hat 293.12 *protective covering*
sunhat 295.15 *headgear,* 634.2 *shelter*
sun-hat 440.6 *shade*
sun helmet 634.2 *shelter*
sunk 244.15 *destroyed,* 277.12 *under,* 322.14 *holed,* 362.19 *fallen,* 722.16 *losing,* 770.6 *depressed*
sunken 276.7 *lowland,* 277.8 *deep,* 317.5 *concave,* 362.19 *fallen*

sunken-eyed 274.2 *emaciated*
sunken eyes 274.8 *emaciation*
sunken garden 69.2 *garden*
sunken reef 635.1 *trap*
sunk line 20.3 *fishing tackle*
sunlamp 408.5 *hot weather*
sun lamp 439.6 *electric light*, 630.14 *hospital*
sunless 440.8 *dark*, 441.5 *dim*
sunlessness 440.1 *darkness*
sunlight 53.15, 55.22 *sun*, 56.23, 439.1 *light*, 439.4 *natural light*
sunlit 439.18 *lit*
sun lounge 256.7 *room*, 408.8 *hot place*
sun lounger 69.3 *ornamental garden*
Sunna 1.8 *tradition*, 7.12 *religious text*
sunned 392.8 *baked*
Sunni 7 *Non-Christian Religions*
sunnier 55.45 *fine*
sunniness 392.14 *desert*, 769.3 *cheerfulness*
sunning 392.13 *drying*
Sunnite 7.6 *non-Christian*
sunny **439**, 55.45 *fine*, 392.5 *rainless*, 408.11 *warm*, 763.2 *likable*, 769.1 *cheerful*, 775.14 *cheering*
sunny period 55.23 *heat*
sunny South 392.14 *desert*
sunny spell 55.23 *heat*
sunny weather 55.23 *heat*
sun oneself 408.16 *feel hot*
sun porch 256.7 *room*
sun print 66.12 *development*
sunray lamp 439.6 *electric light*
sun rise **359**
sunrise 204.1 *morning*, 208.2 *early hour*, 332.4 *compass point*
sunrise and sunset 214.5 *regular thing*
sunrise industry 243.2 *manufacture*
sun roof **71** Motor Vehicle Parts
sun rose **84** Flowers and Flowering Plants
sunscreen 293.12 *protective covering*
sunset 205.1 *evening*, 205.4 *evening thing*, 209.2 *late hour*, 332.4 *compass point*, 360.4 *fall*, 450.7 *red thing*
sunshade 293.12 *protective covering*, 440.6 *shade*, 634.2 *shelter*
sunshine 53.15, 55.22 *sun*, 439.4 *natural light*
sunshine recorder 55.7 *weather instruments*
sunshine-yellow 452.1 *yellow*
sunshiny 439.19 *sunny*
sun spider **82** Arachnids
sunspot 53.15 *sun*, 456.4 *maculation*
sunspot cycle 53.15 *sun*
sun's total eclipse 213.4 *rare things*
sunstroke 55.22 *sun*, 408.5 *hot weather*
sunsuit 295.23 *children's clothes*
suntan 55.22 *sun*, 408.5 *hot weather*, 408.16 *feel hot*, 447.11 *blacken*, 449.3 *brownness*, 449.7 *brown*
suntan lotion 55.22 *sun*, 293.12 *protective covering*, 634.2 *shelter*
suntanned 447.3 *blackened*, 449.2 *browned*
suntanning 55.22 *sun*
suntan oil 634.2 *shelter*
Sun Temple **43** Noted Buildings
sunup 204.1 *morning*, 208.2 *early hour*
sun-up 359.3 *sun rise*
sun visor 440.6 *shade*
sun worship 9.2 *idolatry*
sun-worshipper 9.6 *idolater*, 55.22 *sun*, 408.5 *hot weather*
sun-worshipping 9.10 *idolatrous*
sup 350.24 *have a meal*, 351.2, 351.13 *drink*
Supay **8** Deities
super 51.22 *actor*, 126.12 *superior*, 617.1 *worthy*, 861.1 *good*

Super-8 66.14 *cine film*
superabound 357.4 *exaggerate*, 608.5 *about*, 610.4 *be excessive*
superabundance 132.4 *surplus*, 246.2 *productiveness*, 553.1 *diffuseness*, 608.8 *plenty*, 610.1 *excess*, 755.8 *abundance*
superabundant 132.10 *surplus*, 181.9 *ample*, 553.3 *diffuse*, 608.2 *plentiful*, 610.6 *excessive*, 755.3 *abundant*
superabundantly 132.11 *residually*
superadd 130.6 *add*
superaddition 130.1 *addition*, 130.4 *extra*
superannuate 349.2 *dismiss*
superannuated 200.20 *former*, 600.3 *not wanted*, 600.4 *disused*
superannuation 600.10 *disuse*
superb 126.15 *excellent*, 617.1 *worthy*, 619.1 *perfect*, 655.6 *skilful*, 811.24 *grand*, 861.1 *good*
superbike 33.5 *motorcycle racing*, 71.13 *motorcycle*
superbly 126.16 *superiorly*, 811.40 *grandly*, 861.22 *well*
superbness 861.8 *good*
Super Bowl 19.1 *football*
Supercalc 65.11 *application*
supercharged 235.16 *charged*
supercilious 805.14 *proud*, 809.10 *self-admiring*, 850.13 *contemptuous*
superciliously 809.21 *cockily*, 850.30 *contemptuously*
superciliousness 850.3 *contempt*
superclass 59.17 *taxonomy*
supercluster 53.7 *galaxy*
supercollider 235.8 *nuclear power*
supercomputer 65.3 *computer*
superconducting magnet 56.45 *superconductivity*, 56.60 *magnet*
superconductivity **56**, 235.7 *electrical power*
superconductor 56.45 *superconductivity*, 235.7 *electrical power*, 235.8 *nuclear power*
supercooled 55.43 *atmospheric*
supercooling 55.9 *atmospheric process*
super-duper 617.1 *worthy*
superego 11.7 *spirit*, 61.21 *psyche*, 368.6 *internal world*
supereminence 617.6 *worth*
supereminent 126.14 *best*
supererogation 610.3 *superfluity*
supererogatory 130.9 *extra*, 610.7 *superfluous*
superfamily 59.17 *taxonomy*
superficial **278**, 52.79 *spatial*, 104.8 *intruder*, 104.12 *external*, 145.4 *incomplete*, 248.11 *spatial*, 289.8 *apparent*, 303.7 *outward*, 437.1 *visible*, 457.8 *outer*, 468.11 *perfunctory*, 470.5 *indifferent*, 474.7 *sophistic*, 502.7 *semi-skilled*, 576.2 *changeable*, 612.4 *trivial*, 648.3 *hasty*, 656.4 *bungled*, 660.9 *easy*, 685.4 *uncompleted*, 720.11 *nonobservant*
superficial area 52.38 *surface*
superficiality 104.1 *extraneousness*, 145.1 *incompleteness*, 278.3 *shallowness*, 289.3 *appearance*, 468.1 *inattention*, 470.2 *indifference*, 502.2 *half-knowledge*, 612.7 *triviality*, 660.2 *simplicity*, 685.1 *noncompletion*, 720.1 *nonobservance*
superficially 102.19 *apparently*, 104.18 *extraneously*, 145.6 *incompletely*, 278.8 *shallowly*, 289.15 *externally*, 437.11 *visibly*, 457.15 *apparently*, 526.16 *manifestly*, 612.14 *unimportantly*, 660.21 *easily*, 685.7 *incompletely*, 720.15 *inattentively*
superficial wound 278.4 *shallow thing*
superficies 278.3 *shallowness*, 289.1 *exterior*, 457.3 *external appearance*
superfine 617.1 *worthy*, 861.1 *good*

superfluity **610**, 104.1 *extraneousness*, 130.4 *extra*, 132.4 *surplus*, 246.2 *productiveness*, 553.1 *diffuseness*, 600.8 *nonuse*, 607.3 *waste*, 608.8 *plenty*, 614.3 *uselessness*, 742.7 *opulence*, 754.2 *declining prices*, 757.5 *unrestrainedness*
superfluous **610**, 104.8 *intruder*, 130.9 *extra*, 132.10 *surplus*, 553.3 *diffuse*, 600.3 *not wanted*, 607.9 *waste*, 608.2 *plentiful*, 614.1 *useless*, 754.9 *cheap*
superfluously 104.18 *extraneously*, 130.10 *additionally*, 132.11 *residually*, 132.12 *with a remainder*, 600.12 *out of use*, 607.10 *wastefully*, 610.8 *excessively*
superfluousness 610.3 *superfluity*, 614.3 *uselessness*
superfly 617.1 *worthy*
super-G **18** Sporting Activities
supergiant 53.13 *luminosity*
supergiant elliptical 53.7 *galaxy*
super giant slalom race 41.3 *ski racing*
super giant slalom racing 41.3 *ski racing*
Supergirl 237.6 *muscleman*
superglue 138.3 *adhesive*, 138.7 *cause to adhere*
super G race 41.3 *ski racing*
supergrass 483.7 *person who gives evidence*, 528.10 *informer*, 530.4 *discloser*, 856.3 *accuser*
superheavy 57.34 *elemental*
superheavy element 57.6 *chemical element*
superhero 237.6 *muscleman*, 617.8 *exceller*
superhet receiver 534.18 *radio*
superhighway 71.2, 327.3 *road*
superhuman 659.10 *difficult*
superhumanity 11.2 *the occult*
superhuman task 659.3 *difficult task*
superimpose 130.6 *add*, 293.23 *cover*
superimposed 293.38 *covering*
superimposition 130.1 *addition*, 293.1 *covering*
superintend 166.16 *direct*, 653.1 *manage*
superintendence 653.3 *management*
superintendency 688.5 *position of authority*
superintendent 126.5 *superior*, 653.13 *director*, 653.15 *manager*
superior **126**, **126**, 115.4 *dissimilar*, 154.12 *primary*, 233.11 *influential*, 235.13 *powerful*, 237.10 *potent*, 275.10 *higher*, 611.4 *bigwig*, 611.5 *important*, 611.6 *notable*, 617.1 *worthy*, 627.14 *improved*, 653.13 *director*, 688.10 *person of authority*, 688.12 *authoritative*, 692.15 *self-assured*, 696.5 *company leader*, 861.1 *good*
Superior **94** Lakes, 94.3 *US lakes*
superioress 7.7 *monk*
superiority **126**, 12.3 *governance*, 123.1 *inequality*, 154.2 *priority*, 194.2 *greater importance*, 235.1 *power*, 237.1 *strength*, 611.1 *importance*, 617.6 *worth*, 619.3 *perfection*, 653.4 *directorship*, 688.1 *authority*, 850.3 *contempt*, 861.8 *good*
Superiority **126**
superiority complex 61.18 *complex*
superiorly **126**, 692.16 *commandingly*
superior person **861**, 611.4 *bigwig*
superior planet 53.16 *planet*
superior power 233 *influence*
superjock 617.8 *exceller*
superlative 5.44 *grammatical*, 126.14 *best*, 275.11 *exalted*, 541.1 *exaggeration*, 541.12 *exaggerated*, 617.1 *worthy*, 861.2 *best*, 861.9 *the best*

superlatively 5.52 *grammatically*, 126.16 *superiorly*, 126.17 *supremely*, 541.16 *exaggeratedly*
superman 126.6 *paragon*, 514.5 *surpriser*, 611.4 *bigwig*, 617.8 *exceller*, 682.4 *successful person*, 778.7 *courageous person*, 786.5 *person of wonder*, 861.16 *superior person*
Superman 237.6 *muscleman*
supermarket 350.17 *food shop*, 740.8 *store*
supermom 617.8 *exceller*
supernal 8.14 *heavenly*, 275.9 *high*, 368.8 *nonmaterial*
supernatant 57.33 *crystalline*
supernatant liquid 57.4 *crystal*
supernatural 8.13 *divine*, 11.14 *occult*, 104.12 *external*, 149.12 *extraterrestrial*, 368.9 *parapsychological*
supernatural being 8.5 *deity*
supernaturalism 11.1 *occultism*, 368.3 *spiritual world*
supernaturalist 11.12 *occultist*, 368.7 *believer in a nonmaterial world*
supernaturality 11.2 *the occult*
supernaturally 8.19 *divinely*, 11.25 *occultly*, 104.18, 149.18 *extraneously*, 368.13 *metaphysically*
supernaturalness 11.2 *the occult*
supernatural tale 48.2 *fiction*
supernature 11.2 *the occult*
supernormal 11.14 *occult*, 126.14 *best*
supernormalness 11.2 *the occult*
supernova 53.11 *stellar birth*, 213.4 *rare things*, 439.4 *natural light*
supernova remnant 53.11 *stellar birth*
supernumerary 51.21 *role*, 51.22 *actor*, 130.4, 130.9 *extra*, 605.7 *stored*
superoxide **57** Types of Compounds
superpatriot 481.7 *bigot*
superpatriotic 481.10 *discriminatory*
superpatriotically 481.17 *prejudicially*
superpatriotism 481.4 *social discrimination*
superphysical 11.14 *occult*
superphysicalness 11.2 *the occult*
superposition 130.1 *addition*
superpower 12.5 *political organization*, 91.1 *country*, 233.6 *group influence*, 249.4 *territorial division*
superpower diplomacy 676.1 *war*
superrealism **50** Western Art Styles and Movements
supersaturate 57.25 *solidify*
supersaturated 57.32 *solid*, 610.6 *excessive*
supersaturated solution 57.3 *phase*
supersaturation 610.1 *excess*
superscription 544.3 *means of identification*
supersede 155.22 *succeed*, 222.4 *be a substitute*, 349.5 *take the place of*, 581.2 *discard*, 600.6 *stop using*, 727.9 *dispose of*
superseded 16.57 *null*, 222.8 *substituted*, 600.4 *disused*
superseder 349.26 *ejector*
supersensible 11.14 *occult*, 368.9 *parapsychological*
supersensitiveness 11.2 *the occult*
supersession 222.1 *substitution*
supersonic 70.5 *transportable*, 329.1 *swift*
supersonically 70.6 *commercially*, 329.14 *swiftly*
supersonic flight 329.11 *swift thing*
supersonic speed 56.19 *sound propagation*, 329.8 *speed*
superstar 9.4 *idolized person*, 51.22 *actor*, 126.6 *paragon*, 861.16 *superior person*
superstition 7.1 *religion*, 9.2 *idol-*

atry, 497.2 *religious belief,* 504.6 *fallibility*
superstitious 9.10 *idolatrous*
superstitiously 11.26 *magically*
superstore 740.8 *store*
superstratum 266.1 *layer,* 279.4 *top layer,* 289.1 *exterior*
superstring 56.79 *fundamental interaction*
superstructural 63.32, 382.11 *structural*
superstructurally 382.18 *structurally*
superstructure 74 Parts of a Ship, **63,** 382.6 *construction*
supertanker 74 Ships and Boats
supertax 751.7 *tax*
supertonic 49.16 *musical note*
supervene 195.10 *succeed,* 227.7 *follow from*
supervention 130.1 *addition*
supervise 166.16 *direct,* 435.15 *watch,* 653.1 *manage*
supervised 15.8 *industrial*
supervise staff 653.1 *manage*
supervising 15.8 *industrial,* 332.5 *directions*
supervision 435.3 *observation,* 652.8 *treatment,* 653.3 *management*
supervisor 15.6 *employer,* 435.11 *observer,* 653.15 *manager*
supervisory 653.17 *managerial*
supervisory body 653.6 *governing body*
superwoman 126.6 *paragon,* 402.11 *liberated woman,* 514.5 *surpriser,* 682.4 *successful person,* 778.7 *courageous person,* 786.5 *person of wonder,* 861.16 *superior person*
supinate 28.5 *fence,* 362.8 *sit*
supinated 28.6 *fencing*
supination 28.3 *fencing movements,* 362.16 *courtesy*
supine 236.12 *imminent,* 276.5 *low,* 282.10 *lying,* 325.5, 362.23 *sedentary,* 673.5 *submitting*
supine floating 39.1 *swimming*
supineness 276.1 *lowness,* 282.1 *horizontality,* 673.1 *submission*
supper 350.12 *meal*
supper party 665.7 *social gathering,* 815.5 *party*
supping 350.4 *eating meals,* 351.1 *drinking*
supplant 155.22 *succeed,* 195.11 *follow in office,* 222.4 *be a substitute,* 252.16 *replace,* 349.5 *take the place of*
supplantation 252.3 *replacement*
supplanted 222.8 *substituted,* 252.10 *replaced,* 600.4 *disused*
supplanter 155.13 *replacement,* 222.2 *substitute person,* 349.26 *ejector*
supplanting 222.1 *substitution*
supple 224.13 *changeable,* 374.2 *pliant,* 377.6 *elastic,* 578.11 *equivocating,* 808.6 *servile*
supplely 377.11 *elastically*
supplement 128.1 *increase,* 128.5 *make bigger,* 130.1 *addition,* 130.6 *add,* 144.2 *fullness,* 144.4 *complete,* 155.8 *addition,* 201.5 *fresh start,* 201.20 *make new,* 219.1 *continuity,* 219.3 *continue,* 304.1 *rear,* 354.11 *thing inserted,* 532.4 *newspaper,* 662.26 *be useful,* 751.3 *fee*
supplemental 130.8 *additional,* 219.5 *continual,* 304.4 *rear*
supplementally 219.7 *continually*
supplementarily 128.8 *increasingly,* 130.10 *additionally*
supplementary 662, 128.6 *increasing,* 144.7 *complete,* 155.19 *additional,* 201.14 *renewed*
supplementary angles 52.39 *angle*
supplementary medicine 60.2 *natural medicine*
supplementary unit 75.2 *unit system*

supplementation 130.1 *addition*
supplemented 128.7 *increased*
supplementing 662.30 *helping*
suppleness 224.1 *changeableness,* 374.8 *softness,* 377.1 *elasticity,* 655.1 *skill,* 657.1 *cunning*
suppliant 712.4 *requester*
supplicant 9.5 *worshipper,* 9.9 *worshipful,* 10.17 *worshipper,* 712.4 *requester*
supplicate 10.20 *pray,* 712.6 *request*
supplicating 9.9 *worshipful*
supplication 9.1 *worship,* 10.3 *rite of worship,* 10.9 *prayer,* 712.1 *request*
supplicatory 9.9 *worshipful,* 10.21 *ritualistic*
supplied 606.8 *provisional*
supplier 13.9 *economist,* 606.3 *provider*
supplies 602, 350.7 *food,* 606.1 *provision,* 739.8 *merchandise*
supply 605, 144.6 *fill,* 222.2 *substitute person,* 243.10 *produce,* 594.5 *equip,* 594.11 *fitting out,* 602.6 *find means,* 605.6 *store,* 606.1, 606.5 *provision,* 637.5 *preserve,* 729.5 *give*
supply and demand 13.6 *economic factors*
supply base 605.4 *storage*
supplying 606.1 *provision,* 606.7 *provisioning,* 729.1 *giving*
supply line 606.1 *provision*
supply service 17.4 *military organization*
supply ship 679.24 *warship*
supply-side economics 13.3 *economic statistics*
supply staff 17.5 *military staff*
supply teacher 6.4 *educator,* 222.2 *substitute person*
support 130, 284, 284, 662, 662, 851, 4.22 *propound a philosophy,* 43.8 *column,* 51.22 *actor,* 51.32 *act,* 60.19 *practise medicine,* 116.7, 116.28 *consent,* 219.1 *continuity,* 219.3 *continue,* 225.3 *stabilizer,* 225.7 *make stable,* 230.4 *management,* 230.9 *take action,* 232.1 *instrumentality,* 232.4 *be an instrument,* 237.8 *strengthen,* 280.1, 280.4 *base,* 284.2 *supporting part,* 305.9 *side with,* 361.1 *raise,* 396.20 *support life,* 475.17 *prove,* 480.1 *verify,* 480.2 *prove,* 480.5 *proof,* 483.12 *prove,* 499.4 *assent,* 535.4 *confirmation,* 535.19 *confirm,* 580.3 *side with,* 602.4 *financial resources,* 603.1 *tool,* 606.1, 606.5 *provision,* 608.4 *suffice,* 632.2 *protection,* 632.9 *protect,* 634.1 *refuge,* 637.1 *preservation,* 637.5 *preserve,* 662.3 *sustenance,* 662.9 *patronage,* 662.11 *helper,* 662.20 *sustain,* 662.23 *advise,* 662.29 *finance,* 664.1 *cooperation,* 664.11 *cooperate,* 667.6 *agree with,* 671.22 *plead for,* 718.1 *protection,* 718.10 *secure,* 726.7 *detain,* 729.2 *gift,* 748.3 *donate,* 748.7 *donation,* 755.11 *give,* 767.2 *aid,* 775.4 *comfort,* 819.1 *friendship,* 831.8 *be benevolent,* 835.8 *pity,* 851.1 *approval*
Support 284
supportable 284
support an analogy 107.7 *relate to*
support civil rights 698.14 *be free*
supported 535, 43.16 *columned,* 116.17 *consenting,* 219.5 *continual,* 535.13 *supported,* 851.23 *approved*
support equal rights 698.14 *be free*
supporter 284, 662, 127.6 *inferior,* 138.5 *follower,* 295.18 *underwear,* 499.3 *assenter,* 535.9 *affirmer,* 671.13 *defender,* 729.4 *giver,* 767.5 *helper,* 851.7 *advocate,* 851.8 *admirer*
supporters 544.8 *heraldic device*

supporters' club 851.8 *admirer*
support financially 284
support fleet 17.4 *military organization*
support free love 698.19 *liberalize*
support human rights 698.14 *be free*
supporting 851, 280.3 *base,* 284.9 *supportive,* 662.30 *helping*
supporting actor 51.22 *actor*
supporting cast 51.23 *cast*
supporting character 51.21 *role*
supporting garment 284
supporting member 63.27 *superstructure*
supporting part 284, 51.21 *role*
supporting role 51.21 *role,* 127.1 *inferiority*
supportive 284, 662, 138.10 *tenacious,* 232.6 *instrumental,* 361.11 *raised,* 480.9 *verificatory,* 499.6 *assenting,* 535.10 *affirmative,* 664.17 *cooperative,* 819.11 *devoted,* 851.19 *supporting,* 855.11 *vindicatory*
supportive evidence 855.2 *defence*
supportively 232.9 *instrumentally,* 480.11 *verifiably,* 662.36 *helpfully,* 749.8 *profitably,* 819.19 *devotedly,* 855.15 *in vindication*
supportive statement 535.4 *confirmation*
supportive theory 61.3 *psychiatric treatment*
support life 396
support player 35.4 *rugby player*
support the church 7.19 *be religious*
support unit 17.4 *military organization*
support women's liberation 698.14 *be free,* 700.6 *treat equally*
supposability 518.2 *basis of supposition*
supposable 518.8 *supposed*
suppose 518, 4.20 *philosophize,* 4.22 *propound a philosophy,* 461.16 *have an idea,* 471.17 *theorize,* 472.10 *focus on,* 488.10 *think likely,* 497.8 *be of the opinion,* 516.1 *foresee,* 519.14 *imagine*
supposed 518, 472.7 *focused,* 497.14 *believed,* 800.4 *reputed*
supposedly 518, 4.25 *theoretically,* 472.14 *thematically,* 497.16 *believably*
supposer 518.4 *theorist*
suppose so 518.5 *suppose*
supposing 518, 106.15 *under the circumstances,* 518.7 *suppositional*
supposition 518, 4.1 *philosophy,* 52.65 *theory,* 461.6 *idea,* 471.2 *theory,* 472.1 *topic,* 497.1 *belief,* 535.2 *statement,* 654.1 *advice*
Supposition 518
suppositional 518, 461.10 *speculative,* 471.10 *theoretical,* 519.12 *imaginary,* 535.10 *affirmative*
supposititious 518.7 *suppositional*
suppositive 518.7 *suppositional,* 518.8 *supposed*
suppository 62.9 *pessary,* 354.11 *thing inserted,* 630.10 *surgical dressing*
suppress 690, 147.7 *exclude,* 231.3 *counteract,* 244.8 *destroy,* 362.5 *bear down on,* 525.1 *misinterpret,* 529.12 *keep secret,* 531.8 *conceal,* 546.2 *forget,* 563.15 *strike dumb,* 591.7 *be evasive,* 682.9 *be victorious,* 699.8 *restrain,* 701.7 *defeat,* 709.4 *censor,* 726.7 *detain*
suppressant 699.1 *restraint*
suppressed 690, 61.37 *subconscious,* 362.22 *overthrown,* 424.4 *faint,* 529.9 *secret,* 531.14 *concealed,* 699.13 *restraining*
suppressed desire 61.19 *defence*

mechanism
suppressing 62.14 *counteracting,* 699.13 *restraining,* 701.10 *dominating*
suppression 690, 61.19 *defence mechanism,* 147.1 *exclusion,* 231.1 *counteraction,* 244.1 *destruction,* 362.13 *submergence,* 525.2 *misinterpretation,* 529.1 *secrecy,* 531.4 *silence,* 546.5 *forgetfulness,* 591.15 *evasiveness,* 699.1 *restraint,* 701.2 *domination,* 709.1 *veto,* 726.2 *detention*
suppressive 231.4 *counteracting,* 591.18 *avoiding,* 699.13 *restraining,* 701.10 *dominating,* 709.5 *vetoed*
suppressively 709.7 *by veto*
suppurate 349.14 *let out,* 353.18 *fester,* 628.2 *decay*
suppurated 387.16 *rheumy*
suppurating 387.16 *rheumy,* 626.7 *toxic*
suppuration 353.7 *pus,* 387.3 *body fluid,* 387.6 *flow,* 624.6 *infection,* 626.1 *lack of hygiene*
suppurative 353.27 *purulent,* 387.16 *rheumy*
supramundane 8.13 *divine,* 11.18 *spiritual*
supranatural 11.14 *occult*
supranaturalism 11.1 *occultism*
supranature 11.2 *the occult*
suprarenal gland 352 Endocrine Glands
supremacy 8.2 *divine attribute,* 12.3 *governance,* 126.1 *superiority,* 154.2 *priority,* 166.8 *authority,* 194.2 *greater importance,* 611.1 *importance,* 688.1 *authority,* 861.9 *the best*
suprematism 50 Western Art Styles and Movements
suprematist 50.29 *realist*
supreme 8.13 *divine,* 126.14 *best,* 154.23 *primary,* 166.12 *ruling,* 275.11 *exalted,* 279.5 *top,* 611.5 *important,* 617.2 *best,* 619.1 *perfect,* 688.12 *authoritative,* 696.13 *excellent,* 861.2 *best*
Supreme Being 226.7 *Prime Mover*
supreme control 12.3 *governance,* 653.4 *directorship*
Supreme Court judge 696.3 *leader*
Supreme Court Justice 16.9 *lawmaker*
Supreme Court of Judicature 16.20 *British court*
supreme issue 611.3 *chief thing*
supremely 126, 8.19 *divinely,* 154.23 *primarily,* 611.9 *importantly,* 688.23 *authoritatively,* 696.16 *masterfully*
Supreme Soviet 653.10 *legislative body*
Surabaya 93 Cities
suramin 62 Medication
surbahar 49 Musical Instruments
surcharge 369.6 *displacement,* 610.4 *be excessive,* 750.9 *settle accounts,* 751.3 *fee,* 753.2 *unfair price,* 753.10 *overcharge*
surcoat 295.12 *coat*
surd 52.17 *multiplication,* 169.6 *power,* 169.9 *fractional,* 563.4 *whispering,* 563.9 *voiceless*
sure 199.12 *predictable,* 225.11 *determined,* 480.10 *verified,* 490.1 *certain,* 490.2 *convinced,* 497.11 *believing,* 513.5 *expecting,* 513.7 *expected,* 554.3 *emphatic,* 632.5 *safe,* 688.15 *true,* 714.15 *future,* 718.6 *secure,* 857.4 *honourable*
sure bet 486.3 *strong possibility*
sure defence 632.2 *protection*
sure enough 480.12 *assuredly*
sure-enough 537.19 *authentic*
surefire 682.13 *successful*
sure-fire winner 682.4 *successful person*
surefooted 682.13 *successful*
sure-footed 655.6 *skilful*
surely 718, 480.12 *assuredly,*

490.23 *certainly*, 490.25 *inevitably*, 571.19 *necessarily*, 688.25 *authentically*, 714.18 *potentially*
sureness 490.10 *conviction*
sure sign 543.1 *sign*
sure thing 229.2 *chance*, 486.3 *strong possibility*, 490.12 *something certain*, 589.5 *good chance*, 660.6 *easy thing*
sure-thing 32.7 *horseracing*
surety 16.6 *legal process*, 480.4 *verification*, 490.9 *certainty*, 490.10 *conviction*, 632.2 *protection*, 714.5 *promise-maker*
sure winner 682.5 *victorious person*
surf 54.14, 97.3 *wave*
surface 52, 293, 305, 5.43 *phrasal*, 20.8 *angling*, 54.5 *earth*, 74.10 *sail*, 104.4 *externality*, 248.1 *space*, 248.11 *spatial*, 278.2 *superficial*, 278.3 *shallowness*, 279.4 *top layer*, 289.1, 289.6 *exterior*, 289.8 *apparent*, 289.11 *be exterior*, 303.7 *outward*, 327.4 *road surface*, 347.10 *emerge*, 359.17 *spring up*, 370.9 *be light*, 383.1 *texture*, 437.1 *visible*, 437.6 *visible thing*, 457.3 *external appearance*, 457.8 *outer*, 457.12 *become visible*
surface appearance 289.3 *appearance*
surface area 52.38 *surface*
surface chemistry 57
surface current 54.13 *ocean current*
surface feature 54.7 *landform*
surface integral 52.31 *differentiation*
surface mail 534.2 *postal communication*
surface measurement 52.38 *surface*
surface of revolution 52.45 *curved surface*
surface plug 20.2 *artificial fly*
surface show 303.3 *show*
surface structure 5.24 *phrasing*, 5.29 *grammar*
surface tension 56.10 *force*
surface texture 383.1 *texture*
surface-to-air missile 680.5 *missile weapon*
surface wave 54.23 *seismic wave*, 365.5 *wave*
surface wind 55.12 *wind*
surfacing 293.11 *paving*, 347.15 *outgoing*, 359.1 *ascent*
surfboat 74 Ships and Boats
surfeit 132.4 *surplus*, 610.3 *superfluity*
surf fishing 20.1 *angling*
surficial 54.50 *terrestrial*
surfing 18 Sporting Activities
surge 96.6 *river flow*, 96.7 *flow*, 97.3 *wave*, 97.10 *billow*, 128.2 *spread*, 128.4 *increase*, 161.22 *flood*, 161.40 *crowd*, 347.11 *run out*, 359.2 *upturn*, 359.13 *ascend*, 364.4 *vortex*, 364.10 *swirl*, 423.1 *loudness*, 642.12 *be active*
surge back 97.10 *billow*
surge forward 241.7 *be violent*
surgeon 60.11 *doctor*, 60.13 *medical specialist*, 136.8 *person who separates*, 322.3 *person who opens*, 629.12 *repairer*, 630.15 *healer*
surgeonfish 80 Fishes
surgeon's knot 74 Knots
surgery 60, 630, 60.3 *medical specialty*, 60.8 *treatment*, 60.10, 630.14 *hospital*
surgical 60.22, 630.18 *medical*
surgical air strike 670.13 *air attack*
surgical assistant 60.17 *paramedic*
surgical dressing 630, 293.6 *medical covering*
surgical intervention 60.9 *surgery*
surgical knife 380.10 *knife*
surgically 60.26 *medically*, 630.21 *remedially*

surgical mask 293.6 *medical covering*
surgical operation 60.9, 630.12 *surgery*
surgical registrar 60.11 *doctor*
surgical treatment 60.8 *treatment*, 60.9 *surgery*
surging 96.10 *fluvial*, 97.7 *oceanic*, 423.1 *loudness*
Surinam 91 Countries
Surinam toad 79 Amphibians
surliness 818.1 *discourtesy*, 830.1 *sullenness*
surly 656.3 *clumsy*, 818.5 *discourteous*, 830.6 *sullen*, 830.7 *irritable*
surmisable 518.8 *supposed*
surmise 4.20 *philosophize*, 461.6 *idea*, 461.16 *have an idea*, 492.1 *judgment*, 492.12 *estimate*, 497.1 *belief*, 497.8 *be of the opinion*, 516.1 *foresee*, 518.3 *conjecture*, 518.5 *suppose*
surmised 518.8 *supposed*
surmiser 4.10 *philosopher*, 518.4 *theorist*
surmount 95.9 *tower*, 275.15 *be high*, 279.7 *top*, 357.3 *exceed*, 359.14 *climb*, 682.7 *overcome obstacles*
surmounted 357.14 *surpassing*
surnaj 49 Musical Instruments
surname 560.8 *name*
surpass 123.5 *be unequal*, 126.8 *be superior*, 357.3 *exceed*, 617.9 *be worthy*
surpass belief 786.10 *be wonderful*
surpassing 357, 126.12 *superior*, 674.14 *contending*
surpassingly 126.16 *superiorly*
surplice 7.11 *vestment*
surplus 132, 132, 130.4, 130.9 *extra*, 132.3 *difference*, 143.1 *part*, 357.9 *excessiveness*, 357.12 *excessive*, 608.8 *plenty*, 610.3 *superfluity*, 610.7 *superfluous*
surplusage 610.3 *superfluity*
surprisal 514.3 *shock*
surprise 514, 514, 489.5 *unexpectedness*, 515.6 *disappoint*, 595.8 *lack of preparation*, 595.12 *be unprepared*, 635.1, 635.3 *trap*, 670.1 *attack*, 786.1 *wonder*, 786.10 *be wonderful*
Surprise 514
surprise attack 633.5 *danger*, 670.12 *military attack*
surprise blow 670.12 *military attack*
surprised 514, 595.1 *unprepared*, 786.8 *wondering*
surprise offensive 670.12 *military attack*
surprise party 665.7 *social gathering*, 815.5 *party*
surpriser 514
surprising 514, 786.8 *wonderful*
surprisingly 514, 595.15 *spontaneously*, 786.13 *wonderfully*
surprising thing 514
surreal 547.13 *representational*, 560.13 *representing*
surrealism 48 Literary Groups and Movements, **50** Western Art Styles and Movements
surrealistic 48.16 *literary*, 547.13 *representational*, 560.13 *representing*
surrebuttal 484.1 *counterevidence*
surrejoinder 484.1 *counterevidence*
surrender 598.1 *relinquish*, 598.3 *relinquishment*, 673.1, 673.1 *submission*, 675.1 *submit*, 675.1 *peace*, 675.6 *make peace*, 683.7 *be defeated*, 705.1 *resignation*, 705.5 *resign*, 727.9 *dispose of*, 729.1 *giving*
surrendered 598.5 *relinquished*
surrenderer 667.5 *assenter*, 701.5 *subjected person*
surrendering 673.5 *submitting*, 729.1 *giving*
surrender oneself 7.19 *be religious*

surrender one's life 397.16 *meet one's fate*
surrender one's ticket 344.4 *land*
surrender treaty 667.2 *contract*
surreptitious 529.10 *secretive*, 539.34 *deceiving*
surreptitiousness 539.1 *deception*
surrey 71 Carriages and Carts
Surrey 48 Poets, **92** Counties
surrogacy 222.1 *substitution*, 632.2 *protection*
surrogate 61, 222.2 *substitute person*, 222.7 *substitute*, 293.21 *substitution*, 293.34 *cover for*, 293.40 *substitutive*, 632.7 *tutelary*, 707.2 *alternative*
surrogate mother 222.2 *substitute person*, 293.21 *substitution*
surrogation 222.1 *substitution*
surround 297, 258.20 *extend*, 258.21 *put in a container*, 289.11 *be exterior*, 293.25 *wrap*, 297.7 *surround*, 299.3 *edge*, 301.5 *enclose*, 313.6 *circle*, 334.5 *encircle*, 363.7 *ring*, 670.4 *besiege*, 676.13 *be at war*
surrounded 297, 258.20 *containing*, 633.4 *endangered*
surrounding 297, 106.7, 251.8 *circumstantial*, 256.15 *environmental*
surroundings 297, 106.1 *circumstances*, 256.2 *environment*, 264.3 *near place*, 289.1 *exterior*
Surroundings 297
Sursum Corda 10.9 *prayer*
Surt 8 Deities
surtax 751.7 *tax*
surtax bracket 742.5 *wealth*
Surtees 18 Sporting Personalities
surtitle 49.4 *opera*
surtout 295.12 *coat*
surveillance 435.3 *observation*, 467.3 *carefulness*, 469.5 *watchfulness*, 632.2 *protection*, 653.3 *management*, 671.5 *self-defence*
surveillant 632.3 *protector*
survey 2.2 *sociological research*, 4.4 *philosophical investigation*, 4.20 *philosophize*, 54.65 *map*, 63.30 *engineer*, 142.3 *whole situation*, 250.11 *find*, 268.1 *measurement*, 268.10 *measure*, 299.1, 299.5 *outline*, 435.3 *observation*, 435.14 *inspect*, 467.12 *scrutinize*, 469.11 *care for*, 477.2 *questioning*, 477.17 *question*, 492.1 *judgment*, 492.12 *estimate*, 547.11 *paint*, 561.1 *dissertation*, 561.4 *dissertate*, 562.1 *summary*, 692.7 *overview*
surveyed 250.8 *locational*, 268.13 *measured*, 477.16 *questioned*
surveying 63.17 *civil engineering*, 250.5 *topography*, 268.1 *measurement*, 467.7 *watchful*
survey map 547.7 *map*
surveyor 63.18 *civil engineer*, 170.7 *mathematician*, 268.9 *measurer*, 477.9 *questioner*, 492.5 *judge*
surveyor's chain 75 General Units
surveyor's measure 75.1 *unit*
survivability 237.1 *strength*, 378.6 *toughness*, 396.5 *life cycle*
survival 39.11 *swimming*, 99.6 *continuing existence*, 132.1 *remainder*, 188.4 *long-lastingness*, 200.7 *thing of the past*, 217.1 *permanence*, 219.2 *protraction*, 396.5 *life cycle*
survival device 39.3 *survival swimming*
survival of the fittest 59.16 *evolution*, 674.1 *contention*
survival swimming 39
survive 671, 83.22 *be dormant*, 99.11 *continue to be*, 132.7 *be left*, 188.6 *last*, 217.5 *be permanent*, 219.4 *protract*, 378.10 *be tough*, 396.16 *live*, 575.9 *endure*, 629.4 *be restored*, 632.8 *be*

safe, 638.5 *escape*
survive from the past 202.16 *be old*
survive one's spouse 824.10 *be widowed*
surviving 99.12 *lasting*, 132.9 *remaining*, 217.7 *permanent*, 396.12 *alive*, 575.10 *persevering*
surviving spouse 824
survivor 132.6 *person remaining*, 396.1 *life*, 638.3 *escaper*, 824.6 *surviving spouse*
Surya 8 Deities
Susan B. Anthony dollar 741.8 *American money*
Susa-no-o 8 Deities
susceptibilities 759.3 *feelings*
susceptibility 6.10 *educatability*, 228.6 *suggestibility*, 234.2 *attitude*, 403.2 *ability to sense*, 586.7 *persuadability*, 633.7 *vulnerability*, 760.5 *sensitivity*, 821.3 *lovingness*
susceptible 403, 6.17 *educatable*, 228.13 *suggestible*, 374.7 *impressionable*, 633.3 *vulnerable*, 759.10 *feeling*, 760.1 *sensitive*
susceptibly 6.26 *studiously*, 228.14 *influentially*, 374.18 *softheartedly*
susceptivity 586.7 *persuadability*
sushi 45.54 *other dishes*
suslik 77 Placental Mammals
suspect 471.17 *theorize*, 477.10 *person questioned*, 477.20 *doubt*, 491.18 *be uncertain*, 497.8 *be of the opinion*, 498.7 *disbelieved*, 498.8 *disbelieve*, 518.5 *suppose*, 781.5 *be cautious*, 786.12 *wonder whether*, 856.4 *accused person*
suspected 471.10 *theoretical*, 498.7 *disbelieved*
suspect on the lam 590.7 *the hunted*, 591.17 *avoider*
suspend 283, 16.77 *annul*, 147.8 *eject*, 160.12 *discontinue*, 209.8 *delay*, 218.9 *pause*, 283.12 *interrupt*, 325.9 *make motionless*, 349.2 *dismiss*, 349.3 *disbar*, 600.6 *stop using*, 643.14 *make inactive*, 704.6 *cancel*, 704.7 *terminate*, 709.3 *veto*, 879.1 *punish*
suspended 240, 283, 16.57 *null*, 160.10 *interrupted*, 209.10 *held up*, 236.10 *powerless*, 283.9 *interrupted*, 325.5 *sedentary*, 600.1 *unused*, 641.3 *inactive*, 704.10 *cancelled*, 709.5 *vetoed*
suspended animation 404.2 *unconsciousness*
suspended cymbal 283.3 *suspended object*
suspended note 49.19 *tempo*
suspended object 283
suspender 137.8 *fastening*, 283.4 *hanger*, 295.20 *legwear*
suspender belt 283.4 *hanger*, 295.18 *underwear*
suspenders 137.8 *fastening*
suspend growth 83.22 *be dormant*
suspend hostilities 218.9 *pause*, 677.5 *make peace*
suspendibility 283.1 *suspension*
suspendible 283.7 *suspended*
suspense 325.1 *motionlessness*, 513.1 *expectation*
suspense account 750.1 *accounts*
suspension 71 Motor Vehicle Parts, **283**, 49.19 *tempo*, 133.2 *mixed thing*, 140.4 *compound*, 147.2 *ejection*, 160.4 *interruption*, 209.3 *delayed action*, 218.3 *pause*, 283.6 *interruption*, 325.1 *motionlessness*, 349.18 *dismissal*, 387.10 *solution*, 600.8 *nonuse*, 641.1 *inaction*, 643.5 *inactivity*, 704.1 *cancellation*, 704.2 *termination*, 709.1 *veto*, 879.7 *punishment*
Suspension 283
suspension bridge 63.21 *bridge*, 283.3 *suspended object*, 327.9

bridge

suspension of disbelief 497.3 *believing*

suspension of hostilities 218.3 *pause*, 677.1 *pacification*

suspension system 377.5 *spring*

suspensive 283.7 *suspended*

suspensively 283.13 *pendulously*

suspensiveness 283.1 *suspension*

suspicion 491, 133.4 *admixture*, 182.1 *few*, 471.2 *theory*, 498.1 *disbelief*, 501.2 *information*, 518.2 *basis of supposition*, 518.3 *conjecture*, 542.6 *suggestion*, 781.1 *caution*, 841.2 *distrust*

suspicious 477.14 *questionable*, 491.1 *uncertain*, 498.6 *disbelieving*, 498.7 *disbelieved*, 781.4 *cautious*, 801.4 *disreputable*, 841.5 *distrustful*

suspiciously 477.24 *questionably*, 491.23 *uncertainly*, 498.10 *disbelievingly*, 841.9 *jealously*

suspiciousness 491.10 *suspicion*, 498.1 *disbelief*, 841.2 *distrust*

Susquehanna 96 *Rivers*

suss 471.14 *have an idea*, 501.4 *intellect*, 501.13 *get to know*

sussed 6.19, 501.8 *knowledgeable*

Sussex 68 *Breeds of Cattle*, **68** *Breeds of Fowl*

Sus'sistinnako 8 *Deities*

suss out 787.6 *understand*

sussultatory 365.17 *waving*

sustain 662, 101.12 *establish reality*, 217.6 *make permanent*, 219.3 *continue*, 230.9 *take action*, 237.8 *strengthen*, 284.14 *give moral support*, 350.25 *provide food*, 480.2, 483.12 *prove*, 575.7 *maintain*, 637.5 *preserve*

sustained 212.3 *frequent*, 217.7 *permanent*, 219.5 *continual*, 269.1 *long*

sustained climbing 34.1 *mountaineering*

sustained note 49.21 *tone*

sustainer 284.8 *supporter*

sustaining 284.9 *supporting*, 350.27 *edible*, 662.32 *supportive*

sustainingly 212.1 *frequently*

sustaining pedal 427.5 *resonator*

sustainment 212.4 *frequency*, 284.7 *financial support*, 662.3 *sustenance*

sustentation 662.3 *sustenance*

sustention 662.3 *sustenance*

Susu 5 *Languages and Groups of Languages*

susurrate 428.8 *sound faint*, 429.4 *hiss*

susurration 424.1 *faintness*, 428.4 *faint sound*, 429.1 *hiss*

Sutcliffe 18 *Sporting Personalities*

sutemi-waza 26.7 *judo*

Sutherland 49 *Musicians and Composers*

sutler 606.3 *provider*, 739.11 *pedlar*, 739.14 *street trader*

sutra 7.12 *religious text*

suttee 398.7 *suicide*, 710.7 *martyr*

suture 60.9 *surgery*, 60.20 *practise surgery*, 135.3 *unification*, 135.5 *joint*, 135.10 *link*

Suwa 8 *Deities*

Suwannee 96 *Rivers*

suzerain 688.14 *governmental*, 696.3 *leader*

suzerainty 12.3, 688.4 *governance*, 692.3 *authority*

svelte 274.1 *thin*

Svengali 228.7 *motivator*

Sverdlovsk 93 *Cities*

Svevo 48 *Writers*

swab 392.15 *dryer* , 392.20 *absorb*, 621.10 *cleaning object*,

---

621.13 *clean*, 630.10 *surgical dressing*, 656.10 *unskilled person*, 679.27 *naval man*

swabber 392.15 *dryer* , 621.12 *cleaner*

swabbie 74.7 *nautical person*, 679.27 *naval man*

swabby 676.11 *recruit*

swaddle 135.10 *link*, 295.32 *dress*

swaddling clothes 295.23 *children's clothes*

swag 16.36 *stolen property*, 258.8 *bag*, 360.10 *droop*, 365.4, 365.11 *rock*, 366.25 *pitch*, 681.2 *spoils*, 721.5 *profit*, 734.5 *takings*, 736.4 *stolen goods*, 741.2 *cash*

swagger 324.12 *gait*, 805.27 *be ostentatious*, 807.24 *be vain*, 811.29 *show off*

swaggerer 679.1 *combatant*, 805.13 *proud person*, 807.12 *impudent person*

swaggering 805.22, 809.13 *boastful*, 811.10 *exhibitionism*, 811.25 *vain*

swaggeringly 805.35 *ostentatiously*, 811.41 *vainly*

Swahili 5 *Languages and Groups of Languages*

swain 401.2 *male*, 821.9 *lover*, 826.5 *courting person*

Swale 96 *Rivers*

Swaledale 68 *Breeds of Sheep*

swallow 78 *Birds*, 39.11 *swimming*, 62.19 *administer*, 329.12 *swift animal*, 348.4 *intake*, 348.11 *ingest*, 350.21 *eat*, 351.2, 351.13 *drink*, 497.7 *believe*, 607.1 *waste*

swallow dive 39.6 *diving*

swallow hook, line, and sinker 497.7 *believe*

swallowing 777 *Phobias by Topic*, 348.4 *intake*, 350.1 *eating*, 351.1 *drinking*

swallow insults 808.8 *be servile*

swallow-like 78.23 *avian*

swallow lock, stock, and barrel 482.11 *not discriminate*

swallow one's medicine 840.7 *be punished*

swallow one's pride 806.20 *submit*

swallows 161 *Collective Names by Animal*

swallowtail 176.8 *half*, 544.7 *flag*

swallowtail butterfly 82 *Insects*

swallow the pill 673.4 *succumb*

swallow up 244.12 *consume*

swami 688.10 *person of authority*, 696.9 *educational leader*

Swammerdam 52 *Scientists*

swamp 96.7 *flow*, 98.3 *marsh*, 144.6 *fill*, 181.12 *overcrowd*, 244.12 *consume*, 278.4 *shallow thing*, 389.29 *water*, 391.8 *marsh*, 659.6 *critical situation*

swamp boat 74 *Ships and Boats*

swamp buggy 71 *Motor Vehicles*

swamp cypress 85 *Trees and Shrubs*

swamped 96.11 *flooded*, 144.8 *full*, 236.12 *impotent*, 389.24 *flooded*

swamp eel 80 *Fishes*

swamp-forest 98.3 *marsh*

swampiness 391.7 *bogginess*

swampland 98.3 *marsh*

swampy 98.11 *continental*, 391.11 *marshy*

swan 78 *Birds*, 78.3 *water bird*, 446.9 *white thing*

Swan 52 *Scientists*, **53** *The Constellations*

swan around 811.29 *show off*

swanherd 68.16 *farm worker*

swank 797.2 *pretender*, 797.4 *be affected*, 805.10 *boastfulness*, 805.13 *proud person*, 805.27 *be ostentatious*, 807.24 *be vain*, 809.3 *cockiness*, 809.7 *vain person*, 809.16 *show off*, 811.2

---

airs, 811.15 *showman*, 811.30 *put on airs*

swankily 805.35 *ostentatiously*, 809.21 *cockily*, 811.33 *loftily*, 811.40 *grandly*, 811.41 *vainly*

swankiness 811.9 *grandeur*

swankpot 805.13 *proud person*

swanky 797.3 *affected*, 805.22 *boastful*, 809.11 *cocky*, 811.17 *lofty*, 811.24 *grand*, 811.25 *vain*

Swan Lake 46.11 *classical ballets*

Swan Nebula 53 *Nebulae*

swannery 78.19 *ornithology*

swan's-down 67 *Natural Fabrics*, 78.17 *plumage*, 374.11 *soft thing*, 376.8 *smooth thing*

Swansea 93 *Cities*, 93.4 *British cities*

swan song 155.9 *conclusion*, 157.3 *death*, 397.7 *dying day*, 596.5 *attempt*, 684.2 *conclusion*, 774.2 *lament*

swap 109.1 *interchange*, 109.7 *reciprocate*, 216.4, 216.10 *exchange*, 222.1 *substitution*, 222.6 *give a substitute*, 223.1, 223.5 *exchange*, 326.1, 326.11 *transfer*, 737.1, 737.4 *trade*

swap ideas 624.6 *consult*

swapped 109.4 *reciprocal*, 222.8 *substituted*, 223.7 *exchanged*

swapper 224.4 *editor*

swapping 223.1 *exchange*, 737.13 *mercantile*

sward 87.2 *grassland*, 453.8 *greenness*

swardy 87.9 *grassy*

swarf 143.8 *bits and pieces*

swarm 161 *Collective Names for Birds and Animals*, 82.4 *social insect*, 82.16 *infest*, 128.4 *increase*, 161.20 *crowd*, 161.23 *flock*, 161.40 *crowd*, 181.4 *throng*, 181.11 *crowd*, 246.6 *be fertile*, 273.7 *thicken*, 608.5 *about*

swarm in 346.12 *flood in*

swarming 161.50 *crowded*, 273.2 *dense*, 357.11 *overrun*, 610.6 *excessive*

swarm like ants 181.11 *crowd*

swarm like bees around a honeypot 181.11 *crowd*

swarm like flies 181.11 *crowd*

swarm over 590.12 *aim at*, 734.7 *take*

swarm up 359.13 *ascend*

swarm with 82.16 *infest*, 610.4 *be excessive*

swart 447.2 *dark*

swarthily 447.12 *blackly*

swarthiness 440.3 *dark colour*, 447.7 *blackness*

swarthy 440.10 *dark-coloured*, 447.2 *dark*

swartness 447.7 *blackness*

swash 96.7 *flow*

swashbuckler 679.1 *combatant*, 811.15 *showman*

swashbuckling 811.10 *exhibitionism*

swash-buckling 811.25 *vain*

swash-bucklingly 811.41 *vainly*

swashing 389.8 *watering*

swastika 11.6 *talisman*, 543.1 *sign*

swat 330.3 *hit*, 330.13 *blow*

swatch 143.7 *piece*

swathe 68.11 *farmland*, 68.17 *farm*, 135.10 *link*, 293.25 *wrap*, 295.32 *dress*, 320.9 *enfold*, 630.20 *doctor*

swathed 293.37 *protected*

swather 68.10 *farm tool*

swathing 320.3 *enfoldment*

sway 12.3 *governance*, 123.5 *be unequal*, 126.2 *leadership*, 166.8 *authority*, 214.7 *be regular*, 224.11 *be changeable*, 233.3 *personal influence*, 235.1 *power*, 365.4 *rock*, 365.8 *oscillate*, 365.11 *rock*, 366.11 *stagger*, 366.25 *pitch*, 576.5 *vacillate*, 640.1 *action*, 640.4 *act*, 653.1 *manage*, 688.2 *governance*, 692.3 *authority*

---

swaying 123.3 *unequal*, 224.13 *changeable*, 365.16 *rocking*

sway the crowd 474.11 *practise sophistry*

Swazi 5 *Peoples*, **5** *Languages and Groups of Languages*

Swaziland 91 *Countries*

swear 5.45 *use language*, 483.11 *give evidence*, 535.17 *affirm*, 535.18 *vow*, 714.7 *promise*, 818.8 *get angry*, 822.17 *anger*, 827.5 *curse*

swear a false oath 538.21 *lie*

swear an indictment 856.5 *accuse*

swear an oath 535.18 *vow*

swear an oath of allegiance 535.18 *vow*

swear by 497.7 *believe*

swear by all that is holy 535.18 *vow*

swearer 480.7 *verifier*, 535.9 *affirmer*, 714.5 *promise-maker*

swear falsely 484.8 *reverse*

swear in 535.18 *vow*

swearing 822, 535.1 *affirmation*, 714.1 *promise*, 818.6 *bad-mannered*, 822.13 *angry*, 827.1 *curse*, 827.8 *cursing*

swearing in 535.3 *vow*

swearingly 827

swearing off 727.1 *disposal*

swearing-off 536.4 *renunciation*

swearing on the Bible 535.3 *vow*, 714.1 *promise*

swear like a trooper 827.5 *curse*

swear off 536.9 *renounce*, 578.4 *recant*, 598.1 *relinquish*, 727.9 *dispose of*, 869.5 *be self-restrained*

swear on oath 535.18 *vow*, 714.7 *promise*

swear on one's mother's life 714.7 *promise*

swear on the Bible 535.18 *vow*

swear on the Holy Bible 714.7 *promise*

swear till one is blue in the face 827.5 *curse*

swear to 483.11 *give evidence*

swear to God 535.18 *vow*

swear to tell the truth 16.70 *litigate*

swearword 5, 827.1 *curse*

sweat 353, 353, 347.2 *outflow*, 347.12 *leak*, 349.14 *let out*, 352.2 *secreted substance*, 352.7 *secrete*, 387.3 *body fluid*, 387.25 *flow*, 389.4 *exudate*, 389.32, 391.16 *wet*, 408.1 *heat*, 408.16 *feel hot*, 419.2 *something that makes an unpleasant smell*, 596.2 *try hard*, 636.2 *danger signal*, 640.4 *act*, 644.1, 644.6 *work*, 821.24 *be in love*

sweatband 295.15 *headgear*

sweat blood 644.6 *work*, 644.8 *exert oneself*, 777.14 *worry*

sweatbread 45.31 *offal*

sweater 295, 293.5 *body covering*

sweat for nothing 614.9 *waste effort*

sweat gland 352 *Exocrine Glands*, 77.2 *mammalian characteristic*, 322.4 *body orifice*, 352.3 *gland*

sweatily 352.8 *glandularly*, 353.33 *scatologically*, 387.26 *fluidly*

sweatiness 408.1 *heat*, 419.1 *stench*

sweating 347.2 *outflow*, 352.1 *secretion*, 352.4 *secretory*, 353.8 *sweat*, 353.28 *sweaty*, 391.12 *seeping*, 644.10 *working*

sweating sickness 624.4 *disease*, 624.7 *tropical disease*

sweat like a trooper 353.19 *sweat*

sweat of one's brow 644.1 *work*, 644.4 *exertion*

sweat of one's brows 353.8 *sweat*

sweat scraper 32.14 *horse-riding terms*

sweat shirt 295.4 *informal dress*,

295.8 *shirt*
sweatshop 647.1 *workshop*
sweat socks 295.20 *legwear*
sweaty 353, 55.52 *humid,*
349.29 expulsive, 352.4 secre-
tory, 419.3 *stinking*
sweaty socks 419.2 *something*
that makes an unpleasant smell
swede 45 *Vegetables*
Sweden 91 *Countries*
Swedenborg 4 *Philosophers*
Swedenborgianism 7 Christian
Movements
swedes 68.12 *crop*
Swedish 5 Languages and
Groups of Languages, 30.11
gymnastic
Swedish gymnastics 30.1 *gymnastics*
Swedish Half-bred 32 Breeds of
Horse and Pony
Swedish mile 75 Some Foreign
Units
Swedish Red-and-White 68
Breeds of Cattle
Swedish Warmblood 32 Breeds
of Horse and Pony
sweeny 624.18 *veterinary disease*
sweep 19.9 *play,* 19.15 *play offence,* 27.9 *stroke,* 27.17 *bat,*
33.10 *be on the track,* 36.4,
36.11 *rowing,* 36.12 *canoeing,*
41.16 *bobsled* , 161.40 *crowd,*
229.2 *chance,* 248.7 *range,*
248.20 *extend,* 335.14 *deviating
course,* 338.21 *move forward,*
589.3 *equal chance,* 621.13
clean, 660.19 *go easily,* 682.10
defeat heavily
sweep along 329.4 *be swift*
sweepback 73.7 *miscellaneous
aviation terms*
sweep before one 338.21 *move
forward*
sweep clean 839.10 *absolve*
sweeper 33.6 *motor racing terms,*
38.3 *football player,* 621.12
cleaner
sweeping 33.6 *motor racing
terms,* 41.10 *curling,* 124.1 *average,* 144.7 *complete,* 146.7 *including,* 164.15 *general,* 164.20
generalized, 621.2 *cleaning*
sweepingness 164.3 *nonspecificness*
sweepings 127.7 *inferior thing,*
132.2 *residue,* 614.6 *refuse,*
622.4 *dirt*
sweeping statement 164.8 *generalization*
sweep off one's feet 821.28 *win
the love of*
sweep out 349.11 *void*
sweep problems out of the way
682.7 *overcome obstacles*
sweep rowing 36.4 *rowing*
sweepstake 229.2 *chance,* 589.3
equal chance
sweep stroke 36.6 *canoeing*
sweep the board 617.9 *be worthy,* 682.10 *defeat heavily*
sweep the boards 682.9 *be victorious*
sweep under the carpet 438.8
make invisible, 531.8 *conceal*
sweep up 359.13 *ascend,* 621.13
clean
sweet 86 Nuts, **45**, **414**, 45.9
dish, 45.35 *dessert,* 350.14
mouthful, 350.27 *edible,* 351.17
drinkable, 405.6 *pleasant,* 411.7
tasty, 414.3 *dessert,* 433.6 *melodious,* 763.1 *pleasant,* 789.5
beautiful, 817.7 *courteous,*
821.22 *lovable*
sweet and sour 111.2 *opposites*
sweet-and-sour 414.6 *sweet*
sweet and sour pork 45.48 *Chinese dish*
sweet and twenty 206.11 *young*
sweet as a nut 414.6 *sweet*
sweet bay 85 Trees and Shrubs
sweet briar 84 Flowers and
Flowering Plants
sweet by-and-by 199.1 *future
time*
sweet cherry 86 Fruits

sweet cicely 45 Herbs and
Spices, 418.2 *fragrant thing*
sweet corn 45 Vegetables
sweet dreams 649.1 *ease*
sweet drink 414
sweeten 414, 242.4 *moderate,*
351.13 *drink,* 351.15 *provide
drink*
sweetened 414.6 *sweet*
sweetener 414, 729.2 *gift,*
746.4 *grant,* 878.8 *secret money*
sweetening 414.2 *sweetener*
sweeten the kitty 729.5 *give*
sweeten the pot 586.16 *tempt,*
746.11 *remunerate*
sweet FA 172.2 *nothing*
sweet Fanny Adams 100.2 *nothingness,* 172.2 *nothing*
sweet flag 84 Flowers and Flowering Plants
sweet fuck all 172.2 *nothing*
sweet gum 85 Trees and Shrubs
sweetheart 401.4 *boyfriend,*
402.4 *girlfriend,* 821.9 *lover,*
821.12 *nicknames for lovers,*
826.4 *terms of endearment,*
826.5 *courting person*
sweetheart name 560.8 *name*
sweet herb 69.11 *vegetable*
sweetie 45.41 *sweet,* 821.12
nicknames for lovers, 826.4
terms of endearment
sweeties 414.4 *confectionery*
sweetish 414.6 *sweet*
sweetkins 821.12 *nicknames for
lovers,* 826.4 *terms of endearment*
sweetly 414, 411.11 *tastily,*
433.11 *melodiously,* 817.14
courteously
sweetmeat 45.41 *sweet*
sweetmeats 405.4 *pleasurable
things,* 414.2 *sweetener*
sweetness 414, 405.1 *physical
pleasure,* 411.4 *flavour,* 414.1
sweetness, 817.1 *courtesy,* 821.4
lovability
Sweetness 414
sweet nothings 521.5 *empty talk,*
821.14 *communication of love,*
826.1 *endearment*
sweet on 821.18 *in love*
sweet pea 84 Flowers and Flowering Plants, 418.2 *fragrant
thing*
sweet potato 45 Vegetables,
821.9 *lover*
sweet potato pie 45.36 *cake*
sweet roll 45.36 *cake*
sweets 414.4 *confectionery,*
821.12 *nicknames for lovers,*
826.3 *love token,* 826.4 *terms of
endearment*
sweet-scented 418.4 *fragrant*
sweet sherry 351.9 *wine*
sweet shop 350.17 *food shop,*
414.4 *confectionery*
sweet sixteen 206.11 *young*
sweet sleep 649.1 *ease*
sweet smell 416.1 *odour,* 418.1
fragrance
sweet-smelling 405.6 *pleasant,*
418.4 *fragrant*
sweet smell of success 682.1 *success*
sweetsop 86 Fruits
sweet-sounding 433.6 *melodious*
sweet talk 228.5 *positive stimulus,* 539.3, 540.3 *hypocrisy,*
821.14 *communication of love,*
853.2 *blarney*
sweet-talk 228.9 *motivate,*
474.12 *deceive,* 538.9 *hypocrisy,*
538.24 *pretend,* 540.18 *be hypocritical,* 586.15 *persuade,* 657.5
be cunning, 821.26 *court,* 826.1
endearment, 853.9 *blarney*
sweet-talker 474.6 *sophist*
sweet talking 817.1 *courtesy*
sweet-talking 474.10 *hypocritical,* 538.18 *pretentious,* 540.27
hypocritical, 817.8 *good-mannered,* 853.13 *honeyed*
sweet taste 411.1 *taste,* 411.2
taste of life
sweet tongue 817.1 *courtesy*
sweet-tongued 817.8 *good-man-*

nered
sweet tooth 414.1 *sweetness*
sweet william 84 Flowers and
Flowering Plants
sweet wine 351.9 *wine,* 414.5
sweet drink
swell 54.14, 97.3 *wave,* 97.10
billow, 121.6 *change gradually,*
128.2 *spread,* 128.4, 128.4 *increase,* 130.6 *add,* 144.5 *be complete,* 227.8 *grow,* 261.1 *growth,*
261.5 *make bigger,* 261.6 *become bigger,* 316.5 *be convex,*
318.8 *protrude,* 361.2 *send up,*
366.3 *turbulence,* 366.13 *tempest,* 423.1 *loudness,* 423.8 *be
loud,* 617.1 *worthy,* 807.24 *be
vain,* 861.1 *good*
swelled 261.7 *bigger*
swelled head 805.13 *proud person*
swellelegant 617.1 *worthy*
swelling 97.7 *oceanic,* 128.1 *increase,* 128.2 *spread,* 227.3
growth, 227.11 *growing,* 261.1
growth, 261.3 *enlarged thing,*
261.8 *growing,* 316.1 *convexity,*
316.2 *bulge,* 316.4 *convex,*
318.3 *protuberance,* 318.5 *protuberant,* 423.6 *loud,* 624.3 *symptom,* 624.13 *skin disease,*
624.15 *ulcer,* 793.2 *pimple*
swell out 316.5 *be convex*
swell the ranks 130.7 *support,*
161.41 *band together,* 665.14 *be
a party member*
swell with pride 805.29 *feel pride*
swelter 353.19 *sweat,* 408.16
feel hot
sweltering 55.51 *hot,* 408.11
warm
swelteringly 55.65 *meteorologically*
sweltry 55.51 *hot*
swept 621.17 *cleaned*
swept clean 839.8 *overlooked*
swerve 252.1 *displacement,*
252.14 *displace,* 286.1 *obliqueness,* 286.6 *be oblique,* 331.2 *respond,* 335.1 *deviate',* 335.15 *deviating motion,* 578.2 *equivocate*
swerved 252.8 *displaced*
swerving 252.8 *displaced,*
335.15 *deviating motion,*
335.21 *indirect*
swift 329, 329.12 *swift animal,*
648.3 *hasty*
Swift 48 Writers, **48** Poets
Swiftair 534.2 *postal communication*
swift animal 329
swiftlet 78 Birds
swiftly 329, 191.8 *immediately,*
648.6 *hastily*
swift moth 82 Insects
swift-moving 329.1 *swift*
swiftness 329.8 *speed,* 648.4
haste
Swiftness 329
swift person 329
swift thing 329
swifty 191.5 *immediate*
swig 351.13 *drink,* 874.8 *get
drunk*
swigging 351.1 *drinking,* 874.5
drunken
swill 622, 351.13 *drink,* 393.13
mud, 621.14 *bathe,* 874.8 *get
drunk*
swiller 351.12 *drinker,* 874.17
drunkard
swilling 351.1, 351.16 *drinking,*
874.5 *drunken,* 874.11 *drinking*
swim 39, 36.8 *punting,* 39.11
swimming, 370.9 *be light,*
644.9 *exercise*
swim against the current 659.19
have difficulty
swim against the tide 168.19 *be
independent*
swim-and-tow 39.3 *survival
swimming*
swim bladder 80.5 *fish anatomy*
swim in 608.5 *about,* 610.4 *be
excessive*
swimmer 39
swimming 18 Sporting Activi-

ties, **39, 39,** 74.11 *nautical,*
625.1 *hygiene,* 644.5 *exercise*
Swimming 39
swimming area 39.7 *swimming
pool*
swimming association 39
swimming bath 39.7 *swimming
pool,* 94.2 *small lake,* 621.6 *bath*
swimming beach 39.7 *swimming
pool*
swimming costume 39.8
swimwear, 295.21 *beachwear*
swimming equipment 39.1 *swimming*
swimming hole 39.7 *swimming
pool,* 94.2 *small lake*
swimming in clothes 39.3 *survival swimming*
swimming lake 39.7 *swimming
pool*
swimmingly 655.12 *skilfully,*
682.16 *successfully,* 686.9 *prosperously*
swimming movements 39.2 *swimming technique*
swimming pool 39, 94.2 *small
lake,* 621.6 *bath*
swimming rescue 39.3 *survival
swimming*
swimming stroke 39.1 *swimming*
swimming team 39.1 *swimming*
swimming technique 39
swimming the English Channel
39.1 *swimming*
swimming trunks 39.8 *swimwear*
swimming under water 39.1
swimming
swimsuit 39.8 *swimwear,* 295.21
beachwear
swimsuited 296.10 *in dishabille*
swim under water 39.9 *swim*
swim upstream 659.19 *have difficulty*
swimwear 39, 296.4 *dishabille*
swim with the stream 167.8 *comply,* 660.20 *take it easy*
swim with the tide 808.14 *follow*
Swinburne 48 Poets
swindle 13.12 *cheat,* 515.8 *be
dishonest,* 538.10 *dishonesty,*
538.25 *be dishonest,* 539.10
fraud, 539.28 *trick,* 539.30 *be
fraudulent,* 540.8 *fraud,* 540.21
be fraudulent, 592.3 *expedient
plan,* 657.2 *stratagem,* 657.5 *be
cunning,* 734.3 *taking away,*
734.10 *take away,* 736.7 *dishonesty,* 736.16 *act dishonest,*
747.7 *not pay,* 753.10 *overcharge,* 858.3 *criminality,*
858.10 *be criminal*
swindled 515.10 *deceived,*
736.18 *fraudulent*
swindler 538.12 *cheat,* 539.15
deceiver, 539.17 *cheat,* 540.15
false person, 548.3 *deceiver,*
657.3 *cunning person,* 736.11
dishonest person, 864.9 *wicked
person*
swindling 538.19 *dishonest,*
540.31 *fraudulent,* 747.1 *nonpayment,* 858.7 *criminal*
Swindon 93 Cities
swine 77 Placental Mammals,
161 Collective Names by Animal, 68.8 *livestock,* 864.9
wicked person
swine fever 624.18 *veterinary disease*
swineherd 68.16 *farm worker*
swinepox 624.18 *veterinary disease*
swing 22.7 *play baseball,* 26.2
boxing, 26.11 *do a combat
sport.* 27.8 *delivery,* 27.13 *bowling,* 27.18 *bowl,* 30.5 *horizontal
bar,* 30.7 *stationary rings,* 34.9
mountaineer, 36.16 *row,* 40.2
tennis strokes, 41.2 *cross-country skiing,* 41.14, 41.14 *ski,*
49.8 *jazz,* 49.37 *syncopate,*
123.5 *be unequal,* 214.1 *regularity,* 214.7 *be regular,* 221.4,
221.8 *return,* 224.11 *be changeable,* 230.1 *operation,* 248.6
available space, 283.1 *suspension,* 283.3 *suspended object,*

283.10 *suspend*, 330.3 *hit*, 330.13 *blow*, 330.14 *sporting hit*, 335.10 *slide*, 335.15 *deviating motion*, 364.8 *rotate*, 365.1 *oscillation*, 365.4 *rock*, 365.7 *oscillator*, 365.8 *oscillate*, 365.11 *rock*, 366.11 *stagger*, 366.25 *pitch*, 488.2 *tendency*, 640.1 *action*, 879.6 *be punished*

swing and sway 214.7 *be regular*

swing around 221.8 *return*

swingaround 337.13 *about-turn*

swingback 21.2 *field events*

swing back 221.8 *return*, 331.1 *recoil*

swing bowler 27.4 *team*

swing bridge 63.21 *bridge*

swinger 49.24 *musician*, 405.3 *pleasure-seeker*

swing from 283.10 *suspend*

swinging 30.5 *horizontal bar*, 30.7 *stationary rings*, 34.3 *climbing technique*, 49.33 *jazz*, 123.3 *unequal*, 214.11 *regular*, 283.7 *suspended*, 365.4 *rock*, 365.13 *oscillating*

swingingly 660.21 *easily*

swing in with 664.14 *join with*

swingletree 85.12 *figurative usage*

swing of pendulum 331.4 *recoil*

swing of the pendulum 221.4 *return*, 365.1 *oscillation*

swing on the horizontal bar 30.10 *compete in gymnastics*

swing round 337.9 *turn round*, 364.8 *rotate*

swing to the hill 41.2 *cross-country skiing*, 41.14 *ski*

swing wing 73 *Types of Aircraft*

swingy ice 41.10 *curling*

swinish 77.33 *ungulate*

swink 644.1 *work*

swipe 330.3 *hit*, 330.13 *blow*, 338.5 *throw*, 670.5 *strike*, 670.18 *hit*, 736.12 *steal*

swiping 736.1 *stealing*

swirl 364, 96.6 *river flow*, 96.7 *flow*, 364.3 *reel*, 364.4 *vortex*, 366.3 *turbulence*, 366.22 *agitate*

swirling 364.2 *turning*, 364.11 *rotating*

swish 424.1 *faintness*, 424.5 *sound faint*, 429.1, 429.4 *hiss*

swishingly 429.8 *sibilantly*

Swiss chard 45 Vegetables

Swiss cross 544.6 *national emblem*

Swiss Guard 679.12 *ceremonial troops*

Swiss neutrality 400.11 *nation*

Swiss roll 45.36 *cake*

switch 49 Musical Instruments, 64.28 *plug*, 72.2 *track*, 72.3 *rail*, 143.6 *branch*, 222.1 *substitution*, 222.6 *give a substitute*, 223.1, 223.5 *exchange*, 252.1 *displacement*, 252.14 *displace*, 326.11 *transfer*, 327.10 *railway*, 335.9 *shove aside*, 343.15 *change direction*, 578.3 *apostatize*, 603.1 *tool*, 680.7 *blunt weapon*, 879.3 *hit*, 879.14 *instrument of punishment*

switchback 327.10 *railway*

switchblade 380.10 *knife*

switchboard 51.15 *stage*, 534.12 *public telephone system*

switchboard operator 534.13 *telephoner*

switched 222.8 *substituted*, 223.7 *exchanged*, 252.8 *displaced*

switched off 236.10 *powerless*, 240.6 *suspended*, 421.7 *unheard*

switched on 235.14 *operative*, 403.5 *sensible*

switch grass 87 Grasses

switching 64.15 *circuit function*, 223.1 *exchange*

switching circuit 64.13 *circuit*

switch off 236.8 *overpower*, 404.11 *be unfeeling*, 684.5 *conclude*

switch on 64.35 *conduct*,

156.20, 230.8 *activate*, 235.11 *give power*, 410.11 *fuel*, 439.24 *light*

switch on a light 439.24 *light*

switch over 578.3 *apostatize*

switch yard 72.8 *railway station*

swivel 36.4 *rowing*, 337.9 *turn round*, 364.4 *vortex*, 364.8 *rotate*, 680.12 *historical guns*

swivel chair 47.2 *chair*

swivelling 364.11 *rotating*

swiz 539.10 *fraud*

swizzle 539.10 *fraud*, 539.30 *be fraudulent*

swizzled 539.36 *deceived*

swollen 128.7 *increased*, 259.16 *fat*, 261.7 *bigger*, 273.1 *thick*, 316.4 *convex*, 361.11 *raised*, 557.4 *ornate*, 624.23 *diseased*, 805.22 *boastful*

swollen adenoids 624.9 *respiratory disease*

swollen head 805.13 *proud person*, 809.7 *vain person*

swollen-headed 805.22 *boastful*, 809.8 *vain*

swollen headedness 809.1 *vanity*

swollenness 261.1 *growth*

swoon 236.4 *disability*, 404.2 *unconsciousness*, 650.5 *be fatigued*, 650.7 *fatigue*

swooning 650.1 *fatigued*

swoop 329.4 *be swift*, 329.9 *acceleration*, 360.5 *dive*, 360.12 *drop*

swooping 360.4 *fall*, 360.18 *falling*

swoosh 329.9 *acceleration*, 424.1 *faintness*, 424.5 *sound faint*, 429.1, 429.4 *hiss*

sword 244.7 *agent of destruction*, 380.8 *sharp-pointed thing*, 380.10 *knife*, 679.1 *combatant*, 680.8 *sharp weapon*

sword and sorcery novel 48.2 *fiction*

sword dance 46.4 *historic dancing*

swordfish 80 Fishes, 20.4 *American game fish*, 45.18 *sea fish*

Swordfish 53 The Constellations

sword grass 87 Grasses

Sword Handle 53 Clusters

sword in hand 676.15 *warring*

sword knot 74 Knots

swordlike 380.3 *sharp-edged*

sword of Damocles 571.5 *inevitability*, 633.5 *danger*

Sword of Damocles 777.4 *intimidation*

sword of state 544.4 *insignia*

swordplay 28.1 *fencing*, 28.5 *fence*

sword play 51.2 *play*

swordplay 674.9 *duel*

sword point 380.7 *sharp point*

swordsman 674.10 *contender*, 679.1 *combatant*

swordstick 680.8 *sharp weapon*

swordtail 80 Fishes

swordthrust 670.18 *hit*

sworn 535.12 *vowed*, 714.12 *promised*, 715.7 *contractual*, 847.11 *duty-bound*

sworn enemy 785.3 *disliked person*, 820.5 *hostile person*, 822.8 *hated person*

sworn off 869.8 *self-restrained*

sworn statement 535.3 *vow*, 545.2 *certificate*

sworn testimony 535.3 *vow*

sworn to 535.12 *vowed*, 694.8 *loyal*

swot 6.7 *learner*, 6.23 *learn*, 459.18 *intellectual person*

swotting 6.8 *learning*

swotty 6.18 *educated*

swung dash 543.7 *punctuation*

sybarite 405.3 *pleasure-seeker*, 870.5 *self-indulgent person*

sybaritic 405.7 *pleased*, 870.6 *self-indulgent*

sybaritism 870.1 *self-indulgence*

sycamine 85 Trees and Shrubs

sycamore 85 Trees and Shrubs

syconus 86.2 *botanical fruit*

sycophancy 808, 853, 817.4 *deference*

sycophant 808, 853, 138.5, 155.14 *follower*, 180.9, 195.8 *follower*, 499.3, 667.5 *assenter*, 673.2 *appeaser*, 701.3 *subordinate*, 771.7 *person who humours*, 806.16 *humble person*, 817.6 *courteous person*

sycophantic 808, 853, 138.10 *tenacious*, 376.6 *smooth-mannered*, 673.5 *submitting*, 694.8 *loyal*, 771.11 *humouring*, 817.9 *deferential*

sycophantically 808, 138.12 *tenaciously*, 376.16 *suavely*, 817.16 *deferentially*, 853.17 *flatteringly*

Sydney 93 Cities, 93.6 *other cities*

Sydney to Hobart Race 36.1 *sailing*

syenite 54 Common Rocks

syllabary 5.14 *alphabet*

syllabic 5.41 *lettered*

syllabic metre 48.9 *metre*

syllabic script 5.13 *letter*

syllabification 141.2 *deconstruction*

syllabify 5.47 *word*, 141.4 *deconstruct*

syllable 5.16 *spoken letter*, 5.47 *word*, 564.1 *utterance*

syllabus 6.3 *subject*, 171.2 *table*, 171.5 *list of appointments*, 562.2 *outline*

syllogism 4.5 *philosophical argument*, 4.8 *philosophical term*, 463.2 *reasoning*

syllogist 4.10 *philosopher*, 463.5 *reasoner*

syllogize 4.21 *rationalize*

sylph 11.11 *ghost*, 274.9 *thin person*

sylphic 274.1 *thin*

sylphlike 274.1 *thin*

sylvan 69.16 *horticultural*, 85.16 *wooded*

sylvanite 54 Minerals

sylvatic 85.16 *wooded*

sylvestral 85.16 *wooded*

Sylvestrine 7 Members of Religious Orders

sylvite 54 Minerals

symbiont 59.18 *ecology*, 76.4 *type of animal*

symbiosis 59.18 *ecology*, 89.5 *fungal association*, 90.6 *lichen*, 109.2 *interconnection*, 135.1 *union*, 140.1 *combination*, 180.1 *accompaniment*, 333.2 *middle of the road*, 396.1 *life*, 664.3 *mutual relationship*, 701.1 *subjection*

symbiote 59.18 *ecology*

symbiotic 76.15 *of animals*, 90.7 *algal*, 109.5 *interconnected*, 135.12 *united*, 140.8 *cooperative*, 180.18 *concurrent*, 396.14 *biotic*, 664.17 *cooperative*, 701.9 *subject*

symbiotic alga 90.1 *alga*

symbiotically 89.13 *saprophytically*, 90.9 *algologically*, 109.10 *reciprocally*, 140.10 *in combination*, 180.23 *concurrently*

symbiotic fungus 89.5 *fungal association*

symbol 1.8 *tradition*, 5.13 *letter*, 9.3 *idol*, 11.6 *talisman*, 61.24 *symbolism*, 169.1 *number*, 222.3 *substitute thing*, 543.1 *sign*, 547.6 *image*

symbolic 2.12 *sociological*, 5.39 *of language*, 5.41 *lettered*, 10.21 *ritualistic*, 11.14 *occult*, 520.6 *meaningful*, 526.14 *manifest*, 527.5 *mysterious*, 543.14 *signifying*, 544.12 *identified*, 547.13 *representational*, 560.13 *representing*, 612.4 *trivial*

symbolical 543.14 *signifying*

symbolically 2.16 *sociologically*, 5.48 *linguistically*, 10.23 *ritually*, 50.30 *pictorially*, 520.13 *meaningfully*, 543.18 *indicatively*, 544.14 *identifiably*, 547.14 *representationally*

symbolic anthropology 1.1 *anthropology*

symbolic costume 295.5 *fancy dress*

symbolic interaction 2.3 *social environment*

symbolic language 5.10 *language type*

symbolic logic 52.63 *mathematical logic*

symbolics 10.2 *ritualism*, 11.1 *occultism*

symbolism 61, 543, 10.2 *ritualism*, 11.1 *occultism*, 48.3 *aspect of fiction*, 527.11 *mysteriousness*

Symbolism 48 Literary Groups and Movements, **50** Western Art Styles and Movements

symbolist 48.14 *author*, 50.29 *realist*, 543.8 *signer*

symbolistic 543.14 *signifying*

symbolistically 543.18 *indicatively*

symbolization 61.24 *symbolism*, 526.10 *manifestation*, 527.11 *mysteriousness*, 543.2 *symbolism*, 547.1 *representation*

symbolize 11.20 *occult*, 222.6 *give a substitute*, 520.10 *mean*, 527.14 *imply*, 543.10 *signify*, 547.9 *represent*

symbolizer 543.8 *signer*

symbol list 543.1 *sign*

symbol of death 397

symbol of peace 675

symbological 543.14 *signifying*

symbologist 543.8 *signer*

symbology 543.2 *symbolism*

symmetric 52.79 *spatial*, 109.6 *correlative*, 112.5 *uniform*, 214.11 *regular*, 308.4 *symmetrical*

symmetrical 308, 110.16 *equal*, 114.7 *similar*, 116.13 *harmonious*, 122.6 *equal*, 150.10 *ordered*, 214.11 *regular*, 478.15 *correspondent*, 558.3 *elegant*

symmetrically 308, 109.11 *correlatively*, 112.13 *uniformly*, 114.14 *comparably*, 122.13 *equitably*, 150.27 *methodically*, 214.15 *regularly*, 478.26 *correspondingly*, 558.5 *elegantly*

symmetricalness 308.1 *symmetry*

symmetric figure 52.41 *geometric figure*

symmetric relation 52.63 *mathematical logic*

symmetrize 308, 107.8 *be proportionate to*, 110.8 *make the same*, 116.24 *harmonize*, 124.10 *make average*

symmetrophobia 777 Phobias by Name

symmetry 777 Phobias by Topic, **308,** 52.41 *geometric figure*, 109.3 *correlation*, 110.5 *equality*, 112.1 *uniformity*, 116.4 *harmony*, 122.2 *equilibrium*, 150.7 *method*, 214.1 *regularity*, 478.8 *correspondence*, 558.1 *elegance*, 789.1 *gorgeousness*

Symmetry 308

symmetry element 308.2 *symmetry operation*

symmetry operation 308

sympathectomy 60 Surgical Operations

sympathetic 116.10 *in accord*, 284.9 *supportive*, 374.6 *soft-hearted*, 499.6 *assenting*, 662.35 *benevolent*, 664.25 *of one mind*, 701.10 *in agreeing*, 724.5 *jointly possessing*, 759.12, 760.1 *sensitive*, 784.6 *liking*, 819.8 *friendly*,

821.17 *loving*, 831.6 *benevolent*, 835.6 *pitying*, 859.5 *unselfish*
sympathetically 116.31 *in accord*, 340.14 *attractively*, 662.38 *benevolently*, 667.14 *agreeably*, 724.6 *in common*, 760.12 *sensitively*, 784.11 *admiringly*, 819.17 *in friendship*, 821.30 *lovingly*, 831.10 *benevolently*, 835.13 *pitifully*, 859.9 *unselfishly*
sympathetic magic 11.3 *witchcraft*
sympathetic resonance 427.1 *resonance*
sympathetic vibration 331.4 *recoil*
sympathies 759.3 *feelings*
sympathize 519.16 *have insight*, 662.20 *sustain*, 667.6 *agree with*, 759.18 *feel for*, 760.11 *be sensitive*, 831.8 *be benevolent*, 835.8 *pity*
sympathizer 284.8 *supporter*, 499.3, 667.5 *assenter*, 724.3 *participant*, 759.9 *feeling person*, 760.8 *sensitive person*, 831.5 *benevolent person*, 835.4 *pitying person*
sympathize with 405.10 *comfort*, 784.7 *like*, 821.23 *love*, 835.8 *pity*, 859.7 *be unselfish*
sympathizing 835.6 *pitying*
sympatholytic 62.4 *drug type*, 62.14 *counteracting*
sympathomimetic 62.4 *drug type*, 62.17 *stimulating*
sympathy 116.1 *accord*, 284.6 *moral support*, 340.1 *attraction*, 519.3 *insight*, 662.3 *sustenance*, 664.2 *fellowship*, 667.1 *agreement*, 724.2 *participation*, 759.5 *good feeling*, 760.5 *sensitivity*, 784.1 *liking*, 819.2 *friendly relations*, 821.7 *choice*, 835.1 *pity*, 835.2 *condolence*, 859.2 *unselfishness*
sympathy in grief 835.2 *condolence*
sympathy lock-out 15.4 *industrial dispute*
sympathy strike 15.4 *industrial dispute*, 724.2 *participation*
symphonic 116.13 *harmonious*
symphonically 116.33 *harmoniously*
symphonic music 49.3 *classical music*
symphonious 49.30 *harmonic*, 116.13 *harmonious*
symphonium 49 *Musical Instruments*
symphonize 116.24 *harmonize*, 433.9 *set to music*
symphony 116.4 *harmony*, 243.5 *work of art*
symphony orchestra 49.26 *musical group*, 140.3 *assembly*
symphylan 81.4 *arthropod*
symphysiotomy 60 *Surgical Operations*
symphysis 140.1 *combination*
symphystic 140.7 *combined*
symposiarch 653.14 *leader*
symposium 4.5 *philosophical argument*, 161.5 *conference*, 561.1 *dissertation*, 568.4 *conference*
symptom 624, 180.4 *concomitant*, 483.4 *indication*, 517.5 *omen*, 526.10 *manifestation*, 543.1 *sign*, 636.1 *warning*
symptomatic 60.24 *diagnostic*, 517.13 *predicting*, 543.14 *signifying*, 636.8 *warning*
symptomatically 543.18 *indicatively*
symptomatological 60.24 *diagnostic*, 543.14 *signifying*
symptomatology 60.3 *medical specialty*, 524.5 *science of interpretation*, 543.2 *symbolism*
symptomize 543.10 *signify*
symptomless carrier 626.4 *infectious person*
synaesthesia 48.12 *poetic lan-*

guage, 61.27 *association of ideas*
synagogue 10.11 *place of worship*
synandrous 84.12 *of flowers*
syn–anti isomer 57.13 *structure*
sync 198.3 *synchronism*, 198.7 *synchronize*
syncarpous 86.9 *of a fruit*
synchromesh 603.4 *machine*
synchronic 5.38 *linguistic*, 50.29 *realist*
synchronicity 11.10 *psychic phenomenon*, 110.2 *equivalence*, 140.1 *combination*
synchronic linguistics 5.1 *linguistics*
synchronism 50 *Western Art Styles and Movements*, **180**, **198**, 116.4 *harmony*
synchronization 49.13 *melody*, 116.4 *harmony*, 140.2 *cooperation*, 198.3 *synchronism*, 667.3 *compatibility*
synchronize **198**, 110.8 *make the same*, 116.24 *harmonize*, 122.11 *equalize*, 140.6 *come together*, 150.20 *harmonize*, 180.13 *accompany*, 185.18 *adjust the clock*, 433.8 *harmonize*, 667.8 *be compatible*
synchronized **198**, 39.11 *swimming*, 116.13 *harmonious*, 140.8 *cooperative*, 433.7 *harmonious*, 667.12 *compatible*
synchronized flash 66.19 *flash*
synchronized swimming 18 *Sporting Activities*, 39.1 *swimming*
synchronize watches 185.18 *adjust the clock*, 192.14 *keep time*
synchronous 49.30 *harmonic*, 110.13 *equivalent*, 116.13 *harmonious*, 140.8 *cooperative*, 198.10 *synchronized*, 433.7 *harmonious*
synchronous-induction motor 64.31 *electric motor*
synchronously **198**, 110.18 *identically*, 116.33 *harmoniously*, 140.10 *in combination*, 433.12 *harmoniously*
synchronous motor 64.31 *electric motor*
synchrotron 56.94 *particle accelerator*, 235.8 *nuclear power*
synclastic surface 52.38 *surface*
syncline 54.20 *earth movement*, 320.1 *fold*
syncopal 552.3 *concise*
syncopate 49, 433.9 *set to music*
syncopated 49.33 *jazz*, 433.7 *harmonious*
syncopated steps 46.3 *ballroom dance steps*
syncopation 49.8 *jazz*, 49.19 *tempo*, 185.12 *musical time*, 433.3 *melodiousness*
syncopator 49.24 *musician*
syncope 270.2 *shortening*, 552.1 *conciseness*, 562.2 *outline*
syncretic 133.12 *mixed*, 140.7 *combined*
syncretically 140.10 *in combination*
syncretism 133.1 *mixture*, 140.1 *combination*
syncretize 140.5 *combine*
syncytial 59.23 *cellular*
syncytium 59.7 *cell*
syndeton 5.30 *syntax*
syndicalism 4.7 *school of thought*, 12.1 *government*, 688.7 *type of rule*, 689.2 *anarchism*
syndicalist 4.11 *follower of a doctrine*, 4.14 *of a philosophy*, 12.6 *political party*, 689.3 *anarchist*
syndicalistic 689.7 *anarchistic*
syndicate 140.3 *assembly*, 161.15 *association*, 532.15 *publish*, 533.7 *press agency*, 533.13 *report*, 665.1 *party*, 665.12 *be in league with*
syndicated 665.8 *leagued*
syndicated programme 534.25

broadcast material
syndiotactic 57.44 *polymeric*
syndiotactic polymer 57.21 *polymer*
syndrome 180.4 *concomitant*, 517.5 *omen*, 526.10 *manifestation*, 543.1 *sign*, 624.3 *symptom*
synecdoche 48.12 *poetic language*
synecology 59.18 *ecology*
syneresis 262.1 *contraction*
synergetic 664.17 *cooperative*
synergetically 664.20 *cooperatively*
synergic 116.11 *allied*, 664.17 *cooperative*
synergism 664.1 *cooperation*
synergistic 664.17 *cooperative*
synergistically 664.20 *cooperatively*
synergize 116.22 *form an alliance*
synergy 116.2 *alliance*, 664.1 *cooperation*
syngamy 133.1 *mixture*, 135.4 *sexual union*
Synge 48 *Dramatists*
syngenesis 135.4 *sexual union*
synizesis 262.1 *contraction*
synod 161.5 *conference*, 653.7 *council*
synodal 653.18 *parliamentary*
synodic 53.36 *astronomical*
synonym 5.17 *word*, 122.3 *equalization*, 222.3 *substitute thing*, 520.4 *type of meaning*
synonym dictionary 5.28 *dictionary*
synonymic 5.42 *worded*
synonymity 110.2 *equivalence*, 116.5 *conformity*, 122.3 *equalization*, 520.4 *type of meaning*
synonymous 110.13 *equivalent*, 114.7 *similar*, 116.14 *conforming*, 520.6 *meaningful*, 524.17 *translational*
synonymously 110.18 *identically*, 114.14 *comparably*
synonymousness 110.2 *equivalence*, 520.4 *type of meaning*
synonymy 110.2 *equivalence*, 114.1 *similarity*, 116.5 *conformity*, 520.4 *type of meaning*
synopsis 142.3 *whole situation*, 171.5 *list of appointments*, 270.3 *shortened version*, 299.1, 552.2 *outline*, 562.1 *summary*
synopsize 270.10 *shorten*, 299.5 *outline*, 552.4 *be concise*, 562.8 *summarize*
synopsized 299.6 *outlined*, 562.7 *shortened*
synoptic 55.41 *meteorologic*, 164.15 *general*, 270.7 *short*
synoptically 55.65 *meteorologically*
Synoptic Gospels 7.12 *religious text*
synoptic map 55.4 *weather forecast*
synoptic meteorology 55.1 *meteorology*
synovectomy 60 *Surgical Operations*
synovia 386.4, 395.5 *lubricant*
synpetalous 84.12 *of flowers*
synsepalous 84.12 *of flowers*
syntactic 5.38 *linguistic*, 5.44 *grammatical*
syntactically 5.48 *linguistically*, 5.52 *grammatically*
syntactic analysis 5.30 *syntax*
syntactic meaning 5.30 *syntax*
syntactics 5.1 *linguistics*
syntactic structure 5.30 *syntax*
syntax 5, 65.9 *programming language*
synthesis 57, 4.5 *philosophical*

argument, 4.8 *philosophical term*, 57.1 *chemistry*, 133.2 *mixed thing*, 135.1 *union*, 140.1 *combination*
synthesize 57, 58.25 *metabolize*, 110.8 *make the same*, 140.5 *combine*, 243.10 *produce*, 463.11 *reason*
synthesized 57.40 *synthetic*
synthesizer 49 *Musical Instruments*
synthetic 57, 4.16 *dialectical*, 50.29 *realist*, 57.16 *synthesis*, 57.31 *chemical*, 67.3 *fabric*, 102.12 *not the real thing*, 114.8 *simulated*, 118.13 *imitation*, 243.12 *produced*, 538.14 *unreal*, 539.39 *imitative*
synthetically 57.46 *chemically*, 114.14 *comparably*, 118.14 *imitatively*, 538.28 *dishonestly*, 540.37 *spuriously*
synthetic chemist 57.2 *chemist*
synthetic compound 57.16 *synthesis*
synthetic cubism 50 *Western Art Styles and Movements*
synthetic drug 630.8 *drug*
synthetic dye 67.6 *dye*, 444.4 *pigment*
synthetic fabric 67.3 *fabric*
synthetic fibre 67.1 *fibre*
syntheticness 538.2 *unrealness*
synthetic plasma 387.4 *blood*
synthetic resin 395.10 *resin*, 604.1 *materials*
synthetic rubber 377.4 *rubber*, 539.6 *imitation*
synthetism 50 *Western Art Styles and Movements*
syntone 61.7 *personality type*
syntony 61.7 *personality type*
syphilis 777 *Phobias by Topic*, 624.4 *disease*, 624.14 *venereal disease*
syphilitic 624.23 *diseased*, 626.4 *infectious person*
syphilitic sore 624.14 *venereal disease*
syphilophobia 777 *Phobias by Name*
Syracuse 93 *Cities*
Syria 91 *Countries*
Syriac 5 *Languages and Groups of Languages*
Syrian 98 *Deserts*
Syrian Orthodox 7 *Christian Movements*
syringa 84 *Flowers and Flowering Plants*
syringe 354.11 *thing inserted*, 355.9 *extractor*, 389.11 *wash*, 389.34 *hose*
syrinx 49 *Musical Instruments*, 78.16 *avian anatomy*
syrup 393.9 *jelly*, 394.6 *gelatin*, 414.2 *sweetener*
syrupiness 394.1 *viscosity*, 414.1 *sweetness*
syrupy 393.21, 394.9 *gelatinous*, 414.6 *sweet*
system 54.41 *geological time*, 116.6 *convention*, 142.2 *whole thing*, 150.1 *order*, 150.7 *method*, 152.3 *organization*, 166.6 *custom*, 306.1 *form*, 327.1 *way*, 584.6 *procedure*, 592.2 *policy*
systematic 15.9 *negotiated*, 59.20 *biological*, 59.28 *taxonomic*, 150.10 *ordered*, 150.14 *well-ordered*, 152.22 *organizational*, 166.10 *customary*, 306.9 *formed*, 592.14 *planned*
systematically 59.29 *biologically*, 150.27 *methodically*, 152.28 *in place*, 166.19 *to rule*, 306.13 *formatively*, 584.19 *habitually*, 592.16 *as planned*

systematic error 56.83 *sensitivity*
systematics 59.1 *life science*,
59.17 *taxonomy*, 150.6 *methodicalness*
systematic sampling 52.57 *population*
systematic theology 7.13 *theology*
systematic wage structure 15.2 *industrial negotiations*
systematic zoologist 76.11 *zoologist*
systematic zoology 76.9 *animal science*
systematism 150.6 *methodicalness*
systematization 150.6 *methodicalness*, 152.3 *organization*, 592.7 *planning*
systematize **150**, 116.26 *make uniform*, 152.13 *organize*, 166.14 *regulate*, 214.10 *make regular*, 306.7 *form*, 592.9 *plan*
systematized 152.21 *organized*
systematizer 592.8 *planner*
systematology 150.6 *methodicalness*
Système International d'Unités 268.5 *measuring system*
systemic 5.44 *grammatical*
systemic fungicide 69.8 *weedkiller*
systemic grammar 5.29 *grammar*
systemic herbicide 68.14 *pest control*
systems analysis 52.1 *mathematics*, 65.1 *computing*
systems analyst 52.2 *mathematician*, 65.2 *operator*, 170.6 *calculator*, 592.8 *planner*
systole 262.1 *contraction*
systole and diastole 365.1 *oscillation*
syzygy 53.16 *planet*, 264.1 *nearness*
Szewinska 18 Sporting Personalities
Szilard 52 Scientists
Szondi test 61.5 *psychological test*

T

ta 837.9 *thank you*
taanit 10.16 *religious festival*
tab 130.3 *additional item*, 155.10 *rear*, 544.10 *identify*
tabard 295.11 *jacket*
tabaret 67 Natural Fabrics
Tabasco 351.8 *mixed drink*, 413.2 *seasoning*
Tabasco sauce 45.15 *sauce*
tabby 67 Natural Fabrics, 77 Breeds of Cats, 456.10 *mottled*
tabby cat 456.5 *variegated thing*
tabby-pointed Siamese 77 Breeds of Cats
tabernacle 74 Rigging, 10.11 *place of worship*, 10.13 *shrine*, 10.14 *sacred object*
tabes 274.8 *emaciation*
tabescence 262.1 *contraction*, 274.8 *emaciation*
tabescent 262.8 *contracting*, 274.2 *emaciated*
tabetic 274.2 *emaciated*
tabla 49 Musical Instruments
table **49, 171**, 43.9 *miscellaneous architectural features*, 152.8 *chart*, 170.5 *computer*, 171.1 *list*, 209.8 *delay*, 257.5 *divisions*, 266.1 *layer*, 282.3 *flat thing*, 283.12 *interrupt*, 284.2 *supporting part*, 545.6 *record book*, 591.7 *be evasive*, 598.2 *withdraw*
tableau 50.7 *picture*, 51.5 *show*, 435.7 *view*, 811.14 *show*, 813.3 *formal occasion*
table bird 78
tablecloth 293.1 *protective covering*, 621.11 *cleaning cloth*
tabled 209.10 *held up*, 257.12 *itemized*, 283.9 *interrupted*

table lamp 439.6 *electric light*
tableland 98.7 *upland*, 275.2 *heights*, 282.3 *flat thing*
table manners 350.4 *eating meals*, 584.5 *tradition*
tablemat 621.11 *cleaning cloth*
Table Mountain 53 The Constellations
table of contents 171.2 *table*
tables 170.2 *statistics*
table salt 45.7 *basic ingredient*
table setting 557.1 *ornament*
tablespoon 120.3 *container*, 258.17 *ladle*, 350.16 *eating utensil*
tablet 62.6 *pill*, 266.4 *slice*, 282.3 *flat thing*, 545.6 *record book*, 545.11 *monument*, 630.2 *medicine*
table talk 568.2 *chat*
table tapper 11.2 *occultist*
table tapping 11.1 *occultism*
table tennis 18 Sporting Activities, 40.1 *tennis*
table wine 351.9 *wine*
tabling 209.3 *delayed action*, 283.6 *interruption*
tabloid 532.4 *newspaper*, 630.2 *medicine*
tabloid press 528.4 *mass communication*, 532.3 *journalism*, 533.5 *mass communication*
taboo 1.5 *anthropological concept*, 1.8 *tradition*, 147.1 *exclusion*, 147.7 *exclude*, 147.11 *excluded*, 709.1 *veto*, 709.5 *vetoed*
taboo word 5.19 *swearword*
tabor 49 Musical Instruments
Taborites 7 Christian Movements
Tabriz 93 Cities
tabs 51.17 *stage set*
tabular 52.78 *pictorial*, 152.26 *diagrammatic*, 163.10 *classificatory*, 257.12 *itemized*, 282.8 *horizontal*
tabula rasa 201.5 *fresh start*, 546.4 *eraser*, 704.3 *new beginning*
tabularly 171.13 *inventorially*
tabulate 150.19 *systematize*, 152.15 *categorize*, 163.14 *sort*, 171.8 *list*, 257.9 *itemize*, 545.13 *record*, 545.15 *register*
tabulated 152.24 *categorized*, 171.11 *listed*, 257.12 *itemized*
tabulation 152.5 *categorization*, 171.7 *listing*
tabulation of ballots 580.12 *election*
tabulator 170.5 *computer*
tacamahac 85 Tree Products
tacet 49 Musical Terms
tacheometer 268.8 *meter*
tacheometric 268.16 *micrometric*
tacheometry 268.2 *micrometry*
tachi dori 26.10 *aikido*
tachisme 50 Western Art Styles and Movements
tachi-waza 26.7 *judo*
tachograph 71 Motor Vehicle Parts
tachometer 268.8 *meter*, 329.8 *speed*
tachometric 268.16 *micrometric*
tachometry 268.2 *micrometry*
tachophobia 777 Phobias by Name
tachycardia 624.10 *cardiovascular disease*
tachymeter 268.8 *meter*
tachymetric 268.16 *micrometric*
tachymetry 268.2 *micrometry*
tachyon 185.1 *time*
tacit 422.3 *silent*, 520.6 *meaningful*, 527.4 *unsaid*
taciturn **566**, 422.3, 531.16 *silent*, 552.3 *concise*, 563.11 *speechless*, 591.18 *avoiding*, 816.9 *shy*
taciturnity **566**, 422.4 *silence*, 527.10 *quietness*, 531.4 *silence*, 552.1 *conciseness*, 563.5 *mutism*, 816.1 *unsociability*
Taciturnity **566**
taciturnly **566**, 816.14 *unsocially*
taciturn person **566**

tack 32.14 *horse-riding terms*, 36.1 *sailing*, 36.15 *sail*, 41.14 *ski*, 74.9 *navigate*, 135.10 *link*, 137.8 *fastening*, 137.11 *connect*, 224.11 *be changeable*, 324.15 *walk*, 327.1 *way*, 332.2 *bearing*, 335.1 *deviate*, 335.14 *deviating course*, 350.7 *food*, 380.8 *sharp-pointed thing*, 578.2 *equivocate*, 603.1 *tool*, 603.9 *use tools*
tacked 137.15 *connected*
tackily 394.12 *viscously*, 412.11 *tastelessly*
tackiness 394.1 *viscosity*, 412.4 *bad taste*, 559.3 *ugliness*, 618.8 *inferiority*, 795.2 *tawdriness*
tacking 36.1, 36.10 *sailing*, 41.2 *cross-country skiing*
tackle **137**, **596**, 19.7 *offence*, 35.3 *rugby play*, 35.5 *play rugby*, 36.3 *parts of a sailing boat*, 38.2 *football play*, 38.4 *play soccer*, 156.18 *make a beginning*, 361.9 *lifter*, 574.9 *undertake*, 596.5 *attempt*, 597.1 *undertake*, 603.6 *equipment*, 640.4 *act*, 674.11 *contend*
tackled 35.6 *rugger*, 38.5 *soccer*
tackler 596.7 *attempter*
tackling 35.3 *rugby play*, 38.2 *football play*, 38.5 *soccer*
tack on 130.6 *add*
tacky 138.9 *adhesive*, 391.9 *moist*, 394.8 *viscous*, 412.6 *coarse*, 559.10 *ugly*, 618.2 *inferior*, 754.10 *shoddy*, 793.6 *seedy*
taco 45.50 *Central American dish*
Tacoma 93 Cities
tact 507.1 *wisdom*, 507.8 *skill*, 652.8 *treatment*, 653.3 *management*, 655.1 *skill*, 817.1 *courtesy*
tactful 507.5 *wise*, 817.7 *courteous*
tactfully 817.14 *courteously*, 817.15 *genteelly*
tactfulness 817.1 *courtesy*
tactic 57.44 *polymeric*, 652.9 *tactics*, 657.2 *stratagem*
tactical 17.8 *military*, 592.14 *planned*, 640.6 *effective*, 652.16 *behaving*, 657.4 *cunning*, 676.17 *military*
tactical advantage 652.9 *tactics*
tactical bombing 670.13 *air attack*, 676.8 *warfare*
tactically 17.11 *militarily*, 592.16 *as planned*, 657.6 *cunningly*
tactical nuclear warfare 676.8 *warfare*
tactical nuclear weapon 680.1 *weapon*
tactical unit 17.4 *military organization*
tactical vom 349.23 *vomiting*
tactician 228.7, 586.14 *motivator*, 592.8 *planner*, 655.5 *expert*, 657.3 *cunning person*
tactics **652**, 327.1 *way*, 592.2 *policy*, 640.2 *deed*, 655.1 *skill*, 657.1 *cunning*, 657.2 *stratagem*, 676.6 *art of war*
tactics of war 676.6 *art of war*
tactile 50.25 *sculptural*, 403.8 *sensate*, 407.1 *touch*, 407.8 *touchable*
tactile values 50.4 *treatment*
tactility 407.1 *touch*
tactless 462.10 *inconsiderate*, 585.2 *not customary*, 656.3 *clumsy*, 761.1 *insensitive*, 818.5 *discourteous*
tactlessly 761.8 *unfeelingly*, 818.9 *discourteously*
tactlessness 462.4 *inconsideration*, 656.9 *bungling*, 761.3 *insensitiveness*, 818.1 *discourtesy*
tactual 407.8 *touchable*
tadpole 79.8 *young amphibian*, 206.4 *young animal*
tadpole shrimp 81.4 *arthropod*
Tadzhiki **5** Languages and Groups of Languages
Tadzhikistan **91** Countries
Taegu **93** Cities

tae kwon do **18** Sporting Activities, **26**, 26.1 *combat sports*, 26.15, 674.8 *wrestling*
tae kwon do combinations 26.9 *tae kwon do*
tae kwon do grade 26.9 *tae kwon do*
tae kwon do patterns 26.9 *tae kwon do*
tae kwon do technique 26.9 *tae kwon do*
tael **75** Some Foreign Units
taenia **43** Architectural Decoration, 279.3 *architectural summit*
taeniacide 62.4 *drug type*
Taff **96** Rivers, 96.4 *British rivers*
taffeta 288.4 *textile*
taffy 45.41 *sweet*, 138.4 *adherent*
Taffy **91** Names for Inhabitants, 255.9 *British inhabitant*
tag 130.3 *additional item*, 130.6 *add*, 137.6 *line*, 155.10 *rear*, 505.1 *maxim*, 544.3 *means of identification*, 544.10 *identify*, 560.8 *name*, 731.4 *allot*
Tagalog **1** Peoples, **5** Languages and Groups of Languages
tag along 155.26 *bring up the rear*, 180.16 *attend*, 304.6 *be in the rear*
tag day 729.3 *offering*
tag football 19.1 *football*
tagged 544.12 *identified*
tagging 731.1 *allocation*
tagliatelle **45** Types of Pasta
tag on 130.6 *add*
Iagore **48** Poets
tag-out 22.6 *fielding terms*
tag-team 26.15 *wrestling*
tag-team wrestling 26.5 *wrestling*
Tagula **5** Languages and Groups of Languages, 5.11 *family of languages*
Tagus **96** Rivers
Tahiti **98** Islands
Tahitian **5** Languages and Groups of Languages
Tahltan **5** Languages and Groups of Languages
Tahoe **94** Lakes, 94.3 *US lakes*
tahr **77** Placental Mammals
Tai **1** Peoples
taiga 85.4 *trees*
taiko **49** Musical Instruments
tail **157**, 53.19 *comet*, 130.3 *additional item*, 155.10, 155.20 *rear*, 155.23 *follow close*, 157.25 *hindmost*, 180.9 *follower*, 180.16 *attend*, 264.10 *stay near*, 304.2 *rear end*, 304.4 *rear*, 590.5 *pursuer*, 590.9 *follow*
tailback 159.8 *procession*, 195.1 *succession*
tail beam 43.9 *miscellaneous architectural features*
tail between the legs 806.9 *humiliation*
tail coat 295.3 *formal dress*
tailed amphibian 79.7 *amphibian*
tail end 157.8 *tail*, 304.1 *rear*
tail feather 78.17 *plumage*
tail fin 80.5 *fish anatomy*
tailgate 264.10 *stay near*
tailgate picnic 350.13 *feast*
tail guard 32.14 *horse-riding terms*
tail in a gate 659.7 *awkward situation*
tailing 590.1 *pursuit*
tailless 131.7 *reduced*
tailless amphibian 79.7 *amphibian*
tailless mouse 65.7 *peripheral*
tail light **71** Motor Vehicle Parts, 439.6 *electric light*
tail off 129.4 *decrease*, 157.18 *come to an end*, 218.6 *cease*
tailor 135.7 *joiner*, 216.6 *editor*, 293.17 *coverer*, 295.26 *fashion designer*, 295.35 *make clothing*, 629.12 *repairer*, 646.2 *artisan*, 739.13 *retailer*, 796.8 *fashion*
tailorbird **78** Birds
tailored 295.31 *styled*, 306.9 *formed*
tailoring 295.2 *dressing*, 306.4 *forming*

tailor-made 243.12 *produced*, 295.31 *styled*, 306.10 *prototypical*
tailor-made clothes 295.1 *dress*
tailor-make 295.35 *make clothing*
tailor's dummy 547.6 *image*
tailor's goose 376.9 *smoother*
tailpiece 43.9 *miscellaneous architectural features*, 130.3 *additional item*, 155.10, 304.1 *rear*
tailplane 73 Aircraft Parts
tail rhyme 48.11 *rhyme*
tails 295.3 *formal dress*, 295.11 *jacket*, 580.14 *formal dress*
tailskid 73 Aircraft Parts, 71.21 *miscellaneous motoring terms*
tailspin 71.21 *miscellaneous motoring terms*, 129.2 *decline*
tail wheel 71 Motor Vehicle Parts, **73** Aircraft Parts
tailwind 55.15 *flight*
tail wind 55.15 *wind direction*, 338.12 *propellant*, 390.4 *air flow*, 662.1 *help*
Taine 4 Philosophers
Taino 5 Languages and Groups of Languages
taint 542.6 *suggestion*, 618.10 *poverty*, 620.7 *defect*, 622.2 *uncleanness*, 622.11 *dirty*, 624.6 *infection*, 628.3 *make worse*, 631.15 *poison*
tainted 419.4 *putrid*, 618.4 *poor*, 620.1 *imperfect*, 622.8 *unclean*, 624.23 *diseased*
taipan 79 Reptiles
Taipei 93 Cities
Taiwan 91 Countries, **98** Islands
Taiyuan 93 Cities
tajine 45.6 *kitchen equipment*
Taj Mahal 43 Noted Buildings
takable 730.14 *receivable*
takahe 78 Birds, 78.2 *flightless bird*
take 734, 20.1 *angling*, 66.3 *photograph*, 326.12 *transport*, 518.5 *suppose*, 533.10 *copy*, 593.9 *find necessary*, 607.1 *waste*, 682.9 *be victorious*, 695.7 *force*, 721.4 *earnings*, 730.9 *receive*, 734.5 *takings*, 736.4 *stolen goods*, 737.3 *bargain*, 749.2 *money received*, 749.7 *receive*
take aback 514.9 *surprise*
take a back seat 124.9 *be average*, 127.10 *follow*, 806.19 *be humble*, 810.15 *escape notice*, 859.7 *be unselfish*
take a bath 621.14 *bathe*
take a beating 683.7 *be defeated*
take a bow 51.32 *act*
take a break 218.9 *pause*, 645.4 *have leisure*, 651.2 *be refreshed*
take a breather 218.9 *pause*, 325.8 *be motionless*, 649.2 *take it easy*, 651.2 *be refreshed*
take a bribe 878.13 *get paid*
take account of 146.4 *include*
take a chance 589, 486.7 *make possible*, 488.10 *think likely*, 596.3 *tackle*, 633.9 *face danger*
take a chill 409.10 *be cold*
take a cold bath 699.10 *restrain oneself*
take a commission 676.12 *go to war*
take a corner 38.4 *play soccer*
take a crack at 479.13 *invent*, 597.1 *undertake*
take action 230, 15.12 *have an industrial dispute*, 640.4 *act*, 644.8 *exert oneself*
take a day off 218.9 *pause*, 254.17 *take leave of absence*
take a deep breath 651.2 *be refreshed*
take a dim view of 785.5 *dislike*, 852.14 *disapprove*
take a dip 39.9 *swim*
take a direction 332
take a discount 752
take a dislike to 785.5 *dislike*
take a dive 539.30 *be fraudulent*
take a dose 120.8 *quantify*
take a drubbing 683.7 *be defeated*

take advantage of 539.28 *trick*, 599.3 *exploit*, 601.1 *misuse*, 613.11 *find useful*, 627.1 *improve*, 627.2 *get better*, 640.4 *act*, 652.11 *conduct oneself*, 655.10 *be skilful*, 877.20 *seduce*
take advice 654.6 *consult*
take a fall 360.11 *trip*
take a fancy to 784.7 *like*, 821.24 *be in love*
take a firm grip 233.10 *be a prevailing influence*
take a flier 633.9 *face danger*
take a foul shot 23.6 *play basketball*
take a fresh lease on life 623.6 *get healthy*
take after 114.10 *be similar*, 118.9 *imitate*
take a gander 435.14 *inspect*
take ages 209.6 *be late*
take a guess at 786.12 *wonder whether*
take a header 360.11 *trip*
take a high tone 807.27 *dare*
take a holiday 218.9 *pause*, 645.4 *have leisure*, 649.2 *take it easy*
take a hostage 734.10 *take away*
take a husband 823.15 *marry*
take aim 588.10 *aim*
take a kickback 710.9 *offer*
take a leaf out of one's book 118.9 *imitate*
take a leak 353.17 *urinate*
take a leap in the dark 508.6 *be foolish*, 780.5 *be rash*
take a licking and keep on ticking 575.9 *endure*
take a liking to 821.24 *be in love*
take a long shot 229.4 *chance*
take a maiden voyage 201.19 *begin*
take amiss 828.8 *resent*, 828.10 *be offended*
take an advance on royalties 733.7 *borrow*
take an airing 390.20 *aerate*
take a nap 649.2 *take it easy*
take an aversion to 822.14 *hate*
take an ego trip 860.7 *be egoistic*
take an even chance 229.4 *chance*
take an eye for an eye 109.7 *reciprocate*, 223.5 *exchange*, 746.13 *retaliate*
take an interest in 821.23 *love*
take an opinion poll 580.5 *vote*
take a nosedive 129.4 *decrease*, 360.11 *trip*
take an overdose 398.21 *commit suicide*
take an upturn 359.21 *upturn*
take apart 136.9 *separate*, 141.4 *deconstruct*, 244.9 *demolish*, 600.6 *stop using*
take a pee 767.13 *relieve oneself*
take a penalty kick 35.5 *play rugby*
take a percentage 721.14 *profit*
take a photo 547.9 *represent*
take a photograph 66.21 *photograph*
take a picture 545.13 *record*, 547.9 *represent*
take a plane 327.14 *find one's way*
take a poll 580.5 *vote*
take a position 676.14 *battle*
take a pot shot 338.31 *snipe*, 670.2 *fire*
take a powder 345.4 *hurry off*, 349.33 *go away*
take a profit 721.14 *profit*
take a rain check 222.5 *take a substitute*
take a random sample 229.4 *chance*
take a recess 651.2 *be refreshed*
take a resolution 574.7 *resolve*
take a rest 649.2 *take it easy*
take a ride to Tyburn 879.6 *be punished*
take a risk 229.4 *chance*, 589.12 *take a chance*
take a running jump 349.33 *go away*, 360.11 *trip*

take a sabbatical 160.13 *pause*, 645.4 *have leisure*
take a salary advance 733.7 *borrow*
take as a model 118.9 *imitate*
take a second helping 609.6 *be unsatisfied*
take a share 724.4 *have joint possession*, 731.5 *get one's allotment*
take a shine 439.27 *glaze*
take a shine to 821.24 *be in love*
take a short cut 270.11 *short-cut*, 327.14 *find one's way*
take a shot 24.8 *play billiards*
take a shot at 597.1 *undertake*
take a shot in the dark 229.5 *happen by chance*
take a shower 621.14 *bathe*
take a shufty 435.14 *inspect*
take a ski lift 41.14 *ski*
take a sledgehammer to crack a nut 610.5 *be superfluous*
take as one 482.11 *not discriminate*
take a stand 475.18 *appear*, 526.4 *show oneself*
take a stand against 670.8 *counterattack*
take a stroke 24.8 *play billiards*
take a strong line 692.10 *demand*
take a substitute 222
take a summer holiday 214.7 *be regular*
take a supporting role 127.10 *follow*
take a tiger by the tail 633.9 *face danger*
take a trip 875.10 *drug oneself*
take a trip to the showers 22.7 *play baseball*
take a tumble 360.11 *trip*
take a turn 313.6 *circle*
take a turn at the table 24.8 *play billiards*
take a turn for the better 627.2 *get better*
take a turn for the worse 129.4 *decrease*, 628.1 *deteriorate*, 683.6 *fail*
take authority 12, 688
take a vacation 218.9 *pause*, 645.4 *have leisure*
take a walk 349.33 *go away*
take away 326, 734, 767, 52.91 *add*, 131.3 *subtract*, 136.10 *set apart*, 170.9 *add*, 458.3 *cause to disappear*, 722.9 *lose*, 879.1 *punish*
takeaway 350.15 *eating place*, 599.10 *usable*, 606.1 *provision*, 606.7 *provisioning*
take away one's freedom 701.6 *subject*
take-away window 350.15 *eating place*
take a whack at 597.1 *undertake*
take a wife 823.15 *marry*
take a wild guess 229.5 *happen by chance*
take a wrong turn 335.3 *go astray*
take back 734, 125.6 *be compensated*, 221.7 *restore*, 511.13 *remind*, 536.9 *renounce*, 578.4 *recant*
take back to the drawing board 627.4 *reconsider*
take by force 695.7 *force*
take by storm 586.15 *persuade*, 670.9 *attack successfully*, 682.9 *be victorious*
take by surprise 514.9 *surprise*, 635.3 *trap*
take by the hand 662.23 *advise*
take captive 734.10 *take away*
take care 636.10 *look out*, 781.5 *be cautious*
take care of 293.33 *fix*, 350.25 *provide food*, 469.11 *care for*, 640.4 *act*, 653.1 *manage*, 697.8 *serve*
take care of number one 174.18 *be one*, 860.7 *be egoistic*
take care of oneself 623.5 *be healthy*
take centre stage 811.29 *show off*
take chances 479.13 *invent*

take charge of 469.11 *care for*, 597.1 *undertake*, 632.9 *protect*
take charity 662.18 *receive help*
take cognizance 16.69 *have jurisdiction over*, 16.71 *try a case*
take cognizance of 146.4 *include*
take command 12.12 *take authority*, 126.8 *be superior*, 688.20 *take authority*
take communion 9.7 *worship*
take compassionate leave 848.12 *exempt oneself*
take control 12.12 *take authority*
take courage 778
take cover 531.11 *conceal oneself*
take custody of 699.11 *detain*
take cuttings 69.15 *cultivate*, 245.13 *propagate*
take disciplinary action 879.1 *punish*
take down 350.21 *eat*, 362.1 *lower*, 362.3 *bring down*, 545.14 *inscribe*, 806.23 *abase*
take down a peg 806.23 *abase*
take Draconian measures 690.5 *be severe*
take drugs 875.10 *drug oneself*
take early retirement 645.4 *have leisure*, 705.5 *resign*
take effect 227, 230.7 *be operational*, 640.4 *act*
take evasive action 591.6 *evade*, 671.26 *act on the defensive*
take every course 350.22 *eat well*
take exception 663.15 *object*
take exception to 828.8 *resent*
take fire 828.12 *become angry*
take five 160.13, 218.9 *pause*, 649.2 *take it easy*, 651.2 *be refreshed*
take flight 345.4 *hurry off*, 591.8 *run away*, 638.5 *escape*
take for a ride 398.17 *murder*, 539.28 *trick*, 734.10 *take away*
take for better or for worse 580.3 *side with*, 823.15 *marry*
take for granted 488.10 *think likely*, 497.7 *believe*, 513.9 *predict*, 518.5 *suppose*, 787.5 *not wonder about*
take for oneself 734.7 *take*
take for richer or for poorer 580.3 *side with*
take French leave 254.18 *abscond*, 458.2 *depart*, 591.8 *run away*, 638.5 *escape*, 698.14 *be free*
take fright 777.11 *be afraid*
take guard 27.17 *bat*
take half measures 576.10 *compromise*, 609.5 *be insufficient*
take heart 775.9 *be hopeful*, 778.16 *take courage*
take heed 636.6 *be warned*
take hold 233.10 *be a prevailing influence*
take hold of 138.6 *adhere*, 726.6 *retain*, 734.7 *take*
take hold of one 584.17 *become a habit*
take holy orders 7.21 *ordain*, 825.11 *be monastic*
take home 730.9 *receive*
take-home pay 730.2 *something received*, 746.3 *pay*, 878.4 *reward for service*
take-home work 644.1 *work*
take hostage 699.11 *detain*
take ill 828.10 *be offended*
take in 62.19 *administer*, 130.6 *add*, 146.4 *include*, 262.5 *make smaller*, 346.14 *enrol*, 348.7 *admit*, 497.9 *make someone believe*, 501.13 *get to know*, 522.6 *understand*, 605.6 *store*, 632.9 *protect*, 730.9 *receive*, 734.7 *take*, 734.11 *be hospitable*
take-in 721.4 *earnings*
take in bad part 828.10 *be offended*
take industrial action 15.12 *have an industrial dispute*, 693.15 *be disobedient*, 713.8 *cause mischief*
take in exchange 222.5 *take a substitute*
take in food 350.21 *eat*

take in good part 817.10 *be courteous,* 839.12 *show mercy*
take in hand 150.22 *pacify,* 597.1 *undertake,* 662.23 *advise,* 734.7 *take*
take in one another's washing 223.5 *exchange*
take in one's lap 826.7 *show endearment for*
take in one's stride 655.11 *be expert,* 660.17 *do easily*
take in oxygen 651.2 *be refreshed*
take in sail 328.3 *slow down*
take in sickness and in health 580.3 *side with*
take in supplies 606.5 *provision*
take into account 146.4 *include*
take into consideration 146.4 *include*
take into custody 699.11 *detain,* 734.10 *take away*
take into one's arms 821.27 *kiss*
take into one's head 518.5 *suppose*
take in tow 339.11 *pull,* 662.23 *advise*
take in vain 601.1 *misuse*
take in with one's mother's milk 140.5 *combine*
take issue 500.8 *dissent,* 663.15 *object*
take issue with 536.8 *rebut,* 676.14 *battle*
take it 518.5 *suppose,* 673.4 *succumb*
take it easy 649, 660, 328.1 *move slowly,* 470.6 *be neglectful,* 628.1 *deteriorate,* 698.17 *be informal,* 781.5 *be cautious*
take it from one 673.4 *succumb*
take it from the top 221.7 *restore*
take it into one's head 579.5 *be capricious*
take it in turns 155.24 *alternate*
take it lying down 673.4 *succumb*
take it on the chin 320.10 *close,* 673.4 *succumb*
take it on the lam 345.4 *hurry off,* 638.5 *escape*
take it or leave it 571.16 *be compelled*
take it out of 650.6 *fatigue,* 806.25 *deflate*
take it out on 828.13 *vent one's anger*
take it slowly 781.5 *be cautious*
take it that 4.21 *rationalize*
take judicial notice 16.69 *have jurisdiction over*
take leave 254.16 *absent oneself,* 645.4 *have leisure*
take leave of absence 254
take leave of one's senses 508.6 *be foolish*
take lessons 6.23 *learn*
take liberties 698.19 *liberalize,* 708.5 *be permitted,* 807.22 *be rude,* 807.27 *dare,* 818.7 *be discourteous,* 846.15 *presume*
take liberties with 764.11 *quarrel*
take life 398.16 *kill*
take long odds 229.4 *chance*
take measures 594.1 *prepare,* 640.4 *act*
Takemikazuchi 8 Deities
take minutes 545.14 *inscribe*
take money away 734.10 *take away*
take more grass 25.7 *bowl*
taken 518.8 *supposed,* 730.13, 749.6 *received*
taken aback 514.6 *surprised*
taken as read 518.8 *supposed*
taken away 131.5 *subtracted,* 254.12 *missing*
taken back 839.6 *forgiven*
taken bad 624.22 *sick*
taken by God 397.19 *dead*
taken care of 742.2 *solvent*
taken down a peg or two 806.3 *humbled*
take neither side 783.15 *be impartial*
taken for a ride 539.36 *deceived*
taken for granted 518.8 *supposed,* 787.4 *predictable*
taken ill 624.22 *sick*

taken in 539.36 *deceived,* 730.13 *received*
take no advice 577.9 *be obstinate*
take no chances 632.8 *be safe*
taken off guard 540.1 *unprepared*
take no interest 783.12 *be indifferent*
take no interest in 466.6 *be incurious*
take no note of time 193.3 *mistime*
take no notice of 436.16 *be blind to,* 468.12 *be inattentive,* 470.6 *be neglectful*
take no offence 839.12 *show mercy*
take no part in 254.15 *be absent*
take no precautions 595.12 *be unprepared*
take no prisoners 398.18 *slaughter*
take no risks 781.5 *be cautious*
take note of 467
take nourishment 350.21 *eat*
taken over 730.13 *received*
taken prisoner 701.9 *subject*
taken to the cleaners 515.10 *deceived*
taken with 821.18 *in love*
takeoff 73.5 *flight,* 118.3 *mockery,* 128.2 *spread,* 345.8 *start,* 359.4 *taking off,* 854.6 *ridicule*
take-off 21.2 *field events,* 21.6 *track,* 39.6 *diving,* 771.4 *entertainment,* 850.4 *ridicule*
take offence 820.11 *be hostile,* 828.10 *be offended*
take offence at 785.5 *dislike*
take off for 332.7 *take a direction*
take office 12.12, 688.20 *take authority*
take off in a big way 128.4 *increase*
take off one's hat to 849
take-off point 21.2, 21.2 *field events*
take off someone's hands 730.9 *receive*
take-off strip 327.13 *flight path*
take off the gloves 690.6 *suppress*
take off weight 871.5 *fast*
take on 348.10 *introduce,* 574.9 *undertake,* 596.3 *tackle,* 597.1 *undertake,* 605.6 *store,* 640.4 *act,* 663.16 *confront,* 670.8 *counterattack,* 674.11 *contend,* 674.12 *fight,* 710.11 *volunteer,* 714.8 *guarantee,* 733.8 *adopt,* 734.7 *take,* 828.11 *be angry*
take on all comers 574.8 *brace oneself*
take on a new lease of life 629.4 *be restored*
take on a pilot 74.9 *navigate*
take on board 257.6 *contain,* 734.11 *be hospitable*
take on depth 522.4 *be intelligible*
take one's bearings 332.8 *orient*
take one's breath away 563.15 *strike dumb,* 786.10 *be wonderful*
take one's chance 210.5 *take the opportunity,* 642.14 *push*
take one's coat off 644.6 *work*
take one's commission 752.4 *take a discount*
take one's cue from 654.6 *consult*
take one's cut 731.5 *get one's allotment*
take one's departure 345.1 *depart*
take one's ease 645.4 *have leisure,* 649.2 *take it easy*
take oneself off 345.6 *part*
take oneself to a nunnery 825.11 *be monastic*
take one's fancy 405.9 *give pleasure*

take one's foot off the gas 328.3 *slow down*
take one's gruel 879.6 *be punished*
take one's hat off to 851.15 *compliment*
take one's heritage 682.12 *succeed to*
take one's leave 254.16 *absent oneself,* 345.1 *depart,* 345.6 *part*
take one's life in one's hands 633.9 *face danger*
take one's lumps 673.4 *succumb*
take one's medicine 879.6 *be punished*
take one's own life 398.21 *commit suicide*
take one's percentage 752.4 *take a discount*
take one's pick 580.4 *pick*
take one's place 116.25 *conform,* 150.24 *line up*
take one's pleasure with 877.20 *seduce*
take one's punishment 840.7 *be punished*
take one's revenge 832.19 *be pitiless*
take one step at a time 781.5 *be cautious*
take one's time 209.6 *be late,* 328.2 *hesitate,* 645.4 *have leisure,* 781.5 *be cautious*
take one's turn 214.7 *be regular*
take one up on 668.5 *defy*
take on oneself 588.8 *resolve*
take on one's shoulders 597.1 *undertake*
take on responsibility 222.4 *be a substitute*
take on supplies 606.5 *provision*
take on the responsibility 847.15 *be liable*
take on too much 597.1 *undertake*
take on trust 466.5 *not ask,* 497.7 *believe*
take on water 606.5 *provision*
take orders 694.5 *obey*
take out 25.7 *bowl,* 131.3 *subtract,* 147.8 *eject,* 243.10 *produce,* 355.11 *extract,* 546.1 *obliterate,* 734.10 *take away,* 819.14 *seek the friendship of*
take-out 41.10 *curling*
take out a business loan 733.7 *borrow*
take out a loan 733.7 *borrow,* 744.9 *acquire credit*
take out a mortgage 723.7 *possess,* 733.7 *borrow*
take out a tackler 35.5 *play rugby*
take out a tenancy 723.7 *possess*
take out credit 744.9 *acquire credit*
take out insurance 781.5 *be cautious*
take out membership 665.13 *be a member*
take out of context 309.12 *distort the truth,* 525.1 *misinterpret*
take out of print 546.1 *obliterate*
take out one's spite on 618.14 *ill-treat*
takeover 13.7 *corporation,* 195.4 *accession,* 230.2 *joint operation,* 252.3 *replacement,* 475.6 *mass demonstration,* 728.1 *transfer of property,* 734.1 *taking,* 734.7 *take,* 734.12 *taking,* 737.9 *bargaining,* 738.7 *purchasing*
take over 12.12 *take authority,* 13.11 *deal,* 155.22 *succeed,* 195.11 *follow in office,* 222.4 *be a substitute,* 233.10 *be a prevailing influence,* 252.16 *replace,* 475.19 *protest,* 670.9 *attack successfully,* 679.38 *conquer,* 688.20 *take authority,* 728.3 *transfer property,* 730.9 *receive*
takeover bid 13.7 *corporation,* 710.3 *business offer,* 728.1 *transfer of property,* 734.1 *taking,* 738.7 *purchasing*
take over from 767.11 *assist*
take over the mantle 195.11 *follow in office*

take over the reins 12.12 *take authority,* 195.11 *follow in office,* 688.20 *take authority*
takeover zone 21.1 *track events*
take pains 642.15 *try,* 781.5 *be cautious*
take part 18.6 *participate,* 21.6 *compete in athletics,* 146.5 *be included,* 253.12 *attend*
take part in 640.4 *act,* 724.4 *have joint possession*
take part in an endurance race 33.9 *race*
take part in a survey 477.19 *be questioned*
take part in a training scheme 6.23 *learn*
take pity 835.14 *have pity*
take pity on 835.8 *pity,* 835.10 *show mercy*
take place 227.9 *take effect*
take pleasure in 405.8 *feel pleasure,* 762.6 *enjoy,* 821.23 *love*
take poison 398.21 *commit suicide*
take possession of 734.7 *take*
take pot luck 229.4 *chance*
take potluck 815.11 *be sociable*
take precautions 247.9 *practise birth control,* 516.2 *show prudence,* 594.3 *be prepared,* 632.8 *be safe,* 781.5 *be cautious*
take precedence 154, 126.10 *lead,* 194.8 *be before,* 611.7 *be important*
take pride in 805.25 *be proud of,* 805.29 *feel pride*
take priority 154.16 *take precedence,* 194.8 *be before*
take prisoner 699.11 *detain,* 701.7 *defeat,* 702.9 *imprison*
take profits 734.7 *take*
taker 734, 349.26 *ejector,* 723.5 *possessor,* 730.5 *recipient,* 736.8 *thief,* 738.12 *purchaser*
take refuge 290.14 *go inside,* 632.8 *be safe,* 634.4 *shelter*
take reprisals 672.3 *retaliate*
take responsibility 222.4 *be a substitute*
take responsibility for 714.7 *promise*
take risks 780.5 *be rash*
take rooms 255.14 *inhabit*
take root 83.21 *vegetate,* 217.5 *be permanent,* 225.6 *be stable,* 233.8 *influence,* 584.17 *become a habit*
take second best 222.5 *take a substitute*
take seriously 772, 611.8 *make important*
take sexual possession of 734.7 *take*
take shame 806.24 *be humiliated*
take shape 99.18 *come to be*
take short steps 328.1 *move slowly*
take sides 305.9 *side with,* 493.11 *be unjust,* 580.3 *side with*
take some doing 659.17 *be difficult*
take someone's job and shove it 705.5 *resign*
take someone's word for 497.7 *believe*
take someone's words to heart 636.6 *be warned*
take something off 752.3 *discount*
take soundings 74.9 *navigate,* 277.14 *deepen*
take stance 27.17 *bat*
take statements 16.71 *try a case*
take steps 594.1 *prepare,* 640.4 *act*
take stock 170.11 *number,* 750.8 *audit*
take stock of 435.16 *visualize,* 461.15 *think about*
take sword in hand 594.8 *prepare oneself*
take tentative steps 781.5 *be cautious*
take that 672.7 *revenge*
take the airline 332.7 *take a direction*

take the attitude 4.22 *propound a philosophy*
take the auspices 517.12 *divine*
take the backtrack 337.3 *reverse*
take the bit between one's teeth 574.8 *brace oneself*
take the blame 222.4 *be a substitute*, 852.24 *be open to criticism*
take the bull by the horns 479.13 *invent*, 574.8 *brace oneself*, 596.3 *tackle*, 597.1 *undertake*, 642.14 *push*, 778.15 *be courageous*
take the chair 242.4 *moderate*, 653.2 *direct*
take the championship 682.9 *be victorious*
take the chill off 408.14 *be hot*
take the consequences 879.6 *be punished*
take the cup 682.9 *be victorious*
take the easy way out 660.20 *take it easy*
take the edge off 242.4 *moderate*, 381.10 *blunt*, 587.5 *discourage*
take the fancy of 821.28 *win the love of*
take the field 22.7 *play baseball*, 27.15 *play*, 676.13 *be at war*
take the first step 156.21 *pioneer*
take the floor 564.14 *speak to*, 567.7 *address*
take the gloves off 695.7 *force*
take the good with the bad 717.4 *compromise*
take the guise of 457.11 *appear*
take the heart out of 628.5 *hurt*, 690.5 *be severe*
take the heat 673.4 *succumb*
take the heat off 673.3 *submit*
take the helm 195.11 *follow in office*, 303.10 *be in front*, 653.2 *direct*, 688.20 *take authority*
take the high road 327.14 *find one's way*
take the initiative 156.21 *pioneer*
take the law into one's own hands 16.74 *be lawless*, 689.4 *be anarchic*, 720.10 *violate the law*
take the lead 126.10 *lead*, 194.8 *be before*, 303.10 *be in front*, 611.7 *be important*
take the lid off 437.10 *make visible*, 530.5 *disclose*
take the limelight 611.7 *be important*
take the line of least resistance 660.20 *take it easy*, 673.4 *succumb*
take the long-term view 199.10 *expect*
take the long view 199.10 *expect*
take the Lord's name in vain 827.5 *curse*
take the mantle of 155.22 *succeed*
take the mean 124.10 *make average*
take the measurements of 268.10 *measure*
take the middle way 242.3 *be moderate*
take the oath 483.11 *give evidence*
take the oath of office 535.18 *vow*
take the offensive 670.1 *attack*, 676.13 *be at war*
take the omens 517.12 *divine*
take the opportunity 210, 208.11 *get ahead*
take the opposing side 111.8 *be opposite*
take the part of 662.24 *back*
take the piss 799.6 *deride*
take the place of 349, 155.22 *succeed*, 222.4 *be a substitute*
take the pledge 699.10 *restrain oneself*, 869.5 *be self-restrained*
take the plunge 156.11 *make a beginning*, 574.8 *brace oneself*, 580.3 *side with*, 778.15 *be courageous*, 823.15 *marry*
take the prize 617.9 *be worthy*, 682.9 *be victorious*

take the Queen's shilling 17.10 *enlist*
take the rap 222.4 *be a substitute*, 852.24 *be open to criticism*, 879.6 *be punished*
take the reciprocal course 337.3 *reverse*
take the rise out of 362.4 *debase*
take the role of 155.22 *succeed*
take the shape of 220.8 *be transformed*, 457.11 *appear*
take the shine out of 806.25 *deflate*
take the square root 52.91 *add*
take the stage 51.32 *act*
take the stand 16.70 *litigate*
take the starch out of 628.5 *hurt*, 806.25 *deflate*
take the sting out of 242.4 *moderate*, 614.8 *make useless*, 677.4 *pacify*, 767.9 *relieve*
take the strain 608.4 *suffice*
take the sun 332.8 *orient*
take the train 327.14 *find one's way*
take the veil 7.21 *ordain*, 816.12 *be unsocial*, 825.11 *be monastic*
take the weight of 369.15 *weigh*
take the wind out of one's sails 74.10 *sail*, 362.4 *debase*, 542.21 *detract from*, 661.8 *hinder*
take the wind out of someone's sails 236.8 *overpower*, 325.9 *make motionless*, 628.5 *hurt*, 806.25 *deflate*
take the words out of one's mouth 208.9 *prepare*
take the wraps off 530.5 *disclose*
take things easy 673.3 *submit*
take things slowly 470.6 *be neglectful*
take thought for tomorrow 199.10 *expect*
take time by the forelock 210.5 *take the opportunity*
take time off 254.17 *take leave of absence*, 649.2 *take it easy*
take time out 160.13 *pause*, 645.4 *have leisure*
take time to smell the flowers 645.4 *have leisure*
take to 584.18 *habituate*, 784.7 *like*, 821.24 *be in love*
take to arms 241.7 *be violent*, 676.12 *go to war*
take to bits 244.9 *demolish*
take to court 16.70 *litigate*
take to heart 759.17 *feel deeply*, 760.11 *be sensitive*, 828.10 *be offended*
take to like a duck to water 584.18 *habituate*, 660.17 *do easily*
take to mean 4.21 *rationalize*, 524.8 *interpret*
take too much time 19.18 *be penalized*
take to one's bed 624.24 *be unhealthy*
take to one's bosom 726.7 *detain*
take to oneself 130.6 *add*
take to one's heels 345.4 *hurry off*, 591.8 *run away*, 638.5 *escape*
take to pieces 136.9 *separate*, 141.4 *deconstruct*, 244.9 *demolish*, 614.8 *make useless*
take to task 852.20 *censure*, 879.1 *punish*
take to the cleaners 515.8 *be dishonest*, 734.10 *take away*
take to the hills 531.11 *conceal oneself*, 634.4 *shelter*
take to the limit 142.10 *complete*
take to the masses 164.26 *popularize*
take to the road 289.12 *be outside*, 327.14 *find one's way*
take to the woods 634.4 *shelter*
take turn and turn about 109.7 *reciprocate*, 155.24 *alternate*
take turns 109.7 *reciprocate*, 155.24 *alternate*
take umbrage 764.11 *quarrel*, 820.11 *be hostile*, 828.10 *be offended*

take unawares 514.9 *surprise*
take under one's wing 632.9 *protect*, 662.23 *advise*
take untimely action 211
take up 36.15 *sail*, 195.11 *follow in office*, 270.10 *shorten*, 348.13 *absorb*, 361.4 *gather up*, 567.12 *address oneself to*, 574.9 *undertake*, 580.1 *select*, 584.16 *have a habit*, 597.1 *undertake*, 599.1 *use*, 662.23 *advise*, 730.9 *receive*
take up again 219.4 *protract*
take up an option 580.1 *select*
take up a position 251.9 *be situated*
take up arms 241.7 *be violent*
take up arms for 671.22 *plead for*
take up a thing and drop it 579.5 *be capricious*
take up no room 260.6 *be little*
take upon oneself 597.1 *undertake*, 846.14 *arrogate*
take upon one's shoulders 847.15 *be liable*
take up residence 256, 250.10 *settle*
take up residence in 723.7 *possess*
take-up spool 66.18 *exposure time*
take up the cause 676.12 *go to war*
take up the cause of 671.22 *plead for*
take up the challenge 674.11 *contend*
take up the cudgels 676.12 *go to war*
take up the cudgels for 662.24 *back*, 671.22 *plead for*
take up time 269.10 *lengthen*
take up with 819.13 *befriend*
take vows 7.21 *ordain*
take what's on offer 717.4 *compromise*
take wing 78.27 *fly*, 345.3 *quit*
take with a pinch of salt 498.8 *disbelieve*
take wrong 525.1 *misinterpret*
takin 77 *Placental Mammals*
taking 734, 734, 721.1 *gain*, 723.1 *possession*, 730.1, 730.11 *receiving*, 736.1 *stealing*
Taking 734
taking advantage of 539.7 *tricking*
taking all things together 124.11 *on average*
taking an overdose 398.7 *suicide*
taking a part 51.20 *acting*
taking apart 141.2 *deconstruction*
taking a role 51.20 *acting*
taking away 734, 131.1 *subtraction*, 136.2 *setting apart*, 252.2 *removal*, 722.1 *loss*
taking back 734, 221.2 *restoration*
taking back one's words 578.8 *recantation*
taking by storm 670.14 *siege*, 682.2 *victory*, 734.6 *taker*
taking candy from a baby 612.8 *trifle*
taking counsel 654.2 *consultation*
taking everything into consideration 142.13 *on the whole*
taking food 350.1 *eating*
taking for granted 787.3 *unmoved*
taking hold 734.1 *taking*
taking in 734, 262.1 *contraction*, 348.1 *admittance*, 734.1 *taking*
taking in hand 734.1 *taking*
taking into account 492.14 *considering*
taking issue with 536.3 *rebuttal*
taking it easy 624.22 *sick*
taking it that 106.15 *under the circumstances*
taking liberties 357.8 *transgression*
taking life 398.1 *killing*
taking measures 594.9 *preparation*
taking money away 734.3 *taking away*

taking of evidence 16.7 *legal trial*
taking off 359
taking on 734.1 *taking*
taking one's time 328.5 *unhurried*
taking on responsibility 597.6 *enterprising*
taking out 734.3 *taking away*, 821.6 *courtship*
taking out a loan 733.1 *borrowing*
taking over 195.4 *accession*, 688.3 *acquisition of power*, 734.1 *taking*
taking pains 644.4 *exertion*
taking part 642.21 *meddling*
taking possession 723.1 *possession*, 734.1 *taking*
taking precedence 154.1 *precedence*, 611.5 *important*
takings 734, 721.4 *earnings*, 730.2 *something received*, 749.2 *money received*
taking steps 594.9 *preparation*
taking the auspices 517.2 *divination*
taking the opportunity 208.6 *getting ahead*
taking the plunge 823.1 *marriage*
taking the waters 389.7 *hydrotherapeutics*
taking to task 852.7 *blame*
taking up 36.1 *sailing*
taking up the post of 195.4 *accession*
Taklimakan 98 *Deserts*
Talaing 1 *Peoples*
talambas 49 *Musical Instruments*
talapoin 77 *Placental Mammals*, 7.7 *monk*
Talavera ware 44 *Types of Ceramics*
Talbot 52 *Scientists*
talc 54 *Minerals*, 384.5 *powder*
talcum powder 418.2 *fragrant thing*
tale 538.4 *lie*, 560.3 *narration*
talebearer 528.10 *informer*
talent 75 *Some Foreign Units*, 50.5 *artistry*, 165.7 *special skill*, 234.3 *aptitude*, 235.2, 485.2 *ability*, 507.2 *intelligence*, 655.2 *aptitude*, 660.1 *easiness*, 741.12 *ancient coins*, 861.12 *proficiency*
talented 235.13 *powerful*, 485.9 *qualified*, 501.8 *knowledgeable*, 507.6 *intelligent*, 655.6 *skilful*, 655.7 *gifted*, 861.5 *proficient*
talentless 656.1 *unskilful*
talent spotter 51.31 *theatregoer*
tale of woe 774.2 *lament*
Taliesin 48 *Poets*
talion 672.1 *retaliation*
talipot 85 *Trees and Shrubs*
talisman 11, 10.14 *sacred object*, 517.6 *good-luck sign*, 543.1 *sign*, 637.2 *preserver*
talismanic 11.15 *witchlike*
talk 565, 5.3 *spoken language*, 5.45 *use language*, 420.8 *something heard*, 475.3 *explanation*, 530.6 *divulge*, 534.30 *communicate*, 564.1 *faculty of speech*, 564.11 *speak*, 565.7 *be talkative*, 567.1 *address*, 568.1 *conversation*, 568.9 *converse*
talk about 532.13 *make public*, 854.13 *vilify*
talk about behind one's back 854.13 *vilify*
talkative 565, 528.16 *informative*, 530.11 *disclosing*, 553.3 *diffuse*, 564.19 *speaking*, 568.12 *conversing*
talkatively 565
talkativeness 565, 553.1 *diffuseness*, 564.2 *power of speech*
Talkativeness 565
talk at length 565.7 *be talkative*
talk back 478.18, 807.25 *answer back*
talk big 807.24 *be vain*, 809.16 *show off*
talk bunk 538.23 *talk nonsense*
talk bunkum 521.9, 538.23 *talk nonsense*
talk crap 538.23 *talk nonsense*
talk dirty 827.5 *curse*

talk double Dutch 521.9 *talk non-sense*, 523.7 *be unintelligible*
talk down 73.6 *flight control*
talker 565, 478.10 *answerer*, 564.10 *speaker*, 568.7 *conversationalist*
talk filthy 827.5 *curse*
talk for effect 809.16 *show off*, 811.31 *put on a show*
talk gibberish 521.9 *talk non-sense*
talk guff 538.23 *talk nonsense*
talk hogwash 538.23 *talk non-sense*
talk-in 568.4 *conference*
talk in clichés 426.14 *repeat*
talk in 534.1 *communications*, 564.1 *faculty of speech*, 564.19 *speaking*, 568.12 *conversing*
talking big 557.2 *affectation*
talking bird 78.7 *cagebird*
talking book 436.3 *aid for poor sight*
talking dirty 827.1 *curse*
talking head 534.29 *broadcaster*
talking in superlatives 541.4 *bombast*
talking-to 852.7 *blame*
talking to oneself 569.5 *soliloquizing*
talk in riddles 523.7 *be unintelligible*
talk in superlatives 541.10 *boast*
talk into 228.9 *motivate*, 586.15 *persuade*
talk like an idiot 521.9 *talk non-sense*, 523.7 *be unintelligible*
talk nineteen to the dozen 565.8 *talk too much*
talk nonsense 506, 521, 538, 523.7 *be unintelligible*
talk off the subject 104.13 *be ex-traneous*
talk off the top of one's head 595.13 *improvise*
talk of the town 682.4 *successful person*, 801.2 *disreputable char-acter*
talk one's head off 565.8 *talk too much*
talk on the big white telephone 349.15 *vomit*
talk out of 587.1 *dissuade*
talk out of turn 117.12 *be dispa-rate*, 530.7 *betray*
talk over 568.11 *confer*
talk plainly 312.11 *be straight*
talk privately 568.10 *chat*
talk radio 420.9 *audio device*
talk round 242.4 *moderate*, 586.15 *persuade*, 591.7 *be eva-sive*
talk rubbish 521.9 *talk nonsense*
talks 568, 678.5 *conference*
talk shit 474.12 *deceive*
talk show 534.25 *broadcast mate-rial*
talk straight 312.11 *be straight*, 530.6 *divulge*
talk sweetly 539.26 *be a hypocrite*
talk tête-à-tête 568.10 *chat*
talk the hind leg off a donkey 565.8 *talk too much*
talk the same language 667.6 *agree with*
talk through one's hat 506.6 *talk nonsense*
talk to 564.14 *speak to*, 567.7 *ad-dress*
talk to a brick wall 614.9 *waste effort*
talk together 568.9 *converse*
talk too long 788.6 *be boring*
talk too much 565, 610.4 *be ex-cessive*
talk to oneself 564, 569.3 *solilo-quize*
talk to the wall 569.3 *soliloquize*
talk turkey 520.10 *mean*, 530.6 *divulge*, 552.4 *be concise*, 556.7 *be simple*
talk until one is blue in the face 565.8 *talk too much*
talk with one's fingers crossed 474.12 *deceive*
tall 275, 269.1 *long*, 275.9 *high*
Tallahassee 93 *Cities*

Tallahatchie 96 *Rivers*
tallboy 47.5, 258.3 *cabinet*
tall drink 351.2 *drink*, 874.12 *al-cohol*
taller 275.10 *higher*
tallest 275.10 *higher*
tallharpa 49 *Musical Instru-ments*
tallied 750.11 *accounted*
Tallinn 93 *Cities*
tallith 7.11 *vestment*, 10.14 *sa-cred object*, 295.14 *neckwear*
tall money 742.6 *money*
tallness 259.2 *bigness*, 269.4 *length*, 275.1 *height*
tall order 597.2 *undertaking*, 659.3 *difficult task*
tallow 386.4 *lubricant*, 395.8 *fat*
tallow candle 439.5 *incandescent light*
tallow-faced 445.8 *drained of col-our*
tallow wood 85 Trees and Shrubs
tallowy 386.10, 395.11 *oily*
tall person 259, 275
tall ship 74 Sailing Ships and Boats
tall-ship racing 36.1 *sailing*
tall story 541, 309.4 *distortion of the truth*, 489.6 *implausibil-ity*, 538.4 *lie*, 560.3 *narration*, 771.5 *joke*
tall tale 538.4 *lie*
tall thing 275
tally 52.12 *numeration*, 107.8 *be proportionate to*, 109.3 *correla-tion*, 109.9 *correlate*, 110.7 *be the same*, 114.10 *be similar*, 116.25 *conform*, 122.11 *equal-ize*, 130.2 *mathematical addi-tion*, 167.7 *conform*, 169.4 *mathematical result*, 169.10 *number*, 170.3 *count*, 170.8 *calculate*, 170.11 *number*, 171.1 *list*, 171.10 *score*, 257.5 *divi-sions*, 257.9 *itemize*, 478.7 *nu-merical result*, 478.8 *correspond-ence*, 478.21 *answer to*, 544.3 *means of identification*, 545.1 *re-cord*, 545.15 *register*, 667.8 *be compatible*, 744.1 *credit*, 745.5 *amount owing*, 750.3 *accounting*
tally-ho 431.5 *hunting cry*, 590.2 *chase*, 590.19 *after him*
tallying 170.3 *count*, 478.15 *cor-respondent*
tally stick 52.67 *calculator*
Talmud 1.8 *tradition*, 7.12 *reli-gious text*
Talmud Torah 6.12 *educational institution*
talon 43 Architectural Decora-tion, 380.8 *sharp-pointed thing*, 726.3 *tools for gripping*
talons 78.16 *avian anatomy*
talus 382 Bones
tamale 45.50 *Central American dish*
tam âm la 49 Musical Instru-ments
tamandua 77 Placental Mam-mals
tamanoas 8.5 *deity*
Tamar 96 Rivers
tamarack 85 Trees and Shrubs
tamarillo 86 Fruits
tamarin 77 Placental Mammals
tamarind 85 Trees and Shrubs, **86** Fruits
tamarisk 85 Trees and Shrubs
tamarou 77 Placental Mammals
Tamashek 5 Languages and Groups of Languages
tambour 40.5 *real tennis*, 43.9 *miscellaneous architectural fea-tures*
tambourine 49 Musical Instru-ments
tambura 49 Musical Instru-ments
tame 242.4 *moderate*, 325.5 *sed-entary*, 412.5 *tasteless*, 555.1 *unemphatic*, 584.18 *habituate*, 632.5 *safe*, 673.5 *submitting*, 694.7 *obedient*, 701.6 *subject*

tame animal 76.3 *domesticated animal*
tamed 76.15 *of animals*, 584.14 *habituated*
tamely 555.3 *unemphatically*, 694.10 *obediently*
tameness 412.1 *tastelessness*, 555.2 *lack of emphasis*, 673.1 *submission*, 694.1 *obedience*
Tamil 5 Languages and Groups of Languages
Tamil art 50 Non-Western Art
Tamils 1 Peoples
Tammuz 8 Deities
tam-o'shanter 295.15 *headgear*
tamp 330.2 *collide*, 330.15 *ram*, 371.9 *make dense*
Tampa 93 Cities
tamper 330.15 *ram*, 628.4 *imp-air*, 642.17 *meddle*
Tampere 93 Cities
tamperer 642.11 *meddler*
tampering 642.9 *overactivity*
tampering with 540.9 *falsification*
tamper with 133.8 *mix*, 153.10 *disrupt*, 216.8 *cause change*, 407.11 *touch*, 540.22 *falsify*
Tampico 93 Cities
tamping iron 330.15 *ram*
tampion 323.2 *stopper*, 354.11 *thing inserted*
tampon 323.2 *stopper*, 323.8 *stop*, 354.11 *thing inserted*, 630.10 *surgical dressing*
tam-tam 49 Musical Instru-ments
Tamworth 68 Breeds of Pig
tan 293.24 *coat*, 378.11 *make tough*, 408.5 *hot weather*, 408.16 *feel hot*, 444.15 *colour*, 447.11 *blacken*, 449.1, 449.7 *brown*, 451.1 *orange*, 879.3 *hit*
Tana 94 Lakes
tanager 78 Birds
tandem 36.7, 36.13 *windsurfing*, 71.12 *bicycle*, 176.2 *double*
tandem exchange 534.12 *public telephone system*
tandem race 36.6 *canoeing*
tandoori 45.49 *Indian dish*
tang 413.1 *piquancy*
tanga 295.21 *beachwear*
Tangaloa 8 Deities
Tanganyika 94 Lakes, 94.5 *other major lakes*
Tang dynasty art 50 Non-West-ern Art
tangelo 86 Fruits
tangency 267.1 *juxtaposition*
tangent 52.37 *line*, 52.52 *trigono-metric function*, 267.5 *juxta-posed*, 286.1 *obliqueness*, 286.4 *oblique*, 310.2 *obliquity*, 335.13 *deviation*, 342.5 *focus*, 342.7 *convergent*
tangential 52.80 *linear*, 267.5 *juxtaposed*, 310.8 *oblique*, 342.7 *convergent*
tangentially 267.7 *beside*
tangent rule 52.51 *trigonometry*
tangerine 86 Fruits, 451.3 *or-ange thing*
tangibility 101.1 *reality*, 367.1 *material world*, 407.1 *touch*, 437.3 *visibility*, 537.2 *reality*
tangible 101.6 *real*, 367.7 *mate-rial*, 403.8 *sensate*, 407.8 *touch-able*, 437.1 *visible*, 537.16 *exist-ing*, 725.8 *propertied*
tangible assets 725.5 *personal es-tate*
tangible object 367.5 *object*
tangibles 725.5 *personal estate*
tangibly 367.9 *materially*, 407.14 *palpably*
Tangier 93 Cities
tanginess 413.1 *piquancy*
tangle 151, 113.8 *be diverse*, 133.3 *miscellany*, 151.24 *make disordered*, 375.12 *make rough*, 539.33 *snare*, 659.5 *predicament*
tangled 133.12 *mixed*, 151.18 *muddled*, 371.7 *condensed*
tango 46.2, 46.15 *dance*
Tango 534 Phonetic Alphabet
tango romantica 41.7 *ice-dancing*
tangram 529.4 *brain-teaser*

tang soo do 18 Sporting Activi-ties
Tang ware 44 Types of Ceramics
tangy 413.9 *piquant*, 415.5 *acid*
Tanhoy 532.1 *publication*
Tanit 8 Deities
tank 72.5 *locomotive part*, 258.11 *vessel*, 605.4 *storage*, 679.21 *armoured cavalry*, 702.2 *the inside*
tanka 48.7 *poem*
tankage 259.1 *size*
tankard 258.13 *drinking vessel*, 351.10 *drink container*
tank assault 670.12 *military at-tack*
tank-buster 679.31 *military air-craft*
tanked up 874.1 *drunk*
tank engine 72.4 *locomotive*
tanker 74 Ships and Boats, 72.4 *locomotive*, 74.3 *vessel*
tank farmer 68.15 *agriculturist*
tank farming 68.4 *arable farming*
tank top 295.8 *shirt*
tanktown 10.19 *village*
tank transporter 679.21 *armoured cavalry*
tank trap 635.1 *trap*
tank up 874.13 *get drunk*
tank wagon 72.6 *rolling stock*
tanned 378.2 *toughened*, 447.3 *blackened*, 449.2 *browned*
tanner 293.17 *coverer*, 741.10 *former British money*
Tannhäuser 48 Poets
tannin 352.2 *secreted substance*
tanning 408.5 *hot weather*
Tannoy 420.9 *audio device*
tan one's hide 879.3 *hit*
Tanta 93 Cities
tantalic 57.34 *elemental*
tantalite 54 Minerals
tantalization 515.1 *disappoint-ment*, 586.3 *incentive*
tantalize 228.9 *motivate*, 340.12 *lure*, 515.6 *disappoint*, 586.16 *tempt*, 782.15 *cause desire*, 821.26 *court*
tantalizer 586.13 *tempter*
tantalizing 228.11 *motivational*, 586.19 *persuasive*
tantalizingly 228.14 *influentially*, 515.13 *disappointingly*, 821.30 *lovingly*
tantalous 57.34 *elemental*
tantalum 57 Chemical Elements
tantamount 122.6 *equal*, 520.6 *meaningful*
tantara 430.1 *stridency*
tantivy 329.9 *acceleration*
tanto 49 Musical Terms
Tantrism 7 Non-Christian Reli-gions
tantrum 828.4 *anger*
Tanzania 91 Countries
Taoism 7 Non-Christian Reli-gions, 4.7 *school of thought*
Taoist 4.11 *follower of a doctrine*, 4.14 *of a philosophy*, 7.16 *de-nominational*
tap 330, 85.18 *manage trees*, 323.2 *stopper*, 326.11 *transfer*, 330.13 *blow*, 347.7 *outlet*, 355.14 *suck*, 389.13 *irrigator*, 407.11 *touch*, 420.15 *hear*, 425.2, 425.6 *crack*, 426.11 *knock*, 521.7 *mean nothing*, 605.3 *supply*, 606.5 *provision*, 712.8 *solicit money*, 734.10 *take away*, 826.1 *endearment*
tap dance 46.2 *dance*
tap-dance 46.15 *dance*
tap dancer 46.5, 51.28 *dancer*
tap dancing 46.1 *dancing*
tape 34.4 *climbing equipment*, 135.10 *link*, 137.6 *line*, 137.11 *connect*, 420.9 *audio device*, 420.15 *hear*, 534.26 *recording*, 534.30 *communicate*, 545.6 *re-cord book*, 545.7 *recording*, 545.13 *record*
tape collection 605.5 *collection*
taped 534.34 *communicated*, 545.16 *recorded*
tapedeck cassette 534.26 *recording*

tape grass 87 Grasses
tape machine 545.10 *recording instrument*
tape measure 170.5 *computer*, 268.6 *measuring instrument*
tape punch 65.7 *peripheral*
taper 272.8 *narrow thing*, 272.9 *narrowing*, 272.10 *narrow*, 342.6 *narrowing*, 342.9 *converge*, 342.11 *focus*, 380.15 *make sharp*, 410.2 *lighter*, 439.8 *fire*
tape-record 534.30 *communicate*, 545.13 *record*
tape recorder 114.3 *copier*, 118.6 *photocopier*, 420.9 *audio device*, 534.26 *recording*, 545.10 *recording instrument*
tape recording 118.5 *duplicate*, 534.26 *recording*
tapered 272, 380.1 *sharp*
tapering 121.7 *gradational*, 272.3 *tapered*, 272.9, 342.6 *narrowing*, 342.7 *convergent*, 380.1 *sharp*
taper off 121.6 *change gradually*, 129.4 *decrease*
taper to a point 380.14 *be sharp*
tape streamer 65.7 *peripheral*
tapestry 42 Hobbies and Pastimes, 67 Natural Fabrics, 50.1 *art*, 50.7 *picture*, 293.8 *wall covering*, 792.2 *pattern*
tapeworm 81 Worms, 81.6 *worm*, 81.10 *parasite*
tapioca 45.35 *dessert*
tapir 77 Placental Mammals
tapirs 77.15 *hoofed mammal*
tap one's foot 543.11 *gesture*
tap out a message 543.12 *signal*
tapper 85.8 *forester*, 330.15 *ram*
tapping 85.6 *tree management*, 330.12 *collision*, 349.22 *disgorgement*, 355.4 *sucking*
tapping foot 543.3 *gesture*
taproot 83.7 *root*, 226.3 *rudiment*
taps 399.2 *funeral*, 543.6 *word*
tapster 85.8 *forester*
tap water 389.2 *drinking water*
tar 49 Musical Instruments, 74.7 *nautical person*, 293.11 *paving*, 293.29 *surface*, 394.2 *adhesive*, 395.10 *resin*, 413.7 *tobacco*, 447.9 *black thing*, 631.9 *pollution*, 676.11 *recruit*
tarabuka 49 Musical Instruments
taradiddle 538.4 *lie*
tarak 42 Card Games
taramasalata 45.12 *hors d'oeuvre*, 45.16 *fish dish*, 45.52 *Greek dish*
Taranaki 92 New Zealand Regions and Territories
tar and feather 879.1 *punish*
tarantass 71 Carriages and Carts
tarantella 46.4 *historic dancing*
tarantism 366.8 *spasm*
tarantula 82 Arachnids, 82.2 *arachnid*
Tarantula Nebula 53 Nebulae
Tarapon 5.11 *family of languages*
Tardigrada 81.4 *arthropod*
tardigrade 81.4 *arthropod*, 328.7 *delayed*
tardily 209.15 *late*
tardiness 193.1 *wrong time*, 209.1 *lateness*, 328.12 *hesitation*
tardy 193.6 *too late*, 209.9 *late*, 328.7 *delayed*, 643.3 *not participating*
tare 752.1, 752.3 *discount*
tare and tret 752.1 *discount*
Tarentaise 68 Breeds of Cattle
tares 614.6 *refuse*
Targa Florio 33.3 *sports car race*
target 157.14 *aim*, 332.1 *direction*, 471.4 *purpose*, 471.18 *aim*, 534.28 *radar*, 588.6 *objective*, 671.7 *armour*, 850.9 *butt*
target archery 18 Sporting Activities
target area 588.6 *objective*
targeted 471.12 *purposive*
targeting 471.12 *purposive*
target shooter 338.15 *shooter*
target shooting 37
Targhee 68 Breeds of Sheep

Targum 7.12 *religious text*
tariff 13.6 *economic factors*, 171.4 *bill*, 302.2 *limiting factor*, 749.2 *money received*, 751.1 *price*, 751.8 *levy*
tariff barrier 13.6 *economic factors*, 737.5 *commercial trade*
tariff duty 13.6 *economic factors*
tariff wall 147.3 *exclusion zone*, 699.2 *economic restraint*
tarmac 63.25 *construction material*
Tarmac 280.1 *base*, 293.11 *paving*, 293.29 *surface*, 327.4 *road surface*, 376.8 *smooth thing*, 376.11 *smooth*, 604.2 *building material*
Tarmacadam 327.4 *road surface*
tarn 94.1 *lake*
tarnish 441.1 *murk*, 445.6 *decolour*, 622.11 *dirty*, 793.1 *spot*, 854.12 *defame*
tarnished 441.7 *dimmed*, 622.7 *dirty*
tarnishing 854.5 *scorn*, 854.16 *defamatory*
taro 45 Vegetables
tarogato 49 Musical Instruments
Tarot cards 11.9 *divination*, 517.10 *cards*
Tarot reader 11.13 *diviner*
Tarot-reading 11.9 *divination*
tarp 293.7 *overhead covering*
tarpan 77 Placental Mammals
Tarpan 32 Breeds of Horse and Pony
tarpaulin 67 Natural Fabrics, 293.7 *overhead covering*, 634.2 *shelter*
tarpon 80 Fishes, 20.4 *American game fish*
tarragon 45 Herbs and Spices, 413.5 *herbs*
tarred with the same brush 110.12 *same*
tarring and feathering 879.7 *punishment*
tarry 209.7 *wait*, 325.8 *be motionless*, 328.2 *hesitate*, 395.14 *resinous*
tarsal 382 Bones
tarsal gland 352 Exocrine Glands
tarsectomy 60 Surgical Operations
tarsier 77 Placental Mammals
Tarski 4 Philosophers
Tarsus 93 Cities
tart 45.4 *cake*, 402.7 *prostitute*, 402.9 *woman considered as a sex object*, 411.7 *tasty*, 413.9 *piquant*, 415.5 *acid*, 818.8 *discourteous*, 829.4 *irascible*, 830.7 *irritable*, 832.14 *hostile*, 877.9 *immoral woman*
tartan 74 Sailing Ships and Boats, 456.2 *check*, 456.5 *variegated thing*, 456.8 *checked*, 544.5 *uniform*
tartar 622.4 *dirt*, 829.3 *irascible person*
Tartarean 8.16 *devilish*
tartare sauce 45.15 *sauce*
tartaric acid 415.3 *sour thing*
Tartar Pony 32 Breeds of Horse and Pony
Tartarus 8.11 *heaven*
Tartuffe 117.6 *misfit*, 118.7 *imitator*, 538.12 *cheat*, 539.19 *hypocrite*, 548.3 *deceiver*, 797.2 *pretender*
Tartuffery 474.5, 538.9 *hypocrisy*, 539.3, 540.3 *hypocrisy*

Tartuffian 538.18 *pretentious*, 539.37 *hypocritical*
Tartuffism 538.9, 539.3 *hypocrisy*
tart up 295.33 *dress up*, 457.14 *present*, 789.8 *beautify*, 791.16 *make up*, 792.11 *paint and decorate*
tarty 295.30 *dressed up*, 559.10 *ugly*, 877.13 *unchaste*
Tarzan 237.6 *muscleman*
Tashi Lumpo 10.13 *shrine*
Tashkent 93 Cities
tasimeter 268.8 *meter*
tasimetric 268.16 *micrometric*
tasimetry 268.2 *micrometry*
task 644, 847, 230.3 *business*, 597.2 *undertaking*, 599.1 *use*, 640.2 *deed*, 644.7 *work for*, 650.6 *fatigue*, 703.2 *engagement*, 879.10 *affliction*
task force 17.4 *military organization*, 679.14 *armed forces*
task force commander 17.5 *military staff*
task group 17.4 *military organization*
taskmaster 690.4 *strict person*
taskmistress 690.4 *strict person*
taskwork 644.1 *work*
taslich 10.7 *non-Christian ritual*
Tasman 97 Oceans and Seas
Tasmania 92 Australian States and Territories, 98 Islands
Tasmanian devil 77 Marsupials
Tasmanian shrimp 81.4 *arthropod*
tassel 87.3 *grass plant*, 283.3 *suspended object*
Tasso 48 Poets
tastable 411.7 *tasty*
taste 777 Phobias by Topic, 350, 411, 411, 6.11 *refinement*, 165.3 *characteristic*, 234.1 *tendency*, 351.13 *drink*, 396.4 *biological function*, 403.1 *sensation*, 403.11 *sense*, 481.2 *judiciousness*, 492.1 *judgment*, 542.6 *suggestion*, 558.1 *elegance*, 580.7 *preference*, 782.1 *desire*, 784.3 *likes*, 794.1 *elegance*
Taste 411
taste bad 415.8 *sour*
taste battle 676.13 *be at war*
taste flat 412.7 *be tasteless*
taste foul 415.8 *sour*
tasteful 411, 6.20 *refined*, 411.7 *tasty*, 481.9 *discriminating*, 542.13 *subtle*, 558.3 *elegant*, 763.1 *pleasant*, 789.5 *beautiful*, 789.6 *personable*, 794.5 *refined*, 796.7 *fashionable*
tastefully 6.27 *discerningly*, 411.11 *tastily*, 481.16 *judiciously*, 558.5 *elegantly*
tastefulness 558.1, 794.1 *elegance*
tasteless 412, 238.13 *insufficient*, 412.6 *coarse*, 482.1 *undiscriminating*, 542.17 *insipid*, 559.8 *indecorous*, 559.10 *ugly*, 628.12 *deteriorated*, 788.4 *boring*, 795.8 *discourteous*, 844.13 *improper*
tasteless items 412
tastelessly 412, 238.14 *weakly*, 411.11 *tastily*, 482.13 *unselectively*, 542.26 *insipidly*, 555.3 *unemphatically*, 559.11 *inelegantly*, 788.8 *boringly*
tastelessness 412, 795, 412.4 *bad taste*, 482.6 *lack of discrimination*, 542.8 *insipidness*, 559.2 *impropriety*, 788.1 *boredom*
Tastelessness 412
taste of life 411
taster 411, 154.6 *preview*, 350.18 *eater*
taste stale 412.7 *be tasteless*
taste test 411.5 *taster*
taste treat 411.5 *taster*
tastily 411, 350.29 *edibly*
tastiness 763, 405.1 *physical pleasure*, 411.1 *taste*
tasting 350.3 *delicate eating*, 351.1 *drinking*, 411.3 *appetizer*
tasting cup 411.5 *taster*

tasty 411, 763, 350.27 *edible*
tat 288.8 *interweave*, 754.5 *cheap item*
Tatar 5 Languages and Groups of Languages
Tatars 1 Peoples
Tate 48 Poets
tatouay 77 Placental Mammals
tattered 296.10 *in dishabille*, 743.3 *beggarly*
tatters 143.8 *bits and pieces*, 295.1 *dress*, 296.4 *dishabille*, 743.7 *beggary*
tatting 42 Hobbies and Pastimes, 288.2 *braid*
tattle 520.8 *something heard*, 568.2 *chat*
tattler 528.10 *informer*, 565.4 *talker*, 578.9 *equivocator*
tattling 565.6 *effusive*
tattoo 338.7 *shot*, 426.1 *drumming*, 426.8 *drum*, 543.6 *word*, 544.3 *means of identification*, 544.10 *identify*, 636.2 *danger signal*, 811.14 *show*, 812.8 *salute*, 813.3 *formal occasion*
tattooed 544.12 *identified*
tattooing 792.2 *pattern*
tatty 127.14 *poor*, 628.13 *dilapidated*, 743.3 *beggarly*, 754.10 *shoddy*, 793.6 *seedy*
Tatum 52 Scientists
Tatumen 8 Deities
Tau Ceti 53 Named Stars
Taueret 8 Deities
taught a lesson 636.9 *warned*
taunt 850, 850, 478.18 *answer back*, 668.3 *act of defiance*, 668.6 *be insubordinate*, 807.7 *insult*, 807.29 *ridicule*, 828.9 *offend*, 852.9 *show of disapproval*
taunted 852.35 *hissed*
taunting 850, 807.18 *insulting*
Taunton 93 Cities
tauon 56.77 *elementary particle*
taupe 448.1 *grey*, 448.4 *greyness*
Taupo 94 Lakes
Taurids 53 Meteor Showers
taurine 77.33 *ungulate*
tauromachy 674.9 *duel*
Taurus 53 The Constellations, 53 Zodiac Constellations, 53 Mountains, 95 Mountains
taut 135.15 *tied*, 373.2 *tough*
tauten 135.8 *unite*, 373.9 *harden*
tautly 135.18 *inextricably*, 373.12 *toughly*
tautness 373.5 *hardness*
tautog 80 Fishes
tautologic 110.12 *same*
tautological 52.86 *logical*, 183.12 *repetitious*, 520.6 *meaningful*, 553.3 *diffuse*, 610.7 *superfluous*
tautologically 110.18 *identically*, 553.7 *diffusely*
tautologize 520.10 *mean*, 553.5 *be diffuse*
tautologous 553.3 *diffuse*, 610.7 *superfluous*
tautologously 553.7 *diffusely*
tautology 4.8 *philosophical term*, 5.22 *many words*, 52.64 *reasoning*, 110.1 *sameness*, 183.2 *iteration*, 504.11 *grammatical error*, 553.1 *diffuseness*, 610.3 *superfluity*
tautonym 5.17 *word*, 560.8 *name*
tautonymic 5.42 *worded*
tavern 256.10 *hotel*
tavern's bush 544.3 *means of identification*
Tavghi 5 Languages and Groups of Languages
tawa 85 Trees and Shrubs
tawdriness 795, 412.4 *bad taste*, 559.3 *ugliness*, 618.8 *inferiority*, 811.4 *flashiness*
tawdry 412.6 *coarse*, 559.10 *ugly*, 612.4 *trivial*, 618.2 *inferior*, 754.10 *shoddy*, 795.7 *vulgar*, 811.19 *flashy*
Tawe 96 Rivers
Tawhiri 8 Deities
tawny 449.1 *brown*, 452.1 *yellow*
tawny owl 78 Birds
tawny port 351.9 *wine*

tawse 879.14 *instrument of punishment*

tax 751, 369.8 *weighing down*, 369.14 *make heavy*, 599.1 *use*, 644.7 *work for*, 650.6 *fatigue*, 712.7 *demand*, 729.2 *gift*, 734.5 *takings*, 734.8 *take back*, 746.4 *grant*, 748.5 *expense*, 749.2 *money received*, 751.12 *charge*

taxable 13.13 *economic*, 729.7 *given*, 734.12 *taking*, 751.15 *chargeable*

taxable income 13.6 *economic factors*, 751.7 *tax*

tax assessor 751.10 *taxpayer*

taxation 13.6 *economic factors*, 751.7 *tax*

tax avoidance 13.6 *economic factors*, 638.1 *escape*, 747.1 *nonpayment*

tax benefit 729.2 *gift*

tax collector 161.35, 730.7 *collector*, 751.10 *taxpayer*

tax computation 751.7 *tax*

tax consultant 751.10 *taxpayer*

tax declaration 751.7 *tax*

tax-deductible 751.15 *chargeable*

tax demand 692.2 *demand*, 751.7 *tax*

tax disc 71.21 *miscellaneous motoring terms*

tax dodger 638.3 *escaper*, 747.6 *nonpayer*

tax-dodging 638.1 *escape*

taxed 369.3 *ponderous*

taxes 749.2 *money received*, 751.7 *tax*

tax evader 591.17 *avoider*, 638.3 *escaper*, 711.4 *refuser*, 720.6 *evader*, 736.11 *dishonest person*, 747.6 *nonpayer*

tax evasion 13.6 *economic factors*, 638.1 *escape*, 711.1 *refusal*, 736.7 *dishonesty*, 747.1 *nonpayment*, 858.3 *criminality*

tax-exempt 751.15 *chargeable*

tax exile 747.6 *nonpayer*

tax form 751.7 *tax*

tax-free 848, 751.15 *chargeable*, 754.11 *free of charge*, 848.13 *with impunity*

tax haven 638.1 *escape*, 747.1 *nonpayment*

taxi 71 Motor Vehicles, 71.18 *cab*, 324.15 *walk*, 326.5 *means of transport*

taxicab 71.18 *cab*

taxidermy 637.1 *preservation*

taxi driver 326.7 *transferor*

taxing 369.3 *ponderous*, 369.8 *weighing down*, 734.2 *taking back*, 879.21 *punishing*

taxiplane 73 Types of Aircraft

taxi rank 218.4 *stopping place*

taxiway 73.4 *airport*, 327.13 *flight path*

tax office 751.7 *tax*

taxon 59.17 *taxonomy*

taxonomic 59, 83, 59.20 *biological*, 150.12 *hierarchical*, 152.25 *categorical*, 163.10 *classificatory*, 171.11 *listed*

taxonomically 163, 59.29 *biologically*, 150.25 *in order*, 152.28 *in place*, 171.13 *inventorially*

taxonomic group 59.17 *taxonomy*

taxonomist 59.19 *life scientist*

taxonomy 59, 59.1 *life science*, 150.2 *grouping*, 152.5 *categorization*, 163.1 *classification*, 171.7 *listing*, 396.9 *classifications of life*, 560.7 *nomenclature*

tax owed 751.7 *tax*

taxpayer 751

tax-payer 15.7 *employee*

tax payment 751.7 *tax*

tax-raising 734.2 *taking back*, 734.12 *taking*

tax rate 751.7 *tax*

tax refund 751.7 *tax*

tax return 528.3 *document*, 751.7 *tax*

tax roll 171.6 *list of names*

tax shelter 638.1 *escape*, 747.1 *nonpayment*

tax system 751.7 *tax*

tax table 751.7 *tax*

tax write-off 729.2 *gift*

Tay 94 Lakes, **96** Rivers

tayberry 86 Fruits, 133.5 *hybrid*

Taylor 52 Scientists, **52** Scientists

Taylor series 52 Named Concepts

tayra 77 Placental Mammals

Tayside 92 Counties

T-bar 41.12 *ski*

T-bar lift 41.1 *skiing*

T-beam 63.27 *superstructure*

T-bone 33.10 *be on the track*, 45.22 *beef*

T-boned 33.11 *racing*

T-boning 33.9 *motor racing terms*, 33.11 *racing*

TCA cycle 58.24 *respiration*

TCDD 631.9 *pollution*

Tchaikovsky 49 Musicians and Composers

Tchenaran 32 Breeds of Horse and Pony

t-distribution 52.59 *probability distribution*

tea 351, 350.12 *meal*, 815.3 *meeting*, 875.6 *drug*

teabag 322.6 *porous thing*

tea break 185.6 *interval*, 649.1 *ease*

tea caddy 258.11 *vessel*

teacake 45.39 *loaf*

teach 6.22 *educate*, 167.10 *assimilate*, 501.14 *cause to know*, 526.1 *display*, 528.11 *inform*, 584.18 *habituate*, 594.6 *brief*, 654.5 *advise*, 696.14 *master*

teachability 6.10 *educatability*, 522.9 *intelligibility*

teachable 6.17 *educatable*, 522.1 *intelligible*

teachableness 586.7 *persuadability*

teach an old dog new tricks 487.10 *attempt the impossible*

teacher 4.12 *sage*, 6.4 *educator*, 220.5 *converter*, 465.3 *curious person*, 501.6 *knowledgeable person*, 524.6 *interpreter*, 561.3 *dissertator*, 594.15 *preparer*, 646.1 *worker*, 653.13 *director*, 654.4 *adviser*, 655.5 *expert*, 688.10 *person of authority*, 696.9 *educational leader*

teacher's pet 238.4 *weakling*, 694.4 *obedient person*, 821.11 *loved one*, 826.6 *object of endearment*

teacher training 6.2 *educational system*

tea chest 258.6 *box*

teach freely 698.14 *be free*

teach-in 568.4 *conference*

teaching 4.2 *philosophical system*, 6.1 *education*, 501.3 *learning*, 876.7 *moral*

teaching contract 715.2 *purchase contract*

teaching hospital 60.10 *hospital*

teachings 471.5 *ideology*

teach manners 627.1 *improve*

teach one his place 806.17 *humiliate*

teach one's grandmother to suck eggs 610.5 *be superfluous*, 807.28 *get above oneself*

teach wickedness 864.17 *make wicked*

tea clipper 74 Sailing Ships and Boats

teacup 258.13 *drinking vessel*, 351.10 *drink container*

tea dance 46.1 *dancing*

tea-drinker 873.8 *sober person*

tea-drinking 873.1 *sober*, 873.6 *sobriety*

tea estate 68.6 *farm*

tea for two 350.12 *meal*

tea garden 69.2 *garden*

tea gown 295.7 *frock*

teahouse 350.15 *eating place*

teak 85 Trees and Shrubs, 373.7 *hard substance*

teal 78 Birds, **161** Collective Names by Animal

tea lady 697.5 *office assistant*

tea leaf 864.10 *bad person*

tea-leaf reader 11.13 *diviner*

tea-leaf reading 11.9 *divination*

tea leaves 517.10 *cards*

team 27, 161, 305, 664, 77.21 *assemblage of mammals*, 116.2 *alliance*, 140.3 *assembly*, 146.3 *person included*, 176.1 *two*, 176.14 *pair*, 646.4 *personnel*, 665.1 *party*

team captain 653.14 *leader*

team dinghy racing 36.1 *sailing*

team handball 18 Sporting Activities

team-mates 664.9 *team*

team member 18.3 *sportsman* , 148.5 *member*

team race 674.4 *race*

team spirit 116.1 *accord*, 664.2 *fellowship*

team sports 674.1 *contention*

teamster 653.14 *leader*

team together 665.12 *be in league with*

team up 116.22 *form an alliance*, 161.41 *band together*, 180.14 *keep company with*

team up with 140.6 *come together*, 664.14 *join with*, 665.14 *be a party member*

teamwork 664.4 *joint operation*

tea party 350.12 *feast*, 665.7 *social gathering*, 815.5 *party*

tea plantation 68.6 *farm*

tea planter 68.15 *agriculturist*

teapot 258.15 *pot*

tear 136.3 *separateness*, 136.9 *separate*, 265.2, 265.5 *crack*, 322.1 *opening*, 322.18 *open*, 350.21 *eat*, 387.3 *body fluid*, 406.3 *injury*, 406.11 *inflict pain*, 618.14 *ill-treat*, 620.7 *defect*

tearable 136.19 *separable*, 379.1 *brittle*

tear along 329.4 *be swift*

tear apart 136.9 *separate*, 244.9 *demolish*, 852.17 *criticize*

tear dew 391.6 *dew*

tear down 244.9 *demolish*, 362.2 *flatten*

teardrop 387.3 *body fluid*

tearful 391.12 *seeping*, 759.12 *sensitive*, 770.5 *sad*, 774.4 *lamenting*, 874.2 *slightly drunk*

tearfully 352.8 *glandularly*, 387.26 *fluidly*, 774.8 *mournfully*

tearfulness 774.1 *lamentation*

tear gas 631.10 *warfare*

tearing 355.6 *extorsion*, 379.1 *brittle*

tearing apart 136.3 *separateness*

tearing hurry 648.4 *haste*

tearing one's hair 543.3 *gesture*

tearing out 252.2 *removal*, 355.1 *extraction*

tearing rage 828.4 *anger*

tear into 670.5 *strike*

tear-jerking 774.5 *lamentable*, 835.7 *pitiful*

tearlike 387.16 *rheumy*

tear limb from limb 244.9 *demolish*, 879.5 *execute*

tear loose 700.5 *be liberated*

tear off 294.11 *uncover*, 296.15 *make nude*, 329.6 *accelerate*, 345.4 *hurry off*, 648.2 *make haste*

tear off the mask 526.4 *show oneself*, 530.5 *disclose*

tear oneself away 345.6 *part*

tear oneself away from 705.5 *resign*

tear one's hair 543.11 *gesture*

tearoom 350.15 *eating place*

tea rose 84 Flowers and Flowering Plants

tear out 252.15 *remove*, 355.11 *extract*, 355.16 *extort*

tears 352.2 *secreted substance*, 387.3 *body fluid*, 389.4 *exudate*

tears for oneself 835.1 *pity*

tears of rage 822.5, 828.4 *anger*

tears of self-pity 835.1 *pity*

tears of sympathy 835.2 *condolence*

tear-stained 391.12 *seeping*

tear to bits 136.9 *separate*, 244.9 *demolish*

tear to pieces 244.9 *demolish*

tear to rags 244.9 *demolish*

tear to shreds 244.9 *demolish*, 854.11 *criticize*

tear up 244.8 *destroy*, 598.1 *relinquish*

tear up the road 329.4 *be swift*

tease 506.4 *buffoon*, 515.1 *disappointment*, 515.6 *disappoint*, 579.4 *capricious person*, 579.5 *be capricious*, 586.16 *tempt*, 768.8 *annoy*, 771.6 *humorist*, 771.13 *be humorous*, 821.26 *court*, 828.9 *offend*, 850.24 *ridicule*

teasel 84 Flowers and Flowering Plants

teaser 51.17 *stage set*, 506.4 *buffoon*, 529.4 *brain-teaser*, 532.9 *advertisement*, 659.4 *problem*, 771.6 *humorist*

teaset 258.16 *crockery*

teashop 350.15 *eating place*, 351.11 *drink provider*

teasing 228.2 *inducement*, 228.11 *motivational*, 586.2 *flattery*, 586.19 *persuasive*, 771.3 *wit*, 771.10 *humorous*, 850.6 *taunt*, 850.15 *taunting*

teasingly 228.14 *influentially*

teaspoon 120.3 *container*, 258.17 *ladle*, 350.16 *eating utensil*

teat 77.2 *mammalian characteristic*

tea table 47.4 *table*

tea towel 621.11 *cleaning cloth*

tea tree 85 Trees and Shrubs

tea trolley 71.7 *handcart*

tea urn 258.15 *pot*

technetium 57 Chemical Elements

technical 6.21 *curricular*, 31.8 *hockey*, 165.21 *specialized*, 520.6 *meaningful*, 612.4 *trivial*, 659.12 *problematic*

technical drawing 50.3 *drawing*, 547.2 *reproduction*, 560.9 *representation*

technical foul 23.4 *playing terms*, 23.5 *penalties*, 31.5 *lacrosse*

technical hitch 218.2 *stop*, 661.2 *obstacle*

technicality 592.3 *expedient plan*, 612.8 *trifle*, 638.2 *means of escape*, 654.3 *precept*, 659.1 *difficulty*

technical journal 532.5 *journal*

technical knock-out 26.2 *boxing*

technical knowledge 655.1 *skill*

technical language 165.10 *specialized language*

technically 6.26 *studiously*

technical meaning 520.4 *type of meaning*

technical problems 661.2 *obstacle*

technical rehearsal 51.12 *production*

technical skill 655.1 *skill*

technical subject 561.3 *subject*

technical term 5.20 *jargon word*, 560.8 *name*

technical word 5.20 *jargon word*

technician 63.4 *mechanical engineer*, 230.5 *operator*, 485.8 *qualified person*, 603.7 *machinist*, 646.2 *artisan*, 655.5 *expert*

Technicolor 444.7 *colour painting*

technicoloured 444.10 *coloured*

technics 603.5 *mechanics*

technique 327.1 *way*, 501.2 *information*, 549.1 *style*, 602.1 *means*, 655.1 *skill*

techniques of the aiki jo 26.10 *aikido*

techniques of the bokken 26.10 *aikido*

techno 49.9 *popular music*

technobabble 5.20 *jargon word*, 165.10 *specialized language*, 564.1 *faculty of speech*

technocracy 12.1 *government*

technocratic 12.9 *governmental*

technological 603.8 *mechanical*

technologically 603.10 *instrumentally*

technology 13.6 *economic factors*, 243.1 *production*, 243.2 *manufacture*, 367.6 *natural science*, 501.5 *science*, 602.1 *means*, 603.5 *mechanics*

technospeak 5.20 *jargon word*

tectology 382.8 *science of structure*

tectonic 54, 43.11 *architectural*, 382.11 *structural*

tectonically 43.20 *architecturally*, 382.18 *structurally*

tectonic forces 54.20 *earth movement*

tectonics 43.1 *architecture*, 54.1 *earth science*, 243.2 *manufacture*, 382.1 *structure*

tectosilicate 54.34 *mineral*

tectrix 78.17 *plumage*

tedder 68.10 *farm tool*

teddy 295.18 *underwear*

teddy bear 547.6 *image*

Te Deum 10.8 *hymn*, 812.7 *thanksgiving*, 837.2 *thanks*

tedious 112.8, 183.13 *monotonous*, 553.3 *diffuse*, 556.1 *simple*, 616.1 *inconvenient*, 618.3 *bad*, 650.4 *fatiguing*, 659.13 *inconvenient*, 788.4 *boring*

tediously 112.15 *monotonously*, 616.6 *inconveniently*, 650.9 *tiringly*, 659.28 *awkwardly*, 788.8 *boringly*

tediousness 112.4 *monotony*, 556.4 *simplicity*, 618.9 *badness*, 788.1 *boredom*

tedium 183.3 *repetitiveness*, 553.1 *diffuseness*, 788.1 *boredom*

tee 29.2 *golfing terms*

teed 874.3 *dead drunk*

teed up 594.18 *prepared*

teeing ground 29.1 *golf*

teeing off 29.3 *golf shots*

tee line 41.10 *curling*

teem 55.62 *rain*, 156.26 *produce*, 161.40, 181.11 *crowd*, 246.6 *be fertile*, 608.5 *about*

teeming 161.50 *crowded*, 246.5 *fertile*, 273.2 *dense*, 357.11 *overrun*, 608.3 *filled*, 610.6 *excessive*

teeming with 144.8 *full*

teem with 82.16 *infest*, 610.4 *be excessive*

teenage 206.11 *young*

teenaged 206.11 *young*

teenager 179.7 *double figures*, 206.6 *young person*, 400.7 *person*

teenage runaway 591.17 *avoider*

teen idol 340.6 *charmer*

teens 179.7 *double figures*, 206.1 *youth*

teensy-weensy 612.4 *trivial*

teeny 260.7 *little*, 612.4 *trivial*

teenybopper 206.6 *young person*, 821.9 *lover*

teeny-weeny 260.7 *little*, 612.4 *trivial*

tee off 29.7 *golf*, 156.18 *make a beginning*

Tees 96 *Rivers*, 96.4 *British rivers*

Teeswater 68 *Breeds of Sheep*

teeter 224.11 *be changeable*, 238.6 *be weak*, 365.7 *oscillator*, 365.8 *oscillate*, 366.25 *pitch*, 576.5 *vacillate*

teeterboard 365.7 *oscillator*

teetering 224.13 *changeable*, 238.8 *weak*, 576.4 *unsteady*

teetering on the edge 633.2 *unsafe*

teeter on the edge 633.8 *be in danger*

teeter-totter 365.7 *oscillator*, 365.8 *oscillate*

teetery-bender 365.7 *oscillator*

teeth 777 *Phobias by Topic*, 350.16 *eating utensil*, 446.9 *white thing*, 564.5 *organ of speech*, 680.7 *weapon*, 726.3 *tools for gripping*

teething troubles 659.8 *snag*, 661.2 *obstacle*

teethless 381.4 *toothless*

teetotal 869.8 *self-restrained*, 873.1 *sober*

teetotalism 869.1 *self-restraint*, 873.6 *sobriety*

teetotaller 591.17 *avoider*, 711.4 *refuser*, 869.4 *self-restrained person*, 873.8 *sober person*, 876.6 *moralist*

teetotally 869.11 *with self-restraint*

tee up 594.4 *prepare for action*

tefillin 10.14 *sacred object*

Teflon 57.21 *polymer*, 139.3 *non-adhesive thing*

Tefnut 8 Deities

Tegid 94 Lakes

Tegucigalpa 93 Cities

tegumen 293.13 *casing*

Tehran 93 Cities

Teifi 96 Rivers

Teilhard de Chardin 4 Philosophers

Te Kanawa 49 Musicians and Composers

tektite 53.20 *meteor*

telaesthesia 11.1 *occultism*

telaesthetic 11.12 *occultist*, 11.16 *psychic*

Tel Aviv 93 Cities

telecamera 534.21 *television*

telecast 532.13 *make public*, 534.25 *broadcast material*, 534.30 *communicate*

telecasting 532.2 *mass media*

telecommunication 534, 532.2 *mass media*

telecommunications 64.1 *electronics*, 65.14 *data transfer*, 235.9 *electronics*, 534.1 *communications*

telecommunicator 543.8 *signer*

telecommuting 65.15 *network*

teleconference 716.3, 716.3 *discussion*

teleconferencing 65.12 *electronic office*, 664.8 *conferring*

telecottage 534.6 *telecommunication*

telegram 326.10 *transferred thing*, 528.2 *communication*, 534.8 *data transmission*

telegraph 235.9 *electronics*, 326.10 *transferred thing*, 329.11 *swift thing*, 528.12 *communicate*, 534.8 *data transmission*, 534.31 *correspond*

telegrapher 534.29 *broadcaster*, 543.8 *signer*

telegraphese 5.20 *jargon word*, 552.1 *conciseness*

telegraphic 534.33 *communicational*, 543.16 *signalling*, 552.3 *concise*

telegraphically 543.18 *indicatively*, 552.5 *concisely*

telegraphist 534.29 *broadcaster*, 543.8 *signer*

telegraph messenger 543.8 *signer*

telegraph operator 543.8 *signer*

telegraph pole 275.6, 275.6 *tall thing*, 534.12 *public telephone system*

telegraph signal 543.4 *signal*

telegraphy 534.6 *telecommunication*

Teleia 823.14 *gods and goddesses of marriage*

teleinformatics 534.6 *telecommunication*

telekinesis 11.1 *occultism*, 11.8 *psychic power*

telekinetic 11.12 *occultist*, 11.16 *psychic*

telemark 41.2 *cross-country skiing*, 41.4 *skiing technique*, 41.14 *ski*

Telemark 68 Breeds of Cattle

telemarking 41.4 *skiing technique*

telemessage 528.2 *communication*

Telemessage 534.8 *data transmission*

telemeter 268.8 *meter*

telemetric 268.16 *micrometric*

telemetry 53.32 *satellite*, 56.95 *mensuration*, 268.2 *micrometry*

telemon 43 Architectural Decoration, 50.12 *sculpture*

Telenet 65.15 *network*

teleological 471.12 *purposive*, 588.11 *intending*

teleology 4.6 *branch of philosophy*, 199.4 *looking to the future*, 588.5 *final intention*

teleost fish 80.2 *fish*

telepathic 11.16 *psychic*, 368.9 *parapsychological*, 464.7 *precognitive*, 516.6 *foreseeing*

telepathically 11.25 *occultly*, 368.13 *metaphysically*, 516.8 *foresightedly*

telepathic dream 11.10 *psychic phenomenon*

telepathic hallucination 11.10 *psychic phenomenon*

telepathic transmission 11.1 *occultism*

telepathist 11.12 *occultist*, 368.7 *believer in a nonmaterial world*, 516.5 *predictor*, 517.8 *oracle*

telepathy 11.1 *occultism*, 11.8 *psychic power*, 368.4 *parapsychology*, 403.1 *sensation*, 464.2 *precognition*, 516.3 *foresight*

telephone 777 Phobias by Topic, **534**, **534**, 235.9 *electronics*, 329.11 *swift thing*, 420.9 *audio device*, 420.11 *aural*, 528.12 *communicate*

telephone answering machine 420.9 *audio device*

telephone bell 427.4 *sources of resonance*

telephone book 534.11 *dialling*

telephone booth 534.9 *telephone*

telephone box 534.9 *telephone*

telephone call 534

telephone directory 171.3 *dictionary*, 528.5 *reference book*, 534.11 *dialling*

telephone engineer 534.13 *telephoner*

telephone engineering 534.6 *telecommunication*

telephone exchange 534.12 *public telephone system*

telephone kiosk 534.9 *telephone*

telephoneline 534.12 *public telephone system*

telephone mechanic 534.13 *telephoner*

telephone number 534.11 *dialling*, 544.3 *means of identification*

telephone numbers 181.2 *multitude*, 223.3 *something in exchange*

telephone operator 230.5 *operator*, 534.13 *telephoner*

telephone pole 534.12 *public telephone system*

telephoner 534

telephone receiver 730.8 *receiver*

telephone ring 543.4 *signal*

telephone set 534.9 *telephone*

telephone tap 420.9 *audio device*

telephone tapper 420.2 *hearer*

telephone wire 534.12 *public telephone system*

telephonic 420.11 *aural*, 534.33 *communicational*

telephonically 420.17 *aurally*

telephonist 230.5 *operator*, 534.13 *telephoner*

telephonophobia 777 Phobias by Name

telephony 534.6 *telecommunication*

telephotography 66.1 *photography*

telephoto lens 66.17 *lens*, 435.8 *reflection*

telephoto zoom 66.17 *lens*

teleplay 51.2 *play*

teleport 11.24 *experience psychic phenomena*

teleportation 11.1 *occultism*

teleprinter 534.8 *data transmission*

Teleran 73.6 *flight control*

telergic 11.16 *psychic*

telergy 11.1 *occultism*

telescope 53, 56.32 *optical instrument*, 56.85 *microscope*, 262.5 *make smaller*, 262.6 *become smaller*, 270.10 *shorten*, 435.10 *visual aid*, 437.7 *that which makes visible*, 552.4 *be concise*

Telescope 53 The Constellations

telescoped 262.7 *smaller*

telescopic 53.36 *astronomical*, 262.9 *contractible*, 435.20 *visual*

telescopic loader 68.10 *farm tool*

telescopic rod 20.3 *fishing tackle*

telescopic sight 37.3 *hunting equipment*, 435.10 *visual aid*

Telescopium 53 The Constellations

telescopy 435.10 *visual aid*

teleshop 738.1 *purchase*

teleshopper 738.12 *purchaser*

teleshopping 738.8 *shopping*, 738.14 *buying*

Telesio 4 Philosophers

Teletext 534.8 *data transmission*, 534.25 *broadcast material*

telethon 534.25 *broadcast material*, 712.3 *solicitation*, 833.5 *charity*

teletypewriter 534.8 *data transmission*

Teleut 5 Languages and Groups of Languages

televangelist 7.5 *Christian*, 220.5 *converter*, 534.29 *broadcaster*

televise 526.2 *display something*, 528.12 *communicate*, 532.13 *make public*, 534.30 *communicate*

televised 532.19 *published*, 534.34 *communicated*

television 534, 56.13 *electromagnetic radiation*, 235.9 *electronics*, 528.4 *mass communication*, 532.2 *mass media*, 534.1 *communications*

television broadcaster 534.29 *broadcaster*

television broadcasting 534

television camera 534.21 *television*

television channel 534.24 *television broadcasting*

television director 243.9 *producer*

television drama 51.2 *play*

television dramatist 51.24 *dramatist*

television engineer 646.2 *artisan*

television evangelist 220.5 *converter*

television mast 534.24 *television broadcasting*

television news 533.6 *radio news*

television personality 51.27 *entertainer*

television play 51.2 *play*

television producer 243.9 *producer*

television programme 526.9 *production*

television ratings 532.2 *mass media*

television receiver 64.20 *electron tube*

television reception 534

television review 524.3 *criticism*

television set 534

television station 534.24 *television broadcasting*

television time out 19.5 *game time*

television tower 534.24 *television broadcasting*

television trial 16.7 *legal trial*

television tube 44.9 *industrial ceramics*, 534.21 *television*

telex 326.13 *post*, 528.2 *communication*, 528.12 *communicate*, 534.8 *data transmission*, 534.31 *correspond*

telex machine 118.6 *photocopier*, 534.8 *data transmission*

Telford 52 Scientists

tell 6.22 *educate*, 169.10, 170.11 *number*, 501.14 *cause to know*, 520.10 *mean*, 528.11 *inform*, 528.13 *inform on* , 530.6 *divulge*, 560.15 *recount*, 564.11 *speak*, 611.7 *be important*, 654.5 *advise*
tell a cock-and-bull story 309.12 *distort the truth*
tell a dirty lie 538.21 *lie*
tell a fish story 538.21 *lie*
tell all 530.6 *divulge*
tell a pack of lies 538.21 *lie*
tell a shaggy dog story 538.21 *lie*
tell a story 560.15 *recount*
tell a tale 560.15 *recount*
tell a tall story 541
tell a white lie 538.21 *lie*
tell a whopper 538.21 *lie*
tell dirty jokes 827.5 *curse*
teller 170.6 *calculator*, 528.9 *informant*, 741.18 *treasurer*
Teller 52 Scientists
teller of dirty jokes 622.6 *dirty person*
teller of tales 560.10 *descriptive writer*
tell fortunes 11.23, 517.12 *divine*
telling 170.3 *count*, 232.7 *causal*, 233.11 *influential*, 237.10 *potent*, 520.6 *meaningful*, 522.1 *intelligible*, 586.19 *persuasive*, 611.5 *important*
telling off 766.2 *expression of dissatisfaction*, 852.7 *blame*, 879.7 *punishment*
telling one's dream before breakfast 517.7 *bad-luck sign*
tell it like it is 552.4 *be concise*, 556.7 *be simple*, 857.6 *be honourable*
tell its own story 526.5 *be visible*
tell its own tale 522.4 *be intelligible*
tell lies 538.21 *lie*, 858.8 *be dishonourable*
tell of 520.10 *mean*
tell off 431.14 *hiss*, 852.20 *censure*, 879.1 *punish*
tell on 528.13 *inform on* , 530.7 *betray*
tell oneself 569.3 *soliloquize*
tell one straight to his face 556.7 *be simple*
tell porkies 309.12 *distort the truth*
tell someone where to get off 711.6 *dissent*
tell someone where to go 711.6 *dissent*
telltale 40.8 *squash*, 528.10 *informer*, 530.4 *discloser*, 543.14 *signifying*, 879.9 *equivocator*
tell-tale 472.9 *local*, 483.7 *person who gives evidence*, 483.8 *evidential*, 520.6 *meaningful*
tell tales 483.13 *turn Queen's evidence*, 489.7 *be improbable*
telltale sign 530.2 *divulgence* , 543.1 *sign*
tell-tale sign 483.4 *indication*
tell tales out of school 530.7 *betray*
tell tall stories 538.21 *lie*
tell the half-truth 538.21 *lie*
tell the men from the boys 115.6 *differentiate*
tell the near-truth 538.21 *lie*
tell the same old story 112.12 *be monotonous*, 183.18 *harp*, 788.6 *be boring*
tell the same story 110.7 *be the same*
tell the truth 537.29 *be truthful*
tell the truth and shame the devil 857.6 *be honourable*
tell the whole truth and nothing but the truth 857.6 *be honourable*
tell the world 532.13 *make public*
tell to one's face 526.4 *show oneself*
tell upon 233.8 *influence*, 239.2 *be full of vigour*
tellurian 53.36 *astronomical*, 400.7 *person*, 400.12 *human*

telluric 53.36 *astronomical*, 57.34 *elemental*
tellurium 57 Chemical Elements
tellurometer 268.8 *meter*
tellurous 57.34 *elemental*
Tellus 8 Deities
telly 534.22 *television set*
telophase 59.10 *cell division*
telpher 72.1 *railway*, 327.12 *cableway*
telpherage 326.2 *transportation*
telpher line 327.12 *cableway*
telpher way 327.12 *cableway*
Telstar 53.32 *satellite*, 534.7 *satellite communication*
Telugu 5 Languages and Groups of Languages
temblor 54.22 *seismic activity*
Temne 5 Languages and Groups of Languages
temp 155.13 *replacement*, 707.1 *deputy*
temper 57.30 *extract*, 105.4 *state of mind*, 133.8 *mix*, 203.8 *mitigate*, 237.8 *strengthen*, 242.4 *moderate*, 373.5 *hardness*, 373.9 *harden*, 374.1 *ease*, 378.11 *make tough*, 485.15 *modify*, 591.3 *abstain*, 594.7 *develop*, 767.9 *relieve*, 822.5 *anger*, 869.5 *be self-restrained*
tempera 50.8 *painting*, 50.11 *artist's materials*
temperament 771, 103.4 *nature*, 105.4 *state of mind*, 165.2 *personality*, 578.6 *equivocation*, 579.3 *whim*, 830.3 *irritableness*
temperamental 105.8 *in a state of*, 403.7 *susceptible*, 576.2 *changeable*, 579.1 *capricious*, 759.13 *passionate*, 760.2 *oversensitive*, 829.4 *irascible*, 830.7 *irritable*
temperamentally 105.9 *conditionally*, 760.13 *oversensitively*, 829.9 *irascibly*, 830.14 *irritably*
temperamentalness 829.1 *irascibility*
temperamental person 224.5 *changeable person*
temperance 4.3 *detachment*, 242.1 *moderation*, 591.11 *abstinence*, 699.3 *self-restraint*, 709.1 *veto*, 863.2 *virtues*, 869.1 *self-restraint*, 873.6 *sobriety*, 876.3 *moral purity*
temperance society 873.8 *sober person*
temperate 4.18 *detached*, 55.50 *warm*, 242.6 *moderate*, 408.11 *warm*, 591.19 *abstaining*, 699.14 *self-restrained*, 863.6 *ethical*, 869.8 *self-restrained*, 873.1 *sober*, 876.9 *pure*
temperate climate 55.38 *climate*
temperately 4.27 *stoically*, 242.9 *moderately*, 591.21 *away*, 699.17 *with self-restraint*, 863.10 *ethically*, 869.11 *with self-restraint*, 873.9 *soberly*
temperateness 869.1 *self-restraint*
temperate zone 55.39 *climatic zone*
temperature 56, 408.1 *heat*, 408.2 *heat measurement*, 624.3 *symptom*
temperature scale 56.37 *temperature*, 75.3 *scale*
tempered 133.12 *mixed*, 203.16 *mitigated*, 242.6 *moderate*, 373.3 *hardened*, 378.2 *toughened*, 869.8 *self-restrained*
tempering 237.4 *strengthening*, 373.6 *solidification*, 542.6 *suggestion*
temper oneself 237.8 *strengthen*
temper tantrum 828.4 *anger*
tempest 366, 55.14 *windiness*, 241.5 *violent weather*, 329.11 *swift thing*
tempesta 45 Types of Pasta
tempest in a teapot 666.2 *argument*

tempestuous 55.48 *stormy*, 241.6 *violent*, 329.1 *swift*, 366.17 *turbulent*, 375.4 *bumpy*
Templar 7 Members of Religious Orders
Templars 7 Christian Movements
template 306.2 *prototype*
temple 10.11 *place of worship*, 243.8 *construction*, 305.1 *side*, 634.1 *refuge*
Temple of Apollo Epicurius 43 Noted Buildings
temple state 12.5 *political organization*
tempo 49 Musical Terms, **49**, 185.12 *musical time*, 214.1 *regularity*, 214.5 *regular thing*, 365.2 *vibration*, 433.3 *melodiousness*
temporal 185, 192.17 *timekeeping*
temporal bone 382 Bones
temporalities 725.4 *possessions*
temporally 185.30 *chronologically*
temporarily 189.8 *transiently*, 196.10 *for the present*, 222.9 *instead*
temporary 185.20 *temporal*, 189.7 *impermanent*, 196.7 *occasional*, 222.7 *substitute*, 595.3 *without preparation*, 707.7 *deputizing*, 717.7 *half-measure*
temporary measure 222.1 *substitution*
temporary stoppage 218.2 *stop*
temporary substitute 609.8 *insufficiency*, 717.2 *half-measure*
temporary truce 675.1 *peace*, 677.1 *pacification*
temporary worker 707.1 *deputy*
temporize 209.8 *delay*, 657.5 *be cunning*
temporizing 657.1, 657.4 *cunning*
tempo rubato 49.19 *tempo*
temps de poisson 46.9 *ballet steps*
tempt 586, 226.10 *awaken*, 228.10 *manipulate*, 233.8 *influence*, 340.12 *lure*
tempt 782.15 *cause desire*, 821.26 *court*, 864.17 *make wicked*
temptation 226.1 *cause*, 340.4 *allurement*, 586.2 *flattery*, 784.1 *liking*
tempter 586, 228.7 *motivator*
tempt fate 508.6 *be foolish*, 596.3 *tackle*, 633.9 *face danger*
tempting 228.11 *motivational*, 233.12 *appealing*, 340.9 *attractive*, 586.19 *persuasive*, 763.4 *tasty*, 782.8 *desirable*, 784.5 *likable*, 821.22 *lovable*
temptingly 228.14 *influentially*, 586.21 *persuasively*, 782.17 *desirably*, 784.10 *with great liking*, 821.30 *lovingly*
tempting offer 228.5 *positive stimulus*, 878.4 *reward for service*
tempt providence 596.3 *tackle*, 633.9 *face danger*, 780.5 *be rash*
temptress 228.7 *motivator*, 340.6 *charmer*, 586.13 *tempter*, 821.9 *lover*
temulent 874.6 *intoxicating*
ten 49 Musical Terms, **179**, 179.17 *tenth*
tenable 486.5 *possible*, 497.13 *believable*, 632.6 *invulnerable*
tenably 486.10 *practically*
tenacious 138, 574, 237.11 *strong in spirit*, 378.4 *powerful*, 570.7 *iron-willed*, 575.10 *persevering*, 577.3 *unyielding*, 726.9 *retentive*, 778.12 *self-reliant*
tenaciously 138, 726, 237.14 *strongly*, 378.13 *powerfully*, 394.12 *viscously*, 575.13 *persistently*, 577.9 *be obstinate*, 778.18 *courageously*
tenaciousness 138.2 *tenacity*, 394.1 *viscosity*, 726.1 *retention*
tenacious of life 396.12 *alive*
tenacious person 575

tenacity 138, 574, 135.1 *union*, 237.1 *strength*, 378.8 *physical strength*, 394.1 *viscosity*, 570.2 *willpower*, 575.1 *perseverance*, 577.6 *determination*, 726.1 *retention*, 778.3 *steadfastness*
tenancy 185.3 *duration*, 723.1 *possession*
tenancy in common 724.1 *joint possession*
tenant 255.3 *householder*, 723.5 *possessor*, 725.7 *property man*
tenanted 255.11 *inhabited*
tenant farmer 68.15 *agriculturist*
tenantry 723.1 *possession*
ten-beat crawl 39.2 *swimming technique*
Tenby 93 Cities
ten cents 10c 741.8 *American money*
ten centuries 179.9 *treble figures*
tench 80 Fishes, 20.5 *British game fish*
tenchi nage 26.10 *aikido*
Ten Commandments 16.1 *the law*, 179.6 *ten*, 225.4 *stable thing*, 847.6 *ethics*
tend 234, 60.19 *practise medicine*, 68.18 *practise livestock farming*, 332.7 *take a direction*, 580.2 *prefer*, 630.20 *doctor*, 632.9 *protect*, 637.5 *preserve*, 662.19 *support*, 662.25, 697.8 *serve*
Tendai 7 Non-Christian Religions
tendency 234, 488, 584, 227.4 *significance*, 332.2 *bearing*, 485.2 *ability*, 580.7 *preference*, 588.5 *final intention*, 655.2 *aptitude*, 784.2 *inclination*, 796.4 *design*, 821.7 *choice*
Tendency 234
tendentious 234.5 *tending to*
tendentiously 234.6 *probably*
tendentiousness 588.5 *final intention*
tender 74 Ships and Boats, 36.10 *sailing*, 72.5 *locomotive part*, 370.2 *insubstantial*, 374.6 *softhearted*, 403.7 *susceptible*, 406.5 *painful*, 407.8 *touchable*, 624.23 *diseased*, 679.24 *warship*, 691.4 *lenient*, 729.5 *give*, 737.3 *bargain*, 737.9 *bargaining*, 759.12, 760.1 *sensitive*, 760.3 *sore*, 764.4 *painful*, 821.20 *amorous*, 826.7 *show endearment for*, 835.6 *pitying*
tender age 206.1 *youth*
tender as a spring chicken 374.5 *soft as butter*
tender boat 36.2 *sailing boat*
tendered 737.18 *contractual*
tender feeling 759.5 *good feeling*, 784.1 *liking*, 821.3 *lovingness*
tenderfoot 104.7 *new arrival*, 108.3 *unconnected person*, 149.6 *immigrant*, 156.14 *beginner*, 865.4 *innocent person*
tender heart 835.1 *pity*
tender-hearted 374.6 *softhearted*, 760.1 *sensitive*, 835.6 *pitying*
tender-heartedly 835.13 *pitifully*
tender-heartedness 835.1 *pity*
tenderize 374.13 *soften*
tenderloin 45.23 *beef*, 45.25 *pork*
Tenderloin 93.7 *city district*
tender loving care 469.2 *consideration*, 662.3 *sustenance*
tenderly 370.11 *lightly*, 374.18 *softheartedly*, 469.13 *caringly*, 691.6 *leniently*, 760.12 *sensitively*, 821.30 *lovingly*, 831.10 *benevolently*, 835.13 *pitifully*
tenderness 370.5 *lightness*, 374.12 *gentleness*, 403.2 *ability to sense*, 406.1, 631.5 *pain*, 691.1 *leniency*, 760.5 *sensitivity*, 760.7 *soreness*, 784.1 *liking*, 821.3 *lovingness*, 835.1 *pity*
tender spot 633.7 *vulnerability*, 828.3 *cause of offence*
tending 60.25 *therapeutic*, 488.2 *tendency*, 488.6 *probable*, 613.3 *instrumental*, 662.32 *supportive*, 784.6 *liking*

tending to 234
ten-dollar bill 741.8 *American money*
tendon 137.6 *line*, 382.7 *skeleton*
tendril 83.6 *leaf*, 143.6 *branch*, 726.3 *tools for gripping*
tend to 4.22 *propound a philosophy*, 52.94 *order*
tend to go 332.7 *take a direction*
tendus 46.10 *positions at the barre*
tenebrous 440.8 *dark*, 441.5 *dim*
tenement 256.6 *apartment block*, 725.1 *property*, 725.2 *legal terms*, 727.8 *sink*
tenement building 727.8 *sink*
tenement district 93.7 *city district*
Tenerife 53 Mountains, **98** Islands
tenet 4.1 *philosophy*, 166.4 *guide*, 497.2 *religious belief*, 654.3 *precept*
tenets 471.5 *ideology*
tenfold 179.17 *tenth*, 179.24 *fivefold*
ten-gallon hat 295.15 *headgear*
ten-metre platform 39.6 *diving*
ten million 179.11 *million*
ten-minute penalty 31.3 *ice hockey*
tenne 544.8 *heraldic device*, 544.13 *heraldic*
tenner 179.6 *ten*, 741.8 *American money*, 741.9 *British money*
Tennessee 92 American States, **96** Rivers, 96.3 *US rivers*
Tennessee Walking Horse 32 Breeds of Horse and Pony
tennis 18 Sporting Activities, **40**, 40.5 *real tennis*
tennis ball 40.3 *tennis equipment*, 338.10 *ball*, 377.3 *elastic thing*
tennis court 40.3 *tennis equipment*, 376.8 *smooth thing*
tennis elbow 424.16 *rheumatism*
tennis equipment 40
tennis party 665.7 *social gathering*
tennis player 40
tennis racket 40.3 *tennis equipment*, 330.15 *ram*
tennis shoes 295.19 *footwear*
tennis skirt 295.6 *skirt*
Tennis, Squash, Badminton, Etc. 40
tennis strokes 40
tennis terms 40
Tennyson 48 Poets
tenon 47.10 *carpenter's term*, 47.17 *carpenter*
tenoner 47.11 *woodworking tool*
tenon saw 47.11 *woodworking tool*
tenoplasty 60 Surgical Operations
tenor 49.32 *instrumental*, 121.1 *degree*, 234.1 *tendency*, 332.2 *bearing*, 433.5 *melodist*, 488.2 *tendency*, 520.1 *meaning*, 549.1 *style*
tenor clef 49.17 *notation*
tenorite 57 Minerals
tenotomy 60 Surgical Operations
ten out of ten 619.3 *perfection*
ten pence 741.9 *British money*
ten-per-center 51.25 *producer*
ten-per-cent man 51.25 *producer*
tenpin 25.10 *bowling*
tenpin bowler 25.6 *bowler*
tenpin bowling 18 Sporting Activities, 25.4 *bowling*
ten-pound note 741.9 *British money*
tenrec 77 Placental Mammals
Tenri Kyo 7 Non-Christian Religions
tense 5, 5.30 *syntax*, 135.15 *tied*, 373.2 *tough*, 373.9 *harden*, 642.18 *active*, 777.8 *fearful*, 820.6 *hostile*
ten-second backcourt violation 23.5 *penalties*
ten-second line 23.1 *basketball*
tensely 135.18 *inextricably*, 373.12 *toughly*

tenseness 373.5 *hardness*
tensibility 377.1 *elasticity*
tensible 377.6 *elastic*
tensile 377.6 *elastic*
tensileness 374.8 *softness*
tensile strength 237.1 *strength*
tensimeter 268.8 *meter*
tensiometer 268.8 *meter*
tension 63.14 *load*, 235.4 *energy*, 373.5 *hardness*, 377.1 *elasticity*, 385.9 *irritation*, 777.2 *fearfulness*, 820.2 *personal conflict*
tension traverse 34.3 *climbing technique*
tension wood 85.3 *timber*
tensity 373.5 *hardness*
tens of thousands 181.2 *multitude*
tensor 52.50 *scalar quantity*
tens place 52.8 *number system*
tent 34.4 *climbing equipment*, 256.9 *mobile home*, 293.7 *overhead covering*, 630.10 *surgical dressing*, 630.14 *hospital*
tentacle 403.4 *someone or something that feels*, 407.7 *sense organ*, 726.3 *tools for gripping*
tentation 479.1 *experiment*
tentative 596, 328.6 *hesitant*, 479.8 *experimental*, 656.3 *clumsy*, 781.4 *cautious*
tentative explanation 518.1 *supposition*
tentatively 328.16 *slowly*, 596.10 *ambitiously*, 781.7 *cautiously*
tentativeness 328.12 *hesitation*, 781.1 *caution*
tentative offer 710
tented 293.36 *covered*
tenth 179, 52.75 *equal*, 143.1 *part*, 173.4 *less than one*, 179.6 *ten*, 179.24 *fivefold*
tenthly 179.24 *fivefold*
ten thousand 179.10 *thousand*
tenth part 179.6 *ten*
tenths 751.7 *tax*
ten to one 488.11 *probably*
tenuity 272.7 *fineness*, 372.3 *sparseness*
tenuous 102.8 *unreal*, 260.7 *little*, 272.2 *fine*, 372.1 *sparse*
tenuously 260.8 *in a small way*, 372.7 *sparsely*
tenuousness 260.1 *littleness*, 372.3 *sparseness*
tenure 185.3 *duration*, 187.4 *period of activity*, 723.1 *possession*, 725.2 *legal terms*
tenuto 49 Musical Terms
Tenzing Norgay 18 Sporting Personalities
tenzone 48.7 *poem*
tepee 256.9 *mobile home*, 293.7 *overhead covering*
tephra 54.25 *eruption*
tepid 408.9 *hot*
tepidity 408.1 *heat*
tepidness 408.1 *heat*
teponaztli 49 Musical Instruments
tequila sunrise 351.8 *mixed drink*, 451.3 *orange thing*
tera 75 SI Units
teratologic 541.12 *exaggerated*
teratological 541.12 *exaggerated*
teratologist 60.13 *medical specialist*, 541.6 *exaggerator*
teratology 60.3 *medical specialty*, 541.5 *tall story*, 786.3 *wonderworking*
teratophobia 777 Phobias by Name
terbang 49 Musical Instruments
terbium 57 Chemical Elements
terbutaline 62 Medication
terce 10.4 *public worship*, 204.1 *morning*
tercentenary 179.9 *treble figures*, 511.5 *day to remember*
tercentennial 179.9 *treble figures*
tercentennially 214.16 *cyclically*
tercet 48.8 *part of poem*
terebinth 85 Trees and Shrubs
teredo 81 Molluscs
Terence 48 Dramatists
tergiversant 484.4 *tergiversator*

tergiversate 216.7 *be changed*, 224.12 *be irresolute*, 484.8 *reverse*, 528.13 *inform on*, 530.7 *betray*, 536.9 *renounce*, 576.5 *vacillate*, 578.2 *equivocate*, 598.1 *relinquish*, 628.1 *deteriorate*, 693.15 *be disobedient*
tergiversating 576.1 *vacillating*, 578.11 *equivocating*, 628.12 *deteriorated*
tergiversation 216.2 *change of mind*, 224.2 *irresolution*, 484.2 *reversal*, 530.2 *divulgence*, 576.11 *vacillation*, 578.6 *equivocation*, 628.7 *deterioration*, 693.1 *disobedience*, 858.2 *faithlessness*
tergiversator 484, 220.6 *convert*, 335.19 *deviant person*, 337.21 *backslider*, 500.5 *dissenter*, 576.15 *indecisive person*, 578.9 *equivocator*, 693.10 *seditionist*, 820.5 *hostile person*
tergiversatory 693.13 *disobedient*
term 43 Architectural Decoration, **185**, 5.17 *word*, 52.25 *algebraic expression*, 187.1 *period*, 187.4 *period of activity*, 188.1 *duration*, 203.1 *season*, 560.8 *name*, 567.11 *title*
termagant 241.4 *violent person or animal*, 829.3 *irascible person*
terminal 64, 65.7 *peripheral*, 73.4 *airport*, 157.6 *end point*, 157.20 *ending*, 218.4 *stopping place*, 263.8 *distant*, 344.15 *destination*, 344.19 *approaching*, 397.20, 398.23 *deadly*, 624.22 *sick*, 684.8 *concluded*, 776.5 *past hope*
terminal bud 83.8 *bud*
terminal case 60.18 *patient*
terminal disease 624.2 *illness*
terminal illness 397.5 *ways of dying*, 624.2 *illness*, 687.1 *adversity*
terminally 397.23 *fatally*, 398.25 *lethally*
terminally ill 397.18 *dying*
terminal patient 397.10 *dying person*
terminal point 344.15 *destination*
terminal velocity 73.5 *flight*
terminate 704, 144.4 *complete*, 144.5 *be complete*, 157.16 *cease*, 160.12 *discontinue*, 218.6 *cease*, 227.5 *show an effect*, 244.8 *destroy*, 323.9 *close down*, 574.7 *resolve*, 684.5 *conclude*
terminated 144.7 *complete*, 157.21 *ended*, 160.9 *discontinued*, 684.8 *concluded*, 704.10 *cancelled*
termination 704, 64.28 *plug*, 144.3 *completion*, 155.9 *conclusion*, 157.2 *cessation*, 218.1 *cessation*, 227.1 *effect*, 323.1 *closure*, 684.2 *conclusion*
terminator 53.17 *moon*
terminological inexactitude 309.4 *distortion of the truth*, 538.4 *lie*
terminologically 171.13 *inventorially*
terminologist 5.2 *linguist*
terminology 171.3 *dictionary*, 560.7 *nomenclature*
terminus 72.8 *railway station*, 157.6 *end point*, 218.4 *stopping place*, 327.10 *railway*, 344.15 *destination*
termitarium 82.4 *social insect*
termite 82 Insects, 82.4 *social insect*, 815.10 *social animal*
termite colony 82.4 *social insect*
term of imprisonment 187.4 *period of activity*
term of office 187.4 *period of activity*
term report 528.3 *document*
terms 106.1 *circumstances*, 152.10 *agreement*, 716.2 *basis for negotiations*
terms and conditions 15.1 *industrial relations*
terms of endearment 826, 821.12 *nicknames for lovers*

terms of reference 485.6 *specification*
tern 78 Birds, 78.3 *water bird*
ternary 52.71 *numerical*, 57.35 *combined*, 177.7 *three*
ternary compound 57.7 *chemical compound*
terotechnology 603.5 *mechanics*
terpene 57 Types of Compounds, **58**, 58.6 *lipid*
Terpsichore 46.1 *dancing*
Terpsichorean 51.28 *dancer*, 51.37 *dramatic*
terrace 34.5 *rock face*, 68.11 *farmland*, 69.3 *ornamental garden*, 266.2 *level*, 282.3 *flat thing*, 327.3 *road*, 435.9 *viewpoint*
terraced 34.8 *mountaineering*, 43.12 *structural*, 256.16 *manorial*, 266.7 *layered*
terraced house 43.3 *building*, 256.5 *house*
terracotta 44.1 *ceramics*, 44.9 *industrial ceramics*, 50.12 *sculpture*, 50.14 *sculptor's materials*, 63.26 *masonry*
terra firma 344.15 *destination*
terrain 54.6 *continent*, 249.1 *region*, 256.2 *environment*
terra incognita 529.8 *anonymity*
terrapin 79 Reptiles, 79.4 *chelonian*
terrestrial 54, 53.36 *astronomical*, 76.15 *of animals*, 83.14 *of plants*
terrestrially 53.39 *astronomically*
terrestrial magnetism 54.44, 56.58 *geomagnetism*
terrestrial planet 53.13 *planet*
terrestrial reptile 79.6 *extinct reptile*
terre verte 453.10 *green pigment*
terrible 618.3, 776.8 *bad*, 777.10 *frightening*, 862.7 *evil*, 862.15 *bad luck*
terribleness 862.1 *evil*
terribly 862.12 *evilly*
terrier 77 Breeds of Dogs
terrific 617.1 *worthy*, 861.1 *good*
terrified 777.7 *frightened*
terrify 777.13 *frighten*
terrifying 777.10 *frightening*
terrigenous 54.51 *oceanic*
terriginous 97.7 *oceanic*
terrine 258.16 *crockery*
territorial 2.14 *socioeconomic*, 92.6 *administrative*, 249.16 *regional*, 256.15 *environmental*, 688.14 *governmental*, 725.8 *propertied*
Territorial 632.3 *protector*, 679.8 *soldier*
Territorial Army 17.2 *the military*, 632.3 *protector*, 679.15 *army*
territorial capital 92.5 *administrative headquarters*
territorial division 249
territorial limits 249.3 *regional boundary*
territorially 2.16 *sociologically*, 92.8 *administratively*, 249.19 *geographically*, 256.20 *environmentally*, 725.10 *proprietarily*
territorial waters 249.3 *regional boundary*
territory 12.5 *political organization*, 91.3 *dominion*, 233.7 *sphere of influence*, 249.1 *region*, 249.4 *territorial division*, 249.5 *state*, 249.14 *sphere*, 250.1 *location*, 256.2 *environment*, 688.8 *governmental organization*, 725.1 *property*
terror 241.4 *violent person or animal*, 777.1 *fear*, 832.8 *malefactor*
terrorful 832.11 *cruel*
terrorism 241.2 *physical violence*, 587.7 *deterrence*, 628.10 *impairment*, 669.3 *resistance movement*, 693.3 *subversion*, 693.4 *revolution*, 713.2 *disorder*, 777.4 *intimidation*, 832.2 *cruelness*
terrorist 241.4 *violent person or animal*, 398.10 *killer*, 398.11 *murderer*, 635.2 *troublemaker*,

669.5 *resister,* 669.12 *resisting,* 670.19 *attacker,* 679.9 *guerrilla,* 689.3 *anarchist,* 693.10 *seditionist,* 695.4 *coercive person,* 713.5 *seditionist,* 713.10 *lawbreaking,* 736.8 *thief,* 777.5 *frightener,* 832.8 *malefactor,* 862.6 *evil person,* 864.9 *wicked person*
terrorist attack 670
terrorist bomb 635.1 *trap*
terroristic 832.11 *cruel*
terrorist killing 398.2 *murder*
terrorization 777.4 *intimidation*
terrorize 587.2 *deter,* 670.9 *attack successfully,* 679.38 *conquer,* 690.6 *suppress,* 693.16 *be subversive,* 713.8 *cause mischief,* 777.13 *frighten,* 832.18 *torment*
terrorized 777.7 *frightened*
terror-struck 777.7 *frightened*
terror tactics 670.16 *terrorist attack*
terry 67 Natural Fabrics
terse 270.7 *short,* 552.3 *concise,* 562.6 *summary,* 566.3 *sparing with words*
tersely 270.12 *short,* 552.5 *concisely,* 562.11 *summarily*
terseness 270.1 *shortness,* 552.1 *conciseness,* 562.4 *summariness,* 566.6 *guarded speech*
Tersky 32 Breeds of Horse and Pony
tertian 214.12 *cyclic*
tertiary 177.7 *three*
Tertiary 54 Geological Time Intervals
tertiary chord 49.16 *musical note*
tertiary education 6.2 *educational system*
Tertiary period 200.3 *geological period*
tertiary structure 58.9 *protein*
tervalent 57.35 *combined*
Terylene 67 Synthetic Fibres and Fabrics
terza rima 48.10 *verse form*
Teshekpuk 94 Lakes
Teshub 8 Deities
tesla 75 SI Units, 75 Scientific and Technical Units
Tesla 52 Scientists
Tesla coil 57.20 *surface chemistry*
TESSA 14.4 *personal finance*
tessellate 456.11 *variegate*
tessellated 354.12 *inserted,* 456.8 *checked*
tessellation 140.2 *cooperation,* 354.8 *insertion,* 456.2 *check*
tessera 44.8 *ceramic object,* 456.2 *check,* 544.3 *means of identification*
test 596, 52.66 *proof,* 60.7 *diagnosis,* 268.7 *standard,* 411.9 *taste,* 477.3 *questionnaire,* 477.17 *question,* 479.1 *experiment,* 479.8 *experimental,* 479.11 *experiment,* 535.3 *vow*
Test 96 Rivers
testa 83.9 *seed,* 293.13 *casing*
testament 570.1 *will,* 729.1 *giving*
testamental 729.7 *given*
testamentary 725.8 *propertied,* 729.7 *given*
testate 729.7 *given*
testator 326.7 *transferor ,* 729.4 *giver*
test ban 677.1 *pacification*
test card 534.23 *television reception*
test case 16.5 *litigation,* 119.2 *original*
test design 517.4 *model*
test drive 71.21 *miscellaneous motoring terms*
test-driver 479.5 *experimenter*
tested 479, 617.1 *worthy,* 819.11 *devoted,* 851.23 *approved*
testee 479.7 *experimentee*
tester 411.5 *taster,* 477.9 *questioner,* 479.5 *experimenter,* 492.5 *judge,* 596.7 *attempter*
testes 245.8 *organs of reproduction*

test flight 479.2 *rehearsal*
test for 60.19 *practise medicine*
testicles 245.8 *organs of reproduction,* 316.2 *bulge*
testicular 352.5 *of a secretion*
testificatory 480.9 *verificatory*
testifier 480.7 *verifier,* 528.9 *informant,* 535.9 *affirmer*
testify 480, 483.11 *give evidence,* 528.11 *inform,* 535.18 *vow,* 560.15 *recount,* 714.7 *promise*
testily 830.14 *irritably*
testimonial 475.4 *proof,* 480.6 *evidence,* 483.6 *documentation,* 485.3 *qualifications,* 545.2 *certificate,* 545.11 *monument,* 688.9 *permission,* 708.2 *permit,* 714.12 *promised,* 812.6 *tribute,* 837.3 *recognition,* 851.6 *recommendation*
testimonial banquet 812.6 *tribute*
testimonial evidence 483.5 *legal evidence*
testimony 16.7 *legal trial,* 473.3 *line of argument,* 475.4 *proof,* 483.5 *legal evidence,* 688.9 *permission,* 714.1 *promise*
testiness 829.1 *irascibility*
testing 479.3 *experimentation,* 479.8 *experimental,* 596.9 *tentative*
testis 352 Endocrine Glands
test match 27.1 *cricket match,* 674.2 *contest*
test model 517.4 *model*
test of endurance 674.2 *contest*
test pilot 73.3 *aircraft personnel*
test-pilot 479.5 *experimenter*
test someone's patience 829.8 *make irascible*
test statistic 52.54 *hypothesis testing*
test the alarm system 636.7 *raise the alarm*
test the depth 479.11 *experiment*
test the ground 716.4 *negotiator*
test the water 479.11 *experiment*
test the waters 516.2 *show prudence*
test tube 220.4 *medium of conversion*
test-tube baby 245.3 *propagation*
testudo 671.8 *military defences*
testy 473.8 *argumentative,* 818.5 *discourteous,* 829.4 *irascible,* 830.7 *irritable*
tetanus 624.6 *infection*
tetchily 829.9 *irascibly*
tetchiness 829.1 *irascibility*
tetchy 403.7 *susceptible,* 829.4 *irascible,* 830.7 *irritable*
tête-à-tête 654.2 *consultation,* 815.3 *meeting*
tether 135.10 *link,* 139.9 *yoke,* 137.12 *bind,* 661.4 *restraint,* 661.10 *restrain,* 699.5 *means of restraint,* 699.12 *gag*
tethered 137.16 *bound,* 225.10 *stabilized,* 661.14 *blocked*
tetra 80 Fishes
tetracaine 62 Medication
tetrachord 49.16 *musical note*
tetracycline 62 Medication, 62.4 *drug type*
tetrad 178.1 *four*
tetradactyl 178.3 *foursome*
tetradymite 54 Minerals
tetraethyl lead 57 Common Chemical Compounds
tetragon 52.44 *polygon,* 178.2 *quadrilateral,* 310.3 *angled figure*
tetragonal 52.82 *polygonal,* 57.33 *crystalline*
tetragonal crystal 57.4 *crystal*
tetragram 178.3 *foursome*
tetragrammation 178.3 *foursome*
tetrahedral 178.8 *quadrilateral*
tetrahedrite 54 Minerals
tetrahedron 52.46 *polyhedron,* 178.2 *quadrilateral*
tetrahydrofuran 57 Common Chemical Compounds
tetrahydrozoline 62 Medication, 62 Medication

tetralogy 51.2 *play,* 178.3 *foursome*
tetramerous 178
tetrameter 48.9 *metre,* 178.3 *foursome*
tetraplegia 236.4 *disability,* 624.17 *nervous disorder*
tetrapod 178.3 *foursome*
tetrasaccharide 58.3 *carbohydrate*
tetrastich 48.8 *part of poem*
tetraterpene 58.20 *terpene*
tetravalent 57.35 *combined,* 178.9 *tetramerous*
tetrode 64.20 *electron tube*
tetrose 58.3 *carbohydrate*
tetter 624.13 *skin disease*
Teuso 1 Peoples
Teutates 8 Deities
Teutonic 5 Languages and Groups of Languages, 5.11 *family of languages*
Teutonic Knights 7 Christian Movements
Teutonism 5.26 *dialect*
Teutonophobia 777 Phobias by Name
te-waza 26.7 *judo*
TEX 65.11 *application*
Texas 92 American States
Texas accent 5.26 *dialect*
Texas Leaguer 22.5 *batting terms*
Texas League single 22.5 *batting terms*
Texas Longhorn 68 Breeds of Cattle
Texel 68 Breeds of Sheep
text 51.2 *play,* 143.2 *particular,* 472.1 *topic,* 520.1 *meaning,* 654.3 *precept*
textbook 6.14 *school book,* 532.6 *book publishing*
text editor 65.11 *application*
textile 288, 383, 67.3 *fabric,* 243.7 *produce,* 604.1 *materials*
text transmission 534.8 *data transmission*
texts 517.10 *cards*
textual 537.23 *literal*
textual critic 524.6 *interpreter*
textual criticism 524.3 *criticism*
textualism 537.10 *literalness*
textual note 524.2 *annotation*
textural 383, 382.11 *structural*
texturally 383
texture 383, 54.28 *rock,* 67.4 *weaving,* 382.2 *fabric,* 407.1 *touch*
Texture 383
textured 375.1 *rough,* 383.7 *textural*
textured lighting 66.15 *lighting*
Tezcatlipoca 8 Deities
T-formation 19.7 *offence*
TGV 72.10 *miscellaneous*
thaasophobia 777 Phobias by Name
Thackeray 48 Writers
Thag 7 Non-Christian Religions
Thai 5 Languages and Groups of Languages
Thai boxing 18 Sporting Activities
Thailand 91 Countries
thalamotomy 60 Surgical Operations
thalassic 54.51, 97.7 *oceanic*
thalassographer 97.6 *oceanographer*
thalassographic 97.8 *oceanographic*
thalassography 97.5 *oceanography*
thalassometer 97.2 *tide*
thalassophobia 777 Phobias by Name
Thales 4 Philosophers
Thalia 51.10 *comedy*
thalidomide 62 Medication
thallic 57.34 *elemental*
thallium 57 Chemical Elements
thallium scan 60.7 *diagnosis*
thalloid 90.7 *algal*
Thallophyta 83.4 *lower plant*
thallophyte 83.4 *lower plant,* 90.1 *alga*
thallophytic 83.16 *taxonomic*
thallose liverwort 88.3 *moss*

thallous 57.34 *elemental*
thallus 89.4 *fungal body,* 90.3 *plant body*
Thalna 8 Deities
Thalo purple 455.2 *purple pigment*
Thalo red 450.6 *red pigment*
Thalo yellow green 453.10 *green pigment*
Thames 96 Rivers, 96.4 *British rivers*
Thames Cup 36.5 *Henley trophies*
Thames punt 36.8 *punting*
Thames Valley 92 New Zealand Regions and Territories
thanatophobia 777 Phobias by Name
thanatopsis 774.2 *lament*
Thanatos 8 Deities, 61.22 *libido*
thane 723.6 *lord*
thank 837.6 *be grateful,* 878.9 *reward*
thankful 765.4 *satisfied,* 837.4 *grateful*
thankfully 765.13 *with satisfaction,* 837.8 *gratefully*
thankfulness 765.1 *satisfaction,* 837.1 *gratitude*
thank God 837.7 *give thanks,* 837.9 *thank you*
thank goodness 837.9 *thank you*
thank heaven 837.9 *thank you*
thanking 837
thankless 838, 614.2 *futile*
thanklessly 838.7 *ungratefully*
thanklessness 614.4 *futility,* 838.1 *ingratitude*
thankless person 838
thankless task 644.1 *work,* 838.1 *ingratitude*
thank offering 729.3 *offering,* 837.3 *recognition*
thank one's lucky stars 837.7 *give thanks*
thanks 837, 812.7 *thanksgiving,* 837.9 *thank you,* 845.2 *due,* 878.1 *reward*
thanks a lot 837.9 *thank you*
thanksgiving 812, 9.1 *worship,* 10.3 *rite of worship,* 10.6 *Eucharist,* 773.2 *fanfare,* 837.2 *thanks*
Thanksgiving 812.5 *anniversary*
Thanksgiving Day 214.6 *annually celebrated day*
Thanksgiving party 665.7 *social gathering*
thanks to 232.9 *instrumentally,* 662.37 *in aid of*
thanks to Mother Nature 246.8 *fruitfully*
thank you! 837
thank you 837.2 *thanks*
thank-you card 837.3 *recognition*
thank-you gift 837.3 *recognition*
thank-you letter 837.3 *recognition*
thank you very much 837.9 *thank you*
Thar 98 Deserts
Tharparkar 68 Breeds of Cattle
that being so 106.15 *under the circumstances,* 116.36 *accordingly*
that being the case 106.15 *under the circumstances,* 116.36 *accordingly*
thatch 293.7 *overhead covering,* 293.27 *roof,* 604.2 *building material,* 629.1 *repair*
thatched 293.36 *covered*
thatched cottage 44.3 *building*
thatcher 87.5 *grass-cutter,* 293.17 *coverer,* 646.2 *artisan*
Thatcher's children 809.5 *self-interest*
that is 475.22 *demonstrably,* 524.18 *in other words*
that is to say 165.31 *namely,* 475.22 *demonstrably,* 524.18 *in other words*
that's awful 862.15 *bad luck*
that's enough 218.12 *stop*
that's for sure 537.40 *right*
that's it 218.12 *stop,* 4/1.25 *got it,* 537.40 *right*
that's the idea 471.25 *got it*
that's the one 480.13 *really*
that which makes invisible 438

that which makes visible 437
thaumatology 786.3 *wonder-working*
thaumaturge 11.4 *witch*, 514.5 *surpriser*, 786.5 *person of wonder*
thaumaturgia 11.3 *witchcraft*
thaumaturgic 786.8 *wonderful*
thaumaturgically 11.26 *magically*
thaumaturgics 11.3 *witchcraft*
thaumaturgist 11.4 *witch*
thaumaturgy 11.21 *bewitch*
thaumaturgy 11.3 *witchcraft*, 786.3 *wonder-working*
thaw 55.63 *snow*, 139.6 *come unstuck*, 374.13 *soften*, 387.8 *fluidification*, 387.24 *melt*, 408.5 *hot weather*, 408.14 *be hot*, 835.11 *excite pity*
thawable 387.21 *liquefiable*
thawed 387.19 *liquefied*
thawing 393, 387.8 *fluidification*, 387.20 *liquefying*
the 1,000 Guineas 32.7 *horseracing*
the 18th Amendment 873.7 *prohibition*
the 2,000 Guineas 32.7 *horseracing*
the Absolute Idea 471.1 *idea*
the absolute truth 537.3 *the truth*
the accused 856.4 *accused person*
the Acropolis 33.4 *motor rally*
the actual truth 537.3 *the truth*
the administration 688.4 *governance*
Theaetetus 4 Philosophers
the afterlife 190.3 *life without end*
the age of amphibians 200.3 *geological period*
the age of reptiles 200.3 *geological period*
the aggregate 142.4 *all*
the Alamo 398.15 *slaughterhouse*
the all clear 708.1 *permission*
the Almighty 8.3 *God*
the Alpine 33.4 *motor rally*
the altogether 294.3 *nakedness*, 296.2 *nudity*
the Americans 91.7 *United States*
the America's Cup 36.1 *sailing*
the ancients 200.6 *people of the past*, 400.4 *civilized human*
the ancient world 200.1 *past time*
the angel of death 244.6 *destroyer*
the animal kingdom 396.1 *life*
thearchy 12.1 *government*
the arts 48.1 *literature*, 50.1 *art*, 501.5 *science*
Theatine 7 Members of Religious Orders
the Atlantic Race for Cruisers 36.1 *sailing*
theatre 51, 51.1 *drama*, 63.20 *building*, 228.3 *construction*, 249.14 *sphere*, 435.9 *viewpoint*, 811.3 *dramatics*
theatre craft 51.7 *dramaturgy*
theatregoer 51, 253.5 *someone present*
theatre-in-the-round 51.14 *theatre*
theatre movements 51
theatre nuclear warfare 676.8 *warfare*
theatre nuclear weapon 680.1 *weapon*
theatre of cruelty 51.8 *theatre movements*
theatre of fact 51.8 *theatre movements*
theatre of operations 17.1 *military affairs*
theatre of silence 51.8 *theatre movements*
theatre of the absurd 51.8 *theatre movements*
theatre of war 666.1 *disagreement*, 676.10 *battleground*
theatre review 524.3 *criticism*
theatre sister 60.16 *nurse*
theatre ticket 544.3 *means of identification*
theatre world 51.1 *drama*
theatrical 51.37 *dramatic*, 475.10 *demonstrative*, 797.3 *affected*, 811.18 *dramatic*

theatrical agent 51.25 *producer*
theatrical convention 51.7 *dramaturgy*
theatrical cosmetics 51.19 *stage requisite*
theatrical costume 51.19 *stage requisite*, 295.5 *fancy dress*
theatrical engagement 51.13 *engagement*
theatricality 51.7 *dramaturgy*, 797.1 *affectedness*, 811.3 *dramatics*
theatricalize 51.36 *dramatize*
theatrically 51.42 *dramatically*, 475.21 *demonstratively*, 811.34 *dramatically*
theatrical makeup 51.19 *stage requisite*
theatrical performance 51
theatrical production 243.5 *work of art*
theatricals 51.1 *drama*
theatrical technique 51.20 *acting*
theatrics 51.1 *drama*, 51.7 *dramaturgy*, 475.2 *demonstrativeness*
The Australian Capital Territory 92 Australian States and Territories
the authorities 688.4 *governance*, 696.8 *the power structure*
the autumn of one's life 202.1 *oldness*
the average punter 400.7 *person*
the axe 349.18 *dismissal*, 704.2 *termination*
the ayes 499.3 *assenter*
the back of beyond 263.3 *distant place*
the bad 864.9 *wicked person*
the Band of Hope 873.8 *sober person*
the bar 644.5 *exercise*
the basic fact 99.5 *fact*
the basics 99.5 *fact*, 602.1 *means*, 604.1 *materials*
the battery 22.2 *baseball player*
the beak 16.23 *judge*, 492.6 *justice*
the beasts of the field 76.1 *animals*
the beginning of the end 244.4 *ruin*
the bench 492.3 *place of judgment*, 492.6 *justice*
Thebes 93 Cities
the best 861, 126.7 *the best people*, 580.9 *chosen thing*, 682.15 *victorious*
the best ever 861.9 *the best*
the best people 126
the Betty Ford Clinic 873.8 *sober person*
the beyond 397.1 *death*
the big apple 46.2 *dance*
the Big Apple 93.3 *New York*
the big C 624.12 *cancer*
the big cheese 126.5 *superior*
the big E 147.2 *ejection*, 252.4 *relegation*, 341.6 *repulse*, 704.2 *termination*
the big enchilada 126.5 *superior*
the big house 323.4 *closed place*, 702.2 *the inside*
the big lie 538.4 *lie*
the big picture 588.5 *final intention*
the big sleep 397.1 *death*
the big time 682.1 *success*
the big top 51.4 *show business*
the Big Top 51.5 *show*
the Bill of Rights 225.4 *stable thing*, 698.2 *free speech*
the billow 97.1 *sea*
the bird 713.3 *gesture of protest*, 850.6 *taunt*
the birds 76.1 *animals*
the birds and the bees 245.3 *propagation*
the biz 126.6 *paragon*
the black 744.3 *deposit*
the Black Death 244.7 *agent of destruction*
the blahs 783.1 *indifference*
the Blessed One 8.3 *God*
the Blessed Virgin 8.10 *deified person*

the blind 436.4 *blind people*
the blue 97.1 *sea*
the blues 41.7 *ice-dancing*, 770.2 *depression*, 830.2 *sign of sullenness*
the board 688.4 *governance*, 696.8 *the power structure*
the boards 51.1 *drama*, 51.4 *show business*, 51.15 *stage*
the boat race 36.4 *rowing*
the book 702.4 *prison sentence*
the Book 7.12 *religious text*
the boondocks 263.3 *distant place*
the boonies 263.3 *distant place*
the boot 147.2 *ejection*, 252.4 *relegation*, 349.17 *expulsion*, 349.18 *dismissal*, 704.2 *termination*, 727.1 *disposal*
the bounce 252.4 *relegation*, 349.17 *expulsion*, 704.2 *termination*
the Bowery 93.3 *New York*
the bowler hat 704.2 *termination*
the Bowry 93.3 *New York*
the box 534.22 *television set*
the boys 401.15 *menfolk*
the boys in blue 16.14 *police*
the boys in the back room 401.15 *menfolk*
the brass 126.7 *the best people*
the brass ring 782.5 *object of desire*
the breaks 686.2 *good fortune*
the brightest and best 126.7 *the best people*
the briny 97.1 *sea*, 389.1 *water*
the briny deep 97.1 *sea*
the British 91.8 *Great Britain*
The British Association for Shooting and Conservation 37.2 *hunting*
The British Field Sports Society 37.2 *hunting*
the British Isles 91.8 *Great Britain*
the Broads 94.4 *British lakes*
the Bronx 93.3 *New York*
the brush 50.2 *painting*
the brushoff 349.19 *ostracism*
the bucket 36.8 *punting*
the buff 294.3 *nakedness*, 296.2 *nudity*
the bullet 704.2 *termination*
the bum's rush 349.17 *expulsion*
the burden of years 202.1 *oldness*
theca 90.3 *plant body*
the canvas 674.7 *boxing*
the Capitol 688.6 *place of authority*, 696.8 *the power structure*
the case 99.5 *fact*, 537.3 *the truth*
the case in point 490.18 *particularity*
the cat's pyjamas 861.16 *superior person*
the chair 879.16 *instrument of execution*
the channels 366.1 *agitation*
the choice 674.10 *contender*
the chop 704.2 *termination*, 727.1 *disposal*
the chosen 580.9 *chosen thing*
the chuck 349.17 *expulsion*
the Church 7.9 *priesthood*
the City 93.5 *London*, 740.5 *stock market*
the civilized world 400.4 *civilized human*
the classics 48.1 *literature*
the Classics 674.4 *race*
the claw 25.2 *grip*
the clergy 7.9 *priesthood*
the clerisy 48.15 *literary person*
the cloak of night 205.2 *night*
the cloth 7.9 *priesthood*
the clothing business 295.2 *dressing*
the Coast 249.8 *regions of the US*
the Code of Hammurabi 225.4 *stable thing*
the cold shoulder 349.19 *ostracism*
the collywobbles 777.2 *fearfulness*
The Comedy of Errors 48
Shakespeare's plays

the Common Enemy 8.7 *devil*
the common lot 124.4 *average*
the common people 803
the common rule 15.1 *industrial relations*
the commons 803.2 *the common people*
the common touch 814.3 *familiarity*, 817.1 *courtesy*
the Commonwealth 400.11 *nation*
the Commonwealth of Nations 724.1 *joint possession*
the condemned 397.10 *dying person*
the conscious 368.6 *internal world*
the Conservative Party 217.2 *conservatism*
the contemporary world 196.2 *the present day*
the corridors of power 696.8 *the power structure*
the couch 61.3 *psychiatric treatment*
the country club set 742.11 *the rich*
the county set 742.11 *the rich*
the cover of *Time* 532.7 *publicity*
the covers 27.4 *team*
the crack of doom 199.3 *future condition*
the cream 580.9 *chosen thing*
the cream of society 742.11 *the rich*
the Creation 156.2 *creation*
the Creator 8.3 *God*, 156.16 *originator*, 226.7 *Prime Mover*
the creeps 403.3 *stimulus*
the crowd 815.7 *human society*
the crud 624.4 *disease*
the crunch 611.2 *important matter*, 659.6 *critical situation*
the current situation 196.2 *the present day*
the curse 353.11 *menstruation*
the Curse of Eve 353.11 *menstruation*
the D 24.3 *English billiards*
the dark of night 205.2 *night*
the day after tomorrow 199.1 *future time*
the day before yesterday 200.1 *past time*, 200.22 *in the past*
the dead 397, 397.12 *death count*
the dead and dying 397.12 *death count*
the dead of night 205.3 *midnight*
the Dead Sea 94.1 *lake*
the deaf 421.2 *deaf people*
the deceased 397.11 *dead person*
the deep 97.1 *sea*
the deeps 277.4 *deep thing*
the defensive 671.1 *defence*
the defunct 397.11 *dead person*
the Deity 226.7 *Prime Mover*
the Deluge 96.6 *river flow*
the deprived 743.11 *the poor*
the depths 277.4 *deep thing*
the Derby 32.7 *horseracing*, 674.4 *race*
the Devil 8.7 *devil*
the devil take it 827.16 *euphemisms*
the directorship 688.4 *governance*, 696.8 *the power structure*
the dirt 99.5 *fact*
the disadvantaged 743.11 *the poor*
the distant future 199.1 *future time*
the dogs 674.4 *race*
the doldrums 770.2 *depression*
the dole 13.8 *industrial relations*, 718.1 *protection*, 831.3 *welfare*, 833.4 *welfare state*
the done thing 513.3 *the expected thing*, 584.5 *tradition*, 794.3 *etiquette*
the dope 99.5 *fact*
the Dow 14.2 *stock exchange*
the draft 17.1 *military affairs*, 676.7 *war measures*
the drama 51.1 *drama*
the dregs of society 743.11 *the poor*
the drill 327.1 *way*

the drink 97.1 *sea*
the dumps 770.2 *depression,*
830.2 *sign of sullenness*
the Eight 50 Schools and
Groups of Artists
the elbow 147.2 *ejection,* 252.4
relegation, 704.2 *termination*
the elderly 202.2 *old people,*
207.10 *the old*
the elect 617.7 *elite*
the elements 55.3 *weather*
the elite 126.7 *the best people*
the Emerald Isle 91.10 *Ireland*
the end 144.1 *completeness,*
157.13 *ender,* 684.2 *conclusion*
the end of the rainbow 519.8
dreamland
the end of the world 199.3 *future
condition,* 618.11 *harmfulness*
the end of time 199.3 *future condition*
the enemy 663.8 *the opposition*
the Enemy 8.7 *devil*
the English 91.9 *England*
the English season 203.1 *season*
the environmental movement
627.11 *reformism*
the Erinys 828.7 *gods and
goddesses of anger*
the essentials 99.5 *fact,* 143.5
largest part, 604.1 *materials*
the Establishment 126.7 *the best
people,* 225.4 *stable thing,*
233.6 *group influence,* 688.4
governance, 696.8 *the power
structure*
the Eternal 8.3 *God*
the eternal feminine 402.1 *female sex*
the Eumenides 828.7 *gods and
goddesses of anger*
the Everglades 98.3 *marsh*
the evil eye 618.11 *harmfulness,*
827.4 *malediction,* 862.4 *evil
power*
the Evil One 8.7 *devil,* 862.6 *evil
person*
the exact same 110.1 *sameness*
the exact time 192.3 *chronology*
the exact truth 537.3 *the truth*
the expected thing 513
the exploited 481.8 *victim of discrimination*
the external 104.4 *externality*
the facts 537.3 *the truth*
the faithful 7.3 *religious person*
the fallen 397.12 *death count*
the fancy 674.7 *boxing*
the far future 199.1 *future time*
the far left 665.3 *political grouping*
the far past 200.1 *past time*
the far right 665.3 *political grouping*
the fashion world 295.2 *dressing*
the Father 8.3 *God*
the father of medicine 630.15
healer
the Fearsome Foursome 19.10 *defence*
the fidgets 366.5, 642.7 *restlessness*
the field 32.7 *horseracing,* 663.8
the opposition, 674.10 *contender*
the filth 16.14 *police*
the final blow 157.13 *ender*
the final thrill 397.1 *death*
the finger 713.3 *gesture of protest*
the flavour of the month 532.7
publicity
the flesh 877.3 *sexual immorality*
the Flood 96.6 *river flow*
the footlights 51.1 *drama*
the force 16.14 *police*
the four elements 367.4 *matter*
the Four Freedoms 698.2 *free
speech*
**the Four Horsemen of the Apoca-
lypse** 244.7 *agent of destruction*
the four last things 588.5 *final
intention*
the fourth dimension 185.1 *time,*
438.5 *invisible thing*
the fowl of the air 76.1 *animals*
the Franciscan order 743.8 *renunciation of wealth*

the French disease 624.14 *venereal disease*
the Fringe 51.1 *drama*
the front four 19.10 *defence*
theft 736, 16.39 *crime,* 721.5
profit, 734.3 *taking away,* 736.1
stealing
the fundamentals 99.5 *fact*
the Furies 828.7 *gods and
goddesses of anger*
the future 197.1 *different time,*
199.1 *future time*
the fuzz 16.14 *police,* 718.3 *security officer*
the f-word 5.19 *swearword*
the gate 349.18 *dismissal,* 730.2
something received
the gen 99.5 *fact*
the genuine article 119.2 *original,* 537.6 *authenticity*
the giggles 773.3 *laughter*
the girls 402.13 *womenfolk*
the glitterati 742.11 *the rich*
the globe 54.5 *earth*
the Glorious Koran 7.12 *religious
text*
the go-ahead 708.1 *permission*
the go-by 850.5 *insult*
the gods 8.5 *deity,* 51.16 *auditorium*
the God squad 7.5 *Christian*
the golden rule 652.1 *conduct*
the Good Book 7.12 *religious text*
the good life 106.5 *comfortable
circumstances,* 405.1 *physical
pleasure,* 686.1 *prosperity,* 742.7
opulence
the goods 617.8 *exceller*
the Good Shepherd 8.4 *God the
Son*
**the goose that lays the golden
eggs** 605.3 *supply*
the gospel truth 537.3 *the truth*
the government 688.4 *governance*
the Government 696.8 *the power
structure*
the Grand Challenge Cup 36.5
Henley trophies
the Grand National 674.4, 674.4
race
the grand scheme 588.5 *final intention*
the Grand Slam 29.1 *golf*
the grand style 48.12 *poetic language*
the grape 351.9 *wine*
the great adventure 397.1 *death*
the great American game 22.1
baseball
the great divide 397.1 *death*
the Great Divide 263.3 *distant
place*
the greatest 126.6 *paragon,*
611.4 *bigwig,* 617.8 *exceller*
The Greatest Show on Earth
532.8 *public relations*
the greatest show on earth 617.8
exceller
the Great Lakes 94.3 *US lakes*
the Great Leveller 397.2 *death
personified*
the great outdoors 289.2 *outside,*
390.5 *open air*
the Great Salt Lake 94.1 *lake*
the Great Spirit 8.3 *God*
The Great Train Robbery 736.3
theft
the great unwashed 124.7 *average person,* 161.20 *crowd,*
164.11 *general public,* 419.2
*something that makes an un-
pleasant smell,* 795.6 *vulgar herd*
The Great War 676.1 *war*
the Great Wen 93.5 *London*
the green-eyed monster 820.2
personal conflict, 822.1 *hate*
the green light 708.1 *permission,*
855.1 *vindication*
the green stuff 453.12 *figurative
usage*
the Grim Reaper 244.6 *destroyer,*
397.2 *death personified*
the gross amount 142.4 *all*
the grumps 830.2 *sign of sullenness*
the hand of God 232.3 *assistant*
the hand of time 244.6 *destroyer*

the hands of the clock 185.18 *adjust the clock*
the happy couple 823.9 *married
couple*
the happy hunting ground 714.4
promised land
the happy land 8.11 *heaven*
the hard of hearing 421.2 *deaf
people*
the hard right 217.2 *conservatism*
the hard way 644.4 *exertion,*
644.12 *laboriously,* 659.3 *difficult task,* 659.25 *difficultly,*
661.17 *in the way*
the hare and the tortoise 111.2
opposites
the have-nots 743.11 *the poor*
the haves 686.4 *prosperous person,* 721.8 *wealthy person,*
742.11 *the rich*
the heart of the matter 537.3 *the
truth,* 552.1 *conciseness*
the heave-ho 147.2 *ejection,*
252.4 *relegation*
the heavens 390.1 *air*
the heavies 532.4 *newspaper*
the heebie-jeebies 777.2 *fearfulness*
the height of fashion 196.4 *up-to-
dateness*
the heights 126.4 *summit*
the Henley Royal Regatta 36.4
rowing
the hereafter 190.3 *life without
end,* 199.3 *future condition,*
396.5 *life cycle*
the here and now 101.1 *reality,*
196.1 *present time*
the high command 688.4 *governance,* 696.8 *the power structure*
the Highlands 91.11 *Scotland,*
249.9 *regions of Britain*
the high road 660.6 *easy thing*
the Hill 688.6 *place of authority,*
696.8 *the power structure*
the hoi polloi 161.20 *crowd*
the hole 702.3 *prison cell*
the Holocaust 398.4 *slaughter,*
879.13 *capital punishment*
the Holy Ghost 8.3 *God*
the Holy Spirit 8.3 *God*
the honest-to-God truth 537.3
the truth
the honest-to-goodness truth
537.3 *the truth*
the honest truth 537.3 *the truth*
the horrors 874.16 *alcoholism*
the hots 782.4 *sexual desire*
the hot seat 879.16 *instrument
of execution*
the how 327.1 *way*
the HP 738.7 *purchasing*
the human family 400.9 *group*
the humanities 48.1 *literature,*
501.5 *science*
the hundred days 179.9 *treble figures*
the hunted 590
the ideal 619.3 *perfection*
the idea of 518.1 *supposition*
theileriosis 81.12 *protozoal disease*
the immortals 8.5 *deity*
the Index 709.2 *censorship*
the individual 165.5 *the special*
the in-group 696.8 *the power
structure*
the inner circle 688.4 *governance,* 696.8 *the power structure*
the Inquisition 879.15 *instrument of torture*
the inside 702
the instalment plan 738.7 *purchasing*
the intended 714.6 *someone
promised*
the interior 290.3 *inland*
the in thing 201.2 *trendiness,*
584.4 *custom*
the invisible man 438.5 *invisible
thing*
the Irish 91.10 *Ireland*
the Isle of Dogs 93.5 *London*
theism 4.7 *school of thought,* 7.2
religiousness
theist 4.11 *follower of a doctrine,*
497.5 *believer*

theistic 4.14 *of a philosophy,*
8.13 *divine*
theistically 8.19 *divinely*
the jerks 366.8 *spasm*
the jet set 721.8 *wealthy people,*
742.11 *the rich*
the jimjams 777.2 *fearfulness*
the jitters 777.2 *fearfulness*
the Jockey Club 32.7 *horseracing*
the joint 875.6 *drug*
the judiciary 492.6 *justice*
the jump 300.4 *advantage*
the jumps 777.2 *fearfulness*
the King of Light 8.3 *God*
the kiss off 704.2 *termination*
the know 528.1 *information*
the Kremlin 696.8 *the power
structure*
the Ladies' World Championship
41.10 *curling*
the lads 401.15 *menfolk*
the lady and the tramp 111.2 *opposites*
the Lake District 94.4 *British lakes*
the Land of the Free 91.7 *United
States*
the Land of the Leal 8.11 *heaven*
the Last Day 492.4 *judgment day*
the last debt 397.1 *death*
the last straw 157.13 *ender*
the Last Summoner 397.2 *death
personified*
the last thing one would expect
489.5 *unexpectedness*
the last word 201.2 *trendiness*
the last word in 126.14 *best*
the late lamented 397.11 *dead
person*
the lateness of the hour 209.2
late hour
the latest 796.1 *fashion*
the latest craze 201.2 *trendiness*
the latest fashion 201.2 *trendiness,* 295.2 *dressing*
the latest style 295.2 *dressing*
the latest thing 201.2 *trendiness*
the laugh's on you 672.7 *revenge*
the law 16
the Law West of the Pecos 16.23
judge
the lay of the land 105.3 *state of
affairs*
the lead 154.2 *priority*
the least one can do 593.3 *needfulness*
the left 665.3 *political grouping*
the left wing 665.3 *political
grouping*
the length and breadth 142.4 *all*
the length and breadth of 144.9
completely
the lesser of two evils 222.1 *substitution*
the letter 503.2 *correctness*
the lie of the land 105.3 *state of
affairs*
the life of Riley 405.2 *good time*
the light fails 440.13 *become dark*
the Light of the World 8.4 *God
the Son*
the like of 114.1 *similarity,*
163.4 *type*
the limit 144.1 *completeness,*
157.13 *ender*
the Line 158.4 *midline,* 249.2 *geographical region*
the line of least resistance 675.1
peace
the lion and the lamb 111.2 *opposites*
the literal truth 503.2 *correctness*
the living 396.1 *life,* 400.1 *humankind*
the living and breathing world
396.1 *life*
the Lone Ranger and Tonto
819.7 *famous friendships*
the long and the short of it
143.5 *largest part,* 552.1 *conciseness*
the long run 199.1 *future time*
the long sleep 397.1 *death*
the long term 199.1 *future time*
the long, the short, and the tall
164.10 *everyone*
the loony left 665.3 *political
grouping*

the Lord 8.3 *God*
the Lord of Wisdom 8.3 *God*
the Lord's Prayer 10.9 *prayer*
the lost 397.12 *death count*
the lot 142.4 *all*
the low-down 483.1 *evidence,*
537.3 *the truth*
the lower classes 743.11 *the poor*
the lower regions 397.14 *the spiritual world*
the Lowlands 91.11 *Scotland*
the luck of the draw 229.2 *chance*
the McCoy 537.6 *authenticity*
the Mafia 864.7 *criminality*
the magic word 708.1 *permission*
the magistracy 492.6 *justice*
the Magna Carta 698.3 *independence*
the main 143.5 *largest part*
the main man 126.5 *superior*
the Maker 8.3 *God*
the making of 627.5 *improvement*
the man 400.7 *person,* 611.4 *bigwig*
the Man 702.6 *prison officer*
them and us 161.19 *clique*
the man in black 440.4 *dark thing*
the masses 127.6 *inferior,*
161.20 *crowd,* 400.9 *group,*
803.2 *the common people*
the Masters 29.1 *golf*
thematic 257.12 *itemized,* 472.7
focused
thematically 257, 472
thematic apperception test 61.5
psychological test
theme 48.3 *aspect of fiction,*
49.13 *melody,* 382.9 *artistic
structure,* 433.1 *melody,* 472.1
topic, 473.4 *gist,* 561.1 *dissertation*
the media 528.4 *mass communication,* 532.2 *mass media*
the Melting Pot 91.7 *United
States*
theme park 786.4 *wonder*
The Merchant of Venice 48
Shakespeare's plays
the merry month of May 203.2
spring
The Merry Wives of Windsor 48
Shakespeare's plays
themes 257.5 *divisions*
theme song 433.1 *melody*
the Method 51.20 *acting*
the middle of nowhere 263.3 *distant place*
the Midlands 290.3 *inland*
the Midwest 290.3 *inland*
the military 17
the millennium 199.3 *future condition,* 714.4 *promised land*
the mind's eye 519.1 *imagination*
the ministry 7.9 *priesthood*
the minority 182.2 *least*
the mob 127.6 *inferior,* 864.7
criminality
the modern day 196.2 *the present day*
the modern world 196.2 *the present day*
the month of Maying 203.2 *spring*
the moon 263.3 *distant place*
the mopes 830.2 *sign of sullenness*
the morrow 199.1 *future time*
the most 126.6 *paragon,* 126.17
supremely
the Mother 8.3 *God*
themselves 165.12 *I*
the mulligrubs 830.2 *sign of sullenness*
the mumps 830.2 *sign of sullenness*
the Muse 48.13 *poetic genius*
the Muses 8.5 *deity*
then 155.28 *after,* 185.27 *at
what time,* 197.3 *another time*
the naked ape 400.7 *person*
the naked truth 537.3 *the truth*
Thenard 52 Scientists
thenardite 54 Minerals
The National Rifle Association
37.2 *hunting*
the nature of things 105.3 *state
of affairs*
the nays 500.6 *dissenters*

the near future 199.1 *future time*
the needy 743.11 *the poor*
the Netherlands' Tulip Rally 33.4
motor rally
the never-never 733.4 *credit,*
738.7 *purchasing,* 744.1 *credit*
the new generation 206.10 *the
young*
the new rich 742.11 *the rich*
the New York season 203.1 *season*
the next world 190.3 *life without
end,* 199.3 *future condition*
the nine-to-five 584.3 *way*
the nitty-gritty 226.3 *rudiment,*
367.4 *matter*
the noble animal 400.7 *person*
the noble experiment 873.7 *prohibition*
the nod 499.2 *yes,* 667.1 *agreement,* 708.1 *permission*
the noes 500.6 *dissenters*
the nonce 196.2 *the present day*
the normal 513.3 *the expected
thing*
the North 91.10 *Ireland,* 249.9 *regions of Britain*
the Northern Irish 91.10 *Ireland*
The Northern Territory 92 Australian States and Territories
the North Pole 263.3 *distant
place*
the nouveaux riches 721.8
wealthy people
the nude 294.3 *nakedness,* 296.2
nudity
The Nutcracker 46.11 *classical
ballets*
the Oaks 32.7 *horseracing,* 674.4
race
the objective truth 537.3 *the truth*
theobromine 62 Medication
the Occident 332.4 *compass point*
the occult 11, 368.3 *spiritual
world*
theocracy 8.2 *divine attribute,*
12.1 *government,* 688.7 *type of
rule*
theocratic 8.13 *divine,* 12.9 *governmental*
theocratically 8.19 *divinely*
Theocritus 48 Poets
theodolite 56.32 *optical instrument,* 56.84 *altimeter,* 63.17
civil engineering, 268.8 *meter,*
310.4 *angular measurement*
the OK 499.2 *yes,* 667.1 *agreement,* 708.1 *permission,* 855.1
vindication
the old 207
the Old Adam 864.6 *religious sin*
the old country 91.6 *native land*
the older generation 207.10 *the
old*
the old folks 207.7 *older person*
the old heave-ho 349.17 *expulsion,* 704.2 *termination*
the Old Man 688.10 *person of authority,* 696.7 *military leader*
the old moon in the new moon's
arms 53.14 *solar system*
the old-old story 821.8 *love affair*
the old way 584.1 *custom*
theologer 7.14 *theologian*
theologian 7
theological 7
theological hermeneutics 7.13
theology
theologically 7.23 *religiously*
theological metaphysics 7.13 *theology*
theological virtues 863.2 *virtues*
theologician 7.14 *theologian*
theologist 7.14 *theologian*
theologize 7
theologizer 7.14 *theologian*
theologue 7.14 *theologian*
theology 7, 4.6 *branch of philosophy*
the Olympians 8.5 *deity*
theomachy 674.6 *fight*
theomancer 11.13 *diviner*
theomancy 11.9 *divination*
theomania 510.4 *delusion*
theomorphic 8.13 *divine*
the one and only 119.1 *originality*

Theopaschites 7 Christian
Movements
theopathic 7.15 *religious*
theopathy 7.2 *religiousness*
the open 289.2 *outside*
the Open 29.1 *golf*
the Open Sesame 708.1 *permission*
theophanic 457.7 *appearing*
theophany 8.8 *divine manifestation,* 457.4 *something that appears,* 526.10 *manifestation*
Theophilus 53 Lunar Features
theophobia 777 Phobias by
Name
Theophrastus 4 Philosophers
theophylline 62 Medication
the opposition 663, 500.6 *dissenters*
the oppressed 481.8 *victim of
discrimination*
theorbo 49 Musical Instruments
theorbo-lute 49 Musical Instruments
the ordinary 124.4 *average*
theorem 52.65 *theory,* 56.6 *law,*
472.1 *topic,* 505.1 *maxim,*
518.1 *supposition*
theorematic 52.69 *theoretic*
theoremic 52.69 *theoretic*
theorem proving 65.16 *artificial
intelligence*
theoretic(al 52
theoretical 56, 102, 471, 4.13
of philosophy, 57.31 *chemical,*
461.10 *speculative,* 463.10
causal, 518.7 *suppositional*
theoretical chemist 57.2 *chemist*
theoretical chemistry 57.1 *chemistry*
theoretical framework 52.65 *theory*
theoretical linguistics 5.1 *linguistics*
theoretically 4, 471, 52.87 *mathematically,* 57.46 *chemically,*
102.18 *ideally,* 518.10 *supposedly*
theoretical physics 56.4 *experimental physics*
theoretician 4.10 *philosopher,*
471.9 *person of ideas,* 518.4 *theorist*
the Orient 332.4 *compass point*
theories of life 396
theorist 518, 4.10 *philosopher*
theorization 102
theorize 52, 102, 471, 461.16
have an idea, 463.14 *premise,*
505.3 *aphorize,* 518.5 *suppose*
theorizer 4.10 *philosopher,* 102.6
unrealistic person, 471.9 *person
of ideas,* 518.4 *theorist*
theory 52, 56, 471, 52.1 *mathematics,* 102.4 *theorization,*
310.5 *viewpoint,* 461.6 *idea,*
463.4 *explanation,* 497.1 *belief,*
518.1 *supposition*
theory builder 518.4 *theorist*
theory of everything 56.79 *fundamental interaction*
theory of knowledge 4.1 *philosophy*
theory of probabilities 589.7 *calculation of chance*
theory of relativity 367.6 *natural
science*
theory of social systems 2.2 *sociological research*
theosophical 11.16 *psychic*
theosophist 11.12 *occultist*
theosophy 11.1 *occultism*
the other day 200.22 *in the past*
the other man 130.5 *extra person,* 841.3 *rival*
the other side 289.5 *extraneousness,* 368.3 *spiritual world,*
397.1 *death,* 663.8 *the opposition*
the other side of the tracks 93.7
city district
the other way around 287.4 *inversely*
the other woman 821.9 *lover,*
841.3 *rival*
the outside 147.3 *exclusion zone*

the Oval 27.2 *ground,* 674.3 *stadium*
the over-the-hill gang 207.10 *the
old*
the palm 25.2 *grip*
the paranormal 11.2 *the occult,*
104.4 *externality*
the partially sighted 436.4 *blind
people*
the particular 165.5 *the special,*
490.18 *particularity*
the past 3.8 *past time,* 197.1 *different time,* 200.1 *past time*
the patter of tiny feet 245.3 *propagation*
the peace process 677.1 *pacification*
the peace that passeth all understanding 649.1 *ease*
the Pearly Gates 8.11 *heaven*
the pencil 50.2 *painting*
the Pentagon 696.8 *the power
structure*
the people 795.6 *vulgar herd,*
803.2 *the common people*
the people's 724.5 *jointly possessing*
the persecuted 481.8 *victim of
discrimination*
the person in second place 195.7
subordinate
the pick 674.10 *contender*
the pick of the bunch 126.7 *the
best people*
the picture 99.5 *fact,* 106.1 *circumstances*
the pigs 16.14 *police*
the pill 247.3 *birth control*
the pits 683.1 *failure,* 687.1 *adversity*
the plains 98.6 *lowland*
the plain truth 537.3 *the truth*
the play 51.1 *drama*
the plural 175.1 *plurality*
the political right 217.2 *conservatism*
the poor 743
the portrait of Dorian Gray 396.6
things brought to life
the possible 608.7 *sufficiency*
the pouts 830.2 *sign of sullenness*
the powers that be 233.6 *group
influence,* 688.4 *governance,*
696.8 *the power structure*
the power structure 696, 126.7
the best people, 688.4 *governance*
the present 196.1 *present time*
the present day 196
the present generation 196.2 *the
present day*
the present moment 196.1 *present time*
the present situation 196.2 *the
present day*
the present time 196.2 *the present day*
the Preserver 8.3 *God*
the press 23.4 *playing terms,*
528.4 *mass communication,*
532.3 *journalism,* 534.1 *communications*
the pretty way 363.5 *ringroad*
the prime of life 206.1 *youth,*
207.4 *middle age*
the prince and the pauper 111.2
opposites
the Principality 91.12 *Wales*
the privileged 742.11 *the rich*
the probabilities 589.7 *calculation of chance*
the proles 795.6 *vulgar herd*
the proper thing 847.1 *duty*
the push 147.2 *ejection,* 349.17
expulsion, 704.2 *termination*
the rabid right 665.3 *political
grouping*
the rackets 864.7 *criminality*
the rage 201.2 *trendiness*
the rag trade 295.2 *dressing,*
796.3 *fashion business*
the rains 55.26 *raininess*
the ranks 679.17 *army person*
therapeutic 60, 62.18 *pharmacological,* 630.17 *remedial,* 654.7
advising, 662.34 *beneficial*
therapeutically 630.21 *remedially*

therapeutic radiology 60.8 *treatment*

therapeutics 60.8 *treatment*, 62.1 *pharmacology*, 630.11 *medical art*, 630.13 *therapy*

therapeutist 630.15 *healer*

therapist 60.12 *healer*, 61.29 *psychologist*, 630.15 *healer*, 654.4 *adviser*

therapsid 79.6 *extinct reptile*

therapy 630, 60.8 *treatment*, 624.20 *pathology*, 654.1 *advice*, 662.5 *medical assistance*

Theravada 7.12 *religious text*

the raw 294.3 *nakedness*, 296.2 *nudity*

there 196.8 *available*, 250.12 *where*, 253.15 *here*, 457.7 *appearing*

thereabouts 250.12 *where*, 264.6 *near*

the ready 741.2 *cash*

the real article 119.2 *original*

the realities 99.5 *fact*

the real McCoy 119.2 *original*

the realms of possibility 486.2 *possibleness*

the real Simon Pure 537.6 *authenticity*

the real stuff 235.2 *ability*

the real thing 99.4 *demonstrable existence*, 119.2 *original*, 537.6 *authenticity*, 821.2 *romantic love*

the real world 537.2 *reality*

threat 250.12 *where*

the red 744.1 *credit*, 745.1 *debt*

The Redeemer 8.4 *God the Son*, 700.3 *liberator*, 735.3 *returner*

the red, white, and blue 544.7 *flag*

therefore 116.36 *accordingly*

the remote future 199.1 *future time*

the remote past 200.1 *past time*

the Republic 91.10 *Ireland*

the Republic of Ireland 91.10 *Ireland*

there she blows 590.19 *after him*

there's hope 775.16 *never say die* nil desperandum where there's life

the Resurrection 629.10 *revival*

the revealed truth 537.3 *the truth*

theriac 630.4 *antidote*

theriacal 630.17 *remedial*

therianthropic 76.14 *animalian*

therianthropism 76.7 *legendary beast*

the rich 742

the rich and famous 721.8 *wealthy people*

the right 665.3 *political grouping*

the right man for the job 696.10 *expert*

the right man in the right place 667.5 *assenter*

the right person for the job 667.5 *assenter*

the right stuff 235.2 *ability*

the right thing 847.1 *duty*

the right wing 217.2 *conservatism*, 665.3 *political grouping*

the right word in the right place 558.1 *elegance*

the ring 51.5 *show*, 674.7 *boxing*

theriolater 9.6 *idolater*

theriolatrous 9.10 *idolatrous*

theriolatry 9.2 *idolatry*

theriomorphic 76.14 *animalian*

the riper years 207.4 *middle age*

the rising generation 206.10 *the young*

the rising young 206.10 *the young*

the Riviera 98.4 *coast*

therm 75 Scientific and Technical Units, 408.2 *heat measurement*

thermae 98.10 *miscellaneous*, 408.8 *hot place*, 621.6 *bath*, 625.1 *hygiene*, 630.14 *hospital*

thermal 31.8 *mountaineering*, 55.10 *air movement*, 55.43 *atmospheric*, 56.98 *physical*, 98.11 *continental*, 408.8 *hot place*, 408.9 *hot*, 410.10 *powered*

thermal conductivity 56.36 *heat flow*

thermal efficiency 63.13 *engine cycle*

thermal equilibrium 56.36 *heat flow*

thermal imaging 56.41 *thermometry*

thermal ink jet printer 65.7 *peripheral*

thermally 56.100 *physically*, 98.13 *continentally*, 410.12 *powerfully*

thermal metamorphism 54.32 *metamorphism*

thermal power station 64.32 *power station*

thermal radiation 56.40 *heating effect*

thermal reactor 56.73 *nuclear reactor*, 410.7 *nuclear power*

thermal spring 54.25 *eruption*, 98.10 *miscellaneous*

thermal underwear 34.4 *climbing equipment*, 295.18 *underwear*

thermal wear 408.3 *heater*

thermic 408.9 *hot*

thermionic cathode 64.24 *electron emission*

thermionic emission 56.40 *heating effect*, 64.24 *electron emission*

thermionic valve 64.20 *electron tube*

thermobarometer 268.8 *meter*

thermochemistry 57.1 *chemistry*

thermocouple 56.89 *thermometer*

thermodynamic 56.98 *physical*, 57.31 *chemical*

thermodynamically 56.100 *physically*, 57.46 *chemically*

thermodynamics 56, 56.2 *classical physics*, 57.1 *chemistry*, 367.6 *natural science*

thermodynamic scale 75.3 *scale*

thermodynamic temperature 56.38 *thermodynamics*

thermoelectric 64.36 *electronic*

thermoelectrically 64.37 *electronically*

thermoelectric effect 56.40 *heating effect*, 56.49 *electromagnetic induction*

thermoelectric generator 64.30 *generator*

thermoelectricity 56.40 *heating effect*, 56.42 *electricity*, 235.7 *electrical power*

thermograph 55.7 *weather instruments*, 408.2 *heat measurement*

thermographic 55.42 *barometric*

thermography 60.7 *diagnosis*

thermoluminescence 56.24 *light emission*, 192.3 *chronology*

thermoluminescent dating 185.8 *dating*

thermometer 57 Laboratory Apparatus, **56**, 55.7 *weather instruments*, 268.8 *meter*, 408.2 *heat measurement*, 543.5 *indicator*

thermometric 55.42 *barometric*, 268.16 *micrometric*

thermometry 56, 56.96 *microscopy*, 268.2 *micrometry*

thermonuclear 235.17 *powered*, 408.10 *on fire*, 410.10 *powered*

thermonuclear fusion 56.72 *nuclear fission*

thermonuclear reaction 235.8 *nuclear power*

thermonuclear reactor 56.76 *fusion reactor*

thermophobia 777 Phobias by Name

thermopile 56.89 *thermometer*, 268.8 *meter*

thermoplastic 604.1 *materials*

thermoplastic material 57.21 *polymer*

thermos 258.14 *bottle*

Thermos 351.10 *drink container*, 408.3 *heater*, 637.2 *preserver*

thermoset 604.1 *materials*

thermosetting plastic 57.21 *polymer*

thermosphere 275.8 *high thing*

thermostat 408.3 *heater*

the road to hell 628.7 *deterioration*

the roaring game 41.10 *curling*

the Roaring Twenties 3.10 *past age*

the rough with the smooth 142.4 *all*

the rounds 334.1 *circuit*

the Royal and Ancient Golf Club 29.1 *golf*

the ruling class 126.7 *the best people*, 688.4 *governance*, 696.8 *the power structure*

the run of 698.6 *liberality*

the runs 353.2 *defecation*, 624.8 *indigestion*

the sack 147.2 *ejection*, 252.4 *relegation*, 349.18 *dismissal*, 645.3 *unemployment*, 704.2 *termination*

the St Leger 32.7 *horseracing*, 674.4 *race*

the saints 617.7 *elite*

the same 110.1 *sameness*, 122.2 *equilibrium*

the sands of time 185.2 *passage of time*

the San Remo Rally of the Flowers 33.4 *motor rally*

thesaurus 5.28 *dictionary*, 6.14 *school book*, 65.11 *application*, 133.3 *miscellany*, 171.3 *dictionary*, 528.5 *reference book*, 532.6 *book publishing*, 605.5 *collection*

the Saviour 8.4 *God the Son*

The Saviour 700.3 *liberator*, 729.4 *giver*

the scenes 51.1 *drama*

the scoop 99.5 *fact*

the score 99.5 *fact*, 106.1 *circumstances*

the Scottish 91.11 *Scotland*

the scythe of time 244.6 *destroyer*

the season 203.1 *season*

the Season 203.1 *season*, 203.5 *winter*

the second sex 402.13 *womenfolk*

the secret 524.1 *interpretation*

these days 196.9 *at present*

the senses 403.1 *sensation*

The Serpentine 94.4 *British lakes*

the services 17.2 *the military*

the shades 397.14 *the spiritual world*

the shakes 366.7 *shake*

the shape of things 105.3 *state of affairs*

the shits 353.2 *defecation*

the shivers 403.3 *stimulus*

the shove 147.2 *ejection*, 704.2 *termination*

the sight 435.5 *imagination*

the sightless 436.4 *blind people*

the Silver Broom 41.10 *curling*

the silver screen 51.4 *show business*

the simple truth 537.3 *the truth*

the sincerest form of flattery 118.1 *imitation*

thesis 4.1 *philosophy*, 4.5 *philosophical argument*, 4.8 *philosophical term*, 48.4 *non-fiction*, 56.6 *law*, 472.1 *topic*, 473.3 *line of argument*, 518.1 *supposition*, 535.2 *statement*, 561.1 *dissertation*

thesis novel 48.2 *fiction*

the sisterhood 402.13 *womenfolk*

the Six Counties 91.10 *Ireland*

the sixties 708.1 *permission*

the size of it 105.3 *state of affairs*, 251.2 *circumstances*

the skids 628.7 *deterioration*

the sky 390.1 *air*

The Sleeping Beauty 46.11 *classical ballets*

the slips 27.4 *team*

the small hours 208.2 *early hour*

the Smoke 93.5 *London*, 249.10 *urban area*

Thesmophoria 10.16 *religious festival*

the sober truth 537.3 *the truth*

the Somme 398.15 *slaughterhouse*

the South 91.10 *Ireland*, 249.9 *regions of Britain*

the South Pole 263.3 *distant place*

the special 165

the specific 165.5 *the special*, 490.18 *particularity*

the specifics 99.5 *fact*

Thespian 51.22 *actor*, 51.37 *dramatic*

Thespian art 51.1 *drama*

the spiritual world 397

Thespis 48 Poets

Thespis 51.1 *drama*

the spot 24.3 *English billiards*, 24.5 *snooker*

the Square Mile 93.5 *London*

Thessalian 32 Breeds of Horse and Pony

the stage 51.1 *drama*, 51.4 *show business*

the staggers 123.1 *inequality*

the stake 398.5 *execution*, 408.6 *fire*

the Star Chamber 879.15 *instrument of torture*

the States 91.7 *United States*

the status quo 217.1 *permanence*

the sticks 249.6 *regions*, 263.3 *distant place*

the straight and narrow 863.1 *virtue*

the straight truth 537.3 *the truth*

the subconscious 11.7 *spirit*

the sulks 573.14 *disobedience*, 830.2 *sign of sullenness*

the sullens 830.2 *sign of sullenness*

the sum and substance 142.4 *all*

the sun sets 440.13 *become dark*

the supernatural 11.2 *the occult*, 104.4 *externality*

the supersensible 11.2 *the occult*

the Supreme Being 8.3 *God*

the Supreme Soul 8.3 *God*

the Swedish Midnight Sun 33.4 *motor rally*

the Swinging Sixties 3.10 *past age*

the sword 676.1 *war*

the syndicate 864.7 *criminality*

the system 688.4 *governance*

the talk of the town 532.7 *publicity*

The Taming of the Shrew 48 Shakespeare's plays

the tartan 295.3 *formal dress*

the Teacher 8.3 *God*

The Tempest 48 Shakespeare's plays

The Tempter 8.7 *devil*

the Ten Commandments 654.3 *precept*

the theatre 51.1 *drama*

the Thief in the Night 397.2 *death personified*

the thing 611.3 *chief thing*

the thing to do 813.1 *formality*

the third degree 477.2 *questioning*

the Three Musketeers 819.7 *famous friendships*

the thumbs-up 708.1 *permission*

the time ahead 199.1 *future time*

the time being 196.2 *the present day*

the time now 192.3 *chronology*

the times 106.1 *circumstances*

the tip of the iceberg 527.6 *latency*

Thetis 97.4 *sea god*

the top 688.4 *governance*, 696.8 *the power structure*

the top brass 696.8 *the power structure*

the tops 617.8 *exceller*, 682.4 *successful person*

the total 142.4 *all*

the touch 712.3 *solicitation*

the train 877.7 *sexual assault*

the Trinity 8.3 *God*

the trots 353.2 *defecation*, 624.8 *indigestion*

the truth 537

the Turf 32.7 *horseracing,* 674.4 *race*

the Twelve Tables 654.3 *precept*

the two 176.9 *two*

The Two Gentlemen of Verona 48 Shakespeare's plays

the ultimate truth 537.3 *the truth*

the unalloyed truth 537.3 *the truth*

the unattainable 782.5 *object of desire*

the unborn 155.12 *successor,* 195.6 *posterity*

the unconscious 11.7 *spirit,* 368.6 *internal world*

the underground 689.1 *anarchy*

the underprivileged 743.11 *the poor*

the underprivileged class 743.11 *the poor*

the undersigned 715.4 *contractor*

the underworld 199.3 *future condition*

the unexpected 514.4 *surprising thing*

the unforeseen 489.5 *unexpectedness,* 514.4 *surprising thing*

the unique 165.5 *the special*

the Uniroyal World Junior Championship 41.10 *curling*

the United States Golf Association 29.1 *golf*

the United States Yacht Racing Union 36.1 *sailing*

the unities 51.7 *dramaturgy*

the Universal Self 8.3 *God*

the unknown 104.2 *foreignness,* 502.3 *unknown thing,* 523.11 *unintelligibility*

the unpredictable 514.4 *surprising thing*

the unqualified truth 537.3 *the truth*

the unseen 438.5 *invisible thing*

the unvarnished truth 537.3 *the truth*

the upper class 721.8 *wealthy people*

the upper classes 742.11 *the rich*

the upper crust 721.8 *wealthy people,* 742.11 *the rich*

the upper hand 688.1 *authority*

the upwardly mobile 686.4 *prosperous person*

theurgically 11.26 *magically*

theurgist 11.4 *witch*

theurgize 11.21 *bewitch*

theurgy 11.3 *witchcraft*

the US Open 29.1 *golf*

the US PGA 29.1 *golf*

the usual 124.4 *average,* 513.3 *the expected thing*

the utmost 144.1 *completeness*

the veil 825.3 *monasticism*

the very best 861.9 *the best*

the very same 110.1 *sameness*

the very thing 537.6 *authenticity,* 667.4 *suitability,* 861.17 *good thing*

the very truth 537.3 *the truth*

the very words 110.1 *sameness,* 537.10 *literalness*

the Virgin 8.10 *deified person,* 825.4 *celibate person*

the Virgin Mary 8.10 *deified person,* 876.5 *pure person*

the Virgin Mother 8.10 *deified person*

the visual arts 50.1 *art*

the visually handicapped 436.4 *blind people*

the visually impaired 436.4 *blind people*

the vitals 290.4 *insidesn*

the Wandering Jew 104.7 *new arrival*

the war years 676.4 *belligerency*

the Water Carrier 326.7 *transferor*

the way it is 106.1 *circumstances*

the way it looks 488.2 *tendency*

the way of 327.1 *way*

the way of gentleness 26.7 *judo*

the way of harmony of the spirit 26.10 *aikido*

the way of the empty hand 26.8 *karate*

the way of the foot and fist 26.9 *tae kwon do*

the way of the world 105.3 *state of affairs,* 124.4 *average,* 251.2 *circumstances*

the way the ball bounces 589.2 *luck*

the way the cookie crumbles 195.9 *sequel,* 589.2 *luck*

the Way, the Truth, and the Life 8.4 *God the Son*

the way things are 105.3 *state of affairs,* 124.4 *average*

the way things are going 234.1 *tendency*

the way things pan out 195.9 *sequel*

the way things shape up 105.3 *state of affairs*

the weed 413.7 *tobacco*

the wee small hours 208.2 *early hour*

the welfare 662.4 *social assistance*

the well-heeled 721.8 *wealthy people,* 742.11 *the rich*

the well-made play 51.7 *dramaturgy*

the well-off 742.11 *the rich*

the well-to-do 721.8 *wealthy people,* 742.11 *the rich*

the Welsh 91.12 *Wales*

the West 13.4 *economic development*

the West End 51.1 *drama*

the wet 55.26 *raininess*

the wherewithal 602.1 *means*

the whim-whams 579.3 *whim*

the whip hand 688.1 *authority*

the Whitbread Round the World Race 36.1 *sailing*

the white flag 673.1 *submission*

the White House 688.6 *place of authority,* 696.8 *the power structure*

the whites 387.3 *body fluid*

the whole 142.4 *all*

the whole bang shoot 142.5 *unit*

the whole caboodle 120.4 *total,* 142.5 *unit*

the whole hog 144.1 *completeness*

the whole kit and caboodle 142.5 *unit,* 164.10 *everyone*

the whole lot 142.4 *all*

the whole picture 106.1 *circumstances*

the whole shebang 142.5 *unit,* 164.10 *everyone*

the whole shooting match 142.5 *unit,* 164.10 *everyone*

the whole story 99.5 *fact*

the whole thing 120.4 *total*

the whole time 185.26 *all the time*

the whole truth and nothing but the truth 537.3 *the truth*

the whole world 142.4 *all,* 164.10 *everyone*

the why 226.5 *reason*

the why and wherefore 226.5 *reason*

the wicked 864.9 *wicked person*

the willies 777.2 *fearfulness*

the Winter Olympic gold medal 41.3 *ski racing*

The Winter's Tale 48 Shakespeare's plays

the Wise One 8.3 *God*

the witching hour 205.3 *midnight*

the womb of time 199.1 *future time*

the Woolsack 492.3 *place of judgment*

the Word 7.12 *religious text,* 8.8 *divine manifestation*

the Word made Flesh 8.8 *divine manifestation*

the works 130.3 *additional item*

the world 54.5 *earth,* 142.4 *all,* 400.1 *humankind*

the world and his wife 142.4 *all,* 803.2 *the common people*

the World Championship 41.3 *ski racing*

the World Championships 36.4 *rowing*

the World Cup 41.3 *ski racing*

the World Curling Championship 41.10 *curling*

the world of today 196.2 *the present day*

the world over 164.32 *universally,* 248.16 *extensively*

the world population 400.1 *humankind*

the worse for 628.12 *deteriorated*

the worse for liquor 841.4 *drunk*

the worse for wear 238.9, 628.13 *dilapidated,* 722.16 *losing*

the worst 687.1 *adversity*

the wrong side of forty 158.7 *middle age*

the wrong way 375.14 *roughly*

thews 237.1 *strength*

the year dot 3.9 *distant past*

the years ahead 199.1 *future time*

the young 206

the younger generation 206.10 *the young*

thiacetazone 62 Medication

thiamin 58.12 *coenzyme*

thick 273, 273, 393, 55.56 *foggy,* 120.6 *quantitative,* 158.2 *core,* 273.3 *thick-witted,* 371.6 *dense,* 394.8 *viscous,* 441.6 *murky,* 441.8 *stupid,* 443.1 *opaque,* 443.5, 460.6 *unintelligent,* 502.6 *ignorant,* 622.7 *dirty,* 761.1 *insensitive,* 819.10 *familiar*

thick and fast 181.14 *in crowds,* 212.1 *frequently*

thick-ankled 273.1 *thick*

thick as a plank 443.5 *unintelligent*

thick as flies 161.50 *crowded*

thick as thieves 135.12 *united,* 180.19 *associated,* 819.10 *familiar*

thick as two short planks 460.6 *unintelligent,* 502.6 *ignorant*

thick-barked 273.1 *thick*

thick-bodied 273.1 *thick*

thick cloud 55.19 *cloud cover,* 441.1 *dimness*

thick-coated 273.1 *thick*

thicken 273, 393, 394, 128.4 *increase,* 128.5 *make bigger,* 273.8 *fatten,* 371.8 *be dense,* 373.10 *solidify,* 443.10 *be opaque,* 443.11 *make opaque*

thickened 273.2 *dense,* 393.20 *thick*

thickener 393, 371.5 *condenser*

thickening 393, 128.1 *increase,* 273.6 *denseness,* 371.1 *density,* 371.5 *condenser,* 394.1 *viscosity*

thick enough to be cut with a knife 371.7 *condensed*

thicket 85.4 *trees,* 371.4 *solid body*

thick-fingered 273.1 *thick*

thick fog 55.33 *fog,* 633.6 *danger signal*

thick-growing 371.6 *dense*

thickhead 874.15 *crapulence*

thick head 874.15 *crapulence*

thickheaded 273.1 *thick,* 443.5 *unintelligent,* 460.6 *unintelligent,* 502.6 *ignorant*

thickheadedness 443.9 *stupidity,* 460.2 *unintelligence*

thickie 460.3 *unintelligent person*

thick-jawed 273.1 *thick*

thick-leaved 273.1 *thick*

thick-legged 273.1 *thick*

thick-lipped 273.1 *thick*

thickly 120.7 *quantitatively,* 273.9 *thick,* 371.10 *densely,* 393.27 *slimily,* 394.12 *viscously*

thick mist 55.34 *mist*

thick-necked 273.1 *thick*

thickness 273, 56.7 *space,* 120.1 *quantity,* 266.1 *layer,* 371.1 *density,* 393.4 *pulpiness,* 441.4 *stupidity,* 443.6 *opaqueness*

Thickness 273

thickness of voice 563.2 *inarticulation*

thicko 502.5 *ignorant person*

thick of the action 642.1 *activity*

thick of things 158.2 *core,* 642.1 *activity*

thick on the ground 161.50 *crowded,* 181.9 *ample,* 371.6 *dense*

thick rib 45.22 *beef*

thick-ribbed 273.1 *thick*

thick seam 45.31 *offal*

thickset 259.17 *stocky,* 270.7 *short,* 273.1 *thick,* 371.6 *dense*

thick skin 404.3 *heedlessness*

thick-skinned 273, 273.1 *thick,* 373.4 *mentally hard,* 378.5 *mentally tough,* 761.1 *insensitive,* 783.7 *indifferent*

thick slice 273.5 *thickness*

thick speech 874.10 *drunkenness*

thick-stalked 273.1 *thick*

thick-stemmed 273.1 *thick*

thick-walled 273.1 *thick*

thick with 273.2 *dense*

thick-witted 273

thick-wristed 273.1 *thick*

thief 736, 16.40 *lawbreaker,* 346.8 *intruder,* 693.9 *criminal,* 721.7 *gainer,* 864.9 *wicked person*

thieve 734.10 *take away,* 736.12 *steal,* 858.10 *be criminal*

thievery 736.1 *stealing*

thieving 734.3 *taking away,* 734.12 *taking,* 736.1 *stealing,* 736.17 *stolen,* 858.3 *criminality,* 858.7 *criminal*

thievish 736.17 *stolen*

thievishly 736

thievishness 736.1 *stealing,* 858.3 *criminality*

thighbone 382 Bones

thigh boots 295.19 *footwear*

thigh-high 275.12 *tall*

thimble 74 Rigging

thimblerig 539.9 *sleight of hand,* 539.29 *juggle*

thimblerigger 539.17 *cheat*

thimeracol 62 Medication

thin 274, 274, 55.60 *cloud,* 69.15 *cultivate,* 85.18 *manage trees,* 120.6 *quantitative,* 129.4 *decrease,* 131.3 *subtract,* 145.4 *incomplete,* 162.14 *dilute,* 182.6 *sparse,* 182.8 *reduce,* 238.7 *weaken,* 238.10 *ill,* 238.13 *insufficient,* 260.7 *little,* 262.5 *make smaller,* 262.6 *become smaller,* 262.7 *smaller,* 272.1 *narrow,* 274.16 *make thin,* 278.2 *superficial,* 296.13 *hairless,* 355.12 *displace,* 372.1 *sparse,* 372.6 *make sparse,* 387.23 *dissolve,* 389.30 *dilute,* 390.12 *airy,* 412.5 *tasteless,* 412.8 *dilute,* 442.2 *translucent,* 555.1 *unemphatic,* 609.1 *insufficient,* 609.3 *underfed,* 871.6 *fasting*

thin air 390.1 *air*

thin as a lath 274.2 *emaciated*

thin as a rail 609.3 *underfed*

thin climbing 34.1 *mountaineering*

thin cloud 55.19 *cloud cover*

thin down 274.16 *make thin*

thin end of the wedge 657.2 *stratagem*

thin-faced 274.1 *thin*

thing 99, 101.1 *reality,* 106.6 *aspect,* 165.8 *specialization,* 243.3 *product,* 367.5 *object*

thing deducted 131.2 *subtracted item*

thing excluded 147

thing from outer space 149.5 *extraterrestrial*

thing included 146

thing inserted 354

thing of beauty 789.2 *beautiful thing*

thing of beauty and a joy forever 696.11 *masterpiece*

thing of the past 200, 202.5 *old thing*

thin gruel 238.5 *weak thing*

things 723.4 *possession,* 725.4 *possessions*

things as they are 537.2 *reality*

things brought to life 396

things contained 257.1 *contents*
thing that is not 538.1 *untruth*
thing transported 70
thingumabob 367.5 *object*, 603.1 *tool*
thingumajig 367.5 *object*
thingummy 367.5 *object*, 603.1 *tool*
thin house 51.31 *theatregoer*
thin ice 34.2 *climbing dangers*, 379.3 *brittle thing*, 635.1 *trap*
think **459, 461,** 463.11 *reason*, 471.15 *imagine*, 492.12 *estimate*, 497.8 *be of the opinion*, 513.9 *predict*, 518.5 *suppose*, 519.14 *imagine*, 759.19 *believe*, 786.12 *wonder whether*
thinkable 486.5 *possible*, 519.13 *imaginable*
think about 461, 4.20 *philosophize*
think again 461.14 *have second thoughts*, 484.8 *reverse*, 578.2 *equivocate*, 627.4 *reconsider*, 867.4 *be penitent*
think ahead 592.12 *plan ahead*
think a lot of oneself 805.29 *feel pride*, 809.15 *be vain*
think aloud 569.3 *soliloquize*
think back 511.12 *remember*
think best 570.12 *choose*, 654.5 *advise*
think better of 627.4 *reconsider*, 867.4 *be penitent*
think better of it 578.2 *equivocate*
think deeply 461.12 *think*
thinker **461,** 4.10 *philosopher*, 459.8 *intellectual person*, 463.5 *reasoner*, 471.9 *person of ideas*, 507.3 *wise man*, 518.4 *theorist*, 696.9 *educational leader*
think everything of 611.8 *make important*
think fit 580.2 *prefer*
think freely 698.14 *be free*
think hard 461.12 *think*
think highly of 849.15 *respect*, 851.11 *approve*
think ill of 852.14 *disapprove*
thinking **777** *Phobias by Topic*, 4.17 *thoughtful*, 459.9 *mental*, 461.1 *thought*, 461.8 *thoughtful*, 463.7 *reasoning*, 471.1 *idea*, 507.5 *wise*, 518.2 *basis of supposition*
thinking aloud 569.5 *soliloquizing*
thinking cap 461.5 *creative thought*
thinking on one's feet 583.4 *improvisation*
think it beneath one 805.28 *disdain*
think it best to 580.2 *prefer*
think laterally 602.6 *find means*
think likely 488
think little of 852.14 *disapprove*
think logically 463.11 *reason*
think negatively 776.9 *be hopeless*
think no more of 512.13 *forget*, 839.9 *forgive*
think nothing of 660.17 *do easily*
think of 156.22 *invent*, 243.10 *produce*, 511.12 *remember*, 519.14 *imagine*, 588.7 *intend*, 714.11 *promise oneself*
think of others first 859.7 *be unselfish*
think of the future 199.9 *look ahead*
think one is it 809.15 *be vain*
think one knows it all 809.15 *be vain*
think oneself God Almighty 809.15 *be vain*
think oneself God's gift to mankind 809.15 *be vain*
think oneself the cat's pyjamas 809.15 *be vain*
think only of oneself 860.6 *be selfish*
think on one's feet 583.3 *improvise*, 648.2 *make haste*
think out 4.21 *rationalize*
think over 461.14 *have second thoughts*
think positively 775.8 *be optimistic*

think profoundly 461.12 *think*
think tank 479.6 *place of experimentation*, 653.7 *council*
think the best of 851.11 *approve*
think the world of 784.7 *like*, 821.23 *love*, 849.16 *revere*
think the worst of 776.9 *be hopeless*
think through 4.21 *rationalize*, 652.14 *behave towards*
think too much of oneself 805.26 *be too proud*
think twice 777.12 *be fearful*, 781.5 *be cautious*
think unimportant 612
think up 243.10 *produce*, 471.15, 519.14 *imagine*, 583.3 *improvise*, 592.11 *invent*
think well of 849.15 *respect*, 851.11 *approve*
think well of oneself 809.15 *be vain*
thin-legged 274.1 *thin*
thinly 120.7 *quantitatively*, 182.11 *sparsely*, 238.14 *weakly*, 274.17 *thin*, 372.7 *sparsely*
thinned **274,** 372.2 *rarefied*, 389.22 *diluted*
thinned-out 372.2 *rarefied*
thinner **274,** 50.11 *artist's materials*, 387.9 *solvent*
thinness 274, 120.1 *quantity*, 238.3 *poor health*, 260.1 *littleness*, 272.5 *narrowness*, 370.5 *lightness*, 372.3 *sparseness*, 412.1 *tastelessness*, 442.6 *translucency*, 555.2 *lack of emphasis*
Thinness 274
thinning 274, 85.6 *tree management*, 262.1 *contraction*, 262.8 *contracting*, 355.2 *displacement*, 372.2 *rarefied*, 372.4 *rarefaction*
thinning out 355.2 *displacement*
thin on the ground 182.6 *sparse*, 274.6 *scant*, 609.4 *scarce*
thin on top 294.10 *bald*, 296.13 *hairless*
thin out 69.15 *cultivate*, 129.4 *decrease*, 129.5 *make smaller*, 131.3 *subtract*, 162.14 *dilute*, 182.8 *reduce*, 238.7 *weaken*, 274.16 *make thin*, 355.12 *displace*, 372.6 *make sparse*
thin person 274
thin red line 679.14 *armed forces*
thin rib 45.22 *beef*
thin skin 403.2 *ability to sense*, 829.1 *irascibility*
thin-skinned 403.7 *susceptible*, 760.2 *oversensitive*, 829.4 *irascible*
thin space 265.1 *interval*
thin-spun 383.10 *delicate*
thio alcohol 57 *Types of Compounds*
thio ether 57 *Types of Compounds*
thioguanine 62 *Medication*
Thiokol 377.4 *rubber*
thiopentone 62 *Medication*
thiopropazate 62 *Medication*
thioridazine 62 *Medication*
thiosulphate 57 *Types of Compounds*
Thio violet 455.2 *purple pigment*
third **177, 177,** 25.3 *bowls player*, 49.16 *musical note*, 52.75 *equal*, 143.1 *part*, 173.4 *less than one*, 177.7 *three*
third age 177.6 *third*, 207.5 *old age*
third base 22.1 *baseball*
third-baseman 22.2 *baseball player*
third-base umpire 22.2 *baseball player*
third class 620.5 *imperfection*
third-class 127.12, 618.2 *inferior*, 620.1 *imperfect*, 754.9 *cheap*
third-class mail 534.2 *postal communication*
third degree 177.6 *third*, 879.12 *corporal punishment*
third-degree burn 408.1 *heat*
third eye 11.7 *spirit*, 11.8 *psychic power*, 177.6 *third*

third finger 407.7 *sense organ*
third guard 28.3 *fencing movements*
third law 56.38 *thermodynamics*
thirdly 177.14 *third*
third man 27.4 *team*
Third Market 740.5 *stock market*
third-order 57.38 *reactive*
third part 177.6 *third*
third party 158.9 *middleman*, 177.6 *third*, 333.3 *moderate person*, 678.3 *mediator*
third person 177.6 *third*
third-person narrative 48.3 *aspect of fiction*
third power 177.6 *third*
third rate 620.5 *imperfection*
third-rate 127.12 *inferior*, 612.4 *trivial*, 618.2 *inferior*, 620.1 *imperfect*
third-rater 127.6 *inferior*
third slip 27.4 *team*
third-stream jazz 49.8 *jazz*
Third World 12.5 *political organization*, 13.4 *economic development*, 177.6 *third*, 249.7 *regions of the world*, 620.5 *imperfection*, 743.11 *the poor*
third-world country 91.1 *country*
Thirlmere 94 *Lakes*, 94.4 *British lakes*
thirst **392, 392,** 782.1 *desire*, 782.3 *appetite*, 782.14 *be hungry*
thirst for 392.18 *thirst*, 782.12 *desire*
thirst for blood 832.17 *kill*
thirst for knowledge 465.7 *be curious*
thirstily 392.24 *drily*, 782.19 *hungrily*
thirstiness 392.12 *thirst*, 782.3 *appetite*
thirsting 392.2 *thirsty*
thirsting for blood 398.24 *murderous*
thirst-quencher 351.2 *drink*, 351.6 *soft drink*
thirst-quenching 649.5 *labour-saving*
thirsty **392,** 782.10 *hungry*, 874.5 *drunken*
thirsty soul 874.17 *drunkard*
thirteen **777** *Phobias by Topic*, 179.7 *double figures*
thirteenth 173.4 *less than one*, 179.18 *eleventh*
thirtieth 173.4 *less than one*, 179.19 *twentieth*
thirty-second note 49.17 *notation*
thirty-second suspension 31.5 *lacrosse*
thirtysomething 207.13 *middle-aged*
Thirty Years' War **17** *Major Wars*
this afternoon 185.27 *at what time*, 196.1 *present time*
this big 259.13 *this size*
this day 196.2 *the present day*
this day and age 196.2 *the present day*
this evening 185.27 *at what time*, 196.1 *present time*
this hour 196.1 *present time*
this instant 196.1 *present time*
this is it 397.24 *I'm dying*
this moment 196.1 *present time*
this moment in time 196.1 *present time*
this morning 185.27 *at what time*, 196.1 *present time*
this second 196.1 *present time*
this size 259
this time 196.2 *the present day*
thistle 84 *Flowers and Flowering Plants*, 375.7 *rough thing*, 380.8 *sharp-pointed thing*
thistledown 370.7 *light thing*, 374.11 *soft thing*
thistly 380.2 *spiked*
this very day 196.1 *present time*
this very minute 196.1 *present time*
thither 250.12 *where*
thixotropic 57.32 *solid*
thixotropy 57.3 *phase*
thole 74 *Parts of a Ship*
tholepin 36.4 *rowing*

tholos 200.7 *thing of the past*
Thomas 48 *Poets*, 48 *Poets*, **48** Poets
Thomas Cup 40.10 *badminton*
Thomism 4.7 *school of thought*
Thomist 4.11 *follower of a doctrine*, 4.14 *of a philosophy*
Thompson submachine gun 680.11 *guns*
Thomson 52 *Scientists*
Thomson effect 56 *Named Laws*
thong 137.6 *line*, 296.4 *dishabille*, 879.14 *instrument of punishment*
thongs 295.19 *footwear*
Thor 8 *Deities*
thoracectomy 60 *Surgical Operations*
thoracoplasty 60 *Surgical Operations*
thoracotomy 60 *Surgical Operations*
Thoreau 4 *Philosophers*
thorianite 54 *Minerals*
thorite 54 *Minerals*
thorium 57 *Chemical Elements*
thorn 375.7 *rough thing*, 380.8 *sharp-pointed thing*, 631.6 *source of trouble*
thorn apple 84 *Flowers and Flowering Plants*
thornback 80 *Fishes*
thornbill 78 *Birds*
thorn forest 85.4 *trees*
thorniness 380.6 *sharpness*
thorn in one's flesh 631.3 *burden*, 659.9 *difficult person*
thorn tree 85 *Trees and Shrubs*
thorny 380.2 *spiked*, 659.12 *problematic*
thorny problem 659.4 *problem*
thorough 144.7 *complete*, 469.9 *careful*, 574.2 *tenacious*, 644.10 *working*, 644.11 *laborious*, 684.7 *completed*
thorough bass 433.3 *melodiousness*
thoroughbred **32,** 32.13 *breeding*, 32.17 *equine*, 68.21 *domesticated*, 134.7 *purebred*, 134.13 *pure*, 329.12 *swift animal*, 802.4 *aristocratic*
Thoroughbred 32 *Breeds of Horse and Pony*
thoroughbred racing 674.4 *race*
thoroughfare 327.3 *road*, 356.2 *passing along*
thoroughgoing 144.7 *complete*, 237.10 *potent*, 684.7 *completed*
thoroughly 144.9 *completely*, 277.17 *profoundly*, 469.12 *carefully*, 619.8, 684.9 *completely*
thoroughness 469.1 *carefulness*, 684.1 *completion*
those who have gone before 397.13 *the dead*
Thoth 8 *Deities*
thou 173.4 *less than one*
though 518.11 *supposing*
thought **461,** 4.1 *philosophy*, 461.6, 471.1 *idea*, 473.2 *logical argument*, 497.1 *belief*, 518.2 *basis of supposition*, 519.4 *ideality*, 542.6 *suggestion*, 547.6 *image*, 564.7 *utterance*
Thought 461
thought for others 859.2 *unselfishness*
thoughtful 4, **459, 461,** 507.5 *wise*, 772.1 *solemn*, 817.7 *courteous*, 831.6 *benevolent*, 861.3 *kind*
thoughtfully 4, **461,** 6.26 *studiously*, 459.15 *intelligently*, 471.20 *theoretically*, 473.19 *logically*, 507.9 *wisely*, 772.10 *solemnly*, 817.14 *courteously*, 817.15 *genteelly*, 831.10 *benevolently*
thoughtfulness 459, **461,** 4.3 *detachment*, 772.4 *solemnity*, 817.1 *courtesy*, 831.1 *benevolence*, 861.10 *kindness*
thoughtless 462, **468,** 436.12 *blind to*, 460.6 *unintelligent*, 462.10 *inconsiderate*, 468.7 *inattentive*, 470.4 *negligent*, 482.1

undiscriminating, 512.10 *unthinking*, 595.3 *without preparation*, 648.3 *hasty*, 656.1 *unskilful*, 720.11 *nonobservant*, 780.4 *rash*, 818.5 *discourteous*, 832.15 *inconsiderate*, 838.3 *ungrateful*
thoughtlessly 462, 468.14 *inattentively*, 512.16 *obliviously*, 595.14 *unreadily*, 648.7 *rashly*, 720.15 *inattentively*, 818.9 *discourteously*, 838.7 *ungratefully*
thoughtlessness 468, 436.7 *figurative blindness*, 460.2 *unintelligence*, 462.1 *lack of thought*, 462.4 *inconsideration*, 468.1 *inattention*, 470.1 *negligence*, 482.6 *lack of discrimination*, 508.1 *folly*, 512.4 *unthinkingness*, 595.8 *lack of preparation*, 648.5 *hastiness*, 656.9 *bungling*, 720.1 *nonobservance*, 818.1 *discourtesy*, 832.6 *inconsiderateness*, 838.1 *ingratitude*
thought of 243.12 *produced*
thought process 461.1 *thought*
thought-provoking 413.10 *stimulating*, 472.8 *problematic*, 518.7 *suppositional*, 554.3 *emphatic*
thought reader 11.12 *occultist*
thought transference 11.1 *occultism*
thought-up 519.12 *imaginary*
thousand 179, 181.7 *myriad*
thousandfold 179.21 *thousandth*
Thousand Island dressing 45.15 *sauce*
thousand-leggers 81.4 *arthropod*
thousand million 179.11 *million*
thousands 181.2 *multitude*
thousandth 179, 173.4 *less than one*
Thracian 5 Languages and Groups of Languages
Thraco-Phrygian 5 Languages and Groups of Languages
thraldom 701.1 *subjection*
thrall 697.7 *slave*, 701.5 *subjected person*
thrash 126.8 *be superior*, 161.9 *social gathering*, 330.5 *beat*, 350.13 *feast*, 406.11 *inflict pain*, 682.10 *defeat heavily*, 879.3 *hit*
thrash about 366.21 *be agitated*, 366.25 *pitch*
thrashed 683.11 *defeated*
thrasher 78 Birds
thrashing 241.6 *violent*, 330.12 *collision*, 330.17 *impelling*, 682.2 *victory*, 683.2 *defeat*, 879.12 *corporal punishment*
thrashing of a lifetime 879.12 *corporal punishment*
thrash metal 49.9 *popular music*
thrash out 568.11 *confer*
thread 67.1 *fibre*, 90.3 *plant body*, 135.10 *link*, 137.6 *line*, 159.2 *consecution*, 159.15 *concatenate*, 238.5 *weak thing*, 272.8 *narrow thing*, 383.6 *fibre*
threadbare 296.10 *in dishabille*, 599.9 *used*, 743.3 *beggarly*
threadfin 80 Fishes
threadlike 272.2 *fine*
threads 295.1 *dress*
thread through 135.10 *link*
thread together 135.10 *link*
threadworm 81 Worms
threat 228.4 *negative stimulus*, 586.8 *incentive*, 588.4 *formulated intention*, 633.5 *danger*, 636.1 *warning*, 668.3 *act of defiance*, 687.1 *adversity*, 692.2 *demand*, 695.2 *coercion*, 712.2 *demand*, 827.3 *vilification*, 832.7 *act of malevolence*
threaten 199.7 *be in the future*, 517.11 *predict*, 587.2 *deter*, 588.8 *resolve*, 633.10 *endanger*, 636.5 *warn*, 668.6 *be insubordinate*, 692.10 *demand*, 695.7 *force*, 712.7 *demand*, 827.6 *vilify*, 832.18 *torment*, 862.11 *be evil*
threaten danger 633.10 *endanger*
threatened 712.10 *demanding*

threatening 199.11 *future*, 241.6 *violent*, 244.1 *destruction*, 244.14 *destructive*, 440.11 *benighted*, 633.1 *dangerous*, 636.8 *warning*, 670.21 *aggressive*, 712.10 *demanding*, 777.4 *intimidation*, 827.9 *vituperative*
threateningly 633.11 *dangerously*
threaten one's life 633.10 *endanger*
threat of dismissal 228.4 *negative stimulus*
three 177, 177, 27.10 *score*, 41.6 *ice-skating*, 52.9 *numeral*
Three 177
three abreast 177.13 *in threes*
three-ball match 29.1 *golf*
three by three 177.13 *in threes*
three-card brag 42 Card Games
three-card monte 42 Card Games
three-card trick 539.9 *sleight of hand*
three cheers 773.2 *fanfare*, 851.5 *acclaim*
three-cornered 177.8 *three-sided*
three-course meal 350.12 *meal*
three-cushion 24.9 *billiard*
three-cushion billiards 24.4 *carom*
three-day event 32.11 *eventing*
three-day eventing 18 Sporting Activities
three-decker 177.2 *trident*, 679.25 *historical naval ships*
three-dimensional 52.79 *spatial*, 177.8 *three-sided*, 248.11 *spatial*, 435.20 *visual*
three-dimensionally 248.14 *spatially*, 248.15 *spaciously*
three-dimensional space 52.35 *space*
threefold 177.7 *three*, 177.12 *thrice*
threefoldness 177.3 *threeness*
three-footed 177.8 *three-sided*
three-hander 177.2 *trident*
three hundred 179.9 *treble figures*
three hundred and one 42.6 *darts*
three-leaved 177.8 *three-sided*
three-legged 177.8 *three-sided*
three-man 36.10 *sailing*
three-man combination 31.8 *hockey*
three-man combination attack 31.3 *ice hockey*
three-man keelboat 36.2 *sailing boat*
three-metre springboard 39.6 *diving*
Three Mile Island 56.75 *nuclear accident*, 410.7 *nuclear power*
three-mile limit 302.3 *furthest point*
three-minute suspension 31.5 *lacrosse*
threeness 177
three of a kind 42.3 *card game terms*
three-on-a-side 25.9 *bowls*
three-on-a-side match 25.1 *green bowling*
three-part 177.9 *trisected*
three-parted 177.9 *trisected*
threepenny bit 741.10 *former British money*
three-phase supply 64.34 *power supply*
three-piece suit 295.10 *suit*
three-ply 177.8 *three-sided*, 266.7 *layered*
three-pointed 177.8 *three-sided*
three-pointer 23.4 *playing terms*
three-point landing 73.5 *flight*
three-point turn 71.21 *miscellaneous motoring terms*
three-pronged 177.8 *three-sided*
three-quarter 173.5 *fractional*
three-quarter back 35.4 *rugby player*
three-quarter-length portrait 50.10 *art subject*
three quarters 173.4 *less than one*
three-quarters 173.7 *fractionally*
three-ring circus 532.8 *public relations*
threescore 179.8 *twenty and over*

threescore and ten 179.8 *twenty and over*
threescore years and ten 185.3 *duration*, 207.5 *old age*, 396.5 *life cycle*
three-second lane violation 23.5 *penalties*
three sheets in the wind 874.1 *drunk*
three-sided 177, 52.82 *polygonal*
threesome 29.1 *golf*, 177.1 *three*
three-storeyed 266.7 *layered*
three-tiered 266.7 *layered*
three times 177.12 *thrice*
three times as much 177.7 *three*
three turn 41.7 *ice-dancing*
three-way 177.8 *three-sided*
three-wheeler 177.2 *trident*
thremmatologist 76.10 *animal welfarist*
thremmatology 68.3 *livestock farming*, 76.8 *animal welfare*
threnodic 774.4 *lamenting*
threnodist 774.3 *lamenter*
threnodize 774.6 *lament*
threnody 48.7 *poem*, 774.2 *lament*
threonine 58 Amino Acids
thresh 366.21 *be agitated*
thresher 80 Fishes
threshold 280.2 *foot*, 298.1 *interface*, 302.2 *limiting factor*, 346.6 *means of entry*
threshold of hearing 421.3 *inaudibility*
threshold of pain 403.2 *ability to sense*
thrice 177
thrift 84 Flowers and Flowering Plants, **756**, 637.1 *preservation*
Thrift 756
thriftily 756.7 *economically*
thriftiness 756.1 *thrift*
thriftless 607.8 *wasteful*, 757.1 *extravagant*
thriftlessly 607.10 *wastefully*
thriftlessness 607.3 *waste*
thrift shop 754.7 *discounter*
thrifty 756, 781.4 *cautious*
thrill 366.10 *beat*, 366.24 *shake*, 403.1 *sensation*, 403.3 *stimulus*, 403.13 *arouse sensation*, 405.9 *give pleasure*, 762.2 *fun*, 762.8 *cause joy*
thrilled 403.7 *susceptible*, 762.4 *happy*
thriller 48.2 *fiction*, 532.6 *book publishing*, 560.5 *fiction*
thrilling 403.9 *exciting*, 560.11 *descriptive*
thrips 82 Insects, 69.12 *pests and diseases*
thrive 128.4 *increase*, 239.2 *be full of vigour*, 246.6 *be fertile*, 261.6 *become bigger*, 623.5 *be healthy*, 642.13 *be busy*, 682.6 *be successful*, 686.5 *be prosperous*, 861.21 *do well*
thriving 246.5 *fertile*, 261.1 *growth*, 261.8 *growing*, 623.1 *healthy*, 682.1 *success*, 682.13 *successful*, 686.1 *prosperity*, 686.8 *prosperous*
throat 322.7 *passageway*, 350.16 *eating utensil*, 564.5 *organ of speech*
throat cancer 624.12 *cancer*
throatiness 430.2 *hoarseness*
throaty 430.8 *hoarse*, 564.18 *phonetic*, 624.23 *diseased*
throb 183.6 *reverberation*, 183.22 *resound*, 214.1 *regularity*, 214.7 *be regular*, 365.2 *vibration*, 365.9 *vibrate*, 366.7 *shake*, 366.9 *jolt*, 366.10 *beat*, 366.24 *shake*, 403.3 *stimulus*, 406.1 *pain*, 406.10 *be painful*, 426.8 *drum*, 764.12 *be painful*
throbbing 183.6 *reverberation*, 183.15 *reverberatory*, 214.11 *regular*, 365.2 *vibration*, 365.14 *vibrating*, 366.6 *shaking*, 366.10 *beat*, 366.18 *shaky*, 406.1 *pain*, 406.5 *painful*, 426.1, 426.15 *drumming*
throbbingly 406.13 *painfully*
throe 241.3 *instance of violence*

throes 366.8 *spasm*, 406.1 *pain*
thrombectomy 60 Surgical Operations
thrombosis 371.2 *concentration*, 371.4 *solid body*, 387.4 *blood*
thrombus 323.2 *stopper*, 371.4 *solid body*
throne 16.18 *tribunal*, 353.14 *toilet*, 544.4 *insignia*
thrones 8.6 *angel*
throng 181, 135.1 *union*, 161.20, 161.40 *crowd*, 181.11 *crowd*
thronged 181.10 *crowded*
throng in 346.12 *flood in*
throttle 236.8 *overpower*, 323.8 *stop*, 699.8 *restrain*, 726.6 *retain*
throttle down 328.3 *slow down*
throttling 699.1 *restraint*, 726.9 *retentive*
through 157.21 *ended*, 232.9 *instrumentally*, 271.8 *breadthwise*, 327.15 *accessible*, 327.17 *via*, 356.14 *by the way*, 602.7 *by means of*
through a glass darkly 441.12 *dimly*
through and through 144.10 *fully*
through arbitration 15.13 *industrially*
through bridge 63.21 *bridge*
through charity 831.11 *charitably*
through fire and water 575.13 *persistently*
through ignorance 462.14 *thoughtlessly*
through nature's bounty 246.8 *fruitfully*
through negotiations 15.13 *industrially*
throughout 144.9 *completely*, 185.21 *lasting through time*
throughout eternity 190.11 *eternally*
throughout the world 248.16 *extensively*, 724.6 *in common*
throughput 243.1 *production*, 326.3 *transmission*
through rose-coloured glasses 471.22 *imaginatively*
through self-denial 669.15 *abstemiously*
through street 327.3 *road*
through the courts 16.81 *legally*
through the green 29.1 *golf*
through the instrumentality of 232.9 *instrumentally*
through the legislative process 16.81 *legally*
through the night 205.7 *evening*
through thick and thin 144.10 *fully*, 190.11 *eternally*, 575.13 *persistently*
throughway 327.3 *road*
throw 330, 338, 338, 36.8 *punting*, 36.19 *punt*, 38.4 *play soccer*, 42.5 *dice*, 42.6 *darts*, 42.10 *play*, 44.11 *make ceramics*, 136.9 *separate*, 306.7 *form*, 324.14 *set in motion*, 362.6 *throw down*, 644.4 *exertion*
throw a cat-fit 828.11 *be angry*
throw a completion 19.15 *play offence*
throw a conniption 828.11 *be angry*
throw a conniption fit 828.11 *be angry*
throw a crackback block 19.18 *be penalized*
throw a curve 22.7 *play baseball*
throw a double whammy on 827.7 *wish ill*
throw a fast ball 22.7 *play baseball*
throw a fight 26.11 *do a combat sport*, 539.30 *be fraudulent*
throw a fit 366.21 *be agitated*, 759.17 *feel deeply*, 828.11 *be angry*
throw a lifeline to 639.1 *deliver*, 767.10 *save*
throw a monkey wrench into 236.8 *overpower*
throw a party 665.16 *host*, 773.5 *rejoice*, 812.18 *salute*, 815.11 *be sociable*

throw a pass 19.15 *play offence*
throw a pot 44.11 *make ceramics*
throw around 162.17 *sow*
throw aside 581.2 *discard*
throw a slider 22.7 *play baseball*
throw a spanner in the works 236.8 *overpower*, 614.8 *make useless*, 661.9 *block*
throw a stone 670.7 *stone*
throw at 670.7 *stone*
throw a tantrum 759.17 *feel deeply*, 828.12 *become angry*
throwaway 189.7 *impermanent*, 599.10 *usable*, 607.9 *waste*, 613.1 *useful*, 614.1 *useless*, 614.6 *refuse*
throw away 349, 51.34 *underact*, 244.12 *consume*, 581.2 *discard*, 598.1 *relinquish*, 600.6 *stop using*, 607.1 *waste*, 722.11 *be wasteful*, 727.9 *dispose of*, 748.1 *expend*
throw away an opportunity 211.6 *lose one's chance*
throwaway manner 807.7 *insult*
throw away the scabbard 676.12 *go to war*
throw a whammy on 827.7 *wish ill*
throw a wild pitch 22.7 *play baseball*
throw a wobbly 759.17 *feel deeply*, 779.4 *be a coward*
throw a wrench in one's plans 614.8 *make useless*
throw axel 41.6 *ice-skating*
throwback 337.18 *setback*, 628.7 *deterioration*
throw back 671.24 *parry*
throw bombs 670.3 *bomb*
throw caution to the wind 508.6 *be foolish*, 780.5 *be rash*
throw cold water on 242.4 *moderate*, 587.5 *discourage*, 661.8 *hinder*
throw down 362, 244.9 *demolish*
throw down the gauntlet 574.8 *brace oneself*, 668.6 *be Insubordinate*
throw dust in one's eyes 108.10 *be unrelated*, 591.6 *evade*
thrower 338, 21.3 *athlete*
throw-forward 35.3 *rugby play*
throw further 721.10 *augment*
throw good money after bad 722.10 *have a financial loss*, 757.8 *overspend*
throw in 35.5 *play rugby*, 38.4 *play soccer*, 42.10 *play*
throw-in 38.2 *football play*, 338.5 *throw*
throwing 338, 26.15 *wrestling*, 44.5 *ceramic process*
throwing a fight 26.2 *boxing*
throwing in the towel 705.1 *resignation*
throwing out 349.17 *expulsion*
throwing out time 157.11 *finality*
throwing overboard 349.20 *eviction*
throwing the crosse 31.5 *lacrosse*
throw in irons 699.12 *gag*
throw in one's hand 598.2 *withdraw*
throw in prison 699.11 *detain*
throw in the air 361.2 *send up*
throw in the cooler 702.9 *imprison*
throw in the slammer 323.10 *enclose*
throw in the sponge 598.2 *withdraw*
throw in the tank 702.9 *imprison*
throw in the towel 673.3 *submit*, 705.5 *resign*
throw into a tizzy 153.7 *disturb*
throw into confusion 153.7 *disturb*
throw into disarray 151.21 *disorder*
throw into disorder 153.8 *disarrange*
throw in together 664.13 *work together*
throw into relief 526.3 *reveal*

throw into the melting pot 518.6 *propound*
throw into the shade 126.8 *be superior*
throw in with 664.14 *join with*
throw it all away 211.6 *lose one's chance*
throw light on 439.29 *clarify*, 524.8 *interpret*, 526.3 *reveal*
throw money at 748.1 *expend*
throw money away 757.8 *overspend*
throw mud 852.23 *show disapproval*, 854.12 *defame*
thrown 44.10 *ceramic*, 306.9 *formed*, 361.11 *raised*
thrown away 581.10 *rejected*
thrown out 252.10 *replaced*, 711.8 *refused*
thrown-out case 16.42 *acquittal*
thrown over 785.9 *disliked*
thrown together 656.4 *bungled*
thrown to the lions 633.4 *endangered*
throw off 296.16 *peel*, 349.10 *exterminate*, 585.5 *disaccustom*, 700.5 *be liberated*
throw off balance 123.5 *be unequal*
throw off discipline 151.26 *be disorderly*
throw off the scent 539.27 *be false*, 591.6 *evade*, 638.6 *elude*
throw off the trail 638.6 *elude*
throw off the yoke 700.5 *be liberated*
throw of the dice 229.2 *chance*, 589.3 *equal chance*, 633.5 *danger*
throw one's arms around 821.27 *kiss*
throw oneself at 590.12 *aim at*
throw oneself at the feet of 808.10 *knuckle under*, 826.8 *court*
throw oneself in the arms of 634.4 *shelter*
throw oneself upon another's mercy 835.12 *ask for mercy*
throw one's hat in the ring 668.6 *be insubordinate*
throw one's weight around 233.10 *be a prevailing influence*, 688.19 *be authoritarian*, 805.28 *disdain*, 807.26 *oppress*, 807.28 *get above oneself*
throw open 526.3 *reveal*
throw out 22.7 *play baseball*, 131.3 *subtract*, 147.8 *eject*, 244.8 *destroy*, 330.1 *impel*, 341.2 *eject*, 349.1 *expel*, 349.13 *throw away*, 581.2 *discard*
throw-out 22.6 *fielding terms*
throw out an idea 518.6 *propound*
throwout level 20.1 *angling*
throw out of gear 136.9 *separate*, 252.14 *displace*
throw out of the window 722.14 *go to waste*
throw out on one's ear 349.1 *expel*
throw over 598.2 *withdraw*
throw overboard 349.13 *throw away*, 362.6 *throw down*, 370.10 *lighten*, 600.6 *stop using*
throw rug 293.9 *floor covering*
throw salchow 41.6 *ice-skating*
throw someone a curve 539.29 *juggle*
throw someone a curveball 539.29 *juggle*
throw something together 45.55 *cook*
throwstick 680.6 *historical missile weapon*
throw stones 852.23 *show disapproval*
throw stones at 330.4 *throw*
throw the baby out with the bath water 656.6 *act foolishly*
throw the book at 852.21 *berate*, 856.5 *accuse*, 879.2 *penalize*
throw the book at him 879.24 *string him up*
throw the casting vote 123.5 *be unequal*
throw the crosse 31.9 *play hockey*

throw the dice 229.4 *chance*
throw the double whammy on 822.15 *curse*
throw the javelin 338.23 *throw*
throw the whammy on 822.15 *curse*
throw to an ineligible receiver 19.18 *be penalized*
throw together 135.8 *unite*, 583.3 *improvise*
throw to the dogs 244.12 *consume*
throw to the four winds 607.1 *waste*
throw up 349.15 *vomit*
throw up a roadblock 661.9 *block*
throw up a smoke screen 539.32 *disguise*
throw up one's hands 523.9 *find unintelligible*
throw up the game 598.2 *withdraw*
thrum 49.38 *sound*, 183.22 *resound*, 426.8 *drum*, 434.10 *lack harmony*
thrumming 426.1, 426.15 *drumming*
thrupenny bit 741.10 *former British money*
thrush 78 Birds, 78.6 *songbird*, 89.5 *fungal association*
thrushlike 78.23 *avian*
thrust 28.5 *fence*, 53.35 *rocketry*, 233 *influence*, 235.4 *energy*, 329.9 *acceleration*, 330.1 *impel*, 330.13 *blow*, 332.2 *bearing*, 337.29 *in reverse*, 338.12 *propellant*, 338.20 *propel*, 535.6 *assertiveness*, 535.21 *be assertive*, 624.18 *veterinary disease*, 642.14 *push*, 670.1 *attack*, 670.6 *stab*, 670.12 *military attack*, 670.18 *hit*
thrust ahead 329.6 *accelerate*
thrust at 670.6 *stab*
thrust bearing 364.4 *vortex*
thrust down 362.5 *bear down on*
thruster 338.11 *propeller*, 642.10 *busy person*
thrust fault 54.20 *earth movement*
thrustful 330.17 *impelling*, 535.14 *assertive*, 642.18 *active*
thrust in 354.3 *impar*
thrusting 239.4 *vigorous*, 330.12 *collision*, 330.17 *impelling*, 642.18 *active*
thrustingly 338.34 *forward*
thrusting under 362.13 *submergence*
thrust oneself forward 642.14 *push*
thrust out 147.8 *eject*
thrust stage 51.15 *stage*
Thuban 53 Named Stars
thud 424.1 *faintness*, 424.5 *sound faint*, 425.1 *bang*, 428.5 *dull sound*, 428.9 *be nonresonant*
thug 241.4 *violent person or animal*, 309.5 *defacer*, 398.11 *murderer*, 601.3 *abuser*, 635.2 *troublemaker*, 679.1 *combatant*, 736.11 *dishonest person*, 832.8 *malefactor*, 864.9 *wicked person*
thuggery 241.2 *physical violence*, 398.2 *murder*
thuggish 679.33 *combative*
thuja 85 Trees and Shrubs
Thule 263.3 *distant place*
thulium 57 Chemical Elements
thumb 43 Architectural Decoration, 135.5 *joint*, 407.7 *sense organ*
Thumbelina 260.4 *little person*, 270.5 *short person*
thumbing 543.15 *gestural*
thumb knot 74 Knots
thumbnail 299.6 *outlined*
thumbnail sketch 50.9 *drawing*, 260.2 *little thing*, 299.1 *outline*, 560.2 *brief description*, 562.1 *summary*
thumb one's nose at 850.26 *cock a snook*
thumb piano 49 Musical Instruments
thumbprint 544.3 *means of identification*

thumbscrew 879.4 *torture*, 879.15 *instrument of torture*
thumbs down 16.43 *conviction*, 500.2 *disapproval*, 709.1 *veto*, 711.1 *refusal*, 852.3 *nonacceptance*
thumbs up 16.42 *acquittal*, 324.11 *bodily movement*, 499.2 *yes*, 667.1 *agreement*, 851.1 *approval*
thumbtack 137.8 *fastening*, 380.8 *sharp-pointed thing*
thumb-twiddling 788.1 *boredom*, 788.4 *boring*
thump 330.3 *hit*, 330.13 *blow*, 424.1 *faintness*, 424.5 *sound faint*, 425.1 *bang*, 428.5 *dull sound*, 428.9 *be nonresonant*
thumping 259.15 *big*
Thunar 8 Deities
thunbergia 84 Flowers and Flowering Plants
thunder 777 Phobias by Topic, 55.21 *thunderstorm*, 55.59 *storm*, 241.5 *violent weather*, 423.1 *loudness*, 423.8 *be loud*, 425.5 *bang*, 532.14 *proclaim*, 554.6 *emphasize*, 564.12 *speak loudly*, 827.6 *vilify*
thunder along 329.4 *be swift*
thunder and lightning 241.5 *violent weather*, 543.1 *sign*
Thunder Bay 93 Cities
thunderbolt 55.21 *thunderstorm*, 439.4 *natural light*, 514.3 *shock*
thunderbolts of Thor 423.1 *loudness*
thunderbowl 727.7 *toilet*
thunderbox 53.14, 727.7 *toilet*
thunderclap 55.21 *thunderstorm*, 423.1 *loudness*, 425.1 *bang*
thundercloud 55.18 *cloud*, 440.4 *dark thing*
thunderer 241.4 *violent person or animal*
thundering 259.15 *big*, 423.6 *loud*, 425.8 *banging*, 427.3 *deepness*, 427.8 *deep*, 431.16 *vociferous*, 827.3 *vilification*
thundering storm 423.1 *loudness*
thunderous 423.6 *loud*, 431.16 *vociferous*
thunderous applause 851.5 *acclaim*
thunderously 431.20 *vociferously*
thunder out 431.10 *cry out*
thunderstorm 55, 56.47 *electric storm*
thunderstruck 514.7 *amazed*, 786.6 *wondering*
thundery 55.48 *stormy*, 440.8 *dark*
thundery shower 55.25 *rain*
thundrous 425.8 *banging*
Thurber 48 Writers
thurible 10.14 *sacred object*, 418.3 *incense*
thurifer 418.3 *incense*
thurification 10.5 *Christian rite*
thurifier 7.8 *priest*
thurify 418.6 *perfume*
Thurso 93 Cities
thus 106.15 *under the circumstances*, 116.34 *uniformly*, 116.36 *accordingly*, 327.16 *how*
thusness 103.4 *nature*, 253.1 *presence*
thwack 330.1 *impel*, 330.3 *hit*, 330.13 *blow*, 879.3 *hit*
thwart 515, 36.4 *rowing*, 36.6 *canoeing*, 218.8 *cause to cease*, 231.3 *counteract*, 310.8 *oblique*, 618.13 *be worthless*, 661.8 *hinder*, 663.18 *counteract*
thwarted 515.9 *disappointed*
thwarting 661.13 *hindering*
thylacine 77 Marsupials
thyme 45 Herbs and Spices, 413.5 *herbs*
thymectomy 60 Surgical Operations
thymine 58.10 *nucleoside*, 59.12 *molecular biology*
thymoxamine 62 Medication
thyrocalcitonin 58 Hormones, 62 Medication
thyroglobulin 58 Hormones

thyroidal 352.5 *of a secretion*
thyroidectomy 60 Surgical Operations
thyroid gland 352 Endocrine Glands
thyroid hormone 58 Hormones
thyroid-stimulating hormone 58 Hormones
thyrotomy 60 Surgical Operations
thyroxine 58 Hormones
thyrse 84.4 *flower head*
Thysanoptera 82 Orders of Insects
thysanopteran 82.10 *insectan*
Thysanura 82 Orders of Insects
thysanuran 82.10 *insectan*
Tia Maria 351.7 *alcoholic drink*
Tianjin 93 Cities
Tian Shan 95 Mountains
tiara 7.11 *vestment*, 295.15 *headgear*, 792.6 *jewellery*
Tiber 96 Rivers, 96.5 *other major rivers*
Tibetan 5 Languages and Groups of Languages
Tibetan Pony 32 Breeds of Horse and Pony
Tibeto-Burman 5 Languages and Groups of Languages
tibia 49 Musical Instruments, **382** Bones
tic 309.2 *facial distortion*, 366.8 *spasm*, 436.2 *poor sight*, 543.3 *gesture*, 624.17 *nervous disorder*
tical 75 Some Foreign Units
tic douloureux 624.17 *nervous disorder*
tick 82 Arachnids, 82.2 *arachnid*, 82.3 *pest*, 116.7, 116.28 *consent*, 191.3 *instant*, 214.1 *regularity*, 214.7 *be regular*, 365.9 *vibrate*, 424.1 *faintness*, 424.5 *sound faint*, 426.4 *knocking*, 426.11 *knock*, 544.10 *identify*, 733.4 *credit*, 738.7 *purchasing*, 744.1 *credit*
ticked 116.17 *consenting*
ticker tape 812.8 *salute*
ticker-tape parade 849.5 *presenting arms*
ticker-tape welcome 812.4 *reception*
ticket 130.3 *additional item*, 346.4 *right of entry*, 480.6 *evidence*, 483.6 *documentation*, 544.3 *means of identification*, 544.10 *identify*, 545.2 *certificate*, 580.12 *election*, 592.2 *policy*, 708.2 *permit*, 718.2 *promise*, 730.3 *acknowledgment of payment*
ticket agent 51.25 *producer*, 739.12 *wholesaler*
ticket collector 51.26 *stagehand*
ticket counterfoil 544.3 *means of identification*
ticketholder 346.7 *entrant*
ticket stub 544.3 *means of identification*, 718.2 *promise*
ticking 67 Natural Fabrics, 214.11 *regular*, 426.17 *rattling*
ticking-off 852.7 *blame*
ticking parcel 633.6 *danger signal*
tickle 403.3 *stimulus*, 403.11 *sense*, 405.9 *give pleasure*, 407.3 *press*, 407.11 *touch*, 821.14 *communication of love*, 826.1 *endearment*
tickled pink 405.7 *pleased*, 762.4 *happy*
tickled to death 405.7 *pleased*, 762.4 *happy*
tickle one's fancy 411.9 *taste*, 798.7 *make one laugh*
tickle one's palate 411.9 *taste*
tickle one's palm 746.11 *remunerate*
tickle pink 405.9 *give pleasure*
tickle the ivories 49.38 *sound*
ticklike 82.11 *arachnidan*
tickling 821.14 *communication of love*
ticklish 633.2 *unsafe*, 659.12 *problematic*, 760.3 *sore*
ticklish business 633.5 *danger*
ticklish issue 666.1 *disagreement*

ticklishness 403.2 *ability to sense*, 633.5 *danger*, 760.7 *soreness*
ticklish spot 659.5 *predicament*
tickly 403.9 *exciting*
tick off 136.10 *set apart*, 169.10 *number*, 544.10 *identify*, 852.20 *censure*
tick off names 545.15 *register*
tick over 230.7 *be operational*
ticktack 543.3 *gesture*
ticktacktoe 42 Children's Games and Party Games
ticktock 365.9 *vibrate*, 426.4 *knocking*, 426.11 *knock*
tidal 54.52 *coastal*, 94.9 *lakelike*, 97.7 *oceanic*, 214.11 *regular*, 224.13 *changeable*
tidal barrage 235.6 *source of energy*
tidal bore 96.2 *channel*
tidal current 54.13 *ocean current*, 97.2 *tide*
tidal energy 410.8 *renewable energy*
tidal flats 278.4 *shallow thing*
tidal flood 97.2 *tide*
tidal flow 97.2 *tide*, 214.1 *regularity*
tidally 54.66 *geographically*, 97.11 *nautically*
tidal pool 94.2 *small lake*
tidal power 56.11 *energy*, 97.2 *tide*, 235.6 *source of energy*, 410.8 *renewable energy*
tidal range 54.15, 97.2 *tide*
tidal rise and fall 97.2 *tide*
tidal stream 97.2 *tide*
tidal table 97.2 *tide*
tidal wave 54.14, 97.3 *wave*, 241.3 *instance of violence*, 275.8 *high thing*, 365.5 *wave*, 375.9 *broken water*, 635.1 *trap*
tiddler 260.4 *little person*, 270.5 *short person*
tiddly 260.7 *little*, 874.2 *slightly drunk*
tiddlywinks 42 Children's Games and Party Games
tide 54, 97, 97.1 *sea*, 214.5 *regular thing*, 336.11 *course*
tide chart 97.2 *tide*
tide gate 97.2 *tide*
tide gauge 97.2 *tide*
tideland 97.2 *tide*
tideline 300.1 *edge*
tidemark 268.6 *measuring instrument*, 543.5 *indicator*, 545.12 *vestige*
tide of time 188.2 *time*
tide over 662.29 *finance*
tide race 97.2 *tide*
tide-rode 36.10 *sailing*
tide-rode boat 36.2 *sailing boat*
tidewater 97.2 *tide*
tideway 97.2 *tide*
tidied 152
tidily 150.26 *orderly*, 152.28 *in place*, 621.19 *cleanly*
tidiness 150.5 *orderliness*, 469.4 *fastidiousness*, 651.5 *refreshment*
tidings 528.1 *information*
tidy 150, 152, 150.13 *orderly*, 152.27 *tidied*, 259.15 *big*, 469.9 *careful*, 621.13, 621.16 *clean*, 627.1 *improve*, 651.1 *refresh*, 789.6 *personable*
tidying 621.2 *cleaning*, 627.5 *improvement*
tidying up 651.5 *refreshment*
tidy step 263.2 *great distance*
tidy sum 181.2 *multitude*, 742.6 *money*
tidy up 150.21, 152.19 *tidy*, 312.10 *straighten*, 627.1 *improve*, 651.1 *refresh*
tie 74 Knots, 63.27 *superstructure*, 69.6 *garden tool*, 72.3 *rail*, 107.1 *relatedness*, 107.7 *relate to*, 110.5 *equality*, 122.2 *equilibrium*, 122.10 *be equal*, 135.5 *joint*, 135.10 *link*, 137.4 *means of connection*, 137.6 *line*, 137.11 *connect*, 137.12 *bind*, 198.4 *equal race*, 198.8 *run equally*, 225.7 *make stable*, 295.14 *neckwear*, 295.34 *wear*,

323.11 *restrain*, 327.10 *railway*, 544.5 *uniform*, 629.1 *repair*, 661.4 *restraint*, 661.10 *restrain*, 685.1 *noncompletion*, 699.12 *gag*, 847.7 *commitment*, 847.17 *impose a duty*
tie a fly 20.7 *angle*
tie a game 110.10 *be equal*
tie a knot in one's handkerchief 511.13 *remind*
tie beam 137.4 *means of connection*
tie clasp 137.8 *fastening*, 726.3 *tools for gripping*
tied 135, 20.8 *angling*, 107.4 *related*, 110.16 *equal*, 122.8 *on equal terms*, 137.15 *connected*, 137.16 *bound*, 225.10 *stabilized*, 847.11 *duty-bound*
tied down 135.15 *tied*, 699.13 *restraining*
tie fly 20.2 *artificial fly*
tied game 110.5 *equality*, 122.2 *equilibrium*
tie down 695.6 *compel*
tied score 122.2 *equilibrium*
tied to one's apron strings 701.9 *subject*
tied up 135.15 *tied*, 684.7 *completed*
tied up with 107.4 *related*
tie-dye 67.15 *treat*, 444.15 *colour*
tie-dyed 67.11 *treated*
tie-dyeing 67.7 *dyeing*
tief 49 Musical Terms
tie hand and foot 236.8 *overpower*, 699.12 *gag*
tie in 69.15 *cultivate*, 135.8 *unite*, 664.16 *join*
tie-in 664.7 *association*
tie in knots 151.22 *discompose*
tie into 107.7 *relate to*
tie in with 107.7 *relate to*, 116.25 *conform*
tiemannite 54 Minerals
tie one's hands 661.10 *restrain*
tie-on label 544.3 *means of identification*
tiepin 137.8 *fastening*, 792.6 *jewellery*
tier 163.5 *social class*, 266.2 *level*, 266.10 *layer*
tierce 177.6 *third*
tierceron ridge rib 43.7 *vault*
Tierra del Fuego 98 Islands
tie the knot 715.5 *contract*, 823.15 *marry*
tie the nuptial knot 823.16 *join in marriage*
tie the wedding knot 823.16 *join in marriage*
tie to 130.6 *add*, 135.10 *link*
tie together 107.7 *relate to*, 135.10 *link*
tie up 74.10 *sail*, 107.7 *relate to*, 135.10 *link*, 236.8 *overpower*, 344.4 *land*, 629.1 *repair*, 664.16 *join*, 684.4 *complete*, 699.12 *gag*, 723.7 *possess*
tie-up 107.1 *relatedness*, 135.1 *union*, 664.7 *association*, 823.2 *alliance*
tie up all the loose ends 684.4 *complete*
tie up to 135.10 *link*
tie up with 135.10 *link*, 823.19 *merge*
tiff 473.1 *argument*, 500.1 *dissent*, 666.2 *argument*, 666.6 *argue*, 764.8, 828.5 *quarrel*
tiffany 442.8 *transparent thing*
Tiffany glass 44.1 *ceramics*
tiffin 350.12 *meal*
tig 42 Children's Games and Party Games
tiger 77 Placental Mammals, 241.4 *violent person or animal*, 401.16 *male animal*, 456.5 *variegated thing*, 778.7 *courageous person*
tiger beetle 82 Insects
tiger cowrie 81 Molluscs
tigerfish 80 Fishes
tiger hunt 590.2 *chase*
tiger hunter 590.6 *hunter*
tigerish 77.28 *carnivorous*, 241.6 *violent*

tiger-like 77.28 *carnivorous*
tiger lily 84 Flowers and Flowering Plants
tiger moth 82 Insects
tiger's-eye 456.5 *variegated thing*
tiger shark 80 Fishes
tight 35.6 *rugger*, 135.15 *tied*, 135.18 *inextricably*, 138.9 *adhesive*, 144.8 *full*, 262.7 *smaller*, 272.1 *narrow*, 302.5 *limited*, 373.2 *tough*, 619.1 *perfect*, 632.6 *invulnerable*, 758.1 *mean*, 874.1 *drunk*
tight-arse 758.5 *miser*, 869.4 *self-restrained person*
tight-arsed 758.1 *mean*, 869.8 *self-restrained*
tight corner 659.6 *critical situation*
tighten 36.15 *sail*, 135.8 *unite*, 262.5 *make smaller*, 262.6 *become smaller*, 272.10 *narrow*, 373.9 *harden*
tightened 262.7 *smaller*
tightened headband 879.15 *instrument of torture*
tightening 135.3 *unification*, 262.1 *contraction*, 262.8 *contracting*
tighten one's belt 743.12 *be poor*, 756.6 *save*, 869.5 *be self-restrained*, 871.5 *fast*
tighten one's grip 726.6 *retain*
tighten up on 150.22 *pacify*
tightfisted 726.9 *retentive*, 758.1 *mean*
tightfistedness 758.3 *parsimony*
tight-fitting 135.15 *tied*
tight grip 726.1 *retention*
tight-knit 552.3 *concise*
tight-lipped 422.3 *silent*, 531.17 *noncommittal*, 566.1 *taciturn*
tightly 135.18 *inextricably*, 138.11 *cohesively*, 272.11 *narrowly*, 373.12 *toughly*
tightly packed 135.15 *tied*
tightness 135.1 *union*, 262.1 *contraction*, 272.5 *narrowness*, 373.5 *hardness*, 758.3 *parsimony*
tight rein 690.1 *severity*
tightrope walker 51.29 *circus performer*, 237.5 *athlete*, 811.15 *showman*
tights 295.20 *legwear*
tight scrum 35.3 *rugby play*
tight ship 690.1 *severity*
tight skirt 295.6 *skirt*
tight spot 260.5 *little space*, 659.6 *critical situation*
tight squeeze 260.5 *little space*, 272.6 *narrow place*, 659.6 *critical situation*
tight-wad 758.5 *miser*
tigon 77 Placental Mammals, 133.5 *hybrid*
Tigré 5 Languages and Groups of Languages
tigress 77.18 *female mammal*, 241.4 *violent person or animal*, 402.14 *female animal*, 829.3 *irascible person*, 832.9 *vixen*
Tigrinya 5 Languages and Groups of Languages
Tigris 96 Rivers, 96.5 *other major rivers*
Tijuana 93 Cities
tiki 11.6 *talisman*
tikka 45.49 *Indian dish*
tiktiri 49 Musical Instruments
Tilamook 45 Cheeses
tilbury 71 Carriages and Carts
tilde 5.36 *accent*, 543.7 *punctuation*
tile 44.8 *ceramic object*, 44.11 *make ceramics*, 63.26 *masonry*, 266.4 *slice*, 280.1 *base*, 293.24 *coat*, 293.27 *roof*, 295.15 *headgear*, 327.1 *road surface*, 604.2 *building material*
tiled 293.36 *covered*
tile painter 44.7 *potter*
tiler 293.17 *coverer*, 646.2 *artisan*
tiles 293.7 *overhead covering*, 293.9 *floor covering*
tiling 44.8 *ceramic object*, 293.9 *floor covering*

till **741**, 36.8 *punting*, 54.38 *glacier*, 68.17 *farm*, 170.5 *computer*, 185.26 *all the time*, 605.4 *storage*, 627.1 *improve*
tillable 68.20 *farmable*
tillage 68.5 *cultivation*, 594.13 *development*
till doomsday 190.11 *eternally*
tilled 68.20 *farmable*
tiller **74** Parts of a Ship, 36.3 *parts of a sailing boat*, 68.15 *agriculturist*, 74.5 *navigation*, 603.1 *tool*, 663.4 *guide*
tiller of the soil 68.15 *agriculturist*
till hell freezes over 157.27 *to the end*, 184.12 *eternally*
till now 3.24 *historically*, 194.11 *before*, 200.23 *before now*
till one is blue in the face 188.11 *long*
till the cows come home 184.12 *eternally*, 186.8 *ever*, 188.11 *long*, 575.14 *continually*
till the crack of doom 190.11 *eternally*
till then 194.11 *before*
till the soil 68.17 *farm*
tilt 25.2 *grip*, 123.1 *inequality*, 123.5 *be unequal*, 286.1 *obliqueness*, 286.6 *be oblique*, 310.2 *obliquity*, 310.11 *angle*, 338.23 *throw*, 360.6, 360.14 *slide*, 362.7 *lean*, 674.9 *duel*, 679.37 *fight*
tilt at 590.10 *chase*, 670.1 *attack*
tilt at windmills 614.9 *waste effort*
tilted 310.8 *oblique*
tilter 679.3 *athlete*
tilth 68.5 *cultivation*
tilting 286.4 *oblique*, 674.9 *duel*
tilting at windmills 519.4 *ideality*
tilting of the scales 123.1 *inequality*
tilt the bowl 25.7 *bowl*
tilt with 674.11 *contend*
Tim 192.1 *clock*
timbales **49** Musical Instruments
timber **85**, 47.12 *wood*, 47.17 *carpenter*, 63.25 *construction material*, 604.1 *materials*
timbered 47.16 *joined*, 85.16 *wooded*
timber hitch **74** Knots
timbering 47.12 *wood*, 243.8 *construction*
timber joint 47.10 *carpenter's term*
timberland 85.4 *trees*
timber line 85.4 *trees*
timberman 85.8 *forester*
timber production **85**
timber tree 85.1 *tree*
timber wolf **77** Placental Mammals
timberwork 47.8 *woodwork*, 47.12 *wood*
timber yard 85.7 *timber production*
timbre 564.3 *mode of speech*
Timbuktu **93** Cities, 263.3 *distant place*
time **777** Phobias by Topic, **56**, **185**, **185**, **188**, 49.19 *tempo*, 75.5 *dimension*, 121.4 *interval*, 187.1 *period*, 192.14 *keep time*, 203.1 *season*, 214.10 *make regular*, 244.6 *destroyer*, 248.21 *space*, 268.10 *measure*, 699.4 *detention*, 702.4 *prison sentence*
Time **185**
time after time 183.23 *repeatedly*, 212.1 *frequently*
time allowed 32.9 *jumping*
time and again 183.23 *repeatedly*, 212.1 *frequently*
time and motion study 653.3 *management*
time and tide 185.2 *passage of time*
time badly 211.5 *take untimely action*, 493.10 *misjudge*
time-based 185.20 *temporal*
time beater 192.11 *person keeping time*

time bomb 192.10 *signal*, 635.1 *trap*, 680.16 *bomb*
time clock 185.13 *timer*
time-consuming 607.8 *wasteful*
time copy 533.10 *copy*
timed 41.13 *ice-skating*, 198.10 *synchronized*, 214.11 *regular*
time-division multiplex 534.14 *radio transmission*
time flies 188.2 *time*
time for oneself 645.1 *leisure*
time fuse 192.10 *signal*
time-fuse 410.2 *lighter*
time-honoured 1.14 *societal*, 185.21 *lasting through time*, 202.12 *olden*, 584.11 *normal*, 849.12 *respected*
time immemorial 3.9 *distant past*, 188.5 *long duration*, 200.1 *past time*, 202.3 *antiquity*
time indicator 543.5 *indicator*
time interval 265.1 *interval*
time it right 185.16 *time*
timekeeper **185**
timekeeper **192**, 21.3 *athlete*, 26.7 *judo*, 26.8 *karate*, 192.11 *person keeping time*, 268.9 *measurer*, 543.5 *indicator*, 543.8 *signer*, 545.9 *recorder*
timekeeping **192**, **192**
Timekeeping **192**
timekeeping 185.10 *chronometry*
time-killing 788.4 *boring*
time lag 160.3 *interval*, 209.1 *lateness*
time lapse 248.8 *intervening space*
time-lapse photography 66.1 *photography*
timeless **186**, 190.8 *eternal*
timelessness **186**, 190.1 *eternity*
Timelessness **186**
time limit 32.9 *jumping*
timeliness **210**, 208.1 *earliness*, 615.3 *convenience*, 667.3 *compatibility*
Timeliness **210**
timely **210**, 203.14 *seasonable*, 208.12 *early*, 472.6 *topical*, 615.1 *convenient*
time machine 185.1 *time*
time measurement **185**
time of adversity **687**
time of day 192.3 *chronology*
time off **645**, 218.3 *pause*, 254.5 *leave of absence*, 649.1 *ease*
time of night 192.3 *chronology*
time of plenty **686**
time of sorrow 687.4 *time of adversity*
time of the month 353.11 *menstruation*
Time of Troubles 3.10 *past age*
time of war 676.4 *belligerency*
time of year 203.1 *season*
time one can call one's own 645.1 *leisure*
time on one's hands 641.1 *inaction*, 645.1 *leisure*, 788.2 *boring thing*
time-out 19.5 *game time*, 160.3 *interval*, 185.6 *interval*, 218.3 *pause*, 645.2 *time off*
time out of mind 3.24 *historically*, 200.22 *in the past*, 202.3 *antiquity*
time period **187**
timepiece 185.13 *timer*, 192.5 *timekeeper*
timer **185**, 23.2 *basketball player*, 192.10 *signal*
time-related 185.20 *temporal*
time-rock unit 54.41 *geological time*
timer's desk 23.3 *basketball equipment*
times 52.88 *equal to*, 52.91 *add*
time-saving 649.5 *labour-saving*, 756.4 *thrifty*
time-saving device 662.7 *convenience*
Timese 533.9 *news story*
timeserver 167.6 *conformist*, 539.21 *traitor*, 578.9 *equivocator*, 657.3 *cunning person*, 808.3 *sycophant*

timeserving 578.11 *equivocating*, 615.3 *convenience*, 657.4 *cunning*, 808.2 *sycophancy*, 808.7 *sycophantic*
times gone by 200.1 *past time*
time-share apartment 724.1 *joint possession*
time-share owner 724.3 *participant*
time sharing 65.17 *computing term*, 724.1 *joint possession*
time-sharing 724.5 *jointly possessing*
time shift 197.1 *different time*
time signal 192.10, 543.4 *signal*
time signature 49.17 *notation*, 185.12 *musical time*
timeslip 185.1 *time*
time-space 248.9 *fourth dimension*
time span 185.3 *duration*, 187.1 *period*, 207.1 *age*
times past 200.1 *past time*
time's scythe 244.6 *destroyer*
Times Square 93.3 New York, 291.4 *centre of activity*
time's winged chariot 185.2 *passage of time*
time switch 192.10 *signal*
times without number 212.1 *frequently*
timetable **192**, 6.3 *subject*, 171.5 *list of appointments*, 171.8 *list*, 185.16 *time*, 192.14 *keep time*, 528.5 *reference book*, 592.1 *plan*, 592.10 *plan out*
timetabled 171.11 *listed*
timetabling 192.1 *timekeeping*
time the enemy 185.2 *passage of time*
time the great healer 185.2 *passage of time*
time thrust 28.3 *fencing movements*
time to come 199.1 *future time*
time to kill 641.1 *inaction*, 645.1 *leisure*, 788.2 *boring thing*
time to oneself 645.1 *leisure*
time to spare 208.1 *earliness*, 328.8 *slowness*, 645.1 *leisure*
time travel 185.1 *time*
time-travel paradox 4.9 *philosophical problem*
time up 157.11 *finality*
time warp 160.3 *interval*, 185.1 *time*, 197.1 *different time*
time-wasting 614.2 *futile*
time when the chips are down 106.4 *difficult circumstances*
time without end 190.1 *eternity*
timeworn 202.12 *olden*
time zone **185**, 192.3 *chronology*, 302.4 *boundary marker*
timid **576**, 238.12 *weak-willed*, 491.3 *confused*, 777.8 *fearful*, 779.3 *cowardly*, 810.11, 816.9 *shy*
timidity **576**, 491.12 *confusion*, 779.1 *cowardice*, 810.4, 816.2 *shyness*
timidly 238.14 *weakly*, 777.15 *fearfully*, 779.5 *cravenly*, 810.18 *shyly*, 816.14 *unsocially*
timidness 810.4 *shyness*
timing 41.7 *ice-dancing*, 49.19 *tempo*, 192.1 *timekeeping*, 214.1 *regularity*, 433.3 *melodiousness*
timing device 185.13 *timer*, 192.10 *signal*
timocracy 742.9 *plutocracy*
Timon of Athens **48** Shakespeare's plays
Timor **32** Breeds of Horse and Pony, **97** Oceans and Seas, **98** Islands
timorous 238.12 *weak-willed*, 777.8 *fearful*, 779.3 *cowardly*, 810.11 *shy*
timorously 777.15 *fearfully*, 779.5 *cravenly*, 810.18 *shyly*
timorousness 238.2 *indecisiveness*, 777.2 *fearfulness*, 779.1 *cowardice*, 810.4 *shyness*
timothy **87** Grasses, 68.12 *crop*

timpani **49** Musical Instruments, 49.25 *musical instrument*
tin **57** Chemical Elements, 45.39 *loaf*, 258.6 *box*, 258.21 *put* in a container, 614.6 *refuse*, 637.2 *preserver*, 637.5 *preserve*
Tina **8** Deities
tinamou **78** Birds
tin bath 258.12 *bath*
Tinbergen **52** Scientists
tin can 258.6 *box*
tinct 444.10 *coloured*
tinctorial 444.10 *coloured*
tincture 133.4 *admixture*, 234.2 *attitude*, 444.3 *hue*, 444.15 *colour*
tinder 410.2 *lighter*
tinderbox 258.6 *box*, 410.2 *lighter*
tine 380.7 *sharp point*
tinea 89.5 *fungal association*
tineid moth **82** Insects
tin-enamel 44.11 *make ceramics*
tin-enamelled 44.10 *ceramic*
tin-enamelled ware 44.1 *ceramics*
tin fish 680.16 *bomb*
ting-a-ling 427.2 *ringing*
tinge 133.4 *admixture*, 133.8 *mix*, 444.3 *hue*, 444.15 *colour*, 542.6 *suggestion*
tinged 133.12 *mixed*, 444.10 *coloured*
tin-glaze 44.11 *make ceramics*
tin-glazed 44.10 *ceramic*
tin-glazed earthenware 44.1 *ceramics*
tingle 403.3 *stimulus*, 403.11 *sense*, 406.10 *be painful*, 407.13 *be touched by*
tingling 406.5 *painful*, 760.3 *sore*, 760.7 *soreness*
tingly 403.9 *exciting*
tin god 653.16 *official*, 696.4 *absolute ruler*, 807.12 *impudent person*
Ting ware **44** Types of Ceramics
tin hat 295.15 *headgear*, 671.7 *armour*
tinily 260.8 *in a small way*
tininess 260.1 *littleness*
tinker 407.11 *touch*, 609.5 *be insufficient*, 614.9 *waste effort*, 628.4 *impair*, 629.12 *repairer*, 642.17 *meddle*, 646.2 *artisan*, 656.5 *be unskilful*, 656.10 *unskilled person*, 657.5 *be cunning*, 739.11 *pedlar*
tinkering 609.8 *insufficiency*, 614.5 *waste of effort*, 656.9 *bungling*
tinker's damn 612.8 *trifle*, 827.1 *curse*
tinker with 216.8 *cause change*, 407.11 *touch*
tinkle 424.1 *faintness*, 424.5 *sound faint*, 427.2 *ringing*, 427.10 *ring*, 534.10 *telephone call*, 767.13 *relieve oneself*
tinkling 427.7 *ringing*
tinkling cymbal 521.1 *lack of meaning*
tin lizzie 71.16 *car*
tin mine 647.1 *workshop*
tinned 258.20 *containing*, 637.7 *preserved*
tinned food 350.7 *food*, 637.3 *preserved thing*
tinner 637.4 *preservationist*
tinning 258.20 *containing*, 637.1 *preservation*
tinnitus 420.8 *something heard*
tinny 430.9 *shrill*
Tino **5** Languages and Groups of Languages
tin-opener 322.2 *opener*
Tin Pan Alley **49**
tinpot 754.10 *shoddy*
tinsel 439.2 *quality of light*, 539.6 *imitation*, 540.10 *fake*, 612.9 *bauble*, 811.4 *flashiness*
tinselled 540.33 *fake*
tinselly 439.16 *bright*, 811.19 *flashy*
tinsmith 646.2 *artisan*
tinstone **57** Common Metal Ores

tint 50.19 *paint,* 56.28 *colour,* 444.3 *hue,* 444.4 *pigment,* 444.15 *colour*
tinted 50.27 *painted,* 442.3 *semi-transparent,* 444.10 *coloured*
tinted glasses 435.10 *visual aid*
tinting 50.2 *painting*
tintinnabular 427.7 *ringing*
tintinnabulate 427.10 *ring*
tintinnabulation 427.2 *ringing*
tintometer 268.8 *meter,* 444.8 *chromatics*
tint tool 47.11 *woodworking tool*
tin whistle 49 Musical Instruments, 430.3 *shrillness*
tiny 173.6 *small,* 260.7 *little,* 612.4 *trivial*
tiny tot 206.9 *child*
tip **528,** 130.4 *extra,* 151.4 *litter,* 157.7 *limit,* 228.5 *positive stimulus,* 279.1 *summit,* 286.1 *obliqueness,* 286.6 *be oblique,* 310.11 *angle,* 330.6 *tap,* 330.13 *blow,* 362.7 *lean,* 528.7 *advice,* 586.17 *bribe,* 605.4 *storage,* 614.6 *refuse,* 636.1 *warning,* 636.5 *warn,* 654.1 *advice,* 721.5 *profit,* 727.8 *sink,* 729.2 *gift,* 729.5 *give,* 746.3 *pay,* 746.11 *remunerate,* 755.7 *gift,* 837.3 *recognition,* 837.6 *be grateful,* 878.7 *bounty,* 878.11 *pay*
tipcat 42 Children's Games and Party Games
tip in 23.6 *play basketball*
tip-in 23.4 *playing terms*
tiple 49 Musical Instruments
tip off 6.22 *educate,* 528.14 *tip,* 636.5 *warn*
tip-off 528.7 *advice,* 636.1 *warning*
tipped 279.6 *topped*
tipper 528.10 *informer,* 729.4 *giver*
Tipperary **92** Counties, **93** Cities
tippet 7.11 *vestment,* 295.14 *neckwear*
Tippett 49 Musicians and Composers
Tippex 438.6 *that which makes invisible,* 438.8 *make invisible*
tipple 351.13 *drink,* 874.8 *get drunk,* 874.13 *drink*
tippler 874.17 *drunkard*
tippling 351.16 *drinking,* 874.5 *drunken,* 874.11 *drinking*
tippoo's tiger 49 Musical Instruments
tipsily 874.18 *drunkenly*
tipsiness 874.10 *drunkenness*
tipstaff 16.11 *British law officer*
tipster 32.15 *horse person,* 517.9 *forecaster,* 528.10 *informer*
tipsy 874.2 *slightly drunk*
tip the balance 369.12 *be heavy*
tip the board 36.18 *windsurf*
tip the scale 233.9 *change*
tip the scales 123.5 *be unequal,* 369.12 *be heavy*
tip the wink 116.28 *consent,* 851.12 *accept*
tiptoe 527.13 *hide,* 531.11 *conceal oneself*
tip to one side 286.6 *be oblique*
tip top 20.3 *fishing tackle*
tiptop 126.14 *best,* 279.1 *summit,* 279.5 *top,* 279.8 *on top,* 617.2 *best*
tip-top condition 623.3 *health*
Tipura **5** Languages and Groups of Languages
tip well 755.10 *be generous,* 878.11 *pay*
tirade 553.1 *diffuseness,* 561.1 *dissertation,* 564.8 *speech,* 567.1 *address,* 852.8 *berating*
tiramisu 45.47 *Italian dish*
Tirana 93 Cities
tire 650.5 *be fatigued,* 650.6 *fatigue,* 673.4 *succumb,* 683.6 *fail,* 788.6 *be boring*
tired 236.12 *impotent,* 238.11 *weakened,* 624.21 *unhealthy,* 628.12 *deteriorated,* 650.1 *fatigued,* 650.2, 788.5 *bored*

tired and emotional 874.2 *slightly drunk*
tired bones 628.9 *dilapidation*
tired brain 650.7 *fatigue*
tired-eyed 650.1 *fatigued*
tired-looking 650.1 *fatigued*
tiredly 650
tiredness 236.4 *disability,* 238.3 *poor health,* 650.7 *fatigue*
tired of 788.5 *bored*
tired of living 788.5 *bored*
tired out 236.12 *impotent,* 650.1 *fatigued*
tired to death 650.1 *fatigued,* 788.5 *bored*
tireless 574.2 *tenacious,* 642.20 *industrious,* 644.10 *working*
tirelessness 575.2 *commitment,* 642.8 *assiduity*
tireless worker 642.10 *busy person*
tire oneself out 650.5 *be fatigued*
tire out 650.6 *fatigue*
tiresome 616.1 *inconvenient,* 650.4 *fatiguing,* 659.13 *inconvenient,* 788.4 *boring*
tiresomely 616.6 *inconveniently*
tiresomeness 788.1 *boredom*
tire to death 650.6 *fatigue*
tiring 644.11 *laborious,* 650.4 *fatiguing,* 788.4 *boring*
tiringly 650, 788.8 *boringly*
tiro 6.7 *learner*
tisane 351.3 *tea,* 630.7 *tonic*
Tishah b'Av 871.3 *fast day*
Tisiphone 828.7 *gods and goddesses of anger*
tissue 274.11 *fineness,* 382.2 *fabric,* 383.5 *textile,* 396.2 *living matter,* 621.11 *cleaning cloth*
tissue culture 59.6 *cell biology*
tissue of lies 538.3 *lying*
tissue paper 238.5 *weak thing,* 293.4 *wrapping,* 604.3 *paper*
tissue sample 60.7 *diagnosis*
tissue structure 59.4 *anatomy*
tit 78 Birds, 78.6 *songbird*
Titan 237.6 *muscleman,* 259.10 *big person*
Titaness 259.10 *big person*
Titania 11.11 *ghost*
titanic 57.34 *elemental,* 259.15 *big*
titanium **57** Chemical Elements
titanium white 446.8 *whitener*
titanosaur 79 Fossil Reptiles
titanothere 77 Placental Mammals
titanous 57.34 *elemental*
titbit 350.14 *mouthful,* 411.3 *appetizer,* 617.7 *elite*
titbits 350.7 *food*
titch 260.4 *little person,* 270.5 *short person*
titchy 260.7 *little*
titfer 295.15 *headgear*
tit for tat 107.2 *interrelatedness,* 109.1 *interchange,* 125.2 *counterbalance,* 223.1 *exchange,* 672.1 *retaliation,* 672.6 *with vengeance,* 674.6 *fight*
tithe 143.1 *part,* 179.6 *ten,* 612.8 *trifle,* 729.3 *offering,* 729.6 *give to charity,* 751.7 *tax,* 751.7 *charge*
tithing 92.2 *former British divisions,* 729.1 *giving*
Tithonus 202.2 *old people*
titi 77 Placental Mammals
Titian 450.3 *red-haired,* 451.1 *orange*
Titicaca **94** Lakes, 94.5 *other major lakes*
titillate 403.13 *arouse sensation,* 405.9 *give pleasure,* 413.13 *be piquant,* 782.15 *cause desire*
titillated 405.7 *pleased,* 784.6 *liking*
titillating 403.9 *exciting,* 405.6 *pleasant,* 413.10 *stimulating,* 782.11 *lustful,* 784.5 *likable,* 877.12 *indecent*
titillatingly 784.10 *with great liking*

titillation 403.3 *stimulus,* 405.1 *physical pleasure,* 413.4 *stimulation,* 784.1 *liking*
tit in the wringer 659.7 *awkward situation*
titivate 295.33 *dress up,* 627.1 *improve,* 789.8, 791.15 *beautify*
titivation 627.5 *improvement*
titlark 78 Birds
title **567,** 21.5 *competition,* 544.3 *means of identification,* 545.2 *certificate,* 560.8 *name,* 723.1 *possession,* 725.1 *property,* 792.3 *honour,* 845.3 *prerogative,* 878.1 *reward*
Title **804**
titled 544.12 *identified*
title deed 545.2 *certificate,* 667.2 *contract,* 718.2 *promise,* 845.6 *bond*
titled person 802.1 *nobleman*
titleholder **804**
titleholder 26.4 *boxer,* 617.8 *exceller,* 655.4 *skilled person,* 682.5 *victorious person*
titleless 803.3 *common*
title page 156.10 *introduction*
title part 51.21 *role*
title role 51.21 *role*
title to fame 617.6 *worth*
Titoism 12.1 *government*
titration 57.18 *gravimetric analysis*
titre 57.18 *gravimetric analysis*
tits 316.2 *bulge*
titter 431.2 *cry of joy,* 431.11, 771.14 *laugh,* 773.3 *laughter,* 773.8 *laugh*
titterer 773.4 *rejoicer*
tittering **161** Collective Names for Birds and Animals, 773.3 *laughter,* 773.10 *laughing*
tittle 173.3 *fragment,* 260.3 *little piece,* 612.8 *trifle*
tittle-tattle 420.8 *something heard,* 465.2 *prying,* 465.7 *be curious,* 565.3 *talk,* 568.2 *chat*
tittle-tattler 465.4 *meddler,* 565.4 *talker,* 568.8 *chatterer*
titubant 360.18 *falling*
titubate 360.12 *drop*
titubation 360.4 *fall*
titular 12.10 *governing,* 518.8 *supposed*
titular head 236.5 *powerless person*
Titus Andronicus 48 Shakespeare's plays
ti-tzu 49 Musical Instruments
Tiv **5** Languages and Groups of Languages
Tiw 8 Deities
Tiwa 1 Peoples
tiz-woz 366.4 *fuss*
tizz 366.4 *fuss*
tizzy 366.4 *fuss,* 828.4 *anger*
T-junction 71.3 *carriageway*
Tlaloc 8 Deities
tlapanhuéhuetl 49 Musical Instruments
tlapiztali 49 Musical Instruments
Tlazolteotl 8 Deities
TLC 57.17 *analysis*
Tlingit 1 Peoples, **5** Languages and Groups of Languages
Tloque Nahuaque 8 Deities
TNT 244.7 *agent of destruction,* 680.15 *explosive*
to 327.17 *via,* 346.18 *into*
to a certain extent 143.12 *partly,* 302.8 *within limits*
to a cinder 408.17 *warmly*
toad 79 Amphibians, 808.3 *sycophant*
toadeater 808.3 *sycophant*
to a degree 121, 143.12 *partly,* 242.9 *moderately*
toadfish 80 Fishes
toad-in-the-hole 45.44 *British dish*
toadish 79.13 *amphibian*
toadlet 79.8 *young amphibian*
toadlike 79.13 *amphibian*
toad lily 84 Flowers and Flowering Plants
toadstool 89.2 *mushroom*

to advantage 662.36 *helpfully*
toady 376.13 *smooth over,* 467.14 *be solicitous,* 499.3 *assenter,* 578.9 *equivocator,* 673.2 *appeaser,* 673.4 *succumb,* 771.7 *person who humours,* 808.3 *sycophant,* 808.9 *fawn,* 853.7 *sycophant,* 853.11 *be sycophantic*
toadying 673.5 *submitting,* 771.11 *humouring,* 808.2 *sycophancy,* 808.7 *sycophantic*
toadyish 853.16 *sycophantic*
toadyism 853.5 *sycophancy*
toady to 771.15 *humour,* 817.13 *defer to*
to a finish 684.9 *completely*
to a frazzle 684.9 *completely*
to a great degree 121.11 *to a degree*
to a hair 503.8 *accurately*
to a limited extent 620.11 *imperfectly*
to all appearances 102.19 *apparently,* 289.15 *externally,* 437.11 *visibly,* 457.15 *apparently*
to all intents and purposes 99.22 *really,* 122.12 *equally,* 142.13 *on the whole,* 264.7 *nearly,* 488.11 *probably*
to all places **248**
to a man 499.8 *unanimously*
to and fro **365,** 109.10 *reciprocally,* 214.15 *regularly,* 223.8 *in exchange,* 224.15 *changeably,* 324.17 *directional*
to-and-fro 214.11 *regular,* 365.13 *oscillating*
to-and-fro movement 214.1 *regularity,* 324.5 *circuition*
to a nicety 503.8 *accurately*
to an increasing extent 128.8 *increasingly*
to apologize 867.8 *penitently*
to approval 851.26 *approvingly*
to a small degree 121.11 *to a degree*
toast 45.38 *bread,* 45.55 *cook,* 351.2 *drink,* 351.14 *drink to,* 392.19 *bake,* 408.14 *be hot,* 449.7 *brown,* 511.14 *commemorate,* 812.6 *tribute,* 812.17 *congratulate,* 815.11 *be sociable,* 817.3 *courtesies,* 817.10 *be courteous,* 819.4 *act of friendship*
toasted 45.56 *culinary,* 408.13 *heated,* 449.2 *browned*
toasted sandwich 45.11 *sandwich*
toaster 45.5 *cooker,* 408.4 *burner*
toast from coast to coast 617.8 *exceller*
toasting 45.8 *cooking technique*
toastmaster 653.14 *leader*
toast of the town 617.8 *exceller*
to a T 503.8 *accurately,* 684.9 *completely*
to atone for 735.7 *redemptively*
to a turn 619.7 *perfectly,* 684.9 *completely*
tobacco **413, 413,** 68.12 *crop*
tobacco auctioneer 423.5 *loud person*
tobacco belt 68.11 *farmland*
tobacco leaf 449.5 *brown thing*
tobacconist 413.8 *smoking,* 739.13 *retailer*
tobacco pouch 413.7 *tobacco*
tobacco sachet 413.7 *tobacco*
to be 199.11 *future*
to be blamed 844.16 *in the wrong*
to be clear 524.18 *in other words*
to be counted on one's fingers 182.5 *few*
to be counted on the fingers of one hand 182.5 *few*
to be disposed of 727.14 *for sale*
to be exact 537.39 *accurately*
to be expected 124.11 *on average,* 488.11 *probably*
to be jumped at 580.15 *chosen*
to be specific 165.28 *specially*
to be sure 480.12 *assuredly*
to be taken seriously 611.5 *important*
to bits 136.21 *apart,* 141.7 *to pieces*

to blame 852.36 *blameworthy,* 866.5 *guilty*
toboggan 41.16 *bobsled ,* 71.10 *sled,* 360.14 *slide*
toboggan chute 41.9 *bobsledding*
tobogganing 18 Sporting Activities
tobogganist 41.11 *skier*
toboggan race 41.9 *bobsledding*
toboggan racing 41.9 *bobsledding*
toboggan run 41.9 *bobsledding*
to boot 130.10 *additionally*
Tobruk 93 Cities
toby jug 44.8 *ceramic object,* 258.13 *drinking vessel*
to capacity 144.10 *fully*
Tocharian 5 Languages and Groups of Languages, 5.11 *family of languages*
to coin a phrase 505.4 *proverbially*
to come 199.11, 714.15 *future*
to completion 684.9 *completely*
to convince 228.14 *influentially*
tocophobia 777 Phobias by Name
to crown all 126.17 *supremely,* 611.9 *importantly*
tocsin 636.2 *danger signal*
to cut a long story short 552.5 *concisely*
Toda 5 Languages and Groups of Languages
today 185.27 *at what time,* 196.1 *present time,* 196.9 *at present,* 198.2 *present time*
Todd 52 Scientists
toddle 324.15 *walk*
toddle along 328.1 *move slowly,* 345.1 *depart*
toddler 206.9 *child*
toddling 324.17 *directional*
toddy 351.7 *alcoholic drink,* 413.6 *cordial*
to death 788.8 *boringly*
to design 588.15 *according to plan*
to-do 151.9 *disorder,* 153.5 *commotion,* 366.4 *fuss,* 473.1 *argument,* 541.1 *exaggeration,* 642.1 *activity*
toe 29.4 *golf club,* 135.5 *joint,* 280.2 *foot,* 407.7 *sense organ*
toeclip 71.11 *bicycle part*
toe dance 46.2 *dance,* 46.8 *ballet*
toehold 322.10 *opportunity,* 726.1 *retention*
toe in the door 322.10 *opportunity*
toe in the water 710.2 *tentative offer*
toe jump 41.6 *ice-skating*
toenail 373.7 *hard substance*
toe piece 41.5 *ski equipment*
toe the line 110.11 *be regular,* 112.10, 116.25 *conform,* 166.17 *obey orders,* 167.8 *comply,* 306.8 *be formal,* 694.5 *obey*
toe to toe 111.6 *oppositely*
toe traverse 34.3 *climbing technique*
to excess 610.8 *excessively*
to explain 524.18 *in other words*
to express appreciation 837.8 *gratefully*
toff 802.1 *nobleman*
toffee 45.41 *sweet,* 138.4 *adherent,* 414.4 *confectionery,* 449.5 *brown thing*
toffee apple 45.41 *sweet*
toffeenose 805.13 *proud person,* 809.7 *vain person*
toffee-nosed 805.17 *conceited*
to fill the bill 615.7 *conveniently*
toft 68.6 *farm,* 725.3 *historic property terms*
Toft ware 44 Types of Ceramics
tofu 45.21 *meat substitute*
tog 75 General Units
toga 295.16 *robe*
toga virilis 295.16 *robe*
together 161, 180, 15.13 *industrially,* 116.31 *in accord,* 135.16 *as one,* 140.10 *in combination,* 198.12 *simultaneously,* 342.12 *convergently,* 509.4 *sane,*

664.20 *cooperatively,* 667.16 *compatibly,* 677.7 *pacifically,* 724.6 *in common*
togetherness 180.3 *companionship,* 664.2 *fellowship,* 815.8 *good company,* 819.1 *friendship*
together with 130.10 *additionally,* 180.24, 664.22 *with*
togged 295.30 *dressed up*
toggery 295.1 *dress*
toggle 137.8 *fastening*
toggle pin 137.8 *fastening*
Togo 91 Countries
to good effect 233.14 *influentially*
to good purpose 682.16 *successfully*
togs 295.1 *dress*
to hand 196.8, 253.10 *available,* 253.16 *on the spot,* 264.5 *near*
to hell and back 248.19 *to all places*
Tohi 8 Deities
toil 644.1, 644.6 *work,* 659.3 *difficult task*
toil and trouble 644.4 *exertion*
toile 67 Natural Fabrics
toiler 642.10 *busy person,* 646.1 *worker*
toilet 353, 727, 256.7 *room,* 295.2 *dressing,* 353.13 *lavatory,* 531.6 *privacy,* 621.5 *ablutions,* 791.3 *beauty treatment*
toilet bag 791.5 *make-up box*
toilet bowl 727.7 *toilet*
toilet paper 604.3 *paper,* 621.11 *cleaning cloth*
toiletries 791, 418.2 *fragrant thing*
toilet roll 621.11 *cleaning cloth*
toilet soap 621.9 *cleaning agent*
toilette 295.2 *dressing,* 791.3 *beauty treatment*
toilet tissue 621.11 *cleaning cloth*
toilet-trained 353.26 *urinary*
toilet water 418.2 *fragrant thing,* 791.6 *toiletries*
toilsome 644.11 *laborious,* 659.10 *difficult*
to infinity 184.10 *infinitely,* 190.11 *eternally*
toing and froing 365.1 *oscillation*
to just the right degree 619.7 *perfectly*
tokamak 56.76 *fusion reactor*
tokay 79 Reptiles
Tokay 351.9 *wine*
to keep 726.11 *tenaciously*
Tokelau 5 Languages and Groups of Languages
token 165.3 *characteristic,* 483.4 *indication,* 511.3 *memento,* 526.10 *manifestation,* 526.14 *manifest,* 543.1 *sign,* 544.3 *means of identification,* 612.4 *trivial,* 681.3 *memento,* 729.2 *gift,* 730.2 *something received*
token economy 61.3 *psychiatric treatment*
tokenism 538.8 *pretence,* 539.3, 540.2 *hypocrisy*
tokenistic 538.18 *pretentious,* 539.37 *hypocritical*
token of esteem 729.2 *gift*
token of one's gratitude 837.3 *recognition*
token of remembrance 681.3 *memento*
Tokyo 93 Cities, 93.6 *other cities*
tola 75 Some Foreign Units
tolazamide 62 Medication
tolazoline 62 Medication
told 3.19 *chronicled*
Toledo 93 Cities, **93** Cities, 680.8 *sharp weapon*
to leeward 36.20 *offshore*
to leg 27.20 *in*
tolerability 765.3 *satisfactoriness,* 783.4 *mediocrity*
tolerable 124.3 *mediocre,* 284.10 *supportable,* 617.5 *not bad,* 620.4 *ordinary,* 765.6 *satisfactory,* 783.10 *mediocre*
tolerableness 124.6 *mediocrity*
tolerably 608.9 *enough,* 783.20 *unexceptionally*

tolerance 4.3 *detachment,* 62.3 *drug,* 482.7 *impartiality,* 691.1 *leniency,* 698.1 *freedom,* 708.1 *permission,* 831.1 *benevolence,* 839.2 *forgivingness*
tolerant 4.18 *detached,* 242.7 *politically moderate,* 482.2 *impartial,* 641.3 *inactive,* 660.13 *easygoing,* 675.7 *peaceful,* 691.4 *lenient,* 698.9 *free,* 708.8 *permitting,* 814.10 *free,* 831.6 *benevolent,* 839.5 *merciful*
tolerantly 482.15 *impartially,* 691.6 *leniently,* 698.20 *freely,* 708.9 *with permission,* 831.10 *benevolently,* 839.14 *forgivingly*
tolerate 284.12 *bear,* 482.12 *be fair,* 499.5 *assent to,* 641.4 *not act,* 667.6 *agree with,* 691.3 *be lenient,* 698.14 *be free,* 708.3 *permit,* 831.8 *be benevolent,* 839.12 *show mercy*
toleration 667.1 *agreement,* 691.1 *leniency,* 698.1 *freedom,* 708.1 *permission,* 814.4 *freedom,* 831.1 *benevolence*
to let 710.17 *offered*
to little purpose 683.12 *unsuccessfully*
Tolkien 48 Writers
toll 130.2 *mathematical addition,* 426.12 *ring,* 427.2 *ringing,* 427.10 *ring,* 636.7 *raise the alarm,* 751.8 *levy*
toll bridge 63.21 *bridge,* 137.5 *road,* 327.9 *bridge*
toll call 534.10 *telephone call*
Tollen's reagent 57 Named Reactions, 58.5 *sugar test*
tollgate 346.6 *means of entry ,* 661.2 *obstacle*
tolling 427.7 *ringing*
toll road 71.2, 137.5 *road,* 327.3 *road*
toll the knell 399.8 *bury*
Tolstala 48 Writers
Tolstoy 48 Writers
Toltec 1 Peoples
Toltecs 200.6 *people of the past*
tolu 85 Tree Products
tom 77.10 *cat,* 77.17 *male mammal,* 402.7 *prostitute*
tomahawk 680.8 *sharp weapon*
to make a fresh start 867.8 *penitently*
to make amends 840.8 *penitently*
to matchwood 136.21 *apart*
tomato 45 Vegetables, **86** Fruits, 450.7 *red thing*
tomato juice 351.6 *soft drink*
tomato ketchup 45.15 *sauce*
tomato sauce 45.15 *sauce*
tomato soup 45.13 *soup*
tomb 243.8 *construction,* 323.4 *closed place,* 325.3 *resting place,* 397.8 *after death,* 399.6 *grave,* 545.11 *monument*
tombac 57 Alloys
tomb of an unknown soldier 545.11 *monument*
tombola 133.3 *miscellany,* 229.2 *chance,* 589.3 *equal chance*
tomboy 206.8 *young woman*
tombstone 399.4 *funeral objects,* 545.11 *monument*
Tombstone 93 Cities
tom cat 401.16 *male animal*
Tom Collins 351.8 *mixed drink*
Tom, Dick, and Harry 795.6 *vulgar herd,* 803.2 *the common people*
Tom, Dick, or Harry 124.7 *average person*
tomfoolery 506, 508.2 *act of folly*
tommy 679.8 *soldier*
Tommy 674.10 *contender,* 676.11 *recruit*
Tommy Atkins 679.8 *soldier*
Tommy gun 680.11 *guns*
tommyrot 521.4 *senseless talk*
tomogram 60.7 *diagnosis*
tomography 60.7 *diagnosis*
tomorrow 185.27 *at what time,* 197.3 *another time,* 199.1 *future time,* 199.14 *in the future*

tomorrow afternoon 199.1 *future time*
tomorrow evening 199.1 *future time*
tomorrow morning 199.1 *future time*
tomorrow night 199.1 *future time*
Tom Sawyer and Huckleberry Finn 819.7 *famous friendships*
Tom Thumb 260.4 *little person,* 270.5 *short person*
tom-tom 49 Musical Instruments, 426.1 *drumming*
tom turkey 78.10 *male bird*
ton 75 General Units, 179.9 *treble figures,* 369.9 *avoirdupois weight,* 741.3 *fortune*
Tonacatacuhtli 8 Deities
tonal 5.39 *of language,* 49.30 *harmonic,* 564.18 *phonetic*
tonality 49.21 *tone,* 433.3 *melodiousness*
tonal language 5.10 *language type*
tonally 5.48 *linguistically*
tonal range 66.8 *composition*
tonal sequence 433.3 *melodiousness*
tone 49, 48.3 *aspect of fiction,* 49.16 *musical note,* 50.4 *treatment,* 50.19 *paint,* 56.20 *musical note,* 105.1 *state,* 234.2 *attitude,* 297.3 *atmosphere,* 327.1 *way,* 377.1 *elasticity,* 416.4 *reputation,* 444.3 *hue,* 444.15 *colour,* 488.2 *tendency,* 534.1 *dialling,* 549.1 *style,* 564.3 *mode of speech,* 623.3 *health,* 652.1 *conduct*
to near starvation 871.7 *abstemiously*
tone control 420.10 *sound quality,* 534.18 *radio*
toned 444.10 *coloured*
toned-down 542.19 *downplayed*
tone deaf 421.4 *deaf*
tone-deaf 482.1 *undiscriminating,* 658.1 *naive*
tone deafness 421.1 *deafness*
tone down 242.4 *moderate,* 374.14 *ease,* 441.11 *tarnish,* 444.15 *colour,* 445.6 *decolour,* 485.15 *modify,* 542.22 *play down*
toneless 421.7 *unheard,* 434.9 *unmelodious,* 445.7 *colourless*
tonelessly 421.12 *deafly,* 445.9 *colourlessly*
tone of voice 564.3 *mode of speech,* 652.1 *conduct*
tone row 49.20 *key*
tone up 627.1 *improve*
Tonga 5 Languages and Groups of Languages, **91** Countries
Tongan 5 Languages and Groups of Languages
Tongariro 92 New Zealand Regions and Territories
Tonga Trench 54.16 *ocean floor*
tongs 726.3 *tools for gripping*
tongue 5.3 *spoken language,* 32.8 *hunting,* 45.7 *offal,* 49.38 *sound,* 98.5 *peninsula,* 350.16 *eating utensil,* 564.1 *faculty of speech,* 564.5 *organ of speech*
tongue in cheek 474.10 *hypocritical,* 539.1 *deception,* 540.3 *hypocrisy*
tongue-in-cheek 521.12 *unmeant,* 538.17 *duplicitous,* 538.26 *untruthfully,* 539.35 *deceptive,* 540.27 *hypocritical,* 797.3 *affected,* 853.12 *flattering*
tongue-in-cheek statement 538.7 *duplicity*
tongue-lash 827.6 *vilify,* 852.21 *berate*
tongue-lashing 852.8 *berating*
tongueless 422.3 *silent*
tongue-tied 563.11 *speechless*
tonic 630, 49.16 *musical note,* 62.3 *drug,* 62.4 *drug type,* 62.17 *stimulating,* 228.3 *stimulus,* 237.4 *strengthening,* 351.8 *mixed drink,* 377.6 *elastic,* 413.6 *cordial,* 564.18 *phonetic,*

586.19 *persuasive*, 623.2 *healthful*, 630.17 *remedial*, 651.3 *refreshing*, 651.6 *refresher*
tonic-clonic fit 510.3 *mental deterioration*
tonicity 377.1 *elasticity*
tonic sol-fa 41.9 *notation*
tonic water 351.6 *soft drink*, 630.7 *tonic*
tonight 185.27 *at what time*, 196.1 *present time*, 196.9 *at present*
toning 444.11 *colourful*
tonitrophobia 777 Phobias by Name
tonjon 71.6 *litter*
tonka bean 45 Vegetables
Tonle Sap 94 Lakes
tonnage 257.2 *load*, 259.1 *size*, 369.4 *heaviness*
tonnage and poundage 751.8 *levy*
tonnara 80.7 *fishing*
tonne 75 General Units
to no avail 614.10 *uselessly*
to no extent 100.15 *not at all*
ton of bricks 369.11 *weight*
tonometer 268.8 *meter*
tonometric 268.16 *micrometric*
tonometry 268.2 *micrometry*
tonoplast 59.8 *cell organ*
to no purpose 358.11 *in vain*, 614.10 *uselessly*, 683.12 *unsuccessfully*
Tonqtiuh 8 Deities
tons 181.3 *profuseness*
tonsillectomy 60 Surgical Operations, 630.12 *surgery*
tonsillitis 624.9 *respiratory disease*
tonsillotomy 60 Surgical Operations
tonsure 294.6 *baldness*, 294.13 *remove*, 296.7 *depilation*
tonsured 296.13 *hairless*
tontine 721.4 *earnings*, 724.1 *joint possession*, 730.2 *something received*, 749.3 *income*
ton-up 329.1 *swift*
tonus 377.1 *elasticity*
too 130.10 *additionally*
too bad 612.15 *no matter*, 618.3 *bad*
too bad! 687
too bad to be true 786.8 *wonderful*
too big 259.15 *big*
too big for one's boots 809.13 *boastful*, 809.14 *opinionated*
too clever by half 507.6 *intelligent*, 657.4 *cunning*, 809.11 *cocky*
too clever for 657.4 *cunning*
too early 193, 193.7 *out of chronological order*, 208.16 *premature*, 208.20 *prematurely*
too far 263.10 *distantly*
too few 182.5 *few*, 182.7 *fewer*, 609.1 *insufficient*, 609.8 *insufficiency*
too few to mention 182.1 *few*
to off 27.20 *in*
too good to be true 489.2 *questionable*, 786.8 *wonderful*
too hot to handle 16.59 *stolen*
too human 864.13 *venial*
tool 603, 65.5 *dynamic structure*, 127.6 *inferior*, 232.2 *instrument*, 245.8 *organs of reproduction*, 539.22 *dupe*, 602.1 *means*, 646.3 *agent*, 662.7 *convenience*, 701.3 *subordinate*, 792.10 *decorate*, 808.3 *sycophant*
Tool 603
too late 193, 193.7 *out of chronological order*, 209.16 *at a late hour*, 211.15 *at the wrong time*
toolbox 65.17 *computing term*
toolhouse 603.1 *tool*
too little 609.1 *insufficient*, 609.8 *insufficiency*
tool-kit 603.1 *tool*
toolroom 603.1 *tool*
tools 602.1 *means*, 603.6 *equipment*
tools for gripping 726
tool shed 603.1 *tool*

tools of the trade 602.1 *means*, 603.1 *tool*
tool-user 603.7 *machinist*
tool-using 603.8 *mechanical*
too many 610.1 *excess*, 610.6 *excessive*
too many chiefs and not enough Indians 656.9 *bungling*
too many cooks 656.9 *bungling*
too many irons in the fire 610.2 *overdoing it*
too much 541.17 *excessively*, 608.8 *plenty*, 610.1 *excess*, 610.6 *excessive*, 610.8 *excessively*, 788.4 *boring*, 846.6 *excessiveness*
too much for 236.14 *powerlessly*
too much of a good thing 610.3 *superfluity*, 788.2 *boring thing*
too much on one's plate 610.2 *overdoing it*
toon 85 Trees and Shrubs
to one's advantage 613.4 *profitable*, 615.1 *convenient*
to one's amazement 786.13 *wonderfully*
to one's chagrin 699.17 *with self-restraint*
to one's discredit 864.18 *wickedly*
to one's embarrassment 699.17 *with self-restraint*
to one's face 475.20 *manifestly*, 526.17 *frankly*, 668.9 *defiantly*
to one's fancy 821.22 *lovable*
to one's heart's content 608.9 *enough*
to one side 305.10 *laterally*
to one's liking 405.6 *pleasant*
to one's mind 821.22 *lovable*
to one's own design 588.15 *according to plan*
to one's own specifications 588.15 *according to plan*
to one's sorrow 862.13 *destructively*
to one's surprise 786.13 *wonderfully*
to one's taste 405.6 *pleasant*, 821.22 *lovable*
to one's utmost 644.12 *laboriously*
to one's way of thinking 471.24 *ideologically*
too old to cut the mustard 207.14 *aged*
too precious for words 753.8 *valuable*
to order 667.16 *compatibly*, 692.16 *commandingly*, 694.10 *obediently*
too small 609.1 *insufficient*
too smart for one's own good 809.11 *cocky*
too soon 193.7 *out of chronological order*, 208.16 *premature*, 208.20 *prematurely*, 211.15 *at the wrong time*
toot 49.38 *sound*, 423.1 *loudness*, 427.10 *ring*, 636.2 *danger signal*, 636.7 *raise the alarm*
tooth 380, 319.1 *notch*, 726.3 *tools for gripping*
toothache 406.2 *painful condition*
toothache tree 85 Trees and Shrubs
tooth and nail 241.10 *violently*, 644.12 *laboriously*
toothbrush 621.10 *cleaning object*
tooth carp 80 Fishes
toothed 380, 83.18 *of leaves*, 319.4 *notched*
tooth for a tooth 223.1 *exchange*
tooth fungi 89.3 *fungi*
toothless 381, 77.26 *insectivorous*
toothlessly 381.11 *smoothly*
toothless mammal 77
toothlessness 381
toothless tiger 381.8 *toothlessness*
toothlike 380.4 *toothed*
toothpaste 134.3 *purifier*, 621.9 *cleaning agent*, 630.3 *prophylactic*

toothpick 355.10 *excavator*, 380.8 *sharp-pointed thing*, 621.10 *cleaning object*
tooth powder 630.3 *prophylactic*
tooth shell 81 Molluscs
toothsome 411.7 *tasty*
toothy 380.4 *toothed*
tootle 427.10 *ring*
toot one's own horn 809.17 *be affected*
tootsie roll 875.6 *drug*
top 279, 279, 42.6 *darts*, 69.15 *cultivate*, 85.18 *manage trees*, 87.12 *manage grassland*, 95.9 *tower*, 126.2 *leadership*, 126.4 *summit*, 126.8 *be superior*, 126.14 *best*, 157.7 *limit*, 275.2 *heights*, 275.15 *be high*, 279.1 *summit*, 293.2 *cover*, 293.23 *cover*, 293.24 *coat*, 295.8 *shirt*, 295.24 *part of garment*, 315.5 *cone*, 323.2 *stopper*, 323.8 *stop*, 359.14 *climb*, 364.6 *rotator*, 407.3 *press*, 615.1 *important*, 619.1 *perfect*, 619.3 *perfection*, 861.2 *best*
toparchy 91.3 *dominion*
topaz 54 Minerals, **54** Gemstones, 452.8 *yellow thing*
top banana 617.8 *exceller*, 771.6 *humorist*
top billing 532.8 *public relations*
top boots 295.19 *footwear*
top brass 126.7 *the best people*, 233.5 *influential person*, 611.4 *bigwig*, 617.8 *exceller*, 653.6 *governing body*
topcoat 266.1 *layer*, 295.12 *coat*
top condition 594.14 *preparedness*
top cushion 24.1 *billiards*
top deck 74 Parts of a Ship
top dog 126.5 *superior*, 400.7 *person*, 617.8 *exceller*, 688.10 *person of authority*, 696.5 *company leader*
top drawer 126.7 *the best people*, 617.7 *elite*
top-drawer 126.12 *superior*, 802.4 *aristocratic*
top-dress 68.17 *farm*, 69.15 *cultivate*, 87.12 *manage grassland*, 246.7 *make fertile*
top dressing 246.3 *fertilizer*, 279.4 *top layer*
tope 80 Fishes, 10.13 *shrine*, 351.13 *drink*, 874.8 *get drunk*
topectomy 60 Surgical Operations
topee 293.12 *protective covering*, 634.2 *shelter*
Topeka 93 Cities
toper 351.12 *drinker*, 870.5 *self-indulgent person*, 874.17 *drunkard*
to perfection 619.7 *perfectly*, 865.11 *innocently*
top-flight 126.15 *excellent*, 611.6 *notable*, 617.1 *worthy*, 655.6 *skilful*
top floor 275.8 *high thing*, 279.3 *architectural summit*
topgallant 74 Sails, 279.2 *head*
topgallant mast 275.8 *high thing*, 279.2 *head*
topgallant sail 279.2 *head*
top gear 71 Motor Vehicle Parts
top gun 670.19 *attacker*
top hat 295.15 *headgear*
top-heaviness 123.1 *inequality*
top-heavy 123.1 *unequal*, 259.16 *fat*, 369.3 *ponderous*, 633.2 *unsafe*, 656.3 *clumsy*
Tophet 8.11 *heaven*
top-hole 617.2 *best*, 861.1 *good*
topiarist 69.13 *horticulturist*
topiary 42 Hobbies and Pastimes, 69.3 *ornamental garden*
topic 472, 226.6 *undertaking*, 472.2 *issue*, 472.4 *sphere*, 473.3 *line of argument*, 473.4 *gist*, 518.1 *supposition*, 520.1 *meaning*
Topic 472
topical 472, 196.6 *present*, 201.10 *new*, 257.12 *itemized*, 473.10 *arguable*, 518.8 *supposed*

topical administration 62.13 *administration*
topicality 196.4 *up-to-dateness*, 201.1 *newness*
topically 472, 201.21 *newly*, 257.15 *thematically*, 473.18 *arguably*
topic for discussion 472.3 *matter of interest*
topics 257.5 *divisions*
to pieces 141
toping 351.1 *drinking*, 874.5 *drunken*
topknot 279.2 *head*
top layer 279
to please oneself 689.8 *anarchically*
topless 294.8 *uncovered*, 296.10 *in dishabille*, 296.11 *exposed*
topless dancer 294.4 *exposer*, 296.8 *nude person*
topless dress 295.7 *frock*
toplessness 296.1 *undress*
topless waitress 296.8 *nude person*
top-level 611.5 *important*, 653.17 *managerial*, 655.6 *skilful*
top-level meeting 653.7 *council*
top man 688.10 *person of authority*
top marks 861.9 *the best*
topmast 74 Rigging, 275.8 *high thing*, 279.2 *head*
top minnow 80 Fishes
topmost 95.7 *mountainous*, 126.14 *best*, 275.10 *higher*, 279.5 *top*, 611.5 *important*
topnotch 126.14 *best*, 617.1 *worthy*, 617.2 *best*, 655.6 *skilful*, 861.1 *good*
topnotcher 617.8 *exceller*, 861.16 *superior person*
top off 144.6 *fill*, 279.7 *top*, 684.6 *elaborate*
top of the bill 51.6 *scene*, 51.39 *stagestruck*
top of the class 682.4 *successful person*
top of the division 682.15 *victorious*
top of the inning 22.1 *baseball*
top of the league 682.15 *victorious*
top of the milk 351.5 *milk*, 395.8 *fat*
top of the pops 617.8 *exceller*
top of the pyramid 126.4 *summit*
top of the tree 154.2 *priority*
top of the world 279.1 *summit*
topographer 268.9 *measurer*
topographic 54.50 *terrestrial*, 249.16 *regional*, 268.12 *metrical*, 275.14 *altimetric*
topographical 250.8 *locational*, 251.7 *situational*
topographically 250, 54.66, 251.11 *geographically*, 268.17 *measurably*
topographic poetry 48.6 *poetry*
topographic surveying 63.17 *civil engineering*
topography 250, 54.6 *continent*, 251.1 *situation*, 268.1 *measurement*, 275.5 *height measure*
topological 52.68 *mathematical*
topology 52
top oneself 398.21 *commit suicide*
toponym 560.8 *name*
toponymy 560.7 *nomenclature*
topophobia 777 Phobias by Name
top out 279.7 *top*, 684.6 *elaborate*
topped 279, 293.36 *covered*
topped off 144.8 *full*
topped up 144.8 *full*, 257.11 *loaded*
top people 126.7 *the best people*, 617.7 *elite*
topper 68.10 *farm tool*, 295.11 *jacket*, 295.15 *headgear*
top person 611.4 *bigwig*

topping 43 Architectural Decoration, 85.6 *tree management*, 95.7 *mountainous*, 275.9 *high*, 279.4 *top layer*, 293.1 *covering*, 293.3 *coating*, 617.1 *worthy*
topping lift 36.3 *parts of a sailing boat*
topping-out ceremony 144.3 *completion*
topping-up 606.1 *provision*
topple 244.9 *demolish*, 360.11 *trip*, 362.3 *bring down*, 362.7 *lean*
topple a government 689.4 *be anarchic*
toppled 362.22 *overthrown*
topple over 360.11 *trip*
toppling 123.3 *unequal*, 362.12 *downthrow*, 362.20 *falling*
top pocket 24.3 *English billiards*, 24.5 *snooker*
top priority 154.2 *priority*
top-rank 611.6 *notable*
top-ranked 126.14 *best*
top-ranking 126.14 *best*
top rope 34.9 *mountaineer*
top roping 34.3 *climbing technique*
top rung of the ladder 126.4 *summit*
tops 617.2 *best*, 861.9 *the best*
topsail 74 Sails, 279.2 *head*
top-secret 527.2 *concealed*, 529.9 *secret*, 611.5 *important*, 709.6 *censored*
top-secret clearance 708.1 *permission*
top-secret document 527.8 *concealment*, 709.2 *censorship*
top-secret file 529.1 *secrecy*
top seed 617.8 *exceller*, 655.4 *skilled person*, 660.11 *contender*
top selection 655.4 *skilled person*
top set 802.2 *aristocracy*
top shell 81 Molluscs
topside 45.22 *beef*, 279.4 *top layer*
top side 305.2 *surface*
topsoil 54.36 *soil*, 266.1 *layer*, 279.4 *top layer*, 293.2 *cover*
top speed 329.8 *speed*
top storey 279.3 *architectural summit*
top surface 279.4 *top layer*
topsy-turviness 151.4 *litter*
topsy-turvy 113.11 *irregularly*, 133.12 *mixed*, 151.4 *litter*, 151.18 *muddled*, 151.28 *anyhow*, 287.2 *inverted*, 287.4 *inversely*
topsy-turvydom 133.3 *miscellany*
top-ten 611.6 *notable*
top the charts 682.6 *be successful*
top twenty 49.9 *popular music*
top up 144.6 *fill*, 257.7 *stuff*, 605.6 *store*, 606.6 *replenish*, 608.4 *suffice*
to put it another way 524.18 *in other words*
to put it succinctly 552.5 *concisely*
toque 295.15 *headgear*
tor 95.1, 275.3 *mountain*
Torah 7.12 *religious text*
Torah scrolls 10.14 *sacred object*
torbernite 54 Minerals
torch 34.4 *climbing equipment*, 408.6 *fire*, 408.15 *burn*, 410.2 *lighter*, 439.7 *lantern*
torchbearer 594.15 *preparer*
torchlight 439.7 *lantern*
torchlit 439.18 *lit*
torch singer 49.23 *singer*
torch song 49.9 *popular music*, 433.2 *song*
Torddu 68 Breeds of Sheep
toreador 398.13 *animal killer*, 679.3 *athlete*
toreador pants 295.9 *trousers*
toreutic 50.25 *sculptural*
tori 26.7 *judo*, 26.10 *aikido*
toric 52.83 *spherical*
Toric 32 Breeds of Horse and Pony
toric lens 56.29 *optical element*
Tories 12.6 *political party*

torment 832, 406.1 *pain*, 406.11 *inflict pain*, 618.13 *be worthless*, 618.14 *ill-treat*, 631.4 *strain*, 631.14 *afflict*, 690.6 *suppress*, 770.1 *sorrow*, 777.14 *worry*, 785.7 *cause dislike*, 828.9 *offend*, 862.11 *be evil*, 879.4 *torture*
tormented 406.7 *feeling pain*, 770.5 *sad*, 777.9 *worried*
tormentil 84 Flowers and Flowering Plants
tormenting 406.8 *inflicting pain*
tormentor 51.17 *stage set*, 631.13 *oppressor*
torn 136.15 *separate*, 252.9 *removed*, 265.7 *cracked*, 322.12 *open*, 379.1 *brittle*, 406.6 *injured*, 820.8 *estranged*
tornadic 364.12 *rotary*
tornado 55.16 *wind vortex*, 241.5 *violent weather*, 314.3 *convoluted thing*, 364.4 *vortex*, 375.9 *broken water*, 635.1 *trap*
Tornado class 36.2 *sailing boat*
tornado watch 55.4 *weather forecast*
tornaria 81.13 *invertebrate larva*
Tornarsuk 8 Deities
toroid 52.45 *curved surface*
toroidal 52.83 *spherical*
Toronto 93 Cities, 93.6 *other cities*
torpedo 72.2 *track*, 244.11 *ruin*, 338.8 *missile*, 338.31 *snipe*, 362.3 *bring down*, 670.2 *fire*, 679.26 *naval mine*, 680.5 *missile weapon*, 680.16 *bomb*
torpedo boat 74 Ships and Boats, 679.24 *warship*, 680.5 *missile weapon*
torpedoed 244.15 *destroyed*
torpedo fish 80 Fishes
torpid 99.16 *vegetating*, 240.5 *inert*, 643.3 *not participating*, 643.4 *not awake*, 761.2 *desensitized*
torpidity 240.1 *inertness*
torpor 99.9 *mere existence*, 240.1 *inertness*, 325.1 *motionlessness*, 404.2 *unconsciousness*, 643.7 *idleness*, 761.4 *desensitization*
Torquay 93 Cities
torque 56.10 *force*, 335.17 *torsion*, 364.2 *turning*, 792.6 *jewellery*
torque wrench 603.1 *tool*
torr 75 Scientific and Technical Units
torrefy 392.19 *bake*
Torrens 94 Lakes
torrent 96.6 *river flow*, 329.11 *swift thing*
torrential 55.53 *rainy*, 96.10 *fluvial*
torrentially 96.13 *fluently*
torrential rain 55.23 *rain*
Torricelli 52 Scientists
torrid 55.51 *hot*, 408.12 *warm-hearted*
torse 544.8 *heraldic device*
torsion 335, 56.10 *force*, 63.16 *deformation*, 309.1 *distortion*, 364.2 *turning*
torsional 364.12 *rotary*
torsional strength 237.1 *strength*
torsional wave 56.12 *wave*
torsion balance 56.86 *weighing instrument*
torsion scale 369.10 *scales*
torso 50.12 *sculpture*, 132.1 *remainder*, 143.6 *branch*, 547.6 *image*
tort 16.39 *crime*, 844.7 *sense of wrong*, 866.3 *sin*
torte 45.36 *cake*
Tortelier 49 Musicians and Composers
tortelli 45 Types of Pasta
tortellini 45 Types of Pasta
tortiglioni 45 Types of Pasta
tortilla 45.50 *Central American dish*
tortious 16.58 *unjust*
tortoise 79 Reptiles, 79.4 *chelonian*, 328.14 *slow creature*, 328.15 *slow person*

tortoise beetle 82 Insects
tortoise racing 674.4 *race*
tortoiseshell 77 Breeds of Cats, 456.5 *variegated thing*, 456.8 *checked*
tortoiseshell and white 77 Breeds of Cats
tortoiseshell butterfly 82 Insects, 456.5 *variegated thing*
tortoiseshell cat 456.5 *variegated thing*
tortoiseshell inlay 47.9 *decorative woodwork*
tortoiseshell-pointed Siamese 77 Breeds of Cats
tortoise's pace 328.10 *slow motion*
tortuous 314.4 *convolutional*, 474.7 *sophistic*, 551.2 *obscure*, 557.4 *ornate*, 559.9 *inelegant*
tortuously 314.8 *circularly*, 551.4 *obscurely*
tortuousness 551.1 *obscurity*, 557.2 *affectation*
torture 879, 241.2 *physical violence*, 241.8 *use violence*, 406.1 *pain*, 406.11 *inflict pain*, 477.18 *interrogate*, 618.14 *ill-treat*, 670.9 *attack successfully*, 690.2 *suppression*, 690.6 *suppress*, 695.3 *coercive methods*, 832.7 *act of malevolence*, 832.18 *torment*, 879.12 *corporal punishment*
torture chamber 879.15 *instrument of torture*
tortured 406.7 *feeling pain*, 690.9 *suppressed*, 879.20 *punished*
torture oneself 866.9 *appear guilty*
torturer 631.13 *oppressor*, 695.4 *coercive person*, 832.8 *malefactor*, 879.17 *punisher*
torture the law 16.73 *be illegal*
torturing 406.8 *inflicting pain*
torturous 832.11 *cruel*, 879.21 *punishing*
to rule 166
torus 43 Architectural Decoration, 52.45 *curved surface*, 52.47 *topology*
Torwen 68 Breeds of Sheep
Tory 12.6 *political party*, 217.3 *conservative person*, 665.6 *political party member*
to satisfaction 851.26 *approvably*
to scale 107.10 *relevantly*
Toscanini 49 Musicians and Composers
tosh 506.1 *nonsense*, 521.4 *senseless talk*
to shreds 136.21 *apart*
Tosks 1 Peoples
to smithereens 136.21 *apart*, 141.7 *to pieces*
to some degree 121.11 *to a degree*
to some extent 107.10 *relevantly*, 121.11 *to a degree*, 143.12 *partly*, 242.9 *moderately*
to some purpose 682.16 *successfully*
to spare 132.10 *surplus*
toss 97.10 *billow*, 330.4, 338.5 *throw*, 338.23 *throw*, 360.12 *drop*, 366.11 *stagger*
toss a coin 229.4 *chance*
toss and tumble 366.25 *pitch*
toss and turn 366.21 *be agitated*, 366.25 *pitch*
tossed salad 45.14 *salad*
tosser 338.14 *thrower*
toss in a blanket 879.1 *punish*
tossing 74.11 *nautical*, 365.16 *rocking*, 642.18 *active*
tossing and turning 224.14 *irresolute*, 366.5 *restlessness*
tossing in a blanket 879.7 *punishment*
toss off one's glass 351.13 *drink*
toss of the coin 229.2 *chance*
toss out 349.1 *eject*
tosspot 874.17 *drunkard*
toss up 229.4 *chance*
toss-up 229.2 *chance*, 229.6 *motiveless*, 589.3 *equal chance*

tostada 45.50 *Central American dish*
to such an extent 120.7 *quantitatively*
to summarize 270.12 *short*
to sum up 552.5 *concisely*
tot 260.4 *little person*
total 120, 169, 170, 52.15 *addition*, 120.6 *quantitative*, 130.2 *mathematical addition*, 130.6 *add*, 142.2 *whole thing*, 142.6 *whole*, 142.9 *be whole*, 144.7 *complete*, 169.4 *mathematical result*, 478.7 *numerical result*, 478.20 *solve*, 619.1 *perfect*, 684.7 *completed*
total abstinence 869.1 *self-restraint*
total blank 512.2 *blankness*
total commitment 574.13 *concentration*, 575.2 *commitment*
total deafness 42.1 *deafness*
total defeat 683.2 *defeat*
total destruction 676.1 *war*
total eclipse 440.1 *darkness*
total exhaustion 650.7 *fatigue*
total immersion 10.5 *Christian rite*
total internal reflection 56.29 *optical element*
totalitarian 12.9 *governmental*, 400.13 *national*, 688.14 *governmental*, 690.8 *severe*
totalitarian dictatorship 12.1 *government*
totalitarianism 12.1 *government*, 112.4 *monotony*, 400.11 *nation*, 688.7 *type of rule*, 690.2 *suppression*
totalitarian state 400.11 *nation*
totality 53.3 *universe*, 120.4 *total*, 142.1 *whole*, 142.2 *whole thing*, 144.1 *completeness*, 684.1 *completion*
totalizator 32.7 *horseracing*
totalize 170.9 *add*
totalizer 170.5 *computer*
totalling 130.2 *mathematical addition*, 170.3 *count*
total loss 244.4 *ruin*, 722.1 *loss*
totally 120.7 *quantitatively*, 142.11 *wholly*, 144.9, 619.8 *completely*, 621.20 *clean*, 684.9 *completely*
totally deaf 421.4 *deaf*
total recall 511.1 *memory*
total serialism 434.4 *atonality*
total silence 422.4 *silence*
total situation 106.1 *circumstances*
total sum 142.2 *whole thing*
total theatre 51.8 *theatre movements*
total trust 464.1 *incuriousness*
total up 130.6 *add*
total war 676.1 *war*
totara 85 Trees and Shrubs
to tatters 136.21 *apart*
tote 32.7 *horseracing*, 326.12 *transport*
tote bag 258.8 *bag*
to tell the truth 537.35 *truly*, 857.7 *honourably*
totem 8.5 *deity*, 10.14 *sacred object*, 11.6 *talisman*
totem dance 46.4 *historic dancing*
totemic 9.10 *idolatrous*, 11.15 *witchlike*
totemism 9.2 *idolatry*, 11.3 *witchcraft*
Totemism 7 Non-Christian Religions
totemist 9.6 *idolater*
totemistic 9.10 *idolatrous*, 10.21 *ritualistic*, 11.15 *witchlike*
totemize 9.8 *idolatrize*
totem pole 10.14 *sacred object*
tote up 130.6 *add*, 169.10 *number*
to that place 250.12 *where*
to the amount of 751.16 *at a price*
to the bitter end 144.10 *fully*, 157.27 *to the end*, 188.10 *for the duration*, 575.13 *persistently*
to the boiling point 408.17 *warmly*

to the brim 144.10 *fully*, 257.14 *internally*
to the contrary 484, 536.16 *no*
to the core 144.10 *fully*, 257.14 *internally*
to the effect that 520.13 *meaningfully*
to the end 157, 144.10 *fully*, 188.10 *for the duration*, 684.9 *completely*
to the end of the chapter 144.10 *fully*
to the end of the line 144.10 *fully*
to the end of the road 144.10 *fully*, 157.27 *to the end*
to the ends of the earth 248.19 *to all places*, 263.10 *distantly*
to the fore 303.11 *in front*
to the four corners of the earth 162.31 *everywhere*
to the four winds 162.31 *everywhere*, 248.19 *to all places*
to the full 144.10 *fully*, 608.9 *enough*, 684.9 *completely*, 757.9 *extravagantly*
to the good 662.36 *helpfully*
to the ground 362.24 *down*
to the heart 144.10 *fully*
to the highest degree 126.17 *supremely*
to the last breath 144.10 *fully*
to the last gasp 157.27 *to the end*
to the last man 144.10 *fully*, 575.13 *persistently*
to the letter 118.14 *imitatively*, 537.38 *literally*, 619.7 *perfectly*, 719.8 *observantly*
to the life 118.14 *imitatively*
to the limit 684.9 *completely*
to the marrow 144.10 *fully*
to the maximum 144.10 *fully*
to the minute 208.17 *early*
to the nth degree 503.8 *accurately*
to the point 381.12 *bluntly*, 471.21 *purposively*, 472.14 *thematically*, 552.3 *concise*, 552.5 *concisely*, 611.5 *important*
to the purpose 615.1 *convenient*
to the quick 406.13 *painfully*
to the rear 304.9 *in the rear*
to the rescue! 639
to the same degree 122.12 *equally*
to the second 208.17 *early*
to the side 305.10 *laterally*
to the top 144.10 *fully*, 257.14 *internally*
to the top of one's bent 144.10 *fully*
to the touch 383.15 *texturally*
to the tune of 120.7 *quantitatively*, 751.16 *at a price*
to the utmost 144.10 *fully*
to the wonder of all 786.13 *wonderfully*
totombito 49 Musical Instruments
totter 139.6 *come unstuck*, 224.11 *be changeable*, 238.6 *be weak*, 360.11 *trip*, 365.11 *rock*, 366.11 *stagger*, 366.25 *pitch*, 628.1 *deteriorate*, 633.8 *be in danger*
totter along 328.1 *move slowly*
tottering 224.13 *changeable*, 238.8 *weak*, 328.4 *slow*, 360.16 *descending*, 576.4 *unsteady*, 628.12 *deteriorated*, 633.2 *unsafe*
tottery 238.8 *weak*, 628.13 *dilapidated*
tot up 130.6 *add*, 169.10 *number*, 170.9 *add*
tot up to 170.10 *total*
toucan 78 Birds
Toucan 53 The Constellations
touch 777 Phobias by Topic, **407, 407**, 28.3 *fencing movements*, 28.5 *fence*, 35.1, 35.6 *rugger*, 107.7 *relate to*, 133.4 *admixture*, 135.1 *union*, 165.3 *characteristic*, 267.1 *juxtaposition*, 267.2 *meeting*, 267.3 *juxtapose*, 278.6 *be shallow*, 298.4 *interface*, 330.6 *tap*, 330.13 *blow*,

383.1 *texture*, 396.4 *biological function*, 403.1 *sensation*, 403.11 *sense*, 407.12 *abut*, 501.2 *information*, 542.6 *suggestion*, 543.3 *gesture*, 599.1 *use*, 628.4 *impair*, 642.17 *meddle*, 655.1 *skill*, 835.11 *excite pity*
Touch 407
touchable 407
touch and go 122.2 *equilibrium*, 224.13 *changeable*, 633.2 *unsafe*
touch a raw nerve 403.13 *arouse sensation*, 406.11 *inflict pain*
touch a sore point 407.12 *abut*
touchback 19.12 *special team*
touch bottom 277.14 *deepen*, 360.10 *droop*, 684.4 *complete*
touch depth 360.10 *droop*
touchdown 19.6 *scoring*, 73.5 *flight*, 344.11 *landing*, 360.5 *dive*, 682.3 *successful thing*
touch down 35.3 *rugby play*, 344.4 *land*, 360.12 *drop*
touched 510.11 *insane*
touched up 201.14 *renewed*, 627.14 *improved*, 791.14 *beautified*
touched-up 540.35 *disguised*, 541.12 *exaggerated*
toucher 407, 25.2 *grip*, 407.7 *sense organ*
touch football 19.1 *football*
touchily 829.9 *irascibly*, 830.14 *irritably*
touchiness 403.2 *ability to sense*, 760.6 *oversensitivity*, 805.2 *unapproachability*, 829.1 *irascibility*, 830.3 *irritableness*
touching 407, 407, 107.10 *relevantly*, 135.1 *union*, 267.1 *juxtaposition*, 267.5 *juxtaposed*, 615.2 *nearby*, 733.1 *borrowing*, 734.1 *taking*, 759.14 *emotive*, 835.7 *pitiful*
touching a sailor 517.6 *good-luck sign*
touching ball 24.2 *billiards play*
touchingly 759.20 *with feeling*
touch-in-goal line 35.1 *rugger*
touching one's cap 817.4 *deference*
touching up 50.2 *painting*, 541.1 *exaggeration*
touching-up 540.12 *facade*
touch line 35.1 *rugger*
touchline 38.1 *soccer*
touch-me-not 84 Flowers and Flowering Plants
touch off 226.10 *awaken*, 410.11 *fuel*
touch of frost 55.36 *frost*
touch one's cap 817.13 *defer to*
touch one's forelock 817.13 *defer to*
touch-operated 407.10 *handed*
touchpaper 410.2 *lighter*
touch rock bottom 127.11 *become inferior*
touch-sensitive 407.8 *touchable*
touch someone 733.7 *borrow*
touchstone 268.7 *standard*
touch the surface 278.6 *be shallow*
touch up 50.19 *paint*, 201.20 *make new*, 407.11 *touch*, 540.24 *mask*, 541.7 *exaggerate*, 627.1 *improve*, 629.2 *refurbish*, 734.7 *take*
touch-up 540.12 *facade*
touch upon 107.7 *relate to*
touch wood 775.9 *be hopeful*
touchy 403.7 *susceptible*, 759.13 *passionate*, 760.2 *oversensitive*, 805.15 *unapproachable*, 829.4 *irascible*, 830.7 *irritable*
tough 373, 378, 225.11 *determined*, 237.9 *physically strong*, 237.11 *strong in spirit*, 237.13 *strengthened*, 241.4 *violent person or animal*, 373.4 *mentally hard*, 394.8 *viscous*, 477.13 *problematic*, 595.6 *uncooked*, 650.4 *fatiguing*, 659.10 *difficult*, 659.12 *problematic*, 669.11 *obstinate*, 676.16 *warlike*, 679.1 *combatant*, 679.33 *combative*, 690.8 *severe*, 761.1

insensitive, 778.9 *courageous*, 832.8 *malefactor*, 832.12 *callous*, 836.4 *pitiless*
tough as leather 378.3 *hard*
tough as nails 378.3 *hard*
tough as old boots 373.4 *mentally hard*, 378.3 *hard*
tough assignment 659.3 *difficult task*
tough as steel 574.3 *strong-willed*
tough decision 580.8 *choice*
toughen 203.7 *season*, 237.8 *strengthen*, 373.9 *harden*, 378.10 *be tough*
toughened 378, 203.15 *seasoned*, 237.13 *strengthened*, 373.3 *hardened*
toughened glass 442.9 *glass*, 632.4 *safety device*
toughening 237.4 *strengthening*, 373.5 *hardness*
tough guy 237.6 *muscleman*, 241.4 *violent person or animal*
tough lineup to buck 659.3 *difficult task*
tough luck 589.2 *luck*
toughly 373, 378, 225.13 *determinedly*, 669.14 *resistingly*, 690.11 *severely*, 836.7 *pitilessly*
toughness 378, 225.2 *determination*, 237.1 *strength*, 371.1 *density*, 373.5 *hardness*, 373.8 *mental hardness*, 394.1 *viscosity*, 577.6 *determination*, 659.1 *difficulty*, 669.2 *obstinacy*, 690.1 *severity*, 778.1 *courage*
Toughness 378
tough nut to crack 477.4 *difficult question*
tough proposition 659.3 *difficult task*
tough something out 378.10 *be tough*
tough thing 378
tough time 687.4 *time of adversity*
Toulon 93 Cities
Toulouse 68 Breeds of Fowl, **93** Cities
Tou Mu 8 Deities
toupé 791.10 *wig*
toupee 295.15 *headgear*
tour 51.13 *engagement*, 187.4 *period of activity*, 334.1 *circuit*, 363.3 *orbit*
touraco 78 Birds
Tour de France 674.4 *race*
tourer 71 Motor Vehicles, 71.16 *car*
touring 41.1 *skiing*, 41.2 *cross-country skiing*, 41.12 *ski*
touring company 51.23 *cast*
touring ski 41.2 *cross-country skiing*, 41.5 *ski equipment*
tourist 224.7 *person who moves around*, 293.22 *progression*, 435.11 *observer*, 465.3 *curious person*
tourist-class 754.9 *cheap*
tourist fare 754.4 *bargain*
tourist route 363.5 *ringroad*
tourist season 203.1 *season*
tourmaline 54 Minerals
tournament 18.1 *sport*, 674.2 *contest*, 674.9 *duel*, 811.14 *show*, 813.3 *formal occasion*
tournament casting 20.1 *angling*
Tournefort 52 Scientists
Tourneur 48 Dramatists
tourney 674.9 *duel*
tourniquet 137.6 *line*, 262.4 *contractor*, 323.2 *stopper*, 630.10 *surgical dressing*
tour of duty 185.3 *duration*, 187.4 *period of activity*
Tours 93 Cities
tours en l'air 46.9 *ballet steps*
to us 351.18 *cheers*
tousle 151.24 *make disordered*, 375.12 *make rough*
tousled 151.15 *untidy*
tout 532.10 *publicizer*, 532.16 *publicize*, 712.6 *request*, 739.1 *sell*, 739.12 *wholesaler*
tovarisch 12.6 *political party*, 401.3 *male title of address*

tow 71.21 *miscellaneous motoring terms*, 339.2, 339.11 *pull*, 383.6 *fibre*
towage 339.1 *traction*
to war 676
towards 327.17 *via*
towbar 71 Motor Vehicle Parts
towboat 74 Ships and Boats
towed 70.5 *transportable*
towed log 74.5 *navigation*
towel 392.15 *dryer*, 392.20 *absorb*, 621.11 *cleaning cloth*
towelling 67 Natural Fabrics, 288.4 *textile*, 392.15 *dryer*
tower 95, 43.3 *building*, 63.27 *superstructure*, 225.4 *stable thing*, 243.8 *construction*, 259.19 *be big*, 275.6 *tall thing*, 275.15 *be high*, 339.6 *towline*, 359.20 *hover*, 382.6 *construction*, 634.1 *refuge*, 671.12 *fort*
tower above 95.9 *tower*, 126.8 *be superior*, 275.15 *be high*
tower block 63.20 *building*, 256.6 *apartment block*, 275.6 *tall thing*
tower crane 63.29 *construction equipment*
towering 95.7 *mountainous*, 259.15 *big*, 275.9 *high*
towering inferno 408.6 *fire*
toweringly 275.19 *high*
Tower of Babel 133.3 *miscellany*
Tower of London 43 Noted Buildings
Tower of Pisa 278.2 *oblique line*
Tower of Silence 399.6 *grave*
tower of strength 225.5 *stable person*, 237.6 *muscleman*, 284.8 *supporter*, 535.9 *affirmer*, 632.2 *protection*, 634.1 *refuge*, 662.13 *supporter*
tower over 233.10 *be a prevailing influence*
tow-haired 452.3 *yellow-haired*
towhead 452.6 *yellowness*
tow-headed 439.21 *light*, 446.3 *white-haired*
towhee 78 Birds
to whose advantage? 613.12 *usefully*
towing 70.5 *transportable*, 339.1 *traction*, 339.8 *tractional*
to wit 165.31 *namely*, 524.18 *in other words*
towline 339, 137.6 *line*
town 93, 92.4 *community*, 93.1 *city*, 93.14 *urban*, 249.11 *settlement*
town centre 291.4 *centre of activity*
town council 16.2 *jurisdiction*, 653.8 *British administrative council*, 653.9 *US administrative council*, 706.2 *representative body*
town crier 423.5 *loud person*, 431.9 *crier*
town dump 727.5 *wasteyard*
towndweller 255.4 *townsman*
townee 93.11 *urbanite*, 255.4 *townsman*
Townes 52 Scientists
town gas 410.3 *gas*
town hall 93.13 *municipal building*
townhall clock 84 Flowers and Flowering Plants
town-hall meeting 532.7 *publicity*
town house 43.3 *building*, 256.5 *house*
town meeting 706.2 *representative body*, 724.1 *joint possession*
town plan 299.4, 547.7 *map*, 592.5 *map*
town-planner 592.8 *planner*
Towns 93
townscape 50.10 *art subject*, 435.7 *view*
townsfolk 255.4 *townsman*
township 92.1 *administrative area*, 92.4 *community*, 93.9 *town*, 249.11 *settlement*
township jazz 49.10 *world music*
township jive 49.10 *world music*
townsman 255, 93.11 *urbanite*
townspeople 255.4 *townsman*

townsperson 255.4 *townsman*
townswoman 255.4 *townsman*
town wall 671.11 *fortification*
towny 256.15 *environmental*
to wonder at 786.8 *wonderful*
towpath 327.6 *path*
towrope 137.6 *line*, 339.6 *towline*
Towyn 93 Cities
toxaemia 624.6 *infection*, 631.7 *poisoning*
toxic 626, 398.23 *deadly*, 415.6 *unpalatable*, 618.5 *harmful*, 622.8 *unclean*, 624.23 *diseased*, 631.16 *blighting*, 633.1 *dangerous*, 862.9 *detrimental*
toxicity 618.11 *harmfulness*, 624.6 *infection*, 631.7 *poisoning*
toxicologist 60.13 *medical specialist*
toxicology 60.3 *medical specialty*, 631.11 *intoxicant*
toxin 624.6 *infection*, 631.8 *poison*
toxiphobia 777 Phobias by Name
toxocariasis 81.11 *helminthic disease*, 624.6 *infection*
toxophilite 338.16 *archer*
toxophily 338.6 *shooting*
toxoplasma 81.10 *parasite*
toxoplasmosis 81.12 *protozoal disease*
toy 260.2 *little thing*, 539.22 *dupe*, 612.4 *trivial*, 612.9 *bauble*, 754.5 *cheap item*, 821.26, 826.8 *court*
toy boy 401.4 *boyfriend*, 808.3 *sycophant*
toy dog 77.9 *dog*
toy gun 338.9 *firearm*
toying 821.6 *courtship*, 826.9 *endearing*
toying with one's food 350.3 *delicate eating*
toy theatre 51.14 *theatre*
toy with 407.11 *touch*
toy with one's food 350.23 *taste*
trabeculectomy 60 Surgical Operations
trace 50.20 *draw*, 132.1 *remainder*, 227.2 *visible effect*, 299.5 *outline*, 542.6 *suggestion*, 545.12 *vestige*, 547.11 *paint*, 560.17 *describe a circle*, 792.10 *decorate*
trace back 3.21 *antiquarianize*, 200.15 *look back*, 221.8 *return*
traced 50.27 *painted*
trace element 58.15 *essential element*
trace horse 32.2 *thoroughbred*
trace program 65.9 *programming language*
tracer 670.13 *air attack*
tracery 43 Architectural Decoration, 288.2 *braid*
traces 137.9 *yoke*, 543.1 *sign*
trachea 390.8 *respiration*
tracheitis 624.9 *respiratory disease*
tracheostomy 60 Surgical Operations
tracheotomy 60 Surgical Operations
trachoma 436.1 *blindness*, 624.7 *tropical disease*
trachyte 54 Common Rocks
tracing 50.3, 50.9 *drawing*, 118.5 *duplicate*, 299.1 *outline*, 547.2 *reproduction*, 560.9 *representation*
tracing paper 604.3 *paper*
track 21, 72, 18.2 *sportsground*, 33.6 *motor racing terms*, 37.7 *shoot*, 55.21 *thunderstorm*, 132.1 *remainder*, 137.6 *road*, 163.6 *students*, 180.16 *attend*, 321.6 *furrow*, 327.2 *route*, 327.6 *path*, 327.10 *railway*, 332.2 *bearing*, 356.2 *passing along*, 483.4 *indication*, 543.1 *sign*, 545.12 *vestige*, 590.9 *follow*, 674.3 *stadium*, 674.5 *racecourse*
track and field 21.6 *track*
track down 250.11 *find*, 496.2 *detect*

tracked down 250.7 *found*
tracker 37.4, 590.6 *hunter*
tracker dog 77.9 *dog*
track event 674.2 *contest*
track events 21
tracking 37.2 *hunting*, 37.8 *shooting*, 590.1 *pursuit*
tracking device 332.3 *orientation*
tracking down 250.3 *locating*, 496.7 *detection*
tracking station 53.32 *satellite*
tracklayer 71 Motor Vehicles
trackman 72.9 *railway worker*
trackmarks 875.1 *drug-taking*
track record 3.5 *chronicle*, 652.1 *conduct*
track rod 71 Motor Vehicle Parts
tracks 327.10 *railway*, 875.1 *drug-taking*
tracksuit 21.4 *sports equipment*, 30.2 *gymnastic clothing*, 295.4 *informal dress*, 295.10 *suit*
tracksuits 814.6 *informal dress*
tract 248.1 *space*, 248.3 *geographical space*, 249.12 *plot*, 472.5 *educational topic*, 561.1 *dissertation*, 725.1 *property*
tractability 228.6 *suggestibility*, 374.8 *softness*, 572.8 *acquiescence*, 586.7 *persuadability*, 694.1 *obedience*
tractable 167.13 *compliant*, 228.13 *suggestible*, 374.2 *pliant*, 572.3 *amenable*, 586.20 *persuadable*, 660.12 *wieldy*, 660.13 *easygoing*, 673.5 *submitting*, 694.7 *obedient*, 847.9 *loyal*
tractably 228.14 *influentially*, 694.10 *obediently*
Tractarianism 7 Christian Movements
tractate 561.1 *dissertation*
tractile 374.2 *pliant*
traction 339, 71.21 *miscellaneous motoring terms*, 235.4 *energy*
Traction 339
tractional 339
traction engine 339.6 *towline*
traction unit 72.5 *locomotive part*
tractive 339.8 *tractional*
tractor 71 Motor Vehicles, 68.10 *farm tool*, 71.20 *truck*
tractor 339.6 *towline*
tractor driver 68.16 *farm worker*
tractor shed 68.7 *farm building*
trad 49.8, 49.33 *jazz*
trade 737, 737, 109.7 *reciprocate*, 135.1 *union*, 165.8 *specialization*, 216.4, 216.10 *exchange*, 223.1, 223.5 *exchange*, 326.1 *transfer*, 346.4 *right of entry*, 606.5 *provision*, 644.3 *job*, 728.1 *transfer of property*, 728.3 *transfer property*, 739.1 *sell*, 739.3 *selling*, 746.6 *pay*
Trade 737
tradeable 216.14 *exchangeable*
trade agreement 13.5 *international trade*, 715.3 *alliance*, 737.9 *bargaining*
trade barrier 13.6 *economic factors*, 737.5 *commercial trade*
trade book 532.6 *book publishing*
traded 223.7 *exchanged*
trade delegation 706.2 *representative body*
trade fair 740.2 *fair*
trade gap 745.2 *national debt*
trade in 737.1 *trade*
trade integration 13.5 *international trade*
trade journal 532.5 *journal*
trade language 5.7 *international language*
trademark 44.4 *porcelain mark*, 119.7 *originate*, 165.3 *characteristic*, 543.1 *sign*, 544.3 *means of identification*, 560.8 *name*
trademarked 119.6 *authentic*, 544.12 *identified*
trademarked product 119.2 *original*
tradename 544.3 *means of identification*, 560.8 *name*
trade off 109.7 *reciprocate*, 223.5 *exchange*, 737.1 *trade*

trade-off 109.1 *interchange*, 109.4 *reciprocal*, 122.3 *equalization*, 223.1 *exchange*, 242.1 *moderation*, 716.1 *negotiation*, 716.8 *negotiated*, 717.1 *compromise*, 728.1 *transfer of property*, 737.4 *trade*
trade on 599.3 *exploit*
trade organ 532.5 *journal*
trade paper 532.5 *journal*
trade plate 71.21 *miscellaneous motoring terms*
trader 737, 13.9 *economist*, 224.4 *editor*, 230.5 *operator*, 739.13 *retailer*
trade restriction 737.5 *commercial trade*
tradescantia 84 Flowers and Flowering Plants
trade show 740.2 *fair*
trade sign 544.3 *means of identification*
tradesman 646.2 *artisan*, 739.13 *retailer*
tradesman's entrance 304.1 *rear*, 327.2 *route*
Trades Union Congress 13.8 *industrial relations*
trade supplement 532.4 *newspaper*
trade tariff 632.2 *protection*
trade union 13.8 *industrial relations*, 15.3 *organized labour*, 161.15 *association*, 665.1 *party*, 737.5 *commercial trade*
trade unionist 13.9 *economist*, 646.1 *worker*, 737.11 *chamber of commerce member*
trade union official 15.7 *employee*
trade war 676.1 *war*
trade winds 55.17 *wind system*
trade with 13, 737.1 *trade*
trading 13.2 *economy*, 737.4 *trade*, 737.13 *mercantile*, 739.3 *selling*
trading centre 740.7 *emporium*
trading company 740.8 *store*
trading deficit 745.2 *national debt*
trading house 740.8 *store*
trading post 740.7 *emporium*
trading ring 302.2 *limiting factor*
tradition 1, 202, 584, 3.7 *narrative*, 116.6 *convention*, 166.6 *custom*, 167.5 *convention*, 214.4 *orderliness*, 306.5 *formality*, 513.3 *the expected thing*, 584.4 *custom*
traditional 312, 1.14 *societal*, 3.19 *chronicled*, 49.33 *jazz*, 116.15 *conventional*, 124.1 *average*, 166.10 *customary*, 167.14 *conformist*, 202.12 *olden*, 214.14 *orderly*, 217.8 *conservative*, 306.11 *formal*, 584.11 *normal*, 669.11 *obstinate*, 719.7 *observant*
traditional belief 497.2 *religious belief*
traditional grammar 5.29 *grammar*
traditionalism 167.4 *conventionalism*, 584.6 *procedure*
traditionalist 167.6, 167.14 *conformist*, 217.3 *conservative person*, 217.8 *conservative*, 497.5 *believer*, 584.8 *creature of habit*, 667.5 *assenter*, 669.5 *resister*, 694.4 *obedient person*
traditionalistic 167.14 *conformist*
traditional jazz 49.8 *jazz*
traditionally 1.18 *societally*, 3.25 *reportedly*, 116.37 *conventionally*, 167.19 *according to rule*, 214.17 *orderly*, 217.10 *conservatively*, 306.14 *conventionally*, 584.19 *habitually*, 669.14 *resistingly*, 719.8 *observantly*
traditional medicine 60.2 *natural medicine*
traditionary 584.11 *normal*
traditions 652.6 *way of life*
traditive 584.11 *normal*
traduce 525.1 *misinterpret*, 854.12 *defame*
traducement 525.2 *misinterpretation*, 854.3 *defamation*

traffic 71.21 *miscellaneous motoring terms*, 135.1 *union*, 223.5 *exchange*, 324.2 *momentum*, 356.2 *passing along*, 737.1, 737.4 *trade*, 739.3 *selling*
traffic accident 397.5 *ways of dying*
trafficator 71 Motor Vehicle Parts, 439.6 *electric light*
traffic circle 71.3 *carriageway*, 327.3 *road*, 334.1 *circuit*
traffic controller 356
traffic cop 16.17 *police officer*, 356.7 *traffic controller*
traffic death 398.8 *accidental killing*
traffic engineer 356.7 *traffic controller*
traffic engineering 63.17 *civil engineering*
traffic flow 356.2 *passing along*
traffic in 13.10 *trade with*, 737.1 *trade*, 739.1 *sell*
traffic in drugs 875.10 *drug oneself*
traffic island 634.1 *refuge*
traffic jam 71.21 *miscellaneous motoring terms*, 159.8 *procession*, 356.2 *passing along*, 661.2 *obstacle*
trafficker 739.12 *wholesaler*
trafficking 737.4 *trade*, 739.3 *selling*
traffic lane 327.2 *route*
traffic light 453.15 *green light*, 543.4 *signal*
traffic lights 71.3 *carriageway*, 356.5 *crossing point*, 439.6 *electric light*
traffic load 356.2 *passing along*
traffic of the state 51.1 *drama*
traffic pattern 73.6 *flight control*, 356.2 *passing along*
traffic police 356.7 *traffic controller*
traffic signals 439.6 *electric light*
traffic warden 356.7 *traffic controller*
tragacanth 85 Tree Products
tragedian 51.22 *actor*, 51.24 *dramatist*
tragedienne 51.22 *actor*
tragedy 51, 628.7 *deterioration*, 862.2 *affliction*
tragic 51, 48.19 *narrative*, 687.6 *adverse*, 770.7 *distressing*, 862.8 *afflicted*
tragically 51.42 *dramatically*, 687.12 *in adversity*, 862.13 *destructively*
tragic drama 51.9 *tragedy*
tragic flaw 51.9 *tragedy*, 620.7 *defect*, 633.7 *vulnerability*
tragic loves 821.10 *lovers*
tragic muse 51.9 *tragedy*
tragicomedy 51.9 *tragedy*, 51.10 *comedy*
tragicomic 51.38 *tragic*
tragic poet 48.14 *author*, 51.24 *dramatist*
tragopan 78 Birds
Traherne 48 Writers
trail 36.19 *punt*, 37.7 *shoot*, 127.8 *be inferior*, 132.1 *remainder*, 155.10 *rear*, 155.23 *follow close*, 283.10 *suspend*, 304.6 *be in the rear*, 327.2 *route*, 327.6 *path*, 328.2 *hesitate*, 339.11 *pull*, 416.3 *scent*, 483.4 *indication*, 543.1 *sign*, 545.12 *vestige*, 590.9 *follow*
trailbike 71.12 *bicycle*
trailblaze 156.21 *pioneer*
trailblazer 154.8 *precursor*, 194.6 *person having priority*, 594.15 *preparer*
trailblazing 154.14 *preparatory*
trailer 71 Motor Vehicles, 68.10 *farm tool*, 71.20 *truck*, 154.6 *preview*, 194.7 *foretaste*, 256.9 *mobile home*, 326.5 *means of transport*, 532.9 *advertisement*, 590.6 *hunter*
trail horse 32.1 *horse*
trailing 36.8, 36.14 *punting*, 590.1 *pursuit*
trail shot 25.2 *grip*

train 72, 6.22 *educate,* 6.23 *learn,* 15.11 *conduct industrial relations,* 32.16 *ride,* 69.15 *cultivate,* 77.21 *assemblage of mammals,* 155.2 *series,* 155.10 *rear,* 159.2 *consecution,* 159.8 *procession,* 167.10 *assimilate,* 195.1 *succession,* 243.10 *produce,* 295.24 *part of garment,* 304.1 *rear,* 326.5 *means of transport,* 339.11 *pull,* 501.14 *cause to know,* 584.18 *habituate,* 594.6 *brief,* 594.8 *prepare oneself,* 644.9 *exercise,* 653.2 *direct*
trainable 6.17 *educatable*
train-bearer 823.7 *bridal party*
trained 6.19 *knowledgeable,* 69.19 *ornamental,* 501.8 *knowledgeable,* 584.14 *habituated,* 594.18 *prepared,* 655.8 *expert,* 694.7 *obedient*
trainee 6.7 *learner,* 156.14 *beginner,* 656.10 *unskilled person*
trainee nurse 60.16 *nurse*
trainer 6.4 *educator,* 26.4 *boxer,* 32.15 *horse person,* 594.15 *preparer,* 653.13 *director,* 679.31 *military aircraft*
trainers 295.19, 295.19 *footwear*
training 6.1 *education,* 30.11 *gymnastic,* 584.7 *habituation,* 594.12 *briefing,* 644.5 *exercise*
training and education 15.2 *industrial negotiations*
training camp 19.14 *miscellaneous terms*
training drill 676.6 *art of war*
training officer 15.6 *employer*
training shoes 30.2 *gymnastic clothing*
training staff 17.5 *military staff*
training tracks 32.7 *horseracing*
trainload 257.2 *load*
train of thoughts 461.5 *creative thought*
train robber 736.8 *thief*
train robbery 736.1 *stealing,* 736.3 *theft*
train spotter 72.10 *miscellaneous,* 435.11 *observer*
train spotting 42 Hobbies and Pastimes, 72.10 *miscellaneous*
train station 218.4 *stopping place,* 291.4 *centre of activity*
train ticket 544.3 *means of identification*
train upon 332.7 *take a direction*
traipse 328.1 *move slowly*
trait 103.4 *nature,* 165.3 *characteristic,* 457.3 *external appearance,* 544.1 *identification,* 584.2 *tendency*
Trait du Nord 32 Breeds of Horse and Pony
traitor 539, 220.6 *convert,* 224.6 *fickle person,* 484.4 *tergiversator,* 540.15 *false person,* 578.9 *equivocator,* 693.10 *seditionist,* 720.6 *evader,* 820.5 *hostile person,* 832.8 *malefactor,* 858.4 *dishonourable person,* 862.6 *evil person,* 864.9 *wicked person*
traitorous 224.14 *irresolute,* 578.11 *equivocating*
traitorously 224.15 *changeably,* 578.13 *perfidiously*
traitor's death 879.13 *capital punishment*
traject 330.1 *impel,* 338.20 *propel,* 356.11 *cross*
trajectile 338.8 *missile,* 338.18 *projectile*
trajection 338.3 *throwing*
trajectory 52.40 *curve,* 53.21 *orbit,* 53.35 *rocketry,* 327.2 *route,* 327.13 *flight path*
Trakehner 32 Breeds of Horse and Pony
Tralee 93 Cities
tralineate 335.1 *deviate*
tram 72.1 Motor Vehicles, 72.1 *railway,* 326.5 *means of transport,* 72.10 *railway*
tramcar 72.1 *railway*
tram driver 326.7 *transferor*
tramline 41.1 *skiing,* 68.11 *farmland,* 327.10 *railway*

tramlines 40.4 *tennis terms,* 40.12 *badminton terms,* 584.3 *way*
trammels 699.5 *means of restraint*
tramontane 55 Winds, 104.6 *outsider,* 104.10 *foreign,* 149.4 *foreigner,* 263.8 *distant*
tramp 168.7 *nonconformist,* 224.7 *person who moves around,* 324.12 *gait,* 324.15 *walk,* 622.6 *dirty person,* 643.8 *nonworker,* 687.5 *person in adversity,* 712.5 *beggar,* 743.10 *poor person*
trample 330.7 *kick,* 618.14 *illtreat,* 670.9 *attack successfully*
trampled down 282.9 *flattened*
trample down 282.7 *make horizontal*
trample in the dust 362.2 *flatten*
trample on 701.6 *subject,* 720.10 *violate the law,* 807.26 *oppress*
trample over 570.15 *impose one's will*
trample underfoot 244.9 *demolish,* 618.14 *ill-treat,* 682.10 *defeat heavily,* 720.10 *violate the law*
trampoline 331.5 *reflector,* 359.8 *lift,* 361.10 *elevator,* 377.3 *elastic thing*
trampolining 18 Sporting Activities
tramp steamer 74 Ships and Boats, 326.5 *means of transport*
tramway 72.1 *railway*
trance 61, 11.10 *psychic phenomenon,* 325.1 *motionlessness,* 404.2 *unconsciousness,* 512.1 *oblivion,* 519.6 *reverie,* 643.9 *sleep,* 761.4 *desensitization*
trance dance 46.4 *historic dancing*
trance-like 512.8 *oblivious*
trance speaking 11.1 *occultism*
trance state 61.14 *trance*
tranche 143.2 *particular,* 143.7 *piece*
trannie 534.18 *radio*
tranquil 4.18 *detached,* 150.16 *harmonious,* 242.6 *moderate,* 325.6 *quiescent,* 641.3 *inactive,* 649.4 *at ease,* 675.7 *peaceful,* 787.3 *unmoved*
tranquillity 4.3 *detachment,* 150.8 *harmony,* 325.2 *repose,* 462.1 *lack of thought,* 641.1 *inaction,* 649.1 *ease,* 787.1 *lack of wonder*
tranquillization 242.1 *moderation,* 767.1 *ease*
tranquillize 242.4 *moderate,* 325.9 *make motionless,* 677.4 *pacify,* 767.9 *relieve*
tranquillizer 62.4 *drug type,* 242.2 *moderator,* 404.4 *anaesthetic,* 630.8 *drug,* 631.11 *intoxicant,* 761.6 *desensitizing substance,* 767.3 *reliever*
tranquillizing 62.15 *sedative,* 242.8 *moderating*
tranquilly 325.10 *motionlessly,* 641.5 *without action,* 675.8 *peacefully,* 787.9 *without wonder*
transact 116.23 *arrange,* 223.5 *exchange,* 640.4 *act,* 652.14 *behave towards,* 667.7 *contract,* 737.1 *trade*
transact business 716.4 *negotiator*
transaction 116.3 *arrangement,* 223.1 *exchange,* 640.1 *action,* 640.2 *deed,* 667.2 *contract,* 737.4 *trade,* 739.3 *selling*
transactional analysis 61.3 *psychiatric treatment*
transactionalism 1.5 *anthropological concept*
transactionalist 1.11 *anthropological*
transactions 545.1 *record,* 652.8 *treatment*
transalpine 263.8 *distant*
Transamerica Pyramid 43 Noted Buildings
transaminase 58.11 *enzyme*

transatlantic 36.10 *sailing,* 104.10 *foreign,* 263.8 *distant*
transatlantic racing 36.1 *sailing*
transavantgarde 50 Western Art Styles and Movements
transceiver 420.9 *audio device*
transcend 8.17 *deify,* 126.8 *be superior,* 357.3 *exceed,* 617.9 *be worthy,* 861.19 *be good at*
transcended 357.14 *surpassing*
transcendence 8.1 *divinity,* 126.1 *superiority,* 357.7 *crossing,* 619.3 *perfection*
transcendency 126.1 *superiority*
transcendent 7.15, 7.15 *religious,* 8.13 *divine,* 119.5 *novel,* 126.14 *best,* 184.2 *immeasurable,* 368.8 *nonmaterial,* 619.1 *perfect*
transcendental 8.13 *divine,* 11.16 *psychic,* 52.72 *complex,* 126.14 *best,* 523.1 *unintelligible*
transcendental argument 4.9 *philosophical problem*
transcendental idealism 368.5 *idealism*
transcendentalism 4.7 *school of thought,* 11.1 *occultism,* 368.5 *idealism,* 523.1 *unintelligibility*
Transcendentalism 48 Literary Groups and Movements
transcendentalist 4.11 *follower of a doctrine,* 4.14 *of a philosophy,* 11.12 *occultist*
transcendentally 8.19 *divinely,* 11.25 *occultly,* 126.16 *superiorly*
transcendental meditation 61.3 *psychiatric treatment*
transcendental number 52.6 *complex number,* 169.2 *kind of number*
transcendently 8.19 *divinely,* 126.16 *superiorly,* 368.13 *metaphysically*
transcending 126.14 *best*
transcontinental 263.8 *distant*
transcribe 5.46 *translate,* 49.35 *compose,* 326.16, 524.12 *translate,* 545.14 *inscribe*
transcribed 118.12 *imitative,* 534.34 *communicated*
transcriber 114.4 *person who copies*
transcript 118.5 *duplicate*
transcription 49.15 *composition,* 216.1 *change,* 326.4, 524.4 *translation,* 534.25 *broadcast material*
transcursion 356.1 *passage,* 357.7 *crossing*
transdermal injection 62.12 *injection*
transducer 56.55 *circuit,* 64.22 *transformer*
transducing 356.12 *passing*
transduction 326.3 *transmission,* 356.1 *passage*
transect 176.16 *halve,* 286.6 *be oblique*
transept 10.12 *church,* 43.10 *church architecture*
transeunt 347.15 *outgoing*
transfer 326, 326, 19.14 *miscellaneous terms,* 57.26 *react,* 118.5 *duplicate,* 195.4 *accession,* 216.8 *cause change,* 220.1 *conversion,* 220.7 *convert into,* 221.2 *restoration,* 252.3 *replacement,* 252.14 *displace,* 324.14 *set in motion,* 356.11 *cross,* 570.16 *bequeath,* 598.1 *relinquish,* 598.3 *relinquishment,* 706.4 *delegate,* 715.5 *contract,* 727.1 *disposal,* 728.1 *transfer of property,* 728.3 *transfer property,* 729.1 *giving,* 729.2 *gift,* 729.5 *give,* 739.1 *sell,* 739.3 *selling*
Transfer 326
transferable 326, 220.15 *convertible,* 716.8 *negotiated,* 727.14 *for sale,* 728.5 *transferring,* 729.7 *given*
transferable vote 580.10 *vote*
transfer a decal 44.11 *make ceramics*
transferase 58.11 *enzyme*
transferee 738.12 *purchaser*

transference 61.27 *association of ideas,* 216.1 *change,* 220.1 *conversion,* 252.1 *displacement,* 326.1 *transfer,* 347.5 *export,* 356.1 *passage,* 728.1 *transfer of property*
transference neurosis 61.10 *neurosis*
transfer of property 728
Transfer of Property 728
transferor 326, 739.9 *seller*
transfer orbit 53.35 *rocketry*
transfer ownership 728.3 *transfer property*
transfer printing 44.3 *glaze*
transfer property 728
transferral 326.1 *transfer*
transferred 252.8 *displaced,* 252.10 *replaced,* 520.6 *meaningful,* 728.5 *transferring*
transferred epithet 48.12 *poetic language*
transferred thing 326
transferring 728, 220.14 *converting,* 356.12 *passing,* 729.8 *giving*
transfer RNA 59.13 *genetic material*
transfers 15.2 *industrial negotiations*
transfer thoughts 11.24 *experience psychic phenomena*
transfiguration 791, 216.3 *transformation,* 220.1 *conversion,* 627.5 *improvement*
transfigure 216.9 *transform,* 220.7 *convert into,* 220.9 *transform,* 627.1 *improve,* 789.8 *beautify*
transfigured 220.13 *converted*
transfiguring 220.14 *converting*
transfinite number 52.7 *natural number,* 52.11 *infinity*
transfix 225.7 *make stable*
transfixed 225.10 *stabilized,* 325.4 *motionless,* 786.7 *wide-eyed*
transform 216, 220, 52.96 *represent,* 220.7 *convert into,* 627.1 *improve,* 789.8 *beautify*
transformable 220.15 *convertible*
transformation 52, 216, 52.29 *mathematical function,* 170.1 *calculation,* 220.1 *conversion,* 627.5 *improvement,* 786.3 *wonder-working,* 791.1 *transfiguration*
transformational 5.44 *grammatical*
transformational-generative 5.44 *grammatical*
transformational grammar 5.29 *grammar*
transformation-generative grammar 5.29 *grammar*
transformation scene 51.6 *scene,* 51.17 *stage set*
transformative 216
transformed 220.13 *converted,* 627.14 *improved*
transform energy 235.12 *generate power*
transformer 64, 56.55 *circuit,* 64.34 *power supply,* 216.5 *changer,* 235.7 *electrical power*
transform fault 54.19 *plate tectonics*
transforming 220.14 *converting*
transfusable 326.17 *transferable*
transfuse 60.20 *practise surgery,* 326.11 *transfer,* 354.2 *inject,* 630.20 *doctor*
transfusion 60.9 *surgery,* 133.1 *mixture,* 326.3 *transmission,* 354.9 *injection,* 356.1 *passage,* 630.12 *surgery*
transgress 357, 504, 168.20 *infringe a law,* 693.15 *be disobedient,* 720.10 *violate the law,* 844.21 *do wrong,* 864.16 *be wicked,* 866.10 *sin*
transgressed 720.14 *violating*
transgressing 16.60 *offending,* 693.13 *disobedient,* 720.14 *violating,* 864.11 *wicked,* 866.7 *sinful*

transgression 357, 16.38 *lawbreaking,* 504.8 *moral error,* 693.2 *violation of the law,* 720.4 *infraction,* 844.8 *wrongdoing,* 864.1 *wickedness,* 866.3 *sin*

transgressive 720.14 *violating,* 844.16 *in the wrong*

transgressor 844.10 *wrongdoer,* 864.9 *wicked person*

transience 189, 224.1 *changeableness,* 270.1 *shortness,* 397.1 *death,* 491.15 *unreliability*

Transience 189

transiency 397.1 *death*

transient 189, 57.35 *combined,* 106.7 *circumstantial,* 216.11, 224.13 *changeable,* 270.7 *short,* 347.15 *outgoing,* 397.20 *deadly,* 458.6 *disappearing,* 491.7 *unreliable*

transient current 56.51 *electric current*

transient discharge 56.46, 64.6 *electric discharge*

transient disturbance 56.12 *wave*

transiently 189, 458.8 *fleetingly,* 491.26 *unreliably*

transient thing 189

transilience 357.7 *crossing*

transilient 356.12 *passing*

transistor 64, 56.44 *semiconductor,* 56.55 *circuit,* 235.7 *electrical power*

transistor amplifier 64.19 *transistor*

transistorize 235.11 *give power*

transistor radio 420.9 *audio device,* 534.18 *radio*

transistor switch 64.19 *transistor*

transit 53.21 *orbit,* 53.37 *observe,* 324.2 *momentum,* 326.2 *transportation,* 356.1 *passage,* 356.11 *cross*

transition 21.2 *field events,* 56.37 *temperature,* 56.67 *excited atom,* 216.1 *change,* 220.1 *conversion,* 326.1 *transfer,* 326.2 *transportation*

transitional 43 *Architectural Styles,* 216.11 *changeable,* 324.16 *moving,* 356.12 *passing*

transitionally 216.15 *changeably,* 324.18 *in motion,* 356.14 *by the way*

transition element 57.6 *chemical element*

transition state 57.14 *chemical reaction*

transition temperature 56.37 *temperature,* 56.45 *superconductivity*

transitive 5.44 *grammatical*

transitively 5.52 *grammatically*

transitive relation 52.63 *mathematical logic*

transitive verb 5.35 *part of speech*

transitorily 189.3 *transiently*

transitoriness 189.1 *transience*

transitory 189.6 *transient,* 216.11 *changeable*

Transit system 74.5 *navigation*

transit van 258.10 *cart*

translatable 5.43 *phrasal,* 220.15 *convertible*

translate 5, 326, 524, 52.96 *represent,* 216.8 *cause change,* 220.7 *convert into,* 220.9 *transform,* 356.11 *cross,* 660.16 *make easy*

translated 5, 5.43 *phrasal,* 220.13 *converted,* 524.15 *interpreted*

translate the truth 309.12 *distort the truth*

translating 5.40 *translated,* 5.43 *phrasal*

translation 5, 326, 524, 5.24 *phrasing,* 52.48 *transformation,* 216.1 *change,* 220.1 *conversion,* 308.2 *symmetry operation*

translational 524

translator 5.2 *linguist,* 524.6 *interpreter*

translator's error 525.2 *misinterpretation*

transliterate 5.46, 326.16 *translate,* 524.12 *translate*

transliterated 5.40 *translated*

transliteration 5.12, 326.4 *translation,* 524.4 *translation*

translocate 252.14 *displace,* 326.11 *transfer*

translocation 252.1 *displacement,* 326.1 *transfer*

translucence 442.6 *translucency*

translucency 442, 442.7 *semitransparency*

translucent 442, 44.10 *ceramic,* 442.3 *semitransparent*

translucent ceramics 44.1 *ceramics*

translucently 44.12 *ornamentally,* 442.13 *transparently*

translumbar injection 62.12 *injection*

transmarine 263.8 *distant*

transmigration 326.1 *transfer*

transmigration of souls 216.3 *transformation*

transmissible 326.17 *transferable,* 534.35 *communicable*

transmission 71 *Motor Vehicle Parts,* **326,** 56.15 *wave property,* 330.11 *impulsion,* 356.1 *passage,* 528.2 *communication,* 534.6 *telecommunication,* 534.25 *broadcast material,* 728.1 *transfer of property*

transmissional 534.33 *communicational*

transmission density 66.10 *graininess*

transmission line 64.33 *power distribution,* 534.6 *telecommunication*

transmission of disease 326.3 *transmission*

transmissive 326.17 *transferable*

transmit 64.35 *conduct,* 326.11 *transfer,* 326.12 *transport,* 356.11 *cross,* 420.16 *be heard,* 528.12 *communicate,* 532.13 *make public,* 533.13 *report,* 534.30 *communicate,* 567.10 *send,* 652.15 *conduct,* 729.5 *give*

transmit colour 444.17 *colourcast*

transmit light 442.11 *be transparent*

transmittable 326.17 *transferable,* 534.35 *communicable*

transmittal 326.1 *transfer,* 728.1 *transfer of property*

transmittance 326.1 *transfer*

transmitted 420.11 *aural,* 534.34 *communicated*

transmitted wave 534

transmitter 534, 326.9 *disease carrier*

transmit thoughts 11.24 *experience psychic phenomena*

transmitting antenna 534.17 *antenna*

transmogrification 216.3 *transformation*

transmogrify 216.9 *transform*

transmontane 263.8 *distant*

transmundane 11.18 *spiritual,* 263.8 *distant,* 368.8 *nonmaterial*

transmutable 220.15 *convertible*

transmutation 56.71 *nuclear reaction,* 216.3 *transformation,* 220.1 *conversion*

transmutative 216.13 *transformative*

transmute 216.9 *transform,* 220.7 *convert into,* 220.9 *transform*

transmuted 220.13 *converted*

transmuting 220.14 *converting*

Trans-New Guinea phylum 5 *Languages and Groups of Languages*

transoceanic 263.8 *distant*

transom 74 *Parts of a Ship,* 36.3 *parts of a sailing boat,* 284.2 *supporting part*

transome 43 *Architectural Decoration*

transpacific 263.8 *distant*

transparency 442, 51.17 *stage set,* 66.3 *photograph,* 66.12 *development,* 438.4 *invisibility,* 442.8 *transparent thing,* 522.10 *simplicity,* 550.1 *clarity*

Transparency 442

transparent 442, 44.10 *ceramic,* 438.1 *invisible,* 522.2 *simple,* 530.10 *disclosed,* 550.3 *clear,* 658.1 *naive*

transparent glaze 44.3 *glaze*

transparently 442, 44.12 *ornamentally,* 550.4 *clearly*

transparent pigment 444.4 *pigment*

transparent thing 442

transpersonal theory 61.3 *psychiatric treatment*

transphysical 11.16 *psychic*

transphysical science 11.1 *occultism*

transpicuous 442.1 *transparent*

transpiration 54.10 *water cycle,* 59.5 *physiology,* 326.3 *transmission*

transpire 54.63 *ebb,* 227.9 *take effect,* 326.11 *transfer,* 526.5 *be visible,* 530.9 *be disclosed*

transplacement 326.1 *transfer*

transplant 60.20 *practise surgery,* 69.15 *cultivate,* 222.3 *substitute thing,* 326.11 *transfer,* 354.6 *plant,* 354.8 *insertion,* 630.12 *surgery*

transplantation 60.9 *surgery,* 326.1 *transfer,* 354.8 *insertion*

transplanted 354.12 *inserted*

transplant surgery 630.12 *surgery*

transpolar 263.8 *distant*

transpontine 263.8 *distant*

transport 70, 70, 326, 70.5 *transportable,* 252.14 *displace,* 324.2 *momentum,* 324.14 *set in motion,* 326.2 *transportation,* 349.4 *ostracize,* 356.11 *cross,* 762.1 *happiness,* 821.2 *romantic love,* 879.1 *punish*

Transport 70

transportable 70, 326.17 *transferable*

transportation 326, 70.1 *transport,* 70.5 *transportable,* 324.2 *momentum,* 349.19 *ostracism,* 879.7 *punishment*

transportation corps 17.4 *military organization*

transportation engineering 63.17 *civil engineering*

transportative 326.17 *transferable*

transport box 68.10 *farm tool*

transport café 350.15 *eating place*

transport charges 751.6 *business costs*

transport door-to-door 70.4 *transport*

transported 70.5 *transportable,* 762.4 *happy*

transporter 71 *Motor Vehicles,* **70,** 71.20 *truck,* 326.7 *transferor*

transporter bridge 263.21 *bridge*

transport goods 70.4 *transport*

transporting 70.5 *transportable*

transportive 326.17 *transferable*

transport of love 821.2 *romantic love*

transport plane 679.31 *military aircraft*

transport ship 679.24 *warship*

transport system 70.1 *transport*

transposable 220.15 *convertible,* 326.17 *transferable*

transposal 326.1 *transfer*

transpose 49.35 *compose,* 52.22 *matrix,* 216.10 *exchange,* 220.7 *convert into,* 223.5 *exchange,* 287.3 *invert,* 324.14 *set in motion,* 326.11 *transfer*

transposed 220.13 *converted,* 223.7 *exchanged*

transposition 49.20 *key,* 216.4 *exchange,* 220.1 *conversion,* 223.1 *exchange,* 287.1 *inversion,* 326.1 *transfer*

transpositional 216.14 *exchangeable,* 287.2 *inverted*

transposon 59.13 *genetic material*

transsexual 401, 224.9 *person who changes sex,* 402.10 *homosexual*

transship 70.4 *transport,* 252.14 *displace*

transshipment 70.1 *transport,* 252.1 *displacement,* 326.2 *transportation*

Trans-Siberian Railway 72.10 *miscellaneous*

transubstantial 10.21 *ritualistic,* 216.13 *transformative*

transubstantiate 216.9 *transform*

transubstantiation 10.6 *Eucharist,* 216.3 *transformation*

transudate 353.4 *excrement*

transudating 356.13 *penetrating*

transudation 347.2 *outflow,* 352.1 *secretion,* 353.1 *excretion,* 353.4 *excrement,* 356.3 *passage into*

transudative 347.17 *leaky,* 353.24 *excretory*

transudatory 352.4 *secretory*

transude 352.7 *secrete,* 353.15 *excrete*

transumption 326.4 *translation*

transuranic 57.34 *elemental*

transuranic element 57.6 *chemical element*

transuretero-ureterostomy 60 *Surgical Operations*

transversal 52.37 *line*

transverse 271.1 *broad,* 286.4, 310.8 *oblique*

transverse dune 54.37 *dune*

transverse load 63.14 *load*

transversely 271.8 *breadthwise,* 286.8 *obliquely*

transverseness 286.1 *obliqueness*

transverse ridge rib 43.7 *vault*

transverse wave 56.12, 365.5 *wave*

transvestite 401.11 *transsexual*

Trans World Airways Terminal 43 *Noted Buildings*

Transylvanian Naked Necks 68 *Breeds of Fowl*

tranylcypromine 62 *Medication*

trap 71 *Carriages and Carts,* **635, 635,** 19.19 *play,* 19.15 *play offence,* 38.4 *play soccer,* 51.15 *stage,* 322.4 *body orifice,* 323.4 *closed place,* 398.22 *kill animals,* 514.10 *ambush,* 531.3 *covering up,* 539.13, 539.33 *snare,* 571.15 *compel,* 586.9 *enticement,* 590.3 *hunting and fishing equipment,* 590.11 *hunt,* 592.13 *plot,* 631.6 *source of trouble,* 633.5 *danger,* 657.2 *stratagem,* 659.23 *cause difficulties,* 671.8 *military defences,* 734.10 *take away*

Trap 635

trapa 7.7 *monk*

trap door 346.6 *means of entry,* 539.12 *disguise,* 539.13 *snare,* 635.1 *trap,* 638.2 *means of escape*

trap-door spider 82 *Arachnids*

trapeze 283.3 *suspended object*

trapeze artist 51.29 *circus performer,* 237.5 *athlete*

trapezium 52.44 *polygon,* 178.2 *quadrilateral*

Trapezium 53 *Named Stars*

trapezoid 52.44 *polygon,* 178.2 *quadrilateral*

trap for the unwary 635.1 *trap*

trapped 539, 38.5 *soccer,* 514.6 *surprised,* 633.4 *endangered*

trapper 77.24 *hunter,* 398.13 *animal killer,* 590.6 *hunter*

trapping 38.2 *football play,* 38.5 *soccer,* 77.23 *mammal hunting,* 398.9 *animal killing,* 590.2 *chase*

trappings 130.3 *additional item,* 603.6 *equipment,* 725.4 *possessions*

Trappist 7 *Members of Religious Orders,* 566.7 *taciturn person*

trapshooter 338.15 *shooter*

trapshooting 18 Sporting Activities, 37.1 target shooting, 338.6 shooting

trash 132,2 residue, 143.8 bits and pieces, 151.4 litter, 506.1 nonsense, 607.2 lay waste, 607.5 waste product, 612.9 bauble, 612.10 nonentity, 614.6 refuse, 618.10 inferiority, 622.4 dirt, 727.3 disposable things, 816.7 outsider

trash can 258.11 vessel

trash dump 605.4 storage, 614.6 refuse, 727.8 sink

trashiness 618.8 inferiority

trashing 683.2 defeat

trashy 521.10 meaningless, 612.4 trivial, 614.1 useless, 618.2 inferior, 754.10 shoddy

Trasimeno 94 Lakes

trattoria 350.15 eating place

trauma 61.12 stress, 406.3 injury, 624.4 disease

traumatic 406.5 painful, 630.10 surgical dressing, 630.18 medical

traumatic disease 624.4 disease

traumatic neurosis 61.10 neurosis

traumatism 61.12 stress

traumatize 406.11 inflict pain

traumatized 61.36 psychologically disturbed, 406.7 feeling pain

traumatophobia 777 Phobias by Name

travail 245.7 obstetrics, 644.1 work, 644.8 exert oneself, 687.1 adversity

travel 777 Phobias by Topic, 23.6 play basketball, 104.14 be foreign, 149.16 migrate, 324.2 momentum, 324.15 walk, 336.1 go forward, 336.10 forward motion, 356.9 proceed

travel at maximum speed 329.4 be swift

travel bag 258.9 baggage

travel by water 74.9 navigate

travelcard 754.4 bargain

travel in a circle 313.6 circle

travel in space 53.38 launch

travel in the astral plane 11.24 experience psychic phenomena

travelled out 661.3 fatigued

traveller 74 Rigging, 149.6 immigrant, 168.7 nonconformist, 224.7 person who moves around, 293.22 progression, 465.3 curious person, 496.12 discoverer, 739.10 salesman, 739.11 pedlar

traveller's cheque 741.14 paper money

traveller's joy 84 Flowers and Flowering Plants

traveller's tale 538.4 lie, 541.5 tall story

travelling 23.5 penalties, 104.10 foreign, 168.13 unconventional, 293.41 progressing, 324.16 moving, 698.11 ranging

travelling circus 51.5 show

travelling clock 191 Timepieces and Timers, 192.6 clock

travelling companion 180.11 companion

travelling salesman 739.10 salesman

travelling through 293.22 progression

travelling wave 56.12 wave

travel off season 754.14 buy cheaply

travelogue 48.4 non-fiction, 243.5 work of art, 528.5 reference book, 560.3 narration

travel report 55.4 weather forecast

travel second-class 754.14 buy cheaply

travel-sick 349.30 vomiting

travel through 293.35 progress

travel tourist-class 754.14 buy cheaply

travel-weary 650.1 fatigued

travel with 180.14 keep company with

travel writing 48.4 non-fiction

travers 32.10 dressage

Travers 48 Dramatists

traversal 293.22 progression

traverse 34.9 mountaineer, 41.12, 41.14 ski, 111.8 be opposite, 231.3 counteract, 293.35 progress, 356.1 passage, 356.11 cross, 663.12 oppose

traverse downhill 41.2 cross-country skiing

traverser 293.22 progression

traverse table 74.5 navigation

traversing 41.4 skiing technique, 41.12 ski, 293.22 progression, 356.1 passage, 356.12 passing

travesty 118.3 mockery, 118.9 imitate, 309.4 distortion of the truth, 504.5 misrepresentation, 525.1 misinterpret, 525.2 misinterpretation, 541.1 exaggeration, 541.7 exaggerate, 548.1 misrepresentation, 548.4 misrepresent, 656.9 bungling

travolator 71.4 personal transport, 326.5 means of transport

trawl 80.7 fishing, 80.15 fish, 339.2 pull, 339.12 drag, 539.13, 539.33 snare, 590.11 hunt

trawled 539.42 trapped

trawler 74 Ships and Boats, 74.3 vessel, 74.7 nautical person, 80.7 fishing, 590.6 hunter

trawlerman 20.6 angler, 80.10 fisher, 590.6 hunter

trawling 74.11 nautical

tray 258.16 crockery, 282.3 flat thing

treacherous 539, 491.7 unreliable, 527.5 mysterious, 538.19 dishonest, 540.29 deceitful, 578.11 equivocating, 633.1 dangerous, 633.2 unsafe, 720.13 noncompliant, 858.6 faithless

treacherously 491.26 unreliably, 538.28 dishonestly, 578.13 perfidiously, 633.11 dangerously, 720.16 disobediently, 858.11 dishonourably

treacherousness 224.2 irresolution, 491.15 unreliability, 539.4 false-heartedness, 633.5 danger

treachery 538.10 dishonesty, 539.4 false-heartedness, 540.5 deceitfulness, 578.7 apostasy, 633.5 danger, 720.3 disregard of orders, 858.2 faithlessness

treacle 138.4 adherent, 393.9 jelly, 394.6 gelatin, 414.2 sweetener

treacliness 394.1 viscosity

treacly 393.21, 394.9 gelatinous, 414.6 sweet

tread 36.8 punting, 121.4 interval, 324.12 gait, 324.15 walk, 327.2 route, 359.10 step, 599.1 use

tread a measure 46.15 dance

tread carefully 469.10 be careful, 659.20 be in difficulty

tread downward 360.9 descend

tread flat 282.7 make horizontal

treading water 39.1 swimming

treadle 338.20 propel

treadmill 110.6 regularity, 112.4 monotony, 159.6 continuum, 364.6 rotator, 584.3 way, 644.1 work, 788.2 boring thing, 879.15 instrument of torture

tread on 330.7 kick, 618.14 illtreat, 690.6 suppress, 701.6 subject

tread on dangerous ground 633.8 be in danger

tread on eggs 659.20 be in difficulty

tread on someone's toes 850.22 show disrespect

tread on the heels of 155.21 follow in sequence, 264.10 stay near

treads and risers 359.7 means of ascent

tread the beaten path 584.16 have a habit

tread the boards 51.32 act

tread the primrose path 628.1 deteriorate

---

tread under foot 690.6 suppress

tread warily 469.10 be careful, 573.8 hold back, 781.5 be cautious

tread water 39.9 swim, 325.8 be motionless, 641.4 not act

treason 484.2 reversal, 539.4 false-heartedness, 540.5 deceitfulness, 668.3 act of defiance, 693.3 subversion, 713.2 disorder, 720.3 disregard of orders, 858.2 faithlessness

treasonable 693.14 subversive

treasonable activities 693.3 subversion

treasonist 539.21 traitor

treasonous 539.38 treacherous, 540.29 deceitful, 713.10 lawbreaking, 720.13 noncompliant, 858.6 faithless

treasure 605.1, 605.6 store, 617.8 exceller, 632.9 protect, 637.5 preserve, 696.11 masterpiece, 741.6 funds, 784.4 likable person, 784.7 like, 789.3 attractive female, 821.23 love, 826.7 show endearment for, 849.15 respect, 861.17 good thing

treasure chest 741.20 money store

treasured 617.3 valuable, 637.7 preserved, 821.21 beloved

treasure house 605.4 storage, 741.19 treasury

treasure hunt 674.4 race

treasure map 299.4 map

treasurer 741, 606.3 provider, 741.17 financier, 746.5 payer, 750.6 accountant

treasure-trove 496.10 find, 721.5 profit

treasury 741, 562.3 compendium, 605.4 storage

treasury note 741.14 paper money

treasury of words 528 dictionary

treat 67, 60.19 practise medicine, 230.9 take action, 405.4 pleasurable things, 405.9 give pleasure, 514.4 surprising thing, 599.1 use, 623.7 make healthy, 629.6 cure, 630.19 remedy, 630.20 doctor, 652.14 behave towards, 662.19 support, 729.5 give, 746.8 defray, 748.3 donate, 762.2 fun, 763.10 pleasant thing

treatable 629.14 repairable

treat as 222.5 take a substitute

treat as a leper 816.13 ignore

treat as an outsider 816.13 ignore

treat as a special case 147.7 exclude

treat as routine 787.5 not wonder about

treat cruelly 628.6 pervert

treated 67

treated like dirt 701.9 subject

treated like shit 701.9 subject

treat equally 700

treat in detail 165.23 particularize

treatise 48.4 non-fiction, 472.5 educational topic, 561.1 dissertation

treat kindly 691.3 be lenient

treat lightly 691.3 be lenient

treat like dirt 701.6 subject, 850.27 desecrate

treat like shit 701.6 subject, 850.27 desecrate

treatment 50, 60, 510, 652, 230.1 operation, 243.2 manufacture, 599.6 use, 630.13 therapy, 662.5 medical assistance

treat rough 690.6 suppress

treat rudely 818.7 be discourteous

treat teeth 60.21 practise dentistry

treat unfairly 481.14 discriminate against, 493.11 be unjust

treat well 831.8 be benevolent

treat with a high hand 807.26 oppress

treat with deference 817.13 defer to

---

treat with politeness 817.11 have good manners

treaty 116.3 arrangement, 667.2 contract, 677.1 pacification, 715.3 alliance

treaty-maker 667.5 assenter, 715.4 contractor

treaty-making 568.5 talks, 715.7 contractual, 716.1 negotiation, 716.8 negotiated

Treaty of Paris 715.3 alliance

Treaty of Rome 667.2 contract, 715.3 alliance

Treaty of Versailles 715.3 alliance

treble 32.9 jumping, 42.6 darts, 49.32 instrumental, 177.1, 177.7 three, 177.10 triple, 420.10 sound quality

treble clef 49.17 notation, 49.20 key

treble figures 179

treble hook 20.3 fishing tackle

trebleness 177.3 threeness

treble top 42.6 darts

trebling 128.1 increase, 177.4 triplication

trebly 177.12 thrice

trebuchet 680.6 historical missile weapon

trecento 50 Western Art Styles and Movements

tredecillion 169.3 large number, 179.11 million

tree 85, 69.9 garden plant, 83.2 plant, 659.23 cause difficulties

tree-covered 85.16 wooded

tree creeper 78 Birds, 85.11 tree-related animal

tree disease 85

tree farm 68.6 farm, 85.4 trees, 647.1 workshop

tree farmer 85.8 forester

tree farming 68.4 arable farming, 85.5 forestry

tree felling 85.6 tree management

tree fern 85 Ferns, 85.1 tree, 88.1 fem

tree frog 79 Amphibians, 85.11 tree-related animal

treehopper 82 Insects, 85.11 tree-related animal

tree kangaroo 77 Marsupials, 85.11 tree-related animal

treeless 247.3 birth control

treelike 85, 343.9 branched

treelikeness 343.4 branching

tree line 85.4 trees

tree litter 85.4 trees

tree mallow 85.1 tree

tree management 85

tree moss 88.3 moss

tree mythology 85

treen 47.8 woodwork, 85.5 forestry, 85.15 woody

treenail 137.8 fastening

tree nursery 85.4 trees

treenware 85.5 forestry

tree nymph 8.5 deity, 85.13 tree mythology

tree of heaven 85 Trees and Shrubs

tree of Jesse 85.13 tree mythology

tree of knowledge 85.13 tree mythology

tree of life 85.13 tree mythology

tree part 85

tree planting 85.5 forestry

tree product 85

tree-related animal 85

tree ring 85.3 timber

tree-ring dating 85.3 timber, 185.8 dating

trees 85

Trees 85

tree-shaped 343.9 branched

tree shrew 77 Placental Mammals, 85.11 tree-related animal

tree snake 79 Reptiles, 85.11 tree-related animal

tree sparrow 85.11 tree-related animal

tree stump 85.2 tree part

tree surgeon 85.8 forester

tree surgery 85.6 tree management

tree tomato 86 Fruits

treetop 279.2 head

tree worship 9.2 *idolatry*
tree worshipper 9.6 *idolater*
tree-worshipping 9.10 *idolatrous*
trefoil 43 Architectural Decoration, **84** Flowers and Flowering Plants, 177.2 *trident*, 544.8 *heraldic device*
Tregean 4.11 *follower of a doctrine*
trellis 69.3 *ornamental garden*, 288.2 *braid*
Trematoda 81 Worms, 81.6 *worm*
trematode 81.6 *worm*
tremble 54.64 *fold*, 224.11 *be changeable*, 238.6 *be weak*, 365.9 *vibrate*, 366.24 *shake*, 409.10 *be cold*, 424.5 *sound faint*, 777.11 *be afraid*
tremble in the balance 633.8 *be in danger*
tremble like an aspen leaf 366.24 *shake*
trembling 777 Phobias by Topic, 366.6 *shaking*, 366.18 *shaky*, 777.2 *fearfulness*, 777.8 *fearful*
trembling in the air 424.4 *faint*
trembling in the balance 633.2 *unsafe*
tremblingly 366.28 *shakily*
trembling palsy 366.7 *shake*
tremelloid 394.9 *gelatinous*
tremendismo 48 Literary Groups and Movements
tremendous 259.15 *big*
tremolite 54 Minerals
tremolo 49.16 *musical note*, 426.6 *musical repetition*
tremophobia 777 Phobias by Name
tremor 241.3 *instance of violence*, 365.2 *vibration*, 365.5 *wave*, 366.7 *shake*, 366.9 *jolt*, 624.17 *nervous disorder*, 636.2 *danger signal*
tremors 874.16 *alcoholism*
tremulous 365.17 *waving*, 366.18 *shaky*, 576.3 *timid*, 777.8 *fearful*
tremulously 366.28 *shakily*, 777.15 *fearfully*
tremulousness 366.6 *shaking*, 576.13 *timidity*
trench 69.15 *cultivate*, 265.2, 265.5 *crack*, 301.3 *enclosing thing*, 317.2 *concave land*, 321.1, 321.6 *furrow*, 634.1 *refuge*, 671.8 *military defences*
trenchancy 554.1 *emphasis*
trenchant 237.10 *potent*, 552.3 *concise*, 554.3 *emphatic*, 611.5 *important*
trenchantly 552.5 *concisely*
trench coat 295.12 *coat*
trencher 63.29 *construction equipment*
trencherman 350.18 *eater*, 872.4 *glutton*
trencherwoman 872.4 *glutton*
trench fever 624.6 *infection*
trench gun 680.11 *guns*
trenching machine 63.29 *construction equipment*
trench-mortar 680.11 *guns*
trench warfare 676.8 *warfare*
trend 105.1 *state*, 114.2 *copy*, 159.7 *stability*, 167.5 *convention*, 201.7 *new thing*, 227.4 *significance*, 234.1 *tendency*, 306.5 *formality*, 324.2 *momentum*, 332.2 *bearing*, 332.7 *take a direction*, 335.1 *deviate*, 488.2 *tendency*, 584.4 *custom*, 588.5 *final intention*, 784.3 *likes*
trendily 201, 105.9 *conditionally*
trendiness 201
trending 234.5 *tending to*
trendsetter 154.8 *precursor*, 201.9 *modern person*, 295.27 *model*
trendsetting 201.16 *avant-garde*
trendsetting group 201.6 *avant-garde*
trend upwards 359.21 *upturn*

trendy 105.8 *in a state of*, 201.10 *new*, 201.16 *avant-garde*, 306.11 *formal*
trenette 45 Types of Pasta
Trent 96 Rivers, 96.4 *British rivers*
Trento 93 Cities
Trenton 93 Cities
Treorchy 93 Cities
trepan 322.2 *opener*, 322.20 *hole*, 630.20 *doctor*
trepang 81.3 *echinoderm*
trephination 630.12 *surgery*
trephine 322.2 *opener*, 322.20 *hole*, 630.20 *doctor*
trepidation 777.2 *fearfulness*
trespass 16.38 *lawbreaking*, 16.39 *crime*, 104.16 *be external*, 149.17 *intrude*, 255.15 *settle*, 346.10 *invade*, 357.5 *transgress*, 357.8 *transgression*, 693.2 *violation of the law*, 693.15 *be disobedient*, 720.4 *infraction*, 720.10 *violate the law*, 844.8 *wrongdoing*, 844.21 *do wrong*, 846.3 *arrogation*, 846.14 *arrogate*, 864.1 *wickedness*, 864.16 *be wicked*, 866.3, 866.10 *sin*
trespasser 104.8 *intruder*, 147.5 *excluded person*, 149.10 *intruder*, 255.6 *illegal occupant*, 346.8 *intruder*, 844.10 *wrongdoer*, 846.7 *usurper*
trespassing 16.60 *offending*, 104.4 *externality*, 104.12 *external*, 346.3 *inroad*, 346.16 *invasive*, 357.11 *overrun*, 720.14 *violating*, 864.11 *wicked*, 866.7 *sinful*
trestle 327.10 *railway*
trestle bridge 63.21 *bridge*
trestletree 85.12 *figurative usage*
tresure 544.8 *heraldic device*
Trevino 18 Sporting Personalities
Trevithick 52 Scientists
trews 295.9 *trousers*
trey 42.3 *card game terms*, 177.1 *three*
triable 16.47 *liable to law*, 16.58 *unjust*
triacidic 57.36 *acid*
triacidic base 57.9 *base*
triad 49.16 *musical note*, 177.1 *three*
triadic 177.7 *three*
trial 16.7 *legal trial*, 16.33 *litigation*, 477.3 *questionnaire*, 479.1 *experiment*, 479.2 *rehearsal*, 479.8 *experimental*, 594.10 *preparations*, 596.6 *venture*, 596.9 *tentative*, 631.2 *adversity*, 659.3 *difficult task*, 674.2 *contest*, 879.10 *affliction*
trial and error 479.1 *experiment*
trial at the bar 16.7 *legal trial*
trial ballon 532.1 *publication*
trial balloon 479.2 *rehearsal*, 657.2 *stratagem*
trial by jury 16.7 *legal trial*
trial by law 16.7 *legal trial*
trial by one's peers 16.7 *legal trial*
trial in court 16.7 *legal trial*
triality 177.3 *threeness*
trial judge 492.6 *justice*
trial jury 16.13 *lawyer*, 16.26, 492.7 *jury*
trial marriage 823.3 *types of marriage*
trial of strength 674.2 *contest*
trial run 479.2 *rehearsal*, 594.10 *preparations*
trials 687.1 *adversity*
trials and tribulations 687.1 *adversity*
triamcinolone 62 Medication
triamterene 62 Medication
triangle 49 Musical Instruments, **52**, 24.1, 24.1 *hilliards*, 52.44 *polygon*, 177.2 *trident*, 310.3 *angled figure*, 427.4 *sources of resonance*, 879.15 *instrument of torture*
triangle fortification 671.11 *fortification*

triangular 31.8 *hockey*, 52.82 *polygonal*, 177.8 *three-sided*, 310.9 *angled*
triangular offence 31.3 *ice hockey*
triangulate 177.8 *three-sided*, 250.11 *find*, 268.10 *measure*
triangulated 268.13 *measured*
triangulation 52.51 *trigonometry*, 250.5 *topography*, 268.1 *measurement*
triangulation point 543.5 *indicator*
triangulation station 275.8 *high thing*
Triangulum 53 The Constellations, **53** The Constellations
Triangulum Australe 53 The Constellations
Triangulum Spiral 53 Galaxies
Triassic 54 Geological Time Intervals
Triassic period 200.3 *geological period*
triathlon 18 Sporting Activities, 674.2 *contest*
triatomic 57.35 *combined*
triaziquone 62 Medication
tribade 402.10 *homosexual*
tribal 1.14 *societal*, 255.12 *native*, 400.13 *national*, 665.9 *societal*
tribalism 12.1 *government*, 400.9 *group*, 688.7 *type of rule*
tribal killer 398.10 *killer*
tribally 1.18 *societally*, 665.18 *cliquishly*
tribal memory 1.8 *tradition*, 132.1 *remainder*
tribal system 12.1 *government*
tribal warrior 679.8 *soldier*
tribasic 57.36 *acid*
tribasic acid 57.8 *acid*
tribe 161 Collective Names for Birds and Animals, 1.7 *society*, 59.17 *taxonomy*, 137.3 *associate*, 161.17 *family*, 163.8 *genealogy*, 195.2 *descent*, 255.2 *inhabitants*, 400.9 *group*, 665.2 *society*
tribrach 48.9 *metre*
tribromoethanol 62 Medication
tribulation 659.3 *difficult task*
tribunal 16, 16.2 *jurisdiction*, 16.49 *judicatory*, 492.3 *place of judgment*, 653.7 *council*
tribunal of penance 16.18 *tribunal*
tribune gallery 10.12 *church*, 43.10 *church architecture*
tributary 96.1 *river*, 127.6 *inferior*, 127.15 *subordinate*, 729.4 *giver*, 729.7 *given*
tribute 812, 511.3 *memento*, 729.2 *gift*, 730.2 *something received*, 746.1 *payment*, 746.4 *grant*, 751.8 *levy*, 763.10 *pleasant thing*, 837.3 *recognition*, 845.2 *due*, 851.4 *compliment*, 878.1 *reward*
tribute-payer 729.4 *giver*
triccaballacca 49 Musical Instruments
trice 339.11 *pull*
tricentenary 214.3, 214.13 *anniversary*
tricentennial 812.14 *centennial*
tricentennially 214.16 *cyclically*
triceps 237.1 *strength*
Triceratops 79 Fossil Reptiles
trice up 135.8 *unite*
trichinophobia 777 Phobias by Name
trichinosis 777 Phobias by Topic
trichloromethane 62 Medication
trichoic 456.6 *variegated*
trichologist 791.13 *beautician*
trichology 791.7 *hairdressing*
trichomatic 456.6 *variegated*
trichomoniasis 81.12 *protozoal disease*
trichopathophobia 777 Phobias by Name
trichophobia 777 Phobias by Name
Trichoptera 82 Orders of Insects
trichopteran 82.10 *insectan*
trichotomize 177.11 *trisect*

trichotomous 177.9 *trisected*
trichotomy 177.5 *trisection*
trichroism 456.1 *variegation*
trichromatism 456.1 *variegation*
trick 539, 539, 102.3 *delusion*, 165.3 *characteristic*, 248.8 *intervening space*, 474.2 *sophism*, 474.12 *deceive*, 477.21 *confuse*, 506.3 *tomfoolery*, 515.8 *be dishonest*, 539.27 *be false*, 539.29 *juggle*, 540.21 *be fraudulent*, 584.2 *tendency*, 592.3 *expedient plan*, 635.1, 635.3 *trap*, 638.2 *means of escape*, 644.2 *task*, 652.9 *tactics*, 655.1 *skill*, 657.2 *stratagem*, 657.5 *be cunning*, 771.5 *joke*, 858.1 *improbity*
trick cycle 71.12 *bicycle*
trick cyclist 60.11 *doctor*, 61.30 *psychiatrist*, 510.10 *psychiatrist*
tricked 515.10 *deceived*, 538.16 *misinformed*, 539.36 *deceived*
tricked out 295.30 *dressed up*, 791.14 *beautified*
trickery 531.5 *evasion*, 539.7 *tricking*, 539.9 *sleight of hand*, 540.8 *fraud*, 657.1 *cunning*, 858.1 *improbity*
trickily 477.24 *questionably*
trickiness 474.3 *cunning*, 539.5 *falseness*
tricking 539
trickle 96.7 *flow*, 182.1 *few*, 328.1 *move slowly*, 347.3 *leakage*, 347.12 *leak*, 391.16 *seep*, 612.8 *trifle*
trickling 347.3 *leakage*
trick of fortune 515.2 *bad outcome*
trick of the light 102.3 *delusion*, 515.3 *mirage*
trick play 19.9 *play*
trick question 477.4 *difficult question*
tricks of the trade 539.7 *tricking*, 602.1 *means*, 657.2 *stratagem*
trickster 474.6 *sophist*, 539.15 *deceiver*, 539.17 *cheat*, 548.3 *deceiver*, 655.5 *expert*, 657.3 *cunning person*, 736.11 *dishonest person*
tricksy 657.4 *cunning*
tricky 474.8 *cunning*, 477.13 *problematic*, 539.34 *deceiving*, 539.40 *illusory*, 540.31 *fraudulent*, 633.1 *dangerous*, 657.4 *cunning*, 659.12 *problematic*, 858.5 *dishonourable*
tricky business 736.7 *dishonesty*
tricky situation 251.3 *difficult circumstances*, 659.5 *predicament*
tricky spot 659.5 *predicament*
triclinic 57.33 *crystalline*
triclinic crystal 57.4 *crystal*
triclofos 62 Medication
tricolour 456.5 *variegated thing*
Tricolour 544.7 *flag*
tricorn 177.2 *trident*, 177.8 *three-sided*, 295.15 *headgear*
tricornered 177.8 *three-sided*
tricot 67 Natural Fabrics
tricotine 67 Natural Fabrics
tricycle 71.12 *bicycle*, 177.2 *trident*
tridem 36.7, 36.13 *windsurfing*
trident 177, 177.8 *three-sided*, 343.5 *fork*
Trident 680.5 *missile weapon*
tridentate 177.8 *three-sided*
trident-like 343.9 *branched*
tridimensional 177.8 *three-sided*
tried 479.10 *tested*, 655.8 *expert*
tried and tested 485.9 *qualified*, 490.1 *certain*
tried-and-true 819.11 *devoted*
tried-and-true method 652.7 *way*
triedness 819.3 *familiarity*
triennial 177.2 *trident*, 177.8 *three-sided*
triennium 177.2 *trident*
trier 479.5 *experimenter*, 575.5 *tenacious person*, 596.7 *attempter*
Trieste 93 Cities
trifid 177.9 *trisected*
Trifid Nebula 53 Nebulae

trifle 612, 45.35 *dessert,* 754.5 *cheap item,* 821.26, 826.8 *court*

trifler 579.4 *capricious person,* 612.10 *nonentity*

trifles 612.8 *trifle*

trifle with 579.5 *be capricious,* 628.4 *impair*

trifling 260.7 *little,* 278.2 *superficial,* 521.10 *meaningless,* 612.4 *trivial*

trifling fault 612.8 *trifle*

trifluoperazine 62 Medication

trifold 177.7 *three*

trifoliate 83.18 *of leaves,* 177.8 *three-sided*

triforium 10.12 *church,* 43.10 *church architecture,* 327.7 *arcade*

triforking 343.4 *branching*

triform 177.7 *three*

trifurcate 177.11 *trisect,* 343.9 *branched,* 343.14 *branch*

trifurcated 177.9 *trisected*

trifurcation 177.5 *trisection,* 343.4 *branching*

trig 52.51 *trigonometry*

trigamy 823.3 *types of marriage*

trigeminal neuralgia 624.17 *nervous disorder*

trigger 410.11 *fuel,* 603.1 *tool,* 680.9 *firearm*

Trigger 32.1 *horse*

triggerfish 80 Fishes

trigger-happy 398.24 *murderous,* 679.33 *combative,* 780.4 *rash*

trigger off 156.20 *activate,* 226.10 *awaken*

triglyceride 58.7 *fat*

triglyph 43 Architectural Decoration

triglyphic 43.17 *structured*

trigon 52.43 *triangle*

trigonal 57.33 *crystalline,* 177.8 *three-sided*

trigonal crystal 57.4 *crystal*

trigonometric 52.68 *mathematical*

trigonometrical 170.15 *mathematical*

trigonometrically 52.87, 170.16 *mathematically*

trigonometric function 52, 52.29 *mathematical function*

trigonometrician 170.7 *mathematician*

trigonometry 52, 52.1 *mathematics,* 170.1 *calculation,* 310.4 *angular measurement*

trig point 275.8 *high thing*

trihebdomadary 177.2 *trident*

trihedral 177.8 *three-sided*

trihedron 177.2 *trident*

trihydrate 57.10 *salt*

triiodothyronine 58 Hormones

trike 71.12 *bicycle*

trilateral 177.8 *three-sided,* 305.6 *side,* 310.9 *angled*

trilby 295.15 *headgear*

trilingual 177.8 *three-sided,* 564.19 *speaking*

trill 426, 49.16 *musical note,* 49.39 *sing,* 96.7 *flow,* 364.9 *roll,* 426.6 *musical repetition,* 433.10 *sing,* 564.3 *mode of speech*

Trillick 93 Cities

trillion 169.3 *large number,* 179.11 *million,* 181.7 *myriad*

trillions 181.2 *multitude*

trillionth 179.22 *millionth*

trilobite 54.43 *fossil,* 81.4 *arthropod,* 200.10 *fossilization,* 202.8 *prehistoric animal*

trilogy 51.2 *play,* 177.2 *trident*

trim 47.17 *carpenter,* 73.7 *miscellaneous aviation terms,* 105.5 *physical state,* 121.6 *change gradually,* 129.5 *make smaller,* 150.13 *orderly,* 167.9 *make conform,* 182.8 *reduce,* 262.5 *make smaller,* 270.10 *shorten,* 295.24 *part of garment,* 306.6 *edge,* 306.6 *nature,* 537.31 *be accurate,* 557.5 *ornament,* 578.1 *be equivocal,* 621.13 *clean,* 623.3 *health,* 754.13 *make cheap,* 789.6 *personable,* 791.8 *hair cut*

Trim 93 Cities

trimaran 74 Ships and Boats, **74** Sailing Ships and Boats, 177.2 *trident*

trim back 628.5 *hurt*

trim down to size 612.13 *make unimportant*

trimeprazine 62 Medication

trimester 177.2 *trident*

trimestrial 177.8 *three-sided*

trimeter 48.9 *metre,* 177.2 *trident*

trimethroprim 62 Medication

trimetric 177.8 *three-sided*

trimipramine 62 Medication

trimmed 47.16 *joined,* 262.7 *smaller,* 270.8 *shortened,* 295.31 *styled,* 537.21 *accurate,* 557.4 *ornate,* 621.17 *cleaned,* 791.14 *beautified,* 792.8 *decorated*

trimmed joist 47.10 *carpenter's term*

trimmer 167.6 *conformist,* 262.4 *contractor,* 539.21 *traitor,* 578.9 *equivocator*

trimming 47.10 *carpenter's term,* 47.16 *joined,* 262.1 *contraction,* 270.2 *shortening,* 300.2 *edging,* 537.8 *accuracy,* 557.1 *ornament*

trimmings 130.3 *additional item,* 132.2 *residue*

trimorphic 177.7 *three*

trimorphism 177.3 *threeness*

trim tab 73 Aircraft Parts

trim the sails 74.9 *navigate*

Trimurti 8.3 *God*

trinal 177.7 *three*

trinary 177.7 *three*

Trincomalee 93 Cities

trine 177.1, 177.7 *three,* 310.4 *angular measurement*

trinely 177.12 *thrice*

Trinidad 98 Islands

Trinidad and Tobago 91 Countries

Trinitarian 7 Members of Religious Orders, 7.5 *Christian*

Trinitarianism 7 Christian Movements

trinity 177.1 *three*

trinket 612.9 *bauble,* 754.5 *cheap item*

trinkets 792.5 *decorative articles*

trinomial 52.76 *functional,* 177.2 *trident*

trio 49.26 *musical group,* 140.3 *assembly,* 177.1 *three,* 664.9 *team*

triode 64.20 *electron tube*

triol 57 Types of Compounds

triolet 48.7 *poem,* 48.10 *verse form*

triose 58.3 *carbohydrate*

trioxygen 57 Chemical Elements

trip 360, 23.6 *play basketball,* 31.9 *play hockey,* 35.5 *play rugby,* 38.2 *football play,* 38.4 *play soccer,* 46.15 *dance,* 324.15 *walk,* 356.1 *passage,* 360.4 *fall,* 361.4 *gather up,* 362.7 *lean,* 362.11 *lowering,* 493.10 *misjudge,* 539.33 *snare,* 656.7 *be clumsy,* 661.9 *block,* 864.16 *be wicked,* 875.1 *drug-taking*

triparted 177.9 *trisected*

tripartite 177.9 *trisected*

tripartition 177.5 *trisection*

tripe 45.31 *offal,* 290.4 *insides,* 506.1 *nonsense,* 521.4 *senseless talk*

tripedal 177.8 *three-sided*

tripeptide 58.8 *amino acid*

triphibious war 676.1 *war*

triphylite 54 Minerals

Tripitaka 7.12 *religious text*

triple 177, 21.6 *track,* 22.5 *batting terms,* 22.7 *play baseball,* 25.5 *bowling delivery,* 128.5 *make bigger,* 177.1, 177.7 *three*

triple-A 670.13 *air attack*

Triple-A league 22.1 *baseball*

triple bar 32.9 *jumping*

triple crown 7.11 *vestment,* 35.2 *championship,* 682.3 *successful thing*

Triple Entente 715.3 *alliance*

triple jump 18 Sporting Activities, 21.2 *field events*

triple jumper 21.3 *athlete*

triple jumping 21.2 *field events*

triple metre 48.9 *metre*

tripleness 177.3 *threeness*

triple play 22.6 *fielding terms*

triple point 56.37 *temperature*

triple point of water 56.38 *thermodynamics*

triples 25.9 *bowls*

triples match 25.1 *green bowling*

triplet 48.8 *part of poem,* 177.2 *trident*

triple-tongue 49.38 *sound*

triple vaccine 630.3 *prophylactic*

triplex 177.7 *three*

triplicate 110.4, 110.9 *duplicate,* 110.15 *duplicate,* 177.7 *three,* 177.10 *triple*

triplicating 177.4 *triplication*

triplication 177, 128.1 *increase*

triplicity 177.3 *threeness*

tripling 177.4 *triplication*

triploid 69.5 *gardening*

triply 177.12 *thrice*

tripod 66.18 *exposure time,* 177.2 *trident,* 284.2 *supporting part,* 517.10 *cards*

tripodic 177.8 *three-sided*

Tripoli 93 Cities, **93** Cities

trip out 875.10 *drug oneself*

trip over 656.7 *be clumsy*

tripped 31.8 *hockey,* 38.5 *soccer*

tripping 23.5 *penalties,* 31.1 *hockey,* 31.3 *ice hockey,* 31.5 *lacrosse,* 31.8 *hockey,* 35.3 *rugby play,* 38.5 *soccer,* 360.18, 362.20 *falling,* 433.6 *melodious,* 558.3 *elegant,* 642.18 *active*

trip switch 64.28 *plug,* 323.2 *stopper*

trip the light fantastic 46.15 *dance*

trip to the moon 53.31 *space travel*

triptych 50.8 *painting,* 177.2 *trident*

triptyque 71.21 *miscellaneous motoring terms*

trip up 539.33 *snare,* 661.9 *block,* 806.23 *abase*

tripwire 539.13, 539.33 *snare,* 671.8 *military defences*

trireme 679.25 *historical naval ships*

trisaccharide 58.3 *carbohydrate*

trisect 177

trisected 177

trisection 177

trishaw 71 Carriages and Carts, 71.12 *bicycle*

triskaidekaphobia 777 Phobias by Name

Tristan and Isolde 821.10 *lovers*

tristich 48.8 *part of poem,* 177.2 *trident*

tritanopia 436.2 *poor sight*

tritanopic 436.9 *weak-sighted*

trite 164.22 *commonplace,* 183.13 *monotonous,* 412.5 *tasteless,* 505.2 *proverbial,* 521.10 *meaningless,* 584.10 *familiar,* 788.4 *boring*

trite expression 164.8 *generalization*

tritely 788.8 *boringly*

triteness 412.1 *tastelessness,* 521.1 *lack of meaning,* 788.1 *boredom*

triterpene 58.20 *terpene*

tritiate 57.26 *react*

tritiation 57 Types of Chemical Reaction

triticale 68.12 *crop*

Triton 97.4 *sea god*

Triton among the minnows 126.5 *superior*

triton shell 81 Molluscs

triturable 384.21 *pulverizable*

triturate 384.23 *pulverize*

triturated 384.19 *pulverized*

trituration 384.4 *pulverization*

triturator 384.11 *pulverizer*

triumph 126.8 *be superior,* 682.2 *victory,* 682.9 *be victorious,* 773.1 *rejoicing,* 773.5 *rejoice,* 812.3 *ceremony,* 812.8 *salute*

triumphal 682.15 *victorious,* 812.12 *ceremonial*

triumphal arch 812.4 *reception*

triumphal procession 676.2 *glory of war*

triumphant 126.14 *best,* 682.15 *victorious,* 773.9 *rejoicing*

triumphantly 126.16 *superiorly,* 682.16 *successfully,* 773.11 *rejoicingly*

triumphant success 682.1 *success*

triumph of justice 855.1 *vindication*

triumph over 806.26 *outdo*

triumvirate 12.1 *government,* 177.2 *trident,* 664.9 *team*

triune 177.1, 177.7 *three*

trivalent 57.35 *combined*

Trivandrum 93 Cities

trivet 177.2 *trident*

trivia 612.8 *trifle*

trivial 612, 104.8 *intruder,* 260.7 *little,* 278.2 *superficial,* 521.10 *meaningless,* 783.11 *insignificant*

trivial error 504

triviality 612, 104.1 *extraneousness,* 278.3 *shallowness,* 612.8 *trifle,* 783.5 *insignificance*

trivialize 612.13 *make unimportant,* 850.20 *scorn*

trivialized 850.17 *unrespected*

trivially 104.18 *extraneously,* 612.14 *unimportantly,* 783.20 *unexceptionally*

Trivial Pursuit 42 Board Games

trivia quiz 477.5 *easy question*

tRNA 58.10 *nucleoside*

troat 432.4 *cry*

trochaic 48.20 *metrical*

troche 62.6 *pill*

trochee 48.9 *metre*

trochilic 364.12 *rotary*

trochilics 364.7 *science of rotation*

trochoid 52.40 *curve*

trochophore 81.13 *invertebrate larva*

trodden 327.15 *accessible,* 584.10 *familiar*

trodden flat 282.9 *flattened*

troglodyte 816.6 *unsocial person*

troglodytes 400.3 *uncivilized human*

trogon 78 Birds

troika 71.10 *sled,* 177.2 *trident,* 664.9 *team*

Troilus and Cressida 48 Shakespeare's plays, 821.10 *lovers*

Trojan 642.10 *busy person*

Trojan horse 65.17 *computing term,* 539.14 *fatal gift,* 540.14 *false thing,* 657.2 *stratagem,* 820.5 *hostile person*

tro-khmer 49 Musical Instruments

troll 11.11 *ghost,* 20.7 *angle,* 76.7 *legendary beast,* 338.22 *roll,* 339.12 *drag,* 364.9 *roll*

trolled 20.8 *angling*

trolley 71 Motor Vehicles, 71.7 *handcart,* 258.10 *cart,* 326.5 *means of transport*

trolleybus 71 Motor Vehicles, 71.19 *bus*

trolley line 327.10 *railway*

trolling 20.1, 20.8 *angling,* 364.2 *turning,* 364.11 *rotating*

trollop 877.9 *immoral woman*

Trollope 48 Writers

trombone 49 Musical Instruments

trometamol 62 Medication

trompe l'œil 47.1 *furniture*

trompe l'oeil 102.3 *delusion,* 519.5 *fantasy*

trona 54 Minerals

Trondheim 93 Cities

Troon 93 Cities

troop 17.4 *military organization,* 77.21 *assemblage of mammals,* 161.14 *force,* 161.23 *flock,*

161.40 *crowd,* 181.4 *throng,* 181.11 *crowd,* 665.1 *party,* 679.16 *army unit*
troop carrier 74 *Ships and Boats,* 679.31 *military aircraft*
trooper 32.15 *horse person,* 679.8 *soldier,* 679.20 *cavalryman*
trooping the Colour 811.13 *ceremonial,* 813.3 *formal occasion*
troops 679.14 *armed forces*
troopship 679.24 *warship*
troostite 54 Minerals
trope 5.24 *phrasing,* 48.12 *poetic language,* 520.4 *type of meaning,* 527.6 *latency,* 557.1 *ornament*
trophoplasm 59.7 *cell*
trophy 681, 511.3 *memento,* 544.4 *insignia,* 545.11 *monument,* 588.6 *objective,* 617.7 *elite,* 674.2 *contest,* 721.5 *profit,* 729.2 *gift,* 730.2 *something received,* 782.5 *object of desire,* 878.2 *prize*
Trophy 681
tropic 249.2 *geographical region,* 527.5 *mysterious*
tropical 69.19 *ornamental,* 249.16 *regional,* 408.11 *warm*
tropical air 55.10 *air movement*
tropical climate 55.38 *climate*
tropical disease 624, 624.4 *disease*
tropical fern 88.1 *fern*
tropical fish 80.2 *fish*
tropical forest 85.4 *trees*
tropical hardwood 85.1 *tree*
tropical heat 408.5 *hot weather*
tropically 69.20 *horticulturally,* 249.19 *geographically*
tropical meaning 520.4 *type of meaning*
tropical medicine 60.1 *medicine*
tropical revolving storm 55.16 *wind vortex*
tropical storm 55.16 *wind vortex*
tropical summer rainy zone 55.39 *climatic zone*
tropic bird 78 Birds
Tropic of Cancer 408.8 *hot place*
Tropic of Capricorn 408.8 *hot place*
tropics 55.39 *climatic zone,* 249.2 *geographical region,* 408.8 *hot place*
tropology 524.5 *science of interpretation*
tropopause 55.8 *atmosphere,* 390.3 *atmospheric layers*
troposphere 55.8 *atmosphere,* 390.3 *atmospheric layers*
tropospheric 55.43, 390.13 *atmospheric*
trot 32.16 *ride,* 324.12 *gait,* 328.10 *slow motion,* 329.4 *be swift,* 524.4 *translation*
Trot 12.6 *political party*
trot along 345.1 *depart*
trot out 183.18 *harp,* 526.3 *reveal*
trot out clichés 426.14 *repeat*
Trotskyist 693.11 *rebel*
Trotskyists 12.6 *political party*
trotter 32.2 *thoroughbred,* 45.24 *pork*
trotters 45.31 *offal*
trotting 18 Sporting Activities, 20.1 *angling*
tro-u 49 Musical Instruments
troubadour 48.14 *author,* 49.24 *musician,* 51.27 *entertainer,* 433.5 *melodist*
troubadour poem 48.7 *poem*
trouble 105.2 *predicament,* 106.4 *difficult circumstances,* 151.9 *disorder,* 153.5 *commotion,* 153.7 *disturb,* 251.3 *difficult circumstances,* 366.22 *agitate,* 616.3 *inconvenience,* 616.5 *be inconvenient,* 618.13 *be worthless,* 631.2 *adversity,* 642.17 *meddle,* 644.1 *exertion,* 650.6 *fatigue,* 659.23 *cause difficulties,* 661.2 *obstacle,* 687.11 *cause adversity,* 768.3 *nuisance,* 777.14 *worry,* 862.2 *affliction,* 862.11 *be evil*

trouble ahead 687.1 *adversity*
trouble and strife 180.12 *partner,* 402.12 *woman in the family,* 823.11 *married woman*
troubled 659, 153.12 *disturbed,* 366.15 *agitated,* 777.9 *worried,* 862.8 *afflicted*
troublefree 660.14 *relaxed*
troublemaker 151, 635, 693, 228.7 *motivator,* 473.6 *arguer,* 500.5 *dissenter,* 618.12 *bad person,* 642.11 *meddler,* 657.3 *cunning person,* 659.9 *difficult person,* 661.7 *hinderer,* 666.4 *dissenter,* 679.5 *arguer,* 713.4 *protester,* 764.9 *unpleasant person,* 820.5 *hostile person,* 862.6 *evil person,* 864.9 *wicked person*
troublemaking 679.34 *argumentative*
trouble oneself 644.8 *exert oneself*
troubles 687.1 *adversity,* 862.2 *affliction*
troubleshooter 654.4, 662.14 *adviser,* 678.3 *mediator*
troubleshooting 678.2 *mediation*
troublesome 659, 106.8 *difficult,* 251.8 *circumstantial,* 616.1 *inconvenient,* 642.21 *meddling,* 644.11 *laborious,* 659.13 *inconvenient,* 687.6 *adverse*
troublesomeness 616.3 *inconvenience*
trouble spot 624.6 *infection,* 635.1 *trap*
troubling 659.12 *problematic,* 659.13 *inconvenient*
troublous 366.15 *agitated,* 862.9 *detrimental*
troublously 366.27 *agitatedly*
trough 57 Laboratory Apparatus, 55.11 *weather system,* 68.10 *farm tool,* 97.3 *wave,* 127.5 *inferior state,* 258.12 *bath,* 317.2 *concave land,* 317.3 *cavity,* 321.1, 321.6 *furrow,* 365.5 *wave*
trounce 126.3 *be superior,* 244.11 *ruin,* 330.5 *beat,* 682.10 *defeat heavily,* 879.3 *hit*
trounced 127.18 *outclassed*
trouncing 330.12 *collision,* 682.2 *victory,* 683.2 *defeat,* 879.12 *corporal punishment*
troupe 51.23 *cast,* 161.12 *team,* 665.1 *party*
trouper 51.22 *actor*
trouser press 282.4 *flattener,* 376.9 *smoother*
trousers 295
trouser suit 295.10 *suit*
trousseau 295.1 *dress,* 605.1 *store*
trout 80 Fishes, **161** Collective Names by Animal, 20.4 *American game fish,* 20.5 *British game fish,* 45.17 *freshwater fish,* 80.8 *food fish*
trout farm 68.6 *farm*
trout fishing 590.2 *chase*
trouvère 48.14 *author,* 433.5 *melodist*
trove 721.5 *profit*
trow 11.11 *ghost*
Trowbridge 93 Cities
trowel 69.6 *garden tool,* 258.17 *ladle,* 376.9 *smoother,* 380.9 *sharp-edged thing,* 380.16 *use a sharp tool ,* 603.2 *garden tool*
troxidone 62 Medication
Troy 93 Cities
troy weight 75.1 *unit,* 268.5 *measuring system,* 369.9 *avoirdupois weight*
truancy 254.4 *absenteeism,* 458.4 *disappearance,* 591.16 *desertion,* 598.3 *relinquishment,* 638.1 *escape*
truancy officer 6.5 *educationalist*
truant 254, 254.6 *absentee,* 458.4 *disappearance,* 591.9 *play truant,* 591.17 *avoider,* 598.4 *deserter,* 638.3 *escaper,* 638.8 *escaping,* 711.4 *refuser,* 720.6 *evader,* 720.12 *nonperforming*
truantism 254.4 *absenteeism*

truce 209.3 *delayed action,* 218.3 *pause,* 325.1 *motionlessness,* 639.2 *deliverance,* 675.1 *peace,* 677.1 *pacification*
truceless war 676.1 *war*
truck 71 Motor Vehicles, **74** Rigging, **71,** 70.5 *transportable,* 72.6 *rolling stock,* 223.1, 223.5 *exchange,* 258.10 *cart,* 326.5 *means of transport,* 326.12 *transport,* 544.7 *flag,* 737.1, 737.4 *trade*
truckage 326.2 *transportation*
truck driver 326.7 *transferor*
trucker 326.7 *transferor*
truck farm 68.6 *farm*
truck farmer 68.15 *agriculturist*
truck farming 68.4 *arable farming,* 69.1 *horticulture,* 86.4 *fruit eating*
truck garden 69.2 *garden,* 69.14 *practise horticulture*
truck gardener 69.13 *horticulturist*
truck in 606.5 *provision*
trucking 71.1 *road transport*
truckle 808.9 *fawn*
truckle bed 47.6 *bed*
truckling 808.2 *sycophancy,* 808.7 *sycophantic*
truckload 120.3 *container,* 257.2 *load*
truculence 818.2 *bad manners,* 832.1 *malevolence*
truculency 832.1 *malevolence*
truculent 670.21 *aggressive,* 818.6 *bad-mannered,* 832.14 *hostile*
truculently 832.20 *malevolently*
trudge 328.1 *move slowly,* 328.10 *slow motion*
trudgen 39.11 *swimming*
trudgen stroke 39.2 *swimming technique*
true 537, 688, 3.19 *chronicled,* 16.51 *legitimate,* 52.86 *logical,* 99.13, 101.6 *real,* 119.6 *authentic,* 312.1 *straight,* 433.6 *melodious,* 490.1 *certain,* 501.10 *known,* 535.12 *vowed,* 537.26 *faithful,* 537.31 *be accurate,* 658.1 *naive,* 694.8 *loyal,* 719.7 *observant,* 819.11 *devoted,* 843.8 *correct,* 857.4 *honourable*
true bearing 332.2 *bearing*
true believer 497.5 *believer*
true bill 856.1 *accusation*
true blue 12.6 *political party,* 217.3 *conservative person,* 663.9 *opposer,* 665.6 *political party member*
true-blue 217.8 *conservative,* 537.26 *faithful,* 584.13 *fixed,* 658.1 *naive,* 662.23 *uncooperative,* 665.10 *political,* 694.8 *loyal,* 857.4 *honourable*
trued 537.21 *accurate*
true fern 88.1 *fern*
true fruit 86.2 *botanical fruit*
true fungi 89.2 *fungi*
true gentleman 805.13 *proud person*
true grass 87.1 *grass*
true grit 575.4 *stamina*
true inlay 47.9 *decorative woodwork*
true lady 857.3 *honourable person*
true look 537.12 *true to life*
true love 821.2 *romantic love,* 821.11 *loved one*
truelove knot 74 Knots
true moss 88.3 *moss*
trueness 490.9 *certainty,* 537.1 *truth,* 537.13 *faithfulness,* 819.3 *familiarity,* 843.2 *correctness,* 857.1 *probity*
true picture 547.1, 560.9 *representation*
true report 537.8 *accuracy*
true representation 537.8 *accuracy*
true self 165.11 *identity*
true sound 537.12 *true to life*

true-speaking 564.19 *speaking*
true to form 165.16 *characteristic*
true to life 537, 114.9, 537.25 *lifelike*
true-to-life 101.7 *realistic,* 503.6 *correct,* 547.13 *representational,* 560.11 *descriptive,* 560.13 *representing*
true to nature 114.9 *lifelike,* 537.12 *true to life,* 537.25 *lifelike*
true to scale 537.12 *true to life,* 537.25 *lifelike*
true to the bitter end 575.12 *indomitable*
true to the core 857.4 *honourable*
true to the facts 537.21 *accurate*
true to the letter 537.10 *literalness,* 537.23 *literal*
true-to-the-letter 503.6 *correct*
true to the spirit 537.25 *lifelike*
true to type 114.9 *lifelike*
true wind 36.1 *sailing*
truffle 89 Fungi, 45.33 *vegetable*
truffle hunter 89.8 *study of fungi*
trug 69.6 *garden tool,* 258.7 *basket*
truing 537.8 *accuracy*
truism 537, 426.7 *repeated word,* 505.1 *maxim,* 521.1 *lack of meaning*
truistic 537
truly 537, 99.22 *really,* 101.14 *certainly,* 118.14 *imitatively,* 119.8 *originally,* 490.23 *certainly,* 535.24 *truthfully,* 537.37, 688.25 *authentically,* 719.8 *observantly,* 772.11 *earnestly,* 819.19 *devotedly,* 843.20 *correctly,* 857.7 *honourably*
trumeau 43.9 *miscellaneous architectural features*
trump 42.3 *card game terms,* 126.8 *be superior,* 602.1 *means,* 655.3 *masterpiece,* 682.11 *overmaster*
trump card 592.3 *expedient plan,* 602.1 *means,* 611.3 *chief thing*
trumped-up 540.32 *falsified,* 856.9 *perjurious*
trumped-up charge 856.2 *false accusation*
trumped-up story 538.3 *lying*
trumpery 521.5 *empty talk,* 612.4 *trivial,* 612.9 *bauble*
trumpet 49 Musical Instruments, 49.38 *sound,* 315.5 *cone,* 423.4 *sound maker,* 423.8 *be loud,* 427.4 *sources of resonance,* 427.10 *ring,* 432.4 *cry,* 532.14 *proclaim,* 564.12 *speak loudly,* 676.2 *glory of war,* 811.28 *flourish,* 851.15 *compliment*
trumpet blast 423.1 *loudness*
trumpet call 543.6 *word,* 586.4 *exhortation,* 636.2 *danger signal*
trumpet creeper 84 Flowers and Flowering Plants
trumpeter 78 Birds, 543.8 *signer*
trumpet fanfare 811.12 *magniloquence*
trumpet-tongued 423.6 *loud*
trump hand 126.3 *advantage*
trumping up 540.9 *falsification*
trumps 602.1 *means*
Trump Tower 740.7 *emporium*
trump up 540.22 *falsify*
trump up a charge 856.6 *accuse falsely*
truncate 52.91 *add,* 270.10 *shorten,* 552.4 *be concise,* 562.8 *summarize,* 628.5 *hurt,* 685.5 *not complete*
truncated 145.4 *incomplete,* 270.8 *shortened,* 552.3 *concise,* 562.7 *shortened,* 685.4 *uncompleted*
truncated cone 52.45 *curved surface*
truncated decimal 52.18 *division*
truncated pyramid 52.46 *polyhedron*
truncation 52.18 *division,* 270.2 *shortening,* 552.1 *conciseness,* 562.2 *outline*

truncheon 330.16 *weapons*, 680.7 *blunt weapon*

trundle 324.15 *walk*, 338.22, 364.9 *roll*

trundling 364.2 *turning*

trunk 83.5 *stem*, 85.2 *tree part*, 132.1 *remainder*, 143.6 *branch*, 258.9 *baggage*, 315.4 *cylinder*, 318.3 *protuberance*, 327.15 *accessible*, 605.4 *storage*

trunk exchange 534.12 *public telephone system*

trunkfish 80 Fishes

trunk line 327.10 *railway*, 534.12 *public telephone system*

trunk road 71.2, 327.3 *road*

trunks 39.8 *swimwear*, 295.18 *underwear*

trunkwood 85.3 *timber*

trunnion 364.4 *vortex*

Truro 93 Cities

truss 74 Rigging, 43.9 *miscellaneous architectural features*, 47.10 *carpenter's term*, 47.17 *carpenter*, 63.27 *superstructure*, 135.8 *unite*, 135.10 *link*, 161.27 *bundle*, 161.38 *group*

truss bridge 63.21 *bridge*

trussed 161.49 *grouped*

trussing needle 45.6 *kitchen equipment*

trust 302.2 *limiting factor*, 326.10 *transferred thing*, 490.10 *conviction*, 497.3 *believing*, 497.7 *believe*, 513.1 *expectation*, 658.4 *be naive*, 665.1 *party*, 703.3 *authority*, 715.3 *alliance*, 744.7 *repute*, 775.2 *expectation*, 775.6 *hope*

trustee 696.9 *educational leader*, 703.5 *commissioner*, 707.3 *agent*, 730.5 *recipient*, 741.18 *treasurer*

trusteeship 703.4 *council*

trustful 497.11 *believing*, 819.11 *devoted*

trustfully 497.15 *believingly*, 819.19 *devotedly*

trustiness 857.1 *probity*

trusting 466.3 *incurious*, 490.2 *convinced*, 497.11 *believing*, 658.1 *naive*

trust in God 7.2 *religiousness*, 7.19 *be religious*

trusting person 497

trusting soul 539.22 *dupe*

trust with 703.6 *commission*

trustworthily 819.19 *devotedly*

trustworthiness 490.17 *infallibility*, 497.4 *believability*, 857.1 *probity*

trustworthy 312.5 *honourable*, 490.6 *infallible*, 497.13 *believable*, 632.5 *safe*, 819.11 *devoted*, 857.4 *honourable*

trusty 857.4 *honourable*

trusty blade 680.8 *sharp weapon*

trusty steed 32.1 *horse*

truth 537, 3.14 *historicalness*, 8.2 *divine attribute*, 52.63 *mathematical logic*, 52.64 *reasoning*, 99.4 *demonstrable existence*, 235.1 *power*, 312.8 *directness*, 490.9 *certainty*, 497.1 *belief*, 503.2 *correctness*, 505.1 *maxim*, 530.3 *openness*, 658.2 *naivety*, 843.2 *correctness*, 855.2 *defence*, 857.1 *probity*

Truth 537

truth condition 4.8 *philosophical term*

truthful 537, 101.7 *realistic*, 312.5 *honourable*, 503.6 *correct*, 526.15 *open*, 658.1 *naive*, 843.10 *moral*, 857.4 *honourable*

truthfully 535, 537, 312.13 *straightforwardly*, 857.7 *honourably*

truthfulness 537, 312.8 *directness*, 857.1 *probity*

truthful person 537

truth function 4.8 *philosophical term*

truthless 540.25 *false*

truthlessly 540.36 *falsely*

truthlessness 540.1 *falsehood*

truth table 4.8 *philosophical term*, 52.63 *mathematical logic*

truth value 4.8 *philosophical term*, 52.63 *mathematical logic*

try 642, 16.70 *litigate*, 16.76 *judge*, 35.3 *rugby play*, 243.1 *production*, 411.9 *taste*, 477.17 *question*, 479.1, 479.11 *experiment*, 479.13 *invent*, 492.11 *judge*, 518.3 *conjecture*, 596.1, 596.5 *attempt*, 597.1 *undertake*, 597.2 *undertaking*, 599.1 *use*, 640.4 *act*, 644.8 *exert oneself*, 674.11 *contend*, 682.3 *successful thing*, 856.5 *accuse*

try a case 16, 16.69 *have jurisdiction over*

try a fall 674.11 *contend*

try and try again 575.6 *persevere*, 596.2 *try hard*, 674.11 *contend*

try conclusions with 674.11 *contend*

try for 588.10 *aim*

try for a miracle 487.10 *attempt the impossible*

try hard 596, 642.15 *try*

trying 479.3 *experimentation*, 479.8 *experimental*, 596.8 *attempting*, 650.4 *fatiguing*, 659.13 *inconvenient*, 764.1 *unpleasant*

trying hard 575.10 *persevering*

try in vain 515.4 *be disappointed*

try it on 652.13 *behave badly*

try on 295.34 *wear*

try one's best 644.8 *exert oneself*

try one's hand 479.13 *invent*

try one's hand at 596.1 *attempt*

try one's luck 229.4 *chance*, 479.13 *invent*, 589.12 *take a chance*, 596.3 *tackle*

try one's patience 659.22 *cause trouble*

try one's strength 479.13 *invent*

tryout 479.2 *rehearsal*

try out 479.11 *experiment*, 479.12 *rehearse*

trypanophobia 777 Phobias by Name

trypanosome 81.10 *parasite*

trypanosomiasis 81.12 *protozoal disease*, 624.7 *tropical disease*

tryparsamide 62 Medication

trypsin 58.11 *enzyme*

tryptophan 58 Amino Acids

trysail 74 Sails, 36.3 *parts of a sailing boat*

try scorer 35.4 *rugby player*

try something new 201.18 *be trendy*

try square 268.6 *measuring instrument*, 281.4 *plumb line*

tryst 161.8 *rendezvous*, 815.3 *meeting*

try the latest craze 201.18 *be trendy*

try to put a square peg in a round hole 656.6 *act foolishly*

try to run before one can walk 287.3 *invert*

try to say 520.10 *mean*

tsar 696.2 *sovereign*

tsarina 696.2 *sovereign*

tsetse fly 82 Insects

T-shape 310.1 *angle*

T-shirt 295.4 *informal dress*, 295.8 *shirt*, 295.18 *underwear*

Tsimpshian 1 Peoples

Tsiolkovski 52 Scientists

Tsiolkovsky 53 Lunar Features

tsk 429.9 *sh*

Tsonga 5 Languages and Groups of Languages

T-square 52.49 *geometric construction*, 268.6 *measuring instrument*, 281.4 *plumb line*, 310.4 *angular measurement*

Tshiluba 5 Languages and Groups of Languages

Tsuki-yumi 8 Deities

tsunami 54.14 *wave*, 56.14 *sound wave*, 97.3 *wave*, 275.8 *high thing*, 365.5 *wave*, 375.9 *broken water*

tsuri daiko 49 Musical Instruments

tsuzumi 49 Musical Instruments

Tswana 5 Languages and Groups of Languages

TTL meter 66.18 *exposure time*

TT race 33.5 *motorcycle racing*

Tuamotuan 5 Languages and Groups of Languages

tuart 85 Trees and Shrubs

tuatara 79 Reptiles, 79.2 *lizard*

Tuatha de Danann 8 Deities

tub 258.12, 621.6 *bath*

tuba 49 Musical Instruments

tuba-dupré 49 Musical Instruments

tubbiness 259.5 *fatness*, 273.5 *thickness*, 315.2 *round body*

tubby 259.16 *fat*, 273.1 *thick*, 315.10 *well-rounded*

tube 72.1 *railway*, 235.7 *electrical power*, 272.8 *narrow thing*, 315.4 *cylinder*, 317.2 *concave land*, 322.7 *passageway*, 327.8 *tunnel*, 327.10 *railway*, 427.4 *sources of resonance*, 534.21 *television*

tube dress 295.7 *frock*

tuber 45.33 *vegetable*, 69.9 *garden plant*, 69.11 *vegetable*, 83.5 *stem*, 83.7 *root*, 226.3 *rudiment*

tubercular 624.23 *diseased*

tuberculophobia 777 Phobias by Name

tuberculosis 777 Phobias by Topic, 624.6 *infection*, 624.9 *respiratory disease*

tuberculous 624.23 *diseased*

tuberose 84 Flowers and Flowering Plants, 418.2 *fragrant thing*

tuberous 83.14 *of plants*

tuberous root 83.7 *root*

tuberous-rooted 83.19 *of roots*

tubers 86.1 *fruits*

tube station 218.4 *stopping place*

tubifex 81 Worms

Tübingen School 7 Christian Movements

tub of lard 259.12 *fat person*

tub-thump 564.14 *speak to*, 567.7 *address*

tub-thumper 564.10 *speaker*, 567.6 *public speaker*, 713.4 *protester*

tub-thumping 564.9 *art of public speaking*, 564.20 *eloquent*

tub to a whale 539.12 *disguise*

tubular 315.9 *round*

tubular bells 49 Musical Instruments

tubular furniture 47.1 *furniture*

tubulidentate 77.6 *insect-eating mammal*, 77.26 *insectivorous*

TUC 15.3 *organized labour*

Tucana 53 The Constellations

Tuche 8 Deities

tuck 39.11 *swimming*, 41.4 *skiing technique*, 262.5 *make smaller*, 320.2, 320.8 *pleat*, 350.7 *food*, 680.8 *sharp weapon*

tuckahoe 89 Fungi

tuck dive 39.6 *diving*

tucked 41.12 *ski*, 262.7 *smaller*, 295.31 *styled*

tucked away 527.2 *concealed*

tucker 295.14 *neckwear*, 350.7 *food*

tucker bag 258.8 *bag*

tuckered out 650.1 *fatigued*

Tucker porcelain 44 Types of Ceramics

tucket 427.2 *ringing*

tuck in 33.10 *be on the track*

tucking 41.12 *ski*

tucking in 33.6 *motor racing terms*

tuck in to 350.22 *eat well*

tuck into 872.5 *be greedy*

tuck jump 39.6 *diving*

tuck one's tail 806.20 *submit*

tuck position 39.6 *diving*

tuck shop 350.17 *food shop*

tuck up 320.8 *pleat*

tucotuco 77 Placental Mammals

Tucson 93 Cities

Tudor 43 Architectural Styles, 47.7 *furniture style*, 202.14 *historic*

Tudor arch 43.5 *arch*

Tudor rose 544.8 *heraldic device*

Tudor times 3.10 *past age*

tudum 49 Musical Instruments

tuffoli 45 Types of Pasta

tuft 87.2 *grassland*

tufted hair grass 87 Grasses

tug 74 Ships and Boats, 324.14 *set in motion*, 330.1 *impel*, 339.2, 339.11 *pull*, 339.12 *drag*, 339.13 *pull at*, 340.1 *attraction*, 340.11 *attract*, 355.1 *extraction*, 407.3 *press*, 407.11 *touch*, 644.4 *exertion*, 644.6 *work*

tugboat 339.6 *towline*

tugging 339.1 *traction*, 339.8 *tractional*, 340.8 *attracting*

tugging out 355.1 *extraction*

tug of love 674.2 *contest*

tug of war 18 Sporting Activities, 339.2 *pull*, 674.2 *contest*

tug one's forelock 808.10 *knuckle under*, 849.19 *take off one's hat to*

tug out 355.11 *extract*

tui 78 Birds

tuition 6.1 *education*

tulip 84 Flowers and Flowering Plants

tulip tree 85 Trees and Shrubs

Tull 52 Scientists

Tullamore 93 Cities

tulle 67 Natural Fabrics

Tulsa 93 Cities

Tultec art 50 Non-Western Art

Tulu 5 Languages and Groups of Languages

tumble 30.10 *compete in gymnastics*, 139.6 *come unstuck*, 244.13 *be destroyed*, 360.4 *fall*, 360.11 *trip*, 362.7 *lean*, 362.1 *lowering*, 364.10 *swirl*, 365.11 *rock*, 366.11 *stagger*, 379.4 *be brittle*, 633.8 *be in danger*

tumbledown 141.6 *disintegrating*, 238.9 *dilapidated*

tumble down 244.13 *be destroyed*

tumbledown 244.15 *destroyed*, 360.16 *descending*, 379.1 *brittle*, 628.13 *dilapidated*, 633.2 *unsafe*

tumbledown shack 256.8 *shelter*

tumble-dry 392.23 *drip-dry*, 621.13 *clean*

tumble-dryer 392.15 *dryer*

tumbler 51.29 *circus performer*, 237.5 *athlete*, 258.13 *drinking vessel*, 351.10 *drink container*

tumble to 522.6 *understand*

tumbling 18 Sporting Activities, 30.8 *floor exercises*, 360.16 *descending*, 360.18, 362.20 *falling*

tumbrel 71 Carriages and Carts

tumefaction 261.1 *growth*

tumescence 261.1 *growth*, 316.1 *convexity*

tumescent 261.8 *growing*, 316.4 *convex*

tumid 261.7 *bigger*, 557.4 *ornate*

tumidity 261.1 *growth*

tumidly 261.10 *largely*

tumidness 261.1 *growth*

tumify 261.6 *become bigger*

tummy 258.18 *stomach*, 290.4 *insides*

tummyache 406.2 *painful condition*

tumour 261.3 *enlarged thing*, 316.2 *bulge*, 624.3 *symptom*, 624.12 *cancer*

tump 143.7 *piece*, 275.3 *mountain*

tumult 366, 151.5 *confusion*, 153.5 *commotion*, 241.3 *instance of violence*, 423.2 *outcry*, 434.2 *dissonant noise*, 642.1 *activity*, 693.2 *violation of the law*

tumultation 366.2 *tumult*

tumultuous 241.6 *violent*, 693.13 *disobedient*

tumultuously 693.17 *disobediently*

tumulus 275.3 *mountain*, 399.6 *grave*

tumyr 49 Musical Instruments

tun 258.11 *vessel*

tuna 80 Fishes, 20.4 *American game fish*, 45.18 *sea fish*
tunable laser 56.26 *laser*
tuna sandwich 45.11 *sandwich*
Tunbridge Wells 93 Cities
tundra 55.39 *climatic zone*
tundra climate 55.38 *climate*
tune 49.13 *melody*, 49.22 *phrase*, 49.34 *harmonize*, 433.1 *melody*, 433.8 *harmonize*, 594.4 *prepare for action*, 629.1 *repair*
tuned 594.18 *prepared*
tuned circuit 64.13 *circuit*
tuned radio-frequency receiver 534.18 *radio*
tuneful 49.30 *harmonic*, 433.6 *melodious*
tunefully 433.11 *melodiously*
tunefulness 49.1 *music*
tune in 116.24 *harmonize*, 420.15 *hear*, 534.30 *communicate*
tuneless 434.9 *unmelodious*
tunelessly 434.12 *dissonantly*
tunelessness 434.3 *musical dissonance*
tuneless voice 563.2 *inarticulation*
tune out 421.8 *be deaf*
tuner 534.18 *radio*
tune up 49.34 *harmonize*, 237.8 *strengthen*, 433.8 *harmonize*, 594.4 *prepare for action*
tune-up 629.8 *repair*
tung oil 85 Tree Products
tungstate 57 Types of Compounds
tungsten 57 Chemical Elements
tungsten lamp 56.25 *light source*
tungsten light 66.15 *lighting*
tungstic 57.34 *elemental*
tungstite 54 Minerals
tungstous 57.34 *elemental*
Tungting 94 Lakes
Tungus 5 Languages and Groups of Languages
Tungusic 5 Languages and Groups of Languages
Tunguska 96 Rivers
tunic 295.5 *fancy dress*, 295.11 *jacket*, 295.16 *robe*
Tunica-Biloxi 1 Peoples
tunicate 81.2 *protochordate*
tunicle 7.11 *vestment*
tuning 125.2 *counterbalance*, 534.18 *radio*, 594.9 *preparation*, 629.8 *repair*
Tunis 93 Cities
Tunisia 91 Countries
tunnel 63, 327, 360, 63.19 *structure*, 63.30 *engineer*, 256.13 *lair*, 272.6 *narrow place*, 277.4 *deep thing*, 277.14 *deepen*, 317.2 *concave land*, 317.7 *make concave*, 322.7 *passageway*, 322.20 *hole*, 356.5 *crossing point*, 427.4 *sources of resonance*
tunnel kiln 44.6 *ceramic workshop*
tunnelled 322.14 *holed*
tunneller 317.4 *digger*, 322.3 *person who opens*
tunnelling 360, 63.19 *structure*, 277.1 *depth*
tunnel out 700.5 *be liberated*
tunnel vision 436.2 *poor sight*, 467.4 *diligence*, 493.3 *injustice*
Tunney 18 Sporting Personalities
tup 68.8 *livestock*, 135.11 *make love*, 401.16 *male animal*
tupan 49 Musical Instruments
tupelo 85 Trees and Shrubs
Tupi 1 Peoples, **5** Languages and Groups of Languages
Tupi-Guarani 5 Languages and Groups of Languages
Tupperware 258.16 *crockery*
Tupperware party 665.7 *social gathering*
turaco 78 Birds
Turanian 5 Languages and Groups of Languages, 5.11 *family of languages*
turban 7.11 *vestment*, 295.15 *headgear*
Turbellaria 81.6 *worm*

turbellarian 81.6 *worm*
turbid 393.17 *muddy*, 443.2 *shady*, 622.7 *dirty*
turbidity 366.3 *turbulence*, 393.3 *muddiness*, 443.6 *opaqueness*, 622.1 *dirtiness*
turbidness 393.3 *muddiness*
turbinate 314.4 *convolutional*
turbinated 364.12 *rotary*
turbination 314.2 *coil*, 364.1 *rotation*
turbine 63, 64.32 *power station*, 235.6 *source of energy*, 338.11 *propeller*, 364.6 *rotator*, 410.4 *electricity*, 603.4 *machine*
turbinectomy 60 Surgical Operations
turbo 338.11 *propeller*
turbocharger 235.6 *source of energy*
turbofan 73 Types of Aircraft, **73** Aircraft Parts
turbojet 73 Types of Aircraft
turbojet engine 73 Aircraft Parts
turbojet propulsion 338.2 *method of propulsion*
Turbo language 65.9 *programming language*
turboprop 73 Types of Aircraft
turboprop propulsion 338.2 *method of propulsion*
turbosupercharger 235.6 *source of energy*
turbot 80 Fishes, 45.18 *sea fish*, 80.8 *food fish*
turbulence 366, 56.8 *time*, 73.7 *miscellaneous aviation terms*, 151.5 *confusion*, 241.1 *violence*, 375.6 *roughness*
turbulent 366, 97.7 *oceanic*, 151.20 *disorderly*, 241.6 *violent*, 375.4 *bumpy*
turbulently 375.14 *roughly*
turbulent sea 97.3 *wave*
turd 353.5 *faeces*
turdine 78.23 *avian*
tureen 258.16 *crockery*
turf 32.7 *horseracing*, 69.9 *garden plant*, 87.2 *grassland*, 87.12 *manage grassland*, 143.7 *piece*, 233.7 *sphere of influence*, 249.13 *locality*, 250.1 *location*, 410.2 *lighter*, 453.8 *greenness*
turf accountant 32.15 *horse person*
turf out 349.1 *expel*
turfy 87.9 *grassy*, 374.4 *compressible*
Turgenev 48 Writers
turgescence 261.1 *growth*, 557.2 *affectation*
turgescent 261.8 *growing*
turgid 261.7 *bigger*, 553.3 *diffuse*, 557.4 *ornate*, 559.9 *inelegant*, 811.20 *pompous*
turgidity 261.1 *growth*, 557.2 *affectation*, 559.4 *inelegance of speech*, 811.5 *pomposity*
turgidly 261.10 *largely*, 553.7 *diffusely*, 557.4 *ornately*, 811.36 *pompously*
turgidness 261.1 *growth*
turgite 54 Minerals
Turin 93 Cities
Turing machine 65.3 *computer*
Turishcheva 18 Sporting Personalities
turistas 353.2 *defecation*
Turkana 94 Lakes
turkey 78 Birds, 25.5 *bowling delivery*, 37.5 *game*, 45.20 *meat*, 78.4 *table bird*, 683.4 *unsuccessful thing*
Turkey 91 Countries
turkey buzzard 78 Birds, 621.12 *cleaner*
turkey cock 78.10 *male bird*, 809.7 *vain person*
Turkey oak 85 Trees and Shrubs
Turkey red 450.1 *red*
turkeys 161 Collective Names by Animal
turkey sandwich 45.11 *sandwich*
turkey shoot 590.2 *chase*
turkey trot 46.2 *dance*

Turkic 5 Languages and Groups of Languages, 5.11 *family of languages*
Turkish 5 Languages and Groups of Languages, **77** Breeds of Cats
Turkish bath 408.8 *hot place*, 621.6 *bath*
Turkish baths 621.6 *bath*
Turkish carpet 293.9 *floor covering*
turkish crescent 49 Musical Instruments
Turkish crescent and star 544.6 *national emblem*
Turkish tobacco 413.7 *tobacco*
Turkmen 1 Peoples, **5** Languages and Groups of Languages
Turkmenistan 91 Countries
Turkoman 5 Languages and Groups of Languages, **32** Breeds of Horse and Pony
Turk's-cap lily 84 Flowers and Flowering Plants
Turk's-head 74 Knots
Turku 93 Cities
turmeric 45 Herbs and Spices
turmoil 161 Collective Names for Birds and Animals, 151.5 *confusion*, 153.5 *commotion*, 244.5 *havoc*, 366.2 *tumult*, 423.2 *outcry*, 434.2 *dissonant noise*, 642.1 *activity*, 674.6 *fight*, 689.1 *anarchy*, 693.2 *violation of the law*
turn 161 Collective Names for Birds and Animals, 7.19 *be religious*, 21.2 *field events*, 27.18 *bowl*, 30.5 *horizontal bar*, 30.6 *pommel horse*, 30.10 *compete in gymnastics*, 39.1 *swimming*, 41.7 *ice-dancing*, 41.14 *ski*, 44.11 *make ceramics*, 49.16 *musical note*, 51.6 *scene*, 68.17 *farm*, 73.5 *flight*, 159.2 *consecution*, 187.4 *period of activity*, 195.1 *succession*, 214.2 *cycle*, 214.8 *be cyclic*, 216.1 *change*, 216.7 *be changed*, 221.6 *reverse*, 224.11 *be changeable*, 234.1 *tendency*, 248.8 *intervening space*, 286.1 *obliqueness*, 286.6 *be oblique*, 306.6 *nature*, 306.7 *form*, 311.2 *bend*, 311.6 *curve*, 313.7 *make circular*, 314.2 *coil*, 314.6 *convolute*, 315.6 *round*, 315.11 *make round*, 320.1 *fold*, 332.7 *take a direction*, 334.1 *circuit*, 335.5 *twist*, 335.14 *deviating course*, 337.3 *reverse*, 337.5 *turn back*, 337.16 *countermotion*, 363.2 *circuitousness*, 363.3, 363.6 *orbit*, 364.3 *reel*, 364.8 *rotate*, 381.10 *blunt*, 415.8 *sour*, 514.3 *shock*, 524.1 *interpretation*, 524.8 *interpret*, 525.2 *misinterpretation*, 628.2 *decay*, 640.4 *act*, 652.11 *conduct oneself*, 655.2 *aptitude*, 657.5 *be cunning*, 671.24 *parry*, 784.2 *inclination*, 784.8 *prefer*, 796.8 *fashion*
turn a blind eye 436.16 *be blind to*, 591.1 *avoid*, 641.4 *not act*
turn a blind eye to 470.6 *be neglectful*, 839.11 *condone*
turn a blind eye toward 673.3 *submit*
turn about 221.6 *reverse*, 223.8 *in exchange*, 335.11 *turn round*
turnabout 337.13 *about-turn*, 629.10 *revival*
turn a card 229.4 *chance*
turn a corner 33.10 *be on the track*, 335.1 *deviate*, 363.8 *detour*
turn a deaf ear 421.8 *be deaf*, 577.9 *be obstinate*, 641.4 *not act*, 836.6 *be pitiless*
turn a deaf ear to 711.5 *refuse*
turn against 220.10 *be converted*, 578.2 *equivocate*, 587.4 *put off*, 829.6 *be irascible*, 858.9 *prove false*
turn all to gold 742.12 *be rich*

turn and turn about 109.1 *interchange*, 109.10 *reciprocally*, 159.18 *consecutively*, 214.15 *regularly*, 223.8 *in exchange*
turn an honest penny 721.12 *earn*
turn a phrase 558.4 *be elegant*
turn a pot 44.11 *make ceramics*
turn around 337.9 *turn round*
turnaround 337.13 *about-turn*, 484.2 *reversal*
turn around 484.8 *reverse*
turn a sentence 5.45 *use language*
turn aside 335.8 *sidestep*, 591.1 *avoid*
turn away 335.8 *sidestep*, 349.6 *send away*, 515.7 *thwart*, 573.7 *refuse*, 591.1 *avoid*, 711.5 *refuse*, 785.6 *react against*
turn away from 822.14 *hate*
turn back 337, 216.7 *be changed*, 216.8 *cause change*, 221.6 *reverse*, 335.11 *turn round*, 341.1 *repel*, 345.2 *withdraw*, 671.28 *survive*, 673.3 *submit*
turn back the clock 200.15 *look back*, 221.6 *reverse*
turn back the tide 487.10 *attempt the impossible*
turn back time 3, 200.15 *look back*, 487.10 *attempt the impossible*
turn back to front 287.3 *invert*
turn backwards 221.6 *reverse*, 287.3 *invert*
turn blue 454.9 *blue*
turncoat 220.6 *convert*, 224.6 *fickle person*, 539.21 *traitor*, 576.15 *indecisive person*, 578.9 *equivocator*, 598.4 *deserter*
turn down 129.5 *make smaller*, 374.14 *ease*, 441.10 *make dim*
turndown 573.12 *opposition*
turn down 581.1 *reject*
turndown 709.1 *veto*
turn down 709.3 *veto*, 711.5 *refuse*, 852.15 *withhold approval*
turn down the volume 424.6 *mute*
turned 306.9 *formed*, 415.6, 764.3 *unpalatable*
turned around 287.4 *inversely*, 337.25 *reversed*
turned away 515.9 *disappointed*, 711.8 *refused*
turned comma 543.7 *punctuation*
turned down 581.10 *rejected*, 711.8 *refused*
turned into 220.13 *converted*
turned off 421.7 *unheard*
turned on 405.7 *pleased*, 875.7 *drugged*, 877.14 *lecherous*
turned out 295.29 *dressed*
turned over 320.5 *folded*
turned-up 270.7 *short*, 359.22 *ascending*
turner 44.7 *potter*, 47.13 *carpenter*, 646.2 *artisan*
turn every stone 644.8 *exert oneself*
turn for the better 627.5 *improvement*, 629.11 *recuperation*
turn for the worse 628.7 *deterioration*
turn from sin 867.4 *be penitent*
turn green with envy 842.3 *be envious of*
turn grey 448.8 *grey*
turn head 805.30 *make proud*
turn heads 821.25 *be loved*
turn head-to-wind 36.15 *sail*
turn ideas into profits 737.1 *trade*
turn indicator 543.5 *indicator*
turning 364, 30.6 *pommel horse*, 30.11 *gymnastic*, 36.12 *canoeing*, 68.5 *cultivation*, 216.11 *changeable*, 224.1 *changeableness*, 286.4 *oblique*, 311.4 *curved*, 335.21 *indirect*, 363.1 *orbital motion*, 363.2 *circuitousness*, 363.9 *orbital*, 363.11 *orbiting*, 364.11 *rotating*, 784.6 *liking*
turning back 221.1 *reversion*
turning back to front 287.1 *inversion*

twenty-four 179.8 *twenty and over*
twenty-four carat 537.19 *authentic*
twenty-four-carat gold 537.6 *authenticity*
twenty-one 42 Card Games
twenty pence 741.9 *British money*
twenty-pound note 741.9 *British money*
twerp 612.10 *nonentity*
Twi 5 Languages and Groups of Languages
twice 176
twice a month 214.16 *cyclically*
twice as much 176.19 *twice*
twice a week 214.16 *cyclically*
twice a year 214.16 *cyclically*
twice over 176.19 *twice*, 183.24 *again*
twice the man one was 651.4 *refreshed*
twice-told 183.10 *iterated*
twice-told tale 788.2 *boring thing*
twice-told tales 553.1 *diffuseness*
Twickenham 35.1 *rugger*
twiddle one's thumbs 641.4 *not act*, 788.7 *suffer boredom*
twiddling one's thumbs 641.1 *inaction*, 788.5 *bored*
twig 83.5 *stem*, 85.2 *tree part*, 143.6 *branch*, 206.5 *young plant*, 501.11 *know*, 522.6, 787.6 *understand*
twigginess 274.7 *thinness*
twiggy 274.1 *thin*
twiglets 45.10 *snack*
twilight 157.9 *close*, 205.1, 205.6 *evening*, 440.1 *darkness*, 441.1 *dimness*, 628.7 *deterioration*
twilight of the gods 157.5 *fate*
twilit 441.5 *dim*
twill 67 Natural Fabrics, 67.10 *woven*, 288.4 *textile*
twilled 383.8 *rough*
twill weave 67.4 *weaving*
twin 176, 109.8 *interrelate*, 110.3 *lookalike*, 110.8 *make the same*, 110.14 *lookalike*, 114.2 *copy*, 114.5 *counterpart*, 116.5 *conformity*, 116.14 *conforming*, 122.5 *equal*, 176.12 *double*, 176.14 *pair*, 176.15 *double*, 478.8 *correspondence*, 478.15 *correspondent*, 478.21 *answer to*
twin bed 47.6 *bed*
twin bill 72.7 *train*
twin cable 64.27 *wire*
twine 137.6 *line*, 288.8 *interweave*, 311.6 *curve*, 314.6 *convolute*, 335.5 *twist*
twine around 138.6 *adhere*
twined 67.9 *spun*, 288.6 *interwoven*
twiner 83.2 *plant*
twinge 406.1, 631.5 *pain*
twinge of conscience 866.2 *signs of guilt*, 867.1 *penitence*
twining 67.2 *spinning*, 83.14 *of plants*, 288.1 *interweaving*
twinkle 53.37 *observe*, 224.11 *be changeable*, 366.12, 366.26 *flicker*, 439.2 *quality of light*, 439.25 *light up*, 543.3, 543.11 *gesture*
twinkling 53.21 *orbit*, 191.3 *instant*, 439.2 *quality of light*, 439.16 *bright*
twinklingly 439.30 *lightly*
twinkling of an eye 191.3 *instant*
twin-lens reflex 66.16 *camera*
twinned 107.4 *related*, 116.14 *conforming*, 176.9 *two*, 198.9 *simultaneous*
twinned city 93.1 *city*
twinning 176.4 *doubling*
twins 176, 114.6 *couple*
Twins 53 The Constellations
twin screws 338.11 *propeller*
twinset 295.13 *sweater*
Twin Stars 176.6 *twins*
twin-tub 621.7 *washer*

twirl 96.6 *river flow*, 96.7 *flow*, 314.2 *coil*, 314.6 *convolute*, 364.3 *reel*, 364.8 *rotate*
twirled 314.4 *convolutional*
twirling 334.1 *circuit*, 364.2 *turning*, 364.11 *rotating*
twist 335, 41.13 *ice-skating*, 46.2, 46.15 *dance*, 67.13 *spin*, 79.15 *live as a reptile*, 102.16 *delude*, 135.10 *link*, 220.9 *transform*, 241.3 *instance of violence*, 241.8 *use violence*, 286.1 *obliqueness*, 286.6 *be oblique*, 288.8 *interweave*, 307.3 *make shapeless*, 309.1 *distortion*, 309.9 *distort*, 310.11 *angle*, 314.2 *coil*, 314.6 *convolute*, 335.6 *distort*, 364.9 *roll*, 474.11 *practise sophistry*, 493.10 *misjudge*, 493.12 *bias*, 514.4 *surprising thing*, 524.1 *interpretation*, 524.8 *interpret*, 525.1 *misinterpret*, 525.2 *misinterpretation*, 540.9 *falsification*, 540.22 *falsify*, 548.1 *misrepresentation*, 548.4 *misrepresent*, 628.6 *pervert*, 640.4 *act*, 652.11 *conduct oneself*, 657.5 *be cunning*
twist and turn 314.6 *convolute*, 335.5 *twist*, 366.24 *shake*
twist around one's little finger 701.6 *subject*
twisted 67.9 *spun*, 286.4 *oblique*, 314.4 *convolutional*, 335.23 *oblique*, 493.8 *unjust*, 540.32 *falsified*, 548.6 *misrepresented*, 620.3 *deformed*, 874.3 *dead drunk*
twistedness 309.1 *distortion*, 314.1 *convolution*
twisted pair 64.27 *wire*
twister 55.16 *wind vortex*, 314.3 *convoluted thing*, 364.4 *vortex*, 375.9 *broken water*, 635.1 *trap*
twisting 39.11 *swimming*, 79.12 *snakelike*, 335.17 *torsion*, 335.21 *indirect*, 364.2 *turning*, 525.2 *misinterpretation*, 540.9 *falsification*
twisting dive 39.6 *diving*
twist lift 41.6 *ice-skating*
twist one's arm 586.15 *persuade*, 695.6 *compel*
twist round one's little finger 688.19 *be authoritarian*, 734.10 *take away*
twist someone's arm 228.10 *manipulate*
twist the law 16.73 *be illegal*
twist the words 525.1 *misinterpret*
twist together 314.6 *convolute*
twist-turned leg 47.3 *chair leg*
twist words 309.12 *distort the truth*
twit 238.4 *weakling*, 460.3 *unintelligent person*, 508.3 *foolish person*, 771.13 *be humorous*, 798.3 *object of ridicule*, 850.25 *taunt*
twitch 339.3 *jerk*, 339.13 *pull at*, 366.8 *spasm*, 366.23 *jolt*, 366.24 *shake*, 406.9 *feel pain*, 407.3 *press*, 407.11 *touch*, 543.3 *gesture*, 624.17 *nervous disorder*, 777.12 *be fearful*
twitcher 78.21 *ornithologist*
twitchety 366.19 *convulsive*
twitch grass 87 Grasses
twitchiness 366.5 *restlessness*
twitchy 366.16 *restless*, 366.19 *convulsive*, 777.8 *fearful*
twitter 78.18 *birdsong*, 78.28 *sing*, 366.1 *agitation*, 366.21 *be agitated*, 366.24 *shake*, 432.2 *bird song*, 432.5 *sing*
twittering 432.2 *bird song*, 432.8 *singing*
twittery 432.8 *singing*
two 176, 176, 27.10 *score*, 52.9 *numeral*
Two 176
two abreast 176.9 *two*, 176.20 *two by two*

two and six 741.10 *former British money*
two bangers short of a barbie 460.6 *unintelligent*
two-bit 612.4 *trivial*, 754.10 *shoddy*
two bits 741.8 *American money*
two-by-four 47.12 *wood*, 47.16 *joined*, 260.7 *little*
two by two 176, 176.9 *two*
two centred arch 43.5 *arch*
two cheers 542.2 *detraction*
two-dimensional 52.79 *spatial*, 176.10 *two-sided*, 248.11 *spatial*, 282.8 *horizontal*, 435.20 *visual*
two-dimensional figure 52.38 *surface*
two-dollar piece 741.8 *American money*
two dozen 179.8 *twenty and over*
two-edged 578.10 *equivocal*
two-edged sword 616.3 *inconvenience*, 680.8 *sharp weapon*
two-faced 176.11 *double-edged*, 540.26 *duplicitous*, 578.11 *equivocating*, 858.6 *faithless*
two-facedness 176.3 *duality*, 540.2 *duplicity*
two-faced person 578.9 *equivocator*
twofer 754.4 *bargain*
two-fingered salute 850.7 *sign of disrespect*
two-finger gesture 543.3 *gesture*
two fingers 351.2 *drink*
twofold 176.9 *two*, 176.19 *twice*
two-foot punt 36.8 *punting*
two for the price of one 754.4 *bargain*
two-handed sword 680.8 *sharp weapon*
two-hander 51.2 *play*, 176.2 *double*, 568.1 *conversation*
two-hand shot 23.4 *playing terms*
two-horse race 32.7 *horseracing*
two-hundred 179.9 *treble figures*
two-level 176.10 *two-sided*
two-man 36.10 *sailing*
two-man bobsled 41.9 *bobsledding*
two-man canoe race 36.6 *canoeing*
two-man dinghy 36.2 *sailing boat*
two-man keelboat 36.2 *sailing boat*
two-man trapeze boat 36.2 *sailing boat*
two-masted 36.10 *sailing*
two-masted boat 36.2 *sailing boat*
two minds with but a single thought 819.2 *friendly relations*
two-minute drill 19.8 *huddle*
two-minute offence 19.8 *huddle*
two-minute warning 19.5 *game time*, 23.1 *basketball*
two-one-two 31.8 *hockey*
two-one-two system 31.3 *ice hockey*
two or three 175.1 *plurality*, 182.1 *few*
two-part harmony 49.13 *melody*
two peas in a pod 110.3 *lookalike*, 114.6 *couple*, 819.6 *close friend*
twopence 612.8 *trifle*, 741.9 *British money*
twopenny 612.4 *trivial*, 754.10 *shoddy*
twopenny-halfpenny 612.4 *trivial*, 754.9 *cheap*
two-phase 41.12 *ski*
two-phase glide 41.2 *cross-country skiing*
two-phase supply 64.34 *power supply*
two-phase uphill 41.2 *cross-country skiing*
two-phase walk 41.2 *cross-country skiing*
two-piece 39.11 *swimming*, 176.2 *double*, 295.31 *styled*
two-piece suit 295.10 *suit*
two-piece swimsuit 39.8 *swimwear*, 295.21 *beachwear*

two-ply 176.10 *two-sided*, 266.7 *layered*
two-point conversion 19.6 *scoring*
two-pointer 23.4 *playing terms*
two sandwiches short of a picnic 460.6 *unintelligent*
twoscore 179.8 *twenty and over*
two-seater 176.2 *double*
two-seater toboggan 41.9 *bobsledding*
two-shilling piece 741.10 *former British money*
two shillings and six pence 741.10 *former British money*
two-sided 176, 305.6 *side*
twosome 176.1 *two*
two-star 395.9 *petroleum*
two-step 46.2 *dance*
two-storey 176.10 *two-sided*
two-storeyed 266.7 *layered*
two strings to one's bow 602.5 *reserves*
two-stroke 176.10 *two-sided*
two-stroke cycle 63.13 *engine cycle*
two-tailed test 52.54 *hypothesis testing*
two thirds 173.4 *less than one*
two-thirds 173.7 *fractionally*
two-tiered 266.7 *layered*
two-time 474.12, 539.23 *deceive*, 540.17 *double-deal*, 858.9 *prove false*
two-timer 224.6 *fickle person*, 539.17 *cheat*, 858.4 *dishonourable person*
two times 176.19 *twice*
two-timing 176.11 *double-edged*, 474.10 *hypocritical*
two track 32.10 *dressage*
two-up-two-down 256.5 *house*
two voices 117.1 *disparity*, 578.5 *equivocalness*
two-way 109.5 *interconnected*, 176.10 *two-sided*, 223.6 *in exchange*
two-way communication 534.6 *telecommunication*
two-way mirror 442.9 *glass*
two-way traffic 223.1 *exchange*
two weeks 179.7 *double figures*
two-wheeler 176.2 *double*
txistu 49 Musical Instruments
Tyburn tree 879.16 *instrument of execution*
Tycho 53 Lunar Features
Tycho's star 53 Named Stars
tycoon 611.4 *bigwig*, 686.4 *prosperous person*, 696.5 *company leader*, 721.7 *gainer*, 741.17 *financier*, 742.10 *wealthy person*
tying the knot 823.1 *marriage*, 823.5 *wedding*
tying the tubes 247.2 *making infertile*
tying up 344.11 *landing*
tyke 77.9 *dog*
tylocin 62 Medication
tympani 49 Musical Instruments
tympanic cavity 420.5 *internal ear*
tympanic membrane 420.5 *internal ear*
tympanum 43 Architectural Decoration, 279.3 *architectural summit*, 420.5 *internal ear*
Tyndall 52 Scientists
Tyne 96 Rivers
Tyne and Wear 92 Counties
type 163, 5.13 *letter*, 103.4 *nature*, 116.2 *convention*, 124.4 *average*, 163.13 *class*, 268.7 *standard*, 306.3 *kind*, 400.7 *person*, 517.5 *omen*, 547.1 *representation*, 560.6 *sort*
typecast 51.36 *dramatize*, 51.38 *tragic*, 112.6 *conforming*, 112.10 *conform*
typecasting mould 112.2 *conformity*
type-cutter 50.10 *engraver*
typed 5.41 *lettered*
type metal 57 Alloys
type of animal 76
type of meaning 520
type of penance 867

type of rule 688
typeset 532.15 *publish*
typesetter 532.12 *publisher*
types of marriage 823
type style 5
Typhan 8.7 *devil*
typhoid 624.6 *infection*
typhoid fever 624.4 *disease*
Typhon 259.10 *big person*
typhoon 55.16 *wind vortex*, 241.5 *violent weather*
typhus 624.6 *infection*
typical 163, 103.9 *characteristic*, 116.15 *conventional*, 124.1 *average*, 165.16 *characteristic*, 166.10 *customary*, 167.15 *everyday*, 214.14 *orderly*, 526.14 *manifest*, 543.14 *signifying*, 547.13 *representational*, 584.11 *normal*
typically 116.37 *conventionally*, 124.11 *on average*, 163.16 *taxonomically*, 164.30 *usually*, 543.18 *indicatively*, 547.14 *representationally*
typical value 52.60 *parameter*
typification 526.10 *manifestation*, 547.1 *representation*
typify 110.11 *be regular*, 517.11 *predict*, 543.10 *signify*, 547.9 *represent*
typifying 116.15 *conventional*
typing error 504
typing paper 604.3 *paper*
typist 545.9 *recorder*
typo 504.12 *typing error*
typographer 50.18 *engraver*
typographical error 504.12 *typing error*
Tyr 676.3 *god of war*
tyrannical 16.62 *above the law*, 233.11 *influential*, 241.6 *violent*, 642.21 *meddling*, 653.17 *managerial*, 688.14 *governmental*, 690.8 *severe*, 701.10 *dominating*, 807.16 *arrogant*, 832.10 *malevolent*
tyrannically 16.85 *summarily*, 233.14 *influentially*, 241.10 *violently*, 690.11 *severely*, 832.20 *malevolently*
tyrannicide 398.3 *homicide*, 398.11 *murderer*, 693.2 *violation of the law*, 713.2 *disorder*
tyrannization 852.5 *intolerance*
tyrannize 12.11 *govern*, 233.10 *be a prevailing influence*, 618.14 *ill-treat*, 642.17 *meddle*, 688.19 *be authoritarian*, 690.6 *suppress*, 701.7 *defeat*, 832.18 *torment*
tyrannized 690.9 *suppressed*
tyrannophobia 777 *Phobias by Name*
tyrannosaur 79 *Fossil Reptiles*
tyrannosaurus 202.8 *prehistoric animal*
tyrannously 241.10 *violently*
tyranny 233.3 *personal influence*, 618.11 *harmfulness*, 688.7 *type of rule*, 690.2 *suppression*, 701.2 *domination*, 807.4 *arrogance*
tyrant 7.4 *religionist*, 631.13 *oppressor*, 688.10 *person of authority*, 696.4 *absolute ruler*, 699.6 *law-maker*, 822.8 *hated person*, 832.8 *malefactor*, 864.9 *wicked person*, 879.17 *punisher*
tyrant flycatcher 78 *Birds*
tyrants 777 *Phobias by Topic*
tyre 71 *Motor Vehicle Parts*, 313.3 *circular thing*
tyremark 545.12 *vestige*
tyre stagger 33.6 *motor racing terms*
Tyrian purple 67.6 *dye*, 455.2 *purple pigment*
tyro 156.14 *beginner*, 201.8 *new arrival*
Tyrolean 34.8 *mountaineering*
Tyrolean hat 295.15 *headgear*
Tyrolean traverse 34.3 *climbing technique*
Tyrone 92 *Counties*
tyrosine 58 Amino Acids
tyrothricin 62 *Medication*
Tyson 18 *Sporting Personalities*
tzatziki 45.52 *Greek dish*

U

U 794.5 *refined*, 802.4 *aristocratic*
Uber Cup 40.10 *badminton*
ubiquitous 8.13 *divine*, 164.17 *widespread*, 183.14 *recurrent*, 233.13 *dominant*, 253.7 *present*
ubiquitously 8.19 *divinely*, 164.33 *influentially*
ubiquitousness 253.2 *omnipresence*
ubiquity 164.4 *widespreadness*, 253.2 *omnipresence*
U-boat 679.24 *warship*
uchi-ude-uke 26.8 *karate*
uchiwa daiko 49 *Musical Instruments*
Uchtsiti 8 *Deities*
ud 49 *Musical Instruments*
Udasin 7 *Non-Christian Religions*
udder 77.2 *mammalian characteristic*
udometer 55.7 *weather instruments*, 389.19 *measuring instrument*
udometric 55.42 *barometric*
UFO 53.34 *SETI* , 502.3 *unknown thing*, 786.4 *wonder*
ufological 11.18 *spiritual*
ufologist 11.12 *occultist*
ufology 11.1 *occultism*
UFOs 529.6 *natural mystery*
UFO sighting 11.10 *psychic phenomenon*
Uganda 91 *Countries*
Ugaritic 5 *Languages and Groups of Languages*
Ugashik 94 *Lakes*
ugli fruit 86 *Fruits*
uglify 628.5 *hurt*
ugliness 559, 309.3 *deformity*, 341.5 *repulsion*, 457.3 *external appearance*
Ugliness 790
ugly 559, 790, 55.48 *stormy*, 309.7 *deformed*, 341.8 *repulsive*, 457.10 *aspectual*, 633.1 *dangerous*
ugly customer 635.2 *troublemaker*, 801.2 *disreputable character*, 829.3 *irascible person*, 832.8 *malefactor*, 864.10 *bad person*
ugly duckling 335.19 *deviant person*
ugly person 790
ugly place 790
Ugric 5 *Languages and Groups of Languages*
UHF transmitter 534.16 *transmitter*
UHF ultrahigh frequency 534 *Radio-frequency Bands*
uhlan 679.20 *cavalryman*
UHT milk 351.5 *milk*
uhv 57.20 *surface chemistry*
Uigur 5 *Languages and Groups of Languages*
ujusini 49 *Musical Instruments*
uka 26.7 *judo*
ukase 166.1 *rule*, 532.1 *publication*, 692.1 *command*
uke 26.10 *aikido*
Ukiyo-e 50 *Non-Western Art*
Ukraine 91 *Countries*
Ukrainian 5 *Languages and Groups of Languages*
Ukteni 8 *Deities*
ukulele 49 *Musical Instruments*
Ulan Bator 93 *Cities*
ulcer 624, 406.2 *painful condition*
ulcerate 623.8 *make worse*, 828.14 *make angry*
ulcerated 624.23 *diseased*
ulceration 624.15 *ulcer*, 628.10 *impairment*
ulcerous 624.23 *diseased*
ullage 145.2 *omission*
Ullswater 94 *Lakes*, 94.4 *British lakes*
ulna 382 *Bones*

ulster 295.12 *coat*
Ulster 92 *Counties*, 91.10 *Ireland*
Ulster Democratic Unionist Party 12.6 *political party*
ulterior 104.12 *external*, 263.8 *distant*
ulterior motive 228.1, 586.11 *motive*, 588.1 *intention*
ultimate 126.14 *best*, 157.20 *ending*, 226.13 *causal*, 263.8 *distant*, 279.5 *top*, 619.3 *perfection*, 684.8 *completed*
ultimate aim 588.5 *final intention*
ultimately 157.26 *finally*, 199.14 *in the future*, 226.14 *causally*
ultimate purpose 588.5 *final intention*
ultimate tensile strength 63.15 *strength of materials*
ultima Thule 263.3 *distant place*
ultimatum 588.4 *formulated intention*, 593.1 *requirement*, 636.1 *warning*, 692.2 *demand*, 710.3 *business offer*, 712.2 *demand*
ultrabasic rock 54.30 *igneous rock*
ultracentrifuge 364.6 *rotator*
ultraconservative 577.4 *set*
ultracool 699.14 *self-restrained*
ultracritical 852.28 *fault-finding*
ultra heat treatment 637.1 *preservation*
ultrahigh frequency 212.6 *radio frequency*
ultramafite 54.30 *igneous rock*
ultramarine 263.8 *distant*, 454.1 *blue*, 454.5 *blueness*
ultrametamorphic rock 54.33 *metamorphic rock*
ultramicroscope 56.85 *microscope*
ultramicroscopic 260.7 *little*
ultramodern 201.10 *new*
ultramodernist 201.9 *modern person*
ultramontane 104.6 *outsider*, 104.10 *foreign*, 149.4 *foreigner*, 263.8 *distant*
ultramundane 263.8 *distant*
ultranational 91.16 *national*
ultranationalism 91.14 *nationalism*, 400.11 *nation*, 481.4 *social discrimination*
ultranationalist 91.14 *nationalist*, 481.7 *bigot*
ultranationalistic 91.16 *national*, 481.10 *discriminatory*
ultranationalistically 481.17 *prejudicially*
ultrasonic 56.98 *physical*, 329.1 *swift*, 421.7 *unheard*
ultrasonically 56.100 *physically*, 329.14 *swiftly*
ultrasonic cleaning 56.22 *sounding*
ultrasonic frequency 56.19 *sound propagation*
ultrasonic imaging 56.22 *sounding*
ultrasonics 56.2 *classical physics*
ultrasonic speed 329.8 *speed*
ultrasonic wave 56.14 *sound wave*
ultrasonic welding 56.22 *sounding*
ultrasound 56.17 *sound*, 421.3 *inaudibility*
ultrasound scan 60.7 *diagnosis*
ultrasound scanner 420.9 *audio device*
ultrastructure 59.6 *cell biology*
ultraviolet astronomy 53.1 *astronomy*
ultraviolet light 439.1 *light*
ultraviolet radiation 55.22 *sun*, 56.13 *electromagnetic radiation*
ultraviolet spectrometry 57.17 *analysis*
ultraviolet spectrum 56.68 *emission*
ultrawide lens 66.17 *lens*
ululant 432, 430.7 *strident*, 431.18 *crying*, 770.5 *sad*
ululate 423.8 *be loud*, 430.4 *be strident*, 431.13, 432.4 *cry*, 770.8 *grieve*, 774.7 *weep*
ululation 423.2 *outcry*, 430.1 *stri-*

dency , 431.6 *cry of pain*, 432.1 *animal cry*, 774.2 *lament*
Uma 8 *Deities*
Umatilla 1 *Peoples*
umbel 84.4 *flower head*
umbelliferous 83.16 *taxonomic*, 84.12 *of flowers*
umbilical 291.6 *central*
umbilical cord 137.6 *line*, 245.7 *obstetrics*, 291.2 *central thing*
umbra 56.24 *light emission*
umbrage 764.5 *unpleasantness*, 828.2 *offence*
umbrageous 440.8 *dark*
umbrella 146.7 *including*, 293.12 *protective covering*, 632.2 *protection*, 634.2 *shelter*
umbrella bird 78 *Birds*
umbrella pine 85 *Trees and Shrubs*
umbrella tree 85 *Trees and Shrubs*
Umbrian 5 *Languages and Groups of Languages*
umiak 74 *Ships and Boats*
umlaut 5.36 *accent*, 136.5 *separator*, 543.7 *punctuation*
umpirage 492.1 *judgment*, 678.2 *mediation*
umpire 15.6 *employer*, 16.23 *judge*, 19.2 *football player*, 23.2 *basketball player*, 25.3 *bowls player*, 27.3 *official*, 40.6 *tennis player*, 158.9 *middleman*, 158.19 *mediate*, 242.2 *moderator*, 242.4 *moderate*, 298.3 *interfacer*, 492.5, 492.11 *judge*, 654.4 *adviser*, 678.1 *mediate*, 678.3 *mediator*, 859.3 *impartial person*
umpire's chair 40.3 *tennis equipment*
umpire's mask 22.3 *baseball equipment*
umpteen 169.3 *large number*, 181.2 *multitude*, 181.6 *many*
umpteenth 179.18 *eleventh*
UN 91.2 *union of nations*
unabashed 668.7 *defiant*, 805.17 *conceited*, 807.15 *audacious*
unabashedly 668.9 *defiantly*
unabbreviated 144.7 *complete*
unabetted 174.15 *solo*
unable 236.10 *powerless*, 614.1 *useless*, 656.1 *unskilful*
unable to act 641.3 *inactive*
unable to believe one's eyes 786.6 *wondering*
unable to be seen 438.1 *invisible*
unable to forget 511.8 *remembering*
unable to get by 743.1 *poor*
unable to hack it 609.1 *insufficient*
unable to keep the wolf from the door 743.1 *poor*
unable to make both ends meet 743.1 *poor*
unable to make up one's mind 576.1 *vacillating*
unable to pay 745, 747.13 *non-paying*
unable to pay one's way 743.1 *poor*
unable to say boo to a goose 779.3 *cowardly*
unable to understand 523.6 *confused*
unable to wait 648.3 *hasty*
unabridged 142.7 *uncut*, 144.7 *complete*, 269.1 *long*, 684.7 *completed*
unabridged dictionary 5.28 *dictionary*
unaccented 424.4 *faint*, 564.18 *phonetic*
unacceptable 581.10 *rejected*, 609.1 *insufficient*, 620.1 *imperfect*, 764.1 *unpleasant*, 852.32 *unsatisfactory*
unacceptably 609.10 *insufficiently*
unaccepted 581.10 *rejected*, 852.31 *disapproved*
unaccessibility 487.6 *hopelessness*
unaccessible 487.3 *hopeless*

unacclaimed 656.1 *unskilful*
unaccommodated 609.2 *unprovided*
unaccommodating 832.15 *inconsiderate*
unaccompanied 174.15 *solo*
unaccomplished 656.1 *unskilful*, 685.4 *uncompleted*
unaccountability 229.1 *lack of motive*, 523.11 *unintelligibility*, 589.1 *chance*
unaccountable 229.6 *motiveless*, 523.1 *unintelligible*, 589.9 *causeless*, 689.6 *anarchic*, 786.8 *wonderful*, 848.5 *exempt*
unaccountably 229.8 *by chance*, 523.13 *unintelligibly*, 589.13 *by chance*, 848.13 *with impunity*
unaccused 632.5 *safe*
unaccustomed 585, 656.3 *clumsy*
unaccustomedly 585
unaccustomeness 585
Unaccustomedness 585
unachievable 487.3 *hopeless*
unachieved 685.4 *uncompleted*
unacknowledged 527.1 *latent*, 838.4 *unknown*
unactuality 102.1 *unreality*
unadaptable 117.11 *unfit*, 373.4 *mentally hard*, 656.1 *unskilful*
unadapted 117.11 *unfit*, 656.1 *unskilful*
unadjusted 656.3 *clumsy*
unadmiring 787.3 *unmoved*
unadorned 556, 690, 522.2, 542.14 *simple*, 550.3 *clear*, 658.1 *naive*
unadorned simplicity 556.4 *simplicity*
unadorned style 522.10 *simplicity*
unadornment 556, 690, 522.10 *simplicity*
unadulterated 119.6 *authentic*, 134.13 *pure*, 134.16 *simple*, 142.7 *uncut*, 144.7 *complete*, 537.19 *authentic*, 556.1 *simple*, 621.16 *clean*
unadulterated truth 526.11 *openness*
unadulteration 537.6 *authenticity*
unadventurous 656.1 *unskilful*, 781.4 *cautious*
unadvisable 616.1 *inconvenient*
unaesthetic 559.10, 790.4 *ugly*
unaffected 814.2 *detached*, 134.17 *direct*, 537.18 *truthful*, 542.14, 556.1 *simple*, 556.3 *natural*, 658.1 *naive*, 761.1 *insensitive*, 783.7 *indifferent*, 814.7 *informal*, 814.9 *familiar*
unaffectedly 814
unaffectedness 537.5 *truthfulness*, 542.4 *simplicity*, 556.6 *naturalness*, 658.2 *naivety*, 814.3 *familiarity*
unaffectionate 783.7 *indifferent*
unaffiliated 104.11 *separate*, 108.6 *unrelated*
unaffordable 757.3 *costly*
unafraid 778.12 *self-reliant*
unaggressive 240.5 *inert*, 675.7 *peaceful*
unagitated 325.6 *quiescent*
unagreed 117.10 *disagreeing*
unaided 174.15 *solo*
Unalaska 98 *Islands*
unalienable 103.5 *essential*
unalike 115.4 *dissimilar*
unallied 108.6 *unrelated*
unalloyed 134.16 *simple*, 619.1 *perfect*
unalterable 217.7 *permanent*, 373.4 *mentally hard*
unalterably 217.9 *permanently*, 225.12 *stably*, 373.13 *inflexibly*
unaltered 110.17 *regular*, 225.10 *stabilized*
unamazed 787.3 *unmoved*
unambiguity 520.3 *comprehension*, 522.9 *intelligibility*
unambiguous 312.5 *honourable*, 442.4 *easily seen through*, 490.3 *decided*, 520.6 *meaningful*, 522.1 *intelligible*, 550.3 *clear*
unambiguously 520.13 *meaningfully*, 522.13 *intelligibly*, 550.4 *clearly*, 619.8 *completely*
unambiguousness 520.3 *comprehension*, 550.1 *clarity*, 660.2 *simplicity*
unambiguous passage 520.3 *comprehension*
unambitious 810.12 *self-deprecating*
unambivalence 522.9 *intelligibility*
unambivalent 522.1 *intelligible*
unamiability 820.1 *enmity*
unamiable 820.6 *hostile*, 832.15 *inconsiderate*
unamiably 820.14 *hostilely*
Unamuno y Jugo 4 *Philosophers*
unanimity 116.1 *accord*, 135.2 *agreement*, 499.1 *assent*, 667.1 *agreement*
unanimous 112.7 *agreeing*, 116.10 *in accord*, 135.13 *agreeable*, 174.13 *whole*, 433.7 *harmonious*, 499.9 *assenting*, 667.10 *agreeing*
unanimously 499, 112.14 *equanimously*, 116.31 *in accord*, 135.17 *agreeably*, 174.23 *wholly*, 433.12 *harmoniously*, 664.20 *cooperatively*, 667.14 *agreeably*
unanimousness 116.1 *accord*
unanimous verdict 16.7 *legal trial*
unanimous vote 112.3 *agreement*
unannounced 514.8 *surprising*
unanswerable 848.5 *exempt*
unanswerably 848.13 *with impunity*
unanswered 491.2 *irresolute*
unanticipated 489.3 *unexpected*, 514.8 *surprising*
unapologetic 868.3 *impenitent*
unapologized for 868.4 *unatoned*
unapparent 438.1 *invisible*
unappeasable 577.3 *unyielding*
unappetizing 412.5 *tasteless*, 415.6, 764.3 *unpalatable*
unapplied 4.13 *of philosophy*, 600.1 *unused*
unappreciated 785.9 *disliked*
unappreciation 838.1 *ingratitude*
unappreciative 838.3 *ungrateful*
unappreciatively 838.7 *ungratefully*
unappreciativeness 838.1 *ingratitude*
unappreciative person 838.2 *thankless person*
unapproachability 805, 616.4 *distance*, 816.1 *unsociability*
unapproachable 805, 126.14 *best*, 263.9 *reserved*, 487.3 *hopeless*, 616.2 *distant*, 816.8 *unsociable*
unapproachably 487.12 *hopelessly*
unappropriated 727.15 *unclaimed*
unapproved 766.5 *unsatisfactory*, 852.31 *disapproved*
unapproving 766.4 *dissatisfied*, 852.25 *disapproving*
unapt 521.10 *meaningless*, 614.1 *useless*, 616.1 *inconvenient*, 656.1 *unskilful*
unaptness 614.3 *uselessness*, 656.8 *unskilfulness*
unarm 614.8 *make useless*
unarmed 236.11 *unprotected*, 633.3 *vulnerable*, 675.7 *peaceful*
unarmoured 633.3 *vulnerable*
unaroused 325.5 *sedentary*, 787.3 *unmoved*
unarranged 151.13 *unordered*, 595.1 *unprepared*
unarticulated 527.4 *unsaid*
unartificial 658.1 *naive*
unascertained 491.5 *uncertified*
unashamed 868.3 *impenitent*
unashamedly 868.6 *impenitently*
unasked 825.6 *celibate*
unaspiring 783.10 *mediocre*, 810.8 *modest*
unassailability 237.1 *strength*
unassailable 632.6 *invulnerable*
unassembled 162.21 *disbanded*
unassertive 708.8 *permitting*

unassertively 708.9 *with permission*
unassimilable 136.17 *unjoined*
unassimilated 136.17 *unjoined*, 139.9 *aloof*
unassisted 174.15 *solo*
unassuming 537.18 *truthful*, 542.15 *reserved*, 556.1 *simple*, 556.3 *natural*, 658.1 *naive*, 806.1 *humble*, 810.8 *modest*, 814.7 *informal*
unassumingly 542.25 *reservedly*, 814.15 *unaffectedly*
unassuming nature 810.1 *modesty*
unassumingness 810.1 *modesty*
unatonable 864.11 *wicked*
unatoned 868
unattached 136.17 *unjoined*, 224.13 *changeable*, 333.4 *middle*, 698.10 *independent*, 825.6 *celibate*
unattached female 402.5 *single girl*
unattached male 401.5 *single man*
unattached man 825.5 *single person*
unattackable 632.6 *invulnerable*
unattainability 487.6 *hopelessness*
unattainable 487.3 *hopeless*
unattainably 487.12 *hopelessly*
unattained 685.4 *uncompleted*
unattempted 591.20 *avoidable*
unattended 633.3 *vulnerable*
unattired 296.9 *undressed*
unattractive 457.10 *aspectual*, 559.10 *ugly*, 764.2 *objectionable*, 790.4 *ugly*
unattractiveness 764.6 *objectionability*
unau 77 *Placental Mammals*
unauthentic 538.14 *unreal*, 540.28 *spurious*
unauthentically 538.28 *dishonestly*
unauthenticated 491.5 *uncertified*
unauthenticity 538.2 *unrealness*, 540.4 *spuriousness*
unauthorization 16.35 *illegality*
unauthorized 16, 291.10 *powerless*, 709.5 *vetoed*, 736.18 *fraudulent*, 846.8 *unentitled*
unauthorized absence 254.4 *absenteeism*
unauthorized borrowing 733.3, 736.6 *illegal borrowing*
unauthorized person 236.5 *powerless person*
unavailability 487.6 *hopelessness*, 616.4 *distance*
unavailable 254.8 *absent*, 487.3 *hopeless*, 609.4 *scarce*, 616.2 *distant*
unavailing 614.2 *futile*
unavoidability 490.16, 571.5 *inevitability*
unavoidable 490.5, 571.12 *inevitable*, 695.9 *compelling*, 695.10 *compulsory*, 847.12 *obligatory*
unavoidably 490.25 *inevitably*, 571.19 *necessarily*, 695.11 *compellingly*
unaware 421.5 *unhearing*, 436.10 *blind to*, 502.6 *ignorant*, 512.8 *oblivious*, 514.6 *surprised*, 633.3 *vulnerable*, 761.1 *insensitive*, 783.7 *indifferent*
unawareness 436.7 *figurative blindness*, 462.2, 502.1 *ignorance*, 761.3 *insensitiveness*
unawares 514.13 *surprisingly*, 633.11 *dangerously*, 865.11 *innocently*
unawed 787.3 *unmoved*
unbalance 123.1 *inequality*, 123.5 *be unequal*, 153.11 *derange*, 510.15 *make insane*
unbalanced 123.3 *unequal*, 153.16 *deranged*, 309.6 *distorted*, 510.11 *insane*, 633.2 *unsafe*, 656.3 *clumsy*, 844.11 *wrong*
unbalanced line 19.7 *offence*
unbalanced mind 510.1 *insanity*
unballast 370.10 *lighten*
unballasted 123.3 *unequal*

unbar 322.19 *open up*, 639.1 *deliver*, 660.16 *make easy*
unbarred 322.13 *opened up*
unbearable 406.5 *painful*
unbearable pressure 644.4 *exertion*
unbeatable 126.14, 617.2 *best*, 669.12 *resisting*, 682.15 *victorious*
unbeaten 201.11 *unfamiliar*, 574.4 *undaunted*, 575.12 *indomitable*, 600.2 *new*, 617.2 *best*, 682.15 *victorious*
unbecoming 117.11 *unfit*, 790.4 *ugly*, 844.13 *improper*
unbefitting 117.11 *unfit*, 211.10 *untimely*, 844.13 *improper*
unbefittingly 211.15 *at the wrong time*
unbeing 100.1 *nonexistence*, 254.1 *absence*
unbeknown 502.8 *unknown*
unbelief 498, 536.2 *rejection*
unbelievability 498, 489.6 *implausibility*
unbelievable 487, 489.2 *questionable*, 498.7 *disbelieved*, 786.8 *wonderful*
unbelievably 498, 489.8 *improbably*
unbelieved 498.7 *disbelieved*
unbeliever 498.5 *disbeliever*
unbelieving 491.1 *uncertain*, 498.6 *disbelieving*
unbelievingly 498.10 *disbelievingly*
unbend 312.10 *straighten*, 374.13 *soften*, 649.2 *take it easy*, 806.18 *condescend*, 815.12 *visit*, 835.10, 839.12 *show mercy*
unbending 373.4 *mentally hard*, 574.3 *strong-willed*, 577.3 *unyielding*, 669.11 *obstinate*, 690.8 *severe*, 805.15 *unapproachable*, 836.5 *inflexible*
unbendingly 669.14 *resistingly*
unbendingness 373.8 *mental hardness*
unbenevolent 832.15 *inconsiderate*
unbent 312.1 *straight*
unbiased 4.15 *rational*, 271.3 *broad-minded*, 482.2 *impartial*, 492.9 *judicious*, 537.18 *truthful*, 698.9 *free*, 783.9 *impartial*, 843.7 *right*, 859.4 *disinterested*
unbiased attitude 783.3 *impartiality*
unbidden 572.5 *voluntary*
unbigoted 271.3 *broad-minded*
unbind 136.9 *separate*, 639.1 *deliver*, 698.15 *set free*, 700.4 *liberate*, 727.9 *dispose of*
unbinding 700.1 *liberation*
unblamable 865.5 *innocent*
unblameworthiness 865.1 *innocence*
unblameworthy 865.5 *innocent*
unbleached 446.1 *white*, 448.1 *grey*
unblemished 134.13 *pure*, 619.1 *perfect*, 865.5 *innocent*
unblended 134.16 *simple*
unblessed 687.8 *unlucky*
unblest 827.10 *maledictive*
unblock 322.19 *open up*, 660.16 *make easy*
unblocked 322.13 *opened up*
unblown 595.5 *immature*
unblunted 380.1 *sharp*
unblurred 318.7 *conspicuous*, 522.1 *intelligible*
unblushing 805.17 *conceited*, 807.21 *impudent*, 868.3 *impenitent*, 877.13 *unchaste*
unblushingly 868.6 *impenitently*
unboastful 810.8 *modest*
unboastfulness 810.1 *modesty*
unboat 344.4 *land*
unbolt 322.19 *open up*, 700.4 *liberate*
unbolted 322.13 *opened up*
unborn 595.5 *immature*
unbosom oneself 530.8 *admit*
unbought 600.3 *not wanted*, 754.10 *shoddy*

unbound 638.8 *escaping,* 698.9 *free,* 848.7 *independent*
unbowed 281, 669.12 *resisting,* 682.15 *victorious,* 778.9 *courageous*
unbreakability 378.6 *toughness*
unbreakable 217.7 *permanent,* 371.6 *dense,* 373.2, 378.1 *tough,* 632.6 *invulnerable*
unbreakable glass 293.12 *protective covering*
unbreakableness 378.6 *toughness*
unbridgeable 523.1 *unintelligible*
unbridle 700.4 *liberate*
unbridled 241.6 *violent,* 689.6 *anarchic,* 698.9 *free,* 698.12 *unconditional*
unbridling 700.1 *liberation*
unbroken 112.5 *uniform,* 116.14 *conforming,* 142.7 *uncut,* 144.7 *complete,* 159.11 *continuous,* 219.5 *continual,* 332.15 *direct,* 336.18 *ongoing,* 376.2 *uniform,* 585.1 *unaccustomed,* 619.1 *perfect,* 684.7 *completed*
unbroken line 312.7 *straight line*
unbrokenness 159.5 *continuity*
unbuild 244.9 *demolish*
unburden 349.12 *unload,* 370.10 *lighten,* 639.1 *deliver,* 660.18 *disentangle,* 700.4 *liberate*
unburdening 370.3, 370.6 *lightening,* 660.8 *disentanglement,* 700.1 *liberation*
unburden oneself 530.8 *admit*
unburdensome 660.9 *easy*
unburnished 622.7 *dirty*
unbury 399.9 *exhume*
unbusinesslike 656.1 *unskilful*
unbutton 136.9 *separate,* 294.11 *uncover,* 296.14 *undress*
unbuttoned 595.1 *unprepared,* 649.4 *at ease,* 698.13 *informal*
unbuttoning 136.1 *separation*
uncage 700.4 *liberate*
uncalculated 583.1 *improvised*
uncalled-for 357.12 *excessive,* 807.18 *insulting,* 846.10 *undue*
uncamouflaged 526.14 *manifest*
uncandid 538.18 *pretentious,* 540.27 *hypocritical,* 858.5 *dishonourable*
uncandidly 538.27 *pretentiously,* 540.38 *hypocritically,* 858.11 *dishonourably*
uncandidness 538.8 *pretence,* 540.3 *hypocrisy*
uncandour 540.3 *hypocrisy*
uncanny 11.18 *spiritual*
uncanny silence 422.4 *silence*
uncared for 785.9 *disliked*
uncaring 462.10 *inconsiderate,* 468.9 *thoughtless,* 470.4 *negligent,* 761.1 *insensitive,* 783.7 *indifferent,* 832.15 *inconsiderate,* 836.4 *pitiless*
uncaringly 783.17 *indifferently*
uncaused 589.9 *causeless*
unceasing 186.5 *timeless,* 188.9 *permanent,* 190.10 *continuing forever,* 219.6 *protracted,* 575.11 *steady,* 642.18 *active*
unceasingly 186.8 *ever,* 219.7 *continually*
uncensored 684.7 *completed,* 877.12 *indecent*
unceremonious 814.7 *informal*
unceremoniously 814.12 *informally*
unceremoniousness 814.1 *informality*
uncertain 491, 224.13 *changeable,* 229.6 *motiveless,* 477.14 *questionable,* 489.1 *improbable,* 498.6 *disbelieving,* 523.2 *unexplained,* 551.2 *obscure,* 576.1 *vacillating,* 579.1 *capricious,* 589.8 *chance,* 633.1 *dangerous,* 656.3 *clumsy*
uncertain future 199.3 *future condition*
uncertainly 491, 224.15 *changeably,* 229.8 *by chance,* 489.8 *improbably,* 498.13 *disbelievingly,* 576.16 *irresolutely*
uncertainness 491.9 *uncertainty*
uncertain person 491

uncertainty 477, 491, 224.1 *changeableness,* 224.2 *irresolution,* 229.1 *lack of motive,* 477.1 *question,* 477.7 *questionableness,* 489.4 *improbability,* 498.1 *disbelief,* 502.1 *ignorance,* 513.1 *expectation,* 523.11 *unintelligibility,* 551.1 *obscurity,* 576.11 *vacillation,* 578.5 *equivocalness,* 579.2 *caprice,* 589.1 *chance,* 633.5 *danger,* 786.1 *wonder*
Uncertainty 491
uncertainty principle 56.6 *law,* 56.81 *causality,* 229.1 *lack of motive,* 488.5 *probability theory*
uncertified 491
unchain 136.9 *separate,* 639.1 *deliver,* 698.15 *set free,* 700.4 *liberate*
unchained 136.15 *separate,* 638.8 *escaping,* 698.9 *free*
unchaining 700.1 *liberation*
unchallengeable 490.3 *decided,* 632.6 *invulnerable,* 843.9 *in the right*
unchallenged 667.10 *agreeing*
unchangeability 225.1 *stability*
unchangeable 110.17 *regular,* 217.7 *permanent,* 225.9 *stable,* 574.5 *steady*
unchangeableness 225.1 *stability,* 537.9 *uniformity*
unchanged 110.17 *regular,* 225.10 *stabilized*
unchanging 110.17 *regular,* 112.5 *uniform,* 190.8 *eternal,* 217.7 *permanent,* 225.9 *stable,* 490.6 *infallible,* 537.22 *uniform*
unchaperoned 174.15 *solo*
uncharacteristic 117.8 *contradictory*
unchargeable 754.11 *free of charge*
uncharged 729.7 *given,* 754.11 *free of charge*
uncharitable 690.8 *severe,* 832.15 *inconsiderate,* 860.4 *selfish*
uncharitableness 690.1 *severity,* 832.6 *inconsiderateness*
uncharitably 690.11 *severely,* 860.8 *selfishly*
uncharted 502.8 *unknown*
unchartered 16.56 *unauthorized,* 846.8 *unentitled*
unchaste 877, 864.12 *immoral*
unchastened 868.3 *impenitent*
unchastised 16.63 *acquitted*
unchastity 877.3 *sexual immorality*
unchecked 491.5 *uncertified,* 698.9 *free*
unchivalrous 764.2 *objectionable,* 818.6 *bad-mannered*
unchivalrously 818.9 *discourteously*
unchosen 581.10 *rejected,* 785.9 *disliked,* 822.12 *hated*
unchristian 832.15 *inconsiderate*
uncial 5.15 *type style,* 5.41 *lettered*
uncircumscribed 248.12 *extensive*
uncircumspect 508.5 *foolish,* 780.4 *rash*
uncivil 764.2 *objectionable,* 816.8 *unsociable,* 818.5 *discourteous,* 850.10 *disrespectful*
uncivilized 595.5 *immature,* 658.1 *naive*
uncivilized human 400
uncivilized state 658.2 *naivety*
uncivilly 816.14 *unsociably,* 818.9 *discourteously*
unclad 294.8 *uncovered,* 296.9 *undressed*
unclaimed 727
unclasp 136.9 *separate*
unclassified 133.12 *mixed,* 151.13 *unordered*
uncle 218.12 *stop,* 401.13 *man in the family,* 673.7 *I/we surrender,* 732.3 *lender*
unclean 622, 151.15 *untidy,* 601.4 *misused,* 622.7 *dirty,* 626.5 *unhygienic,* 877.12 *indecent*

uncleaned 622.7 *dirty*
uncleanliness 626.1 *lack of hygiene*
uncleanly 622.8 *unclean,* 622.12 *dirtily,* 626.8 *unhygienically*
uncleanness 622, 151.3 *untidiness,* 622.1 *dirtiness,* 626.1 *lack of hygiene,* 628.10 *impairment,* 877.2 *indecency*
unclear 307.5 *shapeless,* 428.1 *faint-sounding,* 438.2 *difficult to see,* 441.6 *murky,* 443.4 *inscrutable,* 491.6 *indeterminate,* 520.6 *meaningful,* 523.1 *unintelligible,* 523.4 *difficult,* 551.2 *obscure,* 659.12 *problematic*
unclearly 307.6 *shapelessly*
unclearness 307.1 *shapelessness,* 443.8 *obscurity,* 491.14 *indeterminacy,* 523.11 *unintelligibility*
unclench 598.1 *relinquish,* 727.9 *dispose of*
uncle's 732.4 *lending institution*
Uncle Sam 91.7 *United States ,* 255.10 *US inhabitant*
Uncle Sugar 91.7 *United States*
Uncle Tom 91 Names for Inhabitants, 673.2 *appeaser*
Uncle Tom Cobbley and all 124.7 *average person,* 164.10 *everyone*
unclinch 727.9 *dispose of*
uncloak 296.14 *undress,* 530.5 *disclose*
unclog 349.11 *void,* 660.16 *make easy*
unclose 322.18 *open,* 530.5 *disclose*
unclosed 322.12 *open*
unclot 387.23 *dissolve*
unclothe 294.11 *uncover,* 296.14 *undress*
unclothed 294.8 *uncovered,* 296.9 *undressed*
unclothing 294.2 *undressing,* 296.1 *undress*
unclotted 387.14 *fluid*
unclotting 387.8 *fluidification*
uncloud 442.12 *make transparent*
unclouded 439.19 *sunny,* 442.1 *transparent*
unclubability 816.1 *unsociability*
unclutter 660.18 *disentangle*
uncluttered 556.1 *simple*
uncluttering 660.8 *disentanglement*
uncoded 522.2 *simple*
uncoil 269.10 *lengthen,* 312.10 *straighten,* 331.1 *recoil*
uncoloured 134.13 *pure,* 445.7 *colourless,* 556.2 *unadorned*
uncombed 151.15 *untidy*
uncombined 57.34 *elemental,* 134.16 *simple,* 139.8 *nonadhesive,* 141.5 *disintegrated*
uncomfortable 153.12 *disturbed,* 406.5 *painful,* 764.1 *unpleasant*
uncomfortable with 585.1 *unaccustomed*
uncomfortably 585.6 *unaccustomedly*
uncomforting 785.9 *disliked*
uncommendable 616.1 *inconvenient,* 852.32 *unsatisfactory*
uncommended 852.33 *criticized*
uncommitted 333.4 *middle,* 576.1 *vacillating,* 591.18 *avoiding*
uncommitted person 333.3 *moderate person*
uncommitted vote 576.11 *vacillation*
uncommitted voter 576.15 *indecisive person*
uncommon 165.16 *characteristic,* 182.6 *sparse,* 213.2 *infrequent,* 215.5 *unusual,* 585.2 *not customary*
uncommonly 165.21 *uncomformably,* 213.1 *infrequently,* 215.9 *unusually,* 489.10 *rarely,* 585.8 *unusually*
uncommonness 168.4 *unusualness,* 213.3 *infrequency,* 215.2 *unusualness*
uncommunicative 531.17 *noncommittal,* 566.1 *taciturn,* 816.8 *unsociable*

uncommunicatively 566.10 *taciturnly*
uncommunicativeness 566.4 *taciturnity,* 816.1 *unsociability*
uncompact 372.1 *sparse*
uncompanionable 816.8 *unsociable*
uncompassionateness 836.1 *pitilessness*
uncompelled 698.10 *independent*
uncompensated 123.3 *unequal,* 747.14 *unpaid*
uncompetitive 664.19 *associating,* 675.7 *peaceful*
uncomplaining 765.4 *satisfied*
uncompleted 685, 145.4 *incomplete,* 656.4 *bungled*
uncompliant 168.12 *nonconformist,* 711.8 *refused*
uncomplicated 312.2 *straightforward,* 522.2, 556.1 *simple,* 658.1 *naive,* 660.9 *easy*
uncomplicatedness 660.2 *simplicity*
uncomplimentary 818.5 *discourteous,* 852.27 *critical*
uncomplying 693.13 *disobedient*
uncompounded 134.16 *simple*
uncompressed 370.2 *insubstantial,* 372.1 *sparse*
uncompromising 554.3 *emphatic,* 574.3 *strong-willed,* 577.3 *unyielding,* 690.8 *severe*
uncompromisingly 690.11 *severely*
unconcealed 437.1 *visible,* 526.14 *manifest*
unconceived 462.11 *unthought*
unconcern 436.7 *figurative blindness,* 466.2 *lack of interest,* 468.1 *inattention,* 470.1 *negligence,* 783.1 *indifference,* 787.1 *lack of wonder*
unconcerned 4.18 *detached,* 421.5 *unhearing,* 436.12 *blind to,* 466.4 *uninterested,* 468.7 *inattentive,* 470.4 *negligent,* 673.5 *submitting,* 783.7 *indifferent,* 787.3 *unmoved,* 832.15 *inconsiderate*
unconcernedly 466.8 *disinterestedly*
unconcernedly 466.8 *disinterestedly*
uncondemned 16.63 *acquitted*
uncondensed state 139.1 *nonadhesion*
unconditional 698, 708.7 *permitted,* 847.12 *obligatory*
unconditionally 144.9 *completely,* 698.21 *excessively,* 708.9 *with permission*
unconditional surrender 673.1 *submission*
unconditioned 698.12 *unconditional*
unconditioned reflex 61.20 *conditioning*
unconfined 144.7 *complete,* 248.12 *extensive,* 698.9 *free,* 698.11 *ranging,* 700.8 *free*
unconfirmability 491.13 *indemonstrability*
unconfirmable 491.4 *indemonstrable*
unconfirmed report 532.1 *publication*
unconformable 168.11 *nonconforming*
unconformably 168
unconformist 335.19 *deviant person*
unconformity 117.3, 168.1 *nonconformity*
unconfutability 537.6 *authenticity*
unconfuted 537.19 *authentic*
uncongealed 387.14 *fluid*
uncongenial 117.10 *disagreeing,* 816.8 *unsociable*
uncongeniality 117.4 *disagreement,* 816.1 *unsociability*
unconnected 104.8 *intruder,* 108.6 *unrelated,* 136.17 *unjoined,* 139.8 *nonadhesive,* 160.8 *discontinuous*
unconnectedness 104.2 *foreignness,* 108.1 *unrelatedness*
unconnected person 108
unconquerable 575.12 *indomita-*

ble, 671.31 *entrenched,* 682.15 *victorious*
unconquered 574.4 *undaunted,* 575.12 *indomitable*
unconscious 404, 11.16 *psychic,* 61.21 *psyche,* 61.37 *subconscious,* 236.12 *impotent,* 368.11 *internal,* 436.12 *blind to,* 464.4 *instinct,* 502.6 *ignorant,* 512.8 *oblivious,* 643.4 *not awake,* 761.1 *insensitive,* 761.2 *desensitized,* 783.7 *indifferent*
unconsciously 61.39 *psychologically,* 368.14 *subjectively,* 404.13 *insensibly,* 502.12 *ignorantly,* 512.16 *obliviously,* 643.17 *sleepily,* 783.17 *indifferently,* 865.11 *innocently*
unconscious memory 61.23 *memory*
unconscious mind 61.21 *psyche*
unconsciousness 404, 236.4 *disability,* 368.6 *internal world,* 436.7 *figurative blindness,* 502.1 *ignorance,* 512.1 *oblivion,* 624.3 *symptom,* 643.9 *sleep,* 761.4 *desensitization*
unconsenting 573.2 *refusing,* 711.8 *refused,* 713.9 *protesting*
unconsidered 462.11 *unthought*
unconsolidated 54.56 *petrographic,* 139.8 *nonadhesive*
unconsoling 785.9 *disliked*
unconstitutional 16.56 *unauthorized,* 846.8 *unentitled*
unconstrained 658.1 *naive,* 698.13 *informal,* 814.10 *free,* 848.7 *independent*
unconstrainedly 814.15 *unaffectedly*
unconstraint 698.4 *informality,* 708.1 *permission,* 814.4 *freedom*
unconsumed 132.10 *surplus,* 600.1 *unused*
unconsummated 685.4 *uncompleted,* 825.6 *celibate*
uncontaminated 134.13 *pure,* 142.7 *uncut,* 619.1 *perfect,* 621.16 *clean*
uncontentious 675.7 *peaceful*
uncontestable 490.3 *decided*
uncontested 116.20 *agreeable,* 667.10 *agreeing*
uncontradicted 116.20 *agreeable,* 667.10 *agreeing*
uncontrite 868.3 *impenitent*
uncontrived 595.2 *spontaneous,* 658.1 *naive*
uncontrol 870.3 *overindulgence*
uncontrollable 241.6 *violent,* 577.2 *refractory,* 670.23 *attacking*
uncontrollable tremor 366.7 *shake*
uncontrolled 151.20 *disorderly,* 648.3 *hasty,* 689.6 *anarchic,* 698.10, 848.7 *independent,* 870.8 *overindulgent*
uncontrolled imagination 519.4 *ideality*
uncontroversial 667.10 *agreeing*
unconventional 168, 117.9 *nonconforming,* 215.5 *unusual,* 585.2 *not customary,* 698.10 *independent,* 720.11 *nonobservant,* 814.1 *informality,* 814.7 *informal*
unconventional behaviour 168.3 *nonconformism*
unconventionalist 168.7 *nonconformist,* 500.5 *dissenter*
unconventionality 117.3 *nonconformity,* 168.3 *nonconformism,* 215.2 *unusualness,* 585.3 *unaccustomedness*
unconventionally 117.15 *dissimilarly,* 168.21 *unconformably,* 215.9, 585.8 *unusually*
unconventional medicine 60.2 *natural medicine*
unconversant 656.2 *unskilled*
unconverted 600.1 *unused,* 720.11 *nonobservant*
unconvinced 500.7 *dissenting,* 573.2 *refusing*
unconvincing 238.13 *insufficient,* 555.1 *unemphatic*

unconvincingly 555.3 *unemphatically*
uncooked 595
uncooperative 663, 573.3 *cautious,* 661.13 *hindering,* 669.10 *resistant,* 693.13 *disobedient,* 711.8 *refused*
uncooperatively 711, 661.16 *with delay,* 663.23 *opposingly*
uncooperativeness 663, 669.1 *resistance,* 693.1 *disobedience*
uncopied 119.6 *authentic*
uncordial 820.6 *hostile,* 832.15 *inconsiderate*
uncordiality 820.1 *enmity*
uncordially 820.14 *hostilely*
uncork 322.19 *open up*
uncorked 322.13 *opened up*
uncorroborated 491.5 *uncertified*
uncorrupt 134.12 *morally pure,* 863.5 *virtuous,* 865.5 *innocent*
uncorrupted 134.12 *morally pure,* 863.5 *virtuous,* 865.5 *innocent*
uncorruptible 865.5 *innocent*
uncorruptibly 134.18 *virtuously*
uncorruptness 863.1 *virtue*
uncostly 754.9 *cheap*
uncountable 181.8 *numberless,* 184.2 *immeasurable*
uncounted 181.8 *numberless*
uncouple 136.9 *separate*
uncoupling 136.1 *separation*
uncourtliness 818.1 *discourtesy*
uncourtly 818.5 *discourteous,* 818.9 *discourteously*
uncouth 559.8 *indecorous,* 656.3 *clumsy,* 658.1 *naive,* 764.2 *objectionable,* 790.4 *ugly,* 795.8 *discourteous,* 818.6 *bad-mannered*
uncouthly 818.10 *rudely*
uncouthness 559.2 *impropriety,* 658.2 *naivety,* 795.4 *inelegance*
uncover 294, 131.4 *take off,* 243.10 *produce,* 296.14 *undress,* 322.18 *open,* 322.19 *open up,* 435.18, 437.10 *make visible,* 496.2 *detect,* 526.3 *reveal,* 530.5 *disclose*
uncovered 294, 296.9 *undressed,* 322.12 *open,* 322.13 *opened up,* 437.2 *clear,* 496.14 *discovered,* 526.14 *manifest,* 526.15 *open,* 530.10 *disclosed,* 595.7 *unequipped,* 633.3 *vulnerable*
uncovering 294, 296.1 *undress,* 496.7 *detection,* 526.10 *manifestation,* 530.1 *disclosure*
Uncovering 294
uncover one's head 294.11 *uncover,* 849.19 *take off one's hat to*
uncracked 619.1 *perfect*
uncrease 376.11 *smooth*
uncreated 99.14 *self-existent*
uncreated being 99.7 *self-existence*
uncredited 838.4 *unthanked*
uncritical 482.1 *undiscriminating,* 851.18 *approving*
uncritically 482.13 *unselectively*
uncriticalness 482.6 *lack of discrimination*
uncriticizing 482.2 *impartial*
uncrown 689.4 *be anarchic,* 846.16 *disentitle*
uncrowned king 233.5 *influential person,* 611.4 *bigwig*
uncrumpled 376.2 *uniform*
unction 7.2 *religiousness,* 10.5 *Christian rite,* 62.7 *ointment,* 386.3 *anointment,* 386.5 *ointment,* 395.4 *anointment*
unctional 386.10, 395.11 *oily*
unctuosity 386.2, 395.1 *oiliness,* 853.4 *unctuousness*
unctuous 853, 7.15 *religious,* 376.6 *smooth-mannered,* 386.10, 395.11 *oily,* 538.18 *pretentious,* 540.27 *hypocritical,* 771.11 *humouring,* 808.7 *sycophantic,* 817.9 *deferential*
unctuously 376.16 *suavely,* 386.16, 395.20 *oilily,* 538.27

pretentiously, 540.38 *hypocritically,* 817.16 *deferentially,* 853.17 *flatteringly*
unctuousness 853, 7.2 *religiousness,* 376.7 *smoothness,* 386.2, 395.1 *oiliness,* 538.9, 540.3 *hypocrisy,* 817.4 *deference*
uncultivated 247.3 *birth control,* 595.4 *untrained*
uncultured 658.1 *naive,* 795.8 *discourteous,* 803.4 *common,* 818.6 *bad-mannered*
uncurbed 698.9 *free*
uncurl 312.10 *straighten*
uncurled 312.1 *straight*
uncurtain 530.5 *disclose*
uncut 142, 67.10 *woven,* 144.7 *complete,* 307.5 *shapeless,* 595.5 *immature,* 684.7 *completed*
undamaged 142.7 *uncut,* 619.1 *perfect,* 632.5 *safe*
undamped 392.1 *dry*
undated 193.4 *mistimed*
undaunted 574, 575.12 *indomitable,* 778.9 *courageous*
undauntedness 778.1 *courage*
undead 11.11 *ghost,* 11.15 *witchlike*
undecagon 179.7 *double figures*
undecahydrate 57.10 *salt*
undecayed 637.7 *preserved*
undeceitful 857.4 *honourable*
undeceive 528.11 *inform*
undecennial 179.18 *eleventh*
undeceptive 857.4 *honourable*
undecidable 52.73 *numerable*
undecided 472.8 *problematic,* 473.10 *arguable,* 491.2 *irresolute,* 576.1 *vacillating,* 698.7 *free person,* 698.9 *free*
undecided voter 698.7 *free person*
undecillion 169.3 *large number,* 179.11 *million*
undecipherable 523.1 *unintelligible*
undeclared 527.4 *unsaid*
undeclared war 676.1 *war*
undecorated 556.2 *unadorned*
undecorous 117.11 *unfit*
undecorousness 117.5 *unfitness*
undefeated 575.12 *indomitable,* 669.12 *resisting,* 682.15 *victorious*
undefended 236.11 *unprotected,* 633.3 *vulnerable*
undefended part 633.7 *vulnerability*
undefiled 134.16 *simple,* 621.16 *clean,* 857.5 *pure,* 865.5 *innocent,* 876.9 *pure*
undefined 102.8 *unreal,* 307.5 *shapeless,* 438.2 *difficult to see,* 482.5 *vague,* 491.6 *indeterminate,* 523.3 *unrecognizable*
undemanding 660.9 *easy,* 660.13 *easygoing,* 765.4 *satisfied*
undemocratic 123.4 *unjust,* 690.8 *severe,* 805.23 *prejudiced*
undemocratically 123.8 *unjustly*
undeniable 99.13 *real,* 475.12 *demonstrable,* 490.3 *decided*
undeniableness 537.6 *authenticity*
undeniably 537.37 *authentically,* 772.12 *indeed*
undenied 537.19 *authentic*
undependability 573.14 *disobedience,* 858.2 *faithlessness*
undependable 491.7 *unreliable,* 656.1 *unskilful,* 858.6 *faithless*
under 277, 127.19 *inferiorly,* 276.10 *low,* 293.42 *inclusively*
under a ban 827.10 *maledictive*
under a black cloud 830.13 *sullenly*
under a burden 369.17 *burdensomely*
under a charter 708.9 *with permission*
underachievement 620.5 *imperfection*
underachiever 683.5 *failing person*
under a cloud 687.8 *unlucky*
underact 51, 656.5 *be unskilful*

underage 206.11 *young*
underaged 206.11 *young*
under an agreement 717.9 *compromisingly*
under an arrangement 717.9 *compromisingly*
under an emotional strain 821.30 *lovingly*
under an injunction 709.7 *by veto*
under a patent 708.9 *with permission*
underarm 27.13 *bowling*
under arrest 699.15 *detained,* 702.8 *imprisoned*
under a spell 827.10 *maledictive*
under authorization 708.9 *with permission*
under bad weather 34.10 *on a climb*
underbelly 276.4 *low thing*
underbid 42.3 *card game terms,* 737.3 *bargain*
underbody 276.4 *low thing*
underbuilding 382.6 *construction*
under canvas 74.12 *nautically*
undercapitalized 609.2 *unprovided*
undercarriage 73 Aircraft Parts, 276.4 *low thing,* 280.2 *foot,* 284.2 *supporting part*
under censorship 709, 704.11 *invalidly*
under certain conditions 106.16 *relatively,* 716.9 *feasibly*
undercharge 750.9 *settle accounts,* 754.13 *make cheap*
under cloak of darkness 529.16 *stealthily*
underclothed 296.10 *in dishabille*
underclothes 295.18 *underwear*
undercoat 266.1 *layer,* 292.3 *line,* 444.5 *paint*
undercoated 266.8 *coated*
undercoating 292.1 *lining*
under commission 703
under consideration 472.13 *problematically,* 492.10 *judged,* 592.14 *planned,* 594.17 *developing,* 594.22 *in preparation*
under construction 382.19 *in production,* 594.22 *in preparation,* 685.7 *incompletely*
under contract 15.13 *industrially,* 667.15 *contractually*
under control 150.17 *disciplined,* 302.5 *limited,* 302.8 *within limits,* 694.7 *obedient,* 699.13 *restraining,* 869.9 *moderate,* 869.12 *moderately*
under controls 699.16 *under restraints*
undercooked 45.56 *culinary,* 145.4 *incomplete*
under cover 438.9 *invisibly*
undercover 527.2 *concealed,* 529.10 *secretive*
under cover 632.10 *safely*
undercover agent 529.2 *secretiveness,* 531.7 *concealer*
undercrossing 356.5 *crossing point*
under curfew 302.5 *limited*
undercurrent 96.6 *river flow,* 97.3 *wave,* 527.7 *latent things,* 527.8 *concealment,* 663.3 *conflict,* 759.2 *impression*
undercurrent of sound 424.1 *faintness*
undercut 739.1 *sell,* 754.13 *make cheap*
undercut steak 45.22 *beef*
underdeveloped 307.5 *shapeless,* 595.5 *immature,* 685.4 *uncompleted*
under-developed 145.4 *incomplete,* 243.11 *productive*
underdeveloped countries 13.4 *economic development*
underdeveloped world 249.7 *regions of the world*
underdevelopment 527.6 *latency,* 595.10 *immaturity,* 620.5 *imperfection,* 656.8 *unskilfulness,* 685.1 *noncompletion*
under-development 145.1 *incompleteness*
under discussion 472.13 *problem-*

atically, 477.14 *questionable*, 477.24 *questionably*, 592.14 *planned*

under doctor's orders 624.25 *unhealthily*

underdog 481.8 *victim of discrimination*, 683.5 *failing person*, 687.5 *person in adversity*, 722.6 *loser*

underdone 45.56 *culinary*, 145.4 *incomplete*, 595.6 *uncooked*, 685.4 *uncompleted*

underdressed 296.10 *in dishabille*

underdressing 295.2 *dressing*

under duress 573.17 *unwillingly*, 695.11 *compellingly*, 785.10 *discontentedly*

undereat 274.15 *be emaciated*

underemphasis 542.1 *understatement*

underemphasize 542.20 *understate*

underemphasized 542.12 *understated*

underemployed 641.3 *inactive*

underemployment 641.1 *inaction*

underestimate 495, 129.5 *make smaller*, 493.10 *misjudge*, 495.1 *underestimation*, 525.1 *misinterpret*, 542.20 *understate*, 612.12 *think unimportant*, 850.19 *disrespect*, 854.10 *disparage*

underestimated 495, 493.9 *misjudged*, 538.13 *untrue*, 542.12 *understated*, 850.18 *undervalued*

underestimating 495

underestimation 495, 129.1 *decrease*, 493.1 *misjudgment*, 525.2 *misinterpretation*, 538.1 *untruth*, 542.1 *understatement*, 850.2 *disesteem*, 854.1 *disparagement*

Underestimation 495

under examination 479.14 *experimentally*

underexpose 440.14 *make dark*

underexposed 440.8 *dark*, 445.7 *colourless*

underexposed negative 445.3 *pen-and-ink sketch*

underexposed photograph 445.3 *pen-and-ink sketch*

underexposure 66.8 *composition*, 440.2 *darkening*, 445.3 *pen-and-ink sketch*

under false pretences 540.36 *falsely*

underfed 609, 274.2 *emaciated*, 609.1 *insufficient*, 624.21 *unhealthy*, 743.3 *beggarly*, 871.6 *fasting*

underfelt 276.4 *low thing*

underfinanced 609.2 *unprovided*

under fire 633.4 *endangered*, 679.42 *martially*

underfloor heating 408.3 *heater*

underfoot 276.10 *low*

underframe 284.2 *supporting part*, 284.11 *support*

under full steam 329.14 *swiftly*

underfunded 609.2 *unprovided*

under-gardener 69.13 *horticulturist*

undergarments 295.18 *underwear*

undergird 662.19 *support*

underglaze 44.3 *glaze*, 44.11 *make ceramics*

underglazed 44.10 *ceramic*

underglaze decoration 44.3 *glaze*

underglazing 44.10 *ceramic*

undergo 284.12 *bear*, 759.15 *feel*

undergo a change 216.7 *be changed*

undergo a personality change 220.8 *be transformed*

undergo privation 722.12 *lessen*

undergo repairs 629.4 *be restored*

undergo treatment for 624.24 *be unhealthy*

undergrad 6.7 *learner*

undergraduate 6.7 *learner*

underground 8.20 *devilishly*, 54.50 *terrestrial*, 72.1 *railway*, 276.10 *low*, 277.4 *deep thing*, 277.12 *under*, 327.8 *tunnel*, 327.10 *railway*, 458.8 *fleet-*

ingly, 527.2 *concealed*, 679.14 *armed forces*

underground activities 693.3 *subversion*

underground cable 64.33 *power distribution*, 410.4 *electricity*

underground economy 740.3 *sellers' market*

underground fighter 679.9 *guerrilla*

underground literature 48.1 *literature*

underground press 532.3 *journalism*

underground railway 72.1 *railway*

underground river 96.1 *river*

underground shelter 634.1 *refuge*, 671.10 *shelter*

underground stem 83.5 *stem*

underground water 54.9 *groundwater*

undergrowth 85.4 *trees*, 375.8 *rough ground*

under guard 632.5 *safe*

underhand 474.8 *cunning*, 527.5 *mysterious*, 529.10 *secretive*, 539.35 *deceptive*, 657.4 *cunning*, 801.4 *disreputable*

under hand and seal 714.12 *promised*, 714.16 *as promised*

underhand dealing 529.2 *secretiveness*

underhand dealings 858.3 *criminality*

underhanded 540.31 *fraudulent*, 858.7 *criminal*

underhanded deal 539.10, 540.8 *fraud*, 657.1 *cunning*

underhandedly 858.11 *dishonourably*

underhandedness 539.1 *deception*

under hatches 397.19 *dead*

underheated 626.5 *unhygienic*

under house arrest 699.15 *detained*, 879.20 *punished*

under investigation 473.18 *arguably*

underlaid 276.6 *lower*

underlay 266.1 *layer*, 276.4 *low thing*, 276.8 *be low*, 284.2 *supporting part*

underlayer 266.1 *layer*, 280.1 *base*

under licence 708.9 *with permission*

underlie 276.8 *be low*, 280.4 *base*, 290.13 *be interior*, 527.13 *hide*

underline 237.8 *strengthen*, 437.10 *make visible*, 543.13 *punctuate*, 544.10 *identify*, 554.6 *emphasize*, 611.8 *make important*

underlined 535.15 *emphasized*, 543.17 *punctuated*, 554.4 *emphasized*

underling 127.6 *inferior*, 612.10 *nonentity*, 683.5 *failing person*, 697.1 *servant*, 701.3 *subordinate*, 803.1 *plebeian*

underlining 437.7 *that which makes visible*, 543.7 *punctuation*, 554.1 *emphasis*

underloaded 123.3 *unequal*

under lock and key 632.5 *safe*, 632.10 *safely*, 702.8 *imprisoned*, 702.11 *captively*

underlying 276.6 *lower*, 280.3 *base*, 527.1 *latent*

underlying cause 226.1 *cause*

underlying structure 5.29 *grammar*

underman 182.8 *reduce*

undermanned 182.6 *sparse*, 609.2 *unprovided*, 620.2 *incomplete*

undermine 236.7 *remove power from*, 238.7 *weaken*, 287.3 *invert*, 360.15 *tunnel*, 476.8 *refute*, 592.13 *plot*, 628.5 *hurt*, 657.5 *be cunning*, 661.8 *hinder*, 689.4 *be anarchic*

undermined 628.12 *deteriorated*

undermining 287.1 *inversion*, 360.7 *tunnelling*, 476.1 *refutation*

undermost 276.6 *lower*, 280.3 *base*

underneath 276.4 *low thing*, 276.10 *low*, 280.2 *foot*, 438.9 *invisibly*

under no circumstances 100.15 *not at all*

under notice to quit 727.13 *dismissed*

undernourished 274.2 *emaciated*, 609.1 *insufficient*, 609.3 *underfed*, 624.21 *unhealthy*

under oath 535.24 *truthfully*

under obligation 478.16 *answerable*, 597.8 *responsibly*, 837.4 *grateful*

under official sanction 667.14 *agreeably*

under one's belt 718.8 *accomplished*

under one's breath 424.7 *faintly*, 563.17 *voicelessly*

under one's command 701.9 *subject*

under one's hand and seal 715.7 *contractual*

under one's nose 253.10 *available*, 253.16 *on the spot*, 264.6 *near*, 437.2 *clear*, 475.20 *manifestly*

under one's own steam 174.21 *alone*

under one's thumb 694.7 *obedient*, 701.9 *subject*

under orders 694.10 *obediently*, 701.11 *under subjection*, 703.11 *under commission*

underpaid 609.2 *unprovided*, 743.1 *poor*

underpaint 50.19 *paint*

underpainting 50.2 *painting*

under par 127.19 *inferiorly*, 358.10 *not enough*

underpart 276.4 *low thing*

underpass 63.22 *tunnel*, 137.5 *road*, 277.4 *deep thing*, 322.7 *passageway*, 327.3 *road*, 327.8 *tunnel*, 356.5 *crossing point*

underpin 280.4 *base*, 284.11 *support*

underpinning 63.28 *substructure*, 284.1 *support*, 284.2 *supporting part*

under plain cover 438.9 *invisibly*

underplay 542.20 *understate*, 542.22 *play down*

underplayed 542.19 *downplayed*

underplaying 542.9 *down-playing*

under pleasant circumstances 819.17 *in friendship*

underpopulated 182.6 *sparse*

underpopulation 182.3 *fewness*

underpraise 495.3 *underestimate*, 525.1 *misinterpret*, 542.21 *detract from*

under press of sail 329.14 *swiftly*

under pressure 573.17 *unwillingly*, 648.6 *hastily*, 695.11 *compellingly*

under pressure to 695.11 *compellingly*

underprice 495.3 *underestimate*

underpriced 495.5 *underestimated*, 754.9 *cheap*

underprivileged 743.1 *poor*

under protest 573.17 *unwillingly*, 669.14 *resistingly*

underrate 493.10 *misjudge*, 495.3 *underestimate*, 525.1 *misinterpret*, 542.20 *understate*, 612.12 *think unimportant*, 850.19 *disrespect*, 854.10 *disparage*

underrated 493.9 *misjudged*, 495.5 *underestimated*, 542.12 *understated*, 850.18 *undervalued*

underrating 495.1 *underestimation*

underreckon 542.20 *understate*

underreckoned 542.12 *understated*

underreckoning 542.1 *understatement*

under remission 699.13 *restraining*

under restraint 302.5 *limited*, 699.13 *restraining*

under restraints 699

under restrictions 302.8 *within limits*, 699.16 *under restraints*

underripe 595.5 *immature*

under sail 74.12 *nautically*, 324.18 *in motion*

underscore 237.8 *strengthen*, 543.13 *punctuate*, 544.10 *identify*, 554.6 *emphasize*

underscored 535.15 *emphasized*

underscoring 554.1 *emphasis*

undersea 54.51, 97.7 *oceanic*, 277.12 *under*

underseal 71.21 *miscellaneous motoring terms*

undersea warfare 676.8 *warfare*

undersecretary 12.8 *politician*, 653.16 *official*

undersell 754.13 *make cheap*

under sentence 633.4 *endangered*

under sentence of death 397.18 *dying*

under shelter 632.5 *safe*

undershift 19.10 *defence*, 19.16 *play defence*

undershirt 295.18 *underwear*

undershoot 73.5 *flight*, 123.5 *be unequal*

undershot 123.3 *unequal*

underside 276.4 *low thing*, 280.2 *foot*

under siege 633.4 *endangered*, 679.42 *martially*

undersign 544.11 *identify oneself*

undersize 260.1 *littleness*, 260.7 *little*

underskirt 295.18 *underwear*

undersoil 276.4 *low thing*

under someone's influence 233.14 *influentially*

undersown 68.20 *farmable*

understaff 182.8 *reduce*

understaffed 182.6 *sparse*, 609.2 *unprovided*

understand 522, 787, 4.21 *rationalize*, 6.24 *know*, 277.15 *be profound*, 435.16 *visualize*, 463.11 *reason*, 471.14 *have an idea*, 496.3 *find out*, 497.8 *be of the opinion*, 501.11 *know*, 507.7 *be wise*, 518.5 *suppose*, 519.16 *have insight*, 520.11 *infer*, 524.8 *interpret*, 527.14 *imply*, 528.15 *be informed*, 667.6 *agree with*, 696.15 *learn*, 759.15 *feel*, 831.8 *be benevolent*, 835.8 *pity*

understandability 522.9 *intelligibility*, 660.2 *simplicity*

understandable 522.1 *intelligible*

understandably 522.13 *intelligibly*

understand by 520.11 *infer*

understanding 522, 116.10 *in accord*, 152.10 *agreement*, 277.3 *profundity*, 277.11 *wise*, 284.9 *supportive*, 435.4 *visualization*, 439.13 *enlightenment*, 459.3 *intelligence*, 459.10 *intelligent*, 463.1 *reason*, 463.7 *reasoning*, 471.1 *idea*, 496.8 *finding out*, 501.1 *knowledge*, 507.1 *wisdom*, 507.2 *intelligence*, 519.3 *insight*, 524.1 *interpretation*, 667.1 *agreement*, 677.1 *pacification*, 715.1 *contract*, 717.1 *compromise*, 759.1, 759.10 *feeling*, 819.2 *friendly relations*, 819.8 *friendly*, 821.1 *love*, 835.1 *pity*, 835.6 *pitying*, 847.7 *commitment*

understandingly 116.31 *in accord*

understate 542, 495.3 *underestimate*, 540.22 *falsify*, 854.10 *disparage*

understated 542, 444.13 *softhued*, 538.13 *untrue*

understatement 542, 495.1 *underestimation*, 538.1 *untruth*, 540.9 *falsification*, 854.1 *disparagement*

Understatement 542

under steam 74.12 *nautically*

understeer 71.21 *miscellaneous motoring terms*

understood 518.8 *supposed*, 527.4 *unsaid*, 584.12 *established*

understrapper 612.10 *nonentity*
under strength 238.13 *insufficient,* 609.2 *unprovided*
under strict regulations 690.11 *severely*
understructure 382.6 *construction*
understudy 51.22 *actor,* 51.32 *act,* 114.5 *counterpart,* 155.13 *replacement,* 222.2 *substitute person,* 222.4 *be a substitute,* 293.21 *substitution,* 293.34 *cover for,* 478.23 *answer for,* 707.2 *alternative,* 707.4 *substitute for,* 767.5 *helper*
understudy for 767.11 *assist*
under subjection 701
under supervision 15.13 *industrially*
undersupply 182.3 *fewness*
undersurface 276.4 *low thing,* 280.2 *foot,* 290.1 *interior*
undersurfaced 290.7 *interior*
under suspicion 856.8 *accusatory*
undertake 574, 597, 479.13 *invent,* 567.12 *address oneself to,* 588.8 *resolve,* 590.14 *carry on,* 596.3 *tackle,* 640.4 *act,* 667.7 *contract,* 703.7 *engage*
undertaken 597
undertaker 397.9 *person dealing with the dead,* 399.3 *funeral director,* 596.7 *attempter,* 640.3 *doer*
undertake to 714.7 *promise*
undertaking 226, 597, 230.3 *business,* 243.1 *production,* 588.3 *future intention,* 596.6 *venture,* 640.2 *deed,* 642.2 *social activity,* 667.2 *contract,* 703.2 *engagement,* 715.1 *contract,* 737.6 *business*
Undertaking 597
under the aegis of 632.10 *safely*
under the auspices of 662.37 *in aid of*
under the best circumstances 471.23 *ideally*
under the circumstances 106, 116.36 *accordingly,* 251.12 *circumstantially*
under the counter 16.83 *dishonestly,* 529.16 *stealthily,* 727.16 *disposably,* 737.20 *in trade*
under-the-counter 657.4 *cunning*
under-the-counter purchase 657.1 *cunning*
under the doctor 624.25 *unhealthily*
under the eye of heaven 526.16 *manifestly*
under the ground 54.66 *geographically*
under the hammer 727.16 *disposably,* 739.18 *on sale*
under the influence 874.1 *drunk,* 874.18 *drunkenly*
under the open sky 390.26 *out-of-doors*
under the protection of 632.5 *safe*
under the sun 248.16 *extensively*
under the sway of 701.9 *subject*
under the table 873.4 *dead drunk*
under-the-table 657.4 *cunning*
under-the-table deal 657.1 *cunning*
under the terms of one's will 728.6 *by transfer*
under the thumb 699.13 *restraining,* 808.6 *servile*
under the very nose of 668.9 *defiantly*
under the weather 238.10 *ill,* 624.22 *sick*
under the wing of 632.5 *safe*
underthings 295.18 *underwear*
undertone 49.21 *tone,* 297.3 *atmosphere,* 424.1 *faintness,* 428.4 *faint sound,* 527.10 *quietness,* 563.4 *whispering*
undertow 96.6 *river flow,* 97.3 *wave,* 527.7 *latent things,* 635.1 *trap*
under training 594.17 *developing*
under treatment 624.25 *unhealthily*
undertrick 42.3 *card game terms*

underuse 600.5 *not use,* 600.8 *nonuse*
underused 600.3 *not wanted*
underutilization 600.8 *nonuse*
underutilize 600.5 *not use*
undervaluation 129.1 *decrease,* 493.1 *misjudgment,* 495.1 *underestimation,* 542.1 *understatement,* 850.2 *disesteem*
undervalue 129.5 *make smaller,* 493.10 *misjudge,* 495.3 *underestimate,* 542.20 *understate,* 850.19 *disrespect,* 854.10 *disparage*
undervalued 850, 493.9 *misjudged,* 495.5 *underestimated,* 542.12 *understated*
undervaluing the self 810.5 *self-deprecation*
under warrant 632.5 *safe,* 708.9 *with permission*
under warranty 718.7 *guaranteed*
underwater 20.8 *angling,* 20.9 *on the water,* 39.11 *swimming,* 39.12 *by swimming,* 97.7 *oceanic,* 277.12 *under*
underwater breathing tube 39.1 *swimming*
underwater diving 18 Sporting Activities
underwater explorer 97.6 *oceanographer*
underwater mask 39.1 *swimming*
underwater photography 66.1 *photography*
underwater plug 20.2 *artificial fly*
underwater swimmer 39.4 *swimmer,* 360.8 *descender*
underwater swimming 39.1 *swimming*
underway 36.10 *sailing*
under way 74.12 *nautically,* 324.18 *in motion*
underway 336.20 *in progress*
under way 594.22 *in preparation*
underwear 295, 296.4 *dishabille*
underweight 123.1 *inequality,* 123.3 *unequal,* 127.17 *defective,* 274.1 *thin,* 369.7 *weighing,* 370.1 *light*
underwhelming 542.16 *imperceptible*
underwing moth 82 Insects
underwood 85.4 *trees*
underworld 8.11 *heaven,* 277.4 *deep thing,* 368.1 *nonmaterial world,* 397.14 *the spiritual world,* 864.7 *criminality*
under wraps 438.3 *private,* 527.2, 531.14 *concealed*
underwrite 13.11 *deal,* 116.28 *consent,* 284.13 *support financially,* 499.4 *assent,* 714.8 *guarantee,* 715.5 *contract,* 718.11 *promise*
underwriter 284.8 *supporter,* 499.3 *assenter*
underwriting 589.7 *calculation of chance,* 718.2 *promise*
underwritten 116.17 *consenting,* 499.7 *agreed,* 714.13 *guaranteeing*
undeserved 846.10 *undue*
undeservedness 846.5 *undueness*
undeserving 846, 618.4 *poor*
undesigned 589.9 *causeless*
undesigning 658.1 *naive*
undesirability 616.3 *inconvenience*
undesirable 616.1 *inconvenient,* 635.2 *troublemaker,* 785.9 *disliked,* 801.2 *disreputable character,* 844.13 *improper,* 864.9 *wicked person*
undesired 785.9 *disliked*
undesirous 783.7 *indifferent,* 785.8 *disliking*
undetectability 438.4 *invisibility*
undetectable 438.1 *invisible*
undetected 527.2 *concealed*
undetermined 164.20 *generalized,* 229.6 *motiveless,* 490.8 *unspecified,* 576.1 *vacillating*
undeterred 575.12 *indomitable*
undeveloped 145.4 *incomplete,* 206.11 *young,* 206.12 *immature,* 307.5 *shapeless,* 486.6 *po-

tential,* 527.1 *latent,* 595.5 *immature,* 600.2 *new,* 620.2 *incomplete,* 628.12 *deteriorated,* 656.2 *unskilled*
undeveloped world 249.7 *regions of the world*
undevelopment 206.3 *immaturity,* 307.1 *shapelessness,* 595.10 *immaturity,* 620.5 *imperfection*
undeviating 333, 110.17 *regular,* 116.14 *conforming,* 332.15 *direct,* 490.2 *convinced,* 490.6 *infallible,* 537.22 *uniform*
undeviatingly 332.9 *directly,* 537.39 *accurately*
undies 295.18 *underwear*
undifferentiated 110.12 *same,* 112.6, 116.14 *conforming,* 134.16 *simple,* 159.11 *continuous,* 482.5 *vague*
undifferentiating 482.1 *undiscriminating*
undifferentiation 159.5 *continuity*
undignified 559.7 *graceless*
undiluted 134.13 *pure,* 237.12 *strong to the senses,* 351.17 *drinkable,* 874.6 *intoxicating*
undiminished 142.7 *uncut,* 619.1 *perfect*
undine 8.5 *deity,* 62.11 *linctus,* 97.4 *sea god*
undiplomatic 656.1 *unskilful*
undiplomatically 656.11 *unskilfully*
undirected 335
undiscernible 523.1 *unintelligible*
undiscerning 436.12 *blind to,* 482.1 *undiscriminating,* 656.1 *unskilful*
undischarged bankrupt 747.6 *nonpayer*
undisciplined 151.20 *disorderly,* 579.1 *capricious,* 689.6 *anarchic,* 693.13 *disobedient,* 870.8 *overindulgent*
undisclosed 527.2 *concealed,* 529.9 *secret*
undiscouraged 575.12 *indomitable*
undiscoverable 523.1 *unintelligible,* 527.2 *concealed*
undiscovered 527.2 *concealed,* 527.3 *unsolved*
undiscriminating 482, 412.6 *coarse,* 851.18 *approving*
undiscriminating person 482
undisguised 134.17 *direct,* 437.1 *visible,* 442.4 *easily seen through,* 526.14 *manifest,* 537.18 *truthful,* 658.1 *naive*
undisguisedly 526.16 *manifestly*
undismayed 778.9 *courageous*
undisposed of 600.1 *unused*
undisputed 490.3 *decided,* 497.14 *believed,* 535.16 *definite,* 667.10 *agreeing*
undisputedness 535.8 *definiteness*
undissembling 658.1 *naive*
undissolved 371.7 *condensed*
undistinguishable 482.5 *vague*
undistinguished 124.3 *mediocre,* 158.15 *middling,* 482.5 *vague,* 806.1 *humble,* 806.7 *humility*
undistracted 467.8 *diligent*
undistributed middle 4.9 *philosophical problem*
undisturbed 4.18 *detached,* 325.6 *quiescent*
undiversified 110.17 *regular*
undivided 142.7 *uncut,* 144.7 *complete,* 174.13 *whole,* 219.5 *continual*
undivided attention 467.2 *close attention*
undividedness 174.3 *oneness*
undivulged 527.3 *unsolved,* 527.4 *unsaid,* 529.9 *secret*
undo 136.9 *separate,* 139.5 *unstick,* 221.7 *restore,* 231.3 *counteract,* 244.8 *destroy,* 294.11 *uncover,* 296.14 *undress,* 614.8 *make useless*
undocumented 491.5 *uncertified*
undoing 136.1 *separation,* 244.1 *destruction*

undomesticated 585.1 *unaccustomed*
undone 136.15 *separate,* 139.8 *nonadhesive,* 244.15 *destroyed,* 685.4 *uncompleted*
undoubted 488.6 *probable,* 537.19 *authentic*
undoubtedly 101.14, 490.23 *certainly,* 535.23 *affirmatively,* 537.37 *authentically*
undoubting 490.2 *convinced,* 497.11 *believing*
undrained 98.11 *continental,* 626.5 *unhygienic*
undramatic 555.1 *unemphatic,* 556.1 *simple*
undramatically 556.8 *simply*
undrape 296.14 *undress*
undraped 296.9 *undressed*
undreamed-of 462.11 *unthought*
undress 296, 296, 294.2 *undressing,* 294.11 *uncover,* 814.6 *informal dress*
Undress 296
undressed 296, 294.8 *uncovered,* 595.6 *uncooked,* 595.7 *unequipped*
undressing 294, 296.1 *undress*
undrilled 595.4 *untrained*
undrinkable 415.6 *unpalatable,* 626.5 *unhygienic*
undrooping 575.11 *steady*
undue 846, 357.12 *excessive,* 616.1 *inconvenient*
undue liberty 846.4 *presumptuousness*
undueness 846, 616.3 *inconvenience*
undulancy 365.4 *rock*
undulant 365.17 *waving*
undulate 97.10 *billow,* 214.7 *be regular,* 314.6 *convolute,* 365.12 *wave*
undulating 214.11 *regular,* 275.13 *mountainous,* 365.17 *waving*
undulating land 98.7 *upland*
undulatingly 214.15 *regularly*
undulating motion 214.1 *regularity*
undulation 56.12, 97.3 *wave,* 214.1 *regularity,* 311.2 *bend,* 314.1 *convolution,* 365.4 *rock*
undulatory 311.5 *well-rounded,* 314.4 *convolutional,* 365.17 *waving,* 375.1 *rough*
unduly 846
unduplicated 119.6 *authentic*
undutiful 693.13 *disobedient,* 720.12 *nonperforming*
undutifulness 693.1 *disobedience,* 720.2 *nonperformance*
undyed 134.13 *pure,* 446.1 *white,* 448.1 *grey*
undying 184.3 *eternal,* 186.5 *timeless,* 188.9 *permanent,* 190.8 *eternal,* 217.7 *permanent,* 219.6 *protracted*
undyingly 217.9 *permanently*
unearned 846.10 *undue*
unearned income 721.4 *earnings*
unearth 200.16 *excavate,* 250.11 *find,* 355.13 *dig out,* 399.9 *exhume,* 496.2 *detect,* 526.3 *reveal*
unearthed 250.7 *found,* 496.14 *discovered,* 530.10 *disclosed*
unearthing 250.3 *locating,* 355.3 *digging out*
unearthliness 11.2 *the occult,* 368.2 *unworldliness*
unearthly 8.13 *divine,* 11.18 *spiritual,* 149.12 *extraterrestrial,* 368.8 *nonmaterial*
unearthly hour 208.2 *early hour*
unearth the past 200.16 *excavate*
unease 366.1 *agitation,* 642.7 *restlessness,* 777.2 *fearfulness,* 862.2 *affliction*
uneasily 153.19 *distractedly,* 366.27 *agitatedly,* 777.15 *fearfully*
uneasiness 777.2 *fearfulness,* 777.3 *worry*
uneasy 153.12 *disturbed,* 366.15 *agitated,* 656.3 *clumsy,* 777.8 *fearful*

uneasy conscience 867.1 *penitence*
uneasy peace 676.1 *war*
uneasy truce 675.1 *peace*
uneatable 415.6, 764.3 *unpalatable*
uneconomic 607.8 *wasteful*, 614.2 *futile*, 757.1 *extravagant*
uneconomical 607.8 *wasteful*
uneconomically 607.10 *wastefully*, 757.9 *extravagantly*
unedged 381.1 *blunt*
uneducable 656.2 *unskilled*
uneducated 5.39 *of language*, 502.6 *ignorant*, 585.1 *unaccustomed*, 656.2 *unskilled*, 658.1 *naive*
uneducated speech 5.5 *nonstandard language*
unelaborate 542.14 *simple*
unelaborated 685.4 *uncompleted*
unelaborately 542.24 *simply*
unelaborateness 542.4 *simplicity*
unembellished 556.2 *unadorned*
unembellishment 556.5 *unadornment*
unembodied 11.18 *spiritual*, 368.8 *nonmaterial*
unemotional 4.18 *detached*, 404.6 *unfeeling*, 761.1 *insensitive*, 783.7 *indifferent*
unemotionally 4.27 *stoically*, 761.8 *unfeelingly*, 783.17 *indifferently*
unemphatic 555, 424.4 *faint*, 556.1 *simple*
unemphatically 555
unemployability 614.3 *uselessness*
unemployable 600.1 *unused*, 614.1 *useless*
unemployed 236.10 *powerless*, 325.5 *sedentary*, 600.3 *not wanted*, 641.3 *inactive*, 643.2 *not working*, 645.7 *leisurely*
unemployment 643, 645, 13.6 *economic factors*, 581.6 *discarding*, 600.8 *nonuse*, 641.1 *inaction*, 687.2 *economic adversity*
unemployment benefit 662.4 *social assistance*, 833.4 *welfare state*
unemployment benefits 718.1 *protection*, 831.3 *welfare*
unemployment compensation 662.4 *social assistance*
unemployment insurance 13.8 *industrial relations*, 662.4 *social assistance*
unempowered 846.8 *unentitled*
unenclosed 322.13 *opened up*
unending 159.11 *continuous*, 184.3, 190.8 *eternal*, 190.10 *continuing forever*, 219.6 *protracted*
unendingly 219.7, 575.14 *continually*
unendowed 656.1 *unskilful*
unendurable 618.3 *bad*
unengaged 643.2 *not working*
unenjoyable 788.4 *boring*
unenlightened 436.12 *blind to*, 440.11 *benighted*, 502.6 *ignorant*, 656.1 *unskilful*
unenlightenment 436.7 *figurative blindness*, 502.1 *ignorance*
unenthusiasm 573.13 *dissociation*
unenthusiastic 466.4 *uninterested*, 573.3 *cautious*, 787.3 *unmoved*
unenthusiastically 573.17 *unwillingly*, 787.9 *without wonder*
unentitled 846
unequable 123.3 *unequal*
unequal 123, 2.14 *socioeconomic*, 52.75 *equal*, 108.8 *distorted*, 115.4 *dissimilar*, 117.7 *disparate*, 215.4 *irregular*, 309.6 *distorted*, 656.3 *clumsy*, 666.10 *different*
unequalize 123.5 *be unequal*
unequalled 123.3 *unequal*, 126.14, 617.2 *best*, 619.1 *perfect*, 861.2 *best*
unequally 123, 52.87 *mathematically*, 108.13 *disproportionately*, 113.10 *diversely*, 115.7, 117.15 *dissimi-*

larly, 215.8 *irregularly*, 666.12 *differently*
unequalness 215.1 *irregularity*
unequal to 609.1 *insufficient*
unequipped 595, 620.2 *incomplete*, 656.1 *unskilful*
unequivocal 490.3 *decided*, 522.1 *intelligible*, 535.16 *definite*, 554.3 *emphatic*
unequivocally 144.9 *completely*, 535.23 *affirmatively*, 619.8 *completely*, 857.7 *honourably*
unequivocalness 535.8 *definiteness*
unerring 134.12 *morally pure*, 503.6 *correct*, 537.22 *uniform*, 843.8 *correct*, 863.5 *virtuous*, 865.5 *innocent*
unerringly 134.18 *virtuously*, 537.39 *accurately*, 865.11 *innocently*
unerringness 537.9 *uniformity*
unerroneousness 537.1 *truth*
unescorted 174.15 *solo*, 633.3 *vulnerable*
unessayed 600.1 *unused*
unessential 104.8 *intruder*
unethical 844.15 *immoral*, 858.5 *dishonourable*, 877.11 *immoral*
unethically 858.11 *dishonourably*
unethicalness 877.1 *immorality*
uneuphonious 559.9 *inelegant*
unevasive 522.2 *simple*
uneven 113.5 *diverse*, 123.3 *unequal*, 160.8 *discontinuous*, 215.4 *irregular*, 319.4 *notched*, 375.1 *rough*, 620.1 *imperfect*, 844.11 *wrong*
unevenly 113.10 *diversely*, 123.7 *unequally*, 215.8 *irregularly*, 319.7 *jaggedly*, 375.14 *roughly*, 620.11 *imperfectly*
unevenness 113.1 *diversity*, 123.1 *inequality*, 160.1 *discontinuity*, 215.1 *irregularity*, 375.6 *roughness*, 620.5 *imperfection*, 844.1 *unfairness*
uneven parallel bars 30.7 *stationary rings*
uneventful 612.4 *trivial*
unexaggerated 537.18 *truthful*
unexcelled 126.14 *best*
unexceptionable 617.5 *not bad*
unexceptional 124.3 *mediocre*, 164.21 *common*, 167.15 *everyday*, 242.6 *moderate*, 584.10 *familiar*, 783.10 *mediocre*
unexceptionally 783
unexcitable 240.5 *inert*
unexcited 787.3 *unmoved*
unexciting 412.5 *tasteless*, 555.1 *unemphatic*
unexcusable 864.11 *wicked*
unexecuted 685.4 *uncompleted*
unexercised 595.4 *untrained*, 600.1 *unused*
unexisting 536.14 *nonexistent*
unexpected 489, 229.6 *motiveless*, 489.1 *improbable*, 514.8 *surprising*, 523.5 *strange*, 579.1 *capricious*, 589.8 *chance*, 786.8 *wonderful*, 846.10 *undue*
unexpected attack 635.1 *trap*
unexpected event 635.1 *trap*
unexpected gift 514.4 *surprising thing*
unexpected loss of life 397.5 *ways of dying*
unexpectedly 489, 229.8 *by chance*, 514.13 *surprisingly*, 589.13 *by chance*
unexpected occurrence 514.4 *surprising thing*
unexpended 605.7 *stored*
unexpended balance 605.1 *store*
unexpensive 754.9 *cheap*
unexpensively 754.15 *cheaply*
unexpired 132.10 *surplus*
unexplainable 523.1 *unintelligible*, 589.9 *causeless*
unexplained 523, 527.3 *unsolved*
unexploded bomb 240.3 *inert thing*
unexploited 600.2 *new*
unexplored 201.11 *unfamiliar*,

502.8 *unknown*, 527.3 *unsolved*, 816.11 *secluded*
unexposed 527.2 *concealed*, 632.5 *safe*
unexpressed 527.4 *unsaid*
unexpressive 521.10 *meaningless*
unexpurgated 142.7 *uncut*, 144.7 *complete*, 877.12 *indecent*
unextreme 333.4 *middle*
unfading 217.7 *permanent*, 444.10 *coloured*
unfailing 217.7 *permanent*, 219.6 *protracted*, 575.11 *steady*
unfailingly 217.9 *permanently*
unfair 123.4 *unjust*, 481.10 *discriminatory*, 493.8 *unjust*, 548.6 *misrepresented*, 844.11 *wrong*, 858.5 *dishonourable*
unfair advantage 721.1 *gain*
unfair labour practices 15.1 *industrial relations*
unfairly 123.8 *unjustly*, 481.17 *prejudicially*, 493.14 *unjustly*, 548.8 *unrepresentatively*, 844.25 *wrongly*, 858.11 *dishonourably*
unfairly treated 493.9 *misjudged*
unfairness 844, 481.3 *prejudice*, 493.3 *injustice*, 858.1 *improbity*
unfair opponent 785.3 *disliked person*
unfair price 753
unfair representation 548.1 *misrepresentation*
unfaithful 538, 224.14 *irresolute*, 498.6 *disbelieving*, 539.38 *treacherous*, 576.2 *changeable*, 578.11 *equivocating*, 720.13 *noncompliant*, 820.8 *estranged*, 858.6 *faithless*, 877.14 *lecherous*
unfaithfully 224.15 *changeably*, 578.13 *perfidiously*, 820.14 *hostilely*, 858.11 *dishonourably*
unfaithfulness 683.3 *personal fault*, 693.1 *disobedience*, 820.2 *personal conflict*, 821.8 *love affair*, 858.2 *faithlessness*, 877.4 *illicit love*
unfallaciousness 537.1 *truth*
unfallen 876.9 *pure*
unfalseness 537.1 *truth*
unfaltering 575.11 *steady*
unfamiliar 201, 149.11 *foreign*, 479.9 *original*, 502.8 *unknown*, 585.1 *unaccustomed*
unfamiliarity 201.1 *newness*, 479.4 *originality*, 502.1 *ignorance*, 585.3 *unaccustomedness*
unfamiliarly 149.18 *extraneously*
unfamiliar word 5.17 *word*
unfanciness 542.4 *simplicity*
unfancy 542.14 *simple*
unfashionable 457.10 *aspectual*, 559.10 *ugly*, 585.2 *not customary*, 795.8 *discourteous*
unfashionably 559.11 *inelegantly*
unfashioned 595.5 *immature*
unfasten 136.9 *separate*, 139.5 *unstick*, 322.19 *open up*, 639.1 *deliver*
unfastened 136.17 *unjoined*, 322.13 *opened up*
unfastening 136.1 *separation*
unfastidious 482.1 *undiscriminating*, 622.8 *unclean*
unfathomable 184.2 *immeasurable*, 277.8 *deep*, 443.4 *inscrutable*, 523.1 *unintelligible*
unfathomableness 277.1 *depth*
unfathomably 523.13 *unintelligibly*
unfathomed 277.8 *deep*
unfavourable 211.10 *untimely*, 244.14 *destructive*, 517.15 *presageful*, 663.19 *oppositional*, 687.6 *adverse*, 852.27 *critical*, 862.10 *inauspicious*
unfavourableness 211.1 *untimeliness*, 862.3 *bad luck*
unfavourable review 852.5 *criticism*
unfavourable verdict 16.7 *legal trial*, 16.43 *conviction*
unfavourably 211.15 *at the wrong time*, 687.12 *in adversity*, 862.14 *inauspiciously*

unfearing 574.4 *undaunted*, 778.12 *self-reliant*
unfeasibility 487.6 *hopelessness*
unfeasible 487.3 *hopeless*
unfeathered 296.12 *peeling*
unfed 609.3 *underfed*, 871.6 *fasting*
unfeeling 404, 378.5 *mentally tough*, 381.3 *dull*, 574.3 *strong-willed*, 761.1 *insensitive*, 761.2 *desensitized*, 783.7 *indifferent*, 832.12 *callous*, 832.15 *inconsiderate*, 836.4 *pitiless*
unfeelingly 761, 378.14 *single-mindedly*, 404.13 *insensibly*, 783.17 *indifferently*, 836.7 *pitilessly*
unfeelingness 378.9 *mental toughness*, 832.3 *callousness*, 836.1 *pitilessness*
unfeeling person 404
unfeigning 556.3 *natural*
unfeminine 795.7 *vulgar*, 818.5 *discourteous*
unfenced 322.13 *opened up*
unfermented 873.2 *nonalcoholic*
unfertilized 247.5 *rendered infertile*
unfetter 136.9 *separate*, 639.1 *deliver*, 698.15 *set free*, 700.4 *liberate*
unfettered 136.15 *separate*, 698.9 *free*, 698.11 *ranging*, 700.7 *liberated*
unfettering 700.1 *liberation*
unfictitious 537.15 *true*
unfictitiousness 537.1 *truth*
unfilled 254.14 *unoccupied*, 609.2 *unprovided*, 620.2 *incomplete*
unfinished 375, 143.11 *partial*, 145.4 *incomplete*, 307.5 *shapeless*, 358.7 *short*, 595.5 *immature*, 620.2 *incomplete*, 656.2 *unskilled*, 685.4 *uncompleted*
unfinished piece 375.10 *rough idea*
unfinished state 145.1 *incompleteness*, 358.5 *shortfall*
unfinished task 685.1 *noncompletion*
unfit 117, 236.10 *powerless*, 595.7 *unequipped*, 614.1 *useless*, 614.8 *make useless*, 616.1 *inconvenient*, 620.1 *imperfect*, 624.21 *unhealthy*, 656.1 *unskilful*, 844.13 *improper*
unfit for consideration 581.10 *rejected*
unfit for human consumption 581.10 *rejected*
unfitness 117, 236.1 *powerlessness*, 595.8 *lack of preparation*, 614.3 *uselessness*, 616.3 *inconvenience*, 620.5 *imperfection*, 656.8 *unskilfulness*
unfitted 117.11 *unfit*
unfitting 117.11 *unfit*, 616.1 *inconvenient*, 844.13 *improper*
unfittingness 117.5 *unfitness*, 616.3 *inconvenience*, 846.5 *undueness*
unfixed 136.17 *unjoined*
unflagging 378.4 *powerful*, 575.11 *steady*, 642.20 *industrious*
unflagging efforts 575.2 *commitment*
unflanked 633.3 *vulnerable*
unflattering 537.18 *truthful*, 818.5 *discourteous*
unflavoured 134.13 *pure*, 412.5 *tasteless*
unflawed 619.1 *perfect*
unfledged 78.24 *newly hatched*, 156.32 *embryonic*, 206.11 *young*, 294.9 *shed*, 296.12 *peeling*, 595.5 *immature*
unfleshly 368.8 *nonmaterial*
unflinching 574.4 *undaunted*, 778.9 *courageous*
unfluent 559.9 *inelegant*
unfocused 438.2 *difficult to see*
unfold 4.21 *rationalize*, 83.21 *vegetate*, 99.18 *come to be*, 121.6 *change gradually*, 227.7 *follow from*, 243.10 *produce*,

261.6 *become bigger*, 269.10 *lengthen*, 312.10 *straighten*, 322.18 *open*, 475.16 *explain*, 526.3 *reveal*, 530.5 *disclose*
unfolded 261.7 *bigger*, 322.12 *open*
unfolding 84.5 *flowering*, 261.1 *growth*, 261.8 *growing*, 457.1 *appearance*, 457.7 *appearing*, 526.10 *manifestation*
unforced 572.5 *voluntary*, 583.2 *spontaneous*, 710.18 *voluntary*
unforeseeable 489.3 *unexpected*, 589.8 *chance*
unforeseeableness 489.5 *unexpectedness*
unforeseeably 489.9 *unexpectedly*
unforeseen 489.3 *unexpected*, 514.8 *surprising*, 589.8 *chance*
unforeseen result 514.4 *surprising thing*
unforgettable 511.7 *memorable*, 611.6 *notable*
unforgettably 511.16 *memorably*
unforgivable 844, 864.11 *wicked*, 866.5 *guilty*
unforgivably 855.16 *vindictively*, 866.11 *guiltily*
unforgiving 690.8 *severe*, 836.4 *pitiless*, 855.14 *vindictive*
unforgivingly 836.7 *pitilessly*
unforgivingness 836.1 *pitilessness*
unforgotten 511.7 *memorable*
unform 307.3 *make shapeless*
unformed 307.5 *shapeless*, 595.5 *immature*
unforthcoming 566.1 *taciturn*, 591.18 *avoiding*, 816.8 *unsociable*
unfortified 134.13 *pure*, 236.11 *unprotected*, 238.8 *weak*, 633.3 *vulnerable*
unfortunate 117.11 *unfit*, 211.14 *accidental*, 481.8 *victim of discrimination*, 589.8 *chance*, 616.1 *inconvenient*, 683.5 *failing person*, 683.10 *failed*, 687.5 *person in adversity*, 687.8 *unlucky*, 862.10 *inauspicious*
unfortunately 117.17 *unsuitably*, 211.17 *mistakenly*, 229.9 *luckily*, 589.13 *by chance*, 683.12 *unsuccessfully*, 687.12 *in adversity*, 862.14 *inauspiciously*
unfoul 349.11 *void*
unfouling 349.21 *removal*
unfounded 474.7 *sophistic*, 476.6 *refutable*
unfragranced 134.13 *pure*
unfranchised 846.8 *unentitled*
unfrank 538.5 *pretentious*, 540.27 *hypocritical*
unfrankly 538.27 *pretentiously*
unfrankness 538.8 *pretence*, 540.3 *hypocrisy*
unfree 697.9 *serving*, 701.9 *subject*
unfreeze 387.24 *melt*
unfreezing 387.8 *fluidification*, 727.1 *disposal*
unfriendliness 663.1 *opposition*, 816.1 *unsociability*, 818.1 *discourtesy*, 820.1 *enmity*, 832.6 *inconsiderateness*
unfriendly 663.19 *oppositional*, 670.21 *aggressive*, 785.8 *disliking*, 816.8 *unsociable*, 818.5 *discourteous*, 820.6 *hostile*, 832.15 *inconsiderate*
unfrock 147.8 *eject*, 349.3 *disbar*, 704.7 *terminate*, 846.16 *disentitle*, 879.1 *punish*
unfrocked 846.12 *disentitled*
unfrocking 349.18 *dismissal*, 846.2 *disentitlement*, 879.7 *punishment*
unfruitful 247.3 *birth control*
unfuddled 873.1 *sober*
unfuddled brain 873.6 *sobriety*
unfulfilled 358.7 *short*, 609.2 *unprovided*, 645.4 *uncompleted*
unfulfilled expectations 515.1 *disappointment*
unfulfilling 515.11 *disappointing*
unfunny 788.4 *boring*
unfunny joke 788.2 *boring thing*
unfurl 269.10 *lengthen*, 312.10

straighten, 526.3 *reveal*, 530.5 *disclose*
unfurled 526.13 *displayed*
unfurnished 595.7 *unequipped*, 609.2 *unprovided*
unfussily 542.24 *simply*
unfussiness 542.4 *simplicity*
unfussy 482.1 *undiscriminating*, 542.14 *simple*
ungainly 559.7 *graceless*, 656.3, 659.15 *clumsy*, 790.4 *ugly*
ungallant 818.5 *discourteous*
ungallantly 818.9 *discourteously*
ungallantness 818.1 *discourtesy*
ungarbed 296.9 *undressed*
Ungaretti 48 Poets
ungarnished 556.2 *unadorned*, 595.6 *uncooked*
ungathered 600.2 *new*
ungenerosity 758.3 *parsimony*
ungenerous 758.1 *mean*, 832.15 *inconsiderate*, 860.4 *selfish*
ungenerously 758.9 *meanly*, 860.8 *selfishly*
ungenerousness 758.3 *parsimony*, 832.6 *inconsiderateness*
ungenial 820.6 *hostile*, 832.15 *inconsiderate*
ungeniality 820.1 *enmity*
ungenially 820.14 *hostilely*
ungent 62.7 *ointment*
ungentle 818.5 *discourteous*, 832.12 *callous*
ungentlemanlike 818.5 *discourteous*
ungentlemanliness 818.1 *discourtesy*
ungentlemanly 795.7 *vulgar*, 818.5 *discourteous*, 818.9 *discourteously*, 858.5 *dishonourable*
ungentleness 818.1 *discourtesy*
ungently 818.9 *discourteously*
ungenuine 540.25 *false*, 540.28 *spurious*
ungenuinely 540.36 *falsely*, 540.37 *spuriously*
ungenuineness 540.1 *falsehood*, 540.4 *spuriousness*
unget-at-able 263.8 *distant*
ungettable 632.6 *invulnerable*
ungifted 656.1 *unskilful*
ungiving 373.4 *mentally hard*
unglazed 44.10 *ceramic*
unglazed earthenware 44.1 *ceramics*
unglue 139.5 *unstick*
ungodliness 864.6 *religious sin*
ungodly 862.7 *evil*, 864.14 *impious*
ungovernable 16.61 *lawless*, 241.6 *violent*, 577.2 *refractory*, 698.10 *independent*
ungoverned 689.6 *anarchic*, 698.9 *free*, 698.10 *independent*
ungraceful 559.7 *graceless*, 656.3 *clumsy*
ungracious 652.18 *badly behaved*, 764.2 *objectionable*, 805.22 *boastful*, 816.8 *unsociable*, 818.5 *discourteous*, 832.15 *inconsiderate*, 838.3 *ungrateful*
ungraciously 652.20 *badly*, 816.14 *unsociably*, 818.9 *discourteously*, 832.20 *malevolently*, 838.7 *ungratefully*
ungraciousness 652.4 *bad conduct*, 764.6 *objectionability*, 816.1 *unsociability*, 818.1 *discourtesy*, 832.6 *inconsiderateness*, 838.1 *ingratitude*
ungraded 151.13 *unordered*
ungrateful 838, 512.10 *unthinking*
ungratefully 838
ungratefulness 838.1 *ingratitude*
ungrateful wretch 838.2 *thankless person*
ungrateful yob 838.2 *thankless person*
ungregarious 816.8 *unsociable*
ungregariousness 816.1 *unsociability*
ungrown 595.5 *immature*
ungrudging 755.1 *generous*
ungrudgingly 755.12 *generously*
unguarded 236.11 *unprotected*, 238.8 *weak*, 583.2 *spontaneous*,

595.1 *unprepared*, 633.3 *vulnerable*
unguent 386, 395, 62.7, 386.5 *ointment*, 386.14 *anoint*, 395.6 *ointment*, 395.18 *anoint*
unguentary 386.11, 395.12 *unguent*
unguentous 386.11, 395.12 *unguent*
unguentum 386.5 *ointment*
unguessed 489.3 *unexpected*, 527.3 *unsolved*
unguiculate 77.28 *carnivorous*
unguided 335.22 *undirected*, 658.1 *naive*
unguinous 386.10, 395.11 *oily*
ungulant 77.15 *hoofed mammal*
ungulate 77, 77.15 *hoofed mammal*
unguligrade 77.33 *ungulate*
unhabituated 585.1 *unaccustomed*, 656.3 *clumsy*
unhackneyed 585.2 *not customary*
unhallow 622.11 *dirty*
unhallowed 622.8 *unclean*
unhampered 322.13 *opened up*
unhand 700.4 *liberate*, 727.9 *dispose of*
unhandiness 656.8 *unskilfulness*
unhanding 700.1 *liberation*
unhandled 600.2 *new*
unhandy 656.3 *clumsy*
unhappily 687.12 *in adversity*, 770.11 *sadly*
unhappiness 770.1 *sorrow*, 816.1 *unsociability*, 852.1 *disapproval*
unhappy 454.3 *depressed*, 616.1 *inconvenient*, 656.4 *bungled*, 770.5 *sad*, 774.4 *lamenting*, 852.25 *disapproving*
unharboured 252.10 *replaced*
unhardened 238.8 *weak*
unharmed 142.7 *uncut*, 623.1 *healthy*, 632.5 *safe*
unharmonious 136.18 *disagreeable*, 666.9 *disagreeing*, 764.1 *unpleasant*, 820.6 *hostile*
unharmoniously 136.23 *disagreeably*, 820.14 *hostilely*
unharmoniousness 666.1 *disagreement*
unharmonized 434.9 *unmelodious*
unharness 344.4 *land*
unharvested 600.2 *new*
unhatched 595.5 *immature*
unhazardous 632.5 *safe*
unhealthily 624, 626.8 *unhygienically*
unhealthiness 618.11 *harmfulness*, 624.1 *ill health*, 626.1 *lack of hygiene*, 862.2 *affliction*
unhealthy 624, 398.23 *deadly*, 445.8 *drained of colour*, 618.5 *harmful*, 620.1 *imperfect*, 622.8 *unclean*, 626.5 *unhygienic*, 633.1 *dangerous*, 862.8 *afflicted*
unhealthy climate 626.1 *lack of hygiene*
unhealthy conditions 626.1 *lack of hygiene*
unhealthy situation 633.5 *danger*
unheard 421, 810.13 *reserved*
unheard of 201.11 *unfamiliar*, 502.8 *unknown*, 786.8 *wonderful*
unheard-of 119.5 *novel*, 421.7 *unheard*
unhearing 421, 421.4 *deaf*, 641.3 *inactive*
unheated 409.8 *cold*
unheaviness 370.5 *lightness*
unheavy 370.1 *light*
unheedful 832.15 *inconsiderate*
unheeding 421.5 *unhearing*, 468.7 *inattentive*
unhelpful 573.3 *cautious*, 614.1 *useless*, 616.1 *inconvenient*, 661.13 *hindering*, 663.22 *uncooperative*, 832.15 *inconsiderate*
unhelpfully 614.10 *uselessly*, 616.6 *inconveniently*, 661.16 *with delay*, 663.23 *opposingly*
unhelpfulness 573.12 *opposition*, 614.3 *uselessness*, 663.4 *un-*

cooperativeness, 832.6 *inconsiderateness*
unheroic 576.3 *timid*, 620.4 *ordinary*, 779.3 *cowardly*
unhesitant 574.4 *undaunted*
unhesitating 490.2 *convinced*, 497.11 *believing*
unhesitatingly 497.15 *believingly*
unhewn 307.5 *shapeless*, 595.5 *immature*
unhidden 437.1 *visible*
unhindered 322.13 *opened up*, 698.9 *free*
unhinge 153.11 *derange*, 252.18 *disconnect*, 510.15 *make insane*
unhinged 153.16 *deranged*, 252.12 *disconnected*, 510.11 *insane*, 844.14 *abnormal*
unhinging 252.5 *disconnection*
unhistorical 519.12 *imaginary*
unhitch 136.9 *separate*, 344.4 *land*
unholiness 622.2 *uncleanness*
unholy 622.8 *unclean*
unholy joy 832.3 *callousness*
unholy mess 151.4 *litter*, 659.5 *predicament*
unholy terror 777.1 *fear*, 832.8 *malefactor*
unhook 136.9 *separate*, 296.14 *undress*
unhorse 136.9 *separate*
unhostile 819.8 *friendly*
unhouse 349.8 *evict*
unhoused 252.10 *replaced*
unhurried 328, 268.15 *deliberate*, 325.6 *quiescent*, 645.7 *leisurely*, 649.4 *at ease*, 660.14 *relaxed*
unhurriedly 328.16 *slowly*, 645.7 *leisurely*
unhurriedness 328.8 *slowness*
unhurt 142.7 *uncut*, 619.1 *perfect*, 632.5 *safe*
unhygienic 626, 622.8 *unclean*, 624.23 *diseased*, 633.1 *dangerous*
unhygienically 626
unhygienic person 626
unicameral 174.12 *one-sided*, 653.18 *parliamentary*
unicell 59.7 *cell*
unicellular 59.23 *cellular*, 90.7 *algal*, 174.12 *one-sided*
unicellular organism 59.7 *cell*, 396.2 *living matter*
unicorn 76.7 *legendary beast*, 544.8 *heraldic device*
Unicorn 53 The Constellations
unicycle 71.12 *bicycle*, 174.10 *single thing*
unidentical 115.4 *dissimilar*
unidentifiable 438.1 *invisible*, 523.3 *unrecognizable*
unidentifiably 438.9 *invisibly*
unidentified 438.1 *invisible*, 502.8 *unknown*
unidiomatic 521.10 *meaningless*
unidirectional 174.12 *one-sided*, 332.15 *direct*
unification 135, 140.1 *combination*, 664.7 *association*
Unification Church 7 Christian Movements
unified 134.16 *simple*, 135.12 *united*, 140.7 *combined*, 142.6, 174.13 *whole*
unified field theory 56.79 *fundamental interaction*
uniflagellate 90.7 *algal*
uniflorous 69.16 *horticultural*
uniform 19, 112, 166, 376, 537, 544, 23.3 *basketball equipment*, 52.70 *universal*, 110.17 *regular*, 112.6, 116.14 *conforming*, 122.6 *equal*, 134.16 *simple*, 150.14 *well-ordered*, 159.11 *continuous*, 183.13 *monotonous*, 214.14 *orderly*, 285.4 *correlated*, 295.3 *formal dress*, 295.32 *dress*, 295.35 *make clothing*, 308.4 *symmetrical*, 308.5 *even*, 324.17 *directional*, 444.11 *colourful*, 667.12 *compatible*, 788.4 *boring*, 813.4, 813.4 *formal dress*

Uniform 534 Phonetic Alphabet
Uniform Code of Military Justice
17.6 *military law*
uniformed 295.29 *dressed,*
676.15 *warring,* 813.7 *dressed up*
uniformitarian 59.27 *evolutionary*
uniformitarianism 54.41 *geological time,* 59.16 *evolution*
uniformity 112, 166, 537,
110.5 *sameness,* 110.6 *regularity,* 112.2 *conformity,* 114.1 *similarity,* 116.5 *conformity,* 134.8 *simplicity,* 150.7 *method,* 159.5 *continuity,* 167.1 *conformity,* 183.3 *repetitiveness,* 214.4 *orderliness,* 285.1 *parallelism,* 308.1 *symmetry,* 308.3 *evenness,* 376.7 *smoothness,* 667.3 *compatibility,* 788.1 *boredom*
Uniformity 112
uniformlabour law policy 15.5 *labour law*
uniformly 112, 116, 52.87 *mathematically,* 110.20 *regularly,* 122.13 *equitably,* 150.27 *methodically,* 214.17 *orderly,* 308.7 *symmetrically,* 376.14 *smoothly,* 667.16 *compatibly,* 788.8 *boringly*
uniform movement 324.10 *regular movement*
uniformness 112.1 *uniformity,* 116.5 *conformity*
uniform slops 295.3 *formal dress*
uniform with 114.7 *similar*
unify 110.8 *make the same,* 134.11 *simplify,* 135.8 *unite,* 137.11 *connect,* 140.5 *combine,* 142.9 *be whole,* 174.19 *become one,* 382.15 *shape*
unigravida 245.7 *obstetrics*
unilateral 108.6 *unrelated,* 174.12 *one-sided,* 698.9 *free*
unilateral disarmament 677.1 *pacification*
unilateralism 108.1 *unrelatedness,* 174.5 *aloneness*
unilateralist 174.16 *alone*
unilaterality 698.3 *independence*
unilingual 564.19 *speaking*
unilluminated 440.8 *dark*
unimaginability 487.5 *impossibility*
unimaginable 487.1 *impossible,* 786.8 *wonderful*
unimaginably 487.11 *impossibly*
unimaginative 164.22 *commonplace,* 460.6 *unintelligent,* 493.8 *unjust,* 556.1 *simple,* 761.1 *insensitive,* 787.3, 787.3 *unmoved*
unimaginatively 460.11 *unintelligently,* 787.9 *without wonder*
unimaginativeness 460.2 *unintelligence,* 787.1 *lack of wonder*
unimagined 462.11 *unthought*
unimitated 119.4 *original,* 119.6, 537.19 *authentic*
unimolecular reaction 57.14 *chemical reaction*
unimpaired 142.7 *uncut,* 144.7 *complete*
unimpassioned 4.18 *detached,* 555.1 *unemphatic*
unimpeachable 490.3 *decided,* 843.9 *in the right,* 851.21 *praiseworthy*
unimpeded 322.13 *opened up,* 698.9 *free*
unimplied 521.12 *unmeant*
unimportance 612, 127.1 *inferiority,* 521.1 *lack of meaning,* 618.7 *worthlessness,* 783.5 *insignificance,* 806.7 *humility*
Unimportance 612
unimportant 612, 108.7 *illogical,* 127.13 *insignificant,* 260.7 *little,* 278.2 *superficial,* 521.10 *meaningless,* 618.1 *worthless,* 783.11 *insignificant,* 806.1 *humble,* 810.11 *shy*
unimportantly 612, 127.20 *insignificantly,* 260.8 *in a small way,* 783.20 *unexceptionally*
unimportant person 612.10 *nonentity*
unimposing 810.8 *modest*

unimpress 787.7 *not cause wonder*
unimpressed 766.4 *dissatisfied,* 783.7 *indifferent,* 787.3 *unmoved*
unimpressible 761.1 *insensitive*
unimpressionable 761.1 *insensitive,* 787.3 *unmoved*
unimpressive 542.16 *imperceptible,* 620.1 *imperfect,* 656.1 *unskilful,* 787.4 *predictable,* 810.8 *modest*
unimpressively 542.27 *imperceptibly,* 787.10 *predictably*
unimpressiveness 542.7 *imperceptibility,* 787.2 *predictability*
unimproved 628.12 *deteriorated*
uninfectious 625.4 *hygienic*
uninflated 556.1 *simple*
uninfluenceable 698.9 *free*
uninfluenced 577.3 *unyielding,* 698.9 *free,* 698.10 *independent*
uninfluential 240.6 *suspended,* 612.1 *unimportant*
uninformative 531.17 *noncommittal,* 566.3 *sparing with words*
uninformed 502.6 *ignorant,* 656.1 *unskilful*
uninfringeable 103.5 *essential*
uninhabited 254.14 *unoccupied,* 816.11 *secluded*
uninhibited 658.1 *naive,* 698.12 *unconditional,* 698.13 *informal*
uninhibitedness 698.6 *liberality*
uninitiated 502.6 *ignorant,* 656.2 *unskilled,* 658.1 *naive*
uninjured 142.7 *uncut,* 632.5 *safe*
uninquisitive 466.3 *incurious,* 783.7 *indifferent*
uninquisitively 466.7 *incuriously*
uninspire 787.7 *not cause wonder*
uninspired 164.22 *commonplace,* 412.5 *tasteless,* 555.1 *unemphatic,* 556.1 *simple,* 787.3 *unmoved*
uninspiring 555.1 *unemphatic*
uninspiringly 555.3 *unemphatically*
uninstructed 502.6 *ignorant,* 585.1 *unaccustomed,* 595.4 *untrained,* 656.1 *unskilful,* 656.2 *unskilled*
unintelligence 460, 462.2, 502.1 *ignorance,* 508.1 *folly,* 656.8 *unskilfulness*
unintelligent 443, 460, 441.8 *stupid,* 508.5 *foolish*
unintelligently 460, 508.8 *foolishly*
unintelligent person 460
unintelligibility 523, 151.1 *disorder,* 443.8 *obscurity,* 521.1 *lack of meaning,* 527.11 *mysteriousness,* 551.1 *obscurity,* 659.1 *difficulty*
Unintelligibility 523
unintelligible 523, 443.4 *inscrutable,* 521.10 *meaningless,* 527.2 *concealed,* 529.11 *mysterious,* 531.15 *disguised,* 551.2 *obscure,* 563.12 *inarticulate,* 659.12 *problematic*
unintelligible speech 563.3 *speech defect*
unintelligible thing 523
unintelligibly 523, 443.13 *opaquely,* 521.13 *meaninglessly,* 551.4 *obscurely,* 659.27 *problematically*
unintended 229.6 *motiveless,* 521.12 *unmeant,* 589.9 *causeless*
unintentional 229.6 *motiveless,* 521.12 *unmeant,* 589.9 *causeless*
unintentionally 229.8, 589.13 *by chance*
uninterested 466, 643.3 *not participating,* 783.7 *indifferent,* 787.3 *unmoved*
uninteresting 788.4 *boring*
uninterestingly 788.8 *boringly*
uninterrupted 159.11 *continuous,* 219.5 *continual,* 312.3 *continuous,* 332.15 *direct*

uninterrupted course 219.1 *continuity*
uninterruption 159.5 *continuity*
unintoxicated 873.1 *sober*
unintoxicated state 873.6 *sobriety*
uninucleate 59.24 *nuclear*
uninvented 527.3 *unsolved*
uninventive 460.6 *unintelligent*
uninventively 460.11 *unintelligently*
uninventiveness 460.2 *unintelligence*
uninvited 816.10 *lonely*
uninvited guest 104.8 *intruder,* 108.3 *unconnected person,* 149.10 *intruder,* 255.6 *illegal occupant*
uninviting 412.5 *tasteless,* 415.6 *unpalatable,* 764.1 *unpleasant*
uninvolved 108.6 *unrelated,* 136.17 *unjoined,* 466.4 *uninterested,* 522.2 *simple,* 550.3 *clear,* 556.1 *simple,* 660.9 *easy,* 783.7 *indifferent,* 859.4 *disinterested*
uninvolvement 466.2 *lack of interest,* 522.10 *simplicity*
union 15, 15.10 *unionized,* 52.21 *set,* 116.2 *alliance,* 133.1 *mixture,* 137.1 *connection,* 140.2 *cooperation,* 161.15 *association,* 174.3 *oneness,* 180.1 *accompaniment,* 267.1 *juxtaposition,* 342.4 *meeting place,* 664.7 *association,* 665.1 *party,* 665.3 *political grouping,* 715.1 *contract,* 724.1 *joint possession,* 823.1 *marriage,* 823.2 *alliance*
Union 135
union branch 15.3 *organized labour*
union demands 15.3 *organized labour*
union dues 15.3 *organized labour*
Union flag 544.7 *flag*
Union Internationale des Associations d'Alpinisme 34.6 *mountaineering association*
unionism 15.1 *industrial relations*
Unionist Parties 12.6 *political party*
unionize 665.12 *be in league with,* 665.15 *politicize*
unionized 15
Union Jack 544.7 *flag*
union labour 15.1 *industrial relations*
union-management relations 15.1 *industrial relations*
union member 15.7 *employee,* 724.3 *participant*
union of nations 91, 249.4 *territorial division*
union recognition 15.2 *industrial negotiations*
union shop 15.3 *organized labour*
union strike 15.4 *industrial dispute*
union subscriptions 15.3 *organized labour*
union suit 295.18 *underwear*
uniped 174.10 *single thing*
uniplanar 174.12 *one-sided*
unipolar 174.12 *one-sided*
unique 52.70 *universal,* 103.8 *quintessential,* 113.5 *diverse,* 115.4 *dissimilar,* 117.9 *nonconforming,* 119.5 *novel,* 123.3 *unequal,* 126.14 *best,* 147.10 *excluding,* 165.15 *special,* 165.17 *exceptional,* 168.14 *eccentric,* 174.14 *singular,* 213.2 *infrequent,* 215.5 *unusual,* 537.19 *authentic,* 617.3 *valuable*
uniquely 113.10 *diversely,* 117.15 *dissimilarly,* 119.8 *originally,* 123.7 *unequally,* 126.17 *supremely,* 165.30 *characteristically,* 174.21 *alone,* 213.1 *infrequently,* 489.10 *rarely,* 537.37 *authentically*
uniqueness 113.1 *diversity,* 117.3 *nonconformity,* 119.1 *originality,* 165.1 *speciality,* 168.4 *unusualness,* 174.4 *singularity,* 213.3 *infrequency,* 537.6 *authenticity,* 544.2 *identity*
unirrigated 392.1 *dry*

unisex 174.12 *one-sided,* 295.31 *styled*
unisex clothes 295.1 *dress*
unisexual 174.12 *one-sided,* 245.16 *reproductive*
unison 49.13 *melody,* 112.3 *agreement,* 116.4 *harmony,* 135.2 *agreement,* 433.3 *melodiousness,* 667.1 *agreement*
unisonous 116.13 *harmonious*
unit 75, 142, 148, 142.2 *whole thing,* 148.2 *piece,* 161.14 *force,* 161.16 *party,* 174.1 *one,* 258.3 *cabinet,* 400.7 *person,* 679.16 *army unit*
Unitarian 7.5 *Christian*
Unitarianism 7 Christian Movements
unite 135, 110.8 *make the same,* 112.11 *agree,* 116.22 *form an alliance,* 135.9 *agree,* 137.11 *connect,* 138.7 *cause to adhere,* 140.5 *combine,* 142.9 *be whole,* 144.4 *complete,* 161.41 *band together,* 161.44 *put together,* 174.19 *become one,* 342.10 *come together,* 664.5 *join,* 667.6 *agree with,* 823.16 *join in marriage,* 823.19 *merge*
unite closely 135.8 *unite*
united 135, 110.12 *same,* 112.7 *agreeing,* 116.10 *in accord,* 135.13 *agreeable,* 137.15 *connected,* 140.7 *combined,* 144.7 *complete,* 161.48 *cumulate,* 174.13 *whole,* 664.18 *joint,* 667.10 *agreeing,* 715.7 *contractual,* 724.5 *jointly possessing,* 823.21 *married*
united action 664.4 *joint operation*
United Arab Emirates 91 Countries
united front 664.4 *joint operation*
United Kingdom 91 Countries, 91.8 *Great Britain*
unitedly 116.31 *in accord,* 138.11 *cohesively,* 161.51, 180.21 *together,* 724.6 *in common*
United Nations 400.9 *group,* 653.7 *council,* 675.2 *symbol of peace,* 724.1 *joint possession*
United Nations Organization 724.1 *joint possession*
United Nations peacekeeping force 675.3 *pacifist*
United Nations secretary-general 653.16 *official*
United Press International 528.8 *source of information,* 533.7 *press agency*
United States 91
United States Automobile Club 33.7 *racing governing body*
United States Curling Association 41.10 *curling*
United States GP at Phoenix 33.2 *Formula 1 race*
United States Intercollegiate Lacrosse Association 31.5 *lacrosse*
United States Military Academy 17.3 *military training*
United States Naval Academy 17.3 *military training*
United States of America 91 Countries, 91.7 *United States*
United States Professional Golfers Association 29.1 *golf*
United States Women's Lacrosse Association 31.5 *lacrosse*
United Way 712.3 *solicitation,* 729.3 *offering,* 833.5 *charity*
unite efforts 664.13 *work together*
unite in holy wedlock 823.16 *join in marriage*
unite to 130.6 *add*
unite with 135.8 *unite*
unit furniture 47.1 *furniture*
uniting 140.1 *combination,* 342.7 *convergent*
unit of being 367.4 *matter*
unit of electrical power 235.5 *unit of work*
unit of measurement 75.1 *unit*
unit of work 235

Unit One 50 Schools and Groups of Artists
unit pole 75 Scientific and Technical Units
Units 75
units place 52.8 *number system*
unit system 75
unit vector 52.50 *scalar quantity*
unity 110.1 *sameness*, 112.3 *agreement*, 116.1 *accord*, 135.1 *union*, 135.2 *agreement*, 138.1 *adhesion*, 140.2 *cooperation*, 142.1 *whole*, 144.1 *completeness*, 174.1 *one*, 174.3 *oneness*, 382.9 *artistic structure*, 667.1 *agreement*, 684.1 *completion*
UNIVAC 65.3 *computer*
univalent 57.35 *combined*
univalent chromosome 59.14 *chromosome*
univalve 81.19 *molluscan*
universal 52, 164, 36.13 *windsurfing*, 53.36 *astronomical*, 124.1 *average*, 142.6 *whole*, 146.7 *including*, 164.15 *general*, 248.12 *extensive*, 482.4 *wholesale*, 584.10 *familiar*
universal benevolence 833.2 *public spiritedness*
universal constant 56.97 *fundamental constant*
universal indicator 57.18 *gravimetric analysis*
universalism 91.5 *internationalism*
universalist 91.15 *internationalist*
universality 91.5 *internationalism*, 124.4 *average*, 142.1 *whole*, 144.1 *completeness*, 146.1 *inclusion*, 164.1 *generality*, 482.8 *indiscriminateness*
universalize 164.23 *generalize*, 482.11 *not discriminate*
universal joint 36.7 *windsurfing*
universally 164, 53.39 *astronomically*, 142.11 *wholly*, 146.9 *inclusively*, 248.16 *extensively*, 293.42 *inclusively*, 482.14 *indiscriminately*
universal motor 64.31 *electric motor*
universal peace 675.1 *peace*
universal quantifier 52.63 *mathematical logic*
universal set 52.21 *set*
universal solvent 387.9 *solvent*
universal suffrage 580.11 *franchise*
universal symbol 61.24 *symbolism*
Universal Time 192.3 *chronology*
universe 53, 101.2 *real world*, 142.2 *whole thing*
university 6
university hospital 60.10 *hospital*
university president 696.9 *educational leader*
university press 532.12 *publisher*
univocal 520.3 *comprehension*, 520.6 *meaningful*, 522.1 *intelligible*
UNIX 65.8 *software*
unjam 660.16 *make easy*
unjoined 136, 160.8 *discontinuous*
unjust 16, 123, 493, 548.6 *misrepresented*, 618.3 *bad*, 844.11 *wrong*, 858.5 *dishonourable*
unjustifiable 844.17 *unforgivable*, 866.5 *guilty*
unjustifiably 866.11 *guiltily*
unjustified 846.10 *undue*
unjustly 123, 493, 548.8 *unrepresentatively*, 844.25 *wrongly*
unkempt 151.15 *untidy*, 375.3 *barbed*, 622.7 *dirty*, 628.13 *dilapidated*
unkemptness 151.3 *untidiness*
unkennel 349.8 *evict*, 530.5 *disclose*
unkind 462.10 *inconsiderate*, 758.2 *unpleasant*, 764.2 *objectionable*, 818.5 *discourteous*, 832.15 *inconsiderate*, 862.7 *evil*
unkindest cut of all 850.5 *insult*
unkindliness 832.6 *inconsiderateness*

unkindly 818.9 *discourteously*, 820.14 *hostilely*, 832.15 *inconsiderate*, 832.20 *malevolently*, 862.12 *evilly*
unkindness 161 Collective Names for Birds and Animals, 462.4 *inconsideration*, 618.11 *harmfulness*, 764.6 *objectionability*, 832.6 *inconsiderateness*, 862.1 *evil*
unknot 700.4 *liberate*
unknotting 700.1 *liberation*
unknowable 443.4 *inscrutable*, 502.8 *unknown*, 523.1 *unintelligible*, 523.3 *unrecognizable*, 529.11 *mysterious*
unknowing 502.6 *ignorant*
unknowingly 502.12 *ignorantly*, 865.11 *innocently*
unknown 502, 52.25 *algebraic expression*, 104.10, 149.11 *foreign*, 172.5 *nonentity*, 201.11 *unfamiliar*, 491.1 *uncertain*, 523.1 *unintelligible*, 527.3 *unsolved*, 529.11 *mysterious*, 612.10 *nonentity*, 633.1 *dangerous*, 816.11 *secluded*
unknown country 529.8 *anonymity*
unknown disease 624.4 *disease*
unknown man 527.6 *latency*
unknownness 201.1 *newness*
unknown person 502, 529.8 *anonymity*
unknown quantity 52.25 *algebraic expression*, 529.3 *unknown thing*, 529.8 *anonymity*
unknown territory 502.3 *unknown thing*
unknown thing 502
unknown to law 16.56 *unauthorized*
Unknown Warrior 529.8 *anonymity*
unlaboured 558.3 *elegant*
unlace 136.9 *separate*, 294.11 *uncover*, 296.14 *undress*
unlade 349.12 *unload*, 370.10 *lighten*
unlading 370.6 *lightening*
unladylike 795.7 *vulgar*, 818.5 *discourteous*
unlamented 822.12 *hated*
unlatch 136.9 *separate*, 322.19 *open up*
unlatched 322.13 *opened up*
unlavish 756.4 *thrifty*
unlawful 877, 16.55 *illegal*, 709.5 *vetoed*, 720.14 *violating*, 844.16 *in the wrong*, 846.8 *unentitled*, 864.15 *criminal*
unlawful act 864.7 *criminality*
unlawful carnal knowledge 877.4 *illicit love*
unlawful desires 877.4 *illicit love*
unlawful entry 736.1 *stealing*
unlawful killing 398.2 *murder*
unlawfully 16.82 *illegally*, 16.89 *guiltily*, 709.7 *by veto*, 720.16 *disobediently*, 844.28 *immorally*, 846.19 *unrightfully*, 864.21 *criminally*
unlawfulness 844, 16.35 *illegality*, 493.3 *injustice*, 720.4 *infraction*
unleaded 410.10 *powered*
unleaded petrol 395.9 *petroleum*, 410.6 *oil*
unlearn 512.13 *forget*
unlearned 658.1 *naive*
unleash 530.5 *disclose*, 700.4 *liberate*
unleashing 700.1 *liberation*
unleash the war dogs 676.12 *go to war*
unlegislated 16.56 *unauthorized*
unless 106.15 *under the circumstances*
unlettered 502.6 *ignorant*
unlicensed 16.56 *unauthorized*, 846.8 *unentitled*
unlicked 307.5 *shapeless*, 595.5 *immature*
unlighted 440.8 *dark*
unlikable 618.3 *bad*, 785.9 *disliked*

unlike 115.4 *dissimilar*, 123.3 *unequal*, 548.6 *misrepresented*
unlike a gentleman 818.9 *discourteously*
unlikelihood 477.7 *questionableness*, 489.4 *improbability*, 491.13 *indemonstrability*
unlikeliness 489.4 *improbability*, 491.13 *indemonstrability*
unlikely 117.7 *disparate*, 477.14 *questionable*, 489.1 *improbable*, 491.4 *indemonstrable*
unlikeness 115, 117.1 *disparity*, 123.1 *inequality*
unlimited 33.11 *racing*, 144.7 *complete*, 184.1 *infinite*, 698.12 *unconditional*
unlimited class 33.5 *motorcycle racing*
unlimited space 248.2 *empty space*
unlisted securities market 740.5 *stock market*
unlit 440.8 *dark*, 633.1 *dangerous*
unlived-in 254.14 *unoccupied*
unload 349, 70.4 *transport*, 131.3 *subtract*, 326.15 *take away*, 344.4 *land*, 370.10 *lighten*, 660.18 *disentangle*, 739.1 *sell*, 754.13 *make cheap*
unloaded 70.5 *transportable*, 370.3 *lightening*
unloader 70.3 *transporter*
unloading 70.1 *transport*, 70.5 *transportable*, 349.20 *eviction*, 356.2 *passing along*, 370.3, 370.6 *lightening*
unload on the market 739.1 *sell*
unlock 136.9 *separate*, 322.19 *open up*, 639.1 *deliver*, 700.4 *liberate*, 727.9 *dispose of*
unlock a code 524.9 *decipher*
unlocked 322.13 *opened up*, 524.15 *interpreted*
unlooked-for 846.10 *undue*
unloose 639.1 *deliver*, 700.4 *liberate*
unloosen 700.4 *liberate*
unloose the purse strings 746.6 *pay*
unloosing 700.1 *liberation*
unlovable 785.9 *disliked*, 822.12 *hated*
unloved 785.9 *disliked*, 822.12 *hated*
unlovely 790.4 *ugly*
unloyal 720.13 *noncompliant*
unluckily 211.17 *mistakenly*, 229.9 *luckily*, 589.13 *by chance*, 683.12 *unsuccessfully*, 687.12 *in adversity*, 862.14 *inauspiciously*
unlucky 687, 211.14 *accidental*, 229.7 *adventurous*, 589.8 *chance*, 683.10 *failed*, 862.10 *inauspicious*
unlucky choice 580.8 *choice*
unlucky person 481.8 *victim of discrimination*, 687.5 *person in adversity*
unmake 136.9 *separate*, 221.7 *restore*, 244.8 *destroy*, 307.3 *make shapeless*
unmaking 244.1 *destruction*
unmalleability 373.8 *mental hardness*
unmalleable 373.4 *mentally hard*, 669.11 *obstinate*
unman 131.4 *take off*, 236.9 *make impotent*, 247.8 *make infertile*, 614.8 *make useless*, 628.5 *hurt*
unmanageable 151.20 *disorderly*, 577.2 *refractory*, 656.3 *clumsy*, 659.14 *troublesome*, 693.13 *disobedient*
unmanageably 659.28 *awkwardly*
unmanifested 527.2 *concealed*
unmanly 401.17 *male*
unmanned 236.13 *unsexed*, 254.14 *unoccupied*
unmanned crossing 72.2 *track*
unmanned satellite 53.32 *satellite*
unmannered 850.10 *disrespectful*
unmanneriliness 818.2 *bad manners*, 850.1 *disrespect*

unmannerly 816.8 *unsociable*, 818.6 *bad-mannered*
unmarked 438.1 *invisible*, 619.1 *perfect*
unmarked car 71.17 *police car*
unmarketable 754.10 *shoddy*
unmarred 619.1 *perfect*
unmarried 174.17 *single*, 698.10 *independent*, 816.10 *lonely*, 825.6 *celibate*
unmarried condition 825.1 *celibacy*
unmarried man 174.7 *single person*, 401.5 *single man*, 825.5 *single person*
unmarried state 698.3 *independence*
unmarried mother 402.5 *single girl*, 402.5 *single girl*
unmarry 824.7 *divorce*
unmask 435.18, 437.10 *make visible*, 496.2 *detect*, 526.3 *reveal*, 530.5 *disclose*
unmasked 496.14 *discovered*, 530.10 *disclosed*
unmasking 496.7 *detection*
unmask oneself 526.4 *show oneself*
unmatchable 126.14 *best*
unmatchably 126.17 *supremely*
unmatched 119.5 *novel*, 126.14, 617.2 *best*, 619.1 *perfect*
unmated 825.6 *celibate*
unmeaning 521.10 *meaningless*
unmeant 521, 229.6 *motiveless*, 589.9 *causeless*
unmeasured 608.2 *plentiful*
unmediated 464.7 *precognitive*
unmedicated 134.13 *pure*
unmeditated 583.1 *improvised*
unmellowed 595.5 *immature*
unmelodious 434, 430.7 *strident*
unmelodiously 434.12 *dissonantly*
unmelodiousness 434.3 *musical dissonance*
unmelted 371.7 *condensed*, 409.9 *heat-resistant*
unmemorable 512.11 *forgotten*
unmentionable 709.6 *censored*, 795.9 *ribald*, 877.12 *indecent*
unmentionables 295.18 *underwear*
unmentioned 490.8 *unspecified*, 527.4 *unsaid*
unmercifully 836.7 *pitilessly*
unmercifulness 836.1 *pitilessness*
unmerited 846.10 *undue*
unmeriting 846.11 *undeserving*
unmeritorious 846.11 *undeserving*
unmethodical 151.16 *confused*
unmethodically 151.21 *in disorder*, 215.4 *irregular*, 215.8 *irregularly*
unmethodicalness 215.1 *irregularity*
unmeticulous 482.1 *undiscriminating*
unmilitant 675.7 *peaceful*
unmilitary 675.7 *peaceful*
unmindful 404.6 *unfeeling*, 436.12 *blind to*, 468.7 *inattentive*, 470.4 *negligent*, 512.10 *unthinking*, 720.11 *nonobservant*, 832.15 *inconsiderate*, 838.3 *ungrateful*
unmindfully 468.14, 720.15 *inattentively*
unmindfulness 468.1 *inattention*, 470.1 *negligence*, 512.4 *unthinkingness*, 720.1 *nonobservance*, 832.6 *inconsiderateness*
unmingled 134.16 *simple*
unmissable 437.2 *clear*
unmissed 822.12 *hated*
unmistakable 31.10 *potent*, 437.1 *visible*, 490.1 *certain* 522.3 *recognizable*, 526.14 *manifest*
unmistakably 437.15 *acutely*, 522.13 *intelligibly*
unmistaken 490.1 *certain*, 537.15 *true*, 537.25 *lifelike*
unmistakenness 537.1 *truth*
unmitigated 134.17 *direct*, 144.7 *complete*, 241.6 *violent*

unmitigating 144.7 *complete*

unmixed 134.16 *simple,* 136.17 *unjoined,* 556.1 *simple,* 617.1 *worthy,* 619.1 *perfect,* 621.16 *clean,* 874.6 *intoxicating*

unmodern 197.2 *occurring at a different time*

unmoistened 392.1 *dry*

unmolested 632.5 *safe*

unmoor 74.9 *navigate,* 345.5 *set out*

unmotivated 229.6 *motiveless,* 583.2 *spontaneous,* 589.9 *causeless*

unmount 614.8 *make useless*

unmourned 822.12 *hated*

unmovable 325.4 *motionless*

unmoved 787, 325.4 *motionless,* 325.6 *quiescent,* 466.4 *uninterested,* 577.3 *unyielding,* 783.7, 783.7 *indifferent,* 836.4 *pitiless,* 868.3 *impenitent*

unmoving 240.5 *inert,* 325.4 *motionless*

unmuddied 134.13 *pure,* 621.16 *clean*

unmusical 421.4 *deaf,* 430.7 *strident,* 434.9 *unmelodious,* 658.1 *naive*

unmusicality 563.2 *inarticulation*

unmusicalness 421.1 *deafness*

unmuzzled 698.9 *free*

unnamed 490.8 *unspecified,* 502.8 *unknown*

unnatural 117.8 *contradictory,* 168.17 *abnormal,* 538.18 *pretentious,* 539.39 *imitative,* 559.9 *inelegant,* 797.3 *affected,* 832.12 *callous*

unnaturally 117.15 *dissimilarly,* 168.21 *unconformably,* 538.27 *pretentiously,* 540.37 *spuriously*

unnaturalness 168.6 *deviation,* 538.8 *pretence,* 832.3 *callousness*

unnavigable 278.1 *shallow,* 659.11 *rough*

unnecessarily 607.10 *wastefully,* 610.8 *excessively,* 612.14 *unimportantly,* 846.18 *unduly*

unnecessary 585.2 *not customary,* 600.3 *not wanted,* 607.8 *wasteful,* 610.7 *superfluous,* 612.1 *unimportant,* 614.1 *useless,* 846.10 *undue*

unnecessary expenditure 607.3 *waste*

unnecessary roughness 31.5 *lacrosse*

unneeded 600.3 *not wanted,* 614.1 *useless*

unneighbourly 816.8 *unsociable,* 818.5 *discourteous*

unnerve 236.9 *make impotent,* 238.7 *weaken,* 587.2 *deter,* 777.13 *frighten*

unnerved 236.12 *impotent,* 238.12 *weak-willed*

unnerving 777.10 *frightening*

unnoteworthy 124.3 *mediocre*

unnoticeable 438.1 *invisible*

unnoticeably 438.9 *invisibly,* 542.23 *unobtrusively*

unnoticed 438.1 *invisible*

unnumbered 101.8 *numberless,* 184.2 *immeasurable*

unnutritious 626.5 *unhygienic*

unobjectionable 116.20 *agreeable,* 617.5 *not bad*

unobliging 832.15 *inconsiderate*

unoblingingness 832.6 *inconsiderateness*

unobservant 436.12 *blind to,* 468.7 *inattentive,* 720.11 *nonobservant*

unobserved 438.1 *invisible*

unobstructed 322.13 *opened up,* 442.1 *transparent*

unobstructed view 442.5 *transparency*

unobtainability 487.6 *hopelessness*

unobtainable 487.3 *hopeless,* 609.4 *scarce*

unobtrusive 542.12 *understated,* 810.8 *modest*

unobtrusively 542, 810.17 *modestly*

unobtrusiveness 542.1 *understatement,* 810.1 *modesty*

unoccupied 254, 641.3 *inactive,* 643.2 *not working,* 645.6 *leisure,* 645.7 *leisurely*

unofficial 15.10 *unionized,* 16.56 *unauthorized,* 491.5 *uncertified,* 689.6 *anarchic,* 814.1 *informality,* 814.7 *informal*

unofficial action 15.4 *industrial dispute*

unofficially 15.13 *industrially,* 689.8 *anarchically,* 814.15 *unaffectedly*

unofficial strike 15.4 *industrial dispute*

unoiled 430.8 *hoarse*

unopened 323.12 *closed,* 600.2 *new*

unopposed 116.20 *agreeable,* 667.10 *agreeing*

unordered 151, 133.12 *mixed*

unordered arrangement 52.21 *set*

unorganized 151.13 *unordered,* 482.3 *indiscriminate,* 595.1 *unprepared*

unoriginal 118.12 *imitative,* 227.10 *caused,* 460.6 *unintelligent,* 539.39 *imitative,* 584.10 *familiar*

unoriginality 460.2 *unintelligence*

unoriginally 118.14 *imitatively,* 227.12 *with the effect of*

unornamented 556.2 *unadorned*

unorthodox 117.9 *nonconforming,* 168.12 *nonconformist,* 215.5 *unusual,* 500.7 *dissenting,* 504.16 *errant*

unorthodox medicine 60.2 *natural medicine*

unorthodoxy 117.3 *nonconformity,* 168.3 *nonconformism,* 215.2 *unusualness,* 500.3 *dissentience,* 504.7 *errancy*

unostentatious 542.14 *simple,* 810.1 *modesty,* 810.8 *modest*

unostentatiously 542.24 *simply*

unostentatiousness 542.4 *simplicity*

unowned 727.15 *unclaimed*

unpacific 676.16 *warlike*

unpack 349.12 *unload,* 530.5 *disclose*

unpaid 747, 710.18 *voluntary,* 745.9 *in debt,* 754.11 *free of charge,* 845.12 *owed*

unpaid amount 745.5 *amount owing*

unpaid bill 744.1 *credit*

unpaid work 572.10 *voluntary work*

unpaid worker 572.11 *willing worker,* 710.8 *volunteer*

unpainted 556.2 *unadorned*

unpalatability 415, 411.1 *taste,* 764.5 *unpleasantness*

unpalatable 415, 764, 411.7 *tasty,* 764.1 *unpleasant*

unparalleled 119.5 *novel,* 126.14, 617.2 *best*

unpardonable 844.17 *unforgivable,* 864.11 *wicked,* 866.5 *guilty*

unpardonably 864.18 *wickedly,* 866.11 *guiltily*

unparliamentary language 827.2 *offensive language*

unpartnered 825.6 *celibate*

unpasteurized milk 595.11 *natural state*

unpaved road 215.3 *irregular thing*

unpayable 747.14 *unpaid*

unpayable debt 747.5 *insolvency*

unpeaceful 366.16 *restless*

unpeacefully 366.27 *agitatedly*

unpeel 139.5 *unstick*

unpeople 349.9 *depopulate*

unpeopled 254.14 *unoccupied*

unperceivable 438.1 *invisible*

unperceived 438.1 *invisible,* 502.8 *unknown*

unperceptive 381.3 *dull,* 460.6 *unintelligent*

unperceptiveness 460.2 *unintelligence*

unperformed 685.4 *uncompleted*

unperfumed 417.3 *odourless*

unpermissibility 709.1 *veto*

unpersevering 576.2 *changeable*

unperson 102.5 *insubstantial person,* 172.5 *nonentity*

unpersuadable 577.2 *refractory*

unperturbed 4.18 *detached,* 325.6 *quiescent*

unperturbedly 325.10 *motionlessly*

unphilanthropic 832.15 *inconsiderate*

unphysical 11.18 *spiritual,* 368.8 *nonmaterial*

unpick 136.9 *separate*

unpigmented 445.7 *colourless*

unpin 139.5 *unstick*

unpitiful 836.4 *pitiless*

unpitying 836.4 *pitiless*

unplanned 229.6 *motiveless,* 589.9 *causeless,* 595.3 *without preparation,* 656.4 *bungled*

unpleasant 758, 764, 411.7 *tasty,* 415.6 *unpalatable,* 618.3 *bad,* 666.9 *disagreeing,* 818.5 *discourteous*

unpleasant job 644.2 *task*

unpleasantly 764, 415.10 *sourly,* 618.15 *worthlessly,* 666.11 *in disagreement,* 818.9 *discourteously*

unpleasantness 758, 764, 500.3 *dissentience,* 618.9 *badness,* 666.1 *disagreement,* 818.1 *discourtesy*

Unpleasantness 764

unpleasant person 764

unpleasant smell 416.1 *odour,* 419.1 *stench*

unpleasant taste 411.1 *taste*

unpleasing 764.1 *unpleasant*

unpliability 373.8 *mental hardness*

unpliable 373.4 *mentally hard*

unpliant 373.4 *mentally hard*

unplucked 600.2 *new*

unplug 136.9 *separate*

unplugged 136.15 *separate*

unplumbed 277.8 *deep*

unpoetical 556.1 *simple,* 658.1 *naive*

unpointed 381.1 *blunt*

unpolished 375.5 *unfinished,* 441.7 *dimmed,* 559.8 *indecorous,* 595.5 *immature,* 620.2 *incomplete,* 622.7 *dirty,* 656.4 *bungled,* 658.1 *naive,* 795.8 *discourteous*

unpoliteness 818.1 *discourtesy*

unpolluted 134.13 *pure,* 621.16 *clean,* 632.5 *safe*

unpopular 766.5 *unsatisfactory,* 785.9 *disliked,* 816.10 *lonely,* 822.12 *hated*

unpopular cause 581.8 *rejected thing*

unpopularity 822.4 *hatefulness,* 852.1 *disapproval*

unpossessed 727.15 *unclaimed*

unpowered 236.10 *powerless*

unpractical 614.1 *useless,* 656.1 *unskilful*

unpractised 585.2 *not customary,* 595.4 *untrained,* 656.3 *clumsy*

unpraiseworthy 852.32 *unsatisfactory*

unprecedented 115.4 *dissimilar,* 119.5 *novel,* 201.11 *unfamiliar,* 213.2 *infrequent,* 514.8 *surprising,* 585.2 *not customary,* 786.8 *wonderful*

unpredictability 56.81 *causality,* 113.1 *diversity,* 215.1 *irregularity,* 224.1 *changeableness,* 229.1 *lack of motive,* 489.5 *unexpectedness,* 491.15 *unreliability,* 514.1 *surprise,* 579.2 *caprice,* 589.1 *chance*

unpredictable 113.5 *diverse,* 215.4 *irregular,* 224.13 *changeable,* 229.6 *motiveless,* 489.3 *unexpected,* 491.4 *indemonstrable,* 491.7 *unreliable,* 514.8 *surpris-*

ing, 579.1 *capricious,* 589.8 *chance*

unpredictably 113.10 *diversely,* 215.8 *irregularly,* 224.15 *changeably,* 229.8 *by chance,* 489.9 *unexpectedly,* 491.26 *unreliably,* 589.13 *by chance*

unpredicted 489.3 *unexpected*

unprejudiced 4.15 *rational,* 271.3 *broad-minded,* 482.2 *impartial,* 507.5 *wise,* 698.9 *free,* 783.9 *impartial,* 843.7 *right,* 859.4 *disinterested*

unpremeditated 583.1 *improvised,* 589.9 *causeless,* 595.3 *without preparation*

unpremeditatedly 595.14 *unreadily*

unpremeditation 583.4 *improvisation,* 595.8 *lack of preparation*

unprepared 595, 145.4 *incomplete,* 206.12 *immature,* 209.9 *late,* 514.6 *surprised,* 583.1 *improvised,* 595.6 *uncooked,* 633.3 *vulnerable,* 648.3 *hasty,* 656.2 *unskilled,* 656.4 *bungled*

unpreparedly 206.15 *immaturely,* 209.15 *late,* 595.14 *unreadily*

unpreparedness 145.1 *incompleteness,* 206.3 *immaturity,* 209.1 *lateness,* 514.1 *surprise,* 595.8 *lack of preparation*

unprepossessing 785.9 *disliked,* 790.4 *ugly*

unpretending 537.18 *truthful,* 658.1 *naive,* 810.8 *modest*

unpretentious 134.17 *direct,* 537.18 *truthful,* 542.14, 556.1 *simple,* 556.3 *natural,* 658.1 *naive,* 806.1 *humble,* 810.8 *modest*

unpretentiously 134.20 *homogeneously,* 542.24, 556.8 *simply,* 810.17 *modestly*

unpretentiousness 542.4, 556.4 *simplicity,* 556.6 *naturalness,* 658.2 *naivety,* 806.7 *humility,* 810.1 *modesty*

unpreventability 490.16 *inevitability*

unpreventable 490.5 *inevitable*

unprincipled 844.15 *immoral,* 858.5 *dishonourable,* 864.11 *wicked,* 877.11 *immoral*

unprintable 709.6 *censored,* 795.9 *ribald,* 877.12 *indecent*

unprocessed 595.4 *untrained,* 685.4 *uncompleted*

unproclaimed 527.4 *unsaid*

unprocurable 609.4 *scarce*

unproductive 247.3 *birth control,* 614.2 *futile,* 683.10 *failed*

unproductively 247, 683.12 *unsuccessfully*

unproductiveness 247.1 *infertility,* 609.9 *scarcity,* 614.4 *futility,* 683.1 *failure,* 722.3 *waste*

unproductivity 247.1 *infertility*

unprofessed 527.4 *unsaid*

unprofessional 616.1 *inconvenient,* 656.1 *unskilful,* 720.11 *nonobservant*

unprofessional conduct 866.3 *sin*

unprofessionally 656.11 *unskilfully*

unprofitability 247.1 *infertility,* 614.4 *futility*

unprofitable 722, 737, 247.3 *birth control,* 614.2 *futile,* 616.1 *inconvenient,* 838.5 *thankless*

unprofitableness 247.1 *infertility*

unprofitably 247.11 *unproductively,* 614.10 *uselessly,* 739.17 *marketably,* 838.7 *ungratefully*

unprogressive 217.8 *conservative,* 628.12 *deteriorated,* 641.3 *inactive,* 658.1 *naive*

unprogressively 217.10 *conservatively*

unprohibitive 708.8 *permitting*

unprolific 247.3 *birth control*

unpromising 489.1 *improbable,* 656.1 *unskilful*

unpromoted 527.4 *unsaid*

unprompted 572.5 *voluntary,*

583.2 *spontaneous*, 710.18 *voluntary*
unpronounceable 523.1 *unintelligible*
unpronounced 527.4 *unsaid*
unpropitious 211.10 *untimely*, 663.19 *oppositional*, 687.6 *adverse*, 776.6 *inauspicious*
unpropitiously 211.15 *at the wrong time*, 687.12 *in adversity*
unpropitiousness 211.1 *untimeliness*
unprosperous 687
unprotected 236, 238.8 *weak*, 322.13 *opened up*, 633.3 *vulnerable*
unprovability 491.13 *indemonstrability*
unprovable 491.4 *indemonstrable*
unproved 491.5 *uncertified*
unprovided 609
unprovided for 609.2 *unprovided*, 743.1 *poor*
unprovoked 583.2 *spontaneous*
unpublished 527.4 *unsaid*
unpunctual 193.6 *too late*, 209.9 *late*, 211.10 *untimely*
unpunctuality 209.1 *lateness*, 211.1 *untimeliness*
unpunctually 193.7 *out of chronological order*, 209.15 *late*, 211.15 *at the wrong time*
unpunishable 848.5 *exempt*
unpunished 16.63 *acquitted*
unpurified 622.8 *unclean*
unqualified 117.11 *unfit*, 134.17 *direct*, 144.7 *complete*, 236.10 *powerless*, 502.7 *semi-skilled*, 537.19 *authentic*, 581.10 *rejected*, 595.7 *unequipped*, 614.1 *useless*, 616.1 *inconvenient*, 656.2 *unskilled*, 846.8 *unentitled*
unqualifiedness 537.6 *authenticity*
unquelled 669.12 *resisting*
unquestionability 535.8 *definiteness*, 537.6 *authenticity*
unquestionable 103.5 *essential*, 475.12 *demonstrable*, 487.1 *impossible*, 488.6 *probable*, 535.16 *definite*, 537.19 *authentic*
unquestionableness 535.8 *definiteness*, 537.6 *authenticity*
unquestionably 487.11 *impossibly*, 488.11 *probably*, 490.23 *certainly*, 535.23 *affirmatively*, 772.12 *indeed*
unquestioned 497.14 *believed*, 537.19 *authentic*
unquestioning 466.3 *incurious*, 490.2 *convinced*, 497.11 *believing*
unquestioningly 466.7 *incuriously*
unquiet 366.16 *restless*, 642.7 *restlessness*
unquietly 366.27 *agitatedly*
unquietness 642.7 *restlessness*
unquotable 795.9 *ribald*, 877.12 *indecent*
unratified 491.5 *uncertified*
unravel 134.11 *simplify*, 136.9 *separate*, 152.19 *tidy*, 312.10 *straighten*, 376.11 *smooth*, 524.9 *decipher*, 639.1 *deliver*, 660.18 *disentangle*
unravelled 134.16 *simple*, 152.27 *tidied*
unravelling 136.1 *separation*, 639.2 *deliverance*
unreachable 357.15 *out of reach*, 487.3 *hopeless*
unreached 358.7 *short*
unreactive 57.38 *reactive*, 240.5 *inert*
unreadability 523.11 *unintelligibility*
unreadable 523.1 *unintelligible*, 788.4 *boring*
unreadably 523.13 *unintelligibly*
unreadily 595, 206.15 *immaturely*, 209.15 *late*
unreadiness 145.1 *incompleteness*, 206.3 *immaturity*, 209.1 *lateness*, 514.1 *surprise*, 595.8 *lack of preparation*
unready 145.4 *incomplete*, 206.12 *immature*, 209.9 *late*,

595.1 *unprepared*, 633.3 *vulnerable*
unreal 100, 102, 538, 254.8 *absent*, 368.8 *nonmaterial*, 518.8 *supposed*, 519.11 *fantastical*, 519.12 *imaginary*, 539.40 *illusory*, 540.28 *spurious*
unrealistic 102, 115.4 *dissimilar*, 489.1 *improbable*
unrealistically 115.7 *dissimilarly*
unrealistic person 102
unreality 102, 100.5 *nonreality*, 254.1 *absence*, 368.2 *unworldliness*, 487.5 *impossibility*, 519.4 *ideality*
Unreality 102
unrealized 502.8 *unknown*, 685.4 *uncompleted*
unreally 538.28 *dishonestly*
unrealness 538, 540.4 *spuriousness*
unreaped 600.2 *new*
unreason 460.1 *lack of intellect*, 460.4 *nonhuman existence*, 521.1 *lack of meaning*
unreasonable 229.6 *motiveless*, 474.7 *sophistic*, 487.1 *impossible*, 579.1 *capricious*, 753.7 *dear*
unreasonably 229.8 *by chance*
unreasoningly 460.12 *nonhumanly*
unrecanting 868.3 *impenitent*
unreceptiveness 816.1 *unsociability*
unrecognizable 523, 220.13 *converted*, 438.1 *invisible*, 531.15 *disguised*
unrecognizably 438.9 *invisibly*
unrecognized 438.1 *invisible*, 502.8 *unknown*, 531.15 *disguised*, 838.4 *unthanked*
unrecompensed 747.14 *unpaid*
unreconciled 573.2 *refusing*, 868.3 *impenitent*
unrecorded 546.6 *obliterated*
unrecounted 147.11 *excluded*
unredeemed 864.11 *wicked*, 868.3 *impenitent*
unreduced 619.1 *perfect*
unrefined 375.5 *unfinished*, 482.1 *undiscriminating*, 559.8 *indecorous*, 595.4 *untrained*, 620.2 *incomplete*, 622.8 *unclean*, 656.3 *clumsy*, 658.1 *naive*, 795.8 *discourteous*, 818.6 *bad-mannered*
unrefined rubber 595.11 *natural state*
unrefined sugar 414.2 *sweetener*
unrefinement 559.2 *impropriety*
unreflective 462.8 *thoughtless*
unreformed 868.3, 868.3 *impenitent*
unrefreshed 650.1 *fatigued*
unrefutability 537.6 *authenticity*
unrefuted 490.3 *decided*, 537.19 *authentic*
unregarded 850.18 *undervalued*
unregenerated 868.3 *impenitent*
unregistered 546.6 *obliterated*
unregretful 868.3 *impenitent*
unregretfully 868.6 *impenitently*
unregretted 868.4 *unatoned*
unregretting 868.3, 868.3 *impenitent*
unregular 215.4 *irregular*
unregularity 215.1 *irregularity*
unregularly 215.8 *irregularly*
unregulated 698.9 *free*
unrehearsed 583.1 *improvised*, 595.2 *spontaneous*
unreined 689.6 *anarchic*
unrelated 108, 104.8 *intruder*, 104.10 *foreign*, 108.9 *misconnected*, 115.4 *dissimilar*, 117.7 *disparate*, 136.17 *unjoined*
unrelatedness 108, 104.2 *foreignness*, 115.2 *unlikeness*, 117.1 *disparity*, 612.5 *unimportance*
Unrelatedness 108
unrelated thing 108
unrelaxed 373.2 *tough*
unrelenting 219.6 *protracted*, 577.3 *unyielding*, 836.5 *inflexible*

unrelentingly 219.7 *continually*, 690.11 *severely*, 836.7 *pitilessly*
unreliability 491, 224.1 *changeableness*, 477.7 *questionableness*, 573.14 *disobedience*, 579.2 *caprice*, 858.2 *faithlessness*
unreliable 491, 224.13 *changeable*, 474.10 *hypocritical*, 477.14 *questionable*, 498.7 *disbelieved*, 576.4 *unsteady*, 579.1 *capricious*, 633.2 *unsafe*, 858.6 *faithless*
unreliable narrator 48.3 *aspect of fiction*
unreliableness 578.7 *apostasy*
unreliably 491, 224.15 *changeably*, 474.15 *hypocritically*, 477.24 *questionably*, 498.11 *unbelievably*, 858.11 *dishonourably*
unrelieved 112.8 *monotonous*, 159.11 *continuous*
unrelished 785.9 *disliked*
unremarkable 124.3 *mediocre*, 242.6 *moderate*, 656.1 *unskilful*
unremarkableness 124.6 *mediocrity*
unremitting 159.11 *continuous*, 183.14 *recurrent*, 184.3 *eternal*, 219.6 *protracted*, 575.11 *steady*, 644.11 *laborious*
unremittingly 219.7 *continually*
unremorseful 836.4 *pitiless*, 868.3 *impenitent*
unremorsefully 868.6 *impenitently*
unremorsefulness 836.1 *pitilessness*
unremunerated 747.14 *unpaid*
unremunerative 737.16 *unprofitable*
unrepeatable expression 827.1 *curse*
unrepeatable offer 213.3 *infrequency*
unrepeated 160.9 *discontinued*, 174.14 *singular*
unrepentant 868.3 *impenitent*
unrepented 868.4 *unatoned*
unrepenting 868.3 *impenitent*
unreplenished 609.2 *unprovided*
unreported 147.11 *excluded*
unrepresentative 548.6 *misrepresented*
unrepresentatively 548
unreproachful 839.5 *merciful*
unrequired 600.3 *not wanted*
unrequite 838.6 *be ungrateful*
unrequited 581.10 *rejected*, 838.4 *unthanked*
unrequited love 687.1 *adversity*
unresembling 115.4 *dissimilar*
unresentful 839.5 *merciful*
unresentfulness 839.2 *forgivingness*
unreserved 322.16, 526.15 *open*, 530.11 *disclosing*, 568.12 *conversing*, 658.1 *naive*
unreservedly 530.13 *openly*, 568.15 *conversationally*, 698.21 *excessively*
unreservedness 530.3 *openness*
unresisting 673.5 *submitting*, 675.7 *peaceful*, 694.7 *obedient*
unresistingly 694.10 *obediently*
unresolved 434.8 *disagreeing*, 491.2 *irresolute*, 523.2 *unexplained*, 529.11 *mysterious*, 576.1 *vacillating*
unrespected 850
unresponsive 240.5 *inert*, 404.6 *unfeeling*, 464.4 *uninterested*, 761.1 *insensitive*, 783.7 *indifferent*, 832.15 *inconsiderate*, 836.4 *pitiless*
unresponsively 783.17 *indifferently*, 836.7 *pitilessly*
unresponsiveness 61.13 *depression*, 761.3 *insensitiveness*
unrest 324.2 *momentum*, 366.5, 642.7 *restlessness*
unrested 650.1 *fatigued*
unrestrained 757, 241.6 *violent*, 475.10 *demonstrative*, 482.1 *undiscriminating*, 689.6 *anarchic*, 698.9 *free*, 870.8 *overindulgent*

unrestrainedly 848.13 *with impunity*
unrestrainedness 757
unrestraint 689.1 *anarchy*, 698.1 *freedom*, 870.3 *overindulgence*
unrestricted 144.7 *complete*, 164.19 *prevailing*, 248.12 *extensive*, 322.13 *opened up*, 698.12 *unconditional*, 700.8 *free*, 848.7 *independent*
unretractable 535.13 *supported*
unretracted 535.13 *supported*
unrevealed 527.3 *unsolved*, 529.9 *secret*
unrevengeful 839.5 *merciful*
unrevengefulness 839.2 *forgivingness*
unrevered 850.17 *unrespected*
unreverenced 850.17 *unrespected*
unrewarded 614.2 *futile*, 747.14 *unpaid*, 838.4 *unthanked*
unrewarding 614.2 *futile*, 838.5 *thankless*
unrhymed poetry 48.11 *rhyme*
unrhythmic 215.4 *irregular*
unrhythmical 215.4 *irregular*
unrhythmically 215.8 *irregularly*
unriddle 524.9 *decipher*
unrig 614.8 *make useless*
unrigged 595.7 *unequipped*
unrighteous 844.16 *in the wrong*, 864.11 *wicked*
unrighteousness 844, 864.1 *wickedness*
unrightful 846.8 *unentitled*
unrightfully 846
unrinsed 622.7 *dirty*
unripe 86.9 *of a fruit*, 145.4 *incomplete*, 211.10 *untimely*, 415.5 *acid*, 453.3 *raw*, 585.1 *unaccustomed*, 595.5 *immature*, 656.2 *unskilled*, 685.4 *uncompleted*
unripely 211.15 *at the wrong time*
unripened 595.5 *immature*
unripeness 145.1 *incompleteness*, 211.1 *untimeliness*, 415.1 *sourness*, 595.10 *immaturity*, 620.5 *imperfection*, 656.8 *unskilfulness*, 685.1 *noncompletion*
unrivalled 126.14 *best*, 619.1 *perfect*
unrobe 296.14 *undress*
unrobed 296.9 *undressed*
unroll 269.10 *lengthen*, 312.10 *straighten*, 526.3 *reveal*, 530.5 *disclose*
unrolling 526.10 *manifestation*
unrough 376.1 *smooth*
unroughly 376.14 *smoothly*
unruffled 4.18 *detached*, 112.5 *uniform*, 325.6 *quiescent*, 376.2 *uniform*, 783.7 *indifferent*
unruffled surface 376.7 *smoothness*
unruliness 151.8 *lawlessness*, 689.1 *anarchy*, 693.1 *disobedience*, 698.6 *liberality*
unruly 151.20 *disorderly*, 241.6 *violent*, 577.2 *refractory*, 689.6 *anarchic*, 693.13 *disobedient*, 698.12 *unconditional*
unsaddle 370.10 *lighten*
unsaddling 370.6 *lightening*
unsafe 633, 238.8 *weak*, 618.5 *harmful*
unsafely 238.14 *weakly*
unsaid 527, 147.11 *excluded*
unsalable 754.10 *shoddy*
unsalaried 754.11 *free of charge*
unsaleability 614.3 *uselessness*
unsaleable 614.1 *useless*, 754.10 *shoddy*
unsalted 412.5 *tasteless*
unsalvageable 722.16 *losing*
unsanctioned by custom 585.2 *not customary*
unsanctioned 846.8 *unentitled*
unsanitary 625.5 *unhygienic*
unsated 609.2 *unprovided*
unsatisfactorily 238.14 *weakly*, 609.10 *insufficiently*
unsatisfactory 766, 852, 145.4 *incomplete*, 238.13 *insufficient*, 515.11 *disappointing*, 609.1 *insufficient*, 618.2 *inferior*, 620.1 *imperfect*

unsatisfactory work 656.9 *bungling*
unsatisfied 609.2 *unprovided*
unsatisfied hopes 515.1 *disappointment*
unsatisfying 412.5 *tasteless*, 515.11 *disappointing*
unsaturated 57.32 *solid*, 57.35 *combined*
unsaturated compound 57.7 *chemical compound*
unsaturated fat 58.7, 395.8 *fat*
unsaturated solution 57.3 *phase*
unsavouriness 412.1 *tastelessness*
unsavoury 415.6 *unpalatable*, 764.1 *unpleasant*, 785.9 *disliked*
unsay 484.8 *reverse*, 578.4 *recant*
unsayable 709.6 *censored*
unsaying 484.2 *reversal*
unscarred 619.1 *perfect*
unscathed 142.7 *uncut*, 619.1 *perfect*, 632.5 *safe*
unscented 417.3 *odourless*
unscholarly 502.6 *ignorant*
unschooled 502.6 *ignorant*
unscientific 656.2 *unskilled*, 658.1 *naive*
unscoured 622.7 *dirty*
unscramble 4.21 *rationalize*, 134.11 *simplify*, 141.4 *deconstruct*, 312.10 *straighten*, 478.20 *solve*, 524.9 *decipher*, 660.18 *disentangle*
unscrambled 478.14 *solved*, 524.15 *interpreted*
unscrambling 478.6 *solution*, 524.4 *translation*, 660.8 *disentanglement*
unscratched 619.1 *perfect*
unscreen 530.5 *disclose*
unscrubbed 622.7 *dirty*
unscrupulous 470.5 *indifferent*, 858.5 *dishonourable*, 864.11 *wicked*, 877.11 *immoral*
unscrupulously 858.11 *dishonourably*, 864.18 *wickedly*
unscrupulousness 470.2 *indifference*, 858.1 *improbity*, 877.1 *immorality*
unseal 322.19 *open up*, 530.5 *disclose*
unsealed 322.13 *opened up*
unsearchable 523.1 *unintelligible*
unseasonable 117.11 *unfit*, 211.10 *untimely*, 616.1 *inconvenient*
unseasonableness 211.1 *untimeliness*
unseasonably 117.17 *unsuitably*, 211.15 *at the wrong time*
unseasonal 55.46 *seasonal*
unseasoned 134.13 *pure*, 412.5 *tasteless*, 453.3 *raw*, 585.1 *unaccustomed*, 595.5 *immature*, 656.2 *unskilled*
unseat 139.5 *separate*, 139.5 *unstick*, 252.14 *displace*, 252.16 *replace*, 689.4 *be anarchic*
unseating 252.3 *replacement*
unsecure 633.2 *unsafe*
unsecured 732.6 *loaned*
unsecured debt 745.1 *debt*
unsecured loan 732.2, 745.3 *loan*
unseeable 438.1 *invisible*
unseeing 436.8 *blind*, 641.3 *inactive*
unseemliness 616.3 *inconvenience*, 795.3 *grossness*, 801.1 *disrespect*, 844.3 *impropriety*, 864.3 *venial sin*
unseemly 117.11 *unfit*, 559.8 *indecorous*, 616.1 *inconvenient*, 790.4 *ugly*, 795.8 *discourteous*, 844.13 *improper*, 864.13 *venial*
unseen 436.13 *hidden*, 438.1 *invisible*, 502.8 *unknown*, 523.1 *unintelligible*, 527.2, 531.14 *concealed*, 810.13 *reserved*
unseen world 397.14 *the spiritual world*
unsegregated 146.8 *included*
unselected 482.3 *indiscriminate*, 581.10 *rejected*
unselective 482.1 *undiscriminating*
unselectively 482

unselectiveness 482.6 *lack of discrimination*
unselfish 859, 831.7 *charitable*, 863.5 *virtuous*
unselfishly 859, 831.11 *charitably*, 863.9 *virtuously*
unselfishness 859, 831.2 *charity*, 833.1 *philanthropy*, 863.1 *virtue*
unsensational 556.1 *simple*
unseparated 146.8 *included*
unserious 540.27 *hypocritical*
unseriously 540.38 *hypocritically*
unseriousness 540.3 *hypocrisy*
unserviceable 614.1 *useless*
unserviceableness 614.3 *uselessness*
unsettle 141.4 *deconstruct*, 151.22 *discompose*, 153.7 *disturb*
unsettled 55.46 *seasonal*, 151.17 *discomposed*, 153.12 *disturbed*, 224.13 *changeable*, 254.14 *unoccupied*, 473.10 *arguable*, 491.2 *irresolute*, 845.12 *owed*
unsettledness 491.11 *irresoluteness*
unsettling 153.17 *disturbing*, 616.1 *inconvenient*
unsex 236.9 *make impotent*
unsexed 236
unshackle 700.4 *liberate*
unshackled 698.9 *free*, 700.7 *liberated*, 700.8 *free*
unshackling 700.1 *liberation*
unshakable 225.9 *stable*, 574.4 *undaunted*, 490.6 *infallible*, 778.9 *courageous*
unshakably 225.12 *stably*
unshaken 4.18 *detached*, 574.4 *undaunted*, 718.7 *guaranteed*
unshape 307.3 *make shapeless*
unshaped 307.5 *shapeless*
unshapely 790.4 *ugly*
unshared 723.8 *possessing*, 723.9 *possessed*
unsharp 381.1 *blunt*
unsharpened 376.2 *uniform*, 381.1 *blunt*
unsharpness 381.5 *bluntness*
unshatterable 378.1 *tough*
unshaven 375.3 *barbed*
unsheathe the sword 676.12 *go to war*
unshepherded 633.3 *vulnerable*
unshielded 322.13 *opened up*, 633.3 *vulnerable*
unship 349.12 *unload*
unshorn 375.3 *barbed*
unshrinking 574.4 *undaunted*, 778.9 *courageous*
unshriven 868.3 *impenitent*
unshroud 530.5 *disclose*
unsifted 151.13 *unordered*, 375.1 *rough*
unsighted 436.8 *blind*, 438.1 *invisible*
unsightliness 790.1 *hideousness*
unsightly 151.15 *untidy*, 457.10 *aspectual*, 790.4 *ugly*
unsigned 52.71 *numerical*, 491.5 *uncertified*
unsimilarity 115.1 *dissimilarity*
unsinkable 370.2 *insubstantial*
unskilful 656, 117.11 *unfit*, 585.1 *unaccustomed*, 614.1 *useless*
unskilfully 585, 656, 117.17 *unsuitably*, 595.14 *unreadily*
unskilfulness 656, 117.5 *unfitness*, 502.1 *ignorance*, 585.3 *unaccustomedness*, 595.8 *lack of preparation*, 614.3 *uselessness*, 618.8 *inferiority*
Unskilfulness 656
unskilled 656, 15.8 *industrial*, 117.11 *unfit*, 453.3 *raw*, 502.6 *ignorant*, 595.4 *untrained*, 614.1 *useless*, 618.2 *inferior*, 658.1 *naive*
unskilled labourer 646.1 *worker*
unskilled person 656
unskilled worker 15.7 *employee*, 124.7 *average person*, 230.6 *operative*
unsleeping 575.11 *steady*, 642.20 *industrious*

unsmiling 772.1 *solemn*, 818.5 *discourteous*, 830.7 *irritable*
unsmoked bacon 45.30 *bacon*
unsmooth 375.1 *rough*
unsmoothly 375.14 *roughly*
unsmoothness 375.6 *roughness*
unsnarl 152.19 *tidy*, 660.18 *disentangle*
unsnarled 152.27 *tidied*
unsnarling 660.8 *disentanglement*
unsociability 816, 139.2 *aloofness*, 830.1 *sullenness*, 834.1 *misanthropy*
Unsociability 816
unsociable 816, 139.9 *aloof*, 168.16 *solitary*, 531.16 *silent*, 566.1 *taciturn*, 818.5 *discourteous*, 820.6 *hostile*, 834.3 *misanthropic*
unsociableness 816.1 *unsociability*, 834.1 *misanthropy*
unsociably 139.11 *aloofly*, 818.9 *discourteously*, 820.14 *hostilely*
unsocial habits 816.1 *unsociability*
unsocial person 816, 834.2 *misanthrope*
unsocially 816
unsoiled 621.16 *clean*, 865.5 *innocent*
unsold 600.3 *not wanted*
unsolicitous 818.5 *discourteous*
unsolicitousness 818.1 *discourtesy*
unsolvable 52.73 *numerable*, 523.2 *unexplained*
unsolved 527, 523.2 *unexplained*
unsophisticated 134.17 *direct*, 453.3 *raw*, 556.3 *natural*, 595.4 *untrained*, 658.1, 865.7 *naive*
unsophisticated person 658.3 *naive person*
unsophistication 658.2, 865.3 *naivety*
unsorrowful 868.3 *impenitent*
unsorry 868.3 *impenitent*
unsorted 133.12 *mixed*, 151.13 *unordered*, 482.3 *indiscriminate*
unsought 591.20 *avoidable*
unsound 52.86 *logical*, 127.17 *defective*, 238.10 *ill*, 474.7 *sophistic*, 476.6 *refutable*, 491.7 *unreliable*, 618.4 *poor*, 620.1 *imperfect*, 624.21 *unhealthy*, 626.5 *unhygienic*, 633.2 *unsafe*, 656.2 *unskilled*, 844.12 *incorrect*, 844.14 *abnormal*
unsoundable 277.8 *deep*
unsound argument 52.64 *reasoning*
unsounded 277.8 *deep*, 422.3 *silent*
unsound horse 32.1 *horse*
unsoundly 127.21 *badly*, 238.14 *weakly*, 474.14 *sophistically*, 476.12 *refutably*
unsound mind 510.1 *insanity*
unsoundness 474.1 *sophistry*, 476.4 *refutability*, 491.15 *unreliability*, 618.10 *poverty*, 620.5 *imperfection*, 633.5 *danger*, 633.7 *vulnerability*, 743.6 *insolvency*, 844.2 *incorrectness*
unsparing 608.2 *plentiful*, 690.8 *severe*
unsparingly 690.11 *severely*
unspeakable 523.1 *unintelligible*, 618.3 *bad*, 786.8 *wonderful*
unspeakableness 523.11 *unintelligibility*
unspeakably 786.13 *wonderfully*
unspecific 164.20 *generalized*
unspecified 490, 164.20 *generalized*
unspeciousness 537.1 *truth*
unspectacular 124.3 *mediocre*
unspeller 11.12 *occultist*
unspent 132.10 *surplus*, 600.1 *unused*, 605.7 *stored*
unspiced 134.13 *pure*
unspied 527.2 *concealed*
unspirited 555.1 *unemphatic*
unspiritual 367.7 *material*
unspirituality 367.2 *materialization*
unspoiled 142.7 *uncut*, 617.5 *not bad*, 619.1 *perfect*

unspoilt 134.13 *pure*
unspoken 422.3 *silent*, 502.8 *unknown*, 527.3 *unsolved*, 527.4 *unsaid*, 529.9 *secret*
unsportsmanlike 844.11 *wrong*, 858.5 *dishonourable*
unsportsmanlike conduct 19.13 *penalty*
unspotted 619.1 *perfect*, 865.5 *innocent*
unsprung 373.2 *tough*, 378.3 *hard*
unspuriousness 537.1 *truth*
unstable 113.5 *diverse*, 123.3 *unequal*, 153.16 *deranged*, 189.6 *transient*, 215.4 *irregular*, 224.13 *changeable*, 491.7 *unreliable*, 576.2 *changeable*, 579.1 *capricious*, 633.2 *unsafe*, 759.13 *passionate*
unstable equilibrium 56.10 *force*
unstableness 491.15 *unreliability*
unstable person 61.8 *disordered personality*
unstaffed 254.14 *unoccupied*
unstained 619.1 *perfect*, 621.16 *clean*
unstalked 83.18 *of leaves*
unstarched 374.1 *soft*
unstatesmanlike 656.1 *unskilful*
unstatutory 16.56 *unauthorized*
unstaunch 576.4 *unsteady*, 779.3 *cowardly*
unsteadfast 576.4 *unsteady*, 779.3 *cowardly*
unsteadily 113.10 *diversely*, 215.8 *irregularly*, 224.15 *changeably*, 238.14 *weakly*, 366.28 *shakily*, 379.5 *fragilely*, 491.26 *unreliably*
unsteadiness 215.1 *irregularity*, 224.1 *changeableness*, 366.1 *agitation*, 491.15 *unreliability*, 633.5 *danger*
unsteady 576, 215.4 *irregular*, 224.13 *changeable*, 238.10 *ill*, 366.15 *agitated*, 366.18 *shaky*, 379.1 *brittle*, 491.7 *unreliable*, 620.1 *imperfect*, 628.13 *dilapidated*, 633.2 *unsafe*, 656.3 *clumsy*
unsteerable 656.3 *clumsy*
unsterilized 622.8 *unclean*, 626.6 *contagious*
unstick 139, 136.9 *separate*
unstiffen 374.13 *soften*
unstiffened 374.1 *soft*
unstinting 755.1 *generous*
unstirred 466.4 *uninterested*
unstirring 325.6 *quiescent*
unstitch 136.9 *separate*
unstocked 609.2 *unprovided*
unstop 322.19 *open up*
unstoppable 219.6 *protracted*, 490.5 *inevitable*
unstopped 322.13 *opened up*
unstressed 424.4 *faint*, 564.18 *phonetic*
unstring 136.9 *separate*, 374.13 *soften*
unstrung 238.8 *weak*, 374.1 *soft*
unstuck 136.15 *separate*
unstudied 595.2 *spontaneous*, 658.1 *naive*
unstuffy 814.7 *informal*
unsturdiness 379.2 *brittleness*
unsturdy 379.1 *brittle*
unsubdued 669.12 *resisting*
unsubjected 698.10 *independent*
unsubmissive 168.12 *nonconformist*, 669.12 *resisting*
unsubmissively 669.14 *resistingly*
unsubstantial 102.8 *unreal*, 438.1 *invisible*, 519.12 *imaginary*, 542.12 *understated*
unsubstantiality 102.1 *unreality*, 542.1 *understatement*
unsubstantialness 368.2 *unworldliness*
unsuccessful 247.6 *having no effect*, 515.11 *disappointing*, 609.2 *unprovided*, 614.2 *futile*, 656.1 *unskilful*, 683.10 *failed*, 687.6 *adverse*, 722.17 *unprofitable*
unsuccessful applicant 581.9 *re-*

jected person, 683.5 failing person

unsuccessful candidate 683.5 failing person, 722.6 loser
unsuccessful challenger 683.5 failing person
unsuccessful competitor 683.5 failing person
unsuccessful defence 16.43 conviction
unsuccessfully 683, 614.10 uselessly, 656.11 unskilfully, 687.12 in adversity, 722.20 at a loss
unsuccessful thing 683
unsuccessive 160.8 discontinuous
unsuitability 117.5 unfitness, 614.3 uselessness, 616.3 inconvenience
unsuitable 117.11 unfit, 211.10 untimely, 581.10 rejected, 614.1 useless, 616.1 inconvenient, 666.10 different, 844.13 improper
unsuitableness 211.1 untimeliness
unsuitable time 211.1 untimeliness
unsuitably 117, 211.15 at the wrong time, 666.12 differently, 844.27 improperly
unsuited 117.11 unfit, 211.10 untimely
unsullied 134.13 pure, 621.16 clean, 865.5 innocent
unsung 527.4 unsaid
unsupplied 609.2 unprovided
unsupported 174.15 solo, 633.3 vulnerable
unsure 491.1 uncertain, 576.1 vacillating
unsureness 491.9 uncertainty
unsure of oneself 810.11 shy
unsurpassable 126.14, 617.2 best, 619.1 perfect
unsurpassably 126.17 supremely
unsurpassed 126.14, 617.2 best
unsurpassedly 126.17 supremely
unsurprised 513.5 expecting, 783.7 indifferent, 787.3 unmoved
unsurprising 513.7 expected, 787.4 predictable
unsurprisingly 513.13 expectedly, 787.10 predictably
unsusceptibility 761.3 insensitiveness
unsusceptible 761.1 insensitive
unsuspected 527.3 unsolved
unsuspecting 497.11 believing, 514.6 surprised, 658.1 naive
unsuspectingly 497.15 believingly
unsuspicious 658.1 naive
unsweetened 415.5 acid
unswept 622.7 dirty
unswerving 332.15 direct, 333.5 undeviating, 490.2 convinced
unswervingly 312.12 straight, 332.9 directly
unsymmetric 117.7 disparate
unsymmetrical 151.14, 215.4 irregular, 309.6 distorted
unsymmetrically 309.13 asymmetrically
unsymmetry 151.2 irregular order
unsympathetic 573.3 cautious, 663.19 oppositional, 785.8 disliking, 820.6 hostile, 832.15 inconsiderate, 836.4 pitiless
unsympathetically 785.10 discontentedly, 820.14 hostilely, 836.7 pitilessly
unsympatheticness 836.1 pitilessness
unsympathizing 836.4 pitiless
unsynchronized 197.2 occurring at a different time
unsystematic 151.16 confused, 215.4 irregular, 482.3 indiscriminate
unsystematical 215.4 irregular
unsystematically 151.27 in disorder, 215.8 irregularly
untainted 619.1 perfect, 621.16 clean, 865.5 innocent
untalented 656.1 unskilful

untamed 241.6 violent, 585.1 unaccustomed, 591.18 avoiding
untamed horse 32.1 horse
untangle 152.19 tidy, 312.10 straighten, 639.1 deliver, 660.18 disentangle
untangled 152.27 tidied
untangling 639.2 deliverance
untapped 600.2 new
untarnished 134.13 pure, 621.16 clean
untaught 502.6 ignorant, 583.2 spontaneous, 585.1 unaccustomed, 595.4 untrained, 656.2 unskilled, 658.1 naive
untax 370.10 lighten
untaxed 754.11 free of charge
untaxing 370.6 lightening
unteachable 577.4 set, 656.2 unskilled
untearable 378.1 tough
untempered 238.8 weak
untenability 498.2 unbelievability
untenable 236.11 unprotected, 238.8 weak, 474.7 sophistic, 487.3 hopeless, 498.7 disbelieved
untenableness 474.1 sophistry
untenanted 254.14 unoccupied
untested 201.11 unfamiliar, 453.3 raw, 491.5 uncertified
untethered 698.11 ranging
unthanked 838
unthankful 838.3 ungrateful
unthankfulness 838.1 ingratitude
unthawed 371.7 condensed
unthinkability 487.5 impossibility
unthinkable 487.1 impossible
unthinkably 487.11 impossibly
unthinking 512, 460.6 unintelligent, 462.8 thoughtless, 466.4 uninterested, 468.7 inattentive, 468.9 thoughtless, 648.3 hasty
unthinkingly 460.11 unintelligently, 512.16 obliviously
unthinkingness 512
unthorough 620.2 incomplete, 685.4 uncompleted, 720.11 nonobservant
unthought 462
unthoughtful 832.15 inconsiderate
unthreading 136.1 separation
unthreatened 632.5 safe
unthreatening 632.5 safe
unthriftiness 757.4 extravagance
unthrifty 595.3 without preparation, 757.1 extravagant
unthrone 689.4 be anarchic
untidily 113.10 diversely, 622.12 dirtily
untidiness 151, 470.2 indifference, 622.1 dirtiness
untidy 151, 151.24 make disordered, 366.22 agitate, 470.5 indifferent, 622.7, 622.11 dirty, 628.4 impair
untie 136.9 separate, 296.14 undress, 639.1 deliver, 660.18 disentangle, 698.15 set free, 727.9 dispose of
untied 136.15 separate, 638.8 escaping
untie one's hands 700.4 liberate
untie the knot 824.7 divorce
untie the purse-strings 748.1 expend
until 185.26 all the time
until all the seas run dry 184.12 eternally
until hell freezes over 186.8 ever, 190.11 eternally
untilled 595.4 untrained, 600.2 new
untilled ground 595.11 natural state
until now 3.24 historically, 200.23 before now
until one is blue in the face 614.10 uselessly
until the end of time 184.12, 190.11 eternally
until the Greek Calends 186.8 ever, 190.11 eternally
until the rivers run uphill 184.12 eternally
until the sun ceases to shine 184.12 eternally

until the twelfth of never 186.8 ever, 190.11 eternally
untimeliness 211, 117.5 unfitness, 153.4 disruption, 193.1 wrong time, 616.3 inconvenience, 656.9 bungling
Untimeliness 211
untimely 211, 117.11 unfit, 193.4 mistimed, 493.9 misjudged, 616.1 inconvenient
untimely action 211.1 untimeliness
untimely end 397.5 ways of dying
untimely occurrence 211.1 untimeliness
untinged 134.13 pure
untiring 378.4 powerful, 575.11 steady
untiringly 378.13 powerfully
untold 147.11 excluded, 181.8 numberless, 184.2 immeasurable, 502.8 unknown, 527.3 unsolved, 529.9 secret
untold of 527.4 unsaid
untouchable 127.15 subordinate, 263.9 reserved, 816.7 outsider
untouched 142.7 uncut, 600.2 new, 621.16 clean, 783.7 indifferent, 868.3 impenitent, 876.9 pure
untouched by evil 865.5 innocent
untouched by human hand 243.12 produced
untoward 616.1 inconvenient
untraced 527.3 unsolved
untracked 527.3 unsolved
untraditional 585.2 not customary
untrainable horse 32.1 horse
untrained 595, 453.3 raw, 585.1 unaccustomed, 620.2 incomplete, 656.1 unskilful, 656.2 unskilled
untranslatable 523.1 unintelligible
untravelled 325.5 sedentary
untried 201.11 unfamiliar, 453.3 raw, 491.5 uncertified, 600.1 unused
untrimmed 123.3 unequal, 556.2 unadorned, 595.7 unequipped
untrodden 201.11 unfamiliar, 600.2 new
untroubled 242.6 moderate, 325.6 quiescent
untroublesome 660.12 wieldy
untrue 538, 504.15 erroneous, 518.8 supposed, 519.12 imaginary, 540.25 false, 548.6 misrepresented, 720.13 noncompliant, 844.12 incorrect
untrueness 504.3 erroneousness, 538.1 untruth, 540.1 falsehood
untruism 538.1 untruth
untruly 538.26 untruthfully
untrustworthiness 477.7 questionableness, 491.15 unreliability, 578.7 apostasy, 858.2 faithlessness
untrustworthy 477.14 questionable, 491.7 unreliable, 515.12 deceptive, 633.2 unsafe, 858.6 faithless
untruth 538, 504.3 erroneousness, 531.5 evasion, 540.1 falsehood, 578.5 equivocalness, 636.3 false alarm
Untruth 538
untruthful 309.8 exaggerated, 538.15 lying, 540.25 false, 844.12 incorrect, 855.5 dishonourable, 862.7 evil
untruthfully 538, 309.14 distortedly, 540.36 falsely, 844.26 wrong, 858.11 dishonourably, 862.12 evilly
untruthfulness 309.4 distortion of the truth, 538.1 untruth, 538.3 lying, 540.1 falsehood, 844.2 incorrectness, 858.1 improbity, 862.1 evil
untuned 434.9 unmelodious
untuneful 434.9 unmelodious
untutored 502.6 ignorant, 595.4 untrained, 656.2 unskilled, 658.1 naive
untwist 312.10 straighten
untying 136.1 separation

untypical 115.4 dissimilar
unusable 581.10 rejected, 600.1 unused, 614.1 useless
unusably 600.12 out of use
unused 600, 132.10 surplus, 201.11 unfamiliar, 595.4 untrained, 605.7 stored, 607.9 waste, 643.2 not working, 656.3 clumsy
unused thing 600
unusual 215, 113.5 diverse, 115.4 dissimilar, 117.7 disparate, 165.16 characteristic, 168.14 eccentric, 213.2 infrequent, 514.8 surprising, 585.2 not customary, 786.8 wonderful
unusually 215, 585, 113.10 diversely, 115.7 dissimilarly, 168.21 unconformably, 201.21 newly, 213.1 infrequently
unusualness 168, 215, 213.3 infrequency
unutterable 523.1 unintelligible, 786.8 wonderful
unuttered 422.3 silent, 527.4 unsaid
unvalued 822.12 hated
unvanquished 682.15 victorious
unvariable 110.17 regular
unvariableness 110.6 regularity
unvariably 110.20 regularly
unvaried 110.17 regular, 112.8 monotonous, 426.16 humming
unvarnished 556.2 unadorned, 658.1 naive
unvarying 110.12 same, 110.17 regular, 112.5 uniform, 112.8 monotonous, 116.14 conforming, 122.6 equal, 219.6 protracted, 225.9 stable, 788.4 boring
unveering 332.15 direct
unveeringly 332.9 directly
unveil 156.24 open, 201.19 begin, 296.14 undress, 496.2 detect, 526.3 reveal, 530.5 disclose
unveiled 156.37 enrolled, 201.13 inaugurated, 296.11 exposed
unveiling 156.9 premiere, 201.4 beginning, 496.7 detection, 530.1 disclosure
unveil oneself 526.4 show oneself
unvenerated 850.17 unrespected
unventilated 419.3 stinking, 626.5 unhygienic
unveraciously 540.36 falsely
unverifiability 491.13 indemonstrability
unverifiable 477.14 questionable, 491.4 indemonstrable
unverified 491.5 uncertified, 518.7 suppositional
unverified supposition 518.3 conjecture
unverity 540.1 falsehood
unversatile 656.1 unskilful
unversed 656.2 unskilled, 658.1 naive
unviable 487.3 hopeless
unvirtuous 864.2 immoral, 877.13 unchaste
unvirtuousness 864.2 vice
unvisited 816.11 secluded
unvoiced 527.4 unsaid, 563.9 voiceless
unwanted 132.10 surplus, 581.10 rejected, 600.3 not wanted, 607.9 waste, 614.1 useless, 754.10 shoddy, 785.9 disliked, 822.12 hated
unwariness 780.1 rashness
unwarlike 240.5 inert, 675.7 peaceful
unwarmed 595.6 uncooked
unwarned 633.3 vulnerable
unwarrantable 16.58 unjust
unwarranted 16.56 unauthorized, 357.12 excessive, 846.10 undue
unwarrantedness 846.5 undueness
unwary 404.6 unfeeling, 780.4 rash
unwashed 419.3 stinking, 622.7 dirty
unwasteful 756.4 thrifty
unwatered 392.1 dry
unwavering 225.11 determined,

490.6 *infallible*, 574.4 *un-daunted*, 575.11 *steady*
unwaveringly 225.13 *determinedly*
unwearied 575.11 *steady*, 642.20 *industrious*
unwed 825.6 *celibate*
unwed condition 825.1 *celibacy*
unwedded 174.17 *single*, 698.10 *independent*, 816.10 *lonely*, 825.6 *celibate*, 876.9 *pure*
unwed man 825.5 *single person*
unweeded 83.13 *plantlike*
unweighable 370.1 *light*
unweighableness 370.5 *lightness*
unweighting 41.4 *skiing technique*, 41.12 *ski*
unwelcome 764.1 *unpleasant*, 785.9 *disliked*, 822.12 *hated*
unwelcome guest 346.8 *intruder*, 815.6 *social person*
unwelcome necessity 822.7 *hated thing*
unwelcoming 816.8 *unsociable*
unwell 624.22 *sick*, 687.6 *adverse*
unwhetted 381.1 *blunt*
unwholesome 415.6 *unpalatable*, 419.3 *stinking*, 618.5 *harmful*, 626.5 *unhygienic*, 877.12 *indecent*
unwholesomely 626.8 *unhygienically*
unwholesomeness 415.2 *unpalatability*, 626.1 *lack of hygiene*
unwholesome surroundings 626.1 *lack of hygiene*
unwieldily 659.28 *awkwardly*
unwieldiness 259.2 *bigness*, 369.8 *weighing down*, 616.3 *inconvenience*, 659.2 *awkwardness*
unwieldy 123.3 *unequal*, 369.3 *ponderous*, 616.1 *inconvenient*, 656.3, 659.15 *clumsy*
unwilling 573, 328.6 *hesitant*, 500.7 *dissenting*, 587.10 *dissuaded*, 591.18 *avoiding*, 661.13 *hindering*, 663.22 *uncooperative*, 669.10 *resistant*, 693.13 *disobedient*, 711.8 *refused*, 785.8 *disliking*
unwillingly 573, 500.10 *dissentiently*, 591.23 *shyly*, 661.16 *with delay*, 669.14 *resistingly*, 693.17 *disobediently*, 711.11 *uncooperatively*, 785.10 *discontentedly*
unwillingness 573, 328.12 *hesitation*, 591.12 *shyness*, 661.1 *hindrance*, 663.4 *uncooperativeness*, 669.1 *resistance*, 693.1 *disobedience*, 711.1 *refusal*, 785.1 *dislike*
Unwillingness 573
unwind 374.14 *ease*, 641.4 *not act*, 649.2 *take it easy*
unwiped 621.7 *dirty*
unwise 460.6 *unintelligent*, 508.5 *foolish*, 616.1 *inconvenient*, 656.1 *unskilful*
unwisely 460.11 *unintelligently*, 508.8 *foolishly*
unwitnessed 438.1 *invisible*
unwitting 502.6 *ignorant*
unwittingly 502.12 *ignorantly*
unwonted 585.1 *unaccustomed*, 585.2 *not customary*
unwooed 825.6 *celibate*
unworkability 487.6 *hopelessness*, 614.3 *uselessness*
unworkable 236.10 *powerless*, 487.3 *hopeless*, 614.1 *useless*
unworkably 487.12 *hopelessly*
unworked 595.4 *untrained*, 595.5 *immature*
unworldliness 368, 11.2 *the occult*, 658.2, 865.3 *naivety*
unworldly 11.18 *spiritual*, 368.8 *nonmaterial*, 658.1, 865.7 *naive*
unworried 595.3 *without preparation*
unworthily 127.22 *basely*
unworthiness 618.10 *poverty*, 846.5 *undueness*
unworthy 127.12 *inferior*, 618.4 *poor*, 846.11 *undeserving*
unwrap 296.15 *make nude*,

322.18 *open*, 437.10 *make visible*, 530.5 *disclose*
unwrapped 322.12 *open*
unwrinkled 282.8 *horizontal*, 376.2 *uniform*
unwritten 1.14 *societal*, 527.4 *unsaid*, 546.6 *obliterated*, 564.17 *oral*
unwritten agreement 714.1 *promise*
unwritten code 847.6 *ethics*
unwritten constitution 16.1 *the law*
unwritten law 16.1 *the law*, 584.5 *tradition*, 654.3 *precept*
unwrought 595.5 *immature*
unyielding 577, 237.11 *strong in spirit*, 373.4 *mentally hard*, 378.5 *mentally tough*, 490.5 *inevitable*, 570.7 *iron-willed*, 574.3 *strong-willed*, 669.11 *obstinate*, 836.5 *inflexible*
unyieldingly 237.14 *strongly*, 690.11 *severely*, 836.7 *pitilessly*
unyieldingness 373.8 *mental hardness*, 378.9 *mental toughness*, 836.2 *inflexibility*
unzealous 573.3 *cautious*
unzip 136.9 *separate*, 296.14 *undress*
unzipped 136.15 *separate*
up 359, 56.78 *quantum*, 261.5 *make bigger*, 275.20 *higher*, 281.11 *vertically*, 281.12 *perpendicularly*, 327.17 *via*, 361.1 *raise*, 613.1 *useful*, 769.1 *cheerful*, 775.11 *hopeful*
up against a brick wall 661.14 *blocked*, 661.17 *in the way*
up against it 123.7 *unequally*, 687.6 *adverse*, 743.2 *insolvent*
upalong 359.26 *up*
up and about 324.18 *in motion*, 623.1 *healthy*
up-and-coming 642.18 *active*, 686.8 *prosperous*
up-and-coming star 682.4 *successful person*
up and doing 230.10 *operational*, 640.5 *acting*, 642.19 *busy*
up and down 214.15 *regularly*, 281.12 *perpendicularly*, 365.18 *to and fro*
up-and-down 281.8 *vertical*, 365.13 *oscillating*
up and go 345.12 *depart*
up and going 230.10 *operational*
Upanishad 7.12 *religious text*
uparching 359.22 *ascending*
upas 85 Trees and Shrubs
upasaka 7.7 *monk*
upasika 7.7 *monk*
upas tree 631.12 *poisonous plant*
up a tree 659.16 *troubled*
up back 19.7 *offence*
upbeat 49.19 *tempo*, 775.11 *hopeful*
up before the beak 16.54 *litigated*, 492.10 *judged*
upbend 359.2, 359.21 *upturn*
upbraid 852.20 *censure*
upbraided 852.34 *censured*
upbraiding 852.7 *blame*, 852.30 *censuring*
upbringing 6.1 *education*
upbuoy 361.1 *raise*
upbuoyed 361.11 *raised*
upbuoying 361.6 *raising*
upcast 359.2, 359.21 *upturn*, 359.22 *ascending*, 361.1 *raise*, 361.6 *raising*, 361.11 *raised*
upchuck 349.15 *vomit*
upclimb 34.1 *mountaineering*, 34.9 *mountaineer*, 359.6 *mounting*, 359.14 *climb*
upclimber 34.7 *mountaineer*, 359.11 *ascender*
upcoming 199.11 *future*, 209.13 *later*, 359.1 *ascent*, 359.23 *rising*
upcountry 290.3, 290.9 *inland*
up-country 249.17 *national*
upcurve 338.5 *throw*, 359.2, 359.21 *upturn*
update 201.20 *make new*
updateable 201.15 *renewable*
updated 201.14 *renewed*

updated model 627.8 *better thing*
updated version 627.8 *better thing*
updating 201.5 *fresh start*
Updike 48 Writers, **48** Poets
updraught 55.10 *air movement*, 359.2 *upturn*, 390.4 *air flow*
upend 281.6 *make vertical*
upended 281.8 *vertical*
upending 281.2 *making vertical*
up for auction 710.17 *offered*
up for grabs 739.18 *on sale*
up for sale 710.17 *offered*, 739.18 *on sale*
up for trial 16.54 *litigated*, 492.10 *judged*
up front 303.11 *in front*
upfront 312.5 *honourable*
upgang 359.1 *ascent*
upgo 359.1 *ascent*, 359.13 *ascend*
upgoing 359.1 *ascent*, 359.23 *rising*
upgrade 65.19 *abort*, 201.20 *make new*, 336.8 *further*, 359.2 *upturn*, 359.22 *ascending*, 627.1 *improve*, 629.2 *refurbish*
upgradeable 201.15 *renewable*
upgraded 201.14 *renewed*, 361.12 *exalted*
upgrading 201.5 *fresh start*, 361.7 *lift*, 627.5 *improvement*
upgrow 359.13 *ascend*
upgrowth 359.2 *upturn*
uphaul 36.3 *parts of a sailing boat*
upheaval 151.5 *confusion*, 151.8 *lawlessness*, 153.1 *disturbance*, 244.4 *ruin*, 361.6 *raising*, 674.6 *fight*
upheave 359.13 *ascend*, 359.18 *jump*, 361.1 *raise*
uphill 359.1 *ascent*, 359.22 *ascending*, 359.26 *up*, 644.11 *laborious*, 659.10 *difficult*, 659.25 *difficultly*
uphill christie 41.4 *skiing technique*
uphill ski 41.5 *ski equipment*
uphill struggle 659.3 *difficult task*
uphill task 659.3 *difficult task*
uphillward 359.22 *ascending*, 359.26 *up*
uphill work 644.1 *work*
uphoist 361.1 *raise*
uphold 101.12 *establish reality*, 219.3 *continue*, 284.14 *give moral support*, 361.1 *raise*, 637.5 *preserve*, 662.23 *advise*, 851.13 *support*, 855.8 *justify*
upholder 284.8 *supporter*
upholding 284.9 *supportive*
upholster 47.18 *work wood*, 273.8 *fatten*, 293.24 *coat*
upholstered 47.14 *wooden*
upholstered chair 47.2 *chair*
upholsterer 293.17 *coverer*
upholstery 42 Hobbies and Pastimes, 47.1 *furniture*, 273.5 *thickness*, 293.12 *protective covering*, 374.11 *soft thing*, 603.6 *equipment*
up in arms 642.18 *active*, 663.25 *at odds*, 666.9 *disagreeing*, 669.12 *resisting*, 670.22 *militant*, 676.15 *warring*, 679.42 *martially*, 828.15 *resentful*
up in the air 685.4 *uncompleted*
up in the world 686.8 *prosperous*
upkeep 284.7 *financial support*, 637.1 *preservation*, 662.3 *sustenance*
upkick 39.2 *swimming technique*
upland 98, 95.7 *mountainous*, 98.11 *continental*, 248.3 *geographical space*, 275.2 *heights*
upleap 359.2 *upturn*, 359.17 *spring up*
uplift 54.20 *earth movement*, 275.1 *height*, 275.17 *raise*, 359.2 *upturn*, 361.1 *raise*, 361.6 *raising*, 370.10 *lighten*, 627.1 *improve*, 627.5 *improvement*, 769.6 *bring cheer*

uplifted 275.9 *high*, 359.22 *ascending*, 361.11 *raised*
uplifting 361.6 *raising*, 769.2 *cheering*
uplighter 439.12 *highlight*
uplighting 439.12 *highlight*
up line 72.2 *track*
uplong 359.26 *up*
up-market 753.7 *dear*
up-market price 753.1 *high price*
upmost 126.14 *best*, 275.10 *higher*, 279.5 *top*
up north 359.26 *up*
up on 655.8 *expert*
up on a charge 856.8 *accusatory*
upon one's honour 535.24 *truthfully*
upon one's word 535.24 *truthfully*, 714.16 *as promised*
upper 2.14 *socioeconomic*, 52.75 *equal*, 126.15 *excellent*, 275.10 *higher*, 875.6 *drug*
upper atmosphere 55.8 *atmosphere*, 390.3 *atmospheric layers*
upper bound 52.21 *set*
Upper Carboniferous 54 Geological Time Intervals
upper-case 5.41 *lettered*
upper-case letter 5.15 *type style*
Upper Chamber 12.4, 12.4 *governing body*, 653.11 *British government*, 653.12 *US government*
upper circle 51.16 *auditorium*
upper class 2.7 *social stratification*, 126.7 *the best people*, 400.9 *group*, 617.7 *elite*, 802.2 *aristocracy*, 815.7 *human society*
upper-class 802.4 *aristocratic*
upper-class twit 802.1 *nobleman*
Upper Cretaceous 54 Geological Time Intervals
upper crust 126.7 *the best people*, 617.7 *elite*
upper edge 299.3 *edge*
upper extremity 279.1 *summit*
upper hand 126.3 *advantage*, 233 *influence*, 300.4 *advantage*
Upper House 12.4, 12.4 *governing body*, 653.11 *British government*, 653.12 *US government*
Upper Jurassic 54 Geological Time Intervals
Upper Klamath 94 Lakes
upper limit 52.31 *differentiation*, 120.2 *certain amount*, 302.2 *limiting factor*
Upper Lough Erne 94.4 *British lakes*
upper middle class 158.8 *middle class*, 400.9 *group*
uppermost 126.14 *best*, 275.10 *higher*, 279.5 *top*, 611.5 *important*
upper partial 49.21 *tone*
upper regions 279.1 *summit*
uppers and lowers 380.11 *tooth*
upper side 279.4 *top layer*
upper storey 479.7 *brain*
upper surface 279.4 *top layer*
Upper Triassic 54 Geological Time Intervals
upper wind 55.12 *wind*
upping 359.1 *ascent*
uppish 807.16 *arrogant*
uppishness 807.4 *arrogance*
uppitiness 805.3 *conceit*, 807.4 *arrogance*
uppity 805.17 *conceited*, 807.16 *arrogant*
Uppsala 93 Cities
upraise 281.6 *make vertical*, 361.1 *raise*, 370.10 *lighten*
upraised 275.9 *high*, 281.9 *unbowed*, 361.11 *raised*
upraising 281.2 *making vertical*
uprear 275.16 *rise*, 281.5 *be vertical*, 361.5 *arise*
upreared 275.9 *high*, 281.9 *unbowed*, 361.11 *raised*
uprearing 281.2 *making vertical*, 361.6 *raising*
upright 16.50 *law-abiding*, 52.80 *linear*, 281.3 *vertical thing*, 281.8 *vertical*, 281.11 *vertically*, 843.10 *moral*, 847.8 *dutiful*, 849.13 *respectable*, 857.4 *hon-*

ourable, 863.5 *virtuous*, 865.5 *innocent*, 876.8 *moral*
upright fold 54.20 *earth movement*
uprightly 281.11 *vertically*, 863.9 *virtuously*, 865.11 *innocently*
uprightness 281.1 *verticality*, 843.4, 843.4 *righteousness*, 857.1 *probity*, 863.1 *virtue*, 865.1 *innocence*, 876.2 *good morals*
uprights 19.4 *stadium*
uprisal 359.1 *ascent*
uprise 30.7 *stationary rings*, 275.1 *height*, 275.16 *rise*, 281.5 *be vertical*, 359.1 *ascent*, 359.13 *ascend*, 693.16 *be subversive*
uprising 151.8 *lawlessness*, 275.9 *high*, 281.2 *making vertical*, 359.1 *ascent*, 359.23 *rising*, 642.5 *activism*, 669.3 *resistance movement*, 693.4 *revolution*, 713.2 *disorder*
uproar 151.5 *confusion*, 153.5 *commotion*, 241.3 *instance of violence*, 423.2 *outcry*, 431.1 *cry*, 434.2 *dissonant noise*, 674.6 *fight*
uproarious 241.6 *violent*, 423.6 *loud*, 431.16 *vociferous*, 771.9 *funny*
uproariously 423.9 *loudly*, 431.20 *vociferously*
uproot 131.3 *subtract*, 147.8 *eject*, 244.8 *destroy*, 252.15 *remove*, 349.8 *evict*, 355.11 *extract*
uprooted 252.9 *removed*, 355.19 *dislodged*
uprooting 244.2 *destroying*, 252.2 *removal*, 355.1 *extraction*, 355.18 *extractive*
uprush 128.2 *spread*, 359.2 *upturn*, 610.1 *excess*
UPS 57.17 *analysis*
ups and downs 365.1 *oscillation*
upset 123.5 *be unequal*, 151.1 *disorder*, 151.17 *discomposed*, 151.22 *discompose*, 153.1 *disturbance*, 153.7 *disturb*, 153.12 *disturbed*, 244.9 *demolish*, 252.14 *displace*, 287.1 *inversion*, 287.3 *invert*, 341.4 *be repulsive*, 362.3 *bring down*, 362.12 *downthrow*, 362.22 *overthrown*, 366.1 *agitation*, 366.15 *agitated*, 366.22 *agitate*, 515.6 *disappoint*, 515.9 *disappointed*, 616.3 *inconvenience*, 616.5 *be inconvenient*, 661.8 *hinder*, 785.7 *cause dislike*
upset one's applecart 661.8 *hinder*
upset stomach 406.2 *painful condition*, 624.8 *indigestion*
upsetting 153.17 *disturbing*
up shit creek 106.8 *difficult*
upshoot 359.2 *upturn*, 359.17 *spring up*
upshot 25.2 *grip*, 155.5 *consequence*, 157.12 *end result*, 195.9 *sequel*, 227.1 *effect*, 478.6 *solution*, 684.2 *conclusion*
up side 29.2 *golfing terms*
upside 279.4 *top layer*
upside-down 151.18 *muddled*, 151.28 *anyhow*, 287.2 *inverted*, 287.4 *inversely*
upside-down cake 45.36 *cake*
upslope 359.1 *ascent*
upspin 359.13 *ascend*
upspring 261.6 *become bigger*, 359.17 *spring up*
upstage 51.15 *stage*, 51.33 *overact*, 51.41 *onstage*, 811.29 *show off*
upstairs 275.19 *high*, 359.26 *up*, 471.20 *theoretically*
upstairs and downstairs 248.16 *extensively*
upstairs maid 697.6 *domestic servant*
upstanding 281.8 *vertical*, 361.11 *raised*, 843.10 *moral*, 849.11 *in a respectful stance*, 857.4 *honourable*
upstart 30.7 *stationary rings*,

195.8 *follower*, 201.8 *new arrival*, 201.12 *immature*, 336.16 *progressive person*, 359.17 *spring up*, 807.12 *impudent person*
upstarts 30.5 *horizontal bar*
upstate 290.3, 290.9 *inland*
up sticks 345.3 *quit*
upstream 332.11 *in all directions*, 359.13 *ascend*, 359.26 *up*
upstreamward 359.26 *up*
upsurge 128.2 *spread*, 359.2 *upturn*, 359.13 *ascend*, 610.1 *excess*
upsurgence 359.2 *upturn*
upswarm 359.13 *ascend*
upsweep 359.2, 359.21 *upturn*
upsweep method 21.1 *track events*
upswing 29.3 *golf shots*, 128.2 *spread*, 359.2 *upturn*, 627.5 *improvement*
upswinging 361.7 *lift*
upsy-daisy 359.27 *alley-oop*
up the ante 42.10 *play*
up the chute 244.15 *destroyed*
up-the-middle hit 22.5 *batting terms*
up the pole 245.16 *reproductive*, 510.11 *insane*
up the river 699.15 *detained*, 702.8 *imprisoned*
up the spout 245.16 *reproductive*
up the stick 245.16 *reproductive*
upthrow 359.2 *upturn*, 361.1 *raise*, 364.6 *raising*
upthrust 361.6 *raising*
uptight 167.14 *conformist*, 699.14 *self-restrained*, 777.8 *fearful*, 829.4 *irascible*, 869.8 *self-restrained*
uptightness 666.1 *disagreement*
up to 122.9 *adequate*, 235.13 *powerful*
up to date 6.19 *knowledgeable*, 472.12 *topically*, 528.18 *informed*
up-to-date 196.6 *present*, 201.10 *new*, 336.17 *forward*, 472.6 *topical*
up-to-dateness 196, 201.1 *newness*
up to everything 657.4 *cunning*
up to here with 144.8 *full*
up to no good 858.5 *dishonourable*
up to now 194.11 *before*, 200.23 *before now*
up to one's ass 642.19 *busy*
up to one's ass in 608.3 *filled*
up to one's ears 642.19 *busy*
up to one's ears in debt 745.9 *in debt*, 747.13 *nonpaying*
up to one's eyes 277.16 *deep*, 642.19 *busy*
up to one's neck 642.19, 642.19 *busy*
up to one's neck in 608.3 *filled*
up to par 843.12 *all right*
up to snuff 608.1 *sufficient*, 617.5 *not bad*
up to something 592.15 *planning*, 858.5 *dishonourable*
up to that time 194.11 *before*
up to the ears 144.10 *fully*
up to the eyes 144.10 *fully*
up to the knees 275.19 *high*
up to the mark 122.9 *adequate*, 608.1 *sufficient*, 617.5 *not bad*
up to the minute 472.12 *topically*
up to then 194.11 *before*
up to the neck 144.10 *fully*
up to the shoulders 275.19 *high*
up to the waist 275.19 *high*
up to this moment 200.23 *before now*
up to this time 194.11 *before*, 200.23 *before now*
uptown 93.3 *city district*, 93.14 *urban*, 249.10 *urban area*, 249.18 *local*, 332.11 *in all directions*, 332.14 *directed*, 359.26 *up*
uptowner 93.11 *urbanite*
uptrend 359.2 *upturn*
uptrending 361.6 *raising*
upturn 359, 359, 128.2 *spread*,

627.5 *improvement*, 629.11 *recuperation*
upturned 359.22 *ascending*
Upuaut 8 Deities
up-unweighting 41.4 *skiing technique*
uPVC 57.21 *polymer*
upward 2.14 *socioeconomic*, 275.20 *higher*, 324.17 *directional*, 359.22 *ascending*
upward curve 128.2 *spread*
upwardly mobile 686.8 *prosperous*
upward mobility 2.7 *social stratification*, 627.5 *improvement*, 815.2 *social ambition*
upward motion 324.7 *ascending motion*, 359.1 *ascent*
upwards 359.26 *up*
upwards of 175.6 *plural*
upward trend 128.2 *spread*
up-welling 54.13 *ocean current*
upwind 332.11 *in all directions*, 332.14 *directed*, 359.13 *ascend*, 417.7 *odourlessly*
upwind of 417.3 *odourless*
upwith 359.22 *ascending*, 359.26 *up*
up you get 642.23 *rise and shine*
ura 26.10 *aikido*
uracil 58.10 *nucleoside*, 59.12 *molecular biology*
Ural 95 Mountains, **96** Rivers
Ural-Altaic 5 Languages and Groups of Languages, 5.11 *family of languages*
Uralian 5.11 *family of languages*
Uralic 5 Languages and Groups of Languages
uralite 54 Minerals
Urals 275.4 *mountain range*
uramustine 62 Medication
uranic 57.34 *elemental*
uraninite 54 Minerals
uranium 57 Chemical Elements, 56.73 *nuclear reactor*, 410.7 *nuclear power*, 604.1 *materials*
uranium–lead dating 54.42 *dating*
Uraniun 53.36 *astronomical*
uranographer 53.2 *astronomer*
uranographic 53.36 *astronomical*
uranography 53.1 *astronomy*
uranophobia 777 Phobias by Name
uranous 57.34 *elemental*
Uranus 8 Deities, **53** Planets and their Satellites, 53.16 *planet*
uranyl 57.34 *elemental*
urban 93, 2.13 *communal*, 70.5 *transportable*, 249.17 *national*, 255.12 *native*, 256.15 *environmental*
Urbana 93 Cities
urban area 249
urban blight 628.9 *dilapidation*
urban clearway 71.2 *road*
urban complex 93.1 *city*
urban culture 2.5 *society*
urban district 92.1 *administrative area*
urban dweller 93.11 *urbanite*
urbane 6.20 *refined*, 376.6 *smooth-mannered*, 657.4 *cunning*, 794.5 *refined*, 815.15 *sociable*, 817.7 *courteous*, 817.8 *good-mannered*
urbanely 6.27 *discerningly*, 376.16 *suavely*, 817.15 *genteelly*
urban environment 2.5 *society*
urban guerrilla 398.10 *killer*, 693.10, 713.5 *seditionist*
urbanism 2.5 *society*
urbanite 93, 255.4 *townsman*
urbanities 817.3 *courtesies*
urbanity 6.11 *refinement*, 794.1 *elegance*, 817.2 *good manners*
urbanization 2.5 *society*, 93.1 *city*
urbanize 93, 2.15 *socialize*
urbanized 2.13 *communal*
urbanizing 2.13 *communal*
urban planning 2.5 *society*, 63.17 *civil engineering*
urban renewal 2.5 *society*
urban sector 2.5 *society*
urban society 2.5 *society*

urban sociology 2.1 *sociology*
urban sprawl 162.7 *sprawl*, 249.10 *urban area*
urban spread 93.1 *city*
Urbanus 8 Deities
urceole 10.14 *sacred object*
urchin 206.7 *young man*, 622.6 *dirty person*
Urd 8 Deities
Urdu 5 Languages and Groups of Languages
Ure 96 Rivers
urea 353.6 *urine*
urea-formaldehyde 604.1 *materials*
ureter 322.7 *passageway*
ureterectomy 60 Surgical Operations
ureteroenterostomy 60 Surgical Operations
ureteroneocystostomy 60 Surgical Operations
ureteroplasty 60 Surgical Operations
ureteroscope 60.7 *diagnosis*
ureteroscopy 60.7 *diagnosis*
ureterosigmoidostomy 60 Surgical Operations
ureterostomy 60 Surgical Operations
ureterotomy 60 Surgical Operations
urethane 62 Medication, **62** Medication
urethra 322.4 *body orifice*
urethroplasty 60 Surgical Operations
urethrostomy 60 Surgical Operations
urethrotomy 60 Surgical Operations
Urey 52 Scientists
urge 61.15 *compulsion*, 330.1 *impel*, 510.4 *delusion*, 518.6 *propound*, 554.6 *emphasize*, 574.10 *insist*, 586.15 *persuade*, 648.1 *hasten*, 648.4 *haste*, 654.5 *advise*, 695.1 *compulsion*, 695.6 *compel*, 712.6 *request*, 782.1 *desire*
urged 228.12 *motivated*
urge forward 329.7 *hurry someone up*
urgency 154.2 *priority*, 191.1 *immediacy*, 237.3 *intensity*, 554.1 *emphasis*, 571.1 *necessity*, 593.3 *needfulness*, 611.1 *importance*, 633.5 *danger*, 648.4 *haste*, 712.1 *request*
urgent 191.5 *immediate*, 191.6 *allowing no delay*, 237.10 *potent*, 554.3 *emphatic*, 571.9 *necessary*, 574.2 *tenacious*, 593.6 *demanding*, 611.5 *important*, 648.3 *hasty*, 695.9 *compelling*, 712.9 *requesting*
urgently 237.15 *acutely*, 554.7 *emphatically*, 571.20 *with need*, 593.12 *in need*, 611.9 *importantly*, 648.6 *hastily*, 695.11 *compellingly*, 712.12 *by request*
urge on 329.7 *hurry someone up*
urge to set the world to rights 833.2 *public spiritedness*
urging 586.2 *flattery*, 712.1 *request*
Uriah Heep 362.15 *debasement*, 673.2 *appeaser*, 806.16 *humble person*, 808.3, 853.7 *sycophant*
uric acid 353.6 *urine*
uricosumic 62.17 *stimulating*
Uriel 8.6 *angel*
urinal 353.13 *lavatory*, 727.7 *toilet*
urinary 353
urinate 353, 349.14 *let out*, 389.32 *seep*, 767.13 *relieve oneself*
urination 353, 389.4 *exudate*
urinative 353.26 *urinary*
urine 777 Phobias by Topic, **353**, 387.3 *body fluid*, 389.4 *exudate*, 419.2 *something that makes an unpleasant smell*
urine sample 60.7 *diagnosis*
urinometer 353.3 *urination*

Urmia **94** Lakes, 94.5 *other major lakes*
urn 44.8 *ceramic object*, 258.11 *vessel*, 399.4 *funeral objects*, 399.8 *bury*
urn burial 399.1 *burial*
urned 399.10 *buried*
Urochordata 81.2 *protochordate*
urochordate 81.2 *protochordate*, 81.16 *invertebrate*
Urodela *or* Caudata 79.7 *amphibian*
urodele 79.7 *amphibian*
urogenital disease 624.4 *disease*
urological 60.22 *medical*
urologist 60.13 *medical specialist*
urology 60.3 *medical specialty*
uronic acid 58.3 *carbohydrate*
urophobia **777** Phobias by Name
Ursa Major **53** The Constellations
Ursa Minor **53** The Constellations
ursid 77.8 *flesh-eating mammal*
Ursidae 77.8 *flesh-eating mammal*
Ursids **53** Meteor Showers
ursine 77.28 *carnivorous*
Ursuline **7** Members of Religious Orders
urticaria 624.13 *skin disease*
urua **49** Musical Instruments
Uruguay **91** Countries, **96** Rivers
urus **77** Placental Mammals
us 165.12 *I*, 400.1 *humankind*
usability **613**, 615.3 *convenience*
usable **599, 613**, 101.8 *practical*, 230.10 *operational*, 615.1 *convenient*
usably 599.11, 613.12 *usefully*
US administrative council **653**
usage 10.1 *ritual*, 520.4 *type of meaning*, 584.1 *habit*, 584.4 *custom*, 599.6 *use*, 613.5 *usefulness*, 719.3 *performance*
US Air Force 679.29 *air force*
US Army 679.15 *army*
US Capitol **43** Noted Buildings
US Constitution 225.4 *stable thing*
US court **16**
US dish **45**
use **599, 599**, 230.9 *take action*, 232.1 *instrumentality*, 520.5 *point*, 584.1 *habit*, 593.9 *find necessary*, 611.1 *importance*, 613.5 *usefulness*, 613.11 *find useful*, 627.1 *improve*, 640.1 *action*, 640.4 *act*, 652.11 *conduct oneself*, 655.1 *skill*, 662.1 *help*, 748.2 *consume*, 808.15 *sponge*, 861.13 *benefit*
Use **599**
use a compass 74.9 *navigate*
use a condom 247.9 *practise birth control*, 661.9 *block*
use a credit card 733.10 *buy on credit*
use a crib 524.12 *translate*
use a delayed dribble 31.9 *play hockey*
use a diagonal stride 41.14 *ski*
use a diplomatic excuse 538.21 *lie*
use a footpath 327.14 *find one's way*
use aikido techniques 26.13 *do martial arts*
use a pedestrian crossing 327.14 *find one's way*
use a pony 524.12 *translate*
use a pretext 538.24 *pretend*
use as a doormat 701.6 *subject*
use as a meal ticket 808.15 *sponge*
use a sextant 74.9 *navigate*
use a sharp tool **380**
use a sledgehammer to crack a nut 601.1 *misuse*
use as one's own 733.8 *adopt*
use a subterfuge 538.24 *pretend*

use a triangular offence 31.9 *play hockey*
use a trot 524.12 *translate*
use a turning stroke 36.17 *canoe*
use backspin 29.7 *golf*
use bad language 827.5 *curse*
use bait 20.7 *angle*
use billingsgate 827.5 *curse*
use body language 543.11 *gesture*
use brute force 235.11 *be powerful*, 378.10 *be tough*, 690.6 *suppress*
use bully-boy tactics 832.18 *torment*
use cold steel 674.12 *fight*
use combined tactics 34.9 *mountaineer*
use common speech 556.7 *be simple*
used **599, 748**, 584.14 *habituated*, 601.4 *misused*
used car 599.7 *reused product*
use dead reckoning 74.9 *navigate*
use diplomacy 817.11 *have good manners*
used stamp 139.3 *nonadhesive thing*
used up 236.12 *impotent*, 238.9 *dilapidated*, 599.9 *used*, 600.4 *disused*, 748.13 *used*
use earplugs 421.10 *muffle*
use every muscle 644.8 *exert oneself*
use expletives 827.5 *curse*
use few words 566.8 *be taciturn*
use footwork 28.5 *fence*
use force 235.10 *be powerful*, 237.8 *strengthen*, 241.8 *use violence*
use force against 695.7 *force*
useful **613**, 230.11 *workable*, 232.6 *instrumental*, 478.15 *correspondent*, 599.10 *usable*, 611.5 *important*, 615.1 *convenient*, 617.4 *worthwhile*, 640.6 *effective*, 660.10 *feasible*, 662.33 *helpful*, 721.15 *gainful*, 819.12 *favourable*, 861.6 *beneficial*
usefully **599, 613, 861**, 230.13 *operationally*, 232.9 *instrumentally*, 478.26 *correspondingly*, 640.8 *effectively*, 662.36 *helpfully*, 819.20 *favourably*
usefulness **613**, 232.1 *instrumentality*, 478.28 *correspondence*, 599.6 *use*, 611.1 *importance*, 615.3 *convenience*, 662.10 *helpfulness*, 861.13 *benefit*
Usefulness **613**
useful work 63.10 *work*
use gobbledegook 551.3 *make obscure*
use language **9**
use lateral thinking 461.15 *think about*
useless **614**, 236.10 *powerless*, 600.1 *unused*, 607.9 *waste*, 612.4 *trivial*, 616.1 *inconvenient*, 618.1 *worthless*, 628.12 *deteriorated*, 683.10 *failed*, 754.10 *shoddy*, 776.7 *futile*, 838.5 *thankless*
useless exercise 642.9 *overactivity*
useless expenditure 607.3 *waste*
useless gesture 640.2 *deed*
uselessly **614**, 236.14 *powerlessly*, 600.12 *out of use*, 607.10 *wastefully*, 616.6 *inconveniently*, 683.12 *unsuccessfully*, 838.7 *ungratefully*
uselessness **614**, 236.1 *powerlessness*, 610.3 *superfluity*, 612.7 *triviality*, 618.7 *worthlessness*, 683.1 *failure*
Uselessness **614**
useless work 642.9 *overactivity*
use long words 553.5 *be diffuse*, 557.5 *ornament*
use Morse code 543.12 *signal*
use muscle 237.8 *strengthen*
use obscene language 827.5 *curse*
use of machinery 232.1 *instrumentality*

use one's authority 12.11 *govern*
use one's best endeavours 644.8 *exert oneself*
use one's brain 461.12 *think*
use one's brute strength 235.10 *be powerful*
use one's connections 232.5 *find means*
use one's eyes 435.12 *see*
use one's good offices 232.4 *be an instrument*
use one's head 459.13 *be intelligent*, 461.12 *think*, 507.7 *be wise*
use one's imagination 519.14 *imagine*
use one's influence 232.4 *be an instrument*
use one's initiative 507.7 *be wise*
use one's own initiative 698.16 *be independent*
use people 599.3 *exploit*
use physical force 695.7 *force*
use plain English 556.7 *be simple*
use plain words 322.22 *be open*, 520.10 *mean*
use profanity 827.5 *curse*
user **599**
user-friendly 65.20 *on-line*, 660.11 *made easy*
use short words 522.5 *simplify*
use sign language 421.8 *be deaf*, 524.12 *translate*, 543.11 *gesture*, 563.14 *have difficulty speaking*
use signs **543**
use simple language 522.5 *simplify*
use skilfully 655.10 *be skilful*
use soft words 817.10 *be courteous*
use strong words 535.21 *be assertive*
use symbols 543.9 *use signs*
use tact 817.10 *be courteous*
use tactics 640.4 *act*
use terrorist tactics 713.8 *cause mischief*
use the back-and-knee technique 34.9 *mountaineer*
use the backboard 23.6 *play basketball*
use the bathroom 767.13 *relieve oneself*
use the bottom gear 33.10 *be on the track*
use the crossover recovery 36.19 *punt*
use the C-shape shove 36.19 *punt*
use the hockey stop 41.14 *ski*
use the knife 630.20 *doctor*
use therapy 629.6 *cure*
use the services of 599.2 *frequent*
use the side entrance 327.14 *find one's way*
use the tradesman's entrance 327.14 *find one's way*
use the tuck position 41.14 *ski*
use the vernacular 549.9 *style*
use the windmill stroke 36.19 *punt*
use to advantage 599.3 *exploit*
use tools **603**
use to the full 599.3 *exploit*
use tricks of the trade 539.28 *trick*
use unnecessary roughness 31.9 *play hockey*
use up 218.8 *cause to cease*, 236.7 *remove power from*, 593.9 *find necessary*, 599.1 *use*, 599.5 *dispose of*, 628.5 *hurt*, 748.2 *consume*, 757.7 *waste*
use up one's credit 748.1 *expend*
use violence **241**, 695.7 *force*
use wrongly 601.1 *misuse*
US government **653**, 12.4 *governing body*
U-shape 310.1 *angle*
U-shaped valley 54.7 *landform*
Ushas **8** Deities
usher **180**, 51.26 *stagehand*, 180.15 *escort*, 348.8 *show in*, 652.10 *conductor*, 652.15 *con-*

duct, 697.3 *attendant*, 823.7 *bridal party*
ushered 180.20 *accompanied*
usherette 51.26 *stagehand*
usher in 154.19 *forecast*, 348.8 *show in*, 517.11 *predict*, 730.10 *receive someone*
using 602.7 *by means of*
using as one's own 733.2 *adoption*
using force 712.12 *by request*
using racing skis 41.17 *on a ski run*
using short words 522.2 *simple*
using simple language 522.2 *simple*
using strength 378.12 *toughly*
using up 607.3 *waste*
US inhabitant **255**
US judge **16**
Usk **93** Cities, **96** Rivers
US lakes **94**
US law officer **16**
US mountains **95**
US National Guard 17.2 *the military*
US National War College 17.3 *military training*
US of A 91.7 *United States*
US Open 40.1 *tennis*
US police **16**
US Postal Service 534.2 *postal communication*
US rivers **96**
US Savings Bond 741.14 *paper money*
US Soccer Football Association 38.1 *soccer*
US Supreme Court 16.21 *US court*
Ustyurt **98** Deserts
usual 116.15 *conventional*, 124.1 *average*, 150.15 *habitual*, 164.21 *common*, 166.10 *customary*, 167.15 *everyday*, 556.1 *simple*, 584.9 *habitual*, 612.4 *trivial*, 787.4 *predictable*
usually **164**, 116.37 *conventionally*, 124.11 *on average*, 166.18 *as a rule*, 212.1 *frequently*, 584.19 *habitually*, 787.10 *predictably*
usualness 164.5 *averageness*, 201.1 *newness*, 556.4 *simplicity*, 787.2 *predictability*
usual policy 584.6 *procedure*
usual text 524.1 *interpretation*
usual way 327.1 *way*
usufruct 599.6 *use*
usurer 721.7 *gainer*, 732.3 *lender*, 741.17 *financier*, 744.5 *lender*, 753.5 *overcharger*
usurious 732.6 *loaned*, 753.7 *dear*
usuriously 753.12 *dearly*
usurp 12.12 *take authority*, 155.22 *succeed*, 252.16 *replace*, 349.5 *take the place of*, 357.5 *transgress*, 668.6 *be insubordinate*, 689.4 *be anarchic*, 734.7 *take*, 846.14 *arrogate*
usurpation 16.41 *lawlessness*, 357.8 *transgression*, 688.3 *acquisition of power*, 689.1 *anarchy*, 734.1 *taking*, 846.3 *arrogation*
usurpative 846.9 *presumptive*
usurp authority 689.4 *be anarchic*
usurper **846**, 155.13 *replacement*, 668.4 *defiant person*, 734.6 *taker*
usurp power 688.20 *take authority*
usurp the throne 12.12 *take authority*
usury 721.1 *gain*, 732.1 *lending*, 745.4 *interest*, 753.4 *extortion*
US Weather Bureau 55.4 *weather forecast*
Utah **92** American States, **94** Lakes
Ute **1** Peoples, **5** Languages and Groups of Languages
utensil 603.1 *tool*
utensils 258.16 *crockery*, 603.6 *equipment*
uterine 290.10 *visceral*
uterus 77.5 *placental mammal*,

245.8 *organs of reproduction,*
290.4 *insides*
uti 49 Musical Instruments
Utica 93 Cities
utilitarian 4.11 *follower of a doctrine,* 4.14 *of a philosophy,*
101.8 *practical,* 599.9 *used,*
613.1 *useful,* 662.33 *helpful,*
833.3 *philanthropist,* 833.6 *philanthropic*
utilitarianism 4.7 *school of
thought,* 613.5 *usefulness,*
615.3 *convenience,* 833.2 *public
spiritedness*
utilities 751.6 *business costs*
utility 232.1 *instrumentality,*
599.6 *use,* 611.1 *importance,*
613.5 *usefulness,* 615.3 *convenience,* 662.10 *helpfulness*
utility principle 4.8 *philosophical
term*
utility room 256.7 *room*
utilizable 232.6 *instrumental,*
599.10 *usable*
utilization 599.6 *use,* 613.5 *usefulness*
utilize 599.1 *use,* 613.1 *find useful*
utilized 599.9 *used*
uti possidetis 723.2 *legal terms*
utmost 126.14 *best*
utmost height 279.1 *summit*
utmost speed 329.8 *speed*
Uto-Aztecan 5 Languages and
Groups of Languages
utopia 48.2 *fiction*
Utopia 471.6 *ideal,* 494.2 *overestimate,* 519.8 *dreamland,* 714.4
promised land, 775.3 *aspiration,*
786.4 *wonder*
utopian 4.11 *follower of a doctrine,* 4.14 *of a philosophy,*
102.11 *unrealistic,* 471.9 *person
of ideas,* 471.13 *ideal,* 775.5
hoper, 833.3 *philanthropist*
Utopian 519.9 *visionary,* 519.10
imaginative, 627.12 *reformer,*
627.16 *improving*
utopianism 4.7 *school of thought,*
102.4 *theorization,* 471.7 *idealism*
Utopianism 519.7 *idealism,*
627.11 *reformism*
Utrecht 93 Cities
utter 5.45 *use language,* 134.16
simple, 144.7 *complete,* 505.3
aphorize, 530.6 *divulge,* 535.17
affirm, 564.11 *speak,* 619.1 *perfect,* 684.7 *completed,* 741.24
monetize
utterance 564, 535.2 *statement,*
564.4 *articulation*
utter bore 788.2 *boring thing,*
788.3 *boring person*
utter defeat 683.2 *defeat*
utter devotion 574.13 *concentration*
uttered 535.11 *stated,* 564.16
speech
utterer 564.10 *speaker*
utter failure 244.4 *ruin*
utter loss 722.1 *loss*
utterly 142.11 *wholly,* 144.9,
619.8 *completely,* 621.20 *clean,*
684.9 *completely*
utterly bad 618.3 *bad*
utterly detest 822.14 *hate*
utter nonsense 521.4 *senseless
talk*
utter profanities 822.17 *anger*
U-tube 57 Laboratory Apparatus
U-turn 71.21 *miscellaneous motoring terms,* 216.1 *change,*
221.1 *reversion,* 311.2 *bend,*
337.13 *about-turn,* 363.2 *circuitousness,* 363.6 *orbit,* 484.2 *reversal,* 578.6 *equivocation,*
734.2 *taking back,* 858.2 *faithlessness*
UVA 55.22 *sun,* 56.13 *electromagnetic radiation*
UVB 55.22 *sun,* 56.13 *electromagnetic radiation*
UV filter 66.20 *filter*
uvula 564.5 *organ of speech*
uxoricide 398.3 *homicide,*
398.11 *murderer*

uxorious 821.17 *loving*
uxoriousness 821.2 *romantic love*
Uzbek 5 Languages and Groups
of Languages
Uzbekistan 91 Countries
uzi 680.11 *guns*
Uzza 8 Deities

V

V-1 680.5 *missile weapon,*
680.16 *bomb*
V-2 680.5 *missile weapon,*
680.16 *bomb*
V-8 juice 351.6 *soft drink*
vacancy 100.4, 254.3 *emptiness,*
322.10 *opportunity,* 460.1 *lack
of intellect,* 462.1 *lack of
thought,* 512.2 *blankness,* 612.5
unimportance
vacant 254, 100.9 *nonexistent,*
254.14 *unoccupied,* 322.13
opened up, 460.5 *lacking intellect,* 462.8 *thoughtless,* 512.9
blank, 536.14 *nonexistent,*
600.3 *not wanted,* 609.2 *unprovided,* 643.2 *not working*
vacantly 254.20 *absently,* 322.26
openly, 460.11 *unintelligently,*
512.16 *obliviously*
vacant moments 645.1 *leisure*
vacate 254.16 *absent oneself,*
254.19 *leave empty,* 345.2,
598.2 *withdraw,* 705.5 *resign*
vacate one's seat 359.16 *stand
up*
vacation 214.5 *regular thing,*
214.7 *be regular,* 218.3, 218.9
pause, 254.5 *leave of absence,*
645.2 *time off,* 649.1 *ease,*
649.4 *at ease,* 651.6 *refresher,*
702.4 *prison sentence,* 708.2 *permit*
vacation time 15.2 *industrial negotiations*
vaccinate 60.19 *practise medicine,* 354.2 *inject,* 625.6 *make
hygienic,* 630.20 *doctor,* 632.9
protect
vaccinated 354.13 *injected,*
625.4 *hygienic,* 632.5 *safe*
vaccination 60.6 *health care,*
354.9 *injection,* 625.1 *hygiene,*
630.3 *prophylactic,* 632.2 *protection*
vaccine 630.3 *prophylactic*
vaccinophobia 777 Phobias by
Name
vacillate 365, 576, 216.7 *be
changed,* 224.12 *be irresolute,*
484.8 *reverse,* 491.19 *hesitate,*
578.2 *equivocate,* 579.5 *be capricious,* 671.25 *stall*
vacillating 365, 576, 216.11
changeable, 224.14 *irresolute,*
238.12 *weak-willed,* 491.2 *irresolute,* 578.11 *equivocating*
vacillatingly 216.15 *changeably*
vacillation 365, 576, 216.2
change of mind, 224.2 *irresolution,* 491.11 *irresoluteness,*
578.6 *equivocation*
Vacillation 576
vacillatory 365.15 *vacillating*
vacuity 100.4, 254.3 *emptiness,*
372.3 *sparseness,* 460.1 *lack of
intellect,* 462.1 *lack of thought,*
512.2 *blankness,* 521.1 *lack of
meaning,* 536.5 *nonexistence*
vacuole 59.8 *cell organ*
vacuous 254.13 *vacant,* 372.1
sparse, 460.5 *lacking intellect,*
462.8 *thoughtless,* 512.9 *blank,*
521.10 *meaningless,* 536.14
nonexistent
vacuously 254.20 *absently,*
372.7 *sparsely,* 460.11 *unintelligently,* 512.16 *obliviously*
vacuousness 372.3 *sparseness*
vacuum 56.7 *space,* 57.20 *surface chemistry,* 100.4, 254.3
emptiness, 355.14 *suck,* 372.1

sparse, 372.5 *gas,* 536.5 *nonexistence,* 621.13 *clean*
vacuum cleaner 621.10 *cleaning
object*
vacuum-distil 57.25 *solidify*
vacuum filtration 57.5 *process*
vacuum flask 351.10 *drink container,* 637.2 *preserver*
vacuum gauge 56.88 *barometer,*
57.20 *surface chemistry*
vacuuming 355.4 *sucking,* 621.2
cleaning
vacuum-packed 323.12 *closed,*
619.1 *perfect,* 632.6 *invulnerable*
vacuum-packed food 350.7 *food,*
637.3 *preserved thing*
vacuum pump 57.20 *surface
chemistry,* 355.9 *extractor*
vacuum-sealed 632.6 *invulnerable*
vacuum still 57 Laboratory Apparatus
vacuum tube 235.7 *electrical
power*
vade mecum 528.5 *reference book*
Vadodara 93 Cities
vagabond 816.7 *outsider*
vagary 168.6 *deviation,* 506.3
tomfoolery, 519.4 *ideality,*
579.3 *whim*
vagina 245.8 *organs of reproduction,* 322.4 *body orifice*
vaginal 245.16 *reproductive*
vaginoplasty 60 Surgical Operations
vagotomy 60 Surgical Operations
vagrancy 335.16 *wandering*
vagrant 168.7 *nonconformist,*
224.7 *person who moves
around,* 224.13 *changeable,*
335.25 *wandering,* 622.6 *dirty
person,* 643.8 *nonworker,* 712.5
beggar, 743.10 *poor person*
vague 482, 102.8 *unreal,*
164.20 *generalized,* 307.5 *shapeless,* 375.5 *unfinished,* 441.6
murky, 443.2 *shady,* 491.6 *indeterminate,* 523.4 *difficult,*
531.17 *noncommittal,* 542.16
imperceptible, 551.2 *obscure,*
566.3 *sparing with words,*
578.10 *equivocal*
vaguely 375.15 *incompletely,*
441.12 *dimly,* 482.14 *indiscriminately,* 491.25 *indeterminately,*
542.27 *imperceptibly,* 551.4 *obscurely*
vagueness 307.1 *shapelessness,*
375.10 *rough idea,* 441.2 *murk,*
482.8 *indiscriminateness,*
490.19, 491.14 *indeterminacy,*
531.5 *evasion,* 542.7 *imperceptibility,* 551.1 *obscurity,*
578.5 *equivocalness*
vague suspicion 518.3 *conjecture*
vain 809, 811, 358.7 *short,*
521.11 *aimless,* 614.2, 776.7 *futile,* 805.17 *conceited,* 860.5 *egoistic,* 870.9 *self-absorbed*
Vainamoinen 8 Deities
vain attempt 683.1 *failure*
vain expectation 515.1 *disappointment*
vainglorious 805.17 *conceited,*
809.10 *self-admiring*
vaingloriously 809.19 *vainly*
vaingloriousness 809.4 *self-admiration*
vainglory 805.3 *conceit*
vain labour 722.3 *waste*
vainly 809.19, 811, 358.11 *in
vain,* 494.7 *overoptimistically,*
860.9 *egoistically*
vainness 809.1 *vanity*
vain person 809, 526.12 *displayer,* 805.13 *proud person*
vain pride 809.1 *vanity*
vair 544.8 *heraldic device*
Vaisesika 4.7 *school of thought*
Vajrayna 7 Non-Christian Religions
valance 300.2 *edging,* 293.10
bed covering
valanced 300.9 *skirting*
vale 98.6 *lowland,* 98.8 *valley,*
317.2 *concave land*

valediction 345.9 *parting,* 567.2
salutation, 817.3 *courtesies*
valedictorian 682.4 *successful person,* 730.5 *recipient*
valedictory 345.9 *parting,*
345.11 *departing,* 564.8 *speech,*
567.2 *salutation,* 567.14 *vocative*
valedictory address 345.9 *parting,* 567.2 *salutation*
valence 57
valence band 56.44 *semiconductor*
valence bond 57.11 *chemical
bond*
valence-bond theory 57.12 *valence*
Valencia 93 Cities
valency 57.12 *valence*
valentine 821.11 *loved one,*
821.15 *love item,* 826.3 *love
token*
valentines 223.3 *something in exchange*
vale of tears 862.2 *affliction*
valerian 84 Flowers and Flowering Plants
valeric 58 Common Fatty Acids
Valéry 48 Poets
valet 295, 621.13 *clean,* 629.3
restore, 697.3 *attendant*
valeta 46.2 *dance*
valeting 637.1 *preservation*
valetudinarian 624.19 *sick person,* 624.21 *unhealthy*
valetudinarianism 624.1 *ill health*
Valhalla 368.1 *nonmaterial
world,* 714.4 *promised land*
valiance 778.1 *courage*
valiant 778.9 *courageous*
valiant effort 596.5 *attempt*
valiantly 596.10 *ambitiously,*
778.18 *courageously*
valid 3.19 *chronicled,* 16.44
legal, 52.86 *logical,* 101.6 *real,*
116.18 *permitting,* 235.14 *operative,* 463.10 *causal,* 537.19 *authentic,* 613.2 *usable,* 843.8 *correct*
valid argument 52.64 *reasoning*
validate 16.65 *make legal,* 52.89
theorize, 101.12 *establish reality,* 116.28 *consent,* 225.7 *make
stable,* 475.17 *prove,* 480.1 *verify,* 483.12 *prove,* 499.4 *assent,*
535.19 *confirm,* 537.30 *prove
true,* 708.3 *permit*
validated 116.18 *permitting,*
480.10 *verified,* 499.7 *agreed,*
535.13 *supported,* 537.20 *proved*
validating 480.9 *verificatory*
validation 16.31 *legislation,*
52.64 *reasoning,* 480.4 *verification,* 499.2 *yes,* 535.4, 537.7
confirmation, 708.1 *permission*
validatory 535.10 *affirmative*
validity 3.14 *historicalness,*
16.28 *legality,* 52.64 *reasoning,*
101.1 *reality,* 235.1 *power,*
490.9 *certainty,* 537.6 *authenticity,* 843.2 *correctness*
validly 3.25 *reportedly,* 16.81 *legally*
valid point 463.4 *explanation*
valiha 49 Musical Instruments
valine 58 Amino Acids
valise 258.9 *baggage*
Valium 630.8 *drug,* 631.11 *intoxicant*
Valkyrie 679.10 *woman soldier*
Valla 2 Philosophers
Valletta 93 Cities
valley 98, 54.7 *landform,* 265.3
gulf, 276.2 *lowland,* 277.4 *deep
thing,* 317.2 *concave land*
valley floor 54.7 *landform*
Valley Girl 617.7 *elite*
valley glacier 54.38 *glacier*
valley of the shadow of death
397.7 *dying day*
valley wind 55.12 *wind*
vallum 671.11 *fortification*
valorization 751.7 *tax*
valorous 778.9 *courageous*
valour 778.1 *courage*
Valparaíso 93 Cities

valproic acid 62 *Medication*
valuable 617, 753, 611.5 *important*, 613.4 *profitable*, 662.34 *beneficial*, 861.1 *good*
valuableness 753.6 *value*
valuables 725.5 *personal estate*
valuably 753
valuate 751.11 *price*
valuation 121.3 *gradation*, 268.1 *measurement*, 492.1 *judgment*, 751.2 *value*
valuator 268.9 *measurer*
value 751, 753, 52.14 *operation*, 121.1 *degree*, 122.3 *equalization*, 268.4 *size*, 268.10 *measure*, 444.3 *hue*, 492.12 *estimate*, 520.1 *meaning*, 520.5 *point*, 611.1 *importance*, 611.8 *make important*, 613.6 *usability*, 617.6 *worth*, 750.7 *account*, 751.11 *price*, 821.23 *love*, 849.15 *respect*, 851.11 *approve*, 861.8 *good*
value-added tax 13.6 *economic factors*, 749.2 *money received*
valued 121.7 *gradational*, 268.13 *measured*, 617.1 *worthy*, 617.3 *valuable*, 751.14 *priced*, 849.12 *respected*
valued at 751.14 *priced*
value for money 754.1 *cheapness*
value judgment 4.2 *philosophical system*, 4.8 *philosophical term*, 492.1 *judgment*
valueless 612.4 *trivial*, 614.1 *useless*, 618.1 *worthless*, 754.10 *shoddy*
valuer 268.9 *measurer*, 492.5 *judge*
values 2.3 *social environment*, 50.4 *treatment*
value system 2.3 *social environment*, 4.2 *philosophical system*
valuta 14.1, 741.7 *finance*
valve 64.20 *electron tube*, 235.7 *electrical power*, 323.2 *stopper*
valvotomy 60 *Surgical Operations*
valvular lesion 624.10 *cardiovascular disease*
Vaman 8 *Deities*
vambrace 671.7 *armour*
Vamcharin 7 *Non-Christian Religions*
vamoose 254.18 *abscond*, 345.4 *hurry off*, 345.15 *go*, 349.33 *go away*, 458.2 *depart*, 638.5 *escape*
vamoosed 254.9 *away*
vamp 228.7 *motivator*, 340.6 *charmer*, 583.3 *improvise*, 586.13 *tempter*, 821.9 *lover*, 821.26 *court*, 826.5 *courting person*, 826.8 *court*
vampire 11.11 *ghost*, 734.6 *taker*
vampire bat 77 *Placental Mammals*
vampiric 11.15 *witchlike*
vampirish 11.15 *witchlike*
vampirism 11.3 *witchcraft*
vamp up 627.1 *improve*
van 71 *Motor Vehicles*, 40.4 *tennis terms*, 71.20 *truck*, 72.6 *rolling stock*, 201.6 *avant-garde*, 258.10 *cart*, 326.5 *means of transport*, 679.14 *armed forces*
Van 94 *Lakes*
vanadic 57.34 *elemental*
vanadinite 54 *Minerals*
vanadium 57 *Chemical Elements*
vanadous 57.34 *elemental*
Van Allen 52 *Scientists*
Van Allen belt 390.3 *atmospheric layers*
Van Allen belts 53.16 *planet*, 54.47 *radiation belt*
Vancouver 93 *Cities*, 98 *Islands*
vandal 151.11 *troublemaker*, 241.4 *violent person or animal*, 244.6 *destroyer*, 309.5 *defacer*, 607.7 *destroyer*, 832.8 *malefactor*
Vandal 244.6 *destroyer*
vandalism 151.8 *lawlessness*, 241.2 *physical violence*, 244.3 *destructiveness*, 607.4 *destruc-*

tion, 693.2 *violation of the law*, 832.2 *cruelness*
vandalize 244.10, 607.2 *lay waste*, 628.4 *impair*, 693.15 *be disobedient*
Vandals 200.6 *people of the past*
Van de Graaff 53 *Lunar Features*
Van de Graaff accelerator 56.94 *particle accelerator*
Van de Graaff generator 56 *Named Laws*, 64.30 *generator*
Van der Post 48 *Writers*
van der Waals 52 *Scientists*
van der Waals equation 56 *Named Laws*, 56.38 *thermodynamics*
van der Waals force 57 *Named Reactions*, 57.11 *chemical bond*
Vandyke brown 449.4 *brown pigment*
Vandyke collar 295.14 *neckwear*, 319.2 *notched thing*
vane 78.17 *plumage*
Vänern 94 *Lakes*
vang 36.3 *parts of a sailing boat*
vanguard 154.2 *priority*, 154.8 *precursor*, 201.6 *avant-garde*, 303.1 *front*, 632.3 *protector*, 636.4 *warner*, 671.14 *guard*, 679.14 *armed forces*
vanilla 45 *Herbs and Spices*, 413.5 *herbs*, 418.2 *fragrant thing*
Vanir 8 *Deities*
vanish 52.94 *order*, 100.13 *cease to exist*, 162.11 *explode*, 172.8 *not exist*, 189.4 *be transient*, 254.18 *abscond*, 345.3 *quit*, 438.7 *become invisible*, 458.1 *disappear*, 531.11 *conceal oneself*, 638.5 *escape*
vanished 100.11 *no more*, 172.7 *null*, 254.9 *away*, 458.7 *disappeared*
vanisher 438.5 *invisible thing*
vanishing 438.4 *invisibility*, 458.4 *disappearance*, 458.6 *disappearing*, 638.1 *escape*
vanishing cream 134.3 *purifier*, 438.5 *invisible thing*
vanishing into thin air 638.1 *escape*
vanishing point 50.4 *treatment*, 66.18 *exposure time*, 263.3 *distant place*, 342.3 *convergent view*, 438.6 *that which makes invisible*, 458.4 *disappearance*
vanishing trick 458.4 *disappearance*
vanish into thin air 189.4 *be transient*, 531.11 *conceal oneself*, 638.5 *escape*
vanishment 254.2 *disappearance*
vanitas 50.10 *art subject*
vanity 809, 494.1 *overestimation*, 614.4 *futility*, 805.3 *conceit*, 811.10 *exhibitionism*, 860.2 *egoism*, 870.4 *self-absorption*
Vanity 809
vanity of vanities 614.4 *futility*
vanomycin 62 *Medication*
vanquish 682.9 *be victorious*, 696.14 *master*, 701.7 *defeat*
vanquisher 682.5 *victorious person*
vantage 126.3 *advantage*
vantage ground 126.3 *advantage*, 235.1 *power*, 652.9 *tactics*
vantage point 692, 126.3 *advantage*, 275.8 *high thing*
Van't Hoff 52 *Scientists*
van't Hoff factor 57 *Named Reactions*
Vanuatu 91 *Countries*
vapid 542.17 *insipid*, 555.1 *unemphatic*
vapidity 412.1 *tastelessness*, 542.8 *insipidness*, 555.2 *lack of emphasis*
vapidly 542.26 *insipidly*, 555.3 *unemphatically*
vapidness 412.1 *tastelessness*
vaporescent 388.23 *volatile*
vaporific 388.23 *volatile*
vaporimeter 388, 268.8 *meter*
vaporing 388.19 *smoky*

vaporizable 388.23 *volatile*
vaporization 388, 56.37 *temperature*, 162.3 *dilution*, 355.7 *obtaining an extract*, 370.5 *lightness*, 458.4 *disappearance*, 607.3 *waste*
vaporize 57.25 *solidify*, 100.14 *cause not to exist*, 162.14 *dilute*, 244.8 *destroy*, 349.14 *let out*, 355.17 *obtain an extract*, 370.10 *lighten*, 372.6 *make sparse*, 388.25 *gasify*, 392.17 *dry*, 408.15 *burn*, 442.11 *be transparent*, 458.3 *cause to disappear*, 546.1 *obliterate*, 607.1 *waste*
vaporized 162.27 *dilute*, 546.6 *obliterated*
vaporizer 388, 389.12 *sprinkler*
vaporosity 388.7 *gaseousness*
vaporous 372.1 *sparse*, 388.16 *gaseous*, 442.2 *translucent*, 519.12 *imaginary*
vaporously 388.28 *aerily*
vaporousness 388.7 *gaseousness*, 442.6 *translucency*
vapour 388.1 *gas*, 388.7 *gaseousness*, 389.3 *wateriness*, 416.1 *odour*, 442.8 *transparent thing*, 519.5 *fantasy*, 521.9 *talk nonsense*
vapourability 388.8 *volatility*
vapourable 388.23 *volatile*
vapour bath 621.6 *bath*
vapouriness 388.7 *gaseousness*
vapouring 521.5 *empty talk*, 555.1 *unemphatic*
vapourish 388.16 *gaseous*
vapourizability 388.8 *volatility*
vapour-like 388.16 *gaseous*
vapourous 57.32 *solid*
vapour pressure 56.10 *force*
vapour trail 483.4 *indication*
vapoury 388.16 *gaseous*
var 75 *Scientific and Technical Units*
vara 75 *Some Foreign Units*
Varah 8 *Deities*
Varanasi 93 *Cities*
Varèse 49 *Musicians and Composers*
Vargas Llosa 48 *Writers*
variability 113.1 *diversity*, 123.1 *inequality*, 215.1 *irregularity*, 224.1 *changeableness*, 491.16 *capriciousness*, 576.12 *inconstancy*, 579.2 *caprice*
variable 52.25 *algebraic expression*, 52.77 *given*, 106.7 *circumstantial*, 113.5 *diverse*, 120.5 *numbers*, 120.6 *quantitative*, 123.3 *unequal*, 169.1 *number*, 215.4 *irregular*, 216.11 *changeable*, 224.3 *changeable thing*, 224.13 *changeable*, 491.8 *capricious*, 576.2 *changeable*, 579.1 *capricious*
variableness 215.1 *irregularity*
variable point 52.36 *point*
variable resistor 64.17 *resistor*
variable star 53, 53.10 *star*
variable wind 55.13 *wind strength*
variably 106.16 *relatively*, 113.10 *diversely*, 120.7 *quantitatively*, 123.7 *unequally*, 215.8 *irregularly*, 216.15, 224.15 *changeably*, 491.27 *capriciously*
variance 115.1 *dissimilarity*, 117.1 *disparity*, 500.1 *dissent*, 666.3 *difference*
variant 117.7 *disparate*, 168.6 *deviation*, 168.17 *abnormal*, 224.13 *changeable*, 666.10 *different*
variant reading 524.1 *interpretation*
variate 52.77 *given*
variation 52.60 *parameter*, 113.1 *diversity*, 115.1 *dissimilarity*, 216.1 *change*, 335.13 *deviation*, 485.5 *modification*
variational 485.11 *modified*
variational calculus 52.30 *calculus*
varicectomy 60 *Surgical Operations*
varicoloured 456.6 *variegated*

varicose veins 624.10 *cardiovascular disease*
varicotomy 60 *Surgical Operations*
varied 41.13 *ice-skating*, 113.5 *diverse*, 117.7 *disparate*, 216.12 *changed*, 224.13 *changeable*, 485.11 *modified*
variedly 456
variegate 456, 113.8 *be diverse*, 133.8 *mix*, 216.8 *cause change*, 444.15 *colour*
variegated 456, 113.5 *diverse*, 123.3 *unequal*, 133.12 *mixed*, 224.13 *changeable*, 444.10 *coloured*
variegated thing 456
variegation 456, 113.1 *diversity*, 113.2 *assortment*, 133.3 *miscellany*, 216.1 *change*, 224.1 *changeableness*, 442.2 *colourfulness*
Variegation 456
variety 39.11 *swimming*, 41.7 *ice-dancing*, 51.4 *show business*, 59.17 *taxonomy*, 69.5 *gardening*, 113.1 *diversity*, 115.1 *dissimilarity*, 117.1 *disparity*, 133.3 *miscellany*, 133.3 *kingdom*, 163.4 *type*, 175.2 *multiplicity*, 215.1 *irregularity*, 216.1 *change*, 224.1 *changeableness*, 306.3 *kind*, 456.1 *variegation*, 560.6 *sort*, 580.6 *selection*
variety artist 51.27 *entertainer*
variety circuit 51.13 *engagement*
variety diving 39.6 *diving*
variety meat 45.31 *offal*
variety show 51.5 *show*, 133.3 *miscellany*, 534.25 *broadcast material*
variety theatre 51.14 *theatre*
Varilite 51.18 *stage lighting*
Vari-ma-te-takere 8 *Deities*
variola 624.6 *infection*, 624.13 *skin disease*
variola porcina 624.18 *veterinary disease*
variometer 268.8 *meter*
variorum 524.2 *annotation*
various 175, 113.6 *assorted*, 115.4 *dissimilar*, 117.7 *disparate*
variously 113.10 *diversely*, 115.7 *dissimilarly*, 123.7 *unequally*, 175.10 *plurally*
variousness 113.1 *diversity*
various opinions 113.4 *dissension*
variscite 54 *Minerals*
varmint 76.2 *animal*
Varna 93 *Cities*
varnish 50.11 *artist's materials*, 102.16 *delude*, 293.3 *coating*, 293.24 *coat*, 376.10 *polish*, 376.11 *smooth*, 395.10 *resin*, 444.4 *pigment*, 531.8 *conceal*, 538.9 *hypocrisy*, 539.12, 539.32 *disguise*, 540.12 *facade*, 540.24 *mask*, 541.1 *exaggeration*, 541.7 *exaggerate*, 621.9 *cleaning agent*, 637.2 *preserver*, 637.5 *preserve*
varnished 293.36 *covered*, 376.4 *polished*, 395.14 *resinous*, 539.41, 540.35 *disguised*, 541.12 *exaggerated*
varnishing 637.1 *preservation*
varnish tree 85 *Trees and Shrubs*
Varro 48 *Poets*
varsity 19, 6.21 *curricular*
varsity player 19.2 *football player*, 23.2 *basketball player*, 655.4 *skilled person*
Varuna 8 *Deities*, 97.4 *sea god*
vary 52.94 *order*, 113.8 *be diverse*, 115.6 *differentiate*, 117.12 *be disparate*, 123.5 *be unequal*, 215.6 *be irregular*, 216.7 *be changed*, 224.11 *be changeable*, 335.1 *deviate*, 365.8 *oscillate*, 485.15 *modify*, 491.21 *change*, 576.5 *vacillate*, 579.5 *be capricious*, 666.8 *be different*
varying 117.7 *disparate*, 215.4 *irregular*
vascular 83.16 *taxonomic*
vascular bundle 83.5 *stem*

vascular disease 624.10 *cardio-vascular disease*
vascular plant 83.2 *plant*
vas deferens 245.8 *organs of reproduction*
vase 44.8 *ceramic object*, 258.11 *vessel*
vasectomize 236.9 *make impotent*, 247.8 *make infertile*
vasectomized 236.13 *unsexed*, 247.5 *rendered infertile*
vasectomy 60 Surgical Operations, 236.1 *powerlessness*, 247.2 *making infertile*, 630.12 *surgery*
Vaseline 630.9 *balm*
Vaslav Nijinsky 46.14 *famous ballet dancers*
vasoconstrictor 62.4 *drug type*
vasodilator 62.4 *drug type*
vaso-epididymostomy 60 Surgical Operations
vasopressin 58 Hormones, **62** Medication
vasopressor 62.4 *drug type*
vasotocin 58 Hormones
vasotomy 60 Surgical Operations
vasovasostomy 60 Surgical Operations
vassal 127.6 *inferior*, 697.7 *slave*
vassalage 701.1 *subjection*
vast 184.2 *immeasurable*, 248.13 *spacious*, 259.15 *big*
vastly 184.11 *immeasurably*, 248.15 *spaciously*
vast majority 143.5 *largest part*
vastness 184, 248.4 *spaciousness*, 259.2 *bigness*
Vastosh-Pati 8 Deities
vat 258.11 *vessel*, 258.12 *bath*
VAT 751.7 *tax*
Vata 8 Deities
vat dye 67.6 *dye*
vatic 517.13 *predicting*
Vatican 7.10 *priestly dwelling*
Vatican City 93 Cities
vaticinate 517.11 *predict*, 517.12 *divine*
vaticination 517.2 *divination*
vaticinator 517.8 *oracle*
vaudeville 51.4 *show business*, 51.5 *show*
vaudeville artist 51.27 *entertainer*
vaudeville circuit 51.13 *engagement*
vaudeville house 51.14 *theatre*
vaudeville show 51.5 *show*
vaudeville theatre 51.14 *theatre*
vaudevillian 51.27 *entertainer*, 51.38 *tragic*
Vaughan 48 Poets
Vaughan Williams 49 Musicians and Composers
vault 18 Sporting Activities, **43**, 30.5 *horizontal bar*, 30.6 *pommel horse*, 30.10 *compete in gymnastics*, 43.19 *decorate*, 63.27 *superstructure*, 275.8 *high thing*, 277.4 *deep thing*, 316.3 *dome*, 359.5 *jump*, 359.8 *lift*, 359.18 *jump*, 399.6 *grave*, 605.4 *storage*, 718.5 *safe*
vaulted 43, 311.4 *curved*, 316.4 *convex*
vaulter 21.3 *athlete*, 30.9 *gymnasts*
vaulting 30.5 *horizontal bar*, 30.6 *pommel horse*, 30.11 *gymnastic*, 43.7 *vault*, 359.24 *leaping*
vaulting boss 43 Architectural Decoration
vaulting horse 30.6 *pommel horse*
vaulting pit 21.2 *field events*
vault of heaven 53.3 *universe*
vault up 359.17 *spring up*
vaunt 526.1 *display*, 811.28 *flourish*
Vavilov 52 Scientists
Vayu 8 Deities, **8** Deities
V-bottom 36.6, 36,12 *canoeing*
VD 624.14 *venereal disease*
VDU 64.20 *electron tube*, 65.7 *peripheral*
veal 45.20 *meat*
veal calf 68.8 *livestock*

vection 326.2 *transportation*
vectitation 326.2 *transportation*
vector 52.50 *scalar quantity*, 76.4 *type of animal*, 326.9 *disease carrier*, 332.2 *bearing*, 624.6 *infection*, 626.3 *unhygienic person*
vectoring 73.5 *flight*
vector product 52.50 *scalar quantity*
vector quantity 52.50 *scalar quantity*
vector sum 52.50 *scalar quantity*
vecture 326.2 *transportation*
Veda 7.12 *religious text*
Vedantism 7 Non-Christian Religions
V-E Day 214.6 *annually celebrated day*, 812.5 *anniversary*
vedette 679.14 *armed forces*
Vedic 5 Languages and Groups of Languages, **7** Non-Christian Religions
Vedic hymn 10.8 *hymn*
veer 55.58 *blow*, 74.9 *navigate*, 215.1 *irregularity*, 215.6 *be irregular*, 224.11 *be changeable*, 252.1 *displacement*, 252.14 *displace*, 286.1 *obliqueness*, 286.6 *be oblique*, 335.1 *deviate*, 335.15 *deviating motion*, 337.9 *turn round*
veer around 337.9 *turn round*
veered 252.8 *displaced*
veering 55.15 *wind direction*, 215.1 *irregularity*, 215.4 *irregular*, 224.1 *changeableness*, 252.8 *displaced*, 335.21 *indirect*
Vega 53 Named Stars
vegan 86.4 *fruit eating*, 350.18 *eater*, 350.26 *eating*, 869.4 *self-restrained person*, 869.8 *self-restrained*
veganism 350.5 *eating habit*, 869.1 *self-restraint*
vegetable 45, 69, 69.16 *horticultural*, 83.2 *plant*, 83.13 *plantlike*, 240.2 *inert person*, 460.3 *unintelligent person*, 460.8 *nonhuman*
vegetable casserole 45.34 *vegetarian dish*
vegetable chilli 45.34 *vegetarian dish*
vegetable curry 45.34 *vegetarian dish*
vegetable dye 67.6 *dye*, 444.4 *pigment*
vegetable existence 99.9 *mere existence*
vegetable flan 45.34 *vegetarian dish*
vegetable garden 69.2 *garden*
vegetable grower 69.13 *horticulturist*
vegetable growing 69.1 *horticulture*
vegetable juice 351.6 *soft drink*
vegetable kingdom 83.1 *plants*
vegetable life 83.1 *plants*, 396.1 *life*, 460.4 *nonhuman existence*
vegetable market 740.1 *market*
vegetable marrow 45 Vegetables
vegetable mill 45.6 *kitchen equipment*
vegetable oil 45.7 *basic ingredient*, 395.7 *oil*
vegetable pathology 59.1 *life science*
vegetable peeler 45.6 *kitchen equipment*
vegetable physiology 59.1 *life science*
vegetable remedy 630.2 *medicine*
vegetable resin 395.10 *resin*
vegetables 86.1 *fruits*, 180.5 *side dish*
vegetable soup 45.13 *soup*
vegetal 69.16 *horticultural*, 83.13 *plantlike*
vegetarian 86.4 *fruit eating*, 86.8 *fruit-eating*, 350.18 *eater*, 350.26 *eating*, 869.4 *self-restrained person*, 869.8 *self-restrained*
vegetarian cheese 45 Cheeses
vegetarian diet 350.6 *nutrition*

vegetarian dish 45
vegetarianism 86.4 *fruit eating*, 350.5 *eating habit*, 869.1 *self-restraint*
vegetate 83, 83.22 *be dormant*, 99.21 *merely exist*, 240.4 *be inert*, 261.6 *become bigger*, 325.8 *be motionless*, 641.4 *not act*, 643.12 *be inactive*
vegetating 99, 240.5 *inert*, 325.5 *sedentary*
vegetation 83.1 *plants*, 99.9 *mere existence*, 240.1 *inertness*, 261.1 *growth*, 325.1 *motionlessness*, 460.4 *nonhuman existence*, 641.1 *inaction*
vegetation spirit 8.5 *deity*
vegetative 69.16 *horticultural*, 83.13 *plantlike*, 460.8 *nonhuman*
veggie 350.18 *eater*
vehemence 237.2 *healthiness*, 241.1 *violence*, 535.6 *assertiveness*, 554.1 *emphasis*, 642.4 *energy*, 759.4 *emotion*, 828.4 *anger*
vehement 237.10 *potent*, 239.4 *vigorous*, 241.6 *violent*, 408.12 *warm-hearted*, 535.14 *assertive*, 554.3 *emphatic*, 759.13 *passionate*
vehemently 241.10 *violently*, 535.25 *explicitly*, 554.7 *emphatically*, 759.20 *with feeling*
vehicle 51.2 *play*, 62.5 *prescription*, 232.2 *instrument*, 326.5 *means of transport*, 602.1 *means*
vehicles 777 Phobias by Topic
veil 7.11 *vestment*, 11.20 *occult*, 89.4 *fungal body*, 293.5 *body covering*, 293.16 *disguise*, 293.31 *hide*, 295.15 *headgear*, 438.6 *that which makes invisible*, 438.8 *make invisible*, 440.14 *make dark*, 441.2 *murk*, 441.10 *make dim*, 531.8 *conceal*, 539.12 *disguise*
veiled 290.12 *internalized*, 293.37 *protected*, 438.3 *private*, 441.6 *murky*, 527.2 *531.14 concealed*, 539.41 *disguised*
veiled meaning 527.11 *mysteriousness*
veiling 531.3 *covering up*
Veil Nebula 53 Nebulae
veil of cloud 55.20 *cloud appearance*
vein 57.24 *ore*, 83.6 *leaf*, 105.4 *state of mind*, 133.4 *admixture*, 234.2 *attitude*, 266.1 *layer*, 322.7 *passageway*, 456.11 *variegate*, 549.1 *style*, 553.1 *diffuseness*, 605.2 *resource*
veined 456.9 *striped*
Vela 53 The Constellations
Velcro 137.8 *fastening*, 295.24 *part of garment*
veld 87.2 *grassland*, 98.6 *lowland*, 248.3 *geographical space*
veliger 81.13 *invertebrate larva*
velites 679.8 *soldier*
vellicate 366.24 *shake*
vellication 366.8 *spasm*
vellicative 366.19 *convulsive*
vellum 604.1 *materials*
velo 47.11 *woodworking tool*
velocipede 71.12 *bicycle*
velocity 56.8 *time*, 324.8 *rapid motion*, 329.8 *speed*, 642.3 *nimbleness*, 648.4 *haste*
velocity ratio 63.10 *work*
velour 376.8 *smooth thing*
velours 67 Natural Fabrics
velouté 45.15 *sauce*
velure 67 Natural Fabrics
velutinous 383.11 *fluffy*
velvet 67 Natural Fabrics, 288.4 *textile*, 374.3 *smooth*, 374.11 *soft thing*, 376.8 *smooth thing*, 660.6 *easy thing*
Velvet 32.1 *horse*
velveteen 67 Natural Fabrics, 288.4 *textile*, 374.11 *soft thing*, 376.8 *smooth thing*
velvet glove 652.8 *treatment*, 691.1 *leniency*
velvetiness 374.9, 376.7 *smoothness*

velvetlike 374.3 *smooth*
velvet shank 89 Fungi
velvety 374.3, 376.1 *smooth*, 383.11 *fluffy*, 433.6 *melodious*
venal 858.5 *dishonourable*
venality 858.1 *improbity*
vend 727.11 *dispose of property*, 739.1 *sell*
Venda 5 Languages and Groups of Languages
vendee 738.12 *purchaser*
Vendeen 68 Breeds of Sheep
vendetta 764.8 *quarrel*, 820.4 *act of hostility*
vendibility 739.7 *market*
vendible 739.8 *merchandise*, 739.15 *saleable*
vending 739.3 *selling*
vending machine 350.15 *eating place*, 740.9 *stall*
vendition 739.3 *selling*
vendor 737.10 *trader*, 739.9 *seller*
vendue 739.4 *sale*
veneer 47.18 *work wood*, 266.3 *coat*, 266.10 *layer*, 278.4 *shallow thing*, 293.3 *coating*, 293.24 *coat*, 457.3 *external appearance*, 354.3 *hypocrisy*
veneered 266.8 *coated*
veneer furniture 47.1 *furniture*
veneering 47.1 *furniture*
Venera 53.33 *planetary probe*
venerability 805.6 *majesty*
venerable 202.11 *old*, 202.12 *olden*, 207.14 *aged*, 805.19 *stately*, 849.13 *respectable*
venerableness 202.1 *oldness*
venerably 202, 202.21 *archaically*, 207.16 *maturely*, 805.36 *majestically*
venerate 7.19 *be religious*, 9.7 *worship*, 10.19 *offer worship*, 849.16 *revere*
venerated 9.11 *worshipped*
veneration 7.2 *religiousness*, 9.1 *worship*, 10.3 *rite of worship*, 849.2 *admiration*
venerational 9.9 *worshipful*, 849.10 *reverent*
venerative 849.10 *reverent*
venerator 9.5, 10.17 *worshipper*
venereal 135.14 *conjunctive*, 624.23 *diseased*
venereal disease 777 Phobias by Topic, **624**, 624.4 *disease*
venereal ulcer 624.14 *venereal disease*
venereologist 60.13 *medical specialist*
venereology 60.3 *medical specialty*
venerophobia 777 Phobias by Name
venery 77.23 *mammal hunting*, 821.5 *desire*, 877.3 *sexual immorality*
venesection 349.22 *disgorgement*, 355.4 *sucking*, 630.12 *surgery*
Venetian blind 293.12 *protective covering*, 440.6 *shade*, 634.2 *shelter*
Venetian red 450.6 *red pigment*
Venetian school 50 Western Art Styles and Movements
Venetic 5 Languages and Groups of Languages
Venezuela 93 Countries
vengeance 125.2 *counterbalance*, 672.1 *retaliation*, 855.4 *revenge*
vengeful 672.5 *retaliatory*, 832.13 *merciless*, 836.4 *pitiless*, 855.14 *vindictive*
vengefully 125.11 *in compensation*, 836.7 *pitilessly*, 855.16 *vindictively*
vengefulness 832.4 *bitterness*
venial 864, 612.1 *unimportant*, 839.7 *forgivable*, 855.13 *vindicable*
venially 839.14 *forgivingly*, 855.15 *in vindication*
venial sin 864, 612.8 *trifle*, 866.3 *sin*
Venice 93 Cities
venison 45.20 *meat*

Venn diagram 52 Named Concepts, 152.8 *chart*
venoclysis 62.12 *injection*
venogram 60.7 *diagnosis*
venography 60.7 *diagnosis*
venom 618.10 *poverty*, 631.8 *poison*, 820.1 *enmity*, 822.1 *hate*, 832.4 *bitterness*
venomous 618.5 *harmful*, 626.7 *toxic*, 631.16 *blighting*, 820.6 *hostile*, 822.10 *hating*, 832.14 *hostile*, 854.16 *defamatory*, 855.14 *vindictive*
venomously 626.8 *unhygienically*, 820.15 *aggressively*, 822.18 *hatefully*, 855.16 *vindictively*
venomousness 618.11 *harmfulness*, 631.7 *poisoning*, 832.4 *bitterness*
venomous snake 79.3 *snake*
venous 322.15 *providing passage*
venous blood 387.4 *blood*
venously 322.27 *cavernously*
vent 54.24 *volcanic activity*, 322.7 *passageway*, 322.21 *provide passage for*, 347.7 *outlet*, 349.11 *void*, 530.6 *divulge*, 638.2 *means of escape*
ventage 347.7 *outlet*
venter 88.4 *moss plant*
venthole 347.7 *outlet*
ventilate 134.10 *purify*, 390.20 *aerate*, 409.12 *make cold*, 417.5 *deodorize*, 530.6 *divulge*, 532.13 *make public*, 621.15 *purify*, 625.6 *make hygienic*, 651.1 *refresh*
ventilated 390, 417.3 *odourless*, 532.19 *published*, 625.4 *hygienic*
ventilating system 390.7 *ventilator*
ventilation 390, 134.2 *purification*, 417.1 *odourlessness*, 532.1 *publication*, 621.2 *cleaning*, 625.2 *salubrity*, 651.5 *refreshment*
ventilator 390, 409.4 *cooler*, 417.2 *deodorant*
vent one's anger 828
vent one's rancour 828.13 *vent one's anger*
vent one's spleen 828.13 *vent one's anger*
ventriculostomy 60 Surgical Operations
ventriloquism 539.9 *sleight of hand*, 564.4 *articulation*
ventriloquist 51.27 *entertainer*, 118.7 *imitator*
ventriloquize 539.29 *juggle*
Ventura 65.11 *application*
venture 596, 14.5 *invest*, 230.3 *business*, 479.1 *experiment*, 479.13 *invent*, 491.22 *risk*, 589.12 *take a chance*, 596.3 *tackle*, 597.1 *undertake*, 597.2 *undertaking*, 633.5 *danger*, 633.9 *face danger*, 633.10 *endanger*, 642.2 *social activity*, 674.11 *contend*, 737.2 *speculate*, 737.6 *business*, 778.15 *be courageous*
ventured 479.10 *tested*
venture on 597.1 *undertake*
venturesome 479.9 *original*, 596.8 *attempting*, 597.6 *enterprising*, 633.1 *dangerous*, 778.13 *adventurous*
venturesomeness 633.5 *danger*
venture to say 518.6 *propound*
venturous 633.1 *dangerous*
venue 18.2 *sportsground*, 51.14 *theatre*, 251.1 *situation*
Venus 8 Deities, **53** Planets and their Satellites, 53.16 *planet*, 204.2 *morning thing*, 205.4 *evening thing*, 821.16 *gods and goddesses of love*
venus clam 81 Molluscs
Venus flytrap 84 Flowers and Flowering Plants, 539.13 *snare*
Venusian 53.36 *astronomical*
Venus's flower basket 81.8 *sponge*
Veps 5 Languages and Groups of Languages

veracious 490.1 *certain*, 526.15 *open*, 537.15 *true*, 537.18 *truthful*, 537.25 *lifelike*, 556.3 *natural*, 658.1 *naive*, 843.8 *correct*, 857.4 *honourable*
veraciously 857.7 *honourably*
veraciousness 537.12 *true to life*
veracity 490.9 *certainty*, 537.5 *truthfulness*, 556.6 *naturalness*, 658.2 *naivety*, 843.2 *correctness*, 857.1 *probity*
Veracruz 93 Cities
veranda 256.7 *room*
verb 5.35 *part of speech*
verbal 5.40 *translated*, 5.42 *worded*, 5.44 *grammatical*, 520.8 *semantic*, 534.33 *communicational*, 564.17 *oral*
verbal abuse 827.3 *vilification*, 832.7 *act of malevolence*
verbal attack 670.16 *terrorist attack*, 852.8 *berating*
verbal diarrhoea 553.1 *diffuseness*, 564.2 *power of speech*, 565.1 *talkativeness*
verbal intercourse 564.1 *faculty of speech*, 568.1 *conversation*
verbalism 5.24 *phrasing*, 521.1 *lack of meaning*
verbalize 5.45 *use language*, 5.47 *word*, 306.7 *form*, 564.11 *speak*
verbally 5.49 *colloquially*, 564.21 *orally*
verbal translation 5.12 *translation*
verbatim 5.48 *linguistically*, 110.1 *sameness*, 110.12 *same*, 118.14 *imitatively*, 503.6 *correct*, 503.8 *accurately*, 520.13 *meaningfully*, 524.17 *translational*, 537.23 *literal*, 537.38 *literally*, 619.7 *perfectly*
verbatim account 537.10 *literalness*
verbena 84 Flowers and Flowering Plants, 413.5 *herbs*
verbiage 5.22 *many words*, 521.5 *empty talk*, 551.1 *obscurity*, 553.1 *diffuseness*, 564.2 *power of speech*
verbose 5.42 *worded*, 269.1 *long*, 553.3 *diffuse*, 565.5 *talkative*
verbosely 5.50 *lexically*, 553.7 *diffusely*
verboseness 553.1 *diffuseness*
verbosity 5.22 *many words*, 553.1 *diffuseness*, 564.2 *power of speech*, 565.1 *talkativeness*
verb phrase 5.23 *phrase*
verdancy 453.8 *greenness*
Verdandi 8 Deities
verdant 453, 69.17 *botanical*, 83.13 *plantlike*, 87.9 *grassy*, 246.5 *fertile*
verd antique 453.11 *green thing*
verdantly 69.20 *horticulturally*, 87.13 *herbivorously*, 453.18 *greenly*
verderer 16.23 *judge*, 85.8 *forester*
Verdi 49 Musicians and Composers
verdict 492, 16.7 *legal trial*, 16.33 *litigation*
verdict of acquittal 855.1 *vindication*
verdict of guilty 16.43 *conviction*
verdict of innocence 855.1 *vindication*, 865.2 *legal innocence*
verdict of not guilty 16.42 *acquittal*, 855.1 *vindication*
verdict of not proven 16.42 *acquittal*
verdigris 453.11 *green thing*, 628.9 *dilapidation*
verdigris toadstool 89 Fungi
verditer 453.10 *green pigment*
Verdun 93 Cities
verdure 83.1 *plants*, 87.2 *grassland*, 453.8 *greenness*
verdured 87.9 *grassy*
verdurous 69.17 *botanical*
Verethagna 8 Deities
verge 43.9 *miscellaneous architectural features*, 157.7 *limit*, 264.2 *short distance*, 300.1, 300.1 *edge*, 300.5 *border*, 302.3

furthest point, 332.7 *take a direction*
verge on 264.9 *near*, 300.5 *border*, 407.12 *abut*
verger 7.8 *priest*
verging 302.6 *furthest*
verging on 264.6 *near*
veridical 535.12 *vowed*, 537.18 *truthful*
veridically 537.36 *truthfully*
verifiability 475.5 *demonstrability*
verifiable 480, 3.19 *chronicled*, 475.12 *demonstrable*, 479.8 *experimental*, 490.1 *certain*
verifiably 480, 475.22 *demonstrably*, 718.16 *surely*
verification 480, 52.64 *reasoning*, 475.4 *proof*, 479.3 *experimentation*, 483.2 *proof*, 490.13, 535.4 *confirmation*, 537.7 *confirmation*, 544.1 *identification*, 708.1 *permission*, 718.2 *promise*
Verification 480
verification principle 4.8 *philosophical term*
verificative 480.9 *verificatory*
verificatory 480
verified 480, 119.6 *authentic*, 475.13 *proven*, 479.10 *tested*, 483.8 *evidential*, 501.10 *known*, 535.13 *supported*, 537.20 *proved*, 544.12 *identified*
verifier 480, 535.9 *affirmer*
verify 480, 101.12 *establish reality*, 170.12 *check*, 475.17 *prove*, 479.11 *experiment*, 483.12 *prove*, 490.21 *make certain*, 535.19 *confirm*, 537.30 *prove true*, 544.10 *identify*, 708.3 *permit*, 718.12 *certify*
verifying 479.8 *experimental*
verily 537.35 *truly*
verisimilar 537.25 *lifelike*
verisimilitude 101.3 *realism*, 488.3 *plausibility*, 537.12 *true to life*
verism 50 Western Art Styles and Movements
verismo 48 Literary Groups and Movements
verist 50.29 *realist*
veritable 99.13 *real*, 537.15 *true*
veritably 537.35 *truly*
verity 490.9 *certainty*, 537.1 *truth*
Verlaine 48 Poets
vermeil 450.1 *red*
vermicelli 45 Types of Pasta
vermicellini 45 Types of Pasta
vermicidal 62.14 *counteracting*
vermicide 62.4 *drug type*, 398.13 *animal killer*
vermicular 81.20 *wormlike*
vermiculite 54 Minerals
vermiform 81.20 *wormlike*, 314.4 *convolutional*
vermifugal 62.14 *counteracting*
vermifuge 62.4 *drug type*, 630.4 *antidote*
vermilion 450.1 *red*, 450.6 *red pigment*
vermin 82.3 *pest*, 622.4 *dirt*
verminous 82, 626.5 *unhygienic*
verminousness 626.1 *lack of hygiene*
vermiphobia 777 Phobias by Name
Vermont 92 American States
Vermont Sage 45 Cheeses
vermouth 351.8 *mixed drink*, 351.9, 351.9 *wine*
vernacular 43 Architectural Styles, 5.3 *spoken language*, 5.39 *of language*, 164.21 *common*, 549.8 *inelegant*, 556.1 *simple*, 556.4 *simplicity*, 564.1 *faculty of speech*
vernacularism 5.3 *spoken language*, 5.26 *dialect*
vernacularize 5.45 *use language*
vernacular language 5.3 *spoken language*, 5.26 *dialect*
vernal 203.10 *spring*, 453.4 *fresh*
vernal equinox 10.15 *holy day*, 53.5 *celestial sphere*, 203.2 *spring*
vernal grass 87 Grasses

vernally 203.18 *seasonally*
vernal season 203.2 *spring*
Verne 48 Writers
Vernerian 5.38 *linguistic*
Verner's law 5.37 *linguistic theory*
vernier 268.6 *measuring instrument*
vernier scale 56.84 *altimeter*
Verona 93 Cities
veronica 84 Flowers and Flowering Plants, 10.14 *sacred object*
verruca 624.13 *skin disease*
Versailles 43 Noted Buildings, **93** Cities
versatile 113.5 *diverse*, 175.7 *various*, 224.13 *changeable*, 578.11 *equivocating*, 613.1 *useful*, 655.6 *skilful*, 861.5 *proficient*
versatilely 113.10 *diversely*
versatility 113.1 *diversity*, 146.1 *inclusion*, 224.1 *changeableness*, 578.6 *equivocation*, 613.5 *usefulness*, 655.1 *skill*, 861.12 *proficiency*
verse 6.22 *educate*, 48.6 *poetry*, 48.7 *poem*, 48.8 *part of poem*, 143.2 *particular*
versed 6.19 *knowledgeable*, 485.9 *qualified*, 501.8 *knowledgeable*
versed in 655.8 *expert*
verse drama 51.2 *play*
verse epistle 48.7 *poem*
verse form 48, 306.3 *kind*
versemaker 48.14 *author*
versemonger 48.14 *author*
verse paragraph 48.8 *part of poem*
versesmith 48.14 *author*
versicolour 456.6 *variegated*
versification 48.6 *poetry*
versifier 48.14 *author*
versify 48.21 *write*
version 152.9 *musical arrangement*, 163.4 *type*, 524.1 *interpretation*, 524.4 *translation*, 560.1 *description*
vers-librist 48.14 *author*
verso 304.1 *rear*
verst 75 Some Foreign Units
versus 663.27 *opposed to*
vert 453.1 *green*, 544.8 *heraldic device*, 544.13 *heraldic*
vertebra 382 Bones
vertebral column 382 Bones
vertebrate 76.4 *type of animal*, 76.15 *of animals*
vertebrates 396.9 *classifications of life*
vertebrate zoologist 76.11 *zoologist*
vertebrate zoology 76.9 *animal science*
vertex 52.39 *angle*, 279.1 *summit*, 380.7 *sharp point*
vertical 281, 41.12 *ski*, 52.80 *linear*, 279.5 *top*, 281.3 *vertical thing*, 312.1 *straight*, 361.11 *raised*
vertical angles 52.39 *angle*
vertical axis 281.3 *vertical thing*
verticale 41.3 *ski racing*
vertical gate 41.3 *ski racing*
verticality 281
Verticality 281
vertical-lift bridge 63.21 *bridge*
vertical line 281.3 *vertical thing*, 312.7 *straight line*
vertically 281, 41.17 *on a ski run*, 275.20 *higher*, 312.12 *straight*
vertical machine 63.9 *machine tool*
vertical member 63.27 *superstructure*
vertical movement 54.13 *ocean current*
verticalness 281.1 *verticality*
vertical roll 534.23 *television reception*
vertical thing 281
verticillaster 84.4 *flower head*
verticillium 89 Fungi
vertiginous 275.9 *high*, 364.12 *rotary*
vertigo 238.3 *poor health*, 364.1 *rotation*

Vertumnus 8 Deities
vervain 84 Flowers and Flowering Plants
verve 235.3 *vitality*, 239.1 *vigour*, 554.1 *emphasis*, 759.4 *emotion*
vervet 77 Placental Mammals
very 121.11 *to a degree*
very beginning 208.3 *early stage*
very best 617.2, 861.2 *best*
very good 617.1 *worthy*
very high frequency 212.6 *radio frequency*
very image 110.3 *lookalike*, 547.6 *image*
very important person 611.4 *bigwig*
Very Large Array 53.26 *radio telescope*
Very light 439.8 *fire*, 543.4 *signal*
very long baseline interferometry 53.26 *radio telescope*
very many 181.6 *many*
very occasionally 213.1 *infrequently*
very odd 786.8 *wonderful*
very picture 547.6 *image*
Very pistol 543.4 *signal*
very seldom 213.1 *infrequently*
Very signal 636.2 *danger signal*
very small 438.2 *difficult to see*
very steep 281.8 *vertical*
very steeply 281.12 *perpendicularly*
very thing 110.1 *sameness*
very tiring 644.11 *laborious*
very top 279.1 *summit*
vesicant 62.4 *drug type*
vesiculectomy 60 Surgical Operations
Vesper 53.10 *star*
vesperal 205.6 *evening*
vesperine 205.6 *evening*
vespers 10.4 *public worship*, 205.1 *evening*
vespiary 82.4 *social insect*
vessel 74, 258, 44.8 *ceramic object*, 258.1 *container*
vest 16.68 *legislate*, 116.30 *grant*, 295.11 *jacket*, 295.18 *underwear*, 295.32 *dress*, 728.3 *transfer property*, 729.5 *give*
vesta 410.2 *lighter*, 439.8 *fire*
Vesta 8 Deities, **53** Minor Planets
vestal 134.5 *pure person*, 825.4 *celibate person*, 876.5 *pure person*, 876.9 *pure*
vestal virgin 134.5 *pure person*, 825.4 *celibate person*, 876.5 *pure person*
vested 116.19 *granted*, 295.29 *dressed*
vested interest 233 *influence*
vestibular gland 352 Exocrine Glands
vestibule 43.9 *miscellaneous architectural features*, 43.10 *church architecture*, 256.7 *room*, 303.1 *front*, 327.2 *route*, 346.6 *means of entry*
vestige 545, 3.11 *relic*, 132.1 *remainder*
vestiges 200.7 *thing of the past*
vestigial 3.15 *historic*, 132.9 *remaining*, 280.3 *base*
vestigially 3.25 *reportedly*, 132.11 *residually*
vesting 728.1 *transfer of property*
vestiture 295.2 *dressing*
vestment 7, 293.5 *body covering*, 295.3 *formal dress*
vestments 813.4 *formal dress*
vest-pocket 260.7 *little*
vest power in 235.11 *give power*
vestry 10.12 *church*, 653.7 *council*
vesture 7.11 *vestment*, 295.1 *dress*, 295.3 *formal dress*
vesuvian 54 Minerals
vesuvianite 54 Minerals, **54** Gemstones
Vesuvius 95 Mountains, 408.8 *hot place*
vet 32.15 *horse person*, 60.15 *veterinarian*, 76.10 *animal welfar-*

ist, 492.12 *estimate*, 630.15 *healer*, 679.11 *former soldier*
vetch 84 Flowers and Flowering Plants, 68.12 *crop*
veteran 202.11 *old*, 207.7 *older person*, 207.8 *man*, 594.20 *developed*, 655.5, 655.8 *expert*, 676.11 *recruit*, 676.17 *military*, 679.11 *former soldier*
veterinarian 60, 32.15 *horse person*, 76.10 *animal welfarist*, 630.15 *healer*
veterinary 60.15 *veterinarian*, 60.22 *medical*
veterinary clinic 60.5 *veterinary medicine*
veterinary disease 624
veterinary medicine 60
veterinary nurse 60.15 *veterinarian*
veterinary practice 60.5 *veterinary medicine*
veterinary practitioner 60.15 *veterinarian*
veterinary science 76.8 *animal welfare*
veterinary student 60.15 *veterinarian*
veterinary surgeon 60.15 *veterinarian*, 630.15 *healer*
veterinary surgery 60.5 *veterinary medicine*
veterinary technician 60.15 *veterinarian*
vetiver 418.3 *incense*
veto 709, 709, 16.35 *illegality*, 16.75 *make illegal*, 100.14 *cause not to exist*, 147.1 *exclusion*, 147.7 *exclude*, 231.1 *counteraction*, 231.3 *counteract*, 302.2 *limiting factor*, 302.7 *limit*, 536.2 *rejection*, 536.7 *be negative*, 692.1, 692.9 *command*, 699.1 *restraint*, 699.5 *means of restraint*, 699.8 *restrain*, 711.2, 711.6 *dissent*, 846.17 *criminalize*, 852.3 *nonacceptance*, 852.15 *withhold approval*, 869.5 *be self-restrained*
Veto 709
vetoed 709, 536.12 *rejected*, 692.14 *commanding*, 846.12 *disentitled*, 852.31 *disapproved*
vetoer 536.6 *negativist*
vetting 632.2 *protection*
vex 153.7 *disturb*, 616.5 *be inconvenient*, 618.13 *be worthless*, 650.6 *fatigue*, 768.8 *annoy*, 828.9 *offend*, 829.8 *make irascible*
vexation 616.3 *inconvenience*, 768.2 *annoyance*, 828.1 *resentment*
vexatious 153.17 *disturbing*, 616.1 *inconvenient*, 650.4 *fatiguing*, 659.13 *inconvenient*, 768.5 *aggravating*
vexatiously 616.6 *inconveniently*, 768.10 *annoyingly*
vexed 153.12 *disturbed*, 659.16 *troubled*, 828.15 *resentful*
vexed question 659.4 *problem*
vexillary 679.6 *militarist*
vexillum 544.7 *flag*
vexing 659.13 *inconvenient*, 768.5 *aggravating*
VF 534 Radio-frequency Bands
V-groove 34.5 *rock face*
VHF radio 534.18 *radio*
VHF transmitter 534.16 *transmitter*
via 49 Musical Terms, **327,** 232.9 *instrumentally*, 356.14 *by the way*
viability 396.4 *biological function*
viable 59.21 *living*, 116.20 *agreeable*, 230.11 *workable*, 396.12 *alive*, 486.5 *possible*
viableness 396.4 *biological function*, 486.2 *possibleness*
viably 396.22 *vitally*
viaduct 63.21, 327.9 *bridge*, 356.5 *crossing point*
vial 258.14 *bottle*
viands 350.7 *food*
viaticum 10.5 *Christian rite*, 345.9 *parting*

Viatka 32 Breeds of Horse and Pony
vibes 297.3 *atmosphere*, 759.2 *impression*
vibrancy 365.2 *vibration*
vibrant 239.4 *vigorous*, 427.8 *deep*
vibrantly 427.11 *resonantly*
vibraphone 49 Musical Instruments
vibrate 365, 183.22 *resound*, 224.11 *be changeable*, 366.24 *shake*, 426.8 *drum*, 427.9 *resonate*
vibratile 365.14 *vibrating*
vibratility 365.2 *vibration*
vibrating 365, 224.13 *changeable*, 324.17 *directional*, 331.8 *recoiling*, 366.6 *shaking*, 366.18 *shaky*, 427.6 *resonant*
vibrating string 56.14 *sound wave*
vibration 365, 56.12 *wave*, 56.14 *sound wave*, 183.6 *reverberation*, 324.5 *circuition*, 366.6 *shaking*, 407.1 *touch*, 426.1 *drumming*, 427.1 *resonance*
vibrational 183.15 *reverberatory*
vibrations 297.3 *atmosphere*
vibrato 49.16 *musical note*, 426.6 *musical repetition*
vibrator 64.31 *electric motor*, 365.7 *oscillator*, 366.14 *agitator*, 385.6 *massage*
vibratory 365.14 *vibrating*, 366.18 *shaky*
vibrissa 77.2 *mammalian characteristic*
vibrograph 365.6 *measuring instrument*
vibroscope 365.6 *measuring instrument*
viburnum 84 Flowers and Flowering Plants
vicar 7.8 *priest*, 220.5 *converter*, 707.1 *deputy*
vicarage 7.10 *priestly dwelling*, 256.4 *official residence*
vicar-general 707.1 *deputy*
vicariate 7.9 *priesthood*
vicarious 703.9 *commissioned*
vicarious authority 703.3 *authority*
vicariously 703.11 *under commission*
vicariousness 222.1 *substitution*
Vicar of Bray 224.6 *fickle person*, 578.9 *equivocator*
vicarship 7.9 *priesthood*
vice 864, 16.38 *lawbreaking*, 262.4 *contractor*, 618.9 *badness*, 652.4 *bad conduct*, 683.3 *personal fault*, 726.3 *tools for gripping*, 844.8 *wrong-doing*, 862.1 *evil*, 866.3 *sin*, 877.1 *immorality*, 877.5 *prostitution*
vice admiral 679.27 *naval man*, 707.1 *deputy*
Vice Admiral 17 British Military Ranks, **17** US Military Ranks
vice chairman 707.1 *deputy*
vice chancellor 6.4 *educator*, 653.13 *director*, 688.10 *person of authority*, 696.9 *educational leader*, 707.1 *deputy*
vice consul 707.1 *deputy*, 707.3 *agent*
vicelike 726.9 *retentive*
vicelike grip 726.1 *retention*
vicenary 179.19 *twentieth*
vicennial 179.19 *twentieth*
vice president 12.7 *governor*, 653.13 *director*, 707.1 *deputy*
viceregent 707.1 *deputy*
viceroy 696.3 *leader*, 707.1 *deputy*
vice squad 877.5 *prostitution*
vice squad member 632.3 *protector*
vice versa 109.10 *reciprocally*, 111.6 *oppositely*, 223.8 *in exchange*, 287.4 *inversely*
Vichy 93 Cities
vichyssoise 45.13 *soup*
vicinage 264.3 *near place*
vicinal 264.5 *near*
vicinity 249.13 *locality*, 253.4

availability, 264.3 *near place*, 297.1 *surroundings*
vicious 241.6 *violent*, 378.4 *powerful*, 618.3 *bad*, 822.10 *hating*, 832.11 *cruel*, 844.16 *in the wrong*, 862.7 *evil*, 864.11 *wicked*, 864.12 *immoral*, 877.14 *lecherous*
vicious circle 159.6 *continuum*, 661.2 *obstacle*
viciously 822.18 *hatefully*, 862.12 *evilly*, 864.18 *wickedly*
viciousness 378.8 *physical strength*, 618.9 *badness*, 832.2 *cruelness*, 862.1 *evil*, 864.1 *wickedness*, 877.1 *immorality*
vicissitude 216.1 *change*, 224.1 *changeableness*
Vico 4 Philosophers
victim 238.4 *weakling*, 397.11 *dead person*, 493.6 *misjudged person*, 539.22 *dupe*, 590.7 *the hunted*, 683.5 *failing person*, 687.5 *person in adversity*, 722.6 *loser*, 730.5 *recipient*, 850.9 *butt*
victimization 539.7 *tricking*, 690.2 *suppression*, 768.3 *nuisance*, 832.5 *intolerance*, 879.7 *punishment*
victimize 539.28 *trick*, 618.14 *illtreat*, 690.6 *suppress*, 832.18 *torment*, 879.1 *punish*
victimized 539.36 *deceived*, 690.9 *suppressed*
victim of discrimination 481, 147.5 *excluded person*
victim of fate 687.5 *person in adversity*
victim of oppression 481.8 *victim of discrimination*
victor 126.6 *paragon*, 617.8 *exceller*, 682.5 *victorious person*
Victor 534 Phonetic Alphabet
victoria 71 Carriages and Carts
Victoria 92 Australian States and Territories, **93** Cities, **94** Lakes, **98** Islands, 94.5 *other major lakes*
Victoria Cross 17 British Military Medals and Decorations, 544.4 *insignia*, 681.1 *trophy*
Victorian 43 Architectural Styles, 3.15 *historic*, 47.7 *furniture style*, 134.6 *morally pure*, 202.14 *historic*, 225.5 *stable person*, 876.6 *moralist*, 876.10 *moralistic*
Victoriana 3.11 *relic*, 202.5 *old thing*
Victorian Age 3.10 *past age*
Victorian values 134.1 *purity*
victorious 682, 126.14 *best*
victorious candidate 580.13 *electorate*
victorious general 682.5 *victorious person*
victoriously 126.16 *superiorly*, 682.16 *successfully*
victorious person 682
Victor Meyer's method 57 Named Reactions
victory 682
victory arch 545.11 *monument*
victory garden 69.2 *garden*
victory gardens 676.7 *war measures*
victory laurels 544.4 *insignia*
victory roll 73.5 *flight*
victual 350.25 *provide food*, 606.5 *provision*
victualled 606.8 *provisional*
victualler 606.3 *provider*
victualling 606.1 *provision*
victuals 350.7 *food*, 606.2 *provisions*
vicuna 77 Placental Mammals, 288.4 *textile*
vicuña 67 Natural Fabrics
vid 66.21 *photograph*
Vidal 48 Writers
Vidar 8 Deities
video 66.21 *photograph*, 534.23 *television reception*, 534.26 *recording*, 534.30 *communicate*, 547.2 *reproduction*
video camera 66.16 *camera,*

435.8 *reflection*, 534.26 *recording*, 545.10 *recording instrument*
video cassette 534.26 *recording*
video cassette recorder 114.3 *copier*, 118.6 *photocopier*, 534.26 *recording*, 545.10 *recording instrument*
video collection 605.5 *collection*
videodisc 534.26 *recording*
videoed 534.34 *communicated*
video game 42.1 *game*, 65.18 *computer game*, 534.26 *recording*
video nasty 534.26 *recording*, 877.2 *indecency*
videophone 534.9 *telephone*
video piracy 736.6 *illegal borrowing*
video pirate 736.10 *infringer*
video recording 118.5 *duplicate*, 534.26 *recording*
video signal 534.21 *television*
video tape 56.64 *magnetic recording*, 534.26, 545.7 *recording*, 545.13 *record*
video-taped 545.16 *recorded*
video tape recorder 545.10 *recording instrument*
vie 21.6 *compete in athletics*, 617.9 *be worthy*
vielle 49 *Musical Instruments*
Vienna 93 *Cities*, 93.6 *other cities*
Vienna circle 4.7 *school of thought*
Vienna sausage 45.29 *sausage*
Viennese waltz 41.7 *ice-dancing*, 46.2 *dance*
Vierwaldstättersee 94 *Lakes*
Vietnam 91 *Countries*
Vietnamese 5 *Languages and Groups of Languages*
Vietnamese Pot-Bellied 68 Breeds of Pig
Vietnam War 17 *Major Wars*
view 435, 4.1 *philosophy*, 4.22 *propound a philosophy*, 50.10 *art subject*, 253.12 *attend*, 310.5 *viewpoint*, 435.14 *inspect*, 471.5 *ideology*, 492.1 *judgment*, 497.1 *belief*, 588.3 *future intention*, 654.1 *advice*, 759.3 *feelings*
viewable 435.23, 437.1 *visible*
viewdata 528.6 *information technology*, 534.25 *broadcast material*
viewer 253.5 *someone present*, 435.11 *observer*, 730.5 *recipient*
viewership 532.2 *mass media*
viewfinder 66.18 *exposure time*
view halloo 423.1 *loudness*, 431.5 *hunting cry*, 590.19 *after him*
viewing 526.6 *display*
viewing figures 532.2 *mass media*
viewing the body 397.8 *after death*, 399.2 *funeral*
vie with 663.16 *confront*, 674.11 *contend*
viewpoint 310, 435, 4.1 *philosophy*, 251.2 *circumstances*, 275.8 *high thing*, 471.5 *ideology*, 497.1 *belief*, 759.3 *feelings*
view the body 397.17 *bury*
Viewtron 534.25 *broadcast material*
view with a jaundiced eye 841.6 *be jealous*
view with disfavour 852.14 *disapprove*
view with jealousy 841.6 *be jealous*
vif 49 *Musical Terms*
VIFF 73.5 *flight*
vigesimal 179.19 *twentieth*
vigil 469.5 *watchfulness*
vigilance 467.3 *carefulness*, 469.3 *circumspection*, 469.5 *watchfulness*, 719.1 *observance*, 781.1 *caution*, 841.2 *distrust*
vigilance committee 16.2 *jurisdiction*
vigilant 435.21 *seeing*, 467.7 *watchful*, 469.9 *careful*, 513.5 *expecting*, 575.11 *steady*, 594.18 *prepared*, 632.7 *tutelary*,

642.18 *active*, 781.4 *cautious*, 841.5 *distrustful*
vigilante 435.11 *observer*, 469.8 *watchful person*, 632.3 *protector*, 671.14 *guard*, 672.2 *revenger*, 679.2 *defender*
vigilante committee member 590.5 *pursuer*
vigilantism 16.41 *lawlessness*
vigilantly 435.26 *watchfully*, 467.15 *attentively*, 594.22 *in preparation*, 841.9 *jealously*
vigil light 10.14 *sacred object*
vigils 10.9 *prayer*
vigintillion 169.3 *large number*, 179.11 *million*
vignette 43 *Architectural Decoration*, 48.2 *fiction*, 50.9 *drawing*, 51.21 *role*, 560.2 *brief description*
Vignotte 45 *Cheeses*
Vigny 48 *Poets*, 48 *Dramatists*
vigorous 239, 235.15 *full of energy*, 237.9 *physically strong*, 241.6 *violent*, 329.2 *mentally quick*, 396.13 *lively*, 453.4 *fresh*, 535.14 *assertive*, 554.3 *emphatic*, 574.2 *tenacious*, 623.1 *healthy*, 642.18 *active*
vigorously 235.19 *energetically*, 237.15 *acutely*, 239.6 *with vigour*, 241.10 *violently*, 535.25 *explicitly*, 554.7 *emphatically*, 642.22 *actively*
vigorousness 378.8 *physical strength*, 535.6 *assertiveness*, 554.1 *emphasis*, 642.4 *energy*
vigour 239, 206.2 *youthfulness*, 235.3 *vitality*, 237.2 *healthiness*, 241.1 *violence*, 378.8 *physical strength*, 535.6 *assertiveness*, 554.1 *emphasis*, 557.2 *affectation*, 574.13 *concentration*, 623.3 *health*, 642.4 *energy*
Vigour 239
vihuela 49 *Musical Instruments*
Vijnanavada 4.7 *school of thought*
Viking 53.33 *planetary probe*, 74.7 *nautical person*, 244.6 *destroyer*
vilanelle 48.7 *poem*, 48.10 *verse form*
vile 822.12 *hated*, 827.8 *cursing*, 862.7 *evil*, 864.11 *wicked*
vile language 827.2 *offensive language*
vilely 827.12 *swearingly*, 864.18 *wickedly*
vileness 618.9 *badness*, 652.4 *bad conduct*, 862.1 *evil*, 864.1 *wickedness*
vilification 827, 670.16 *terrorist attack*, 852.8 *berating*, 854.5 *scorn*
vilify 827, 854, 670.10 *criticize*, 766.7 *be dissatisfied*, 852.22 *vituperate*
vilifying 827.9 *vituperative*
villa 256.4 *official residence*, 256.5 *house*, 725.1 *property*
villadom 124.8 *middle classes*
village 93, 92.4 *community*, 93.1 *city*, 93.14 *urban*, 249.11 *settlement*
village cricket 27.1 *cricket match*
village green 93.10 *village*, 453.8 *greenness*
village-like 93.14 *urban*
village pond 94.2 *small lake*
villager 93.11 *urbanite*, 255.5 *countryman*
villain 16.40 *lawbreaker*, 51.21 *role*, 832.8 *malefactor*, 844.10 *wrongdoer*, 858.4 *dishonourable person*, 862.6 *evil person*, 864.9 *wicked person*
villainous 16.60 *offending*, 447.5 *black-hearted*, 618.3 *bad*, 858.5 *dishonourable*, 864.11 *wicked*
villainousness 618.9 *badness*, 858.1 *improbity*
villainy 16.38 *lawbreaking*, 618.9 *badness*, 858.1 *improbity*, 864.1 *wickedness*
villein 701.5 *subjected person*, 803.1 *plebeian*
villeinage 701.1 *subjection*,

723.3 *medieval ownership*, 725.3 *historic property terms*
villeinhold 723.3 *medieval ownership*, 725.3 *historic property terms*
Villon 48 *Poets*
villosity 375.5 *roughness*
villous 375.2 *coarse*
villously 375.14 *roughly*
Vilnius 93 *Cities*
vim 237.2 *healthiness*, 239.1 *vigour*, 554.1 *emphasis*, 778.1 *courage*
vina 49 *Musical Instruments*
vinaigrette 45.15 *sauce*, 413.2 *seasoning*, 415.3 *sour thing*
vinblastine 62 *Medication*
Vincennes ware 44 *Types of Ceramics*
vincristine 62 *Medication*
vinculum 52.25 *algebraic expression*
vindaloo 45.49 *Indian dish*
vin de table 351.9 *wine*
vindicable 855
vindicate 855, 4.21 *rationalize*, 16.78 *acquit*, 473.16 *plead*, 478.18 *answer back*, 480.1 *verify*, 671.22 *plead for*, 839.10 *absolve*
vindicated 16.63 *acquitted*, 473.12 *apologetic*, 478.13 *retaliatory*, 839.6 *forgiven*
vindicating 478.13 *retaliatory*, 671.29 *defending*, 839.4 *forgiving*, 855.11 *vindicatory*
vindication 855, 16.42 *acquittal*, 473.5 *plea*, 478.5 *counterstatement*, 839.3 *absolution*
Vindication 855
vindicator 855, 855.6 *avenger*, 879.17 *punisher*
vindicatory 855
vindictive 855, 618.5 *harmful*, 672.5 *retaliatory*, 822.10 *hating*, 832.14 *hostile*, 836.4 *pitiless*, 862.7 *evil*, 879.19 *punitive*
vindictively 855, 822.18 *hatefully*, 836.7 *pitilessly*, 862.12 *evilly*, 879.23 *punitively*
vindictiveness 618.11 *harmfulness*, 832.4 *bitterness*, 862.1 *evil*
vin du pays 351.9 *wine*
vine 83.2 *plant*
vinegar 45.7 *basic ingredient*, 415.3 *sour thing*, 829.1 *irascibility*
vinegar eel 81 *Worms*
vinegariness 415.1 *sourness*
vinegary 415.5 *acid*, 830.7 *irritable*
vine grower 69.13 *horticulturist*
vine snake 79 *Reptiles*
vineyard 69.2 *garden*
vingt-et-un 42 *Card Games*
vinho verde 351.9 *wine*
vinicultural 69.16 *horticultural*
viniculture 69.1 *horticulture*
viniculturist 69.13 *horticulturist*
vino 351.9 *wine*, 874.12 *alcohol*
vin ordinaire 351.9 *wine*
vinous 351.16 *drinking*, 351.17 *drinkable*, 874.5 *drunken*, 874.6 *intoxicating*
vinousness 874.11 *drinking*
vin rosé 351.9 *wine*
vintage 202.12 *olden*, 243.7 *produce*, 351.17 *drinkable*, 605.1 *store*, 617.1 *worthy*, 617.6 *worth*, 721.6 *yield*
vintage-car racing 33.1 *motor racing*
vintage crop 721.6 *yield*
vintage harvest 608.8 *plenty*
vintage port 351.9 *wine*
vintage wine 351.9 *wine*, 721.6 *yield*
vintner 606.3 *provider*
vinyl 293.9 *floor covering*
vinyl disc 420.9 *audio device*
vinyl ether 62 *Medication*
viol 49 *Musical Instruments*
viola 49 *Musical Instruments*, 84 Flowers and Flowering Plants
viola bastarda 49 *Musical Instruments*

violaceous 455.6 *purple*
viola da gamba 49 *Musical Instruments*
viola d'amore 49 *Musical Instruments*
violate 168.20 *infringe a law*, 241.8 *use violence*, 244.10 *lay waste*, 357.5 *transgress*, 601.1 *misuse*, 618.14 *ill-treat*, 734.7 *take*, 844.21 *do wrong*, 846.14 *arrogate*, 862.11 *be evil*, 877.20 *seduce*
violated 601.4 *misused*, 720.14 *violating*
violate orders 693.15 *be disobedient*, 720.9 *disregard orders*
violate the law 720, 16.73 *be illegal*, 693.15 *be disobedient*
violating 720, 16.60 *offending*
violation 16.38 *lawbreaking*, 241.2 *physical violence*, 357.8 *transgression*, 601.2 *misuse*, 720.4 *infraction*, 734.1 *taking*, 844.6 *unlawfulness*, 846.3 *arrogation*, 877.7 *sexual assault*
violation of contract 15.2 *industrial negotiations*
violation of orders 693.1 *disobedience*
violation of the law 693
violative 844.16 *in the wrong*, 846.9 *presumptive*
violence 241, 601.2 *misuse*, 618.11 *harmfulness*, 676.8 *warfare*, 695.2 *coercion*, 828.4 *anger*, 832.2 *cruelness*
Violence 241
violent 241, 16.61 *lawless*, 55.48 *stormy*, 235.13 *powerful*, 601.5 *abusive*, 618.5 *harmful*, 648.3 *hasty*, 670.23 *attacking*, 695.9 *compelling*, 828.16 *angry*, 832.11 *cruel*
violent change 216.1 *change*
violent charging 38.2 *football play*
violent death 397.5 *ways of dying*, 398.8 *accidental killing*
violently 16.84 *lawlessly*, 235.18 *powerfully*, 330.18 *dynamically*, 601.6 *abusively*, 695.11 *compellingly*
violent person 601.3 *abuser*
violent person or animal 241
violent storm 55.13 *wind strength*
violent weather 241
violet 84 Flowers and Flowering Plants, 56.28 *colour*, 418.2 *fragrant thing*, 455.3 *purple thing*, 455.6 *purple*
violetta 49 *Musical Instruments*
violin 49 *Musical Instruments*
violoncello 49 *Musical Instruments*
violone 49 *Musical Instruments*
viomycin 62 *Medication*
VIP 126.5 *superior*, 400.7 *person*, 611.4 *bigwig*, 653.13 *director*, 653.15 *manager*, 682.4 *successful person*, 686.4 *prosperous person*, 696.5 *company leader*, 800.2 *person of repute*
viper 79 *Reptiles*, 79.3 *snake*, 631.6 *source of trouble*, 832.8 *malefactor*, 875.5 *drug pusher*
viper in one's bosom 820.5 *hostile person*
viper in the bosom 635.2 *troublemaker*
viperish 79.12 *snakelike*, 832.14 *hostile*
viper-like 79.12 *snakelike*
viperous 79.12 *snakelike*
virago 237.6 *muscleman*, 241.4 *violent person or animal*, 402.2 *female*, 759.9 *feeling person*, 822.8 *hated person*, 829.3 *irascible person*, 832.9 *vixen*
virago-like 402.15 *female*
viral 59.21 *living*
viral pneumonia 624.6 *infection*
virelay 48.7 *poem*
Viren 18 Sporting Personalities
virescence 453.8 *greenness*
virescent 453.1 *green*
Virgil 48 *Poets*
Virgilian 48.19 *narrative*

virgin 134.5 *pure person*, 142.7 *uncut*, 201.12 *immature*, 206.8 *young woman*, 402.5 *single girl*, 595.4 *untrained*, 600.2 *new*, 825.4 *celibate person*, 825.7 *virginal*, 863.4 *virtuous person*, 865.4 *innocent person*, 876.5 *pure person*, 876.9 *pure*
Virgin 53 The Constellations
virginal 49 Musical Instruments, **825**, 134.12 *morally pure*, 201.12 *immature*, 206.11 *young*, 446.5 *pure*, 621.16 *clean*, 857.5 *pure*, 863.6 *ethical*, 865.5 *innocent*, 876.9 *pure*
Virginal 10.10 *religious manual*
virginally 134.18 *virtuously*, 201.24 *immaturely*, 206.14 *youthfully*, 825.12 *celibately*, 863.10 *ethically*, 865.11 *innocently*
virgin birth 245.3 *propagation*
virgin forest 85.4 *trees*
Virginia 77 Placental Mammals, **92** American States
Virginia Beach 93 Cities
Virginia reel 46.4 *historic dancing*
Virginia tobacco 413.7 *tobacco*
Virginia Wade 40.7 *famous tennis players*
virginity 825, 134.1 *purity*, 201.3 *immaturity*, 600.9 *newness*, 857.2 *purity*, 863.2 *virtues*, 865.1 *innocence*, 876.3 *moral purity*
Virgin Mary 351.6 *soft drink*, 825.4 *celibate person*
virgin soil 595.11 *natural state*
virgin territory 249.6 *regions*
Virgo 53 The Constellations, **53** Zodiac Constellations
virgo intacta 134.5 *pure person*, 825.4 *celibate person*, 876.5 *pure person*
virgule 286.2 *oblique line*, 543.7 *punctuation*
viridescence 453.8 *greenness*
viridescent 453.1 *green*
viridian 453.10 *green pigment*
viridity 453.8 *greenness*
virile 235.13 *powerful*, 237.9 *physically strong*, 239.4 *vigorous*, 401.17 *male*
virilism 401.1 *male sex*
virility 235.1 *power*, 237.1 *strength*, 401.1 *male sex*, 778.2 *heroism*
virion 59.3 *organism*
viroid 59.3 *organism*
virologist 59.19 *life scientist*, 60.13 *medical specialist*
virology 59.1 *life science*, 60.3 *medical specialty*
virtu 50.5 *artistry*
virtual 235.13 *powerful*, 486.6 *potential*, 527.1 *latent*
virtual image 56.31 *lens element*
virtuality 486.1 *possibility*, 527.6 *latency*
virtually 142.13 *on the whole*, 235.18 *powerfully*, 264.7 *nearly*, 486.11 *potentially*, 527.15 *latently*
virtue 863, 134.1 *purity*, 235.2 *ability*, 613.6 *usability*, 617.6 *worth*, 652.2 *good conduct*, 802.3 *nobleness*, 810.3 *bashfulness*, 843.4 *righteousness*, 857.2 *purity*, 861.10 *kindness*, 865.1 *innocence*, 876.2 *good morals*
Virtue 863
virtueless 864.12 *immoral*
virtues 863, 8.6 *angel*
virtuosity 126.1 *superiority*, 617.6 *worth*, 655.1 *skill*
virtuoso 49.24 *musician*, 49.29 *musical*, 126.6 *paragon*, 485.8 *qualified person*, 655.4 *skilled person*, 688.11, 696.10 *expert*, 861.16 *superior person*
virtuous 863, 134.12 *morally pure*, 617.1 *worthy*, 652.17 *well-behaved*, 810.10 *bashful*, 843.10 *moral*, 847.8 *dutiful*, 857.5 *pure*, 861.3 *kind*, 865.5 *innocent*, 876.8 *moral*
virtuous conduct 863.1 *virtue*

virtuously 134, 863, 652.19 *well*, 810.18 *shyly*, 857.8 *purely*, 865.11 *innocently*
virtuous man 825.4 *celibate person*
virtuousness 843.4 *righteousness*, 861.10 *kindness*, 863.1 *virtue*
virtuous person 863, 876.5 *pure person*
virtuous woman 825.4 *celibate person*
virulence 241.1 *violence*, 618.11 *harmfulness*, 631.7 *poisoning*, 820.1 *enmity*, 822.1 *hate*, 832.4 *bitterness*
virulent 241.6 *violent*, 618.5 *harmful*, 631.16 *blighting*, 820.6 *hostile*, 822.10 *hating*, 828.15 *resentful*, 832.14 *hostile*
virulently 631.17 *banefully*, 822.18 *hatefully*, 828.17 *resentfully*
virus 59.3 *organism*, 65.17 *computing term*, 260.2 *little thing*, 504.14 *computer error*, 624.2 *illness*, 624.6 *infection*, 626.2 *germ*, 631.7 *poisoning*
virus disease 624.4 *disease*
viruses 396.9 *classifications of life*
visa 346.4 *right of entry*, 356.6 *passport*, 480.6 *evidence*, 483.6 *documentation*, 544.3 *means of identification*, 688.9 *permission*, 708.2 *permit*, 718.2 *promise*
VISA 732.4 *lending institution*, 733.4 *credit*, 744.2 *credit card*
Visacocha 8 Deities
visage 303.2 *face*, 457.3 *external appearance*
vis-à-vis 71 Carriages and Carts, 111.4 *opposite*, 111.6 *oppositely*
Visayan 5 Languages and Groups of Languages
viscacha 77 Placental Mammals
viscera 290.4 *insides*
visceral 290 *insides*
visceral leishmaniasis 624.7 *tropical disease*
viscid 138.9 *adhesive*, 378.3 *hard*, 393.16 *semiliquid*, 394.8 *viscous*
viscidity 378.6 *toughness*, 393.2 *semiliquidity*, 394.1 *viscosity*, 726.1 *retention*
viscidly 378.12 *toughly*, 393.27 *slimily*, 394.12 *viscously*
viscometer 268.8 *meter*
viscometric 268.16 *micrometric*
viscometry 268.2 *micrometry*
viscose 67 Synthetic Fibres and Fabrics, 394.8 *viscous*
viscosity 394, 56.10 *force*, 273.5 *thickness*, 273.6 *denseness*, 385.1 *friction*, 393.2 *semiliquidity*
Viscosity 394
viscount 802.1 *nobleman*
viscountcy 802.2 *aristocracy*
viscountess 802.1 *nobleman*
viscounty 802.2 *aristocracy*
viscous 394, 138.9 *adhesive*, 273.2 *dense*, 393.16 *semiliquid*
viscously 394, 138.11 *cohesively*, 393.27 *slimily*
viscousness 394.1 *viscosity*
Vishnu 8 Deities
visibility 55, 437, 56.23 *light*, 457.2 *being in view*, 483.3 *evidentness*, 526.10 *manifestation*
Visibility 437
visible 435, 437, 322.12 *open*, 403.8 *sensate*, 457.7 *appearing*, 457.8 *outer*, 483.9 *evident*, 522.1 *intelligible*, 526.13 *displayed*, 526.14 *manifest*, 530.10 *disclosed*
visible earnings 737.5 *commercial trade*
visible effect 227
visible goods 737.5 *commercial trade*
visible horizon 437.3 *visibility*
visibleness 437.3 *visibility*
visible radiation 56.13 *electro-*

magnetic radiation, 437.6 *visible thing*, 439.1 *light*
visibles 737.5 *commercial trade*
visible spectrum 56.13 *electromagnetic radiation*, 439.1 *light*
visible thing 437
visible to the naked eye 437.1 *visible*
visible trade 13.5 *international trade*, 737.5 *commercial trade*
visibly 435, 437, 318.10 *protuberantly*, 322.25 *obviously*, 483.15 *evidently*
Visicale 65.11 *application*
Visigoths 1 Peoples, 200.6 *people of the past*
vision 435, 8.8 *divine manifestation*, 56.23 *light*, 102.2 *illusion*, 253.6 *ghostly presence*, 435.5 *imagination*, 457.4 *something that appears*, 471.6 *ideal*, 516.4 *prudence*, 519.1 *imagination*, 519.5 *fantasy*, 588.6 *objective*, 775.3 *aspiration*, 789.3 *attractive female*
Vision 435
visional 102.9 *illusory*, 435.20 *visual*
visionariness 471.7 *idealism*
visionary 519, 4.10 *philosopher*, 4.13 *of philosophy*, 102.6 *unrealistic person*, 102.11 *unrealistic*, 435.11 *observer*, 435.21 *seeing*, 457.9 *ostensible*, 471.9 *person of ideas*, 471.13 *ideal*, 516.5 *predictor*, 517.8 *oracle*, 519.11 *fantastical*, 519.12 *imaginary*, 591.17 *avoider*, 627.12 *reformer*, 833.3 *philanthropist*, 833.6 *philanthropic*
visionless 436.8 *blind*
visit 815, 253.12 *attend*, 255.14 *inhabit*, 256.19 *frequent*, 344.6 *stop at*, 346.9 *enter*, 631.14 *afflict*, 815.3 *meeting*, 879.1 *punish*
Visitandine 7 Members of Religious Orders
visitant 346.7 *entrant*
visitation 8.8 *divine manifestation*, 624.2 *illness*, 631.1 *affliction*, 687.1 *adversity*, 815.3 *meeting*, 879.10 *affliction*
visiting 253.2 *omnipresence*, 815.3 *meeting*
visiting card 544.3 *means of identification*
visiting nurse 60.16 *nurse*
visiting often 212.5 *frequenting*
visiting rights 824.3 *divorce court*
visiting side 305.5 *team*
visit often 212.8 *frequent*
visitor 253.5 *someone present*, 255.3 *householder*, 346.7 *entrant*, 723.5 *possessor*, 815.6 *social person*
Visitors' Cup 36.5 *Henley trophies*
visor 293.12 *protective covering*, 539.12 *disguise*, 671.6 *protective clothing*, 671.7 *armour*
visored 539.41 *disguised*
vista 435.7 *view*
Vistula 96 Rivers
visual 435, 437.2 *clear*, 457.8 *outer*, 547.6 *image*
visual acuity 56.23 *light*, 435.1 *vision*
visual aid 435, 437.7 *that which makes visible*, 547.6 *image*
visual appeal 457.5 *impression*
visual artist 50.16 *artist*
visual binary 53.9 *constellation*
visual distortion 436
visual fallacy 519.5 *fantasy*
visual handicap 436.2 *poor sight*
visual imagination 519.1 *imagination*
visualization 435, 471.8, 519.1 *imagination*
visualize 435, 4.20 *philosophize*, 50.23 *design*, 101.11 *make real*, 471.15, 519.14 *imagine*
visualized 471.11 *ideational*
visualizing 519.10 *imaginative*
visually 435, 50.30 *pictorially*
visually handicapped 436.9 *weak-sighted*

visually impaired 436.9 *weak-sighted*
visual record 545.1 *record*
visual sense 435.1 *vision*
Visva-Karma 8 Deities
Visvesvara 8 Deities
vita 545.1 *record*
vital 59.21 *living*, 103.5 *essential*, 233.11 *influential*, 239.4 *vigorous*, 290.10 *visceral*, 396.12 *alive*, 591.4 *necessary*, 593.4 *required*, 611.5, 772.3 *important*
vital air 396.3 *life requirements*
vital body 11.7 *spirit*
vital concern 611.2 *important matter*
vital flame 396.1 *life*
vital force 61.22 *libido*, 396.1 *life*
vital functions 59.5 *physiology*
vitalism 4.7 *school of thought*
vitalist 4.11 *follower of a doctrine*, 4.14 *of a philosophy*
vitality 235, 237.2 *healthiness*, 239.1 *vigour*, 378.8 *physical strength*, 396.1 *life*, 554.1 *emphasis*, 623.3 *health*, 642.4 *energy*
vitalization 396.1 *life*, 651.5 *refreshment*
vitalize 396.19 *give birth to*, 651.1 *refresh*
vitally 396, 233.14 *influentially*, 571.20 *with need*, 593.12 *in need*
vital necessities 396.3 *life requirements*
vitalness 593.3 *needfulness*
vital organs 290.4 *insides*
vital role 233 *influence*
vital spark 396.1 *life*
vital statistics 13.3 *economic statistics*, 52.53, 170.2 *statistics*
vital supplies 602.2 *supplies*
vital to the occasion 210.7 *critical*
vitamin 58, 630.7 *tonic*
vitamin A 58.13 *vitamin*, 58.20 *terpene*
vitamin B₁ 58.13 *vitamin*
vitamin B₁₂ 58.13 *vitamin*
vitamin B₂ 58.13 *vitamin*
vitamin B₆ 58.13 *vitamin*
vitamin B complex 58.13 *vitamin*
vitamin C 58.13 *vitamin*
vitamin D₂ 58.13 *vitamin*
vitamin D₃ 58.13 *vitamin*
vitamin deficiency 609.8 *insufficiency*
vitamin deficiency disease 58
vitamin E 58.13 *vitamin*, 58.20 *terpene*
vitamin K 58.13 *vitamin*, 58.20 *terpene*
vitamins 350.11 *food content*
vitelline membrane 78.15 *eggs*
vitiate 628.6 *pervert*, 877.19 *corrupt*
vitiated 624.23 *diseased*
vitiation 628.8 *perversion*, 864.1 *wickedness*
viticultural 69.16 *horticultural*
viticulture 69.1 *horticulture*
Viti Levu 98 Islands
vitiligo 624.13 *skin disease*
vitrectomy 60 Surgical Operations
vitreosity 442.5 *transparency*
vitreous 373.1 *hard*, 442.1 *transparent*
vitreous humour 435.2 *eye*
vitreousness 442.5 *transparency*
vitrification 373.6 *solidification*
vitrified 373.3 *hardened*
vitrify 373.10 *solidify*
vitriol 820.1 *enmity*, 832.4 *bitterness*
vitriolic 820.6 *hostile*, 827.9 *vituperative*, 832.14 *hostile*
vitriolically 820.15 *aggressively*
vittles 350.7 *food*
Vittorini 48 Writers
vituperate 852, 670.10 *criticize*, 827.6 *vilify*
vituperation 564.9 *art of public speaking*, 827.3 *vilification*, 852.8 *berating*
vituperative 827, 670.25 *critical*,

818.5 *discourteous,* 852.27 *critical*
vituperatively 827, 818.9 *discourteously*
viva 477.3 *questionnaire*
vivacious 235.15 *full of energy,* 396.13 *lively,* 554.3 *emphatic,* 642.18 *active,* 769.1 *cheerful*
vivaciously 396.22 *vitally*
vivaciousness 554.1 *emphasis,* 642.4 *energy*
vivacity 235.3 *vitality,* 396.1 *life,* 554.1 *emphasis,* 642.4 *energy,* 769.3 *cheerfulness*
Vivaldi 49 Musicians and Composers
vivandiere 739.14 *street trader*
viva voce examination 477.3 *questionnaire*
vivement 49 Musical Terms
viverrid 77.8 *flesh-eating mammal*
Viverridae 77.8 *flesh-eating mammal*
viverrine 77.28 *carnivorous*
Vivès 4 Philosophers
vivid 114.9 *lifelike,* 437.2 *clear,* 439.16 *bright,* 444.11 *colourful,* 519.10 *imaginative,* 522.1 *intelligible,* 547.13 *representational,* 554.3 *emphatic,* 560.11 *descriptive*
vivid imagination 519.1 *imagination*
vividly 48.23 *descriptively,* 114.14 *comparably,* 439.30 *lightly,* 547.14 *representationally,* 560.18 *descriptively*
vividness 437.4 *clarity,* 439.1 *light,* 522.9 *intelligibility,* 554.1 *emphasis*
vivification 396.1 *life*
vivified 396.12 *alive*
vivify 396.19 *give birth to*
vivifying 396.12 *alive*
viviparous 245.16 *reproductive*
vivisection 398.9 *animal killing,* 479.3 *experimentation*
vivisectionist 398.13 *animal killer,* 479.5 *experimenter*
vixen 832, 77.18 *female mammal,* 402.14 *female animal,* 829.3 *irascible person*
vixenish 829.4 *irascible,* 830.7 *irritable*
vixenishness 829.1 *irascibility*
viz 165.31 *namely,* 524.18 *in other words*
vizier 653.16 *official*
vizsla 77 Breeds of Dogs
V-J Day 214.6 *annually celebrated day*
Vladimir Heavy Draught 32 Breeds of Horse and Pony
VLSI 64.13 *circuit*
V-neck 295.15 *sweater*
vocabular 5.42 *worded*
vocabulary 171.3 *dictionary,* 549.4 *literary style,* 564.1 *faculty of speech*
vocal 5.41 *lettered,* 49.32 *instrumental,* 431.16 *vociferous,* 564.16 *speech*
vocal chords 423.4 *sound maker,* 564.5 *organ of speech*
vocal folds 564.5 *organ of speech*
vocalic 5.41 *lettered*
vocalise semiotics 5.5 *nonstandard language*
vocalism 5.3 *spoken language*
vocalist 49.23 *singer,* 49.24 *musician*
vocalization 564.4 *articulation,* 564.7 *utterance*
vocalize 5.45 *use language,* 49.39, 433.10 *sing*
vocalized 564.16 *speech*
vocally 5.48 *linguistically,* 431.20 *vociferously,* 564.21 *orally*
vocal organs 564.5 *organ of speech*
vocation 165.8 *specialization,* 228.1, 586.11 *motive,* 644.3 *job,* 652.1 *conduct,* 737.6 *business*
vocational 737.17 *professional*

vocational therapy 61.3 *psychiatric treatment*
vocational training 6.2 *educational system*
vocative 567, 5.31 *case*
vociferate 423.8 *be loud,* 431.10 *cry out*
vociferation 423.2 *outcry,* 431.1 *cry*
vociferous 431, 423.6 *loud*
vociferously 431, 423.9 *loudly*
Vodaphone 534.9 *telephone*
vodka 351.7 *alcoholic drink*
vodka and tonic 351.8 *mixed drink*
vogue 5.42 *worded,* 167.5 *convention,* 796.1 *fashion*
vogue word 5.21 *catchword*
Vogul 5 Languages and Groups of Languages
Vohu Manah 8.6 *angel*
voice 5, 5.30 *syntax,* 5.45 *use language,* 423.4 *sound maker,* 564.1 *faculty of speech,* 564.3 *mode of speech,* 564.5 *organ of speech,* 564.11 *speak,* 580.10 *vote,* 652.1 *conduct*
voice box 423.4 *sound maker,* 564.5 *organ of speech*
voiced 5.41 *lettered,* 564.16 *speech,* 564.18 *phonetic*
voiced consonant 5.16 *spoken letter,* 564.7 *utterance*
voiceless 423.3 *silent,* 424.4 *faint,* 564.18 *phonetic,* 566.2 *silent*
voiceless consonant 563.4 *whispering*
voicelessly 563, 566.10 *taciturnly*
voicelessness 563, 422.4 *silence,* 424.1 *faintness,* 566.5 *silence*
Voicelessness 563
voiceless person 563
voiceless speech 563
voice of conscience 636.1 *warning,* 876.2 *good morals*
voice of one's conscience 867.1 *penitence*
voice of opposition 475.8 *protester*
voice of reason 509.3 *sane person*
voice of the tempter 586.3 *incentive*
voice quality 564.3 *mode of speech*
voice synthesizer 65.7 *peripheral*
voice vote 580.10 *vote*
voicing 564.4 *articulation*
void 777 Phobias by Topic, **349,** 53.7 *galaxy,* 100.4 *emptiness,* 100.9 *nonexistent,* 131.3 *subtract,* 145.2 *omission,* 172.7 *null,* 248.2 *empty space,* 254.3 *vacant,* 265.3 *gulf,* 352.7 *secrete,* 353.16 *defecate,* 362.6 *throw down,* 372.1 *sparse,* 536.5 *nonexistence,* 598.2 *withdraw,* 598.5 *relinquished,* 614.1 *useless,* 704.6 *cancel*
voidance 337.12 *reversal,* 347.2 *outflow,* 349.21 *removal,* 352.1 *secretion,* 353.2 *defecation*
voided 704.10 *cancelled*
voiding 349.21 *removal*
voidness 254.3 *emptiness,* 372.3 *sparseness*
voile 288.4 *textile,* 442.8 *transparent thing*
voiturette 71 Carriages and Carts
Volans 53 The Constellations
volant 329.1 *swift*
Volapuk 5 Languages and Groups of Languages
volatile 388, 189.6 *transient,* 224.14 *irresolute,* 370.2 *insubstantial,* 388.1 *gas,* 491.8, 579.1 *capricious,* 759.13 *passionate*
volatile memory 65.6 *memory*
volatileness 370.5 *lightness,* 372.3 *sparseness,* 491.16 *capriciousness*
volatile oil 395.7 *oil*

volatility 388, 189.1 *transience,* 224.2 *irresolution,* 370.5 *lightness,* 372.3 *sparseness,* 491.16 *capriciousness*
volatilizable 372.1 *sparse,* 388.23 *volatile*
volatilization 162.3 *dilution,* 388.10 *vaporization*
volatilize 162.14 *dilute,* 370.10 *lighten,* 372.6 *make sparse,* 388.25 *gasify*
volatilized 372.1 *sparse*
vol-au-vent 45.12 *hors d'oeuvre*
volcanic 54, 54.56 *petrographic,* 98.11 *continental,* 241.6 *violent,* 322.14 *holed,* 347.15 *outgoing,* 408.10 *on fire*
volcanic activity 54
volcanically 54.66 *geographically,* 98.13 *continentally,* 322.27 *cavernously*
volcanic cone 54.24 *volcanic activity*
volcanic gas 54.25 *eruption*
volcanic island 54.16 *ocean floor*
volcanic lake 94.1 *lake*
volcanic mountain 54.21 *mountain building*
volcanic rock 54.30 *igneous rock*
volcanism 54.24 *volcanic activity*
volcano 54.24 *volcanic activity,* 98.10 *miscellaneous,* 322.5 *hole,* 349.28 *propellant,* 408.8 *hot place,* 635.1 *trap*
volcanological 54.48 *geological*
volcanologist 54.3 *geologist,* 54.4 *geophysicist*
volcanology 54.1 *earth science,* 54.2 *geophysics*
vole 77 Placental Mammals
Volga 96 Rivers, 96.5 *other major rivers*
Volgograd 93 Cities
volition 4.9 *philosophical problem,* 570.1 *will*
volitional 570.6 *willed,* 580.14 *selecting,* 588.12 *intended*
volitive 570.6 *willed*
volley 40.2 *tennis strokes,* 40.5 *real tennis,* 40.13 *serve,* 161.22 *flood,* 330.10 *bat,* 338.5 *throw,* 338.7 *shot,* 338.23 *throw,* 338.28 *shoot,* 425.1 *bang,* 670.2 *fire,* 670.15 *firing*
volley and thunder 338.28 *shoot,* 670.2 *fire*
volleyball 18 Sporting Activities, **18** Sporting Activities
volleyer 40.6 *tennis player*
volley of abuse 827.3 *vilification*
Volos 8 Deities
Volscian 5 Languages and Groups of Languages
Volstead Act 709.1 *veto,* 869.1 *self-restraint*
volt 75 SI Units, **75** Scientific and Technical Units, 235.5 *unit of work*
volta 46.4 *historic dancing*
Volta 52 Scientists, **94** Lakes, **96** Rivers, 94.5 *other major lakes*
voltage 56.52, 64.10 *electric potential,* 235.5 *unit of work*
voltage amplifier 64.21 *rectifier*
voltage regulator 64.34 *power supply*
voltage transformer 64.22 *transformer*
Voltaic 5 Languages and Groups of Languages
voltaic cell 57.19 *electrochemistry,* 64.5 *electrolytic conduction*
voltaic electricity 235.7 *electrical power*
Voltaire 48 Writers
voltameter 268.8 *meter*
voltametric 268.16 *micrometric*
voltammeter 268.8 *meter*
volt-ampere 75 Scientific and Technical Units
volte 32.10 *dressage*
volte-face 221.1 *reversion,* 578.6 *equivocation,* 858.2 *faithlessness*
voltmeter 56.90 *ammeter,* 64.23 *electrical instrument,* 268.8 *meter*

Voltumna 8 Deities
Volturno 96 Rivers
volubility 564.2 *power of speech,* 565.1 *talkativeness*
voluble 564.19 *speaking,* 565.5 *talkative*
volubly 565.10 *talkatively*
volume 52.35, 56.7 *space,* 56.38 *thermodynamics,* 120.1 *quantity,* 143.2 *particular,* 146.1 *inclusion,* 248.1 *space,* 259.1, 268.4 *size,* 534.22 *television set*
volume control 420.9 *audio device,* 534.18 *radio*
volume strain 63.14 *load*
volumeter 268.8 *meter*
volumetric 57.41 *analytic,* 248.11 *spatial,* 268.16 *micrometric*
volumetric analysis 57.18 *gravimetric analysis*
volumetric flask 57 Laboratory Apparatus
volumetry 268.2 *micrometry*
voluminous 120.6 *quantitative,* 248.13 *spacious,* 259.15 *big,* 553.3 *diffuse*
voluminously 120.7 *quantitatively,* 248.15 *spaciously,* 259.20 *largely*
voluminousness 248.4 *spaciousness,* 259.2 *bigness*
voluntarily 572, 588.13 *intentionally,* 710.20 *persuasively*
voluntary 572, 710, 583.2 *spontaneous,* 588.12 *intended,* 729.7 *given,* 754.11 *free of charge*
voluntary aid 572.10 *voluntary work*
voluntary arbitration 15.4 *industrial dispute*
voluntary commitment 714.1 *promise*
voluntary hospital 60.10 *hospital*
voluntaryism 572.10 *voluntary work*
voluntary payment 746.1 *payment*
voluntary poverty 743.8 *renunciation of wealth*
voluntary resignation 705.1 *resignation*
voluntary retirement 15.2 *industrial negotiations*
voluntary service 572.10 *voluntary work*
voluntary work 572, 597.2 *undertaking,* 729.1 *giving,* 754.6 *absence of charge*
voluntary worker 646.1 *worker,* 710.8 *volunteer,* 833.3 *philanthropist*
volunteer 572, 597, 710, 710, 17.9 *enlisted,* 572.11 *willing worker,* 596.7 *attempter,* 597.1 *undertake,* 642.10 *busy person,* 642.16 *be sociable,* 646.1 *worker,* 676.11 *recruit,* 676.12 *go to war,* 679.8 *soldier,* 729.6 *give to charity,* 833.3 *philanthropist*
volunteer army 17.2 *the military,* 679.15 *army*
volunteering 572.5 *voluntary,* 642.2 *social activity,* 676.7 *war measures*
volunteer snooker 24.5 *snooker*
volunteer work 754.6 *absence of charge*
voluptuary 405.3 *pleasure-seeker,* 763.12 *pleasure-loving person,* 870.5 *self-indulgent person*
voluptuous 405.6 *pleasant,* 405.7 *pleased,* 763.5 *pleasure-loving,* 870.6 *self-indulgent,* 877.14 *lecherous*
voluptuousness 405.1 *physical pleasure,* 763.7 *pleasure,* 870.1 *self-indulgence*
volutation 364.2 *turning*
volute 43 Architectural Decoration, **81** Molluscs
volute spring 377.5 *spring*
volution 364.1 *rotation,* 366.11 *stagger*
volva 89.4 *fungal body*
vomer 382 Bones

vomit 349, 347.11 *run out,* 349.23 *vomiting,* 624.24 *be unhealthy,* 785.6 *react against*
vomit forth 387.25 *flow*
vomiting 777 Phobias by Topic, **349, 349,** 624.3 *symptom,* 624.8 *indigestion,* 785.4 *sign of dislike,* 785.8 *disliking*
vomition 349.23 *vomiting*
vomitive 349.30 *vomiting*
vomitory 349.30 *vomiting,* 630.17 *remedial*
Vonnegut 48 Writers
voodoo 11.3 *witchcraft,* 233.2 *occult influence,* 497.2 *religious belief,* 618.11 *harmfulness,* 687.11 *cause adversity,* 862.4 *evil power*
Voodoo 7 Non-Christian Religions
voodoo curse 822.2 *curse*
voodoo doll 618.11 *harmfulness*
voodooed 862.10 *inauspicious*
voodooism 11.1 *occultism,* 11.3 *witchcraft*
voodooist 11.4 *witch*
voodooistic 11.15 *witchlike*
voodoo spell 827.4 *malediction*
voracious 350.26 *eating,* 609.3 *underfed,* 782.9 *desirous,* 872.6 *gluttonous*
voracious eating 350.2 *appetite*
voraciously 350.28 *carnivorously,* 872.7 *gluttonously*
voraciousness 350.2 *appetite,* 872.1 *gluttony*
voracity 350.2 *appetite,* 782.1 *desire,* 872.1 *gluttony*
Voronezh Harness Horse 32 Breeds of Horse and Pony
vortex 364, 96.6 *river flow,* 314.3 *convoluted thing,* 366.13 *tempest,* 635.1 *trap,* 642.1 *activity*
vortical 96.10 *fluvial,* 364.12 *rotary*
vortically 96.13 *fluently*
vorticism 50 Western Art Styles and Movements
Vorticism 48 Literary Groups and Movements
vorticist 50.29 *realist*
vorticose 364.12 *rotary*
vorticular 364.12 *rotary*
Vosges 95 Mountains
Vostok 53.31 *space travel*
votary 7.3 *religious person,* 9.5 *worshipper*
vote 580, 580, 16.68 *legislate,* 492.1 *judgment,* 703.6 *commission,* 851.1 *approval*
Vote 5 Languages and Groups of Languages
vote against 111.9 *oppose,* 113.9 *dissent,* 147.7 *exclude,* 581.1 *reject,* 663.14 *be against,* 711.6 *dissent,* 785.6 *react against*
vote-catcher 586.12 *persuader*
vote-catching 580.16 *elective*
vote counting 580.12 *election*
voted 16.46 *legislated*
voted in 667.10 *agreeing*
vote down 147.7 *exclude,* 580.5 *vote,* 699.8 *restrain*
vote for 499.4 *assent,* 580.5 *vote*
vote in 580.5 *vote*
vote independent 698.16 *be independent*
vote in the affirmative 667.6 *agree with*
vote of confidence 580.10 *vote*
vote of no confidence 580.10 *vote*
vote of thanks 564.8 *speech,* 837.3 *recognition*
vote out 147.7 *exclude,* 580.5 *vote*
voter 580.13 *electorate,* 698.7 *free person*
voters 580.13 *electorate*
votes for women 580.11 *franchise*
vote-snatcher 586.12 *persuader*
vote unanimously 112.11, 135.9 *agree*
vote with one's feet 218.7 *stop working,* 254.15 *be absent,* 580.5 *vote*

voting 580.12 *election,* 580.16 *elective,* 703.1 *commission*
voting list 171.6 *list of names,* 580.12 *election*
voting machine 580.12 *election*
voting paper 580.12 *election*
voting precinct 93.7 *city district*
votive 714.12 *promised,* 729.7 *given*
votive candle 10.14 *sacred object*
votively 714.16 *as promised,* 729.9 *as a gift*
votive offering 710.6, 729.3 *offering,* 840.2 *apology*
Votyak 5 Languages and Groups of Languages
vouch 535.1 *affirmation,* 535.17 *affirm*
vouched 535.12 *vowed*
vouched for 535.12 *vowed*
voucher 480.7 *verifier,* 483.6 *documentation,* 535.9 *affirmer,* 545.1 *record,* 708.2 *permit,* 714.2 *guarantee,* 730.3 *acknowledgment of payment,* 749.1 *receipt*
vouch for 535.18 *vow,* 632.9 *protect,* 714.8 *guarantee,* 718.11 *promise*
vouching 535.1 *affirmation*
vouchsafe 116.28 *consent,* 729.5 *give*
vouchsafed 116.18 *permitting*
vouchsafement 116.7 *consent*
voussoir 43.7 *vault,* 43.9 *miscellaneous architectural features*
vow 535, 535, 597.1 *undertake,* 597.3 *contract,* 714.1, 714.7 *promise,* 729.5 *give,* 847.7 *commitment*
vowed 535
vowel 5.16 *spoken letter,* 564.7 *utterance*
vowel point 543.7 *punctuation*
vower 535.9 *affirmer*
vow of loyalty 819.4 *act of friendship*
vow of poverty 743.8 *renunciation of wealth*
vox populi 12.1 *government,* 16.18 *tribunal,* 116.1 *accord,* 164.11 *general public,* 492.1 *judgment*
voyage 74.1 *water travel,* 356.1 *passage,* 356.9 *proceed*
voyager 224.7 *person who moves around*
Voyager 53.33 *planetary probe*
voyaging 74.1 *water travel*
voyeur 435.11 *observer,* 465.4 *meddler*
voyeurism 435.3 *observation,* 465.2 *prying,* 877.2 *indecency*
vroom 329.4 *be swift,* 329.9 *acceleration*
V-shape 36.13 *windsurfing,* 310.1 *angle,* 343.5 *fork*
V-shaped 310.7 *angular,* 343.9 *branched*
V-shaped valley 54.7 *landform*
V-shaped hull 36.7 *windsurfing*
V-sign 310.1 *angle,* 324.11 *bodily movement,* 543.3 *gesture,* 675.2 *symbol of peace,* 713.3 *gesture of protest,* 807.7 *insult,* 818.3 *act of discourtesy,* 850.7 *sign of disrespect*
VSO 710.8 *volunteer*
VTOL 73.7 *miscellaneous aviation terms*
Vulcan 8 Deities
vulcanite 57.21 *polymer,* 377.4 *rubber*
vulcanization 373.6 *solidification*
vulcanize 67.15 *treat,* 373.9 *harden,* 377.9 *make elastic,* 378.11 *make tough*
vulcanized 67.11 *treated,* 378.2 *toughened*
vulcanized rubber 377.4 *rubber*
vulcanizing 67.8 *fabric treatment*
vulgar 795, 5.39 *of language,* 127.16 *ordinary,* 164.21 *common,* 411.8 *tasteful,* 412.6 *coarse,* 482.1 *undiscriminating,* 559.8 *indecorous,* 559.10 *ugly,*

585.2 *not customary,* 618.4 *poor,* 658.1 *naive,* 803.4 *common,* 811.21 *blatant,* 818.6 *bad-mannered,* 827.8 *cursing,* 844.13 *improper,* 864.12 *immoral,* 877.12 *indecent*
vulgar fraction 52.18 *division,* 169.5 *ratio,* 173.1 *fraction*
vulgar herd 795, 803.2 *the common people*
vulgarian 482.9 *undiscriminating person,* 795.5 *vulgar person*
vulgarism 5.3 *spoken language,* 5.19 *swearword,* 559.4 *inelegance of speech*
vulgarity 127.4 *poor quality,* 411.2 *taste of life,* 412.4 *bad taste,* 482.6 *lack of discrimination,* 559.2 *impropriety,* 559.3 *ugliness,* 559.4 *inelegance of speech,* 618.10 *poverty,* 658.2 *naivety,* 754.3 *shoddiness,* 818.2 *bad manners,* 827.1 *curse,* 844.3 *impropriety,* 864.2 *vice,* 877.2 *indecency*
Vulgarity 795
vulgarization 628.8 *perversion*
vulgarize 795, 164.26 *popularize,* 628.6 *pervert,* 660.16 *make easy*
vulgar language 5.19 *swearword*
vulgarly 411.11 *tastily,* 412.11 *tastelessly,* 811.37 *blatantly,* 818.10 *rudely,* 827.12 *swearingly,* 864.20 *immorally*
vulgarness 844.3 *impropriety*
vulgar person 795
vulgar tongue 5.3 *spoken language,* 564.1 *faculty of speech*
vulgate 5.3 *spoken language,* 524.1 *interpretation*
vulnerability 633, 236.3 *helplessness,* 238.1 *weakness,* 379.2 *brittleness,* 403.2 *ability to sense,* 620.5 *imperfection*
vulnerable 633, 236.11 *unprotected,* 379.1 *brittle,* 595.1 *unprepared,* 620.1 *imperfect,* 864.13 *venial*
vulnerable point 620.7 *defect,* 633.7 *vulnerability*
vulnerably 864, 379.5 *fragilely,* 633.11 *dangerously*
vulnerary 630.18 *medical*
Vulpecula 53 The Constellations
vulpecular 77.28 *carnivorous*
vulpine 77.28 *carnivorous,* 657.4 *cunning,* 858.5 *dishonourable*
vulture 78 Birds, 78.5 *bird of prey,* 621.12 *cleaner,* 734.6 *taker,* 832.8 *malefactor*
vulturine 78.23 *avian*
vulva 245.8 *organs of reproduction*
vulvar 245.16 *reproductive*
vulvectomy 60 Surgical Operations
vulvitis 624.10 *cardiovascular disease*
VX 631.10 *warfare*
vying 663.3 *conflict,* 674.14 *contending*
Vyrnwy 94 Lakes, 94.4 *British lakes*

W

Wa 5 Languages and Groups of Languages
Wabash 96 Rivers
wack down 362.2 *flatten*
Wacker process 57 Named Reactions
wacko 61.8 *disordered personality,* 168.10 *eccentric*
wacky 117.9 *nonconforming,* 229.6 *motiveless,* 510.11 *insane,* 769.2 *cheering*
Waco 93 Cities
wad 161.27 *bundle,* 259.7 *mass,* 292.4 *fill,* 323.2 *stopper,* 680.13 *ammunition*
wadding 257.4 *stuffing,* 292.2

filling, 323.2 *stopper,* 374.11 *soft thing*
waddle 324.12 *gait,* 324.15 *walk,* 328.10 *slow motion,* 365.11 *rock*
waddling 328.4 *slow*
Wade 18 Sporting Personalities
wade across 356.11 *cross*
wade in 674.12 *fight*
wade in blood 398.18 *slaughter*
wade into 607.1 *waste*
wader 78.3 *water bird*
waders 295.19 *footwear*
wade through 324.13 *be in motion,* 644.8 *exert oneself,* 652.14 *behave towards*
wadi 96.1 *river*
wading 39.11 *swimming*
wading bird 78.3 *water bird*
wading pool 39.7 *swimming pool*
wad of notes 742.6 *money*
Wado Kyu 26.8 *karate*
wads 181.2 *multitude*
wads of money 741.3 *fortune*
wafer 45.39 *loaf,* 266.4 *slice,* 274.11 *fineness*
wafer-thin 274.4 *fine,* 379.1 *brittle*
waffle 45.39 *loaf,* 102.16 *delude,* 183.2 *iteration,* 521.9 *talk nonsense,* 553.1 *diffuseness,* 553.5 *be diffuse,* 565.3 *talk,* 565.7 *be talkative,* 578.1 *be equivocal,* 591.7 *be evasive,* 591.15 *evasiveness*
waffle house 350.15 *eating place*
waffle iron 45.5 *cooker,* 408.4 *burner*
waffler 474.6 *sophist,* 565.4 *talker*
waffling 553.3 *diffuse*
waft 326.2 *transportation,* 326.12 *transport,* 370.9 *be light,* 416.1 *odour*
waftage 326.2 *transportation*
wag 365.4 *rock,* 365.12 *wave,* 366.7 *shake,* 366.22 *agitate,* 506.4 *buffoon,* 771.6 *humorist*
wage 640.4 *act,* 746.3 *pay,* 878.4 *reward for service*
wage a campaign 679.36 *combat*
wage bill 751.6 *business costs*
wage council 15.1 *industrial relations*
waged 746.19 *receiving pay,* 749.6 *received*
wage earner 15.7 *employee,* 646.1 *worker,* 721.7 *gainer,* 730.5 *recipient*
wage-earning 15.8 *industrial,* 730.11 *receiving,* 746.19 *receiving pay*
wager 589.12 *take a chance,* 674.11 *contend*
wage rates 15.2 *industrial negotiations*
wager of battle 676.1 *war*
wages 13.6 *economic factors,* 228.5 *positive stimulus,* 721.4 *earnings,* 749.3 *income,* 751.6 *business costs,* 878.4 *reward for service*
wages and salaries 13.8 *industrial relations*
wage scale 878.4 *reward for service*
wage slave 646.1 *worker*
wage war 674.12 *fight,* 676.13 *be at war,* 713.8 *cause mischief,* 820.12 *oppose*
wage worker 15.7 *employee,* 721.7 *gainer*
wagging forefinger 543.3 *gesture*
waggish 506.5 *nonsensical,* 771.10 *humorous*
waggle 365.4, 365.11 *rock,* 366.7 *shake,* 366.22 *agitate,* 366.25 *pitch*
waggonage 326.2 *transportation*
waggoner 326.7 *transferor*
waging war 676.8 *warfare,* 676.15 *warring*
Wagner 49 Musicians and Composers
Wagnerian costume 295.5 *fancy dress*
wagon 71 Carriages and Carts,

71 Motor Vehicles, 71.17 *police car*, 71.20 *truck*, 72.6 *rolling stock*, 258.10 *cart*

wagonette 71 Carriages and Carts

wagon stage 51.15 *stage*

wagon train 71.9 *animal transport*

wagon wheel 364.6 *rotator*

wagtail 78 Birds, 20.2 *artificial fly*, 78.6 *songbird*

Wahhabi 7.6 *non-Christian*

Wahhabiyah 7 Non-Christian Religions

wahoo 80 Fishes, **85** Trees and Shrubs

Wahran 93 Cities

waif 252.7 *displaced person*, 816.7 *outsider*

Waikato 92 New Zealand Regions and Territories, **96** Rivers

wail 55.58 *blow*, 406.12 *express pain*, 430.1 *stridency* , 430.4 *be strident*, 431.6 *cry of pain*, 431.13, 432.4 *cry*, 564.13 *speak in a particular way*, 770.8 *grieve*, 774.6 *lament*, 774.7 *weep*

wailer 774.3 *lamenter*

wailful 432.7 *ululant*

wailfully 432.10 *howlingly*

wailing 431.18 *crying*, 432.1 *animal cry*, 432.7 *ululant*, 774.1 *lamentation*, 774.4 *lamenting*

Wailing Wall 10.13 *shrine*

wain 71 Carriages and Carts

Wain 48 Writers

wainscot 280.2 *foot*, 292.1 *lining*, 292.3 *line*

wainwright 646.2 *artisan*

Wairarapa 92 New Zealand Regions and Territories

waist 158.4 *midline*, 272.8 *narrow thing*

waistband 137.10 *band*, 313.3 *circular thing*

waist belay 34.3 *climbing technique*

waist belt 34.4 *climbing equipment*

waistcloth 295.25 *accessories*

waistcoat 295.11 *jacket*

waist-deep 277.8 *deep*, 278.1 *shallow*

waist-high 275.12 *tall*

waist-length 269.1 *long*

waistline 158.4 *midline*, 295.24 *part of garment*

wait 209, 513, 209.3 *delayed action*, 248.21 *space*, 325.8 *be motionless*, 641.4 *not act*, 876.11 *be moral*

wait and see 209.8 *delay*, 491.18 *be uncertain*, 641.4 *not act*

wait-and-see 641.3 *inactive*

wait-and-see policy 781.1 *caution*

waiter 606.3 *provider*, 697.3 *attendant*

wait for 199.10 *expect*, 513.10 *wait*, 594.3 *be prepared*

wait for the command 694.5 *obey*

waiting 199.4 *looking to the future*, 199.11 *future*, 356.2 *passing along*, 513.1 *expectation*, 513.5 *expecting*, 534.10 *telephone call*

waiting for the bomb to drop 777.8 *fearful*

waiting for the other shoe to fall 777.8 *fearful*

waiting game 781.1 *caution*

waiting in the wings 199.11 *future*

waiting list 171.6 *list of names*, 545.1 *record*

waiting on 697.9 *serving*

waiting room 72.8 *railway station*, 218.4 *stopping place*

wait on 180.16 *attend*, 662.25 *serve*, 701.8 *be subject to*, 808.11 *pander to*, 826.8 *court*

wait on hand and foot 697.8 *serve*, 808.11 *pander to*

waitress 606.3 *provider*, 697.3 *attendant*

wait upon 694.5 *obey*, 697.8 *serve*

waive 598.1 *relinquish*, 600.5 *not use*, 727.9 *dispose of*

waived 598.5 *relinquished*, 600.3 *not wanted*

waiver 19.14 *miscellaneous terms*, 598.3 *relinquishment*, 704.1 *cancellation*, 704.6 *cancel*, 708.2 *permit*

waive the rules 814.11 *not stand on ceremony*

waiving 598.3 *relinquishment*

wakan 8.5 *deity*

Wakashan 5 Languages and Groups of Languages

wake 96.6 *river flow*, 132.1 *remainder*, 155.10 *rear*, 195.1 *succession*, 227.2 *visible effect*, 304.1 *rear*, 397.8 *after death*, 399.2 *funeral*, 403.13 *arouse sensation*, 483.4 *indication*, 642.14 *push*, 774.1 *lamentation*, 835.2 *condolence*

wake course 36.1 *sailing*

wakeful 642.18 *active*

wakefulness 642.7 *restlessness*

wake the dead 11.22 *conjure*, 423.8 *be loud*

wake up 403.12 *awake*, 403.13 *arouse sensation*, 642.12 *be active*

waking time 204.1 *morning*

Waksman 52 Scientists

Walcott 48 Poets, **48** Dramatists

Walden universion 57 Named Reactions

Waldorf salad 45.14 *salad*, 45.43 *US dish*

Waler 32 Breeds of Horse and Pony

Wales 91

walk 324, 21.1 *track events*, 22.7 *play baseball*, 23.6 *play basketball*, 249.13 *locality*, 324.12 *gait*, 328.10 *slow motion*, 334.1 *circuit*, 349.33 *go away*, 363.3 *orbit*, 644.9 *exercise*, 652.1 *conduct*

walk a punt 36.19 *punt*

walk as quiet as an Indian 590.9 *follow*

walk away 345.1 *depart*

walked off one's feet 650.1 *fatigued*

walker 21.3 *athlete*, 284.3 *body support*

walk hand in hand with 815.13 *fraternize*

walk humbly with one's God 863.8 *be virtuous*

walkie-talkie 34.4 *climbing equipment*, 420.9 *audio device*, 534.18 *radio*

walking 21.1 *track events*, 21.6 *track*, 23.5 *penalties*, 71.4 *personal transport*, 324.1 *motion*, 328.4 *slow*, 356.2 *passing along*, 625.1 *hygiene*, 644.5 *exercise*

walking a man in 22.4 *pitching terms*

walking bass 433.3 *melodiousness*

walking boots 295.19 *footwear*

walking disaster 628.9 *dilapidation*

walking encyclopedia 461.7 *thinker*, 501.6 *knowledgeable person*, 655.5, 688.11 *expert*, 696.10 *expert*

walking events 18 Sporting Activities

walking fern 88 Ferns

walking frame 284.3 *body support*

walking gentleman 51.21 *role*

walking lady 51.21 *role*

walking out 821.6, 826.2 *courtship*

walking papers 704.2 *termination*

walking part 51.21 *role*

walking race 21.1 *track events*

walking shoes 295.19 *footwear*

walking skeleton 274.9 *thin person*

walking steps 46.3 *ballroom dance steps*

walking stick 82 Insects, 284.3 *body support*

walking the plank 879.7 *punishment*

walking under a ladder 517.7 *bad-luck sign*

walk in the shoes of 118.11 *emulate*

walk into a trap 633.8 *be in danger*

Walkman 420.9 *audio device*, 534.18 *radio*

walk off 347.9 *exit*

walk-off 347.1 *exit*

walk off with 682.10 *defeat heavily*, 736.12 *steal*

walk off with all the prizes 617.9 *be worthy*

walk of life 105.1 *state*, 652.1 *conduct*

walk on 51.34 *underact*, 701.6 *subject*

walk on eggshells 469.10 *be careful*

walk one's beat 214.8 *be cyclic*

walk one's daily beat 112.12 *be monotonous*

walk on hot coals 659.19 *have difficulty*

walk-on part 51.21 *role*

walk on tiptoe 527.13 *hide*

walk on water 487.10 *attempt the impossible*

walkout 15.4 *industrial dispute*

walk out 15.12 *have an industrial dispute*

walkout 218.2 *stop*

walk out 218.7 *stop working*, 347.9 *exit*, 347.14 *be dismissed*

walkout 500.3 *dissentience*

walk out 500.8 *dissent*, 598.2 *withdraw*

walkout 669.1 *resistance*

walk out 669.6 *resist*, 824.8 *desert*

walk-out 347.1 *exit*, 598.3 *relinquishment*

walk out with 135.8 *unite*, 821.26, 826.8 *court*

walkover 32.7 *horseracing*

walk over 618.14 *ill-treat*

walkover 660.6 *easy thing*, 682.2 *victory*

walk over 690.6 *suppress*, 701.6 *subject*

walk over the course 660.17 *do easily*

walk slowly 328.1 *move slowly*

walk the earth 396.16 *live*

walk the plank 397.16 *meet one's fate*

walkthrough 51.12 *production*

walk through 51.35 *rehearse*

walk up 359.14 *climb*

walkway 63.21 *bridge*

wall 726, 32.9 *jumping*, 34.5 *rock face*, 41.1 *skiing*, 43.9 *miscellaneous architectural features*, 136.6 *boundary*, 147.3 *exclusion zone*, 281.3 *vertical thing*, 284.2 *supporting part*, 284.11 *support*, 301.3 *enclosing thing*, 301.5 *enclose*, 371.4 *solid body*, 634.1 *refuge*, 634.2 *shelter*, 661.3 *barrier*, 661.9 *block*, 671.9 *barrier*, 671.11 *fortification*, 671.18 *fence*, 879.16 *instrument of execution*

wallaby 77 Marsupials

Wallace 48 Writers, **52** Scientists

wallah 646.1 *worker*

wallaroo 77 Marsupials

wallboard 293.8 *wall covering*

wall clock 191 Timepieces and Timers, 192.6 *clock*

wall covering 293

wallcreeper 78 Birds

walled 671.30 *defended*

walled garden 301.2 *enclosed place*, 323.4 *closed place*

walled in 293.37 *protected*, 661.14 *blocked*, 726.10 *retained*

walled-in 301.7 *enclosed*

walled up 293.37 *protected*

Waller 48 Poets

wallet 258.5 *packet*, 258.9 *baggage*, 741.20 *money store*

walleye 80 Fishes, 20.4 *American game fish*, 436.2 *poor sight*

walleyed 436.9 *weak-sighted*

wallflower 84 Flowers and Flowering Plants, 581.9 *rejected person*, 641.2 *nonacting person*, 722.6 *loser*

wall in 301.5 *enclose*, 726.7 *detain*

walling in 293.1 *covering*

walling up 293.1 *covering*

Wallis 52 Scientists

wall knot 74 Knots

wall light 439.6 *electric light*

wall moss 88.3 *moss*

wall off 147.7 *exclude*

Walloons 1 Peoples

wallop 239.1 *vigour*, 330.5 *beat*, 366.25 *pitch*, 879.3 *hit*

walloping 259.15 *big*

wallow 98.3 *marsh*, 362.9 *bow*, 364.10 *swirl*, 365.12 *wave*, 366.11 *stagger*, 366.25 *pitch*, 369.12 *be heavy*, 405.8 *feel pleasure*, 622.5 *swill*, 622.10 *be dirty*

wallower 622.6 *dirty person*

wallow in 608.5 *about*, 610.4 *be excessive*, 870.10 *indulge oneself*

wallowing 74.11 *nautical*, 622.2 *uncleanness*

wallow in ignorance 502.9 *be ignorant*

wallow in riches 742.12 *be rich*

wallow in the mud 98.12 *be marooned*

wall painting 50.8 *painting*

wallpaper 292.1 *lining*, 292.3 *line*, 293.8 *wall covering*, 293.28 *face*, 792.11 *paint and decorate*

wallpapered 293.36 *covered*

wallpaperer 293.17 *coverer*

wallpapering 792.4 *decorating*

wall rue 88 Ferns

wall safe 718.5 *safe*, 741.20 *money store*

Walls of Limerick 46.4 *historic dancing*

Wall Street 93.3 *New York*, 740.5 *stock market*

wall tile 44.9 *industrial ceramics*

wall tiles 293.8 *wall covering*

wall-to-wall 146.7 *including*

wall-to-wall carpet 293.9 *floor covering*

wall-to-wall carpeting 405.4 *pleasurable things*

wall-to-wall coverage 146.1 *inclusion*

wall unit 258.3 *cabinet*

wall up 398.17 *murder*, 531.8 *conceal*, 661.9 *block*

wall writing 545.4 *inscription*

wally 460.3 *unintelligent person*, 508.3 *foolish person*, 656.10 *unskilled person*

walnut 85 Trees and Shrubs, **86** Nuts, 449.1 *brown*

Walpole 48 Writers

Walpurgis Night 11.3 *witchcraft*

walrus 77 Placental Mammals

Walter Mitty 468.3 *absent-mindedness*

Walton 48 Writers, **49** Musicians and Composers

waltz 46.2 *dance*, 46.3 *ballroom dance steps*, 46.4 *historic dancing*, 46.15 *dance*, 364.8 *rotate*

waltz away with 682.10 *defeat heavily*

waltzer 46.5 *dancer*

waltz hold 41.7 *ice-dancing*

wamble 364.9 *roll*

wampum 741.1 *money*, 741.2 *cash*

wan 397.21 *deathly*, 445.8 *drained of colour*, 555.1 *unemphatic*, 624.21 *unhealthy*, 790.4 *ugly*

wand 65.7 *peripheral*, 544.4 *insignia*

wander 104.14 *be foreign*, 108.10 *be unrelated*, 149.16 *migrate*, 160.15 *lose one's train of*

thought, 324.15 *walk*, 335.3 *go astray*, 553.6 *be circuitous*
wander away 633.8 *be in danger*
wanderer 149.6 *immigrant*, 224.7 *person who moves around*, 293.22 *progression*
Wanderers 50 Schools and Groups of Artists
wandering 335, 335, 104.10 *foreign*, 162.25 *sprawled*, 168.13 *unconventional*, 224.13 *changeable*, 324.16 *moving*, 512.8 *oblivious*, 553.2 *circumlocution*, 553.4 *circumlocutory*
wandering eye 436.2 *poor sight*
wandering mind 335.16 *wandering*
wandering minstrel 149.6 *immigrant*
wandering star 53.16 *planet*
wanderlust 642.7 *restlessness*
wander off the point 363.8 *detour*
wandoo 85 Trees and Shrubs
wane 121.6 *change gradually*, 129.4 *decrease*, 252.1 *contraction*, 324.13 *be in motion*, 441.9 *be dim*, 458.1 *disappear*, 458.4 *disappearance*, 607.1 *waste*, 628.1 *deteriorate*, 628.7 *deterioration*, 722.12 *lessen*
wane level off 262.6 *become smaller*
wanga 11.3 *witchcraft*, 11.5 *spell*
Wanganui 92 New Zealand Regions and Territories
wangateur 11.4 *witch*
wangle 539.10 *fraud*, 539.30 *be fraudulent*, 540.9 *falsification*, 540.22 *falsify*, 592.3 *expedient plan*, 657.5 *be cunning*, 858.8 *be dishonourable*
wangling 539.34 *deceiving*
waning 121.7 *gradational*, 129.1 *decrease*, 129.6 *decreasing*, 207.12 *ageing*, 238.3 *poor health*, 262.1 *contraction*, 262.8 *contracting*, 441.5 *dim*, 458.6 *disappearing*, 722.4 *lessening*
waning moon 53.17 *moon*, 129.3 *decreasing thing*
waning of the moon 441.1 *dimness*
Wankel cycle 56.38 *thermodynamics*
Wankel engine 63.11 *engine*, 603.4 *machine*
wanness 555.2 *lack of emphasis*
want 127.11 *become inferior*, 145.1 *incompleteness*, 145.2 *omission*, 145.5 *be incomplete*, 254.2 *disappearance*, 358.1 *fall short*, 358.5 *shortfall*, 513.11 *demand*, 570.11 *wish*, 571.1 *necessity*, 571.4 *need*, 571.14 *necessitate*, 593.2 *need*, 593.3 *needfulness*, 593.7 *require*, 609.5 *be insufficient*, 609.6 *be unsatisfied*, 609.9 *scarcity*, 620.5 *imperfection*, 687.2 *economic adversity*, 687.10 *need money*, 712.1, 712.6 *request*, 714.11 *promise oneself*, 743.5 *poverty*, 743.12 *be poor*, 782.1, 782.12 *desire*, 782.13 *like*, 784.8 *prefer*
want ad 532.9 *advertisement*
wanted 254.12 *missing*, 593.4 *required*, 782.7 *desired*
wanter 782.6 *desirer*
wanting 145.4 *incomplete*, 238.13 *insufficient*, 254.12 *missing*, 358.7 *short*, 513.5 *expecting*, 609.1 *insufficient*, 620.2 *incomplete*, 743.1 *poor*, 782.9 *desirous*
wanting in respect 850.10 *disrespectful*
wanting to know 465.5 *curious*
want no forgiveness 868.5 *be impenitent*
want nothing 144.5 *be complete*
want of alacrity 573.13 *dissociation*
want of chivalry 818.2 *bad manners*
want of excitement 783.1 *indifference*

want of practice 595.8 *lack of preparation*
want of respect 850.1 *disrespect*
want of skill 656.8 *unskilfulness*
want of zeal 783.1 *indifference*
wanton 405.7 *pleased*, 579.1 *capricious*, 698.12 *unconditional*, 877.13 *unchaste*
wanton destruction 244.3 *destructiveness*
wanton destructiveness 244.3 *destructiveness*
want one's own way 577.9 *be obstinate*
wantonly 698.21 *excessively*
wantonness 698.6 *liberality*, 821.5 *desire*, 877.3 *sexual immorality*
want practice 595.12 *be unprepared*
want something to do 645.4 *have leisure*
want to 784.9 *like to*
want to know 465.7 *be curious*, 712.6 *request*
want to vomit 785.5 *dislike*
wapentake 92.2 *former British divisions*, 249.5 *state*
wapiti 77 Placental Mammals
war 676, 17.1 *military affairs*, 36.12 *canoeing*, 117.4 *disagreement*, 398.4 *slaughter*, 500.1 *dissent*, 640.1 *action*, 663.3 *conflict*, 666.2 *argument*, 674.1 *contention*, 674.6 *fight*, 676.8 *warfare*, 676.13 *be at war*, 693.4 *revolution*, 713.2 *disorder*, 820.4 *act of hostility*
War 676
war against 676.13 *be at war*
warble 49.39 *sing*, 78.18 *birdsong*, 78.28 *sing*, 426.13 *trill*, 432.2 *bird song*, 432.5, 433.10 *sing*, 564.13 *speak in a particular way*
warble fly 82 Insects
warbler 78 Birds, 78.6 *songbird*, 433.5 *melodist*
warbling 432.8 *singing*
war bride 823.8 *spouse*
war canoe 36.6 *canoeing*
war cloud 636.1 *warning*
war college 676.6 *art of war*
war correspondent 532.11 *newspaper man*, 560.10 *descriptive writer*
warcraft 17.1 *military affairs*, 676.6 *art of war*
war cry 431.1 *cry*, 543.6 *word*, 636.2 *danger signal*, 676.2 *glory of war*
ward 60.10 *hospital*, 93.7 *city district*, 143.1 *part*, 249.5 *state*, 630.14 *hospital*, 632.2 *protection*, 632.9 *protect*, 634.1 *refuge*, 671.12 *fort*, 671.17 *defend*, 699.4 *detention*, 699.7 *charge*, 701.4 *dependent*
Ward 48 Writers
war dance 10.7 *non-Christian ritual*, 46.4 *historic dancing*, 636.2 *danger signal*, 676.2 *glory of war*
warden 632.3 *protector*, 653.15 *manager*, 671.15 *protector*, 699.6 *law-maker*, 702.6 *prison officer*
wardenship 632.2 *protection*
warder 322.3 *person who opens*, 323.5 *person who closes*, 632.3, 671.15 *protector*, 699.6 *law-maker*, 702.6 *prison officer*
warding off 671.1 *defence*
wardmote 16.18 *tribunal*
ward off 341.13 *fend off*, 591.6 *evade*, 671.24 *parry*
ward orderly 60.17 *paramedic*
Wardour Street English 5.9 *ancient language*
wardrobe 47.5 *cabinet*, 51.19 *stage requisite*, 295.1 *dress*, 295.2 *dressing*
wardrobe mistress 51.26 *stagehand*, 295.28 *valet*
wardroom 74 Parts of a Ship
wardship 206.1 *youth*, 632.2 *protection*, 701.1 *subjection*
ward sister 60.16 *nurse*

warehouse 63.20 *building*, 605.4 *storage*, 605.6 *store*, 632.9 *protect*, 637.5 *preserve*, 740.7 *emporium*, 754.7 *discounter*
warehousing 605.4 *storage*
wares 243.7 *produce*, 603.6 *equipment*, 725.5 *personal estate*, 739.8 *merchandise*
warfare 631, 676, 663.3 *conflict*, 674.1 *contention*, 674.6 *fight*, 676.1 *war*
warfarin 62 Medication, 68.14 *pest control*, 631.8 *poison*
war fever 676.5 *bellicosity*
war-fevered 676.16 *warlike*
war footing 676.7 *war measures*
war galley 679.25 *historical naval ships*
war games 676.6 *art of war*
war gas 631.10 *warfare*
Wargentin 53 Lunar Features
warhammer 680.7 *blunt weapon*
warhead 680.15 *explosive*
warhorse 32, 655.5 *expert*, 679.19 *cavalry*
warily 467.15 *attentively*, 469.12 *carefully*, 573.17 *unwillingly*, 781.7 *cautiously*
wariness 467.3 *carefulness*, 469.5 *watchfulness*, 573.13 *dissociation*, 657.1 *cunning*, 781.1 *caution*
war in heaven 423.1 *loudness*
warlike 676, 17.8 *military*, 237.11 *strong in spirit*, 241.6 *violent*, 473.9 *hostile*, 500.7 *dissenting*, 642.18 *active*, 668.8 *defying*, 670.22 *militant*, 674.15 *contentious*, 679.33 *combative*, 778.11 *militant*
warlike habits 676.5 *bellicosity*
warlike people 679.7 *militarist nation*
warlock 11.4 *witch*, 517.8 *oracle*
warlord 696.4 *absolute ruler*
war-loving 676.16 *warlike*
Warlpiri 5 Languages and Groups of Languages
warm 55, 408, 264.5 *near*, 405.6 *pleasant*, 405.7 *pleased*, 405.10 *comfort*, 408.9 *hot*, 408.14 *be hot*, 444.11 *colourful*, 475.10 *demonstrative*, 496.13 *discovering*, 554.3 *emphatic*, 759.12 *sensitive*, 815.15 *sociable*, 819.8 *friendly*, 821.25 *be loved*, 828.16 *angry*
warm air 55.10 *air movement*
warm as toast 408.10 *on fire*
warm-blooded 77.25 *mammalian*, 408.12 *warm-hearted*
warm-blooded animal 77.1 *mammal*
warm-bloodedness 403.2 *ability to sense*, 408.1 *heat*
warm current 408.8 *hot place*
war measures 676
war medal 681.1 *trophy*
warmed through 408.13 *heated*
warmed up 408.13 *heated*
warmed-up 183.11 *reprinted*
war memorial 399.4 *funeral objects*, 545.11 *monument*
warmer 55.50 *warm*, 408.3 *heater*
warm feeling 642.4 *energy*
warm friendship 819.3 *familiarity*
warm front 55.10 *air movement*, 408.5 *hot weather*
warm heart 835.1 *pity*
warm-hearted 408, 374.6 *softhearted*, 759.12 *sensitive*, 819.8 *friendly*, 831.6 *benevolent*, 835.6 *pitying*
warm-heartedly 819.17 *in friendship*, 835.13 *pitifully*
warm-heartedness 819.1 *friendship*, 835.1 *pity*
warm hue 444.3 *hue*
warming 408.9 *hot*
warming of the earth's atmosphere 408.5 *hot weather*
warming pan 258.15 *pot*, 408.3 *heater*
warmly 408, 55.65 *meteorologically*, 405.11 *pleasingly*, 450.10 *ruddily*, 475.21 *demonstratively*,

759.20 *with feeling*, 815.18 *sociably*, 819.17 *in friendship*, 828.18 *angrily*
warmness 408.1 *heat*, 819.1 *friendship*
warm occlusion 55.10 *air movement*
warmonger 679.6 *militarist*, 679.36 *combat*
warmongering 670.22 *militant*, 674.15 *contentious*, 676.16 *warlike*
warm reception 815.9 *welcome*
warm sector 55.11 *weather system*
warm spell 55.23 *heat*, 408.5 *hot weather*
warm spring 98.10 *miscellaneous*
warmth 56.35, 408.1 *heat*, 444.3 *hue*, 450.5 *redness*, 554.1 *emphasis*, 759.5 *good feeling*, 815.1 *sociability*, 815.9 *welcome*, 819.1 *friendship*
warm the cockles of one's heart 405.9 *give pleasure*
warm through 45.55 *cook*
warm to 819.13 *befriend*, 821.24 *be in love*
warm up 183.20 *renew*, 408.14 *be hot*, 584.18 *habituate*, 594.4 *prepare for action*, 594.8 *prepare oneself*, 644.9 *exercise*
warm-up 644.5 *exercise*
warm-up lap 33.6 *motor racing terms*
warm weather 55.23 *heat*
warm welcome 815.9 *welcome*
warm work 644.1 *work*
warn 636, 154.19 *forecast*, 516.1 *foresee*, 517.11 *predict*, 543.12 *signal*, 587.1 *dissuade*, 654.5 *advise*, 713.6 *protest*, 781.6 *caution*, 852.20 *censure*
warned 636, 594.18 *prepared*
warner 636, 517.8 *oracle*, 718.3 *security officer*
warning 636, 636, 154.6 *preview*, 517.3 *plan*, 517.5 *omen*, 528.7 *advice*, 543.16 *signalling*, 587.6 *dissuasion*, 587.9 *dissuasive*, 654.1 *advice*, 654.3 *precept*, 654.7 *advising*, 713.1 *protest*, 781.2 *insurance*, 852.7 *blame*
Warning 636
warning alarm 636.2 *danger signal*
warning cry 432.1 *animal cry*
warning example 636.1 *warning*
warning flag 543.4 *signal*
warning flare 636.2 *danger signal*
warning light 439.6 *electric light*, 543.4 *signal*, 636.2 *danger signal*
warning notice 692.2 *demand*
warning shot 517.3 *plan*, 636.2 *danger signal*
warning sign 517.3 *plan*, 543.1 *sign*, 636.2 *danger signal*
warning signal 543.4 *signal*
warning sound 543.4 *signal*
warning voice 636.1 *warning*
warn off 147.7 *exclude*
War of 1812 17 Major Wars
War of American Independence 17 Major Wars
war of attrition 670.16 *terrorist attack*, 674.6 *fight*, 676.1 *war*
war of conquest 676.1 *war*
war of containment 676.1 *war*
war of expansion 676.1 *war*
war of independence 676.1 *war*
war of liberation 676.1 *war*
war of nerves 676.1 *war*, 777.4 *intimidation*
War of the Austrian Succession 17 Major Wars
war of the elements 241.5 *violent weather*
War of the Spanish Succession 17 Major Wars
war of words 674.1 *contention*, 676.1 *war*
war on all fronts 676.1 *war*
war on want 676.1 *war*
warp 74 Rigging, 36.3 *parts of a sailing boat*, 67.4 *weaving*,

74.10 *sail*, 216.8 *cause change*, 288.3 *weaving*, 288.8 *interweave*, 309.1 *distortion*, 309.9 *distort*, 309.11 *deform*, 310.11 *angle*, 335.6 *distort*, 335.17 *torsion*, 339.11 *pull*, 382.2 *fabric*, 474.11 *practise sophistry*, 481.13 *prejudge*, 493.12 *bias*, 540.22 *falsify*, 628.5 *pervert*
war paint 444.9 *complexion*, 791.4 *cosmetics*
warp and woof 383.4 *weave*
warpath 676.8 *warfare*
warped 493.8 *unjust*, 620.3 *deformed*
warping 540.9 *falsification*
warplane 679.31 *military aircraft*
war plans 17.1 *military affairs*
war policy 676.5 *bellicosity*, 676.7 *war measures*
war preparations 676.7 *war measures*
warrant 16.6 *legal process*, 16.29 *legalization*, 16.65 *make legal*, 116.8, 116.29 *permit*, 480.1 *verify*, 483.6 *documentation*, 490.14 *guarantee*, 490.21 *make certain*, 632.1 *safety*, 632.9 *protect*, 654.3 *precept*, 688.9 *permission*, 692.2, 692.10 *demand*, 703.3 *authority*, 703.8 *authorize*, 708.2 *permit*, 714.2, 714.8 *guarantee*, 718.2, 718.11 *promise*, 741.14 *paper money*, 845.6 *bond*, 845.14 *be entitled*, 845.16 *entitle*, 855.8 *justify*
warrantable 855.13 *vindicable*
warranted 16.44 *legal*, 116.18 *permitting*, 490.4 *guaranteed*, 632.5 *safe*, 688.16 *authorized*, 703.9 *commissioned*, 708.7 *permitted*, 714.13 *guaranteeing*, 718.7 *guaranteed*, 845.8 *entitled*
warrant of arrest 692.2 *demand*
warrant officer 679.17 *army person*
Warrant Officer 17 British Military Ranks, **17** British Military Ranks, **17** US Military Ranks, **17** US Military Ranks
warrantor 490.15 *guarantor*
warranty 116.8 *permit*, 483.6 *documentation*, 490.14 *guarantee*, 545.2 *certificate*, 632.1 *safety*, 703.3 *authority*, 708.2 *permit*, 714.2 *guarantee*, 718.2 *promise*, 845.6 *bond*
war readiness 676.7 *war measures*
warren 256.13 *lair*, 317.2 *concave land*, 634.3 *animal shelter*
warring 676, 117.10, 666.9 *disagreeing*, 670.22 *militant*, 674.15 *contentious*, 676.8 *warfare*
Warrington 93 Cities
warrior 670.19 *attacker*, 674.10 *contender*, 679.1 *combatant*, 679.8 *soldier*, 778.7 *courageous person*
warrior for God 679.6 *militarist*
Warsaw 93 Cities
Warsaw Pact 715.3 *alliance*
warship 679, 74.3 *vessel*
war skills 676.6 *art of war*
Wars of the Roses 17 Major Wars
war song 676.2 *glory of war*
war strategy 676.6 *art of war*
wart 149.2 *impurity*, 316.2 *bulge*, 373.7 *hard substance*, 624.13 *skin disease*
warthog 77 Placental Mammals
wartime 676.4 *belligerency*
wartime censorship 676.8 *warfare*
wartime conditions 676.4 *belligerency*
wartime propaganda 676.8 *warfare*
wartime rations 350.7 *food*
war to end all wars 676.1 *war*
war to the end 676.1 *war*
war to the knife 674.1 *contention*, 674.2 *fight*, 676.1 *war*
warts and all 144.9 *completely*, 537.5 *truthfulness*, 537.36 *truthfully*

warts-and-all 537.18 *truthful*
wart snake 79 Reptiles
warty 375.2 *coarse*
war upon 676.13 *be at war*
war vessel 679.24 *warship*
war-weary 675.7 *peaceful*
war whoop 636.2 *danger signal*, 676.2 *glory of war*
Warwick 93 Cities
Warwickshire 92 Counties
war widow 824.6 *surviving spouse*
war work 676.7 *war measures*
wary 467.7 *watchful*, 573.3 *cautious*, 636.9 *warned*, 657.4 *cunning*, 781.4 *cautious*
war zone 676.10 *battleground*
wash 389, 50.8 *painting*, 50.19 *paint*, 62.11 *linctus*, 67.15 *treat*, 94.2 *small lake*, 96.6 *river flow*, 96.7 *flow*, 134.10 *purify*, 389.34 *hose*, 444.4 *pigment*, 444.15 *colour*, 446.13 *whiten*, 537.27 *be true*, 608.4 *suffice*, 615.6 *be convenient*, 621.5 *ablutions*, 621.8 *laundry*, 621.13 *clean*, 621.15 *purify*, 630.9 *balm*, 651.6 *refresher*
wash and brush up 651.6 *refresher*, 791.3 *beauty treatment*
wash-and-wear clothes 295.1 *dress*
wash bag 791.5 *make-up box*
washbasin 258.12, 621.6 *bath*
washboard 74 Parts of a Ship, 41.1 *skiing*, 321.3 *furrowed thing*, 375.7 *rough thing*, 621.7 *washer*
washbowl 621.6 *bath*
wash clean 134.10 *purify*, 621.13 *clean*
wash down 351.13 *drink*, 621.13 *clean*
washed 50.27 *painted*, 67.11 *treated*, 96.11 *flooded*, 621.17 *cleaned*
washed out 445.7 *colourless*
washed up 157.21 *ended*, 650.1 *fatigued*, 683.10 *failed*
washed-up 687.8 *unlucky*
washer 621
washer-drier 621.7 *washer*
washerman 621.12 *cleaner*
washer-up 621.12 *cleaner*
washerwoman 621.12 *cleaner*
washin 73.7 *miscellaneous aviation terms*
washing 50.2 *painting*, 67.8 *fabric treatment*, 96.6 *river flow*, 134.2 *purification*, 389.11 *wash*, 621.2 *cleaning*, 621.5 *ablutions*, 621.8 *laundry*
washing machine 621.7 *washer*
washing one's hands 848.3 *self-exemption*
washing out 134.2 *purification*, 621.2 *cleaning*
washing powder 134.3 *purifier*, 621.9 *cleaning agent*
washing soap 395.8 *fat*
washing soda 57 Common Chemical Compounds, 134.3 *purifier*, 621.9 *cleaning agent*
Washington 92 American States, **93** Cities, 93.2 *American cities*, 688.6 *place of authority*, 696.8 *the power structure*
Washington palm 85 Trees and Shrubs
washing up 621.8 *laundry*
washing-up 621.2 *cleaning*
washing-up liquid 134.3 *purifier*, 621.9 *cleaning agent*
Washoe 1 Peoples
wash off 546.1 *obliterate*, 621.13 *clean*
wash one's dirty linen in public 526.4 *show oneself*
wash one's hands of 136.13 *diverge*, 578.2 *equivocate*, 621.15 *purify*, 641.4 *not act*, 729.9 *dispose of*, 848.12 *exempt oneself*
washout 96.6 *river flow*
wash out 134.10 *purify*, 445.6 *decolour*, 546.1 *obliterate*, 621.13 *clean*, 621.15 *purify*
washout 683.4 *unsuccessful thing*, 683.5 *failing person*

washroom 256.7 *room*, 353.13 *lavatory*, 621.6 *bath*, 727.7 *toilet*
washstand 621.6 *bath*
washtub 258.12 *bath*, 621.7 *washer*
wash up 621.13 *clean*
washwoman 621.12 *cleaner*
washy 445.7 *colourless*
wasp 82 Insects, 82.1 *insect*, 82.4 *social insect*, 815.10 *social animal*
Wasp 91 Names for Inhabitants
waspish 241.6 *violent*, 829.4 *irascible*, 832.14 *hostile*
waspishly 829.9 *irascibly*
waspishness 829.1 *irascibility*, 832.4 *bitterness*
wasps' nest 82.4 *social insect*
wasp waist 262.3 *contracted thing*, 274.7 *thinness*
wasp-waisted 274.1 *thin*
wassail 874.8 *get drunk*
wassailing 874.5 *drunken*
wastage 129.1 *decrease*, 607.3 *waste*, 614.6 *refuse*, 722.3 *waste*
waste 247, 607, 607, 607, 722, 757, 129.1 *decrease*, 132.2 *residue*, 243.3 *product*, 244.10 *lay waste*, 244.12 *consume*, 247.1 *infertility*, 247.3 *birth control*, 248.3 *geographical space*, 262.5 *make smaller*, 262.6 *become smaller*, 347.2 *outflow*, 353.4 *excrement*, 398.17 *murder*, 458.3 *cause to disappear*, 599.1, 599.6 *use*, 600.5 *not use*, 601.1, 601.2 *misuse*, 609.7 *make insufficient*, 610.1 *excess*, 614.4 *futility*, 614.6 *refuse*, 628.4 *impair*, 628.10 *impairment*, 722.11 *be wasteful*, 748.2 *consume*, 870.11 *overindulge*
Waste 607
waste an opportunity 211.6 *lose one's chance*, 493.10 *misjudge*
waste away 129.4 *decrease*, 141.3 *disintegrate*, 262.6 *become smaller*, 274.15 *be emaciated*, 607.1 *waste*, 624.24 *be unhealthy*, 722.12 *lessen*
wastebasket 258.7 *basket*, 727.4 *wastebin*
wastebin 727
wasted 238.9 *dilapidated*, 238.10 *ill*, 247.3 *birth control*, 262.7 *smaller*, 274.2 *emaciated*, 600.1 *unused*, 601.4 *misused*, 614.2 *futile*
wasted day 683.4 *unsuccessful thing*
wasted effort 614.5 *waste of effort*, 642.9 *overactivity*, 656.9 *bungling*, 722.3 *waste*
waste disposal 56.74 *nuclear waste*
waste disposal unit 621.10 *cleaning object*, 727.4 *wastebin*
waste disposer 727.4 *wastebin*
wasted labour 614.5 *waste of effort*
waste effort 614, 358.2 *fail*, 601.1 *misuse*, 607.1 *waste*, 642.13 *be busy*, 656.6 *act foolishly*
wasteful 607, 601.5 *abusive*, 614.2 *futile*, 722.17 *unprofitable*, 757.1 *extravagant*, 870.8 *overindulgent*
wastefully 607, 601.6 *abusively*, 722.20 *at a loss*, 757.9 *extravagantly*
wastefulness 607.3 *waste*, 614.4 *futility*, 722.3 *waste*, 757.4 *extravagance*, 870.3 *overindulgence*
wasteful person 722.6 *loser*
wasteland 244.5 *havoc*, 247.1 *infertility*, 249.6 *regions*, 392.14 *desert*
waste matter 353.4 *excrement*
waste no more time 598.2 *withdraw*
waste no words 552.4 *be concise*
waste no words over 566.9 *lapse into silence*
waste of breath 614.5 *waste of effort*, 722.3 *waste*

waste of effort 614, 247.1 *infertility*
waste of space 614.5 *waste of effort*
waste of time 247.1 *infertility*, 614.5 *waste of effort*, 722.3 *waste*
waste of waters 247.1 *infertility*
waste one's breath 614.9 *waste effort*, 722.11 *be wasteful*
waste one's efforts 628.5 *hurt*, 722.11 *be wasteful*
waste one's time 722.11 *be wasteful*
wastepaper 614.6 *refuse*
wastepaper basket 258.7 *basket*, 727.4 *wastebin*
waste pipe 621.10 *cleaning object*, 727.4 *wastebin*
waste processing 56.74 *nuclear waste*
waste product 607, 243.3 *product*, 614.6 *refuse*
waster 607, 722.6 *loser*, 757.6 *spendthrift*
waste reprocessing 235.8 *nuclear power*
waste time 209.7 *wait*, 211.5 *take untimely action*, 328.2 *hesitate*, 487.10 *attempt the impossible*, 614.9 *waste effort*, 643.12 *be inactive*
wasteyard 727
wasting 262.1 *contraction*, 262.8 *contracting*, 274.8 *emaciation*, 398.2 *murder*, 609.3 *underfed*, 618.5 *harmful*
wasting away 129.1 *decrease*, 129.6 *decreasing*, 274.2 *emaciated*, 607.3 *waste*, 624.22 *sick*, 628.12 *deteriorated*, 722.4 *lessening*, 871.6 *fasting*
wasting disease 624.4 *disease*
wasting no time 329.1 *swift*
wasting time 328.8 *slowness*
wastrel 607.6 *waster*, 748.9, 757.6 *spendthrift*, 864.9 *wicked person*
West Water 94 Lakes, 94.4 *British lakes*
wat 10.11 *place of worship*
watch 161 Collective Names for Birds and Animals, **192, 435**, 16.17 *police officer*, 74.7 *nautical person*, 185.13 *timer*, 187.4 *period of activity*, 253.12 *attend*, 467.11 *take note of*, 469.5 *watchfulness*, 469.10 *be careful*, 496.1 *discover*, 534.30 *communicate*, 543.5 *indicator*, 632.3 *protector*, 636.4 *warner*, 641.4 *not act*, 642.14 *push*, 671.14 *guard*, 671.17 *defend*, 718.3 *security officer*, 847.2 *task*
watchable 435.23 *visible*
watch and wait 641.4 *not act*
watch and ward 632.2 *protection*
watchcase 293.13 *casing*
watch committee 16.2 *jurisdiction*
Watch Committee 134.6 *prude*, 876.6 *moralist*
watchdog 77.9 *dog*, 435.11 *observer*, 632.3 *protector*, 636.4 *warner*, 654.4 *adviser*, 876.6 *moralist*
watchdog group 586.14 *motivator*
watcher 253.5 *someone present*, 435.11 *observer*, 632.3 *protector*
watchface 192.8 *face*
watch fire 439.8 *fire*, 543.4 *signal*
watchful 467, 435.21 *seeing*, 469.9 *careful*, 513.5 *expecting*, 632.7 *tutelary*, 642.18 *active*, 719.7 *observant*, 781.4 *cautious*, 841.5 *distrustful*
watchfully 435, 467.15 *attentively*, 632.10 *safely*, 719.8 *observantly*, 781.7 *cautiously*, 841.9 *jealously*
watchfulness 469, 435.3 *observation*, 467.2 *close attention*, 469.3 *circumspection*, 642.7 *restlessness*, 781.1 *caution*, 841.2 *distrust*
watchful person 469

watchglass 57 Laboratory Apparatus

watch glass 293.12 *protective covering,* 442.8 *transparent thing*

watching 253.8 *attendant,* 435.3 *observation,* 435.21 *seeing,* 469.5 *watchfulness,* 469.9 *careful*

watching one's figure 274.10 *diet*

watching the world go by 641.1 *inaction*

watch it 636.10 *look out*

watch like a hawk 435.15 *watch*

watchmaker 185.14 *time keeper,* 192.12 *chronologist,* 646.2 *artisan*

watchmaking 185.10 *chronometry,* 192.4 *horology*

watchman 435.11 *observer,* 632.3 *protector,* 636.4 *warner,* 671.14 *guard,* 718.3 *security officer*

watch one's step 166.17 *obey orders,* 636.6 *be warned,* 781.5 *be cautious*

watch one's weight 274.14 *become thin*

watch out 636.10 *look out*

watch out for 435.15 *watch,* 513.10 *wait*

watch over 293.30 *protect,* 435.15 *watch,* 469.11 *care for,* 632.9 *protect,* 653.1 *manage*

watch the clock 185.19 *clock on,* 192.16 *measure time*

watch the float 20.7 *angle*

watch the pennies 743.12 *be poor*

watch the world go by 641.4 *not act*

watchtower 275.6 *tall thing,* 435.9 *viewpoint,* 692.8 *vantage point*

watchword 505.1 *maxim,* 543.6 *word,* 676.8 *warfare*

water 777 Phobias by Topic, **389, 389,** 50.8 *painting,* 68.18 *practise livestock farming,* 69.15 *cultivate,* 70.1 *transport,* 70.5 *transportable,* 74.11 *nautical,* 87.12 *manage grassland,* 133.8 *mix,* 134.3 *purifier,* 238.5 *weak thing,* 246.7 *make fertile,* 350.11 *food content,* 351.6 *soft drink,* 351.15 *provide drink,* 353.6 *urine,* 372.6 *make sparse,* 387.1 *fluid,* 387.2 *juice,* 396.3 *life requirements,* 442.8 *transparent thing,* 606.5 *provision,* 621.9 *cleaning agent,* 627.1 *improve*

Water 389

water at the mouth 347.12 *leak,* 350.22 *eat well,* 353.20 *salivate*

water balance 55.9 *atmospheric process*

water bear 81.4 *arthropod*

Water Bearer 53 The Constellations

water bed 47.6 *bed*

water beetle 82 Insects

water bird 78

water biscuit 45.39 *loaf*

water boatman 82 Insects

waterborne 70.5 *transportable,* 74.11 *nautical*

waterborne disease 624.4 *disease*

water bowl 68.10 *farm tool*

water boy 326.7 *transferor*

waterbuck 77 Placental Mammals

water buffalo 77 Placental Mammals

water bug 82 Insects

Waterbury 93 Cities

water butt 69.3 *ornamental garden*

water carrier 389, 326.7 *transferor*

water cart 389.16 *water carrier*

water chestnut 45 Vegetables, **86** Nuts

water chinquapin 86 Nuts

water clock 191 Timepieces and Timers, 192.6 *clock*

water closet 256.7 *room,* 727.7 *toilet*

water cloud 55.18 *cloud*

watercolour 50.8 *painting,* 50.16 *artist,* 444.15 *colour,* 547.2 *reproduction*

watercolourist 444.6 *painter,* 547.4 *person who makes a representation*

watercolour pigments 444.5 *paint*

watercolours 50.11 *artist's materials,* 444.5 *paint*

water-cooled 409.9 *heat-resistant*

water-cooled reactor 410.7 *nuclear power*

water course 36.6 *canoeing*

watercourse 96.1 *river,* 327.11 *channel*

watercress 45 Vegetables

water cure 389.7 *hydrotherapeutics*

water cycle 54, 389

water-divine 11.23 *divine*

water diviner 389.20 *hydrologist,* 496.12 *discoverer,* 517.9 *forecaster*

water-divining 11.9 *divination*

water down 129.5 *make smaller,* 133.8 *mix,* 162.14 *dilute,* 238.7 *weaken,* 274.16 *make thin,* 362.4 *debase,* 372.6 *make sparse,* 389.30, 412.8 *dilute,* 542.22 *play down*

water-drinker 873.8 *sober person*

water-drinking 873.1 *sober,* 873.6 *sobriety*

water-driven 410.10 *powered*

watered 69.19 *ornamental,* 372.2 *rarefied,* 412.5 *tasteless,* 456.7 *iridescent*

watered-down 133.12 *mixed,* 162.27 *dilute,* 274.5 *thinned,* 372.2 *rarefied,* 389.22 *diluted,* 412.5 *tasteless,* 542.17 *insipid,* 542.19 *downplayed*

watered-down soup 238.5 *weak thing*

watered silk 456.5 *variegated thing*

waterfall 96.2 *channel,* 235.6 *source of energy,* 347.2 *outflow,* 360.3 *downflow*

water filter 134.3 *purifier,* 621.10 *cleaning object*

water flea 81.4 *arthropod*

water flow 96.6 *river flow*

Waterford 92 Counties, **93** Cities

waterfowl 78.3 *water bird*

waterfowl shooting 37.2 *hunting*

waterfront 300.1 *edge,* 300.8 *edging,* 303.1 *front*

water garden 69.2 *garden*

Watergate 531.5 *evasion*

water gun 338.9 *firearm*

water hazard 29.1 *golf*

water hole 94.2 *small lake*

water hydrant 389.13 *irrigator*

water ice 45.35 *dessert*

wateriness 389, 139.1 *nonadhesion,* 274.12 *thinning,* 387.5 *fluidity,* 391.1 *moisture,* 412.1 *tastelessness,* 442.3 *transparency,* 542.8 *insipidness,* 555.2 *lack of emphasis*

watering 389, 69.5 *gardening,* 389.26 *wetting,* 412.1 *tastelessness*

watering can 69.6 *garden tool,* 258.11 *vessel,* 389.12 *sprinkler*

watering cart 389.16 *water carrier*

watering down 133.1 *mixture,* 162.3 *dilution,* 274.12 *thinning,* 389.5 *dilution,* 412.1 *tastelessness,* 542.9 *down-playing,* 628.10 *impairment*

watering eyes 624.9 *respiratory disease*

watering place 630.14 *hospital*

waterish 389.21 *watery*

water jug 389.16 *water carrier*

water jump 21.1 *track events,* 32.9 *jumping*

waterless 392.1 *dry*

waterlessness 392.11 *dryness*

water level 282.2 *horizontal surface*

water lily 84 Flowers and Flowering Plants

water line 74 Parts of a Ship,

water log 389.29 *water*

waterlogged 98.11 *continental,* 236.12 *impotent,* 389.23 *wet,* 391.11 *marshy,* 393.17 *muddy,* 633.2 *unsafe*

Waterloo 244.4 *ruin,* 683.2 *defeat*

water loss 638.4 *leak*

water louse 81.4 *arthropod*

waterman 36.9 *sailor,* 74.8 *boatman*

watermark 268.6 *measuring instrument,* 543.5 *indicator,* 544.3 *means of identification*

water meadow 98.6 *lowland*

watermelon 86 Fruits

water meter 268.8 *meter*

water mill 410.8 *renewable energy*

water moccasin 79 Reptiles

water mould 89 Fungi

water nymph 8.5 *deity*

water of life 874.12 *alcohol*

water pipe 389.13 *irrigator,* 413.7 *tobacco*

water pistol 389.12 *sprinkler*

water pocket 94.2 *small lake*

water polo 18 Sporting Activities

water power 96.6 *river flow,* 235.4 *energy*

waterproof 392, 34.8 *mountaineering,* 67.11 *treated,* 67.15 *treat,* 295.12 *coat,* 323.12 *closed,* 392.22 *keep dry,* 632.6 *invulnerable,* 637.5 *preserve*

waterproofed 392.10 *waterproof*

waterproofing 67.8 *fabric treatment,* 637.1 *preservation*

waterproof matchbox 34.4 *climbing equipment*

waterproof paper 604.3 *paper*

water rat 77 Placental Mammals

waters 245.7 *obstetrics*

water sapphire 54 Minerals, **54** Gemstones

water scorpion 82 Insects

water's edge 96.2 *channel,* 300.1 *edge*

watershed 54.8 *drainage,* 221.3 *turning point,* 275.4 *mountain range*

water shrew 77 Placental Mammals

waterside 96.2 *channel,* 300.1 *edge,* 300.8 *edging*

water skiing 18 Sporting Activities

water snake 79 Reptiles

Water Snake 53 The Constellations

watersoaked 389.23 *wet*

waters of the earth 54.5 *earth*

water spider 82 Arachnids

water spirit 8.5 *deity,* 97.4 *sea god*

waterspout 55.16 *wind vortex,* 364.4 *vortex*

water sprite 97.4 *sea god*

water start 36.7 *windsurfing*

water strider 82 Insects

water supply 606.1 *provision*

water-supply engineering 63.17 *civil engineering*

water-supply system 63.24 *water system*

water system 63, 96.1 *river*

water table 54.9 *groundwater*

water tank 389.16 *water carrier*

watertight 323.12 *closed,* 392.10 *waterproof,* 619.1 *perfect*

water tower 72.2 *track,* 275.6 *tall thing,* 605.4 *storage*

Water Transport 74

water travel 74, 324.2 *momentum*

water trough 72.2 *track*

water turbine 63.12 *turbine,* 410.8 *renewable energy*

water vapour 388, 389.3 *wateriness*

water vole 77 Placental Mammals

water wave 56.14 *sound wave*

waterway 74, 96.1 *river,* 327.11 *channel*

water wheel 235.6 *source of energy,* 364.6 *rotator*

water wings 39.3 *survival swimming,* 632.4 *safety device*

water witch 11.4 *witch*

waterworks 621.10 *cleaning object,* 647.1 *workshop*

waterworn 376.2 *uniform*

watery 389, 139.8 *nonadhesive,* 238.13 *insufficient,* 274.5 *thinned,* 353.29 *salivating,* 387.15 *flowing,* 391.10 *misty,* 393.19 *juicy,* 442.1 *transparent,* 542.17 *insipid,* 555.1 *unemphatic,* 609.1 *insufficient*

watery-eyed 436.9 *weak-sighted*

watery grave 397.5 *ways of dying*

watery waste 97.1 *sea*

Watson 52 Scientists, 61.29 *psychologist*

Watsonian 61.33 *Freudian*

Watsonian psychology 61.1 *psychology*

Watson-Watt 52 Scientists

watt 75 SI Units, 235.5 *unit of work*

Watt 52 Scientists

wattage 235.5 *unit of work*

watt-hour 75 Scientific and Technical Units

watt-hour meter 64.34 *power supply*

wattle 85 Trees and Shrubs, 288.2 *braid*

wattle and daub 243.8 *construction,* 604.2 *building material*

wattmeter 56.90 *ammeter,* 64.23 *electrical instrument*

Waugh 48 Writers

wave 54, 56, 97, 365, 365, 97.1 *sea,* 97.10 *billow,* 139.5 *come unstuck,* 212.6 *radio frequency,* 224.11 *be changeable,* 311.2 *bend,* 314.6 *convolute,* 324.11 *bodily movement,* 324.15 *walk,* 365.4, 365.11 *rock,* 366.22 *agitate,* 366.26 *flicker,* 526.1 *display,* 543.3, 543.11 *gesture,* 811.28 *flourish,* 817.5 *sign of courtesy,* 817.12 *greet*

Wave 679.27 *naval man*

wave a red flag before a bull 241.9 *make violent*

wave a wand 11.21 *bewitch*

waveband 534.14 *radio transmission*

wave banners 811.28 *flourish*

wave by 543.11 *gesture*

wave crest 56.16 *waveform,* 97.3 *wave*

waved 526.13 *displayed*

wave equation 365.5 *wave*

wave erosion 54.35 *weathering*

waveform 56, 64.14 *terminal*

wave frequency 214.1 *regularity*

wave goodbye 545.6 *part*

waveguide 64.27 *wire*

wave in the wind 224.11 *be changeable*

wave-jump 36.18 *windsurf*

wave jumping 36.7 *windsurfing*

wavelength 56.16 *waveform,* 212.6 *radio frequency,* 365.5 *wave*

wavelet 97.3 *wave*

wavellite 54 Minerals

wave mechanics 56.3 *modern physics,* 56.80 *quantum theory*

wave motion 56.12 *wave,* 214.1 *regularity,* 365.4 *rock*

wave number 56.16 *waveform,* 365.5 *wave*

wave on 543.11 *gesture*

wave one's hat 543.11 *gesture*

wave–particle duality 56.80 *quantum theory*

wave pool 39.7 *swimming pool*

wave power 56.11 *energy,* 235.6 *source of energy,* 410.8 *renewable energy*

wave-powered 235.17 *powered*

wave propagation 56.12 *wave*

wave property 56

waver 215.1 *irregularity,* 215.6 *be irregular,* 224.12 *be irresolute,* 365.4 *rock,* 365.10 *vacil-*

late, 365.11 *rock*, 366.12, 366.26 *flicker*, 484.8 *reverse*, 491.19 *hesitate*, 498.8 *disbelieve*, 576.5 *vacillate*
waverer 576.15 *indecisive person*, 641.2 *nonacting person*
wave-ride 36.18 *windsurf*
wave riding 36.7 *windsurfing*
wavering 215.1 *irregularity*, 215.4 *irregular*, 216.11 *changeable*, 224.2 *irresolution*, 224.13 *changeable*, 238.12 *weak-willed*, 365.3 *vacillation*, 365.15 *vacillating*, 491.2 *irresolute*, 491.8 *capricious*, 491.11 *irresoluteness*, 491.16 *capriciousness*, 576.1 *vacillating*
wavering loyalty 858.2 *faithlessness*
waveringly 215.8 *irregularly*, 224.15 *changeably*, 366.28 *shakily*
wavery 366.20 *flickering*
waves 777 Phobias by Topic
wavesail 36.18 *windsurf*
waveshape 56.16 *waveform*
waves of nausea 624.3 *symptom*
wave speed 56.16 *waveform*
wave the big stick 690.5 *be severe*
wave theory of light 56.5 *theory*
wave through 443.11 *gesture*
wave to 543.11 *gesture*
wave to and fro 365.12 *wave*
wave trough 56.16 *waveform*
wave up and down 365.12 *wave*
wavily 311.7 *curvedly*, 314.8 *circularly*
waviness 97.3 *wave*
waving 365, 139.8 *nonadhesive*, 365.4 *rock*, 812.8 *salute*
waving plumes 811.14 *show*
wavy 311.5 *well-rounded*, 314.4 *convolutional*
wavy navy 679.27 *naval man*
wax 50.14 *sculptor's materials*, 58.6 *lipid*, 85.9 *tree product*, 121.6 *change gradually*, 128.4 *increase*, 220.8 *be transformed*, 261.6 *become bigger*, 293.3 *coating*, 293.9 *floor covering*, 293.24 *coat*, 296.7 *depilation*, 373.9 *harden*, 374.11 *soft thing*, 374.13 *soften*, 376.10 *polish*, 376.11 *smooth*, 385.12 *rub*, 386.4 *lubricant*, 386.13 *lubricate*, 394.2 *adhesive*, 395.5 *lubricant*, 395.7 *oil*, 395.8 *fat*, 395.17 *oil*, 395.18 *anoint*, 457.12 *become visible*, 621.9 *cleaning agent*, 828.4 *anger*
wax and wane 216.7 *be changed*, 224.11 *be changeable*, 365.1 *oscillation*, 365.8 *oscillate*
wax a ski 41.14 *ski*
wax bean 45 Vegetables
waxbill 78 Birds
wax candle 439.5 *incandescent light*
wax cap 89 Fungi
waxed 376.4 *polished*
waxed paper 45.6 *kitchen equipment*
wax eloquent 553.5 *be diffuse*
waxen 395.11 *oily*, 446.4 *pale*
waxer 376.9 *smoother*
wax figure 547.6 *image*
waxily 374.17 *softly*
waxiness 386.2 *oiliness*
waxing 121.7 *gradational*, 128.1 *increase*, 128.6 *increasing*, 261.1 *growth*, 261.8 *growing*, 457.1 *appearance*, 457.7 *appearing*
waxing and waning 216.1 *change*, 216.11 *changeable*
waxing moon 53.17 *moon*, 128.3 *increasing thing*
wax lyrical 851.15 *compliment*
wax modeller 50.17 *sculptor*
wax modelling 50.12 *sculpture*
wax moth 82 Insects
wax palm 85 Trees and Shrubs
wax paper 293.4 *wrapping*, 604.3 *paper*
waxplant 84 Flowers and Flowering Plants

wax polish 418.2 *fragrant thing*
wax tree 85 Trees and Shrubs
waxwing 78 Birds
waxwork 50.12 *sculpture*, 547.6 *image*
waxworks 605.5 *collection*
waxy 374.2 *pliant*, 386.10 *oily*, 394.8 *viscous*, 395.11 *oily*, 828.16 *angry*
way 327, 584, 652, 105.1 *state*, 166.6 *custom*, 332.2 *bearing*, 336.11 *course*, 549.1 *style*, 567.4 *approach*, 592.2 *policy*, 602.1 *means*
Way 327
way back 3.9 *distant past*
way back when 202.19 *anciently*
way behind 263.10 *distantly*
waybill 544.3 *means of identification*, 750.4 *statement*
way down 360.1 *descent*
wayfaring tree 85 Trees and Shrubs
way forward 336.11 *course*
way in 327.2 *route*, 346.5 *entrance*
way in front 263.10 *distantly*
waylay 539.33 *snare*, 657.5 *be cunning*
way of doing things 327.1 *way*
way off 115.4 *dissimilar*
way off the mark 504.17 *mistaken*
way of life 652, 7.1 *religion*, 327.1 *way*, 396.10 *lifestyle*, 584.3 *way*
way of putting something 524.1 *interpretation*
way of things 166.6 *custom*
way out 347, 115.4 *dissimilar*, 327.2 *route*, 585.2 *not customary*, 592.3 *expedient plan*, 638.2 *means of escape*, 639.2 *deliverance*
way-out 165.17 *exceptional*, 168.14 *eccentric*, 617.1 *worthy*
way over 327.2 *route*, 327.9 *bridge*
way-rad 617.1 *worthy*
ways 584.3 *way*
ways and means 327.1 *way*, 602.1 *means*
wayside 264.5 *near*, 300.1 *edge*, 300.8 *edging*
ways of dying 397
ways of the fathers 1.8 *tradition*
ways of thinking 459
way things are 166.6 *custom*
way through 327.2 *route*
way to 327.2 *route*
way under 327.8 *tunnel*
wayward 224.14 *irresolute*, 570.8 *wilful*, 577.2 *refractory*, 579.1 *capricious*, 659.14 *troublesome*
waywardly 224.15 *changeably*, 659.29 *perversely*
waywardness 570.3 *wilfulness*, 579.2 *caprice*
way with 653.3 *management*
way with words 564.2 *power of speech*
wayworn 650.1 *fatigued*
WC 256.7 *room*, 353.13 *lavatory*, 727.7 *toilet*
W chromosome 59.14 *chromosome*
we 165.12 *I*
weak 238, 57.36 *acid*, 127.17 *defective*, 236.12 *impotent*, 242.6 *moderate*, 274.5 *thinned*, 351.17 *drinkable*, 372.2 *rarefied*, 379.1 *brittle*, 389.22 *diluted*, 412.5 *tasteless*, 424.4 *faint*, 428.1 *faint-sounding*, 441.6 *murky*, 476.6 *refutable*, 555.1 *unemphatic*, 576.3 *timid*, 609.1 *insufficient*, 612.2 *obscure*, 620.1 *imperfect*, 624.21 *unhealthy*, 633.2 *unsafe*, 650.1 *fatigued*, 683.10 *failed*, 864.13 *venial*
weak acid 57.8 *acid*
weak alkali 57.9 *base*
weak as a baby 238.10 *ill*, 609.1 *insufficient*
weak as a child 238.10 *ill*

weak as a kitten 238.10 *ill*, 609.1 *insufficient*
weak as water 238.10 *ill*
weak bladder 353.3 *urination*
weak coffee 412.3 *tasteless items*
weak constitution 624.1 *ill health*
weak effort 620.6 *imperfect item*
weak ego 810.5 *self-deprecation*
weaken 238, 129.5 *make smaller*, 133.8 *mix*, 207.17 *age*, 216.8 *cause change*, 236.7 *remove power from*, 238.6 *be weak*, 242.4 *moderate*, 274.16 *make thin*, 372.6 *make sparse*, 412.8 *dilute*, 445.6 *decolour*, 607.1 *waste*, 624.24 *be unhealthy*, 628.1 *deteriorate*, 628.5 *hurt*, 650.6 *fatigue*
weakened 238, 133.12 *mixed*, 628.12 *deteriorated*, 628.13 *dilapidated*, 650.1 *fatigued*
weakened state 238.3 *poor health*
weakening 129.1 *decrease*, 207.12 *ageing*, 412.1 *tastelessness*, 628.11 *hurt*
weaker sex 402.1 *female sex*
weakfish 80 Fishes
weak foundation 238.1 *weakness*
weak heart 624.10 *cardiovascular disease*
weak interaction 56.79 *fundamental interaction*
weak-kneed 238.12 *weak-willed*, 576.3 *timid*, 673.5 *submitting*, 779.3 *cowardly*
weakliness 238.3 *poor health*, 624.1 *ill health*
weakling 238, 260.4 *little person*, 274.9 *thin person*, 576.15 *indecisive person*, 624.19 *sick person*, 687.5 *person in adversity*
weak link in the chain 620.7 *defect*
weakly 238, 127.21 *badly*, 236.14 *powerlessly*, 238.10 *ill*, 238.14 *weakly*, 242.9 *moderately*, 379.5 *fragilely*, 412.10 *without taste*, 476.12 *refutably*, 555.3 *unemphatically*, 624.21 *unhealthy*, 624.25 *unhealthily*, 650.8 *tiredly*, 683.12 *unsuccessfully*
weak-minded 576.3 *timid*
weakness 777 Phobias by Topic, 238, 234.2 *attitude*, 236.3 *helplessness*, 236.4 *disability*, 274.12 *thinning*, 372.4 *rarefaction*, 379.2 *brittleness*, 412.1 *tastelessness*, 476.4 *refutability*, 555.2 *lack of emphasis*, 576.13 *timidity*, 609.8 *insufficiency*, 612.6 *obscurity*, 620.5 *imperfection*, 620.7 *defect*, 624.1 *ill health*, 624.2 *illness*, 624.3 *symptom*, 628.11 *hurt*, 633.7 *vulnerability*, 650.7 *fatigue*, 683.1 *failure*, 683.3 *personal fault*, 779.1 *cowardice*, 782.1 *desire*, 784.1 *liking*, 864.3 *venial sin*
Weakness 238
weakness for liquor 874.11 *drinking*
weakness of the flesh 683.3 *personal fault*, 864.3 *venial sin*
weakness of will 4.9 *philosophical problem*
weak nuclear interaction 56.79 *fundamental interaction*
weak person 612.10 *nonentity*
weak personality 61.8 *disordered personality*
weak point 620.7 *defect*, 864.3 *venial sin*
weak side 19.7 *offence*
weak-sighted 436
weak style 555.2 *lack of emphasis*
weak sun 55.22 *sun*
weak thing 238, 379.3 *brittle thing*
weak will 576.13 *timidity*
weak-willed 238, 576.3 *timid*
weal 309.3 *deformity*, 309.11 *deform*, 686.1 *prosperity*, 793.1 *spot*
weald 98.6 *lowland*

wealth 742, 246.1 *fertility*, 602.4 *financial resources*, 608.8 *plenty*, 682.1 *success*, 686.1 *prosperity*, 698.3 *independence*, 721.5 *profit*, 725.5 *personal estate*, 741.3 *fortune*
Wealth 742
wealthily 742, 721.20 *gainfully*, 741.28 *financially*
wealthy 742, 682.13 *successful*, 686.8 *prosperous*, 721.17 *well-off*, 741.23 *solvent*
wealthy people 721
wealthy person 742, 721.7 *gainer*
wean 68.18 *practise livestock farming*
wean away from 587.3 *deflect*
weaner 68.8 *livestock*, 77.19 *young mammal*
wean from 585.5 *disaccustom*
wean oneself 598.1 *relinquish*
weapon 680, 244.7 *agent of destruction*, 245.8 *organs of reproduction*, 338.8 *missile*, 603.1 *tool*, 632.2 *protection*
Weapon 680
weaponless 236.11 *unprotected*
weaponry 680.2 *arms*
weapons 330, 680.2 *arms*
wear 295, 36.15 *sail*, 74.9 *navigate*, 129.1 *decrease*, 141.1 *disintegration*, 238.1 *weakness*, 238.6 *be weak*, 244.7 *agent of destruction*, 295.1 *dress*, 385.2 *wearing away*, 385.14 *erode*, 599.1, 599.6 *use*, 607.1 *waste*, 650.6 *fatigue*, 722.12 *lessen*
Wear 96 Rivers
wear a catching glove 31.9 *play hockey*
wear a face mask 31.9 *play hockey*
wear a hair shirt 866.9 *appear guilty*, 867.5 *do penance*
wear a helmet 31.9 *play hockey*
wear a macintosh 392.22 *keep dry*
wear and tear 129.1 *decrease*, 131.1 *subtraction*, 141.1 *disintegration*, 244.7 *agent of destruction*, 599.6 *use*, 607.3 *waste*, 628.9 *dilapidation*, 722.4 *lessening*
wear a sackcloth 867.5 *do penance*
wear a shinguard 31.9 *play hockey*
wear a skisuit 41.14 *ski*
wear a smile 296.14 *undress*
wear away 129.4 *decrease*, 141.3 *disintegrate*, 385.14 *erode*, 607.1 *waste*, 722.12 *lessen*
wear down 384.29 *weather*, 586.15 *persuade*
wearied 238.11 *weakened*, 650.1 *fatigued*, 788.5 *bored*
wearily 650.8 *tiredly*, 788.8 *boringly*
weariness 238.3 *poor health*, 650.7 *fatigue*, 788.1 *boredom*
wearing 36.1 *sailing*, 650.4 *fatiguing*, 722.4 *lessening*, 788.4 *boring*
wearing a hair shirt 867.2 *type of penance*
wearing a sackcloth 867.2 *type of penance*
wearing away 385, 458.4 *disappearance*, 722.4 *lessening*
wearing earplugs 421.4 *deaf*
wearisome 644.11 *laborious*, 650.4 *fatiguing*, 659.10 *difficult*, 788.4 *boring*
wearisomely 650.9 *tiringly*
wear mourning 440.12 *be dark*
wear one's heart on one's sleeve 526.4 *show oneself*
wear one's heart upon one's sleeve 658.4 *be naive*
wear out 141.3 *disintegrate*, 238.6 *be weak*, 599.1 *use*, 601.1 *misuse*, 607.1 *waste*, 628.1 *deteriorate*, 628.5 *hurt*, 650.6 *fatigue*
wear the cloth 7.21 *ordain*
wear the crown 12.11 *govern*, 126.8 *be superior*, 166.16 *direct*,

682.9 be victorious, 688.18
have authority
wear the laurels 682.9 *be victorious*
wear the laurel wreath 682.9 *be victorious*
wear the pants 233.10 *be a prevailing influence,* 688.19 *be authoritarian*
wear the trousers 233.10 *be a prevailing influence,* 653.2 *direct,* 688.19 *be authoritarian*
wear thin 238.6 *be weak,* 379.4 *be brittle*
wear well 623.5 *be healthy*
weary 238.11 *weakened,* 644.11 *laborious,* 650.1 *fatigued,* 650.2 *bored,* 650.6 *fatigue,* 788.4 *boring,* 788.5 *bored,* 788.6 *be boring*
wearying 650.4 *fatiguing,* 788.4 *boring*
Weary Willie 643.11 *sleeper*
weasel 71 Motor Vehicles, **77** Placental Mammals, 71.10 *sled,* 578.1 *be equivocal,* 578.9 *equivocator*
weaselly 77.28 *carnivorous*
weasel word 578.5 *equivocalness*
weather 55, 384, 74.9 *navigate,* 241.5 *violent weather,* 444.15 *colour,* 594.7 *develop,* 628.2 *decay*
weather balloon 55.5 *weather station*
weather-beaten 238.9 *dilapidated,* 378.4 *powerful,* 628.13 *dilapidated*
weatherboard 74 Parts of a Ship, 47.12 *wood,* 293.8 *wall covering*
weather bureau 55.4 *weather forecast*
weathercock 55.7 *weather instruments,* 224.3 *changeable thing,* 275.8 *high thing,* 543.5 *indicator,* 576.15 *indecisive person,* 578.9 *equivocator*
weather data 55
weather deck 74 Parts of a Ship
weathered 54, 444.13 *soft-hued,* 445.7 *colourless,* 594.20 *developed*
weather forecast 55, 517.1 *prediction*
weather forecaster 55.2 *meteorologist,* 517.9 *forecaster,* 528.9 *informant*
weather forecasting 55.1 *meteorology*
weatherglass 55.7 *weather instruments*
weather house 389.19 *measuring instrument*
weathering 54, 445.1 *colourlessness,* 628.9 *dilapidation*
weather instruments 55
weather lore 55.3 *weather*
weatherman 55.2 *meteorologist,* 517.9 *forecaster*
Weatherman 693.10 *seditionist*
weather map 55.4 *weather forecast*
weather observer 55.2 *meteorologist*
weatherproof 632.6 *invulnerable*
weather prophet 11.13 *diviner,* 55.2 *meteorologist*
weather radar 55.7 *weather instruments,* 534.28 *radar*
weather satellite 53.32 *satellite,* 55.5 *weather station*
weather science 55.1 *meteorology*
weather ship 74 Ships and Boats, 55.5 *weather station*
weather sign 543.1 *sign*
weather situation 55.3 *weather*
weather station 55
weather symbols 55.4 *weather forecast*
weather system 55
weather the storm 74.10 *sail,* 225.8 *show determination,* 629.4 *be restored,* 632.8 *be safe,* 638.5 *escape,* 682.7 *overcome obstacles*
weather vane 55.7 *weather instruments,* 224.3 *changeable thing*
weather vane 275.8 *high thing,* 543.5 *indicator*
weather-wise 516.6 *foreseeing,* 517.13 *predicting*
weatherwoman 55.2 *meteorologist*
weave 67, 383, 67.4 *weaving,* 135.10 *link,* 243.10 *produce,* 288.8 *interweave,* 324.15 *walk,* 335.5 *twist,* 356.9 *proceed,* 382.2 *fabric*
weave a plot 657.5 *be cunning*
weave one's way 336.7 *make one's way*
weaver 67.4 *weaving,* 135.7 *joiner,* 288.3 *weaving,* 646.2 *artisan*
Weaver 96 Rivers
weaverbird 78 Birds, 78.6 *songbird,* 288.3 *weaving*
weaverfinch 78 Birds
weaver's knot 74 Knots
weave together 314.6 *convolute*
weaving 42 Hobbies and Pastimes, **67, 288,** 135.3 *unification,* 288.1 *interweaving,* 306.4 *forming,* 383.4 *weave*
weaving frame 67.4 *weaving*
weazen 392.21 *dry up*
weazened 392.3 *dried-up*
web 67.4 *weaving,* 82.6 *spinner,* 151.7 *tangle,* 288.2 *braid,* 288.8 *interweave,* 383.4 *weave,* 539.13 *snare,* 592.4 *plot,* 657.2 *stratagem*
Webb 48 Writers
webbed 288.6 *interwoven,* 539.42 *trapped*
webbed feet 78.16 *avian anatomy*
webbing 67 Natural Fabrics, 67.4 *weaving,* 288.1 *interweaving,* 288.2 *braid*
webby 288.6 *interwoven*
web connection 63.27 *superstructure*
weber 75 SI Units, **75** Scientific and Technical Units
Weber 49 Musicians and Composers, **52** Scientists
web of cunning 657.2 *stratagem*
web of deceit 657.2 *stratagem*
web of intrigue 592.4 *plot*
webspinner 82 Insects
Webster 48 Dramatists
wed 135.10 *link,* 135.11 *make love,* 140.6 *come together,* 715.5 *contract,* 823.15 *marry*
wedded 107.4 *related,* 135.12 *united,* 180.19 *associated,* 584.14 *habituated,* 823.21 *married*
wedded bliss 823.1 *marriage*
weddedness 823.1 *marriage*
wedded state 823.1 *marriage*
wedded to 821.18 *in love*
Weddell 97 Oceans and Seas
wedding 823, 135.4 *sexual union,* 813.3 *formal occasion*
wedding anniversary 214.6 *annually celebrated day,* 812.5 *anniversary*
wedding announcement 823.6 *general terms*
wedding banns 823.6 *general terms*
wedding bells 821.8 *love affair,* 823.6 *general terms*
wedding breakfast 161.9 *social gathering,* 350.13 *feast,* 665.7 *social gathering,* 823.6 *general terms*
wedding cake 45.36 *cake,* 823.6 *general terms*
wedding canopy 823.6 *general terms*
wedding caterer 606.4 *caterer*
wedding ceremony 823.5 *wedding*
wedding clothes 295.1 *dress*
wedding dance 46.4 *historic dancing*
wedding day 823.6 *general terms*
wedding dress 295.7 *frock,* 823.6 *general terms*
wedding invitation 823.6 *general terms*
wedding march 823.6 *general terms*
wedding morning 823.6 *general terms*
wedding music 823.6 *general terms*
wedding party 665.7 *social gathering,* 815.5 *party*
wedding photographs 823.6 *general terms*
wedding present 823.6 *general terms*
wedding reception 161.9 *social gathering,* 350.13 *feast,* 665.7 *social gathering,* 815.3 *meeting,* 823.6 *general terms*
wedding rehearsal 823.6 *general terms*
wedding ring 823.6 *general terms,* 826.3 *love token*
wedding service 823.5 *wedding*
wedding shower 823.6 *general terms*
wedding song 823.6 *general terms*
wedding veil 823.6 *general terms*
Wedekind 48 Dramatists
wedge 29.4 *golf club,* 39.11 *swimming,* 44.11 *make ceramics,* 52.46 *polyhedron,* 63.6 *simple machine,* 74.10 *sail,* 85.7 *timber production,* 135.10 *link,* 143.7 *piece,* 272.8 *narrow thing,* 310.2 *obliquity,* 323.2 *stopper,* 380.9 *sharp-edged thing,* 603.1 *tool*
wedged 44.10 *ceramic,* 135.15 *tied*
wedge heels 295.19 *footwear*
wedge in 346.12 *flood in,* 354.5 *inset*
wedge kick 39.2 *swimming technique*
wedge-shaped 34.8 *mountaineering,* 52.82 *polygonal,* 52.84 *cubic,* 272.3 *tapered,* 380.1 *sharp*
wedge-shaped equipment
wedge-shaped nut 34.4 *climbing equipment*
wedgies 295.19 *footwear*
wedging 44.5 *ceramic process*
Wedgwood blue 454.1 *blue*
Wedgwood ware 44 Types of Ceramics
wedgy 380.1 *sharp*
wedlock 135.4 *sexual union,* 715.1 *contract,* 823.1 *marriage*
wee 260.7 *little,* 353.3 *urination,* 353.6 *urine,* 353.17 *urinate,* 387.3 *body fluid,* 389.4 *exudate,* 389.32 *seep*
weed 68.17 *farm,* 69.15 *cultivate,* 83.2 *plant,* 87.12 *manage grassland,* 131.3 *subtract,* 238.4 *weakling,* 627.1 *improve,* 779.2 *coward,* 875.6 *drug*
weed-choked 69.17 *botanical,* 83.13 *plantlike*
weediness 274.7 *thinness*
weeding 68.5 *cultivation,* 69.5 *gardening,* 355.2 *displacement*
weedkiller 69, 68.14 *pest control,* 398.14 *plant killer,* 631.8 *poison*
weed out 129.5 *make smaller,* 134.11 *simplify,* 182.8 *reduce,* 355.12 *displace,* 621.15 *purify*
weeds 614.6 *refuse,* 824.5 *widowhood*
weedy 83.13 *plantlike,* 274.1 *thin*
Wee Free 7.5 *Christian*
week 179.3 *seven,* 185.4 *term,* 187.2 *time period,* 269.8 *measure of time*
weekday 187.2 *time period*
weekend 815.12 *visit*
weekend market 740.1 *market*
weekend party 815.5 *party*
weekend warrior 632.3 *protector,* 679.8 *soldier*
week in week out 185.26 *all the time*
weekly 110.17 *regular,* 110.20 *regularly,* 185.22 *periodic,*
187.7, 187.8 *periodical,* 187.13 *for specified periods,* 214.12 *cyclic,* 214.16 *cyclically,* 532.5 *journal,* 584.9 *habitual*
weekly market 740.1 *market*
weekly newspaper 533.5 *mass communication*
weekly paper 532.4 *newspaper*
weenie 45.29 *sausage*
weenie roast 350.13 *feast*
weeny 260.7 *little*
weenybopper 206.6 *young person*
weep 774, 85.19 *grow,* 347.3 *leakage,* 347.12 *leak,* 352.7 *secrete,* 353.15 *excrete,* 353.18 *fester,* 387.25 *flow,* 389.32, 389.32 *seep,* 391.16 *seep,* 431.13 *cry,* 770.8 *grieve*
weeper 399.3 *funeral director,* 774.3 *lamenter*
weep for 774.6 *lament,* 835.9 *sorrow*
weepily 352.8 *glandularly,* 387.26 *fluidly,* 389.35 *wetly*
weeping 347.3 *leakage,* 347.17 *leaky,* 352.1 *secretion,* 352.4 *secretory,* 353.7 *pus,* 387.16 *rheumy,* 389.4 *exudate,* 389.25, 391.12 *seeping,* 431.6 *cry of pain,* 431.18 *crying,* 774.1 *lamentation,* 774.4 *lamenting*
weeping and wailing 399.2 *funeral,* 431.6 *cry of pain*
weeping and wailing and gnashing of teeth 770.1 *sorrow,* 774.1 *lamentation*
weeping willow 85 Trees and Shrubs
weep over 774.7 *weep*
weep with 835.9 *sorrow*
weep with rage 828.11 *be angry*
wee small hours 205.3 *midnight,* 209.2 *late hour*
weever 80 Fishes
weevil 82 Insects, 69.12 *pests and diseases,* 82.3 *pest*
weevilly 82.12 *verminous*
wee-wee 353.6 *urine,* 353.17 *urinate*
weft 67.4, 288.3 *weaving,* 382.2 *fabric*
weftage 383.4 *weave*
Wegener 52 Scientists
weigh 369, 120.8 *quantify,* 268.10 *measure,* 361.4 *gather up,* 611.7 *be important*
weigh anchor 74.9 *navigate,* 345.5 *set out*
weigh a ton 369.12 *be heavy*
weighbridge 71.21 *miscellaneous motoring terms,* 268.7 *standard,* 369.10 *scales*
weigh down 369.14 *make heavy,* 687.11 *cause adversity*
weighed 120.6 *quantitative,* 369.1 *heavy,* 582.4 *deliberate*
weighed down 369.3 *ponderous*
weigh equally 704.9 *cancel out*
weigh heavy upon 369.13 *weigh on*
weigh in 32.7 *horseracing,* 233.8 *influence,* 369.15 *weigh*
weigh-in 369.1 *heavy,* 369.7 *weighing*
weighing 369, 120.1 *quantity,* 120.6 *quantitative,* 122.3 *equalization,* 369.1 *heavy*
weighing down 369
weighing-in 369.7 *weighing*
weighing instrument 56
weighing little 370.1 *light*
weighing machine 268.7 *standard,* 369.10 *scales*
weighing-out 369.7 *weighing*
weighing room 32.7 *horseracing*
weighing up 122.3 *equalization*
weigh in the balance 369.15 *weigh*
weigh light upon 612.11 *be unimportant*
weigh little 370.9 *be light*
weigh on 369, 362.5 *bear down on*
weigh one down 369.13 *weigh on,* 369.14 *make heavy*
weigh oneself 369.15 *weigh*
weigh out 32.7 *horseracing,*

268.11 *measure out,* 369.15
weigh
weigh-out 369.1 *heavy,* 369.7
weighing
weight 369, 25.2 *grip,* 56.10
force, 120.1 *quantity,* 232.1 *instrumentality,* 233 *influence,*
235.1 *power,* 237.3 *intensity,*
268.4 *size,* 367.1 *material
world,* 369.4 *heaviness,* 537.11
pedantry, 554.2 *seriousness,*
611.1 *importance*
weight allowance 32.7 *horseracing*
weight cloth 32.7 *horseracing*
weighted 369.1 *heavy,* 844.11
wrong
weighted mean 52.60 *parameter*
weigh the same 369.12 *be heavy*
weightily 369.16 *heavily*
weightiness 369.4 *heaviness,*
611.1, 772.6 *importance,* 813.1
formality
weighting 52.60 *parameter*
weighting down 369.8 *weighing
down*
weightless 370.1 *light,* 390.12
airy
weightlessness 53.31 *space
travel,* 370.5 *lightness,* 390.9 *airiness*
weightlifter 237.5 *athlete*
weightlifting 18 Sporting Activities, 644.5 *exercise*
weight loss 129.1 *decrease,*
624.3 *symptom,* 722.1 *loss,*
871.1 *fasting*
weight of numbers 235.1 *power*
weight on one's mind 867.1 *penitence*
weight on one's shoulders 661.6
burden
weights 32.7 *horseracing,* 879.15
instrument of torture
weight watcher 274.9 *thin person,* 350.18 *eater,* 722.7 *dieter,*
871.4 *fasting person*
Weightwatchers 722.7 *dieter,*
869.1 *self-restraint,* 871.1 *fasting*
weight-watching 274.3 *slimming,*
274.10 *diet,* 350.6 *nutrition,*
722.1 *loss,* 871.1 *fasting*
weighty 232.7 *causal,* 237.10 *potent,* 367.7 *material,* 369.1
heavy, 371.6 *dense,* 520.7 *significant,* 537.24 *pedantic,* 554.5 *serious,* 611.5, 772.3 *important,*
813.6 *formal*
weigh up 461.15 *think about,*
473.14 *discuss,* 492.12 *estimate*
weigh up against 704.9 *cancel
out*
weigh up the pros and cons
576.8 *balance*
Weil 4 Philosophers
Weill 49 Musicians and Composers
Weimaraner 77 Breeds of Dogs
weir 63.23 *dam,* 347.7 *outlet,*
661.3 *barrier*
weird 11.5 *spell,* 11.18 *spiritual,*
117.9 *nonconforming,* 168.14
eccentric, 487.2 *unbelievable,*
510.11 *insane,* 523.5 *strange,*
579.1 *capricious,* 786.8 *wonderful*
weird and wonderful 514.8 *surprising,* 786.8 *wonderful*
weirdly 11.26 *magically,* 117.15
dissimilarly, 786.13 *wonderfully*
weirdness 117.3 *nonconformity,*
168.4 *unusualness*
weirdo 104.5 *nonconformist,*
117.6 *misfit,* 168.10 *eccentric,*
335.19 *deviant person*
weird sister 11.4 *witch*
Weismann 52 Scientists
Weismannism 59.16 *evolution*
Weiss 48 Writers
Weissmuller 18 Sporting Personalities
welcome! 344
welcome 348, 815, 815,
203.14 *seasonable,* 210.6
timely, 344.12 *reception,* 348.2
receptivity, 405.6 *pleasant,*

499.4 *assent,* 667.6 *agree with,*
730.10 *receive someone,* 763.1
pleasant, 782.8 *desirable,*
782.12 *desire,* 812.18 *salute,*
815.11 *be sociable,* 815.16 *popular,* 817.3 *courtesies,* 817.10 *be
courteous,* 817.12 *greet,* 819.15
be hospitable, 849.6 *greeting,*
849.20 *salute*
welcomed 730.13 *received*
welcomed with open arms
815.16 *popular*
welcome end 397.5 *ways of dying*
welcome guest 815.6 *social person*
welcome home 817.12 *greet*
welcome with open arms 348.9
welcome, 815.11 *be sociable,*
817.12 *greet,* 819.15 *be hospitable*
welcoming 344, 348.2 *receptivity,* 348.15 *receptive,* 730.4 *reception,* 730.12 *receptive,*
812.13 *congratulatory,* 815.9
welcome, 815.15 *sociable,* 817.7
courteous, 819.8 *friendly*
welcoming address 564.8 *speech*
welcoming ceremony 730.4 *reception*
welcoming embrace 815.9 *welcome*
welcomingly 348.18 *receptively*
welcoming with open arms 348.2
receptivity
weld 63.27 *superstructure,* 135.5
joint, 135.10 *link,* 138.7 *cause
to adhere,* 408.14 *be hot,* 452.7
yellow pigment
welded joint 135.5 *joint*
weldel 41.4 *skiing technique*
welder 135.7 *joiner,* 646.2 *artisan*
welding 135.3 *unification,* 138.1
adhesion
welding torch 50.14 *sculptor's
materials*
welfare 831, 2.10 *social services,*
91.16 *national,* 632.1 *safety,*
662.4 *social assistance,* 686.1
prosperity, 718.1 *protection,*
729.2 *gift,* 833.1 *philanthropy,*
861.13 *benefit*
welfare economics 13.1 *economics*
welfare institution 634.2 *shelter*
welfare officer 15.6 *employer*
welfare organization 2.10 *social
services*
welfare payment 662.4 *social assistance,* 729.2 *gift*
welfare services 662.4 *social assistance*
welfare state 833, 2.10 *social
services,* 12.5 *political organization,* 400.11 *nation,* 632.1
safety, 634.2 *shelter,* 662.4 *social assistance,* 718.1 *protection,*
831.3 *welfare*
welfare work 831.3 *welfare*
welfare worker 831.5 *benevolent
person,* 833.3 *philanthropist*
welfarism 831.3 *welfare,* 833.1
philanthropy
welfarist 831.5 *benevolent person*
welkin 8.11 *heaven,* 53.3 *universe,* 390.1 *air*
well 652, 861, 36.6 *canoeing,*
106.9 *comfortable,* 142.8 *sound,*
277.4 *deep thing,* 322.5 *hole,*
347.2 *outflow,* 362.14 *depression,* 389.13 *irrigator,* 605.2
resource, 617.11 *worthily,* 623.1
healthy, 655.12 *skilfully,*
682.16 *successfully,* 742.16
wealthily, 843.12 *all right,*
857.7 *honourably*
well-adapted 485.9 *qualified*
well-advised 507.5 *wise*
well-affected 662.35 *benevolent*
well-aimed 332.14 *directed,*
537.21 *accurate*
well-appointed 594.18 *prepared,*
606.8 *provisional*
well-armed 237.13 *strengthened*
well-baby clinic 60.10 *hospital*
well-balanced 308.4 *symmetrical,* 590.5 *rational*
well-behaved 652, 861, 150.17

disciplined, 694.7 *obedient,*
817.8 *good-mannered*
well-behaved child 694.4 *obedient person*
well-behaved person 652
well-being 106.5 *comfortable circumstances,* 405.1 *physical
pleasure,* 623.3 *health,* 625.2 *salubrity,* 649.1 *ease,* 686.1 *prosperity,* 861.13 *benefit*
well-beloved 821.11 *loved one,*
821.21 *beloved*
well-born 802.4 *aristocratic*
well-bred 6.20 *refined,* 304.5
bred, 652.17 *well-behaved,*
794.5 *refined,* 802.4 *aristocratic,*
817.8 *good-mannered*
well-bred person 400.4 *civilized
human*
well-brushed 376.1 *smooth*
well-built 237.13 *strengthened,*
259.17 *stocky,* 789.5 *beautiful*
well-cared for 150.13 *orderly*
well-chosen 580.15 *chosen*
well-cooked 594.20 *developed*
well-crafted 655.9 *well-made*
well-cut 295.31 *styled*
well-defended 632.5 *safe*
well defined 318.7 *conspicuous*
well-defined 522.3 *recognizable*
well-deserved 845.10 *due*
well-deserving 851.21 *praiseworthy*
well-directed 332.14 *directed*
well-disposed 284.9 *supportive,*
662.35 *benevolent,* 819.8
friendly
well done 617.12 *fantastic,*
684.7 *completed,* 851.27 *bravo*
well-done 45.56 *culinary,*
594.20 *developed*
well-drawn 48.18, 560.11
descriptive
well-dressed 295.30 *dressed up,*
457.10 *aspectual,* 796.7 *fashionable*
well-drilled 150.17 *disciplined*
well-earned 845.10 *due*
well-educated 501.9 *literate*
well-endowed 259.16 *fat,* 655.7
gifted, 742.1 *wealthy*
wellerism 506.2 *solecism*
well-established 217.7 *permanent,* 225.10 *stabilized,* 237.10
potent
well-fed 259.16 *fat,* 273.1 *thick,*
350.26 *eating*
well-filled 144.8 *full,* 608.3 *filled*
well-finished 794.5 *refined*
well-formed formula 52.63 *mathematical logic*
well-fought 674.16 *competitive*
well-founded 225.9 *stable,*
237.10 *potent,* 490.1 *certain*
well-furnished 608.3 *filled*
well-greased 386.8, 395.16 *lubricated,* 660.12 *wieldy*
well-groomed 150.13 *orderly,*
558.3 *elegant,* 621.16 *clean,*
796.7 *fashionable*
well-grounded 6.19 *knowledgeable,* 490.1 *certain*
well-grounded hope 488.4 *chance*
wellhead 226.2 *source*
well-heeled 686.8 *prosperous,*
721.17 *well-off,* 742.1 *wealthy*
well-housed 742.1 *wealthy*
well hung 141.5 *disintegrated*
wellies 295.19 *footwear*
well-inclined 831.18 *approving*
well I never 514.14 *good heavens,* 786.14 *wonderful*
well-informed 501.8 *knowledgeable*
Wellington 92 New Zealand Regions and Territories, **93** Cities
Wellington boots 295.19 *footwear*
wellingtonia 85 Trees and
Shrubs
well-intended 819.8 *friendly*
well-intentioned 662.35, 831.6
benevolent
well-judged 210.8 *in time*
well-kept 150.13 *orderly,* 637.7
preserved
well-known 99.13 *real,* 532,

501.10 *known,* 526.14 *manifest,* 584.10 *familiar,* 599.9 *used*
well-laid 327.15 *accessible,*
657.4 *cunning*
well-liked 821.21 *beloved*
well-lined 144.8 *full*
well-lined purse 742.5 *wealth*
well lit 437.2 *clear*
well-lit 327.15 *accessible,* 439.18
lit
well-lubricated 874.1 *drunk*
well-made 655, 789.5 *beautiful*
well-made play 51.2 *play*
well-mannered 376.6 *smooth-
mannered,* 652.17 *well-behaved,*
763.2 *likable,* 794.5 *refined,*
861.4 *well-behaved*
well-mannered person 652.3 *well-
behaved person*
well-matched 122.8 *on equal
terms*
well-meaning 662.35 *benevolent,*
819.8 *friendly,* 831.6 *benevolent*
well-meant 662.35, 831.6 *benevolent*
well-merited 845.10 *due*
well-nigh 264.7 *nearly*
well-nourished 350.26 *eating,*
872.6 *gluttonous*
well-off 721, 686.8 *prosperous,*
742.1 *wealthy*
well-oiled 386.8, 395.16 *lubricated,* 660.12 *wieldy,* 874.1
drunk
well-ordered 150, 122.6 *equal*
well-organized 150.14 *well-ordered*
well out 347.11 *run out*
well over 610.4 *be excessive*
well-paid 742.1 *wealthy*
well-paved 327.15 *accessible*
well-paying 721.15 *gainful*
well-pitched 433.6 *melodious*
well-planned 657.4 *cunning*
well-practised 655.8 *expert*
well-prepared 594.18 *prepared,*
655.8 *expert*
well-preserved 207.14 *aged,*
217.7 *permanent,* 637.7 *preserved*
well-proportioned 308.4 *symmetrical,* 315.10 *well-rounded,*
558.3 *elegant,* 789.5 *beautiful*
well-protected 237.13 *strengthened*
well-provided 608.3 *filled*
well provided for 721.17 *well-off*
well-provisioned 608.3 *filled*
well-qualified 501.9 *literate*
well-read 4.19 *learned,* 6.18 *educated,* 48.16 *literary,* 293.41 *progressing*
well-reasoned 4.15 *rational,*
471.12 *purposive*
well-received 730.13 *received*
well-regulated 150.17 *disciplined*
well-rehearsed 594.18 *prepared*
well respected 849.12 *respected*
well-rooted 225.10 *stabilized*
well-rounded 311, 315, 5.43
phrasal
well-rounded shape 315.2 *round
body*
Wells 48 Writers, **93** Cities
well-situated 742.1 *wealthy*
well-spoken 522.2 *simple,*
564.19 *speaking,* 794.5 *refined,*
817.8 *good-mannered*
wellspring 156.3, 226.2 *source*
well-sprung 377.6 *elastic*
well-stocked 144.8 *full,* 608.3
filled
well thought of 800.3 *reputable,*
849.12 *respected,* 851.24 *admired*
well-thought-out 4.15 *rational*
well-thumbed 599.9 *used*
well-tied 135.15 *tied*
well-timed 203.14 *seasonable,*
210.8 *in time,* 615.1 *convenient*
well-to-do 686.8 *prosperous,*
721.17 *well-off,* 742.1 *wealthy*
well-trained 6.19 *knowledgeable,*
694.7 *obedient*
well-trodden 282.9 *flattened,*
599.9 *used*

well-turned 5.43 *phrasal*, 315.10
well-rounded, 558.3 *elegant*
well turned out 295.30, 813.7
dressed up
well-turned phrase 5.24 *phrasing*, 558.1 *elegance*
well up 54.63 *ebb*, 387.25 *flow*
well-upholstered 259.16 *fat*
well up on 655.8 *expert*
well-used 327.15 *accessible*,
599.9 *used*
well-ventilated 390.17 *ventilated*,
625.4 *hygienic*
well versed 501.8 *knowledgeable*
well-versed 4.19 *learned*, 6.19
knowledgeable
well water 389.1 *water*
well-wisher 284.8 *supporter*,
662.15 *benefactor*, 831.5 *benevolent person*, 861.15 *good person*
well-wishing 861.3 *kind*, 861.10
kindness
well-woman clinic 60.10 *hospital*
well-worn 5.42 *worded*, 584.10
familiar, 599.9 *used*, 628.13 *dilapidated*
well-worn phrase 5.21 *catchword*
welly 239.1 *vigour*
wels 80 Fishes
welsh 745.8, 747.7 *not pay*
Welsh 5 Languages and Groups
of Languages, **68** Breeds of Pig
Welsh accent 5.26 *dialect*
Welsh Black 68 Breeds of Cattle
Welsh Cob 32 Breeds of Horse
and Pony
Welsh corgi 77 Breeds of Dogs
Welsh daffodil 544.6 *national
emblem*
Welsh dresser 47.5, 258.3 *cabinet*
welsher 591.17 *avoider*, 747.6
nonpayer
Welsh Grand Committee 12.4 *governing body*
Welsh Guard 679.12 *ceremonial
troops*
Welsh Harlequin 68 Breeds of
Fowl
Welsh Hill Speckled Face 68
Breeds of Sheep
Welsh leek 544.6 *national emblem*
Welshman 91.12 *Wales*, 255.9
British inhabitant
Welsh Mountain 68 Breeds of
Sheep
Welsh Mountain Pony 32 Breeds
of Horse and Pony
Welsh mountains 95.5 *British
mountains*
Welshness 91.12 *Wales*
Welsh Pony 32 Breeds of Horse
and Pony
Welshpool 93 Cities
Welsh poppy 84 Flowers and
Flowering Plants
Welsh rarebit 45.44 *British dish*
Welsh terrier 77 Breeds of
Dogs
Welsumer 68 Breeds of Fowl
welt 309.3 *deformity*, 309.11 *deform*, 793.1 *spot*, 879.3 *hit*
welter 151.5 *confusion*, 362.9
bow, 364.10 *swirl*, 366.11 *stagger*, 366.25 *pitch*
weltering 389.24 *flooded*
welterweight 26.3 *boxing weight
divisions*, 26.4 *boxer*, 26.14 *combat*, 369.7 *weighing*, 679.3 *athlete*
Wembley 674.3 *stadium*
wen 5.13 *letter*
wench 697.6 *domestic servant*
wenching 877.3 *sexual immorality*
W'en-ch'ung 8 Deities
Wendish 5 Languages and
Groups of Languages
Wensleydale 45 Cheeses, **68**
Breeds of Sheep
wentletrap 81 Molluscs
werecat 11.11 *ghost*
werewolf 11.11 *ghost*
wergild 125.1 *compensation*,
677.2 *peace offering*, 840.1
atonement

wernerite 54 Minerals
wersh 542.17 *insipid*, 555.1 *unemphatic*, 609.1 *insufficient*
Wertherism 48 Literary Groups
and Movements
Weschler Adult Intelligence Scale
61.6 *intelligence test*
Weschler-Bellvue intelligence test
61.6 *intelligence test*
**Weschler intelligence scale for
children** 61.6 *intelligence test*
Weser 96 Rivers
we shall overcome 669.16 *fight
on*
Wesker 48 Dramatists
Wesleyan 7.5 *Christian*
west 332.4 *compass point*,
332.12 *north*, 332.13 *directional*
West 48 Writers, **48** Writers,
53 Comets
West Atlantic 5 Languages and
Groups of Languages
westbound 332.13 *directional*
West Coast 92 New Zealand Regions and Territories
West Country 249.9 *regions of
Britain*
Westcountryman 255.9 *British inhabitant*
West End 51.4 *show business*,
93.5 *London*
westerly 55.15 *wind direction*,
55.47 *windy*, 332.12 *north*,
332.13 *directional*
western 48.2 *fiction*, 249.16 *regional*, 305.6 *side*, 332.13 *directional*, 560.5 *fiction*
Western Australia 92 Australian
States and Territories
Western bloc 91.2 *union of nations*
Westerner 255.10 *US inhabitant*
Western Hemisphere 249.7 *regions of the world*
western hemlock 85 Trees and
Shrubs
Western Isles 92 Counties
westernize 220.12 *naturalize*
westernized 220.17 *naturalized*
westernly 332.12 *north*
westernmost 332.13 *directional*
Western nation 91.1 *country*
western red cedar 85 Trees and
Shrubs
Western roll style 21.2 *field
events*
Western Samoa 91 Countries
West Germanic 5 Languages and
Groups of Languages
West Glamorgan 92 Counties
West Highland 68 Breeds of Cattle
West Highland white terrier 77
Breeds of Dogs
westing 332.4 *compass point*
Westlander 255.10 *US inhabitant*
Westmeath 92 Counties
Westminster 12.4 *governing
body*, 93.5 *London*, 653.11 *British government*, 688.6 *place of
authority*, 696.8 *the power structure*
Westminster Abbey 43 Noted
Buildings
Westminster Cathedral 43 Noted
Buildings
Westminster waltz 41.7 *ice-dancing*
Weston cell 57.19 *electrochemistry*
Weston standard 56 Named
Laws
Westphal 53 Comets
west side 305.3 *side direction*
West Side 93.3 *New York*
West Sussex 92 Counties
West Virginia 92 American
States
westward 332.4 *compass point*,
332.13 *directional*
westwardly 332.12 *north*
westwards 332.12 *north*
west wind 55.15 *wind direction*
westwork 43.10 *church architecture*
West Yorkshire 92 Counties
wet 389, 12.6 *political party*,

55.53 *rainy*, 238.4 *weakling*,
353.17 *urinate*, 389.3 *wateriness*, 389.29 *water*, 391.8
marsh, 391.9 *moist*, 391.13
moisten, 576.3 *timid*, 576.15 *indecisive person*, 620.4 *ordinary*,
665.6 *political party member*,
673.2 *appeaser*, 691.2 *lenient
person*, 779.3 *cowardly*
wet-and-dry bulb thermometer
389.19 *measuring instrument*
wetback 91 Names for Inhabitants
wet battery 605.4 *storage*
wet behind the ears 453.3 *raw*,
497.12 *gullible*, 595.5 *immature*, 656.2 *unskilled*, 658.1
naive
wet blanket 242.2 *moderator*,
587.8 *cautionary person*, 661.7
hinderer, 770.4 *depressing person*, 783.6 *indifferent person*,
788.3 *boring person*, 852.13 *pessimist*
wet cell 57.19 *electrochemistry*,
64.29 *power source*, 235.7 *electrical power*
wet chinook 55 Winds
wet-eyed 774.4 *lamenting*
wet fish 80.8 *food fish*
wet-fly 20.8 *angling*
wet-fly fishing 20.1 *angling*
wether 68.8 *livestock*
wetland 391.8 *marsh*
wetlands 98.3 *marsh*, 278.4 *shallow thing*
wet-look 791.8 *hair cut*
wetly 389, 55.65 *meteorologically*, 391.17 *moistly*
wetness 55.26 *raininess*, 389.3
wateriness, 391.1 *moisture*
wet nurse 606.3 *provider*
wet oneself 353.17 *urinate*,
779.4 *be a coward*
wet one's lips 351.13 *drink*
wet one's whistle 351.13 *drink*
wet rot 89.1 *fungus*, 244.7 *agent
of destruction*, 391.4 *seepage*,
622.4 *dirt*
wet season 55.26 *raininess*
wet snow 55.30 *snow*, 409.5 *ice*
wet suit 295.10 *suit*, 295.21
beachwear
wetter 55.53 *rainy*
wet the bed 353.17 *urinate*
wetting 389, 389.8 *watering*
wetting agent 68.14 *pest control*,
389.6 *hydrate*
wetting-out agent 389.6 *hydrate*
wettish 391.9 *moist*
wettishness 389.3 *wateriness*,
391.1 *moisture*
wet weather 391.2 *mistiness*
wet with sweat 353.28 *sweaty*
wetwood 85.3 *timber*
Wexford 92 Counties, **93** Cities
Weymouth 93 Cities
whack 120.2 *certain amount*,
143.1 *part*, 187.4 *period of activity*, 425.1 *bang*, 479.1 *experiment*, 596.5 *attempt*, 650.6 *fatigue*, 879.3 *hit*
whacked 650.1 *fatigued*
whacking 259.15 *big*
whale 77 Placental Mammals,
76.5 *aquatic animal*, 259.9 *big
thing*, 590.11 *hunt*
Whale 53 The Constellations
whale beaching 398.9 *animal
killing*
whaleboat 74 Ships and Boats
whalebone 377.3 *elastic thing*
whaleboned 373.2 *tough*
whalelike 77.29 *cetacean*
whale louse 81.4 *arthropod*,
81.10 *parasite*
whale of a time 405.2 *good time*
whaler 74.3 *vessel*, 74.7 *nautical
person*, 80.10 *fisher*, 590.6
hunter
whales 161 Collective Names
by Animal
Whalesbury 68 Breeds of Fowl
whale shark 80 Fishes
whaling 77.23 *mammal hunting*,
80.7 *fishing*, 590.2 *chase*
wham 425.1, 425.5 *bang*

whammy 11.5 *spell*, 822.2 *curse*,
827.4 *malediction*, 862.4 *evil
power*
wharf 63.24 *water system*, 605.4
storage, 647.1 *workshop*, 740.7
emporium
wharfage 751.6 *business costs*
Wharton 48 Writers
what? 477
what 164.14 *whatever*, 786.14
wonderful
what cannot be 487.5 *impossibility*
whatever 164
whatever comes 589.2 *luck*
whatever happens 589.1 *chance*,
589.14 *perchance*
whatever next 786.14 *wonderful*
what fate has in store 199.3 *future condition*
what for 879.9 *retribution*
what have you 164.14 *whatever*
what is coming to one 879.9 *retribution*
what is contained 257.1 *contents*
what is owing 593.2 *need*
what it takes 235.2, 485.2 *ability*
what it will fetch 751.2 *value*
what makes one tick 228.1 *motive*
what matters 611.3 *chief thing*
what must be 571.5 *inevitability*
whatnot 47.5, 258.3 *cabinet*,
603.1 *tool*
what one can call one's own
725.4 *possessions*
what one deserves 845.2 *due*
what one has coming 845.2 *due*
what one has to one's name
725.4 *possessions*
what one is worth 725.5 *personal
estate*
what one merits 845.2 *due*
what one owes 745.1 *debt*
what rot 521.14 *nonsense*
what's in 201.2 *trendiness*
whatsit 603.1 *tool*
what's-its-name 367.5 *object*
whatsoever 164.14 *whatever*
what's what 99.5 *fact*
what the doctor ordered 625.4
hygienic
what the future brings 199.3 *future condition*
what the future holds 199.3 *future condition*
what you will 164.14 *whatever*
wheat 87 Grasses
wheat belt 68.11 *farmland*
wheatear 78 Birds
wheaten 87.8 *grasslike*
wheatfield 68.11 *farmland*
wheat germ 45.40 *breakfast cereal*
wheatmeal 45.7 *basic ingredient*
wheat pit 740.1 *market*
Wheatstone 52 Scientists
Wheatstone bridge 56 Named
Laws, 64.13 *circuit*
wheat straw 68.9 *animal feedstuff*
wheedle 586.15 *persuade*,
586.16 *tempt*, 657.5 *be cunning*, 808.12 *beg*, 853.10 *cajole*
wheedler 586.12 *persuader*,
853.6 *flatterer*
wheedling 228.2 *inducement*,
586.2 *flattery*, 853.3 *cajolery*,
853.14 *cajoling*
wheel 71 Motor Vehicle Parts,
74 Parts of a Ship, 36.3 *parts
of a sailing boat*, 44.6 *ceramic
workshop*, 63.8 *machine element*, 71.11 *bicycle part*, 71.12
bicycle, 74.5 *navigation*, 313.3
circular thing, 335.11, 337.9
turn round, 338.11 *propeller*,
338.20 *propel*, 363.3, 363.6
orbit, 364.3 *reel*, 364.6 *rotator*,
364.8 *rotate*, 603.1 *tool*, 653.5
guide, 879.15 *instrument of torture*
wheel about 578.2 *equivocate*
wheel and axle 63.6 *simple machine*
wheel and deal 233.8 *influence*,
539.28 *trick*, 592.13 *plot*

wheel animacule 81.6 *worm*
wheel-back chair 47.2 *chair*
wheelbarrow 69.6 *garden tool*, 71.7 *handcart*, 258.10 *cart*
wheelbase 71.21 *miscellaneous motoring terms*
wheel clamp 661.4 *restraint*
wheeler-dealer 233.5 *influential person*, 592.8 *planner*, 611.4 *bigwig*, 642.10 *busy person*, 657.3 *cunning person*, 715.4 *contractor*
wheeler-dealing 592.15 *planning*
Wheeler Peak 95 Mountains, 95.4 *US mountains*
wheelie 33.6 *motor racing terms*
wheelie bin 258.11 *vessel*
wheeling 334.1 *circuit*, 363.1 *orbital motion*, 363.11 *orbiting*, 364.2 *turning*, 364.11 *rotating*
Wheeling 93 Cities
wheeling and dealing 539.7 *tricking*, 652.9 *tactics*, 657.1 *cunning*
wheel lock 680.10 *historical gun*
wheelman 74.7 *nautical person*
wheel of fortune 224.3 *changeable thing*, 229.2 *chance*, 364.6 *rotator*, 589.2 *luck*
wheel of life 214.2 *cycle*
wheels 71.16 *car*
wheel-shaped 334.6, 363.10 *circular*
wheels within wheels 603.4 *machine*
wheel throwing 44.5 *ceramic process*
wheel-track 321.1 *furrow*
wheel-tracked 321.4 *furrowed*
wheelwise 363.12 *circuitously*
wheel wobble 71.21 *miscellaneous motoring terms*
wheelwork 603.4 *machine*
wheelwright 47.13 *carpenter*, 646.2 *artisan*
wheesh 429.9 *sh*
wheeze 424.5 *sound faint*, 429.1, 429.4 *hiss*, 592.3 *expedient plan*
wheezily 429.8 *sibilantly*
wheezing 429.1 *hiss*, 650.3 *panting*
wheezy 424.4 *faint*, 429.6 *hissing*
whelk 81 Molluscs, 45.19 *shellfish*
whelmed 389.24 *flooded*
whelp 74 Rigging, 77.9 *dog*, 77.19 *young mammal*, 77.35 *give birth*, 206.4 *young animal*, 245.11 *have young*
when 185.27 *at what time*
when? 477.25 *what?*
when all is said and done 142.13 *on the whole*, 157.26, 218.11 *finally*
when and how one pleases 570.17 *at will*
whence 116.36 *accordingly*
whence? 477.25 *what?*
when forbidden 302.8 *within limits*
when it comes to the crunch 101.13 *really*
when the chips are down 101.13 *really*, 106.17 *difficultly*, 157.26 *finally*
when the push comes to the shove 101.13 *really*
when the time is right 199.14 *in the future*
when the time is ripe 199.14 *in the future*
where 250, 253.15 *here*
where? 477.25 *what?*
whereabouts 250.1 *location*, 250.12 *where*, 567.5 *place of residence*
wherefore 116.36 *accordingly*
wherefrom 116.36 *accordingly*
where it's at 105.3 *state of affairs*, 291.4 *centre of activity*
where the action is 291.4 *centre of activity*
where the earth meets the sky 263.3 *distant place*
where the rainbow ends 157.7 *limit*
whereupon 185.27 *at what time*

wherever you look 162.31 *everywhere*
wherewith 602.7 *by means of*
wherewithal 741.6 *funds*
wherry 74 Ships and Boats
wherryman 74.8 *boatman*
whet 241.9 *make violent*, 380.15 *make sharp*, 403.13 *arouse sensation*
whether one will or not 571.19 *necessarily*
whet one's appetite 782.15 *cause desire*
whetstone 380.12 *sharpener*
whet the knife 594.4 *prepare for action*
whet the sword 676.12 *go to war*
whey 68.9 *animal feedstuff*, 387.2 *juice*
which 164.14 *whatever*
whicker 432.4 *cry*
whidah 78 Birds
whiff 416.1 *odour*, 416.8 *have odour*, 419.1 *stench*, 419.5 *stink*
whiffle 224.11 *be changeable*
whiffy 416.5 *odorous*, 419.3 *stinking*
Whigs 12.6 *political party*
while 185.26 *all the time*, 198.15 *as*, 248.8 *intervening space*
while away 645.4 *have leisure*
while confined to bed 699.16 *under restraints*
while ill 238.14 *weakly*
while in captivity 699.16 *under restraints*
while in love 831.10 *benevolently*
while in one's power 701.11 *under subjection*
while in prison 702.11 *captively*
while keeping watch 719.8 *observantly*
while seeing red 828.18 *angrily*
while under a spell 827.14 *damningly*
whilst 185.26 *all the time*
whim 71 Carriages and Carts, **579**, 224.2 *irresolution*, 519.4 *ideality*, 578.6 *equivocation*, 784.3 *likes*
whimbrel 78 Birds
whimper 406.12 *express pain*, 431.6 *cry of pain*, 431.13 *cry*
whimpering 431.18 *crying*
whimsical 215.5 *unusual*, 216.11 *changeable*, 224.14 *irresolute*, 491.8 *capricious*, 519.11 *fantastical*, 576.2 *changeable*, 578.11 *equivocating*, 579.1 *capricious*, 771.10 *humorous*
whimsicality 215.9 *unusualness*, 216.15, 224.15 *changeably*, 491.27 *capriciously*, 771.16 *humorously*
whimsical notion 519.4 *ideality*
whimsy 215.2 *unusualness*, 519.4 *ideality*, 579.3 *whim*, 784.3 *likes*
whim-wham 519.4 *ideality*
whinchat 78 Birds
whine 428.4 *faint sound*, 428.8 *sound faint*, 431.6 *cry of pain*, 431.13, 432.4 *cry*, 432.6 *buzz*, 434.10 *lack harmony*, 564.13 *speak in a particular way*, 713.7 *complain*, 766.7 *be dissatisfied*, 808.12 *beg*, 830.9 *be sullen*
whiner 713.4 *protester*, 766.3 *dissatisfied person*, 770.4 *depressing person*, 830.5 *sullen person*
whinge 713.7 *complain*, 766.7 *be dissatisfied*, 830.9 *be sullen*
whingeing 766.4 *dissatisfied*
whinger 713.4 *protester*, 766.3 *dissatisfied person*, 770.4 *depressing person*, 830.5 *sullen person*
whininess 830.1 *sullenness*
whining 428.4 *faint sound*,

432.3 *insect noise*, 808.7 *sycophantic*
whinny 432.1 *animal cry*, 432.4 *cry*
whip 49 Musical Instruments, 12.8 *politician*, 25.2 *grip*, 39.11 *swimming*, 45.55 *cook*, 69.5 *gardening*, 161.34 *assembler*, 228.4 *negative stimulus*, 228.10 *manipulate*, 241.9 *make violent*, 330.5 *beat*, 330.13 *blow*, 330.16 *weapons*, 366.22 *agitate*, 374.13 *soften*, 390.23 *whisk*, 393.25 *thicken*, 586.8 *incentive*, 590.6 *hunter*, 648.1 *hasten*, 648.4 *haste*, 653.15 *manager*, 682.10 *defeat heavily*, 688.10 *person of authority*, 696.3 *leader*, 879.3 *hit*, 879.14 *instrument of punishment*
whip antenna 534.17 *antenna*
whipbird 78 Birds
whipcord 137.6 *line*
whip hand 12.3 *governance*, 126.3 *advantage*, 233 *influence*, 300.4 *advantage*
whip in 161.43 *herd*
whip kick 39.2 *swimming technique*
whip off 345.4 *hurry off*
whipped 228.12 *motivated*, 370.2 *insubstantial*
whipped cream 414.3 *dessert*
whipper 879.17 *punisher*
whipper-in 32.15 *horse person*, 161.34 *assembler*, 590.6 *hunter*, 653.15 *manager*
whippersnapper 206.9 *child*, 807.12 *impudent person*
whippet 77 Breeds of Dogs
whipping 330.12 *collision*, 682.2 *victory*, 832.14 *hostile*, 879.12 *corporal punishment*
whipping boy 222.2 *substitute person*, 707.2 *alternative*, 840.3 *atoner*
whipping cream 395.8 *fat*
whipping in 161.2 *herding*
whipping post 879.14 *instrument of punishment*
Whipple 53 Comets
whippletree 85.12 *figurative usage*
whippoorwill 78 Birds
whip-round 729.2 *gift*, 746.1 *payment*
whipsaw tactics 15.4 *industrial dispute*
whip scorpion 82 Arachnids
whip snake 79 Reptiles
whip something up 45.55 *cook*
whipstall 73.5 *flight*
whip up 241.9 *make violent*, 366.22 *agitate*
whip up on 674.12 *fight*
whipworm 81 Worms
whir 364.2 *turning*, 427.9 *resonate*
whirl 46.15 *dance*, 96.6 *river flow*, 96.7 *flow*, 324.13 *be in motion*, 364.2 *reel*, 364.4 *vortex*, 364.8 *rotate*, 596.5 *attempt*, 642.1 *activity*, 648.4 *haste*
whirlabout 364.3 *reel*
whirlblast 364.4 *vortex*
whirl by 648.2 *make haste*
whirligig 82 Insects
whirling 329.1 *swift*, 334.1 *circuit*, 364.2 *turning*, 364.11 *rotating*
whirl like a dervish 364.8 *rotate*
whirlpool 96.6 *river flow*, 314.3 *convoluted thing*, 364.4 *vortex*, 364.10 *swirl*, 635.1 *trap*
whirlpool bath 385.6 *massage*, 389.11 *wash*
Whirlpool Galaxy 53 Galaxies
whirlwind 55.16 *wind vortex*, 364.4 *vortex*, 366.13 *tempest*
whirlwindish 364.12 *rotary*
whirlwindy 364.12 *rotary*
whirr 424.1 *faintness*, 424.5 *sound faint*, 426.2 *humming*, 426.9 *hum*, 432.5 *sing*
whirring 364.2 *turning*, 426.2, 426.16 *humming*, 427.1 *resonance*, 427.6 *resonant*

whish 23.4 *playing terms*
whisht 429.9 *sh*
whisk 390, 45.6 *kitchen equipment*, 45.55 *cook*, 133.6 *mixer*, 326.12 *transport*, 329.4 *be swift*, 330.6 *tap*, 330.13 *blow*, 364.6 *rotator*, 366.14 *agitator*, 366.22 *agitate*, 621.10 *cleaning object*, 621.13 *clean*
whisked 370.2 *insubstantial*
whisker 77.2 *mammalian characteristic*, 403.4 *someone or something that feels*, 407.7 *sense organ*
whiskers 375.7 *rough thing*
Whiskey 534 Phonetic Alphabet
whiskey sour 351.8 *mixed drink*
whisky and soda 351.8 *mixed drink*
whisky mac 351.8 *mixed drink*
whisky sour 415.3 *sour thing*
whisper 55.58 *blow*, 85.19 *grow*, 424.1 *faintness*, 424.5 *sound faint*, 428.4 *faint sound*, 428.8 *sound faint*, 429.1, 429.4 *hiss*, 527.10 *quietness*, 527.14 *imply*, 528.7 *advice*, 528.14 *tip*, 563.4 *whispering*, 563.16 *speak in a low voice*, 564.7 *utterance*, 564.13 *speak in a particular way*, 854.13 *vilify*
whispered 424.4 *faint*, 428.1 *faint-sounding*, 563.10 *low-voiced*
whispering 563, 429.6 *hissing*, 563.10 *low-voiced*, 854.16 *defamatory*
whisper in one's ear 563.16 *speak in a low voice*
whisper sweet nothings 821.26, 826.8 *court*
whisper together 568.10 *chat*
whist 42 Card Games, 429.9 *sh*
whistle 49 Musical Instruments, 49.38 *sound*, 55.58 *blow*, 327.10 *railway*, 423.4 *sound maker*, 423.8 *be loud*, 429.4 *hiss*, 430.3 *shrillness*, 430.6 *be shrill*, 432.5 *sing*, 543.3 *gesture*, 543.4 *signal*, 543.11 *gesture*, 543.12 *signal*, 636.2 *danger signal*, 671.5 *self-defence*, 713.3 *gesture of protest*, 713.7 *complain*, 766.2 *expression of dissatisfaction*, 786.2 *sign of wonderment*, 786.9 *wonder*, 851.16 *acclaim*
whistle at 766.7 *be dissatisfied*
whistle-blower 528.10 *informer*, 530.4 *discloser*, 856.3 *accuser*
whistle flute 49 Musical Instruments
whistler 78 Birds
whistle stop 72.8 *railway station*, 93.10 *village*
whistle-stopping 580.12 *election*
whistle-stop tour 580.12 *election*
whistling 429.1 *hiss*, 430.3 *shrillness*, 430.9 *shrill*, 543.15 *gestural*, 851.5 *acclaim*
Whistling Dick 680.12 *historical guns*
whistling duck 78.3 *water bird*
whit 173.3 *fragment*, 612.8 *trifle*
Whitby 93 Cities
white 446, 78.15 *eggs*, 134.14 *purified*, 351.17 *drinkable*, 439.21 *light*, 441.6 *murky*, 445.8 *drained of colour*, 446.13 *whiten*, 621.16 *clean*, 624.21 *unhealthy*, 865.5 *innocent*, 876.9 *pure*
White 48 Writers, **48** Writers, **52** Scientists, **68** Breeds of Fowl, **97** Oceans and Seas, 1.6 *race*, 1.13 *racial*
white admiral 446.9 *white thing*
white alkali 54 Minerals, 446.8 *whitener*
white ant 82 Insects, 82.4 *social insect*, 446.9 *white thing*
white around the gills 445.8 *drained of colour*
white arsenic 446.8 *whitener*
white as a lily 446.1 *white*
white as a sheet 238.10 *ill*, 397.18 *dying*, 445.8 *drained of*

colour, 446.4 *pule*, 624.21 *unhealthy*, 777.7 *frightened*
white as marble 446.1 *white*
white as milk 446.1 *white*
white as snow 621.16 *clean*
white as the driven snow 446.1 *white*
White Austrian 68 Breeds of Fowl
whitebait 80 Fishes, 45.18 *sea fish*, 80.8 *food fish*, 446.9 *white thing*
white ball 24.3 *English billiards*, 24.4 *carom*, 24.5 *snooker*
whitebeam 85 Trees and Shrubs
white blood cell 387.4 *blood*, 446.9 *white thing*
white Bordeaux 351.9 *wine*
White Brand 29.5 *golf ball*
white bread 45.38 *bread*, 446.9 *white thing*
white cabbage 45 Vegetables
whitecap 54.14, 97.3 *wave*, 446.9 *white thing*
white cedar 85 Trees and Shrubs
white chocolate 414.4 *confectionery*
White Cliffs of Dover 446.9 *white thing*
white clover 68.12 *crop*, 446.9 *white thing*
white coffee 351.4 *coffee*, 446.9 *white thing*
white-collar 15.10 *unionized*
white-collar class 158.8 *middle class*
white-collar crime 864.7 *criminality*, 866.3 *sin*
white-collar criminal 736.11 *dishonest person*
white-collar union 15.3 *organized labour*
white-collar worker 15.7 *employee*, 124.8 *middle classes*, 400.10 *member of society*, 446.10 *figurative usage*, 646.1 *worker*
white cue ball 24.1 *billiards*
whitecurrant 86 Fruits
white deal 47.12 *wood*
whited sepulchre 446.10 *figurative usage*, 538.12 *cheat*, 539.19 *hypocrite*, 540.15 *false person*
white dwarf 53.11 *stellar birth*, 446.9 *white thing*
white elephant 446.10 *figurative usage*, 631.3, 661.6 *burden*, 727.3 *disposable things*, 754.5 *cheap item*
White Ensign 544.7 *flag*
white-eye 78 Birds
whiteface 51.19 *stage requisite*
Whiteface Dartmoor 68 Breeds of Sheep
Whiteface Woodlands 68 Breeds of Sheep
white feather 446.10 *figurative usage*, 779.1 *cowardice*
whitefish 80 Fishes
white fish 446.9 *white thing*
white flag 446.9 *white thing*, 544.7 *flag*, 675.2 *symbol of peace*, 677.2 *peace offering*
white flour 446.9 *white thing*
white fly 82 Insects, 69.12 *pests and diseases*, 446.9 *white thing*
white foam 54.14 *wave*
White Friar 7 Members of Religious Orders, 446.9 *white thing*
white frost 55.36 *frost*, 409.5 *ice*
White Fulani 68 Breeds of Cattle
White Galloway 68 Breeds of Cattle
white gas 395.9 *petroleum*
white gold 57 Alloys, 446.9 *white thing*, 741.16 *bullion*
white goods 243.7 *produce*, 446.9 *white thing*, 739.8 *merchandise*
white-haired 446, 202.11 *old*, 207.14 *aged*
Whitehall 688.6 *place of authority*, 696.8 *the power structure*
Whitehall farce 51.10 *comedy*
white hat 446.10 *figurative usage*
whitehead 793.2 *pimple*
Whitehead 4 Philosophers

white heat 408.1 *heat*, 439.8 *fire*, 446.9 *white thing*
white hole 53.11 *stellar birth*
White Holland 68 Breeds of Fowl
white hope 446.10 *figurative usage*, 655.4 *skilled person*
white horse 446.9 *white thing*
white horses 54.14, 97.3 *wave*
white-hot 408.9 *hot*, 446.2 *whitened*
Whitehouse 93 Cities
White House 43 Noted Buildings, 256.4 *official residence*, 446.9 *white thing*
white hunter 77.24 *hunter*
white knight 446.10 *figurative usage*, 632.3 *protector*, 671.13 *defender*, 737.10 *trader*, 861.15 *good person*, 863.4 *virtuous person*
white lady 351.8 *mixed drink*
white lead 446.8 *whitener*
white lie 446.10 *figurative usage*, 578.5 *equivocalness*, 657.2 *stratagem*
white light 56.28 *colour*, 66.15 *lighting*, 446.9 *white thing*
white lightning 446.10 *figurative usage*
white like ivory 446.1 *white*
white line 543.5 *indicator*
white-line 47.15 *woodcrafted*
white-line woodcut 47.8 *woodwork*
whitely 446
white magic 11.3 *witchcraft*
white meat 45.20 *meat*, 45.28 *poultry*, 446.9 *white thing*
white metal 57 Alloys, 446.9 *white thing*
white meter 64.34 *power supply*
White Mountains 446.10 *figurative usage*
whiten 446, 439.28 *bleach*, 444.15 *colour*, 445.5 *lose colour*, 445.6 *decolour*, 621.13 *clean*
whitened 446, 621.17 *cleaned*
whitener 446, 445.4 *colour remover*
whiteness 446, 445.1 *colourlessness*, 621.1 *cleanness*, 865.1 *innocence*
Whiteness 446
White Nile 446.10 *figurative usage*
whitening 445.1 *colourlessness*
white noise 56.17 *sound*, 429.1 *hiss*, 434.5 *atmospheric dissonance*, 534.19 *radio reception*
white notes 49.16 *musical note*
white oak 85 Trees and Shrubs, 446.9 *white thing*
white object ball 24.4 *carom*
white of the eye 435.2 *eye*
whiteout 55.30 *snow*
white out 438.8 *make invisible*, 546.1 *obliterate*
white-out 409.5 *ice*, 436.1 *blindness*
white paint 446.8 *whitener*
white paper 446.9 *white thing*, 528.3 *document*
White Park 68 Breeds of Cattle
white pepper 45 Herbs and Spices, 413.2 *seasoning*, 446.9 *white thing*
white phosphorus 57 Chemical Elements
white pine 85 Trees and Shrubs
white poplar 85 Trees and Shrubs, 446.9 *white thing*
white port 351.9 *wine*
white rhinoceros 77 Placental Mammals
white rose 446.9 *white thing*
white rum 351.7 *alcoholic drink*
White Russia 446.10 *figurative usage*
White Russian 693.12 *reactionary*
whites 27.6 *pad*, 295.3 *formal dress*, 446.9 *white thing*
white sale 446.9 *white thing*, 739.4 *sale*
white sapphire 54 Gemstones
white sauce 45.15 *sauce*, 446.9 *white thing*
White Sea 446.10 *figurative usage*

white shark 80 Fishes, 446.9 *white thing*
white-skinned 445.8 *drained of colour*
white slave 701.5 *subjected person*
white slavery 701.1 *subjection*
white slave trade 877.5 *prostitution*
white slave traffic 737.4 *trade*
white spirit 50.11 *artist's materials*
white spruce 85 Trees and Shrubs, 446.9 *white thing*
white stick 436.3 *aid for poor sight*
White Stilton 45 Cheeses
white stuff 446.10 *figurative usage*, 875.6 *drug*
white supremacy 12.3 *governance*, 805.11 *prejudice*
White supremacy 688.7 *type of rule*
whitetail 446.9 *white thing*
white-tailed deer 446.9 *white thing*
white thing 446
whitethorn 446.9 *white thing*
whitethroat 78 Birds, 446.9 *white thing*
white tie 446.9 *white thing*, 813.4 *formal dress*
white-tie 813.7 *dressed up*
white tie and tails 295.3, 813.4 *formal dress*
white trash 743.11 *the poor*
White Volta 446.10 *figurative usage*
white wall 446.9 *white thing*
white walnut 86 Nuts
whiteware 44.1 *ceramics*
whitewash 102.16 *delude*, 293.8 *wall covering*, 293.24 *coat*, 293.28 *face*, 309.12 *distort the truth*, 444.4 *pigment*, 444.15 *colour*, 446.8 *whitener*, 446.13 *whiten*, 474.11 *practise sophistry*, 531.8 *conceal*, 538.8 *pretence*, 538.24 *pretend*, 539.12 *disguise*, 540.12 *facade*, 540.21 *be fraudulent*, 540.24 *mask*, 621.9 *cleaning agent*, 621.13 *clean*, 637.2 *preserver*, 637.5 *preserve*, 682.10 *defeat heavily*, 855.3 *cover-up*, 855.9 *cover up*
whitewashed 293.36 *covered*, 446.2 *whitened*, 539.41 *disguised*, 540.31 *fraudulent*
whitewasher 293.17 *coverer*, 855.5 *vindicator*
whitewashing 309.4 *distortion of the truth*, 539.7 *tricking*, 539.34 *deceiving*, 855.3 *cover-up*
whitewash job 540.8 *fraud*
white water 36.12 *canoeing*, 446.9 *white thing*, 615.1 *trap*
white water rafting 18 Sporting Activities
white water running 36.6 *canoeing*
white wedding 823.5 *wedding*
White Welsh 68 Breeds of Cattle
white whale 77 Placental Mammals, 446.9 *white thing*
white wine 351.9 *wine*, 446.9 *white thing*
white witch 11.4 *witch*
white with dust 446.2 *whitened*
whitey 91 Names for Inhabitants
whither 250.12 *where*
whiting 80 Fishes, 45.18 *sea fish*, 446.8 *whitener*, 621.9 *cleaning agent*
whitish 439.21 *light*, 444.13 *soft-hued*, 445.7 *colourless*, 446.1 *white*
whitishness 446.7 *whiteness*
Whitman 48 Poets
Whitney 52 Scientists, 95 Mountains
Whitsun 10.16 *religious festival*, 203.3 *summer*
Whitsunday 10.15 *holy day*
Whitsuntide 203.3 *summer*
whittle 47.18 *work wood*, 50.21

sculpt, 129.5 *make smaller*, 306.7 *form*, 380.10 *knife*, 380.16 *use a sharp tool*
Whittle 52 Scientists
whittle away 262.5 *make smaller*
whittled 47.15 *woodcrafted*
whittle down 121.6 *change gradually*
whittling 47.8 *woodwork*, 50.12 *sculpture*
whiz 429.1, 429.4 *hiss*, 642.10 *busy person*, 861.16 *superior person*
whiz-bang 680.5 *missile weapon*
whiz kid 126.6 *paragon*, 336.16 *progressive person*, 640.3 *doer*, 642.10 *busy person*, 655.5 *expert*, 682.4 *successful person*, 786.5 *person of wonder*, 861.16 *superior person*
whiz off 345.4 *hurry off*
whizz 329.4 *be swift*, 329.9 *acceleration*, 762.2 *fun*
whizz by 329.6 *accelerate*
whizzing 329.1 *swift*
whoa 218.12, 325.11 *stop*, 431.5 *hunting cry*
who cares?, who gives a shit ? 612.15 *no matter*
whodunit 48.2, 560.5 *fiction*
whoever 164
who knows? 502
whole 142, 142, 174, 52.12 *numeration*, 52.71 *numerical*, 120.4 *total*, 120.6 *quantitative*, 144.7 *complete*, 164.15 *general*, 169.4 *mathematical result*, 169.8 *odd*, 619.1 *perfect*, 632.5 *safe*, 637.7 *preserved*, 684.7 *completed*
Whole 142
wholefood 350.7 *food*, 625.2 *salubrity*
wholefood restaurant 350.15 *eating place*
wholehearted 134.17 *direct*, 574.2 *tenacious*
wholeheartedly 134.20 *homogenously*
wholeheartedness 642.8 *assiduity*
whole hog 574.2 *tenacious*
whole list 142.5 *unit*
wholely 120.7 *quantitatively*
wholemeal 45.7 *basic ingredient*
wholemeal bread 45.38 *bread*, 449.5 *brown thing*
wholeness 142.1 *whole*, 144.1 *completeness*, 174.3 *oneness*, 619.3 *perfection*, 684.1 *completion*
whole number 52.6 *complex number*, 142.2 *whole thing*, 169.2 *kind of number*
whole picture 251.2 *circumstances*
wholesale 482, 13.13 *economic*, 144.7 *complete*, 146.7 *including*, 608.2 *plentiful*, 737.13 *mercantile*, 739.1 *sell*, 739.3 *selling*, 754.15 *cheaply*
wholesale merchant 739.12 *wholesaler*
wholesale murder 398.4 *slaughter*
wholesale price 751.1 *price*
wholesaler 739, 606.3 *provider*, 646.3 *agent*, 737.10 *trader*, 754.7 *discounter*
wholesaling 13.2 *economy*
whole situation 142
wholesome 350.27 *edible*, 617.4 *worthwhile*, 623.2 *healthful*, 625.4 *hygienic*
wholesomely 625.7 *hygienically*
wholesomeness 623.4 *healthfulness*, 625.2 *salubrity*
whole thing 142
wholly 142, 174, 144.9 *completely*, 164.31 *overall*, 619.8 *completely*, 621.20 *clean*, 684.9 *completely*
whomever 164.13 *whoever*
whomp 330.2 *collide*
whomsoever 164.13 *whoever*
whoop 423.2 *outcry*, 431.2 *cry of joy*, 431.3 *cry of praise*, 431.11 *laugh*, 432.2 *bird song*, 590.10 *chase*, 769.5, 769.8 *cheer*

ties, **48** Poets, **48** Dramatists, **49** Musicians and Composers, **86** Fruits

Williamson 48 Writers

Williamson's process 57 Named Reactions

Williamson's synthesis 57 Named Reactions

willing 572, 6.17 *educatable,* 167.13 *compliant,* 228.13 *suggestible,* 499.6 *assenting,* 570.1 *will,* 570.6 *willed,* 583.2 *spontaneous,* 642.18 *active,* 662.35 *benevolent,* 664.17 *cooperative,* 667.10 *agreeing,* 694.7 *obedient,* 698.13 *informal,* 784.6 *liking,* 847.9 *loyal,* 861.4 *well-behaved*

willing and able 572.2 *eager*

willing giver 755.9 *generous person*

willing hands 572.11 *willing worker*

willing horse 642.10 *busy person*

willingly 572, 6.26 *studiously,* 167.16 *adaptably,* 228.14 *influentially,* 499.8 *unanimously,* 594.22 *in preparation,* 662.38 *benevolently,* 667.14 *agreeably,* 694.10 *obediently,* 698.22 *informally,* 784.11 *admiringly,* 861.24 *obediently*

willingness 572, 228.6 *suggestibility,* 586.7 *persuadability,* 642.3 *nimbleness,* 662.10 *helpfulness,* 667.1 *agreement,* 694.1 *obedience,* 782.1 *desire,* 784.2 *inclination,* 847.4 *sense of duty,* 861.11 *good behaviour*

Willingness 572

willingness to learn 6.10 *educatability*

willing sacrifice 710.7 *martyr*

willing servant 817.6 *courteous person*

willing worker 572, 575.5 *tenacious person*

williwaw 55 Winds

will-making 729.1 *giving*

will of Allah 571.5 *inevitability*

will of one's own 570.3 *wilfulness*

will-o'-the-wisp 11.11 *ghost,* 102.2 *illusion,* 435.5 *imagination,* 439.9 *firefly,* 539.5 *falseness*

willow 85 Trees and Shrubs, 27.7 *bat*

willow grouse 85.11 *tree-related animal*

willowherb 84 Flowers and Flowering Plants

willowiness 274.7 *thinness,* 374.8 *softness*

willow tit 85.11 *tree-related animal*

willow wands 34.4 *climbing equipment*

willow warbler 78 Birds, 85.11 *tree-related animal*

willowy 85.14 *treelike,* 274.1 *thin,* 374.2 *pliant*

willpower 570, 574.15 *will*

Wills 18 Sporting Personalities

will to 729.5 *give*

will to live 188.4 *long-lastingness,* 396.5 *life cycle*

willy 245.8 *organs of reproduction*

Willy Brandt 675.4 *Nobel Peace Prize*

willy-nilly 113.11 *irregularly,* 571.19 *necessarily,* 695.11 *compellingly*

willy-willy 55.16 *wind vortex*

Wilson 48 Writers, **48** Writers, **52** Scientists, **52** Scientists, **95** Mountains

Wilson Trophy 36.1 *sailing*

wilt 69.12 *pests and diseases,* 83.22 *be dormant,* 85.10 *tree disease,* 238.6 *be weak,* 353.19 *sweat,* 392.21 *dry up,* 607.1 *waste,* 628.1 *deteriorate,* 673.4 *succumb,* 770.9 *despair*

wilting 69.17 *botanical,* 353.28 *sweaty*

Wilton 67.3 *fabric*

Wiltshire 92 Counties

Wiltshire Horn 68 Breeds of Sheep

wily 538.19 *dishonest,* 539.34 *deceiving,* 540.29 *deceitful,* 657.4 *cunning*

wily person 657.3 *cunning person*

Wimbledon 40.1 *tennis,* 674.3 *stadium*

wimp 65.11 *application,* 238.4 *weakling,* 576.15 *indecisive person,* 612.10 *nonentity,* 673.2 *appeaser,* 779.2 *coward,* 806.16 *humble person*

wimpish 576.3 *timid*

wimple 7.11 *vestment,* 295.15 *headgear*

Wimshurst machine 56 Named Laws

win 21.6 *compete in athletics,* 22.4 *pitching terms,* 32.7 *horseracing,* 57.30 *extract,* 126.8 *be superior,* 319.6 *notch up,* 679.38 *conquer,* 682.2 *victory,* 682.9 *be victorious,* 696.14 *master,* 718.13 *secure one's objective,* 721.9 *gain,* 734.7 *take*

Winabojo 8 Deities

win a downhill race 41.14 *ski*

win an award 721.14 *profit*

win a point 682.9 *be victorious*

win a prize 721.14 *profit,* 878.12 *be rewarded*

win a scrum 35.5 *play rugby*

win at a canter 660.17 *do easily*

win a trophy 721.14 *profit*

win a victory 682.9 *be victorious*

win by a landslide 682.9 *be victorious*

win by a TKO 26.11 *do a combat sport*

win by a whisker 682.9 *be victorious*

wince 331.2 *respond,* 331.6 *response,* 406.9 *feel pain*

winch 74 Parts of a Ship, 339.12 *drag,* 361.9 *lifter*

Winchester 93 Cities, 65.7 *peripheral,* 680.9 *firearm,* 680.12 *historical guns*

wincing 406.7 *feeling pain*

wind 777 Phobias by Topic, **55,** 102.4 *theorization,* 224.3 *changeable thing,* 236.8 *overpower,* 335.5 *twist,* 349.24 *belch,* 364.9 *roll,* 372.5 *gas,* 388.5 *belch,* 390.4 *air flow,* 521.5 *empty talk,* 594.4 *prepare for action,* 624.8 *indigestion,* 650.6 *fatigue*

windage 248.6 *available space*

wind around one's little finger 233.10 *be a prevailing influence*

windbag 102.5 *insubstantial person,* 541.6 *exaggerator,* 565.4 *talker,* 568.8 *chatterer*

wind band 140.3 *assembly*

windblown 151.15 *untidy*

windbreak 634.2 *shelter*

windbreaker 295.11 *jacket*

windcheater 295.11 *jacket*

wind-chill 55.13 *wind strength*

wind-chill factor 55.6 *weather data,* 55.13 *wind strength,* 409.7 *cold weather*

wind cone 55.7 *weather instruments*

wind crust 41.1 *skiing*

wind direction 55

wind-dried 392.8 *baked*

wind-driven 235.17, 410.10 *powered*

wind-driven generator 64.30 *generator*

wind-dry 392.17 *dry*

winded 650.3 *panting*

winder 364.6 *rotator*

Windermere 94 Lakes, 94.4 *British lakes*

wind erosion 54.35 *weathering*

windfall 130.4 *extra,* 514.4 *surprising thing,* 721.5 *profit,* 721.15 *gainful,* 729.2 *gift,* 861.17 *good thing*

windfall money 721.5 *profit*

windfall profit 721.5 *profit*

windfall profits tax 751.7 *tax*

wind farm 235.6 *source of energy*

wind force 55.13 *wind strength*

wind gauge 55.7 *weather instruments,* 268.8 *meter,* 329.8 *speed meter*

wind generator 410.8 *renewable energy*

windier 55.47 *windy*

windily 55.65 *meteorologically,* 811.36 *pompously*

wind in 339.12 *drag*

wind in and out 286.6 *be oblique*

wind-induced current 54.13 *ocean current*

windiness 55, 372.3 *sparseness,* 388.5 *belch,* 565.1 *talkativeness*

winding 147 *resistor,* 96.10 *fluvial,* 314.4 *convolutional,* 335.21 *indirect*

winding course 335.14 *deviating course*

winding sheet 295.17 *grave clothes,* 399.4 *funeral objects*

winding up 684.3 *elaboration*

windings 64.30 *generator*

windjammer 74 Sailing Ships and Boats

windlass 74 Parts of a Ship, 339.6 *towline,* 361.9 *lifter*

windless 55.45 *fine,* 325.4 *motionless*

windlessness 325.2 *repose*

windmill 73 Aircraft Parts, 36.14 *punting,* 235.6 *source of energy,* 275.6 *tall thing,* 364.6 *rotator,* 410.8 *renewable energy*

windmill stroke 36.8 *punting*

wind of change 224.3 *changeable thing*

window 439, 43.9 *miscellaneous architectural features,* 65.11 *application,* 171.2 *table,* 322.7 *passageway,* 435.9 *viewpoint,* 442.8 *transparent thing,* 442.9 *glass*

window box 69.3 *ornamental garden*

window case 382.4 *framework*

window cleaner 621.12 *cleaner*

window display 740.9 *stall*

window-dress 540.24 *mask,* 811.27 *show*

window-dressing 532.8 *public relations ,* 538.9 *hypocrisy,* 540.12 *facade,* 811.10 *exhibitionism,* 811.16 *showy*

window envelope 442.8 *transparent thing*

window glass 44.9 *industrial ceramics,* 442.9 *glass*

windowless 443.1 *opaque,* 626.5 *unhygienic*

window light 442.9 *glass*

window manager 65.11 *application*

windowpane 379.3 *brittle thing,* 439.10 *window,* 442.9 *glass*

Windows 65.11 *application*

window shade 634.2 *shelter*

window-shopping 519.6 *reverie*

window tax 751.9 *historical taxes*

windpipe 322.7 *passageway,* 390.8 *respiration*

wind power 56.11 *energy,* 235.6 *source of energy,* 410.8 *renewable energy*

wind-powered 235.17, 410.10 *powered*

windproof 34.8 *mountaineering*

windproof clothing 34.4 *climbing equipment*

wind-propelled 338.19 *propelled*

wind propulsion 338.2 *method of propulsion*

wind pump 410.8 *renewable energy*

wind-rode 86.10 *sailing*

wind-rode boat 36.2 *sailing boat*

wind rose 55.7 *weather instruments*

windrow 68.11 *farmland*

Windrush 96 Rivers

Windscale 410.7 *nuclear power*

wind scorpion 82 Arachnids

windscreen 71 Motor Vehicle Parts, 435.9 *viewpoint,* 442.9 *glass,* 634.2 *shelter*

windscreen wiper 621.10 *cleaning object*

wind shear 73.7 *miscellaneous aviation terms*

windshield 71 Motor Vehicle Parts, 442.9 *glass*

wind shift 55.15 *wind direction*

windslab 41.1 *skiing*

wind sleeve 55.7 *weather instruments,* 543.5 *indicator*

windsock 55.7 *weather instruments,* 543.5 *indicator*

Windsor 45 Cheeses, **93** Cities, **93** Cities

Windsor Castle 256.4 *official residence*

Windsor chair 47.2 *chair*

Windsor green 453.10 *green pigment*

Windsor Grey 32 Breeds of Horse and Pony

Windsor knot 74 Knots

Windsor red 450.6 *red pigment*

Windsor tie 295.14 *neckwear*

Windsor violet 455.2 *purple pigment*

Windsor yellow 452.7 *yellow pigment*

wind speed 55.6 *weather data,* 55.13 *wind strength*

wind storm 55.12 *wind*

wind strength 55, 55.6 *weather data*

windsurf 36, 36.13 *windsurfing*

windsurfer 36.9 *sailor*

windsurfing 18 Sporting Activities, **36, 36**

windsurfing classes 36.7 *windsurfing*

windsurfing techniques 36.7 *windsurfing*

windsurfing terms 36.7 *windsurfing*

windsurf racing 36.7 *windsurfing*

wind system 55

wind together 314.6 *convolute*

wind tunnel 73.7 *miscellaneous aviation terms*

wind turbine 410.8 *renewable energy*

wind up 157.15 *end,* 218.7 *stop working,* 230.8 *activate,* 239.3 *invigorate,* 323.9 *close down,* 339.12 *drag,* 594.4 *prepare for action,* 683.6 *fail,* 684.5 *conclude,* 739.1 *sell,* 747.9 *be unable to pay,* 764.11 *quarrel*

wind-up 22.4 *pitching terms,* 118.3 *mockery,* 157.1 *end,* 684.2 *conclusion*

wind up accounts 750.9 *settle accounts*

wind vortex 55

windward 74 Parts of a Ship, 36.20 *offshore,* 332.10 *clockwise*

windward side 305.3 *side direction*

windy 55, 372.1 *sparse,* 388.20 *flatulent,* 390.15 *breezy,* 521.10 *meaningless,* 553.3 *diffuse,* 565.5 *talkative,* 612.4 *trivial,* 779.3 *cowardly,* 811.20 *pompous*

wine 351, 351.7 *alcoholic drink,* 351.15 *provide drink,* 405.2 *good time,* 874.12 *alcohol*

wine and dine 350.25 *provide food,* 405.9 *give pleasure,* 665.16 *host*

wine-bibber 874.17 *drunkard*

wine-bibbing 351.1 *drinking,* 874.5 *drunken,* 874.11 *drinking*

wine bottle 258.14 *bottle*

wine cask 258.11 *vessel*

wine cellar 605.4 *storage*

wine-coloured 450.1 *red*

wined and dined 815.16 *popular*

wineglass 258.13 *drinking vessel,* 351.10 *drink container*

wine lake 68.2 *Common Agricultural Policy ,* 246.2 *productiveness,* 605.1 *store*

wine list 171.4 *bill*

wine making 42 Hobbies and Pastimes

wine merchant 606.3 *provider*

wine palm 85 Trees and Shrubs

wineskin 258.14 *bottle,* 874.17 *drunkard*

wine steward 322.3 *person who opens,* 697.3 *attendant*
wine taster 351.12 *drinker,* 411.5 *taster*
wine tasting 351.1 *drinking*
wine vinegar 45.7 *basic ingredient*
win fame 686.5 *be prosperous*
win fame and glory 686.5 *be prosperous*
win for Christ 7.20 *preach*
win freedom 638.5 *escape*
win friends 819.13, 819.13 *befriend*
win friends and influence people 819.13 *befriend*
wing 71 Motor Vehicle Parts, **73** Aircraft Parts, 17.4 *military organization,* 32.9 *jumping,* 36.7 *windsurfing,* 45.28 *poultry,* 51.17 *stage set,* 78.13 *assemblage of birds,* 78.27 *fly,* 130.3 *additional item,* 140.3 *assembly,* 143.4 *component,* 161.16 *party,* 326.12 *transport,* 329.4 *be swift,* 634.2 *shelter,* 679.14 *armed forces,* 679.30 *air force unit*
wing area 31.5 *lacrosse*
wingback 19.7 *offence*
wing chair 47.2 *chair*
Wingco 679.32 *airman*
wing commander 679.32 *airman*
Wing Commander 17 British Military Ranks
wingcut 51.17 *stage set*
winged 77.27 *chiropteran,* 329.1 *swift*
winged horse 32.1 *horse*
winged insect 82.1 *insect*
winged messenger 326.8 *messenger*
winger 31.4 *ice hockey player,* 38.3 *football player*
wing feather 78.17 *plumage*
wing flap 225.3 *stabilizer*
wing-footed 329.1 *swift*
wing half 31.2 *hockey player,* 38.3 *football player*
wing it 51.33 *overact,* 595.13 *improvise*
winglet 73 Aircraft Parts
wing loading 73.7 *miscellaneous aviation terms*
win glory 686.5 *be prosperous*
wing mirror 56.29 *optical element,* 435.8 *reflection*
win going away 682.10 *defeat heavily*
wingover 73.5 *flight*
wings 51.15 *stage,* 78.16 *avian anatomy,* 544.4 *insignia*
wingspan 73.7 *miscellaneous aviation terms,* 271.4 *breadth*
win hands down 660.17 *do easily,* 682.10 *defeat heavily*
win in a walk 660.17 *do easily*
win in record-breaking time 21.6 *compete in athletics*
win in straight sets 682.10 *defeat heavily*
wink 436.14 *be blind,* 439.25 *light up,* 528.7 *advice,* 543.3, 543.11 *gesture,* 636.1 *warning,* 636.5 *warn,* 821.14 *communication of love,* 821.26 *court,* 851.1 *approval,* 851.12 *accept*
wink at 436.16 *be blind to,* 720.7 *not observe,* 839.11 *condone*
winker 71 Motor Vehicle Parts, 439.6 *electric light,* 543.5 *indicator*
winking 436.2 *poor sight,* 436.9 *weak-sighted,* 439.15 *lucent,* 543.15 *gestural*
winkle 81 Molluscs, 45.19 *shellfish*
winkle out 355.11 *extract*
winkle-pickers 295.19 *footwear*
Winkler 18 Sporting Personalities
wink murder 42 Children's Games and Party Games
Winnebago 1 Peoples, **5** Languages and Groups of Languages, **94** Lakes
winner 126.6 *paragon,* 490.12

something certain, 617.8, 617.8 *exceller,* 682.4 *successful person,* 682.5 *victorious person,* 721.7 *gainer,* 730.5 *recipient,* 861.17 *good thing*
winner's enclosure 32.7 *horseracing*
Winnibigoshish 94 Lakes
winning 126.14 *best,* 586.19 *persuasive,* 617.2 *best,* 682.13 *successful,* 682.15 *victorious,* 721.1 *gain,* 734.1 *taking,* 821.22 *lovable*
winning by a mile 682.2 *victory*
winning card 592.3 *expedient plan*
winning hazard 24.3 *English billiards*
winning position 126.3 *advantage*
winning post 588.6 *objective*
winnings 749, 681.2 *spoils,* 721.4 *earnings,* 730.2 *something received,* 734.5 *takings*
winning streak 686.2 *good fortune*
winning ways 586.3 *incentive,* 821.4 *lovability*
Winnipeg 93 Cities, **94** Lakes, 94.5 *other major lakes*
winnow 134.10 *purify,* 580.4 *pick*
wino 351.12 *drinker*
win one's spurs 682.6 *be successful,* 778.15 *be courageous*
win on moves 682.9 *be victorious*
win on points 682.9 *be victorious*
win over 220.11 *persuade,* 228.9 *motivate,* 497.9 *make someone believe,* 586.15 *persuade,* 677.4 *pacify*
win power 235.10 *be powerful*
win praise 851.17 *meet with approval*
win renown 640.4 *act*
winsome 789.5 *beautiful,* 821.22 *lovable*
winsomeness 821.4 *lovability*
winter 203, 203, 203.6 *spend the season,* 214.5 *regular thing,* 409.7 *cold weather,* 687.4 *time of adversity,* 815.12 *visit*
winter aconite 84 Flowers and Flowering Plants
winter barley 68.12 *crop*
winter bud 83.8 *bud*
winter climbing 34.1 *mountaineering*
winter clothes 408.3 *heater*
winter feed 350.8 *animal food*
winter garden 69.2 *garden*
winter horse 32.1 *horse*
winter jasmine 84 Flowers and Flowering Plants, 452.8 *yellow thing*
winterlike 203.13 *winter*
winter melon 86 Fruits
winter monsoon 55.17 *wind system*
winter oats 68.12 *crop*
winter of discontent 687.4 *time of adversity*
winter of one's life 207.5 *old age*
Winter Olympics 674.2 *contest*
winter quarters 409.6 *Arctic*
winter sale 739.4 *sale*
winter solstice 10.15 *holy day,* 203.5 *winter*
Winter Sports 41
wintertide 203.5 *winter*
wintertime 203.5 *winter*
winter wheat 68.12 *crop*
winter woollies 408.3 *heater*
wintery 203.13 *winter*
win the affection of 821.28 *win the love of*
win the ball 35.5 *play rugby*
win the battle 682.9 *be victorious*
win the blue ribbon 126.8 *be superior*
win the championship 126.8 *be superior*
win the cup 126.8 *be superior*
win the game 682.9 *be victorious*
win the heart of 821.28 *win the love of*
win the last battle 682.9 *be victorious*
win the lottery 721.14 *profit,* 742.13 *get rich*

win the love of 821, 821.28 *win the love of*
win the match 682.9 *be victorious*
win the pools 721.14 *profit,* 742.13 *get rich*
win the prize 126.8 *be superior*
win the race 329.6 *accelerate,* 682.9 *be victorious*
win through 718.13 *secure one's objective*
wintrily 203.18 *seasonally,* 409.13 *coldly*
wintriness 55.31 *coldness,* 409.7 *cold weather*
wintry 55.46 *seasonal,* 203.13 *winter,* 409.8 *cold*
wintry shower 409.5 *ice*
winy 874.6 *intoxicating*
wipe 392.20 *absorb,* 442.12 *make transparent,* 458.3 *cause to disappear,* 621.13 *clean*
wipe away one's tears 835.9 *sorrow*
wipe clean 134.10 *purify,* 621.13 *clean*
wiped away 839.8 *overlooked*
wiped out 100.11 *no more,* 244.15 *destroyed,* 683.11 *defeated,* 704.10 *cancelled,* 743.2 *insolvent,* 874.3 *dead drunk*
wipe dry 392.20 *absorb*
wipe off 546.1 *obliterate,* 621.13 *clean*
wipe off the face of the earth 398.18 *slaughter*
wipe off the map 244.8 *destroy,* 546.1 *obliterate*
wipe one's feet on 618.14 *illtreat*
wipe out 36.18 *windsurf,* 100.14 *cause not to exist,* 157.17 *kill,* 172.9 *annihilate,* 244.8 *destroy,* 398.18 *slaughter,* 458.3 *cause to disappear,* 546.1 *obliterate,* 607.2 *lay waste,* 682.10 *defeat heavily*
wipeout 683.4 *unsuccessful thing*
wipe out 704.6 *cancel*
wipe-out 36.7 *windsurfing*
wipe out a score 672.3 *retaliate*
wipe the floor with 682.10 *defeat heavily*
wipe the plate clean 872.5 *be greedy*
wipe the slate clean 201.17 *become new,* 704.8 *be reborn,* 747.10 *forgive a debt,* 839.10 *absolve,* 867.4 *be penitent*
wipe the smile off one's face 772.8 *be serious*
wipe up 392.20 *absorb,* 621.13 *clean*
wiping out 36.7 *windsurfing*
wiping up 621.2 *cleaning*
wire 64, 64.35 *conduct,* 137.6 *line,* 272.8 *narrow thing,* 528.2 *communication,* 528.12 *communicate,* 534.8 *data transmission,* 534.31 *correspond*
wire basket 258.7 *basket*
wired 137.15 *connected*
wire-drawn 272.2 *fine,* 383.10 *delicate*
wire grass 87 Grasses
wire-haired pointing griffon 77 Breeds of Dogs
wireless 420.9 *audio device,* 420.11 *aural,* 534.18 *radio*
wire-mesh 28.6 *fencing*
wire-mesh mask 28.2 *fencing equipment*
wire netting 68.11 *farmland*
wirepuller 527.9 *backstage manipulator,* 586.14 *motivator,* 653.13 *director,* 657.3 *cunning person,* 688.10 *person of authority*
wirepulling 233.4 *indirect influence,* 592.4 *plot,* 688.1 *authority*
wire ropeway 327.12 *cableway*
wires 233.4 *indirect influence*
wire sculpture 50.12 *sculpture*
wire service 528.8 *source of information,* 533.7 *press agency*
wiretap 420.9 *audio device,* 420.15 *hear,* 545.10 *recording instrument*

wireway 327.12 *cableway*
wireworm 82 Insects, 69.12 *pests and diseases,* 81.6 *worm,* 82.3 *pest,* 82.5 *larva*
wiriness 274.7 *thinness,* 378.8 *physical strength*
wiry 274.1 *thin,* 378.4 *powerful*
Wisconsin 92 American States
wisdom 507, 8.2 *divine attribute,* 277.3 *profundity,* 277.7 *deep thinking,* 459.4 *cleverness,* 463.1 *reason,* 492.1 *judgment,* 501.3 *learning,* 654.4 *prudence,* 654.1 *advice,* 781.1 *caution*
Wisdom 507
wisdom literature 48.1 *literature*
wisdom tooth 380.11 *tooth*
wise 277, 507, 4.19 *learned,* 6.18 *educated,* 327.1 *way,* 459.10 *intelligent,* 463.7 *reasoning,* 492.9 *judicious,* 501.8 *knowledgeable,* 516.6 *foreseeing,* 615.1 *convenient,* 654.8 *advisable,* 655.6 *skilful,* 657.4 *cunning,* 849.14 *awe-inspiring*
wiseacre 809.7 *vain person*
wise-arsed 807.14 *cheeky*
wisecrack 506.2 *solecism,* 771.5 *joke,* 771.13 *be humorous*
wisecracker 506.4 *buffoon,* 771.6 *humorist*
wised up 528.18 *informed*
wise guy 4.12 *sage,* 501.6 *knowledgeable person,* 507.4 *intellectual,* 655.5 *expert,* 807.12 *impudent person,* 809.7 *vain person*
wise in one's own conceit 809.13 *boastful*
wisely 4, 507, 6.25 *educationally,* 459.15 *intelligently,* 501.15 *knowledgeably,* 516.8 *foresightedly,* 654.9 *advisably*
wise man 507, 4.12 *sage,* 277.7 *deep thinking,* 459.8 *intellectual person,* 461.7 *thinker,* 501.6 *knowledgeable person,* 654.4 *adviser,* 688.10 *person of authority,* 696.9 *educational leader*
wisent 77 Placental Mammals
wiser 627.14 *improved*
wise to 501.8 *knowledgeable*
wise up 528.11 *inform,* 787.6 *understand*
wise woman 11.13 *diviner,* 277.7 *deep thinking,* 507.3 *wise man*
wish 570, 513.11 *demand,* 519.6 *reverie,* 570.1 *will,* 712.1, 712.6 *request,* 775.3 *aspiration,* 775.7 *aspire,* 782.1 *desire,* 784.3 *likes,* 784.7 *like*
wishbone 11.6 *talisman,* 36.13 *windsurfing,* 45.28 *poultry,* 78.16 *avian anatomy,* 343.5 *for*
wishbone boom 36.7 *windsurfing*
wished for 782.7 *desired,* 784.5 *likable*
wished on one 827.10 *maledictive*
wisher 782.6 *desirer*
wish for 782.12 *desire*
wish for oneself 784.7 *like*
wishful 775.13 *aspirant,* 782.9 *desirous*
wishfully 782.18 *desirously*
wishful thinker 519.9 *visionary*
wishful thinking 61.19 *defence mechanism,* 102.4 *theorization,* 471.6 *ideal,* 471.7 *idealism,* 504.6 *fallibility,* 519.6 *reverie,* 539.2 *self-deception,* 775.1 *hope*
wish ill 827
wishing 784.1, 784.6 *liking*
wishing for 782.9 *desirous*
wishing stone 11.6 *talisman*
wishing well 11.6 *talisman*
wish the best for 831.8 *be benevolent*
wish to 784.9 *like to*
wish undone 867.4 *be penitent*
wish well 284.14 *give moral support,* 831.8 *be benevolent*
wishy-washiness 412.1 *tastelessness,* 542.8 *insipidness,* 576.13 *timidity*
wishy-washy 238.13 *insufficient,* 242.7 *politically moderate,*

389.22 diluted, 412.5 tasteless, 445.7 colourless, 542.17 insipid, 555.1 unemphatic, 576.3 timid

wisp 143.7 piece, 260.4 little person, 272.8 narrow thing

wispiness 272.7 fineness, 372.3 sparseness

wisp of cloud 55.20 cloud appearance

wisp of smoke 388.3 miasma

wispy 143.11 partial, 272.2 fine, 372.1 sparse

wispy cloud 55.20 cloud appearance

wisteria 84 Flowers and Flowering Plants

wistful 4.17 thoughtful, 782.9 desirous

wistfully 4.28 thoughtfully, 782.18 desirously

wistfulness 782.1 desire

wit 771, 459.3 intelligence, 459.4 cleverness, 501.4 intellect, 506.4 buffoon, 507.2 intelligence, 771.1 humorousness, 771.6 humorist

witch 11, 133.7 person who mixes, 402.8 nasty woman, 507.3 wise man, 517.8 oracle, 786.5 person of wonder, 829.3 irascible person, 830.5 sullen person, 832.9 vixen

witchcraft 11, 11.1 occultism, 233.2 occult influence, 235.1 power, 539.7 tricking, 618.11 harmfulness, 864.6 religious sin

witch doctor 7.8 priest, 11.4 witch, 630.15 healer, 636.4 warner

witchery 11.3 witchcraft, 586.3 incentive

witches' broom 85.10 tree disease

witches' butter 89 Fungi

witches' Sabbath 11.3 witchcraft

witch hazel 85 Trees and Shrubs

witch-hunt 7.20 preach, 477.18 interrogate, 481.14 discriminate against, 590.1 pursuit

witch-hunter 7.4 religionist, 481.7 bigot, 879.17 punisher

witch-hunting 7.2 religiousness, 7.15 religious, 481.4 social discrimination

witching hour 11.3 witchcraft

witchlike 11

witchman 11.4 witch

witch master 11.4 witch

Witch of Endor 11.4 witch, 517.8 oracle

witch's brew 133.2 mixed thing

witch's broom 396.6 things brought to life

witch's broomstick 11.6 talisman

witch's hat 295.15 headgear

witchweed 84 Flowers and Flowering Plants

witchwoman 11.4 witch

witchwork 11.3 witchcraft

with 180, 664, 232.9 instrumentally, 602.7 by means of

with a bad grace 573.17 unwillingly

with abandon 698.21 excessively

with a big heart 831.11 charitably

with a break 265.8 apart

with a bun in the oven 245.16 reproductive

with a cable car 41.17 on a ski run

with a cheerful heart 769.9 cheerfully

with a clean slate 704.11 invalidly

with a clear conscience 865.11 innocently

with a clear head 873.1 sober, 873.9 soberly

with a come-hither look 821.30 lovingly

with a coquettish look 826.10 endearingly

with a courteous manner 819.17 in friendship

with a cox 36.20 offshore

with a credit card 733.13 on loan

with a deafening roar 423.9 loudly

with a difference 119.8 originally

with a disappointing result 515.13 disappointingly

with a dishonourable discharge 704.11 invalidly

with a dominating manner 126.16 superiorly

with a dowry 725.10 proprietarily

with a drink problem 874.5 drunken

with affection 784.10 with great liking, 819.17 in friendship, 821.30 lovingly, 826.10 endearingly

with a fine-tooth comb 106.19 meticulously

with a flight of fancy 519.17 imaginatively

with a forgiving heart 839.14 forgivingly

with a free spirit 700.8 free

with a frog in one's throat 563.10 low-voiced

with a frown 829.9 irascibly

with a fuzzy tongue 874.4 crapulous

with a generous heart 730.15 receptively

with a glib tongue 657.6 cunningly

with a golden handshake 704.11 invalidly

with a good heart 831.10 benevolently

with a good nature 831.10 benevolently

with a grateful heart 837.8 gratefully

with agreement 667.14 agreeably

with a grimace 829.9 irascibly

with a guilty conscience 866.11 guiltily, 867.8 penitently

with a handicap 123.7 unequally

with a hangover 874.4 crapulous

with a heavy hand 407.15 insensitively, 690.11 severely

with a heavy heart 573.17 unwillingly

with a helping hand 819.20 favourably

with a hook 137.17 in connection with

with a hop 366.29 jerkily

with a jealous heart 828.17 resentfully, 841.9 jealously, 842.4 enviously

with a J turn 36.20 offshore

with a lick and a promise 278.8 shallowly

with a light hand 691.6 leniently

with a light rein 691.6 leniently

with a light touch 370.11 lightly, 407.16 sensitively

with a likeable manner 784.10 with great liking

with all documents 480.11 verifiably

with all due respect 849.22 respectfully

with all haste 648.6 hastily

with all its faults 620.11 imperfectly

with all one's heart 134.20 homogenously, 572.16 willingly, 759.20 with feeling

with all one's love 821.30 lovingly

with all one's might 235.18 powerfully, 596.10 ambitiously, 644.12 laboriously

with all respect 849.22 respectfully

with all speed 329.14 swiftly

with all the trimmings 144.10 fully

with a lock 137.17 in connection with

with a long face 573.17 unwillingly, 770.12 joylessly

with a lot of nerve 668.9 defiantly

with a loving heart 863.10 ethically

Witham 96 Rivers

with amendments 216.15 changeably

with a monopoly 665.18 cliquishly

with a motive 582.4 deliberate

with an acid tongue 830.14 irritably

with an advantage 126.16 superiorly

with an aim in mind 471.21 purposively

with an architect 43.20 architecturally

with a natural look 114.14 comparably

with an easy conscience 865.11 innocently

with an empty stomach 871.6 fasting

with an eye to 588.14 for

with an eye to the main chance 597.6 enterprising

with anger 713.11 disapprovingly, 818.9 discourteously, 829.9 irascibly

with an ill nature 822.18 hatefully, 830.14 irritably

with an independent manner 108.12 irrelevantly

with an indifferent attitude 698.20 freely

with an intermission 265.8 apart

with an interval 265.8 apart

with an intrusive manner 104.18 extraneously

with an iron hand 690.11 severely

with an offwind 36.20 offshore

with a noose round one's neck 633.4 endangered

with an open heart 658.5 naively

with an open mind 730.15 receptively, 783.19 impartially, 859.8 disinterestedly

with antagonism 668.10 in defiance, 820.15 aggressively

with an unapproachable manner 263.11 reservedly

with a pin 137.17 in connection with

with aplomb 655.12 skilfully

with appropriate papers 480.11 verifiably

with approval 667.14 agreeably

with a price on one's head 16.64 convicted

with a remainder 132

with a right to 845.11 entitled to

with a rope 137.17 in connection with

with a sad face 770.11 sadly

with a scowl 829.9 irascibly

with a search party 590.18 pursuant to

with a sick headache 874.4 crapulous

with a single mind 667.14 agreeably

with a single oar 36.20 offshore

with a sledge hammer 244.16 destructively

with a sparing hand 756.7 economically

with a sprint 21.7 fast

with assurance 714.16 as promised, 718.16 surely

with a steady pace 122.13 equitably

with a stiff upper lip 859.8 disinterestedly, 869.13 calmly

with a straight face 772.10 solemnly, 783.17 indifferently

with a stroke 640.7 actively

with a strong tendency 234.6 probably

with a thick head 874.4 crapulous

with a tight fist 726.11 tenaciously

with a tongue in one's head 564.19 speaking

with a trumpet flourish 811.32 showily

with authenticity 667.15 contractually

with authority 126.16 superiorly, 233.14 influentially, 688.23 authoritatively

with avarice 734.13 avariciously

with a vengeance 130.10 additionally, 144.10 fully, 239.6 with vigour, 241.10 violently

with a view to 471.21 purposively, 588.14 for

with a volley of abuse 818.10 rudely

with a warm heart 819.17 in friendship

with a warm welcome 730.15 receptively

with a weight of 369.1 heavy

with a whole skin 632.5 safe

with a will 239.6 with vigour, 572.16 willingly

with bad grace 830.14 irritably

with balance 30.12 competitively

with bated breath 428.10 faintly, 513.12 expectantly, 563.17 voicelessly, 806.28 subserviently

with beat of drum 811.32 showily

with bits missing 143.11 partial

with bitterness 820.14 hostilely, 828.17 resentfully

with body and soul 574.17 resolutely

with both oars in the water 509.4 sane

with British Rail 70.6 commercially

with brotherhood 665.18 cliquishly

with brute force 378.13 powerfully

with candour 698.22 informally

with cap in hand 808.16 with servility

with care 469.12 carefully

with certainty 490

with charity 729.9 as a gift, 821.30 lovingly

with child 245.16 reproductive, 513.6 expectant

with clarity 522.13 intelligibly

with clean hands 865.5 innocent, 865.11 innocently

with cleated boots 34.10 on a climb

with cohesion 135.16 as one

with compassion 374.18 softheartedly, 831.10 benevolently, 833.8 philanthropically, 835.13 pitifully

with complications 133.14 in the midst

with compliments 851.25 approvingly

with conditions 699.16 under restraints

with confidence 692.16 commandingly

with consent 116, 715.8 contractually

with consistency 667.16 compatibly

with contempt 822.18 hatefully

with controls 699.16 under restraints

with conviction 554.7 emphatically

with cooperation 667.14 agreeably

with courtesy 817.14 courteously

with crushing effect 244.16 destructively

with deception 734.13 avariciously, 736.19 thievishly

with deference 817.16 deferentially

with delay 661

with deletions 709.8 under censorship

with designs on 588.11 intending

with determination 225.13 determinedly

with devotion 819.19 devotedly

with different parts 133.14 in the midst

with difficulty 659.25 difficultly, 661.17 in the way

with dignity 805, 817.15 genteelly

with diplomacy 653.19 managerially, 706.8 representatively

with discretion 139.11 aloofly, 481.16 judiciously

with disdain 816.14 unsocially

with dissent 136.23 *disagreeably*
with downcast eyes 810.18 *shyly*
with dragging feet 573.17 *unwillingly*
withdraw 345, 598, 131.3 *subtract,* 174.18 *be one,* 221.6 *reverse,* 254.16 *absent oneself,* 337.2 *retreat,* 339.14 *draw in,* 347.9 *exit,* 355.11 *extract,* 458.2 *depart,* 476.9 *deny,* 578.2 *equivocate,* 578.4 *recant,* 591.8 *run away,* 600.6 *stop using,* 673.3 *submit,* 704.6 *cancel,* 705.5 *resign,* 741.25 *demonetize,* 741.26 *bank,* 783.12 *be indifferent,* 816.12 *be unsocial*
withdrawal 875, 61.13 *depression,* 61.19 *defence mechanism,* 131.1 *subtraction,* 136.2 *setting apart,* 218.1 *cessation,* 221.1 *reversion,* 324.4 *backward motion,* 337.11 *retreat,* 345.7 *departure,* 355.1 *extraction,* 458.4 *disappearance,* 476.2 *denial,* 500.3 *dissentience,* 512.1 *oblivion,* 578.6 *equivocation,* 578.8 *recantation,* 591.12 *shyness,* 598.3 *relinquishment,* 638.1 *escape,* 683.1 *failure,* 705.1 *resignation,* 816.1 *unsociability*
withdrawal of the charge 16.42 *acquittal*
withdrawal sickness 875.3 *withdrawal*
withdrawal symptoms 875.3 *withdrawal*
withdraw a statement 734
withdraw from circulation 741.25 *demonetize*
withdraw from currency 614.8 *make useless*
withdrawing 734.2 *taking back*
withdrawing a statement 734.2 *taking back*
withdraw into the background 127.10 *follow*
withdrawment 337.11 *retreat*
withdrawn 61.34 *introverted,* 131.5 *subtracted,* 136.17 *unjoined,* 174.16 *alone,* 512.8 *oblivious,* 531.16 *silent,* 566.1 *taciturn,* 598.6 *apathetic,* 741.22 *monetary,* 783.7 *indifferent,* 816.8 *unsociable*
withdrawn coinage 741.15 *false money*
withdraw the charge 855.7 *vindicate*
with dry eyes 783.17 *indifferently*
with due deference 806.28 *subserviently*
with due respect 849.22 *respectfully*
withe 137.6 *line*
with ears burning 465.5 *curious*
with ease 649
with efficiency 230.13 *operationally*
with eloquence 554.7 *emphatically*
with embarrassment 661.18 *inhibitively,* 699.17 *with self-restraint*
with emendations 216.15 *changeably*
with empathy 667.14 *agreeably*
with emphasis 535.23 *affirmatively,* 668.9 *defiantly*
with emptiness 372.7 *sparsely*
with empty pockets 609.2 *unprovided*
with energy 235.19 *energetically*
with enmity 820.14 *hostilely*
with envy 820.14 *hostilely,* 841.9 *jealously,* 842.4 *enviously*
with equal chance 700.8 *free*
with equal force 704.11 *invalidly*
with equal measures 114.14 *comparably*
wither 83.22 *be dormant,* 129.4 *decrease,* 202.17 *grow old,* 207.17 *age,* 262.6 *become smaller,* 392.21 *dry up,* 408.14 *be hot,* 607.1 *waste,* 628.1 *deteriorate,* 631.14 *afflict*
withered 238.9 *dilapidated,* 247.3 *birth control,* 262.7

smaller, 274.2 *emaciated,* 392.3 *dried-up,* 628.12 *deteriorated*
withering 262.1 *contraction,* 392.13 *drying*
witherite 54 Minerals
withershins 332.10 *clockwise,* 337.29 *in reverse*
with evil intent 832.20 *malevolently*
with evil intentions 864.18 *wickedly*
with exactitude 469.12 *carefully*
with excess 698.21 *excessively*
with expertise 696.16 *masterfully*
with expression 543.18 *indicatively*
with eyes on stalks 786.7 *wide-eyed*
with faith 134.18 *virtuously*
with fatal results 862.13 *destructively*
with fear and trembling 777.15 *fearfully*
with feeling 759, 760.12 *sensitively*
with few words 552.5 *concisely*
with fingers crossed 474.15 *hypocritically*
with firmness 371.10 *densely,* 373.13 *inflexibly*
with flair 549.10 *stylistically*
with flying colours 682.16 *successfully,* 811.32 *showily*
with folded arms 641.5 *without action*
with fondness 821.30 *lovingly*
with footwork 26.16 *professionally,* 28.7 *on guard*
with forbearance 669.15 *abstemiously*
with force 712.12 *by request*
with foresight 516.8 *foresightedly*
with forethought 588.13 *intentionally*
with full knowledge 588.13 *intentionally*
with full play 698.21 *excessively*
with full powers 235.13 *powerful*
with fury 828.18 *angrily*
with gaping mouth 786.13 *wonderfully*
with gentleness 370.11 *lightly*
with giant leaps 329.14 *swiftly*
with giant strides 329.14 *swiftly*
with give-and-go 31.10 *on the field*
with good cheer 769.9 *cheerfully,* 815.18 *sociably*
with good effect 682.16 *successfully*
with good grace 572.16 *willingly,* 763.15 *pleasantly,* 817.14 *courteously*
with good intentions 863.9 *virtuously*
with good results 682.16 *successfully*
with good will 833.8 *philanthropically*
with gratitude 837.8 *gratefully*
with great admiration 784.11 *admiringly*
with great charm 815.18 *sociably,* 821.30 *lovingly*
with great effect 233.14 *influentially*
with great emotion 821.30 *lovingly*
with great liking 784
with great weight 369.16 *heavily*
with gusto 572.16 *willingly*
with haste 642.22 *actively*
with hate 832.20 *malevolently,* 862.12 *evilly*
with hat in hand 806.28 *subserviently*
with head held high 805.32 *proudly*
with heart and soul 644.12 *laboriously*
with heat 98.13 *continentally*
with heels dug in 577.3 *unyielding*
withheld 283.9 *interrupted,* 711.8 *refused,* 726.10 *retained*
with high spirits 769.9 *cheerfully*

with hindsight 3.24 *historically,* 200.24 *retrospectively*
withhold 209.8 *delay,* 283.12 *interrupt,* 487.8 *make impossible,* 529.12 *keep secret,* 637.5 *preserve,* 726.7 *detain*
withhold approval 852
withhold assent 711.6 *dissent*
withhold consent 711.6 *dissent*
withholding 283.6 *interruption,* 711.8 *refused*
withhold payment 747.8 *stop payment*
withhold permission 709.3 *veto*
with honesty 863.10 *ethically*
with honeyed words 853.17 *flatteringly*
with hope 714.17 *auspiciously,* 775.15 *hopefully*
with hostility 136.23 *disagreeably,* 666.11 *in disagreement,* 670.26 *aggresively,* 713.11 *disapprovingly,* 822.18 *hatefully*
with humility 673
with idealism 368.14 *subjectively*
with imagination 119.8 *originally,* 519.17 *imaginatively*
with immunity 698.20 *freely*
with impunity 848, 632.10 *safely*
within 146.9 *inclusively,* 257.14 *internally,* 368.14 *subjectively*
within bounds 242.9 *moderately,* 463.15 *reasonably,* 699.16 *under restraints,* 869.9 *moderate,* 869.12 *moderately*
within call 264.6 *near,* 420.17 *aurally*
within earshot 264.6 *near,* 420.14 *hearable,* 420.17 *aurally*
within hearing 264.6 *near,* 420.17 *aurally*
with inhibitions 661.18 *inhibitively*
with inhumanity 834.5 *misanthropically*
within limits 302, 242.6 *moderate,* 242.9 *moderately,* 699.16 *under restraints*
within living memory 200.22 *in the past*
within one's depth 278.8 *shallowly*
within one's means 754.9 *cheap*
within one's power 486.10 *practically*
within one's rights 843.21 *in the right*
within range 242.9 *moderately,* 264.6 *near,* 420.14 *hearable,* 420.17 *aurally*
within reach 253.10 *available,* 253.16 *on the spot,* 264.6 *near,* 486.10 *practically,* 615.7 *conveniently,* 615.8 *nearby*
within reason 242.6 *moderate,* 242.9, 869.12 *moderately*
within reasonable limits 869.9 *moderate,* 869.12 *moderately*
within sight 264.6 *near,* 435.24 *visually,* 486.10 *practically*
within someone's orbit 233.14 *influentially*
with insularity 98.13 *continentally*
with interest 130.10 *additionally,* 749.8 *profitably*
with interference 31.10 *on the field*
within the bounds of 121.7 *gradational*
within the law 16.44 *legal,* 16.81 *legally*
within the time limit 210.8, 210.11 *in time*
with irreverence 787.9 *without wonder*
with irritation 830.14 *irritably*
with it 6.19 *knowledgeable,* 201.16 *avant-garde,* 584.12 *established*
with-it 796.7 *fashionable*
with justice 122.13 *equitably*
with justification 855.15 *in vindication*
with kid gloves 691.6 *leniently*
with kindness 691.6 *leniently,*

with 817.14 *courteously,* 819.17 *in friendship,* 831.10 *benevolently*
with knobs on 130.10 *additionally,* 144.10 *fully*
with larceny in one's heart 736.19 *thievishly*
with legal protection 708.9 *with permission*
with light fingers 736.19 *thievishly*
with little thought 595.3 *without preparation*
with love 784.11 *admiringly,* 815.18 *sociably,* 821.30 *lovingly,* 826.10 *endearingly,* 831.10 *benevolently*
with loyalty 819.19 *devotedly*
with luck 686.9 *prosperously*
with lust 821.30 *lovingly*
with malice 822.18 *hatefully,* 828.17 *resentfully,* 832.20 *malevolently,* 855.16 *vindictively,* 862.12 *evilly,* 862.13 *destructively*
with malice aforethought 588.13 *intentionally,* 832.20 *malevolently*
with many changes 106.16 *relatively*
with many words 553.7 *diffusely*
with material 367.9 *materially*
with maturity 207.16 *maturely*
with meaning 520.13 *meaningfully,* 543.18 *indicatively*
with meditation 588.13 *intentionally*
with mercy 835.13 *pitifully*
with might and main 235.18 *powerfully,* 237.14 *strongly,* 574.17 *resolutely,* 642.22 *actively,* 644.12 *laboriously*
with misgivings 785.10 *discontentedly*
with moderation 242.9, 869.12 *moderately*
with modesty 699.17 *with self-restraint,* 859.9 *unselfishly*
with momentum 330.18 *dynamically*
with much ado 659.25 *difficultly,* 661.16 *with delay*
with mud 98.13 *continentally*
with need 571
with no admiration 787.9 *without wonder*
with noble intentions 859.9 *unselfishly*
with nobody the wiser 529.15 *in secret*
with no expense spared 755.12 *generously*
with no frills 788.8 *boringly*
with no guilt 865.11 *innocently*
with no holds barred 530.13 *openly,* 698.21 *excessively*
with no interest 783.17 *indifferently*
with no letup 219.6 *protracted,* 219.7 *continually*
with no questions asked 708.9 *with permission*
with no regrets 868.6 *impenitently*
with no remorse 868.6 *impenitently*
with no strings attached 698.21 *excessively,* 710.20 *persuasively*
with no surprises 787.10 *predictably*
with not a moment to lose 648.6 *hastily*
with nothing on 296.17 *nakedly*
with nothing to hope for 743.1 *poor*
with no thought for others 860.9 *egoistically*
with objectivity 367.9 *materially*
with obligations 597.5 *undertaken*
with observance 719.8 *observantly*
with offence 827.12 *swearingly,* 864.21 *criminally*
with official approval 688.25 *authentically,* 703.11 *under commission*
with one accord 116.31 *in ac-*

cord, 499.8 *unanimously,*
664.20 *cooperatively*
with one bite 872.7 *gluttonously*
with one blow 244.16 *destructively*
with one foot in the grave
207.14 *aged,* 207.16 *maturely,*
397.18 *dying*
with one hand tied behind one's
back 660.21 *easily*
with one's back to the wall 633.4
endangered, 661.14 *blocked,*
661.17 *in the way,* 687.7 *unprosperous*
with one's cards on the table
526.16 *manifestly*
with one's dander up 828.18 *angrily*
with one's eyes closed 660.21
easily
with one's eyes open 588.13 *intentionally*
with one's eyes starting out of
one's head 786.7 *wide-eyed*
with one's hands 15.13 *industrially*
with one's hands in one's pockets 641.5 *without action*
with one's head in the clouds
462.14 *thoughtlessly,* 519.17
imaginatively
with one's heart in one's mouth
777.8 *fearful*
with one's monkey up 828.18 *angrily*
with one's nose in the air 805.32
proudly
with one's nose out of joint
828.17 *resentfully*
with one's tail between one's
legs 806.28 *subserviently*
with one's trousers down 595.1
unprepared
with one thought 667.14 *agreeably*
with one voice 116.10, 116.31 *in*
accord, 198.13 *synchronously,*
499.8 *unanimously,* 664.20 *cooperatively,* 667.10 *agreeing,*
667.14 *agreeably*
with open arms 348.18 *receptively,* 572.16 *willingly,* 815.18
sociably, 819.17 *in friendship*
with open doors 532.22 *publicly*
with open hands 755.12 *generously,* 831.11 *charitably*
with openness 730.15 *receptively*
with oppression 369.17 *burdensomely*
with others in mind 859.9 *unselfishly*
without 106.15 *under the circumstances,* 131.8 *by subtraction,*
145.6 *incompletely,* 289.15 *externally,* 722.16 *losing*
without a bean 743.2 *insolvent*
without a care 700.8 *free*
without a care in the world
462.14 *thoughtlessly*
without a case 16.64 *convicted*
without a cent 743.2 *insolvent*
without a change of pace 788.8
boringly
without a change of scenery
788.8 *boringly*
without acknowledgment 838.5
thankless, 838.7 *ungratefully*
without a clue 523.2 *unexplained*
without a conscience 868.3 *impenitent*
without a cooperative spirit
711.11 *uncooperatively*
without a cox 36.20 *offshore*
without action 641
without adhesion 139.10 *noncohesively*
without ado 660.21 *easily*
without adornment 690.12 *plainly*
without a doubt 466.7 *incuriously*
without affectation 658.5, 865.12
naively
without affiliation 698.20 *freely*
without a hangover 873.1 *sober*
without a hitch 660.21 *easily*
without airs 806.1 *humble*
without a job 641.3 *inactive*
without a leg to stand on 16.64

convicted, 236.10 *powerless,*
476.6 *refutable,* 476.12 *refutably*
without an inheritance 727.16
disposably
without any qualms 868.6 *impenitently*
without any scruples 868.6 *impenitently*
without a pang of regret 868.3
impenitent
without a penny 593.5 *necessitous,* 727.16 *disposably*
without a penny to one's name
747.15 *without paying*
without application 104.18 *extraneously*
without appreciation 838.5 *thankless,* 838.7 *ungratefully*
without approval 713.11 *disapprovingly*
without art 658.1 *naive*
without artifice 658.1 *naive,*
658.5 *naively*
without a second thought 466.7
incuriously
without a shadow of doubt
490.23 *certainly*
without a sign of life 641.3 *inactive*
without a solution 523.2 *unexplained*
without a sou 743.2 *insolvent*
without a spot 134.19 *purely*
without assimilation 139.11
aloofly
without assistance 661.16 *with*
delay, 816.14 *unsocially*
without a stain 619.1 *perfect*
without a stain on one's character 16.63 *guiltily*
without a stitch on 296.9 *undressed,* 296.17 *nakedly*
without a twinge of conscience
836.7 *pitilessly*
without authority 16.56 *unauthorized,* 16.82 *illegally,* 236.14
powerlessly, 689.8 *anarchically*
without authorization 709.7 *by*
veto
without a word 566.10
taciturnly, 816.14 *unsocially*
without a worry 783.18 *carelessly*
without ballast 576.2 *changeable*
without batting an eye 836.7 *pitilessly*
without bearing a grudge 839.14
forgivingly
without beginning or end 184.3
eternal
without bias 4.26 *rationally,*
843.19 *equally,* 859.8 *disinterestedly*
without blame 863.9 *virtuously*
without blemish 619.1 *perfect,*
863.5 *virtuous*
without body 368.8 *nonmaterial*
without ceasing 212.1 *frequently*
without ceremony 810.17 *modestly,* 814.12 *informally*
without chains 700.8 *free*
without charge 754.11 *free of*
charge
without charm 818.9 *discourteously*
without cheer 830.13 *sullenly*
without commitment 717.10 *irresolutely*
without comparison 115.7 *dissimilarly,* 119.8 *originally,* 126.17
supremely
without compassion 836.4 *pitiless*
without complaints 765.4 *satisfied*
without compromise 690.11 *severely*
without compunction 868.3 *impenitent,* 868.6 *impenitently*
without concern 787.9 *without*
wonder
without conditions 708.9 *with*
permission
without consistency 113.10 *diversely,* 666.12 *differently*
without content 254.13 *vacant*
without control 698.21 *excessively*
without cooperation 666.11 *in*
disagreement

without courteousness 818.9 *discourteously*
without credit 838.5 *thankless,*
838.7 *ungratefully*
without defect 619.1 *perfect*
without delay 191.8 *immediately,* 208.17 *early,* 648.3
hasty, 648.6 *hastily*
without demur 572.16 *willingly*
without design 229.8 *by chance*
without difficulty 660.21 *easily*
without discrimination 700.8 *free*
without distinction 843.19 *equally*
without effect 238.14 *weakly*
without embarrassment 668.9 *defiantly*
without emotion 869.13 *calmly*
without employment 641.3 *inactive*
without end 181.8 *numberless,*
184.10 *infinitely,* 188.12 *everlastingly,* 190.11 *eternally,*
269.1 *long,* 269.11 *lengthily*
without enemies 675.7 *peaceful*
without enthusiasm 573.17 *unwillingly*
without equal 115.7 *dissimilarly,*
126.14 *best*
without equality 375.14 *roughly*
without equivocation 857.7
honourably
without exception 110.20 *regularly,* 112.13 *uniformly,* 116.35
consistently, 142.11 *wholly,*
146.7 *including,* 164.30 *usually*
without excess 869.11 *with self-*
restraint
without excitement 788.8 *boringly*
without excuse 866.5 *guilty,*
866.11 *guiltily*
without exemption 142.11 *wholly*
without fairness 123.8 *unjustly*
without fault 655.12 *skilfully*
without fear 675.8 *peacefully*
without fear of contradiction
535.23 *affirmatively*
without fear or favour 843.19
equally
without feelings 783.17 *indifferently,* 836.4 *pitiless,* 836.7 *pitilessly*
without flexibility 373.13 *inflexibly,* 379.5 *fragilely*
without food 871.6 *fasting,*
871.7 *abstemiously*
without fuss 810.17 *modestly*
without gloss 445.7 *colourless*
without good fortune 862.14 *inauspiciously*
without grounds 476.12 *refutably*
without guile 658.5 *naively*
without guilt 863.9 *virtuously*
without harmony 666.11 *in disagreement*
without hearing 421.4 *deaf*
without help 139.11 *aloofly,*
661.16 *with delay*
without hesitation 572.17 *spontaneously,* 667.14 *agreeably*
without holes 371.6 *dense*
without honour 717.10 *irresolutely,* 858.11 *dishonourably*
without hope 776.1 *hopeless*
without illusion 537.19 *authentic*
without imagination 787.9 *without wonder*
without importance 612.1 *unimportant*
without intelligence 460.11 *unintelligently*
without interruption 219.7 *continually*
without issue 247
without justice 123.8 *unjustly*
without law 16.61 *lawless*
without legal backing 16.56 *unauthorized,* 16.82 *illegally*
without let or hindrance 660.21
easily
without limit 181.8 *numberless,*
184.1 *infinite,* 184.10 *infinitely*
without looking 436.17 *blindly*
without looking back 868.6 *impenitently*
without loss 619.1 *perfect*
without love 785.8 *disliking*

without manners 585.2 *not customary*
without mass 368.8 *nonmaterial*
without meaning 520.6 *meaningful,* 521.10 *meaningless*
without meeting expectations
515.13 *disappointingly*
without mercy 832.20 *malevolently*
without morals 783.18 *carelessly,*
864.12 *immoral,* 864.20 *immorally*
without movement 641.5 *without*
action
without moving 135.18 *inextricably,* 718.17 *fastly*
without notice 208.18 *soon*
without number 184.2 *immeasurable*
without obligations 825.12
celibately
without offspring 247.12 *without*
issue
without omission 146.7 *including*
without one's husband 824.13
without one's spouse
without one's spouse 824
without one's wife 824.13 *without one's spouse*
without order 113.11 *irregularly*
without overdoing it 869.11 *with*
self-restraint
without patience 829.9 *irascibly*
without pausing for breath
188.12 *everlastingly*
without paying 747
without payment 729.9 *as a gift*
without permission 709.7 *by veto*
without pity 832.20 *malevolently,* 836.1 *pitilessness,* 836.7
pitilessly
without planning 595.3 *without*
preparation
without prejudice 4.26 *rationally,*
122.13 *equitably,* 859.8 *disinterestedly*
without preparation 595, 595.14
unreadily
without pretence 134.20
homogenously
without pretensions 658.5 *naively*
without prompting 572.18 *voluntarily*
without prospects 743.1 *poor*
without question 490.23 *certainly*
without rationality 460.12 *nonhumanly*
without reason 460.8 *nonhuman,*
460.12 *nonhumanly*
without reference 108.12 *irrelevantly*
without regard 108.12 *irrelevantly*
without regard for honesty
858.11 *dishonourably*
without regard to feelings
864.18 *wickedly*
without regard to morality
693.17 *disobediently*
without regret 868.6 *impenitently*
without regrets 868.3 *impenitent*
without regularity 375.14 *roughly*
without regulations 700.8 *free*
without relevance 108.12 *irrelevantly*
without remorse 868.3 *impenitent,* 868.6 *impenitently*
without resistance 673.6 *with humility*
without resolution 717.10 *irresolutely*
without resource 236.11 *unprotected*
without respect 818.10 *rudely*
without respite 219.6 *protracted,*
219.7 *continually*
without restraint 698.21 *excessively*
without rhyme or reason 151.27
in disorder, 521.10 *meaningless*
without rights 846.8 *unentitled*
without risk 632.5 *safe,* 632.10
safely, 718.6 *secure,* 718.16
surely
without roughness 376.14
smoothly

without seeing the error of one's ways 868.6 *impenitently*
without shame 668.9 *defiantly*, 877.21 *immorally*
without shape 375.15 *incompletely*
without side 806.1 *humble*
without significance 104.18 *extraneously*, 783.20 *unexceptionally*
without similarities 108.13 *disproportionately*
without similarity 666.12 *differently*
without sin 863.9 *virtuously*
without skill 776.8 *bad*
without speaking 566.10 *taciturnly*
without stint 608.2 *plentiful*, 698.21 *excessively*
without stop 212.1 *frequently*
without stopping 112.13 *uniformly*, 159.19 *continuously*, 188.12 *everlastingly*, 212.1 *frequently*
without strings 698.12 *unconditional*, 708.7 *permitted*, 708.9 *with permission*
without substance 370.11 *lightly*
without success 683.12 *unsuccessfully*
without sympathy 820.14 *hostilely*
without taste 412
without thanks 838.5 *thankless*, 838.7 *ungratefully*
without thinking 460.11 *unintelligently*, 404.22 *wrongly*, 584.19 *habitually*
without title 846.8 *unentitled*
without tricks 658.1 *naive*
without trouble 376.15 *soothingly*
without validity 704.11 *invalidly*
without variety 788.8 *boringly*
without violence 675.8 *peacefully*
without warmth 818.9 *discourteously*
without warning 380.19 *suddenly*, 489.9 *unexpectedly*, 514.13 *surprisingly*
without wasting words 552.5 *concisely*, 562.12 *in brief*
without weight 370.1 *light*
without wonder 787
with patience 839.14 *forgivingly*
with permission 708, 116.39 *with consent*, 712.12 *by request*
with pleasure 405.11 *pleasingly*, 762.9 *joyfully*, 763.15 *pleasantly*
with plenty of time 208.17 *early*
with power 330.18 *dynamically*, 688.23 *authoritatively*
with praise 851.25 *approvingly*
with precise measurements 268.17 *measurably*
with precision 469.12 *carefully*
with prejudice 862.12 *evilly*
with promise 714.17 *auspiciously*, 819.20 *favourably*
with propriety 652.19 *well*
with provisions 106.16 *relatively*, 716.9 *feasibly*
with prudence 869.12 *moderately*
with pure greed 872.7 *gluttonously*
with pure intentions 857.8 *purely*, 865.11 *innocently*
with qualification 485
with qualifications 855.15 *in vindication*
with reason 483.14 *as evidence*
with recourse to 602.7 *by means of*
with regret 573.17 *unwillingly*, 867.8 *penitently*
with regularity 584.19 *habitually*
with relevance 667.17 *suitably*
with repentance 867.8 *penitently*
with reproach 827.13 *vituperatively*, 828.17 *resentfully*, 866.11 *guiltily*
with resentment 828.17 *resentfully*, 829.9 *irascibly*, 830.14 *irritably*
with reservations 147.12 *exclusively*
with resistance 711.11 *uncooperatively*

with resolution 726.11 *tenaciously*
with respect 817.15 *genteelly*
with responsibility 703.11 *under commission*
with restraint 542.28 *moderately*
with restrictions 147.12 *exclusively*, 709.8 *under censorship*
with rhythm 30.12 *competitively*
with rocks 98.13 *continentally*
with romance 821.30 *lovingly*
with rudeness 816.14 *unsocially*
with satisfaction 765
with sealed lips 566.3 *sparing with words*
with self-control 699.17, 869.11 *with self-restraint*
with self-discipline 699.17 *with self-restraint*
with self-love 860.9 *egoistically*
with self-motivation 698.20 *freely*
with self-reliance 698.20 *freely*
with self-restraint 699, 869
with servility 808
with sexual undertones 135.16 *as one*
with skill 655.12 *skilfully*, 688.26 *expertly*
with skis 41.17 *on a ski run*
with sobriety 873.9 *soberly*
with softness 374.17 *softly*
with sorrow 866.11 *guiltily*
with spite 822.18 *hatefully*
withstand 663, 231.3 *counteract*, 668.5 *defy*, 669.6 *resist*, 670.8 *counterattack*, 671.28 *survive*, 674.11 *contend*, 711.6 *dissent*
withstanding 669.3 *resistance movement*, 669.10 *resistant*
withstand testing 608.4 *suffice*
with statesmanship 653.19 *managerially*
with sticky fingers 736.19 *thievishly*
with stiffness 373.12 *toughly*
with strings attached 485.18 *with qualification*, 699.13 *restraining*
with style 549.10 *stylistically*
with suffering 624.25 *unhealthily*
with superiority 126.16 *superiorly*
with supervision 15.13 *industrially*
with suppleness 377.11 *elastically*
with swordplay 28.7 *on guard*
with sympathy 667.14 *agreeably*
with synchronization 39.12 *by swimming*
with tears in one's eyes 770.11 *sadly*
with telling effect 235.18 *powerfully*, 239.6 *with vigour*
with tender loving care 831.10 *benevolently*
with tenderness 370.11 *lightly*, 374.18 *softheartedly*
with thanks 837.8 *gratefully*
with the aid of 232.9 *instrumentally*, 602.7 *by means of*
with the back-and-foot technique 34.10 *on a climb*
with the back-and-knee technique 34.10 *on a climb*
with the best intentions 865.11 *innocently*
with the crowd 660.9 *easy*
with the current 660.9 *easy*
with the effect of 227
with the exact touch 114.14 *comparably*
with the exception of 131.8 *by subtraction*, 147.12 *exclusively*
with the help of 232.9 *instrumentally*
with the innocence of a newborn babe 865.12 *naively*
with the intention of 588.14 *for*
with the lark 204.8 *in the morning*
with the merchant navy 70.6 *commercially*
with the object of 588.14 *for*
with the odds stacked against one 123.7 *unequally*

with the proviso 485.18 *with qualification*
with the rest 132.12 *with a remainder*
with the result that 227.12 *with the effect of*
with the sun 204.8 *in the morning*
with the throttle wide open 239.6 *with vigour*
with the wisdom of hindsight 200.24 *retrospectively*
with the worst intentions 832.20 *malevolently*
with time to spare 208.17 *early*
with tongue in cheek 474.15 *hypocritically*, 771.17 *jokingly*
with tooth and nail 574.17 *resolutely*
with truth 537.35 *truly*, 857.7 *honourably*
with two oars 36.20 *offshore*
with two wives 823.24 *matrimonially*
with urgency 648.6 *hastily*, 712.12 *by request*
with velocity 21.7 *fast*
with vengeance 672
with vigour 239
with warmth 819.17 *in friendship*
with whip and spur 329.14 *swiftly*
witless 460.6 *unintelligent*, 460.7 *intellectually subnormal*
witlessness 460.2 *unintelligence*
witness 253.5 *someone present*, 253.12 *attend*, 435.11 *observer*, 435.12 *see*, 477.10 *person questioned*, 480.2 *prove*, 480.3 *testify*, 480.7 *verifier*, 483.7 *person who gives evidence*, 483.11 *give evidence*, 528.9 *informant*, 535.9 *affirmer*, 856.5 *accuse*
witness box 16.27 *courtroom*, 492.3 *place of judgment*
witnessed 253.8 *attendant*, 480.8 *verifiable*, 483.8 *evidential*
witness for the prosecution 856.3 *accuser*
witness to 543.10 *signify*
wits 459.3, 507.2 *intelligence*, 509.2 *rationality*
witter 426.9 *hum*, 565.3 *talk*, 565.7 *be talkative*
Wittgenstein 4 Philosophers
Wittgensteinian 4.11 *follower of a doctrine*, 4.14 *of a philosophy*
witticism 505.1 *maxim*, 506.2 *solecism*, 552.1 *conciseness*, 771.5 *joke*
wittily 771.16 *humorously*, 815.18 *sociably*
wittiness 771.1 *humorousness*
wittingly 588.13 *intentionally*
witty 505.2 *proverbial*, 771.10 *humorous*, 798.5 *ridiculous*, 815.15 *sociable*
witty repartee 478.1 *answer*
wive 823.15 *marry*
wizard 11.4 *witch*, 617.1 *worthy*, 655.4 *skilled person*, 655.6 *skilful*, 786.5 *person of wonder*, 861.1 *good*
wizard-like 11.15 *witchlike*
wizardly 11.15 *witchlike*
wizardry 11.3 *witchcraft*, 655.1 *skill*
wizard's cap 11.6 *talisman*
wizard's hat 295.15 *headgear*
wizard wheeze 471.3 *plan*
wizen 207.17 *age*, 262.6 *become smaller*, 262.7 *smaller*, 392.21 *dry up*
wizened 207.14 *aged*, 260.7 *little*, 262.7 *smaller*, 274.2 *emaciated*, 392.3 *dried-up*
woad 67.6 *dye*, 444.4 *pigment*, 454.5 *blueness*, 454.9 *blue*
wobble 25.2 *grip*, 215.1 *irregularity*, 215.6 *be irregular*, 224.11 *be changeable*, 328.1 *move slowly*, 335.10 *slide*, 366.25 *pitch*, 576.5 *vacillate*
wobbler 539.13 *snare*, 576.15 *indecisive person*
wobbliness 215.1 *irregularity*, 224.1 *changeableness*

wobbling 215.4 *irregular*, 576.1 *vacillating*
wobbly 215.4 *irregular*, 224.13 *changeable*, 238.8 *weak*, 366.18 *shaky*, 576.1 *vacillating*, 620.1 *imperfect*
wobbly-legged 656.3 *clumsy*
Wodehouse 48 Writers
wodge 143.7 *piece*, 259.7 *mass*
woe 618.10 *poverty*, 631.2 *adversity*, 770.1 *sorrow*, 774.1 *lamentation*, 862.2 *affliction*
woebegone 770.5 *sad*, 774.4 *lamenting*
woeful 618.4 *poor*, 862.8 *afflicted*
woefully 862.13 *destructively*
woe is me 862.15 *bad luck*
wog 91 Names for Inhabitants
Wöhler 52 Scientists
Wöhler's synthesis 57 Named Reactions
wok 45.6 *kitchen equipment*, 258.15 *pot*
wold 87.2 *grassland*, 98.7 *upland*, 275.2 *heights*
wolf 77 Placental Mammals, 241.4 *violent person or animal*, 350.18 *eater*, 350.22 *eat well*, 734.6 *taker*, 821.9 *lover*, 872.4 *glutton*, 872.5 *be greedy*
Wolf 48 Writers, **53** The Constellations, **53** Named Stars
wolf at the door 743.5 *poverty*
wolf down 348.11 *ingest*
Wolfe 48 Writers, **48** Poets
Wolff 4 Philosophers
wolf fish 80 Fishes
wolfing 872.6 *gluttonous*
wolf in sheep's clothing 117.6 *misfit*, 538.12 *cheat*, 539.15 *deceiver*, 635.1 *trap*, 657.3 *cunning person*, 666.4 *dissenter*
wolfish 77.28 *carnivorous*, 350.26 *eating*, 872.6 *gluttonous*
wolfishly 872.7 *gluttonously*
wolfishness 350.2 *appetite*, 872.1 *gluttony*
wolflike 77.28 *carnivorous*
wolframite 54 Minerals
wolfsbane 84 Flowers and Flowering Plants, 631.12 *poisonous plant*
wolf spider 82 Arachnids
wolf whistle 430.3 *shrillness*, 543.3 *gesture*
wolf-whistle 430.6 *be shrill*
wollastonite 54 Minerals
Wollaston prism 56 Named Laws
Wollongong 93 Cities
Wolof 5 Languages and Groups of Languages
Wolverhampton 93 Cities
wolverine 77 Placental Mammals
woman 207, 400.7 *person*, 402.1 *female sex*, 402.2 *female*
woman behind the man 233.4 *indirect influence*
woman-chaser 821.9 *lover*, 826.5 *courting person*
woman considered as a sex object 402
woman-crazy 877.14 *lecherous*
woman-hater 820.5 *hostile person*, 822.9 *hater*, 834.2 *misanthrope*
woman-hating 834.3 *misanthropic*
womanhood 207.2 *adulthood*, 402.1 *female sex*
woman in the family 402
womanish 402.15 *female*
womanishness 402.1 *female sex*
womanize 877.17 *be sexually immoral*
womanizer 821.9 *lover*, 826.5 *courting person*, 877.8 *immoral man*
womanizing 877.3 *sexual immorality*
womankind 400.1 *humankind*, 402.1 *female sex*
womanliness 402.1 *female sex*
womanly 402.15 *female*
woman-mad 877.14 *lecherous*

woman of her word 857.3 *honourable person*
woman of letters 48.15 *literary person*
woman of taste 794.4 *refined person*
woman of the world 207.9 *woman*
woman sailor 679.27 *naval man*
Woman's Christian Temperance Union 869.1 *self-restraint*, 873.8 *sober person*
woman soldier 679
woman's quarters 821.13 *abode of love*
womb 156.3, 226.2 *source*, 245.4 *development*, 245.8 *organs of reproduction*, 290.4 *insides*
wombat 77 *Marsupials*
women 777 *Phobias by Topic*, 402.13 *womenfolk*, 646.4 *personnel*
Women 727.7 *toilet*
women and song 405.2 *good time*
womenfolk 402
women's 100m hurdles race 21.1 *track events*
women's 200m hurdles 21.1 *track events*
women's 3000m race 21.1 *track events*
women's 80m hurdles 21.1 *track events*
Women's Alliance 12.6 *political party*
women's clothing 295.1 *dress*
women's hospital 60.10 *hospital*
women's judo 26.7 *judo*
women's lib 402.1 *female sex*, 698.1 *freedom*, 700.2 *equal opportunity*
women's libber 402.11 *liberated woman*, 693.7 *protester*, 698.7 *free person*, 700.3 *liberator*
Women's Liberation 402.1 *female sex*, 698.1 *freedom*, 700.2 *equal opportunity*
women's magazine 532.5 *journal*
Women's Movement 402.1 *female sex*
women's penitentiary 702.1 *prison*
women's quarters 402.13 *womenfolk*
women's rights 402.1 *female sex*, 845.3 *prerogative*
Women's Room 727.7 *toilet*
Women's Royal Air Force 679.29 *air force*
Women's Royal Army Corps 679.15 *army*
Women's Royal Naval Service 679.22 *navy*
women's suffrage 580.11 *franchise*
womenswear 295.1 *dress*
won 718.8 *accomplished*, 741.11 *national coins*
Won 7 *Non-Christian Religions*
wonder 786, 786, 786, 4.20 *philosophize*, 477.17 *curiosity*, 477.17 *question*, 489.5 *unexpectedness*, 514.2 *amazement*, 514.4 *surprising thing*, 523.9 *find unintelligible*, 617.8 *exceller*, 786.5 *person of wonder*, 861.16 *superior person*
Wonder 786
wonder about 491.18 *be uncertain*
wonder boy 786.5 *person of wonder*
wonder drug 62.3, 630.8 *drug*
wonderful 786
wonderful! 786
wonderful 617.1 *worthy*, 762.5 *delightful*, 861.1 *good*
wonderfully 786, 861.22 *well*
wonderfulness 861.8 *good*
wonderful to relate 786.13 *wonderfully*
wonderful works 786.3 *wonderworking*
wondering 786, 477.12 *questioning*, 523.6 *confused*, 849.10 *reverent*

wonderland 519.8 *dreamland*, 786.4 *wonder*
wonderless 787.3 *unmoved*
wonderman 514.5 *surpriser*
wonderment 786.1 *wonder*
wonder of the world 617.8 *exceller*
wonders will never cease 786.14 *wonderful*
wonder whether 786
wonder woman 126.6 *paragon*
wonderwoman 514.5 *surpriser*, 617.8 *exceller*
wonder woman 786.5 *person of wonder*
Wonder Woman 237.6 *muscleman*
wonder-working 786, 786.8 *wonderful*
wondrous 786.8 *wonderful*
wondrously 786.13 *wonderfully*
wonky 238.8 *weak*, 628.13 *dilapidated*
Wŏnsan 93 *Cities*
wont 166.6 *custom*, 584.1 *habit*, 599.6 *use*
wonted 124.1 *average*, 166.10 *customary*, 584.9 *habitual*
wontedly 584.19 *habitually*
won ten 45.48 *Chinese dish*
woo 590.12 *aim at*, 712.6 *request*, 782.13 *like*, 819.14 *seek the friendship of*, 821.26, 826.8 *court*
wood 77 *Placental Mammals*, **47**, 25.1 *green bowling*, 29.4 *golf club*, 63.25 *construction material*, 74.4 *shipbuilding*, 85.3 *timber*, 85.4 *trees*, 85.15 *woody*, 338.10 *ball*, 338.13 *fuel*, 373.7 *hard substance*, 410.1 *fuel*, 410.2 *lighter*, 604.1 *materials*
Wood 49 *Musicians and Composers*
wood alcohol 85.9 *tree product*, 351.7 *alcoholic drink*
wood ant 85.11 *tree-related animal*
wood block 49 *Musical Instruments*, 47.8 *woodwork*
wood-block 50.15 *engraving*
wood-blocked 47.15 *woodcrafted*
wood-block printing 47.8 *woodwork*
woodborer 82 *Insects*, 82.3 *pest*, 85.11 *tree-related animal*
woodburned 47.15 *woodcrafted*
woodburning 47.8 *woodwork*, 408.13 *heated*, 410.10 *powered*
woodcarved 47.15 *woodcrafted*
woodcarver 47.13 *carpenter*
woodcarving 47.8 *woodwork*, 50.1 *art*, 50.12 *sculpture*
woodchat 78 *Birds*, 85.11 *tree-related animal*
woodchuck 77 *Placental Mammals*, 85.11 *tree-related animal*
woodchuck hunting 590.2 *chase*
wood club 29.4 *golf club*
wood coal 85.9 *tree product*
woodcock 78 *Birds*, 45.20 *meat*, 78.4 *table bird*, 85.11 *tree-related animal*
woodcraft 47.8 *woodwork*, 85.5 *forestry*
woodcrafted 47
woodcraftsman 47.13 *carpenter*
woodcreeper 78 *Birds*
woodcut 47.8 *woodwork*, 47.15 *woodcrafted*, 50.7 *picture*, 50.15 *engraving*
woodcut illustration 47.8 *woodwork*
woodcutter 47.13 *carpenter*, 85.8 *forester*, 410.9 *power-worker*
wood duck 78 *Birds*, 85.11 *tree-related animal*
wooded 85, 83.13 *plantlike*
wooden 47, 26.15 *wrestling*, 41.12 *ski*, 85.15 *woody*, 559.9 *inelegant*, 577.3 *unyielding*
wooden chair 47.2 *chair*
wood-engraved 47.15 *woodcrafted*
wood engraver 47.13 *carpenter*, 50.18 *engraver*

wood engraving 47.8 *woodwork*, 50.15 *engraving*
wood-engraving tool 47.11 *woodworking tool*
wooden mask 295.5 *fancy dress*
woodenness 577.6 *determination*
wooden shoes 295.19 *footwear*
wooden ski 41.5 *ski equipment*
wooden spoon 45.6 *kitchen equipment*, 133.6 *mixer*, 258.17 *ladle*, 656.8 *unskilfulness*, 878.2 *prize*
wooden walls 679.22 *navy*
woodenware 47.8 *woodwork*
wood fire 408.6 *fire*
wood furniture 47.1 *furniture*
woodgrain 47.12 *wood*
woodgrouse 85.11 *tree-related animal*
wood hedgehog 89 *Fungi*
wood inlay 47.9 *decorative woodwork*
woodland 85.4 *trees*, 85.16 *wooded*, 453.8 *greenness*
woodlander 85.8 *forester*
woodland stalking 37.2 *hunting*
woodlark 85.11 *tree-related animal*
wood lot 85.4 *trees*
woodlouse 81.4 *arthropod*, 85.11 *tree-related animal*
woodman 85.8 *forester*
wood meadow grass 87 *Grasses*
wood moss 88.3 *moss*
woodnote 432.2 *bird song*
wood nymph 8.5 *deity*, 85.13 *tree mythology*
woodpecker 78 *Birds*, 85.11 *tree-related animal*
woodpeckers 161 *Collective Names by Animal*
wood pigeon 78 *Birds*, 85.11 *tree-related animal*
wood pitch 85.9 *tree product*
woodprint 47.8 *woodwork*
woodprinted 47.15 *woodcrafted*
wood rat 85.11 *tree-related animal*
Woodrow Wilson 675.4 *Nobel Peace Prize*
woodrush 87 *Grasses*
woods 85.4 *trees*
wood-sculpted 47.15 *woodcrafted*
wood sculpting 47.8 *woodwork*
wood sculpture 47.8 *woodwork*
wood shot 29.3 *golf shots*
woodsia 88 *Ferns*
woodsman 85.8 *forester*
Wood's metal 57 *Alloys*
wood sorrel 84 *Flowers and Flowering Plants*
wood spirit 85.9 *tree product*
wood stove 408.6 *fire*
wood sugar 85.9 *tree product*
woodsy 85.16 *wooded*
wood tar 85.9 *tree product*
wood texture 47.12 *wood*
wood tick 82 *Arachnids*, 82.3 *pest*
wood-turned 47.15 *woodcrafted*
wood turning 47.8 *woodwork*
wood vinegar 85.9 *tree product*
wood warbler 85.11 *tree-related animal*
woodwasp 82 *Insects*, 85.11 *tree-related animal*
woodwind 49.25 *musical instrument*
wood woollyfoot 89 *Fungi*
woodwork 42 *Hobbies and Pastimes*, **47**
woodworker 646.2 *artisan*
woodworking 47.8 *woodwork*
woodworking tool 47
woodworm 82 *Insects*, 81.6 *worm*, 82.3 *pest*, 85.11 *tree-related animal*, 244.7 *agent of destruction*
woody 85, 69.17 *botanical*, 83.14 *of plants*, 378.3 *hard*, 410.10 *powered*
woody perennial 83.2 *plant*
woody plant 69.9 *garden plant*, 83.2 *plant*
woody tissue 85.3 *timber*
wooer 821.9 *lover*, 826.5 *courting person*

woof 288.3 *weaving*, 432.1 *animal cry*
wooing 712.1 *request*, 712.9 *requesting*, 821.6, 826.2 *courtship*, 826.9 *endearing*
wool 67 *Natural Fabrics*, 67.12 *natural*, 77.2 *mammalian characteristic*, 288.4 *textile*, 374.11 *soft thing*, 604.1 *materials*
Woolf 48 *Writers*
woolgather 468.12 *be inattentive*
woolgatherer 468.6 *inattentive person*
woolgathering 462.6 *daydream*, 468.3 *absent-mindedness*, 468.8 *absent-minded*
woollen 67.12 *natural*, 288.6 *interwoven*
woolliness 374.9 *smoothness*
woolly 67.12 *natural*, 288.6 *interwoven*, 295.13 *sweater*, 374.3 *smooth*, 375.3 *barbed*, 376.1 *smooth*, 383.8 *rough*
woolly aphid 69.12 *pests and diseases*
woolly bear 82.5 *larva*
woolly hat 295.15 *headgear*
woolly mammoth 202.8 *prehistoric animal*
woolly monkey 77 *Placental Mammals*
woolly rhinoceros 77 *Placental Mammals*
woolly spider monkey 77 *Placental Mammals*
woolsack 16.18 *tribunal*, 16.27 *courtroom*
woomera 680.6 *historical missile weapon*
woopies 207.10 *the old*
wooziness 874.10 *drunkenness*
woozy 404.10 *sleepy*, 874.2 *slightly drunk*
wop 91 *Names for Inhabitants*
Worcester 93 *Cities*, **93** *Cities*
Worcester porcelain 44 *Types of Ceramics*
Worcester sauce 45.15 *sauce*, 351.8 *mixed drink*
Worcestershire sauce 413.2 *seasoning*
word 5, 5, 543, 143.2 *particular*, 528.1 *information*, 528.7 *advice*, 535.2 *statement*, 535.3 *vow*, 549.9 *style*, 564.7 *utterance*, 636.1 *warning*, 654.1 *advice*, 692.1 *command*, 718.2 *promise*, 887.7 *commitment*
Word 65.11 *application*
word association 61.27 *association of ideas*
word-association test 61.5 *psychological test*
wordbook 5.28 *dictionary*
word-coiner 5.2 *linguist*
worded 5, 549.6 *styled*
word form 5.17 *word*, 306.3 *kind*
word for word 118.14 *imitatively*, 503.8 *accurately*, 520.13 *meaningfully*, 537.38 *literally*, 619.7 *perfectly*
word-for-word 5.40 *translated*, 5.48 *linguistically*, 524.17 *translational*, 537.23 *literal*
word-for-word translation 5.12, 524.4 *translation*, 537.10 *literalness*
word game 42.1 *game*
wordily 5.50 *lexically*
wordiness 5.22 *many words*, 553.1 *diffuseness*, 564.2 *power of speech*, 565.1 *talkativeness*
wording 5.24 *phrasing*, 5.42 *worded*, 549.4 *literary style*
word in one's ear 420.8 *something heard*
word in the ear 528.7 *advice*, 636.1 *warning*, 654.1 *advice*
wordless 422.3 *silent*, 786.7 *wide-eyed*
wordlessness 422.4 *silence*
word list 171.3 *dictionary*
word magic 549.4 *literary style*
word of advice 654.1 *advice*
word of a gentleman 535.3 *vow*
word of command 543.6 *word*, 676.8 *warfare*

work with 180.14 *keep company with*

work without pay 644.1 *work*, 710.11 *volunteer*

work wonders 617.10 *do good*, 642.15 *try*, 682.6 *be successful*, 786.11 *do wonders*

work wood 47

world 53.3 *universe*, 142.2 *whole thing*

world atlas 547.7 *map*

World Bank 13.4 *economic development*, 732.4 *lending institution*, 741.7 *finance*

world-beater 126.6 *paragon*, 617.8 *exceller*, 682.5 *victorious person*

world-beating 126.14, 617.2 *best*, 682.15 *victorious*

World Bowl 19.1 *football*

World Boxing Association 26.2 *boxing*

world champion 26.4 *boxer*, 26.14 *combat*, 655.4 *skilled person*, 682.5 *victorious person*, 786.5 *person of wonder*

world champions 22.1 *baseball*

World Championship points 33.1 *motor racing*

World Cup 38.1 *soccer*

world fair 740.2 *fair*

World Federation of Trade Unions 15.3 *organized labour*

World Games 21.5 *competition*

world government 12.1 *government*

World Grand Prix of Cross-country Skiers 41.2 *cross-country skiing*

world-hater 834.2 *misanthrope*

worldliness 367.2 *materialization*, 860.1 *selfishness*

worldly 367.7 *material*, 501.9 *literate*, 860.4 *selfish*

worldly goods 725.4 *possessions*

worldly man 401.7 *libertine*

worldly wisdom 655.1 *skill*

world map 299.4, 547.7 *map*

world music 49

world of 181.4 *throng*

World of Art group 50 Schools and Groups of Artists

world of experience 367.1 *material world*

world of finance 14.1, 741.7 *finance*

world of nature 367.1 *material world*

world of spirits 368.3 *spiritual world*, 397.14 *the spiritual world*

world picture 142.3 *whole situation*

world price 751.1 *price*

world's end 263.3 *distant place*

World Series 22.1 *baseball*

world-shattering 233.11 *influential*, 611.5 *important*, 611.6 *notable*

worlds of 181.4 *throng*

world soul 8.3 *God*

World Team Racing Championship 36.1 *sailing*

World Trade Center 43 Noted Buildings

World Trade Center twin towers 285.2 *parallel thing*

world view 4.2 *philosophical system*, 142.3 *whole situation*, 164.7 *global view*

world war 676.1 *war*

World War I 17 Major Wars

World War II 17 Major Wars

world-weariness 788.1 *boredom*

world-weary 788.4 *boring*, 788.5 *bored*

worldwide 142.6 *whole*, 146.7 *including*, 164.16 *universal*, 248.12 *extensive*, 482.4 *wholesale*

world without end 190.11 *eternally*

worm 81, 20.1 *angling*, 68.18 *practise livestock farming*, 76.4 *type of animal*, 127.6 *inferior*, 624.6 *infection*

worm-eaten 628.13 *dilapidated*

worm gear 63.7 *gear*, 364.6 *rotator*

worm grass 87 Grasses

wormlike 81

wormlike invertebrate 81.6 *worm*

worm lizard 79 Reptiles

worm oneself into 808.9 *fawn*

worm oneself into the affections 821.28 *win the love of*

worm one's way in 356.10 *enter*

worm out 355.15 *draw out*, 496.2 *detect*

worms 777 Phobias by Topic, 624.18 *veterinary disease*

Worms 93 Cities

worm's-eye view 435.9 *viewpoint*

worm shell 81 Molluscs

wormwood 84 Flowers and Flowering Plants, 413.5 *herbs*, 415.3 *sour thing*, 618.11 *harmfulness*, 631.4 *strain*

Wormwood Scrubs 702.1 *prison*

worn 131.7 *reduced*, 238.9 *dilapidated*, 381.1 *blunt*, 526.13 *displayed*, 599.9 *used*, 628.13 *dilapidated*, 650.1 *fatigued*

worn away 458.7 *disappeared*

worn clothes 295.1 *dress*

worn out 236.12 *impotent*, 238.9 *dilapidated*, 238.11 *weakened*, 599.9 *used*, 600.4 *disused*, 614.1 *useless*, 628.12 *deteriorated*, 628.13 *dilapidated*, 650.1 *fatigued*

worn to a frazzle 628.13 *dilapidated*, 650.1 *fatigued*

worn to a fritter 628.13 *dilapidated*

worn to a shadow 274.2 *emaciated*, 628.13 *dilapidated*

worn to the threads 628.13 *dilapidated*

worried 777, 153.12 *disturbed*, 491.3 *confused*, 659.16 *troubled*

worrier 491.17 *uncertain person*

worries 687.1 *adversity*

worrisome 659.13 *inconvenient*

worry 777, 777, 153.1 *disturbance*, 153.7 *disturb*, 350.21 *eat*, 366.22 *agitate*, 491.20 *make uncertain*, 631.4 *strain*, 631.14 *afflict*, 659.4 *problem*, 659.23 *cause difficulties*, 687.1 *adversity*

worrying 153.17 *disturbing*, 491.3 *confused*, 659.13 *inconvenient*

worryingly 153.18 *disturbingly*, 491.24 *confusingly*

worse 628, 216.11 *changeable*, 362.17 *lowered*, 628.12 *deteriorated*

worse alternative 222.1 *substitution*

worse and worse 628.12 *deteriorated*

worse element 143.1 *part*

worsen 127.11 *become inferior*, 216.8 *cause change*, 362.1 *lower*, 628.1 *deteriorate*, 628.3 *make worse*, 768.6 *aggravate*, 768.7 *become aggravated*

worsened 628.12 *deteriorated*, 768.4 *aggravated*

worsening 127.2 *deficiency*, 362.11 *lowering*, 628.7 *deterioration*, 628.12 *deteriorated*, 768.1 *aggravation*

worship 9, 9, 7.19 *be religious*, 10.1 *ritual*, 694.3 *obeisance*, 694.6 *show obeisance to*, 719.5 *observe religious ceremony*, 821.1, 821.23 *love*, 849.2 *admiration*, 849.16 *revere*

Worship 9

worship freely 698.14 *be free*

worshipful 9, 804, 7.15 *religious*, 849.10 *reverent*

worshipfully 9, 7.23 *religiously*, 10.23 *ritually*, 849.22 *respectfully*

worship idols 9.8 *idolatrize*

worshipped 9

worshipper 9, 10, 7.3 *religious person*, 497.5 *believer*, 729.4 *giver*, 782.6 *desirer*

worshipping 10, 9.9 *worshipful*, 694.9 *obeisant*, 849.10 *reverent*

worship the almighty dollar 742.14 *seek riches*

worship the golden calf 742.14 *seek riches*

worship the ground one walks on 849.16 *revere*

worsted 67 Natural Fabrics, 127.18 *outclassed*

worst intention 832.1 *malevolence*

worst luck 589.2 *luck*

wort 83.2 *plant*

worth 617, 863, 520.5 *point*, 611.1 *importance*, 613.6 *usability*, 751.2 *value*, 751.14 *priced*, 753.6 *value*, 861.8 *good*

Worth 617

worth a bundle 742.1 *wealthy*

worth a fortune 753.8 *valuable*

worth a king's ransom 617.3, 753.8 *valuable*

worth a lot 742.1 *wealthy*

worth a million 613.4 *profitable*, 617.3 *valuable*

worth a mint 613.4 *profitable*, 617.3 *valuable*, 742.1 *wealthy*

worth a packet 742.1 *wealthy*

worth a pretty penny 753.8 *valuable*

worth buying 738.13 *bought*

worth choosing 580.15 *chosen*

worth considering 611.5 *important*

worthily 617, 863, 485.17 *capably*, 805.33 *with dignity*

worth imitating 617.1 *worthy*

worthiness 805, 485.1 *qualification*, 617.6 *worth*, 861.8 *good*, 863.3 *worth*

worth its weight in gold 617.3, 753.8 *valuable*

worthless 618, 127.14 *poor*, 236.10 *powerless*, 521.11 *aimless*, 607.9 *waste*, 612.4 *trivial*, 614.1 *useless*, 620.1 *imperfect*, 628.12 *deteriorated*, 754.10 *shoddy*, 776.7 *futile*, 850.12 *disregardful*, 858.5 *dishonourable*, 862.7 *evil*, 864.11 *wicked*

worthlessly 618, 127.20 *insignificantly*, 236.14 *powerlessly*, 858.11 *dishonourably*

worthlessness 618, 127.4 *poor quality*, 521.2 *aimlessness*, 612.7 *triviality*, 614.3 *uselessness*, 620.5 *imperfection*, 858.1 *improbity*, 862.1 *evil*

Worthlessness 618

worth millions 721.17 *well-off*, 742.1 *wealthy*

worth one's keep 613.4 *profitable*

worth one's salt 613.4 *profitable*

worth one's weight in gold 613.4 *profitable*

worth watching 435.23 *visible*

worthwhile 617, 243.11 *productive*, 611.5 *important*, 613.4 *profitable*, 621.1 *convenient*, 682.14 *rewarding*, 708.7 *permitted*, 746.18 *profitable*, 782.8 *desirable*, 851.22 *approvable*, 861.6 *beneficial*

worthwhileness 861.13 *benefit*

worthy 617, 863, 485.9 *qualified*, 782.8 *desirable*, 804.5 *entitled*, 805.19 *stately*, 845.8 *entitled*, 845.9 *meritorious*, 849.13 *respectable*, 851.21 *praiseworthy*, 861.1 *good*

worthy aim 655.9 *meritorious*

worthy cause 226.6 *undertaking*, 833.5 *charity*

worthy of 845.9 *meritorious*

worthy of discussion 472.8 *problematic*

Wotan 8 Deities, 676.3 *god of war*

Wotton 48 Poets

would-be 588.11 *intending*, 782.9 *desirous*

would like 580.2 *prefer*

would rather 580.2 *prefer*

wound 160.4 *interruption*, 238.7 *weaken*, 406.3 *injury*, 406.11 *inflict pain*, 618.14 *ill-treat*, 628.5, 628.11 *hurt*, 828.9 *of-*

fend, 862.2 *affliction*, 862.11 *be evil*

wounded 406.6 *injured*, 806.3 *humbled*, 862.8 *afflicted*

Wounded Knee 398.15 *slaughterhouse*

wounded pride 806.9 *humiliation*

wounding 806.6 *humiliating*

wound up 157.21 *ended*, 323.14 *closed down*, 684.8 *concluded*

woundwort 84 Flowers and Flowering Plants

woven 67, 135.15 *tied*, 288.6 *interwoven*, 383.7 *textural*

woven cloth 288.4 *textile*

woven fabric 67.3 *fabric*

woven through 135.12 *united*

wow 434.5 *atmospheric dissonance*, 617.8 *exceller*, 682.3 *successful thing*, 682.4 *successful person*, 786.5 *person of wonder*, 786.14 *wonderful*

wowser 134.5 *pure person*, 876.6 *moralist*

WPC 632.3 *protector*

WRAC 679.10 *woman soldier*

wrack 90 Algae, 90.1 *alga*, 244.4 *ruin*

WRAF 679.10 *woman soldier*

wraith 11.11 *ghost*, 102.2 *illusion*, 274.9 *thin person*, 435.5 *imagination*

wraithlike 11.18 *spiritual*, 274.2 *emaciated*

wraithy 11.18 *spiritual*

Wran 74.7 *nautical person*, 679.27 *naval man*

Wrangel 98 Islands

wrangle 68.18 *practise livestock farming*, 117.4 *disagreement*, 117.14 *disagree*, 473.1 *argument*, 473.13 *argue*, 666.2 *argument*, 666.5 *disagree*, 666.6 *argue*, 674.1 *contention*, 679.40 *argue*, 764.8, 764.11 *quarrel*

wrangler 68.16 *farm worker*, 463.6, 473.6 *arguer*, 679.5 *arguer*, 764.9 *unpleasant person*

wrangling 117.4 *disagreement*, 117.10 *disagreeing*, 473.7 *arguing*, 666.1 *disagreement*, 666.9 *disagreeing*, 716.1 *negotiation*, 716.8 *negotiated*, 858.5 *dishonourable*

wrap 293, 301, 135.10 *link*, 161.38 *group*, 258.21 *put in a container*, 295.25 *accessories*, 295.32 *dress*, 320.9 *enfold*, 457.14 *present*, 632.9 *protect*

wrapped 161.49 *grouped*, 258.20 *containing*, 293.37 *protected*, 295.29 *dressed*, 297.5 *surrounded*

wrapped up 161.49 *grouped*, 684.7 *completed*

wrapped up in oneself 860.5 *egoistic*

wrapper 301, 258.5 *packet*, 293.4 *wrapping*, 295.4 *informal dress*, 295.16 *robe*, 814.6 *informal dress*

wrapping 293, 258.20 *containing*, 293.1 *covering*, 301.4 *wrapper*, 320.3 *enfoldment*

wrapping paper 293.4 *wrapping*, 301.4 *wrapper*, 604.3 *paper*

wrap round 293.25 *wrap*

wraparound skirt 301.4 *wrapper*

wrap up 144.4 *complete*, 157.15 *end*, 293.25 *wrap*, 531.8 *conceal*

wrap up in clean linen 457.14 *present*

wrasse 80 Fishes

wrath 822.5, 828.4 *anger*

wrathful 822.13, 828.16 *angry*

wrathfully 828.18 *angrily*

wrathfulness 828.4 *anger*

wreak havoc 244.10 *lay waste*, 670.9 *attack successfully*

wreak havoc on 862.11 *be evil*

wreak one's malice on 618.14 *ill-treat*

wreak one's spite 832.16 *be malevolent*

wreath 84.1 *flower*, 288.2 *braid*, 313.3 *circular thing*, 399.4 *funeral objects*, 544.4 *insignia*,

544.8 *heraldic device*, 588.6 *objective*, 681.1 *trophy*
wreathe 792.10 *decorate*, 792.12 *honour*, 817.12 *greet*
wreathed 288.6 *interwoven*
wreck 74.10 *sail*, 141.4 *deconstruct*, 216.8 *cause change*, 244.4 *ruin*, 244.9 *demolish*, 244.11 *ruin*, 607.4 *destruction*, 628.4 *impair*, 628.9 *dilapidation*, 877.19 *corrupt*
wreckage 132.1 *remainder*, 244.4 *ruin*
wrecked 244.15 *destroyed*
wrecker 244.6 *destroyer*, 635.2 *troublemaker*, 736.9 *plunderer*, 832.8 *malefactor*
wreckfish 80 *Fishes*
wreck one's chances 211.6 *lose one's chance*
wren 78 Birds, 78.6 *songbird*
Wren 74.7 *nautical person*, 679.10 *woman soldier*, 679.27 *naval man*
wren babbler 78 Birds
wrench 136.9 *separate*, 241.3 *instance of violence*, 241.8 *use violence*, 330.1 *impel*, 339.3 *jerk*, 339.13 *pull at*, 355.1 *extraction*, 355.6 *extorsion*, 355.10 *excavator*, 355.16 *extort*, 525.1 *misinterpret*, 603.1 *tool*, 603.9 *use tools*, 726.3 *tools for gripping*
wrenching 355.6 *extorsion*, 525.2 *misinterpretation*
wrenching out 355.1 *extraction*
wrench out 355.11 *extract*
wrest 355.6 *extorsion*, 355.16 *extort*
wrested 252.9 *removed*
wresting 355.6 *extorsion*
wresting out 355.1 *extraction*
wrestle 26, 26.5, 674.8 *wrestling*, 674.11 *contend*, 679.37 *fight*
wrestle freestyle 26.12 *wrestle*
wrestler 26, 237.5 *athlete*, 674.10 *contender*, 679.3 *athlete*
wrestling 18 *Sporting Activities*, **26**, **26**, **674**, 25.9 *bowls*, 26.1 *combat sports*
wrestling hold 26.5 *wrestling*
wrestling match 26.5, 674.8 *wrestling*
wrestling ring 26.5 *wrestling*
wrestling shot 25.2 *grip*
wrestling toucher 25.2 *grip*
wrestling weight divisions 26.5 *wrestling*
wrest out 355.11 *extract*
wretch 770.3 *sad person*
wretched 612.2 *obscure*, 618.4 *poor*, 770.5 *sad*, 774.4 *lamenting*, 862.7 *evil*
wretchedness 612.6 *obscurity*, 618.10 *poverty*, 687.1 *adversity*, 770.1 *sorrow*, 774.1 *lamentation*, 862.1 *evil*
Wrexham 93 *Cities*
wriggle 314.2 *coil*, 314.6 *convolute*, 366.7, 366.24 *shake*, 657.5 *be cunning*
wriggling 314.4 *convolutional*, 366.18 *shaky*
wriggly 366.18 *shaky*
wright 646.2 *artisan*
Wright 48 *Writers*, **52** *Scientists*
wring 355.6 *extorsion*, 355.16 *extort*, 392.23 *drip-dry*, 406.11 *inflict pain*, 621.13 *clean*
wringer 355.9 *extractor*, 376.9 *smoother*, 392.15 *dryer*
wring from 695.7 *force*
wringing 355.6 *extorsion*, 389.23 *wet*
wringing hands 543.3 *gesture*
wringing wet 389.23 *wet*
wring one's hands 236.6 *be powerless*, 543.11 *gesture*
wring out 355.12 *displace*, 621.13 *clean*
wring the neck of 398.17 *murder*
wrinkle 321, 321, 207.17 *age*, 262.5 *make smaller*, 262.6 *become smaller*, 320.2, 320.8 *pleat*, 375.12 *make rough*, 383.14 *go against the grain*,

539.8 *trick*, 628.1 *deteriorate*, 628.5 *hurt*, 657.2 *stratagem*
wrinkled 207.14 *aged*, 262.7 *smaller*, 321.5 *wrinkly*, 375.1 *rough*
wrinkleproofing 67.8 *fabric treatment*
wrinklies 202.2 *old people*
wrinkliness 375.6 *roughness*
wrinkling 262.1 *contraction*
wrinkly 321, 207.7 *older person*, 375.1 *rough*
wrist 135.5 *joint*
wristband 295.25 *accessories*, 313.3 *circular thing*
wrist bandage 30.2 *gymnastic clothing*
wristbone 382 Bones
wristwatch 191 Timepieces and Timers, 192.7 *watch*
writ 16.6 *legal process*, 16.33 *litigation*, 654.3 *precept*, 692.2 *demand*, 703.3 *authority*
write 48, 5.45 *use language*, 49.35 *compose*, 51.36 *dramatize*, 65.19 *abort*, 243.10 *produce*, 519.14 *imagine*, 532.15 *publish*, 533.13 *report*, 534.30 *communicate*, 534.31 *correspond*, 545.14 *inscribe*
write a bestseller 682.6 *be successful*
write about 561.4 *dissertate*
write a cheque 741.26 *bank*
write a column 524.13 *interpret news*
write a leader 524.13 *interpret news*
write a lyric 48.21 *write*
write an account of 560.15 *recount*
write an editorial 524.13 *interpret news*
write a portrait of 519.14 *imagine*
write a purple patch 541.7 *exaggerate*
write a sonnet 48.21 *write*
write a story about 560.15 *recount*
write a thesis 535.17 *affirm*
write a treatise on 561.4 *dissertate*
write bawdy poems 827.5 *curse*
write down 171.8 *list*, 545.14 *inscribe*, 750.7 *account*
write-enabled 65.20 *on-line*
write for the layman 522.5 *simplify*
write in a let-out clause 716.6 *make conditions*
write in letters of gold 611.8 *make important*
write into 525.1 *misinterpret*
write notes for 524.10 *annotate*
write off 125.5 *counterbalance*, 598.1 *relinquish*, 600.6 *stop using*, 704.6 *cancel*, 747.10 *forgive a debt*, 776.9 *be hopeless*
write-off 244.4 *ruin*, 704.1 *cancellation*, 745.5 *amount owing*, 776.2 *hopeless situation*
write off accounts 750.9 *settle accounts*
write one's memoirs 511.12 *remember*
write one's name 544.11 *identify oneself*
write one's signature 544.11 *identify oneself*
write over 546.1 *obliterate*
writer 5.2 *linguist*, 48.14 *author*, 243.9 *producer*, 532.12 *publisher*, 545.9 *recorder*, 560.10 *descriptive writer*, 561.3 *dissertator*, 646.1 *worker*
write ring 65.17 *computing term*
write up 532.15 *publish*, 750.7 *account*
write-up 532.3 *journalism*, 561.2 *article*
write well 558.4 *be elegant*
writhe 314.6 *convolute*, 366.21 *be agitated*, 406.9 *feel pain*
writhing 406.7 *feeling pain*
writing 777 Phobias by Topic, 5.13 *letter*, 48.1 *literature*, 243.1 *production*, 534.1 *commu-*

nications, 545.3 *notes*, 545.8 *registration*, 547.1 *representation*
writing desk 47.4 *table*, 258.3 *cabinet*
writing on the wall 517.5 *omen*, 636.2 *danger signal*
writing over 546.3 *obliteration*
writing paper 604.3 *paper*
writing table 47.4 *table*
writ of summons 692.2 *demand*
written 5.39 *of language*, 48.16 *literary*, 534.34 *communicated*
written acknowledgement of payment 749.1 *receipt*
written all over one for all to see 526.14 *manifest*
written authority 692.4 *authorization*, 703.3 *authority*
written character 5.13 *letter*
written constitution 16.1 *the law*, 225.4 *stable thing*
written discharge 746.1 *payment*
written down 545.16 *recorded*
written guarantee 714.2 *guarantee*
written in stone 225.9 *stable*
written language 5.6 *official language*
written law 16.1 *the law*
written letter 5.13 *letter*
written music 49
written off 125.10 *counterbalancing*, 600.4 *disused*
written order 654.3 *precept*
written permission 708.2 *permit*
written reply 478.2 *acknowledgment*
written statement 16.5 *litigation*, 535.4 *confirmation*
written terms 716.2 *basis for negotiations*
written unit 5.17 *word*
Wroclaw 93 *Cities*
wrong 844, 844, 844, 16.39 *crime*, 16.58 *unjust*, 117.11 *unfit*, 476.13 *no*, 493.7 *misjudging*, 493.9 *misjudged*, 504.15 *erroneous*, 504.17 *mistaken*, 525.3 *misinterpreted*, 548.6 *misrepresented*, 616.1 *inconvenient*, 616.3 *inconvenience*, 618.3 *bad*, 618.9 *badness*, 618.14 *ill-treat*, 828.2 *offence*, 844.7 *sense of wrong*, 844.8 *wrong-doing*, 862.1, 862.7 *evil*, 862.11 *be evil*, 862.12 *evilly*, 864.1 *wickedness*, 864.11 *wicked*, 866.3 *sin*, 877.1 *immorality*, 877.11 *immoral*
Wrong 844
wrong association 108.5 *misconnection*
wrong conviction 16.4 *bad law*
wrong course 335.13 *deviation*
wrong date 193.1 *wrong time*, 197.1 *different time*
wrong day 193.1 *wrong time*
wrongdoer 844, 16.40 *lawbreaker*, 832.8 *malefactor*, 862.6 *evil person*, 864.9 *wicked person*, 866.4 *guilty person*
wrongdoing 844, 16.39 *crime*, 504.7 *errancy*, 640.2 *deed*, 864.1 *wickedness*, 864.11 *wicked*, 866.3 *sin*, 877.1 *immorality*
wrong end of the stick 493.1 *misjudgment*, 525.2 *misinterpretation*
wrong execution 16.4 *bad law*
wrong explanation 525.2 *misinterpretation*
wrongful 16.58 *unjust*, 618.3 *bad*, 844.11 *wrong*
wrongfully 844.25 *wrongly*
wrongfulness 618.9 *badness*
wrong-headed 493.7 *misjudging*
wrong-headedness 577.5 *obstinacy*
wrong impression 493.1 *misjudgment*
wrong instruction 525.2 *misinterpretation*
wrong interpretation 525.2 *misinterpretation*
wrong in the head 844.14 *abnormal*

wrongly 504, 844, 16.82 *illegally*, 117.17 *unsuitably*, 493.13 *misguidedly*, 525.4 *mistakenly*, 548.8 *unrepresentatively*, 601.6 *abusively*, 618.15 *worthlessly*, 862.12 *evilly*, 864.18 *wickedly*
wrongly accused 493.9 *misjudged*
wrongly dated 193.4 *mistimed*
wrongly timed 616.1 *inconvenient*
wrongness 117.5 *unfitness*, 504.3 *erroneousness*, 616.3 *inconvenience*, 844.1 *unfairness*, 862.1 *evil*
wrong no-one 865.8 *be innocent*
wrong note 434.3 *musical dissonance*
wrongous 16.58 *unjust*
wrong place 252.6 *misplacement*
wrong reference 108.5 *misconnection*
wrong side of forty 207.4 *middle age*
wrong side of the tracks 249.10 *urban area*
wrong side out 221.13 *reversibly*
wrong time 193, 197.1 *different time*, 211.1 *untimeliness*
Wrong Time 193
wrong turning 504.1 *mistake*
wrong'un 539.9 *sleight of hand*, 864.10 *bad person*
wrong use 599.6 *use*, 601.2 *misuse*
wrong verdict 16.4 *bad law*
wrong way 337.25 *reversed*
wrong way in 287.2 *inverted*
wrong way out 287.2 *inverted*
wrong way round 337.25 *reversed*
wrong words 525.2 *misinterpretation*
wrought 594.20 *developed*
wrought iron 57 Alloys, 63.25 *construction material*, 373.7 *hard substance*
wrought-iron 373.1 *hard*
wrought-up 828.15 *resentful*
wrybill 78 Birds
wry face 830.4 *sign of irritableness*
wryneck 78 Birds
Wuhan 93 *Cities*
wulfenite 54 *Minerals*
Wurlitzer 49 *Musical Instruments*
Württemberg 32 *Breeds of Horse and Pony*
Wurtz reaction 57 *Named Reactions*
Wyandotte 68 *Breeds of Fowl*
Wyatt 48 *Poets*
wych-elm 85 *Trees and Shrubs*
Wycherley 48 *Dramatists*
Wye 96 *Rivers*
Wyfold Cup 36.5 *Henley trophies*
wynd 327.3 *road*
Wyoming 92 *American States*
wysiwyg 65.17 *computing term*
wyvern 76.7 *legendary beast*

X

X 529.8 *anonymity*, 531.7 *concealer*
xanthene 452.7 *yellow pigment*
xanthine dye 67.6 *dye*
xanthophyll 58.18 *pigment*, 90.3 *plant body*, 452.7 *yellow pigment*
Xanthophyta 90.2 *algae*
xanthophyte 90.2 *algae*
xanthous 452.2 *yellowish*
x-block 26.9 *tae kwon do*
X chromosome 59.14 *chromosome*
xebec 74 *Sailing Ships and Boats*
xenobiology 59.1 *life science*
xenolith 54.28 *rock*, 149.1 *foreign body*
xenolithic 149.11 *foreign*
xenolithically 149.18 *extraneously*
xenon 57 *Chemical Elements*
Xenophanes 48 *Poets*
Xenophanes of Colophon 4 *Philosophers*

xenophobe 91.14 *nationalist*, 481.7 *bigot*, 493.5 *misjudging person*, 820.5 *hostile person*, 822.9 *hater*

xenophobia 777 Phobias by Name, 91.4 *nationalism*, 147.4 *exclusiveness*, 481.4 *social discrimination*, 493.3 *injustice*, 785.1 *dislike*, 805.11 *prejudice*, 822.3 *race hatred*

xenophobic 147.10 *excluding*, 481.10 *discriminatory*, 493.8 *unjust*, 805.23 *prejudiced*, 820.7 *intolerant*, 822.11 *racist*

xenophobically 481.17 *prejudicially*

Xenopus 79 Amphibians

xerically 392.24 *drily*

xeroderma 392.16 *dry skin*

Xerography 66.2 *photoreproduction*

xeromorphic 392.7 *adapted to drought*

xerophilous 392.7 *adapted to drought*

xerophthalmia 58.14 *vitamin deficiency disease*, 392.16 *dry skin*

xerophyte 83.2 *plant*

xerophytic 83.14 *of plants*, 392.7 *adapted to drought*

xerophytically 83.24 *herbaceously*, 392.24 *drily*

xerostomia 392.12 *thirst*

Xerox 66.7 *photocopy*, 110.4, 110.9 *duplicate*, 114.12 *imitate*, 118.5 *duplicate*, 245.1 *reproduction*, 245.9 *reproduce*, 545.5 *copy*, 547.2 *reproduction*, 560.9 *representation*

Xerox copy 545.5 *copy*

Xeroxed 110.15 *duplicate*

Xerox machine 114.3 *copier*

Xhosa 1 Peoples, 5 Languages and Groups of Languages, 7 Non-Christian Religions

Xi An 93 Cities

Xilonen 8 Deities

Xipe 8 Deities

Xiuhtecuhtli 8 Deities

Xochiquetzal 8 Deities

XPS 57.17 *analysis*

X-rated 296.11 *exposed*, 618.4 *poor*

X-rated film 296.3 *pornography*

X-rated movie 709.2 *censorship*, 877.2 *indecency*

X-ray 534 Phonetic Alphabet, 60.7 *diagnosis*, 60.19 *practise medicine*, 66.3 *photograph*, 547.9 *represent*

X-ray astronomy 53.1 *astronomy*

X-ray binary 53.9 *constellation*

X-ray crystallography 57.4 *crystal*

X-ray eye 435.2 *eye*

X-ray film 66.9 *film*

x-rays 437.7 *that which makes visible*

X-rays 56.13 *electromagnetic radiation*, 56.70 *radioactivity*

X-ray satellite 53.32 *satellite*

X-ray spectroscopy 57.17 *analysis*

X-ray spectrum 56.68 *emission*

X-ray telescope 53.26 *radio telescope*

x-unit 75 Scientific and Technical Units

xylem 83.5 *stem*

xylene 57 Common Chemical Compounds

xylograph 47.8 *woodwork*

xylographer 47.13 *carpenter*

xylographic 47.15 *woodcrafted*

xylography 47.8 *woodwork*, 50.15 *engraving*

xylometazoline 62 Medication

xylon 58.4 *polysaccharide*

xylophone 49 Musical Instruments

xylopyrographer 47.13 *carpenter*

xylopyrographic 47.15 *woodcrafted*

xylopyrography 47.8 *woodwork*

xylorimba 49 Musical Instruments

xylose 58 Common Sugars

x-y plotter 65.7 *peripheral*

Y

Yacatecutli 8 Deities

yacht 74 Sailing Ships and Boats, 36.2 *sailing boat*, 74.3 *vessel*

yacht class 36.2 *sailing boat*

yacht designer 36.9 *sailor*

yachting 36.1, 36.10 *sailing*, 74.11 *nautical*

yachting association 36.1 *sailing*

yacht race 36.1 *sailing*

yacht racing 18 Sporting Activities, 36.1 *sailing*, 674.4 *race*

yachtsman 36.9 *sailor*, 74.8 *boatman*

yacht tender 36.2 *sailing boat*

yackety-yak 521.5 *empty talk*, 521.9 *talk nonsense*

Yaghuth 8 Deities

Yagi antenna 534.17 *antenna*

YAG laser 56.26 *laser*

yahoo 818.4 *discourteous person*

yahrzeit 10.4 *public worship*

Yahtzee 42.5 *dice*

Yahweh 8.3 *God*

Yahwistic 8.13 *divine*

Yahwistically 8.19 *divinely*

Yajurveda 7.12 *religious text*

yak 77 Placental Mammals, 565.3 *talk*

yakkety-yak 564.1 *faculty of speech*, 565.3 *talk*, 565.12 *rhubarb rhubarb*

yakking 564.1 *faculty of speech*, 565.6 *effusive*

Yakut 5 Languages and Groups of Languages, 32 Breeds of Horse and Pony

Yakutsk 93 Cities

yak yak 565.12 *rhubarb rhubarb*

Yale key 137.8 *fastening*

Yale lock 137.8 *fastening*

Yalta 93 Cities

yam 45 Vegetables

Yama 8 Deities

Yamm 8 Deities

yammer 431.13 *cry*, 521.5 *empty talk*, 521.9 *talk nonsense*

Yanauluha 8 Deities

yang 407.3 *press*

yangchin 49 Musical Instruments

Yangtze 96 Rivers

yangum 49 Musical Instruments

yank 339.3 *jerk*, 339.13 *pull at*, 407.11 *touch*

Yank 91 Names for Inhabitants, 91.7 *United States* , 255.10 *US inhabitant*

Yankee 534 Phonetic Alphabet, 91.7 *United States* , 255.10 *US inhabitant*

Yankeeland 249.8 *regions of the US*

Yankee polka 41.7 *ice-dancing*

yan tan tethera 170.3 *count*

Yaoundé 93 Cities

yap 432.1 *animal cry*, 432.4 *cry*

yapok 77 Marsupials

Yarborough 42.3 *card game terms*

yard 75 General Units, 36.3 *parts of a sailing boat*, 68.7 *farm building*, 72.8 *railway station*, 179.10 *thousand*, 269.7 *measure of length*, 301.2 *enclosed place*, 322.8 *open space*, 647.1 *workshop*

yardage 19.14 *miscellaneous terms*, 269.4 *length*

yardbird 702.5 *prisoner*

yard marker 19.4 *stadium*

yard-on 25.2 *grip*, 25.9 *bowls*

yard sale 754.7 *discounter*

yardstick 124.4 *average*, 154.4 *precedent*, 170.5 *computer*, 268.6 *measuring instrument*, 268.7 *standard*

Yare 96 Rivers

yarmulke 7.11 *vestment*

yarn 67.1 *fibre*, 364.9 *roll*, 383.6 *fibre*, 538.4 *lie*, 541.5 *tall story*,

560.3 *narration*, 604.1 *materials*, 771.5 *joke*

yarner 539.16 *liar*

yarn-spinner 538.11, 539.16 *liar*

yarran 85 Trees and Shrubs

yarrow 84 Flowers and Flowering Plants

yashmak 295.15 *headgear*, 438.6 *that which makes invisible*

yassa 45.53 *African dish*

yataghan 680.8 *sharp weapon*

yaupon 85 Trees and Shrubs

Yavapai 1 Peoples

yaw 74.9 *navigate*, 224.11 *be changeable*, 335.1 *deviate*, 335.15 *deviating motion*

yawing 73.5 *flight*, 74.11 *nautical*

yawl 74 Ships and Boats, 74 Sailing Ships and Boats, 36.2 *sailing boat*, 430.4 *be strident*, 431.1 *cry*, 431.10 *cry out*, 432.4 *cry*

yawling 432.1 *animal cry*

yawn 277.14 *deepen*, 643.13 *sleep*, 650.5 *be fatigued*, 783.12 *be indifferent*

yawning 277.8 *deep*, 643.4 *not awake*, 650.1 *fatigued*

yawn-making 183.13 *monotonous*

yawp 430.1 *stridency* , 430.4 *be strident*, 431.10 *cry out*, 432.1 *animal cry*, 432.4 *cry*

yaws 624.7 *tropical disease*, 624.13 *skin disease*

Y chromosome 59.14 *chromosome*

yea 499.2 *yes*, 580.10 *vote*

yeah 499.2 *yes*

yeanling 77.19 *young mammal*

year 163.6 *students*, 185.4 *term*, 187.2 *time period*, 269.8 *measure of time*

year after year 183.23 *repeatedly*

yearbook 171.3 *dictionary*, 528.5 *reference book*, 605.5 *collection*

year daemon 8.5 *deity*

year-group 163.6 *students*

year in year out 183.23 *repeatedly*

yearling 32.1 *horse*, 68.8 *livestock*, 206.4 *young animal*

yearly 110.17 *regular*, 110.20 *regularly*, 185.22 *periodic*, 187.8 *periodical*, 187.13 *for specified periods*, 214.12 *cyclic*, 214.13 *anniversary*, 214.16 *cyclically*

yearly cycle 214.2 *cycle*

yearn 775.7 *aspire*, 784.7 *like*

yearned for 782.7 *desired*

yearn for 609.6 *be unsatisfied*, 782.12 *desire*, 821.24 *be in love*

yearning 775.3 *aspiration*, 775.13 *aspirant*, 782.1 *desire*, 782.9 *desirous*, 784.1, 784.6 *liking*, 821.5 *desire*, 821.20 *amorous*

yearningly 784.11 *admiringly*

years 188.5 *long duration*

years ago 200.22 *in the past*

years gone by 200.1 *past time*

years of discretion 207.4 *middle age*

years on end 188.5 *long duration*

yeast 89 Fungi, 45.7 *basic ingredient*, 216.5 *changer*, 361.10 *elevator*, 370.8 *leavening*, 390.11 *aeration*

yeastiness 370.5 *lightness*

yeasty 89.9 *fungal*, 370.4 *leavening*, 390.18 *bubbly*

Yeats 48 Poets, 48 Dramatists

yegg 736.8 *thief*

yell 406.12 *express pain*, 423.8 *be loud*, 430.1 *stridency* , 430.4 *be strident*, 431.1 *cry*, 431.10 *cry out*, 564.12 *speak loudly*, 769.5, 769.8 *cheer*, 773.2 *fanfare*, 773.7 *dance*

yell at 785.6 *react against*

yeller 431.9 *crier*

yelling 423.2 *outcry*, 423.6 *loud*, 431.16 *vociferous*

yellow 452, 56.28, 56.28 *colour*, 238.12 *weak-willed*, 444.15 *colour*, 452.5 *cowardly*, 452.10 *make* **yellow**, 624.21 *un-*

healthy, 779.3 *cowardly*, 841.4 *jealous*, 875.6 *drug*

Yellow 96 Rivers, 97 Oceans and Seas, 96.5 *other major rivers*

yellow ball 24.5 *snooker*

yellow-bellied 779.3 *cowardly*

yellow-belly 452.9 *figurative usage*, 779.2 *coward*

yellow brass 57 Alloys

yellow-brown 449.1 *brown*

yellow cake 604.1 *materials*

yellow card 452.8 *yellow thing*

yellow colour 452.6 *yellowness*

yellow edge 69.12 *pests and diseases*

yellow-eyed 841.4 *jealous*

yellow-faced 452

yellow fever 452.6 *yellowness*, 624.7 *tropical disease*

yellowfin tuna 80 Fishes

yellow flag 544.7 *flag*, 636.2 *danger signal*

yellow-green 453.1 *green*

yellow-green algae 90.2 *algae*

yellow hair 452.6 *yellowness*

yellow-haired 452

yellowhammer 78 Birds, 452.8 *yellow thing*

yellowish 452, 445.7 *colourless*

yellowish-red 451.1 *orange*

yellow jacket 82 Insects, 82.4 *social insect*, 452.8 *yellow thing*, 875.6 *drug*

yellow journalism 452.9 *figurative usage*

Yellowknife 93 Cities

yellowlegs 78 Birds

yellow line 452.8 *yellow thing*

yellowly 452

yellow metal 452.8 *yellow thing*, 741.16 *bullion*

yellowness 452

Yellowness 452

yellow ochre 452.7 *yellow pigment*

Yellow Pages 171.3 *dictionary*, 452.8 *yellow thing*, 528.5 *reference book*, 532.9 *advertisement*, 534.11 *dialling*

yellow pepper 45 Vegetables

yellow perch 20.4 *American game fish*

yellow peril 452.9 *figurative usage*, 635.2 *troublemaker*

yellow pigment 452

yellow poplar 85 Trees and Shrubs

yellow press 452.9 *figurative usage*, 528.4 *mass communication*, 532.3 *journalism*, 533.5 *mass communication*

yellow rain 452.8 *yellow thing*

yellows 452.8 *yellow thing*

Yellow Sea 452.9 *figurative usage*

yellow skin 452.6 *yellowness*

yellow spot 452.8 *yellow thing*

Yellowstone 94 Lakes, 96 Rivers, 94.3 *US lakes*

Yellowstone National Park 452.9 *figurative usage*

yellow streak 452.9 *figurative usage*, 779.1 *cowardice*

yellow sunshine 452.8 *yellow thing*, 875.6 *drug*

yellowtail 80 Fishes, 20.4 *American game fish*, 452.8 *yellow thing*

yellow thing 452

yellowthroat 452.8 *yellow thing*

yellow underwing 452.8 *yellow thing*

yellowwood 85 Trees and Shrubs

yelp 406.12 *express pain*, 430.1 *stridency* , 430.4 *be strident*, 432.1 *animal cry*, 432.4 *cry*, 564.13 *speak in a particular way*

Yemaja 8 Deities

Yemen 91 Countries

yen 741.11 *national coins*, 782.1 *desire*

Yengishiki 7.12 *religious text*

Yenisei 5 Languages and Groups of Languages, 96 Rivers

Yeo 96 Rivers

ye olde 202.12 *olden*

yeoman 32.15 *horse person*,

68.15 *agriculturist*, 679.20 *cavalryman*
yeomanry 679.19 *cavalry*
Yerevan 93 Cities
yerk 339.3 *jerk*, 339.13 *pull at*
yes 499
yes! 499
yes-and-no 617.5 *not bad*
Yesenin 48 Poets
yeshiva 6.12 *educational institution*
yes man 667.5 *assenter*
yes-man 167.6 *conformist*, 499.3 *assenter*, 808.3, 853.7 *sycophant*
yesterday 3.8 *past time*, 3.24 *historically*, 185.27 *at what time*, 191.8 *immediately*, 197.3 *another time*, 200.1 *past time*, 200.22 *in the past*
yesterday afternoon 200.1 *past time*
yesterday evening 200.1 *past time*, 200.22 *in the past*
yesterday morning 200.1 *past time*
yesterday's news 3.18 *in the past*
yesteryear 3.8 *past time*, 3.24 *historically*, 200.1 *past time*, 200.22 *in the past*
yestreen 200.22 *in the past*
yet 3.24 *historically*, 200.23 *before now*
yet again 176.19 *twice*
yet another 100.18 *additional*
yeti 95.3 *mountaineer*
Yeti 76.7 *legendary beast*, 529.6 *natural mystery*
yet to be 199.11 *future*
yet to come 199.11 *future*
Yevtushenko 48 Poets
yew 85 Trees and Shrubs
Yezidi 7 Non-Christian Religions
Y-fronts 295.18 *underwear*
Yggdrasil 85.13 *tree mythology*
yid 91 Names for Inhabitants
Yiddish 5 Languages and Groups of Languages
yield 374, 721, 86.1 *fruits*, 86.10 *fruit*, 167.8 *comply*, 238.6 *be weak*, 243.7, 243.10 *produce*, 377.10 *be adaptable*, 499.5 *assent to*, 576.10 *compromise*, 586.18 *be persuaded*, 598.1 *relinquish*, 606.1, 606.5 *provision*, 673.3 *submit*, 694.5 *obey*, 721.13 *be profitable*, 727.9 *dispose of*, 729.5 *give*, 749.7 *receive*
yield a return 746.12 *be profitable*
yielder 598.4 *deserter*
yielding 721, 167.13 *compliant*, 224.14 *irresolute*, 374.2 *pliant*, 377.2 *adaptability*, 377.6 *elastic*, 377.7 *adaptive*, 598.3 *relinquishment*, 660.12 *wieldy*, 673.1 *submission*, 694.1 *obedience*, 694.7 *obedient*, 835.6 *pitying*
yieldingly 167.16 *adaptably*
yield oneself 673.3 *submit*
yield strength 63.15 *strength of materials*
yield the palm 673.3 *submit*
yield to 127, 694.5 *obey*
yield to others 810.14 *be modest*
yield to pressure 695.8 *be compelled*
yield to temptation 858.8 *be dishonourable*
yield to the pressure 673.4 *succumb*
yield up 629.3 *restore*
yield with a good grace 673.3 *submit*
yigdal 10.8 *hymn*
Yin and Yang 111.2 *opposites*
yippee 431.2 *cry of joy*, 773.12 *hurrah*
ylang-ylang 85 Trees and Shrubs
yob 401.2 *male*, 635.2 *troublemaker*, 795.5 *vulgar person*, 818.4 *discourteous person*, 832.8 *malefactor*
yobbishly 818.10 *rudely*
yobbo 832.8 *malefactor*

Yob Tom 10.15 *holy day*
yodel 431.8 *musical cry*, 431.15 *sing out*, 433.2 *song*
yodeller 431.9 *crier*
yoga 11.1 *occultism*, 627.9 *physical improvement*, 644.5 *exercise*
Yoga 4.7 *school of thought*
Yogacara 7 Non-Christian Religions
yoga trance 11.10 *psychic phenomenon*, 512.1 *oblivion*
yoghurt 45.35 *dessert*, 243.7 *produce*, 393.8 *pulp*
yogi 11.12 *occultist*
yogism 11.1 *occultism*
Yogism 7 Non-Christian Religions
yohimbine 85 Tree Products
yoicks 431.5 *hunting cry*, 590.19 *after him*
yoke 137, 68.18 *practise livestock farming*, 135.1 *union*, 135.10 *link*, 137.4 *means of connection*, 137.12 *bind*, 140.5 *combine*, 176.1 *two*, 176.14 *pair*, 295.24 *part of garment*, 699.5 *means of restraint*, 699.12 *gag*
yoked 135.15 *tied*, 137.16 *bound*, 140.7 *combined*, 176.9 *two*
yokel 93.12 *rural dweller*, 255.5 *countryman*, 658.3 *naive person*, 795.5 *vulgar person*, 803.1 *plebeian*
yokeldom 249.6 *regions*
yoke to 130.6 *add*
yoke together 135.10 *link*
yoko-geri 26.8 *karate*
Yokohama 68 Breeds of Fowl, **93** Cities
yolk 74 Rigging, 78.15 *eggs*
Yom Kippur 10.15 *holy day*, 840.2 *apology*, 871.3 *fast day*
yon 263.8 *distant*, 263.10 *distantly*
yonder 263.8 *distant*, 263.10 *distantly*
Yonge 48 Writers
yoni 9.3 *idol*, 246.4 *fertility cult*
Yonkers 93 Cities
yonks 188.5 *long duration*
yonkyo 26.10 *aikido*
york 27.18 *bowl*, 338.23 *throw*
York 93 Cities, 93.4 *British cities*
yorker 27.8 *delivery*, 338.5 *throw*
Yorkshire accent 5.26 *dialect*
Yorkshire fog 87 Grasses
Yorkshire pudding 45.44 *British dish*
Yorkshire terrier 77 Breeds of Dogs
Yoruba 1 Peoples, **5** Languages and Groups of Languages, **7** Non-Christian Religions
you and me 400.9 *group*
you can say that again 499.9 *yes*
you could have knocked me down with a feather 514.14 *good heavens*
you don't say 514.14 *good heavens*
you must be joking 536.17 *never*
young 206, 156.32 *embryonic*, 201.12 *immature*, 203.10 *spring*, 206.4 *young animal*, 243.7 *produce*, 245.6 *progeny*, 453.4 *fresh*, 595.5 *immature*, 656.2 *unskilled*, 658.1 *naive*
Young 52 Scientists
young adult 206.6 *young person*
young amphibian 79
young animal 206
youngberry 86 Fruits
young bird 78
young blood 206.2 *youthfulness*, 206.10 *the young*
young buck 401.2 *male*
young creature 243.7 *produce*
young days 206.1 *youth*
younger 127.6 *inferior*
younger days 206.1 *youth*
younger generation 201.6 *avant-garde*
young fish 80
young generation 201.6 *avant-garde*

young girls 777 Phobias by Topic
young hopeful 206.6 *young person*, 494.3 *optimist*, 775.5 *hoper*
young lady 206.8 *young woman*
youngling 206.6 *young person*
young love 821.2 *romantic love*
young mammal 77
young man 206, 401.2 *male*, 821.9 *lover*
young matron 823.7 *bridal party*
youngness 206.2 *youthfulness*
young offender institution 702.1 *prison*
young people 206.10 *the young*
young person 206
young plant 206
young pup 206.7 *young man*, 807.12 *impudent person*
Young's experiment 56 Named Laws
young shaver 206.7 *young man*
youngster 206.6 *young person*, 206.9 *child*
Youngstown 93 Cities
young thing 453
young Turk 168.8 *dissenter*, 401.2 *male*
young'un 206.6 *young person*
young woman 206, 402.2 *female*
Your Excellency 696.3 *leader*
your Honour 16.23 *judge*
your Lordship 16.23 *judge*
Your Majesty 696.2 *sovereign*
Your Royal Highness 696.2 *sovereign*
yourself 165.12 *I*
yourselves 165.12 *I*
yours to command 694
yours truly 165.12 *I*, 368.6 *internal world*
youth 206, 156.4 *conception*, 201.3 *immaturity*, 206.6 *young person*, 206.7 *young man*, 206.10 *the young*, 237.2 *healthiness*, 396.5 *life cycle*, 401.2 *male*, 595.10 *immaturity*, 658.2 *naivety*, 658.3 *naive person*, 686.3 *time of plenty*
Youth 206
youth custody centre 627.10 *reformatory*, 702.1 *prison*
youthen 206.17 *make young*
youthful 201.12 *immature*, 206.11 *young*, 453.4 *fresh*
youthfully 206, 201.24 *immaturely*, 453.18 *greenly*
youthfulness 206
youth hostel 256.10 *hotel*
you've got it 537.40 *right*
yowl 406.12 *express pain*, 423.8 *be loud*, 431.10 *cry out*, 432.4 *cry*
yowling 432.1 *animal cry*, 432.7 *ululant*, 432.4 *dissonant noise*
yo-yo 34.9 *mountaineer*
yo-yoing 34.3 *climbing technique*
Ypres 93 Cities
Y-shape 343.5 *fork*
Y-shaped 343.9 *branched*
ytterbium 57 Chemical Elements
yttrium 57 Chemical Elements
yü 49 Musical Instruments
yuan 741.11 *national coins*
Yuan dynasty art 50 Non-Western Art
yucca 84 Flowers and Flowering Plants, **85** Trees and Shrubs, 380.8 *sharp-pointed thing*
yuck 622.8 *unclean*
yucky 618.4 *poor*, 622.8 *unclean*, 785.9 *disliked*
yueh ch'in 49 Musical Instruments
Yuh-hwang-shangte 8.3 *God*
Yukawa 52 Scientists
Yukon 96 Rivers, 96.3 *US rivers*
Yukon Daylight Time 185.9 *time zone*
Yukon Standard Time 185.9 *time zone*
Yukon Territory 92 Canadian Provinces and Territories
yule 203.5 *winter*
yule log 45.36 *cake*

Yule log 410.2 *lighter*
yuletide 203.5 *winter*
Yuletide 10.16 *religious festival*
Yuman 5 Languages and Groups of Languages
Yum Kaax 8 Deities
yummy 411.7 *tasty*
yun lo 49 Musical Instruments
yun ngao 49 Musical Instruments
Yupik 1 Peoples
yuppie 201.9 *modern person*, 642.10 *busy person*, 686.4 *prosperous person*, 742.10 *wealthy person*
Yurak 5 Languages and Groups of Languages
Yurok 1 Peoples

Z

zabaglione 45.47 *Italian dish*
Zadkiel 8.6 *angel*
Zagreb 93 Cities
Zagros 95 Mountains
Zaïre 91 Countries, 96.5 *other major rivers*
Zambezi 96 Rivers
Zambia 91 Countries
zampogna 49 Musical Instruments
zaniness 798.1 *ludicrousness*
zanthoxylum 85 Trees and Shrubs
zany 51.30 *clown*, 771.10 *humorous*, 798.5 *ridiculous*
Zanzibar 93 Cities, **98** Islands
zap 157.17 *kill*, 244.8 *destroy*, 329.9 *acceleration*, 425.1 *bang*
zap along 329.4 *be swift*
Zapotec 1 Peoples, **5** Languages and Groups of Languages
zareba 671.9 *barrier*, 671.12 *fort*
Zátopek 18 Sporting Personalities
Z chromosome 59.14 *chromosome*
zeal 161 Collective Names for Birds and Animals, 7.2 *religiousness*, 237.2 *healthiness*, 572.7 *eagerness*, 574.13 *concentration*, 759.4 *emotion*, 782.1 *desire*
zealot 7.4 *religionist*, 168.8 *dissenter*, 490.11 *opinionist*, 495.5 *misjudging person*, 577.8 *obstinate person*, 642.10 *busy person*
zealotry 572.7 *eagerness*, 577.7 *opinionatedness*
zealous 7.15 *religious*, 237.11 *strong in spirit*, 572.2 *eager*, 574.2 *tenacious*, 642.18 *active*, 759.13 *passionate*
zealously 7.23 *religiously*, 237.15 *acutely*, 759.20 *with feeling*
zealousness 572.7 *eagerness*
zeatin 58.17 *plant hormone*
zebra 77 Placental Mammals, 19.2 *football player*, 456.5 *variegated thing*, 702.5 *prisoner*
zebra crossing 71.3 *carriageway*, 327.5 *crossing*, 356.5 *crossing point*, 634.1 *refuge*
zebra finch 78 Birds
zebra fish 80 Fishes
zebras 161 Collective Names by Animal
zebrawood 85 Trees and Shrubs
zebu 77 Placental Mammals
zed bed 47.6 *bed*
Zeebrugge 93 Cities
Zeeman 52 Scientists
zegeni 45.53 *African dish*
Zeisel reaction 57 Named Reactions
zelophobia 777 Phobias by Name
Zemaituka 32 Breeds of Horse and Pony
zemi 8.5 *deity*
zemitot 10.8 *hymn*
zemstvo 653.7 *council*
Zem-Zem 10.13 *shrine*